# CANADIAN WHO'S WHO

# CANADIAN
# WHO'S
# WHO

## 1994

VOLUME XXIX

Kieran Simpson
Editor

UNIVERSITY OF TORONTO PRESS

Toronto  Buffalo  London

© University of Toronto Press Incorporated 1994
Toronto  Buffalo  London
Printed in Canada
ISBN 0-8020-4677-0
ISSN 0068-9963

**Canadian Cataloguing in Publication Data**

The National Library of Canada has catalogued
this publication as follows:

Main entry under title:

The Canadian who's who

v. 1–    ; 1910–
Prelim. matter in English and French with some
biographies in French.
ISSN 0068-9963
ISBN 0-8020-4677-0 (v. 29)

I. Canada – Biography.

FC25.C35        920'.071        C76-031588-4
F1005.C35

# CONTENTS

# CANADIAN WHO'S WHO
# 1994

*Canadian Who's Who* is the largest and most authoritative publication of its kind in Canada, offering instant access to more than fourteen thousand prominent Canadians in all walks of life. Published annually to provide current and accurate information, the familiar bright-red volume is recognised as the standard reference source of contemporary Canadian biography.

Until University of Toronto Press acquired publication rights in 1978, the *Canadian Who's Who* was issued triennially, with five supplementary booklets (the *Canadian Biographical Service*) published at intervals between editions of the main volume. This publication policy was found on examination to have many drawbacks. Because purchase of the main volume was separate from subscription to the supplementary booklets, librarians and others were never quite sure if their holdings were complete. Also, with the three-year period between editions, the biographies in the main volume became too dated and the current information, scattered in the supplements, was not easily accessible. An annual edition obviated the need for such supplements by locating the most recent information conveniently in one place. Thus while the *Canadian Who's Who* 1979 was cumulative for the years 1976–9, the 1980 edition was the first to cover a one-year period.

In 1985 University of Toronto Press also published *Canadian Who's Who Index* 1898–1984, compiled by Evelyn McMann, a complete index of the entire backlist of *Canadian Who's Who* volumes which includes full name, year of birth, profession or occupation, and the volume or volumes in which each biography appears. Also indexed are the 1898 and 1912 editions of *Canadian Men and Women of the Time*, edited by Henry J. Morgan. In addition, backlist volumes are available in a microfiche set under the title, *Canadian Who's Who in Microfiche* 1898–1975, and *Canadian Who's Who in Microfiche*, 1979–1988.

*Canadian Who's Who* 1994 includes more than fourteen thousand biographies of persons who are of current national interest for reference or inquiry. Over five thousand individuals were invited to complete questionnaires from which new biographies were compiled. Those already listed in earlier editions were given two opportunities to update their biographies.

*The Canadian Who's Who* was first published in 1910 by *The Times Publishing Company* of London, England, and contained some two thousand biographies of important living Canadians. The late A. L. Tunnell acquired copyright from *The Times* in 1932, and in 1936 published a substantially larger second edition which incorporated *Canadian Men and Women of the Time*, a parallel reference work edited by Henry J. Morgan. Beginning with the 1936 edition, the *Canadian Who's Who* was published under the continuous editorial direction of A. L. Tunnell for forty-two years, until his retirement in 1978 and the acquisition of the work by University of Toronto Press.

The guiding principle governing selection for inclusion has not changed since the first edition was published. There is no charge, nor is there any obligation whatsoever, for the inclusion of a biography in the *Canadian Who's Who*. Biographees are chosen on merit alone.

Since the biographies document the achievements of Canadians from all walks of life, *Canadian Who's Who* serves as a record and overview of culture in Canada.

Kieran Simpson
May 1994

# ACKNOWLEDGMENTS

Supervising Editor: Elizabeth Lumley
Chief Researcher: Gwen Peroni
Chief Copy Editor: Lynn Burdon
Research Editor: Lesley Fairfield
Researchers: Nancy Passy
Nancy Love Bianchi
Lisa Wuohela
Janet Ritvo

# BIOGRAPHIES

# A

**AARON, Joseph;** health organization executive; b. Toronto, Ont. 23 Sept. 1915; s. Reuben and Dora (Goldman) A.; e. Jarvis C.I. & several courses; m. Gladys d. Joshua and Ita Zuckert 5 Apr. 1941; children: Susan, Raymond; PRES., CANDN. NATURAL HYGIENE SOC. 1960– ; the society is a vegetarian soc. advocating a total approach to healthful living; Bd. Mem., Am. Natural Hygiene Soc. 6 years; operated fleet of 6 taxis; self-employed in auto supply industry for 20 years; Past Big Brother; Boston marathon runner in his 50s; recently won 2 firsts in speed walking for seniors; Home: 14 Lynn Haven Rd., Toronto, Ont. M6A 2K8.

**AARON, Raymond Leonard,** B.Sc.; professional speaker, motivator, real estate entrepreneur; b. 18 Sept. 1944; s. Joseph and Gladys (Zuckert) A.; e. Bathurst Heights C.I. 1962 (Ontario Scholar); Univ. of Toronto, B.Sc. (Hons.) 1966; separated; daughter: Juli-Ann Elizabeth; step-daughters: Lori Lea, Lisa Lyn; PRES., THE RAYMOND AARON GROUP 1981– ; Mngt. Cons., Kates Peat Marwich 1966–67, 1973–78; Math. Teacher, Newtonbrook S.S. 1969–71; Computer Teacher, Waikato Technical Inst., New Zealand 1972; started real estate investments 1973; creator/teacher 12–hour Real Estate Course across Can. 1983– ; opened a real estate bookstore 1984; launched the Library Club 1986; real estate syndictor 1987– ; launched the Millionaire Club 1988; launched The Raymond Aaron Group VISA Card jointly with Royal Bank of Can. 1989; taught the Fire Walk 1990; launched 'Biz U' business college 1992; launched Class Action Lawsuit against Bloc Quebecois Members of Parliament including injunction request that they not be allowed to sit as Official Opposition 1993; Maurice Hutton Alumni scholarship 1962; Candn. Achievers Award 1988; finalist, Internat. Entrepreneur of the Year Award 1988; Life Mem., Candn. Natural Hygiene Soc.; author: 'A Programmed Instruction Course in the Techniques of Calculus' 1967; 'You Can Make a Million in Canadian Real Estate' 1987; 'Vast Profits for the 1990's' 1990; 'Springboard to Success' 1990; 'Beware the Big Bad Syndicator' 1991; 'The Future of Canada' 1992; 'Bloom Where You're Planted' 1993; 'The Turning Point' 1993; recreations: reading, walking, jogging (previously marathoning, nordic skiing, caving, rock climbing, mountaineering); Office: 482 Queen St., Newmarket, Ont. L3Y 2H4.

**ABBEY, Lloyd Robert,** B.A., M.A., Ph.D.; writer; b. London, Ont. 4 Apr. 1943; s. Edward Lloyd and Madeleine (Riddell) A.; e. McMaster Univ., B.A. 1966; Univ. of Western Ont., M.A. 1968; Univ. of Toronto, Ph.D. 1971; English Professor, McMaster Univ. 1971–72; Univ. of B.C. 1972–77; Univ. of Toronto 1977–80; Honourable Mention, Woodrow Wilson Fellowship 1966; Included in Best Poems of 1972; Finalist, 1983 CBC Lit. Competition; Contbr., Salvaide of Can.; East Timor Alert Network; author: 'The Last Whales' (novel) Canada 1989, U.S. & England 1990; 'Selected Poems' 1989, 'The Antlered Boy' 1984, 'Braindances' 1979 (poetry); 'Destroyer and Preserver: Shelley's Poetic Skepticism' 1979 (lit. crit.); co-author: 'Flies' 1973, 'The Antlered Boy' 1970 (poetry); recreations: bird watching, arranging music; clubs: Writer's Union of Can.; Amnesty Internat.; Address: c/o Random House, 1265 Aerowood Dr., Mississauga, Ont. L4W 1B9.

**ABBIS, Hon. Mr. Justice Joseph Chaiker,** B.C.L.; b. Beirut, Lebanon 24 Nov. 1914; s. Michael and Mary (Farah) A.; came to Can. 1914; e. Edmundston (N.B.) Pub. Sch. 1924; Seminaire de Qué. 1931; St. Francis Xavier Univ. B.A. 1935; McGill Univ. B.C.L. 1948; JUDGE, COURT OF QUEEN'S BENCH, N.B. until retirement 1982; Teacher, Edmundston High Sch. 1935–45; called to Bar of N.B. 1948; cr. Q.C. 1968; practised law Edmundston, N.B. 1948–73; Chrmn., N.B. Study Comte. on Nursing Educ. 1970; rec'd George Findlay Stephens Award, Candn. Hosp. Assn. 1971; Citation for Meritorious Services, Am. Hosp. Assn. 1976; 'Judge Chaiker Abbis Award' estbd. by N.B. Hosp. Assn. 1977; recipient Queen's Silver Jubilee Medal 1977; Hon. Fellowship, Amer. Coll. of Hospital Executives 1985; served with Carleton & York Regt. (Reserve); Pres., N.B. Hosp. Assn. 1953–58, Candn. Hosp. Assn. 1966–68; Del.-at-Large, Am. Hosp. Assn. 1966–79; Estbd. and funded Hosp. Governance Research Fund 1984; author various articles on trusteeship, health; Liberal; R. Catholic; recreations: travel, reading, golf, collecting first editions; Home: 8 Nineteenth Ave., Edmundston, N.B. E3V 2A8.

**ABBOTT, Hon. Anthony C.,** P.C.; lawyer; business consultant; b. Montreal, Que. 26 Nov. 1930; s. Douglas Charles and Mary Winifred (Chisholm) A.; e. Bishop Univ. B.A. 1952; Osgoode Hall Law School LL.B. 1961; m. Naomi d. E. Norman Smith 19 Feb. 1955; children: Douglas Chisholm, Hilary Smith, Timothy Alexander; el. to H. of C. 1974; Min. of Consumer and Corporate Affairs 1976; Min. of National Revenue 1978; Past Pres., Retail Council of Canada; Anglican; Clubs: Union (Victoria); Home: 2631 Mill Bay Rd., Mill Bay, B.C. V0R 2P0.

**ABBOTT, Elizabeth,** M.A., Ph.D.; historian; writer; editor; b. Ottawa, Ont.; d. William Richard and Margaret Langley (Griggs) Abbott; e. Sir George Williams Univ. B.A. 1963; McGill Univ. M.A. 1966, Ph.D. 1971; one s. Ivan; DEAN OF WOMEN, TRINITY COLLEGE, DEAN OF ST. HILDA'S COLL., UNIV. OF TORONTO; Editor-in-Chief, The Urban Pet (newspaper) 1991–93; Rsch. Dir., Centre d'Etude du Québec, Concordia Univ. 1966–84; Prof. of Hist. Dawson Coll. Montreal 1972–84; Reuters reporter for Haiti 1986–88; Ed.-in-Chief Chronicle Publications 1989–91; Ed.-in-Chief Chronicle of Canada 1990; author 'Haiti: The Duvaliers and their Legacy' 1988; 'Tropical Obsession' (play) 1986; co-compiled 'Bibliographie pour Servir à L'Etude de l'Histoire du Canada Français' 1966; 'l'inventaire de la Collection Louis-Hippolyte LaFontaine' 1968; ed. 'Racism or Responsible Government? The French Canadian Dilemma of the 1840's' 1967; 'Debates of the Legislative Assembly of United Canada 1841–1854' Vols. 1–19 1970–83; recipient Lt. Gov.'s Silver Medal Hist. Sir George Williams Univ. 1963; Arthur C. Tagge Mem. Fellowship McGill 1964–65; McConnell Mem. Fellowship McGill 1966–70; Bd. of Dirs., St. Patrick's Benevolent Soc.; Volunteer, Toronto Humane Soc.; mem., Candn. Writers' Union; Anglican; recreations: skating, bicycling, swimming; Address: 44 Devonshire Place, Toronto, Ont. M5S 2E2.

**ABBOTT, Martin G.,** B.A., LL.B.; lawyer; b. Regina, Sask. 25 July 1952; s. Brian Martin A.; e. Univ. of Alta. B.A. (R.O.T.P.) 1973, LL.B. 1981; m. Jane d. John and Arlene England 25 Aug. 1979; children: Simon, Alexandra, Emily, Samantha; joined BLAKE, CASSELS & GRAYDON 1991, partner 1992; Fighter Pilot, 439 Squadron Baden-Soellingen, W. Germany 1974–79; articled with Milner Fenerty 1981, Partner 1988; Capt., Cdn. Armed Forces Supp. Reserves 418 Squadron; Dir., Ballistic Energy Corp.; Oryx Energy Can. (Indonesian Holdings) Ltd.; and several priv. oil & gas cos.; City of Moose Jaw/Prov. of Sask. trophies for highest standing basic and advanced pilot training, CFB Moose Jaw 1973; Flt. Lt. Barker Trophy for highest standing advanced pilot training, CFB Cold Lake 1974; Bd. of Gov., Calgary Parks Found.; Past Chrmn., Natural Resources Section, Candn. Bar Assn.; mem. U.C.C.; author: 'Fundamental Issues and Practical Requirements Affecting the Purchase and Sale of Producing Resource Properties' Alberta Law Review 1990; recreations: skiing, hockey, hunting; club: Calgary Petroleum; Home: 20 Baycrest Pl., Calgary, Alta. T2V 0K6; Office: 35th fl., Banker's Hall E., 855 – 2 St., Calgary, Alta. T2P 4J8.

**ABBOTT-NAMPHY, Elizabeth;** see ABBOTT, Elizabeth.

**ABEL, Allen Joel,** B.Sc.; journalist; b. Brooklyn, N.Y. 31 Jan. 1950; s. Benjamin and Henrietta (Jacobson) A.; e. Rensselaer Polytechnic Inst., B.Sc. 1971; m. Linda Joy d. James and Agnes Deyo 20 Apr. 1974; REPORTER, CBC PRIME TIME NEWS 1992– ; documentaries incl.: 'The Fires of Kuwait' 1991; 'The Price of Freedom' (East Germany); 'The Two Cubas' 1990; 'Crime and Punishment in the USSR'; 'Romanian Journey'; 'The Murder, the Mayor, the Movie' (New York racial politics) 1989; 'The Mirror That Remembers - 150 Years of Photography'; 'Tienan'men Square' 1989; 'Dreams of Amazonia' 1988; 'The Rio Café' 1987; 'Abel's Korea' 1988 Summer Olympics; 'Abel's New Zealand' 1990 Commonwealth Games; 'Abel's Savoie' 1992 Winter Olympics; Sports Writer, The Times Record (Troy, N.Y.) 1972–75; The Times-Union (Albany, N.Y.) 1974–77; Sports Commentator, WTRY (Troy, N.Y.) 1973–77; Sports Columnist, The Globe and Mail 1977–83; Sports Commentator, CFRB (Toronto) 1982–83; Peking Correspondent, Globe and Mail 1983–85; Reporter, Producer, The Journal, CBC Television 1986–92; winner National Newspaper Award 1980; Hearst Newspaper Award 1974, 1975, 1975; N.Y. State Associated Press Award 1972, 1973, 1974, 1975, 1976; author: 'But I Loved It Plenty Well' 1983; 'Scaring Myself Again' 1992; Office: 100 Carlton St., Toronto, Ont. M5W 1A0.

**ABEL, Elie,** B.A., M.Sc., LL.D.; journalist; educator; b. Montreal, Que. 17 Oct. 1920; s. Jacob and Rose (Savetsky) A.; e. Baron Byng High Sch., Montreal, 1933–37; McGill Univ. B.A. 1941; Columbia Univ. M.Sc. 1942; LL.D. McGill 1971; LL.D. Univ. W. Ont. 1976; m. Corinne, d. Clifford A. Prevost, 28 Jan. 1946; children: Mark, Suzanne (Abel-Vidor); MARY LOU AND GEORGE BOONE CENTENNIAL PROFESSOR & DIRECTOR, STANFORD IN WASHINGTON 1993– ; Harry and Norman Chandler Professor of Communication, Stanford Univ. 1979–91; Vice Chrmn., Nat. News Council, New York 1982–84; mem., Intl. Cmsn. for the Study of Communication Problems at UNESCO 1977–79; U.S. delegation to UNESCO's 21st Gen. Conf. at Belgrade, Yugoslavia 1980; Dean, Sch. of Journ., Columbia Univ. 1970–1979; Reporter, 'Windsor Daily Star' 1941; Asst. City Ed., 'Montreal Gazette' 1945; Foreign Corr., North American Newspaper Alliance 1946–47; U.N. Corr. Overseas News Agency 1947–49; Reporter and Foreign Corr., 'New York Times' 1949–59; Washington Bureau Chief, 'The Detroit News' 1959–61; Reporter-Commentator, Nat. Broadcasting Co. Inc. 1961–70; served with RCAF 1942–45; co-author (with W. Averell Harriman) Special Envoy to Churchill and Stalin, 1941–46 (Random House, NY); co-author 'Roots of Involvement: The U.S. in Asia 1784–1971'; 'The Shattered Bloc: Behind the Upheaval in Eastern Europe 1990; author 'The Missile Crisis' 1966; ed. 'What's News: The Media in American Society' 1981; 'Leaking: Who Does It? Who Benefits? At What Cost' 1987; rec'd. George Foster Peabody Award for 'outstanding radio news' 1967; Overseas Press Club Award for 'best interpretation of foreign news' 1969; Jewish; Clubs: The Century (New York); Office: Stanford in Washington, 2661 Connecticut Ave., NW, Washington, DC 20008.

**ABELLA, Irving Martin,** C.M., M.A., Ph.D., F.R.S.C.; educator; b. Toronto, Ont. 2 July 1940; s. Louis and Esther (Shiff) A.; e. Univ. of Toronto B.A. 1963, M.A. 1964, Ph.D. 1969; m. Rosalie d. Jacob and Fanny Silberman 8 Dec. 1968; two s. Jacob Julian, Zachary Joshua; PROFESSOR OF HISTORY, YORK UNIVERSITY 1968– ; (and Gov. 1984– ;); Dir., Goldfarb Corp.; Baycrest Centre; Founding Chrmn. Ctte. Candn. Labour Hist. 1970–76; Chrmn., Candn. Professors for Peace in the Middle East; Chrmn. Candn. Jewish Archives 1980–92; Pres., Candn. Jewish Congress 1992– ; Chrmn., Holocaust Documentation Project 1986– ; recipient Guggenheim Meml. Fellowship 1979–80; Nat. Jewish Book Award U.S.A. 1983; John A. Macdonald Book Award Candn. Hist. Assn. 1983; Joseph Tannebaum Lit. Award Toronto Jewish Cultural Counc. 1985; Meml. Found. Jewish Culture Award Geneva 1985; Walter L. Gordon Research Fellow 1985–86; Fellow, Royal Soc. of Canada 1993; Mem., Order of Canada 1994; author 'A Coat of Many Colours: Two Centuries of Jewish Life in Canada' 1990; 'Nationalism, Communism and Canadian Labour' 1973; 'On Strike: Six Major Industrial Disputes in Canadian History' 1974; 'The Canadian Labour Movement' 1976; 'The Canadian Worker in the Twentieth Century' 1978; co-author 'None is Too Many: Canada and the Jews of Europe 1933–48' 1982; 'Twentieth Century Canada! 1983; various articles learned and popular journs.; ed. 'Middle East Focus' 1981–92; Founding Ed. 'Canadian Labour History Bulletin' 1970–75; recreations: tennis, squash, reading; Office: Glendon Coll., 2275 Bayview Ave., Toronto, Ont. M4N 3M6.

**ABELLA, Rosalie Silberman,** B.A., LL.B.; b. Stuttgart, Germany 1 July 1946; d. Jacob Sumer and Fanny (Krongold) Silberman; e. Bathurst Hts. S.S., Toronto 1964; Univ. Coll., Univ. of Toronto B.A. 1967, LL.B. 1970; LL.D. (Hon.) Dalhousie Univ. 1985, Queen's Univ. 1985, McMaster Univ. 1986; Univ. of Windsor 1988; Univ. of Ottawa 1988; Univ. of New Brunswick 1989; Mount St. Vincent Univ. 1989; Univ. of Calgary 1990; Univ. of B.C. 1990; Univ. of Toronto 1990; Univ. of Waterloo 1990; Concordia Univ. 1991; York Univ. 1991; Univ. of Western Ont. 1991; Univ. of Victoria 1992; m. Irving Martin A. 8 Dec. 1968; two s. Jacob Julian, Zachary Joshua; JUSTICE, ONTARIO COURT OF APPEAL 1992– ; called to Bar of Ont. 1972; private law practice 1972–76; Comnr. Ont. Human Rights Comn. 1975–80; Co-Chrmn. Univ. of Toronto Acad. Discipline Tribunal 1976–84; Judge, Ont. Family Court 1976–87; mem. Ont. Pub. Service Labour Relations Tribunal 1975–76; mem. Premier's Adv. Comte. on Confed. 1977–82; Chrmn. Study on Access to Legal Services by Disabled 1982–83; Sole Comnr. Royal Comn. on Equality in Employment which created concept of 'employment' equity 1983–84; Chair, Ont. Labour Relations Bd. 1984–89; Chair, Ont. Law Reform Comn. 1989–92; Moderator, 1988 Leader's Debate; Boulton Visiting Prof., Fac. of Law, McGill Univ. 1988–92; Sr. Fellow, Massey Coll. 1989–92; Continuing Fellow, Massey Coll. 1992– ; Rosalie S. Abella Annual Lecture Series estbl. at Univ. of Guelph 1989; Mem., Candn. Judicial Council Inquiry Ctte. re Donald Marshall, Jr. Reference 1990; Programme Chair, Gov. General's Candn. Study Conf. 1990–91; Chief Rapporteur (Halifax) and Co-Chair (Vancouver) Candn. Constitutional Conferences; Dir. Internat. Comn. Jurists (Candn. Sect.); Dir. Candn. Inst. Adm. Justice; Dir., Inst. for Rsch. on Public Policy; B'Nai Brith Woman of Yr. 1977; Honor Roll Medal, Maclean's 1990; Candn. Bar Assoc. (Ont.) Distinguished Service Award 1992; author 'Access to Legal Services by the Disabled' 1983; 'Equality in Employment' 1984; various articles legal jours.; co-ed. 'Family Law: Dimensions of Justice' 1983; 'Justice Beyond Orwell' 1985; Bd. of Trustees, McGill Institute for the Study of Canada 1993– ; recreations: music, reading; Home: 375 Glengrove Ave. W., Toronto, Ont. M5N 1W4; Office: 130 Queen St. W., Toronto, Ont. M5H 2N5.

**ABILDGAARD, Paul;** executive; b. Denmark 30 Jan. 1930; s. Ole Hjalmer and Katrine (Ornholm) A.; e. Technicum, Finance, Commerce Denmark; m. Elinor d. Johannes and Algunda (Jakobsen) 7 Dec. 1952; children: Susanne, Jeanette, John, Peter, Erik, Charlotte; FOUNDER, C.E.O., THE ALBERT; Founder, C.E.O. Alberta Investment & Doll Co. Inc.; Albert Investments Ltd.; Linen House Inc.; Lady Godiva Oats, Pellets & Cubes Ltd.; Pres., C.E.O., Halcyon Discovery Ltd.; Founder, Nanton Soft Drink; Nanton Food; Appaloosa Beer; Nanton Interbrew; Owner, Crown A Ranches; recreation: horse breeding; Clubs: Rotary (Past Pres.); Ranchmen's; Address: P.O. Box 656, Nanton, Alta. T0L 1R0.

**ABLEY, Mark James Chapman,** M.A.; writer; b. Leamington, Engl. 13 May 1955; s. Henry Thomas and Mary Muriel (Collins) A.; e. City Park Coll., Saskatoon 1971; Univ. of Saskatchewan B.A.(Hons.) 1975; Oxford Univ. B.A.(First-Class) 1977, M.A. 1983; Rhodes Scholar 1975–78; m. Ann d. R.J.S. and A.O. Beer 15 Aug. 1981; two d.; literary editor, Montreal 'Gazette' 1989–91; feature writer, Montreal 'Gazette' 1987– ; freelance writer (literary journalism) 1978–87; researcher CBC-TV 1978–79; tutor, St. John's Coll., Oxford Univ. 1981, 1982; judge, poetry comp., Stroud and Oxford Festivals 1982; awarded Gov.-Gen.'s Medal 1971; Gov.-Gen.'s Gold Medal 1975; Fiona Mee Prize for Literary Journalism 1980; Eric Gregory Award for Poetry 1981; Mark Harrison Prize 1991; Anglican; Bd. mem., Fed. English-Language Writers of Quebec; mem. Candn. Nature Fed.; Candn. Assn. of Rhodes Scholars; Writers' Union of Canada; League of Candn. Poets; P.E.N.; Canada-Tibet Ctte.; author: 'Beyond Forget: Rediscovering the Prairies' 1986; 'Blue Sand, Blue Moon' (poetry) 1988; 'Heartland' 1989; writer/narrator CBC radio series 'Ideas' 1981, 1983, 1984, 1987; Contrib. Ed. 'Saturday Night' 1986–92; contrib.: 'Canada and the Nuclear Arms Race' 1983; ed.: 'The Parting Light: Selected Writings of Samuel Palmer' 1985; recreations: travel, the arts, nature, cats; Home: 38 Drayton Rd., Pointe-Claire, Qué. H9S 4V2.

**ABOUD, Frances Elaine,** Ph.D.; university professor; b. Toronto, Ont. 7 Feb. 1947; d. Henry Lloyd and Laurice Adele (Bassett) A.; e. Univ. of Toronto B.A. 1969; McGill Univ. M.A. 1970, Ph.D. 1973; m. Charles P. s. Margaret and Charles Philip Larson 5 April 1983; children: Charles Philip, Leila Margaret; PROF., DEPT. OF PSYCHOL., MCGILL UNIV. 1975– ; Asst. Prof., Ctr. for Cross-Cultural Rsch., Western Washington Univ. 1973–75; rsch. into social/psychol. devel. in children & prejudice 1975– ; rsch. & teaching in Ethiopia as part of McGill-Ethiopia Community Health Project 1988–89 and 1990–91; Fellow, Candn. Psychol. Assn.; Mem., Soc. for Rsch. in Child Devel.; Soc. for Exper. Social Psychol.; author: 'Children and Prejudice' 1988; recreations: horseback riding, reading; Home: 59 Arlington Ave., Montreal, Qué. H3Y 2W5; Office: 1205 Dr. Penfield Ave., Montreal, Qué. H3A 1B1.

**ABOUHAIDAR, Mounir G.,** M.Sc., Ph.D.; university professor; b. Baskinta, Lebanon 9 April 1948; s. Georges Habib and Nabiha T. (Rmaily) A.; e. Lebanese Univ. B.Sc. 1971, M.Sc. 1972; Univ. of Strasbourg Ph.D. 1976; m. Margaret d. F.E. Tester 1 Sept. 1972; one d.: Nina; PROFESSOR, DEPT. OF BOTANY, UNIV. OF TORONTO 1990– ; High School Teacher 1969–70; Postdoctoral Fellow, Univ. of Western Ont. 1976–77; Research Assoc. 1977–78; Asst. Prof., Univ. of Toronto 1979–84; apptd. to Grad. Faculty 1979; Assoc. Prof., Dept. of Botany 1984–90; cross-apptd. Dept. of Microbiology, Fac. of Med., Univ. of Toronto; Chair, Safety Ctte., Dept. of Botany 1989–91; Virology Ctte., Candn. Phytopathological Soc. 1988–90; elected rep., Univ. of Toronto Faculty Assn. 1989– ; Mem. of several cttes. at dept. & univ. levels; Min. of Edn. (Lebanon) Honour Awards 1966–70; Nat. Research Council Lebanon 1970–76; Pres., King George Neighbourhood Assn., City of York 1989– ; Office: Univ. of Toronto, Toronto, Ont. M5S 3B2.

**ABRAHAM, S. Clifford,** B.A., M.B.A.; shipping executive; b. Toronto, Ont. 8 Aug. 1956; s. Sheldon Duncan and Elizabeth Anne (Leitch) A.; e. Lakefield Coll. Sch. 1974; Trinity Coll., Univ. of Toronto, B.A. 1978; York Univ., M.B.A. 1981; m. Dorothy d. Robert and Helen Bolder 25 Oct. 1985; children: Sean, Kalyn; PRES. & C.E.O., UPPER LAKES GROUP 1993– ; Mktg. Mngt. Prog., North Am. Life Assur. 1978; Analyst, Upper Lakes Shipping Ltd. 1981; Corp. Sec. 1982; Commercial Mgr., ULS Internat. 1984; Dir. of Mktg. 1986; Exec. Vice-Pres. 1988; Vice-Pres. & Dir., Thornmark Corp. Mngt. Inc.; Upper Lakes Shipping Ltd.; Upper Lakes Group Inc.; Thornmark Capital Corp.; Dir., ULS Marbulk Inc. (Salem, Mass.); Sec. & Dir., A.D.&K. Found.; recreations: golf, skiing, squash; clubs: Granite, Ontario; Office: 49 Jackes Ave., Toronto, Ont. M4T 1E2.

**ABRAHAMS, Cecil Anthony,** B.A., M.A., Ph.D., F.A.S.L.; educator; writer; b. Johannesburg, S.A. 29 Aug. 1940; s. Thomas and Elizabeth Stella A.; e. Pius XII Univ. College, Univ. of S. Africa, B.A. 1963; Univ. of N.B., M.A. 1965; Univ. of Alta., Ph.D. 1977; m. Rosemary d. Quintin and Barbara Gwyn 1 March 1986; children: Vanya, Pierre, Alexei; VICE-PRES. ACADEMIC and PROF. OF ENGLISH, ACADIA UNIVERSITY 1993– ; Teacher, Lenasia High Sch., Johannesburg 1963; Teaching Asst., Univ. of Alta. 1965–67; Lectr., Univ. of N.B. 1967; Asst. Prof., Bishop's Univ. 1969; Assoc. Prof. 1976; Prof. 1981; Vis. Prof., Loyola Coll. 1972; Univ. of the W. Indies 1981; Bayero Univ., Nigeria 1983; McGill Univ. 1984; Dean of Humanities & Prof. of English, Brock Univ. 1987–93; Publisher, Kumalo Publications; Abrahams Consulting & Writing Services; Commonwealth Fdn. Vis. Prof. to Africa 1976; Fellow, African Soc. of Lit.; Assoc. Fellow, Australian Lit. Soc.; mem. African Lit. Assn. (Pres. 1986–87); Candn. Assn. for Commonwealth Lit. & Lang. Studies (Pres. 1976–80); Vice-Chrmn. & Ed., Assoc. for Commonwealth Lit. & Lang. Studies 1980–83; Ed., ACLALS Bulletin 1980–83; Nat. Assn. of S. Africans in Can. (Pres. 1975– ;); Dir., Candn. Univ. Service Overseas; Humanities Rsch. Counc. of Can.; Candn. Fedn. for the Humanities; Shastri Indo-Canadian Inst.; The Africa Network; Trustee, S. African Assn. of Can.; author: 'William Blake's Fourfold Man' 1978; 'Alex La Guma' 1985; 'Essays in Literature' 1986; 'Don't Mourn, Mobilize' (novel) 1988; ed.: 'Memories of Home: The Writings of Alex La Guma' 1991; 'Critical Essays on La Guma' 1993; 'The Tragic Life: Bessie Head and the Literature of Southern Africa' 1990; co-ed. 'The Future of the Canadian University' 1972; recreations: tennis, squash, soccer, cricket; Home: 1330 Belcher St., Port Williams, N.S. B0P 1T0; Office: Wolfville, N.S. B0P 1X0.

**ABRAHAMS, Vivian Cecil,** B.Sc., Ph.D., D.Sc.; educator; b. London, Eng. 19 Oct. 1927; s. Woolf Shusterman A.; e. City of London Sch. 1945; Edinburgh Univ. B.Sc. 1952, Ph. D. 1955, D.Sc. 1978; m. Pamela Phyllis Julia d. Ewart Dance, Swallowfield, Berks., Eng. 10 Sept. 1955; children: Graham, Mark, Carolyn, Jennifer; Professor of Physiology; Fulbright Fellow, Univ. of Pa. 1955–56; Beit Mem. Fellow, Med. Research Council, Nat. Inst. for Med. Research 1956–59, mem. scient. staff 1959–63; Assoc. Prof. 1963, Prof. 1967, Queen's Univ.; M.R.C. Visiting Scient. Univ. Coll. London 1970–71; Head of the Dept., Queen's Univ. 1976–88; Dir., Med. Rsch. Counc. of Can. Group in Sensory-Motor Physiology 1990– ; Chrmn. Ont. Grad. Scholarship Bd. 1977–78; served with RA 1945–48; author various articles in prof. journs.; mem. Scitec (Past-Pres.); Candn. Physiol. Soc. (Pres. 1983–84); Internat. Assn. for Study of Pain (Founder-mem.), Physiol. Soc.; Soc. Neuroscience (Finance Comte. 1983–86; Nominating Comte. 1985–86; Governmental and Public Affairs Ctte. 1987–90); Can. Assn. for NeuroSci. (Pres. 1981–82; Chrmn., Nominating Comte. 1986–90); Am. Physiol. Soc.; Vice Pres., Comte. of Parl., Sci. and Eng. (1979–83); Med. Rsch. Counc. 1984–90 (Mem., Comte. on Neuroscience 1982–85; Standing Comte. on Public Affairs 1985–89; Working Group on Research Involving Animals 1986–89; Standing Comte. on Rsch. and Personnel Funding 1987–89, Budget Comm. 1988–90, Exte. mem. 1988–90); Bd. mem., Candn. Fed. of Biological Societies 1982–85 (Science Policy Comte. 1983–85); mem., Organizing Comte., Internat. Union of Physiological Sciences, Vancouver Mtg. 1984–86; mem., Scientific Comte., Muscular Dystrophy Assoc. of Can. 1982–91; Chrmn., Scientific Adv. Ctte. and Medical Adv. Ctte., Mem. of Bd. and Extve. of Muscular Dystrophy Assoc. of Can. 1988–91; Organizing Ctte., Internat. Brain Rsch. Orgn., 1987–91; mem., Council of Scientists, Human Frontiers Science Program Organization 1989– ; Principal Investigator, Networks of Centres of Excellence Node in Neural Regeneration and Functional Recovery; mem., Bd. of Dirs. NCE; Chrmn., Scientific Adv. Ctte., NCE 1990– ; recreations: golfing; Home: 259 Fairway Hills Cres., Kingston, Ont. K7M 2B5; Office: Dept. of Physiol., Queen's Univ., Kingston, Ont. K7L 3N6.

**ACHEN, Norman Charles,** B.Sc.; banker; e. Mont. State Univ. B.Sc.1966; SR. VICE PRES. & DEPUTY, LENDING, MULTINATIONAL, CREDIT RISK MANAGEMENT, ROYAL BANK OF CANADA 1993– ; Mgmt. Trainee present Bank, Regina 1966, Special Asst. to Chrmn. and Pres., Montréal 1970, Asst. Inspr. Loans, Candn. Loans, Montréal 1971, Vice Pres. RoyMarine Leasing Ltd. Montréal 1973, Mgr. Project Finance Dept. Montréal 1976, Exec. Dir. Orion Bank Ltd. London, Eng. 1978, Vice Pres. Nat. Accts. Ont., Toronto 1981; Sr. Vice Pres. Comm. Banking & Nat. Accts., Royal Bank of Can. 1983–86, Sr. Vice Pres., Comm. Banking, Product Mgmt. & Mktg. 1986–88; Sr. Vice Pres., Corp. Banking, Financial Institutions 1988–91; Sr. Vice Pres., Corp. Banking, Operating Services 1991–93; Sr. Vice Pres., Corporate Bkg., Marketing 1993; mem., Bd. Trade Metrop. Toronto; Treas., Pres. Ont. Division, Candn. Cancer Soc.; Clubs: National; Empire; Office: F8, South Tower, Royal Bank Plaza, Toronto, Ont. M5J 2J5.

**ACKMAN, Roger S.,** B.A., B.C.L.; executive; b. Montréal, Qué. 31 Dec. 1938; s. Douglas F. and Cornelia L. (Hayes) A.; e. Mount Allison Univ. B.A. 1960; McGill Univ. B.C.L. 1963; m. Valerie d. Douglas and Leila Roberts 15 June 1963; two d. Linda, Susan; VICE PRES., GEN. COUNSEL & SECY., IMPERIAL TOBACCO LTD. 1989– ; private law practice Montréal 5 yrs.; joined Imasco Ltd. 1970–89; mem. Bd. Graduate Soc. McGill Univ.; mem. Candn. Bar Assn.; Assn. Candn. Gen. Counsel; recreations: golf, sailing, skiing; Clubs: Montreal Badminton & Squash; Royal Montreal Golf (mem. Bd.); Home: 773 Upper Lansdowne, Westmount, Qué. H3Y 1J9; Office: 3810 St. Antoine St., Montréal, Qué. H4C 1B5.

**ACTON, William L.,** B.Sc., F.S.A., F.C.I.A.; actuary; b. Ottawa, Ont. 10 Nov. 1952; s. Donald Beach and Marian E. (Thompson) A.; e. Queen's Univ., B.Sc. 1975; m. Susan Ruth d. Norman and Ruth Loube 15 July 1978; children: Karen, Samuel; VICE PRES. & DIR., IRISH DIV., CANADA LIFE ASSURANCE CO. 1991– ; joined Canada Life 1975; Asst. Actuary in British & Irish Div. 1979; Assoc. Actuary in Group Div. 1982; Group Insur. Actuary 1985; Gen. Mgr. & Chief Actuary 1986; Head, Group Creditor Insur., Can. Life Assur. 1984–91; Pres. & Chief Operating Offr., Canada Life Casualty Insurance Co. 1988–91; recreations: golf; Club: St. Andrew's Golf; Office: Republic of Ireland Canada Life Hse., Temple Rd., Blackrock, Co. Dublin, Ireland.

**ACZÉL, János Dezső,** M.A., Ph.D., D.Sc., Dr.h.c., F.R.S.C.; mathematician, educator; b. Budapest, Hungary 26 Dec. 1924; s. late Dezső and Irén (Adler) A.; e. Primary Sch. 1930–34, Eng. Sch. 1934–35 and Berzsenyi High Sch. 1935–43, 2Budapest; Pázmány Univ. of Budapest B.A. 1946, M.A. 1947, Ph.D. 1947; m. Susan Kende d. late Lajos Kende 14 Dec. 1946; children: Catherine (Mrs. S. Boivie), Julie (Mrs. M. More); PROFESSOR EMERITUS OF MATH. UNIV. OF WATERLOO; author 'Funktionalgleichungen der Theorie der geometrischen Objekte' (with S. Gołąb) 1960; 'Vorlesungen über Funktionalgleichungen und ihre Anwendungen' 1961; 'Ein Blick auf Funktionalgleichungen und ihre Anwendungen' 1962; 'Lectures on Functional Equations and their Applications' 1966; 'On Applications and Theory of Functional Equations' 1969; 'On Measures of Information and their Characterizations' (with Z. Daróczy) 1975; 'A Short Course on Functional Equations Based upon Recent Applications to the Social and Behavioral Sciences' 1987; 'Functional Equations in Several Variables with Applications to Mathematics, Information Theory and to the Natural and Social Sciences' (with J. Dhombres) 1989; author over 240 articles; ed. 'Functional Equations: History, Applications, and Theory' 1984; Ed.-in-Chief 'Aequationes Mathematicae'; ed. 'Journal of Geometry'; 'Results of Mathematics'; 'Mathematica Japonica'; 'Rendiconti di Matematica'; 'Utilitas Mathematica'; Ed., 'Encyclopedia of Mathematics and Its Applications'; 'Theory and Decision Library Series B'; rec'd M. Beke Award 1961; Hungarian Acad. Sciences Award 1962; Distinguished Prof. 1969; fellow, Royal Soc. Can. 1971; Cajal Medal (Nat. Counc. of Scientific Rsch., Spain) 1988; Hon. degree (Dr. h.c.), Univ. Karlsruhe 1990; Foreign fellow, Hungarian Acad. of Sciences 1990; mem. Candn. Math. Soc. (Council 1971–73, Organizer of Special Meeting); Am. Math. Soc. (Organizer of Special Meeting; Plenary Speaker on Joint Mathematics Meeting); Royal Soc. Can. (Convenor Math. Div. 1974–75, Chrmn. Acad. Science Ed. Comte. 1977–78, Ed. Math. Reports 1978–91);

N.Y. Acad. Science; Oesterr. Math. Ges.; recreations: swimming, reading; Home: 97 McCarron Cr., Waterloo, Ont. N2L 5M9; Office: Aequationes Math, Dept. of Pure Math., Univ. of Waterloo, Waterloo, Ont. N2L 3G1.

**ADAIR, James Allen;** politician,; b. Edmonton, Alta. 13 May 1929; s. late James Wilfred and late Beatrice (Shewfelt) A.; e. Athabasca, Mayerthorpe, Edmonton (Westglen High Sch.); State Seed Lab. St. Paul, Minn.; m. Joyce Helen d. the late Rev. C. Alvin and Mrs. Elsie Johnson, Wetaskiwin, Alta. 31 Oct. 1960; children: Richard, Catherine, Robert; Minister of Transportation and Utilities Alta. also responsible for the Northern Alberta Development Counc. 1986–92; Feed Mill Operator and Grain Buyer, Searle Grain Co. 1948–49; Seed Buyer, Peace Milling Co., Peace River 1953–59; Catering Supvr., Fortier & Associates Catering, Peace River 1960–64; Salesman and Sports Dir. CKYL Radio, Active Partner and Secy. Treas. Peace River Broadcasting Corp. 1964–71; el. P. Cons. mem. for Peace River Alta. g.e. 1971, re-el. since; apptd. Min. without Portfolio for N. Devel. and Indian-Metis Liaison 1971, Min. of Recreation, Parks and Wildlife 1975–79; Min. of Tourism and Small Business Alta. 1979–1986; Min. of Consumer and Corporate Affairs 1986; Past Sr. Councillor, Un. Comm. Travellers of Am. 1958–59; Dir. Alta. Wildlife Foundation 1970–71; Pres. Peace River & Dist. Assn. Mentally Retarded 1969–70; mem. Alta. Adv. Council Air Cadet League Can. 1972–73; Registrar, Alta. Amateur Hockey Assn. Peace Country 1967–70; Peace River Campaign Chrmn. Red Shield 1967; Secy.-Treas. and Stat., N. Peace Hockey League 1965–70; former Dir. Alta. Golf Assn.; P. Conservative; Anglican; recreations: golf, swimming, baseball, fishing; Clubs: Peace River Toastmaster (Charter Pres. 1966–67); Optimist (Peace River Past Pres. and Past Lt. Gov. 1955–57); Peace River Curling (Pres. 1959); Home: 9634 - 83 Ave., Peace River, Alta. T8S 1A4; Office: Room 208, Legislature Bldg., Edmonton, Alta. T5K 2B6.

**ADAM, Gordon Stuart,** B.J., M.A., Ph.D.; university professor; b. Toronto, Ont. 25 Jan. 1939; s. Alexander Crawford and Dorothy Mary (Midgley) A.; e. Bedford Park Public Sch. 1953; Lawrence Park Collegiate 1956; Trinity Coll. Sch. 1957; Carleton Univ., B.J. 1963, M.A. 1967; Queen's Univ., Ph.D. 1978; children: Mark, Julie, Sara; DEAN, FACULTY OF ARTS, CARLETON UNIV. 1992– ; Reporter, Ottawa Journal 1961–62; Deskman, Toronto Star 1963–66; Editorial writer, Ottawa Journal 1967; joined Carleton Univ. as Asst. Prof. 1968–69, 1971–73; Assoc. Prof. 1973; Prof. since 1979; Dir., Sch. of Journalism, Carleton Univ. 1973–87; Chair, Centre for Mass Media Studies, Grad. Sch. of Journalism, Univ. of Western Ont. 1987–89; ed. 'Journalism, Communication and the Law' 1976; 'A Sourcebook of Canadian Media Law' 1989; 'Notes Towards a Definition of Journalism' 1993; author numerous articles and papers; rec'd. Kenneth R. Wilson Award in Journalism 1963; Student Counc. Honour Award, Carleton Univ. 1963; Canada Counc. Doctoral Fellowships 1969–70; Dean's Honour Roll, Queen's Univ. 1969–70; mem., Senate, Carleton Univ. (Senate Extve. 1980–83); Inst. Candn. Studies (Mgmt. Comte. since 1973); Consultant to newspapers and governmental agencies; Freelance writing, broadcasting, lecturing; Visiting Fellow Western Australian Inst. Tech. (Perth); Visiting Scholar, Poynter Inst. for Media Studies, St. Petersburg, Fla.; mem., Assn. for Education in Journalism; Candn. Communication Assn.; Club: Ottawa Athletic Club; recreations: racquets; Office: Paterson Hall, Carleton Univ., 1125 Colonel By Drive, Ottawa, Ont. K1S 5B6.

**ADAMOWSKI, Thomas H.,** Ph.D.; professor; b. Wilmington, Delaware 30 July 1941; s. Henry J. and Frances M. (Skibicka) A.; e. Univ. of Delaware, B.A. 1963; Indiana Univ., M.A. 1966, Ph.D. 1969; m. Eleanor d. Charles and Ellen Chetkowski 1 Sept. 1962; children: Rebecca M. and Natalie A.; PROF., DEPT. OF ENGLISH, UNIV. OF TORONTO 1967– ; CHRMN., DEPT. OF ENGLISH 1985–90, 1991–97; recipient of 2 SSHRCC leave fellowships author of scholarly articles on William Faulkner, D.H. Lawrence, Jean-Paul Sartre; editor 'University of Toronto Quarterly' 1985–90; recreation: hunting; Home: 160 Colbeck St., Toronto, Ont. M6S 1V7; Office: Dept. of English, Univ. of Toronto, Toronto, Ont. M5S 1A1.

**ADAMS, Bryan;** vocalist, composer; b. Kingston, Ont. 1959; Vocalist 1976– ; composer, various bands incl. Prism, Bachman-Turner-Overdrive, Bob Welch, Kiss 1977– ; albums include 'You Want It, You Got It' 1982, 'Cuts Like a Knife' 1983, 'Reckless' 1985, 'Into the Fire' 1987, 'Waking up the Neighbors' 1991; singles include 'Straight from the Heart,' 'Cuts Like a Knife' 1983, 'Heaven,' 'One Night Love Affair,' 'It's Only Love' 1985, 'Heat of the Night,' 'Victim of Love,' 'Only the Strong Survive,' 'Hearts On Fire' 1987, (Everything I Do) I Do It for You,' 'Can't Stop this Thing We Started,' 'There Will Never Be Another Tonight,' 'Thought I Died and Gone to Heaven' 1991; decorated with Order of B.C., Order of Canada; recipient multi-platinum record, No. 1 single in Am., Can., U.K., Sweden, Finland, Denmark, Norway; named Artist of Decade, Candn. Recording Industry; nom. for 6 Grammys and 7 Juno awards and Acad. Motion Picture Sci. & Arts 1992; many other music awards.

**ADAMS, George Allen,** B.A.Sc., M.A.Sc., Ph.D.; university professor; b. Ottawa, Ont. 18 Mar. 1951; s. John James and Florence Margarette (Wells) A.; e. Nepean H.S. 1969; Univ. of Waterloo, B.A.Sc. 1975, M.A.Sc. 1976; McMaster Univ., Ph.D. 1976–80; m. Elizabeth d. John and Jane Fyles 2 Sept. 1972; children: Jennifer, Nathan; Fac., Surgery/Biochemistry, Univ. of Ottawa 1984– ; Pres., Hemo-Stat Inc. 1988– ; MRC Fellow, Baylor Coll. of Med. 1981; Sr. Sci., Candn. Red Cross 1982–88; Program Mgr., EVAD Heart Project 1988–91; Dir., Artificial Heart Rsch. Lab., Univ. of Ottawa Heart Inst. Rsch. Ctr. 1989–91; cons. to numerous biomed. cos.; Reviewer, 'Med. Res. Counc. of Can.; Ont. Heart & Stroke Found.; mem., Am. Heart Assn.; Candn. Biomaterials Soc. (Pres.); Candn. Med. & Biol. Engrs. Soc.; Am. Assn. of Artificial Internal Organs; Candn. Artherosclerosis Soc.; Am. Soc. for Biomaterials; author of 104 sci. pubns. in nat. & internat. jours. incl. 6 book chaps. on the properties of blood; Home: 543 Broadview Ave., Ottawa, Ont. K2A 2L3.

**ADAMS, Hon. George W.;** judge; b. Hamilton, Ont. 30 June 1945; s. Howard Miller and Beatrice Helen (Fletcher) A.; e. McMaster Univ. B.A. 1967; Osgoode Hall Law Sch. LL.B. 1970 (Bronze Medal); Harvard Law Sch. LL.M. 1971; m. Mara d. John and Velta Melbardis 28 July 1967; children: Paul, Sandra, David, Michael; JUSTICE, ONTARIO COURT OF JUSTICE (GENERAL DIVISION) 1991– ; called to Bar of Ont. 1973; cr. Q.C. 1981; Assoc. Prof. Osgoode Hall Law Sch. Toronto 1971–77; Vice-Chair Ont. Labour Relations Bd. 1974, Chrmn. 1979–84; Asst. Dep. Min. of Labour Ont. Policy Analysis 1975–76; Chrmn. Ont. Grievance Settlement Bd. 1977–79; Vice Chrmn. Ont. Edn. Relations Comn. 1977–79; mem. Pub. Review Bd. Un. Automobile Workers 1977–79; Pub. Service Staff Relations Bd. 1975–79; Partner Cassels, Brock & Blackwell 1978–79; Sr. Partner Fasken Campbell Godfrey and Head of Labour & Employment Law Dept. 1985–90; Prof. of Common Law, Univ. of Ottawa 1990–91; Graduate of the Year (1970) Phi Delta Phi Legal Frat.; recipient McKenzie King Travelling Scholar 1971; Harvard Law Sch. Scholarship 1971; Candn. Legal Inst. Award 1987; author 'Canadian Labour Law' 1985, 2nd ed. 1993; mem. Candn. Bar Assn.; Phi Delta Phi Legal Frat.; Candn. Ind. Relations Assn.; Internat. Bar Assn.; Home: 12 Bryce Ave., Toronto, Ont. M4V 2B2; Chambers: Court House, 361 University Ave., Toronto, Ont. M5G 1T3.

**ADAMS, J. Bruce,** B.A.Sc., M.B.A.; executive; b. Toronto, Ont. 13 Feb. 1925; s. Andrew Hepburn Syme and Janet Barr (Macaulay) A.; e. Univ. of Toronto Schs. 1942; Univ. of Toronto B.A.Sc. (Mech. Eng.) 1948, M.B.A. 1957; m. Shirley d. Cyril and Kathleen DeMara 5 June 1954; children: Kathleen Janet (Mrs. J.D. Gray), Jeffrey Bruce, Judith Elizabeth (Mrs. N.A.R. Beveridge); CHRMN., WAINBEE LTD. 1988– ; Sales Engr. The Torrington Co. Ltd. 1948–56; Sales Rep. Blackwood Hodge Ltd. 1956–60; Sales Mgr., Exec. Vice Pres. and Dir., Canadian Pollard Bearings Ltd. 1960–69; Exec. Vice Pres., Pres., Chrmn. and Dir. Canadian Bearings Inc. 1969–82; Sr. Operating Exec. (1980), Chrmn. and Dir. TEK Bearing Co. Inc. (U.S.A.) 1976–82; Pres., Power Transmission Group and Dir. Hugh Russel Inc. 1976–82; Pres. & Dir., Wainbee Ltd. 1982–87; Dir.: MonoLino Typesetting Ltd. 1969–85; R & J Dick (Canada) Ltd. 1970–79; Dir., Profit Sharing Counc. of Can. 1987– ; served with RN Fleet Air Arm 1944–45; Elder Knox Presb. Ch.; Life mem., St. Andrews Soc.; Am. Soc. Mech. Engrs. (Past Chrmn. Ont. Sec.); mem., Bearing Specialists Assn. (Past Pres. & Hon. mem.); Bd. Trade Metrop. Toronto; Clubs: Rotary (Past Pres. Oakville; Paul Harris Fellow); Oakville Golf; Home: 1124 Lakeshore Rd. E., Oakville, Ont. L6J 1L2; Office: 5789 Coopers Ave., Mississauga, Ont. L4Z 3S6.

**ADAMS, John David Vessot,** B.Eng., M.B.A., P.Eng.; executive; b. Ottawa, Ont. 7 Jan. 1934; s. Albert Oliver and Estelle Priscilla (Vessot) A.; e. Nepean High Sch. Ottawa; Carleton Univ.; McGill Univ. B.Eng. 1955; Univ. of W. Ont. M.B.A. 1958; m. Dorothy d. Annie and David Blyth 27 June 1959; children: Nancy, Joel, Louis; PRESIDENT, QUALITY PERFORMANCE ENGINEERING INC., Owen Sound, Ont. 1988– ; Project Engr., Abitibi Paper Co., Cockshutt Farm Equipment Co. Ltd. and Canadian Industries Ltd. 1957–63; Financial Analysis & Planning, Rio Tinto Zinc Group London, Eng. 1963–66; Mgr. Adm. and Planning, Candn. Gypsum Co. Ltd. Toronto, Ont. 1966–72; Mgr. Logistics & Finance, Massey Ferguson Co. Ltd. Toronto 1972–79; Pres. and Owner, The Canada Spool & Bobbin Co. Ltd. 1979–88; mem. Assn. Prof. Engrs. Prov. Ont.; United Church; recreations: curling, golf, skiing; Clubs: Curling; Rotary; Home: 386 14th Ave., Hanover, Ont. N4N 2Y1; Office: 3195 3rd Ave. E., Owen Sound, Ont. N4K 5N3.

**ADAMS, John Lawrence,** CMM, CD, B.Eng., B.A., P.Eng.; public servant; b. Saint John, N.B. 31 May 1942; s. Lawrence Hugh and Jean Marjorie (Poley) A.; e. Royal Military College B.Eng. 1965; Oxford Univ. B.A. 1967; m. Marilyn d. Reginald and Olive Walton 23 July 1966; children: Derek, Ryan, Erin; ASSISTANT DEPUTY MINISTER, INFRASTRUCTURE & ENVIRONMENT, NAT. DEFENCE HEADQUARTERS 1990– ; Officer, 3 Field Eng. Squadron Chilliwack B.C. 1967–70; Commanding Officer 1974–76; Staff Officer, Nat. Defence H.Q. 1971–74; various staff appointments, Candn. Forces 1976–85; Commander, Special Service Force Petawawa Ont. 1989–90; Dir., Defence Construction Canada; Mem., Candn. General Standards Bd.; Rhodes Scholar; Grad. Candn. Army Staff College and Nat. Defence College; Canada 125 Medal; Dir., Gloucester-Ottawa Swim Club; Mem., Military Eng. Assn. of Canada; St. Peters Soc.; Royal Military College Club; recreations: hockey, swimming official; Home: Nat. Defence H.Q., MGen G.R. Pearkes Bldg., Ottawa, Ont. K1A 0K2.

**ADAMS, Karen G.,** B.A., M.L.S.; librarian; b. Eriksdale, Man. 3 May 1946; d. Everet Harold and Margaret Anna (Goranson) Sidwall; e. Eriksdale Collegiate 1963; Univ. Man., B.A. (Hons.) 1967; Univ. Western Ont., M.L.S. 1975; children: Karina Jarry & Richard Everet; EXTVE. DIR., CANADIAN LIBRARY ASSN. 1991– ; Policy & Special Projects Dir., Evergreen Sch. Div. 1975–76; Librarian, Teshmont Consultants 1977–78; Cataloguer, Public Library Services 1977–78; Consultant, Public Library Services, Evening Instructor Red River Community Coll. Lib. Tech Prog. 1978; Acting Dir., Public Library Services, Prov. of Man. 1979, Dir. 1981; Sask. Provincial Librarian 1984–90; Chair, Advisory Group on Nat. Library Services for Handicapped Persons; mem. Candn. Library Assn.; Sask. Library Assn.; author various articles; co-author 'Kidstuff' 1979; recreations: skiing; reading; cycling; gardening; Home: 501 Metcalfe St., Ottawa, Ont. K1S 3P2; Office: 602 – 200 Elgin St., Ottawa, Ont. K2P 1L5.

**ADAMS, Mark Edward,** M.Sc., M.D., F.R.C.P.(C); physician; researcher; scientist; b. Jacksonville, Fla. 1 May 1946; s. Mark Elbert and Anna-Marie Clara (Kuntz) A.; e. Univ. of Okla. B.S. 1968; Univ. of Toronto M.Sc. 1971, M.D. 1974; m. Elaine d. Frank and Valma Stokes 14 June 1975; two s. Jeffrey Michael, Jonathan David; PROF. OF MED. UNIV. OF CALGARY 1992– , Arthritis Soc. Chair 1990– , Assoc. Prof. of Med. 1989; Rsch. Assoc. in Pathol. Mount Sinai Hosp. 1977–78; Visiting Sci. in Biochem. Kennedy Inst. of Rheumatol. 1978–80; Assoc. Prof. of Med. Univ. of B.C. 1980–86, Assoc. in Pathol. 1983–86; Head of Clin. Investig. CIBA-Geigy Canada Ltd. 1986–89; Assoc. Prof. of Pathol. & Med. Univ. of Toronto 1986–89; Acting Chair, Ctte. on Research 1992; Active Med. Staff Foothills Hosp.; recipient C.S. Wainwright Meml. Scholarship 1973; Roy J. Simpson Prize in Paediatrics 1973; K.M. Hunter Found. Fellowship in Rheumatol. 1977–80; H.H. and Kathleen MacKenzie Award Pathol. & Bacteriol. 1977, 1978; Helen L. Vanderveer Fellowship 1978–79; Alpha Omega Alpha; mem. Arthritis Soc. Manpower Panel 1986–92, Chrmn. 1989–92; Arthritis Soc. Med. Planning Ctte. 1989–92; Arthritis Soc. (Bd. of Dirs., Alta. Div. 1991); author or co-author numerous manuscripts, book chapters, addresses; recreations: alpine skiing, gardening; Club: Sunshine Ski; Office: 3330 Hospital Dr. N.W., Calgary, Alta. T2N 4N1.

**ADAMS, Michael John,** M.A.; market and opinion research executive;b. Walkerton, Ont. 29 Sept. 1946; s. William Eldridge and Florentine Catherine (Weiler) A.; e. Queen's Univ. B.A.(hons.) 1969; Univ. of Toronto M.A. 1970; PRESIDENT, ENVIRONICS RESEARCH GROUP LTD. 1970– ; author numerous articles on public opinion; frequent media commentator and public speaker; Home: 165 Collier St., Toronto, Ont. M4W 1M2; Office: 45 Charles St. E., Ste. 200, Toronto, Ont. M4Y 1S2.

**ADAMS, Peter Frederick,** M.Eng., Ph.D.; educator; b. Halifax, N.S. 4 Feb. 1936; s. Gordon Vincent and Freda (Fraser) A.; e. Dalhousie Univ. Dipl. in Engn. 1956; N.S. Tech. Coll. B.Eng. 1958, M.Eng. (Civil Engn.) 1961; Lehigh Univ. Ph.D. (Civil Engn.) 1966; m. Barbara Elaine Dickey; three s.; EXTVE. DIR., CANDN. INSTITUTE FOR PETROLEUM INDUSTRY DEVELOPMENT 1993– ; Design Engr. Gen. Engn. Dept. Internat. Nickel Co. of Canada, Copper Cliff, Ont. 1958–59; Asst. Prof. of Civil Engn. Univ. of Alta. 1960–63; Research Asst. Fritz Engineering Laboratory, Lehigh Univ. Bethlehem, Pa. 1963–66; Assoc. Prof. 1966–70, Prof. of Civil Engn., Univ. of Alta. 1970–89 (Dean of Engn. 1976–84); Design Engr., Project Planner, Dominion Bridge Co. Toronto (sabbatical leave) 1973–74; Pres., C-FER (Centre for Frontier Engineering Research) 1984–89; Pres., Technical Univ. of Nova Scotia 1989–92; Dir. Petroleum Recovery Inst.; Computer Modelling Group; Coal Mining Research Centre (Extve. Comte.); Mang. Adv. Inst.; Hydrocarbon Research Centre (Chrmn.); Candn. Welding Bureau; mem. organ. comtes. various confs.; mem., Nat. Sci. and Eng. Resch. Council 1982–86; Nat. Adv. Com. on Mining and Metall. Resch. 1982– ; National Marine Counc. 1988– ; rec'd Cert. of Merit Candn. Soc. Civil Engn. 1978; rec'd A.B. Sanderson Award Candn. Soc. Civil Engn. 1986; co-author 3 maj. texts instr. structural steel design; contrib. various monographs aspects structural stability & steel design; author or co-author over 100 publs.; presented over 80 lectures, addresses; mem. Assn. Prof. Engrs., Geols. & Geophysicists Alta.; Candn. Council Prof. Engrs.; Hon. Mem., Internat. Assn. Bridge & Structural Engn. (Vice Pres. Internat.; Fellow, Candn. Soc. Civil Engrs. mem.-at-Large Structural Stability Research Council; mem. Candn. Standards Assn.; Internat. Standards Organ.; Chrmn. Candn. Standards Assn. Steering Comte. on Offshore Structures; Community League; Salvation Army (Red Shield Appeal Extve. 1979–87, Chrmn. 1986–87); Club: Skyscraper Toastmasters; Address: Alberta International, Univ. of Alberta, 222 Campus Towers, Edmonton, Alta. T6G 2E1.

**ADAMS, Roy J.,** B.A., M.A., Ph.D.; professor of industrial relations; b. Philadelphia, Pa. 28 June 1940; s. Robert George and Marie (Gaughran) A.; e. Penn State Univ. B.A. (summa cum laude) 1967 (Phi Beta Kappa & Marshal, Coll. of Lib. Arts); Univ. of Wisconsin M.A. 1970, Ph.D. 1973; m. Marilyn d. Kenneth and Edyth Whittaker 5 Jan. 1964; children: Jennifer, Emily; PROFESSOR OF INDUSTRIAL RELATIONS, MCMASTER UNIV. 1973– ; Chrmn., Industrial Relations Dept. 1975–76; Chrmn. & Chief Extve. Offr., Nat. Comn. on Educ. Leave & Productivity 1978; Mem., Ont. Task Force on Literacy & Occup. Health & Safety 1980–84; Advisor to var. govt. & quasi-govt. agencies; frequent conference speaker & univ. lecturer; Visiting Prof., Rutgers Univ. 1980; Inst. for Internat. Studies & Training Japan 1985; Eur. Inst. of Bus. Admin. France 1987; Univ. of Sci. & Tech. Beijing China 1989; Victoria Univ. N.Z. 1992; Visiting Scholar, Internat. Inst. of Labour Studies Switz. 1988; Candn. Pacific Distinguished Visiting Prof., Univ. of Toronto 1990; Visiting Fellow, Inst. for Labour Rsch. Hungary 1991; Co-ord., Internat. Working Group of Researchers & Teachers of Comp. Indus. Relns.; Editor, 'Comparative Industrial Relations Newsletter'; Ed. Bd. Mem. of several profl. journals; Pres., Candn. Indus. Relns. Assn. 1981–82; recipient of several teaching awards, McMaster Univ. incl. most recent MBA Teacher of the Year 1990; 1st Dallas M. Young Disting. Visiting Lectr., Case-Western Reserve Univ. 1989; Raporteur, World Cong. of Indus. Relns. Belgium 1989; Mem., Internat. Indus. Relns. Assn.; Indus. Relns. Rsch. Assn.; Candn. Assn. of Univ. Teachers; author: 'White-Collar Union Growth in Britain and Sweden' 1975, 15 book chapters & over 70 profl. & popular pubns.; co-author: 'Education and Working Canadians' 1979; editor: 'Comparative Industrial Relations 1991; co-editor: 'Industrial Relations Theory' 1993; recreations: running, mountaineering, scuba diving, tennis; clubs: Bruce Trail, Sierra, Marlins Underwater; Home: 50 Whitton Rd., Hamilton, Ont. L8S 4C7; Office: Hamilton, Ont. L8S 4M4.

**ADAMS, Stephen Norman,** Q.C., F.R.S.A., LL.B., C.L.J., F.Inst.D.; lawyer; b. Toronto, Ont. 3 July 1942; s. George D. (C.M.G.) and Helen M. (Field) A.; e. Appleby Coll. Oakville, Ont. 1950–60; Neuchâtel Jr. Coll. Switzerland 1960–61; Huron Coll. Univ. of W. Ont. 1961–63, Fac. of Law LL.B. 1966 (Gold Medalist); Osgoode Hall 1968; m. Linda d. Charles E. and Edythe Frosst 15 Aug. 1964; two d. Susan Patricia, Jennifer Anne; PARTNER, HARRISON, ELWOOD 1971– ; Dir. and Chrmn. Audit Comte., mem. Extve. Ctte., Firan Corp. 1979– ; Harding Carpets Ltd. 1983; Dir. O-Pee-Chee Co. Ltd. 1982– ; Sec. Timberland Equipment Ltd. 1985–89; Dir., Mem. Extve. Ctte., Audit Ctte., Comp. Ctte., and Sec. Coronet Carpets Inc. 1986–92; Corp. Sec., Air Ontario Inc. 1993– ; articled Tory Tory DesLauriers & Binnington, Toronto 1966–67; called to Bar of Ont. 1968; cr. Q.C. 1981; law practice present firm 1968– ; Sr. Instr. Income Tax Law (London) Law Soc. U.C. Bar Admission Course 1976–82; Lectr. in Advanced Corporate Law, Univ. of W. Ont. 1980–92; apptd. Adjunct Prof. of Law, Univ. of W. Ont. 1991; mem. Bd. Comnrs. Police London 1983–85; Dir. Ang. Foundation Can. 1978–88, 1989–92; Univ. Hosp. London 1980–86 (Vice Chrmn. 1984–86); mem. Adv. Bd. London Psychiatric Hosp. 1976–88 (Chrmn. 1985–88); Dir. and Sec. Transplant Internat. (Canada) 1985– ; Dir., London-Middlesex Children's Aid Soc. 1990– , Vice Pres. 1992– ; author: 'Annotated Ontario Business Corporations Act' 1990 (updated twice yearly) and numerous legal articles; Past Dir., Thames Valley Crippled Children's Treatment Centre 1969–79 (Pres. 1975–79); Dir. Univ. Hosp. Found. 1986–91; Mem. Exec. Ctte., Diocese of Huron 1981– ; Chancellor, Anglican Diocese of Huron 1990– ;(Vice-Chancellor 1988–90); Mem., Corp. of Huron Coll. 1978– ; el. F.R.S.A. 1991; el. Fellow, Inst. Dirs. 1988; apptd. C.L.J. 1992; Assessor, 1992 General Synod, Anglican Ch. of Can.; mem. Central Advisory Grp., Pension Ctte., Anglican Ch. of Can. 1992– ; recreations: reading, music, hiking; Clubs: London; Albany (Toronto); Home: 52 Doncaster Pl., London, Ont. N6G 2A5; Office: PO Box 3237, 450 Talbot St., London, Ont. N6A 4K3.

**ADAMS, Hon. William Gilbert,** LL.B.; provincial supreme court justice; b. St. John's, Nfld. 17 June 1923; s. James Palmer and Mary (Cooze) A.; e. Bishop Field Coll. St. John's; Dalhousie Univ. LL.B. 1952; JUSTICE, SUPREME COURT OF NFLD. 1986– ; (previously Chief Judge, Dist. Court of Nfld. 1982–86, when court merged with Supreme Court of Nfld.); law practice St. John's 1953–78, Q.C. 1963; el. twice to Nfld. House of Assembly; St. John's Mun. Council 1961–73; Mayor of St. John's 8 yrs; apptd. Judge, Dist. Court of Nfld. 1978, Supreme Court of Nfld. 1986; Anglican; recreations: yachting, winter fishing; Club: Royal Nfld. Yacht (Past Commodore); Home: Elizabeth Towers, 100 Elizabeth Ave., Apt. 413, St. John's, Nfld. A1B 1R9; Office: 317 Duckworth St., St. John's, Nfld. A1C 5M3.

**ADAMS, William Peter,** Ph.D.; university professor; b. U.K. 17 April 1936; s. William Albert and Ellen Julia (Dickinson) A.; e. Univ. of Sheffield, B.A. (Hons.) 1958; McGill Univ., M.Sc. 1962, Ph.D. 1966; m. Jill d. Florence and Samuel Smith 23 September 1960; children: Joanne, Michèle, Annette, William; M.P.P. (LIBERAL) FOR PETERBOROUGH 1993– ; M.P.P. (Liberal) for Peterborough 1987–90 and Parliamentary Asst. to the Min. of the Environment 1989–90; Dir., McGill Subarctic Rsch. Lab. 1963–66; Founder Chrmn., Dept. of Geog., Trent Univ. 1968–77; variously Dean of Grad. Studies, Assoc. Dean for Science, Assoc. Vice-Pres. 1977–85; Prof., Dept. of Geog., Trent Univ. & Extve. Dir., Assn. of Candn. Univ. for Northern Studies 1985–87; Prof. invité, Univ. du Qué. à Qué. 1984–87; Chair, Standing Ctte. on Social Development, Ont. Legislature 1987–88; Carnegie Arctic Scholar, McGill Univ. 1959–61; Fellow, Arctic Inst. of N. Am.; Citizen of the Year, Peterborough; Prov. of Ont. Citation for Sport; Past Bd. Mem., Trent-Peterborough-Malawi Project; Peterborough Co. Bd. of Edn.; Mem., Internat. Glaciological Soc.; Candn. Assn. of Geog.; Sigma Xi; E. Snow Conf. (Pres. 1984–85); Past Hon. Pres. OAGEE: Nat. Adv. Counc. for Fitness & Amateur Sport; Past Chrmn., Participaction Peterborough; Ont. Summer Games; Energy Savers Peterborough; Peterborough Mid Winter Half Marathon; Cancer Campaign and United Way Peterborough; author of many scientific articles; author: 'Canada and Polar Science Revisited' 1992; co-author: 'Canada and Polar Science' 1987; editor: 'International Geography/La Géographie Internationale' 1972, 'Peterborough and the Kawarthas' 1992; 'Snow and Ice Chemistry and the Atmosphere' 1985; 'Education, Research, Information Systems and the North' 1987; 'Canada's Subarctic Universities/Les universités canadiennes du moyen nord' 1987; recreations: running, skiing; Home: 779 Aylmer St. N., Peterborough, Ont. K9H 3X7; Office: House of Commons, Ottawa, Ont. K1A 0A8.

**ADAMSON, Agar Cawthra Lazier,** M.A.; educator; b. Toronto, Ont. Sept. 1933; s. Rodney and Rosemunde (Lazier) A.; e. Ridley Coll. St. Catharines, Ont.; Carleton Univ. 1962; Queen's Univ. 1966; Univ. of Toronto ABD; m. Mary-Elizabeth d. Daniel and Flora Conway Oct. 1958; children: Geoffrey, Andrea, Blair, Ashley; PROF. OF POL. SCI. ACADIA UNIV. 1966– ; Summer Sch. Univ. of Victoria 1978; Commentator Pub. Affairs Radio and TV; Pres. Pub. Legal Edn. Soc. N.S. 1982–86; mem. N.S. Barristers' Soc. Council 1985–88; Acad. Dir. N.S. Legis. Intership Prog. 1985– ; Dir. Neptune Theatre Found. 1982–85; Chrmn. Fundy Mental Health Centre 1981–83; Chair, Kings Municipal Reform Adv. Ctte. 1993– ; recipient Japan Found. Fellowship 1987; author various articles acad. publs. on Candn. politics; mem. Candn. Pol. Sci. Assn.; commentator (radio & TV) on politics and political life in Canada and Japan; Internat. Pol. Sci. Assn.; Candn. Study Parlt. Group; IPAC; recreations: skiing, walking; Anglican; Home: R.R. 1 Wolfville, N.S. B0P 1X0; Office: Wolfville, N.S. B0P 1X0.

**ADAMSON, Anthony,** O.C. (1974), M.A., LL.D., F.R.A.I.C.; b. Toronto Ont. 7 Oct. 1906; s. Col. Agar, D.S.O., and Mabel (Cawthra) A.; e. Elementary School, Port Credit, Ont.; Wellington College, England; Cambridge Univ., M.A.; London Univ., Eng. (Post-Grad.); LL.D.: Queen's Univ. 1975, Univ. of Windsor 1985; m. Augusta, d. Judge Angus Bonnycastle, 11 Sept. 1931; children: Adrian C., Inigo H.T.C.(d.), Jeremy E.A.; Assoc. Prof. of Town Planning 1955–65, Univ. of Toronto; Vice-Chrmn., Nat. Capital Comn., Ottawa, 1959–67; served for ten yrs. as el. municipal offr. in Twp. of Toronto, Sch. Bd. and Councillor; Reeve 1953–54; Chrmn. of Public Utilities Comn., 1955–56; Pres., Children's Aid Soc., Peel Co., 1956; Pres. (1964), Ont. Welfare Council; Pres. (1946, 1951), Town Planning Inst. Can.; Dir., Nat. Theatre Sch. 1967–69; mem. Ontario Heritage Foundation 1975–81; Ont. Council for Arts (Chrmn. 1969–74); co-author 'The Ancestral Roof'; 'The Gaiety of Gables'; 'The Hallowed Walls' (Gov. Gen.'s Award for non-fiction) 1975; 'Cornerstones of Order' 1983; awarded Coronation Medal; Jubilee Medal; Award of Merit, City of Toronto 1978; Gabrielle Leger Medal, Heritage Can. 1981; Conservative; Anglican; Home: 23 Rosedale Road, Toronto, Ont. M4W 2P1.

**ADAMSON, Barry;** management consultant; b. Halifax, N.S. 10 Aug.1944; s. George and Nesta (Brett) A.; e. Port Credit Secondary Sch. 1963; McMaster Univ. B.A. 1966; m. Margaret d. Russell and Peggy West of Vermont 1967; children: Daniel, Christy; PRES., MURRAY AXMITH & ASSOC. 1980– ; Mktg. Rsch., Advertising and Human Resources, Dominion Stores 1966–71; Mgr. Staff Devel. and Mgr. Planning and New Programs Ont. Govt. 1971–80; author: 'Recovering from Downsizing' Financial Post 1984; co-author (with Murray Axmith) 'Managing Large Scale Staff Reductions' Univ. of W. Ont. Bus. Quar. 1983; recreations: hockey, skiing, birdstudy, tennis; Home: 1 Arkendo Dr., Oakville, Ont. L6J 5T8; Office: 130 Bloor St. W., Ste. 800, Toronto, Ont. M5S 1N5.

**ADAMSON, Walter Robert;** retired graphic arts executive; b. Toronto, Ont. 16 Apr. 1914; s. William Robert and Ethel May (Hunter) A.; e. Howard Park Pub. Sch. Toronto 1927; Oakville (Ont.) High Sch. 1932; Carnegie Inst. of Technol. B.Sc. in Printing 1936; m. Dorothy d. Acton Larter 26 June 1943; children: Robert Martin, Donna Marilyn (Wright), Luella May (Frazer); joined Mono Lino Typesetting Co. Ltd. 1936, Secy.-Treas. 1944, Vice Pres. and Gen. Mgr. 1948, Pres. and Gen. Mgr. 1958, Chrmn. and Pres. 1967–85; Pres. and Dir. Lettering Designs Ltd. 1964–85; served with Royal Candn. Army Service Corps 1942–44; Dir. Oakville-Trafalgar Mem. Hosp. 1951–57; mem. Bd. Mgrs. Knox Presb. Ch. Oakville 1945–51, Chrmn. 1950–51, Elder 1946, Clk. of Session 1961–89; Dir., Toronto Graphic Arts Assn. 1951–60, Pres. 1957–59; Typographers Internat. Assn. 1954–70, Pres. 1958–59; Graphic Arts Industries Assn. 1959–69, Treas. 1963–65, Vice Pres. 1965–68; Council Printing Industries Can. 1970–84, Chrmn. 1977–78; Secy.-Treas. Toronto Typographic Assn. 1945–52, Pres. 1953; mem. Bd. Trade Metrop. Toronto, Educ. Comte. 1972–81, Publs. Adv. Comte. 1977–85; Presbyterian; recreations: golf, curling; Clubs: Oakville Golf; Oakville Curling; Bd. of Trade Country Club; Home: 22 Brookfield Rd., Oakville, Ont. L6K 2Y5.

**ADASKIN, Gordon,** R.C.A.; painter; educator; b. Toronto, Ont. 7 June 1931; s. Harry Adaskin; e. apprentice of Frank Lloyd Wright 1951; Vancouver Sch. of Art grad. 1952 (Drawing & Painting Hons.); Prov. Normal Sch. Vancouver grad. 1955; children: Jon, Susan; Docent and Asst. Curator Vancouver Art Gallery 1955–56; Art Teacher and Counsellor Vancouver Sch. System 1956–62; Instr. in Drawing, Painting, Anat. and Art Hist., Alta. Coll. of Art Calgary 1963–66; Painting Instr. Banff Sch. of Fine Art summers 1964, 1965, 1970, Instr. in Drawing summers 1975, 1976, Lectr. in Basic Design Banff Centre Theatre Crafts 1972–77, Educ. Program Consultant to Theatre Div. 1977; Instr. in Design Univ. of Alta. summers 1963, 1966; Asst. Prof. of Environmental Studies Univ. of Man. 1966, Prof. 1971, Chrmn. of Basic Design (5 yrs.) 1975; Guest Lectr. Univ. of B.C.

1973; considerable radio and TV experience as commentator, interviewer, script writer and program consultant; solo exhns. incl.: London (Eng.) House 1953; Maison Canadienne Paris 1954; Tempus Gallery Vancouver 1963, Little Gallery 1966; Applied Arts Centre Calgary 1965; Banff Sch. of Fine Arts 1964, 1965; Univ. of Man. 1967, 1969, 1980; Griffiths Gallery Vancouver 1967, 1968, 1969; Studio Gallery West Vancouver 1973; Private Studio Shows Vancouver 1973, Banff 1975, Winnipeg 1976; Peter Whyte Gallery Banff 1976; Bau-Xi Gallery Vancouver 1981; Melnychenko Gallery Winnipeg 1981; rep. in numerous group shows Can. and USA, pub. and private colls.; mem. Council Royal Candn. Acad. Arts; Home: 375 Lilac St., Winnipeg, Man. R3M 2S8; Office: Faculty of Architecture, Univ. of Manitoba, Winnipeg, Man. R3T 2N2.

**ADASKIN, Harry,** O.C.; LL.D.(Dalhousie), LL.D.(Simon Fraser), LL.D.(U.B.C); violinist; b. 1901; m. Frances Marr (C.M.); original of Hart House String Quartet 1923–38 and toured with them in Can., U.S., U.K., France, Italy, Holland, Denmark and Sweden; made N.Y. solo debut Feb. 1947; for some yrs. C.B.C. Intermission Commentator on the Sunday Afternoon N.Y. Philharmonic broadcasts; Prof. of Music, Univ. of B.C., Head of Dept. of Music, 1946–58 (retired 1972); autobigraphy 'A Fiddler's World' Vol. 1, 1977; 'A Fiddler's Choice' Vol. 2, 1981; jury member, violin contest, Naumberg Award, New York City, June 1984; Address: 4958 Angus, Vancouver, B.C. V6M 3M5.

**ADASKIN, Murray,** O.C., LL.D. (Univ. of Lethbridge 1970, Univ. of Saskatchewan 1984, on the occasion of its Diamond Jubilee), D.Mus. (Brandon Univ. 1972, Univ. of Windsor 1977, Univ. of Victoria 1984); composer; b. Toronto, Ont. 28 Mar. 1906; s. Samuel and Nisha (Perstnov) A.; e. Royal Conserv. of Music, Toronto; Paris, France; Music Acad. of the West, Calif.; Aspen Sch. of Music, Colo.; m. Frances (dec. 22 Aug. 1988), d. Frederick William James. 16 July 1931; m. Asta-Dorothea, d. Lars Christian and Sigrid Knudsen-Trautman Larsen 7 May 1989; Composer-in-Residence, (the first in Canada) Univ. of Sask., since 1966 (Prof. and Head of Dept. of Music 1952–66); mem. Canada Council 1966–69; for many years Violinist with Toronto Symphony Orchestra; composer of over 100 publ. and recorded vocal, chamber music and orchestral works, incl. Centennial opera 'Grant Warden of the Plains' and many commissioned works, incl. 'Of Man and the Universe' for Expo, 'Coronation Overture' and 'Algonquin Symphony'; two hr. CBC broadcast, 'Profile of Murray Adaskin at 65' 1971; 'The Travelling Musicians' narrative by P.K. Page premiered Jan. 1984; six hr. CBC broadcast 1989, 'Murray Adaskin - A Canadian Music Retrospective' repeat broadcast 1990; Premiere, 'Concerto for Orchestra' commissioned by Victoria Sym. Orch. (Can. Council grant) dedicated to Myfanwy Pavelic, Candn. Painter; 'Concerto for Viola and Orchestra' dedicated to violist, Rivka Golani, 1991; Woodwind Quintet No. 2 (1993) commissioned by CBC Ottawa; Quartet No. 2 (1994) dedicated to Lafayette String Quartet; 'Murray Adaskin Retrospective' CJRT-FM (Toronto) broadcast 1993; rec'd. Sr. Arts Fellowship, Canada Council 1960–61, to work in Europe; chosen 'Citizen of the Year' Saskatoon 1969; Bd. mem. Saskatoon Art Centre 1966–67; apptd., Officer of the Order of Canada' 1980; Hon. Life mem., Saskatoon and Toronto Musicians' Assns.; mem. Candn. League of Composers since founding; Royal Soc. of Arts; SOCAN; Centennial Medal, 1967; Lifetime Award for Excellence in the Arts, Saskatchewan Arts Bd. 1991; 1994 featured Candn. Composer, Saskatchewan Music Festival Assn.; Club: Joel (Saskatoon); Address: 3020 Devon Rd., Victoria, B.C. V8R 6C9.

**ADDY, The Hon. George Arthur,** LL.B., B.A., E.D., C.D.; retired judge; b. Ottawa, Ont. 28 Sept. 1915; s. late Frederick William and Clorida Richer de la Flèche A.; e. Univ. of Ottawa, B.A.; Osgoode Hall Law Sch., Toronto; m. Joyce Rose Sylvia, d. late John Head, April 1942; children: Paul, Clive, Nicole, Vincent, George; mem. Court Martial App. Bd. 1953–59; app. Sup. Court of Ont. 1967; Fed. Court of Canada, 1973; Court Martial Appeal Court, 1974–90; called to Bar of Ont. (in absentia) 1942; Q.C. 1960; Partner Vincent & Addy 1945–55; Partner Vincent, Addy & Charbonneau 1955–60, Sr. Ptner. 1960; served with Militia (Regt. de Hull) 1934–40, active service Eng. and Aleutian Islands) 1940–45; Commdr. Univ. Ottawa C.O.T.C. 1945–56; C.O. Regt. de Hull (21st Armoured) 1956–58; retired rank Lt.-Col.; apptd. Hon. Col. Regt. de Hull 1973; Past Pres. and Life mem. R.C.A.C. Assn.; mem., Roy. Candn. Mil. Inst., Toronto; Founding mem. (Hon. mem. and Past Pres.) Cercle Universitaire d'Ottawa; Hon. Gov. Ottawa Univ.; Heart Inst. Adv. Bd., Civic Hosp.; R. Catholic; recreation: yachting; Home: 737 Island Park Dr., Ottawa, Ont. K1Y 0B9.

**ADDY, George,** B.A., LL.B.; public servant, lawyer; b. Ottawa, Ont. 31 May 1953; s. George Arthur and Joyce Rose Sylvia (Head) A.; e. Univ. of Ottawa B.A. 1974, LL.B. 1977; m. Lyse Hélène d. Eugène and Hélène Marchand; children: George Keith, Emilie Kate; DIRECTOR OF INVESTIGATION AND RESEARCH (COMPETITION ACT), GOVT. OF CANADA 1993– ; Acting Vice-Pres. of Legal Serv., Extve. Interchange, Canada Ports Corp., Govt. of Can. 1985; Special Counsel, Dept. of Justice Can. 1988–89; Partner, Gowling, Strathy & Henderson 1979–89; Sr. Dep. Dir. of Investigation & Research (Mergers), Bur. of Competition Policy, Industry Can. 1989–93; Mem., Law Soc. of U.C.; Candn. Bar Assn.; Internat. Bar Assn.; Lecturer, Univ. of Ottawa; author/co-author of several articles, reports & newsletters; recreations: skiing; Office: Place du Portage, Ottawa, Ont. K1A 0C9.

**ADELL, Bernard Leo,** B.A., LL.B., D. Phil.; university professor; b. Edmonton, Alta. 26 Aug. 1939; e. Univ. Alta., B.A. 1960; LL.B. 1961; Oxford Univ., D.Phil 1967; married; children: Simon, Rebecca, Elena; PROF. LAW, QUEEN'S UNIV.; joined present univ. 1964; Assoc. Dean, Faculty of Law 1969–71; Dean, 1977–82; labour arbitrator since 1966; Visiting scholar, Univ. Aix-Marseille 1971–72; Consultant on law of strikes, Dept. of Justice (Can.) 1975; labour legislation expert, Internat. Labour Office (Swaziland 1976); Visiting scholar, Internat. Inst. Labour Studies (Geneva) 1982–83; Consultant to Ont. Task Force on Inflation Protection for Employment Pension Plans 1987; Project Dir., Ont. Law Reform Comn. Study on Adjudication of Workplace Disputes 1990; Visiting scholar, Univ. of Montreal School of Industrial Relations 1992–93; author books and articles on labour relations and employment law; Rhodes scholar for Alta. 1961; mem. Law Soc. Upper Can.; Office: Queen's Univ., Kingston, Ont. K7L 3N6.

**ADELMAN, Howard,** B.A., M.A., Ph.D.; university professor; b. Toronto, Ont. 7 Jan. 1938; s. Harry and Frances (Duviner) A.; e. Univ. of Toronto, B.A. 1960, M.A. 1963, Ph.D. 1971; 2nd m. Nancy Jean d. Gary and Jean Garrett 25 June 1984; children: Daniel Jacob, Gabriel Benjamin (2nd m.); Jeremy Ian, Shonagh Esther, Rachel Eva, Eric Reuben (1st m.); PROFESSOR OF PHILOSOPHY, YORK UNIV. 1980– ; Lectr., Univ. of Toronto 1963–64; Asst. Prof., York Univ. 1966–70; Assoc. Prof. 1970–80; Assoc. & Acting Dean, Atkinson Coll. 1969–71; Chrmn., Philos. Dept. 1974–77; Dir., Grad. Prog. in Philos. 1980–83; Nat. Chrmn., Candn. Profs. for Peace in the Middle East 1983–84; Dir., Refugee Documentation Project 1982–86; Dir., Centre for Refugee Studies 1988–93; Vice-Chrmn., York Univ. Senate 1980–81; Chrmn. 1981–82; Mem., Holy Blossom Synagogue; author numerous articles in books and journals on refugees and immigration policy; author: 'The Beds of Academe' 1970; 'The Holiversity' 1973; 'Canada and the Indochinese Refugees' 1982; editor: 'The Indochinese Refugee Movement in Canada' 1980; 'Refuge' 1983–86, 1988–93; 'Refugee Policy: Canada and the United States' 1991; 'Hungarian Refugees' 1993; 'Legitimate and Illegitimate Discrimination' forthcoming; co-editor: (with Dennis Lee) 'The University Game' 1968; (with C. Michael Lanphier) 'Refuge or Asylum? A Choice for Canada' 1990; (with Lois Foster, Meyer Burstein & Allan Borowski) 'Immigration and Refugee Policy: Australia and Canada Compared' 1993; (with John Sorenson) 'African Refugees' 1993; Home: 64 Wells Hill Ave., Toronto, Ont. M5R 3A8; Office: Rm. 322, York Lanes Bldg., Centre for Refugee Studies, York Univ., 4700 Keele St., Downsview, Ont. M3J 1P3.

**ADES, David Samuel,** B.Sc.; executive; b. Cairo, Egypt 19 Nov. 1929; s. Raphael Ezra and Jeanne (Yayon) A.; e. Eng. Sch. Cairo; Manchester Univ. B.Sc.; A.M.C.T. 1951; children: Rochele Lee, Ralph Michael; CHRMN., PRES. & DIR. REALCAP HOLDINGS LTD. 1957– ; Pres. & Dir. RealCap, Inc. (U.S.); RealCap Funds, Inc. (U.S.); Dir.: Standrue Investments Ltd. 1981– ; recreations: swimming, cross-country skiing, reading; Club: Granite; Home: 4005 Bayview Ave., PH#5, Willowdale, Ont. M2M 3Z9; Office: Ste. 604, 2161 Yonge St., Toronto, Ont. M4S 3A6.

**ADILMAN, Sid;** newspaper columnist; b. Saskatoon, Sask. 27 Oct. 1937; s. Lawrence and Clarice (Goldstein) A.; e. Tecumseh Pub. Sch., South Coll. Inst., Central Coll Inst., London, Ont.; Univ. of W. Ont. B.A. work in Eng. and Sociol. plus degree course in Journalism; m. Toshiko Suzuki, Japan 1 May 1965; two s. Mio, Nobu; Entertainment Editor, Toronto Star 1987–91; columnist since 1971; Candn. Bureau Chief, Variety 1964–91; joined Toronto Star 1960–63; rejoined 1971; Toronto Telegram 1963–71; co-author 'Dining Out in Toronto'; contrib. to various books; author articles Candn. and U.S. mags. and newspapers; Jewish; recreation: reading; Home: 74 Albany Ave., Toronto, Ont. M5R 3C3.

**ADITYA, Gora,** B.Sc.; biochemist, executive; b. India 5 Dec. 1940; s. Suhas Kumar and Subarna Prova A.; e. Univ. of Calcutta, Univ. of Toronto B.Sc. 1960; m. Phyllis d. John and Zelma Gideon 10 April 1965; children: Peter, Paul, Jennifer; FOUNDER & PRESIDENT, MED-CHEM LABORATORIES LIMITED 1970– ; emigrated to Canada 1964; Jr. Chemist, then Chief Technologist, Dept. of Biochem., Sunnybrook Hosp. 1964–72; Med-Chem was started as a diagnostic clinical lab (now 4th largest in Ont. with over 600 staff members serving over 1500 physicians, 80 nursing homes; processes over 150,000 blood samples per month); Vice-Pres., MCTU Diagnostics Ltd.; Pres., Philo Investments Ltd.; Med-Chem Florida; Dir., Polar Latex India (mfr. of latex condoms); Methodist; Mem., Candn. Soc. of Clin. Chemists; Candn. Soc. of Lab. Technol.; Ont. Assn. of Med. Labs.; recreations: badminton, Indian music esp. Tagore's songs; club: Club 8150; Home: 34 Cobblestone Dr., Thornhill, Ont. L3T 4E4; Office: 8510 Sheppard Ave. E., Scarborough, Ont. M1B 5K2.

**ADRIAN, Donna Jean,** M.L.S.: librarian; b. Morden, Man. 28 Aug. 1940; d. William Gordon and Dorothy Jean (Gregory) Frazer; e. Brandon (Man.) Coll. Inst.; Brandon Coll. B.A. 1962; McGill Univ. B.L.S. 1963, M.L.S. 1968; Que. Class I Teacher's Cert.-Lib. Science 1965; Laubach Literacy Canada Tutor Certificate 1982; Master Tutor Certificate 1984; m. James Ross Adrian 17 July 1965; LIBRARIAN, ROSEMERE HIGH SCHOOL (part-time) 1980– ; Lib. Consultant (part-time) Laurenval Sch. Bd. 1980– ; Lectr. (part-time) Concordia Univ. Lib. Studies Program 1974– ; Lib., Rosemere High Sch. and Supvr. Laurenvale Elem. Sch. Libs. 1963–66; Lib.-Dept. Head, Rosemere High Sch. 1966–74; Lib. Consultant (part-time) North Island Regional Sch. Bd. and Lib. (part-time) Rosemere High Sch. 1974–79; Lib. Consultant, Laurenval Sch. Bd. 1979–80; Literacy tutor, Laurenval School Board 1982–; mem. ed. bd. 'Canadian Materials'; 'Emergency Librarian'; mem. Copyright Ctte., Que. Dept. of Educ. 1989– ; mem. Candn. Lib. Assn. (Pres. CSLA); Que. Assn. Sch. Libs. (Pres.); Corp. Prof. Libs. Que.; Am. Lib. Assn.; Internat. Assn. Sch. Librarianship (Conf. Co-Chrmn.); Protestant; recreations: scuba diving, bridge, bowling, swimming; Home: 194 Roi Du Nord, Ste-Rose, Laval, Qué. H7L 1W5; Office: 530 Northcote Rd., Rosemere, Qué. J7A 1Y2.

**AFFLECK, Ian Keith,** B.Sc., A.M., Ph.D., F.R.S.C.; physicist; b. Vancouver, B.C. 2 July 1952; s. William Burchill and Evelyn Mary Colenso (Carter) A.; e. Trent Univ., B.Sc. 1975; Harvard Univ., A.M. 1976, Ph.D. 1979; m. Glenda d. Sydney and Marguerite Harman 2 July 1977; children: Geoffrey Roger, Ingrid Katherine; PROF. OF PHYSICS, UNIV. OF B.C. 1987– ; Jr. Fellow, Harvard Soc. of Fellows 1979–81; Asst. Prof., Princeton Univ. 1981–87; Vis. Scientist, C.E.N. Saclay France 1984–85; rsch. on theory of elementary particles, condensed matter; Gov. Gen.'s Medal 1975; Fellow, Sloan Foundation 1983–87; Fellow, Candn. Inst. for Advanced Rsch. 1987– , (Confederation Fellow 1988– ;); Stacey Prize 1988; Herzberg Medal 1990; Rutherford Medal 1991; U.B.C. Killam Prize 1991; author of var. articles in sci. jours. and proc.; recreations: swimming, windsurfing; Home: Vancouver, B.C.; Office: Dept. of Physics, Univ. of B.C., Vancouver, B.C. V6T 1Z1.

**AFFLECK, W. Bruce,** Q.C., B.A., LL.B.; lawyer; b. Oshawa, Ont. 3 May 1931; s. William Affleck; e. O'Neill Coll. & Vocational Inst. Oshawa 1950; Univ. of Toronto Victoria Coll. B.A. 1953; Osgoode Hall Law Sch. Toronto LL.B. 1957; m. Frances Myrtle Walker 14 Feb. 1981; two s. Robert Bruce (dec. 27 July 1986), William John; step-children: Derek William, Kelly April, Jason Michael; PARTNER, AFFLECK, SOSNA & SHAUGHNESSY; called to Bar of Ont. 1957; cr. Q.C. 1970; Asst. Crown Atty. Co. Ont. 1959–61; Crown Atty. Co. Ont. Region Durham 1961–77; Dir. Crown Attys. E. Central Ont. Region 1975–77; Chrmn. Bail Comte. Ont. Crown Attys. Assn. (brief 1967), Secy. of Assn. 1965–67; Dir. and former Secy.-Treas. Oshawa Gen. Hockey Club 1962–86; Vice Pres. Whitby Warriors Sr. 'A' Hockey Club 1973–74; Dir. Oshawa Falcon TV Sr. 'A' Softball Club 1975–77; Pres. Cardiac Rehabilitation Assn. 1976–77; Dir. Oshawa Green Gaels 1977–79; Nat. Pres. Candn. Assn. Children Learning Disabilities 1969–71; Pres. Ont. Assn. Children Learning Disabilities 1964–68, 1968–69; Pres. Boy Scouts Can. Oshawa & Dist. 1974–75; Guest Lectr. Queen's Univ. Law Sch., Windsor Univ. Law Sch., Osgoode Hall Law Sch., Univ. of Toronto Law Sch.; Lectr., RCMP Coll. Ottawa 1966–77; Ont. Prov. Police Coll. 1962–74;

Candn. Fire Investigator's Sch. 1967; Coroners for Prov. Ont. on Inquest Evidence 1962–77; Prov. Judge's Assn. 1976–83; named Hon. Col. State of Miss. 1964; one of top 3 Crown Attys. in Can. (Candn. Mag.) 1977; recipient Outstanding Young Man Award Jr. Chamber Comm. 1968, named Hon. Life mem.; Queen's Medal for Outstanding Performance 1977; author various articles prof. journs.; el. Bencher Law Soc. Upper Can. 1979–83 and 1983–87; Dir. Criminal Lawyers Assn. 1981–83; Certified as a Specialist in Criminal Law, Law Soc. of Upper Can. 1988; Ont. Fed. Prog. Conserv. Assn.; mem. Candn. Bar Assn.; P. Conservative; Protestant; recreations: public speaking, reading, hiking, swimming; Home: R.R.1, Hampton, Ont. L0B 1J0; Office: 214 Colborne St. W., Whitby, Ont. L1N 1X2.

**AGASSI, Joseph,** M.Sc., Ph.D., F.R.S.C.; professor; b. Jerusalem 7 May 1927; s. Samuel Meïr and Fruma Hassida (Reichmann) Birnbaum; e. Hebrew Univ., M.Sc. 1951; Univ. of London, Ph.D. 1956; m. Judith d. Margarete Buber-Neumann and Rafael Buber 10 Aug. 1949; children: Tirzah, Aaron; PROF., YORK UNIV. 1983– ; (Fall semesters) & TEL-AVIV UNIV. 1971– ; (Spring semesters); Rsch. Assoc., Ctr. for Adv. Study in Behavioural Sci. 1956–57; Lectr., London Sch. of Econ. 1957–60; Reader & Philos. Dept. Head, Hong Kong Univ. 1960–63; Assoc. Philos. Prof., Univ. of Illinois 1963–65; Philos. Prof., Boston Univ. 1965–84; Fellow AAAS; Fellow, World Academy of Arts, Science and Letters; Rsch. Fellow, Alexander-von-Humboldt Found., res. at Zentrum für Interdisz. Forschung, Bielefeld 1977–78 and at the Economics Dept. Frankfurt Univ. 1987; Visiting Bean Prof. of Science, Technology and Public Policy and Visiting Cowling Prof. of Philos., Carleton Coll., MN, winter 1989; Visiting Prof. of Phil. Sci., Universidad Antonoma de Mexico, Iztapalapa, Mexico, summer 1990; Visiting Rsch. Prof., Hadassah Med. Center, Hebrew Univ. 1990; Visiting Prof., Karl-Franzen Universität Graz, spring 1991; offered Rockefeller fellowship but declined 1959; Fellow, Royal Soc. of Can.; Fellow, World Acad. of Art and Science; author: 'Towards an Historiography of Science' 1963, 'The Continuing Revolution' 1968, 'Faraday as a Natural Philosopher' 1971, 'Science in Flux' 1975, 'Towards a Rational Philosophical Anthropology' 1977, 'Science and Society' 1981, 'Technology' 1985, 'The Gentle Art of Philosophical Polemics' 1988; 'The Siblinghood of Humanity: Introduction to Philosophy' 1991; 'Radiation Theory and the Quantum Revolution' 1993; 'A Philosopher's Apprentice' 1993; co-author: 'Paranoia' 1976, 'Psychiatry as Medicine' 1983; 'Diagnosis: Philosophical and Medical Perspectives' 1990; editor: 'Philosophical Forum (Vol. 1)' 1968, 'Psychiatric Diagnosis' 1981; co-editor: 'Scientific Philosophy Today' 1982, 'Rationality: The Critical View' 1987, and about 400 contributions to the learned press; recreations: music, walking; Office: Dept. of Philos., York Univ., North York, Ont. M3J 1P3 and Tel-Aviv Univ., Tel-Aviv 69978.

**AGNAÏEFF, Michel**; union executive; b. Cairo, Eqypt 16 Sept. 1939; s. Constantin Kambulatovitch and Vera Anatolevna (Kahanskaya) A.; e. Coll. de La Salle Cairo Bacc. français 2ème partie 1958; Centre pédagogique La Sallien Cairo Certificat d'aptitude pédagogique 1959; Min. of Edn. Qué. Brevet A 1967; Univ. of Montréal studies in French Lit. & Linguistics 1967–69; Laval Univ. post-graduate studies in Policy Analysis 1981–83; m. Normande d. Joseph-Aimé and Jeannette Villeneuve 30 Dec. 1985; children: Constantin, Vladimir, Igor (by previous mariage), Tanya; DIR.-GEN. CENTRALE DE L'ENSEIGNEMENT DU QUEBEC (CEQ) 1976– ; teacher 1959–63 and mem. film ind. 1963–66 Cairo; secondary sch. teacher and head French dept. Can. 1966–70; Union Offr. and Exec. mem. Alliance des professeurs de Montréal 1968–71; Sec. CEQ 1971–72, Dir. of Communications 1972–76; past Assoc. Pres. NDP Can.; Vice Pres., Candn. Comn. for UNESCO and past Chair, Subcomn. for Educ.; General Secy., Comité syndical francophone de l'éducation et de la formation 1990– ; Home: 1037 J.J. Joubert, Duvernay, Laval, Qué. H7G 4J5; Office: 9405, Sherbrooke E., Montréal, Qué. H1L 6P3.

**AGNEW, Gordon,** B.A.Sc., Ph.D.; university professor; b. Milton, Ont. 22 May 1954; e. Milton Dist. H.S. 1973; Univ. of Waterloo B.A.Sc. 1978, Ph.D. 1982; ASSOCIATE PROF., UNIV. OF WATERLOO; joined present univ. 1982; Teacher, Swiss Fed. Inst. of Technol. 1984; Dir., Computer Communication Network Group, U. of W. 1987–91; Co-founder, Möbius Encryption Technologies (Data Security co.) 1985; Fellow, Inst. for Combinations and its Applications 1990; Dir., Internat. Assn. for Cryptologic Rsch. (IACR); Dir. & Sec., Candn. Jiu Jitsu Assn.; Mem., IEEE; IACR; ICA, APEO; recreations: martial arts (4th degree black belt), golf, skiing, fishing, sailing, hiking; Office: Waterloo, ON N2L 3G1.

**AGOSTINI, Lucio;** composer; conductor; b. Fano, Italy 30 Dec. 1913; s. Guiseppe A.; e. began musical studies with father (woodwinds) continuing with Louis Michiels and Henri Miro (harmony and composition) and Peter Van der Meerschen (cello); m.; children: Lola, Elio; came to Can. 1916; at 15 played tenor saxophone, bass clarinet and cello in father's theatre orchestra and at 16 played cello in Eugène Chartier's Montreal Philharmonic; conducted Red and White Revue McGill Univ. 1929 and 1930 and first radio show on CFCF; began composing film scores for Associated Screen News 1932–44, latterly as Music Dr.; completed scores over 150 shorts incl. monthly instalments for NFB's 'Canada at War' and 'The World in Action' series; began conducting CRBC radio network 1934 and subsequently CBC; programs incl. 'Mantilles et castagnettes,' 'The Little Review' and 'Carnival in Venice'; composed and conducted incidental music for Andrew Allan's CBC radio drama series 'Stage' 1944–55, CBC 'Wednesday Night' Shakespeare productions, CBC radio's 'Ford Theatre' 1949–55 and several variety programs incl. own 'Strictly for Strings' 1951–52 and 'Appointment with Agostini' 1954–55, 1958–61; became conductor and arranger for CBC TV 'Front Page Challenge' 1957; other programs incl. 'Music Album' 1968, 'Collage' 1969, 'Music to Remember' 1970; compositions incl. 'Shakespearean Suite for Strings' 1948, 'Piano Concerto' 1948, 'Willie the Squowse' 1968, 'Gibraltar' 1975, 'Divorce' 1976; scores for feature films 'Inside Out' 1975, 'Ragtime Summer' 1977, 'The Little Brown Burro' 1978 and 'Ichabod Crane' 1978; 'Flute Concerto' (1960) recorded by Nicholas Fiore with Albert Pratz Orchestra; 'Trio Québécois' (1970) written for Avrahm Galper; in preparation an opera based on life of Haitian 'Papa Doc' Duvalier; has written arrangements for various recordings; Winner of the ACTRA 'John Drainie Award' (for distinguished contribution to broadcasting) 1983; recipient Nice (France) Music Festival Award 1957; mem. Composers, Authors & Publ. Assn. Can.; Address: #402, 80 Inverlochy Blvd., Thornhill, Ont. L3T 4P3.

**AGRO, John L.,** Q.C.; barrister and solicitor; b. Vinemount, Ont. 4 Dec. 1919; s. Sam and Grace (Guagliano) A.; e. Cathedral H.S.; Univ. of Toronto, B.A. 1942; called to Bar 1949; m. (1) Mary Anna d. Paul & Anna Bonk 10 Sept. 1949 (dec. 19 Oct. 1961); m. (2) Frances Willemene d. Harold and Frances Gallagher 20 Oct. 1962; children: Marjoh, Brenda Ellen, Charles, David, Hugh, Frances; Chrmn., Hamilton Harbour Comn. 1976–89; appointed Q.C. 1959; elected Bencher, certified as a Specialist in Civil & Criminal Litigation, Law Soc. of Upper Can. 1983; served in U.K. & Europe, CDA, Lieut. & a/Capt.May 1942–Dec. 1945; Counsel & founder of Candn. Football League Players' Assn.; formerly Counsel to Ont. Harness Horsemen's Assn.; Horsemen's Benevolent & Protective Assn.; named Italo-Canadian Citizen of the Year 1984; named to Gallery of Distinction, City of Hamilton 1989; Emilius Irving Award, Hamilton Law Assoc. 1989; Life Mem., Candn. Ports & Harbour Assoc. 1991; awarded Law Society Medal 1992.

**AHERN, T. Sean,** B.Sc., M.B.A.; financial executive; b. Campbelleton, N.B. 30 Aug. 1940; s. Philip Charles and Constance Mary (Cluffe) A.; e. St. Mary's Univ. B.Sc. 1963; Queen's Univ. M.B.A. 1966; m. Donna d. Donald and Stella Bruce 22 Aug. 1964; children: Stephen, Kelly, Michaeline; SR. VICE-PRES. & CHIEF FINANCIAL OFFR., MONTREAL TRUST, FINANCIAL INSTITUTION 1993– ; Systems Analyst, John Labatt Ltd. 1966–68; Asst. to Sr. Partner, Price Waterhouse 1969–71; Supvr., Mktg. & Planning, Mercantile Bank of Can. 1971–72; Gen. Mgr. and Chief Accountant 1972–75; Vice-Pres. & Gen. Mgr. 1975–76; Sr. Vice-Pres., Admin. 1976–80; Corp. Devel. 1980–81; Vice-Pres. & Chief Financial Offr., Canterra Energy Ltd. 1981–88; Sabbatical (travelling) 1988–92; recreations: squash, skiing, golf; clubs: Montreal Badminton & Squash, Royal Montreal Golf; Home: 1335 Redpath Cres., Montreal, Que. H3G 1A1; Office: 1800 McGill College, 17th floor, Montreal, Que. H3A 3K9.

**AHIAKPOR, James Cobla Willington,** M.Sc., M.A., Ph.D.; educator; b. Keta, Ghana 11 Dec. 1945; s. John Kwami Ahiakpor and Paula Dofi (Hlogbe); e. Univ. of Ghana B.Sc. 1971, M.Sc. 1974; Univ. of B.C. M.A. 1977; Univ. of Toronto Ph.D. 1981; m. Olivia d. Victor Akabutu and Gladys Anima (George) 1974; children: Michael Dodzi, Andrew Kafui, Daniel Edem; PROF. OF ECON., CALIFORNIA STATE UNIV. 1993– ; Tutor in Money & Banking Sch. of Continuing Edn. Univ. of Toronto 1979–91; Rsch. Fellow/Lectr. Univ. of Ghana 1973–81; Asst. Prof. Saint Mary's Univ. 1981–86, Assoc. Prof. 1986–93; Assoc. Prof. of Econ., California State Univ. 1991–93; recipient Univ. of Ghana Post-Graduate Scholarship 1972–73; Nat. Best Essay Award Ghana Assn. Mfrs. 1972; Univ. of Toronto Rsch. Fellowship 1980; Univ. of Toronto Doctoral Fellowship 1979–81; Inst. for Humane Studies Summer Fellowship 1986; Koch Fellowship 1992; Award of Excellence (Hon. Mention) conf. paper Adm. Sci's Assn. Can. 1984; author 'The Economic Consequences of Political Independence: The Case of Bermuda' 1989; 'Multinationals and Economic Development: An Integration of Competing Theories' 1990; numerous articles acad. jours., books and other mags.; interviewed CBC radio progs. & local newspapers; mem. Candn. Econ. Assn.; W. Econ. Assn.; Hist. Econ. Soc.; R. Catholic; recreations: music, reading; Home: 3163 Christopher Way, San Ramon, CA 94583; Office: Hayward, CA 94542.

**AHRONHEIM, Gerald Alexander,** B.Sc., M.D.; physician; educator; b. Jackson, Mich. 13 Feb. 1941; s. Jacques Heinz, M.D., F.C.A.P. and Sylvia Edith (Hirschhorn) A., M.D.; e. pub. and high schs. Jackson Mich. 1958; Univ. of Mich. B.Sc. 1962, M.D. 1966; m. Naomi B., M.D. d. Nathan and Ida Stein 7 May 1978; children: Sara, Devorah, Anna-Leah; MEM. DEPT. OF MICROBIOL. & IMMUNOL. (SECTS. INFECTIOUS DISEASES & VIROL.) AND DEPT. OF PEDIATRICS, STE-JUSTINE'S HOSP. 1979– ;and HEAD, INFECTIOUS DISEASES CONSULTATION SERVICE; Prof. adjoint de clinique, Dept. de Microbiologie, Univ. de Montréal 1982–88, Prof. agrégé de clinique 1988– ; Attending staff Montréal Children's Hosp. 1975– ; (Infectious Diseases Div. 1975–79); Rotating Intern Philadelphia Gen. Hosp. 1966–67; Capt. USAF Med. Corps Chanute AFB Ill. and K–2 AB Taegu, Korea 1967–69; gen. med. and surg. practice Jackson, Mich. 1967, 1969; Trainee in Pediatrics Ohio State Univ. 1970; Resident in Pediatrics Children's Hosp. Boston 1970–72; Fellow in Pediatric Infectious Diseases Duke Univ. 1972–75; Guest Worker LPD/NIAID Bethesda, Md. 1973; Asst. Prof. of Pediatrics McGill Univ. 1975–83; Fellow in Medical Microbiol. Univ. de Montréal 1980–81; author or co-author 40 publs. and abstracts; mem. Candn. Infectious Diseases Soc.; Infectious Diseases Soc. Am.; Am. Soc. Microbiol.; Candn. Pediatric Soc.; Pediatric Infectious Diseases Society; Office: Hôpital Ste-Justine, 3175 Cote Ste-Catherine, Montréal, Qué. H3T 1C5.

**AHUJA, Hira Nand,** M.A.Sc.; university professor; b. Bannu, India 15 March 1929; s. Chand Ram and Parbati A.; e. Brit. India Tech. Coll. C.C.E. 1946; Panjab Univ. B.A. 1952; Univ. of Waterloo M.A.Sc. 1969; m. Kamal d. Tehl Ram and Bhranwa 14 Oct. 1951; children: Neel, Lalit, Sunil; ADJUNCT PROF., FACULTY OF APPLIED SCIENCE & ENGINEERING, UNIV. OF TORONTO and PRES., EPIC EDUCATIONAL PROGRAM INNOVATIONS CENTER; Prof. & Dir. of Cont. Edn. Div., Tech. Univ. of N.S. 1984–92; Res. Engr., Karam Chand Thapar and Bros. Ltd., India 1952–66; Prof., Civil Engr., Memorial Univ. of Nfld. 1969–84; scheduling/cost cons. on several priv. & govt. projects; Fellow, Cand. Soc. of Civil Engr. (Tech. Prog. Chrmn., Atl. Reg. 1988); Mem., Assn. of Profl. Engrs. of N.S.; Candn. Construction Rsch. Bd. 1983–87; Chrmn., Constr. Cost Mngt. Ctte., Am. Assn. of Cost Engrs. 1982–86; thesis supvr.; author: 'Construction Performance Control' 1979; 'Successful Construction Cost Control' 1980; 'Project Management – Techniques in Planning and Controlling Construction Projects' 1984; co-author: 'Successful Methods in Cost Engineering' 1983, 'Construction Estimating' 1987; author/co-author of 30 papers in tech. jours., conf. proceedings; conf. presenter; keynote speaker; specialist in devel. & orgn. of tech. advancement seminars & short courses (organized over 1000 seminars & short courses); Home: 119 Lincoln Cross, Halifax, N.S. B3M 3S8; Office: Suite B10, 3034 Windsor St., Halifax, N.S. B3K 5G1.

**AIKEN, Gordon Harvey,** Q.C., LL.B.; b. Ripley, Ont. 26 Sept. 1918; s. late Albert Henry and Rhetta (Treleaven) A.; e. Pub. & Continuation Sch., Allenford, Ont.; Owen Sound Collegiate, Ont.; Osgoode Hall, Toronto, Ont. (Grad. Hons.) 1940; m. Marie Kathrine Miller, Prince George, B.C., 7 Dec. 1945; children: Carol Jane, Anne Shirley, George Arthur Miller, Clare Ruth; m. 2ndly, Ingrid Krall, 26 Aug. 1978; son, Roger Lee; Chrmn., Ont. Comm. on Election Finances 1983–86; Family Mediation; cr. K.C. (Q.C.) 1952; practised law Tara, Bracebridge & Gravenhurst, Ont. 1940–83; Judge, Family Court, Muskoka 1951–56; served as officer in Candn. Army 1941–1946, Signals, Mil. Intelligence and Platoon Commander R.H.L.I. overseas; el to H. of C. 1957, re-elected 1958, 1962, 1963, 1965 and 1968, not a candidate subsequently; del. to U.N. Gen. Assembly 1961; Chrmn. Banking & Commerce Comte., H. of C. 1962; leader Cdn. Delegation to Rome, I.P.U. 1972; author 'The Backbencher' 1974; 'Returning Officer'

1982; 'Looking out on the 20th Century' 1993; mem. Royal Canadian Legion (past Pres., Tara Br.); United Church; recreations: camping, outdoor life; Clubs: Rotary International since 1946 (Pres. Grav. Club 1952–53); Home: Orillia, Ont.; Office: Box 2436, Orillia, Ont. L3V 7A3.

**AIMERS, John Lathrop,** B.A.; monarchist; schoolmaster; b. Dublin, Ireland 18 Dec. 1951; s. Jeffrey Jenner-Fust and Katharine Lathrop (Mayer) A.; e. Selwyn House Sch. and Lower Can. Coll. Montréal 1968; Sir George Williams Univ. B.A. 1972; McGill Univ. Dip. Ed. 1974; FOUNDER (1970) AND DOMINION CHRMN. THE MONARCHIST LEAGUE OF CAN. 1970–72, 1975– ; Head of English, Avon Old Farms School 1993– ; Master, The Allen-Stevenson School 1992–93; Asst. to the Headmaster, The Toronto French Sch. 1991–92; Adm. Asst. to Rt. Hon. J.G. Diefenbaker 1969–70, to R. Coates, M.P. 1972, S. Schumacher, M.P. 1973; Ind. Cand. Que. Prov. Elec. 1973, def.; Schoolmaster, Selwyn House Sch. 1974–78; Special Asst. to Hon. Donald Johnston, P.C., M.P. 1979–80; Dir. of Admissions, Laurentian Univ. Sudbury 1980; Resident Master, St. John's-Ravenscourt Sch. Winnipeg 1980–83, Dir. of Devel. 1981–83; Housemaster, Appleby Coll. Oakville 1983–91; Founding Dir. Qué. High Sch. Debating Fedn. 1976; Founder, Internat. Independent Sch. Pub. Speaking League 1982; Pres. Fulford Cup League 1985–87; Nat. Pres. P. Cons. Youth Fedn. 1977; Pres. Old Boys' Assn. and Gov. Lower Can. Coll. 1975–77, member of Corporation 1970– ; Pub. 'Monarchy Canada' mag. 1975– ; mem., Royal Sch. of Ch. Music; Episcopal Synod of Am.; Prayer Book Soc. of Can.; recreations: reading, travel; Home: 49 St. Clair Ave. W., Apt. 505, Toronto, Ont. M4V 1K6; Office: P.O. Box 1057, Oakville, Ont. L6J 5E9.

**AINEY, Lloyd Arthur William;** technology executive; commercial real estate broker; construction manager; b. Toronto, Ont. 20 Sept. 1951; s. Arthur Joseph and Shirley Elizabeth (Ray) A.; e. Candn. Meml. Chiropractic Coll. 1979; Univ. of Toronto; PRES. INTERFACE TECHNOLOGIES INC. 1982– ; Pres., Park Group Inc. 1987; Lloyd Ainey Realty Inc. 1982– ; Empire Leaseholds Inc.; PG Commercial Real Estate Services; Propr., Eastern-Ainey Enterprises 1974–77; Knowlton Realty Ltd. 1979–82; recreations: flying, swimming; Clubs: Air One; YMCA; Home: 1107 – 280 Simcoe St., Toronto, Ont. M5T 2Y5; Office: 111 Richmond St. W., Ste. 318, Toronto, Ont. M5H 2G4.

**AIRD, Alexander Ross,** B.A., F.C.M.C.; management consultant; b. Toronto, Ont. 2 Apr. 1936; s. William Hugh and Margaret Grace (Cameron) A.; e. Lower Canada Coll., Montreal; McGill Univ. B.A. 1958; m. Margot Knox d. Herbert Knox McLean, 13 Dec. 1958; one s. William Cameron; three d. Wendy Birks, Linda McLean, Philippa Ross; SENIOR PARTNER, DELOITTE & TOUCHE MANAGEMENT CONSULTANTS; Managing Dir., Braxton Associates; Assoc. Managing Partner, Deloitte & Touche; joined Payne Ross Ltd., Montreal 1958; Partner-in-Charge, P.S. Ross & Partners, Winnipeg 1964–68, Toronto 1968–70, Mng. Partner 1972–79; Chrmn. 1979–85, an associate managing partner of Deloitte & Touche 1990– ; Reserve Officer, Black Watch (R.H.R.) of Canada 1957–64; Fellow, Inst. Mgmt. Consultants of Ont.; mem., Inst. Mgmt. Consultants of U.S.; Alpha Delta Phi; Presbyterian; Clubs: York; Toronto Golf; Mount Bruno Country; Badminton and Racquet Club of Toronto; Home: R.R. #1, Terra Cotta, Ont. L0P 1N0.

**AIRD, Hugh H.;** business executive; b. Toronto, Ont. 7 Dec. 1953; s. John B. and Jane (Housser) A.; e. Harvard Univ.; Upper Canada College; m. Virginia d. Robert G. and Elizabeth Bertram 14 June 1975; 3 children; PRES. & C.E.O., TRILON SECURITIES CORP.; Dir., Trilon Financial Corp.; Royal Lepage Limited; mem., Order of St. John; Office: BCE Place, 181 Bay St., Ste. 4420, P.O. Box 771, Toronto, Ont. M5J 2T3.

**AIRD, Capt. (N) The Hon. John B.,** C.C., O.Ont., Q.C., B.A., LL.B., LL.D.(Hon.), D.Litt.S.; b. Toronto, Ont. 5 May 1923; s. late Hugh Reston and May (Black) A.; e. Upper Can. Coll.; Trinity Coll. B.A. 1946; Osgoode Hall Law Sch.; m. Lucile Jane, d. Harry Housser 27 July 1944; one s. Hugh Housser, three d. Lucille Elizabeth (Mrs. W.J. Menear), Jane Victoria (Mrs. T.G. Blackmore), Katherine Black (Mrs. D.S. Porter); CHANCELLOR EMERITUS, UNIV. OF TORONTO 1991– ; COUNSEL AND HONORARY CHAIRMAN, AIRD & BERLIS; Hon. Counsel, St. Paul's Anglican Ch., Toronto; Dir. 1985– : Algoma Central Corp. (Chrmn. & Dir. 1959–80; Depy. Chrmn. 1990–91; Hon. Chrmn. 1991– ;); The Molson Companies Ltd. (Dir. 1974–80; 1985–93; Hon. Dir. 1993– ;); Reed Stenhouse Companies Ltd. (Chrmn. & Dir. 1968–80, 1985–93); Dir. 1986–93: Power Corporation of Canada (Vice-Chrmn.); Dir. 1986– : Economic Investment Trust Limited; Inco Limited; The Consumers' Gas Co. Ltd. (Chrmn. & Dir. 1987–91; Hon. Chrmn. 1991– ;); Dir. 1988– : Mercedes Benz Canada Inc.; Nova Corp. of Alta.; Chrmn. Emeritus, Candn. Inst. for Advanced Rsch. 1990; representative, Bermuda Commercial Bank Ltd. 1993– ; read law with Wilton & Edison, assoc. with same 1949–53; Partner, Edison, Aird & Berlis 1953–74; Partner, Aird Zimmerman & Berlis 1974–78; Partner, Aird & Berlis 1978–80; Lieut. Gov. of Ont. 1980–85; Sr. Partner, Aird & Berlis 1985–93; Hon. Chrmn., Aird & Berlis 1990– ; Counsel, Aird & Berlis 1993; served as Lt. R.C.N.V.R. 1942–45; enrolled in Supplementary Reserve 1981, promoted to rank of Captain (N) Candn. Forces; installed as Hon. Col. 49th Field Regiment (RCA) (Sault Ste. Marie) 1983–86; Hon. Col., The 78th Fraser Highlanders 1989; cr. Q.C. 1960; mem. Senate of Can. 1964–74; Chrmn. Candn. Sec., Can.-U.S. Perm. Jt. Bd. on Defence 1971–79; Mem., Ctte. of Nine (North Atlantic Assembly) 1973; Chrmn., Inst. for Research on Public Policy 1974–80; Offr., Order of Can. 1976; Companion, Order of Can. 1993; Chancellor, Wilfrid Laurier Univ. 1977–85 (Chancellor Emeritus); Chancellor, Univ. of Toronto 1986–91; Kt. of Justice of the Most Venerable Order of the Hospital of St. John of Jerusalem 1987; Kt. Commdr., Mil. and Hospitaller Order of St. Lazarus of Jerusalem 1977; Great Lakes Man of the Yr. 1977; 4th Hon. Fellow, Trinity Coll. 1981; Hon. Commr., Ont. Provincial Police 1983; Human Relations Award, Candn. Counc. of Christians & Jews 1983; Gillette Lectr., Univ. of W. Ont. 1984; Hon. Sr. Fellow, Renison Coll., Univ. of Waterloo 1985; Distinguished Service Award, Ont. Police Comn. 1985; Hon. Jr. Citizen of Yr. 1985; 35th Humanitarian Award, Beth Shalom Brotherhood 1985; Kt. of Merit, Internat. Constantinian Order 1985; Silver Acorn, Boy Scouts of Canada 1986; 1985 Provincial Sport Citation; 6th Recipient Family Service Assoc. of Metro Toronto Award 1986; apptd. Officer Order of Red Cross 1986; Award of Merit, City of Toronto 1987; First Recipient, Order of Ontario 1987; Paul Harris Award, The Rotary Foundation of Rotary International 1987; Promise of Hope Award, Candn. Children's Found.; King Clancy Award, Candn. Found. for Physically Disabled Persons 1990; Gold Award, Naval Officers' Assn. of Can. 1990; Distinguished Service Award, The Easter Seal Soc. 1992; Commemorative Medal for the 125th Anniversary of Candn. Confedn. 1992; Third Visitor, Massey Coll., Univ. of Toronto 1990; LL.D. (Hon.): Wilfrid Laurier Univ. 1975, Royal Military Coll. of Can. 1980, Univ. of W. Ont. 1983, Lakehead Univ. 1984, Univ. of Toronto 1984; D.Litt.S. (Hon.) Wycliffe Coll. 1985; D.S.L. (Hon.) Univ. of St. Michael's Coll. 1992; Hon. Chrmn.: United Way of Greater Metrop. Toronto 1987–91; Candn. Liver Found.; Hon. Gov., Variety Village; Hon. Pres. Naval Offrs. Assn. of Can.; Hon. Pres. & Patron, Famous People Players; Patron and Hon. Trustee, Sunnybrook Medical Centre; Chief Patron, Sculptor's Soc. of Can.; Hon. Co-Chrmn., The Mandarin Club; Dir., Candn. Special Olympics; Hon. Dir., Gordon Sinclair Journalism Foundn.; Hon. Patron: City of Toronto Children's Network; Candn. Mental Health Assn.; Sports for Disabled, Ont.; Mandarin Golf and Country Club; Patron: Grenville Christian Coll.; Cheshire Homes Foundn.; Lester B. Pearson Coll. of the Pacific; Community Assoc. of Riding for the Disabled; The National Mental Health Fund; Muskoka Heritage Found.; HMCS HAIDA Assoc.; South Muskoka Memorial Hosp.; Hon. Life Mem., Toronto Press Club; Nat. Counc., Boy Scouts of Canada; Clubs: York; Toronto; Toronto Golf; Royal Candn. Yacht; Royal and Ancient Golf Club of St. Andrews; Royal Bermuda Yacht; Office: Aird & Berlis, BCE Place, Ste. 1800, Box 754, 181 Bay St., Toronto, Ont. M5J 2T9.

**AIRD, Paul Leet,** B.Sc.Agr., M.S., Ph.D., R.P.F.; professor; conservationist; b. Toronto, Ont. 11 Jan. 1930; s. Douglas Maiben and Perle (Leet) A.; e. Macdonald College, McGill Univ. B.Sc.Agr. 1952; Cornell Univ. M.S. 1953, Ph.D. 1957; m. Margaret d. Florence and Ross Murray 26 June 1954; children: Joan Rosslyn, Diana Jean; PROFESSOR, FACULTY OF FORESTRY, UNIV. OF TORONTO 1981– ; teaching and conducting research on forest policy and conservation of renewable natural resources; Rsch. Assoc. Industrial Celluose Research Ltd. 1953; Rsch. Forester 1955 and Asst. Mgr. 1959, Woodlands Rsch. Div., Canadian International Paper Co.; Rsch. Scientist, Pulp & Paper Research Inst. of Canada 1968; joined present univ. as Assoc. Prof. 1974; mem. Gov. Counc., Univ. of Toronto 1984–87; Associate, Inst. for Environmental Studies 1978– ; mem., Niagara Escarpment Commission 1993– ; recipient J.A. Bothwell Award, Candn. Pulp and Paper Assn. 1971; Vice-prés., Conseil québecois de l'environnement 1972–73; Dir. Argenteuil County Historical Soc. and Museum 1965–68; mem. Candn. Inst. of Forestry; Federation of Ont. Naturalists; Conservation Counc. of Ont.; Royal Candn. Institute; Ont. Forestry Assn.; Ont. Profl. Foresters Assn.; Kirtland's Warbler Recovery Team, Dept of the Interior, U.S.; author and editor numerous reports, articles, fables and nature poems published in sci. journs., scholarly periodicals and newspapers; Club: Brodie; Office: Faculty of Forestry, Earth Sciences Centre, 33 Willcocks St., Toronto, Ont. M5S 3B3.

**AITKEN, Douglas George;** real estate executive; b. Regina, Sask. 28 Aug. 1937; s. Robert and Pauline A.; e. Univ. of Sask. (Business Adm.); m. Rita N. d. George Bell; children: Cathy, Bruce, Dyan, Nancy; PRES. AND C.E.O., MARATHON REALTY CO. LTD. 1990– ; Pres., Marathon U.S. Realties, Inc.; joined Marathon Realty Co. Ltd. 1969; Vice-Pres., Opns 1976; Sr. Vice-Pres., Western Canada 1981; Extve. Vice Pres. 1983; Pres. and C.E.O. 1990; Dir., Candn. Inst. of Public Real Estate Cos.; Mem., Candn. Ctte., Internat. Counc. of Shopping Centres; recreation: squash; Clubs: Cambridge; Royal Candn. Yacht; Hollyburn Country; Home: 175 Cumberland St., Toronto, Ont. M5R 3M9: Office: 1100, 123 Front St. W., Toronto, Ont. M5J 2M2.

**AITKEN, Leslie Marilynn,** B.A., B.L.S., M.L.I.S.; university librarian; b. Edmonton, Alta. 24 March 1940; d. Tom and Emma (Newman) Flint; e. Univ. of Alta. B.A. 1963, B.L.S. (with distinction) 1971, M.L.I.S. 1988; m. Loren George s. Laurence George and Helen Lucy Hepler 2 July 1993; one d.: Alison Rae; UNIVERSITY LIBRARIAN, ATHABASCA UNIV. 1992– ; Children's Librarian, Western Counties Regional Library 1971–72; Instructor, Grant MacEwan Lib. Tech. Prog. 1972–73; Ref. Librarian, Edmonton Public Lib. 1973–76; Librarian, Materials Resource Centre for the Blind & Visually Impaired Alta. Edn. 1976–80; Curriculum Lib., Univ. of Alta. 1980–86; Collections Lib., Coutts Lib., Univ. of Alta. 1986–91; Mem., Can. Lib. Assn. CACUL Div.; editor: 'School Libraries in Canada' 1991; Selection Ctte. for Adult, Young Adult Series, Alta. Heritage Learning Resources 1979; Home: Box 3567, Athabasca, Alta. T0G 0B0; Office: Box 10,000, Athabasca Alta. T0G 2R0.

**AITKEN, Mary S.;** business executive; b. St. Thomas, Ont. 10 Feb. 1948; d. Grover Alexander and Ila Maynard (Zavitz) McArdle; e. Woodstock C.I. 1967; divorced; children: Jason, James; PRES. & DIR., RENAISSANCE SECURITIES INC. 1984– ; Founder, Pronto Toronto 1977–81; Pres., Mary S. Aitken & Assoc. 1981–84; Dir., Advanced Material Resources Limited; Gov., Trinity Coll. Sch., Port Hope; Home: 130 South Dr., Toronto, Ont. M4W 1R8; Office: 121 King St. W., Toronto, Ont. M5H 3T9.

**AKENSON, Donald Harman,** Ph.D., F.R.S.C., F.R.Hist.S.; F.R.S.A.; historian; educator; b. Minneapolis, Minn. 22 May 1941; s. Donald Nels and Fern L. (Harman) A.; e. Yale Univ. B.A. 1962; Harvard Univ. Ed.M. 1963, Ph.D. 1967; PROF. OF HIST. QUEEN'S UNIV. since 1974; publisher and owner, Langdale Press ('Canadian Papers in Rural History'); Allston Burr Sr. Tutor, Dunster House, Harvard Coll. 1966–67; Asst. Prof. of Hist. and Asst. Dean, Yale Coll. 1967–70; Assoc. Prof. 1970–74, Prof. of Hist., Queen's Univ. 1974– ; Hon. Research Fellow, Inst. Irish Studies, Queen's Univ. of Belfast 1976–77; Hon. Prof. of Educ. Trinity Coll. Dublin 1976–77; Sr. Editor, McGill-Queen's Univ. Press 1982– ; Guest Artist, Yaddo Colony 1985; Hon. Lectr. History and Demography, Australian National Univ. 1985; Guest writer, Bellagio Centre, Italy 1993; comm. sheep farmer; rec'd Am. Council Learned Socs. Research Award 1976–77; SSHRC Major Research Award 1981–84, 1991–94; Guggenheim Fellow 1984–85; Chalmers Prize 1985; Landon Prize 1987; Lansdowne Lectr., Univ. of Victoria, B.C. 1987; John David Stout Rsch. Fellow, Victoria Univ., Wellington, N.Z. 1988–89; University Fellow, Inst. of Social and Economic Rsch., Rhodes Univ., Grahamstown, S. Africa 1990; Writer-in-Residence, Village Servelloni, the Rockeffler Found., Bellagio, Italy 1993; Grawemeyer World Order Award 1993; author 'The Irish Education Experiment: The National System of Education in the Nineteenth Century' 1970; 'The Church of Ireland: Ecclesiastical Reform and Revolution 1800–1885' 1971; 'Education and Enmity: The Control of Schooling in Northern Ireland 1920–50' 1973; 'The United States and Ireland' 1973; 'A Mirror to Kathleen's Face: Education in Independent Ireland 1922–60' 1975; 'Local Poets and Social History: James Orr, Bard of Ballycarry' 1977; 'Between Two Revolutions: Islandmagee, County Antrim, 1798–1920' 1979; 'The Lazar House Notebooks' 1981; 'A Protestant in Purgatory: Richard Whately, Archibishop of Dublin'

1981; 'The Irish in Ontario: A Study in Rural History' 1984; 'Brotherhood Week in Belfast' 1984; 'Being Had: Historians, Evidence, and the Irish in North America' 1985; 'The Orangeman: The Life and Times of Ogle Gowan' 1986; 'The Edgerston Audit' 1987; 'Small Differences: Irish Catholics and Irish Protestants, 1815–1922' 1988; 'Half the World from Home: Perspectives on the Irish in New Zealand' 1990; 'At Face Value. The Life and Times of Eliza McCormack/John White' 1990; 'Occasional Papers on the Irish in South Africa' 1991; 'God's Peoples: Covenant and Land in South Africa, Israel and Ulster' 1992; 'The Irish Diaspora: A Primer' 1993; Phi Beta Kappa; Clubs: Yale (N.Y.C.); Co. Antrim Yacht (N. Ireland); R.R. 1, Gananoque, Ont. K7G 2V3.

**AKINCI, His Excellency Ugurtan;** diplomat; b. Istanbul, Turkey 25 Aug. 1938; e. Saint Joseph H.S. 1956; Fac. of Pol. Sci., Ankara Univ. 1961; married; one child; foreign languages: French, English; AMBASSADOR OF TURKEY TO CAN. 1992– ; Candidate Career Offr. & Third Sec., Dept. of Cultural Affairs, Min. of Fgn. Affairs 1968–70; Third, Second & First Sec., Turkish Embassy Rabat 1970–72; First Sec. & Counsellor Turkish Embassy, Bucharest 1972–75; Chief of Section, Dept. of Pol. Affairs, Min. of Fgn. Affairs 1975–77; Counsellor, Turkish Embassy, Copenhagen 1977–81; Dir., Multilateral Cultural Relns., Dir. Gen. of Cultural Affairs, Min. of Fgn. Affairs 1981–84; Consul Gen. of Turkey, Frankfurt 1984–87; Dir. of Admin. & Finan. Affairs, Min. of Fgn. Affairs 1987–89; Ambassador of Turkey, United Arab Emirates 1989–91; Office: 197 Wurtemburg St., Ottawa, Ont. K1N 8L9.

**AKPALIAPIK, Manasie;** sculptor; b. Arctic Bay, N.W.T. 23 Aug. 1955; raised in family of sculptors Lazaroosee and Kakyuraq Akpaliapik; adopted grandparents were artists Peter and Elisapee Kanangnaq Ahlooloo; e. great aunt Paniluk Qamanirq taught him to carve at 10 years of age; 11 group exbns. incl. most recent: Winnipeg Art Gallery 1993, 1992; 'Le Nouveau Monde Nouveau Territoires ...' Montreal 1992; Salon International Europ'art '92, Geneva, Switz. 1992; Nat. Gallery of Canada 1992; solo exbns.: Winnipeg Art Gallery 1990, Images Art Gallery Toronto 1989; works in 4 collections incl. art galleries of N.S., Ontario (Sarick Coll.), and Winnipeg, National Gallery of Canada; Canada Council Explorations Grant for 'North Baffin Island Legends' 1989; one of Canada's reps. at Ainu Cultural Soc. conf. Japan 1989; Bd. Mem., Inuit Art Found. 1990; appeared on cover of spring issue of 'Inuit Art Quarterly' 1990; workshop participant, Candn. Mus. of Civilization held by Om niiak Native Arts Group 1990; subject of articles and catalogues; Home: Toronto, Ont. Office: c/o Ingo Hessel, Indian and Northern Affairs Canada, Les Terrasses de la Chaudière, Ottawa, Ont. K1A 0H4.

**AKRIGG, George Philip Vernon,** M.A., Ph.D., F.R.H.S., F.R.S.C.; Shakespeare scholar and historian; b. Calgary, Alta. 13 Aug. 1913; s. George Straker and Rose Edith (Norton) A.; e. Central Sch. and Lethbridge (Alta.) Coll. Inst.; Calgary (Alta.) Normal Sch.; Univ. of B.C. B.A. 1937, M.A. 1940; Univ. of Cal. Berkeley Ph.D. 1944; m. Helen Brown d. late E. C. Manning 2 Sept. 1944; children: Marian, Daphne, George; PROF. EMERITUS OF ENG., UNIV. OF B.C. 1979– ; Prof. of Eng. Univ. of B.C. 1958–79; Dir. Discovery Press; Research Fellow, Folger Shakespeare Lib. Washington, D.C. 1946–47; Can. Council Leave Fellowship 1970–71, 1975–76; Pres. Vancouver Inst. 1963–64; author 'Jacobean Pageant or the Court of King James I' 1962; 'Shakespeare and the Earl of Southampton' 1968; co-author '1001 British Columbia Place Names' 1969; 'British Columbia Chronicle 1778–1846' 1975; 'British Columbia Chronicle 1847–1871' 1977; 'British Columbia Place Names' 1986; editor, 'Letters of King James VI & I' 1984; 'H.M.S. "Virago" in the Pacific 1851–1855' 1992; numerous articles on Shakespeare, Eng. lit. and hist. of Renaissance; mem. Modern Lang. Assn.; Anglican; recreations: travel, gardening; Homes: (Spring & Summer) Box 64, Celista, B.C. V0E 1L0; (Winter) 2575 Tolmie St., #8, Vancouver, B.C. V6R 4M1.

**ALARIE, Pierrette (Madame Simoneau);** O.C. (1967); soprano; teacher; b. Montréal, Que. 9 Nov. 1921; d. Sylva et Amanda (Plante)Alarie; é. primary and secondary schools; m. Léopold Simoneau 1 June 1946; children: Isabelle, Chantal; studied with Jeanne Maubourg, Albert Roberval and Elizabeth Schumann, and in the studio of Salvator Issaurel; as a soloist, with her husband, sang on great European and N. American stages; co-recipient (with husband) Prix de musique Calixa-Lavallée 1959; Diploma of Honour, Candn. Conference of the Arts 1983; Chevalière de l'Ordre des arts et des lettres de France 1990; (for recording 'Mozart Concert Arias and Duets') Grand Prix du disque, Académie Charles-Cros, Paris 1961; co-founded (with husband) Canada Opera Piccola (Victorian chamber opera co.) 1978; Advanced Training Opera Centre 1982; Catholique; recreations: theatre, lecture, haute cuisine, walking.

**ALBERT, Richard,** B.B.A.; financial executive; b. Fredericton, N.B. 7 March 1947; e. Bishop's Univ. B.B.A. 1969; PRESIDENT, NORFOLK FINANCIAL GROUP INC.; Office: 510, 940 – 6 Ave. S.W., Calgary, Alta. T2P 3T1.

**ALBERTI, Peter William,** M.B., B.S., Ph.D., F.R.C.S.(C), F.R.C.S.; otolarygologist; b. Coblence, Germany 23 Aug. 1934; s. William Peter and Edith Elizabeth (Lachmann) A.; e. Royal Grammar Sch., Newcastle upon Tyne; Univ. of Durham, M.B., B.S. 1957; Washington Univ. Ph.D. 1963; Post-Grad. Training Otolaryngology, Univ. of Newcastle upon Tyne; Medical training, R.V.I., Newcastle upon Tyne, Emory Univ., Washington Univ.; F.R.C.S. 1965; F.R.C.S.(C) 1968; SR. STAFF OTOLARYNGOLOGIST, TORONTO GENERAL HOSPITAL 1982– ; Prof. and Chrmn., Dept. of Otolarygology, Univ. of Toronto 1982–92; Otolaryngologist-in-Chief, Mt. Sinai Hosp. 1970–88; Toronto General Hosp. 1982–89; joined clinical faculty present univ., Sunnybrook Hosp. 1967; Asst. Prof. 1968; Assoc. Prof. 1970; Prof. 1977; Consultant, Workers Compensation Appeals Tribunal; profl. interests: occupational hearing loss, laser microsurgery of larynx; Gen. Secy., Internat. Fed. of Oto-Rhino-Laryngological Socs. 1991– ; Hon. Mem., Brazilian Otolaryngolical Soc.; Assoc. of Otolaryngologists of India; Irish Otolaryngology Soc.; South African Otolaryngological Soc.; mem. Candn. Otolaryngological Soc.; Candn. Med. Assn.; Royal Soc. of Medicine; Amer. Soc. for Rhinology, Otology and Laryngology; Amer. Otological Soc.; Amer. Acad. Otolaryngology; C.O.R.L.A.S.; Sigma Xi; co-author: 'Clinical Otoscopy' 1984; ed.: 'Personal Hearing Protection in Industry' 1981; co-ed.: 'Centennial Conf. on Laryngeal Cancer' 1975; 'Otological Medicine and Surgery' 1988; author numerous scholarly articles; recreations: yachting, antique books; Club: Royal Canadian Yacht; Home: 259 Glencairn Ave., Toronto, Ont. M5N 1T8; Office: 7.219 Eaton W. N., 200 Elizabeth St., Toronto, Ont. M5G 2C4.

**ALBINO, William Michael,** B.A., M.B.A.; business executive; b. United States 12 Dec. 1951; s. George Robert and Julianne Ellen (Fogarty) A.; e. St. Andrew's College 1970; Univ. of Toronto B.A. 1973; Univ. of Western Ont. M.B.A. 1975; m. Catherine d. Dr. Donald and Jean Brown 20 July 1973; children: Mary, Laura, Emily; VICE-PRESIDENT, MARKETING & PLANNING, XEROX CANADA LTD. 1990– ; numerous marketing & sales assignments, Xerox Canada Ltd. 1975–82; Manager, Business Planning 1982–84; Mgr., S.W. Ont. Dist., residing in London, Ont. 1984–88; Dir., Customer Service 1988; Office Products Buisness 1989; Mem., United Church; Ont. Historical Soc.; recreations: tennis, skiing; clubs: Timberlane Tennis & Country; Home: 7 Karindon Court, Aurora, Ont. L4G 6K8; Office: 5650 Yonge St., North York, Ont. M2M 4G7.

**ALBOIM, Elly,** B.A., M.Sc.; professor; b. Montreal, Que. 7 July 1947; s. Samuel and Helen (Gold) A.; e. McGill Univ., B.A. (Hons.) 1968; Columbia Univ., M.Sc. 1970; m. Kathleen d. John and Clytie Moore 15 Aug. 1971; children: Jennifer, Jesse, Jaime; CONSULTANT, EARNSCLIFFE STRATEGY GROUP, OTTAWA; Lineup Ed., Montreal, CBC TV 1970–76; Nat. Assignment Ed., Toronto, CBC TV 1976–77; Bureau Chief, Parliament Hill, Ottawa, CBC TV 1977–93; Assoc. Prof., Carleton Univ., Sch. of Journalism 1987– ; Sess. Lectr. 1979–87; Concordia Univ., Grad. Dept. of Communications 1985–88; Dir., Nat. Press Gallery, Ottawa, Ont. 1982–88; Dir., Candn. Journalism Found.; Home: 2111 Montreal Rd., #183, Ottawa, Ont. K1J 8M8; Office: 150 Wellington St., 8th fl., Ottawa, Ont. K1P 1A5.

**ALBOINI, Victor Philip Michael,** B.A., LL.B., LL.M.; restructuring, mergers and acquisitions advisor; b. Hamilton, Ont. 29 March 1948; s. Vince and Christina (Grottoli) A.; e. Univ. of Toronto B.A. 1969, LL.B. 1972; Osgoode Hall Law Sch. York Univ. LL.M. 1977; m. Lesley d. James Ross and Elizabeth Ann LeMesurier 25 May 1981; PRESIDENT, STATURE INC. 1990– ; Managing Partner, Mergers & Acquisitions, Loewen, Ondaatje, McCutcheon 1988–90; Pres. & C.O.O., Prenor Financial Ltd. 1987–88; Partner, McCarthy & McCarthy 1980–86; called to Bar of Ont. 1974; Assoc. McCarthy & McCarthy 1974–79; Part-time Lectr. in M.B.A. Program, Univ. of Toronto 1980–87 and in Executive M.B.A. Program, Univ. of Toronto 1986–87 and in Comm. and Finance 1980–82; Seminar Leader Bar Admission course 1974–76; Quarterback, Univ. of Toronto Blues 5 years; author 'Ontario Securities Law' (text) 1980; 'Securities Law and Practice' (securities law service) 1984; various legal articles; recreations: tennis, piano, golf; Clubs: Albany; Cambridge; Toronto Lawn Tennis; Home: 95 Glengowan Rd., Toronto, Ont. M4N 1G5.

**ALBRIGHT, Wilfred Paul,** B.A., M.B.A., Ph.D.; university professor; b. Hamilton, Ont. 3 Jan. 1922; s. Wilfred Leroy and Beatrice Levina (Church) A.; e. McMaster Univ., B.A. 1947, M.B.A. 1962; State Univ. of N.Y. at Buffalo, Ph.D. (Bus. Admin.) 1970; m. Priscilla Mary d. Anthony and Florence Yantha 22 Apr. 1978; PROF. & CHRMN. DEPT OF BUS., WILFRID LAURIER UNIV. 1964– ; personnel offr., Studebaker of Canada 1952–63; Asst. Prof., Wilfrid Laurier Univ. 1964–68; Chrmn., Univ. Senate Task Force on Trends & University Strategy 1978; mem. Bd. of Govs. 1981–82; repeated terms in Senate; Pres., Fac. Assn. 1986–87; Professor Emeritus 1988; Dir. of Project Rsch., Joint Nat. Manpower Rsch. Ctte. of the Mech. Constrn. Ind. in collaboration with Fed. Dept. of Manpower & Immigration 1970; Mem., Ethics Ctte., Freeport Hosp. 1989– ; author: 'Collective Bargaining: A Simulation' 1973; 'The Impact of Technology on the Manpower Needs of the Canadian Piping Industry in the 1970s' 1971; recreations: collecting antique tools and scientific instruments, preservation of heritage bldgs.; Home: 52 Hill St., West Montrose, Ont. N0B 2V0.

**ALCOCK, Alfred John,** B.A.Sc., D.Phil., F.R.S.C.; scientist; b. Glasgow, Scot. 3 Feb. 1938; s. Alfred Kelvin and Agnes Susan (MacFeat) A.; e. Glasgow Acad. 1955; Univ. of Toronto B.A.Sc. 1959; Oxford Univ. D.Phil. 1965; m. Denise d. John and Victoria Platschorre 1962; children: Deborah Anne, Douglas John; HEAD, ADVANCED LASER TECH. & APPLICATIONS, INST. FOR MICROSTRUCTURAL SCIENCES, NAT. RESEARCH COUNCIL OF CAN. 1991– , Sr. Research Offr. 1975–85, Principal Rsch. Offr. 1985– ; postdoctoral Fellow present Council 1965, Asst. Research Offr. 1966, Assoc. Research Offr. 1968, Head, Laser & Plasma Physics Sect. 1974–90; recipient Herzberg Medal, Candn. Assn. Phys. 1975; author over 80 publs. sci. journs.; Fellow, Inst. Elec. & Electronics Engrs.; mem. Candn. Assn. Phys.; Am. Phys. Soc.; Optical Soc. of Amer.; Anglican; recreations: swimming, cross-country skiing; Home: 1 Massey Lane, Gloucester, Ont. K1J 6C7; Office: Ottawa, Ont. K1A 0R6.

**ALCOCK, Charles Benjamin,** Ph.D., D.Sc., F.R.S.C.; educator; consultant; b. London, Eng. 24 Oct. 1923; s. Arthur Charles and Margaret (Francis) A.; e. Imp. Coll., B.Sc. 1944; Univ. of London, Ph.D. 1955, D.Sc. 1969; m. Valerie Marie Daniel Robinson 20 Aug. 1949; children: Deborah Susan, Martin Charles, James Benjamin; PROF. OF METALLURGICAL CHEM., IMPERIAL COLL. 1964– ; EMERITUS PROF. METALL. AND MATERIALS SCIENCE, UNIV. OF TORONTO; Extractive Metall. Lectr., Am. Inst. Metall. Engrs. 1974; Visiting Prof., Carnegie Inst. of Tech 1961; N. Carolina State Univ. 1964; Univ. of Penn. 1968; Univ. of Notre Dame, U.S. 1986; Imperial College London 1992; Freimann Chaired Prof., Univ. of Notre Dame 1987; Dir., Center for Sensor Materials, Univ. of Notre Dame 1987; Author, 'Principles of Pyrometallurgy'; co-author, 'Metallurgical Thermochemistry' (5th ed.); 'Electromotive Force Measurements in High Temperature Systems' and author of over 150 tech. papers; Le Beau Medallist, Soc. des Hautes Températures, 1976; Kroll Medallist, Ins. Metals London 1983; Fellow, Royal Soc. of Can.; Royal Soc. of Chemistry (U.K.); Amer. Inst. Met. Engrs.; Royal Soc. Arts; Anglican; recreations: sports, music; Home: Ste. 1106, 130 Carlton St., Toronto, Ont. M5A 4K3; Office: 160 College St., Toronto, Ont. M5S 1A4.

**ALCOCK, James,** B.Sc., Ph.D.; university professor; b. Central Butte, Sask. 24 Dec. 1942; s. Albert Edward and Ruth Hildegarde Charlotte (Nelson) A.; e. McGill Univ. B.Sc. (Hons.) 1963; McMaster Univ. Ph.D. 1972; PROFESSOR, DEPT. OF PSYCHOLOGY, GLENDON COLLEGE, YORK UNIV.; joined present univ. 1973; Partner, Fleming, Alcock & Vigna, Reg. Psych.; Fellow, Candn. Psych. Assn.; author: 'Parapsychology: Science Or Magic?' 1981, 'Science and Supernature' 1990; co-author: 'A Textbook of Social Psychology' 2nd ed. (3rd ed. forthcoming 1994); Office: 2275 Bayview Ave., Toronto, Ont. M4N 3M6.

**ALCOCK, Norman Zinkan,** B.Sc., M.S., Ph.D.; physicist; b. Edmonton, Alta., 29 May 1918; s. late Joseph Benjamin and late Edith Alma (Zinkan) A.; e. Queen's Univ., B.Sc. (Elect. Eng.) 1940; Cal. Tech., M.S. (Elect. Eng.) 1941; McGill Univ., Ph.D. (Physics) 1949; m. Patricia Christian Sinclair Hunter, 29 June 1948;

children: Stephen, Christopher, David, Nancy; Research Eng. (ground radar), Nat. Research Council Can., 1941; Telecommunications Research Estab., Great Malvern, Eng. (airborne radar), 1943; McGill Univ., Research Physicist (cyclotron design), 1946; Atomic Energy of Canada Ltd. (neutron diffraction research), 1947; Vice-Pres. and Dir., Isotope Products Ltd., Oakville, Ont., 1950; Gen. Mgr. of Isotopes Products Div., Canadian Curtiss-Wright, 1957, and Dir. of Eng. there 1958; founded and directed Cdn. Peace Research Inst. 1961–81; commissioned in R.C.A.F. 1942; Fellow, Ryerson Poly. Inst. 1990; Address: Miller Lake, Ont. N0H 1Z0.

**ALDANA, Patricia,** B.A.; publisher; b. Guatemala 13 Nov. 1946; d. Fernando and Barbara (Kidder) A.; e. Concord Acad.; Stanford Univ. B.A. 1968; Bryn Mawr Coll.; children: Carlota and Seth McAllister, Daniel and Madeleine Cohen; PUBLISHER, GROUNDWOOD BOOKS 1978– ; Partner and Dir. Douglas and McIntyre 1981– ; Pres. Assn. Candn. Publishers 1977–79; Pres., Orgn. of Book Publishers of Ont. 1989–91; Office: 585 Bloor St. W., 2nd Flr., Toronto, Ont. M6G 1K5.

**ALDERSON, Evan W.,** B.A., M.A., Ph.D.; educator; b. Philadelphia, Pa. 27 April 1938; s. Wroe and Elsie Star (Wright) A.; e. Westtown School (Pa.) 1956; Haverford College B.A. 1961; Univ. of Calif. at Berkeley M.A. 1964, Ph.D. 1972; m. Elizabeth Ingrid d. Mervyn and Ilse Sprung 27 June 1987; children: Rebecca D., Kai H.; DEAN, FAC. OF ARTS, SIMON FRASER UNIV. 1992– ; Research Asst. & Acting Instr., Univ. of Calif. 1962–67; Dept. of English, Simon Fraser Univ. 1967–83; Acting Chairman 1974–75; Founding Dir., Centre for the Arts (now Sch. for the Contemporary Arts) 1976–80; Assoc. Prof. 1981– ; Associate Dean, Fac. of Arts 1985–88; Acting Dean of Arts summers 1988, '89; Founding Dir., Graduate Liberal Studies Program, Simon Fraser Univ. 1991–92; Canada Council Doctoral Fellowship 1968–69; Bd. Chrmn., Paula Ross Dance Co. 1981–83; Adv. Ctte., Vancouver Playhouse Acting Sch. 1987–90; Mem., Soc. of Dance History Scholars; Assn. for Dance in Univs. & Colleges in Canada; Congress on Research in Dance; author of essays reviews & schol. papers on Am. lit. & lit. criticism, dance history & aesthetics & cultural policy; Co-editor, 'Reflections on Cultural Policy'; recreations: cooking, tennis; Home: 2403 w. 34th Ave., Vancouver, B.C. V6M 1G8; Office: Dean of Arts, SFU, Burnaby, B.C. V5A 1S6.

**ALDERSON, Sue Ann,** B.A., M.A.; university professor; b. New York, N.Y. 11 Sept. 1940; d. Eugene Leonard and Ruth Edith (Schuchowsky) Hartley; e. Antioch Coll. B.A. Eng. 1962; Ohio State Univ. M.A. Eng. Lit. 1964; Univ. of Calif. Berkeley Eng. Lit. 1967; m. Evan A. 12 Feb. 1965 (now divorced); children: Rebecca, Kai; PROF. OF CREATIVE WRITING, UNIV. OF BRITISH COLUMBIA 1992– ; Instr. Eng. Dept. Simon Fraser Univ. 1967–71; Instr. Eng. Dept. Capilano Coll. 1973–80; Asst. Prof. present univ. 1980–84, Assoc. Prof. 1984–92, Prof. 1992– ; author children's picture books: 'bonnie mcsmithers you're driving me dithers' 1974; 'The Finding Princess' 1977; 'The Adventures of Prince Paul' 1977; 'hurry up, bonnie!' 1977; 'bonnie mcsmithers is at it again!' 1979; 'anne-marie maginol tu me rends folle' 1981; 'Ida and the Wool Smugglers' 1987; 'Sure as Strawberries' 1992; juvenile novels and novellas: 'Comet's Tale' 1983; 'The Not Impossible Summer' 1983; 'The Something in Thurlo Darby's House' 1984; 'Maybe You Had To Be There, By Duncan' 1989; 'Chapter One' 1990; 'Sure As Strawberries' 1992; 'A Ride for Martha' 1993; poetry for adults appearing in 'New West Coast' anthology (ed. F. Candelaria) 1977; initiator and sole instr. Writing for Children Prog., U.B.C. (only univ. to offer M.F.A. in Writing for Children); Home: 4004 W. 32 St., Vancouver, B.C. V6S 1Z6; Office: Vancouver, B.C. V6T 1W5.

**ALDOUS, John Gray,** M.A., Ph.D.; university professor; b. Bristol, Eng. 16 Nov. 1916; s. Frederick Gray and Mary Ursula (Macfarlane) A.; came to Can. 1919; e. Univ. of B. C., B.A. 1939, M.A. 1941; Univ. of Toronto, Ph.D. 1945; m. 1stly the late Elsie Eileen Hooley 22 July 1944; m. 2ndly Florence Jean White 26 Oct. 1985; children: Joleen, Peter, Donald; PROF. EMERITUS OF PHARMACOLOGY, DALHOUSIE UNIV. 1981– ; Asst. in Gen. Physiol. and Biol., Univ. of B.C. 1939–41; Demonst. in Gen. Physiol., Univ. of Toronto 1941–45; Asst. Prof. of Pharmacol., Dalhousie, 1945–48 and Assoc. Prof. 1948–50; Prof. & Head of Dept. 1950–75; Alpha Omega Alpha; mem., Candn. Physiol. Soc.; Pharmacol. Soc. of Can. (Pres. 1970); N.S. Inst. of Science (Hon. Life mem.; Pres. 1956–58); Biol. Council Can. (Treas. 1973, Vice Pres. 1974); N.S. Comn. on Drug Dependency (Bd. mem. 1972–81); Hon. mem., N.S. Pharm. Soc. 1977; Drugs & Therap. Comm., N.S. Dept. Health (Chrmn. 1978–85); recreations: photography, music, philately, sports; Address: #903 – 2008 Fullerton Ave., N. Vancouver, B.C. V7P 3G7.

**ALDRIDGE, Gordon James,** M.A., M.S.W., Ph.D.; university professor; b. Toronto, Ont. 19 Oct. 1916; s. Eugene Froyard and Alicia Louisa (Jourdan) A.; e. N. Toronto Coll. Inst., 1934; Univ. of Toronto, B.A. (Sociol.) 1938, Dipl. in Social Science 1939, M.A. (Psychol.) 1948, M.S.W. 1949; Univ. of Mich., Ph.D. (Community Devel.) 1955; Univ. of London, Dipl. in Educ. 1963; m. Gladys Parker, d. late Rev. Joseph Fletcher Chapman, 21 June 1941; one s., Dr. Ronald Gordon; PROF. EMERITUS OF SOCIAL WORK, ARIZONA STATE UNIV.; Social Caseworker, Big Brother Movement, Toronto, 1939–41; Casework Supvr., 1946–50 (Asst. Extve. Dir. 1949–50); Lectr. in Psychol., Univ. of Toronto, 1946–50; Dir., Ont. summer camp for emotionally disturbed boys, 1947–49; Assoc. Prof. of Social Welfare and Dir. of Human Relations Inst., Fla. State Univ., 1950–52; Assoc. Prof. to Prof., Michigan State Univ. 1952–78; Dir., Sch. of Social Work, 1959–66; Prof. of Social Work, Arizona State Univ. 1978–86; Prof. Emeritus of Social Work 1986; Consultant on social work educ. incl. Inst. of Higher Educ., Columbia Univ., periodic consultant with state and nat. organs. concerning programs and services in aging and retirement; served with Candn. Army in Can. and Europe 1941–46; rank Maj. on discharge; author 'Social Issues and Psychiatric Social Work Practice' 1959; co-author 'Social Welfare and the Aged' 1959; 'Social Welfare of the Aging' (Vol. II of 'Aging Around the World') 1962; 'Liberal Education and Social Work' 1965; 'Undergraduate Social Work Education' 1972; many articles and book reviews; mem., Council Social Work Educ.; Nat. Assn. Social Workers; Gerontol. Soc. of Amer.; Internat. Assn. Gerontol.; Can. Assn. on Gerontol.; Protestant; recreations: music, theatre, swimming; Home: 2625 East Southern Ave., C251, Tempe, Ariz. 85281; Office: Tempe, Ariz. 85282.

**ALEXANDER, Andrew;** theatre, movie and television producer/entrepreneur; b. London, England 24 March 1944; s. Fredrick and Barbara (Watson) A.; e. Central Peel H.S. 1964; Tri-State Coll. 1965; Ryerson Polytech. 1965; m. Diane d. Ruth and Don Titmarsh 8 July 1983; CO-OWNER and C.E.O., SECOND CITY INC. 1974– ; Producer, 'Spring Thaw' 1971; opened Second City in Canada 1974; Co-developed & Extve. Produced 'SCTV' 1976; Emmy Award Nominee 1982, 1983; acquired 'Chicago Second City' 1985; 1st Cand. Producer to sell a TV series to an Am. Network (NBC); 1st series to go from syndication to Network (NBC, CBC) to Pay TV (HBO, Superchannel) and back to syndication; set up full scale TV/Film production company with Imagine Films, Los Angeles 1989; Address: Second City, 110 Lombard St., Toronto, Ont. M5C 1M3.

**ALEXANDER, Bruce Bingham;** Q.C., B. Comm., LL.B.; b. Montreal, Que. 8 April 1938; s. Clarence Henry and Ruth Eleanor (Bingham) A.; e. Oakville-Trafalgar H.S.; Queen's Univ., B. Comm. 1960; London Sch. of Econ. 1960–61; Dalhousie Law Sch., Dunn Scholar 1962–63; Univ. of Toronto, LL.B. 1965; Harvard Univ., Adv. Mgmt. Prog. 1985; m. Andrea d. Don and Chris Lough 20 July 1963; one s.: Christopher; Special Advisor to the Federal Minister responsible for Constitutional Affairs; Lawyer, Osler, Hoskin & Harcourt 1967–72; Extve. Asst. to Min. of Transp. & Commun., Ont. 1972–73 (Dir., Legal Br. 1973–75; Extve. Dir., External Relations 1975–77; Actg. Asst. Dep. Min. 1977–78); Chrmn., Ont. Highway Transport Bd. 1978–83; Asst. Dep. Min., Fin. & Admin., Min. of Transp. & Commun. 1983–86; Asst. Depy. Min., Ops., Min. of Community & Soc. Services 1986–87; Mng. Dir., Fraser & Beatty 1987–92; United Church; mem., University Counc., Queen's Univ.; recreations: cross country skiing, canoeing; Home: 106 Birch Ave., Toronto, Ont. M4V 1C8.

**ALEXANDER, Dan C.;** paper industry executive; b. Paris, Texas 26 Mar. 1947; s. Chester C. and Lola B. A.; e. Eastern Ill. Univ., B.S. 1974; m. Margaret d. William and Ruth Andersen 22 June 1968; one d.: Bethanny; PRES. & CHIEF EXTVE. OFFR., ST. MARYS PAPER INC. 1984– ; Dir., Indus. Devel. (4 counties), State of Ill. 1974–76; Extve. Dir., Somerset Co. Indus. Devel. 1976–77; Mgr., Indus. Relns. & Pub. Affairs, Madison Paper Industries 1977–79; Vice-Pres., Mktg. 1979–83; Madden International Corp.; Pres. & Chief Extve. Offr., D.C. Northam, Inc. 1983– ; Founding Mem. & Chrmn., SC Council New York, NY (non-profit assn. of 15 Eur. and N. Am. paper co.'s); Mem., Premier's Council - Ont.; Home: 6386 Blackhawk Trail, Indian Head Park, Ill. 60525; Office: 75 Huron St., Sault Ste. Marie, Ont. P6A 5P4.

**ALEXANDER, David,** B.F.A., M.F.A.; artist; b. Vancouver, B.C. 1947; e. Vanc. Art Sch. 1967–70; Vanc. City Coll. 1971–72; Notre Dame Univ. B.F.A. 1978; Emma Lake Artist Workshop 1979; Univ. of Sask. M.A. 1980; grad. rsch., London, Paris, N.Y. 1981–83; Paris, Aix-en-province Givery (Sask. Arts Bd.) 1984; Workshop Coord., Emma Lake 1982, '83, '84; Guest Curator, Emma Lake Now, Sask. Lib. Gall. 1982; Instr. of Drawing, Univ. of Sask. 1982; of Painting 1985; Guest Artist, Boston Mus. Sch. 1982; Can. Counc. Visiting Artist, Kamloops Art Gall. 1985; Dundas Sch. of Art 1986; McMaster Univ. 1986; Instr. of Painting, Nova Scotia Coll. of Art and Design (Intersession), Halifax, N.S. 1987; Visiting Artist, Guelph Univ., Guelph, Ont. 1989; Visiting artist, Beaverbrook Art Gall., Fredericton, N.B. 1990; Drawing Instr., St. Peters Coll., Sask. 1991–92; solo exhibitions incl.: Heffel Gall. Limited Vanc. 1985, '87, '89 & '91, Feheley Fine Arts Toronto 1989 & '91, Waddington & Schiell Gall. Toronto 1985, '86, '87; Eva Cohen Chicago 1987, Elca London Art Gall. Montreal 1983, '86 & '88, Mendel Art Gall. Sask. 1985, Scottish Gall., Edinburgh, Scotland 1991; group exhibitions incl.: Peter Ohler Gall., Richmond, B.C. 1969, 'Saskatchewan Open,' Mendel Art Gall. Saskatoon 1984, 'Fourteen Saskatchewan Painters,' McKenzie Art Gall. Regina 1985, Chicago Art Fair 1986, 'Out of Saskatchewan,' Expo '86 1986, Grace Borgenicht Gall. N.Y. 1988, Robert McLaughlin Gall. Oshawa Ont. 1990, Editions, Basil Switzerland 1991, Hope & Optimism Portfolio, Oxford Eng. 1992; represented by 5 galleries; 53 permanent corp. & public collections incl.: Mendel Art Gall., Dept. of External Affairs, Edmonton Art Gallery, Canada Counc. Art Bank, Univ. of Sask., Notre Dame Univ., City of Trail B.C., Burnaby Art Gall., Shell Resources, Sask. Telecommunications, Pan Oil, Armak Chem., Mendel (Public) Art Gall. Sask., Sask. Potash Corp., McMaster Univ., Univ. of Toronto, Univ. of Lethbridge, Robert McLaughlin Gall., Concordia Univ., Beaverbrook Art Gall.; scholarships & awards: City of Nelson B.C. 1976; Notre Dame Univ. 1978; Univ. of Sask. 1980–82; Can. Council projects 1981; Sask. Arts Bd. Individual Asst. 1982, '84; Sask. Open, Mendel Art Gall. (purchase) 1982; Sask. Arts Bd. Individual Assistance (drawing trips to high Arctic and Scotland) 1988, 1990; Office: 318 – 4th St. E., Saskatoon, Sask. S7H 1J3.

**ALEXANDER, Donald Ross,** F.I.I.C.; reinsurance executive; b. St. Lambert, Que. 14 July 1938; s. James Black and Grace Elizabeth (Davidson) A.; e. Chambly Co. H.S. 1955; McGill Univ. 1955–58; m. Judith d. John and Mary Sangster 17 Apr. 1965; children: Jennifer, David; PRES., SKANDIA CAN. REINSUR. CO. 1983– ; Inspector, Candn. Underwriters Assn. 1958–61; Underwriter, Fed. Mutual Insur. Co. 1961–66; Vice-Pres., The Candn. Surety Co. 1966–78; Pres., The Insur. Shop 1978–80; Vice-Pres. & Gen Mgr., The Home Insur. Co. 1980–83; Chrmn., The Reinsur. Rsch. Counc.; Mem., Insur. Inst. of Can.; Soc. of Fellows of the Insur. Inst.; recreations: golf, skiing; Clubs: National; Summit Golf & Country; Toronto Ski; Home: 25 Salonica Rd., Don Mills, Ont. M3C 2L6; Office: 55 University Ave., Toronto, Ont. M5J 2H7.

**ALEXANDER, Ernest Raymond;** construction executive; b. Barrie, Ont. 10 Feb. 1927; s. Charles Raymond and Eva Belle (Emery) A.; e. Barrie Central Coll. Inst. 1946; Central Tech. Sch. Arch. Drafting & Constr. 1947; m. June L. d. Kenneth and Virginia Morrison 1 Oct. 1949; children: Robert, Barbara, John; PRESIDENT, E.R. ALEXANDER CONSTRUCTION CO. LTD. 1959– ; worked for father in constr. 1948–50; formed partnership Chas. Alexander & Son 1951, assumed business 1954; inc. present Co. 1959; Ald., Barrie Council 1951; Commr., Barrie Pub. Utilities Comn. 1959–94, Comn. Chrmn. 18 yrs.; Chrmn. Ont. New Home Warranty Registration Comte. 1976–90; Barrie Indust. Comn. 1977–84; Dir. Municipal Financial Corp. 1981–94; Municipal Savings & Loan Corp. 1973–94; Mun. Trust Co. 1988–94; recipient, Queen's Silver Jubilee Medal 1977; 125th Anniversary, Confederation of Canada, Commemorative Medal 1992; Pres., Candn. HOME Builders' Assn. 1964; Dir., Ont. Mun. Elect. Assn. 1985–88 (Pres. 1973); Georgian Bay Mun. Elect. Assn. (Dir. 1979–83, Vice Pres. 1985); Chrmn., Municipal Electric Assoc. (District 2) 1986–87; Pres., Barrie Flyers Intermediate Hockey Club 1981–82; Shriner; Past Chrmn. Bd. Stewards Collier St. Un. Ch.; Home: 288 Codrington St., Barrie, Ont. L4M 1S8; Office: 8 Eccles St. N. (P.O. Box 514), Barrie, Ont. L4M 4T7.

**ALEXANDER, Harold H.,** B.A., C.A.; executive, chartered accountant; b. Ont. 24 Sept. 1926; s. Arthur James and Mary (Hardie) A.; e. Burk's Falls H.S. 1944; Univ. of Toronto B.A. 1949; C.A.; PRESIDENT, ROBINTIDE INVESTMENTS INC.; Robintide Farms Ltd.; Gen. Mgr., Muttart Organ. for 10 yrs.; Vice Pres. and Treas.,

Konvey Construction Co. Ltd. and Engineered Structures for 25 yrs.; Trustee and Elder, West Ellesmere Un. Ch.; Past Pres., Candn. Diabetic Assn.; Clubs: Bd. of Trade; Empire; Home: R.R. #1, King City, Ont. L0G 1K0; Office: 100 University Ave., Suite 507, Toronto, Ont. M5J 1V6.

**ALEXANDER, James Kenneth,** B.A., LL.B.; barrister & solicitor; b. Barrie, Ont. 13 Nov. 1942; s. Flt. Lt. Orlin Ronald ('Jake') (dec.) and Grace Wylie (McChesney) A. (stepfather: the late William Norman Sparrow); e. Kirkland Lake C.V.I. 1961; Univ. of Western Ont. B.A. 1965, LL.B. 1969; articled with Malcolm Robb, Q.C. at Toronto 1969–70; called to Ont. Bar 26 March 1971; m. Anda d. Zenta & Vilis Griis 27 May 1967; children: Mark, Laura; PARTNER, ALEXANDER BARBER 1989– ; practiced law at Timmins, Iroquois Falls, & Matheson, Ont. 1971– ; emphasis on civil & criminal litigation at both trial & appellate levels & in admin. tribunals; Partner, Alexander & Girones 1971–73; sole practitioner until 1979; Partner, Cousineau, Alexander & Fournier (Robert N. Fournier now judge) until 1980; and J. André Cousineau (now judge) until 1985; with Jo-Anne Barber 1985– ;and Maureen Tomlin 1986–89; Mem., Area Ctte., Ont. Legal Aid Plan (Former Chair) 1975– ; Pres., Candn. Bar Assn. (Ont.) 1991–92 (Vice-Pres. 1990–91; Membership Chair, Ont. 1982–84, Nat. 1984–86); Chair, Timmins & Dist. Hosp. (elected 1991– ;); Vice-Chair 1986–91; Bd. Mem. 1984– ; Vice-Chair, Timmins & Dist. Hosp. Foundation 1990– ; Dir., Timmins Symphony Orch. 1982–86; Dir., Spruce Needles Inc. 1976–81; Timmins C. of C. 1974–76; Mem., Un. Ch.; Liberal Party; Law Soc. of U.C. 1971– ; Candn. Bar Assn.; Cochrane Law Assn. (Pres. 1973–74) 1971– ; Advocates Soc. 1980– ; County of York Law Assn. 1971– ; Royal Canadian Legion (Assoc. Mem.) 1991– ; recreations: skiing, golf, running, aviation, piano, reading; clubs: Porcupine Ski Runners, Spruce Needles Golf, Nighthawk Flying; Home: 704 Richelieu St., Timmins, Ont. P4N 5G6; Office: 192 Third Ave., Timmins, Ont. P4N 1C8.

**ALEXANDER, Jon,** M.A., Ph.D.; educator; b. Carbondale, Ill. 2 Jan. 1940; s. Orville Burris and Ola Ivoh (Anderson) A.; e. S. Ill. Univ. B.A. 1961, M.A. 1962; Univ. of Kansas Ph.D. 1966; children: Jon Burris, Gern Alexander; ASSOC. PROF. OF POL. SCI., CARLETON UNIV. 1983– ; Public Information Offr., Acad. Staff Assn.; Visiting Scholar Center for Study of Democratic Instns. 1965–66, 1968; Visiting Asst. Prof. Emory Univ. 1966–67, Columbia Univ. summer 1967; Asst. Prof. of Pol. Sci. present Univ. 1967; Guest Lectr. Inst. for Policy Studies 1969; Science Advisor, Sci. Council of Can. 1973–74; co-founder, Caucus for a New Political Science 1968; co-founder, Centretown Community Health Centre 1971; co-founder 'Let X =X' radio program CKCU 1985; Co-founder and Editor, Science, Technology & Politics 1985; Co-founder and Dir., Technology Policy Inst. 1986; Consultant: Wadsworth Publishing Co.; Univ. Press of Ky.; Candn. Fed. Youth Hostel Task Force; Can. Council; Dept. of Justice and of Supply & Services; Sci. Council of Can.; Dir. Ottawa Valley Homebuilders Assn.; Pestalozzi Coll.; Ottawa Homebuilders Co-op.; collab. 'Cultural Affairs and Foreign Relations' 1964; 'Science for What?' 1974; 'Science and Technology Policy Evaluation' 1990; 'Science, Technology & Politics Yearbook' 1990; contrib. various mags. and journs.; co-ed. 'Survival'; mem. Candn. Pol. Sci. Assn.; Internat. Studies Assn.; Midwest Pol. Sci. Assn.; Am. Pol. Sci. Assn.; Internat. Pol. Sci. Assn.; recreations: charitable fundraising, sailing, reading; Home: Lac Gauvreau, R.R. 2, Masham, Qué. J0X 2W0; Office: Ottawa, Ont. K1S 5B6.

**ALEXANDER, Col. The Hon. Lincoln MacCauley,** P.C., C.C., K.St.J., O. Ont., Q.C., B.A., LL.B., LL.D. (Hon.), D.Litt.S. (Hon.); b. Toronto, Ont. 21 Jan. 1922; s. Lincoln MacCauley and Mae Rose (Royale) A.; e. McMaster Univ. B.A. 1949; Osgoode Hall Law Sch. 1953; m. Yvonne Phyllis d. the late Robert and the late Edythe (Lewis) Harrison 10 Sept. 1948; one s. Keith; CHANCELLOR, UNIV. OF GUELPH 1991; Dir., George Weston Limited; Royal LePage Limited; Bd. Mem., Upper Canada Coll., Massey Hall/Roy Thomson Hall, Doctors' Hosp.; Shaw Festival; Hamilton Philharmonic Soc.; called to Bar of Ont. 1953; cr. Q.C. 1965; formerly Partner, Millar, Alexander, Tokiwa & Isaacs, Hamilton, Ont. 1963–79; el. to H. of C. for Hamilton W. g.e. 1968, re-el. 1972, 1974, 1979, 1980; U.N. Observer 1976, 1978; Min. of Labour Can. 1979–80; other former parlty. assns.: mem. Inter-Parlty. Union (Candn. Group); Commonwealth Parlty. Assn. (Candn. Br.); Candn. NATO Parlty. Assn.; Can.-U.S. Parlty. Delegation; Chrmn., Ont. Workers' Compensation Bd. 1980–85; 24th Lieutenant Governor of Ont. 1985–91; Hon. Dir., Ont. League, Royal Candn. Army Cadets; Hon. Life Mem.: Navy League of Can.; Ont. Chamber of Comm.; Mem. and Past Pres., Hamilton Optimist Club; mem.: Hamilton Lawyers Club; Wentworth County Law Assn.; Candn. Bar Assn.; McMaster Univ. Alumni Assn.; Scottish Rite, Hadji Temple Shrine, 33rd (PHA); Past Pres.: Internat. Assoc. of Industrial Accident Bds.; Assn. of Workers' Compensation Bds. of Can.; served with RCAF 1942–45, rank Cpl.; apptd. Hon. Col. 2 Tactical Aviation Wing, Toronto 1989; recipient: St. Ursula Award 1969; Officer, Order of the Hospital of St. John of Jerusalem 1981, Comdr. (Brother) 1983, Knight of Grace 1985; Man of the Year Award, Ethnic Press Council of Canada Inc. 1982; Cultural Achievement Award, Caribana Cultural Comte. 1984; Certificate of Service Award, House of Commons 1984; Honorary Counsel, Stewart Meml. Ch. Hamilton 1985; Candn. Award, John G. Diefenbaker Meml. Foundn. 1985; Paul Harris Fellow (The Rotary Found. of Rotary Internat.) 1986; received the 36th Annual Humanitarian Award of Beth Sholom Brotherhood 1986; Honoree of the Year, 1986 Hamilton Negev Dinner (Jewish National Fund of Canada) 1986; LL.D. (hon. causa): Univ. of Toronto 1986; McMaster Univ. 1987; Univ. of Western Ont. 1988; York Univ. 1990; Royal Mil. Coll. 1991; D.Litt.S. (hon. causa): Univ. of Trinity Coll. 1993; awarded Boy Scouts of Canada Silver Acorn by the Gov. Gen. of Can. 1988; Provincial Sport Citation in the Humanities Category, Govt. of Ont. 1988; Outstanding Citizen Award and Mel Osborne Fellow, Kiwanis Found. 1989; Hon. Sr. Fellow, Renison Coll.; Canadian Unity Award (1st recipient), Thornhill Secondary Sch. 1989; Human Relations Award, Candn. Counc. of Christians and Jews 1989; Hon. Chief of Police, Metro. Toronto Police, 1989; Hon. Fellow, Candn. Sch. of Mgmt. 1989; Outstanding Candn. Award, Armenian Community Ctr. of Toronto 1990; Knight of The Military and Hospitaller Order of St. Lazarus of Jerusalem 1990; as an Osgoode Hall graduate between the years 1889–1960, awarded LL.B. degree by the Senate of York Univ. 1991; Commissioner (Hon.), Ont. Provincial Police 1991–94; Hon. Commander, Ordo Sancti Constantini Magni 1991; apptd. Officer, Order of Ont. 1992; invested by the Pres. of Senegal as an Officer of the Nat. Order of the Lion 1992; el. Hon. Bencher, Law Soc. of Upper Canada 1992; apptd. Companion of the Order of Canada by His Excellency the Right Hon. R. J. Hnatyshyn 1992; Baptist; P. Conservative; recreations: music, gardening; Home: 30 Proctor Blvd., Hamilton, Ont. L8M 2M3.

**ALEXANDER, Norman J.;** investment consultant; b. Regina, Sask. 1909; Former Vice-Pres. James Richardson & Sons Ltd. and Former Mang. Partner Richardson Securities of Canada; Past Pres. B.C. Bond Dealers Assn.; Vancouver Stock Exchange; Investment Dealers Assn. of Can.; Clubs; Manitoba; St. Charles Country; Winnipeg Winter; Vancouver; Capilano Golf & Country; Home: 66 Wilton St., Winnipeg, Man. R3M 3C1; Office: Suite 1220, One Lombard Place, Winnipeg, Man. R3B 0X3.

**ALEXANDER, Ruth Marion,** B.A.; volunteer executive; b. Hamilton, Ont. 12 Jan. 1929; d. Rev. W. Frederick J. and Mary Allen (Gardiner) Manning; e. Grimsby H.S.; Univ. of Toronto (Victoria Coll.) B.A.; m. William Gordon s. Gordon P. and Edith H. A. 11 Apr. 1953; Chairman, Bd. of Regents, Victoria Univ. 1989–93; Pres., Bd. of IODE Children's Hosp., NYGH 1975–78; Nat. Pres., IODE 1980–82; Queen's Jubilee Medal; Bd. Mem., Gardiner Mus. of Ceramic Art 1989– ; Fdn. of North York Gen. Hosp. 1980– ;(Bd. of Gov. 1973–78); Belmont House 1969–79; Pilot Place 1985– ; Mem., Trinity York Mills Presbyn. Ch.; club: Toronto Ladies; Home: 414 - 4005 Bayview Ave., Willowdale, Ont. M2M 3Z9.

**ALEXANDER, Stuart Jeffery,** M.Sc.; executive; b. St. Albans, Herts., Eng. 26 Apr. 1942; s. Marcus and Pearla (Rose) Alexander; e. St. Albans Grammar Sch. 1961; Univ. of Sheffield B.Sc. (Hons) (Physics) 1964; Univ. of London M.Sc. (Microwave Physics) 1972; m. Linda d. Harry and Bertha Ross 25 Nov. 1967; children: Rachel Jane, James Peter; DIR., CORPORATE PROGRAMS, SPAR AEROSPACE LTD. 1983– ; joined Marconi Elliott Avionics as Research Physicist 1964, set up and headed Laser Dept. 1974; joined Spar Aerospace Ltd. Toronto 1977, Elect. Engn. Mgr. 1979, Asst. to Chrmn. of Bd. 1981; Vice Pres. Bus. Develop., Northway Gestalt Corp. 1982; author or co-author various tech. papers microwaves, radar and lasers; Bd. of Govs., Beth Tikvah Synagogue; mem. Inst. Elect. Engrs. (UK); Assn. Prof. Engrs. Prov. Ont.; recreations: cross-country skiing, jogging, hiking, cycling, puzzles; Home: 115 Newport Square, Thornhill, Ont. L4J 7N3; Office: Suite 900, 5090 Explorer Dr., Mississauga, Ont. L4W 4X6.

**ALFORD, Gregory George,** B.A.; corporate and government affairs manager; b. Chaffey's Lock, Ont. 30 Jan. 1956; s. James Edward and Mary Kathryn (Murphy) A.; e. McMaster Univ., B.A. 1977; m. Christine Kenopic 1 Oct. 1988; SR. VICE PRES., THYSSEN BHI 1989– ; Gen. Mgr., Corporate and Government Affairs; Econ., Planning & Prioirities Sec., Govt. of Nfld. & Lab. 1977; Mktg., Grew Corp. 1978; F.M.H. Can. Ltd. 1979–83; Sr. Cons. & Dir., Client Serv., Alta Nova 1984; joined Government Consultants International 1985, Pres. & C.O.O. 1985–88, Vice Chrmn. 1988; Mem., Candn. Nat. Bobsled Team 1981–84; Chef d'Equipe, Candn. Olympic Bobsled Team, Calgary Olympics 1988; Dir., & Sec., Extve. Ctte., Candn. Bobsleigh Assn.; fundraiser, var. charities; recreations: cycling, golf, bobsledding, skiing; Home: 640 Broadway Ave., Toronto, Ont. M4G 2S7.

**ALFRED, Braxton M.,** B.A., M.A., Ph.D.; educator; b. Houston, Texas 3 June 1933; s. Basil and Lillian (Henderson) A.; e. Univ. of Houston B.A. 1958; Univ. of Colo. M.A. 1963, Ph.D. 1965; Stanford Univ. Nat. Insts. of Health Post-doctoral Fellow 1965–66; m. Diane d. Hugh and Elsie Wiebe 14 Aug. 1987; one s. Peter; PROF. OF ANTHROP. UNIV. OF B.C. 1966– ; joined Univ. of B.C. 1966; Univ. of Cal. San Francisco Med. Sch. 1969–73; Forensic and Acturial Cons.; Martin-Denver, Data Reduc Group Leader; Stanley Aviation, Static Test Lab. Asst. Eng. Oper. Dir.; Dir. Stat. Centre present Univ. 1966–69; Exec. Sec. XI Internat. Cong. Anthrop. & Ethnol. Sci. 1980–81; mem. Bd. Dirs., Treas. and Dir. Samosa Project S. Vancouver Neighbourhood House; author 'Elements of Statistics for the Life and Social Sciences' 1987; ed. Candn. Review Phys. Anthrop.; mem. Am. Assn. Phys. Anthrop.; Candn. Assn. Phys. Anthrop. (Sec.-Treas. 1973–76); Soc. Study Human Biol.; Sigma Xi; recreations: sailing, flying, hiking, fishing, fencing, martial arts; Clubs: Experimental Aircraft Assn.; Sailing; Home: 304, 5880 Hampton Pl., Vancouver, B.C. V6T 2E9; Office: 6303 N.W. Marine Dr., Vancouver, B.C. V6T 1Z1.

**ALIA, Valerie,** M.A., Ph.D.; educator; journalist; b. New York, N.Y. 20 Dec. 1942; d. Julius Abraham and Bertha (Fenyves) Graber; e. Univ. of Cincinnati B.A. 1965; Mich. State Univ. M.A. 1967; York Univ. Ph.D. 1989; children: David Owen and Daniel Olam Restivo; ASST. PROF., GRAD. SCH. OF JOURNALISM, UNIV. OF W. ONT. 1989– ; arts writing Boston Phoenix 1970–71; Dance Critic Boston Herald Traveller 1971–72; Music & Dance Critic Albany Times Union and Knickerbocker News 1974–79; arts prodn. WMHT-TV Schenectady 1976–77; arts writing, reportage, photog. UPI, Arctic Circle, Globe and Mail, CBC Radio and TV, CTV, Up Here, Rutland (Vt.) Herald; Sessional appt., Sociol. Dept. Univ. of Toronto 1989; SSHRC funded rsch. n. media 1990–91; Co-ord. Media Info. Project UN 2nd Special Session on Disarmament 1982; participant, Native Geog. Names Symposia (Fed. Govt. and McGill Univ.) 1985–87; SSHRC funded rsch., journalism ethics 1992–94; cons. Royal Comn. Electoral Reform 1990; Inuit Tapirisat of Can.; Ont. Task Force Vocational Rehab.; Inst. Environ. Rsch.; Native News Network of Can. (Adv. Bd.); Yukon Govt. Women's Directorate 1990–91; Candn. Museums Assn.; Can. Federation for the Humanities 1992– ; recipient AAUW Am. Fellowship for arctic rsch. 1986–87; Ont. Grad. Scholarship 1986; Candn. Woman Studies Writing Award 1983; Schmidlapp Fellowship 1965; Nat. Endowment on Arts (U.S.) Fellowship Dance Criticism 1972; Strauss and Elliston Poetry Prizes 1965; Elliston Poetry Fellow 1965; mem. Nat. Honor Soc.; author 'The Politics of Naming' in progress; 'Project Surname: Inuit & the Politics of Naming in Canada' 1994; co-author '1982' 1978; 'Arms Control and Disarmament Bibliography' 1984; co-author 'Canada - North of Sixty' 1991; editor 'Journalism Ethics in Canada' (in progess); Aboriginal Peoples & Humanities Scholarship; jour. and mag. articles, radio and TV broadcasts; mem. Am. Assn. Univ. Women (AAUW) (Internat. Fellowship Awards Panel, Internat. Mem.-at-large); Assn. Cinema, TV & Radio Artists; Assn. Professional & Practical Ethics; Westminster Inst. for Ethics and Human Values (Fellow); Candn. Communication Assn.; Candn. Studies Assn.; Periodical Writers Assn. Can. (Toronto Exec. 1989–90); Internat. Arctic Social Sci. Assn. (Founding mem.); Dance Critics Assn. (Founding mem.); Vt. Acad. Arts & Sci's; Couchiching Inst. Pub. Affairs; Candn. Soc. Study Names; recreations: photography, music, travel, poetry, irreverence; Office: Middlesex Coll., London, Ont. N6A 5B7.

**ALLAIRE, Yvan,** B.Sc.Comm., M.B.A., Ph.D.; mem. of Académie des lettres et des sciences humaines, Royal Soc. of Can.; Soc. of Sigma Xi (M.I.T. chapter), Strategic Mgmt. Soc., Mensa Internat.; university professor; b. Latuque, P.Q. 3 July 1941; s. Leopold and Georgine

(Lauzon) A.; e. Univ. Sherbrooke, B.Sc.Comm. (summa cum laude) 1967; M.B.A. 1969; Sloan Sch. Mgmt., M.I.T., Ph.D. 1973; children: Catherine, Mylène; m. Prof. Mihaela E. Firsirotu 1984; CO-FOUNDER, SECOR GROUP INC.; Prof. of Strategy, Univ. du Qué. à Montréal; Asst. Prof., Univ. Sherbrooke 1969; Asst. Prof., Univ. Ottawa 1971–73; Dir. Grad. Studies 1971–72; joined present univ. as Assoc. Prof. 1973; Full Prof. 1974; Chrmn. of Ph.D. Program 1982–86; Visiting Prof., Université de Grenoble and Sloan Sch. of Management, M.I.T. (Cambridge, Mass.); author numerous and prize-winning articles and papers strategy and socio-political subjects; author: 'La gestion stratégique des organisations' 1984; co-author: (with Mihaela Firsirotu) 'Theories and Strategies for Radical Change in Complex Organizations' 1983; 'L'entreprise stratégique' 1993; 'The Making of Strategy' forthcoming; rec'd. Pres.'s Scholarship, Bank of Montreal; Bronfman Foundation Fellowship; Candn. Advertising Advisory Bd. Doctoral Dissertation Award; Sloan Fellowship; Hydro-Québec Fellowship; Bd. Mem., École de Tech. Supérieure 1973–79; Candn. Arsenals Ltd. 1977–86; Mem., Conseil des universités du Québec 1975–77; Conseil canadien de la recherche en sciences sociales 1980–82; recreations: tennis, reading, hiking; Office: 555 René Lévesque Blvd. West, 9th Flr., Montréal, Qué. H2Z 1B1.

**ALLAN, David Geoffrey Peter;** executive; b. Buenos Aires, Argentina 28 Jan. 1942; s. Denis Creswell (deceased) and Joan Cecil (Spanton) A.; e. Oundle Sch., Northants, Eng.; McGill Univ.; m. Judith Frances d. William O. (dec.) and Frances Helen Twaits 22 June 1973; children: Gwenael, Vanessa, Trevor, Ashley; EXECUTIVE DIRECTOR, YORKTON SECURITIES INC. 1992– ; Pres. & Dir., Proteus Bio-Research Corp.; Pres. & C.E.O. Mead & Co. Ltd. 1966–80; Sr. Vice Pres. and Dir., Walwyn Stodgell Cochran Murray Ltd. 1980–86; Dir., Loewen Ondaatje McCutcheon 1987–91; Clubs: Beaver Valley Ski; Rosedale Golf; Toronto Lawn Tennis; University; Home: 40 Scholfield Ave., Toronto, Ont. M4W 2Y3; Office: 40 King St. W., Suite 5500, P.O. Box 1006, Toronto, Ont. M5H 3Y2.

**ALLAN, Douglas Henry Wilson,** B.A.Sc., P.Eng.; b. Toronto, Ont. 18 Nov. 1919; s. late Thomas Henry and late Edna Mae (Wilson) A.; e. Univ. of Toronto, B.A.Sc. (Metall.) 1942; m. Evelyn Anne Grace, d. late W.A. and late Beatrice Wagner, Richmond Hill, Ont.; children: Marilyn Grace Giekes, Warren Douglas; retired Pres., Doug Allan International Consulting Services Inc. 1983–91; held various metall. positions, Hamilton Works, The Steel Co. of Canada Ltd. 1945–55; Metall. Engr., American Iron and Steel Inst., N.Y., 1955–64; Chief, Iron and Steel Div., Materials Br., Dept. of Industry, Ottawa, 1964–68; Mgr. of Marketing, Peace River Mining and Smelting Ltd., Amherstburg, Ont., 1968–71; Vice-Pres. & Gen. Mgr. Industrial Research Inst., Univ. of Windsor 1971–75; Assistant to President of Co-Steel International Ltd. 1975–76; Chief Engr., Export Dev. Corp., Ottawa 1976–84; Fellow Am. Soc. for Quality Control; mem. Assn. of Profl. Engrs. of Ont.; Amer. Inst. of Mining Metall. and Petroleum Engrs.; Freemason; United Church; Address: 2325 Shaver Rd., R.R. 2, Ancaster, Ont. L9G 3L1.

**ALLAN, Duncan McCallum,** M.A.; retired civil servant; b. North Easthope Twp., Ont. 17 Dec. 1936; s. Headrick and Arnetta (Dahmer) A.; e. Queen's Univ. B.A. 1959; Univ. of Toronto M.A. 1963; m. Diana Bayne d. John and Marian Plunkett 27 June 1959; children: James, Margaret; PRESIDENT, ALLANWAY CONSULTING INC. 1992– ; joined Ford Motor Co. 1959–61; Ministry of Treasury and Econ. Ont. 1961–72; Asst. Depy. Min. of Ind. and Tourism 1978; Secy., B.I.L.D. 1980; Depy. Min. of Agric. and Food 1981; Deputy Min. of Energy 1984; Special Advisor for Toronto Waterfront Development 1987; Office: 1001 Bay St., #1313, Toronto, Ont. M5S 3A6.

**ALLAN, Vice-Admiral (ret.) John,** C.M.M., O.M.M., O.St.J., C.D., B.Sc., P.Eng.; b. Kirkland Lake, Ont. 31 March 1928; e. Queen's Univ. B.Sc. (Elect. Engn.) 1955; m. Isabel Anne (Jamieson); children: Sandra, Kathryn, James, William; PRESIDENT, J & IA CONSULTANTS INC.; joined RCN 1946; commanded HMCS Qu'Appelle; Proj. Mgr. DDH 280 Prog.; Apptd. Offr. in Order of Military Merit for serv. in DDH 280 prog.; Cmmdr. First Destroyer Sqdn.; Chief of Staff Mar. Cmmd. Hdqts.; Dir. Gen. Mar. Engin. and Maint.; Assoc. Asst. Dep. Min. Materiel; apptd. Commander of Order of Military Merit; promoted Vice-Admiral July 1979 and in Aug. appt. Cmmdr. of Mar. Cmmd. in Halifax, N.S.; Depy. Chief of Defence Staff in Ottawa 1980; Extve. Vice-Pres. Aviation Electric Ltd. 1982; Marine Administrator, Transport Canada 1983; Pres., MIL Systems Engineering Inc. 1985; Sr. Partner, CFN Consultants 1987; Office: 1969 Mulberry Cr., Gloucester, Ont. K1J 8J8.

**ALLAN, John R.,** B.A., A.M., Ph.D.; university professor and administrator; b. Glasgow, Scotland 24 March 1932; e. Hamilton Central C.I.; McMaster Univ. B.A. (Hons.) 1955; Princeton Univ. A.M. 1961, Ph.D. 1965 (Dean's Honour List 4 years); highest standing in Economics); married with two daughters; VICE-PRESIDENT (ADMINISTRATION), UNIV. OF REGINA 1993– ; Lecturer, Univ. of Sask. 1961–62; Asst. Prof., Queen's Univ. 1962–65; Assoc. Prof. McMaster Univ. 1965–69; Principal, Woods Gordon & Company 1969–70; Dir., Fiscal Policy, Dept. of Finance Canada 1970–73; Tax Policy 1973–77; Vice-Pres., Admin. & Treas. and Adjunct Prof., Econ., Univ. of Windsor 1977–80; Dir., Interpretations & Appeals Div., Alta. Corp. Tax Admin. 1981–93; Princeton Univ. Fellowship; Canada Council Pre-Doctoral Fellowship; Ford Found. Doctoral Fellowship; several past executive appointments and assignments; bilingual; Mem., Candn. Econ. Assn.; Candn. Tax Found.; Nat. Tax Found.; Inst. of Public Admin. of Canada; Edmonton Tax Lawyers and Accountants Discussion Group; author of several articles and papers; Home: 14319 – 48 Ave., Edmonton, Alta. T6H 5A3; Office: Regina, Sask. S4S 0A2.

**ALLAN, The Hon. Mme. Justice Marion Jean,** B.A., M.A., LL.B.; judge; b. Torpoint, Cornwall, England 6 July 1946; d. William Allan and Doris (Dyson) Douglas; e. St. Ann's Acad. 1963; Univ. of B.C., B.A. 1967, LL.B. 1977; Univ. of Alta. M.A. 1970; divorced; one d.: Michelle Marie Alblas; JUDGE, SUPREME COURT OF B.C. 1990– ; articled Russell & DuMoulin Vanc. 1977–78; called to Bar of B.C. 10 July 1978; practiced Russell & DuMoulin 1978–88; Partner 1985–88; Judge, County Court of Vancouver 1988–90; taught civil procedure, Law Sch., Univ. of B.C. 1984, 85, 86, 88 (4 spring terms); Dir., Vanc. Bar Assn. 1985–87; Dir., Continuing Legal Education 1991– ; Office: Law Courts, 800 Smithe St., Vancouver, B.C. V6Z 2E1.

**ALLAN, Ralph Thomas Mackinnon,** B.Com.; insurance executive; b. Montréal, Qué. 17 Feb. 1942; s. Ralph Percival Hall and Margaret Hunter (Lawrie) A.; e. Mount Allison Univ. B.Com. 1963; m. Suzanne Patricia d. François and Alison Delaute 18 May 1968; two d. Alison, Margaret; EXTVE. VICE PRES. INVESTMENTS AND CORPORATE SERVICES, LONDON LIFE INSURANCE CO. 1992– ; Chrmn. & Dir. (1987), Internat. Care Corp. 1992– ; RLMC Holdings Ltd. 1992– ; Royal Lepage Mortgage (Broker) Co. 1991– ; Depy. Chrmn. & Dir. (1981), Toronto College Park Ltd. 1992– ; London Reinsurance Group Inc. 1991– ; Pres. and Dir., London Life Financial Corp. 1981– ; London Life Insurance. Co. of Michigan 1990– ; Extve. Vice Pres., Investments, London Insurance Group Inc. 1989– ; Vice Pres. & Dir., Lonvest Equities Ltd. 1989– ; Vice Pres., Invests. Trilon Financial Corp. 1982– ; Dir., LonLife Data Services 1983– ; Devan Properties Ltd. 1986– ; Coscan Development Corp. 1989– ; London Life & Casualty Reinsurance Corp. 1989– ; London Life Internat. Reinsurance Corp. 1989– ; Intrawest Development Corp. 1990– ; Security National Insur. Co. 1991– ; Longroup Insur. Co. 1992– ; London Life Bank Corp. 1992– ; London Life & General Reinsurance Co. 1992– ; Meloche Monnex Inc. 1992– ; Primmum Insur. Co. 1992– ; Wellington Insur. Co. 1992– ; Trojan Technologies Inc. 1993– ; Assoc. Treas. & Head of Private Placement Operation; Sun Life Assurance Co. of Canada, Hamilton & Montréal 1974–78; Vice-Pres., Commercial Lending, Central Trust Co., Halifax 1979–80; Vice Pres. Investments present Co. 1981–86; Sr. Vice Pres. Investments 1986–89; Extve. Vice Pres. Investments 1989–92; mem. Invest. Ctte. (1982) and Mem. Bd., London Community Found. 1993; City of London 1982– ; Adv. Bd., St. Joseph's Hosp., London; Clubs: London; London Hunt & Country; National (Toronto); Home: R.R. 3, London, Ont. N6A 4B7; Office: 255 Dufferin Ave., London, Ont. N6A 4K1.

**ALLAN, Robert William,** B.Comm., C.A.; financial executive; b. Vancouver, B.C. 24 July 1946; s. Charles M. and Edith G. (Chittenden) A.; e. Univ. of Toronto 1969; m. Judy d. Roy and Evelyn Allaby Sept. 1969; children: Angela, Heather; VICE-PRESIDENT, CORPORATE SERVICES, UNITEL COMMUNICATIONS INC. 1990– ; Price Waterhouse Toronto 1969–72; Vice-Pres. Finance & Public Affairs, Rothmans Inc. 1972–87; Vice-Pres. Finance, Dinnerex Inc. 1987–90; Home: 2301 Pyramid Cres., Mississauga, Ont. L5K 1C8; Office: 200 Wellington St. W., Toronto, Ont. M5V 3C7.

**ALLAN, Robyn Louise,** B.A., M.A.; financial executive; b. Vancouver, B.C. 14 Aug. 1955; d. Norman Campbell and Diane Louise (Yates) A.; e. Univ. of B.C. B.A. 1976, M.A. 1978; children: Karl, Harris; Pres., C.E.O. & Dir., Insurance Corp. of B.C. 1992–..; Analyst, Crown Investments Corp. of Sask. 1978; Mgr., Financial Planning & Budget Control, Sask. Govt. Insur. 1980; Consultant 1982–85; Economics Teacher, Univ. of Regina; Teacher, Kwantlen College & Econ., B.C. Central Credit Union 1985; Sr. Economist, B.C. Central 1989; Extve. Dir., VanCity Community Found. 1990; Bd. of Dir., Western Inst. for Public Policy; Vancouver Planetarium; Past Co-chair, Globe 92 Conference; author of numerous articles; recreations: choreogapher, dancer, producer.

**ALLAN, Spence A.,** M.B.E., E.D., B.A.; b. Hamilton, Ont. 20 Feb. 1906; s. George and Clara Mabel (Carey) A.; e. Hamilton College Inst.; Univ. of Toronto B.A. (Pol. Econ.) 1929; m. Dorothy Walker, d. Alexander F. Zimmerman, 20 June 1931; children: George A., Mrs. Charles E. Parker, Mrs. D. M. Catto; Past Pres. Chedoke Hospitals (retired); joined Reid Press Ltd. 1929 as Plant Superindt;. Asst. to Mang. Dir., 1945–51; Pres. 1954; served with Argyll & Sutherland Highlanders, N.P.A.M., 1930–40 (now Hon. Col.); 2nd World War with R.C.A.F. 1940–45, Adm. Br. trans. to Reserve with rank of Group Capt.; awarded M.B.E.; Past. Pres., Candn. Paper Box Mfrs. Assn.; Past Chrmn., Hamilton Br., Candn. Inst. Internat. Affairs; Past Chrmn. Bd. of Govs., Art Gallery of Hamilton; Senator Stratford Shakespearean Festival Foundation; mem. Extr. Comte., Royal Botanical Gardens; Hon. Col., 91st Argyll Sutherland Highlanders of Can.; Kappa Alpha; Conservative; Presbyterian; recreations: boating, horticulture; Clubs: The Hamilton; Royal Hamilton Military Institute; Tamahaac; Badminton & Racquet (Toronto); Home: 53 Markland St., Hamilton, Ont. L8P 2J5.

**ALLAN, Ted;** playwright and author; b. Montreal, P.Q. 25 Jan. 1916; s. Harry and Anne (Elias) Herman; e. Elementary Schs., Montreal, and Baron Byng High Sch. there; m. Kate Schwartz, 25 Aug. 1939, (divorced 1966); children: Julia Iona, Norman Bethune; Member of Internat. Bgde., Spanish Civil War; Political and Press Offr., Spanish-Candn. Blood Transfusion Inst., Madrid 1937; stage plays: 'The Money Makers' (produced in Toronto 1954); 'The Ghost Writers' (prod. at Arts Theatre, London 1955); 'Legend of Pepito' (Theatre Workshop, London 1956); (with Roger MacDougall) 'Double Image' (prod. by Lord Olivier at Savoy Theatre, London 1957, and at Michodière Theatre, Paris 1959–64 under title 'Gog et Magog'); 'Secret of the World' (prod. Theatre Royal, Stratford East 1962; 'Oh What a Lovely War' – stage treatment – (prod. by Joan Littlewood, London and N.Y. 1965); 'Chu Chem – A Zen Buddhist-Hebrew Musical' (prod. by Albert Marre, Philadelphia 1965; Jewish Rep. Theatre, Ritz Theatre, N.Y. 1988); I've Seen You Cut Lemons' (prod. by Fortune Theatre, London 1970); 'My Sister's Keeper' (prod. at Lennoxville Festival, 1974); 'Willie, The Squowse' (Young Peoples' Theatre, Toronto 1988); books: 'This Time a Better Earth' 1940; 'The Scalpel, The Sword: The Story of Dr. Norman Bethune' (in collab. with Sydney Gordon) 1955; 'Willie the Squowse' 1977 and 1992; 'Love is a Long Shot' (novel) 1984; (Stephen Leacock Award – Best Humourous Novel 1985) 'Don't You Know Anybody Else' (short story coll.) 1985; also short stories in 'New Yorker,' 'Harpers,' 'Mademoiselle,' 'Colliers,' etc.; Academy Award Nom. Best Orig. Screen Play, 'Lies My Father Told Me' (1975); Golden Globe 'Best Foreign Film Award' 1976 co-author with John Cassavetes, 'Love Streams' 1984; screenplay 'Bethune: The Making of a Hero' 1990; Address: 9 Tennis Cres., Apt. B24, Toronto, Ont. M4K 1J4.

**ALLAN, William,** B.Sc., P.Eng.; mining executive; b. Kirkland Lake, Ont. 23 May 1934; e. Queen's Univ. B.Sc. 1958; m.; 3 children; SR. VICE PRES. & C.O.O., CAMECO CORPORATION 1992– ; served various mining co's 8 yrs., Noranda Inc. 25 yrs.; Sr. Vice Pres. Operations, Cameco Corporation 1990–91; Office: 2121 – 11th St. W., Saskatoon, Sask. S7M 1J3.

**ALLAN, William Norman,** B.A., M.Com. (M.B.A.), F.R.Econ.S.; executive; b. Toronto, Ont. 30 May 1925; s. Leslie Brown and Anne Lillian (Morrison) A.; e. Allenby Public School; Lawrence Park Coll. Inst.; Univ. of Toronto (Victoria Coll. B.A. 1948), (Grad. Sch. of Business Adm., M.Com. (M.B.A.) 1951); m. Jean Mary, d. Louis and Agnes Pryzdial, 22 May 1965; CHRMN. AND PRES., FISCAL INVESTMENTS LTD. 1961– ; Great Lakes Commercial & Holdings Corp. Ltd.; Great North Uranium & Energy Resources Inc.; Chrmn. & C.E.O., Fairstone Financial Corp. Ltd.; Founder, Anglo-Permanent Corporate Holdings Ltd.; Pres., grad. Bus. Admin. Course, University of Toronto 1950–51; Economist, Ont. Govt. (Treas.) 1949–52; Business Consultant and Econ., 1952–57; Extve. Asst. to The Hon. Donald M. Fleming (Candn. Min. of Finance, Receiver Gen., Gov. World Bank, Founding Chrmn. O.E.C.D.) Govt. of Can. 1957–61; Former Pres., Toronto Audubon Soc.; Life Gov., Royal Humane Soc.; Chrmn. & Gov., Fidelity Charitable Foundation; mem., Nat. Trust for Scotland; Life Member, Acad. of Pol. Sci. (Columbia Univ.); Life Fellow, Roy. Commonwealth Soc.; Roy. Econ. Soc., London, Eng. (el. 1951); mem., Ont. Hist. Soc.; Bd. of Trade of Metro Toronto; Life mem., Empire Club of Can.; St. Andrew's Soc. Tor.; Candn. Econ. Assn.; Life mem., Kappa Sigma Fraternity (Internat.); Am. Internat. Acad.; 32 degree Freemason (Scottish Rite); Shriner; Protestant; P. Conservative; recreations: comparative religion, fishing, ornithology, world history, astronomy, mycology; Clubs: Albany; Board of Trade of Toronto; Home: 157 Golfdale Road, Toronto, Ont. M4N 2C1.

**ALLARD, (Joseph) Claude,** B.Com., C.A.; retired accountant and management consultant; b. St. Constant, P.Q. 22 May 1926; s. Joseph Normand and Marie Jeanne (Lefebvre) A.; e. McGill Univ., B.Com. (Hon. Econ.) 1949; Inst. Chart. Accts. Que., C.A. 1951; m. Kathleen Isabel, d. late Denis John McCarthy, 18 June 1951; children: Claudette, Richard, Nicole; with Price Waterhouse & Co., Chartered Accountants, Montreal, 1949–60; joined Dom. Steel & Coal Corp., Ltd. as Asst.-Comptroller 1960; Vice-Pres., Finance, and Treas., Dosco Industries Ltd., and Dominion Coal Co. Ltd., 1964–68; Partner, Price Waterhouse & Co., Price Waterhouse Assoc., and Mineau, Allard, Mantha et Associes, Montreal 1968–81 (ret.); served in 2nd World War with R.C.C.S. 1945–46; Alderman, Town of St. Bruno, 1962–68; Mayor 1968–69; mem., Order of Chart. Accts. of Que.; R. Catholic; recreation: golf, travel; Home: 117 De Touraine, St. Lambert, Que. J4S 1H3.

**ALLARD, Sébastien,** K.C.H.S., A.I.I.C.; retired insurance executive; b. Montréal, Qué. 10 July 1922; s. René and Rose (Léger) A.; e. St. Stanislas and St. Agnes, Montréal; m. Denise d. Eugène and Bernadette Chartrand 10 June 1946; children: René, Robert, André, François, Michel, Denis; Pres. (1982–86), Gov. and Dir., Conseil du Patronat du Québec; Chrmn., Fonds d'Assurance Responsabilité Professionnelle du Barreau du Québec; Dir., Candn. Labor Market and Productivity Centre; Commissioner, Commission des Droits de la Personne du Québec; Knight Commander, Equestrian Order of the Holy Sepulchre of Jerusalem; Gov., Hôpital Notre-Dame; Associate, Insurance Institute of Canada (recipient Award of Merit 1974); mem., Insurance Institute of Qué. (Pres. 1965–66); recreations: skiing, reading; Club: St-Denis; Home: 10525 Chambord St., Montréal, Qué. H2C 2R6.

**ALLATT, David H.,** B.A.Sc., P.Eng.; service industry executive; b. Weston, Ont. 1 Apr. 1934; s. Frank and Kathleen (Bellamy) Allatt; e. Royal Roads 1956; Royal Military College, dipl. E.E. 1958; Univ. of Toronto B.A.Sc. 1959; m. M. Gail d. Clarence and Stella Ford 7 Jan. 1967; children: M. Annice, Emily M., Daniel D. Allatt; VICE PRESIDENT & MGR., CANDN. SERV. DIV., WESTINGHOUSE CANADA INC.; Flying Offr., Royal Candn. Air Force 1958–63; various management roles, present firm 1963– ; Mem., Assn. of Profl. Engrs. Ont.; Home: 73 Sunrise Cres., Dundas, Ont. L9H 3S1; Office: P.O. Box 2510, Hamilton, Ont. L8N 3K2.

**ALLCOCK, William F.,** B.A.; economic development executive; b. St. Catharines, Ont. 1 June 1950; s. Fred and Daisy Margaret (Windibank) A.; e. Brock Univ., B.A. 1973; Carleton Univ., Univ. of Waterloo Cert. in Econ. Devel. 1980; m. Christine d. Matt and Olga Baraniuk 12 July 1975; children: Amy, Adam; CHIEF ADMINISTRATIVE OFFICER, CITY OF STONEY CREEK, ONT. 1993– ; Mgmt. Trainee North American Life Assurance Co. 1973; Tourism Devel. Cons. Ont. Ind. & Tourism Dept. 1973, Econ. Analyst 1975, Ind. Devel. Cons. 1977–79; Sr. Bus. Devel. Offr. St. Catharines, Ont. 1979–82; Gen. Mgr. Business Devel. Dept. Cambridge, Ont. 1982–87; Gen. Mgr. Edmonton Econ. Devel. Authority 1987–90; Assoc. Deputy Min., Sask. Economic Development 1990–93; Dir. Ont. Ind. Devel. Council 1985–87; World Trade Center Edmonton 1987–89; mem. Ind. Developers Assn. Can. (IDAC), Dir., Pres. 1988–89, Chrmn. Profl. Devel. Ctte. 1985–87, Lectr. IDAC/Univ. of Waterloo 1985–89; recreations: matchbook collecting, tennis, jogging, cross-country skiing; Club: Optimist; Home: 5 Portofino Place, Stoney, Ont. L8E 5E8; Office: Box 9940, Stoney Creek, Ont. L8G 4N9.

**ALLEMANO, Gregory O.,** B.Com., M.B.A., C.A.; executive; b. Huntsville, Ont. 9 Apr. 1951; s. Oreste Luigi and Elena (Lasci) A.; e. Huntsville High Sch.; Univ. Toronto, B.Com. 1974; M.B.A. 1977; Chartered Accountant 1977; m. Alessandra, d. Ferdinando and Bruna Lanzalone, 20 May 1974; two s. Michael, David; VICE-PRES. AND GEN. MGR. NORTH AMERICA, THE WHEELABRATOR CORPORATION 1992– ;and VICE-PRES. AND GEN. MGR. WHEELABRATOR CANADA INC. 1984– ; C.A., Arthur Andersen & Co. 1974; joined present firm as Secy.-Treas. 1977; Past Dir. & Treas., Milton Distr. Hosp.; Past Acctg. Instr., Sheridan Coll.; recreations: racquet sports, golf; Club: Trafalgar Golf & Country; Home: 1403 Winterberry Dr., Burlington, Ont. L7P 4T3; Office: 4501 Corporate Dr., Unit. 3, Burlington, Ont. L7L 5T9.

**ALLEN, Charlotte Vale;** author; b. Toronto, Ont. 19 Jan. 1941; e. Harbord Coll. and Northview Hts. Coll. Insts. Toronto; m. Walter Bateman Allen Jr. 21 July 1970; divorced; one d. Kimberly Jordan; actress, singer London, Eng. 1961–64; actress, singer, cabaret performer Toronto 1964–66; nightclub singer USA 1966–70; full-time writer 1975– ; part-time lectr., seminars, workshops incest/child abuse; author 'Love Life' 1976; 'Hidden Meanings' 1976; 'Sweeter Music' 1976; 'Gentle Stranger' 1977; 'Another Kind of Magic' 1977; 'Mixed Emotions' 1977; 'Running Away' 1977; 'Meet Me In Time' 1978; 'Julia's Sister' 1978; 'Becoming' 1978; Believing in Giants' 1978; 'Gifts of Love' 1978; 'Acts of Kindness' 1979; 'Moments of Meaning' 1979; 'Times of Triumph' 1979; 'Promises' 1980; 'Daddy's Girl' 1980 (autobiography); 'Marmalade Man' 1981 ('Destinies' in paperback); 'Perfect Fools' 1981; 'Intimate Friends' 1983; 'Pieces of Dreams' 1984; 'Matters of the Heart' 1985; 'Time/Steps' 1986; 'Illusions' 1987; 'Dream Train' 1988; 'Night Magic' 1989; 'Painted Lives' 1990; 'Leftover Dreams' 1992; 'Dreaming in Color' 1993; writing as Katharine Marlowe: 'Heart's Desires' 1991; 'Secrets' 1992; 'Nightfall' 1993; mem. Authors Guild (NY); Writers' Union of Can.; recreations: photography, needlework, travel; Home: 144 Rowayton Woods Dr., Norwalk, Conn. 06854.

**ALLEN, Clive Victor,** B.A., B.C.L.; lawyer and executive; b. Montreal, Que. 11 June 1935; s. John Arthur and Norah (Barnett) A.; e. McGill Univ., B.A. 1956, B.C.L. 1959; m. Barbara Kantor, 22 Feb. 1964; two s. Drew Keith, Blair John; SR. VICE-PRESIDENT & GENERAL COUNSEL, NORTHERN TELECOM LIMITED 1982– ; read law with Hackett, Mulvena, Drummond & Fiske and an Assoc. there 1960–63; called to Bar of Que. 1960; Partner, Fiske, Emery, Allen & Lauzon 1964–66; Asst. Secy., Allied Chemical Canada, Ltd. (now Allied-Signal Canada Inc.) 1966–69, Secy. 1969; Vice-President & Secy. 1972–74; joined Northern Telecom Limited (then Northern Electric Company, Limited) May, 1974; Lect. in Mgmt., Concordia Univ. 1961–74; Adv. Ctte., Internat. Business & Trade Law Prog., Univ. of Toronto; mem., Candn. Adv. Bd., Allendale Ins.; Adv. Bd., Can.-U.S. Law Inst.; mem., Candn. Bar Assn.; Bar of Quebec (Montreal Sec.); Assn. of Can. Gen. Counsel; International Bar Assn.; Protestant; Clubs: Montreal Badminton & Squash; St. James's (Montreal); Granite (Toronto); Home: 18A Deer Park Cres., Toronto, Ont. M4V 2C2; Office: 3 Robert Speck Parkway, Mississauga, Ont. L4Z 3C8.

**ALLEN, Derek Pearson Henderson,** B.A., B.Phil., M.A., D.Phil.; university professor; b. Hamilton, Ont. 19 June 1947; s. Wilfred Alfred and Muriel Kathleen (Robertson) Henderson (stepfather: Thomas John Allen); e. Univ. of Toronto Schools 1965; Univ. of Toronto B.A. 1969, M.A. 1972; Univ. of Oxford B.Phil. 1971, D.Phil. 1979; m. Margaret d. Elisabeth and Ronald Woollard 11 July 1987; ASSOCIATE PROFESSOR OF PHILOSOPHY, TRINITY COLLEGE, UNIV. OF TORONTO 1980– ; Lectr. in Phil., Trinity Coll., Univ. of Toronto 1973–79; Asst. Prof. of Phil., Trinity Coll., Univ. of Toronto 1979–80; Inaugural Ashley Fellow 1977–80; Counselling Co-ord. 1979– ; Co-ord., Ethics, Society & Law Prog.; Chair, ctte. overseeing implementation of recommendations for future of Trinity Coll. 1993–94; Assoc. Chair & Undergrad. Co-ord., Philos., Univ. of Toronto 1980–81, 1983–85;– ;Ont. Rhodes Scholarship Selection Ctte. 1979–83, 1988; Gov. Gen. Medal for Highest Standing in Humanities, Trinity Coll. 1969; Rhodes Scholar Ont. 1969; Woodrow Wilson Fellowship 1969 (declined); Ont. Confed. of Univ. Fac. Assns. Award for Outstanding Contbn. to Univ. Teaching 1992; Univ. of Toronto Fac. of Arts & Sci. Outstanding Teaching Award (an inaugural recipient) 1993; Ont. Lt.-Gov. Award for Teaching Excellence 1993; Bd. of Dir., Visiting Homemakers Assn. of Toronto 1987–90; Chair, Workshop on Long-Term Care in Ont. 1991; Ont. Chair, Long-Term Care Interaction Ctte. 1991– ; author of journal articles; Office: 6 Hoskin Ave., Toronto, Ont. M5S 1A1.

**ALLEN, Fraser Hall,** B.A.Sc., M.S., Ph.D.; petroleum consultant; b. Toronto, Ont. 19 Oct. 1918; s. Russell James and Edna (Bryans) A.; e. Univ. of Toronto Schs. 1937; Univ. of Toronto B.A.Sc. 1941; Univ. of Texas at Austin M.S. 1943, Ph.D. 1947; m. Eloise d. late James H. McCabe 22 Dec. 1942; children: Joanne Victoria Walker, Douglas Fraser, Stephen James; PRESIDENT & FOUNDER, PETRO-ECONOMICS, INC., 1982– ; Dir., Rigel Energy Corp.; held various engn. assignments 1941–51 Stanolind Oil & Gas and Pan American Petroleum Corp.; became Dist. Engr. latter Co. Corpus Christi, Texas 1951, Div. Engr. Oklahoma City 1955, Chief Engr. Tulsa 1960, Div. Production Supt. Fort Worth 1961–62; Co-ordinator Crude Oil Production Purchasing & Transport. Amoco Corp. Chicago 1962–66; Mgr. Production Amoco International Oil Co. N.Y. 1966, Mgr. Operations Co-ordination Chicago 1968; Pres. and Gen. Mgr. Amoco Argentina, Buenos Aires 1969; Vice Pres. Production Amoco International 1972; Pres., Amoco Can. Petroleum, Co., 1975; Distinguished Lectr. (Internat.), Soc. of Petroleum Engineers 1987–88; military service U.S. Naval Research Lab. Washington 1943–46; Dir. Calgary Philharmonic Society 1978–81; Couchiching Inst. on Public Affairs, Toronto 1979– ; Pres., Cordillera Presidents Foundn., Denver 1983–85; Dir. & V.P., Canada Colorado Society, Denver; Chrmn. Tulsa Boy Scout Circus; Dir. Jr. Achievement S. Alta.; mem. Adv. Comte. Internat. Oil & Gas Educ. Center; S.W. Legal Foundation Dallas; Petroleum Engn. Visiting Comte. Univ. of Texas; Dir., Univ. of Okla. Research Inst.; Candn. Petrol. Assn. (Gov. 1975–81, Hon. Life Mem. 1982); Soc. Petrol. Engrs. (Dir. 1963–66; Distinguished lectr. 1988–89); Registered Prof. Engr., Alberta and Texas; Fellow, Inst. of Dirs., London; Fellow, Inst. of Petroleum, London; AAPG; Sigma Xi; Presbyterian; recreations: golf, fishing, skiing, canoe tripping, scuba diving; Clubs: Calgary Petroleum; University (Denver and Chicago); Gormandizers (Buenos Aires); Hiwan Golf; Office: 325 Inca Parkway, Boulder, Colorado 80303; Summer Address: Cache Lake, Algonquin Park, Ont.

**ALLEN, John P.;** musician, recording artist; b. London, Ont. 25 Nov. 1953; s. Harry Walden and Evelyn Alice (Adair) A.; e. Sir Wilfrid Laurier S.S. (Hons.) 1972; Trent Univ. 1972–73; Reich College of Auctioneering (Mason City, Iowa) grad. 1973; m. Wendy d. F/L E. Alex Campbell (DFC) and Hazel Campbell 24 June 1978; children: Wesley, Taylor, Beverly; MEMBER (FIDDLE, MANDOLIN, GUITAR, VOCALS), PRAIRIE OYSTER 1984– ; profl. debut (age 5) at Kilworth Pie Social (near London, Ont.) accompanied by his father Waldie Allen; Concertmaster, high sch. orch. 1972; performed with Good Brothers 1974–75; Ian Tyson & the Great Speckled Bird 1976; Big Redd Ford 1977–78; session musician for jingles, recordings & network TV 1979–81; Dixie Flyers 1981–84; entertained Candn. Military Personnel in Germany, Cyprus, Israel & Egypt 1981, '86; Fiddler, Tommy Hunter Show, CBC, 1990 season; Prairie Oyster is an award-winning group of the Juno & Candn. Country Music Assn. (C.C.M.A.); won Juno for Country Group of the Year 1985–86, 1987–87, 1990, 1991; numerous C.C.M.A. awards including Group of the Year 1990, 1991, 1992; Album of the Year ("Everybody Knows") certified Platinum 1992; Fiddle Play of the Year 1991, 1992; nominated Best New Group or Duo 1991, (U.S.) Acad. of Country Music (1st Canadians so honoured); the Toronto-based band is signed to BMG Canada; celebrity auctioneer at fundraising events; comnd. a Kentucky Colonel 1990; performed for Her Majesty Queen Elizabeth II, during 'Canada 125' celebrations, Parliament Hill, 1 July 1992; sang 'O Canada' prior to game 5 of the World Series, Skydome, Toronto 1992; mem. SOCAN, C.C.M.A., C.M.A. (U.S.), A.C.M. (U.S.); United Church; recreations: gourmet cooking, sport fishing, reading, corresponding, gardening, politics, media watching, rooting for the Toronto Blue Jays; Home: R.R. #3, Lambeth, Ont. N0L 1S0; Office: A.M.K. Management, 49 Ontario St., 2nd Floor, Toronto, Ont. M5A 2V1.

**ALLEN, Lowell Archibald,** B.A., LL.B.; retired lawyer; b. Summerside, P.E.I. 8 Apr. 1926; s. William Arthur and Louise (MacKinnon) A.; e. Acadia Univ. B.A. 1948; Dalhousie Univ. LL.B. 1952; m. Anne d. Dr. Duncan and Tina MacRae; children: Susan, David; Dir., Brascade Resources Inc.; Brascade Holdings Inc.; former Vice-Pres., Brascan Limited 1964–91; Solicitor, Can. Mortgage & Housing Corp. 1953–57; Extve. Asst. to Min. of Fisheries 1957–59; Solicitor, Candn. Pacific 1959–64; Dir., various Brascan subs.; P.Admin., Inst. of Chartered Sec. & Admin.; Candn. Infantry Corps 1943–45; Presbyn.; P.C.; mem., Law Soc. of U.C.; Candn. Bar Assn.; Inst. of Chartered Sec. & Admin.; Home: 140 Chatsworth Dr., Toronto, Ont. M4R 1S2.

**ALLEN, Orville Brian**, Ph.D.; statistician; educator; b. Smith Falls, Ont. 12 Sept. 1950; s. Seymour Howard and Anna Bernice (Munro) A.; e. Univ. of Guelph B.Sc. 1972, M.Sc. 1973; Cornell Univ. Ph.D. 1979; m. Linda d. James and Victoria Foran 27 May 1972; children: Eric Andrew, Anna Elizabeth; ASSOC. PROF. OF BIOSTATISTICS, UNIV. OF GUELPH 1986– , Dir. Ashton Stat. Lab. 1988– ; Asst. Prof. present Univ. 1979, Dir. Alumni Assn. (Sec. 1981–83) 1980–83; Visiting Fellow Cornell Univ. 1985–86; Cons. Subctte. Microbiol. Criteria, Ctte. Food Protection, Food & Nutrition Bd. Nat. Rsch. Council (US) 1983–84; mem. Ont. Forest Resources Inventory Ctte. 1986–87; Asst. Ed., Candn. J. Soil Science 1992–94; recipient Natural Sci's & Eng. Rsch. Council Postgrad. Scholarship 1972–73; author or co-author over 50 papers and book chapters; mem. Stat. Soc. Can.; Am. Stat. Assoc.; Inst. of Mathematical Statistics; Internat. Environmetrics Soc.; Fellow, Royal Stat. Soc.; Sigma Xi; recreations: running, canoeing; Home: 30 Floral Dr., Guelph, Ont. N1G 1R1; Office: Guelph, Ont. N1G 2W1.

**ALLEN, Peter A.**, B.A.Sc., P.Eng.; mining executive; b. Toronto, Ont. 18 Mar. 1940; s. John Charles L. and Francis Louise (Ackerman) A.; e. Upper Canada Coll. 1947–54; Trinity Coll. Sch. 1954–58; Univ. of Toronto 1958–62, B.A.Sc., P.Eng. (Civil); m. Jocelyn d. Dr. Edmund and Margaret Botterell 27 June 1968; children: Eric, Geoffrey, Christopher; PRES., C.E.O. & DIR., LAC MINERALS LTD.; Dir., Bell Canada Enterprises; Dir., Mercantile and General Reinsurance Co. of Canada; Montreal Trust; Dir. & Past Chrmn., Candn. Inst. for Advanced Research; Past Gov., Trinity Coll. Sch.; Chrmn., The Royal Conservatory of Music; joined Imperial Oil Ltd. Pipeline Division 1962–65; Partner, John C.L. Allen Ltd. 1965–74; joined LAC Mining Group 1974; Dir., World Wildlife Fund Canada; Mining Assn. of Can.; mem., C.D. Howe Inst.; Candn. American Ctte.; Corporate Higher Education Forum; Assn. of Prof. Engrs. of Ont.; Candn. Inst. of Mining and Metallurgy; recreations: sailing, tennis, skiing; Clubs: Royal Canadian Yacht; Badminton & Racquet; York; The Toronto; Office: PO Box 156, North Tower, Suite 2100, Royal Bank Plaza, Toronto, Ont. M5J 2J4.

**ALLEN, (Alexander) Richard**, M.A., Ph.D.; educator; author; politician; b. Vancouver, B.C. 10 Feb. 1929; s. Harold Tuttle and Ruby Rhoda (Reilly) A.; e. Fernie (B.C.) High Sch. 1947; Univ. of B.C. 1947–50; Toronto Teachers Coll. 1954; Univ. of Toronto B.A. 1956; Univ. of Sask. M.A. 1961; Duke Univ. Ph.D. 1967; m. 1stly Margaret Jane Ritchie 1951; m. 2ndly Nettie d. Daniel Shewchuk, Hamilton, Ont. 24 Apl. 1965; children: Daniel Richard, Philip Andrew; MINISTER WITHOUT PORTFOLIO (in Economic Development) ONTARIO 1993– ; Pub. Sch. Teacher, Ottawa 1954–55, Crystal Bay, Ont. 1956–57; Gen. Secy. Student Christian Movement Can., Univ. of Sask. 1957–61; mem. Dept. Hist. Univ. of Regina 1964–74, Dir. Candn. Plains Area Studies Program 1968–74; joined McMaster Univ. 1974, mem. Senate 1976–78; Prof. of Candn. History, McMaster Univ. 1976–87; Min. of Colls. and Univs. and Min. of Skills Development in first Ont. NDP Govt. 1990–93 (lead min. among provincial labour market ministers); rec'd Can. Council Sr. Leave Fellowships 1971–72, 1978–79 (Fellow, Faculty Religious Studies McGill Univ.); Principal Founder Candn. Plains Research Center Univ. of Regina; Nat. Student Chrmn., Student Christian Movement Can. 1952–53; sometime rep. on Social Science Research Council Can.; past mem. Archives Comte. Un. Ch. of Can., Consultant on Ch. and Labour; author 'The Social Passion: Religion and Social Reform in Canada 1914–1928' 1971; Ed. 'A Region of the Mind: Interpreting the Western Canadian Plains' 1973; 'The Social Gospel in Canada' 1975; 'Man and Nature on the Prairies' 1976; various articles, biog. studies and colls. religion and soc. in post-confed. Can.; mem. Program Comte. and Council Candn. Hist. Assn. 1972–74; past mem., Candn. Meth. Hist. Soc.; John Howard Soc.; mem. Amnesty International; Project Ploughshares; Pollution Probe; el. June 1982, NDP Member Ontario Legislature for Hamilton West, re-el. 1985, 1987, 1990; mem., Federal Counc., NDP 1989–91; Vice Chair, Counc. of Ministers of Educ. of Can. 1991–92; mem. Candn. Parly. Assn.; Assn. Interparlementaire de Langue Française; United Church; recreations: skiing, log cottage restoration, music, French; Home: 85 Haddon Ave. N., Hamilton, Ont. L8S 4A4; Offices: Hamilton, Ont. L8P 4B4 and Queen's Park, Toronto, Ont. M7A 1A1.

**ALLEN, Robert Pearson**, B.A.; arts administrator; b. Montréal, Qué. 28 Dec. 1945; s. Gordon Wallace and Ella Curtis (Wheeler) A.; e. Univ. of B.C. B.A. 1968; THEATRE OFFICER, ARTS AWARDS, CANADA COUNCIL 1993– ; Asst. Adm. Dir. Vancouver Playhouse 1969–73; Theatre Critic and Arts Reporter Vancouver Province 1973–83; Media Relations Mgr. and Ed. Dir. Stratford Festival, Ont. 1984–87; Communications Cons. Nat. Arts Centre Ottawa 1988; Eng. Ed. Candn. Museum of Civilization, Hull 1988–89; Nat. Co-ord., National Book Festival, Canada Council 1989–93; recreations: sports, cooking, reading; Home: 2 - 304A Nelson St., Ottawa, Ont. K1N 7S4; Office: 350 Albert St., Ottawa, Ont. K1P 5V8.

**ALLEN, Warren Edwin**, B.A.Sc., M.A.Sc., M.B.A., P. Eng., C.M.C., PMP; consultant; b. Toronto, Ont. 15 Oct. 1936; s. George Henry and Lilian (Robinson) A.; e. Univ. of Toronto B.A.Sc. 1959, M.A.Sc. 1964; York Univ. M.B.A. 1970; m. Elizabeth d. Gerald and Ethel Sutton 6 Dec. 1958; children: Deborah Lynn, Jonathan Kirby, Barbara Joanne, Janice Elizabeth; MANAGING DIRECTOR, PM ASSOCIATES INC. 1986– ; AND PRES., WARREN E. ALLEN & ASSOC. LTD. 1983– ; Offr., R.C.E. 1955–62, Capt. 1962; Professional Engineer & Project Mgr., Stone & Webster (Can.) Ltd. 1964–69; Management Consultant & Partner, Woods Gordon, 1969–83; Prof., Univ. of Calgary 1984–86; mem., A.P.E.G.G.A.; A.P.E.O.; Inst. of Management Consultants of Alta.; Inst. of Man. Consult. of Ont.; Project Management Inst.; recreations: curling, golf, skiing; Clubs: Calgary Petroleum; Calgary Winter; Home: 5003 Norris Rd., N.W., Calgary, Alta. T2K 5R6.

**ALLEYNE, Andrew Douglas**, B.Comm., M.A.; insurance executive; b. Bridgetown, Barbados 10 March 1950; s. Douglas Herbert and Lucille Marion A.; e. McMaster Univ. B.Comm. 1972; York Univ. M.A. 1975; m. Sonia Grisonich 16 April 1983; children: Nicholas, Victoria, Daniel; VICE-PRES., INVESTMENT POLICY AND RESEARCH, THE GREAT-WEST LIFE ASSUR. CO. 1989– ; Royal Bank of Canada 1972–74; Prof., Ryerson Polytechnical Inst. 1975–88; Sr. Econ., Toronto-Dominion Bank H.Q. 1978–89; Chair, Winnipeg C. of C. Debt/Deficit Ctte.; Mem., Candn. C. of C. (Extve. Policy Ctte.); Nat. Statistics Council; Man. Assn. of Business Economists (Past Pres.); Canadian Club; C.D. Howe Inst.; Can. West Found.; Man. Task Force on Capital Markets; recreations: sailing, squash, badminton, swimming; club: Winnipeg Winter; Home: 89 Queenston St., Winnipeg, Man.; Office: 100 Osborne St. N., Winnipeg, Man. R3C 3A5.

**ALLIN, Patrick Joseph**, B.Comm., C.A.; business executive; b. Toronto, Ont. 25 Aug. 1951; s. Leonard H. and Rita A. (McCloskey) A.; e. Univ. of Toronto B.Comm. 1974; m. Anne Smisko 8 Oct. 1977; three children; DIRECTOR, MOORE U.S. DIVISION, MOORE BUSINESS FORMS SYSTEMS 1993– ; Partner, Price Waterhouse 1974–87; Vice-Pres. & Treas., Moore Corp. Limited 1987–88; Vice-Pres. & Controller, Moore U.S. Forms Div. 1988–91; Pres., Moore Canadian Div., Moore Business Forms & Systems 1991–93; Dir., Moore Business Forms Inc.; Moore Business Forms & Systems Ltd.; Lectr., Univ. of Toronto 1976–81; OICA, School of Accountancy 1983–85; C.A. 1976, Certified Information Systems Auditor 1979; Dir., Toronto Symphony; Dir., Nat. Ballet School; Vice-Pres. of Certification, EDPAA 1980–87; recreations: running, squash, golf; clubs: National, Devil's Pulpit, Toronto Bd. of Trade; Office: 275 North Field Dr., Lake Forest, IL 60045.

**ALLISON, Russell Stafford**, B.Sc., P.Eng.; transportation executive; b. Tichborne, Ont. 1 June 1924; s. William Russell and Gertrude (Stafford) A.; e. Tichborne and Clarendon pub. schs.; Parham and Tamworth Continuation Schs. 1942; Queen's Univ. B.Sc. (Civil Engn.) 1946; m. Jean Edith d. John and Cela McKillop 5 Mar. 1949; children: Joan, John; Pres., CP Rail 1984–89; joined CP Rail 1945, Div. Engr. 1950, Asst. Supt. 1957, Supt. 1962, Gen. Mgr. & Regional Mgr. Operation and Maintenance, Pacific Region 1966, Vice-Pres. Prairie Region 1969, Vice-Pres. Eastern Region 1974; Extve. Vice-Pres. CP Rail 1981–84; Pres., CP Rail 1984–89; mem. Am. Assn. Railroad Superintendants; Am. Railway Engn. Assn.; Assn. Profl. Engrs. Prov. Ont.; Hon. Mem., Candn. Inst. of Traffic and Transportation; Fellow, Engn. Inst. Can.; Fellow of Chartered Inst. of Transport; Knight, The Order of St. John; recreation: swimming; Clubs: London; Toronto Railway; Candn. Railway; Mount Stephen; Home: 448 Grangeover Cres., London, Ont. N6G 4P7.

**ALLMAND, Hon. Warren**, P.C.; b. Montreal, Que. 19 Sept. 1932; s. Harold W. and Rose Irene (McMorrow) A.; e. Loyola High Sch., Montreal; St. Francis Xavier Univ.; McGill Univ.; Univ. de Paris; children: Patrick, Julianne, Robin; called to Bar of Que. 1958; el. to H. of C. for Montreal-N.D.G. in g.e. 1965, 1968 1972, 1974, 1979, 1980, 1984, 1988; Min. Consumer & Corporate Affairs 1977–79; Min. Indian & Northern Affairs 1976–77; Sol. Gen. of Canada 1972–76; mem.: Que. Bar Assn.; Liberal; recreations: skiing, hockey, tennis, distance running; Club: Mount Royal Tennis.

**ALLNUTT, Alan Ernest;** newspaper editor; b. Montreal, Que. 15 Nov. 1951; s. Albert Ernest and Helen Scott (Thomson) A.; e. Sir Winston Churchill H.S.; Sir George Williams Univ.; m. Janet d. Joseph and Annette Takefman 25 May 1975; one d.: Erica Heather; EXECUTIVE EDITOR, THE GAZETTE 1993– ; Reporter / Photographer / Editor, various weeklies 1971–75; Reporter, Montreal Star 1975–77; Desk Editor 1977–78; City Editor 1978–79; City Editor, Ottawa Journal 1979–80; Assignment Editor, The Gazette 1980–82; Extve. Sports Ed. 1982–86; Graphics Editor 1986–89; Assoc. Mng. Editor 1989–91; Managing Editor 1991–93; Dir., Canadian Managing Editors Conf.; Mem. Editorial Ctte., Candn. Daily Newspaper Assn.; Office: 250 St-Antoine ouest, Montreal, Que. H2Y 3R7.

**ALLOOLOO, Hon. Titus**, M.L.A.; politician; b. near Pond Inlet, N.W.T. 1953; e. schools in Pond Inlet & Churchill, Man.; Algonquin College; travelled across Canada to broaden his knowledge of the country as a whole; MEMBER, LEGISLATIVE ASSEMBLY OF THE NORTHWEST TERRITORIES FOR AMITTUQ 1987– ;and MEMBER OF THE EXTVE. COUNCIL, GOVT. OF THE NORTHWEST TERRITORIES 1987– ; currently responsible for Renewable Resources and Municipal and Community Affairs, previous responsibilities were Culture and Communications, Transportation, Education and Assoc. Minister of Aboriginal Rights and Constitutional Development; worked in electronics with Dept. of Energy, Mines & Resources Canada until 1973; worked in Municipal Offices and as Supvr., Dept. of Public Works and Highways Pond Inlet 1973; while operating his own outfitting & guiding business entered municipal politics 1974; elected Mayor 1975; Founding Mem., Baffin Regional Council; Past Mem., Beaufort Sea Environ. Assessment Panel; Chair, Lancaster Sound Land Use Planning Comn. and Vice-Chair, N.W.T. Land Use Planning Comn.; Members' Asst. to all non-ministerial Members of the Legislative Assembly with special duties for Inuit Members 1984; Extve. Asst. to Min. of Culture and Communications 1987; Office: Yellowknife, N.W.T. X1A 2L9.

**ALLOWAY, Donald Miller**, B.A.Sc., P.Eng.; company executive; b. Oshawa, Ont. 9 June 1921; s. late Arthur Roy and Mary Kelly (Sickle) A.; Reg'd Prof. Engr., Prov. of Ont.; children: Heather Elizabeth, Donald Miller Jr., Wendy Jane, Robert Raymer, Graham Frederick; CHRMN., PRES. & C.E.O., CAIRN CAPITAL INC.; Chrmn., Consolidated Graphics Inc.; DCP Limited; Maranatha Found. (Toronto); Mistwood Inc., Delaware; Dir., Graphics Arts Mutual Insurance Co. (N.Y.); The Toronto General and Western Hosp. Found.; Past Pres., Graphic Arts Industries Assn. Can.; Dir. of Graphic Arts Technical Found. (USA) 1978–79; rec'd Centennial Medal 1967; mem. Governing Counc., Univ. of Toronto 1985–88; affil.: Yorkminster Baptist Church, Toronto; recreations: golf, boating; Clubs: Granite; National; Muskoka Lakes Golf & Country; Home: 211 Queen's Quay West, Suite 908, Toronto, Ont. M5J 2M6; Summer: Port Carling, Ont.; Office: 41 Valleybrook Dr., Suite 201, Don Mills, Ont. M3B 2S6.

**ALMOND, Paul**, M.A. (Oxon); cineaste; b. Montreal, Que. 26 Apr. 1931; s. Eric and Irene Clarice (Gray) A.; e. B.C.S.; McGill Univ.; Balliol Coll., Oxford B.A. 1952, M.A. 1954; m. Angela Leigh, 1956; m. Geneviève Bujold, 1967; one s. Matthew James; m. Joan Harwood Elkins, Sept. 1976; Producer Dir. with CBC 1953–66 and TV co's in New York, London and Hollywood of over 125 TV productions; wrote, produced, and directed feature film 'Isabel' 1968; 'Act of the Heart' 1970; 'Journey' 1972; 'Ups & Downs' 1982; 'The Dance Goes On' 1991; Dir. 'Captive Hearts' 1987; Subject of book by Janet Edsforth 'The Flame Within,' Publ. Cdn. Film Inst.; Canadian Film Award Best Feature Director 1970 (ETROG); Best TV Director, 1979 (GENIE); Coq d'Or, Best Fr. TV Commercial 1981; mem., Dirs. Guild Can. (Hon. Life); Royal Acad. of Art; Address: Quest Film Productions Ltd., 1272 Redpath Cres., Montreal, Que. H3G 2K1.

**ALOFS, Paul S.**, B.Comm., B.A., M.B.A.; music industry executive; b. Windsor, Ont. 13 Feb. 1956; s. Omer F. and Pat A.; e. Univ. of Windsor B.Comm. 1978, B.A. 1978; York Univ. M.B.A. 1982; m. Martha Proudfoot 10 Oct. 1981; children: Sarah, James; PRESIDENT, HMV CANADA; HMV Canada has been recognized by num. awards incl.: Innovative Retailer of the Year, Retail Council of Canada; Service Marketing Winner, Am. Mktg. Assn.; Business Excellence Award, HMV Group;

Music Retailer of the Year from the record industry; Store Design, Internat. Council of Shopping Centres; formerly with Colgate Palmolive; Grey Advertising, Vice-Pres., Client Serv., Marketing & Promotion Group; Lectr., York Univ. Business School & Univ. of Toronto's Communication Studies Dept.; Mem., Young Pres. Orgn.; Bd. Mem., Retail Council of Canada; Office: 5401 Eglinton Ave. W., #110, Toronto, Ont. M9C 5K6.

**ALONZO, Anne-Marie,** B.A., M.A., Ph.D.; author, publisher, journalist; b. Alexandria, Egypt 13 Dec. 1951; d. Noël and Héliane Raymonde (Baindeky) A.; e. Univ. of Montreal B.A. 1976, M.A. 1978, Ph.D. 1986; Co-founder, Les Editions TROIS 1985; Founder & Co-ordinator, Festival de TROIS, Laval an annual arts & literary festival 1989– ; Co-founder & Dir. TROIS review 1985– ; Founder, Productions AMA 1987; Co-founder & Vice-Pres., AUTO/GRAPHE theatre & prodn. co. 1981–87; Mem., Union des écrivains du Qué. 1980; SOCAN 1985; Soc. littéraire de Laval 1985; CEAD 1985; Amnesty Internat. 1988; Artistes pour la paix 1989; Greenpeace Found. 1989; Prix Lizette-Gervais 1990; author: 'Une Lettre rouge orange et ocre' 1984 (play); 'Bleus de mine' 1985, Écoute, Sultane' 1987, 'Seul le désir' 1987, 'Esmaï' 1987, 'Le Livre des ruptures' 1988 (fiction); 'L'Immobile' 1990 (epistolary fiction); 'Lead Blues' 1990 (trans. by W. Donoghue); 'Galia qu'elle nommait Amour' 1992 (fiction), rec'd Grand Prix d'excellence artistique en creation littéraire 1992; 'Margie Gillis, La Danse des marches' 1993 (poetry); co-author: 'Linked Alive' 1990 (renga-poetry); of texts, articles, interviews, literary & arts reviews for magazines such as 'NBJ,' 'Possibles,' 'Des femmes en mouvements,' 'Moebius,' 'Estuaire,' 'Canadian Fiction Magazine,' '(f)Lip,' 'Arcade,' 'Tessera,' etc.; texts for theatre and radio; Prix Emile-Nelligan for 'Bleus de mine' 1985; Home: 2033 Jessop, Laval, Que. H7S 1X3.

**ALPER, Howard,** B.Sc., Ph.D., F.R.S.C.; educator; b. Montreal, Que. 17 Oct. 1941; s. Max and Frema (Weinstein) A.; e. Concordia Univ. B.Sc. 1963; McGill Univ. Ph.D. 1967; m. Anne d. Jack and Emma Fairhurst 4 June 1966; two d. Lara, Ruth; PROF. OF CHEM. UNIV. OF OTTAWA 1978– , Chrmn. of Chem. 1982–85, 1988– , Assoc. Prof. 1975; NATO Postdoctoral Fellow Princeton Univ. 1967–68; Asst. Prof. State Univ. of N.Y. Binghamton 1968, Assoc. Prof. 1971–74; Group Chrmn. Chem. NSERC 1987–90; Convenor Chem. Royal Soc. Can. 1989–92; Chrmn. Inorganic Div. Candn. Soc. for Chem. 1986–88, Alfred Bader Award in Organic Chem. 1990; Alcan Award Inorganic Chem. Chem. Inst. Can. 1980, Catalysis Award 1984; E.W.R. Steacie Fellow NSERC 1980–82; J.S. Guggenheim Fellow 1985–86; Killam Rsch. Fellow 1986–88; author or co-author over 310 publs., ed. two books; holds 23 patents; Office: Ottawa, Ont. K1N 6N5.

**ALPERT, Herbert S.,** A.S.C., C.S.C.; investor, film producer; b. New Haven, Conn. 26 Nov. 1918; s. Meyer and Gussie (Lipkovitz) A.; m. Patricia d. Oscar Pattenick 5 Dec. 1957; children: Lisa, Nancy; PRESIDENT, ULTIMUS FILMS LTD.; Dir. & Vice-Pres., First Mercantile Currency Fund Financial Corp.; Vice-Pres., Patjoy Investments Ltd.; Office: 347 Bay St., Ste. 404, Toronto, Ont. M5H 2R7.

**ALSOP, David John,** B.Comm., M.B.A.; truck building executive; b. Winnipeg, Man. 19 Jan. 1944; s. Cyril Henry and Kathleen Adele (Reid) A.; e. Univ. of Man. B.Comm. 1964; Harvard Univ. M.B.A. 1970; m. Dorothy Anne d. Reginald and Dorothy Neville 29 Oct. 1966; two d. Meredith Jane, Erin Elizabeth; Pres. & C.E.O., Pacific Truck & Trailer Ltd. (N. Vancouver) 1989–.; Pres. & C.E.O., Versatile Pacific Shipyards Inc. 1986–89 (previously served in various senior mgmt. positions with same co. 1973–86); Dir. Southern Gold Resources Ltd.; Asst. Group Supr. Great-West Life Assurance Winnipeg 1964–68; Assoc. McKinsey & Co. Toronto 1970–73; Pres. N. Vancouver C. of C. 1981–82, Treas. 1979–80; recreations: golf, outdoors; Club: Capilano Golf & Country; Address: 389 Ventura Cres., North Vancouver, B.C. V7N 3G7.

**ALSTON, Jan Millward,** B.A., LL.B.; lawyer; b. Calgary, Alta. 12 Aug. 1955; s. John Millward and Val A.; e. Cheltenham Coll. 1974; Univ. of Alta. B.A. (Econ.) 1978, LL.B. 1981; m. Vanessa (dec'd. 3 Jan. 1991) d. Stan and Ellen Reid 4 Sept. 1987; children: Lauren Leanne, Reid Alexander; PRES., SEC. TREAS. & DIR., CANADIAN NORTHCOR ENERGY INC. 1989– ; admitted to Law Soc. of Alta. 1982 concentrating in corp., commercial & securities regulation areas; Gen. Couns., present firm 1986–91; Dir. & Sec. Treas., Savanna Resources Ltd.; Dir., Visionwall Corp.; Home: 328 Edgemont Place N.W., Calgary, Alta. T3A 2K2; Office: 1015, 600 – 6th Ave. S.W., Calgary, Alta. T2P 0S5.

**ALTON, Harvey M.,** B.Sc., P.Eng.; provincial civil servant; b. Lloydminster, Sask. 8 Aug. 1939; s. Morris and Ella (Steenson) A.; e. Univ. of Alta. B.Sc. 1962; m. Jacqueline d. Jack and Violet Wall 1960; children: Joan, Cindy, Bradley; DEP. MIN. OF ALTA. TRANSPORTATION & UTILITIES 1987– ; Asst. Dist. Eng. Peace River 1962–67; Dist. Transport. Eng. Red Deer Dist. 1967–73; Mun. Service Eng. H.O. Edmonton 1973–77; Exec. Dir. Regional Coordination 1977–80; Dep. Min. Regional Transport. 1980, Dep. Min. of Transport. 1983; Dir., Alta. Resources Railway; Internat. Road Fedn.; Past Pres. Roads & Transport. Assn. Can.; mem. Assn. Profl. Engs., Geols. & Geophysicists; Office: Twin Atria Building, 4999 – 98 Ave., Edmonton, Alta. T6B 2X3.

**ALTON, Thomas R.,** C.A.; financial executive; b. Walkerton, Ont. 29 July, 1939; e. C.A. 1962; m. Janet Ann, 21 April, 1962; children: Sharon, Linda, Carol Ann; PRES. & C.E.O., BANK OF MONTREAL MORTGAGE CORP. 1983– ; articled with Coopers & Lybrand, Toronto becoming Mgr. 1957–63, trans. to London, Eng. 1963–64; Gen. Mgr. Scotia Mortgage Corp. 1964–71; Pres. & C.E.O., Scotia Mortgage Corp. 1971–83; Gen. Mgr. Mortgages and Investments, The Bank of Nova Scotia 1980–83; Past Pres. Candn. Scholarship Trust Found.; Chrmn., Oakville Trafalgar Memorial Hosp.; mem. Economic Rsch. Counc., Candn. Home Builders Assn.; Past Chrmn., Mortgage Ctte., Candn. Banekrs Assoc.; Co-Chair (with Fed. Housing Min. Alan Redway), Canada's First Housing Finance Conference; Clubs: Albany; Oakville; Alpine Ski; Office: 55 Bloor St. W., Toronto, Ont. M4W 3N5.

**ALVAREZ, Frank S.;** b. Arbo, Spain 12 Apl. 1944 (emigrated to Portugal 1952); s. Avelino L. and Encarnacao R. (Alvarez) Sestelo; e. High Sch. and Hotel Mgmt. Lisbon, Portugal; George Brown Coll. TV Prodn.; m. Dolores S. 1 Nov. 1964; children: Carmen, Frank Lewis; PRES. SALVA ORGANIZATIONS 1974– ; Pres. CIRV Radio Multicultural 1986– ; served hotel mgmt. and community orgns. many yrs.; Exec. Dir., Sottomayor Bank of Can.; Dir., Doctor's Hosp. Corp.; mem. Adv. Ctte. Fed. Bus. Devel. Bank; Past Vice Pres. and Founder, Vila Gaspar Corte Real Inc.; Pres., Festival Portuguese Friendship Club Inc.; Pres., Magazine Imagens; Past Pres., Fedn. Portuguese Candn. Business Professionals; Past Exec. Dir. & Founder, Canada-Portugal Chamber of Commerce 1989; recipient, 125th Anniversary, Candn. Confederation, Commemorative Medal 1992; numerous awards incl. those from Candn. Red Cross Soc. 1979; Metro Toronto Soccer Centennial 1981; Molson Toronto Star 1983; Sofadeca 1987; Candn. Ethnic Media 1988; Min. of Citizenship and Min. Responsible for Race Relations 1988; Candn. Multilingual Press Fedn. 1988; Doctor's Hosp. 1989; recreations: sports, music; Home: 9 Ashwood Cres., Islington, Ont. M9A 1Z2; Office: 1087 Dundas St. W., Toronto, Ont. M6J 1W9.

**ALWAY, Richard M.,** C.M., M.A., Phil.M., D.Litt.S.; university administrator; foundation executive; b. Hamilton, Ont. 22 Oct. 1940; s. Bruce Mowbray and Elizabeth Lannan (Battle) A.; e. Westdale Secondary Sch. Hamilton; Univ. of Toronto B.A. 1962 (Cardinal Mercier Gold Medal Philos.), M.A. 1965 (Can. Council Fellowship), Phil.M. 1967 (IODE War Meml. Fellowship), D.Litt.S. St. Michael's Coll. 1989; PRES. AND VICE CHANCELLOR, UNIV. OF ST. MICHAEL'S COLL. 1990– ; Chrmn., C.D. Howe Memorial Found., Montreal 1991– ; Chrmn. and C.E.O., The Ont. Heritage Found. 1987–92; Chrmn. Natural Heritage League 1987–92; James C. Cumming Fellow Trinity Coll. Univ. of Toronto 1970–73, Dean of Men 1973–75, mem. Corp. 1970– ;and Council 1978–1990; Dir. of Rsch. Univ. Toronto Sesquicentennial Hist. Project 1971–73, Warden and Chrmn. Bd. Stewards Hart House 1977–90, mem. Univ. Affairs Bd. Governing Council 1987–90; Sr. Policy Cons. Can. Studies Found. 1973–75, Trustee & Exec. Ctte. 1969–76; News Analyst & Commentator CFRB Toronto 1976–86; Acting Dir. Nat. Gallery of Can. 1986–87; Trustee and Exec. Ctte. Nat. Museums of Can. 1979–86, Chrmn. Nat. Progs. Adv. Ctte. 1983–86; Acting Publisher 'The Catholic Register' 1988–90; Bd. of Govs., The Candn. Educational Standards Inst.; Bd. of Dirs., Candn. Opera Co.; Chrmn. Capital Campaign St. Michael's Coll. 1988, Chrmn. of Found. 1990– ; mem. Michaelmas Conf. Pontifical Inst. Medieval Studies Toronto 1978– ; Founding Chrmn. Cath. Council St. Michael's Cath. Toronto 1968–73; Knight of Magistral Grace, Sovereign and Military Order of Malta 1991; apptd. to Order of Canada 1989; awarded 125th Anniversary of Confederation Commemorative Medal 1992; author various articles and reviews learned jours. and popular press; over 700 broadcast commentaries; R. Catholic; Office: 81 St. Mary St., Toronto, Ont. M5S 1J4 and 77 Bloor St. W., Toronto, Ont. M7A 2R9.

**AMABILE, George,** M.A., Ph.D.; writer; educator; b. Jersey City, N.J. 29 May 1936; s. Anthony Thomas and Josephine (Masi) A.; e. Princeton (N.J.) High Sch., 1953; Amherst Coll., A.B. 1957; Univ. of Minn., M.A. 1961; Univ. of Conn., Ph.D. 1969; PROF. OF ENGLISH, UNIV. OF MANITOBA since 1987; joined the Univ. as Lectr. 1963, Asst. Prof. 1966–68, 1969–71; Assoc. Prof. 1972–86; Visiting Writer in Residence, Univ. of B.C. 1968–69; Dir. Can. Periodical Pub. Assn.; Dir., Reach Out today (ex-convict employment & re-entry organ.); mem. Comte. of Artists to advise Min. of Tourism & Culture; has given readings of own work at Man. Theatre Centre and on radio, TV and at the Montreal Olympics 1976; rec'd Hunter Prize; Anna Von Helmholz Phelan Prize, Univ. of Minn. 1961; Can. Council Grants 1968, 1969, 1981–82; Can. Authors Assn. National Prize for Poetry, 1983; Third Prize, CBC National Literary Competition 1992; author, 'Blood Ties,' 1972; 'Open Country,' 1976; 'Flower and Song,' 1977; 'Ideas of Shelter,' 1981; 'The Presence of Fire' 1982; other writings published in numerous anthols., journs. and periodicals; co-founder and Ed., 'The Far Point'; Ed. 'Northern Light'; has ed. 'The Ivory Tower'; 'The Penny Paper'; W. Candn. Publishers' Assn. (Founding & Constitutional Comte.); League Candn. Poets; recreations: fishing, tennis, guitar, raquetball, carpentry, baseball; Home: 907 Merriam Blvd., Winnipeg, Man. R3T 0V2; Office: Dept. of English, Univ. of Man., Winnipeg, Man. R3T 2N2.

**AMATO, Lanfranco,** C.M., K.M., K.C.L.J., K.G.C.T.L., F.R.S.A.; company executive; b. Rovereto, Italy 19 Apr. 1922; s. Joseph and Adile (Valdagni) A.; e. Univ. of Bocconi, Milan, Italy, degree in Comm. and Finance; m. Dr. Liliana, d. Joseph Conte, 23 Oct. 1954; one s. Sergio; PRES., L. AMATO ASSOCIATES LTD. 1978– ; Pres., C.E.O. & Dir., Riello Corp. of America; Pres., G.M. & Dir., Riello Canada Inc.; Dir.: Moog-Canada Ltd.; Banca Commerciale Italiana of Canada; Hon. Chrmn & Dir., Olivetti Canada Ltd.; began as Sales Rep for Olivetti in Italy, 1950; apptd. Special Rep. for the market devel. of overseas agents in 1952, during the course of which gained an intimate knowledge of many countries in the Far East, W. and N. Africa and in Europe; i/c Agent-Dealer Operations for the newly formed Candn. subsidiary of Olivetti, 1955; following merger of Underwood and Olivetti, apptd. Gen. Sales Mgr. and Dir., Underwood Ltd. 1960; Vice-Pres., Marketing 1962; Extve. Vice-Pres. 1965; Pres. and Gen. Mgr. Olivetti Underwood Ltd. 1966, Chrmn. 1973; Associate, Bregman & Hamann 1975–78; served in 2nd World War with Italian Army (Lieut., 1st Regt. of Grenadiers); with U.S. Army from Sept. 1943; Mentioned in Dispatches by Gen. Sir Harold Alexander; awarded Kt. of Obedience, Sovereign Mil. Order of Malta; Kt. Grand Cross, Sovereign Mil. Teutonic Order of Levant; Grand Offr., Order of Merit, Republic of Italy; Grand Offr., Order of Merit, Republic of San Marino; Serving Brother, Order of St. John; Kt. Commander, Mil. Order St. Lazarus of Jerusalem; Knight of Corona D'Italia; Princely Household Order of Lippe (Order of the Rose); Golden Mercury 'Ad Honorem' (Italian Oscar for Commerce & Industry); Academician, Accademia Degli Incamminati (Italy); Academia Tiberina (Itlay); Fellow, Royal Soc. of Arts of Gt. Brit.; Fellow, Royal Soc. of Antiquaries of Scotland; European War Cross (France); Royal Yugoslavian War Cross; Internat. Ambassador for Aviation Hall of Fame (Canada); other decorations and honours from govts. Japan, Portugal, Canada, U.S.; Former Gov.: Central Hospital; York-Finch Gen. Hosp.; Toronto Arts Production; Italian Cdn. Benevolent Corp.; Former Trustee: MacLaren Found.; Trustee, Cdn. Mediterranean Inst.; Italian Chamber of Comm. of Toronto (Pres. 1963–66); Ont. Council for the Arts; Hon. Patron, Metro Internat. Caravan; former Dir.: Toronto Symphony Orch.; Candn. Opera Co.; National Youth Orchestra Assn. of Canada; Cdn. Business Equipment Mfrs. Assn.; mem. Cdn. Italian Business and Profl. Men's Assn.; Swiss Cdn. Business Assn. Inc.; Adv. Comte., Heritage Ont. 1972; R. Catholic; Clubs: Canadian (Toronto); Empire; Arts and Letters; Rotary Internat.; Chevalier de la Confrerie du Tastivin (Burgundy); Gotha Internat.; recreations: swimming, reading; Home: 108 Sandringham Drive, Downsview, Ont. M3H 1C9.

**AMBER, Arnold,** B.Pol.Sci., M.A.; television producer; b. Montreal, Que. 29 Oct. 1939; s. Joseph and Bella (Goldberg) A.; e. Univ. of Ottawa B.Pol.Sci. 1960; McGill Univ. 1961; Queen's Univ. M.A. 1963; m. Phyllis d. Emerine and Edward Mullings 1 Sept. 1964; children: Jeannine, Gillian, David; EXTVE. PROD., TV NEWS SPECIALS, CBC 1980– ; Reuters News Agency London 1963; Fgn. Corr. Zaire 1964–66; Ghana, Nigeria, Biafra 1966–68; Ed./Corr. London/Eur. 1968–69; Reporter, Toronto Star 1969; News Ed/Reporter, CBC 1969–74; Sr. News Prod., CBLT 1975–77; Prod., CBC 1977–79; Sr. Prod. 1979–80; Pres., Assn. of Television Prod. & Dir. 1986– ; Ed./Pub., the Toronto Citizen 1970–74; Tutor/lecturer, Queen's Univ., Atkinson Coll., York Univ.; Gemini Award 1987, 1990, and 1991 for Best Canadian Television Special Event Coverage; Jewish; Pres., Candn. Ctte. to Protect Journalists 1993– ; mem., Candn. Diabetes Assn.; Candn. Assn. of Journalists; Candn. Civil Liberties Assn.; Children's Aid Soc. of Metro. Toronto; major contbr.: 'The New Africans, Reuters Guide to the Contemporary History of Emergent Africa and its Leaders' 1967; recreations: coaching hockey, community involvement; Office: Box 500, Stn. A., Toronto, Ont. M5W 1E6.

**AMBRIDGE, Charles,** B.Sc.; petrochemical executive; b. Barry, South Wales 21 May 1924; e. Univ. of Wales B.Sc. 1951; m. Joan Bury; children: David, Jacqueline, Vivian, Trevor; Group Vice-President, Polysar Ltd. 1985–88; Rsch. Chemist, Polysar Ltd. 1954, Mgr. Strategic Planning 1968, Gen. Mgr. New Products Group 1972, Gen. Mgr. Polysar France, Strasbourg 1976, Vice Pres. Polysar, Brussels 1978, Pres. & C.E.O., Petrosar Ltd. 1982; Home: Box 581, Forest, Ont. N0N 1J0.

**AMBROSE, John Daniel,** M.S., Ph.D.; botanist; curator; b. Detroit, Mich. 20 June 1943; e. Univ. of Mich. B.S. 1965, M.S. 1966; Cornell Univ. Ph.D. 1975; m. Cherry Booth 1971; one child: Robin; CURATOR OF BOTANY, METRO TORONTO ZOO 1991– ; Curator, The Arboretum, Univ. of Guelph 1974–91; Grad. Fac., Dept. of Botany, Univ. of Guelph 1988– ; Steering ctte., Ont. Chapter, Soc. for Ecological Restoration; Bd. of Dirs., Eastern Native Plant Alliance; Ctte. Status Endangered Wildlife Can.; Scientific Adv. Ctte., Nature Conservancy of Can.; Sigma Xi; author or co-author numerous publs. sci. jours., reports, mags.; Office: P.O. Box 280, West Hill, Ont. M1E 4R5.

**AMBROZIC, Aloysius Matthew,** S.T.L., S.S.L., Th.D.; bishop; b. Gabrje, Slovenia 27 January 1930; s. Aloysius and Helena (Pečar) A.; e. klasična gimnazija, Ljubljana; St. Augustine's Seminary; Univ. San Tommaso, S.T.L. 1958; Pontificio Inst. Biblico, S.S.L. 1960; Univ. of Würzburg, Th.D. 1970; ARCHBISHOP, ROMAN CATHOLIC ARCHDIOCESE OF TORONTO 1990– ; ordained 1955; Prof., St. Augustine's Sem. 1960–67; Toronto Sch. of Theol. 1970–76; Dean of Studies, St. Augustine's Sem. 1971–76; Aux. Bishop, Roman Catholic Archdiocese of Toronto 1976–86; Coadjutor Archbishop of Toronto 1986–90; apptd. to the Pontifical Counc. for the Pastoral Care of Migrants and Itinerant People 1990, Congregation for Clergy 1991 and Pontifical Council for Culture 1993; one of four Bishops representing Can. at the 1990 Synod on the Formation of Priests, Rome; Mem., Catholic Biblical Assn. of Am.; ACEBAC; author: a monthly column in 'The Catholic Register'; author: 'The Hidden Kingdom' 1972; 'Remarks on the Canadian Catechism' 1974; 'Oče, posvečeno bodi tvoje ime' 1980; recreations: hiking, swimming; Office: 355 Church St., Toronto, Ont. M5B 1Z8.

**AMERONGEN, Gerard Joseph,** Q.C., B.A., LL.B.; lawyer; b. Winnipeg, Man. 18 July 1914; s. Maximilian Ernest and Maria (Waas) Taets von Amerongen; e. Univ. of Alta., B.A. 1943, LL.B. 1944; m. Elizabeth Fetherstonhaugh, 6 Dec. 1943; children: Mary, Peter, Margaret, Monica, Helen, Michael, Elizabeth, John; called to the Bar of Alta. 1946; appointed Q.C. 1966; elected to Legislative Assembly 1971, re-el. 1975, 1979, 1982, and served as Speaker 1971–86; Chrmn. Constitution Ctte., Legislative Assembly 1981; Chrmn. Members' Services Ctte.; Legislative Internship Advisory & Selection Ctte.; Cand. Rep.; Extve. Ctte. of the Commonwealth Parliamentary Assoc. 1981–84; Mem., Bd. of Trustees, St. Joseph's Hosp. 1987– ; Dir., Edmonton City Ctr. Church Corp. 1987–93; Bd. of Trustees, Forum for Young Albertans 1986–93; Founding Dir., Alberta's first Candn. Native Friendship Ctr. (personnel dir., 6 yrs.); past mem., 3 Edmonton hosp. bds.; past mem., Nat. Extve., P.C. Assoc. of Canada; Alta. P.C. Assoc. (past Pres.); mem., Law Soc. of Alta.; recreations: hiking, reading, woodworking; Home: 10236 Connaught Dr., Edmonton, Alta. T5N 3J2; Office: 2170 Sun Life Place, 10123 – 99 St., Edmonton, Alta. T5J 3H1.

**AMES, Michael,** B.A., Ph.D.; museum director, university professor; b. Vancouver, B.C. 19 June 1933; s. Ernest Oliver Francis and Elsie (McClean) A.; e. Univ. of B.C., B.A. (Hons.) 1952; Harvard Univ., Ph.D. 1961; separated; children: Daniel J., Kristin J.; DIR., U.B.C. MUSEUM OF ANTHROPOLOGY 1974– ; Asst. Prof. of Sociol., McMaster Univ. 1962–64; Asst. Prof. to Prof. of Anthropol., present univ. 1964– ; Research among Indians of B.C. 1954–55, 1980– ; in Sri Lanka 1959–60, 1963; in India 1967–68; Past Gov., Shastri Indo-Candn. Inst.; Candn. Mus. Assn.; B.C. Mus. Assn.; Counc. for Mus. Anthropol.; occasional cons. for univs., mus. & mus. training prog. incl. McCord Mus., Univ. of Toronto Mus. Studies Prog., Expo '86 pavilions & several others; The Simon Guggenheim Fellowship 1970–71; Fellow, Royal Soc. of Can. 1979; author: 'Museums, The Public and Anthropology' 1986; co-editor: 'Manlike Monsters on Trial' 1980; 'Cannibal Tours and Glass Boxes' 1992, 1993; Office: 6393 N.W. Marine Dr., Vancouver, B.C. V6T 1Z2.

**AMIEL, Barbara,** B.A.; writer; b. Herts., Eng.; d. Col. Harold Joffre and Vera Isserles (Barnett) A.; e. N. London Coll. Sch. Canons Park, Eng.; Univ. of Toronto B.A. 1963; m. George Jonas 11 Oct. 1974 (m. dissolved); m. Conrad M. Black 21 July 1992; Ed., 'Toronto Sun' 1983–85; Columnist, 'Maclean's' 1976– ; Columnist 'The Times' (London, Engl.) 1986–90; Sr. Pol. Columnist 'The Sunday Times' (London, Engl.) 1991– ; rec'd Can. Council Grant 1974; Media Club of Can. Award 1976; Periodical Publishers Assn. Award 1977; co-author 'By Persons Unknown' 1977; author of 'Confessions' 1980; winner Mystery Writers of America Edgar Allan Poe Award for best fact crime book; commended British Press Award 1987; Women of Distinction 1989 (Britain); Jewish; Address: c/o The Telegraph plc, 10 Toronto St., Toronto, Ont. M5C 2B7.

**AMIOT, Patrick;** artist; b. Montreal, Que. 1959; self-taught; all works have been produced in collaboration with Brigitte Laurent; selected exhibitions: Nancy Poole's Studio 1988, 89, 90; Galerie Franklin Silverstone Montreal 1988, 89, 90; Doheny Gall. Vancouver 1990; Grace Gall. Vanc. 1984–86; group exhibitions: New Art Forms Exhib. Chicago 1989; 'Abreath of Canadian Life,' Sunlife of Canada Calgary 1989; collections: Burlington Cultural Ctr.; McDonald's Restaurants; Claridge Investments Limited Montreal; Coca Cola Limited; Hees Internat. Toronto; Bombardier Found. Montreal; Power Corp.; Lignum Indus.; Washington State Art Bank; General Foods Corp. N.Y.; Apple Computers; numerous priv. collections in Can., U.S., Japan, Hong Kong; commissions & awards: winner Business and the Arts Found. award 1986; Washington State Arts Comn. (incl. 2 murals & 3 standing figures) 1986; The Land Plaza Comp. Expo '86 1985; Comn., B.C. Pavillion, Expo '86, ceramic mural 120 sq. ft. 1985; Comn., Govt. of Can. (Can. Harbour Place Pavillion Expo '86) 5 murals, 50 sq. ft. & 5 large portrait sculptures of Candn. Inventors; Office: c/o Nancy Poole's Studio, 16 Hazelton Ave., Toronto, Ont. M5R 2E2.

**AMORE, Roy C.,** B.A., B.D., Ph.D.; educator; b. Newark, Ohio 10 Sept. 1942; s. Ralph C. (dec.) and Mary Ellen (Wyckoff) A. (dec.); e. Ohio Univ., B.A. 1964; Drew Univ. Madison, N.J., B.D. 1967; Columbia Univ., Ph.D. 1970; m. Michelle Morrison; children (from previous marriage): Allison Amore Lee, Justin; PROF. OF RELIGIOUS STUDIES, UNIV. OF WINDSOR 1981– , Head of Dept. 1986–88; part-time Lectr. Drew Univ. 1968–69; Visiting Lectr. Upsala Univ., N.J. summer 1969; Instr. Bard Coll. 1969–70; joined present Univ. 1970, Asst. Prof. 1970, Assoc. Prof. 1974, Co-ordinator Asian Studies Prog. 1980–81, 1982–86; Wilson-Craven Prof. Southwestern Univ. 1978–79; mem. Candn. Council for Southeast Asian Studies, Pres. 1980–82; Candn. Asian Studies Assn., Vice Pres. 1980–82; Candn. Soc. Studies in Religion; Sec. Candn. Corp. Studies in Religion 1976–78; author 'Two Masters, One Message' 1978, Asian ed. 1985; co-author 'Lustful Maidens and Ascetic Kings: Buddhist and Hindu Stories of Life' 1981; ed. 'Developments in Buddhist Thought: Canadian Contributions to Buddhist Studies' 1979; co-ed. 'Culture and Development in Southeast Asia' 1987; recreations: golf, racquetball, basketball; Home: 385 Lakeside Rd., R.R. 5, Box 59, Harrow, Ont. N0R 1G0; Office: 401 Sunset Ave., Windsor, Ont. N9B 3P4.

**AMYOT, Léopold H.,** C.V.O., B.L.Sc., B.A., B.Sc.S.; diplomat; b. Québec, Qué. 25 Aug. 1930; s. S. Eugène and Juliette (Gagnon) A.; e. Laval Univ., B.L.Sc. 1952; Univ. of Ottawa, B.A. 1953; course on Internat. Inst., Geneva, Switz. 1956; Laval Univ., B.Sc.S. 1956; m. Marie Jeanne 'Andrée' d. Dr. Jean-Baptiste and Jeannette Jobin 11 Oct. 1958; children: Christian, Annick, Chantal; Ambassador to Lebanon (accreditation to Syria, Jordan, Iraq) 1974; Asst. Sec. Gen., Agence de Coop. culturelle et technique, Paris, France 1976; Chief of Protocol, Dept. of External Affairs 1980; Extve. Dir., Task Force on Pope's Visit to Can. 1983; Ambassador to Morocco 1983; Secretary to the Governor General of Canada, 1985–90; also Sec. Gen., Order of Canada, Sec. Gen. of the Order of Military Merit 1985–90 and First Herald Chancellor of Canada 1988– ; Chrmn., Official Residence Collections Adv. Ctte.; 'Prix d'honneur de la Section de Qué. de l'Inst. canadien des Affaires internat.' Quebec 1985; apptd. Commander of the Royal Victoria Order by Her Majesty Queen Elizabeth the Second July 1st 1990; recreations: tennis, golf, swimming, contemporary art collector; clubs: Five Lakes, Le Cercle univ. d'Ottawa; Home: 15–140 Rideau Terrace, Ottawa, Ont. K1M 1Z2.

**AMYOT, René,** Q.C., B.A., LL.L., M.B.A.; barrister; b. Quebec City, Qué. 1 nov. 1926; s. Omer Amyot and Caroline (Barry) L'Espérance; e. Coll. Des Jesuites De Que., B.A. 1946; Laval Univ. Law Sch., LL.L. 1949; Harvard Univ. Grad. Sch. of Business Adm., M.B.A. 1951; COUNSEL, JOLIN, FOURNIER, MORISSET; Dir. Fidusco Ltd.; Ferme Charlevoix Inc.; Logistec Corp.; Rothmans Inc.; Palmar Inc.; Counc. of Business and the Arts in Can.; Le Groupe Chab Inc.; Expand Images Canada Inc.; called to Bar of Que. 1949; cr. Q.C. 1965; rec'd Chevalier de l'ordre de Léopold, 1985; joined Procter & Gamble, Montreal, 1951; Bouffard & Associates, Quebec, 1952; Asst. Prof., Fac. of Admin. Sciences, Laval Univ. 1954–69; Asst. Prof., Fiscal Law, Laval Univ. Law Sch. 1960–70; Consul for Belgium 1966–82; Dir. & Mem. Extve. Ctte., Centre de Recherche Industrielle of Que. 1971–76; Pres., Que. District Chamb. of Comm. 1972; Founding Pres., CIREM (Centre International Recherches et études en management) 1972; Dir., Bank of Nova Scotia 1972–81; Chrmn., Air Canada 1981–83; Gov., Fac. of Admin. Sciences, Laval Univ.; mem., Candn. Bar Assn.; Que. Bar Assn.; Candn. Tax Foundation; Internat. Chamber Comm.; Assn. des MBA du Québec; Liberal; R. Catholic; recreations: skiing, swimming, tennis, farming; Clubs: Quebec Garrison; Toronto Club; Office: Edifice Iberville 3, Suite 500, 2960 Boul. Laurier, Ste-Foy, Qué. G1V 4S1.

**ANAND, Raj,** B.A., LL.B.; barrister and solicitor; b. New Delhi, India 20 Apr. 1955; s. Tilak Raj and Kailash Kumari (Dhall) A.; e. St. John's-Ravenscourt Sch. Winnipeg 1972; Queen's Univ. B.A. 1975; Univ. of Toronto LL.B. 1978; called to Bar of Ont. 1980; m. Anne d. Aba and Evelyn Bayefsky 6 July 1986; three d. Rachel Lisa, Sarah Dana, Michelle Jessica; PARTNER, SCOTT & AYLEN; articled Cameron, Brewin and Scott 1978–79, Partner 1980–83; Partner, Jack, Harris, Anand 1983–85, Cavalluzzo, Hayes and Lennon 1985–87; Chief Comnr. Ont. Human Rights Comn. 1988–89; Researcher/Writer, Royal Comn. N. Environment and Ont. Law Reform Comn. 1977–79; Chrmn. Task Force Law Concerning Trespass to Publicly Used Property Youth & Minorities 1986–87; Instr. Bar Admission Course Law Soc. Upper Can. 1982–83, 1985, Lectr. Cont. Legal Edn. 1985– ; Candn. Judicial Council 1993; recipient Gov. Gen.'s Medal 1972; Univ. of Toronto Prizes Civil Procedure 1976, Internat. Law 1977, Best Oralist Jessup Meml. Internat. Law Moot Court Competition 1977, Dean's Key 1978; author or co-author various legal publs.; speaker on various human rights, administrative and employment law issues; member, Human Rights Bd. of Inquiry; mem. C.C.L.A.; Amnesty Internat.; Candn. Bar Assn.; Minority Advocacy and Rights Council; Organization of South Asian Canadians; Editorial Bd., Nat'l. Journal of Constitutional Law; recreations: piano, reading; Office: F34, Royal Trust Tower, Toronto-Dominion Ctr., Toronto, Ont. M5K 1H6.

**ANCTIL, Pierre,** M.A., Ph.D.; educator; b. Quebec City, Que. 28 July 1952; s. Jean-Louis and Constance (Barry) A.; e. Univ. Laval B.A. 1973, M.A. 1975; New Sch. for Social Rsch. New York Ph.D. 1980; m. Monique d. Ernest and Hermine Drapeau 28 June 1979; children: Gabriel, Liliane, Philippe; AGENT DE RECHERCHE ET DE PLANIFICATION SOCIO-ÉCONOMIQUE, MINISTÈRE DES COMMUNAUTÉS CULTURELLES ET DE L'IMMIGRATION, GOUVERNEMENT DU QUÉBEC 1993– ; Researcher, l'Institut québécois de recherche sur la culture, Montreal 1980–88; Dir. French Can. Studies and Asst. Prof. of Jewish Studies, McGill Univ. 1988–91; Conseiller en services aux communautés culturelles, Ministère de l'Éducation, Gouvernement du Québec 1991–93; Vice Pres. Candn. Multiculturalism Adv. Ctte. 1990–91; Can. Rsch. Fellow (postdoctoral) Social Sci's & Humanities Rsch. Council Can. 1988–91; mem. Bd. Govs. Montreal Holocaust Meml. Centre 1990–91; author: 'Pòemes Yiddish' 1992; 'Le Rendez-vous manqué, les Juifs de Montréal face au Québec de l'entre-deux-guerres' 1988; 'Le Devoir, les Juifs et l'immigration. De Bourassa à Laurendeau' 1988; ed.: 'Un Homme Grand. Jack Kerouac at the Crossroads of Many Cultures' 1990; 'An

Everyday Miracle, Yiddish Culture in Montreal' 1990; 'If One Were to Write a History... Selected Writings by Robert F. Harney' 1991; Founding mem., Dialogue St-Urbain 1989– ; mem. Candn. Christian-Jewish Consultation 1987–92; Candn. Ethnic Studies Assn. (Pres. 1985–87); recreation: philately; Office: 360 McGill, Montréal, Qué. H2Y 2E9.

**ANDERSEN, Marguerite,** Ph.D.; writer, former university professor; b. Magdeburg, Germany 15 Oct. 1924; d. Theodor and Martha (Bohner-Seeberg) Bohner; e. Cert. d'études sup. Sorbonne 1953; Staatsexamen, Freie Univ. Berlin 1957; Univ. of Montreal Ph.D. 1964; children: Christian and Marcel Nouvet, Tinnish Andersen; has taught in France, Germany, Tunisia, Ethiopia and the U.S.; Prof., Loyola (Concordia Univ.) 1965–72; Univ. of Guelph 1972–89; Chair, Dept. of Lang. & Lit. 1972, 1989; Nancy Jackman Chair in Women's Studies, Mount Saint Vincent Univ. 1987–89; Pres., Assn. des professeurs de français dans les univ. et coll. canadiens 1990–92; Soc. des écrivains canadiens (Toronto) 1990– ; France-Canada Exchange Fellowship 1982–83; Mem., N.D.P.; Amnesty Internat.; Union des évriv. et écriv. Qué.; The Writers' Union of Canada; Internat. P.E.N.; Candn. Rsch. Inst. for the Advancement of Women; author: 'La Chambre noire du bonheur' 1994; 'L'Homme-papier' 1992; 'Courts métrages et instantanés' 1991; 'L'Autrement pareille' 1984; 'De mémoire de femme' 1983 (Prix du 'Journal de Montréal' 1983); 'Paul Claudel et l'Allemagne' 1965; co-author: 'Mécanismes structuraux' 1967; editor: 'Mother was not a person' 1972; co-editor: 'Paroles rebelles' 1992; articles, book reviews, poetry and short stories pub. in num. magazines and journals; Office: c/o The Writers' Union of Canada, 24 Ryerson Ave., Toronto, Ont. M5P 2T3.

**ANDERSEN, Peter Russell,** A.M., Ph.D.; consulting economist; b. Toronto, Ont. 1 Sept 1939; s. William A. Burkart and Elizabeth Olive (Russell) Andersen; e. Univ. of Toronto B.A. 1962; Harvard Univ. A.M., Ph.D. 1967; m. Katharine d. Douglas and Mildred Kearns 16 Sept. 1963; children: Jennifer, Brian, Mark; PRES. ANDERSEN ECONOMIC RESEARCH LTD. 1984– ; Rsch. Offr., Asst. Chief Rsch. Dept., Bank of Canada 1965–72; Partner, Woods Gordon 1972–80; Vice Pres. & Dir., Heritage Securities Corp. 1980–81; Chief Economist, Burns Fry Ltd. 1981–84; Lectr. Univ. of Western Ont. 1963; Columnist, Home Builder Mag.; recipient J. Reginald Adams Gol Medal 1962; Ford International Fellowship 1962; Can. Council Fellowship 1963; Duerr Fellowship 1963; Bd. of Govs., Royal St. George's Coll. 1986– ; Dir. Arts Etobicoke 1977–80; co-author 'Sales Forecasting, A Handbook of Business Problem-Solving' 1980; 'Supply Relationships in the Canadian Economy' 1972; various articles; mem. Candn. Home Builders Assn. (Chief Econ. 1983– ;); Bd. Trade Metrop. Toronto (Econ. Policy Ctte. 1978–85); Candn C. of C. (Econ. Policy Ctte. 1982); Humber Valley Hockey Assn. (Vice Pres. 1980); Delta Tau Delta (Pres. 1962); recreations: tennis, platform tennis; Clubs: Kingsway Platform Tennis; Lambton Golf; Home: 77 Strath Ave., Toronto, Ont. M8X 1R6; Office: Royal Bank Plaza, P.O. Box 63, South Tower, Suite 2300, Toronto, Ont. M5J 2J2.

**ANDERSON, Bruce,** M.Arch., F.R.A.I.C.; architect; educator; b. Montreal, Que. 8 Jan. 1941; s. Ralph Fritjof and Doris Amy (Smith) A.; e. King's Sch., Westmount High Sch.; McGill Univ. B.Arch. 1964; Harvard Univ. M.Arch. 1966; m. Bissera d. Yanko and Donna Doneff 23 June 1971; two d. Diana Celina, Christina Julia; PROF. OF ARCH., McGILL UNIV. 1981– , Dir. Sch. of Arch. 1985–90; Prin. Anderson Architects 1982– ; Lectr. in Arch. present Univ. 1964, Asst. Prof. 1966, Assoc. Prof. 1969; Prin. Anderson, Covo Architects 1980; Dir. St. Andrew's Sch. Westmount 1985–89; Miss Edgar's and Miss Cramp's Sch. Westmount 1989– ; Pres. McGill Faculty Club 1976; co-author 'Fort George' 1981; mem. O.A.Q.; Office: Montreal, Que. H3A 2T5.

**ANDERSON, D.J. Carl,** B.A., B.Ed., M.Ed., FOTF; energy executive / educator; b. Toronto, Ont. 14 Apr. 1931; s. David Joseph and Frieda Mae (Quinn) A.; e. Jarvis Coll. & Hornepayne Cont. Sch.; Univ. of Toronto, B.A. 1956, B.Ed. 1965, M.Ed. 1967; m. Thelma d. William and May (Gray) 1976; children: Gregory, Karena; CHAIRMAN, NORTH YORK HYDRO 1976– ; Chrmn., Municipal Elec. Assoc. 1988–90; Acct. Rep., Industrial Acceptance Corp. 1956–59; Principal (Elem.), North York Bd. of Edn. 1959–87; operates coin & antique business; Past Extve., Ont. Public Sch. Teachers' Fed.; Past Bd. of Gov., Ont. Teachers' Fed.; Dir., Am. Public Power Assn. 1989– ; Past Extve. Mem., North York Coin Club, Schoolmasters Curling Club, Newtonbrook Un. Ch.; Hon. Life Mem., OPSTF (Ont. & North York); Fellow, Ont. Teachers' Fed.; author of numerous educational articles; recreations: curling, coins, antiques; Home: 121 Clansman Blvd., North York, Ont. M2H 1Y2; Office: 5800 Yonge St., North York, Ont. M2M 3T3.

**ANDERSON, Hon. David Alexander Hebden,** LL.B., P.C., M.P.; politician; b. Victoria, B.C. 16 Aug. 1937; s. James William and Sheila Jutta (Gillespie) A.; e. St. Michael's 1945–47; Central British School HK, Aiglon College Switz.; Victoria H.S. 1953–55; Inst. of Oriental Studies, Univ. of Hong Kong Mandarin Lang. Prog. 1964–67; Univ. of B.C. LL.B. 1962; m. Sandra, d. Archibald and Kathleen McCallum 5 Nov. 1982; children: James William David, Zoe Kathleen Sheila; MINISTER OF NATIONAL REVENUE, CANADA 1993– ; External Affairs Officer 1962–68; elected M.P. for Esquimalt-Saanich 1968; Provincial M.L.A., Victoria & Leader of B.C. Liberal Party 1972–75; Environmental Consultant 1976–78; Visiting Prof., Sch. of Public Admin., Univ. of Victoria 1979–84; Mem., Immigration Appeal Bd. 1984–88; Environmental Consultant 1989–93; Special Advisor to Premier of B.C. on Oil Spills 1990–91; Commissioner, Inquiry into Petroleum Exploration in Fraser Valley, B.C. 1991–92; Silver Medal, Olympics 1960; Silver Medal, Pan American Games Chicago 1959; Captain of the Rowing Team, Univ. of B.C.; Mem., Anglican Ch.; Liberal Party; recreations: rowing, sailing; clubs: Victoria City Rowing Club, Royal Hong Kong Yacht, Royal Victoria Yacht; Home: 3195 Exeter Rd., Victoria, B.C. V8R 6H7; Office: 135 East Block, House of Commons, Ottawa, Ont. K1A 0A6.

**ANDERSON, Donald G.;** insurance broker; b. Dublin, Ireland 1 June 1950; s. George W.D. and Violet Myrtle A.; e. Hibernian Marine Coll. Dublin; Chart. Ins. Broker; m. Patricia d. Edward and Nessa Grieve 14 Feb. 1974; children: Sean, Heather; PRES. FIRSTBROOK, CASSIE & ANDERSON 1989– ; began ins. career Ireland 1967; came to Can. 1970; joined present firm 1973, Dir. and Shareholder 1980; Sec. Treas. Toronto Ins. Conf.; Dir. Ins. Inst. Can.; mem. Reg'd Ins. Brokers Ont.; Bd. Trade Metrop. Toronto; Office: 124 Eglinton Ave. W., Toronto, Ont. M4R 2G8.

**ANDERSON, Doris Hilda,** O.C. (1974), B.A.; writer, editor; author; columnist; b. Calgary, Alta. 10 Nov. 1921; d. Thomas and Rebecca (Laycock) McCubbin; e. Crescent Heights (Alta.) High Sch.; Univ. of Alta., B.A. 1945, hon. LL.D. 1975; m.; children: Peter David, Stephen Robert, Mitchell Richard; Pres., National Action Committee on the Status of Women 1982–84; Pres., Candn. Adv. Council on the Status of Women 1979–81; Editor, Chatelaine Magazine 1958–77; former Dir., Maclean-Hunter Publishing Co.; MacMillan Publishing Co. Can. Ltd.; Canadian Film Development Corp.; former Dir., Bd. of Candn. Civil Liberties; Metropolitan Children's Aid; former Gov., York Univ.; mem., Ontario Press Council 1977–84; Dir., North South Inst.; Trustee, Inst. of Resch. on Public Policy Planning; Mem., Judicial Counc. of Ont. 1986–92; Bd. Mem., Harbourfront; Chancellor, University of Prince Edward Island 1992– ; author 'Two Women' 1978; 'Rough Layout' 1981; 'Affairs of State' 1988; 'Unfinished Revolution' 1991; commenced as Edit. Asst., Star Weekly 1945; Claire Wallace radio programme scriptwriter 1946; with T. Eaton Co., Advertising Dept. 1946–50; joined Chatelaine 1951 and held positions of Edit. Asst., Asst. Ed., Assoc. Ed. and Mang. Ed. prior to Editor; awarded Centennial Medal 1967; City of Toronto Award 1981; Can. Press Club Hall of Fame 1981; YWCA Woman of Distinction Award 1982; Persons' Award 1991; recreations: reading, travel; Home: Toronto, Ont.

**ANDERSON, Douglas J.,** H.B.Sc., A.I.C.B., M.B.A., F.I.C.B.; business executive; b. Huntsville, Ont. 1 Oct. 1951; s. John Edward and Margaret Edith (Brown) A.; e. Univ. of Toronto, H.B.Sc. 1974; McMaster Univ., A.I.C.B. 1975, M.B.A. 1976; Univ. of Toronto, F.I.C.B. 1978; m. Caroline Ruth d. Walter James and Nora Lennard Mizen 31 Dec. 1977; children: Johnathon James, Iain Douglas; PRES. & DIR., ACTCO LIMITED 1985– ; Asst. Mgr., Co-op Prog., Royal Bank of Can. 1974–76; Accounting and Economic Lectr., Univ. of Toronto 1977–80; Regional Mgr., Citibank of Can. 1977–79; Devel. Offr., Cadillac Fairview 1979–80; Dir. of Residential Group, Bramalea Limited 1980–85; Dir. & Officer, Oakstone Homes Limited; Past Chrmn. Continuing Care Ctte., Past Mem. Extve. Ctte., & Dir., Ont. Hosp. Assn.; Dir., Ont. Blue Cross; Dir., Health Counc. of Greater Toronto Area; Past Chrmn., Bd. of Gov., Northwestern Gen. Hosp.; Chrmn. & Founder, Northwestern Health Serv.; Vice Chrmn. and Co-Founder, Northwestern Health Campus Corp.; Past Dir., the Administrator of the Hosps. of Ont. Pension Plan; Dir., Past Chrmn. & Co-founder, The Harold & Grace Baker Ctr.; Dir., Northwestern Health Centre Foundation; Past Dir., Georgian Peaks Club; Anglican; Mem., Anglican Diocese of Toronto Bishop's Papers; Member, Bishop's Co.; Past Chrmn., Bd. of Mngt., Church of the Redeemer; Chrmn., Task Force, Chronic Care Hosp. of Ont. and Ont. Hospital Assn.; Mem., H.C.G.T.A. Chair's Task Force on Excellence in Governance; Mem., Human Resource Ctte., Ont. Blue Cross; Patrons Counc., Ryerson Polytechnical Inst., Ballet for Books; Chrmn., Bldg. Ctte., The Harold and Grace Baker Ctr.; Chrmn., Earlscourt Child and Family Centre 80th Anniversary; Past Chrmn., Georgian Peaks Long Range Planning Ctte.; Past mem., Univ. of Toronto Standards and Awards Ctte.; Past Chrmn., Pres. Trayco Bank and Manufacturing Co., Junior Achievement; recreations: tennis, skiing, squash, woodworking, reading historic biographies; clubs: Toronto Lawn and Tennis; Georgian Peaks; Stoney Lake Yacht; Albany; Home: R.R. #4, Tottenham, King Twp., Ont. L0G 1W0; Office: 1575 The Queensway, Etobicoke, Ont. M8Z 1T9.

**ANDERSON, Edwin Orlando,** B.B.A., M.A.; educator; b. Mankato, Minn. 20 July 1934; s. Edwin Oswald and Martha Helena (Torgerson) A.; e. Univ. of Minn. B.B.A. 1956; Univ. of Man. M.A. 1971; Wash. State Univ.; m. Joan Townsend d. Turner and Pauline Broom 14 Aug. 1970; stepchildren: Joe Wayne and Paula Lynn Townsend; SECY. OF SENATE, UNIV. OF MAN. 1986– ; ASSOC. PROF. OF ADULT EDN. UNIV. OF MAN. 1981– ; advertising and retailing 1956–68; Part-time Lectr. in Anthrop. present Univ. 1971, Asst. Prof. of Adult Edn. 1974, Pres. Faculty Assn. 1980–81; Chrmn. Bd. Govs. Man. Museum of Man & Nature 1981–83, Bd. Govs. 1977–83, Hon. Life mem.; Pres. Candn. Assn. Univ. Teachers 1985–86, Vice Pres. 1983–85, Dir. 1980–83; recreations: music, travel; Home: 85 Tunis Bay, Winnipeg, Man. R3T 2X2; Office: Senate Secretariat, 244 Engineering Bldg. Winnipeg, Man. R3T 2N2.

**ANDERSON, Eiliv Howard;** corporate executive; b. Robsart, Sask. 20 July 1934; s. Thore Albert and Randine (Hanson) A.; e. Robsart H.S. S.S.G.D. 1951; Univ. of Saskatchewan, Sch. of Agric.; Extve. Program, Sch. of Bus., Queen's Univ., Kingston, Ont.; m. Joy Sheila d. Sigurd and Ethel Brekhus 20 July 1962; one s. Jordan; President, Anderson Consultants, Ottawa, Ont.; farmer, rancher Robsart, Sask. 1954–81; co-owner and Secy. Border Land & Cattle Co. Ltd., Maple Creek, Sask. 1970–81; co-owner and Pres. Lanta Enterprises Ltd., Medicine Hat, Alta. 1975–81; co-owner and Pres. Warlodge Enterprises Ltd., Maple Creek, Sask. 1972–80; M.L.A. Shaunavon, Sask. 1975–78; Exec. Dir. Sask. Liberal Assn., Fed. and Prov. 1981; Chrmn. & C.E.O., Farm Credit Corp. Can. 1982–87; Pres., Anderson Consultants, North Gower, Ont. 1988– ; Personnel Mgr. and Cash Book Clerk, Bank of Montreal, Maple Creek, Sask. 1952–53; Dept. of Regional Econ. Expansion, PFRA, Consul, Sask. 1951–52; Conservation and Devel. Br., Dept. of Agric., Sask. 1950–51; author: 'Constituency Orgn. Manual for Candidates for the Liberal Party of Saskatchewan' 1981; co-author: 'An Evaluation of the Beef Industry for Canada' 1981–82; Exec. Dir. Sask. Stock Growers Assn. 1957–75; Dir. Sask. Fed. of Agric. 1968–74; Dir. Nat. Beef Info. Centre 1972–74; Dir. Sask. Beef Info. Centre 1970–74; mem. Adv. Comte. Sask. Dept. of Agric. 1961–66; past Master, Masonic Lodge, Eastend Sask. 1967; mem. Mensa Can. 1977; Lutheran; awarded Queen's Silver Jubilee Medal; recreations: skiing, photography, hiking, sketching; Clubs: Canadian; Home: Box 527, North Gower, Ont. K0A 2T0.

**ANDERSON, Elizabeth Gay,** B.Sc.; business executive; b. Huntsville, Alabama 8 Oct. 1956; d. William Turner and Virginia Dare (Adkins) A.; e. Auburn Univ. B.Sc. (Bus. Admin.) 1977; m. Donald s. Roy and Emory Nosé 18 July 1992; VICE-PRESIDENT FINANCE, COCA-COLA LTD. (CANADA); Audit Manager C.P.A., Price Waterhouse 1977–83; Controller & Dir. of Finan. Planning, Johnstown American Cos. 1983–84; Vice-Pres., North Riverside Capital Corp. 1984–86; Manager, Bus. Devel., The Coca Cola Company (USA & Corp.) 1986–..; presently on foreign service tour of duty in Canada from U.S.; Home: 80 Lowther Ave., Toronto, Ont. M5R 1E1; Office: One Concorde Gate, Suite 500, Don Mills, Ont. M3C 3N6.

**ANDERSON, Gail Scott,** B.Sc., M.P.M., Ph.D.; university professor; b. Cleveland, England 7 Nov. 1961; d. Alexander Scott and Pamela MacNay (MacDonald) A.; e. Manchester Univ. B.Sc. (Hons.) 1983; Simon Fraser Univ. M.P.M. 1986, Ph.D. 1992; m. Gregory Leo s. Timothy and Margaret St. Hilaire 19 Dec. 1987; ASST. PROF., FORENSIC ENTOMOLOGY, SIMON FRASER

UNIV. 1992– ; Teaching Asst. & Rsch. Asst. 1984–91; Forensic Entomological Cons., B.C. Coroner's Service, R.C.M.P. & City Police 1988– ; Fac. Mem., Ctr. for Pest Management & Dept. of Biological Sciences, Simon Fraser Univ. 1992– ; Consultant, Motion Picture Indus. 1988; first full-time forensic entomologist in Canada; Guest Instructor, Major Crime Police Course, Forensic Odontology & Forensic Anthropology courses; Grad. Fellowship, Simon Fraser Univ. 1990; Ph.D. Stipend, S.F.U. 1990; Candn. Wild Horse Soc. Award 1985; U.K. Sci. & Engr. Rsch. Council Award, tenable overseas 1984–87; Pres. Rsch. Stipend, S.F.U. 1984; Zoology Dept. Prize, Manchester Univ. 1983; Mem., Entomological Soc. of Am.; Am. Acad. of Forensic Science; Candn. Soc. of Forensic Sci.; Pacific N.W. Forensic Study Group; B.C. Entomological Soc.; author of 7 scientific papers; Home: 25352 72nd Ave., Aldergrove, B.C. V4W 1H6; Office: Dept. of Biological Sciences, Simon Fraser Univ., Burnaby, B.C. V5A 1S6.

**ANDERSON, George D.,** M.A.; financial executive; e. Carleton Univ. B.A. 1969; Univ. of Regina M.A. 1973; PRES. AND CHIEF EXEC. OFFR., INSURANCE BUREAU OF CANADA 1992– ; Chrmn., Adv. Bd., Dynatek Automation Systems; Chrmn., Toronto Civic Employees Pension Fund; Chrmn., Central Guaranty Trust Co. 1990–91; Pres. and C.E.O., Canada Mortgage and Housing Corp. 1986–90; Dir. Mortgage Insurance Co. of Canada 1991; Dir. Rsch. & Planning Sask. Housing Corp. Regina 1972–73; Dir. Direct Lending, Canada Mortgage and Housing Corporation Ottawa 1974, Dir. Policy & Rsch. and Exec. Dir. Corporate Planning 1975, Regional Gen. Mgr. Saskatoon 1978, Vice Pres. Ottawa 1981–83, National Trust Co. Toronto 1983–86; Award of Excellence Candn. Home Builders Assn. 1990; selected Communicator of Yr. 1991 Internat. Assn. Bus. Communications; Chrmn., Federal Public Service United Way 1987; Dir. Nat. Mental Health Fund 1991; Trustee, Danny Grossman Dance Co.; Gov., Candn. Comprehensive Audit Found.; recreations: golf, tennis, skiing; Clubs: University; Summit Golf & Country; Royal Ottawa Golf; Royal Nova Scotia Yacht Squadron; United Church; Office: 180 University Ave., Toronto, Ont. M5H 3M7.

**ANDERSON, George R.M.,** B.A., M.Litt.; federal civil servant; b. Belleville, Ont. 11 Feb. 1945; s. Dr. Reginald Moore and Alice Calder (McIntosh) A.; e. Queen's Univ. B.A.; Nuffield Coll. Oxford M.Litt.; Ecole Nationale d'Adm. Paris Diplôme; m. Charlotte d. Robert and Elizabeth Gray 27 Oct. 1979; three s. Alexander, Nicholas, Oliver; Fellow, Center for International Relations, Harvard University 1992–93; Exec. Asst. to Dep. Min. Indian & N. Affairs 1972–75; Treasury Bd. Analyst 1976–77; Adv. Fed. Provl. Relations Office 1977–79; Policy Analyst and Dir. W. Eur. Div. External Affairs 1979–83; Dep. Adm. Can. Oil & Gas Lands Adm. 1983–86; Asst. Dep. Min. Energy Mines & Resources 1986–89; Asst. Dep. Min. Econ. Devel. Policy, Finance Can. 1990–92; Clubs: Five Lakes; Cave Reginam; Home: 51 Spring Valley Road, Belmont, Ma. 02178.

**ANDERSON, Harry Sheldon,** Ph.D.; b. Pittsburgh, Pa. 22 Apr. 1931; s. William Clark and Sarah King (Harris) A.; e. Univ. of Pittsburgh, B.A. 1953, M.Litt. 1956; Temple Univ., Ph.D. 1971; m. Michela d. Helen and Salvatore DiPietro 23 Dec. 1958; children: Eric Christopher, Alexander William, Michael Francis; ASSOC. PROF., DEPT. OF ENGLISH, MCGILL UNIV. 1972– ; Lectr., Delaware State Coll. 1958–60; Temple Univ. 1960–65; Lectr., Asst. Prof., present univ. 1965–72; Dir., Humanistic Studies Prog. 1987– ; Examiner: Baccalaureate International; Dir., (acad.), Drama & Theatre Prog. 1980–84, 1988–89; Dir. (theatre), Delaware State & Temple Univ.; Arts Westmount 1985; Dir., P.L.S. (Univ. of Toronto) 1986; Dir. & Teacher, Pa. Counc. for the Arts 1987; Dir., numerous McGill prodns.; Bd. of Dir., The Painted Bird Theatre Co.; Danse Icarus; co-author: 'Staging Symbolic Action in the Medieval Cycle Play' 1988; general editor: 'McGill Studies in Drama'; recreations: travel, bridge; Home: 58 Somerville Ave., Westmount, Que. H3Z 1J5; Office: Montreal, Que. H3A 2T5.

**ANDERSON, Isabel Beatrice,** M.A.; information broker; b. Unity, Sask. 28 May 1939; d. James and Barbara Ethel (Dickson) A.; e. Univ. of Sask. B.A. 1960, (Hons.) 1961, M.A. 1963; Univ. of Mich. Horace H. Rackham Sch. Grad. Studies 1963–64; Queen's Univ. Ph.D. (ABD) 1972; Centre Universitaire d'Etudes Française à l'Univ. Domaine Grenoble, France 1980–81; m. Frederick Frazer s. George Burwash and Irene Beryl Langford 24 Apl. 1982; children: Lesley Ann, Georgina Louise Melvin, Elizabeth Margaret; PRES. & RSCH. DIR., AAL INFOSERVE 1993– ; Dir. Potash Corp. of Sask. Inc. (Extve. Ctte. 1990– ;); Researcher Econ. Council Can. 1964–66; Prof. of Econ., Univ. of Sask. 1968–93; Visiting Asst. Prof. Univ. of Victoria, B.C. 1972–73; Candn. NGO Del. UN Conf. Trade & Devel. Nairobi 1976; Candn. Del. UN Conf. Sci. & Technol. Vienna 1979; Budget Cons. Dept. Finance Sask. 1983–85; Trade Comnr. Pub. Hearings Can.-US Bilateral Trade Negotiations Sask. 1986; pub. speaker, panelist and commentator radio and TV nat. and internat. econ.; Dir. Candn. UNICEF Ctte. 1979–82; Sask. Council Internat. Co-op. 1976–79; mem. Sask. Environmental Adv. Council 1975–77; author or co-author; mem. Saskatoon Nutana Rotary (Dir. 1990–92; 1993–94); Paul Harris Fellow; Home: 1212 Colony St., Saskatoon, Sask. S7N 0S6; Office: Saskatoon, Sask. S7N 0S6.

**ANDERSON, John Ansel,** Ph.D., D.Sc., LL.D., F.R.S.C., F.C.I.C., F.A.I.C., F.A.A.C.; chemist; b. Sidcup, Kent, Eng. 16 Aug. 1903; s. Alfred William and Agnes (Hanna) A.; e. Univ. of Alta. B.Sc. 1926, M.Sc. 1928, LL.D. 1965; Leeds Univ. Ph.D. 1930; Univ. of Graz (Austria); Univ. of Birmingham; Univ. of Sask. D.Sc. 1964; Univ. of Man. LL.D. 1978; m. Isla Doune d. T.J. Scott 1931; children: Garet Sean, Jason Alfred; Biol. Div. Applied Biol. & Agric. Nat. Rsch. Council Can. Ottawa 1930–39; Dir. Grain Rsch. Lab. Candn. Grain Comn. 1939–62; Dir. Winnipeg Rsch. Stn. Agric. Can. 1962–63, Dir. Gen. Rsch. Br. 1963–68; Rsch. Prof. of Plant Sci. Univ. of Man. 1968–71; recipient Thomas Burr Osborne Medal Am. Assn. Cereal Chems. 1957; ed. 'Enzymes and Their Role in Wheat Technology' 1946; 'Storage of Cereal Grains and Their Products' 1954; mem. Am. Assn. Cereal Chems. (Pres. 1952–53); Internat. Assn. Cereal Chems. (Pres. 1959–60); Protestant; recreations: golf, chess.

**ANDERSON, John Bateman,** M.D.; association executive; family physician; b. Victoria, B.C. 8 Apl. 1946; s. John Burton and Agnes Elizabeth (Proudfoot) A.; e. Univ. of B.C. M.D. 1972 (Gold Medal); m. Barbara-Rae d. Edward and Grace Pridham 29 June 1968; children: Christina, Bryan, Patricia; Pres., B.C. Medical Assn. 1989; Pres. Gen. Practice Sec. 1983–84; Pres. Med. Staff Victoria Gen. Hosp. 1981–82; Pres. Greater Victoria Un. Way; mem. Candn. Med. Assn. (Dir. 1978–89); Candn. Coll. Family Phys.; recreations: skiing, music; Home: 908 Hillside Ave., Victoria, B.C. V8T 1V8.

**ANDERSON, John H.,** B.B.A.; advertising executive; b. Brantford, Ont. 30 Apr. 1943; s. Harold and Greta A.; e. Univ. of W. Ont., B.B.A. 1967; m. Janet d. Mary Ward 10 July 1970; children: Melinda, Bronwyn; SR. VICE PRES., MACLAREN LINTAS ADVT. LTD. 1986– ; Acct. Dir., MacLaren Advt. 1967–72; Sr. Coordinator, Automotive Advt., Imperial Oil Ltd. 1972–78; Corp. Advt. Mgr. 1978–81; Pres., Foote, Cone & Belding Can. 1981–86; Dir. and Vice Pres., Marketing, Ont. Heart and Stroke Found.; recreations: tennis, golf, rowing; Clubs: Hanlan Boat; Lytton Park; Office: 20 Dundas St. West, Toronto, Ont. M5G 2H1.

**ANDERSON, John Harold Cameron,** B.A.Sc.; retired manufacturer; b. Perth, Ont. 17 Apr. 1924; s. John McLaren and Irene F. (Cameron) A.; e. Perth (Ont.) Coll. Inst. 1946; Univ. of Toronto B.A.Sc. 1950; m. Willa Florence Ward 6 Sept. 1952; children: W. Darlene, John B.; Vice-Chrmn., Jenkins Canada Inc. 1985–89; Indust. Engr., Orange Crush Ltd. 1950–52, Advertising Mgr. 1953–55; Sales Rep. Toronto present Co. 1955, Sales Engr. H.O. Montreal 1960, Vice Pres.-Mfg. and Dir. 1970, Pres. 1978; mem. Assn. Profl. Engrs. Prov. Ont.; Anglican; recreations: golf, workshop hobbies; Club: Smiths Falls Golf and Country; Home: 22 Cedar Lane, Smiths Falls, Ont. K7A 4S5.

**ANDERSON, John Murray,** B.Sc.F., Ph.D., LL.D., D.Ped.; educator; b. Toronto, Ont. 3 Sept. 1926; s. Murray Alexander and Eleanor Montgomery (Valentine) A.; e. Jarvis Coll. Inst., Toronto; Univ. of Toronto, B.Sc.F. 1951, Ph.D. 1958; St. Thomas Univ., LL.D. 1974; Univ. of Maine, D.Ped. 1976; LL.D. Dalhousie Univ., 1979; m. Eileen Anne, d. Dr. A. M. McFaul, Collingwood, Ont., 3 Nov. 1951; children: Nancy, Susan, Peter, Katherine; remarried Sylvia Ella Hébert 10 May 1986; stepchildren: Tanya, Tracy; PRES., J.M. ANDERSON CONSULTANTS INC. 1980– ; Dir. Rsch. & Education, Atlantic Salmon Federation 1984–86, Vice Pres., Operations 1986– ; Asst. Prof. Biol., U.N.B. 1958; Assoc. Prof. Biol., Carleton Univ. 1963; Dir. Fisheries Research Bd. Can. Biol. Stn., St. Andrews, N.B. 1967; Dir.-Gen., Research and Devel. Fisheries & Marine Service, Dept. of Environment, Ottawa 1972; Pres., Univ. of New Brunswick 1973–79; mem. Scient. Adv. Comte., World Wildlife Fund (Can.); Pres. & Chrmn. of Bd. Huntsman Marine Lab., St. Andrews, N.B. 1973–77, Dir. 1985– ; Dir., Assn. of Univ. and Coll. of Canada 1975–79; Fraser Inc. 1975–79; Bd. of Govs., Inst. Candn. Bankers; Rothesay Coll. School; Kenya Technical Teachers Coll., Nairobi, Kenya; Extve. Comte., N.B. Museum; Vice-Pres. Biolog. Council of Canada; Chrmn. Assn. of Atlantic Univ. 1978–79; John R. Bradford Ed. Fund (Noranda) 1979–86; Pres. Aquaculture Assn. of Can. 1983–85; Mem. Bd. of Trustees, Sunbury Shores Arts and Nature Inc. 1970— ; (Chrmn., Bd. of Trustees 1982–84); Mem., Bd. of Dirs., Nature Trust of New Brunswick Inc. 1986–90; Chrmn., Bd. of Trustees, W.L. Mackenzie King Scholarships 1986– ; Mem., Science Counc. of Can. 1988–92; Pres., Atlantic Aquaculture Fair 1993– ; served with RCNVR 1945; author over 40 scient. publs. in area animal physiol.; mem. Candn. Soc. Zools. (Past Pres.); Sigma Chi; Unitarian; recreations: skiing, boating, tennis; Home: P.O. Box 547, St. Andrews, N.B. E0G 2X0; Office: Atlantic Salmon Federation, P.O. Box 429, St. Andrews, N.B. E0G 2X0.

**ANDERSON, John Oliver,** B.Sc., B.Ed., M.Ed., Ph.D.; university professor; b. Winnipeg, Man. 27 Dec. 1944; s. Kristian Eyolfur and Allie (Swainson) A.; e. Univ. of Man. B.Sc. 1965, B.Ed. 1969, M.Ed. 1971; Univ. of Alta. Ph.D. 1978; m. Jean Nemis Aug. 1966; CHAIR, PSYCHOLOGICAL FOUNDATIONS OF EDUCATION, UNIV. OF VICTORIA 1993– ; High School Teacher, Manitoba until 1970; Dir., Rsch. Services, Educational Rsch. Inst. of B.C. 1978–87; Prof., Univ. of Victoria 1987– ; Home: 2551 MacDonald Dr., Victoria, B.C. V8N 1X7; Office: Box 3010, Victoria, B.C. V8W 3N4.

**ANDERSON, Admiral John R.,** CMM, CD, B.Sc.; b. Trail, B.C. 9 Sept. 1941; e. Univ. of B.C., B.Sc. 1963; Long Operations Offrs. course, Command and Staff Coll.; m. Anne Penwarden 4 Jan. 1964; three children: Ian, Karen, Jennifer; CANDN. PERMANENT REPR. AND AMBASSADOR TO NORTH ATLANTIC COUNCIL 1994– ; commissioned in 1963; served in HMC ships in both Atlantic and Pacific fleets; Commanding Offr., HMCS 'Restigouche' 1978; Naval Captain 1982; Cmdr., First Cdn. Destroyer Squadron 1982; Staff, Nat. Defence HQ 1982; Commodore 1986; Dir., Maritime Doctrine and Operations 1986; Rear-Admiral 1987; Head, Candn. Nuclear Submarine Acquisition Project 1987; Chief, Maritime Doctrine and Opns. 1989; Vice-Admiral 1991; Commander of Maritime Command, Halifax 1991; Vice Chief of the Defence Staff 1992; Admiral 1993; Chief of the Defence Staff, National Defence HQ, Ottawa 1993; Apptd. Commander of the Order of Military Merit in 1989 and Principal Commander in 1993; Address: Delegation of Canada, Léopold III Blvd., 1110 Brussels, Belgium.

**ANDERSON, Judith Catherine,** B.A., LL.B., LL.M.; lawyer; b. Hardisty, Alta. 28 March 1946; d. Stewart and Bertha Sophie (Carbon) Wright; e. Univ. of Alta. B.A. 1968, LL.B. 1969; Univ. of Ottawa LL.M. 1983; m. James Anderson 14 April 1977; children: Jill Abeline, Catherine Isabel; LAWYER, HARRIS & CO. 1991– ; Dir., Legal Services, Alta. School Trustees Assn. 1972–90; Adjunct Prof., Simon Fraser Univ.; Office: 2200-1111 West Georgia St., Vancouver, B.C. V6E 4M3.

**ANDERSON, Logan Bruce,** B.Comm., A.C.A.; financial executive; b. New Zealand 13 June 1954; e. Univ. of Otago (Dunedin, N.Z.) B.Comm. 1977; New Zealand Soc. of Accountants, Mem., ACA; INDEPENDENT FINANCIAL CONSULTANT; Accountant, Coopers & Lybrand 1977–82; Dir., various public & private companies 1982– ;.

**ANDERSON, Margaret E. Seguin,** M.A., Ph.D.; educator; b. St. Clair, Mich. 12 June 1945; d. Ralph Carl and Vera Evelyn (Guyitt) Welser; e. Univ. of Mich. B.A. 1967, M.A. 1968, Ph.D. 1977; m. Clarence s. Alfred and Louisa Anderson 10 July 1984; two s. Ralph Paul and Michel Roland Seguin; DIRECTOR OFFICE OF FIRST NATIONS ACTIVITIES AND CHAIRPERSON, FIRST NATION STUDIES, UNIVERSITY OF NORTHERN BRITISH COLUMBIA 1992– ; joined Univ. of Western Ont. 1973, Assoc. Prof. 1985, Chair of Anthropol. 1986–89, Dir. Centre for Rsch. & Teaching Candn. Native Langs. 1984–91; author 'Interpretive Contexts For Traditional And Modern Coast Tsimshian Feasts' 1985; contbr. 'Handbook Of North American Indians' Vol. 7 1990; numerous jour. articles; ed. 'The Tsimshian: Images Of The Past, Views For The Present' 1984; series ed. 'Text Plus+ Series' Studies in the Interpretation of Candn. Native Langs. & Cultures; ed. 'Culture' Jour. Candn. Anthrop. Soc. 1990–93; mem. Candn. Anthrop. Soc./Société Canadienne d'anthropologie (Sec.-Treas. 1980–83); Office: Bag 1950, Stn. A, Prince George, B.C. V2L 5P2.

**ANDERSON, Michael James,** B.A., LL.B.; lawyer; b. Leicestershire, Eng. 22 Jan. 1944; s. Thomas Harvey and

Ada Elizabeth (Day) A.; e. London Central Coll. Inst. 1961; Univ. of W. Ont. B.A. 1964, LL.B. 1967; m. Mary d. John and Martha Mikula 12 Aug. 1967; children: Michael Kevin, Helen Marie, James Peter; LAWYER, SMITH, LYONS, TORRANCE, STEVENSON & MAYER 1985– ; called to Bar of Ont. 1969; law practice W. Laird Thomas, London, Ont. 1969–71; Asst. Secy. John Labatt Ltd. and Secy. Ogilvie Mills Ltd., London, Ont. 1971–79; Vice Pres. and Gen. Counsel Swift Canadian Co. Ltd. Toronto 1980–81; Gen. Counsel & Secy., Denison Mines Ltd. 1981–85; Club: Toronto Cricket Skating & Curling; Home: 17 Inglewood Dr., Toronto, Ont. M4T 1G7; Office: Suite 6200, Scotia Plaza, 40 King St. W., Toronto, Ont. M5H 3Z7.

**ANDERSON, Morris A.,** B.A., B.Ed., M.A., LL.D., educator; college administrator; b. Saskatoon, Sask. 12 Aug. 1930; e. Univ. of Sask. B.Ed. 1953; B.A. 1956; Univ. of Oregon M.A.; Capital Univ. LL.D.; m. Bergliot Charstad 20 Aug. 1953; children: Susan; Stephen; Philip; Past President, Luther College, Univ. of Regina 1964–86; High Sch. Teacher, Bedford Rd. Collegiate, Saskatoon 1953–54; Teacher, Luther Coll. 1956–62, Vice-Princ. 1963; Mem., Sask. Comm. on Directions in Health Care; Dir., Lutheran Life Insurance Soc. of Can.; Interim Pres., Augustana University Coll.; past Pres., various organizations, including Sask. Div., Arthritis Soc. of Can.; Lutheran Educational Conference of N. Amer.; Sask. Assn. of Private Schools; Chair, Canada World Youth; mem. (past Pres.) Regina Gyro Club; Chrmn., Regina Public Lib. Bd. 1976–86; Chrmn., Sask. Lib. Development Bd. 1974–84; Hon. LL.D., Capital Univ. 1977; recreations: golf; reading; Home: 5022 10th Ave., Regina, Sask. S4T 7P4.

**ANDERSON, Myles Norman,** B.Sc.; geological engineer, business executive; b. Flin Flon, Man. 22 Jan. 1931; e. Flin Flon schools; Univ. of Manitoba B.Sc. 1953; m. Tania Lorette Babienko; children: Kristopher, Paul, Kathryn; PRESIDENT, ANDERSON & ASSOCIATES; Dir., BGR Precious Metals Inc.; Finning Ltd.; Gulf Canada Resources; Homestake Mining Co.; Prime Resources Group Inc.; Solv-Ex Corp.; The Toronto Dominion Bank; started at Cominco Ltd.: EIT Sullivan Mine 1953; Engr. H.B. Mine 1955–57; Dev. Supt., Mines Div. Kootenay Florence-Ainsworth 1957; various jobs, Sullivan 1957–61; Mine Supt., Wedge Mine 1961; Bluebell Mine 1962; Mining Engr., Mines Div., Trail 1964; Mgr. Magmont Mine 1965–70; Vice-Pres. and Gen. Mgr., Buick Operations, AMAX 1970–73; Vice-Pres., Lead Operations and Mining, AMAX Lead-Zinc Inc. 1973; Vice-Pres., Cominco Amer. Inc. (Spokane) 1974; Pres. and C.E.O., Fording, Calgary 1974; Group Vice-Pres., Calgary, Cominco 1975; Vice-Pres. and Asst. C.O.O., Vancouver 1976; Exec. Vice-Pres. and C.O.O. 1977; Pres. and C.O.O. 1978; Chrmn. & C.E.O. 1980–86; mem. C.I.M.M.; I.M.M.; A.I.M.E.; B.C. Prof. Engrs.; Coal Assn. of Can.; recreations: hunting, fishing, curling, golf; Office: 502 – 455 Granville St., Vancouver, B.C. V6C 1V2.

**ANDERSON, The Hon. N. Robert,** LL.B.; judge; b. Sherbrooke, Guysborough Co., N.S., 30 Nov. 1930; s. Robert Clarence and Ida Lyll (Morris) A.; e. Elem. and High Sch., Sherbrooke, N.S.; Dalhousie Univ. Law Sch., LL.B.; m. Edith Louise, d. H. E. Pyle, Boylston, N.S., 14 Jan. 1961; children: Shirley L., Katherine I., Caroline M., John M.; SUPREME COURT JUSTICE OF NOVA SCOTIA 1993– ; Judge, Co. Court District No. 1, Nova Scotia 1971– ; read law with A. W. Cameron, Q.C.; called to Bar of N.S. 1957; in law practice, Sherbrooke, N.S. 1957–65; apptd. Dir. (Criminal), Dept. Atty. Gen., N.S., Halifax 1965; def. Cand., Prov. Lib. Party 1960; mem. N.S. Barrister Soc.; Candn. Bar Assn.; Freemason; Presbyterian; recreations: fishing, hunting, camping, reading; Office: Court House, Halifax, N.S. B3J 1S7.

**ANDERSON, Philip Robley;** construction executive; b. Newcastle, Eng. 4 May 1921; s. Joseph Walton and Vida Caroline (Robley) A.; e. Jordanhill Coll. Sch., Glasgow, Scot.; Glasgow Univ.; m. Audrey Jewel, d. late William Broadbridge, 22 March 1947; children: Jane, Blair, Lois; PRES., P.R. ANDERSON CONSTRUCTION SERVICES INC. 1982– ; Chrmn., Walsim Develop. Corp.; Field Engr., The Foundation Co. Ltd., Toronto, 1947–48; Project Mgr., Toronto, 1948–50; Gen. Supt., Toronto, 1950–53; Br. Mgr., Calgary, 1953–57; W. Div. Mgr. and Vice-Pres., Calgary, 1957–63; Extve. Asst. to Pres., EGM Cape & Co. Ltd., Montreal 1963–64, V.P. Operations 1964–68, V.P. & Gen. Mgr. 1969–77, Pres. 1978–80; Vice-Pres., R.G. Kirby & Sons Ltd. 1981–82; Past Pres. Calgary Construction Assn.; Past Pres. Ont. General Contractors; Past Pres. Alta. Construction Assn.; Dir. Candn Construction Assn. 1977–81; served with R.E. in Europe during 2nd World War; rank Maj.; Anglican; recreations: golf, swimming; Clubs: Rosedale Golf; St. Andrews Golf (Scotland); Home: 65 Spring Garden Ave., Suite 604, Willowdale, Ont. M2N 6H9.

**ANDERSON, Raymond Cecil,** B.A., LL.B.; international affairs consultant; b. Wetaskiwin, Alta. 6 June 1929; s. Rudolph Thure and Alice Woodrow (Shantz) A.; e. Univ. of Alta., B.A. 1952, LL.B. 1957; Harvard Univ. (Advanced Business Mgmt.) 1971; m. Joyce Ralphene, d. J. Russell Love, Edmonton, Alta., 21 Aug. 1954; children: Douglas Russell, Calvin Blair, Catharine Alice, Doris Dorothy; Founding Pres., Asia Pacific Foundation of Canada 1985–90; Dir., Niagara Inst.; joined Trade Commr. Service, Dept. Industry, Trade & Comm. 1957; Vice Consul, São Paulo, Brazil 1959; Vice Consul and Trade Commr., Los Angeles 1961; Chargé d'Affaires, Manila 1963; Consul and Sr. Trade Commr., Boston 1965; Dir. (Personnel) Trade Commr. Service, Dept. External Affairs 1968, Dir. Personnel Operations 1971–74, Consul Gen., Seattle; Asst. Depy. Min. Industry, Trade and Commerce 1974–76; Consul General Los Angeles 1978; Candn. High Commr. to Australia 1980; Asst. Depy. Min. Internat. Trade Devel., Dept. of External Affairs 1983–85; International Affairs Advisor, Swinton & Co., Barristers and Solicitors, Vancouver; with R.C.A.F., Course Dir. Univ. Flying Trainees 1955–56; Zeta Psi; United Church; recreations: music, bridge; Clubs: Harvard Business; Vancouver; Rotary; Candn. Soc. of Los Angeles; Royal Commonwealth Soc.; Vancouver.

**ANDERSON, Reid Bryce;** artistic director; b. New Westminster, B.C. 1 Apl. 1949; e. Kirkwood Acad. of Performing Arts Burnaby, B.C.; Royal Ballet Sch. London, Eng.; Ecole de Danse Princess Grace Monte Carlo, Monaco; apptd. ARTISTIC DIR., NATIONAL BALLET OF CANADA 1990– ; Dir., Ballet British Columbia 1987– ; joined Stuttgart Ballet W. Germany 1969 becoming Prin. Dancer; leading ballet roles incl. 'Romeo and Juliet,' 'Onegin,' 'Taming of the Shrew,' 'Carmen,' 'Lady of the Camelias,' 'Orpheus,' 'Voluntaries'; apptd. Ballet Master Stuttgart 1983, retired from stage 1985; choreographed ballets for Stuttgart Ballet, Anna Wyman Dance Theatre, Alberta Ballet, Ballet British Columbia; co-produced CBC TV prodn. John Cranko's 'Onegin' Nat. Ballet of Can.; danced 2 pas de deux with Natalia Makarova BBC series 'Ballerina'; awarded 'Bundesverdienstkreuz' (Order of Fed. Repub. W. Germany) for services to Arts 1986; Office: 157 King St. E., Toronto, Ont. M5C 1G9.

**ANDERSON, Hon. Richard Philip,** B.A., LL.B.; lawyer; b. Victoria, B.C. 1 Jan. 1921; s. Herbert Glass A.; e. Univ. of B.C., B.A., LL.D.; m. Margaret Chapman d. Foster Bingham, Seattle, Wash., 4 Feb. 1965; children: Kathryn, Marion, Christine, Graeme, Heather; step d. Pamela, Susan; BOUGHTON, PETERSON, YANG, ANDERSON; read law with law A. R. McDougall; called to Bar of B.C. 1949: cr. Q.C. 1969; former Justice, Supreme Court, B.C.; former Justice, Court of Appeal, B.C.; served with Candn. Army and RCAF during World War II, Flight Lt.; mem., Law Soc. B.C.; Candn. Bar Assn.; Phi Gamma Delta; recreation: golf; Clubs: Vancouver; Point Grey Golf & Country; Home: #5, 1063 West 7th Ave., Vancouver B.C. V6P 1W4; Office: 1055 Dunsmuir St., P.O. Box 49290, 2500 Four Bentall, Vancouver, B.C. V7X 1S8.

**ANDERSON, Robert Davis,** Q.C., B.A., LL.M.; lawyer; executive; b. Evergreen Park, Ill. 22 June 1934; s. Carlyle Fairfax and Ellen Elizabeth (Davis) A.; e. Ross Pub. Sch. Welland, Ont. 1948; Phillips Acad. Andover 1952; Univ. of Wis. B.A. 1956; Osgoode Hall Law Sch. Call to Bar, 1960, LL.M. 1977; m. Ellyn d. Verner and Jean McCord 1 June 1957; children: Christopher (d. 1982), Mary; GENERAL COUNSEL & SECRETARY, PROCTER & GAMBLE INC. 1975– ; and mem. Mang. Comte. 1976– ; Legal Counsel present Co. 1963, Secy. 1965; called to Bar of Ont. 1960; cr. Q.C. 1975; private law practice Bassel, Sullivan, Toronto prior to 1963; Dir., Procter & Gamble Inc. 1987– ; Assn. Candn. Gen. Counsel; Patent & Trademark Inst. Can.; Beta Theta Pi; Anglican; recreation: tennis; Clubs: Granite; Home: 72 Cheltenham Ave., Toronto, Ont. M4N 1P7; Office: 4711 Yonge St., North York, Ont. (P.O. Box 355, Stn. 'A,' Toronto, Ont.) M5W 1C5.

**ANDERSON, Robert Newton,** B.A., B.Ed., M.A., Ph.D.; educator; b. Saskatoon, Sask. 14 March 1929; s. George W. and Bertha M. (Sloan) A.; e. Univ. of Sask. B.A. 1949, B.Ed. 1951; Univ. of Minn. M.A. 1959, Ph.D. 1963; m. Shirley Anne Bennett 24 March 1951; children: Janis, Ellen, Jeffrey, Paul, David; Professor and Dean of Educaiton, Univ. of Lethbridge 1986–87; Hist. Teacher and Head of Dept. Regina Coll. System 1950–58; Assoc. Dir. of Curriculum Prov. Sask. Dept. Educ. 1958–59; Prof. of Educ. Foundations and Head of Dept. Univ. of Calgary 1959–65; Prof. of Secondary Educ. and Head of Dept. Univ. of Sask. Regina 1965–69; Candn. Rep. to World Conf. on Educ. Asilomar, Calif. 1970; Visiting Prof. Univ. of Lagos and Advisor to Govt. of Nigeria 1970–71; mem. Bd. of Govs., Univ. of Lethbridge 1970–74 and 1988–90; Prof. of Educ. since 1969 and Dean of Educ. there 1974–79, Professor Emeritus 1990– ; Visiting Fellow, Univ. of Aberdeen, Scotland 1979–80; Dir. of Grad. Studies (Educ.) Univ. of Lethbridge 1982–85; Research Fellow, Univ. of Exeter, 1985–86; author 'Institutional Analysis of Mount Royal College' 1964; 'Two White Oxen: A Perspective on Early Saskatoon' 1972; co-author 'Foundation Disciplines and the Study of Education' 1968; 'Trends in Teacher Education' 1977; 'Lifelong Education in a World Perspective' 1978; 'International Perspectives for Classroom Teachers' 1984; 'Thinking Skills, Achievement, and Sense of Efficacy' 1988; rec'd. Distinguished Teacher Award, Univ. of Lethbridge 1988; contrib. to educ. journs.; Fellow, Philos. Educ. Soc.; mem. Comparative & Internat. Educ. Soc.; World Council on Curriculum (Founder and mem. Bd. Dirs.); Candn. Soc. Studies Educ.; Candn. Assn. African Studies; Candn. Educ. Assn.; Candn. Coll. Teachers; Candn. Foundations Educ. Assn. (Founding Pres. 1962, 1970); N.W. Regional Philos. Educ. Soc. (Pres. 1965–66); rep. of N. Am. at World Conf. on Curriculum in Istanbul Aug. 1977; United Church; Address: 101 Chippewa Cres., Lethbridge, Alta. T1K 5B4.

**ANDERSON, Roy Clayton,** B.Sc., M.A., Ph.D.; university professor; b. Camrose, Alta. 26 Apr. 1926; s. Leslie and Nina (Wager-Keller, U.E.L.) A.; e. Pub. and High Schs., Camrose, Alta.; Univ. of Alta., B.Sc. 1950; Univ. of Toronto, M.A. 1952, Ph.D. 1956; Univ. of London, 1956–57; Univ. of Paris, Dipl. Helminthology 1958; m. Phylliss Cathleen, d. Addison Brox, 1948; children: Douglas Roy, Michel Brock; PROF. OF ZOOL., UNIV. OF GUELPH 1965– ;(Chrmn. of Zool. 1979–89); Research Assoc. and Sr. Research Scientist, Ont. Research Foundation, 1958–65; served with R.C.N.V.R. 1943–45; Co-ed., 'Systematic Parasitology'; Official Correspondent, Commonwealth Inst. of Parasitology (Commonwealth Agric. Bureaux), St. Albans, Eng.; Ed. Bd., 'Bulletin Museum Natl. d'Histoire Naturelle' (France); Ed. Bd., 'Annales de Parasitologie' (France); Ed. Bd. 'Folia Parasitologica' (Czechoslovakia); Ed. Bd., 'Proceedings of Helminthological Soc. of Washington, DC'; rec'd Henry Baldwin Ward Medal, Am. Soc. Parasitologists, 1968; Rec'd Sigma Xi Award, Guelph Chapt. 1973; Rec'd Distinguished Service Award, Wildlife Disease Assoc. 1978; el. 'Correspondant du Museum,' Museum National d'Histoire Naturelle, Paris 1987; rec'd Wardle Medal, Parasitology Sect., Candn. Soc. Zool. 1988; rec'd Directors Award, Friends of Algonquin Park 1992; Emeritus Prof., Guelph 1992; author of over 200 scient. papers and Ed. of two books on wildlife diseases and Commonwealth Inst. of Helminthology 'Keys to the Nematode Parasites of Vertebrates'; author: 'Nematode Parasites of Vertebrates, their development and transmission'; has contrib. to understanding of helminths of wild and domesticated animals; mem., Am. Soc. Parasitol. (Vice-Pres. 1977); Helminthol. Soc. Washington, D.C.; Candn. Soc. Zool. (Pres. 1975 Chrmn. Parasitol. Sectn. 1982); Wildlife Society; Wildlife Disease Assn. (Pres. 1981–83); Linnean Society (Fellow); mem., Sigma XI; Protestant; recreation: literature; Home: 40 Westminster Ave., Guelph, Ont. N1E 4C1.

**ANDERSON, Russell C.,** M.B.A., P.Eng.; business executive; b. London, Ont. 2 Dec. 1942; s. Calvin G. and Mary E. (Whally) A.; e. General Motors Inst. Bach. Ind. Eng. 1967; Univ. of W. Ont., M.B.A. 1969; m. Sharon d. George and Joyce Freethy 26 July 1985; children: Greg, Mike, Peter (by previous marriage); V.P. Manufacturing, Consumers Glass 1991– ; Eng. Co-op. General Motors Diesel, London, Ont. 1962–67; Otis Elevator 1969–84, Plant Mgr., Vice Pres. Operations, Dir. Mfg. Operations World Wide; Pres. Rail Trans Ind. (UTDC) 1984–86; Group Pres. Innopac Packaging Inc. 1987–89; Mgmt. Consulting, Principal, Ernst & Young 1990–91; Dir. Hamilton C. of C. 1980–82; Home: 33 Rollscourt Dr., Willowdale, Ont. M2L 1X6.

**ANDERSON, Thomas W.,** B.A.; association executive; b. Toronto, Ont. 26 Aug. 1946; s. Thomas and Ellen May (Cain) A.; e. Univ. of Toronto B.A. 1969; VICE-PRESIDENT, SPECIAL SERVICES, CANADIAN BANKERS ASSN.; Bd. Mem., Internat. Business Council of Can.; Mem., Standards Council of Canada; Candn. General Standards Bd.; Am. Nat. Standards Inst.; Chrmn., Candn. Nat. Ctte. on the Orgn. for Internat. Standardization; extensive experience in Canadian banking standards and policies; club: Cambridge; Home:

390 Wellesley St. E., #20, Toronto, Ont. M4X 1H6; Office: P.O. Box 348, Commerce Court West, Toronto, Ont. M5L 1G2.

**ANDERSON, Lt. Gen. William Alexander Beaumont,** O.B.E. (1945), C.D., D. Mil.Sc. (1977); is descended of a family many yrs. active in Candn. Mil.; b. Montreal P.Q., 7 May 1915; s. Maj.-Gen. William Beaumont and Lois Winnifred (Taylor) A.; e. Rothesay Coll., N.B.; Queen's Univ., B.A. 1937; Roy. Mil. Coll., Grad. 1936; Staff Coll., Camberley, Eng., 1941; U.S. Army and Navy Staff Coll., 1945; Nat. Defence Coll., 1950; Imp. Defence Coll., Eng., 1956; m. 1stly late Caroline Jane, d. Col. R.H. Waddell, Kingston Ont., 4 Nov. 1939; m. 2ndly Frances Helen Diana Birkett, d. H.A.K. Drury, Ottawa, Ont. 12 Apr. 1982; two s. Robert (died 1956), Anthony; Col. Commandant, Royal Regt. Candn. Arty. 1986–91; joined Candn. Mil., Roy. Candn. Horse Arty. 1936; trans. from Kingston to Winnipeg 1938; served in World War 1939–45 with Canadian Army Overseas; appts. incl. Personal Asst. to Gen. Crerar 1942; Cmdg. Offr., 15 Fd. Regt., R.C.A. 1943–44; Gen. Staff Offr., 1st Grade (Operations) in N.W. Europe 1944–45; Chief Instr., R.M.C., 1945; Dir. of Mil. Intelligence, Ottawa, 1946–49; Dir., Canadian Army Staff Coll., 1950–51; Comdr. W. Ont. Area, 1952–53; Commdr., 1st Candn. Inf. Bgde., Germany, 1953–55; Vice-Adj. Gen. 1957–59; Depy. Chief of Gen. Staff, Ottawa, 1959–60; Comdt. Royal Mil. Coll., 1960–61; Adj.-Gen., 1962–64; Depy. Chief Reserves 1965–66; Commdr., Mobile Command, 1966–69; apptd. Chrmn. Ont. Civil Service Comn. 1969 and Depy. Min. Ont. Dept. Civil Service 1971; Secy., Mang. Bd., Ont. Cabinet 1974; Depy. Prov. Secy., Resources Development 1979; Spec. Adviser to federal govt. on Lambert and d'Avignon Reports 1980–82; Vice-Chrmn., Ont. Inflation Restraint Bd. 1982–85; Pres., Roy. Life Saving Soc. Can. 1982–85; Mentioned in Despatches (N.W. Europe) 1944; Offr., Belgian Order of Leopold (1948); Offr. Belgian Order of the Crown with Palm (1946); Belgian Croix-de-Guerre with Palm (1946); Anglican; Clubs: Rideau; York; Home: 16–140 Rideau Terrace, Ottawa, Ont. K1M 0Z2.

**ANDERSON, The Honourable William Joseph;** b. Oakville, Man. 20 Apr. 1918; s. William Victor and Adeline (Whitmore) A.; e. Gladstone Pub. Sch., Winnipeg and Teulon (Man.) High Sch.; Univ. of Man.; Osgoode Hall Law Sch.; m. Alison Rosamond, d. late Dr. Charles L. Morgan, 2 July 1951; two s., William Hugh, Charles Edward; JUDGE, HIGH COURT OF JUSTICE FOR ONTARIO apptd. 1977, retired 1993; read law with H. Fred Parkinson, Q.C.; called to Bar of Ont. 1948; cr. Q.C. 1960; practised law with Gardiner, Roberts or predecessor firms from 1948; served with Candn. Army Reserve 1939–42; Active Service 1942–45; mem., Advocates' Soc.; Candn. Bar. Assn.; York Co. Law Assn.; Phi Delta Phi; Anglican; recreations: reading, fishing, liturgical music; Clubs: Lawyers, National; Home: 3 Castle Frank Rd., Toronto, Ont. M4W 2Z3.

**ANDERSON, William M.,** B.A., B.B.A.; executive; b. Seattle, Wash. 16 July 1931; e. Univ. of Wash. B.A. 1954; Am. Grad. Sch. Internat. Mgmt. (Thunderbird) 1957; Univ. of Minn. B.B.A. 1959; m. Claudia Sims 1955; children: Britt Arick, W. Mathew; Pres. & Chief Extve. Offr., Thomas Lighting Inc. 1990–93; Mgr. Finance & Adm. Honeywell Eur. Region 1959–65; Controller, Bell & Howell (Inc.) (E.C.E.) 1966–68; Dir. Mfg., Planning & Adm. Hyster Co. 1968–75; Pres. Hyster Canada 1975–81; Pres. & C.E.O., Canadian Manoir Industries Ltd. 1981–89; recreations: racquet sports, gardening, skiing; Club: Granite; Home: 21 Knightswood Rd., Toronto, Ont. M4N 2G9.

**ANDIAPPAN, Palaniappan,** B.A., M.A., M.Litt., M.S., Ph.D.; university professor; b. Melasivapuri, India 25 Jan. 1944; s. Palaniappan and Valliammai A.; e. Univ. of Madras, India B.A. 1963, M.A. 1965, M.Litt. 1967; Univ. of Massachusetts, M.S. 1973; Univ. of Iowa, Ph.D. 1977; m. Kay d. Muthu and Meena Muthiah 2 Sept. 1966; children: Jasmine Valliammai, Meena Rose; ASSOCIATE DEAN AND PROF. OF BUS., UNIV. OF WINDSOR 1985– ; Rsch. Scholar, Indian Sch. of Internat. Studies 1967–70; Rsch. Assoc., Indian Inst. of Mgmt. 1970–71; Asst. Prof., Sch. of Admin., Univ. of N.B. 1977–1980; Assoc. Prof., Fac. of Bus., Univ. of Windsor 1980–85; Area Head, Admin. Studies Area 1982–85; Fulbright Fellowship 1971; Vice Pres., Admin Sciences Assn. of Can. (Co-Prog. Chair, Internat. Bus. Div. 1984–85; Div. Chrmn., Personnel & Human Resources 1987–88); author 'Women and Work' 1980; co-author 'Readings in Canadian Industrial Relations' 1978; author and ed. var. articles and proceedings; Home: 5873 Bishop, Windsor, Ont. N9H 2K4; Office: Windsor, Ont. N9B 3P4.

**ANDRACHUK, Brenda Jean;** advertising executive; b. Collingwood, Ont. 15 Aug. 1941; d. Lloyd Albert and Margaret Elizabeth (Gould) Gilbert; e. Ryerson Inst. of Technol. Journalism; m. John Stanley s. John and Catharine Andrachuk 1963; divorced; one d. Leslie Ann; GROUP VICE PRES., MGR., THE ONT. GOVT. AGENCY OF RECORD, MEDIA BUYING SERVICES LTD. 1989– ; Broadcast Supr. Ogilvy & Mather Canada Inc. 1975–79; Broadcast Supr., Bristol-Myers Canada Inc. 1979, Mgr. Media & Prog. Services 1980, Dir. Advt. Services 1982–89; Pres. Broadcast Rsch. Council Can. 1984; mem. TV Exec. Ctte., BBM Bureau Broadcast Measurement; mem. Assn. Candn. Advertisers (Past Chrmn. Broadcast Ctte.; Sr. Vice Chrmn. 1986 (First woman), Chrmn. 1988 (First woman); recreations: skiing, tennis; Clubs: Toronto Ski; Parkview Sports; Home: 110 Cottingham St., Apt. 101, Toronto, Ont. M4V 1C1; Office: 150 Bloor St. W., Toronto, Ont. M5S 2X9.

**ANDRAS, Kenneth Bertram;** stock broker; b. Toronto, Ont. 5 Apr. 1909; s. Edward Bertram Gay and Gwendolyn Osler (Francis) A.; e. Brown Pub. Sch., Toronto, Ont.; Univ. of Toronto Schs., 1920–27; m. Elizabeth Boyd, d. late Dr. Joseph Graham, 12 Sept. 1936; children: Kenneth, John, Jane, Elizabeth; HON. CHAIRMAN, ANDRAS RESEARCH CAPITAL INC.; Founding Chrmn. and now Director, CARE of Can.; Dir., The Canadian Hearing Society; The Donwood Institute; CNIB Amateur Radio Club; Fort York Branch, Royal Candn. Legion; Pres., Tippet Foundation; Hon. Extve. Ctte., St. George's Soc.; commenced career as Jr., Mara & McCarthy, Toronto, Ont., 1927; became Partner, 1939 (firm name changed to Stanton, Hatch & McCarthy in 1941, to Andras, Hatch & McCarthy in 1952 and to Andras, Hatch & Hetherington Ltd. 1963); served in 2nd World War, 1941–45 with R.C.A.F.; Overseas, 1941–44; retired with rank of Sqdn. Ldr.; Mentioned in Despatches; Univ. Toronto Schs. Old Boys' Assn. (Past Pres.); Hon. Chrmn. 1967 Jr. Bd. of Trade; Past Pres., Bureau Municipal Research; past Chrmn., Metro Toronto Hospital Planning Council; Adv. Comte., Boy Scouts Assn.; Officer, Hospitaller and Military Order of St. Lazarus; Conservative; Anglican; recreations: fishing, photography, amateur radio (Stn. VE3UU); Clubs: Rotary Club of Toronto (Past Pres.)(Paul Harris Fellow); Progressive Conservative Business Men's; Badminton & Racquet (Hon. Mem.); National; Home: 2 Rose Park Cres., Toronto, Ont. M4T 1P9; Office: P.O. Box 265, Ernst & Young Tower, Toronto-Dominion Centre, Toronto, Ont. M5K 1J5.

**ANDRAS, Kenneth William,** B.A.; investment advisor; b. Toronto, Ont. 3 May 1942; s. Kenneth Bertram and Elizabeth Boyd (Graham) A.; e. Rosethorne P.S. 1953; Upper Canada College 1961; Oakwood Collegiate 1962; Waterloo Lutheran Univ. B.A. 1965; m. Margaret d. Ken and Marjorie Beeby 16 Sept. 1966; children: William, Peter, Janet; SENIOR VICE PRESIDENT, RESEARCH CAPITAL CORPORATION (formerly Andras Group Research Capital Corp.) 1969– ; Floor Trader, Andras Hatch & Hetherington 1965–67; Bond Dealer & Investment Advisor, Bartlett Cayley 1967–69; Extve. Vice-Pres., Lawrence Park Ratepayers Assn.; Dir., Downtown Churchworkers Moorelands Camp 1971–81; Aquarians 1967–85; Rotary Club of Toronto 1971– ; Probus Club 1979–84; Core of North York 1978–81; Marketing Care Canada 1987– ; Lawrence Park Ratepayers Assn. 1988– ; Anglican; clubs: Albany, Board of Trade, Rotary; Home: 22 St. Leonards Ave., Toronto, Ont. M4N 1J9; Office: Toronto Dominion Centre, Suite 1500, P.O. Box 265, 222 Bay St., Toronto, Ont. M5K 1J5.

**ANDRE, Harvie,** P.C., M.P., B.Sc., M.S., Ph.D., P.Eng.; politician; b. Edmonton, Alta. 27 July 1940; s. John and Doris (Ewasiuk) A.; e. Univ. of Alta. B.Sc. 1962, Ph.D. 1966; Cal. Inst. of Technol. M.S. 1963; m. Joan Roberta d. Robert and Ivy Smith 15 May 1965; children: Coryn, Lauren, Peter; Min. of State (to assist the Prime Minister) and Government House Leader 1990–93; Assoc. Prof. of Chem. Eng., Univ. of Calgary 1966–72; el. to H. of C. g.e. 1972, re-el. 1974, 1979, 1980, 1984; Min. of Supply & Services, Can. 1984; Assoc. Min. of Defence Canada 1985; Min. of Consumer and Corporate Affairs 1986–89; Min. of Regional Indust. Expansion and Min. of State, Science, 1989–90; former Dir. Clifford E. Lee Foundation; Past Vice Pres. Social Planning Council of Calgary; mem. Chem. Inst. Can. (Chrmn. Calgary Sect. 1970); United Church; recreations: gardening, politics, golf; Clubs: Calgary Petroleum; Calgary Commerce; Office: 819 Crescent Blvd. S.W., Calgary, Alta. T2S 1L3.

**ANDRE, Marion;** theatre director; playwright; b. Le Havre, France 12 Jan. 1920; s. Emil Tenenbaum and Renata (Liebling) C.; e. Fac. of Law and State Conservatory Drama Dept., Lwow, Poland 1940–41; m. Ina d. Joe and Nora Rubin 13 Nov. 1970; children: Tom, Krystian, Jennifer, John; Dir. and writer for theatre, radio and television, Poland 1950–56; transl. and adapted several Eng. plays produced in all media; moved to Can. 1957; Drama Specialist Protestant Sch. Bd. of Greater Montreal 1958–62; Dir. prodns. at McGill Univ.; Founder 'Frelancers' (profl. co. at Theatre Club, St. Luc, Montreal) 1958; Artistic Dir. Saidye Bronfman Centre Theatre 1967–72; Founder and Artistic Dir., Theatre Plus 1973–85; directed prodns. at Nat. Theatre Sch. 1974–75; Lectr. and Dir. York Univ. 1972, 1979; transl./adapt. Carl Sternheim's 'The Snob' (prod. by Theatre Plus 1976; publ. 1982); co-author 'The Invented Lover' (prod. by Theatre Plus 1980; publ. 1982); author: (play) 'The Aching Heart of Samuel Kleinerman' (prod. by Theatre Plus 1984; River West theatre, N.Y. 1989); Holocaust-oriented short stories in 'The Gates' and play 'The Aching Heart of Samuel Kleinerman' 1984 (publ. 1986); play 'Skinny Dip of an Aging Professor' 1985 (public reading Stratford Festival 1985); 'The Sand' (prod. at York Univ. Theatre Dept., also public reading by Medina Theatre Ensemble 1986, 1987, 1992); Holocaust oriented play 'Soldat Hans Stumpf' 1987 (public reading at Leah Poslun's theatre, dir. by Robin Phillips 1988; publ. in Germany 1989; prod. at The Man on the Moon Theatre, London, Eng. under the title 'Savage Storm' 1992; staged reading at the Actors Studio, N.Y. 1993); 'A Road to Freedom' (play) 1988; short stories and 'The Skinny Dip of an Aging Professor' publ. in 'The Verdict of Fate' 1988; 'Maria B.' (novel) publ. 1990; 'Captive of Yesteryear' (play) 1989; 'Glu Glub or Power of Persuasion' (tragic farce) 1990; Dir., Chekhov's 'The Three Sisters' Cleveland Play House 1987; radio and TV dramas produced by CBC incl. 'The Scorn of Fate'; 'Recollection'; 'The Value of Fifty'; 'The Fate of a Poet'; 'Two Faces of Love'; 'The Betrayer'; documentaries for CBC Radio and CBC-TV; recipient Toronto Drama Bench Award for Distinguished Contrib. to the Candn. Theatre 1985; Life Mem., ACTRA; mem., Equity; Playwright's Union of Can.; Internat. P.E.N.; The Candn. Centre; Address: 59 Clifton Rd., Toronto, Ont. M4T 2E8.

**ANDREACHUK, Lori G.,** Q.C., B.A., LL.B.; lawyer; mediator; b. Lethbridge, Alta. 27 July 1953; d. William and Joyce M. (Pizzey) A.; e. Univ. of Lethbridge B.A. (Hon. Econ.) 1977; Univ. of Alta. LL.B. 1977; PARTNER, NORTH PETERSON LINT ANDREACHUK, BARRISTERS AND SOLICITORS 1977– ; Dir. Lethbridge C. of C.; Lecturer and mem. Action Comte. Status of Women, Univ. of Lethbridge, Lethbridge Community Coll.; mem. Candn. Bar Assn.; Lethbridge Bar Assn.; Alta. Adv. Counc. on Women's Issues; Univ. of Lethbridge Found.; named Woman of Distinction for S. Alta. 1991; recreations: reading, athletics; Club: Henderson Lake Golf; Home: 14 Kings Rd., Lethbridge, Alta.; Office: 220–4th St. S., Chancery Court, Lethbridge, Alta. T1K 5E3.

**ANDREW, Arthur Julian,** M.A., D.C.L.; retired Canadian public servant; b. Pictou, N.S., 20 Nov. 1915; s. late Rev. Canon Albert Edward and Ethel (Sinclair) A.; e. Kings Coll. Sch., Windsor, N.S.; Dalhousie Univ., B.A. 1937, M.A. 1947; Kings Coll., Halifax, D.C.L. 1971; m. Joyce Mowbray, d. Lieut-Col. G. C. Sircom, Halifax, N.S., 24 Oct. 1940; two d.: Stephanie, Victoria; apptd. Asst. Under-Sec. of State for Ext. Affairs in 1974 (formerly Dir.-Gen., Asia & Pacific Bur. 1971–74); joined Dept. of Exter. Affairs, Aug. 1947; 2nd and 1st Secy., Candn. Embassy, Bonn, 1950–52; 1st Secy. and Chargé d'Affaires, Candn. Legation, Vienna, 1953–54; Head of Information Div., Ottawa, 1955–57; Counsellor and Chargé d'Affaires, Candn. Legation, Prague, 1957–60; Head of Inspection Service, Ottawa, 1961–62; Candn. Ambassador to Israel & High Commr. to Cyprus, 1962–65; Candn. Ambassador to Sweden, 1965–69; Foreign Service Visitor, Univ. of Toronto, 1969–70; Ambassador to the Hellenic Republic; Dir.-Gen., Asia and Pacific Bur. 1971–74; Asst. Under-Sec. of State for Ext. Affairs 1974–79 (ret.); Foreign Service Visitor, Visiting Prof., Univ. of Kings Coll., Halifax, 1978–93; author: 'Defence by Other Means: Diplomacy for the Underdog' 1970; 'The Rise and Fall of a Middle Power' 1993; sub-editor Canadian Press, Atlantic Bureau 1937–39; served in 2nd World War; Princess Louise Fusiliers (MG); Lieut., Sept. 1939; retired as Capt., March 1946; Anglican; Club: Halifax; Address: 990 McLeon St., Apt. 202, Halifax, N.S. B3H 2V1.

**ANDREW, James Vernon;** writer; publisher; b. Port Arthur, Ont. 9 June 1929; s. Oswald Edward and Helen Mary (Stewart) A.; e. Kirkland Lake Coll. & Vocational Inst. 1946; Royal Candn. Naval Coll. Victoria 1948; Royal Naval Eng. Coll. Plymouth, Eng. 1953; m. Joan d. Ralph and Elizabeth Batten 9 June 1973; children: Gillian, Robin; Owner, Andrew Books Ltd. 1988–93; trained as naval cadet and served as eng. offr. with RCN 1946–74; author 'Bilingual Today, French Tomorrow' 1977; 'Backdoor Bilingualism' 1979; 'Enough!' 1988; recreations: bridge, choral music, reading, golf, bagpipe; Address: 804, 1061 Queens Blvd., Kitchener, Ont. N2M 1C1.

**ANDREWS, Douglas Guy,** M.A., Sc.D., P.Eng., C.Eng., F.I.Mech.E., F.R.S.A.; professor emeritus; b. Boston, Eng. 17 Oct. 1917; s. John Thomas and Lydia (Pine) A.; e. Boston Grammar Sch.; King's Coll. (Scholar) Cambridge B.A. 1939, M.A. 1943 (Eng. Sci.); m. Robina d. John and Mary Dobbins 5 Sept. 1942; children: Glenys Willys Pyne, Douglas Gordon Harrison, Randall Keith; PROF. EMERITUS OF NUCLEAR ENG., UNIV. OF TORONTO 1983– ; Exper. Asst. and Offr. RN Sci. Service, magnetic fields capital ships, magnetic & acoustic torpedoes, naval & mil. intelligence, part-time Lt. Home Guard Arty., Lt. RNVR, 1939–49; Eng. II and I, precursor UK Atomic Energy Authority, basic design thermal & fast neutron reactors, isotope enrichment plant, chem. plant & radioactive waste storage plant, 1949–57; Assoc. Prof. of Nuclear Eng. present Univ. 1957–63, Prof. 1963–83; 1st Candn. Prof. of Nuclear Eng. and 1st Candn. holder licence for civilian nuclear reactor installation; set up nuclear training progs. for Candn., Indian and Pakistani engs.; Co-founder Univ. of Toronto Radiation Protection Authority; mem. USA Objective Criteria Ctte. for Nuclear Eng. Edn. 1960–64; Rsch. Fellow, Centre d'Etudes Nucléaires, Grenoble, France 1969–70; Visiting Prof. Univ. of Adelaide, Australia 1982; Dir. Chem. Eng. Rsch. Consultants Ltd. 1963–84; Pres. Youth Sci. Found. Can. 1971–73; Vice Pres. N. Am. Region, Internat. Coordinating Ctte. for Presentation of Sci. UNESCO Cat. 'B' 1972–73; radiation adv. Ont. Red Cross, to 1983; recipient Pro Mundi Beneficio Medal, Brazilian Acad. Humane Sci's 1976; co-founder sch. for learning-disabled students; founded and chaired various Scout groups; participant over 100 radio and TV progs.; author or co-author over 100 sci. publs. nuclear eng.; Vice Chrmn. Founding Ctte. Candn. Nuclear Assn. 1959–60; Fellow, Inst. Mech. Engs. (Br. Chrmn. & mem. Council 1973–74); Sc.D., Univ. of Cambridge 1992; Co-founder Candn. Soc. Mech. Engrg.; mem. Candn., Brit. and Am. Nuclear Soc's; Assn. Prof. Engs. Prov. Ont.; Imp. Offrs. Assn.; Internat. Order St. Luke (Past-Convenor); Freemason (Life mem.); Anglican (former warden and lay mem. Synod); recreations: tennis, skiing, Scottish dancing; Home: 703, 2185 Marine Dr., Oakville, Ont. L6L 5L6.

**ANDREWS, Hon. Harry Tedford Gee,** B.A., LL.B.; provincial court judge; b. Sault Ste. Marie, Ont. 9 Dec. 1927; s. the late Rev. Thomas Wesley Ferguson Gee and Erma Isabel (Hooper) A.; e. Univ. of Toronto Victoria Coll. B.A. 1949; Osgoode Hall Law Sch. 1954; m. Judith Patricia d. Jack and Eileen Ryan 22 Dec. 1981; two s. Robert Thomas, James Bruce; law practice Bowyer, Beatty, Andrews 1954–60; Andrews and Webber 1960–62; Judge, Juvenile and Family Court, Co. of Peel and Prov. Magistrate 1962–68; Chief Judge, Provincial Court (Family Div.) 1968–90; Past Mem., Judicial Council Ont.; Rules Ctte., Prov. Ct.; Justice of the Peace Review Counc.; Ont. Courts Adv. Council; Ont. Ctte. of Bench & Bar Member; Ont. Assn. Prov. Court Judges (Family Div.); Ont. Assoc. for Family Mediation; Candn. Council of Juvenile & Family Court Judges (planned & organized 1st meeting 1967; now amalgamated with Candn. Assoc. of Prov. Ct. Judges); Candn. Inst. for the Admin. of Justice; Candn. Assn. Prov. Court Judges; Nat. Council Juvenile Court Judges U.S.A.; Nat. Council Crime & Delinquency U.S.A.; Internat. Counc. on Family Law; Internat. Assoc. of Youth Magistrates; formerly Associate Dir., National Judicial Institute; Advisor to Candn. Internat. Institute of Applied Negotiation; practitioner and teacher of techniques of negotiation, mediation and arbitration; recipient Honour Award & Gold Key, Univ. of Toronto 1949; Candn. Centennial Medal 1967; Queen's Silver Jubilee Medal 1977; author of some book chapters, short stories & articles in var. jours. & mags.; ed. 'Family Law in the Family Courts' 1973; 'The Unified Family Court' 1977; recreations: white-water canoeing, skiing, karate, crafts and piano; Office: 491 Steeles Ave. E., Milton, Ont. L9T 1Y7.

**ANDREWS, Janice Margaret (Jan),** M.A.; writer; storyteller; special events co-ordinator; editor; researcher; b. Shoreham-By-Sea, England 6 June 1942; d. Sydney Frederick and Georgina Beatrice (Welsman) Ellins; e. Univ. of Reading, B.A. (Hons.) 1963; Univ. of Sask., M.A. 1969; m. Christopher J. s. John and Greta A. 10 Aug. 1963; children: Miriam Paula (Mim), Kieran Mark, Elaine Piché (Foster); emigrated to Can. 1963; Copywriter, CFQC Radio, Sask.; Prog. Offr., Dept. of Sec. of State, Native Citizens Prog. 1973–75; Multiculturalism 1976; Acting Head, Acad. & Cult. Resources 1984; exclusively freelance 1984– ; incl. 2 pamphlets on multicult. in edn. 1985; 'Coming of Age,' a dramatic montage for Internat. Youth Year 1985 for Nat. Lib.; 'Out of the Everywhere' Expo '86 storytelling prog.; 'The Chance to Give' exhibit at Nat. Lib. 1987; 'The Secret Self' exhibit at Nat. Lib. 1988; programming for Nat. Gall. amphitheatre 1988; programming for Cultures Canada 88 festival, National Capital Comn. 1988; Co-coordinator/founder, The Chance to Give/Une Chance à Donner, non-profit orgn. providing multicultural programming to schools 1989; Mem., Writers' Union of Can.; Candn. Soc. of Children's Authors, Illustrators & Performers; author: 'Fresh Fish - and Chips' 1973, 'Ella, an Elephant, un Elephant' 1976, 'Very Last First Time' 1985; 'The Auction' 1990; 'Pumpkin Time' 1990; editor: 'The Dancing Sun' 1981; provided significant number of stories used in lang. arts material; worked with children in formal edn. environ. giving creative writing workshops & standing as Co-ord. for Alternative Parent Co-op. Sch. 1981, 1984–85; recreations: wilderness activities, canoeing, solo kayak trips, skiing; Office: c/o Groundwood / Douglas & McIntyre Children's Books, 2nd Floor, 585 Bloor St. W., Toronto, Ont. M6G 1K5.

**ANDREWS, John Hobart McLean,** M.A., Ph.D.; educator; b. Kamloops, B.C. 15 May 1926; s. John Ernest and Cynthia Maria (Robinson) A.; e. Univ. of B.C. B.A. (Physics) 1947, M.A. (Educ.) 1954; Univ. of Chicago Ph.D. (Educ.) 1957; m. Doris Deborah d. late Wilfrid Reid Payne 28 Aug. 1948; children: William J., Donald W., Jeffrey P., Lorraine D.; DEAN EMERITUS OF EDUC., UNIV. OF BRIT. COLUMBIA since 1988, Prof. of Educ. 1973–88; Dean, Faculty of Educ. there 1973–79; Prof. of Educ. Univ. of Alta. 1957–65; Prof. of Educ. and Asst. Dir. Ont. Inst. for Studies in Educ. Toronto 1965–73; Unitarian; Home: #703 – 1835 Morton Ave., Vancouver, B.C. V6G 1V3.

**ANDREWS, Raymond A.,** B.Sc.; public servant; b. Port de Grave, Nfld. 17 April 1941; s. Alfred Gordon and Rita (Ward) A.; e. St. Luke's H.S. 1958; Memorial Univ. of Nfld., B.Sc. 1970; m. Joyce d. Walter and Ida Stevens 19 August 1961; children: Beverley, Lindsey; Extve. Asst. to Min. of Fisheries & Oceans; former Dep. Min., Dept. of Fisheries, Nfld. & Lab. 1982–89; Prin., Port de Grave and Port Anson, Nfld. 1959–62; Fish Insp. Offr., various locations in Nfld. 1962–72; Dist. Insp. Offr., Fisheries & Oceans Can., Grand Falls, Nfld. 1972–76; Area Mgr. 1976–79; Asst. Dep. Min., Prov. Dept. of Fisheries, Fisheries Devel. 1979–80; Policy Planning 1980–82; Chrmn., Nfld. & Lab. Fisheries Devel. Corp.; former Dir., Candn. Saltfish Corp.; Nfld. & Lab. Inst. of Fisheries & Marine Tech.; Fisheries Loan Bd. of Nfld. & Lab. 1979–82; Exploits Valley Devel. Assn. mid-70s; Pres., Windsor, Nfld. Br., Candn. Red Cross 1978–79; recreation: reading; Home: 5 MacPherson Ave., St. John's, Nfld. A1B 2B8.

**ANDREWS, Stephen James,** R.C.A.; painter; b. Saskatoon, Sask. 16 May 1922; s. Samuel James and Ida Gertrude (Atkinson) A.; e. Windsor Sch. and Glenlawn Coll. Inst. St. Vital, Winnipeg 1940; The Winnipeg Sch. of Art 1942; Chelsea Polytechnic Sch. of Art 1946; Camberwell Sch. of Art & Crafts 1948; Académie Julian Paris 1948–49; studied with Martin Bloch, London, Eng. 1950; Scuola del Mosaico Ravenna, Italy 1953; solo exhns. incl. Librairie Paul Morihien, Palais-Royal Paris 1952; Hanover Gallery London, Eng. 1957; Winnipeg Art Gallery 1958; Montreal Museum of Fine Arts 1959, 1963; Ritchie Hendriks Gallery Dublin 1961; Opus Gallery London 1962; Overseas Press Club of Am. New York 1964; Roberts Gallery Toronto 1964; Lidchi Gallery, Johannesburg 1967; Jacox Galleries Edmonton 1968; Walter Phillips Gallery Banff 1977; S. African Assn. Arts Cape Town, Pretoria, Durban 1979; Gump's Art Gallery San Francisco 1980; Galeria Kreisler Dos Madrid 1981; Theo Waddington Gallery Montreal 1983; Waddington & Shiell Galleries, Toronto 1982, 1984, 1989; Thomas Gallery Winnipeg 1978, 1989, 1992; Galerie Guinière, Angers, Anjou, France 1989; Equinox Gallery Vancouver 1991; Galerie Barbara Silverberg, Montreal 1992; Leo Kamen Gall., Toronto 1992; group exhns. incl. Exhn. Candn. Paintings Fortnum & Mason London 1955; John Moores Liverpool Exhn. I 1957–58; Grosvenor Gallery London 1964; Candn. Artists South London Art Gallery 1965; 50 Years Michaelis Sch. of Fine Art, S. African Nat. Gallery 1975; 2nd Candn. Biennale Prints & Drawings touring 1980–82; rep. in various pub., corporate and private colls. incl. Adverb Werbeagentur PR GmbH, Hamburg; Aikens Macauley, Toronto; Aluminum Co. of America, Pittsburg; Art Gallery of Hamilton; Art Group Inc. Montreal; Bull, Houser & Tupper, Vancouver; Can. Council Art Bank Ottawa; Consortian Toronto; Durban Art Gallery; Eric Harvie Theatre Banff; Esso Canada Calgary; Faculty of Fine Arts York Univ.; F.M. Corporation, Santa Clara, Calif.; General Foods Ltd. Toronto; Guaranty Trust Toronto; Gutenberg Electronic Hamburg; Hamburger Werbe Agentur Hamburg; Herbert Art Gallery & Museum Coventry; Jost Investments Montreal; Kaneko Coll. Toronto; Konica BM International GmbH, Hamburg; Kowatul Islam Mosque Cape Town; MacLeod, Young & Weir, N.Y.C.; McLean Hunter, Toronto; Mendel Art Gallery Saskatoon; Montair Inc. Montreal; Montreal Museum of Fine Arts; Museo Etnográfico de Grandas de Salime, Asturias; Nabisco Brands Ltd. Toronto; Nat. Gallery Can.; Nat. Museum of Amer. Art, Smithsonian Inst. Washington, D.C.; Nissho Iwai Canada Ltd., Vancouver; Noranda Forest, Toronto; Norsk Hydro, Oslo; Ottawa Civic Hospital; Panroyal Wuppertal Germany; Pekarsky Noble Assoc., Vancouver; Peter Whyte Foundation Banff; Petro Canada, Calgary and Montreal; Pretoria Art Museum; Provid Finance Inc., Toronto; Rothschild Canada Ltd., Toronto; Royal Bank Coll.; Sasclaw Mgmt. Ltd. Toronto; Saskatoon City Hosp. Found.; Sask. House London, Eng.; S. African Nat. Gallery; Steinberg Collection Inc., Montreal; Theatre Museum, Covent Garden, London, Eng.; Toronto Dominion Bank Toronto; Toronto Dominion Bank Winnipeg; Tory Tory Deslauriers & Binnington, Toronto; Toyku Corp., Vancouver; Univ. of Calgary; Univ. of Winnipeg; Winnipeg Art Gallery; toured India in 1955 and 1961 and studied under Maharishi Mahesh Yogi; Visiting Lectr. St. Paul's Sch. London; Univ. of Alta.; Univ. of Cape Town; McMaster Univ.; York Univ.; Banff Sch. Fine Arts; Univ. Calgary; has designed for theatre and film; Artist-in-Residence and Head of Winter Studio Art Program, Banff Centre Sch. Fine Arts 1976–77; author various art and travel articles; served with RCNVR 1942–45; recreations: playwriting, collecting; Address: Finca La Jordana, 29690 CASARES, Málaga, Spain.

**ANGEL, Aubie,** B.Sc. (Med.), M.D., M.Sc., FRCP(C); educator; b. Winnipeg, Man. 28 Aug. 1935; s. Benjamin and Minnie (Kaplan) A.; e. Univ. of Man. B.Sc. (Med.) 1959, M.D. 1959; McGill Univ. M.Sc. 1963; m. Esther-Rose d. Jack and Fannie Newhouse 21 June 1961; children: Jennifer, Jonathan, Suzanne, Steven, Michael; H.E. SELLERS PROF. and HEAD OF DEPT. OF INTERNAL MEDICINE, UNIVERSITY OF MANITOBA and PHYSICIAN-IN-CHIEF, HEALTH SCIENCE CENTRE, Winnipeg 1991– ; Jr. and Sr. Intern Winnipeg Gen. Hosp. 1959–61; Resident in Diabetes & Endocrinol. Montreal Gen. Hosp. 1961–62; Med. Rsch. Council Fellow in Exper. Med. McGill Univ. 1962–63, Asst. Prof. of Pathol. 1965–68; Asst. Resident in Med. Royal Victoria Hosp. Montreal 1963–64, Staff Phys. 1965–68; Med. Rsch. Council Scholar Univ. of Toronto 1965–71, Asst. Prof. of Med. 1968, Assoc. Prof. 1972, Prof. 1982; Dir. Inst. Med. Sci. & Clin. Sci. Div. 1983–91; Sr. Staff Endocrinol. Toronto Gen. Hosp. 1968–90; Prof. and Head Dept. of Med. Univ. of Man. 1991; Phys.-in-Chief Health Sci's Centre Winnipeg 1991; recipient Outstanding Service Award Heart & Stroke Found. Ont. 1985; Joe Doupe Visiting Prof. 1986; Project Dir. Candn. Internat. Devel. Agency Toronto, Costa Rica 1987–94; Hon. Bd. mem. Juvenile Diabetes Found. Internat. 1987; Fellow, Trinity Coll. Toronto 1989; co-ed. various profl. jours.; mem. Candn. Soc. Clin. Investig. (Councillor 1977–80); Candn. Soc. Endocrinol. & Metabolism (Pres. 1980–82); Am. Soc. Clin. Investig.; Internat. Assn. Study Obesity (Gov. 1986); N.Am. Assn. Study Obesity (Pres. 1986–87); Candn. Inst. Acad. Med. (Founding Pres. 1990); Fellow, Royal Soc. of Medicine, London 1991– ; mem. Bd. of Dirs., Manitoba Heart and Stroke Foundation 1991– ; Chair, Advisory Bd., Diabetes Rsch. and Treatment Centre, Univ. of Manitoba 1991– ; Home: 121 Lamont Blvd., Winnipeg, Man. R3P 0E7; Office: Dept. of Internal Medicine, Health Science Centre, 820 Sherbrook St., Winnipeg, Man. R3A 1R9.

**ANGELL, Harold M.,** B.A., M.A.; university professor; b. London, England 2 Mar. 1930; s. Woolf and Rebecca (Rubenstein) A.; e. Strode's Sch.; Hebrew Univ. of Jerusalem; Sir George Williams Univ., B.A. 1958; McGill Univ., M.A. 1960; m. Sylvia d. Eli and Pearl Endler 1 Sept. 1955; one s.: David J.R.; ASSOC. PROF., CONCORDIA UNIV. 1974– ; Lectr., Asst. & Assoc. Prof., Pol. Sci., Sir George Williams Univ. 1962–74; Chrmn. 1971–74; cons. for fed. & prov. govts., Que. Liberal Fed., journalists & news media; Vis. Prof., McGill; community lectr.; mem., Candn. & Am. Pol. Sci. Assns.; Soc. québécoise de sci. pol.; Internat. Pol. Sci. Assn. (Rsch. Ctte. on Pol. Finan. 1982– ;); Concordia Fac. Club Assn. (Pres. 1978–84); fellowships: Woodrow Wilson 1958–60; McGill Grad. & Can. Counc. 1960–62; Que. Rsch. 1966–67; author: 'Electoral Reform in the Prov. of Quebec' 1961 and several articles, book chaps., conf. & other papers; co-author: 'Rapport sur la revision de la carte electorale de la province de Québec' 1962; recreations: reading, swimming, soccer, table tennis; Home: 640 Grosvenor, Westmount, Qué. H3Y 2S8; Office: 1455 de Maisonneuve Blvd. W., Montreal, Qué. H3G 1M8.

**ANGENOT, Marc**, D.Phil., F.R.S.C.; educator; b. Brussels, Belgium 21 Dec. 1941; s. Marcel and Zoé Marthe (De Clercq) A.; e. Univ. libre de Bruxelles L.Phil 1962, D.Phil. 1967; m. Nadia Khouri 1975; children: Olivier, Valérie, Maya; PROF. OF FRENCH & COMPARATIVE LIT. McGILL UNIV. 1981– ; joined present Univ. 1967; Dir., Inter-University Centre for Discourse Analysis, Montreal; recipient Prix Biguet (Académie française) 1983; Killam Award 1987; author 'Le Roman populaire' 1975; 'Les Champions des femmes' 1977; 'Glossaire pratique de la critique contemporaine' 1979; 'La Parole pamphlétaire' 1982; 'Critique de la raison sémiotique' 1985; 'Le Cru et le faisandé' 1986; 'Ce que l'on dit des Juifs en 1889' 1989; 'Topographie du socialisme' 1989; 'Le Centenaire de la Révolution' 1989; 'Mille huit cent quatre-vingt neuf' 1990; 'L'Oeuvre poétique du Savon du Congo' 1992; 'L'Utopie collectiviste' 1993; ed. 'Social Discourse'; Home: 4572 Harvard Ave., Montreal, Qué. H4A 2X2; Office: 3460 McTavish St., Montreal, Qué. H3A 1X9.

**ANGERS, Bernard**, M.Sc.; rector; b. Jonquière, Qué. 16 April 1939; s. Joseph and Lucienne (Hudon) A.; e. Laval Univ. M.Sc.So.(Rel. Ind.) 1963; London Sch. of Econ. M.Sc.(Econ.) 1965; m. Monique d. Thomas Louis and Simone Tremblay Caron 25 Aug. 1962; children: Lucie, Paul, Isabelle, Christine, Sylvie; RECTOR, UNIVERSITÉ DU QUÉBEC À CHICOUTIMI 1993– ; joined Min. of Edn. Qué. 1966–69; Dir. of Remuneration Min. of Pub. Service 1969–72; Asst. Dep. Min. of Financial Instns., Co's and Co-ops. 1972–74 and of Mun. Affairs 1974–77; Dep. Min. of Pub. Works & Supplies 1977–79; Del. of Qué. Govt. to Nat. Defence Coll. 1979–80; Assoc. Sec. Gen. Conseil exécutif 1980–81; Pres. Quebec Housing Corp. 1981–86; Dep. Min. of Revenue 1986–93; mem. Inst. Pub. Adm. Can. (Regional Pres. Qué. 1974–75, mem. Nat. Exec. 1975–78); Mem. of the Bd.: La Caisse populaire des fonctionnaires 1988–90; La Mutuelle des Fonctionnaires du Qué. 1984–86, 1993– ; La Capitale 1984–86; mem. Candn. Assn. Friends London Sch. Econ.; Corp. des Conseillers en relations industrielles; Am. Mgmt. Assn.; Am. Soc. Pub. Adm.; Internat. Fiscal Assn.; Candn. Tax Found.; Nat. Tax Assn. – Tax Inst. Am.; recreations: reading, travel, golf, hockey, fishing; Home: 1724, Du Portage, Chicoutimi, Qué. G7H 7L3; Office: 555, boul. de l'Université, Chicoutimi, Qué. G7H 2B1.

**ANGERS, Hon. Joseph Alexandre Jean-Claude**, B.C.L.; judge; b. Valleyfield, Que. 30 March 1942; s. Alexandre and Gabrielle (LePage) A.; e. Univ. St. Louis (Edmunston, N.B.) B.A. 1961; Univ. of N.B. B.C.L. 1965; m. Joan Marie d. Adolphus Gerard MacDonald 19 Aug. 1967; children; Joseph Alexandre Paul, Marielle Joan, Marie-Claude Nicole; JUDGE, COURT OF APPEAL, N.B. since 1982; called to Bar of N.B. 1965; cr. Q.C. 1977; Solr., Dept. Justice N.B. 1965; Crown Prosecutor, Edmunston, N.B. 1967; mem. Rice & Angers, Edmunston 1968; apptd. Judge, Co. Court N.B. 1979; Court of Queen's Bench, 1979–82; part-time Lectr. in Law, Univ. of N.B. 1976–77; Lectr. Bar Admission Course; Bd. Govs. Univ. of Moncton 1977–80; mem. Extve. Bd. Dirs. Coll. St. Louis Edmundston 1976–77; def. Lib. Cand. for Edmunston prov. g.e. 1974; Vice Pres. Organ. Comte. N.B. First Summer Games; rep. N.B. Lawyers CBC TV 'On the Evidence'; Offr., N.B. Barristers' Soc. 1971–72, 1976–77; Prov. Offr. Candn. Bar Assn. 1973; mem. N.B. Legal Aid Comte. 1971–79; R. Catholic; recreation: sports; Office: P.O. Box 6000, Justice Bldg., Fredericton, N.B. E3B 5H1.

**ANGEVINE, Gerry Edwin**, B.Comm., Ph.D.; economist; consultant; b. Saint John, N.B. 25 Feb. 1941; s. the late Douglas and late Gwendolyne (MacLeod) A.; e. Saint John H.S.; Mount Allison Univ., B.Comm. 1962; Dalhousie Univ., M.A. 1965; Univ. of Mich., Ph.D. 1973; m. Sherie d. Molly and Gordon Cobham 1965; children: Jill, Lauri, Derek, Gregory; PRESIDENT & DIRECTOR, CANDN. ENERGY RSCH. INST. 1980– ; var. positions ending as Sr. Econ., Canadian Imperial Bank of Commerce 1974–79; Mem., Am. Econ. Assn.; Candn. Assn. for Bus. Economics; recreation: skiing, tennis; Home: Site 36, Box 11, RR2, Calgary, Alta. T2P 2G5; Office: #150, 3512 – 33rd St. N.W., Calgary, Alta. T2L 2A6.

**ANGHIK, Abraham Apakark;** artist; b. Paulatuk, N.W.T. 1951; medium: sculpture, drawings, printmaking; 21 group exbns. incl. most recent: Surrey Art Gallery B.C. 1992, Vancouver Inuit Art Soc. 1991, Bunkamura Art Gall. Tokyo, Japan 1991, Candn. Mus. of Civilization Hull, Que. 1990; solo exbns.: Alaska Gall. of N.Y. 1991, Images for a Canadian Heritage Vancouver 1981, Bayard Gall. N.Y. 1980, Pollock Gall. Toronto 1977, 1978, 1979, 1980, Langlois Gall. Yellowknife, N.W.T. 1976, Arctic Arts Gall. Edmonton, Alta. 1973; cultural grant 1974, 1979, 1980; drawing of an owl adopted for coat-of-arms of Soc. for the Encouragement of Northern Talent 1975; attended opening at Pollock Gall. Toronto 1977; comnd. by Nahanni Chapter, Imperial Order of the Daughters of the Empire to sculpt 'Children of the Light' donated to Prince of Wales Northern Heritage Centre Yellowknife 1979; one of six artists incl. in a commemorative portfolio of prints pub. to assist Royal Ont. Mus. Renovation/Expansion Fund; subject of several articles and catalogues; Home: Salt Spring Island, B.C.; Office: R.R. 2, Toynbee C-31, Ganges, B.C. V0S 1E0.

**ANGLESIO, Franco J.;** hotel executive; b. Italy 14 Sept. 1943; m. Mary C. Bartlett 22 Aug. 1970; children: Marco P., Michael S.; PRESIDENT, COAST HOTELS & RESORTS VCR 1992– ; General Manager, Chateau Laurier 1980–83; Hotel Vancouver 1983–86; Vice-Pres., Coast Hotels VCR 1986–91; Exec. Vice-Pres., Coast Hotels & Resorts 1991–92; Pres., Coast Hotels & Resorts 1992– ; Dir., Coast Hotels & Resorts; Mem., Skal Club of VCR; Châine des Rôtisseurs; recreations: skiing, hiking, golf; clubs: Swan-e-Set Bay Country; Home: 1278 Bracknell Place, North Vancouver, B.C. V7R 1V5; Office: 900 – 1090 W. Georgia St., Vancouver, B.C. V6E 3V7.

**ANGLIN, Douglas G.**, M.A., D.Phil.; university professor; b. Toronto, Ont. 16 Dec. 1923; s. George Chambers and Ruth Cecilia (Cale) A.; e. Forest Hill Village (Ont.) Schs., 1929–41; Univ. of Toronto, B.A. (Hons., Pol. Science & Econ.) 1948; Univ. of Oxford (Rhodes Scholar for Ont., 1948), Corpus Christi Coll. and Nuffield Coll., B.A. (Philos., Pol. Econ.) 1950, M.A. 1954, D.Phil. 1956; m. Mary Elizabeth, d. Orville Pierce Watson, Toronto, Ont. 26 June 1948; two d., Margaret Alice, Deirdre Ruth; PROFESSOR EMERITUS, CARLETON UNIV. 1993– ; Asst. and Assoc. Prof. of Pol. Sci. and Internat. Relations, Univ. of Manitoba, 1951–58; Assoc. Prof. of Pol. Sci., Carleton Univ., 1958–65, Prof. 1965–89; Assoc. Research Fellow, Nigerian Inst. of Soc. & Econ. Research, Univ. of Ibadan, Nigeria, 1962–63; Vice-Chancellor, Univ. of Zambia, 1965–69; Research Assoc. with Center of Internat. Studies, Princeton Univ. 1969–70; Consultant on 'Education for Democracy,' South African Council of Churches, Johannesburg 1992– ; served with R.C.N.V.R. as Lt. 1943–45; co-ed. 'Africa: The Political Pattern' 1961; 'Canada, Scandinavia and Southern Africa' 1979; 'Conflict and Change in Southern Africa' 1979; co-author 'Zambia's Foreign Policy: Studies in Diplomacy and Dependence' 1979; author 'The St. Pierre and Miquelon Affaire of 1941' 1966; author numerous articles for various learned journs.; mem., African Studies Assn. (U.S.A.); Candn. Inst. Internat. Affairs; Candn. Pol. Science Assn.; Candn. Assn. of African Studies (Pres. 1973–74); United Church; Address: Dept. of Political Science, Carleton Univ., Ottawa, Ont. K1S 5B6.

**ANGLIN, James P.**, Q.C., B.C.L.; retired executive; b. Westmount, Que. 28 Jan. 1912; s. James Penrose and Florence E. (Christy) A.; e. Westmount High Sch. 1929; McGill Univ., B.A. 1933, B.C.L. 1936; Univ. of Paris, France, Faculty of Law; m. 1stly Julia Elizabeth, d. H.M. Moore, Montreal, 1938; 2ndly Doris Harrison, d. Dr. Harold Brown, Vancouver 1983; children: Susan Elizabeth (Mrs. Eric W. Winn), Julia Christine, James Penrose; read law with Gordon W. MacDougall, K.C.; called to Bar of Que. 1936; Partner, Smith, Anglin, Laing, Weldon & Courtois and predecessor firms, (Montreal) 1937–70; Lectr., Faculty of Law, McGill Univ. 1945–55; mem. Bd. of Bar Examiners of Que. 1947–55; mem. Council, Bar of Montreal 1955–58; Past Pres., Montreal Boy's Assn.; Past. Pres. 1956 and Hon. Life Gov. Royal Candn. Golf Assn. 1978 (Chrmn., Rules of Golf Comte. 1960–70); mem. Rules of Golf Comte., Royal & Ancient Golf Club 1960–70; Rules of Golf Comte., U.S. Golf Assn. 1960; Past Pres., Candn. Cancer Soc. B.C. & Yukon Div.; mem., Candn. Bar Assn. (mem. Extve. 1966–70); recreations: golf, fishing, ornithology; Clubs: Shaughnessy Golf and Country; Royal Montreal Golf; Royal & Ancient Golf (St. Andrews, Scot.); Home: 1855 Acadia Road, Vancouver, B.C. V6T 1R2.

**ANGLIN, John Perry**, B.A., M.Sc.; public servant; b. South Porcupine, Ont. 15 June 1940; s. the late John Farquhar and Olive Locke (Logan) A.; e. Univ. of Toronto B.A. 1962; Columbia Univ. M.Sc. 1964; Oxford Univ.; U.K. Civil Service College; m. Aimée d. Paul Lefebvre; ASSISTANT DEPUTY MINISTER, ARTS & HERITAGE SECTOR, DEPT. OF COMMUNICATIONS 1991– ; various positions in Consumer & Corp. Affairs, Treasury Bd. and Indian & Northern Affairs, Govt. of Canada; Asst. Dep. Min., Consumer & Corp. Affairs, Govt. of B.C. 1977–79; served twice with Treasury Bd. Sec. since 1980 (recently as Asst. Sec. resp. for social & cultural sector, 1988–91); Asst. Sec., Communications Policy, Privy Council 1981–84; Min. of State for Social Devel. 1984; Asst. Dep. Min., Legis. & Intergovt. Affairs, Revenue Canada, Taxation 1984–88; recreations: arts, heritage, golf, nordic skiing; clubs: Larrimac Golf; Home: 71 Geneva St., Ottawa, Ont. K1Y 3N6; Office: 300 Slater St., Room 516, Ottawa, Ont. K1A 0C8.

**ANGUS, Elisabeth (Lis) Anne**, B.A., M.A., M.B.A.; consultant, writer, editor, lecturer; b. Rimbey, Alta. 6 Sept. 1946; d. Baron Bernhard and Alma Bertine (Eritsland) von Tettenborn; e. Eckville H.S. 1963; Carleton Univ. B.A. 1968; York Univ. M.A. 1978, M.B.A. 1988; m. Ian C. s. K.C. and Margaret (Thomas) A. 22 Feb. 1969; children: Jessica Margaret, Amanda Katherine; EXECUTIVE VICE-PRES., ANGUS TELEMANAGEMENT GROUP 1980– ; expert witness, CRTC long-distance comp. proceedings 1991; frequent public speaker and guest lecturer; Bd. Mem., Candn. Telecommunications Cons. Assn.; Mem., Ont. Telecommunications Adv. Ctte.; Internat. Soc. of Telecommunications Consultants; Chair Adv. Bd. Sheridan Coll.; Adv. Bd. Mem., Ryerson Polytechnic Univ.; Co-recipient, Candn. Bus. Telecomm. Alliance Honorary Award 1990; co-editor: 'Telemanagement'; author of 1 book chapter and 8 books incl. 'Future Applications for Telecommunications Technology' 1992; co-author: 'Telecommunications and Business Competitiveness in Canada and the U.S.' 1992, 'Long Distance Alternatives in Canada' 1993, 'Long Distance Resale in Canada' 1991; recreations: gardening, reading; Home: 718 Pebble Ct., Pickering, Ont. L1V 3Z4; Office: 8 Old Kingston Rd., Ajax, Ont. L1T 2Z7.

**ANGUS, Harry G.**, B.Sc.; consulting engineer; b. Toronto, Ont. 11 Oct. 1949; s. Donald L. and E. Katherine (Gordon) A.; e. Upper Canada College; Queen's Univ. B.Sc. 1974; m. Dianne; children: Megan, Shaun, Scott; PRESIDENT, H.H. ANGUS & ASSOCIATES LTD. 1985– ; director of 6 related companies in Canada, USA and UK; Mem., Adv. Bd., Inst. for Rsch. in Construction, NRC; Past Pres., Profl. Engrs. Ont. 1992–93; Past Chair, Mech. Engr. Adv. Bd., Queen's Univ.; Trustee, McMichael Candn. Collection; Office: 1127 Leslie St., Don Mills, Ont. M3C 2J6.

**ANGUS, Ian Cole**, M.A.; telecommunications consultant; lecturer; author; b. Vancouver, B.C. 14 Aug. 1945; s. Keith Cole and Margaret (Thomas) A.; e. Carleton Univ., B.A. (Hons.) 1970; Univ. of Toronto, M.A. 1972; m. Elisabeth Anne d. Baroness Alma and Baron Bernhard von Tettenborn 22 Feb. 1969; children: Jessica Margaret, Amanda Katherine; PRES. & CHIEF EXTVE. OFFR., ANGUS TELEMANAGEMENT GROUP INC. 1979– ; Mktg., Bell Can. 1972–79; Mem., Soc. of Telecomm. Cons. 1979– (Dir. 1981–83, 1985–; Vice-Pres. 1982–83; Mag. Ed. 1981–83); Cand. Bus. Telecomm. Alliance 1980– ;(Conf. speaker 1980, 81, 83, 84, 85, 86, 87, 89); Candn. Telecomm Consultants Assoc. 1987– ; Secy., N. American ISDN Users Forum 1989–90; editor: 'The TeleManagement Report' 1982–88, 'Telecom Systems and Strategies' 1984–88, 'Telemanagement' 1988– ; contbr.: 'ComputerData,' 'Teleconnect'; author: 'Preparing for Interconnection' 1980; 'Telephone Cost Control' 1981; 'Users Guide to Bell Canada Rates' 1982; 'Contemporary Issues in Telephone System Management' 1984; 'ISDN in the Real World' 1988; 'ISDN: A Managers Guide' 1989; 'The Angus TeleManagement Guide to Meridian 1' 1990; 'The Angus TeleManagement Guide to Long Distance Resale in Canada' 1991; 'Long Distance Competition in Canada' 1991; 'The angus Telemanagement Guide to Long Distance Alternatives in Canada' 1993; 'Phone Pirates' 1993; co-recipient, Honorary Award, Candn. Business Telecommunications Alliance 1990; Home: 718 Pebble Court, Pickering, Ont. L1V 3Z4; Office: 8 Old Kingston Rd., Ajax, Ont. L1T 2Z7.

**ANGUS, Margaret**, C.M., B.A., LL.D.; author; conservationist; b. Chinook, Mont. 23 May 1908; d. Ulysses S. Grant and Cora (Krauss) Sharp; e. Univ. of Mont. B.A. 1930; Queen's Univ. LL.D. 1973; m. William Angus 28 Aug. 1929; children: Barbara (Mrs. Owen Morgan), James; Dir. of Radio, Queen's Univ. 1957–1968, museum curator 1968–85; Chrmn. Kingston Centennial Comte. 1966–67; Kingston Comte. Arch. Review 1970–72; Dir. Ont. Hist. Studies Series 1972–88; Pres. Frontenac Hist. Foundation 1973–1976, 1979–81; Gov. Heritage Can. 1974–79; Dir. Ont. Heritage Foundation 1975–81; Gov. Kingston Gen. Hosp. since 1972; Consultant Candn. Hist. Sites Div.; named 'Citizen of the Year' by Kingston Jaycees 1968; Queen's Univ. Alumni Award 1968 and Medal 1975; Cruikshank Gold Medal 1974; Heritage Can. Travel Award 1975; Silver Jubilee Medal 1977; Ont. Assoc. of Architects' Allied Arts Award 1989; Member, Order of Canada 1992; 125th Anniversary Medal 1992; author 'The Old Stones of Kingston' 1966; 'The Story of Bellevue House' 1967; 'History of Kingston General Hospital' 1972, volume II 1994; contrib. 'Oliver Mowat's Ontario' 1972; 'Kingston 300' 1973; 'John A. Lived Here' 1984; 'Queen's History in Names' 1991; over 30 short stories on hist. subjects for CBC, 4 documentaries, radio plays and hist. studies; series ed., 'Buildings of Architectural and Historic Significance in Kingston'; mem. Ont. Hist. Soc. (Pres. 1969–71); Arch. Conservancy Ont.; Kingston Hist. Soc. (Pres. 1972–74); Dir. Cataraqui Archaeological Research Foundation 1983–84; Home: 191 King St. E., Kingston, Ont. K7L 3A3.

**ANGUS, Hon. W. David,** A.B., B.C.L., Q.C.; barrister & solicitor; b. Toronto, Ont. 21 July 1937; s. Melvyn Graham and Ada Madeline (Hutchison) A.; e. Lower Canada College 1954; Princeton Univ. A.B. (cum laude) 1959; McGill Univ. B.C.L. (1st Class Hons.) 1962; children: Jacqueline, Gregor; PARTNER, STIKEMAN EL-LIOTT 1968– ; joined Stikeman Elliott 1962; specialist in Maritime Law; Mem., Canadian, Quebec and Montreal Bar Assns.; Pres., Candn. Maritime Law Assn. 1989–92; Pres. & Dir., Madeg Holdings Inc.; Dir., Air Canada (Chair, Human Resources & Compensation Ctte.); Reed Stenhouse & Cos. Ltd.; Eastern Canada Towing Ltd.; Le Groupe M.I.L. Inc.; MPact Immedia Inc.; Eastern Candn. Tug Owners' Assn.; Q.C. 1984; Senator, Senate of Canada 1993; Chair, P.C. Canada Fund 1983–93; Pres., Montreal Gen. Hosp. Corp.; Vice-Chair, Montreal Gen. Hosp. Centre; Pres., St. Andrew's Presbyn. Homes Found.; recreations: golf, skiing; Home: 3491 Redpath, Montreal, Que. H3G 2G7; Office: 3700 – 1155 René Lévesque Blvd. W., Montreal, Que. H3B 3V2; Senate Office: Room 624, Victoria Bldg., Ottawa, Ont. K1A 0A4.

**ANGUS, William,** B.S., A.M., Ph.D., LL.D.; professor emeritus; b. Dundee, Scotland 22 Mar. 1897; s. James and Eliza (Black) A.; e. Bowdoin Coll., B.S. 1919; Harvard Univ. 1921–22; Northwestern Univ., A.M. 1928; Cornell Univ., Ph.D. 1935; New York Univ. and Columbia Univ. 1945; Queen's Univ., LL.D. 1990; m. Margaret, d. late U.S. Grant Sharp, 28 Aug. 1929; children: Mrs. (Barbara) Morgan, James Grant; taught at Northwestern Univ., 1922–25; Indiana Univ. Extension Dept., 1923–25; Grinnell Coll., Iowa, 1925–27; State Univ. of Montana, 1927–32; Cornell Univ., 1934–35; N. Illinois State Teachers Coll., 1935–37; joined staff of Queen's Univ., 1937; Visiting Prof., Univ. of Hawaii, 1956; taught at Mayville (N.D.) State Coll., 1965–66; St. Hilda's and St. Hugh's Sch. (N.Y.) 1966–67; mem., Theatre Arch. Comte. of Amer. Educ. Theatre Assoc., 1950–53; three times Regional Chrmn. of Dom. Drama Festival for E. Ont.; Founder and Dir., Queen's Summer Radio Inst., 1945–49; Guest Dir., Community Theatre; Rockefeller Foundation Fellowship, 1945; rec'd Candn. Drama Award, 1948; Nuffield Foundation Research Grant, 1958; Centennial Medal, 1967; 125th Anniversary Medal 1992; served in U.S. Army, Depot Bgde., Camp Devens, Mass., 1918; mem. Heritage Canada; Frontenac Hist. Foundation; Kingston Gaelic Soc.; Ont. Hist. Soc.; Kingston Hist. Soc.; Bd. of Dir. Seasoned Spirits Sr. Cit. Theatre of Kingston; Bd. of Dir., Kingston Summer Theatre; Publications: numerous contrib. to scholarly and prof. journs.; 'Death With Dessert' (a short whodunnit); 'Dove é Fumo é Fuoco: Where there's Smoke there's Fire' (libretto of one-act light opera); Ed. of 'Historic Kingston' 1976–85; Home: 191 King St. E., Kingston, Ont. K7L 3A3.

**ANGUS, William Roger,** B.A., LL.B.; business executive, barrister & solicitor; b. Oshawa, Ont. 2 July 1949; s. William Henry and Doris Madeline (Croghan) A.; e. Oshawa Cent. Coll. 1968; Univ. of Toronto B.A. 1971; Queen's Univ. LL.B. 1974; Osgoode Hall, Law Soc. of U.C. call to Ont. Bar 1976; m. Lynette d. Yvonne and Eric Berry 7 Nov. 1987; VICE-PRES., HUMAN RE-SOURCES, CANADA MALTING CO. LIMITED 1990– ; Staff Cons., Ont. Lib. Party on Labour Matters 1976; Admin., Ont. Liquor Bd. Employees' Union 1976–80; Labour Relns. Cons., Peel Bd. of Edn. & Ont. Pub. Sch. Trustees' Assn. 1980–82; Corp. Offr. & Personnel Dir., Am. Dist. Telegraph Co. 1982–88; Vice-Pres., Human Resources, Lily Cups Inc. 1988–90; develops & teaches courses: grade school, coll. & univ. levels; former Instr., Sheridan Coll.; presented several

seminars; lectr. on drug abuse; has developed innovative personnel functions, procedures & programs; Mem., Law Soc. of U.C.; Candn. Bar Assn.; Human Resources Profls. Assn. of Ont.; Bd. of Trade of Metro. Toronto; Ont. Soc. for Training & Devel.; author of numerous scholarly articles; recreations: archaeology, golf, tennis; Office: 10 Four Seasons Pl., Ste. 600, Etobicoke, Ont. M9B 6H7.

**ANHALT, Istvan,** D.Mus. (Hon.), LL.D.; composer; educator; b. Budapest, Hungary 12 Apr. 1919; s. Arnold and Katalin (Herzfeld) A.; e. D. Berzsenyi, Realgymnasium, Budapest 1929–37; Hungarian Acad. of Music 1936–41; forced labour service, Hungarian Army 1942–44; Conservatoire Nat. de Musique, Paris, 1946–48; private study with N. Boulanger and S. Stravinsky; D.Mus. (Hon.) McGill Univ. 1982; LL.D. Queen's Univ. 1991; m. Beate, d. Paul and Emma Frankenberg, Jan. 1952; two d., Helen, Carol; Asst. Conductor, Hungarian Opera 1945; Asst. Prof. (Lady Davis Fellow), Assoc. Prof. and Prof., McGill Univ. 1949–71 (also served as Chrmn., Dept. of Theory, Faculty of Music 1963–69; Dir. of Electronic Music Studio 1964–71; mem. Senate 1968–71); Visiting F. Slee Prof. of Composition, State Univ. of N.Y., Buffalo 1969; Head Music Dept. Queen's Univ. 1971–81; Professor Emeritus 1984– ; rec'd Centennial Medal 1967; Commemorative Medal for 125th Anniversary of Candn. Confederation 1993; John B. Stirling Medal 1993; compositions incl. 'Comments'; 'Symphony No. 1'; 'Cento'; 'Fantasia'; 'Foci'; 'Symphony of Modules'; 'Trio'; 'Sonata for Piano'; 'Sonata for Violin and Piano'; 'La Tourangelle'; 'Four Electronic Compositions'; 'Winthrop'; 'Thisness'; 'Simulacrum'; 'SPARKSKRAPS'; 'Sonance • Resonance (Welche Töne?)'; 'Doors... Shadows (Glenn Gould in memory)'; numerous recordings; author 'Alternative Voices' 1984; 'Oppenheimer' 1990; 'A Weave of Life Lines' 1992; and other texts; most recent work an opera: 'Traces (Tikkun)' a pluri-drama 1994; mem., Candn. League of Composers; Address: 274 Johnson St., Kingston, Ont. K7L 1Y4.

**ANISMAN, Philip,** B.A., LL.B., LL.M., J.S.D.; lawyer; b. Toronto, Ont. 12 Sept. 1941; s. Louis and Mary (Rubenstein) A.; e. Univ. of Toronto B.A. 1964, LL.B. 1967; Univ. of Cal. Berkeley LL.M. 1971, J.S.D. 1974 (recipient Walter Perry Johnson Fellowship, Boalt Hall, Sch. of Law there 1967–68); SOLE PRACTITIONER; called to Bar of Ont. 1970; Asst. Prof. of Law, Univ. of W. Ont. 1968–71; Research Offr. Law Reform Comn. Can. 1971–73; Dir. Corporate Research, Dept. Consumer & Corp. Affairs Can. 1973–78; Prof. of Law, Osgoode Hall Law Sch., York Univ. 1978–85; Visiting Prof. Monash Univ., Melbourne, Australia 1983; Special Counsel on Corporation, Securities and Constitutional Law, Goodman and Carr 1985–87; author 'Takeover Bid Legislation in Canada: A Comparative Analysis' 1974; 'A Catalogue of Discretionary Powers in the Revised Statutes of Canada 1970' 1975; 'Insider Trading Legislation for Australia: An Outline of the Issues and Alternatives' 1986; 'Insider Trading in Canada: Recommendations and Guidance on Boardroom Practice' 1988; co-author 'Proposals for a Securities Market Law for Canada' 3 vols. 1979; co-editor 'The Media, the Courts and the Charter' 1986; various articles learned journs.; mem. Law Soc. of Upper Can.; Office: Suite 1905, 80 Richmond St. W., Toronto, Ont. M5H 2A4.

**ANKA, Paul Albert;** singer; composer; actor; b. Ottawa, Ont. 30 July 1941; s. late Andrew Emile and late Camelia (Tannis) A.; e. Connaught Sch. and Fisher Park High Sch., Ottawa, Ont.; D.Mus., St. John's Univ. N.Y.C. 1978; m. Anne Alison, d. Charles De Zogheb, Paris, France, 16 Feb. 1963; 5 children: Amelia, Anthea, Alicia, Amanda, Alexandra; Co-owner of the Ottawa Senators (the National Hockey League franchise); estbd. Paul Anka Productions; recipient of 15 Gold Records (rec'd when single record sells 1 million copies); has written 800 songs registered by BMI; has sold over 50 million records internationally; has rec'd over 22 Citations for writing from BMI; Young Can. Award 1961; invited to White House 1967 and 1986; Alsac Service Award (St. Jude Children's Research Hosp. for Leukemia Foundation) 1968; Chevalier de l'Ordre des Arts et des Lettres 1991; composer: 'Diana,' 'You Are My Destiny,' 'Puppy Love,' 'Lonely Boy,' 'Put Your Head On My Shoulder,' 'Having My Baby,' 'One Man Woman,' 'I Don't Want To Sleep Alone,' 'Let Me Try Again,' 'Times Of Your Life' (theme song for Kodak commercials), 'Hold Me 'Til The Morning Comes,' 'My Way' (for Frank Sinatra), 'She's A Lady' (Tom Jones), 'It Doesn't Matter Anymore' (Buddy Holly), 'Jubilation' (Barbra Streisand), Tonight Show theme, 'The Longest Day' for movie of same name (Acad. Award nomination), theme song for Louis Malle film 'Atlantic City' (1st place, Venice Film Festival); 'No Way Out' for

movie of same name; Catholic; recreation: tennis; Club: Friars; Address: 10100 Santa Monica Blvd., Ste. 1300, Los Angeles, CA 90067.

**ANKNEY, Claude Davison,** B.S.; Ph.D.; university professor; b. Cleveland, OH 20 Sept. 1946; s. Claude Davison and Grace Arlene (Krohn) A.; e. Michigan State Univ. B.S. 1968; Univ. of Western Ont. Ph.D. 1974; m. Sandra d. Karl and Hattie Johnson July 1976; one d.: Theresa; PROFESSOR, ZOOLOGY, UNIV. OF WESTERN ONTARIO; supervised rsch. of 7 Ph.D. and 21 M.Sc. students who are now involved in teaching, rsch. and wildlife mngt. across N. Am.; Sci. Advisor, Inst. for Waterfowl and Wetlands Rsch.; Long Point Waterfowl and Wetlands Rsch. Fund; Long Point Biosphere Reserve; Dir., Soc. for Academic Freedom and Scholarship; Fellow, Am. Ornithol. Union 1992; 'Citation Classic' awarded 1992; Pres., Ont. Fed. of Anglers and Hunters 1991–94; Dir., Candn. Wildlife Fed.; Mem., Am. Assn. for the Adv. of Sci.; Am. Ornithol. Union; Candn. Soc. of Zool.; The Wildlife Soc.; Candn. Soc. of Ornithol.; Soc. for Study of Human Behavior and Evolution; co-editor: 'Ecology and Management of Breeding Waterfowl' 1992; author/co-author of over 90 sci. papers; recreations: hunting, birdwatching, fishing; club: Long Point Waterfowlers; Home: 1249 Hillcrest Ave., London, Ont. N5Y 4N2; Office: London, Ont. N6A 5B7.

**ANNABLE, Robert Graham,** B.A.; executive; b. Moose Jaw, Sask. 10 Mar. 1927; s. George Reynolds and Muriel (Horg) A.; e. Prince of Wales High Sch., 1945; Univ. of B.C., B.A. 1951; m. Janice Elizabeth, d. Douglas Rowley McColl, 24 Nov. 1951; children: Blake Malcolm, Tanyss Jane, Peter Douglas, Mark Graham; CHRMN. AND CHIEF EXTVE. OFFR., ANCORE INTERNATIONAL (CANADA) LTD. (founded Co. 1961; trading, shipping ins.); The East Asiatic Co. (export lumber marketing) 1951–61; has founded many cos in Can. and abroad; past mem., Economic Counc. of Can.; past Dir., Federal Business Development Bank; past Chrmn. and Pres., Capilano Golf & Country Club; Gov., Brentwood College; past Trustee, Vancouver Art Gallery; West Vancouver Found.; Phi Delta Theta; Anglican; recreations: golf, tennis, skiing, bridge; Clubs: Vancouver; Capilano Golf & Country; Hollyburn Country; Royal and Ancient Golf of St. Andrew, Scotland; Home: PTH #11–3085 Deer Ridge Close, W. Vancouver, B.C. V7S 4W1; Office: P.O. Box 91608, West Vancouver, B.C. V7V 3P3.

**ANNAU, Ernest,** Dipl. Ing., O.A.A., F.R.A.I.C., R.C.A.; architect; b. Szeged, Hungary 24 Dec. 1931; s. Ernest and Ilona (Antos) A.; e. Ont. Coll. of Art 1953–57; Acad. of Fine Arts (Munich, W. Germany) 1957–59; Univ. of Toronto 1951–53; Tech. Univ. of Munich, Dipl. Ing. 1959–63; m. Patricia d. Arthur and Gladys Harding 21 Sept. 1962; children: Catherine, Marion, Adrienne; private practice, ANNAU ASSOC. ARCHITECTS INC. 1972– ; numerous nat. and internat. design awards for architecture and scholarships & awards for drawing & painting; coloured lino-cut print 'Saturday Night' acquired by Art Gall. of Ont.; winner of the internat. competition for the design of China's first enclosed hockey stadium in Changchun; important projects incl. Bedford Glen, Rosegarden Mews, Balmoral Club Retirement Home, Winona Housing Co-op., National Yacht Club, prop. Solar Office Bldg., Min. of Ont. Attorney Gen. (all in Toronto), Concorde Corporate Centre and Concorde Park Condominiums, (Don Mills), South Common Leisure Pool (Mississauga), 7th Street Juniour School and Child Care Ctr., Etobicoke; Port Union Rec. Ctr. & Library (Scarborough), Parkway Mall (St. John, N.B.); designer of Ont. Hosp. Assn. Ctr. – Blue Cross (Don Mills); Brochure in the coll. of Candn. Ctr. for Arch.; Profl. Adv., Ont. Masonry Design Awards 1984–86; Chrmn., Heritage Markham 1977–81; R.A.I.C. Mission to China, Lecture Tour 1983; Chrmn., Competitions Ctte., Ont. Assn. of Archit. 1970–72, mem. 1985–89; Design critic, Univ. of Toronto; Univ. of Waterloo; McGill Univ.; Mem., Royal Candn. Acad. of Arts (Chrmn. Exhbn. Ctte. 1987–89); mem., Toronto Historical Bd. 1990– ;(Chair Preservation Ctte. 1992–93, Vice Chair Toronto 200 Ctte.); Fellow, Royal Archit. Inst. of Can.; mem., Ont. Assn. of Archit.; Contrib. ed.: 'Canadian Interiors' 1971–82; contrib. to numerous archit. mags.; recreations: sketching, cross country skiing; Home: 120 Imperial St., Toronto, Ont. M5P 1C6; Office: 819 Yonge St., 2nd Flr., Toronto, Ont. M4W 2G9.

**ANNETT, John C.,** B.A.Sc., M.B.A.; distributor; b. Detroit, Mich. 30 Jan. 1937; s. Francis C. and Cecile M. (Dwyer) A.; e. St. Michael's Coll. Sch., Toronto, 1954; Univ. of Toronto, B.A.Sc. (Elect. Engn.) 1958; York Univ., M.B.A. 1974; m. Gail R., d. Alex Stewart, 20 June 1959; children: Matthew, Kirsten, Megan; PRESI-

DENT, ELECTRONIC INDUSTRIES CORP. 1989– ; Applications Engr., Andrew Antenna Co. Ltd. 1958; Sales Mgr., Douglas Randall Canada Ltd. 1964; Pres. Amerace Ltd. 1981; Mgr., Corp. Develop., Jannock Ltd. 1981–83; Pres., Electrical Group, Jannock Ltd. 1983–88; mem., Assn. Prof. Engrs. Ont.; recreations: golf, fitness programs; Clubs: Bayview Golf & Country; Canadian; Address: 6338 Viscount Rd., Mississauga, Ont. L4V 1H3.

**ANNETT, Kenneth Hugh,** C.D., D.C.L., F.C.C.T.; historian; Gaspé, Que. 18 Aug. 1914; e. High Sch. New Carlisle, Que.; Macdonald Coll. McGill Univ. teaching educ.; Bishop's Univ. B.A., post-grad. M.Ed. courses; Columbia and Harvard Univs. post-grad. M.Ed. courses; m. Velma Law; three s.; Counsellor Superior Council of Educ. Que. 1974–79; Supvr. of Schs. R-D-A Central Sch. Bd. 1958–62; Dir. of Guidance Protestant Schs. Que. Dept. of Pub. Instr. 1962–65; Asst. Dir. Guidance Bureau Que. Dept. Educ. 1965, Asst. Dir. Gen. Elem. and Secondary Educ. Br. 1966, Counsellor Office Depy. Min. Educ. 1973–74; served with RCAF Active Service Radar 1942–45; Secy. and Pres. St. Francis Teachers' Assn.; mem. Sr. Adms. Group; Chief Instr. Cadet Services Can.; Author 'Huguenot Influence in Quebec'; 'The Annett Family of Gaspé'; 'Saga I'; 'Saga II'; 'Gaspé of Yesterday' Vol. 1–8 incl.; Columnist 'Huguenot Trails'; Contributor, CBC 'Québec A.M.'; Fellow Candn. Coll. Teachers; founding mem. Candn. Guidance & Counselling Assn. and Richmond Hist. Soc.; mem. Que. Assn. Sch. Adms.; Vice-Pres. Lit. & Hist. Soc. Que.; mem. Corp. of the Wales Home; mem. Holy Trinity Cathedral Parish; Anglican; Hon. Life Mem., Huguenot Soc. of Can.; Hon. Mem., Gaspesian Channel Islands Soc.; recreations: travel, hist. research, photography; Home: 1225 Lavigerie, Ste. Foy, Qué. G1W 3W8.

**ANSARY, Hassan J.,** B.A., M.B.A., Ph.D.; crown corporation executive; b. Tehran, Iran 3 May 1949; s. A.J. and R.J. (Naimi) A.; e. Univ. of Tehran B.A. 1971; Memorial Univ. of Nfld. Grad. Studies in Econ. 1973–75; Pittsburg State Univ. M.B.A. 1976; Cal. W. Univ. Ph.D. 1982; one d. Farrah Roxanne; EXEC. VICE PRES., CANADA PORTS CORP. 1988– ; Policy Adv., Communications Br., Min. of Transp. & Communications, Ont., Toronto 1977–78; Mgr. Strategic Planning Domtar Inc., Montréal, Qué. 1978–80; Mgr. Planning Coordination, Corporate Strategic Planning, Polysar Ltd., Sarnia, Ont. 1981–83; Mgr. Planning & Devel., Styrenics Div. 1983–84; Dir. Corporate Devel., present Corp., Ottawa 1984–85; Vice Pres., Corporate Services, present Corp. 1985–88; Chrmn., EDI Council of Can.; Dir., Van Horne Inst.; Dir., Containerization & Intermodal Inst.; First Vice-Chrmn., ICHCA International Secretariat; Dir., EDI Inst.; Fellow, Chartered Inst. of Transport; Mem., Adv. Group, Canada-Florida Inst.; Past Dir., Ridley Teminals Inc., Prince Rupert, B.C.; Pres., Internat. Cargo Handling Coord. Assn.; Chrmn., Planning & Rsch. Ctte., Am. Assn. of Port Authorities; Chrmn., EDI Counc. of Can.; Dir., CCC–375; Dir., Canada Grains Counc.; past Chrmn., Candn. Port Dev. Forum; Founding mem. Strategic Mgmt. Soc. and World Economic Forum; Candn. Film Inst.; recreations: theatre, films, skiing; Home: 2201 – 160 George St., Ottawa, Ont. K1N 9M2; Office: 99 Metcalfe, Ottawa, Ont. K1A 0N6.

**ANSTEY, Everett,** M.Eng.; computer hardware manufacturer; b. Nfld.; e. Tech. Univ. of N.S. B.Eng. 1965, M.Eng. 1967; m. Maureen Kerr; PRES. SUN MICROSYSTEMS OF CANADA INC. 1989– ;Corporate Dir. Sun Microsystems Inc. Cal.; former Vice Pres. & Gen. Mgr. Datagraphics Ltd.; Vice Pres./Partner Digital Systems Associates Ltd.; joined Digital Equipment of Canada Inc. 1977 becoming Vice Pres. Sales; joined present Co. as Vice Pres. Sales 1988; mem. Info. Technol. Assn. Can. (Bd.); York Technol. Assn.; recreation: boating; Office: 100 Renfrew Dr., Markham, Ont. L3R 9R6.

**ANTHONY, Brian Paul;** arts administrator; b. London, Eng. 21 June 1944; s. Frederick and Gladys Ellen (Wye) A.; e. Ottawa Teachers Coll. Ont. Teaching Cert. 1964; Carleton Univ. 1967–69; m. Nancy d. Maurice and Ruth Hughes 7 Apl. 1979; children: Eon (by previous marriage), Elizabeth, David; ASSOCIATE DIRECTOR, THE CANADA COUNCIL 1992– ; Press Offr. Nat. Arts Centre Ottawa 1976, Sec. of Corp. and Special Asst. to Dir. Gen. 1976–77; Exec. Asst. to Asst. Under Sec. of State (Arts & Culture) Dept. Sec. State Ottawa 1977–78; Policy Adv. Arts & Culture Br. Dept. Communications Ottawa 1978–80; Dir. of Info., Canadian Conference of the Arts 1980–83; Nat. Dir., CCA 1983–86; Extve. Dir., Confederation Centre of the Arts, Charlottetown 1986–89; Chief of Staff to the Federal Min. of Communications 1989–90; Consultant, Anthony and Associates 1990–92; Dir., Governor General's Performing Arts Awards Found. 1992– ; mem. Nat. Adv. Ctte. Culture Stats. 1984–88; Adv. Ctte. on Training and Employment Opportunities in the Cultural Sector (CEIC) 1984–86; Nat. Innovations Adv. Ctte. (CEIC) 1986; Mem., Sectoral Adv. Group on Internat. Trade (Arts and Cultural Industries), External Affairs 1986–89; Nat. Statistics Counc. (Stats Can) 1986–88; Dir. Ottawa Arts Centre Found. 1983–86; Contbg. Ed. 'Performing Arts in Canada' 1982–84; awarded Commemorative Medal for 125th Anniversary of Candn. Confederation 1993; Club: MENSA; Office: P.O. Box 1047, Ottawa, Ont. K1P 5V8; Home: 109 Powell Ave., Ottawa, Ont. K1S 2A2.

**ANTHONY, G.F. Kym,** B.A., M.B.A.; investment dealer; b. Montreal, Que. 5 Apr. 1955; s. George Herbert and Dorothy Inace (Sadler) A.; e. Simon Fraser Univ., B.A. 1977 (scholarships 1973, 75, 76, 77); Univ. of West. Ont., M.B.A. 1980 (Gold medallist 1979, 1980; selected to exchange prog. London Grad. Sch. of Bus.); m. Allison d. Jon and Hettie Vickers 5 Dec. 1981; three children: Michael, Callen, Evelyne; Sr. Vice Pres., Risk Management, CIBC and Wood Gundy Inc. 1991; joined Wood Gundy 1980; Vice-Pres., New Issues Dept. & Br. Mgr., Tokyo 1984; Bd. of Dir. 1986– ; Dir., Capital Markets 1988–91; Mem., Can.-Japan Businessmen's Soc.; Bd. of Mgs., Knox Presbyterian Ch.; recreations: classical music, squash, golf; Home: Oakville, Ont.

**ANTOFT, Kell,** B.A., M.A.; b. Roskilde, Denmark 24 July 1923; s. Otto Hugo and Asta Sigrid (Rump) A.; e. Dalhousie Univ., B.A. 1967; M.A. 1977; m. Mary Lou, d. Basil and Margaret Courtney, 19 Dec. 1980; children (from previous m.): Asta Ellen; Susan Kirsten; Nicholas Kevin; Timothy Steven; PROFESSOR (Part-time), HENSON COLLEGE, DALHOUSIE UNIV. 1984– ; Pres., Viking Air Service Ltd. 1946–56; Pres. Nordic Biochemicals Ltd. 1951–66; Asst. Extve. Dir., Nat. Cancer Inst. Can. and Candn. Cancer Soc. 1966–69; Asst. Dir., Inst. Public Affairs, Dalhousie Univ. 1969–76, Dir. 1977–84; Head, Municipal Admin. Program 1969–78; Special Lectr., Sch. Public Administration since 1972, Professor 1984–89; editor: 'Guide to Local Government in Nova Scotia' 1977 (3rd ed. 1992); author numerous papers and studies on local govt.; served as Air Navigator, R.C.A.F., 1943–46; rec'd. Scholarship in Pub. Admin. 1942–43; Overseas League Essay Prize 1943; Hon. Life Mem., Candn. Hostelling Assn.; Outstanding Achievement Award, Maritime Municipal Training and Development Bd. 1979; rec'd Lt.-Gov. (N.S.) Award for Excellence in Public Administration 1986; Hon. Life Mem., Candn. Cancer Soc. 1990; Chrmn., N.S. Jt. Labour Mgmt. Study Comte. 1974–79; Past Pres., Inst. Pub. Admin. Can.; Secy., Atlantic Mgmt. Inst.; Cofounder and Chrmn., Nancy Greene Ski League 1968–72; Dir. Opcan (Katimavik), Chrmn. of Bd. of Dir. 1986–89; Candn. Cancer Soc. N.S. Div. 1970–84, Hon. V.P., N.S. Div. 1984–91; mem. Counc. of Trustees, Inst. for Research on Public Policy 1982–86; Clubs: Royal Candn. Legion; Wentworth Valley Ski; Veterans Against Nuclear Arms; N.S. Seniors Ski Club (Chrmn.); recreations: skiing; canoeing; reading; Office: Henson College, Dalhousie Univ., 1261 Seymour St., Halifax, N.S. B3H 3J5.

**ANTON, Frank Robert,** C.D., B.Sc. (Econ.), M.A., Ph.D.; educator; b. Leix, Ireland 22 July 1920; s. Norman James and Teresa Beatrice (Baker) A.; e. London Sch. of Econ. B.Sc. 1950; Univ. of Calif. Los Angeles M.A. 1956; Univ. of London Ph.D. 1961; Professor Emeritus, Univ. of Calgary 1986; Research Econ., Govt. Can. Ottawa 1950–51; Inst. Indust. Relations UCLA 1953–56; Prof. of Econ., Univ. of Calgary 1957–86; Head of Econ. 1967–73, mem. Senate 1966–68; Visiting Prof. Middle E. Tech. Univ. Ankara (OECD Sponsorship) 1964; recipient various Can. Council and Killam Fellowships; Chrmn. numerous Arbitration, Adjudication & Conciliation Bds. Govts. Alta., Can.; Assessor, Can. Council Killam Fellowships; served with RAF Bomber Command Navig. 1940–43, P.O.W. Germany 1943–45; author 'Government Supervised Strike Voting' 1961; 'The Role of Government in the Settlement of Industrial Disputes in Canada' 1962; 'Wages and Productivity: The New Equation' 1969; 'Worker Participation: Prescription for Industrial Change' 1980; 'The Canadian Coal Industry: Challenge in the Years Ahead' 1981; co-author 'Economics in a Canadian Setting' 1964; articles various internat. journs.; Founding mem. and Dir. Econ. Soc. Alta. 1966–68; Town & Gown Calgary; Liberal; Anglican; recreations: swimming, hiking, music, travel, theatre; Home: P.O. Box 1, Site 9, S.S. 3, Calgary, Alta. T3C 3N9; Office: Calgary, Alta. T2N 1N4.

**ANTONIO, Juan;** artistic director; choreographer; dancer; b. Mexico City 4 May 1945; s. Juan Antonio and Ofelia (Rodea) Jimenez; e. Colegio Madrid 1963, Mexico City; N.Y. Univ.; ARTISTIC DIR. CONFIDANSE 1988– ; Prin. Dancer Ballet Nacional and Ballet Folklo Rico de Mexico; Co-Founder, Prin. Dancer, Assoc. Artistic, Resident Choreog., co. teacher, Louis Falco Dance Co. , New York City 1967–83; Guest Artist Netherlands Danse Theater, Jose Limon Dance Co., Joffrey Ballet Co.; Asst. Choreog. Broadway Prodns. 'Indians Dude' and 'Garden of Earthly Delights'; Prin. Dancer Glen Tetley Dance Co.; Artist-in-Residence (First) York Univ. 1985–88; staged Glen Tetley ballet Royal Swedish Ballet Co. 1987; Artistic Dir. Toronto Dance Centre 1983; Choreog. George Brown Coll. and Ryerson Polytech.Inst. 1988; recipient various grants Nat. Endowment Arts, Ont. Arts Council, Creative Arts Pub. Services New York City (choreog.); Adjudicator Dora Moore Dance Awards; Address: 106 Sumach St., Toronto, Ont. M5A 3J9.

**ANTONIO, Marlene Joan Elaine,** B.Ed., B.A., M.Ed.; educator; b. Moose Jaw, Sask. 24 Apr. 1936; d. John Ewan and Ruby Irene (Bagg) Lauder; e. Univ. of Saskatchewan B.Ed. 1956, B.A. 1957; Univ. of Calgary M.Ed. 1972; Nat. Counc. of Jewish Women Scholarships; Grad. Teaching Asst., Univ. of Calgary; m. Harry s. John and Annie Antonio 27 Apr. 1957; children: Jolaine, Ann; MEMBER, CITY OF CALGARY PARKS AND RECREATION BOARD 1993– ;and MEMBER, DEAN OF SCIENCE AND TECHNOLOGY ADVISORY CTTE., MT. ROYAL COLLEGE 1993– ; Texaco Expl. Ltd., Nat. Resch. Counc. 1957; teacher, var. parts of Alta. 1960–66; Instr., Mt. Royal Coll. 1966–70; Univ. of Calgary and Mt. Royal Coll. 1972–76; Calgary Bd. of Educ. 1976–81; apptd. to Alta. Human Rights Comn. 1979 (Chrmn. 1981–85; Mem., Chairman's Counc. 1989–92); mem. Min. of Educ. Ctte. on Tolerance and Understanding 1983–84; Pres., Candn. Assn. of Statutory Human Rights Agencies 1984–85, Past Pres. 1985–86; Treas., Calgary Home and Sch. Assn. 1976–78; mem. Alta. Teachers Assn. 1956–66, 1968–70, 1976–80; Recipient, Candn. Counc. of Christians and Jews 'Good Servant Medal'; Hon. mem., Assn. Prof. Engr., Geol. & Geophys., Alta. 1986; APEGGA Practice Review Bd. 1986, 1987– ; APEGGA General Counc. 1987–92; Calgary Bd. of Educ. 1986–92; Co-Chair, Bowmont Natural Park Ctte. 1992– ; Office: 5115 Varscliff Rd. N.W., Calgary Alta. T3A 0G2.

**ANTONSON, Richard Alvin;** tourism executive; b. Vancouver, B.C. 12 August 1949; s. Alvin and Elsie Elizabeth (Bailey) A.; e. Burnaby South H.S. 1967; Simon Fraser Univ. 1967–69; m. Wendy d. Stanley and Marjorie Lyons 14 Dec. 1968 (separated 1990); children: Brent Richard, Sean Kelly; EXTVE. DIR. & C.E.O., TOURISM VANCOUVER 1993– ; Pres. & Pub., Antonson Publishing Ltd. 1970–77; Mng. Dir., S.W. B.C. Tourist Assn. 1977–82; Founding Extve. Dir., Tourism Indus. Assn. of B.C. 1980–82; Vice-Pres., Douglas & McIntyre, Pubs. 1982–87; Pres. & C.E.O., Edmonton Convention & Tourism Authority 1987–90; Vice Pres., Sales & Marketing, Great Candn. Railtour Co. Ltd. 1990–93; Wise Old Owl Award and Dive B.C.'s President's Award for outstanding indiv. contrib. to tourism devel.; Co-chair, B.C. Spec. Olympic Games 1984; Initiator & Co-chair, Conf. on Vancouver's Future 1984, 85 and 86; Chrmn., Prov. Leader's Ctte., B.C. Liberal Party 1985, 86; Pres., Assn. of Book Pubs. of B.C. 1984–86; Dir., Assn. of Candn. Pubs. 1984–86; Tourism Indus. Assn. of Can. 1980–82; Vice-Pres., Cand. Periodical Pubs. Assn. 1977; Vice Chair, Candn. Assoc. of Convention & Visitor Bureaux 1988–90; Vice Chrmn., Pacific Asia Travel Assn. (PATA) Travel Mart 1990; apptd. Adv. Counc. for Pacific Asia Travel Assoc.; apptd. Chrmn., Adv. Ctte., Tourism, B.C. Inst. of Technology; apptd. Extve. Ctte., Counc. of Tourism Assoc. of B.C.; mem., Adv. Counc., PATA 1992–92; mem. Extve. Ctte., Counc. of Tourism Assoc. of B.C.; mem., Pacific Asia Adv. Group, Tourism Canada 1991–93; Co-Founder, 'Canada Train Week' 1991; part-time lecturer & public speaker; author: 'The Fraser Valley' 1981; co-author: 'In Search of a Legend' 1972; author of numerous articles & papers; recreations: hiking, travel; Home: 3359 Flagstaff Place, Vancouver, B.C. V5S 4K9.

**APPEL, A. Bram,** B.Com., C.A.; chartered accountant; b. Montreal, Que. 13 Jan. 1915; s. Israel and Sophia (Hecht) A.; e. McGill Univ. B.Com. 1935; C.A. 1936; m. Bluma d. Joseph Levitt 11 July 1940; children: David Harry, Mark Gordon; PRESIDENT A. BRAM APPEL CONSULTANTS INC. 1976– ; Chrmn., Electroline Television Equipment Inc.; Canmont Investment Corp. Ltd.; Dir., Pall Corp.; Ultra Lasertech Inc.; O H Plastics Inc.; Canada Israel Chamber of Commerce and Industry; Sr. Partner, Appel & Partners 1936–75; Extve. Asst. to Min. of Energy, Mines & Resources, Ottawa 1966–67; Consultant to Secy. of State 1968–69, to Min. of Industry, Trade & Comm. 1970–72; Dir. and Chief Financial Offr. Interimco Ltd. Ottawa 1973–79; Consultant to 'Labyrinth' Project Nat. Film Bd. Expo '67; Gov., Mt. Sinai Hosp. Toronto; rec'd Centennial Medal 1967; Address: 18A Hazelton Ave., Suite E406, Toronto, Ont. M5R 2E2.

**APPEL, Bluma,** C.M.; executive; b. Montreal, Que.; d. Jack and Dora (Blitz) Levitt; m. A. Bram Appel; children: David Harry; Mark Gordon; CHAIRMAN, APPEL CONSULTANTS INC. 1977– ; suit designer, Chester Reed Clothes 1948–52; var. N.Y. theatre productions 1952–62; Dir. and co-owner, Waddington Galleries 1957–65; Chargée de Mission to Sec. of State (Gerard Pelletier) 1970–72; Liaison to Min. Responsible for the Status of Women (Marc Lalonde) 1975–79; Liberal fed. cand. H. of C. 1979; Dir. Canmont Investment Corp. Ltd.; Canmont Realty Corp.; Dir. and Sec. Treas. Electroline Television Equipment inc.; Founder and Exec. Dir. Am. Friends of Canada Ctte.; Dir. Couchiching Inst. of Pub. Affairs; theatre in St. Lawrence Centre, Toronto, named after her 1983; apptd. to Bd. of Trustees of the ROM (Royal Ont. Mus.) 1990; Founder 'Partners in Research' 1988; Bd. of Dirs.: McMichael Gall. 1986–90; 'Necessary Angel' Theatre Co. 1987–90; Brock Univ. 1988; Ont. Crafts Counc. 1987; Prime Mentors of Can. 1987; The Shakespeare Globe Ctr. of Can. 1989; Bd. of Advs., Second Harvest 1991; Chrmn. of Bd., Candn. Found. for AIDS Rsch. (CanFAR); Past Dir., Nat. Gallery, Ottawa 1973–77; Candn. Opera Co. 1981–88; Candn. Psychiatric Rsch. Found. 1980–89; Candn. Centre for Advanced Film Studies 1986–91; Metro Toronto Community Found. 1987–91; Toronto Arts Awards 1988–90; Trustee, National Symphony Orch., Kennedy Ctr. for Performing Arts, Washington; apptd. Member of the Order of Canada 1988; awarded Commemorative Medal for 125th Anniversary of Candn. Confederation; 1993 'Hero' Metro Toronto Community Church; recreations: walking, swimming, cross-country skiing; Home: 18A Hazelton Ave., Apt. 406, Toronto, Ont. M5R 2E2; Office: 18A Hazelton Ave., Apt. 405, Toronto, Ont. M5R 2E2.

**APPELT, David Clemens,** M.A., A.B.L.S.; librarian; b. Upper Moutere, New Zealand, 3 Aug. 1915; s. Arthur and Margaret (Darsow) A.; came to Canada, 1925; e. Univ. of Alberta, B.A. (Hons. Eng.) 1936, M.A. 1937; Univ. of Michigan, A.B.L.S. (Hons.) 1940; m. Natalie, d. Fred Schmidt, Duval, Sask., 22 July 1946; children: Jane Elizabeth, Timothy James; Instr. in Eng., Mount Royal Coll., Calgary, Alta., 1937–39; Head Cataloguer, Univ. of Alberta Lib., 1941–45; University Librarian, Univ. of Sask. 1945–80; Pres., Candn. Assn. of Coll. and Univ. Libs., 1966–67; mem. Candn. Lib. Assn.; Royal Candn. Coll. of Organists; Lutheran; recreation: music; Home: 18 Sunnyside Dr., St. Catharines, Ont. L2M 2A1.

**APPLE, Barnabas William Nixon,** Q.C., B.A., LL.B.; barrister and solicitor; b. Toronto, Ont. 29 Jan. 1924; s. Elmer Albert and Beatrice Muriel (Nixon) A.; e. Pickering Coll. 1936–40; Univ. of Toronto B.A. 1946; Osgoode Hall Law Sch. 1949 (Bronze Medal); m. Sonia Jane d. Vera and John Skinner 14 June 1947; children: Heather Elizabeth, William Nixon, Sara Jane, Derek Phin; SR. PARTNER, SALTER APPLE COUSLAND AND KERBEL; called to Bar of Ont. 1949; cr. Q.C. 1964; served with RCNVR 1943–45; author 'Filing of Prospectuses by Mining Companies' 1964; 'Shareholders' Agreement' 1968; 'Financing through the Toronto Stock Exchange' 1972; and Osgoode Hall Cont. Legal Ed. Series; Conservative; Church of England; recreations: golf, farming; Clubs: National; York Downs Golf & Country; Home: RR 3, Uxbridge, Ont. L9P 1R3; Office: 1000, 67 Yonge St., Toronto, Ont. M5E 1J8.

**APPLE, Heather Elizabeth,** B.Sc.; horticulturist; b. Toronto, Ont. 9 Oct. 1948; d. B. Nixon and Sonia Jane (Skinner) A.; Branksome Hall 1967; e. Univ. of Toronto B.Sc. (Hons.) 1972; single; Teacher and Speaker at local, prov. & nat. levels; creator of edn. displays; radio-guest on local & nat. programs; guest radio host, local gardening show; Subject & Cons. 'Organic Gardening' home study course & 'Field of Greens' Roger Cable TV; Subject, TV series 'Millenium'; Canada 125 Medal; Pres., Heritage Seed Program; Rep. for nongovt. orgns. on Agric. Canada's Expert Ctte. on Plant Gene Resources; Nat. Extve., Candn. Organic Growers; dedicated to the preservation of heirloom & endangered varieties of food crops and a wide range of eco activities; Mem., Seed Savers Exchange; Garden Writers Assn. of Am.; Ont. Profl. Women in Hort.; Assn. of Living Hist. Farms & Agric. Museums; Henry Doubleday Rsch. Assn.; N. Am. Fruit Explorers; Flower and Herb Exchange; Soc. of Ont. Nut Growers; Commercial Assn. of Nut Growers of Ont.; Northern Nut Growers Assn.; author: 'How to Save Your Own Vegetable Seeds' 1990, '92; editor: 'Heritage Seed Program' mag.; Garden Columnist, 'Cognition' mag.; author of numerous mag. articles; recreations: crafts, reading, movies; Address: R.R. 3, Uxbridge, Ont. L9P 1R3.

**APPLEBAUM, Louis,** O.C., LL.D; composer; conductor, Arts Administrator; b. Toronto, Ont. 3 Apr. 1918; s. Morris Abraham and Fanny (Freiberg) A.; e. Harbord Coll. Inst., Toronto, 1931–36; Univ. of Toronto, 1940; Toronto Conserv. of Music 1928–40; private study under scholar. in N.Y. with Bernard Wagenaar and Roy Harris, 1940–41; m. Janet, d. Lewis Hershoff, Toronto, 19 July 1940; one s. David Hersh; Chrmn. Fed. Culture Policy Review Comte. 1980–82 (Applebaum/Hebert Report published 1982); Extve. Dir., Prov. of Ont. Council for the Arts, 1971; Pres., Group 4 Productions; Music Consultant, C.B.C.-TV; joined staff of National Film Board of Can. as Composer 1941; Music Dir., 1943, composing and cond. scores for about 200 theatrical and non-theatrical documentary films; invited to Hollywood 1945, to compose and conduct score for 'Tomorrow the World,' produced by Lester Cowan for Un. Artists; returned 1946 to score 'The Story of G.I. Joe,' same studio; later returned to Can. to continue work at Nat. FilmBd.; resigned in 1947 to engage in study and research in N.Y.; composed scores for many documentary producers, incl. UNO, U.S. Army, March of Time, Nat. Film Bd., etc.; also writing lect. and teaching film music; won two prizes in Candn. Performing Right Soc. competition 1938 and 1939; score for 'Tomorrow the World' won special citation from Hollywood Writers Mobilization; score for 'Story of G.I. Joe,' nominated for an Acad. Award; has contributed to 'Film Music Notes,' 'Journ. of Aesthetics and Art Criticism,' 'Music in Canada,' 'The Stratford Scene,' 'Film Music'; Music Director, Stratford Festival 1953–60; Canadian Film Award 1968; Wilderness Award 1973; Canadian Film Award, 1975; Anik Award, 1977; concert works have beenperformed by orchestras in many countries, over CBC, BBC (U.K.), by the League of Composers, New York, and in recital in Canada, the U.S.A. and England; Chrmn., Composers, Authors & Publishers Assn. of Can. Comte. for Promotion of Candn. Music, 1964–71; Music Consultant, Nat. Arts Centre, Ottawa, 1964–67; mem. Adv. Panel, Can. Council, 1965–69; Lecturer, York Univ. 1974–78; mem. Bd. of Directors, Candn. Music Centre; Candn. League of Composers; SOCAN; Planning Council of OECA; Nat. Ballet Sch.; Candn. Conf. for the Arts; Candn. Music Council; mbr. Royal Soc. of Arts; Clubs: Arts & Letters; Cercle Universitaire; awarded Centennial Medal 1967; Order of Canada 1977; Queens Jubilee Medal, 1977; LL.D.(Hon) York U. 1979; Hon. Fellow, Ont. Coll. of Art. 1981; Beta Sigma Rho; Hebrew.

**APPLETON, Thomas Edmund;** aerospace executive; b. Ipswich, Eng. 16 Oct. 1941; s. Thomas Edmund and Violet Ellen (Cousins) A.; e. Fisher Park High Sch., Ottawa 1960; McGill Mgmt. Inst. 1981; m. Heather d. Beryl Kilgour 16 Dec. 1967; children: Duncan, Nicholas; EXTVE. VICE PRES., BOMBARDIER REGIONAL AIRCRAFT DIVISION, BOMBARDIER INC. 1991– ; Pilot, Spartan Air Services, Survair Ltd., 1960–66; joined de Havilland as Test & Demonstration Pilot 1966; Mgr., Mktg. Projects 1979; Dir., Tech. Services 1980; Vice Pres., Customer Support 1981; Vice Pres., Marketing & Sales 1986; Vice Pres., Mktg., Sales & Govt. Affairs, de Havilland Canada 1986–91; holds six world (FAI) records for time to height, Turboprop Aircraft (1975); mem. Soc. of Experimental Test Pilots; Home: 2230 All Saints Cres., Oakville, Ont. L6V 5N2.

**APPLEYARD, Edward Clair,** M.Sc., Ph.D.; geologist; educator; b. Strathroy, Ont. 22 June 1934; s. Harold Frederick Gaviller and Muriel Chanter (Jarvis) A.; e. Meaford (Ont.) High Sch.; Brantford (Ont.) Coll. Inst. 1952; Univ. of W. Ont. B.Sc. 1956; Queen's Univ. M.Sc. 1960; Cambridge Univ. Ph.D. 1963; m. Elizabeth Ann d. Albert Edward Curtis 28 July 1962; children: Gregory David Jarvis, Mary Louise Desborough; ASSOC. PROF. OF EARTH SCIENCES, UNIV. OF WATERLOO; mem. Geol. Assn. Can.; Mineral. Assn. Can.; Anglican; Home: 61 Larkspur Cres., Kitchener, Ont. N2M 4W8; Office: Univ. of Waterloo, Waterloo, Ont. N2L 3G1.

**APPLEYARD, James Stuart;** real estate executive; b. Stretford, Lancashire, U.K. 21 April 1933; s. Eric Bentley and Elsie (Thurlby) A.; e. Ashford, Middlesex County Grammar Sch.; Assoc. Mem., Royal Inst. of Chartered Surveyors (U.K.) 1960; Fellow 1972; m. Alexandria d. Margaret and Alexander Brown 4 April 1975; children: Eric Samuel, Ian James, Stuart John; PRESIDENT & CHIEF EXECUTIVE OFFICER, SLOUGH ESTATES CANADA 1972– ; worked in U.K. with London County Council & Birmingham City Council where he started new Town of Daventry; Chief Estates Officer, East Kilbridge Devel. Corp. in Scotland prior to moving to Canada in early 1970s; Dir., SDK Developments; Dir., Royal Life Canada; Past Chrmn., Royal Inst. of Chartered Surveyors, East Candn. Group 1984–86; Past Pres., Brit. Candn. Trade Assn. 1981–83; Econ. Devel. Council of Ont. 1987; Mem., Inst. of Housing (U.K.) 1954; Fellow 1981; Corp. Mem., Inst. of Revenues, Rating & Valuation (U.K.0 1969; Mem., Professional Land Economist 1971; Anglican; clubs: Lambton Golf & Country, National; Home: 3 Concorde Place, #1502, Don Mills, Ont. M3C 3K7; Office: Ste. 4803, P.O. Box 303, 40 King St. W., Toronto, Ont. M5H 3Y3.

**APPLEYARD, Peter,** O.C.; composer; vibraphonist; percussionist; b. Cleethorpes, Eng. 26 Aug. 1928; drummer Brit. dance and Central RCAF Bands prior to moving to Bermuda 1949 and to Toronto 1951 where he began playing vibraphone; performed with Billy O'Connor, Colonial Tavern 1953; Park Plaza Hotel, CBC Radio & with Cal Jackson 1954–56; formed own group 1957 travelling widely in N. Am.; co-host CBC Radio 'Patti and Peter' 1961–62; Music Dir. for Gloria DeHaven on tour U.S. early 1960's; CBC TV 'Mallets and Brass' with Guido Basso 1969; served as Music Dir. various Toronto nightclubs and cocktail lounges incl. Park Plaza Hotel, Sutton Place Hotel, Toronto-Dominion Centre, Delta Chelsea; performed as leading percussionist in theatre, radio and TV, recording orchestras; toured Middle E. & Ellesmere Island through CBC and UN; joined Benny Goodman's sextet early 1970's touring Europe 1972, 1974, Australia 1973; joined an orchestra incl. Count Basie Band for special Broadway (Uris Theatre) engagement accompanying Frank Sinatra & Ella Fitzgerald 1975; appeared in concert annually 1976–79 Ont. Place; Host 'Peter Appleyard Presents' (TV jazz and variety program) Toronto and syndicated in N.Am. 1977–79; toured Europe with Barney Kessel & Sacha Distel, Buddy DeFranco, Herbie Mann late 80's & early 90's; toured Japan with Mel Tormé 1993; composer incidental music radio shows and themes for his jazz groups; various recordings incl. Juno nominated & Gold Record Swing Fever All Star Swing Band 1983; Sarasota Jazz Festival Most Popular Musician 1990; Honorary Citizen of Moncton; Civic Award of Merit, City of Scarborough; Keys to City of North York; Benno Haussmann Award, City of Cork, S. Ireland 1992; Officer, Order of Canada 1992; mem. SOCAN.

**APPLIN, Anne-Marie Haig,** B.A.; consulting executive; b. Toronto Ont. 10 Jan. 1952; d. Edward Patrick and Anne Veronica (McDermott) Haig; e. Univ. of Toronto B.A. 1974; m. Michael Robert s. Morgan Ashton and Margaret (Reid) A. 5 Aug. 1978; children: Stephanie Margaret Haig and Katherine Anne Haig Applin; PRES. APPLIN MKTG. & COMMUNICATION 1981– ; Nat. Training Dir. Clinique Labs. 1974–78; Instr. George Brown Coll. 1978–88; Dir. of Mktg., Convention & Visitors Assn. Metro Toronto 1978–80 and World Trade Ctr. Toronto 1980–81; Partner Music by Appointment 1987– ; Assoc. Dir. Optimum Communications 1988–92; Speaker ACAA-O Inst. for Candn. Alumni Admin. 1989 and CAIS Independent Sch. Development Officers 1992; guest speaker, broadcast interviews radio & TV 1975– ; Founding Mem. Toronto Culinary Guild 1986– ; Mem. The Fashion Group 1987– ; Alumni Serv. Award, U. of Toronto 1989 (active member since 1978; several extve. posts); Paul W. Fox Award for 'outstanding contrib. to Erindale Coll.' 1986; Mem., Royal Ont. Museum Curatorial Ctte. 1990– ; Gov. Univ. of Toronto 1987–90; Mem. Coll. of Electors 1978–80, 1984–85, 1990–92; Bd. Extve., St. Margaret's Towers Inc. Non-Profit Housing; Dir., Centennial Coll. Retail Adv. Bd. 1988–93; Oolagen Community Serv. 1986– ; Mem., Toronto Symphony Women's Ctte. 1979– , The Parkinson Found. of Can. 1989– , Stratford Fest. Express 1988, '89, '90, '91, '92, '93, '94, Mississauga Symphony Gala Project 1990, 1991, and several other cttes. involved in fundraising activities; Dir., The Kidney Found. of Can. (Ont.) 1981–86; Co-Chair Advertising/Public Relations, Juvenile Diabetes Found. Fundraising Gala 1988, '89; recreations: golf, painting, design, gardening, music; Address: 512 Briar Hill Avenue, Toronto, Ont. M5N 1M9.

**APSEY, Thomas Michael,** R.P.F.; forestry executive; b. Vernon, B.C. 1 Apr. 1938; e. Univ. of B.C., B.S.F. 1961; m. Sharon Meagher 1962; two d. Susan, Jill; PRESIDENT & C.E.O., COUNCIL OF FOREST INDUSTRIES 1984– ; Dir., Candn. Forest Industries Counc.; Pacific Salmon Found.; mem., B.C. Round Table on the Environment and the Economy; Econ. and Forest Ind. Analyst B.C. Dept. Ind. Devel., Trade and Comm. 1961–63; Sr. Market Analyst Pulp & Paper Grp., MacMillan Bloedel Ltd. 1963–68; Forestry Offr. Forest Inds. UN Food & Agric. Orgn., Turkey 1968–70; Econ.

present Coun. 1970, Vice Pres. Forestry 1972–74; Sr. Econ. and Vice Pres. F.L.C. Reed and Assoc. 1974–78, mem. Forest Policy Adv. Ctte., conducted studies forest inds. Colombia, Ghana, Honduras and various Eur. and Latin Am. countries; Depy. Min. of Forests B.C. 1978–84, served as Vice Chrmn. B.C. Dep. Mins.' Ctte. on Econ. Devel.; mem., Internat. Task Force on Tropical Forests convened by the World Resources Inst., the World Bank and the United Nations Development Program 1984–85; awarded the Rielle Thomson Award for outstanding contribution to public knowledge of the forest, Candn. Pulp & Paper Assn. 1985; awarded Chevalier de l'Ordre du Mérite Agricole, for contribution to world forestry, Govt. of France 1991; mem. Vancouver Bd. Trade; Assn. Prof. Econs. B.C.; Assn. B.C. Profl. Foresters; Clubs: Vancouver, Canadian; Office: 1200 – 555 Burrard St., Vancouver, B.C. V7X 1S7.

**AQIGAAQ, Mathew;** sculptor; b. near the Kazan River Falls, N.W.T. 14 Aug. 1940; 47 group exbns. incl. most recent: National Gallery of Canada Ottawa 1991, Vancouver Inuit Art Soc. 1990, 1991, Candn. Mus. of Civilization Hull, Que. 1990, Art Gall. of Ont. Toronto 1989; solo exbns.: The Innuit Gall. of Eskimo Art Toronto 1991, The Upstairs Gall. Winnipeg 1982, Waddington's Toronto 1980, Theo Waddington N.Y. 1980, Inuit Galerie Mannheim, Germany 1980, Theo Waddington London, Eng. 1979; works in 14 collections incl. art galleries of Windsor, Edmonton, Ontario (Klamer Family and Sarick colls.), Winnipeg (Swinton and Twomey colls.), Candn. Mus. of Civilization, Inuit Cultural Inst. Rankin Inlet, N.W.T., National Gall. of Can., Dennos Mus. Ctr., N.W. Michigan Coll. Traverse City, Mich.; participant, experimental graphics workshop Baker Lake 1965; attended opening 'Masters of the Arctic' N.Y. 1989; subject of several articles and catalogues; Home: Baker Lake, N.W.T.; Office: c/o Candn. Arctic Producers, 1645 Inkster Blvd., Winnipeg, Man. R2X 2W7.

**ARANDA, Jacob Velasco,** M.D., Ph.D.; pharmacologist; pediatrician; educator; b. Isabela, Philippines 29 Dec. 1942; s. late Anacleto T. and Gorgonia (Velasco) A.; came to Can. 1969; e. Manila Central Univ. M.D. 1965; McGill Univ. Ph.D. 1975; m. Dr. Betty I., d. late Frederic Sasyniuk 29 Dec. 1974; children: Kenneth Frederic; Christopher James; PROF. OF PEDIATRICS, PHARMACOLOGY & THERAPEUTICS MCGILL UNIV. 1984– ; Dir., Developmental Pharmacology & Perinatal Research, McGill Univ./Montreal Children's Hosp. Research Inst.; mem. attending staff in neonatology Royal Victoria Hosp.; Montreal Gen. Hosp.; Jewish Gen. Hosp.; St. Mary's Hosp.; Intern, Washington Hosp. Center and Children's Hosp., Washington, D.C. 1965; Resident, State Univ. of N.Y. Upstate Medical Center, Syracuse 1966; Clinical and Research Fellow, Case Western Reserve Univ. at Cleveland Metropolitan Hosp. 1968; Clinical and Research Fellow, McGill Univ. – Montreal Children's Hosp. 1969–71; Asst. Prof. Pediatrics, McGill Univ. 1974–77; Assoc. Prof. of Pediatrics 1977–83; Assoc. Prof. of Pharmacology & Therapeutics 1979–83; Mem. Amer. Acad. of Pediatrics; Amer. Soc. for Clinical Pharmacology and Therapeutics; Amer. Soc. for Toxicology; Amer. Fed. of Clinical Research; Amer. Coll. of Clinical Pharmacology; Amer. Thoracic Soc.; Fed. of Medical Specialists (Que.); Candn. Pediatric Soc.; Candn. Assn. for Research in Toxicology; Candn. Thoracic Soc.; Candn. Pharmacological Soc.; Candn. Soc. for Clinical Investigations; N.Y. Acad. of Sciences; Soc. for Pediatric Research; Ed.-in-Chief 'Developmental Pharmacology and Therapeutics'; author more than 100 scientific papers and book chapters on pediatrics, neonatology and pharmacology; Queen Eliz. II Research Scientist for Diseases in Children 1976–82; Fellow, Med. Research Council of Can. 1971–75; Beta Sigma; Protestant; recreations: music (piano, voice), swimming, running, skiing, skating, cycling; Club: Canadian; Home: 3800 Grey Ave., Montreal, Qué. H4A 3N7; Office: 2300 Tupper Ave., Montreal, Qué. H3H 1P3.

**ARASON, Greg S.;** agricultural executive; b. Winnipeg, Man. 27 Sept. 1946; s. Skapti and Edith J. (Avery) A.; e. Univ. of Manitoba; Banff Sch. of Adv. Management; m. Margaret d. Colin and Marion Barlow 20 June 1970; children: Colin, Cade; CHIEF EXECUTIVE OFFICER, MANITOBA POOL ELEVATORS 1988– ; Resource Cons., Central Plains Reg. Devel. Corp. 1970; Econ. Analyst, Govt. of Man. 1970–71; Dist. Supervisor, Man. Pool Elevators 1971–76; Mgr., Field Serv. 1976–80; Corp. Sec. 1980–85; Gen. Mgr., Serv. & Devel. 1985–88; Dir., XCAN Grain Pool Ltd.; Canamera Foods Ltd.; Prince Rupert Grain; Pacific Elevators Ltd.; Western Pool Terminals Ltd.; Can-Oat Milling Ltd.; Chair, Western Grain Elevator Assn.; Advisor, Univ. of Man. Transport Inst.; Red River Community College; Guest Lectr., Univ. of Man., Fac. of Agric.; Past Chair, Sr. Grain Transp. Ctte. 1990–93; Past Dir., Kidney Found. (Man.) 1990–92; Dir., Winnipeg C. of C. 1992– ; Man. Co-op. Council 1980– ; Mem., Canadian Club of Winnipeg; Graint Elevator & Processing Soc.; recreations: cottage, golf, squash, hockey; clubs: Carleton, Windsor Community, Winnipeg C. of C.; Home: 440 Kingston Cres., Winnipeg, Man. R2M 0T9; Office: 500 – 220 Portage Ave., Winnipeg, Man. R3C 3K7.

**ARBOUR, Hon. Louise,** B.A., LL.L.; judge; b. Montreal, Que. 10 Feb. 1947; e. Univ. de Montréal B.A. 1967, LL.L. 1970; JUDGE, COURT OF APPEAL FOR ONT. 1990– ; Judge, Supreme Court of Ontario (High Court of Justice) 1987–90; Office: 130 Queen St. W., Toronto, Ont. M5H 2N5.

**ARBOUR, Pierre;** business executive; b. Shawinigan, Que. 30 Aug. 1935; s. William and Alida (Ayotte) A.; e. Univ. de Montréal B.A. 1956, McGill Univ., B.Comm. 1959; m. Chantal d. Roland Gilbert; children: Christine, Philippe, Eric; PRES., ALKEBEC INC. 1990– ; London Life 1959–62; Finan. Analyst, Morgan Ostiguy 1962–66; Caisse de Depôt et Placement du Que. 1966–75; Sr. Corp. Advisor 1975–79; Pres., Monterey Capital Inc. 1979–90; Dir., Regional Cablesystems Inc.; CABLE 2000 Inc., New Brunswick; Sportscene Restaurants Inc., Montreal; Centre d'art contemporain; clubs: M.A.A.A., Montreal Hill-Side Tennis Club; Home: 1275 Redpath Cres., Montreal, Qué. H3G 1A1; Office: 1155 Boul. René Lévesque Ouest, Montreal, Qué. H3B 4T3.

**ARCAND, Denys;** écrivain-réalisateur; né Québec 1941; e. Univ. de Montréal, M.A.; Réal., 'Le Declin de l'Empire Americain' 1985 (Prix de la Féd. Internat. de la Presse Cinématograph., Cannes (Quinzaine des Réal), le Prix John Labatt Classic pour le film le plus populaire et le Prix CITY, Meilleur Film Candn., Fest. du Film de Toronto 1986, eight Genies, incl. best picture, supporting actor and actress, director and screenplay and the Golden Reel Award as the most commercially successful Candn. film of the year 1987), 'Le Crime d'Ovide Plouffe' 1983, 'Empire Inc.' (3 eps.) 1983, 'Le Confort et l'indifference' 1980 (Prix Ouimet – Molson), 'Jésus de Montréal' 1988 (Winner, Jury Prize, Cannes Film Festival 1989), 12 Genies & Golden Reel, et divers autres films et TV.

**ARCAND, Robert,** B.Com., D.H.C.; administrator; b. St-Roch, Qué. 12 Feb. 1945; s. Richard and Bibiane (Laverdière) A.; e. Univ. of Ottawa B.Com. 1968; Univ. du Qué. Abitibi-Temiscamingue D.H.C. 1987; m. Pierrette d. Raoul Duchesne 20 May 1967; children: Annie, Marie-Claude, Sebastien; Pres. Fondation D'Entrepreneurship du Québec 1987–..; Dir. Télébec Ltée; Domco Inc.; joined Bank of Commerce 1968–74; Fédération des Sociétés d'Entraide Economiques du Québec, Pres. 1982–85; Société d'Entraide Economique du Québec, Pres. 1985–88; La Financière Entraide-Coopérant Inc., Pres. 1988–89; recipient Paul Harris Fellowship Rotary Internat. Found.; Trudeau Medal, Administration Faculty, Univ. of Ottawa; Sec. Treas. Innocentre Inc.; Dir. Qué. C. of C.; Clubs: Le Blainvillier Golf; St-Denis.

**ARCAND, Theodore Jean,** B.A.; diplomat; b. Bonnyville, Alta. 25 June 1934; s. Louis and Marie-Anne (Ayotte) A.; e. McMaster Univ., B.A. 1957; Laval Univ.; m. Jennifer Marjorie d. Leslie Garner-Ashmore 21 June 1958; one s.: Jean-Louis; Canadian Ambassador to the Holy See 1990–93; Jr. Admin. Offr., Dept. of Citizenship and Immigration 1957–58; joined External Affairs 1958; 3rd Sec., Candn. Legation, Prague 1959–62; Personnel Div., Ottawa 1962; 2nd Sec., Candn. Embassy, Yaounde 1963–65; 1st Sec., Candn. Embassy, Copenhagen 1965–68; Information Div., Ottawa 1968–70; Counsellor, Candn. High Comn., Dar-es-Salaam 1970–72; Couns./Chargé d'Affaires, Candn. Embassy to the Holy See 1972–76; Dir., Commonwealth Affairs, Ottawa 1976–77; Dir., Francophone Africa & Maghreb Affairs, Ottawa 1977–78; Ambassador concurrently to Lebanon, Syria and Jordan 1979–82; to Hungary 1982–85; Chief of Protocol of Can. 1985–89; Grand Cordon of the Order of Pius IX; Grand Cordon de l'Ordre du Cèdre (Lebanon); Knight Commander of the Order of St. Gregory the Great; Mem., Royal Commonwealth Soc.; Candn. Inst. for Internat. Affairs; Candn. Mediterranean Inst.; Hon. Mem., Assn. of Goldsmiths of Valenza (Italy); recreations: history, goldsmithing, travel; Home: 209 MacKay St., Ottawa, Ont. K1M 2B6; Office: Government House, Ottawa, Ont.

**ARCHAMBAULT, André,** B.A., B.Sc.Phm., D. Pharm.; educator; b. St. Antoine-sur-Richelieu, Que. 22 May 1928; s. Wilfrid and Aline (Jacques) A.; e. Univ. of Montreal, B.A. 1949, B.Sc. Phm. 1954; Univ. of Paris (Grad. studies and research in Biochem.), D.Pharm. (Rsch.) 1956; m. Fleur-Ange, d. late Rosario Chrétien, 2 Oct. 1954; two s.; PROF. OF HEALTH AND PHARMACY ADMIN., UNIV. OF MONTREAL 1981– ; Dir., Poulenc Canada Lté; Asst. Prof. of Biochem., Faculty of Pharm., Univ. of Montreal, 1956–60; Vice-Dean and Dir. of Studies, 1960; Assoc. Prof. of Biochem. and Dir. of Research, Univ. of Montreal, 1960–65, Prof. June 1965; Dean and Dir. of Studies (Pharm.), 1965–68; Pres., Comn. of Grad. Studies there, 1962–68; Vice-Pres., Academic, Univ. of Montreal 1968–80; Sabbatical leave, Dept. of Medical Care Organization, Univ. of Michigan 1980–81; mem. of Bd., Med. Research Council, P.Q. 1964–69; Dir., Candn. Foundation for Advanc. of Pharm. and three major teaching hospitals in Montreal; mem., Coll. of Pharmacists of Que. Prov.; Pres., Pharmacy Examining Bd. Can. 1987; Mem., Internat. Pharm. Fed.; Brit. Pharm. Comn.; Am. Assn. Coll. Pharm.; Candn. Acad. of Hist. of Pharm.; Am. Acad. of Hist. of Pharm.; Am. Pub. Health Assn.; many Candn. pharm. and scientific orgs.; mem. Conseil supérieur de l'éducation du Qué. 1968–76; Fellow, Am. Assn. Advanc. Science; Hon. mem., Am. Bd. of Diplomates in Pharm.; del. to a no. of Internat. Congs. (Pharm.); mem. Med. Rsch. Counc. of Can. 1986; consultant to various health and governmental orgns.; has rec'd a number of Hon. distinctions, prizes and memberships incl. Ltd. Gov's Medal of P.Q., Centennial Medal 1967; Publications: over 45 research papers and/or reports, over 75 prof. articles; Home: 650 Dollard, Outremont, Qué. H2V 3G3; Office: Faculty of Pharmacy, Univ. of Montreal, P.O. Box 6128, Stn. A, Montreal, Qué. H3C 3J7.

**ARCHAMBAULT, Louis,** O.C., B.A., D.B.A., A.R.C.; sculpteur; né Montréal 4 avril 1915; é. Coll. des Jésuites Jean-de-Brébeuf, Montréal; Ecole des Beaux-Arts; ép. Mariette Provost, 1941; enfants: Aubert, Eloi, Eve, Patrice; carrière pédagogique: à Montréal: Ecole du Meuble, Ecole du Musée des Beaux-Arts, Ecole des Beaux-Arts, Coll. Jean-de-Brébeuf, Univ. McGill, UQAM, Concordia; à Vancouver: U.B.C.; a reçu: Médaille des Arts connexes, Inst. Royal d'Architecture du Can. 1958; Diplôme d'Honneur, Conférence Canadienne Des Arts, 1982; expositions particulières: 'Les Sculptures Urbaines de Louis Archambault' Musée D'Art Contemporain, Montréal 1972; 'Essai de Renouvellement Formel de Quelques Symboles Mystiques,' Centre Culturel Canadien, Paris et itinèrante en Grande Bretagne 1980–81 (Ces cinq oeuvres sont aujourd'hui répertoriées dans la collection permanente du Musée des Beaux-Arts de Montréal); expositions collectives: Festivals de Gde-Bretagne, Londres, 1951; X[e] et XIe Triennale de Milan, 1954 et 1957; XXVIIIe Biennale de Venise, 1956; Internationale de Pittsburgh, 1958; 300 Ans d'Art Canadien, Musée des Beaux-Arts du Canada 1967; Exposition Internat. de Sculpture Contemporaine, Expo 67; Ve Expo Internat. de sculpture, Legnano, Milan, Italie, 1969; 11e Biennale de Middleheim, Anvers, 1971; Bourses: gouv. can., Séjour en France 1953–54; Conseil des Arts du Can., 1959, 1962 et 1969; Ministère de l'Education du Québec, recherche, 1969–70, 1970–71; Collaborations importantes: Pavillon du Can., Bruxelles 1958; aéroport d'Ottawa 1960; Place des Arts, Montréal 1963; aéroport de Toronto 1964; ésplanade, Galerie d'Art, Expo 67, Montréal; Pavillon du Can., Expo 67, Montréal; The Macdonald Block, Queen's Park, Toronto 1969; Palais de Justice de Québec, Québec 1983; Faculté de Médecine Vétérinaire, Univ. de Mtl., à St. Hyacinthe 1985; Centre d'accueil René Lévesque, Longueuil, Qc 1987; Centre hospitalier Anna Laberge, Chateauguay, Qué. 1989; Atelier; 278 avenue Sanford, St-Lambert, Qué. J4P 2X6.

**ARCHAMBAULT, Louis,** B.A., LL.B., F.T.C.I.; executive; b. Montreal, Que. 18 Dec. 1928; s Auguste and Georgette A.; e. Loyola Sch. Montreal; Coll. Ste-Marie, Montreal B.A. 1949; Univ. of Montreal LL.B. 1953, post-grad. Law Sch. 1954; m. Monique LL.L.d. late Paul-Emile Gagnon, Q.C. Rimouski, Que. 27 Aug. 1955; children: Nicole, Louis Jr., Marie; former Pres. & C.E.O., Trust Général du Canada 1978–82 (Dir. & mem. Extve. Comte. 1976–82); former Pres. and C.E.O., Sherbrooke Trust 1978–82 (Dir. & mem. Extve. Comte. 1978–82); former Dir. RoyNat; Prêt Ville-Marie Inc.; Canadian Equitable Corp.; Stérling Trust Corp.; called to Bar of Que. 1954; joined present co. as Legal Counsel 1955, Founding Mgr. Trois-Rivières Br. 1957, Mgr. Que. Br. 1966, Gen. Mgr. 1970, Extve. Vice Pres. and Gen. Mgr. 1976; mem. Law Faculty Council Univ. of Montreal; mem. Extve. Cloutier of Cap-de-la-Madeleine and Ste-Thérèse of Shawinigan Hosps.; Co-Founder Que. Heart Foundation (Quebec City 1967–68), Dir. 1970, Campaign Pres. Quebec City Sec. 1968–69; Fellow, Trust Co's Inst.; Pres. Young Bar Assn. Trois-Rivières 1964; mem. Counsel and Executive Comte.

Trust Co's Assn. Can. Que. Sec. (Secy. 1971–73, Treas. 1973–75, Vice Pres. 1975–77, Pres. 1977–79); R. Catholic; recreations: swimming, tennis; Clubs: Chambre de Comm.; St-Denis; St. James's Club of Montreal; Home: 90 Berlioz, #1603, Ile des Soeurs, Verdun, Qué. H3E 1N1.

**ARCHAMBAULT, Hon. Maurice;** b. St. Hyacinthe, P.Q. 5 Apr. 1914; s. Sylvanie and Emma (Beaudry) A.; e. Acad. du Sacré-Coeur, Granby, Qué.; Séminaire de St-Hyacinthe, B.A. 1935; Univ. of Montréal (Law) 1935–38; called to the Bar of Qué., 1938; cr. Q.C. 1950; m. Rolande, d. Aimé De Laboursodière, 8 June 1940; children: Nicole, Ghislaine, Andrée, Maryel, Louise; Justice, Superior Court of Que. 1962–89; retired since 5 Apr. 1989; Crown Prosecutor Dist. of Bedford, Que., 1950–60; formerly Counsel for many Mun. and Sch. Corps.; Pres., Rural Bar Assn. of P.Q., 1961; awarded Mérite universitaire, Univ. of Montréal; R. Catholic; recreations: golf, travel; Home: 115 Chemin de la Côte Ste-Catherine, app. 708, Outremont, Qué. H2V 4R3.

**ARCHAMBAULT, Monique,** B.C.L.; lawyer; b. Montreal, Que.; e. McGill Univ. B.C.L. 1981; called to Quebec Bar 1982; PARTNER, MARTINEAU WALKER 1990– ; Mgr., Treasury, Finan. Instruments for a major Candn. bank; Partner, Fasken Martineau Davis 1990– ; main practice: public & private internat. financing & off-balance-sheet finan. instruments; primary contact for Fasken Martineau Davis at Internat. Swap Dealers Assn.; Mem., Quebec Bar Assn.; Candn. Bar Assn.; Internat. Finance Club of Montreal; Quebec-Japan Business Forum; Japanese Soc. of Canada; recreations: skiing, horseback riding, flying (pilot); club: Aeroclub of Montreal; Office: Box 242, 3400 Stock Exchange Tower, Montreal, Qué. H4Z 1E9.

**ARCHDEACON, Maurice Dunstan;** federal public servant; b. Liverpool, UK 8 Jan. 1934; s. Robert Maurice and Henriette Rose (O'Toole) A.; e. St. Edward's Coll. Liverpool 1949; Univ. of London Inter., B.Sc. 1952; Aerospace Systems Winnipeg 1963; m. Jean Margaret d. Ronald and Edna Trory 19 Oct. 1957; children: Sally, Stephen, Phillip, Susan; EXEC. DIR., SECURITY INTELLIGENCE REVIEW CTTE. 1985– ; served with RAF 1952–56, Pilot; RCAF 1957–85, Pilot; Exec. Asst. to Chief Defence Staff 1975–77, 1977–80 (rank Col.); Chef de cabinet Chrmn. NATO Mil. Ctte. Brussels 1980–83 (Brig. Gen.); Dep. Asst. Sec. to Cabinet Foreign & Defence Policy 1983–85; mem. Prime Min.'s Peace Initiative Task Force 1983–84; mem. Council Advs. Centre for Global Security; mem. Mensa Can.; recreations: tennis, sailing, sail boarding, bridge; Clubs: Cercle de la Garnison de Québec; Home: 99 Fraser Beach, Aylmer, Qué. J9H 2H1; Office: P.O. Box 2430, Postal Station D, Ottawa, Ont. K1P 5W5.

**ARCHER, Angus McDonald,** B.A.; association executive; b. Ayr, Scot. 27 July 1942; s. John Gillies and Catherine Emma (McDonald) A.; e. Glenlyon Sch. for Boys Victoria; Fisher Park High Sch. Ottawa; Carleton Univ. B.A. 1963; EXEC. DIR. UN ASSN. IN CAN. 1989– ; Prog. Offr. Overseas Inst. Can. Ottawa 1963–66; Special Prog. Offr. Freedom From Hunger Campaign UN Food & Agric. Orgn. Rome 1966–69; Exec. Dir. Candn. Council Internat. Coop. Ottawa 1969–75; Coord. UN Non-Govt'al Liaison Service New York 1975–89; mem. Govt. Relations Ctte. YMCA; ed. 'Scanning Our Future' 1975; Home: 89 Ivy Cres., Ottawa, Ont. K1M 1Y1; Office: 808, 63 Sparks St., Ottawa, Ont. K1P 9Z9.

**ARCHER, Georges,** B.Sc.A., M.Sc., F.E.I.C., F.C.S.C.E.; consulting engineer; b. Quebec, Que. 20 Sept. 1938; s. Maurice and Cécile (Giroux) A.; e. Univ. of Ottawa B.A. 1956; Laval Univ. B.Sc.A. 1961; McGill Univ. M.Sc. 1964; m. Louise d. Gilles Payette 27 June 1970; children: Julie, Dominik; SENIOR PARTNER, ARCHER Consulting Engineers 1972– ; Pres. Standards Council of Can. 1984– ; mem. firm Lalonde, Valois, Consulting Engineers 1961; Cartier, Côté et Piette 1965–67; Surveyer, Nenniger et Chênevert 1968–70; Publ Works Can. 1971; served as Lt. Can. Artillery; Former Pres. Candn. German Chamber Ind. & Comm.; former Vice Pres. Eng. Inst. Can.; Mem. Bd. of Dirs., National Quality Institute 1993– ; Order of Engineers of Que.; Home: 72 Sunnyside, Westmount, Qué. H3Y 1C2.

**ARCHER, John Andrew,** B.A.; insurance and financial services broker, writer, columnist; b. Wrightville, Que. 26 Jan. 1959; s. George H. and Helen M. (Tingley) A.; e. McGill Univ. B.A. 1982; m. Hélène P. Hamel d. Roger and Louise Hamel 11 July 1987; one d.: Gabrielle; VICE-PRESIDENT, ARCHER DESORMEAU 1984– ; columnist, 'RRIF-Annuity Q & A' The Gazette Montreal 1993– ; Mem., Assn. des intermédiaires en assurance de personnes du Qué.; Annuity and RRIF Brokers Assn.; author: 'Understanding Annuities and RRIFs' 1992; and several newspaper articles & newsletters on retirement income options & mutual fund investing; recreations: badminton, golf, squash, tennis, composing music, piano, reading, writing; clubs: Montreal Badminton & Squash; Home: 322 Prince Albert Ave., Westmount, Que. H3Z 2N7; Office: 1827 Baile St., Montreal, Que. H3H 1P5.

**ARCHER, John H.,** O.C., S.O.M., B.L.S., M.A., Ph.D., D.C.L.; educator; b. Broadview, Sask. 11 July 1914; s. Charles H. and Mary (Archer) A.; e. Broadview (Sask.) High Sch.; Scott Coll. Inst., Regina, Sask.; Univ. of Sask., B.A. (Hons) 1947 and M.A. 1948; McGill Univ. Library Sch., B.L.S. 1949; Queen's, Ph.D. 1969; LL.D. Univ. of Regina 1981; D.C.L. Univ. of Emmanuel Coll. 1982; m. Alice Mary, d. late Leonard Widdup, Kipling, Sask., 24 Aug. 1939; children: John Widdup, Alice Mary-Lynn; Pres. Univ. of Regina 1974–76; Pres. Emeritus Univ. of Regina 1976; Saskatchewan Pres. Council for Can. Unity, 1979 (Pres. 1983); Queen's Silver Jubilee Medal, 1978; Off., Order of Can. 1981; Lt. Gov.'s Can. Heritage Foundation 1982; Sask. Order of Merit 1987; Candn. ed., Project Offr. Comn. on Govt. Organ. (Can.) 1961–62; Dir., Univ. Libs., McGill Univ.; Archivist and Assoc. Prof. of Hist., Queen's Univ. 1967–69; won Undergrad. Scholarship, Univ. of Sask., 1946 and Dafoe Scholarship 1947; served in 2nd World War, U.K. and Mediterranean Theatres 1940–45, 1st Candn. Survey Regt., R.C.A.; Comn. Overseas 1943; Hon. Col. 10th Fld. Reg't, R.C.A., Regina; author 'Historic Saskatoon,' 1948; 'Saskatchewan: A History' 1980; co-author 'The Story of a Province' (jr. hist. of Sask.) 1955; 'Footprints in Time: Saskatchewan' 1965; Ed. 'West of Yesterday,' 1965; 'Land of Promise' 1969; mem. Candn. Lib. Assn. (Pres. 1966–67); Chrmn. Comte. on Intellectual Freedom 1962–65; Res. Off., Freedom of Information Com., Sask. 1982; Dir., Candn. Centenary Council; mem. Candn. Hist. Assn.; Inst. Pub. Adm. of Can.; Candn. Citizenship Fed.; Royal Candn. Legion; Anglican; recreations: bridge, golf, football spectacles, curling; Clubs: Canadian; Men's University; Royal United Services Inst.; Inst. of Strategic Studies; Home: 1530 MacPherson Ave., Regina, Sask. S4S 4C9.

**ARCHER, Keith Allan,** M.A., Ph.D.; educator; b. Windsor, Ont. 28 Sept. 1955; s. John Gordon and Joan Marie (Cannon) A.; e. Kennedy Coll. Inst. 1974; Univ. of Windsor B.A. 1979, M.A. 1980; Duke Univ. Ph.D. 1985; m. M. Lisa d. Evelyn and Noah Hurst 17 Feb. 1979; children: Justin Noah David, Caitlin Hurst, Benjamin Reid, William Hurst, Isaiah Randall John; ASSOC. PROF. OF POL. SCI., UNIV. OF CALGARY 1988– ; Partner, Pollstar Research Inc., Calgary; R. Taylor Cole Instr. Duke Univ. 1983–84; Asst. Prof. present Univ. 1984; Visiting Prof. Univ. of P.E.I. 1990–91; Pres., Calgary Waldorf Sch.; Bd. of Dirs., Candn. Political Science Assn. 1993–95; author 'Political Choices and Electoral Consequences' 1990; co-author 'Canadian Political Life: An Alberta Perspective'; mem. Candn. Pol. Sci. Assn.; recreations: camping, handball, skiing, hiking; Home: 2403 Chicoutimi Dr. N.W., Calgary, Alta. T2L 0W2; Office: Dept. of Political Sci., Univ. of Calgary, Calgary, Alta. T2N 1N4.

**ARCHER, Brig.-Gen. Maurice,** M.B.E., C.M., E.D., B.Sc.; civil engineer; b. Quebec, Que., 4 Oct. 1910; s. Edouard and Juliette (Hudon) A.; e. Comm. Acad., Quebec City; Royal Mil. Coll., Kingston, Ont. (Grad. 1932); McGill Univ., B.Sc. (Civil Engn.), 1933; m. Cécile Giroux, d. Jean-Baptiste Giroux, 22 Oct. 1937; children: Georges, Joan, Edouard, André, Isabelle; Sr. Vice-Pres. Candn. Nat. Railways, 1971–76 (Vice Pres. Research & Devel. 1963–71); Mount Royal Rice Mills Ltd.; Consulting Engr. with Archer & Dufresne, Quebec City (except for war yrs.) 1937–52; Vice-Chrmn., Nat. Harbours Bd., July 1952–58, Chrmn., 1958–61; Extve. Asst. to Pres., E. G.M. Cape & Co. Ltd., 1961–63; served in 2nd World War in 4 M.E.D. Regt., R.C.A. in N.W. Europe; awarded M.B.E.; Pres., Royal Candn. Arty. Assn., 1954; Fellow, Engn. Inst. Can., mem. Corp. Prof. Engrs., Que., Roman Catholic; recreations: golf, tennis; Home: Stockwell St., C.P. 803, Knowlton, Qué. J0E 1V0.

**ARCHER, Richard Elliott,** B.Comm.; financial executive; b. Winnipeg, Man. 2 Feb. 1940; s. Edgar J.B. and Gunda L. (Bloomquist) A.; e. Univ. of Man., B.Comm. (Hons.) 1962; m. Elaine d. James and Gertrude Adair 27 Nov. 1964; children: Chris, Tim, Colleen; EXTVE. VICE-PRES., INVESTMENTS & TRUST, INVESTORS GROUP 1987– ; Vice-Pres. Investments, The Monarch Life Assur. Co. 1978–83; Pres., Investors Syndicate Realty Ltd. 1983–86; Sr. Vice-Pres. Investments, present firm 1986–87; Chrmn., Man. Civil Serv. Superannuation Bd.; Dir., Winnipeg Enterprises Corp.; Winnipeg Jets Hockey Club; C.F.A.; recreations: squash, tennis, golf; Clubs: Manitoba; Winnipeg Squash & Racquet; St. Charles Country; Home: 46 River Rd., Winnipeg, Man.; Office: One Canada Centre, 447 Portage Ave., Winnipeg, Man. R3C 3B6.

**ARCHER, Violet B.,** C.M., D.Mus.; composer; educator; pianist; organist; university professor; adjudicator; b. Montreal, P.Q. 24 Apr. 1913; d. Balestreri Cesare Angelo and Beatrice (Azzi) A.; e. McGill Univ., Teacher's Licentiate in Piano, 1934, B.Mus. 1936; Yale Univ., B.Mus. 1948, M.Mus. 1949; McGill Univ., D.Mus. (Hon.) 1971; Instr. in Music, McGill Univ. 1943–47; Resident Composer, N. Texas State Coll., Denton, Texas, 1950–53; visiting Prof. of Music, Cornell Univ. 1952; Asst. Prof. of Music, Univ. of Oklahoma 1953–61; Assoc. Prof. of Music, Univ. of Alberta, 1962, Prof. there 1970–78, Prof. Emeritus since 1978; Chrmn. Div. Theory and Composition 1962–1978, Composer in residence, Banff School of Fine Arts 1978, 79; Co-ordinator of Music Programs for 'Canada Music Week' and 'International Music Day' in Edmonton since 1962; Mem. Adv. Bd., Celebration of Women in the Arts, Edmonton, Alta. 1988– ; works have been performed at Internat. Festival of Edinburgh, Brussels World Fair, Osaka Festival (Japan), Expo 67, Stratford Shakespearean Festival, Vancouver Festival, also throughout Can., U.S., France, Belgium, Switzerland, Eng., Ireland, Scotland, Italy, Spain, Portugal, Germany, Finland, Austria, Czechoslovakia, Russia, Israel, China, Japan, Australia, New Zealand, Thailand, Chile, Greece, Hungary, Poland, Estonia, Latvia, Lithuania, the Ukraine, and in several networks in these countries incl. many Composers' Symposia in U.S.; comnd. by Internat. House of New Orleans for 1st Inter-Am. Music Festival (1st Candn.) 'Trio for Piano, Violin and Cello' in 1958; by Montreal Brass Quintet for 100th concert of Sarah Fischer Series, 'Divertimento for Brass Quintet,' 1963; by C.B.C. (1964, '65, '67, '72, '78, '80, '81, '84, '85, '87, '88); by Can. Council (1965, '78, '79, '92); by Montreal Jr. Symphony Orchestra, Edmonton Symph. Orch., and Saskatoon Symph. Orch. etc.; composer numerous works (chamber, orchestral, opera, keyboard, organ, choral, songs a capella, electronic music and others); awarded Composition Trophy, Que. Music Festival Competition 1939; won several scholarships and awards from 1948–59; Charles Ditson Fellowship, Yale Univ. 1948; Woods-Chandler prize for composition, Yale Univ., 1949; Ladies' Morning Musical Club of Montreal, 1949 (for work abroad); rec'd Fellowship, MacDowell Colony, Peterborough, N.H. 1956; Can. Council Sr. Fellowship, 1958–59; nominated recipient of Alumni Award for distinguished service in field of music by Extve. Comte., Yale Sch. of Music Alumni Assn. 1968; rec'd Merit Award, Govt. Alta. for contrib. to music in Prov., 1971; Queen's Jubilee Silver Medal 1978; award for Outstanding Music 1980–81; Performing Rights Org. of Can. Award for Outstanding Success in the Concert Music Fields 1981; Award of Merit, McGill Alma Mater Fund 1982; 125th Anniversary, Candn. Confederation, Commemorative Medal 1992; The Violet Archer Fellowship named in her honour by the Dept. of Music, Univ. of Alta. 1992; author over 60 articles on music in journs., publications, incl. 'Prelude and Allegro for Violin & Piano' 1954; 'Fanfare and Passacaglia for Orchestra' 1956; 'Three Sketches for Orchestra' 1966; 'Sonata for Clarinet and Piano' 1973; 'Sganarelle' (opera) 1973; 'Psalmody' (for orchestra, chorus and baritone voice) 1978; 'Sonata for Alto Saxophone and Piano' 1972; 'Sonata for Oboe and Piano' 1973; 'Four Duets for Violin and Cello,' 1979; 'Piano Sonata No. 2' 1979; two film scores: 'Someone Cares' 1977; 'Whatsoever Things Are True' 1980; many Song Cycles 1979–83; 'String Quartet no. 3' 1981; opera 'The Meal' 1983; 'Ikpakhuaq' for violin, cello & piano 1985; 'Miniatures from the Chinese' and 'Epigrams' (song cycles for tenor voice & piano) 1985; 'Divertimento' (for piano and string orch.) 1985; 'Improvisations on a Name' for chamber orchestra 1987; 'Carillon for a Festal Day' 1988; 'Evocations' for Two Pianos and Orchestra 1988 (Russian première, Kiev Festival of Ukrainian and Internat. Composers 1990 and performed on Kiev Radio 1990); 'Four Miniatures' for classical accordion 1988; 'Three Essays' for solo soprano and alto saxophone 1988; 'Variations on an Original Theme' for violin and piano 1988; 'Twenty-third Psalm and Ninety-sixth Psalm,' anthems for a cappella mixed choir 1988; 'The Ninety-eighth Psalm' for a cappella SATB 1989; 'Four Dialogues for Classical Guitar and Chamber Orchestra' 1989; 35 compositions recorded commercially; 83 works published; more than 293 works composed; mem., Candn. League of Composers; Music Educators' Nat'l Conf. Assoc.(U.S.A.); Internat. Folk Music Council; Candn. Folk Music Soc.; Am. Music Centre; Candn. Music Centre; Edmonton Musician's Assn.; Candn. Fed. Music Teachers; Alta. Reg'd

Music Teachers' Assn., Assn. Acad. Staff of Univ. of Alta., Candn. Univs. Music Soc.; Edmonton Chamber Music Soc.; Composer member, Frau und Musik, Internationaler Arbeitskreis (Cologne, Germany) 1979; Amer. Soc. of Univ. Composers; Amer. Women Composers Inc.; Soc. of Composers Inc., U.S.A.; Assoc. of Can. Women Composers; Candn. Music Educators' Soc.; Founder and Vice Pres., Edmonton Composers' Concert Soc.; D.Mus. (hon. causa), McGill Univ. 1971; rec'd Creative & Performing Award from City of Edmonton 1972; nominated Life Academic Member, Accademia Tiberina of Rome, Italy 1979; Honour Certificate for contribution to Alta's Musical Heritage 1980; Special Award in honour of outstanding contribution to the cultural life of Alta., presented by Celebration of Women in the Arts 1983; Hon. Life Mem., Latitude 53, Soc. of Artists 1983; mem. Order of Canada 1983; chosen 'Composer of the Year,' Candn. Music Counc. 1984; Hon. Fellow, Royal Candn. Coll. of Organists 1985; ornamental park named in her honour, Edmonton 1985; 'The Violet Archer Festival' Edmonton 1985 (a festival entirely of her music, the first Candn. composer and the first North Am. female composer to have been thus honoured); Mus.D(oc.) hon. causa: McGill Univ. 1971, Univ. of Windsor 1986, Mt. Allison Univ. 1992; Cultural Hall of Fame, City of Edmonton 1987; Hon. mem., Candn. Music Centre 1987; awarded Sir Frederick Haultain Prize, Govt. of Alta., for excellence as a composer, educator, performer 1987; Special Mention for contribution to the promotion of Candn. Music awarded by Candn. Music Counc. 1989; Hon. LL.D., Univ. of Calgary 1989; Life Achievement Award, 'On behalf of all Albertans in Recognition of Outstanding Contbn. in the Arts in Alta.' CBC and Prov. of Alta. 1990; Candn. Music Centre - Prairie Region 10th Anniv. Citation Honouring 'Outstanding Contributions of Violet Archer' 1990; Presidential Serv. Award, Candn. Fed. of Music Teachers' Assn. 1991; Candn. Univ. Music Soc. honours Violet Archer, Queen's Univ. 1991; The McGill Alma Mater Fund Award of Merit in appreciation of 20 yrs of active service on behalf of the Alma Mater Fund 1991; subject of 'Violet Archer – A Bio-Bibliography' by Dr. Linda Hartig 1991; included in publication 'Contemporary Composers' 1992; Hon. Mem. Sigma Alpha Iota; Home: 10805–85th Ave., Edmonton, Alta. T6E 2L2.

**ARCHIBALD, Adams Gordon,** O.C., B. Com., D.C.L., LL.D.; retired public utility executive; b. Truro, N.S. 7 Jan. 1911; s. Harry Adams and Wilanna (Archibald) A.; e. Colchester Co. Acad., 1924–27; Dalhousie Univ., B.Com. 1933; m. Marion Dean, d. George D. Muggah, 14 Sept. 1938; children: Mrs. Murray Fraser, David Dean, George Gordon, William Harry; Chrmn., ICG Scotia Gas Ltd. 1979–93, retired; Dir., Dover Industries Ltd.; joined Maritime Telegraph & Telephone Co. Ltd. 1934 as a Salesman; Chief Clrk. in Sydney, N.S. 1935–38, trans. to Amherst, N.S. as Local Mgr., Feb. 1939; trans. to H.O. as Comm. Supervisor, Feb. 1940; apptd. Gen. Comm. Mgr. 1943, Gen. Plant Mgr. 1956, Gen. Mgr. 1958, Vice-Pres. 1959, Pres. 1963, Chrmn. and Pres. 1968, Chrmn. and C.E.O. 1975, Chrmn. 1976–81; Chrmn., Bd. of Govs., Dalhousie Univ. 1980–85; Pres., Candn. Chamber of Comm. 1970–71; Hon. Pres. Halifax YMCA; Chrmn. Scottish Societies Assn. of N.S. 1978–89; Chrmn., Victorian Order of Nurses, Halifax 1988; United Church; Hobbies: riding, fishing, skiing; Clubs: Halifax; Saraquay; Home: 63 Wyndrock Dr., Halifax, N.S. B3P 2N7; Office: PO Box 880, Halifax, N.S. B3J 2W3.

**ARCHIBALD, George Christopher,** M.A., B.Sc.(Econ.), F.R.S.C.; economist; b. Glasgow, Scot. 30 Dec. 1926; s. George, Lord Archibald of Woodside and Dorothy Holroyd (Edwards), Lady Archibald of Woodside; e. Phillip's Exeter Acad. 1943; King's Coll. Cambridge B.A. 1945, M.A. 1950; London Sch. of Econ. & Pol. Sci. B.Sc.(Econ.) 1951; m. Daphne d. George Henham 1971; EMERITUS PROF. OF ECONOMICS, UNIV. OF B.C. 1991, Prof. 1971–91; Lectr. in Econ., Univ. of Otago 1952–55; Leon Research Fellow, Univ. of London 1955–56; Asst. Lectr. and Lectr., London Sch. of Econ. 1956–64; Reader, Univ. of Essex 1964–67, Prof. 1967–71; Visiting Assoc. Prof., Univ. of Calif. Berkeley 1962–63; Visiting Prof. and Ford Foundation Faculty Fellow, Northwestern Univ. 1967–68; Visiting Prof., Univ. of B.C. 1970–71, Killam Sr. Fellow 1975–76; Can. Council Killam Fellow 1981, 1982; co-author 'Introduction to a Mathematical Treatment of Economics' 1967, 3rd ed. 1977; U.S.A. ed. 'Introduction to Mathematical Economics' 1976; ed. 'The Theory of the Firm' 1971; 'Information, Incentives and the Economics of Control' 1992; author over 40 papers learned jours.; Fellow, Econometric Soc.; recreations: fishing, gardening; Office: U.K.

**ARCHIBALD, Harold David,** C.M., M.S.W., D.Sc., F.R.H.S.; association executive; b. Truro, N.S. 22 July 1919; s. Harry Adams and Willanna A.; e. Colchester Co. Acad. Truro 1936; N.S. Agric. Coll. Truro 1939; Univ. of W. Ont. B.A. (Social Science) 1946; Univ. of Toronto M.S.W. 1948; Acadia Univ. D.Sc. 1974; m. Ruth d. William and Ethel May Jackman 31 Aug. 1946; children: Lynda, Janet, Gordon, Susan; PAST CHAIRMAN, CANADIAN CENTRE ON SUBSTANCE ABUSE 1989– ; Past Pres., Internat. Counc. on Alcohol & Addictions 1981– ; Chrmn., Royal Commn. to Enquire into Illicit Drugs and Alcohol, Govt. of Bermuda 1983–84; Consultant, World Health Organ. and various internat. organs. 1954– ; Chrmn., Jellinek Memorial Fund; Consultant, Govt. of Can. for Development of Nat. Policy & Program on Alcohol & Illicit Drugs 1987; Chrmn., Archibald Task Force, National Drug Program, Can.; founded Addiction Research Foundation 1949 and served as Extve. Dir. 27 yrs. becoming Extve. Vice Chrmn. 1976; Dir. Development, Nat. Drug Strategy, Govt. of Bermuda 1990–91; Consultant to govts. in Can., U.S.A., Europe, S.E. Asia, Latin Am. and Caribbean Region; one-man comn. (W.H.O.) Thailand re devel. programs to provide health care in jungle region; mem. Internat. Bd. on Alcohol, Drugs & Traffic Safety; Co-Founder and Hon. Life mem. Candn. Addictions Foundation; Past Pres. Alcohol & Drug Problems Assn. N.Am.; Assoc. Ed. 'Journal on Alcoholism and Related Addictions' (Yugoslavia); mem. Ed. Bd. 'Excerpta Medica Foundation' (The Netherlands); mem. Senate Univ. of Toronto 1960–71; named Man of Yr. Alcohol & Drug Problems Assn. N.Am. 1971; recipient Distinguished Service Award Candn. Addictions Foundation 1975; Candn. Centennial Medal 1967; Queen's Silver Jubilee Medal 1977; Edward W. Browning Achievement Award 1980; E.M. Jellinek Memorial Award 1986; apptd. Mem., Bd. of Fame, Univ. of Toronto 1992; Member, Order of Canada 1989; Annual H. David Archibald Lecture Series F Distinguished Rsch. in the Addictions, estab. 1993; mem. Candn. Pub. Health Assn.; Am. Assn. Advanc. Science; United Church; recreations: fishing, boating, carpentry; Clubs: Canadian; Empire; Home: #603 - 1300 Bloor St., Mississauga, Ont. L4Y 3Z2; Office: 33 Russell St., Toronto, Ont. M5S 2S1.

**ARCHIBALD, Raymond Douglas,** B.A., LL.B.; barrister and solicitor; b. Saskatoon, Sask. 10 Mar. 1921; s. Raymond and Jane (McPhee) A.; e. Univ. of Sask., B.A. 1940 and LL.B. 1942; m. Jocelyn Fallis, d. W.G. Yule, Regina, Sask., 24 Mar. 1945; children: Peter D., Edna Jane, Jocelyn Joan; retired Partner, Lang Michener Lawrence & Shaw; read law with Estey, Moxon & Schmidt, Saskatoon, Sask.; called to Bar of Sask. 1945 & Ont. 1972; Secy., Dom. Textile Co. Ltd., 1951–60; Vice-Pres. and Gen. Mgr., Caldwell Linen Mills Ltd. 1960–69; retired Dir., CBS Records Canada Ltd.; CBS Broadcast International of Canada Ltd.; Central States Can of Canada Ltd.; Canadian Locker Co. Ltd.; EMI April Music (Canada) Ltd.; EMI Blackwood Music (Canada) Ltd.; served in 2nd World War with Calgary Tank Regt. and Candn. Grenadier Guards as Lieut.; wounded in action at Falaise, 1944; mem., Law Soc. of Upper Can. (retired); The Royal Cdn. Legion; H.R.H. Duke of Edinburgh's Study Conf. Oxford 1956; United Church; recreation: golf; Home: 16 Victoria St., Iroquois, Ont. K0E 1K0.

**ARCHIBALD, Thomas Ross,** B.A., M.B.A., Ph.D., F.C.A.; educator, researcher, writer; b. Toronto, Ont. 29 May 1935; s. Thomas and Janet McPherson (Laidlaw) A.; e. John L. Forster C.I.; Univ. of W. Ont. B.A. (Hons.) 1958; Inst. of C.A.s of Ont. C.A. 1961; Univ. of Chicago M.B.A. 1964, Ph.D. 1969; m. Yvonne Salisbury d. Christopher and Barbara Mortimer 14 May 1966; children: Nicole Jane, Jennifer Lynne; PROFESSOR, WESTERN BUSINESS SCHOOL, UNIV. OF W. ONT. 1966– ; Audit Staff, Clarkson Gordon 1958–62; Research Assoc., Univ. of Chicago 1963–66; Technical Serv., Price Waterhouse 1978–79; Co-ord., Managerial Acctg. & Control Area Group 1968–70, 1974–92; Founding Course Dir., Mngt. for Acctg. & Financial Executives 1975–82; Co-ord., Gender Equity Ctte., Western Bus. Sch. 1989–92; Founding Pres., C.A. Students' Assn. of W. Ont. 1960–61; Bd. of Examiners, Candn. Inst. of C.A.s 1969–72; Technical Advisor, Acct. Standards Ctte. 1982–86; Edn. Ctte., Inst. of C.A.s Ont. 1982– ; Comm. Corp. Rep., Financial Extves. Inst. Can. 1991– ; Financ. Extve. Rsch. Found. Rsch. Consortium 1992– ; Sr. Wrestling Champion, 167 lbs., CIAU 1957; Bus. Sch. Hon. Award, UWO 1958; Doctoral Program Fellow, Univ. of Chicago 1963–66; Walter J. MacDonald Memorial Award 1971; Fellow, Inst. of C.A.s of Ont. 1973; Dir., FEIC, S.W. Ont. Ch. 1980–82; Consultant to over 30 private & public sector orgns.; Mem., Candn. Inst. of C.A.s; Inst. of C.A.s of Ont.; Am. Acct. Assn.; Candn. Acad. Acctg. Assn.; Fin. Extve. Inst. Can.; Pacioli Soc. 1992; Soc. for Acad. Freedom & Scholarship 1993; author: 'Accounting for Pension Costs and Liabilities' 1980 and over 30 rsch. papers; co-author: 'Survey of Pension Plans in Canada' 7th ed. 1988, 8th ed. 1990, 9th ed. 1992, 'The Management of Change in the Canadian Securities Industry' (8 vols) 1972–77; recreations: running, birding, nordic skiing; clubs: Delta Upsilon Alumni Assn. (Treas. 1969–84), Univ. Club of London (Pres. 1975–76); Home: 9 Woodgate Court, London, Ont. N6K 4A3; Office London, Ont. N6A 3K7.

**ÁRDAL, Páll Steinthórsson,** M.A., Ph.D., D.Phil.; educator; b. Akureyri, Iceland 27 June 1924; s. Steinthór Pálsson and Hallfridur (Hannesdóttir) A.; e. Menntaskolinn A Akureyri 1944; Univ. of Edinburgh M.A. 1949, M.A. (Hons.) 1953, Ph.D. 1961; D.Phil. (hon. causa), Univ. of Iceland 1991; m. Harpa Asgrimsdottir d. late Asgrimur Petursson 7 Sept. 1946; children: Hallfridur, Maja, Steinthór, Grimur; JOHN AND ELLA G. CHARLTON PROF. OF PHILOS., QUEEN'S UNIV. 1981– ; teacher Menntaskolinn Á Akureyri 1944–45, 1949–51; Univ. of Edinburgh 1955–69; Visiting Prof. Dartmouth Coll. 1963, 1971; Visiting Prof., Univ. of Toronto 1966; Prof. of Philos. Queen's Univ. 1969–81; author 'Passion and Value in Hume's Treatise' 1966 (2nd ed. in paper 1989); 'Sidferdi Og Mannlegt Edli (Virtue and Human Nature)' Reykjavik, Iceland, 1982; various book chapters, papers, reviews, critical studies; book ed.; mem. Hume Soc.; Candn. Philos. Assn.; Parkinson Foundation Can. (Past Pres. Kingston Chapter); NDP; Lutheran; recreation: bridge; Home: 277 Welborne Ave., Kingston, Ont. K7M 4G7; Office: Kingston, Ont.

**ARDELL, William E.,** B.Com.; retail executive; b. Calgary, Alta. 14 February 1944; s. Wilbert D. and Marjorie T. (Kells); e. Lower Canada Coll. 1962; Sir George Williams Univ., B.Com. 1966; Harvard A.M.P. 1989; m. Sherry d. Randal and Marguerite Dumoret, 24 Sept. 1966; children: Randal, Keleigh; PRESIDENT, C.E.O. & DIR., SOUTHAM INC. 1992– ; Nat. Merchandising Mgr., Spalding Canada 1968–78; Vice-Pres. & Gen. Mgr., Shakespeare Canada 1978; Nat. Sales Mgr., T.S. Simms 1978–79; Gen. Mgr., Graphic Web 1979–82; Pres. & C.E.O., Coles Book Stores 1982–90; Pres. & C.E.O., Southam Business Communications Inc. 1990–91; Exec. V.P. & C.O.O. Southam Inc. 1991–92; Chrmn., ABC CANADA (Literacy Found.); recreations: squash, skiing, golf; Home: 20 Oriole Gardens, Toronto, Ont. M4V 1V7; Office: 1450 Don Mills Rd., Don Mills, Ont. M3B 2X7.

**ARDIEL, June Victoria M.,** M.A.; advertising executive; b. London, Ont. 24 May 1921; d. late John Joseph Lorne and Daisy Blanche (Robinson) A.; e. Bishop Strachan Sch., Toronto, Ont. (Grad. 1939); University Coll., Univ. of Toronto, B.A. (Fine Art) 1943, M.A. 1968; PRES., JUNE ARDIEL LTD.; Dir., Leidra Lands Ltd.; Toronto Mutual Ins. Co.; joined Ardiel Advertising Agency Ltd. in 1943 as a Junior; former Creative Dir., Delta Delta Delta; Anglican; recreations: painting, reading; Club: Granite; Home: 33 Harbour Sq., Apt. 410, Toronto, Ont. M5J 2G2.

**ARENDS, Ronald George,** B.A.Sc., M.B.A., P.Eng.; manufacturing executive; b. Toronto, Ont. 11 Mar. 1945; s. Richard and Violet May (Cupit) A.; e. East York Coll., Toronto, Ont. Sr. Matric. 1963; Univ. of Toronto B.A.Sc. Ind. Engr. 1967; M.B.A. 1969; Harvard Univ. Grad. Sch. of Bus. Admin., Advanced Mgmt. Prog. 1984; m. Janet d. Ward and Mae Hallman 14 June 1968; children: Kirk, Jason; Pres., Tremco Ltd. 1988–94; Profl. Football player, Toronto Argonauts 1966–71; Honeywell Controls 1967–68; joined Canada Wire and Cable Ltd. 1968, Vice-Pres. 1977–80, Exec. Vice-Pres. 1980–87; Exec. Vice Pres., present co. 1987–88; Dir. Electrical and Electronic Mfrs. Assn. of Can. 1984–87; mem. Assn. of Profl. Engrs. of Ont.; Univ. of Toronto Alumni; Harvard Bus. Sch. Alumni; Profl. Engr. 1969; Home: R.R. #1, Claremont, Ont. L0H 1E0.

**ARÈS, Georges Armand,** B.A., LL.B.; lawyer; b. Zénon Park, Sask. 6 Jan. 1944; s. Louis Aimé and Anna (Courteau) A.; e. St. Francis Xavier High Sch. Edmonton; Coll. St. Jean Edmonton B.A. 1966; Univ. of Ottawa LL.B. 1970; children: Chantal, Laurent, François, Mireille; Partner, Arès & Lynass 1984–88; Pres. Arès Food Services Ltd.; articled with Brower Johnson law firm Edmonton 1970–71, Assoc. 1971–73; called to Bar of Alta. 1971; Assoc. and Partner Durocher Arès Manning & Lynass 1974–84; Pres. and Dir.: Caisse Francalta Credit Union Ltd. Edmonton 1972–76; Centre d'Expérience Pre-Scolaire 1980–84; Soc. de Parents pour les Écoles Francophones d'Edmonton 1984–86; Pres. Assn. Canadienne Française de l'Alberta 1986–89; Treas. and Dir. Comm. Nationale des Parents Francophone 1985–88; Extve. Dir., Assn. Canadienne Française de l'Alberta 1990– ; R. Catholic; recreations: travel, reading; Office: 200, 8923 – 82 Ave., Edmonton, Alta. T6C 0Z2.

**ARGYLE, A. Raymond;** communications executive; b. St. Boniface, Man. 4 Sept. 1929; s. late Percy and Katherine (Connor) A.; e. Creston (B.C.) Elem. Sch. and Creston Valley High Sch.; m. Marie d. late Andrew and Helen Holowack 2 Sept. 1950; three d. Sharon, Brenda, Roanne; PRES. & CHRMN., ARGYLE COMMUNICATIONS INC. 1979– ; Reporter, Regina Leader-Post 1950; News Ed. South Edmonton Sun 1950–51; W. Mgr. British United Press 1952–54, Business Mgr. Toronto 1955–58; Ed. and Mgr. Toronto Telegram Syndicate 1959–69; Gen. Mgr. Inland Publishing Co. (subs. Telegram Corp.) 1967–69; Vice Pres. and Gen. Mgr. Carleton Cowan Public Relations (div. MacLaren Advertising) 1969–71; Pres. The Argyle Syndicate Ltd. 1971–76; Prin., Tisdall Clark & Partners 1977–79; Chrmn., Industry Strategies Inc. 1986–90; Informedia Inc. 1987–90; OEB Internat. Ltd. 1989–90; Pres., Video Marketers of Canada Ltd. 1989–90; Chrmn., XII Public Relations World Congress 1991; Sec.-Treas. Found. Advanc. Candn. Letters 1976– ; Trustee Scarborough Bd. Edn. 1974–78; Pres.: Cand. Prof. Chapter Sigma Delta Chi 1965–68; York-Scarborough Lib. Assn. 1974–75; Dir. Candn. Pub. Relations Soc. 1978–79; author 'Canadian Issues Analysis' 1984–87; Ed. 'Education Reports ' 1977–79; Ed., 'Communications in the New Millennium' 1991; Mem. of the Bd., Internat. Public Relations Assoc.; mem., Candn. Publ. Relations Soc.; Inst. of Corporate Dirs. in Can.; recreations: boating, fishing; Club: Toronto Press; Home: 109 Collingsbrook Blvd., Agincourt, Ont. M1W 1M5; Office: 2 Berkeley St., Toronto, Ont. M5A 2W3.

**ARIANO, Louis Raymond,** B.A., M.A.; university administrator; b. Sault Ste. Marie, Ont. 7 Oct.1954; s. Raymond V. and Gabrielle L. (Charron) A.; e. Gonzaga Univ. B.A. 1981; Univ.of Regina M.A. 1988; m. Carol d. Herbert and Juliette Powell 1 Aug. 1981; children: Tara Christina, Leah Janine; REGISTRAR, BROCK UNIVERSITY 1993– ; Instructor, Sask. Indian Fed. Coll., Univ. of Regina 1981–82; Registrar 1982–89; Assoc. Registrar (Services), Brock Univ. 1989–93; Mem., Assn. of Registrars of the Univs. & Colleges of Can. (Member-at-large 1984–88; Sec.-Treas. 1988–90); Ont. Univ. Registrars Assn.; Am. Assn. of Coll. Registrars & Admission Officers; recreations: officiating ringette, reading; Home: 26 Crestcombe Rd., St. Catharines, Ont. L2S 2J4; Office: St. Catharines, Ont. L2S 3A1.

**ARISS, Herbert Joshua;** painter; art teacher; b. Guelph, Ont. 29 Sept. 1918; s. William Minno and Wilhemina Helen (Zinger) A.; e. Toronto (Ont.) Public and High Schs., Ont. Coll. of Educ. (1947); Ont. Coll. of Art (1940); m. Margot Joan, d. Earl D. Phillips, London, Ont., 5 July 1950; two s. Joshua Herbert Jr., Jeffrey Earl; began as Designer for Vibra-Lite Co. (outdoor adv.); Illustrator and book Designer, Copp Clark, Macmillans, Longmans, Green, etc., 1947–62; Head of Art Dept., H.B. Beal Secondary School, London, Ont., 1966; taught painting, Doon Sch. of Fine Arts, 1952–56; Lect. widely throughout Ont. to art socs., awarded Can. Council Sr. Fellowship for Painting, 1960–61; served in 2nd World War with Candn. Army (Engrs.), 1942–46; Trustee, London Lib. & Art Museum, 1956–59; rep. in colls. of Nat. Gallery, Ottawa, Art Gallery of Toronto, London Art Gallery, Winnipeg Art Gallery, ACA Gallery, Calgary, Alta., Vancouver Art Gallery, N.B. Museum, Saint John, N.B., etc., mem., Ont. Soc. Artists; Candn. Soc.Painters in Water Colour (2nd Vice-Pres.) Candn. Group of Painters; Past Pres., Western Art League; Candn. Graphic Arts; el. to Roy. Candn. Acad. of Arts 1978; Anglican; Address: 770 Leroy Crescent, London, Ont. N5Y 4G7.

**ARKELL, Hon. Kenneth Frederick,** B.A., LL.B.; judge; b. Calgary, Alta. 6 Dec. 1930; s. Frederick Peter and Charlotte Lorimer Daisy (Scotchmer) A.; e. Hillhurst High Sc. Calgary; Clinton (Ont.) Coll. Inst.; Univ. of W. Ont. B.A. 1956; Univ. of B.C. LL.B. 1959; m. Olivia d. Jesse and Tone Tofteland 23 July 1960; children: Kathryn Ann, Frederick James, Karyn Jane, Thomas Jesse; JUSTICE, SUPREME COURT OF B.C. 1990– ; served with RCMP 1950–52; played Professional Football, B.C. Lions 1956–59; called to Bar of B.C. 1960; Alta. 1970; Partner, Lewin, Arkell & Callison, City Solr. & Prosecutor City of Dawson Creek 1960–69; Dist. Judge, Prov. Court of B.C. 1970–72, Dep. Chief Judge 1972–75; Assoc. Chief Judge 1975–76; Co. Court Judge & Local Judge Supreme Court of B.C. 1976–90; mem. and Vice Chrmn. Judicial Council B.C. 1970–76; Vice Chrmn. and Trustee St. Joseph's Hosp. Bd. 1962–71; mem. Vernon Jubilee Hosp. Bd. 1971–72; Dir. John Howard Soc. 1971–73; Judicial Council Study & Report on Role & Salaries Prov. Court Judges; drafted Prov. Court Act 1975; Hon. mem. Royal Candn. Legion; Pres. Dawson Creek C. of C. 1966–67; Pres. Cariboo Bar Assn. 1968; mem. Candn. Bar Assn. (Council B.C. Sect. 1968–70); Candn. Inst. Adm. Justice; Candn. Judges Conf.; Kappa Alpha; recreations: golf, skiing; Clubs: Kalamalka Country; Vernon Golf & Country; Office: Courthouse, 3001 – 27th St., Vernon, B.C. V1T 4W5.

**ARLESS, Steven George,** B.Sc. (Chem.); executive; b. Montréal, Qué. 23 July 1949; s. George and Laurice (Shadeed) A.; e. McGill Univ. B.Sc. (Chem.) 1971; m. Lina Simard 8 Dec. 1979; one s. Dustin, one d. Anne Michelle; Pres., Consulmed Inc. 1990– ; Product Mgr. Burroughs Wellcome Inc. 1971–74; joined Smith & Nephew Inc. 1974 serving as Mktg. Devel. Exec., Mktg. Mgr., Vice Pres. Mktg. & Sales and Pres. 1986–90; named Chrmn. of Yr. Advertising & Sales Execs. Club Montréal 1984; Bd. of Dirs.: Candn. Wholesale Drug Assn. 1989, 1990; MEDEC 1987, 1988, 1989, 1990; Candn. Advanced Technology Assoc. 1989; recreations: tennis, squash, skiing, biking; Clubs: Southwest I Racquet; Summerlea Golf; Home: 10 Garrison Lane, Beaconsfield, Qué. H9W 5C2.

**ARLUK, George;** sculptor; b. Winnipeg, Man. 5 May 1949; 50 group exbns. incl. most recent: l'Iglou Art Esquimau, Douai (toured 17 cities) France 1987–91, Snow Goose Assoc. Seattle, Wa. 1991, Maison Hamel-Bruneau Ste-Foy, Que. 1990–91, Images of the North San Francisco, Ca. 1990, Feheley Fine Arts Toronto 1990, Candn. Mus. of Civilization Hull, Que. 1990; solo exbns.: Northern Reflections Eskimo Art Gall. La Jolla, Ca. 1988, Inuit Galerie Mannheim, Germany 1982, Candn. Guild of Crafts Que. Montreal 1980, Images of the North San Francisco, Ca. 1979, The Innuit Gall. of Eskimo Art Toronto 1972, Univ. of Alberta 1969, Winnipeg Art Gall. 1968; works in 17 collections incl. art galleries of Ontario (Klamer Family, Sarick and Williamson colls.), Vancouver, Winnipeg (Millard, Swinton and Twomey colls.), Candn. Mus. of Civilization, Eskimo Mus. Churchill, Man., Inuit Cultural Inst. Rankin Inlet, N.W.T., Musée des beaux-arts de Montréal, Nat. Gallery of Can. (Stillwell Coll.); attended openings: Inuit Gall. of Eskimo Art Toronto (Canada Council travel grant) 1972, 'Abstract in Stone' La Jolla, Ca. 1988; comnd. to create sculpture for auction in aid of Keith Rawlings Memorial Scholarship Fund; presented a carving demonstration, Winnipeg Folk Festival 1991; subject of several articles and catalogues; Home: Arviat, N.W.T.; Office: c/o Candn. Arctic Producers, 1645 Inkster Blvd., Winnipeg, Man. R2X 2W7.

**ARMATAGE, Elizabeth Kay,** B.A., M.A., Ph.D.; university professor; filmmaker; curator; b. Sask. 15 Jan. 1943; d. Trenholm Porter and Agnes Elizabeth (Lawrence) A.; e. Queen's Univ., B.A. (Hons.) 1965; Univ. of Toronto, M.A. 1967, Ph.D. 1974; one d. Alexis Elizabeth Armatage House; Dir., Women's Studies Program, New College, Univ. of Toronto 1988–92; joined Univ. of Toronto 1971, has taught women's studies & cinema studies since 1972; independent filmmaker 1975– ; Sr. Programmer, Curator, Toronto Festival of Festivals 1981– ; media cons. and lectr.; Chicago Film Festival Award 1981, 1984; Toronto Film Festival Award 1987; Toronto Women and Film Special Merit Award 1988; YWCA Woman of Distinction 1989; has exhibited films in internat. festivals in N. Am. and Europe; author of many articles in Candn. jours.; 16 mm. films: 'Jill Johnston' 1977; 'Gertrude & Alice In Passing' 1978; 'Bed and Sofa' 1979; 'Speak Body' 1979; 'Striptease' 1980; 'Storytelling' 1983; 'Artist on Fire' 1987; Home: 53 Brunswick Ave., Toronto, Ont. M5S 2L8; Office: New College, Univ. of Toronto, Toronto, Ont. M5S 1A1.

**ARMENI, Silvia;** artist; b. Bari, Italy 17 July 1952; d. Enzo and Olga (Paladino) A.; e. Liceo Artistico of Rome dipl. 1970; main shows (one-woman): Italy: Dei Leoni Gallery Rome 1975, '76, Della Tartaruga Gallery Rome 1977, '78; Canada: Danielli Gallery 1979, Elajana Gallery 1979, '80, Lourie Gallery 1985, '88, Gallery Phillip 1987 (all Toronto), Mihalis Gallery Montreal 1989; Back Cover 'Reader's Digest' 1985 (Canada), 1986 (Italy); Address: c/o The Gallery on the Lake, Box 10, Buckhorn, Ont. K0L 1J0.

**ARMENIAN, Raffi,** C.M., B.Sc., LL.D.; music director; b. Cairo, Egypt 4 June 1942; s. Barour and Marguerite (Podimatas) A.; e. Imp. Col. Univ. of London B.Sc. (Metall.) 1965; Acad. of Music Vienna 1962, 1968, 1969; Univ. of Waterloo LL.D. 1983; m. Agnes d. Ferdinand and Maria Grossmann 27 March 1984; Music Dir., Kitchener-Waterloo Symphony 1971–93; Music Dir. Opera Studio Opera de Montréal 1986–89, Montréal Conservatoire Orch. 1980– ; Music Dir. Stratford Festival 1973–76; Founder, Candn. Chamber Ensemble 1974, internat. tours incl. Spain 1984, 1986, S. Am. 1985, USA 1986, S.Am. 1989, Holland, Switzerland, E. & W. Germany 1990, USSR 1991; Conductor, Candn. Opera Co. 1974, 1975, 1977; Montréal Opera 1982, 1985, 1986; Opera Columbus 1986, 1988, 1989; has conducted maj. Candn. orchs., Brussels Radio, Bucharest Philharmonic; recipient Queen's Silver Jubilee Medal 1977; Member Order of Canada 1987; Home: 300 Regina St. N., Waterloo, Ont. N2J 3B8.

**ARMERDING, William Horsey,** A.B., M.T.I., R.I. (B.C.); consultant; b. Boston, Mass. 8 Oct. 1934; s. the late Howard Sherman and the late Grace Stratton (Horsey) A.; e. Wheaton Coll, Illinois, A.B. 1955; m. Joy d. Ray (dec.) and Evelyn Butler 23 June 1956; children: Lois Ann, Laurel Beth (Sheppard), Linda Cheryl (Tatchell), Leslie Joy; PRES., EQUITICORP CAPITAL LIMITED AND EQUITICORP VENTURE CAPITAL (VCC) CORP. 1987– ; Pres. and Dir., Equiticorp Investments Ltd. 1986– ; C.E.O. & Dir., Schloss Mittersill Christian Conferences Inc. 1989–92; Dir. and mem., Extve. Comte., Inter-Varsity Christian Fellowship of Can. 1977– ; Data Processing Management, John Hancock Mutual Life Insurance Co., Boston 1959–69; Mgr., Data Processing and Operations, Houghton Mifflin Publishers, Burlington, Mass. 1969–74; came to Can. 1974; Vice-Pres., Fidelity Trust Co., 1974–79; Vice Pres., Columbia Trust Co. 1979–86; Vice-Pres., Guardian Trust Co. 1986–87; mem., Trust Companies Inst.; Real Estate Inst. of B.C.; Member, Granville Chapel; recreations: golf, skiing, sailing; Home: 12071 Hayashi Court, Richmond, B.C. V7E 5W2.

**ARMITAGE, John Murray,** B.A., C.A.; merchant banking executive; b. Montreal, Que. 30 Mar. 1940; s. John Leonard and Edith A. (Hodge) A.; e. Univ. of Toronto (Victoria Coll.), B.A. 1962; C.A. 1966; m. Susan d. Mary and Bill Ortved 2 Oct. 1964; children: Kirsten, Kevin; CO-CHIEF EXECUTIVE OFFICER, BEDFORD CAPITAL CORP. 1989– ; Clarkson Gordon 1963–73; Toronto Dominion Bank 1973–74; Founding Partner, Crosbie Armitage & Co. 1978–85; Sr. Vice-Pres. & Dir., Merrill Lynch Canada Inc. 1985–89; Dir., Merchant Private Limited; Halton Reinsur. Co. Limited; Pet Valu Inc.; Bedford Capital Finan. Corp.; Chrmn. & Dir., Anford Inc.; Vice Chrmn. & Dir., Brita International Holdings Inc.; clubs: Granite, Albany, Osler Bluff Ski; Home: 4 Donino Ave., Toronto, Ont. M4N 2W5; Office: Ste. 4712, Scotia Plaza, Toronto, Ont. M5H 3Y2.

**ARMSON, Kenneth Avery,** B.Sc.F., R.P.F.; educator; b. Newton Brook, Ont. 19 Feb. 1927; s. Harold P. and Gladys D. (Wraight) A.; e. Royal Grammar Sch., Worcester, Eng., Univ. of Toronto, B.Sc.F. 1951; Oxford Univ., Dipl. Forestry 1955; D.Sc.(Hon.), Lakehead Univ. 1991; m. Harriett E. C., d. late James T. Coltham, 12 Apr. 1952; one child, Erling J.T.; FORESTRY CONSULTANT 1989– ; Consultant in Silviculture and Forest Soils to indust. and govt.; joined Research Div., Ont. Dept. of Lands and Forests, 1951–52; Prof. of Forestry, Univ. of Toronto 1952–78; Chief Forester, Ont. Min. of Nat. Resources 1978–83; Extve. Coordinator, Forest Resources 1983–86; Provincial Forester, Ont. Min. of Natural Resources 1986–89; served with Candn. Army 1945–46; Can. Forestry Achievement Award, 1978; Ont. Forestry Achievement Award, 1990; author, 'A Manual of Forest Tree Nursery Soil Management' 1974; 'Forest Soils: Properties and Processes' 1977; also over 45 papers in scient. journs; mem. Ont. Prof. Foresters Assn.; Candn. Inst. Forestry; Soc. Am. Foresters; Soil Science Soc. Am.; Ont. Forestry Assn.; United Church; Home: 446 Heath St. E., Toronto, Ont. M4G 1B5.

**ARMSTRONG, Alayne,** B.A.H., M.A. in progress; foundation executive; b. RCAF Cold Lake, Alta. 17 Jan. 1965; d. Cameron T. and Edith M. A.; e. Queen's Univ. B.A.H. 1988; currently Univ. of Manitoba; PRES., JOHN H. MCDONALD JOURNALISM FOUNDATION 1993– ; Entertainment editor 'The Queen's Journal,' Queen's Univ. 1986–87; Managing editor 'The Queen's Journal,' Queen's Univ. 1987–88; Entertainment editor 'The Manitoban,' Univ. of Manitoba 1990–91; Managing editor 'The Manitoban,' Univ. of Manitoba 1991–92; Prairie Regional Co-ord., Canadian Univ. Press 1992–93; Pres., Canadian Univ. Press 1993–94; Chair, Canadian Univ. Press Media Serv. Ltd., Campus Plus 1993–94; Home: 643 King Edward Ave., Ottawa, Ont. K1N 7N8; Office: 126 York St., Ste. 408, Ottawa, Ont. K1N 5T5.

**ARMSTRONG, Christopher,** B.A., A.M., Ph.D.; professor; b. Toronto, Ont. 23 Jan. 1942; s. Charles Harold Algeo and Agnes Honoria (Wrong) A.; e. Univ. of

Toronto, B.A. (Hons.) 1963, Oxford Univ., B.A. 1965; Harvard Univ., A.M. 1966; Univ. of Toronto, Ph.D. 1972; m. Valerie d. Charles H.W. Cane 27 Aug. 1966; one d.: Emily Anne; PROF., HISTORY DEPT., YORK UNIV. 1984– ; Asst. Prof. of Hist., Brock Univ. 1969–71; York Univ. 1971–75; Assoc. Prof. 1975–84; Prof. 1984– ; author: 'The Politics of Federalism' 1981; co-author: 'The Revenge of the Methodist Bicycle Company' 1977, 'Monopoly's Moment, the Organization and Regulation of Canadian Utilities 1830–1930' 1986; 'Southern Exposure: Canadian Promoters in Latin America and the Caribbean 1896–1930' 1988; Home: 82 Chatsworth Dr., Toronto, Ont. M4R 1R7; Office: Dept. of Hist., York Univ., 4700 Keele St., North York, Ont. M3J 1P3.

**ARMSTRONG, David William,** M.Sc., Ph.D.; research scientist b. Ottawa, Ont. 29 Jan. 1954; s. Robert Crosby and Margaret Theresa (Larose) A.; e. Univ. of Ottawa, B.Sc. 1978, M.Sc. 1980; Carleton Univ., Ph.D. 1984; Mass. Inst. Technol., Univ. of Minn. Advanced Training in Animal Cell; Reg'd Specialist Microbiol. 1982; m. Elaine d. Wilbert and Audrey Robertson 10 June 1978; one d. Laura Lynne; HEAD, CELL CULTURE FACILITY, INST. BIOL. SCIENCES, NAT. RESEARCH COUNCIL 1985– ; Adv. Biotechnol. Candn. Space Life Sciences Ctte. 1985–88; joined present Council 1979; Patentee in Biotechnol.; Ont. Grad. Scholar 1978; mem. Candn. Coll. Microbiols.; Tissue Culture Assn.; recreation: ballroom dancing; Home: 952 Winnington Ave., Ottawa, Ont. K2B 5C7; Office: 100 Sussex Dr., Ottawa, Ont. K1A 0R6.

**ARMSTRONG, Donald Eugene,** B.A., B.Com., Ph.D.; management consultant; educator; b. Nanton, Alta. 10 May 1925; s. Samuel Timothy and Laura (Bridges) A.; e. Univ. of Alta., B.A., B.Com. 1950; McGill Univ. Ph.D. 1954; m. Muriel Gladys d. Dr. Frank G. Buchanan 14May 1947; children: Susan Deryl, Joanne Patricia, Terrence Bruce; PRES., MADATA INC.; Prof. of Econ., Faculty of Management McGill Univ.; founding Dir., Grad. Sch. of Bus.; founding Pres., Financial Research Inst.; mgmt. consultant practice 1954– ; author 'Competition Versus Monoply: Combines Policy In Perspective' 1982; 'Education and Achievement' 1970; various articles transport., econ. forecasting, energy; served with Candn. Inf. Corps 1943–45, rank Lt.; mem. Candn. Chamber Comm. (various nat. comtes.); Candn. Econ. Assn.; recreations: swimming, dancing; Address: 3 Westland Dr., Montreal, Qué. H4X 1M1.

**ARMSTRONG, Frederick Henry,** M.A., Ph.D.; educator; writer; b. Toronto, Ont. 27 March 1926; s. late Silas Henry and Dorothy Lillian (Goode) A.; e. Parkdale Coll. Inst. 1946; Univ. of Toronto B.A. 1949, M.A. 1951, Ph.D. 1965; m. Josephine Joan. d. late Ladislas Biberovich 6 Aug. 1960; children: Dale Henry, Irene Eleanor; PROF. EMERITUS OF HISTORY, UNIV. OF W. ONT. 1991– ; in business 1951–60; Instr. in Hist., Univ. of Toronto 1962–63; Univ. of W. Ont. since 1963, Prof. 1975–89, Rsch. Prof. 1989–91; Chrmn. Local Arch. Conserv. Adv. Comte., London, Ont. 1979, mem. 1973–79; various Can. Council and Soc. Sci. & Humanities Counc. Fellowships; Univ. of W. Ont. Pres.'s Medal 1979; Am. Soc. for State and Local History Award of Merit 1984; author 'Handbook of Upper Canadian Chronology' 1967 (2nd ed., rev. and enlarged 1985); 'Organizing for Preservation' 1978; 'Toronto: The Place of Meeting' 1983; 'The Forest City: An Illustrated History of London Canada' 1986; 'A City in The Making' 1989; co-author 'Reflections on London's Past' 1975; Ed. or Co-ed.: (Henry Scadding) 'Toronto of Old' 1966, (2nd ed., rev. 1987); 'Approaches to Teaching Local History Using Upper Canadian and Ontario Examples' 1969; 'Aspects of Nineteenth Century Ontario: Essays Presented to James J. Talman' 1974; 'Old Ontario: Essays in Honour of J.M.S. Careless' 1990; author over 125 articles, 50 reviews nineteenth century Ont. and urbanization; 50 papers and presentations as mem. of panels learned socs., univs.; mem. Candn. Hist. Assn.; Champlain Soc. (Council 1974– , Vice Pres. 1980–88, Pres. 1988–91); Ont. Hist. Soc. (Dir. 1963–65, 1972–80, Pres. 1977–79); Royal Hist. Soc.; recreations: photography, gardening, music, travel; Home: 1 Franklin Ave., London, Ont. N6C 2G6; Office: London, Ont. N6A 5C2.

**ARMSTRONG, Henry Conner,** B.Sc., M.B.A., P.Eng.; consultant; b. Winnipeg, Man. 16 June 1925; s. William Arthur Laird and Archena May (Conner) A.; e. St. John's Coll. Sch. Winnipeg 1943; Queen's Univ. B.Sc. (Metall. Engn.) 1949; Univ. of Toronto M.B.A. 1954 (Kresge Fellow); Internat. Mgmt. Inst. Geneva, Dipl. Internat. Business 1958 (Alcan Fellow); m. Barbara Fay d. Forrest Lyle Jackson, Kingston, Ont. 20 May 1950; children: Barbara Elizabeth (Marosi), Nancy Margaret (Ridler), Scott Jackson; various sales and marketing positions Aluminum Co. of Canada Ltd. 1954–64; Commodity Offr. Dept. Trade & Comm. Ottawa 1964–66; Counsellor (Metals & Minerals) Candn. High Comn. London 1965; Comm. Counsellor Candn. Embassy Washington 1966–74; Chief, Research & Planning Div. Resource Industries Br. Dept. Industry, Trade & Comm. Ottawa 1974–75; Dir. Minerals & Metals Div., Dept. of Energy, Mines & Resources 1975–81, Acting Dir.-Gen. Mineral Devel. Br. 1981, Exec. Dir., Internat. Minerals Div. 1981–82; Mgr., Special Projects, Mineral Policy Sector 1982–83; Counsellor (Metals, Minerals & Energy) Canadian High Commission Canberra 1983–86; Counsellor (Commercial), Candn. Embassy, Washington, D.C. 1986–89; CIM Distinguished Lectr. 1981–82; guest speaker on minerals various groups and organs.; mem. various Candn. dels. meetings internat. organs. incl. Internat. Tin Council, Internat. Lead-Zinc Study Group, UNCTAD Copper negotiations; participated meetings Can./Japan Econ. Comte., Can./EC Jt. Econ. Comte.; Pacific Economic Cooperation Conf.; mem. Assn. Prof. Engrs. Prov. Ont.; Candn. Inst. Mining & Metall.; Am. Soc. Metals (Extve. 1964–66); Queen's Alumni Assn. (Extve. 1955–57); served in Canada & U.K. in R.C.A.F. and Royal Navy (Fleet Air Arm) 1944–45; United Church; recreations: skating, skiing, swimming, bridge; Address: 2159 Delmar Dr., Ottawa, Ont. K1H 5P6.

**ARMSTRONG, J.D. (Jack),** M.D.; pediatrician/association executive; b. Winnipeg, Man. 4 Sept. 1939; e. Norwood Coll.; United Coll., Univ. of Man., B.A. 1961; Univ. of Man. Med. Coll., M.D. 1966; m. Glenda Paul; children: Jeanne, Carolyn; priv. practice Winnipeg 1971– ; active staff, St. Boniface, Winnipeg Children's; Jr. internship St. Boniface Gen. Hops. 1966–67; Pediatric residency 1967–71; Winnipeg Children's Hosp. and Univ. of Colorado Med. Ctr.; cert. Pediatric Specialist 1971; Pres., Man. Med. Assn. 1987–88; Mem. Manitoba Health Adv. Network 1989– ; Rep. of Man. Med. Assoc. to Bd. of Candn. Med. Assoc. 1989– ; Chrmn. of Bd., Manitoba Med. Assn. 1990– ; Mem.-at-large, past mem., Med. Adv. Ctte., St. Boniface Hosp.; Assoc. Prof. of Pediatrics, Univ. of Man. 1991– ; a past Chrmn., Man. Chap. Candn. Pediatric Soc.; Chair, Ctte. on Aboriginal Health MMA 1991– ; Bd. Mem., United Way of Winnipeg 1992– ; Bd. Mem., Project Opikihiwawin 1989– ; CMA Bd. Rep. to National Steering Ctte. Enhancing Prevention in the Practice of Health Professionals 1990– ; past Bd. Mem. & Chrmn., St. Vital United Ch.; Home: 108 Southmoor Rd., Winnipeg, Man. R2J 2P4.

**ARMSTRONG, J. Wray,** B.A., B.S.L.; artists' manager; b. Carrot River, Saskatchewan 2 Aug. 1950; s. James Shire and Elizabeth Elsie (Boyle); e. University of Saskatchewan, B.A. 1971; Laurentian Univ. B.S.L. (Hons.) (High Distinction) 1975; French Translator, Dept. of Secretary of State 1975–77; Mngmt. Apprentice, David Haber Artist Mngmt. Inc. 1977–78; joined The Toronto Symphony as Asst. Orch. Mgr. 1978, Music Admin. 1980, Asst. Gen. Mgr. 1982, Mng. Dir. 1987–91; Past Directorships: 1991 Glory of Mozart Festival; Adv. Ctte. Mem., CFMX-FM; Adv. Ctte. Mem., Metro Toronto Public Participation/Cultural Plan Development; 1983 Toronto Intnl. Festival, Toronto Arts Awards, 1989 Intnl. Choral Festival; Producer, Big Valley Jamboree (1984); recreations: karate, travel, opera, drawing, painting; Address: c/o ICM Artists (London) Inc., Oxford House, 76 Oxford St., London W1R 1RB England.

**ARMSTRONG, Jack Irwin,** M.A.; retired; b. Hamilton, Ont. 21 June 1914; s. Frank Irwin and Edna Banks (Green) A.; e. Delta Coll. Inst., Hamilton, Ont.; McMaster Univ., B.A. 1935, M.A. 1936; Osgoode Hall Law Sch., Toronto, Ont.; m. Rowena Mary, d. late Rev. E. J. Etherington, 5 July 1941; one s. John Gibsone; President, Canadian Textiles Institute, 1970–80; Deputy Services Adm., W.P.T.B., 1943; Deputy Wool Adm., W.P.T.B., 1944–46; Gen. Mgr., Candn. Textiles Inst. 1946–70; read law with Roebuck & Bagwell, Toronto, Ont.; called to the Bar of Ont. 1939; Past Pres. and mem., Inst. of Assn. Extves.; Delta Chi; Conservative; Protestant; recreations: woodworking, music, sports; Home: 2180 Marine Dr., Suite 2008, Oakville, Ont. L6L 5V2.

**ARMSTRONG, Joe C.W.,** B.A., F.R.G.S., F.R.G.S.(C); author; historian; heritage publicist; b. Toronto, Ont. 30 Jan. 1934; s. James S.P. and Helen Strawn (Woodland) A.; e. Upper Can. Coll.; Trinity Coll. Sch.; Bishops Univ. B.A. 1958; m. Barbara d. Walter and Lois Johnson 18 July 1970; children: Geoffrey James, Jill Anne, Katherine Margaret, James Walter; SR. INDUST. DEVEL. OFFICER, GOVT. OF CAN. 1972– ; Nominee Investment Dir., Charterhouse Can. Limited 1963; Extve. Vice-Pres. and Dir., Candn. Manoir Industries Limited 1968; Pres., Port Franks Properties Limited 1971; Sr. Indust. Devel. Gov. of Can., Expo '86 Vancouver 1986; Dir., Econ. Devel., Candn. Counc. for Native Bus. 1987; Owner, Publicist, 'Canadiana Collection, Art & Discovery Maps of Can.'; publicist for var. insts. & corp. celebrations; sponsor: hist. map reproductions/ Assoc. of Candn. Map Libs. 1983; Creator/Narrator, 'The Explorer Series,' CBC Morningside 1981; Founder, The Ctte. of One for One Canada 1992 (re Oct. 1992 referendum); Fellow, Royal Geog. Soc., U.K. 1980; Can. 1981; Hon. Dir., Candn. Inst. of Surveyors 1983; Dir., Galiano Cult. & Hist. Soc., B.C. 1986; Ont. Heritage Found. (Hist. Ctte., Archeology Ctte.) 1987; Adv. Ctte. on Land Registry Office Records, Ont. Min. of Culture & Communications 1989; mem. Champlain Soc.; Anglican; Freemason; Appointed Hon. membre Le Mouvement Francité (Québec) 1990; cartographic consultant: 'Black Robe' 1991; author: 'From Sea Unto Sea/Art & Discovery Maps of Canada' 1982, 'Champlain' (Eng. ed.) 1987, (Fr. ed.) 1988 and a brief to Senate of Can.: 'The Meech Lake Accord, An Hist. & Phil. Perspective'; 'Meech Plus: The Charlatan Accord'; 'Legitimize Dissent Or Lose The Federation' 1993; briefs on Canadian constitution to Beaudoin-Edwards Special Joint Ctte. and to Ont. Leg. Ctte. on Ont. in Confed. 1991; recreations: Lambton Heritage Museum, travel, photography, swimming, piano, banjo, heritage TV & radio broadcasting; Home: 347 Keewatin Ave., Toronto, Ont. M4P 2A4.

**ARMSTRONG, John B.,** M.D., F.R.C.P.(C), D.I.M. (McGill); b. Toronto, Ont. 19 Oct. 1918; s. Charles Henry and Olive May (Buchanan) A.; e. Univ. of Toronto Schs. (1930–37); Univ. of Toronto, M.D. 1943; m. Dorothy Green 27 May 1944; children: Robert, Stanley, Sheila, Mary; retired Prof. in Preventive Medicine and Biostatistics, Univ. of Toronto; Res. Training, Royal Victoria Hosp., Montreal, P.Q. 1946–48; Fellow in Med., Duke Univ., Durham, N.C., 1948–49; Registrar, Roy. Post-grad. Med. Sch. of London, Hammersmith Hosp., 1949–50; Asst. Prof., Physiol. and Med. Rsch., Univ. of Manitoba 1950–56; Assoc. Prof. Pharmacol. Univ. of Toronto 1957–69 and Univ. of Ottawa 1969–75; Exec. Dir., Candn. Heart Found. 1957–75; Sr. Consultant in Chronic Disease Epidemiol., Ont. Govt. 1975–83; Gov. for Ont., Am. Coll. of Cardiol. 1966–68; mem., Admissions Comte., Duke Univ. Med. Sch.; served in 2nd World War, Capt.; mem., No. 1 Rsch. Lab., R.C.A.M.C.; Fellow, Candn. Life Ins. Offrs. Assn. 1950–52; Markle Scholar in Med. Sciences 1952–56; Queen's Silver Jubilee Medal 1977; Lic., Med. Counc. of Can.; mem., Candn. Cardiovascular Soc. (Councillor 1956–59); Pharm. Soc. Can. (Pres. 1972–3); Candn. Med. Assn.; Candn. Soc. for Clinical Investig. (founder mem.); Am. Heart Assn.; United Ch.; Home: #401, 151 Bay St., Ottawa, Ont. K1R 7T2.

**ARMSTRONG, John Edward,** M.A.Sc., Ph.D., F.R.S.C. (1950), F.G.S.A. (1945); geologist; Canadian public servant (ret.); b. Cloverdale, B.C., 18 Feb. 1912; s. David Edward and Mary Ellwood (White) A.; e. Univ. of British Columbia, B.A.Sc. (Geol. Engn.) 1934, M.A.Sc. (Geol. Engn.) 1935 (Carnegie Scholarship, 1935; Nicholson Scholarship 1936); Univ. of Toronto, Ph.D. 1939; m. Constance Lilian, d. Harold Crump, Vancouver, B.C., 2nd Oct. 1937; one s. John B.; former Sec.-Gen., XXIV Int. Geol. Congress; entered Geol. Survey of Can. in 1934; retired 1976; publications: over 135 papers by Govt. of Can., and in various scient. journals; Roy. Soc. Can. (Past Convener); Hon. Life mem. Geol. Soc. of America; Hon. Life mem. and Past Pres., Vancouver Natural Hist. Soc.; Permanent mem., Steering Comte., Internat. Geological Congress; Hon. Vice-Pres., XII Internat. Quaternary Congress; Gold Medalist, 24th Internat. Geol. Congress 1972; Merit Award, Pub. Service of Can. 1973; Queen's Jubilee Medal 1978; Medal and Diploma, XXVI Int. Geol. Congress (France), 1980; recreations: golf, natural history; Home: 206–2298 McBain Ave., Vancouver, B.C. V6L 3B1; Office: 2298 McBain Ave., Vancouver, B.C. V6L 3B1.

**ARMSTRONG, Neil Mackenzie,** C.M., B.A.; educational director, retired; b. St. Catharines, Ont. 14 Oct. 1925; s. Garnet McDermid and Beatrice Martha (Mackenzie) A.; e. St. Catharines Coll. Inst. 1944; Univ. of W. Ont. B.A. 1949; m. Marjorie Joan d. George and Joanna Swan 14 Aug. 1948; children: Lori, Blair, Cindi, Renee; Dir. Banff Sch. of Fine Arts 1977–91; Dir. Banff Festival of the Arts 1972–91; Vice Pres. Edn. The Banff Centre 1982–91; served with RCN 41st Minesweeping Flotilla HMCS Fort William 1944–45; Adm./Teacher Sch. of Bus. Adm. Univ. of W. Ont. 1950–72, Adm. Dir. Mgmt. Devel. Prog. 1955–72; Assoc. Dir. the Banff Centre 1972–82; Pres. Univ. Placement & Counselling Assn.

Can. 1963–65, Life Mem.; mem. Bd. and Exec. Coll. Placement Council U.S.A. 1963–66; Dir. Jr. Achievement of Can. London 1960–65; Founding Dir.: Candn. Festival Youth Orchs. 1973, Pres. 1973–80; Cand. Assn. Youth Orchs. 1975, Pres. 1975–80, Dir. Emeritus; New West Film & TV Found. and Banff TV Festival, Dir. 1978–82; Vice Pres. Cand. Conf of Arts 1979–82; Founding Chrmn. Internat. Symposium on Arts 1985; Dir. Am. Symphony Orch. League, Youth Orch. Div. 1975–78; Dir. Candn. Assn. Orchs. 1975–80; mem. Downey Comn. Fine Arts Edn. 1975; Trustee, Village of Byron 1953–56; Dir. and Chrmn. Ski Runners Candn. Rockies 1974–76; Charter mem. Ind. Devel. Comn. London 1970–72; Pres. Scot. Country Dance Soc.; mem. Internat. Council Fine Arts Deans; Candn. Assn. Fine Arts Deans; Member, Order of Canada 1989; Donald Cameron Gold Medal 1990; Commemorative Medal, 125th Anniversary of Candn. Confedn.; United Church; recreations: photography, fishing, golf, skiing, hiking; Club: Canmore Golf and Curling; Home: 105 China Close, P.O. Box 2624, Canmore, Alta. T0L 0M0.

**ARMSTRONG, Paul Wayne,** B.A., M.D., F.R.C.P.(C), F.A.C.C.; academic cardiologist; b. Port Arthur, Ont. 27 Mar. 1942; s. Kenneth James and Anne Gladys (Stewart) A.; e. Queen's Univ. B.A. 1963; Queen's Univ. M.D. 1966; F.R.C.P. Cardiology 1972; F.A.C.C. 1974; m. Beverley Anne d. Lloyd and Averill Dawson 25 Mar. 1967; children: Lisa Christine, Kevin Drew; PROFESSOR & CHAIRMAN, DEPT. OF MEDICINE, UNIV. OF ALBERTA 1993– ; Intern Toronto Gen. Hosp. 1966–67; Asst. Resident in Med. Kingston (Ont.) Gen. Hosp. 1967–69; Cardiac Fellow Massachussetts Gen. Hosp. (Boston) 1969–71; Cardiac Fellow St. George's Hosp. (London, Eng.) 1971–72; Dir. Coronary Care Unit Kingston Gen. Hosp. 1972–84; Prof. of Med. Queen's Univ. 1981–84; Prof. of Med., Univ. of Toronto 1984–93; Chief of Cardiology, St. Michael's Hosp. 1984–93; Chrmn., Medical Advisory Ctte., Heart and Stroke Foundation of Canada; Co-Chrmn., Organizing Ctte., Candn. Task Force for Cardiovascular Science; Candn. Co-ordinator and Mem. Internat. Steering Ctte., Global Utilization of Streptokinase and +PA in Occluded Vessels (GUSTO I) 1991–93; Extve. Ctte., Steering Ctte. and Candn. Co-ordinator, Global Utilization of Strategies to Open Occluded Coronary Arteries (GUSTO II) 1993– ; recipient: Basmajian Award for excellence in medical rsch., Queen's Univ. 1980; William Goldie prize, Dept. of Medicine, Univ. of Toronto 1987; Tony Graham Award, Outstanding Volunteer, Heart and Stroke Foundation of Ont. 1990; Rsch. Achievement Award, Candn. Cardiovascular Soc. 1993; Home: 15315 44 Avenue, Edmonton, Alta. T6H 4Z9; 2Fl.30 W.C. Mackenzie HSC, Edmonton, Alta. T6G 2R7.

**ARMSTRONG, Richard Gary,** B.Com., C.H.R.P.; transportation executive; b. North Bay, Ont. 22 Aug. 1938; s. Richard William and Reida M. (Daly) A.; e. North Bay Coll. (Scollard Hall); St. Patrick's Coll. Ottawa B.Com. 1963; CHRMN., PRES. AND C.E.O., GREAT LAKES PILOTAGE AUTHORITY LTD. 1978– ; Dir. Seaway International Bridge Corp. Ltd. (Secy. 1977–78); Dir., Welland Canal Twinning Project Contractor's Assn. 1968–72; Dir. of Personnel & Indust. Relations 1972–77, Dir. of Adm. 1977–79, St. Lawrence Seaway Authority; Vice Pres., Laurencrest Youth Services of SD & G Inc.; Dir. and Chrmn. Cornwall Youth Residence Inc. 1969–88; Treas. Cornwall-United Counties Basketball Assoc. 1984–87; Former Dir. Kiwanis Club; Chrmn., St. Francis de Sales Parish Council 1979–80; Past Chrmn., Treas., Cornwall Library Bd.; former Trustee, S. Ont. Lib. Service – Rideau; mem. Human Resources Professionals Assoc. of Ont.; Home: 1217 Princess St., Cornwall, Ont. K6J 1S2; Office: 202 Pitt St. (P.O. Box 95), Cornwall, Ont. K6H 5R9.

**ARMSTRONG, Robin Louis,** B.A., M.Sc., Ph.D., F.R.S.C.; physicist; educator; b. Galt, Ont. 14 May 1935; s. Robert Dockstader and Beatrice Jenny (Grill) A.; e. Hespeler (Ont.) Pub. Sch. 1949; Preston (Ont.) High Sch. 1954; Univ. of Toronto B.A. 1958, M.Sc. 1959, Ph.D. 1961; Oxford Univ. post-doctoral studies 1961–62 (Nat. Research Council Fellowship, Rutherford Mem. Fellowship Royal Soc. Can.); m. Karen Elisabeth d. Carl Frederick Feilberg Hansen 8 July 1960; children: Keir Grill, Christopher Drew; PRESIDENT, UNIV. OF NEW BRUNSWICK 1990– ; Asst. Prof. of Physics, Univ. of Toronto 1962, Assoc. Prof. 1968 and of Engn. Science 1969, Prof. of Physics 1971–90, Adjunct Prof. 1990– , Prof. of Engn. Science 1971–74, Prof. of Radiology 1985–90, Assoc. Chrmn. of Physics 1969–74, Chrmn. 1974–82, Dean of Arts and Science, Univ. of Toronto 1982–90; Prof. of Physics, present univ. 1990– ; Affiliated Scientist (Radiology), Dr. Evertt Chalmers Hosp., Fredericton, N.B. 1991– ; Candn. Inst. Advanced Studies (CIAR) 1981– ;(Founding Dir. 1981–82, Mem. of Rsch. Counc. 1982– ;); Dir. Huntsman Marine Lab. 1983–87; Pres. Candn. Assoc. for Neutron Scattering 1985–86; Pres. Candn. Inst. for Neutron Scattering 1986–89; Vice-Pres., Candn. Assn. Physicists 1989–90; Pres., Candn. Assn. Physicists 1990–91; Mem., Triumf-KAON Ventures Office Bd. 1991– ; NSERC Council 1991– ;(Mem. of Extve. 1992– ;); rec'd Herzberg Medal, Candn. Assn. Physicists 1973; Visitante Distinguido, Univ. of Cordoba, Argentina 1987; Medal of Achievement, Candn. Assn. Physicists 1990; awarded Commemorative Medal for 125th Anniversary of Candn. Confederation 1992; co-author 'Mechanics, Waves and Thermal Physics' 1970; 'The Electromagnetic Interaction' 1973; over 150 research publs. condensed matter physics various tech. journs.; mem. Candn. Assn. Physicists; Soc. Magnetic Resonance; Soc. Magnetic Resonance in Medicine; recreations: gardening, skiing, golf; Home: 58 Waterloo Row, Fredericton, N.B. E3B 1Y9; Office: University of N.B., Box 4400, Fredericton, N.B. E3B 5A3.

**ARMSTRONG, Sally Wishart,** B.Ed.; journalist; b. Montreal, Que. 16 July 1943; d. William and Mary Alma (Wishart) Saddler; e. McGill Univ., B.Ed. (phys. ed.) 1966; m. Ross s. John Grant and Lillian A. 19 Aug. 1967; children: Heather, Peter, Anna; EDITOR-IN-CHIEF, HOMEMAKER'S MAGAZINE 1988– ; freelance writer 1975–79; Contbg. Ed., Canadian Living Magazine 1975 (launch issue) to 1982; Assoc. Ed. 1983–87; Video Documentary Co-prod., 'Reason to Live' 1987, 'Human Rights – Human Wrongs' 1987, 'Broken Trust' 1988; author 'Mila' (biography) 1992; Office: 50 Holly St., Toronto, Ont. M4S 3B3.

**ARMSTRONG, Stephen Cooley,** B.Sc.Eng., C.Eng., MIMechE, P.Eng, CMC; professional engineer, management consultant; b. Belfast, N. Ireland 29 Feb. 1956; s. Brian and Elizabeth (Hutchinson) A.; e. Lisburn Coll. of Technol., N. Ireland 1977; Full Technological Cert. Mech. Eng., City & Guilds of London Inst.; Univ. of Westminster, London, U.K., B.Sc., Mech. Engr. (Hons.) 1980; aeronautical eng. apprenticeship, Short Bros. 1972–77; m. Dr. Pamela d. Bill and Althea Letts 24 May 1986; PRESIDENT, ARMSTRONG MANAGEMENT GROUP INC. 1993– ; Cons. Mech. Engr., aerospace indus. 1980–83; Mgr., Mfg. Engr., BBC Brown Boveri 1983–86; Mktg. Mgr. & Mktg. Cons., Honeywell Infor. Serv. 1986–88; Principal Management Consultant, Peat Marwick Stevenson & Kellogg 1988–93; Adv. Ctte., Centennial Coll. of Technol.; Past Teacher, Centennial Coll.; Young Outstanding (under 35) Engr. 1990; Pres. Award, Soc. of Mfg. Engrs. USA 1986; Mem., Eur. Fedn. d'Assn. Nat. d'Ingen. 1990; Inst. of Cert. Mngt. Cons. Ont. 1988; Assn. of Profl. Engrs. Ont. 1983; Sr. Mem., Soc. of Mfg. Engrs. 1982 (Chrmn. Toronto Chap. 26 1989–90); Corp. Mem., Inst. of Mech. Engrs. (MIMechE.) 1979; recreations: squash, soccer, reading, theatre, movies, music; clubs: Raquet Sports Group of Can.

**ARMSTRONG, Thomas E. (Tim),** Q.C., B.A., LL.B.; lawyer; public administrator; b. Toronto, Ont. 3 Dec 1931; s. Thomas Wellington and Greta Isabel (Grosskurth) A.; e. Univ. of Toronto Schs. 1950; Victoria Univ., Univ. of Toronto 1954; Osgoode Hall Law Sch. 1958; m. Betty d. Pearl and Everett Spafford 10 Aug. 1957; children: Michael, James, Katie; COUNSEL, MCCARTHY, TÉTRAULT 1993– ; Depy. Min., Ont. Ministry of Industry, Trade & Tech. 1991–92; Chrmn., Asia/Pacific Study Group 1990; Ontario's Agent Gen., Asia/Pacific Region, Tokyo, Japan 1986–90; Depy. Min. of Labour, Ont. 1976–86; Mem., Civil Service Commn. 1978–86; Chrmn., Ont. Construction Industry Adv. Bd. 1977–85; Mem., Candn. Bar Assn. (Labour Rel. Subctte.); Niagara Inst. (Dir. 1976–86); Chrmn., Ont. Labour Relations Bd. 1974–76; Partner, Messrs. Armstrong and Maclean 1969–74; Assoc., Messrs. Jolliffe, Lewis & Osler 1959–69; Couns., Civil Lit. Section, Fed. Dept. of Justice 1958–59; Mem., Bd. of Dirs., de Havilland Holdings Inc., Asia Pacific Foundation and Intercedent Ltd.; Mem., Canada-Japan Society; Home: 35 Lowther Ave., Toronto, Ont. M5R 1C5; Office: Suite 4700, Toronto Dominion Bank Tower, Toronto-Dominion Centre, Toronto, Ont. M5K 1E6.

**ARMSTRONG, William T.,** B.A.; broadcasting executive; b. Wakefield, Que. 8 Dec. 1929; s. Francis Kenneth and Lillian Amy Daisy (Orme) A.; e. Wakefield (P.Q.) Consol. Sch.; Glebe Coll. Inst., Ottawa, Ont., Sr. Matric. 1947; Carleton Univ., B.A. 1952; m. Margaret, d. George Pilmer, Victoria, B.C., 4 June 1955; children: Andrew, Jessica; Dir. for the Province of Ont., C.B.C. 1989–92; Gen. Mgr., New Massey Hall (Toronto) 1981–83; Hon. Gov., Roy Thomson Hall; with E. B. Eddy. Co., Hull, P.Q. 1952–58 in Indust. Relations Div. and finally (1956–58) Public Relations Offr.; joined C.B.C., Apl. 1958 as Audience Relations Coordinator; Dir. of Information Services, 1959–62; Secy., Commonwealth Broadcasting Conf. 1962–63; Extve. Asst. to Pres. 1963–65; Dir., Centennial Program Planning 1965–67; Dir., Corporate Relations 1967–69; Dir. Ottawa Area 1969; Vice Pres. Public Relations 1973; Managing Dir. Radio. CBC 1975–1979; Asst. Gen. Mgr., Eng. Serv. Div. 1979–81; Extve. Vice-Pres., CBC 1983–89; has been active in Ottawa theatrical circles, former Dir. of Ottawa Little Theatre, Organist and Choir-master, St. Matthias Ch., Ottawa, 1955–64; Founding mem., Candn. Public Relations Soc. (mem. Nat. Council, 1959–61, Nat. Secy., 1961–62); Anglican; recreations: music, theatre; Home: 141 Roehampton, Apt. 903, Toronto, Ont. M4P 1P9.

**ARMSTRONG, William Walton,** B.A.; artist; b. Toronto, Ont. 9 Nov. 1916; s. William Charles Earl and Claribel (Walton) A.; e. Glebe Coll. Inst. Ottawa; Univ. of Toronto Victoria Coll. B.A. 1939, Univ. Coll. 2 yrs. Fine Arts 1941; teacher in associaiton with Arthur Lismer, Montreal Art Assn. 1945–52; McGill Univ. Adult Edn. 1949–52; Accademia Florence drawing & painting, studying in Venice and Genoa 1951–57; exhns. incl. (award best painting Spring Show 1946) Montreal with Paul Beaulieu and Gooderich Roberts 1951–57; Waldorf Gallery & Waddington Gallery exhns., and Saggittarius Gallery, New York City 1959; Sun Dance Gallery, Calgary 1975; Gallery House Sol Georgetown, Ont. 1980–90; Field Gallery Thornhill 1980; Cambrian Rose Gallery Ottawa 1985–86; Gallerie Westmount 1988; Virginia Christopher Galleries, Calgary 1989–91 and Kyoto, Japan 1992; rep. Nat. Gallery and Parlt. Bldgs. Ottawa, various private colls. N.Y., London, England, Austria, Montreal, Paris & Geneva; mem. Art Gallery Ont.; Royal Ont. Museum; Thornhill Village Artists; recreations: reading, walking; Address: P.O. Box 239, Thornhill, Ont. L3T 3N3.

**ARNELL, Gordon Edwin,** B.A., LL.B.; realty executive; b. Calgary, Alta. 19 Feb. 1935; e. Univ. of Alta., B.A. 1956, LL.B. 1957; called to Bar of Alta. 1958; m. Reta; children: Patrick, Kevin, Paul, Dana; PRES., C.E.O. & DIR., CARENA DEVELOPMENTS LTD. 1988– ; law practice 1958–70; Vice-Pres., Allarco Devel. Ltd. 1970–73; Pres., Seaboard Life Ins. Co. & Pres., North West Trust Co. 1973–75; Extve. Vice-Pres., Oxford Devel. Group Ltd. 1975–80; Pres., Dover Park Devel. Corp. Ltd. 1980–84; Extve. Vice-Pres., Corp. Devel. Trizec Corp. Ltd. 1984–86; Pres. & C.O.O., Trilea Centres Inc. 1986–87, Pres. & C.E.O., 1987–88; Dir., Bramalea Limited; Coscan Ltd.; Carma Ltd.; Trizec Ltd.; mem., Candn. Bar Assn.; Alta. Law Soc.; recreations: hunting, fishing, trail riding; Clubs: Cambridge, Founders, Bow Valley; Office: 181 Bay St., Ste. 4200, Toronto, Ont. M5J 2T3.

**ARNETT, Emerson James,** B.A., LL.B., LL.M., Q.C.; senior law partner; b. Winnipeg, Man. 29 Sept. 1938; s. Emerson Lloyd and Elsie Audrey (Rhind) A.; e. Kelvin H.S.; Univ. of Man. B.A. 1959, LL.B. 1963; Harvard Univ. LL.M. 1964; m. Alix d. Mr. & Mrs. W.L. Palk, Q.C. 16 June 1964; children: Shanly, Netannis, William, Charles; SR. PARTNER, STIKEMAN, ELLIOTT 1973– ; read law with (now) Rt. Hon. Brian Dickson, former Chief Justice of Can. 1959–63; MacKenzie King Travelling Scholarship 1963–64; Dept. of Justice, Ottawa 1964–65; practised law with Pitblado & Hoskin 1965–66; Extve. Asst. to Extve. Vice-Pres., Vickers & Benson Advtg. 1966–67; Assoc., Davies, Ward & Beck, Solicitors 1968; Partner 1970; Partner, Stikeman, Elliott 1973; Can. Chrmn., Harvard Law Sch. Fund 1985–87; Pres., Harvard Law Sch. Assn. of Ont. 1990–91; Q.C. (Ont.); Spec. Couns. to Govt. of Can. in connection with Investment Canada Act 1984; Mem., Zeta Psi Soc.; Internat. & Candn. Bar Assns.; Law Socs. of Upper Can. & Man.; Candn. Counc. on Internat. Law; co-editor: 'Doing Business in Canada' 1984; author of several articles; recreations: shooting, skiing; clubs: Duck Island, Royal Lake-of-the-Woods Yacht; Home: 3220 Highland Place NW, Washington, D.C. 20008; Office: Suite 1210, West Tower, 1300 I Street, N.W., Washington, D.C. 20005.

**ARNGNA'NAAQ, Silas;** politician; cabinet minister; b. Baker Lake 20 April 1957; s. Luke and Myra (Kukiiyaut) A.; e. Sir John Franklin H.S.; Dalhouse Univ. diploma Public & Bus. Admin.; m. Teri J. d. David and Maureen Thayer 9 April 1984; children: Nathan Kigyougalik, Sarah Maureen, Laura Margaret; Manager, Inuit Pitgosii Baker Lake 1979; Dept. of Economic Devel. & Tourism 1981–87, 1989–91; Dept. of Edn., Formation of Keewatin Div. Bd. of Edn. 1987–89; Mem., Hamlet Council Baker Lake; Chair, Community Edn. Council Baker Lake; Treasurer, Anglican vestry Baker Lake (one year); elected to Legislative Assemply of the N.W.T. as member for Kivalivik 1991; Chrmn. Standing Ctte. on Legislation 1991–93; apptd. to Extve. Council as Min. of Municipal and Community Affairs 1993; recreations: hunting, fishing, dogteaming; Home: 45 Gold City Crt., Yellowknife, N.W.T. X1A 3P7; Office: Box 1320, Yellowknife, N.W.T. X1A 2L9.

**ARNOLD, Armin Herbert,** Dr. ès Lettres, F.R.S.C.; educator; author; b. Zug, Switzerland 1 Sept. 1931; s. Franz and Ida (Baumgartner) A.; e. Univ. of Fribourg 1951–53, 1955–56 Dr. ès Lettres 1956; Univ. of Zurich 1953–54; Univ. of London 1954–55; AUX. PROF. OF GERMAN, McGILL UNIV. 1984–89; Asst. Prof. of German, Univ. of Alta. 1959–61; Asst. Prof. McGill Univ. 1961, Assoc. Prof. 1964, Prof. 1968, Chrmn. German Dept. 1965–70, 1971–74; author: 'D.H. Lawrence and America' 1958; 'Heinrich Heine in England and America' 1959; 'James Joyce' 1963, Eng. transl. 1969; 'D.H. Lawrence and German Literature' 1963; 'G.B. Shaw' 1965; 'Die Literatur des Expressionismus' 1966, 2nd ed. 1971; 'Felix Stümpers Abenteuer und Streiche' 1967; 'Friedrich Dürrenmatt' Berlin 1969, 2d ed. 1971, 3rd ed. 1974, 4th ed. 1979, 5th ed. 1986; Eng. transl. 1972; 'D.H. Lawrence' 1972; 'Prosa des Expressionismus' 1972; co-author: (with J. Schmidt) 'Reclams Kriminalromanführer'; editor: 'D.H. Lawrence: The Symbolic Meaning' 1962; 'Kriminalerzählungen aus drei Jahrhunderten' 1978; 'Interpretationen zu Georg Kaiser' 1980; 'Sherlock Holmes auf der Hintertreppe' 1981; 'Westerngeschichten aus zwei Jahrhunderten' 1981; 'English Crime Stories' 1990; 'American Crime Stories' 1991; co-editor: 'Kanadische Erzähler der Gegenwart' 1967; 'Studien zur Germanistik, Anglistik und Komparatistik' 110 vols. 1969– ; 'Canadian Studies in German Language and Literature' 33 vols. 1969– ; 'Das Goethe-Haus Montreal 1962–70' 1970; 'Interpretationen zu Friedrich Dürrenmatt' 1982; 'Caesar von Arx: Briefe an den Vater' 1982; 'The Popular Novel in the 19th Century' 1982; 'Spionagegeschichten aus zwei Jahrhunderten' 1984; 'Die verschlossene Tür' 1984; 'Hermann Böschenstein: Die Mutter und der neutrale Sohn' 1984; 'Studien und Texte zur Literatur der deutschen Schweiz' 1984– ; 'Cäsar von Arx – Walter Richard Ammann: Briefwechsel 1929–1949' 1985; 'Cäsar von Arx – Philipp Etter: Briefwechsel und Dokumente 1940–1941' 1985; 'Cäsar von Arx: Werke 1' 1986; 'Werke 3' 1987; 'Der gesunde Gelehrte' 1987; 'Dictionary of Literary Themes and Motifs' 2 vol. 1988; Lit. Critic: 'Neue Zürcher Zeitung' 1955–70; 'Die Welt' 1964–71; numerous prefaces, introductions and articles in books, Candn. and foreign prof. journs.; R. Catholic; Summer Home: 9e rang, Ste-Anne de la Rochelle, Qué. J0E 2B0; Winter Home: Rauchlenweg 332, 4712 Laupersdorf, Switzerland.

**ARNOLD, G. Jeff,** B.A., C.A.; financial executive; b. Liverpool, England 31 Jan. 1949; s. of the late George W. and the late Sarah E. (Webster) A.; e. Univ. of Western Ont. B.A. (Hons.) 1973; C.A. 1976; m. Hanne, d. Erling and Else Pedersen, 22 May 1976; children: Kris, Erik; VICE-PRES. & CHIEF FINANCIAL OFFR., CAMPBELL SOUP COMPANY LTD 1991– ; Mgr., Arthur Andersen & Co. C.A.s 1974–85; Dir., Financial Planning, Campbell Soup Co. Ltd 1985–86; Controller 1986–89; Vice-Pres., Chief Financial Officer and Controller 1989–91; Office: 60 Birmingham St., Toronto, Ont. M8V 2B8.

**ARNOLD, Hugh James,** B.A., M.A., Ph.D.; university professor; b. Lethbridge, Alta. 9 Nov. 1949; s. Hugh Alexander and Islay May (Brown) A.; e. Univ. of Alta., B.A. 1970; Oxford Univ., M.A. 1972; Yale Univ., M.A. 1974, Ph.D 1976; m. Clara d. John and Agnes Fergusson 2 Sept. 1978; children: Jennifer Lee, Christine Marie, Hugh Robert Craig; DEAN, AND MAGNA INTERNATIONAL PROF. OF BUSINESS STRATEGY, FAC. OF MGMT., UNIV. OF TORONTO 1992– ; Chair of Organizational Behaviour 1983–85; Founding Dir., Centre for Organizational Effectiveness 1984–85; Assoc. Dean (Exec. Progs.) and Dir., Exec. M.B.A. Prog. 1985–87, 1991–92; Assoc. Dean (Soc. Sciences), Sch. of Grad. Studies 1987–88; Magna Internat. Prof. of Business Strategy 1988–91; mem. Ed. Bd., Acad. of Mgmt. Jour. 1983–85, Org. Dynamics 1989– ; Chair, Rsch. Methods Div., Acad. of Mgmt. 1987–88; Prog. Ctte. Chair, Pan-Pacific Bus. Assoc. 1985, Acad. of Mgmt. 1986, Decision Sciences Inst. 1986; consultant to numerous bus. orgns.; Associate, Candn. Inst. for Advanced Rsch.; Treas., York Mills Valley Assn. 1985–87; author: 'Organizational Behaviour: A Canadian Perspective' 1992; 'Organizational Behaviour' 1986; 'Managing Individual and Group Behaviour in Organizations' 1983; ed. 'Organizational Behaviour: Cases and Readings' 1983, 2nd ed. 1986, 3rd. 1988; recreations: skiing, tennis; Clubs: Granite; Devil's Glen Ski; Home: 54 Plymbridge Rd., Willowdale, Ont. M2P 1A3; Office: 246 Bloor St. W., Toronto, Ont. M5S 1V4.

**ARNOLD, Hugh Peter,** B.A., B.Ed.; human resources executive; b. Peterborough, Ont. 4 Dec. 1951; s. Hugh Pickering and Jean Eleanor A.; e. Trent Univ. B.A. 1974; Univ. of Toronto B.Ed. 1978; m. Maria d. Hendrik and Klaasje Kooiman 21 Aug. 1976; children: Ryan Peter, Laura Ashley; VICE-PRESIDENT, HUMAN RESOURCES AND CORPORATE SERV., CANADIAN OCCIDENTAL PETROLEUM LTD. 1982– ; Branch Admin. Mgr., Bank of Montreal 1974–77; Employee Relns. Advr., Imperial Oil Ltd. 1978–79; Sr. Advr., Training & Devel., Husky Oil Opns. Ltd. 1979–81; joined present firm as Sr. Advr., Training & Devel. 1982; Mem., Corp. Council on Edn., Conf. Bd. of Can.; Extve. Mem., Council of HR Executives (West), Conf. Bd. of Can.; recreations: sports (golf, baseball), coaching (kids baseball and hockey); Home: Calgary, Alta.; Office: 1500, 635 – 8th Ave. SW, Calgary, Alta. T2P 3Z1.

**ARNOLD, John Malcolm Owens,** B.Sc., M.D., F.R.C.P.Edin.; F.R.C.P.(C).; F.A.C.P.; F.A.C.C.; physician; b. Belfast, N. Ireland 12 Feb. 1951; s. John and Elizabeth (Owens) A.; e. Queen's Univ., Belfast, B.Sc. 1973, M.B., B.Ch., B.A.O. 1976; M.D. 1983; m. Colleen d. Robert and Betty Crooks 3 April 1980; children: David, Paul, Michael; STAFF CARDIOLOGIST, VICTORIA HOSP., LONDON; ASSOC. PROF. OF MED., PHARMACOLOGY & TOXICOLOGY, UNIV. OF W. ONT. 1989– ; Sr. Tutor, Queen's Univ., Belfast 1977–78; Clinical Rsch. Fellow Harvard Med. Sch. 1983–85; Asst. Prof. of Med., 1985-89 & Lectr. in Pharmacology, Univ. of W. Ont. 1986–89; Brit. Am. Fellow, Brit. & Am. Heart Founds. 1983–84; rec'd Career Sci. Award, Pharm. Mfrs. Assn. of Can. 1987–92; rec'd K.M. Piafsky Young Investigator Award of Candn. Soc. of Clinical Pharmacology 1988; recipient, Pierre Bois Rsch. Presentation Runner Up Award, PMAC Health Rsch. Found. 1992; Fellow, Ulster Med. Soc.; Fellow, Royal Coll. of Phys. of Edinburgh; Fellow, Royal Coll. of Phys. of Canada; Fellow, Am. Coll. of Physicians; Fellow, Am. Coll. of Cardiology; Mem., Brit. Pharmacological Soc.; Candn. Cardiovascular Soc.; Candn. Soc. for Clinical Investigation; Candn. Soc. for Clinical Pharmacology; Candn. Hypertension Soc.; Am. Soc. of Clinical Pharmacology & Therapeutics; co-author 'Arterial Disease in the Elderly' 1984; author of more than 60 papers on cardiovascular disease; recreations: family, church, golf; Home: 64 McStay Rd., London, Ont. N6G 2K8; Office: Victoria Hosp., South St., London, Ont. N6A 4G5.

**ARNOTT, Gordon R.,** B.Arch., F.R.A.I.C., F.A.I.A. (Hon.); b. Winnipeg, Man. 1 Aug. 1926; e. Univ. of Man. B.Arch. (Khaki Mem. Bursaries, R.A.I.C. Gold Medal) 1948; PRES., ARNOTT KELLEY O'CONNOR ASSOCS. LTD. formerly Arnott MacPhail Assocs. Ltd. since 1974; Princ., Gordon Ryan Arnott 1950–51; Community & Regional Planning Central Mortgage & Housing Fellowship Univ. of B.C. 1951–52; Townsite Planning & Liaison Arch., Aluminum Co. of Canada, Vancouver-Kitimat 1952–53; Partner, Izumi & Arnott, Regina 1954, Izumi, Arnott, Sugiyama 1954–68; Princ., Gordon R. Arnott & Assoc. 1968–74; awards and comns.: Massey Medal Hon. Mention 1958; Vincent Massey Award of Excellence in Urban Environment (Midtown Plaza, Saskatoon) 1971; T.C. Douglas Bldg., Wascana Centre, Regina; First place, Wascana Centre Restaurant & H.Q. competition 1975; Addition to Western College of Veterinary Medicine, Saskatoon; Air Terminal Bldg. expansion, Regina; Saskatchewan Pavilion, Vancouver, EXPO 1986; Queen's Jubilee Medal 1977; Pres. (1970–71) Royal Arch. Inst. Can., mem. Sask. Assn. Archs. (Past Pres.); Candn. Inst. Planners; Nat. Design Council Can. (1973–79); Pres. Assiniboia Club, Regina 1977–78; Hon. mem. Mexican Soc. Archs.; Dir. Regina Exhbn. Assn. 1982; Dean, Royal Arch. Inst. Can. Coll. of Fellows 1987–89; Chrmn., Adv. Design Ctte., National Capital Commn., Ottawa 1993; Bd. Mem., Can. Extve. Service Organization (CESO) 1989– ; Office: 2275 Albert St., Regina, Sask. S4P 2V5.

**ARNOTT, John,** I.D.S.A., A.O.C.A., A.C.I.D.; industrial designer, entrepreneur; b. Frittenden, England 27 Nov. 1944; s. George Cyril Metcalfe and Elspeth Rosamond (Huggard) A.; e. Ontario College of Art, Assoc.; one d. Alexandra; PRES., THE ARNOTT DESIGN GROUP INC. 1972– ; Dir. of Design, Wesco Products, Hong Kong 1974–76; Vice-Pres., 430603 Ontario Ltd. 1976– ; Pres., Furnitech Systems Inc. 1980–88; Interlearn Inc. 1986–90; Founder, Hydra Communications Inc. 1992– ; Dir., The Design Exchange; The Group for Design in Business; Former Dir., The Performing Arts Devel. Fund; Past Pres., Assn. of Candn. Indus. Designers; Mem., The Indus. Designers Soc. of Am.; recreations: sailing, skiing, tennis; clubs: Waterfront Tennis, Royal Candn. Yacht, Caledon Ski; Office: 33 Davies Ave., Toronto, Ont. M4M 2A9.

**ARNUP, Hon. John Douglas,** O.C., Q.C., LL.D., D.Litt.S.; retired judge; b. Toronto, Ont. 24 May 1911; s. Jesse Henry and Ella Maud (Leeson) A.; e. Oakwood Coll. Inst., Toronto, Ont.; Victoria Coll., Univ. of Toronto, B.A. 1932; Osgoode Hall, Toronto, Ont. 1935; LL.D.: Queen's Univ. 1967; York Univ. 1969; Law Soc. of Upper Can. 1984; D.Litt.S.: Victoria Univ. 1976; m. Caroline Dora, d. Jan Ulrichsen, Beaverton, Ont., 2 Aug. 1941; children: Judith Ann (Dickson), Carol Elizabeth (Andrews), Mary Katherine, Caroline Jane; Judge, Court of Appeal, Ont. 1970–85; Bencher, Law Soc. of Upper Can. 1952–70 and 1985– ; called to the Bar of Ont., Sept. 1935; cr. K.C. 1950; former partner, Arnup, Foulds, Weir, Boeckh & Morris; mem. of Senate, Univ. of Toronto 1945–50; Bd. of Regents, Victoria Univ. 1960–70; Treas., Law Soc. of Upper Can. 1963–66; author 'Middleton – The Beloved Judge' 1988; mem. Candn. Bar Assn.; Officer of the Order of Canada 1989; United Church; recreations: curling, golf; Clubs: Toronto Cricket, Skating, Curling; Lawyers (Past Pres.); Sturgeon Point Golf; Address: 88 Stratford Cres., North York, Ont. M4N 1C6.

**ARONOFF, Samuel,** Ph.D.; educator; b. Brooklyn, N.Y. 27 Feb. 1915; s. Esa and Sonia (Berchofsky) A.; e. Univ. of Calif. (Los Angeles) A.B. 1936, (Berkeley) Ph.D. 1942; m. Edith Elizabeth, d. Everett R. and Ruth Ames Moyer, Syracuse, N.Y., 1936; three d., Zena Katherine, Elizabeth Anne, Margaret Ruth; Prof. Emeritus of Biochem., Simon Fraser Univ.; mem. Am. Soc. Biol. Chems.; Candn. Soc. Biol. Chem.; Am. Chem Soc.; Am. Soc. Plant Physiols.; Am. Soc. Advanc. Science; Home: Langley, B.C. V3A 5G3.

**ARONOVITCH, Michael,** B.Sc., M.D., C.M., F.R.C.P.(C); retired physician; b. Montreal, P.Q. 15 Apr. 1910; s. Isaac and Minnie (Miller) A.; e. McGill University, B.Sc. (Arts) 1931; M.D., C.M., 1935; m. Katherine Louisa, d. S. Silver, Montreal, P.Q. 30 Dec. 1945; children: Jane Ellen, Stephen Arnold, Carole Anne, Isaac Lawrence; Consultant, Mt. Sinai Hosp. Montreal; former Consultant, Montreal Chest Hospital Centre; Honorary Phys., Royal Victoria Hosp.; former Chest Consultant, Herbert Reddy Mem. Hosp. and Bellechasse Hosp., Montreal; Former Assoc.Prof. of Med. and Clinical Med., McGill Univ.; former Chrmn. of Bd., Fulcrum Investment Co. Ltd.; Pres. Armika Ltd.; former Dir. and Chrmn. of Bd., Alphatext Ltd.; Past Consultant, Grace Dart Hospital, Montreal and Dept. Veterans Affairs; specialized in Internal Medicine and Chest Diseases; Major, R.C.A.M.C., 1942–46; author of many articles mostly on internal medicine; mem., Candn. Med. Assn.; Montreal Clinical Soc. (Pres., 1952–53); Fellow Royal Coll. of Physicians; Fellow Am. Coll. of Phys.; Fellow Am. Coll. of Chest Phys.; Assoc. mem., Roy. Coll. of Phys., London, Eng.; Treas., M.S.H. Found.; Home: 92 Cambridge Cr., Richmond Hill, Ont. L4C 6G2.

**ARRELL, Hugh Anthony,** B.Sc.A., M.B.A.; executive; b. Hamilton, Ont. 20 Dec. 1944; s. Hugh Cameron and Grace Louise A.; e. Univ. of Guelph B.Sc.A. 1967; York Univ. M.B.A. 1968; m. M. Suzanne 14 May 1968; children: Laura, Cameron, Ashleigh, Nicole; Dir. Scotts Hospitality Inc.; Woodwards Stores Ltd.; Fairfax Financial Holdings Ltd.; Garbell Holdings Ltd.; joined Pitfield McKay 1969–70; Brown, Baldwin Nisker 1972–76; Gardiner Watson Ltd. 1976–83; Wood Gundy Inc. 1983–85; Wood Gundy Corp., New York City 1985–88; Chrmn. & C.E.O. Midland Walwyn Inc. 1988–90; Past Pres. Cystic Fibrosis Foundation; United Church; recreation: cattle breeding; Clubs: National; Metropolitan (N.Y.); Home: 33 Rose Park Dr., Toronto, Ont. M4T 1R2.

**ARROTT, Anthony Schuyler,** B.Sc., M.S., Ph.D., F.R.S.C.; professor; b. Pittsburgh, Pa. 1 Apr. 1928; s. Charles Ramsey and June (Scheffler) A.; e. Carnegie Inst. of Technol., B.Sc. 1948, Ph.D. 1954; Univ. of Pa., M.S. 1950; m. Patricia d. Helen and George Graham 6 June 1953; children: Anthony Patterson, Helen Graham, Matthew Ramsey, Elizabeth; PROF. OF PHYSICS, SIMON FRASER UNIV. 1968– ; Brown Instrument Div., Minn. Honeywell 1948–50; Asst. Prof., Carnegie Inst. of Technol. 1955–56; Sci., Ford Motor Co. 1956–69; Adjunct Prof., Univ. of Michigan 1967–69; Chrmn., Physics Dept., Simon Fraser Univ. 1977–80; Vis. Sci., Brookhaven Nat. Lab. 1956, 1962, 1965, 1986; Atomic Energy Rsch. Establishment 1964; Argonne Nat. Lab. 1967; TRIUMF 1976–77; Weizmann Inst. 1982; Univ. of Tokyo 1985; Mem., Magnetism Comn. Int. Union of Pure and Applied Physics 1977–83; NSERC Grants Selection Ctte. 1979–81; Ctte. for Internat. Coop. 1984–88; Review Cttes., Argonne Nat. Labs. 1979–86; NRC Physics Div. 1981; Fellowships: Allis Chalmers 1951–53; Guggenheim 1964; Japan Soc. for the Promotion of Sci. 1985; Sci. Counc. of B.C. Gold Medal for Phys. Sci.

1982; F.R.S.C. 1983; Univ. Rsch. Prof., Simon Fraser Univ. 1983–84; Medal of Achievement, Candn. Assn. of Physicists 1986; Pres., Sci. for Peace 1988–90 (Dir. 1982–91, founding Mem., B.C. chapt. 1982); Adv. Bd., Physicians for Social Responsibility 1983– ; Orgn. Ctte., Nuclear War: The Search for Solutions 1984; Mem.-at-large, Vancouver Inst. 1983– ;(Pres. 1991–93); Mem., Candn. Assn. of Phys.; Am. Phys. Soc. (Fellow); Ed. Bds.: 'International Journal of Magnetism' 1970–74; 'Journal of Magnetism and Magnetic Materials' 1974– ; 'Journal of Applied Physics' 1983–85; 'Applied Physics Letters' 1983–85; author of more than 200 articles; Office: Dept. of Physics, Simon Fraser Univ., Burnaby, B.C. V5A 1S6.

**ARSHINOFF, Rena,** RN, B.A., M.H.Sc.; research nurse co-ordinator; b. Montreal, Que. 15 Sept. 1953; d. Ben and Ann (Huberman) Shames; e. Bancroft Sch.; Northmount H.S.; Vanier Coll., RN 1973; Concordia Univ., cert. in community nursing 1977, B.A. 1978; Univ. of Toronto, M.H.Sc. 1983; m. Stephen s. Morton and Bernice A. 9 Mar. 1975; children: Michael, Rachel, Jessica; Co-ordinator of Epidemiologic Rsch. Studies, Preventive Med. & Biostat. Dept., Univ. of Toronto 1985–..; cross-apptd. at Addiction Rsch. Found.; Hosp. Nurse Montreal 1973–76; public health nurse 1976–80 (worked in all areas of public health, developing & implementing several programs); involvement with Bereaved Families of Ont. to help families who have lost a baby; Mem., Miscarriage Adv. Ctte., Women's Coll. Hosp.; Nat. Counc. of Jewish Women Hadar Branch (Prog. Chrmn. 1986–88); author/co-author of several health articles and manuals; Address: 167 Lord Seaton Rd., Willowdale, Ont. M2P 1K8.

**ARTAUD, Gérard,** Ph.D.; psychotherapeute; ecrivain; né Bretignolles sur/mer, France 19 mai 1926; f. Gabriel et Florentine (Bouchereau) A.; é. Univ. de Poitiers France B. Phil. 1945; Univ. Gregorienne Rome L.Th. 1952; Ecole des Hautes Etudes Paris Diplôme Psychologie 1968; Univ. La Sorbonne Paris Ph.D. 1971; ép. Marie-Anne f. Paul et Marie-Ange Paillat 19 mai 1969; enfants: Laurence, Janick; Professeur Univ. d'Ottawa 1969–93; Professeur de Philosophie Institution Jean XXIII France 1952–60, Directeur 1960–64; Chercheur Centre de Recherche en Psychologie Comparative de l'Ecole des Hautes Etudes Paris 1966–69; Psychotherapeute, Dept. de Psychiatrie Hôpital Général d'Ottawa 1969–79; Directeur de l'Institut de Pédagogie de langue française Univ. de Fribourg 1979–80; Prix d'excellence en enseignement de l'Univ. d'Ottawa 1984; auteur 'Se connaitre soi- même: La crise d'identité de l'adulte' 1979; 'L'adulte en quête de son identité' 1985; 'La récreation du savoir' 1985; 'L'intervention educative' 1990; récreations: ski, natation; Bureau: 39 - 100 Hillside Dr., Ottawa, Ont. K1K 4J3.

**ARTHUR, James Greig,** Ph.D., F.R.S.C., F.R.S.; educator; b. Hamilton, Ont. 18 May 1944; s. John Greig and Katherine Mary Patricia (Scott) A.; e. Upper Can. Coll. Toronto 1962; Univ. of Toronto B.Sc. 1966, M.Sc. 1967; Yale Univ. Ph.D. 1970; m. Dorothy Pendleton d. George and Dorothy Helm 10 June 1972; two s. James Pendleton, David Greig; UNIVERSITY PROFESSOR, MATHEMATICS, UNIV. OF TORONTO 1979– ; Instr. Princeton Univ. 1970–72, Visiting mem. Inst. for Advanced Study 1976–77; Asst. Prof. Yale Univ. 1972–76; Prof. Duke Univ. 1976–79; Sloan Fellow 1975–77; E.W.R. Steacie Memorial Fellow 1981–83; John L. Synge Award, Royal Soc. of Can. 1987; Fellow, Royal Soc. of London 1992; author various articles math. jours.; mem. Candn. Math. Soc.; Am. Math. Soc.; recreations: tennis, squash; Home: 23 Woodlawn Ave. W., Toronto, Ont. M4V 1G6; Office: Toronto, Ont. M5S 1A1.

**ARTHUR, Mark Leslie,** B.Admin., M.B.A., C.F.A.; b. Ottawa, Ont. 17 March 1956; s. Charles Douglas and Eleske Irene (Van Berkum) A.; e. Brock Univ. B.Admin. 1977; Univ. of Western Ont. M.B.A. 1980; Univ. of Virginia C.F.A. 1984; EXTVE. VICE-PRES., C.I.O. & DIRECTOR, ROYAL BANK INVESTMENT MANAGEMENT 1989– ; Research, Institutional Sales, Mktg. Dept., Royal Bank of Canada-Dominion Securities 1980–84; Vice-Pres., Manager Mktg. Dept. 1984–88; Vice Chairman, Investment Strategy Ctee. 1984–91; Vice-Pres. & Dir. 1988–92; Pres. & Dir., Dominion Securities Investment Management 1988–89; Dir., Barbican Properties; Home: 18 Hartfield Rd., Etobicoke, Ont. M9A 3C7; Office: Royal Bank Plaza, 4th Floor, N.T., Toronto, Ont. M5J 2J2.

**ARTHUR, Paul Rodney,** C.M., B.A., RCA, SEGD(F); design consultant; b. Liverpool, Eng. 20 Dec. 1924; s. Eric Ross and Deborah Doris (Debert) A.; e. Upper Can. Coll. Toronto; Univ. Coll., Univ. of Toronto B.A. 1948; m. Dinah d. Archibald S. and Margery Kerr 31 May 1981; children: Carolyn Rose, Jonathan, Laura Haggart (step-d.); PRINCIPAL, PAUL ARTHUR VISUCOM LIMITED (a generalist design consulting firm that specializes in developing wayfinding solutions for the built environment); Partner, Newton Frank Arthur Inc. 1976–88; Asst. Ed. 'Graphis' mag. Zurich, Switzerland 1951–56; estbd. Paul Arthur & Associates Ltd. Ottawa 1956; Dir. of Publs. Nat. Gall. of Can. Ottawa also Designer, Art Dir., Ed. and subsequently Publisher 'Canadian Art' mag. 1956–68; estbd. PA & A Ltd. Toronto and began extensive practice in U.S. with offices in N.Y.C. and Portland, Ore. 1968–74; estbd. Paul Arthur VisuCom Ltd. to supervise design and distribution of the firm's 'Picto'grafics' Toronto 1974; designer colour system for 31,000 U.S. post offices 1972; designer bilingual communications for U.S. border stns. 1972; Design Dir. Nat. Museum's 'Discovery Train' 1978; recipient Centennial Award 1967; Mem., Order of Canada 1994; chair CAN Z-321 Cttee. on Signs and symbols in the workplace; co-author, with Romedi Passini, 'Wayfinding: People, Signs, and Architecture' 1992; designer, national signs and symbols program for Canada Post Corp. 1988–90; mem. Nat. Rsch. Counc. Washington, D.C.; Candn. Standards Assn.; Candn. Govt. Standards Bd.; Founding mem. and Fellow (F) Soc. for Environmental Graphic Design (SEGD) Cambridge, Mass.; Home: 30 St. Andrews Gdns., Toronto, Ont.; Office: 950 Yonge St., Toronto, Ont. M4W 2J4.

**ARTHURS, Harry William,** O.C., B.A., LL.M., LL.D., D.Litt., F.R.S.C.; educator; b. Toronto, Ont., 9 May 1935; s. Leon and Ellen (Dworkin) A.; e. Oakwood Coll. Inst., Toronto 1952; Univ. of Toronto, B.A. 1955, LL.B. 1958; Harvard Law Sch., LL.M. 1959; LL.D. (Sherbrooke, Brock, Law Soc. of Upper Canada); D.Litt. (Lethbridge); PRESIDENT EMERITUS, YORK UNIVERSITY 1992– , President 1985–92; Prof. of Law, Osgoode Hall Law School since 1968; read law with S.L. Robins, Q.C., Toronto; called to the Bar of Ont. 1961; Asst. Prof., Osgoode Hall Law Sch. 1961, Assoc. Prof. 1964, Prof. 1968, Assoc. Dean 1968–70, Dean 1972–77; Visiting Lectr.: Faculty of Law, Univ. of Toronto 1965–66; Faculty of Law, McGill Univ. 1967–68; Visiting Fellow: Clare Hall, Cambridge 1971; Centre for Socio-Legal Studies, Oxford, 1977–78; Killam Fellow and Visiting Prof.: University Coll., London 1984; Arbitrator and Conciliator in Labour disputes since 1962; Impartial Chrmn., Men's (1967–83) and Ladies' (1967–81) Garment Industry, Toronto; Pres. Candn. Civil Liberties Assn. 1976–77; Chief Adjudicator, Public Service of Can. 1967–69; mem. Candn. Bar Assn.; Candn. Assn. Law Teachers; Assn. Am. Law Schs.; Candn. mem. Un. Auto Workers Public Review Bd. 1967–77; mem. Economic Counc. of Can. 1978–81; Bencher, Law Soc. of Upper Can. 1979–83; Chrmn. Consultative Group on Legal Research and Educ. S.S.H.R.C. 1980–83; Chrmn., Counc. of Ont. Univs. 1987–89; Fellow, Roy. Soc. of Can. 1982; Officer, Order of Canada 1989; author of numerous articles and monographs on labour relations law, civil liberties, adm. law, legal history and educ. in learned and prof. journs.; Home: 11 Hillcrest Park, Toronto, Ont. M4X 1E8; Office: York Univ., 4700 Keele St., North York, Ont. M3J 1P3.

**ARTIBISE, Alan Francis Joseph,** B.A., Ph.D.; educator; b. Dauphin, Man. 23 Jan. 1946; s. Henry Damian and Alma Ann (Farenhurst) A.; e. St. Joseph's Coll. Yorkton, Sask. 1964; Univ. of Man., B.A. 1967; Univ. of B.C., Ph.D. 1972; m. Sonja Karen d. Ray and Hallie Cunningham 17 Feb. 1990; children: Henri Yuri, Anna Alma; PROF., SCH. OF COMM. & REG. PLANNING, UNIVERSITY OF B.C. 1988– ;and EXEC.-DIR., INTERNAT. CENTRE FOR SUSTAINABLE CITIES, VANCOUVER; Lectr. in Hist. & Candn. Studies, Cariboo Coll. Kamloops, B.C. 1971, Chrmn. Social Sci's Div. and Coordinator Candn. Studies Prog. 1973–75; Head, W. Can. Sect. Hist. Div. Candn. Museum of Civilization Ottawa 1975–76; mem. Hist. Dept. Univ. of Victoria 1976, Prof. 1982; Prof. of Hist., Univ. of Winnipeg 1983–88; Dir., Inst. of Urban Studies, Univ. of Winnipeg 1983–88; Dir., Sch. of Comm. & Reg. Planning, Univ. of B.C. 1988–93; Past Vice Pres. Bd. Govs. Man. Museum of Man and Nature; Past Pres. Social Sci. Fedn. Can.; Past Pres. Internat. Council for Candn. Studies; Past Chrmn. Nat. Capital Comn. Planning Ctte.; mem. Acad. Adv. Ctte. Prog. for Candn. Studies in Israel; Adv. Ctte. Bus. Fund for Candn. Studies in USA; mem. Lambda Alpha International, Vancouver; Bd. Mem., Glacier Resorts Ltd.; mem. Candn. Del. to Group on Urban Affairs, Orgn. for Econ. Coop. & Devel. Paris; Bd. Mem., Inst. for the Study of Internat. Cities; Past Chrmn., National Capital Comn. Adv. Ctte. on Marketing and Programming; Past Bd. Mem., Candn. Inst. for Historical Microreproductions; served Bds. Age & Opportunity Centre Inc.; Rossbrook House Inc.; Srs. Transp. Service Inc.; Man. Multicultural Resources Centre; Woodsworth House Hist. Soc.; Man. Record Soc.; Champlain Soc. Can.; Vice Chrmn. comn. reviewing City of Winnipeg Act 1984–85; Exec. mem. Internat. Planning Hist. Group; mem. Bd. Forks Renewal Corp. 1987–88; nat. & internat. lectr. Candn. hist. & urban studies; regular CBC Radio commentator; recipient numerous fellowships & awards incl. 3 medals Man. Hist. Soc.; Awards of Merit Candn. Hist. Assn., Am. Assn. for State & Local Hist., Assn. Candn. Studies in USA; Internat. Council for Cdn. Studies; Excellence in Planning Award, Planning Inst. of B.C.; Media Club of Canada Award; Marie Tremaine Medal Bibliog. Soc. Can.; Hon. Citizen City of Winnipeg; Citation for Citizenship presented by Secy. of State for Can. 1988; awarded Commemorative Medal for 125th Anniversary of Candn. Confederation 1992; author 'Winnipeg: A Social History of Urban Growth' 1975; 'Winnipeg: An Illustrated History' 1977; 'The Canadian City: Essays in Social and Urban History' 1977, 2nd ed. 1984; 'The Usable Urban Past' 1979; 'Shaping the Canadian Urban Landscape' 1982; 'Town and City: Aspects of Western Canadian Urban Development' 1981; 'Western Canada Since 1870: A Bibliography and Guide' 1978; 'Canada's Urban Past: A Bibliography and Guide to Urban Studies' 1981; 'Power and Place: Canadian Urban Development in the North American Context' 1986; 'Canadian Regional Development: The Urban Dimension' 1989; 'The Pacific Fraser Region: Towards 2010' 1991; ed.-in-chief 'Urban History Review/Revue d'histoire urbaine' 1975–88; assoc. ed. 'Prairie Forum,' 'America: History and Life,' 'Urban Affairs Quarterly' and 'Journal of Urban Affairs'; gen. ed. 'History of Canadian Cities Series'; urban cons. 'The Canadian Encyclopedia'; Pres. Assn. Candn. Studies 1982–86; Vice Pres., Pacific Rim Council on Urban Development; Bd. mem. International Downtown Assn.; Past Pres. Candn. Regional Sci. Assn.; former Bd. mem. Candn. Hist. Assn.; Candn. Fedn. Humanities; Gov. N.Am. Urban Affairs Assn.; Office: University of British Columbia, 6333 Memorial Rd., Vancouver, B.C. V6T 1Z2.

**ASBIL, The Rt. Rev. Walter Gordon,** B.A., L.Th., B.D., S.T.M., D.D.; bishop; b. Rawdon, Que. 3 Oct. 1932; s. John and Violet (Tracey) A.; e. Concordia Univ. B.A. 1954; Montreal Diocesan Theol. Coll. L.Th. 1957; McGill Univ. B.D. 1957, S.T.M. 1967, D.D., Montreal Diocesan Theological Coll. 1991; m. Mavis d. Walter and Myrtle Shaver 20 July 1957; children: Brent, Andrew, Mark, Cynthia; BISHOP, DIOCESE OF NIAGARA 1991– ; ordained Deacon, Dioc. of Montreal May 1957; Priest Dec. 1957; Incumbent of Aylwin, River Desert Parish 1957; Montreal South Shore Parish 1960; Rector, St. Stephen's Westmount 1965; St. George's Ste. Anne de Bellevue 1965; St. George's St. Catharines 1970; Dean of Ottawa, Rector, Christ Ch. Cathedral 1986; Canon, Christ's Ch. Cath. 1972; Archdeacon, Dioc. of Niagara 1981; Prolocutor, Gen. Synod, Anglican Con. Counc. 1983; Priest Del. from Can. in Nigeria, Singapore, Wales 1984–90; Coadjutor Bishop, Diocese of Niagara 1990–91; Diocesan Bishop of Niagara Nov. 1991; Founding Dir., Volunteers Bur.; St. Catharines Un. Way; Bd. Mem., St. Catharines Gen. Hosp. 1983–86; Home: 26 Terrace Dr., Dundas, Ont. L9H 3X2; Office: 67 Victoria Ave. S., Hamilton, Ont. L8N 2S8.

**ASH, Stuart Bradley,** RCA, AGI, AIGA, GDC; design consultant; b. Hamilton, Ont. 10 July 1942; s. Clifford and Margaret A.; e. Western Tech. Sch. (graphic design); Ont. Coll. of Art (graphic design) grad. 1962; PRINCIPAL, GOTTSCHALK & ASH INTERNATIONAL DESIGN CONSULTANTS TORONTO, MONTREAL, ZURICH since 1966; design work has been published, exhibited, and given awards internationally; Instructor at Ontario Coll. of Art (Advanced Typography) 1978–80; recipient, Canada Centennial Medal; recreations: sailing, skiing; Home: 48 Hazelton, Toronto, Ont. M5R 2E2; Office: 11 Bishop St., Toronto, Ont. M5R 1N3.

**ASHBY, Roger Arthur,** B.Sc.(Comm.), R.I.A./C.M.A., F.C.G.A.; executive; b. Marieville, Que. 2 Nov. 1940; s. Emmett and Aurore (Ledoux) A.; e. Univ. of Montreal B.Sc.(Comm.) 1963; R.I.A./C.M.A. 1966, C.G.A. 1967; m. Marguerite d. Louis Kelly 12 Feb. 1966; children: Eric, Alexandre; PRESIDENT & C.E.O., ROLLAND INC. 1991; Dir., Sintra Inc.; PWA Decor Inc.; Q.F.I.A. (Qué. Forest Industries Assoc.); Pres. & C.E.O., Spruce Falls Power and Paper Co. Ltd. 1976–78; Extve. Vice Pres. and Chief Operating Offr., Rolland Inc. 1978–80; Pres., Domtar Pulp and Paper 1981–90; served one year Royal Military Coll. – Navy; mem., Candn. Pulp and Paper Assn. (Technical Section); Catholic; Club: St. James; Mount Bruno Country; recreations: skiing, tennis, golfing, cycling; Home: 65 Pagnuelo, Outremont, Qué. H2V 3B8.

**ASHE, George Lyle;** former politician; b. Ottawa, Ont. 5 Oct. 1932; s. late Elmer Lyle and Marjorie Laura (Constantineau) A.; e. S.S. Hon. Grad. Dipl. 1950, Chartered Life Underwriter 1964; m. Margaret d. late Frank and late Agnes Conroy 10 July 1954; children: Steven, Cheryl, Kevin, Brian; Pres., G.A. Consultants Ltd. and Pres., Ashe-Allen Productions Inc. 1987–92; Vice Pres., Land Development Steele Valley Developments Ltd. 1989–93; former M.P.P., Ont. and Party Critic for Financial Institutions; Life Ins. Agent, Field Mgr., Prudential Ins. Co. of Am. 1956–66; Agency Mgr. and Brokerage Mgr., Northern Life of Can. 1967–77; Sep. Sch. Trustee, Gloucester, Ont. 1956–57; Sep. Sch. Bd. Chrmn., Nepean Twp. 1961–65; Dep. Reeve, Twp. of Pickering, Ont. 1970–73; First Mayor of New Town of Pickering 1974–77, re-el. by acclamation 1976; el. M.P.P., Durham West, Ont. June 1977, re-el. Mar. 1981, May 1985; Parl Asst., Treasurer & Min. of Econ. & Intergovt. Affairs 1977–79; Parl Asst., Min. of Energy 1979–81; Min. of Revenue, Ont. Apr. 1981–July 1983; Min. of Govt. Services July 1983–Feb. 1985; Min. of Energy Feb.–May 1985; Chrmn. Mgmt. Bd. of Cabinet May–June 1985; Queen's Jubilee Medal 1977; P. Conservative; Roman Catholic; recreation: tennis; Home: 417 Victor Court, Pickering, Ont. L1W 3J7.

**ASHEVAK, Kenojuak,** C.C., R.C.A., LL.D.; graphic artist; b. Ikerrasak, S. Baffin Island Oct. 1927; m. the late Johnniebo A.; children: Adamie, Anago, Jamasie, Pee, Pudloo, Shelaky; medium: drawings, prints, sculpture, crafts; 165 group exhbns. incl. most recent: Cape Dorset Graphics 1990, 1991, Snow Goose Assoc. Seattle, Wa. 1991, Bunkamura Art Gall. Tokyo, Japan 1991, Albers Gall. San Francisco, Ca. 1991, l'Iglou Art Esquimau, Douai (toured ten galleries) France 1991–92, The McMichael Candn. Art Coll. Kleinburg, Ont. 1991–92, Nat. Gall. of Canada Ottawa 1992, Marion Scott Gall. Vanc. 1992; solo exhbns.: Arctic Artistry Hartsdale, N.Y. 1988, McMichael Candn. Coll. 1986, Waddington & Shiell Galleries Ltd. 1983, Canadian Galleries Edmonton 1982, Waddington Galleries 1979, 1980, Walter Phillips Gall. Banff 1979; The Innuit Gall. of Eskimo Art Toronto 1971, 1986, National Library 1967; works in 47 collections incl. art galleries of Edmonton, Greater Victoria, Hamilton, Kitchener-Waterloo, London Region, Nova Scotia, Ontario (Klamer Family Coll.), Vancouver, Windsor, Winnipeg, Amon Carter Mus. of Western Art Fort Worth, Texas, Canada Council Art Bank Ottawa, Candn. Mus. of Civilization Hull, Que., National Gallery of Can. Ottawa, Inuit Cultural Inst. Rankin Inlet, N.W.T., New Brunswick Mus., Royal Ont. Mus., Tate Gallery and Victoria & Albert Mus. London, Eng., World Wildlife Fund Coll. Switzerland; attended openings at Nat. Lib. of Can. 1967, (gala opening) 1988, N.S. Technical Coll. 1974 (travel grant), World Wildlife Fund 1977, 'Inuit Print' exhbn. Rotterdam, Holland 1980, Godard Editions Gall. 1981, Nat. Gall. of Canada 1988, 'Masters of the Arctic' N.Y. 1989; Order of Canada 1967; Companion 1982; R.C.A. 1974; 'Enchanted Owl' (1960) reproduced on stamp commemorating N.W.T. centennial 1970; 'Return of the Sun' stamp 1980; 'Kenojuak: A Retrospective Exhibition' McMichael Candn. Coll. 1986; limited ed. lithograph 'Nunavut Qajanartuk' comnd. by INAC to commemorate the Tungavik Fed. of Nunavut's land claim agreement 1990; Hon. LL.D. Queen's Univ. 1991; Univ. of Toronto 1992; subject: 'Graphic Masterworks of the Inuit: Kenojuak' 1981; subject of numerous articles, catalogues and one film by NFB 1962; Home: Cape Dorset, N.W.T.; Office: c/o Dorset Fine Art, 33 Belmont St., Toronto, Ont. M5R 1P9.

**ASHFORD, Mary-Wynne,** B.Sc., B.Ed., M.D.; family physician; b. Indian Head, Sask. 17 March 1939; d. Jack and Katherine Elizabeth (Wilson) Moar; e. Edmonton Strathcona H.S. 1956; Univ. of Alta. B.Sc. 1960, B.Ed. 1961 (Mamie Shaw Simpson Award for Outstanding Woman Student 1960; Honor Prize, Golden Key Soc.); Univ. of Calgary M.D. 1981; Internship, Victoria Gen. Hosp. 1981–82; m. David. s. Rev. Ray and Belinda A. 29 Aug. 1959; divorced 1981; children: Karen Ann, Graham Allan Ray, Patrick Robert; High School Teacher, Bonnie Doon Composite 1960–65; homemaker, freelance writer, volunteer with Calgary Zoo & Pres., Suzuki Violin Prog. 1965–74; Weekly Columnist, Calgary Herald & Editor, Dinny's Digest 1975; Family Practitioner, Victoria, B.C. 1982–92; writer & speaker on issues of peace & disarmament; Victoria YMCA Peace Medal 1989; Pres., Victoria YM-YWCA 1987–89; Candn. Physicians for Prevention of Nuclear War 1988–90; Vice-Pres., N. Am. Internat. Physicians for Prevention of Nuclear War 1991–93 (Nobel Emissary to France 1988; Pres., World Congress Montreal 1988); Keynote speaker Forum for a Nuclear Free World for the Survival of Mankind in Moscow 1987; 1990 Lucyk Lectr., T. Eaton Un. Ch.; Special Advr. to External Affairs for UN Spec. Session on Disarmament III 1988; Mem., Cons. Group to Canada's Ambassador for Disarmament 1988– ; Nat. Bd. Mem., YWCA of/du Canada 1991–92; Voice of Women; Group of 78; Chair Adv. Counc., Ctr. for Studies in Religion and Soc., Univ. of Victoria 1992– ; PhD. candidate, Simon Fraser Univ. 1992– ; (Simons Found. Doctoral Entrance Fellowship; Arthur and Ancie Foulks Grad. Entrance Award in Public Service); Bd. of Govs., Univ. of Victoria 1993– ; awarded Commemorative Medal for 125th Anniversary of Candn. Confederation 1993; Anglican; recreations: theatre, community cable production; Home: 1644 Rockland Ave., Victoria, B.C. V8S 1W7; Office: 1625 Oak Bay Ave., Victoria, B.C. V8R 1B1.

**ASHMAN, Robert Anthony;** company executive; b. Bromley, Kent, U.K. 13 Jan. 1945; s. Leslie Ernest Walter and Dorothy Gertrude (Pain) A.; e. Hayesbrook School Tonbridge, Kent 1958–61; Dartford College, Kent 1961–64; m. Patricia d. Archibald and Kathleen Bessant 7 Oct. 1967; children: Stuart David, Philip James; Pres., GEC Plessey Telecommunications (Canada) Ltd. 1985–..; Apprentice Field Engr., Int. Computers Ltd., U.K. 1961–64; joined GEC Telecoms 1964 as Communications Engr., Coventry, U.K.; on secondment as Site Supervisory Engr., Capetown, S.A. 1970–72; Area Mgr. 1972–76; Tech. Mgr., Gen. Mgr., Managing Dir., GEC Telecoms Nigeria 1976–85; Pres., Electronic Inds. Assn. of Manitoba; Dir., GEC Canada Ltd.; Miconex Inc.; mem. Candn. Inst. of Corporate Dirs.; Inst. of Electrical & Electronics Engrs.; Winnipeg Chamber of Commerce; recreations: jogging, squash, sailing, classic car rallies; Clubs: Winnipeg Hash House Harriers; Northern Harbour Yacht; Carleton.

**ASHOONA, Kaka;** sculptor; b. 18 Sept. 1928; 77 group exbns. incl. most recent: Arctic Artistry Hastings-on-Hudson, N.Y. 1990, 1992, Inuit Gallery of Vancouver 1991, Vancouver Inuit Art Soc. 1991, Arctic Inuit Art Richmond, Va. 1991, Virginia Mus. of Fine Arts Richmond, Va. 1990–91, Winnipeg Art Gall. 1990–92, Feheley Fine Arts Toronto 1990, Candn. Mus. of Civilization Hull, Que. 1990; solo exbns.: Inuit Gall. of Vancouver 1981, 1990, Theo Waddington N.Y. 1981, Zwickers Gall. Halifax 1973, Gallery of the Arctic Victoria 1973; works in 24 collections incl. art galleries of Windsor, Edmonton, Kitchener-Waterloo, Winnipeg (Lindsay and Twomey colls.), Ontario (Sarick Coll.), Canada Council Art Bank, Candn. Mus. of Civilization, Inuit Cultural Inst. Rankin Inlet, N.W.T., Kroller Muller Museum Holland, Musée des beaux-arts de Montréal, Nat. Gallery of Can., N.B. Museum Saint John; short term grant Canada Council 1973; attended openings: Nat. Gallery of Can. (gala) 1988, 'Masters of the Arctic' N.Y. 1989; travelled to Vancouver for solo exhbn. & featured on CTV National News; subject of several articles and catalogues; Home: Cape Dorset, N.W.T.; Office: c/o Dorset Fine Arts, 33 Belmont St., Toronto, Ont. M5R 1P9.

**ASHOONA, Kiawak;** sculptor; b. 16 Sept. 1933; 81 group exhbns. incl. most recent: Arctic Artistry, Hastings-on-Hudson N.Y. 1991, 1992, Nat. Gallery of Canada Ottawa 1992, McMichael Candn. Art Coll. Kleinburg, Ont. 1991–92, Vancouver Inuit Art Soc. 1991, Feheley Fine Arts Toronto 1991, Arctic Inuit Art Virginia Mus. of Fine Arts Richmond, Va. 1990–91, Inuit Gall. of Vanc. 1990, Candn. Mus. of Civilization Hull, Que. 1990; solo exhbns.: Marion Scott Gallery Vancouver 1991, Houston North Gallery Lunenburg, N.S. 1986, Inuit Galerie Mannheim, Germany 1985, Waddington Galleries Toronto 1980, Theo Waddington N.Y. 1980; works in 23 collections incl. art galleries of Ontario (Klamer Family & Sarick colls.), Winnipeg (Abbott & Twomey colls.), Canada Council Art Bank Ottawa, Candn. Mus. of Civilization Hull, Que., National Gallery of Can. Ottawa, Inuit Cultural Inst. Rankin Inlet, N.W.T., Metro. Mus. of Art N.Y., Nunatta Sunaqutangit Mus. Iqaluit, N.W.T.; attended openings: Stratford Festival 1959, 'Sculpture / Inuit' Vancouver 1971, 'Masters of the Arctic' N.Y. 1989; on cover of 'Sculpture / Inuit' catalogue 1971; 'Sedna' sculpture featured on Canadian stamp 1980; carving presented to U.S. pres. Ronald Reagan at Summit meeting 1987; subject of several articles and catalogues; Home: Cape Dorset, N.W.T.; Office: c/o Dorset Fine Arts, 33 Belmont St., Toronto, Ont. M5R 1P9.

**ASHWOOD-SMITH, Michael John,** M.Sc., Ph.D.; educator/researcher; b. London, UK 19 June 1932; s. Arthur George and Elsie Mary (Simmons) Smith; e. St. Paul's Sch. London; Kings Coll. Durham Univ. B.Sc. 1953, M.Sc. 1959; Nat. Inst. Med. Rsch. Univ. of London Ph.D. 1962; m. Barbara d. Oswald and Eira Spencer-Jones; children: Martin, Peter, Hannah; PROF. OF BIOL. UNIV. OF VICTORIA 1972– ; Sci., Med. Rsch. Council UK 1959–69; Sci. in Residence US Naval Radiol. Defence Lab. San Francisco 1962–63; Chrmn. of Biol., Univ. of Victoria 1974–77; Chief Sci. Bourn Hall Clinic Cambridge, UK 1985–87; Prof. Univ. of Dijon (ENSBANA) France 1977–78; Sr. NATO Rsch. Fellow France 1977–78; DFG Prof. Univ. of Ulm FRG 1982–83; Visiting Guest Prof. Free Univ. of Brussels 1988–90; mem. Bd. Mgmt. Victoria Gen. Hosp. 1972–77; co-ed. and co-author 'Low Temperature Preservation in Medicine and Biology' 1980; numerous sci. papers and reviews; Fellow, Royal Soc. Med., UK; recreations: music, gardening, fishing, cooking; Home: 9230 Ardmore Dr., R.R. 2, Sidney, B.C. V8L 3S1; Office: Victoria, B.C. V8W 2Y2.

**ASHWORTH BARTLE, Jean,** B.A., A.R.C.T.; choral conductor, musician, teacher; b. Lancashire, England 7 March 1947; d. George and Iris (Clement) Ashworth; e. Parkdale C.I. 1965; Lakeshore Teachers' College 1966; A.R.C.T. Singing (Performers) 1970, (Teachers) 1973; Royal Conservatory of Music; Univ. of Toronto B.A. (Hons.) 1977; m. Donald Ernest s. Ernest and Flora Bartle 21 April 1984; step-children: Elinor, Geoffrey, Andrew; grandchildren: Kimberly, Andrew, James, Erin, David; FOUNDER & MUSIC DIRECTOR, TORONTO CHILDREN'S CHORUS; Primary School Teacher 1966–70; Music Teacher, Howard P.S. 1970–89; Blythwood School 1989– ; Soprano Soloist, Dir. of Jr. & Youth Choirs, Kingsway Lambton Un. Ch. 1970–87; Soprano, Toronto Mendelssohn Choir 1975–91; Founder & Music Dir., Toronto Children's Chorus 1978–87 (regarded by musicians & critics alike as one of the finest children's choirs in the world; Juno Award winner); has taken this chorus on 5 internat. tours: Gt. Brit. 1982, W. Europe and Yugoslavia 1984, Australia and New Zealand 1988, Finland and Russia 1990, England and France 1992; on sabbatical, visited Hong Kong, the Franz Liszt Acad. in Budapest, the Yehudi Menuhin Sch. and Purcell Schs. in Engl. 1992; Choral Clinician, Lectr., Adjudicator, Guest Conductor of children's choirs throughout the world; Mem., Extve. Ctte., Toronto Mendelssohn Choir 1976–87; Dir., Children's Choirs, Assn. of Candn. Choral Conductors; Ont. Music Edn. Assn. 1972–76; Candn. Music Educators Assn. (Sec. 1973); Leslie Bell Conducting Scholarship 1977; Sir Ernest MacMillan Conducting Scholarship 1982; Roy Thomson Hall Award for outstanding contbn. to the musical life of Metro. Toronto 1986; Toronto Children's Chorus prizes: 1st Prize, Llangollen Internat. Eistedd fod, Wales 1982; 1st Prize, CBC Competition 1982, '84, '90; Healey Willan Prize (Canada Council) 1983; 'Let The People Sing' 1st Prize 1993; author: 'Lifeline for Children's Choir Directors' 1987 and numerous articles; editor: Toronto Children's Chorus Series and Jean Ashworth Bartle Series for Treble Voices; recreations: travelling, gardening, bridge, reading, swimming, aerobics; clubs: Boulevard; Home: 31 Ridgevalley Cres., Islington, Ont. M9A 3J8; Office: 2180 Bayview Ave., Toronto, Ont. M4N 3K7.

**ASIMAKOPULOS, Athanasios (Tom),** M.A., Ph.D., F.R.S.C.; educator; b. Montreal, Que. 28 May 1930; s. Antonios and Paraskevi (Sepentzis) A.; e. Montreal High Sch. 1947; McGill Univ. B.A. 1951, M.A. 1953; Cambridge Univ. Ph.D. 1959; m. Marika d. Nicholas and Efrosini Salamis 18 Aug. 1961; two d. Anna, Julia; William Dow Professor of Political Economy, McGill Univ. 1988– ; Asst. Prof. Royal Mil. Coll. Kingston 1957–59; Asst. Prof. present Univ. 1959, Assoc. Prof. 1963, Prof. 1966, Chrmn. of Econ. 1974–78; Visiting Prof. Monash Univ. Australia 1973–74; me. Research Staff, Royal Comn. on Govt. Orgns. 1961, Royal Comn. on Banking & Finance 1962; author 'The Reliability of Selected Price Indexes as Measures of Price Trends' 1964; 'An Introduction to Economic Theory: Microeconomics' 1978; 'The Nature of Public Pension Plans: Intergenerational Equity, Funding and Saving' 1980; 'Investment, Employment and Income Distribution' 1988; ed. 'Theories of Income Distribution' 1988; 'Economic Theory, Welfare and the State' 1990; 'Keynes's General Theory and Accumulation' 1991; co-ed. Candn. Pol. Sci. Assn. Confs. on Stats. 1962–63, Papers 1964; mng. ed. 'Canadian Journal of Economics' 1968–72; mem. mng. bd. eds. 'Journal of Post-Keynesian Economics'; mem. Candn. Econ. Assn. (Extve. Council 1967–72); Home: 3230 The Boulevard, Westmount, Qué. H3Y 1S3; Office: 855 Sherbrooke St. W., Montreal, Qué. H3A 2T7.

**ASKA, Warabé (Masuda, Takeshi);** artist, writer; b. Kagawa, Japan 3 Feb. 1944; s. Satoru and Miyoko (Fujimoto) Masuda; e. Takamatsu Technol. Sch. Kagawa 1963; m. Keiko d. Nobuo and Yoshii Inouye 17 Oct. 1979; children: Yohyoh, Mari, Kohta; Founder and Pres. Ad House (design studio) Tokyo 1964–78; came to Can. 1979; solo oil painting exhns. incl. Konohana Gallery

Tokyo 1972; Mitsukoshi Gallery Kagawa 1973; Madden Gallery London, Eng. 1975, 1982; Tokai Gallery Nagoya, Japan 1978; Gustafsson Gallery Toronto 1982; Shayne Gallery Montréal 1984; Colborn Lodge Toronto 1984; Art Emporium Vancouver 1986; Royal Candn. Acad. of Arts 1991; selected group shows incl. UNESCO Exhbn., Tokyo 1966; Discovering High Park, Market Gallery Toronto 1983; Biennale of Graphic Design Brno 1984, 1988, 1992; Poster of the Year Bologna 1985; The Best of the 80's, Soc. of Graphic Designers of Can. 1985; Internat. Book Design Exhbn. Leipzig 1985, 1989; Biennale of Illustrations Exhbn. Bratislava 1985, 1987, 1991; Biennale of Illustration Barcelona 1986, 1992; Illustrators Exhbn. Bologna 1986, 1992; Once Upon a Time, Vancouver Art Gallery 1988; Magic Places, La Maison de la Culture, Glendon Coll. Toronto 1989, Canada at Bologna 1990; pub. colls. incl. Hino Motors. Co. Ltd., Tokyo; Corp. of the coll. of the City of Toronto; Osborn Coll., Toronto Public Lib.; work selected for UNICEF greeting card 1985; Hon. Mention Best Designed Books Leipzig 1986; commissioned Earth Day 1993 official poster; author 'Discovering Japan in Eighty Days' 1973; 'A Midsummer Night's Dream' 1976; 'Ma Vlast and Harry Janos' 1977; 'Dandelion Puffs' (picture book, juvenile) 1981; 'P-yororo O-yororo' (picture book, juvenile) 1982; 'Who Goes to the Park' 1984 (City of Toronto Book Award 1985, reproduced video cassette, Prisma Open Book I 1985); 'Who Hides in the Park' 1986; (Hon. Diploma Best Designed Books Leipzig 1989, reproduced video cassette, Prisma Open Book III 1987); 'Seasons' (art book; shortlisted for Gov. Gen.'s Award; Mr. Christie's Award; Studio Magazine Gold Award) 1990; 'Aska's Animals' (picture book; Silver Medal for Biennale of Graphic Design Brno; Runner-up for Amelia France Howard-Gibbon Illustrator's Award) 1991; 'Aska's Birds' (picture book) 1992; 'Aska's Sea Creatures' (picture book) 1994; Shintoist; recreations: driving, swimming, skiing; Address: 1019 Lorne Park Rd., Mississauga, Ont. L5H 2Z9.

**ASPELL, Peter;** artist; b. Vancouver, B.C. 25 Dec. 1918; e. Vancouver Sch. of Art; Acad. de Ghent Belgium; Instr., Vanc. Sch. of Art 1948–70; Extension Dept., U.B.C. 1965–84; Dir., Peter Aspell Sch. of Art 1970–78; solo exhibitions: Heffel Gallery Limited Vanc. 1987, '88, '89, '90, Goldman-Kraft Gall. Chicago 1990; Moos Gall. Toronto 1987, '89, Galerie 1900/2000 Paris 1988, Wade Gallery Los Angeles 1987, Kenneth G. Heffel Fine Art Inc. 1982, '83, '84, '85, '86, Mahalas Gall. Montreal 1985, Bau-Xi Gall. Vanc. & Toronto 1977; Vanc. Art Gall. 1955; group exhibitions: Montreal & Bundy Art Gall. Vermont 1965, North-West Artists Group 1958–68, Canadian Group 1952–65, Group of Eight (across Canada) show 1965; selected collections: National Gall. of Can., Vanc. Art Gall, Univ. of B.C., Hamilton Art Gall., Imperial Oil, Stern Collecton Chicago, Mr & Mrs J Hunter Chicago, Burnaby Art Gall., Bundy Art Gall. Vermont, O.J. Firestone Collection Ottawa, Cineplex Odeon Comn. Marina Del Rey, Calif.; awards: Emily Carr Scholarship 1956; Can. Counc. Fellowship 1965; Gold Medal Candn. Group Show 1968; Office: c/o Heffel Gallery Limited, 2247 Granville St., Vancouver, B.C. V6H 3G1.

**ASPER, Israel Harold,** Q.C., B.A., LL.B., LL.M., LIEUT. COL. (HON.); b. Minnedosa, Man. 11 Aug. 1932; s. Leon and Cecilia Asper; e. Univ. of Man., B.A. 1953, LL.B. 1957, LL.M. 1964; m. Ruth Miriam, Winnipeg, Man. 27 May 1956; children: David, Gail, Leonard; CHRMN. AND C.E.O., CANWEST GLOBAL COMMUNICATIONS CORP.; Chrmn. & C.E.O., The CanWest Capital Group Inc.; Founder & Chrmn., CanWest Broadcasting Ltd. (CKND-TV, Winnipeg), which has won more national & internat. awards than any other independent TV Stn. in Canada incl. Enterprise of the Year, Manitoba C. of C.; Chrmn., Global Television Network, Toronto; SaskWest Television Inc. (CFRE-TV and CFSK-TV); CanWest Pacific Television Inc. (U.TV, Vancouver); CanWest Trust Co. of Can.; TV3, New Zealand; Dir., The Ten Television Network, Australia; called to Bar of Man. 1957; Counsel to Buchwald, Asper, Henteleff, Barristers 1970; former M.L.A. and Leader of Liberal Party in Man. 1970–75; author 'The Benson Iceberg: A Critical Analysis of the White Paper on Tax Reform in Canada' 1970; newspaper columnist on subject of taxation, nationally syndicated through Toronto Globe & Mail 1966–77; Gov., Univ. of Jerusalem; mem. Council, Canada West Found.; Dir., Associates of Faculty of Admin. Studies, Univ. of Man.; Mem. Bd. of Govs., Jewish Found. of Man.; Co-Chrmn., Internat. Advisors, Banff Television Festival; Bd. Mem., Manitoba Indian Business Development Corp.; Nat. Youth Parliament Assn.; Mem., Mayor's Adv. Ctte. on Winnipeg 2000; Candn. Inst. of Internat. Communications; Friends of Univ. of Man. Law School; Candn. Women in Radio & Television; estabd. The Asper Foundation 1983; Hon. Patron, Misericordia General Hospital Rsch. Found.; mem. Candn. Bar Assn.; Candn. Tax Foundation; Man. Bar Assn.; Man. Law Soc.; Internat. Institute of Communications; apptd. Q.C. 1975; rec'd. Univ. of Man. Alumni Jubilee Award, outstanding 25 year graduate, 1979; Hon. Fellow, Hebrew Univ.; Lt.-Col. (Hon.), Candn. Militia 1986; Hon. Pres., Youth Parliament of Man.; Man. Business Entrepreneur of the Year 1989 and 1991; Candn. Assn. of Broadcasters Gold Ribbon (broadcast excellence) 1992; B'nai Brith Award of Merit 1993; recreations: music, travel, tennis; Home: 1063 Wellington Cres., Winnipeg, Man. R3N 0A1; Office: 31st Floor, TD Centre, 201 Portage Ave., Winnipeg, Man. R3B 3L7.

**ASPINALL, Gerald Oliver,** Ph.D., D.Sc., F.R.S.C., F.R.S.E., F.R.I.C., F.C.I.C.; educator; b. Chesham Bois, Bucks., Eng. 30 Dec. 1924; s. Leonard and Catherine Martha (Black) A.; e. Merchant Taylors' Sch. Herts. Eng. 1942; Univ. of Bristol, B.Sc. 1945, Ph.D. 1948; Univ. of Edinburgh, D.Sc. 1958; m. Joyce, Ph.D. d. Thomas and Elizabeth Brading 25 June 1953; children: John Jillian; Distinguished Rsch. Prof. of Chem. 1988, 1992– ; Lectr. in Chem. Univ. of Edinburgh 1948–61, Sr. Lectr. 1961–63, Reader 1963–67; Prof. of Chem. Trent Univ. 1967–72; Prof. of Chem., York Univ. 1972–82; recipient C.S. Hudson Award Carbohydrate Chem. Am. Chem. Soc. 1986; John Labatt Award Organic Chem./Biochem. Candn. Soc. Chem. 1987; author one book, ed. 5 books incl. 'The Polysaccharides' Vols. 1, 2 and 3, 1982, 1983, 1985; author or co-author over 180 tech. papers and reviews chem./biochem. complex carbohydrates; Fellow, Royal Soc. Chem.; mem. Biochem. Soc.; Anglican; recreations: music, travel, golf; Home: 6–296 Torresdale Ave., Willowdale, Ont. M2R 3N3; Office: 4700 Keele St., North York, Ont. M3J 1P3.

**ASPLER, Tony,** B.A.; writer; wine consultant; b. London, England 12 May 1939; s. Izak and Mimi (Young) A.; e. Oakfield Sch. 1947–52; Epsom Coll. 1952–56; McGill Univ., B.A. 1959; children: Annabel, Guy; WINE COLUMNIST, TORONTO STAR 1981– ; BBC 1961–64; freelance 1964–73; Radio Prod., CBC 1973–82; Freelance writer/broadcaster 1982– ; Wine Cons.; Founding Chrmn., Crime Writers of Can. 1982–84; Bd. of Govs., Sommelier Guild of Canada; author: 'Vintage Canada' 1992; 'Tony Aspler's Wine Lover's Companion' 1991; 'Tony Aspler's International Guide to Wine' 1986, 'The Wine Lover Dines' 1986; 'Vintage Canada' 1983 (non-fiction); 'Blood is Thicker Than Beaujolais' 1993; 'Titanic' 1989; 'One of My Marionettes' 1973; 'The Streets of Askelon' 1972 (novels); co-author: (with Rose Murray) 'Cellar and Silver' (non-fiction); (with Gordon Pape) 'The Music Wars' 1982, 'The Scorpion Sanction' 1980, 'Chain Reaction' 1978 (novels); Home: 27-B Claxton Blvd., Toronto, Ont. M6C 1L7.

**ASSELIN, Rt. Hon. Martial,** P.C., Q.C.; lieutenant governor; b. La Malbaie, P.Q. 3 Feb 1924; s. Ferdinand and Eugénie (Tremblay) A.; e. Acad. St. Etienne, La Malbaie; Semy. Chicoutimi, B.A.; Laval Univ., LL.L.; m. 1stly Pierette Bouchard d. Albert Bouchard Beauport, 14 Feb. 1953; three s. Bernard, Jean-Louis, François; m. 2ndly Ginette d'Auteuil 17 Sept. 1976; LIEUTENANT GOVERNOR OF QUEBEC 1990– ; called to the Bar of Que., 1951; cr. Q.C. 1967; Mayor of La Malbaie, P.Q. 1957–63; Pres., Laval Univ. Student Council 1949–1950; Legal Adv., Charlevoix Chamber of Commerce 1951; Dir., Saguenay Bar 1955; mem. of H. of C. for Charlevoix 1958–63; sworn to Privy Council and apptd. Min. of Forestry in Diefenbaker Cabinet March 1963; def. in g.e. Apl. 1963; re-el. g.e. 1965, 1968; Del. of Can. to N.A.T.O. Parliamentary Assembly, London 1959; represented Canada at Commonwealth & international conferences 1960–61; Del. of U.N. to Africa (Rwanda-Burundi) 1961 for Independence Elections; summoned to Senate of Can. 1972; apptd. Min. of State responsible for the Candn. International Development Agency and Francophonie 1979; Partner, Jolin, Fournier, Morisset 1980–90; Depy. Speaker of the Senate 1984–88; Pres., Internat. Assn. of French speaking Parliamentarians 1988; Dir., La Laurentienne Générale, Banque Laurentienne, Sphynx et Memisca and La Laurentienne-Vie 1976–90; Knight of Columbus, 3rd Degree; named Grand-Croix de l'Ordre de la Pléiade 1988; named Grand de Charlevoix 1989; Knight of the Order of St. John of Jerusalem 1990; honoured with Commemorative Medal, 125th Anniversary, Confed. of Canada 1992; mem. Lions Club, Clermont-La Malbaie-Pointe-au-Pic; Hon. Mem., Quebec Garrison Club; Clubs: Murray-Bay Golf; Manoir Richelieu Golf; P. Conservative; Roman Catholic; Address: 1050 St. Augustin St., Quebec, Qué. G1A 1A1.

**ASTER, Jeannette,** B.Mus.; freelance opera/artistic director; b. Linz, Austria 4 Jan. 1948; d. Igor Ignace and Tatiana (Braitman) Kuchinsky; e. Monkland H.S. 1964; Ecole Normale de musique, lauriat mus. 1966; McGill Univ. B.Mus. 1969; London Opera Centre dipl. opera prodn.; m. Howard s. Ida and Sam A. 7 Sept. 1969; children: Misha, Samara Shira; ARTISTIC DIRECTOR, OPERA LYRA OTTAWA 1988– ; made profl. Candn. debut as stage dir. National Arts Centre Opera Festival 1977 with Mozart's 'The Magic Flute'; 1st live opera telecast on CBC TV; has directed operas for all major cos. across country; made U.S. debut Houston Grand Opera 1982 with Alban Berg's 'Wozzeck'; Co-dir., 'Otello' with Placido Domingo & Tippett's 'New Year' (World Premiere & European Premiere) with Sir Peter Hall & Bill T. Jones; other U.S. credits incl. Lyric Opera Chicago, San Francisco Opera, Washington Opera, Cincinnati Opera & 8 prodns. with Los Angeles Music Ctr.; European credits: Royal Opera House London, Vienna State Opera, Paris Opera, Glyndebourne Festival; frequent collaborator on special film & stage projects with Sir Peter Hall & Götz Friedrich; Staff Dir., Netherlands Opera, Hamburg State Opera, Deutche Oper Berlin 1974–78; Asst. Dir., Candn. Opera Co. 1978–80; First Resident Dir. 1980–82; Assoc. Dir. & Resident Stage Dir., Los Angeles Music Centre Opera 1986–90; Tyrone Guthrie Award, Stratford Fest. 1972; Co-recipient, Internat. Critics Prize for best production in Italy for 'Tristan & Isolde' Florence 1990; Mem., Canadian Actors Equity, ACTRA, AGMA, British Actors Equity; recreations: cooking, fishing, drawing; Home: 319 Allan St., Oakville, Ont. L6J 3P4; Office: 2 Daly Ave., Ottawa, Ont. K1N 6E2.

**ASTLEY, Robert Murray,** B.Sc., F.C.I.A., F.S.A.; insurance exec.; b. Winnipeg, Man. 26 Dec. 1944; s. Cyril and Barbara Donalda (Maxwell) A.; e. Neepawa (Man.) Area Coll. Inst. 1962; Univ. of Man. B.Sc.(Hons.) 1966; m. Judith d. James and Vera Armour 6 June 1970; children: Derek, Jennifer; PRESIDENT & C.E.O., THE MUTUAL LIFE ASSURANCE CO. OF CANADA 1985– ; Dir., The Mutual Trust Co., Toronto; Dir. & Chrmn., The Mutual Group (U.S.) Inc.; Mutual Diversico Ltd.; Mutual Investco Inc.; Dir., Mu-Cana Investment Counselling Ltd.; Mutual Financial Planning Ltd.; joined present co. 1966–70, 1973– ; Cons. Actuary Towers, Perrin, Forster & Crosby 1970–73; Vice Pres., Candn. Inst. Actuaries 1982–84, mem. Council 1976–78; Past Chair, Wilfrid Laurier Univ.; Home: 82 McCarron Cres., Waterloo, Ont. N2L 5N1; Office: 227 King St. S., Waterloo, Ont. N2J 4C5.

**ATACK, Douglas,** B.Sc., Ph.D.; consultant; retired research executive; b. Wakefield, Eng. 16 Aug. 1923; e. Leeds Univ., B.Sc. 1942, Ph.D. 1945; m. Nancy Lynn Hull 5 Aug. 1950; one s. Christopher; Vice-Pres. & Dir. of Rsch., Pulp & Paper Inst. of Can. 1987–89; former Auxiliary Prof., Dept. of Mech Engr., McGill Univ.; joined Pulp & Paper Inst. in 1954; cond. studies on friction of wood in Cavendish Lab., Cambridge Univ. 1955–56; Weldon Medal 1962, 1981; TAPPI Fellowship 1975; Walter Brecht Medal of Zellcheming 1982; Arne Asplund Award 1987; Fellow, Royal Soc. of Can. 1989; John S. Bates Meml. Gold Medal 1992; Past Chrmn. & Prog. Chrmn., Internat. Mech. Pulping Conf.; Home: 2180 Marine Dr., Ste. 2204, Oakville, Ont. L6L 5V2.

**ATCHEALAK, Davie;** artist; b. Ikirasaq, down coast from Dorset, N.W.T. 1947; medium: sculpture, drawings, prints, paintings; 20 group exbns. incl. most recent: Westdale Gallery Hamilton, Ont. 1992, Vancouver Inuit Art Soc. 1991 (2), 'Masters of the Arctic' New York, N.Y. 1989; solo exbns.: Inukshuk Galleries Waterloo, Ont. 1980, The Snow Goose Ottawa, Ont. 1979; collections: Amway Environ. Found. Collection, Art Gall. of Ont., Dennos Mus. Ctr. N.W. Michigan College Traverse City, Mich., Inuit Cultural Inst. Rankin Inlet, N.W.T., National Gallery of Canada Ottawa; attended opening: 1st solo exbn. at Snow Goose Ottawa 1979; submitted sketches to Dept. of Public Works Canada for carvings for exterior of Centre Block of Parl. Bldgs. Ottawa 1980; established record auction price for an Inuit carving Waddington's 1989; subject of articles and catalogues; Home: Iqaluit, N.W.T.; Office: c/o Polar North, 5823 St. François, Qué. H4S 1B6.

**ATHANASSOULAS, His Grace Sotirios,** B.D., M.A.; bishop; b. Lepiana Arta, Greece 19 Feb. 1936; s. George and Anastasia (Skabardonis) A.; e. Univ. of Athens B.D. 1961; Univ. of Montreal M.A. 1971; BISHOP OF THE GREEK ORTHODOX CHURCH IN CANADA 1974– ; Deacon 1962; Priest 1962; pastorates: St. George Greek Orth. Ch., Edmonton 1962–65; Montreal 1965–75; has established 33 Greek Orth. churches in Canada; has introduced social services, a monthly newspaper & a weekly nat. TV prog.; Mem., Holy Synod of the Greek Orthodox Archdiocese of N. and S. Am.; Chair, Synodal Ctte. on Worship, Min. of Sermons &

Publications; Mem., Archdiocesan and Diocesan Councils; Extve. Ctte., Candn. Council of Churches (delegate to China 1981); Centennial Medal of Canada; Queen's Jubilee Award; 125 Canada Award; Hon. Pres., Thelassemia Found.; Mem., Gov. Council, Univ. of Toronto 1975–79; Vice-Pres., Christian Pavillion, Expo 67; Mem., Orgn. Ctte., World Council of Churches 1983; fluent in Greek, English and French; author: 'Catechism: Basic Teaching of the Orthodox Faith' 1991, 'Verses: An Orthodox Catechism' 1992; Office: 27 Teddington Park Ave., Toronto, Ont. M4N 2C4.

**ATHANS, George S., Jr.,** C.M. (1974), B.A.; athletic champion; b. Kelowna, B.C. 6 July 1952: s. George D., M.D. and Irene (Hartzell) A.; e. Concordia Univ. Sir George Williams Campus B.A. 1975, Communications-Pub. Relations Cert. 1975; McGill Univ. post-grad. courses in M.B.A. program; one d. Shawn Sacha; Pres. Athans Communications (film, video and corporate communication production co.), Montreal; mem. Can.'s Nat. Water Ski Team 1966–75; holder World Slalom Record 1969–72; World and Candn. Champion 1965–75; Candn. Champion 33 times; winner over 100 water ski titles; Loyola Univ. Award Modern Sculpture 1970; named to Can.'s Amateur Hall of Fame Ottawa 1971 and Can.'s Sports Hall of Fame Toronto 1974; B.C. Athlete of the year 1971; Candn. Amateur Athlete of the Yr. 1972, 1973; Que. Athlete of the Yr. 1973; Order of Can. 1974; author 'Water Skiing' 1975 (also published in French and Russian); Hon. Life mem. Candn. Water Ski Assn.; nominated for Foster Hewitt Award for Excellence in Sportscasting, ACTRA 1983 and 1984; recreations: swimming, running, snow skiing, film, music; Club: Le Sanctuaire; Address: 65 St. Paul St. W., #103, Montreal, Qué. H2Y 3S5.

**ATHERLEY, Gordon,** M.B., Ch.B., M.D., LL.D. (h.c.), F.R.S.A.; association executive; b. Manchester, Eng. 8 June 1933; s. John Campbell and Kathleen Eleanor A.; e. Univ. of Manchester M.B.,Ch.B. 1957, rsch. doctorate in med. 1967; Simon Fraser Univ. LL.D. (h.c.) 1983; m. Audrey d. Fred and Hilda Lowe 15 June 1968; children: Peter, Anthony, Paul, Simon, Julian, Kate; PARTNER, ATHERLEY, O'CONNELL & ASSOCIATES 1990– ; PRES., OBERON COMPOSER SOFTWARE, Oakville; Prof., Dept. of Health Admin., Univ. of Toronto 1990– ; Partner ARTIMPORT; Mng. Dir. Linglen Ltd. 1963–67; Flight Lt. RAF and Sqdn. Leader RAF Reserve 1959–61; Part-Time Staff Phys. and Cons. in Toxicol. Bell Canada 1978–79; Prof. and Head of Safety & Hygiene Dept., Univ. of Aston, Birmingham, Eng. 1975–78; Prof. of Med. Univ. of Toronto 1978–79; Pres. & C.E.O., Candn. Centre for Occupational Health and Safety 1979–89; Chrmn. Ctte. Experts Safe Use Asbestos Internat. Labour Office 1983; mem. Council Fellows Collegium Ramazzini 1986; Vice Pres. Can., Am. Pub. Health Assn. 1986–87; O.St.J. 1978; Hon. Fellow Inst. Occupational Safety & Health UK; author: 'Occupational Health and Safety Concepts' 1978; Home: 100 Lakeshore Rd. E., Suite 303, Oakville, Ont. L6J 6M9.

**ATHERTON, David L.,** B.A., M.A., P.Eng., F.Inst, NDT; professor of physics; b. Chelsea, England 22 Feb. 1935; s. William and Eleanor Mary (Taylor) A.; e. Cambridge Univ. M.A. 1963, B.A. 1959; Royal Air Force Tech. Coll. Debden 1955; Gresham's Sch. Norfolk 1948–53; m. Joanna d. Terrence and Belinda Banham 9 Dec. 1964; children: Tamsin Carol Susan, Heather Jane Bridget; PROFESSOR OF PHYSICS, QUEEN'S UNIV. 1975– ; Head, Superconductivity Rsch., Ferranti-Packard Ltd. 1959–71; Assoc. Prof., Queen's Univ. 1971–75; Leader, Candn. Magnetic Levitation Project 1970–80; Applied Magnetics Rsch. Group 1980– ; Founding Chrmn., Candn. Assn. for Rsch. in NDE 1987–89; Dir., Can. Superconductor Cryogenics 1971–74; Tech. Adv. Bd., Urban Transp. Devel. Corp. 1971–83; Internat. Cons. & Specialist Advr. on Magnetics to several cos.; Major Open Scholars, and Exhib., Clare Coll. 1956–59; E.I.C. Ross Medal 1979; Queen's Univ. Prize for Excellence in Rsch. 1982; Fellow, Brit. Inst. for Non-Destructive Testing 1988; Am. Soc. for Nondestructive Testing 1990 Achievement Award; Mem., Assn. of Profl. Engrs. of Ont.; Can. Assn. of Physicists; I.E.E.E.; Am. Phys. Soc.; Sigma Phi; Can., Am. & Brit. socs. for Nondestructive Testing; author of more than 150 refereed sci. pubns.; recreations: beef farmer; Home: R.R. 2, Perth Road, Ont. K0H 2L0; Office: Kingston, Ont. K7L 3N6.

**ATKEY, Ronald G.,** P.C., Q.C.; lawyer; b. Saint John, N.B. 15 Feb. 1942; s. late Osborne Lorne George and late Mary Agnes (Hills) A.; e. Univ. of Western Ontario, B.A. 1962, LL.B. 1965; Yale Univ. LL.M. 1966; called to Ont. Bar 1969; m. Marie d. Elmer and Catherine Rounding 8 Oct. 1976; children: Jennifer, Matthew, Jonathan, Erin; PARTNER, OSLER HOSKIN & HARCOURT 1976– ; Chrmn., Security Intelligence Review Comte. 1984–89; Dir., Daiwa Bank Canada; Nikon Canada Inc.; Warner Communications (Canada) Limited; Student-at-Law with Sidney L. Robins Q.C. 1966–67; Prof. of Law, Univ. of Western Ont. 1967–70; Counsel, Ont. Law Reform Commission 1970–71; Prof. of Law, Osgoode Hall Law Sch. 1971–73; M.P. for St Paul's and Opposition Critic for Corp. Affairs 1972–74; Prof. of Law, Univ. of Toronto 1974–77; Partner, Osler Hoskin & Harcourt 1976–79; Min. of Employ. & Immigration and M.P. for St Paul's 1979–80; cr. Q.C. 1980; Mem. of Minister's Adv. Ctte. on Competition Policy 1985–86; Dir., Internat. Comn. of Jurists; Candn. Civil Liberties Assn.; Trustee, Motion Picture Foundation of Can.; Past Pres., Univ. of Western Ont. Law Assn.; mem., Kappa Alpha Soc.; co-author (with J. Noel Lyon) 'Canadian Constitutional Law in a Modern Perspective' 1970; numerous law review articles on bus. law & regulation, communications, federal-provincial relations, the Canada/U.S. Free Trade Agreement, NAFTA, the Candn. Charter of Rights & Freedoms and immigration; P. Conservative; Protestant; recreations: skiing, squash, tennis, piano, music, travel; Clubs: Albany (Dir.); Rideau; Craigleith Ski; Home 77 Hudson Dr., Toronto, Ont. M4T 2K2; Office: Ste. 6600, Box 50, First Canadian Place, Toronto, Ont. M5X 1B8.

**ATKIN, Elliot Harvey;** actor; b. Toronto, Ont. 18 Dec. 1942; s. Murray and Ida (Garshon) A.; e. Northview Heights S.S. 1961; m. Celia d. Manley and Sonia Tessler 25 Aug. 1963; children: Lisa, Daniel; worked as construction foreman before starting own construction co. and land devel. & real estate brokerage firm while doing amateur acting in commercials; became profl. actor 1968: movies, series, commercials; Dir., Aurelian Developers Ltd.; Pres., Cansell Realty Ltd.; Mgr./Dir., Surrey Glen Devel.; Pelican Prodns.; real estate broker; pilot; prod./dir. TV shows/commercials; ACTRA award winner; Assoc. of Candn. Cinema nominee; Int'l. Clio Award winner; Calif. commercial award winner; Mich. Award winner; Mem., ACTRA; SAG; AFTRA; Toronto Real Estate Bd.; Assoc. of Candn. Cinema/TV; Office: The Characters Talent Agency, 150 Carlton St., 2nd fl., Toronto, Ont. M5A 2K1.

**ATKINS, David Hedley,** M.A., F.C.A.; chartered accountant; b. London, England 29 Apr. 1935; s. Hedley John Barnard and Gladwys Gwendoline (Jones) Atkins; e. Sherborne Sch. 1953; 2nd Lt. 8th K.R.I. Hussars 1953–55; Trinity Coll., Oxford, M.A. 1958; m. Jane d. John and Mary McGreevy 6 Jan. 1961; children: William, Chloé; MANAGING PARTNER, INTERNATIONAL, COOPERS & LYBRAND 1988– ; qualified as C.A., England & Wales 1961; joined Coopers & Lybrand, Can. 1962; Mem., Ont. Inst. of C.A.'s 1968; Partner, Coopers & Lybrand 1968; F.C.A. Ont. 1976; Cons., Insur. Bur. of Can. 1970–80; Chrmn., Coopers & Lybrand Insur. Ctte. 1979–85; Mem., Partnership Bd. 1986; Chrmn. & Mem., var. cttes. of Candn. & Ont. Insts. of C.A.'s 1970–87; Mem., Slater Task Force on Insur. in Ont. 1986; Cons. to Supt. of Fin. Insts., Can. 1987; Lectr., Concordia Univ. 1965–68; Chrmn., The Clarke Inst. of Psychiatry Found.; Benefactor, The Royal Ont. Mus.; Anglican; former dir., various arts orgns.; co-author of var. rsch. studies as follows: Chrmn., 'Extent of Audit Testing' (CICA), Mem., 'Financial Reporting for Property and Casualty Insurers' (CICA), 'Relationship of the Actuary and Auditor' (CIA & CICA); recreations: tennis, travel, squash; Clubs: York, Garrick; Home: 433 Russell Hill Rd., Toronto, Ont. M5P 2S4; Office: 145 King St. W., Toronto, Ont. M5H 1V1.

**ATKINS, Gordon Lee,** B.Arch., R.C.A.; architect; b. Calgary, Alta. 5 March 1937; s. Grant Lee Kearl and Dorothy A.; e. Univ. of Wash. B.Arch. 1960 (Faculty Medal for Design Excellence; Am. Tile Inst. Award); m. C. Joan Lecoq 21 March 1956; children: Lisa, Laura, Drew, Ryan, Murray, Seth; PROP., GORDON ATKINS AND ASSOCIATES ARCHITECTS LTD. 1963– ; Partner with Alton McCaul Bowers (religious works) 1961–62; sessional instr. Mount Royal Coll., S. Alta. Inst. of Technol.; lectr. Univ. of Calgary 4 yrs.; solo exhn. Edmonton Art Gallery 1970; recipient many design awards incl. Massey Medal (Melchin Summer Homes); Hon. Mention Design for Candn. Flag; 2nd Place Calgary Centennial Planetarium Competition; award & nat. exhn. R.C.A. Drahanchuk Studios, A.G.T. Elbow Park; Mayland Hts. Sch. display Nat. Schs. Conf., Union Internationale Archs. Budapest; Eighth Ave. Mall Design Award Candn. Arch.; Urban Design Awards Leavitt Residence 1979, Varsity Estates Condominiums Calgary 1979, Calgary Indian Friendship Center 1980; Pinebrook GolfClub Exhn. Olympic Games Montreal; Stoney Adm. Bldg. Hon. Mention Candn. Arch. 1978; Shouldice Athletic Change Pavilion Calgary, Candn. Arch. Yearbook Award 1980; Practice Profile Award, Alta. Assn. of Arch., 75th Anniversary; Gov. Gen.'s Medal 1981 Stoney Admin. Bldg.; subject various TV programs; Exhn. Nickle Arts Gallery Univ. of Calgary 1980; served as Bishop of Mormon Ch.; mem. Bd. Examiners Univ. Alta.; Dir. Calgary Centennial Comte.; Council Community Services; Gov. Calgary Allied Arts Centre; mem. Alta. Assn. Archs. (Pres. Calgary Br.); Royal Arch. Inst. Can.; Mid-Can. Corridor Foundation; Rural Devel. Assn. (Dir.); Mormon; recreations: books, music, skiing; Home: 1008 Durham Ave. S.W., Calgary, Alta. T2T 0P7; Office: 1909 – 17th Ave. S.W., Calgary, Alta. T2T 0E9.

**ATKINSON, Edward Arthur,** B.A., C.A.; chartered accountant; b. Moose Jaw, Sask. 12 Aug. 1948; s. Fredrick Francis and Virginia Elaine (Petz) A.; e. Simon Fraser Univ. B.A. 1971; C.A. 1975; m. Laura d. John and Kathleen Bray 25 Sept. 1948; children: John, Lynne; CONTROLLER, HUSKY INJECTION MOLDING SYSTEMS LTD. 1993– ; Comptroller, Federal Pioneer Limited 1981–90; The Enfield Corp. Limited 1987–90; Management Consultant 1990; Mgr., Financial Opns., Federal Pioneer Limited 1991–93; Residence: 92 Charnwood Place, Thornhill, Ont. L3T 5H3.

**ATKINSON, George F.,** M.A., Ph.D., C.Chem, FRSC(UK), FCIC; university professor; b. Toronto, Ont. 25 Feb. 1932; s. Francis Howard and Hazel Pearl (Roberts) A.; e. Humberside C.I. 1949; Univ. Coll., Univ. of Toronto B.A. 1953, M.A. 1954, Ph.D. 1960; m. Lorraine d. Archibald and Agnes McGowan 9 Sept. 1961; children: Sheila Jean, Arwen Christine, James Clark, David George; ASSOC. PROF. & UNDERGRAD. OFFR., UNIV. OF WATERLOO 1961– ; Lectr., Univ. of Western Ontario 1960–61; Dir., Liberal Sci. Prog. 1983–91; Ctr. for Soc., Technol. & Values 1989–91; FRSC(UK); FCIC; Chartered Chem. (Ont. & U.K.); Visiting Prof., Univ. of Southampton 1969–70, 1975–76; Univ. of East Anglia 1988–89; Mem., Univ. of Waterloo Senate 1978–83, 1984–88, 1990–; Bd. of Gov. 1982–83, 1990–92; Dir., Kitchener Public Lib. Bd. 1981–88 (Chrmn. 1984); Mem., Anglican Ch. of Can.; Sigma Xi; Am. Assn. for Advancement of Sci.; Soc. for Rsch. into Higher Edn.; Am. Chem. Soc.; recreations: hiking, photography, music, pastel drawing; Home: 18 Cyprus Dr., Kitchener, Ont. N2M 4R5; Office: Waterloo, Ont. N2L 3G1.

**ATKINSON, Lloyd C.,** Ph.D.; banker; b. Hamilton, Ont. 20 Feb. 1942; s. Harold C. and Mary A. (Fowler) A.; e. Univ. of Windsor B.A. 1965 (Gold Medal Econ. & Pol. Sci., Woodrow Wilson Fellowship 1965); Univ. of Mich. Ph.D. 1969 (Rackham Dissertation Prize 1968); children: Scott, Stefan; EXEC. VICE PRES. AND CHIEF ECONOMIST, BANK OF MONTREAL 1990– , Sr. Vice Pres. & Chief Economist 1982–90; prior to joining Bank served 2 yrs. as Dep. Asst. Dir. U.S. Congressional Budget Office, Washington, D.C. and 2 yrs. as Sr. Econ. Jt. Econ. Ctte. U.S. Congress; lectr. various U.S. univs. incl. Univ. of Mich., Univ. of Md., Miami Univ. (Oxford, Ohio), Am. Univ. (Washington, D.C.); served as cons. to N.Y. and Md. State Govts. and to U.S. Del. to IMF, World Bank, IFC; author 'Economics: The Science of Choice' 1982; various scholarly articles; Bd. of Dirs., Candn. C. of C.; Mem. Adv. Counc., C.D. Howe Inst.; recreations; squash, swimming; Office: 21, First Canadian Place, Toronto, Ont. M5X 1A1.

**ATKINSON, Michael Arthur Charles,** B.A., LL.B.; construction executive; b. Toronto, Ont. 15 April 1954; s. Gordon Arthur and Elaine Nancy (Derose) A.; e. Univ. of Ottawa B.A. 1975, LL.B. 1979; m. Rachelle M. d. André and Renee Lapointe 16 Feb. 1985; step-children: Nathalie, Corey Bennett; PRESIDENT, CANADIAN CONSTRUCTION ASSOCIATION 1993– ; Staff Officer, Candn. Construction Assn. 1981–87; Dir. of Indus. Practices 1987–90; Sr. Dir. 1990–93; Edit. Adv. Bd., The Construction Law Letter; Mem., Construction Law Section, Candn. Bar Assn.; Office: 85 Albert St., 10th fl., Ottawa, Ont. K1P 6A4.

**ATKINSON, Michael M.,** B.A., M.A., Ph.D.; professor; b. Edmonton, Alta. 5 Dec. 1947; s. Peter and Margaret Mary (Lofthouse) A.; e. Univ. of Alta., B.A. 1968; Carleton Univ., M.A. 1972, Ph.D. 1978; m. Pamela d. Ralph and Elizabeth Stone 3 July 1971; one s.: Stephen Douglas; PROF., DEPT. OF POL. SCI., McMASTER UNIV., Chrmn. of Dept. 1986–92; joined McMaster faculty 1976; main area of rsch.: institutions and public policy; Visiting Prof., Duke Univ. 1989–90; Mem., Senate & Bd. of Govs., McMaster Univ. 1986–89; Senate 1992– ; Bd. of Dir., Candn. Pol. Sci. Assn. 1980–82; co-author: 'The Canadian Legislative System' 1980; 'The State, Business and Industrial Change in Canada' 1989; ; editor: 'Governing Canada: Institutions and Public Policy' 1993; co-editor: 'The Politics of Canadian Public Policy' 1983; Governance: An Internat. J. of Policy and Administration; recreations: squash, tennis, canoeing; contbr., acad. jours., newspaper, radio & television; Office: Hamilton, Ont. L8S 4M4.

**ATKISON, Paul Robert,** B.Sc., M.Sc., M.D., Ph.D., FRCP(C); physician; b. Hamilton, Ont. 24 Dec. 1951; s. William 'George' and Mabel Rose (Jackson) A.; e. Univ. of Waterloo B.Sc. 1975, M.Sc. 1977; Univ. of Calgary Ph.D. 1980, M.D. 1984; Univ. of Western Ont. F.R.C.P.(C) Paed. 1987; m. Brenda d. William and Marjorie Cooke 11 Aug. 1972; children: Larissa, Jesse, Ryan; DIRECTOR, PAEDIATRIC TRANSPLANT PROGRAM, UNIV. OF WESTERN ONT. (CHILDREN'S HOSP. OF WESTERN ONT.) 1992– ; Asst. Prof. Paediatrics, Univ. of Western Ont. 1988– ; Dir., Cellular Transplant Unit, Multi-Organ Transplant Serv., Univ. Hosp. 1988– ; Assoc. Scientist, Immunology Group, Robarts Rsch. Inst. 1988– ; scholarships: Alta. Grad. 1978–79; Wm. H. Davies Med. Rsch. 1979–80; fellowships: Alta. Heritage Found. for Med. Rsch. (AHFMR) Postdoctoral 1980–81; AHFMR part-time Post Doctoral 1981–84; Med. Rsch. Counc. of Canada Postdoctoral 1987–88; Studentship Awards, Candn. Soc. of Clin. Investig. 1979, '80; Nat Christie Found. Med. Entrance Award 1981–84; Mem., Am. Diabetes Assn.; author of numerous sci. articles & articles on islet transplantation for the lay press; recreations: golf, swimming, skiing; Home: 243 Ambleside Dr., London, Ont. N6G 4P4; Office: 339 Windermere Rd., London, Ont. N6A 5A5.

**ATTRELL, Robert Beverley;** automotive dealer; b. Orillia, On. 27 June 1940; s. Gordon Campbell and Marjorie Elinor (Stubbs) A.; e. Winston Churchill S.S.; Pickering H.S.; Danforth Tech.; m. Hazel Robertson d. Rev. Victor and Beryl Mornan 14 March 1959; children: Linda Ann, John Allan, David Henry, Robert Vincent; PRESIDENT, ATTRELL AUTO HOLDINGS LTD. 1975– ; Auto Technician, General Motors; Toyota Canada Head Office 1969–75; acquired Toyota dealership Brampton 1975 (now one of the most successful Toyota franchises in Canada); launched Hyundai franchise Brampton 1991; Founding Pres., Candn. Assn. of Japanese Auto. Dealers; Chrmn., Toyota Nat. Dealer Council; Pres., Toronto Auto. Dealers Assn.; Pres., Toronto Internat. Car Show 1992; Chrmn. of Bd., Co-Auto (dealers buying co-operative) 1993; Founding Chrmn. of Bd., Candn. Motorsport Hall of Fame 1993; prominent promoter & participant in Candn. Motor Sports competing in num. Ice Races, Rallies & Track Races across Canada & internationally; clubs: British Auto Racing Club of Canada (Past Pres.; organizer, sponsor & Pace Car Driver at several internat. races, incl. Molson Indy), Canadian Racing Drivers Club; Home: 22 Casper Cres., Brampton, Ont. L6W 4N3; Office: 247 Queen St. E., Brampton, Ont. L6W 2B5.

**ATTRIDGE, George Norman;** executive; b. Carlisle, Ont. 25 July 1928; s. Norman Leslie and Stella Jane (Cairns) A.; e. Westdale Coll. Inst. Hamilton, Ont. 1946; m. Colleen d. Izon and Flo Landers 23 Apr. 1940; three s. Norman, Michael, Gregory; VICE-CHRMN., GARLAND COMMERCIAL RANGES LTD. 1991– ; Chrmn., Garland Catering Equipment Ltd. (Eng.); Dir. Garland Commercial Industries Inc. (Pa.); joined Royal Bank of Canada 1946–53; present Co. 1953, Asst. Gen. Mgr. 1955–62, Vice Pres. 1962–70, Extve. Vice Pres. 1970–79, Pres. 1979–91; mem. Candn. Gas Assn. (Dir. 1983–84); Candn. Mfrs. Assn.; Bd. Trade City of Mississauga; Home: 326 Bethune Dr., P.O. Box 1607, Gravenhurst, Ont. P0C 1G0 and in U.S.; Offices: 1177 Kamato Rd., Mississauga, Ont. L4W 1X4 and in U.S.

**ATWOOD, Harold Leslie,** M.A., Ph.D., D.Sc., F.R.S.C.; educator; b. Montreal, Que. 15 Feb. 1937; s. Carl Edmund and Margaret Dorothy (Killam) A.; e. Univ. of Toronto B.A. 1959; Univ. of Cal. Berkeley M.A. 1960; Univ. of Glasgow Ph.D. 1963, D.Sc. 1978; m. Lenore d. Sheir and Eva Mendelson 23 Dec. 1959; children: David Malcolm, Robert Carl, Evan Douglas; PROF. OF PHYSIOL. AND DIR., MEDICAL RSCH. COUNCIL GROUP IN NERVE CELLS AND SYNAPSES 1991– ; Research Assoc., Univ. of Ore. 1962–64; Research Fellow Cal. Inst. of Tech. 1964–65; Asst. Prof. of Zool. present Univ. 1965, Assoc. Prof. 1968, Prof. 1972– ; Prof. & Chrmn. of Physiol., Univ. of Toronto 1981–91; Guggenheim Fellow 1972; Forchheimer Professor, Israel 1977–78; ed. 'Biology of Crustacea' vols. 3 and 4, 1982; ed., Candn. Journal of Physiology and Pharmacology, 1987–91; author or co-author over 120 sci. books and papers; Fellow, Am. Assn. Advanc. Sci.; Fellow, Royal Soc. of Can.; mem. Soc. Neurosci.; Am. Physiol. Soc.; Candn. Physiol. Soc.; recreation: wilderness travel; Home: 602 Castlefield Ave., Toronto, Ont. M5N 1L8; Office: Medical Sciences Bldg., Toronto, Ont. M5S 1A8.

**ATWOOD, Margaret,** C.C., A.M., D.Litt., LL.D., F.R.S.C.; poet and book author; b. Ottawa, Ont. 18 Nov. 1939; d. Dr. Carl Edmund and Margaret Dorothy (Killam) A.; e. Victoria Coll., Univ. of Toronto, B.A., 1961; Radcliffe Coll., A.M., 1962; publications (poetry): 'Double Persephone' 1961; 'The Circle Game' 1964; 'Kaleidoscopes Baroque: a poem' 1965; 'Talismans for Children' 1965; 'Speeches for Doctor Frankenstein' 1966; 'The Animals in That Country' 1968; 'The Journals of Susanna Moodie' 1970; 'Procedures For Underground' 1970; 'Oratorio for Sasquatch, Man and Two Androids' Poems for Voices CBC 1970; 'Power Politics' 1971; 'You Are Happy' 1974; 'Selected Poems' 1976; 'Marsh Hawk' 1977; 'Two-Headed Poems' 1978; 'True Stories' 1981; 'Notes Towards A Poem That Can Never Be Written' 1981; 'Snake Poems' 1983; 'Unearthing Suite' 1983; 'Interlunar' 1984; 'Selected Poems II: Poems Selected and New 1976–1986' 1986; 'Selected Poems 1966–1984' 1990; 'Margaret Atwood Poems 1965–1975' 1991; publications (fiction): 'The Edible Woman' 1969; 'Surfacing' 1972; 'Lady Oracle' 1976; 'Dancing Girls' (short stories) 1977; 'Life Before Man' 1979; 'Bodily Harm' 1981; 'Encounters with the Element Man' 1982; 'Murder in the Dark' (very short fiction) 1983; 'Bluebeard's Egg' 1983; 'The Handmaid's Tale' 1985; 'Cat's Eye' 1988; 'Wilderness Tips' 1991; 'Good Bones' (very short fiction) 1992; 'The Robber Bride' 1993; publications (children's books): 'Up in the Tree' 1978; 'Anna's Pet' 1980; 'For the Birds' 1990; publications (non-fiction): 'Survival, A Thematic Guide to Canadian Literature' 1972; 'Days of the Rebels 1815–1840' 1977; 'Second Words: Selected Critical Prose' 1982; television scripts: 'The Servant Girl' 1974; 'Snowbird' 1981; 'Heaven on Earth' (with Peter Pearson) 1986; radio script: 'The Trumpets of Summer' 1964; co-editor, with Shannon Ravenel: 'The Best American Short Stories 1989'; recordings: 'The Poetry and Voice of Margaret Atwood' 1977; 'Margaret Atwood Reads From A Handmaid's Tale'; Awards rec'd: E.J. Pratt Medal 1961; President's Medal, Univ. of W. Ont. 1965; Gov. Gen. Award (for 'The Circle Game') 1966; 1st Prize, Centennial Comn. Poetry Competition, 1967; Union Poetry Prize, Chicago 1969; Bess Hoskins Prize, poetry, Chicago 1974; City of Toronto Book Award 1977; Candn. Booksellers' Assn. Award, 1977; Periodical Distributors of Canada Short Fiction 1977; St. Lawrence Award for Fiction 1978; Radcliffe Graduate medal 1980; Molson Award 1981; Guggenheim Fellowship 1981; Companion of the Order of Canada 1981; Welsh Arts Council Internat. Writers Prize 1982; Periodical Distributors of Canada and the Foundation for the Advancement of Canadian Letters Book of the Year Award 1983; Ida Nudel Humanitarian Award 1986; Toronto Arts Award 1986; Governor General's Award (for 'The Handmaid's Tale') 1986; Los Angeles Times Fiction Award 1986; Ms. Magazine, Woman of the Year 1986; shortlisted for the Booker Prize, England, 1987 and Ritz Hemingway Prize, Paris 1987; Arthur C. Clarke Award for best Science Fiction 1987; Commonwealth Literary Prize, Regional winner 1987; Council for Advancement and Support of Education, Silver Medal, Best Article of the Year 1987; Humanist of the Year Award 1987; Fellow, Royal Soc. of Can. 1987; YWCA Women of Distinction Award 1988; Nat. Magazine Award for Environmental Journalism, First Prize 1988; Am. Acad. of Arts and Sciences, Foreign Hon. Mem., Literature 1988; 'Cat's Eye' Torgi Talking Book (CNIB) 1989; Awards for 'Cat's Eye': City of Toronto Book Award 1989; Coles Book of the Year 1989; Candn. Booksellers Assoc., Author of the Year 1989; Foundation for the Advancement of Candn. Letters in conjunction with the Periodical Marketers of Can., Book of the Year 1989; Trillium Award for excellence in Ontario Writing 1992 for 'Wilderness Tips'; Book of the Year Award, Periodical Marketers of Can. 1992 for 'Wilderness Tips'; John Hughes Prize, Welsh Development Bd. 1992; rec'd Order of Ontario 1990; Centennial Medal, Harvard Univ. 1990; Commemorative Medal for the 125th Anniversary of Candn. Confederation; Honourary degrees: D. Litt. Trent Univ. 1973; LL.D. Queen's Univ. 1974; D. Litt. Concordia 1980; Smith Coll. Northampton, Mass. 1982; Univ. of Toronto 1983; Univ. of Waterloo 1985; Univ. of Guelph 1985; Mount Holyoke Coll. 1985; Victoria College 1987; Université de Montréal 1991; recreation: canoeing; Address: c/o McClelland & Stewart, 900 - 481 University Ave., Toronto, Ont. M5G 2E9.

**AUBIN, Jane Esther,** B.Sc., Ph.D.; educator; b. Cornwall, Ont. 3 March 1950; d. J. Leonard and M. Nora (Broderick) A.; e. Queen's Univ. B.Sc. 1972; Univ. of Toronto Ph.D. 1977; PROF., UNIV. OF TORONTO 1988– , Chair, Dept. of Anatomy and Cell Biology 1994– ; Postdoctoral Fellow Molecular Biol. & Biochem. Max Planck Inst. for Biophys. Chem. Gottingen, FRG 1977–79; Asst. Prof. present Univ. 1979, Assoc. Prof. 1984, Prof. 1988– , Chair Grad. Dept. of Dentistry and Dir. Div. Postgrad. Dental Edn. 1989–94; mem. Sci. Adv. Bd. (Progs. Bone Rsch. & Devel.) Allelix Pharmaceuticals; Cons. & Reviewer Med. Rsch. Council Can. (mem. Council); BC Health Care Found.; Nat. Insts. Health/NIDR, NIGMS, NIAMS (USA); Fonds nat. Suisse de la recherches scientifiques; Binat. Sci. Found.; Israel Acad. Sci. & Humanities Basic Rsch. Found.; recipient Gold Medal Chem. Queen's Univ. 1972; Oral Biol. Rsch. Award Internat. Assn. Dental Rsch. 1985; author or co-author over 100 sci. publs.; mem. various ed. bds.; mem. Am. Soc. Bone & Mineral Rsch. (Council); Candn. Fedn. Biol. Soc's; Am. Soc. Cell Biol.; Internat. Soc. Differentiation; Internat. Assn. Dental Rsch.; N.Y. Acad. Sci's; Office: 4384 Medical Sciences Bldg., Toronto, Ont. M5S 1A8.

**AUBIN, Paul;** historian; b. Montréal, Qué. 15 Dec. 1933; s. Adrien and Evelina (Cocher) A.; e. Univ. de Montréal Hist. 1968; PROFL. HISTORIAN, INSTITUT QUÉBÉCOIS DE RECHERCHE SUR LA CULTURE 1981– ; Teacher of Hist. 1968–72; Profl. Hist. Qué. Dept. of Cultural Affairs 1972–81; Co-Producer Computerized Data Bank HISCABEQ: Hist. of Qué. & Can.; author 'Bibliography of the History of Québec and Canada' 1946–65, 1966–75, 1976–80, 1981–85; Bibliog. Sect. 'Revue d'Histoire de l'Amérique Française' since 1967; 'Register of post-graduate dissertations in progress in history and related subjects' since 1986; mem. Candn. Hist. Assn.; Assoc. of Candn. Studies/Assoc. des études canadiennes; Bibliographical Soc. of Can.; Assoc. for the Bibliography of Hist.; Société canadienne d'histoire de l'Eglise catholique/Candn. Catholic Historical Assn.; Home: 2014, Hélène-Boulé, Sainte-Foy, Qué. G1V 2B8; Office: 14 rue Haldimand, Québec, Qué. G1R 4N4.

**AUBREY, Larry Craig,** B.A., O.T.C.; actor/director; teacher; b. Ottawa, Ont. 15 Aug. 1944; s. Frederick George and Margaret Gage (Fitchpatrick) A.; e. Rockcliffe Park P.S. 1957; Lisgar C.I. 1962; Carleton Univ. B.A. 1965; Ont. Teachers Cert., Univ. of Toronto 1993; FOUNDING DIR/ADMIN., SUDBURY THEATRE CTR. TOURING CO. 1985– ; Mem., Stratford Shakespeare Fest. Co. 1964–67; resided in London & co-starred with Lynn Redgrave (London stage), Joan Greenwood (Richmond stage), Franco Nero (Italian film) 1967–73; film and TV 1973– ;includes: 'For the Record,' 'Adderly,' 'Escape From Iran,' 'The Vindicator,' 'The Gate II,' 'Cardinal Sins,' 'Married to it,' 'Top Cops,' 'Maniac Mansion,' 'Secret Service,' 'Clarence' and stage across Can. incl.: Nat. Arts Ctr., Shaw Fest., St. Lawrence Centre, Toronto; Past Ctte. Mem., Ont. Arts Counc.; Children's Aid Soc.; Head Boy, Rockcliffe Park P.S. 1957; the Sudbury Theatre Ctr. Touring Co. is the 1st profl. theatre co. to tour remote native communities accessible by air only; a documentary film of the Touring Co. has been made by Canamedia Prodns. in association with the British Broadcasting Corporation; Mem., Actors' Equity Assn.; OPSEU; OSSTF; Assn. of Candn. TV & Radio Artists; Brit. Equity; Home: 33 Conway Ave., Toronto, Ont. M6E 1H1.

**AUBRY, (Joseph Charles Noël) Yves;** air traffic controller; human resources specialist; b. Ottawa, Ont. 26 June 1952; s. (Joseph) Charles (Edouard Frédéric Georges) and (Madeleine Antoinette) Pauline (deBellefeuille) A.; e. St-Rédempteur, Gauvin, Polyvalente and St-Jean Baptiste, Hull, Qué. 1970; Carleton Univ. Elect. Engn. 1970–71; Dept. of Transport Air Traffic Control Licence 1973; Hull Music Conserv. 1968–69; m. (Marie) Jocelyne (Ann) d. Jacques Emond, Lac Ste-Marie, Qué. 27 May 1972; two d. Julie Sonia, Annick Pauline; Nat. Vice Pres., Candn. Air Traffic Control Assn. Inc. 1979–80; mem. Bargaining Team 1979–80 Contract, Rep. on NJC Fed. Govt.; Côte-Nord Br., Sept-Iles, Qué. (Secy. Treas. 1975–76, Chrmn. 1977, 1981–85); CATCA, Chrmn. of Br. 1977, Qué. Regional Dir. 1978–79; mem. Ottawa Guitar Soc. 1969–71; Drum Corps: Amicalists de Hull 1965–66, Les Troubadours Hull 1966–68; recreations: classical and flamenco guitar, woodworking, electronics, computer programming; Address: 87 de Richmond, Gatineau, Qué. J8R 1Y1.

**AUBUT, Marcel,** C.M., Q.C., B.ès A., LL.M.; lawyer; sports association executive; b. St. Hubert de Riviere-du-Loup, Que. 5 Jan. 1948; s. Roland and Omerine (Proulx) A.; e. Academie de Québec B.ès A. 1968; Univ. Laval LL.B. 1970, LL.M. 1975; m. Francine Vallée 15 Aug. 1970; children: Melanie, Julie, Catherine; SR. PARTNER AND DIR. AUBUT & CHABOT 1983– ; Pres. & Chief Exec. Offr. Que. Nordiques Hockey Club 1978– , Chrmn. 1980– ; Gov. NHL Que. 1979– ; Chief Exec. Offr. Trans-Am. Prodns. Montreal 1984– ;

Dir. Major Can. Corps.; called to Bar of Que. 1971; cr. Q.C. 1987; Assoc. Tremblay, Beauvais, Bouchard, Truchon & Morisset, Quebec 1972, Sr. Partner 1976–83; Legal Adv., Sec.-Treas. Que. Nordiques Hockey Club, Que. 1976–78; Chrmn., Chief Exec. Offr. Internat. Festival Sports, Culture & Arts Rendez-Vous 87, Que.; Pres. La fête du Can. 1985; recipient C.M. 1986; Extve. of Yr. Award NHL 1987; mem. Candn. Bar Assn.; Que. Bar Assn.; Que. Jr. Bar Asn.; Que. C. of C.; Lions (Sillery & St-Foy); Clubs: Garnison; Royal 22nd Regt. (Hon. mem.); Office: 736, 2 Place Quebec, Quebec City, Qué. G1R 2B5 and 2205 Ave. du Colisee, Quebec City, Qué. G1L 4W7.

**AUCH, Susan;** athlete; MEMBER, CANADIAN SPEED SKATING TEAM; Silver Medal Winner, Women's 500-m long-track speed skating, 1994 Olympics, Lillehammer, Norway; 6th place, 500-m race, 1992 Games, Albertville; holds Canadian record for 500-m race; Student, Broadcast Journalism, Univ. of Calgary; Home: Winnipeg, Man.; Office: c/o Speed Skating Canada, 1600 James Naismith Dr., Gloucester, Ont. K1B 5N4.

**AUCLAIR, Denis,** B.Comm., M.Comm.; marketing executive; b. Quebec City 16 June 1943; s. Mathieu and Madeleine (Renaud) A. e. Laval Univ. B.Comm. 1964, M.Comm. 1965; m. Michèle d. Aline and Emile Marier 1 June 1965; children: Charles, Isabelle; VICE-PRESIDENT, MARKETING, WHITE PAPER GROUP 1993– ; Nat. Marketing Mgr., Container Div., C.P. Forest Products 1978–79; Gen. Mgr., Single Serv. Div. 1980–84; Gen. Mgr., Canexel Hardboard Div. 1984–88; Vice-Pres., Papers Div., Rolland Inc. 1989–90; Vice-Pres. Marketing, White Paper & Paperboard, Candn. Pacific Forest Products Ltd. 1991–93; clubs: Montreal Amateur Athletic Assn.; Home: 640 Habitat 67, Cité du Havre, Montréal, Qué.; Office: 1250 René Lévesque Blvd. W., Montréal, Qué. H3B 4Y3.

**AUCLAIR, Michel,** B.A., M.Comm., C.A.; food industry executive; b. Montreal, Que. 21 June 1950; e. Univ. of Montreal B.A. 1970; Univ. of Sherbrooke M.Comm. 1973; C.A. 1974; single; PRESIDENT, GROCERY GROUP, CULINAR INC. 1991– ; Vice-Pres., Finance, La Brasserie Labatt Limitée (Quebec subs.) 1980–83; Partner resp. for planning & bus. devel., Raymond Chabot Martin Pare & Partners 1983–88; Asst. to Pres. 1986; Vice-Pres., Finance, Culinar Inc. 1988–91; Mem., Montreal C. of C. (Bd. Mem. 1983–86; Extve. Ctte. Mem. & Treas. 1986–90); Gov., Admin. Faculty, Univ. of Sherbrooke; Mem., Que., Ont. & Candn. Insts. of C.A.s; Financial Executives Inst.; Planning Forum; recreations: tennis, skiing; Office: 4945 Ontario St. E., Montreal, Qué. H1V 1M2.

**AUCOIN, Peter Charles,** M.A., Ph.D.; educator; b. Halifax, N.S. 3 Oct. 1943; s. Charles A. and Kathleen G. (Doyle) A.; e. St. Mary's Univ. H.S.; St. Mary's Univ. B.A. 1964; Dalhousie Univ. M.A. 1966; Queen's Univ. PhD. 1971; m. Margot d. Everett and Margaret Flemming 5 Aug. 1967; children: Nicole, Paul, Richard; McCULLOCH PROFESSOR IN POLITICAL SCIENCE & PROFESSOR OF PUBLIC ADMINISTRATION, DALHOUSIE UNIV. 1979– ; Asst. Prof. of Pol. Sci. present Univ. 1970, Assoc. Prof. 1974; Assoc. Dir. Sch. of Pub. Adm. 1975–80, Dir. 1980–85, Chair, Dept. of Pol. Sci. 1992– ; Sci. Adv., Sci. Council of Can. 1973–74; mem. Fed. Electoral Boundaries Comn. (N.S.) 1982–83; Research Co-Dir. Halifax Comn. on City Govt. 1982–83; Research Co-ordr., Royal Comn. on the Economic Union and Development Prospects for Can. 1983–85; Dir. of Rsch., Royal Comn. on Electoral Reform and Party Financing 1990–91; mem. Adv. Counc., Can. Centre for Mgmt. Devel., Govt. of Can. 1988–91; mem., Fed. Electoral Boundaries Comn. (N.S.) 1993–94; recipient Can. Council Leave Fellowship 1976–77; Social Sciences & Humanities Research Council Leave Fellowship 1983–84; author 'Public Accountability in the Governing Professions' 1978; co-author 'Knowledge, Power and Public Policy' 1974; 'The Centralization-Decentralization Conundrum' 1988; ed. 'The Politics and Management of Restraint in Government' 1981; 'Regional Responsiveness and the National Administrative State' 1985; 'Regional Representation and Party Government in Canada' 1985; 'Institutional Reforms for Representative Government' 1985; 'Middle Managers: The Crucial Link'; co-ed. 'The Structures of Policy-Making in Canada' 1971; 'Public Policy in Canada' 1979; mem. Candn. Pol. Sci. Assn. (Dir. 1974–76; Vice Pres. 1979–80); Inst. Pub. Adm. Can. (Journ. Ed. Bd. 1974–76; Case Program Bd. 1976–78; Research Comte. 1983–87; N.S. Group 2nd Vice Chrmn. 1981–83; 1st Vice Chrmn. 1983–85; Chrmn. Schools and Programs Comte. 1985–87; mem. Nat. Extve. 1987–90; Vice Pres. 1989–90); mem. Ed. Bd., 'Governance: An International Journal of Policy and Administration' 1987– ; 'Public Sector Management' 1991– ; R. Catholic; recreation: tennis; Club: Waegwoltic; Home: 6571 Norwood St., Halifax, N.S. B3H 2L7; Office: Halifax, N.S. B3H 4H6.

**AUDCENT, Mark Anthony,** B.A., LL.B.; lawyer, public servant; b. Lytham-St. Annes, Eng. 13 June 1950; s. Gerard Arthur and Eileen Winnifred (Kenway) A.; e. Univ. of Ottawa B.A. (Hons.) 1971, LL.B. 1975, Cert. in Legislative Drafting 1982; Univ. de Lille France Cert. d'études sup., 2e cycle, Lettres modernes 1972; ASSISTANT LAW CLERK & PARLIAMENTARY COUNSEL, THE SENATE OF CANADA 1982– ; Law Soc. of Alta. 1976; Assoc. Counsel, Bennett, Jones 1976–79; Ast. Prof., Law, Univ. of Sask. 1979–81; Pres., Assn. of Parly. Counsel in Canada 1985, '93; Sec. 1984, '92; Chair, United Way Senate Campaign 1990–91; Vice-Chair, Found. for the Study of the Processes of Govt. in Canada 1993; Sec. 1991, '92; Lectr., Law, Univ. of Ottawa 1989– ; recreation: curling; club: Les Balayeux; Home: 90 Concord St. N., Ottawa, Ont. K1S 0Y8; Office: 907 – 140 Wellington St., Ottawa, Ont. K1A 0A4.

**AUDET, Henri,** C.M. (1984), B.A., B.Sc.A., M.Sc., D.Sc.; communications executive; b. Montréal, Que. 7 Aug. 1918; s. Victor F. and Alice (Turgeon) A.; e. Jean-de-Brébeuf Coll., B.A.; Ecole Polytech. B.A.Sc.; Mass. Inst. Technol., M.Sc.; Univ. de Qué., D.Sc. m. Marie, d. Henri-S. Labelle, 24 June 1950; children: Louis, François, Denise, Bernard, Geneviève; CHAIRMAN, COGECO, INC.; STÉRÉO LAVAL INC.; Chrmn., Cogeco Telecom; CJMF-FM Ltd.; Cablestrie Inc.; Beauce Video Ltée; Télécable BSL Inc.; Thetford Video Inc.; Publications Dumont; Dir., Télévision St-Maurice Inc.; Télévision St-François Inc.; La Belle Vision Inc.; Intervision de la Mauricie; Spectavision; with La Soc. Radio-Canada 1945–57; Past Chrmn., Que. Univ. (Trois-Rivières); Candn. Assn. Broadcasters; ACRTF; TV Bureau of Advertising; Caisse Populaire de Normanville; Comité Trifluvien des Concerts Symphonique de Qué.; Cultural Centre; past Dir. La Laurentienne Insurance Co.; Broadcast News; Symphonic Concerts of Que.; Centre Hospitalier Ste-Marie; mem., Order of Engineers; Eng. Inst. of Can.; Broadcast Extve. Soc.; I.E.E.E.; Acad. can. du génie; Club des ambassadeurs de la CEDIC; Pres. Club & Thelma Finlayson Soc., Simon Fraser Univ.; Cons. des gouv. assoc. de l'Univ. de Montréal; Gov. Mem., Fond. univ. du centre du Qué.; Dir., Fond. des ingén. du Qué.; Hydro-Qué.; Hon. Counc., Montreal Symphonic Orch.; Chrmn., Fond. du Théâtre du Rideau Vert; Chambre de Commerce du Qué.; Chambre de Commerce du Montréal Métropolitain; Montreal Bd. of Trade; (and past Dir.) Festivals de Musique of Qué.; r. catholique; Recreation: sailing; Clubs: St. Denis; Mount-Royal; St.-Maurice Yacht; Laviolette; Radisson; Ki-8–Eb Golf; Home: 169 Maplewood Ave., Outremont, Qué. H2V 2M6; Office: 1, Place Ville-Marie, #3636, Montreal, Qué. H3B 3P2.

**AUDET, Fr. Léonard,** D.Th., L.S.S.; educator; b. Maria, Qué. 26 Nov. 1932; s. Ernest Nicolas and Emilie (Loubert) A.; e. Univ. of Montreal B.A. 1954, D.Th. 1962; Pontificium Institutum Biblicum Rome L.S.S. 1964; SUPERIOR GENERAL OF THE CONGREGATION OF THE CLERICS OF SAINT VIATOR 1988– ; Prof. of Holy Scripture Sch. of Theol. Joliette, Qué. 1965–67; Prof. of New Testament Lit., Univ. of Montreal 1967–88 (Dir. of Bible Dept. 1973–77; Dean of Theology 1977–85); Priest, The Clerics of Saint Viator (Dir. 1971–74); Dir. Cath. Soc. of Bible 1981–83; mem. Société Canadienne de théologie; Assn. Catholique des études Bibliques au Can. (Treas. 1968–77); co-author 'Résurrection. Espérance humaine et don de Dieu' 1971; 'Jésus? De l'histoire à la foi' 1974; 'Neuve est ta Parole' 1974; 'A Companion to Paul' 1975; 'Vivante est ta parole' 1975; 'Après Jésus. Autorité et liberté dans le peuple de Dieu' 1977; 'Je crois en Dieu' 1989; and article in 'La Vie des communautés religieuses' 1992; Home: Chierici di San Viatore, Casella Postale 10793, 00144 Roma, Italia.

**AUDET, Luc,** LL.B.; attorney; b. Montréal, Qué. 10 Aug. 1956; s. Charles-Henri and Lucette (St-Cyr) A.; e. Sherbrooke Univ. LL.B. 1980; Qué. Bar School 1981; one d.: Véronique; VICE PRESIDENT, CORPORATE AFFAIRS & GENERAL COUNSEL, RADIO-QUÉBEC, 1991– ; private practice until 1982; Legal Couns., Coopérants, Life Insurance Company 1982–88; Chief Legal Couns. & Corp. Sec. 1988–89; Chief Legal Counsel & Corp. Secy., Coopérants Group Inc. 1989–91; Dir. & Pres. of several private real estate companies; Sec.-Treas., Assn. for Tele-Education in Canada; Mem., Quebec Bar Assn.; Candn. Bar Assn.; Home: 2570, rue de Lotbinière, Laval, Qué. H7E 5B4; Office: 1000, Fullum St., Montréal, Qué. H2K 3L7.

**AUDET, Maurice G.,** B.A., M.A.; insurance broker; b. New Westminster, B.C. 24 Oct. 1946; s. George J. and Simone Marie (Touchette) A.; e. Simon Fraser Univ. B.A. 1969, M.A. 1971; m. Lorna d. Ron and Margaret Makepeace 4 Sept. 1972; children: Michael, Carolyn; SR. ACCT. MGR., REED STENHOUSE 1990– ; joined Marsh & McLennan as Trainee 1973; var. positions in Claims and Ins. Brokering Depts.; appt. Vice Pres. 1987; Mgr., Ins. Broking, Masters Insurance Limited 1987–91; Past Pres., Toronto Ins. Conf., Alternate; Dir., Candn. Fedn. of Ins. Agts. & Brokers Assns.; author numerous articles on property & liability insurance; Home: 523 Downland Dr., Pickering, Ont. L1W 3B1; Office: 20 Bay St., Toronto, Ont. M5J 2N9.

**AUDET, Paul-A.;** retired newspaperman; b. Québec, Qué. 14 Mar. 1923; s. Sylvio and Rose-Aimee (Cloutier) A.; e. Acad. de Québec (Que.); Laval Sch. of Comm.; m. Michèle Richard, 13 Sept. 1947; children: Francine, André, Marc; former Pres. & Gen. Mgr., Le Soleil (Div. of UniMedia Quebec Inc.); Hon. Col., Les Voltigeurs de Qué.; Doctorate hon. causa Univ. de Qué. 1985; Consultant to BCP Advertising Agency; Vice-Pres., Québec Military Institute; Dir., Inst. canadien de Qué.; formerly: Pres. Edimedia Inc.; Les Quotidiens du Québec Inc.; Past Pres., Newspaper Advertising Extve. Assn. Can.; Dir., Opéra de Québec; mem., Cercle de la Garnison; R. Catholic; recreations: swimming, golf, fishing, skiing; Home: 9 Jardins Merici, Apt. 1803, Québec, Qué. G1S 4N8; Office: 1220 Taché, Québec, Qué. G1R 3B4.

**AUDETTE, Louis de la Chesnaye,** O.C. (1974), Q.C. (1953), B.A., L.Ph., LL.B., D.Sc.Mil.(hon.); Canadian public servant (retired); b. Ottawa, Ont. 7 Apr. 1907; s. Hon. Justice Louis Arthur and Mary Grace (d. Hon. Justice Sir Andrew Stuart) A.; e. Univ. of Ottawa, B.A., L.Ph.; Univ. of Montreal LL.B.; Royal Roads Mil. College, D.Sc.Mil. (hon.); called to Bar of Qué. 1931; practised law with Audette & OBrien 1931–39; R.C.N. 1939–45, commanding various ships in N. Atlantic and Mediterranean; retired as Commdr. R.C.N.(R); mentioned in Despatches; 1st Secy., Dept. of External Affairs 1945–1947; Commr. Candn. Maritime Comn. 1947–1953, Chrmn. 1954–59; mem. Comm. of Inquiry into R.C.N. 1949; Dir. Export Devel. Corp. 1946–71; Dir. Crown Assets Disposal Corp. 1953–60; Dir. 1948–1959 and Pres. 1954–59 Park Steamship Co. Ltd.; mem. N.W.T. Council 1947–59; Court Martial Appeal Bd. 1951–59; Chrmn. Prep. Comte. U.N. Inter-govt. Maritime Consultative Organ.1954–59 and Pres. First Assembly (London, 1959); Chrmn. Tariff Bd. of Can. 1959–72; Administrator, Maritime Pollution Claims Fund 1973–78 and 1983–88; Dir. Ottawa Handicapped Assn. 1967–79; Candn. Cerebral Palsy Assn. 1971–82; mem. Comte. for the Transportation of the Disabled (Ottawa) 1972–91; Gov., Participation House Projects International (Ont. Fed. for the Cerebral Palsied) 1976–77; mem. 1977–85 and Chrmn. 1980–82 Ottawa-Carleton Adv. Bd., Ont. March of Dimes (Rehabilitation Foundation for the Disabled); Dir. Rehabilitation Inst. of Ottawa 1980–91; Past Pres. Canadian Club (Ottawa) and of Ottawa Philharmonic Orchestra; mem. Que. Bar; R.C.; Club: Cercle Universitaire; Residence: 451 Besserer St., Ottawa, Ont. K1N 6C2.

**AUGER, Fred S.,** B.Sc.; b. Calgary, Alta., 7 June 1907; s. Albert Raymond and Mabel Christine (Saunders) A.; e. Calgary Pub. and High Schs.; Univ. of Idaho, B.Sc. (Business); m. Dorothy Kathleen, d. late Norman Colin Hill, Calgary, Alta., 18 June 1934; children: Barry Norman, Timothy Frank; Hon. Dir., Southam Press Ltd.; Past Pres., Ducks Unlimited, Can.; Publisher 'Vancouver Province' and 'Winnipeg Tribune'; Phi Gamma Delta; United Church; recreations: hunting, fishing; Clubs: Vancouver; Shaughnessy Golf; Vancouver; Black Watch of Canada (Montreal); Home: 4266 Staulo Cres., Vancouver, B.C. V6N 3S2.

**AUGER, Jacques G.;** transportation executive; b. Montreal, Que. 31 Aug. 1941; s. Gerard and Georgette (Aboussafy) A.; e. Univ. of Montreal, Hautes Etudes Commerciales mngt. acctg. 1968; m. Claudette d. Thomas and Leanne Roussel 13 June 1964; children: Pascal, Stephane, François; PRESIDENT & CHIEF EXECUTIVE OFFICER, AÉROPORTS DE MONTRÉAL; Former Chair, Consultative Ctte. on The Railway Industry; Vice Chrmn., Quebec Central Railway; Hon. Pres., Fond. Dr. Maurice Bertrand; Fellow, Chartered Inst. of Transport; Dir., EDICOM, Space Camp Canada, General Secretariat for the Internat. Civil Aviation Celebrations; clubs: Mount-Royal, Rideau; Home: 366 Brookfield, TMR, Montreal, Qué. H3P 2A8; Office: 1100 René Lévesque Blvd. W., Montreal, Qué. H3B 4X8.

**AUGER, Paul Emile,** O.C., B.A., D.Sc., F.R.S.C., F.G.S.A.; geologist; b. St. Croix, Lotbinière Co., P.Q. 30 Sept. 1908; s. Arthur and Valeda (Boisvert) A.; e. Laval Univ., B.A. 1929, B.Sc. 1933; Queen's Univ., B.Sc. 1936; Mass. Inst. of Tech., D.Sc. 1940; m. Gabrielle, d. Joseph Hébert, 3 Feb. 1940; childen: Jacques, Louise, Michèle; named to Que. Prov. Econ. Council, July 1961; former Prof. of Econ. Geol. and of Structural and Engn. Geol., Fac. of Sciences, Laval Univ.; Geol., Que. Bur. of Mines 1940–60; Deputy-Min., Dept. of Natural Resources, Govt. of Que. 1960–71; has written many reports and papers on minerals in Que.; Wing Commdr., C.O. Laval Univ. Sqdn., R.C.A.F.; mem., Candn. Inst. of Mining & Metall. (Pres. 1968–69); Corp. Prof. Engrs. Que.; Cong. of Candn. Engrs.; Geol. Assn. of Can. (Pres. 1962); Soc. of Econ. Geols.; R. Catholic; Address: 250 Grande Allée, O. – 1701, Quebec, Qué. G1R 2H4.

**AUGUSTINE, Jean Magdalene,** B.A., M.Ed.; school principal; b. Grenada, W.I. 9 Sept. 1937; d. Ossie Oswald and Olive (John) Simon; e. St. Joseph's Convent High Sch. 1954; Univ. of Toronto B.A. 1973, M.Ed. 1980; Ont. Inst. Studies in Edn. Supervisory Offrs. Cert. 1983; m. Winston D. s. C.J. Augustine 29 June 1968; children: two d. Valerie, Cheryl; LIBERAL CANDIDATE, ETOBICOKE LAKESHORE FEDERAL RIDING; began teaching career Grenada, W.I. 1955; former Principal, St. Gregory's Separate Sch. 1985–88 (now on leave of absence); Corporate Services, M.S.S.B.; Past Chair, Metro Toronto Housing Authority; conducts workshops & seminars pertaining to multiculturalism, race relations, visible minorities & women's issues; Mem., Bd. of Govs., York Univ.; Past Dir. Harbourfront Corp.; Dir. Cath. Children's Aid Soc.; Trustee, Toronto Hosp. for Sick Children; mem. Bd. Metro Action Ctte. Violence Against Women & Children; Urban Alliance Race Relations (Past Vice Pres. & Past Treas.); Past mem. Ont. Judicial Council; Past Nat. Pres., Cong. Black Women Can.; Past Mem. Candn. Adv. Council Status Women; Past Pres. Grenada Assn. Toronto; recipient Y.W.C.A. Women of Distinction 1987 and the Kay Livingstone Award; Cariban Achievement Award 1984; Home: Rayside Dr., Etobicoke, Ont. M9C 1T1.

**AUGUSTYN, Frank Joseph,** O.C., dancer; b. Hamilton, Ont., 27 Jan. 1953; s. Walter and Elizabeth (Schmider) A.; student Nat. Ballet Sch., 1965–70; LL.D. (hon.), York U., 1977, McMaster U., 1979; ARTISTIC DIRECTOR, THEATRE BALLET OF CANADA & OTTAWA BALLET 1989– ; Mem. Corps de Ballet, Nat. Ballet Co. of Can., Toronto 1970–71, soloist, 1971–72, prin., 1972– ; co-founder Ballet Revue; has performed in Can., U.S., London Festival Ballet, Germany, France, Holland, Monaco, Belgium, USSR, Italy, Switzerland, Cuba; TV appearances include Giselle (CBC), 1975, La Fille Mal Gardé (CBC), 1979 Pleasure of Your Company, Magic Show; Winner best couple award 2d Internat. Ballet Competition, Moscow, 1973; decorated Order of Can. Author: Kain-Augustyn, 1977; Office: Ottawa Ballet, 142 Bank St., Ottawa, Ont. K1P 5N8.

**AULD, Douglas Allen Lauriston,** B.A., M.A., Ph.D.; b. London, Ont. 15 March 1941; s. James Lauriston and Margaret Lillian (Seager) A.; e. Univ. of W. Ont., B.A. (Hon.) 1964; Univ. of Toronto, M.A. 1965; Australian Nat. Univ., Ph.D. 1969; m. Margaret d. Sidney and Edna Lonie 29 June 1968; children: Robyn Elizabeth, Christopher James; PRESIDENT & C.E.O., LOYALIST COLLEGE, Belleville, Ont. 1988– ; Rsch. Econ., Imperial Oil 1965; Asst. Prof., Univ. of Guelph 1968–70; Assoc. Prof. 1970–73; Prof. 1974– ; Chrmn., Dept. of Econ., 1980–86; Principal & Extve. Dean, Sch. of Natural Resources (Lindsay) 1986; Conjunct Prof. of Economics, Trent Univ. 1987– ; Vis. Asst. Prof., Univ. of B.C. 1969–70; Vis. Scholar, Univ. of York (U.K.) 1974; Vis. Prof., Duke Univ. 1976; Pres., DALA Inc. 1984– ; Mem., Counc. of Ont. Univ. 1980–86; Ont. Econ. Counc. 1984–85; Bd. of Trustees, Wellington Co. Edn. 1985–86; author: 'Economic Thinking & Pollution Problems' 1970, 'Contemporary Issues in Economics' 1971, 'Evaluating Australian Fiscal Policy' 1971, 'Study Guide to Accompany Economics' 1973, 1976, 1979, 1982, 1985, 'Macroeconomic Foundations' 1978, 'Principles of Public Finance' 1979, 1983; seventy-five scientific journal publications 1968–90 incl. J. of Pol. Econ., Quart. J. of Econ., J. of Public Economics; Home: RR #1 Foxboro, Ont. K0K 2B0; Office: Box 4200, Belleville, Ont. K8N 5B9.

**AULD, Frank,** M.A., Ph.D.; psychologist; educator; b. Denver, Colo. 9 Aug. 1923; s. Benjamin Franklin and Marion Leland (Evans) A.; e. Drew Univ. A.B. 1946; Yale Univ. M.A. 1948, Ph.D. 1950; m. Elinor Florence (dec.) d. Rev. Jacob Ellis James 29 June 1946; children: Mary Elinor, Robert Franklin, Margaret Elizabeth; PROF. EMERITUS OF PSYCHOL., UNIV. OF WINDSOR 1992– ;(Prof. 1970–90, Adjunct 1990–91); Instr. and Asst. Prof. of Psychol. Yale Univ. 1950–59; Assoc. Prof. and Prof. of Psychol. Wayne State Univ. 1959–67; Prof. of Psychol. Univ. of Detroit 1967–70; Chrmn. Dearborn (Mich.) Community Council 1963; Consultant Advertising Research Detroit Un. Fund 1965–68;mem. Adv. Comte. Coll. Work Epis. Diocese Mich. 1963–71; mem. Psychol. Licensing Bd. State of Mich. 1968–71; served with U.S. Army 1943–46; author 'Steps in Psychotherapy' 1953; 'Scoring Human Motives' 1959; 'Resolution of Inner Conflict: An Introduction to Psychoanalytic Therapy' 1991; over 40 papers psychotherapy and psychol. testing; mem. Accreditation Council Ont. Psychol. Assn. 1976–91 (Convenor 1981–82); mem. Candn. Psychol. Assn.; Am. Psychol. Assn.; Brit. Psychol. Soc.; recreations: hiking, music; Home: 1340 Pierce St., Birmingham, Mich. 48009; Office: 401 Sunset Ave., Windsor, Ont. N9B 3P4.

**AUMENTO, Fabrizio,** M.Sc., Ph.D.; geothermal energy consultant; b. Rome, Italy 19 Jan. 1940; s. Romualdo and Alda (Veronesi) A.; e. Univ. of London B.Sc. 1961; Dalhousie Univ. M.Sc. 1962, Ph.D. 1965; children: Paul, Lara, Patrick; GEOSCIENTIFIC CONSULTANT; joined Geol. Survey of Can. 1965–69; Dalhousie Univ. 1969–78, Chrmn. of Geol. 1973–75; Visiting Prof. Univ. of Geneva 1977, Instituto de Geociencias Dos Acores 1978; rec'd Nat. Research Council Steacie Fellowship 1976; APICS Young Scient. Award 1975; author 'Initial Reports of the Deep Sea Drilling Project' Vol. 37 1977; over 110 publs. on geothermics, marine geol. and assoc. topics; Fellow Royal Soc. Can.; recreation: sailing; Office: Site 24, Box 118, R.R. 6, Armdale, N.S. B3L 4P4.

**AUNE, J. Brian,** C.A.; investment executive; b. Vancouver, B.C. 12 Nov. 1939; s. Ornulf and Louella (Stangland) A.; e. C.A. 1965; one s. Jonathan; CHRMN., ST. JAMES FINANCIAL CORP. INC. 1990– ; Dir.: The Nesbitt Thomson Corp. Ltd., Toronto; Taiga Forest Products Ltd., Burnaby, B.C.; Ventures West Technologies Ltd., Vancouver; Haley Industries Ltd., Haley, Ont.; MacDonald Dettwiler and Associates Ltd., Richmond, B.C.; Prudential Corp. Can., Kitchener, Ont.; Peerless Carpet Corp., Montreal, Que.; Chrmn., Teleglobe Inc., Montreal, Que.; C.A., Clarkson Gordon & Co. 1965–66; Nesbitt, Thomson Inc. 1966–90, Chrmn. & C.E.O. 1980–90; Gov., Concordia Univ.; Chrmn. Invest. Dealers Assn. Can. 1982–83; Gov., The Montreal Exchange 1983–88; recreation: golf; Clubs: Mount Royal; Mount Bruno Golf & Country; Shaughnessy Golf & Country; Home: 640 Clarke Ave., Westmount, Qué. H3Y 3E4; Office: #300, 910 Sherbrooke St. W., Montreal, Qué. H3A 1G3.

**AUSTEN, John;** newspaper editor; b. Cowansville, Qué. 17 Apr. 1959; s. Patrick M. and Constance Joyce (Rudd) A.; e. Macdonald High Sch. 1976; John Abbott Coll. Degree Social Sci. 1979; ED. THE CHRONICLE 1986– ; Sports Ed. 1979–86, Asst. Ed. 1984–86; recipient Jack Sanderson Award Best Nat. Editorial 1987 Candn. Community Newspapers Assn.; mem. Bd. West Island Big Brothers & Big Sisters Assn. 1982; hockey & baseball coach; recreations: hockey, baseball, golf; Home: 104, 9 Kirkland Blvd., Kirkland, Qué. H9J 1N2; Office: 15 E Cartier Ave., Pointe Claire, Qué. H9S 4R7.

**AUSTENSON, Herman M.,** B.S.A., M.Sc., Ph.D., F.A.I.C.; research foundation executive; educator; b. Viscount, Sask. 28 Nov. 1924; s. John Oscar and Inger Louise (Soland) A.; e. Univ. of Sask. B.S.A. 1946, M.Sc. 1948; Wash. State Univ. Ph.D. 1951; m. Marilyn d. Harold and Edna Steel 3 June 1973; children: John N., Mary A., Paul C.; EXEC. DIR. WESTERN GRAINS RSCH. FOUND. 1989– ; Prof. of Crop Sci. Univ. of Sask. 1966–92, Head of Dept. and Dir. Crop Devel. Centre 1975–83; Asst. Agron. Wash. State Univ. 1951–53; Asst. Prof. Cornell Univ. 1953–54; Agron. W. Wash. Exper. Stn. 1955–65; Exec. and mem. Bd. Govs. Agric. Inst. Can. Rsch. Found.; mem. Council Agric. Inst. Can. 1986–88; mem. Candn. Soc. Agron. (Pres. 1984–85); Sask. Inst. Agrols.; Regent Augustana Univ. College (Alta.); Home: 13 Spruce Pl., Saskatoon, Sask. S7N 2N8; Office: 118 Veterinary Rd., Saskatoon, Sask. S7N 2R4.

**AUSTIN, Hon. Jacob (Jack),** P.C., Q.C., B.A., LL.B., LL.M., Sc.Soc.D.(h.c.); Senator; b. Calgary, Alta. 2 Mar. 1932; s. Morris and Clara Edith A.; e. Crescent Hts. High Sch., Calgary; Univ. of B.C.; Harvard Law Sch.; Univ. of Cal. (Berkeley); B.A.; LL.B. 1955; LL.M. 1957; m. Natalie Veiner Freeman, d. Harry Veiner, 4 Feb. 1978; three d.: Edith, Sharon, Barbara; CANADIAN SENATOR 1975– ; read law with N.T. Nemetz, Q.C.; called to Bar of B.C. 1958 and Yukon 1966; cr. Q.C. 1970; Asst. Prof. of Law, Univ. of B.C. 1955; Law Partner, Nemetz, Austin & Co., Vancouver 1958; Extve. Asst. to Min. of N. Affairs & Nat. Resources, Ottawa 1963; Lib. Cand. for Vancouver-Kingsway g.e. 1965; Law Partner, J. Austin, Vancouver 1966; Andrews, Swinton, Margach, Austin & Williams 1966; Pres., Giant Mascot Mines Ltd., Vancouver 1968; Brameda Resources Ltd. 1970; Depy. Min., Energy, Mines and Resources 1970–74; Principal Secretary to the Prime Minister 1974–75; summoned to Senate of Can. 1975; apptd. to Fed. Cabinet as Min. of State 1981; Min. of State for Social Devel. 1982–84; Min. of State for Canada Devel. Investment Corp.; Min. of State for Expo 86, 1982–84; Chrmn., Ministerial Sub-Comte. on Broadcasting and Cultural Affairs 1982; Pres., Internat. Div., Bank of B.C. Jan.-Nov. 1985; Bd. Chrmn., Elite Insurance Mgt. Ltd. 1986–90; Associate Counsel, Boughton, Peterson, Yang, Anderson, Vancouver 1992; Pres., Canada China Trade Council 1992; Chrmn., North American Institute 1988; author 'Canadian-United States Practice and Theory Respecting the International Law of International Rivers'; co-author 'Canadian View of Territorial Seas and Fisheries'; recreations: boating, reading; Clubs: Vancouver (Vancouver); Canadian (N.Y.); Rideau; Cercle Universitaire d'Ottawa: Home: 3439 Point Grey Road, Vancouver, B.C.; Office: Senate of Canada, Rm. 304, Victoria Bldg., 140 Wellington St., The Senate, Ottawa, Ont. K1A 0A4.

**AUSTIN, Paul Murray,** B.A., M.A., Ph.D.; university professor; b. China 17 May 1941; s. John Alfred and Lilian Maud (Reeks) A.; e. Chefoo Sch. (China), Felpham Sch. (Eng.); Harbord & Parkdale Coll.; Univ. of Toronto, B.A. 1963; Cornell Univ., M.A. 1964; Univ. of Moscow 1965–66; Univ. of Toronto, Ph.D. 1970; m. Mary d. Albert and Helen Campbell 25 July 1964; children: Peter, Nancy, Karen; CHRMN., DEPT. OF RUSSIAN & SLAVIC STUDIES, MCGILL UNIV. 1981– ; Brock Univ. 1967–68; McGill Univ. 1968– ; Assoc. Prof. 1974; Dir., Boy Scouts of Can. 1980–85; Mem., Anglican Ch. of Can.; Candn. Assn. of Slavists (Extve. Ctte., Pres. 1986–87); author of numerous articles in scholarly journals; recreations: photography; Office: 1001 Sherbrooke St. W., Montreal, Qué. H3A 1G5.

**AVERY, Colin,** B.Comm., C.M.A., M.B.A.; financial executive; b. London, England 5 Sept. 1942; s. Harold Francis and Freda Alma A.; e. Elmbridge Boarding Sch. (H.S.) 1958; Mid Essex Technical Coll. 1967; Chartered Mgmt. Accountant (UK) 1968; Sir George Williams Univ. B.Comm. C.M.A. 1973; Concordia Univ. M.B.A. 1976; m. Ann d. Jim and Eleanor Park 23 March 1967; children: Karen, Susan; VICE-PRES. FINANCE & TREASURER, LUMONICS INC. 1986– ; Budget Officer, The Marconi Co. (U.K.) 1963–67; Controller, Telecommunications Div., Canadian Marconi Co. (Montreal) 1967–74; Asst. Controller, Molson Breweries of Can. 1974–76; Controller, Apparel Prod. Div., Dominion Textile 1976–81; Vice-Pres. & Controller, AES Data 1981–82; Vice-Pres. Finance (C.F.O.) 1982–84; Vice-Pres. Finance, Ault Dairies (Toronto) 1984–86; recreations: tennis; clubs: Manotick T.C.; Home: 5616 Whitewood Ave., Manotick, Ont. K4M 1E1; Office: 105 Schneider Rd., Kanata, Ont. K2K 1Y3.

**AVERY, Maurice,** B.A., B.Sc., Ph.D.; university professor and administrator; b. Granby, Que. 5 Sept. 1942; s. Aimé Donat and Margaret (Hoar) A.; e. Univ. de Montréal B.A. 1963, B.Sc. 1967; Univ. Laval Ph.D. 1971; m. Micheline d. Maurice and Jeanne (Meloche) Lambert 18 Aug. 1967; children: Mathieu, Annabelle; VICE-RECTOR FOR PLANNING AND GEN. SEC., UNIV. DU QUEBEC A RIMOUSKI 1988– ; Postdoctoral Fellow, MRC Lipid Metabolism Unit (U.K.) 1971; Prof. of Biochem., Univ. du Qué. à Rimouski 1972; Univ. Laval 1973; Asst. to V.P. for Rsch., Univ. du Qué. Sainte-Foy 1974–76; Dean of Grad. Studies & Rsch., Inst. nat. de la rech. scientifique 1976–81; Mem., Ordre des chim. du Qué.; past mem. & chair grant cttes. of Que. & Candn. rsch. councils; Mem., Candn. Assn. for Grad. Studies (Extve. Ctte. 1988–89) 1981–89; Com. des sec. gén., Conf. des recteurs et des principaux des univ. qué. 1988– ; postgrad. fellowships: Candn. MRC, NRC & Que. Govt. 1967–70; postdoctoral fellowship: Candn. MRC 1971; Hoffman-Laroche Prize for PH.D. thesis 1971; mem. of various councils incl. Conseil rég. de dév. du Bas-Saint-Laurent; Conseil rég. de la santé et des serv. soc. du Bas-Saint-Laurent et Gaspésie, les Iles; Conseil d'admin. du CEGEP de Matane; Mem., Assn. can. française pour l'avancement des sci.; Assn. des admin. de rech. industrielle du Qué.; Assn. des admin. de rech. univ. du Qué.; Assn. des sec. gén. des univs.; author of sci. pubs. in internat. renowned journals; recreations: reading, cuisine; Home: 17, chemin de la Mer, C.P. 655, St-Fabien, Qué. G0L 2Z0; Office: 300, allée des Ursulines, Rimouski, Qué. G5L 3A1.

**AVERY, William Francis,** B.Com., C.A.; financial executive; b. Andover, England 25 Sept. 1938; s. Frederick William and Fredricka deSilva (Pritchard) A.; e. Bedford Modern School (U.K.) 1957; Univ. of Leeds B.Com. (Hons.) 1960; VICE-PRES., FINANCE & ADMIN., UMA GROUP (and subsidiaries) 1986– ; C.A. student, Turquand Young, London, Eng. 1960–63; Clarkson Gordon, Toronto & Rio de Janeiro 1964–71; various positions, Falconbridge Ltd. 1971–79; Controller, Patino Group 1979–82; Vice-Pres., Finance & Admin., Potash Corp. of Sask. 1982–86; C.A. England 1963, Ont. 1964, Sask. 1984, B.C. 1987; recreations: nordic skiing, gardening; clubs: Terminal City (Vancouver); Home: 483 Eastcot Rd., West Vancouver, B.C.; Office: 1700, 1066 West Hastings St., Vancouver, B.C. V6E 3X2.

**AVIO, Kenneth Louis,** M.S., Ph.D.; educator; b. Portland, Ore. 25 Sept. 1942; s. Joseph and Monica Mercedes (Moore) A.; e. Univ. of Ore., B.S. 1966; Purdue Univ., M.S. 1971, Ph.D. 1972; children: Julie Louise, Jackson Louis; PROF. OF ECON., UNIV. OF VICTORIA 1991– ; Assoc. Prof., present Univ. 1978–91; Lectr. Univ. of W. Ont. 1970–72, Asst. Prof. 1972–74; Asst. Prof. present Univ. 1975–78, Acting Chrmn. and Chrmn. of Econ. 1981–86; Visiting Scholar: Purdue Univ. (Econ.) 1972, Univ. of Toronto (Law) 1986–87, Oxford Univ. (Law, Centre for Socio-Legal Studies) 1987; named Nat. Defence Edn. Act Fellow 1966; David Ross Fellow 1969; co-author 'Property Crime in Canada: An Econometric Study' 1976; various articles aspects criminal justice; mem. Canada Econ. Assn.; Am. Econ. Assn.; Phi Eta Sigma Nat. Hon.; Phi Beta Kappa; recreations: racquet sports, opera; Home: 1277 Rockland Ave., Victoria, B.C. V8V 3J3; Office: P.O. Box 3050, Victoria, B.C. V8W 3P5.

**AVIS, Jeannette,** B.Ed., M.Ed.; special education teacher; b. Coleman, Alta. 23 Dec. 1914; d. James Dunn and Elizabeth Anne (Cherry) Young; m. John s. Margaret and John A. 11 Nov. 1937; children: Jacqueline, Elizabeth; retired in 1975 after a 30-year career in remedial teaching lastly as a remedial teacher for special needs children for a period of 13 years; placements incl. Russian (Doukhobor) General, Cranbrook Remedial & Jr. Sr. High, Creston Elem., Japanese Internment (High School), Langford Elem., Powell River Remedial, Slocan City General, Winlaw General, Gibson's Creek, General, N. Vancouver Remedial-adjustment; Mem., United Church, Social Credit (B.C.), Conservative (Canada); recreations: sports, walking, gardening, motoring through B.C., music appreciation; Home: 1968 Brunette Ave., Coquitlam, B.C. V3K 1H9.

**AVIS, Judith Myers,** B.A., M.S.W., Ph.D.; educator; family therapist; b. Toronto, Ont. 27 Aug. 1944; d. John Chandler and Jessie Ellis (Baker) M.; e. Queen's Univ. B.A. 1966; Univ. of Toronto M.S.W. 1968; Purdue Univ. Ph.D. 1986; two s. Andrew, Michael; PROF. OF FAMILY STUDIES UNIV. OF GUELPH 1986– ; private practice individual, couple, family & group therapy; Social Worker Dept. Corrections Toronto and Community Mental Health Clinic Fredericton, N.B. 1968–74; Supr. Life Line Crisis Center Melbourne, Australia 1975–76; Instr. and Asst. Prof. St. Thomas Univ. Fredericton 1974–5, 1976–86; Nat. Welfare Fellow, Purdue Univ. 1983–86; Coll. Family & Consumer Studies Teaching Award Univ. Guelph 1987, Faculty Assn. Distinguished Prof. Teaching Award 1989; Nat. Health & Welfare Rsch. Grant 1989–91; author numerous profl. articles; co-author 'Group Treatment For Sexually Abused Adolescents' 1992; mem. various ed. bds.; mem. Am. Family Therapy Acad.; Am. Assn. Marriage & Family Therapy; Am. Orthopsychiatric Assn.; recreations: travel, hiking, music, friends, yoga; Home: 47 Keats Cres., Guelph, Ont. N1G 3B1; Office: Guelph, Ont. N1G 2W1.

**AWAD, A. George,** M.B., B.Ch., Ph.D., F.R.C.P.(C); psychiatrist/university professor; b. Cairo, Egypt 23 June 1934; s. George Youssef and Lisa A. (Hanna) A.; e. Cairo Univ., M.B., B.Ch. 1957; Acad. of Med. Sci. Moscow, Ph.D. 1964; F.R.C.P.(C) 1974; m. Lara F. d. Sergie and Nina Fokina 1964; one s.: Michel; PSYCHIATRIST-IN-CHIEF, WELLESLEY HOSP. 1985– ; Gen. Physician 1957–60; Dir. & Lectr., Nat. Rsch. Inst., Cairo; Post-doctoral fellow, Inst. Superiore de Sanita, Italy 1968; Rsch. Assoc., Dept. of Pharmacology, Univ. of Toronto 1969–70; Residency Prog. 1970–74; Psychiatrist & Dir., York Reg. Serv., Lakeshore Hosp. 1974–76; Chief, S.W. Serv., Queen St. Mental Health Ctr. 1976–80; Dir., Psychobiol. Unit, Toronto Western Hosp. 1980–84; Cons., Clarke Inst. of Pyschiatry, Princess Margaret Hosp., Queen St. Mental Health Ctr.; author: 'Evaluation of Quality of Care in Psychiatry' 1980; 'Disturbed Behaviour in the Elderly' 1986; Home: 34 Eden Valley Dr., Islington, Ont. M9A 4Z7; Office: Rm. 307, E.K. Jones Bldg., 160 Wellesley St. E., Toronto, Ont. M4Y 1J3.

**AWENDER, Michael A.B.J.,** Ph.D.; university administrator; b. Kitchener, Ont.; s. Andrew P. and Catherine (Koch) A.; e. Univ. of Windsor, B.A. 1970, M.A. 1973; Univ. of Toronto, M.Ed. 1972; Claremont Grad. Sch., Ph.D. 1975 (fellowship 1974–75); m. Judith d. Jack and Mary Primeau 14 Aug. 1965; children: Todd, Darren; DEAN, FAC. OF EDN., UNIV. OF WINDSOR 1988– ; Elementary, then Secondary School Teacher 1964–67; Principal 1967–68; Supt. of Schools, Kent Co. Sep. Sch. Bd. 1970–75; Assoc. Prof., present univ. 1975–84; Prof. 1984– ; Chrmn., Grad. Edn. Admin. Concentration 1976; Coord., Pre-Serv. B.Ed. Prog. 1978–88; Supvr., Grad. M.Ed. Prog. 1987–88; Assoc. Prof., O.I.S.E. summer 1976; Mem., Bd. of Gov., Ont. Counc. for Leadership in Edn. Admin. 1989– ; Univ. Copyright Ctte. 1988– ; Ont. Assn. of Deans of Edn. 1988– ; and past & present mem. of numerous committees; Can. Counc. Rsch. grant 1972–73, 1977–78; U.S. Govt. grant 1972–73; scholarships: Can. Counc. 1975; Phi Beta Kappa 1974; Phys. & Health Edn., Ont. Min. of Edn. 1964; Mem., CASEA, CAUT, CAPE, CSSE, OERC, OCUFA, OADE, AERA, Politics of Edn. Assn.; author of several articles; Hockey Scout, Vancouver Canucks 1983–84; Chicago Black Hawks 1984–89; N.Y. Rangers 1989– ; Gen. Mgr., Windsor Spitfires Hockey Club - Junior A 1993– ; Dir. of Hockey Opns., Windsor Bulldogs 1989–91; recreations: coaching minor hockey & baseball; Home: 297 Gordon Ave., St. Clair Beach, Ont. N8N 2Y8; Office: Faculty of Education, Sunset Ave., Windsor, Ont. N9B 3P4.

**AXELSON, R. Dean,** D.V.M.; veterinarian; publisher; b. Owen Sound, Ont. 3 Oct. 1934; s. Thomas Alexander and Anna Ingeborg (Hedvall) A.; e. East Elgin H.S. grade XIII 1954; Ont. Vet. Coll., Guelph, Doctor of Vet. Med. (D.V.M.) 1960; m. Judith M. d. Boynton and Grace Fisher 4 July 1959; children: Richard Dean Jr., Gregory Allen; OWNER, THE LINKS ROAD ANIMAL AND BIRD CLINIC; CANAVIAX PUBLICATIONS LTD.; AXELSON HOLDINGS LIMITED; practiced large animal med. with Dr. Stuart Foster, Fergus, Ont. 1960; practiced small animal med. and surgery with Dr. Colin Comfort, London (Ont.) 1961–65; practiced small animal med. and surg. with Dr. Allan Secord and initiated primary clinical resch. with birds and exotic pets while there, Toronto 1965–73; purchased Links Rd. Animal Clinic, Willowdale, Ont. now having 3 vets. and working with 80% birds, reptiles and exotic pets and 20% dogs and cats; pioneered the devel. of avian (bird) and exotic med. in Can.; also specializes in dentistry in animals such as orthodontal work, root canal work, capping teeth etc.; Pres. Axelson Holdings Ltd.; Lectr. at many vet. and avian assn. conventions and vet. colls. across N. Amer.; author 'The Indian Occupation of Ontario' 1975; 'Caring For Your Pet Bird' 1981 (rev. 1984), French ed. 1986; 43 minute colour video 'So You Want a Bird' 1987; colour videos on bird care 1990 'Choosing the Right Bird,' 'Cages,' 'Cage Environment,' 'Nutrition for Small Birds,' 'Nutrition for the Parrot Family' and 'Food and Water Dishes' (all short edn. films); Past Pres., Assn. of Avian Vet.; mem. A.F. & A.M. Lodge; Dir. Vet. Emergency Clinics of Toronto; mem. numerous profl. assns.; has appeared on 55 television and 27 radio interview shows and been subject of numerous mag. and newspaper articles; avian and exotic pet cons. for Am. Animal Hosp. Assn.; Past Pres.: Ont. Assn. of Avian Vet.; Assoc. Avian Vets. (U.S.); mem.: Candn. Vet. Med. Assn.; Toronto Acad. of Vet. Med.; Am. Vet. Med. Assn.; Am. Animal Hosp. Assn.; Amer. Assn. Zoo Veterinarians; Toronto Parrot Club; Golden Triangle Parrot Club; Am. Fed. of Aviculture; Am. Assn. of Avian Pathologists; Upper Can. Rifles; Ont. Arms Collector's Assn.; Ont. Archeol. Soc.; Royal Ont. Mus.; Metro Toronto Zoo; Candn. Brewerianist; Nat. Muzzle Loading Rifle Assn.; Ont. Handgun Assn.; Nat. Geog. Soc.; Un. Ch. of Can.; listed in: 'Who's Who in Veterinary Science & Medicine'; 'Men of Achievement'; 'The International Register of Profiles'; 'Five Thousand Personalities of the World' and 'Personalities of America'; recreations: camping, muzzle-loading rifle shooting, photography, archaeology, knife making, silversmithing, flint knapping, paleontology, geology, pottery making, travelling, antique bottle collecting; Home: 237 Lord Seaton Rd., Willowdale, Ont. M2P 1L2; Office: 41 The Links Rd., Willowdale, Ont. M2P 1T7.

**AXFORD, Donald W.,** B.Sc.; resource consultant; b. Winnipeg, Man. 16 Sept. 1920; s. Gudmunder and Ethel Lara (Middal) A.; e. Univ. of Man. B.Sc. 1948; m. Ruth, D. Thomas and Christine Hartig 31 Mar. 1951; children: Janet; d. Jon; Robert; Eric; PRES. & MGR., D.W. AXFORD AND ASSOC. LTD. 1977– ; Columbia Basin Energy Corp. 1982– ; DB & K Oils Ltd.; Pres., C.E.O. & Chrmn. of the Bd., Trax Petroleums Ltd.; Dir. Highridge Exploration Ltd.; Canada Nova Scotia Offshore Petroleum Bd. 1990– ; Geologist, Mobil Oil Canada Ltd. 1948; Advisor, Candn. Exploration, Mobil Oil Corp., N.Y. 1956; Chief Research Geologist, Mobil Oil Canada Ltd. 1957; Division Geologist, Mobil Oil Corp., Texas 1960; Sr. Exploration Analyst Mobil Oil Corp., N.Y. 1964; Vice Pres. Exploration & Dir., Mobil Oil Canada Ltd. 1967; Vice-Pres. Exploration, Petro-Canada 1976; mem., Candn. Soc. of Petroleum Geologists; Amer. Assn. of Petroleum Geologists (recipient, Distinguished Service Award; Vice Pres. 1992); Geological Assn. of Can.; Geol. Soc. of Amer.; Soc. of Economic Paleontologists & Mineralogists; Assn. of Profl. Engrs.; Geologists & Geophysicists of Alberta; recreation: golfing; Club: Earl Grey Golf Club; Home: 30 Massey Place S.W., Calgary, Alta. T2V 2G3; Office: #2170, 250 – 6 Ave. S.W., Calgary, Alta. T2P 3H7.

**AXWORTHY, Hon. Lloyd,** P.C., M.P., M.A., Ph.D.; politician; b. North Battleford, Sask. 21 Dec. 1939; s. Norman Joseph and Gwen Jane A.; e. Univ. of Winnipeg B.A.; Princeton Univ. M.A., Ph.D.; m. Denise Ommanney 3 August 1984; one child: Stephen; HUMAN RESOURCES MINISTER and WESTERN DEVELOPMENT MINISTER 1993– ; Liberal Critic on External Affairs 1988–93; Min. of Employment and Immigration, Can. 1980–83 and Min. of State for Status of Women 1980–81; Min. of Transportation, Can. 1983–84; Critic on Internat. Trade for the Official Opposition 1984–88; Chrmn., Liberal Caucus Ctte. on External Affairs and Nat. Defence 1988– ; Vice-Chrmn., Standing Ctte. of External Affairs and Internat. Trade 1991– ; Dir. Univ. Research Inst.; Assoc. Prof.; def. cand. fed. g.e. 1968; el. M.L.A. Man. g.e. 1973, re-el. 1977; el. to H. of C. for Winnipeg-Fort Garry g.e. 1979, re-el. 1980–84; re-el. new riding of Winnipeg South-Centre 1988; Liberal; United Church; Office: House of Commons, Ottawa, Ont. K1A 0A6.

**AXWORTHY, Thomas Sydney,** B.A., M.A., Ph.D.; political scientist; b. Winnipeg, Man. 23 May 1947; s. Norman J. and Gwen J. (Thomas) A.; e. Univ. of Winnipeg B.A. 1968; Queen's Univ. M.A. 1970; Ph.D. 1979; Visiting Student, Nuffield Coll., Univ. of Oxford, England 1972–73; m. Roberta Dojack d. Charles E. Dojack 23 July 1971; EXTVE. DIR., THE CRB FOUNDATION 1989– ;(Vice Pres. 1986–88) and Associate of the Centre for Internat. Affairs, Harvard Univ. 1986–92; Adjunct Lectr. in Public Policy, John F. Kennedy School of Govt., Harvard Univ. 1990–92; joined in 1974 as Special Asst. on Urban Policy to Min. of State for Urban Affairs and Spec. Asst. (Cabinet Briefing) to Min. of Nat. Rev.; Consultant, The Canada Consulting Group, 1975; Spec. Asst., Office of the P.M. 1975–76; Policy Advisor 1977–78; Asst. Princ. Secy. (Policy) 1978–79; Sen. Policy Adv., Office of the Leader of the Opposition, 1979–80; Acting Dir., Lib. Caucus Research Bur., 1979–80; Instr., Dept. of Pol. Studies, Queen's Univ. (part-time) 1979–80; Princ. Secy. to the Prime Minister of Canada 1981–84; Fellow, Inst. of Politics, Kennedy Sch. of Govt., present Univ. 1984–85; Mackenzie King Professor of Candn. Studies, present univ. 1985–86; author various articles; mem. Amer. Pol. Sci. Assn.; Candn. Pol. Sc. Assn.; Candn. Inst. of Internat. Affairs; Oxford Union Soc.; Liberal Party; United Church; Home: 241 Stanstead, Town of Mount Royal, Qué. H3R 1X4; Office: 1170 Peel St., Montreal, Qué. H3B 4P2.

**AYCOCK, Burl N.,** B.Sc.; professional engineer, oil executive; b. Canyon, Texas 27 Aug. 1948; s. Haley West and Lee (Pauw) A.; e. Univ. of Alberta B.Sc. 1971; m. Linda d. Don and Barbara Baker 12 Feb. 1971; children: Kirstin, Davis, Scott; PRESIDENT & DIR. (CHAIR), MAXX PETROLEUM LTD. 1987– ; Extve. Vice-Pres. & Dir., Sundance Oil Co. 1980–84; recreations: skiing, squash, golf, horses, Charolais cattle; club: Glenco; Office: Suite 1000, 112 – 4th Ave. S.W., Calgary, Alta. T2P 0H3.

**AYE, Maung Tin,** M.A., M.B.B.Chir., Ph.D., F.R.C.P.(C); physician/scientist/university professor; b. Rangoon, Burma 9 Aug. 1941; s. Dr. Maung and Daw San Kyi E.; e. Meth. English H.S. 1957; Cambridge Univ. B.A. 1963; Cambridge Univ. & St. Thomas Hosp. M.B. (with distinction in pathol.) 1966; Univ. of Toronto, Ph.D. 1974; F.R.C.P.(C) 1982; m. Barbara-Ann d. Joseph and Marie-Anna Egan 19 July 1968; children: Mary Christina, Andrew Bertrand; NATIONAL DIRECTOR, BLOOD SERVICES, CANADIAN RED CROSS SOCIETY 1991– ; Investigator, Univ. of Ottawa 1974; MRC Scholar 1976–81; Panel Mem. & Sci. Offr., MRC Peer Review Panel on Cancer 1982–87; Chrmn., Human Experimentation Ctte., Ottawa Gen. Hosp. 1975–86; Univ. of Ottawa AIDS Study Group 1988; Project Dir. & Co-author, Royal Soc. of Can.

Study on Impact of AIDS in Canada 1988; Head, Hematology, Univ. of Ottawa & Ottawa Gen. Hosp. 1988–91; Med. Dir., Candn. Red Cross Blood Transfusion Service, Ottawa Centre 1989–91; Pres. & Founder, Tanda Software Inc. 1982–86; Queen's Coll. (Cambridge) book prize 1966; MRC Fellow 1970–74; recipient, Centennial Medal, Royal Soc. of Can. 1988; Commemorative Medal for 125th Anniversary of Candn. Confederation; Mem., Candn. Hematol. Soc.; Am. Soc. of Hematol.; Internat. Soc. of Exper. Hematol.; Am. Assn. for Adv. of Sci.; sole author: 'Word Wand/L'Editexte' (French/English word proc. program for IBM personal computer) 1982 and other sci. pubs.; recreations: swimming, computer programming; Home: 50 Whitemarl Dr., Rockliffe Park, Ottawa, Ont. K1L 8J6; Office: 1800 Alta Vista Dr., Ottawa, Ont. K1G 4J5.

**AYER, William A.,** B.Sc., Ph.D., F.C.I.C., F.R.S.C.; educator; b. Middle Sackville, N.B. 4 July 1932; s. Charles Frederic and Elizabeth Main (Harper) A.; e. Sackville (N.B.) High Sch. 1949; Univ. of N.B., B.Sc. 1953, Ph.D. 1956; m. Dorothy d. Howard and Margaret Monteith 10 May 1954; children: Susan, Stephen, Judith, Andrew, Katherine, Carol; UNIVERSITY PROFESSOR 1992– ; PROF. OF CHEM., UNIV. OF ALTA. 1967– ; Asst. Prof. present Univ. 1958, Assoc. Prof. 1963, Prof. 1967–00, McCalla Research Prof. 1983–84; Fellow, A.P. Sloan Foundation 1965–67; Visiting Prof. Japan Soc. for Promotion of Sci. 1976; Visiting Prof. Univ of Western Ont. 1977; Job Visiting Prof., Memorial Univ. of Nfld. 1983; Peoples Republic of China Academy of Science Visiting Prof. 1983; Van Cleave Lectr., Univ. of Regina 1985; recipient Merck, Sharpe, Dohme Award Chem. Inst. of Can. 1970, John Labatt Award 1981; Alta. Achievement Award 1980; E.W.R. Steacie Award, Candn. Soc. for Chem. 1994; author or co-author over 160 sci. publs.; Pres., Candn. Soc. for Chem. 1988–89; Sr. Ed. 'Canadian Journal of Chemistry' 1983–87, Organic Chem. Ed. 1976–83; mem. Am. Chem. Soc.; mem. Chem. Inst. Can.; Candn. Soc. for Chem.; recreations: camping, horse racing; Home: 8440 – 117 St., Edmonton, Alta. T6G 1R4; Office: Edmonton, Alta. T6G 2G2.

**AYKROYD, Daniel Edward;** writer, actor; b. Ottawa, Ont. 1 July 1952; s. Peter Hugh and Lorraine G. (Gougeon) A.; m. Donna Dixon 1984; Mem., Toronto Co. of Second City Theatre; starred in CBS TV series 'Coming Up Rosie'; writer & actor, NBC's Saturday Night Live 1975–79; other TV appearances incl. 'All You Need is Cash'; motion picture appearances incl. '1941' 1979, 'Mr. Mike's Mondo Video' 1979, 'Blues Brothers' 1980 (also screenwriter), 'Neighbors' 1981, 'Doctor Detroit' 1985, 'Trading Places' 1983, 'Twilight Zone' 1983, 'Ghostbusters' 1984, 'Nothing Lasts Forever' 1984, 'Into the Night' 1985, 'Spies Like Us' 1985 (also screenwriter), 'Dragnet' 1987 (also co-screenwriter), 'Caddyshack II' 1988, 'The Great Outdoors' 1988, 'My Stepmother is an Alien' 1988, 'Ghostbusters II' (also co-writer) 1989, 'Driving Miss Daisy' 1989, 'My Girl' 1991; performed with John Belushi as the Blues Brothers; albums incl. 'Made in America'; recipient Emmy Award 1976–77; Mem., Writers Guild Am. West, AFTRA; Office: c/o Fred Specktor, 9830 Wilshire Blvd., Beverly Hills, Ca. 90212-1825.

**AYLESWORTH, John;** TV and film writer-producer; b. Toronto, Ont. 18 Aug. 1928; s. Dr. Fredrick Allen and Thelma Marie (Bansley) A.; e. Forest Hill Coll. Inst., Toronto; children: Linda, Robert, John, Cynthia, William, Thomas; performer-writer, CBC 'After Hours'; 'The Big Review'; 'On Stage'; creater-writer, 'Front Page Challenge'; writer, 'Cross Canada Hit Parade'; 'The Andy Williams Show'; 'The Judy Garland Show'; 'Hullabaloo'; 'Kraft Music Hall'; 'Frank Sinatra – A Man and His Music'; 'Julie Andrews Show'; producer-writer, 'The Jonathan Winters Show'; 'Hee Haw'; 'Herb Alpert Special'; 'Happy Days'; 'Don Adams Special'; 'Sonny and Cher' series; 'Shields and Yarnell' series; 'Dorothy Hammill Presents Winners' special; 'Hee Haw Tenth Anniversary' special; 'The Grady Nutt Show,' 'The Nashville Palace,' NBC; 'Dolly,' ABC; 'Hee Haw Twentieth Anniversary Special'; rec'd Emmy and Peabody Awards for 'Frank Sinatra – A Man and His Music'; author: 'Fee Fi Fo Fum' 1961; 'Service!' 1971; 'Durante - The Musical' 1989; Anglican; recreations: travel, reading, writing novels; Home: 1549 Twin Palms Dr., Palm Springs CA; Office: 601, 11777 San Vicente Blvd., Los Angeles, CA 90049.

**AYLESWORTH, Samuel William,** B.Sc., S.T.B., M.Sc.; anglican priest, investment manager, community development advocate; b. Calgary, Alta. 25 Apr. 1940; s. Robert Wesley and Agnes Alice (Nickle) A.; e. Univ. of Alta. B.Sc. 1961; Anglican Theol. Coll. of B.C. L.Th. 1964, S.T.B. 1968; Univ. of Calgary M.Sc. 1973; m. Diane d. Cecil and Edel Parson 10 Sept. 1960; children: Samuel Vernon (dec'd), William Derek, Suzanne Darlene; VICE PRES. & MGR., NICKLE FAMILY FOUNDATION 1983– ; Parish Priest, Anglican Dioc. of Kootenay 1964–65; Social Worker, City of Calgary 1968–69; Staff Psychol., Woods Christian Homes 1972–73; Psychol., Educator & Commun. Devel. Worker, Serv. for Handicapped, Govt. of Alta. 1974–79; Founding shareholder, Penta Holdings Ltd. 1978– ; Vice-Pres. & Extve. Dir., Nickle Family Found. (which grants $650,000 annually to Alta. char. orgns.) 1983– ; NRC scholarships 1970–73; Hon. Asst. Priest, Anglican Cath. of Calgary 1991– ; former Hon. Asst., St. Laurence & St. Peter's Anglican churches; recreations: hiking, extensive reading; Home: 140 Valley Ridge Green N.W., Calgary, Alta. T3B 5L5; Office: #401, Highstreet House, 933 – 17th Ave. S.W., Calgary, Alta. T2T 5R6.

**AYOUB, Norman N.,** B.Comm., C.L.U.; insurance executive; b. Montreal, Que. 5 Oct. 1949; s. Thomas G. and Olga (Salhani) A.; e. Concordia Univ. (Sir George Williams) B.Comm. 1970; m. Francine d. Emile and Madeline Charlebois 30 Sept. 1972; children: Jeffrey; VICE-PRES., INDIVIDUAL LIFE, MARITIME LIFE ASSURANCE 1991– ; Life Agent, London Life 1970–72; Supvr., Univ. Recruiting 1973–77; Agency Mgr. 1977–80; R.V.P. Que.-Maritime 1980–82; Agency Mgr., 1982–86; R.V.P. Toronto 1986–88; Vice-Pres., Mktg., MacDougall-MacDougall-Mactier 1988–89; Vice-Pres., Mktg., Individual Life, Maritime Life 1989–90; Dir., Balanced Planning Inc.; Former Chrmn., Medic-Alert Campaign Toronto; Former Teacher, Continuing Edn., Univ. of Toronto and McGill Univ.; recreations: golf, hockey: clubs: Lambton Golf & Country (Toronto); Saraguay; Ashburn Golf & County; Granite Springs Golf & Country (Halifax); Home: 5 Wendover Ct., Halifax, N.S. B3M 4E8; Office: P.O. Box 1030, Halifax, N.S. B3J 2X5.

**AYRE, Anthony Green,** O.B.E.; Chevalier De L'Ordre De Leopold (Belgium); Knight, Order of the Oranj-Nassau (Dutch); consultant; b. St. John's Nfld. 20 Nov. 1916; s. late James Garfield Green and late Carlotta P. (Glassey) Ayre; stepson late Hon. C.P. Ayre; e. Holloway and Prince of Wales Schs. Nfld.; Caldecott Prep. Sch. Eng. 1929–31; Ley's Pub. Sch. Cambridge, Eng. 1931–33; Macdonald Coll. McGill Univ. Dipl. Agric. 1937; PRES., TRAILS END DEVELOPMENT LTD.; self-employed Anthony G. Ayre Associates; Company Director; former Consul for Belgium and for the Netherlands 1965; joined RCN and comnd. 1941, service various naval vessels Pacific Coast and Atlantic 1942–45, joined HMCS Cabot as Reserve Offr. and promoted Lt. Commdr. 1949, C.O. Memorial Univ. Naval Training Div. 1949, Chief of Staff to Commodore Nfld. rank Acting Commdr. 1950, Area Offr. Sea Cadets Nfld. 1952–55; Extve. Mgr. Nfld. Bd. Trade 1959–70; Pres., Chamber of Commerce Executives of Canada, and Dir., Am. Chamber of Commerce Executives, 1968–69; Gen. Mgr. St. John's Bd. Trade 1970–71; Secy. St. John's Shipping Assn. Ltd. 1959–78; Extve. Secy. Nfld. Real Estate Bd. 1973–75; former mem. Bd. Referees Unemployment Ins. Comn.; Area Supply Offr. Emergency Measures Organ, 1962–75; mem. Nfld. Labour Relations Bd. 1959–74; Court of Revision City of St. John's 1976–79; former Dir. St. John's Tourist Comn.; mem. and past Chrmn., Bd. of Govs., Nfld. Div. Candn. Corps of Commissionaires; former Chrmn. Pub. Libs. Bd. Nfld.; Regional Drama Festival Soc. Nfld.; former Dir. John Howard Soc.; has farmed in Eng., Nfld., Que. and Ont.; free lance writer and broadcaster; mem. ACTRA; Royal Candn. Legion; Anglican; recreations: agriculture, reading, broadcasting, walking; Clubs: Crow's Nest Officers'; Naval (London, Eng.); Address: Trail's End, Topsail Rd., PO Box 1506, St. John's Nfld. A1C 5N8.

**AYRE, John David,** B.A.; writer; b. Toronto, Ont. 24 Nov. 1947; s. Charles Alan and Joan Collins Crawford (Wilson) A.; e. Victoria Coll., Univ. of Toronto, B.A. 1971; m. Mary Ann d. Milton and Hilda Evans 10 May 1974; children: Evelyn, Edward, Eleanor; freelance journalist/critic 1970– ; contbr. editor, 'Maclean's' 1977–83; has concentrated mostly on literary & dance subjects; published most frequently in 'Saturday Night,' 'Weekend,' and 'Maclean's'; Author's Award 1978 (Periodical Distrib. of Can.); author: 'Northrop Frye: A Biography' 1989; Home: 35 Tiffany St. W., Guelph, Ont. N1H 1X9.

**AYRE, Miller H.,** B.A., M.B.A.; investment executive; b. St. John's, Nfld. 27 Dec. 1941; s. Lewis H.M., C.M. and Olga Rogers (Crosbie) A.; e. Holloway Sch. St. John's; Bishop's Coll. Sch. Lennoxville, Qué.; Harvard Univ. B.A. 1964; McGill Univ. M.B.A. 1968; m. Susan B. d. F. Allen Sherk; children: Andrew, Deirdre; PUBLISHER, ST. JOHN'S EVENING TELEGRAM; Dir. Ayre & Sons Ltd.; Mansbord Inc.; Chrmn. Nfld. Medicare Comn. 1971–73; mem. St. John's Mun. Council 1974–78; Adv. Bds. Memorial Univ. of Nfld. Inst. Social & Econ. Rsch. 1974–79 and Sch. Bus. Adm. & Comm. 1975–77; Pres. Nfld. Div. Candn. Cancer Soc. 1978–80, Nat. Dir. of Soc. 1977–81; Dir. Harvard Alumni Assn. 1979–81; Past Chrmn. Retail Council Can.; Vice Chrmn., Nat. Theatre Sch. Montréal; Chrmn., Candn. Chamb. of Comm.; mem., Econ. Council Can.; Distributive Trades Adv. Ctte. Ind. Trade & Comm., Can.; Dir., Candn. Council Christians & Jews; United Church; Club: Rotary (Pres. 1982 St. John's); Home: P.O. Box 5005, St. John's, Nfld. A1C 5V3; Office: P.O. Box 70, St. John's, Nfld. A1C 5H8.

**AZIZ, David,** M.A.Sc., Ph.D.; chemical engineer; b. Toronto, Ont. 1924; e. Univ. of Toronto, B.A.Sc. 1945, M.A.Sc. 1946, Ph.D. 1949; m. 1952; 3 children: SENIOR VICE PRESIDENT, IGI INTERNATIONAL WAXES 1993– ; Dir. of Production, and Research, present co., 1950; Vice-Pres. Production 1954; Pres. 1955; Chrmn. 1966; Pres. 1981–93; Club: Scarborough Golf; Home: Don Mills, Ont.; Office: 50 Salome Dr., Agincourt, Ont. M1S 2A8.

**AZIZ, Khalid,** B.S.E., B.Sc., M.Sc., Ph.D.; engineer; educator; b. Pakistan 29 Sept. 1936; s. Aziz ul Hussan and Rashida Atamohammed; came to Can. Jan. 1957; e. Univ. of Michigan B.S.E. 1955; Univ. of Alta. B.Sc. 1958; M.Sc. 1961; Rice Univ. Ph.D. 1966; m. Mussarrat, d. late M.S. Rizwani 12 Nov. 1962; children: Natasha; Imraan; PROF. OF PETROLEUM ENGR., STANFORD UNIV. 1982– ; OTTO N. MILLER PROFESSOR OF EARTH SCIENCES, STANFORD UNIV. 1989– ; Jr. Design Engr., Massey Ferguson, Detroit 1955–56; Distribution Engr., Karachi Gas Co., Pakistan 1958–59; Instr., Asst. Prof., Petroleum Engineering, Univ. of Alta. 1960–62; Chief Engr., Karachi Gas Co., Pakistan, 1962–63; Asst. Prof., Assoc. Prof. and Prof., Dept. of Chem. and Petroleum Engrg., Univ. of Calgary 1965–82; Mgr. & Dir., Computer Modelling Group 1977–82; Prof., Petroleum Engr. 1982– , Assoc. Dean for Research, Stanford Univ. 1983–86, Chrmn., Petroleum Engr. 1986–91; author and co-author of over 150 articles, books and research papers in field; Fellow, Chemical Inst. of Can.; awarded APEGGA Gold Medal (Univ. of Alta.); Ralph Budd Award (Rice Univ.); Ferguson Award (S.P.E.); Best Paper Award (C.N.G.P.A.); Distinguished Service Award (Petroleum Soc.); Reservoir Engineering Award (S.P.E.) 1987; Lester C. Uren Award (SPE) 1988; Distinguished Achievement Award for Petroleum Engineering Faculty (SPE) 1990; Amer. Inst. of Chem. Engrs.; Distinguished Mem., Soc. of Petroleum Engrs. of A.I.M.E. since 1983; Soc. of Industrial and Applied Mathematics; recreations golf, bridge; skiing, travel; Home: 112 Peter Coutts Circle, Stanford, Calif. 94305; Office: Stanford Univ., Stanford, Calif. 94305.

**AZIZ, Philip John Andrew Ferris,** B.F.A., M.F.A.; painter, sculptor, designer (of jewelry, celature, furniture, stained-glass windows), graphic artist, architectural designer, liturgical artist; b. St. Thomas, Ont.; e. Yale Univ. B.F.A. 1947, M.F.A. 1949; Fogg Museum, Harvard Univ., 1949 post-grad. work; numerous field & study trips to Europe and Middle East; exhibits in leading galleries, museums, etc. in chief cities in U.S. & Canada; Instr. of Art, Yale Univ. 1948–49; Lectr. in Art, Univ. of W. Ont. 1950–55; lectures extensively at colleges, museums & institutions in U.S.; pioneer use of egg-tempera medium; first public exhbn. Detroit, Mich. 1950; selected one-man Shows: Eaton Fine Art Gallery 1950–57; Montréal Museum of Art 1952, 1967; Seattle World's Fair 1961; Gall. Hervé, NY 1964; Royal Soc. of Portrait Painters, London, Eng. 1966, 1967, 1968; National Gall. of Art, Ottawa 1967; Univ. of Waterloo Art Gall. 1967; New York Culture Centre, 1968–69; New York Culture Centre 1969 (retrospective); 9th Internat. Exhbn., Gall. Internat., NY 1969; Sign of Mermaid Gall., Grosse Pointe, Mich. 1971; War Meml. Ctr., Grosse Pointe, Mich. 1971; Minnesota Museum of Art 1972; Tribute to Paul Tillich exhbn. St. John Univ. Collegeville, Minn. 1972; Artist-in-residence, exhbr., Aspen Inst. of Humanistic Studies 1972–76; William Beadleston Gall., NY 1973; Albert White Gall., Toronto 1974; London Arts Gall., Detroit 1975; David Findlay Gall., NY 1976; Tom Gruenebaum Gall., NY 1978; Detroit Inst. of Arts 1982; Theo Waddington Gall., Toronto 1981; Waddington & Shiell Gall., Toronto 1984; Exhbn., Office of Premier David Peterson, Queen's Park, Toronto 1985; President's gift of an Aziz painting to Francois Mitterand of France on behalf of the Govt. of Ont. 1985; Ontario Pavilion, Vancouver, Expo' 86; Ontario House, Paris, France 1986; Ontario House, Tokyo, Japan 1987; Selections from W. Hawkins Ferry Coll. Detroit Inst. of Arts 1987; rep. in selected permanent collections: Detroit Inst. of Arts; Montréal Museum of Arts; Metropolitan Opera, Lincoln Centre

Plaza, NY; Minnesota Museum of Art; K-Mart Administrative Centre, Troy, Mich.; Detroit Receiving Hospital; Robert McLaughton Gallery, Oshawa; Vatican Museum, Rome; and numerous private collections Can., U.S., Gt. Brit., Europe; portraits incl.: Eugene Cardinal Tisserant (Dean, Coll. of Cardinals, Rome); Risë Stevens (Metropolitan Opera, NY); Yousuf Karsh; Lady Eaton; Erik Bruhn; mems. of Ford and Du Pont families, etc.; cr. Lady Chapel, St. Peter's Basilica, London, Ont. 1958–59; also St. Joseph Chapel and Chapel of Christ The King; cr. Timothy Eaton Meml. Chapel 1960–61; Nativity Altar piece, Motherhouse of St. Joseph, Hamilton, Ont. 1952; Pieta altar piece, Trinitarian Monestary, St. Bruno, Qué. 1951; Panels of The Four Seasons for Mich. Consolidated Gas Co. Bldg., Detroit 1962; Permanent Coll.: Norton Simon Inc., NY; Univ. of Toronto; Vanier Inst. for the Family; Univ. of Western Ont.; London Free Press Publishing Co.; National Archives, Ottawa - 'Portrait of Solange Karsh' 1991; subject CBC Documentary 'Aziz: The Modern Renaissance Artist' 1981; numerous scholarly articles and critical essays in periodicals and art journals U.S., Can., Europe & Middle East; designer of a private country residence in Ont. 1980–90; Architectural Designer and consultant on numerous projects, incl.: Landmark Centre, St. Paul, Minn. 1972–74; Middlesex Court Centre, London, Ont. 1969–78; Ontario Place, Toronto 1973–73; St. Peter's Lutheran Church, NY 1978–80; selected memberships: The American Biographical Inst. 1987; Internat. Biographical Center, (Cambridge, England) 1987; Friends of Modern Art; (Patron) Detroit Inst. of Arts 1984; Heritage Canada 1975; Who's Who in the World 1974; National Register of Prominent Americans 1972; National Trust for Historic Preservation, Washington, DC 1972; Internat. Platform Soc., U.S. 1971; Directory of Internat. Biography (English) 1971; Admiral, Texas Navy 1970; Vice Pres., Yale Alumni Assn. of Can. 1969; The Blue Blook (for outstanding profl. achievement in English-speaking world) 1969; Trustee, National Pollution Control Foundn., NY 1968; Vice Pres., Yale Club of Canada, Toronto 1968; Am. Directory of Arts 1965; Internat. Dir. of Arts (German ed.) 1963; Who's Who in Art (English ed.) 1958; Fellow, Internat. Inst. of Arts & Letters, Switzerland 1957; Clubs: Yale of N.Y.C. (since 1947); University Club, Toronto (since 1965); Address: 1180 Western Rd., London, Ont. N6G 1G8.

**AZIZ, Rashid A.;** biopharmaceutical executive; b. Peshawar, Pakistan 28 Jan. 1954; s. Abdul Aseem and Brenda (Hull) A.; e. Aitchison Chiefs Coll. 1961–71; articling student 1972–76; children: Jordana, Rebecca; EXEC. VICE PRES. & DIR., INFLAZYME PHARMACEUTICALS INC. 1993– ; Chartered Acct., Chantrey Button & Co. 1976; Controller, Kadhoda Chicken Co. 1976–79; Mgr., Deloitte Haskings & Sells 1980–87; Vice-Pres. & Chief Finan. Offr., Quadra Logic Technol. Inc. 1988–92; F.C.A., Inst. of Ch. Accts. in England & Wales; C.A., Inst. of Ch. Acct. in B.C.; Former Mem., Med. Devices Sector Initiative, Indus. Sci. & Technol. Can.; Counc., Finan. Sect., Pharm. Mfg. Assn. Can.; Camp Coord. for French Camps in B.C. 1989–90; Mem., Fin. Ctte. Childrens Telethon 1988–89; Dir., St. Johns Ambulance (Burnaby) 1993– ; recreations: squash, swimming; club: The Vancouver; Address: 3842 Pentland Court, Burnaby, B.C. V3N 4L4.

# B

**BAAR, Carl,** M.A., Ph.D.; educator; b. Los Angeles, Cal. 22 Sept. 1940; s. Tim and Ella B.; e. UCLA B.A. 1961; Univ. of Chicago M.A. 1963, Ph.D. 1969; m. Ellen d. Lewis and Frances Samuels 26 Aug. 1963; two s. David William, Keith Richard; PROF. OF POLITICS, BROCK UNIV. 1982– ; Asst. Prof. of Pol. Sci. Univ. of B.C. 1966–68, James Madison Coll. Mich. State Univ. 1968–70; Visiting Asst. Prof. Cornell Univ. 1971–72, Univ. of Mich. 1972–73; Visiting Asst. Prof. present Univ. 1974, Assoc. Prof. 1975, Founding Dir. Prog. Judicial Adm. 1980–85; Faculty mem. Inst. for Court Mgmt. Denver, Colo. 1973–92; Visiting Prof. Prog. Law & Soc. York Univ. 1985–86; Special Lectr. Univ. of Toronto Law Sch. 1985; Rsch. Fellow, Osgoode Hall Law Sch., York Univ. 1987–88; Visiting Prof. Pol. Sci., Univ. of Toronto 1988–89; Legis. Intern Cal. State Assembly 1962–63; Congressional Fellow US House and Senate 1965–66; cons. court adm. various govt. and legal orgns. Can., USA and Australia; pol. analyst 'Canada AM' CTV Network; Woodrow Wilson Fellow 1961–62; Fellow Inst. Court Mgmt.; Russell Sage Fellow Yale Law Sch. 1970–71; Jackson Lectr. Nat. Judicial Coll. 1979; author 'One Trial Court: Possibilities and Limitations' 1991; 'Separate But Subservient: Court Budgeting in the American States' 1975; co-author 'Judicial Administration in Canada' 1981; collaborator, 'Maitre chez eux/Masters in Their Own House' 1981; author or co-author 40 profl. articles, book chapters, reports court orgn. & mgmt., judicial process; Ed.-in-Chief 'The Justice System Journal' 1974–77; Dir. Am. Judicature Soc. 1978–82; mem. Acad. Freedom & Tenure Ctte. Candn. Assn. Univ. Teachers 1982–85; mem. Candn. Pol. Sci. Assn.; Am. Pol. Sci. Assn.; Law & Soc. Assn.; Inst. Pub. Adm. Can. (Dir. Toronto Regional Group 1979–81); Internat. Pol. Sci. Assn. (Exec. Ctte. Rsch. Ctte. Comparative Judicial Studies 1976–88); Candn. Inst. Adm. Justice; Candn. Law & Soc. Assn.; Phi Beta Kappa; Unitarian; Home: 706 Drury Lane, Burlington, Ont. L7R 2X7; Office: Dept. of Politics, Brock Univ., St. Catharines, Ont. L2S 3A1.

**BABCOCK, James M.,** B.A., M.B.A.; banker; e. Univ. of Toronto B.A. (Hons.) 1962; Univ. of Western Ont. M.B.A. 1966; m. Ruth; children: Benjamin, Shawna, Kimberley; SR. VICE-PRES., MANITOBA & SASK. DIV., THE TORONTO-DOMINION BANK 1990– ; var. positions in internat. & domestic divisions, London, UK & Vanc., The Toronto-Dominion Bank 1966–73; Area Supt. Hong Kong 1973–78; Asst. Gen. Mgr., Comm. Devel. Toronto 1978–80; Nat. Accounts Div. 1980; Gen. Mgr., Western Reg., USA Div. 1980–84; North Am. Credit Toronto 1984–87; Sr. Vice-Pres., Atlantic Div. Halifax 1987–90; Mem., Candn. Bankers Assn.; Crocus Investment Fund (Adv. Council); Bd. of Dir., Royal Winnipeg Ballet; Candn. Council for Aborigial Business (Man. Ch.); Bd. of Gov., Manitoba Mus. of Man & Nature; clubs: St. Charles Golf & Country, Manitoba Club & Winter Club; Office: P.O. Box 7700, 18th Floor, 201 Portage Ave., Winnipeg, Man. R3C 3E7.

**BABIUK, Lorne A.,** Ph.D., D.Sc.; educator; research director; b. Sask. 25 Jan. 1946; s. Paul and Mary (Mayden) B.; e. Univ. of Sask. B.S.A. 1967, M.Sc. 1969, D.Sc. 1987; Univ. of B.C., Ph.D. 1972; m. Betty Lou d. Harold and Agnes Wagar 29 Sept. 1973; children: Shawn, Kimberley; DIRECTOR, VETERINARY INFECTIOUS DISEASE ORGN., UNIV. OF SASKATCHEWAN 1993– ; (Assoc. Dir. Research 1984–93) and PROFESSOR 1979– ; Postdoctoral Fellow, Univ. of Toronto 1972–73; Asst. Prof. present Univ. 1973; Cons. Genentech Inc. 1981–85; Molecular Genetics 1980–85; Biostar Inc. 1986–93; named Teacher of Yr. 1978; Preclin. Teacher of Yr. 1979; Distinguished Agric. Grads. Award 1980; CSM Award 1990; Bill Snowden Award 1990; Rotarian Wheel Award in Science & Technology 1991; Am. Assoc. Vet. Immunol. Award 1992; Xerox-Canada Forum Award; author over 300 book chapters, sci. articles; mem. Am. Soc. Microbiol.; Am. Soc. Virol.; Candn. Soc. Microbiol.; recreation: skiing; Home: 245 East Place, Saskatoon, Sask. S7J 2Y1; Office: 124 Veterinary Rd., Saskatoon, Sask. S7N 0W0.

**BACHAND, André,** C.M., B.A., LL.L., L.Sc.Com., M.S.; consultant; b. Sherbrooke, Que., 1 April 1917; s. Charles Emile and Emilie (Codère) B.; e. St-Charles Borromée, Sherbrooke, B.A.; Univ. de Montréal, LL.L. 1941, L.Sc.Com. 1942; Harvard Grad. Sch. of Business Adm. 1942–43; Columbia Univ., M.S. 1944; two s. Claude, Raymond; Asst. to Pres., Quebecor Inc. 1985–90; Consultant, Development Fund, Univ. de Montreal 1982–87; Dir., Renault Automobiles (Canada) Ltd.; called to Bar of Que. 1941; trained with C.A. firm Montreal 1943–44; managed, reorganized and subsequently acquired Robin Frères Ltée 1945–52; joined present Univ. as Lectr. in Accounting, Sch. of Comm., 1945–52 and Faculty of Law 1952–56; Dir. of Pub. Relations and Asst. to Secy. Gen. 1952–62; Asst. to Rector 1962–67; Director Development fund 1967–82; TV and Radio regular series, guest panelist and moderator; Founder, Town of Mount Royal Mun. Lib.; Community Concerts Assn.; Dir., Candn. Automobile Assn. (Extve. 1972–74); Touring Club Montreal (Pres. 1972–73); Atelier Libre de Recherches Graphiques Inc.; Musées Nationaux du Can. (Vice Prés. 1974–78); Vice pres., Festival International du Film sur l'Art; SOGAM; former Bd. mem. Soc. Canadienne de la Croix-Rouge (Montréal); La Comédie Canadienne; Montreal Museum of Fine Arts; Past Vice Pres., Festivals de Montréal; Past Co-Chrmn. du Maurier Council in Performing Arts; First Pres., Town of Mount Royal Chamber Comm.; Past mem. Bd., Chambre de Comm. Française au Can.; Chambre de Comm. du Dist. Montréal; former member St. James's Club (Comte. 1965–67) mem. Soc. Canadienne des Relations Publiques; Am. Alumni Council; Am. Coll. Pub. Relations Assn. (Past Dir.-1st Candn.); Candn. Assn. Univ. Devel. Offrs.; Certified Mem., Nat. Soc. of Fund Raising Extves.; Asst. to Gen. Secy., Assn. des Univs. entièrement ou partiellement de langue française 1961–86; Mem. Order of Can. 1979; Clubs: St. Denis; Canadian (Pres. 1961–62); Address: Maison des étudiants canadiens, 31 boul. Jourdan, 75014 Paris, France.

**BACHAND, Jean-Claude,** M.B.A., LL.L., B.èsA.; business executive, lawyer; b. Sherbrooke, Que. 22 Feb. 1945; s. André and Madeleine (Vien) B.; e. Coll. de Saint-Laurent B.èsA. 1963; Univ. de Montréal LL.L. 1966; Univ. of W. Ont. M.B.A. 1969 (S. Bronfman scholarship 1967; Dean's Hon. List 1969); Candn. Secur. Inst. (partners, dir. & offr. qualifications); m. Nathalie d. Raymond and Marguerite Eudes 8 June 1968; children: Geneviève, Frédéric; EXTVE. VICE-PRES., ADMIN. & GEN. COUNS., MONTREAL TRUST 1984– ; Lawyer, Stikeman, Elliott, Tamaki, Mercier & Robb 1969–70; Extve. Asst. to C.E.O. (Paris), Capital Mngt. Internat. Ltd. 1970–71; Banque Nat. de Paris Group 1972–84 (last post held Sr. Vice Pres.); Bd. Mem. & Secy., French Chamb. of Comm. in Can. 1983; Dir. & Mem. Extve. Ctte., Montreal Symphony Orch.; OSM Chrmn. of Corp. Funding Campaign 1991–92; Mem., Candn. Bar Assn.; Barr. du Qué.; Que. MBA Assn. (Founding Mem. 1971); Assoc. of Candn. Gen. Counsel; Clubs: University Club of Montreal; Club Saint-Denis; Vallée du Richelieu Golf; Home: 30 Elmwood Ave., Outremont, Qué. H2V 2E2; Office: 1800 McGill College Ave., 17th fl., Montreal, Qué. H3A 3K9.

**BACHINSKI, Walter Joseph Gerard,** M.A.; artist; educator; b. Ottawa, Ont. 6 Aug. 1939; s. Walter Michael and Antonia Mary (Domanski) B.; e. Ont. Coll. of Art A.O.C.A. in Drawing & Painting; Univ. of Iowa M.A. 1967; children: Sarah, Matthew, Una, Michael; Prof. of Fine Art, Univ. of Guelph 1967–94; solo exhns. incl. Mazelow Gallery Toronto 1971, 1974; Peter Hess Gallery Hamilton 1974; Gallery 1640 Montreal 1975; Gallery Moos Toronto 1977, 1979, 1980, 1982, 1984, 1986, 1987; Art Gallery of Hamilton 1981; Galerie l'Art Français Montreal 1984; Robertson Gallery Ottawa 1986, 1989; Heffel Gallery Vancouver 1989, 1991; Drabinsky Gallery 1992; Kitchener-Waterloo Art Gallery: Bachinski, Approaching Classicism 1991; McLaren Art Ctr., Barrie: Bachinski, Still Life 10 years; Galerie de Bellefeville 1993; pub. comns. incl. Univ. of Waterloo 1975, Kitchener Court House 1977, Mohawk Coll. Health Sci's Centre 1980, Maclean Hunter Bldg. Toronto 1984, Donald Forster Sculpture Park Macdonald-Stewart Art Centre Guelph 1985, Cineplex Odeon Theatre Kitchener 1988; Mines and Minerals Rsch. Ctr., Laurentian Univ., Sudbury; rep. group & travelling exhns. incl. IX Bienniele Prints & Drawings Lugano 1972, IVth Internat. Biennal of Graphic Arts Florence 1974 (Premio Dell'Instituto Bancario S. Paolo di Torino), Vth Bienal Americana De Artes Graficas Museo de Arte Moderno Cali, Colombia; rep. pub. and corporate colls. incl. Uffizi Gallery Florence, Can. Council Art Bank, Montreal Museum of Fine Art, Saidye Bronfman Centre Montreal; recipient T. Eaton Travelling Scholarship 1965; Can. Council Grants 1969–70, 1978–79, 1982; Albert Dumochel Prize Internat. Exhn. Graphics Montreal 1971; Merit Prize Los Angeles Printmaking Soc. Internat. Exhn. 1973; Univ. of Guelph Rsch. Adv. Bd. Grants 1971, 1973; Arts Council Ont. Grants 1978, 1979; recreations: walking, cycling, travel; Studio: R.R. 2, Shanty Bay, Ont. L0L 2L0.

**BACHYNSKI, Morrel Paul,** B.E., M.Sc., Ph.D., F.A.P.S., F.C.A.S.I., F.R.S.C., F.I.E.E.E.; scientist; executive; b. Bienfait, Sask. 19 July 1930; s. Nickolas and Karoline B.; e. Univ. of Sask. B.E. 1952, M.Sc. 1953; McGill Univ. Ph.D. (Physics) 1955; m. Slava Krkovic, Arvida, Que. 30 May 1959; children: Caroline Dawn, Jane Diane; FOUNDER, PRES. AND DIR. MPB TECHNOLOGIES INC. since 1977; Dir. Bytek Electronics; Lab. Dir. Microwave & Plasma Physics RCA Ltd. 1958, Dir. Research & Devel. 1965, Vice Pres. Research & Devel. 1975–76; rec'd David Sarnoff Outstanding Achievement Award in Engn. 1963; Prix Scientifique Du Qué. 1973; Can. Enterprise Award 1977; Queen's Silver Jubilee Medal; CAP Medal for Achievement in Physics 1984; Candn. Rsch. Mgmt. Assoc. Medal 1988; Prix PME (Que.) 1989; Can. Awards for Business Excellence - Entrepreneurship 1989, 1990; ADRIQ Research Mgmt. Award 1992; LL.D. (hon.) Univ. of Waterloo 1993; author 'The Particle Kinetics of Plasmas' 1968; over 80 scient. articles various journs.; Fellow, Inst. Elect. & Electronic Engrs.; Am. Phys. Soc.; Can. Aeronautics and Space Inst.; Can. Acad. of Engrg.; Hon. Mem., Engineering Inst. of Can. 1987; mem. Candn. Assn. Physicists (Pres. 1968–69); SCITEC (Pres. 1974–75); Royal Soc. Can. (Vice Pres. Acad III 1984); Am. Inst. Aeronautics & Astronautics; Am. Geophys. Union; Chrmn., Candn. Res. Mgmt. Assoc. (Pres. 1986); apptd. to Sci. Counc. of Can. 1983–90; recreation: tennis; Home: 78 Thurlow Rd., Montreal, Qué. H3X 3G9; Office: 1725 North Service Road, Dorval, Qué. H9P 1J1.

**BACHYNSKY, John A.,** B.S.P., M.Sc., Ph.D.; educator; b. Flin Flon, Man. 13 Feb. 1937; s. Alexander and Nellie B.; e. Univ. of Sask. B.S.P. 1959; Philadelphia Coll. of Pharm. & Sci., M.Sc. 1962; Univ. of Wisc., Ph.D. 1967; m. Lois d. James and Phyllis Webb 30 Apl. 1960; children: James, Carol, Ronald; formerly Dean of Pharm. & Pharm. Sciences, Univ. of Alta. and Prof. of Pharm. 1981–.; Dir. of Pharm. Swift Current Union Hosp. 1960–61; Instr. in Pharm. Univ. of Sask. 1962–64; Rsch. Offr. health & Welfare Can. 1967–72, Sr. Planning Offr. Long Range Health Planning 1972–77, Dir. Gen. of Health Planning 1978–80; Past Pres., Assn. Faculties Pharm. Can.; Assn. Deans Pharm. Can.; Rho Chi; recreation: curling; Home: 4714 – 147 St., Edmonton, Alta. T6H 5E7; Office: 3118 Dent/Pharm. Centre, Edmonton, Alta. T6G 2N8.

**BACK, Frédéric,** R.C.A., O.C.; animated film producer; interior decorator; painter; b. Sarrebruck, Territoire de la Sarre 8 Apr. 1924; s. Jean and Guillemette (Siegel) B.; e. Ecole de l'Académie Strasbourg, France 1937; Ecole Estienne Paris, France 1939; Fine Arts Rennes, France 1939–43; m. Ghylaine d. Lucien Paquin 2 July 1949; children: Christian, Süzel, Francis; Prof., Ecole du Meuble Montreal 1948–53; Prof., Fine Art Sch. Montreal 1948–51; Free-lance work Radio-Canada T.V. 1953–56; Illustrator, Film Animator, small scale sets for film 1959– ; Set Designer for Niagara Films 1956–59; interior decorator for restaurants; La Saulaie, Hélène de Champlain; churches: Pierreville, Aylmer, Ste-Agathe, Qué., South-Colton, Chateauguay, Brushton (USA); stained glass mural Metro Place des Arts Montreal; rec'd Can. Council Art Scholarship for study animation film in Europe 1963; Employee, Société Radio Canada since 1964, animation section since 1968; various prizes internat. animation film festivals; Academy Award ('Oscar') for 'Crac!' (animated film) 1982; Annie Award, ASIFA, Hollywood 1986; 'The man who planted trees' (30 min. animation film) 1987; Grand prizes at Festivals of Annecy (France), Hollywood (U.S.A.), Royan (France), Hiroshima (Japan) and Academy Award 88 (Oscar) in Hollywood; 'The Mighty River' (24 min. animation film) Grand Prix at Annecy International Animation Film Festival 1993; 1988 Prize, Internat. Animated Film Assn. ASIFA; Albert Tessier Prize, Cultural Affairs, Prov. of Que. 1991; Chevalier de l'Ordre du Québec 1989; Officer of the Order of Canada 1990; Officier des arts et des lettres, France 1993; mem., Internat. Animated Film Assn.; Acad. of Motion Picture Arts & Sciences (U.S.A.); Cinémathèque Québécoise; Royal Candn. Acad. of Arts; (hon. mem.) Soc. des Décorateurs Ensembliers du Qué.; hon. mem. Soc. des illustrateurs du Québec; mem. Soc. québécoise pour la défense des animaux (Adm.); GreenPeace; Soc. pour vaincre la pollution; Nature Can.; recreations: gardening, tree planting, caring for animals, drawing; Home: 3514 ave. Kent, Montréal, Qué. H3S 1N2; Office: Société Radio-Canada, 1400 est blvd. René Lévesque, Montréal, Qué. H2L 2M2.

**BACKELAND, Gerald H.,** B.A., LèsL.; industrial utilities executive; b. Winnipeg, Man. 21 Feb. 1945; s. Eva B.; e. Univ. of Man. B.A. 1966; Univ. of Montreal LèsL. 1969; m. Jeannette Bourgoin; VICE-PRES., WESTCOAST ENERGY INC. 1992– ; Vice-Pres., Union Energy Inc.; various posts with Government of Manitoba, 1969–81, ending as Extve. Dir., Admin. & Internal Serv., Indus. & Comm.; Dir of Gas Supply, Gaz Inter-Cite Que. Inc. 1981–84; Gas Supply Cons., SOQUIP, SOQUIP Alta. & Gaz Metro. Inc. 1984–85; Sr. Mgr., Gas Supply Gaz Metro. Inc. 1985–88; Vice-Pres., Centra Gas Ont. Inc. 1988–92; Dir., Natural Gas Exchange Inc.; Westcoast Gas Services Inc.; witness, Nat. Energy Bd.; Que. Elect. & Gas Bd.; Ont. Energy Bd.; NWT Public Util. Commission; Home: 4575 Capilano Rd., N. Vancouver, B.C. V7R 4K2; Office: 1333 W. Georgia St., Vancouver, B.C. V6E 3K9.

**BACKHOUSE, Constance Barbara,** LL.M.; educator; b. Winnipeg, Man. 19 Feb. 1952; d. Edward Alexander and Olga Helena (Czechowski) B.; e. Kelvin High Sch. 1969; Univ. of Man. B.A. 1972; Osgoode Hall Law Sch. LL.B. 1975; Harvard Law Sch. LL.M. 1979; children: Diana Nancy, Mark Edward; ASSOC. PROF. OF LAW, UNIV. OF W. ONT. 1984– ; Rsch. Assoc. Ralph Nader's Centre for Auto Safety, Washington, D.C. 1972; Law Clk. B.C. Labour Relations Bd. 1974, Ont. Labour Relations Bd. 1975–76; Exec. Asst. to Ont. Dep. Min. of Labour 1976–77; Asst. Prof. of Law present Univ. 1979; Cons. women's issues govt., bus. & labour orgns. Can. and USA; mem. Bd. Women's Edn. & Rsch. Found. Ont. 1982– ; mem. Candn. Adv. Council Status Women 1981–84; Dir. London Battered Women's Advocacy Clinic 1983–86; mem. Exec. Ctte. Western's Caucus on Women's Issues 1987– ; mem. London Status Women Action Group 1979– ; Candn. Assn. Re-

form Abortion Law 1979– ; recipient Augusta Stowe-Gullen Affirmative Action Medal S.W. Ont. Assn. Advanc. Learning Opportunities for Women 1981; co-author: 'The Secret Oppression: Sexual Harassment of Working Women' 1979; 'Sexual Harrassment on the Job' 1981; 'Petticoats & Prejudice: Women and Law in Nineteenth Century Canada' 1991; numerous scholarly articles women's issues; Office: London, Ont. N6A 3K7.

**BACON, David Walter,** B.A.Sc., M.S., Ph.D.; educator; b. Peterborough, Ont. 12 Sept. 1935; s. Arthur and Eleanor Winifred (Bothwell) B.; e. Univ. of Toronto B.A.Sc. 1957; Univ. of Wis. M.S. 1962, Ph.D. 1965; m. Lucille d. Neil and Georgia Parks 6 July 1963; children: Ann Marie, David Eric; PROF. OF CHEM. ENGN., QUEEN'S UNIV. 1973– ; Computations Analyst, Canadian General Electric Co. 1957–60; Research Group Leader, Du Pont Canada Inc. 1965–67; Assoc. Prof. of Chem. Engn. present Univ. 1968–73, Dean of Applied Science 1980–90; Visiting Prof., Univ. of Wis., Univ. of Havana, Univ. of Sydney, Stanford Univ.; Consultant, General Mills, Council for Continuous Improvement; recipient Award for Excellence in Teaching Ont. Confed. Univ. Faculty Assns.; author or co-author various tech. publs.; Fellow, Am. Stat. Assn.; Fellow, Can. Soc. Chem. Eng.; Past Chair, Comm. Ont. Deans of Engn.; Past Chrmn. Nat. Comte. Deans of Engn. & Applied Science; mem. Assn. Prof. Engrs. Prov. Ont.; Candn. Soc. Chem. Engrs.; Am. Stat. Assn.; Stat. Soc. Can.; Royal Stat. Soc.; United Church; recreations: sailing, swimming, cycling; Home: R.R. 1, Picton, Ont. K0K 2T0; Office: Dept. of Chem. Eng., Queen's University, Kingston, Ont. K7L 3N6.

**BACON, Larry Douglas,** B.Comm., M.B.A.; banker; b. Stouffville, Ont. 25 May 1953; s. Douglas L. and Edith F. (Corbett) B.; e. Laurentian Univ. B.Comm. (Hons.) 1976; Univ. of Western Ontario M.B.A. 1982; m. Colleen; two children; VICE-PRESIDENT & HEAD OF CORPORATE FINANCE, ONTARIO, CITIBANK CANADA 1991– ; Vice-Pres. & Dir., Loewen, Ondaatje, McCutcheon 1990; Merrill Lynch Canada Inc. 1982–90; Dir., Citibank Canada Securities Limited; Mem., Leaside United Church; Office: 123 Front St. W., Toronto, Ont. M5J 2M3.

**BACON, Peter J.H.,** B.Comm., M.B.A.; banking executive; b. Colne, England 3 Apr. 1948; s. Claude J. and Joy M.B. (Pedersen) Hickman; e. Concordia Univ. B.Comm. 1969; Univ. of Toronto M.B.A. 1980; Cdn. Sec. Inst., Cdn. Sec. Course 1970, '88; P.O.D. 1989; m. Heather d. Keith and Ella MacKeen 28 Dec. 1970; children: Andrew J.K., Sarah J.E.; DIR. & PRES., BANK OF MONTREAL INVESTOR SERVICES LTD. 1988– ; various posts, Nesbitt Thomson 1969–73; Mastercard Div., Bank of Montreal 1973–80; Sr. Mgr., Mastercard Opns. 1981–83; Vice-Pres., Domestic Opns., Bank of Montreal 1984–88; Mem., Indus. Adv. Group, Baycom Inc. 1988–91; Dir., Credit Grantors Assoc. of Canada, Toronto 1981–83; Pres., Fac. of Mngt. Alumni Assn., Univ. of Toronto 1991–92 (Dir. 1990–91 & 1992– ;); Mem., Concordia Alumni Assoc.; Mem., Toronto Corporations Ctte., Concordia Univ. 1990– ; Mem., Extve. Ctte., Treas., Lorne Park Scout Group 1990–93; recreations: swimming, tennis, gardening, genealogical research; Clubs: Tecumseh Tennis; Oxford; Office: 302 Bay St., 6th Fl., Toronto, Ont. M5X 1A1.

**BACON, Hon. Roger Stuart,** M.L.A.; politician; b. Upper Nappan, N.S. 29 June 1926; s. Robert Clinton and Lillian May (Smith) B.; e. Upper Nappan schs.; m. Clara Emily d. Albert Hawthorne, St. Stephen's, N.B. 30 Nov. 1944; children: Douglas, Diana, Deborah; Min. of Housing & Min. Responsible for the Emergency Measures Organization Act 1989–91; dairy farmer; auctioneer; former Councillor, Depy. Warden Cumberland Co.; former mem. and Chrmn. Amherst Mun., Vocational and Regional High Sch. Bds.; Cumberland Co. and Towns Jt. Expenditure Bds.; Past Pres. Cumberland Co. P. Cons. Assn.; Life Mem., N.S. Fruit Growers Assoc.; Life Mem., N.S. Blueberry Growers Assoc.; Hon. Assoc., N.S. Agricultural Coll.; el. M.L.A. for Cumberland East prov. g.e. 1970, re-el. since; Min. of Tourism, Min. of the Environment and Min. Responsible for Adm. Emergency Measures Organ. N.S. Act and Regulations, Govt. of Nova Scotia 1978; Min. of Agriculture and Min. of the Environment 1979; Min. of Agriculture and Marketing 1979–89; Depy. Premier 1989–90; Premier 1990–91; Hon. Senator, Nova Scotia Fedn. of Agriculture 1992; P. Conservative; United Church; recreations: curling, golf, auctioneering; Club: Curling; Home: Upper Nappan, N.S.; Office: R.R. #6, Amherst, N.S. B4H 3Y4.

**BACOPULOS, John George;** real estate executive; b. Keene, New Hampshire 28 May 1947; s. Rev. George

John and Evelyn G. (Bardis) B.; e. C.W. Post Coll.; Pace Univ.; m. Sheila J. d. John Kennedy and Wilhelmina Bateman 6 Nov. 1976; children: Christine, George John, Alyce, Sarah, Jessica, Stephanie; CHRMN., CHIEF EXTVE. OFFR. & DIR., BEDFORD HOUSE INVESTMENT LTD. 1986– ; Vice-Pres.: Gulf & Western (Can.) Ltd. 1975–77; Famous Players Limited 1977–80; Chrmn. & Dir.: Famous Players Devel. Corp. Limited 1982– ; Data Networking Services Ltd. 1988– ; Bedford House Publishing Corp. 1989– ; Dir., Web Offset Publications Ltd. 1986; Partner, St. Thomas Street Restaurant; Dir., Simcoe Disposal and Recycling Inc.; Home: 44 North Dr., Islington, Ont. M9A 4P9; Office: Bedford House, 10 Carlson Court, Ste. 600, Etobickoe, Ont. M9W 6L2.

**BACQUE, James Watson,** B.A.; writer; b. Toronto, Ont. 19 May 1929; s. Frederic Harold and Edith Macintyre (Watson) B.; e. Upper Can. Coll. 1948; Trinity Coll., Univ. of Toronto, B.A. 1952; m. Elisabeth d. Constance and Ferdinand Marani 22 July 1955; children: Susan Elisabeth, Catherine Mary, James Benson, Andrew Watson; Reporter, Stratford Beacon-Herald 1954–55; Asst. Ed., Saturday Night Magazine 1955; Stagehand, CBC TV 1955–58; Asst. Ed. 'Canadian Packaging,' Maclean Hunter 1958–59; 'Canadian Homes' 1959–61; Ed., Macmillan of Can. 1961–68; Pres. & Co-founder, New Press 1969–75; Ed., Seal Books, McClelland & Stewart 1975–76; First Prize, Bull-dancing, Assn. des Courses-Landaises (France) 1965; Founding Mem., Assn. of Candn. Pubs.; Writers' Union of Can. (Sec. Treas. 1980–81); author: 'The Lonely Ones' 1969, 1970, 'A Man of Talent' 1972, 'Big Lonely' 1978, 'The Queen Comes to Minnicog' 1979, 'Other Losses: An investigation into the mass deaths of German prisoners at the hands of the French and Americans after World War II'; ('Der Geplante Tod' 1989; 'Morts Pour Raisons Diverses' 1990); 'Just Raoul' 1990; 'Crimes and Mercies' in preparation; 'Dear Enemy' in preparation; Contbr.: 'Canada' 1964, 'Creation' 1973, 'Marked by the Wild' 1973; recreations: tennis, sailing, canoeing; Club: Badminton; Home: Toronto, Ont.

**BADER, Richard F.W.,** F.R.S.C., F.C.I.C., Ph.D.; professor; b. Kitchener, Ont. 15 Oct. 1931; s. Albert Joseph and Alvina Gerloff B.; e. McMaster Univ., B.Sc. 1953, M.Sc. 1955, M.I.T., Ph.D. 1958; m. Pamela Loi d. Alexander and Loi Kozenof 8 Sept. 1958; children: Carolyn Patricia, Kimberly Jane, Suzanne Katherine; PROF., DEPT. OF CHEMISTRY, McMASTER UNIV. 1966– ; post-doct. fellow, M.I.T. 1958; Univ. of Cambridge 1958–59; Asst. Prof. 1959–62, Assoc. Prof., Univ. of Ottawa 1962–63; Assoc. Prof. 1963–66, Prof., McMaster Univ. 1966– ; Fellowships: NRC Postdoctoral Fellowship 1958–59; A.P. Sloan Rsch. 1964–66; E.W.R. Steacie Meml., NRC 1967–69; John Simon Guggenheim Meml. 1979–80; F.R.S.C. 1980; F.C.I.C. 1970; Mem., Am. Physical Soc.; author: 'An Introduction to the Electronic Structure of Atoms and Molecules' 1970; 'Atoms in Molecules - A Quantum Theory' 1990; and 120 sci. articles; Home: 126 Birett Dr., Burlington, Ont. L7L 2T1; Office: Dept. of Chem., McMaster Univ., Hamilton, Ont. L8S 4M1.

**BADGLEY, Robin Francis;** educator; sociologist; b. Montreal, Que. 6 May 1931; s. Clement Montagu and Joan Gordon (Coles) B.; e. McGill Univ., B.A. 1952, M.A. 1954; Yale Univ. M.A. 1955, Ph.D. 1957 (Sr. Sterling Fellow); m. Jean Winifred, d. George Duncan, Northumberland, UK, 18 June 1959; children: Anne Duncan, Mary Elizabeth, Peter Francis; CHAIR, GRAD. DEPT. OF COMMUNITY HEALTH, FACULTY OF MED. 1992– , and PROF. OF BEHAVIOURAL SCIENCE, FACULTY OF MED., UNIV. OF TORONTO and Prof. of Sociol. 1968– ; Prof. Family and Community Medicine 1993– ; Chrmn. Dept. of Behavioural Sci. 1968–76 and 1987–88; Russell Sage Foundation Post-Doctoral Fellow, Yale Univ. 1957–58; Assoc. Prof., Dept. of Social and Preventive Med., Univ. of Sask. 1959–63 (Acting Chrmn. 1962–63); Sr. mem. Milbank Mem. Fund, N.Y. 1963–68; Visiting Lectr., Dept. of Epidemiol., Yale Univ. 1963–68; Visiting Lectr., Sch. of Pub. Health, Columbia Univ. 1965–82; Consultant, Expert Adv. Comte. on Health Manpower, World Health Orgn. 1969–70); mem. Research & Demonstration Grants Program, Welfare Adm., Washington, 1966–69; Rev-Comm., Nat. Inst. Child Health & Human Devel., U.S. Pub. Health Service, Washington 1966–70; Comm. on Candn. Public Health Assn. 1967–69; Health Services Committee, Ontario Council of Health, 1974–81; Health Promotion Committee, Conference of Federal-Provincial Health Ministers, 1974–76; Chrmn. Committee on the Operation of the Abortion Law, Privy Council, Govt. of Canada 1975–77; mem. Adv. Comte. on Med. Rsch., World Health Orgn. (PAHO) 1976–84; Chrmn., Task Force on User Charges, Ont. Council of

Health, 1978–79; Fellowship, World Health Orgn. 1978; Chrmn., Comte. on Social Sci-Health Research, World Health Orgn. 1979–82; Chrmn., Comte. on Sexual Offences Against Children, Dept. of Justice & Nat. Health & Wel., Govt. of Can. 1981–84; Working Group on Collective Bargaining, Ont. Council of Health 1980–81; Expert Consultant for World Health Orgn. to Israel, Nicaragua and Dominican Republic 1981, and on health manpower, Indonesia 1984; consultant, Development Co-operation for Health in Commonwealth Countries, Commonwealth Secretariat/Internat. Develop. Rsch. Centre 1984–87; mem. Adv. Comte., Nat. Inst. of Public Health, Govt. of Mexico 1984–92; Expert Comte. on Malaria, World Health Orgn. 1985–88; Consultant, Caribbean-Canadian Partnership for Health 1989–90; Chrmn., Task Force on Sustainable Development, Candn. Public Health Assoc. 1989–90; Consultation Group on the Future of Public Health, World Health Orgn. (PAHO) 1990–92; Chrmn. Advisory Ctte. on Community Health Framework, Ont. Min. of Health 1993– ; co-author, 'Doctors' Strike: Medical Care and Conflict in Saskatchewan' 1967, 2nd ed. 1971; 'The Family Doctor' 1972 (US), 1973 (Can.); Ed. 'Milbank Memorial Fund Quarterly' 1963–68; 'Behavioural Science and Medical Education in Latin America' 1966, Spanish transl. 1967; 'Social Science and Health Planning: Culture, Disease and Health Services in Columbia' 1968, Spanish transl. 1968; 'Social Science and Health in Canada' 1971; co-author 'Report of the Comte. on the Operation of the Abortion Law' 1977; 'User Charges for Health Services' 1979; 'Bibliography on Social Science Health Research in Latin America (WHO)' 1981; co-author, 'Report of the Committee on Sexual Offences Against Children' (2 vols.) 1984; 'Development Co-operation for Health in Commonwealth Countries' (2 vols). 1986; author of book chapters, articles and reviews in prof. journs.; mem. Am. Sociol. Assn. (Secy.-Treas. Med. Sociol. Sec. 1965–68); Internat. Sociol. Assn. (Secy.-Treas. Comte. Med. Sociol. 1970–81); Home: 298 Watson Ave., Oakville, Ont. L6J 3V4; Office: Toronto, Ont. M5S 1A8.

**BADLEY, Bernard W.D.,** M.D., F.R.C.P., F.R.C.P.(C); hospital administrator; educator; b. London, Eng. 21 Dec. 1933; s. George and Eva (Parkhouse) B.; e. St. Bartholomew's Hosp. Med. Coll. England; Univ. of London M.D. 1957; m. Ingeborg d. Rudolf and Trudi Mayer 26 March 1960; children: Jennifer, Andrew; PRES. AND CHIEF EXTVE. OFFR., VICTORIA GENENERAL HOSPITAL 1988– ; Prof. of Med. Dalhousie Univ. 1982– ; postgrad. training in Internal Med. Eng. and Can.; served with Royal Candn. Army Med. Corps 1960–63 followed by two and a half yrs. gen. practice rural N.S.; Physician, present Hosp. 1969– , Chief of Gastroenterol. Service 1976–81, Exec. Dir. 1981–82, Head of Med. 1982–86; Asst. Prof. present univ. 1969, Assoc. Prof. 1974, Vice Dean Fac. of Med. 1986–88; Chrmn. Dalhousie Faculty Ctte. on Undergrad. Med. Edn. 1972–77; Pres., N.S. Soc. of Internal Med. 1980–81; Dir. & Vice Pres. Candn. Rugby Union 1982–88; musical dir., conductor, Tupper Concert Bank; R.S. McLaughlin Fellowship 1968; Lea C. Steeves Award for Med. Edn. 1990; author or co-author over 30 sci./med. publs.; recreation: golf; Club: Ashburn Golf; Home: 5890 Chain Rock Dr., Halifax, N.S. B3H 1A1; Office: 1278 Tower Rd., Halifax, N.S. B3H 2Y9.

**BADUN, Walter R.,** P.Eng., M.B.A.; real estate executive; b. Poland 2 Jan. 1930; s. Alexander and Mary (Semeniuk) B.; e. Univ. of Alta. B.Sc. 1952; Univ. of Western Ont. M.B.A. 1957; m. Jean d. Evelyn and Don Barton 18 Sept. 1954; children: Robert, Maryanne, Carol, Monique, Graham; CHAIRMAN & CHIEF EXTVE. OFFR., PENREAL ADVISORS LTD. 1982– ; Sr. Vice-Pres., Abbey Glen Prop. Corp. 1969–74; Chrmn., Morguard Properties Ltd. 1974–82; Dir., B.C. Housing Mngt. Comn. 1988–92; Chrmn. B.C. Buildings Corp. 1978–81; Director & Chrmn., Construction Ctte., Expo 86 1981–86; One Man Royal Comn., Prov. of Alta. to investigate school construction problems in N. Alta. 1964; Mem., Assn. of Profl. Engrs. of Alta.; recreations: golf; club: Shaughnessy Golf & Country; Home: 2292 Yewbrook Place, Vancouver, B.C. V6P 6K4; Office: #700, 1090 West Georgia St., Vancouver, B.C. V6E 3V7.

**BADYK, Joseph Stanley;** executive; b. Saskatoon, Sask. 3 June 1925; s. Peter and Lena (Yurach) B.; e. St. Peters Coll., Muenster, Sask.; m. Patricia F. d. Frank and Mary Sandgathe 1 Dec. 1951; children: David, Patricia; CHRMN. OF THE BD. AND DIR., PRUDENTIAL STEEL LTD. 1966– ; Chrmn. (Owner) Badco Energy Inc.; Acct., CP Hotels (Banff Springs, Palliser, Chateau Lake Louise) 1946–51; Mgr. & Dir., Canada-Cities Service 1951–66; Dir. and Past Campaign Chrmn. Calgary Un. Way; past Dir. and Chrmn. Camp Cadicasu, Bragg Creek; Past Chrmn. and Gov., Oilmen's; Past Pres. & Dir., Earl Grey Golf Club; Corporate Campaign Chrmn., Candn. Cerebral Palsy Assoc. 1987; recreations: golf, gin rummy; Clubs: Calgary Golf & Country; Calgary Petroleum (Past Pres. and Dir.); Home: 1619 Senlac St. S.W., Calgary, Alta. T3C 2J8.

**BAECKER, Harry David,** M.A.; educator; b. Prague, Czechoslovakia 6 June 1931; s. Fritz and Marianne (Toders) B.; e. Czech State Schs. 1939; Culford Sch. Bury St. Edmunds, U.K. 1942; Abingdon (Roysse's) Sch. U.K. 1949; Jesus Coll. Cambridge B.A. 1954, M.A. 1956; Social Sciences Research Centre, Univ. of Edinburgh 1954–56; m. Dana d. John and Jean Lower 31 March 1984; two s. Mark, Allan; Assoc. Prof. of Computer Sci., Univ. of Calgary 1968–91; Programmer, Info. Processing Div. Standard Telephones & Cables Ltd. Newport, Wales 1956–60; Project Mgr. C-E-I-R (UK) Ltd., London 1960; Co-founder and Tech. Dir. Computer Analysts & Programmers Ltd. 1961–66; Sr. Lectr. Imp. Coll. of Sci. & Technol. 1966–68; Pres. Calgary Chapter Credit Unions 1976–78, Dir. 1975–81; Fellow, Brit. Computer Soc.; mem. W. Candn. Sunbathing Assn.; recreations: science-fiction, music; Home: 108 River Rd., Box 474, Lake Cowichan, B.C. V0R 2G0.

**BAEKER, Gregory G.,** B.A., M.M.St.; cultural executive; b. London, Ont. 14 Dec. 1954; s. George Alfred and June Elizabeth (Work) B.; e. Univ. of Western Ont., B.A. 1977; Univ. of Toronto, M.M.St. 1981; PARTNER, APPLIED CULTURAL PRINCIPLES (consulting firm specializing in community and cultural development) 1993– ; doctoral candidate, Urban and Regional Planning, Univ. of Waterloo (focusing on community cultural planning) 1993– ; Extve. Coordinator, Ont. Heritage Policy Review, Min. of Culture & Communications, Ont. 1987–91 (This cross-government review of heritage policies, legislation and programs resulted in Ontario's adoption of the first overall heritage policy and strategy in Canada); Mgr., Strategic Planning, Min. of Culture and Communications 1992–93; Extve. Dir., Ont. Mus. Assn. 1982–86; Founding Partner, Museum Programs Collaborative (museum consulting firm) 1981; Pres., Children's Discovery Mus. of Toronto; Chrmn., Mus. Labour Market Study (Candn. Mus. Assn.); mem., Adv. Ctte., Univ. of Toronto Masters of Museum Studies Prog.; Chair, Adv. Ctte., Univ. of Toronto (Scarborough Campus) Arts Admin. Prog.; author of wide range of articles for profl. jours.; Home: 105 Winchester St., Toronto, Ont. M4X 1B3.

**BAETZ, Reuben C.,** M.A., B.S.W., LL.D.; b. Chesley, Ont. 9 May 1923; s. Harry William and Alice F. (Henrich) B.; e. Univ. of W. Ont., B.A. (cum laude) 1947; Columbia Univ., M.A. 1948; Univ. of Toronto, B.S.W. 1957; Extve. Devel. Sch., Am. Red Cross, 1960; LL.D. (hon. causa) Sir Wilfrid Laurier Univ.; LL.D. (hon. causa) Univ. of Windsor; m. Jule Annette, d. Dr. George Anderson, Minneapolis, Minn., 5 Aug. 1950; children: Mark Conrad, Annette Alice, Carla Patricia; Ontario Minister of Intergovernmental Affairs 1985; Min. of Culture & Recreation 1978–82; Min. of Tourism & Recreation 1982–85; Gov., Waterloo Lutheran Univ.; Pres., Internat. Council on Social Welfare; Asst. Dir., Lutheran World Fed. worldwide Operation, Geneva 1952 (Dir. 1953); appt. Asst. Nat. Commr., Candn. Red Cross, Toronto, Ont. 1956; Extve. Dir., Candn. Counc. on Social Develop., Ottawa 1962; el. to Ont. Leg. June 1977; Parlty. Asst. to Attorney-Gen. Sept. 1977; Min. of Energy Jan. 1978; served in 2nd World War, Candn. Active Service Force, Oct. 1939–Nov. 1942; mem., Bd. of Social Ministry, Lutheran Ch. in Am.; Ont. Econ. Council; Trustee, Candn. Inst. for Rsch. on Policy; Lutheran; recreations: golf, fishing, gardening; Clubs: Rideau; Albany.

**BAGLOW, John Sutton,** M.A., Ph.D.; writer; labour unionist; public sector worker; b. London, Eng. 10 Dec. 1946; s. Robert Lloyd and Lucy Elizabeth (Sutton) B.; e. Carleton Univ. B.A. 1969, M.A. 1970; Univ. of Glasgow Ph.D. 1973; author 'Emergency Measures' (poetry) 1976; 'Hugh MacDiarmid: The Poetry of Self' (criticism) 1987; contbr. 'Grey Matters: The Peace Arts Anthology' 1985; poetry and articles various mags.; presently Nat. Dir. Nat. Capital Region Pub. Service Alliance Can.; Vice Pres., Ont. Fed. of Labour 1988– ; Sec. Ottawa & Dist. Labour Council 1984–90, Recording Sec. 1990–91, Vice Pres. 1991– ; Bd., Ottawa-Carleton Labour Community Services, 1989– ; Bd., Labour Studies Inst. (ODLC/Algonquin Coll.) 1989– ; Grants Prog. Offr. Social Sci's & Humanities Rsch. Council 1974– ;(Can. Council prior to 1978); Bd. of Dir., Candn. Abortion Rights Action League 1976–86; recreations: reading, cooking, walking, conversation, sailing, scuba diving, music, films, writing; Home: 53 Simcoe St., Ottawa, Ont. K1S 1A3; Office: 10F, 255 Albert St., Ottawa, Ont. K1P 6G4.

**BAGNALL, Graham Edward,** B.A., M.B.A., C.A.; business executive; b. Birmingham, Eng. 20 Jan. 1948; s. Herbert Edward and Marie Lily (Hall) B.; e. Univ. of Manchester, B.A. 1970; York Univ., M.B.A. 1975; C.A. 1973; m. Christine d. Robert and Kathleen Walker 14 Oct. 1972; one d. Sarah; VICE PRES. AND COMPTROLLER, MONTREAL TRUSTCO INC. 1991– ; Vice-Chrmn., The Montreal Children's Hosp. Found.; Clarkson Gordon 1970–74; Bell Canada 1974–82; Bell Canada Enterprises 1983, Asst. Treas. 1984–86, Vice Pres. and Treas. 1986–91; ; recreations: squash, badminton; Clubs: MAAA; University; Home: 57 Thornhill Ave., Westmount, Qué. H3Y 2E3; Office: 1800 McGill College Ave., Montréal, Qué. H3A 3K9.

**BAGNELL, Kenneth,** B.A., B.D.; journalist, public speaker; b. Glace Bay, N.S. 9 Sept. 1934; s. William George and Mary Margaret (Andrews) B.; e. Mount Allison Univ., B.A. 1956; Pine Hill Divinity Hall, B.D. 1958; m. Barbara d. William and Leone Robar June 1958; children: Paul, David, Andrea; began his career in journalism in 1961 as a writer & subsequently Mng. Ed., Un. Ch. Observer; Ed. Bd. Mem., Toronto Star; joined Globe & Mail 1969 as Ed. Bd. Mem., then Ed., Globe Magazine, then daily columnist; also active as radio & TV commentator; Editor, Imperial Oil Review 1974–90; Contbr., numerous mags. & speaker on wide variety of subjects at various conventions in Can. & U.S.; Speaker & Counsellor, bereavement field for many years; Mem., Ont. Bd. of Funeral Services 1970s; Dir., Loewen Group Inc. 1989– ; has received various awards for mag. writing & editing; Mem., United Ch. of Can.; author: 'The Little Immigrants' 1980, 'Canadese' 1989; recreations: jogging, traveling, reading; club: YMCA of Metro. Toronto; Home: 74 Redpath Ave., Toronto, Ont. M4S 2J7.

**BAGULEY, Robert,** M.A., Ph.D.; economist; b. Niagara Falls, Ont. 28 Jan. 1942; s. Donald and Jean Marian (Stringer) B.; e. Univ. of W. Ont. B.A. 1963; Harvard Univ. M.A. 1966, Ph.D. (Econ.) 1969; m. Nancy Louise, d. Wilfred Samuel Ratz, 12 Oct. 1968; two d. Karen Jane Louise, Jocelyn Suzanne; DEPUTY CHIEF ECON., THE ROYAL BANK OF CANADA; Asst. Prof of Econ. Univ. of W. Ont. 1967–71; Chief Econ., Econ. Analysis and Fiscal Policy Div., Dept. of Finance Ottawa 1971–73; mem. Am. Econ. Assn.; Candn. Econ. Assn.; Am. Stat. Assn.; Am. Management Assoc.; Can. Inst. Internat Affairs; Nat. Assoc. Bus. Economists; Nat. Planning Assoc.; Can. Bankers Assoc.; mem. Bd. Dirs., Inst. of Applied Econ. Research, Concordia Univ. Montreal Econ. Assn.; Clubs: University; Canadian; Harvard (Montreal); Home: 403 Walpole Ave., Beaconsfield, Qué. H9W 2G6; Office: P.O. Box 6001, Montreal, Qué. H3C 3A9.

**BAHNMAN, Al;** electronics executive; b. Davidson, Sask. 28 June 1946; s. Susan (Dahl) B.; e. Moose Jaw, Sask. 2 yr. prog. STI (Electronics) 1965; m. Marilyn d. Howard and Muriel Wills; children: Jason, Kim; CHRMN., CHIEF EXEC. OFFR., PRES. AND DIR. TEE-COMM ELECTRONICS INC. 1986– ; Pres. Tee-Comm Distribution Inc.; Envirofan Energy Systems Inc.; Vice Pres. Tee-Com Inc.; Pres. Banvil Ltd. 1974–86; mem. Candn. Mfrs. Assn.; C.S.A.; CHHMA; recreations: golf, travel, curling; Office: 775 Main St. E., Milton, Ont. L9T 3Z3.

**BAILEY, Alfred Goldsworthy,** O.C., M.A., Ph.D., LL.D., D.Litt., F.R.S.C.; educator; author; b. Quebec, P.Q. 18 Mar. 1905; s. Loring Woart and Ernestine Valiant (Gale) B.; e. Univ. of New Brunswick, B.A. 1927, D.Litt.; Univ. of Toronto, M.A. 1929, Ph.D. 1934; awarded Roy. Soc. Can. Fellowship for Research, 1934; Sch. of Econ. and Pol. Science, Univ. of London, Eng., 1934–35; St. Thomas Univ., LL.D.; McGill U., D.Litt.; Mount Allison, LL.D.; Officer of the Order of Canada, 1978; m. Jean Craig, d. Samuel Alexander Hamilton, Moose Jaw, Sask., 8 Sept. 1934; Prof. Emeritus of Hist. and formerly Prof. of Hist. and Head of Dept., and Vice Pres. (Acad.) Univ. of New Brunswick; Asst. Dir. and Assoc. Curator, N.B. Museum, 1935–38; Univ. of N.B., Lecturer in Anthrop., 1941–50; Dean of Arts, 1946–64; Hon. Librarian, Bonar Law Bennett Lib., 1946–59; mem. Hist. Sites & Monuments Bd. of Canada, 1951–62; former mem., Nat. Lib. Adv. Council; Harold Innis Visiting Prof., Univ. of Toronto, 1955–56; former Pres. of the St. John Art Club, 1936 former Gov., Lord Beaverbrook Art Gallery; former Chrmn., Bd. of Govs., Beaverbrook Playhouse; former Chrmn., Prov. Tree Comn. for N.B.; former mem., Gov.-Gen's Lit. Awards Comte.; Humanities Research Council of Can.; Extve. Comte. of Social Science Research Council of Can.; former Pres., York-Sudbury Hist. Soc.; Hon. Life Mem., League of Candn. Poets; Hon Pres., N.B. Writers Fedn.; Freeman of the City of Fredericton; author 'Songs of the Saguenay and Other Poems' 1927; 'Tao: A Ryerson Poetry Chap Book' 1930; 'The Conflict of European and Eastern Algonkian Culture 1504–1700: A Study in Canadian Civilization' 1937 (2nd ed. 1969); 'Border River' 1952; 'Culture and Nationality: Essays' 1972; 'Thanks for a Drowned Island' 1973; 'Miramichi Lightning' short-listed for Gov.-Gen. Lit. Award, 1981; his poems have appeared in 'Candn. Poetry Mag.' Vol.1; 'Dalhousie Review'; 'Canadian Forum'; 'Preview'; 'Voices'; 'Here and Now'; 'Oxford Book of Canadian Verse'; 'Book of Canadian Poetry'; 'First Statement'; 'Northern Review'; 'Penguin Book of Canadian Verse'; 'Ninety Seasons: Modern Poems of the Maritimes'; 'Wascana Review'; 'Canadian Literature'; 'Contemporary Verse'; 'Poems of a Snow-Eyed Country; 'Anthology of Common Wealth Verse'; 'Reflections on a Hill Behind a Town; 'Antholgy Commemorating the 35th Anniversary of the founding of the Fiddlehead Magazine; 'Anthology of Magazine Verse and Handbook of American Poetry'; etc.; Anglican; Home: 2 Acacia Court, Fredericton, N.B. E3B 1Y7.

**BAILEY, Brig. Gen. Anthony John Beswick,** D.S.O., O.B.E., E.D., C.D.; b. Sandwick, B.C. 16 Apr. 1914; s. Maj. John Beswick, D.S.O. and Ida Gertrude Barrow (Mogg) B.; e. Pub. and High Schs., Vernon, Chemainus and Duncan, B.C.; Jr. War Staff Coll. 1941–42; Imp. Defence Coll. 1964; m. Rosemary Dorothy, d. George Edward and Mary Botting, 28 Nov. 1938; children: Christopher John Beswick, Barbara Patricia (Mrs. Robert Longe); enlisted NPAM as Boy Signaller 1930; comnd. 2nd Lt. RCA 1936; served in various regt'al and staff appts. 1939–45 in Can., U.K., Italy and N.W. Europe incl comd. 3rd Fd. Regt. RCA; and in sr. staff appts. in Can. 1945–50; commanded 2 RCHA in Korea, May–Nov. 1951; promoted Col. to Command Royal Candn. Sch. of Arty., Camp Shilo, Man. 1951; Dir. of Arty, Ottawa 1954–57; Chief of Staff, W. Command, Edmonton 1957–59; Dir. of Mil. Operations and Plans, Ottawa 1959–60; promoted Brig. and Commdr., E. Ont. Area, Kingston 1960; Commdr., 2 Candn. Inf. Bgde. Group, Camp Petawawa 1962–63; Chief of Staff, Training Command, Winnipeg 1965–66; Dir., Nat. Defence Coll. 1966–68 when retired; Vice. Pres., Adm., Mt. Allison Univ. 1969–75; awarded M.B.E. 1944, D.S.O. 1945, O.B.E. 1951; Mentioned in Despatches 1944; Anglican; recreation: Arabians; gardening; Address: 1605 Rockland Ave., Victoria, B.C. V8S 1W6.

**BAILEY, David;** editor; b. Rothwell, England 25 Sept. 1950; s. Lancelot Leonard and Joan Mary B.; e. Kettering Grammar Sch.; Harlow College; m. Johanna d. Reginald and Norma Powell 18 April 1980; children: Garron, Heather; EXECUTIVE EDITOR, FINANCIAL POST 1991– ; Reporter, East Midland Allied Press, Corby Evening Telegraph 1968; Peterborough Evening Telegraph (Northants, Eng.) 1973; Winnipeg Tribune 1975; Sunday Editor, Toronto Sun 1975; News Editor, Edmonton Sun 1978; Editor-in-Chief 1981; Office: 333 King St. E., Toronto, Ont. M5A 4N2.

**BAILEY, David George,** B.Sc.Phm., M.Sc., Ph.D.; clinical pharmacologist; b. Toronto, Ont. 17 March 1945; s. the late George Herbert and Barbara Frances (Smith) B.; e. Univ. of Toronto B.Sc.Phm. 1968, M.Sc. 1970, Ph.D. 1973; m. Barbara Jean d. Walter and Jean Gillespie 30 May 1970; children: Karen Joanne, Brian David, Scott Andrew; RESEARCH SCIENTIST, DEPT. OF MEDICINE, VICTORIA HOSPITAL 1989– ; Post-Doctoral Fellow, Univ. of Sask. 1973; Scientific Adviser, Sask. Prescription Drug Plan 1976; Sr. Investigator, Drug Rsch. & Devel., Smith Kline & French (Canada) 1978; Cardiovascular Rsch. Dir., Astra Pharm. Canada 1982; area of research expertise: pharmacokinetics and pharmacodynamics; major scientific discovery of a new & important type of food-drug interaction involving inhibition of drug metabolism by constituents in grapefruit juice & possibly other foods; Asst. Prof., Dept. of Pharm. & Toxicology, Univ. of Western Ont.; Canada's first sub 4-minute miler (San Diego, Calif. 1966); World Univ. Games Tokyo 1967 1500m silver medalist; Pan Am. Games Winnipeg 1967 1500m bronze medalist; awarded Candn. Univ. Track & Field Athlete of the Year 1965, '67; rep. Canada at Olympic Games Mexico City 1968 & Commonwealth Games Kingston, Jamaica 1966; Mem., Candn. Soc. for Clin. Pharm.; Candn. Soc. for Clin. Investigation; Am. Soc. for Clin. Pharm. & Therapeutics; Candn. Soc. of Hosp. Pharm.; Ont. Coll. of Pharm.; author of over twenty peer-reviewed sci. pubns.; recreations: coaching baseball, hockey; Home: 31 Notre Dame Court, London, Ont. N6J 2G3; Office: 375 South St., London, Ont. N6A 4G5.

**BAILEY, Donald Atholl,** B.A., M.A., Ph.D.; educator; b. Rochester, Minn. 24 Feb. 1940; s. Allan Archibald, M.D. and Mary Emily (Marshall), M.D., B.; e. Univ. of Sask. B.A. 1962; Oxford Univ. B.A. 1964, M.A. 1968; Univ. of Minn. Ph.D. 1973; m. Leuba Sonia d. Daniel Z. and Kathleen Daniels 28 July 1963; children: Monica Ruth, Marshall Charles; PROF. OF HIST. UNIV. OF WINNIPEG 1988– ; part-time instr. Carleton Coll. Northfield, Minn. 1966–67; part-time Instr. Extension Div. Univ. of Minn. 1966; Univ. of Sask. sessional instr. 1964–65, spring 1965, summer 1967; joined present Univ. 1969; sabbaticals in France 1975–76, 1984–85, 1991–92; Bd. of Dir.: Health Sci's Centre Winnipeg 1973–75; Mount Carmel Clinic 1974–75; Vice Pres., Manitoba Assoc. for Rights and Liberties 1992– ; Pres., Aurora Musicale 1992– ; Pres., Osborne NDP 1992–93; Steering Ctte., City of Winnipeg's Year for Racial Harmony 1993– ; author various book chapters, articles hist. jours. on French and Canadian history; freelance writing Winnipeg Free Press 1983–90; CBC Commentary; mem. W. Soc. French Hist. (Pres. 1988–89); Soc. French Historical Studies; Candn. Hist. Assn.; Man. Hist. Soc.; Collegium; Unitarian Ch. (Chair Bd. Mgmt. Winnipeg 1972–74); NDP (cand. for Osborne Man. prov. el. 1990); recreations: theatre, concerts, golf, swimming; Home: 86 Wildwood Park, Winnipeg, Man. R3T 0C8; Office: 515 Portage Ave., Winnipeg, Man. R3B 2E9.

**BAILEY, Donald Gilbert (Don);** writer; producer; b. Toronto, Ont. 7 Oct. 1942; s. Edward and Dorothy (Miller) B.; e. D.B. Hood Pub. Sch. and Oakwood Coll. Inst. Toronto; Candn. Urban Training Centre, Toronto, grad. Soc. Change Prog.; m. Daile d. Richard and Thelma Unruh 21 Dec. 1985; children: Daniel, Rebecca, Estelle; author (fiction) 'If You Hum Me A Few Bars I Might Remember the Tune' 1971; 'In the Belly of the Whale' 1974; 'Replay' 1975; 'The Sorry Papers' 1979; 'Making Up' 1981; 'Swim For Your Life' 1984; 'Bring Me Your Passion' 1986; (poetry) 'My Bareness Is Not Just My Body' 1972; 'The Shapes Around Me' 1973; 'How Will We Know When We Get There' 1986; 'Homeless Hearts' 1989; (memoir) 'Margaret Laurence: Friend and Mentor' 1989; various mag. articles, many radio plays, several stage plays; numerous TV progs. incl. 'Seer Was Here' (nominated ACTRA Best Drama 1978); 'Are You Happy' (drama) 1986; 'All Sales Final' 1986; latter 2 plays produced by own film co. Real Special Productions Inc., first 2 plays directed by Claude Jutra; Teacher in Creative Writing Red River Coll. 1984– ; recipient 3 sr. Can. Council Arts Grants; Ont. Arts Council Award; Man. Arts Council Award; mem. ACTRA; Writer's Union Can.; Playwrights' Assn. Man.; Man. Writers' Guild (Treas. 1985–86); recreations: racquet ball, fishing, photography; Address: c/o Writers' Union of Canada, 24 Ryerson Ave., Toronto, Ont. M5T 2P3.

**BAILEY, Franklin Truman,** B.Com., LL.B.; lawyer; executive; b. Regina Sask. 12 Apl. 1946; s. Truman Albert amd Jessie (Blakley) B.; e. Univ. of Sask. B.Com. 1969; Univ. of B.C. LL.B. 1970; m. Goldie d. Anton and Anna Smukavich 11 Apl. 1991; VICE PRES. AND GEN. COUNSEL, BOVAR CHEMICAL SECURITY 1994– ; Dir. Kenting Apollo Drilling Inc.; Kenting Drilling Co. Ltd.; Kenting Services Ltd.; Liquid Transporters Inc.; Quality Service Tank Lines Inc.; Rentway Inc.; Trimac Transportation Inc.; Trimac Transportation Services Ltd.; Triway Truck Leasing Inc.; called to Bar of Alta. 1972; served Crosland & Co. to 1974; Corporate Solr. Trimac Ltd. 1974, Sec. & Gen. Counsel 1977, Vice Pres. Adm., Sec. & Gen. Counsel 1980, Vice Pres. Corporate Affairs, Sec. and Gen. Counsel 1984–93; Home: 2204 – 18A St. S.W., Calgary, Alta. T2T 4W4; Office: 4 Manning Close N.E., Calgary, Alta. T2E 7N5.

**BAILEY, John Michael;** publisher; b. Blackpool, Eng. 23 Feb. 1947; s. Capt. Joseph Edward, M.B.E., M.C. and Eileen (Thomas) B.; e. Grace Dieu Prep. Leicester, Eng. 1959; Ratcliffe Coll. Leicester 1964; Simon Fraser Univ. 1967–70; m. Lina d. Giovanni and Maria Conceita D'Ambrosio 17 Oct. 1981; one d. Danielle, one s. Julian; PRES. FOXWOOD INTERNATIONAL LTD. 1988– ; Dir., Millbank Books Ltd. (U.K. Publishing Co.); served Am. pharm. co. Central and Latin Am. 1971–76; Dist. Mgr. C.B.S. Books W. Coast 1976–77; served Brit. pharm. co. U.K. and Africa 1977–80; Pres., Cupress (Canada) Ltd. 1983–88; author 'The Mercenary' novel 1987; R. Catholic; recreations: writing, sports, photography; Home: Foxwood House, 230 McLaren Rd., Campbellville, Ont. L0P 1B0; Office: P.O. Box 523, Milton, Ont. L9T 4Z1.

**BAILEY, Leuba Sonia,** M.Ed.; teacher; writer; b. Canora, Sask. 17 Sept. 1940; d. Daniel Zederayko and Kathleen (Franko) Daniels; e. Canora Elem. and Composite High Schs. 1958; Univ. of Sask. B.A. 1961, B.Ed. 1965; Univ. of Man. M.Ed. 1976, Advanced Cert. in Edn. 1984; m. Donald Atholl s. Allan A. and Mary E. Bailey 28 July 1963; children: Monica Ruth, Marshall Charles; teacher of Eng., French and Drama Winnipeg Adult Edn. Centre 1970–72, River Heights Jr. High Sch. 1972–73, Gordon Bell Coll. Inst. 1974, Westwood Coll. Inst. 1975–76, Kelvin High Sch. 1978–84, Daniel McIntyre Coll. Inst. 1985– , all of Winnipeg; Intern Supr. Student Teachers Univ. of Man. 1989; author 'A Teachers' Resource Guide: The Immigrant Experience' 1976; 'The World of the Novel: Nineteen Eighty–Four' 1984; ed. 'The Immigrant Experience in Canadian Literature' 1975; co-ed. 'An Integrated and Multicultural Approach to Literature and Language Study for Secondary Schools' 1984; mem. Candn. Council Teachers Eng.; Man. Assn. Teachers Eng. (Pres. 1974–75); Delta Kappa Gamma; Unitarian; NDP; recreations: Ikebana, madrigal singing, swimming; Home: 86 Wildwood Park, Winnipeg, Man. R3T 0C8; Office: 720 Alverstone St., Winnipeg, Man.

**BAILEY, Nigel Geoffrey,** B.A.; telecommunication executive; b. Liverpool, U.K. 16 Feb. 1948; s. Norman Louden and Olive May (Gore) B.; e. Upper Canada College 1965; Univ. of Victoria B.A. 1972; m. Ona Darlene d. Cordell and Bernice Swinarton 22 Sept. 1973; children: Sarah Elizabeth Frances, Andrew Geoffrey Louden; GENERAL MANAGER, TECHNOLOGY, VICTORIA COMMONWEALTH GAMES SOC. 1992–94; Controller, B.C. Development Corp. 1977–81; Co-Founder, Discovery Enterprise Prog. 1982–86; Vice-Pres., Discovery Found. 1981–86; Partner, The Nexus Group of Companies 1988– ; Vice-Pres. & Dir., Nexus Engineering Corp. 1987–92; Founder & Pres., Infosat Telecommunications Ltd. 1986–92; Mem., Indonesian Candn. Bus. Assn.; Vancouver Bd. of Trade; Electronic Mfrs. Assn. of B.C.; Candn. Exporters Assn.; Pacific Telecommunications Council; Commissioned Officer, Royal Canadian Naval Reserve 1978; author: 'Venture Investing in Technology Companies' 1984; 'Rural Telecommunications in Developing Countries' 1992; recreations: golf, coordinator of youth soccer & baseball; clubs: Wardroom, HMCS Discovery, Capilano Power Squadron; Home: 4472 Cottontree Lane, Victoria, B.C. V8X 4G1; Office: P.O. Box 1994, 4400f West Saanich Rd., Victoria, B.C. V8W 3M8.

**BAILEY, Norma Elsie,** B.A.; film producer, director; b. Winnipeg, Man. 30 Aug. 1949; d. Allan Douglas and Muriel (Clayton) B.; e. Gimli H.S.; Univ. of Manitoba, B.A. (Architecture) 1967; m. Ian s. Nathan and Rose Elkin; 2 sons: Ben, Will; PRODUCER, DIRECTOR, FLAT CITY FILMS INC.; Prod. & Dir., 'Bordertown Cafe' (feature film) 1990; Dir., 'Women in the Shadows' 1991; filmography awards: 'The Performer' Special Jury Award Cannes Film Fest. 1980; 'Nose and Tina' Best Dir., Best Film, Bijoux Awards 1982; 'Daughters of the Country' Best Picture, Best Script, Yorkton Film Fest. 1988, Best TV series Gemini 1988, Best Film, Am. Film Fest. 1987; Best TV series Women in Film Fest. 1987; Bd. Mem., Man. Arts Counc.; YWCA Woman of the Year 1988; mem., Man. Film Prod. Assn.; Candn. Film & TV Assn.; Acad. of Candn. Film & TV; Home: 336 Queenston St., Winnipeg, Man. R3N 0W8.

**BAILEY, Peter A.,** B.Comm., C.A.; financial executive; b. Montreal, Que. 29 May 1942; s. Gerard A. and Vera E. (Legere) B.; e. Loyola College B.Comm. 1965; C.A. 1970; m. Joan E. Garand 15 Dec. 1972; CHIEF OPERATING OFFICER & SECRETARY, GORDON CAPITAL CORP. 1989– ; various positions, investment industry 1974–82; Extve. Dir., Toronto Stock Exchange 1982–85; Chief Financial Offr., Dean Witter Reynolds (Canada) Inc. 1986–89; recreations: antique boating; clubs: Antique Boat Soc. (Past Pres.); Home: 80 Front St. E., Toronto, Ont. M5E 1T4; Office: Toronto-Dominion Centre, Toronto, Ont. M5K 1E7.

**BAILEY, Richard R.,** B.Sc.; association executive; b. Rouyn-Noranda, Que. 31 July 1938; s. Bernard Bruce and Francis Celia (McIver) B.; e. George William Coll. Chicago B.Sc. (Hons.) 1962; Harvard Univ., Adv. Mngt. Program 1991; m. Nancy d. Archie and Sara Carlyle 31 Aug. 1968; children: Coleen Nancy, Sean Bruce; PRESIDENT & CHIEF EXECUTIVE OFFICER, YMCA OF GREATER TORONTO 1992– ; Dir., Camping & Youth, YMCA of Edmonton 1964–66; Extve. Dir. 1966–69; Dir., Programs 1969–73; Gen. Sec., YMCA of Lethbridge 1973–78; Extve. Dir., Urban Group & Dir., Personnel Serv., YMCA Canada 1978–82; C.E.O., YMCA of Edmonton 1982–86; C.E.O., YMCA Canada 1986–91; C.E.O., YMCA Ont. 1992– ; Chair, Nat. Voluntary Orgns. 1990–92; Dir., Nat. Bd., YMCA Can. 1984–93; Vice Chair, YMCA Retirement Fund 1987–91; Pres., Student Union 1962; George Williams Coll. 1964;

Extve. Council, Royal York Rd. Un. Ch.; recreations: running, biking, reading; Home: 79 Glenaden Ave. E., Toronto, Ont. M8Y 2L5; Office: 15 Breadalbane St., Toronto, Ont. M4Y 1C2.

**BAILEY, Terence William,** Mus.Bac., M.F.A., Ph.D., F.R.S.C.; educator; music scholar; b. Toronto, Ont. 12 July 1937; s. James Alexander and Marie Azile (Gauvin) B.; e. Riverdale Coll. Inst.; Univ. of Toronto Mus.Bac. 1958; Princeton Univ. M.F.A. 1960; Univ. of Washington Ph.D. 1968; m. Kathryn Ann d. Elwood and Margaret Compton 12 Dec. 1964 (div. 1989); children: Gauvin Alexander, Sara Rebecca; PROF. OF MUSIC HIST. UNIV. OF W. ONT. 1978– ; Lectr. Univ. of Regina 1963–64; Asst. Prof., Assoc. Prof. Univ. of B.C. 1964–74; Assoc. Prof. present Univ. 1974, Chrmn. of Music Hist. 1975–85; author 'The Fleury Play of Herod' 1965; 'The Processions of Sarum and the Western Church' 1971; 'The Intonation Formulas of Western Chant' 1973; 'Commemoratio Brevis' 1979; 'The Ambrosian Alleluias' 1983; 'The Ambrosian Cantus' 1987; (with Paul Merkley) 'The Antiphons of the Ambrosian Office' 1989; (with Paul Merkley) 'The Melodic Tradition of the Ambrosian Office -Antiphons' 1990; 'Antiphon and Psalm in the Ambrosian Office' 1994; Home: 904 – 549 Ridout St. N., London, Ont. N6A 5N5; Office: London, Ont. N6A 3K7.

**BAILEY, William (Bruce) Currie,** B.A., LL.B., LL.M.; investment banker and lawyer; b. Toronto, Ont. 14 Mar. 1953; s. William Henry Currie and Jessie Lindsay (Browning) B.; e. Queen's Univ., B.A. (Hons.) 1976; Dalhousie Univ., LL.B. 1979; called to Ont. Bar 1980; Columbia Univ., LL.M. 1987; m. Gillian d. John and Patricia MacKay 15 Aug. 1981; one s. Sam; OF COUNSEL, GROVER T. WICKERSHAM, ATTORNEYS AT LAW, Palo Alto, CA; articled clerk, Leonard Kitz of Kitz, Matheson 1978; Osler, Hoskin & Harcourt 1979–80; Solr., Osler, Hoskin & Harcourt 1980–82, 1984–86; Acting Legal Adv., Ont. Securities Comn. 1983; Dir., Bailey & Co. Inc.; Sanderling Ventures Limited; Zeta Music Systems, Inc.; Hague Acad. of Internat. Law Scholarship 1979 and 1987 (declined); Pres., Dalhousie Law Sch. Alumni Assn. (S. Ont.) 1982–87; Dir., Jessie's Ctr. for Teenagers 1986–87; The Law Inst. of the Pacific Rim 1982–86; jour. contbr.; recreations: horses, art, opera; Club: The Dog; Home: 74 Willcocks St., Toronto, Ont. M5S 1C8; Office: #550 - 300 Hamilton Ave., Palo Alto CA 94301-2542.

**BAILIE, Warren R.;** officer of the legislature; b. York Co., Ont. 4 Dec. 1928; s. Samuel Robert and Ethel Lile (Atkins) B.; e. Vaughan Rd. C.I.; Ryerson Inst. of Technol.; m. Elizabeth d. John and Edith Whaley 14 May 1949; children: Lynda Dianne, Warren Robert Jr., Samuel Randall, Brian James, Catherine Anne; CHIEF ELECTION OFFICER OF ONTARIO 1982– ; Federal Returning Offr. 1958–65; Prov. Returning Offr. 1966–75; Asst. to Chief Election Offr. 1974–76; Asst. Chief Election Offr. 1977–81; Sec., Counc. on Govt. Ethics Laws 1981–82; Comnr., Election Finan. Comn. 1982– ; Vice-Chrmn., Electoral Bound. Comn. of Ont. 1983–85; Official Candn. Observer, Zimbabwe Elections 1979; El Salvador 1984; Guatamela 1985; U.N. Supvr., Namibia Elections 1990; U.N. election survey team in Cambodia 1991; Official Candn. Observer, Ethiopian Elections 1992; Observer, Provincial Council Elections, Sri Lanka 1993; Observer, Malawi's first national referendum 1993; Partner, Publishing & Printing Co. 1958–64; Pres., Roberts-Bailie Lithographing Co. 1964–70; Vice-Pres., Carbon-Set Forms Co. Ltd. 1964–70; Ont. Rep., Candn. C. of C. 1970–72; Trustee, Vaughan Twp. Area Sch. Bd. 1960–67 (Vice-Chrmn. 1965–66; Chrmn. 1967); York Co. Bd. of Edn. 1968–75; Chrmn., York So. Reg. Edn. Comn. 1966; Mem., Thornhill Presbyn. Ch.; AF & AM # 54 Vaughan Lodge; L.O.L. # 28 Woodbridge Lodge; Irish Regiment of Canada Veterans Assoc.; Candn. Assn. of Veterans in United Nations Peace-Keeping; co-author of 4 articles; recreations: hiking, fishing; Office: 51 Rolark Dr., Scarborough, Ont. M1R 3B1.

**BAILLIE, A. Charles, Jr.,** B.A., M.B.A.; bank executive; b. Orillia, Ont. 20 Dec. 1939; s. A. Charles and Jean (Gibson) B.; e. Trinity Coll., Univ. of Toronto, B.A. (Hons.) 1962; Harvard Grad. Sch. of Bus. Admin., M.B.A. 1964; Fellow, Inst. of Candn. Bankers 1967; m. Marilyn Jane d. Charles E. and Audrey J. Michener 25 June 1965; children: Charles, Matthew, Jonathan, Alexandra; VICE CHAIRMAN, CORPORATE & INVESTMENT BANKING GROUP, THE TORONTO DOMINION BANK 1992– ; Co-Chrmn.: TD Securities Inc.; Toronto Dominion Securities (USA) Inc.; Pres.: TD Mortgage Corp.; Dir.: Green Line Investor Serv. Inc.; TD Australia Limited; Aetna Life Insur. Co. of Can.; Aetna Casualty & Surety Co. of Can.; Bd. of Govs., Treasurer & Chrmn. Finance & Audit Cttee., Shaw Festival; Mem., Finan. Ctte. & Investment Sub-Ctte., Nat. Cancer Inst.; Mem., Corp. of Trinity Coll.; Hon. Treasurer, St. George's College Bldg. Fund; Clubs: The Toronto Club Limited; Badminton & Racquet Club, Toronto; University Club (N.Y.); Office: 55 King St. W. & Bay St., 7th Fl., TD Tower, Toronto, Ont. M5K 1A2.

**BAILLIE, Duncan,** B.Com.; investment executive; b. Timmins, Ont. 14 Nov. 1941; s. Robert Thomas and Mina (Hulf) B.; e. Univ. of Toronto Schs.; Univ. of Toronto B.Com. 1965; m. Alexandra Dover 26 Oct 1984; three s. (prev. marr.) Robert, Peter, Paul; PRES., O'DONNELL INVESTMENT MANAGEMENT 1993– ; joined Bank of Canada, Ottawa 1965–67; Invest. Offr. Canadian Imperial Bank of Commerce 1967, Special Asst. to Chief Gen. Mgr. 1971–72; Sr. Portfolio Mgr. Canada Trust Co. 1972, Mgr. Fixed Income Invests. & Econ. 1974, Vice Pres. and Treas. 1978; Vice Pres., Investments and Treas., Victoria and Grey Trust Co. Ltd. 1981–84; Extve. Vice-Pres. – Investments, The National Trust Co. 1984–88; Partner, Laurentian Investment Management 1990–92; Sr. Vice-Pres. & Chief Investment Offr., Ondaatje Managed Investments 1992–93; Phi Gamma Delta; United Church; recreations: skiing, tennis; Home: R.R. 2, Caledon East, Ont. L0N 1E0.

**BAILLIE, James Cameron,** B.A., LL.B., LL.M., Q.C.; lawyer; b. Toronto, Ont. 6 Aug. 1938; s. Donald Ross and Jean Elizabeth (Cameron) B.; e. Upper Can. Coll.; Univ. of Toronto B.A., LL.B. 1961; Harvard Univ. LL.M. 1964; called to Bar of Ont. 1963; cr. Q.C. 1977; PARTNER, TORY, TORY, DESLAURIERS & BINNINGTON, TORONTO 1980– ; Assoc. present firm 1963–77; Chrmn. Ont. Securities Comn. 1978–80; Dir.: Continental Bank of Canada; FPI Ltd.; Manufacturers Life Insurance Co.; Midland Walwyn Inc.; Clubs: University (Toronto); National (Toronto); York (Toronto); Home: 35 Church St., Ste. 816, Toronto, Ont. M5E 1T3; Office: 3000, PO Box 270, Aetna Tower, Toronto-Dominion Centre, Toronto, Ont. M5K 1N2.

**BAIN, George Charles Stewart;** journalist; b. Toronto, Ont. 29 Jan. 1920; s. William Stewart and Mary (Ross) B.; e. pub. and high schs. Toronto; Carleton Univ. (Honorary) Litt.D. 1983; Univ. of King's Coll. (Honorary) D.C.L. 1986; m. Marion Jene Breakey 16 Dec. 1944; one s. Christopher George Stewart; Freelance columnist, Macleans magazine (Media Watch); former Gen. reporter & City Hall Reporter, Toronto Telegram; Gen. reporter, City Hall, Provincial Affairs, National Affairs reporter and columnist, correspondent London and Washington, The Globe and Mail; Editorial Page Editor, European correspondent, Ottawa columnist, Toronto Star; served with RCAF W.W. II, pilot: #6 (Cdn) Bomber Group; author 'I've Been Around, and Around, And Around' 1964; 'Nursery Rhymes to be Read Aloud by Young Parents with Old Children' 1965; 'A Guide to Canadian Parliamentary Procedure' 1970; 'Champagne is for Breakfast' 1972; 'Letters from Lilac' 1979; mem. Un. Services Inst.; recreation: gardening; Address: Oakland, R.R. 2, Mahone Bay, N.S. B0J 2E0.

**BAIN, Richard Anthony,** Q.C.; lawyer; b. Toronto, Ont. 22 Mar. 1942; s. Alexander Elias and Ruth Lynn (Baker) B.; e. Michigan State Univ., B.A. Hons. (magna cum laude) 1965; Univ. Toronto Law Sch., LL.B. (magna cum laude) 1968; cr. Q.C. 1982; m. Harriet, d. Ruby and Molly Wohl 3 Oct. 1991; children: Vanessa Ellen; H. David; PARTNER, FOGLER, RUBINOFF; Dir., Dynacare Inc.; Jewish; Home: 406 Vesta Dr., Toronto, Ont. M5P 3A5; Office: Ste. 4400, P.O. Box 95, Royal Trust Tower, Toronto-Dominion Centre, Toronto, Ont. M5K 1G8.

**BAINES, William Douglas,** B.Sc., M.S., Ph.D.; mechanical engineer; university professor; b. Edmonton, Alta. 11 Feb. 1926; s. Cyril John Douglas and Mary Winifred (Neale) B.; e. Univ. of Alta., B.SC. (Engn. Physics) 1947; Univ. of Iowa, M.S. 1948, Ph.D. 1950; m. Alaine Mae, d. Arthur Holmes Barrett, Peekskill, N.Y., 10 Aug. 1950; children: Ian Douglas, Janice Linell, Ross Barrett, Marc Douglas; PROF. OF MECH. ENGN., UNIV. OF TORONTO since 1966 and Chrmn. of that Dept. 1971–76; Fellow, Massey College; Asst. Prof. of Civil Engn., Mich. State Univ. 1950–51; Research Offr., Nat. Research Council 1951–59; Head of Hydraulics Lab. 1954–59; joined present Univ. as Assoc. Prof. of Mech. Engn. 1959–66; Acting Dean of Grad. Studies 1970–71; Acting Dir., Sch. of Continuing Studies 1985–87; Associate, Kings Engineering Associates Ltd.; mem. Gloucester Twp. Sch. Bd. 1957–59; mem. Bd. of Govs., Ont. Inst. for Studies in Educ. 1978–83; rec'd J.C. Stevens Award, Am. Soc. Civil Engs. 1953; author of over 60 papers in scient. and engn. journs.; mem. Assn. Prof. Engrs. Ont.; Internat. Assn. Hydraulic Research; Internat. Union Theoretical & Applied Mech.; Lambda Chi Alpha; Anglican; recreations: skiing, swimming, sketching, hiking; Home: 1675 Wedmore Way, Mississauga, Ont. L5J 2J7; Office: 5 King's College Rd., Toronto, Ont. M5S 1A4.

**BAIRD, Charles F.,** B.A.; executive; b. Southampton, N.Y. 4 Sept. 1922; s. George White B.; e. Middlebury (Vt.) Coll., B.A. 1944; New York Univ. Grad. Sch. of Business Adm.; Advanced Mang. Program, Harvard Univ. Grad. Sch. of Business Adm.; m. Norma Adele White; children: Susan F., Stephen W., Charles F. Jr., Nancy W.; Former Dir., Inco Ltd.; Bank of Montreal; Aetna Life & Casualty Co.; Trustee, Logistics Management Inst.; Bd. Chrmn., Center for Naval Analyses; Financial Extve., Standard Oil Co. of New Jersey 1948–65 (Depy. European Financial Rep., London, 1955–58; Asst. Treas. 1958–62; Dir. and mem. Extve. Comte. Esso Standard S.A. Française, Paris, 1962–65); Asst. Secy. (Financial Mang.) U.S. Navy 1965–67; Under Secy. of the Navy 31 July 1967–20 Jan. 1969; Vice Pres. Finance, Inco Ltd. 1969–74, Sr. Vice Pres. 1974–76, Vice Chrmn. 1976–77, Pres. 1977–80, Chrmn. & C.E.O. 1980–87; served U.S. Marine Corps 1943–46, 1951–52 (Capt.); mem., Council on Foreign Relations; Trustee, Bucknell Univ.; Clubs: Chevy Chase, (Washington, D.C.); Maidstone (East Hampton, N.Y.); Bridgehampton (N.Y.); International Lawn Tennis Club; Home: 4423 Boxwood Rd., Bethesda, MD 20816 and Bullhead Lane, Bridgehampton, N.Y. 11932.

**BAIRD, David Carr,** Ph.D.; scientist; educator; b. Edinburgh, Scotland 6 May 1928; s. David and Jessie (Rule) B.; e. Univ. of Edinburgh B.Sc. 1949; Univ. of St. Andrews Ph.D. 1953; m. Margaret, d. Dr. William and Mary Sheridan 27 Dec. 1954; children: David Bruce; Michael Andrew; Christopher Sheridan; Jennifer Mary; PROFESSOR OF PHYSICS, ROYAL MILITARY COLLEGE; conducting ongoing research in archaeological sci. and cryogenic engrg.; participated in archaeological excavations, U.K. and Ont., 1947–53; Correspondent, Ordnance Survey, Ancient Monuments Div., U.K. 1950–52; joined present institution 1952 as Instr., Dept. of Physics; Lectr. 1954; Asst. Prof. 1955; Assoc. Prof. 1958; Prof. 1965; Head of Dept. 1972–78; Dean of Science 1980–90; Visiting Prof., Univ. of St. Andrews 1966–67; Exchange Prof., Royal Mil. Coll. of Sci., England 1979–80; Visiting Scientist, Lab. for Archaeological Sci. and the Hist. of Art, Oxford Univ. 1980– ; conducted research in low temperature Physics 1949– ; mem. Candn. Assn. of Physicists (Chrmn. of Lectures 1964–66; Councillor and Chrmn. Physics Educ. 1975–77; Chrmn. Physics & Soc. 1980–81); active in science educ. with Ont. Min. of Educ.; author 'Experimentation' 1962, 2nd ed. 1987; co-author 'Physics of Engineering Solids' 1963; 'Electrical Experiences' 1972; charter mem. Kingston Symphony Assn. (Dir. 1955); founding mem. Kingston Film Soc.; founding mem. and first Pres., Kingston Choral Soc. (1953–55); Fellow, Soc. of Antiquaries of Scotland; mem. Amer. Assn. for the Advancement of Sci.; recreations: music; old books; ancient history and archaeology; mythology and history of religion; Home: 46 Watts Cres., Kingston, Ont. K7M 2P3; Office: Royal Military College, Kingston, Ont. K7K 5L0.

**BAIRD, David McCurdy,** O.C., Ph.D., D.Sc., F.R.S.C. (1958); geologist; b. Fredericton, N.B. 28 July 1920; e. Univ. N.B., B.Sc. 1941; Univ. Rochester, M.Sc. 1943; McGill Univ., Ph.D. 1947; D.Sc.: Memorial Univ. 1972; Univ. of N.B. 1973; LL.D.: Univ. of Calgary 1985; MUSEUMS CONSULTANT & DIR., RIDEAU CANAL MUSEUM Smiths Falls, Ont. 1986– ; Teach. Asst., Univ. of Rochester 1941–43; Demonst., McGill Univ. 1943–46 and Lectr., Dawson Coll. there, summer session 1947; Asst. Prof. of Geol., Mount Allison Univ. 1946–47 and Univ. of N.B. 1947–50; Assoc. Prof. 1950–52; Prov. Geol. for Nfld., 1952–58; Prof. of Geol., Memorial Univ. of Nfld. 1953–54; Head of Dept. and mem. of Univ. Senate 1954–58; Prof. of Geol. and Chrmn. of Dept., Univ. of Ottawa 1958–66; Secy., Faculty of Science and mem. of Senate 1960–62; prof. and field experience incl. N.B. Dept. of Mines., Geol. Survey of Can., Geol. Survey of Nfld. 1939–66; mem. and Chrmn., Pub. Sch. Bd., Township of Gloucester, 1960–66; Dir., Nat. Museum of Science and Tech. 1966–81; Dir, Tyrell Museum of Palaeontology 1981–86; has appeared on nat. radio and T.V. programs; rec'd. Past Pres.' Medal of Candn. Inst. Mining and Metall. 1965; author of guidebooks to geol. and scenery of Nat. Parks of Can.; mem., Geol. Assn. Can. (Councillor 1956–58); Candn. Inst. Mining & Metall. (Chrmn., Nfld. Br. 1954–55; Councillor 1955–57); Am. Assn. Advance. Science.; Nat. Assn. Geol. Teachers; Candn. Museums Assn.; Nat. Adv. Comte. on Research in Geol. Sciences 1953–58; Secy.,

Geol. Sec., Royal Soc. Can. 1960–63 (winner of Barlow Award 1970); Massey Medal, Royal Candn. Geographic Soc. 1986; Officer, Order of Canada 1986; Office: 9 Glen Abbey Cres., Stittsville, Ont. K2S 1R6.

**BAIRD, Donald Alexander,** B.A., M.S.; librarian; archivist; screenwriter; b. Edmonton, Alta. 29 Jan. 1926; s. Alexander and Elizabeth Morrison (Thompson) B.; e. Univ. of B.C., B.A. 1950; Columbia Univ., M.S. 1951; Pub. Arch. of Can. certificate, 1978; m. Sydney Irene, d. late Sydney Thompson Barlow, 18 May 1957; children: Alexis Rawlings, Brenan Thompson; HONORARY UNIVERSITY ARCHIVIST, SIMON FRASER UNIV. 1991– ; Cataloguer, Vancouver Pub. Lib. 1951–54; Head, Cataloguing Dept., Victoria Pub. Lib. 1954–57 and Univ. of Alta. 1957–60; Asst. Lib., Univ. of Alta. Libraries 1960–64, Alta. Lib. Bd. Mem. 1959–1962, Chrmn. 1963–64; Univ. Librarian, Simon Fraser Univ. 1964–77; Univ. Archivist, Simon Fraser Univ. 1978–91; Dir. of Public Hist. there 1980–83, and Adjunct Prof. of Hist. 1981–84; rec'd Can. Medal; co-author 'The English Novel, 1578–1956' 1958; 'The English Novel, 1578–1956' 1974; 'Canadian University Archives Survey' 1975; 'Canadian University Archives Survey, 1980'; 'Proposed Standards for Canadian University and College Archives' 1983; 'Canadian University Archives Survey, 1985' 1987; joint producer 'A Manual for Small Archives' 1988; 'A Handbook for Records Management and College Archives' 1989; author, 'Jump for the Gold' (screenplay) 1991; 'On Account' (screenplay) 1991; 'Museums' (screenplay) 1992; 'The Red Haired Man' (screenplay) 1992; 'Bricks and Mortar' (Teleplay) 1992; 'Chicken, Chicken' (Teleplay) 1993; 'The Lion of Summer' (screenplay) 1993; Other writings incl. articles in prof. journs.; mem. Assn. of B.C. Archivists (Pres. 1982–83; Ed. 1983–84; Chair, Educ. Ctte. 1985–86; Chair, Archives Manual Ctte. 1987–88); Assn. of Candn. Archivists (Chair, Univ. and College Archivists 1979–83); Univ. Archives Survey Ctte. (Chair, 1984–87); Task Force for College Archives (Chair) 1986–89; Soc. of Archivists; Soc. of Amer. Archivists; Candn. Assn. Univ. Teachers; NDP; recreations: gardening, golf; Home: 3052 Armada St., Port Coquitlam, B.C. V3C 3S3.

**BAIRD, George,** B.Arch.; architect; educator; b. Toronto, Ont. 25 Aug. 1939; s. George Charles and Gertrude Mary (Baines) B.; e. Toronto B.Arch. 1962; postgrad. rsch. Univ. Coll., London, Eng. 1964–67; m. Elizabeth Carol d. Frank and Olive Davis 20 Dec. 1963; Prof. of Architecture, Univ. of Toronto 1968–92; Acting Chrmn. Dept. of Architecture, Univ. of Toronto 1983–85; Prof. of Architecture, Harvard Univ. 1992–93; Partner Baird/Sampson Architects 1968–91; Curator Architecture Sec. Okanada 1978–80; Ed. Trace Magazine 1979–80; author: 'Alvar Aalto' 1969; co-ed. 'Meaning in Architecture' 1968; Fellow, Royal Arch. Inst. of Can.; Home: 20 Elgin Ave., Toronto, Ont. M5R 1G6; Office: 35 Brilain St., Toronto, Ont. M5A 1R7.

**BAIRD, John D.,** M.A., Ph.D.; university professor; b. Glasgow, Scotland 9 May 1941; s. Gerald Fortay and Easter (Clifton) B.; e. Larchfield School, Helensburgh; Merchiston Castle Sch., Edinburgh; St. Andrews Univ. M.A. 1963; McMaster Univ. M.A. 1964; Princeton Univ. M.A. 1967, Ph.D. 1970; m. Eileen d. Albert and Melba Coumont 31 May 1975; children: three daughters; PROF. OF ENGLISH LITERATURE, VICTORIA COLLEGE & UNIV. OF TORONTO 1981– ; joined present univ. 1967; Dir. of Grad. Studies 1985–89; Assoc. Dean, Humanities, Sch. of Grad. Studies 1992– ; Co-editor: 'The Poems of William Cowper' 1980– ; author of various articles and reviews in learned journals; recreations: music; Office: Victoria Coll., Univ. of Toronto, Toronto, Ont. M5S 1K7.

**BAIRD, Keith Alexander,** B.A.; publisher; b. Kitchener, Ont. 19 Aug. 1925; s. James Roy and Myrtle Adelaide (Waldron) B.; e. Univ. of W. Ont. B.A. 1949; m. Constance Mary d. Benjamin Franklin Hamel 5 Aug. 1949; one d. Judith Leigh Yormak; Publisher, Kitchener-Waterloo Record Ltd. 1975–90; joined Co. 1949, Asst. Publisher 1969, Vice Pres. 1971; served with RCN 1942–45; contrib. 'Historic Heights' 1967; recipient W. Ont. Press Awards 1967, 1969, 1972, 1974; Chairperson, W. Ont. Newspaper Awards; formerly: Chrmn. Extve. Comte., The Presbyterian Record; mem., Candn. Daily Newspaper Publishers Assn. (former Chrmn.); Candn. Press (Dir.); Internat. Press Inst. (Candn. Dir.); Commonwealth Press Union; Ont. Press Council; Presbyterian; recreation: power-boating; Clubs: Toronto Press; Westmount Golf & Country (Kitchener); Home: 429 St. Leger St., Kitchener, Ont. N2H 4M8.

**BAIRD, Patricia Ann,** B.Sc., M.D., C.M., F.R.C.P.(C), F.C.C.M.G.; professor; b. Lancashire, England; d. Harold and Winifred Cainen Holt; e. Queen Mary Sch. for Girls, Lytham, Lancashire; McGill Univ. B.Sc. 1959; M.D., C.M. 1963; D.Sc. (hon. causa), McMaster Univ. 1991; D.Univ. (hon. causa), Univ. of Ottawa 1991; Order of B.C. 1992; m. Robert Merrifield Baird 22 Feb. 1964; children: Jennifer Ellen, Brian Merrifield, Bruce Andrew; PROFESSOR OF MEDICAL GENETICS, UNIVERSITY OF B.C. 1982– ; Head, Dept. of Medical Genetics, Univ. of B.C. 1979–89; Head, Depts. of Med. Genetics, Grace Hosp. and Children's Hosp. of B.C. 1981–89, University Hospital 1986–89; Intern, Royal Victoria Hosp. 1963–64; Pediatric Resident Vancouver Gen. Hosp. 1964–68; Instr. in Pediatrics, Div. of Med. Genetics 1968; Asst. Prof. of Med. Genetics present univ. 1972; Assoc. Prof. 1977; Dept. Head 1979; Acting Dir., Centre for Molecular Genetics there 1982–87; Bd. of Gov. Univ. of B.C. 1984–90; author numerous scientific articles on genetics; Dir. Candn. Coll. of Med. Geneticists 1982–86 (Vice-Pres. 1984–85); Med. Cons., Health Surveillance Registry of B.C. 1977–90; mem. Nat. Consultative Ctte. on Epidemiology of Mental Retardation 1984–86; Chrmn., Genetics Grant Ctte., Medical Rsch. Counc. of Can. 1983–87; Mem., Med. Rsch. Counc. of Can. 1987–90; Mem., Nat. Adv. Bd. on Science & Technology to Fed. Govt. 1987–91; Co-Chair, National Forum of Science & Technology Councils 1991; Vice Pres., Candn. Inst. for Advanced Rsch. 1991– ; Mem., Sci. Counc. of Can., Study Ctte. on genetic predisposition 1987–90; Ethics Panel, Internat. Pediatric Assn. 1990–95; Mem., Adv. Bd., Genetic Epidemiology 1991–94; YWCA Woman of Distinction Award 1988; Chairperson, Royal Comn. on New Reproductive Technologies 1989–93; Bd. of B.C. Medical Services Found. 1984–90; Royal Coll. of Physicians & Surgeons of Can.; Am. Soc. of Human Genetics; Western Soc. for Pediatric Rsch.; Genetics Soc. of Can.; recreations: skiing, gardening, bicycling; Office: 226–6174 University Blvd., Vancouver, B.C. V6T 1Z3.

**BAIRD, Ronald A.,** A.O.C.A., R.C.A.; sculptor; b. Toronto, Ont. 29 Mar. 1940; s. Cyril and Nellie (Arnott) B.; e. Art Coll. of Ont., A.O.C.A. 1964; m. Lynda M. d. Ross and Virginia Hunt, 4 Aug. 1977; children: Emory, Zachary, Melissa, Patrick, Jessie; works: Dragon Tree and Gazebo, Casa Loma, Toronto; Sculptural Memorial, Science North, Sudbury, Ont.; Bell Tower, Uxbridge, Ont.; Spirit Catcher, Barrie, Ont.; Sea Monster, Horseshoe Valley, Ont.; Spirit Catcher III, Uxbridge, Ont.; Carillon Tower, St. John's Church, Oakville; Kinetic Outdoor Sculpture, Church of the Good Shepherd, Scarborough; two major works, Expo '86; Rivera Park, Kinetic Mobile, Lindsay, Ont.; Philco-Ford, Park Sculpture, Markham, Ont.; Lyndhurst Hosp., Kinetic Sculpture, Toronto, Ont.; Bell Canada, Atrium Mobile, Scarborough, Ont.; Bronze Flower, Garden Sculpture, Manhattan, N.Y.; Winter Fountain, Waterfront, Sarnia, Ont. 1990; Icon Design for ICOMM, Brantford, Ont.; Mural, Newmarket Town Office, Newmarket, Ont.; Garden Sculpture, Valhalla Inn, Markham, Ont.; Creature Design for feature film; West Park Hosp., Recognition Rainbow, Toronto; Garden Screen, Seller's Residence, Toronto; Spiral of Sharing (Donor Recognition Piece), Markham Stouffville Hosp. 1990; Entrance Doors, Beth Sholom Synagogue, Toronto 1991; Donor Mural, Markham Stouffville Hosp. 1991; Garden Sculpture (Donor Recognition Piece), St. Peter's Hosp., Hamilton, Ont. 1992; Crucifix, Cardinal Carter Chapel 1992; Design for Wall Mural, Legislature, Yellowknife, N.W.T. 1993; Tibetan Dream Pony, Interasia Trading Co., New York, NY; Donor Recognition Dream Ship Sculpture & Key People Mural Oakville Centennial Memorial Hosp., Oakville, Ont. 1993; Sculpture Pergola for Gerome Markson Architect, Cabbagetown, Toronto 1994; has been collaborating on projects with Lynda Baird since 1986; approx. 100 major works over 30 years; numerous books and prints (etchings); graphics for C.B.C.; 30–min. film for O.E.C.A. 'Ron Baird's Friendship Shape'; Sculptor in Residence, Univ. of Toronto 1965–66; Seneca Coll. 1970; Lectr., Univ. of Toronto, Sch. of Architecture; recreations: skiing, sailing, kayaking; Address: R.R. #3, Stouffville, Ont. L4A 7X4.

**BAIRD, Ronald J.,** B.Sc., M.D., M.S., F.R.C.S.(C), F.A.C.S.; b. Toronto, Ont. 3 May 1930; s. Robert Whitney and Mary Agnes (Williamson) B.; e. Univ. of Toronto M.D. 1954, B.Sc. 1956, M.S. 1964; F.R.C.S.(C), Gen. Surg. 1959, Cardiovascular & Thoracic Surg. 1964; m. Fern E. d. Roy and Fern Sarles 23 July 1955; children: Ronald, Fraser, Catherine; SR. CARDIOVASCULAR SURGEON, TORONTO GEN. HOSP.; PROF. OF SURGERY, UNIV. OF TORONTO 1973– ; Head, Cardio. Surg., Toronto West. Hosp. 1972–77; Dir. of Rsch., Dept. of Surg., Univ. of Toronto 1972–77; Head, Div. of Cardio. Surg., Univ. of Toronto and Toronto Gen. Hosp. 1977–87; Pres., Candn. Cardio. Soc. 1976–78; Candn. Soc. of Cardio. & Thor. Surg. 1982–83; Internat. Soc. for Cardio. Surg. 1988–89; described new methods of revascularization of heart, kidneys & legs; performed first heart transplants in Toronto 1968; world's first heart-lung bypass with new anticoagulant from snake venom 1988; several past extve. & advisory posts; Royal Coll. of Surg. Medal in Surg. 1969; Gold Medal, Univ. of Toronto 1954; Lister Award in Surg. 1964; Hon. Guest Lectr., Japanese Soc. for Thor. Surg. 1985; Hon. Dir., Candn. Soc. for Egyptian Antiquities; Hon. Mem., Southern Assoc. for Vascular Surgery; Maritime Vascular Soc.; Tulane Surgical Assn.; Bd. of Dir., Ont. Heart & Stroke Found.; Candn. Heart Found.; author of over 200 sci. papers & book chaps.; Ed. Bd., 'Review of Surgery' 1977–91, 'Journal of Vascular Surgery' 1984– ;and Can. J. Surgery, Surgery, & Journal of Thoracic & Cardiovascular Surgery 1965–82; recreations: family, fishing, skiing; Club: York; Home: 72 Clarendon Ave., Toronto, Ont. M4V 1J3; Office: Eaton 14N–224, Toronto, Ont. M5G 2C4.

**BAIRSTOW, Frances,** B.S.; professor; arbitrator; b. Racine, Wis. 19 Feb. 1920; d. William Kanevsky and Minnie (Dubow); e. Univ. of Wis. B.S. 1942; m. David S. s. William Bairstow 17 Dec. 1954; children: Dale Owen, David Anthony; Dir., Industrial Rlns. Centre and Prof. of Labour Rlns., Faculty of Mgmt., McGill Univ. until 1985; concurrently arbitrator of ad hoc labour disputes since 1964; consultant, prodn. of labour-mgmt. films, Nat. Film Bd. of Can. 1955–75; cons., labour-mgmt. films, Australian Film Unit 1969–70; Chrmn. Govt. of Can. Fed. Inquiry Comn. on structure of bargaining in airlines, airports, grain handling 1978; Cons. on European bargaining structures, Orgn. for Econ. Coop. and Devel., Paris, France 1979; Rsch. Econ. Candn. Pacific Railway, Montreal 1956–58; Chief, Wage Data Unit, Wage Stablization Bd., Washington, B.C. 1951–53; Labour Educ. Specialist, Univ. of Puerto Rico 1950–51; Rsch. Econ. U.S. Senate Labour Ctte., Washing, D.C. 1949–50; Visiting Prof. Univ. of New South Wales, Australia 1983; Mediator, Publ. Service Staff Relations Bd., Ottawa 1970–78; Essential Services Comnr. Prov. of Que. 1978; Mediator and Labour Disputes Facilitator, Air Can. and Assn. of Flight Attendants for Can. 1980–85; Special Master, Florida Public Employees Relations Comn. 1985–95; Mediator, Southern Bell Telephone & Communcations Workers of Am. 1985– ; Mediator, American Telephone & Telegraph Co. 1989– ; Arbitrator, United Airlines and Assoc. of Flight Attendants 1989– ; Arbitrator, State Univ. System of Florida 1990– ; Contrib. of columns on labour matters to Montreal Gazette; frequent speaker on labour relations issues to local and nat. radio and TV; author: 'Grievance Arbitration in U.S. & Canada' in Labour Arbitration Yearbook, Canada 1993; 'The Trend Toward Centralized Bargaining: A Patchwork Quilt of International Diversity' Columbia Jnl. of World Bus. 1985; (with Prof. L.B. Sayles) 'Bargaining over Work Standards by Professional Unions' 1975; 'Employment Security in Civil Aviation' 1977; 'Labour Relations in Quebec' Financial Times of London 1978; 'Rethinking Bargaining Structures' Labour Law Jnl. 1980; 'Avoiding Confrontation in Labour-Mgmt. Relations' 1982; mem. Nat. Acad. of Arbitrators 1972– ; (Gov. 1977–80; Prog. Chrmn. 1983, Vice Pres. 1986–88); Nat. Coordinator of Regions 1987–90; founding charter mem. Soc. for Profls. in Dispute Resolution 1964; Fulbright Scholar, Oxford Univ. 1953–54; mentioned in 'World's Who's Who of Women'; 'Who's Who in the South & Southwest'; 'Who's Who of American Women'; 'Two Thousand Notable Americans'; 'Who's Who in American Education'; 'Who's Who of Women in Canada' 1985; 'Foremost Women of the Twentieth Century' 1984; 'Most Admired Woman of the Decade'; recreations: travel, swimming, reading; Address: 1430 Gulf Blvd., #507, Clearwater, FL 34630.

**BAKAN, Joel Conrad,** B.A., LL.B., LL.M.; university professor; b. East Lansing, MI 13 May 1959p; s. Paul and Rita (Feierstein) B.; e. Eric Hamber S.S. 1977; Simon Fraser Univ. B.A. 1981; Univ. of Oxford B.A. 1983; Dalhousie Univ. LL.B. 1984; Harvard Univ. LL.M. 1986; m. Marlee Kline d. Carol and Terry Kline 10 Aug. 1986; ASSOC. PROF., FACULTY OF LAW, UNIV. OF B.C. 1990– ; Law Clerk to Chief Justice Brian Dickson, Supreme Court of Canada 1985; Student-at-Law, Gowling and Henderson 1986; Asst. Prof., Osgoode Hall Law Sch. 1987–90; Visiting Asst. Prof., Fac. of Law, Univ. of B.C. 1989–90; teaching specialty: constitutional law and theory; Rhodes Scholarship 1981; Governor General's Medal 1981; Killam Research Prize 1991; author of num. articles on Candn. constitutional law; recreations: music (jazz and rhythm & blues); Home: 3115 West 5th Ave., Vancouver, B.C. V6K 1V1; Office: 1822 East Mall, Vancouver, B.C. V6T 1Z1.

**BAKER, Barnaby John;** business owner; b. Andover, Eng. 11 June 1940; s. Sir John Wakeling and Katherine Hilary Margaret (Bonham-Carter) B.; e. Winchester Coll., U.K. 1953–58; Univ. of B.C., B.Sc. 1962; Harvard Univ. M.B.A. 1964; divorced; children: Alan G., Christropher M., Darcy T.; PRESIDENT, FACTOR FORMS LIMITED 1971– ; Pres., Erynall Holdings Ltd. 1977– ; Pres., LASART Services Inc. 1988– ; Res. Analyst, Eaton's of Canada 1964–65; Acct. Extve., McLaren Advertising 1965–66; Spitzer, Mills & Bates 1966–67; Mktg. Mgr., ABF Automated Business Forms 1967–69; Gen. Mgr., ABF (Western) 1969–71; Vice-Pres., Edmonton Concert Hall Found.; Dir., Edmonton Symphony Soc.; Shareholder, Edmonton Klondike Days Assn.; recreations: sailing, travel theatre; Home: 6815 – 95th Ave., Edmonton, Alta. T6B 1A9.

**BAKER, Bob,** B.F.A.; artistic director; b. Edmonton, Alta. 11 May 1952; s. Kenneth Edwin and Mabel Molly (Boyd) B.; e. Ross Shepherd High Sch. Edmonton 1970; Univ. of Alta. B.F.A. (Honours) 1974; ARTISTIC DIR. CANDN. STAGE CO. 1990– ; dancer Les Feux Follets 1974–75, toured Can. and U.S.A.; actor Stratford (Ont.) Festival Co. 1975–79; freelance dir./teacher Vancouver 1979–82; Artistic Dir. Phoenix Theatre, Edmonton 1982–87; freelance dir. Toronto, Vancouver, Calgary, Ottawa, Cleveland, Edinburgh, Boston 1987–90; teacher: Vancouver Community Coll. Langara Campus (acting/voice) 1979–82; Univ. of Alta. Drama Dept. 1982–83; Ryerson Theatre Sch. Toronto 1989–90; Bd. mem.: Profl. Assn. Candn. Theatres 1985–87, 1990– ; Toronto Theatre Alliance; P.A.I.S. Toronto; recipient Dora Mavor Moore Award (directing) 1987; co-author 'North Shore Live' play 1981; recreation: bicycling; Home: 11 Wilkins Ave., Toronto, Ont. M5A 3C2; Office: 26 Berkeley St., Toronto, Ont. M5A 2W3.

**BAKER, Bruce Earle,** D.Sc.; of U.E.L. descent; b. Stanbridge E., P.Q. 1 Aug. 1917; s. Harry Arnold and Blanche Vivian (Soule) B.; e. Bedford (P.Q.) High Sch., 1937; Fessenden Scholarship for Math. 1939; Bishop's Univ. B.Sc. 1940; Laval Univ. D.Sc. 1943; m. late Saxe Clare. d. Earl Currie Cornell, Stanbridge E., 22 May 1948; children: Peter Cornell, Susan Jane, Philip Bruce, Robert Saxe, Jeffrey Arnold; PROF. FACULTY OF AGRIC. MACDONALD COLL. OF McGILL UNIV., since 1964; Chrmn., Dept. Agric. Chem. 1972–76; began as Research Chemist, Mallinckrodt Chemicals, 1944–45; Monsanto Chemicals, 1945–46; Lectr. Agric. Chem., McGill Univ. 1946–48; Asst. Prof., 1948–57; Assoc. Prof. 1957–64; devel. methods of producing sulfanilythioureas; process for hydrolysis of proteins; author and co-author of more than 100 scient. articles on milk and seed proteins, protein hydrolysates, milk chemistry, pharmaceuticals, pollution of soil and water with pesticides and industrial chemicals, radioactive fallout in arctic and sub-arctic regions, constitution of milks from arctic animals, and forage preservation; consultant, Comet Confectionary, St. Hyacinthe, Que. and other food industries; Dir., Missisquoi Historical Soc.; Counsellor, Township of Stanbridge, Que.; Citizen of the Year Award 1992; mem., Nat. Dairy Council of Canada; Candn. Inst. Food Technol.; Am. Dairy Sc. Assn.; Am. Chem. Soc.; Candn. Inst. Chem.; Sigma Xi; Anglican; recreations: travel, farming, wine making, reading; Address: Stanbridge East, Qué. J0J 2H0.

**BAKER, Lt. Col. Charles;** executive; b. Toronto, Ont. 10 June 1920; s. late Charles Robert and late Frances Gladys (Stipe) B.; e. Upper Can. Coll., Toronto; Univ. of Toronto; m. Susanne Elizabeth, d. late Frederick Arthur Gaby; children: Charles, (Mrs.) Susanne Young; TRUSTEE, THE ONTARIO JOCKEY CLUB; CHRMN., CHARLES BAKER ADV. LTD; Dir., AGF Japan Fund Ltd.; AGF Money Market Fund; AGF Option Equity Fund; Canadian Trusteed Income Fund; AGF Special Fund Ltd.; American Growth Fund Ltd.; Canadian Security Growth Fund Ltd.; Canadian Gas and Energy Fund Ltd.; Corporate Investors, Ltd.; Corporate Investors Stock Fund Ltd.; Growth Equity Fund Ltd.; Hi Teck Fund Ltd.; Steward, Jockey Club of Canada; Dir. of Thoroughbred Racing Associations; member the Jockey Club, N.Y.; joined Candn. Armoured Corps, Gov. Gen.'s Horse Guards 1940; served overseas as Lt., Italy, France, Belgium and Holland; twice wounded; rank Lt. Col. on discharge; thrice Mentioned in Despatches; Trustee, Gov. Gen.'s Horse Guards; Past Pres. and mem. Extve. Comte. Royal Agric. Winter Fair; recreations: farming, thoroughbred horses; Clubs: Toronto; York; Toronto & North York Hunt; Home: Norcliffe Farms, R.R. 3, King, Ont L0G 1K0; Winter Residence: 12 Heronsnest, Sewell's Point, Stuart, Florida 34996; Office: P.O. Box 156, Rexdale, Ont. M9W 5L2.

**BAKER, Donald Noel,** B.A., A.M., Ph.D.; university professor and administrator; b. Vancouver, B.C. 24 Dec. 1936; s. Jack Sydney and Joyce Marie (Heap) B.; e. Univ. of B.C. B.A. (Hons.) 1958; Stanford Univ. A.M. 1960, Ph.D. 1965; m. Heather d. Grant and Luella McLeod; children: Janet, Noel, Carol; VICE-PRESIDENT, ACADEMIC & PROF. OF HISTORY, WILFRID LAURIER UNIVERSITY 1989– ; Instructor, History, Stanford Univ. 1962–65; Asst., then Assoc. Prof., History, Michigan State Univ. 1965–70; Assoc. Prof. of History, Univ. of Waterloo 1970–80; Trustee, Waterloo County Bd. of Education 1972–74, 1978–80; Pres., Mount Royal College 1980–89; Chair, Council of Pres., Public Colleges of Alta. 1984–86; Chair, Steering Ctte., Joint Planning Council, Presidents of Universities and Colleges of Alta. 1984–86; Dir., Sec. to the Bd., Candn. Ctr. for Learning Systems 1984–89; Adv. Bd., Calgary Econ. Devel. Authority 1982–89; Bd. of Dirs., Big Country Edn. Consortium 1981–84; Candn. Assn. of Youth Orchestras 1980–83; Calgary United Way 1984–87; Calgary Consortium for Tourism and Hospitality Studies 1987–89; Steering Ctte., Calgary Tourism Adv. Bd. 1988–89; Counc. of Ont. Universities' Standing Ctte. on College-University Relations 1991– ; COU Task Force on a Distance Educ. Network 1991–92; coordinator, COU study of credit transfer among Ont. universities 1991–92; author: numerous articles in French history; co-editor: 'Landmarks in Western Culture: Commentaries and Controversies,' 2 vols. 1968; co-editor: 'The Making of Frenchmen: Current Directions in the History of Education in France, 1679–1979' 1980; Fellow, National Humanities Foundation 1967–68; Canada Council Leave Fellowship 1976–77; recipient of grants from the Canada Council, Social Sciences and Humanities Rsch. Council, Am. Philosophical Soc., and Social Science Rsch. Council; Home: 528 Colonial Dr., Waterloo, Ont. N2K 1Z6; Office: Waterloo, Ont. N2K 3C5.

**BAKER, Eric E.,** B.Sc., M.Sc.; business executive; b. Spencerville, Ont. 27 Aug. 1933; s. Herman E. and Flora (Shannon) B.; e. Queen's Univ. B.Sc. 1956; M.I.T. M.Sc. 1958; m. Ann d. Thomas Relyea 1 July 1955; children: Rebecca, Charles, Melanie; PRESIDENT, MIRALTA CAPITAL INC. 1992– ; Chrmn., Alta Genetics Inc., Calgary; Biomira Inc., Edmonton; Intertape Polymer Inc.; Dir., Hands Fireworks Inc.; Moneysworth & Best Corp.; R & M Metals Inc.; Proj. Engineer, Cities Service Oil Co. Ltd., Oakville 1958–59; Bus. Mgr. (Plastics) & Operations Mgr. (Plastics and Chemicals Union Carbide Can. 1959–71; Kauser, Lowenstein & Meade Ltd. and Innocan Investments Ltd. 1972–83; Chrmn., AES Data Ltd. 1978–79; Pres., Sentrol Systems Ltd. (portfolio holding of Innocan) 1975; Pres., Altamira Capital Corp. 1984–92; United Church; recreations: breeding race horses, outdoor activities, collecting antique carriages; Home: Robin Rd., Long Sault, Ont. K0C 1P0; Office: 475 Dumont Ave., Ste. 300, Dorval, Qué. H9S 9Z7.

**BAKER, Frank P.;** wallcovering company executive; b. London, Eng. 29 Jan. 1929; s. Frank P., M.B.E. and E.A. (McDermott) B.; came to Can. 1968; e. St. Peters Sch., York, Eng.; Royal Mil. Acad., Sandhurst, Eng., grad. 1948; m. Anne, d. A. Gilmour, C.M.G. June 1957; div. 1983; children: Francis, Catherine; m. 2ndly Gillian Dupre, June 1984; CHRMN. & C.E.O., INTERNATIONAL WALLCOVERINGS LTD.; CHRMN., I. LAPPIN WALLCOVERINGS INC., Wayne, Pa.; Chrmn., Decorlux Ltd., Montreal; commenced with Pinchin Johnson Paints, Eng., Far East Rep. 1955–58; Mang. Dir. Shalimar Paints Ltd., India 1958–68; Pres. & Mng. Dir. of Roxalin of Can. 1968–86; joined International Paints Canada Ltd. as Extve. Vice-Pres. and Dir., at amalg. with Roxalin of Canada Ltd. 1969; Pres. and Mang. Dir. 1971–83; retired as Depy. Chrmn. & Pres. 1986; Pres. & Chrmn., Internat. Wallcoverings Manufacturing Assoc., Brussels 1989–90; with Brit. Regular Army 1946–55; retired 1955, rank of Capt.; Anglican; recreations: polo, fencing, hunting, golf; Club: Oriental (London, Eng.); Home: RR #2, Erin, Ont. N0B 1T0; Office: 151 East Dr., Brampton, Ont. L6T 1B0.

**BAKER, Fred L.,** B.A.; public servant; b. Mountain, Ont. 8 Dec. 1949; s. James B. and Clara B. (Bell) B.; e. Mountain Dist. H.S.; Brock Univ. B.A. 1972; children: T. Kate, Emma-Ruth, Jesse; CHAIRMAN, ONTARIO SHEEP MARKETING AGENCY 1993– ; Information Specialist, Statistics Can. 1972–92; Bd. of Dir., Ont. Sheep Mktg. Agency 1989–92; Instructor, OATI; Dir., Candn. Sheep Fed.; Ont. Indus. Rep., Nat. Tripartite Stabilization Ctte. 1991, '92, '93; author: 'Guide to Managing Statistics Canada Publications in Libraries' 1991; recreations: many interests incl. music, skiing, hiking, canoeing, photography, puttering; Home: R.R. 3, Mountain, Ont. K0E 1S0; Office: 50 Dovercliffe Rd., Unit 13, Guelph, Ont. N1G 3A6.

**BAKER, Gordon Roy,** Q.C., B.A., M.A., LL.B.; lawyer; b. Geraldton, Ont. 14 Apr. 1943; s. Roy Herbert and Anna Jean (Poustie) B.; e. McMaster Univ. B.A. Hons. 1966; Univ. Western Ont., M.A. 1967; Queen's Univ., LL.B. 1970; m. Katheryn, d. Gordon Ward and Evelyn Hunter, 7 Aug. 1971; children: Leigh Anne; Kristin; PARTNER, WEIR & FOULDS, BARRISTERS & SOLICITORS 1983– ; Dir. DAY International (Canada) Ltd.; Marriott Corporation of Canada Ltd.; Everest & Jennings Canadian Ltd.; Scitex Canada Inc.; E.K. Williams & Co. Ltd.; The Conservation Found. of Greater Toronto; Mason Windows Ltd.; Pineal Lake Lumber Co. Ltd.; Lakeside Controls Ltd.; I-Corp Security Services Inc.; called to the Bar Ont. 1972; Assoc. Robertson, Lane, Perrett, Frankish & Estey 1972; Partner Robertson, Lane Perrett 1974–81; Instr., Bar Ad. Course 1977–85; Beaches Fed. Prog. Conservative Assn.; Dir. and Extve., Metrop. Toronto Region Conservation Foundation; Mem., Candn. Bar Assn. Ont. Comte. on Taxation; Candn. Tax Foundn.; United Church; Clubs: Bd. of Trade Metrop. Toronto; Albany; Empire; Balmy Beach Canoe; Beaver Valley Ski; Ashbridges Bay Yacht; recreations: water skiing; wind-surfing; snow skiing; running; sailing; theatre; Home: 56 Beaufort Rd., Toronto, Ont. M4E 1M9; Office: Weir & Foulds, Exchange Tower, 16th Floor, P.O. Box 480, 2 First Canadian Place, Toronto, Ont. M5X 1J5.

**BAKER, J. Richard,** B.A.; construction executive; b. Montreal, Que. 26 Feb. 1931; s. William Edward and Audrey Gertrude (McKechnie) B.; e. Univ. of B.C., B.A. 1952; m. Lorna Calderwood 28 Dec. 1957; children: Susan, Jeffrey, Stephen, Hugh; PRESIDENT AND DIR., OCEAN EQUIPMENT LTD. and WEST OCEAN CONSULTANTS LTD.; Dir., Seaboard Life Insur. Co.; Pres., C.E.O. and Dir., Dillingham Construction Ltd. 1983–89; Pres. and C.E.O. Dillingham Corp. Canada Ltd. 1980–82; Vice Pres. Dillingham Corp. Canada Ltd. 1973–80; Gov., Business Council of B.C.; Chrmn., Construction Industry Devel. Counc.; Dir., B.C. Rehabilitation Soc.; Gov., Workers' Compensation Bd. of B.C.; recreations: skiing, boating; Clubs: Vancouver; Royal Vancouver Yacht; Home: 2367 Bellevue Ave., West Vancouver, B.C. V7V 1C9.

**BAKER, Michael Allen,** MD, FRCPC, FACP; physician, haematologist-oncologist, professor of medicine; b. Toronto, Ont. 24 Jan. 1943; s. Saul and Esther (Bruner) B.; e. Univ. of Toronto, MD 1966; Nat. Bd. of Med. Exam (USA) Dipl. 1967; FRCPC Haem. 1971; Am. Bd. of Internal Med. and Am. Bd. of Haem. Dipls. 1972; m. Barbara d. Agnes and Bruce Woods 27 June 1967; children: Jeffrey, Jillian; PROF. OF MED., UNIV. OF TORONTO 1982– ; Dir., Oncol. Prog. 1989; Physician-in-Chief, The Toronto Hosp. 1992– ; Cons., Princess Margaret Hosp.; Addiction Rsch. Found.; Mem., Inst. of Med. Sci. 1986; Sch. of Grad. Studies, Toronto 1974– ; Alpha Omega Alpha Hon. Med. Soc.; Am. Assn. for the Adv. of Sci.; for Cancer Rsch.; FACP; Am. Fed. for Clin. Rsch.; Am. Soc. for Clin. Oncol.; of Hematol.; Candn. Med. Assn.; Candn. Soc. for Clin. Invest.; Ont. Med. Assn.; FRCPC; Ont. Scholar 1960; Fulford Scholarship 1962; Med. Alumni Assn. Prize 1962; B'Nai Br'th Scholarship 1963 (all Univ. of Toronto); Vis. Prof., Univ. of W. Ont. 1979; Hebrew Univ. 1985; Past Chair of several panels & cttes.; Pres., Nat. Cancer Inst. 1992–94; Bd. of Trustees, The Toronto Hosp. 1990; co-author: 'Clinical Medicine' and 'Clinical Sciences: Oncology' 2nd ed. 1983, book chapters and more than 90 med. articles; recreations: tennis, music; Home: 14 Wells Hill Ave., Toronto, Ont. M5R 3A6; Office: Toronto Hospital, Bell Wing, 585 University Ave., Toronto, Ont. M5G 2C4.

**BAKER, Ronald James,** O.C., M.A., LL.D.; University Professor and president emeritus; b. London, Eng. 24 Aug. 1924; s. James Herbert Walter and Ethel Frances (Miller) B.; e. Chistlehurst and Sidcup Grammar Sch. Eng.; Univ. of B.C., B.A. 1951, M.A. 1953; Grad. work, Sch. of Oriental and African Studies, Univ. of London 1954–56; LL.D. (hon.) Univ. of N.B. 1970; LL.D. (hon.) Mount Allison Univ. 1977; LL.D. (hon.) Univ. of P.E.I. 1989; LL.D. (hon.) Simon Fraser Univ. 1990; came to Can. with R.A.F. 1944 and then permanently 1947; m. 1stly Helen Gillespie, d. late Thomas Elder, East Lothian, Scot., 3 Sept. 1949; children: Sharon Ann, Lynn Frances, Ian James, Sarah Jane, Katherine Jean; m. 2ndly Frances Marilyn Frazer; one s. Ralph Edward; University Professor and President Emeritus, Univ. of P.E.I. 1978–91 (President and Vice-Chancellor 1969–78); Distinguished Visiting Professor, Univ. of New England, Australia, and universities in Bangkok, Kuala Lumpur, Australia and New Zealand 1984; Dir., Inst. for Departmental Leadership, Atlantic Provinces; Lectr. in Eng., Univ. of B.C. 1951, Assoc. Prof. 1962; first faculty mem. apptd. as Prof. and Head of Eng. Dept. and Dir. of Acad.

Planning, Simon Fraser Univ. 1964, Prof. 1968–69; First Pres., Univ. of P.E.I. 1969–78; apptd. University Prof. 1978; The David MacDonald Stewart Prof. of Canadian Studies 1988–91; Co-ordr. Atlantic Inst. of Education, Univ. of P.E.I. Grad. Prog. in Education 1979–82; consults on univ. organization (e.g. Universidad Privada Del Valle, Bolivia 1989); served with RAF in Eng. and Germany, 1943–47 as Navig./Flying Controller, Liaison Offr. on Disarmament in Germany; rank Flight Lt.; Candn. Linguistic Assn. (Extve. 1958–60); Nat. Council of Teachers of Eng. (U.S.A.); Assn. of Candn. Univ. Teachers of Eng. (Pres. 1967–68); B.C. Council of Teachers of Eng. (Extve. 1967–68); Comte., Conf. on Coll. Composition and Communication (U.S.A.) (Extve. 1967–70); Candn. Assn. of Univ. Teachers 1954–77; Candn. Council of Teachers of Eng. (Prog. Comte. 1968, Dir.-at-Large 1969–71); Fellow, Royal Soc. of Arts 1971–90; Royal Commonwealth Soc. 1972– ; Candn. Soc. for Study of Higher Educ. (Pres. 1975–76); Humanities Assn. of Can.; Candn. Soc. for Study of Educ.; Bd. of Examiners, B.C. 1964–66; Acad. Bd., B.C. 1964–69; Bd. of Govs., N.S. Tech. Coll. 1969–78; Holland Coll., Charlottetown 1969–78; Mem., Interim Adv. Counc., Univ. of Northern B.C. 1990; mem. Can. Council 1970–76; Assn. of Univs. and Colls. of Can. (Dir. 1972–75, 1975–78; Chrmn. and mem. of various Comtes.); Assn. of Atlantic Univs. (Pres. 1976–78; Chrmn. and mem. various Comtes.); mem. Official Candn. Del. on Educ. to People's Rep. of China 1974; mem. Joint Evaluation Comte. of Federal Lang. Progs., Secy. of State and Council of Ministers in Educ. 1976–78; Assoc. Ed., 'The Canadian Journal of Higher Education' 1980–92; Chrmn., SSHRC Leave Fellowship Ctte. (English & Linguistics) 1981–83; mem., Killam Prize and Fellowship Ctte. 1985–87; mem., Molson Prize Ctte. 1987; Chrmn., Nat. Defence Strategic Studies Ctte. 1986– ; Mem., Minister's Cttee. on Canadian Military Colleges 1993; part-time mem. Candn. Radio-Television and Tele-Communications Comn. (CRTC) 1982–87; rec'd Centennial Medal 1967; Queen's Jubilee Medal 1977; Commemorative Medal for 125th Anniversary of Candn. Confederation 1992; Offr., Order of Can. 1978; The 1988 Distinguished Member Award of Can. Soc. for the Study of H.E.; author of numerous articles in acad. and educ. journs.; recreations: fishing, photography, music, conversation; Clubs: 1864 (Charlottetown); Canadian (Pres. 1974–75); Home: #2 – 13957 70th Ave., Surrey, B.C. V3W 0A3.

**BAKER, Warren Edward,** B.A.Sc., Sc.D.; university professor; b. Toronto, Ont. 1 Mar. 1940; s. John Arthur and Gabrielle (Warren) B.; e. Leaside H.S. 1958; Univ. of Toronto B.A.Sc. 1962; M.I.T. Sc.D. 1966; m. Mary Ann d. Michael and Mary Martucci 1 Apr. 1970; children: Susanna Madlyn, Michael Warren; PROFESSOR, CHEMISTRY DEPT., QUEEN'S UNIV. 1985– ; Rsch. Engr., DuPont Can. 1966–67; Rsch. Mgr. & later Vice-Pres., LECO Indus. 1968–82; Pres., Vista Polymerics Inc. 1982– ; cons. to many chem. & polymer processing cos. incl. Colortech Inc. & DuPont Can. Inc.; Dir., Vista Polymerics Inc.; Colortech Corp.; Gold Medal, Chem. Engr. 1962; NSERC-DuPont funded Professorship 1985; Mem., Candn. Soc. of Chem. Engrs.; Soc. of Chem. Indus.; Internat. Polymer Processing Soc.; N. Am. Rep., Assn. of Profl. Engrs. of Ont.; Soc. of Plastics Engrs.; author of 27 refereed articles in var. engr. & polymer sci. journals; editor, 'Progress in Polymer Processing'; recreations: canoeing, travel; Home: 32 Hilldowntree Rd., Islington, Ont. M9A 2Z8; Office: Kingston, Ont. K7L 3N6.

**BAKER, Hon. Winston,** M.H.A.; politician; b. Grand Bank, Nfld. 17 Dec. 1939; s. Eli and Violet B.; e. elem. sch. Springdale, Nfld.; high sch. Gander, Nfld. 1955; Meml. Univ. of Nfld. 1961, grad. work in Fisheries & Environmental Biol.; Univ. of Toronto grad. studies in Edn.; Queen's Univ.; m. Beverley d Graham and Myrtle LeDrew 17 Nov. 1961; one s. John; PRES. TREASURY BD., GOVT. OF NFLD. AND LABRADOR 1989– ; & MIN. OF FINANCE 1992– ; Pres. Exec. Council, sch. teacher Twillingate, Springdale, St. John's and Espanola, Ont. prior to returning to Gander 1977 to teach; Dep. Mayor Gander Town Council 1981–85; twice unsuccessful cand. prior to el. as M.H.A. 1985, re-el. for Gander 1989, 1993; served as Opposition Spokesman for Finance and Newfoundland Hydro, Chrmn. Pub. Accts. Ctte.; Home: 11 Calgary St., St. John's, Nfld. A1A 3W1; Office: P.O. Box 8700, St. John's, Nfld. A1B 4J6.

**BAKHSHI, Narendra Nath**, Ph.D., P.Eng., C.Eng., MI Chem E; university professor; b. New Delhi, India 27 July 1928; s. Jog Raj and Raj Wanti B.; e. Banaras Hindu Univ., B.Sc. 1946, M.Sc. 1948; Virginia Polytech. & State Univ., Ph.D. 1956; m. Nirmal d. Lekhram and Leela Wanti Tara Sharma 25 Apr. 1951; children: Ranju, Neena, Arun, Rajesh; PROF., CHEMICAL ENGR., UNIV. OF SASKATCHEWAN 1974– ; Acoustics Div., Nat. Physical Lab, New Delhi 1950–53; U.S.: Process Engr., Hydrocarbon Rsch. Inc. 1956–59; Sr. Chem. Engr., Air Prod. & Chem. Inc. 1959–60; U.K.: Sr. Process Engr., Air Products Ltd. 1960–62; British Oxygen Co. 1963; Asst. Prof., Chem. Engr., Univ. of Sask. 1963; Assoc. Prof. 1967; Cons., Sask. Minerals; Can. Packers; Fellow, Chem. Inst. of Can.; Pres., Vedanta Soc. of Sask. 1985–86; author of 90 sci. papers; has presented numerous sci./tech. papers before sci. societies; recreations: photography, hiking, comparative philosophy; Home: 159 A.E. Adams Cres., Saskatoon, Sask. S7K 5M6; Office: Saskatoon, Sask. S7N 0W0.

**BAKHT, Baidar,** P.Eng., B.Sc.Eng, M.Sc., D.Sc., F.CSCE, F.I.E.,F.E.I.C.; reserach civil engineer, educator; b. Delhi, India 4 Sept. 1940; s. Mukhtar and Anwar Jehan Chishti B.; e. Aligarh Univ. B.Sc. 1962; Imperial College London M.Sc. 1972; London Univ. D.Sc. 1990; m. Anita Das 11 Sept. 1968; children: Natasha, Sacha; arrived in Can. 1973; PRINCIPAL RSCH. ENGR., MIN. TRANSP. ONT. 1974– ; Registered profl. engr. Ont.; Asst. Engr., Heavy Engr. Corp. (India) 1962–66; Engr., Environ. Dept. London 1967–73; Adjunct Prof., Civil Engr., Univ. of Toronto 1991– ; co-author: 'Bridge Analysis Simplified' 1985, 'Bridge Analysis by Microcomputer' 1988, 'Soil-Steel Bridges' 1993; translator of 9 books of Urdu poetry to English 1985–94; author of over 150 articles on structural engr. & Urdu lit.; co-inventor, unique deck slab of bridges; Moisseif Award, ASCE 1982; Pres. Medal, Road & Transp. Assn. of Can. 1985; Inst. Engrs. (India) cert. of merit 1990; Candn. Soc. for Civil Engrg. (Vice-Pres. Tech. Activiteis; Pratley Award 1988); Engr. Inst. Can. (Gzowski Medal 1983); Chair, Candn. Highway Bridge Design Code; avocation: translating Urdu poetry into English; Home: 21 Whiteleaf Cres., Scarborough, Ont. M1V 3G1; Office: 1201 Wilson Ave., Downsview, Ont. M3M 1J8.

**BAKISH, David,** B.Sc., M.D., F.R.C.P.(C), C.S.P.Q.; psychiatrist; b. Istanbul, Turkey 1 May 1948; s. Marko and Dora B.; e. McGill Univ. B.Sc. 1971; Univ. Louis Pasteur (Strasbourg, France) M.D. 1980; Univ. of Ottawa, dipl. in psych. 1985; F.R.C.P.(C) 1985; m. Margaret d. Klas & Ingrid Hellstrom 20 July 1974; children: Jaimie, Nicholas, Joseph; ASSOC. PROF., UNIV. OF OTTAWA / HEAD, PSYCHOPHARMACOLOGY UNIT, ROYAL OTTAWA HOSPITAL 1993– ; Internship, Pasqua Hosp. (Sask.) 1981; Internal Medicine Residencey 1982; Res. in Psych., Univ. of Ottawa 1983–84; Staff Psych. & Dir., Post Grad. / Clin. Investigator, Pierre Janet Hosp. 1985–87; Asst. Prof., Univ. of Ottawa 1987–93; Staff Psych., Adult Outpatient, Clin. Coord. of Drug Trials in Anxiety & Depression, Royal Ottawa Hosp. 1987–93; Consultant Psych. to pharm. industry 1987– ; interests: psychopharmcology studies; special interest in anxiety & depressive disorders; area of expertise: neurotransmitter rsch. in affective disorder; new generation antidepressants; Teaches psychopharm. to residents & med. students; Eli Lilly Award, Ont. Psych. Assn. Lecture 1992; recreations: skiing, baseball, tennis; clubs: Lac Marois Country; Home: 1785 Devlin Cres., Ottawa, Ont. K1H 5T5; Office: 1145 Carling Ave., Ottawa, Ont. K1Z 7K4.

**BAKKER, Barend (Bard) Hendrik,** M.A., Ph.D.; educator; b. Hilversum, Holland 12 Sept. 1934; s. Cornelis Marinus and Anna Maria (van Ammers) B.; e. Univ. of Toronto B.A. 1956, M.A. 1958, Ph.D. 1968; m. Sonia d. Reginald (Nik) and Marjorie Cavell 29 Aug. 1958; children: Michael, Pamela, Gillian; PROF. OF FRENCH, YORK UNIV. (GLENDON COLL.) 1975– ; Dir. Zola Research Prog., Univ. of Toronto 1973– ; Principal Investigator and Sr. Ed., The Zola Research Project 1976– ; Master, Trinity Coll. Sch. Port Hope 1958–59; Lectr. Wilfrid Laurier Univ. 1959–60; Instr. Univ. of Toronto 1960–63; Lectr. Ind. Univ. 1964–65; Asst. Prof. present Univ. 1965, Assoc. Prof. 1970; Visiting Fellow Wolfson Coll. Cambridge 1983; Visiting Prof. Waseda Univ. (Tokyo), Aïchi Univ. (Nagoya), Univ. of Kyoto 1985; Visiting Prof., Univ. of California at Santa Barbara 1987; Can. Council Fellow 1966–68, 1972–73; Reader and Assessor for Can. Council, Social Sci. and Humanities Research Council Can., Univ. of Toronto Press, Nat. Endowment for Humanities, Brit. Acad., Brit. Council; author 'Naturalisme pas mort. Lettres inédites de Paul Alexis à Emile Zola 1871–1900' 1971; various articles learned journs.; ed. 'Emile Zola: Correspondence' Vols. 1–9 1978–93; mem. Modern Lang. Assn. Am.; Assn. Profs. French Univs. & Colls. Can.; Société littéraire des Amis d'Emile Zola; Etobicoke Philharmonic Orchestra; recreations: music (flute), swimming, cycling, walking; Home: 12 De Vere Gardens, Toronto, Ont. M5M 3E5; Office: Zola Research Program, 14038K Robarts Library, 130 St. George St., Toronto, Ont. M5S 1A1.

**BAKKER, Martin,** B.A., M.B.A.; financial executive; b. Netherlands 4 July 1945; s. Jan Willem and Hermina (Bruins) B.; e. McMaster Univ. B.A. 1967, M.B.A. 1970; m. Anne Wright 2 May 1987; children: Karen, Deborah, Janice, Jennifer; SENIOR VICE-PRES., FINANCE & CHIEF FINANCIAL OFFICER, EXPORT DEVELOPMENT CORP. 1989– ; Asst. Mgr., Internat. Trade and Finance (Montreal) / Rep. (Dusseldorf, Germany) / Mgr., Govt. Banking, Internat. Banking Div., Bank of Montreal 1970–75; Asst. Regional Mgr., Middle-East & S.E. Africa, Export Devel. Corp. 1975; Asst. Reg. Mgr., Asia 1976; Mgr., Far East 1977; Asst. Vice-Pres., Export Financing Group 1980; Vice-Pres., Corp. Affairs & Chair, Risk Assessment Panel 1984; Sr. Vice-Pres., Export Financing Group 1985; Mem., Exec. Mngt. Ctte., Export Devel. Corp.; Home: 64 Lillico Dr., Ottawa, Ont. K1V 9L6; Office: 151 O'Connor St., Ottawa, Ont. K1A 1K3.

**BALA, Nicholas M.C.,** B.A., LL.B., LL.M.; law professor; b. Montréal, Qué. 14 Mar. 1952; s. Karel Charles and Vera Judith (Lowenbach) B.; e. Univ. of Toronto, B.A. (Hons.) 1974; Queen's Univ. LL.B. 1977; Harvard Univ. LL.M. 1980; m. Martha d. Ken and Hilda Gunn 5 July 1980; children: Emily Anne, Katherine Mary, Andrew John; LAW PROF., QUEEN'S UNIVERSITY 1978– ; Associate Dean 1994– ; Articling student, Burke-Robertson, Chadwick & Ritchie 1977–78; Vis. Prof., Faculty of Law, McGill Univ. 1982; Duke Law Sch., Duke Univ. 1985; Fac. of Law, Univ. of Calgary 1989; teaching & rsch. interests: family law, children's law, juvenile justice; Prin. Invest., Ont. Child Abuse Register Review 1987–88; Legal cons. to var. bodies incl. Min. of the Solicitor Gen. of Can.; Dept. of Justice Can.; Health & Welfare Can.; Ont. Inst. for the Prevention of Child Abuse; Ont. Counc. of Indian Chiefs; Manitoba Aboriginal Justice Inquiry; extensive speaker; co-author: 'The Child & The Law' 1982, 'Canadian Children's Law' 1982, 'Young Offenders Act Annotated' 1984, 'Juvenile Justice in Canada' 1985; 'Canadian Child Welfare Law' 1991; 'Juvenile Justice in Canada: A Theoretical and Analytical Assessment' 1992; 'Rethinking Decisions About Children' 1993; co-editor: 'Young Offenders Service' 1984–87; recreations: hockey, running, soccer; Club: Queen's Faculty; Office: Kingston, Ont. K7L 3N6.

**BALAKRISHNAN, Tattamangalam R.,** B.A., M.A., Ph.D.; university professor; b. Palghat, India 8 Apr. 1932; s. Tattamangalam S. and Chitoor N. (Sankaram) Raman; e. Univ. of Madras B.A. (Hons.) 1952, M.A. 1953; Univ. of Michigan Ph.D. 1963; m. Ruth d. Richard and Margaret Sager 23 June 1970; PROFESSOR, DEPT. OF SOCIOLOGY, THE UNIV. OF WESTERN ONTARIO 1971– ; Statistician, Indian Stat. Inst. Calcutta 1955–58; Asst. Prof., Indian Inst. of Mngt. Calcutta 1963–65; The Univ. of West Ont. 1965–67; Assoc. Prof. 1967–71; Chrmn., Sociology Dept. 1989–92; Dir., Population Studies Ctr. 1974–84; Visiting Prof., Indiana Univ. 1969–70; Visiting Scholar, Univ. of Calif. Berkeley 1972; U.N. Latin Am. Population Ctr. Santiago Chile 1973; Fellow, East-West Population Inst. Hawaii 1980–81; cons. to Stats. Can., CIDA, IDRC, Sec. of State for Multiculturalism; Royal Comn. for New Reproductive Technologies; Fulbright Fellow 1958–59; Population Counc. Fellow 1959–61; Fac. Rsch. Professorship 1988–89; Mem., Candn. Population Soc. (Vice-Pres. 1976–78; Pres. 1978–80; Internat. Union for the Sci. Study of Population (elected); Population Assn. of Am.; Candn. Sociol. & Anthropol. Assn.; co-author: 'Fertility and Family Planning in a Canadian Metropolis' 1975, 'Patterns of Fertility in Canada 1971' 1979; 'Family and Childbearing in Canada' 1993; co-editor: 'Family in Crisis? A Population Crisis?' 1989; recreations: golf, tennis; Home: 759 North Mile Rd., London, Ont. N6H 2X7; Office: London, Ont. N6A 5C2.

**BALANYK, Thomas Elie**, D.D.S., D.D.P.H., M.Sc.; public health dentist; dental researcher; general practitioner; b. Niagara Falls, Ont., Aug. 1954; s. Elie and Nellie B.; .e. Stamford Coll. Inst. Niagara Falls 1973; Univ. of Toronto D.D.S. 1979, D.D.P.H. 1981, M.Sc. 1986; m. Ksenija d. Ilija and Bosa Isajev, Nov. 1985; children: Peter Daniel, Olivia Marina; VICE PRES. BIO SCI RESEARCH CANADA LTD. 1989– ; Dental Rsch. Northam Dental Sciences Inc.; gen. dental practice Port Colborne and Toronto, Ont. 1979– ; Dental Adv. City of Toronto Pub. Health Dept. 1983–85; Dental Dir. Med-Check Canada 1985–87 and Hazelton Laboratories Canada 1987–88; co-holder U.S. Patent Benzoin Antimicrobial Dental Varnishes (assigned to Univ. of Toronto Innovations Found.) 1985; co-inventor Chlorzoin ® dental varnish (recipient Can. Bus. Award 1988); Bronze Award Inventions Min. Ind., Sci. & Tech. Can. 1988; author or co-author various profl. publs.; recreations: bicycling, swimming, guitar, harpsichord; Address: 605 Royal York Rd., Toronto, Ont. M8Y 4G5.

**BALANZINO, Sergio Silvio,** LL.M.; diplomat; b. Bologna, Italy 20 June 1934; s. Guido and Fulvia (Beraud) B.; e. Univ. of Rome LL.M. 1958; Fullbright Scholar, Univ. of Wisconsin; m. Emanuella d. Maurizio and Sofia Bettoja; one s. Guido; AMBASSADOR OF ITALY TO CAN. 1990– ; joined foreign service Rome 1959, Desk Offr. Press & Info. Service Min. of Foreign Affairs (M.F.A.) 1960; Attaché 1960; Third Sec. 1962; Second Sec. Perm. Mission to OECD Paris 1962; Vice Consul Neuchâtel 1966; First Sec. 1966; Consul Zurich 1967; Counsellor 1968; Counsellor Nairobi 1969; Bureau Chief Tech. Coop. Service Devel. Countries M.F.A. Rome 1972; First Counsellor 1973; First Counsellor Athens 1975; Ottawa 1978; Envoy Extraordinary and Min. Plenipotentiary 2nd Class 1980; Min. Counsellor Ottawa 1980; Dept. Devel. Coop. M.F.A. Rome 1982; Envoy Extraordinary and Min. Plenipotentiary 1st Class 1986; Depy. Dir. Gen. Cultural Relations 1986; Dir. Gen. Cultural Relations 1988; Named Grand Offr. Italian Order of Merit; Clubs: Royal Ottawa Golf; Cercle Universitaire d'Ottawa; Rideau; Muthaiga Country (Nairobi); Home: 1475 Aylmer Rd., Aylmer, Qué. J9H 5E1; Office: 275 Slater St., 21st Floor, Ottawa, Ont. K1P 5H9.

**BALDOCK, J. Bruce;** financial executive; b. Toronto, Ont. 25 Aug. 1937; s. late Joseph George and Marion Elizabeth B.; e. John Fisher P.S.; London South Collegiate; Univ. of Western Ont.; m. Anne d. Elmer and Mary Reddon 23 July 1960; children: Joanne, Steven, Gregory; PRES. COMMERCIAL CAPITAL CORP. 1980– ; various positions in Canada and the US, The Bank of N.S. 1958–72; Vice-Pres., TKM (Canada) Ltd. 1972–76; Shareholder, Commercial Capital Corp. 1976– ; Dir., The Commercial Capital Corp.; PCC First Capital Corp.; Larr Capital Corp. (Alta. Stock Exchange); Advisor, Brock Univ. Burgoyne Ctr. for Entrepreneurship; Anglican; recreations: fishing; clubs: Albany Club of Toronto (Dir.); Home: R.R. 1, Bolton, Ont. L7E 5R7; Office: 4211 Yonge St., Ste. 305, Willowdale, Ont. M2P 2A9.

**BALDREY, Keith Donald;** journalist; b. North Vancouver, B.C. 26 Aug. 1958; s. Donald Sheldon and Patricia June B.; m. Anne Katherine Mullens 1990; BUREAU CHIEF VICTORIA, THE VANCOUVER SUN 1990– ; Pres. B.C. Legis. Press Gallery 1990–92; joined present newspaper as journalist 1984; regular CBC-Radio commentator; magazine writer; co-author 'Fantasyland: Inside the Reign of Bill Vander Zalm' 1989; Home: 1326 Thurlow Rd., Victoria, B.C. V8S 1L6; Office: Press Gallery, Parliament Buildings, Victoria, B.C. V8V 1X6.

**BALDWIN, Barry,** B.A., Ph.D.; university professor; b. Lincoln, England 24 Sept. 1937; s. Harry Clement and Ethel (Baxter) B.; e. The Lincoln School (England) 1948–56; Univ. of Nottingham B.A. (1st class hons.) 1959, Ph.D. 1962; m. Janet Kathleen d. Ellis and Kathleen Agnew 10 May 1968; children: Alexander James, Martha Kathleen; PROFESSOR OF CLASSICS, THE UNIV. OF CALGARY 1965– ; Asst. Lectr. in History, Loughborough Coll. (Engl.) 1960–62; Lectr. in History, Univ. of New England (Australia) 1963–65; Head, Classics Dept., Univ. of Calgary 1968–73, 1975–80; author: 'Studies in Lucian' 1973, 'Studies in Aulus Gellius' 1975, 'The Roman Emperors' 1980, Suetonius: Biographer of the Caesars' 1983, 'Philogelos' or 'Laughter Lover' 1983, 'Timarion' 1984, 'Studies on Late Roman & Byzantine History' 1984, 'An Anthology of Byzantine Poetry' 1985, 'Studies on Greek & Roman History & Literature' 1985, 'An Anthology of Later Latin Literature' 1987, 'Roman & Byzantine Papers' 1989; recreations: upsetting left-wingers and liberals; clubs: none: I am in the words of Dr Johnson, 'a thoroughly unclubbable man'; Home: 3917 Edison Cres., Calgary, Alta. T2S 0X1; Office: 2500 University Dr. N.W., Calgary, Alta. T2N 1N4.

**BALDWIN, John Russel,** B.A., M.A., B.Litt., D.C.L.; retired transportation executive; b. Toronto, Ont. 7 Aug. 1912; s. John Russell and Florence M. (Byers) B.; e. McMaster Univ. B.A. 1933; Univ. of Toronto M.A. 1934; Rhodes Scholar, Ont. 1934; Oxford Univ., M.A. B.Litt. 1937; Acadia Univ. D.C.L. 1971; m. Dorothy d. Richard Pearson 24 June 1944; children: John, Richard, Blair; staff mem., History Dept., McMaster Univ. 1937–38; Exec. Sec., Candn. Inst. for Internat. Affairs 1938–41; Dept. of External Affairs 1941–42; Asst. Sec., War Ctte. of Cabinet, Ottawa 1942–45; Sr. Asst. Sec. to Cabinet 1945–49; Chrmn. Air Transport Bd. Ottawa 1949–54; Depy. Min. of Transport 1954–68; Pres. Air Canada 1968 until ret. 1974; part-time transp. consultant to business; awarded Sir Sefton Brancker Medal for Aeronautics, Roy. Inst. for Aeronautics, U.K. 1971; Hon. Commodore, Candn. Coast Guard 1973; C.D. Howe Award for Aeronautics 1974; author several publications; recreations: oenology; Home: 165 Ontario St., Apt. 805, Kingston, Ont. K7L 2Y6.

**BALDWIN, R. George,** M.A., Ph.D.; educator; b. Vancouver, B.C. 13 Jan. 1927; s. late Sidney George and Vera Berkeley (Bailey) B.; e. Vernon (B.C.) Public Sch. and Preparatory Sch. 1938; Point Grey Jr. and Prince of Wales High Schs. Vancouver, B.C. 1944; Univ. of Brit. Columbia B.A. (Hons. Eng.) 1948; Univ. of Toronto, M.A. 1949, Ph.D. 1957; m. Barbara Kathleen, d. late Joseph Vernor and Anna Kathleen (Carson) Chew 28 Aug. 1948; children: Christopher George, John Robert (deceased), Janet Kathleen (Werner); EMERITUS PROF. OF ENGLISH, UNIV. OF ALBERTA 1985– ; joined present Univ. as Lectr. 1951, Asst. Prof. 1954, Assoc. Prof. 1958, Prof. 1963, Chrmn. Dept. of Eng. 1967–71, Assoc. Dean Arts 1971, Dean of Arts 1972–79, Vice-Pres. (Academic) 1979–84; mem. B.C., Genealogical Soc.; Can. Council Sr. Fellow 1966–67; Recipient Univ. of Alberta Alumni Golden Jubilee Award 1986; Past Gov. Univ. of Alta.; Alpha Delta Phi; Anglican; Home: 1200 Island Park Walk, Vancouver, B.C. V6H 3T4.

**BALESTRA, Roger A.,** C.M.A.; financial executive; e. Okanagan College; Soc. of Management Accountants C.M.A.; VICE-PRES., FINANCE & SECRETARY, CABRE EXPLORATION LTD. 1988– ; North Canadian Oils Limited 1982–84; Canadian Roxy Petroleum Ltd. 1984–88; Controller and Secretary, Cabre 1993 Ltd.; Dir., Iris Petroleum Software Ltd.; Office: Suite 1400, 700 – 9th Ave. S.W., Calgary, Alta. T2P 3V4.

**BALFOUR, R. James,** Q.C.; b. Regina, Sask. 22 May 1928; s. Reginald McLeod and Martha (McElmoyle) B.; e. Luther Coll., Regina; Univ. of Sask., LL.B.; m. Beverly Jane, d. Charles Roberts Davidson, Q.C., Regina, Sask. 6 June 1951; children: John Alan, James Roberts, Reginald William (dec'd), Beverly Ann; PARTNER, BALFOUR, MOSS, MILLIKEN, LASCHUK; Dir., Ducks Unlimited (Canada); Colonial Oil & Gas Ltd.; read law with R.M. Balfour, Q.C.; called to Bar of Sask. 1952; cr. Q.C. 1969; el. M.P. for Regina East 1972–79; apptd. to Senate 1979; mem. Regina Bar Assn. (Pres. 1956); Sask. Law Soc.; Candn. Bar Assn.; Royal United Services Inst.; Freemason; P. Conservative; Protestant; recreations: sailing, skiing, shooting; Clubs: Assiniboia; Regina; The Country Club (Aylmer, Que.); Home: 175 Lansdowne Rd. S. Ottawa, Ont. K1M 0N8; Office: #700 – 2103 – 11th Ave., Regina, Sask. S4P 4G1 or The Senate of Can., Parl. Bldgs., Ottawa, Ont. K1A 0A4.

**BALFOUR, St. Clair,** O.C., D.S.C., B.A., LL.D.; executive; b. Hamilton, Ont. 30 Apr. 1910; s. St. Clair and Ethel May (Southam) B.; e. Highfield Sch., Trinity Coll. Sch., Port Hope, Ont.; Trinity Coll., Univ. of Toronto, B.A., 1931; m. Helen Gifford, d. E.G. Staunton, Toronto, Ont., Jan. 1933; children: Elizabeth Staunton, St. Clair; Pres., Berriedale Ltd.; Balgarnie Investments Inc.; 867167 Ontario Ltd.; Chairman, Southam Inc. 1975–85; Hon. Life mem., Commonwealth Press Union; Canadian Press; Hon. Fellow, Woodsworth College, Univ. of Toronto; served in 2nd World War; Commander R.C.N.(R.); awarded D.S.C.; Zeta Psi; Anglican; Clubs: Hamilton; Toronto; Toronto Golf; York; Badminton & Racquet; Faculty; Address: 17 Ardwold Gate, Toronto, Ont. M5R 2W1.

**BALIKCI, Asen,** Ph.D.; anthropologist; educator; b. Istanbul, Turkey 30 Dec. 1929; s. Cosma and Nidela (Janeva) B.; e. Internat. Sch. of Geneva 1948; Univ. of Geneva licence ès sciences géographiques 1953; Columbia Univ. Ph.D. (Anthrop.) 1962; m. Verena Ossent (divorced); children: Nicolas, Anna; PROF. OF ANTHROP., UNIV. OF MONTREAL; anthropol. field work: Macedonian Ethnic Group Toronto 1955; Candn. Eskimos 1957–61; Vunta Kutchin Indians, Y.T. 1961; Peasants in S. Yugoslavia 1962; anthropol. films Netsilik Eskimos 1963–68; Danakil pastoralists in Ethiopia 1969–70; pastoral nomads Afghanistan 1973–76; films incl.: 'The Netsilik Eskimo Film Series'; 'Sons of Haji Omar' (Nat. Film Bd.); 'Man: A Course of Study'; recipient Can. Council, Harvard Univ., Smithsonian Inst., NEH, NSF, Nat. Geographic Soc. grants; author 'Vunta Kutchin Social Change' 1962; 'The Netsilik Eskimo' 1972; over 50 scholarly articles various anthropol. subjects; mem. Candn. Ethnol. Soc.; Am. Anthropol. Assn.; Greek Orthodox; Office: P.O. Box 6128, Montreal, Qué. H3C 3J7.

**BALKE, Mary Noel,** B.A.; retired librarian; b. Londonderry, N. Ireland, 25 Dec. 1918; d. Maj. William, M.M. and Jenny (Wilson) Schoales; e. Londonderry (N. Ireland) High Sch., Belvedere and Godolphin Schs., Eng.; Sheffield Univ., B.A. 1939; m. Maj. Nicholas Balke, C.D., 2 Sept. 1944; children: William Greer, Jennifer Mary Eileen; trained in Sheffield (Eng.) Pub. Libs.

1939–40; Asst. Lib., Patents and Alloys, Brown-Firth Research Labs., Sheffield, 1940; Research Asst. X-Ray Crystallography, 1942; Lib. and Information Offr., Ministry of Supply, Signals Research & Devel. Estab., Christchurch, Hants., 1943–44; Cataloguer, UN Information Office, London 1945; freelance writing and broadcasting 1948–58; Reference Lib., Ottawa Pub. Lib. 1959–61; Asst. Head, Business & Technol. Dept., 1962–63; Chief Librarian, Nat. Gallery of Can. 1964–79 (ret.); author of various newspaper articles, scripts and interviews for CBC; rec'd. Mem. Award, Candn. Women's Press Club, 1956; mem., Lib. Assn. Gt. Brit. (el. Assoc. 1942); Candn. Lib. Assn. (founding mem. and chrmn., Art Libraries Comte. 1967–69); Special Libraries Assn. (Chrmn. Museums, Arts & Humanities Div. 1974–75); Int. Fed. of Library Assns. & Insts. (Secy., Art Librarians Round Table 1978–79); Anglican; recreations: walking, reading, Tai Chi, writing, theatre; Home: Box 27, Sea Dog, Nanoose Bay, B.C. V0R 2R0.

**BALKIND, Alvin,** B.A.; curator; b. Baltimore, Md. 28 Mar. 1921; s. Benjamin and Nessie (Bers) B.; e. Johns Hopkins Univ., B.A. 1953; Univ. of Paris, Sorbonne, 1954–55; Curator of Contemp. Art, Art Gallery of Ont. 1973–75; Chief Curator Vancouver Art Gallery 1975–78; co-curator, exhibition, 'Fragments, Content, Scale,' London (Ont.), 49th Parallel (N.Y.C.), & Emily Carr Coll. of Art (Vancouver); Candn. Commissioner, Paris Biennale, 1980; mem. Arts Adv. Panel of Can. Council; Dir., New Design Gallery, Vancouver, 1955–62; Fine Arts Gallery, Univ. of B.C., Vancouver, 1962–73; Chief Curator, Vancouver Art Gallery 1975–78; Head, Visual Arts Studios, Banff Sch. of Fine Arts 1985–87; served in USN 1943–46; former prof. Univ. of B.C.; past mem. Visiting Comte., Nat. Gallery; Arts Adv. Panel, Canada Counc.; author of various catalogues and articles for art journs.; 'Escaping Gas' (book); essay in book 'Visions' 1983; essay in catalogue 'Vancouver: Art and Artists, 1931–83' 1984; essay in book 1992; exhbn. Harbourfront, Toronto July 1984 '6 Vancouver Artists'; exhbn. 'Ex Academe,' Contemporary Art Gall., Vancouver Nov. 1984; Co-Curator, 'Jeu D'Histoire' Exhbn., New Harbourfront Gall. May 1987; Contributor, 'Vancouver Forum I' 1992; Hon. Diploma, Emily Carr Coll., Vancouver 1991; $50,000 Award, Vancouver Inst. for the Visual Arts 1992; recreation: travel; Home: 4416 West 11th Ave., Vancouver, B.C. V6R 2M3.

**BALKWILL, John Andrew,** D.D.S.; dentist, corporation director; b. Perth, Ont. 26 July 1945; s. Joseph Andrew and Elizabeth Ellen (Nichols) B.; e. Univ. of Western Ont.; Univ. of Toronto D.D.S. 1971; m. Janet d. Dr. Charles and Elizabeth Millar 25 Sept. 1971; children: (Elizabeth) Anne, Kristy Jane; DIR., CANADA PORTS CORPORATION 1986– ; private dental practice 1971– ; Chairman, Ports Canada Police; Chairman, E.D.I.; National Vice-Pres., P.C. Party of Canada 1981–86; Office: 99 Metcalfe St., Ottawa, Ont. K1A 0N6.

**BALL, Dennis Percy,** Q.C., LL.B.; lawyer; b. Edmonton, Alta. 9 May 1944; s. Percy D. and Anne C. (Mix) B.; e. Univ. of Sask. LL.B. 1968; m. Lynn d. Einar and Gladys Fagerheim 29 June 1984; children: David, Michelle, Jodi-Lynn; PARTNER, MACPHERSON LESLIE AND TYERMAN 1989– ; called to Bar of Sask. 1969; cr. Q.C. 1986; Partner, Hill, McLellan, Ball & Co. Estevan, Sask. 1969–82; el. Bencher, Law Soc. Sask. 1982–85; Chrmn. Sask. Labour Relations Bd. 1982–89; Chrmn., Law Found. Sask. (Law Soc. Rep. 1984–92); Chrmn., Literacy Found. of Sask. 1991– ; Ed. Bd. Mem., Labour Times (Canada Law Book); mem. Candn. Bar Assn.; mem. Adv. Council, Salvation Army; Club: Rotary; Home: 2363 Brodie Bay E., Regina, Sask. S4V 0V1; Office: 1500 – 1874 Scarth St., Regina, Sask. S4P 4E9.

**BALL, Harold Graham,** CD, Major (retired); association executive; b. Kidderminster, Worcestershire, England 16 Dec. 1926; s. Charles and Lilian Victoria (Smith) B.; emigrated to Canada 1928; e. Alexander Muir School 1939; military qualification of grade 12 equivalent; m. Doris Margaret d. Fred and Mary Schmuland 10 June 1949; children: Pamela Jane, Stanley Graham, Melanie Margaret; NATIONAL SECRETARY, ARMY BENEVOLENT FUND 1981– ; delivery boy & labourer 1939–42; Engr. Dept., Candn. Gen. Electric 1942, 1945; enlisted Canadian Army (R) 1943, trans. to Candn. Army Active Serv. Force; Candn. Army Interim Force 1946; Sergeant, Royal Candn. Reg. Korea 1952–53; Lt. 1957; retired as Captain 1971; Prov. Sec. (Ont.), Army Benevolent Fund 1971; Major (Reserves) & Aide to Chief of Reserves 1982; served NATO Forces (Germany) 1959–62; served Airborne 1947–53; Mgr., Candn. Forces Personnel Assistance Fund; Guest speaker, Dept. of Nat. Defence & Royal Candn. Legion seminars; Candn. Forces Decoration with 2 bars for 32 years hon. military serv.; Candn. Centennial Medal 1967; Queen's Silver Jubilee Medal 1977; Sec., Toronto Br., Royal Commonwealth Soc. & Dir., Good Neighbours Club 1972–80; Dep. Comnr., Ottawa Br., St. John's Ambulance 1981; Dir. & Pres., N.E. Region, Ont. Football Assn. 1990–91; Mem., Royal Candn. Legion; Royal Candn. Regiment Assn.; Candn. Guards Assn.; recreations: golf, skating, spectator sports; clubs: Royal Candn. Military Inst., Army Officers' Mess; Home: 1450 Meadowbrook Rd., Gloucester, Ont. K1B 5G6; Office: 245 Cooper St., Ottawa, Ont. K2P 0G2.

**BALL, John James,** B.A., B.Ed., LL.B.; lawyer; b. Halifax, N.S. 2 Feb. 1943; s. The Late Rev. John G. E.and Jeanette Elizabeth (Taylor) B.; e. Mount Allison Univ. B.A., B.Ed. 1966 (Don Norton Meml. Award 1966); Dalhousie Univ. LL.B. 1969; m. Eleanor K. d. Jennie and late Clarke Heckman 24 Aug. 1968; children: Michael, J.J.; PARTNER, KEYSER MASON BALL 1984– ; Dir. Hoke Controls Ltd.; Ilsco of Canada Ltd.; Zimmer Canada Inc.; Purolator Products Ltd.; United Canadian Directories Inc.; Ginsey Industries Inc.; Glazing Technology Industries Limited; Minit Holdings Canada Ltd.; Minit of Canada Ltd.; called to Bar of N.S. 1970, Ont. 1971; joined McMillan Binch 1971–75; Partner, Broadhurst & Ball 1975–84 and present firm 1984– ; mem. Candn. Bar Assn. (Exec.-Ont.); Ed. Bd., National, CBA; Candn. Bar Communications Ctte.; Instr. Bar Admission Course 1991–93; Bd. Regents Mount Allison Univ. 1973–81; Past Chrmn. Vanier Cup; Past Dir. Mississauga Bd. Trade; United Church; Clubs: Mississaugua Golf & Country; Caledon Ski; Home: 1312 Lakeshore Rd. E., Oakville, Ont. L6J 1L6; Office: 701, 201 City Centre Dr., Mississauga, Ont. L5B 2T4.

**BALL, Melvyn J.,** M.D., F.R.C.P.(C); university professor; b. Toronto, Ont. 1940; s. Louis E. and Rose (Goldstein); e. Univ. of Toronto, M.D. 1963; m. Elaine d. of Louis and Malka Kagan; children: Lawrence, Tamara, Robert; PROFESSOR OF PATHOLOGY AND NEUROLOGY, DIR. OF NEUROPATHOLOGY, OREGON HEALTH SCIENCES UNIV.; Prof. of Pathology, Univ. of Western Ont. 1969–92; Staff Pathologist, Toronto Gen. Hosp. and Univ. of Toronto 1968–69; Dir., Univ. of Western Ont. Dementia Study Group 1977– ; Dir., Alzheimer Soc. of Canada; mem., Scientific Advisory Bds., Sandoz Found. for Gerontological Rsch., Gerontology Res. Counc. of Ont.; Nicholas and Hedy Munk Geriatric Award 1978; Assoc. Ed.: 'Canadian Journal on Ageing,' 'Alzheimer Disease and Related Disorders'; Ed.: 'First Canadian Symposium on the Organic Dementias' Candn. Jour. of Neurological Sciences 1986; Co-author: 'Syringomyelia' 1973; Office: Oregon Health Sciences Univ., L-113, 3181 S.W. Sam Jackson Park Rd., Portland, Oregon 97201–3098.

**BALLACHEY, Frank George,** B.A.; retired; b. High River, Alta. 31 July 1920; s. Alec Addington, Q.C., and Florence Genevieve (Macdonnel) B.; e. High River (Alta.) High Sch. (1938); Oxford Univ. 1944–45; Univ. of California (Berkeley) B.A. 1947; Nat. Defence Coll., Kingston, Ont. 1957–58; m. Kathleen Beatrice, d. Charles Rivet, Dallas, Texas 3 Oct. 1959; President, F. Ballachey Associates Inc. 1985–93; began as Reporter, Calgary, Alta. 1945–46; with Dept. of External Affairs of Can. 1947–60; Consul, Shanghai 1948–51; Acting Commr., Internat. Supervisory Comm. Laos 1954; Pol. Advr. to Candn. Commrs. in Indo-China 1955–56; Candn. Del. to Malayan Independence Celebrations 1957; First Secy. and Consul, Stockholm 1958–59 and Chargé d'Affairs there 1959; Extve. Asst., Canadian Imperial Bank of Commerce 1960–70; Regional Mgr., Export Financing, The Royal Bank of Can. 1970–80; Chief Advr., Govt. Affairs, Royal Bank of Canada 1980–85; served in 2nd World War with R.C.A.F. 1942–45, Flying Offr. (Pilot); Dir., P.C. 500; Vice-Chrmn., Chimo Group; mem., Candn. Inst. Internat. Affairs; RCAF Assoc.; Canada Korea Soc.; Kappa Alpha; R. Catholic; recreations: golf, fishing, bridge; Club: Rideau (Ottawa); Penticton Golf & Country; Home: 119 – 1634 Carmi Ave., Penticton, B.C. V2A 6Z1.

**BALLANTYNE, Robert Henry,** B.A.Sc., P.Eng.; association executive; b. Toronto, Ont. 5 Feb. 1935; s. Robert Law and Hazel Idella (Whitlow) B.; e. Univ. of Toronto, B.A.Sc. 1960; m. Marlene d. Ira and Clarice Luttrell 28 July 1962; children: David, Deborah; PRES., THE RAILWAY ASSN. OF CAN. 1988– ; Jr. Engr., CP Rail 1960; Systems Engr. 1965; Asst. Mgr., Systems & Procedures 1966; Dir., Transp. Planning 1970; Asst. Gen. Mgr., CP Consulting Serv.; Vice-Pres. 1981; Dir., Can. Safety Council; Nat. Transp. Week Inc.; Mem., Assn. of Profl. Engrs. of Ont.; Order of Engrs. of Que.; Am. Railway Engr. Assn.; Home: R.R. #1, Martintown, Ont. K0C 1S0; Office: Suite 1105, 800 Rene Levesque Blvd. W., Montreal, Qué. H3B 1X9.

**BALLARD, Geoffrey E. H.,** B.Sc., Ph.D.; executive; b. Niagara Falls, Ont. 16 Oct. 1932; s. Archibald Hall and Jessie Marguerite Mildred B.; e. Queen's Univ. B.Sc. 1956; Univ. of Washington Ph.D. 1963; Harvard AMP 1974; Georgetown Univ. Post Doctoral Math. & Physics; m. Shelagh d. William Ivan and Phyllis Glenn 26 May 1956; three s. A. Curtis, William Mark, Edward; CHAIRMAN, BALLARD POWER SYSTEMS 1988– ; Field Geol. Alta. 1956–60; Rsch. Eng. Cold Regions Rsch. & Eng. Labs. Hanover, N.H. 1963–69; Visiting Prof. Dartmouth Coll. and summer studies Nat. Acad. Sci's Woodshole 1965–66; Sec. U.S. Army pub. law appt., Hon. Fellow Inst. Electronics Command 1967; Dir.: Inst. for Exploratory Rsch. Fort Monmouth 1969; Advanced Telecommunications Office Fort Huachuca 1971; Office of Energy Conservation, Fed. Energy Office, Washington, D.C. Comnr. for Oil & Gas State of Ariz., Cons. to American Energizer Corp. Ariz. and to Horton Maritime Explorations Vancouver, B.C. 1974; Pres. Southern Arizona Manufacturing Co. 1974; Exec. Vice Pres. Maritime Commercial & Trading Corp. Vancouver, B.C. 1976; Pres. Ultra Energy Inc. 1977; Pres. Ballard Research Inc. 1979–88, Pres., Ballard Technologies Corp. 1985–89; Wheeler Fellow 1960–63; U.S. Army Decoration for Meritorious Civilian Service 1969, 1971; active pub. speaker tech. symposium forums edn. & technol.; author over 100 mgmt./sci. presentations, reports, articles; holds various patents; P. Eng. 1963–89; Anglican; recreations: tennis, skiing; Office: 980 West 1st St., Unit 107, North Vancouver, B.C. V7P 3N4.

**BALLARD, Michael E.P.,** B.A., F.I.C.B.; association executive; b. Montreal, Que. 17 March 1939; s. Michael James and Mary Ellen (Walsh) B.; e. Sir George Williams Univ. B.A. 1974; F.I.C.B. 1980; m. Lorraine d. Charles and Emily Whitewick 4 April 1959; children: Gary John, Michael Charles; VICE-PRESIDENT, QUEBEC DIVISION, CANADIAN BANKERS ASSN. 1991– ; joined present firm 1971; Vice-Pres., Security 1985–91; Bd. Chairman, Internat. Banking Security Assn. Inc. (N.Y.); clubs: Ontario, United Services; Home: 6275 Lasalle Blvd., Verdun, Que. H4H 1P8; Office: 1002 Sherbrooke St. W., Suite 900, Montreal, Que. H3A 3M5.

**BALLEM, John Bishop,** Q.C., M.A., LL.M., LL.D. (Hon.); b. New Glasgow, N.S. 2 Feb. 1925; s. John C., M.D. and Flora (Miller) B.; e. Dalhousie Univ., B.A., 1946, M.A. 1948, LL.B. 1949; Harvard Univ. Law Sch., LL.M. 1950; LL.D. (Hon.) Univ. of Calgary 1993; m. Grace Louise, d. Aird Flavelle, Vancouver, B.C., 31 Aug. 1951; children: Flavelle Bishop, Mary Mercedes, John Flavelle; PARTNER, BALLEM, McDILL, MacINNES & EDEN; Pres., Scotia Oils Limited; served as pilot, Royal Navy Fleet Air Arm 1944–45; author of several novels incl. 'The Moon Pool', 'Alberta Alone', 'Sacrifice Play', 'The Marigot Run', 'Oilpatch Empire', 'Death Spiral', and 'The Barons'; a legal textbook 'The Oil and Gas Lease in Canada' (2nd ed. 1985), and numerous articles in various legal journs. and nat. mags.; mem. Phi Delta Theta; Presbyterian; Clubs: Calgary Golf & Country; Petroleum; The Ranchmen's Club; Pinebrook Golf & Country Club; Address: 4000, 150 – 6 Ave. S.W., Calgary, Alta. T2P 3Y7.

**BALLINGALL, Sally Patricia,** B.Ed.; association executive; student at law; b. St. Helier, Jersey, Channel Islands 30 March 1946; d. Frederick James and Mary McCraith (Gemmell) Bryant; e. Univ. of B.C. B.Ed. 1977; m. Brian s. Francis and Jim B. 29 Nov. 1969; children: Sara, Jane; STUDENT AT LAW, MCCARTHY TÉTRAULT; Bd. Mem., Candn. Centre for Global Security; Gen. Mgr. of a Toronto-based real estate, property mngt. co. prior to entering law school; Bd. Mem., Task Force on Churches & Corp. Responsibility; Bd. Mem., Candn. Ctte. for UNIFEM; Past Pres., YWCA of/du Canada; Home: 32 Browning Ave., Toronto, Ont. M4K 1V7; Office: 80 Gerrard St. E., Toronto, Ont. M5B 1G6.

**BALLINGER, Paul,** B.A., M.B.A.; management consultant; b. Montreal, Que. 11 Oct. 1947; s. Robert and Margaret Dudley (Bigham) B.; e. Simon Fraser Univ. B.A. 1969; Univ. of W. Ont. M.B.A. 1983 (Dean's Honour List); m. Sandra d. Harry and Irene Gawne 24 Feb. 1973; two s. Robert, Marc; VICE PRES., BUSINESS DESIGN & SUPPORT, BC TEL MOBILITY CELLULAR 1993– ; Mgr. Financial Systems Pemberton Securities Inc. 1987, Vice Pres. Mgmt. Info. Systems 1988–89; Sr. Vice Pres. Finance & Adm. Canadian Western Bank 1989–90; Dir., Mgmt. Consulting, DMR Group Inc. 1991–93; served Candn. Forces various acctg. and control positions Can., Eur., Cyprus 1966–80, rank Capt.; Sr. Staff Offr. Acctg. & Finance, Audit & Non-Pub. Fund Acctg. Air Command HQ 1980–81, rank Maj., Directorate Costing Services Nat. Defence HQ 1983–86; Dir. of Pay System Automation 1986–87, rank Lt. Col.; mem. Vancouver Bd. Trade; Candn. Club; recreation: skiing; Home: 657 Folsom St., Coquitlam, B.C. V3J 5A4.

**BALLMANN, Franz;** banker; b. Germany 11 November 1924; s. Wilhelm Karl and Elsa (Gruener); e. Dilthey School, Wiesbaden, Germany; Goethe University, Frankfurt-Main; First Legal State Examination 1950, Great Legal State Examination 1953; m. Kwee Fong How, Singapore; 3 sons 1 daughter; VICE PRES. AND SR. ADVISOR, INTERNATIONAL CAPITAL FLOWS, BANK OF MONTREAL 1985– ; Dir. and Pres., Les Amis de l'Ecole Alexander von Humboldt, Montreal; Assoc. Atty. at Law, Wiesbaden 1953; Assoc. Counsellor, Hessian Ministry of Econ. & Transport 1954; Assoc. Counsellor, Fed. Ministry of Econ., Bonn 1955; Counsellor: Fed. Ministry of Econ., Bonn 1958; Legal Dep't. I.M.F. Washington 1960 to 1967; Special Consultant on Currency, Banking & Foreign Exchange to Depy. Prime Min. and Min. for Finance, Singapore 1967–70; Temporary Alternate Gov. IBRD. for Singapore 1968; Dir. Fed. Min. Econ. Bonn (on leave of absence) 1969; Financial Adv. Bank of America NT and SA, London, Eng. 1970; Vice Pres. and Chief Financial Adv. 1971; resigned from German Civil Service 1971; Sr. Banking Adv. The Monetary Authority of Singapore 1974; Vice Pres. Internat. Banking Bank of Montreal, London, Eng. 1975; Served in Second World War 1943–45 as Company Commander; rec'd Order of Merit (First Class) of the Federal Republic of Germany 1986; mem. Internat. Law Assn.; Candn. Inst. of Internat. Affairs (C.I.I.A.); Société Universitaire Européenne de Recherches Financiéres (S.U.E.R.F.); Recreations: Deep sea fishing; scuba diving; underwater photography; Home: 757 Victoria Park Ave., Suite 901, Toronto, Ont. M4C 5N8.

**BALLOCH, Anthony Edward,** O.B.E., B.A., D.C.L., LL.D.; retired paper manufacturing executive; b. Woking, England 29 Mar. 1916; s. Gideon and Muriel Sutcliffe Montagu (Mort) B.; e. Winchester Coll., 1929–34; Magdalen Coll., Oxford, B.A. (Hons.) 1937; D.C.L. Acadia 1967; LL.D., St. Francis Xavier 1968; m. Mary Chase, d. Admiral H. S. Howard, U.S.N., Washington, D.C., 1946; children: Patricia Ann (Tuff), Josephine Mary Chase (Ahrens), Howard Robert, Hugh McCauley; with Bowater Paper Corp. 1938–80 in various capacities in Britain, U.S.A. and Canada; Commd. in Royal Arty. (T.A.) 1936; served in 2nd World War; London A.A. Defences, Brit. Army Staff in Washington, and 15th Army Group and 5th U.S. Army in Italy; retired as Lieut.-Col.; O.B.E.; Mentioned in Despatches; U.S. Legion of Merit; U.S. Bronze Star Medal; Anglican; recreations: golf, tennis, photography; Clubs: Conanicut Yacht (Jamestown, R.I.); Home: 7 Glen Hill Lane, Wilton, Conn. 06897.

**BALLS, Herbert Ryan,** B.A., D.M.Sc. (Ottawa 1973); b. Winnipeg, Man. 24 May 1910; s. George Herbert and Alma Myrtle (Ryan) B.; e. Kelvin High Sch., Winnipeg, Man.; Univ. of Manitoba, B.A. (Hons.) 1931; Post-grad. studies in Pol. Science and Econs. at Univ. of Manitoba and Univ. of Toronto; m. Evelyn Marjorie, d. James Alexander Clarke, Ottawa, Ont., 7 Sept 1937; Dir. Northern Ont. Pipeline, Crown Corp., 1956–68; Dir., Candn. Nat. (W.I.) Steamships Ltd., 1960–71; staff of Auditor-Gen. of Can.; 1931–50; mem. of Research Staff, Royal Comm. on Dom.-Prov. Relations, 1938; Special Asst. to Dir. of Public Accounts Enquiry for Dom.-Prov. Conf., 1941–42; Special Asst. to Deputy Min. of Finance, 1950–54; Dir. of Financial Adm. and Accounting Policy Div., Dept. of Finance, 1954–58; Pres., Civil Service Co-op. Credit Society Ltd., 1957–59; Comptroller of the Treasury, 1958–68; Deputy Min. of Services and Deputy Rec. Gen. for Can. 1968–75, Skelton Clark Fellow, Queens Univ. (1975–76); Research Fellow, Inst. of Public Admin. of Canada; mem. Bd. of Govs., Candn. Council on Social Devel.; mem. Bd. of Govs., Huntington Univ. 1968–71; Pres. Un. Appeal of Ottawa and Dist., 1963–65; Chrmn., Community Funds and Councils of Can., 1965–69; Chrmn. Nat. Agency Review Comte, 1971–74; Dir., Ont. Share and Deposit Insur. Corp. 1976–85; mem., Inst. of Public Adm. Can. (Nat. Pres. 1960–61); United Church; recreations: painting, writing, gardening; Club: Rideau; Home: 2026 Thistle Cres., Ottawa, Ont. K1H 5P5.

**BALLSTADT, Carl Paul Arthur,** M.A., Ph.D.; educator; writer; b. Sault Ste. Marie, Ont. 28 Dec. 1931; s. Paul Adolph and Rheinhilda Christina (Liedtke) B.; e. Sault Ste. Marie elem. and high schs.; North Bay Normal Sch. 1952–53; Univ. of W. Ont. B.A. 1957, M.A. 1959; Univ. of London Ph.D. 1965; m. Dorothy d. Harry and Edith Copeland 8 July 1967; children: Kurt Paul Alexander, Marnin Rochelle; PROF. OF ENGLISH, McMASTER UNIV. 1986– ; teacher Sault Ste.

Marie schs. 1953–57, 1959–60; Univ. of Sask. 1962–66; Guelph Univ. 1966–67; joined present Univ. 1967; author 'The Search for English Canadian Literature' 1975; 'Catherine Parr Traill and Her Works' 1983; co-author 'Susanna Moodie: Letters of a Lifetime' 1985; ed. Susanna Moodie's 'Roughing it in the Bush' 1988; several essays Dictionary Candn. Biog.; articles nineteenth-century Candn. lit.; mem. Assn. Cand. Studies; Candn. Assn. Am. Studies; Lutheran; recreations: hobby farm & woodlot maintenance, cottage, cross-country skiing; Home: 115 Hwy. #8, Dundas, Ont. L9H 4V7; Office: Dept. of English, 1280 Main St. W., Hamilton, Ont. L8S 4L8.

**BALMAIN, Keith George,** Ph.D., P.Eng., F.I.E.E.E.; university professor; b. London, Ont. 7 Aug. 1933; s. William and Laeta Marguerite (Whaley) B.; e. Univ. of Toronto B.A.Sc. 1957; Univ. of Illinois M.S. 1959, Ph.D. 1963; m. Shirley d. Frank and Margaret Ebbutt 16 Aug. 1958; PROF., DEPT. OF ELECTRICAL ENGINEERING, UNIV. OF TORONTO 1973– ; Rsch. Assoc., Univ. of Illinois 1963–64; Asst. Prof. 1964–66; Univ. of Toronto 1966–67; Assoc. Prof. 1967–73; Chrmn., Div. of Engr. Sci. 1985–87; Chrmn., Rsch. Bd. 1987–90; Sr. Chairholder, NSERC/Bell Can. Indus. Rsch. Chair in Electromagnetics 1991–96; Mem., Admin. Ctte., IEEE Antennas & Propagation Soc. 1973–76; Dir., EEC Ltd. 1977–81; Chrmn., Electr. Engr. Grant Selection Ctte., NSERC 1984–85; F.I.E.E.E. 1987; Best Paper of the Year for 1970 award, IEEE Antennas & Prop. Soc.; Mem., Assn. of Profl. Engrs. of Ont.; Assoc. Ed., 'Radio Science' 1978–80; co-author: 'Electromagnetic Waves and Radiating Systems,' 2nd ed. 1968; Office: 10 King's College Rd., Toronto, Ont. M5S 1A4.

**BALON, Eugene Kornel,** RNDr., C.Sc. (=Ph.D.); university professor; b. Orlova, Czechoslovakia 1 Aug. 1930; s. Josef and Jaromira (Zavičaková) B.; e. Polské realné gymnasium, Orlova 1949; Charles Univ., Prague B.Sc. 1952, RNDr. 1953, C.Sc. 1962; m. Christine d. Eugen and Margarete Flegler 1 Aug. 1980; one s.: Janusz S. Balon; PROF. OF ZOOLOGY, UNIV. OF GUELPH 1976– ; Rsch. Sci., Lab. of Fish. Res., Bratislava 1954–67; Fish Biol., UNDP/FAO Rsch. Inst., Zambia 1967–71; Rsch. Assoc., Univ. of Toronto 1971–72; Assoc. Prof., Univ. of Guelph 1972–76; Rsch. Assoc., Royal Ont. Mus. 1972– ; Proj. Danube, Senckenberg Inst., Frankfurt 1976–87; Vis. Rsch. Fellow, J.L.B. Smith Inst. of Ichthyology & Rhodes Univ. on Hugh Kelly Fellowship 1986–87; Cons., IDRC, Borneo 1980; Rsch. Expdns. to Cuba 1965, Tanzania 1969, '91, '92, Kenya 1970, Costa Rica 1973, Danube River, Germany, Austria 1976, '84, Borneo 1980, American deserts 1981, Okawango, Botswana 1987, Comoro Islands 1987, '90, Chernobyl, USSR 1990, Zanzibar 1992; mem., Am. Soc. of Zool.; Sigma Xi; Am. Soc. of Ichthyol. & Herpetol.; Euro. Ichthyol. Union; Am. Fish. Soc.; Fish. Soc. of Brit. Isles; Coelacanth Conserv. Counc. & others; author: 'Fishes of Slovakia' 1967, 'Fishes of Lake Kariba' 1974,'Early Life Histories, New Perspectives' 1985; co-author: 'Expedition Cayo Largo' 1967; 'Evolution of Organisms' 1969; significant essays: 'Kariba: the Dubious Benefits of Large Dams' 1978 (in German 1978, in Japanese 1989), 'Epigenetic Mechanisms: Reflection on Evolutionary Processes' 1983', 'Saltatory Ontogeny and Evolution' 1986, 'The Tao of Life: From the Dynamic Unity of Polar Opposites to Self-Organization' 1989, 'Epigenesis of an Epigeneticist' 1990; editor: 'Charrs, Salmonid fishes of the genus Salvelinus' 1980; co-editor: 'Lake Kariba, the Man-Made Ecosystem in Central Africa' 1974; 'The Biology of 'Latimeria chalumnae' and evolution of coelacanths' 1991; editor of 2 book series: 'Developments in Environ. Biol. of Fishes,' 'Perspectives in Vertebrate Science'; editor-in-chief & founder intern. journ., 'Environ. Biol. of Fishes' 1976– ; author of over 300 sci. papers, book chapters & 7 books in fish ecology, ecomorphology, systematics, embryology, epigenetics, evolution and philosophy; recreations: photography, scholarly contemplation, illustration, reading; Home: R.R. 3, Rockwood, Ont. N0B 2K0; Office: Inst. of Ichthyology and Dept. of Zoology, Univ. of Guelph, Guelph, Ont. N1G 2W1.

**BALTHAZAR, Louis,** Ph.D.; educator; b. Montreal, Que. 25 March 1931; s. Elzéar and Laure (Jolicoeur) B.; e. Coll. Ste-Marie Montréal B.A. 1950; Univ. de Montréal M.A. 1955; Jesuit Faculties Montréal 1956 L.Phil., 1963 L.Th.; Harvard Univ. Ph.D. 1971; div.; one s. Martin; PROF. OF POL. SCI. UNIV. LAVAL 1982– ; mem. Jesuit Order 1950–69; taught drama, speech, French, Latin and Greek Coll. des Jésuites Québec City 1956–59; joined present Univ. 1969, Chrmn. of Pol. Sci. 1970–73, 1979–80; Visiting Prof.: Univ. de Bordeaux Institut d'études politiques 1973, 1986; Glendon Coll. York Univ. 1974–75; Johns Hopkins Univ. Sch. Advanced Internat. Studies 1980; Visiting scholar, Ctr. for Internat. Affairs, Harvard Univ. 1990; mem. Qué.'s Superior Council Edn. 1982–86; Assoc. mem. Bd. Dirs. Assn. Candn. Studies in U.S. 1977–81; Mem. of Bd. of Dir., Quebec Center Internat. Relations 1977– ; Researcher Candn. Royal Comn. Bilingualism & Biculturalism 1965–66; author 'Bilan du nationalisme au Québec' 1986 (Air Canada Prize 1987); 'French-Canadian Civilization' 1989; co-author 'L'École détournée' 1989; 'Contemporary Quebec and the United States' 1988; co-editor 'International Perspectives' 1974–79; numerous articles; frequent lectr. Can., USA and Eur. Québec nationalism and US-Can. relations; mem. Candn. Pol. Sci. Assn.; Assn. Candn. Studies in U.S.; Home: 7, Couillard, Québec, Qué. G1R 3S6; 184 Morel, Kamouraska, Qué. G0L 1M0; Office: Québec City, Qué. G1K 7P4.

**BALTZAN, Marc,** M.D., F.R.C.P.(C); physician; b. Saskatoon, Sask. 31 Oct. 1929; s. David M. and Rose (Cristall) B.; e. Nutana Collegiate Inst. 1946; McGill Univ., B.Sc. 1949; M.D., C.M. 1953; m. Nahid 21 Mar. 1992; children: Marcel, Frances, Elizabeth; PRES., CANADIAN MEDICAL ASSN. 1982–83; post-grad. work in internal medicine, McGill and Johns Hopkins Univ.; private practice, Saskatoon; Dir. Kidney Transplantation Unit, Univ. Sask. since 1963; Chrmn., Dept. Med., Univ. Sask. 1974–79; author articles on internal medicine, kidney transplantation, medical economics; mem. Sask. Med. Assn. (Pres. 1966–68); Candn. Med. Assn. (Pres. 1982–83) (Chrmn. Counc. on Economics 1976–80); club: Saskatoon; recreations: golf; jogging; Home: 303 Saskatchewan Cres. W., Saskatoon, Sask. Office: 200 - 366 3rd Ave. S., Saskatoon, Sask. S7K 1M5.

**BAMBERGER, Jonathan,** B.Sc., C.A.; business executive; b. South Yemen 8 Nov. 1955; e. Univ. of Manchester B.Sc. 1977; Inst. of C.A.s in England & Wales C.A. 1980; m. Diane; children: James, Victoria; PRES., CANDN. MALTING OPNS., CANADA MALTING CO. LIMITED 1991– ; Royal Air Force 1974–77; Coopers & Lybrand 1977–82; Controller, Treas., Vice-Pres. Finan. & Corp. Devel., present firm 1982–91; recreations: squash, skiing; Home: R.R. #4, Rockwood, Ont. N0B 2K0; Office: 325 – 21 Four Seasons Place, Toronto, Ont. M9B 6J8.

**BAMBROUGH, Noel Raymond;** cable television executive; b. Toronto, Ont 15 February 1938; s. Raymond Howard and Ruby Frances (Towns) B.; e. Univ. of Toronto, B.Sc. 1963; York Univ., M.B.A. 1970; Harvard Univ. Grad. Sch. of Bus. Adv. Mgmt. Prog.; m. Darlene d. John and Wanda Jenkins 14 Feb. 1974; one son: Jonas; two d.: Jennifer, Aimée; SENIOR VICE PRESIDENT, SHAW COMMUNICATIONS 1993– ; Vice-Pres., Opns., Cablecasting Ltd. 1976–79; Extve. Vice-Pres., Cable Am. Inc. 1979–84; Pres. & C.E.O., Cablecasting Ltd. 1984–..; Past Chrmn. & Dir., Candn. Cable TV Assn.; Dir., Ont. Cable Telecommunication Assoc.; Dir., Greater Winnipeg Cablevision Ltd.; Cablecasting Ltd.; YTV Ltd.; Clubs: Granite; Royal Candn. Military Inst.; Cherokee Town & Country (Atlanta); Manitoba Club (Winnipeg); Home: 25 St. Edmund's Dr., Toronto, Ont. M4N 2P7; Office: Royal Bank Plaza, South Tower, Box 97, Suite 2525, Toronto, Ont. M5J 2J2.

**BAMFORTH, John Stephen George,** M.B., B.S., F.R.C.P.(C.); educator; b. Halifax, Yorks., Eng. 30 July 1952; s. John Howard and Enid Moira (Holdsworth) B.; e. Woodhouse Grove Sch. Bradford, Yorks.; Guys Hosp. Med. Sch. Univ. of London M.B., B.S. 1975; m. Fiona d. Allan and Mary Odle 3 July 1976; children: Bryony, Emily, Owain, Lucy; ASST. PROF. OF PEDIATRICS (MED. GENETICS) UNIV. OF ALTA. 1988– ; Sr. House Offr. (Pediatrics) Sydenham Children's Hosp., Lewisham Hosp., Guys Hosp. and Hosp. for Sick Children Great Ormand St. London 1976–79; Registrar training in Pediatrics Liverpool 1980–83; Sr. Registrar in Med. Genetics Univ. of Wales 1984–86; Fellow in Med. Genetics Univ. of B.C. 1986–88; author various sci. papers clin. genetics, pediatrics; Fellow, Candn. Coll. Med. Genetics; mem. Royal Coll. Phys. UK; Clin. Genetics Soc. UK; Am. Soc. Human Genetics; Skeletal Dysplasia Group UK; Garrod Soc.; Diplomate Am. Bd. of Medical Genetics; Fellow, Royal Coll. of Physicians (Can.); Home: 688 Romaniuk Rd., Edmonton, Alta. T6R 1A5; Office: B–139 CSB, 8440 – 112 St., Edmonton, Alta. T6G 2G3.

**BANADYGA, Walter Kirk,** B.Arch., P.P./FRAIC, Hon. FAIA; architect; b. Wadena, Sask. 16 June 1946; s. Steven and Margaret (Marwick) B.; e. Wadena Comprehensive H.S.; Univ. of Man., B.Arch. 1971; m. Sherry Anne (Anderson) Jan. 1957; one s. Kirk Jr.; PRES. & MNG. PRINC., ARCHITECTS IN ASSOCIATION, BANADYGA, MITCHELL, OKUMURA, PHILLIPS LIMITED 1985– ; Past Pres. & Fellow, Royal Archit. Inst. of Can. 1985; Vice-Pres. 1984; Counc. Rep. 1979–83; Pres., Sask. Assn. of Archit. 1979; Hon. Fellow, Am. Inst. of Archit. 1985; Dir., Construction Specifications Can. 1976; Assiniboia Club 1979–80 (Pres. 1981); Senate Mem., Univ. of Regina, 1980–83; recreations: golf, skiing; Club: Wascana Country; Home: 25 Tibbitts Rd., Regina, Sask. S4S 1N5.

**BANASCHEWSKI, Bernhard,** F.R.S.C.; university professor; b. Munich, Germany 22 Mar. 1926; s. Adalbert Schremmer and Anna Magdalena B.; e. Hamburg Univ.; Dr. rerum naturarum; came to Canada, 1955; Asst., Hamburg Univ., 1953–55; Asst. Prof., McMaster Univ., 1955–57; Assoc. Prof., 1957–59; Prof., 1959; Dept. Chrmn. 1961–67; M[c]Kay Prof. of Math. 1964; Dept. Chrmn. 1982–87; Emeritus 1991; served in 2nd World War in German army (Wehrmacht) 1944–45; prisoner-of-war, 1945–47; Assoc. Ed., Candn. Journal of Math. 1968–79; Ed. Bd., Topology and Its Applications 1970–93; Ed. Bd., Quaest. Math. 1987; author of over 120 papers on algebra, gen. topology and related fields; mem., Candn. Math. Soc. (Vice-Pres. 1983); Nat. Sci. and Eng. Research Council of Can. 1981–88; Home: 100 Bay St. S., Apt. 503, Hamilton, Ont. L8P 3H3.

**BANCROFT, John Basil,** B.A., Ph.D., F.R.S.C.; university professor; b. Vancouver, B.C. 31 Dec. 1929; s. John Stanley and Marjorie (White) B.; e. Univ. B.C., B.A. 1952; Univ. Wisconsin, Ph.D. 1955; m. Mary, d. George and Mary Ross, 28 Aug. 1954; children: Leslie Ann; Ian David; Graham John; Jane Elizabeth; PROFESSOR OF PLANT SCIENCE, UNIV. OF WESTERN ONTARIO 1973– ; Dean of Science, Univ. of Western Ontario 1979–..; mem. faculty Purdue Univ. 1955–70; NSF sr. postdoctoral fellow, Virus Research Unit, Cambridge, Eng. 1965–66; Head, Dept. Virus Research, John Innes Inst. (Norwich, Eng.) 1970–73; Chrmn. Dept. 1973–78; author about 100 papers in field; rec'd. Ruth Allen Award 1970; McCoy Award 1971; Fellow, Royal Soc. Can. 1979; Fellow, Am. Phytopath. Soc., mem. Am. Soc. Virology; Soc. Gen. Microbiology; Sigma Xi; Phi Kappa Phi; Home: 21 Scarlett Ave., London, Ont. N6G 1Z3; Office: Natural Sciences Centre, Univ. of Western Ont., London, Ont. N6A 5B7.

**BANDEEN, Robert Angus,** O.C., K.St.J., Ph.D., LL.D., D.C.L.; management executive; b. Rodney, Ont., 29 Oct. 1930; s. John Robert and Jessie Marie (Thomson) B.; e. Univ. of W. Ont., B.A. (Hons.) 1952; Duke Univ., (1952–55) Ph.D. 1959; Univ. of Western Ont. LL.D. 1975; Dalhousie Univ. LL.D. 1978; Bishop's Univ. D.C.L. 1978; Queen's Univ. Hon. LL.D. 1982; Syracuse Univ. Salzberg Medal 1982; m. Mona Helen, d. S.M. Blair, Bolton, Ont., 31 May 1958; children: Ian Blair, Mark Everett, Robert Derek, Adam Drummond; CHRMN. & PRES., CLUNY CORP. 1986– ; Pres., Crownx Inc. 1984–85; Vice Chrmn., Crownx Inc. 1985–86; and Chrmn., Pres. & C.E.O., Crown Life Insurance Co. 1982–85; former Pres., C.E.O. & Dir., Canadian National Railways; Dir., BP Canada Inc.; Counsel Corp.; Diversicare Inc.; Greyvest Financial Services Inc.; Greyvest Inc.; Newfoundland Capital Corp.; Hope Brook Gold Inc.; Vice Chrmn., The Inst. for Research on Public Policy; Lester B. Pearson Coll. of the Pacific; Senator, Stratford Shakespearean Festival; Former Chancellor, Bishop's Univ. (Dir. of Foundation, mem. of Corp.); Vice Pres., Art Gallery of Ont.; mem., British-North American Comte.; Howe Inst. Policy Analysis Comte.; Adv. Comm., Candn. Ski Counc.; Gov.: Sport Participation Can.; Olympic Trust of Canada; recreations: tennis, squash, skiing; Officer, The Order of Canada; Knight, The Order of St. John; Clubs: M.A.A.A.; Mount Royal; York; Toronto; Delta Upsilon Fraternity; Office: 57 Cluny Dr., Toronto, Ont. M4W 2R1.

**BANDLER, John William,** B.Sc.(Eng.), Ph.D., D.Sc.(Eng.); university professor; b. Jerusalem 9 Nov. 1941; e. Univ. of London, B.Sc. (Hons.) 1963, Ph.D. 1967, D.Sc. 1976; m. Beth Budd 1990; children: Lydia, Zoe; PROF. OF ELECTRICAL & COMPUTER ENGR. 1974– ; & DIR., SIMULATION OPTIMIZATION SYSTEMS RES. LAB., MCMASTER UNIV. 1983– ; Engr., Mullard Rsch. Labs. 1966–67; Post-doct. fellow & sess. lectr., Univ. of Man. 1967–69; Asst. Prof., McMaster Univ. 1969; Assoc. Prof. 1971; Chrmn., Dept. of Elect. Engr. 1978–79; Dean, Fac. of Engr. 1979–81; Pres., Optimization Systems Assoc. Inc. 1983– ; Pres., Bandler Research Inc. 1989– ; Fellow, Royal Soc. of Can. 1986– ; Fellow, Inst. of Electr. & Electronics Engrs. 1978– ; Fellow, Inst. of Electr. Engrs. 1978– ; Assn. of Profl. Engr. of Ont.; Mem., The Electromagnetics Acad. 1990– ; recognized as one of the 'young Canadians who have achieved excellence in the Arts & Sciences,' Queen's Silver Jubilee dinner 17 Oct. 1977; num. referee & cons. positions; extensive work on cttes. (acad. & others), confs., panels, workshops & seminars;

Mem., IEEE Circuits & Systems Soc., Control Systems Soc., Microwave Theory & Tech. Soc., Power Engr. Soc.; Math. Prog. Soc.; author of 250 pub. articles; Mem., Ed. Bd., 'IEEE Transactions on Microwave Theory and Techniques' (Assoc. Ed. 1969–74; Guest Ed., spec. issue on Computer-Oriented Microwave Practices, March 1974; Guest Co-Ed., spec. issue on Process-Oriented Microwave CAD and Modeling, July 1992), 'International Journal of Numerical Modelling' 1987– ; 'International Journal of Microwave and Millimeter-wave Computer-Aided Engineering' 1989– ; Computer & Electrical Engineering, McMaster Univ., Hamilton, Ont. L8S 4L8.

**BANERJEE, Diponkar,** M.B., Ch.B., F.R.C.P.C., Ph.D.; university professor; b. Calcutta, India 16 Nov. 1946; s. Rabindranath and Renuka (Mukherjee) B.; e. Makerere Med. Sc., Kampala, Uganda, M.B., Ch.B. 1971; Univ. of Minnesota Med. Sch., post-grad. training 1973–74; Univ. of Ottawa post-grad. training and Ph.D. 1974–78; m. Maheshwari d. Yeshwantsinh and Rajendra Yeshwantsinh 11 May 1973; children: Gautam, Preetam; PROF. OF PATHOL., UNIV. OF TORONTO 1991– , CHIEF OF ONCOLOGIC PATHOL., ONTARIO CANCER INST., PRINCESS MARGARET HOSP. 1991– ; Asst. Prof. of Pathol., Univ. of W. Ont. and Cons. Pathol., Univ. Hosp. 1978–83, Assoc. Prof. 1983–91; Dir., Immunopathol. Lab., Univ. Hosp. 1980–86; Chief of Pathology, St. Joseph's Health Ctr. 1986–91; Mem., Candn. Assn. of Pathol.; Ont. Assn. of Pathol.; Ont. Med. Assn.; U.S. & Candn. Acad. of Pathol.; author of 51 journal pubns., 60 abstracts and 5 book chapters; Home: 108 Kimbark Blvd., Toronto, Ont. M5N 2Y2.

**BANFIELD, Alexander William Francis,** M.A., Ph.D.; professor emeritus; b. Toronto, Ont. 12 March 1918; s. Rev. Alexander Woods and Althea (Priest) B.; e. Univ. of Toronto, B.A. 1942, M.A. 1946; Univ. of Michigan, Ph.D 1952; research fellow, Univ. Edinburgh 1975–76; m. Martha Fern, d. Fraser Duncan Munro, Lancaster, Ont., 3 Oct. 1942; children; Brian Alexander, Candace Anne, Martha Kim; PROFESSOR EMERITUS, BROCK UNIVERSITY 1980– ; joined Canadian Civil Service as Mammalogist, Nat. Parks Bureau, 1946–47; Chief Mammalogist, Candn. Wildlife Service, 1947–57; joined Nat. Museum of Natural Sciences, Ottawa as Chief Zoologist 1957; Dir., 1964–69; Prof. of Biol. Sciences, Brock Univ. 1969, Dir. Inst. of Urban & Environmental Studies 1974–79; Pres., Rangifer Associates Environmental Consultants 1979–83; served in 2nd World War; enlisted Apr. 1942; discharged Oct. 1945; Overseas service with rank of Capt., Signal Corps and later Arty.; Publications: 'Mammals of Canada' 1974, 2 books and over 130 scientific articles dealing with mammalogy, ornith, and wildlife management; Fellow, Arctic Inst. N.Am.; Am. Assn. Advance. Science; mem., Am. Soc. of Mammal; Candn. Soc. of Zool.; Centennial Medal 1967; Phi Sigma; Sigma Psi; United Church; Address: 37 Yates St., St. Catharines, Ont. L2R 5R3.

**BANFIELD, Charlotte Jane,** B.A., LL.B., M.A., Ph.D.; educator; b. Vancouver, B.C. 13 July 1930; d. William Orson and Beatrice Maud (Timmins) B.; e. Univ. of B.C. B.A., LL.B. 1954; Univ. of Toronto M.A. 1959; Univ. of London, London Sch. of Econ. & Pol. Sci. Ph.D. 1973; m. Robert Hall s: James and Lillian Haynes 2 June 1966; ASSOCIATE PROFESSOR OF SOCIAL SCIENCE, YORK UNIV. 1974– ; articled Clerk at Law, Davis & Co. 1954–55; Extve. Sec., World Univ. Serv. of Canada 1955–58; Program Offr., Candn. Nat. Comn. for UNESCO 1960–62; Commonwealth Scholar, Makerere Univ. Kampala Uganda 1962–64; Asst. Prof. of Pol. Sci., Loyola Coll. 1964–65; and at Calif. State Univ. at Hayward 1965–68; Asst. Prof. of Soc. Sci., York Univ. 1968–74; Chair, Div. of Soc. Sci. 1977–81; First Adviser to York Univ. on the Status of Women 1975–77; Consultant on Women's Rights, York-Thailand Project (Thammassat Univ. Bangkok) 1991; Founding Dir., Law & Soc. Program 1974– ; Mem., Bd. of Gov. 1990–92; Chair, Bd. of Dir., Inst. for Feminist Legal Studies 1990– ; Mem., Council of Ont. Univs. 1979–81; Dir., The Osgoode Soc. for Candn. Legal History 1979– ; Mem., The Ontario Econ. Council 1976–79; numerous Candn. Human Rights Tribunals (employment equity, sex discrimination) 1978–92; Candn. Bar Assn.; Candn. Pol. Sci. Assn.; Law & Soc. Assn.; editor: 'Readings in Law and Society' 1987; author of various articles on law & politics; recreations: travel; Home: 15 Queen Mary's Dr., Toronto, Ont. M8X 1S1; Office: North York, Ont. M3J 1P3.

**BANIASSAD, Essy,** B.Arch., M.A., Ph.D.; university professor/administrator; b. Tehran, Iran 29 Nov. 1936; s. Assad and Esmat B.; e. Univ. of Illinois, B.Arch. 1962; Univ. of Manchester, M.A. 1967, Ph.D. 1978; m. Cynthia d. Helen and Martin Riser; one d.: Elisa; PROF. & DEAN, FAC. OF ARCH., TECHNICAL UNIV. OF N.S. 1981– ; practiced, Chicago & Manchester, England; taught, U.K. & Can. & helped in redirection of arch. edn. & rsch. in Can. & the Commonwealth countries through activities at the RAIC & the Commonwealth Assn. of Arch.; Fellow & President, RAIC; Hon. Fellow, Am. Inst. of Architects; Principal Researcher & Consultant, IDRC; various design articles on arch. theory, crit. & edn.; recreations: sailing, riding, climbing; Home: 1540 Carleton St., Halifax, N.S. B3H 3B9; Office: P.O. Box 1000, Halifax, N.S. B3J 2X4.

**BANISTER, Eric W.,** B.Sc., M.P.E., Ph.D., F.A.C.S.M.; educator, scientist; b. Kirby-in-Furness, Lancs. Eng., 18 May 1932; s. Eric and Alice Ann (Halshall) B.; e. Manchester Univ., B.Sc. 1953; Loughborough Coll., Dipl. (PE) 1954; Univ. of B.C., M.P.E. 1962; Univ. of Ill., Ph.D. 1964; m. Maureen, d. Stanley Landless, N. Wales, 6 Aug. 1960; children: Simon John, Fiona Jane, Susan Pia; PROF. OF KINESIOLOGY, FACULTY OF APPLIED SCIENCES, SIMON FRASER UNIV. and Chrmn. of Dept. 1970–82, 1987–88; Dir., Inst. for Human Performance 1980– ; Dir., Geraldine and Tong Louie Human Performance Ctr. 1992– ; Environmental Physiology Unit 1981–88; Altero Technologies Inc., Vancouver 1987–91; Pres., Western Fitness Consultants Ltd., Vancouver 1972–75; mem. Med. Adv. Comte., Remedial Gymnast Association (B.C.) 1971–73 and Candn. Soccer Assn. 1972–85; Co-Chrmn. Symposium on Gravitational Physiology, XXX Internat. Congress Physiological Sciences Vancouver 1986; Orgn. Ctte. and Symposium Chrmn., (Modeling Physiological Response to Exercise) 1st Internat. Conf. Human-Environment System, Tokyo, Japan, Dec. 1991; joined Univ. of B.C. as Asst. Prof.; Dept. of Phys. Educ. 1964–67; joined present Univ. as Asst. Prof. Dept. of Phys. Devel. Studies, 1967–69, Assoc. Prof. of Kinesiology, 1970; Research Prof. Dept. Naval & Aviation Med, Karolinska Institutet Stockholm 1969–70; Research Prof. Dept. Physiology, Schl. Med., Univ. of Hawaii 1975–76; served with Parachute Regt., Brit. Army, 1954–56; rank 2nd Lt.; Ed. Chrmn., Proceedings 5th Internat. Hyperbaric Conf., 1973; author of book chapters, reviews and over 80 articles in scient. journs.; 'Experiments in Human Performance' (with I.B. Mêkjavic, G. Asmundson and R. Ward) 1990; 'Contemporary Health Issues' (with M. Allen, S. Fadl, G. Bhakthan and D. Howard) 1988; 'Environmental Ergonomics' (with I.B. Mêkjavic and J.B. Morrison) 1988; editor 'Human Factors: Health Concerns Working with VDT's'; Fellow, Am. Coll. Sport Med.; mem., Undersea Med. Soc.; Candn. Ass. Sports Sciences (Pres. 1977–78); Vice Pres., Sport Med. Council Can. 1978; Ed., Candn. Journal of Applied Sports Sciences 1980–83; Assoc. Ed., Annals of Physiological Anthropology 1985– ; Ed. Bd., Undersea Biomedical Rsch. 1985–92; Ed.-in Chief, Sports Medicine, Training and Rehabilitation: an International Journal 1989– ; Harwood Academic Publishers N.Y.; rec'd first Illinois Writing Fellowship, Human Kinetics Publishers, Inc. & Univ. of Illinois Coll. of Applied Life Studies Jan. 1987; Anglican; Home: 2651 Haywood Ave., W. Vancouver, B.C. V7V 1Y7; Office: Burnaby B.C. V5A 1S6.

**BANISTER, Harold Bertram,** B.Com., M.B.A.; construction executive; b. Edmonton, Alta. 1 Jan. 1951; s. Ronald Kitchener and Inez Adelaide (Thorson) B.; e. Univ. of Alta. B.Com. 1973; Concordia Univ. M.B.A. 1976; m. 2ndly Linda C. (Taylor) Banister; children: Taylor Harold and (from previous marriage): Brooke A., Dallas I.; CHRMN. & C.E.O., GREAT WESTERN GROUP INC. 1992– ; President, K.R. Ranches Ltd. 1991– ; Extve. Asst., Corp. Planning, Banister Continental Ltd. 1977–78; Mgr., Corp. Planning & Bus. Devel. 1978–80; Vice-Pres. 1980–83; Vice-Pres., Planning, Equipment & Bus. Devel. 1983–87; Extve. Vice-Pres. 1987–90; Acting Pres., Banister Pipelines Ltd. 1989– ; Pres. and C.E.O., The Foundation Co. of Canada 1988–90; Sr. Vice Pres. Corp. Services & Asst. to Pres., PCL Construction Inc. 1990–91; Pres. Edmonton C. of C. 1986; Chrmn. Edmonton Un. Way 1988; Dir. Candn. Equestrian Team 1989; recreations: golf, running, skiing; Club: Mayfair Golf & Country (Edmonton); Office: 11631 Saskatchewan Dr., Edmonton, Alta. T6G 2B5.

**BANKES, John F.,** B.A. (Hons.), LL.B., M.B.A., LL.M.; investment banker; b. Calgary, Alta. 14 Sept. 1951; s. John Maxwell and Betty Jean (Ingraham) B.; e. Westmount (Que.) High Sch. 1968; Neuchatel Jr. Coll. Switzerland 1969; Queen's Univ. B.A. (Hons.) 1973; York Univ. M.B.A., LL.B 1977 (Silver Medal 1977); Harvard Univ. LL.M. 1979; m. Pamela M. d. Donald G. and Marian M. Gibson 25 May 1984; PRESIDENT, NOVA BANCORP CAPITAL MANAGEMENT LTD. 1992– ; articled with Davies, Ward & Beck Toronto 1977–78, Assoc. 1980–81, Partner 1981–83; Assoc. Corporate Finance, Morgan Stanley & Co. Inc. N.Y. 1983–84; Vice Pres. Invest. Banking Services (Can.), Goldman, Sachs & Co. N.Y. 1984–87; Vice Pres. Invest. Banking Dept., The First Boston Corp. N.Y. & Toronto 1987–90; Exec. Vice Pres. and Dir., Head of Invest. Banking, Richardson Greenshields of Canada Ltd. 1990–92; Dir., Silcorp Limited; Security Home Mortgage Investment Corp.; Gov. and Vice Chrmn., York Univ.; Gov., Royal Life Saving Soc. Can.; Corp. of Massey Hall and Roy Thomson Hall; Dir., Sunnybrook Found.; The Toronto Symphony; Candn. Coun. of Christians and Jews; mem. Council Bd. Trade Metrop. Toronto; Law Soc. Upper Can.; recreations: competitive sailing, racquet sports, fly-fishing; Clubs: Empire (Past Pres.); Granite; Toronto; Toronto Lawn Tennis; Rosedale Golf; Harvard (N.Y.C.); Metropolitan (N.Y.C.); Larchmont Yacht; Home: 137 Teddington Park Ave., Toronto, Ont. M4N 2C7; Office: 1805 – 40 King St. W., Toronto, Ont. M5H 3Y2.

**BANKES, John Maxwell;** banker (ret.); b. Victoria, B.C. 28 June 1915; s. Stanley Fownes and Frances Victoria (McArthur) B.; e. Monteray at Oak Bay, Victoria; Oak Bay High Sch.; Victoria Coll.; m. Betty Jean, d. George Ingraham, Calgary, Alta., 2 Nov. 1950; one s.; two d.; Chrmn. Emeritus, Drivers Jonas, Canada Ltd.; commenced with the Royal Bank in Canada in 1934 at Victoria, B.C.; served at various brs. in B.C. and at Supv. Dept., Vancouver till 1941 when attached to Asst. Gen. Mgrs. Dept., Toronto; Asst. Mgr., Hamilton, Ont. 1946; Mgr. Bus. Devel. Dept., Calgary 1950; Mgr., Portage Ave. Winnipeg 1952; Ottawa 1953; at Toronto Main Br. 1957; apptd. Asst. Gen. Mgr. 1961; Depy. Gen. Mgr. 1964–71; Vice-Pres. 1971–75; served in Royal Candn. Navy, 2nd World War 1942–45; mem. R.C.N.V.R.; Protestant; recreations: tennis, golf, swimming, boating, Clubs: Toronto; Granite; Rosedale Golf; Royal Poinciana Golf (Naples, Fla.); Naples (Fla.) Yacht; Address: 31 Stratheden Rd., Toronto, Ont. M4N 1E5.

**BANKS, Tommy (Thomas Benjamin),** O.C. LL.D.; pianist; conductor; composer; b. Calgary, Alberta. 17 Dec. 1936; Hon. Diploma of Music, Grant MacEwan Coll. 1979; Hon. Doctorate of Laws, Univ. of Alta. 1987; Chrmn., Music Programme, Grant MacEwan College 1983–87; Chrmn., Alta. Found. for Performing Arts 1978–86; Bd. of Govs. & Chrmn., Music Ctte., Alberta Coll. 1977–79; Chrmn., Edmonton Concert Hall Found. 1989–91; Mem., Canada Council 1989– ; Prop. Tommy Banks Music Ltd., music production and publishing; affiliate SOCAN; Host, pianist, arranger and conductor 'The Tommy Banks Show' (CBC-TV 1968–74, ITV International syndication 1974–76, CBC-TV 1980–83); Conductor or music co-ordinator of various internationally-syndicated TV specials; performed Montreux Internat. Jazz Festival Switzerland 1978 (double LP of concert rec'd Juno Award 1979); concert tour Japan, Hong Kong, Malaysia, first foreign jazz band to tour People's Republic of China 1983; producer of numerous stage show incl. Royal Command Performance 1978; guest conductor Hamilton Philharmonic, National Arts Centre, Winnipeg Symphony, Regina Symphony, Saskatoon Symphony, Calgary Philharmonic, Edmonton Symphony and Vancouver Symphony orchestras; Mus. Direction, Commonwealth Games 1978, World University Games 1983, gala state visit of Pres. Reagan 1981, visit of John Paul II (Vancouver) 1984, Opening Ceremonies EXPO '86, XV Olympic Winter Games 1988; Film actor ('The Red Dress,' 'Conspiracy of Silence,' 'Running Brave,' 'The Wild Pony,' 'Small Sacrifices'); Achievement Awards Prov. of Alberta 1971 & 1978; City of Edmonton 1975 & 1979; Hon. member Cosmopolitan Internat. 1979; Grand Prix du Disque – Canada 1979; Sir Frederick Haultain Prize 1990; Officer of the Order of Canada 1991; Address: 2nd Flr., National Bank Bldg., 10150 – 100th St., Edmonton. Alta. T5J 0P6.

**BANNERMAN, Eugen,** B.A., M.A., M.Th., Ph.D.; university professor, minister; b. Poland 16 May 1935; s. Teofil and Waldina (Kublik) Fandrich; e. Fulton Sr. High 1954; Univ. of Alta. B.A. 1957; Wheaton College M.A. 1961; Knox College M.Th. 1967; Univ. of St. Michael's, Univ. of Toronto Ph.D. 1986; m. Iris d. Joan Harcourt and Ronald Potter 26 Feb. 1983; children: Fiona Siobhan (adopted), Justin (step-son); PROFESSOR OF PSYCHOLOGY, RYERSON POLYTECHNIC UNIV. 1967– ; Pres., Bannerman Holdings 1985– ; Minister, Seaforth United Ch. 1989–93; Dir., Bd. of Gov., Ryerson 1992– ; Ryerson Fac. Assn. Extve. 1987–91; Project Dir. & Design Coord., Howard Kerr Memorial Mace Ctte. (ceremonial mace donated by citizens of Seaforth to Ryerson) 1991–94; athletic & literary awards in high school; high school records in track & field; nom. Professor-of-the Year, Ryerson 1987, '88; Pres., Stratford Children's Theatre 1981–85; Pres. &

Founder, Catacomb Players 1969–72; Pres. & Prod., Theatre-in-the-Home 1972–75; Mem., Stratford Friends of the Festival 1993– ; Stratford Shakespearean Festival Found. 1993– ; author of var. journal & mag. articles dealing with psych., religion & the biography of Kerr (founder of Ryerson); recreations: reading, classical music, travel; clubs: Arts and Letters Club; Home: 220 Hibernia St., Stratford, Ont. N5A 5V7; Office: 350 Victoria St., Toronto, Ont. M5B 2K3.

**BANNERMAN, Robert Smith;** business executive; b. Toronto, Ont. 17 Apr. 1940; s. William Ewart and Charity Katharine (Smith) B.; e. Trinity Coll. Sch. Port Hope 1959; McGill Univ. 1959; Upper Can. Coll. Toronto 1960; m. Joan Elizabeth d. Austin F. and Grace Sanderson 15 Aug. 1969; children: William Robert Bryant, Christina Joan; PRES., CHIEF EXEC. OFFR. AND DIR., BOB BANNERMAN MOTORS LTD. 1963– ; PRES., CHIEF OPER. OFFR. AND DIR.: REGAL GOLDFIELDS LTD.; Pres., C.E.O. & Dir.: Burns, Bannerman & Associates Inc.; Eagle Crown Investments of Texas Inc.; Pres., C.E.O. and Dir., R.S. Bannerman Investment Corp.; joined Ken Seager Motors Ltd. and became Partner 1960; Dir. and maj. shareholder Carrol and Reed Ltd. 1969; estbd. B.I.G. Super Save Drugs Ltd. 1982 and served as Chrmn., C.E.O. and Dir.; estbd. Bannerman Security Systems Corp. becoming Chrmn., C.E.O. and Dir. 1983–87; co-estbd. Goldteck Mines Ltd. serving as Vice Chrmn. and Dir. 1986–87; co-estbd. Bob Bannerman Motors (Hamilton) Inc. serving as Chrmn. and C.E.O. 1987–88; Gov. Trinity Coll. Sch., Port Hope (mem. Ctte. of Convocation during 1960's and 1983–87; Vice-Chrmn. 1988–89; Chrmn. 1989–90); Vice Chrmn., T.C.S. Capital Campaign; Trustee, The Country Day School Found., King City; Dir.: Toronto Automobile Dealers Assn. 1969–74; Better Bus. Bureau Metrop. Toronto 1972–81; Victorian Order Nurses Metrop. Toronto Br. 1977–81; apptd. mem. Comm. Registration Appeal Tribunal by Ont. Premier 1971– ; Knight of the Sovereign Order of St. John of Jerusalem Knights Hospitaller; Knight of the Military and Hospitaller Order of Our Lady of Mount Carmel; recreations: swimming, tennis, skiing, golf, sailing, canoeing; Clubs: Granite; Antique & Classic Boat Soc.; Toronto & N. York Hunt; Tanbark; Hidden Valley Highlands Ski; Home: P.O. Box 488, Aurora, Ont. L4G 3L6; Office: 1730 Eglinton Ave. E., Toronto, Ont. M4A 1J7.

**BANTING, Peter Myles,** B.A., M.B.A., Ph.D.; educator; marketing consultant; b. Hamilton, Ont. 17 March 1936; s. Joseph Maitland and Beatrice Aline (Myles) B.; e. McMaster Univ., B.A. 1958, M.B.A. 1965; Mich. State Univ., Ph.D. 1971; m. Wendy Sharon Papple 24 Apr. 1981; PROF. OF MARKETING, FACULTY OF BUSINESS, McMASTER UNIV. 1967– ; Ed., 'The Harvester,' Internat. Harvester Co. of Canada Ltd., 1959–64; Instr., Mich State Univ., 1965–66; Consultant, Prov. Fed. and Foreign Govts. and Indust.; author 'Marketing in Canada' 1973; 'Canadian Marketing: A Case Approach' 1977; co-author 'Canadian Cases in Marketing' 1968; 'Business Marketing' 1993; other writings incl. monographs and articles in learned and prof. journs.; Past Vice Pres., Acad. of Marketing Science; Past Vice Pres., Symphony Hamilton; Past Pres., The Hamilton Assoc. for the Advancement of Literature, Science and Art; Beta Gamma Sigma; Sr. Fellow, Acad. of Mktg. Sci.; Anglican; Office: Hamilton, Ont. L8S 4M4.

**BANZ, George,** Dipl.Arch., M.Sc., R.C.A.; architect; b. Lucerne, Switzerland 21 Dec. 1928; s. Robert and Josephine (Simeon) B.; e. elem. and secondary schs. Lucerne 1947; Swiss Fed. Inst. of Technol. Zurich Dipl. Arch. 1951; Okla. State Univ. (U.S.-Swiss Exchange Fellowship) M.Sc. (Arch. Engn.) 1952; m. Josette d. late Paul Charmillot 3 Sept. 1958; children: Eric, Caroline; Pres. Urbanprobe Associates Ltd.; part-time mem. Univ. of Toronto Sch. of Arch. Faculty 1960–64, 1970–75, 1978–85, Adjunct Prof. 1986–87; Assoc., Inst. for Environmental Studies 1971–84; Special Consultant to Min. of State for Urban Affairs, Ottawa 1972–74; Part-time mem. Faculties of Ont. Coll. of Art (Indust. Design) 1980–94; Univ. of Waterloo (Sch. of Arch.) 1980–81; recipient numerous arch. design awards and distinctions; author 'Elements of Urban Form' 1970; 'Computer Aids in Building Design' 1983; articles and papers on computer simulation, design automation, planning and architecture; mem. Comte. of Adjustment City of Toronto 1980–89 (Vice Chair 1987–89); Delegate, R.A.I.C. Mission to China 1983; OCA Mission to Brazil 1987; Mem. Ont. Assn. Archs. 1957–93; Mem., Royal Arch. Inst. Can.; Royal Candn. Acad. of Arts; Home: 498 St. Clair Ave. E., Toronto, Ont. M4T 1P7; Office: P.O. Box 12, Station Q, Toronto, Ont. M4T 2L7.

**BARAKETT, Mr. Justice Frank G.;** judge; b. Trois-Rivières, Que. 15 March 1943; s. Georges Thomas and Alice Mary (Salany) B.; e. Bishop Univ. history, philosophy 1965; Laval Univ. law 1968; London Univ., London School of Econ.; JUDGE, SUPERIOR COURT, PROVINCE OF QUEBEC; formerly practiced law in Quebec City and lectured at the Law Faculty, Laval Univ.; Former Dir., Bd. of Trade of Quebec City; Past Pres., Canadian Red Cross Quebec City; Home: 193 de la Chaudière, St. Nicolas, Que. G0S 2Z0; Office: 300 boul. Jean Lesage, R-320, Quebec, Que. G1K 8K6.

**BARANOWSKI, Russell M.,** B.Com.; business executive; b. Selkirk, Man. 14 March 1938; s. late Harry and Jessie B.; e. Univ. of Man. B.Com. 1959; m. Gail d. Frederick and Catherine Hemming 15 Sept. 1965; children: Tanya Jennifer, Michael Jason; Dir. Merlin Gerin Canada; joined Canadian General Electric 1959, Mktg. Mgr. Maj. Appliances Montreal 1970–74, Vice Pres. and Gen. Mgr. Housewares & Home Entertainment Dept. Barrie 1974–81, Vice Pres. and Gen. Mgr. Lighting Products Dept. Toronto 1982–86; Pres., Chief Extve. Offr. and Dir., Federal Pioneer Ltd. 1987–92; mem. Elect. & Electronic Mfgs. Assn. Can. (Dir.); R. Catholic; recreations: fitness, squash, tennis, skiing; Clubs: Toronto Cricket Skating & Curling; Fitness Inst.; Home: 87 Teddington Park Ave., Toronto, Ont. M4N 2C5.

**BARBARO, Ron D.;** insurance executive; b. Ottawa, Ont. 28 Oct. 1931; s. Joseph and Margaret (Menchini) B.; m. Ginetta d. Gino and Maria Cusinato 14 May 1955; children: Maria, Catherine, Richard; PRES., PRUDENTIAL INS. CO. OF AM.; Mgr., N. Am. Life Assur. Co. (Detroit) 1959–60; Br. Mgr. (Toronto) 1960–70; Partner, Win-Bar Ins. Brokers Ltd. 1970–85; Pres. & C.E.O., The Prudential Ins. Co. of Am., Candn. Opns. 1985–90; el. to Bd. of Trustees, Life Underwriting Training Council (LUTC) 1991; Mem. Bd. of Dirs., Equifax, Inc.; Canbra Foods; Candn. Life and Health Insurance Assoc. 1988–89; Pres., Million Dollar Round Table 1984–85 (1st non-Am. Pres.); Toronto Life Mgrs. Assn. 1970; Dir., Nat. Life Underwriters Assn. of Can. 1966; Toronto Life Underwriters Assn. 1963; Founding Chrmn., Ont. Life Mgrs. Conf. 1963; Campaign Chrmn., St. Francis Xavier Univ. Bldg. Campaign; Co-Chrmn., Metro. Toronto Santa Claus Parade; Cand. Assn. of Chiefs of Police Rsch. Found. of Ont. 'Cops & Kids'; Mem., Bd. of Govs., St. Francis Xavier Univ.; Canada's Sports Hall of Fame; Mem., Found. Ctte., Candn. Centre for Advanced Film Studies; Adv. Counc., Second Harvest; Former Chrmn., Bd. of Mgmt., Metro Toronto Zoo 1977–86 (negotiated with People's Republic of China to allow 1st visit of Giant Pandas to Canada); Candn. Children's Found. 'Kids Help Phone' Campaign 1989; Ambassador for the City of Scarborough 1989; Campaign Chrmn., Un. Way of Gter. Toronto 1990; Mem., Bd. of Trustees, Art Gallery of Toronto 1990–93; former Mem., Bd. of Dirs., Ronald McDonald Children's Charities of Canada; Equifax Canada Inc.; Health Systems Group Ltd.; Molson Indy; United Way of Greater Toronto; Past Dir., Northwestern Gen. Hosp., resp. for arranging 1st annual 'Medic Alert Month' for Can.; Honours: selected by Jr. Bd. of Trade as one of the 'Men of the Year,' Toronto, 1969; citation from Red Cross for fundraising; a chair in veterinary med. dedicated in his name; Univ. of Jerusalem's Scopus Award of humanitarianism 1986; Ron Barbaro Day proclamations by Metro Chrmn. Denis Flynn 1986, 1987; 1989 Citizen of the Year Gardiner Award and 1989 Humanist Award for setting precedent within industry by establ. special assistance to terminally ill policyholders 1989; Governor's Award, Leonardo da Vinci Acad. of Arts & Sciences, for outstanding achievements in education, culture and other humanitarian pursuits 1991; Ursaski Award, Sales & Mktg. Man of the Year, Can. 1991; Nat. Recognition Award, Creative Thinking Assoc. of Am. 1992; Catholic Big Brothers Man of the Year 1992; D.H.L., Eastern Coll. 1992; author of numerous articles; motivational speaker in 15 countries, 49 states, 10 provinces; recreations: jogging, tennis; Clubs: York Racquet; Bd. of Trade; Home: Toronto, Ont.; Office: 213 Washington St., Newark, N.J. 07102.

**BARBEAU, Hubert;** executive; b. Montréal, Qué. 31 Oct. 1929; e. Univ. de Montréal Bus. Adm. & Acctg. degree 1954; CHRMN. OF THE BD. & C.E.O, MULTI-MARQUES INC.; mem. Les Chefs Mailleurs du Québec; Ecole des Hautes Etudes Commerciales Con. Adm.; Tremplin '2000' Inc.; Office: 510, 1600 boul. Henri-Bourassa O., Montréal, Qué. H3M 3E2.

**BARBEAU, Jacques,** Q.C., B.A., LL.B., L.L.M., C.G.A.; b. Montreal, Que. 20 May 1931; s. Alphonse and Marguerite (Beaulieu) B.; e. Univ. of B.C. B.A. (Econ.), LL.B.; Harvard Law Sch. LL.M. 1960, Dipl. Internat. Program in Taxation 1960; m. Margaret Ann d. The Hon. Walter S. Owen, Q.C., LL.D., Victoria, B.C., 12 Apr. 1958; children: Jean, Paul, Monique, Jacqueline; BARBEAU & CO. and CHRMN. BARBEAU & COMPANY CAPITAL MANAGEMENT INC.; Dir., The Laurentian Bank of Canada; Western International Communications Ltd. (WIC); Atlantic Foundation: An Educational Trust (U.K.); The North Atlantic Foundation (Bermuda); Kwik Lok Ltd.; Beaumont Timber Co. Ltd.; The Shepard Bank; Glamis Gold Ltd.; read law with Thomas E. Ladner, Q.C.; called to Bar of B.C. 1957; Solr. Taxation Div. Dept. Nat. Revenue Ottawa 1957–60; Finance Offr. Taxation Div. Dept. of Finance Ottawa 1960–61; Dir. of Research Candn. Tax Foundation 1961–62; Lectr. Banff Sch. of Advanced Mgmt. and Faculty Chrmn. Banff Tax Seminar, Banff Centre; Vice-Chrmn., Emily Carr College of Art; Trustee Vancouver Sch. Bd. of Vancouver 1973–74; mem. Candn. Bar Assn.; B.C. Law Soc.; Candn. Tax Foundation; Delta Kappa Epsilon; Clubs: Vancouver; Mount Royal; Arbutus; Home: 1998 Hosmer St., Vancouver, B.C. V6J 2S8, 1499 Edwards Dr., Point Roberts, Wash. 98281 and #8 Cross Bay Rd., Southampton, Bermuda; Office: The Toronto Dominion Bank Tower, P.O. Box 10019 Pacific Centre, 1450 - 700 West Georgia St., Vancouver, B.C. V7Y 1A1.

**BARBEAU, Marcel,** ARC; artiste peintre; sculpteur; né à Montréal, Qué. 18 février 1925; f. Philippe et Elisabeth (St-Antoine) B.; é. Diplôme de l'école du meuble de Montréal (design) 1947; étudié avec le peintre Paul-Emile Borduas, l'architecte Marcel Parizeau et l'historien d'art Maurice Gagnon; dév. Suzanne Meloche 1974; ép. Ninon, fille de Gérard Gauthier et Fleurette Rose 26 avril 1975; enfants: Manon, François; co-signataire du 'Refus Global,' il participe à toutes les manifestations du groupe 'Automatiste' 1946–54; séjour à Paris 1962–64, New York 1964–68; séjour en Californie 1970–71 et Paris 1971–74, 1993– ; représenté par la Galerie Michel Ange à Montréal; Galerie J. et J. Donguy, Paris; Galerie Gray, Cannes; Westgrige Gallery, Vancouver; Art South, Philadelphia; expositions individuelles: Foyer de l'Art et du Livre Ottawa 1951, 1953; Wittenborn and Shutz New York 1952; Galerie Agnès Lefort Montréal 1952, 1953, 1955, 1956; Palais Montcalm Qué. 1955; Galerie de l'Actuelle Montréal 1955; Centre d'Art de Ste-Adèle 1957; Musée des Beaux Arts Montréal 1962; Galerie Denise Delrue Montréal 1961, 1962, 1963; Galerie Iris Clert Paris 1964; Galerie Dorothy Cameron Toronto 1963, 1964; Galerie du Siècle Montréal 1964, 1965, 1967; East Hampton Gallery New York 1965, 1966; Jerold Morris Toronto 1965; Carmen Lamana Gallery Toronto 1967, 1968; Nouvelle Galerie Denise Delrue Montréal 1969; Retrospective: Winnipeg Art Gallery, Musée d'Art Contemporain Montréal et, Scarborough Coll. Toronto 1969; Centre Culturel Canadien Paris 1971; Relais Culturel Aix-en-Provence 1971; Galerie St-Georges Lyon 1971; Galerie 'Le Point d'Or' Grenoble 1972; Hôtel de Ville de Poitiers 1972; Théâtre de Caen 1972; Galerie III Montréal 1972; Centre Culturel Français Luxembourg 1972; Centre Culturel Asselt, Namur, Liège 1972; Galerie Yala Tunis 1974; Galerie de l'Union des Arts Plastiques Alger 1974; Galerie de Marseille 1974; Musée de Québec 1975; Musée d'Art Contemporain Montréal 1975; Bau-Xi Gallery Toronto 1977; 'Dessins de Marcel Barbeau 1957–62' Musée des Beaux Arts de Montréal 1977; Centre Culturel, Université de Sherbrooke, Sherbrooke 1978; Galerie Dresdnere, Toronto, 1980, 1981; Galerie Pierre Bernard, Hull, 1981; Galerie Gilles Corbeil, Montreal, 1981; Galerie Sherbrooke, Sherbrooke, 1981; Centre d'exposition Drummond, Drummondville 1982; Galerie Cultart, Montréal 1982; Centre d'exposition l'Imagier, 1982; Galerie Esperanza, 1984, 1985; Salon national des Galeries d'Art, Montréal, 1984; Galerie des Arts Contemporains 1987; Galerie du Grand Théatre, Québec 1988; Kaspar Gallery, Toronto 1989, 1991; Galerie Michel-Ange, Montréal 1990–91; Galerie Estampe, Plus Québec 1990; Centre Socio-Culturel, Chicoutimi 1991; Vieux-Presbytère de Saint-Bruno 1991; Galerie J. et J. Donguy, Paris 1991; Maison de la culture du Plateau Mont Royal 1991; Centre d'Artiste, Bishop's Univ. 1992; Pavillon des Arts, Ste-Adèle 1992; collections publiques: Galerie Nationale du Can.; Musée Stedelijk Amsterdam; Musée Chrysler Norfolk, Va.; Musée du Nouveau Brunswick; Musée des Beaux Arts de Montréal; Art Gallery of Ontario; Musée d'Art Contemporain Montréal; Musée du Québec; Musée de Vancouver; Agnes Etherington Art Centre, Queen's University; Univ. du Mass.; Amherst; Musée Rose Hart, Brandeis Univ., Waltham, Mass.; Winnipeg Art Gallery; Conseil des Arts du Canada; Ministère des Affaires extérieures du Canada; Banque d'oeuvres d'art, C.A.C.; Hart House Univ. de Toronto; Maison des étudiants canadiens Cité Universitaire Paris; Confederation Centre Art Gallery and Museum P.E.I.; Centre Culturel de Poitiers, France; Musée des Beaux-Arts de Lyon; Edmonton Art Gallery; Musée de Joliette; Kitchener Art Gallery, Kitchener; Toronto City Corp.; Municipalité de St. Laurent; Concordia Univ., Montréal; Municipalité de Joliette; Municipalité de Lachine; Musée de Lachine; Municipalité de Montréal-Est; Greater Victoria Art Gallery; Hamilton Art Gallery; Owen Art Gallery, Sackville, N.B.; Musée Louis Hémont, Péribonca, Que.; Collection Prêt D'Oeuvres d'Art, Gouv. de Qué.; Univ. du Québec à Montréal; Ecoles des Hautes Etudes Commerciales; Archives de l'Univ. du Qué. à Montréal; Univ. de Montréal; Univ. McGill; Univ. de Sherbrooke; National Gallery, Washington; Bibliothèque nationale de France; Univ. of Lethbridge Art Gall.; Esso Collection; INCO Collection; Northern Central Collection; Aird & Berlis Collection, Tor.; Shell Collection; Collection Teleglobe, Montreal; Union-Vie; Richard Brown Baker Coll., N.Y.; McDonald's Restaurants Canada, Toronto; Gaz Metropolitain, Montréal; Reader's Digest, Montréal; IST, Montréal; Banque Nationale, Montréal; Casses Populaires Desjardins; General Electric, Canada; nombreuses expositions collectives et symposiums au Can. et à l'étranger dans des musées et galeries universitaires, des années quarante à ca jour; concepteur et producteur du film 'Désirs mouvements' et concepteur du film 'Instants privilégiés'; autres activités: nombreuses conférences et séminaires; participation à plusieurs émissions de radio et de télévision au Canada et en France; dont 'A Passionate Harmony' de la série 'Visions' de Don Thompson de T.V. Ontario; initiation à la Sculpture Centre d'art de Saint-Adèle 1954–56; prof. d'arts plastiques: expression plastique et initiation à l'histoire de l'art: enseignement privé et au Centre culturel canadien à Paris 1971–73; artiste résident, Bishop Univ., 1977–78 et 1978–79; bourses et prix: ler prix de peinture de la Royal Can. Acad. 1963; Séminaire Internat. des Arts de l'Université Fairleigh-Dickinson 1965; Bourse Lynch-Staunton, Conseil des Arts du Canada 1973; Prix de sculpture du concours d'art McDonald's 1985; certificat d'excellence, pour réalisation exceptionnelle en peinture à l'International Art Competition de New York 1988; mention d'excellence Art Horizon, New York 1989; selectionné par le concours national de murales de Via Rail pour réaliser une des 12 murales des Voitures Park 1988; hombreuses oeuvres publiques dont Lachine, Montréal-Est, Joliette, Université McGill; divers catalogues et livres d'art au Canada et à l'étranger dont 'Marcel Barbeau: le regard en Fugue' par Carolle Gagnon et Ninon Gauthier 1990; Traduction 'Fugato' par Liliane Busby; Editions CECA, 1990 et Édition Le Cercle d'Art, Paris 1994; mem. Cons. des Artistes Peintres du Qué.; conseil de la sculpture du Québec; Candn. Conf. Arts; Royal Candn. Acad. of the Arts; récréations: lecture, musique, opéra, cinéma, spectacles de danse, ski de fond, marche, golfe, tennis, canoë; résidence: 31 Blvd. Jourdan, Apt. 83, Paris 75014 France.

**BARBEAU, Victor,** D.Phil., O.C. (pseud. T U R C); professeur, journaliste, écrivain; né. Montréal, Qué. 17 août 1894; f. Zotique et Victoria (Beaudoin) B.; é. Univ. de Paris D.Phil. 1924; ép. Lucile Clément 4 oct. 1919; enfants: Michèle, Nicole, Pierre-Valéry, Claudine, François; Ancien élève, Ecole des Hautes Etudes urbaines (Paris); Prof.,lang. et litt. française, École des Hautes Etudes Comm. de Montréal 1925–63; Prof., l'Univ. McGill 1939–42; L'Univ. Laval à Qué. 1939–43; Prés-fond., 'La Familiale' coop. de consommation 1937–60; l'Alliance des Coop. de consom.; ancien prés./executif de nombreuses sociétés inclus l'Acad. canadienne-française 1944–72; Lt. d'aviation, Royal Air Force, Angleterre 1917; British War Medal (Guerre de '14–18); Lauréat, Acad. française Paris; Prix Duvernay 1959; Docteur 'honoris causa' des univs.: Aix-en-Provence, Laval (Qué.), Montréal; Officier, Ordre du Canada 1970; Grand officier, Ordre nat. du Qué.; auteur: 'Le choix de Victor Barbeau dans l'oeuvre de Victor Barbeau' 1981, 'La tentation du passé' 1977, 'Le français du Canada' 1963, 1970, 'Grammaire et linguistique' 1968, 'Le Face et l'envers' 1966, 'La réalité épicière' 1961, 'Libre examen de la démocratie' 1960 et six autres; co-auteur: 'Hommage à Berthe Chaurès-Louard, 1889–1968' 1982, 'Dictionnaire bibliographique' 1974 et trois autres; revues et périodiques: 'Les Cahiers de TURC' 1921–22, 1926–27, 'L'Économiste' 1929–40, 'Le Coopérateur' 1940–43, 'Liaison' 1946–50, 'Cahiers de l'Acad. canadienne-française' 1956–72; collab. aux journaux: 'Le Devoir,' 'La Presse,' 'L'Action,' 'Le Nationaliste,' 'Le Nouveau Journal'.

**BARBER, Clarence Lyle,** O.C., M.A., Ph.D., LL.D. (h.c.); economist; university professor; b. Wolseley, Sask. 5 May 1917; s. Richard Edward and Lulu Pearl (Lyons) B.; e. Wolseley High Sch., 1930–34; Univ. of Sask., 1937–40 (B.A. 1939); Clark Univ., M.A. 1941; Univ. of Minnesota, 1941–43 (Ph.D. 1952); m. Barbara Anne, d. Ernest Luther Patchet, Toronto, Ont. 10 May 1947; children: Paul Edward, Richard Stephen, David Stuart, Alan Gordon; PROFESSOR EMERITUS, UNIVERSITY OF MANITOBA, 1985– ; Commr., Royal Comn. on the Economic Union and Devel. Prospects for Canada 1982–85; mem., Nat. Comn. on Inflation 1979; Commr., Royal Comn. on Farm Machinery; served R.C.A.F. 1943–45; Economist, Dom. Bureau of Stat., 1945–48; Asst. Prof., McMaster Univ. 1948; Assoc. Prof., Univ. of Manitoba 1949, Prof. of Economics 1956, Head of Econ. 1963, Distinguished Prof. 1982; visiting Prof., Queen's Univ., 1954–55, McGill Univ., 1964–65; Dir., Research, Royal Comn. on Flood, Cost Benefit, Manitoba, 1957–59; Special Adviser on Nat. Income to Govt. of Philippines, U.N. Tech. Asst. Adm., 1959–60; co-author (with J.C.P. McCallum) 'Controlling Inflation: Learning from Experience in Canada, Europe and Japan' 1982; other publications incl. 'Inventories & The Business Cycle'; 'On the Origins of the Great Depression'; The Canadian Electrical Manufacturing Industry (Royal Comn. on Can. Econ. Prospects), Canadian Tariff Policy; Pres., Candn. Assn. of Univ. Teachers, 1958–59; Pres. (1972–73) Candn. Econ. Assn.; Fellow Roy. Soc. of Canada 1977; Officer, Order of Canada 1987; LL.D. (hon. causa), Univ. of Guelph 1988; Protestant; recreations: lawn bowling, bridge; Address: 766 Richmond Ave., Victoria, B.C. V8S 3Z1.

**BARBER, Douglas E.,** C.G.A.; financial executive; b. Toronto, Ont. 6 June 1953; s. Roy and Marion P. (Cooper) B.; e. Seneca College 1974; C.G.A. 1979 m. Renate d. Frank and Anita Stanisz 1975; children: Carley, Jillian, Alexis; CHIEF FINANCIAL OFFICER, LATIN AMERICAN DIVISION, MEDTRONIC OF CANADA LTD. 1981– ; Asst. Controller, G.D. Searle Ltd. 1974–79; Fireco Sales Ltd. 1979–81; Dir., Medtronic of Canada Ltd.; Home: 24 Moffat Ave., Brampton, Ont.; Office: 6733 Kitimat Rd., Mississauga, Ont. L5N 1W3.

**BARBER, Katherine Patricia Mary,** B.A., M.A.; lexicographer; b. Ely, Cambridgeshire, England 8 Sept. 1959; d. Gordon Maitland and Patricia Frances (Clarke) B.; e. Univ. of Winnipeg B.A. 1980, B.A. (Hons.) 1986; Univ. of Ottawa M.A. 1990; EDITOR-IN-CHIEF, CANADIAN DICTIONARIES, OXFORD UNIVERSITY PRESS CANADA 1991– ; Lecturer, Sch. of Translation & Interpretation, Univ. of Ottawa 1984–91; Rsch. Assoc., Bilingual Candn. Dictionary, Univ. of Ottawa 1989–91; Roman Catholic; Mem., Euralex (Eur. Assn. for Lexicography); Dictionary Soc. of N. Am.; Office: 70 Wynford Dr., Don Mills, Ont. M3C 1J9.

**BARBER, Lloyd I.,** C.C., B.A., B.Comm., M.B.A., Ph.D., LL.D., Hon. C.A.; university president emeritus; b. Regina, Sask. 8 Mar. 1932; s. the late Lewis Muir & the late Hildred (Ingram) B., e. Regina Beach Sch., 1948; Luther Coll., Regina, 1949; Univ. of Sask., B.A. (Econ.) 1953, B.Comm. 1954; Univ. of Cal., Berkeley, M.B.A. 1955; Univ. of Wash., Ph.D. 1964; m. Muriel Pauline, d. late F. MacBean, 12 May 1956; children: Muir, Brian, Kathy, David, Susan, Patti; PRESIDENT EMERITUS, UNIV. OF REGINA, SASKATCHEWAN; President and Vice Chancellor, Univ. of Regina, Sask. 1976–90; Past Chrmn., Corporate Higher Education Forum; Dir., Muir Barber Ltd.; Burns Foods Ltd. 1971–85; Bank of Nova Scotia; Can. Arctic Co-operative Federation Ltd. 1974–78; SED Systems Ltd. 1972–87; OPCAN (Katimavik) 1977–78; Molson Companies; Husky Oil Ltd. 1979–91; Indian Equity Foundation (1977–79); Sask. Computer Utility Corp. 1973–75; Cominco; Candn. Pacific Ltd. 1983– ; Inst. for Saskatchewan Enterprise 1988– ; Investment Corporation of Saskatchewan 1992– ; Winnipeg Commodities Exchange 1990–91; The North West Company Inc. 1990– ; Council for Candn. Unity 1990– ; STV 1990– ; Crown Mngmt. Bd. 1990–91; Can West Global Communications Corp.; Bd. of Dirs. & mem., Candn. Polar Comn. 1991– ; CP Ltd.; Past Trustee, Candn. Schenley Football Awards; Candn. Scholarships Trust Fund; Wascana Centre Authority; Past mem., N. W. Terr. Leg. Council (1967–70); Natural Sci. Engn. Research Council (1979–81); Instr. in Comm., Univ. of Sask., 1955; Asst. Prof. 1959; Assoc. Prof., 1964, Dean of Comm. 1965–68, Vice-Pres. 1968–74; Commr., Sask. Royal Comn. on Govt. Adm., 1964; Chrmn., Sask. Prov. Youth Review Comte., 1965; Indian Claims Comr., (apptd. by Privy Council of Can.) 1969–77; Special Inquirer for Elder Indian Testimony (apptd. by Privy Council of Canada) 1977–81; Chrmn., Sask. Energy Comn. 1989; Chrmn., Advisory Council for the Sask. Order of Merit 1990– ; Bd. of Dirs., Working Ventures Candn. Fund, Inc. 1990– ; The Arms Control Centre 1990– ; Bd. of Trustees, Candn. Museum of Nature 1990– ; author of Brief to Carter Comn. for Retail Merchants Assn. Can. and several articles for learned journs.; awarded Can. Council pre-doctorial Fellowship; Ford Foundation Dissertation Grant; Centennial Medal; Vanier Medal; Hon. Sask. Indian Chief; Concordia Univ.'s Advisory Ctte. to the Rector on Public Affairs Award 1983; Hon. Chartered Accountant awarded by the Inst. of C.A.s. of Sask. 1984; Hon. Doctor of Laws, Univ. of Alta. 1983; Hon. Doctor of Laws, Concordia Univ. 1984; Aboriginal Order of Canada 1985; Hon. Prof., Shandong Univ. 1986; Mem., Candn. Inst. of Advanced Rsch. 1986– ; Amer. Econ. Assn; Cdn. Econ. Assn.; Inst. of Pub. Admin. of Can.; Assn. Candn. Schs. of Business (Pres. 1967–68); Pres. Assn. of Univs. & Colls. of Can. 1981–83; Hon. Lt.-Col., 16 Serv. Battalian (M), Regina; Mem. at Large, Candn. Red Cross Soc. 1990– ; Past Dir., Regina United Way; Freemason; Liberal; United Church; recreations: hunting, fishing, sailing, swimming, reading, travel; Clubs: Regina Beach Yacht; Assiniboia; Faculty; Roy. United Serv. Inst.; Regina Officers Mess; Home: P.O. Box 510, 800 Green Ave., Regina Beach, Sask. S0G 4C0.

**BARBER, Maj. Gen. (Ret'd) R. Russell,** CD; freelance writer; b. Brandon, Man. 7 June 1926; s. William Clarence and Inez Isobel (Purse) B.; e. Maryfield, Sask. 1942; Aerospace Systems Course 1957; RCAF Staff College 1963; m. Shirley M. d. Wilson and Alma Bearance 19 July 1949; wartime service overseas as Air Gunner; Regular Forces 1945–79; Active Reserve Forces 1979–91; Dir., Electronics Training Aerospace Systems Course 1957–59; RCAF Exchange Offr. USAF Academy, Colorado Springs 1959–61; Sr. Nav. Offr. Air Transport Command 1961–63; Dir. Air Plans, Nat. Defence HQ 1973–75; Base Commdr. CFB Toronto 1975–76; Chief of Staff, Airforce Operations, Air Command HQ 1976–77; Chief of Staff, Plans & Progs., NORAD HQ, Colorado Springs 1977–79; recipient, C.V.S.M. and Clasp, War Medal 1939–45; Candn. Centennial Medal 1967; Queen's Jubilee Medal 1977; Can. Forces Decoration with 2nd Clasp; Air Member Can./US Permanent Joint Board of Defence, Air Member Can./US Military Cooperation Ctte., Air Member NATO Can./US Regional Planning Group 1975–77; Pres., Vancouver Island Dist. Can. Cancer Soc. 1987–89 (Campaign Chrmn. 1984–87); Pres.-elect, B.C. & Yukon Div., Can. Cancer Soc. 1989–91; Vol. Driver Cowichan Valley Unit, Can. Cancer Soc.; Chrmn. Sponsoring Ctte., 744 Air Cadet Sqdn., Duncan 1983–88; Bd. of Mgrs., St. Andrews Presbyterian Church, Duncan 1982–85; Dir. Agapeland Christian Nursery Sch., Duncan 1983–85; author military articles; mem., Royal Cdn. Legion; Air Gunners Assn.; RCAF Commonwealth Air Training Plan Museum; Home: 1432 Kingsview Rd., R.R. #5, Duncan, B.C. V9L 4T6.

**BARBER, Thomas Kelly,** B.A., M.B.A.; business executive; b. Toronto, Ont. 6 Sept. 1955; s. Timothy William and Margaret Elizabeth (Kelly) B.; e. Univ. of Toronto Schools 1973; Trinity College, Univ. of Toronto B.A. (Hons.) 1977; Univ. of Western Ont. M.B.A. 1979; m. Colette Marie Richardson 8 Feb. 1986; children: Michael, Mary Elizabeth, Graeme; PRESIDENT AND CHIEF EXECUTIVE OFFICER, MORGAN STANLEY CANADA LIMITED; joined Morgan Stanley Canada Limited Montreal 1979; Vice-Pres., Morgan Stanley & Co. Inc. New York 1984; Principal 1986; Pres., Morgan Stanley Canada 1988; Managing Dir., Morgan Stanley & Co. Inc. 1989; recreations: sailing, fishing, skiing; clubs: Royal Candn. Yacht, Islington Golf, Mount Royal; Home: 57 King Georges Rd., Toronto, Ont. M8X 1L6; Office: 40 King St. W., Suite 3010, Toronto, Ont. M5H 3Y2.

**BARBÈS, Hon. Charles Noël,** B.A., C.R.; juge; né Hull, Qué. 25 déc. 1914; f. Victor et Delphine (Bédard) B.; é. Coll. St-Alexandre de Limbour, Qué. B.A. 1935; Univ. de Montréal LL.B. 1938; ép. Yvette f. Georges Terrien & Yvonne Fortin 21 oct. 1939; enfants: Hélène, Louise, Pierre, Suzanne, Jean-René, Jacques, François; JUGE DE LA COUR SUPÉRIEURE 1965–90; admis au Barreau d'abord en 1939 et de nouveau en 1990; Membre du Centre d'arbitrage commercial national et international du Québec 1991; Bâtonnier (Abitibi-Témiscamingue) 1955; élu Chambre des Communes 1957; Procureur de la Couronne 1960; Juge Provincial 1962; Cathol. Romain; loisirs: lectures, voyages; Club: Richelieu; Adresse: 122, 2e Avenue Est, Amos, Qué. J9T 3A5; Bureau: 4, 1 ière Avenue Ouest, Amos, Qué. J9T 3A4.

**BARBOUR, Douglas Fleming,** B.A., M.A., Ph.D.; writer; professor; b. Winnipeg, Man. 21 Mar. 1940; s. Harold Douglas and E. Phyllis (Wilson) B.; e. Acadia Univ., B.A. 1962; Dalhousie Univ., M.A. 1964; Queen's Univ., Ph.D. 1976; m. Sharon d. Anna and Wesley Nicoll 21 May 1966; PROF., DEPT OF ENGLISH, UNIV. OF ALTA. 1982– ; Mem., English Dept., Alderwood C.I. 1968–69; Asst. Prof., Univ. of Alta. 1969; Assoc. Prof. 1977; Mem., Ed. Bd., NeWest Press; Writers Guild of Alta. award to recognize excellence in writing:

Stephan Stephansson Award for Poetry 1984 (Visible Visions); author: 'Story for A Saskatchewan Night' 1990; 'Visible Visions' 1984, 'The Harbingers' 1984, 'Shore Lines' 1979, 'Visions of My Grandfather' 1977, 'He. &. She. &.' 1974, 'Songbook' 1973, 'White' 1972, 'A Poem As Long As the Highway' 1971, 'Land Fall' 1971 (poetry); 'Michael Ondaatje' 1993; 'John Newlove and his Works' 1992, 'Daphne Marlatt and her Works' 1992, 'bp nichol and his Works' 1992, 'Canadian Poetry Chronicle (1984)' 1985, 'Worlds Out of Words' 1979 (scholarly/critical); co-author: 'The Pirates of Pen's Chance' 1981; editor: 'Three Times Five' 1983, 'Richard Sommer: Selected and New Poems' 1983, 'The Story So Far Five' 1978; 'Beyond Tish' 1991; co-editor: 'Tesseracts II' 1987, 'Writing Right' 1982, 'The Maple Laugh Forever' 1981; Home: 11655 72nd Ave, Edmonton, Alta. T6G 0B9; Office: Univ. of Alta., Edmonton, Alta. T6G 2E5.

**BARCLAY, Ian Andrew,** B.C.L., M.P.A., LL.D.; consultant; b. Montreal, Que. July 3 1921; s. Gregor and Jean Gertrude (Fleck) B.; e. Ashbury College; McGill Univ. B.C.L. 1948; Harvard Univ. M.P.A. 1949; m. Ann d. Geoffery and Gwyneth Hadrill 22 Sept. 1951; one d.: Deborah Ann Rollins; OWNER, IAN A. BARCLAY & ASSOC. (BUSINESS BROKER); Barrister, Scott Hugessen Macklaier & Hyde; Vice-Pres. & Sec., Columbia Cellulose & Celgar Limited; Past Chrmn. & C.E.O., B.C. Forest Products Limited; Can. Harbour Place Corp.; Candn. Pulp & Paper Assn.; Pulp & Paper Rsch. Inst. of Can.; Counc. of Forest Indus. of B.C.; Forest Indus. Advr. Ctte., fed. govt.; Past Pres., United Community Serv. of Greater Vanc.; Gov., Olympic Trust of Can.; Dir., Forintek Canada Corp.; Hudson's Bay Co.; Pres., Physical Med. Rsch. Found.; R.C.N.V.R. 1941–45; recreations: golf, reading; clubs: Vancouver; Shaughnessy Golf & Country; Home: 5925 Chancellor Blvd., Vancouver, B.C. V6T 1E6; Office: Suite 2500, Three Bentall Ctr., P.O. Box 49200, 595 Burrard St., Vancouver, B.C. V7X 1L1.

**BARCLAY, Lawrence 'Ross' Coates,** B.Sc., M.Sc., Ph.D.; university professor; b. Wentworth, N.S. 24 Oct. 1928; s. Neil and Mary Jenette (Clancy) B.; e. Colchester Co. Academy 1946; Mount Allison Univ. B.Sc. 1949, M.Sc. 1951; McMaster Univ. Ph.D. 1957; m. Helen May d. Willis and Jean Fraser 28 Aug. 1950; children: Gregor, Michael, Nancy; PROFESSOR 1959– ;& CARNEGIE PROFESSOR OF CHEMISTRY, MOUNT ALLISON UNIV. 1967– ; Asst. Prof., Mt. Allison Univ. 1951–55; Assoc. Prof. 1956–59; Head, Chemistry Dept. 1967–82; Visiting Rsch. Officer, Nat. Rsch. Council 1979–80; Visiting Prof., Univ. of Alta. summer 1961; Visiting Lectr., McMaster Univ. 1955–56; Lord Beaverbrook Overseas Scholar 1950–51; Fellow, Chem. Inst. of Canada; Syntex Award; Lectr., Chem. Inst. of Canada 1992; Tucker Award for Excellence in Teaching, Mount Allison Univ. 1993; Mem., United Ch.; Candn. Soc. for Chemists; Chair, Organic Chemistry Div., Chem. Inst. of Canada; author of 75 scientific pubns. in refereed Candn. & fgn. chem. jours.; recreations: coaching provincial level minor hockey, recreational tennis; Home: 74 York St., Sackville, N.B. E0A 3C0; Office: Sackville, N.B. E0A 3C0.

**BARCZA, Peter Josef;** baritone, classical opera; b. Stockholm, Sweden; s. Josef and Katherine Elizabeth (Tamasi) B.; e. Royal Conservatory of Music, Toronto; Univ. of Toronto, Diploma, Faculty of Music; postgrad training, Villa Schifanoia, Florence, Italy; m. Constance Adorno; CLASSICAL OPERA SINGER; leading roles incl. Canadian Opera Co.; Toronto Symphony; CBC Radio and TV; Guelph Spring Festival; Manitoba Opera; Opera In Concert (Toronto); Calgary Opera; Theatre Royal de Wallonie (Belgium); Rochester Opera; Rainbow Stage; Regina Symphony; Algoma Festival; Paris Opera; Kentucky Opera; Memphis Opera; Vancouver Opera; Comus Music Theatre; Pacific Opera; Connecticut Opera; New Orleans Opera; Opera Lyra, Ottawa; Opéra de Montréal; Opera Hamilton; Opera Orchestra of New York; Seattle Opera; New York City Opera; Centro Internacional de Opera, Mexico City; major Candn. symphony orchestras, Bad Hersfeld Festival (Germany); has appeared on TV, Radio-France; mem., Actors Equity; ACTRA: AGMA (USA); Home: 17 Strathallan Blvd., Toronto, Ont. M5N 1S8.

**BARD, Jean-Marc,** F.C.A.; public servant; b. La Sarre-Abitibi, Que. 30 June 1941; s. Louis-Philippe and Madeleine (Marcoux) B.; e. Laval Univ., B.Comm. 1964, M.Comm. 1965, M.Accting. 1967; C.A. 1967; SENIOR DEPUTY MINISTER OF TRANSPORT, GOVT. OF QUEBEC 1989– ; Arthur Andersen & Co. C.A.s 1967–73; Comptroller, Treas., Lavalin Internat. Inc. 1979–85; Asst. Dep. Min., Treasury Bd. 1986; Sr. Dep. Min., Dept. of Supply & Serv. 1986–89; Pres., Montreal Olympic Installation Bd. 1988–89; Bd. of Dir. & Pres., Offices des autoroutes du Québec 1989– ; Bd. of Dir., Société québécoise des Transports 1989– ; Fellow, Order of C.A. 1989; Home: 1213 Marie-Victorin, La Prairie, Qué. J5R 1G8; Office: 700 boul. St-Cyrille est, 28ieme étage, Quebec, Qué. G1R 5H1.

**BARDON, Vicki Lynn,** B.A.; designer; b. Halifax, N.S. 27 June 1947; d. Dr. J. Bruce and Jessie Bowlby (Armstrong) Crowe; e. Acadia Univ. B.A. 1968; New York Sch. of Interior Design; m. Gary C. d. John and Viola Bardon 4 June 1977; children: Andrew Bruce, Alexander David, Alma Beth; FOUNDER AND DESIGNER, SUTTLES & SEAWINDS OF NOVA SCOTIA LTD. 1973– ; Asst. Ed. Interior Design American Home Mag. New York 1969–72; recipient Design Can. Award 1974; Tommy Award Am. Printed Fabrics Council N.Y. 1978; awarded Commemorative Medal for 125th Anniversary of Candn. Confederation 1992; Home: 794 S. Main St., Mahone Bay, N.S. B0J 2E0; Office: 466 Main St., Mahone Bay, N.S. B0J 2E0.

**BARFOOT, Joan Louise,** B.A.; author; journalist; b. Owen Sound, Ont. 17 May 1946; d. Robert Scott and Helen Isabel (MacKinnon) B.; e. Univ. of W. Ont. B.A. 1969; Reporter/Editor, London Free Press 1976–94; Reporter, Windsor Star 1967–69; Mirror Publications, Toronto 1969–73; Toronto Sunday Sun 1973–75; author (novels): 'Abra' 1978 (Books in Can. First Novel Award 1978); 'Dancing in the Dark' 1982; 'Duet For Three' 1985; 'Family News' 1989; 'Plain Jane' 1992; recipient Women of Distinction Award London YM-YWCA 1985; Marian Engel Award 1992; mem. Writers Union of Can.; Women & Words; P.E.N. Internat.; Home: 286 Cheapside St., London, Ont. N6A 2A2.

**BARFORD, Ralph Mackenzie,** B.Comm., M.B.A., LL.D.; investment executive; b. Toronto, Ont. 6 July 1929; s. Ralph Alexander and Geraldine Edna (Mackenzie) B.; e. Univ. of Toronto B.Comm. 1950; Harvard Univ. M.B.A. 1952; m. Elizabeth (dec. Nov. 14 1991); children: Ralph M. Jr., Anne E. (Dunlop), John A., Patricia S. (Mann), Elizabeth J. (Malcolm), Jane M. (Manolakas); PRES., VALLEYDENE CORP. LTD. 1972– ; Rsch. Asst., Harvard Univ. 1953; Analyst, Am. Rsch. & Devel. 1954; Pres., Nat. Merchandising Corp. 1954–60; Beatty Bros. 1960–62; G.S.W. Inc. 1962–72; Chrmn., GSW Inc.; Camco Inc.; Dir., Advanced Technology Labs Inc.; Algoma Steel Corp.; Bank of Montreal; BCE Inc.; Garbell Holdings Ltd.; Hollinger Inc.; Molson Indus. Inc.; Morton Internat. Inc.; Spacelabs Medical Inc.; Templeton Growth Fund Ltd.; LL.D., Univ. of West. Ont. 1988; recreations: golf, skiing; clubs: York, Rosedale Golf, Granite; Home: 11 Valleyanna Dr., Toronto, Ont. M4N 1J7; Office: 1903, 20 Eglinton Ave. W., Toronto, Ont. M4R 1K8.

**BARG, Stephan R.,** B.Sc., M.Phil.; executive; b. Vancouver, B.C. 26 May 1947; s. Peter and Edna Mae (Webber) B.; e. McGill Univ. B.Sc. 1968; Univ. of York, Eng., M.Phil. 1974; m. Judith d. Melvin and Hazel Holling 16 May 1970; children: Andrew, Michael, Carolyn; TREASURER, INTERNAT. INST. FOR SUSTAINABLE DEVELOPMENT; Sask. Dept. of Finance 1974–77; Vice-Pres., Finance & Corp. Planning, Crown Investments Corp. of Sask. 1977–83; Vice Pres., Admin. & Develop., Prince Albert Pulp Co. Ltd. 1983–86; Pres., Stephan Barg & Associates Ltd. 1986–87; Pres., Public Investments Corp. of Manitoba 1988–89; Home: 93 Harrow St., Winnipeg, Man. R3M 2X8.

**BARGE, Brian L.,** B.A., M.Sc., Ph.D.; research executive; b. Lucky Lake, Sask. 24 March 1946; e. Univ. of Sask. B.A. 1966; McGill Univ. M.Sc. 1968, Ph.D. 1972; m. Wendy 14 July 1979; children: Blake, Mark, Christina; PRES., C.E.O. & DIR., ALBERTA RESEARCH COUNCIL 1991– ; Dir., Calgary Research & Development Authority; Co-Chair, Assn. of Prov. Res. Org.; Candn. Rsch. Mgmt. Assn.; Rsch. Assoc. becoming Group Leader Atmospheric Sci's Dept. present Council 1972, Head of Dept. 1981, Head Advanced Technols. Dept. 1984, Vice Pres.: Energy & Biotechnol. 1988, Advanced Technols. 1990, Devel. & Planning 1990; recipient Ducie Award in Physics 1965; Univ. Undergrad. Scholarship 1965–66; Postgrad. Scholarship NRC 1968–71; Sir Andrew Thompson Award Applied Meterol. Candn. Meteorol. & Oceanographic Soc. 1981; mem. Adv. Ctte. Calgary Econ. Devel. Authority; Candn. Exec. Service Overseas; recreations: sports, travel, reading; Home: 10006 – 97 Ave., Edmonton, Alta. T5K 0B1; Office: 250 Karl Clark Rd., P.O. Box 8330 Stn. F, Edmonton, Alta. T5H 5X2.

**BARIBEAU, Michel;** executive; b. Lévis, Qué. 4 May 1931; s. Herve and Cecile (Despres) B.; e. St. Louis de Conzague, Qué.; Acad. de Qué.; Laval Univ., Business Adm., R.I.A. 1953; m. Marielle, d. Arthur Simoneau, St-Agapit, Qué., 13 Oct. 1956; children: Louis, Jean, Alain, Bernard; PRES., BARIBEAU & FILS INC.; Prés., Radio Saguenay Ltée.; C.J.A.B.-FM Inc.; Inter Québec Publicité Inc.; R. Catholic; Home: 654 St. Augustin, Breakeyville, Lévis, Qué. G6V 6L5.

**BARKER, Clifford Albert Victor,** C.M., C.D., D.V.M., M.Sc., D.V.Sc.; university professor emeritus; veterinarian; b. Ingersoll, Ont. 5 Jan. 1919; s. Albert Pelerin and Martha (Hansler) B.; e. Ingersoll (Ont.) Pub. and High Schs.; Univ. of Toronto, D.V.M. 1941 (Gold Medal), D.V.Sc. 1948; McGill Univ., M.Sc. 1945; m. Lily Jean, d. late Lorne Healy, 19 Sept. 1942; children: Ian K., Eric J., Graham Edward; Lectr., Animal Husbandry, Macdonald Coll., McGill Univ., 1941–45; Asst. Prof. 1948–51; Assoc. Prof. 1951–53; Prof. (Theriogenology) Dept. of Clinical Studies, Ont. Veterinary Coll., Univ. of Guelph 1953–84; served with Ont. Agric. Coll. C.O.T.C. and McGill Univ. C.O.T.C.; Personnel Offr., Central Command Personnel Selection Unit attached 11 Field Arty. Regiment with rank of Major, 1953–65, awarded Canadian Forces Decoration (1960); Past Chrmn., Wellington-Waterloo Airport Commission; former Trustee, Animal Welfare Found. of Canada; Past Pres., Candn. Soc. for Study of Fertility; Univ. of Guelph Alumni Assn.; author of over 75 pub. scientific papers; rec'd Mary A. Farley Award from Am. Dairy Goat Assn. 1962; Carlo Del Bo Award, Italy 1964; Spallanzani Research Inst. Medal, Italy 1964; Soc. Award, Candn. Soc. Study Fertility 1955, 1965, 1971; Distinguished Alumnus Award, Ont. Veterinary Coll. 1977; Jason A. Hannah History of Medicine Medal, Royal Soc. of Can. 1985; co-author, two books on Candn. veterinary med. hist.; Hon. mem., Coll. of Veterinary Med. of Venezuela; mem., Foreign Soc. (Italy, Spain, Brazil); Pres., Candn. Veterinary Med. Assn. 1965–66; Past Pres., Ont. Veterinary Assn.; Ont. Vet. Coll. Alumni Assn.; mem. Roy. College of Veterinary Surgeons; Charter mem., Cryo-biol. Soc.; Soc. for Study of Reproduction; Internat. Lectr. on Animal Reproduction; Hon. mem., Omega Tau Sigma; former Business Mgr., Candn. Veterinary Journ. 1963–65; former mem. Ed. Bd., Candn. Journ. Comp. Med.; former Ed., Ont. Veterinary Coll. Alumni Bulletin; Chart. Diplomate, Am. Coll. of Theriogenologists (1971); Chrmn., Guelph Civic Museums Bd. of Mgmt. 1983, 1984; Founder and Dir., C.A.V. Barker Museum of Candn. Veterinary Hist.; Mem., Order of Canada 1986 (first Candn. veterinarian to receive this honour); Protestant; recreation: sailing; Home: 61 Dean Ave., Guelph, Ont. N1G 1L3.

**BARKER, E. Conyers,** RC.A., O.S.A. C.S.P.W.C.; visual artist; b. Toronto, Ont. 18 March 1909; s. Charles Ernest and Gertrude (Scatcherd) B.; e. Central Technical School 1923–27; Scholarship 1925, Diploma 1927; Ont. College of Art 1928, 1941–42; m. Hughina d. Robert and Elizabeth McGowan 28 Nov. 1964; first exhibited a watercolour, Ont. Soc. of Artists 1928 and in later years with Royal Candn. Academy & Candn. Soc. of Painters in Water Colour (CSPWC); elected to CSPWC 1931; Interim Pres. 1935; Life Mem. 1991; elected to Candn. Soc. of Graphic Art 1938; Sec. then Pres. 1940s; elected Ont. Soc. of Artists 1970s; elected an academician, Royal Candn. Academy 1990; Art Teacher, Collingwood Dist. C.I. 1952–56; Barrie Dist. C.I. 1960–62; Georgian College summer 1976; watercolour in the Royal Library, Windsor Castle, England; in Russian Cultural Exchange 1945; Purchase Awards, Ont. Soc. of Artists 1977, '78; watercolours in many private collections in Canada, U.S., Great Britain; corp. collections incl.: St. Hilda's College, Univ. of Toronto; Weston Corp. Toronto; Hiram Walker Toronto; Stelco Corp. Hamilton; Toyota Motor Car Corp. Japan; Art Gall. of Ont.; Candn. Imperial Bank of Commerce; City of Toronto, Public Archives; Pacific Art Services Award for Outstanding Water Colour 1992; Geneva Conf. Ctr. Orillia; City of Barrie, Simcoe Co. Admin. Ctr.; commercial artist for 43 years 1927–70 with Batten, Ltd. Toronto; subsequent employers: Toronto Star, Reliance Engravers, Imperial Oil Ltd., CKVR TV Barrie; religion: Order of St. Luke the Physician, headquarters in San Antonio, Texas; recreations: photography, canoeing; Home: 102 Shakespeare Cres., Barrie, Ont. L4N 6B6.

**BARKER, Robert M.,** B.A., B.Ed.; teacher; b. The Pas, Manitoba 15 Aug. 1938; S. Edward Stanislaus and Ethel Mildred (Coan) B.; e. St. Thomas More Coll., Univ. of Sask. B.A. 1960; Fac. of Ed. B.Ed.; m. Betty Jo d. Luigi and Mary Antonini 21 July 1962; children: Thomas Martin, Louise Joan, Stephen William, Kenneth James; DIRECTOR, INTERNAT. PROGRAMS, CANADIAN TEACHERS' FED. 1970– ; Teacher, Campion Coll. 1961–66; Dir., Humanities & Fine Arts, Miller Comp. H.S. (Regina) 1966–69; Head, English Dept., O'Neill

H.S. 1969; Mem., Candn., Comn., Internat. Year of the Child; Merit Award, Ghana Nat. Assn. of Teachers; Cons. to teacher unions in Africa, Asia, the Caribbean & Latin Am.; Dir., Internat. Devel. Assistance Program, Candn. Teachers' Fed.; Home: 21 Firwood Cres., Nepean, Ont. K2B 6K2; Office: 110 Argyle Ave., Ottawa, Ont. K2P 1B4.

**BARKER, Warren T.,** B.Comm., C.A.; financial executive; b. Calgary, Alta. 17 Feb. 1957; s. Robert George and Phyllis Lorraine (Grierson) B.; e. Univ. of Calgary B.Comm. 1978; Inst. of C.A.s of Alta. C.A. 1980; m. Erika d. Anton and Edith Brenner 18 June 1983; children: Leighton, Matthew, Andrew; CHIEF FINAN. OFFR. & CONTROLLER, SUN ICE LIMITED 1987– ; Controller, Green Drop Limited 1983–86; Staff C.A., Dunwoody & Co. 1986; Teacher, S. Alta. Inst. of Technol. 1990– ; Cons., Fuzzy Pickles Playschool of Airdrie 1988– ; Mem., Licensing Extves. Soc.; verbal presentations to rural communities regarding agricultural credit; recreations: golf, squash, reading, refereeing hockey & football, cub leader; Home: 65 Hawkbury Close N.W., Calgary, Alta. T3G 3N2; Office: 1001 1st St. S.E., Calgary, Alta. T2G 5G3.

**BARKHOUSE, Hon. Ronald Theodore,** M.H.A.; politician; b. New Ross, Lunenburg Co., N.S. 22 Apr. 1926; s. the late Alfred Simpson and Annie (Meister) Barkhouse; e. New Ross Pub. Sch.; Horton Acad. Wolfville, N.S.; m. Eleanor P. Grant d. late Ernst Grant 1 Nov. 1951; children: Dawn, Robert, Lesley, Jimmie; VICE-PRES., BD. OF DIRS. & TREAS. OF FINANCE CTTE., BONNY LEA FARM (a training facility for the mentally and physically disabled); owned and operated wholesale lumber business and gen. store until 1974; mem. Chester Mun. Council 1952–67; mem. Chester Mun. Sch. Bd. 1952–61; mem. Bldg. Ctte., New Ross Elementary Sch. 1954; New Ross Consolidated School 1959; el. M.H.A. for Lunenburg E. 1974, '78, '81; apptd. Min. of Mines and Min. in charge Nova Scotia Energy Council 1978; apptd. Min. of Mines and Energy 1979 and Min. in charge, The Nova Scotia Power Corp.; retired from extve. council and portfolio 1983; Past positions: Chrmn. & C.E.O., Tidal Power Corp. 1984; Pres., C.E.O. & Dir., Tidal Power Corp. 1986; Pres., Lunenburg-East P.C. Assoc. 1971–74, 1989–91; Vice Pres., Fed. South Shore P.C. Assoc. 1971–74, 1989–91; Commnr., Supreme Court of Nova Scotia; Eleanor Pew Morris memorial rink, Chester; Vice-Pres., South Shore Tourist Assn.; Depy. Warden, Municipality of Chester; Chrmn. 150th Anniv. Ctte., New Ross 1966; Chrmn. Centennial Ctte., New Ross 1967; Charter Pres., New Ross Dist. Museum Soc. (Founders of Ross Farm Museum opened 1970); Secy., New Ross Fire Dept.; Vice-Chrmn. & Dir., Nova Scotia Adv. Bd. on Learning Disabilities; Charter Pres., New Ross Historical Soc.; currently: mem. Heritage Adv. Ctte., Municipality of Chester; Genealogical Assoc., Royal N.S. Historical Soc.; Honours: rec'd Centennial Medal 1967; Queen's Silver Jubilee Medal 1976; Commemorative Medal, 125th Anniversary of Candn. Confedn. 1992; Hon. Patron, Ross Farm Museum; Hon. mem., New Ross Fire Dept.; Hon. Kentucky Colonel 1979; Hon. Mem. South Shore Genealogical Soc.; Hon. Chrmn., Cancer Campaign, Municipality of Chester 1985; Award, outstanding contrib. and dedication to New Ross Hist. Soc. 1991; Charter mem. & Past Master, Norwood Masonic Lodge, New Ross; mem. Royal Arch, Bridgewater, Mount Zion Preceptory, Kentville, and Philae Shrine, Halifax; Freemason (P.M.); recreations: collecting records & tapes pre-1955 jazz; genealogy; Home: 336 Lake Lawson Rd., R.R. 2, New Ross, Lunenburg Co., N.S. BOJ 2MO.

**BARKIN, Martin,** M.D., B.Sc. (Med.), M.A., F.R.C.S.(C); b. Toronto, Ont. 20 July 1936; s. Jack and Freda (Spivak) B.; e. Forest Hill Coll. Inst. 1954; Univ. of Toronto M.D. 1960 (Cody Medal 1960), B.Sc. 1962, M.A. 1963; m. Carol d. Sam and Dora Kohm 9 June 1957; children: Tim, Jeff, Kerry, Risa, Dana, Robert; PRESIDENT, DEPRENYL RESEARCH LIMITED; Prof. of Surgery, Univ. of Toronto 1982– , Prof. of Health Admin. 1986– ; Depy. Min., Ont. Min. of Health 1987–91; Partner and National Practice Leader, Health Care and Social Services, KPMG Peat Marwick Stevenson & Kellogg 1991–92; Gallie Course in Surgery 1961–66; McLaughlin Fellow to London, Eng. and Harvard 1967; Chief Urologist Sunnybrook Medical Centre 1972–84; Pres. of Med. Staff and Chrmn. of Sunnybrook, Univ. of Toronto Clinics 1980–83; Pres. and C.E.O., Sunnybrook Medical Centre 1984–87; Cons. Urologist to Hosp. for Sick Children, St. Michael's Hosp., Hugh MacMillan Centre; recipient Queen's Silver Jubilee Medal 1977; Dir., Ont. Med. Assn.; Candn. Med. Assn.; Am. Urol. Assn. (Pres. N.E. Sect. 1985); Candn. Urol. Assn.; recreations: tennis, hunting; Clubs: Granite; Goodwood; Home: 54 Old Forest Hill Rd., Toronto, Ont. M5P 2P9; Office: 337 Roncesvalles, Toronto, Ont. M6R 2M8.

**BARKLEY, William Donald (Bill),** B.Sc., M.A.; museum director; b. New Westminster, B.C. 4 Apr. 1941; s. Donald MacMillan and Ethel Margaret (Mines) B.; e. Lester Pearson H.S. New Westminster; Univ. of B.C., B.Sc.(Hons. Zoology) 1964, M.A. 1972; Univ. of Victoria P.B. (Sec.) 1965; m. Gayle d. Jack and Alvina Alanson 29 Aug. 1964; children: Warren, Colleen; EXTVE. DIR., ROYAL B.C. MUSEUM 1984– ; Biol. Teacher Salmon Arm (B.C.) H.S. 1964–68; Chief Naturalist, Wye Marsh Wildlife Centre, Midland, Ont. 1968–72; Chief, Wildlife Interpretation, Ottawa 1972–77; Asst. Dir. present Museum 1977–84; Dir. Tourism Victoria; Past Dir. Candn. Nature Fedn.; Fedn. B.C. Naturalists; Advr., Acad. Counc. Cultural Resource Mgmt. Prog. Univ. of Victoria; recipient Commonwealth Inst. Fellowship, London, Eng. 1982; Distinguished Service Award, Interpretation Can. 1983; Commemorative Medal for 125th Anniversary of Candn. Confederation; author numerous papers and articles; Past Pres. Candn. Museums Assn.; Past Dir. B.C. Museums Assn.; United Ch.; recreations: ornithology, stained glass, backpacking, jogging, photography; Club: Victoria A.M.; Home: 4809 Sea Ridge Dr., Victoria, B.C. V8Y 3B6; Office: 675 Belleville St., Victoria, B.C. V8V 1X4.

**BARKOW, Jerome,** B.A., M.A., Ph.D.; university professor; b. Brooklyn, N.Y. 18 Jan. 1944; s. Philip and Rebecca (Gendler) B.; e. Brooklyn Coll., CUNY, B.A. 1964; Univ. of Chicago, M.A. 1967, Ph.D. 1970; m. Irma d. Toivo and Marjatta Juuti 1979; children: Philip, Sarah; COORDINATOR, INTERNATIONAL DEVELOPMENT STUDIES, 1991–92, 1993– ;and PROF., DEPT. OF SOCIOL. & SOCIAL ANTHROPOL., DALHOUSIE UNIV. 1980– ; postdoctoral fellow, Duke Univ. Med. Ctr. 1970–71; Asst. Prof., Dalhousie Univ. 1971; Assoc. Prof. 1975; fieldwork in Nigeria 1968–69, 1977, 1979–80 among the Hausa and the Migili (Koro); fieldwork in Maradi (Rep. of Niger) 1972, 1973–74; fieldwork in Ifugao, Philippines 1993; Partner, SSDCC 1979–81; Ed. Bd., 'Anthropologica' 'Ethology and Sociobiology'; Phi Beta Kappa; Fellow, Am. Assn. for the Advancement of Sci.; Royal Anthropol. Inst. of Gt. Britain & Ireland; author: 'Darwin, Sex, and Status' 1989; 'Once More for Children' and 'Health and the Health Care Delivery System' unpub. reports; co-editor: 'The Adapted Mind' 1992; editor/co-editor of two published proceedings; recreations: gardening, aquaculture; Home: 2112 Beech St., Halifax, N.S. B3L 2X8; Office: Halifax, N.S. B3H 1T2.

**BAR-LEWAW, Itzhak Isaac,** Ph.D.; professor; linguist; writer; b. Nriow, Poland 9 Feb. 1922; s. Menachem and Sarah (Mühlstock) B.; e. Hebrew Univ., M.A. 1953; Nat. Univ. (Mexico), Ph.D. 1959; m. Lea Laura d. Aaron and Helen Goldman 12 Nov. 1942; children: Michael, Helen Ilana, Henry Oscar; PROF., YORK UNIV. 1967– ; Lectr., Hebrew Univ. 1953–55; Univ. of Chile 1960; Univ. of Ecuador (summer) 1962; Asst. Prof., Univ. of Kansas 1961–63; Univ. of Florida 1963–64; Assoc. Prof., Univ. of Sask. 1964–67; Vis. Lectr., Indiana Univ.; Carleton Univ.; McGill Univ.; Laval Univ.; Univ. of Calgary; Couns. & Ph.D. Adv., McMaster Univ. 1972; recipient several univ. & Can. Counc. grants; Jewish; Mem., Internat. Assn. of Hispanists; author: 'Gabriel de la Concepción Valdés' 1959, 'Plácido, Vida y Obra' 1960, 'Temas Literarios Iberoamericanos' 1961, 'Introducción Critico-biográfica a José Vasconcelos' 1965, 'José Vasconcelos, Vida y Obra' 1966, 'La Revista "Timón" y José Vasconcelos' 1971; 'La Obra Períodistica de José Vasconcelos' 2 vols. 1991, vol. 3 1992; co-author: 'Pedro de Toledo, El primer traductor español del Moré Nebujim' 1966; author: many articles on Candn. bilingualism published in several Candn. publications; community lectr.; extensive lit. contbr.; Latin Am. correspondent for El Universal, Mexico City, Mexico; has attended five internat. congs.; Home: 39 Golfwood Heights, Weston, Ont. M9P 3L8; Office: 250 Winters Coll., York Univ., 4700 Keele St., Downsview, Ont. M3J 1P3.

**BARLOW, Curtis Leonard,** B.Sc., LL.M.; cultural executive; lawyer; diplomat; b. Middleton, N.S. 2 May 1947; s. Curtis Francis and Patricia Mary (Trask); e. Mount Allison Univ. 1964–66; Univ. of Western Ont. 1966–67; Carleton Univ., B.Sc. 1968; Univ. of Ottawa, LL.B. 1972; Osgoode Hall Bar Admission 1974; University Coll. (U.K.), LL.M. 1976; COUNSELLOR, CULTURAL AFFAIRS, CANADIAN EMBASSY, Washington, D.C. 1990– ; articled with Thomson, Rogers, Toronto 1972–73; Solicitor, Ont. Min. of Treasury, Economics & Intergovernmental Affairs 1974–75; Extve. Dir., Professional Assoc. of Candn. Theatres 1977–86; Dir., Canada House Cultural Centre and Couns., Cultural Affairs, Candn. High Comn., London, Eng. 1986–90; Pres., Candn. Conference of the Arts 1984–86; Pres., Candn. Centre of the Internat. Theatre Inst., English-language 1981–86; mem., Extve. Ctte. Internat. Theatre Inst. 1983–86; Pres. World Encyclopedia of Contemporary Theatre (Canada) 1984–86; Co-Pres., XXIst World Congress of the Internat. Theatre Inst. 1985; Soc. of West End Theatres Olivier Awards Theatre Panel, London 1988; Public Relations Ctte., Duke of Edinburgh's Award Internat. Secretariat, London, 1987–90; Counc., Br. Centre of the Internat. Theatre Inst. 1989–90; Awards Panel, Helen Hayes Theatre Awards, Washington 1992– ; mem., Law Soc. of Upper Canada; Assoc. of Cultural Executives; Co-ed.: 'Playwrights Guide to Canadian, non-profit, professional theatres, PACT' 1984; recreations: travel, literature, languages; Office: The Canadian Embassy, 501 Pennsylvania Ave. N.W., Washington, D.C. 20001.

**BARLOW, Elizabeth,** B.Sc., B.L.S.; librarian; b. Drumheller, Alta. 19 Dec. 1950; d. Ernest William and Anna Teresa (Guidolin) B.; e. Drumheller Comp. H.S. 1968; Univ. of Alta., B.Sc. 1971, B.L.S. 1972 (both with distinction); HEAD, PUBLIC SERVICES, CALGARY PUBLIC LIBRARY 1992– ; Cataloguer, Univ. of Man. Library 1972–74; Health Sci. Ref. Librarian, Univ. of Sask. 1974–78; Govt. Pubs. Dept. Head, Univ. of Sask. 1978–81; Head, Information Serv., Saskatoon Public Library 1981–89; Dept. Head, Humanities, Calgary Public Library 1989–91; Gov.-Gen. Bronze Medal 1968; Pres., Bd. of Dir., Public Legal Edn. Assn. of Sask. 1985–87; Sask. Open Door Soc. 1984–85; Pres., Candn. Library Assn. 1989–90; Candn. Assn. of Special Libraries & Inform. Serv. 1977–78; Mem., Candn. Libr. Assn.; Libr. Assn. of Alta.; Sask. Libr. Assn.; Home: 9 – 140 Point Dr. N.W., Calgary, Alta. T3B 4W3; Office: c/o Calgary Public Library, 616 Macleod Trail S.E., Calgary, Alta. T2G 2M2.

**BARLOW, Leonard Edgar,** B.A., C.F.A.; investment dealer (ret.); b. Hamilton, Ont. 27 Aug. 1914; s. Edgar and Minerva (Laforce) B.; e. McMaster Univ., B.A., 1937; m. Margaret Olive, d. Col. H.C. Craig; Hon. Dir., Global Communications Ltd.; Pres., Toronto Soc. of Financial Analysts, 1962–63; Pres., Inst. of Chart. Financial Analysts, 1969–70; Dir., Financial Analysts' Fed., 1965–66 and 1969–70; Trustee, Research Foundation, Financial Analysts 1971–74; United Church; recreations: golf, gardening, sailing; Club: Royal Canadian Yacht; Ontario; York Downs Golf & Country; Home: 3800 Yonge St., Toronto, Ont. M4N 3P7.

**BARLOW, Maude Victoria,** B.A.; political activist; b. Toronto, Ont. 24 May 1947; d. William Thomas and Flora MacDonald (Wilkie) McGrath; e. Carleton Univ. B.A. 1974; m. Andrew Davis s. Norman and Beverly Shaffran; two s. Charles Garnet and William Joel Barlow; Nat. CHAIRPERSON, COUNCIL OF CANADIANS 1988– ; Vice Pres. Women Associates Consulting Inc. 1975–80; Dir. Office of Equal Oppportunity City of Ottawa 1980–83; Sr. Adv. Women's Issues to Prime Min. of Can. 1983–84; Co-Founder Pro Canada Network; Visiting Scholar-in-Residence, Queen's Univ. and Univ. of Ottawa 1991; Cons. Family Violence Prevention Project Ont. Min. Edn.; mem. Council Advs. Candn. Centre Arms Control & Disarmament; Foundng mem. Ctte. '94; Past Pres. Amethyst Women's Drug & Alcohol Abuse Centre; former Social Justice Adv. to Fed. Lib. Party; chaired nat. Lib. conf. social policy 1987; Hon. Fellow Ont. Teachers' Fedn.; author 'Parcel of Rogues: How Free Trade is Failing Canada' 1990; 'Take Back the Nation' 1991; Home: C, 525 Bay St., Ottawa, Ont. K1R 6B4.

**BARMA, Oscar;** fonctionnaire; né Québec 4 avril 1929; f. Siméon et Eva (Beaudin) B.; é. Coll. Saint-Thomas Chatham, N.B. 1952; Univ. Laval 1954; ép. Marie f. Dr. Roland et Béatrice Miller Desmeules 13 juillet 1957; enfants: Sylvie, Pierre, Louise, Marie-José, Lucie, Robert; ATTACHÉ D'ADMINISTRATION, BIBLIOTHÈQUE DE L'ASSEMBLÉE NATIONALE 1987– ; Vice-prés. Barma Automobiles Inc. 1955–60; Prés. Husk Air Inc., Directeur Grande Allée Construction Inc. et de Belleroute Construction Inc., Prés. Ray-Car Enterprises Ltd. 1960–70; Ministère du Travail 1970; Recherchiste à l'Assemblée nationale à la direction du personnel des députés et des partis 1983; Participer à l'élaboration et à l'application d'un système de gestion des documents 1985; Vice-prés. de Ski Can. et de Ski Qué.; Prés. du Club de Ski Acrobatique du Lac Beauport; Coordonateur de Centraide 1987–89; Collaborer à la cueillette de fonds comme bénévole pour La Société Canadienne du Cancer 1990; R. Catholique; Parti libéral du Canada (PLC) et Parti libéral du Québec (PLQ); loisirs: ski alpin, camping, natation, voile, golf, chasse, pêche, tennis; Adresse: 6 Jardins Mérici, #317, Ville de

Québec, Qué. G1S 4N7; Bureau: Hôtel du Parlement, Edifice Pamphile-LeMay, Québec, Qué. G1A 1A5.

**BARNARD, Michael C.,** F.C.I.I., B.Comm., M.Ed.; insurance executive; b. Horsham, Sussex 3 May 1932; s. Frederick and Dorothy B. (both dec.); e. Ch. Insur. Inst. (U.K.) F.C.I.I. 1959; Sir George Williams Univ. B.Comm. 1964; Ont. Inst. for Studies in Education M.Ed. 1973; 2nd m. Janet Doreen Bedbrooke 3 Jan. 1987; children: Chris, Claire, Jon, Jo-Anne (from prev. marriage); EXTVE. VICE-PRES., CORP., ROYAL INSURANCE CO. OF CANADA 1988– ; joined Royal Insur. England 1953; transferred to Canada 1957; Training Offr. 1965; Personnel Mgr. 1974; Vice-Pres. Personnel 1978; seconded to U.K. as Dep. Group Personnel Mgr. 1983; returned to Canada 1986; Vice-Pres., Corp. 1986; Vice-Pres. & Corp. Sec. 1987; Mem., Ch. Insur. Inst. of G.B.; Insur. Inst. of Can. (Past Chair, Edn. Ctte.); Dir., Royal Life Insur. Co. of Can.; (Chair, Investment Ctte.); Roins Holding Limited; Western Assurance Co.; Royal Insur. Co. of Can.; Anglican; recreations: skiing, tennis, hiking, theatre, travel, cooking; clubs: Albany, Donalda, The Fitness Inst.; Home: 58 Willow Ave., Toronto, Ont. M4K 3K2; Office: 10 Wellington St. E., Toronto, Ont. M5E 1L5.

**BARNARD, Peter Robert,** B.Sc., Ph.D., P.Eng.; management consultant; b. Montreal, Que. 29 May 1938; s. Robert T. and Florence M. (Callaghan) B.; e. Willingdon Pub. and Westmount Jr. High Schs. Montreal; Oakville (Ont.) Trafalgar High Sch.; Queen's Univ. B.Sc. 1960; Cambridge Univ. (Athlone Fellow) Ph.D. 1963; Harvard Bus. Sch. Advanced Mgmt. Prog. 1982; m. Despina d. Nicholas Callis 26 June 1965; two s. Robert, Christopher; MANAGEMENT CONSULTANT; Partner, Bradstock Reicher & Partners cons. engs. 1963–67; Pres. Peter Barnard Associates, Toronto, mgmt. cons. 1967–85; Mgr. Can., Cresap, management consultants, a Towers Perrin Co. 1985–91; Pres. & C.E.O., Peat Marwick Stevenson & Kellogg, management consultants 1991–93; mem. Univ. Council, Queen's Univ.; Former Dir. Dellcrest Children's Centre Toronto; Past Pres. Badminton and Racquet Club, Toronto; Chrmn., Cambridge Candn. Trust; Dir., Candn. Arctic Beverage Corp.; Jr. Candn. Tennis Doubles Champion 1955, third ranking Ont. sr. player and Capt. Candn. Jr. Davis Cup Team 1959; Blue, Cambridge 1960–63; Capt. Cambridge Hockey 1962; mem. Assn. Prof. Engs. Prov. Ont.; Inst. Mgmt. Cons. Ont.; recreations: tennis, golf, squash, sketching, croquet; Clubs: Toronto; Mad River Golf; Badminton & Racquet; Queen's; Internat. Lawn Tennis of Can.; Internat. Lawn Tennis of Gt. Brit.; Home: 103 Ridge Dr., Toronto, Ont. M4T 1B6; Office: Toronto, Ont.

**BARNES, Christopher J.,** M.A., Ph.D.; university professor; b. Sheffield, England 10 March 1942; s. William and Doris (Oxley) B.; e. King Edward VII Sch. Sheffield 1960; Corpus Christi Coll. Cambridge B.A. 1963, M.A. 1967, Ph.D. 1971; Moscow Univ. 1963–64; m. 1975; children: Nicola, Julia; PROFESSOR AND CHAIRMAN, DEPT. OF SLAVIC LANGUAGES AND LITERATURES, UNIV. OF TORONTO 1989– ; Lecturer in Russian, St. Andrews Univ. Scotland 1967–89; Adv. Bd. Mem., 'Scottish Slavonic Review' 1982– , 'Elementa' 1992– ; Editor, Radio Liberty Research Bulletin 1974–75; Manners Scholarship in Modern Languages, Corpus Christi Coll. 1960; Chair, Academy Concerts Toronto 1991– ; Anglican; Mem., Brit. Scriabin Soc.; Royal Musical Assn.; Brit. Univ. Assn. of Slavists (Ctte. 1984–87); Assn. of Teachers of Russian; Candn. Assn. of Slavists; Am. Assn. for Advancement of Slavic Studies; Royal Candn. Coll. of Organists; author: 'Boris Pasternak: A Literary Biography' vol. I 1989; editor and translator: 'Boris Pasternak and European Literature' 1991, 'Boris Pasternak: Collected Short Prose' 1977, 'Boris Pasternak: The Voice of Prose' vol. I 1986, vol. II 1991, 'Studies in Twentieth Century Literature' 1975; co-translator: 'Red Square' Edward Topol 1983, 'Russian Seven' Edward Topol 1990, 'The Blind Beauty' Boris Pasternak 1969; Home: 53 Alberta Ave., Toronto, Ont. M6H 2R5; Office: 21 Sussex Ave., Toronto, Ont. M5S 1A1.

**BARNES, Christopher Richard,** F.R.S.C., Ph.D.; university professor; b. Nottingham, Eng. 20 Apr. 1940; e. Univ. of Birmingham B.Sc. 1961; Univ. of Ottawa Ph.D. 1964; m. Susan; children: Penny, Joanne, Allison; DIRECTOR, CENTRE FOR EARTH AND OCEAN RESEARCH, UNIV. OF VICTORIA 1989– ; DIR., SCH. OF EARTH AND OCEAN SCIENCES, UNIV. OF VICTORIA 1992– ; N.A.T.O. Rsch. Fellow, Univ. of Wales (Swansea) 1964–65; Asst. Prof., Univ. of Waterloo 1965–70; Sr. Rsch. Fellow (sabbatical), Univ. of Southampton, U.K. 1971–72; Univ. of Waterloo: Assoc. Prof. 1970–76, Prof. and Chrmn. 1976, cross-appt. in Biology Dept. 1973–81, Adjunct Prof. 1981–82; Univ. of Cambridge, U.K. (sabbatical) 1980–81; Prof. and Head, Dept. of Earth Sciences 1981–87, and Acting Dir., Centre for Earth Resources Research 1983–87, Memorial Univ. of Nfld.; Dir. Gen., Sedimentary and Marine Geoscience, Geological Survey of Can. 1987–89; Pres., Geol. Assn. of Can. 1983–84; Pres., Can. Geoscience Counc. 1979; Chrmn., I.U.G.S. Subcomn. on Ordovician Stratigraphy 1982–89; Pres., Acad. of Sci., Royal Soc. of Can. 1990–93; mem., Sci. Counc. of B.C. 1991–94; recvd. GAC Past Presidents Medal 1979; Bancroft Award, R.S.C. 1982; Willis Ambrose Medal 1991; Fellow, Royal Soc. of Can. 1982; author of numerous scientific papers, and ed. of two symposium volumes; Office: CEOR, Univ. of Victoria, P.O. Box 1700, Victoria, B.C. V8W 2Y2.

**BARNES, Leslie William Charles Seaman,** M.A.; economist, author; b. London, Eng. 13 Feb. 1920; s. William and Ada Minnie Amy (Seaman) B.; m. Dorothy Mary Waters; two s. Charles, Michael; e. Shooters Hill Sch., London, Eng.; London Univ.; Cambridge Univ.; Univ. of Zurich; B.A. 1949, M.A. 1952; served with Brit. War Office and Ministry of Supply; Dir. of Proof & Ballistics, Dept. of Nat. Defence 1951–65; Exec. Dir., Prof. Inst. Public Service of Canada 1965–74; Gov., Ashbury Coll., Ottawa 1965–75; rec'd Centennial Medal 1967; Commemorative Medal for 125th Anniversary of Candn. Confederation 1992; lately Visiting Sr. Research Fellow, Ind. Relations Centre, Queen's Univ.; Past Chrmn. Int. Affairs Ctte., Ang. Diocese of Ottawa; First Vice-Pres., Federal Superannuates National Assn.; Past Pres., Prof. Inst. Public Service of Can.; Former Dir., Friends of the Canadian War Museum; mem., Public Service Arbitration Tribunal 1980–89; author: 'Consult and Advise'; 'Canada's Guns,' etc.; mem., Cambridge Soc.; Anglican; Address: 60 McLeod St., Apt. 801, Ottawa, Ont. K2P 2G1.

**BARNES, Timothy David,** M.A., D.Phil., F.R.S.C.; educator; b. Yorks., Eng. 13 March 1942; s. David and Margaret (Baxter) B.; e. Queen Elizabeth Grammar Sch. Wakefield 1949–60; Oxford Univ. B.A. (Balliol) 1964, M.A. 1967, D.Phil. 1970; m. Anne Jenifer d. John K.S. and Phyllis (Beniston) Dixon 16 July 1965; four s. Thomas, Christopher, Alexander, Dunstan; PROF. OF CLASSICS, UNIV. OF TORONTO 1976– ; Harmsworth Sr. Scholar Merton Coll. Oxford 1964–66, Jr. Rsch. Fellow The Queen's Coll. 1966–70; Asst. Prof. of Classics Univ. Coll. present Univ. 1970, Assoc. Prof. 1972, Assoc. Chrmn. of Classics 1979–83, 1986–89, Connaught Sr. Fellow in the Humanities 1984–85; Visiting mem. Inst. Advanced Study Princeton 1976–77; Visiting Fellow Wolfson Coll. Oxford 1983–84; Fellow, Trinity Coll., Univ. of Toronto 1989– ; Townsend Lectr., Cornell Univ. 1994; recipient Conington Prize Oxford 1974; Philip Schaff Meml. Prize Am. Soc. Ch. Hist. 1984; Charles Goodwin Award of Merit Am. Philol. Assn. 1984; author 'Tertullian. A Historical and Literary Study' 1971, 2nd ed. 1985; 'The Sources of the Historia Augusta' 1978; 'Constantine and Eusebius' 1981; 'The New Empire of Diocletian and Constantine' 1982; 'Early Christianity and the Roman Empire' 1984; 'Athanasius and Constantius, Theology and Politics in the Constantinian Empire' 1993; 'From Eusebius to Augustine: Selected Studies 1982-1992' 1994; Office: Trinity Coll., Toronto, Ont. M5S 1A1.

**BARNETT, Henry Joseph Macaulay,** O.C., M.D., F.R.C.P.(C), F.A.C.P. F.R.C.P.; educator; b. Eng. 10 Feb. 1922; e. Univ. of Toronto M.D. 1944; PROFESSOR EMERITUS, DEPT OF CLIN. NEUROL. SCIENCES, UNIV. OF WESTERN ONT. 1991, Prof. 1974–91; Residency and Grad. training Toronto Gen. Hosp., Banting Inst. Univ. of Toronto, Sunnybrook Hosp. Toronto, Nat. Hosp. London, Eng., Oxford Univ. (Research Asst. Neurol.) 1944–52; Phys., Toronto Gen. Hosp. 1952–67; Consultant in Neurol. Sunnybrook Hosp. 1953–66, Chief Div. of Neurol. 1966–69; Consultant in Neurol. Clarke Inst. Psychiatry 1953–68 and Toronto Hosp. Weston, Ont. 1954–66; Chief Div. of Neurol. Victoria Hosp. London, Ont. 1969–72 and Univ. Hosp. London 1972–74; Clin. Teacher, Univ. of Toronto 1952, Assoc. (Med.) 1954, Asst. Prof. 1963, Assoc. Prof. 1966; Prof. of Neurol. Univ. of W. Ont. 1969; Chief, Dept. Clin. Neurol. Sciences, Univ. Hosp. London, Ont. 1974–85; Pres. and Scientific Dir., Robarts Rsch. Inst. 1984–92; has held numerous guest lectr. and visiting prof. positions incl.: Jacobson Visiting Prof. Newcastle-Upon-Tyne 1976; Willis Lectr., Montreal Neurol. Inst. 1978; Wartenberg Lectr., Am. Acad. Neurol. 1979; Allison Meml. Lectr., Queens Univ. Belfast 1979; G. Robinson Meml. Lectr., Toronto 1979; J.S. Simpson Meml. Lectr., Toronto 1980; S. Harrington Goldwater Meml. Visiting Prof., Barrows Neuro. Inst., Phoenix 1981; Squires Prof., Univ. of Toronto 1981; J.N. Allen Meml. Lectr., Ohio State Univ. 1982; Paterson Meml. Lectr., Sunnybrook Hosp., Toronto 1983; 14th J.J. Gitt Visiting Prof., St. Louis 1983; A.B. Baker Lectr., Minneapolis 1983; Botterell Lectr., Toronto Gen. Hosp. 1983; Louis Gross Meml. Lectr., Montreal 1984; Murray Robertson Meml. Lectr., Toronto 1984; Raymond Adams Visiting Prof., Boston 1985; E. Graeme Robertson Meml. Lectr., Singapore 1985; Sir Hugh Cairns Lectr., Adelaide, Australia 1985; Parke-Davis Visiting Prof., Vanderbilt Univ. Med. Ctr., Nashville, Tennessee 1986; Dr. W.E. Upjohn Lect., CMA Annual Meeting, Charlottetown, P.E.I. 1987; Willis Lectr., Am. Heart Assoc., San Diego, CA 1988; Mayfield-Aring Lectr., Cincinnati, Ohio 1988; The Robert Clark Dickson Lectr. in Med., Dalhousie Univ., Halifax, N.S. 1988; Allan A. Bailey Meml. Lectr., Saskatoon, Sask. 1988; The First Frederick and Lotte Stern Stroke Lectr., The Stern Stroke Ctr., Albert Einstein Coll. of Med., Montefiore Med. Ctr., New York, N.Y. 1989; Royal Coll. Lectr., Royal Coll. of Physicians & Surgeons of Can., Edmonton, Alta. 1989; Emanuel Goldberg Family Lectr., Univ. of Rochester, Rochester, N.Y. 1989; Koret Visiting Prof., San Francisco, CA 1991; Ned Atack Neurology Lectr., Univ. of Ottawa, Ottawa, Ont. 1991; Fred Plum Lectr., Univ. of Washington, Seattle, Washington 1991; William S. Fields Lectr., Univ. of Texas Med. Sch. at Houston, Houston, Texas 1991; Seventh Annual Joseph A. Provenzano, M.D. Meml. Lectr., The Fairfax Hosp., Fairfax, VA 1992; co-ed.: 'Syringomyelia' 1973; 'Cerebrovascular Diseases: New Trends in Surgical and Medical Aspects' 1981; 'ASA: New Uses for an Old Drug' 1982; 'Cerebral Ischemia: Clinical and Experimental Approach' 1982; ed. 'Neurologic Clinics' 1983; (with J.P. Mohr, B.M. Stein and F.M. Yatsu) 'Stroke: Pathophysiology, Diagnosis and Management' 2 vols. 1986, 2nd ed. 1992; (with Dr. V.C. Hachinski) 'Neurologic Clinics' 1992; author or co-author 85 book chapters, 94 articles/papers/abstracts/conf. proceedings; mem. various ed. bds., med. journs.; Hon. Fellow, Am. Coll. Physicians; Royal Coll. Physicians (London); Med. Soc. of London; Hon. Mem., Hungarian Neurosurg Soc.; Hon. Pres., Bishin-kai Rsch. Inst. for Brain and Blood Vessels, Japan; present research: Project Dir. and Princ. Investigator, North Am. Symptomatic Carotid Endarterectomy Trial; mem. Candn. Neurol. Soc. (Secy. 1964–68, Vice Pres. 1974–75, Pres. 1975–76); Toronto Neurol. Soc. (founding Pres. 1968); Am. Assn. Neurol. Surgs.; Am. Neurol. Assn. (1st Vice-Pres. 1984); Am. Heart Assn. (Extve. Comte., Stroke Counc.); London Neurosciences Assn. (Past-Pres.); Candn. Stroke Soc. (Pres.); Heart and Stroke Foundation, Can. (Dir.); Ont. Heart Foundation (Sr. Adv. Counc.); Ont. Deafness Research Foundation (Past Chrmn., Scient. Adv. Comte.); Royal Coll. Physicians & Surgeons (mem. Council 1981–84, Chrmn. Rsch. Comte.); Dir., J.P. Robarts Rsch. Inst.; Siebens-Drake Rsch. Inst.; World Wildlife Fund of Can.; Dir., London Convention Centre; Editor-in-Chief, 'Stroke' (Journal) 1982–86; co-recipient Royal Bank Award 1983; Officer, Order of Canada 1984; Hon. LL.D., Dalhousie Univ. 1984; Hon. D.Sc., N.Y. Inst. of Technol. 1985; Isaak Walton Killam Prize, Can. Counc. 1988; Hon. Mem., Am. Neurological Assoc. 1990; Distinguished Achievement Award, Am. Heart Assoc. 1990; J. Allyn Taylor International Prize in Medicine; Home: 1571 Gloucester Rd., London, Ont. N6G 2S5; Office: J.P. Robarts Inst., P.O. Box 5015, London, Ont. N6A 5K8.

**BARNICKE, Joseph John,** C.M., K.C.S.G., LL.D., D.S. Litt.; real estate executive; b. Cudworth, Sask. 6 Apl. 1923; e. Oakville (Ont.) Pub. and High Schs.; Univ. of W. Ont. 1949; Univ. of Toronto Honorary LL.D. 1989; m. Justina Marie (dec.) 25 Sept. 1949; children: Peter, Paul, Andrew, Anne, Carroll; CHRMN. AND FOUNDER J.J. BARNICKE LTD. 1959– ; Dir. George Wimpey (Canada) Ltd.; Viking-Rideau Corp.; Barbican Properties Inc.; various mgmt. positions Canadian Breweries; Sales Mgr. O'Keefe Brewing Co. 1947–57; Vice Pres. Gibson Bros. 1957–59; Hon. Doctorate in Sacred Letters, Univ. of St. Michael's Coll.; Order of Canada; Knight Commander, The Order of St. Gregory; Hon. Degree of Doctor of Laws, Univ. of Toronto; Award of Merit, City of Toronto 1985; Human Relations Award, Candn. Council of Christians and Jews 1986; mem. and Past Council mem. Bd. Trade Metrop. Toronto; Past Dir.: Toronto Real Estate Bd.; Appraisal Inst. Can.; Past Pres. Ont. Jr. C. of C.; Dir. Candn. Council Christian & Jews; Chrmn. St. Joseph's Hosp. Found.; former Ont. and Nat. Campaign Chrmn. Candn. Cancer Soc.; Past Corporate Chrmn. Share Life; served with RCAF 1941–45, Flying Offr.; R.Catholic; recreations: golf, music; Clubs: Griffith Island; Muskoka Lakes Golf & Country; Albany; RCYC; Granite; Craigleith Ski; National (Dir.); Home: 20 Montclair Ave., Toronto, Ont. M4V 1W1; Office: 3100, 401 Bay St., Toronto, Ont. M5H 2Y4.

**BARNIM, (Roger) Scott,** M.A.; craftsperson, potter; b. Brantford, Ont. 20 Oct. 1957; s. Verne and Helen (Hammond) B.; e. Cardiff Inst. of Higher Edn. M.A. 1985; OWNER, BARNIM POTTERY 1987– ; apprenticed with Donn Zver 1976–78; Barnim Pottery employs 2 full-time potters & produces a complete range of domestic pottery marketed across Canada; gallery exbns. in Canada & abroad; num. workshops & lectures throughout Ont.; Teacher, Sheridan College Sch. of Art & Design; Acquisition Ctte. Mem., Burlington Cultural Ctr. Ceramic Collection; works incl. in num. public & private collections; Pres., Ont. Crafts Council 1991–92; recreations: travel and study of Mediterranean culture; Home & Studio: 15 Park St. E., Dundas, Ont. L9H 1C9.

**BARNOR, Nah-Amakuma,** M.D., F.R.C.P.(C); paediatrician; b. Accra, Ghana 25 June 1949; d. Joseph Daniel and Christiana Diana (Bampoe-Addo) B.; e. Achimota Sch.; Univ. of Toronto, B.Sc. 1970, M.D. 1974; Hosp. for Sick Children Toronto, F.R.C.P.(C) Paed. 1979; m. Kojo Lamptey; children: Nakoshie, Nii-apa, Arakua; CHIEF OF PAEDIATRIC PROGRAMME, HUMBER MEMORIAL HOSPITAL 1985– ; worked at Rusholme Clinic to 1980, then opened own office; Humber Hosp. 1984; St. Joseph's Hosp. 1980– ; Courtesy Staff, Women's Coll. Hosp. 1981– ; Teacher, St. Joseph's Health Ctr.; Vice-Pres., Nat. Counc. of Ghanaian Candns. 1987–90; Home: 502 Christie St., Toronto, Ont. M6G 3C8; Office: 2545 Eglinton Ave. W., Toronto, Ont. M6M 1T2.

**BARNUM, John,** Mus.Bac.; conductor; educator; b. Guelph, Ont. 24 June 1947; s. Donald Alfred and Doris Arleen (Young) B.; e. Univ. of Toronto Mus.Bac. 1969; various specialized courses & study France, Italy, USA, Can.; m. H. Rochelle d. James H. Sturgeon 7 Aug. 1971; children: Julia Marie, Alisdair Andrew; Conductor & Music Dir. Mississauga Symphony & Sinfonia 1978– ; Teacher of Conducting Univ. of Toronto 1983– ; Supervisor, Royal Conserv. of Music Division, Mississauga, Oakville, Brampton 1992– ; Resident Conductor Thunder Bay Symphony 1970–72; Asst. Conductor Edmonton Symphony 1973–76, Conductor & Music Dir. Youth Orch. 1973–78 and Symphony Chorus 1973–76, Chorus Master Edmonton Opera 1977–78; Music Cons. Alta. Culture 1976–78; Violist Toronto freelance, Hamilton Philharmonic, Edmonton Symphony 1969–85; Conductor & Music Dir. Halton-Peel Youth Orch. 1981–83; Exec. Asst. to Prin. & Ensemble Dir. 1978–82; Conductor & Music Dir. Orpheus Choir Toronto 1981–87; Coord. of Ensembles, Orch. Dir. Royal Conserv. of Music 1986–92; recipient Heinz Unger Award 1970; Mississauga Musician of Yr. 1970; mem. Bd. Mississauga Music Edn. Found. 1983– ; Ont. Fedn. Symphony Orchs. 1979–82; Toronto Symphony, Youth & Edn. Ctte. 1986–90; Toronto Early Music Soc. 1987–91; recreations: tennis, swimming; Home: 3642 Sawmill Valley Dr., Mississauga, Ont. L5L 2P6; Office: 273 Bloor St. W., Toronto, Ont. M5S 1W2.

**BAROLET, Ralph Yvon,** B.Sc., B.Eng., D.D.S., M.S.D.; educator; b. Montréal, Qué. 4 Oct. 1929; e. Loyola Coll. Montréal B.Sc. 1952; McGill Univ. B.E. (Chem.) 1954; Univ. de Montréal D.D.S. 1970; Ind. Univ. M.S.D. 1972; m. Lorraine Raby 26 Nov. 1955; one d. Frances; DEAN AND PROF. OF DENTISTRY, McGILL UNIV. 1987– ; Assoc. Prof. Univ. Laval 1974–82, Prof. 1982–87, Assoc. Dean 1980–83; Visiting Prof. Univ. de Rennes, France 1981, Univ. of Alta. 1981, McGill Univ. 1984, 1986; Fellow, Internat. Coll. Dentists; Acad. Internat. Dental Studies; Acad. Dental Materials; Am. Coll. of Dentists; Acad. Dentistry Internat.; Pierre Fauchard Acad.; Home: 16 Arlington, Westmount, Qué. H3Y 2W4; Office: 3640 University St., Montréal, Qué. H3A 2B2.

**BARONE-ADESI, Giovanni,** Ph.D.; university professor; b. Reggio Calabria, Italy 29 Sept. 1951; s. Vittorio and Liliana (Rizzo) B.; e. Univ. of Padova, laurea in El. Eng. 1974; Univ. of Chicago, M.B.A. 1978, Ph.D. 1982; m. Kristine d. Edward and Lois Phelps 3 May 1981; children: Katerina, Victoria; PROF. OF FINANCE, BUSINESS FAC., UNIV. OF ALTA. 1981– ; Vis. Assoc. Prof., Univ. of Texas at Austin 1987; McCalla Rsch. Prof. 1989–90; Dir., Northern Finance Assn.; author/co-author of several models for the valuation of finan. assets, options, and commodity futures and several articles; recreations: sailing, ethnic foods; Home: 12444 28th Ave., Edmonton, Alta.; Office: Edmonton, Alta. T6G 2R6.

**BAROOTES, Hon. Efstathios William,** B.A., M.D., F.R.C.S.(C), F.A.C.S.; senator; b. Winnipeg, Man. 15 Nov. 1918; s. William Efthemios and Anastasia (Makasiki) B.; e. Buena Vista Pub. Sch. and Nutana High Sch. Saskatoon; Univ. of Sask. B.A.; Univ. of Toronto M.D., post-grad. Janes' Surg. Course; m. Betty Lorraine d. Thomas and Gladys Stewart 28 March 1948; children: Barbara Elaine Hughes, Barrie Allan, Bryan Gordon, Brenda Diane, Brent Stewart; Mem., The Senate of Canada 1984–..; Dir.: (and mem. Exec. Ctte.) Producers Pipeline Inc.; Westspur Pipeline Inc.; Professional Properties Ltd.; Counc. for Candn. Unity; mem. Adv. Ctte. (Regina) Royal Trust; Professor Emeritus of Surg. (Urology) Univ. of Sask. Med. Coll.; summoned to Senate of Canada 1984; Urological Surg. Regina, Sask. 1951–79; recipient Candn. Med. Assn. Medal of Service 1980; mem. Gen. Counc., Candn. Med. Assn. (Depy. Pres. 1977–78); Vice Pres. and mem. Counc. Candn. Med. Protective Assn.; mem. Anglo-Hellenic Educational & Progressive Assn. (AHEPA); P. Conservative; Anglican; Club: Assiniboia; Home: 3315 Robinson St., Regina, Sask. S4S 1V9.

**BARR, Brian W.,** B.Comm.; business executive; b. Hamilton, Ont. 22 Jan. 1943; s. Robert M. and Christine P. (Simpson) B.; e. Ridley Coll. St. Catharines, Ont. 1961; Acadia Univ. B.Com. 1965; m. B. Joan Oates 30 June 1966; children: Patricia Lynn, Michael Brian; CHRMN. AND CHIEF EXEC. OFFR. FIRECO INC. 1982– ; Chrmn., Norwich Union Life Insurance Soc.; Dir., Shaben Internat. Inc.; Wash Rack Supply Ltd.; Select Disposal Systems Ltd.; Gov. Ridley Coll.; recreation: golf; Clubs: National Golf; Mariner Sands Country; Beacon Hall; Toronto Golf; Loxahatchee Golf; Home: 47 The Kingsway, Toronto, Ont. M8X 2S9; Office: 1280 Courtney Park Dr., Mississauga, Ont. L5T 1N6.

**BARR, David Wallace,** B.Sc., Ph.D.; cultural manager; b. Toronto, Ont. 1 Jan. 1943; s. David Wallace and Clara Mae (Cowieson) B.; e. Univ. of Toronto B.Sc. (Hons.) 1965; Cornell Univ. Ph.D. 1969; Univ. of Calif. at Berkeley, Museum Mngt. Inst. 1985; children: Heather Ann, James Wallace; ASSOCIATE DIR., PROJECT MANAGEMENT, ROYAL ONTARIO MUSEUM 1991– ; Asst. Curator, Royal Ontario Museum 1969; Assoc. Curator 1973; Curator 1980; Curator-in-charge, Entomology 1980; Assoc. Dir., Curatorial 1984; Assoc. Prof., Zoology, Univ. of Toronto; Mem., Candn. Museums Assn.; Candn. Fed. of Friends of Museums; Visitor Studies Assn.; recreations: computer programming, photography, interpretive writing, film/video history; Home: 2768A Danforth Ave., Toronto, Ont. M4C 1L7; Office: 100 Queens Park, Toronto, Ont. M5S 2C6.

**BARR, John Jay,** M.A.; management communication consultant; b. Edmonton, Alta. 27 Aug. 1942; s. Victor Jack and Juanita Inez (Taylore) B.; e. Univ. of Alta., M.A. 1965; m. Janis d. Victor and Edna Heeks 3 Sept. 1988; one d.: Laura Francine; NATIONAL PUBLIC AFFAIRS PRACTICE LEADER, BURSON-MARSTELLER LTD. 1987– ; Edit. Commentator, Edmonton Journal 1965–68; Chief of Staff, Alta. Min. of Edn. 1969–71; Dir. of Public Affairs, Syncrude Can. Ltd. 1972–86; Vice-Pres., The Martland Group 1986–87; Extve. Advr., Metro. Toronto Community Found.; Dir., Alternatives to Racism Soc.; Chrmn., Pacific Found. for Econ. and Social Co-operation; author: 'Dynasty: The Rise and Fall of Social Credit in Alberta' 1975; co-author: 'The Making of the Modern West' 1984; editor: 'The Unfinished Revolt: Essays on Western Independence' 1971; contbr.: 'The New Canadian Encyclopedia'; recreations: tennis, skin-diving; club: Mayfair; Home: 440 Sandbar Place, Delta, B.C. V4L 2L1; Office: 1100 Melville St., Vancouver, B.C. V6E 4A6.

**BARR, The Hon. John Roderick,** Q.C., LL.B., LL.D.; b. Toronto, Ont. 9 Sept. 1921; s. Peter and Anne (Peardon) B.; e. Hillfield Sch. Hamilton to 1938; Westdale Coll. Inst. Hamilton 1939; Osgoode Hall Law Sch. Toronto 1945–48; m. Rhoda Henrietta d. Robert James and Elizabeth Marshall, Stella, Ont. 9 Oct. 1948; children: Peter Marshall, Rhoda Elizabeth Anne; COUNSEL, BARR GIANNOTTI & LEACH (St. Catharines); called to Bar of Ont. 1948; cr. Q.C. 1961; practice civil litigation St. Catharines 1948–83; el. Bencher, Law Soc. Upper Can. 1979–83; Judge, High Court of Justice, Supreme Court of Ont. 1983–89; Lectr., Brock Univ. (Administration of Justice) 1993– ; Instr. Central Flying Sch., RCAF, and Pilot, RAF Bomber Command 1940–45; mem. Advocates' Soc. (Past Vice Pres.); Candn. Bar Assn.; Hon. Doctor of Laws degree, Brock Univ. 1984; Presbyterian; Clubs: St. Catharines; St. Catharines Rowing; St. Catharines Golf; Royal Candn. Mil. Inst. (Toronto); Home: 33 Hillcrest Ave., St. Catharines, Ont. L2R 4Y2.

**BARR, Maj. Gen. (ret.) John Wilmer Browning,** C.M.M., C.D., K.St. J., Q.H.P., M.D., C.M., D.H.A.; b. Lanark, Ont. 7 Dec. 1916; s. late James and late Mary Allen (Browning) B.; e. Lanark (Ont.) Cont. Sch., 1933; Perth (Ont.) Coll. Inst., 1934; Queen's Univ., M.D., C.M. 1940; Candn. Army Staff Coll., psc 1947; Royal Army Med. Coll., London, Eng., 1952–53; Univ. of Toronto, Dipl. in Hosp. Adm. (Robert Wood Johnson Award) 1959; Nat. Defence Coll., 1964–65; m. late Marion Sarah, d. late James Crawford, Thedford, Ont., 10 May 1945; Internship: Nichols' Hosp., Peterborough, Ont., 1939, Ottawa Civic Hosp. 1940; Gen. Duty Med. Offr., various units of 3 Candn. Inf. Div. 1940–44; C.O. 23 Candn. Field Ambulance and 6 Candn. Field Dressing Stn. 1945–46; various med. staff appts. Candn. Army 1947–50; C.O., RCAMC Sch., 1950–52; C.O., 2 Field Ambulance and Sr. Candn. Med. Offr., Europe, 1953–54, Asst. Dir. Med. Services, Army HQ 1954–57; C.O., Candn. Forces Hosp. Kingston, 1959–61; Dir. of Med. Personnel, Candn. Forces HQ 1961–64; Depy. Surg. Gen. (Operations) 1966–70; Surg. Gen., Candn. Forces, 1970–73; Col. Com. Can. Forces Medical Services 1976; Chief Med. Off., Order of St. John, Priory of Canada 1977–81; Registrar Emeritus, Med. Council Can. 1982 (Registrar 1973–81); Queen's Hon. Physician, 1967–73 and since 1977; Kt. of Grace, Order of St. John of Jerusalem, 1978; Hon. Vice-Pres., Def. Med. Assn. of Can., 1978; Sr. Mem., Candn. Med. Assoc. 1987; Member Emeritus, Coll. of Physicians and Surgeons of Ont. 1988; Freemason; United Church; recreations: philately, gardening; Home: 429 Huron Ave. South, Ottawa, Ont. K1Y 0X3.

**BARR, Murray Llewellyn,** O.C. (1968), B.A., M.Sc., M.D., LL.D., D.Sc., F.R.C.P. (C), F.R.C.O.G., F.A.C.P., F.R.S.C., F.R.S. (London); b. Belmont, Ont., 20 June 1908; s. William Llewellyn and Margaret (McLellan) B.; e. Univ. of W. Ont., B.A. 1930, M.D. 1933, M.Sc. 1938; m. Ruth Vivian, d. Wallace King, Ashtabula, Ohio, 1934; Children: Hugh, Robert, Carolyn, David; Prof. Emeritus of Anatomy, U. of W.O.; served with Res. R.C.A.M.C., 1936–39; 2nd World War on active service with R.C.A.F. 1939–45; on Res. with rank of Wing Commdr.; main interest is cytol. research as it applies to sex anomalies and mental retardation; author of numerous publs. in field of cytol., principally cytol. of the nervous system and human cytogenetics; mem., Candn. Neurol. Soc.; Anatomical Soc. of Gt. Brit. & Ireland; Am. Assn. of Anatomists; Assn. for Research in Nervous & Mental Diseases; Candn. Assn. Anat.; awarded Flavelle Medal by Royal Soc. Can., 1959; the Charles Mickle Fellowship, 1960; rec'd from Pres. Kennedy one of the first Joseph P. Kennedy Jr. Foundation Awards 1962; Ortho Medal, Am. Soc. for the Study of Sterility (1962); Medal, Am. Coll. of Physicians (1962); Award of Merit, Gairdner Foundation (1963); Papanicolaou Award, Am. Soc. of Cytology (1964); F.N.G. Starr Medal, Candn. Med. Assn. (1967); Maurice Goldblatt Award, Internat. Acad. Cytology 1968; Alpha Omega Alpha; Protestant; Clubs: Harvey; Cajal; Home: 411–312 Oxford St. W., London, Ont. N6H 4N7.

**BARR, Peter G.,** B.A.Sc., M.B.A.; investment executive; b. Montreal, Que. 18 May 1939; s. James and Marjory B.; e. Queen's Univ., B.A.Sc. 1963; Univ. of West. Ont. M.B.A. 1969; one d.: Laurie Elizabeth; PRES., ROYAL TRUST ENERGY CORP. 1985– ; Vice-Pres., Nesbitt Thomson Securities 1977–80; Dome Petroleum Limited 1980–84; Dir./Pres., RTER Holding Corp.; Royal Trust Energy Resources Corp.; Royal Trust Energy Resources II Corp.; recreations: skiing, golf, sailing; clubs: Calgary Petroleum, Bow Valley, Montreal Badminton & Squash; Home: 2605 – 10th St. S.W., Calgary, Alta. T2T 3H1; Office: 3300, 700 – 2nd St. S.W., Calgary, Alta. T2P 2W2.

**BARRACLOUGH, Kathleen Ash,** B.A., M.Mus.; professor of music; orchestral conductor; b. Vancouver, B.C. 5 Dec. 1939; d. Kenneth James and Ida Rose (Lightfoot) Ash; e. Univ. of Washington, B.A. (Music) 1961; Univ. of Calif., M.Mus. (Dean's Hon.) 1967; one s.: Rex; Conductor of Orchestra York & Camerata York; Conductor Emeritus, South Valley Symphony; Guest Conductor, Huronia Symphony; Saratoga Chamber Orch.; Valley del Sur Chamber Orch.; Vallejo Symph.; El Camino Opera Co.; Saratoga Drama Group; West Valley Light Opera Assn.; Recitalist & 1st violinist, Carmel Back Fest., Carmel CA; Asst. Concertmaster & 1st violniist, San Jose Symphony 1968–75; Pres., Arts Advisory Alliance (CA); Bd. of Dir., Arts Counc. of Santa Clara Co. (CA); private teaching in Toronto & San Jose; Woman of Achievement Award – Arts, Santa Clara Co. Calif. 1986; 'Golden Bell' award nominee (CA); Mu Phi Epsilon (Hon.); music & scholarship, Univ. of So. Calif.

**BARRETT, Allan James,** CD, rmc, B.Sc., M.Sc., Ph.D.; university professor and administrator; b. St. John's, Nfld. 8 March 1943; s. Allan James and Verda Maud (Hilchey) B.; e. Coll. militaire royal de St. Jean 1959–62; Royal Military College of Canada B.Sc. 1964,

M.Sc. 1971; Univ. of London, King's College Ph.D. 1975; m. Cornelia d. Willem and Cornelia van Westernbrugge 21 Nov. 1964; children: Michael, David, Sydny; PROFESSOR, MATHEMATICS, ROYAL MILITARY COLLEGE OF CANADA 1985– ; Flying Officer, RCAF 1964–67; Captain, Candn. Armed Forces 1967–72; Lecturer, Math., Royal Military College 1967–71, 1973–75; Asst. Prof. 1975–80; Assoc. Prof. 1980–85; Dean of Science 1990– ; Visiting Scholar, Dartmouth College 1981–82; Mem., United Ch. of Canada; Home: 306 Glen Cairn Terrace, Kingston, Ont. K7M 4A5; Office: Kingston, Ont. K7K 5L0.

**BARRETT, Hon. David,** B.A., M.S.W., LL.D. (Hon.), M.P.; politician; b. Vancouver, B.C. 2 Oct. 1930; s. Samuel and Rose (Hyatt) B.; e. Britannia High Sch., Vancouver 1948; Seattle Univ. B.A. 1953; St. Louis Univ., Mo. M.S.W. 1956; Hon. LL.D., St. Louis Univ. 1974; m. Shirley Hackman, 16 Oct. 1953; children: Daniel Alexander, Joseph Samuel, Jane Rosanne; Mem. of Parliament, House of Commons 1989–93; Candidate for leadership of New Democratic Party 1990; formerly engaged in social work, Probation Office, St. Louis 1956; Supervisor, Social Training, Haney Correctional Inst. 1957–59; Supvr., Counselling Services, John Howard Soc. of B.C., Vancouver 1959–64; Extve. Dir., Jewish Family Service Agency, Vancouver 1965–70; first el. to B.C. Leg. g.e. 12 Sept. 1960; re-el. g.e. 1963, 66, 69, 72, 76, 79; Leader of the Opposition 1969; Premier of B.C., Pres., Extve. Council and Min. of Finance 1972–75; Leader of the Opposition 1976–84; Public Affairs Broadcaster, Vancouver 1985–88; Fellow, John F. Kennedy Sch. of Govt., Harvard Univ. fall 1987; Visiting Lectr. Univ. of McGill Pol. Sci., spring 1988; N.D.P.; Jewish.

**BARRETT, John Ernest,** M.A., Ph.D.; executive; b. Toronto, Ont. 13 May 1951; s. David Ernest and Jane (Jennie) Hannah B.; e. Gravenhurst (Ont.) Pub. & High Schs.; Univ. of Toronto, Univ. Coll. B.A. 1973, M.A. 1974; London Sch. of Econ. & Pol. Sci Ph.D. 1982; m. Maurie Leigh Holland 4 Jan. 1992; INTERNATIONAL STAFF, POLITICAL AFFAIRS DIVISION, NATO HQ, Brussels, Belgium; Dep. Dir., Candn. Centre for Arms Control & Disarmanent 1986–89; Internat. Security and Arms Control Bur., Candn. Dept. of External Affairs 1989–91; Ed. 'Millennium: Journal of Interantional Studies' London 1977–78; Visiting Researcher, Institut für Politikwissenschaft, Univ. of Tübingen, Federal Repub. of Germany and Ed. Cons. Inst. for Sci. Co-op. with Developing Countries, Tübingen 1981–83; Post-Doctoral Rsch. Assoc. Mil. & Strategic Studies Prog. Inst. Internat. Relations Univ. of B.C. 1983–85; recipient Ont. Grad. Fellowship; Can. Council Doctoral Fellowship; Dir.'s Award Internat. Centre Econ. & Related Disciplines (LSE); author numerous articles and commentary arms control, security policy & internat. relations; Founding mem. Brit. Internat. Studies Assn.; mem., Candn. Assoc. of Friends of the London Sch. of Economics and Pol. Sci.; recreations: ice skating, golf, crossword puzzles; Home: 281 Clarence St., Ottawa, Ont. K1N 5R2.

**BARRETT, Matthew W.;** banker; b. County Meath, Ireland 20 Sept. 1944; e. Harvard Business School Adv. Mngt. Program; m. Irene Korsak; children: Tara, Kelly, Andrea, Jason; CHAIRMAN & CHIEF EXTVE. OFFR., BANK OF MONTREAL 1990– ; joined Bank of Montreal 1962; Vice-Pres., Management Services, Bank of Montreal 1978; Vice-Pres., B.C. Div. & Sr. Vice-Pres., Eastern & N. Ont. 1979; Sr. Vice-Pres. & Dep. Gen. Mgr., Internat. Banking 1981; Sr. Vice-Pres. & Dep. Group Extve., Treasury 1984; Extve. Vice-Pres. & Group Extve., Personal Banking 1985; Pres. & Chief Op. Offr. 1987; Chief Extve. Offr. 1989; Dir., Molson Companies Ltd.; Bank of Montreal; Harris Bankcorp Inc.; The Nesbitt Thomson Corp.; The Montreal Bd. of Trade Heritage Found.; Canadian Council for National Unity; Policy Ctte. & Dir., Business Council on Nat. Issues; Co-Chair, Royal Victoria Hosp.; Trustee and Finance Ctte. Mem., The Toronto Hosp.; York University Adv. Council, Fac. of Admin. Studies; Univ. of West. Ont. Program Adv. Ctte.; Chrmn., Capital Campaign for Univ. of Waterloo; Mem., Policy Ctte., Founding Dir., Bd. of Harvard Business Sch. Alumni (Ottawa); Dir., Conference Board of Canada; mem. of Bd. of Govs., Junior Achievement of Canada; recreations: fly-fishing, tennis or a good book: Office: P.O. Box 1, First Canadian Place, Toronto, Ont. M5X 1A1

**BARRETT, Pam,** B.A., M.Phil., M.L.A.; economist/political scientist; b. Brandon, Man. 26 Nov. 1953; d. Raymond Phillip and Agatha Mary (Trainor) B.; e. Univ. of Alta. B.A. 1979; Glasgow Univ. M.Phil. 1981; N.D.P. HOUSE LEADER AND CONSTITUTIONAL SPOKESPERSON, ALBERTA LEGISLATURE; worked for A.G.T. and Edmonton Telephones 1971–75; part-time property mngt. employment 1975–81; Freelance (contract) researcher 1981–83 (Organizer, Alta. Fed. of Labour/Solidarity Alta.); Sr. Rsch., Official Opposition, New Democrat Caucus, 1983–86; Founding Partner, Brian's Bazaar and Exchange 1982–86; Roman Catholic; first affiliation with NDP commencing in 1968; el. g.e. 1986; M.L.A. Edmonton Highlands & Official Opposition House Leader, Govt. of Alta. 1986–..; re-el. g.e. 1989; Mem., Edmonton Tenants' Assn. 1975–77; Free S. Africa Ctte. 1975–78; Edmonton Learner Ctr. 1976– ; Candn. Cancer Soc. 1973–77; Project Alternative Childcare Edmonton 1983–85; Tools for Peace 1984– ; Sundance Housing Co-op 1986–91; Anti (Vietnam) war/peace activist movement 1967–71; recreations: patron of theatre (esp. Theatre Network & The Fringe Fest.); symphony & opera; reading statistics & political books/journals; Office: 202 Legislature Bldg., Edmonton, Alta. T5K 2B6.

**BARRETT, Richard E.,** B.Sc.; mining engineer; b. Cobden, Ont. 20 June 1905; s. Lawrence Atholstane and Etta June (McCrum) B.; e. McGill Univ., B.Sc. (Mining Eng.) 1926; m. Margaret Robertson, d. late William MacNairn Shaw, Walkerton, Ont., 16 June 1934; one s., Lawrence Shaw; with Cerro de Pasco Copper Corp., Peru, S.A., 1926–29; Indust. Engr., Preston Furniture Co., 1929–33; Mgr., Parkhill Gold Mines, Wawa, Ont., 1933–36; Mgr., Central Patricia Gold Mines, N.W. Ont., 1936–47; Prof. of Mining and Head, Dept. of Mining Engn., Univ. of Toronto, 1947–53; Mgr., Beaverlodge Operation, Eldorado Mining & Refining Co. Ltd., Uranium City, Sask., 1953–55; Dir., Ore Procurement, Eldorado Mining & Refining Co. Ltd., 1955–63; Extve. Dir., Candn. Inst. of Mining & Metall., 1963–65; mem., Candn. Inst. Of Mining and Metall.; Assn. Prof. Engrs. of Ont.; Freemason; Anglican; Home: 3 Silver Crescent, Port Hope, Ont. L1A 2C4.

**BARRETT, Spencer Charles Hilton,** B.Sc., Ph.D.; university professor; b. Bushey, Herts., England 7 June 1948; s. Arthur Charles and Doris (Boorer) B.; e. Pinner Co. Grammar Sch., England; Univ. of Reading, B.Sc. 1971; Univ. of Calif. at Berkeley, Ph.D. 1977; m. Suzanne d. Douglas and Pamela Whittaker 1 Sept. 1973; children: Rowan Douglas Hilton, Seth Vincent Arthur; PROF., DEPT. OF BOTANY, UNIV. OF TORONTO 1986– ; Weed Biol., Commonwealth Devel. Corp., Swaziland Irrigation Scheme 1969–70; Mem., Univ. of Reading Plant Collecting Expedition to N.E. Brazil 1971–72; Aquatic Weed Cons., Internat. Rsch. Inst., Jari, Lower Amazon, Brazil 1974, 1977; Asst. Prof., present univ. 1977; Vis. Rsch. Sci., Commonwealth Scientific and Industrial Rsch. Orgn., Canberra, Australia 1983–84; main rsch.: plant ecological & evolutionary genetics, conservation biology, reproductive biol. of plants, genetics of weed invasions; Chrmn., NSERC Grant Selection Ctte. in Population Biol. 1986–87 (mem. 1984–88); NSERC E.W.R. Steacie Mem. Fellowship 1988–89; Mem., Soc. for the Study of Evolution; Brit. Ecological Soc.; Botanical Soc. of Am.; The Genetical Soc.; author of 90 sci. rsch. papers & 20 book chaps.; editor, 1 book; trained 10 grad. students; invited lectr. worldwide; Assoc. Ed., 'Evolution' 1989–92; recreations: gardening, photography, canoeing, tropical travel; Home: 182 Humbervale Blvd., Etobicoke, Ont. M8Y 3P8; Office: Toronto, Ont. M5S 3B2

**BARRETT-CRAMER, Raymond Joseph,** LL.B.; provincial judge; b. Winnipeg, Man. 26 Apr. 1930; s. Phillip and Anne (Singer); e. Univ. of Winnipeg, B.A. 1954, B.A. (Hons.) 1958; Manitoba Law Sch. 1958; Office: 5th Flr., 408 York Ave., Winnipeg, Man. R3C 0P9.

**BARRETTE-JONCAS, Hon. Madam Justice Claire,** B.A., LL.L.; b. Montreal, Que. 18 May 1933; d. Hon. Jean and Cécile (Guindon) Barrette; e. Acad. St-Paul; Pensionnat d'Outremont; Coll. Jésus-Marie, B.A. 1953; Univ. de Montréal, LL.L. (cum laude) 1956; m. Judge Claude Joncas, s. late Louis E. Joncas, Westmount, Que., 21 Dec. 1963; children: Louis, Lucie; JUSTICE, SUPERIOR COURT OF QUEBEC 1975– ; Judge in Charge of Criminal Assizes, District of Montreal 1984– ; mem. Bd. Dirs., Univ. of Montreal 1985–89; called to Bar of Que. 1957; cr. Q.C. (fed.) 24 Dec. 1971; first woman to preside over Jr. Bar of Montreal (1961–62), first to sit on Bar Council of Montreal (1962–63), first to sit on Bar Council of Que. 1962–63 and first to plead before the Criminal Assizes in Quebec (Montreal 1958); former Dir., John Howard Soc. of Montreal; Treas., Inst. Philippe Pinel de Montréal (until 1975); former Secy., Legal Aid Bureau, Bar of Montreal; former Pres., Comte. of Criminal Affairs of Former Bureau; Elder, St-Viateur Ch., Outremont, Que. (1971–74); French Secy., Jr. Assocs. Montreal Museum Fine Arts 1960–61; Past Pres., Assn. Women Lawyers, P.Q.; Jr. Bar Assoc. of Montreal; Past mem. Council, Bar of Montreal and Bar of P.Q.; Lectr. in Criminal Law, Univ. of Montreal 1962–64 and McGill Univ. 1967–70; part-time mem. Law Reform Comm. of Canada 1971–75; R. Catholic; recreations: geneology, reading, travel; Home: 261 Côte Ste-Catherine Rd., Outremont, Qué. H2V 2B2; Office: Court House, 1 est. rue Notre Dame, Ch. 16.66, Montreal, Qué. H2Y 1B6.

**BARRIGAR, Robert H.,** Q.C.; barrister; b. Smiths Falls, Ont. 4 June 1937; s. John Wellington and Carol Adelaide (Hubbell) B.; e. Univ. Toronto, B.A.Sc. 1959; Dalhousie Univ., LL.B. 1963; Harvard Law Sch., LL.M. 1964; m. Evelyn, d. Peter and Eva Neufeld, 8 Sept. 1962; children: Jennifer; Stephen; Diana; John; COUNSEL, BARRIGAR & OYEN since 1974; admitted Ont. Bar 1966; B.C. Bar 1975; Alta. Bar 1978; Univ. B.C. Faculty Law 1977–78; cr. Q.C. 1981; Pres., FICPI Can. 1985–91; Pres., Patent & Trademark Inst. Can. 1991–92; author 'The Canadian Patent Act Annotated' and numerous articles in legal journals; Sir James Dunn Scholar (Dalhousie Law Sch.); Harvard Law Sch. Scholar; Fellow, Foundation for Legal Research; Home: 393 Maple Lane, Rockcliffe, Ont. K1M 1H7; Offices: 81 Metcalfe St., Ottawa, Ont. K1P 6K7, 1250 Two Robert Speck Parkway, Mississauga, Ont. L4Z 1H8 and 480 - 601 West Cordova St., Vancouver, B.C. V7X 1M3.

**BARRINGTON, J. Douglas,** B.Comm., M.B.A., C.A.; financial executive; b. Montreal, Que. 22 July 1943; s. Thomas John and Eileen Telford (Walker) B.; e. McGill Univ. B.Comm. (Hons.) 1964; Harvard Grad. School of Business Admin. M.B.A. 1966; C.A. 1967; m. Kathryn d. Ralph and Winnifred Tees 16 Sept. 1967; children: Cynthia, Christopher, Amanda; CHAIRMAN, DELOITTE & TOUCHE 1992– ; joined Touche Ross 1966; Partner 1973; Partner in Charge, Nat. Capital Region 1978; Dep. Mng. Partner, Eastern Canada 1988; Dep. Mng. Partner, Deloitte & Touche 1990; Dir. and Vice-Chrmn., Canadian Comprehensive Auditing Foundation; editor: 'Comprehensive Audit Reporting – Concepts Issues Practice' 1991; recreations: gardening; Club: York; Home: 220 Blythwood Ave., Toronto, Ont. M4N 1A6; Office: 150 King St. W., Toronto, Ont. M5H 1J9.

**BARRON, John Christopher;** financial executive; b. Toronto, Ont. 21 Sept. 1931; s. John A. and Isobel E. (Cassels) B.; e. Upper Canada College 1950; m. Janet C. d. Dr. & Mrs. Jamison Martin; children: Cecil Cassels, Claire Ruth; CHRMN., NATIONAL TRUST and CHRMN., CASSELS BLAIKIE & CO. LIMITED; Chrmn., Cassels Blaikie & Co. Limited 1969– , Partner 1959; Chrmn., Economic Investment Trust; Dir., Canadian & Foreign Securities Co. Ltd.; The Debenture and Securities Corp. of Can.; Dominion and Anglo Investments Ltd.; The Dominion of Canada General Insur. Co.; E-L Financial Corp. Ltd.; Ellis-Don Limited; Empire Life Insurance Co.; National Trust Co.; National Trustco Inc.; Past Chrmn., Toronto Stock Exchange; Chrmn., Bd. of Dir., The Young Naturalist Found.; Chrmn., Presidential Investment Adv. Ctte., Univ. of Toronto; recreations: fishing, hunting, skiing, tennis, ornithology; Home: Terra Cotta, Ont. L0P 1N0; Office: Ste. 200, 33 Yonge St., Toronto, Ont. M5E 1S8.

**BARRON, John Philip,** M.Mus.; music consultant; b. Kimberley, B.C. 20 Dec. 1939; s. Philip Lewis and Marguerite Jean (Beasley) B.; e. J. Lloyd Crowe, Trail, B.C. 1957; Univ. of Toronto Mus.Bac. 1960, M.Mus. 1966; m. A. Lowell d. Edwin and Ruth Jarmain 15 July 1967; children: Jennifer, Naomi, Julie, Katie; MUSIC CONSULTANT, MIDDLESEX COUNTY BOARD OF EDUCATION 1972– ; Music Teacher, Eastern H.S. of Commerce, Toronto 1962–64; Lawrence Park Collegiate, Toronto 1965–70; Westminster S.S., London 1970–71; Overseas study in Hungary 1976–77 to study the music edn. system developed by Zoltán Kodály; Dir., Ont. Youth Choir 1975–76 (winner, CBC Candn. Amateur Choral Comp. 1976 & BBC Internat. Choral Comp. 'Let the People Sing' 1976 – best choir from 18 countries in the competition); Founding Conductor, London Pro Musica 1970–73; Musical Dir., Toronto Chamber Soc. 1977–80; Co-Dir., Amabile Youth Singers 1985– ;(winner, CBC Choral Comp. 1986, '88, '90, '92; finished 2nd in Arnham, The Netherlands 1987 (youth choir category) & 4th overall of 84 choirs; won, 'Youth and Music' comp., Vienna, Austria 1989); Kodaly Centennial Medal 1983 presented by Hungarian Govt. for outstanding contbn. to the knowledge of the work of Zoltán Kodály in Canada; Pres., Ont. Choral Fed. 1973–74; Dir. 1970–76; Mem., OMEA, CMEA, KSC, IKS, CCCA, ACDA, OCF; author: 'Kodály and Education' 1979; editor: 'Reflections of Canada' vol. I 1985, vol. II 1986, vol. III 1987, 'Reflet du Canada' 1991; 'Ride With Me' 1993; recreations: golf; Home: 88

Main St., Komoka, Ont. N0L 1R0; Office: 1120 Hyde Park Blvd., London, Ont. N0M 1Z0.

**BARROW, Jack C.;** company director; b. Toronto, Ont. 9 Jul. 1914; s. John and Alice E. B.; e. Riverdale Coll., Toronto, Ont.; m. Margaret E. (Betty), d. George A.J. Cook, 19 Nov. 1941; children: Peter C., Mary E.; HON. DIR., SEARS CANADA INC.; Past Chrmn., Candn. Centre for Philanthropy; Pirelli Canada Inc.; Bus. Counc. on Nat. Issues; Past Pres., Retail Council of Can.; Chrmn. Corporate Div., Un. Appeal Metrop. Toronto, 1965; Pres., Un. Community Fund of Greater Toronto, 1968, Chrmn. Bd. Trustees, 1969–70; Asst. Buyer, Women's Ready-to-Wear. Mail Order Div., The Robert Simpson Co. Ltd., 1946–49; Buyer, Girls' Wear, 1950–52; Mail Order Sales Mgr., Simpsons-Sears Ltd., 1953–55; Merchandise Supvr., Men's Wear, 1955–58, Men's and Boys' Wear, 1958–60; Gen. Retail Merchandise Mgr., 1960–62; Extve. Asst. to Pres., 1962; Extve. Vice-Pres., 1962–66; Chrmn. and C.E.O., 1966–79; served during 2nd World War with Candn. Army 1941–44; recreation: golf; Clubs: Canadian; Toronto; York; Lambton Golf & Country; Toronto Hunt; The Country (Fla.); Home: Apt. 1001, 150 Heath St. W., Toronto, Ont. M4V 2Y4 and 400 South Ocean Blvd., Manalpan, Palm Beach, Florida; Office: 222 Jarvis St., Toronto, Ont. M5B 2B8.

**BARROW, Robin St. Clair,** B.A., M.A., Ph.D.; university professor; b. Oxford, England 18 Nov. 1944; s. Arthur Hugh Duncan and Awdry Gilchrist (Wrightson) B.; e. Dragon School, Oxford 1957; Westminster School, London 1963; Christ Church, Oxford M.A. (Hons.) 1967; Univ. of London Ph.D. 1972; P.G.C.E. 1968; 1st m. Hilary d. Sir Paul and Lady Eila Mallinson 1965; one s.: Paul; 2nd m. Lynn d. Captain Charles and Joan Hansen 1976; children: Alexandra, Natasha; DEAN OF EDUCATION, SIMON FRASER UNIV. 1992– ; Asst. Master, Elliott Comprehensive School London 1968; City of London School for Boys 1968–72; Lecturer in Philosophy of Edn., Univ. of Leicester 1972–80; Visiting Prof., Univ. of W. Ont. 1977–78; Reader, Univ. of Leicester 1980–82; Prof. of Edn., Simon Fraser Univ. 1982– ; Dir. of Grad. Programs 1987–90; Assoc. Dean of Education 1990; Vice Chair, Philosophy of Edn. Soc. of Great Britain 1980–83; Pres., N.W. Phil. of Edn. Soc. 1988; Candn. Phil. of Edn. Soc. 1990–93; author: 'Language, Intelligence and Thought' 1993, 'Utilitarianism' 1991, 'Understanding Skills' 1990, 'A Critical Dictionary of Educational Concepts' 1986, 'Giving Teaching Back to Teachers' 1984, 'The Philosophy of Schooling' 1983, 'Injustice, Inequality and Ethics' 1982, 'Language and Thought' 1982, 'Happiness' 1979, 'Radical Education' 1978, 'The Canadian Curriculum' 1978, 'Plato's Apology' 1978, 'Common Sense and the Curriculum' 1978, 'Plato and Education' 1976, 'Greek and Roman Education' 1976, 'Moral Philosophy for Education' 1975, 'Plato, Utilitarianism and Education' 1975, 'Sparta' 1975, 'Introduction to Philosophy of Education' 1974, 'Athenian Democracy' 1973; recreations: music, soccer, literature; Home: 830 Ranch Park Way, Coquitlam, B.C. V3C 2H3; Office: Burnaby, B.C. V5A 1S6.

**BARRY, David G.,** Q.C., B.Sc., M.Sc., LL.B.; lawyer; b. Saint John, N.B. 2 Aug. 1944; s. Hon. John Paul and Rita Marie (Feeney) B.; e. St. Francis Xavier Univ. B.Sc. (Hons.) 1966; Univ. Alta., M.Sc.(Computer Sci.) 1968; Univ. of N.B., LL.B. 1972; m. Jane (M.L.A.), d. John W. and M. Constance Baird; children: Patrick, Jonathan, Colin, Ryan, Gregor; PARTNER, BARRY & O'NEIL; admitted N.B. Bar 1972; former Council mem., Bar Admission Course Ctte., Chrmn., Automation Ctte., Law Soc. of N.B.; former Counc. mem., Saint John Law Soc.; Candn. Bar Assn. (former mem. Council and Profl. Services Comte.; former mem. & Chrmn. Law, Sci. & Tech. Comte.); mem. Am. Bar Assn.; Candn. Information Processing Soc.; Assn. for Computing Machinery; New York Academy of Sciences; former Chrmn., Candn. Law Information Counc.; former Gov., Candn. Tax Foundation; Lectr. Business Law, Univ. N.B. (1973–75); Lectr. Company Law (1973–76) Law Office Mgmt. (1976–84), & Drafting (1989–92), Bar Ad. Course, Law Soc. of N.B.; Commissioner, Greater Saint John Economic Development Commn.; former Pres., Saint John Bd. of Trade; former Pres., N.B. Museum; former Dir., United Way Saint John; former Vice Pres., Assn. for Community Living, Saint John Br.; former Vice-Pres., Assn. for Community Living, N.B. Div.; former Dir., Housing Alternatives Inc. and Rehabitat Inc.; former Pres., Saint John Co-operative Supply Depot Inc.; former Pres. Saint John Liberal Assn.; former Dir., Saint John Transit Comn.; Vice-Pres., YM-YWCA Saint John; Vice-Pres., Candn. Federation of Friends of Museums; Chrmn., The Enterprise Centre (YM-YWCA); former Dir., Saint John Learning Exchange; former Vice-Pres. & Dir., Family Services of Saint John; former Dir., Junior Achievement Saint John; recreations: golf; tennis; cross-country skiing; Clubs: Westfield Golf & Country; Union; Home: 807 Anderson Dr., Saint John, N.B. E2M 4G2; Office: Royal Bank Bldg., 85 Charlotte St., P.O. Box 6010, Stn.A, Saint John, N.B. E2L 4R5.

**BARRY, Lieut.-Col. Eric Lawrence,** C.D.; association executive; b. Montreal, P.Q. 15 April 1927; s. William Henry and Beatrice Dillon (Lawrence) B.; e. St. Leo's Acad., Westmount, P.Q. 1933–45; McGill Univ. Sch. of Comm. 1945–49; Sir Geo. Williams Univ. B.A. (Econ.) 1966; m. Mae Christine d. John Joseph O'Brien 11 Oct. 1952; children: Christopher John, Lisa Maureen, Mary Catherine, Erica Jane, David William; PRES., CANADIAN TEXTILES INSTITUTE 1980– ; joined Can. Paint Mfrs. Assn. as Asst. to Pres. & Gen. Mgr. Jan. 1952; apptd. Secy., Sept. 1957; Gen. Mgr. 1958, Extve. Vice-Pres., 1964–79; served Canadian Army (Militia) 1949–65; Lieut.-Col. and C.O. Royal Canadian Hussars 1960–64; mem. Order of St. John, Priory of Canada since 1971; Chancellor 1993– ; Canadian Society of Association Executives; Dir., Standards Council of Canada 1977–83; mem., International Trade Advisory Committee (ITAC) 1988– ; mem., Textiles, Footwear and Leather, Sectoral Advisory Group for International Trade (SAGIT) 1986–88, Chrmn. 1988–91; Chrmn., Textiles, Fur and Leather, SAGIT 1991– ; R. Cath.: Knight, Order of St. John of Jerusalem (1983); Club: Rideau; Office: 66 Slater St., Suite 1720, Ottawa, Ont. K1P 5H1.

**BARRY, Francis Leopold (Frank),** M.A., R.C.A.; artist; educator; b. London, Eng. 16 Apr. 1913; s. Hubert Charles and Olive (Armstrong) B.; e. Ealing Sch. of Art London, Nat. Dipl. in Design 1950; Hornsey Sch. of Art London, Art Teachers Dipl. 1951; Sir George Williams Univ. M.A. (Art Educ.); m. Hilda Patricia d. Pat Rawlinson 1945; children: Christopher, Ailsa; rep. in Nat. Gallery, McGill, Carleton and Concordia Univs. and in private colls.; monograph publ. Yvan Boulerice 'Frank Barry'; served with R.A.F. (Intelligence) 1943–46; Dir., Mississauga Arts Counc.; mem. Royal Candn. Acad.; Anglican; recreations: cross-country skiing, swimming; Home: 54 Eaglewood Blvd., Mississauga, Ont. L5G 1V4.

**BARRY, Ivor,** B.A.; actor and writer; b. Merthyr Tydfil, Glamorganshire, S. Wales, 12 April 1919; s. William John and Lily Maude (Phillips) B.; e. Univ. Coll. of Wales, B.A. (Hons. in French Lang. and Lit.), 1947; m. Helen Joy, d. Geoffrey Brameld of Somerset, Eng. and Mysore, India, 23 June 1950; one d. Bronwen Anne; began as Secondary Sch. Teacher and Pte. Tutor in London, Eng., 1948–52; came to Canada, 1953 and has since been engaged as a TV, Film, Radio, and Stage Actor, and as a script writer for these media, specializing in translation adaptations from the French (most work in close assoc. with CBC); served in 2nd World War, Royal Arty., 1940–46; Commnd. 1941, Overseas service (1941–46) in Middle E. and Italy; demob. with rank of War Subst. Lieut.; Pres., Assn. of Candn. Television & Radio Artists, 1961–62 (Council mem. 1959–61 and 1962–63, Dir. 1965); Dir., Candn. Council of Authors and Artists, 1962; mem. Acad. Motion Picture Arts and Sciences, Hollywood; recreation: retirement; Address: 1219 Alamo Creek Terrace, Paso Robles, CA 93446-5070.

**BARRY, (Pamela) Jane,** B.Sc., M.L.A.; legislator; b. Halifax, N.S. 10 July 1944; d. John Wesley and Marion Constance (McGrath) Baird; e. Convent of the Sacred Heart; Mount St. Vincent Univ.; St. Francis Xavier Univ., B.Sc. cum laude 1965; m. David Gerard s. Rita and Paul B. 3 Sept. 1966; children: Patrick, Jonathan, Colin, Ryan, Gregor; MIN. OF ENVIRONMENT, GOVT. OF NEW BRUNSWICK 1991– ; Pres./Chair, Candn. Council of Ministers of the Environment 1993– ; mem., Cabinet Ctte. on Policy & Priorities 1989– ; mem., Premier's Round Table on Economy & Environment 1991– ; first elected M.L.A. for Saint John West 1987; Co-Chair, Task Force on Parents & Early Childhood Edn. 1985; Co-Chair, Select Cttee., N.B. Legis. on 1987 Constitutional Accord 1989; Min. of State for Childhood Services, Govt. of N.B. 1989–91; Chair, Gulf of Maine Counc. on the Marine Environment 1991–92; Chair, Atlantic Environment Ministers 1992; serves on several legis. cttes.; formerly Chemist, Atlantic Sugar; Rsch. Asst., Fac. of Pharm., Univ. of Alta.; Bd. of Gov., United Way; Chrmn. 1990 & 1991 Red Shield Appeal (Salvation Army), St. John; Past Dir., Loyalist Days Inc.; Past Pres., Saint John Co-op Supply Depot; Past Pres., West Saint John Co-op Presch.; Former mem., N.B. School Trustees Assn.; Mem. & Past Pres., Univ. Women's Club; St. Francis Xavier Alumni Assn.; Former Trustee, Dist. 20 Sch. Bd.; recreations: boating, tennis; Home: 807 Anderson Dr., Saint John, N.B. E2M 4G2; Office: P.O. Box 6000, Fredericton, N.B. E3B 5H1.

**BARRY, John E.,** B.A.; investment executive; b. Wilmington, Mass. 1 Aug. 1928; s. Michael H. and Anna R. (Fitzgerald) B.; e. Univ. of Notre Dame B.A. 1952; m. Paula d. Edward and Edna Long 20 Sept. 1952; children: Michael, Shauna, Ellen, Patrick, Timothy, Kevin; PRES. & CHIEF EXTVE. OFFR., JEB INVESTMENT LTD. 1980– ; District Rep. Vancouver & Toronto, Caterpillar Tractor Co. 1952–60; Vice-Pres. Sales – Senior Vice-Pres., R. Angus Alberta Limited 1960–80; Dir., Vencap Equities Alberta Ltd. 1982– ; Bd. Chrmn., Misericorda Hosp. 1971–79; Bd. Mem., Alta. Catholic Hosp. Found. (Chrmn. 1989– ;) 1981– ; Bd. of Governors, Univ. of Alta. 1978–84; Pres., Edmonton United Community Fund 1969–70; Edmonton C. of C. 1977; Edmonton Area Hosp. Planning Counc. 1978; recreations: golf, tennis; clubs: Mayfair Golf & Country, Ironwood Country Club (Palm Desert, Calif.); Home/Office: 1002 – 10045 118 St., Edmonton, Alta. T5K 2K2.

**BARRY, Leo,** B.A., B.Sc., LL.M., Q.C.; b. Red Island, Placentia Bay, Nfld. 7 Aug. 1943; s. Leo Maurice & Elizabeth (Ryan) B.; e. High Sch. Brigus, Conception Bay, Nfld. (Gov. Gen.'s Medallist, Imperial Oil and Electoral Scholar) 1958; Memorial Univ. B.Sc. 1962, B.A. 1963; Dalhousie Law Sch. LL.B. 1967; Yale Univ. LL.M. 1968; divorced; children: Sheila, Diana; JUDGE OF SUPREME COURT OF NEWFOUNDLAND, TRIAL DIVISION 1989– ; called to Bar of Nfld. 1969; practised law with firm of Thoms, Fowler, Rowe & Barry 1969–72, with Halley, Roberts, Barry 1981–87 and with Kendell & Crosbie 1987–89; el. M.H.A. March 1972, apptd. Depy. Speaker 1972; Min. of Mines and Energy, Nfld., 1972–75, 1979–81; assoc. Prof. of Law, Dalhousie Law Sch. 1977–79; re-el. M.H.A. June 1979, April 1982 and April 1985; Leader of the Liberal Party of Nfld. and Labrador and Leader of the Opposition 1984–87; mem. Candn. Human Rights Foundation; Law Soc. of Nfld.; Candn. Bar Assn.; Am. Soc. Internat. Law; Fellow, Foundation for Legal Research in Can.; R. Catholic; recreations: squash, golf, chess, reading, bridge; Home: 46 Circular Rd., St. John's, Nfld. A1C 2Z1; Office: Supreme Court, 317 Duckworth St., P.O. Box 937, St. John's, Nfld. A1C 5M3.

**BARSHAI, Rudolf,** D.Mus., H.C.; symphony conductor; b. USSR 28 Sept. 1924; s. Boris and Maria (Alexeyeva) B.; e. Moscow Conserv., D.Mus. 1949; m. Helena d. Sofia and Sergei Raskov Jan. 1979; children: Lev, Walter, Takeshi; Viola-Solo, Chamber Ensembles with D. Shostakovich, S. Richter, D. Oistrakh, E. Gilels & others 1946–70; mem., Borodin Quartet 1946–53; Tchaikovsky Quartet 1953–55; Founder & Music Dir., Moscow Chamber Orch. 1955–77; cond. all major USSR orchs. & most major European orchs.; emigrated 1977; Music Dir., New Israel Orch. 1977–79; Prin. Cond., Bournemouth Symphony 1982–88; Music Dir., Vancouver Symphony 1985–88; Jury Pres., Arturo Toscanini Conductors Competition, Parma, Italy 1990– ; compl. & instrum. Bach's 'Art of Fugue' 1972, 1985; decoded & instrum. Bach's 'Das Musikalische Opfer' 1970; instrumen., Shostakovich's 'Chamber Symphonies No 1 & No 2' 1968; a symphony for wind and strings 1988; 'Chamber Symphony Op 83a' 1989; Prokofiev's 'Visions Fugitive' 1960; numerous recordings on Melodia, Decca, D.G. and EMI labels; Address: c/o Allied Artists, 42 Montpelier Square, London SW7 1JZ England.

**BARSOUM, Khalil E.,** B.Sc.; financial executive; b. 14 July 1944; e. Univ. of Montreal, B.Sc. 1966; m. Lucille Tessier; children: Jean-Francois, Caroline; Vice-Pres., Finance & Planning, IBM Canada Ltd. 1988–93; joined IBM as Sales Trainee 1966; progressed through various mktg. & br. mngt. positions then Asst. to Chrmn. & Pres.; assignment in N.Y. as Extve. Asst. to Corp. Chrmn. followed; Vice-Pres., Mktg. Staff, Toronto 1986; Bd. of Dirs., ISM Information Systems Mgmt.; Mem., Conf. Bd. of Can.; Home: 30 Valentine Dr., Don Mills, Ont. M3A 3J8.

**BART, Christopher Kenneth,** B.A., M.B.A., Ph.D., C.A.; educator; inventor; b. St. Catharines, Ont. 6 Jan. 1952; s. John and Alexandra (Savriga) B.; e. York Univ. B.A. 1974, M.B.A. 1975; C.A. 1977; Univ. of W. Ont. Ph.D. 1982; m. Julie Mary d. Edmond and Rita Desjardins 6 May 1978; children: Madeleine, Veronica, Miriam; ASSOC. PROF. OF BUS. POLICY McMASTER UNIV. 1981– ; Coordinator, Innovation Rsch. Working Group, McMaster Univ. 1991– ; Sr. Acct. Coopers & Lybrand 1975–77; Rsch. Fellow Nat. Centre Mgmt. Rsch. & Devel. Univ. of W. Ont. 1987–88; 'International Speaker' Australian Soc. Accts. 1990 World Cong.; Visiting Fellow in Acctg. Monash Univ. Melbourne 1990; Co-inventor of Computer Assisted Strategic Evaluation (C.A.S.E.) software 1991; Dir.: Hamilton Entertainment & Convention Facilities Inc. 1986–88; E.D.I.C. Inc. 1986– ; Marken Associated Consultants 1986– ; Visiting Lectr.: Grad. Sch. of Bus. Univ. of Cape Town 1984, 1986; Sch. of Mgmt. Cranfield Inst. Technol. 1989; Sch. of Bus. Leadership, Univ. of Pretoria 1991; I.A.T.A. 1991, 1993; Czechoslovakian Mgmnt. Centre 1993; Cons. to sr. execs. maj. Candn. and internat. corps.; Recipient: Can. Council Doctoral Fellowship 1977; Social Sci. Humanities Rsch. Council Doctoral Fellowships 1978 & 1979; Ontario Graduate Scholarship 1974; Gulf Oil Grad. Fellowships 1978 & 1979; Inst. of Citizenship Fellowships 1979 & 1980; Rsch. Prizes: Found. Adm. Rsch. 1985; Adm. Sci's Assn. Can. 1988 & 1992; Named: Outstanding Undergrad. Bus. Prof. 1982 and M.B.A. Prof. of Yr. 1984, 1989 & 1991 McMaster Univ.; Reviewer, Case Research Journal; Dir.: Harshman Found. 1982–88 (currently mem.); Planning Execs. Inst. Toronto Chapter 1982–84; author numerous scholarly and profl. mgmt. articles various nat. and internat. jours.; Mem.: North Am. Case Rsch. Assn.; Inst. C.A.'s Ont.; R.Catholic; Recreations: travel, Italian gourmet cooking; Home: 1432 Bridgestone Lane, Mississauga, Ont. L5J 4E2; Office: Hamilton, Ont. L8S 4M4.

**BARTEL, Frank,** B.Com., M.B.A.; financial executive; b. Germany 28 Apr. 1937; s. Erich and Eva (Wittke) B.; e. Concordia Univ. B.Com. 1965, M.B.A. 1975; m. Dorothea d. Erich and Hildegard Bendig 24 May 1959; two s. Colin, Derrick; Hoechst. Canada Inc., Dir. 1984–., Corp. Vice-Pres., 1982–.., Secy.-Treas. 1972–..; CELANESE CANADA INC., Vice-Pres., Controller-Treas. 1989– ; HCCI Management Services Inc., Vice Pres. & Chief Financial Offr. 1989– ; recreations: outdoors, soccer, tennis, reading; Home: 288 Willowtree, Rosemere, Qué. J7A 2E3.

**BARTEL, Lee R.,** B.A., B.Mus., A.Mus., L.Mus., M.Ed., Ph.D.; university professor; b. Steinbach, Man. 4 April 1948; s. Peter and Margaret (Rempel) B.; e. Univ. of Manitoba B.A. 1973; Brandon Univ. B.Mus. 1975; Western Bd. of Music Assoc. Dipl. in Music-Singing 1981, Lic. in Music-Singing 1983; Univ. of Manitoba M.Ed. 1984; Univ. of Illinois Ph.D. 1988; m. Grace d. Geordie and Sophie Brown 18 July 1969; children: Melanie, Lucas; ASSOC. PROF. OF MUSIC, UNIV. OF TORONTO 1987– ; Jr. & High School & Univ. Music Specialist-Teacher 1969–76; private instructor in guitar, voice, violin 1970–90; Sessional Lecturer, var. univs. 1976–83; Music Dept. Chair & Prof., Steinbach Bible Coll. 1975–85; Dir. of Devel. 1986–87; Founder & Dir., Candn. Music Edn. Rsch. Ctr., Univ. of Toronto; Chair, Rsch. Comn., Candn. Music Educators' Assn. 1993– ; Editor, 'Can. J. of Res. in Music Edn.' 1993– ; Rsch. Assoc., John Adaskin Project 1990– ; Research Staff, Hugh MacMillan Rehab. Ctr. 1990– ; Assoc., Ctr. for Health Promotion, Univ. of Toronto 1990– ; Rsch. Council of the Candn. Music Educators Assn. 1990–93; Outstanding Dissertation in Music Edn. Award, Council for Rsch. in Music Edn. 1990; Man. Arts Council Scholarship 1980; Lola McQuarrie Music Scholarship 1974; Man. Teachers Soc. Scholarship 1972; Man. Sci. Teachers Award 1969; Conductor & Artistic Dir., Pax Christi Chorale 1988–92; Singer, soloist, choir pres. & bd. mem., Winnipeg Singers 1983–85; Mem., Am. Edn. Rsch. Assn.; Candn. Univ. Music Soc.; Internat. Soc. for Musi Edn.; Musi Educators Nat. Conference; Ont. Music Eduators Assn.; Phi Delta Kappa; co-author: 'A Guide to Provincial Music Curriculum Documents since 1980' 1993, 'Get Into Guitar' 1973; editor: 'Research Perspectives on Music Education' monograph series; 'A College Looks Forward' 1987; Home: 115 Fontainbleau Dr., Willowdale, Ont. M2M 1P1; Office: Toronto, Ont. M5S 1A1.

**BARTHOLOMEW, Gilbert Alfred,** Ph.D., F.A.P.S., F.R.S.C., F.A.A.A.S.; retired nuclear physicist; b. Nelson, B.C. 8 Apr. 1922; s. Alfred Bartholomew; e. Univ. of B.C. B.A. 1943; McGill Univ. Ph.D. 1948; m. late Rosalie May d. late Edwin Hugh Dinzey 19 Apr. 1952; m. Anna Teresa Lubicz-Luba 24 July 1992; Jr. Research Offr. Nat. Research Council, Ottawa 1943–44; joined Atomic Energy of Canada Ltd. Chalk River 1948, Head of Neutron Physics Br. 1962–71; Research Dir., Physics Div., Atomic Energy of Can. Research Co. 1971–83 (ret.); Mem. 1978–87 and Sec. 1981–87 Nuclear Physics Comn., Int'l Union of Pure & Applied Physics; Chrmn. AECL/IREQ Tokamak de Varenne Advisory Ctte. 1982–92; Vice Chrmn. Science and Technology Seminar, Assn. for Baha'i Studies 1991– ; author over 100 scient. publs. incl. 7 review articles neutron capture $\gamma$-rays, neutron physics and low energy nuclear physics and advanced systems for nuclear power; mem. Candn. Assn. Physicists; Sigma Xi; Candn. Nuclear Soc.; recreations: canoeing, sailing, hiking; Home: P.O. Box 150, Lions Bay, B.C. V0N 2E0.

**BARTKIW, Roman,** R.C.A.; artist; b. Montreal, Que. 8 March 1935; s. Ivan and Annastasia B.; e. Beamsville (Ont.) High Sch. 1956; Ont. Coll. of Art A.O.C.A. 1960 (Henry Birks Medal; Gov. Gen. Medal; J.S. McClean Scholarship 1960); Sheridan Sch. of Design Mississauga glass blowing 1969; Alfred Univ. N.Y. glass blowing 1970, glass technol. and arch. glass concepts 1974–75; one d.; owned and operated pottery studio Toronto and Markdale, Ont. 1961–71; glass blowing studio Combermere, Ont. 1975–77; estbd. pottery studio in N.S. 1981; created glass-blowing studio (uses high energy conservation and waste reclaim glass) 1984; pottery teacher own studio Toronto 1961–62; Northern Coll. Inst. Toronto 1962; Head of Ceramics Ont. Coll. Art 1968–69; instr. in ceramics and glass blowing Georgian Coll. Applied Arts 1971–74; estbd. arts & crafts program Chesterfield Inlet, N.W.T. 1978; instr. various summer and night courses; res. mastercraftsman potter, St. Clair College, Chatham, Ont. Demonst. and Panel mem. Internat. Glass Symposium Denmark 1976; pottery workshop Cambrian Coll. 1977; solo ceramic exhns. incl. Candn. Guild of Crafts Gallery Toronto 1964; Candn. Guild of Potters 1967; 'The Past is Flowing into the Future' (homage to the Bowl and Fertility Symbol) Wells Gallery (Ottawa) and Dresden Gallery (Halifax) 1985; solo glass exhns. incl. Wells Gallery Ottawa 1976; Thomas Gallery Winnipeg 1976; Alice Peck Gallery Hamilton 1976; recipient Candn. Guild Crafts Design Award Ceramics 1965; Carling Festival of Arts Award Toronto 1969; Can. Council Award 1969; Candn. Scandinavian Foundation Travelling Scholarship 1974; Candn. Guild Crafts Travel Grant to Sweden 1975; Marriott Award for hand blown glass 'Man' 1977; Ont. Arts. Council Grant 1979; Can. Council Grant 1973; rep. glass exhn. Umea and Gothenburg Museums, Sweden, Denmark and Finland 1974–76; Masters Exhn. Toronto 1976; rec'd Dept. of Culture grant, N.S. Prov. Govt. as Candn. Rep. for Inauguration of Internat. Art Glass Museum, Ebeltoft, Denmark 1986 where he presented glass works for permanent coll. (4 major sculpture pieces: Fire, Water, Earth, Air); Craft Consultant, Upper Clements Park (a historical and cultural theme park, opened 1989); Head Master Craftsman, Glass, Blower and Presser, Upper Clements Pk. N.S. 1989, 1990; rep. in various perm. colls. incl. Royal Ont. Museum, Umea and Gothenburg Museums Sweden, Museum of Decorative Arts Copenhagen, N.S. Dept. of Culture & Recreation, Cultural Centre Japan, Massey Coll., Indus. Min. Coll., Seagram Coll.; mem. R.C.A. 1980; Visual Arts Ontario; N.S. Designer's Craftsman; Candn. Crafts Council; Ont. Crafts Council; Candn. Ceramic Soc.; Ont. Potters Assn.; Ont. Arts Council; Address: Box 100, Paradise, N.S. B0S 1R0.

**BARTLEMAN, James Karl;** diplomat; b. Orillia, Ont. 24 Dec. 1939; s. Percy Scott and Maureen Florence (Simcoe) B.; e. Port Carling Continuation Sch.; London Central Coll.; Univ. of West. Ont.; m. Marie-Jeanne d. Octave Rosillon 12 Sept. 1975; children: Anne Pascale, Laurent William, Alain-André; CANDN. PERMANENT REPR. AND AMBASSADOR TO NORTH ATLANTIC COUNCIL 1990– ; joined External Affairs 1966; service abroad: Bogota Colombia 1968–70; Dacca Bangladesh 1972–73; Nato Brussels 1973–77; Ambassador to Cuba 1981–83; Ambassador to Israel and High Commn. to Cyprus 1986–90; Home: P.O. Box 489 (BNATO), Ottawa, Ont. K1N 8T7.

**BARTLETT, Donald Sinclair,** M.Sc.; executive; b. Beamsville, Ont. 21 April 1929; s. Harry Alfred Benjamin and Anne Spence (Sinclair) B.; e. Mich. State Univ. B.Sc. 1949; Wash. State Univ., M.Sc., 1951; m. Lilly Malene, d. Omil Thorstvedt, 29 Sept. 1951; children: Inger Anne, Margaret Lynn, Donald Benjamin Sinclair, Brenda Louise; PRES., DONALD S. BARTLETT INVESTMENTS LTD. and CONSULTANT, BARWELL FOOD SALES INC., London, Ont.; past Pres., Arctic Gardens Inc.; Past Dir., Candn. Food Processors. Assn.; Dist. Mgr., Continental Can Co. of Canada Ltd., 1951–56; Clark Foods from 1956 to 1966 retired as Vice President; former mem., Can. Cham. of Comm.; Can. U.K. Cham. of Comm.; Bus. and Admin., Montreal Bd. of Trade; Faculty of Concordia; mem., Amer. Frozen Food Inst.; Sigma Chi; Freemason; United Church; recreations: skiing, golf; Clubs: Mississaugua Golf & Country (Port Credit, Ont.); M.A.A.A.; Royal Montreal Golf; Home: 1779 Laird Blvd., Town of Mount Royal, Qué. H3P 2V1.

**BARTLETT, Glenn Sargent,** M.D., F.R.C.S.(C), C.H.E.; b. Beamsville, Ont. 13 Sept. 1932; s. Clemens Jordison and Elizabeth Sargent (Best) B.; e. Univ. of Toronto M.D. 1958; m. Linda d. John and Grace Lapp 22 Dec. 1990; two d. Lisa Anne, Julie Lynn; CHIEF OPERATING OFFR. VICTORIA HOSP. 1990– ; Surg. Toronto E. Gen. Hosp. 1965–82, Chief of Staff 1977–82, Vice Pres. Med. 1982–1987 and present Hosp. 1987–90; Chrmn. Provl. Adult Cardiac Care Ctte.; recreations: hobby farming, cycling, travel, photography; Club: Highland Golf & Country; Home: 551 Country Club Dr., London, Ont. N6C 5R3; Office: 800 Commissioners Rd. E., London, Ont. N6A 4G5.

**BARTLETT, Lloyd Cleveland,** M.D., F.R.S.C.(C); surgeon; association executive; b. Stratford, Ont. 3 Oct. 1917; s. Reginald Cleveland and Olive (Masters) B.; e. Stratford Coll. Vocational Inst. 1935; Univ. of W. Ont. M.D. 1941; Univ. of Man. postgrad. surgical training 1949–52; m. Desta d. William and Kathleen Buse 8 Oct. 1942; children: Lorna, Sheila, Robert, Rex, Ellen; ASST. PROF. OF SURG. UNIV. OF MAN. 1953– ; Staff Surg. Grace Gen. Hosp. 1954– ; internship Ottawa Civic Hosp. 1941–42; remote n. practice Favourable Lake, Ont. 1942–49; Curator Pathol. Museum Univ. of Man. 1952–62, Dir. Postgrad. Surg. Edn. 1959–67; Staff Surg. Health Sci's Centre Winnipeg 1953–72; inventor numerous med. devices, procedures, systems; private med. practice; recipient Distinguished Service Award MMA 1984; author 'Exams Are For Passing' 1972; 'If You Lose, You Win' 1982; co-author 'Foot Notes, A Guide to Foot Care' 1988; numerous jour. publs.; Fellow, Am. Coll. Nutrition; Dir., Man. Medical Assn. (Pres. Greater Winnipeg Dist. 1982–83, Hon. Treas. 1987–88, Pres. 1989–90, Chrmn. numerous cttes.); Candn. Med. Assn. (Dir. 1986–89, Chrmn. Ctte. Tobacco Legis. and Rep. to Candn. Council on Smoking & Health 1988–93); Candn. Assn. Clin. Surgs.; recreations: fitness, cottage, photography, inventing, innovating, writing; Office: 1620 - 233 Kennedy St., Winnipeg, Man. R3C 3J5.

**BARTLETT, The Honourable Mr. Justice Rupert W.;** b. St. John's, Nfld. 23 Jan. 1921; s. Lewis Goodison and Clara (Thompson) B.; e. Prince of Wales College and Memorial Univ.; read law with Hon. L.R. Curtis Q.C.; admitted to Nfld. Bar 1944; 1st m. Mabel Hiscock; children: Robert, Janet; 2nd m. Marion Hutchings (nee Wright); JUSTICE OF THE SUPREME COURTS OF NFLD. 1985– ;AND OF THE NORTHWEST TERRITORIES 1993– ; Former Sr. Partner, Bartlett, Chalker, Marshall, Rowe, and Green; Q.C. 1963; Bencher, Law Soc. (Pres. 1969–74); Master, Supreme Court of Nfld. 1969; Mem., Nfld. House of Assembly 1971–72; apptd. to Central Dist. Court 1974; past director of several Nfld. businesses; Past Pres., Nfld. Hist. Soc.; Past Chair, Avalon Consolidated School; Founding Chair, Agnes Pratt Home for Senior Citizens; Mem., Explorers Club of New York (he accompanied his uncle Capt. Robert A. Bartlett on 5 of his sci. expeditions to the High Arctic under the aegis of the Nat. Geog. Soc., Smithsonian Inst., Am. Musuem of Nat. Hist., etc. 1936–40); Residence: 1 Dartmouth Pl., St. John's, Nfld. A1B 2W1.

**BARTLETT, William Hedley,** B.A., C.L.U.; insurance benefits consultant; b. London, Ont. 5 May 1928; s. William Taylor and Florence Gwendolyn (Scandrett) B.; e. Ridley Coll. St. Catharines, Ont.; Univ. of Toronto Schs.; Univ of W. Ont. B.A. 1950; C.L.U. 1958; m. Sally d. Tom and Jean Rigby 11 Oct. 1952; children: Jean, Bill, Charles, Mary; MLH + A; joined Confederation Life as Mgmt. Trainee becoming Dir. of Agencies 1966; Vice Pres. Mktg. Eaton Life 1970; Vice Pres. Reed Stenhouse Ltd. 1973; Pres. Bartlett Trihey & Co. Ltd. 1977–..; frequent lectr. market trends and future product requirements; Kappa Alpha; Anglican; recreations: golf, tennis, squash; Clubs: Caledon Ski; Badminton & Racquet; Toronto Golf; Office: 1 Eglinton Ave. E., Ste. 320, Toronto, Ont. M4P 1A1.

**BARTLIFF, Charles E.;** bank executive; b. Clinton, Ont. 1942; e. Univ. of Western Ont., Bus. Mngt. 1981; m. Donna; three children; SR. VICE-PRES., NON-FINANCIAL INSTITUTIONS, CORP. & GOVT. BANKING, BANK OF MONTREAL 1987– ; Vice-Pres., Domestic Money Mngt., Bank of Montreal 1979; Vice-Pres., Treasury, N.Y. 1982; Sr. Vice-Pres. & Branch Mgr. N.Y. 1984; recreations: sports, reading, travel; clubs: Cambridge, Canadian (Toronto & N.Y.); Office: First Canadian Place, Toronto, Ont. M5X 1A1.

**BARTNIKAS, Ray,** B.A.Sc., M.Eng., Ph.D., P.Eng., F.I.E.E.E., F.Inst.P., F.A.S.T.M., F.R.S.C.; electrical engineer; educator; b. Kaunas, Lithuania 25 Jan. 1936; s. Andrius and Eugenia (Kanisauskas) B.; e. St. Michael's Coll. Sch. Toronto 1954; Univ. of Toronto B.A.Sc. 1958; McGill Univ. M.Eng. 1962, Ph.D. 1964; m. Margaret d. Walter and Margaret McLachlan 19 Aug. 1967; children: Andréa, Thomas; DISTINGUISHED SR. SCI. INSTITUT DE RECHERCHE D'HYDRO-QUÉBEC 1983– ; Adjunct Prof. of Elect. Eng. Univ. of Waterloo

1969– ; Adjunct Prof. of Elect. Eng. McGill Univ. 1968– ; Professeur Associé Eng. Physics Ecole Polytechnique 1980– ; Rsch. Eng. Cable Engineering Labs. Northern Electric Co. (now Northern Telecom) 1958–63; mem. Sci. Staff Northern Electric R & D Labs. (now Bell-Northern Research) 1963–68; Sr. Sci. present Inst. 1968, Sci. Dir. Materials Sci. 1970-83; cons. proposed submarine cables Straight of Belle Isle crossing and P.E.I.-N.B. cable link; cons. planning & constrn. CEPEL Labs. Rio de Janeiro; Candn. Del. CIGRÉ Cttee. Elect. Insulating Materials 1970–76; Pres., IEEE Dielectrics and Electrical Insulation Soc. 1976–78; Chrmn., ASTM Cttee. on Electrical and Electronic Insulating Materials 1979–85; Chrmn., IEC Cttee. on Endurance Tests 1993– ; recipient IEEE Thomas Dakin Sci. Achievement Award 1980; Centennial Medal 1984; Whitehead Meml. Award 1987; Morris Leeds Award 1989; McNaughton Gold Medal 1993; IEE (Japan) Distinguished Honorary Lectr. SEIM 1983; ASTM Award of Merit 1985; Charles Dudley Medal 1985; Arnold Scott Award 1985; CSA Award of Merit 1986; John Jenkins Award 1989; Standards Council of Canada J.P. Carrière Award 1992; Assn. canadienne française pour l'avancement des sciences Urgel-Archambault Prize 1993; Univ. of Toronto Engineering Medal 1993; author or ed. various sci. publs. & books; mem. Internat. Electrotech. Comm.; Candn. Standards Assn.; Candn. Elec. Assn.; Ordre des Ingénieurs du Qué.; IEEE Energy Policy Cttee.; IEEE Insulated Conductors Cttee.; Commission de la Recherche Univ. (Qué.); R.Catholic; Home: 640 Pine Beach Blvd., Dorval, Qué. H9P 2K4; Office: 1800 Montée Ste-Julie, Varennes, Qué. J0L 2P0.

**BARTON, John,** B.A., M.L.I.S.; poet; librarian; b. Edmonton, Alta. 6 March 1957; s. Richard Charles and Nancy Fitzgerald (Preston) B.; e. Univ. of Victoria B.A. 1981; Columbia Univ. 1983 (incomplete M.F.A.); Univ. of W. Ont. M.L.I.S. 1986; LIB. NAT. AVIATION MUSEUM 1987– ; writing instr. YM-YWCA and Co-dir. Streetaccess Reading Series Victoria 1982–83; Instr. Carleton Bd. Edn. Festival of Arts 1987–88; Programme Dir., Tree Reading Series 1989–91; recipient Can. Council Arts B Award 1983; Patricia Hackett Prize for Poetry Univ. W. Australia 1986; Archibald Lampman Award for Poetry Ottawa Ind. Writers 1988; author: 'A Poor Photographer' 1981; 'Hidden Structure' 1984; 'West of Darkness' 1987; 'Great Men' 1990; 'Notes Toward a Family Tree' 1993; various poems, articles and book reviews nat. and internat. mags. and anthols.; Poetry ed.: 'Wot' Victoria 1981–83; Assoc. ed. 'Arc' Ottawa 1987–89, Co-Ed. 1990– ; mem. League Candn. Poets; Address: c/o League of Canadian Poets, 24 Ryerson, Toronto, Ont. M5T 2P3.

**BARTON, John Stafford,** M.A., B.D., D.D.; priest; b. Crowthorne, Engl. 4 Jan. 1930; s. Frederick Sherbrooke and Violet Irene (Hedges) B.; e. Univ. of Toronto B.A. 1952; Cambridge Univ. M.A. 1954; McGill Univ. B.D. 1957; Wycliffe Coll., D.D. 1984; m. Barbara d. Alfred and Marianne Rothe 15 July 1961; children: Dominic, Kristiana, Antony; Dir., World Mission, Anglican Church of Canada 1982–94; Gen. Secy., Student Christian Movement, McGill Univ. 1957–61; Vice-Prin., Bishop Tucker Coll. 1961–68; Vicar, St. James' Cathedral 1968–71; Parish Priest, St. Thomas' Chilliwack 1971–82; School Trustee 1979–81; recreations: gardening, canoeing, clarinet; Home: 1259 Sprucelea Dr., Oakville, Ont. L6J 2E7; Office: 600 Jarvis St., Toronto, Ont. M4Y 2J6.

**BARTON, William Hickson,** C.M., B.A., L.L.D.; retired; b. Winnipeg, Man. 10 Dec. 1917; s. Ernest James and Norah (Hickson) B.; e. Univ. of Brit. Columbia, B.A. (Hons.) 1940, Mt. Allison U., L.L.D., 1978; m. Jeanie, d. late Florence and Frederick B. Robinson, 27 Dec. 1947; one s., Scott Donald; Ambassador and Permanent Rep. of Can. to U.N. 1976–80; joined Defence Research Bd., Secy. 1946; Secy., Nat. Aeronautical Research Comte. 1950 until seconded to Dept. External Affairs 1952; joined that Dept. 1954 serving abroad in Vienna and Geneva, and at UN, New York; Alternate Gov. for Can., Internat. Atomic Agency 1957–59; External Affairs mem., Permanent Jt. Bd. Defence 1959; Head, UN Div., Dept. External Affairs, Ottawa 1964, Asst. Under-Secy. State for External Affairs 1970; Ambassador to UN in Geneva 1972; Ambassador to the UN in New York 1976–80; Pres., UN Security Council 1977 and 1978; served in World War, R.C.A. 1940–46; Chrmn., Bd. of Dirs., Candn. Inst. for Int'l. Peace & Security 1984–89; Member of the Order of Canada 1994; mem. Candn. Inst. Internat. Affairs; recreations: reading, swimming; Address: 13 Kilbarry Cr., Ottawa, Ont. K1K 0G9.

**BARTRAM, Edward John,** M.A., R.C.A.; artist; educator; b. London, Ont. 21 Mar. 1938; s. Edward Alexander and Olive (English) B.; e. Neuchatel, Switzerland 1958; Univ. of W. Ont. B.A. 1961; Univ. of Toronto M.A. (Fine Arts) 1964; m. Mary Elizabeth d. William E. Bromley and Helen (Doig) 8 June 1980; Printmaking Instr. Ont. Coll. of Art Toronto; solo exhns. incl. Univ. of Guelph 1966; York Univ. 1969; Univ. of Toronto 1972; Aggregation Gallery Toronto 1975; 1640 Gallery Montreal 1975; 2719 Gallery Dallas, Texas 1975; Mira Godard Gallery Toronto 1977, 1983; 10–yr. Retrospective, Nat. Travelling Exhbn. 1979–82; rep. in numerous group exhbns. incl. Internat. Printmakers Annual Seattle 1969, 1971; Salon Internat. de La Gravure Montreal 1971; Pratt Invitational N.Y. 1971; Cdn. Artists Invitational Art Gallery Hamilton 1972; Candn. Heritage Art Gallery Ont. 1973; Premio Internazionale Biella, Italy 1973; 5 Printmakers Can. House London, Eng. and Centre Culturel Paris 1974–75; Norwegian Print Biennale 1980; 10 Contemporary Print Artists Japan 1981; New Work from Can., World Print Counc., San Francisco 1981; Listowel Internat. Print Biennale, Ireland 1982; 7th Brit. Internat. Print Biennale, Bradford, Engl. 1982; Cdn. Contemporary Printmakers, Bronx Museum, N.Y. (travelling to Mexico City) 1982; rep. in various pub., corporate and private colls. incl. Art Gallery Ont., Can. Council Art Bank, Dept. External Affairs Ottawa; recipient Graphex II Purchase Award 1974; Editions I Ont. Arts Council Publ. & Purchase Award; G.A. Reid Award C.P.E. Annual, Sir George Williams Univ.; Ont. Soc. Artists 103rd and 105th Annual Purchase Awards; 'Imprint' Praga Industries Award, Print & Drawing Council Can. 1976; Graphex IV Ont. Arts Council Editions Award 1976; mem. Ont. Soc. Artists; Print & Drawing Council Can.; Roy. Can. Acad.; Address: P.O. Box 188, King City, Ont. LOG 1KO.

**BARWIN, B. Norman,** B.Sc., M.B., Ch.B., B.A.O., M.D., F.R.C.O.G., F.A.C.O.G., F.S.O.G.C.; obstetrician, gynecologist, association executive; b. Benoni, S. Africa 3 Aug. 1938; s. Aaron and Rita (Miller) B.; e. Univ. of Stellenbosch, B.Sc. Med. 1962; Queen's Univ. (Ire.), M.B., Ch.B., B.A.O. 1965, M.D. 1972; Royal Coll. of Obs/Gyn, D.R.O.G. 1967, M.R.C.O.G. 1969, F.R.C.O.G. 1983; Am. Coll. of Obs/Gyn, F.A.C.O.G. 1975; Soc. of Obs/Gyn of Can., F.S.O.G.C. 1985; m. Myrna d. Percy and Bella Zelikow 1962; children: Gary, Kevin, Alan, Lynn, Beth, Jackie; private practice in gynecology in Ottawa; formerly Assoc. Prof. of Obs/Gyn, Univ. of Ottawa & Co-Dir., Fertility Ctr., Ottawa Gen. Hosp.; Cons., Children's Hosp. of East. Ont. & Royal Ottawa Hosp.; Chair, Human Sexuality Prog., Univ. of Ottawa; Teacher, Reproductive Ethics Course; Chrmn., Candn. Standards Ctte. on Barrier Contraception; Dir., Pan Am. Androl. Soc.; Adv. Bd. Mem., Fed. Min. of Health & Welfare on Medicated Devices; Hon. Pres., Soc. for the Advancement of Contraception (also Dir.); Past Pres., Planned Parenthood Fed. of Can.; Candn. Fertility Soc.; Best Clin. Prof. for 4 consecutive yrs., Univ. of Ottawa; awarded Barbara Cass Beggs Meml. Award 1992–93; Knight of the Order of Columbus 1983; Chair, Profl. Adv. Bd., Bereaved Families of Ont.; Fallopius Soc.; Mem., Soc. of Obs/Gyn of Can. & U.S.; Candn. Med. & Ont. Med. Soc.; Assn. of Univ. Profs. of Obs/Gyn; co-author: 'Advances in Contraception' 1990, 'Adolescent Gynecology and Sexuality' 1982, 'Andrology' 1980 plus 3 earlier books, over 20 book chapters, and over 80 med. articles; extensive guest lectr. in Can. & abroad; serves on 4 Ed. Bds.; Ed., Soc. for Advancement of Contraception Newsletter; Rsch. Reviewer, MRC; Extve., Infertility Awareness Assoc. of Can. (IAAC); Pres., Canada Israel Cultural Found. (CICF), Ottawa; recreations: tennis, skiing, cycling, gourmet cooking, music; Home: 73 Loch Isle Rd., Nepean, Ont. K2H 8G7; Office: 770 Broadview Ave., Ottawa, Ont. K2H 3Z3.

**BASACCHI, Andy Arduino,** P.Eng., M.A.Sc.; electrical engineer; b. Palermo, Sicily 6 April 1956; s. Antonio and Maria (Coraci) B.; e. Univ. of Toronto M.A.Sc. Engr. Sci. 1979, Biomed. Engr. 1981; m. Dorothy d. Rocco and Elizabeth Mazzone 12 July 1980; children: Daniela, Diana, Jean-Paul; ELECTRICAL ENGINEER, TRIAX INFRASTRUCTRE MANAGEMENT CORP. (IBM spin off co.) 1993– ; Programmer, Analyst Trainee, IBM Canada Ltd. 1981; Systems Mgr., Rental Billing Application; Programmer, Analyst Assoc. Programmer-Analyst 1982; programmed bldg. automation system control for IBM H.Q.; Construction Engineer for renovations within bldg.; IBM Internal Admin. Achievement Award for Special Contbn., Major Suggestion & 'GPAX Automation Internat.' awards; Roman Catholic; Mem., Assn. of Profl. Eng. of Ont.; I.E.E.E.; Instrument Soc. of Am.; co-author: 'Interacting Communication Aid for the Non-Verbal Physically Handicapped Child' 1980; recreations: Wado Kai Karate; Home: 22 Bridwell Cres., Richmond Hill, Ont. L4C 9C4; Office: 251 Consumers Rd., Suite 300, North York, Ont. M2J 4R3.

**BASCH, Joseph David;** hotel/motel executive; b. Montreal, Que. 9 June 1939; s. Arthur and Elaine (Tabak) B.; e. Wilfrid Laurier Univ.; m. Sylvia Marilyn d. Theodore and Nellie Schwab 3 Feb. 1963; children: Michael Andrew, Robin Heather; Co-Founder, Pres. & Chief Fin. Offr., Journey's End Corp.; joined family retail business & ran operation for several years; Journey's End Corp. has largest number of hotels/motels in Can.; Former Dir., Belleville C. of C.; Ont. C. of C. Business Award; recreations: Life Master Bridge; clubs: Sales & Ad, Belleville; Home: 44 Briarwood Cres., Belleville, Ont. K8N 5K9.

**BASFORD, Hon. S. Ronald,** P.C., Q.C, B.A., LL.B.; b. Winnipeg, Man. 22 Apr. 1932; s. Douglas and Elizabeth (Menagh) B.; e. Gen. Steele Elem. Sch., Fort Garry, Man.; Comox (B.C.) High Sch.; Univ. of B.C., B.A. 1955, LL.B. 1956; m. Madeleine Nelson Kirk, 3 June 1967; two children: Daniel, Megan; PARTNER, DAVIS & CO., BARRISTERS & SOLICITORS since 1979; Dir. and mem. Extve. Comte., Canadian Imperial Bank of Commerce; Past Dir., North East Coal Development Project; Gendis Inc.; I.T.T. Industries; mem., Bd. of Mgmt., B.C. Research Council; Vancouver Public Aquarium Assn. (Past Pres.); Vancouver Gen. Hosp. Foundation; Univ. of B.C. Resources Council; practised law as partner in a Vancouver firm prior to el. to H. of C., def. cand., for Vancouver-Burrard, g.e. 1962; el. 1963, re-el. 1965; el. 1968, 1972, 1974 for riding of Vancouver Centre; Parlty. observer 18th Session of U.N. Gen. Assembly, 1963; Special Adviser to Govt. Del., 49th Conf. of the Internat. Labour Organ., Geneva, 1965; Leader, Candn. Del., 11th Commonwealth Parlty. Assn. Conf., Wellington, N.Z., 1965; Del., 12th Conf., Ottawa, 1966; Co-Chrmn. with Senator David Croll of Special Joint Comte. of Senate & H. of C. on Consumer Credit & Cost of Living, 1967; Min. Consumer & Corporate Affairs 1968, Urban Affairs 1972, Nat. Revenue 1974, Justice and Attorney-General 1975; resigned from Cabinet Aug. 1978 and from H. of C. Feb. 1979; mem., Vancouver Bar Assn.; Vancouver Bd. Trade; Law Soc. of B.C.: recreation: fishing; Club: Vancouver; Home: P.O. Box 152, Sechelt, B.C. V0N 3A0; Office: 2800 Park Place, 666 Burrard St., Vancouver, B.C. V6C 2Z7.

**BASINGER, James Frederick,** M.Sc., Ph.D.; educator; paleobotanist; b. Edmonton, Alta. 19 Sept. 1951; s. W. James Frederick and Phyllis Joan (Watson) B.; e. Victoria Composite High Sch. Edmonton 1969; Univ. of Alta. B.Sc. 1973, M.Sc. 1976, Ph.D. 1979; one d. Claire Olivia; PROF. OF GEOL. SCI., UNIV. OF SASK. 1985–, N.S.E.R.C. Univ. Rsch. Fellowship 1981–91; post-doctoral fellowships Ind. Univ. 1979–80, Univ. of Adelaide, Australia 1980–81, Univ. of Calgary 1981; rsch. evolution fossil floras w. and n. Can.; mem. Candn. Bot. Assn.; Bot. Soc. Am.; Geol. Assn. Can.; Office: Saskatoon, Sask. S7N 0W0.

**BASINSKI, Zbigniew Stanislaw,** O.C., M.A., D.Phil., D.Sc. (Oxon.), F.R.S., F.R.S.C.; research scientist; b. Wolkowysk, Poland 28 Apr. 1928; s. Antoni Basinski and Maria Z.A. Hilferding Basinska; e. Lyceum of Krzemieniec, Poland; Univ. Oxford B.Sc. 1952, M.A. 1954, D.Phil. 1954, D.Sc. 1966; m. 1 Apr. 1952; children: Stefan Leon Hilferding, Antoni Stanislaw Hilferding; PROFESSOR EMERITUS, DEPT. OF MATERIALS SCIENCE AND ENGINEERING, INSTITUTE FOR MATERIALS RESEARCH, McMASTER UNIV.; Research Scient. Div. Physics, Nat. Research Council 1956–87; Ford Distinguished Visiting Prof. Carnegie Inst. Technol. 1964; Commonwealth Visiting Prof. Metall. & Materials Science, Univ. Oxford, Visiting Fellow, Wolfson Coll. 1969–70; Visiting Rsch. Scientist, Cavendish Laboratory Cambridge, and Overseas Fellow, Churchill College Cambridge 1980–81; First recipient (1977) Candn. Metal Physics Medal; Fellow, Royal Soc. of London 1980; Fellow, Royal Soc. of Can. 1978; Officer, Order of Canada 1985; Doctor Honoris Causa (DHC) Mining & metallurgy Academy, Stanisław Staszic Univ., Kraków, Poland 1991; author many scient. research articles various internat. journs.; service Polish Army Cadet Sch. Camp Barbara, Palestine 1943–47; Home: 98 Bluebell Cres., Ancaster, Ont. L9K 1G1; Office: Inst. for Materials Rsch., McMaster Univ., 1280 Main St. W., Hamilton, Ont. L8S 4M1.

**BASKEN, Reginald Charles;** trade union executive; b. Churchbridge, Sask. 13 Sept. 1937; s. Reginald Robert Stanley and Margaret Isobel (Fraser) B.; e. Langenburg H.S. 1957; Univ. of Sask. 1 yr.; divorced; children: Kevin, Colleen; EXTVE. VICE-PRESIDENT, COMMUNICATIONS, ENERGY & PAPERWORKERS UNION

OF CANADA (CEP) 1992– ; Staff, Candn. Labour Cong. 1963; Oil, Chem. & Atomic Workers Internat. Union 1963–80; Pres., Alta. Fed. of Labour 1972–77 (1st V.P. 1972; 2nd V.P. 1971); Extve. Counc. Mem., Candn. Lab. Cong. 1972–77; Vice-Pres. at Large 1986; Pres., Energy and Chemical Workers Union 1984–92; has held extve. positions with Can. Safety Counc., Candn. Cancer Soc., United Way, Canada West Found., Gov. Gen. Candn. Study Conf., Nat. & Alta. Round Tables on the Econ. & the Environ.; 1st grad. Labour Coll. of Can. 1963; Senate, Univ. of Alta. 1979–81; mem., NDP; Candn. Found. for Econ. Edn.; recreations: gardening, golfing; Home: 9220 Ottewell Rd., Edmonton, Alta. T6B 2C7; Office: Suite 1900, 350 Albert St., Ottawa, Ont. K1R 1A4.

**BASMAJIAN, John V.,** O.Ont., M.D., F.A.C.A., F.R.C.P.(C), F.A.C.R.M., F.R.C.P.S.(Glasg.), F.S.B.M., F.A.B.M.R.; university professor and medical scientist; b. Constantinople (of Armenian parentage) 21 June 1921; s. Mihran and Mary (Evelian) B.; e. (came to Canada, 1923) Univ. of Toronto, M.D. (with Hons.) 1945; St. Thomas's Hosp., London, Eng., Post-grad. studies, 1953; Saddington Medal, Univ. of Toronto, 1943, and Cody Silver Medal, 1945; m. Dora, d. Samuel Lucas, Leamington, Ont., 4 Oct. 1947; children: Haig Lucas, Nancy, Sally Ann; DIR. OF RESEARCH AND TRAINING GRANTS, EASTER SEAL RESEARCH INST. 1990– ; Emeritus Prof. of Medicine and Anatomy & Former Dir. of Rehabilitation Medicine Programs, McMaster Univ. since 1986; Dir. Regional Rehab. Research & Training Centre & Prof. of Anat., Physical Med. & Psychiatry, Emory Univ. 1969–77; Dir. of Neurophysiol., Georgia Mental Health Inst. 1969–77; Research Assoc., Hosp. for Sick Children, Toronto, 1955–57; Hon. Secy.-Treas., Banting Research Foundation, Toronto, 1955–57; Demonst. of Anat., Univ. of Toronto, 1946–47; Post-grad. work at Sunnybrook Hosp., and Hosp. for Sick Children, Toronto, 1947–48; Lect. in Anat., Univ. of Toronto, 1949–51, Asst. Prof., 1951–54, Assoc. Prof., 1954–56; Prof., 1956–57; Prof. and Head of Anat., Queen's Univ. 1957–69; awarded Starr Medal for Research, Univ. of Toronto, 1956; served in R.C.A.M.C., 1943–45 with rank of Capt.; N.R.C. exchange scientist to Soviet Acad. of Sciences, 1963; publications: 'Primary Anatomy' (8th ed.) 1982; 'Surface Anatomy' 1977; 'Muscles Alive: Their Functions Revealed By Electromyography' (4th ed.) 1979; 'Grant's Method of Anatomy' (10th ed.) 1980, (11th ed. with C. Slonecker) 1989; 'Clinical Electroneurography' (with M. Smorto; 2nd ed.) 1980; 'Computers in Electromyography' (with H. Clifford, W. McLeod and N. Nunnally); 'Electrodiagnosis' (with M. Smorto) 1977; 'Therapeutic Exercise' (4th ed.) 1984, (5th ed. with S.L. Wolf) 1990; 'Biofeedback' (2nd ed.) 1983; 'Electrode Placement in EMG Biofeedback' (with R. Blumenstein) 1980; Neuromotor Examination of the Limbs' (with M. Smorto) 1980; 'Therapeutic Exercise – Student Edition' 1980; 'Medical Rehabilitation' (with R.L. Kirby) 1984; 'Stroke Rehabilitation' (with M.E. Brandstater) 1987; 'Rational Manual Therapies' (with R. Nyberg) 1992; 'I.O.U. - Adventures of a Medical Scientist' 1993; many scientific articles in various medical journals; mem., Am. Assn. of Anats. (Extve Comte. 1975–79, Pres. 1985–86); Anat. Soc. of Gt. Brit. & Ireland; Biofeedback Res. Soc. (Extve. Comte 1975–77, Pres. 1979–80); Candn. Neurol. Soc.; Acad. of Med., Toronto; Fellow, N.Y. Acad of Med., mem., Ont. Coll. of Phys. & Surg.; Candn. Assn. Anats. (mem. Extve. Council and Secy., 1965–68); Am. Acad. Neurol.; Cajal Club (Neurol.); Hon. mem., Mexican Assn. of Anats.; Am. Assn. Advance. Science; Neuroscience Soc.; Soc. for Psychophysiol.; Biomed. Engn. Soc.; Am. Cong. of Rehabilitation; Internat. Soc. of Electromyographic Kinesiol. (Pres. 1968–72); Internat. Soc. Biomechanics (Extve. Comte. 1974–76); Biofeedback Soc. of America (Pres. 1979); mem., Ed. Bd., Candn. Journal of Surgery (1957–68); the International Journal 'Electromyography'; the 'Queen's Quarterly' (1961–68); Am. Journ. of Phys. Med.; Assoc., Ed., Am. Journ. of Anat.; Anatomical Record; mem. of Senate, Queen's Univ., (1965–68); Chrmn., subcomte. on Med. Electronics and Electrotherapy, Comte. on Electrical Definitions, Candn. Standards Assn. (1960–67); Dir., Ont. Div., Candn. Cancer Soc. (mem., Med. Adv., Publicity & Educ. Comtes.; Chrmn., sub-comte. on sch. ed. programmes); mem., Nat. Fitness Research Review Comte. (Chrmn., 1967–69) Dept. of Health and Welfare, Ottawa, Trustee, Kingston Bd. of Educ. (Chrmn. of Bd., 1964, 1965); mem. Fitness Council of Can. 1968–69; Study Sec. on Orthopedics and Applied Physiology, Dept. Health, Educ. Welfare, Washington; rec'd Kabakjian Award for Contributions to Science, New York 1967; named to '2000 Men of Achievement' 1973, 1974; Gold Key Award, Am. Congress of Rehabilitation Medicine 1977; Honorary Fellow, Roy. Coll. of Phys. and Surgeons 1978; visiting professor award, Alberta Heritage Fndn. 1982; J.C.B. Grant Award of Can. Assoc. Anatomists 1985; Hon. Fellow, Australian Coll. of Rehab. Med. 1987; Coulter Lectr., Am. Congress of Rehab. Med. 1988; Henry Gray Laureate, Am. Assoc. Anatomists, 1991; Recipient, Order of Ont. 1991; Hon. Fellow, Royal College of Physicians and Surgeons, Glasgow 1992; visiting lecturer in many universities in Europe, Japan, Australia, New Zealand, etc; United Church; recreations: travel, gardening; Home: 106 Forsyth Ave. N., Hamilton, Ont. L8S 4E4.

**BASSETT, Charles Philip,** B.A.; federal civil servant; b. Clydach, Wales 8 Jan. 1937; s. Philip and Elsie (Jones) B.; e. Ystalyfera Grammar Sch.; Univ. of Poitiers; Univ. of Wales B.A. 1960, Dip. P.M. 1961; m. Sandra d. Maldwyn and Eileen Jones 11 Aug. 1962; children: Caroline, Christopher, Matthew; VICE PRESIDENT, CORPORATE AFFAIRS, CANDN. INTERNAT. DEVELOPMENT AGENCY (CIDA) 1993– ; Labour Relations & Training Offr. Imperial Chemical Industries, Manchester 1961–68; Training Offr. CAP Mgmt. Course, Pub. Service Comn. Can. 1968–70; Mgr. Mgmt. Devel. & Training Can. Post 1970–72; Sr. Personnel Secretariat, Privy Council Office 1972–73; Dir., Adm. Staffing Prog. Pub. Service Comn. 1973–76; Dir.-Gen. Personnel, Candn. Internat. Devel. Agency (CIDA) 1976–78, Dir.-Gen. Personnel & Adm., CIDA 1978–82; Vice Pres. Anglophone Africa Br., CIDA 1982–89; High Commissioner of Canada to Zimbabwe 1989–93; Lectr. in Bus. Adm. Manchester Univ. 1966–68; mem. Univ. Students Pres. Assn. (UK); Royal Commonwealth Soc.; N.Am. Gymanfa Ganu Assn.; recreations: music, theatre, food, wine; Office: 200 Promenade du Portage, Hull, Qué. K1A 0G4.

**BASSETT, Douglas Graeme,** O.C., CStJ, LL.D.; executive; b. Toronto, Ont. 22 June 1940; s. John White Hughes and Eleanor (Moira) B.; e. Bishop's Coll. Sch., Lennoxville, Que.; Upper Can. Coll., Toronto; Univ. of New Brunswick, Fredericton, N.B.; m. Susan Joan Temple, d. C.R. Douglas, 19 Oct. 1968; three d.: Deborah Elizabeth, Stephanie Alexandra, Jennifer Moira; PRES., C.E.O. AND DIR., BATON BROADCASTING INC.; CFTO-TV Ltd.; Nation's Capital Television Inc.; Dir., Glen-Warren Productions Ltd.; Telegram Corporation Ltd.; Russwood Broadcasting Ltd.; Eaton's of Canada Ltd.; Canadian Imperial Bank of Commerce; Norcen Energy Resources Ltd.; South Western Ontario Broadcasting Inc.; Cooper Corporation Ltd.; CTV Television Network Ltd.; Mid-Canada Communications (Canada) Corp.; Mercedes-Benz Canada Inc.; Gov., National Ballet of Canada; Olympic Trust of Canada; Pres., Candn. Robert F. Kennedy Memorial; Vice Pres., The Candn. Soc. for Weizmann Inst. of Sci. (Toronto Chapt.); Dir., Counc. for Cdn. Unity; Hospital for Sick Children Found.; Cdn. Counc. of Christians and Jews; World Wildlife Fund Canada; Honours: LL.D. (hon. causa) Univ. of New Brunswick; Comdr. of The Order of St. John; Comdr. Ont., The Nobiliary Order of the Niadh Nask; Kt. Comdr. of the Military and Hospitaller Order of St. Lazarus of Jerusalem; Ordo Constantini Magni; Pro Ecclesia Et Pontifice Cross; awarded Human Relations Award, C.C.C.J.; McGill Mgmt. Achievement Award, McGill Univ.; Humanitarian Award, Beth Shalom Brotherhood; Honouree, Jewish Nat. Fund Negev Tribute 1988; Officer of the Order of Canada 1991; Commemorative Medal for the 125th Anniversary of Cdn. Confederation 1992; recreations: squash, tennis, boating, golf; Clubs: The Toronto; York; Toronto Golf; Badminton & Racquet (Toronto); London (London, Ont.); Muskoka Lakes Golf & Country; Albany (Toronto); Canadian (Toronto); Lyford Cay (Nassau); North Hatley (Que.); Variety (Toronto); Empire (Toronto); Mount Royal (Montreal); Rideau (Ottawa); Caledon Ski; Mill Reef Club (Antigua); Offices: P.O. Box 9, Stn. O, Toronto, Ont. M4A 2M9 and 9 Channel Nine Court, Scarborough, Ont. M1S 4B5.

**BASSETT, Isabel Glenthorne,** M.A.; television producer and reporter; d. Ranald Ian and Janet Marjorie (MacKinnon) Macdonald; e. St. Clement's Sch. Toronto 1957; Queen's Univ. B.A. 1960; Ont. Coll. of Edn. Cert. Eng. & French 1961; York Univ. M.A. 1973; m. John White Hughes s. John and Marion Bassett 17 July 1967; children: Avery Isabel, Sarah Glenthorne, Matthew Macdonald; Eng. and French Teacher Humberside Coll. Inst. Toronto 1961–64; Reporter, Toronto Telegram 1964–67; Eng. Teacher Calabar High Sch. Kingston, Jamaica 1967; Lectr. York Univ. 1974–75; Reporter 'W5' CTV 1976–77; Host & Reporter 'Hourlong' CFTO-TV 1977–84; Co-Host CFTO-TV Ont. Prov. Els. 1985, 1987, Ont. Tory Leadership Convention 1985, Lib. 1982 and NDP 1982; Co-Host 'Survival 2000' 1982; Co-Host and Assoc. Producer 1983 'Children Take Care' (Bronze Medal 1983 Internat. Film & TV Festival N.Y.; Gold Medal Can Pro Awards 1984); Reporter and Interviewer 'No Place to Hide' 1985 (Gold Medals Can Pro Awards 1986, Candn. Film & TV Assn. 1986); Reporter 'Missing' 1986; Producer & Reporter 'Growing Up in the 80's' 1987, 'Quebec Today' 1987 and 'No Fixed Address' 1988, 'Something Old, Something New' 1988, 'Beyond the Blues' 1989, 'Teen Gangs - Kids in Turmoil' 1989, all documentaries CFTO-TV; Mem. of Bd. of Govs. Trinity Coll. Sch., Port Hope, Ont.; Dir. Internat. Readings Harbourfront Toronto; Gov. Ryerson Polytech. Inst.; Patron, Toronto Arts Awards; Scarborough Women's Centre; Council of Patrons Outward Bound; Mem., Bd. of Govs. and Vice-Chair, Ryerson Polytechnical Inst.; author 'The Parlour Rebellion' 1975; 'The Bassett Report: Career Success of Canadian Women' 1985; recreations: reading, riding, jogging; Home: 76 Binscarth Rd., Toronto, Ont. M4W 1Y4; Office: 1206, 101 Richmond St. W., Toronto, Ont. M5H 1T1.

**BASSETT, Maj. The Hon. John White Hughes,** P.C., C.C., O.Ont., B.A.; broadcasting executive; b. Ottawa, Ont. 25 Aug. 1915; s. John and Marion Wright (Avery) B.; e. Ashbury Coll., Ottawa, Ont.; Bishop's Coll. Sch., Lennoxville, P.Q.; Univ. of Bishop's Coll., B.A. 1936; m. Eleanor Moira, d. Dr. F. H. Bradley, Sherbrooke, Que., 26 Apl. 1938; children: John, Douglas, David; 2ndly Isabel Glenthorne, d. Dr. Ian Macdonald, 17th July 1967; children: Avery, Sarah, Matthew; CHAIRMAN OF EXTVE. COMTE., BATON BROADCASTING INC.; Chrmn. Security Intelligence Review Ctte., Ottawa; served in 2nd World War as Major, Seaforth Highlanders of Can.; saw action in Italy and N.W. Europe; def. cand to H. of C. for Sherbrooke, Que. 1945 and Toronto Spadina, g.e. June 1962; mem., Candn. Legion; Hon. Trustee, Hosp. for Sick Children; Companion of the Order of Canada; Order of Ontario; Member of the Privy Council; P. Conservative; Anglican; recreations: riding, tennis; Clubs: York; Canadian; International Lawn Tennis; Rideau (Ottawa); Home: 76 Binscarth Road, Toronto, Ont. M4W 1Y4; Office: Suite 1206, 101 Richmond St. W., Toronto, Ont. M5H 1T1.

**BASSNETT, Peter J.,** F.L.A.: librarian; b. Sutton Coldfield, Engl. 16 Nov. 1933; s. Lionel and Phyllis (Maw) B.; e. Steyning Grammar Sch. matric. 1951; Hammersmith Sch. of Arch. & Bldg. Intermediate A.I.Q.S. 1956; North-Western Poly-tech. Sch. of Librarianship 1961–63; m. Ann Gorham 12 Dec. 1959; two d. Madeline, Sarah; C.E.O., SCARBOROUGH PUBLIC LIBRARY BD. 1975– ; Quantity Surveyor Godfrey & Burgess, London, Eng. 1955–58; Librarian-in-Charge Haringey, London, Eng. 1964–66; Calgary Pub. Lib. Bd. 1966–72, Adm. Asst. to Dir.; Dir. Systems & Mang. Services N. York Pub. Lib. Bd. 1972–75; Extve. Co-ord., Ont. Pub. Libraries Programme Review for the Min. of Citizenship and Culture 1980–82; served with RAF 1952–54; author various articles pub. lib. adm. and research; Pres. Alta. Lib. Assn. 1968–69; mem. Lib. Assn. (Eng.); Candn. Lib. Assn.; Ont. Lib. Assn.; Private Libs. Assn.; recreations: bibliography, horticulture, musicophile, art appreciation; Home: 29 Highbridge Place, Scarborough, Ont. M1V 4R7; Office: Administration Centre, 1076 Ellesmere Rd., Scarborough, Ont. M1P 4P4.

**BASSO, Guido;** flugelhornist; trumpeter; arranger; composer; conductor; b. Montreal, Que.; began playing trumpet at 9; played in dance and show bands and at 18 was heard by Vic Damone at club El Morocco and subsequently toured with him; toured throughout N. Am. with Pearl Bailey and her husband (Louis Bellson's) orchestra 1957–60; settled in Toronto 1960 becoming a first-call studio musician and leader; Music Dir. CBLT 'Nightcap' 1963–67 and CBC TV 'Barris and Company' 1968–69; co-starred with Peter Appleyard in CBC TV 'Mallets and Brass' 1969; Music Dir. CBC Radio 'After Noon' 1969–71 and led orchestras for 2 CBC TV series on big band era 'In the Mood' 1971–72 and 'Bandwagon' 1972–73; organized CNE big band concerts with Dizzy Gillespie, Quincy Jones, Woody Herman and Benny Goodman 1975; also performed in Toronto nightclubs and hotel lounges with his own groups; soloist with Rob McConnell and The Boss Brass; recordings incl. several pop instrumental LPs; many Jazz LP's with the Boss Brass, Singers Unlimited, Hi Lo's and others; studio musician for numerous radio & TV jingles; Leader, The Guido Basso dance band and the Guido Basso jazz quintet.

**BASTABLE, Colum Patrick,** F.C.A.; b. Dublin, Ireland 9 Dec. 1946; s. Michael and Kathleen (Wills) B.; e. Christian Brothers Coll., Monkstown Park, Dublin; Assoc. Inst. of C.A.s in Ireland 1971; Fellow 1982; m. Elizabeth d. Arthur and Kathleen Ashley 18 Mar. 1972; children: Sarah, Brian; PRES., ROYAL LEPAGE LIM-

ITED 1993– ; Audit Mgr., Peat Marwick Mitchell 1972; Controller, NTI Bus. Equipment & Systems 1974; V.P. Finan. & Dir., A.E. LePage (Que.) Inc. 1976; A.E. LePage (Ont.) Ltd. 1979; Extve. V.P. Finan., Chief Finan. Offr. & Dir., A.E. LePage Limited 1980, Royal LePage Limited 1984; Extve. Vice Pres., Investment & Profl. Serv., Royal LePage Ltd. 1987–92; Extve. Vice-Pres., Commercial Real Estate Serv., Royal LePage Ltd. 1992–93; Dir., Royal LePage Real Estate Services Ltd.; Dir. & Past Chrmn., The Ireland Fund of Can.; Dir. & Vice-Chrmn., The Nat. Ballet Sch.; recreations: tennis, golf, squash; club: Granite; Home: 23 Beaverhall Dr., North York, Ont. M2L 2C6; Office: Suite 1000, 33 Yonge St., Toronto, Ont. M5E 1S9.

**BASTARACHE, J.E. Michel;** lawyer; b. Québec, P.Q. 10 June 1947; s. Alfred and Madeleine (Claveau) B.; e. Univ. Moncton, B.A. 1967; Univ. Montréal, LL.L. 1970; Univ. Nice (France), D.E.S. 1972; Univ. Ottawa, LL.B. 1978; m. Yolande, d. Edmond and Stella Martin, 17 Aug. 1968; children: Emilie; Jean-François (dec.); PRESIDENT AND C.E.O., ASSUMPTION MUTUAL LIFE 1989– ; Chrmn., Mountain States Life Insurance Co. of America; Louisbourg Investments; Place Beauséjour; Legal Translator, Prov. New Brunswick 1970–71; Gen. Secy., Nat. Soc. Acadians 1973; Asst. to Pres., Assumption Mutual Life 1974; Dir. Sales, 1975; Vice-Pres. Marketing 1976; joined Univ. of Moncton as Law Prof. 1978; Dean of Law Sch. there 1980–83; Dir. Gen., Promotion of Official Langs., Dept. of Secy. of State, 1983–84; Assoc. Dean, Common Law Sect., Faculty of Law, Univ. of Ottawa, 1984–87; Assoc., Lang Michener Lash Johnston 1987–88, Partner 1988–91; mem., Law Soc. of Upper Can.; N.B. Barrister's Soc.; Corp. Translators and Interpreters of N.B.; Candn. Bar; ed. 'Egalité'; recreations: tennis; golf; Office: P.O. Box 160, Moncton, N.B. E1C 8L1.

**BASTIAN, Donald N.,** B.A., B.D.; bishop; b. Estevan, Sask. 25 Dec. 1925; s. Josiah and Esther Jane (Millington) B.; e. Greenville (Ill.) Coll. B.A. 1953, Dr. Sacred Theol. 1974; Asbury Theol. Semy. Wilmore, Ky., B.D. 1956, Distinguished Service Award 1973, D.D. 1991; Seattle Pacific Univ. D.D. 1965; Roberts Wesleyan Coll. DHL 1990; m. Kathleen G. d. John and Norma Swallow 20 Dec. 1947; children: Carolyn Dawn, Donald Gregory, Robert Wilfrid, John David; Bishop, Free Methodist Church in Canada 1974–93; Pastor, Lexington, Ky. 1953–56; New Westminster, B.C. 1956–61; Greenville Coll. Ch. 1961–74; el. Bishop 1974; author 'The Mature Church Member' 1963; 'Belonging' 1977; 'The Joy of Christian Fathering' 1980; 'Managing Tainted Money' 1986; 'Counterfeit: The Lie of Living Together Unmarried' 1988; Exec. Ed. Light & Life Mag. 1981–86; recipient Citation for Service Greenville Ill. Police Dept. 1974; Mem. Wesleyan Theol. Society (Am); Candn. Methodist Hist. Society; Past Pres., Evangelical Fellowship of Can.; Address: 63 Adirondack Cres., Brampton, Ont. L6R 1E5.

**BASTIAN, Michael A.;** financial executive; b. Shanghai, China 16 Nov. 1944; e. Bishop's College School 1961; m. Jacqueline Rogers 29 Oct. 1982; PRESIDENT, ROYAL BANK INVESTOR TRADING INC. 1992– ; Vice-Pres. & Treas., Bank of America, Canada 1982–86; Dir., Bank of America Options Inc. 1983–86; Vice-Pres., Treasury Div., Royal Bank 1986–92; Chief Foreign Exchange Trader, Royal Bank London, Eng. 1972–75; Toronto 1975–82; Office: 200 Bay St., 16th Floor, Toronto, Ont. M5J 2J5.

**BASTIEN, Richard,** B.Sc.Econ., FLMI; financial executive; b. St-Léonard, Qué. 30 Sept. 1948; s. Noel and Noella (Dagenais) B.; e. Univ. de Mont. B.Sc.Econ. 1971; m. Denise 5 June 1971; children: Frédéric, Stéphanie; EXTVE. VICE-PRES., GROUPE COOPERANTS INC. 1991– ; Dir. of Admin., Investments, Les Coopérants; Vice-Pres. 1983–86; Sr. Vice-Pres., Investments, Finan. & Devel., Groupe Cooperants Inc. 1986–91; Dir., Finan. Coopérants Inc.; First Internat. Life Inc.; Gestion d'Investissements Coop. Inc.; Premier Life Inc.; Coopdev Inc.; Mem., F.L.M.I.; Assn. des Econ. de Montréal; Cercle Finan. et Placement; Home: 21 boul. Prud'Homme, Repentigny, Qué. J5Y 1G1; Office: 2075 Université, Montréal, Qué. H3A 2L1.

**BASTOMSKY, Charles Henry,** M.B.,B.Ch., F.R.C.P.; physician; educator; b. Johannesburg, S. Africa 28 Feb. 1935; s. Boris and Millie B.; e. Orange Grove Primary Sch. and Highlands North High Sch. Johannesburg 1951; Univ. of Witwatersrand M.B.,B.Ch. 1957; M.S.Q. (Specialty Med. Biochem) 1974; MED. BIOCHEM., ROYAL VICTORIA HOSP. and Assoc. Prof. of Exper. Med. McGill Univ. 1974– ; Internship, Johannesburg 1958–59; Registrar in Neurol. Maida Vale Hosp. London, U.K. 1960; Fellow in Med., Seton Hall Univ. N.J. 1961–63, Boston Univ. 1963–65, McGill Univ. 1965–68; Scholar, Med. Research Council Can., Royal Victoria Hosp. and McGill Univ. 1968–74; Visiting Scient. (Welcome Trust) Univ. of Glasgow 1971–72; Consultant in Thyroid Testing, Endocrinol. Div. Royal Victoria Hosp., Teacher Postgrad. Med. Biochem.; author or co-author over 45 articles thyroid Patho-Physiol. and Lab. Med. various books and med. journs.; mem. Endocrine Soc.; Am. Thyroid Assn.; Candn. Soc. Clin. Investigation; Home: 3450 Drummond St., Apt. 1722, Montreal, Qué. H3G 1Y2; Office: 687 Pine Ave. W., Montreal, Qué. H3A 1A1.

**BASZTYK, William Alexander (Marquis de BlancheGarde),** M.B.A., Ph.D., F.C.I.S.; executive, educator, author; b. Toronto, Ont. 20 July 1955; s. Alex and Frances Dorothy (Radik) B.; e. Bloor C.I. 1973; Chartered Sec. 1982; Candn. Sch. of Management, Northland Open Univ. M.B.A. 1984; P.W.U. (Calif.) Ph.D. 1984; PRESIDENT, GLAM CORP. 1987– ; Accountant, insurance industry 1974–78; Co-ord. Author, Insur. Inst. of Can. 1978–80; Gen. Mgr., Candn. Jewellers Assn. 1980–81; Extve. Dir., Candn. Insolvency Assn. 1981–83; Prof., Faculty of Business, George Brown College 1985– ; Pres., Wm. Basztyk & Assoc. Ltd. 1974– ; Prof. (part-time), Seneca Coll. 1985– ; Asst. Prof., Candn. Sch. of Mngt. 1985– ; Assoc. Prof., Northland Open Univ. 1986– ; Hereditary Marquis de Blanchegarde, Baron de Nephin; Knight Grand Commander of St. Andrew 1992; comnd. Colonel on Staff of Gov. of Kentucky 1992; Pres. & Dir., Ont. Centre for Mngt. Studies 1993– ; Sec.-Treas., Ont. Watchmakers & Jewellers Assn. 1992– ; Fellow, Inst. of Chartered Secs. 1992 (ACIS 1982); Credit Inst. of Can. 1979; Insur. Inst. of Can. 1978 (AIIC 1976); Cert. Admin. Managers 1991 (CAM 1984); Inst. of Dirs. 1989; Guild of Accountants 1985 (ICIA 1976); Ont. Ctr. for Mngt. Studies 1993; author: 'Retailing in Canada' 1993, 'Caution Office Ahead' 1987, 'Motivation and Recruitment' 1986, 'How to Recognize a Potential Insolvency' 1984 and num. articles in journals, var. seminars for assns.; Home: Willowdale, Ont.; Office: 260 Adelaide St. E., No. 177, Toronto, Ont. M5A 1N0.

**BATA, George Lewis,** B.A.Sc., M.Sc.; chemist; b. Budapest, Hungary 18 Nov. 1924; e. Univ. of Budapest B.A.Sc. (Chem. Engn.) 1946, M.Sc. (Chem.) 1947; Univ. of Utah Tutorial Extr. Metall. 1972; Mass. Inst. of Technol. Turorial Polymer Rheology 1981; m. Judith Eve Belgrader 25 March 1950; one d. Catherine; ADJUNCT PROF., MCGILL UNIV., MONTREAL 1990– ;and DIR., INDUST. MATERIALS RESEARCH INST., NAT. RESEARCH COUNCIL OF CAN. 1978– ; Works Engr. Monoplast Ltd. Budapest 1947–49; Consultant New Product Devel. Société Gentia, Vincennes, France 1949–50; Devel. Group Leader, Arborite Ltd., LaSalle, Que. 1950–53; Dir. and Vice Pres. Resinous Products Inc., Dorval, Que. 1953–54; R & D Mgr. Varcum Chemicals Ltd. Lindsay, Ont. 1954–55; Staff Asst. Union Carbide Canada Ltd. 1955, Assoc. Dir. of Devel. 1956, Dir. of Devel. 1958, Dir. of Technol. 1968–78; Assoc. Prof., Dept. of Metallurgical Eng. of Ecole Polytechnique; Mem., Candn. Res. Mgmt. Assn. (CRMA)/Science Counc. Working Ctte.; Conseil de la Science et de la Technologie du Québec; Exec. of COPSE (Ctte. of Parliamentarians, Scientists & Engs.); Bd. of Dir., Candn. Welding Bureau; Nat'l. Conf. on the Advancement of Research (NCAR); mem., Int'l. Polymer Processing Group; Candn. Counc. of the Int'l. Inst. of Welding; Advisory Ctte. to the Metallurgical Eng. Dept. of Ecole Polytechnique; Candn. Del. to Int'l. Org. of Standardization and to VAMAS (Versailles Project on Advanced Materials & Standards); mem. Adv. Panel Strategic Grants, Nat. Sciences & Engn. Research Council Can. 1980–84; mem. Assoc. Ctte. on Tribology NRCC 1978–79, Task Force Study Que. Lab. on Engn. Materials 1977, Adv. Ctte. Biomed. Engn. 1976–81; Gov., Sodalitas Danubiana Foundation & Lib. Inc. 1974– ; Dir. Physico-Med. Systems Corp. 1968–78; Chrmn. Consultative Comte. Coll. Educ. in Plastics, Ministry Educ. Que. 1966–73; Chrmn. Candn. Chem. Engn. Conf. (25th); Treas. II World Cong. Chem. Engn. Montreal 1981; holds 27 nat. and internat. patents; author numerous publs., book chapters; rec'd Candn. Research Mang. Assn. Awards: 1979 Médaille de Vermeil La Société d'encouragement de la recherche et de l'invention Paris, France; 1980 Candn. Research Management Assn.; 1984 Cross of the Order of the Knights of Malta; mem. Chem. Inst. Can.; Am. Soc. Testing & Materials; Candn. Inst. Mining & Metall.; Assn. Scient., Engn. & Technol. Community Can. (Pres. 1981); Candn. Research Mang. Assn. (Chrmn. 1977–79); Soc. Plastic Engrs. (Chrmn. Internat. Relations Comte. 1967–68); Candn. Soc. Chem. Engn. (Vice Pres. 1970–71, Dir. 1967–68); l'Ordre des chimistes du Qué. (Past Dir.); Sigma Xi; R. Catholic; recreations: archaeology Central Asia, biomedical engineering, ocean sailing, Canadian science policy; Club: Mount Royal Tennis; Home: 40 Terrase Les Hautvilliers, Outremont, Qué. H2V 4P1; Office: 75 De Mortagne Blvd., Boucherville, Qué. J4B 6Y4.

**BATA, Sonja Ingrid,** O.C., LL.D., L.H.D.; director; b. Zurich, Switzerland 8 Nov. 1926; d. Dr. George, C.B.E. and Pati (Suter) Wettstein; e. Swiss Fed. Inst. of Technol. Zurich; Honorary Degrees: York Univ. LL.D.; Wilson Coll. Pa. LL.D.; Loyalist Coll. Belleville Hon. Dipl. for Applied Arts & Technol.; Mount St. Vincent Univ., Halifax, N.S. L.H.D.; m. Thomas J. Bata, 26 Oct. 1946; children: Thomas G., Christine, Monica, Rosemarie; Dir. Bata Ltd.; Chrmn., Bata Shoe Museum Found.; Dir., Alcan Aluminium Ltd.; CT Financial Services Inc.; The Canada Trust Co.; Canada Trust Realtor; Canada Trustco Mortgage Co.; Chrmn., Governor's Council, North York Gen. Hosp.; Dir., Council for Business and the Arts in Can.; Council for Candn. Unity; Jr. Achievement of Can. (Chrmn. 1985–88); Dir., World Wildlife Fund (Can.) (Chrmn. 1983–85); Trustee, World Wildlife Fund (Internat.); Mem. Bd. Advisors, Community Found. of Greater Toronto; Hon. Capt.(N), Fifth Candn. Destroyer Squadron; Hon. Gov. Toronto French Sch.; mem. Candn. Adv. Council Shastri-Indo Candn. Inst.; Dir., Canadian Commercial Corporation 1978–91; Canadian Club of Toronto 1984–90 (Vice Pres. 1986–88); Gov., York Univ. 1976–85; mem. Nat. Bd. Candn. C. of C. 1976–80 (mem. Extve. Counc. 1976–78); mem. Nat. Design Counc. Can. 1964–76 (Chrmn. 1973–75); Bd. Trustees Art Gallery Ont. 1968–74; active in Girl Guide World Assn. (mem. W. Hemisphere Comte. and World Finance Comte.) 1953–64; Home: 44 Park Lane Circle, Don Mills, Ont. M3C 2N2; Office: 59 Wynford Dr., Don Mills, Ont. M3C 1K3.

**BATA, Thomas J.,** C.C. (1971); manufacturer; b. Praha, Czechoslovakia, 17 Sept. 1914; s. Thomas and Marie B.; e. Elem. Schs., Zlin, Czechoslavakia; Private Schs., Eng. and Switzerland; Acad. of Comm., Uherske, Hradiste; m. Sonja Ingrid, d. Dr. George Wettstein, Zurich, Switzerland, 26 Oct. 1946; CHRMN. BATA LTD.; Mem., Adv. Grp. on Private Sector Development Rsch., World Bank Group; Operation Enterprise Adv. Ctte., Am. Mgmt. Assoc.; Adv. Bd., Pres.'s Assoc., Am. Mgmt. Assoc.; Adv. Counc., CESO (Candn. Extve. Service Overseas); Dir., International Business Counc. of Can.; Dir. at large, Bd. of Dirs., National Retail Fedn., N.Y.; Hon. Chrmn. Canada-India Bus. Council; Hon. Gov., Trent Univ.; mem. Bd. Govs. Candn. Export Assn.; Chrmn. Comte. on Development for Business & Industry Adv. Comte. to OECD; Chrmn., Commission on Multinational Enterprises, International Chamber of Commerce; Chrmn., Advisory Council, International MBA Program, York Univ.; Co-Chrmn., Czech & Slovak Business Council of Canada; Chrmn., Bohemiae Foundation, Czech Republic; Chrmn., Business & Industry Adv. Ctte. BIAC to the OECD 1969–71; Candn. Assn. of Latin Am. & Caribbean 1975–79; mem. Adv. Ctte. East/West Enterprise Exchange, York Univ., Toronto; mem., National Ballet Guild of Canada; Fellow, Internat. Acad. Mang.; mem.: Chief Extves. Organization; Young Pres. Organ. (Founding mem. and Past Dir.); Business Council on National Issues (BCNI); Advisory Bd. of African Project Development Facility - APDF (an IFC affiliate); Former Mem.: International Trade Adv. Ctte. to the Govt. of Can.; Business Adv. Council, IFC (World Bank); former Dir.: IBM Canada Ltd; IBM World Trade Americas/Far East Corp.; CP Airlines; Expert Advisor, UN Cttee. on Transnational Corporations 1985–88; came to Can. 1939; under his leadership, new plant built up at Batawa, Ont.; served in Candn. Reserve Army as Capt., Hastings & Prince Edward Regt.; D.Sc. (hon.) Univ. of Economics, Prague; Holder of the Order of Tomas Garrick Masaryk; R. Catholic; recreations: tennis, skiing, scuba-diving, riding, aviation; Clubs: Rotary (Trenton); Granite; Royal Can. Yacht.; Royal Automobile (London, Eng.); Rideau (Ottawa); Canadian (N.Y.); Home: 44 Park Lane Circle, Don Mills, Ont. M3C 2N2; Office: 59 Wynford Drive, Don Mills, Ont. M3C 1K3.

**BATCHELOR, Barrington de Vere,** B.Sc., D.I.C., Ph.D., P.Eng., F.C.S.C.E., F.E.I.C.; civil engineer; b. Lucea, Jamaica 2 July 1928; s. Reginald Augustus and Vera Louise (O'Connor) B.; e. Kingston (Jamaica) Tech. High Sch. 1948; Univ. of Edinburgh B.Sc. (Civil Engn.) 1956; Imp. Coll. of Science & Technol. Univ. of London D.I.C. 1961, Ph.D. 1963; Nat. Defence Coll. Can. 1982–83; m. Alison Yvonnie d. late J. Johnston, Jamaica 14 Sept. 1960; children: Roger Dwight, Nicola Anne, Wayne Barrington; PROF. OF CIVIL ENGN., QUEEN'S UNIV. 1972– ; civil service Jamaica 1948–53; Engr., Sir William Halcrow and Partners, London, Eng. 1956–58; Extve. Engr. Govt. Jamaica 1958–63, Sr. Extve. Engr.

1963–64; Princ., Franks & Batchelor, Consulting Engineers, Jamaica and Chrmn. Caribbean Consulting Engineers Ltd. 1964–66; Asst. Prof. of Civil Engn. present Univ. 1966, Assoc. Prof. 1968; Visiting prof. Cornell Univ., Washington Univ. 1974–75; consultant Florida Dept. of Transportation; Mem., Task Force for Developing Draft of New Design Code for Am. Assoc. of State and Highway Officials (AASHTO); recipient Commonwealth Scholarship (U.K.) Award 1960; various papers prof. journs.; Fellow, Engn. Inst. of Can.; Candn. Soc. Civil Engn.; Founding mem., Jamaica Inst. Engrs.; mem., Assn. Prof. Engrs. Prov. Ont.; Am. Soc. Civil Engrs.; Am. Concrete Inst.; recreations: golf, boating, gardening, woodworking; Home: 150 Collingwood St. Kingston, Ont. K7L 3X5; Office: Kingston, Ont. K7L 3N6.

**BATE, Derek Andrew,** Mus.Bac.; musician; b. Toronto, Ont. 29 Nov. 1953; s. Charles Derek Stewart and Catherine Elizabeth (Catto) B.; e. Royal Conservatory of Music Toronto ARCT (piano) 1971, ARCT (organ) 1972 (Gold Medal); Univ. of Toronto Mus.Bac. 1975; Musical Dir., 'Phantom of the Opera' Canadian Nat. Tour 1991–93; Musical Dir., 'Les Miserables' Toronto prod. 1989–90; Conductor over 20 prodns. Candn. Opera Co. incl. (in Toronto) 'Carmen' 1979, 1984, 'Die Fledermaus' 1982, 1987, 'La Traviata' 1982, 1986, 'Falstaff' 1982, 'Cosi fan tutte' 1985; touring prodns. incl. 'Le Nozze di Figaro' 1970, 'La Cenerentola' 1980, 1986, 'La Boheme' 1984, 'Tales of Hoffmann' 1987; Conductor, Calgary Opera, Edmonton Opera, Alta. Ballet Co., Nat. Arts Centre; Opera Piccola; Comus Music Theatre; Toronto Operetta Theatre; Opera Grand Rapids, Mich. ('La Boheme' 1984); Gilbert & Sullivan Soc. Toronto; concert appearances with Symphony N.S., Edmonton Symphony, Orch. London, L'Orchestre Mondial des Jeunesses Musicales, Fla. Music Festival; Coach Opera Dept. Univ. of Toronto 1975–78; Coach Opera Div. Banff Sch. of Fine Arts 1976–81, Head Coach 1979–81; Chorus Master, Candn. Opera Co. 1980–85; Resident Conductor, Candn. Opera Co. Ensemble 1980–83; Music Advisor, Candn. Opera Co. Orch. 1984–87; Music Dir., Summer Opera Lab. 1987–88; recipient Jean Chalmers Award Candn. Opera Co. 1975; mem. Toronto Musicians' Assn.; Gilbert & Sullivan Soc. Toronto; Amnesty Internat.; recreations: tennis, badminton, bridge; Home: 281 Silver Birch Ave., Toronto, Ont. M4E 3L6.

**BATEMAN, Leonard A.,** P.Eng.; consultant; b. Winnipeg, Man. 14 Jan. 1919; e. Lord Roberts, Riverview and Kelvin High Schs., Man.; United Coll.; Univ. of Man., B.Sc. (Elect. Engn.) 1942, M.Sc. 1948; Banff Sch. of Advanced Mang. (Business Adm.); Macro Eng. Seminar, M.I.T.; m.; three children, one s., two d.; PRES., BATEMAN & ASSOCIATES LTD.; design and operating responsibilities, City of Winnipeg 1942, Gen. Supt. i.c. Power Production when resigned 1956; joined Manitoba Hydro Electric Bd. as Systems Planning Engr. 1956, Dir. of Production 1961, Dir. Systems Planning 1967, Asst. Chief Engr. 1970, Asst. Gen. Mgr. (Engn.) and Chief Engr. 1971; Gen. Mgr. Engineering 1971; apptd. Chrmn. and Chief Extve. Offr. 1972; formed Bateman Consulting Services Jan. 1979, Bateman & Associates, 1980; Chrmn., CIGRE Study Comte. 14 (H.V.DC Links) 1976–82; Candn. Rep., World Power Conf., Moscow, Aug. 1968 and New Delhi 1984; Candn. Elect. Assn. Rep. on Tech. Adv. Comte., Hydro-Quebec Inst. Research 1971–74; Past Dir., Banff Sch. Advanced Mang.; Sr. Life Mem., Inst. Elect. & Electronic Engrs.; mem. Candn. Elect. Assn. (Past Pres.); Fellow & Life Mem., Engn. Inst. Can. (Past Vice-Pres. Can. Nuclear Assoc.; mem., World Energy Conference; Conf. International des Grands Réseaux Electriques (CIGRE); Chrmn. Can. National Comte of CIGRE, 1980–85; mem., Winnipeg Ch. of Commerce; Assn. Prof. Engrs. Man. (Past Pres.); author of numerous papers in prof. journs.; recipient Queen's 25th Anniversary medal 1977; Address: 23l Brock St., Winnipeg, Man. R3N 0Y7.

**BATEMAN, Robert McLellan,** O.C., B.A., LL.D.; artist; b. Toronto, Ont. 24 May 1930; s. Joseph Wilbur and Anne (McLellan) B.; e. Forest Hill High Sch. Toronto 1950; Univ. of Toronto B.A. 1954; Ont. Coll. of Educ. 1955; m. Birgit Ilse d. Ulrich Freybe, West Vancouver, B.C. 1 Aug. 1975; children of 1st marriage: Alan, Sarah, John; of 2nd marriage: Christopher, Robbie; high sch. art teacher 20 yrs.; guest lectr. art, photography, nature, conserv. various educ. and service groups; frequent tour leader and lectr.; films incl. 'Robert Bateman' CBC TV 'This Land' 1972; 'Images of the Wild: A Portrait of Robert Bateman' Nat. Film Bd. Can. 1978; 'The Nature Art of Robert Bateman' 1981; 'Robert Bateman – Artist/Naturalist' CBC Spectrum 1984; 'A Day in the Life of Robert Bateman' CBC 1985; 5 postage stamps Candn. Govt. Endangered Species Series 1976–81; Metrop. Toronto Bd. Trade painting 'Window Into Ontario' 1977; Candn. Govt. wedding present to Prince Charles 'Northern Reflections – Common Loon Family' 1981; Platinum Polar Bear Series, Royal Candn. Mint 1990; named American Artist Magazine Artist of Yr. 1980; Master Artist Leigh Yawkey Woodson Art Museum 1982, Wausau, Wisc.; rec'd Excellence Award in Arts for Contrib. to Artistic Community Wentworth Co.; D.Sc. (hon. causa) Carleton Univ. 1982; LL.D. (for Fine Arts, hon. causa) Brock Univ. 1982; D.Litt. (for Fine Arts, hon. causa) McMaster Univ. 1983; LL.D. (hon. causa) Univ. of Guelph 1984; LL.D. (hon. causa) Laurentian Univ. 1987; D.F.A. (hon. causa) Colby Coll., Maine 1989; D.F.A. (hon. causa) Northeastern Univ., Boston 1991; biog. 'The Art of Robert Bateman' by Ramsay Derry 1981 (French ed. 1982; German ed. 1984); 2nd. biog. 'The World of Robert Bateman' by Ramsay Derry 1984; 3rd biog. 'Robert Bateman: An Artist in Nature' by Rick Archbold 1990; publ. in 'Ten Top Wildlife Artists' Watson-Guptil U.S.A. 1982; 'Wildlife Artists at Work' by Patricia Van Gelder 1982; 'Twentieth Century Wildlife Artists' by Nicholas Hammond 1986; 'From the Wild' by Christopher Hume 1986; 'Painting Birds' by Susan Rayfield 1988; major retrospective at the Smithsonian, Wash. 1987; maj. Candn. travel Exhn. Nat. Museum of Natural Sciences Ottawa 'Images of the Wild' 1981 through 1982; rec'd Queen's Silver Jubilee Medal 1977; Officer, Order of Can. 1984; Member of Honour Award, World Wildlife Fund (presented in Geneva by HRH Prince Philip) 1985; Past Dir., Hamilton Naturalist Assn., and Fed. Ont. Naturalists; Hon. Life mem.: Audubon Soc.; Cdn. Nat. Wildlife Fed.; Sierra Club; Burlington Cultural Centre; Fedn. of Ont. Naturalists; Hon. Dir., Niska Wildlife Foundation, and Long Point Bird Observatory; Hon. Chrmn., Harmony Found.; Address: Gulf Islands, B.C.

**BATEMAN, William Maxwell,** D.F.C., B.A.Sc., P.Eng.; retired executive; b. Winnipeg, Man. 7 May 1920; s. Norman Silver and Veda (Maxwell) B.; e. Bayside High Sch. (L.I., N.Y.); Univ. of Toronto, B.A.Sc. 1949; m. Gaye Marjorie, d. late Frederick George Lister, 22 Oct. 1949; children: Kathryn, Paul, Anne, Leslie; PRES., WILLIAM M. BATEMAN CONSULTING LTD. 1985– ; Project Engr., C.A. Pitts General Contractors Ltd. 1949, Chief Engr. 1957, Vice Pres. and Chief Engr. 1963, Dir. 1967, Sr. Vice Pres. 1971; Pres. and Dir., Lake Ont. Cement 1972; Pres., Genstar Constr. Ltd. 1979; Pres. and Dir., Banister Continental Ltd. 1981–85 and 1990–91, Dir. 1981–86; Dir. Bantrel Group Engineers 1983–85; served in 2nd World War, R.C.A.F.; rank at discharge Flight Lt.; mem. Assn. of Prof. Engrs. Ont.; Assn. of Prof. Engrs. Geologists & Geophysicists of Alta.; author of various tech. articles and contrib. to 'Heavy Construction'; awarded Officer, Royal Order of St. John; Anglican; recreations: boating, golf; Clubs: Mayfair Golf and Country (Edmonton); Mississaugua Golf and Country (Past Pres.); Home: 5039 – 154 St., Edmonton, Alta. T6H 5P1.

**BATER, Basil Robert,** M.A., S.T.M., Ph.D.; university professor; b. Stony Beach, Sask. 2 June 1928; s. Charles Mayne and Florence Gertrude (Abbot) B.; e. Univ. of Sask. B.A. (Great Distinction) 1948; Univ. of Oxford B.A. (Hons.) 1952; St. Andrew's Coll. B.D. 1953; Union Theol. Seminary S.T.M. (summa cum laude) 1959, Ph.D. 1962; m. Ellen d. Herb and Grace Brooker 19 Mar. 1982; children: Clark, Craig, Barbara, Phyllis; Prof., New Testament, Queen's Theological College and Queen's University 1974–..; Min., N. Portal-Bienfait Un. Ch. 1953–55; Prof., St. Andrew's Coll. & Lectr., Univ. of Sask. 1957–70; Sr. Min., Eglinton Un. Ch. 1970–74; Prin., Queen's Theol. Coll. 1974–83; Head, Dept. of Studies in Religion, Queen's Univ. 1974–83; Rhodes Scholar of Sask. 1950; McGeachy Mem. Sr. Scholarship 1983; Scholar, Tantur Ec. Inst., Israel 1985; Min., Un. Ch. of Can.; mem., The Westar Inst.; Candn. Soc. of Bib. Studies; Soc. of Bib. Lit.; Catholic Bib. Soc.; Candn. Soc. for the Study of Rel.; Citizen's Adv. Ctte., Kingston Women's Prison; author: 'All This and Christian Too' 1970; recreations: skiing, curling, swimming, skating, sailing; Club: Saturday (Kingston); Home: 1419 Tamarac St., Kingston, Ont. K7M 7J2.

**BATES, Albert E.,** B.Comm., F.C.I.B.; insurance executive; b. Loon Lake, Sask. 30 June, 1937; s. Edward & Doris (Lockyer); e. Western Canada High School, Calgary; McGill Univ., Montreal B.Comm. (Gold Medal) 1969; m. Constance Jo-Anna d. the late C.A. Wear, 8 March 1958; children: Jo-Anne, Cathy, Kevin; PRES., C.F.M. CONSULTING; Trustee, Graceland Coll.; Gov., Candn. Red Cross (Mem. Compensation Ctte.); joined Bank of Montreal June 1955, held various positions in Alta.; attended McGill Univ.; returned to bank, various exec. positions to Oct. 1973; VP Master Card 1973–76; VP Retail Banking 1976–78; VP Retail Operations 1978–79; VP E. & N. Ont. 1979–80; Sr. Vice Pres. Man. & Sask. Div. 1980–82; Sr. VP, Central Reg., Domestic Banking 1982–84; Sr. Vice Pres. & Depy. Group Exec., Personal Banking 1984–87; joined Metropolitan Life Oct. 1987; Pres., Candn. Subsidiaries, Metropolitan Life Insurance Co. 1989–92 (Retired); Home: Box 18, Ennisclaire Dr., R.R. #2, Rockwood, Ont. N0B 2K0.

**BATES, David Vincent,** M.D., F.R.C.P., F.R.C.P. (C), F.A.C.P., F.R.S.(C); educator; b. West Malling, Kent, Engl. 20 May 1922; s. Dr. John Vincent and Alice Edith (Dickins) B.; e. Rugby Sch. 1935–39; Pembroke Coll., Cambridge 1939–41; St. Bartholomew's Hosp., Univ. of London 1941–44; M.B. Cambridge 1945, M.D. 1954; m. Gwendolyn Margaret, d. W. F. Sutton, 24 March 1948; children: Anne Elizabeth, Joanna Margaret, Andrew Vincent; Dean, Faculty of Med., Univ. of Brit. Columbia 1972–77; Prof. of Medicine and Physiology since 1972; sometime Sr. Phys., Roy. Victoria Hosp., Montreal, Prof. Exper. Med., McGill Univ., Chrmn. Dept. of Physiol. and Assoc. Dean, Grad. Studies there; Chrmn., Adv. Panel on Aviation, Defence Research Bd. Can.; Chrmn., Roy. Comn. on Uranium Mining, Prov. of B.C. 1979–80; Visiting Prof: Univ. N.C.; Univ. of Otago, N.Z.; Univ. of Cal.; Johns Hopkins Univ.; Harvard Med. Sch.; Univ. of Wisc.; Dalhousie; Univ. of Melbourne, Australia; served in Royal Army Med. Corps. 1945–48; service in India, Japan and Malaya; Fellow Roy. Coll. of Phys.; Physiol. Soc. of London; Med. Research Soc.; Am. Physiol. Soc.; Candn. Physiol. Soc.; Am. Soc. for Clin. Investig.; Candn. Soc. for Clin. Investig.; Roy. Soc. Med.; Candn. Thoracic Soc. (Pres. 1973); Candn. Assn. for Club of Rome; Air Pollution Control Assn.; Fellow of Collegium Ramazzini; awarded Robert A. Cooke Medal, Am. Acad. of Allergy 1966; Queen's Jubilee Medal 1978; Certificate of Special Merit, Candn. Meteorol. Soc. 1973; Ramazzini Medal 1985; Connaught Award, Candn. Lung Assoc. 1991; Trudeau Medal, Am. Thoracic Soc. 1993; author: 'A Citizen's Guide to Air Pollution' 1972; 'Respiratory Function in Disease' 1989; over 200 papers in scient. journs.; recreation: gardening, poetry; Office: Dept. of Health Care & Epidemiology, Univ. of Brit. Columbia, Vancouver, B.C. V6T 1W5.

**BATES, Donald George,** M.D., Ph.D.; professor; b. Windsor, Ont. 18 Mar. 1933; s. George Harley and Sarah Hughena (Stephenson) B.; e. Walkerville Coll.; Univ. of West. Ont., M.D. 1958, B.A. 1960; Johns Hopkins Univ, Ph.D. 1975; m. Mary Catherine d. Mary and Reginald Young 1 June 1957 (divorced); children: Gregory Howard, Jennifer Ann; THOMAS F. COTTON PROF. OF HIST. OF MED., DEPT. OF SOC. STUDIES OF MED., McGILL UNIV. 1975– ; Intern, Victoria Hosp. 1958–60; N.I.H. fellow, Inst. of Hist. of Med., Johns Hopkins Univ. 1960–62; Inst./Asst. Prof. 1962–66; Assoc. Prof., Dept. of Hum. & Soc. Stud. in Med., McGill Univ. 1966–75; Chrmn. 1966–82, 1987–88; Assoc. Prof., Dept. of Epidem. & Health 1971–84; Norman Bethune Exch. Prof., Beijing Med. Coll. 1978; Rsch. Assoc., Oxford Univ. 1979–80; Vis. Lectr., Life Planning Ctr., Japan 1982; Chrmn., McGill Study Group for Peace & Disarmament 1981–88; Cons., Royal Soc. of Can., Environ. Implications for Can. of Nuclear War Ctte.; Mem., Ed. Bd., 'Medicine and War,' 'Comparative Studies in Health Systems and Medical Care' series; Bd. of Dir., Candn. Phys. for Prevention of Nuclear War (Candn. Rep. when assn. awarded Nobel Peace Prize 1985); Gov. Counc., Internat. Phys. for Prev. of Nuclear War 1985–86, Vice Pres., 1987–88; var. named acad. lectureships; Mem., Am. Assn. for Hist. of Med.; Am. Assn. for Adv. of Sci.; Candn. Soc. for Hist. of Med.; Soc. for Social Hist. of Med.; author & publ.: 'Thoughts on Peace and Security' 1985–87; articles in profl. jours., newspapers; radio & TV presentations; Home: The 4300, Apt. 702, 4300 Blvd. de Maisonneuve, Westmount, Qué. H3Z 3C7; Office: Dept. of Soc. Studies of Med., McIntyre Med. Sci. Bldg., 3655 Drummond St., Montreal, Qué. H3G 1Y6.

**BATES, Paul Kevin;** b. London, England 29 Dec. 1950; s. Charles Ernest and Violet Ruth (Ryan) B.; e. Cornwall Tech. Coll. 1968; m. Sally d. Stanley and Marcia Collier 4 Nov. 1969; children: Rachel, Elizabeth, Charlotte; PRES., MARATHON BROKERAGE 1988– ;and PRES., GREEN LINE INVESTOR SERVICES 1993– ; var. positions, Nat. Westminster Bank U.K. & Scotiabank 1968–73; Retail Stockbroker, Richardson Greenshields 1973–76, 1983–85; var. sales and mgmt. positions, Xerox Can. 1976–83; Dir., Nat. Sales, Royal Trust 1985; Vice Pres., Investments, Personal Fin. Serv., Royal Trust 1986–88; author: 'Sales Force Management in The Financial Service' 1989; contbg. author: 'Through the Mutual Funds Maze' 1988; Dir., Jr. Achievement of Metro Toronto; Dir. & Past Chrmn., National Mental Health Fund; Nat. Mental Health Fund; Dir., Candn. Psychiatric Research Foundation;

Mem. Nat. Counc., Duke of Edinburgh's Award Scheme; Office: P.O. Box 41, Toronto, Ont. M5X 1K1.

**BATES, Peter John Henry,** B.Sc.; information scientist; b. Maidenhead, Berks, Eng. 22 Dec. 1940; came to Can. 1967; s. Richard Henry and Eleanor (Milson) B.; e. Merchant Taylors' Sch., London 1959; London Univ. B.Sc. 1964; divorced; m. 2ndly Louise S. Fortier 1986; children: Alexander Richard, Evan Daffyd; step-children: Michelle, Christine, Lisa; INFORMATION SPECIALIST, SYNCRUDE CANADA LTD. 1972– ; Asst. Librarian, Associated Lead Mfrs. 1964–67; Library Asst., Univ. of Sask. 1967–68; Librarian, Alta. Rsch. Counc. 1968–72; Ed., Alta. Oil Sand Index 1972; recreations: photography, poking about, reading, model railways, travelling; Office: 10120 – 17th St., Edmonton, Alta. T6P 1V8.

**BATTEN, Alan Henry,** D.Sc., Ph.D., F.R.S.C., F.R.A.S.; astronomer; b. Whitstable, Eng. 21 Jan. 1933; s. late George Cuthbert and Gladys (Greenwood) B.; e. Wolverhampton Grammar Sch. 1950; Univ. of St. Andrews B.Sc. (Astron.) 1955, D.Sc. 1974; Univ. of Manchester Ph.D. 1958; m. Lois Eleanor d. late Albert Ernest Dewis, Bedworth, Eng. 30 July 1960; children: Michael Henry John, Margaret Eleanor; Sr. Rsch. Offr., Dominion Astrophysical Observatory 1976–91; Research Asst. and Jr. Tutor, St. Anselm Hall of Residence, Univ. of Manchester 1958–59; Nat. Research Council Fellow, Dom. Astrophys. Observatory 1959–61, staff mem. 1961–91, Guest worker since 1991; Part-time Lectr. in Astron. Univ. of Victoria 1961–63; Guest Investigator Vatican Observatory 1970 and Instituto de Astronomia/Fisica Del Espacio Buenos Aires 1972; rec'd Queen's Silver Jubilee Medal 1977; Pres. Parent-Teacher Assn. Willows Elem. Sch. 1971–73; mem. Synod Diocese of B.C. 1967–69, 1974; Gov. Ang. Theol. Coll. Vancouver 1967; author 'Binary and Multiple Systems of Stars' 1973; 'Resolute and Undertaking Characters: The Lives of Wilhelm and Otto Strave' 1988; Ed. 'Extended Atmospheres and Circumstellar Matter in Spectroscopic Binary Systems' 1973; 'Algols' 1989; co-ed. 'Determination of Radial Velocities and Their Applications' 1967; trans. 'L'Observation des Etoiles Doubles Visuelles' (par P. Couteau) 1980; 2 correspondence courses in Astron. for B.C. Dept. Educ.; over 130 research papers and articles in prof. journs.; 3 catalogues Orbital Elements of Spectroscopic Binary Systems; mem. Am. Astron. Soc.; Astron. Soc. Pacific (Vice Pres. 1965–68); Council mem. Royal Soc. of Can. 1980–81; Royal Astron. Soc. of Can.; Pres. Victoria Centre 1970–72, Nat. Pres. 1976–78; Ed. Journal of Royal Astron. Soc. of Can. 1981–88; Candn. Astron. Soc. (Charter mem. 1971, Pres. 1972–74); Internat. Astron. Union (Vice-Pres. 1985–91; Pres. Comn. 30, Radial Velocities 1976–79; Pres. Comn. 42, Close Binary Stars 1982–85; mem. Candn. Nat. Comte. 1964–70 and 1976–82, Chrmn. Nat. Organ. Comte. XVII Gen. Assembly Montreal 1976–79); Fellow, Explorers Club 1979; Member, Ancient Soc. of Coll. Youths 1988; Mem., Adv. Counc., Centre for Studies in Religion & Soc., Univ. of Victoria 1993– ; Anglican; Home: 2987 Westdowne Rd., Victoria, B.C. V8R 5G1; Office: 5071 W. Saanich Rd., Victoria, B.C. V8X 4M6.

**BATTEN, Jack Hubert,** B.A., LL.B.; author, journalist, radio broadcaster; b. Montreal, Que. 23 Jan. 1932; s. Jack Hubert Sr. and Mary Kathleen (Soward) B.; e. Univ. of Toronto Schools; Univ. of Toronto B.A. 1954, LL.B. 1957; Osgoode Hall Law Sch. 1959; m. 2ndly Marjorie Harris 20 Apr. 1968; children (by 1st m.): Russell Bradshaw, Sarah Jane; FREELANCE JOURNALIST, AUTHOR, BROADCASTER since 1968; called to the Bar of Ontario 1959; lawyer, McLaughlin, Macaulay, May and Soward 1959–63; writer, Maclean's Magazine, The Canadian, and managing ed., Saturday Night Magazine 1963–68; author of twenty books incl. 'The Honest Ed Story' 1972; 'The Leafs in Autumn' 1975; 'Lawyers' 1980 (on which a CBC-TV serial was based in 1985); 'In Court' 1982; 'Robinette' 1984; 'Judges' 1986; 'Crang Plays The Ace' 1987; 'On Trial' 1988; 'Straight No Chaser' 1989; 'Riviera Blues' 1990; several articles for Chatelaine, Toronto Life, Saturday Night, etc.; mem. Writers' Union of Can.; Kappa Alpha; Protestant; recreations: tennis, jazz; Address: 199 Albany Ave., Toronto, Ont. M5R 3C7.

**BATTEN, Reginald A.;** film executive; b. Toronto, Ont. 19 Apr. 1932; s. Alexander and Helen (Wallace) B.; e. Forest Hill Pub. Sch., Cantab Coll. and Upper Canada Coll., Toronto, Ont.; Appleby Coll., Oakville, Ont.; McMaster Univ.; children: Reginald Jr., Kim Alexandra, Deborah Louise; retired Pres., Rabko Television Productions and Medallion Film Laboratories Ltd.; studied in Radio and T.V., N.Y. City, 1954; with Batten Films Ltd.; Soc. Motion Picture & T.V. Engrs.; Anglican; recreations: golf, skiing; Club: Craigleith Ski; Home: 19 Edgehill Rd., Islington, Ont. M9A 4N1.

**BATTEN, W. Howard,** B.A., F.C.I.I.M.E.; graphic arts executive; b. Toronto, Ont. 23 June 1929; s. W. Howard and Margaret Grace (Banfield) B.; e. Upper Canada Coll. (1939–46) and Cantab Coll. (1946–48), Toronto, Ont.; Univ. of Toronto, B.A. 1951; m. Sharon R., d. Gary Roggen, Melbourne, Fla. 5 Sept. 1976; children: Bill, Tom, Tim, Bob (Wilkins); Kathryn Ullian; Wendy Bromley; Chip Howard, Geoffrey (Batten); former Chrmn. & C.E.O., Jannock Imaging Companies Ltd., Toronto, Ont. 1986–87, retired; Pres., Hobat Ltd.; Batten Industries Ltd.; Dir.: Brights Wines Ltd.; Keswick Sharon Inc.; Hobat Holdings Ltd.; mem. Adv. Bd., Fiscal Investments Ltd.; with Rapid Grip & Batten Ltd., 1951–71 (Mgr., Ottawa Br. 1954–65; Extve. Vice Pres. 1965–71); formed Batten Graphics Ltd. 1971 (Pres. to 1986); formed Batten Gravure Ltd. 1977 (Pres. to 1986); Pres. Ottawa Bd. Trade, 1963–64; Pres., Ottawa Advt. & Sales Club 1961–62; Ottawa Extves. Assn. (1961); Pres., Internat. Pre-press Assn. 1990–92; Hon. Dir., Nat. Adv. Benevolent Assoc.; Dir., Toronto Symphony Orch.; Hon. Fellow, Inst. of Comm. & Indust. Mgrs., Birmingham, Eng.; Kappa Alpha; United Church; recreations: golf, music; Clubs: Granite; John's Island Golf; Toronto Golf; Home: 164 Cumberland St., Apt. 608, Toronto, Ont. M5R 1A8; Office: 553 Richmond St. W., Toronto, Ont. M5V 1Y6.

**BATTISTE, Charles A. (Art),** B.A., Ed.Dip.; civil servant; b. Carlsbad, New Mexico 14 Dec. 1942; s. Charles B. and Phyllis M. (Hoose); e. Univ. of Saskatchewan B.A. 1966, Ed.Dip. 1966; m. Angeline L. Hull 14 April 1968; children: Angeline Gabrielle, Katherine Alexandra, C. Robert Shaun P., Chirstopher W. Arthur E.; DEP. MIN. DEPT. OF ECONOMIC DEVELOPMENT AND TOURISM, GOVT. OF NOVA SCOTIA 1994– ; Teacher, Stoon Sep. Schools 1965–67; various positions with Govt. of Sask. ending as Research Co-ord., Sask. Econ. Devel. Bd. 1967–71; Admin. ARDA Programs, Sask. Nat. Resources, then Devel. Officer, Tourism, Northlands, Min. Expl., Dept. of Regional Econ. Expansion 1971–75; various positions with Govt. of Canada Secretary of State ending as Acting Director General, Management Info. 1975–82; various positions with Govt. of Sask. ending as Vice-Pres., Saskatchewan Property Management Corp. 1982–92; private consulting practice 1991–93; Regl. Dir., Sask. Abilities Council 1991–93; clubs: Knights of Columbus, PGK, Christ the King Players: Office: World Trade Centre, Suite 710, 1800 Argyle St., Halifax, N.S. B3J 2R7.

**BATTLE, Edward Gene,** B.Sc.; company executive; b. Mont Belvieu, Texas, 19 June 1931; s. Paul E. and Annie-Mae B.; e. Texas A & M Univ. B.Sc. (Petrol. & Geol. Engn.); CHRMN. AND DIR., NORCEN ENERGY RESOURCES LIMITED 1990– ; Dir., Liquid Carbonic Inc.; Hollinger Inc.; joined Continental Oil Co., Texas 1954; Evaluation Engr. Medallion Petroleums Ltd. (subsequently Canadian Industrial Gas & Oil Ltd. 1965) 1957, Vice Pres. Production 1965, Extve. Vice Pres. 1966, Pres. 1973; Pres. and Chief Operating Offr. Northern and Central Gas Corp. Ltd. (subsequently present Co. 1975) 1974; Pres., C.E.O. & Dir. 1975–90; mem. Assn. Prof. Engrs. Geols. & Geophysicists Alta.; Assn. Prof. Engrs. Ont.; Soc. Petrol. Engrs.; Am. Inst. Mining Metall. & Engn.; recreations: golf, tennis; Club: Calgary Golf & Country; Rosedale Golf (Toronto); Toronto; Home: 6128 Belvedere Rd., S.W., Calgary, Alta. T2V 2E1; Office: #3200, 715 – 5th Ave., S.W., Calgary, Alta. T2P 2X7.

**BATTLE, Helen Irene,** M.A., Ph.D., D.Sc., LL.D.; professor emeritus; b. London, Ont. 31 Aug. 1903; d. Edward Barrow and Elizabeth Ida (Hodgins) B.; e. Univ. of W. Ont. B.A. 1923, M.A. 1924, LL.D. 1971; Univ. of Toronto, Ph.D. 1928; D.Sc. Carleton 1971; joined Univ. of W. Ont. 1923 as Demonst. in Zool.; Instr. 1924; Asst. Prof., 1929; Assoc. Prof., 1933; Prof. 1949–72; Fellow, Am. Assn. for Advanc. of Science; Hon. Life mem. Nat. Assn. Biol. Teachers; awarded Centennial Medal 1967; Pres. (1962–63) Candn. Soc. Zool. (Hon Life Mem. 1969); Fry Medallist, Can. Soc. Zool. 1977; J.C.B. Grant Award, Can. Soc. Anat. 1977; has written scient. papers with special reference to teleosts in the field of embryology, exper. biol., spawning rhythms, embryological effects of carcinogens; Inheritance of Mackinder's brachydactyly; history of Zoology in Canada; Pi Beta Phi; Anglican; Clubs: University Women's; Soroptomist; Address: Helen I. Battle Agency, c/o The Canada Trust Company, P.O. Box 5703, Terminal A, London, Ont. N6A 4S4.

**BATTLE, Kenneth Robert,** B.A., M.Phil.; social policy expert; b. Calgary, Alta. 29 July 1947; s. Robert Felix and Lois Victoria (Morrison) B.; e. Bell High Sch. 1966; Queen's Univ. B.A. 1970; Oxford Univ. M.Phil. 1972; Commonwealth Scholar, Woodrow Wilson Fellow, Medalist in Pol. Studies; PRESIDENT, THE CALEDON INST. OF SOCIAL POLICY 1992– ; Rsch. Assoc. Queen's Univ. 1972–73; Policy Analyst, Dept. Secy. of State 1973–74; Evaluation Offr., Dept. Manpower & Immigration 1974–76; Asst. Dir. present Counc. 1976–80; Dir., National Council of Welfare 1980–92; author 'Jobs and Poverty' 1977; 'Working Together' 1978; 'In the Best Interests of the Child' 1979; 'The Working Poor' 1981; 'Medicare' 1982; 'Family Allowances for All?' 1983; 'Poverty and Public Policy' 1983; 'A Pension Primer' 1984; 'Opportunity for Reform' 1985; 'Giving and Taking: The May 1985 Budget and the Poor' 1985; 'Poverty Profile' 1985; 'The Impact of the 1985 and 1986 Budgets on Disposable Income' 1986; 'Indexation and Social Policy' 1987; 'Testing Tax Reform' 1987; 'The 1987 White Paper on Tax Reform'; 'Child Benefits in Decline'; 'Welfare Reform'; 'Social Spending and the Next Budget'; 'The 1989 Budget and Social Policy'; 'The Demise of Universality in the Canadian Welfare State'; 'Clawback'; 'Social Policy by Stealth'; 'The Privatization of Poverty'; 'Poverty Myths'; 'White Paper Whitewash: the New Child Tax Benefit'; 'Federal Social Programs: Setting the Record Straight'; 'Opening the Books on Social Spending'; Home: 17 Waterton Cres., Kanata, Ont. K2M 1Y8; Office: 620 – 1600 Scott St., Ottawa, Ont. K1Y 4N7.

**BATTLE, Robert Felix,** O.C. (1974); retired public servant. b. Delia, Alta. 9 Apr. 1916, s. John and Fay (Friedley) B.; e. Mount Royal Coll. and Univ. of Alta. 1934–37, Cooper Inst., Higher Accountancy & Business Adm. 1950; Banff Sch. of Advanced Mgmt. 1954; Nat. Defence Coll. 1969–70; m. Lois Morrison, 4 Oct. 1942; children: Kenneth, Murray, Ellen; with Albertan Publishing Co. 1937–38; Delia Crown Lumber Co. Ltd. 1938–41; International Harvester Co. 1941–42; joined fed. civil service, Indian Affairs Br., Alta., 1945; served as Field Agt., Indian Supt., Regional Supvr. of Indian Agencies (Alta., N.W.T.); Chief, Econ. Devel., Ottawa, 1960; apptd. Asst. Dir., Operations then Dir., Indian Affairs; subsequently Asst. Depy. Min., Indian & Eskimo Affairs (made Hon. Chief, 'Mountain Chinook Wind,' Stoney Tribe); Asst. Depy. Min., Dept. Indian & N. Affairs (Finance & Adm.) 1970 until retirement; served in Brit. and N.W. Europe 1942–45; recreation: sailing; Home: #21 – 909 Carolwood Dr., Victoria, B.C. V8X 3T9.

**BATTS, Michael Stanley,** B.A., D.Phil., M.L.S., D.Litt., F.R.S.C.; educator; b. Mitcham, Eng. 2 Aug. 1929; s. Stanley George and Alixe (Watson) B.; e. Sir Walter St. John Sch. London 1947; Univ. of London B.A. 1953, D.Litt. 1973; Univ. of Freiburg D.Phil. 1957; Univ. of Toronto M.L.S. 1974; m. Misao d. Ryuichi Yoshida, Victoria, B.C. 19 March 1959; one d. Anna Yuri; PROFESSOR EMERITUS OF GERMANIC STUDIES, UNIV. OF B.C.; teaching positions Univs. Mainz, Basle, Wurzburg, Calif. (Berkeley); served with Brit. Army 1947–49; Pres. Cdn. Counc. of Teachers of German 1983–86; author 'Die Form der Aventiuren im Nibelungenlied' 1961; 'Bruder Hansens Marienlieder' 1963; 'Studien zu Bruder Hansens Marienliedern' 1964; 'Gottfried von Strassburg' 1971; 'Das Nibelungenlied: Paralleldruck der Hss A, B und C nebst Lesarten der übrigen Handschriften' 1971; 'A Checklist of German Literature 1945–75' 1977; 'The Bibliography of German Literature: An Historical and Critical Survey' 1978; 'A History of Histories of German Literature: Prolegomena' 1987; co-author 'Scandinavian Literature in English Translation 1928–77' 1978; Ed. 'Essays on German Literature in Honour of G. Joyce Hallamore' 1968; 'A Short Account of a Northwest Voyage Performed in the Years 1796, 1797 and 1798' 1974; 'Translation and Interpretation: the Multi-cultural Context' 1975; 'The Canadian Settlers Guide' Part 2 1975; 'In Praise of Scribes' 1977; 'Echoes and Influences of German Romanticism' 1987; various articles and reviews on medieval and modern lit., bibliog., book hist.; mem. Canadian Assn. of Univ. Teachers of German (Pres. 1982–84); Internationale Vereinigung für germanische Sprach – und Literaturwissenschaft (Pres. 1990–95); Modern Humanities Research Assn.; Philol. Assn. Pacific Coast (Pres. 1984); Gesellschaft für interkulturelle Germanistik; recreations: tennis, gardening; Home: 8415 Granville St., Dept. 30, Vancouver, B.C. V6P 4Z9; Office: Germanic Studies, Univ. of B.C., 1873 East Mall, Vancouver, B.C. V6T 1Z1.

**BATTY, Helen Patricia,** M.D., C.C.F.P., M.Ed., F.C.F.P.; academic family physician; b. London, England 24 Feb. 1949; d. Donald John and Leah (Broadhurst) B.; e. Univ. of Toronto M.D. 1973; Ont. Inst. for Studies in Edn. M.Ed. 1982; m. John David s. R. Norman and Elinore Beattie 20 Oct. 1973; ASSOC. CHIEF, WOMEN'S COLLEGE HOSP., DEPT. OF FAMILY & COMMUNITY MEDICINE 1987– ; Medical Intern, Toronto East Gen. 1973–74; Family Practice Resident, Women's College Hosp. 1974–75; Cert., Coll. of Family Physicians of Canada 1975; Active Mem., Medical Staff, Women's College Hosp. 1975– ; Lecturer, Family & Community Med., Univ. of Toronto 1975–79; Asst. Prof. 1979–90; Assoc. Prof. 1990– ; Dir., Acad. Fellowship Program, Family & Community Med., Univ. of Toronto 1990– ; Dir., Women's Health Fellowship Program, Women's Coll. Hosp. 1992– ; Medical Co-ord., Regional Women's Health Ctr. 1991– ; Fellow, Coll. of Family Physicians of Can. 1985; Invited Expert Mem., Task Force on Healthy Lifestyles 1988–89; Invited Physician Mem., Subctte. on Smoking Reduction, Candn. Cancer Soc. 1988–90; Mem., Coll. of Family Physicians of Canada (Extve. Mem. incl. Pres., Metro Chapter 1978–83); Metro Dist. Health Council, Health Protection & Protection Ctte. 1985–90; recreations: gardening, reading, walking; Office: 76 Grenville St., Toronto, Ont. M5S 1B2.

**BAUDOUIN, Jean-Louis,** Q.C., B.A., B.C.L., Ph.D.; educator; lawyer; judge; b. Paris, France 8 Aug. 1938; s. Louis M. and Marguerite (Guérin) B.; e. Univ. de Paris B.A. 1955, Ph.D. 1962; McGill Univ. B.C.L. 1958; Univ. de Sherbrooke Doc. en droit 1990; m. Renee d. René and Marguerite Lescop 15 Dec. 1966; children: Christine, Stéphanie, Véronique, Marie-Louise; PROF. OF LAW, UNIV. DE MONTREAL 1962– ; JUDGE, COURT OF APPEAL 1989– ; Counsel to law firm Leduc-Lebel 1986–89; called to Bar of Que. 1959; cr. Q.C. 1978; Comnr. Law Reform Comn. Can. 1976–78, Vice Chrmn. of Comn. 1978–80, Special Cons. on Bioethics 1980–89; Counsel to law firm Geoffrion and Prud'homme 1980–83; to law firm Aquin-Chénard 1983–86; to Leduc-Lebel 1986–89; Vice Chrmn. Institut des Droits d'Expression Française; Chrmn. Assn. Henri Capitant; Dir. Candn. Inst. for Adm. Justice; el. to Royal Soc. of Can. 1979; mem. Candn. Bar Assn.; Assn. des Médecins de Langue Française du Can. (Bioethics Comte. 1980– ;); Dir. Instituto de Derecho Comparado de Puerto Rico; author: 'Ethique de la mort et droit à la mort' 1993; 'Produire l'Homme: de Quel Droit?' 1987; 'La Responsabilité Civile Délictuelle' 1973, 1985; 'Les Obligations' 1970, 1983, 1989, 1993; 'Terrorisme et Justice' 1970; 'Secret Professionnel et Droit au Secret' 1965; Co-Editor 'Canadian Bar Review' (1980–89); mem. various wine testing socs.; recreations: windsurfing, tennis, fishing; Club: Winchester; Home: 186 Bloomfield, Montreal, Qué. H2V 3R4; Office: Court House, 1, est Notre Dame, Montréal, Qué. H2Y 1B6.

**BAUER, Nancy Luke,** B.A.; writer; b. Chelmsford, Mass. 7 July 1934; d. Wendell Denton and Grace Elizabeth (Bridgeford) Luke; m. William s. Alfred and Virginia B. 9 June 1956; children: Ernest, Grace, John; Editor, N.B. Chapbooks 1967–83; Founder, Maritime Writers' Workshop 1976 (Teacher 1976–83, 1986); Instr., Univ. of N.B. 1975–87; Writer-in-Res., Bemidji State Univ., Minn. 1987; Cape Cod Writers Conf., summer 1983; Writer-in-Residence, Univ. of N.B. 1989–90; Jury, Explorations, The Can. Counc. 1984–85; Instr., writers' workshops throughout N.B.; Mem., Founding Ctte., WFNB 1982–83; Mem., Lit. Adv. Ctte., Prov. of N.B. 1977–82 (Chrmn. 1982); McCord Hall Writers Group 1967–83; Second Prize, CBC Lit. Comp., Short Story 1982; Mem., Un. Ch.; Writers' Union of Can.; Writers' Fed. of N.B.; Gallery Connexion Co-op (Vice-Pres., 1985–86); author: 'Flora, Write This Down' 1982, 'Wise-Ears' 1985, 'The Opening Eye' 1988, 'Samara The Whole Hearted' 1991, 'The Irrational Doorways of Mr. Gerard' 1994 (novels) & numerous articles about artists & writers in the Maritimes; Home: 252 Stanley St., Fredericton, N.B. E3B 3A3.

**BAUM, Bernard Rene,** M.Sc., Ph.D., F.R.S.C., F.L.S.; research scientist; b. Paris, France, 14 Feb. 1937; s. Kurt and Marta (Berl) B.; e. Hebrew Univ., Jerusalem Ph.D. 1966; m. Danielle, d. Robert and Raymonde Habib, 24 May 1961; 1 d.: Anat; PRINCIPAL RESEARCH SCIENTIST, CENTRE FOR LAND AND BIOLOGICAL RESOURCES RESEARCH 1991– ; Principal Research Scientist, Biosystematics Research Centre, Agriculture Canada 1980– ;and Section Head 1980–88; Agric. Canada: rsch. scientist, Plant Rsch. Inst. 1966; section head, Vascular Plants Sect. and sr. rsch. scientist Biosystematics Rsch. Inst. 1974; Principal rsch. scientist, Biosystematics Rsch. Ctr. 1980–90; Principal rsch. scientist, Centre for Land and Biological Resources Rsch. 1990– ; Mem., Internat. Comn. for the Nomenclature of Cultivated Plants 1987– ; maj. spkr. at various internat. symposia; U.S.D.A. Merit Award 1966; Lawson Medal, Can. Bot. Assn. 1979; Fellow, Royal Soc. of Can. Academy III; Assoc. Ed. Can. Jour. of Bot. 1974–79, 1986– ; Assoc. Ed. Euphytica 1987– ; Assoc. Ed. G.R.A.C.E. 1991– ; Assoc. Ed. Plant Systematics and Evolution 1991– ; author: 'Material for an international oat register' 1972; 'Oats: wild and cultivated. A monograph of the genus Avena' 1977; 'The genus Tamarix' 1978; 'Barley Register' 1983; 150 research publs.; recreation: swimming; Home: 15 Murray St., Ottawa, Ont. K1N 9M5; Office: Centre for Land and Biological Resources Research, Saunders Bldg., Central Experimental Farm, Agriculture Canada, Ottawa, Ont. K1A 0C6.

**BAUM, Gregory G.,** M.A., Th.D. (R.C.), O.C.; university professor; author; b. Berlin, Germany, 20 June 1923; s. Franz S. and Bettie (Meyer) B.; came to Canada (from Eng.) 1940; e. McMaster Univ., B.A. (Math and Phys.) 1946; Ohio State Univ., M.A. (Math) 1947; Univ. of Fribourg, Switzerland, Th.D. 1956; Hon. Doctorates; Huron Coll., St. Francis Xavier, Ohio Wesleyan, Lafayette, Waterloo Lutheran, McMaster & Dubuque; PROF. OF RELIGIOUS STUDIES, McGILL UNIV.; mem. Edit. Comte., Relations; author of 'That They May Be One' 1958; 'The Jews and the Gospel' 1961 (rev. ed. paperback under title 'Is the New Testament Anti-semitic'); 'Progress and Perspective' 1962 (paperback ed. under title 'Catholic Quest for Christian Unity' 1965); 'Ecumenical Theology Today' 1965; 'Ecumenical Theology No. 2' 1967; 'The Credibility of the Church Today' 1968; 'Faith and Doctrine' 1969; 'Man Becoming' 1970; 'New Horizon' 1972; 'Religion and Alienation'1975; 'The Social Imperative' 1978; 'Catholics and Canadian Socialism' 1980; 'The Priority of Labour' 1982; 'Ethics and Economics' 1984; 'Theology and Society' 1987; 'Compassion and Solidarity' 1988; 'The Church in Quebec' 1991; Officer of the Order of Canada 1990; mem., Candn. Theol. Soc.; Candn. Soc. for Study of Religion; Cath. Theol. Soc. of America; Address: Religious Studies, McGill Univ., Montreal, Qué. H3A 2A7.

**BAUMANN, Alexander Sasa;** student; athlete (swimmer); b. Prague, Czechoslovakia 21 Apr. 1964; s. Dr. Bedrich and Vera Eva (Vanura) B.; e. Laurentian Univ., Hons. B.A. in Pol. Sci. (cum laude) 1990; TWO GOLD MEDALS IN 1984 OLYMPICS; TWO WORLD RECORDS IN 200M AND 400M INDIVIDUAL MEDLEY 1984; Bronze Medal 400m individual medley Pan Am Games 1979; World Record for 200m Individual Medley, Germany 1981; World Swimmer of the Year 1981, 1984; Ontario Athlete of the Year 1981, 1984; Two Gold Medals and World Record for 200m Individual Medley Commonwealth Games 1982; Two Gold Medals, one Silver and three Bronze, World Universide 1983; World record in 400m Individual Medley Olympic Trials 1984; Order of Can. 1984; Athlete of the Year 1984; one of five recipients Young Canadians Award 1984; Candn. Sports Hall of Fame 1988; Candn. Amateur Sports Hall of Fame 1987; Order of Ontario 1988; Home: 48 Minnie St., South Port, Queensland 4215, Australia.

**BAUMGART, Alice Jean,** B.S.N., M.Sc., Ph.D.; university professor and administrator; b. Edmonton, Alta. 7 Feb. 1936; d. George A. and Amanda B.; e. Univ. of B.C. B.S.N.; McGill Univ. M.Sc.; Univ. of Toronto Ph.D.; Vice-Principal (Human Services), Queen's University 1988–..; Prof., Univ. of B.C. 1964–73; Prof. & Dean, School of Nursing, Queen's Univ. 1977–88; Pres., Canadian Nurses Assn. 1990–92; Candn. Assn. of Univ. Schools of Nursing 1986–88; Western Region 1968–70; Ont. Region 1981–83; Dir., VON Canada 1986–92; extensive involvement with govt. & assns. as external liaison, extve. & sci. ctte. mem., etc.; Her Majesty the Queen, 25th anniversary medal; Milbank Found. Faculty Assn. Fellowship; One of the Women of the Year, 'Vancouver Province' 1970; Canadian Nurses Found. Fellowship 1962–63; Kellogg Found. Grad. Awards 1963–64; fellowships: 3M Internat. Council of Nurses 1973–74; involved in var. research projects; acts as consultant to other research projects; Mem., Candn. Public Health Assn.; Candn. Research Inst. for the Advancement of Women; Registered Nurses Assn. of B.C.; Registered Nurses Assn. of Ont.; author of over 80 pubns. incl. journal articles, conf. proceedings, comnd. reports, etc.; over 80 keynote addresses, invitational lectures, seminars & workshops to profl. nursing & health related groups worldwide; Home: 223 East Plum St., Elizabethtown, PA 17012.

**BAXENDALE, Michael Stanley;** publisher; b. Brighouse, Yorks., Eng. 27 Sept. 1937; s. Stanley and Dora Maria (Day) B.; e. King Edward VI Sch. Chelmsford, Eng.; Univ. of Toronto, Comm.; Univ. of Sask., Hist. & Eng.; two s.: Dean, Bradley; 1 d.: Alison; CHRMN. & C.E.O., OPTIMUM PUBLISHING INTERNATIONAL INC., EDITIONS OPTIMUM INTERNATIONAL INC. 1975– ; Dir. Optimum Publishing USA Inc.; Atwater Press Inc.; Hamdale Publishing Co.; Asst. to Vice Pres. Kelvinator Canada 1958–60; Market Analyst Montreal Standard Publishing Co. 1960–62, Sales and Mktg. Mgr. 1962–67, Asst. Dir. 1967–71; Dir. Info. Service Div. Montreal Star 1971–75; Founder, Optimum Publishing International Inc. 1975– ; served with RCR 1955–58, Parachutist, mem. Special Combat Force (MSF); 1st Vice Pres. Montréal Internat. Book Fair; Founding mem. Montréal Publishers Roundtable; mem. Book Publishers Counc.; Dir. Am. Mktg. Assn. (Past Vice Pres.); author: 'The Role of Marketing in Corporate Growth' 1965; 'This Land is Our Land: The Mohawk Revolt at Oka' 1990; mag. articles Candn. & Internat. pub.; co-author various publs.; Anglican; recreations: sailing, gliding, skiing, fishing; Home: 437 Grosvenor Ave., Westmount, Qué.

**BAXTER, James Douglas,** M.D., C.M., M.Sc., F.R.C.S.(C); educator; otolaryngologist; b. Montreal, Que. 2 Oct. 1923; e. Mem. Univ. Coll. Nfld. 1940–42; McGill Univ. M.D., C.M. 1947, M.Sc. 1952; m. Dorothy Rowena Hardy 7 June 1947; two d. Carolyn Ann, Barbara Hardy; EMERITUS PROF. OF OTOLARYNGOLOGY, McGILL UNIV., Chrmn. 1970–89, Prof. 1972–90; Otolaryngol.-in-Chief, Royal Victoria Hosp. 1970–90; Montreal Gen. Hosp. 1977–90; Dir. Inst. of Otolaryngol. McGill Univ. and Royal Victoria Hosp. 1970–90; Consultant, Reddy Mem. Hosp., Queen Elizabeth Hosp., Montreal Chest Hosp., Jewish Gen. Hosp.; Resident, Royal Victoria Hosp., Queen Mary Veterans' Hosp., Grad. Hosp. Univ. of Pa., Children's Hosp. of Philadelphia 1947–53; rec'd J.B. Collip Fellowship in Med. Research 1951–52; joined McGill Univ. 1954; apptd. to Dept. Otolaryngol. Royal Victoria Hosp. 1953, The Children's Mem. Hosp. (now Montreal Children's Hosp.) 1954; apptd. to Med. Staff Shriner's Hosp. for Crippled Children as Otolaryngol. 1969; Dir. of On-Going Survey and Project of Ear Disease and Hearing Loss Inuit Population Candn. Arctic under auspices McGill Baffin Program since 1972; mem. CPHA Task Force on the Health Effects of Increased Flying Activity in the Labrador area 1985–87; awarded Commemorative Medal for 125th Anniversary of Candn. Confederation; author or co-author numerous articles, papers, reports; Dir. SEVEC (Soc. for Educ. Visits and Exchanges in Canada) 1981–84 (Adv. Counc. 1984–93); Fellow, Am. Acad. Otolaryngol.; Am. Laryngol. Assn. (2nd Vice Pres. 1971–72); Am. Broncho-Oesophaol. Soc. (Vice Pres. 1978–79); mem. Candn. Med. Assn.; Candn. Otolaryngol. Soc. (Council 1968–76, Program Chrmn. 1970, Secy. 1970–72, Vice Pres. 1972–74, Pres. 1974–75); Montreal Medico-Chirurgical Soc. (Pres. Otolaryngol. Sec. 1965–67); Pan Am. Assn. Oto-Rhino-Laryngol. & Broncho-Esophagol. (Vice Pres. 1974–76, 1980–84); Internat. Assn. Bronchol. & Esophagol.; Assn. Otolaryngols. Prov. Que. (Vice Pres. 1971–72); Am. Laryngol., Rhinol. & Otol. Soc. Inc. (Secy. E. Sec. 1979–80); Collegium Oto-Rhino-Laryngologicum Amicitiae Sacrum; Protestant; Home: Apt. #12 – 1509 Sherbrooke St. W., Montreal, Qué. H3G 1M1.

**BAXTER, Judith Dianne;** artist; writer; b. Saint John, N.B. 26 June 1942; d. Arthur G. and Margaret S. (MacVicar) Barnes; e. Saint John Vocational Sch. 1960; m. Glendon s. Sydney and Florence Baxter 7 March 1964; three d. Cherylynn Leigh, Wanda Lynn, Jennifer Joan; studied art with Ted Campbell and Fred Ross; fashion illus. MRA Saint John 1962; Head Artist Robert Simpson Co. Halifax 1964; set designer Rothesay Playhouse 1969; freelance illus. since 1969; assoc. with Boyce Gallery Saint John; art rep. numerous private, corporate and pub. colls.; cons. N.B. Dept. Tourism, Recreation & Heritage; visiting artist Dist. 19 Sch. Bd.; Dir.: John Fisher Meml. Museum; Candn. Museum of Civilization; Kingston Farmers Market; author '845 Kingston Peninsula, A Pencil Sketch Tour' 1983; co-author 'Magic Seagull' children's 1978; Vice Pres. Atlantic Nat. P. Cons. Women's Fedn.; N.B. Writers Fedn.; Assn. Museums N.B.; mem. Clifton Royal Recreation Council; Presbyterian; Address: R.R.1 Clifton Royal, Kings Co., N.B. E0G 1N0.

**BAXTER, Malcolm R.;** executive; b. Saint John, N.B. 16 Jan. 1935; s. Robert W. and Mary A. (Lamb) B.; e. Saint John High Sch. 1953; Acadia Univ 1953–55; m. Kathryn d. W. Gordon and Thelma Ross 21 Sept. 1957; children: Robert, Wendy, Kathy; CHRMN., PRES. & C.E.O., BAXTER FOODS LTD. and subsidiary companies 1973– ; Chrmn., Atcan Capital Corp.; Pres. and Dir., Charisma Holdings Ltd.; BMC Ltd.; Kelly Tire Ltd.; Pres. & Dir., Atlantic Insurance Agency Ltd.; Dir., Bank of Nova Scotia; mem. Engn. Dept., City of Saint John 1955–57; Sales Mgr. present Co. 1957, Vice Pres. and Gen. Mgr. 1961; Past Pres. N.B. Prot. Orphans' Home & Children's Foundation; Gov. Olympic Trust of Canada; Dir. & Past Chrmn. Nat. Dairy Council Can.;

Dir. Milk Industry Foundation Washington, D.C.; Freemason; Shriner; United Church; mem. Saint John Bd. of Trade; recreations: yachting, fishing, hunting; Clubs: Royal Kennebeccasis Yacht (Past Commodore); Riverside Country; Union; Royal Ocean Racing, London, Eng.; Home: 5 Maple Grove Terrace, Saint John, N.B. E2K 2H9; Office: 91 Millidge Ave., Saint John, N.B. E2K 2M3.

**BAY, Eli David,** B.A.; entrepreneur; transformation catalyst; b. Dauphin, Man. 13 June 1947; s. Harry and Sadie (Kovnats) B.; e. Dauphin Coll. & Tech. Inst. 1965; Univ. of Man. B.A. 1968; m. Masza d. Wolf and Sara Szechter 16 Apr. 1975; children: Ariel, Daniel; FOUNDER & PRES., THE RELAXATION RESPONSE LTD. 1978– ; Personnel Offr., Xerox of Can. 1969–70; Extve. Asst., Min. of Fin., Govt. of Man. 1970–72; Ind. Futures Rscher. (U.K.) 1972; Rsch. Fellow, IJA (UK) 1972–73; Teacher, Bor. of North York 1974; Consultant, Min. of Fin., Govt. of Man. 1975; Personnel Offr., Ont. Min. of Rev. 1976–78; Host, TVOntario Series 'Beyond Stress,' 'Well-Being'; pioneering rschr., synthesizer & trainer of psychotechnologies for personal & social transformation; work recommended in 'Superlearning,' 'Healthier Workers,' 'Stress for Success', 'Curing Nuclear Madness,' 'Supermemory'; Panentheist; pol.: Green; Dir., Inst. of Cultural Affairs; mem., Assn. Humanistic Psychology; Inst. of Noetic Sci.; Inst. for the Adv. of Health; Greenpeace; Global Family; recreations: reading, parenting, music, collecting quotations, meditation; Home: 226 Wychwood Ave., Toronto, Ont. M6C 2T3; Office: 858 Eglinton Ave. W., Toronto, Ont. M6C 2B6.

**BAYCROFT, The Right Rev. John Arthur,** M.A., D.D., D.S.Litt., E.G.C.L.J., CMLJ; anglican bishop; b. Redcar, Yorkshire, England 2 June 1933; s. Robert and Mary Alice (Williams) B.; e. Sir Wm. Turner Sch.; Christ Coll., Cambridge (Synge sch.) B.A. 1954, M.A. 1958; Ripon Hall, Oxford (G.O.E.) 1955; Trinity Coll., Toronto B.D. 1959; m. Joan d. V. Lake 8 June 1955; children: John Michael, Sally Elizabeth, Anne Victoria; BISHOP OF OTTAWA, ANGLICAN CHURCH OF CANADA 1993– ; Rector, Loughborough 1955–57; Asst. Rector, St. Matthew's Ch., Ottawa 1957–62; Rector, Perth, Ont. 1962–67; St. Matthias Ch., Ottawa 1967–84; Christchurch Cathedral & Dean of Ottawa 1984–86; Suffragan Bishop of Ottawa, Anglican Ch. of Can. 1985–93; formerly Archdeacon of Ottawa W.; Canon Theol. of the Diocese of Ottawa; Mem., Anglican/R. Cath. Internat. Comn.; Angl. Co-Chrmn., Angl./R. Cath. Dialogue of Can.; lectr., Carleton Univ.; Mem., Fac. of Theol., St. Paul Univ. (Owen Meml. Lectr. 1987); Hon. D.D. Montreal Diocesan Theol. Coll.; D.S.Litt.(jur. dig.), Thornloe Univ.; Mem., Am. Acad. of Religion; Soc. of Bib. Lit.; Candn. Ch. Hist. Soc.; author: 'The Anglican Way' 1980, 'The Eucharistic Way' 1982, 'The Way of Prayer' 1983 and others as well as num. scholarly articles; recreations: theatre, art, ballet; club: Nat. Press; Home: 97 Java St., Ottawa, Ont. K1Y 3L5; Office: 71 Bronson Ave., Ottawa, Ont. K1R 6G6.

**BAYDA, Hon. Edward Dmytro,** B.A., LL.B., LL.D. (Hon.); judge; b. Alvena, Sask. 9 Sept. 1931; s. Dmytro Andrew and Mary (Bilinski) B.; e. Alvena (Sask.) High Sch.; City Park Coll. Inst., Saskatoon, Sask., 1948; Univ. of Sask. B.A. 1951, LL.B. 1953; m. Marie Thérèse Yvonne, d. Joseph Rosaire Gagné, 28 May 1953; children: Paula, Christopher, Margot, Marie-Thérèse, Sheila, Kathryn; CHIEF JUSTICE OF SASKATCHEWAN, 1981– ; called to Bar of Sask. 1954; cr. Q.C. 1966; practised law in Regina, Sask. 1953–72; Sr. Partner, Bayda, Halvorson, Scheibel & Thompson 1966–72; Queen's Bench 1972; Justice of Appeal 1974; Past Nat. (Can.) Registrar, Assn. Kinsmen Clubs (Past Pres., Regina Kinsmen); K. of M.; R. Catholic; Club: Assiniboia (Past Dir.); Home: 3000 Albert St., Regina, Sask. S4S 3N7; Office: Court House, Regina, Sask. S4P 3V7.

**BAYEFSKY, Aba,** C.M., R.C.A.; artist; b. Toronto, Ont. 7 Apr. 1923; s. Samuel and Hetty (Simon) B.; e. Central Tech. Sch., Art. Dept., Toronto, Ont.; Acad. Julian, Paris, France; m. Evelyn, d. of Paul and Bessie Swartz, Oshawa, Ont.; children: Anne, Edra, Eban; Staff mem., Ont. Coll. Art, Toronto 1957–88; Dir., art classes, Hart House, Univ. of Toronto 1957–69; awarded French Govt. Scholar., 1947–48; Can. Council Fellowship for travel and study in India; mem., Internat. Jury for 2nd Internat. Exhn. prints, Tokyo; won first Purchase Prize of Candn. Soc. of Painters in Watercolour, 1953; J.W.L. Forster award of Ont. Soc. Artists, 1958; Work in war art coll. of Nat. Gallery Ottawa; Nat. Gallery of Victoria, Melbourne, Australia; Art Gallery of Ont.; Hamilton; London (Ont.); Sarnia; Metropolitan Museum, N.Y.; Library of Congress, Wash.; Hebrew Univ., Jerusalem; École des Beaux Arts, Que.; Loyola Coll., Que.; Concordia Univ., Montreal; Hart House, Univ. of Toronto; Beaverbrook Gallery, Fredericton, N.B.; and various colls. in Can., U.S.A., India; 35 one-man exhns. since 1942 including 'Bayefsky's Toronto: A Celebration of the City and its people,' The Market Gallery, Toronto, 1982; 'Bayefsky at the Market,' Ont. Coll. of Art 1976; Exhibition of Portfolio 'Legends' and 'Forces of Earth and Sky,' Candn. Consulate, N.Y. 1973; and Candn. Embassy, Washington, D.C. 1971; Retrospective Exbn. Art Gallery of Hamilton 1973; Albert White Gallery, Toronto 1966; three months of painting, drawing and travel in Japan and Korea; principally in the studio of Master Tattoo Artist, Mitsuaki Ohwada, in Yokohama, Japan 1982–83; 'A Japanese Sketchbook' one-man exhibition, Gustafsson Gallery, Toronto, 1983; Major Portrait Retrospective, Justina M. Barnicke Gallery, Hart House, Univ. of Toronto 1986; 'Aba Bayefsky Revisited' 40 year retrospective, Koffler Gall. 1989; awarded Order of Can. 1979; awarded Commemorative Medal for 125th Anniversary of Candn. Confederation 1992; served in 2nd World War with R.C.A.F. as Official War Artist, 1942–46; mem. Candn. Soc. Graphic Art (Past Pres.); Candn. Soc. Painters in Watercolour; Candn. Group of Painters (Past Pres.); Fed. of Candn. Artists (Past Pres., Ont. Region); Home: 7 Paperbirch Dr., Don Mills, Ont. M3C 2E6.

**BAYEFSKY, Anne Fruma,** M.A., LL.B., M.Litt.; educator; b. Toronto, Ont. 8 Nov. 1953; d. Aba and Evelyn D. (Swartz) B.; e. Univ. of Toronto B.A. 1975, M.A. 1976, LL.B. 1979; Oxford Univ. M.Litt. 1982; m. Raj Anand 6 July 1986; three d. Rachel, Sarah, Michelle; ASSOC. PROF. OF LAW, UNIV. OF OTTAWA 1981– ; called to Bar of Ont. 1983; legal research/cons. to Candn. Human Rights Comn. 1978, Ont. Human Rights Comn. 1979, Law Reform Comn. Can. 1985, 1990; Stagiaire, Eur. Comn. Human Rights, Strasbourg 1981; Special Adv. to Candn. Del. UN Gen. Assembly 1984; Special Observer to Candn. Delegation UN General Assembly 1989; Advisor to the Candn. Delegation to the UN World Conference on Human Rights 1993; Fellow, Centre for Study Human Rights Columbia Univ. 1985; Chair, Bds. of Inquiry under Ont. Human Rights Code 1986– ; mem. Exec. Bd. Candn. Council on Internat. Law 1984–88; Adv. Council Interights, Internat. Centre for Legal Protection Human Rights, London, Eng. 1986– ; Pres. Candn. Sect., Internat. Assn. Philos. Law & Social Philos. 1985–87; mem., Extve. Counc., Am. Soc. of Internat. Law 1987–90; Bd. of Review and Develop., Am. Soc. of Internat. Law 1992– ; mem., Ctte. on Internat. Law in Municipal Courts, Internat. Law Assn. 1989– ; Ctte. on the Enforcement of Human Rights Law, Internat. Law Assn. 1993– ; Recipient, 1992 Bora Laskin National Fellowship in Human Rights Research, SSHRC; author: 'International Human Rights Law: Use in Canadian Charter of Rights and Freedoms Litigation' 1992; 'Canada's Constitution Act 1982 and Amendments: A Documentary History' 1989; Ed. 'Legal Theory Meets Legal Practice' 1988; Assoc. Ed. 'Canadian Yearbook of Human Rights' Vols. 1–4 (1983–87); Co-ed. 'Equality Rights and the Canadian Charter of Rights and Freedoms' 1985; Consulting Ed., 'The Canadian Journal of Law and Jurisprudence' 1992– ; mem. ed. bd. 'Canadian Journal of Women and the Law' 1985–87 (mem. Adv. Bd. 1987–93); author various articles internat. & constitutional law, human rights; Office: Ottawa, Ont. K1N 6N5.

**BAYER, Fern Patricia,** B.A., M.A.; curator; b. Montreal, Que. 23 Oct. 1949; d. Dr. George James and Catherine Marie Gloria (Boucher) B.; e. Internat. Sch. of Sacred Heart; McGill Univ. B.A. 1971; Univ. Internaz. dell'Arte, Italy, dipl. Museum Sci. 1972; Univ. of Toronto M.A. 1975; CHIEF CURATOR, GOVT. OF ONT. ART COLLECTION 1977– ; curator for major internat. contemporary art exhbns. in Middle East, Japan, Korea and Europe; Teaching Asst., Univ. of Toronto 1975–76; freelance art cons. 1975–77; R. Catholic; author: 'The Ontario Collection' 1984, and various articles; contrib. (with Eric Arthur): 'From Front Street to Queen's Park' 1979; Home: 131 Bloor St. W., Apt. 1017, Toronto, Ont. M5S 1S3; Office: c/o Fitzhenry & Whiteside, 9 Granton Ave., Richmond Hill, Ont. L4B 2N5.

**BAYLEY, C.C.,** M.A., Ph.D., F.R.S.C. (1961); university professor; b. Congleton, Eng. 5 March 1907; s. Harry and Hannah (Calvert) B.; e. Univ. of Manchester, B.A. 1928, M.A. 1929; Univ. of Marburg (1930); Univ. of Chicago, Ph.D. 1938; m. Ethel Mary, d. U. B. Woolliscroft, 11 Sept. 1936; two d. Ann Margaret, Susan Nancy; PROF. DEPT. OF HISTORY, McGILL UNIV. (Chrmn. of Dept. 1961–65); Lectr. in Hist., Univ. of Toronto, 1931; Asst. Prof. of Colorado Coll., 1932; Univ. Fellow, Univ. of Chicago, 1935; joined McGill Faculty, 1935; Guggenheim Fellowship 1948; Can. Council Sr. Fellowship 1966; Killam Fellowship 1970; publications: 'The Formation of the German College of Electors' 1949; 'War and Society in Renaissance Florence' 1961; 'Mercenaries for the Crimea: The German, Swiss, and Italian Legions in British Service, 1854–1856' 1977; Anglican; recreation: travel; Home: 3610 McTavish St., Apt. 34, Montreal, Qué. H3A 1Y2.

**BAYLEY, Stanley Thomas,** B.Sc., Ph.D.; scientist; educator; b. Grays, Essex, Eng. 5 Nov. 1926; s. Thomas James and Grace Furber (Manwaring) B.; e. Palmer's Boys Sch. Grays 1943; King's Coll. Univ. of London B.Sc. 1946, Ph.D. 1950; m. Betty Evelyn d. Thomas William and Edith Florence Cole 9 Sept. 1950; two d. Elizabeth Grace, Valerie Anne; PROFESSOR EMERITUS, McMASTER UNIV. 1992– ; Prof. of Biol. 1967–92; Interim Dir. Inst. for Molecular Biol. & Biotechnol. 1985–88, Chrmn. of Biol. 1968–74; Nuffield Rsch. Fellow King's Coll. Univ. of London 1951–52; Rsch. Offr. Div. Biosciences Nat. Rsch. Council, Ottawa 1952–67; Visiting Sci. Imp. Cancer Rsch. Fund London, Eng. 1974–75; recipient Candn. Centennial Medal 1967; Queen's Silver Jubilee Medal 1977; author or co-author over 70 papers internat. sci. jours.; recreations: music, photography; Home: 163 Dromore Cres., Hamilton, Ont. L8S 4B3; Office: McMaster Univ., 1280 Main St. W., Hamilton, Ont. L8S 4K1.

**BAYLY, John Uniacke,** B.A., LL.B., Q.C.; barrister and solicitor; b. Toronto, Ont. 20 Apr. 1945; s. George Henry Uniacke and Fay Mavis (Anderson) B.; e. Upper Can. Coll. (primary); Trinity Coll. Sch. Port Hope (jr. matric.); N. Toronto Coll. Inst. (sr. matric. 1964); Univ. of Toronto B.A. 1967; Osgoode Hall Law Sch. LL.B. 1971; m. Cristine d. Camillo and Lois (Darroch) Milani 29 Dec. 1967; children: Jennifer, Melissa, Timothy, Katherine; private law practice, counsel to Dene Nation and Metis Assn. of N.W.T. 1981–88; called to Bar of Ont. 1973; Asst. Crown Atty. Thunder Bay, Ont. 1973–74; assoc. with Brand & Co., Yellowknife 1974–78, Counsel to Inuit groups Mackenzie Valley Pipeline Inquiry 1974–76; Asst. Crown Atty. and Dir. of Pub. Prosecutions N.W.T. 1978–79; Extve. Dir. Legal Services Bd. N.W.T. 1979–80; Counsel on Staff of Dene Nation 1980–82; Principal, Bayly and Associates, currently Bayly Williams Barristers and Solicitors 1982– ; Chrmn., Task Force on Spousal Assault in N.W.T. 1984–85; Dir. Great Slave Sledging Co.; mem. Bd. Internat. Comn. Folk Law & Legal Pluralism; Chrmn., Denendeh Conservation Bd. 1987–91; mem., Historic Site & Monuments Bd. of Can. 1989–91; R.C.M.P. Public Complaints Comn. 1989– ; columnist weekly newspapers 'News/North' (Yellowknife) 1979–91, 'The Hub' (Hay River) 1981– ; Nunatsiaq News (Iqaluit) 1979–90; author various articles legal journs.; completed commemorative dog sled mail run N.W.T. (450 miles) 1980; Co-winner, Cadogan Award as outstanding journalist in a Cdn. weekly newspaper 1983; mem. Law Soc. N.W.T. (Chrmn. Discipline Comte. 1978– ;); Law Soc. Upper Can.; Candn. Bar Assn.; Anglican; Chancellor, Anglican Diocese of the Arctic 1993– ; recreations: canoeing, dog sledding, reading, gardening; Home: (P.O. Box 2882) 1 Bayly Burrow, Yellowknife, N.W.T. X1A 2R2; Office: (P.O. Box 2882) #203 – 5102 – 50th Ave., Yellowknife, N.W.T. X1A 2R2.

**BAYNE, James Ronald Douglas,** B.A., M.D., F.R.C.P.(C), F.A.C.P.; educator; physician; b. Sherbrooke, Que. 25 Jan. 1923; s. Henry Douglas and Lillian Frances (Younger) B.; e. Bishops Coll. Sch. 1935–40; McGill Univ. B.A., M.D./C.M. 1940–47; Fellow Royal Coll. of Physicians and Surgeons of Can. 1972; m. Barabara d. Herbert and Elsie Sheard 7 June 1954; children: Jennifer, Lillian, Jessica, Sarah; PROF. OF MED. EMERITUS, MCMASTER UNIV.; post-grad. training Internal Med. Roy. Victoria Hosp., Montreal and New England Med. Centre 1948–53; post-grad. training in Geriatrics, West Middlesex Hosp., Engl. 1953–56; Gen. Practice Sherbrooke Que. 1956–59; Physician-in-Chief Gerontology and Chief of Med. Ste. Ann's Veterans Hosp., Montreal 1960–70; co-ed. 'Research Issues in Aging' 1980; author 'Use of Geriatric Evaluation & Placement Service as a Resource for Teaching' in Geriatric Medicine Collamore Press 1981; 'Strengthening Research - Policy Relations in the Field of Aging and Health' in Aging and Health, Linking Research and Public Policy 1989; Chrmn. Gerontology Rsch. Counc. of Ont. 1979–90; Vice-Chrmn. Nat. Adv. Counc. on Aging 1980–81; Pres. Candn. Assn. on Gerontology 1983–87; Chrmn., Candn. Coalition of Nat. Organizations with Interest in Medication Use and Elderly Persons 1989–90; Life Mem., Ont. Med. Assoc. 1990; Fellow, Am. Coll. of Physicians; Gerontological Soc. of Am.; Am. Geriatrics Soc.; Surveyor, Candn. Counc. on Health Facilities Accreditation 1973–92; Honoured by the Ontario Gerontology Assn. who established the Bayne-Galloway Annual Rsch. Lectureship in Gerontology; Honoured by McMaster Univ. in setting up the Bayne Annual Gerontology Internship, and the Ronald Bayne Lecture in Geriatrics; awarded Commemorative Medal for 125th Anniversary of Candn. Confederation by the Governor General in recognition of significant contribution to compatriots, community and to Canada; recreations: gardening; Home: 69 Dromore Cres., Hamilton, Ont. L8S 4B1.

**BAYNE, Sir Nicholas Peter,** , M.A., D.Phil., KCMG; british diplomat; b. London, England 15 Feb. 1937; s. Ronald Christopher and Elizabeth Margaret (Ashcroft) B.; e. Christ Church, Oxford M.A. 1959, D.Phil. 1964; m. Diana d. Thomas and Florence Wilde 16 Sept. 1961; children: Thomas, Charles (dec.), Richard; BRITISH HIGH COMMISSIONER, OTTAWA 1992– ; entered British Diplomatic Service 1961; served in Manila, Bonn, Paris, Foreign & Commonwealth Office and HM Treasury, London 1961–82; attached to Royal Inst. of International Affairs, London 1982–83; British Ambassador to Zaire and (non-resident) Congo, Rwanda, Burundi 1983–84; UK Rep. to OECD, Paris 1985–88; Economic Dir., Foreign & Commonwealth Office 1988–92; co-author: 'Hanging Together: The Seven Power Summits' 1984, 2nd ed. '87 (also German, Japanese & Italian versions); Office: 80 Elgin St., Ottawa, Ont. K1P 5K7.

**BAZAN, Bernardo Carlos,** M.A., Ph.D.; university professor; b. Mendoza, Argentina 26 Oct. 1939; s. Bernardo Samuel and Delfina (Sosa) B.; e. Univ. of Cuyo (Argentina) M.A. 1962; Univ. of Louvain (Belgium) Ph.D.Phil. 1967, Ph.D.Med. Studies 1972; m. Agueda s. Pedro and Aurora Reus 17 Feb. 1963; children: Guillermo, Maria Victoria, Mariela; PROFESSOR, UNIV. OF OTTAWA 1979– ; Full Prof., Univ. of Cuyo 1969; Assoc. Prof., Univ. of Ottawa 1977; Chair, Dept. of Philosophy 1980; Dean, Faculty of Arts 1991– ; Visiting Prof., Catholic Univ. of America 1983; Pres., Soc. de Philosophie de l'Outaouais 1987–89; Mem. of the Bureau, Soc. for Mediaeval Philosophy 1989–93; Soc. internat. de Philosphie Médiévale 1987–97; Office: Ottawa, Ont. K1N 6N5.

**BAZERGUI, André,** B.Sc.A., Ph.D.; educational administrator; b. Cairo, Egypt 8 Sept. 1940; e. Ecole Polytechnique B.Sc.A. 1963; Univ. of Sheffield Ph.D. 1966; m. Maria Palffy; children: Aline, Marc-André, Nives; DEAN AND DIRECTOR GENERAL, ECOLE POLYTECHNIQUE 1990– ; Assistant Prof., Ecole Polytechnique 1966–71; Assoc. Prof. 1971–78; Head, Applied Mechanics Section, Dept. of Mech. Engr. 1978–85; Prof. 1978– ; Mem., Order of Eng. of Qué.; Candn. Acad. of Engr.; Candn. Soc. for Mech. Engr.; Am. Soc. of Mech. Eng.; Soc. for Exp. Mech.; Soc. of Automotive Engr.; Fellow, CSME 1990; G.H. Duggan Medal (CSME) 1987; Fellow, E.I.C. 1981; NATO Scholarship 1965; Athlone Fellowship (UK) 1963; Kennecott Cooper Corp. Scholarship 1962; Principal (co)author, 'Résistance des matériaux' 1985, 2nd ed. 1993; Home: 20 Russell, Ville Mont Royal, Qué. H3P 1A8; Office: C.P. 6079, Succ. A., Montréal, Qué. H3C 3A7.

**BEACH, Donald Irving,** F.C.A.; chartered accountant; b. New Liskeard, Ont. 11 June 1937; s. Howard Harkness and Ida Irene (Irving) B.; e. New Liskeard High Sch.; Queen's Univ. C.A. 1960; m. Patricia d. Clarence and Marjorie Wadge 20 May 1961; children: Carol-Anne, John Elmer; Nat. Tax Partner, Coopers & Lybrand 1987–..; joined Ont. Treasury Dept. 1960–63; Candn. Tax Found. 1963–65; present firm 1965; author 'Business and Securities Valuation' 1971; 'Tax Guide for Construction Contractors' 1974; 'Tax Guide for the Real Estate Professional' 1977; contbg. ed. 'Financial Times of Canada'; Pres. Inst. C.A.'s Ont. 1987–88; Gov. and mem. Exec. Ctte. Candn. Inst. C.A.'s; mem. Candn. Assn. Bus. Valuator's; Bd. Trade Metrop. Toronto; Treas. Official Bd. Greenwood Un. Ch.; Club: Ontario; Home: Greenwood, Ont. L0H 1H0.

**BEACH, Russell J.;** manufacturer; b. Cupar, Sask. 5 June 1910; s. Olin A. and Charlotte (Wolfe) B.; e. pub. and high schs. Ottawa, Ont.; m. Beryl d. Charles and Anne Sheffield 20 May 1933; two d. Jill Porter, Lynda Smith; Pres., Beach Industries Ltd. 1949–87; Vice Pres. Beach Motors Ltd. 1929–49; Pres. Candn. Owners & Pilots Assn.; Sr. Vice Pres. Internat. Council Aircraft Owners & Pilots Assn.; Past Pres., Smiths Falls Rotary; Ottawa Ad and Sales Club; Address: P.O. Box 9, Smiths Falls, Ont. K7A 4S9.

**BEAGRIE, George Simpson,** D.Sc. (Hon.), D.D.S., F.D.S., R.C.S. (Edin. & Eng.), F.R.C.D.(C), F.I.C.D., F.A.C.D.; educator; b. Peterhead, Scot. 14 Sept. 1925; s. late Eliza Lawson and George B.; came to Canada 1968; e. High Sch. Lasswade, Scot. 1943; Dental Sch. Edinburgh 1947; Royal Coll. Surgs., (Edinburgh), L.D.S. 1947, F.D.S. 1954; Univ. of Edinburgh, D.D.S. 1966; D.Sc. (Hon.) McGill Univ. 1985; D.D.S. (Hon.), Edinburgh Univ. 1987; Hon. Doctorate, Univ. of Montreal 1991; m. Marjorie Ena, d. late John McVie 30 Sept. 1950; children: Jennifer Hunter, Lesley Elizabeth, Ailsa Marjorie, Elspeth Simpson; DEAN EMERITUS, FAC. OF DENTISTRY, UNIV. OF B.C. 1989; Prof. and Head, Dept. Clinical Sciences, Fac. of Dentistry, Univ. of Toronto 1968–78; Dean, Fac. of Dentistry, Univ. of Br. Col. 1978–88; formerly Prof. and Head (1st) Dept. Restorative Dent., Edinburgh Univ.; served in R.A.F. as Dental Offr. 1948–50, rank Flight Lt.; mem. Council, Royal Coll. Dent. of Can. (elected Pres. 1977–79); mem. Candn. Dental Assn. (Counc. on Educ.); Hon. Mem., Am. Dental Assoc. 1990; Nat. Dental Examining Bd. of Can.; Brit. Dental Assn.; Féd. Dentaire Internat. (Vice-Chrmn. Comn. on Dent. Educ. 1976–80, Chrmn. 1981–87); Cons., Oral Health, World Health Orgn. 1976– ; mem. Internat. Assn. Dent. Research, (Pres. 1977–78); Candn. Acad. Periodontists; Brit. Soc. Periodontol.; Ont. Soc. Periodontists; Med. Research Council Can. (mem. Dent. Sciences Comte., Scient. Offr. Dent. Science 1971–76); Pierre Fauchaud Academy; Fellow, Amer. Coll. of Dentists; Past Council mem. Brit. Soc. Periodontol.; Past mem. Dent. Council Royal Coll. Surgs. Edinburgh; Dent. Ed. (Cont. Educ.) Candn. Dent. Assn.; Liberal; United Church; recreations: golf, riding, music, travel, gardening; Office: Faculty of Dentistry, Univ. of British Columbia, Vancouver, B.C. V6T 1W5.

**BEAIRSTO, Frederick James,** B.Sc., C.E., M.B.A., P.Eng.; mechanical contractor, petroleum equipment distributor; b. Fredericton, N.B. 26 Sept. 1939; s. Walter Joseph and Margaret Esther (Steeves) B.; e. Univ. of N.B. B.Sc.C.E. 1963; Univ. of Western Ont. M.B.A. 1965; m. Dixie d. Arnold and Maxine Astle 3 Sept. 1960; children: Karen, Kelly, Eric, Jeffrey; OWNER & PRES., W.J. BEAIRSTO CO. LTD. & P.E.S. SALES LTD.; formerly Dir. & Bd. Chair, J.W. Bird and Co. Limited and Bird Holdings Limited; Alumni Award of Honour, Univ. of N.B.; McDonald Cartier Award for P.C. Party (Fredericton York Sunbury Riding); Mem., Bd. of Gov., Univ. of N.B.; Federal Business Development Board (Reg. Adv. Ctte.); has served as Pres., Univ. of N.B. Alumni Assn.; Pres., Fredericton C. of C.; Pres., Fredericton Construction Assn.; Pres., IFAW; Co-Chair, Citizens Ctte. on Language and Culture and several other past executive positions; Mem., Wilmot Un. Ch. (Former Chair, Bd. of Trustees); Former Dir., Prov. Riding Assn. & Federal Riding Assns. of P.C. Party; Dir., Fed. P.C. Party (current); Campaign Manager for var. ridings 1988–92; N.B. Campaign Manager, YES Ctte. 1992 Referendum; recreations: sailing, skiing; Home: 949 York St., Fredericton, N.B. E3B 3S1; Office: P.O. Box 1509, Fredericton, N.B. E3B 5G2.

**BEAKBANE, Thomas,** B.Sc.; marketing executive; b. Kidderminster, UK 9 Feb. 1957; s. Henry Renault and Joan Robina (Hornby) B.; e. Leighton Park Sch. Reading, UK 1975; Durham Univ. B.Sc. 1979; m. Margaret Jane Esplen 11 Dept. 1987; one d. Stephanie Margaret Joan; PRES. BEAKBANE MARKETING INC. 1987– ; Chrmn., Beakbane Marketing Internat. Inc.; joined United Biscuits PLC 1979–81; Pepsi-Cola Canada 1982–84, Product Mgr.; Alberto-Culver Canada 1985–87, Mktg. Mgr.; author 'Getting The Best From Suppliers, A Guide To Purchasing Marketing And Creative Services' 1991; ed. 'The Boffin And The Book-Keeper, Beakbane of Lancaster 1936–1988' 1988; Hon. Life mem. Durham Univ. Students' Union; Past Pres. Electronic Desktop Publishing Assn.; mem. Electronic Composition & Imaging (Ed. Bd.); Am. Mktg. Assn.; Soc. Graphic Designers Can.; Group for Design in Business; Museum for Promotional Arts; Toronto Bd. Trade; Taxpayers Coalition Ont.; Religious Soc. Friends; recreations: tennis, triathlons, cross country skiing; Office: 130 Bridgeland Ave., Toronto, Ont. M6A 1Z4.

**BEALL, Herbert Wilson,** B.Sc.F.; b. Ottawa, Ont. 29 Sept. 1908; s. Herbert Pelton and Gertrude Helen Evelyn (Wilson) B.; e. Pub. Sch. and Lisgar Coll. Inst., Ottawa, Ont.; Queen's Univ.; Univ. of Toronto, B.Sc.F. 1932; m. Mary Gertrude, d. late Hon. Robert Forke, 20 Oct. 1934; children: Elma Gertrude, James Herbert Forke; Forest Fire Research Offr., Candn. Public Service 1932–40; in charge of Forest Fire Research, 1946–50; Chief, Forestry Operations Divn., Dept. N. Affairs and Nat. Resources, 1951–60; Dir. Adm. Br., Dept. of Forestry, 1961–64; Special Advisor 1965–69, since when retired; served in R.C.A.F., 1941–45 (Radar duties in U.K.; Radar staff appts in Middle East); retired with rank of Sqdn. Leader; Mentioned in Despatches; mem. Candn. Inst. of Forestry; Ont. Prof. Foresters Assn.; author or jt.-author of some 30 publ. and articles on devel. of forest fire danger rating techniques and fire control planning methods; Freemason; Psi Upsilon; Anglican; recreations: target shooting, photography, fishing; Home: #522 Robertson House, 1 Mill Hill Rd., Nepean, Ont. K2H 9L6.

**BEAM, Carl,** B.F.A.; artist; e. Residential Sch. Espanola 1957–65; Elem. Sch. West Bay 1957–65; Kootenay Sch. of Art 1971–73; Univ. of Victoria 1973–79, B.F.A. 1975; Grad. Assistantship, Grad. Studies, Univ. of Alta. 1975–76; m. Anne Weatherby 1979; one d.: Anong; Labourer in Toronto 1957–65; over fifty exbns. incl. most recent: 'The Columbus Project Phase 1' Artspace Peterborough, Ont., The Art Gall. of Peterborough; 'A Piece of My Life: Prints by Carl Beam' Agnes Etherington Art Ctr., Kingston, Ont.; 'Political Landscapes' Tom Thomson Mem. Art Gall., Owen Sound, Ont.; 'Beyond History' Art Gall. of Vancouver; 'In the Shadow of the Sun' Candn. Mus. of Civilization, Hull, Que. 'Indian Art '89' Woodland Indian Cultural Edn. Ctr., Brantford, Ont.; works appear in 16 collections incl. cities of Buffalo, Revelstoke and Sudbury, Albright-Knox Art Gall. Buffalo, N.Y., Art Gall. of Hamilton, Dept. of Indian & Northern Devel. Toronto/Ottawa, Nat. Gall. of Canada, Govt. of Ont. Art Coll. Sudbury, Ont.; comn.: 'Exorcism' a 7' x 20' multimedia construction for Thunder Bay Nat. Exbn. & Ctr. for Indian Art 1984; subject of num. articles and catalogues; Canada Council Artist's grants 1984, '88, '89; Ont. Arts Council Artist-in-Residence, Artspace, Peterborough, Ont. 1989; Ont. Arts Council exbn. assistance grant; Home: West Bay, Manitoulin Island, Ont. P0P 1G0; Office: c/o The Arnold Gottlieb Gallery, 80 Spadina Ave., Suite 313, Toronto, Ont. M5V 2J3.

**BEAMENT, George Edwin,** O.B.E. (1943), C.M. (1986), K.St.J. (1964); E.D., C.D., Q.C., L.S.M., LL.D.; b. Ottawa, Ont. 12 Apr. 1908; s. Thomas Arthur and Edith Louise (Belford) B.; e. Roy. Mil. Coll. of Can. 1929; Univ. of Toronto, B.A.Sc. (M.E.) 1931; Osgoode Hall, grad. 1934; m. Brenda Yvonne Mary, d. Henry James Macthomas Thoms, Scot., 22 Feb. 1941; children: Justin Geoffrey, Meriel Virginia Mary Bradford; COUNSEL, BEAMENT, GREEN, DUST since 1968; called to the Bar of Ont. 1934; cr. K.C. 1948; Assoc. Beament & Beament 1934; Offr. Commdg., 2 Field Batty., Roy. Candn. Arty. 1939; Offr. Commdg., 2/14 Field Batty., do., 1940; proceeded to U.K. 1940; Bdge. Maj., 1st Candn. Armoured Bgde. 1941; Lt.-Col., Commdg. Offr., 6th Candn. Field Regt., Roy. Candn. Arty. 1942; G.S.O. 1, 4th Canadian Armoured Divn. 1942; G.S.O. 1 (Ops.) First Candn. Army 1943; Col., Gen. Staff, First Candn. Army 1943; Brig., Gen. Staff, 1st Candn. Army 1945; Pres., Khaki Univ. of Can. in U.K. 1945–46; Mentioned in Despatches; Croix de Guerre (avec Palme); Order of the White Lion; Mil. Cross (Czechoslovakia); Hon. Pres., Ottawa YM-YWCA 1968–73; Hon. Gov., Corps of Commissionaires (Ottawa); Law Soc. of Upper Can., Bencher 1964–75, Life Mem. 1984; Commr., Nat. Capital Comm., 1961–1966; Chancellor, Priory of Canada, Order of St. John of Jerusalem 1975–78; Hon. Col 30 Field Regt. R.C.A. 1968–78; L.S.M. (Medal of Law Soc. of Upper Canada) 1987; LL.D. (Hon. causa) 1984; Kappa Alpha; Conservative; Anglican; Club: Rideau (Life Mem. 1988); Home: Snowberry, Notch Rd., Old Chelsea, Qué. J0X 2N0; Office: 14th Floor, 155 Queen St., Ottawa, Ont. K1P 6L1.

**BEAMENT, Tib.,** M.A., R.C.A.; artist; b. Montreal, Que. 17 Feb. 1941; s. Harold and Ida Lawson (McDougall) B.; e. Fettes Coll. Edinburgh, Scot. (Crerar Scholarship) 1959; Beaux-Arts Montreal Dipl. 1963, post grad. studies Print Making 1964–66; Specialist's Dipl. Art Ed. 1969; Accademia Delle Belle Arti, Rome 1963–64; Sir George Williams Univ. M.A. (Art Ed.) 1972; Art Teacher, Miss Edgars Sch. 1966–79; Concordia Univ. (Design) 1975–83; McGill Univ. (Drawing) 1973–82; exhbns. Can., USA, Europe for more than 30 yrs.; solo exhbns. Can. since 1965, Zurich 1981; rep. pub. and private colls. Can., USA, S. Am., Europe; rec'd Italian Govt. Grant 1963, 1964; Can. Council Grant 1966; Que. Govt. Grant 1966, 1973; Greenshields Foundation Grant 1971, 1975; Royal Can. Acad. (Chrmn. Centennial Comm., Que. 1978–80); mem. Extve. Comte. and Dir. Greenshields Foundation; mem. Print & Drawing Council Can.; Accademia Delle Arti Italia; Protestant; recreations: sailing, garden design, scuba diving; Address: RR #1, Ayers Cliff, Qué. J0B 1C0.

**BEAMISH, Frederick William Henry,** B.A., Ph.D.; university professor; b. Toronto, Ont. 31 July 1935; s. Frederick Earl and Dorothy Naomi (Grasser) B.; e. North Toronto C.I.; Univ. of Toronto B.A., Ph.D.; m. Lois Woolley 8 Nov. 1958; children: Cynthia Ann, Robert Burk, Eric William; PROFESSOR, DEPT. OF ZOOLOGY, UNIV. OF GUELPH 1970– ; Asst. Scientist, Dept. of Fisheries & Oceans, St. Andrews N.B.

1962–65; Asst. Prof., present univ. 1965–67; Assoc. Prof. 1967–70; Prof. & Chair 1974–79; Candn. Comnr., Great Lakes Fishery Comn. 1989– ; Dir., Atlantic Salmon Fed. 1990– ; Home: 5 Drummond Place, Guelph, Ont.; Office: Dept. of Zoology, Univ. of Guelph, Guelph, Ont. N1G 2W1.

**BEAMISH, Robert E.,** C.M., B.A., B.Sc., M.D., D.Sc., F.R.C.P. (Can) (Edin) (London), F.A.C.P., F.A.C.C., F.C.C.P., F.I.C.A.; b. Shoal Lake, Man. 9 Sept. 1916; s. William Henry and Margaret May (McLeod) B.; e. Shoal Lake (Man.) Pub. Sch. 1930; McConnell High Sch. 1933; Brandon Coll. McMaster Univ. B.A. 1937; Univ. of Man. M.D. 1942, B.Sc.(Med.) 1944; m. Mary Kathleen, d. late Abel Seneca Weekes, 26 June 1943; three d., Catherine Margaret, Judith Millicent, Mary Anne; Consultant, St. Boniface Rsch. Centre (Div. of Cardiovascular Sciences); Assoc. Prof. of Med. Univ. of Manitoba 1964–81; Prof. of Med. 1981–88; Emeritus Prof. Med. 1989– ; Assoc. Phys. Health Sciences Centre, Winnipeg 1957–88; Nuffield Dominion Travelling Fellow Gt. Brit. 1947–48 subsequently part-time Tutor in Med. Univ. of Man.; Phys. and Cardiologist, Man. Clinic 1948–70; apptd. Med. Dir. Great West Life Assurance Co. 1970; Vice Pres., Underwriting and Medical 1975–81; Consultant, The Great-West Life Assurance Co. 1981–92; served with RCAMC 1944–46, rank Capt.; Distinguished Service Award, Brandon Univ. 1979; Candn. Heart Found. 1980; Distinguished Service Award, Manitoba Medical Assn. 1985; Community Service Award, City of Winnipeg 1984; Hon. D.Sc., Brandon Univ. 1988; Hon. D.Sc., Univ. of Manitoba 1989; Mem., Order of Canada 1990; Gen. Chrmn. Winnipeg Centennial Symposium on Dilemmas of Modern Man; Co-Chrmn., Int'l. Symp. on Stress and Heart Disease, 1984; Co-Chrmn., Internat. Symposium on Heart Metabolism in Health and Disease 1986; Chief, Ed. Bd., Canadian Journ. of Cardiology, 1984– ; Dir. Candn. Heart Found.; Man. Heart Found.; Health Sciences Rsch. Found.; Man. Medical College Found.; Man. Paraplegic Found.; Trustee Am. Coll. Cardiology 1975–80; mem. Candn. Assn. for the Club of Rome; Coll. Phys. & Surg.'s Man. (Pres. 1960–61); Man. Med. Assn. (Pres. 1970–71); Candn. Med. Assn. (Gen. Council 1966–72); Candn. Cardiovascular Soc. (Pres. 1968–70); Am. Coll. Phys. (Gov. Man.-Sask. 1972–76); Interam. Soc. Cardiol. (1st Vice Pres. 1972–76–80; Hon. Pres., 12th Interam. Congress of Cardiol., Vancouver 1985); Candn. Life Ins. Med. Offrs. Assn. (Pres. 1978–79); past Pres., U.N. Assn. in Can.; past Pres., Candn. Inst. of Internat. Affairs (Winnipeg Br.); Pres., Bd. Dirs., Brandon Univ. Found. 1980–87; United Church; recreations: medical history, philosophy; Club: Manitoba; Home: 176 Oxford St., Winnipeg, Man. R3M 3J6.

**BEAN, Daryl T.;** union executive officer; b. Shawville, Que. 19 July 1942; s. Thomas E. and Jenny B. (Dale) B.; e. Shawville H.S.; children: Kimberly Ann, Shelley Denise; NAT. PRES., PUBLIC SERV. ALLIANCE OF CAN. 1985– ; Public Works Can. 1960–82; Public Serv. Alliance of Can. 1982– ; joined Civil Serv. Assn. of Can. Stationary Engrs. & Assoc. Group 1960–65 (elected Shop Steward); Chrmn., Grievance Ctte. (HP) Local 70023 1965–68; Pres. 1968–72; Third Nat. Vice-Pres., Public Works Component of PSAC 1972–75; Nat. Pres. 1975–82; Extve. Vice-Pres., PSAC 1982–85; Gen. Vice-Pres., Candn. Labour Cong. 1985– , Candn. Titular Member, Extve. Ctte., Pub. Serv. Internat. 1987, 1989, 1993; Mem., Pub. Serv. Superannuation Adv. Ctte.; Mem. Bd. of Mgmt., Public Service Health Care; Mem. Bd. of Mgmt., Public Service PSAC Dental Plan; Vice-Chrmn., Nat. Joint Counc.; Chrmn. & Dir., PSAC Holdings Ltd.; Gov., Labour Coll. of Can.; Dir., United Way of Ottawa-Carleton 1987–91; Home: 83 Tartan Dr., Nepean, Ont. K2J 3V6; Office: 233 Gilmour St., Ottawa, Ont. K2P 0P1.

**BEAN, W. Donald,** B.A., M.B.A.; investment banker; b. Kitchener, Ont. 13 June 1939; s. Walter Alexander and Eleanore Elizabeth (Fearman) B.; e. Kitchener-Waterloo Coll. Inst. ; Univ. of Toronto B.A. 1962; Univ. of W. Ont. M.B.A. 1964; m. 2ndly Irene W. Babbin 14 Dec. 1984; children: Mary, Tupper, Bryan; Dir., Lancaster Group 1988– ; Banker, Mercantile Bank of Canada, Halifax and Winnipeg 1965–69; joined Wood Gundy Inc. 1969, Asst. Vice Pres. 1973, Vice Pres. 1973, Mgr. Corporate Finance Dept. 1974, Dir. 1976, Gen. Mgr. and C.O.O. 1980; Pres., C.O.O. and Dir., Wood Gundy Inc. 1982–88; Mem. Bd. of Govs., Renison College; Past Pres., St. Christopher House 1973–74, 1976–77; Trustee, Toronto Gen. Hosp. 1979–89; Delta Kappa Epsilon; recreations: skiing, tennis, sailing; Clubs: Toronto; York; Craigleith Ski; Office: One First Canadian Place, Ste. 5700, P.O. Box 18, Toronto, Ont. M5X 1A9.

**BEAN, Walter Alexander,** C.B.E., E.D., C.D., LL.D., B.Com; retired trust company extve.; b. Kitchener, Ont. 26 July 1908; s. late David Alexander and Rose Anna (Winter) B.; e. Kitchener-Waterloo Coll. Inst.; Univ. of Toronto, B.Comm. 1930; m. Eleanore Elizabeth, (died May 1971), d. late George D. Fearman, 30 May 1934; children: Douglas A., W. Donald; Hon. Dir., Economical Mutual Insurance Co. of Canada; Mutual Life Ins. Co. of Canada; Waterloo Ins. Co.; Electrohome Ltd.; with B. F. Goodrich Co. of Canada, 1925–26; joined Waterloo Trust now merged with Canada Trust as Statistician, 1930; apptd. various offices 1935–1957; Dir. 1957; Pres. and Gen. Mgr. 1964; Depy. Chrmn. and Vice Pres., Canada Trustco and Huron-Erie Mortgage Corp., 1968; retired 1978; Lieut. and Capt., Scots Fusiliers of Can., N.P.A.M., 1930–40; served in 2nd World War, 1940–45; Capt. Highland Light Inf. of Can.; Capt., Major, Lieut.-Col. and Brig. various hdqrs.; Commanded 2nd Candn. Inf. Bde. (Reserve) 1949–52; Hon. Col. Highland Fusiliers of Can; 1966–72; Past Pres., K-W Gyro Club; Past Pres., Trust Co's Assn. of Can.; Kitchener Chamber of Comm.; Delta Kappa Epsilon; Conservative; Anglican; recreation: golf; Clubs: Westmount Golf & Country; Muskoka Lakes Golf & Country; Rotary; Gyro; Home: 238 Stanley Drive, Waterloo, Ont. N2L 1H8 Office: 305 King St. W., Kitchener, Ont. N2E 4B9.

**BEANLANDS, Donald S.,** M.D.C.M., F.R.C.P.(C); cardiologist; b. Halifax, N.S. 27 Dec. 1932; s. Stewart Allison and Frances Vera (Hubley) B.; e. Queen Elizabeth H.S. Halifax; Dalhousie Univ. M.D.C.M. 1958; FRCP(C) 1962; postgrad. training Dalhousie Univ. & Univ. of Toronto; m. Rhona d. B.G. Rawdon 27 July 1958; children: Rob, Heather, Bruce, Ian; CHIEF CARDIOLOGIST, UNIVERSITY OF OTTAWA HEART INST. 1975– ; Toronto Western Hosp. 1962–75; active cardiologist in demand by patients across Canada; outstanding teacher; received PAIRO Award as outstanding teacher, Sch. of Med., Univ. of Ottawa; mem. of more than 40 med. assns. both nat. & internat.; author/co-author of more than 100 pub. papers; extensive public speaker; Annual Lecturer, Candn. Cardiovascular Soc.; selected as Dupont Lecturer 1992; Dep. Director-General, Univ. of Ottawa Heart Inst. and Chief, Div. of Cardiology, Univ. of Ottawa; Office: Ottawa Heart Inst. H202, 1053 Carling Ave., Ottawa, Ont. K1Y 4E9.

**BEARDMORE, Harvey Ernest,** B.Sc., M.D., C.M., F.R.C.S.(C), F.A.C.S.; surgeon; educator; b. Windsor, Ont. 4 Feb. 1921; s. Harold Beardmore; e. McGill Univ. B.Sc. 1946, M.D., C.M. 1948; m. Frances Seymour d. Kenneth Seymour Barnes 1 Sept. 1945; children: Richard Murdoch, Ann Elizabeth, Patricia Louise, Ian Harold, Carol Harvey, Diane Frances; Paediatric Gen. Surgeon, The Montreal Children's Hosp. 1954–92, retired; Assoc. Prof. of Surgery McGill Univ. 1972–92; served with P.P.C.L.I. 1943–45, Italy & N.W. Europe, rank Lt.; R.C.A.M.C. 1949–59 (Reserve Active Offrs.), rank Capt., Supplementary Reserve 1959; Fellow, Am. Acad. of Pediatrics; Protestant; Home: 4501 Sherbrooke St. W., Apt. 5B, Montreal, Qué. H3Z 1E7.

**BEARDSLEY, John Douglas,** M.A.; poet; educator; b. Montreal, Que. 27 Apl. 1941; s. Ivan and Alice Muriel (Winsborrow) B.; e. Univ. of Victoria B.A. 1976; York Univ. M.A. 1978; one d. Anna Maura Bouey; SENIOR INSTRUCTOR IN ENGLISH, UNIV. OF VICTORIA 1981– ; Instr. Inst. Candn. Bankers Extension Dept. 1983–85; Instr. in Community Edn. Camosun Coll. Victoria 1984–85; joined Gregson Graham Ltd. (communications) Victoria 1978–82, Chief Ed. Tech., Occupational & Bus. Writing 1980–82; Osborne, Beardsley & Associates 1982–85; Beardsley & Assocs. 1985–91; recipient numerous awards incl. Can. Council 1975, 1978; Ont. Arts Council 1977–78; Pres.' Scholarship 1975 and Petch Meml. Award in Creative Writing 1976 Univ. of Victoria; Rsch. Grad. Scholarship York Univ. 1977; Social Sci's & Humanities Rsch. Council Doctoral Fellowship 1979; Tech. Writing & Editing Awards Nat. Soc. Tech. Communications 1982–83; nominated B.C. Book Prize for Poetry 1989; numerous nat. and internat. readings contemporary poetry; TV, radio and print interviews; Artist-in-the-Sch. Prog. Greater Victoria Sch. Dist. 1986–87; author 'Going Down Into History' 1976; 'The Only Country in the World Called Canada' 1976; 'Six Saanich Poems' 1977; 'Play on the Water: The Paul Klee Poems' 1978; 'Pacific Sands' 1980; 'Kissing the Body of My Lord: The Marie Poems' 1982; 'Country on Ice' 1987, paperback 1988; 'A Dancing Star' 1988; co-author 'Premonitions and Gifts' 1979; 'Poems' 1979; ed. 'The Rocket, The Flower, The Hammer, And Me' 1988; 'Inside Passage' 1993; recreations: music, squash, tennis, racquetball, biking; Address: 1074 Lodge Ave., Victoria, B.C. V8X 3A8.

**BEARE-ROGERS, Joyce L.,** C.M., Ph.D., D.Sc., F.R.S.C.; nutrition scientist; b. Pickering, Ont. 8 Sept. 1927; d. Frederick John and Sarah May (Michell) B.; e. Univ. of Toronto B.A. 1951, M.A. 1952; Carleton Univ. Ph.D. 1966; Univ. of Man. Hon. D.Sc. 1985; Univ. of Guelph, Hon. D.Sc. 1993; m. Dr. Charles G. Rogers 30 Dec. 1961; one d. Anne Catherine; Adjunct Prof. of Biochem. Univ. of Ottawa 1980–92; Rsch. Assoc. Univ. of Toronto 1952–54; Instr. in Physiol. Vassar Coll. Poughkeepsie 1954–56; Food & Drug Directorate Ottawa 1956–65, Rsch. Sci. 1965–75; Chief, Nutrition Rsch. Div. Health and Welfare Can. 1975–91; recipient Bordon Award 1972; Queen's Silver Jubilee Medal 1977; Chevreul Medal (France) 1984; Crampton Award McGill Univ. 1986; Normann Award (Germany) 1987; Fellow, Royal Society of Canada 1989; Mem., Order of Canada 1992; Earle Willard McHenry Award, Can. Soc. Nutritional Sciences 1993; author over 100 articles mostly in lipid nutrition; ed. 'Methods for Nutritional Assessments of Fats' 1985; 'Dietary Fat Requirements in Health and Development 1988; mem. Candn. Soc. Nutr. Sci. (Pres. 1984–85); Candn. Biochem. Soc.; Am. Inst. Nutrition; Candn. Inst. Food Sci. & Technol. (Chrmn. Nutrition Interest Group 1979–81); Am. Oil Chems. Soc. (Sec. 1981–84, Vice Pres. 1984–85, Pres. 1985–86); Internat. Soc. for Fat Rsch. (Pres. 1991–92); recreations: hiking, canoeing, reading; Home: 41 Okanagan Dr., Nepean, Ont. K2H 7E9; Office: Ottawa, Ont. K1A 0L2.

**BEATH, Ronald J.,** B.E.Sc., M.B.A.; financial executive; e. Univ. of Western Ont. B.E.Sc.(Mech.Eng.) 1966, M.B.A. 1968; VICE-PRESIDENT, FINANCE, MONSANTO CANADA INC.; Controller, Canada-Latin America,Corning Glass Works 1973; Materials Mgr., Greb Industries Ltd. 1976; Mgr., Operations Acctg. & Credit, Monsanto Canada Inc. 1978; Office: 2330 Argentia Rd., P.O. Box 787, Mississauga, Ont. L5M 2G4.

**BEATON, George H.,** M.A., Ph.D.; educator; b. Oshawa, Ont. 20 Dec. 1929; s. late John H. and Madeline I. (Rogerson) B.; e. elem. and high sch. Oshawa; Univ. of Toronto B.A. 1952, M.A. 1953, Ph.D. 1955; m. Mary P. d. late James C. Clarke 15 Aug. 1953; children: James H., Patricia M., Dorcas E.; PROF. OF NUTRITIONAL SCIENCES, FACULTY OF MEDICINE UNIV. OF TORONTO; Chrmn. of Dept. 1975–81; joined Univ. of Toronto 1955, Head, Dept. Nutrition Sch. of Hygiene 1963–75, Acting Dir. Sch. of Hygiene 1973–75, Acting Dean Faculty of Food Sciences 1975–78; rec'd Borden Award of Nutrition Soc. of Can.; Atwater Memorial Lectureship, E.W. McHenry Award of Candn. Soc. Nutritional Sciences 1983; E.V. McCallum Memorial Lectureship (U.S.); Boyd Orr Memorial Lectureship (U.K.) 1986; Raymond Pearl Memorial Lectureship (U.S.) 1990; Co-ed. 'Nutrition: A Comprehensive Treatise' 3 Vols. 1965; Co-ed. and author 'Nutrition in Preventive Medicine' 1977; author over 100 scient. papers in field of nutrition; mem. Nutrition Soc. Can. (Secy., Pres.); Am. Inst. Nutrition (Council); Am. Soc. Clin. Nutrition; Candn. Physiol. Soc.; Office: FitzGerald Bldg., Univ. of Toronto, Toronto, Ont. M5S 1A8.

**BEATON, William Henry,** B. Eng.; consulting engineer; b. Montreal, Que. 4 May 1921; s. William Alexander and Cécile (Décarie) B.; e. Loyola Coll. 1938; McGill Univ. B. Eng. (Civil Engn.) 1947; m. Annah Jean, d. Russell Meikle, 29 Sept. 1951; children: Karen, Marilyn, Gordon (dec.), Gregory; Retired founding Partner & Dir., Beauchemin-Beaton-Lapointe Inc.: Past Chrmn. Cansult Ltd.; in 1951, Project Engr. with Beauchemin & Hurter on projects for Dept. of Nat. Defence; in 1954 became an Associate of J.A. Beauchemin & Assocs. engaged on various defence and pub. works developments in E. and N. Can.; joined present partnership on formation 1956 since when has contrib. to management technical & devel. aspects of the firm incl. feasibility studies and masterplans for three USAF air bases projected for Que.; the complete devel. of new resource towns in Que. and Labrador; also been engaged in internat. devel. projects which include: conceptual planning and project management of a new internat. airport, a harbour development and extensive dredging and reclamation works for navigation channels and industrial sites in the United Arab Emirates; airport extensions in several Caribbean islands; environmental engn. projects for cities of Riyadh and Medinah, Saudi Arabia; highway projects in Saudi Arabia, in the U.A.E., and in the Sultanate of Oman; also became engaged on project management for the new Montreal International Airport, Mirabel, Que., the CFB Megastructure in St. Jean, Que. and various industrial projects in Que.; served in RCAF (Pilot Offr.) 1942–44; mem. Engn. Inst. Can.; Am. Inst. Civil Engrs.; Order of Engrs. Que.; Assn. of Consulting Engrs. Can.;

Christian; recreations: reading, music, writing; Home: 79 Lakeshore Rd., Beaconsfield, Qué. H9W 4H7.

**BEATTIE, Allan Leslie,** C.M., Q.C., B.A., LL.B.; b. Copper Cliff, Ont., 25 March 1926; s. Robert Leslie and Amelia Edna (Allen) B.; e. Copper Cliff Pub. and High Schs., 1944; St Andrew's Coll. Aurora, Ont. 1944–45; Trinity Coll., Univ. of Toronto, B.A. 1948; Osgoode Hall Law Sch. 1948–51; m. Elizabeth Agnes Mary, d. late Maurice Ogilvie Tremayne, 20 July 1951; four d., Elizabeth Anne, Barbara Allen, Mary Louisa, Leslie Anne; VICE CHRMN. & CHRMN, EXTVE. CTTE., EATON'S OF CANADA LTD.; formerly Chrmn. of the Firm and its Exec. Ctte., Osler, Hoskin & Harcourt; Chrmn. & Dir.: Baton Broadcasting Inc.; Laurentian Group of Mutual Funds; Chrmn., Pres. & Dir.: Telegram Corn Ltd.; Dir., Laurentian Financial Services Ltd.; Desjardins Laurentian Financial Corporation; Imperial Life Assurance Co. of Can.; read law with Osler, Hoskin & Harcourt; called to Bar of Ont 1951; Sr. Partner 1965, retired 1986; cr. Q.C. 1962; apptd. Member, Order of Canada 1993; Honorary Chrmn., Bd. of Trustees, Hospital for Sick Children, Toronto; Chrmn., Bd. of Dirs., Hospital for Sick Children Found.; Trustee, Timothy Eaton Mem. Ch.; R. Samuel McLaughlin Found.; Chrmn. Eaton Retirement Annuity Plan; mem., Candn. Bar Assn.; Candn. Tax Foundation; United Church; recreations: golf, skiing, cottaging; Clubs: York; The Toronto; Toronto Golf; Craigleith Ski; Briars Golf; Home: 80 Chestnut Park Rd., Toronto, Ont. M4W 1W9; Office: 15th Fl., 250 Yonge St., Toronto, Ont. M5B 1C8.

**BEATTIE, John Maurice,** Ph.D.; university professor; b. Newcastle-upon-Tyne, England 7 March 1932; s. Frank William and Mary Eva (Aspery) B.; e. Blaydon Grammar Sch., England 1949; Univ. of San Francisco B.S. 1954; Univ. of Calif., Berkeley M.A. 1956; Univ. of Cambridge Ph.D. 1963; m. Susan d. Basil and Eva Mills 9 Aug. 1958; children: Roger, Allison, Katherine; PROF., DEPT. OF HIST., UNIV. OF TORONTO 1972– ; Lectr., Dept. of Hist., Univ. of Toronto 1961–63; Asst. Prof. 1963–67; Assoc. Prof. 1967–72; cross-appt. to Ctr. of Criminology 1972, Acting Dir. 1986–87, Dir. 1989– ; University Professor 1988; awards: Gershoy Prize, Am. Hist. Assn. 1986; Ferguson Prize, Candn. Hist. Assn. 1987; Snow Prize, N.A. Conf. on Brit. Studies 1987; Gottschalk Prize, Am. Soc. for 18th-Cent. Studies 1987; Garneau Prize, Candn. Hist. Assn. 1990; Killam Sr. Fellowship 1979–81; Guggenheim Fellowship 1987–88; author: 'The English Court in the Reign of George I' 1967, 'Crime and the Courts in England, 1660–1800' 1986; editor: 'Attitudes Towards Crime and Punishment in Upper Canada, 1830–1850: A Documentary Study' 1977; recreations: music; Home: 143 Farnham Ave., Toronto, Ont. M4V 1H7; Office: Toronto, Ont. M5S 1A1.

**BEATTIE, Owen Beverly,** B.A., Ph.D.; university professor; b. Victoria, B.C. 3 June 1949; s. Beverly John and Alice Elizabeth (Martin) B.; e. Simon Fraser Univ. B.A. 1972, Ph.D. 1981; Univ. of B.C. grad. study 1973–74; m. Lynda d. Samuel and Delphine Hergert 29 Jan. 1972; children: Matthew, Jennifer, Megan; PROF., UNIV. OF ALTA. 1991– ; Sess. Lectr., Simon Fraser Univ. 1974–75; Instr., Fraser Valley Coll. 1975–76; Douglas Coll. 1976–78; Vis. Asst. Prof., Univ. of Alta. 1979–80, Asst. Prof. 1980–86, Assoc. Prof. 1986–91; rsch. interests: human skeletal biol. & forensic anthropol.; rsch. in Candn. Arctic on 18th and 19th cent. Brit. explorations for N.W. Passage 1981– ; excavations along coastal B.C. with rsch. focus on phys. anthropol. of prehist. inhabitants 1971–80; Cons., Archaeol. Surv. of Alta.; Off. of the Chief Med. Exam. (Edmonton); R.C.M.P.; Mem., Candn. Archaeol. Assn.; Candn. Assn. for Phys. Anthropol.; co-author 'Frozen in Time: Unlocking the Secrets of the Franklin Expedition'; 'Buried in Ice: The Mystery of a Lost Arctic Expedition'; 'Dead Silence: the Greatest Mystery in Arctic Discovery'; associate prod. of film documentary 'Frozen in Time/Buried in Ice'; author & co-author of 37 pub. sci. papers, reviews, chapters & 110 govt. reports; Alta. Achievement Award 1989; Honourable Mention, Rolex Awards for Enterprise 1990; Premier's Award for Excellence 1989; recreations: soaring, photography; Office: Dept. of Anthropol., Univ. of Alta., Edmonton, Alta. T6G 2H4.

**BEATTIE, Peter Greer,** Q.C., B.A.; lawyer; b. Toronto, Ont. 21 Jan. 1933; s. Oliver Mowat and Elva Elizabeth (Giffen) B.; e. Victoria Coll., Univ. of Toronto, B.A. 1954; Osgoode Hall Law Sch. 1958; Q.C. 1971; m. H. Joan d. Clarence D. and Aileen L. Carruthers 1958; children: Mark, Paul, Katherine, Beth; PARTNER, McCARTHY TÉTRAULT, BARRISTERS & SOLICITORS 1968– ; Assoc. 1958–68; Dir., Foster's Brewing Group Canada Inc.; Trustee, First Candn. Mutual Funds; Dir., Candn. Hearing Soc. Found.; Former Dir., Ont. Trillium Found.; The Nat. Ballet of Can.; Gov., St. George's Coll.; Former Gov., The Bishop Strachan Sch.; mem., Law Soc. of Upper Can.; Candn. Bar Assn.; clubs: Toronto, The York, The Caledon Mountain Trout; Home: 313 Russell Hill Rd., Toronto, Ont. M4V 2T7; Office: Suite 4700, Toronto Dominion Bank Tower, Toronto-Dominion Centre, Toronto, Ont. M5K 1E6.

**BEATTY, David K.,** B.A., M.B.A., C.G.A.; financial executive; b. London, Ont. 24 Dec. 1942; s. David and Elaine Fleming (Kennedy) B.; e. Univ. of Western Ont. B.A. 1966, M.B.A. 1968; m. Rose V. d. James and Sophie Sadowey 19 Aug. 1967; children: Shannon, Cheryl; VICE-PRES. FINANCE & ADMIN., FISHER SCIENTIFIC LTD. 1987– ; Mgr., Financial Systems & Devel. / Product Analysis & Pricing, Chrysler France 1976–80; Mgr. Material Cost & Product Analysis / Organ. & Systems, Chrysler Canada Limited 1968–76; Dir. Finance & Operations, G.D. Searle & Co. of Canada 1980–87; Mem., Financial Extves. Inst.; Home: 35 Blue Heron Court, Ottawa, Ont. K1L 8J7; Office: 112 Colonnade Rd., Nepean, Ont. K2E 7L6.

**BEATTY, David Ross,** O.B.E., B.A., M.A., C.F.A.; executive; b. Toronto, Ont. 19 March 1942; s. David S. Beatty; e. Upper Can. Coll. Toronto 1960 (Pat Strathy Memorial Scholarship); Trinity Coll. Univ. of Toronto B.A. 1965; Queens' Coll. Cambridge M.A. 1967; (ODI/Nuffield Fellowship); m. Deborah Ann d. late Kenneth W. and late Helen Elizabeth Peacock 10 June 1965; children: Andrew, Kenneth, Deborah Elise, Charles; PRES., WESTON FOODS, GEORGE WESTON LTD. 1985– ; Dir. and Vice Chrmn. Old Canada Investment Corp. Ltd.; Dir., George Weston Limited; Bank of Montreal; Spar Aerospace; Sr. Transport Econ., Ministry of Devel. Planning, Govt. of Un. Repub. of Tanzania 1967–70; Mgmt. Cons. McKinsey & Co. Inc. 1969–70; Chrmn. The Canada Consulting Group 1970–73; Econ. Advisor to Prime Min. and Dir. Central Planning Office Govt. of Papua New Guinea 1973–77; Pres., Dabed Enterprises Ltd. 1977–81; Pres., Garbell Holdings Ltd. 1982–85; Vice Pres. Invests., Gardiner Group of Companies 1982–85; Chrmn. of the Bd., Upper Can. Coll.; Mem. Adv. Bd., Peter F. Drucker Foundation; recipient Independence Medal, Papua New Guinea; Canadian Citizenship Award; Order of the British Empire 1993; Hon. Consul for Canada, Papua New Guinea; recreations: jogging, rowing, fishing, skiing; Clubs: Franklin; Toronto; B & R; Rosedale Golf; Osler Bluffs Ski; Toronto; Home: 98 Teddington Park, Toronto, Ont. M4N 2C8; Office: 22 St. Clair Ave. E., Ste. 1901, Toronto, Ont. M4T 2S7.

**BEATTY, David S.,** C.M.; financial consultant; b. Toronto, Ont. 11 May 1915; s. Harold Eastwood and Ann Lois (Duggan) B.; e. Upper Can. Coll., Toronto; m. Eugenie Isabel, 19 July 1979; children: David Ross. Barbara Elise; Pres., Beatinvest Ltd.; Chrmn., Old Canada Investment Corp. Ltd.; Dir. CSA Management Ltd.; Goldcorp Inc.; Gold Trust Ltd.; with Dominion Securities, 1932–39; Burns Bros. and Denton Ltd. 1939–67 (Pres. 1952–65, Depy. Chrmn. 1965–67); served Overseas with Royal Regt. Can. in 2nd World War; demob. with rank Maj.; awarded C. in C. Cert. of Gallantry; Past Hon. Col., R. Reg't. C.; Past Pres., Invest. Dealers' Assn. Can.; Bd. Govs., Toronto Stock Exchange; Mem., Order of Canada; Anglican; recreations: fishing, music, nature study; Clubs: Toronto; Glenmajor Angling; York; Home: Ste. 301, 616 Avenue Rd., Toronto, Ont. M4V 2K8; Office: Suite 2700, 145 King St. W., Toronto, Ont. M5H 1J8.

**BEATTY, (Henry) Perrin,** P.C., M.P., B.A.; politician; b. Toronto, Ont. 1 June 1950; s. George Ernest and Martha L. (Perrin) B.; e. James McQueen Pub. Sch. Fergus, Ont. 1962; Upper Can. Coll. Toronto 1968; Univ. of W. Ont. B.A. 1971; m. Julia Florence Carroll Kenny d. late Robert Allen Kenny and Mrs. David Jones, Ottawa, Ont. 23 Feb 1974; two sons: Christopher, Patrick; Minister of External Affairs 1993; el. to H. of C. g.e. 1972, re-el. 1974, 1979, 1980, 1984, 1988; mem. Comte. on Univ. Affairs Govt. of Ont. 1971–72; Asst. to Min. of Health Ont. 1971–72; Min. of State (Treasury Bd.) June 1979–Feb. 1980; Min. of National Revenue & Min. responsible for Canada Post Corp. Sept. 1984–Aug. 1985; Solicitor General of Canada Aug. 1985–June 1986; Min. of National Defence 1986–89; Min. of National Health & Welfare 1989–91; Min. of Communications 1991–93; Hon. mem. Royal Candn. Legion; P. Conservative; United Church; recreations: reading, swimming, music; Home: P.O. Box 33, Fergus, Ont. N1M 2W7.

**BEATTY, Robert Lawler,** B.A.; retired; b. Yellow Grass, Sask. 24 June 1916; s. William Alexander and Eva Mary (Small) B.; e. Swift Current, Sask., Univ. of Toronto, B.A. (Math. and Phys.) 1938; Ont. Coll. of Educ., High Sch. Specialist standing in Math. and Phys. 1939; m. Helen Elizabeth, d. late Kenneth McLeod Munro, 20 Dec. 1941; children: Jane Weir, David Munro, Kenneth William Robert, John Edward; SPECIAL ADVISER, UNEMPLOYMENT INSURANCE COMN.; Dir. General Insurance Service 1970; Teacher, Toronto Coll., 1939–40; joined federal govt. 1947 holding various positions in Unempl. Insur. Comm., Dept. of Nat. Health and Welfare and Privy Council office; Asst. Dir. of Unemployment Ins., 1962; apptd. Dir. Gen. 1966; Special Adviser to Comm. 1972–77; Trustee Ottawa Bd. of Education 1972–88, Chrmn. 1973, 1974, 1983; Pres., Large School Bds. of Ont., 1980–81; sessional Lectr. in Math, Carleton Univ. 1950–75; served as an Officer with RCN in N. Atlantic and with RN, 1940–45; Chrmn., Group Comte. of Boy Scouts Assn.; Vice Chrmn., World Ctte. on Unemployment Insurance, Internat. Social Social Security Assn. 1970–77; Elder, Parkdale Un. Ch.; Dir., Inst. Gen. Mang.; recreations: travelling, golf, tennis, curling, skiing; Home: 2397 Georgina Dr., Ottawa, Ont. K2B 7M9.

**BEATY, Ross J.,** B.Sc., M.Sc., LL.B.; geologist; b. Vancouver, B.C. 18 July 1951; s. John David and Jean Margaret (Macleod) B.; e. Prince of Wales S.S. 1969; Univ. of B.C., B.Sc. (Hons.) 1974; Univ. of London, Royal Sch. of Mines, M.Sc. (Dist.) 1975; Imperial Coll., dipl. 1975; Univ. of B.C., LL.B. 1979; m. Patricia d. Edwin and Patience Fockler 10 May 1980; children: Carolynn, John, Heather, Shannon, Fiona; PRES., EQUINOX RESOURCES LTD. 1983– ; Exploration geol., var. mining & cons. geol. firms 1974–79; Articled law student, Ladner, Downs 1979–80; Pres., Beaty Geol. Ltd. 1980– ; Dir., Long Bay Resources Ltd.; Consolidated Silver Standard Mines Ltd.; Fellow, Geol. Assn. of Can.; mem., Assn. Profl. Engrs.; Geoscientists of B.C.; Candn. Inst. of Mining & Metal.; BC-Yukon Ch. of Mines; recreations: mountaineering, skiing; Clubs: Alpine Club of Can.; Natural Hist. Soc.; Office: 1500 – 625 Howe St., Vancouver, B.C. V6C 2T6.

**BEATY, William Harvey;** food industry executive; b. Trafalgar Twp., Ont. 9 Sept. 1916; s. William Stanley and Hazel Irene (Fox) B.; e. Milton H.S.; Univ. of Toronto 1939; m. Erma A. d. Alfred and Eusebia (Russel) McFadden 29 March 1955; CHAIRMAN & CHIEF EXECUTIVE OFFICER, COLD SPRINGS FARM LIMITED; Founded Cold Spring Farm 1949; currently comprised of 17 companies involved in prodn. & processing of turkeys, prodn. of hogs & processing pork, prodn. of beef, crop prodn. & proc. in co. elevators & feed mill facilities; interests in farm equip. & high volume fertilizer blending & distbn.; Mem. & Past Dir., Oxford Fed. of Agric.; Past Dir., Ont. Food Council; Poultry Prod. Inst. of Can.; Candn. Turkey Fed.; Candn. Egg Prod. Council; Past Dir. & Chrmn., Ont. Egg Mktg. Bd.; Ont. Turkey Mktg. Bd.; Poultry Indus. Conf. & Exhbn.; Past Dir. & Pres., Ont. Broiler Chicken Assn.; Ont. Poultry Council; Award of Merit, Ont. Poultry Council 1982; Max Weiner Award, Candn. Hatchery Fed. 1990; First Patron, Poultry Indus. Ctr. for Rsch. & Edn. 1991; Dir., Western Fair Assn.; Dir., Covent Garden Market Authority 1985– ; Mem., Oxford P.C. Assn. (Past Pres.); Thamesford Village Council (Mem. 11 yrs; Chrmn. 5 yrs); Official and Bd. Mem., Westminster Ch. 13 yrs; Home: 175 Dundas St., Thamesford, Ont. N0M 2M0; Office: 149 Brock St., Thamesford, Ont. N0M 2M0.

**BEAUBIEN, Rév. Irénée,** S.J., B.A., L.Ph., D.D. (R.C.); n. Shawinigan, Qué. 26 janv. 1916; é Sém. des Trois-Rivières, P.Q.; études en lettres, sciences, philosophie et théologie chez les Pères Jesuites, Montréal, P.Q.; ordonné prêtre en 1949; fit séjours d'études spéciales aux Etats-Unis et en Europe en vue de mieux comprendre le problème des relations entre catholiques et non-catholiques; fonda en 1952 à Montréal le Catholic Inquiry Forum (centre de renseignements sur le catholicisme); a collaboré à l'organisation de plusieurs centres d'information catholique au Canada et à l'étranger; a contribué des articles à plusieurs revues et journaux; en 1958 inaugure dialogue mensuel entre pasteurs protestants et prêtres catholiques; en 1962 nommé par S.E. le cardinal Léger président de la Commission d'oecuménisme de Montréal et, en 1963, directeur-fondateur du Centre d'oecuménisme; président du Pavillon Chrétien à l'Expo 67 de Montréal; en 1966, nommé par l'épiscopat canadien au poste de directeur de l'Office national d'oecuménisme; 1968–73, consulteur au Secrétariat pour l'Unité des Chrétiens, Rome; 1971–83, membre de dialogues interconfessionnels; en 1975, fusion du Centre et de l'Office national d'Oecuménisme qui deviennent, sous sa direction, le Centre Canadien d'Oecuménisme; en 1984, fonde 'Sentiers de Foi,' exclusivement au service des baptisés chrétiens qui ne vont plus à l'église; en 1989 est introduit par l'American Biographical Inst. au temple international de la renommée; Résidence: 25 ouest, rue Jarry, Montréal, Qué. H2P 1S6; Bureau: Sentiers de Foi, 7400 boulevard St-Laurent, suite 224, Montréal, Qué. H2R 2Y1.

**BEAUBIEN, Philippe de Gaspé,** O.C.(1967), B.A., M.B.A., LL.D. (h.c.); broadcasting and publishing executive; b. Montreal, Que. 12 Jan. 1928; s. Philippe de Gaspé and Lucille (Mercier) B.; e. Univ. of Montreal, B.A.; Harvard Sch. Business Adm., M.B.A.; York University, LL.D.; m. Nan-bowles d. Michael Frederick O'Connell 29 Jan. 1956; children: de Gaspé, Nanon, François; CHRMN. & C.E.O, TELEMEDIA CORP. 1971– ;(owner of 26 radio stns. in Que. and Ont.; incl. a News & Sports Network; Publisher TV GUIDE INC./TV HEBDO INC. (publishes TV GUIDE, TV HEBDO, CANADIAN LIVING, TV PLUS, HARROWSMITH, EQUINOX, COUP DE POUCE, ELLE QUEBEC, etc.); Dir.: Bombardier Inc., McDonald's Restaurants of Can. Ltd., Toronto Dominion Bank, Innocan Inc.; Past Dir.: Reitman's (Canada) Ltd., Candn. Devel. Corp. (CDC), York Univ. (Adv. Comte.); Chief Extve. Organ.; Candn. Satellite Communications Inc.; Founder and Pres., Beaubien Distribution Co. Ltd. 1960–63; Dir. of Operations, Candn. Corp. for 1967 World Exhbn. (Mayor of Expo '67) 1963–67; Pres. Télémédia (Que.) Ltd. 1968–71; Founder and Hon. Chrmn., ParticipAction; Founder and Co-chair, Internat. Centre for Family Enterprises; awarded Centennial Medal 1967; Czechoslovakia Gold Medal 1968; B'nai Brith Award of Merit; R. Catholic; recreations: all sports; Clubs: Mount Royal; York; St. Denis; Home: Surrey Gardens, Westmount, Que H3Y 1N5; Office: 1010 Sherbrooke W., Suite 1610, Montreal, Qué. H3A 2R7.

**BEAUBIER, David Wilson,** B.A., LL.B., LL.M.; judge; b. Regina, Sask. 18 June 1932; s. Beaty Frederick and Evangeline Lenore (Maher) B.; e. Univ. of Sask. B.A. 1954, LL.B. 1960; Univ. of Toronto LL.M. 1961; m. Otillia d. Frank and Margaret Lerner Aug. 1958; one s.: Beaty Frederick; JUDGE, TAX COURT OF CANADA 1990– ; admitted to Bar of Sask. 1962; Mem. & Partner, Cuelenaere, Beaubier & Co. 1962–90; Pres., Sask. Br., Candn. Bar Assn. 1973–74; Bencher, Law Soc. Sask. 1975–78; Lectr. in taxation, Univ. of Sask. 1964–69; Q.C. 1981; Gov., Candn. Tax Found. 1987–90; Mem., Rules Ctte., Tax Court of Can. 1989–90; Founder & Pres., Estate Planning Counc. of Saskatoon; Founder & Dir., Elmwood Residences Limited; author of a number of articles on law & taxation in var. law journals; club: Saskatoon; Office: 200 Kent St., Ottawa, Ont. K1A 0M1.

**BEAUCHAMP, Claude,** B.A., LL.L.; publisher; b. Montréal, Qué. 9 July 1939; s. Rosaire and Yvette (Dufresne) B.; e. St-Viateur Coll. Outremont; Univ. de Montréal B.A. 1960, med. studies 1960–61, LL.L. 1964; Ecole des Hautes Etudes Commerciales de Montréal Applied Econ. 1965–66; Harvard Bus. Sch. M.B.A. Cert. 1987; m. Céline d. Pierre and Amanda Paquette Gélinas 1 Sept. 1962; three d. Dominique, Pascale, Geneviève-Annick; PRES. AND OWNER EDITUS INC. 1990– ; Dir. and mem. Exec. Ctte. G.T.C. Transcontinental Group Ltd. 1985– ; News Dir. 'Les Affaires' financial weekly 1963–64; Financial Ed. 'La Presse' Montréal 1965, Nat. Assembly Bureau Chief 1967, Ed. Dir. Econ., Pol. & Internat. News Sects. 1971–74; Ed.-in-Chief and Dep. Publisher 'Le Soleil' Québec City 1974–80; Pres., Publisher & Co-owner Transcontinental Publications Inc. 1980–90; regular TV host and commentator CBC and TVA French network; recipient Prix des communications du Québec 1984; Bene Merenti De Patria Award Soc. Saint-Jean-Baptiste and Prix du journalisme Olivar-Asselin 1986; Annual Merit Award Assn. des diplômés de l'Univ. de Montréal 1986; Pres. La Fédération professionnelle des journalistes du Québec 1972–73; Founding mem. and Dir. Que. Press Council 1973–74; mem. ed. ctte. Candn. Daily Newspapers Assn. 1976–80; Chrmn. Forum des communications du Québec 1986–89; Pres. 1989 Telethon Assn. de paralysie cérébrale du Québec; Co-Chrmn., Comité Relance PME, Govt. of Qué. 1991–93; Chrmn., Que. Assoc. of Magazine Publishers 1991; Mem., Permanent Adv. Ctte. on Internat. Trade, Indus. Sci. & Internat. Trade, Canada 1991–93; Pres., Assn. on the Economy and the Constitution 1991–92; Found. Conseil de Presse du Québec; Candn. Jewish-Christian Council; recreations: tennis, squash, golf, skiing; Clubs: Club de tennis Ile-des-Soeurs; Montreal Country Club; Address: 608, 2500 av. Pierre-Dupuy, Cité du Havre, Qué. H3C 4L1.

**BEAUCHAMP, Marc,** B.A., M.B.A.; financial executive; b. Montreal, Que. 7 May 1945; s. Edouard C. and Simone (Comtois) B.; e. Univ. of W. Ont. B.A. (Hons.) 1967; Columbia Univ. M.B.A. 1969; m. Marie-Françoise d. Jean and Claudine Bocquillon 26 June 1970; children: Alphée, Coralie, Aude, Renaud; PRESIDENT & FOUNDER, NOVACAP INVESTMENTS INC. 1981– ; Stock Rsch. & Bond Trading, Harris & Partners 1969–72; Inst. & Stock Rsch., Brault, Guy, O'Brien Inc. 1972–74; Sec. Treas. & Cons., UFICO Limitée 1974–76; Vice-Pres. & Founding Shareholder, Westhill Indus. Ltd. 1976–80; Investment Offr., Innocan 1980–81; Dir., Memotec Data Inc.; Teleglobe Can. Inc.; Mercuriades "Finance" award 1987; Mem., Assn. of Candn. Venture Capital Cos.; C. of C. of Montreal & Que.; Young Pres. Assn.; recreations: nordic skiing, swimming, windsurfing; Home: 190 Pine St., St-Lambert, Qué. J4P 2N4; Office: 1981 McGill College Ave., #515, Montreal, Qué. H3A 2X1.

**BEAUCHAMP, Pierre J.,** FRI(E); real estate executive; b. Ottawa, Ont. 17 Dec. 1943; s. the late Adrien and Simone (Poirier) B.; e. Ottawa Univ.; EXECUTIVE VICE-PRESIDENT, CANADIAN REAL ESTATE ASSN. 1983– ; promoter of Candn. lumber products to Candn. & Am. consumers (a joint project of fed. govt. & Candn. Lumbermen's Assn.); Former Chrmn., Candn. Real Estate Assn. (CREA) Extve. Offrs. Council; Dir., CREA 1 term; Extve. Dir., Real Estate Bd. of Ottawa-Carleton 1980–83; Sec.-Gen., Internat. Real Estate Fed.; Fellow, Real Estate Inst.; clubs: Cercle Univ. d'Ottawa, Ottawa Athletic; Home: 52 Huntersfield, Ottawa, Ont.; Office: 320 Queen St., Suite 2100, Tower A, Ottawa, Ont. K1R 5A3.

**BEAUCHAMP, Sylvie,** B.Sc., M.Sc.; sociologue; née. Montréal, Qué. 12 mai 1950; f. Albert et Rita (Chouinard) B.; é. Univ. de Montréal B.Sc. 1971, M.Sc. 1975; ép. Michel f. Gerald et Irene Sirois 4 mai 1984; enfants: Katia, Alexis, Catherine, Louis-Michel; SECRETAIRE GENERALE ET ADJOINTE AU DIR. GEN., L'ECOLE NATIONALE D'ADMINISTRATION PUBLIQUE (ENAP); A l'ENAP depuis 1984, elle a occupé successivement les postes de chercheure au CEPAQ, d'adjointe au Dir. du perfectionnement et de Dir. par intérim du perfectionnement; antérieurement à son entrée à l'ENAP, elle a été active dans le secteur privé comme dirigeante d'une firme de rech. soc. appliquée; elle a également oeuvré à titre de responsable de rech. à l'Univ. de Montréal; rés.: 2410 Adolphe Chapleau, Sillery, Qué. G1T 1M6; bureau: 945 ave Wolfe, Ste-Foy, Qué. G1V 3J9.

**BEAUCHEMIN, Francine L.,** B.Comm.; securities regulation executive; b. Quebec City, Que. 13 July 1951; e. B.Comm. (Accountancy) 1975; m. François; SENIOR VICE-PRESIDENT, THE MONTREAL EXCHANGE; Office: 800 Victoria Square, Montreal, Que. H4Z 1A9.

**BEAUCHEMIN, Micheline,** O.C. (1973), F.R.S.C., R.C.A.; tapestry weaver; b. Longueuil, Qué.; e. Ecole des Beaux Arts, Montreal, Qué.; studied with Ossip Zadkine in Paris 1953, working on stained glass windows, Chartres, France; took up embroidery and tapestry, Greece 1955; returned to Can. 1957 working as wardrobe keeper and designer C.B.C.; full-time tapestry and weaving 1958; specialized in tapestry weaving, Japan 1962; created Curtain, Nat. Arts Centre, Ottawa; exhns. incl. Montreal and Toronto (all one-woman); 1959; Mexico, Tokyo and Paris; rec'd. Can. Council Grants 1959, 1965, 1973; Centennial Medal 1967; mem. Candn. Council of Esquimaux Arts; has travelled widely in China and India; researched weaving with Andes and Jungle Indians, S.Am. 1973; Address: 22 Chemin du Roy, Les Grondines, Qué. G0A 1WO.

**BEAUCHEMIN, Paul T.,** B.A.Sc.; consulting engineer and urbanist; b. Montreal, Que. 26 Mar. 1931; s. Jules Armand and Marie-Anne (Gervais) B.; e. Coll. de Montréal, B.A.; Ecole Polytechnique, B.A.Sc., C.E., P.Eng.; m. Lise, d. Paul-Henri Roy, 8 Oct. 1955; children: Louis, Sophie, Patrick; PRESIDENT, BEAUCHEMIN-BEATON-LAPOINTE INC.; Pres., Cartier– ;Monenco Inc., Chrmn., Cartier Group; SOMER (multi-disciplinary planning & research group); La Société d'Ingénierie Cartier Limitée; Dir. Cansult Ltd.; mem. Construction Ind. Dev. Council (past Chrmn.); Assn. of Consulting Engrs. of Can. (Pres. 1976–77); Assn. Consulting Engrs. Que. (Pres. 1974–76); Order of Engrs. Que.; Prof. Corp. of Urbanists of Que.; Candn. Inst. of Planners; Engn. Inst. Can.; R. Catholic; recreations: flying, fishing, swimming, boating; Club: Cercle Universitaire; Mount Stephen Club; M.A.A.A.; Home: 754 Upper Lansdowne, Westmount, Qué. H3Y 1J8; Office: 2045 Stanley St., Montreal, Qué. H3A 2V4.

**BEAUCHEMIN, Roger Olivier;** consulting engineer; executive; b. Donnacona, Que. 20 May 1923; s. Jules Armand and Marie-Anne (Gervais) B.; e. Coll. Mont Saint-Louis; Ecole Polytechnique, Univ. de Montréal, B.A.Sc. 1950; m. Andrée, d. Dr. Noël Décarie, 29 June 1950; children: François, Denys, Anne Marie; Roger; PRESIDENT, ROGER O. BEAUCHEMIN & ASSOCIES INC.; Chrmn. & C.E.O., R.C.I., Rocon Containers Internat. Inc.; Vice Chrmn., Rocon Co. Ltd., Poland; Chrmn., AXA Assurances Inc.; Transit II; Dir., Candn. Marconi Co.; Nat. Westminster Bank of Can.; mem. Econ. Counc. of Can. 1982–85; Engr., Tech. Sales Dept., Canada Cement Co. 1950; Partner, J.A. Beauchemin & Associates 1955; Sr. Partner, Beauchemin-Beaton-Lapointe Inc. 1956–86; responsible for transp., structural and certain engn. projects such as: the Macdonald-Cartier Bridge and other bridges in Que. and Cameroons, several freeways and parkways Que., transport and parking facilities Expo '67; consultant to French Govt. re transport. planning for Grenoble Winter Olympic Games 1968; conducted study for Lebanese Govt. on devel. Mt. Hermon summer and winter resort complex; Councillor, Mun. of Mont Tremblant 1965–74; Pres., Chambre de Comm. du Dist. de Montréal 1969–70; Montreal Heart Inst. 1977–78; Chrmn. Montreal Port Counc. 1970–71; Chrmn. Montreal Port Auth. 1977–80; C.E.O. Port of Montreal 1978–80; mem. Order of Engrs. (Que.); Assn. Consulting Engrs. Can.; Inst. of Transport Engrs. (Pres. 1971); Engn. Inst. Can.; Kt. Order of St. Lazarus of Jerusalem; Chrmn. Au Carrefour des Cèdres 1983– ; R. Catholic; recreations: golf, history, skiing, travel; Clubs: Mount Royal; St-Denis; Mont Bruno; Home: 4345 Westmount Ave., Westmount, Qué. H3Y 1W4.

**BEAUDIN, Guy A.,** B.Com., C.A.; financial executive; b. Montreal, Que. 31 Aug. 1928; s. J. Albert Aimé and Esméralda (McGowan) B.; e. St-Joseph de Bordeaux; Coll. Mont St-Louis Montréal; Ecole des Hautes Etudes Commerciales B.Com., C.A. 1954; m. Lise d. Jean and Germaine Courtois De Serres 7 Nov. 1953; children: Michel, Christian, Marie-José, Nicolas, Patrice, Valérie; Pres. and Gen. Mgr., F-I-C Fund Inc. 1972–86; Dir. Unigesco Inc.; Excelco Inc.; joined Raymond, Chabot, Martin & Paré 1950–54; Auditor Corps. Dept. Revenue Can. Taxation 1954–55; Internal Auditor Crédit Foncier Franco-Canadien 1955–58; Comptroller Corp. de Valeurs Trans-Canada 1958–67; Treas. Les Entreprises SNC Ltée 1967–72; mem. Order C.A.'s Que.; recreations: tennis, sailing, skiing; Clubs: St-Denis; M.A.A.A.; Home: 5 Redpath Pl., Montreal, Qué. H3G 1C9.

**BEAUDIN, Yves E.,** B.A., B.Ed., M.Ed.; association executive; educator; b. St. Eustache, Man. 8 Feb. 1944; s. Roland and Alfreda (Lachance) B.; e. St. Mary's Univ., San Antonio, Texas B.A. 1968; Laval Univ. B.Ed. 1973, M.Ed. 1976; m. Judith d. Lionel and Alberta Simard 22 Aug. 1970; children: Sarah, Yves Patrice; PRES., UNITED WAY/CENTRAIDE CANADA 1988– ; High School Teacher 1969–74; H.S. Vice-Principal 1974–78; Principal 1978–80; Dir. Gen., Outaouais Reg. School Bd. 1980–86; Outaouais-Hull Sch. Bd. 1986–88; Vice-Chair, Coalition of National Voluntary Orgns.; Roman Catholic; Mem., Candn. Soc. of Assn. Executives; Home: 336 Radisson, Aylmer, Qué. J9J 2H5.

**BEAUDOIN, François,** M.B.A.; banking executive; b. Montreal, Que. 12 Jan. 1951; s. Léon and Madeleine (Cormier) B.; e. École des Hautes Études Commerciales, Montreal B.B.A. 1972; Columbia Univ. M.B.A. 1973; m. Manon d. Bernard and Madeleine Laverdure 18 Aug. 1974; two d. Marie-Caroline, Chantal; PRESIDENT AND CHIEF EXECUTIVE OFFICER, FEDERAL BUSINESS DEVELOPMENT BANK 1993–; Vice-Pres. Bank of Montreal Ottawa Dist. 1983–85, W. Que. Dist. 1985–90; Exec. Vice-Pres. & Chief Operating Offr., Federal Business Development Bank 1990–93; Vice-Pres. St. Mary's Hosp. Montreal; Dir., St. Mary's Hosp. Foundation, Montreal; author 'Le Zero Base Budgeting: L'outil dans le cadre dynamique d'une organisation' 1979; Beta Gamma Sigma; Clubs: Royal Montreal Golf; Club St-Denis; Board of Trade of Metro. Montreal; Office: P.O. Box 335, Tour de la Place-Victoria, Montreal, Qué. H4Z 1L4.

**BEAUDOIN, Hon. Gérald-A.,** O.C., C.R., M.S.R.C., B.A., M.A., LL.L., D.E.S.D., LL.D. (h.c.); avocat; professeur de droit; sénateur; né Montréal, Qué. 15 avril 1929; f. Armand et Aldéa B.; é. études primaires, Montréal, secondaires chez les Jésuites, Montréal; Univ. de Montréal, B.A. 1950, LL.L. 1953 (Prix du doyen), M.A. (droit) 1954, études post-graduées; Univ. Toronto Law Sch. (boursier Carnegie) 1954–55; Univ. d'Ottawa, D.E.S.D. 1958; LL.D. (hon. causa), Univ. de Louvain-La-Neuve 1989; ép. Renée, f. E. Desmarais, Montréal, Qué. 11 sept. 1954; enfants: Viviane, Louise, Denise, Françoise; MEMBRE DU SÉNAT DU CANADA depuis le 26 septembre 1988– ; Conseiller juridique au Min. de la Justice, Ottawa, 1956; Conseiller parlementaire adjoint de la Chambre des communes 1965; nommé c.r. 1969; Doyen, Univ. d'Ottawa, Faculté de droit, Sec. de droit civil, 1969–79; Vice-Prés. (Can.) de l'Inst. international de droit d'expression française depuis 1973; mem. Barreau du Qué. depuis 1954; Assn. du Barreau candn. 1954 (Prés. nat., Sec. de droit constit. 1971–73, 1986–87); Gouverneur de l'Inst. candn. d'études juridiques supérieures depuis 1979; membre de la Comm. sur l'Unité can. (Comm. Pepin-Robarts) 1977–79; membre du Conseil de la Section canadienne de la Comm. internat. des juristes depuis 1979 (Vice-prés. 1987–90 et Prés. 1990–92); mem. titulaire de l'Académie internationale de droit comparé 1984; mem. de la Société Royale du Canada, 1977; Officier de l'Ordre du Canada, 1980; mem. de l'Académie des lettres du Québec 1983; Directeur du Centre des droits de la personne, Univ. d'Ottawa 1986–88; Professeur titulaire de droit constitutionnel 1969–89; Professeur invité depuis 1989; mem. du Comité de la rédaction française de la Constitution 1985–89; Co-Prés. du comité mixte spécial de la Chambre des communes et du Sénat sur la formule d'amendement (Rapport Beaudoin-Edwards); membre et co-président du Comité spécial mixte du Sénat et de la Chambre des communes sur le renouvellement du Canada (Rapport Beaudoin-Dobbie) 1991–92; Prés. du Comité sénatorial permanent des Affaires juridiques et constitutionnelles 1993– ; a donné un grand nombre de conférences sur la Constitution, au Canada, en Europe, aux Etats-Unis, en Amérique du Sud, en Afrique, et en Australie; auteur d'un grand nombre d'articles en droit constitutionnel et des ouvrages intitulés 'Essais sur la Constitution' 1979; 'Le partage des pouvoirs' 1980 (3e éd., 1983); 'La Constitution du Canada' 1990; co-auteur de 'Mécanismes pour une nouvelle Constitution' 1981, 'Les quotidiens et la loi' 1981, et de plusieurs autres ouvrages sur la Constitution; Co-éditeur avec W.S. Tarnopolsky de: 'La Charte canadienne des droits et libertés' 1982; 'Canadian Charter of Rights and Freedoms' 1982; Co-éditeur avec Ed Ratushny de: 'Charte canadienne des droits et libertés' 2ème éd. 1989, et de 'Canadian Charter of Rights and Freedoms' 2nd ed. 1989; Co-éditeur avec Daniel Turp de: 'Perspectives canadiennes et européennes des droits de la personne' 1986; éditeur des ouvrages: 'Conférence sur la Cour suprême du Canada - Conference on the Supreme Court of Canada' 1986; 'Charter Cases - Causes invoquant la Charte' 1987; 'Vos clients et la Charte - Your Clients and the Charter' 1988; 'As the Charter evolves - Ainsi évolue la Charte' 1990; 'La Charte: Dix ans après - The Charter: ten years later' 1992; éditeur de l'ouvrage collectif: 'Vues canadiennes et européennes des droits et libertés' 1989; Professeur invité à La Sorbonne, à Paris, au printemps 1985; à Tunis, en août 1993 (pour l'Académie int. de droit const.); Conférencier invité à Cambridge au Royaume-Uni en 1979, 1981 et 1983 et à Strasbourg en 1984 et en 1988; titulaire du Prix de l'Acfas, en sciences humaines, en mai 1987; catholique r.; loisirs: lectures, voyages, natation; Club: Cercle Universitaire; résidence: 4 St-Thomas, Hull, Qué. J8Y 1L4.

**BEAUDOIN, Gérard,** M.D.; psychiatrist; university professor; b. Montreal, Que. 4 Feb. 1922; s. Médéric and Blandine (Brûlé) B.; e. Coll. de St-Jean, 1935–40 and Coll. Ste-Marie, Montreal, B.A. 1942; Univ. de Montréal, P.C.B. 1943, M.D. 1948; m. Ruth, d. J. Théo Legault, Montreal, Que., 31 July 1950; one d., two s.; Dir. Dept. of Psychiatry, Univ. de Montréal and mem., Council Faculty of Med. 1965–.; Dir., Dept. of Psychiatry, Hôpital Général du Christ-Roi, Verdun, Que., since 1953; residency: Hôpital Général de Verdun, 1948–49; Montefiore Hosp., N.Y., 1950–51; N.Y. Hosp., White Plains, N.Y., 1951–53; C.S., P.Q., 1955; Asst. Prof., Dept. Psychiatry, Univ. de Montréal, 1956–64; Assoc. Prof. 1964; mem. 'Comité Consultatif,' since 1965; mem., Candiac Catholic Sch. Comn.; Candn. Psych. Assn. (Dir. since 1963); Que. Psych. Assn. (Dir. since 1962); Candn. Med. Assn.; Assn. des Médecins de Langue Française du Can.; Société Médicale de Montréal; R. Catholic; Home: 58 Place de Bretagne, Candiac, Qué. J5R 3M9; Office: 3875 St. Urbain, Suite 405, Montréal, Qué. H2W 1C1.

**BEAUDOIN, Jacques;** b. Sainte-Brigitte de Laval, Qué. 8 Apr. 1935; e. Univ. of Michigan; Univ. du Qué.; N.Y. State Police Academy; FBI Academy; DEPUTY MINISTER, PUBLIC SECURITY, 1988– ; Agent, Sûreté du Qué. 1958–68; Lieutenant (Offr.) 1968–73; Depy. Dir. Gen. 1973–74; Dir. Gen., 1974–88; Medal, Order of St. John of Jerusalem; Centennial Medal; mem., Assn. of Chiefs of Police; Am. Mgmt. Assn.; recreations: horse-breeding; Club: Saint-Denis; Office: 1200, Route de l'Eglise, Sainte-Foy, Qué. G1V 4T4

**BEAUDOIN, Laurent,** O.C. (1973), M.Com.; industriel; né à Laurier Station, comté de Lotbinière, Qué. 13 mai 1938; f. P.A. et Yvonne (Rodrigue) B.; é. Coll. Ste. Anne, B.A. 1957; Univ. de Sherbrooke, maîtrise en commerce 1960; Institut des Comptables Agréés, Comptable agréé 1961; Docteur (hon. causa) en science de l'administration, Univ. de Sherbrooke 1971; Docteur (hon. causa) en économie, Univ. Sainte-Anne, Pointe-de-l'Eglise, Nouvelle-Ecosse 1983; Mgmnt. Achievement Award, McGill Univ. 1984; Fellow de l'Ordre des Comptables Agrées du Qué. 1984; Doctor (hon. causa) of civil law, Bishop's Univ. 1989; Doctorat (hon. causa), Univ. de Montréal 1989; Doctorat (hon. causa) York Univ. 1992; Doctor (hon. causa) of Sci., Queen's Univ. of Belfast 1992; ép. Claire, f. J.-Armand Bombardier 29 août 1959; enfants: Nicole, Elaine, Denise, Pierre; pratique privée, Beaudoin, Morin, Dufresne et Ass., Qué. 1961–63; contrôleur, Bombardier 1963; Prés. et Dir. Gén. 1966; Prés. du Conseil et Chef de la Dir. 1979; Membre du Conseil d'Admin. de: The Conference Bd.; membre: Institut des Comptables Agréés; Clubs: Mont-Royal; Loisirs: motoneige, golf, équitation, tennis; Bureau: 800 Boul. René Levesque Ouest, Montréal, Qué. H3B 1Y8.

**BEAUDOIN, Louise;** historienne; née Québec, Qué. 26 septembre 1945; f. Jean-Robert et Louise (Des Rivières) Beaudoin; é. Univ. Laval Licence en Histoire 1967, Maîtrise en Histoire 1972; Sorbonne, Paris Licence de Sociologie 1969; ép. François f. Joseph et Marie-Antoinette Dorlot 11 août 1973; DIRECTRICE GÉNÉRALE, SOCIÉTÉ DU PALAIS DE LA CIVILISATION 1990– ; Administratrice, Vie Optimum, Paris; Théâtre expérimental des femmes (Espace Go), Montréal; Domaine Forget de Charlevoix Inc., St-Irénée; Directrice adjointe des Etudes, Ecole Nationale d'Adm. Publique Univ. du Québec 1971–76; Directrice du Cabinet du Ministre des Affaires intergouvernementales Québec 1976–81; Directrice des Affaires françaises, Ministère des Relations internationales Québec 1981–84; Déléguée générale du Québec, France 1984–85; Chargée de mission, en France, auprès des PDG de Lavalin et Canadair 1986–87; Directrice Distribution, Marketing et Affaires Internationales, Telefilm Canada 1987–90; Officier de la Légion d'Honneur; auteure 'La formation des cabinets provinciaux 1867–1967' 1967; en collaboration 'Le Québec dans le monde' 1977; 'La francophonie en direct' Tome I 1987; Bureau: 275, rue Notre-Dame est, Montréal, Qué. H2Y 1C6.

**BEAUDOIN, Nicole,** B.A., M.B.A., F.C.A.; business executive; b. Montréal, Qué. 19 July 1939; d. Ovide and Gilberte (Giroux) Beaudoin; e. Univ. de Montréal B.A. 1960; Ecole des Hautes Etudes Commerciales B.B.A. 1978, M.B.A. 1985; C.A. 1978; m. André (d. 1986) s. Joseph and Marie-Anne Sauvé 30 May 1960; children: Jasmin, Pascale, Benoit; GENERAL MANAGER, EASTERN MANUFACTURING DIV., SCOTT PAPER LTD. 1992– ; Dir. Vidétron Ltée; Mgr. Emaco Canada Ltd. 1969–74; Asst. Controller and Office Mgr. Le Roi des Bas Prix de la région de Montréal 1974–76; Auditing Trainee Samson Bélair 1978–81; Controller Lavo Ltd. 1981–84; Controller Shirtmate Apparel Group Ltd. 1984–86, Vice Pres. Finance & Adm. 1987; Vice Pres. Finance & Adm. Via Rail Canada Inc. 1987–89; Vice Pres., Finance and Mem. Mgmt. Ctte., Perkins Papers Ltd. 1990–92; mem. Bd. Order Chart. Accts. Prov. Qué. 1984–88; Dir. Ordre des Ingénieurs du Qué.; mem. YMCA Found. Greater Montréal; Centre Marie Vincent; recreations: golf, alpine skiing, music, theatre; Home: 203, 4560 Promenade Paton, Laval, Qué. H7W 4W2; Office: 100 – 1st Ave., C.P. 500, Crabtree, Qué. J0K 1B0.

**BEAUDOIN, Pierre,** LL.L., LL.M.; lawyer; b. Quebec City, Que. 28 Feb. 1943; s. J.-Robert and Louise (des Rivières) B.; e. Laval Univ. LL.L. 1965, LL.M. 1967; Ecole Nat. d'Admin. Paris 1966; m. Helene d. Jules Gauvin 21 Feb. 1981; children: François, Sandrine; PARTNER, LAVERY, de BILLY; Nat. Assembly, Govt. of Que. 1966–70; joined present firm 1970; Dir., Reseau Pathonic Inc. 1984– ; Laïterie Laval Ltée. 1982–86; L'Unique General Insur. Co. 1980–85; Teacher, Fac. of Law, Laval Univ. 1968–75; Dir., Coll. des Jésuites de Qué. 1970–80; Gouv., The Que. Bar Found.; Pres., Qué. Young Bar Assn. 1972; Mem., Gen. Counc., Qué. Bar 1971–74; recreations: travel, skiing; clubs: Garrison; Home: 2375 Perodeau, Sillery, Qué.; Office: 925 chemin St-Louis, Bur. 500, Quebec City, Qué. G1R 4W8.

**BEAUDOIN-ROSS, Jacqueline,** B.A., M.A.; curator, costume historian; b. Montreal, Que. 15 Aug. 1931; d. Leopold Joseph and Eliza Mae (Squires) B.; e. McGill Univ. B.A. (Hons.) 1952, M.A. 1975; m. the late Ian s. Muriel and Donald Ross 30 Nov. 1955; children: Ian Beaudoin, Heather Diana; CURATOR OF COSTUME AND TEXTILES, MCCORD MUSEUM OF CANADIAN HISTORY 1979– ; curated 16 in-house costume or textile exbns. for McCord Mus.; Lectr. on Candn. Costume Hist., Concordia Univ. 1980, '81; McGill Univ. 1986; author of various journal articles; co-author: 'Costume in Canada: An Annotated Bibliography' 1984, 'Costume in Canada: The Sequel' 1991; clothing entry for 'The Canadian Encyclopedia' 1985; 'Form and Fashion: Nineteenth Century Monteal Dress' (exbn. catalogue) 1992; recreations: the arts, tennis; clubs: Hillside Tennis; Home: 24 Thornhill Ave., Westmount, Qué. H3Y 2E1; Office: 690 Sherbrooke St. W., Montreal, Qué. H3A 1E9.

**BEAUDRY, Jean;** arbitrator; b. St-Julienne, Que. 14 Aug. 1929; e. Labour Coll. of Can.; Arbitrator and Mediator of Labour/Management disputes 1990– ; trade union career began Noranda Mines, N. Que.; Asst. Geol. for 7 yrs.; joined Internat. Union of Mine, Mill and Smelter Workers 1947; el. departmental steward; joined Canadian Congress of Labour Volunteers' Organ. Comte. 1948; el. Recording Secy., Local 4278, Un. Steelworkers of Am., 1949; served on various local comtes. during next 5 yrs.; also served as Secy., N.W. Que. Mining Council for several terms; apptd. Internat. rep., Un. Steelworkers of Am. 1954–85 (formerly Extve. Vice Pres. Candn. Labour Cong. 1970–74); retired 1 Jan. 1985; has also worked on various comtes of Que. Fed. of Labour and travelled overseas on behalf of Steelworkers and Candn. labour movement; Labour Rep. on Royal Comm. on Safety and Health of Miners in Ontario 1974–76; Sr. Advisor to C.E.O., Candn. Labour Market and Productivity Centre 1985–88; R. Catholic; Club: Canadian; Home: 1219 Whitmore Ave., Ottawa, Ont. K2C 2N6.

**BEAUGRAND, Kenneth Louis,** B.A., LL.B., LL.M.; business executive; b. New York 19 Oct. 1938; e. Brown Univ., Providence, R.I. B.A. 1960; Columbia Law School, N.Y. LL.B. 1963; Univ. of London, England LL.M. 1964; m.; 3 children; SR. VICE PRES. AND GEN. MGR., U.S. OPNS., THE MANUFACTURERS LIFE INSURANCE CO. 1992– ; Dir., Chrmn. & Pres., The Manufacturers Life Insurance Co. (U.S.A.); Dir. & Chrmn., The Manufacturers Life Insurance Co. of Am.; Dir., Manulife Holding Corp.; The Manufacturers Life Insurance Co. of Michigan; Wilkie, Farr & Gallagher, Solicitors, N.Y. 1964–68; I.O.S. Ltd., Financial Services, Geneva, Switzerland 1968–72, Solicitor 1968–69, Secretary 1969–71, Vice-Pres., General Counsel & Dir. 1971–72; Value Capital Services, Amsterdam, Holland, Financial Services, Vice-Pres., General Counsel & Dir. 1972–73; Aird, Zimmerman & Berlis, Solicitors, Toronto 1973–77; joined Eaton Financial Services Ltd. in 1977 as Vice-Pres., Secy. & General Counsel; Sr. Vice-Pres., Secy. and General Counsel 1979; Sr. Vice Pres., Insurance and Fund Divisions 1981; Sr. Vice Pres., Operations 1984; Exec. Vice Pres., 1985–86; joined The Imperial Life Assur. Co. of Can. as Sr. Vice Pres., Investments 1986; Extve. Vice Pres. & C.O.O., The Imperial Life Assurance Co. of Canada 1987–89; Chrmn. & C.E.O., Imbrook Properties Ltd. 1986–89; joined The Manufacturers Life Insurance Co. as Sr. Vice Pres. and Gen. Mgr., Canada Operations 1989; recreations: tennis, skiing, sailing; Clubs: Toronto Lawn Tennis; University; Westmount Golf & Country; Home: 427 Russell Hill Rd., Toronto, Ont. M5P 2S4; Office: 200 Bloor St. E., Toronto, Ont. M4W 1E5.

**BEAUJOT, Roderic P.,** B.A., Ph.D.; professor of sociology; b. Whitewood, Sask. 22 April 1946; s. Leon P.R. and Dorothy (Mullie) B.; e. College Mathieu Gravelbourg Sask. B.A. 1967; Univ. of Alta. Ph.D. 1975; m. Elisabeth J.M. d. Sipke and Betty Vandermeer 13 July 1974; children: Ariel, Natalie, Damien; SOCIOLOGIST / DEMOGRAPHER, UNIV. OF WESTERN ONTARIO 1976– ; Demographer, Statistics Canada 1974–76; Pres., Fed. of Canadian Demographers 1987–90; author: 'Population Change in Canada: The Challenges of Policy Adaptation' 1991; Office: Dept. of Sociology, Univ. of Western Ont., London, Ont. N6A 5C2.

**BEAULAC-BAILLARGEON, Louise,** B.A., B.Pharm., Ph.D.; university professor, pharmacologist, scientist; b. Shawinigan, Que. 21 Feb. 1944; d. Auray L. and Cécile (Allard) Beaulac; e. Coll. Marie de l'Incarnation B.A. 1964; Laval Univ. B.Pharm. 1968, Ph.D. 1974, post-doctoral studies 1978–82; m. Michael s. Thomas and Rita (Parrot) Baillargeon 2 Aug. 1967; children: Emilie, Grégoire (Baillargeon); ASSOC. PROF. & CHAIR OF PHARMACOLOGY, SCHOOL OF PHARMACY, FACULTY OF MEDICINE, LAVAL UNIV. 1978– ; Asst. Prof., Laval Univ. 1974–78; Assoc. Prof. & Chair of Pharm. 1978; nomination: Full Prof. 1994; Chair, Foetal & Perinatal Pharm., conducts continuing education courses; fields of rsch.: estimation of milk to plasma ratios by an in vitro methodological approach; pharmacokinetics during pregnancy & post-partum; caffeine cigarettes interaction on birth weight; Mem., Rsch. Ctr., Hôp. St-François d'Assise 1987; Comn. de la rech. & Bd. of Dir., Fac. des études sup., Laval Univ.

1990– ; Bd. of Dir. & Sec., School of Pharm. 1992– ; Dir., Master Degree Prog. in Hospital Pharm. 1980–88; Soc. can. pour l'avancement des sci. pharm. summer 1967; MRC scholarship 1968–72; Visiting Scientist, Unité de rech. mère enfant, INSERM Paris France 1988; Mem., Assn. of Faculties of Pharm. of Canada; Club de rech. clin.; author and editor: 'Mortalité et morbidité périnatales et infantiles' 1989; co-author and editor: 'Médicaments pendant la grossesse et la lactation' forthcoming; author of many communications, articles, 2 book chapters & peer-reviewed sci. papers; co-author of 1 chapter in 'Médicaments pour personnes âgées' 1991; recreations: computers, painting, music, travelling, alpine and nordic skiing, biking; Home: 1850, Côte du Verger, Sillery, Que. G1T 2P4;; Office: Quebec, Que. G1K 7P4.

**BEAULIEU, Charles E.,** Ph.D.; executive/educator; b. Amqui, Que. 5 July 1930; s. J. Antoine and M. Luce (Tremblay) B.; e. Laval Univ. B.A. 1951, B.Sc. 1956, Ph.D. 1960; m. Madeleine d. Armand St. Pierre 5 May 1956; children: Ann-Louise, Jean C., Stephane Eric; CHRMN. & CHIEF EXTVE. OFFR., NAT. OPTICS INST. 1988– ; Prof. of Metallurgy, Univ. Laval 1961–68; Head, Dept. of Mining & Metallurgy 1966–69; founded Campus of Rimouski (Univ. du Qué.), 1st Dir. 1969–70; Founding Dir., Nat. Inst. of Sci. Rsch., Univ. du Qué. 1970–76; Vice-Pres. Edn. & Rsch., Univ. du Qué. 1976–79; Assoc. Dep. Min. (Mines), Dept. Energy & Resources, Que. 1979–82; Dep. Min., Dept. of Indus. & Comm., Que. 1982–88; Dir., Sidbec 1982–88; NRC 1976–79; CRIQ 1969–74; Comm. Adv. Bd., Doc Ottawa 1976–78; Gov., Univ. du Qué. 1969–79; post-doct. fellowship, NATO 1960; Mem., Inst. de Cardiol. de Qué.; CRMA; Ordre des Ingénieurs du Qué.; Candn. Academy of Engineering; Hon. doctorate, Univ. du Qué. 1991; recreations: skiing, golf, fishing; club: Revermont Golf; Home: 999 Beauregard, App. 601, Ste-Foy, Qué. G1V 4T9; Office: 369 Franquet, Ste-Foy, Qué. G1P 4N8.

**BEAULIEU, Hon. Lucien Arthur,** B.A., M.S.W., LL.B.; judge; b. Mutrie, Sask. 10 Sept. 1933; s. Magloire and Elodie (Boudreau) B.; e. Philomath Sch. Mutrie, Sask.; Maison St. Joseph, Otterburne, Man. 1950; Coll. Mathieu, Gravelbourg, Sask. 1951; Univ. of Ottawa B.A. 1955, M.S.W. 1960; Osgoode Hall Law Sch. LL.B. 1966; m. Joan Patricia d. Edmond J. Andrecheck, Barry's Bay, Ont. 13 Aug. 1962; children: André J., Noël W.; JUSTICE, ONTARIO COURT (GENERAL DIV.) Toronto 1993– ; Sr. Judge, Ontario Court (Provincial Div.) Ottawa 1990–93; Sr. Judge, Provincial Court (Family Div.) York, York Region and Peel 1977–90, apptd. Prov. Judge Family Div. 1973; Chrmn. Task Force on Vandalism 1979–81 (author of report); called to Bar of Ont. 1968; Social Worker, Sask. Dept. Social Welfare 1956–58; Cath. Children's Aid, Toronto 1960–63, Case-worker and Dept. Supvr.; Group Home Supvr. 1961–69; Asst. Crown Atty. Toronto 1968–71; Asst. Prov. Dir. and Prov. Dir. Appeals Legal Aid Ont. 1971–73; Commr. Royal Comn. on Violence in Communications Industry 1975–77 (co-author 7 vol. Report 1977); editor & author various articles on young offenders, violence in the family; winner Jaycees Effective Speaking Contest, 1957 Nat.; Winner, Impromptu Debates, Osgoode Hall; served with Candn. Militia, rank 2nd Lt.; mem. Prov. Family Court Assn. (Dir. and Pres.); Special Projects Dir., Youth and Family Court Ctte., Candn. Assn. of Provincial Court Judges 1984–93; Internat. Youth Magistrate Assn. (Dir., Sec. Gen., Depy. Pres.); Candn. Bar Assn.; Candn. Assn. Corrections & Criminology; Thomas More Lawyers Guild; Lawyers Club; Ont. Assn. of Family Mediation; Candn. Assn. of Family Mediators; Assn. of Conciliation Courts; Ass. de juristes d'expression française; K. of C.; R. Catholic; recreations: tennis, music, reading, walking, theatre; Home: 435 Sackville, Toronto, Ont. M4X 1T1; Office: 361 University Ave., Toronto, Ont. M5G 1T3.

**BEAULIEU, Hon. Mario,** B.A., LL.L.; notary and Title Attorney; b. Plantagenet, Ont. Feb. 1930; s. Henri de Montpellier-Beaulieu and Berthe (Lalonde) B.; e. Coll. St-Ignace & Coll. Ste-Marie (Montréal) B.A.; Univ. Montréal, LL.L. 1955; m. Louise, d. René Thomas Montréal, Qué. 8 sept. 1956; children: François, Martine, Louis, Stephane, Charles; FORMER SENIOR PARTNER, ESPOSITO-COCCIARDI BEAULIEU; Chrmn., Simard Beaudry Inc.; La Societé d'Adm. Place d'Armes Inc. (S.A.P.A.); Dir., Daigle Lumber Ltd.; Epicerie en Gros Métropolitaine Inc.; Paurad Inc.; Winzen (Toronto) Ltd.; Gov., Youth and Music of Canada 1981; Former Chrmn., Fondation Wilfrid Pelletier 1986; Former Vice-Chrmn. Opcan-Katimavik 1985; Dir., Canada Post Corp. 1984–87; notary and Title Attorney 1956; Union Nationale Candidate in gen. el. Laurier, 1962; Pres., Union Nationale electoral campaign 1966; Chief of Staff, Premier Daniel Johnson and Depy. Min. of Extve. Counc. 1966; Gen. Dir. Union Nationale 1968; el. M.P.P. Dorion, 1969; Min. Immigration (Mar.), Min. Fin. Inst. (Apr.), Min. Finance (July); Vice-Pres., P.C. electoral campaign (Que.) 1984; Chrmn., P.C. electoral campaign 1988; mem., Candn. Bar Assn.; Apptd., Senate of Canada 1990; R. Catholic; recreation: golf; Clubs: Chambre Commerce (Montréal and Laval); Laval-sur-le-Lac; BOCA Hotel and Club (Boca-Raton, Fla.); Le Club Colette, Palm Beach, Fla.; Balmoral; Residence: 1139 Blvd Mont-Royal, Outremont, Qué. H2V 2H6; Office: 4230 St. Elzear Blvd. E., Laval, Qué. H7E 4P2.

**BEAULIEU, Hon. Roland,** M.L.A., B.Com.; politician; b. Kilburn, N.B. 21 Dec. 1944; s. Ida B.; e. Cormier High Sch.; Centre Universitaire Saint-Louis-Maillet B.Com. 1986; Univ. of Waterloo Cert. in Econ. Devel.; m. Monique d. Ronald and Cecile Carrier 23 Sept. 1973; one d. Michelle; Min. of Tourism, Recreation & Heritage N.B. 1987–91; various bus. positions N.B. 1970–86; el. M.L.A. for Edmunston 1986; Home: 62 Vimy St., Edmunston, N.B. E3V 1A4; Office: P.O. Box 6000, Fredericton, N.B. E3B 5H1.

**BEAULNE, Guy,** C.M., B.A., B.Ph.; actor and director; b. Ottawa, Ont. 23 Dec. 1921; s. Léonard Elie and Yvonne (Daoust) B.; e. Univ. of Ottawa, Normal Sch. Teacher Dipl. 1941, B.A., B.Ph. 1945; Conservatoire Nat. Supérieur d'art dramatique Paris 1948–49; m. Pauline d. Laurent J. and Jeanne (de Varennes) Beaudry 15 Sept. 1948; children: Pascale, Martine, Vincent; Dir., Conservatoire d'Art Dramatique de Montréal 1981–87; retired 1988; Drama and Arts Critic 'Le Droit' Ottawa 1945–52; Theatre Reviewer 'Points de vue' Montréal 1955–61; Drama Prod. Radio and TV, Radio-Canada Montréal 1950–63; Dir. Gen. of Artistic Training and of Theatre, Dept. Cultural Affairs Qué. 1963–70; Dir. Gen. Le Grand Théâtre de Qué. 1970–76; Cultural Couns. Délégation générale du Qué. Paris 1976–79; mem. Exec. and Drama Adjudicator Dominion Drama Festival 1950–70; Pres. and mem. Exec. Candn. Theatre Centre (ITI-Unesco); Founder and Dir. Assn. canadienne du théâtre d'amateurs 1958; Qué. Comnr. Prague Quadriennal 1967; recipient Candn. Drama Award 1955; Candn. Centennial Medal 1967; Member of the Order of Canada 1975; Confederation Medal 1992; el. to Royal Soc. Can. 1972; Pres. Académie des lettres et des sciences humaines 1982–84; Hon. mem. Assn. for Candn. Theatre Rsch. 1982; Hon. Mem., Société québécoise d'études théâtrales 1990; Chevalier de l'Ordre national du Québec 1993; author 'Notre théâtre - Conscience d'un peuple' 1967; 'Le théâtre canadien-français' 1976; contr. 'History of Theatre' 3rd ed. 1968; numerous articles various nat. and internat. theatre publs.; Home: 3710 Jeanne Mance St., Montréal, Qué. H2X 2K5.

**BEAULNE, Jean-Pierre,** Q.C., B.A., B.Ph., LL.B., Dipl.E.S.D.; judge; b. Ottawa, Ont. 19 Sept. 1925; s. Léonard Elie and Yvonne (Daoust) B.; e. Univ. of Ottawa B.A., B.Ph. 1949; Osgoode Hall Law Sch., called to Bar 1955; Univ. of Ottawa D.E.S.D. 1969; m. Louise d. Lorenzo and Yvonne Lafleur 17 Sept. 1955; children: Emmanuelle, Philippe, Brigitte; CHRMN., RCMP PUBLIC COMPLAINTS COMMISSION 1992– ; Judge of the Ontario Court of Justice 1967–92, Retired; Navigator, RCAF (Can. & U.K.) 1943–45; Candn. Army (Korea) 1950–52; joined Lafleur & Aubin (later Lafleur, Aubin & Beaulne) 1955; Pro-tem Mem., Immigration Appeal Bd. 1958–63; Crown Couns. (on request) 1957–62; Jr. Couns., Norris Inquiry 1963; extensive practice in crim. & civil litigation; Q.C. 1966; Lectr., Univ. of Ottawa 1967–92; Past Chrmn./Extve./Mem. of several health, justice, arts/theatre & edn. orgns.; Hon. Mem., Bd. of Gov., Univ. of Ottawa 1983– ; Dir., Candn. War Corres. Assn.; clubs: Cercle Univ. d'Ottawa, Nat. Press (Life mem.); Office: P.O. Box 3423, Stn. D, Ottawa, Ont. K1P 6L4.

**BEAUMONT, Donald A.,** B.A.; retail executive; b. Hamilton, Ont. 19 Jan. 1935; s. Bert and Jessie Dorothea B.; e. Brantford (Ont.) Coll. Inst. 1954; McMaster Univ. B.A. 1957, Extension Retail Adm. 1961; m. Marilyn d. William and Myrna Flight 24 June 1961; children: Robert Scott, Linda Catherine, Carol Diane; PRESIDENT & CHIEF EXECUTIVE OFFICER, KMART CANADA LIMITED 1991; Asst. Dept. Mgr. T. Eaton Co. Ltd. Hamilton, Ont. 1957–62, Group Sales Mgr. 1962–65, Store Mgr. Toronto 1965–66, Group Mdse. Mgr. 1966–74, Nat. Group Mdse. Mgr. 1974–77; Vice Pres. Mktg., Towers Department Stores Inc. 1977–89, Extve. Vice Pres. & C.O.O. 1989–91; Exec. Cttee. & Bd. of Dirs., Retail Council of Can.; Dir., Ravel Church Properties; Mem., Metro Toronto Bd. of Trade; Internat. Senator, Junior Chamber of Commerce; Council of Business Leaders for Region of Peel United Way; Bd. of Dirs., Kids' Help Foundation; Home: 5 Chipstead Rd., Don Mills, Ont. M3B 3E5.

**BEAUPRE, Odette;** lyrique artist; b. Rivière-du-Loup, Qué. 5 Apr. 1952; d. Maurice and Eméline (Pelletier) B.; e. Laval Univ.; Cons. of Music of Qué.; children: Geneviève Desjardins, Andreane Beaupré; mem., Candn. Opera Co. Ensemble 1983–85; repertoire incl. 'Dorabella' Cosi fan tutte, 'Siebel' Faust, 'Suzuki' Madame Butterfly, 'Zozo' The Merry Widow, 'Lucy May Lockit' The Beggar's Opera and 'Carmen' Carmen; performed title role in Carmen with the Opera of Qué. 1985; 'Lola' in Cavaleria Rusticana 1985 and 'Stephano' in Romeo and Juliette 1986 with the Montreal Opera; 'Siebel' in Faust with the Edmonton Opera 1985; 'Maddalena' in Rigoletto with Candn. Opera Co. 1987; 3rd prize Indiana Opera Theatre MacAllister Award Competition 1985; 1st award, International Festival of Toronto; 1st award, Chalmer's Found., Ont. Art Counc. 1986; rec'd Canada Counc. grant for an audition tour in Europe 1987; performed with Que. Symphony Orch., Montreal Symphony Orch., Les Jeunesses Music. du Can.; Catholic.

**BEAUREGARD, Hon. Jules,** B.A., B.C.L.; judge; b. Montréal Qué. 11 Aug. 1922; s. Georges Louis and Cécile Marie (Cousineau) B.; e. Jéan de Brebeuf B.A. 1940; McGill Univ. B.C.L. 1945; m. Andrée d. Dr. L.H. Gariepy 16 Aug. 1947; children: Christiane, Julie, Louis, Alain; JUDGE, SUPERIOR COURT OF QUE. 1975– ; Jr. Partner, Beauregard, Brisset, Reycraft & Lalande, Montréal 1947–56; Mun. Judge, City of Dorval 1950–60; Sr. Partner, Pagé, Beauregard, Duchesne & Renaud, Montréal 1957–75; cr. Q.C. 1960; Legal Counsel to L'Oeuvre des Enfants Oubliés; Gouverneur Hôpital Marie Enfant; recreations: golf, tennis, cross country skiing; Club: Knowlton Golf & Country; Home: 672 Chemin Marie Leber, Ile des Soeurs, Qué. H3E 1T3; 4300 ouest, de Maisonneuve, #909, Montréal, Qué. H3Z 3C7; Office: 12.43 Court House, 10 St. Antoine St. E., Montréal, Qué. H2Y 1A2.

**BEAUREGARD, Luc,** B.A., A.P.R.; public relations executive; b. Montreal, Que. 4 Aug. 1941; s. François and Gertrude (Lévesque) B.; e. Coll. Stanislas B.A. 1959; m. Michelle d. Roland and Simonne Lafleur; children: Valérie, Stéphanie, François, Philippe (from previous m.); PRESIDENT, NATIONAL PUBLIC RELATIONS LTD. 1976– ; Reporter, Parliamentary Corr. in Ottawa, City Ed. Montreal Daily La Presse 1961–68; Pres. Sec. Que. Min. of Edn. 1968–69; Founding Partner Beauregard, Landry, Nantel & Assoc. Pub. Relations Cons. 1970–73; Pres. and Publisher Montreal-Matin Daily Newspaper 1973–76; Sec. of Info. Comn. Que. Liberal Party 1978, 1979, 1980; Chrmn. Amarc, City of Montreal Corp. managing Man and His World (formerly Expo '67) 1982–86; Dir. St. Hubert BBQ; Chrmn. Montreal Island School Council Found. 1991– ; Dir., Montreal Museum of Contemporary Art 1987– ; Chrmn. Montreal Better Bus. Bur. 1983–84; Dir. and mem. Exec. Ctte. Que. Heart Found. 1983–85; Dir. Nouvelle Compagnie Theatrale; Chrmn., Found. of Montreal Museum of Contemporary Art 1987–90; Pres. Candn. Pub. Rlns. Soc. 1984–85 (Chrmn. Cons. Inst. 1982–83); Chrmn. N. Am. Pub. Rlns. Counc. 1985–86; recreations: golf, tennis; Club: des Quinze, Mount-Royal, Knowlton; Home: 3430 Peel St., Montreal, Qué. H3A 3K8; Office: 770 Sherbrooke St. W., Suite 1600, Montreal, Qué. H3A 1G1.

**BEAUREGARD, Hon. Marc,** B.A., B.C.L.; judge; b. Montreal, Que. 14 July 1937; s. François and Gertrude (Levesques) B.; e. Stanislas Coll. Montreal; B.A.(Paris) 1956; McGill Univ. B.C.L. 1959; m. Mireille d. Conrad Lefebvre, Montreal, Que., 17 Sept. 1960; children: Patrick, Charles, Emmanuelle; JUSTICE, COURT OF APPEAL OF QUE.; called to Bar of Que. 1960; Council mem. Jr. Bar of Montreal 1965–66; Bar of Montreal 1967–68; Bar Prov. of Que. 1967–68; Que. Sec. Candn. Bar Assn. 1974–75; R. Catholic; recreations: bridge, hunting, tennis, fishing; Home: 1175 Ave. Bernard W., app. 52, Outremont, Qué. H2V 1V5; Office: Court House, 1 Notre Dame E., Montreal, Qué. H2Y 1B6.

**BEAVERBROOK, Lady,** LL.D.; b. Sutton, Surrey, Eng., 27 July 1910; d. John Christoforides and Mildred Nightingale-Boyes; came to Can. 1932; Dalhousie Univ., LL.D. (honoris causa) 1967; m. 1stly Sir James Dunn, Bt., Q.C. 7 June 1942; 2ndly The Rt. Hon. Lord Beaverbrook 7 June 1963; recreation: horse racing; Address: Dayspring, Saint Andrews, N.B. E0G 2X0.

**BECA, Peter,** B.A., F.S.A., F.C.I.A., M.A.A.A.; consulting actuary; b. Rotenburg, Germany 1 May 1948; s. Ilko and Natalia (Sudanowa) B.; e. New Toronto S.S. 1967; Univ. of Toronto B.A. 1971; m. Judith d. Dr. George and Cissy Yeung 7 June 1980; children: Christine Marie, Jaclyn Marie; MANAGING PRINCIPAL, MLH + A INC. 1988– ; F.S.A. 1975; F.C.I.A. 1975; Enrolled Actuary 1976; Mem., Am. Academy of Actuaries 1978; various positions ending as Assistant Vice-President, Manulife Financial 1971–88; Mem., Health & Welfare Ctte., Canadian C. of C.; Bd. Mem., Catholic Family Services of Toronto; Roman Catholic; recreations: books, travel, cottage; clubs: Boulevard Club; Home: 62 Cosmic Dr., Don Mills, Ont. M3B 3G2; Office: 1 Eglinton Ave. E., Suite 320, Toronto, Ont. M4P 1A1.

**BECHTEL, Stephen Davison, Jr.,** B.Sc.E., M.B.A., D.Eng., D.Sci.; engineering-construction executive; b. Oakland, Cal. 10 May 1925; s. Stephen Davison and Laura (Peart) B.; e. Purdue Univ. B.Sc.E. 1946, D.Eng. 1972 (Hon.); Stanford Grad. Sch. of Business M.B.A. 1948; Univ. of Colo. D.Sci. (Hon.) 1981; m. Elizabeth Hogan; 5 children; CHRMN. EMERITUS, BECHTEL GROUP INC. 1990– ; Chrmn., The Fremont Group & Sequoia Ventures, Inc.; former Dir. International Business Machines Corp.; Am. Soc. of French Legion of Honor; Grad. mem. and former Chrmn. The Business Council; Life Councillor and former Chrmn. The Conf. Bd. Inc.; joined Bechtel 1941; held variety of field and head office positions; Dir. 1951; Vice Pres. and Dir. 1952; Sr. Vice Pres. and Dir. 1955; Extve. Vice Pres. and Dir. 1957; Pres. and Dir. 1960; served various USA Presidential Comtes. 1967–74; Trustee, Cal. Inst. Technol. & mem. & Past Chrmn., Bldg. & Grounds Ctte., Caltech; mem. Pres.'s Council Purdue Univ.; mem. Adv. Counc., Inst. for Internat. Studies, and Bd. of Visitors; Stanford Univ.; former charter mem. Adv. Counc., Grad. Sch. of Bus., Stanford Univ.; Hon. Chrmn., Nat. Engineers Week, Nat. Soc. of Profl. Engrs. 1990; rec'd Purdue's Distinguished Alumnus Award 1964; Ernest C. Arbuckle Distinguished Alumnus Award Stanford Grad. Sch. of Business 1974; Distinguished Alumnus Award 1978 and Distinguished Engn. Alumnus Award 1979 Univ. of Colo.; Engn. News Record's Constr.'s Man of Yr. Award 1974; Moles' Award Outstanding Achievement in Constr. 1977; ASCE Civil Engn. Mgmt. Award 1979; Herbert Hoover Medal 1980; AAES Chairman's Award 1982; ASCE's President's Award 1985; Washington Award Western Soc. Engrs. 1985; Am. Jewish Ctte's Inst. of Human Relations Nat. Award 1987; National Medal of Technology (from Pres. Bush) 1991; Golden Beaver Award from the Beavers 1992; author various publs.; served with U.S. Marine Corps Reserve 1943–48; U.S. Navy Reserve 1948–59; Offr., French Legion of Honour; Fellow, Am. Soc. Civil Engrs.; Mem., Am. Soc. of Engr. Educ.; Foreign mem., Royal Acad. of Engn.; Royal Acad. of Engn., UK; mem. & Former Chrmn., Nat. Academy of Engn.; Am. Inst. Mining, Metall. & Petroleum Engrs.; Hon. Trustee, Cal. Acad. Sciences; Fellow, Am. Acad. of Arts & Sciences; Beta Theta Pi; Tau Beta Pi; Hon. Mem. Chi Epsilon 1990; Protestant; recreations: golf, tennis, fly fishing, bird shooting, cross-country skiing, horseback riding, hiking, photography; Clubs: Mount Royal (Montreal); Vancouver (B.C.); York (Toronto) and many social and business clubs USA; Home: P.O. Box 193809, San Francisco, CA 94119–3809; Office: 45 Fremont St., Suite 300, San Francisco, CA 94105.

**BECK, Howard Leighton,** Q.C., B.A., LL.B., LL.M.; b. Vancouver, B.C. 15 March 1933; s. late Ralph J. and Freda R. B.; e. Univ. of B.C. B.A., LL.B.; Columbia Univ. LL.M.; m. Delores Wright 9 Sept. 1971; Partner, Davies, Ward & Beck 1963–89; Dir., American Barrick Resources Corporation; The Horsham Corp.; Benvest Capital Inc.; Bramalea Ltd.; Canadian German Chamber of Industry and Commerce Inc.; Canadian Manoir Industries Ltd.; Citibank Canada; Maclean Hunter Ltd.; Paragon Petroleum Corp.; Philip Environmental Inc.; Premdor Inc.; Revenue Properties Co. Ltd.; read law with Lawson, Lundell, Lawson & McIntosh; called to Bar of B.C. 1957, Ont. 1963; cr. Q.C. 1971; Assoc. Lawson, Lundell, Lawson & McIntosh Vancouver 1957–61; Jt. Secy. Atty. Gen.'s Comte. on Securities Leg. (Kimber Comte.) 1963–65; Lectr. Mergers and Acquisitions Course, Univ. of Toronto Extension; Seminar on Corporate Finance, Osgoode Hall Law Sch., York Univ.; Candn. Inst. C.A.'s Mergers and Acquisitions; Going Public, Univ. of Toronto Extension 1969; co-author 'McDonald's Current Taxation to 1966'; Assoc. Ed. 'McDonald's Canadian Income Tax to 1966'; contrib. author to 'Acquisitions and Mergers in 'Canada' 1977; Home: 3 Ormsby Cres., Toronto, Ont. M5P 2V2.

**BECK, James Murray,** M.A., Ph.D., LL.D., F.R.S.C.; professor emeritus, researcher, writer; b. Lunenburg, N.S. 2 Dec. 1914; s. Allan Clyde and Florence Louise (Silver) B.; e. Lunenburg (N.S.) Acad.; Acadia Univ. B.A. 1934, M.A. 1938; Univ. of Toronto M.A. 1946, Ph.D. 1954; Hon. LL.D.: Dalhousie Univ. 1981; St. Francis Xavier Univ. 1985; Royal Mil. Coll. of Can. 1985; PROF. EMERITUS OF POL. SCIENCE, DALHOUSIE UNIV. 1963– ; teacher pub. and high schs. N.S. 1934–41; Instr. in Pol. Science Univ. of Toronto 1948–50; Asst. Prof. of Pol. Science and Hist. Acadia Univ. 1950–52; Asst., Assoc. and Full Prof. of Pol. Science, Royal Mil. Coll. of Can. 1952–63; Full Prof. of Dalhousie Univ. 1963–80; Consultant to N.S. Govt. on constitutional matters 1967–70; served with RCAF 1941–45, radar officer, rank Flight Lt.; author 'Government of Nova Scotia' 1959; 'Pendulum of Power: Canada's Federal Elections' 1968; 'The History of Maritime Union: A Study in Frustration' 1969; Ed. 'Joseph Howe: Voice of Nova Scotia' 1964; 'The Shaping of Canadian Federalism: Central Authority or Provincial Right?' 1971; 'Joseph Howe Vol. 1: Conservative Reformer 1804–1848' 1982; 'Joseph Howe Vol. II: The Briton Becomes Canadian 1848–1873' 1983; 'Politics of Nova Scotia 1710–1896' vol. 1; 'Politics of Nova Scotia 1896–1988' vol. 2; contrib. to 'Dictionary of Canadian Biography'; over 50 booklets and articles on Candn. govt. and politics; mem. Candn. Pol. Science Assn.; Candn. Hist. Assn.; United Church; Address: Box 563, Lunenburg, N.S. B0J 2C0.

**BECK, John Christian,** M.Sc., M.D.C.M., Ph.D.(hon.), F.R.S.(C.) (1970), F.R.C.P.(C), F.R.C.P.(London), F.A.C.P.; physician; educator; b. Audubon, Iowa 4 Jan. 1924; s. Wilhelm and Marie (Brandt) B.; e. McGill Univ., B.Sc. 1944, M.D., C.M. (Holmes Gold Medal) 1947, M.Sc. 1951, Dipl. in Med. 1952; Ph.D. (Hon.) Ben Gurion Univ. of the Negev, Israel 1981; one s., Philip; PROFESSOR OF MEDICINE, UNIV. OF CALIFORNIA, LOS ANGELES 1979– ; Dir., Multicampus Div. of Geriatric Medicine and Gerontology 1979–92; Dir., UCLA/USC Long-Term Care Gerontology Center 1980–85; Dir., Academic Geriatric Resource Center, Univ. of California, Los Angeles 1984–89; Dir., California Geriatric Education Center 1987– ; Center Dir., Long-Term Care National Resource Center at UCLA/USC 1988–91; Dir., Older Americans Independence Center (OAIC) 1991–93; Sr. Consultant in Med., Queen Mary Veteran's Hosp.; Hon. Consultant, Lakeshore Gen. Hosp.; Consultant in Med., Royal Edward Chest Hosp.; postgrad. work Royal Victoria Hosp., Cleveland Clinic (Ohio), New Eng. Med. Center (Boston), Rigshospitalet (Copenhagen) and Univ. Coll. Hosp. (London, Eng.) 1949–53; Lectr. in Med. and Clin. Med., McGill Univ., 1954–55; Asst. Prof. of Med. 1955–57; Asoc. Prof. 1957–64; Prof. 1964–74; Chrmn. Med., McGill Univ., and Dir., Univ. Clinic, 1964–74; Research Assoc., McGill Univ. Clinic, 1954–55; Research Fellow since 1955; Markle Scholar in Med. Sciences 1954–59; Clin. Asst., Royal Victoria Hosp., 1952–54; Asst. Phys. 1955–59; Phys. 1960–64; Phys.-in-Chief 1964–74; Chief, Endocrine-Metabolic Unit, 1964; Sr. Physician, Dept. of Med., Royal Victoria Hosp. 1974–81; Attending Staff, UCLA Medical Center 1979– ; Attending Staff, Jewish Homes for the Aging, Los Angeles 1982– ; Physician & consultant, V.A. Medical Center, West Los Angeles (Wadsworth Div.) 1985– ; mem. Ed. Bd., 'Journal of Clinical Endocrinology and Metabolism'; 'Current Topics in Experimental Endocrinology'; 'Society for Experimental Biology and Medicine'; 'Psychiatry in Medicine'; 'Recent Progress in Hormone Research'; 'Journal of the American Geriatrics Society'; 'Health Policy and Education'; Consulting Ed. 'Roche Laboratory Series on Geriatrics and Gerontology'; Ed. 'Year Book of Geriatrics and Gerontology' 1986– ; Ed., Geriatric Review Syllabus: A Core Curriculum in Geriatric Medicine 1988– ; Hon. Ed. 'Geriatric Medicine Issue' of 'Western Journal of Medicine'; Dir., Que. Camp for Diabetic Children; Mem., Bd. of Govs., Jewish Services for the Aging 1988– ; Mem. Awards Ctte., The Gerontological Soc. of Am.; Mem., Public Policy ctte., Assoc. for Gerontology in Higher Educ. (AGHE) 1990–91; Dir. and Chrmn., Am. Bd. Internal Med.; Pres., Am. Bd. of Med. Specialties; Inst. of Med.; Secy.-Gen., Internat. Soc. for Endocrinology, Inc.; Hon. Fellow, Royal Soc. of Med. (London) 1971; mem., Am. Soc. Clin. Investigation; Assn. Am. Phys.; mem. of council, Roy. Coll. of Physicians; Candn. Soc. Clin. Investigation (Pres.); Endocrine Soc. (Vice Pres., Chrmn., Post-grad. Assembly); Am. Fed. Clin. Research (Council, E. Div.); Candn. Med. Assn. (post-grad. educ. comte.); Am. Diabetes Assn.; Candn. Diabetes Assn.; McGill Osler Reporting Soc. (Secy.); Montreal Physiol. Soc.; Montreal Med. Chirurg. Soc.; Candn. Physiol. Soc.; mem. Bd. of Dirs., Laurentian Hormone Conf.; Candn. Assn. Profs. Med.; Am. Assn. for Advancement of Sci.; Am. Clinical and Climatological Assn.; Am. Coll. of Physicians (Master); Am. Physiological Soc.; Assn. of Am. Medical Colls.; Candn. Medical Protective Assn.; Internat. Soc. of Neuroendocrinology; McGill Assn. of Univ. Teachers; N.Y. Acad. of Sciences; Peripatetic Club; Que. Med. Assn.; Soc. for Experimental Biology and Medicine; Western Assn. of Physicians; Hon. mem., Peruvian Endocrine Soc.; Sigma Xi; Alpha Omega Alpha; Ronald V. Christie Award, Candn. Assoc. of Professors of Med.; Milo F. Leavitt Memorial Award, Am. Geriatrics Soc. 1988; Allan T. Bailey Meml. Lectr., Univ.of Sask., Can.; Bruce Hall Meml. Lectr., Garvan Inst. of Med. Rsch., Univ. of N.S.W., Sydney, Australia; Duncan Graham Award., Royal Coll. of Phys. & Surg. 1990; Joseph T. Freeman Award, Gerontological Soc. of Am. 1990; Irving S. Wright Award, Am. Fed. of Aging Rsch. 1991; Lutheran; Office: 10833 Le Conte Ave. (32–144 CHS), Los Angeles, CA 90024–1687.

**BECK, John Ryder,** B.A.; EC official; b. Munich, Germany 14 Sept. 1934;– ;e. Michael Hall School; Lincoln College, Oxford Univ. B.A. (Hons.) 1958; m. Helen Mary Pugh 4 April 1964; children: Toby, Thomas; AMBASSADOR, HEAD OF DELEGATION TO CANADA, COMN. OF THE EUROPEAN COMMUNITIES 1993– ; Head, East Eur. Div., London C. of C. 1960–66; Cons. Dir., Economist Intelligence Unit 1966–73; Senior Administrator European Commission 1973–83; Head of Div. for GATT & Multilateral Trade Policy, EC Comn., Brussels 1983–88; Deputy Head, EC Comn., Perm. Del., Geneva 1988–93; recreations: mycology, cooking, hiking; Home: 767 Acacia Lane, Rockcliffe, Ont. K1M 0M9; Office: 350 Sparks St., Ste. 1110, Ottawa, Ont. K1R 7S8.

**BECK, Nuala,** B.A.; economist; b. Montreal, Que. 20 Oct. 1951; d. William J. and Elizabeth C. (Hendrick) Broughal; e. Le Couvent Anglais, Bruges, Belgium 1967; Carleton Univ. 1974; m. Frank J. s. Frank and Juliana Beck 6 July 1974; PRES., NUALA BECK & ASSOC. INC. 1984– ; Economist, The Bank Credit Analyst 1974–77; Vice-Pres. & Sr. Econ., McLeod Young Weir Limited 1977–81; Vice-Pres. & Dir., Pitfield Mackay Ross Limited 1981–84; Dir., Pitfield Mackay Ross Limited 1981–84; YWCA 1984–87; Regent, Candn. Investment Seminar (Univ. of W. Ont. & Candn. Finan. Analysts Fed.) 1983–86; Dir., Couchiching Inst. on Public Affairs 1988; Mem. of Council & Chair, Econ. Policy Ctte., Bd. of Trade of Metro. Toronto 1985–89; Dir., Ontario Hydro 1993– ; National Rsch. Council IMD Adv. Bd.; pioneered a new framework for contemporary econ. & finan. analysis; developed 25 new finan. ratios & 160 new econ. indicators; best known for her groundbreaking work on 'The New Economy'™; frequent speaker & guest lecturer; author: 'Shifting Gears: Thriving in the New Economy' 1992, 'The End of Financial History' 1991, 'Sunrise Statistics' 1989, 'Financial Disinflation' 1988, 'Who Owns America' 1987, 'Free Trade' 1985, 'Collision' 1985, '87, 'Economic & Capital Markets' vol. I 1983, 'Industry Economics' 1981, 'Canada at the Crossroads' 1980; regular column on the New Economy for 'Globe & Mail'; recreations: travel, theatre, symphony, avid reader; Home: 5160 Montclair Dr., Mississauga, Ont.; Office: BCE Place, 161 Bay St., Suite 1300, Toronto, Ont. M5J 2S1.

**BECK, Roger Lyne,** M.A., Ph.D.; educator; b. London, Eng. 11 Jan. 1937; s. Henry Wolfestan and Mathilda Genevieve (Lyne) B.; e. Radley Coll. Eng. 1955; New Coll. Oxford Univ. B.A. 1961; Univ. of Ill. M.A. 1963, Ph.D. 1971; m. Janet d. Carl Coffin 20 Apl. 1968; one d. Winifred; PROF. OF CLASSICS, ERINDALE COLL., UNIV. OF TORONTO; Lectr. in Classics Univ. of Man. 1963–64; Univ. Coll. Univ. of Toronto 1964–65; Asst. Prof. of Classics present Coll. 1968 becoming Assoc. Prof. and Prof.; mem. Gov. Council Univ. of Toronto 1979–81, 1985–88, 1990–96 (Chrmn. Acad. Affairs Comte. 1980, 1987; Chair Budget Comte. 1993); Assoc. Dean (Humanities) Erindale Coll. 1985–88, 1989–91, Vice Princ. (Academic) 1986–88, 1989–91, Acting Principal 1991–92; 'Phoenix' Review Ed. 1978–81, Assoc. Ed., 1982–86; author, 'Planetary Gods in the Mysteries of Mithras' 1988; and various articles classical topics especially Petronius and the ancient novel, the cult of Mithras; served with R.A. 1955–57, rank 2nd Lt.; mem. Classical Assn. Can. (Secy. 1977–79); Am. Philol. Assn.; Anglican; recreations: astronomy, antique collecting (china), travel; Home: Lislehurst, Erindale Coll., Mississauga, Ont. L5L 1C6.

**BECK, Stanley M.,** Q.C., LL.M.; educator; b. Vancouver, B.C. 9 Aug. 1934; s. Ralph J. and Freida R. (Walfish) B.; e. Univ. of B.C., B.A. 1957, LL.B. 1958; Yale Univ. LL.M. 1959; m. Barbara d. Harry and Sharne Burke 1969; children: Carolyn Elizabeth, Lindsay Nicole; COMMERCIAL ARBITRATOR, CHRMN., CENTRAL CAPITAL CORP. 1989– ; Chrmn., Ont. Securities Comn. 1985–89; Asst. Prof. of Law Univ. of B.C. 1959–63; Assoc. Prof. of Law Queen's Univ. 1964–67; Prof. of Law, Osgoode Hall Law Sch., York Univ. 1967–85 (and Dean of Law 1977–82); Comnr. Ont. Securities Comn. 1971–82; recipient MacKenzie King Travelling Scholarship 1958–59; Visiting Fellow All Souls Coll. Oxford 1975; Assoc. Ed. 'Canadian Business Law Journal' 1975– ; co-author 'Cases and Materials on Business Associations' 1983; ed. 'Canada and the Constitution: The Unfinished Agenda' 1983; numerous articles various journs.; Jewish; recreations: tennis, skiing; Club: University; Caledon Ski; Home: 50 Binscarth Rd., Toronto, Ont. M4W 1Y4; Office: 70 Bond St., Suite 200, Toronto, Ont. M5B 1X3.

**BECKEL, William Edwin,** B.A., M.S., Ph.D.; retired university president; b. Kingston, Ont. 11 Apr. 1926; s. Elmer Ernest and Beatrice Mary (Driver) B.; e. Kingston (Ont.) Coll. & Vocational Inst.; Queen's Univ., B.A.; State Univ. of Iowa, M.S.; Cornell Univ., Ph.D.; m. Dorothy Kathleen, d. E. W. Brown, Claresholm, Alta., 3 Sept. 1953; children: John, Margaret, Julia, Millie; Pres. and Vice Chancellor, Carleton Univ. 1979–89, retired 1989; Head, Entom. Sec., Defence Research N. Lab., 1948–54; Physiol. Ecol., Entom. Lab., Chatham, Ont., 1955; Asst. Prof. of Zool., Univ. of Toronto, 1956–60; Assoc. Prof. 1960–63; Prof. 1963; Dean of Science, Scarborough Coll., Univ. of Toronto, 1963–64 and of Coll. 1964–68; Vice-Pres., Acad. and Finance of Univ. of Lethbridge 1968–71; Pres. and Vice Chancellor 1971–79; pioneered educ. TV in Can. for higher educ.; rec'd Allied Dye and Chem. Fellowship, Cornell Univ.; D.U., Univ. of Ottawa 1989; LL.D., Carleton Univ. 1989; author of over 50 publs. for prof. journs.; mem., Candn. Soc. Cell Biols.; Candn. Soc. Zool.; recreations: skiing, hunting; Home: 3884 Lewister Rd., North Vancouver, B.C. V7R 4C3.

**BECKER, Edward S.,** M.S., Ph.D., F.C.I.C., P.Eng.; research manager; b. Bisbee, Ariz. 8 Sept. 1929; s. Otto Carl and Fanny Elizabeth (Hunter) B.; e. Oregon State Univ. B.S. 1951, M.S. 1953, Ph.D. 1957; m. Norma d. Paul and Vernon Kloster 18 March 1951; children: Keith, Alan (d. 1977), Kathy; PRES. ECONOTECH SERVICES LTD. 1972– , Owner 1987– ; Pres. and Dir. Double K Investments Ltd.; Sect. Leader Rayonier Inc. Shelton, Wash. 1957–64; Group Leader Union Camp Princeton, N.J. 1964–65; Dir. Tech. & Environmental Control Columbia Cellulose Vancouver, B.C. 1966–72; author numerous tech. jour. reports; Bd. of Dirs.: Food on the Corner; PR 39 Charitable Foundation; Campus Crusade for Christ Canada; Deacon, South Delta Baptist Church; Home: 5243 Upland Dr., Delta, B.C. V4M 2G3; Office: 852 Derwent Way, New Westminster, B.C. V3M 5R1.

**BECKER, Henry Aron,** B.E., M.Sc., Sc.D., FCIC; educator; b. Castor, Alta. 15 Apr. 1929; s. Aron and Helen (Neustadter) B.; e. Rosthern (Sask.) Jr. Coll. 1947; Univ. of Sask. B.E. 1952, M.Sc. 1955; Mass. Inst. of Technol. Sc.D. 1961; m. Margaret d. Alexander and Susanna Venichenko 1 June 1957; divorced 1978; three d. Karen Alexandra, Helen Susanna, Juliet Anne; PROF. OF CHEM. ENG., QUEEN'S UNIV. 1968– ; Jr. Rsch. Offr. Nat. Rsch. Council Can. Saskatoon 1952–58; Asst. Prof. of Chem. Eng. Mass. Inst. of Technol. 1961–63; Asst. Prof. of Chem. Eng. present Univ. 1963, Assoc. Prof. 1964, Head of Dept. 1977–87; Dir., Centre for Advanced Gas Combustion Tech., Queen's Univ. 1992– ; British Gas; Consumers Gas; NSERC Industrial Rsch. Professor of Gas Combustion Engineering 1993– ; Visiting Prof. and Sr. Visiting Fellow Univ. of Sheffield 1973; Dir. Combustion Inst. (former Dir. & Chrmn. Candn. Sect., Distinguished Service Award); Chrmn. CSA Ctte. Incinerator Performance; Assoc. mem. Brit. & Am. Flame Rsch. Cttes.; recipient: Prize for Excellence in Rsch. Queen's Univ. 1989; Engineering Medal, Assn. of Prof. Engrs. of Ont. 1990; Izaac Walton Killam Memorial Prize 1992; author: 'Dimensionless Parameters' 1976; contbg. author 'Studies in Convection' Vol. 2 1977; mem. ed. bds. various publs.; mem. Candn. Soc. Chem. Engs.; Am. Inst. Chem. Engs.; Am. Soc. Eng. Edn.; Am. Assn. Advanc. Sci.; Sigma Xi; Phi Lambda Upsilon; Unitarian-Universalist Assn. (Council 1973–76, Vice Pres. 1975–76); recreations: jogging, swimming, reading, violin, music; Home: 365 King St. W., Kingston, Ont. K7L 2X3; Office: Kingston, Ont. K7L 3N6.

**BECKER, Laurence Edward,** M.D., FRCP(C), FACP; neuropathologist; professor; b. Edmonton, Alta. 30 Mar. 1943; s. Emanuel Jacob and Doris Johanna (Krebs) B.; e. Eastglen H.S. 1961; Univ. of Alta., M.D. 1967; postgrad.: McGill Univ. 1967–68, Univ. of Toronto 1968–72, Johns Hopkins Univ. 1972–74; m. Edna d. William and Mina Whitmore 7 Aug. 1971; children: Lisa Michelle, Andrea Lynn, Mia Suzanne; PEDIATRIC NEUROPATHOLOGIST, HOSP. FOR SICK CHILDREN & PROF. & HEAD, DIV. OF NEUROPATHOLOGY, UNIV. OF TORONTO 1981–91; PROF., DEPT. PATHOLOGY AND PEDIATRICS; Dir., Training Prog. in Neuropathol., Univ. of Toronto 1981–90; active rsch. in mental retardation (Down's Syndrome), sudden infant death syndrome & childhood brain tumors; Consultant Neuropathol., Toronto Gen. Hosp.; Women's Coll. Hosp.; Alpha Omega Alpha Hon. Med Soc.; Mem., Candn. Med. Assn.; Am. Assn. of Neuropathol.; Soc. for Pediatric Pathol.; Candn. Assn. of Neuropathol.; College of Am. Pathol.; author of over 200 pubs. in med. lit.; recreations: squash, swimming, skiing; Office: 555 University Ave., Toronto, Ont. M5G 1X8.

**BECKET, Ralph Wilson,** Q.C., B.A., B.C.L.; b. Montreal, P.Q. 3 June 1909; s. Ralph Alexander and Laura Eliza (Langhoff) B.; e. King's Sch.; Westmount (P.Q.) High Sch.; McGill Univ., B.A. 1931, B.C.L. 1934; m. Mary Evelyn, d. late Rev. J.W. MacKenzie, 30 Nov. 1938; children: Heather, Joanna, Wilson; retired Vice-Pres. and Gen. Counsel, Canadian International Paper Company; RETIRED GEN. COUNSEL, THE IMPERIAL TRUST CO.; Dir., Dascon Investments Ltd.; Strew Investments Ltd.; called to the Bar of Que. 1935; cr. Q.C. 1955; Manager, Prince Edward Island Trust Co., 1936–39; mem., Montgomery, McMichael, Common, Howard, Forsyth & Ker, 1945–50; served in 2nd World War, 1939–45; Adjt., P.E.I. Highlanders (Black Watch); Lieut.-Col. and O.C., 3rd Regt. First Special Service Force (Parachute); awarded U.S. Silver Star; Protestant; recreations: fishing, numismatics; Home: 4377 Grand Blvd., Montreal, Qué. H4B 2X7.

**BECKETT, Hon. Mr. Justice Thomas A.,** B.A., LL.B.; judge; b. Windsor, Ont. 23 Dec. 1925; s. Harold Champ and Josephine (Toull) B.; e. Edith Cavell Pub. Sch., Walkerville Coll. Inst., Assumption Coll., Windsor, Ont.; Univ. of Toronto B.A. (Honour Law) 1949, LL.B. (Hons.) 1950; m. E. Joan Baden-Powell; m. 2ndly Meralee Joyce Wheaton d. Frank and Mona Ferguson 1986; children (by previous marriage): John Thomas Baden, Elizabeth Ann (Plashkes), Mary Jo (Land); apptd. to ONT. COURT OF JUSTICE (GENERAL DIVISION) 1990; articles: Nolan, Chambers & Co., Calgary, Alta.; called to Bar of Alta. 1952 and Ont. 1952; private practice Hamilton, Ont. 1952–84, Sr. Partner, Beckett, Harris & Henderson; cr. Q.C. 1974; appt. to District Court of Ont. June 1984; assigned to Unified Family Court 1984; Ancaster Township Counc. 1958–65; Wentworth County Counc. 1960–65; Chrmn. Hamilton Region Conserv. Authority 1966–71; former Pres. Inst. of Ecology, Washington, D.C.; former Pres. Hamilton Social Planning and Rsch. Council; former Dir., Conservation Counc. of Ont., Algonquin Wildlands League; Home: 300 Mill Rd., Etobicoke, Ont. M9C 4W7; Office: 55 Main St. W., Hamilton, Ont. L8P 1H4.

**BECKLEY, Michael John,** M.H.C.I.M.A.; hotelier; b. Watford, England 24 March 1942; s. Reginald George and Elsie Louise (Hart) B.; e. Westminster Hotel School of London 1961; m. Janet Brandon; children: Justin, Julian; PRESIDENT & CHIEF OPERATING OFFICER, COMMONWEALTH HOSPITALITY LTD. 1987– ; Trainee/Mgr., British Transport Hotels in France, Germany & U.K. 1961–66; Mgr., Pink Beach Club Bermuda 1966–68; Gen. Mgr., Discovery Bay Hotel Barbados 1968–71; Area Mgr., St. James Beach Hotels Barbados & Bermuda 1971–76; Operations Dir., U.K. Div., Commonwealth Hospitality Ltd. 1976–81; transferred to Canada as Vice-Pres., Operations 1981; Extve. Vice-Pres. Canada 1987; Bd. of Trustees, Educational Inst. of A.H. & M.A.; Chrmn., Policy Adv. Bd., AMPHI, Univ. of Guelph 1991–93; Chrmn., Experience Canada; Chrmn., Ministers Policy Adv. Ctte. on the Development of a Tourism Strategy for the Province of Ontario; recreations: golf, tennis; Home: 20 Cherry Post Crescent, Etobicoke, Ont.; Office: 31 Fasken Drive, Etobicoke, Ont. M9W 2K1.

**BECKMAN, Henry**; actor; writer; director; b. Halifax, N.S. 26 Nov. 1921; s. H.F.W. and Harriet Beatrice (Helm) B.; e. Royal Mil. Coll. Kingston, Ont. 1941; Am. Acad. Dramatic Arts New York City B.A. Equiv. 1946; U.C.L.A. Extension 1970–88; m. Cheryl Maxwell d. Frederick and Sara Myres 25 Nov. 1955; two s. Brian Christopher, Stuart Francis; Stage-Mgr., Performer 9 Broadway plays, over 800 TV progs.; co-star (regular) 'Peyton Place,' 'McHale's Navy,' 'I'm Dickens, He's Fenster,' 'Here Come the Brides' (Captain Clancy); sitcom 'Check it Out' (with Don Adams); Guest Star dozens of sitcom and drama series; Character lead CBC feature film 'Family Reunion' 1987; feature films incl. 'The Undefeated' (with John Wayne), 'The Stalking Moon' (with Gregory Peck etc.); 'Stuck With Each Other' (with Tyne Daley & Richard Crenna) 1989; Lawrence Kasdan's 'I Love You to Death' 1989; Georg Stanford Brown's (Nexus Films) 'Garwood, The Last P.O.W.?', Movie-of-the-week; C.B.S. TV M.O.W. 'Blood River' (with Wilferd Brimley) 1990; 'The Man Upstairs' CBC M.O.W. (with Katherine Hepburn & Ryan O'Neal); Trustee & C.E.O., TELEKINETIX FILMS, Vancouver, B.C. & L.A.; Founder/Dir. V.O.T.E. (Voice Of The Electorate) voter's activist org.; 'Emmy' nominee for 'Crazy' George Anderson, 'Peyton Place', 20th Cent. Fox series; Member, Blue Ribbon Panel, Am. Acad. TV Arts & Sci's; Queen Elizabeth II Jubilee Medal (contrib. to Candn. culture - esteem of peers'); twice winner Genie Award Best Actor, Supporting Role - (great book-ends); Genie Nominee, 1988; Golden Halo Award for Pub. Service, S. Cal. Motion Picture Soc.; author: 'How To Sell Your Film Project' 1979; 'Actors I Have Worked With' (and a few I wish I'd never met!) Filmography 1992, Fourth Corner Pub.; Charter mem. Candn. Acad. TV Arts & Sci's; Am. Film Inst.; A.C.T.R.A.; Dirs. Guild Can.; Vice-Admiral, Texas Navy; Knighted by Sovereign Order of St. John of Jerusalem (Knights of Malta) World's oldest order of Knighthood, dubbed Chevalier (Sir Henry) 1990; recreations: cooking, fishing, playing jazz bagpipes; conceptor / developer / director / producer / sole actor - definitive 'auteur' project, 'THE SCREEN TEST', first totally one-man film; Address: 3906 Nelson Rd., Deming, WA 98244.

**BECKMAN, Margaret Lilas Armstrong,** B.A., B.L.S., M.L.S., LL.D.; librarian; b. Hartford, Conn. 1926; d. Ewen Cameron and Anne Armstrong; e. Kitchener-Waterloo (Ont.) Coll. Inst.; Univ. of Western Ont., B.A. 1946; Univ. of Toronto, B.L.S. 1949, M.L.S. 1969; Univ. of Western Ont., LL.D., (hon. causa) 1987; m. Arthur Kenneth B. 16 Sept. 1950; children: Christopher, Susan, David; PRESIDENT, BECKMAN ASSOCIATES LIBRARY CONSULTANTS INC.; Lectr. in Lib. Planning Sch. of Lib. and Information Science, Univ. of W. Ont. since 1970; Lib. Bldg. Consultant to several acad., public and govt. libs.; Head Cataloguing Dept. Univ. of Waterloo 1960, Dir. Tech. Services 1964; joined Univ. of Guelph as Systems Lib. 1966, Depy. Lib. 1970, Chief Librarian 1971–84; Exec. Dir. for Information Technology, Univ. of Guelph 1984–88; mem. Candn. Assn. Coll. and Univ. Libs. (Past Pres.); Ont. Lib. Assn.; Candn. Library Assn.; Am. Lib. Assn.; Past Pres. (1980–84), Adv. Bd. on Scient. and Tech. Information, National Rsch. Council; Nat. Lib. Task Force on Nat. Union Catalogue; author numerous books, book chapters and articles in prof. journs.; Past Chrmn. Waterloo Public Lib. Bd.; Presbyterian; recreations: hiking, skiing, swimming, canoeing; Address: 168 John Blvd., Waterloo, Ont. N2L 1C5.

**BECKWITH, John,** C.M., Mus.D., Mus.M.; composer; writer; retired university professor; b. Victoria, B.C. 9 Mar. 1927; s. Harold Arthur and Margaret Alice (Dunn) B.; e. Victoria Coll. 1944–45; Royal Conservatory of Music, Toronto, private piano study with Alberto Guerrero 1945–50; Univ. of Toronto Fac. of Music Mus.B. 1947, Mus.M. 1961; private composition study with Nadia Boulanger, Paris 1950–52; children: Robin Jane Goodale, Jonathan, Symon, Lawrence; Continuity Writer CBC Radio 1953–55; Special Lectr., Fac. of Music, Univ. of Toronto 1952–55; Lectr. 1955–61; Asst. Prof. 1961–66; Assoc. Prof. 1966–70; Prof. 1970–90; Dean 1970–77; Dir. Inst. for Candn. Music 1984–90; Composed over 90 works; Reviewer and Columnist Toronto Star 1959–62, 1963–65; Assoc. Ed. 'Candn. Music Journal' 1957–62; Contbr. 'Dictionary of Contemporary Music' 1974; Ed. 'Canadian Composers' study series 1975–90; Candn. Cons. and Contbr. 'The New Grove' 1980; Contbr. and Exec. Bd. mem. 'Encyclopedia of Music in Canada' 1981 and 1993; Princ. works: 'Music for Dancing' 1948; 'Night Blooming Cereus' 1958; 'Concerto Fantasy' 1959; 'Flower Variations and Wheels' 1962; 'Jonah' 1963; 'The Trumpets of Summer' 1964; 'Canada Dash, Canada Dot' 1967; 'Place of Meeting ' 1967; 'Circle, with Tangents' 1967; 'Taking a Stand' 1972; 'Quartet' 1977; 'The Shivaree' 1978; 'Keyboard Practice' 1979; 'A Little Organ Concert' 1982; 'A Concert of Myths' 1983; 'Etudes' 1983; 'Harp of David' 1985; 'Crazy to Kill' 1988; 'Peregrine' 1989; 'Round and Round' 1992; 'Taptoo!' 1993; 20 recorded works and 30 pub. works; co-Ed. 'The Modern Composer and His World' 1961; 'Contemporary Canadian Composers' 1975; 'Musical Canada' 1988; Ed. 'The Canadian Musical Heritage, v.5: Hymn tunes' 1986; mem. Bd. Candn. Opera Co. 1970–77; mem. Bd. Candn. Music Centre 1970–77, 1978–80; mem. Bd. New Music Concerts 1970–84; Ed. Bd. Candn. Musical Heritage Soc. 1981– ; mem. Toronto Musicians Assoc. 1947– ; mem. Candn. League of Composers 1951– ; composer, arranger and performer at 'Music at Sharon' festivals 1981–86, 1988, 1989, 1991; Candn. Music Counc. annual medal 'for services to Candn. music' 1972; Mus.D. (honoris causa) Mount Allison Univ. 1974; Mus.D. (h.c.) McGill Univ. 1978; Univ. of Toronto Sesquicentennial Award 1977; Candn. Music Counc. 'Composer of the Year' 1985; Member, Order of Canada 1987; Richard S. Hill Award, (US) Music Library Assn. 1990; recreations: Scottish country dancing, bicycle touring; Home: 121 Howland Ave., Toronto, Ont. M5R 3B4; Office: c/o Faculty of Music, University of Toronto, Toronto, Ont. M5S 1A1.

**BEDARD, George Bryan,** B.Comm., M.B.A., C.M.C.; management consultant; b. Montreal, Que. 26 Aug. 1939; s. Joseph Hermenegilde and Jeannette Elizabeth (Bryar) B.; e. Loyola H.S. 1957; Loyola Coll., Univ. of Montreal, B.Comm. 1961; Univ. of W. Ont., M.B.A. 1965; m. Jane Ellen d. William and Mary McGillivray 25 June 1966; children: Paul Bryan, Phillip Anthony; PRES., BEDARD McGILLIVRAY & ASSOC. 1978– ;and CHRMN., COLONIAL PUBLICATIONS INC. 1992– ; Product Mgr. & Gen. Sales Mgr., Gillette of Can. 1965–67; Mktg. Mgr., Gillette de Puerto Rico 1967–68; Venezuela 1968–69; Extve. Mktg. Dir., Gillette Europe 1969–71; Internat. Mktg. Coord., Gillette Corp. 1971–73; Gen. Mgr., Mktg. & AVP, Bus. Devel., Bell Can. 1973–76; Pres. & C.O.O., Wilkinson Match Group Can. 1976–78; Nat. Dir., Deloitte Haskins & Sells 1984–91; Dir. several Candn. & U.S. companies; mem., Economic Development Commission of Mid-Florida; Greater Orlando Chamber of Commerce; Candn.-Am. Business Assn.; Rotary Club of Orlando; Candn. Inst. of Internat. Affairs; Internat. Soc. for Strategic Mgmt. & Planning; recreations: golf, squash, modern jazz, travel; clubs: Univ. Club of Toronto; Univ. Club of Winter Park; Citrus Club of Florida; The Royal Montreal Golf, Lambton Golf & Country; Office: 2127 Forest Club Dr., Orlando, Florida 32804.

**BEDARD, Myriam;** athlete; b. Loretteville, Que.; d. Francine and Pierre Bedard; MEMBER, BIATHLON CANADA; Winner of 2 gold medals, 1994 Olympics, Lillehammer, Norway: 15 km. biathlon and 7.5 km. biathlon; first North American to win Olympic biathlon gold; bronze medal, Albertville Olympics 1992; former Canadian army cadet; Address: c/o Biathlon Canada, 1600 James Naismith Dr., Gloucester, Ont. K1B 5N4.

**BEDARD, Robert P.,** B.A., B.Ed.; teacher/headmaster; b. St. Hyacinthe, Que. 13 Sept. 1931; s. Georges Stephen and Estelle Lucille (Massé) B.; e. Sem. St. Charles Borromée; Loyola Coll. B.A. 1951; Sir George Williams; U.C.L.A.; Univ. of Sherbrooke B.Ed. 1966; m. Anne d. Helen and Weldie Stacey 6 Apr. 1957; children: Mark, Paul, Michael, Peter; HEADMASTER, ST. ANDREW'S COLLEGE (AURORA, ONT.) 1981– ; Teacher & Coach, Bishop's College School 1958–72; Housemaster 1962–72; Dir. & Admin., French Summer School 1966–72; Teacher, Head of Guidance & Coach, St. Andrew's College 1972–81; Asst. Headmaster 1973–81; Mem., Nat. Fitness Counc., Min. of Health & Welfare 1970–72; Fed. Grants-in-Aid Prog. 1970–74; Chrmn., Davis Cup Selection Ctte. 1970–76; Pres., Que. Lawn Tennis Assn. 1967–70; Vice-Pres., Candn. Lawn Tennis Fed. 1973–77; Trustee, Clarke Inst. of Psych. 1982–87; Sportsmanship Trophy, Loyola Coll. 1951; Candn. Davis Cup Team 1953–61, 1967; elected Loyola Coll. Hall of Fame 1971; elected Candn. Amateur Athletic Hall of Fame 1974; Laureamus Alumnus, Sherbrooke Sem. 1977; Province of Que. Sports Hall of Fame 1991; Tennis Canada Hall of Fame 1991; Queen's Jubilee Award 1977; No. 1 ranked tennis player in Can. 1955–65; Father & Son Canadian Champion 1989 and 1991; MVP, Sherbrooke Beavers, Hockey 1956; author: 'History of Lacrosse,' 'Coaching and Training Methods of Ice Hockey' (The Olympic Library series); Roman Catholic; recreations: reading, philately, sports; Home: St. Andrew's Coll., Aurora, Ont. L4G 3H7.

**BEDASSE, Ken,** B.Sc.; business executive; b. Jamaica, W.I. 23 July 1950; s. Charles and Dorothy B.; e. Univ. of the West Indies B.Sc. 1972; m. Marjorie d. Clarence and Connie Newland 23 April 1972; children: Jason, Stephanie; VICE-PRES., OPERATIONS, McNEIL CONS. PRODUCTS 1989– ; Asst. Mgr., Research & Devel., Cooper Labs Canada 1977–82; Sr. Project Leader, Research & Devel., Johnson & Johnson 1982–86; Mgr., Quality Assur., McNeil Cons. Product 1986–87; Mem., Bd. of Gov., Univ. of Guelph 1992– ; Chair, Pensions & Benefits Ctte. 1993– ; Mem., Finance Ctte. 1992; Campaign Chair, United Way of Guelph 1992; Dir., Guelph C. of C. 1991– ; Home: 18 Bridle Path, R.R. 3, Guelph, Ont. N1H 6H9; Office: 890 Woodlawn Rd. W., Guelph, Ont. N1K 1A5.

**BEDDOES, John Michael,** B.Sc.; electrical engineer; b. Kidderminster, Eng. 2 Sept. 1929; s. John and Edith B.; e. Univ. of London B.Sc. 1954; Carleton Univ. course work M.Eng. 1966; Univ. of Mich. Solid State Physics 1963; McMaster Univ. Advanced Math., several short courses Mang., Finance & Business; m. Priscilla d. Albert Wacker, Eng. and Germany; children: Ursula, Jonathan, Rebecca, Matthew; VICE PRES., ELECTRONICS NETWORK OF ALBERTA 1989– ; Dir., Omni Rand Inc. 1989– ; Circuit Design Engr. Decca Radar, Eng. 1954–57 and Racal Engineering Ltd. Eng. 1956–57; Part-time Lectr. in Electronics, Hamilton Inst. Technol. 1961–62; Sr. Engr. Canadian Westinghouse Co. Ltd. Hamilton 1957–63; mem. Scient. Staff Northern Electric Co. Ottawa 1963–65, Mgr. Applications Engn. & Design 1965–68, Mgr. Tech. Resources Advanced Devices Centre 1968–69; Tech. Dir. Microsystems International Ltd. Ottawa 1969–70, Acting Gen. Mgr. 1970–71, Operations Mgr. Data Products 1972–73, Vice Pres. Tech. Devel. 1970–73; Product Mgr. Memories/Microprocessors, General Instrument Microelectronics Div., Hicksville, Long Island, N.Y., Dir. of Technol. 1974–75; Extve. Vice Pres. Commercial Products, Atomic Energy of Can. Ltd. 1975–82; Consultant National Health and Welfare 1982–83; Pres., Intercontinental Data Control Corp. 1983–85; Dir. of Business Devel., Electronics Test Centre 1985–89; Dir. Edmonton Council Advanced Tech. 1986–89; Dir., Healthcare Opportunities Alberta 1988–92; Chrmn., Candn. Telecommunications Adv. Bd. 1992– ; Mem., Pro Coro Canada 1987–90; served with Brit. Army 1948–50; holds 3 patents, 8 disclosures accepted; author various papers, articles; Queen's Jubilee Medal 1977; mem. Assn. Prof. Engrs. Prov. Ont.; Assn. Prof. Engrs. Geologists and Geophysicists, Alta.; Royal Candn. Coll. Organists; Protestant; recreations: music, equestrian sports, farming; Home: R.R. 3, Almonte, Ont. K0A 1A0; Office: 1810 - 45 O'Connor St., Ottawa, Ont. K1P 1A4.

**BEDDOME, John M.;** petroleum executive; b. Vernon, B.C. 20 Sept. 1930; e. Univ. of B.C., B.Sc. 1952; m. Barbara McCarthy; children: Maureen, David; PRES. & C.E.O., ALBERTA NATURAL GAS LTD. 1991– ; Dir., Ipsco Inc. 1986– ; Morgan Hydrocarbons Inc. 1989– ; PanCanadian Petroleum 1992– ; various pos., Gulf Oil Canada 1952–71; Dome Petroleum Limited 1971–88 (Pres. & C.O.O. 1983–88); Dir. & Chrmn., TransCanada PipeLines Limited 1979–83; Dir., PanArctic Oils 1981–88; Pres. & C.E.O., Polar Gas Ltd. and Polar Delta Project 1989–91; Mem., Bd. of Govs., Canadian Petroleum Assn. 1986–88; Dir. & Vice-Pres., Ind. Petroleum Assn. of Can. 1980–85; Mem., Assn. of Profl. Engrs., Geologists & Geophysicists of Alta.; recreations: badminton, skiing, photography, reading; Clubs: Calgary Petroleum; Canyon Meadows Golf & Country; Ranchmen's; Office: 2900, 240 Fourth Ave. S.W., Calgary, Alta. T2P 4L7.

**BEDELL, Graysanne Lyla,** B.A., LL.B.; lawyer/food industry executive; b. Toronto, Ont.; e. Trent Univ. B.A. 1976; Osgoode Hall Law Sch. LL.B. 1979; m. Allan s. Gary and Gizelle Bogler 30 Dec. 1985; VICE PRES., LAW, SCOTT'S HOSPITALITY INC. FOOD SERVICES DIV. 1991– ; called to Ontario Bar 1981; articled clerk, assoc. of Kingsmill, Kennings law firm 1981–86; Partner 1986–88; offr. of most major food service subs. of Scott's Hosp. Inc.; Sec. & Assoc. Gen. Couns., Scott's Hospitality Inc. 1988–91; Dir. & Vice-Pres., Streethaven at the Crossroads (char. orgn. serving women in need); Mem., Law Soc. of U.C.; Candn. Bar Assn. (Corp. Couns. Conf.); recreations: nordic skiing; Office: 500 Hood Rd., Markham, Ont. L3R 0P6.

**BEDESKI, Robert E.,** Ph.D.; educator; b. Detroit, Mich. 3 Nov. 1937; s. Edward John and Mary Regina (Guzowski) B.; e. Univ. of Cal. Berkeley B.A. 1964, M.A. 1965, Ph.D. 1969; m. Kathleen d. Chi Ching Chi and Chi Dong Zheng-yin 1962; one d. Pamela; PROF. OF POL. SCI., UNIV. OF VICTORIA 1989– ; Cons. Dept. Nat. Defence Ottawa, Asst. Prof. Ohio State Univ. 1969–73; Asst. Prof. Carleton Univ. 1973, Assoc. Prof. 1975; rsch. grants & awards incl. Nat. Defense Foreign Lang. Fellowship in Japanese 1965–66, 1966–67; Sr. Rsch. Fellow Center Chinese Studies Univ. Cal. Berkeley 1967–68, 1968–69; Social Sci. Rsch. Council Grant Contemporary China 1971–72; Japan Found. Rsch. Fellowship 1981–81; SSHRCC Leave Grant 1980–81; Pacific Cultural Found. Writing & Travel Grant 1982–83; Bilateral Exchange Grant SSHRCC & Chinese Acad. Social Sci's 1983–84, 1986; Rsch. Fellow, Kyungnam Univ. Inst. for Far Eastern Studies, Seoul, Korea, summer, 1988; Rsch. Fellow, Internat. Cultural Soc. of Korea Grant, Seoul, summer 1990; Visiting Prof., Meiji Univ., Tokyo 1993–94; Japan Foundation Fellow 1993–94; author 'State-Building in Modern China: The Kuomintang in the Prewar Period' 1981; SSHRCC Rsch. Grant 1992–93, 'The Post-Industrial State in East Asia: Japan, Taiwan, South Korea, and Malaysia'; 'The Fragile Entente: the 1978 Japan-China Peace Treaty in a Global Context' 1983; 'The People's Republic of China - Relations in Asia: The Strategic Implications' 1984; Canadian Cooperative Security Grant, (with J. Bayer, RRMC) 'Arms Control on the Korean Peninsula' 1993; 'The Transformation of South Korea: Reform and Reconstitution in the Sixth Republic Under Roh Tae Woo 1987–93' 1994; Dir., Program in Human Security, Pacific Region, Univ. of Victoria; Mem., Bd. of Dirs., Candn. Soc. for Chinese Studies; mem. Candn. Pol. Sci. Assn.; Candn. Asian Studies Assn.; Internat. Pol. Sci. Assn.; Candn. Inst. of Strategic Studies; recreations; cross-country skiing, rock climbing, long distance running; Home: 4689 Boulderwood Dr., Victoria, B.C. V8Y 2P8; Office: Dept of Pol. Sci., Univ. of Victoria, Victoria, B.C. V8W 2Y2.

**BEDFORD, (Charles) Harold,** M.A., Ph.D.; educator; b. Toronto, Ont. 31 Oct. 1929; s. Victor Edwin and Winnifred (Farmer) B.; e. Parkdale Coll. Inst. and Etobicoke High Sch. Toronto; Univ. of Toronto, Univ. Coll. B.A. 1951, M.A. 1952; Univ. of London Ph.D. 1956; m. Hannele d. Torsten and Inkeri Malmio 12 Aug. 1961; children: Susan Kristina, Hannele Melanie; PROF. OF SLAVIC LANGS. & LIT. UNIV. OF TORONTO 1975– ; Lectr. present Univ. 1955, Asst. Prof. 1959, Assoc. Prof. 1964, Assoc. Chrmn. 1966–71, Acting Chrmn. 1984–85, Chrmn. 1971–79, 1985–88, mem. Grad. Centre Study Drama and Centre Russian & E. Eur. Studies; author 'The Seeker: D.S. Merezhkovskiy' 1975; mem. Candn. Assn. Slavists (Sec.-Treas. 1958–59); Candn. Friends of Finland; Home: 3264 Havenwood Dr., Mississauga, Ont. L4X 2M1; Office: Toronto, Ont. M5S 1A1.

**BEECROFT, Norma Marian;** composer, producer (music), educator; b. Oshawa, Ont. 11 Apr. 1934; d. Julian Balfour and Eleanor Chambers (Norton) B.; e. Royal Conserv. of Music, Toronto (piano, flute & composition) 1950–58; Berkshire Music Centre, Tanglewood, composition with Aaron Copland and Lukas Foss, 1958; Acad. of Saint Cecilia, Rome, grad. in composition, 1961; private studies in Darmstadt, Germany and Dartington, Eng, 1960–61; major compositions incl.: 'Tre Pezzi Brevi' 1960–61; 'Improvvisazioni Concertanti' 1961; 'Contrasts for Six Performers' 1962; 'From Dreams of Brass' (Jane Beecroft) 1963–64; 'Elegy and Two Went to Sleep' (Leonard Cohen) 1967; 'Piece Concertante No. 1.' 1966; 'Undersea Fantasy' (electronic score) 1967; 'The Living Flame of Love' (St. John of the Cross) 1967; 'Rasas I' (Commission) 1968; 'Soc. de Musique contemp. du Qué.'; 'Improvvisazioni Concertanti No. 2,' Nat. Arts Centre Commission 1971; 'Rasas II' CBC Commission 1972–73 for contralto, chamber ensemble and tape; 'Three Impressions from Sweetgrass' (Wayne Keon) Ontario Youth Choir Commission 1973 for mixed choir and percussion; 'Improvvisazioni Concertanti No. 3,' Toronto Symphony Women's Committee commission, 1973, for flute, timpany and orch.; 'Rasas III,' New Music Concerts commission, 1974, for soprano, chamber ensemble and tape; '11 and 7 for 5+,' 1975 CBC commission for Canadian Brass quintet and tape; 'Piece for Bob,' 1975, CBC commission for solo flute and tape; 'Collage '76' for solo flute, chamber ensemble and tape, Ont. Arts Council Comm. 1976; 'Consequences for Five,' Candn. Electronic Ensemble commission, 1977, for piano, 3 brass, synthesizers and electronics; 'Collage '78,' Music Inter Alia Commission, 1978, for bassoon solo, ensemble and tape 1978; 'Quaprice,' 1979–80, commissioned by James MacDonald for solo horn, percussion and tape; 'Cantorum Vitae,' 1980–81, commissioned by Days, Months & Years to Come (Vancouver) for flute, cello, 2 pianos, percussion & tape; 'Hedda' 1981–82, ballet score for orchestra and tape, Nat. Ballet of Can. comm.; 'Troissonts' 1982, comm. by Rivka Golani; 'Jeu de Bach,' 1985, Chamber orchestra and tape, commissioned by Bach 300 Festival; 'Jeu II,' 1985, solo flute and solo viola, digital tape and live electronics, commissioned by New Music Concerts; Incidental Music for TV Ontario 13 week series 'FISH ON' 1985–86; 'Images' 1987, wind quintet, commissioned by York Winds; 'Jeu III,' 1987, solo viola & tape, commissioned by Rivka Golani; 'The Dissipation of Purely Sound,' 1988, text by Sean O'Huigin, electronic work for radio, commissioned by David Olds, CKLN Radio; 'Accordion Play' 1988, for accordion and percussion, CBC commission for Joseph Petric; Producer, Music Dept. (Radio), CBC; since 1969 free-lance commentator on contemporary music (host of CBC-FM series 'Music of Today') and documentarist on Canadian composers, music and technology); Course Dir., Electronic Media Workshop, York Univ. 1984–85; Course Dir., Music Writing Workshop, York Univ. 1986–87; rec'd schols. in composition Royal Conserv. of Music, Berkshire Music Centre, Canada Council, Italian Ministry of Foreign Affairs; Armstrong Award for Excellence in FM Broadcasting; Victor M. Lynch-Staunton Award (Can. Council) for distinguished artists, 1978–79; producer of SOCAN/RCI (formerly CAPAC/RCI) record series 'Music Canada' etc.; producer of electronic music scores for Stratford Festival productions of 'Macbeth' 1983 and 'Midsummer Night's Dream' 1984; other comns.; Charlottetown Festival, 1966; Ten Centuries Concerts (Pres.) 1967; Expo '67; Waterloo Lutheran Univ., 1967; Crest Theatre Hour Co., 1967; Pres., New Music Concerts, Toronto, 1971; Secy., Candn. League Composers, 1966–67; mem., SOCAN; Address: 1866 Glendale Dr., Pickering, Ont. L1V 1V5.

**BEEFORTH, Douglas William,** B.A.A.; broadcasting executive; b. Hamilton, Ont. 23 April 1955; s. Harry Douglas and Merne Lila (Anderson); e. Ryerson Polytech. Inst. B.A.A. (Radio & Television) 1976; m. Carol d. Carl and Doreen Parker 22 Dec. 1980; children: Michael, Mackenzie, Harrison; DIRECTOR OF SPORTS, CTV TELEVISION NETWORK 1993– ; Broadcaster, CFRB Radio 1975–80; Producer, Hockey Night in Canda 1980–86; Supervising Producer, CTV Host Broadcast Unit, XV Olympic Winter Games 1986–88; Prod., NBC TV, Seoul Olympic Games 1988; Prod., ABC TV, World Alpine Championships 1989; Vice-Pres., RMA TV 1988–90; Prod., Turner Broadcasting, Seattle Goodwill Games 1990; Exte. Prod., CTV Sports 1990–93; Exte. Prod., CTV, 1992 Olympics (Barcelona); Exte. Prod., CTV, 1994 Olympics (Norway); Guest Lectr., Ryerson Polytech. Inst., Syracuse Univ.; Emmy Award 1988; nom., Gemini Award 1989, '92, '93; nom., Emmy Award 1988; nom., US Ace Award 1990; Mem., Internat. Olympic Ctte. Radio & TV Commission; Academy of Candn. Cinema & Television; Internat. Sports Press Assn.; Office: 42 Charles St. E., Toronto, Ont. M4Y 1T5.

**BEELER, Byron E.,** B.Sc., M.S.A., P.Ag.; agricultural executive; b. Upper Canard, N.S. 11 Aug. 1936; s. Clifford A. and Gladys E. (Porter) B.; e. McGill Univ. B.Sc. 1958; Univ. of Toronto M.S.A. 1963; m. Katherine d. Ralph and Edith Marshall 10 April 1957; children: Sharon Elizabeth, Carolyn Jean, Janet Christine; VICE-PRES. & HEAD, ANIMAL HEALTH DIV., CIBA-GEIGY CANADA LTD. 1991– ; Sales Manager / General Manager, Stewart Seeds 1971–75; General Manager, Ciba-Geigy Seeds 1975–85; Director of Public Affairs 1985–89; Vice-Pres., Agricultural Div. 1989–91; Hon. Life Member., Candn. Seed Growers Assn. 1991; Pres., The Royal Agricultural Winter Fair 1992–94; Candn. Agric. Hall of Fame Extve., Agric. Inst. of Canada 1958–92; Pres., Ont. Inst. of Agrologists 1990–91; Dir., Candn. Seed Growers Assn. 1968–71; Chair, Official Bd., First St. Andrews Church 1981–82; Chair, Bd. of Dir., William Proudfoot House 1982–84; recreations: gardening; Home: 4 Bannisdale Way, Carlisle, Ont. L0R 1H0; Office: 6860 Century Ave., Mississauga, Ont. L5N 2W5.

**BEER, (John) Charles (McWaters),** M.P.P., M.A.; politician; b. Toronto, Ont. 24 Nov. 1941; s. Harry and Elizabeth G. (Holmes) B.; e. Pickering Coll. Newmarket 1959; Univ. of Toronto B.A. 1964; Laval Univ. Postgrad. Studies Hist. & French 1964–66; Nat. Defence Coll. Kingston 1972–73; York Univ. M.A. 1986; m. Mary Anna d. Stanley and Jane True 21 Aug. 1965; children: Stephanie, Gregory; LIBERAL OPPOSITION CRITIC FOR EDUCATION AND CHILDREN'S SERVICES 1992– ; Prov. g.e. Lib. Cand. Scarborough 1977, 1981, el. M.P.P. York North 1987; mem. Select Ctte. Constitutional Reform 1988; Parlty Asst. to the Min. of Educ., Oct. 1988; Min. of Community and Social Services and Min. Responsible for Francophone Affairs 1989–90; Exec. Sec. Ont./Qué. Perm. Comn. Federal/Provincial Constitutional Review 1968–72; Sr. Intergovt'al Affairs Adv. Min. of Treasury, Econ. & Intergovt'al Affairs 1972–75; Dir. of Citizenship for Ont. 1975–77; Exec. Dir. Office Leader of Opposition 1977–81; Asst. Headmaster Pickering Coll. 1981–86; Dir. Ont. Conf. Independent Schs. and Dir. Candn. Ednl. Standards Inst. 1986–87; Home: 1189 Kingdale Rd., Newmarket, Ont. L3Y 4W1; Office: Suite 1303, Whitney Block, Queen's Park, Toronto, Ont. M7A 1A4.

**BEER, Josh David George,** B.A., M.A.; university professor; b. St. Albans, England 14 Sept. 1941; s. Henry Charles and Doris May (Otton) B.; e. The Eardley 1953; Battersea Grammar Sch. 1960; Bristol Univ., B.A. 1963; McMaster Univ., M.A. 1964; Univ. of Toronto 1964–66; Am. Sch. of Classical Stud., Athens 1966; m. Carmel Anne d. Curt Conrad and Marie Rose Isenschmid 9 Nov. 1979; one s.: Barnaby Tristan; Chrmn., Fine Arts Ctte., Carleton Univ. 1983–88; Teaching Asst., Classics, Univ. of Toronto 1965–66; Asst. Lectr., Hum., York Univ. 1965–66; Lectr., Classics, Carleton Univ. 1966–68; Asst. Prof. 1968–82; Assoc. Prof. 1983– ; Chrmn., Dept. of Classics 1975–83; attended Brit. Theatre Assn. Sept.–Dec. 1984; Panel Mem., Ont. Grad. Scholarship Ctte. in Fine Arts 1987; McMaster Grad. Fellowship 1963–64; Ont. Grad. Scholarship 1964–66; Sec./Treas., Candn. Assn. of Fine Arts Deans 1986–89; Mem., Internat. Counc. of Fine Arts Deans 1984– ; (Chrmn., Ottawa Programme Planning Ctte. 1989); Soc. for the Promotion of Hellenic Stud. 1967– ; Candn. Mediterranean Inst. 1987– ; contbr.: 'Florilegium' 1981, 'Mélanges Étienne Gareau' 1982; 'Essays in Theatre' 1990; co-editor 'Lives of the Theatre' series; recreation: theatre; Home: 25 Willard St., Ottawa, Ont. K1S 1T4; Office: Classics Dept., Carleton Univ., Ottawa, Ont. K1S 5B6.

**BEESTON, Paul M.,** B.A., C.A.; sports executive; b. Welland, Ont.; e. Univ. of Western Ont. B.A. 1968; C.A. 1976; PRESIDENT AND CHIEF EXECUTIVE OFFICER, THE TORONTO BLUE JAYS (WORLD SERIES CHAMPIONS 1992 and 1993) 1989– ; various positions, Toronto Blue Jays 1976–89; Dir., The Toronto Sun Publishing Corp.; Home: 202 Strathgowan Ave., Toronto, Ont. M4N 1C5; Office: 3200, 300 Bremner Blvd., Toronto, Ont. M5V 3B3.

**BÉGIN, Catherine;** comédienne; n. Bois-Colombes, France 22 avr. 1939; f. Lucien et Marie-Louise (Van Havre) B.; e. Conserv. Nat. d'Art Dramatique, Montréal; 30 ans de services comme comédienne sur les scènes de Montréal et à la télévision Canadienne; membre du Conseil d'Admin. de la Cie de Théâtre Albert-Millaire; Vice-Prés. de l'Assn. des Anciens du Conserv. d'Art Dramatique du Qué. Prés. du Conseil Québécois du Théâtre; Porte-parole officiel de la Coalition du Monde des Arts et des Affaires Culturelles; Bureau: 426 rue Sherbrooke Est, Montréal, Qué. H2L 1J6.

**BÉGIN, Hon. Monique,** P.C., M.A.; b. Rome, Italy 1 March 1936; d. Lucien and Marie-Louise (Vanhavre) B.; e. Notre-Dame-de-Grâce Elem. Sch. Montreal; Esther Blondin High Sch. Montreal; Teachers' Coll. Rigaud, Que.; M.A. in Soc., Univ. of Montreal; doctoral stuides, Univ. of Paris; McGill Univ.; Hon. Ph.D. St. Thomas Univ., N.B. 1977; Hon. Doctorate, Mount St. Vincent Univ., N.S. 1982; LL.D. (hon. causa), Dalhousie Univ. 1987; Queen's Univ. 1987; Laurentian Univ. 1988; Fac. of Med., Univ. of Toronto 1988; Univ. of Alta. 1989; D.Sc. (hon. causa), McGill 1991; DEAN OF THE FACULTY OF HEALTH SCIENCES, UNIV. OF OTTAWA 1990– ; Founding mem. Fed. de Femmes du Qué. 1965–67; Extve. Secy. Royal Comn. on Status of Women in Can. 1967–70; mem. Candn. Human Rights Foundation; el. to H. of C. for Montréal-St-Michel (later Saint-Léonard-Anjou) g.e. 1972 (First Quebec woman elected to federal parliament), re-el. 1974, 1979, 1980; apptd. Parlty. Secy. to Secy. of State for External Affairs 1975; Min. of Nat. Revenue and Sworn of Privy Council 1976; Min. of Nat. Health & Welfare 1977–79, 1980–84; Visiting Prof. and Chair in Economics, Univ. of Notre Dame, In. 1984–85; Visiting Lectr., Dept. of Sociology, McGill Univ. 1985–86; Joint Chair in Women's Studies, Carleton and Ottawa Univ. 1986–90; Distinguished Service Award, Candn. Soc. for Clinical Investigation, 1979; 1st Dr. Brock Chilsholm Medal, Med. Soc. of WHO, Geneva 1984; mem., Bd., McGill-Queen's Univ. Press, Montreal/Kingston 1986– ; Bd. of Govs., McGill Univ. 1986–90; Adv. Counc., Kellogg Inst. for Internat. Studies, Univ. of Notre Dame, Indiana 1987–91; Liberal; R. Catholic; Office: 451 Smyth Rd., Ottawa, Ont. K1H 8M5.

**BÉGIN, Robert,** F.S.A.; b. Giffard, Que. 20 Oct. 1925; s. Joseph and Germaine (Blais) B.; e. Primary Sch., Giffard, Que.; Academie de Québec; Laval Univ.; Univ. of Manitoba; m. Marie, d. Gaston Cancade, Findlay, Man., 8 Oct. 1949; children: Lorraine, André (deceased), Gisèle, Danielle, Céline; CHRMN. OF THE BOARD, INDUSTRIAL-ALLIANCE LIFE INSURANCE CO.; Dir., Industrial-Alliance Financial Corp. and its subsidiaries; Industrial-Alliance Life Management Corp. and its subsidiaries; General Trustco of Canada; The National Life Assurance Co. of Can.; The North West Life Assurance Co. of Can. and The North West Life Assurance Co. of Am.; joined co. in 1947, Asst. Actuary 1954, Actuary 1958, Vice-Pres. and Controller 1966, Extve. Vice Pres. 1967, Pres. & C.E.O. 1977, Chrmn. & C.E.O. 1988; mem., Candn. Inst. of Actuaries; Candn. Life & Health Assn.; Life Office Mang. Assn. (Atlanta, Ga.); Que. Chamber of Comm.; R. Catholic; recreations: hockey, fishing, hunting, gardening; Home: 3445 Hawey Blvd., Quebec, Qué. G1E 1P4; Office: 1080 St. Louis Rd., Quebec, Qué. G1K 7M3.

**BÉGIN-HEICK, Nicole,** B.Sc.D., M.S., Ph.D.; educator; b. Lac Etchemin, Qué. 30 Oct. 1937; d. Joseph and Madeleine (Perron) B.; e. Coll. Notre-Dame de Bellevue, Qué.; Univ. Laval B.Sc.D. 1957; Cornell Univ. M.S. 1960; McGill Univ. Ph.D. 1965; m. Hans s. Otto and Charlotte Heick 15 Jan. 1965; children: Caroline Elizabeth, Christopher; DEAN, SCH. OF GRAD. STUDIES AND RSCH. UNIV. OF OTTAWA 1989– ; Post Doctoral Fellow Univ. of Toronto 1964–65, Duke Univ. 1965–67; Asst. Prof. Univ. Laval 1968, Assoc. Prof. 1971–72; Assoc. Prof. present Univ. 1972, Prof. 1980– , Vice Dean of Health Sci's 1987–89; mem. Bd. Assn. Univs. & Colls. Can. 1972–74, Standing Ctte. Status Women in Univs. 1972–75, Chair 1973–75; Chair Candn. Council Animal Care 1972–75; Rep. to Nat. Cancer Inst. Can. 1972–80; mem. Med. Rsch. Council Can. 1977–84, mem. 1977–78 and Chair 1979–84 Fellowship Selection Ctte., mem. Standing Ctte. Rsch. Personnel 1982–86; Natural Sci's & Eng. Rsch. Council Can. 1987–93, Exec. 1988–93, Internat. Ctte. 1988–93, mem. 1979–82 and Chair 1982 Selection Ctte. 1967 Scholarships, Mem. 1991 Selection Ctte. for Silver Medal; Chair, E.W.R. Steacie Fellowship Selection Ctte. 1991 & 1992; Chair, Ont. Council on Graduate Studies 1993 (Vice-Chair 1992); author numerous articles biochem. and physiol. jours.; mem. Candn. Biochem. Soc. (Sec. 1971–74, Council 1976–79); Candn. Fedn. Biol. Socs. (Vice Pres. 1991, Chair Sci. Policy Ctte. 1991, Pres. 1992; Past Pres. 1993– ;); Candn. Soc. Nutritional Sci's; Am. Inst. Nutrition; member-at-large, Candn. Assn. of Graduate Studies 1993– ; recreations: jogging, swimming, reading, music; Home: 340 Roger Rd., Ottawa, Ont. K1H 5C4; Office: 115 Séraphin-Marion, Ottawa, Ont. K1N 6N5.

**BEGUN, David R.,** B.A., M.A., Ph.D.; university professor; b. Croix Chapeau, France 24 Sept. 1959; s. Sanford Harold and Huguette Elise (Besse) B.; e. Brandeis Univ. 1977–79; Univ. of Pennsylvania B.A. 1981, M.A. 1984, Ph.D. 1987; m. Dana L. Bovee d. David and Barbara Bovee 5 June 1982; children: André, Alyx, Mara; ASSOC. PROF., ANTHROPOLOGY, UNIV. OF TORONTO 1993– ; Research Fellow, Anthropology, Smithsonian Inst. 1986–89; Post-doctoral Rsch. Fellow, Cell Biol. & Anat., Johns Hopkins Univ. Sch. of Med. 1988–89; Asst. Prof., Anthropol., Univ. of Toronto 1989–93; Rsch. Assoc., Anthropol., Smithsonian Inst.; Vertebrate Paleontology, Royal Ont. Mus.; Mem., Can. & Am. assns. of Physical Anthropology; author of articles in scholarly journals; recreations: home renovation; Home: 21 Lawlor Ave., Toronto, Ont. M4E 3L8; Office: Toronto, Ont. M5S 1A1.

**BEHIELS, Michael D.,** B.A., M.A., Ph.D.; university professor; b. Edmonton, Alta. 8 June 1946; s. Emile Pierre and Dorothy (Brown) B.; e. Univ. of Ottawa; Univ. of Alta, B.A. 1967, M.A. 1969; York Univ., Ph.D. 1978; m. Linda d. Vernon and Eileen Cox 3 July 1967; children: Marc Steven, Justin Emile-Pierre; PROF. OF HISTORY, UNIV. OF OTTAWA 1986– ; Chrmn., Dept. of History 1988–93; taught at Univ. of Toronto 1973–75; Acadia Univ. 1975–86; Vis. Prof., Univ. of Alta. 1982–83; Vis. Prof., Univ. of Augsburg, Germany 1992; served on various cttes. since 1976; Pres. & Past-Pres., Acadia Univ. Fac. Assn. 1979–81; Can. Counc. Doctoral Fellowship 1969–73; Ont. Grad Fellowship 1971–72; Harvey T. Reid Award 1976; nom. for Gov. Gen's Award 1985; mem. Candn. Hist. Assn.; Shastri Indo-Canadian Inst.; author: 'Prelude to Quebec's Quiet Revolution, 1945–1960' 1985; 'Quebec since 1945' 1987; 'The Meech Lake Primer: Conflicting Views of the 1987 Constitutional Accord' 1989; ed. (with R. Cook) 'The Essential Laurendeau' 1976; numerous articles on intellectual & pol. devels. in 20th Century Que.; recreations: skiing, cycling; Home: 1758 Windflower Way, Orleans, Ont. K1C 5Y5; Office: Ottawa, Ont. K1N 6N5.

**BEHRENDS, Wolfgang,** LL.B., M.Comp.L.; retired diplomat; b. Oberhausen, Germany 12 Jan. 1926; s. Heinrich and Meta (Henkel) B.; e. Univ. of Göttingen, LL.B. 1949; George Washington Univ. Law Sch., M.Comp.L. 1951; children: Sabine, Martina, Kathrin; Ambassador of the Fed. Rep. of Germany 1983–91; joined German Fgn. Serv. 1952; postings: Hong Kong 1954–58; Del. to NATO in Paris 1958–62; Fgn. Min., Bonn 1962–71; Min., New Delhi 1971–73; Ambassador & Head of Del. to MBFR-Negs. in Vienna 1973–78; Ambassador to Egypt 1978–79; Head, Fgn. Dept., Press & Info. Office, Bonn. 1979–83; Ambassador & Rep. to U.N. Comn. on Human Rights, Geneva 1983; Mem., IISS London; recreations: skiing, riding; Address: c/o German Embassy, P.O. Box 379, Postal Stn. A, Ottawa, Ont. K1N 8V4.

**BEHRENS, Jack,** M.Sc., Ph.D.; educator; composer; pianist; b. Lancaster, Pa. 25 March 1935; s. Burt Augustus and Elizabeth Martha (Kranch) B.; e. Juilliard Sch. of Music New York B.Sc. 1958, M.Sc. (Composition) 1959; Harvard Univ. Ph.D. (Composition) 1973; m. Sonja d. Emil and Catherine Peterson 31 Aug. 1962; Head, Theory Dept. Affiliated Conserv. Univ. of Regina 1962–66; Acting Chrmn. Centre Communications & Arts Simon

Fraser Univ. 1966–67; Chrmn. Fine Arts Dept. Cal. State Coll. Bakersfield 1973–76; Chrmn. of Theory & Composition Univ. of W. Ont. 1976–80, Dean of Music, 1980–86; composer numerous comns. incl. Am. Dance Festival, Sask. House Summer Festival, Regina Orchestral Soc., Can. Council, Candn. Pavilion Expo '67, Candn. Centennial Comn. Festival Can., Kern Philharmonic Soc., Ont. Arts Council, CBC; lecture-recitals (piano) Can., U.S.A., Eng.; recipient Va. Center Creative Arts Grant 1972; Helene Wurlitzer Foundation Grant New Mexico 1975, 1976; Wolf Trap Farm Park Performing Arts Grant 1978, 1979; Univ. of W. Ont. Foundation Inc. Grant 1985; Candn. Council Project Grant 1991; Artistic Dir., 'Trillium Plus Music and Letters' 1983– ; composer, 'The Old Order Amish' (film score) 1961; 'The Feast of Life' (record) 1976; 'Fiona's Flute,' 'Dialogue' (record) 1983; 'Aspects' (record) 1985; 'In a Manger' (SATB chorus) 1962; author various articles, reviews; mem. Candn. Univ. Music Soc. (Vice-Pres. 1983–85; Chrmn. Council Mem. Schs. 1981–83); Candn. League Composers; Assoc. Composer, Candn. Music Centre; Candn. Music Centre Ont. Regional Council 1984– , Vice-Chrmn. 1989–90, Chrmn. 1990–92; Candn. Music Centre National Bd. 1987–92; Soc. of Composers Inc.; Composer/USA Nat. Counc.; Am. Soc. Composers, Authors & Publishers; Club: Arts and Letters (Toronto); Home: P.O. Box 115, Thorndale, Ont. N0M 2P0; Office: Fac. of Music, Univ. of W. Ont., London, Ont. N6A 3K7.

**BEIGIE, Carl E.,** A.B., economist; b. Cleveland, Ohio 9 Apr. 1940; s. George C. and late Carol Elizabeth (Chamberlin) B.; e. Cleveland Heights (Ohio) High Sch. 1958; Muskingum Coll. A.B. 1962; Mass. Inst. Technol. Grad. work in Econ. 1962–66 (Woodrow Wilson Fellow 1962; Presb. Fellow 1962, 1964); m. Mary Catherine d. Late William H. Hall 3 June 1961; children: David P., Darin E.; DIRECTOR AND CHIEF ECONOMIST, DOMINION SECURITIES INC. 1983– ; Dir. Oakwood Petroleums Ltd.; Ontario Housing Corp. 1986– ; Professor (part-time), Fac. of Mgmt. Studies, Univ. of Toronto; Assoc. Prof. (Part-Time) Faculty of Mgmt. McGill Univ.; Dir. John Howard Soc. of Ont.; Lectr. Dept. Econ. Univ. W. Ont. 1966–68; Asst. Vice Pres. and Internat. Econ. Irving Trust Co. New York City 1968–71; Extve. Dir. C.D. Howe Inst. 1971–77 (Pres. 1978–82); Dir., Candn. Foundation for Econ. Educ. 1980– ;(and Chrmn. 1984– ;); Zinor Holdings Ltd. 1979–82; Industrial Bank of Japan (Canada) 1982–83; Fraser Companies Ltd., 1975–86; frequent speaker and media commentator on Econ.; business consultant; participant govt. adv. groups; mem., Dept. of Communications' Consultative Comte. on the Implications of Telecommunications for Candn. Sovereignty, 1979; author 'The Canada-U.S. Automotive Agreement: An Evaluation' 1970; 'Inflation Is a Social Malady' 1979; co-author 'The Disappearance of the Status Quo' 1975; author or co-author numerous articles in fields of telecommunications policy, energy issues, trade policy and gen. econ. conditions; mem. Time Canada's Bd. of Econs. 1973–75; Candn. Econ. Assn. (Extve. Council 1972–75); Nat. Assn. Business Econs. (Adolph G. Abramson Award 1971); Candn. Assn. Business Econs.; Am. Econ. Assn.; United Church; recreations: reading, philately, athletics.

**BEÏQUE, Jean F.,** B.Sc.Econ.; investment executive; b. Quebec City, Que. 12 March 1941; s. Henri F. and Madeleine (Carignan) B.; e. Univ. of Montreal B.Sc.Econ. 1965; m. Hélène d. Eloi and Berthe Gendron 30 Dec. 1965; children: Sophie, Anne, Jean-Philippe; GENERAL MANAGER, CN INVESTMENT DIVISION 1979– ; Jones Heward & Co. 1965–74; Brault, Guy & O'Brien 1974–75; with CN Investment Division since 1975; Chair, Novacap Investments Inc.; Vice-Pres., Sec. & Dir., Canapen Group, Canapen Investments Ltd.; Dir., Cambridge Shopping Centres Ltd.; Princeton Devel. Ltd.; Toronto College Park Ltd.; Public Gov., The Montreal Exchange; Mem., Assn. of Investment Management & Research; Cercle finance et placement du Québec; Home: 1695 Montpellier St., St. Bruno, Qué. J3V 4P4; Office: P.O. Box 11002, 5 Place Ville Marie, Suite 1515, Montreal, Qué. H3C 4T2.

**BEIRNE, Brian Desmond, B.A.;** theatre administrator; b. Toronto, Ont. 26 Feb. 1964; s. Patrick F. and Simonne Cecile (Cyr) B.; e. Our Lady of Perpetual Help Sch.; Neil McNeil H.S.; Victoria Coll., Univ. of Toronto; ADMINISTRATIVE DIR., VANDERHEYDEN ASSOCIATES 1990– ; Front of House, St. Lawrence Ctr. for the Arts 1983–85; Admin., Toronto Free Theatre 1984–86; Theatre Mgr., 'CATS', Elgin Theatre, Toronto 1985–87; House Mngt. Cons., Toronto Arts Awards 1986–87; Asst. to Artistic Dir., Toronto Free Theatre 1986–87; Scene Shop Supervisor, The Canadian Opera Co. 1987–88; Production Mgmt. Asst. 'The Phantom of the Opera,' The Live Entertainment Corp. of Canada 1988–90; Admin. Dir., 'Bugs Bunny World Tour'; Bd. of Mgmt., St. Lawrence Centre for the Arts 1989– ; Bd. of Dirs., The Canadian Stage Co. 1992– ; Bd. of Dirs., The Fringe of Toronto Theatre Festival 1993– ; Delta Upsilon Internat. Frat., Indianapolis, IN, Undergrad. Adv. Bd. and Toronto Chap. Sec. 1983–84; Roman Catholic; Office: Ste. 1100, 119 Spadina Ave., Toronto, Ont. M5V 2L1.

**BEIRNE, Bryan Patrick,** M.A., M.Sc., Ph.D.; entomologist; educator; b. Rosslare, Co. Wexford, Ireland, 22 Jan. 1918; s. late Patrick James and late Mabel (Kelly) B.; e. Trinity Coll., Univ. of Dublin, B.Sc., M.Sc., M.A., Ph.D.; m. Elizabeth, d. late James Curry, 12 Apr. 1948; children: Patrick J., Anne M.; PROF. EMERITUS OF PEST MGMT., SIMON FRASER UNIV.; Dir. of Pestology Centre 1967–79 and Dean of Grad. Studies 1979–82 there; Lectr. in Entomol., Univ. of Dublin, 1945; Research Scientist (Insect Systematics), Can. Dept. of Agric., Ottawa, 1949; Dir., Research Inst. (Biol. Control), Belleville, Ont., 1955; participant in various internat. confs. and symposia on biol. pest control and pest mang incl. FAO, WHO, IBP and IACBC (Chrmn.); Mem. R. Irish Acad. 1943; Gold Med. Entomol. Soc. of Canada 1976; Career Achievement Award, Science Council, B.C. 1993; author 'The Origin and History of the British Fauna' 1952; 'British Pyralid and Plume Moths' 1952; 'Pest Management' 1968; 'The Leafhoppers of Canada and Alaska' 1956; 'Collecting, Preparing and Preserving Insects' 1955; 'Irish Entomology: The First 100 Years' 1985; also over 180 research papers on insect systematics and morphology, pest ecology, biol. and integrated controls, zoogeog.; Fellow, Entomol. Soc. Can.; mem., Entomol. Soc. Am.; Office: Burnaby, B.C. V5A 1S6.

**BEISSEL, Henry Eric,** M.A.; educator; author; b. Cologne, Germany 12 Apr. 1929; s. Walter and Joanna (Dillgen) B.; e. Cologne and London (Eng.), studies in philos.; Univ. of Toronto M.A. 1960; m. Arlette d. Ange-Marie and Suzanne Francière 3 Apl. 1981; children: (by previous marriage) two; Clara; PROF. OF ENG. CONCORDIA UNIV. 1966– ; previously Prof. of Eng. Univ. of Alta., Univ. of Trinidad; author poetry: 'Witness the Heart' 1963; 'New Wings For Icarus' 1966; 'Face on the Dark' 1970; 'The Salt I Taste' 1975; 'Cantos North ' (deluxe ed.) 1980, (regular ed.) 1982; 'Season of Blood' 1984; 'Poems New and Selected' 1987; 'Ammonite' 1987; 'Stones to Harvest' (deluxe ed.) 1991, (regular ed.) 1993; 'Dying I Was Born' 1992; drama: 'Skinflint' 1969, premiere Gesu Theatre Montréal 1969; 'Inook and the Sun' 1973, premiere Stratford Festival 1973; 'For Crying Out Loud' 1975, premiere Char-Lan Theatre Workshop, Williamstown 1975; 'Goya' 1976, premiere Montreal Theatre Lab 1976; 'Improvisations for Mr. X' 1978; 'Under Coyote's Eye' 1979, premiere Chicago 1979; 'Hostages' Banff 1983; 'The Noose' premiere Winnipeg 1985; 1989; 'The Noose & Improvisations for MRX' publ. 1989; 'Cues and Entrances' (anthology of plays, incl. 'For Crying Out Loud') rev. ed 1993; poetry transls. incl. 'The Price of Morning' 1969, 'A Different Sun' 1976, both by Walter Bauer; 'A Thistle in his Mouth' by Peter Huchel 1987; drama transls. incl. 'Three Plays By Tankred Dorst' 1976; 'Are You Afraid of Thieves?' 1978, by Louis-Dominique Lavigne; 'The Emigrants' 1984, by Slawomir Mrozek; 'Hedda Gabler' 1983, by Ibsen; 'All Corpses Are Equal' and 'Sacrifices' 1986, by Shie Min; co-transl. 'The Glass Mountain' 1989, by Tor Åge Bringsvaerd; 'Waiting For Gaudreault' 1978, by André Simard; children's poetry 'The World Is A Rainbow' set to music by Wolfgang Bottenberg 1968; 'Inook and the Sun' opera by Wolfgang Bottenberg 1987; prose: 'Kanada' 1981; 'Der Flur' short story 1985; 'Raging Like a Fire: Celebrating Irving Layton' 1993; ed. 'Edge' pol. and lit. jour. 1963–69; contbr. numerous mags., anthologized various publs. incl. 'Modern Canadian Verse,' 'The Penguin Book of Canadian Verse' and 'The Poets of Canada'; recipient Epstein Award 1958; Davidson Award 1959; DAAD Fellowship 1977; several awards and grants Can. Council (incl. 1979 Sr. Arts Grant), Ministère des Affaires culturelles du Qué. and Ont. Arts Council; Pres. League Candn. Poets 1980–81; mem. Writers' Union; Playwrights Can.; Theatre Ont.; P.E.N.; Assn. Candn. Univ. Teachers Eng.; Assn. Comparative Lit.; Candn. Authors & Composers Assn.; Candn. Wildlife Assn.; Candn. Civil Liberties Assn.; Internat. Theatre Inst.; Home: (P.O. Box 339) Alexandria, Ont. K0C 1A0; Office: 1455 De Maisonneuve Blvd. W., Montréal, Qué. H3G 1M8.

**BÉLAND, Pierre,** B.A. B.Sc., Ph.D.; research scientist, administrator; b. Quebec City 4 Oct. 1947; s. René and Andrée (Boulanger) B.; e. Jesuits College B.A. 1967; Laval Univ. B.Sc. 1971; Dalhousie Univ. Ph.D. 1974; Univ. of Queensland, postdoctoral fellow 1975; m. Marie d. Marcel and Denise Cloutier 15 Nov. 1990; children: Martine, Éliane; RESEARCH SCIENTIST & SCIENCE DIRECTOR, ST. LAWRENCE NATIONAL INST. OF ECOTOXICOLOGY 1987– ; Consulting Biologist 1976–77; Rsch. Sci., Paleobiology, Nat. Mus. of Natural Sciences 1977–80; Rsch. Sci. & Section Head, Marine Ecosystems, Fisheries & Oceans Canada 1981–82; Rsch. Sci. & Dir., Fisheries Ecology Rsch. Ctr. 1982–87; Invited Prof., Ctr. Oceanographique de Rimouski, Univ. of Que. 1983; Dir., Mus. de la mer de Rimouski 1985–91; Assoc. Prof., Fac. Veterinary Medicine, Univ. Montreal 1991– ; Mem., Conseil cons. de la conservation et de l'environ., Govt. of Que. 1990– ; Mem., Extve. Ctte., Bd. of Dir., Internat. Ctr. for Ocean Devel. 1990– ; Host, Weekly TV series 1990–91; Best Candn. Francophone Sci., CBC Radio 1988; 1st Prize, Que. Soc. of Public Relns. 1989; Environ. Merit, Que. Regional Environ. Council 1989; ACFAS Prize, Environmental Sciences 1992; author of over 60 mag. & journal articles; Office: 460, du Champ-de-Mars, Suite 504, Montreal, Qué. H2Y 1B4.

**BÉLANGER, André-J.,** B.Comm., M.A., Ph.D., FRSC; university professor; b. Montreal, Que. 17 June 1935; s. Jacques and Jeanne (Fauteux) B.; e. McGill Univ., B.Comm. 1959, M.A. 1961; Laval Univ., Ph.D. 1973; m. Ghyslaine d. Paul-Emile and Marie-Paule Guertin 12 Aug. 1967; children: Mathieu, Guillaume; PROF., UNIV. OF MONTREAL 1973– ; Prof., Laval Univ. 1965–73; Pres., Candn. Political Science Assn. 1989–90; FRSC; author: 'L'apolitisme des idéologies québécoises 1934–36' 1974, 'Ruptures et Constantes' 1977, 'Framework for a Political Sociology' 1985; Office: P.O. Box 6128, Stn. A., Montreal, Qué. H3C 3J7.

**BELANGER, Gérard,** M.A., M.Soc.Sc., F.R.S.C.; educator; economist; b. St. Hyacinthe, Qué. 23 Oct. 1940; s. Georges and Cécile (Girard) B.; e. Univ. de Montréal B.A. 1960; Princeton Univ. M.A. 1966; Univ. Laval M.Soc.Sc. 1967; one child: Marie-José; PROF. OF ECON., UNIVERSITE LAVAL 1967– ; Research Coordr., C.D. Howe Inst. 1977–79; mem. Que. Govt. Task Force on Urbanization 1974–76; mem. Finance Comte. Que. Council Univs. 1971–73; author 'Croissance du secteur public et fédéralisme' 1988; 'L'économique du secteur public' 1981; 'Le financement municipal au Québec' 1976; co-author 'The Price of Health' 1974; 'Le prix du transport au Québec' 1978; 'Taxes and Expenditures in Quebec and Ontario: A Comparison' 1978; various articles; mem. Royal Soc. Can.; Candn. Econ. Assn.; Am. Econ. Assn.; Société canadienne d'économique; Comité scientifique de la Revue française de finances publiques; R. Catholic; Home: 3384 Gaspareau, Ste-Foy, Qué. G1W 2N2; Office: Québec, Qué. G1K 7P4.

**BELANGER, Leo R.,** B.Sc., M.B.A.; information technology executive; b. Windsor, Ont. 6 May 1942; s. Leo Paul and Ella May B.; e. Univ. of Windsor B.Sc. 1965; York Univ. M.B.A. 1972; m. Audrey d. Norman G. Reid 11 Sept. 1965; children: Tracy, Brent; Vice Pres., STM Systems/Westbridge 1987–..; Dir. Manitoba Data Services; CSB Systems; Infocorp.; Rescom; joined Ont. Hydro 1965–70, latterly Mgr. Systems Support Services, Mgr. Prodn. Services 1973–74; Mgmt. Cons. Urwick Currie & Partners 1970–72; Gen. Mgr. Computer Services Control Data Canada 1974–75; Exec. Dir. Computer Services Ont. Govt. 1975–79; Vice Pres. and Gen. Mgr. Canadian ADP 1979–87; contbr. various trade jours.; recreations: golf, tennis; Clubs: Ontario Racquet; Mississaugua Golf; Wyldewood Golf; Home: 1692 Sherwood Forest Circle, Mississauga, Ont. L5K 2G7.

**BELANGER, Marcel,** O.C. (1974), F.C.A.; b. Montreal, P.Q. 2 June 1920; s. late Victorien and Alice (Beaudet) B.; e. Laval Univ., B.A. 1940, M.Comm. 1943; Harvard Univ., M.A. (Econ.) 1948; Hon. Ph.D. (Adm.) Sherbrooke and Laval; m. Simone, d. late J.E. Gagnon, Quebec City, P.Q., 17 July 1948; one d. Marie Veitch; PRES., GAGNON & BÉLANGER INC.; formerly mem., Royal Comn. on Coastal Trade (1955–58); Study Comte. on Public Assistance in Que. (1962–63); Ind. Review Comte. on Office of Auditor Gen. (1974–75); Chrmn. Que. Prov. Roy. Comn. on Taxation, 1963–65; mem. Que. Comn. on Trade of Alcoholic Beverages 1968–71; Dir., Commerce Group Insurance; La Fondation J. Armand Bombardier; Hudson's Bay Co.; Hon. Dir., John Labatt Ltd.; Past Pres., Candn. Inst. Chart. Accts. (1975–76) R. Catholic; recreations: swimming, fishing, skiing; Home: 839 Eymard Ave., Quebec, Qué. G1S 4A3; Office: 140, Grande Allée Est, Bur. 200, Quebec, Qué. G1R 5M8.

**BÉLANGER, Michel Ferdinand,** C.C., B.A., B.Sc.; b. Lévis, Que. 10 Sept. 1929; s. Ferdinand and Jeanne (Blouin) B.; e. Coll. de Lévis (Que.) B.A. 1949; Univ.

Laval, B.Sc. Social Science (Econ.) 1952; McGill Univ. Post-Grad. Studies (Central Mortgage & Housing Corp. Schol.) 1952–54; married, 6 children; Chrmn., Pres. and C.E.O., National Bank of Canada 1981–..; Dir. Nat. Bank of Canada; Simpson-Sears Ltd.; Banque de l'Union Occidentale Française et Canadienne; CIP Inc.; Power Corp of Can.; MICC Investments Ltd.; joined Dept. Finance (Ottawa) 1954; (Quebec City) 1960; Resources 1960; Dir. Planning, Que. Dept. Nat. Resources 1961; Asst. Depy. Min. Nat. Resources 1961; Depy. Min., Que. Dept. Indust. and Comm. 1966; Econ. Adv. to the Que. Extve. Council 1969; Secy. Treasury Bd. 1971; Pres. and Ch. Exec. Off. Montreal Stock Exchange 1973; Pres. Provincial Bank of Canada 1976; Pres. and C.E.O. 1977; Pres. & C.E.O., Nat. Bank of Canada 1979; mem. Régie de la Place des Arts; Dir., St. Mary's Hospital; Clinical Research Inst. of Montreal; C.D. Howe Inst.; Companion, Order of Canada 1994; Address: 615 Dunlop Ave., Outremont, Qué. H2V 2W1.

**BÉLANGER, Paul Raoul,** B.Com., LL.B.; provincial judge; b. Ottawa, Ont. 30 Sept. 1942; s. Gérard A. and Alice (Brisson); e. Univ. of Ottawa, B.Com., 1962; Osgoode Hall Law Sch., LL.B. 1968; m. Lyse d. Roger & Simone Charbonneau, 2 Sept. 1967; children: Danielle, Michelle, Julie; SENIOR PROVINCIAL COURT JUDGE, OTTAWA 1984– ; Offr., Royal Candn. Navy 1958–65; Called to the Bar of Ontario 1970; Pres., County of Carleton Law Assoc. 1977; appointed Provincial Judge, Criminal Div. 1978; Hon. Dir., Thomas More Lawyers Guild of Ottawa; Founding Pres., Coll. Catholique Samuel Genest 1979–84; mem., Extve. Ctte., Ont. Provincial Judges Assoc.; Candn. Bar Assoc.; Assoc. des Juristes d'Expression Francaise de l'Ontario; Ottawa Flying Club; County of Carleton Law Assoc.; The Osgoode Soc.; recreations: flying, sailing, computers, etc.; Home: 920 Plante Dr., Ottawa, Ont. K1V 7E2; Office: The Court House, 161 Elgin St., Ottawa, Ont. K2P 2L1.

**BÉLANGER, Pierre Rolland,** B.Eng., S.M., Ph.D.; educator; b. Montréal, Qué. 18 Aug. 1937; s. Pierre H. and Lucille (Rolland) B.; e. McGill Univ. B.E. 1959; Mass. Inst. of Technol. S.M. 1961, Ph.D. 1964; m. Margaret d. Henry and Florence Clark 24 Aug. 1963; children: Mark, Suzanne, David; DEAN OF ENGINEERING, McGILL UNIV. 1984– , Prof. of Elect. Eng. 1976– ; Asst. Prof. of Elect. Eng. Mass. Inst. Technol. 1964–65; Systems Analyst, The Foxboro Co. 1965–67; Assoc. Prof. of Elect. Eng. present univ. 1967–76, Chrmn. of Elect. Eng. 1978–84; co-author 'Introduction to Circuits with Electronics – An Integrated Approach' 1985; Fellow, IEEE (Centennial Medal 1984); mem., Order Engs. Qué.; Nat. Adv. Bd. for Sci. and Technol. 1987–90; Candn. Acad. of Eng.; Vice-Chrmn., Defense Science Adv. Bd. 1989– ; 817 Sherbrooke St. W., Montréal, Qué. H3A 2K6.

**BELBECK, Kenneth George,** B.A.; management consultant; b. London, Ont. 11 Feb. 1928; s. George Jerald and Lily May (Jolliffe) B.; e. London (Ont.) Central Coll. Inst., 1941–46; Univ. of W. Ont., Sch. of Business Adm., B.A. 1950; m. Patricia Ann, d. Murray Leslie McCulloch, London, Ont., 19 May 1951; children: Gregory, Jeffrey, David, Susan; CHRMN., PEAT MARWICK STEVENSON & KELLOGG, since 1986; Dir., Humber Memorial Hosp.; Pallett Pallett Inc.; Comptroller, Geo. Pattison & Co. Ltd., 1950–53; joined present Co. 1953; apptd. Consultant and subsequently Princ. and Pres.; Founding mem., Inst. Mang. Consultants Ont.; Past Pres., Candn. Assn. Mang. Consultants; Zeta Psi; United Church; recreations: skiing; Club: Granite; Home: 27 Pettit Dr., Weston, Ont. M9R 2W6; Office: 2300 Yonge St., Toronto, Ont. M4P 1G2.

**BELCHER, Stanley Dennis Norman,** A.I.B.; banker; b. Birmingham, England 18 Sept. 1940; s. Stanley Vernon and Edith (Fitzgerald) B.; e. Harrow Co. Grammar School 1958; Assoc., Inst. of Bankers (UK); Stonier Grad. School of Banking (US) grad.; m. Carole d. John Waters 29 Feb. 1964; one d: Ruth Carole; EXECUTIVE VICE-PRESIDENT, THE BANK OF NOVA SCOTIA 1991– ; employed U.K. bank until 1972; various positions, Bank of N.S. until 1983; Sr. Vice-Pres. 1983; Adv. Bd. of Am. Grad. School of Internat. Business Management; Dir., Insolvency Inst. of Canada; Shieldings Inc.; author of two book chapters; recreations: golf; clubs: St. Georges Golf & Country, The Fitness Inst., The National; Home: 1278 Monks Passage, Oakville, Ont. L6M 1R4; Office: 44 King St. W., Toronto, Ont. M5M 1H1.

**BELCOURT, Herbert Clifford;** business executive; b. Lac St. Anne, Alta. 6 July 1931; s. Wilfred and Florence B.; e. Univ. of Alta.; m. Lesley M. Fouthrop d. Alan and Lily Tarrant 30 June 1973; children: David, Kim, Colin, Jolene; PRES. HERBEL HOLDINGS LTD. 1980– ; Pres. Tara Bel Inc. 1989– ; Sword & Shield Movie Theatres 1983– ; Pres., Herb's Upholstery Ltd. 1957; Mutual Phone Line Service 1960; Belcourt Construction 1965–80; Canative Housing Corp. 1971–86, Treas. 1986– ; Lord Belcourt Formal Wear 1974–80; News Building Syndicate 1980–88; recipient Queen's Silver Jubilee Medal 1977; mem. C. of C. Edmonton, Sherwood Park (Treas.); mem. Bd. Sr. Citizens Home Gunn, Alta.; Pres. Nat. Urban Native Housing Assn. 1975; N. Pres. Motion Picture Assn. Alta. 1986–88; Chrmn. Bus. Assistance Native Albertans 1981–84; mem. Alta. Art Found. 1980–83, Vice Pres. 1980–81; Adv. Council CESO 1986– ; Bd. of Govs., Univ. of Athabasca; Pres. Pembina P. Cons. Assn. 1976–77; mem. Prov. and Fed. P. Cons. Parties since 1956; prov. and fed. P. Cons. Cand. 1977–88; mem. Outreach Ctte. All Saints Cath. 1983, Vestry 1983; Bd. Mem., Festival Place 1991; Chrmn., UIC Appeal Bd., Edmonton, Alta. 1991– ; Mem., Sherwood Park Lions Club 1992– ; Freemason; recreations: golf, theatre, dog walking; Clubs: Lions; Rotary; Address: 406 Evergreen St., Sherwood Park, Alta. T8A 1K3.

**BELFORD, John A.,** B.Com.; retired company executive; b. Ottawa, Ont. 16 Jan. 1918; s. John Alexander and Lillian Jane (Wingfield) B.; e. Glebe Coll. Inst., Ottawa, Ont.; McGill Univ, B.Com. 1941; m. Jeanne, d. Thomas Nelson Woods, 13 Sept. 1945; children: John Alexander Jr., Glenys Jane; Vice Pres. Personnel & Indust. Relations, Massey-Ferguson Ltd. from 1957, retired as Corp. Vice Pres. 1978; Personnel Mgr., Belding-Corticelli Ltd., Montreal, P.Q., 1946–50; Asst. to Vice Pres. Personnel, Brazilian Traction, Rio de Janeiro, 1951; Asst. Labour Relations Mgr., Canadian Nat. Rlys., Montreal, P.Q., 1952–56; Lect. in Indust. Relations and Dir. of Field Work, Grad. Sch. of Indust. Relations, Univ. of Montreal, 1947–50; Pres., Montreal Personnel Assn., 1950; served in 2nd World War; enlisted as Cadet, R.C.A., Candn. Army, Apr. 1941; overseas service, U.K. and N.W. Europe, 1941–45; retired with rank of Maj., 1946; Chrmn., Citizens' Advisory Ctte., Ont. Medical Assn. 1973–76; Home: 1097 Lakeshore Road E., Oakville, Ont. L6J 1K9.

**BELHUMEUR, David,** B.A., L.Sc.Com., D.B.A. (H.C.), F.C.A.; executive; b. St-Guillaume, Que. 21 Apr. 1919; s. Omer and Annette (Bonin) B.; e. Laval Univ., B.A. 1940; Univ. of Montreal, L.Sc.Com. 1945, D.B.A. (H.C.) 1975; m. Andrée, d. Raoul Cavet, Quebec, P.Q., 10 Sept. 1951; children: Jean, Hélène, Pierre, Josée; Pres. Fonds D.B. Inc.; Vice-Pres. SOGERO Inc.; Dir., Trust Général du Canada 1970–81; Inst. de Cardiologie de Montréal 1970–79; Advisor, Export Credit Insurance Corp. 1959–63; Gov., Faculty of Adm., Univ. of Sherbrooke; Marie-Enfant Hosp.; Dir., Symphonic Orchestra of Québec 1966–68; Prov. Chamber Comm. 1964–66; Pres., Trois-Rivières Chamber of Comm. 1963–64, Chevalier de l'Ordre Equestre du St-Sepulcre de Jerusalem (1974); R. Catholic; recreation: yachting, golf; Clubs: St.-Denis; Montreal Yacht; Laval-Sur-Le-Lac Golf; Address: 6000 Ch. Deacon, PH E, Montréal, Qué. H3S 2T9.

**BÉLISLE, His Excellency the Most Rev. Gilles;** Catholic bishop; b. Clarence Creek, Ont. 7 Oct. 1923; s. Hermile and Clara (Charlebois) B.; e. Le Petit Sém. d'Ottawa; Le Grand Sém. d'Ottawa; Angelicum and Gregorian Universities in Rome; AUXILIARY BISHOP OF OTTAWA, CATHOLIC ARCHDIOCESE OF OTTAWA 1977– ; ordained priest 1950; co-ord. of pastoral works, French sector, Ottawa archdiocese; Mem., Ont. Conf. of Catholic Bishops; Conf. of Catholic Bishops of Can.; Home: 143 St. Patrick, Apt. 25, Ottawa, Ont. K1N 5J9; Office: 1247 Kilborn Ave., Ottawa, Ont. K1H 6K9.

**BÉLISLE, J. Denis,** B.Comm., M.Comm.; diplomat; b. Drummondville, Que. 27 June 1942; s. René and Marie-Jeanne (Bédard) B.; e. Univ. de Sherbrooke B.Comm. 1963; M.Comm. 1964; Graduate Inst. of Intl. Studies Geneva, 1965–66; m. Micheline d. Alcide Labrecque 30 Dec. 1967; children: Jean-Christophe, Jean-François; AMBASSADOR OF CANADA TO COTE D'IVOIRE, MALI, NIGER AND BURKINA FASO 1991– ; Pension Trust Offr., Royal Trust 1964; Co-ord., Expo 67 1966–67; Asst. Trade Comnr., Industry, Trade & Comm. 1968; Commercial Sec., Candn. Embassy Washington 1968–72; var. mngt. positions, Candn. Pacific Consulting Services 1972–88; Vice-Pres., Bus. Coop., Candn. Internat. Devel. Agency 1988–91; Past Dir. of five companies; Chair, Com. cons. du comm. extérieur et du dével. tech. du Gouv. du Qué. 1985–88; Conseiller du comm. etérieur du Qué. 1987–88; Rotary Internat. Found. Scholarship 1965–66; Prix Codère & Walter M. Loneys' Scholarship 1964; Bourse des jeunesses musicales du Can. 1958; recreations: golf, skiing; Office: P.O. Box 500 (ABDJN), Ottawa, Ont. K1A 0G2.

**BELIVEAU, Jean Arthur;** executive; hockey player (retired); b. Trois-Rivieres, Que. 31 Aug. 1931; m. Elise (Couture); one d. Helene; Sr. Vice Pres. and Dir. Rel., Club de Hockey Canadien Inc. (Retired); Dir., The Molson Co.'s Ltd.; Canadian Reassurance International Group; Acier Leroux; Carena Developments; played with Montreal Canadiens 1953–71; Captain 1961–71; scored 507 regular season goals, 79 more in playoffs; 712 regular seas. assists, and 162 playoff hockey games; on 10 Stanley Cup winners; mem. Hockey Hall of Fame; Winner of Art Ross Trophy; twice Hart Trophy (MVP); Conn Smythe Trophy; Address: 155 Victoria St., Longueuil, Qué. J4H 2J4.

**BELL, Alistair Macready;** artist-printmaker; b. Darlington, Eng. 21 Oct. 1913; s. Archibald and Gladys Mary (Vassie) B.; e. elem. schs. Darlington, Eng., Toronto, Ont. and Galt, Ont.; Galt Coll. Inst. & Vocational Sch. 1928; m. Lorna Beatrice d. Kenneth Rivers Streatfeild 5 July 1941; one s. Alan Streatfeild; full-time artist-printmaker since 1967; rep. in various internat. graphics exhns. particularly Xylography; many one-man exhns. Can.; retrospective prints exhn. (with completely illustrated cat. of all prints to end of 1981) Art Gallery of Greater Victoria 1982; rep. in pub., corporate and private colls. incl. Nat. Gallery Can., Museum of Modern Art New York, Victoria and Albert Museum, Museo Ugo da Carpi Italy; Co-Trustee Emily Carr Scholarship Trust 6 yrs.; rec'd Can. Council Sr. Artists' Fellowship 1959, 1967; Past Pres. B.C. Soc. Artists; Candn. Group of Painters; Address: 2566 Marine Dr., West Vancouver, B.C. V7V 1L4.

**BELL, Allan Gordon,** B.A., M.Mus.; composer, professor; b. Calgary, Alta. 24 May 1953; s. Gordon Albert and Gloria Doris Thorene (McKay) B.; e. Univ. of Alta., B.A., M.Mus. 1980; m. Trudy d. Frances and Eric Work 6 Nov. 1982; children: Caitlin, Jameson; PROF., DEPARTMENT OF MUSIC, UNIV. OF CALGARY 1983– ; created works for solo instruments, voice, choir, orchestra, band, & electroacoustic media; comnd. by orgns. such as Can. Council, CBC, Candn. Band Dir. Assn., Soc. de musique contemporaine du Que. (SMCQ); works performed by the Calgary Philharmonic Orch., the Esprit Orch., Candn. Chamber Orch., Purcell String Quartet, Orford String Quartet, the ensembles of Toronto New Music Concerts, ARRAYMUSIC, & SMCQ & many others worldwide; has composed scores for award-winning film & TV prodns.; Pres., Candn. Music Ctr. 1984–88; composer: 'Kinesis' 1980, 'Arche' 1980, 'Five Rituals' 1980, 'Monashee' 1982, 'Mistaya' 1983, 'From Chaos to the Birth of a Dancing Star' 1983, 'Gaia' 1984, 'Concerto for Percussion & Orchestra' 1984, 'In the Eye of Four Winds' 1986, 'Innua: Three Masks' 1987, 'Concerto for Two Orchestras' 1988, 'Sonora borealis' 1989, 'Arche II' 1989, 'Orca' 1989, 'Symphony No 1' 1989, 'Prairie II' 1989; 'Lumen' 1990, Office: Calgary, Alta. T2N 1N4.

**BELL, C. Randolph;** executive; b. St. John's, Nfld. 30 May 1944; s. Charles Renfrew and Ruth (Hickman) B.; e. Bishop Field and Bishop's Coll., St. John's; Memorial Univ. of Nfld.; m. Mary Virginia, d. Col. H.E.C. Price, Ottawa, Ont., 15 Apl. 1966; children: Christopher, Timothy, Andrew, Ruth; PRES. & DIR., CHARLES R. BELL LTD. since 1972; Bell Holdings Ltd.; Campanelle Ltd.; Cohen's Home Furnishings Ltd.; Frog Pond Holdings Ltd.; Northview Ltd.; Dir., National Sea Products Ltd., Halifax, N.S.; Nfld. Offshore Services Ltd.; joined present firm 1964; Treas., Internat. Grenfell Assn.; mem. Adv. Bd., Royal Trust Co.; Chrmn., The Salvation Army St. John's Adv. Bd.; Mem. Bd., Grace General Hosp., St. John's; Presbyterian; recreations: tennis, gardening; Clubs: Royal Nfld. Yacht; York Club, Toronto; Home: Frog Pond Farm, Topsail, C.B., Nfld. A0A 3Y0; Office: 81 Kenmount Rd., St. John's, Nfld. A1B 3P8.

**BELL, David Victor John,** A.M., Ph.D.; educator; b. Toronto, Ont. 9 Apr. 1944; s. Herbert McLean and Violet Eudora (Bryan) B.; e. Northview Heights Coll. Inst. Toronto 1962; York Univ./Univ. of Toronto B.A. 1965; Harvard Univ. A.M. 1967, Ph.D. 1969; m. Kaaren d. John Barfoot and Beatrice K. Macdonald 30 Aug. 1966; children: Kristin Cassandra, Jason David; DEAN OF ENVIRONMENTAL STUDIES, YORK UNIV. 1992– , Prof. of Pol. Science 1981– , Chair, Dept. of Pol. Science 1991–92 and Coordinator, Alternative Security Studies, York Center for Strategic Studies 1988–92; Acting Dir. Robarts Centre for Candn. Studies 1983–85, Dean of Grad. Studies 1981–87; lectr. Harvard Univ. 1968–69; Asst. Prof. Mich. State Univ. 1969–71; Asst. Prof. present Univ. 1971, Assoc. Prof. 1973, Dir. Grad. Program Pol. Science 1973–76; Founding mem. Extve. LaMarsh

Research Program on Violence & Conflict; served Task Force on Pub. Educ., Addiction Research Foundation 1979–81; Ont. Scholar 1962; Woodrow Wilson Fellow 1965; Harvard Grad. Prize Fellow 1965–69; Chrmn. Leave Fellowship Selection Comte. 2, Social Sciences & Humanities Research Council Can. 1978–79; Pres. Grindstone Co-operative Ltd. 1976–81; Vice Pres. Thornhill Minor Soccer Club 1982–83, Pres. 1983–85; Mem., Ontario Round Table on the Environment and the Economy 1993– ; author 'Resistance and Revolution' 1973; 'Power, Influence and Authority: An Essay in Political Linguistics' 1975; 'The Roots of Disunity: A Study of Canadian Political Culture' 1992; co-author 'Alcohol: Public Education and Social Policy' 1981; 'Reaching the Voter: Constituency Campaigning in Canada' 1991; ed. 'Language and International Politics' 1979; co-ed. 'Issues in Politics and Government' 1971; 'Canada in Transition' series (8 books publ.) 1973–87; 'Reaching the Voter: Constituency Campaigning in Canada' 1991; mem. various ed. bds.; wrote and presented 5 one-hour 'Ideas' programs CBC-FM Radio series 'The Roots of Disunity'; wrote scripts for 2 programs in TVOntario series 'Left, Right and Center'; mem. Candn. Pol. Science Assn.; Assn. Cinema, TV & Radio Artists; recreations: soccer coaching, squash, sailing, cross-country skiing, jazz bassist; Home: 5 Shaindell St., Thornhill, Ont. L3T 3X5; Office: N925 Ross Bldg., 4700 Keele St., Downsview, Ont. M3J 1P3.

**BELL, Douglas Leslie Dewey, C.M.;** retired commissioner; b. Moose Jaw, Sask. 15 June 1926; s. Douglas C. and Irene M. (Dewey) B.; e. Central Coll. Inst. Moose Jaw; m. Pearl L. d. John and Margaret Gray 25 Sept. 1946; children: Linda L., Douglas B.C., Robert G.; PUBLISHER, YUKON NEWS, Whitehorse 1986– ; served as Radio Operator, Radio Technician, Offr.-in-Charge and Area Mgr. Transport Can. 1946–77; el. City Council Ald. Whitehorse, Y.T. 1976; apptd. Depy. Comnr. Yukon Govt. 1977; Comnr. 1980–86 (ret.); former mem. Lib. Bd. Medicine Hat, Alta.; served with RCAF 1943–46, Sgt. Wireless Air Gunner; recipient Distinguished Life Membership RCMP Offr. and NCO Messes; Member, Order of Canada 1989; Commemorative Medal, 125th Anniversary of the Confed. of Canada 1992; Past Pres. Yukon Scout Counc.; recreation: photography; Club: Chamber of Commerce; Toastmasters; Home: 1 Kluhini Cres., Whitehorse, Yukon Y1A 3P3.

**BELL, J.A. Gordon;** retired banker; b. Rivers, Man. 16 Aug. 1929; s. John Edwin, D.D. and Mary MacDonald (McIlraith) B.; e. Pub. and High Schs. at Man., Nfld., Ont.; LL.D. (Hon.): Brock Univ., St. Mary's Univ.; Depy. Chrmn., Pres. & Chief Operating Offr., The Bank of Nova Scotia 1982–93, retired; Dir., The Bank of Nova Scotia; Bosch Inc.; Bramalea Limited; Devtek Corp.; Domtar Inc.; Hudson's Bay Company; D.A. Stuart Ltd.; Trustee, Spencer Hall Fndn.; joined The Bank of Nova Scotia, Queen and Church Branch, Toronto 1948; Inspection Staff, General Office, 1953; transferred to London, Eng. as Special Rep., 1955; Mgr., W. End, London, 1957; Asst. Mgr., Toronto Br., 1959; Mgr., Halifax Br. 1962, Ottawa Br. 1964, Kingston, Jamaica 1965; Asst. Gen. Mgr., Kingston, Jamaica, 1966; Mng. Dir., The Bank of Nova Scotia Jamaica Ltd. 1967; Gen. Mgr., Metrop. Toronto Branches 1968; Deputy Chief Gen. Mgr. 1969; Exec. V.P. and Chief Gen. Mgr. 1972; Pres. & Chief Operating Offr. 1979; Clubs: National; Granite; Toronto; Office: Scotia Plaza, Suite 900, 44 King St. W., Toronto, Ont. M5H 1H1.

**BELL, J. Milton,** O.C., D.Sc., F.R.S.C., F.A.I.C.; b. Islay, Alta. 16 Jan. 1922; s. Milton Wilfred and Elsie Joyce (Larmour) B.; e. High Sch., Scott, Sask.; Sch. of Agric., Vermilion, Alta., 1940; Univ. of Alta., B.Sc.A. 1943; Macdonald Coll., McGill Univ., M.Sc. 1945; Cornell Univ., Ph.D. 1948; McGill Univ., D.Sc. 1986; m. Edith Margaret Joan, d. Charles William Smith, 21 Sept. 1944; three s., two d; Emeritus Prof. Animal Science, Coll. of Agric.; named Can.'s (first) Laureate of Agric., 1970; rec'd Borden Award, Nutrition Soc. Can., 1962; Fellow, Agric. Inst. Can., 1966; Fellow, Royal Soc. of Canada, 1973; Officer, Order of Canada, 1972; Jas. McAnsh Award 1988; Mem., Sask. Agric. Hall of Fame 1989; mem., Am. Inst. Nutrition; Candn. Soc. Animal Sci.; Am. Soc. Animal Sci.; United Church; recreation: photography; Home: 1530 Jackson Ave., Saskatoon, Sask. S7H 2N2.

**BELL, James Allan;** advertising executive; b. Angusville, Man. 1 Oct. 1928; s. Thomas Hedley and Constance Gwendolyn (Ewens) B.; e. Gladstone (Man.) Coll. Inst. 1945; m. Edna d. William and Grace Websdale 8 Feb. 1951; children: Alan Jeffrey (dec. 1972), Jennifer, Maureen, Lisa; Sr. Vice Pres., Mediacom Inc. 1986–.; joined Claude Neon Ruddy Kester Ltd. Winnipeg 1946–50, 1952, Fort William, Ont. Br. Mgr. 1953; Local Sales Mgr. E.L. Ruddy Co. Toronto 1962 becoming Operations Mgr., Vice Pres. Operations, Sr. Vice Pres. 1986; served with Candn. Army Special Force 1950–52, Korea; Dir. Ont. Safety League; Outdoor Advt. Assn. Can. (Past Chrmn. Operations Ctte.); mem. Bd. Trade Metrop. Toronto; former Steward and Chrmn. Finance Ctte. Bloordale Un. Ch. Etobicoke; Club: Rotary; Home: 82 Toledo Rd., Etobicoke, Ont. M9C 2H9.

**BELL, John Charles,** B.A.; writer, editor, archivist; b. Montreal, Que. 4 May 1952; s. Arnold Vincent and Mary Eileen (Curley) B.; e. Dalhousie Univ. B.A. (Hons.) 1975; m. Suanne d. Peter and Jean Rogers 22 June 1973; children: Natasha Christine, Nicholas Tyler; ARCHIVIST, MANUSCRIPT DIVISION, NAT. ARCHIVES OF CANADA 1985– ; Dalhousie Univ. Archives 1975–81; Diefenbaker Project, Univ. of Sask. 1982–85; Publisher and Editor, 'Borealis' 1978–79; Edit. Bd. Mem., 'Arc' 1982–90; Co-chair, 10th World Fantasy Convention 1984; Curator, Candn. Mus. of Caricature Exbn. Guardians of the North: The National Superhero in Candn. Comic-Book Art 1992; Mem., Writers' Fed. of N.S.; Cartophilic Soc. of Canada; Cartophilic Soc. of G.B.; Ephemera Soc. of Can.; author: 'Canuck Comics' 1986, 'Guardians of the North / Protecteurs du nord' 1992; co-author: 'Canadian Science Fiction and Fantasy' (bibliography) 1979; editor: 'At the Harbour Mouth' Archibald MacMechan 1988, 'Halifax: A Literary Portrait' 1990, 'Ottawa: A Literary Portrait' 1992, 'The Grand-Slam Anthology of Canadian Baseball Writing' 1993; co-editor: 'Visions from the Edge' 1981 Home: 168 Florence St., Ottawa, Ont. K1R 5N4; Office: P.O. Box 902, Stn. B., Ottawa, Ont. K1P 5P9.

**BELL, John Kim,** C.M., D.Mus., LL.D.; conductor; composer; foundation president; b. Kahnawake, Que. 8 Oct. 1952; s. Carl Donald and Beth Isabelle (Hamilton) B.; e. Ohio State Univ. B.M. 1975; Acad. of Music Siena, Italy Cert. of Performance 1981; Lakehead Univ. D.Mus. 1990; FOUNDER AND PRES. CANDN. NATIVE ARTS FOUND. 1988– ; began career as Broadway Musical Conductor; Guest Conductor Nat. Ballet of Can.; Conductor Eglevsky Ballet Co. and Dance Theatre of Harlem N.Y.C.; Asst. Conductor and Conductor U.S.A. tour Soviet Ballet team 'The Panovs' 1972; Apprentice Opera Coach Chautauqua Opera Assn. 1974; Apprentice Conductor Toronto Symphony 1980; produced and co-composed first Native ballet 'In the Land of Spirits', premiered Nat. Arts Centre Ottawa 1988; composed scores PBS docudrama 'The Trial of Standing Beer'and CFTO 'Divided Loyalties' 1989; Producer/Dir./Co-Composer, 1992 National Tour 'In the Land Of Spirits'; Music Dir., Canada Day Official Ceremonies 1991, 1992, 1993; Guest Conductor, National Arts Centre Orchestra; Dir., Institute for Rsch. on Public Policy; Hugh Macmillan Rehabilitation Centre; Friends of Candn. Broadcasting; mem., National Sectoral Council for Cultural; mem. Fed. Task Force Profl. Training Cultural Sector Can.; mem. Adv. Bd. Mktg. & Programming Nat. Capital Comn. 1989–91; mem. External Affairs Sagit Ctte. Arts & Cultural Inds.; recipient Can. Council Grant 1980; William Oxley Thompson Alumni Award 1987 Ohio State Univ.; Four Seasons Music Festival Ont. Award 1989; C.M. 1991; Successors Award Candn. Bus. Mag. (1 of 12 'outstanding young Candn. entrepreneurs'); awarded Commemorative Medal for 125th Anniversary of Candn. Confederation 1992; LL.D. (honoris causa) Trent Univ. 1992; Office: 77 Mowat Ave., Ste. 508, Toronto, Ont. M6K 3E3.

**BELL, John P.,** B.Comm.; diplomat; b. Montreal, Que. 26 Apr. 1938; s. Jack T. and Dorothy L. (Platt) B.; e. Univ. of B.C., B.Comm. 1962; CANADIAN HIGH COMMISSIONER, CANDN. HIGH COMMISSION KUALA LUMPUR, MALAYSIA 1993– ; joined Trade Comn. Serv. 1962; 2nd Sec., Comml., Stockholm 1963–67; Office of ADM, Trade Promo., ITC, Ottawa 1967–68; Trade Promo. & Planning 1968–69; Extve. Asst. to Gen Dir., TCS 1969; 1st Sec., Comml. Accra 1969–70; Abidjan 1970–71; Couns., Comml., Paris 1971–74; Consul, Sydney 1974–75; Consul & Sr. Trade Comnr., Sao Paulo, Brazil 1975–79; Dir., Personnel, TCS, Ottawa 1979–81; Acting Dir. Gen., TCS/CRO 1981–82; Depy. Consul Gen., N.Y. 1982–84; Ambassador of Can. to Ivory Coast, Mali, Niger & Burkina Faso 1984–87 (Hon. Chieftan of 27 villages in Ivory Coast, Mali & Niger); Ambassador of Canada to Brazil 1987–90; Adjunct Prof., Sustainable Development Rsch. Institute, Univ. of B.C. 1992–93; Special Advisor to the Secretary of State for External Affairs on the Environment 1990–93; recreations: tennis, scuba; clubs: var. worldwide; Home: 195, Acacia Ave., Ottawa, Ont. K1M 0L6; Office: Ottawa, Ont.

**BELL, John R.;** food industry executive; b. United Kingdom 1946;; e. Ryerson Polytech. Inst. Bus.Admin. 1968; Univ. of West. Ont. MTC 1984; m. Jasmin; 2 children; PRES. & CHIEF EXTVE. OFFR., NABOB FOODS LIMITED 1988– ; Sales Rep., Bristol Myers 1968–70; Prod. Mgr., Beecham Can. 1970–73; Acct. Supvr., Leo Burnett Co. 1973–75; Partner, Palmer Bell & Assoc. 1975–77; Mktg. Mgr., present firm 1977–80; Vice-Pres., Mktg. 1980–85; Extve. Vice-Pres. & Gen. Mgr. 1986–88; Dir., Coffee Assn. of Can. (Chrmn. 1992–93); Nabob Foods Ltd.; Lifestream Natural Foods Ltd.; Grocery Products Mfrs. of Can.; National Institute of Nutrition; Past Pres., Am. Mktg. Assn.; Gov., Science World B.C.; Trustee, Outward Bound Western Canada; Adv. Counc., UBC Faculty of Agric. & Food Sci.; Simon Fraser Univ., Faculty ofBusiness Administration External Advisory Board; Office: 3131 Lake City Way, Burnaby, B.C. V5A 3A3.

**BELL, Hon. Madam Justice Judith Miriam,** B.A., LL.B.; judge; b. Ottawa, Ont. 7 Feb. 1940; d. Hon. Richard Albert Bell, P.C., Q.C., LL.D. and Winnifred Osborne (Sinclair) Bell; e. Nepean High Sch. Ottawa; Dalhouse Univ. B.A. 1960, LL.B. 1962; JUDGE, ONTARIO COURT OF JUSTICE, GENERAL DIVISION 1986– ; law practice Fraser & Beatty Toronto 1964–65; Assoc. and Partner, Bell, Baker Ottawa 1965–86; cr. Q.C. 1975; Bencher, Law Soc. Upper Can. 1983–86; Lectr. in Community Planning & Land Use Ottawa Univ. Law Sch. 1976–83; Lectr. in Mun. Law Algonquin Coll. 1986; Past mem. Bd. Govs. Carleton Univ.; Past mem., Univ. of Ottawa Heart Inst. Adv. Bd.; Past Dir., Candn. Judges Conf.; Past Chrmn. Bd. Trustees Ottawa Civic Hosp.; Past Chrmn. Hosp. Adv. Bd. Ottawa-Carleton Regional Dist. Health Council; past Hon. Dir. Ottawa YM-YWCA; Past Pres. Univ. Women's Club Ottawa; former mem. Council Ont. Br. and Nat. Council Candn. Bar Assn.; Club: Britannia Yacht; Office: 161 Elgin St., Ottawa, Ont. K2P 2K1.

**BELL, Malcolm C.,** M.A.Sc., Ph.D., P.Eng.; metallurgist; b. Noranda, Qué. 31 Jan. 1939; s. Archibald M. and Dorothea (Evert) B.; e. Univ. of Toronto B.A. Sc. 1961, M.A.Sc. 1962, Ph.D. 1964; NRC Postdoctoral Scholar Royal Sch. of Mines, London, Eng. 1965; m. Michelle d. Fernand and Kelly Lettner 1962; children: Cameron, Kelly, Michaela; VICE PRES. INCO LTD. 1986– ; Pres. IncoTech; joined Inco 1965, Mgr. Process Technol. Copper Cliff, Ont. 1973, Dir. J. Roy Gordon Lab. Sheridan Park 1976, Vice Pres. Inco Metals Co. 1981, Vice Pres, Inco Ont. Div. Sudbury 1984; holds 25 patents; author or co-author over 12 tech. publs.; mem. Candn. Inst. Mining & Metall.; Home: 1371 Gallery Hill, Oakville, Ont. L6M 2N3; Office: P.O. Box 44, Royal Trust Tower, Toronto-Dominion Centre, Toronto, Ont. M5K 1N4.

**BELL, (Philip) Michael,** M.A.; art administrator; historian; b. Toronto, Ont. 31 Dec. 1942; s. William Harvey and Alice W. (Stone) B.; e. Aurora (Ont.) & Dist. High Sch. 1961; Univ. of Toronto B.A. 1966, M.A. (Fine Arts) 1967; m. Natalie Maria d. Prof. George N. Luckyj 15 Aug. 1977; DIRECTOR, CARLETON UNIV. ART GALLERY, Ottawa, Ont. 1992– ; Teacher, Dr. G.W. Williams Secondary Sch. Aurora, Ont. 1967–68; Hist. Research Offr. and Head, Paintings, Drawings & Prints Sec. Pub. Archives of Can. 1968–73; Dir. Agnes Etherington Art Centre, Kingston, Ont. 1973–78; Visual Arts Offr. Ont. Arts Council Toronto 1978–79; Asst. Dir. Pub. Programs Nat. Gallery Can. 1979–81, Acting Dir. 1981; Dir. & CEO McMichael Canadian Collection 1981–86; Assoc. Curator, Agnes Etherington Art Centre, Queen's Univ. 1986–92; author 'Painters In A New Land' 1973 (Gov. Gen.'s Award Non-Fiction 1974); numerous articles, papers, reviews, exhn. catalogues; mem. Candn. Conf. of Arts; Vice Pres. and Secy.-Treas. Ont. Assn. Art Galleries 1976–78, 1979–80 (Past Chrmn. various comtes.); mem. Counc., Candn. Museums Assn. 1983–86; Ed. Bd., Inuit Art Quarterly 1986–88; Trustee, National Museums of Canada 1987–90; Trustee, National Gallery of Can. 1990–91; Home: 306 – 499 Sunnyside Ave., Ottawa, Ont. K1S 0S8.

**BELL, Michael R.,** B.Com.; diplomat; b. Montréal, Qué. 27 Jan. 1939; s. Harry Heartz and Elizabeth Charlotte (Brown) B.; e. Bishop's Coll. Sch. 1957; Queen's Univ. B.Com. 1961; m. Christine d. Ronald and Margaret McCook 22 Feb. 1969; children: Katherine A., Hugh T.; CANDN. AMBASSADOR TO THE NETHERLANDS 1993– ; Trade Comnr. Service assignments Norway, UK, Peru, Spain and USSR 1962–75; Treas. Bd. Secretariat 1975–77; Dir., Policy & Planning, Indus. Trade & Comm. 1978–79; Min.-Couns. (Comm), Candn. Embassy, Moscow 1979–81; Candn. Ambassador to Peru and Bolivia 1981–84; Asst. Depy. Min., Latin Am. & Caribbean, Dept. of External Affairs 1985–88; Asst. Depy. Min., Special Projects, Dept. of External Affairs 1988–90; Candn. Ambassador to Russia, Belarus, Georgia, Armenia, Azerbaijan, Uzbekistan,

Kazakhstan, Turkmenistan, Kirghizstan, Tadjikistan 1990–92; Pres., Candn. Univ. Soc., London, Eng. 1968–69; recreations: golf, cross-country skiing; Home: 809 Eastbourne Ave., Ottawa, Ont. K1K 0H8; Office: Candn. Embassy, Sophialaan 7, The Hague, Netherlands.

**BELL, Norman Brooke,** B.A.; b. Toronto, Ont. 8 Nov. 1920; s. late Norman Brooke and late Helen Monro (Murray) B.; e. Upper Can. Coll., Toronto, 1929–39; Trinity Coll., Univ. of Toronto, B.A., 1942; m. Cicely Barlow d. late Douglas White Ambridge, Toronto, 18 Sept. 1953; children: Mrs. Patricia Brooke Reid, Douglas Ambridge Brooke; Dir., Bell Gouinlock Ltd. 1957–86; Dir., Zurich Life Ins. Co. 1967–90; Chrmn. Emeritus, Sunnybrook Health Science Centre; served with 48th Highlanders of Can., 1941–45; Zeta Psi; Anglican; Clubs: University; Badminton & Racquet; Home: 3 Drumsnab, Toronto, Ont. M4W 3A4.

**BELL, Norman Henry;** corporate executive; b. Brantford, Ont. 21 Nov. 1911; s. Frederick Wallace and Mary (Tunnicliffe) B.; e. Brantford (Ont.) Pub. Sch. and Coll. Inst. and Vocational Sch.; Univ. of Toronto (Sch. of Applied Science) 1931–32; Mang. Training, Univ. of W. Ont. 1955; m. Winnifred, d. late Robert James Miller, St. Thomas, Ont., 26 July 1941; one d. Kathryn Joanne; Gen. Mgr. and Dir. (1955–58) in Brantford Coach and Body Ltd. 1938–58; Pres., White Motor Corp. of Can. Ltd. 1958–76; served in 2nd World War (1942–1946, R.C.A.F.); Navigator's Wing and Flying Offr., June 1944; posted Overseas Sept. 1944; returned to Can. Jan. 1946 and discharged with rank of Flying Offr.; Hon. Dir., Can. Safety Council; Lambda Chi Alpha; Freemason (Scot. Rite); Anglican; Clubs: Mississaugua Golf & Country; Home: Ste. 607, 1700 The Collegeway, Mississauga, Ont. L5L 4M2.

**BELL, Robert Gordon,** O.C., M.D., LL.D., I.C.A.D.C.; b. St. Mary's, Ont. 11 July 1911; s. Robert and Elizabeth (Oliver) B.; e. St. Mary's Coll. Inst.; Univ. of Toronto M.D.; m. Mary Irene d. Ernest P. and Anastasia Donihee Lamping, Ridgeway, Ont. 18 June 1938; children: Ronald Gordon, Janice Marie Hambley, Mary Linda Kennedy, Mary Elizabeth Plouffe, Brian Joseph; Pres., Glenmaple, Highland Creek 1946–47; Shadow Brook Health Foundation, Willowdale 1948–54; Willowdale Hosp. 1951–54; The Bell Clinic, Willowdale 1954–67; The Donwood Inst. 1967–83; Bellwood Health Services Inc. 1983–90; Hon. Chrmn. & Sr. Consultant 1990– ; served with R.C.A.M.C. 1942–46, dir. psychol. retraining and rehabilitation centres; rec'd Honour Award, Students' Adm. Council Univ. of Toronto 1943; Citation of Merit, Malvern Inst., Pa. 1958; Centennial Medal 1967; Queen's Silver Jubilee Medal 1977; Officer, Order of Can. (1979); Royal Bank Award 1985; LL.D. (hon. causa), York Univ. 1986; Hon. Mem., Candn. Med. Soc. on Alcohol and Other Drugs, 1989; Provincial Award of Distinction, Addiction Rsch. Found. 1989; Pioneer Award, Oxford Inst., U.S.A. 1990; Humanitarian Award, Ont. Psychological Found. 1991; author 'Escape from Addiction' 1970; 'A Special Calling' 1989; over 20 educational films; over 100 articles for clin. and lay publs.; Chrmn. Emeritus, The Donwood Inst.; mem. Cdn. Medical Assn. (sr. mem.); Ont. Med. Assn. (life mem.); recreations: reading, gardening, bridge, travel; Clubs: Aesculapian; Civic Garden Centre; Home: 47 York Rd., Willowdale, Ont. M2L 1H7; Office: 1020 McNicoll Ave., Scarborough, Ont. M1W 2J6.

**BELL, Robert Murray,** Q.C., B.A., LL.B.; insurance executive; b. Aurora, Ont. 11 Sept. 1913; s. Robert Norman and Agnes R.T. (Alexander) B.; e. Univ. of Alta., B.A. 1934; Osgoode Hall Law Sch. 1938; York Univ. LL.B. 1991; m. Ann Elizabeth, d. Harold C. Walker, Q.C., Toronto, Ont., 5 Nov. 1955; one s., one d.; read law with Messrs. Fraser and Beatty; called to the Bar of Ont. 1938; cr. Q.C. 1962; joined Fraser, Beatty, Palmer & Tucker 1938; entered Legal Dept. of Confederation Life Insurance Co. 1946, Extve. Asst. 1953, Gen. Counsel 1957, Vice-Pres. and Gen. Counsel 1961 retired as Vice-Pres., Gen. Counsel and Secy. 1978; Comnd. in Q.O.R. of Can. 1940 serving overseas; later with Candn. Intelligence Corps. in N. Africa, Italy and N.W. Europe; mem. Assn. Life Ins. Counsel; Bd. Trade Metrop. Toronto; Champlain Soc.; Phi Delta Phi; United Church; Club: Lawyers; Home: 134 Forest Hill Rd., Toronto, Ont. M4V 2L9.

**BELL, Ross,** B.Comm., F.S.A., F.C.I.A.; insurance executive; b. Winnipeg, Man.; e. Univ. of Manitoba B.Comm. 1967; m. Patricia; children: Tracy, Kristin; SR. VICE-PRES., PROPERTY & CASUALTY OPERATIONS, THE PRUDENTIAL INSURANCE CO. OF AMERICA (CANADA) 1992– ; joined Candn. Head Office, Prudential Insurance 1967; transferred to corp. home office Newark, N.J. 1968; Sr. Actuarial Asst., Group Insur. Dept. 1970; returned to Canada 1972; Assoc. Actuary in Group Insur. 1973; Vice-Pres., Group Insur. 1979; trans. to Property & Casualty Operations 1988; Pres., Prudential of America General Insur. Co. (Canada) 1991; Dir., Prudential of America General Insurance Co.; Policy Management System Canada; OTIP/RAEO Insurance Co. Inc.; recreations: squash, golf; Home: Willowdale, Ont.; Office: 200 Consilium Place, Scarborough, Ont. M1H 3E6.

**BELL, Thomas Johnston,** O.C., M.C., C.D., B.Comm., LL.D.; company executive; b. Southampton, Ont. 26 June 1914; s. Charles M. and Hazel (Hamilton) B.; e. Ridley Coll., St. Catharines, Ont. (Grad. 1932); Univ. of Toronto, B.Com. 1936, LL.D. 1979; m. Gertrude, d. late George Alexander Harshman, 2 Apr. 1948; two s. and four d.; Past C.E.O., Abitibi Price Inc.; Past Chrmn. Bd. of Trustees, Toronto General Hospital; joined Federal Wire & Cable Co. Ltd., Guelph, Ont. 1936, Vice-Pres. 1951; Pres., Fiberglas Canada Inc., Toronto, Ont. 1956–67; Pres. & C.E.O., Abitibi Paper Co. 1967–73, Chrmn. & C.E.O. 1973–79, Chrmn. 1979–83; served in 2nd World War; 12th Field Regt., R.C.A., 1942–46; awarded M.C.; Lieut.-Col., 11th Field Reg. (Reserve), 1946–52; Conservative; Anglican; recreations: golf, skiing; Clubs: Rosedale Golf; York; Augusta National Golf; Home: 175 Teddington Park, Toronto, Ont. M4N 2C7.

**BELL, William Edwin,** B.A., M.A., B.Ed., M.Ed.; editor, writer, teacher; b. Toronto, Ont. 27 Oct. 1945; s. William Bratty and Irene (Spowart) B.; e. Trinity College, Univ. of Toronto B.A. 1968, M.A. 1969, B.Ed. 1970; Ontario Inst. for Studies in Education M.Ed. 1984; m. 1970; divorced 1991; children: Dylan, Megan, Brendan; HEAD, ENGLISH DEPT., ORILLIA COLLEGIATE 1988– ; English Teacher, Orillia Collegiate 1970–78; English Dept. Head, Innisdale S.S. (Barrie) 1978–82, 1983–85; Instructor, English & Teaching Methodology, Harbin Univ. of Science & Technology (Harbin, China) 1982–83; English Instructor, Foreign Affairs College (Beijing, China) 1985–86; English Teacher, Innisdale S.S. 1986–88; Mem., Amnesty International; Greenpeace; author (novels): 'Crabbe' 1986; 'Metal Head' 1987; 'The Cripples' Club/Absolutely Invincible' 1988; 'Death Wind' 1989; 'Five Days of the Ghost' 1989 (Manitoba Young Reader's Choice Award 1992); 'Forbidden City' 1990 (Ruth Schwartz Award for Excellence in Children's Literature 1991); 'No Signature' 1992 (Belgium Award for Excellence in Children's Literature 1992); 'The Golden Disk' 1994; editor: 'Contours' 1992 (anthology of Canadian drama); Home: Orillia, Ont.; Office: 2 Borland St. E., Orillia, Ont. L3V 2B4.

**BELLAMY, Denise,** B.A., LL.B.; lawyer; b. Saskatoon, Sask. 20 Jan. 1949; d. Arthur Henry and Aline Blanche (Buckley) B.; e. Carleton Univ. B.A. 1975; Osgoode Hall Law Sch. LL.B. 1978; Bar Admission Course, Osgoode Hall 1980; spouse: William George Thorpe; DIRECTOR, LEGAL SERVICES BRANCH, MINISTRY OF THE SOLICITOR GENERAL AND CORRECTIONAL SERVICES 1990– ; Secretary, House of Commons 1969–72; Asst. Crown Attorney 1980–84; Sr. Policy Advisor for Justice Issues, Ont. Women's Directorate 1984–86; Crown Counsel, Criminal Law Policy 1986–88; Mem., Court Reform Task Force, Min. of Attorney Gen. 1988–90; Bencher, Law Soc. of U.C.; Vice-Pres., Ont. Centre for Advocacy Training; Dir., Fed. of Law Societies; Ont. Rep. in Vienna, Austria at U.N. Ctte. on the Elimination of All Forms of Discrimination against Women; Bencher, Law Soc. of U.C. 1988– ; Mem., Candn. Bar Assn.; L'Assn. des Juristes d'expression française de l'Ont.; Women's Law Assn.; recreations: wine tasting, gardening, cycling; clubs: T.O. Bicycle Network; Office: 175 Bloor St. E., Suite 400, North Tower, Toronto, Ont. M4W 3R8.

**BELLAMY, Robert E.,** B.Com., C.A.; investment dealer; b. Lindsay, Ont. 6 Aug. 1933; s. Clifford C. and Evelyn B. (Burgess) B.; e. Univ. of Toronto B.Com. 1954; C.A. 1958; m. Shirley Jeanne d. Stanford and Marion Pitts 16 June 1956; children: Karen, Jane, John, Michael; VICE CHRMN. AND DIR. BURNS FRY LTD. 1982– ; Dir. Canadian Mini Warehouse Properties Ltd.; Sema Associates Ltd.; Repap Enterprises Corp. Inc.; Real/Data Ontario Inc. (RDO); Sec., Treas. and Dir. Charterhouse Canada Ltd. 1963–68; A.E. Ames & Co. Ltd. 1968–81, Dir. 1971, Pres. 1980; Vice Chrmn. Dominion Securities Ames Ltd. 1981–82; Sigma Chi; Baptist; recreations: golf, curling; Clubs: Toronto; Cambridge; Granite; Home: 403 Glencairn Ave., Toronto, Ont. M5N 1V2; Office: P.O. Box 150, 1 First Canadian Place, Toronto, Ont. M5X 1H3.

**BELLAN, Ruben Carl,** B.A., M.A., Ph.D.; professor emeritus; b. Winnipeg, Man. 2 Oct. 1918; s. Hyman Baruch and Lillian (Kolovson) B.; e. Univ. of Man., B.A. 1938; Univ. of Toronto, M.A. 1941 (McKenzie Fellow); Columbia Univ., Ph.D. 1958; m. Ruth d. Louis and Minnie Lercher 1 June 1947; children: Paul, Susan, Lorne; PROF., UNIV. OF MANITOBA; RCAF 1941–45; Mem., Econ. Dept., Univ. of Man. 1946–88; Dean of Studies, St. John's Coll. 1970–76; served in var. capacities on num. local cttes. & comns. 1950–77; Pres., Man. Econ. Assn. 1973–74; Can. Counc. Fellow & Leverhulme Fellow, Manchester Univ. 1965–66; Japan Exch. Scholar 1982; Chrmn., Winnipeg Br., John Howard & Eliz. Fry Soc. 1963–64; Candn. Inst. of Internat. Affairs 1968–69, 1989–90; Hum. Assn. of Can. 1970–71; author: 'Principles of Economics and the Canadian Economy' 1960, 1985, 'Fundamentals of Economics' 1962, 'The Evolving City' 1971, 'Winnipeg First Century' 1978, 'The Unnecessary Evil' 1986; co-author: 'The Canadian Economy' 1981; freelance edit. writer var. newspapers, mags. & jours.; recreations: curling, swimming, golf; Home: 628 Niagara St., Winnipeg, Man.; Office: 400 Dysart Rd., Winnipeg, Man. R3T 2M5.

**BELLAN, Susan Riva,** B.A.; import and retail executive; b. Winnipeg, Man. 5 July 1952; d. Dr. Ruben Carl and Ruth (Lercher) Bellan; e. Univ. of Man., B.A. 1973; McGill Univ., B.A. 1974; m. William P. s. Walter and Anne Molson 1 Sept. 1981; children: Adam, Melissa, Monica; OWNER/MGR. FRIDA CRAFT STORES 1979– ; Buyer and Econ. Nat. Handicraft Mktg. Corp. Botswana 1974–76; travelled extensively Africa, India, S.E. Asia 1976–77; Cons. to World Bank and Commonwealth Secretariat crafts projects India, Rwanda, Mauretania, Madagascar 1977–78; Cons. to Novib, Holland handcrafts Zimbabwe 1980, Min. of N. Devel. Dene handicrafts N.W.T. 1981; occasional cons. Royal Ont. Museum; winner Jr. Musical Club Trophy (piano) Winnipeg Music Festival 1968; Chair, Banking Issues Ctte., Candn. Organization of Small Business; mem. Candn. Inst. Internat. Affairs; Beaches Hebrew Inst.; Home: 2A Fernwood Park Ave., Toronto, Ont. M4E 3E7; Office: 39 Front St. E., Toronto, Ont. M5E 1B3.

**BELLEHUMEUR, Ghislain;** L.Sc.C., C.A.; executive; b. Lorrainville, P.Q. 20 Sept. 1937; s. Leonard and Aldea (Paquin) B.; e. Ottawa Univ. High Sch. 1955; Ottawa Univ., B.Com. 1959; Laval Univ., L.Sc.Com. 1960; L.Sc.C. 1960; Chartered Accountant 1960; m. Michele, d. André and Rosana Bellemare; 2 July 1962; children; Judith; Claudine; PRES. AND DIR., TEMISKO (1983) INC. since 1974; auditor, Price Waterhouse & Co. 1960; comptroller, Meubles Bellehumeur Ltée. 1964; asst. to the Pres. and comptroller; Brazeau Transport Inc. 1967; chief extve., Air Brazeau 1973; mem. Candn. Truck & Trailer Manufacturers Assn.; recreations: fishing; hunting; skiing; golf; Home: P.O. Box 416, Notre-Dame du Nord, Qué. J0Z 3B0; Office: P.O. Box 460, Notre-Dame du Nord, Qué. J0Z 3B0.

**BELLEMARE, Daniel A.,** Q.C., B.A., LL.L., LL.M., OStj; lawyer, author, teacher; b. Drummondville, Que. 2 May 1952; s. J. Martial and Geneviève (Vigneault) B.; e. Univ. of Ottawa B.A. 1972, LL.L. (magna cum laude) 1975; Univ. of Montreal LL.M. 1980; called to Quebec Bar 1976; ASSISTANT DEP. ATTORNEY GENERAL (CRIMINAL LAW), FED. DEPT. OF JUSTICE 1993– ; articled with Fed. Dept. of Justice Montreal 1976; Federal Prosecutor (mainly under Narcotic Control and Food and Drug acts) 1976–83; Dep. Dir. then Director, Criminal Law Policy Section, Fed. Dept. of Justice Ottawa 1983–88; Uniformity Commissioner for Canada 1983–87; Sec., Criminal Law Section 1985; Dept. of Justice Rep., Duff-Rinfret Scholarship Jury 1985–86; Sr. Gen. Counsel & Head, Legal Serv. Unit, Min. of Solicitor-Gen. of Can. 1988–93; guest lecturer, Ottawa & McGill universities; Duff-Rinfret Scholarship, Dept. of Justice 1975; Canada Art Council Scholarship 1975 (declined); Federa; Q.C. 1990; Canada 125 Medal 1993; Order of St. John 1993; Vice-Pres. (Public & Legal Affairs), Extve. Ctte. Mem. & Bd. Mem., St. John Ambulance Quebec Council; Deputy Min. of Justice Award for Humanitarian Excellence 1993; Teacher, Que. Bar Admission Courses 1976–90; Candn. Police Coll. and others; author: 'L'Hébertisme au Québec' 1976, Ed. Le Jour; 'L'Ecoute électronique au Canada' 1981, Ed. Yvon Blais 'How to Testify in Court' 1984, Ed. Yvon Blais 'Comment déposer devant les Tribunaux' 1984, Ed. Yvon Blais Index to the Dubois Annotated 'Criminal Code' 1990 and over 50 journal articles; recreations: jogging, judo, canoeing, antique furniture refinishing; Office: Justice Bldg., Room 462, 239 Wellington St., Ottawa, Ont. K1A 0H8.

**BELLEMARE, Raymond,** D.B.A., R.C.A., A.I.G.A.; graphic designer; b. Nicolet, Que. 25 Jan. 1942; s. Jean-Baptiste and Rita (Dubuc) B.; e. primary sch. Nicolet,

Que. 1954; Coll. l'Assomption, Que. classical course 1958; Montreal Sch. of Fine Arts grad. Graphic Design 1962; PRES., RAYMOND BELLEMARE DESIGNERS INC.; Part time teacher, Université du Québec à Montréal; Member of the stamp advisory committee at Canada Post 1983–84–85; Dir. Graphic Design Dept. Olympic Ctte. 1976; Design Consultant, CBC; awards: Graphis Press, Packaging Assn. Can.; Graphica Club of Montreal; Soc. Graphic Designers Can.; Communication Arts Mag. USA; Deco Press Italy; Design Canada; Arts. Dirs.' Club N.Y.; VII Miedzynarodowe Biennale Plakatu, Warsawa; Symbols of the World, Japan; corporate image designs, Cdn. postage stamps, posters, signalling, printed material; mem., Royal Cdn. Academy of Arts; Am. Inst. Graphic Arts; recreations: farming, cycling, fishing, travel; Home and Business Address: 703 Road 225, Noyan, Qué. J0J 1B0.

**BELLEW, Geoffrey Ronald,** M.B.A., F.I.C.B.; banker; b. London, England 30 Jan. 1950; s. Robert and Ethel (Gold) B.; e. Univ. of Toronto M.B.A. 1989; F.I.C.B. Gold Medal 1983; m. Marilyn d. Ewart and Dorothy Vallis July 1974; children: Kimberley, Richard, Matthew, Andrew, David; SENIOR VICE-PRESIDENT, RETAIL MARKETING, THE BANK OF NOVA SCOTIA; Chief Cashier, Mitton Butler Priest (U.K.) 1969–71; joined Scotiabank 1971; 10 years Branch Management; 10 years var. extve. positions incl. Nat. Accts. Mgr. (Sales), Group Product Mgr. (Mktg.), Dir. Strategic Planning (Planning), Vice-Pres., Govt. Relns. (Deregulation Task Force); Mem., Planning Forum, Bayfair Baptist Ch.; recreations: squash, soccer; Club: Fitness Institute; Home: 1552 Eagleview Dr., Pickering, Ont. L1V 5H6; Office: 8th Fl., 100 Yonge St., Toronto, Ont. M5H 1H1.

**BELLINI, Francesco,** B.Sc., Ph.D.; pharmaceutical executive; b. Ascoli Piceno, Italy 20 Nov. 1947; e. Ascoli Piceno, Italy, Dip. (Chem. Eng.) 1967; Loyola Coll. Montreal B.Sc. (Chem.) 1972; Univ. of N.B. Ph.D. (Organic Chem.) 1977; m. Marisa; two s. Roberto, Carlo; PRES., CHIEF EXEC. OFFR. AND DIR., IAF BIOCHEM INTERNATIONAL INC. renamed BIOCHEM PHARMA INC. 1986– ; Rsch. Asst. Ayerst Labs. Montreal 1968–74, Nat. Rsch. Council Industrial Post-doctoral Fellowship 1977–79, Sr. Sci. 1979–81, Rsch. Assoc. Ayerst Labs. 1981–84; Dir. Biochemicals Div. Institut Armand-Frappier Univ. du Québec 1984–86; Pres., C.E.O. & Dir., IAF Biochem International Inc., renamed Biochem Pharma Inc. 1986– ; Dir.: Biocapital Inc.; IAF BioVac Inc.; Ivax Corp.; North American Vaccine, Inc. (NAVA); discovered a product 'Tolrestat' which is currently being developed at Wyeth Ayerst for the treatment of complications of diabetes; named 'Successor' Candn. Bus. Mag. 1987; 'Man of the Month' Commerce Mag. 1991; Lectr. of the E. Le Sueur Award 1993; author or co-author 20 patents, numerous publs.; member of many Clubs & Assns.; Office: 2550 Daniel-Johnson Blvd., Suite 600, Laval, Qué. H7T 2L1.

**BELL-IRVING, Hon. Henry Pybus,** O.C. (1984), D.S.O., O.B.E., O.B.C., D.Sc.M., E.D., C.D., LL.D.; b. Vancouver, B.C. 21 Jan. 1913; s. Henry Beattie and Annie Hilda (Pybus) B-I; e. Shawnigan Lake Prep. Sch. Vancouver Is. 1927; Loretto Sch. Musselburgh, Scot. 1930; Univ. of B.C. 1931; m. Nancy Isobel d. Reginald Symes 8 Apl. 1937; three s. Henry Symes, Roderick, Donald Reginald; Lieut. Seaforth of C., N.P.A.M., 1933–39; C.A.S.F., 1939–45, U.K., Sicily, Italy, N.W. Europe. Commanded in turn, Canadian O.C.T.U., Battle School, in U.K., Loyal Edmonton Regt., Seaforth of C. in Italy, 10 Cdn. Inf. Bde. in N.W. Europe promoted Lt. to Brig., awarded D.S.O. and bar, O.B.E., m.i.d.x2; Post War: Honorary Colonel Seaforth Highlanders of Canada; Chrmn. and Pres. Bell-Irving Realty Ltd. 1948–72; Chrmn. and Pres. A. E. LePage Western Ltd.; Dir. A. E. LePage Ltd. Toronto; Boy Scouts: Akela, Dist. Commr, Hon. Pres. B.C. and Yukon 1949– ; Chrmn. B.C. Real Estate Agents Licencing Bd. 1954–58; Gov. rep. on Board of Vancouver Children's Hospital 1962–78; B.C. Corps Commissionaires C.O. 1967–71, Trustee 1971–78; Pres. Vancr. Real Estate Bd. 1958; Cdn. Real Estate Assn. 1972; a founding Fellow, Cdn. Inst. of Realtors (F.R.I.); accredited appraiser, Cdn. and U.S. Institutes, (A.A.C.I., M.A.I.); Vancouver Board of Trade Council 1965 (President, 1974); Lt. Gov. of B.C. 18 May 1978–15 July 1983; K.St.J.; LL.D. (Hon.) U.B.C. 1984; apptd. Freeman of the City of Vancouver 1986; awarded Order of British Columbia 1990; Anglican; recreations: boating, fishing, shooting; Clubs: Vancouver; Terminal City; Union (Victoria); Address: 42–2236 Folkestone Way, W. Vancouver, B.C. V7S 2X7.

**BELLIVEAU, Robert Pierre,** M.D.; physician; b. Yarmouth, N.S. 1 Aug. 1926; s. Pierre Elizée and Angèle Marie (Robichaud) B.; e. Univ. of Ste-Anne, Church Point, N.S., B.A. 1947; Univ. Laval M.D. 1952; L.M.C.C. 1952; m. Rose Alma d. Robert and Suzanne Preston 16 June 1952; children: Jean-Paul, André, Guy, Gilles, Daniel, Nicole, Christine, Aline, Alain; SR. PHYSICIAN, CLARE MEDICAL CENTRE; Past Chrmn. Bd. Dirs. Univ. Ste-Anne; Past Pres. N.S. Med. Soc. Br. Soc. (W.Br.); former mem. Bd. Maritime Medical Care Inc.; mem. Med. Soc. Yarmouth Regional Hosp.; a Dir., Clare Golf & Country Club Assoc.; recreations: swimming, fishing, racquetball, gardening, philately, golf; Address: P.O. Box 20, Meteghan River, N.S. B0W 2L0.

**BELLON, Jean-Paul,** B.A.; travel executive; b. Montreal, Que. 5 Nov. 1941; s. Georges and Germaine (Robitaille) B.; e. Coll. Jean-de-Brébeuf B.A. 1963; Univ. Laval, law studies 1963–66; children: Marie-Michelle, Dominique; FOUNDER & PRES., CLUB JEUNESSE AND CONSULTOUR / CLUB VOYAGES INC.; Consultour/Club Voyages Inc. is a retail travel network of 200 agencies in Que.; Bd. Mem. & Dir., Groupe Transat A.T. Inc.; Mem., Montreal Bd. of Trade; Bd. Mem., La Fondation St-Laurent; club: Skal; Home: 2691 Hill Park Circle, Montreal, Qué. H3H 1S8; Office: 300, Leo Pariseau, Suite 200, Montreal, Qué. H2W 2P6.

**BELLRINGER, Stephen T.,** B.Comm., M.B.A.; business executive; b. Birmingham, England 5 July 1946; m. Katherine; PRESIDENT & C.E.O., TRANS MOUNTAIN PIPE LINE CO. LTD.; Dir., B.C. Gas; Vice-Pres., Union Gas 1976–85; Pres. & C.E.O. 1985–93; Past Chrmn., Candn. Gas Assoc.; Past Chrmn., Ont. Natural Gas Assoc.; Past Chrmn., Bd. of Govs., Univ. of Windsor; Dir., Timber West Forest Limited; Dir., Vancouver Bd. of Trade; Office: 1333 West Broadway, Suite 900, Vancouver, B.C. V6H 4C2.

**BELLWARD, Gail Dianne,** B.Sc. (Pharm.), M.Sc., Ph.D.; university professor; b. Brock, Sask. 27 May 1939; d. Eric Harvey and Mildred Eleanor (Cyr) B.; e. Univ. of B.C., B.Sc. (Pharm.) 1960, M.Sc. 1963, Ph.D. 1966; Emory Univ. (U.S.A) Fellow in Medicine 1968–69; Royal Postgrad. Med. Sch. (U.K.) Visiting Scientist 1975; PROF. OF PHARMACOLOGY AND TOXICOLOGY, FAC. OF PHARMACEUTICAL SCIENCES, UNIV. OF B.C.; Asst. Prof. present Univ. 1967, Assoc. Prof. 1973, Prof. 1979, Chrmn. Div. of Pharmacol. and Toxicol. 1981–85, Asst. Dean 1985–88, Assoc. Dean, Rsch. and Grad. Studies 1988 to 1989; active on various univ. cttes.; consultant to various levels of govt., legal profession, education bodies; mem. Pharmacy Examing Bd. of Canada 1976–79; M.R.C. Pharm. Sci. Grants Ctte. 1970–74; M.R.C. Visiting Prof. Univ. of Toronto 1971–72, Univ. of Sask. 1975–76, Dalhousie Univ. 1975–76; M.R.C. Pharmacology and Toxicology Grants Ctte. 1992–93; Award of Merit, Lambda Kappa Sigma Internat. Prof. Frat. 1980; I.W. Killam Sr. Fellow 1989; speaker and external examiner for many univ. and sci. meetings; referee for numerous sci. journals; mem. Fed. of Am. Soc. for Experimental Biology; Soc. of Toxicology of Can.; Am. Soc. for Pharmacol. and Experimental Therapeutics; Pharmacol. Soc. of Canada (Sec. 1977–80, Nom. Ctte. 1982, Upjohn Award Ctte. 1983–86, scrutineer 1985, Vice-Pres. 1985–87, Pres. 1987–89, Past Pres. 1989–91); Candn. Fed. of Biological Soc. (Dir. 1977–80 and 1987–89); author numerous sci. publs.; Bd. mem., Science Council of B.C. 1992–95; Chair, 10th International Symposium on Microsomes and Drug Oxidations; recreations: music, travel, gardening, bicycling; Office: 2146 East Mall, Vancouver, B.C. V6T 1Z3.

**BELMER, Michael H.,** B.Comm., MCIT; business executive; b. Brighton, U.K. 13 Oct. 1943; s. Walter and Josephine (Boyle) B.; e. McGill Univ. C.A. 1964; Loyola College B.Comm. 1972; Concordia Univ. M.B.A. 1977; m. Patricia Lynn d. Patricia and Emil Adamyk 29 April 1978; children: Stephanie, Ashley, Chelsea; EXECUTIVE VICE-PRESIDENT & DIR., MONTREAL SHIPPING INC. 1991– ; Auditor, Weir, Duncan & Co., Chartered Accountants 1962–64; Voyage Accountant, Montreal Shipping Inc. 1964–65; General Accountant 1965–66; Chief Accountant 1966–69; Assistant Comptroller 1969–72; Comptroller 1972–77; Treasurer 1977–83; Vice Pres., Traffic 1983–91; Mem., Concordia Transp. Mgr. Ctr. (Extve. Council); Shipping Fed. of Canada (former Ctte. Chair); Dir., Mariner's House of Montreal; Montreal Bd. of Trade; Canadian Export Assn. (Past Dir., Chair, Transp. Ctte.); Chartered Inst. of Transportation; recreations: golf, curling; clubs: Kanawaki Golf, Montreal Thistle Curling, Montreal Badminton & Squash; Home: 219 Wolseley North, Montreal West, Qué. H4X 1W1; Office: 360 St. Jacques St. W., Montreal, Qué. H2Y 1R2.

**BELONOGOV, Ambassador Alexander M.,** Ph.D.; diplomat; b. Moscow 1931; e. Moscow State Inst. of International Relations Ph.D. international law; AMBASSADOR TO CANADA OF THE RUSSIAN FEDERATION 1992– ; joined Ministry of Foreign Affairs 1954; served with Treaty & Law Dept. then Dept. of Internat. Econ. Orgns.; Third, Second, then First Sec. of the USSR Embassy in the U.K. of Great Britain and N. Ireland 1962–67; Counsellor, Sr. Counsellor, Chief Counsellor, Dir. of the Div., then Deputy Dir., Foreign Policy Planning Dept. 1967–84; Ambassador Extraordinary and Plenipotentiary of the USSR to the Arab Republic of Egypt 1984; Perm. Rep. of the USSR to the UN & USSR Rep. to the UN Security Council 1986–90; Deputy Minister of Foreign Affairs 1990–92; State decorations; Office: 285 Charlotte St., Ottawa, Ont. K1N 8L5.

**BELSHAW, Cyril Shirley,** M.A., Ph.D., F.R.S.C.; anthropologist; educator; b. N.Z. 3 Dec. 1921; s. Prof. Horace Belshaw; e. Auckland Grammar Sch.; Auckland Univ. Coll., Univ. of N.Z. M.A. 1945; London Sch. of Econ. Ph.D. 1949; m. (late) Betty Joy Sweetman; children: Diana Marion, Adrian William; EMERITUS PROF. OF ANTHROP. UNIV. OF B.C.; Head of Anthrop. present univ. 1968–74, mem. Senate 1963–72 and 1975–78, Secy. Faculty Assn. 1957–58, Extve. 1959–64, Pres. 1960–61; mem. Extve., Internat. Social Science Council 1973–77, Vice Pres, 1976–77; mem. Extve. Social Science Research Council of Can. 1968–71, Vice Pres. 1970–72; Del. to Assembly, Int. Council Philos. & Humanistic Studies 1977 and 1979; Candn. Del. UNESCO Gen. Conf. 1972, 1974; Extve., Cdn. Comn. UNESCO 1971–72, Mem.-at-Large 1973–86; Consultant variously to UNESCO, UN Bureau of Social Affairs, UN ECOSOC, OECD, IDRC, Spanish Nat. Comn. for UNESCO; Dir. UN Training Centre Vancouver 1961–62; mem. UN ECOSOC Mission Thailand 1965; Dir., East African Workshop, Internat. Soc. Sci. Writing, Nairobi 1985; Colonial Service, Brit. Solomon Islands 1943–46; field work in Solomon Islands, New Caledonia, New Hebrides, New Guinea, Fiji, B.C., Thailand, Switzerland; mem. Acad. Bd. for Higher Educ. B.C. 1971–72; Emslie Horniman Scholar 1947–49; Sr. Scholar in Econ. Univ. N.Z. 1942; John Simon Guggenheim Fellow 1965–66; Gorjanović Kramberger medal of the Croation Anthropological Soc. 1988; Wenner-Gren Found., Sr. Rsch. Stipend 1987; Hon. Life Fellow, Royal Anthropological Inst.; Hon. Life fellow, Assn. of Soc. Anthropologists in Oceania; Hon. Life mem., Pacific Sci. Assoc.; author 'Island Administration in the South West Pacific' 1950; 'Changing Melanesia' 1954; 'In Search of Wealth' 1955; 'The Great Village' 1957; 'Under the Ivi Tree' 1964; 'Anatomy of a University' 1964; 'Traditional Exchange and Modern Markets' 1965; 'Comercio Tradicional y mercados modernos' 1973; 'The Conditions of Social Performance' 1970; 'Towers Besieged: The Dilemma of the Creative University' 1974; 'The Sorcerer's Apprentice: An Anthropology of Public Policy' 1976; 'Complete Good Dining Guide to Greater Vancouver Restaurants' 1984; co-author 'The Indians of British Columbia' 1958; various articles and reports; Ed. 'Current Anthropology' 1974–85; Pres., Int. Union of Anthropological and Ethnological Sciences 1978–83 (Past Pres. 1983–88); Pres., XIth Int. Congress of Anthropological and Ethnological Sci. 1983; Pres., XLIII Int. Congress. of Americanists, 1979; Extve. Am. Anthrop. Assn. 1969–71; Pres., Educational Foundation for Anthropology and the Public 1981–83; Founding mem. Candn. Univ. Service Overseas. Internat. Assn. Scient. Eds' Assn. (Exec. 1978), Internat. Assn. Anthrop. Eds.; Vice Pres. Int. Fedn. Scientific Editors' Assns. 1983–87; Pacific Science Assn. (Cdn. Nat. Ctte., Chrmn. Social Sciences & Humanities 1968–77); Restaurant critic 'Plus' Magazine, Vancouver 1987–90; Office: c/o 34 Bloem Ave., Toronto, Ont. M6E 1S1.

**BELTON, Edward F. 'Ted';** writer; consultant; b. Toronto, Ont. 4 March 1931; s. Francis S. and Margaret A. (Malone) B.; e. De La Salle Coll. 'Oaklands' Toronto 1949; m. Joan Marie, d. Albert Drury 23 Oct. 1954; children: Kelly-Ann, Gregory Scott, Lisa Marie, Edward Patrick; Consultant, Tillinghast, a Towers Perrin co.; Pres. & C.E.O., Edward F. Belton Enterprises Inc.; joined Halifax Insurance Co. Toronto 1949 serving in Fire, Casualty, Auto. and Claims Depts.; Toronto Field Rep. 1953; Field Rep. Federation Insurance Co. 1956, Service Office Supv. Windsor, Ont. 1956, Ont. Br. Casualty Supv. 1958; Casualty Mgr. for Can., Halifax Insurance Co. 1959, Chief Underwriter 1960, Supt. of Brs. 1962, Mgr. W. and E. Divs. 1964, Vice-Pres. Marketing 1972; Mgr. for Can. Safeco Insurance Cos. 1973; Pres. & C.E.O., Insurers' Advisory Organ. Inc. 1974; Pres. & C.E.O., Candn. Insurance Exchange 1987; Extve. Vice Pres., Pafco Financial Holdings Ltd.; Vice Chrmn. & C.E.O., Pafco Insurance Co., Pafco General Ins. Co., Pafco General Ins. Co. (Indiana) 1988; author: 'The Belton Report' a quarterly analysis of property and casualty insurance in Canada; 'The Dynamics of the P&C

Marketplace'; mem., Ins. Inst. of Ont.; Int'l Ins. Soc.; Dir., Skandia Canada Reinsurance Co.; Catholic Family Services of Metro. Toronto; Providence Centre, Scarborough; Clubs: National (Toronto); recreations: sailing, jogging, reading; Home: 13620 Weston Rd., Keswick, Ont. L7B 1K4.

**BELZBERG, Brent Stanley,** B.Com., LL.B.; executive; b. Calgary, Alta. 1 Jan. 1951; s. Hyman and Jenny B.; e. Queen's Univ. B.Com. 1972; Univ. of Toronto LL.B. 1975; m. M. Lynn d. Michael and Mildred Rosen 6 Jan. 1979; children: Bram David, Kate Sonja, Zachary William; PRES. & C.E.O., HARROWSTON CORPORATION (formerly First City Financial Corp. Ltd.) 1991– ;and Dir. 1979– ; Pres. & C.O.O., Talborne Capital Corp. (formerly First City Trustco Inc.) 1988– ; Chrmn. & C.E.O. Harrowston Development Corp. (formerly First City Development Corp. Ltd.) 1979– ; Chrmn. & C.E.O., First City Capital Markets Ltd. 1986– ; Chrmn. & C.E.O., Wokingham Capital Corp. (formerly Pioneer Lifeco Inc.) 1988– ; Chrmn., First City Trust Co. 1989–92 and Dir. 1979–92; Dir., Westar Group Ltd.; Marsulex Inc.; Solr. Tory, Tory, Deslauriers & Binnington 1975–79; Dir.: Olympic Trust of Can.; United Jewish Appeal Campaign; Jr. Achievement of Canada; The Weizmann Inst.; Mount Sinai Hosp.; mem. Extve., President's Ctte., Univ. of Toronto; Bd. of Dirs., Crescent Sch.; Home: 186 Warren Rd., Toronto, Ont. M4V 2S5; Office: 150 York St., Ste. 1300, Toronto, Ont. M5H 3T1.

**BELZBERG, Samuel,** C.M., B.Com.; financial executive; b. Calgary, Alta. 26 June 1928; e. Cliff Bungalow Pub. Sch., Rideau Park Jr. High and Central High Sch., Calgary; Univ. of Alta., B.Com. 1948; LL.D. (hon. causa); m. Frances, d. late David Cooper, Los Angeles, Cal. 8 Oct. 1950; children: 1 s., 3 d.; PRES., BEL-FRAN INVESTMENTS LTD.; Dir., Franklin Supply Company Ltd.; CVD Capital Corp.; Chrmn., Bd. of Trustees, Yeshiva Univ., Los Angeles (and Founder, Simon Wiesenthal Center there); Founder & Chrmn., Dystonia Medical Research Foundation; Chrmn., Simon Fraser Univ. Bridge to The Future Campaign 1986–89; Mem., Simon Fraser Univ. Found.; Cdn. Soc. for the Weizmann Inst. of Sci.; Canada-Israel Found. for Academic Exchanges; Cdn. Friends of Haifa Univ.; Jerusalem Found. of Can., Inc.; mem. Nat. Bd., Cdn. Council of Christians and Jews; mem., Rockefeller Univ. Council; Adv. Council, Fac. of Commerce and Business Admin., Univ. of B.C. 1987–91; recreations: golf, tennis; Clubs: Richmond Golf & Country; Vancouver Lawn Tennis and Badminton; Tamarisk Country, Palm Springs; Office: 1177 W. Hastings St., Suite 2000, Vancouver, B.C. V6E 2K3.

**BELZILE, Hervé,** B.A., M.Com., F.C.A., Dr. Com.Sc.; insurance executive; e. Rimouski (Que.) Semy. B.A. 1942; Univ. of Montreal M.Com. 1945, Dr.Com.Sc. 1970; C.A. 1948; Harvard Business Sch. AMP 1959; Dir., Sodarcan; Trustco Général du Canada Inc.; Prof., Ecole des Hautes Etudes Commerciales 1945–52; joined present co. as Controller 1952, Secy. 1955, Mang. Dir. and mem. Bd. 1957, mem. Extve. Comte. 1962, Pres. 1963, Chrmn. 1985; Clubs: Saint-Denis; Laval-sur-le-Lac.

**BEMBRIDGE, Wayne Richard,** B.Ed., M.A.; educator; school principal; b. Winnipeg, Man. 5 March 1943; s. Albert Addison and Bertha Emily (Clark) B.; e. Univ. of Man. B.A. 1964, Cert. Ed. 1965, B.Ed. 1968; Univ. of B.C. M.A. 1970; m. Teresa d. Joseph and Jean Klasz 22 Dec. 1984; children: Richard Addison, Jennifer Anne; PRIN. UPPER SCH. ST. JOHN'S RAVENSCOURT SCH. 1988– ; Consultant, Home Study Skills Program 1991– ; high sch. teacher Oakville, Man. 1964–68; Dir. of Edn. & Training Man. Training Sch. Portage la Prairie, Man. 1966–70; Prin. Winnipeg Sch. Div. Ellen Douglas Sch. 5 yrs., Tyndall Park Community Sch. 5 yrs., Hugh John Macdonald Jr. High Sch. 4 yrs. 1973–87; Sales Rep. Sun Life of Canada 1987; O.C.O.D. (C.I.D.A.) volunteer cons. ednl. adm. Grenada, W.I. several summer terms; sessional lectr. Univ. of B.C., Univ. of Man.; recipient Grad. Fellowship Univ. B.C. 1971–73; Nat. Inst. Mental Retardation Rsch. Fellowship 1972; Florence S. Dunlop Fellowship 1973; mem. Candn. Bd. Govs. Council for Exceptional Children, Man. Pres. & Gov. 1979–82; mem. Nat. Assn. Secondary Sch. Princ's 1988; Exec. Offr. Advanced Placement Council Man. 1990–92; Dir. Children's Home of Winnipeg 1984–88; ed. 'A Social Living Curriculum for Retarded Persons' 1979; recreations: golf, alpine skiing; Home: 2, 1692 St. Mary's Rd., Winnipeg, Man. R2N 1L8; Office: 400 South Dr., Winnipeg, Man. R3T 3K5.

**BENARROCH, Georges,** B.Sc., M.Sc.; investment banker; b. Morocco 16 Feb. 1947; s. David and Simy (Hassan) B.; e. Faculté de Droit, Toulouse, France 1968; Univ. of Montréal B.Sc. 1970; Univ. de Nice, Faculté de Droit, Institut Européen des Hautes Etudes Internationales, Institut du Droit de la Paix et du Developpement Economique M.Sc. 1972; Univ. de Paris Doctorat de Droit Internat. (3 Cycle) 1974; CHRMN. AND CHIEF EXEC. OFFR., CREDIFINANCE SECURITIES LTD. 1991– ; Lectr., Institut Européen des Hautes Etudes Internationales, Univ. de Nice; mem. Academie de la Paix; Home: 78 Hazelton Ave., Toronto, Ont. M5R 2E2.

**BENAYON, Jaime;** business executive; b. Tangiers, Morocco; e. Univ. of Morocco; m. Rami; 4 children; PRESIDENT & CHIEF OPERATING OFFICER, ONTARIO STORE FIXTURES INC., METAL DIV.; Pres. & C.E.O., Benwind Industries; clubs: Cambridge, Richmond Hill Golf & Country; Office: 400 Fenmar Dr., North York, Ont. M9L 1M6.

**BENCHIMOL, Michel R.;** auto industry executive; b. Casablanca, Morocco 23 March 1945; s. Albert and Ricca B.; e. Concordia University; m. Anna Rosalie; children: Eric, Amanda; SENIOR VICE-PRES. AND GENERAL MANAGER, MAZDA CANADA INC.; Office: 2075 Kennedy Rd., Ste. 400, Scarborough, Ont. M1T 3V3.

**BENDEL, Michael,** LL.B.; labour arbitrator; b. London, Eng. 19 Dec. 1944; s. Isaac and Rose (Goldstein) B.; e. Manchester Univ. LL.B. 1966; Univ. of Ottawa, LL.B. 1975; m. Miriam d. Herman and Mina Davidovich 8 Apr. 1979; children: Isaac, Samuel, Malca, Joseph; PRIN. MICHAEL BENDEL ARBITRATION SERVICES 1987– ; called to Bar of Ont. 1977; Legal Offr. Internat. Labour Office Geneva 1966–69; Legal Offr., Negotiator, Coordinator Collective Bargaining, Profl. Inst. Pub. Service of Can. Ottawa 1969–74; Prof. of Common Law Univ. of Ottawa 1977–84; Dep. Chrmn. Pub. Service Staff Relations Bd. Ottawa 1984–87; part-time Vice Chair, Ont. Labour Relations Bd. Toronto; part-time mem. Pub. Service Staff Relations Bd.; Pres. Young Israel of Ottawa 1988–90; mem. Bd. Dirs. Ecole Maimonides Torah Day Sch. Ottawa 1984–92; Vice Pres. Cong. Beth Shalom of Ottawa 1981–83; author various articles law jours.; Address: 40 Glen Cres., Thornhill, Ont. L4J 4W6.

**BENDER, Graham Ivan,** B.Sc., M.B.A., AMP; forest products executive; b. Radisson, Sask. 26 Nov. 1939; s. Elmer Ivan and Jeanetta (McMillan) B.; e. Univ. of Saskatchewan B.Sc. 1961; McGill Univ. M.B.A. 1967; Harvard Univ. AMP 1984; m. Marion d. Barton and Madaleine Jackson 20 Oct. 1962; children: Joyce Elizabeth, John Barton, Marnie Jo; PRESIDENT & CHIEF EXECUTIVE OFFICER (and Director), WELDWOOD OF CANADA LTD. 1993– ; Engineering Economist, Canadian National Railways 1961–66; Mktg. Officer 1967–8; various positions ending as General Manager, Powell River Division, MacMillan Bloedel Ltd. 1968–89; Sr. Vice-Pres., Pulp & Paper, Weldwood of Can. 1989–92; Pres. & C.O.O., Weldwood Canada Limited 1992–93; Dir., Weldwood of Canada Limited; CanWel Distbn.Ltd.; Seaboard Lumber & Shipping Co. Ltd.; Bd. of Gov., Business Council of B.C.; Pres., Cariboo Pulp & Paper Co.; recreations: squash, skiing, boating; clubs: Vancouver, Hollyburn; Home: 5350 Westhaven Wynd, West Vancouver, B.C. V7W 3E8; Office: P.O. Box 2179, Vancouver, B.C. V6B 3V8.

**BENEDICT, Michael Christopher,** M.A.; journalist; b. New York City, N.Y. 20 Jan. 1947; s. Peter C. (dec.) and Felice B.; e. McGill Univ., B.A. 1968; Sir George Williams Univ., M.A. 1971; children: Nicholas Peter, Matthew Ross; ASST. MANAGING ED., MACLEAN'S, 1989– ; St. John's Evening Telegram, Nfld., 1972–75; Toronto Star Ottawa Bureau, 1975–77; CTV Nat. News, Ottawa 1977–80; Dir. Communications, Ont. Min. Ind. & Tourism, Toronto, 1980–83; Dir. Corporate Communications (York Div.) Can. Post Corp., Toronto, 1983–86; Sr. Ed., Maclean's, 1986–89; Candn. Direct Mktg. Assn. RSVP Award 1984; Parl. Press Gallery 1975–80; ed. 'Postmark: Toronto' 1984; Home: 262 Pacific Ave., Toronto, Ont. M6P 2P5; Office: 777 Bay St., Toronto, Ont. M5W 1A7.

**BENEDIKTSON, Stephan Vilberg,** B.Sc., P.Eng.; oil and gas executive, rancher; b. Innisfail, Alta. 22 June 1933; s. Sigurdur Vilberg and Rosa Sigulah (Stephansson) B. (grandson of Icelandic Candn. poet Stephan G. Stephansson); e. Univ. of Alberta B.Sc., C.E. 1962; m. Audrey d. Henry and Gloria Jones of London, England 1 Dec. 1956; children: Stephan Robert, Susan Rosa, Paul David; PRESIDENT, BENSON PETROLEUM LTD. 1986– ; worked in oil fields 1953–62; worked for Esso (Canada, U.S., Australia, Indonesia) 1962–71; Chief Offshore Engr., Northern Devel. Govt. of Canada 1971–73; Petroleum Eng. & Prod. Opns., Aramco (Saudi Arabia) 1973–77; Vice-Pres., Drilling & Prod. then Vice-Pres. in charge, United Arab Emirates, Amerada Hess Corp. 1977–81; Founder, Benson Internat. Oil and Gas Serv. Ltd. 1981; Dir. Gen., Bridas SAPIC (Argentina) 1983–86; also operated Benson Ranch Inc.; Dir., Austar Resources Corp.; Mem., CIMM (Charter Dir., Ottawa Petroleum Branch); Mem., Soc. of Petroleum Engrs. (Charter Dir., United Arab Emirates); recreations: squash, polo, skiing; clubs: Calgary Ranchman's, Calgary Polo; Home: Box 18, Site 35, R.R. 2, Calgary, Alta. T2P 2G5; Office: 521-3rd Ave. SW, Ste. 1070, Calgary, Alta. T2P 3T3.

**BENIDICKSON, Agnes McCausland,** O.C., O.Ont., B.A., LL.D.; b. Kingston, Ont. 19 Aug. 1920; d. James Armstrong and Muriel (Sprague) Richardson; e. Riverbend Sch. (now Balmoral Hall) Winnipeg; Queen's Univ., B.A. 1941; m. Hon. William Moore s. Christian and Gertrude B. 29 Nov. 1947; now widowed; 3 children; CHANCELLOR, QUEEN'S UNIV. & DIR., JAMES RICHARDSON & SONS LIMITED; Dir., The Mutual Group 1976–94; The National Trust Co. Limited 1976–91; Pres., Candn. Counc. on Social Devel. 1972–75 (now Hon. Pres.); Assn. of Candn. Clubs 1979–83; Hon. Pres. (former Pres.), Friends of the Nat. Gall. of Can.; Hon. LL.D., Queen's 1979, U.B.C. 1987, R.M.C. 1991; Univ. of Manitoba 1992; Officer of the Order of Canada 1987; Order of Ont. 1991; Dir., Comm. Found. of Ottawa-Carleton 1988–93; Nat. Capital Region Mem. Canadiana Fund; Mem., Rideau Club, Royal Lake of the Woods Yacht Club; Home: 2903, 1785 Riverside Dr., Ottawa, Ont. K1G 3T7; Office: Queen's Univ., Kingston, Ont. K7L 3N6.

**BENMERGUI, Raphael (Ralph);** broadcaster; b. Tangeir, Morocco 13 Dec. 1955; s. Meir and Rachel (Bengio) B.; e. Forest Hill C.I.; York Univ.; Univ. of Alberta; Ryerson (journalism, 2 years); m. Kathryn d. Elizabeth Lander and Guy Swinnerton 24 Oct.1985; children: Jonah, Chas; HOST, 'FRIDAY NIGHT WITH RALPH BENMERGUI,' CBC 1992– ; Researcher, Current Affairs Radio, CBW Winnipeg 1985; Host, CBC Stereo's 'Nightlines' 1986–87; CBC Radio's 'Prime Time' 1987–89; CBC Stereo's 'The Entertainers' 1987–89; CBC TV 'Midday' 1989–92; Lead Singer, 'The Stingers' Rock Band 1978–80; Stand-up Comic, Yuk Yuk's Internat. 1979–89; Host 1991 Gemini Awards; Gemini nom. 1992 for 'Friday Night with Ralph Benmergui'; Gemini nom. 1991 for Best Host / Interviewer; Office: Box 500, Station A, Toronto, ON– ;M5W 1E6.

**BENMORE, Richard Carlile,** C.A.; real estate executive; b. Vancouver, B.C. 1 Nov. 1946; s. John Carlile and Ruth Evelyn (Hamlin) B.; e. C.A. 1971; one d. Meaghan; CHIEF OPERATING OFFICER, FIRST PROFESSIONAL MANAGEMENT INC. 1988– ; joined Bank of Montreal 1964–65; Tax Mgr., Arthur Andersen & Co. 1965–77; Sr. Vice Pres. Daon Development Corp. 1977–82; Sr. Vice Pres. & C.F.O., Coscan Development Corp. (formerly Costain Ltd.) 1983–88; Dir. Family Services Greater Vancouver 1980–83, Treas. 1982–83; Clubs: Summit Golf & Country; Arbutus (Vancouver); Point Grey Golf & Country (Vancouver); Home: 227 Ranleigh Ave., Toronto, Ont. M4N 1X3.

**BENN, Carl Eric,** B.A., M.Div.; museum curator; b. Toronto, Ont. 4 March 1953; e. Univ. of Toronto B.A. 1980, M.Div. 1983; m. Ann Joan Procyk 1981; children: Andrew, Elizabeth; CURATOR, MIL. & MARINE HIST. TORONTO HIST. BD. 1985– ; Part-time Teacher, Univ. of Toronto; Hist. Interpreter present Bd. 1969, 1971–75; Sr. Hist. Interpreter, Borough of Etobicoke 1975–80; Curator of Collections, Regional Mun. of Waterloo 1983–85; author 'The King's Mill on the Humber' 1979; 'The Battle of York' 1984; 'Historic Fort York, 1793–1993' 1993; various articles; mem. Ont. Museum Assn. (Council 1986, Chrmn. Publs. Ctte. 1979–80); Candn. Museums Assn.; Candn. Historical Assn.; Co. of Military Historians (U.S.); Ont. Historical Soc. (editorial advisory ctte. for Ontario History); Anglican; Home: 254 Indian Rd., Toronto, Ont. M6R 2X2; Office: 205 Yonge St., Toronto, Ont. M5B 1N2.

**BENN, Daniel L.J.,** B.Sc.; software industry executive; b. Brussels, Belgium 5 Jan. 1949; s. Philip and Alice (Ginas) B.; e. Massachusetts Inst. of Technol. B.Sc. 1969; m. Elaine d. Jack and Catherine Cassidy 12 Jan. 1982; children: Trevor, Michael, Caitlin; FOUNDER, PRESIDENT & CHIEF EXECUTIVE OFFICER, COMPUTERTIME NETWORK CORP. 1979– ; Computer Systems Engr., McGill Univ. 1973–76; Sr. Software Cons., Digital Equipment 1976–79; Home: Pointe Claire, Que. H9S 4Y1; Office: 10340 cote de Liesse, Lachine, Que. H8T 1A3.

**BENNATHAN, Serge;** artistic director; choreographer; b. L'Aigle, France 14 Aug. 1957; s. Alfred and Regine (Bouvry) B.; e. Academie internat. de danse Paris; ARTISTIC DIR. DANCEMAKERS 1990– ; freelance choreographer since 1987; created first full-length work 'The Song of the Nightingale' 1989; profl. dancer Roland Petit's Ballet de Marseille 1975–81; formed own troupe 'Compagnie Serge Bennathan' 1982; emigrated to Can. 1985; profl. dancer and choreographer Le Groupe de la Place Royale 1985; Home: 5 Ozark Cres., Toronto, Ont. M4K 1T4; Office: 927 Dupont St., Toronto, Ont. M6H 1Z1.

**BENNETT, A. Dwight;** conductor; b. Peterborough, Ont. 28 Dec. 1945; s. Donald Dwight and June Winnifred (Burgis) B.; e. Univ. of Toronto 1963–69; Royal Conserv. Toronto; Sch. of Mus., Indiana Univ. 1969–73; Academia Chigiana, Siena, Italy; m. Margaret Helleiner 19 Dec. 1982; Music Dir. & Conductor, Windsor Symphony Orchestra 1986–90; Music Dir. & Conductor, Thunder Bay Symphony Orchestra 1974–89; Artistic Dir., Mississauga City Centre Opera 1993– ; Conductor, Candn. Opera Company 1993– ; Guest conductor, most Candn. orchestras, CBC orchestras & opera cos.; 2 CBC Vanc. Orchestra recordings released; First Prize Heinz Unger Conducting Competition, Canada; Address: 102 Briar Hill Ave., Toronto, Ont. M4R 1H9.

**BENNETT, Allan,** M.B.A., A.M.C.S.T., A.I.Q.S.; consultant; b. Thelwall, England 26 March 1933; s. Albert and Lillian (Haines) B.; e. Boteler Grammar Sch.; Manchester Coll. of Sci. & Tech., A.M.C.S.T. 1956; Univ. of B.C., M.B.A. 1980; m. Jean d. Fred and Ruth Bagnall 16 July 1955; children: Susan, Marie; PRESIDENT, A. BENNETT & ASSOCIATES 1993– ; var. mngt. posts, Laing Construction 1957–73; Cons./Project Mgr. for major children's hosp. & ancillary devel., Mng. design, constr., commissioning 1977–81; Mgr., Projects, A & B Constr. Co. Ltd. 1973–77, 1981–83; Pres., Amalgamated Construction Assn. of B.C. 1983–93; Chrmn., Nat. Adv. Bd., Institute for Rsch. in Construction, National Rsch. Council; Candn. Construction Rsch. Counc.; Chrmn. SPARK Ctte. of BC Science Counc., Construction Sector; Chrmn., B.C. Chapt., Candn. Construction Rsch. Bd.; Judge, Internat. Design/Constr. comp. for excellence in sports facilities (Germany) 1987; Trustee, St. Vincent's Hosp. Soc./Found./Arbutus Soc.; Comnr. (Past Chrmn.), Vanc. Park Bd. (elected office) 1980–90; Past Pres., Candn. Parks & Rec. Assn.; Trustee, Vancouver Botanical Gardens Assn.; Anglican; recreations: fishing, walking, bird- & marine animal-watching; club: B.C. Club; Home: 203 - 2108 West 38th Ave., Vancouver, B:C. V6M 1R9.

**BENNETT, Claude Frederick;** former politician; b. Ottawa, Ont. 19 Sept. 1936; e. Ottawa, Ont.; m. Deborah; children: Natalie, Winston; CHRMN., BD. OF DIRS., CANADA MORTGAGE AND HOUSING CORP. 1990– ; Advisor to Sedgwick, Insurance Lenders; Bd. Mem., Nationa's Capital Television (NCTI) - CJOH Ottawa; el. Ald. Ottawa City Council 1961; re-el. 1963, 1965, 1967; mem. first Ottawa-Carleton Regional Govt. 1968–70; el. to Ottawa Bd. of Control 1970 serving as Sr. Controller and Acting Mayor; mem. Exec. of Ottawa-Carleton Regional Council 1970 and Chrmn. Ottawa Planning Bd.; el. M.P.P. for Ottawa S. 1971–87; apptd. Parlty. Asst. to Min. of Treasury, Econ. & Intergovernmental Affairs 1972; Min. Without Portfolio 1972; Min. of Industry & Tourism 1973; Min. of Housing 1978; Min. of Mun. Affairs & Housing 1981; Min. of Tourism & Recreation 1985; Chrmn. of Cabinet (and mem. of its Policy & Priorities Bd.) 1985; Dir. & Vice. Pres., Central Can. Exhn. Assn.; Mem.-at-large, Lambda Alpha Internat.; Dir., Ottawa Lynx Triple 'A' Baseball Co.; Dir., Bd. of Govs., Ashbury Coll., Ottawa; Bd. Mem., National Boy Scout Counc.; as an independent ins. agt. rec'd Three Outstanding Young Men Award, Ont. Jr. Chamber of Comm. 1968; voted Man of the Yr. by Ottawa Shrine Club 1979; Address: CMHC, 700 Montreal Rd., Ottawa, Ont. K1A 0P7.

**BENNETT, Hon. Colin E.,** Q.C.; executive; b. Meaford, Ont. 5 March 1908; s. Thomas Emerson and Ellen Haggart (Stewart) B.; e. Univ. of Toronto (Pol. Econ.), 1931; Osgoode Hall, 1936; m. late Mary Dorothy, d. Franklyn H. Tindale, 16 April 1938; children: Cynthia, Laurence, Mary Ellen; 2ndly Fern Eleda Butchart, d. Jasper A. Stuart, 28 Aug. 1965; HON. CHRMN., THE NATIONAL TRUST CO. 1984– ; Pres. and C.E.O. Victoria and Grey Trust Co. 1974–78; Partner, Love & Bennett Ltd., Sporting Goods, Maple Leaf Gardens 1931–34; called to Bar of Ont., 1936; Dir. (1975–83): Casualty Co. of Canada, Dom. of Can. General Insur. Co., Empire Life Insur. Co., E-L Financial Corp. Ltd.; Judge, Co. Court of Grey 1957–69; Chief Judge, Ont. Co. and Dist. Courts 1969–73; served in 2nd World War 1941–45 with R.C.A.F., retiring as Group Cap.; Town Clerk and Solicitor, Meaford 1945–49; 1st el. to H. of C. for Grey N., g.e. 1949; re-el. g.e. 1953; Parlty. Asst. to Minister of Veterans' Affairs, 1953–57; Canada's Rep. on Legal Comn. and Alt. Del. General Assembly, United Nations, Paris 1951; First Chrmn. Criminal Injuries Compensation Board 1968–71; Under Treasurer, Law Soc. of Upper Can. 1982; Past Dir., John Howard Soc. of Ont.; Freemason; United Church; Clubs: University; R.C.M.I.; Empire; Lawyers; Canadian; Address: Apt. 201, 2 Clarendon Ave., Toronto, Ont. M4V 1H9.

**BENNETT, Colin John,** B.Sc., M.Sc., Ph.D.; university professor; b. London, England 17 June 1955; s. John Samuel and Margaret Lillian B.; e. Univ. of Wales B.Sc. 1977, M.Sc. 1981; Univ. of Illinois at Urbana-Champaign Ph.D. 1986; ASSOC. PROF., POLITICAL SCIENCE, UNIV. OF VICTORIA 1991– ; Asst. Prof., Univ. of Victoria 1986–91; Cons., Nat. Survey on Privacy from Ekos Rsch. Assn.; contbr. of articles on privacy 'Ottawa Citizen; Mem., Am. Pol. Sci. Assn.; Candn. Pol. Sci. Assn.; author: 'Regulating Privacy: Data Protection and Public Policy in Europe and the United States' 1992 (Charles H. Levine Memorial Book Prize, Internat. Pol. Sci. Assn.) and several articles and presentations; Home: 5120 – 75 Gorge Road W., Victoria, B.C. V9A 7A9; Office: P.O. Box 3050, Victoria, B.C. V8W 3P5.

**BENNETT, Gilbert Stuart,** LL.B.; business executive; b. Sudbury, Ont. 10 May 1938; s. Wilbur Sydney and Vera Mae (Cooke) B.; e. Univ. of Toronto 1957–59; Osgoode Hall Law Sch., LL.B. 1962; m. Audrey d. Christopher and Nora Pope 3 June 1961; children: Martha Jean, Anne Katherine, James Stuart; CHAIRMAN AND DIRECTOR, SHIELDINGS INCORPORATED 1992– ; barrister & sol., Fraser & Beatty 1964–66; partner, Aird & Berlis 1966–79; Pres., Comstock Internat. Ltd. 1979–83; Pres., Canadair Limited 1983–86; Consultant 1986; Sen. Vice-Pres., Gulf Canada Resources Ltd. 1986–88; Vice Chrmn., CIC Canadian Investment Capital Ltd. 1988–90; Pres., Lundrigans Limited 1990–92; Dir., Canadian Tire Corporation, Limited; Algoma Steel Inc.; Fortis Inc.; de Havilland Holdings Inc.; Air Nova Inc.; National Community Tree Found.; mem., Law Soc. of Upper Can.; recreations: squash, golf, fishing, hiking; Clubs: Lambton Golf & Country; Granite; Cambridge; Home: 9 Highland Ave., Corner Brook, Nfld. A2H 2Y4; Office: Suite 1714, 130 Adelaide St. W., Toronto, Ont. M5H 3P5.

**BENNETT, Hon. Gordon Lockhart,** O.C., M.Sc., D.C.L. LL.D.; b. Charlottetown, P.E.I. 10 Oct. 1912; s. J. Garfield and Annie (Lockhart) B.; e. Elem. Schs. Charlottetown, P.E.I.; Prince of Wales Coll.; Acadia Univ. B.Sc. 1937, M.Sc. (Chem.) 1947, D.C.L. 1976, LL.D. Univ. of P.E.I. 1980; m. the late Doris L., d. the late H. Bruce Bernard 10 Aug. 1937; one d. F. Diane (Mrs. David Campbell); m. E. Muriel Deacon 20 Aug. 1985; Teacher (elem., secondary and univ.) 1932–66; el. to Prov. Leg. P.E.I. 1966, re-el. 1970, 1974; Pres. Extve. Council 1966–74, Min. of Educ. 1966–72, Min. of Justice and Attorney Gen. 1970–74; Lieut. Gov., Prov. of P.E.I. 1974–80; Prov. Secy. 1970–74; Candn. Del. to UNESCO, Paris 1972, to Commonwealth Parlty. Assn., Sri Lanka 1974; Nat'l. Pres., Cdn. Bible Soc.; Pres., P.E.I. Br., Council for Cdn. Unity; Prov. Pres., Terry Fox Centre; Chancellor, Univ. of P.E.I. 1985–92; Officer, Order of Canada 1983; Mason (PGM); Grand Comdr., Scottish Rite Masonry of Can.; Rotarian, Paul Harris Fellow; Liberal; United Church; recreations: gardening, golf, curling (Past Pres. Dom. Curling Assn., mem. & Builder, Candn. Curling Hall of Fame); Address: 13 Carriage Lane, Charlottetown, P.E.I. C1A 9B7.

**BENNETT, Harry;** insurance executive; b. Staten Isld., N.Y. 14 Jan. 1923; s. William and Annie (Thomson) B.; e. William Penn Charter Sch. 1940; Univ. of Penna., grad. 1947; m. Carol, 8 May 1954; PRES., OSBORN & LANGE, INC.; with Fire Assn. of Philadelphia 1947–49; Ocean Marine Ins. Co., London, Eng. 1949–50; L. Hammond & Co. 1950–51; F.B. Hall & Co., N.Y. 1951–52; Osborn & Lange (U.S.A.), Inc. 1952–54; served during 2nd World War with U.S.N.R.; discharged with rank of Lieut.; mem., Candn. Comte. of Lloyds Register of Shipping; Past Pres. of Corp., Bishop's Univ.; Bishop's Univ. Found.; Candn. Maritime Law Assn.; Past Pres., Montreal YMCA; recreations: golf, travel; Clubs: St. James's; Royal and Ancient Golf Club of St. Andrews; Pine Valley Golf (U.S.A.); Mt. Bruno Country; Toronto Golf; National (Toronto); Hawk's Nest Golf (Vero Beach, Fla.); Moorings (Vero Beach, Fla.); Home: 30 Holton Ave., Westmount, Qué. H3Y 2E8; Office: 360 St. James St., Montreal, Qué. H2Y 1P5.

**BENNETT, Ian Cecil,** D.D.S., M.S.D., F.A.C.D., F.I.C.D.; educator; b. Bebington, Eng. 2 Aug. 1931; s. Arthur Cecil and Gladys (Davies) B.; e. Birkenhead Sch. Eng. 1950; Liverpool Univ. B.D.S. 1956; Univ. of Toronto D.D.S. 1959; Univ. of Wash. M.S.D. 1964; m. Marcia A. Boyd d. Ernest and Eloise Jackson 11 June 1993; children: Davis Bayer, Alessandra Lee; CLINICAL PROFESSOR OF PEDIATRIC DENTISTRY, UNIV. OF BRITISH COLUMBIA 1992– ; gen. dental practice Greasby, Cheshire, Eng. 1956; Med. Offr. Oxford Univ. Geol. Expdn. to W. Greenland 1956; Dental Offr. Fed. Civil Service Aklavik, N.W.T. 1956–58; Pedodontic practice Vancouver, B.C. 1959–61; Dental Offr. E. Sector Cdn. Div. Distant Early Warning Line 1961–62; Asst. Prof. of Pedodontics Univ. of Ky. 1965, Assoc. Prof. 1968, Asst. Coordr. Med. Center TV 1966–67 and Div. Med. Center Communications & Services 1967, Dir. of Medical Center Communications & Services 1967–68; Assoc. Dean Coll. of Dentistry and Assoc. Prof. of Pedodontics N.J. Coll. of Medicine & Dentistry 1968–69 (subsequently Univ. of Medicine & Dentistry of N.J., N.J. Dental Sch.), Dean & Prof. of Pedodontics 1969–76; Head of Dental Dept. Halifax Children's Hosp. 1963–65; Consultant East Orange (N.J.) Veterans' Adm. Hosp. 1969–76; Assoc. Prof. and Head Div. Pedodontics, Dalhousie Univ. 1963–65, 1988–89; Consultant, Izaak Walton Killam Hosp. for Children Halifax 1976; Prof. of Pediatric Dentistry, Dalhousie Univ. 1976–92 and Dean of Dentistry 1976–86; Visiting Prof., Dept. of Growth & Development, Univ. of California at San Francisco 1987–88; Visiting Prof., Dept. of Clinical Dental Sciences, Univ. of B.C. 1991; recipient Co. Maj. Univ. Scholarship 1950–56; Am. Acad. Pedodontics Research Award 1966; various research and educ. grants; author or co-author numerous publs.; Extve. Dir., Can. Acad. Pediatric Dentistry 1990– ; Fellow, Am. Acad. Pediatric Dentistry; mem. Am. Acad. Hist. Dentistry; Am. Assn. Dental Schs.; Am. Assn. Advanc. Sci.; Am. Assn. Univ. Profs.; Am. Dental Assn.; Am. Soc. Dentistry Children; Candn. Acad. Pediatric Dentistry (Vice Pres. 1978–80; Pres. 1980–85; Imm. Past Pres. 1985–87); Candn. Assn. Dental Research; Candn. Dental Assn.; Fed. Dentaire Internationale; Internat. Assn. Dental Research; N.Y. Acad. Sciences; N.S. Dental Assn. (Extve. Comte. 1976–86); recreations: skiing, travel; Clubs: Climbers; Wayfarers; Home: 4095 Puget Dr., Vancouver, B.C. V6L 2V3; Office: Vancouver, B.C. V6T 1W5.

**BENNETT, Jalynn H.,** B.A.; consultant; b. Toronto, Ont. 12 March 1943; d. Alfred W. and Elizabeth H. (Lumbers) Rogers; e. Wellesley Coll. 1962–63; Univ. of Toronto Trinity Coll. B.A. 1965; PRES. JALYNN H. BENNETT & ASSOCIATES LTD. 1989– ; Dir. Bank of Canada; St. Marys Cement; Sears Canada Inc.; Commissioner, Ont. Securities Comn. 1990– ; mem. Ont. Teachers Pension Plan Bd. Investment Ctte.; mem. Candn. Nat. Ctte. Pacific Econ. Coop. 1990– ; Ont. Govt. Asia-Pacific Study Group 1990–91; Ont. Premier's Council Econ. & Quality of Life 1990– ; Chair, Sectorial Adv. Group Internat. Trade: Financial Services 1986–91; Internat. Trade Adv. Ctte. 1988–91; Fed. Adv. Council on Adjustment 1988–89; Vice-Chrmn., Trent Univ. Bd. of Govs.; Dir. Laidlaw Found.; Wellesley Hosp.; mem. Candn. Assn. Bus. Econs.; Toronto Soc. Financial Analysts; Candn. Inst. Corporate Dirs.; Candn. Coalition of Svc. Cos.; Office: 303, 247 Davenport Rd., Toronto, Ont. M5R 1J9.

**BENNETT, Keith John,** B.Com.; labour relations executive; b. New Westminster, B.C. 6 June 1933; s. Alfred Cecil and Annie (Done) B.; e. Univ. of B.C., B.Com. 1956; m. Mary d. Michael and Doris Kitt 14 Feb. 1959; children: Bradley, Sandra, Grant; PRES. FOREST INDUSTRIAL RELATIONS LTD. 1979– ; joined CIL 1956–57; Lenkurt Electric 1957–60; present Co. 1960, Asst. Mgr. 1967, Vice Pres. 1973; Fraser Burrard Hosp. Assn.; recreation: golf; Club: Vancouver Golf & Country; Home: 522 Lyn Court. Coquitlam, B.C.; Office: 880, 505 Burrard St., Vancouver, B.C. V7X 1M3.

**BENNETT, Marcia Joslin,** F.C.S.I.; investment banker; b. London, Ont. 13 Mar. 1948; d. John Frederick and Norah Elaine Joslin (Hall) B.; e. Burlington Central H.S.; Inst. of Chartered Secs.; Univ. of Toronto; Candn. Securities Inst.; m. John A.D. Weston s. David and Doreen Weston 12 April 1990; one d.; Robin Joslin Bennett Payzant; DIR., GORDON CAPITAL CORP. 1982– ; Yorcan Communications Ltd. 1989– ; New York Investors Funding, New York; Bovis Holdings, London U.K.; Partnership, Pacific, Australia, Harris & Partners; Nesbitt Thomson; Burns Fry; Mem., PC Can.; Dir., Bus. Club; recreations: tennis, swimming; Club: Cricket; Home: 16 Wychwood Park, Toronto, Ont. M6G 2V5; Office: Box 67, Toronto-Dominion Ctr., Toronto, Ont. M5K 1E7.

**BENNETT, Brig.-Gen. Robert Taylor,** O.B.E. 1945, C.D. 1951, O.St.J. 1970, B.A. 1979; Canadian Forces (retired), b. Ottawa, Ont. 15 July 1918; s. late Charles Herbert and Winnifred Gwendolyn Alice (Dawson) B.; e. Glebe Coll. Inst., Ottawa, 1935; Royal Mil. Coll., Hon. grad. 1939; Royal Mil. Coll. of Science, 1940 (I.O.O.); Candn. Army Staff Coll. 1943 (psc); U.S. Command & Gen. Staff Coll. 1945; NATO Defence Coll. 1952 (NADC); Nat. Defence Coll. 1962 (NDC); Univ. of Man., B.A. 1979; m. Evelyn Mary, d. late Harry Albert Underwood, 18 Dec. 1947; three s., Geoffrey Taylor, Robert George, Richard James; overseas, 1st, 2nd and 5th Divs., 1st & 2nd Candn. Corps, 1st Candn. Army, CMHQ and Pacific Force World War II; Lt. 1939; Capt. 1940; Maj. 1941; Lt. Col. 1943 (youngest in Candn. Army); Col. 1953; Brig. Gen. 1971; Mentioned in Despatches; Instr., Army Staff Coll., Kingston, 1946–50; Army HQ, QMG Br., Ottawa, 1950–51; SHAPE, Paris, 1952–53; Mil. Asst. to Secy. Gen., NATO HQ, 1953–56; Chief of Staff, Central Command, Oakville, 1956–58; Garrison Commdr., Longue Pointe, Montreal, 1958–61; C.O., Cdn. Del. to Internat. Control Comn., Indo-China, 1961–62; Dir. Ordnance Services, AHQ/CFHQ, Ottawa, 1963–67; Dir. of Organ., CFHQ, 1967–71; Sr. Candn. Mil. Offr. Indo-China and Sr. Mil. Adviser and acting Commissioner, Internat. Control Comn., Viet-Nam, 1971–72; Dir.-Gen. Restructuring CFHQ 1973; retired 1974; man. cons., E.A.C. Amy and Sons, Ltd. Ottawa 1974–84; Commandant, Can. Army Bisley Cadet Rifle Team 1966–69; mem. Que. and Federal Dists. Councils St. John of Jerusalem 1959–75; Ottawa Anglican Diocesan Extve. Comte. 1975–77; Pres. Nat. Supply Comte., Boy Scouts of Can. 1963–81; mem. Boy Scout Gen. Council, 1980–81; Medal of Merit, Boy Scouts of Can. 1984; Pres., Can. Youth Publications 1981–85; Secy.-Treas., Un. World Coll. (Candn. Comte.) 1967–70; Mil. Lay Del. Gen. Synod 1959, 1969; Delegate to Ottawa Anglican Synod 1965–70, 1972–77; Warden, St. Matthias Church, Ottawa 1968–70; Extve. Comte. and Gen. Council Royal Mil. College Club Can., 1968–71, 1982– ; Adjutant, RMC Old Brigade 1985– ; Pres. RMC Club of Can. (Ottawa branch) 1978; Pres., Carleton Condominium Corp. 1980–83; Hon. ADC to Gov. Gen. of Can. 1959–61; Granted Honorary Degree of Doctor of Military Science, Royal Military College of Canada 1993; Anglican; recreations: racquetball, golf, gardening; Club: RMC Club of Canada; NATO Defence College Club (Founder Member); Amberwood Golf and Country; Home: 20 Kittansett Court, Amberwood Village, Stittsville, Ont. K2S 1B9.

**BENNETT, Ross C.,** M.D.; coroner; b. London, Ont. 21 Aug. 1928; s. Arnold Gibson and Marjorie Kathleen (Brown) B.; e. Mimico High Sch. 1946; Univ. of W. Ont. M.D. 1954; m. Janet d. Willard and Rose Mace 30 June 1955; children: David, Nancy, Marjorie, Stephanie, Thomas; Chief Coroner for Ont. 1982–90; Lectr. in Med. Jurisprudence Univ. of Toronto; interned S. Pacific Hosp. San Francisco and Tuscon; family practice Beach Clinic 1955–72; Coroner Metrop. Toronto 1969–72; Depy. Chief Coroner Prov. Ont. 1972–82; Fellow, Am. Acad. Forensic Sciences, Vice Pres.; Vice Pres. Internat. Assn. Coroners & Med. Examiners; Toronto Medico-Legal Soc.; co-author 'Drugs in Fatally Injured Drivers and Pedestrians in Ontario' 1980; recreations: sailing, cross-country skiing, cottage; Office: 26 Grenville St., Toronto, Ont. M7A 2G9.

**BENNETT, Roy Frederick,** F.C.A.; executive; b. Winnipeg, Man. 18 Mar. 1928; s. Charles William and Gladys Mabel (Matthews) B.; e. N. Toronto Coll. Inst.; Inst. Chart. Accts. Ont. 1953, F.C.A. 1973; LL.D. (hon. causa), York Univ. 1989; m. Dr. Gail C.A. Cook; children: Bruce Roy, Brenda Laurie, Lynne Susan, Christopher William; PRES., BENNECON LTD.; Dir., Jannock Limited; Bell Canada; Midland Walwyn Inc.; (and Former Chrmn. and C.E.O.) Ford Motor Co. of Canada Ltd.; Talisman Energy Inc.; Toronto Medical Corp.; mem., Bus. Counc. on National Issues; Protestant; recreations: golf, tennis, skiing; Clubs: Mississauga Golf & Country; Toronto; Office: Ste. 3404 Royal Trust Tower, P.O. Box 59, Toronto Dominion Bank Tower, Toronto, Ont. M5K 1E7.

**BENNETT, William John,** B.A., LL.B.; business executive; b. Ottawa, Ont. 11 May 1945; s. William John and Elizabeth Josephine (Palleck) B.; e. Loyola H.S. 1962; St. Michael's Coll., Univ. of Toronto, B.A. (Hons.) 1967; Fac. of Law, LL.B. 1970; m. Diana d. Hon. Justice & Mrs. Frederick T. Collins 2 Oct. 1976; children: Carl Edward, William John Patrick, Juliana Elizabeth; CHRMN. & C.E.O., BENVEST CAPITAL INC.; joined Scotia McLeod Inc. 1972; Vice-Pres. 1974; Vice-Pres. & Dir. 1976; Extve. Vice-Pres. 1988; Sr. Vice-Pres., Imasco Limited 1989–91; Dir., Weider Europe B.V.; Lunetterie 'New Look' Inc.; Lafayette Paper L.P.; Continental Pharma Cryosan Inc.; M3i Systems Inc.; Candn. Council for Aboriginal Business; St. Mary's Hospital Centre; Vice Chrmn. & Treas., C.D. Howe Memorial Foundation; Trustee, St. Michael's Coll. Foundation; mem., Law Soc. of Upper Can. 1972; clubs: Mount Royal, Montreal Racket; Home: 36 Church Hill, Westmount, Qué. H3Y 2Z9; Office: 3230, 1 Place Ville-Marie, Montreal, Qué. H3B 3Y2.

**BENNETT, Hon. William Richards,** P.C.; former politician; b. Kelowna, B.C. 14 Apr. 1932; s. late Hon. William Andrew Cecil Bennett (former Premier of B.C.) and Annie Elizabeth May (Richards) B.; e. Kelowna (B.C.) Pub. Schs.; m. Audrey Lyne d. late Jack James, Vesuvius Bay, B.C., 16 Apr. 1955; children: Bradford, Kevin, Stephen, Gregory; Dir., Imasco Ltd.; Canadian Pacific Forest Products; Teck Corp.; Prime Resources; joined B.C. Social Credit Party 1952; el. mem. Leg. Assembly B.C. for S/ Okanagan 1973; el. Leader B.C. Social Credit Party 1973; Premier, Prov. of Brit. Columbia 1975–86; Past Pres. Kelowna Chamber Comm.; Past Pres. Kelowna Toastmasters Club; Campaign Dir., Kelowna & District Chamber of Comm.; Dir., Counc. for Candn. Unity; Gov., Olympic Trust of Can.; United Church; Clubs: Kelowna Gyro (Past Dir.); Kelowna; Kelowna Golf and Country.

**BENNETT, Winslow Wood;** executive; b. Minneapolis, Minn. 18 March 1925; s. Russell H. and Miriam von S. (Fletcher) B.; e. Phillips Acad. Andover, Mass. 1943; Univ. of Minn. Bachelor of Mech. Engn. 1949; m. Adele d. Lucien Wulsin, Cincinnati, Ohio 20 Oct. 1951; children: Winslow Wood Jr., Peter W., Frank B., Russell H.; Dir., Princeton Mining; Equity Silver Mines; MacDonald Dettwiler; Fairfax Financial, Xillix Corp.; recreations: fishing, tennis, skiing; Clubs: Vancouver; Shaughnessy Golf; Home: 3739 Angus Dr., Vancouver, B.C. V6J 4H6; Office: Suite 1880, 505 Burrard St., Vancouver, B.C. V7X 1M6.

**BENOIT, André,** M.Sc.Com.; insurance executive; b. Montreal, Que. 13 Apr. 1938; s. Benoit and Gilberte (St-Germain) B.; e. Univ. of Ottawa B. Com. 1960; Sherbrooke Univ. M.Sc.Com. 1961; m. Suzanne d. Robert Lafrance 6 Aug. 1960; children: Diane, Eric, Christine; BD. CHRMN. & DIR., LE GROUPE COMMERCE COMPAGNIE D'ASSURANCES 1979– ; Pres., Groupe de Placements Benoit; Hydro Maska Inc.; Dir., Annoit Inc.; Belair Insurance Co.; C.D.M.V. Inc.; Halifax Insurance Co.; Hydraska; ING Canada; Insuan Inc.; Placements Ger-Ben Inc.; joined Lévesque Beaubien 1961–62; Bolton Tremblay & Cie 1962–64; Portfolio Mgr. present Co. 1964, Vice Pres. & Secy. 1966; Dir. Chambre de Comm. de St-Hyacinthe; Inst. Cycle; Cercle Finance Placements; recreations: skiing, sailing, swimming, tennis; Clubs: St-Denis; Home: 615 rue Benoit, St-Hyacinthe, Qué. J2S 1L8; Office: 1177 Després, #102, St. Hyacinthe, Qué. J2S 6L6.

**BENOIT, Maj. Gen. Jean J.,** Q.H.P., C.D., B.A., M.D., C.R.C.P., C.S.P.Q.; physician; b. Rivière-du-Loup, Qué. 14 Feb. 1932; s. Joseph Octave and Germaine Marie (Soucy) B.; e. Laval Univ. B.A. 1952, M.D. 1958; m. Claudette d. Adrien Poitras 7 Sept. 1957; children: Guy, Marie-Josée, Richard, Julie; former Surgeon General, National Defence Headquarters; post-grad. studies in Anaesthesia, Toronto 1964–67; Chief of Anaesthesia, Oromocto Pub. Hosp. 1967–68; Candn. Forces Hosp. Halifax 1968–74; Candn. Forces Hosp. Valcartier (also Commandant) 1974–76; Nat. Defence Med. Centre 1976–85 (Chief of Anaesthesia; Physician; Commandant 1985–89); Commander, Candn. Forces Hosp. and Med. Supply System (CFHMSS) 1989–90; holds appt. Queen's Hon. Phys.; Cdr. Mt. Venerable Order St-John Jerusalem; mem. Candn. Anaesthetists Soc.; Coll. Phys. & Surgs. Prov. Qué.; AMQ; CMA; recreation: golf; Club: Hylands Golf; Home: 131 Chambord Private, Ottawa, Ont. K1V 0L3.

**BENOLIEL, Barbara,** B.A., M.B.Sc.; retail executive, researcher, counsellor, consultant; b. Toronto, Ont. 4 April 1954; d. Marvin and Evelyn (Lipton) Goodman; e. Univ. of Toronto B.A. (Hons.) 1976; George Brown College, Addiction Counselling 1979; Univ. of Tel Aviv M.B.Sc. 1988; Ph.D. Fellow, The Fielding Institute; m. Dan s. Henrietta and Leon B. 18 May 1976; children: Talia, Atara, Tamar; PRESIDENT, PREFERRED SOLUTIONS INC.; specialist in organizational behaviour & devel.; cert. addiction counsellor; Advr. to the Armed Forces 1982–84; publisher researcher in 'Family Business,' 'Women in Business,' 'Human Resource Professional'; Mem., Human Resource Profl. Assn. of Ont.; Candn. Assn. of Addiction Counsellors; Bd. Dir., Candn. Assn. of Family Enterprise (Ont.); Chair, Ctte. on Personal Advisory Groups; twice awarded Univ. of Toronto Award of Excellence; Mem., Darchai Noam; author and co-author of var. articles in journals in Canada & abroad; recreations: sailing, tennis; Office: 29 – 2 Connell Court, Toronto, Ont. M8Z 5T7.

**BENSLEY, Edward Horton,** M.B.E. (1946), B.A., M.D., D.Sc., F.R.C.P.C., F.C.I.C., F.A.C.P. educator; b. Toronto, Ont., 10 Dec. 1906; s. Benjamin Arthur and Ruth (Horton) B.; e. Univ. of Toronto, B.A. 1927, M.D. 1930 (1st Alex T. Fulton Scholar, in Natural & Phys. Sciences (1924), Jean Balmer Scholar. Science (1924), Edw. Blake Scholar. in Biol. and Med. Sciences (1925), Daniel Wilson Scholar. in Biol. and Med. Sciences (1926), Brit. Assn. for Advanc. of Science Bronze Medal (1927), Gold Medal for highest aggregate standing in med. course (1930); D.Sc. Acadia 1964; Emeritus Prof. of Med. and Hon. Osler Librarian, McGill Univ.; Consulting Phys., Montreal Gen. Hosp.; mem., Staff of Montreal Gen. Hosp. since 1932, and of McGill Univ. since 1941; formerly Vice Dean, Faculty of Med.; Publications: approx. 200 articles in med. and other journs.; Chrmn. Nutrition Panel, Def. Res. Bd. of Canada 1949–52; mem. Can. Council on Nutrition 1948–58; Chrmn. Comm. on Nutrition, C.M.A., 1951–54; Consult. in Nutrition, Can. Forces Med. Council 1957–60; Pres. Nutrition Soc. of Canada 1961–62; Pres. Can. Soc. of Clinical Chemists 1957–58; Hon. Sec. Can. Fed. of Biol. Societies 1957–61; Hon. Pres. Osler Soc. of McGill Univ. 1956–57, 1980; Pres. James McGill Soc. of McGill U. 1978–80; Hon. Consultant Royal Victoria Hospital 1962–67; Consultant in Metabolism and Toxicology, Reddy Memorial Hospital 1950–61; awarded Centennial Medal 1967; John B. Neilson Award (for contributions to medical history) Associated Medical Services 1985; Hon. or Emeritus Mem.: Amer. Assn. for History of Medicine; Amer. Osler Soc.; Beaumont Medical Club, Yale Univ.; Candn. Physiological Soc.; Candn. Soc. of Clinical Chemists; Candn. Soc. for Clinical Investigation; Candn. Soc. for History of Medicine; James McGill Soc., McGill Univ.; Osler Soc., McGill Univ.; Pharmacological Soc. of Can.; Sr. Mem., Candn. Medical Assn.; served in 2nd World War, Major, R.C.A.M.C. (Advisor in Nutrition); Alpha Omega Alpha; Unitarian; Home: 157 Morrison Ave., Montreal, Qué. H3R 1K5.

**BENSON, Crandall Adair,** B.ScF., M.Sc., M.ScF.; university professor; b. Palmerston, Ont. 24 June 1941; s. John Ivan and Opal Eileen (Ingram) B.; e. Ripley Dist. H.S. 1961; Univ. of Toronto B.Sc.F. 1966; Coll. of Environ. Sci. & Forestry Syracuse M.Sc., M.ScF. 1969; m. Evadne d. Dan Ward 1966; children: Dylan Ward, Laurel Heather; ASSOC. PROF., SCHOOL OF FORESTRY, LAKEHEAD UNIV. 1975– ; Unit Forester, Ont. Min. of Natural Resources 1969–71; Forestry Cons., Teme-Augama Anishnabai 1981– ; Forests for Tomorrow & expert witness, Environmental Assessment Hearings 1988–91; Bd. of Examiners, Ont. Profl. Foresters 1988– ; Chair, Forest Mngt. Working Group, Candn. Inst. of Forestry; cert. of appreciation, Fed. of Ont. Naturalists; author of 1 book chapter and several technical reports; recreations: nordic skiing, photography; club: Nordic Trails; Home: 624 Rosewood Cres., Thunder Bay, Ont. P7E 2R7; Office: School of Forestry, Lakehead Univ., Thunder Bay, Ont. P7B 5E1.

**BENSON, Eugene,** Ph.D.; educator; writer; b. Larne, N. Ireland 6 July 1928; s. John Joseph and Isobel (Green) B.; e. Nat. Univ. of Ireland B.A. 1950; Univ. of W. Ont. M.A. 1958; Univ. of Toronto Ph.D. 1966; m. Renate d. Walter and Elisabeth Niklaus 30 Apl. 1968; children: Ormonde, Shaun; PROF. OF ENGLISH, UNIV. OF GUELPH 1971– ; Lectr. Royal Mil. Coll. Kingston, Ont. 1960–61; Asst. Prof. of Eng. Laurentian Univ. 1961–64; Asst. Prof. present Univ. 1965, Assoc. Prof. 1967; mem. Ctte. Ont. Univs. 1970–72; Lectr. 5 N.Z. univs. as Vice Chancellors of N.Z. Univs. Visitor 1986; Dir. The Edward Johnson Music Found. and Guelph Spring Festival 1966–86, Pres. 1971–72, 1987–88; author 'The Bulls of Ronda' novel 1976; 'Power Game, or the Making of a Prime Minister' novel 1980; 'J.M. Synge' critical study 1982; 'The Summoning of Everyman' libretto, performed Stratford Festival 1974; 'Heloise and Abelard' libretto, performed Candn. Opera Co. 1973; 'Psycho Red' libretto, performed Guelph Spring Festival 1978; 'The Ram' one-act play 1967; 'The Gunner's Rope' and 'Joan of Arc's Violin' one-act plays CBC Studio '70 1970, Backdoor Theatre Toronto 1972; 'The Doctor's Wife' CBC Sunday Theatre 1973; co-transl. various Qué. plays and 'Beethoven: The Man and His Times' (F. Grasberger) 1970; ed. 'Encounter: Canadian Drama in Four Media' anthology 1973; co-author 'English-Canadian Theatre' critical study 1987; co-ed. 'Oxford Companion to Canadian Theatre' 1989; ed. 'Canadian Drama, L'Art dramatique canadien' 1980–90; mem. Writers' Union Can. (Chrmn. 1983–84); P.E.N. (Co-Pres. -Eng. Can. 1984–85, Vice Pres. 1985–90); Assn. Candn. Theatre Hist.; Candn. Assn. Irish Studies;

recreations: travel, sailing; Home: 55 Palmer St., Guelph, Ont. N1E 2P9; Office: Guelph, Ont. N1G 2W1.

**BENSON, Kenneth Peter,** C.A.; forestry executive; b. Vancouver, B.C. 1 March 1927; s. Lawrence Benson; e. Univ. of B.C.; C.A. 1953; m. Joyce d. Charles Heino 5 Nov. 1949; children: David, Sally; CHRMN. AND CHIEF EXTVE. OFFR., FINLAY FOREST INDUSTRIES LTD. 1992– ; joined Powell River Co. 1955, Asst. Controller 1958; BC Forest Products Co. 1962 Comptroller, Vice Pres. Finance 1967, Dir. 1970, Exec. Vice Pres. Operations 1972, Sr. Exec. Vice Pres. 1974, Pres. and Chief Operating Offr. 1976, Pres. & C.E.O. 1979, Chrmn. & C.E.O. 1984–87; Chrmn. 1987–91; Club: Vancouver; Home: 6329 Angus Dr., Vancouver, B.C. V6M 3P4; Office: #680 Bentall One, 505 Burrard St., Vancouver, B.C. V7X 1M4.

**BENSON, Kenneth Samuel,** B.Comm., LL.B.; executive; b. Vancouver, B.C. 12 Aug. 1937; s. Samuel and Ruby Gertrude (Poole) B.; e. Univ. of B.C., B.Comm. 1961, LL.B. 1962; m. Inara Blums 8 Aug. 1964; VICE PRES. PERSONNEL & ADM. CANADIAN PACIFIC LIMITED 1986– ; Dir.: The Fraser Inst.; Extve. Ctte., Inst. for Donations and Public Affairs Rsch.; Mount Royal College Found.; Montreal General Hosp. Rsch. Inst.; The McGill Graduate Studies and Rsch. Advisory Bd.; called to Bar of B.C. 1963; Petrol. Land Man, The Atlantic Refining Co. Vancouver 1963; Barrister & Solr., Guild, Yule & Co. Vancouver 1965; Barrister, Solr. & Corporate Sec., Bulkley Valley Forest Industries Ltd. 1968; Barrister, Solr. & Asst. Corporate Sec., Cominco Ltd. 1972, Corporate Sec. 1980, Vice Pres., Corporate Sec. 1984; Vice Pres. Canadian Pacific Enterprises Ltd. Calgary 1985, Vice Pres. Adm. & Sec. 1985; Vice Pres. Adm. present Co., Calgary 1985; mem. Conf. Bd. Can.; Conf. Bd. USA; Law Soc. B.C.; Candn. Bar Assn.; Human Resource Planning Soc.; recreations: music, hiking; Club: Sporting Club du Sanctuaire Montréal; Office: 800 Place du Canada, P.O. Box 6042, Station A, Montréal, Qué. H3C 3E4.

**BENSON, Michael,** B.Sc., C.L.U.; life underwriter; b. Alta. 20 July 1929; s. John and Anna (Stoyka) Benca; e. Wayne State Univ. Detroit B.Sc. 1953; C.L.U. 1955; m. Patricia Burger 20 Nov. 1955; children: Barbara, Jo-Ann, Robert, William, Richard; PRIN. MICHAEL BENSON & ASSOCIATES LTD. 1952– ; Pres. Benway Insurance Brokers; served Prudential Assurance Co. 35 yrs., Leading Agt., mem. Adv. Council 1984–87; Charter Pres. Windsor Chapter Chart. Life Underwriters Inst. 1966; Charter mem. Windsor Estate Planning Council 1976; Dir. Life Underwriters Assn. Can. 1985, Chrmn. Taxation & Legis. Ctte. 1986; mem. Windsor C. of C. Tax & Finance Ctte. 1986; Div. Vice Pres. Million Dollar Round Table 1985, 1987, Speaker, Chrmn. Internat. mem. Task Force 1984, Life & Qualifying mem.; Pres. Life Underwriters Assn. Can. 1987; mem. Faculty Ont. Life Ins. Sch. 1983–84; Internat. Speaker Sales Cong. & Ind. Meetings; Fund Raising Campaign Chrmn. Most Precious Blood Ch. 1975; recreations: golf, curling; Club: Beach Grove Golf & Country (Treas.); Home: 7250 Riverside Dr. E., Windsor, Ont.

**BENSON, Robert L.,** P.Eng., B.Sc.; engineering company executive; b. Winnipeg, Man. 16 May 1947; s. Leslie W. and Glenna C. (McCarthy) B.; e. Univ. of Manitoba B.Sc. 1969; m. Patricia L. d. Robert and Lillian Hughes 16 Aug. 1969; children: Robert C., Scott L.; EXECUTIVE VICE-PRESIDENT, CORPORATE DEVELOPMENT & MARKETING, MONENCO AGRA INC.; Staff Gas Engineer, Shell Canada 1969–79; joined Monenco Group Limited 1979; held positions of Vice-Pres. Corp. Planning, Vice-Pres. Marketing, Extve. Vice-Pres. Western Region; Mem., 1991 Campaign Cabinet, Calgary United Way; Pres., Energy Project Engineering Contractors Assn. 1989; Mem., Assn. of Profl. Engr., Geologists & Geophysicists of Alta.; recreations: golf, skiing; clubs: Pinebrook Golf & Country (Vice Pres. 1989–90), Calgary Petroleum Club; Home: 47 Oakmount Court S.W., Calgary, Alta. T2V 5B9; Office: 400, 801 – 6 Ave. S.W., Calgary, Alta. T2P 3W3.

**BENSON, Susan,** N.D.D., A.T.D.; theatre designer; painter; b. Bexley Heath Kent 22 Apr. 1942; d. John and Nella B.; e. Talbot Heath Sch., Bournemouth; N.D.D. 1958–62; West of England Coll. of Art Bristol A.T.D. 1963; came to Can. 1966; m. Michael s. Al and Joan Whitfield 5 June 1971; Designer, Stratford Festival 1974–87; productions incl. 'Twelfth Night' 1975; 'A Midsummer Night's Dream' with Jessica Tandy, Maggie Smith 1976–77; 'The Mikado' 1982–84; The Old Vic., London, Eng. 1984; 'The Gondoliers' 1983–84; U.S. Tour 1986–87; Cabaret 1987; Head of Design, Stratford Festival 1981–82; Asst. Prof. Univ. of Illinois 1970–74; Lectr. Nat. Theatre Sch., Banff Sch. of Fine Arts; York Univ.; Resident Designer Krannert Centre for the Performing Arts 1970–74; Designer for: Candn. Opera Co.; Nat. Ballet of Can.; Nat. Arts Centre; Manitoba Theatre Centre; Vancouver Playhouse; Theatre New Brunswick; Young People's Theatre; St. Lawrence Centre; Neptune Theatre; Roundabout Theatre, N.Y. City; Denver Centre Theatre Co., Col.; designer, 'Jeanne' Birmingham Repertory Theatre England 1985; 'Steps' Royal Winnipeg Ballet 1986; 'Don Quichotte' New York City Opera 1986; solo exhbns. of paintings 1980–84; portraits incl. Maureen Forrester, William Hutt, Nicholas Pennell; illus. incl. Toronto Symphony Poster 1983–84; mem. Assoc. Designers of Can.; Un. Scenic Artists; Can. Counc. Grant 1970; winner Dora Mavor Moore Award 1980, 1981, 2 in 1987; Ace Television Award for Costume Design 1986; rep. Can. at Prague Quadrennial 1979, 1983; el. to Royal Candn. Acad. 1985.

**BENTALL, David Clark,** B.comm.; real estate developer; b. Vancouver, B.C. 22 June 1955; s. H. Clark and Phyllis Emily (Weedon) B. ; e. Univ. of B.C., B.Comm. 1979; m. Alison Margaret d. Margaret and Lewis O'Leary 2 June 1978; children: Christine, Jonathan, Jennifer, Stephanie; PRES. & C.E.O., THE DOMINION COMPANY 1993– ; Extve. Asst. to the C.E.O., The Bentall Group 1980–81; Bus. Devel. Offr., Dominion Constr. Co. Ltd. 1981–82; Devel. Offr., Bentall Investments Ltd. 1982–84; Cadillac Fairview Corp. Ltd. 1984–86; Vice-Pres., The Bentall Group, Calif. 1986–88; Extve. Vice Pres. & C.O.O., The Dominion Co. 1988–91; Pres. & C.O.O. 1991–93; His Royal Highness Duke of Edinburgh Commonwealth Study Conf. participant 1980; Gov., Business Council of B.C.; Bd. Mem., St. George's School; Bd. Mem., Pearson College of the Pacific; Trustee, Langham Trust; Home: 2825 West 30th Avenue, Vancouver, B.C. V6L 1Z1; Office: 400 – Two Bentall Ctr., 555 Burrard St., Vancouver, B.C. V7X 1S9.

**BENTALL, Harold Clark,** O.C., B.A.Sc., LL.D., P.Eng.; company executive; b. Vancouver, B.C. 4 May 1915; s. Charles and Edna Olive (Gilmour) B.; e. Univ. of British Columbia, B.A.Sc. 1938; m. Phyllis Emily Weedon, 16 June 1938; children: Mrs. Helen Burnham, Charles Ernest, Mrs. Mary George, David Clark; HONORARY CHRMN., THE DOMINION CO.; Dir., Internat. Forest Products Ltd.; joined Dominion Construction in 1938, el. a Dir. 1943, Vice-Pres. 1950, Pres. & C.E.O. 1955–80, Chrmn. 1980– ; Baptist; recreations: yachting; Clubs: Vancouver; Shaughnessy Golf & Country; Royal Vancouver Yacht; Home: 2610 West 50th Ave., Vancouver, B.C. V6P 1B7; Office: Suite 300, Two Bentall Centre, Vancouver, B.C. V7X 1S9.

**BENTALL, Robert G.,** B.A.Sc., P.Eng.; company executive; b. Vancouver, B.C. 6 Nov. 1922; s. Charles and Edna Olive (Gilmour) B.; e. Univ. of B.C., B.A.Sc. 1944; m. Lynda L. Wager; children: Robert, Laura Nelson, Mrs. Ruth Anderson; CHRMN. & C.E.O., THE BENTALL CORPORATION; Clubs: Vancouver; Capilano Golf & Country; Home: Penthouse 11, 111–18th St., West Vancouver, B.C. V7V 3V3; Office: 3100, 3 Bentall Centre, Vancouver, B.C. V7X 1B1.

**BENTLEY, C. Fred,** M.Sc., Ph.D., D.Sc.; university professor Emeritus; b. Cambridge, Mass., 14 March 1914; s. Charles Fred and Lavina Ann (MacKenzie) B.; e. Victoria High Sch. (1932), and Edmonton Normal Sch. (1933), Edmonton, Alta; Univ. of Alberta, B.Sc. 1939 M.Sc. 1942; Univ. of Minnesota, Ph.D. 1945; Univ. of Guelph, D.Sc. 1984; Univ. of Alta. D.Sc. 1990; m. Helen Signe, d. Thorwald Petersen, 16 Sept. 1943; children: Ann Catherine, Theodore Carl; PROF. EMERITUS UNIV. OF ALBERTA, since 1979; Bd. Govs., Internat. Devel. Research Centre 1970–74; taught school, 1933–36; Instr. in Soil Science, Univ. of Minn., 1942–43; Instr. and Asst. Prof., Soil Science, Univ. of Sask., 1943–46; Asst. Prof., Assoc. Prof., Prof. of Soil Science, Univ. of Alta., 1946–79; Can. Colombo Plan Specialist in Ceylon, 1952–53; Dean, Faculty of Agric., Univ. of Alta., 1959–68; F.A.O. Consultant in Thailand, 1962; Centennial Lect., Agric. Inst. of Can., 1967; Leader, Can. Agric. Task Force to India, 1967; Agric. Advisor External Aid Office, Ottawa, 1968–69; Leader, Can. Agric. Team to Sri Lanka, 1979 and 1980; Leader, Can. Teams Agric. Educ. to China 1983; Chrmn. Bd. Trustees, Internat. Bd. Soil Res. and Mgt. 1983–87; mem. and Chrmn. Gov. Bd. ICRISAT, Hyderabad, India 1972–82; Fellow, Royal Society of Canada; Fellow, Am. Soc. of Agronomy; Fellow, Soil Science Soc. of America; Fellow, Am. Assn. Adv. Science; Agric. Inst. Can. (Pres. 1963–64); Fellow, Cdn. Soc. Soil Science (Past Pres.); Fellow, Nat. Acad. Agric. Scis., India 1991; Honor Award, Soil Cons. Soc. Amer. 1984; mem. Alta. Inst. Agrols. (Past Pres.); Am. Soc. Soil Science; Am. Soc. Agron.; Past Pres. Int. Soc. Soil Sci. (Pres. 1974–78); Klink Lecturer, Agric. Inst. Can. 1981–82; author of some 100 scient. papers, and invited major addresses; awarded Centennial Medal; Queen's Jubilee Medal; recipient, Univ. of Minn. Outstanding Achievement Award; Alberta Premier's Award for Excellence 1979; Agronomy Merit Award, Prairie provinces 1982; Alta. Agricultural Hall of Fame 1985; Alberta Order of Excellence 1987; Hon. Mem., World Assn. for Soil and Water Conservation 1989; H.H. Bennett Award for excellence in conservation, Soil and Water Cons. Soc. 1989; Internat. Recognition Award, Agric. Inst. Can. 1992; Distinguished Agrologist Award, Alberta Inst. Agrologists 1993; Home: 13103 – 66 Ave., Edmonton, Alta. T6H 1Y6.

**BENTLEY, David Michael Reid,** M.A., Ph.D., M.A. (Candn. Studies), F.R.S.A.; educator; b. Kitale, Kenya 14 Aug. 1947; s. Michael Archibald and Margaret Morrison (Reid) B.; e. Shawnigan Lake Sch. B.C.; Univ. of Victoria B.A. 1969; Dalhousie Univ. M.A. 1970; Univ. of London King's Coll. Ph.D. 1974; Carleton Univ. M.A. (Candn. Studies) 1976; m. Susan d. F.A.J. and E.M. Wakeman-Long 27 May 1972; children: Michael John David Reid, Simon Thomas David Wakeman, Diana Margaret Susan; PROF. OF ENG., UNIV. OF WESTERN. ONT. 1983– , Asst. Prof. 1975; Fellow, Westminster Inst. for Ethics and Human Values; mem. Econ. Rsch. Council London, Eng.; Pres. Candn. Inst. Hist. Microreproductions, Ottawa 1988–92; author numerous publs. Candn. and Victorian lit. including 'The Gay Grey Moose: Essays on the Ecologies and Mythologies of Canadian Poetry, 1690-1990' 1992; 'Mimic Fires: Accounts of Early Long Poems on Canada' 1994; Ed. and Founder 'Canadian Poetry: Studies, Documents, Reviews' 1977– ; Ed. Candn. Poetry Press Series Early Candn. Long Poems 1986– ; recipient, Edward G. Pleva Award for Excellence in Teaching 1993; mem. Assn. Candn. Teachers Eng.; Assn. Candn. & Que. Lits.; Am. Soc. Aesthetics; Bibliographical Soc. of Canada; Nat. Consultative Ctte. Hist. Lit. Instn. Can.; Anglican; recreations: gardening, carousing; Club: Farmers (London, Eng.); Home: 34 Mayfair Dr., London, Ont. N6A 2M6; Office: London, Ont. N6A 3K7.

**BENTLEY, G. Firman,** B.Com., B.Ed.; executive; b. Truro, N.S. 12 Feb. 1934; s. William Wilkinson and Hazel Mary (Crowe) B.; e. Mt. Allison Univ. B.Com. and B.Ed. 1957; Harvard Univ. Grad. Advanced Mgmt. Course 1984; m. Nancy Lee d. Morley and Helen Roberts 18 May 1957; children: Paul, LeeAnn, Craig; CHRMN. & C.E.O., ADAMAC MANAGEMENT GROUP INC. 1992– ; Personnel Mgr. Polysar Ltd., Sarnia, Ont. 1964, Dir. of Personnel 1968, Gen. Mgr. Polysar Belgium, Antwerp 1971, Vice Pres. Eur. Operations 1974, Vice Pres. Rubber Operations N. & S. Am. 1978, Group Vice Pres. Global Rubber & Plastics 1981; Group Vice Pres., Basic Petrochemicals 1985; Pres., Basic Petrochemicals 1988; Pres. and C.E.O., Petrosar Ltd. 1985–88; Sr. Vice Pres., Nova Corp. of Alberta 1988–91; Chrmn. Sectoral Adv. Group Internat. Trade Energy, Chemicals & Petrochemicals; mem. Internat. Trade Adv. Counc. (Govt. of Can.); Soc. Chem. Ind.; Dir., Learning for a Sustainable Future; Ontario Waste Management Corp.; Chrmn., Sarnia Found.; Mem., Bd. of Regents, Mt. Allison Univ.; Home: R.R. 1, Camlachie, Ont. N0N 1E0; Office: 265 N. Front St., Suite 505, Sarnia, Ont. N7T 7X1.

**BENTLEY, Gerald Eades Jr.,** B.A., B.Litt., D.Phil., D.Litt., F.R.S.C.; b. Chicago, Ill. 23 Aug. 1930; s. Gerald Eades and Esther (Felt) B.; e. Princeton Univ., B.A. 1952; Oxford Univ., B.Litt. 1954, D.Phil. 1956; D.Litt. 1985; m. Anne Elizabeth Kathryne Louise, d. Raymond Budd, 22 June 1952; two d., Sarah Elizabeth Esther, Julia Greenwood; PROF. OF ENGLISH, UNIVERSITY OF TORONTO; Teacher, Univ. of Chicago 1956–60, Univ. d'Alger (Algeria) 1967–68; Univ. of Poona (India) 1975–76; Fudan Univ. (Shanghai, China) 1982–83; joined present Univ. 1960; Visiting Lectr., Eng., Japan, Australia, New Zealand, China, Thailand, Sri Lanka, India, Wales, Hong Kong, Spain, Canada, Italy, Korea, U.S.A.; Guggenheim Fellow 1958–59; Can. Council Fellow 1963–64, 1970–71, 1977–78; S.S.H.R.C. Fellow 1982–85, 1991–94; Harold White Fellow, Nat. Lib. of Australia 1989; Fulbright Lectr. 1967–68, 1975–76, 1982–83; Connaught Fellow 1991–92; Rockefeller Found. (Bellagio Fellow) 1991; Visiting Prof., University Coll., Swansea, 1985; Univ. of Hyderabad (India) 1988; Fudan Univ. (China) 1988; Visiting Rsch. Prof., Princeton Univ. 1992; Visiting Rsch. Fellow, Merton Coll., Oxford 1993; research also in France, Austria, Germany, Switzerland, Italy, Taiwan, Iran, Scotland, Egypt, Tanzania; ed.: Wm. Blake's 'Vala or the Four Zoas' 1963; 'The Early Engravings of Flaxman's Classical Designs' 1964; ed. Wm. Blake's 'Tiriel' 1967; 'Blake Records' 1969; 'The Blake Collection of Mrs. Landon K. Thorne' 1971; ed. Wm. Blake's 'America' 1974; 'William Blake: The Critical

Heritage' 1975; ed. 'Editing Eighteenth-Century Novels' 1975; 'A Bibliography of George Cumberland' 1975; ed. Wm. Blake's 'Europe' 1975; 'Blake Books' 1977 (Jenkins Award for Bibliography 1979); ed. 'William Blake's Writings' 2 vols. 1978; ed. 'William Blake's Writings in Conventional Typography' 1984; 'Blake Records Supplement' 1988; ed. George Cumberland, 'The Captive of the Castle of Sennaar' 1991; author of articles in various lit. journs.; mem., Modern Lang. Assn.; Bibliog. Soc.; Oxford Bibliog. Soc.; Conf. Ed. Problems (sometime Chrmn.); Fellow, Royal Soc. of Can. 1986; recreations: travel, dam building, book collecting; Home: 246 MacPherson Ave., Toronto, Ont. M4V 1A2.

**BENTLEY, Kenneth Chessar,** D.D.S., M.D.,C.M., F.I.C.D., F.A.C.D., (Hon.) F.R.C.D.(C.); oral and maxillofacial surgeon; educator; b. Montreal, Que. 22 Sept. 1935; s. Albert Edwin and Lilian Beatrice (Hoare) B.; e. McGill Univ. D.D.S. 1958, M.D.,C.M. 1962; m. Jean d. Campbell and Margaret Benvie Wadsworth 19 Aug. 1961; children: Douglas, Margaret; PROF. OF DENTISTRY, McGILL UNIV. 1975– ; Dental Surg.-in-Chief Montreal Gen. Hosp. 1970– ; internship and residency Montreal Gen. Hosp. and Bellevue Hosp. New York 1962–66; Asst. Prof. McGill Univ. 1966, Assoc. Prof. 1967, Prof. 1975, Dean of Dentistry 1977–87; Jr. Asst. Dental Surg. Montreal Gen. Hosp. 1966, Assoc. Dental Surg. and Assoc. Dir. Dept. Dentistry 1968; consultant in oral and maxillofacial surg. Montreal Children's Hosp., Reddy Mem. Hosp., Royal Victoria Hosp., St. Mary's Hosp.; co-author 'Advanced Oral Radiographic Interpretation' 1979; Fellow, Pierre Fauchard Acad.; Fellow, Internat. College of Dentists; Fellow, Am. College of Dentists; Fellow, Royal College of Dentists of Canada; Fellow, Academy of Internat. Dental Studies; Fellow, Academie Dentaire du Qué.; Assn. Oral & Maxillofacial Surgs. Que.; Bellevue Soc. Oral Surgs.; Candn. Dental Assn. (Chrmn. Council Hosp. Services 1971–75 and Council on Educ. 1982–85); Candn. Assn. Oral & Maxillofacial Surgs. (Secy.-Treas. 1970–71); Internat. Assn. Study Pain; Internat. Assn. Oral Surgs.; Lafleur Reporting Soc.; Montreal Dental Club (Secy. 1968, Pres. 1992); Nat. Dental Examining Bd. Can.; Council on Dental Accreditation of Canada; Order Dentists Que.; United Church; recreations: music, pipe organ; Home: 23 Anwoth Rd., Westmount, Qué. H3Y 2E6; Office: 1650 Cedar Ave., Montreal, Qué. H3G 1A4.

**BENTLEY, Lorne Kenneth,** B.Comm., C.A.; chartered accountant; b. Montreal, Que. 15 Dec. 1933; s. Archibald Frederick and Kate Phillis (Mennenga) B.; e. Lower Canada College Montreal 1951; Sir George Williams Univ. (Concordia) B.Comm. 1957; m. Dorothy Joan d. John and Marjorie Riches 6 Oct. 1962; children: John, Scott, Martha; DIRECTOR, ONTARIO WASTE MANAGEMENT CORPORATION 1984– ; Cooper & Lybrand 1957–65; Asst. Treas., Quebec Iron & Titanium Corp. 1965–71; Asst. Gen. Mgr., Admin., Manitoba Div., Inco Limited 1971–75; Vice-Pres., Finance & Sec., The Quebec & Ontario Paper Co. Limited 1975–80; Deputy Comptroller, The Bank of N.S. 1980–82; Vice-Pres. & Chief Financial Offr., Campbell Resources Inc. 1982–84; Mem., Financial Extves. Inst.; Candn. Inst. of C.A.s; Inst. of C.A.s of Ont.; Pres., Que. Assn. of Protestant School Bds. 1970–71; club: Toronto Bd. of Trade; Home: 30 Dalhousie Ave., St. Catharines, Ont. L2N 4W4; Office: 2 Bloor St. W., 11th Floor, Toronto, Ont. M4W 3E2.

**BENTLEY, Peter John Gerald,** O.C., LL.D.; executive; b. Vienna, Austria 17 March 1930; s. Leopold Lionel Garrick and Antoinette Ruth Bentley; e. St. George's Sch., Vancouver, B.C.; Univ. of Brit. Columbia Sch. of Forestry; Banff Sch. Advanced Mang.; m. Sheila Farrington McGiverin, 23 May 1953; four d. Barbara Ruth, Susan Patricia, Joan Katherine, Lisa Maria; one s. Michael Peter; CHRMN., C.E.O. & DIR., CANFOR CORPORATION; CANADIAN FOREST PRODUCTS LTD.; Co-Chrmn. & Dir., Howe Sound Pulp & Paper Ltd.; Canfor-Weldwood Distribution Ltd.; Mem. International Adv. Bd., Chemical Bank, N.Y.; Dir.: Bank of Montreal; Shell Canada Limited; Seaboard Shipping Co. Ltd.; Past Chrmn. & Trustee, Vancouver General Hosp. Foundation; Dir., Jr. Achievment of Can.; Past Chrmn., Business Counc. of B.C.; Vice Chrmn., Business Council on Nat. Issues, Ottawa; Advisory Council, Fac. of Comm. and Bus. Admin, Univ. of B.C.; mem., Univ. of BC Forestry Advisory Ctte.; Trustee, Forest Alliance of B.C.; Past Pres., Hon. Dir. and Hon. life mem. Canadian Forestry Assn. of B.C.; Trustee B.C. Sports Hall of Fame and Museum; Hon. Dir., Candn. Prof. Golfers Assn.; Gov., Olympic Trust of Can.; Officer, Order of Canada; Honorary Doctor of Laws (LL.D.); Clubs: Capilano Golf & Country; Marine Drive Golf; Vancouver Lawn Tennis & Badminton; Vancouver; Thunderbird Country (Palm Springs, Calif.); Royal and Ancient Golf Club of St. Andrews, Scotland; The Morningside (Rancho Mirage, California); Office: 2900–1055 Dunsmuir St., P.O. Box 49420, Bentall Postal Stn., Vancouver, B.C. V7X 1B5.

**BÉRARD, André;** banker; b. Bedford, Que. 13 Aug. 1940; e. Coll. Viateur 1956; Inst. of Candn. Bankers, Fellow's Dipl. 1967; Mem., Wyman Task Force, Special Mngt. Program, Harvard Univ. 1985; CHAIRMAN OF THE BOARD & CHIEF EXECUTIVE OFFICER, NATIONAL BANK OF CANADA 1990– ; Asst. Mgr., International Credit, National Bank of Canada 1972; Supt. & Mgr. International 1973; Asst. Gen. Mgr. International 1975; Vice-Pres. International 1977; Senior Vice-Pres. & Gen. Mgr. International 1980; Sr. Vice-Pres. & Gen. Mgr. Credit Div. 1981; Extve. Vice-Pres., National Accounts 1982–84; Senior Executive Vice-Pres., Banking 1984; Pres. & Chief Operating Offr. 1986; Pres. & Chief Executive Offr. 1989; Dir. & Chrmn., NBC Export Devel. Corp. Inc.; National Bank Export Finance Co. Inc.; Dir., National Bank of Canada; Natcan Internat. Trade Financing Co. Limited; Natcan Finance (Asia) Ltd.; The Macdonald Stewart Fdn.; Dir. & Mem., Audit Ctte., Le Groupe Vidéotron Ltée.; Télé-Métropole Inc.; Noranda Inc.; Mem., Bd. of Gov., Conseil du Patronat du Qué.; C. de C. du Qué.; Mem., Policy Ctte. of the Business Council on Nat. Issues; International Trade Advisory Ctte.; Mem., Cons. des gouv. assoc. de l'Univ. de Montréal; Canada / France Business Relns. Club; Adv. Ctte. to the Prime Minister on the Bus./Govt. Extve. Exchange Program; Chrmn., Extve. Council, Candn. Banker's Assn. 1986–89; Univ. of Ottawa, hon. doctorate 1991; Office: 600 de La Gauchetière Ouest, Montréal, Qué. H3B 4L2.

**BERCHARD, Morris,** B.A.; employee assistance consultant; b. Winnipeg, Man. 10 Aug. 1955; s. Simon and Eva (Szmulewicz) B.; e. Univ. of Winnipeg B.A. 1976; EXECUTIVE VICE-PRES., WARREN SHEPELL CONSULTANT CORP. 1982– ; Researcher-Developer, Age & Opportunity, Inc. 1977–78; Assessor, Visiting Homemakers Assn. 1979–82; develops and markets employee assistance programs; Mem., Bd. of Trade; Employee Assistance Soc. of N. Am.; Am. Mngt. Assn.; Human Resource Professionals Assn. of Ont.; recreations: tennis, cycling, swimming, music; Home: 12 Playter Blvd., Toronto, Ont. M4K 2V9; Office: 170 Bloor St. W., Suite 600, Toronto, Ont. M5S 1T9.

**BERCHEM, Frederick Ronald,** C.D., B.A., M.A.; shipmaster, author, artist; b. Saltcoats, Ayrshire, Scotland 6 Aug. 1931; s. Frederick William and Nannie-May Cuthbertson (Bowman) B.; e. Rossall Sch., Lancashire, England; Univ. of Toronto, B.A. (Hons.) 1964, M.A. 1968; m. Patricia d. Frank and Elizabeth Beckwith 15 Aug. 1959; children: Anthony, Fiona, Isabel; MASTER OF SCIENTIFIC RESEARCH VESSELS, FED. DEPT. OF FISHERIES & OCEANS, ON GREAT LAKES & EAST COAST OF CAN. 1977– ; served Royal Navy & Royal Candn. Navy, specializing in submarines (Lt.) 1954–60; Royal Candn. Naval Reserve (Commanding Offr. H.M.C. ships Porte St. Louis, Porte St. Jean 1962, 1971–74 & H.M.C.S. Porte Dauphine 1974–75) 1960–76; Rank of Commander 1970; H.S. Hist. Teacher 1964–67, 1969–72; Commanding Offr., H.M.C.S. York, Toronto & Hon. A.D.C. to His Excellency the Gov. Gen. of Can. 1971–73; One-man exhib. of watercolours at Gall. Ingénu, Toronto 1978; at Alice Peck Gall., Burlington 1984; several works sold to priv. collections; Mem., Naval Offr. Assn. of Can.; author: 'The Yonge Street Story (1793–1860) 1977, 'Ships in Bottles' 1989, (Italian ed.) 1992; recreations: reading, walking, travel, model-making; club: Royal Candn. Military Inst.; Office: c/o Ship Div., Bedford Inst. of Oceanography, P.O. Box 1006, Dartmouth, N.S. B2Y 4A2.

**BERCUSON, David Jay,** M.A., Ph.D.; educator; b. Montreal, Que. 31 Aug. 1945; s. Joseph Myer and Sylvia (Green) B.; e. Monklands High Sch. Montreal 1962; Sir George Williams Univ. B.A. 1966; Univ. of Toronto M.A. 1967, Ph.D. 1971; children: Michael Solomon, Sharon Rena; m. Barrie Bercuson Keel d. Gordon and Anne K.; DEAN, FACULTY OF GRADUATE STUDIES 1989– ;and PROF. OF HISTORY, UNIV. OF CALGARY 1978– ; Visiting Asst. Prof. Univ. Calgary 1970, Asst. Prof. 1971, Assoc. Prof. 1975, Pres. Faculty Assn. 1974–75, mem. Gen. Faculties Council 1977–80; Pres. Calgary Hebrew Sch. 1986–88; rec'd Lt. Gov.'s Silver Medal for Hist. 1966; Can. Council Doctoral Dissertation Fellowships 1966–70 and Leave Fellowship 1975; Social Science & Humanities Research Council Leave Fellowship 1979; Killam Resident Fellowship 1981; Killam Rsch. Fellowship 1985–87; Ed. 'Canadian Historical Review' 1977–83; author 'Confrontation at Winnipeg' 1974; 'Winnipeg Strike: 1919' 1974; 'Canada and the Burden of Unity' 1977; 'Fools and Wise Men' 1978; 'The Secret Army' 1983; 'The Great Brain Robbery' 1984; 'Canada and the Birth of Israel' 1985; 'True Patriot: The Life of Brooke Claxton' 1993; various articles w. Candn. labour & social hist., the middle e., Candn. regionalism, Candn. defence and foreign policy in numerous mags., newspapers, freelance broadcaster; mem. Candn. Hist. Assn.; Fellow, Royal Soc. of Can.; Jewish; Office: 2500 University Dr. N.W., Calgary, Alta. T2N 1N4.

**BERCUVITZ, Judith Singer,** M.M.A.; art school administrator; b. Amsterdam, N.Y. 22 May 1938; d. Herbert Theodore and Ruth (Sack) Singer; e. Cornell Univ., B.A. 1960; McGill Univ., M.M.A. 1975; m. Mark s. Mabel and Max B. 20 Dec. 1959; children: Richard, Jeffrey, Debra; Dir., Sch. of Fine Arts, Saidye Bronfman Centre 1988–91; Music Specialist, PSBGM (teacher) 1960–61; Instr. of music theory, McGill Univ. 1976–84; Dir. of Volunteers, YWCA of Montreal 1984–88; private piano teacher 1960–69; choral conductor 1985–89; Bd. of Dir., Caldwell Residence for the Elderly, Montreal; Home: 786 Upper Lansdowne, Montreal, Qué. H3Y 1J8.

**BERCZI, Andrew,** B.Sc., B.A., M.B.A., Ph.D.; educator; b. Budapest, Hungary 15 Aug. 1934; s. Stephan and Iren (Bartha) B.; e. Univ. of Tech. Sciences, Budapest, Indust. & Electr. Engn. 1951–56; Sir George Williams Univ. B.Sc. 1961; B.A. 1963; McGill Univ. M.B.A. 1965; Ph.D. 1972; m. Susan; d. Zoltan Bartok; two s. Thomas Edgar, Peter Alexander; VICE-PRESIDENT, FINANCE AND ADMINISTRATION, WILFRID LAURIER UNIV.; served as Engr., Supvr. Engn., Supvr. Computer Systems in Engn., HQ-Accounting and Business Information Systems Depts., Bell Telephone Co. of Canada 1956–65; Prof. of Quantitative Methods and Chrmn. of Dept., Sir George Williams Univ. 1965–72; Dean, Fac. of Comm. and Adm., Concordia Univ. 1972–78; Dean, Faculty of Grad. Studies, Wilfrid Laurier Univ. 1978–87; Vice-Pres., Planning, Finance and Information Services, Wilfred Laurier Univ. 1987–92; rec'd Can. Council and Prov. Que. Scholarships; McConnell Fellowship; NSERC and SSHRC research grants; author several textbooks, monographs and over 50 articles and papers in mang. science and info. systems areas, various journs. and confs.; mem. Data Processing Mang. Assn.; Assn. Computing Machinery; Systems & Procedures Assn.; Candn. Operations Research Soc.; Operations Research Soc. Am.; Inst. Mang. Science; Am. Mang. Assn.; Fellow, Am. Assn. Advanc. Science; Inst. of Electric. and Electron. Engrs. (IEEE); R. Catholic; recreations: tennis, skiing, sailing, swimming; Home: 76 McCarron Cresc., Waterloo, Ont. N2L 5N1; Office: 75 University Ave. W., Waterloo, Ont. N2L 3C5.

**BERENG, His Excellency Nehemia Sekhonyana,** B.A., M.P.A.; diplomat; b. Lesotho 16 April 1948; s. Cranmer Theko and Caroline Malira (Lerotholi) B.; e. Eagle's Peak H.S. 1967; Univ. of Botswana, Lesotho and Swaziland B.A. 1972; Univ. of Pittsburgh M.P.A. 1981; m. Ntee d. Tšekelo and 'Mamoroesi Moshoeshoe 25 Feb. 1976; children: Mpona, Lerato; HIGH COMMISSIONER FOR LESOTHO 1992– ; Higher Extve. Offr., Civil Serv. of Lesotho 1972; a flyer promoted to higher responsibilities in 1972, '75, '77 Permanent Sec. 1982; Govt. Sec. 1990; Mem., African Methodist Episcopal Ch.; Vice Sec., Matlama Football Club 1991–92 (Tse Putsoa); recreations: jogging; Home: 2 Crescent Rd., Rockcliffe Park, Ottawa, Ont. K1M 0N1; Office: 202 Clemow Ave., Ottawa, Ont. K1S 2B4.

**BERESFORD-HOWE, Constance Elizabeth,** Ph.D.; (Mrs. C.W. Pressnell); writer; b. Montreal, P.Q., 10 Nov. 1922; d. Russell and Marjory Mary (Moore) B.-H.; e. West Hill High Sch., Montreal, P.Q.; McGill Univ., B.A. 1945 (with Shakespeare Gold Medal for Eng. Lit. and Dorothy Peterson Prize for creative writing), M.A. 1946 (with $1200 scholar. from P.Q.); Brown Univ. Ph.D. 1950; m. Christopher W. Pressnell, M.A., 1960; one s., Jeremy Howe; author: (novels) 'The Unreasoning Heart' 1946; 'Of This Day's Journey' 1947; 'The Invisible Gate' 1949; 'My Lady Greensleeves' 1955; 'The Book of Eve' 1973; 'A Population of One' 1976; 'The Marriage Bed' 1978; 'Night Studies' 1985; 'Prospero's Daughter' 1988; 'A Serious Widow' 1991; (CBC-TV Drama) 'The Cuckoo Bird' 1981; awarded Dodd, Mead Intercoll. Lit. Fellow. 1945; Candn. Booksellers Award 1973; Can. Council Sr. Arts Award 1975; Ont. Arts Council Grants 1976, 1983 and 1985; short stories have appeared in 'Saturday Night,' 'Candn. Home Journal,' 'Chatelaine' and 'Maclean's,' articles in 'The Writer' and 'The Montrealer'; mem., The Writers' Union of Canada; Internat. P.E.N. Club (Past Pres. Montreal Centre); Phi Beta Kappa; Anglican; Address: 225 Moore Ave., Toronto, Ont. M4G 1C6.

**BERG, Ronald J.;** artist; b. Niagara-on-the-Lake, Ont. 10 Apr. 1952; s. John and Susan (Rempel) B.; e. Grantham High Sch. St. Catharines; Sheridan Coll. Oakville Dip. Graphic Design 1972; Ont. Coll. of Art, Toronto Dip. Fine Arts 1976; m. Josie d. Antonio and Maria Ciccone 20 Nov. 1976; children: Jennifer, Christopher; freelance illustrator 1976– ; illustrator (children's books) 'The King's Loon' 1979; 'A Proper Acadian' 1980; 'The Tin Lined Trunk' 1980; 'Goodbye Sarah' 1981; 'Michi's New Year' 1980; 'The Owl and the Pussycat' 1984; 'Wynken, Blynken and Nod' 1985; mem. Candn. Assn. Photographers & Illustrators in Communications; Candn. Soc. Children's Authors, Illustrators & Performers; recreation: tennis; Club: Mayfair; Address: 71 Hewitt Ave., Toronto, Ont. M6R 1Y4.

**BERGEN, William Edward,** B.Com., B.A.; b. Swift Current, Sask. 5 Jan. 1928; s. Wilhelm Henry and Maria (Enns) B.; e. Rosthern Jr. Coll. 1947; Univ. of W. Ont. 1949; Univ. of Sask. B.Com. and B.A. 1952; m. Elma d. Cornelius and Emma Friesen 20 Aug. 1949; children: Valerie J. Strom, Sandra L., William D., Lorna G.; self-employed cons. 1982–93; joined Federated Co-operatives Ltd. 1952, Chief Exec. Offr. 1970–79; Univ. lectr. and cons. 1979–82; Past Dir.: The National Bank of Canada; The Mercantile Bank of Canada; Interprovincial Co-operatives Ltd.; Western Co-operative Fertilizer Ltd.; Rosthern Jr. Coll.; Candn. Council Christians & Jews; Saskatoon Un. Way; Banff Sch. Advanced Mgmt.; Cooperative Energy Development Corp.; Mennonite (Gen. Conf.); recreations: golf, reading, travel; Home: 128 Riel Cres., Saskatoon, Sask. S7J 2W6.

**BERGER, Carl,** M.A., Ph.D.; educator; b. The Pas, Man. 25 Feb. 1939; e. Univ. of Man. B.A. 1961; Univ. of Toronto M.A. 1962, Ph.D. 1967; two d. Rachel, Clare; PROF. OF HISTORY, UNIV. OF TORONTO; author 'The Sense of Power: Studies in the Ideas of Canadian Imperialism 1867–1914' 1970; 'The Writing of Canadian History' 1976 (rec'd. Gov. Gen.'s Award for Non-Fiction 1977); 'Science, God, and Nature in Victorian Canada' 1983; mem. Royal Soc. Can.; Home: 20 Tilson, Rd., Toronto, Ont. M4S 1P4; Office: Toronto, Ont. M5S 1A1.

**BERGER, David Lawrence,** B.Tech., M.B.A., P.Eng., C.M.C.; management consultant; b. Toronto, Ont. 30 May 1954; s. Bernard and Barbara A. (Hyde) B.; e. Univ. of Toronto Eng. Sci. 2 yrs. 1977; Ryerson Polytech. Inst. B.Tech. 1980; York Univ. M.B.A. 1982; m. Eileen d. Harry and Elka Rubenstein 27 Aug. 1975; children: Michael, Avi, Joshua, Aron; PARTNER (INFO. SYSTEMS & OPERATIONS MGMT. GROUP) PRICE WATERHOUSE 1990– ; Ind. Mfg. Eng. Ferranti-Packard Electronics Ltd. Mississauga 1978–82; Cons. Woods Gordon Mgmt. Cons. Calgary 1982–83; Sr. Cons. Ind. Eng. Services Dept. Canada Packers Inc. Toronto 1983–86; Pres. and Co-founder The Lamus Group Inc. Toronto 1986–89; Mng. Dir. Info. Systems & Ind. Services Divs. Laventhol & Horwath Toronto 1988–90, Prin. 1990; Lectr. Ind. Eng. Prog. Ryerson Polytech. Inst. 1988– , mem. Ind. Adv. Ctte. 1987– ; Adjunct Prof. of Adm. Studies Univ. of Toronto 1986– , mem. Adv. Ctte. Eng. Cont. Edn. Prog. 1990– ; Lectr. Mount Royal Coll. Alta. 1982; Dir. Children's Private Day Sch. 1988–93; Dir., Not-For-Profit Children's & Sr. Citizens' Camp/Lodge 1988– ; author over 55 profl. publs.; monthly columnist PEM Plant Engineering & Maintenance Mag., Operations ed. 1989– ; monthly columnist Plant Services, U.S.A.; Founder and Past Pres. Plant Eng. & Maintenance Assn. Can. 1990– ; Regional Vice-Pres., Canada Region, Institute of Industrial Engrs. 1993– ; Pres. Toronto Chapter Inst. Ind. Engs. 1990–92, Dir. 1982– ; recreations: swimming, cycling, camping; Home: 26 Croydon Rd., Toronto, Ont. M6C 1S7; Office: 1600, 2 Robert Speck Parkway, Mississauga, Ont. L4Z 1H8.

**BERGER, Gerald A.,** B.A., M.B.A.; Canadian public service; b. Toronto, Ont. 31 Dec. 1937; s. Louis and Salome (Lubetsky) B.; e. Forest Hill Coll. Inst., Toronto, 1956; Univ. of Toronto, B.A. 1959; Columbia Univ., M.B.A. 1961; m. Ruth Bryna, d. late Phillip Cohen and Doris Edelstein, 25 June 1967; children: Michael Robert, Lisa Miriam; FEDERAL COORDINATOR AND SPECIAL ADVISOR TO THE MINISTER, OFFICE FOR THE 1994 COMMONWEALTH GAMES; joined Fed. Pub. Service as Project Offr., Dept. of Trade and Commerce 1961; Mang. Control Group, Dept. of Defense Production 1963; Extve. Asst. to Asst. Depy. Min., Finance and Adm. of Dept. Defense Production and Dept. Industry 1964; Extve. Asst. to Asst. Depy. Min. of Operations, Dept. Industry 1965 and to Depy. Min. of Industry 1966; Extve. Asst. to Secy. of Treasury Bd. 1968; Sr. Program Offr., Treasury Bd. Secretariat 1969; Secy., Prices and Incomes Comn. 1969; Dir. Gen. (Supply Planning) Dept. of Supply and Services 1972; Asst. Depy. Min. (Comm. Supply) 1974–82; Dir. Crown Assets Disposal Corp. 1974–85 (and Pres. 1983–84); Asst. Depy. Min., Operations, Dept. of Supply and Services 1982–84; Sr. Asst. Depy. Min., Dept. of Supply and Services 1984–88; seconded as Fed. Coordinator, Government of Canada Office for the 1988 Olympic Winter Games 1984–88; Apptd. Chrmn., Procurement Review Bd. of Canada 1989–92; author 'Canada's Experience with Incomes Policy – 1969–70'; Jewish; Home: 384 Hamilton Ave. S., Ottawa, Ont. K1Y 1C7; Office: P.O. Box 1533, Stn. B, Ottawa, Ont. K1P 6P6.

**BERGER, Hon. Thomas Rodney,** O.C., Q.C., B.A., LL.B.; barrister and solicitor; b. Victoria, B.C. 23 Mar. 1933; s. Maurice Theodore and Nettie Elsie Perle (McDonald) B.; e. Univ. of B.C., B.A. 1955, LL.B. 1956; m. Beverley Ann, d. Joseph O. Crosby, 5 Nov. 1955; children: Erin Frances, David Bruce; called to Bar of B.C. 1957; practised law in Vancouver 1957–71; Judge, Supreme Court of B.C. 1971–83; Chrmn., Royal Comn. on Family and Children's Law (B.C.) 1973–74; Commr., Mackenzie Valley Pipeline Inquiry (Can.) 1974–77; Comr., Indian and Inuit Health Consultation 1979–80; Chrmn., Alaska Native Review Comm. 1983–85; Depy. Chrmn., Independent Review (commissioned by World Bank) of Sardar Sarovar Projects in India 1992–93; served as M.P. (NDP) for Vancouver-Burrard 1962–63; M.L.A. for Vancouver-Burrard 1966–69; Hon. degrees: Queen's, Simon Fraser, Victoria, Manitoba, St. Thomas Aquinas, Guelph, Notre Dame (Nelson), Waterloo, York, Trent, Saskatchewan, McMaster; Officer, Order of Canada 1990; Anglican; Club: Jericho Tennis; Office: #300, 171 Water St., Vancouver, B.C. V6B 1A7.

**BERGERON, Hon. Anthime;** juge; né Montréal, Qué. 22 Jan. 1925; fils Donat et Aline (Héneault); é. Coll. Ste-Marie B.A. 1945; Univ. de Montréal LL.B. 1948; ép. Thérèse Parizeau 27 juin 1949; enfants: Yves, Luc; JUGE, COUR SUPERIEURE DU QUEBEC depuis septembre 1973; admis au Barreau du Québec, 12 juillet 1948; Président, Jeune Barreau de Montréal 1953; nommé C.R. 1958; 'Associate,' Lacoste & Lacoste 1948–54; Associé sr. (1955–73), Tansey, de Grandpré, Bergeron, Monet, Lavery, (Lavery, de Billy); Catholique romain; Clubs: St. Laurent-Kiwanis de Montréal (Prés. 1967); Club de Golf Laval-sur-le-Lac (Prés. 1993); Résidence: 4540 Promenade Paton, Laval, Qué. H7W 4W6; Bureau: Palais de Justice, 1 Notre Dame Est, Montréal, Qué. H2Y 1B6.

**BERGERON, Hon. Camille L.,** B.A., Ph.B., Th.B., LL.L.; judge; b. LaReine, Qué. 7 Dec. 1928; s. Ernest and Alexina (Doyle) B.; e. Univ. of Ottawa B.A. 1950, Ph.B. 1950, Th.B. 1952; Laval Univ. LL.L. 1956; m. Huguette d. J.A. Oscar Bellemare 7 Sept. 1957; children: Louise, Claire, Denis, Diane; PUISNE JUDGE, SUPERIOR COURT OF QUE.; called to Bar of Que. 1957; Appointed to the Bench, 1969; mem. Candn. Judges Conf.; R. Catholic; recreations: oil painting, woodcarving; Home: 79 Trémoy Rd., Noranda, Qué. J9X 1W2; Office: Court House, 2 Ave. du Palais, Rouyn, Qué. J9X 2N9.

**BERGERON, Catherine Marie Yvette,** M.D., F.R.C.P.(C); physician; neuropathologist; b. La Tuque, Que. 6 Apr. 1950; d. Leo E. and Germaine L. (Jalbert) B.; e. Coll. des Jesuites, Que. D.E.C. 1969; Laval Univ. M.D. 1973; Univ. of Toronto internship and training in med., neurology, neuropathology 1973–79; Royal Coll. certification in Neuropathology 1979; m. John Gordon s. Beatrice and William Edmeads 18 Aug. 1979; PRINCIPAL INVESTIGATOR, CENTER FOR RESEARCH IN NEURODEGENERATIVE DISEASES, UNIV. OF TORONTO 1990– ; Staff Pathologist Toronto Gen. Hosp. 1981– ; Fellow Med. Rsch. Counc. of Can. 1980–83; Co-ordinator, Candn. Brain Tissue Bank 1981–86; Staff Neuropathologist Princess Margaret Hosp. and Wellesley Hosp. 1983–86; author and co-author scientific publs. in a number of med. journs. incl.: Am. Jour. of Pathology, Neurology, Archives of Internal Med., Candn. Jour. of Neurological Sci., Annals of Neurology, Neurosurgery, Science; Asst. Prof. Dept. of Pathology, Univ. of Toronto 1983; Fellow, Coll. of Am. Pathologists; mem.: Scientific Advy. Counc., Huntington Soc. of Can.; Rsch. Policy Ctte., Amyotrophic Lateral Sclerosis Soc. of Can.; Candn. Assn. of Pathologists; Candn. Assn. of Neuropathologists; Ont. Med. Assn.; Ont. Assn. of Pathologists; Am. Acad. of Neurology; Am. Assn. of Pathologists; Society for Neuroscience; Am. Assn. for the Advancement of Sci.; recipient R.N. Starr Medal in Med., Univ. of Toronto; Fellow Roy. Coll. of Physicians and Surgeons of Can.; recreations: birdwatching, photography, reading; Home: 20 Boswell Ave., Toronto, Ont. M5R 1M4.

**BERGERON, Jean-Marc,** B.A., B.Ped., B.Sc., M.B.A.; financial executive; b. Trois-Rivières, Qué. 1944; e. Univ. Laval B.A. 1964; Univ. of Montreal B.Ped. 1968; McGill Univ. B.Sc. 1976; Ecole des Hautes Etudes Comm. M.B.A. 1978; divorced; 3 children; Chief Executive Officer, Cooperative Fédérée de Quebec 1988–92; Gen. Mgr., Horticultural Div., Union des producteurs agricoles 1978; Mgr., Communications & Corp. Affairs, Dairy Div., Coopérative fédérée de Qué. 1979–82; Gen. Mgr. 1982–88; Mem., Assn. des MBA du Qué.; Montreal Bd. of Trade; Ordre des agronomes du Qué.; author of various articles & conf. papers; Eminent Grad. MBA, Ecole des Hautes Etudes Commercials, 20th anniv.; recreations: golf, reading.

**BERGERON, Laurent A.,** C.M.A.; executive; b. Drummondville, Qué. 28 June 1935; s. Réal and Angeline (Prince) B.; e. McGill Univ. 1954–60; Exec. Devel. Inst. 1962–64; R.I.A. Inst. 1965–67; Cdn. Inst. Chart. Accts. (taxation) 1972–73; m. Marcelle d. Stanislas and Elizabeth Macé 18 Sept. 1959; one child: Danièle; EXTVE. VICE PRES., CANADIAN SPACE AGENCY 1989– ; Systems and Procedures Analyst Dominion Textile Co. 1954–60; Asst. Controller N. Bourassa Ltd. 1960–64; Div. Controller, Dosco Steel Co. Ltd. 1964–68; Corp. Controller Ingersoll-Rand (Canada) Ltd. 1968–74; Vice Pres. and Chief Fin. Offr. International Paints (Canada) Ltd. 1974–76; Pres. & Gen. Mgr. Desourdy Entreprises Inc. 1976–77; Pres. & C.E.O., Canadian Arsenals Ltd. 1977–86; Extve. Vice Pres., SNC Group and Pres., SNC Defence Products Ltd. 1986–87; Pres., (Defense Group) Canadair Inc. (Div. of Bombardier) 1987–88; mem. CMA Corp.; Presidents Assoc.; Adv. Bd., Military Colleges of Canada; Conseil de la Science et de la Technologie, Govt. of Québec; Outstanding Achievement Award, Public Service of Canada 1985; Home: 1986 chemin des Hirondelles, R.R. #2, St-Jovite, Qué. J0T 2H0; Office: 6767 Route de l'Aéroport, Saint-Hubert, Qué. J3Y 8Y9.

**BERGGREN, His Excellency Håkan A.,** M.A., Ph.D.; diplomat; b. Orebro, Sweden 7 June 1936; e. Univ. of Uppsala M.A. 1958, Ph.D. 1963; m. Marianne Wangemann 1977; AMBASSADOR OF SWEDEN TO CAN. 1989– ; rsch. and teaching positions Uppsala Univ. 1959–66; Visiting Prof. Univ. of Wisc. 1965; joined Min. of Foreign Affairs Sweden 1966 serving in New York 1968–73, New Delhi 1977–80, Singapore & Brunei, Ambassador 1980–85, Perm. Undersec. M.F.A. 1985–89; author various publs. Swedish, Am. and Asian hist. & devel.; Office: 377 Dalhousie St., Ottawa, Ont. K1N 9N8.

**BERGGREN, John Lennart,** M.Sc., Ph.D.; educator; b. Spokane, Wash. 16 Feb. 1941; s. Thorsten Nelson and Evelyn Hildegard (Soderberg) B.; e. Univ. of Wash. B.Sc. 1963, M.Sc. 1965, Ph.D. 1966; m. Tasoula d. Michael and Myrianthe Saparilla 2 Jan. 1966; children: Thorsten Michael, Karl Kimon; PROF. OF MATH. SIMON FRASER UNIV. 1984– ; Asst. Prof. present Univ. 1966, Assoc. Prof. 1973, Pres. Faculty Assn. 1980–81, mem. Bd. Govs. 1984–90; Visiting Fellow Yale Univ. 1972–73, 1975–76; Visiting Scholar, Harvard Univ. 1990–91 and 1992; co-editor 'From Ancient Omens to Statistical Mechanics' 1987; author 'Episodes in the Mathematics of Medieval Islam' 1986; co-author 'The History of Mathematics from Antiquity to the Present' 1985; 'Euclid's 'Phaenomena'' 1993; mem. Candn. Ed. Adv. Bd. Encyclopaedia Britannica; Pres. Confederation of Univ. Faculty Assns. B.C. 1982–83; mem. Candn. Soc. Hist. & Philos. Math. (Pres. 1977–79, Pres. 1988–90); Hist. Sci. Soc.; recreations: gardening, winemaking; Club: Diamond University; Home: 435 Donald St., Coquitlam, B.C. V3K 3Z9; Office: Burnaby, B.C. V5A 1S6.

**BERGMAN, Richard Allan,** B.Sc., M.Sc.; police executive; b. Flin Flon, Man. 22 June 1940; s. Agnar Johann and Evelyn Margurite (Eymundson) B.; e. Univ. of Sask. B.Sc. (Hons.) 1972, M.Sc. 1974; m. Teresa d. John and Alice Bill 27 June 1964; children: Richard, Lorie; DEPUTY COMMISSIONER, LAW ENFORCEMENT & PROTECTIVE SERVICES, RCMP HQ OTTAWA 1993– ; joined RCMP 1962; post to Prov. of Man. after recruit training; gen. police duties; Forensic Lab. Regina; Forensic Toxicologist, Vancouver Lab.; Asst. Officer in charge of Vanc. Lab. 1977; Toxicology Rsch. Offr. and then Offr. in Charge of Forensic Labs. Admin. Ottawa H.Q.; french-language training 1981; Officer in Charge of Staffing & Personnel Br., Personnel Directorate; Asst. Comnr. & Dir. of RCMP Forensic Labs. 1987; Commanding Offr., RCMP 'D' Div. (Man.) 1991–93; Mem., Internat. Assn. of Chiefs of Police; Candn. Assn. of Chiefs of Police (Mem., Forensic Identification & Labs. Ctte.; Vice Chair, Operational Rsch. Ctte. 1977–91); Candn. Soc. of Forensic Science 1987–

92; Am. Academy of Forensic Science 1987–92; Bd. of Dir., Am. Soc. of Crime Lab. Directors & Chair, Internat. Liaison Ctte. 1987–91; RCMP Long Service Medal; Salvation Army Citizens Adv. Bd. 1991, '92; St. John Ambulance Awards Ctte. 1991, '92; Bd. of Govs., Manitoba Corps of Commissionaires; Hon. Mem., Scouts Canada 1991–92, 1992–93; Branch Devel. Ctte. 1992– ; recreations: golf; clubs: Charleswood Golf, Carleton Golf & Country, Arbutus Ridge Golf & Country; Office: 1200 Vanier Parkway, Ottawa, Ont. K1A 0R2.

**BERGSMA, John,** M.A.Sc., M.B.A., P.Eng.; manufacturer; b. The Netherlands 11 Nov. 1945; s. Folkert and Antje (Brouwer) B.; came to Canada 1953; e. St. Catharines (Ont.) Coll. Inst. 1964; Univ. of Waterloo, B.A.Sc. (Mech. Engn.) 1969, M.A.Sc. (Civil Engn.) 1971; McMaster Univ. M.B.A. 1973; m. MargAnn Pierson; children: Glynis Rachelle, Katharine June, Robert Andrew, Jon Graham; SR. VICE-PRES., UNION GAS 1987– ; PRES., ST. CLAIR PIPELINES LTD. 1988– ; Extve. Vice-Pres., Massey Combines Corp. 1986–87; Pres., Gen. Mgr. & Dir., Columbus McKinnon Ltd. 1975–85; mem. Engn. Inst. Can.; Assn. Prof. Engrs. Ont.; Candn. Soc. Mech. Engrs.; Am. Soc. Mech. Engrs.; Conference Bd. of Can.; Can. Gas Assn.; Bd. of Govs., Univ. of Waterloo; Home: 500 King St. W., Chatham, Ont. N7M 1G9; Office: 50 Keil Dr. N., P.O. Box 2001, Chatham, Ont. N7M 5M1.

**BERKHOLD, Gerald Andrew,** B.Comm.; executive; b. Medicine Hat, Alta. 28 Aug. 1938; s. George Edward and Caroline (Ewen) B.; e. Medicine Hat High Sch. 1956; Univ. of Alta. B.Comm. 1960; m. Beverly Faye d. Gordon and Joann Simmons 1964; two s. Gordon Andrew, Graham George; PRESIDENT ATLAS CONCRETE INC. (Calgary, Alta.) 1989– ; Pres. and Dir. Redi-Mix Inc. (Dallas, Texas); Dir., Ince Holdings Ltd.; Monarch Communications Inc.; CalGas Inc.; Calgary Philharmonic; Property & Devel. Soc. Un. Ch.; joined Canadian Imperial Bank of Commerce 1960–70; Triarch Corp. Ltd. 1970–72; Extve. Vice Pres., Revelstoke Companies Ltd. 1972–86; Pres., Revelstoke Concrete Inc. 1986–89; Club: Glencoe; Home: 10707 Willowgreen Dr. S.E., Calgary, Alta. T2J 1P7.

**BERLAND, Alwyn,** M.A., M.Litt.; academic administrator; b. Chicago, Ill. 31 July 1920; s. Jacob and Elizabeth (Berg) B.; e. Univ. of Chicago, M.A. 1948; Cambridge Univ., M.Litt. 1953; m. Jayne Epstein, 3 Aug. 1941; 4 children; CHRMN., BD. OF MGMT.; MANAGING EDITOR, BERTRAND RUSSELL EDITORIAL PROJECT 1977–86; Prof. of English, McMaster Univ. 1973– ; Dean of Humanities there 1973–81; Visiting Prof., Nanjing, China 1988–89; Prof. and Chrmn., Dept. of English, Univ. of Saskatchewan 1963–67; Dean of Arts and Science there 1967–68; Extve. Dir. Candn. Assn. Univ. Teachers 1968–72; served as Ensign with U.S.N. during 2nd World War; Fulbright Scholar 1951–52, 1952–53; rec'd Can. Council Grant 1968; Can. Council Fellowship 1978–79; author: 'William Faulkner's "Light in August": A Study in Black and White' 1992; 'Culture and Conduct in the Novels of Henry James,' 1981; Ed., 'The Wascana Review'; author of numerous articles for journs. in Eng., U.S. and Can.; Pres., Humanities Assn. Can.; Hon. Life Mem., Candn. Assn. Univ. Teachers; mem., Assn. Candn. Univ. Teachers Eng.; Humanities Research Council Can.; Soc. of Friends; Home: 11 Roanoke Rd., Hamilton, Ont. L8S 3P6; Office: Hamilton, Ont. L8S 4L9.

**BERLET, Frederick G.W.,** M.B.A.; executive; b. Monkton, Ont. 7 Oct. 1928; s. Walter H. and Anna (Schmidt) B.; e. Mitchell High Sch.; Univ. of W. Ont., M.B.A. 1953; m. Donna, d. Judge C.L. (Roy) and Willa Austen, 11 Sept. 1954; children: Debra; David, Susan, Gregory; DEPUTY CHRMN., FLECK MFG. INC. since 1986; Pres., S.W.O. Mgmt. Consultants Ltd.; Treas. & Dir., Margate Industries Inc. (U.S.A.); Dir., Waterloo Scientific Inc.; Gen. Mgr. L. McBrine Co. Ltd. 1947; joined present firm as Gen. Mgr. 1960; Charitable Gov., Lutherwood; Past Pres., Tillsonburg District Memorial Hosp. Foundation; Lutheran; Club: Tillsonburg Golf and Country; recreation: golf; Home: 35 Parkwood Dr., Tillsonburg, Ont. N4G 2B7; Office: 80 Brock St. E., Tillsonburg, Ont. N4G 1Z9.

**BERLINGUETTE, Vincent Raymond,** B.Com.; retired public servant; statistician; b. Ottawa, Ont., 28 Jan. 1919; s. Edgar and Rosa (Sayer) B.; e. Univ. of Ottawa, B.Com. 1941; m. Marie (deceased), d. late Joseph Rubben, 25 May 1946; three children; m. Ellen, d. late Arthur P. Nugent; Acct. & Stat., Imperial Tobacco Co. Ltd., Montreal, 1941–42; joined former Dom. Bureau of Statistics as Stat. and subsequently Chief, Business Stat. Sec., Research & Devel. Div., 1945–59; Asst. to Dir., Indust. & Merchandising Div., 1959–63; Dir., Indust. Div., 1963–67; Dir.-Gen., Econ. Stat. Br. 1967–73; Asst. Chief Stat. (Bus. Stat.), Statistics Can. 1973–78 (ret.); served Overseas as Arty. Offr. with 1st Medium Regt., RCA, 1942–45; R. Catholic; Home: 1890 Louisiana Ave., Ottawa, Ont. K1H 6V1.

**BERLIS, Douglas Albert,** Q.C., B.A., LL.B.; barrister and solicitor; b. Toronto, Ont. 25 Dec. 1920; s. Henry Albert and Annie Jean (Henderson) B.; e. Trinity Coll., Univ. of Toronto, B.A. 1942; Osgoode Hall; COUNSEL, AIRD & BERLIS (Established 1974); Chrmn. and Dir., Canada Tungsten Mining Corporation Limited; Canadian Worcester Controls Ltd.; Dir. and Secy., Hamilton Kent of Can. Ltd.; Dir., Algoma Central Corp.; Cdn. Overseas Packaging Industries Ltd.; Old Canada Investment Corp. Ltd.; read law with Manning, Mortimer & Kennedy, Toronto, Ont.; called to the Bar of Ont., 1949; cr. Q.C. 1961; Partner, Edison, Aird & Berlis 1953–74; Partner, Aird & Berlis 1974–86; served in 2nd World War; Pilot in R.C.A.F., 1941–45, Can., Eng., N. Africa, Italy, Flight Lieut.; Trustee, Bank of Nova Scotia Pension Fund; Hon. Chrmn., N. York Gen. Hosp.; Presbyterian; recreations: golf; Clubs: Toronto; Toronto Golf; Toronto Hunt; Granite; Home: 1 Suncrest Drive, Don Mills, Ont. M3C 2L1; Office: P.O. Box 754, Ste. 1800, BCE Place, North Tower, 181 Bay St., Toronto, Ont. M5J 2T9.

**BERLIS, Norman Frederick Henderson,** B.A.; barrister-at-law; diplomat; b. Toronto, Ont. 8 Apr. 1914; s. Henry Albert and Annie Jean (Henderson) B.; e. Trinity Coll., Univ. of Toronto, B.A. 1937; Osgoode Hall Law Sch., Toronto, grad. 1940; m. Oriel Louise Pollock, 11 March 1949 (deceased 1975); children: Michael Ernle, Anna Louise; read law with Joy & Chitty and with Mason, Foulds, Davidson, Carter & Kellock, Toronto; called to Bar of Ont. 1946; joined Dept. of External Affairs, Can. 1947; Offr. i/c Perm. Mission of Can. to European Office of U.N., Geneva, 1948–52; Depy. Head of European Div., Ottawa, 1952–54; Head of Estabs. & Organ. Div., 1954–56; Counsellor, Candn. Embassy, Rome, 1956–59; Head of Information Div., Ottawa, 1960–62; High Commr. to Tanzania, 1962–65 and concurrently accredited as High Commr. to Uganda, 1962–65 and to Kenya, 1963–65; Ambassador to Poland, 1965–67; Chief of Protocol, Ottawa, Ont. 1967–69; Ambassador to Austria 1969–73 and concurrently Perm. Rep. of Can. to the U.N. Indust. Devel. Organ., and to Internat. Atomic Energy Agency, also Candn. Gov. on I.A.E.A. Bd. of Govs., Vienna, 1970–73; Ambassador and Rep. of Can. to U.N. Econ. & Social Council N.Y. and Geneva, and concurrently Dir. U.N. Econ. & Social Affairs Div., Dept. External Affairs, Ottawa 1973–75; Ambassador to Denmark 1975–79; retired from diplomatic service 1979; served with RCNVR 1943–46; enlisted as Ordinary Seaman; discharged with rank of Lt.; awarded Centennial Medal, 1967; Home: 6A Egerton Gardens, London SW3 2BP, England.

**BERMAN, Brigitte (Ursula),** B.A., B.Ed.; film director, producer, writer; b. Frankfurt, W. Germany 15 Jan.; e. York Mills Coll. Inst. Toronto; Queen's Univ. B.A. 1972, McArthur Coll. B.Ed. 1973; PRES. BRIDGE FILM PRODUCTIONS INC. 1979– ; Researcher CBC current affairs progs. 'Weekend' and 'Up Canada' 1973–75; Producer/Dir. CBC 'In Good Company,' 'This Monday,' 'Quarterly Report,' 'Take 30' 1975–84; Producer/Dir./Writer/Film Ed. present Co. 1979– ; 'Dramatic Feature' Dir. Resident, Candn. Centre for Advanced Film Studies 1988–89; Dir. Resident, 2nd year Feature Film Development Program 1989; Writer/Dir./Producer 'The Circle Game' (dramatic feature film) 1993–94; Producer, Dir. and Ed. 'Bix: "ain't none of them play like him yet"' (also co-writer), 'Artie Shaw: Time Is All You've Got' (also writer); CBC Documentaries incl. 'The Many Faces of Black' 1977, 'Elmira' 1975, 'The Osbornes: A Very Special Family' 1982, 'Judy Chicago' 1982; recipient Acad. Award (Oscar) for Best 1986 Documentary Feature 1987; Internat. Film Festival awards incl. First Prize (World Hist.) Valladolid, Spain 1986; Bronze Hugo Award Chicago 1981; Hon. Mention San Francisco 1981; Merit Award Athens 1983; Chris Plaque Columbus 1983; Nomination Golden Sheaf Award Yorkton 1983; Cert. of Appreciation St. Catharines City Centennial 1976; mem. Am. Acad. Motion Picture Arts & Sci's; Acad. Candn. Cinema & TV; recreations: film, music, theatre, arts; Address: 44 Charles St. W., Toronto, Ont. M4Y 1R7.

**BERMAN, Bruce Josef,** Ph.D.; university professor; b. New York, N.Y. 14 April 1942; s. Jack M. and Frances (Stern) B.; e. Horace Mann Sch. 1959; Dartmouth Coll. A.B. 1963; London Sch. of Econ. M.A. 1965; Yale Univ. M.Phil. 1968, Ph.D. 1974; m. Elaine d. Joseph and Ruth Shapiro 16 July 1967; one s.: Daniel; one d.: Erica; PROF., QUEEN'S UNIV. 1991– ; Rsch. Assoc., Inst. for Devel. Studies, Univ. of Nairobi 1968–69; Lectr., Dept. of Pol. Studies, Queen's Univ. 1971–74; Asst. Prof. 1974–77; Assoc. Prof. 1977–91; Vis. Prof., Univ. of Cambridge 1977–78; Univ. of Pennsylvania 1984; Sussex Univ. 1985; History of Sci. Soc.; Candn. Assn. of African Studies (Conf. Chair 1987–88, Extve. Ctte. 1987–92, Pres. 1990–91, Past Pres. 1991–92); fellowships: Can. Counc. 1977–78; SSHRC 1984–85; SSHRC grant 1986, 1987; mem.: Cong. Iyr Ha-Melech (Reform Synagogue) (Pres. 1986–88); Jewish Comm. Counc. of Kingston (Pres. 1988–90); Ctte. on Race Relations, Kingston Police Services Bd. (Depy. Chair 1989–91); author: 'Control and Crisis in Colonial Kenya' 1990 (Joel Gregory Prize 1991); co-author: 'Unhappy Valley' 1992; Co-editor & co-author: 'Africa and Eastern Europe: Crises and Transformations' 1993; 'African Capitalists in African Development' 1993; author/co-author of over 25 chapters, articles & reviews in books & profl. jours.; Home: 331 Union St. W., Kingston, Ont. K7L 2R3; Office: Kingston, Ont. K7L 3N6.

**BERMINGHAM, John Thomas,** B.Com.; executive; b. Montréal, Qué. 20 June 1932; s. Thomas Charles and Mary Angusena (McDonald) B.; e. Concordia Univ. B.Com. 1953; m. Helen d. Dymitro and Marie Dzus 14 Aug. 1968; Secy.-Treas. Pom Bakery Ltd. 1970–..; Co-founder (1981), Dir. and Treas. Kelligrews Resources Ltd.; served 4 yrs. as Asst. Secy.-Treas. Supervised Investments Ltd.; Adm. Mgr. Canadian Appraisl Co. Ltd. 1967–69; Dist. Mgr. and Corp. Secy. MIS Computer Services Ltd. 1969–70; mem. Qué. del. food ind. France 1976; Dir. and past Treas. St. Patrick's Soc. Montréal; past Dir. Planning Execs. Inst. Montréal Br.; Charter mem. Nat. Corporate Cash Mgmt. Assn.; mem. Cash & Treasury Management Assn.; Centraide Montréal; Canadian Club of Montréal; Montréal Bd. Trade; recreations: travel, history; Home: 358 Olivier Ave., Montréal, Qué. H3Z 2C9.

**BERNARD, Alain M.,** M.B.A.; banker; b. La Rochelle, France 16 July 1947; e. McGill Univ. M.B.A. 1978; m. Evelyne Bernard; one child: Loïc; MEMBER OF SENIOR MANAGEMENT AND BRANCH MANAGER, CRÉDIT SUISSE CANADA 1980– ; Montreal Stock Exchange 1971; Bank of Montreal 1973; Mercantile Bank of Canada 1976; recreations: sailing, reading, music; Office: 1250 René-Lévesque ouest, Suite 3935, Montreal, Qué. H3B 4W8.

**BERNARD, Hon. J. Leonce,** MLA; politician; b. Abram Village, P.E.I. 23 May 1943; s. Antonin Joseph and Emma Marie (Cormier) B.; e. Evangeline H.S.; m. Florence d. Albenie Gallant 27 July 1968; children: Michel, Pierre, Francine, Charles; Gen. Mgr., Le village Tourist complex; Mgr., Evangeline Credit Union 1970–86; elected Liberal MLA 1975; re-el. 1978, 1979, 1982, 1986, 1989; Min. of Industry, Prov. of P.E.I. and Chrmn. of P.E.I. Development Agency 1986–89; Min. of Community and Cultural Affairs, Min. of Fisheries and Aquaculture, Prov. of P.E.I. 1989–92; former Extve. Dir., Baie Acadienne Venture Capital Group; Past Pres., Conseil Co-op de l'Ile (P.E.I. Rep., Candn. Counc. of Co-ops.); Past Vice-Pres., United Way; mem., var. community orgns.; Roman Catholic; Home: 101 Mill Rd., Wellington, P.E.I. C0B 2E0; Office: P.O. Box 2000, Charlottetown, P.E.I. C1A 7N8.

**BERNARD, Jean-Thomas,** Ph.D.; educator; b. Montmagny, Qué. 30 June 1946; s. Edouard and Ena (Roy) B.; e. Coll. Ste-Anne-de-la-Pocatière B.A. 1966; Univ. d'Ottawa B.A. 1968; Univ. of Pa. Ph.D. 1973; m. Lise d. Valère Biron 9 Aug. 1969; children: Jean-Stéphane, Marie-Christine; PROF. OF ECON., UNIV. LAVAL 1983– ; Asst. Prof. Queen's Univ. 1973–76; Asst. adjoint present Univ. 1976, Assoc. Prof. 1978–83, Chrmn. Green Center 1988– , Chrmn. Grad. Studies Econ. 1982–84, Chrmn. of Econ. 1977–78; Rsch. Fellow Harvard Univ. 1987–88; recipient William Polk Carey Prize in Econ. Univ. Pa. 1974; Médaille d'or du Doyen de la Faculté des Sci's sociales à l'Univ. d'Ottawa 1968; author various articles and papers; mem. Assn. canadienne d'économie; Am. Econ. Assn.; Econometric Soc.; Soc. canadienne de sci. économique; Home: 1700 chemin Gomin, Sillery, Qué. G1S 1N9; Office: GREEN, Dépt. d'économique, Pavillon JA De Sève, Université Laval, Québec, Qué. G1K 7P4.

**BERNARDI, Mario,** C.C. (1972); b. Kirkland Lake, Ont. 20 Aug. 1930; s. Leone and Rina (Onisto) B.; e. Coll. Piox, Treviso, Italy; Benedetto Marcello Conserv., Venice, Italy; Mozarteum, Salzburg, Austria; Royal Conserv., Toronto; m. Mona d. Philip T. Kelly 12 May 1962; Head, Calgary Symphony Orchestra 1984– ; Former Musical Dir., Sadler's Wells Opera Co.; has guest conducted the Royal Philharmonic, the London Symphony, the Quebec City, Montreal, Toronto, Edmonton,

Vancouver, Indianapolis, Chicago and Pittsburgh Orchestras, as well as L'Orchestre de la Suisse roman de, the Los Angeles Chamber, the BBC Welsh, the Slovak Philharmonic Orchestras; as NAC Music Dir. & Conductor has toured Canada, the USA, Mexico, Europe and USSR; Music Dir. & Conductor, National Arts Centre Orchestra, 1979–83; Guest Conductor, Handel's 'Rinaldo,' Metropolitan Opera 1984; Verdi's 'Aida,' English National Opera 1986; Massenet's 'Cendrillon,' Kennedy Centre, Washington 1987; 'Don Giovanni,' Opéra de Montréal 1987; various orchestras; Asst. Conductor, Toronto Opera Festival (later Candn. Opera Co.); conducted for radio and television; first worked as coach at Sadler's Wells on schol., 1962; makes annual performances at Stratford, Ont. Music Festival; U.S. debut, San Francisco Opera, Nov. 1967; annual appearances Vancouver Opera Assn. and C.B.C.; rec'd CM Council Medal 1981; CCA's Diplôme d'honneur 1982; Club: Savage.

**BERNIER, Bernard,** B.A., Ph.D.; university professor; b. Lévis, Que. 15 July 1942; s. Maurice and Lucienne (Gaumond) B.; e. Univ. Laval, B.A. 1962; Univ. of B.C.; Cornell Univ., Ph.D. 1970; m. Chantal d. Emile and Louisette Kirsch 21 Oct. 1975; PROF. OF ANTHROPOLOGY, UNIV. OF MONTREAL 1980– ; Rsch. Asst., Hawthorn Comn. on the Candn. Indians 1964–65; McGill Univ., McGill Cree Project 1967; Asst. Prof., Anthropol., Univ. of Montreal 1970–75; Assoc. Prof. 1975–80; Dir. d'études, Ecole des Hautes Etudes en Sci. Soc., Paris 1983–84; Interim Dir., Ctr. d'études de l'Asie de l'Est, Univ. of Montreal 1984–85; Bobbs-Merrill Award in Anthropol., Cornell Univ. 1967; Mem., Candn. Asian Studies Assn.; CSAA; Japan Soc. Sci. Assn. of Can.; ACSALF; Assn. for Asian Studies; Candn. Anthropol. Soc.; author: 'Capitalisme, société et culture au Japon' (Canada-Japan Book Ward 1989) 1988, 'Breaking the Cosmic Circle' 1975; co-editor: 'Le Japon face à l'internationalisation' 1988, 'L'Etat et le capitalisme au Japon' 1987, 'Travail, industries, classes ouvrières' 1986, 'Le Japon' 1980; recreations: tennis, painting; Home: 3550, Northcliffe, Montreal, Qué. H4A 3K7; Office: Montreal, Qué. H3C 3J7.

**BERNIER, Hon. Leo;** former politician; b. Sioux Lookout, Ont. 12 Aug. 1929; s. Joseph and Leah (Jubinville) B.; e. Sioux Lookout (Ont.) Cont. Sch.; m. Marjorie, d. Dallas Gastmeier and Ellen Lalonde, 22 Aug. 1949; children: Janice (Mrs. Brian Evans), Karen (Mrs. Ralph Cast Jr.), Donald, John; el. M.P.P. for Kenora 1966–85; apptd. Min. of Mines & Northern Affairs 1971 and served additionally as Min. of Lands & Forests and Min. of Natural Resources until 1977; apptd. Ontario's first Min. of Northern Affairs 1977–85; served as govt. Whip for 2 yrs.; mem. Management Board of Ont. Cabinet; mem. three policy field comtes. (Resources Develop.; Justice and Social Develop.); presently Chrmn., Fed. Govt. Economic Development Initiative for North. Ont.; LL.D. (hon. causa), Lakehead Univ.; recipient, Bud Thomas Leadership Award 1990; mem. Jr. Chamber Comm.; Hudson Public Sch. Bd.; hon. mem. Royal Cdn. Legion; K. of C.; P. Conservative; R. Catholic; recreations: hunting, fishing, curling; Home: P.O. Box 70 – 23 West Lane, Hudson, Ont. P0V 1X0.

**BERNIER, Roger B.;** librarian; b. Drummondville, Qué. 28 Sept. 1942; s. Armand W. and Jeanne (Ouellette) B.; e. Seminaire de Sherbrooke B.A. 1964; Univ. de Montréal B.Bibl. 1965; Univ. de Sherbrooke 1966; m. Denise d. Gerard Marquis 26 Sept. 1967; divorced; one d. Hélène; HEAD, BIBLIOTHEQUE DES SCIENCES, UNIV. DE SHERBROOKE 1981– ; Head of Cataloging & Classification Seminaire de Sherbrooke Bibliotheque 1965–67; Supvr. of Classification Univ. de Sherbrooke Bibliotheque 1967–69; Head, Service du Catalogage Univ. du Qué. à Montréal Bibliotheque 1969–70; Head, Bibliotheque des Sciences Univ. de Sherbrooke 1970–72, 1981–00; Head, Centres de documentation de la Bibliotheque 1972–76, Head, Bibliotheque Générale 1976–77, Head, Informatheque Du Programme de Recherche sur l'Amiante 1977–81; Teacher, Lib. Congress Classification, Stage en Bibliothéconomie de La Pocatière summers 1966, 1967, 1969, 1970; CEGEP Maisonneuve 1969; author 'Classification Library of Congress: Manuel Pratique d'Utilisation (traduction) 1969; 'Abrégé de la Classification Library of Congress' 1970; 'La Classification Library of Congress: Cours et Exercices' 1973; Prés. de la Comn. de Crédit, Caisse Populaire Ste-Jeanne d'Arc, Sherbrooke; L'Association des Propriétaire de la Plage Southière, Magog; Assoc. du Parti Conservateur du Comte. de Sherbrooke (Dir. 1990– ;); owner Marina du Grand Boisé Enr., Magog; Corp. des Bibliothécaires Professionels du Qué.; R. Catholic; recreations: skiing, sailing; Club: Optimist (Pres. 1989–90); Home: 420 Duvernay, Sherbrooke, Qué. J1L 1J1; Office: Sherbrooke, Qué. J1K 2R1.

**BERNIER, Hon. Yves,** C.D., B.A., LL.L., B.Sc.Soc.; judge, retired; b. Lévis, Qué. 17 Feb. 1916; s. late Henri and late Yvonne (Picard) B.; e. Coll. de Lauzon; Séminaire de Qué. B.A. 1937; Univ. Laval LL.L. 1940, B.Sc.Soc. 1941; m. Victoire d. late Joseph T. Bernier 8 June 1942; children: Josée, Simon, Pierre; Judge, Court of Appeal, Que. 1973–91, retired; called to Bar of Que. 1940; cr. Q.C. 1956; law practice Bernier & Bernier 1940; Moraud, Alleyn, Labreque & Bernier 1951; mun. Judge, City of Lauzon 1956–61; Judge, Superior Court Que. 1961–73; Prof. of Law (Bankruptcy) Laval Univ. 1961–72, Qué. Bar Sch. 1972–73; Depy. Judge, Admiralty Court 1965–70; apptd. to Court Martial Appeal Court 1961; Chrmn. Royal Comn. on Pilotage 1962–70; active service Candn. Army 1940–46, rank Lt. Col.; Reserve Army 1946–57, rank Lt. Col. (35e A/tk Régt. R.C.A.); mem. Candn. Bar Assn.; R. Catholic; Home: 1510 Beau-Lieu Ave., Apt. 607, Sillery, Qué. G1S 4R3; Office: Court House, 300 Blvd. Jean-Lesage, Québec, Qué. G1K 8K6.

**BERNSTEIN, Alan,** Ph.D., F.R.S.C.; scientist; professor; b. Toronto, Ont. 25 June 1947; s. Max and Shirley (Spivak) B.; e. Univ. of Toronto, B.Sc. 1968, Ph.D. 1972; children: Andrew Michael, Gillian Sarah; HEAD, DIV. OF MOLECULAR & DEVEL. BIOL. AND ASSOC. DIR., MOUNT SINAI HOSP. RSCH. INST. 1985– ; post-doct. fellow, Imperial Cancer Rsch. Fund Labs. 1972–74; Sr. Staff Sci., Div. of Biol. Rsch., Ont. Cancer Inst. 1974–85; Asst. Prof., Dept. of Med. Biophys. and Med. Genetics, Univ. of Toronto 1974–79; Assoc. Prof. 1979–84; Prof. 1984– ; Mem., Bd. of Dirs., Nat. Cancer Inst. of Can. 1989– ; Chrmn., Adv. Ctte. on Rsch., Nat. Cancer Inst. of Can. 1986–88 (Mem., Strategic Planning Ctte. 1986); Mem., Scientific Adv. Bd., Biomedical Rsch. Ctr., Univ. of B.C.; Spec. Revr., Nat. Inst. of Health & Nat. Cancer Inst. U.S.A. 1984, 1985, 1986; Mem., Mgmnt. Ctte., Can. Genome Program 1992– ; Mem., Ed. Bds., 'Molecular and Cellular Biology' 1982– ; 'Blood' 1992– ; 'Cell Growth & Diff.' 1992– ; James Loudon Gold Medal in Math. & Phys. 1968; King George V Jubilee Cancer Rsch. Fellowship (Nat. Cancer Inst. of Can.) 1972–73; Internat. Rsch. Scholar, Howard Hughes Med. Inst. 1991–96; Fellow, Royal Soc. of Can. 1991; Mem., Am. Soc. for Microbiol.; Candn. Soc. for Cell Biol.; Candn. Genetics Soc.; author & co-author of over 120 sci. pubns. dealing with retrovirology, hematopoiesis, leukemia, gene transfer, transgenic mice, oncogenes, tumour suppresser genes and developmental biology; Home: Toronto, Ont.; Office: 600 University Ave., R. 885, Toronto, Ont. M5G 1X5.

**BERNSTEIN, Mark Aaron,** M.D., F.R.C.S.(C); neurosurgeon; b. Ottawa, Ont. 23 May 1950; s. Harold Joseph and Dorothy (Snipper) B.; e. Univ. of Toronto, B.Sc. 1972; Univ. of Ottawa, M.D. 1976; Neurosurgery Residency, Toronto 1976–85 (2 yrs. 1980–82, in rsch. training, Univ. of Calif.); m. Lee d. John and Olive Rolnick 28 Feb. 1981; children: Lauren, Andrea, Jody; HEAD, DIVISION OF NEUROSURGERY, THE TORONTO HOSP. & ASSOC. PROF., DEPT. OF SURGERY, UNIV. OF TORONTO; spec. rsch. interest: malignant brain tumours; Home: 66 Highland Cres., Willowdale, Ont. M2L 1G6; Office: 2 McLaughlin Pavilion, Toronto Hosp., 399 Bathurst St., Toronto, Ont. M5T 2S8.

**BERRETT, Tim,** M.A., M.P.A.; athlete; lecturer; b. Tunbridge Wells, Eng. 23 Jan. 1965; s. Roger and Doris (Beale) B.; e. The Skinners' Sch. Tunbridge Wells 1983; Brazenose Coll. Oxford B.A. 1986; Queen's Univ. Kingston M.A. 1989, M.P.A. 1989; Ph.D. Student, Univ. of Alta. 1992; Econ. Analyst Nat. Econ. Rsch. Associates London, Eng. 1986–87; Resource Econ. Centre for Resource Studies, Queen's Univ. 1989–90, Coach Track & Field/Cross Country; Lectr., Dept. of Economics, Univ. of Sask. 1991; internat. athlete race walking (Commonwealth Record 5Km Indoor 1993, Candn. Record 20Km Track 1992, Candn. Record 50Km Track 1991); Candn. Olympic Games Team 1992; recipient several scholarships: Oxford Open Exhn. Scholarship 1985–86; Candn. Rhodes Found. Scholar 1987–89; Univ. of Alta. Ph.D. Scholarship 1991–93; Candn. Olympic Assn. Petro-Canada Olympic Torch Scholarship 1991–93; Izaak Walton Killam Memorial Scholar 1993– ; author or co-author various sci. articles; Office: Dept. of Physical Education & Sport Studies, Univ. of Alberta, Edmonton, Alta. T6G 2H9.

**BERRIDGE, John (Joe) David,** B.A., M.A.; urban planner; b. Newport, Wales, U.K. 11 Sept. 1946; s. William Edward and Mary Christine B.; e. Exeter Sch. 1965; Univ. of Sussex, B.A. 1968; Univ. of Toronto, M.A. 1971; m. Antoinette d. Claire Jennings 1968; children: Sarah, Amy, David; PARTNER, BERRIDGE LEWINBERG GREENBERG 1986– ; Urban Rsch., Univ. of Sussex 1969; City Planner, City of Toronto, Planning & Devel. Dept. 1973–75; Mgr., Housing Dept. 1975–78; Partner, Coombes, Kirkland, Berridge, 1978–86; cons. to large scale downtown & waterfront developments in Toronto, N.Y., London, Manchester, Puerto Rico, Chicago & N.J.; Juror, Prog. Architecture Annual Awards 1987; Toronto Arts Awards; Atlanta & Mississauga Urban Design Awards; Adv. Ctte. Mem., Nat. Capital Comn. 1986–88; Dir., Candn. Urban Institute; Expansion Cttee., Women's College Hosp.; frequent radio, T.V. and newspaper articles on urban planning; Mem., Candn. Inst. of Planners; recreations: walking, talking; club: Sabbatical Soc.; Home: 88 Kendal Ave., Toronto, Ont. M5R 1L9; Office: 111 Queen St. E., Ste. 200, Toronto, Ont. M5C 1S2.

**BERRISFORD, Nigel Edward Francis;** corporate executive; b. Buxton, Eng. 8 July 1945; s. Clifford and Iris (Heyhoe) B.; e. Kents Bank Sch.; m. Louise d. Jean-Paul and Therese Lefebvre 31 May 1969; children: Martin, Nicholas; PRES., KEY PORTER BOOKS LTD. 1992– ; joined W.H. Smith in England as Mgmt. Trainee 1961; Store Mgr., Montreal 1967; Area Mgr., Ottawa 1974; Area Mgr., Montreal 1977; Buying Mgr., Head Off. 1980; Book Mktg. Dir. 1987; Vice Pres. W.H. Smith Inc. 1988–92; judge, Books in Canada Best Candn. First Novel Award; Dir., Candn. Booksellers Assoc. 1988–90; mem., Candn. Found. for Ileitis & Colitis; recreations: reading, classical music, cricket; Home: 1381 Hastings Rd., Oakville, Ont. L6H 2T6; Office: 70 The Esplanade, Toronto, Ont. M5E 1R2.

**BERRY, Edmund Grindlay,** M.A., Ph.D., F.R.S.C.; educator; b. Leslie, Aberdeenshire, Scot. 12 Mar. 1915; s. Rev. James Garrow and Agnes (Henderson) B.; e. Dumfries Acad. 1925–26; Fredericton, N.B. 1926–32; Univ. of N.B. 1932–33; Queen's Univ. B.A. 1936, M.A. 1937; Univ. of Chicago Ph.D. 1940; m. Virginia d. Fred J. Gingerick, North Manchester, Ind. 25 Aug. 1943; children: Julia, Margaret; EMERITUS PROF. OF CLASSICS, UNIV. OF MAN.; Lectr. present univ. 1940, Asst. Prof. 1946, Assoc. Prof. 1949, Prof. 1957–80, Head of Classics Dept. 1961–78, Dir. of Summer Sch. 1946–49, Asst. Dean of Arts & Sci. 1949–51; mem. Queen's Univ. Council 1963–75; Candn. Council Acad. Panel 1966–69; Chrmn. Humanities Research Council 1972–74; mem. St. John's Coll. Council 1972–76; rec'd Guggenheim Fellowship 1951–52; Nuffield Foundation Research Grant 1969; author 'Emerson's Plutarch' 1961; articles on Plutarch, Anacreon, classical influences on Am. and Eng. lit.; Chrmn. Ed. Bd. 'Mosaic' 1976–80; mem. Classical Assn. Can. (Pres. 1970–72); Humanities Assn. (Pres. 1961–63); Hellenic Soc.; Am. Philol. Assn.; Classical Assn. Middle W. and S.; Anglican; recreations: reading, travel; Home: 310 Dromore Ave., Winnipeg, Man. R3M 0J5.

**BERRY, Harold Townsend,** B.Sc.; consulting metallurgist; b. 30 Dec. 1917; e. Queen's Univ. B.Sc. (Metall. Engn.) 1940; m. Betty Isabel Colles, 14 Sept. 1942; children: Brian, Michael, Jane; joined Cominco, Trail, B.C. 1945; Falconbridge Nickel Mines Ltd., Falconbridge, Ont. 1953, Toronto 1969–82; recreations: golf, skiing; Office: 4 Lauderdale Dr., Willowdale, Ont. M2L 2A9.

**BERRY, John Widdup,** B.A., Ph.D.; educator; b. Montreal, Que. 20 May 1939; s. William Macfarlane and Harriet Evelyn (Huycke) B.; e. Westmount High Sch. 1956; Sir George Williams Univ. B.A. 1963; Univ. of Edinburgh Ph.D. 1966; m. Joan d. Arthur and Joyce Melkman 1 July 1961; children: Heather, Susan, Michael; PROF. OF PSYCHOL. QUEEN'S UNIV. 1978– ; Merchant Seaman 1956–59; Lectr. Univ. of Sydney 1966–69; Asst. Prof. present Univ. 1969–72, Assoc. Prof. 1972–78; Fellow, Netherlands Inst. Advanced Study 1974–75; Visiting Prof. Univ. de Nice 1979–80, Univ. de Genève 1986–87; Cons. World Health Orgn. 1986–87; Pres. Cross-Cultural/Multi-Cultural Associates; mem. Candn. Task Force Mental Health Immigrants & Refugees; author 'Human Ecology and Cognitive Style' 1976; co-author 'Multiculturalism and Ethnic Attitudes in Canada' 1977; 'On the Edge of the Forest' 1986; 'Human Behavior in Global Perspective' 1990; 'Cross-Cultural Psychology: Research and Applications' 1992; co-ed. 'Handbook of Cross-Cultural Psychology' 1980; 'Multiculturalism in Canada' 1983; 'Human Abilities in Cultural Context' 1988; 'Ethnicity and Culture in Canada: The Research Landscape' 1993; Co-chair Waterfront Users Assn. Kingston; Chair Nonsmokers Assn. Kingston; Fellow, Candn. Psychol. Assn.; Past Pres. & Sec. Gen. Internat. Assn. Cross-Cultural Psychol.; recreations: sailing, music; Club: Kingston Yacht; Home: 36 Wellington St., Kingston, Ont. K7L 3C1; Office: Kingston, Ont. K7L 3N6.

**BERRY, L. Michael,** B.A.; diplomat; b. Bolton, U.K. 28 Sept. 1937; s. Leonard and Margaret (Wynne) B.; e. McGill Univ. B.A. 1961, grad. studies internat. relations 1963–64; m. Linda Kathleen d. Alan M. and Frederica Randal, Ottawa, Ont. 17 Aug. 1963; children: Elizabeth, Mark, Kathryn; CANADIAN HIGH COMMISSIONER TO AUSTRALIA 1991– ; Dept. of Finance 1961; Special Asst. to Min. of Justice 1961–63; joined Dept. External Affairs 1964, Second Secy. Berlin 1966–68, Counsellor (Econ.) London 1971–75, Dir. Comm. & Econ. Policy Div. Ottawa 1977–79; Can. High Commr. to Singapore 1979–82; Dir. Gen., Internat. Energy Relations, Dept. of Energy Mines & Resources 1982–83; Dir. Gen., Economic Policy, Dept. of External Affairs 1983–85; Dir. Gen., Asia Pacific South Bureau, Dept. of External Affairs 1985–88; Canadian Ambassador & Permanent Rep. to the Orgn. for Economic Cooperation & Development (OECD) 1988–91; Protestant; recreations: squash, cricket; Home: 32 Mugga Way, Canberra, ACT 2603, Australia; Office: Commonwealth Avenue, Canberra, ACT 2600, Australia.

**BERRYMAN, Jeffrey Bruce,** LL.B., M.Jur., LL.M.; university professor and administrator; b. Auckland, N.Z. 3 March 1955; s. David and Hazel Rachel (Worner) B.; e. Kelston Boys H.S.; Univ. of Auckland LL.B. (Hons.) 1977, M.Jur. (with distinction) 1978; LL.M. (with distinction) 1981; m. Carol d. Florence and Louis McDermott 15 June 1985; children: Owen and Kiri Fiona McDermott-Berryman; DEAN OF LAW, UNIV. OF WINDSOR 1990– ; Jr. Lectr. in Business Law, Massey Univ. N.Z. 1979; Judges' Clerk, High Court of N.Z. at Auckland 1979–80; Asst. Prof., Fac. of Law, Univ. of Windsor 1981–85; Assoc. Prof. 1985; admitted as Barrister & Solicitor, High Court of N.Z. 1979; Spencer Mason Travelling Scholarship in Law 1980; Dalhousie Grad. Scholarship 1980; Dir., Windsor Centre for Seniors 1990; Mem. Bd. of Govs., Univ. of Windsor Cand. Assn. of Law Teachers; Candn. Assn. of Univ. Teachers; Law Soc. of U.C. Legal Edn. Ctte. & Equity Ctte.; author of num. scholarly articles; co-author: 'Remedies: Cases and Materials' 2nd ed. 1992; editor: 'Remedies: Issues and Perspectives' 1991; Editor-in-Chief, 'Windsor Yearbook of Access to Justice' 1987–89; recreations: golf; Home: 238 Sunset Ave., Windsor, Ont. N9B 3A7; Office: Sunset Ave., Windsor, Ont. N9B 3P4.

**BERTALANFFY, Felix D.,** M.Sc., Ph.D., F.R.M.S.; educator; b. Vienna, Austria, 20 Feb. 1926; s. late Prof. Ludwig and late Maria (Bauer) von B.; e. Univ. of Vienna Med. Sch. 1945–48; McGill Univ. M.Sc. 1951, Ph.D. 1954; m. Gisele Lavimodière, 20 Jan. 1954; PROF. EMERITUS OF ANATOMY, UNIV. OF MANITOBA since 1991; joined present Univ. as Asst. Prof. 1955, Assoc. Prof. 1959, Prof. 1965–91; med. and biol. research incl. cell div. and kinetics, cancer and carcinogenesis, regeneration, exfoliative cancer cytol., fluorescence microscopy and histochem., histophysiol. and pathol. of respiratory system, cancer chemotherapeutic agts.; developed acridine orange fluorescence microscopy for exfoliative cancer diagnosis (clin. application); writings incl. over 120 contribs. to biol. and med. journs. publ. in 6 langs.; over 150 articles on Japanese philately and postal hist. in various Eng. and German philatelic publs.; Hon. Fellow, Pan Am. Cancer Cytol. Soc.; Fellow, Roy. Microscopical Soc. (London); Amer. Philatelic Soc., Writers Hall of Fame; mem. Am. Assn. Anatomists; Candn. Assn. Anatomists; Am. Assn. Cancer Research; Candn. Soc. Cytol.; Internat. Soc. Stereol.; Internat. Soc. Chronobiology; Sigma Xi; R. Catholic; recreation: Japanese philately; Home: 886 Lindsay St., Winnipeg, Man. R3N 1H8; Office: Dept. of Anatomy, Univ. of Manitoba, 730 William Ave., Winnipeg, Man. R3E 0W3.

**BERTELL, Rosalie,** B.A., M.A., Ph.D., D.Hum.Lit., D.Sc., LL.D.; b. Buffalo, N.Y. 4 Apl. 1929; d. Paul G. and Helen J. (Twohey) B.; e. D'Youville Coll. B.A. 1951; Cath. Univ. M.A. 1959, Ph.D. 1966; PRES. INTERNAT. INST. OF CONCERN FOR PUB. HEALTH 1987– ; Registrar & Assoc. Prof. Math Dept. Sacred Heart Junior Coll., Pennsylvania 1958–68; Co-ord., High Sch. Math Teachers Diocese of Atlanta 1968–69; Assoc. Prof. Math Dept. D'Youville Coll., Buffalo 1969–72, Co-ord. of Inst. Rsch. 1971–72; Sr. Cancer Rsch. Sci. Roswell Park Mem. Inst. 1970–78; Visiting Prof., State Univ. of NY 1972–73, Asst. Rsch. Prof. Graduate Sch., 1974–78; Dir. of Rsch. & Biostatistical Radiation Health Cons., Min. of Concern for Public Health, Buffalo 1978–80; Energy/Public Health Specialist, Jesuit Centre for Social Faith & Justice, Toronto 1980–84; Dir. of Rsch., Dir. Bd. Internat. Inst. of Concern for Public Health 1984–87; Pres. IICPH 1987– ; Founding mem., Internat. Comm. of Health Profls. 1985– ; apptd. to Sci. Adv. Bd. on the Great Lakes, Internat. Joint Comn. 1991–93; Cons. U.S. Nuclear Regulatory Comn. and U.S. Environmental Protection Agency; Cons. to Consumers Assn. Penang, Malaysia; Centre for Ind. Safety & Environmental Concerns Kerala, India; Inst. Energy Rsch. Heidelberg, Germany; Japanese Assn. Sci's; recipient Right Livelihood Award 1986; Women of Distinction Award 1987; World Peace Award 1988; Fellow, Ryerson Polytech. Inst. 1988; Fellow, Ont. Inst. for Studies in Education 1990; named to Honor Role, UNEP Global 500 Award 1993; Honorary degrees: Mount St. Vincent Univ. Halifax D.Hum.L. 1985; D'Youville Coll., Buffalo D.Sc. 1988; Laurentian Univ., Sudbury LL.D. 1988; Univ. of Windsor D.Sc. 1988; mem. Bd. Global Edn. Associates; Food & Water Inc.; ed.-in-chief 'International Perspectives in Public Health' jour. 1984– ; ed. 'Handbook for Estimating the Health Effects of Ionizing Radiation' 1984, revised ed. 1986; Fellow, Indian Soc. Naturalists; mem. Grey Nuns of Sacred Heart; numerous profl. assns.; Kappa Gamma Pi; Sigma Xi; Office: 830 Bathurst St., Toronto, Ont. M5R 3G1.

**BERTHIAUME, Pierre,** M.A., Doctorat d'Etat; educator; b. Montréal, Qué. 19 Dec. 1946; s. Euclide and Hectorine (Desjardins) B.; e. Univ. de Montréal B.A. 1968; McGill Univ. M.A. 1972; Univ. de Grenoble Doctorat de Troisième Cycle 1974, Doctorat d'Etat 1987; PROF. DES LETTRES FRANÇAISES UNIV. D'OTTAWA 1977– ; Prof. Coll. Ahuntsic Montréal 1969–76; Prof. of French McGill Univ. 1976–77; author 'Le Journal Piège' 1981; 'L'Aventure Américaine au XVIIIe Siécle' 1990; co-author: 'Foi et Légendes - La Peinture Votive au Québec (1666–1945)'; ed. 'Prévost, Contes Singuliers' 1985; co-ed. 'Prévost, Mémoires et Aventures d'un Homme de Qualité' 1978; Office: Ottawa, Ont. K1N 6N5.

**BERTON, Pierre,** C.C. (1986), B.A., LL.D., D.Litt., Doctor of A.U., LL.D., D.F.A.; author; b. Whitehorse, Yukon 12 July 1920; s. Francis George and Laura Beatrice (Thompson) B.; e. Victoria Coll., Victoria, B.C.; Univ. of B.C., B.A. 1941; m. Janet Constance, d. A. L. Walker, Haney, B.C., 22 Mar. 1946; children: Penny Margaret, Pamela Beatrice, Patricia Dorothy, Peter Andrew, Paul Francis, Peggy Ann, Perri Robin; Panelist, 'Front Page Challenge' (CBC-TV); Pres., Pierre Berton Enterprises Ltd.; My Country Productions Ltd.; City Editor, Vancouver 'News Herald' 1941–42; Feature Writer, 'Vancouver Sun' 1946–47; Assistant Editor, 'Maclean's' Mag. 1947–51; Assoc. Ed. 1952, and Mng. Ed. 1953–59; Assoc. Editor & Columnist, 'Toronto Star' 1958–62; rejoined 'Maclean's' Mag. 1962–63; Editor-in-chief, Canadian Centennial Library 1964–68; served in 2nd World War with Cdn. Inf. Corps. as Pte., Cpl., 2nd Lt. and Lt.; Royal Mil. Coll. (Intelligence Staff as Acting Capt., G.S.O. III); author of 'The Royal Family' 1954; 'The Golden Trail' 1955; 'The Mysterious North' 1956 (Gov. Gen. Award for Creative Non-Fiction 1956) rev. 1989; 'Klondike' 1958 (Gov. Gen. Award for Creative Non-Fiction 1958); 'Just Add Water and Stir' 1959 (Leacock Medal for Humour 1960); 'Adventures of a Columnist' 1960; 'The New City' 1961; 'The Secret World of Og' 1961, 1974 and (30th anniversary ed.) 1991; 'Fast, Fast, Fast Relief' 1962; 'The Big Sell' 1963; 'The Comfortable Pew' 1965; 'The Smug Minority' 1968; 'The National Dream' 1970; 'The Great Railway' (Illustrated) 1972; 'The Last Spike' (Gov. Gen. Award for Non-Fiction) 1971; 'Drifting Home' 1973; 'Hollywood's Canada' 1975; 'My Country' 1976; 'The Dionne Years: A Thirties Melodrama' 1977; 'The Wild Frontier' 1978; 'The Invasion of Canada 1812–13' 1980; 'Flames Across the Border 1813–1814' 1981; 'Why We Act Like Canadians' 1982; 'The Klondike Quest, A Photographic Essay 1896–1899' 1983; 'The Promised Land' 1984; 'Vimy' 1986; 'Starting Out' 1987; 'The Arctic Grail: The Quest for the North West Passage and the North Pole 1809–1909'; 'The Great Depression 1929 – 1939' 1990; series of 40 books for juveniles, 'Adventures in Canadian History'; 'Niagara: A History of the Falls' 1992; 1982 Nat. Newspaper Awards for Feature Writing and Staff Corresponding, 1961; ACTRA award (best public affairs broadcaster in radio, 1978); ACTRA'S Gordon Sinclair Award – Integrity and Outspokenness in Broadcasting – 1972; Stephen Leacock Medal for Humour 1960; Cdn. Authors Assn. Award, 1981; Cdn. Booksellers Award, 1982; Alumni Award of Distinction, U.B.C., 1981; Beefeater Club Prize for Literature ('The Invasion of Canada' and 'Flames Across the Border'), 1982; OHASSTA Perspective Award, 1982; World Tourism Day Medal, 1982; Cdn. Newsman's Hall of Fame 1983; Companion of the Order of Canada 1986; Gabriel Leger Heritage Medal 1989; Coles Book Award 1989; Order of Mariposa 1990; U.B.C. Trekker Award 1990; Periodical Marketers of Canada 'Book of the Year' Award (The Arctic Grail) 1990; Periodical Marketers of Canada, Author's Award (The Great Depression) 1991; Periodical Marketers Award, Authors Award for Leadership 1992; Commemorative Medal, 125th Anniversary of Candn. Confedn. 1992; recreations: painting, bird watching, gardening, sketching, conversation; Home: R.R. 1, Kleinburg, Ont. L0J 1C0; Office: 21 Sackville St., Toronto, Ont. M5A 3E1.

**BERTRAND, Charles Lloyd,** B.A., M.A., Ph.D.; vice-rector; b. Spokane, Wash. 17 March 1939; s. George Lestor and Dorothy Alice (Baumgartner) B.; e. Western Washington Univ. B.A. 1961; Univ. of Oregon M.A. 1962; Univ. of Wisconsin Ph.D. 1969; one d.: Rachel Susan; VICE-RECTOR, SERVICES, CONCORDIA UNIV. 1992– ; Lecturer in History, Sir George Wiliams Univ. 1967–69; Asst. Prof. 1969–72; Assoc. Prof., Concordia 1972– ; Chair, Dept. of History 1981–85; Dean, Fac. of Arts and Sci. 1985–92; Mem., Bd. of Dir., Greater Montreal YMCA; Comnr., Candn. Comn. on Military History 1992–96; Mem., Candn. Historical Assn.; Am. Historical Assn.; Soc. for Italian Historical Studies; author of journal articles; editor: 'Revolutionary Situations in Europe, 1917–1922' 1977; recreations: squash, tennis, cycling; club: Monteal Amateur Athletic Assn.; Home: 1080 – 36th Ave., Lasalle, Que. H8P 3A8; Office: 1455 de Maisonneuve Blvd. W., Montreal, Que. H3G 1M8.

**BERTRAND, Claude,** C.C. (1971), B.A., M.D., F.A.C.S., F.R.C.S.(C); neurosurgeon; b. Sherbrooke, Que. 28 March 1917; s. Stella (Gamache) B.; e. St. Charles Borromée Semy., Sherbrooke, B.A. 1934; Univ. de Montréal, M.D. 1940; Rhodes Scholar elect; grad. and post-grad. training in Can. and USA; Research Assoc., Dept. of Anat., Oxford Univ., 1946–47; m. Claire Paradis, 16 May 1942; children: Hélène, Denise (Mrs. Luc Pelland), Lucie (Mrs. Charles Wheeler), Louis; EMERITUS PROF. SURGERY (NEUROSURGERY), UNIV. DE MONTRÉAL; Emeritus Chief of Neurosurgery, Hôpital Notre-Dame; Pres. of Extve., Med. Bd., Univ. de Montréal in 1969; joined Hôpital Notre-Dame as Acting Chief, Dept. of Neurosurg., 1947; mem. Med. Research Comte. in Surg. 1965–66; joined Univ. de Montréal as Asst. Prof. of Surg. (Neurosurg.), 1947; Assoc. Prof. 1952, Prof. 1969; ; consulting neurosurg.; Montreal Neurol. Inst.; Barrie (Ont.) Mem. Hosp.; Hôtel-Dieu (Montreal and Sherbrooke); Santa Cabrini Hosp., Montreal (Hon.); Visiting Prof., Nat. Inst. of Health, Bethesda, Md., 1962; Bowman-Gray Sch. of Med., Winston-Salem, N.C., 1962; Univ. of Vermont 1966; Univ. of Alta. 1968; Dartmouth Univ. 1971; Exchange Prof., Univs. of Strasbourg, Paris, Marseille, Lyon, 1961; Univ. of Mexico 1964; Max Planck Inst., Frankfurt, 1969; served with RCAMC 1943–45; rank Capt. (Acting Maj.); Traveler for James IVth Assn. 1969; mem. Med. Research Council Can. 1969–71; rec'd Lawrence Poole Prize, Univ. of Edinburgh, 1970–71; Bd. of Dir., Digital Equipment; mem., Am. Assn. Neurol. Surgs.; Soc. Neurol. Surgs.; Neurosurg. Soc. Am. (Founding mem.; Pres. 1963); Soc. de Neurochirurgie de Langue Française Paris (Pres. 1964); Assn. des Neurochirurg. de la Prov. de Qué.; Candn. Neurosurg. Soc. (Pres. 1961); Soc. Brit. Neurol. Surgs. (Hon. mem. 1970); Montreal Neurol. Soc. (Pres. 1952); Am. Acad. Neurol. (Assoc. mem. 1956): Soc. Neurol. de Paris (Hon. mem.); Candn. Med. Assn. and other med. assns.; R. Catholic; recreations: skiing, tennis, golf; Clubs: Montreal Tennis; Mount Stephen; Address: 129 Rue de l'Épee, Montréal, Qué. H2V 3T1.

**BERTRAND, Françoise,** B.A., M.E.S.; b. Montreal, Que. 6 Aug. 1948; s. Gaston and Laurette (Armand) B.; e. Coll. Ste-Marie Montreal B.A. 1968; York Univ. M.E.S. (Master Environmental Studies) 1975; one d. Julie; C.E.O., SOCIÉTÉ DE RADIO-TÉLÉVISION DU QUÉBEC (RADIO-QUÉBEC) 1988– ; Administrative Dean, Univ. du Quebec A MONTREAL 1984– ; Journalist, CBC French Network Toronto 1975–76; Dir. of Communications, Soc. des Jeux du Qué., Montréal 1976–78; Cons. in Advertising, TV Programming; Rsch. Pub. Surveys Environmental Field Sorecom, Montreal 1978–80; Asst. to Vice Pres. Acad. Affairs present univ. 1980–82, Assoc. Dean 1982–83; mem. Inquiry Fed. Water Policy 1984–85; Vice-pres., Consortium TV5 Québec-Canada; mem., Assemblée des Gouverneurs 1990; Mem., Ecole nationale de l'humour 1991; Mem., Revue Voir 1991; Office: 800 Fullum, Montreal Qué. H2K 3L7.

**BERTRAND, Gérard,** Q.C., B.A., LL.L; b. Donnacona, Que. 13 Apr. 1927; s. Joseph Alfred and Yvonne (Gravel) B.; e. Ecole du Sacré coeur Donnacona, Que.; Coll. de Lévis; Séminaire de Qué.; Laval Univ. B.A., LL.L.; Royal Candn. Sch. Inf.; Univ. of Toronto and York Univ. M.B.A. course 1971 (Pub. Service Bicultural Devel. Fellow); children: Louis, Anne Pascale; DIRECTEUR DU PROGRAMME DE DIPLÔME EN RÉDACTION LÉGISLATIVE, ÉTUDES SUPÉRIEURES,

FACULTÉ DE DROIT, UNIV. OF OTTAWA 1988– ; called to Bar of Que. 1952; cr. Fed. Q.C. 1975; rec'd comn. (COTC) 1950, Staff Learner H.Q.E. Que. Area 1951–52; joined Dept. External Affairs 1952–63 serving in Ottawa, Tokyo (1953–56), Paris (Second and First Secy. 1958–62); Candn. Corp. for 1967 World Exhn. 1963–67 serving as Extve. Asst. to Pres. and Commr. Gen. and Project Offr. 'Man in the Community' Pavilion; Gen. Mgr. Nat. Film Bd. Can. 1968–71; Asst. Secy. to Cabinet (Leg. and House Planning) Privy Council Office 1972–76; Registrar, Supreme Court of Can. 1976–78; Assoc. Chief Leg. Counsel, Leg. Sec., Dept. of Justice 1978–80; Chief Leg. Counsel, Dept. of Justice 1980–87; Mem., Statute Revision Comn. of Can. 1982–87; Prés., Conseil régional Ottawa-Carleton, Assn. canadienne française de l'Ontario (ACFO) 1983–87; Gov., Univ. of Ottawa 1984–87; Dir., The Ottawa-Carleton Learning Found. 1985–87, 1989–91; Dir., Théâtre du Trillium 1989– ; Sec., Commonwealth Assn. of Legislative Counsel 1986–87; Chrmn., Ontario French-Language Services Commission 1987–88; mem. Hull Bar; Bar Prov. Que.; R. Catholic; recreations: cycling, reading; Clubs: Cercle Universitaire d'Ottawa (Founding mem.); Home: 10–333 Metcalfe St., Ottawa, Ont. K2P 1S5; Office: Faculté de Droit, Univ. of Ottawa, 57 Louis-Pasteur, Ottawa, Ont. K1N 6N5.

**BERTRAND, Gilles,** O.C., B.A., M.Sc., M.D., F.R.C.S.(C) (1956); neurosurgeon; b. Montreal, Que. 5 Aug. 1924; s. Albert and Françoise (Demers) B.; e. Univ. de Montréal, Coll. Jean-de-Brebeuf, B.A. 1943; Univ. de Montréal, M.D. 1949; McGill Univ., M.Sc. 1954; m. Louise, d. late Napoleon Lafleur, 20 June 1953; children: Maryse, François, Martin; CONE PROF. OF NEUROSURGERY, McGILL UNIV. 1988; Lect. neurosurg. there 1955; Asst. Prof. 1960, Assoc. Prof. 1963, Prof. 1971; Neurosurgeon-in-Chief, Montreal Neurol. Hosp. (1973); Consultant Neurosurg., Hosp. Jean-Talon, Montreal; Brome Missisquoi Perkins Hosp.; Montreal Gen. Hosp.; Past Pres., Candn. Assn. Neurol. Surg.; mem. Am. Assn. of Neurosurgs.; Am. Acad. Neurol. Surg.; Soc. of Neurological Surgeons; Soc. de neurochirurgie de langue française; Montreal Neurol. Soc. (Past Pres.); Assn. des neurochirurgiens Prov. Que. (Sec., Pres. 1965–69); R. Catholic; recreations: sailing, skiing; Home: 1317 Redpath Cresc., Montreal, Qué. H3G 1A1; Office: 3801 University, Montreal, Qué. H3A 2B4.

**BERTRAND, Guy,** B.A., B.Eng., M.Sc.; university executive; b. Montreal, Que. 13 Feb. 1942; s. Raymond and Juliette (Laberge) B.; e. Coll. Ste-Marie B.A. 1961; Ecole Polytechnique Montreal B.Eng. 1965; Univ. de Montréal M.Sc. 1972; m. Danielle d. Blandine and Adrien Villeneuve 8 May 1971; children: Christine, Jean-Patrick; DIRECTOR, PLANNING & DEVELOPMENT, UNIV. OF QUEBEC 1988– ; Service Engineer, Cdn. Westinghouse 1965–67; Prof. of Computer Sci., Cégep Maisonneuve 1968–69; Consultant, S.M.A. Montreal 1969–72; Dir., Computer Systems, Univ. of Que. 1972–74; Communications Systems 1974–82; Vice-Pres. Communications 1982–88; Dir., Univ. of Que. Press; Sci. Dir., Centre Francophone de Rech. Inform. des Orgns.; Pres., Soc. Qué. de Communication et de Rech. en Informatique; Pub., Tech. Information & Soc.; Sr. Mem., Observatoire Qué. des Industries de la Langue; Mem., Ordre des ingénieurs du Qué.; Planning Forum; Inst. of Electrical & Electronical Engs.; Candn. Information Processing Soc.; Assn. can.-française pour l'avancement des sci.; recreations: tennis; clubs: Club de Tennis Montcalm; Home: 3017 de la Seine, Ste-Foy, Que. G1W 1H8; Office: 2875 boul. Laurier, Ste-Foy, Que. G1V 2M3.

**BERTRAND, Rev. Hector-L.,** C.M., S.J., Ph.D., D.Sc. (R.C.); priest; educator; b. Warren, Ont. 10 March 1907; s. William James and Eugénie (Gervais) B.; e. Sacred Heart Coll., Sudbury, Ont., B.A. 1928; S.J. 1928; Georgetown Univ., D.Sc.; VICE PRES.-ADM., UNIV. OF SUDBURY since 1965; Publisher and Ed., 'Le Voyageur' (weekly French paper) since 1975; o. 1939; Prof. of Apologetics and Dean of Discipline (Prefectus Disciplinae), Sacred Heart Coll. of Sudbury (now present univ.) 1941; Founder, 1st Conv. and Exhn. for Hosps., Prov. Que. 1948; Founder and Dir., L'Ecole Supérieure d'Administration Hospitalière, 1948; 'L'Hopital d'Aujourd'Hui' (journ.), 1955; Founder, Med. Dirs. course, 1957; Hosp. and Med. Adm. courses (evening), 1961; Regent, Coll. of Medicine, Bangalore, India, 1963–65; consultant in hosp. adm.; during World War II served as Chaplain, Parachutists Corps (Candn.) 1943; Maj. and Commdg. Chaplain, Mil. Dist. No. 10, Can., 1944; rec'd George Findlay Stephens Mem. Award for 'Outstanding services to Hospitals of Canada,' citations from various prof. assns.; Pres. and Extve. Dir., Cath. Hosp. Assn. Can. 1945–52; Founder, Pres. and 1st Extve. Dir., Comité des Hôpitaux du Qué. 1947; Gov., Candn. Hosp. Assn., 1947–63 (with 2 yrs. exception; Chrmn. Comte. on Educ.); Founder, Assn. Med. Dirs. Prov. Que., 1957; Assn. Hosp. Adms. Prov. Que., Assn. Practical Nurses Prov. Que. (Hon. mem.), Assn.: Baby-Nurses Prov. Que.; Assn. Med. Record Librarians Prov. Que., 1960; Co-founder, Candn. Council on Hosp. Accreditation; Hon. Fellow, Am. Coll. Hosp. Adms.; Hon. mem., Que. Assn. Hosp. Adms.; Candn. Med. Record Librarians; Life mem., Assn. Consultants in Indust. Relations; mem., Acad. Hosp. Counsellors; Member, Order of Canada; Address: Univ. of Sudbury, Sudbury, Ont. P3E 2C6.

**BERTRAND, J. Richard,** B.Sc., M.B.A., A.P.R.; government relations consultant; b. Hull, Que. 2 Sept. 1942; s. Gerard Scott and the late Marguerite (Ennis) B.; e. McGill Univ., B.Sc. 1964; Univ. of Ottawa, M.B.A. 1985; m. Hella d. the late Kazick and Anni Zarudzka 7 Aug. 1965; children: Paul, Rebecca; VICE CHRMN., EXTVE. CONS. LIMITED 1980– ; Captain, Candn. Armed Forces 1959–67; Information Services, Min. of Nat. Defence 1967; Cons., Govt. & Bus. 1968–69; Vice-Pres., Ottawa Cablevision 1969–80; Pres., Ottawa-Brennan Ltd.; Accredited Public Relations; Chrmn., Extve. Ctte. and Vice Chrmn., Bd. of Govs., Univ. of Ottawa; Trustee, Royal Ottawa Hosp.; Adv. Bd., Royal Trust, Ottawa; recreations: summer and winter sports; Clubs: Country; Rideau; Royal Ottawa Golf; Candn.; Univ. of Ottawa Faculty; Home: 32 Selwyn Cr., Kanata, Ont. K2K 1N8; Office: 155 Queen St., Ste. 1100, Ottawa, Ont. K1P 6L1.

**BERTUZZI, Lawrence Albert,** B.Sc., LL.B.; lawyer; b. Hamilton, Ont. 29 Jan. 1948; s. Peo Joseph and Ida Theresa (Ferroni) B.; e. Michael Power High Sch. 1966; Univ. of W. Ont. B.Sc. 1969, LL.B. 1972; m. Norma d. William and Jean Stevenson; children: Shannon Norma, Michael Stevenson; PARTNER, MILLER THOMSON 1979– , Chrmn. & C.E.O. 1988–92; Rsch. Asst. Dispute Settlement Services 1971; articled with Miller, Thomson, Sedgewick, Lewis & Healy 1972–73; called to Bar of Ont. (with honours) 1974; Assoc. present firm 1974–79; seconded to Fed. Anti-Inflation Bd. as Policy & Interpretation Offr. Compensation Br. 1976; Guest Lectr. in Labour Law Univ. of W. Ont.; apptd. Special Arbitrator under National Hockey League Constitution 1992; Cubmaster 93rd Toronto Wolf Cub Pack 1984– ; mem., Bd. of Dirs., The Bethany Hills Sch. 1991, 1992; mem. Bd. of Dirs., Hockey Hall of Fame; mem. Bd. Trade Metrop. Toronto (Labour Relations Subctte. 1980–90); Candn. Bar Assn. (Labour Law Subsect. 1974– ;); Ont. Trucking Assn.; United Church; recreation: athletics; Club: Granite; Home: 51 Coldstream Ave., Toronto, Ont. M5N 1X7; Office: P.O. Box 27, 20 Queen St.W., Toronto, Ont. M5H 3S1.

**BÉRUBÉ, Adrien,** Ph.D.; educator; b. Edmundston, N.B. 16 May 1944; s. Charles and Jeannette (Moreau) B.; e. Univ. de Moncton B.A. 1964, B.Ed. 1972; Simon Fraser Univ. M.A. 1977; Univ. Laval Ph.D. 1991; m. Constance d. Roland G. Martin 14 Sept. 1964; children: Elaine, Dominique, Maryse, Jean-François, Claude-Eric; DEAN OF STUDIES CENTRE UNIV. SAINT-LOUIS-MAILLET UNIV. DE MONCTON 1991– , Prof. of Geog. 1987– ; Lectr. in Geog. present Centre 1966, Asst. Prof. 1973, Assoc. Prof. 1977, Dir. Secteur des Sci's Humaines 1980–86, 1991, Pres. Assn. professeurs & bibliothécaires 1976–78; mem. Bd. Govs. present Univ. 1977–78, Senate 1980–86, 1991– ; Pres. and Pub. Marévie Inc. 1988– ; mem. Candn. Assn. Geogs. (Exec. Ctte. 1978–79); Social Sci's & Humanities Rsch. Council Can. 1990– ; Comité d'orientation, Cahiers de géographie du Qué. 1989– ; Comité de rédaction, Revue de la Société historique du Madawaska 1980– ; mem. Assn. québécoise de cartographie; Edmundston C. of C. (Dir. 1982–83); co-author 'J'apprivoise L'Explorateur: Pour découvrir les relations interpersonnelles à l'intérieur de groupes avec un ordinateur' 1990; 'Thomas Albert, Histoire du Madawaska: Entre l'Acadie, le Québec et l'Amérique' 1982; Home: 141 39e ave., Edmundston, N.B. E3V 2X4; Office: Edmundston, N.B. E3V 2S8.

**BERUBE, Jean-Yves,** C.M. (1979); homme d'affaire; né Cap Chat, Qué. 5 mars 1928; f. Ephrem et Marie Leda Isabelle Bérubé; é. Ecole Cap-Chat cours primaire; Collège St-Alexandre et Gaspé cours classique; Université du Québec cours adm. 1972–75; ép. Blandine f. Edouard Coulombe 23 octobre 1967; enfant: Louise; PRÉS. FONDATEUR: LIGUE NAVALE DE CAP-CHAT 1972–90; membre du conseil Duc Edimbourg; Syndicat Minier Boisbuisson; du Festival Folklorique inter-ethnique 1975–78; de l'Office d'Habitation Municipale de Cap-Chat; Prés.: Commission de Développement de la ville de Cap-Chat; de la Ligue Navale du Canada, div. Québec 1985–87; de la Ligue Navale du Canada, div. Cap-Chat 1962–77; des Pecheries Cartier Inc.; Administrateur Cegep de Matane, Soc. des arts Traditionnels du St-Laurent; Décoration: Ordre du Canada 1977; Médaille de la Reine Elizabeth 1977; Médaille 125 Canada 1992; Echevin: à la ville de Cap-Chat 1972–74; Commissaire: Commission scolaire Régionale des Monts: Gérant personnel et traffic chez Ungava Transport Inc. 1951–63, agence Maritime Inc. 1963–68, service de la paie Gaspé Construction; Exécutif: Conseil régional de Développement de l'Est du Qué. 1970–77; Vice-prés.: Assoc. Touristique de la Gaspésie 1988–90; Mem.: Soc. des Arts Traditionnels du St-Laurent, Chevalier de Colomb, Club Lion; Secrétaire: Actionnaire de la Soc. Minière Boisbuisson (Mines Madeleine); Catholique; récreations: tennis, skiing, ping-pong, baseball, hockey; adresse: C.P. 10, Cap-Chat, Qué. G0J 1E0.

**BESANT, Derek Michael,** B.F.A., R.C.A.; artist; educator; b. Fort MacLeod, Alta. 15 July 1950; e. Univ. of Calgary B.F.A. 1973, grad. studies 1974; m. Alexandra Haeseker 1 Aug. 1974; INSTR., ALTA. COLL. OF ART 1977– , Drawing Chrmn. 1978–88; Exhbn. Designer, Glenbow-Alta. Inst. Art Gallery & Museum 1973–77 (design and layout for new museum location Calgary opening 1976); Guest Lectr., S.W. Texas State Univ., San Marcos, USA 1982; recent exhbns. incl. Candn. Rep. Brit. Internat. Biennale 1979; 'Contemporary Candn. Printmakers' (Invit. Tour, Bronx Museum, NY); 'Perspectives on Architecture' (Calgary Arch. and Urban Studies Alliance); Cabo Frio Internat. Biennial (Brazil); Premio Internat. Biella per L'Incisione (Italy); Salon des Nations (Paris, France); Biennale Internat. de Gravure (Yugoslavia); 4th Internat. Seoul Biennale (Korea); British Drawing Biennale (Middlesborough, Engl.); Int'l. Print Exhibit (China) 1983; Norske Internasjonale Biennale 1984 (Norway); 10th Krakow Int'l Biennale 1984 (Poland); Cdn. Contemporary Printmaking (Australia) 1984; Fredrikstad Biennale (Norway) 1984; 7th Tokyo Video Festival (Japan) 1985; Ethiopia Exhbn., Akron (Ohio) Art Museum 1985; Ibiza International (Spain) 1985; 6th Internat. Impact, Kyoto (Japan) City Museum 1985; Interaction, Queensland College of Art Australian Tour 1985; Artists' Response to Architecture, Victoria, Texas 1986; Art Plastyk Warynskiego, Para Museum of Art, Poland 1986; Diagrams, Mira Godard Gallery, Toronto 1986; Asian/Pacific, Univ. of New Delhi, India 1986; Contemporary Realists, Glenbow Museum, Banff, Alta. 1986; 5th Seoul Internat. Biennale, The Dong-A Ilbo, Korea 1986; Premio Biella Internazionale, Italy 1987; Galantal. Artpool, Museum of Fine Arts, Budapest, Hungary 1987; Lodz 87 Poland, 5th Internat. Exhbn. Gallery Arts Bureau 1987; Northern Lights: Contemporary Canadian Art, various galleries, U.S.A. 1987; XV Olympic Arts Festival, Calgary 1988; 12th International Biennale, Krakow, Poland 1988; Metropolitan Museum, Miami, Fla. 1988; International Buchkunst, Leipzig 1989; Southwest Texas Artforum 1989; Mira Godard, Toronto 1989; Wolujen/Udell/Vancouver 1989; Gütersloh, West Germany 1989; Premio Biella, Italy 1990; Art Gall. of Hamilton 1990; 3rd Biennale International, Cuba 1990; British International Biennale 1991; Kharkov Art Museum, USSR 1991; recent works incl.: 'Flatiron Mural' W. wall Gooderham Flatiron Bldg. Toronto 1980; Video Documentation 'Christo – Surrounded Islands' (Miami); commissions: Cineplex Odeon, New York City 1989; Scotia Plaza, Toronto 1989; Mount Royal Coll., Calgary 1989; rec'd 2nd Prize Miami Internat. Biennale 1977; World Culture Prize for Letters, Arts & Science' 1984, Centro Studi e Ricerche delle Nazioni (Italy); Alta. Achievement Award 1984; Canada Counc. Grant 1985; West. Canada Art Assoc. Publication Awards 1986; Alberta Culture, Visual Arts Project Grant 1987; Olympics Exhbn. Comte., Calgary 1985–86; Bd. of Govs., Alta. College of Art 1985–87; Art Ctte., Nickle Arts Bd. 1986; Home: Box 48081, Midlake Postal Outlet, 40 Midlake Blvd. S.E., Calgary, Alta. T2X 3C0; Office: 1407 – 14 Ave. N.W., Calgary, Alta. T2N 4R3.

**BESEN, Joan Lori;** musician, songwriter, writer; b. Chicago, Ill. 12 June 1951; d. Irvin and Eleanor Shirley (Wolfe) B.; e. Bathurst Heights C.I. 1969; Toronto Teachers' College 1970; one s.: Sunny Besen Thrasher; MEMBER, PRAIRIE OYSTER 1982– ; started playing music professionally in 1969; Teacher, French & Theatre Arts, North & East York Bds. of Edn. 1970–74; played with Sylvia Tyson & The Great Speckled Bird 1978–82; Prairie Oyster is an award-winning group of the Juno & Candn. Country Music Assn. (CCMA); the Toronto-based band is signed to RCA Nashville/BMG Canada; awards: 1st Juno nom. for Country Group of the Year 1984–85; won Juno for Country Group of the Year 1985–86, 1986–87, 1990; Juno nomination for Songwriter of the Year 1992; CCMA Group of the Year 1990, 1991; CCMA Single of the Year 1990; CCMA

Keyboard Player of the Year 1990, 1991; CCMA Song of the Year (writer) 1991; CMPA Country Song of the Year (1st runner-up) 1991; 7 RPM Big Country Awards: Group of the Year 1991; Entertainer of the Year, Group of the Year, Album of the Year, Single of the Year, Song of the Year (written by Keith Glass & Joan Besen) 1992, and Country Composer of the Year 1993; 4 CCMA Awards: Group of the Year, Album of the Year, Song of the Year (written by Joan Besen), Keyboard Player of the Year 1992; SOCAN Country Song of the Year (with Keith Glass) 1992; has written music for Prairie Oyster for film & TV; regular performer & contbr. on var. CBC radio shows; Script Editor on CBC / Nelvana / Disney show 'The Edison Twins' in which her son starred; 2nd Place Stephen Leacock Limerick Contest 1989, honourable mention 1990; Mem., Soc. of Candn. Authors & Composers; Candn. Country Music Assn.; Country Music Assn. (U.S.); Candn. Songwriters' Assn.; ECO (Earth Communications Office – entertainment indus. envir. orgn.); author of chapter in Peter Gzowski's 'The Morningside Papers' 1985; recreations: cryptic crossword puzzles, reading, writing, listening to music; Home: 156 Hiawatha Rd., Toronto, Ont. M4L 2X9.

**BESSE, Ronald Duncan;** executive; b. Stayner, Ont. 7 Dec. 1938; s. Josiah R. and Annie Mae (Buie) B.; e. Ryerson Polytech. Inst., Bus. Admin. 1960; m. Barbara Jane Low 26 Jan. 1963; children: Christopher, Alison; Chrmn., PRES. & C.E.O., CANADA PUBLISHING CORP. 1984– ; Vice-Pres., Edn. Div., McGraw-Hill Ryerson 1969–70; Mng. Dir., Libros McGraw-Hill de Mexico 1970–73; Pres. & C.E.O. McGraw-Hill Ryerson 1973–76; Pres., Consolidated Graphics 1976–78; Pres. & C.E.O., Gage Pub. Ltd. 1978–84; Young Pres. Orgn. (Past Chrmn. Ont. & Upper Can. chapters; Internat. Dir. 1981–87); Past Pres., Candn. Book Pub. Counc.; Chrmn. & C.E.O., Macmillan Can.; Chrmn. & Pres., RDB Capital Corp.; Chrmn., Gage Edn. Pub. Co.; Diffulivre Inc.; Global Press; Gage Distribution; Past Gov., The Shaw Festival; Past Dir., The Canadian Club; Dir., MDC Corp.; Rogers Communications Inc.; Luxembourg Cambridge Holding Group, Luxemourg; Samcor Inc., Toronto; Past Gov., Bishop Strachan Sch.; Ryerson Polytech. Inst.; West Park Hosp.; Past Chrmn., Heritage Dinner, Ont. Liberal Party; Mem., Chief Extves. Organization; World President's Organization; recreations: flying, tennis, fishing; Clubs: The Granite (Chrmn.; Past Pres. 1992–93); Muskoka Lakes Golf & Country; Bd. of Trade; National; 4872 (Past Chrmn.); Ocean Reef (Key Largo, Fla.); Racquet Club (Ocean Reef, Florida); Home: 18 Valleyanna Dr., Toronto, Ont. M4N 1J8 (summer: The Crow's Nest, Port Sandfield, Ont.; winter: Ocean Reef Club, Key Largo, Florida); Office: 164 Commander Blvd., Agincourt, Ont. M1S 3C7.

**BESSELL, D. Hugh,** B.Comm., F.C.A.; chartered accountant; b. Calgary, Alta. 30 May 1941; s. Leslie W. and Flora M. (Robertson) B.; e. Univ. of Alberta B.Comm. 1964; m. Patricia Minniss 1972; children: Jennifer, Allison; DEPUTY CHAIRMAN & CHIEF OPERATING OFFICER, KPMG PEAT MARWICK THORNE 1993– ; C.A. 1966; Partner, Thorne Riddell Calgary 1972; Audit Partner, Calgary Office & Partner-in-Charge, Profl. Practice for the Prairies Reg. 1976–82; Partner-in-Charge, Audit 1982–88; Calgary Office Mng. Partner, KPMG Peat Marwick Thorne 1988–93; Partnershp Bd. 1988– ; Chair 1992–93; Mem., Council, Inst. of C.A.s of Alta. 1978–83; Mem., Extve. Ctte. 1980–83; Pres. 1982–83; Mem. Bd. of Gov. 1981–83; Fellow, Inst. of C.A.s of Alta. 1984; Life Mem. 1985; Founding Mem. & Past Pres., Univ. of Calgary Alumni Assn.; Former Mem., The Senate, Univ. of Calgary; Former Bd. Mem. & Past Chair, Calgary Housing Authority; Bd. Mem., Acctg. Foundation of Alberta; clubs: National Club, Toronto, Glencoe, Glencoe Golf & Country, Ranchmen's, Calgary; Home: 40 Kings Lynn Rd., Etobicoke, Ont. M8X 2N2; Office: Box 122, Scotia Plaza, 40 King St. W., Toronto, Ont. M5H 3Z2.

**BESSETTE, Gérard,** M.A., L.ès L., D.ès L., F.R.S.C., university professor; b. Sabrevois, Que., 25 Feb. 1920; s. Jean-Baptiste and Victoria (Bertrand) B.; e. Univ. de Montréal, B.A. 1941; M.A. 1946, L.ès L. 1946, D.ès L. 1950; m. Irene, d. Jan Bakowski, 3 Sept. 1971; Univ. of Sask., 1946–49; Duquesne Univ., Pittsburgh, Pa., 1951–58; Royal Mil. Coll., Kingston, Ont., 1958–60; Prof. of French, Queen's Univ. 1960–79; publications: 'Poèmes Temporels' 1954; 'La Bagarre' (novel) 1958; 'Le Libraire' (novel) 1960; 'Les Images en poésie canadienne-française' 1960; 'Les Pédagogues' (novel) 1961; 'Not For Every Eye' (trans. of 'Le Libraire') 1962; Ed., 'Anthologie d'Albert Laberge' 1962; 'L'Incubation' (novel) 1965; 'Incubation (trans. of 'l'Incubation') 1967; rec'd Gov. Gen.'s Lit. Award for French Fiction, 1966 and 1972; Ed., 'De Québec à Saint-Boniface' (anthol. of French-Candn. short stories) 1968; 'Une Litérature en ébullition' (criticism) 1968; 'Histoire de la litérature canadienne-française' (in collab.) 1968; 'Le Cycle' (novel) 1971; 'Trois romanciers québécois' (criticism) 1974; 'La Commensale' (novel) 1975; 'The Brawl' (trans. of 'La Bagarre') 1976; 'Les Anthropoïdes' (novel) 1977; 'Mes romans et moi' (memoirs) 1979; 'Le Semestre' (novel) 1979; 'La Garden-party de Christophine' (short stories) 1980; received Le Prix David du Québec 1980; 'Les Dires d'Omer Marin' (novel) 1985; 'The Cycle' (trans. of 'Le Cycle') 1987; Mem., l'Académie canadienne-française; Address; 270 Frontenac St., Kingston, Ont. K7L 3S8.

**BEST, Brian Desmond,** M.D., F.R.C.S. (Edin.), F.R.C.S. (C); b. Chandlers Ford, Eng. 20 Aug. 1910; s. Robert Moore and Ann (McBride) B.; came to Canada 1911; e. Killarney Pub. and High Schs., Man. (Gov.-Gen.'s Medal 1927); Univ. of Manitoba, M.D. 1934 (Univ. Gold and Silver Medals in Medical Course 1934); Lic., Med. Council of Can. 1934; F.R.C.S. (Edin.) 1937; F.R.C.S.(C.) 1949; m. Jean Margaret, d. Herman Prior, Portage la Prairie, Man., June 1940; children: Robert, Shelagh; EMERITUS PROF. OF OBSTET. AND GYNAECOL., UNIV. OF MANITOBA; retired from practice 1980; Hon. Obstet. and Gynaecol., Winnipeg Gen. Hosp.; mem., Candn. Med. Assn.; Winnipeg Med. Soc.; Coll. of Phys. & Surg. of Man. (Pres. 1946–47); Past Pres. Soc. of Obstet. & Gynaecols. of Can.; Past Pres. Candn. Gynaecol. Soc.; former mem. of Bd., Cancer Found. of Manitoba; has contrib. scient. papers to various med. publs.; Home: 204–1 Evergreen Pl., Winnipeg, Man. R3L 0E9.

**BEST, Edward Willson,** B.Sc., Ph.D.; geologist; b. Windsor, Ont. 15 Apr. 1927; s. William and Della Pearl (Willson) B.; e. Univ. of W. Ont., B.Sc. 1949; Univ. of Wis., PhD. 1953; m. Bette Ilene Rushlow, 1951; children: Wendy Elizabeth, Alan Randall, Carolyn Leslie; PARTNER, FOSTER RESEARCH 1985– ; Chrmn., Oil and Gas Ctte., Govt. of Can.; Chrmn. of the Bd. of Dirs., Transwest Energy Inc.; Mem. Bd. of Dirs., Fishery Products International Ltd.; retired 1985 as Pres. Oil and Gas Div. & Dir. BP Canada Inc.; Address: 116 Roxboro Rd. S.W., Calgary, Alta. T2S 0R1.

**BEST, Henry Bruce Macleod,** M.A., Ph.D.; educator; b. Toronto, Ont. 9 Oct. 1934; s. late Dr. Charles Herbert and Margaret (Mahon) B.; e. Upper Can. Coll. Toronto; Univ. of Toronto B.A. 1956; Laval Univ. M.A. 1957, Ph.D. 1969; m. Janna Mairi de Grasse d. the late Iain Ramsay, younger of Kildalton, and Freda Landen Ramsay, Isle of Islay, Scot. 28 Dec. 1964; children: Mairi, Bruce; PAST PRES. AND PROF. OF HISTORY, LAURENTIAN UNIV. OF SUDBURY 1977– ; Extve. Asst. to Secy. of State for External Affairs 1958–59; Extve. Asst. to Leader of Opposition Nfld. 1960; Extve. Secy. Internat. Diabetes Fed. 1963–64; Office of the Pres. and Dept. of Hist., York Univ. 1964–69; Academic Assoc. Dean and Acting Coordinator of Candn. Studies, Atkinson Coll. 1969–77; Pres. Laurentian Univ. 1977–84; Visiting Prof. of Candn. Studies, University Coll., Cork; Hebrew Univ. of Jerusalem; Univ. of Edinburgh; and British Counc. 1984–85; mem. Sudbury 2001 Comte. 1977–85; Chrmn. First Special Council Ont. Univs. Comte. on Support of Bilingualism (francophones) 1978, Chrmn. Univs. Centennial Comte. Ont. 1965–67; Chrmn. Centennial Programme in Arts AUCC 1965–67; regular commentator in French and Eng. on pol. and cultural affairs radio and TV Toronto and Montreal 1965– ; mem. Governing Council Ont. Coll. Art 1972–74 (Chrmn. 1973–74); Course Dir. New Horizons Programme Fed. Govt. 1973–74; mem. Planning Bd. Twp. Nassagaweya 1970–73 (Chrmn. Comte. Adjustment 1973–74); Dir. Ont. Educ. Communications Authority 1978–82; Sudbury & District Chamber of Commerce; Laurentian Hospital; Elliot Lake Centre; awarded Knight of the Order of Italy 1984; Commander of the Order of St. Lazarus of Jerusalem 1990; author various acticles, papers, book chapters, contrib. to 'The Dictionary of Canadian Biography' Vols. 1 and V; mem. Candn. Assn. Scot. Studies; Candn. Professors for Peace in Middle E.; Adv. Bd., 'Language and Society'; P. Conservative; Presbyterian; Address: Dept. of Hist., Laurentian Univ., Sudbury, Ont. P3E 2C6.

**BEST, James Calbert,** B.A.; management consultant; b. New Glasgow; s. Albert T. and Carrie Mae (Prevoe) B.; e. New Glasgow (N.S.) High Sch., 1943; King's Coll., Dalhousie Univ., B.A. 1948, Dipl. Journalism 1948, post-grad. work, Pol. Science-Pub. Adm. 1949; m. Barbara Doreen (dec.), d. Isaac Charles Phills and Mary Phills (Alda), Sydney, N.S., 17 Oct. 1957; children: Christene, Jamie, Stephen, Kevin; Canadian High Commissioner to Trinidad and Tobago 1985–88; Nat. Pres., Civil Service Assn., Can. 1957–66; Dir., Personnel & Adm., Office of Comptroller of Treasury, Can. 1966–69; Dir.-Gen., Adm., Dept. Supply & Services, Can. 1969–70; Asst. Depy. Min. (Operations) 1970–73; Asst. Dep. Min. (Adm.), Dept. of Manpower and Immigration 1974–75; Dir. Applied Studies in Govt. Prog., Commonwealth Secretariat, London, Eng. 1975–77; Special Policy Advisor to Dep. Min./Chrmn. Can. Employment and Immigration Comm./Dept. 1978; Extve. Dir., Immigration 1978–85; former mem. Bd. of Govs., King's Coll., Halifax; Chrmn., Minister's Task Force ONSPORT 1991–92; co-author: (with M. Blackhurst & L. Makosky) 'Sport - The Way Ahead' 1992; mem. Bd. of Dirs., Children's Aid Found. of Ottawa; rec'd Centennial Medal 1967; mem., Inst. Pub. Adm. Can.; Anglican; recreations: reading, photography, music; Address: Ste. 1804, 1510 Riverside Dr., Ottawa, Ont. K1G 4X5.

**BEST, Patricia Margaret,** B.A.; writer; editor; b. Toronto, Ont. 31 Dec. 1953; d. Norman Cyril and Margaret Ellen (Casey) B.; e. Univ. of Toronto; Ryerson Polytech. Inst. B.A. (Jour.) 1975; m. Carlo s. Domenic and Santina Liconti 1975; Asst. Managing Editor, Financial Times of Canada 1988–91; Business Ed. Maclean's 1985–87; writer, Daily Commercial News 1975–78; Sr. Writer, Financial Post 1978–84; recipient Nat. Bus. Book Award 1985; Nat. Bus. Writing Awards 1983; co-author 'A Matter of Trust' 1985; 'The Brass Ring' 1988; Address: c/o Random House of Canada Ltd., Suite 210, 33 Yonge St., Toronto, Ont. M5E 1G4.

**BEST, Robert Brian,** B.A., M.P.A., C.H.R.P.; insurance executive; b. Winnipeg, Man. 26 Feb. 1943; s. Brian Desmond M.D. and Jean Margaret (Prior) B.; e. Univ. of Manitoba B.A. 1964; Univ. of Winnipeg M.P.A. 1980; Univ. of Manitoba Cert. Personnel-Ind. Relations 1972; m. Joyce d. Rudolph and Emily Miller 20 Sept. 1969; children: Raina, Heather; VICE-PRES. HUMAN RESOURCES, THE MANITOBA PUBLIC INSURANCE CORP. 1991– ; Personnel Offr. Prov. of Manitoba 1964–71; Dir. of Personnel Prov. of Manitoba 1971–79; Exec. Dir. Manitoba Human Rights Comn. 1980–81; Vice-Pres. Human Resources, Great-West Life Assurance Co. 1981–91; contrib. author 'The Meaning of Merit' in 'Canadian Public Administration: Problematical Perspectives' 1982; pub. articles on human resource mgmt.; mem. Adv. Bd. 'Canadian HR Reporter' 1988–90; mem. Internat. Personnel Mgmt. Assn. (Pres. Winnipeg Chapter 1978; Dir. Candn. Region); Adv. Counc. Compensation Rsch. Centre, Conf. Bd. of Can.; Council of Human Resources Extves. (West) 1990– ; Manitoba Inst. of Mgmt. (Dir. 1982–91, Chrmn. 1985–87); Candn. Life and Health Ins. Assn. (Ctte. on Educ. Relations 1984–90); mem., LOMA Human Resources Council 1990–91; mem., Life Mgmt. Inst. Counc. 1987–90; Winnipeg C. of C.; Adv. Bd. Inst. for Social & Econ. Rsch., Univ. of Man. 1982–84 (Lectr. Continuing Edn. Div. there 1976–80; past Pres. Alumni Assn. 1981–82; Senator and mem. Senate Ctte. on Hon. Degrees 1981–82); Candn. Cancer Soc. (Pres. Manitoba Div. 1987–89); Nat. Dir., Candn. Cancer Soc. 1987–90; Bd. Mem., Manitoba Inst. of Cell Biology 1988–91; Candn. Counc. of Native Business (Man.) 1987–91; Dir. Age & Opportunity Centre, Winnipeg 1971–78; recreations: golf, squash; Clubs: Southwood Golf & Country; Winnipeg Squash Racquet; Home: 26 Cass St., Winnipeg, Man. R3R 2M4; Office: 330 Graham Ave., Winnipeg, Man. R3C 4A4.

**BEST, Thomas Harold,** B.A.; publishing executive; b. Toronto, Ont. 26 Oct. 1953; s. Douglas Wilson and Betty Jane (Kirby) B.; e. The Candn. Jr. Coll. Lausanne 1972; Univ. of Toronto B.A. 1976; Radcliffe-Harvard Publ. Prog.; m. Margaret d. Donald and Gwen Sutherland 1 May 1982; children: Alexander Kirby, Hilary Evans, Rebecca Catherine; CO-PUBLISHER, HARPER-COLLINS CANADA LTD. 1993– ;and PRES., ONTARIO PUBLISHING CO. 1990– ; Sales & Mktg. Dir. Raincoast Books and Book Express, Vancouver 1983–85; Vice Pres. Mktg. & Sales Key Porter Books Ltd. Toronto 1985–89; Vice Pres. Mktg. & Sales and Assoc. Publisher, HarperCollins Canada Ltd. 1989–93; Chrmn., Word on the Street 1994– ; Co-Fundraising Chrmn., The Candn. Give the Gift of Literacy Found. 1993–94; mem. Book Publishers' Profl. Assn. (Pres. 1989–90); Alpha Delta Phi Literary Fraternity; Un. Ch. of Can.; Liberal; recreations: skiing, tennis, squash; Club: Granite; Home: 10 Southlea Blvd., Toronto, Ont. M4G 3L2.

**BETHUNE, Brian A.,** B.A., M.A., Ph.D.; financial economist; b. Hamilton, Ont. 27 Oct. 1954; s. Kenneth Macdonald and Ruth Elizabeth (Summerlin) B.; e. McMaster Univ. B.A. (Hons.) 1977, M.A. 1979; Univ. of Geneva, Grad. Inst. of Internat. Studies Ph.D. 1983; m. Eva d. Trinidad and Carl Marich 21 Sept. 1983; children: Adrian, Adam; SENIOR ECONOMIST, BANK OF MONTREAL 1987– ; Economist, Gen. Agreement on Tariffs and Trade (GATT) 1982; Internat. Econ., Royal Bank of Can. 1983–87; Internat. Economist (seconded), Inst. of Internat. Finance Washington DC 1984; Mem., Econ. Policy Ctte., Cdn. C. of C. (elected 1992) and Toronto Board of Trade 1993; Friends Extve., Candn. Inst. of Advanced Rsch.; 1977 Grad. Gold Medal; 1990 Am. Express Essay Book Prize; 1983 Mackenzie King Scholarship; Home: 95 Perry Cres., Islington, Ont.; Office: P.O. Box 1, First Canadian Place, Toronto, Ont. M5X 1A1.

**BETTERIDGE, Lois Etherington,** M.F.A., R.C.A.; silversmith and goldsmith; b. Drummondville, Que. 6 Nov. 1928; d. Alfred George and Dorothy May (Young) Etherington; e. Ont. Coll. of Art 1948; Univ. of Kans. B.F.A. 1951; Cranbrook Acad. of Art Mich. M.F.A. 1957; m. Keith James Betteridge, Hants., Eng. 10 Sept. 1960; children: Eric Beasley, Lise Miranda; rep. 17 solo exhns. and over 100 group exhns.; rep. in various pub. colls. incl. Royal Scot. Museum; Massey Foundation Coll. of Contemporary Candn. Crafts; Nat. Museum of Natural Sciences Ottawa; Candn. Museum of Civilization; Candn. and Ont. Crafts Councils Perm. Works; R. Abramson, Washington D.C.; Charles Bronfman, Montreal; Pres. Karamalis of Greece; Cranbrook Art Gallery, Michigan; lectr. USA, Gt. Brit., Scandinavia and Can.; Juror, Workshops Can. and abroad; secular and ecclesiastical holloware; gold and silver jewelry; el. Distinguished mem. Soc. N. Am. Goldsmiths 1974; recipient Citation for Distinguished Prof. Achievement Univ. of Kans. 1975; Saidye Bronfman Award for Excellence in Crafts 1978; el. to Royal Candn. Acad. of Arts 1978; Can. Council Travel Grant to attend opening of her exhn. at Candn. Cultural Centre Paris 1979; Fellowship, New Brunswick Craft Sch., Fredericton 1988; M. Joan Chalmers Award 1991; Hon. Mem., Ont. Coll. of Art, Toronto, Ont. 1992; Debeers Ring Competition Award; Craft Dimensions Award; cited various publs.; author various articles; mem., Ont. Crafts Council; Candn. Crafts Council; Alpha Delta PI (Vice Pres. 1950–51); Protestant; recreations: swimming; Address: 9 Kirkland St., Guelph, Ont. N1H 4X7.

**BETTERIDGE, Mark Stephen,** B.Sc., M.A.; real estate developer; b. Epsom, England 9 May 1953; s. John Edward and Jean Valerie (Long) B.; e. King Edward VI Royal Grammar Sch., England; Marlboro H.S., New Jersey; Trent Univ., Ontario B.Sc. (Hons.) 1974; Univ. of Waterloo, Ontario M.A. 1977; children: Mark Edward, Christopher David, Andrew James; PRESIDENT, UBC REAL ESTATE CORP. 1988– ; Corporate Planner, Norcom Homes (Mississauga) 1977–78; Project Mgr., Nu-West Development Corp. (Edmonton) & Extve. Mem., Edmonton C. of C. 1978–82; Town Manager, Town of Stony Plain, Alberta 1982–85; Asst. to Municipal Mgr., Dist. of Surrey, B.C. 1985–88; Co-Chrmn., Residential Ctte., UDI Edmonton 1979–81; Mem., Edn. Ctte., UDI Vancouver 1989– ; Extve. Dir., Discovery Parks Inc. 1991– ; Mem., Vancouver Bd. of Trade 1988– ; Alberta Planning Award 1984 from Alta. Assn., Candn. Inst. of Planners; established municipal twinning relations with Shikaoi, Japan and Zhu-hai, China; Mem., Candn. Inst. of Planners 1978– ; recreations: squash, nautilus training; Home: 14970 Buena Vista Ave., White Rock, B.C. V4B 1X7; Office: Suite 400 – 1727 W. Broadway, Vancouver, B.C. V6J 4W6.

**BETTS, Donald Drysdale,** B.Sc., M.Sc., Ph.D., F.R.S.C.; university professor; b. Montreal, Que. 6 May 1929; s. Wallace Havelock and Mary (Drysdale) B.; e. Dalhousie Univ. B.Sc. (Physics) 1950, M.Sc. (Physics) 1952; McGill Univ., Ph.D. (Physics) 1955; m. Vilma Florence, d. late Horace Mapp, 5 June 1954; div. 1980; children: Malcolm R., Sylvia M., Eric K., Douglas R.; m. Patricia McWilliams 1986 d. late Ronald Giles; EDITOR, CANADIAN JOURNAL OF PHYSICS 1992– ; Asst. Prof. 1956–61, Assoc. Prof. 1961–66, Prof. 1966–80, Univ. of Alta.; Prof. of Physics 1980–90, Dean of Arts and Science 1980–88, Dean of Science 1988–90, Dalhousie Univ.; Dir., Theoretical Physics Inst. 1972–78; mem. of organizing comte. of internat. summer schs. in physics, 1957, 1961, 1965 and 1968; rec'd. Nat. Research Council of Can. Post-doctoral Fellowship, 1955–56 and Grants; NATO Science Fellow 1963–64; Nuffield Foundation Fellow, 1970–71; Fellow of the Royal Society of Canada 1982– ; mem., Candn. Assn. Physicists (Vice Pres. 1968–69; Pres. 1969–70); recreations: camping, game of go, badminton, gardening; Office: Dept. of Physics, Dalhousie Univ., Halifax, N.S. B3H 3J5.

**BEUG, Lorne Arthur,** B.A.; visual artist; b. Regina, Sask. 7 Nov. 1948; s. Arthur Otto and Emma (Focht) B.; e. Univ. of Regina B.A. (great distinction) 1969; B.C. Inst. of Technol.; Banff Sch. of Fine Arts; solo exhibitions: McIntosh Gall., Univ. of W. Ontario, London 1994; Hart House, Univ. of Toronto 1994; Nickle Arts Museum, Univ. of Calgary 1992; Portals Gall. Chicago 1991; Dunlop Gall. Regina 1989 (installation of 'Two Pavilions'); Mendel Gall. Sask. 1987; Comn. for ceramic mural, City of Regina Fieldhouse 1987; Mackenzie Gall. Regina 1985; Susan Whitney Gall. Regina 1980, 84, 88, 92; Bau-XI Gall. Vancouver 1976, 78, 81; numerous group exhibitions incl. 'A Treasury of Canadian Craft' Canadian Craft Museum, Vancouver 1992; Los Angeles Internat. Art Fair 1990–93; Chicago New Art Forms Exhib. 1987–93; Liberty's (U.K.); collections incl.: Canada Council Art Bank; Glenbow-Alberta Inst.; Meml. Univ. of Nfld.; Univ. of Lethbridge; etc.; Lt. Gov. Medal Grade XII; Canada Council Arts Grant; C.C. project grants; individual assistance grants, Sask. Arts Bd.; Mem., 'The Folly Fellowship' (U.K.); catalogues: 'Two Pavilions' 1990, Dunlop Art Gall., Regina; 'Glass Architecture / Cultured Stones' 1987, Mendel Art Gall.; 'Lorne Beug: Artists with their Work' 1985, Mackenzie Art Gall.; recreations: industrial archaeology, graphic design, electronics; Addresses: 2026 Alexandra St., Regina, Sask. S4T 4P5 or c/o Susan Whitney Gallery, 2220 Lorne St., Regina, Sask. S4P 2M7.

**BEUGNOT, Bernard A.H.,** M.A., Ph.D., F.R.S.C.; educator; b. Paris, France 3 July 1932; s. Raoul and Gripray (Germaine) B.; e. Ecole Normale Supérieure 1954; Sorbonne Paris B.A. 1955, M.A. 1957, Ph.D. 1969; m. Brigitte L'Hermite 11 June 1960; children: Marie-Christine, Nicolas, Sophie; PROF. OF FRENCH UNIV. DE MONTRÉAL 1970– , Chrmn. of French 1985–91; service French Army 1958–60, rank Lt.; Teacher Coll. of Chartres 1960–62; joined present Univ. 1962; recipient Academie Française Halphen Prize 1974; Chevalier Ordre Nat. du Mérite et Palmes Academiques 1976 and 1989; Killam grant 1991–93; author twelve books; over 100 articles French lit. 17th Century and some modern authors; mem. Soc. d'Etude du XVIIe Siecle; Soc. d'Histoire Litteraire de la France; Home: 4720 Grosvenor Ave., Montréal, Qué. H3W 2L8; Office: Montréal, Qué. H3C 3J7.

**BEVAN, (Joseph) Tal,** B.A.; communications executive; b. Comox, B.C. 1 July 1957; s. Major Joseph David and Elsie (Lepine) B.; e. Widdifield S.S.; York Univ. B.A. (Hons.) 1980; m. Michelle d. Joseph Donald and Yvette Tobin 9 Aug. 1980; DIRECTOR OF SALES, BUSINESS SYSTEMS DIVISION, OCTEL COMMUNICATIONS CANADA INC. 1993– ; Instructor & Counsellor, Metro Toronto Assn. for the Mentally Retarded 1980–81; Sales Rep., Xerox Can. 1981–82; Acct. Extve. then Sr. Sales Rep., Bell Can. 1982–87; Industry Market Mgr. 1987–89; Nat. Acct. Mgr. 1989–91; Area Mgr., Octel Communications 1990–91; Mktg. Dir. 1991–93; Dean's Honour Roll, York Univ.; Ontario Scholar; Coach, Special Olympics Floor Hockey Program (Scarborough, Variety Village); recreations: golf, basketball; Home: 217 Erskine Ave., Toronto, Ont. M4P 1Z5; Office: 4110 Yonge St., Suite 506, Willowdale, Ont. M2P 2B7.

**BEVERIDGE, James MacDonald Richardson,** O.C., Ph.D., M.D., LL.D., D.Sc., F.R.S.C. (1960); b. Dunfermline, Scotland, 17 Aug. 1912; s. James and Margaret (Spence) B.; e. Dunfermline High Sch.; came to Can., 1927; Horton Acad., Wolfville, N.S. (1933); Acadia Univ., B.Sc. 1937, and D.Sc. 1962; Univ. of Toronto, Ph.D. 1940; Univ. of W. Ont., M.D. 1950; LL.D. Mount Allison 1966; D.Sc., Queen; Univ. 1978; m. Jean Frances, d. Rev. Dr. F. H. Eaton, 26 Dec. 1940; children: Catherine, James, Alexander, Robert, Duncan, William, Elizabeth; Pres. Acadia Univ. 1964–78; Craine Prof. of Biochem., Queen's Univ. and Head of Dept., 1950–64; Chrmn., Bd. of Grad. Studies there, 1960–63; Dean of School 1963–64; mem., Candn. Nat. Comte. of Internat. Union of Biochem., since 1955 (Chrmn. 1959–62); Chrmn., Defence Research Bd. Panel on Nutrition & Metabolism, 1961–65; Dir., C.B.C., 1965–68; mem., Fisheries Research Bd. Can., 1959–68; Research Asst., Univ. of Toronto, 1940–44; Scient. Asst. and later Assoc. Biochemist, Pacific Fisheries Exper. Stn., Vancouver, 1944–46; Lectr., Univ. of W. Ont., 1946–50; Publications; about 100 scient. papers; Hon. Mem., Candn. Atherosclerosis Soc. 1993; Mem., Am. Inst. Nutrition; Am. Soc. for Clinical Nutrition; Candn. Biochem. Soc.; Candn Physiol. Soc (Secy. 1953–56); Candn. Soc. for Clinical Chem; Chem. Inst. Can.; Council on Arteriosclerosis; Nutrition Soc. Can. (Pres., 1964–65); Science Council of Can. 1968–71; Alpha Omega Alpha; United Church; recreations: golf, fishing, bridge; Clubs: Ken-Wo Golf & Country; Home: R.R. 1, Canning, N.S. B0P 1H0.

**BEVERIDGE, Terrance J.,** M.Sc., Ph.D., F.R.S.C.; educator; b. Toronto, Ont. 29 Apl. 1945; s. Fredrick Charles and Doris Elizabeth B.; e. Univ. of Toronto B.Sc. 1968, Dip. Bact. 1969, M.Sc. 1970; Univ. of W. Ont. Ph.D. 1974; m. Janice Elizabeth d. Edison and Hazel Barnett 9 Oct. 1970; children: Braden Charles, Jennifer Bree; PROF. OF MICROBIOL., COLL. OF BIOLOGICAL SCIENCE, UNIV. OF GUELPH 1986– ; Dir. NSERC Guelph Regional STEM Facility 1981– ; Dir., Life Sciences, Royal Soc. Can. 1992– ; Ivey Rsch. Found. Assoc. 1975–78; Asst. Prof. present Univ. 1978, Assoc. Prof. 1983; Visiting Prof. Universität fur Bodenkultur Vienna 1987; Visiting Prof. Biozentrum Universität der Basel, Switzerland 1987; mem. Centre of Excellence on Bacterial Disease 1989; recipient Steacie Award 1984; Fellow, Royal Society of Canada; Fellow, Candn. Institute of Advanced Rsch.; Fellow, Am. Academy of Microbiology; ed. Jour. of Bacteriol. 1988– ; assoc. ed. Candn. Jour. Microbiol. 1982–87; Biorecovery 1986– ; co-ed. 'Metal Ions and Bacteria' 1989; mem. Candn. Soc. Microbiol.; Am. Soc. Microbiol.; Microscopial Soc. Can.; Electron Microscopic Soc. Am.; recreations: cross-country skiing, skating, hiking; Home: 101 Chalmers St., Elora, Ont. N0B 1S0; Office: Guelph, Ont. N1G 2W1.

**BEVERLEY, Perry Seafield Grant;** editor; publisher; b. Brockville, Ont. 28 June 1940; d. Malcolm Seafield and Helen Lois (Graham) Grant; e. Brockville Collegiate Inst., Carleton Univ.; m. David Taylor 16 Sept. 1961; divorced; children: David, Dorcas, Hunter; m. Michael Beverley 18 June 1983; ED.-IN-CHIEF & CO-PUBLISHER, BROCKVILLE RECORDER & TIMES 1980– ; co-pub. since 1968; mem. St. Lawrence Islands Nat. Park Adv. Ctte. (Vice-Chrmn. 1976–78); Candn. Press; Inter-Am. Press Assn.; Commonwealth Press Union; Candn. Daily Newspaper Assn.; Anglican; recreations: sailing, gardening; Club: Brockville Yacht; Home: 'The Farm,' R.R. 4, Brockville, Ont. K6V 5T4; Office: P.O. Box 10, Brockville, Ont. K6V 5T8.

**BEVERSDORF, Wallace Dale,** M.Sc., Ph.D.; educator; scientist; b. Antigo, Wis. 29 Oct. 1949; s. Willis and Ruth B.; e. Univ. of Wis. B.Sc. 1972, M.Sc. 1974, Ph.D. 1975; m. Lynn Marie d. William and Dorothy Smith 30 Aug. 1969; children: Chandra, Thad; Chrmn. and Prof. of Crop Science, Univ. of Guelph 1987–..; Vice Pres. & Sci. Mgr., Allelix Inc. Mississauga, Ont. 1986–87; Asst. Prof. present Univ. 1976, Assoc. Prof. 1981; Chrmn. and mem.: Genetics Ctte.-USA Soybean Breeders Group 1984–86; Ont. Oil & Protein Crop Rsch. Ctte.; Prog. Ctte. 1986 Crucifer Improvement Conf.; Chrmn., Ont. Field Crops Rsch. Ctte.; CARC Standing Ctte. on Biotechnol.; Bd. of Govs., NRC Plant Biotech Inst. Saskatoon; Candn. Expert Ctte. Grain Breeding; Ont. Field Bean Rsch. Ctte.; Candn. Seed Growers Assn.; holds various patents hybridization process; author or co-author numerous book chapters, articles, papers; Home: 36 Forster Dr., Guelph, Ont. N1G 3X3.

**BEWERS, Patricia Anne,** B.Sc., F.L.M.I., I.S.P.; financial executive; b. Glasgow, Scotland 17 Sept. 1945; d. James and Babs (MacMillan) Smith; e. Univ. of Glasgow, B.Sc. (Hons.) 1967; F.L.M.I. 1983; I.S.P. 1989; m. Dr. J. Michael s. Gladys and Samuel John B. 8 Dec. 1967; children: Jean-Paul, Marc; VICE-PRES., SYSTEMS DEVELOPMENT, CENTRAL GUARANTY TRUST 1988– ; Programmer/Analyst, Dalhousie Univ. 1967–72; Systems Analyst 1972–74; Mgr. Personnel/Payroll Serv. 1976–80; Mgr., Systems Devel., Maritime Life Assur. 1981–85; Asst. Vice-Pres., Systems Devel., Central Trust 1985–88; mem., F.L.M.I.; Candn. Information Processing Soc. (Past Pres., Nat. Pres., Vice-Pres., Atlantic Reg.; Dir., Past Pres. Halifax Section); recreations: tennis, walking; club: YMCA; Home: 30 Litchfield Cres., Halifax, N.S. B3P 2N3; Office: P.O. Box 2343, Halifax, N.S. B3J 3C8 and 1770 Market St., Halifax, N.S. B3J 3M3.

**BEWICK, Howard Albany,** M.A., Ph.D.; consultant; retired chemist; b. Toronto, Ont. 9 Sept. 1916; s. Albany and Maude (Coupland) B.; e. Univ. of Toronto, B.A. 1940, M.A. 1941, Ph.D. 1945; m. Lenore, d. Karl D. Knechtel, Hanover, Ont. 28 Apr. 1945; children: Brenda, Paul, David, Brian; Chemist, Imperial Oil, Sarnia, Ont. 1943–44; Research Chem., Nat. Research Council, Toronto and Ottawa 1944–45; Research Supv., Solvay Process Div., Allied Chemical Corp., Syracuse, N.Y. 1946–52, Asst. Dir. Research 1952–58; Dir., Devel., Allied Chemical Canada Ltd., Montreal 1959–67; Vice-Pres. Development and Planning (Pte. Claire) 1967–73; Technical Dir. (Amherstburg) 1973–75; Dir. Environment Services (Amherstburg) 1975–76; Dir. Special Projects (Amherstburg) 1976–80; mem. Am. Chem. Soc.; Protestant; Home: 68 Roseland Dr., Carrying Place, Ont. K0K 1L0.

**BEWLEY, J. Derek,** Ph.D., D.Sc., F.R.S.C.; researcher and educator; b. Preston, U.K. 11 Dec. 1943; s. Clifford and Marion (Garner) B.; e. King Edward VI Sch. Stafford 1962; Queen Elizabeth Coll. Univ. of London B.Sc. 1965, Ph.D. 1968, D.Sc. 1983; m. Christine d. Robert and Kathleen Kite 3 Sept. 1966; children: Alexander, Janette Louise; PROF. OF BOTANY, UNIV. OF GUELPH 1985– , Dir., Plant Biology Program 1993– , Chrmn. of Botany 1985–90; Postdoctoral Fellow Fox Chase Cancer Research Inst. Philadelphia 1968–70; Asst. Prof. of Biol. Univ. of Calgary 1970, Assoc. Prof. 1973, Prof. (with Plant Physiol. Rsch. Group) 1977; mem. Adv. Panel NSERC Strategic Grants 1981–83; mem. Grant Selection Ctte., NSERC Plant Biology 1986–90 (Chrmn. 1988–90); Internat. Bd. for Plant Genetic Resources Adv. Group on Seed Storage 1981–87; E.W.R. Steacie Memorial Fellow NSERC 1979–81; C.D. Nelson Award Candn. Soc. Plant Physiols. 1978; Society Gold Medal Award 1992; Killam Resident Fellow Univ. Calgary 1978, 1982; co-author 'Physiology and Biochemistry of Seeds in Relation to Germination' vols. I and II 1978, 1982; 'Seeds. Physiology of Develop. & Germination' 1984; ed. 'Nitrogen and Carbon Metabolism' 1981; ed./mem. ed. bd. 'Plant Physiology,' 'Planta,' and 'Seed Science Research'; author or co-author over 190 sci. research articles and reviews; mem. Candn. Soc. Plant Physiols. (Secy. 1983–85, Vice Pres. 1987–88, Pres. 1988–89 & Past Pres. 1989–90); Convener, Plant Biol. Div., Royal Soc. of Can. 1985–87; Sigma Xi; recreations: squash, golf, gardening, reading, travel; Home: 26 Waverley Dr., Guelph, Ont. N1E 6C8; Office: Guelph, Ont. N1G 2W1.

**BEXON, Robert Lance,** B.A.; tobacco industry executive; b. London, On. 22 May 1952; s. Howard John and Merle Nan (Latta) B.; e. Univ. of Toronto B.A. 1972; m. Anne Marie d. Theresa and Theophilus Slaney 21 Oct. 1972; children: Jennifer, Emily, Natalie; VICE-PRESIDENT, MARKETING, IMPERIAL TOBACCO LTD.; positions in Sales, Marketing Research, Marketing Planning, Communications, Product & Packaging Development, Imperial Tobacco Ltd.; Home: 10 Old Forest Rd., Kirkland, Qué. H9J 2Z8; Office: 3810 St. Antoine St., Montreal, Qué. H4C 1B5.

**BEZANSON, Keith A.,** B.A., Ph.D.; international development executive; b. Kingston, Ont. 12 May 1941; s. Walter Millen and Eileen Mary (Burke) B.; e. Carleton Univ. B.A. 1964; Stanford Univ. Ph.D. 1972; m. Monique d. Emilien and Pauline Ouellet 18 Sept. 1982; children: Kathryn, Sarah, Julia; PRESIDENT, INTERNATIONAL DEVELOPMENT RESEARCH CENTRE 1991– ; S.S. Teacher, Nigeria, Candn. Univ. Serv. Overseas 1964–66; 5-mo. special assignment, Min. of Edn., Nigeria 1966; doctoral program, Internat. Devel. Edn. Ctr. & thesis rsch. in Ghana 1966–72; Project Dir., School Leavers Rsch. Project, Ghana 1970–73; Chief Planning Offr., Econ. & Tech. Coop. in Anglophone Africa, Candn. Internat. Devel. Agency 1973–77; Reg. Dir., E. Afric Program 1977–78; Director General, Multilateral Prog. 1978–81; Vice-Pres. Americas Branch 1981–85; Candn. Ambassador to Peru and Bolivia 1985–88; Admin. Mgr., Inter-Am. Devel. Bank, Washington, D.C. 1988–91; Medal of Bravery, Governor-General of Canada for a civilian act of bravery 1981; Advanced Doctoral Fellowship, Canada Council 1969–70; Ford Found. Fellowship 1966–68; Honour Award, Carleton Univ. (1 of 6 annual awards for acad. excellence & contbns. to the life of the Univ.) 1964; Trustee, African Ctr. for Devel. & Strategic Studies; Mem., Soc. for Internat. Devel.; author of num. papers & pubns.; Home: 49 Kenora St., Ottawa, Ont. K1Y 3K7; Office: P.O. Box 8500, Ottawa, Ont. K1G 3H9.

**BHERER, Wilbrod,** C.M., Q.C.; lawyer; b. St-Fidèle, Qué. 11 Aug. 1905; s. Wilbrod and Laure (Lapointe) B.; e. St. Mary's Coll., Montreal B.A.; Laval Univ., Faculty of Law studies; m. Françoise d. A. O. Pruneau 13 Oct. 1931; one d. Hélène (Mrs. Jean Pelletier); COUNSEL, GRONDIN POUDRIER BERNIER 1989– ; called to Bar of Que. 1930; cr. K.C. 1945; law practice 1930–58; Pres., George T. Davie & Sons Ltd. 1958–64; Depy. Chrmn. Canadian Vickers Ltd. 1964–67, Chrmn. 1967–76; mem. Extve. Comte., Tele-Capital 1976–78, Pres. & C.E.O. 1978–83; Partner, Bherer Bernier 1983–89; Chrmn. R. Cath. Sch. Bd. City Quebec 1958–71; mem. Bd. Laval Univ. 1967–72, Chrmn. Med. Center 1968–79; Kt. Commander Ordre Equestre du St-Sépulcre de Jérusalem; Dr. (honoris causa), Université Laval, Qué. 1975; Member, Order of Canada 1977; served with Que. Regt., rank Lt. Col.; mem. Candn. Bar Assn.; R. Catholic; recreation: gardening; Club: Cercle de la Garrison; Home: 835 des Braves, Quebec City, Qué. G1S 3C5; Office: Édifice Mérici, 801, Chemin St-Louis, Bureau 200, Québec, Qué. G1S 1C1.

**BIANCHINI, Lucian,** M.A.L.S.; retired librarian; b. Ferrara, Italy 15 March 1929; s. Amedeo and Jole (Bruni) B.; e. Cermenate, Como, Italy; Aquinas Coll. 1950–51 and Rosary Coll., M.A.L.S. 1954; Sacred Heart Semy., Melrose Park, Ill., 1951–54; Gregorian Univ., Rome, 1960–61; M.P.A., Dalhousie Univ. 1981; LIBRARIAN EMERITUS, MOUNT ST. VINCENT UNIV. since 1992; Cataloguer, Univ. of Calgary Lib., 1967, Head, Humanities Div., 1969; Librarian, Mount St. Vincent Univ. 1973–92; mem., Candn. Lib. Assn.; Atlantic Provs. Lib. Assn.; R. Catholic; Home: 17 Tangmere Cres., Halifax, N.S. B3M 1K2.

**BIBEAU, Fernand R.;** executive; b. Montreal, Que. 27 Sept. 1931; s. Louis Joseph and Aurore (Duquette) B.; e. Coll. St-Viateur; Ecole Beaux-Arts de Montréal; Hautes Etudes Commerciales; m. Hélène d. Camille Beaupré 19 Sept. 1953; children: Robert, Marc, Suzanne (Mrs. J.F. Taillefer); PRES., BEAUWARD SHOPPING CENTRES LTD. 1964– ; PRES., SCHOKBETON QUEBEC INC., 1962–00; EXEC. V.P., ARGO CONSTRUCTION LTD.; Dir. Chrysler Canada Ltd.; Shell Canada Ltd.; Xerox Canada Inc.; Paribas Bank of Canada; Scott Paper Ltd.; Prudential Corp. Can.; Société d'Énergie de la Baie James; Foundation de l'Hôpital du Sacré-Coeur de Montréal; mem. Mil. & Hospitaller Order St. Lazarus Jerusalem; Internat. Order Alhambra; former mem. YPO; mem. XPO; recreations: golf, boating, painting; Clubs: Mount-Royal Club; Laval-sur-le-Lac Curling Club; Laval-sur-le-Lac Golf (currently Pres.); Lost Tree Club Inc. (Palm Beach, Fla.); Home: 4 Ile Roussin, Laval-sur-le-Lac, Qué. H7R 1E7; Office: 576 Boul. Sauvé, St-Eustache, Qué. J7R 4K5.

**BIBEAU, Gilles,** M.A., Ph.D.; educator; b. Montréal, Qué. 22 Apl. 1934; s. Louis-Philippe and Rosa (Brissette) B.; e. Univ. de Montréal M.A. 1961; Univ. d'Aix-Marseille, France Doctorat 3e cycle 1970; m. Yvette d. René and Cécile Filiatrault 2 Aug. 1958; separated; children: Michel, Christiane, Sylvain, Natalie; PROF. OF LANGUAGE DIDACTICS, UNIV. DE MONTRÉAL 1981– ; Secondary Sch. Teacher 1956–64; Lectr. in Linguistics present Univ. 1964–70, Asst. Prof. (Chargé ens.) 1970–73, Asst. Prof. (Adjoint) Faculty of Edn. 1973–81, Dean of Studies 1978–81, Chrmn., Dept. of Didactics 1990– ; Guest Lectr. Univ. of Victoria 1967, Univ. de Grenoble 1970; Dir. Evaluation Lang. Training Prog. Pub. Service Can. 1975–76; Cons. Conseil de la langue française du Qué., Office de la langue française du Qué., Ministère de l'édn. du Qué.; recipient Whitworth Trophy (CEA) 1985; author 'Nos enfants parleront-ils français?' 1966; 'Introduction à la phonologie générative du français' 1975; 'Report of the Independent Study of the Language Training Programme of the Public Service of Canada' 12 vols. 1976; 'L'éducation bilingue en Amérique du Nord' 1982; co-author 'L'enseignement du français langue maternelle: perceptions et attentes' 1987; 'Les perceptions et les attentes des Québécois à propos de l'enseignement du français dans les écoles' (Vol. I, II, III) 1987, 1988, 1990; Chief Ed. Professional Review (Québec Français) 1980–84; ed. 'L'éducation et le français au Québec' 1984; co-ed. 'Le statut culturel du français au Québec' 1984; 'La qualité en éducation: enjeux et perspectives' 1985; preface writer 6 books; over 50 articles sci. and profl. jours.; mem. Candn. Assn. Applied Linguistics (Pres. 1972–75); Home: 154 Tailhandier, Boucherville, Qué. J4B 2T7; Office: C.P. 6128 Succ. A, Montréal, Qué. H3C 3J7.

**BICKERTON, James Parker,** M.A., Ph.D.; educator; b. Berwick, N.S. 8 Jan. 1954; s. John Irvine and Evelyn Harriet (Rice) B.; e. Sydney (N.S.) Acad. 1972; Acadia Univ. B.A. 1976; Carleton Univ. M.A. 1980, Ph.D. 1987; m. Theresa d. Frank and Mary MacNeil 4 Aug. 1981; three s. Neil, Benjamin, Luke; ASSOC. PROF. OF POL. SCI. ST. FRANCIS XAVIER UNIV. 1990– ; Asst. Prof. present Univ. 1984–89; Visiting Fellow Western Societies Prog. Cornell Univ. 1991–92; author 'Ottawa and the Politics of Regional Development' 1990; co-author 'The Almanac of Canadian Politics' 1991; co-ed. 'Canadian Politics' 1990, 1994; mem. Candn. Pol. Sci. Assn. (Dir. 1989–91); St. Francis Xavier Assn. Univ. Teachers (Exec. mem. 1989–91); recreations: tennis, squash, hockey; Home: 27 Highland Dr. Antigonish, N.S. B2G 1N7; Office: Antigonish, N.S. B2G 1C0.

**BICKFORD, James G.;** banker; b. Huntingdon, Que. 22 July 1928; s. Harold Gordon and Jean Forbes (Stark) B.; e. Huntingdon (Que.) Acad. 1945; m. Jetta Florence Georgina, d. Merlin Aubrey Goodger-Hill, Toronto, Ont., 6 Aug. 1951; Exec. Vice Pres., Office of the Chrmn., & C.E.O., Canadian Imperial Bank of Commerce, retired 1989; Dir., CIBC Trust Corp.; Great Lakes Re. Management Corp. (N.Y.); joined present bank 1945; served at various brs. Que. Region until 1959; Mgr., Lachine, Que. 1959, Regional Gen. Mgr.'s Dept., Montreal, special assignment 1961, Mgr., Kingston, Jamaica 1964–66, London, Eng. 1967, Vice Pres., Internat. 1970; Senior Vice-Pres., Internat 1973; Exec. Vice-Pres., Int'l., 1978; Exec. Vice Pres., Admin., 1980; mem. St. Andrews Soc.; Toronto Black Watch Assn.; 48th Highlanders of Can. Offrs. Assn.; Presbyterian; recreations: shooting, fishing, photography, chess; Clubs: Royal Candn. Mil. Inst.; National; (Toronto) City of London (Eng.); Overseas Bankers (London, Eng.); Home: 55 Harbour Square, Ste. 1013, Toronto, Ont. M5J 2L1.

**BIDWELL, Roger Grafton Shelford,** B.Sc., M.A., Ph.D., F.R.S.C.; biologist; educator; b. Halifax, N.S., 8 June 1927; s. late Adm. Roger Edward Shelford and Mary Grafton (Bothamly) B.; e. Dalhousie Univ., B.Sc. 1947; Queen's Univ., B.A., M.A., Ph.D. 1954; m. Shirley Mae Rachael, d. late Ernest Mason, 1 July 1950; children: Barbara Mary Grafton, Alison Deborah, Roger John Shelford, Gillian Frances; PROFESSOR EMERITUS, QUEEN'S UNIV. 1979– ;and ADJUNCT PROFESSOR, MOUNT ALLISON UNIV., Sackville, N.B. 1987– ; Tech. Offr., Defence Research Bd. of Can., Kingston, Ont. 1951; Asst. Research Offr., Nat. Research Council, Halifax 1956; Assoc. Prof. of Bot., Univ. of Toronto, 1959; Prof. of Biol., Case W. Reserve Univ., Cleveland, 1965–69 (Chrmn. of Dept. 1966–69); Prof. of Biology, Queen's Univ. 1969–79; I.W. Killam Research Prof. and Prof. of Biology, Dalhousie Univ. 1981–85; Founder and Exec. Dir., Atlantic Inst. of Biotechnology 1985–88; External Examiner in Botany, Nanyang Univ. Singapore 1974–77; Sc. Exch. Visitor, People's Republic of China, 1975 and 1977; Visiting Prof., Cornell Univ., summers 1961–63; Visiting Scientist, NRC, Halifax, 1966, 1976–77; mem. Adv. Bd., Atlantic Regional Lab. of NRC (1972–75); mem. Nat. Adv. Comte. on Biotechnology 1983–88; Past Dir. and Sr. Partner, Atlantic Research Associates Ltd.; Past Dir., North Nova Forest Owners' Co-Operation Ltd.; has participated in internat. confs. on plant science in China, USA, Brit., Poland, Australia and Can.; conducted research in photosynthesis, plant metabolism, seaweed metabolism, nitrogen and proteins in plants; author 'Plant Physiology' 1974, 1979; Assoc. Ed. 'Canadian Journal of Botany' 1970–1980; Ed. 'Biological Council of Canada Newsletter' 1972–76; co-ed. 'Plant Physiology: A Treatise' Vols. VII, VIII and X; other writings incl. over 120 scient. papers, book chapters; Fellow, Royal Soc. of Can. 1972; Convener, Plant Sciences Sec., 1975–77; Pres., Halifax Br., Civil Service Assn. 1959; mem., N.S. Inst. Science; Candn. Soc. Plant Physiols. (Founding Comte.; Secy.-Treas. 1963–65, Pres. 1972–73); Fellow, Am. Assn. Advanc. Science 1987; Biol. Council Can. (Secy. 1972–76); Fellow, Explorers Club 1978; Queen's Jubilee Medal 1977; Candn. Soc. of Plant Physiols. Gold Medal 1979; Anglican; recreations: bicycling, skiing, walking, music; Office: Atlantic Research Associates, R.R. #1, Wallace, N.S. B0K 1Y0.

**BIELBY, Hon. Myra B.,** B.A., LL.B.; judge; b. Port Colborne, Ont. 8 July 1951; d. Richard Ross and Kathryne Faye B.; e. Univ. of Alta. B.A. 1974, LL.B. 1974; m. Gordon R. s. Wilfred and Isobel Thomas 1 Apl. 1989; two d. Sandra T. Woo, Jennifer B. Woo; JUSTICE, COURT OF QUEEN'S BENCH ALTA. 1990– ; Assoc. Field & Field 1975, Partner 1978–90; cr. Q.C. 1990; Bencher Law Soc. Alta. 1990; Pres. Edmonton Bar Assn. 1986–87; Dir. Alta. Law Reform Inst. 1986–90; Office: Law Courts Building, 1A Sir Winston Churchill Sq., Edmonton, Alta. T5J 0R2.

**BIELER, Ted,** B.F.A.; sculptor; b. Kingston, Ont., 23 July 1938; s. André and Jeannette A. (Meunier) B.; m. Marina (Hahn) B.; three children: Kolya, Tashi, Andrew; e. studied sculpture with Ossip Zadkine, Paris, 1953–54; painting, with Singier at Academie Ranson, Paris; tapestry design, under Jean Lurcat at St. Céré, France; graphic art, under John Buckland-Wright at the Slade Sch. of Art, Univ. of London, 1954; Summer Sch. of Fine Arts, Queen's Univ. (under Gentile Tondino and Alex Millar) 1956; Kingston Coll. and Vocational Inst. 1957; Cranbrook Acad. of Art, Bloomfield Hills, Mich., B.F.A. (Fine Arts) 1961; schol. Summer Sch. of Painting, Saugatuck, Mich. 1960; PROF. OF FINE ARTS, YORK UNIV. 1969– ; Dir., Grad. Studies Prog. in Visual Arts there 1981–83, 1986– ; Chrmn., Dept. of Visual Arts 1987– ; 6 months tour Europe and Asia, Can. Council Award, 1967–68; Lecturer, Dept. of Fine Arts, Univ. of Toronto, 1962–68; Instr. in Sculpture. Albright Sch. of Art, Univ. of Buffalo, 1961; one-man shows: Isaacs Gallery 1964; York Univ. 1977; Univ. of Rochester 1977; Geraldine Davis Gallery 1986; group shows: Four Man Show, Art Gall. of Toronto 1959; Four Man Show, Isaacs Gall. 1962; Albright-Knox Art Gall., Buffalo, NY 1964; Outdoor Sculpture Exhbn., Toronto City Hall 1967; Candn. Govt. Pavilion, Expo '67; Canadian Artists '68, Art Gall. of Ont. 1968; A Plastic Presence, Jewish Museum, NY; Milwaukee Art Center; San Francisco Museum of Art 1970; The Wall: Art for Architecture, Art Gall. of Ont. (travelling) 1971; Faculty Exhbn., York Univ. 1970, 1975, 1976, 1980, 1982, 1986; Signs and Symbols, Art Gall. of Ont. (travelling); Artario '72, many locations 1972; Sculpture Stratford, Gall. Stratford 1976; Outdoor Sculpture, Art Gall. of Windsor 1976; Rehearsal, Harbourfront Art Gall., Toronto 1977; Contemporary Sculpture, Civic Centre, Sault Ste. Marie 1976; Big Ballot for Sculpture, Ontario Place 1977; We Among Others, exhbn. of Ont. Artists, Writers, Composers, Directors, etc. sponsored by Ont. Govt., toured Europe 1978–79; Performance, Harbourfront Art Gall., Toronto 1978; Sculpture Walk, National Capital Comn., Ottawa/Hull 1978; Sculpture Today/Canada Multi-Media Show, Ont. Place 1978; Survey of Contemp. Candn. Sculpture, MacDonald Gall., Toronto 1978; Monumental Sculpture, Toronto Dominion Centre 1978; Contemp. Candn. Sculpture, Burlington Cultural Centre, Burlington 1980; Drawings, Harbourfront Art Gall. 1981; Contemp. Outdoor Sculpture at the Guild, Scarborough 1982; The Building of Architectural Vision, City Gallery, Dept. of Cultural Affairs, (N.Y., NY) 1986–87; Princeton Univ. 1987; major commissions: 'Sleeping Giant' sculpture (Lakehead Terminal Airport, Thunder Bay, Ont.) 1964; Relief Walls for News and Admin. Bldg. (Expo '67) 1965; Wall Relief Agnes Etherington Art Centre (Kingston, Ont.) 1965; 'Ontario Waterways' fountain (Ont. pavilion, Expo '67) 1966; Modular Concrete Exposed Structure, Dr. Joseph O. Ruddy Meml. Hosp. (Whitby, Ont.) 1966; 'Helix of Life' sculpture (Medical Sciences Bldg., Univ. of Toronto, Ont.) 1967; 'Bieler Block Walls' circulation corridors modular wall relifs (Health Sciences Centre, McMaster Univ., Hamilton, Ont.) 1968–71; set for 'The Shining People of Leonard Cohen' (ballet for Royal Winnipeg Ballet; premiered in Paris at Theatre de la Ville 1970); 'Rib Cage' (Engn. Bldg., Univ. of Waterloo, Ont.) 1972; sets for 'Star-Cross'd' (ballet choreographed by Brian Macdonald for Festival Canada, National Arts Centre, Ottawa) 1973; 'Mudra' sculpture (Drew Building, Govt. of Ont. 1975); 'Tetra' sculpture (Portsmouth Harbour, Kington, Ont.; site of 1976 Sailing Olympics; comnd. by Dept. of Secy. of State as gift to City of Kingston, Ont.) 1976; 'Lotus,' 'Spiral,' 'Triple A,' 'White Caps,' 'Boats' sculptures (Govt. of Canada Bldg., Toronto) 1977; 'Canyons' relief sculpture (Wilson Station, Spadina Subway Line, TTC, Toronto) 1978; 'Wings' fountain (Scarborough Centenary Hosp.) 1979; 'Boat Bridge' relief wall (Govt. of Ont. Bldg., Kingston) 1984; 'Triad' sculpture (comnd. by Marathon Realty Co., dedicated to City of Toronto on its Sesquicentennial) 1984; rep. in collections: Agnes Etherington Art Centre, Queen's Univ., Kingston, Ont.; Univ. of Toronto, Ont.; McMaster Univ., Hamilton; Montreal Museum of Fine Arts; York Univ., Toronto; Canada Counc., Ottawa; City of Toronto and many others private and corporate; awarded Allied Arts Medal, Royal Architectural Assn. of Can. 1969; Silver Jubilee Medal, 1977; mem. Counc., Royal Candn. Acad. of Arts 1975–76, 1976–77; Vice-Chrmn. Advisory Bd., Internat. Sculpture Centre, Lawrence, Kansas 1977–78, 1978–79; mem. Extve. Comte., 10th Internat. Sculpture Conf., Toronto 1978; mem. Bd. of Dirs.: Sculpture Garden, King St. E., Toronto 1981–84; Harbourfront Art Gall., Toronto 1980–84 (and Chrmn., New Gall. Comte. 1982–84); Selection Ctte., Visual Arts, Toronto Arts Awards 1987; Address: Glenstreams, R.R. #1, Locust Hill, Ont. L0H 1J0.

**BIENENSTOCK, Harvey,** B.Sc., C.A., M.B.A.; business executive; b. Montreal, Que. 7 June 1949; s. Leon and Regina (Weiser) B.; e. McGill Univ. B.Sc. 1970, M.B.A. 1975; m. Roslyn d. Issie and Esther Chrzastowski 1 June 1975; children: Leonard, Eric; VICE-PRESIDENT (CONTROLLER), CONTINENTAL PHARMA CRYOSAN INC. 1982– ; Corporate consolidations, Northern Telecom 1975–78; Controller, First Quebec Corp. 1978–82; Office: 5485 Paré St., Mount-Royal, Qué. H4P 1P7.

**BIENENSTOCK, John,** M.R.C.S., F.R.C.P., F.R.C.P.(C)., FRS(C); physician; university professor; b. Budapest, Hungary 6 Oct. 1936; s. Maurice and Anne (Horn) B.; e. St. Paul's School, London 1949–54; m. Audrie d. Leo and Nancy Sanders 24 Nov. 1961; children: Jimson Andrew, Adam Sebastian, Robin Anne; DEAN, HEALTH SCIENCES 1992– , VICE PRES. 1989– ; PROF. OF MED. & PATH., McMASTER UNIV. 1974; Fellow, Harvard Med. Sch. 1964–66; Buswell Fellow, State Univ. of N.Y. at Buffalo 1966–68; Asst. Rsch. Prof. of Med., State Univ. of N.Y. 1967–68; joined McMaster as Asst. Prof. 1968; Assoc. Dean for Rsch. 1972–78; Chrmn., Dept. of Path. 1978–88; D.W. Harrington Lectr., State Univ. of N.Y. 1986; Rayne Vis. Prof., Univ. of W. Australia 1987; Founding mem., AB Biol. Supplies Inc.; Agritech Rsch. Inc.; cons. to many pharm. cos.; Chrmn., Candn. Red Cross Nat. Blood Services Adv. Ctte. 1985–89; mem. Sci. Adv. Ctte., Ottawa Civic Hosp. Loeb Inst. 1987; Chrmn. Candn. Arthritis & Rheumatism Rsch. Projs. Panel 1988; Scholar Candn. Med. Rsch. Counc. 1969–74; Order of the Red Cross 1990; Fellow, Royal Soc. of Canada 1991; Hon. Mem., Swiss Soc. of Allergology & Immunology; Secy., Collegium Internat. Allergologicum 1988– ; Pres., Candn. Soc. for Immunology 1985–87; Chrmn., Dundas Valley Sch. of Art 1984–86; author and co-author of more than 300 sci. papers & publs.; ed. 'Immunology of the Lung and Upper Respiratory Tract'; 'Mast Cell Differentiation and Heterogeneity' 1986; 'Recent Advances in Mucosal Immunology – Part A & B' 1987; recreation: painting; Home: 50 Albert St., Dundas, Ont. L9H 2X1.

**BIENVENU, Paul Alfred,** company president; b. Sherbrooke, Que. 23 Dec. 1931; s. Lionel and Maximilienne (Gregoire) B.; e. St. Patrick's High Sch., Quebec City; Royal Mil. Coll., Kingston B.A. 1955; Univ. Laval, Quebec City M. Com.; London Sch. of Economics and Pol. Sci.; Inst. of Chartered Fin. Analysts, Univ. of Virginia, U.S.A., C.F.A.; m. Francine, d. Alphonse and Aline Poupart, 18 Aug. 1962; children: Charles, Sylvie, Marc; PRES., HOWARD BIENVENU INC. since 1976; with Greenshields Inc. 1957–61; Vice-Pres., Bolton Tremblay 1961–76; Club: Saint Denis; Home: 747 Boissy, St. Lambert, Qué. J4R 1K1.

**BIENVENUE, Jean;** business executive; b. Upton, Que. 20 Sept. 1941; s. Olivier and Imelda (Touchette); e. Casavant H.S. 1961; m. Huguette d. Jean-Maurice Lacoste 19 Sept. 1964; children: Edith, Vicky, Claudia; CHIEF EXECUTIVE OFFICER, OLYMEL, SOCIÉTÉ EN COMMANDITE 1991– ; employed in family business Abattoir Bienvenue 1961–78; Dir., Salaison Olympia 1978–86; Vice-Pres., Fresh Meats Div., Olympia Ltée. 1987; Olympia Ltée. merged with Turcotte & Turmel to form present firm 1991; recreations: golf, skiing, tennis; clubs: Club Optimiste St-Valérien, Private Club Maskoutain; Home: 1010 Milton, St-Valérien, Qué. J0H 2B0; Office: 400, 2200 ave. Leon Pratte, St. Hyacinthe, Qué. J2S 4B6.

**BIERWAGEN, Ottmar;** photographer; b. Eltze, W. Germany 11 Aug. 1948; s. Otto and Melusine (Harmel) B.; e. Sheridan Coll. Journalism & Photog.; Mohawk Coll. Computer Prog.; Trent Univ. Eng. & German Lit.; Photog. Hamilton Spectator and Toronto Sun 1978–81; Photo Ed. Winnipeg Free Press 1981–83; freelance/contract photog. National Geographic 1984–86; Picture Ed. Toronto Star 1987–88; one of 2 Candn. photogs. rep. by Black Star, New York; named Photog. of Yr. 1977 Nat. Press Photogs. Assn. (sole Candn. to do so); Photog. of Yr. 1977, 1988 Ont. News Photogs. Assn.; won 2 silver & 2 gold Awards in Travel Photography for S.A.T.W. 1990; Found. Award Photojournalism 1985 Nat. Mag. Awards Found.; author: 'Canada' Time-Life Book Series 1987; 'Calgary - Heart of the West' 1987; 'The XV Winter Olympic Games' 1988; 'Heartland - Prairie Portraits and Landscapes' 1989; 'Canada - The Great Lone Land' 1989; mem. Am. Soc. Mag. Photogs.; Candn. Assn. Photogs. & Illustrators in Can.; Nat. Press Photogs. Assn. Soc. Am. Travel Writers; Home: 60 Withrow Ave., Toronto, Ont. M4K 1C9.

**BIETENHOLZ, Peter Gerard,** D.Phil.; university professor; b. Basel, Switzerland 7 Jan. 1933; s. Alfred and Mary (Gerhard) B.; e. Univ. of Basel, D.Phil. 1958; m. Doris S., d. Franz Huber, Basel, Switzerland, 26 Aug. 1958; children: Michael F., I. Balthasar, Samuel A.; came to Can. 1963; Professor, Dept. of History, Univ. of Sask.; author: 'Der italienische Humanismus und die Blütezeit des Buchdrucks in Basel' 1959; 'Pietro Della Valle (1586–1642)' 1962; 'History and Biography in the Work of Erasmus of Rotterdam' 1966; 'Basle and France in the Sixteenth Century' 1971; Ed., Mino Celsi 'In haereticis coërcendis quatenus progredi liceat' (poems & correspondence) 1982; Ed., 'Collected Works of Erasmus' vols. 5–8, 1979–88; Ed. 'Contemporaries of Erasmus' 1985–87; mem. Ed. Bd., 'Les Index des livres interdits du XVIe siècle'; mem. Ed. Bd., 'Canadian Journal of History/Annales Canadiennes d'Histoire'; mem., Candn. Hist. Assn.; Rennaissance Soc. Am.; Am. Soc. Reformation Research; Home: 117 Albert Ave., Saskatoon, Sask. S7N 1E6.

**BIGELOW, Charles Cross,** B.A.Sc., M.Sc., Ph.D., F.C.I.C.; educator; b. Edmonton, Alta. 25 Apr. 1928; s. Sherburne Tupper and Helen Beatrice (Cross) B.; e. Univ. of Toronto Schs. 1946; Royal Mil. Coll. 1952; Univ. of Toronto B.A.Sc. 1953; McMaster Univ. M.Sc. 1955, Ph.D. 1957; m. Elizabeth d. Jack and Edna Sellick 22 Aug. 1977; children (by previous marriage): Ann K. Siess, David C.; PROF. OF CHEM. UNIV. OF MAN. 1979– ; post-doctoral Fellow, Carlsberg Lab. Copenhagen, Denmark 1957–59; Assoc., Sloan-Kettering Inst. for Cancer Research, New York 1959–62; Asst. Prof. of Chem. Univ. of Alta. 1962, Assoc. Prof. 1964; Visiting Prof. of Chem. Fla. State Univ. Tallahassee 1965; Assoc. Prof. of Biochem. Univ. of W. Ont. 1965, Prof. 1969–74; Visiting Prof. of Biochem. Univ. of Toronto 1973–74; Prof. and Head of Biochem. Mem. Univ. of Nfld. 1974–76; Dean of Science and Prof. of Chem. St. Mary's Univ. Halifax 1977–79; Dean of Science, Univ. of Man. 1979–89, Dean Emeritus 1990– ; Visiting Scientist, Nat'l Inst. for Medical Research, Mill Hill, London Eng. 1984–85; mem. Bd. Govs., Univ. of W. Ont. 1972–73; Univ. of Man. 1982–84; Man. Museum of Man and Nature 1986–91; mem. Bd. of Dirs., Candn. Assn. for the Club of Rome 1982–84; mem. Bd. of Mgmt., TRIUMF (Tri-Univ. Meson Facility), Vancouver 1987–89; Prov. Secy. Nfld. NDP 1974–76; Pres. N.S. NDP 1978–79; Pres. Man. NDP 1982–84; author numerous scient. papers protein chem.; Chrmn. Ont. Confed. Univ. Faculty Assns. 1970–71; Pres. Candn. Assn. Univ. Teachers 1972–73; recreations: book collecting, reading; Home: 701 South Dr., Winnipeg, Man. R3T 0C2; Office: Winnipeg, Man. R3T 2N2.

**BIGELOW, Wilfred Gordon,** O.C., B.A., M.D., M.S., LL.D., F.R.C.S.(C) (E (Hon.)), F.A.C.S.; surgeon; educator; b. Brandon, Man., 18 June 1913; s. Wilfred Abram and Grace Ann Carnegie (Gordon) B.; a direct descendent of Isaac B., emigrated from New. Eng. to N.S. 1761; e. Brandon (Man.) Coll.; Brentwood Coll., Victoria, B.C.; Brandon College 1931; Univ. of Toronto, B.A. 1935, M.D. 1938, M.S. 1938; LL.D., Brandon Univ. 1967; m. Ruth d. William Arthur Jennings, 9 July 1941; children: Mary, John, Dan, William; Retired Head, Cardiovasc. Surg., Toronto Gen. Hosp. and Prof. Emeritus, Dept. of Surg., Univ. of Toronto; started as Research Fellow, John Hopkins, Baltimore, Md. 1946–47; joined staff, Toronto Gen. Hosp. and apptd. Assoc., Dept. Surg., Univ. of Toronto 1948 ret'd as Sr. Surg. 1984; served in R.C.A.M.C., Field Transfusion Unit 1941–42; Graded Surg., 6th Candn. C.C.S., Eng. and N.W. Europe 1942–45; mem. Defence Research Bd. 1967–72; mem. Bd. Dirs., Ont. Heart Foundation, Nature Conservancy of Canada; Hon. Fellow, Royal Coll. of Surgs. (Eng.); rec'd Lister Prize and Peters Prize, Univ. of Toronto 1949; Gairdner Award, Toronto 1959; Centennial Medal 1967; Charles Mickle Fellowship 1973; Nat. Heart Foundation of Canada, Award of Merit and Queen's Medal 1977; Award of Merit, City of Toronto 1978; Offr., Order of Canada 1981; Hon. Mem., Candn. Soc. CV and T Surg. and 'Bigelow Lecture' Royal College 1984; Hannah Medal for scientific book, Royal Soc. of Can. 1986; Hon. Dr. Med. Hamburg 1990; Commemorative Medal, 125th Anniversary of Candn. Confedn. 1992; D.Sc. (hon. causa), Univ. of Toronto 1992; Starr Medal, Candn. Med. Assoc. 1992; Hon. Mem., Soc. Thoracic Surg. 1993; mem. Candn. Med. Assn.; Ont. Med. Assn. (Hon. mem.); Coll. of Physicians & Surgs. of Ont.; Central Surg. Assn.; Soc. of Univ. Surgs.; Am. Surg. Assn.; Am. Heart Association; Am. Assn. Thoracic Surg. (Pres. 1975); James IV Assn. of Surgs.; Candn. Soc. Clin. Surgs.; Internat. Cardiovasc. Soc. (Vice-Pres. 1971); Candn. Cardiovasc. Soc. (Pres. 1970–72); Soc. for Vascular Surg. (Pres. 1968–69); current occupation: writing and nature conservation; recreations: family, birding, riding, fishing, hunting, skiing; Clubs: University; Osler Bluff; Home: 7 Castle Frank Rd., Toronto, Ont. M4W 2Z3.

**BIJL, Willem Jacob,** B.Sc.; business executive; b. Numansdorp, Holland 11 May 1940; s. Arnoldus Pieter and Elisabeth (deKluiver) B.; e. Hotel Training Coll. Maastricht, Holland 1960; Cornell Univ. Sch. Hotel Adm. B.Sc. 1966; Insead, Eur. Sch. of Bus. Adm. I.E.P. 1974; children: Floris Willem, Sara Maria Charlotte; PRES., LE SOLEIL INNS - RESORTS 1991– ; Operations, Hilton International, Amsterdam Hilton, Rotterdam Hilton, Holland 1966–70; Dir. Operations Analysis, Inter-Continental Hotels Eur., Africa, Middle E. Div., Paris, France 1970–71, Asst. to Pres. 1971–73, Dir. Adm. 1973–75; Vice Pres. Canadian Pacific Hotels, Toronto 1975–79; Vice Pres. and Gen. Mgr. York-Hannover Hotels 1979–80, Pres. and Chief Operating Offr. 1980–81; Pres. & Dir., Kanata Hotels Ltd. 1981–90; Pres. and Dir. Kanata Hotels International Inc. 1986–90; Pres. and Dir., Nedcan Investments Ltd. 1986–91; Admissions Office Interviewer Insead, Eur. Sch. Bus. Adm.; mem. and Past Pres. Toronto Chapter Cornell Soc. Hotelmen; Manorial Soc. of Great Britain; recreations: piano, horses; Address: 2 First Canadian Place, Suite 2345, P.O. Box 75, Toronto, Ont. M5X 1B1.

**BILBROUGH, Walter Heslop,** B.A.; textiles executive; b. York, Yorkshire, England 17 Nov. 1907; s. Norman Heslop and Emilie Mary (Martin) B.; e. Upper Can.

Coll.; Trinity Coll. B.A. 1930; Univ. of Toronto; London Sch. of Econ.; Univ. of London; PRES., W.H. BILBROUGH & CO. LTD. 1933– ; imports & distributes fine furnishing fabrics; wholesale showrooms in Toronto, Calgary & Vancouver; served with RCAF & RAF in Middle East, N. AFrica & S.E. Asia during World War II; mem., 1st trade mission to People's Republic of China 1972 & later led a delegation to Hong Kong, the P.R.C., Taiwan & S. Korea; Dir., Candn. Importers Assn. 4 yrs.; mem., Internat. Trade Ctte., Toronto Bd. of Trade 4 yrs; served on Corp. of Trinity Coll. & U.C.C. Found.; London House (a residence in London, England for grad. students from the Commonwealth, U.S.A. & E.U.) built a special V.I.P. visitors' suite named in his honour; Anglican; Life Mem., Toronto Bd. of Trade; Dir., London Goodenough Assn. of Can. (Hon. Sec. 20 yrs.); recreations: tennis, sailing, bicycling; clubs: R.C.Y.C., Royal Candn. Military Inst., North York Winter Tennis; Home: 50 Hillsboro Ave., Toronto, Ont. M5R 1S8; Office: 326 Davenport Rd., Toronto, Ont. M5R 1K6.

**BILD, Fred;** diplomat; b. Leipzig, Germany 7 Aug. 1935; s. late Joseph and Ida B.; e. Sir George Williams Univ. B.A. 1957; Univ. Coll., London, U.K., Dipl. 1958–60; Ecole Nationale d'Adm. Dipl. 1968; m. Eva d. late W.A. Kornpointer; children: Eva, Maia, Sarah; AMBASSADOR OF CANADA TO THE PEOPLE'S REPUBLIC OF CHINA 1990– ; diplomatic assignments: Cdn. Embassy, Tokyo 1963; Internat. Control Comn. in Laos 1966; Cdn. Embassy, Paris 1968; Extve. Asst. to Under-Secy. of State for External Affairs Ottawa 1970; Economic Counsellor, Paris 1972; Dir. Personnel Operations, Ottawa 1977; Ambassador to Thailand, The Socialist Republic of Vietnam and the Lao Democratic Peoples Republic 1979–83; Min. Plenipotentiary, Cdn. Embassy, Paris 1984–87; Asst. Depy. Min., Political and Internat. Security Affairs, Dept. of External Affairs, Ottawa, Ont. 1987–90; Chrmn. of U.N. Working Group on Verification of Arms Limitation & Disarmament Agreements, United Nations 1988–90; Secy. Gen., Ottawa Conf. on Open Skies, Jan. to Mar. 1990; recreations: billiards, cycling, reading; Clubs: Martel Mem. Billiards; Address: Box 500 (Pekin), Postal Stn. A, Ottawa, Ont. K1N 8T7.

**BILJAN, Robert;** court administrator; b. Zagreb, Yugoslavia 26 Oct. 1942; s. the late Mato and late Sofia (Heini) B.; e. Scollard Hall, North Bay Coll., Algonquin Coll., Mgmt. Studies cert. 1977; Carleton Univ. B.A. 1976; m. Angele d. Napoleon (dec.) and Alice Pelchat; children: Kathleen, Stephan, Christine; ADMIN. OF FED. COURT OF CAN. & COURT MARTIAL APPEAL COURT OF CAN. 1982– ; Extve. Asst. to Chief Justice, Fed. Court of Can. 1971; Clerk of Process, Court of Appeal 1972; Asst. Admin. 1974; Asst. Admin. of the Court 1978; Depy. of the Comn. for Fed. Judicial Affairs & Deputy Head of Staff, Fed. Court of Can. 1981; Acting Admin. of the Court 1981; Registrar of Appeals, Pesticide Residue Compensation Act, Health of Animals Act & Plant Protection Act 1982; Pres., Assn. of Candn. Court Administrators 1990–92; Office: Fed. Court of Can., Supreme Court of Can. Bldg., Kent & Wellington Sts., Ottawa, Ont. K1A 0H9.

**BILLARD, Allan Robert,** B.Sc.; business executive; b. Halifax, N.S. 24 Apr. 1949; s. Robert and Renée B. (Collins) B.; e. Dalhousie Univ. B.Sc. 1970; Univ. de Moncton; m. Dona d. George and Geneva Roberts 1969; children: Robert, Nicole; PRES. SAND DOLLAR PRODUCTIONS INC. 1979– ; Alderman, Dartmouth City Council 1985–91; Dir. Fish Prices Support Bd.; recipient Lt. Gov.'s Award for Journalism 1979; author several plays, and articles on marine life E. Can.; Pres. Phi Kappa Pi 1971; recreations: water and racquet sports; Home: 714 Brookdale Ct., Dartmouth, N.S. B3A 4P7.

**BILLING, Randall (Randy) Charles,** C.A.; chartered accountant; b. Calgary, Alta. 22 Oct. 1946; s. Clement Joseph and Blanche Alice (DePatie) B.; e. Univ. of Calgary B.Comm. 1969; m. Patricia S. d. Kathleen and Ernest Hollingshead 30 Aug. 1968; children: Lindsey, Courtney; PRESIDENT, ENVIRONMENTAL SERVICES INC., ERNST & YOUNG 1993– ; joined Ernst & Young, Calgary 1969; obtained C.A. designation 1971 (Alta.), 1976 (Ont.); Partner 1980; National Indus. Dir., Mining 1987–93; Chair, Candn. Inst. of Chartered Accountants (CICA) Rsch. Report 'Environmental Auditing and the Role of the Accounting Profession' 1992; Chair, CICA Rsch. Report 'Environmental Performance Reporting' 1993; Chair, Candn. Standards Assn. Ctte. 'Environmental Auditing' 1992– ; Mem., Bd. of Trustees, United Way of Toronto 1985–93; recreations: golf, skiing; clubs: University Club of Toronto, Toronto Golf; Pawley's Plantation Golf & Country, S.C.; Home: 1592 Bramsey Dr., Mississauga, Ont. L5J 2H6; Office: P.O. Box 251, Ernst & Young Tower, Toronto-Dominion Ctr., Toronto, Ont. M5K 1J7.

**BILLINGSLEY, Robert William,** B.Sc.; industrialist; b. Toronto, Ont. 26 Apr. 1937; s. William Benson and Marjorie Eileen (Munro) B.; e. Univ. of Pa., B.Sc. (Econ.) 1960; m. Sandra Lynn, d. Nelson B. Kulz, 30 Sept. 1961; one d. Anne Elizabeth; Pres., Billvest Ltd.; Chrmn., Sunroot Energy Ltd.; Canadian Wallpapers Manufacturers Ltd.; Pres. and C.E.O., Anglo-Canadian Pulp and Paper Mills Ltd.; Dir., Canadian Glassine Co. Ltd.; Intercontinental Pulp Co.; Reed-Ingram Corp.; Reed International Ltd.; Takla Forest Products Ltd.; Takla Logging Co.; Prince George Pulp and Paper Ltd.; started as Sales Representative, Broad Base Retailing, Marketing Research, Information Systems, Shell Canada Ltd. 1960; Area Mgr.-E., Pulp & Paper Div., Div. Mgr. Pulp & Paper, Erco Chemicals (Electric Reduction Co. of Canada Ltd.) 1967; with Hooker Chemical Corp., Prod. and Sales Mang., Engn., Tech. Sales and Devel. 1970; former Chrmn., C.E.O. and Dir., BCM Technologies Ltd.; former Pres. & C.E.O., Reed Paper Ltd.; former Dir., Bramalea Ltd.; mem. C.D. Howe Inst.

**BILLINTON, Roy,** Ph.D., D.Sc., F.I.E.E.E., F.R.S.C., F.E.I.C., P.Eng.; educator; b. Leeds Eng. 14 Sept. 1935; s. Edwin and Nettie (Skidmore) B.; e. Univ. of Man. B.Sc. 1960, M.Sc. 1963; Univ. of Sask. Ph.D. 1967, D.Sc. 1975; m. Alice Joyce d. Joseph and Gertrude McKenna 21 July 1956; children: Leslie Jane, Kevin William, Michael Robert, Christopher John, Jeffrey Edwin; PROF. OF ELEC. ENG., & ASSOC. DEAN, COLL. OF ENGINEERING, UNIV. OF SASKATCHEWAN; C.J. McKenzie Prof. of Eng.; Pres. Power Comp. Associates Ltd.; apprentice electrician-journeyman Man. 1956; Man. Hydro, System Operations, Prodn. Div., Planning Div. 1960–64; Asst. Prof. present Univ. 1964; Sir George Nelson Award 1965–67 and Ross Medal, Eng. Inst. Can. 1972; Engineering Achievement Award, A.P.E.S. 1986; Centennial Distinguished Service Award, Candn. Electrical Assoc. 1991; Outstanding Power Engineering Educator Award, IEEE 1992; co-author: 'Power System Reliability Evaluation' 1970; 'Power System Reliability Calculations' 1973; 'System Reliability Modelling and Evaluation' 1977; 'Reliability Evaluation of Engineering Systems' 1983; 'Reliability Evaluation of Power Systems' 1983; 'Reliability Evaluation of Large Electric Power Systems' 1988; 'Applied Reliability Assessment in Electric Power Systems' 1990; Fellow, Inst. Elec. & Electronics Engrs.; Fellow, Eng. Inst. of Canada; Royal Soc. of Canada; Fellow, Safety and Reliability Soc. (U.K.); mem. Candn. Elec. Assn.; Assn. Prof. Engs. Prov. Sask.; recreations: sports; Home: 3 Maclean Cres., Saskatoon, Sask. S7J 2R6; Office: Saskatoon, Sask. S7N 0W0.

**BILLO, Edward J.,** B.A.; broadcasting executive; b. Stratford, Ont. 28 May 1942; s. Edward J. and Madeline A. (Nicholson) B.; e. Univ. of W. Ont. B.A. 1964; m. Susan, d. Frank and Lorraine Hayward 9 Oct. 1965; children: Kevin, Craig; GENERAL MANAGER, MITV MARITIMES; Dir., Candn. Assn. of Broadcasters; Industrial Relations Specialist; Ford Motor Co. 1964; Adm. Asst., Baton Broadcasting Ltd. (CFTO-TV) 1967; Program Mgr., 1970; Vice Pres. & Gen. Mgr., CFGO Radio Ltd. (Ottawa) 1975; Pres. & Dir., Bushnell Communications Ltd. 1978–85; Vice Pres., Standard Broadcasting Corp. Ltd.; Program Comte., CTV Network; Vice-Pres., Lavalin Defence Inc.; Consultant, Lavalin Communications Inc. 1988–92; R. Catholic; recreations: golf; gardening; Club: Royal Ottawa Golf; Home: 80 Chipstone Close, #415, Halifax, NS B3M 4L4.

**BILODEAU, Michel,** B.A., L.és.L., M.P.A.; health executive; b. Quebec, Que. 25 Mar. 1947; s. Roland and Madeleine (Auger) B.; e. Laval Univ., B.A. 1967, L.és.L. 1970; ENAP, M.P.A. 1986; m. Jocelyne d. Florian and Lorette Bourgon 5 Oct. 1973; one s. Francis Bourgon; PRES. AND C.E.O., SCO HEALTH SERVICE 1993– ; Extve. Dir., Elisabeth-Bruyère Health Centre, Ottawa 1991–92; Vice-Pres., Professional Serv., Ottawa Gen. Hosp. 1984–90; Dir., Human Resources, Ottawa Gen. Hosp. 1983–84; Laval Univ. Hosp. 1977–82; Dir., Language Training Prog., Public Serv. Comn.; author of num. articles; Office: 43 Bruyère St., Ottawa, Ont. K1N 5C8.

**BILODEAU, Paul,** M.Comm.; business executive; b. Jonquière, Qué. 28 Apr. 1931; e. Université Laval M.Comm. 1953; Chartered Administrator, Prov. of Québec; PRES. & GEN. MGR., WYETH LTD./LTÉE.; Mem., Bd. of Trade, Toronto; L'Association des médecins de langue française du Canada, Montreal (Assoc. Mem.); Office: 1120 Finch Ave. W., North York, Ont. M3J 3H7.

**BILODEAU, Rodrigue J.,** B.Eng., LL.D., D. Admin.; corporate director; b. Levis, Que. 23 Apr. 1921; s. Theodore H. and May (Shink) B.; e. St. Patrick's High Sch., Quebec City; St. Francis Xavier Univ. (Eng. Cert.); McGill Univ. (B.Eng.); Harvard Business Sch. (A.M.P.); LL.D. (Hon.), St. Francis Xavier Univ. 1983; D. Admin. (Hon.), Northland Open Univ. 1986; Hon. Fellow, (F.C.S.M.), Candn. Sch. of Mgmt. 1986; m. Betty June Parker, 3 June 1950; children: Carol, Dale, Patricia, Anita; Dir., Honeywell Ltd.; joined Honeywell in 1950; Eastern Cdn. Sales Mgr., Comml. Div. 1953; Nat. Sales Mgr., Indust. Div., Toronto 1956; transferred to Europe as Gen. Mgr. Indust. Products Group (Europe), Honeywell Inc., Frankfurt, Germany 1959; apptd. Asst. Dir., European Operations 1961 and Pres., Honeywell S.A., Paris, France 1964; returned to Canada as Vice Pres., Mktg. and Dir., Honeywell Ltd. 1968; Pres., Honeywell Ltd. 1970; Chrmn. & C.E.O. 1974–86; Chrmn. 1986–90; Served in World War II, R.C.A.F.; Pilot (Flying Offr., 407 Sqdn.); Past Pres. Cdn. Mfrs. Assn.; Past Pres. & mem. Extve. Comte., Cdn. Council of the Internat. Chamber of Commerce; mem. Assn. of Prof. Engrs. of the Prov. of Ont.; recreations: golf, skiing, tennis; Clubs: Bayview Country; RioVerde Golf Club (Arizona); Delta Sigma Phi; Home: 65 Spring Garden Ave., Ste. 303, Willowdale, Ont. M2H 6H9.

**BILODEAU, Roger J.,** C.G.A.; financial executive; b. Province of Quebec 6 April 1947; s. E. and T. (Carrier) B.; e. Univ. Laval cert. in Business Admin. 1970; cert. in Acctg. 1970, C.G.A. 1973; children: Audrey, François; VICE-PRES. FINANCE, ADMINISTRATIVE SERVICES & TREAS., MFQ VIE, CORP. D'ASSURANCE; LA PERSONNELLE VIE, CORP. D'ASSURANCE; TREAS., CORP. FINANCIÈRE M.F.Q.; SOGEFONDS MFQ INC.; VICE-PRES. FINANCE, ADMINISTRATIVE SERVICES, GROUPE MFQ INC. 1988– ; Dir., Société Bon Pasteur Enr.; Gestion Capidem Inc.; Auditor, Caron Bélanger Dallaire Gagnon 1970–74; Dept. Chief Acct., Asst. Mgr., Finances Mgr., Mutuelle des Fonctionnaires du Québec, La Capitale, compagnie d'assurance générale 1974–85; Finances Mgr., Mutuelle des Fonctionnaires du Québec 1985–88; Mem., Cert. Gen. Accountants' Assn.; recreations: swimming, tinkering, reading; Home: 53, Gravel, Lévis, Qué. G6V 4X4; Office: 625, rue Saint-Amable, Québec, Qué. G1R 2G5.

**BILODEAU, Ronald,** B.A., M.A.; public servant; b. Montreal, Que. 16 March 1943; s. the late Harold and Clairette (Hébert) B.; e. Coll. Sainte-Marie de Montréal B.A. 1964; Univ. of Montreal M.A. 1969; Ecole nat. d'admin. Paris 1974; m. Suzanne Laviolette 10 July 1967; children: Annick, Catherine, Valérie, Alexandre; DEPUTY MINISTER, NATURAL RESOURCES CANADA 1993– ; various positions, public service 1967–81 (incl. 7 years in Dept. of Regional Econ. Expansion); Asst. Dir. & Dir. positions, Min. of State for Economic Development 1981–84; Dir., Indus., Transp. & Nat. Resources Div. then Asst. Sec., Treas. Bd. Secretariat 1984–87; Privy Council Office, Asst. Sec. to Cabinet for Govt. Operations & Labour Relations then Asst. Sec. to Cabinet for Econ. & Regional Development Policy 1987–90; Dept. Sec. to Cabinet (Operations) 1990–93; Dep. Min., Energy, Mines and Resources 1993; Home: 847 Acadian Garden, Orléans, Ont. K1C 2V7; Office: 580 Booth St., 21st Floor, Ottawa, Ont. K1A 0E4.

**BILTON, Kent Norman,** B.A., LL.B.; lawyer; b. Hamilton, Ont. 9 Dec. 1942; s. Lloyd Harrison and Jessie Mae (Atkinson) B.; e. Hagersville Secondary Sch. 1960; McMaster Univ. B.A. 1964; Ont. Coll. of Educ. 1965; Univ. of Toronto LL.B. 1971; one d. Natasha Maria; CHIEF SOLICITOR, CANADA MORTGAGE AND HOUSING CORP. 1991– ; Teacher, Ont. Secondary Schs. 1964–66; Instr., George Brown Coll. Toronto 1968–69; private legal practice London, Ont. 1973–81; various legal positions with Canada Mortgage and Housing Corp. 1981–91; Instr. in Creditors' and Debtors' Rights, Ont. Bar Admission Course 1978–81; mem., Ctte. for an Independent Canada (Dir. 1974–77; Chrmn. London Chapter 1975–77); London Chamber Comm. (Chrmn. Prov. & Nat. Affairs Ctte. 1980–81); co-author 'The Anatomy of the Cable Television Licensing Policy of the CRTC' (Broadcaster, Feb. 1971); Home: 6122 Willowbark Dr., Orleans, Ont. K1C 5T6; Office: 700 Montreal Rd., Ottawa, Ont. K1A 0P7.

**BINDA, Pier Luigi,** Ph.D.; geologist; university professor; b. Sergnano (Cr), Italy 31 Mar. 1935; s. Carlo and Emilia (Bonomi) B.; e. Liceo Cesare Beccaria, Milano 1955; Univ. Degli Studi, Pavia, D.S.G. 1961; Univ. of Alberta, Ph.D. 1970; m. Mona d. Harry and Sylvia Cass 5 Sept. 1987; children: Francesca Chantal, Carlo Hugh Ernesto; PROF., DEPT. OF GEOL., UNIV. OF REGINA 1992– ; Lectr., Univ. of Pavia 1962–63; Sr. Geol., Roan Selection Trust, Zambia 1967–70; Rsch.

Geol., Roan Consolidated Mines Ltd. 1970–75; Principal Econ. Geol., Saudi Arabian Min. of Petroleum & Minerals 1975–76; Prof., King Abdulaziz Univ., Jeddah, Saudi Arabia 1976–81 (Head, Sedimentol. Dept. 1976–79); Vis. Prof., Univ. of Padova; Assoc. Prof., present Univ. 1982–92; Geol. Cons. to internat. exploration & mining cos. and to UNESCO; guest speaker at univs. & insts. in N. Am., Eur., Africa & Middle East; Italian N.R.C. Bursary for Alpine Rsch.; Univ. of Alta. Dissertation Fellowship; Mem., Soc. of Econ. Paleontol. & Mineralog.; Candn. Soc. of Petrol. Geol. (Nat. Liaison Ctte. 1988– ;); Assn. of Geosci. for Internat. Devel.; Soc. of Mining Engrs. of A.I.M.E.; Sask. Geol. Soc. and others; author/co-author of more than 50 sci. articles; Assoc. Ed. of four volumes on Evolution & Mineralization of the Arabian-Nubian Shield; recreations: golf, lapidary; Home: 1624 Grant Dr., Regina, Sask. S4S 4N2; Office: Regina, Sask. S4S 0A2.

**BINDON, Kathryn,** M.A., Ph.D.; university administrator; b. Toronto, Ont. 8 Jan. 1949; d. Ralph and Marion (Staples) Schultz; e. Jarvis Coll. Inst. Toronto 1967; Sir George Williams Univ. B.A. 1971; Queen's Univ. M.A. 1973, Ph.D. 1978; Nat. Defence Coll. Can. 1986–87; one s. Jeremy Edouard; PRINCIPAL AND PROFESSOR OF HISTORY, SIR WILFRED GRENFELL COLL., MEMORIAL UNIV. OF NFLD.; Lectr., Asst. and Assoc. Prof. of Hist. Concordia Univ. 1978–87, Prin. Sch. of Community and Pub. Affairs/Ecole des affaires communautaires et publiques 1981–84, Exec. Asst. to Rector 1984–86; Vice Pres. Acad. Mount Saint Vincent Univ. 1987–91; mem. Gov. Gen.'s Candn. Study Conf. 1983; Maritime Provs. Higher Edn. Comn. 1989–91; N.S. Council Higher Edn. 1989–91; Treas. World Univ. Service Can. 1987–92; Vice-Pres., World Univ. S.C. 1992–93; mem., Min.'s Adv. Bd. Women in Candn. Forces 1990–93; Chair, Min.'s Adv. Bd. on Gender Integration in the Candn. Forces 1993– ; mem., Consultative Cttee. on Social Change in the Candn. Forces 1991– ; Min.'s Adv. Group on Defence Infrastructure 1991–92; Woodrow Wilson Fellow 1971–72; Sir John A. Macdonald Fellow 1972–74; author 'Queen's Men, Canada's Men: The Military History of Queen's University, Kingston' 1978; 'More than Patriotism: Canada at War 1914–1918' 1979; mem. Candn. Hist. Assn.; Champlain Soc. Can.; recreations: scuba diving, piano, cello; Home: 1 Cobb Lane, Corner Brook, Nfld. A2H 2V3; Office: University Dr., Corner Brook, Nfld. A2H 6P9.

**BINDON, Norman Stanley;** association executive; airline captain; b. Edmonton, Alta. 5 May 1941; s. Walter Hugh and Elaine Frances (Smith) B.; m. Elizabeth d. the late Norman and Hazel Holliss Mar. 1990; children: Scott Allan, Lisa Leanne, Sheila Lindsay; Pres., Candn. Air Line Pilots Assn. 1987–..; Capt. Air Canada 1978– ; served with RCAF 1959–66; rec'd wings 1960; posted Cold Lake, Alta. CF-100 All Weather Fighter Operational Training 1960; trans. to 419 All Weather Fighter Sqdn. Baden Sollingen, Germany 1961; rtn'd Can. 1963; Flying Instr. Penhold, Alta. 1963–65; flew with 418 City of Edmonton Reserve Sqdn. one yr.; Second Offr. Air Canada 1966, First Offr. 1967; Chrmn. of Bd. St. John's Sch. Ont. 1986–87; Sec.-Treas. present Assn. 1983–86; recreations: wilderness canoeing, snowshoeing; Home: 1380 Winglos Court, Mississauga, Ont. L5C 1R1.

**BINGHAM, Stephen Richard Baston,** B.A.; business executive; b. Ottawa, Ont. 14 July 1949; c. Carleton Univ. B.A. (Hons.) 1978; divorced; CHRMN. & C.E.O., ALIAS RESEARCH INC. 1983– ; Dir., National Film Theatre 1980–83; Mem., A.C.M.; I.T.A.C.; Festival of Festivals (Board); Office: 110 Richmond St. E., Toronto, Ont. M5C 1P1.

**BINHAMMER, Helmut Herbert Frederick,** B.A., M.A., Ph.D.; professor; b. Argentina 6 June 1927; s. Herbert Karl and Marianna (Ratzel) B.; e. Univ. of Western Ontario B.A. 1948; Queens Univ. M.A. 1957; McGill Univ. PhD. 1961; National Defence College of Canada, 1982–83; m. Frances Mary d. Robert and Frances Chambers 31 Aug. 1957; one d.: Jane; Dean of Arts, Royal Military Coll. 1980–90; Lecturer & Bus. Administrator, Waterloo Coll. 1950–55; Instr. McGill Univ. 1960–61; Research Bureau, Univ. of Dar Es Salaam, Tanzania, 1968–69; R.M.C. 1955–58, and 1961 to present, Head of Dept. of Econ. & Political Sc. 1976–80; has been Econ. Consultant to U.N., World Bank, various governments & their agencies & financial institutions; Earhart Fellow; awards by Can. Council and Soc. Sc. & Humanities Research Council; Dir., Cataraqui Cemetery Co.; author 'The Development of a Financial Infrastructure in Tanzania' 1975; 'Money, Banking and Canadian Financial System, 6th Ed.' 1993; (with J.P. Cairns & R.W. Boadway); 'Canadian Banking and Monetary Policy, 2nd Ed.' 1972; (with Jane Williams) 'Deposit-Taking Institutions: Innovation and the Process of Change' 1977; various articles, reports and book reviews; mem., St. Georges Cathedral, served in various positions of Cathedral and Anglican Synod of Ont.; Candn. Econ. Assn.; Am. Econ. Assn.; recreations: fishing, skiing; Home: 61 Mackenzie Cres., Kingston, Ont. K7M 2S2; Office: Royal Military College of Canada, Kingston, Ont. K7K 5L0.

**BINKLEY, Clark Shepard,** A.B., M.Sc., Ph.D.; university professor and administrator; b. Salt Lake City, Utah 1 Dec. 1949; s. Otto Francis and Emily (Shepard) B.; e. Harvard Univ. A.B. (cum laude ) 1971, M.Sc. 1976; Yale Univ. Ph.D. 1979; m. Nadine b. Alex and Alice Bonda 1 July 1972; children: Clayton Bonda, Emily Elizabeth, Alex Francis; DEAN & PROF., FACULTY OF FORESTRY, UNIV. OF B.C. 1990– ; Asst. / Assoc. / Full Prof., School of Forestry & Environmental Studies, Yale Univ. 1979–90; named Frederick K. Weyerhaeuser Prof. of Forest Resource Management 1990; Mem., Bd. of Dir., West Fraser Timber Ltd.; Pacific Forest Products; Mngt. Ctte., Nelson Forests Joint Venture; Cons. to many govt. agencies, private non-profit conservation groups & cos.; lectured on forestry throughout the world; Mem., Adv. Bd., Ecotrust Internat.; Marcus Wallenberg Prize Ctte.; elected Mem., Bd. of Finance, Guilford, Connecticut 1988–90; author of over 75 papers & five books related to forestry & natural resource econ.; recreations: fishing; Home: 3183 West 42nd Ave., Vancouver, B.C. V6N 3H1; Office: 270 – 2357 Main Mall, Vancouver, B.C. V6T 1Z4.

**BINKS, The Honourable Kenneth C.,** B.A., LL.B.; justice; b. Ottawa, Ont. 19 May 1925; s. Russell Stuart and Kathleen Emily (Webster) b.; e. Ottawa public & high schools; Queen's Univ. B.A. (Hons.) 1948 (winner of Debating Cup 1948; tutored in Hist. Dept.); Cambride Univ. 1949–50; Univ. of Sask. LL.B. 1952; m. Jean Donalda d. William and Georgina Holman 7 May 1949; children: Georgina, Charles, Andrew, Martha; JUSTICE, ONTARIO COURT OF JUSTICE (GEN. DIV.) 1991– ; Mem., Bars of Ont. & Sask. 1953– ; single Asst. Crown Attorney, Carleton Co. 1954–56; Partner, Binks, Chilcott & Simpson 1958–91; Member of Parliament 1979–80; Sessional Lectr., Carleton Univ. 1974–75; Dir., Ottawa Litte Theatre 1971– ; Grace Hosp. (Chair, Grace Hosp. Found.); Founding Mem., St. Timothy's Presbyn. Ch. & Chair, Bd. of Managers; author: 'Canada's Parliamentary Library' French & English eds. 1978; recreations: walking, reading, music appreciation; clubs: National Press, Cercle Universitaire, Cambridge Union (Life Mem.), St. Catherines Soc., Candn. Bar Assn. Advocates' Soc., Internat. Bar Assn., Candn. Judicial Conf.; Home: 553 Thessaly Circle, Ottawa, Ont. K1H 5W8; Office: Court House 6040, 161 Elgin St., Ottawa, Ont. K2P 2K1.

**BINNIE, W. Ian C.,** Q.C., B.A., LL.B., LL.M.; barrister; b. Montreal, Que. 14 Apr. 1939; s. James Corneil and Phyllis Low (Mackenzie) B.; e. Lakefield Coll. Sch., Trinity Coll. Sch. 1957; McGill Univ. B.A. (Hon.) 1960; Univ. of Cambridge, B.A. 1962, LL.B. 1963, LL.M. 1988; Univ. of Toronto LL.B. 1965; m. Susan d. Malcolm and Barbara Strickland 28 May 1965; children: Daniel, Matthew, Alexandra and Mackenzie; PARTNER, McCARTHY TÉTRAULT, Barristers etc. Toronto 1986– ; articled with Wright and McTaggart; called to Bar of England 1966, Ont. 1967, Yukon Terr. 1984, Alberta 1991; Legal Advr. to Treasury, Govt. of Tanzania 1970–71; Q.C. 1979; in recent years has been counsel in the Supreme Court of Canada in several leading constitutional and civil cases; of legal counsel to Canada before the Internat. Court of Justice at the Hague in Gulf of Maine dispute with the U.S. 1984; Assoc. Deputy Minister, Dept. of Justice, Canada 1982–86; Legal Counsel to the Joint Ctte. of Parliament on the 1987 Constitutional Accord; Legal Counsel to the H. of C. Special Ctte. to Study the Proposed Companion Resolution to the Meech Lake Accord 1990; of legal counsel to Canada before Internat. Court of Arbitration in dispute with France over St. Pierre and Miquelon 1991; Fellow, Am. College of Trial Lawyers; mem. Law Soc. of Upper Canada; Middle Temple; Candn. Bar Assn.; Advocates Soc.; first Candn. Pres., Cambridge Univ. Union Soc. 1963; Gov., Lakefield Coll. Sch. 1971–80; Dir., Nelson Small Legs Foundation 1977–80; Cambridge Candn. Trust 1984– ; mem., Toronto Planning Bd. 1973–75; part-time Lectr., Osgoode Hall Law Sch. 1975–79; Dir., Internat. Comn. of Jurists 1978– ; author, various articles; recreations: gardening, skiing, squash; Clubs: University; Royal Canadian Yacht; Home: 6 Donino Ave., Toronto, Ont. M4N 2W5; Office: Suite 4500, Toronto Dominion Bank Tower, Toronto-Dominion Centre, Toronto, Ont. M5K 1E6.

**BINNS, Patrick George,** B.A., M.A.; management consultant; b. Weyburn, Sask. 8 Oct. 1948; s. Stanley Ernest and Phyllis Mae (Evans) B.; e. St. Dominic Savio, Weyburn, Sask.; Meridian Sch. Lloydminster, Sask.; Univ. of Alta. B.A., M.A.; m. Carol Isobel d. M.J. (Buster) MacMillan, Charlottetown, P.E.I. 8 May 1971; children: Robbie, Mark, Bradley, Lilly Ann; MANAGEMENT CONSULTANT, PAT BINNS & ASSOCIATES and CO-OWNER, ISLAND BEAN LTD.; Parlty. Sec. to Min. of Fisheries and Oceans 1986–88; family farm operator Hopefield, P.E.I. 1972– ; Devel. Offr., Govt. Alta. 1971–72; Devel. Offr. & Asst. Mgr., Rural Devel. Counc. of P.E.I. 1972–75; Co-ordinator, Kings Co. Regional Services Centre 1975–78; el. M.L.A. for Dist. of Kings 1978, re-el. 1979 and 1982; apptd. to provl. cabinet 1979; held portfolios incl. Industry, Fisheries, Community Affairs; Mem. of Parliament for Cardigan, P.E.I. 1984–88; former Chrmn. of P.E.I. Development Agency; rec'd Queen's Silver Jubilee Medal 1978; Phi Kappa Pi (Pres., Univ. of Alta. chapter 1970–71); P. Conservative; R. Catholic; recreations: hockey, skiing; Home: R.R. #4, Murray River, P.E.I. C0A 1W0.

**BIRCH, Anthony Harold,** Ph.D., F.R.S.C.; university professor; b. Ventnor, England 17 Feb. 1924; s. Frederick Harold and Rosalind Dorothy (Noblett) B.; e. William Ellis Sch., London; Univ. Coll., Nottingham; London Sch. of Econ., B.Sc. 1945, Ph.D. 1951; m. Dorothy d. Robert and Madeleine Overton 7 Jan. 1953; children: Peter Anthony, Tanya Dorothy Rosalind; Lectr. in Gov., Univ. of Manchester 1947–61; Commonwealth Fund Fellow, Harvard Univ. & Univ. of Chicago 1951–52; Prof. of Pol. Studies, Univ. of Hull 1961–70; Prof. of Pol. Sci., Univ. of Exeter 1970–77; Univ. of Victoria 1977–89; Prof. Emeritus 1989– ; Cons. to govt. of Western Reg. of Nigeria 1956–58; Vis. Prof., Tufts Univ. 1968; Vice-Pres., Internat. Pol. Sci. Assn. 1976–79; Vice-Pres., U.K. Pol. Studies Assn. 1976– ; F.R.S.C. 1988– ; author: 'Federalism, Finance and Social Legislation' 1955, 'Small-Town Politics' 1959, 'Representative and Responsible Govenment' 1964, 'The British System of Government' 1967, 9th ed. 1993, 'Representation' 1971, 'Political Integration and Disintegration in the British Isles' 1977, 'Nationalism and National Integration' 1989; 'The Concepts and Theories of Modern Democracy' 1993; recreations: bridge, music, camping; Home: 1901 Fairfield Rd., Victoria, B.C. V8S 1H2.

**BIRCH, Daniel R.,** M.A., Ph.D.; educator; b. Ganges, B.C. 1 Sept 1937; s. George Alfred and Grace Lilian (Poland) B.; e. Delta High Sch., Ladner, B.C. 1954; Northwest Bapt. Theol. Coll., Dipl. in Theol. 1958, B.R.E. 1960; Univ. of B.C., B.A. 1963, M.A. 1968; Univ. of Cal. (Berkeley) Ph.D. 1969; m. Rose Arlene, d. late Donald McDonald, 1962; one d., Carol Leah; PROF., VICE PRESIDENT, ACADEMIC, AND PROVOST, UNIV. OF B.C. 1986– ; Teacher of Hist. 1959–61 and High Sch. Counsellor 1961–63, Maple Ridge, B.C.; Social Studies Dept. Head and Vice Princ. 1964–65; Assoc. Sch. of Educ., Univ. of Cal. (Berkeley) 1968–69; joined Simon Fraser Univ. as Assoc., Educ. Foundations Centre 1966–67, Asst. Prof. of Educ. 1969–71; Chrmn., Prof. Devel. Centre 1970–71; Dean, Faculty of Education 1971–75; Prof. of Educ. and Assoc. Vice Pres. (Academic) 1975–80; Prof. and Dean of Educ. U. of B.C. 1981–86; co-dir. research training programs in U.S. and Can. on guided self-analysis and teacher educ.; Pres., Candn. Assn. of Deans of Educ. 1984–86; Dir., Candn. Educ. Assn. 1983–92; Trustee, Shaughnessy Hospital 1982–88, Chrmn., Bd. of Trustees 1985–88; Trustee, University Hospital 1988–92; Pres., Candn. Soc. Study Higher Educ. 1992–93; author: 'Gandhi'; 'Life in Communist China'; 'Asia' (all 1969); 'Early Indian Cultures of North America'; 'Voyages of Discovery'; 'Life in Early North America'; 'Growth of a Nation'; 'Culture Realms of the World' (all 1974); also prof. articles in various educ. journs.; mem., Am. Educ. Research Assn.; Candn. Soc. Study Educ.; Home: 945 Esquimalt Ave., West Vancouver, B.C. V7T 1J9; Office: 6328 Memorial Rd., Vancouver, B.C. V6T 1Z2.

**BIRD, Hon. Florence Bayard,** C.C. (1972); senator, journalist, broadcaster, and author (pen name Anne Francis); b. Philadelphia, Pa. 15 Jan. 1908; d. Dr. John H.W. and Elizabeth (Kane) Rhein; e. Agnes Irwin Sch., Philadelphia; Bryn Mawr Coll.; m. John Bird (d. 1978), 14 Nov. 1928; member Canadian Del. to UNESCO Conf., New Delhi, 1956; produced documentaries for CBC in Germany, Denmark, France, Switzerland, Belgium, Netherlands, U.S. and Hungary, 1958–66; news commentator on nat. and internat. service of CBC, 1946–66; Chrmn., Royal Comn. on Status of Women in Can., 1967–70; consultant to Task Force on Status of Women in CBC, 1974; Special CIDA Consult. to the Govt. of Jamaica 1975–76; to Govt. of Barbados 1977; Mem., Senate of Can. 1978–83; mem. Adv. Comte. on the Status of Refugees, Dept. of Immigration 1983–85; author 'Anne Francis: An Autobiography' 1974; 'Holiday in the Woods' 1976; Companion of the Order of Canada 1972; LL.D. (Hon.) York Univ. 1972; D.Hum.L. (Hon.) Mt. St. Vincent Univ. 1974; Award of Merit, the Art Directors' Club of Toronto 1973–74; LL.D. (Hon.) Carleton Univ. 1975; LL.D. (Hon.) Queen's Univ. 1975; two Women's National Press Club Awards; Governor General's Persons Award 1983; D.Hum.L. (Hon.) Univ. of Windsor 1989; Distinguished Citizen Award, Univ. of Regina 1989; mem. Candn. Inst. Internat. Affairs (Past Chrmn., Winnipeg and Ottawa Women's Br.); Hon. Life Mem., Cdn. Res. Inst. for the Adv. of Women; Dir. Cdn. Writers' Foundation Inc.; Patron, MATCH; Adviser, Inst. of Cultural Research; United Nations Assn.; mem., The Group of 78; Patron, Lester B. Pearson Coll. of the Pacific; Hon. Patron, Elsie Gregory MacGill Memorial Fund; Hon. Mem., Media Club of Ottawa 1991; recreations: swimming, walking, reading; Address: 201, 333 Chapel St., Ottawa, Ont. K1N 8Y8.

**BIRD, Ian D.,** B.Sc., R.P.F.; forest industries executive; b. Ottawa, Ont. 31 Jan. 1929; s. Frederick George (dec.) and Jane Margaret (Currie) B. (dec.); e. Lawrence Park Coll. 1947; Univ. of N.B., B.Sc. 1952; m. Roberta d. Herbert and Sereta Meehan 19 May 1952; children: Jane, Michael, Keith, Peter; President, Ontario Forest Industries Assn. 1985–92, Retired; Ontario Paper 1952–67; various mgmt. positions ending as Gen. Woodlands Mgr. QNS Paper 1968–75; Founding Gen. Mgr., Algonquin Forestry Authority 1975–85; Dir., Candn. Forest Industries Counc.; Consultant, CIDA 1979, 84; J.A. Bothwell Award for Forest Conservation, Candn. Pulp & Paper Assn. 1977; mem., Woodlands Counc.; Candn. Pulp & Paper Assn.; Ont. Professional Foresters Assn. (Pres. 1979); Candn. Inst. of Forestry; recreations: golf, canoeing, skiing; Club: Huntsville Downs Golf & Country; Home: R.R. 1, Huntsville, Ont. P0A 1K0.

**BIRD, Richard Miller,** M.A., Ph.D., F.R.S.C.; economist; educator; b. Fredericton, N.B. 22 Aug. 1938; s. Robert Bruce and the late Annie Margaret (Miller) B.; e. Sydney (N.S.) Acad. 1954; Univ. of King's Coll. B.A. 1958; Columbia Univ. M.A. 1959, Ph.D. 1961; London Sch. of Econ. 1960–61; m. Marcia Gladys d. the late Alfred Abbey, Littleover, Eng. 10 May 1958; children: Paul, Marta, Abbey; PROF. OF ECON. UNIV. OF TORONTO 1970– ; Instr. Harvard Univ. 1961–63; Sr. Research Assoc. Columbia Univ. 1963–64; Adv., Ministry of Finance, Govt. of Colombia 1964–66; Lectr. Harvard 1966–68; Assoc. Prof. present Univ. 1968–70, Dir. Inst. for Policy Analysis 1980–85; Chief, Tax Policy Div. Internat. Monetary Fund 1972–74; Killam Fellow 1969–70; Lincoln Inst. of Land Policy Fellow 1976–77 and 1986–87; Visiting Prof., Monash Univ. 1979, 1986, Univ. of York, and Erasmus Univ., Rotterdam 1987; Visiting Fellow, Australian National Univ. 1986–87 and Nat. Inst. of Public Finance and Policy, India 1987; Japan Soc. for the Promotion of Science 1987; Tinbergen Prof., Erasmus Univ. 1988; Research Fellow, World Bank 1990–91; Consultant to numerous foreign countries and internat. organs.; Dir. Commission on Intergovernmental Finance, Colombia, 1980–81; author 'Financing Urban Development in Mexico City' 1967; 'Taxation and Development' 1970; 'Growth of Government Spending in Canada' 1970; 'Taxing Agricultural Land in Developing Countries' 1974; 'Charging for Public Services' 1976; 'Residential Property Tax Relief in Ontario' 1978; 'Growth of Public Employment in Canada' 1979; 'Financing Canadian Government' 1979; 'Urban Public Finance in Canada' 1983, 2nd ed. 1993; 'Intergovernmental Finance in Colombia' 1984; 'Federal Finance in Comparative Perspective' 1986; 'Industrial Policy in Ontario' 1986; 'Public Finance in Theory and Practice' 1987; 'Government Policy and the Poor in Developing Countries' 1989; 'Taxation in Developing Countries' 1990; 'Tax Policy and Economic Development' 1992; and numerous papers on pub. finance and econ. devel.; mem. Internat. Inst. Pub. Finance; Ctte. on Taxation Resources and Economic Devel.; Nat. Tax Assn./Tax Inst. Am. (Dir.); Internat. Seminar in Pub. Economics (Chrmn.); Am. Econ. Assn.; Candn. Econ. Assn.; Candn. Tax Foundation; Home: 1065 Stockwell Ave., Mississauga, Ont. L5H 1B5; Office: 150 St. George St., Toronto, Ont. M5S 1A1.

**BIRD, Roger A.,** B.A., M.A., Ph.D.; university professor, news editor; b. Toronto, Ont. 2 May 1938; s. Norman Sylvester and Dora Anne (Bradshaw) B.; e. Lisgar Coll. 1957; Carleton Univ., B.A. 1961; Univ. of Minn., M.A. 1963, Ph.D. 1969 (all English lit.); m. Ann d. James and Aileen Finlay 29 Aug. 1964; children: Stephen, Sarah; ASSOC. PROF. OF JOURNALISM, CARLETON UNIV. 1974– ; Reporter, Ottawa Journal 1965; Reporter & Editor, Montreal Gazette 1966–68; Asst. Prof. of English, Sir George Williams Univ. (now Concordia) 1968–74; part-time news editor for variety of media incl. Financial Times of Canada, Montreal Star, Ottawa Citizen, Southam News, Globe and Mail, CBC TV, and The Easy Reader (Calif.); mem. ed. adv. ctte., Candn. Geographic magazine; mem., Candn. Communication Assn.; Assn. for the Study of Candn. Radio & TV; Candn. Assoc. of Journalists; editor: 'Documents of Canadian Broadcasting' 1988; Fellow, Royal Candn. Geographical Soc.; recreations: gardening, bird-watching, winter sports; Home: P.O. Box 4098, Stn. E., Ottawa, Ont. K1S 5B1; Office: Ottawa, Ont. K1S 5B6.

**BIRD, Terence Carl,** B.A.; telecommunications executive; b. Saint John, N.B. 4 March 1945; s. George Carl Watters and Evelyn Ann (McElwain) B.; e. Univ. of N.B. B.A. 1967; m. Margaret Jane d. William and Constance Giggey 16 May 1967; children: Jennifer, Kristin, Cameron; CHRMN., PRES. AND CHIEF EXEC. OFFR. BRUNCOR INC. 1988– ; Chrmn. N.B. Telephone Co. Ltd.; Dir. Brunswick Square; V & A Properties; Bruncor Leasing and other Bruncor subsidiaries; Canada Life; Chancellor Corp., RVM & G Inc.; Vice Pres. Day and Ross Inc. 1977, Pres. & C.E.O. 1977, Vice Chrmn. and Chief Exec. Offr. 1988; Chrmn., Business Advisory Council for Univ. of New Brunswick, Saint John; Chrmn., Literacy New Brunswick Inc.; Past Chrmn. Atlantic Provs. Econ. Council; mem. Young Pres's Orgn.; Bus. Council Nat. Issues; Corporate Higher Edn. Forum; Adv. Bd. Huntsman Marine Sci. Centre; past mem. Un. Way Greater Saint John; Family Services Saint John Inc.; Saint John YM-YWCA; recreations: tennis, golf, skiing; Clubs: Riverside Golf & Country; Union; Home: 21 Elizabeth Parkway, Renforth, N.B. E2H 1E7; Office: P.O. Box 5030, Saint John, N.B. E2L 4L4.

**BIRDSALL, William F.,** M.A., Ph.D.; librarian; b. Farmington, Minn. 30 Oct. 1937; s. Herman Elden and Mae Elizabeth B.; e. Univ. of Minn. B.A. 1959, M.A. 1964; Univ. of Wis. Ph.D. 1973; m. Ann d. Boyd and Helen Page 20 Dec. 1965; children: Sarah, Stephanie, Thomas; UNIV. LIBRARIAN, DALHOUSIE UNIV. 1981– ; Reference Lib. Iowa State Univ. 1961–63; Head of Pub. Services Wis. State Univ. Lib. 1965–70; Asst. Dir. Pub. Services Univ. of Man. Libs. 1973–77, Assoc. Dir. 1977–81; author various articles prof. journs.; Pres. Man. Lib. Assn. 1981; Pres. Atlantic Provs. Lib. Assn. 1984; mem. Candn. Lib. Assn. (Council 1981–84); Home: 54 Village Cres., Bedford, N.S. B4A 1J2; Office: Killam Library, Dalhousie Univ., Halifax, N.S. B3H 4H8.

**BIRINGER, Paul Peter,** M.A.Sc., Ph.D.; educator; consultant; b. Marosvasarhely, Hungary 1 Oct. 1924; s. Arpad Biringer; e. Tech. Univ. Budapest Dipl. Engn. 1947; Royal Inst. of Technol. Stockholm M.A.Sc. 1951; Univ. of Toronto Ph.D. 1956; m. Eva Barbro Gunnarsdotter, M.A. d. Axel Gunnar Rengman 15 Apr. 1952; two d. Anne Barbro, M.D., Monica Eva, B.A., LL.B.; PROFESSOR EMERITUS, UNIV. OF TORONTO 1990– ; Head, Research & Devel., Hatch Associates Ltd., Toronto 1980– , Consulting Engr. 1970– ; Dir. Electrical Engineering Consociates Ltd.; Consulting Engr., Ajax Magnethermic Corp. Warren, Ohio 1958– ; General Engineering Co. Ltd. Toronto 1953–58; Asst. Prof. Univ. of Toronto 1957, Assoc. Prof. 1961, Prof. 1965; Gov., George Brown Coll. Applied Arts & Technol. 1972–78; recipient Pleyel Award for Research 1951; Candn. Dist. Prize AIEE 1958; Order of Honour, Assn. Prof. Engrs. Prov. Ont. 1968; Prize Paper Award Indust. Appl. Soc. of IEEE 1979; Centennial Medal IEEE 1980; Erskine Fellow, Univ. of Canterbury, Christchurch 1987; Achievement Award, Magnetics Soc., IEEE, 1988; Fellow, Candn. Acad. of Engr. 1989; Advisory Prof. of Shanghai Jiao Tong Univ., Shanghai, People's Republic of China 1991; Distinguished Lectr., Magnetics Soc., IEEE 1991–92; Internat. Union for Electroheat Medal of Honour 1992; author over 100 publs.; holds over 40 patents in fields of magnetic frequency changers, solid state frequency changers, indust. electroheat; participant several internat. projects designing and bldg. electrometallurgical plants and electric furnaces; Sr. Research Fellow, Japan Soc. Promotion Science; Fellow, Inst. Elect. & Electronics Engrs.; Chrmn. Awards Comte., Magnetics Soc.; Chrmn. Cdn. Nat. Comte., Internat. Electric Comn.; mem. Assn. Prof. Engrs. Prov. Ont.; recreations: tennis, skiing; Clubs: Toronto Lawn Tennis; Empire; Home: 6 Lumley Ave., Toronto, Ont. M4G 2X4; Office: 10 King's College Rd., Toronto, Ont. M5S 1A4.

**BIRKENMAYER, Sandra A.,** B.A., M.B.A.; business executive; b. Glace Bay, N.S. 14 Sept. 1941; d. George Henry and Isabella (Irvine) Saunders; e. Carleton Univ. B.A. 1962; Queen's Univ. M.B.A. 1971; m. John A. Hill Aug. 1990; President & C.E.O., Ontario Training Corp. 1988–..; Supply Officer (Captain), Royal Canadian Air Force 1963–68; Systems Commodity Analyst, Federal Dept. of Supply & Services 1968–69; Research Fellow, Queen's Univ. 1970; Policy Analyst / Extve. Co-ord., Policy Secretariat, Ont. Ministry of Health 1971–75; Gen. Mgr., Corp. Div. / Managing Dir. / Sr. Managing Dir., Corp. Devel., TVOntario 1975–88; Chair, The Migraine Found. 1992– ; Bd. of Gov., YMCA of Metro. Toronto 1988– ; Volunteer Counsellor, Candn. Cancer Soc. 1988– ; Mem., Am. Soc. for Training & Devel. 1988– ; Conf. Bd. of Canada 1988– ; World Futures Soc. 1975– ; Toronto Bd. of Trade 1980– ;(Edn. Ctte. 1991– ;); Ont. Ctte. on Status of Women 1971–75; Ont. Advisory Council on the Status of Women (Comnr.) 1973–75; Agency for Tele-Edn. in Canada (Dir. & Treas.) 1975–88; Broadcast Extves. Soc. 1974–88; recreations: extensive travel, adventurous hiking, avid reader, cottage and family activities; Home: 72 Duggan Ave., Toronto, Ont. M4V 1Y2.

**BIRKENSHAW, David John,** B.A.; investment executive; b. Toronto, Ont. 29 July 1955; s. John Thomas and Isabel Lois (Sutherland) B.; e. N. Toronto Coll. Inst.; Glendon Coll. York Univ. B.A. 1976; m. Nancy Alison d. Louis and Shirley Sampson 12 Sept. 1987; one s. Geoffrey David; PRES. BIRKENSHAW & CO. LTD. 1989– ; Stockbroker L.A. Brenzel Securities Ltd. 1976–82, Gardiner Watson Ltd. 1982–83; Partner Brenzel Birkenshaw Capital Ltd. 1983–87; Assoc., Lancaster Financial 1987–89; Chairman, Atlas Corporation; Vice-Chrmn., Cangold Resources Ltd.; Pres., Phoenix Financial Holdings Inc.; Dir., Aurizon Mines Ltd.; Trustee The Gershon Iskowitz Found.; Dir. Toronto Arts Awards Found.; Dir. Big Brothers Metrop. Toronto; Fellow, Candn. Securities Inst.; Clubs: RCYC; Toronto Hunt; National; Craigleith Ski; Muskoka Lakes Golf & Country; Rosedale Golf; Badminton & Raquet; Home: 30 Rosedale Rd., Toronto, Ont. M4W 2P3; Office: 5306 Scotia Plaza, 40 King St. W., Toronto, Ont. M5H 3Y2.

**BIRKS, George Drummond,** C.M., LL.D., B.Com.; executive; b. Montreal, P.Q. 18 Feb. 1919; s. Henry Gifford and Lilian Cockshutt (Drummond) B.; e. Selwyn House Sch., Montreal, P.Q.; St. Andrew's Coll., Aurora, Ont.; McGill Univ. B.Comm.; m. 1stly late Muriel Anne, d. late T.J. Scobie, M.D.; five children; m. 2ndly Charlotte Anne Lohéac; Dir., Monarch Development Corp.; United Corporations Ltd.; Formula Growth Ltd.; Trustee, Montreal Childrens Hospital Foundation; mem. Territorial Adv. Bd., Salvation Army; served with Black Watch (R.H.R.) of Canada; Mentioned in Despatches; United Church; Clubs: Mount Royal; Mount Bruno Country; National (Toronto); Home: 3577 Atwater Ave., Apt. 1401, Montreal, Que. H3H 2R2.

**BIRKS, Henry Jonathan,** B.A., LL.L.; retail jeweller; b. Ottawa, Ont. 17 Dec. 1945; s. George Drummond and the late Muriel Ann (Scobie) B.; e. Selwyn House Sch., Montreal; Trinity Coll. Sch., Port Hope; Univ. of Lausanne, Lausanne, Switzerland; McGill Univ., B.A. 1967; Diploma in Private Internat. Law, City of London Coll., London, England 1969; Univ. Laval, LL.L. 1970; m. Maria del Carmen Denegri Boza d. Dr. Felix Denegri Luna, Lima, Peru 24 July 1970; children: Alexandra Maria; Henry Patrick; Francesca Victoria; Cristina Andrea; Ryan Christian Jonathan; PRES. C.E.O. & DIR., HENRY BIRKS & SONS (1993) INC. and BIRKS JEWELLERS INC.; Dir. & Mem. Extve. Ctte., Stone & Webster (Canada) Ltd.; Dir., La Société de Fiducie Lombard Odier; Reitmans (Canada) Ltd.; Montreal Gen. Hosp. Foundn.; Montreal YMCA Found.; American Gem Soc.; Quebec Easter Seal Society; Bd. of Trustees, The Hotchkiss Sch., Lakeville, Ct.; articled with Smith, Anglin, Laing, Weldon & Courtois; Internal Auditor, Henry Birks & Sons Ltd., Montreal 1970; Branch Mgr., Ottawa 1973; Merchandise Mgr., Ottawa-Hull 1974; Area Mgr., Ottawa-Hull 1976; Pres., Henry Birks and Sons (Montreal) Ltd. 1979; Former Dir., Univa Ltd.; Gov., Montreal Gen. Hosp.; Douglas Hosp.; mem., World Wildlife Fund (Can.); Stratford Shakespearean Festival Foundation (Can.); Montreal Bd. of Trade; Que. Chamber of Commerce; Candn. Bar Assn.; Young Presidents' Orgn.; Commanderie de Bordeaux; recipient Canadian Award, John G. Diefenbaker Memorial Foundation 1984; Personnalité du mois de la Revue Commerce 1989; Registered Jeweller, Am. Gem Soc.; Delta Kappa Epsilon; United Church; recreations: tennis, swimming, skiing; Clubs: Mount Royal; St. James's; Montreal Indoor Tennis; Hillside Tennis; Office: 1240 Phillips Sq., Montreal, Que. H3B 3H4.

**BIRKS, Thomas Massey,** M.B.A.; merchant banker; b. Montreal, P.Q. 15 Dec. 1946; s. George Drummond and Muriel Ann (Scobie) B.; e. Selwyn House Sch. (Montreal); Trinity Coll. Sch. (Port Hope, Ont.); Univs. Lausanne; Freiburg; McGill; Paris; Harvard; m. Linda, d.

Julius Hanek, 22 May 1969; children: Randall Drummond; Caroline Anne; Heather Lilian; Bradley Massey; PRES. & DIR., BIRINCO HOLDINGS INTERNATIONAL INC.; Home: 809 Upper Belmont, Westmount, Qué. H3Y 2K5; Office: 2000 Peel St., Montreal, Qué. H3A 2W5.

**BIRMINGHAM, Bruce R.,** B.Comm., M.B.A.; banker, b. Montreal, Que. 22 Dec. 1941; e. Sir George Williams Univ. B.Comm. 1970; Univ. of B.C. M.B.A. 1971; VICE CHAIR, BD. OF DIR., BANK OF NOVA SCOTIA 1992– ; various positions, Bank of Nova Scotia 1971–79; Sr. Vice-Pres., Corp. Banking & Gen. Mgr., N. Am. Internat. Regional Office 1980–83; Extve. Vice-Pres., Corp. Banking 1983–91; Sr. Extve. Vice-Pres. 1991–92; Dir., Scotia Leasing; Scotia Securities Inc.; Bank of N.S. Jamaica Limitd; Scotiabank Jamaica Trust & Merchant Bank Limited; The West India Co. of Merchant Bankers Limited; Bank of N.S. Trinidad & Tobago Limited; Bank of N.S. Trust Co. of Trinidad & Tobago Limited; Scotia Investment Mngt. Limited; Trustee & Mem., Extve. Ctte., Bd. of Trustees, Scotiabank Pension Plan; Office: 44 King St. W., Toronto, Ont. M5H 1H1.

**BIRNBAUM, Eleazar,** B.A., Dipl. O.A.S.; educator; b. 23 Nov. 1929; s. late Solomon Asher and Irene (Grunwald) B.; e. Holt Sch. Liverpool, Eng. 1946; City of London (Eng.) Sch. 1947; Univ. of London Sch. Oriental & African Studies Dipl. Hebrew Palaeography & Epigraphy 1949, B.A. (Arabic) 1950, B.A. (Turkish) 1953; m. Rebecca d. late Moszek Pardes, Brussels, Belgium 30 May 1962; children: Nathan J., Samuel M., Abraham U., Sarah M. Eisen, Miriam D.; PROF. OF MIDDLE EAST & ISLAMIC STUDIES, UNIV. OF TORONTO 1970– ; Asst. Lib., Oriental Sec. Durham Univ. Lib. (Eng.) 1953–60; Near E. Bibliog. Dept. Near E. Langs. & Lits. Univ. of Mich. 1960–64, Head of Lib.'s Near E. and S. Asian Unit 1960–64; Assoc. Prof. Univ. of Toronto 1964–70; Co-ordinator of Graduate Studies, Dept. of Middle East and Islamic Studies, Univ. of Toronto 1983–90; Assoc. Chrmn., Middle East & Islamic Studies, Univ. of Toronto 1990–93; Consultant to research fund granting agencies Can. and U.S.A.; Consultant and book reviewer scholarly journs.; author 'Books on Asia, from the Near East to the Far East' 1971; 'The Islamic Middle East' 1975; '"The Book of Advice" by King Kay-Ka'us Ibn Iskandar: The Earliest Old Ottoman Turkish "Kabusname"' 1981; 'From Manuscript to Printed Book in the Islamic World' 1989; co-author 'Introduction to Islamic Civilisation' 1976; numerous articles Orientalist, Turkish, and Jewish studies scholarly journs.; Dir., Eitz Chaim Schs., Beth Jacob High Sch., Maimonides Coll., Toronto; mem. Am. Oriental Soc.; Middle E. Studies Assn. N. Am.; Turkish Studies Assn.; Middle E. Librarians Assn.; Am. Research Inst. Turkey; Am. Assoc. of Teachers of Turkish; recipient of Fellowships and Research Awards from Canada Counc. (1969, '70, '72); SSHRC (1979–82; 1986–89; 1991–93); Am. Rsch. Inst. in Turkey (1986–87); Univ. of Toronto Rsch. Bd. (1967, '71, '74, 1976–80, 1982–94); Specialist in Turkish and Middle Eastern Studies; Expert in manuscripts in Middle Eastern languages; extensive rsch. travel in Middle East, Europe and Central Asia; Jewish; recreations: research Middle E. langs., lits., hist. & bibliog., swimming; Clubs: Faculty; Oriental; Home: 132 Invermay Ave., Downsview, Ont. M3H 1Z8; Office: Dept. of Middle East & Islamic Studies, Univ. of Toronto, Toronto, Ont. M5S 1A1.

**BIRNEY, Alfred Earle,** O.C. (1970), Ph.D., D.Litt., LL.D., F.R.S.C. (1954); author; b. Calgary, Alta. 13 May 1904, of a Western pioneer family, his father having arrived in Alta. on horseback, 1883, later prospecting in various parts of the Rockies; s. William George and Martha Stout (Robertson) B.; e. Univ. of B.C., B.A. 1926; (scholar. to Univ. of Toronto 1926–27); Univ. of Toronto, M.A. 1927; Ph.D. 1936; Univ. of California (grad. sch.) 1927–30; Univ. of London (Roy. Soc. of Can. Fellowship) 1934–35; LL.D., Univ. of Alta. 1965; D.Litt., McGill 1979; D.Litt., Univ. of W. Ont. 1984; D.Litt., Univ. of B.C. 1987; m. Esther, d. Emmanuel Bull, Hampstead Garden Suburb, London, 6 Mar. 1940, divorced 1977; one s., William; began career as Teaching Fellow, Univ. of California, 1927–30; Lectr. Summer Sch., Univ. of B.C., 1927 and eight other summers; Instr. Univ. of Utah 1930–32, 1933–34; Leonard Fellow, Univ. of Toronto 1932–33; Lect. in Eng., Univ. Coll., Univ. of Toronto, 1936–41; Asst. Prof. 1941–42; Supervisor of European Foreign Lang. Broadcasts, Internat. Shortwave Service, CBC 1945–46; Prof. of Eng. Univ. of B.C. 1946–63, and Head, Dept. of Creative Writing there 1963–65; Writer-in-Residence, Univ. of Toronto 1965–67; Univ. of Waterloo 1967–68; Univ. of Western Ont. 1981–82; Univ. of Alaska (Fairbanks) 1984; Lit. Ed., 'Canadian Forum' 1936–40; Editor-in-Chief, 'Canadian Poetry Magazine' 1946–48; Editor-in-Chief, 'Prism International' 1964–65; Advisory Ed., 'New Canadian & American Poetry' 1964–68; served with Reserve Army (C.O.T.C.) 1940–42, with rank of Lieut.; served in World War 1942–45 with Inf. Personnel Selection Service, Overseas 1943–45; Maj. in charge, Personnel Selection for Candn. Army Belgium and Holland; invalided home; winner of Gov.-Gen's Award in Poetry, 1942 and 1945; author of 'David and Other Poems' 1942; 'Now is Time' 1945; 'Strait of Anian' 1948; 'Turvey' (a military picaresque novel) 1949; 'Trial of a City' 1952; 'Twentieth Century Canadian Poetry' (anthology) 1953; 'Down the Long Table'(novel) 1955; (ed.) U.B.C. 'Record of Service in Second World War' 1955; 'Ice Cod Bell or Stone' (poems) 1962; (ed.) 'Selected Poems of Malcolm Lowry' 1962; 'Near False Creek Mouth' (poems) 1964; 'Selected Poems' 1966; 'The Creative Writer' 1966; 'Memory no Servant' (poems) 1968; co-ed., 'Lunar Caustic,' Malcolm Lowry 1968; 'pnomes, jukollages & other stunzas' 1969; 'poems of earle birney' 1969; 'rag & bone shop' (poems) 1971; 'The Cow Jumped Over the Moon/ the writing & reading of poetry' 1972; 'The Bear on the Delhi Road' (poems) 1973; 'What's so Big about Green?' (poems) 1973; 'Collected Poems 1920–74' 1975; 'Alphabeings' (visual poems) 1976; 'The Rugging and the Moving Times' (poems) 1976; 'The Damnation of Vancouver' (stage play) 1977; 'Ghost in the Wheels' (sel. poems) 1977; 'Fall by Fury' (poems) 1978; 'Big Bird in the Bush' (sel. stories and sketches) 1978; 'Spreading Time – Book I 1904–49' (essays and memories) 1980; 'The Mammoth Corridors' (poems) 1980; 'Music & Poetry: Earle Birney & Nexus' (3 albums, digital recording) 1982; 'Words on Waves' (sel. radio plays) 1985; 'Essays on Chaucerian Irony' 1985; 'Copernican Fix' (new poems) 1985; 'Last Makings' (poems) 1991; numerous poems, stories, essays, lit. articles, book reviews, etc. to Candn., Am. and Brit. publs.; awarded Borestone Poetry Award (U.S.A.) 1951; Lorne Pierce Gold Medal for Lit. (Royal Soc. Can.) 1952; Leacock Medal for Humour by Stephen Leacock Mem. Comte., 1949; Candn. Govt. Overseas Fellowship to France, 1953; Nuffield Scholar, England, 1958–59; Visiting Prof., Univ. of Oregon, 1961; Regents Prof., Univ. of California, 1968; Can. Council Sr. Arts Fellowship, 1962–63, 1968–69, 1975, 1978–81; mem., Writers Union of Canada; Assoc. of Can. Television and Radio Artists; awarded Can. Council Medal 'for outstanding cultural achievement' 1968; recreations: swimming, gardening, cycling; Address: #1204, 130 Carlton St., Toronto, Ont. M5A 4K3.

**BIRNIE, David Alexander George,** B.A., LL.B.; barrister & solicitor; b. Vancouver, B.C. 17 Dec. 1945; s. George Frederick and Mary Helen (Wilson) B.; e. West Vancouver Sr. Secondary Sch. 1962; Univ. B.C., B.A. 1966; LL.B. 1969; m. Roberta, d. Robert and Doreen Knill, 2 Sept. 1967; children: Douglas; Paige; SR. TAX PARTNER, KOFFMAN, BIRNIE & KALEF; Student, Meredith & Co. 1969; Assoc. 1970; Assoc., Barbeau, McKercher, Collingwood & Hanna 1971; Partner 1973; Partner, Birnie, Sturrock & Co. 1975; author several reports and articles mostly on aspects of Candn. Income Tax; rec'd. Diana & P.A.E. Irving Scholarship; Farris, Farris, Vaughan, Taggart Wills & Murphy Scholarship; Class of 53 Scholarship; Internat. Moot Shield; Can. Permanent Mortgage Corp. Prize; Allen S. Gregory Memorial Prize; mem. Minister's Adv. Counc. on Tax Admin.; Depy. Min.'s Adv. Ctte. on GST; former Gov., Cdn. Tax Foundn.; mem., Cdn. Bar Assn. (Chrmn., National Taxation Sect.; Chrmn., Taxation Sect., B.C., 1982–84; Secy. 1980–82); Chrmn., Fed. Jt. Ctte. on Taxation, C.B.A.-C.I.C.A.; Am. Bar Assn. (Taxation Sectn.); B.C. Jt. Ctte. on Taxation, C.B.A.-C.I.C.A.; Clubs: Royal Vancouver Yacht; recreations: boating; tennis; squash; Home: 875 Aubeneau Cr., W. Vancouver, B.C.; Office: 19th Flr., 885 W. Georgia St., Vancouver, B.C. V6C 3H4.

**BIRNIE DANZKER, Jo-Anne,** B.A., Dip.Ed., B.Ed.; arts executive; b. Brisbane, Australia 1945; d. Colin Maxwell and Margaret Dorothy B.; e. Univ. of Queensland, B.A. 1966, Dip.Ed. 1967, B.Ed. 1971; m. Otfried Zimmermann 25 Apr. 1987; Teaching Asst., York Univ. 1973–74; Curator, The Electric Gallery 1973–74; Visual Arts. Cons., Dept. of Cult. Affairs, Canada House (UK) 1974; Exhib. Prog., Galleria Arte Borgogna (Italy) 1975–76; Mng. Ed., 'Flash Art' 1975–76; Orgn., 1st. Nat. Conf. of Candn. Art Mags. 1977; Curator, Vancouver Art Gallery 1977–84; Acting Dir. 1984; Dir. 1985–87; Comnr. for Can., 'Toyama Now '87: New Art Around the Pacific' Toyama, Japan Feb.–Oct. 1987; Dir., KULTUR Inc. 1988– ; Dir., MBD Associates 1991– ; Head Moderator for B.C., Citizens' Forum on Canada's Future; mem., Candn. Museum Assn. 1985–90; Am. Assn. of Art Mus. Dir.; Vancouver Bd. of Trade 1986; Counc. of Assoc. Mus. Dir.; Candn. Art Mus. Dir. Orgn.; Am. Assn. of Mus.; Assn. Internat. des Critiques d'Art 1985–90; Chrmn., Bd. of Dirs., Anna Wyman Dance Theatre Found. 1989–90; Vice-Chrmn., Special Counc. Ctte. on the Arts, City of Vancouver 1989–93; Chrmn., Subctte. on Cultural Diversity, City of Vancouver 1989–91; Adv. Counc., Vancouver Dance Centre 1990–92; Adv. Bd. 'Artropolis '90' exhbn. and the 'Wells Project' 1990; Curator, 'Graphothek' exhbn. 1990; art columnist, 'Vancouver' mag. 1989– ; author of num. catalogues, most recent: 'Graphothek,' 'Away from Utopia: Graham Gillmore, Angela Grossmann, Derek Root' 49th Parallel, New York 1989; 'Edvard Munch,' 'Luxe, calme et volupte' 1986; 'Gathie Falk,' 'Gum San/Gold Mountain' 1985; articles, most recent: 'Cultural Convergence' Canadian Art 1990, 'Cultural Apartheids' Muse 1990 and Third Text 1991; 'Ken Lum' Artscribe 1991; 'Three Modern Masters' in Western Living Magazine 1989; 'Stan Douglas' in Canadian Art 1989; 'Kunst des Unsagbaren' in Wolkenkratzer Art Journal 1989; 'New Art around the Pacific' in Toyama Now '87, 'Box of Daylight,' 'Smokey Top' in Vanguard 1984; Address: 1477 Fountain Way, Suite 101, Vancouver, B.C. V6H 3W9.

**BIRON, André,** B.A.Sc., M.A.Sc., Ph.D.; educator; b. Montréal, Qué. 21 July 1934; s. Marcel and Marthe (Hurtubise) B.; é. Ecole Polytechnique, Mech.-Elec. Engr. B.A.Sc. 1958, Mech. Engr. M.A.Sc. 1963; Illinois Inst. of Tech. Ph.D. 1967; children: Paule, Michel, Pascale; Assoc. Dir., Centre for Rsch. on Computation and its Applications (CERCA) 1992– ; teaching, rsch. in Mech. Engrg. Ecole Polytechnique 1958–91 inc. plastic behaviour of structures (limit analysis), fatigue and creep of materials; Prof. Dept. of Mech. Engr., Ecole Polytechnique, Montreal 1958–93; cons., mem. team of Engr. stress analysis group involved in stress and vibration analysis and seismic behaviour analysis for nuclear power plants 1961–79; Head, Section of Applied Mech. 1970–78; Head, Dept. of Mech. Engr. 1978–84; responsible for Aeronautical Engr. programs, Ecole Polytechnique 1980–87; Assoc. Dir. of Rsch. and Grad. Studies 1985–93; Visiting Rsch. Offr. NSERC 1984–85; author or co-author over 50 tech. papers and one book; Fellow Engr. Inst. of Can. 1980; Fellow Am. Soc. of Mech. Engr. 1980; Fellow, Candn. Soc. for Mech. Engr. 1987; Fellow, The Inst. of Engrs. of Ireland 1990; Eur. Ing. 1990; mem. Order of Engrs. of Que.; Am. Soc. Mech. Engr.; Candn. Soc. Mech. Engr. (Pres. 1975–76); Counc. NSERC 1982–86; Candn. Engr. Accreditation Bd., Candn. Counc. of Prof. Engr. 1984 (Chrmn. 1990–91); Adv. Ctte. on Nuclear Safety 1984– ; Mem., Conseil de la Science et de la Technologie (Que.) 1986–91; Pres. Parents' Assn., Ecole Notre-Dame-de-Grâce 1970–71; Bd. of Admin. Coll. Marie de France 1975–84; Manoir Notre-Dame-de-Grâce 1978–80; recreations: jogging, tennis, hiking, cross-country skiing; Home: 4110 Harvard, Montreal, Que. H4A 2W7; Office: 5160 Décarie, Suite 400, Montréal, Qué. H3X 2H9.

**BIRON, Hon. Jacques,** B.A., LL.L.; judge; b. Drummondville, Que. 29 Sept. 1935; s. Antoine and Thérèse (Gendron) B.; e. Brébeuf Coll. B.A. 1956; Univ. de Montréal LL.L. 1959; m. Louise d. Armand and Bibiane Thibodeau 15 Aug. 1959; children: Yves, Marie Claude; JUDGE (1980), QUEBEC COURT (civil division), PRESIDENT OF THE PROFESSIONS TRIBUNAL; called to Bar of Que. 1960; law practice Drummondville 1960–80; Crown Atty. 1966; Juvenile Court Atty. 1966–70; Atty. for City of Drummondville 1964–80; served as mem. various comtes. Que. Bar Assn., Candn. Bar Assn.; R. Catholic; recreations: fishing, skiing; Home: 195 Chemin de la Côte Ste-Catherine, Apt. 1709, Outremont, Que. H2V 2B1; Office: The Court House, Rm. 13.26, 1, Notre-Dame E., Montreal, Que. H2Y 1B6.

**BIRT, Ronald Gordon,** B.A., D.H.A.; health service executive; b. Winnipeg, Man. 12 Apl. 1941; s. Charles Taylor and Maree Kathleen (Mathews) B.; e. Winnipeg Gen. Hosp. Reg'd Technol. 1963; N.D. State Univ. B.A. 1968; Univ. of Toronto Dip. Hosp. Adm. 1970; m. Margaret d. Albert and Rose Franklin 5 Aug. 1970; children: Amanda, Peter; PRES. MAN. HEALTH ORGNS. INC. 1991– ; Lab. Technol. Winnipeg Gen. Hosp. 1963–67; Adm. Resident Humber Meml. Hosp. 1969–70; Exec. Asst. Sanatorium Bd. Man. 1970, Exec. Dir. 1973–80; Asst. Exec. Dir. Seven Oaks Gen. Hosp. 1980, Exec. Dir. 1985–90; Exec. Dir. present Orgn. 1990–91, Dir. 1986–90; mem., Review Ctte. Sustaining Grants Prog. Nat. Voluntary Health Orgns. Min. Health & Welfare 1985–87; Chrmn. Task Force Extended Treatment Bed Review Man. Health 1989–90; mem. Working Group Health Promotion Health Care Facilities Health & Welfare Can. 1988–90; mem., Provincial Health Information Ctte. 1992; mem. Min. Council Nursing Edn. 1992–93; Urban Health Advisory Council; Rural Health Advisory Coucil; Man. Health Work Restructuring Extve. Ctte.; TQM Coordinating Ctte. 1992–93; Affiliate, Am. Coll. of Healthcare Extves. 1988– ; Candn. Soc. Assn. Execs.; Pres. Man. Pub. Health Assn. 1982–83; Dir. Candn.

Pub. Health Assn. 1982–84; Dir., Candn. Lung Assn. 1976–79, 1984–86; Gov., Manitoba Museum of Man and Nature 1991–93; mem. Rotary Internat. since 1975, Dir. Winnipeg 1976–78 and N. Winnipeg 1981–82, 1986–88; recreations: photography, reading, music, nature; Home: 2 Waterview Cove, Winnipeg, Man. R2N 3C8; Office: 360 Broadway, Winnipeg, Man. R3C 4G6.

**BISAILLON, J. Guy,** M.B.A.; banker; b. 10 Oct. 1936; e. University of Montreal (H.E.C.) M.B.A. 1986; SENIOR VICE-PRES., QUEBEC, THE BANK OF NOVA SCOTIA 1987– ; various functions, The Royal Bank of Canada 1953–81; Vice-Pres. 1981–87; Dir., Conseil Candn. des chrétiens et des juifs; Festival internat. du film sur l'art; Fond. québécoise en environnement; Dir., La Fond. de la Maison Trestler; Dir., Société des Musees de Sciences Naturelles de Montréal; Mem., Assn. des anciens des H.E.C.; Assn. des banquiers canadiens; Assn. des M.B.A. du Qué.; recreations: swimming, golf; clubs: Le Sanctuaire, Laval-sur-le-Lac, Mont-Royal, Saint-Denis; Office: 1002 ouest, rue Sherbrooke, Bureau 430, Montréal, Qué. H3A 3M3.

**BISHOP, Charles Johnson,** B.Sc., A.M., Ph.D., D.Sc (Hon.) F.R.S.C., F.A.S.H.S., F.A.I.C.; retired horticulturist; b. Semans, Sask. 6 Jan. 1920; s. Lewis Leander and Nellie Erdine (Illsley) B.; e. elem. schs. Wolfville, Berwick and Somerset (N.S.); high schs. Berwick, Kentville (N.S.); Acadia Univ. B.Sc. 1941; Univ. of W. Ont. 1941–42; Harvard Univ. A.M., Ph.D. 1947; Acadia Univ. D. Sc. (Hon.) 1982; m. Katherine Adele d. late Frank L. Corey 19 June 1951; one s. John; Weather Forecaster (RCAF) Dept. Transport 1942–45, Flying Offr. 1945; Research Scient. Tree Fruit Breeding Exper. Stn. Can. Dept. Agric. Kentville, N.S. 1947–52; Supt. Exper. Stn. 1952–58; Acting Supt. Exper. Stn. Summerland, B.C. 1958–59; Assoc. Dir. Program (Crops) Research Br. Can. Dept. Agric. Ottawa 1959–63, Research Coordinator (Hortic.) 1963–78; Rsch. Co-ordr. (Crop Production) Rsch. Br. Agriculture Can. 1978–85 (ret.); rec'd Candn. Hortic. Council Merit Award and Hon. Life Membership; Queen's Silver Jubilee Medal; Vavilof Centenary Medal; author over 25 papers scient. research genetics & fruit breeding; Fellow, Am. Soc. Hortic. Science; Fellow, Agric. Inst. Can. (Past Hon. Secy.); Hon. Life mem. W. Candn. Soc. Hortic.; Fellow (Past Pres. & Secy.) Science Acad., Royal Soc. Can.; Past Pres. and Hon. Pres. Candn. Soc. Hortic. Science; Past Mem., Internat. Bd. for Plant Genetic Resources; Past Pres., Genetics Soc. Can.; past mem. Internat. Soc. Hortic. Science (Council); Genetics Soc. Am.; Baptist; recreations: curling, photography, gardening; Club: West Ottawa Rotary; Granite Curling; Address: 1968 Bel Air Dr., Ottawa, Ont. K2C 0W9.

**BISHOP, Claude Titus,** B.Sc., B.A., Ph.D., F.R.S.C.; retired; scientist; Canadian public servant; b. Liverpool, N.S., 13 May 1925; s. Claude Wetmore and Elva (Titus) B.; e. Acadia Univ., B.Sc. 1945, B.A. 1946; McGill Univ., Ph.D. (Chem.) 1949; m. Pierrette Marie Therese (deceased 1975), d. late Eugene Picard, 8 July 1951; one s., Scot; m. Joan M. Marshall, 5 May 1983; Editor-in-Chief, Research Journals, Nat. Research Council 1970–90 and Secy. Gen., N.R.C. 1987–89; joined NRC as Jr. Research Offr. 1949; served as Asst., Assoc., Sr. and Princ. Research Offr. 1949–65; Asst. Dir., Biochem. Lab., 1969–72; Assoc. Dir., Div. of Biol. Sciences 1972–78; Dir., Div. Biol. Sci. 1978–87; Asst. Ed. and Ed., Canadian Journal of Chemistry, 1964–70; Hon. Ed., Royal Soc. Can. 1991– ; author of over 85 scient. papers; Chrm., USA Nat. Acad. Sciences Comte. on Specifications & Criteria for Biochem. Compounds, 1965–68; mem. Royal Soc. of Canada; D.Sc. (hon. causa) Univ. of Western Ont. 1986; recreations: golf, skiing; Home: 63 Holborn Ave., Nepean, Ont. K2C 3H1.

**BISHOP, David Michael,** B.Sc., Ph.D., D.Sc., F.R.S.C.; university professor of chemistry; b. London, England 19 Sept. 1936; s. Jack Montague and Margery Edith (Faggeter) B.; e. Caterham School Surrey 1954; Univ. College London B.Sc. 1957, Ph.D. 1960, D.Sc. 1972; PROFESSOR, DEPT. OF CHEMISTRY, UNIV. OF OTTAWA 1972– ; research in theoretical chem., Carnegie Inst. of Technology 1960–63; Asst. Prof., Univ. of Ottawa 1963–72; rsch. interests are based on very accurate calculations of properties of small molecules; results widely used to calibrate experiments most recently in field of non-linear optics; F.R.S.C.; author: 'Group Theory and Chemistry' 1973, 1993; recreations: cryptic crossword puzzles, music; club: Goats; Home: 714 – 200 Rideau Terrace, Ottawa, Ont. K1M 0Z3; Office: Ottawa, Ont. K1N 6N5.

**BISHOP, Olga Bernice,** M.A., A.M.L.S., Ph.D., LL.D.; professor emeritus; b. Dover, N.B. 24 June 1911; d. Thomas Cochrane and Minnie Earle (Colpitts) B.; e. Mount Allison Univ., B.A. 1938, M.A. 1951, LL.D. 1971; Carleton Univ., B. Pub. Admin. 1946; Univ. of Michigan, A.M.L.S. 1952, Ph.D. 1962; PROF. EMERITUS, UNIV. OF TORONTO FACULTY OF LIBRARY AND INFORMATION SCI. 1977– ; Volunteer Librarian, Metropolitan United Ch., London 1981–92; Secy., Mount Allison Mem. Lib., Sackville, N.B. 1932–40; Asst. Lib., 1946–53; apptd. Gen. Lib., Univ. of Western Ont., 1953–54; Med. Lib., 1954–65; Assoc. Prof., Univ. of Toronto Faculty of Library and Information Sci. 1965–70; Prof. there 1970–77; served during 2nd World War as Sr. Adm. Offr. R.C.A.F. Record of Service, Can. Civil Service, Ottawa, 1940–46; Dir., London Community Concert, 1963–66; author of 'Publications of the Governments of Nova Scotia, Prince Edward Island, New Brunswick 1758–1952' 1957; 'Publications of the Government of the Province of Canada 1841–1867' 1963; 'Publications of the Government of Ontario 1867–1900' 1976; 'Bibliography of Ontario History, 1867–1976: Cultural, Economic, Political, Social' 1980; 'Canadian Official Publications' 1981; 'Publications of the Province of Upper Canada and of Great Britain relating to Upper Canada 1791–1840' 1984; ed. 'Growing to Serve: A History of Victoria Hospital, London, Ontario' 1985; 'North Talbot Road, Westminster Township' 1986; 'Glanworth, Westminster Township' 1987; 'Westminister Township Southeast of the Thames' 1988; compiled: 'History of the English-Speaking Union of Canada: London and Western Ontario Branch 1967–87' 1990; has written articles and book reviews for various lib. journs.; mem., Candn. Lib. Assn. (Convenor Awards and Scholarships Ctte. 1986–88); Candn. Assn. Coll Univ. Libs. (Secy. 1965–66); Ex Libris Assn. (Dir. 1986–88); Ont. Lib. Assn.; Ont. Assn. Coll. Univ. Libs. (Councillor 1963–65, Vice Chrmn. 1965–66, Chrmn. 1966–67); Inst. Prof. Libs. Ont. (Dir. 1964–68, Pres. 1966–67); Candn. Assn. Univ. Teachers (UTFA Toronto Councillor 1968–1973): Med. Lib. Assn.; Bibliog. Soc. Can. (Dir. 1974–80; Pres. 1976–78); Ont. Historical Soc.; Assn. for Candn. Studies; Heritage Canada; Westminster Historical Soc.; Architectural Conservancy of Ont. London Region Br.; rec'd Birk's Gold Medal, Highest Average Scholarship, Mount Allison Ladies Coll. 1927–28; Marie Tremaine Medal in Can. Bibliography 1981; CASLIS Award 1981; Univ. of Mich. Sch. of Library Sci. and Library Sci. Alumni Soc. Alumni Recognition Award in recognition of international leadership in library profession 1985; Ont. Coll. and Univ. Assoc. Merit Award 1987; recipient, Dictionary of International Biography illuminated plaque for distinguished service in the field of Librarianship, Bibliography, Teaching, 1991; Beta Phi Mu; Metropolitan United Church Plaque of Appreciation for Volunteer Services 1993; Progressive Conservative; United Church; recreation: handicrafts; Club: Women's Canadian; University Women's (Chrmn., Canadiana Grp. 1983–87); English Speaking Union; Home: 62 Thornton Ave., London, Ont. N5Y 2Y3.

**BISSELL, Claude Thomas,** C.C. (1969), M.A., Ph.D., D.Litt., LL.D., F.R.S.C.; ex-univ. president and administrator; b. Meaford, Ont., 10 Feb. 1916; s. George Thomas and Maggie Editha (Bowen) B.; e. Runnymede Coll. Inst., Toronto, Ont.; Univ. Coll., Univ. of Toronto, B.A. 1936 and M.A. 1937; Cornell Univ., Ph.D. 1940; D. Litt. of Univ. of Manitoba, Univ. of Western Ont., Lethbridge, Leeds, Toronto, LL.D. of McGill Univ., Queen's, New Brunswick, Carleton, Montreal, St. Lawrence Univ. (Canton, N.Y), Brit. Columbia, Michigan, Columbia, York, Prince of Wales Coll., Windsor, St. Andrew's (Scotland), Dalhousie Univ.; Docteur ès Lettres, Laval; m. Christina Flora, d. William Gray, Glasgow, Scot., 12 Sept. 1945; one d., (Mrs.) Deirdre Macdonald; Instr. in Eng., Cornell Univ. 1938–41; Lectr. in Eng., Univ. Coll. Univ. of Toronto 1941; Dean of Residence, University Coll., 1946–56; Asst. Prof. 1947; Assoc. Prof. 1951; Prof. 1962 and since July 1971; Asst. to the Pres., Univ. of Toronto 1948–52; Vice-Pres., 1952–56; President, Carleton Univ., 1956–58; Pres., Univ. of Toronto 1 July 1958–30 June 1971; Professor there 1971–83; President and Professor Emeritus 1983; Dir., Confed. Life Ins. Co.; served in 2nd W.W. with Candn. Inf. Corps 1942–46; with Argyll and Sutherland Highlanders of Can. in N.W. Europe campaign; discharged with rank of Capt.; Award of Merit, City of Toronto 1962; Hon. Mem. Am. Acad. of Arts and Science 1968; ed.: 'University College: A Portrait' 1953; 'Canada's Crisis in Higher Education' and 'Our Living Tradition' 1957; 'Great Canadian Writing' 1966; author: 'The Strength of the University' 1968; 'Halfway Up Parnassus: A Personal Account of the University of Toronto 1932–71' 1974; 'The Humanities in the University' 1977; 'The Young Vincent Massey' 1981 (Co-winner of City of Toronto annual book award 1982; winner Candn. Authors Assn. Literary Award for Non-Fiction); 'The Imperial Canadian' 1986 (Winner of Univ. of Columbia Medal for Biography 1986); 'Ernest Buckler Remembered' 1989 (Winner of City of Dartmouth Literary Award for non-fiction 1990); named Chrmn., Canada Council 1960–62; Pres., World University Service of Can. (2 yr. term) Nov. 1962; Pres., Nat. Conf. of Candn. Univs. and Colls. 1962–63; Chrmn., Candn. Universities Foundation 1962–63; Chrmn. Carnegie Foundation for the Advancement of Teaching 1966; Pres. World University Service of Canada 1962–63; Chrmn. Comm. of Presidents of Universities of Ontario 1962–66; Visiting Prof. of Candn. Studies, Harvard Univ. 1967–68; Commonwealth Fellow, Sch. of English, Leeds Univ. 1973; Aggrey-Fraser-Guggisberg Memorial Lecturer, Univ. of Ghana 1976; mem. Council of the Arts (Ont.) 1972–75; author of various articles on Candn. and Eng. lit. in Candn. and Am. journals; United Church; Clubs: Arts and Letters; York; Address: 229 Erskine Ave., Toronto, Ont. M4P 1Z5.

**BISSET, Ronald J.,** B.Comm., M.B.A.; retired bank executive; b. Toronto, Ont. 9 Aug. 1934; s. Norman Peter and Kathleen Isobel (Reid) B.; e. Queen's Univ. B.Comm. 1966; Harvard Univ. M.B.A. 1968; m. Nettie d. Michael and Anne Kaban 7 Sept. 1957; children: Robert James, Melanie Kathleen; Executive Vice-Pres., Individual Bank, Credit Management, Canadian Imperial Bank of Commerce 1991–93, Retired; joined CIBC Toronto 1951; Vice-Pres. & Reg. Gen. Mgr., Toronto 1976; Hamilton 1979; Sr. Vice-Pres. & Reg. Gen. Mgr., Alta. & N.W.T., Calgary, Alta. 1985; Extve. Vice-Pres., Eastern Canada & West Indies 1986; Extve. Vice-Pres., Domestic Delivery Systems Implementation Team (Project Delta) 1987; Dir., Bank of Commerce, Trinidad & Tobago Ltd.; recipient, Gold Medal, Queen's Univ. 1966; United Church; Mem., HBS Club of Toronto; Queen's Business School Club of Toronto; recreations: golf, curling; clubs: Granite, Aurora Highlands Golf & Country; Home: 108 Cranberry Lane, Aurora, Ont. L4G 5Z3.

**bissett bill** poet paintr singr b. halifax, nova scotia 23 nov 1939 s. fred and catherine (covert) b e. dalhousie univ ubc 1956 one dottr michelle 59 books uv poetree 7 wun person shows van art galleree wintr 84 author: recent books seagull on yonge street northern birds in color pomes for yoshi beyond even faithful legends medicine my mouths on fire nobody owns erth first book we sleep inside each othr all 1966 canada gees mate for life 1986 animal uproar 1987 what we have 1989 (Milton Acorn Peopuls Poets Award 1990) hard 2 beleev 1990 latest book inkorrect thots 1992 th last photo uv th human soul 1993; recordings: awake in th red desert northern birds in color sonic horses 1 & 11 & luddites– ;cassett– ;nu music– ;vocals with– ; gerry collins– ; peter denny– ; n murray favro– ;1989 book– ; <u>what we have</u> & LUDDITES 1p– ;& shining spirit– ; tape (with chris meloche)– ;canada council grants 67 69 70 75 79 writer in residens western universities 85–86 sound poetree festivals london england st john's nufoundland paris france glasgow scotland nu york publishr blewointmentpress 63–83 recent wun prson art shows embassy cultural hous 86 pizzariccos 86 neoartism galleree 86 382A powell st studio 86 othr recent art shows– ;forest city galleree london ontario rezoning group show vancouvr art galleree– ; 89– ; wun prson show van art galleree 84– ; - selby hotel art galleree toronto 89–90 not just deserts– ; vancouvr– ;91– ;latest luddite cassett– ;dreemin uv th nite with gerry collins & murray favro =nu LONDON LIFE cassett with chris meloche– ; c/o talon books 201–1019 east cordova st vancouver bc v6a 1m8.

**BISSON, André,** C.M., B.A., M.B.A., M.Com., d.h.c., F.I.C.B.(hon.); executive; b. Trois-Rivières, P.Q. 7 Oct. 1929; s. Roger and Marcelle (Morin) B.; e. Séminaire de Trois-Rivières, B.A. 1950; Univ. Laval, M.S.C. 1953; Harvard Univ. M.B.A. 1955; m. Reine, d. Helen and Arthur Lévesque, 13 June 1953; children: Hélène; Isabelle; CHAIRMAN OF THE BOARD, BURSON-MARSTELLER QUÉBEC; Chancellor & Chrmn. of Bd., Univ. de Montréal; Chrmn., Bd. of Dirs., Hôpital Notre-Dame; Candn. Found. for Internat. Mgmt.; Société d'investissement jeunesse; Bd. Mem., Acme Canada Inc.; Axa Assurances (Canada) Inc.; Donohue Inc.; European Inst. of Business Admin. (INSEAD, Fontainebleau, France); Pirelli Canada Inc.; Power Financial Corp.; The Council for Canadian Unity; Mem. Bd. of Govs., Conseil du Patronat du Qué.; Mem. Adv. Bd., SpencerStuart Canada; Hon. Chrmn., Czech and Slovak Business Counc. of Qué.; formerly: Pres., Macmillan Investments Canada Inc.; OAG Canada; SRDS Canada; Maxwell Communications Canada; Logistec Corp.; Sr. Vice Pres. & Gen. Mgr., Qué., Bank of Nova Scotia; Dir., Inst. Candn. Bankers; Chrmn., Dept. Bus. Admin., Chrmn., Div. of Rsch., Assoc. Prof. of Bus. Admin., Fac. of Admin. Sciences, Laval Univ.; distinctions: Member of the Order of Canada 1982; Man of the Month, Revue Commerce 1979; Médaille 'Gloire de l'Escolle,' Laval Univ. Alumni Assn. 1982; Hon. Doctorate, Univ. du Québec 1985; Hon. Fellow, Inst. of Candn. Bankers 1988; recipient, Hermès Trophy, Laval Univ. 1988; Ordre des francophones d'Amérique 1992; Commemorative Medal for 125th Anniversary of Candn. Confederation 1992; R. Catholic; Clubs: Forest & Stream; Mount-Royal; St. Denis; Saint James's; Terminal City; Toronto; Winchester; recreation: swimming, photography; Home: 2 Poplar Place, Baie d'Urfé, Qué. H9X 3H5; Office: 1155 René Lévesque Blvd. W., Montréal, Qué. H3B 3T6.

**BISSON, Hon. Claude,** B.A., LL.L.; juge; né Trois-Rivières, Qué. 9 mai 1931; f. Roger Bisson, C.R., et Marcelle (Morin) B.; é. Univ. Laval, Québec, B.A., 1950; Univ. Laval, LL.L., 1953; ép. Louisette, f. Gaston Lanneville, 12 Oct. 1957; enfants: Alain, Marie, Louis; JUGE EN CHEF DU QUÉBEC depuis le 24 mai 1988; JUGE DELA COUR D'APPEL DU QUEBEC depuis 1980; Juge Puine de la Cour Superieure du District de Montreal, du 27 fév. 1969 au 1 Mai 1980; admis au Barreau du Québec, 1954; Catholique; Bureau: Palais de Justice, Montreal, Qué. H2Y 1B6.

**BISSON, Frank Joseph,** B.Comm., F.C.A.; construction executive; b. Woodslee, Ont. 31 March 1939; s. Earl Benedict and Caroline Serene (Voakes) B.; e. Univ. of Windsor, B.Comm. 1961; Inst. of C.A.'s of Ont. C.A. 1965, Fellow 1988; m. Sandra d. Harry and Virginia Sheardown 20 May 1961; children: Lori-Anne, Brad; PRES. & DIR., SANFRANBISCO HOLDINGS LIMITED 1992– ; articled with Price Waterhouse & Co. 1961–65; Controller, Eastern Constr. Co. Ltd. 1965–81; Extve. Vice-Pres. & Dir., Vanbots Const. Corp./Treas. & Dir., Venture Metalcrafts Limited/Controller & Dir., Lenworth Metal Products Limited; Treas. & Dir., Buttcon Limited/Partner, Carrier Dr. Joint Venture 1981–86; Sr. Vice-Pres., Chief Fin. Offr. & Sec., Eastern Construction Company Limited 1986–92; Pres., Construction Industry Advisory Council of Ont. 1989– ; Chrmn., Economic Development and Taxation Ctte. for the Council of Ontario Construction Assns.; Extve. Mem., Building Indus. Strategy Bd. 1986–88 (Chrmn., Constr. Productivity Improvement Ctte.); Mem., Building Project Adv. Ctte., Inst. of C.A.'s of Ont. 1987– ; Mem., Premises Ctte., Candn. Inst. of C.A.'s and numerous past extve. positions for various assns.; recipient, 'Construction Man of the Year' Award, Toronto Construction Assoc. 1988; 'Construction Man of the Year' Award, Gen. Contractors Section, Toronto Construction Assoc. 1991; recreations: basketball, squash, running, golf; clubs: Blue Springs Golf; Burlington Racquet; Home: 1 MacArthur Dr., R.R. 2, Campbellville, Ont. L0P 1B0.

**BISSOONDATH, Neil,** B.A.; writer; b. Trinidad, W.I. 19 Apl. 1955; s. Crisen S. and Sati G. (Naipaul) B.; e. St. Mary's Coll. Trinidad G.C.E. 'A' Level 1973; York Univ. B.A. 1977; Instr. in French and Eng. Inlingua Sch. of Lang. 1977–80, The Lang. Workshop 1980–85; author 'Digging Up The Mountains' short story coll. 1985 (short listed City of Toronto Book Awards 1986); short story 'Dancing' awarded McClelland & Stewart Award for Fiction (Gold), Nat. Mag. Awards 1986; author 'A Casual Brutality' novel 1988 (shortlisted Trillium Award, and W.H. Smith/Books in Canada First Novel Award); 'On the Eve of Uncertain Tomorrows' short story coll. 1990; 'The Innocence of Age' novel 1992; awarded Candn. Authors Assn. Fiction Award 1993; recipient Banff Sch. Fine Arts writing scholarship 1984; Address: c/o The Lucinda Vardey Agency, 297 Seaton St., Toronto, Ont. M5A 2T6.

**BISWAS, Asit Kumar,** Ph.D.; scientist; b. Balasore, India 25 Feb. 1939; s. Anil Kumar and Asha Rani B.; e. Indian Inst. of Technol., Kharagpur, B.Tech. (Hons, Civil Eng.) 1960, M. Tech.(Water Resources Eng.) 1961; Univ. of Strathclyde, Glasgow, Ph.D.(Water Mgmt.) 1967; Dr. Tech. (Honoris Causa), Univ. of Lund, Sweden, 1984; m. Margaret Rose, d. Edward and Susannah Peitsch, 24 June 1971; DIR., BISWAS AND ASSOCIATES, (International consultants on resources and environment) 1976– ; senior policy and scientific advisor to four heads of U.N. Agencies, N.A.T.O., O.E.C.D., Asian Inst. of Tech., Asian Develop. Bank, World Bank, and Govts. of Bhutan, Cameroun, Canada, China, Egypt, Greece, India, Japan, Jordan, Mexico, Nepal, Pakistan, Qatar, Sudan, Sri Lanka, Thailand, Turkey, Venezuela; Rsch. Fellow, Loughborough Univ. of Technol., U.K. 1962–63; Assoc. and Asst. Prof., Univ. of Strathclyde, Glasgow, 1963–67; Visiting Prof., Queen's Univ., Kingston 1967–68; Visiting Prof., Univ. of Ottawa 1968–70; Chief, Resources Mgmt. Div., Dept. of Environ., Ottawa 1968–72; Dir., Environmental Systems Br., Dept. of Environ., Ottawa 1972–76; Sr. Fellow, Internat. Inst. for Applied Systems Analysis, Laxenburg, Austria 1978–79; teaching appts. at Univ. of Lund, Sweden 1982 to present and Univ. of Tech., Twente, Netherlands 1985 to present; rsch. appt., Queen Elizabeth House, Univ. of Oxford, Engl. 1988– ; Chrmn., Ctte. on Water Resources Systems, Int'l. Assn. for Hydraulic Rsch. 1969–72; Chrmn., Ctte. on New Developments, Int'l. Comn. on Irrigation and Drainage 1974–78; Pres., Int'l. Soc. for Ecological Modelling 1976– ; Vice-Pres., Internat. Assoc. for Clean Tech. 1987– ; Pres. 1988–91, Vice-Pres. 1980–82 and Chrmn., Ctte. on Internat. Waters 1991– , Internat. Water Resources Assn.; Walter Huber Award for outstanding rsch., American Soc. of Civil Engs. 1974; First Rockefeller Foundation Fellow in Int'l. Relations 1974–75; Hon. Life Mem., Indian Water Resources Soc. 1982; Hon. Mem., Egyptian Engr. Acad. 1989; Chrmn., U.N. Task Force on Long-Distance Water Transfer 1983–85; Mem., WHO/FAO/UNEP Internat. Panel of Experts on Environmental Mgmt. 1989– ; Special Adv., Internat. Lake Environment Ctte. Found., Japan 1989– ; Mem., Water Adv. Group, U.N. Environment Programme 1981–93 (Chrmn. 1988–90); Vice-Chrmn. and Secy., Internat. Panel of Eminent Persons on Economic Policies for Sustainable Development of Asian Development Bank 1990–91; Mem., Scientific Cttee., Stockholm Water Symposium 1991– ; Mem. Bds. of Govs., Hydrocontrol Inst., Cagliari, Italy 1990– ;and Globetree Foundation, Stockholm, Sweden 1991– ; Chrmn., Middle East Water Commission 1993–95; Doctor of Technology (Hon.), Univ. of Lund, Sweden 1984; author of 500 sci. papers and 42 books, incl. 'History of Hydrology' 1970; 'Systems Approach to Water Management' 1976; 'Food, Climate and Man' 1979; 'Models for Water Quality Management' 1981; 'Renewable Sources of Energy and the Environment' 1981; 'Climate and Development' 1984; 'Integrated Rural Energy Planning' 1985; 'Environmental Impact Assessment' 1987; 'Hazardous Wastes Management' 1988; 'Modelling of Environmental Systems' 1990; 'Earth and Us' 1991; 'Climatic Fluctuations and Water Management' 1992; Ed. of Internat. Jour. of Ecol. Modelling, Internat. Jour. of Water Resources Devel.; former Ed., Mazingira; mem. Ed. Bds., 16 internat. scientific and technical jours.; works transl. into 13 languages; recreations: classical music, painting; Club: United Kenya; Office: #87 - 3691 Albion Rd. S., Gloucester, Ont. K1T 1P2.

**BITOVE, John Louis Nicholas;** corporate executive; b. Toronto, Ont. 19 Mar. 1928; s. Nicholas Louis and Vana (Anastasov) B.; e. Danforth Tech. Sch.; m. Dotsa d. Thomas and Elena Lazoff 30 Oct. 1949; children: Vonna, Nicholas Louis, Thomas John, John Ivan, Jordan Lazo; CHRMN. & C.E.O., THE BITOVE CORP. 1987– ; Bd. Mem., Fahnestock Viner Holdings Inc.; Java Shoppe Restaurants 1949–59; Quality Craft Interiors 1960–69; Big Boy Family Restaurants of Can. 1969–79; Petro Inc. Resources Ltd. 1980–83; Pres. & Chrmn., York County Quality Foods Ltd. 1983–87; Bd. mem., Dome Consortium Investments Inc. 1986– ; Bd. mem., Toronto Chapter, Candn. Soc. for the Weizmann Inst. of Sci.; Hon. Citizen, Metro Toronto 1979; Member, Order of Canada 1989; Commemorative Medal, 125th Anniversary of Candn. Confedn. 1992; Founder & Chrmn., Candn. Macedonian Place (Sr. Citizen Housing Project); Bd. Chrmn., Candn. Macedonian Fedn. 1990; Bd. Chrmn., PROACTION 1990; Chrmn., Macedonian World Congress 1992 and 1993; Former Dir., Royal Ont. Mus.; Mem., St. George's East. Orthodox Ch.; King Solomon's Lodge; Toronto Gen. Hosp.; Candn. Cystic Fibrosis; Univ. of Western Ont.; Club: Boca Raton Golf & Country; Home: 61 St. Clair Ave. W., Toronto, Ont. M4V 2Y8; Office: 41 Peter St., 3rd Floor, Toronto, Ont. M5V 2G5.

**BITTORF, Donald George,** M.Arch., R.C.A., F.R.A.I.C.; retired architect; b. Edmonton, Alta. 13 Aug. 1926; s. George Nicholas and Edna Elizabeth (Seibel) B.; e. Eastwood High Sch. Edmonton; 1945; Univ. of Wash. B.Arch. 1954; Harvard Univ. Grad. Sch. Design M.Arch. 1955; m. Loa Rae Mackenzie 9 June 1956; children: Donald Blair, Graeme Reed, Elizabeth Ann, Marin Rae; Pres., Bittorf Thorkelsson Architectural Associates Inc. 1989–92, Retired; Assoc. Partner, K.C. Stanley and Co. Edmonton 1956–59; Green Blankstein Russel & Associates Winnipeg 1959–70; Annett and Bittorf Architects Edmonton 1959–64; Bittorf Wensley Architects Edmonton; D.G. Bittorf Architect Ltd. 1970– ; Bittorf Holland and Company Architects Ltd. 1976–82; exhns. incl. Nickle Gallery Calgary 1980; City of Edmonton Design Awards, 1979, 1980, 1981; rec'd Am. Inst. Archs. Scholarship 1951; Grad. Award 1954; Univ. of Wash. Arch. Alumni Travel Scholarship 1953; Structural Clay Products Inst. Award 1954; Winnipeg City Hall Competition co-recipient 1st Prize 1960; Alta. Assn. Archs. Design Award 1965 (Edmonton Art Gallery); Dir., Fort Edmonton Hist. Foundation; Northern Lights Theatre; Devonian Gardens 1988– ; Trustee, Govt. House Foundation 1982–84, Chrmn. 1984–91; mem. Alta. Assn. Archs. (Council 1963–65, Bd. Examiners 1971–75, 1979); Bd. mem. Edmonton Art Gallery 1960–72; Phi Beta Kappa; Tau Sigma Delta; P. Conservative; Unitarian; recreations: skiing, wilderness hiking, canoeing; Clubs: Faculty; Calgary Professional; Harvard Club of Edmonton; Home: (P.O. Box 14.3) R.R. #5, Edmonton, Alta T5P 4B7.

**BJARNASON, Harold Frederick,** B.A., M.Sc., M.A., Ph.D.; federal civil servant; b. Gimli, Man. 13 Aug. 1938; s. Harold T. and Agustina H. (Finnson) B.; e. Gimli Coll. Inst. 1957; Univ. of Man., B.A. 1960; Univ. of Iceland 1961–62; S. Dakota State Univ., M.Sc. 1964; Univ. of Wis., M.A. 1966, Ph.D. 1967; m. Brenda d. Edmund and Jessie Matthes 21 May 1971; children: Lee Anne, Benjamin John; ASSOC. DEP. MIN. AGRICULTURE AND AGRI-FOOD CANADA 1987– ; Adjunct Prof. of Agric. Econ. Univ. of Man.; Board Econ. Candn. Wheat Board 1967, Gen. Dir. Mkt. Analysis & Devel. Dept. 1970, Mgr. Brussels Office 1972, Sr. Econ. 1976, Exec. Dir. 1980–85; Asst. Dep. Min. Agric. Can. 1985–87; Lutheran; Home: 1599 Featherston Dr., Ottawa, Ont. K1H 6N9; Office: 930 Carling Ave., Ottawa, Ont. K1A 0C5.

**BJERKELUND, Toralf (Ted),** B.Sc., P.Eng.; association executive; b. Three Rivers, Qué. 7 Apr. 1927; s. Carl and Gudrun (Johansen) B.; e. Queen's Univ. B.Sc. 1949; m. Manuella d. Franciszek and Klementyna Wolny 9 Oct. 1954; children: Ingrid, Cathryn, Erik, Lissa; EXEC. DIR. INDUSTRIAL GAS USERS ASSN. 1982– ; held various tech., prodn. & mgmt. positions chem ind. 1949–82; Past Pres., Bd. Dirs., Queen's Univ. Alumni Assn.; mem. Assn. Prof. Engs. Prov. Ont.; Candn. Soc. Assn. Execs.; Internat. Assoc. for Energy Economics; Club: Rideau; Home: 63 Ashburn Dr., Nepean, Ont. K2E 6N4; Office: 900, 170 Laurier Ave. W., Ottawa, Ont. K1P 5V5.

**BLACHFORD, C.W.,** B.E., M.S., Ph.D., F.E.I.C.; educator; e. Univ. of Sask. B.E. 1953; Univ. of Ill. M.S. 1959, Ph.D. 1963; PROFESSOR OF ENGINEERING, UNIV. OF REGINA 1967– ; Athlone Fellow UK 1953–55; joined English Electric Co. St. Catharines and Toronto 1956–58; Assoc. Prof. Queen's Univ. 1963–67; Assoc. Vice Pres. and Dean, Graduate Studies and Research, Univ. of Regina 1967–92; Past Pres., Candn. Assn. Grad. Schs.; Past Pres., Candn. Assoc. Univ. Research Administrators; Past Pres., Candn. Soc. for Elect. & Computer Engrg.; Assn. Prof. Engrs. Sask.; recreations: reading, curling, skiing; Club: Rotary; YMCA; Office: Regina, Sask. S4S 0A2.

**BLACHFORD, Peter Carl Howard,** B.B.A., M.B.A., CHE; medical executive/management consultant; b. North Bay, Ont. 28 Apr. 1949; s. Howard Arnold and Mary Greenlees (Rous) B.; e. Ridley Coll.; Oakville Trafalgar H.S.; York Univ., B.B.A. 1972, M.B.A. 1973; m. secondly, Heather Elizabeth Rae; children: Courtney Patricia, Lauren Alexandra, Matthew Adam, Derek Alexander, Alysia Rae; PRESIDENT, PCHB 86 MGMT. CONSULTANTS; Owner, B. & C. Landscape Co. & Mgmt. Cons. 1968–73; Sr. Corp. Planner, Imperial Oil Ltd. 1973–75; Sr. Mngt. Cons., Toronto Gen. Hosp. 1975–76; Asst. Admin., Oaklands Rgn. Ctr. for the Developmentally Handicapped 1976–78; Sr. Cons., Woods Gordon Mngt. Cons. 1978–80; Pres. & C.E.O., Queensway Gen. Hosp. 1980–86; Preceptor & Lectr., Faculty of Medicine, Univ. of Toronto 1981–92; Sec., Bd. of Govs., Toronto E. Gen. & Orthop. Hosp. Inc. 1986–91; Pres. & Chief Extve. Offr., Toronto East Gen. & Orthopaedic Hosp. 1986–91; Dir., Centennial Hosp. Linen Serv. 1981–86; Bd. Mem., Hosp. Counc. of Metro. Toronto; Dir., Toronto E. Gen. Hosp. Found.; Toronto E. Gen. Hosp. Rsch. Found.; CHE Designation 1984; Candn. Coll. of Health Serv. Extves. 1976– ; Rotary Club of Etobicoke 1983–86; Muskoka Lakes Assn. 1967– ; contbr. medical and health care mags.; recreations: tennis, skiing, golf, boating, reading, cycling, music; Clubs: Port Credit Yacht; Address: 2373 Conquest Dr., Mississauga, Ont. L5C 2Z1.

**BLACHUT, Teodor Josef,** M.Sc., Dr.Sc.Techn., F.R.S.C., F.PAN.; scientist; b. Czestochowa, Poland 10 Feb. 1915; s. Aleksander Blachut; e. Tech. Univ. of Lwow, Poland M.Sc. (Geodesy) 1938; Tech. Univ. of Zurich Dr.Sc.Techn. 1971; Tech. Univ. of Mining & Metall. Krakow, Hon. Dr. Degree 1974; m. Schawalder 28 Dec. 1948; children: Jan. Daniel, Piotr; joined Wild Co., Switzerland 1946; came to Can. 1951; Head of Photogrammetry Rsch. Sec., National Rsch. Counc. 1951–80; invented and was responsible for devel. no.

photogrammetric concepts and instruments; holds several patents; his concept of integrated surveying and mapping operations based on cadastre and stereo-orthophoto technique gained international attn. – pilot projects in Colombia (1976) and Peru (1983) and presently under consideration in several African countries and China; Mem. various Candn. and internat. comtes.; invited lectr. various acads. of science, univs. and learned socs. Europe, N. and S. Am., Australia and Asia; Visiting Scient., Univ. of Brasilia 1970; Pres., Comte. on Large Scale and Urban Surveying & Mapping, Pan Am. Inst. Geog. & Hist. 1969–77; initiated and promoted devel. photogrammetric instrument mfg. in Can.; organizer numerous scient. and prof. internat. confs. Can. and abroad; rec'd Hon. Medal Tech. Univ. of Milan 1960; Photogrammetric Award and Luis Struck Award, Am. Soc. Photogrammetry 1973; served with Polish Armed Forces in France during World War II; editor and main author 'Urban Surveying and Mapping' 1979, published in three languages; author over 130 publs. geodetic, photogrammetric and cartographic subjects in Eng., Polish, French, Spanish and German; Editor and co-author of 'History of Photogrammetry' Vol. 1, published in eight languages; Past Ed. 'The Canadian Surveyor'; Mem. Candn. Inst. Surveying (Past Pres.); Am. Soc. Photogrammetry, MOLDS (Dir.); Pan Am. Inst. Geog. & Hist.; Internat. Soc. Photogrammetry; Corr. Mem. Polish Geodetic Soc.; Hon. Mem. Corp. des Arpenteurs-Géomètres Prov. Qué.; Brazilian Cartographic Soc.; Candn. Inst. of Surveying and Mapping 1987; Polish Photographic Soc.; Hon. Mem., Pan Am. Inst. Geography & History 1993; R. Catholic; Home: 61 Rothwell Dr., Ottawa, Ont. K1J 7G7.

**BLACK, The Hon. Conrad M.,** P.C., O.C., B.A., M.A., LL.L., Litt.D., LL.D.; businessman; publisher; b. Montreal, Que. 25 Aug. 1944; s. late George Montegu and late Jean Elizabeth (Riley) B.; e. Carleton Univ. B.A. 1965; Laval Univ. LL.L. 1970; McGill Univ. M.A. 1973; LL.D. (Hon.), St. Francis Xavier Univ. 1979, McMaster Univ. 1979, Carleton Univ. 1989; Litt.D. (Hon.), Univ. of Windsor 1979; m. Barbara Amiel 1992; CHRMN. OF BD., CHRMN. EXEC. COMTE. & C.E.O., HOLLINGER INC.; Chrmn. & C.E.O. Ravelston Corp. Ltd.; Chrmn. & C.E.O., Argus Corp. Ltd.; Chrmn., The Telegraph plc, London, Eng.; Saturday Night Magazine Inc.; Depy. Chrmn., American Publishing Co.; John Fairfax Holdings Limited (Sydney, Australia); Dir., Cdn. Imp. Bank of Comm.; Dir., Brascan Limited; Eaton's of Can. Ltd.; The Financial Post Co. Ltd.; Hees International Bancorp Inc.; Key Publishers Co. Ltd.; Southam Inc.; The Spectator (1828) Ltd.; UniMédia Inc.; Mem. Advisory Bd., The National Interest (Washington, D.C.); Mem.: Chairman's Counc. of the Americas Society; The Trilateral Commission; Internat. Inst. for Strategic Studies; Mem., Adv. Bd., St. Mary's Hosp. West Palm Beach, Fla.; Mem., Steering Ctte. and Adv. Group, Bilderberg Meetings; Patron, The Malcolm Muggeridge Found.; author 'Duplessis' 1977; 'A Life In Progress' 1993; recipient Order of Canada 1990; apptd., Privy Council of Canada 1992; Clubs: Granite; Toronto; York; Toronto Golf; University (Montreal); Mount Royal Club (Montreal); Everglades (Palm Beach); Office: 10 Toronto St., Toronto, Ont. M5C 2B7.

**BLACK, Donald Wayne;** investment executive; b. Regina, Sask. 18 Feb. 1947; s. Douglas James and Edna Lillian (Bickel) B.; e. Martin C.I. 1965; Univ. of Regina; m. Gail Barbara d. Pauline and Robert Hoff 21 June 1980; children: Dustin Scott, Dallas James; PRES., CHIEF EXTVE. OFFR. & DIR., THE INVESTMENT CORPORATION OF SASKATCHEWAN 1992– ; var. posts ending as Pres. & Chief Op. Offr., Houston Willoughby (now RBC Dominion Securities) 16 years; Pres. & Chief Extve. Offr., Sask. Govt. Ins., 2 1/2 years; Pres., C.E.O. & Dir., Pioneer Life Assur. Co. 1985–90; Pres. & Gen. Mgr., Regina Volkswagen (1988) Ltd. 1990–92; Dir., Candn. Scholarship Trust; Regina Health District; Hosp. of Regina Found. Inc.; McDowell Found.; Life Mem., Jaycees Internat. Senate; recreations: trap shooting, downhill skiing, upland game & migratory bird hunting, squash; clubs: Health (YMCA), Wascana Country; Home: 31 Forbes Pl., Regina, Sask. S4S 6P9.

**BLACK, Eldon Pattyson,** B.C.L., diplomat; b. Montreal, Que. 15 Oct. 1925; s. Charles Eldon and Eva (Kingman); e. McGill Univ. B.C.L. 1949; m. Francine Welter, d. late Dr. Georges Welter, 24 Sept. 1949; children: Catherine Anne, Kristina, Claudia, Charles Eldon; R.C.N.V.R. 1943–45; called to Que. Bar 1949; joined Dept. of External Affairs 1949; served abroad in Moscow, Stockholm, London, Brussels and Paris; various positions in Ottawa incl. Dir. Gen. Bureau of European Affairs; Asst. Depy. Min. (Policy, Dept. Nat. Defence); Asst. Depy. Min. (Security and Intelligence), Dept. of External Affairs; Ambassador to the Holy See, June 1985 – May 1989; Chrmn., Candn. Counc. for European Affairs 1990; Address: 12 – 140 Rideau Terrace, Ottawa, Ont. K1M 0Z2.

**BLACK, Harry Samuel,** B.A., B.Tech; b. Toronto, Ont. 30 July 1934; s. Edward Colman and Elizabeth Regina (Milligan) B.; e. Ryerson Polytechnical Inst. grad. Archt. 1957; McMaster Univ. grad. Hist. 1966; York Univ. postgrad. Hist. 1970; m. Susanne d. Charles and Olive Anderson Oct. 1960; children: Annelise; NAT. EXEC. DIR. UNICEF CANADA/THE UNITED NATIONS CHILDREN'S FUND 1973– ; Supr. Candn. Red Cross Soc. Blood Donor Service 1958–60; Dir. Toronto Blood Depot 1960–63; Fund Raising Dir. Candn. Red Cross Soc. 1963–73; served with Red Cross in Lebanon and Jordan following 1967 Arab-Israeli War; disaster relief worker on Internat. Staff; author and Ed. UNICEF 'Communique' 1979–83; author and Ed. Fund Raising Manual Candn. Red. Cross Soc. 1967; rep. Canada at many internat. UNICEF meetings; Dir. Internat. Devel. Exec. Assn.; South Asia Partnership (Can.); Mem. Assn. of UNICEF Nat. Dirs. (Geneva); former Dir. Un. Nations Asssn. of Can.; recreations: tennis, squash, canoeing; Club: Mayfair; Home: R.R. #1, Gormley, Ont. L0H 1G0; Office: 443 Mount Pleasant Rd., Toronto, Ont. M4S 2L8.

**BLACK, Rev. J. Bernard,** B.A., M.L.S., S.T.B.; librarian; b. Toronto, Ont., 31 May 1926; s. Frederick Gerald and Alma Helen (Sampson) B., e. St. Michael's Coll. Sch. (1939–44); St. Michael's Coll. Univ. of Toronto, B.A. 1949, B.L.S. 1952, M.L.S. 1956, S.T.B. 1955; Univ. of Mich. 1959–61; Counsellor, Emmanuel Convalescent Centre 1983–87; Librarian, St. Michael's Coll., Univ. of Toronto 1961–85; Mem., Tor. Public Library Board 1979–84, Chrmn. 1981, 1982; Instr., Univ. of Toronto Lib. Sch. 1963–65; Univ. of Western Ont. Sch. Lib. and Info. Science 1971; Asst. Lib., St. Basil's Semy., 1953–56; Lib. and Asst. Prof of Eng., St. Thomas More Coll. in Univ. of Sask. 1956–59; Mem. of Adv. Council. Sask. Lib. Assn., 1958–59; served in Royal Candn. Inf., 1944–45; Mem., Candn. Coll. of Teachers; Roman Catholic; joined Basilian Fathers, 1946; Address: 95 St. Joseph St., Toronto, Ont. M5S 2R9.

**BLACK, James Thompson,** F.C.A.; b. Montreal, P.Q. 16 July 1925; s. James and Agnes Lang (McCartney) B.; e. High Sch. of Montreal (Matric. 1941); C.A. 1949; HON. CHRMN., THE MOLSON COMPANIES LTD. 1988– ; Dir., Ivaco Inc.; The Molson Companies Limited; Monac Internat. Corp.; Mutual Trust Co.; Mutual Life Assurance Co. of Canada; Rio Algom Ltd.; with McDonald Currie & Co., Chart. Accts., Montreal, P.Q., 1941–49 (except war service); joined Molsons Brewery Ltd. 1949; served in 2nd World War with RCAF; Flying Offr.-Navigator, 1943–45; Gov., Adv. Ctte., Niagara Inst.; Gov., Candn. Centre for Management Development; LL.D. (hon. causa) Wilfrid Laurier Univ. 1982; LL.D. (hon. causa) Univ. of New Brunswick 1986; Member of the Order of Canada 1989; Club: The Toronto; Address: P.O. Box 931, Niagara-on-the-Lake, Ont. L0S 1J0.

**BLACK, John Buchanan,** M.A., Ph.D.; library administrator; educator; b. Guelph, Ont. 5 Aug. 1940; s. William Henry and Mary Adelaide (Buchanan) B.; e. Milton (Ont.) High Sch. 1958; Univ. of W. Ont. B.A. 1962, M.A. 1964; Univ. of London (London Sch. of Econ.) Ph.D. 1969; m. Elizabeth d. Robert and Margaret McNaught 20 July 1966; children: Christopher, Alice; CHIEF LIBRARIAN, UNIV. OF GUELPH 1984– , Prof. of Political Studies 1994– ; Lectr. in Pol. Studies present Univ. 1966, Asst. Prof. 1969, Assoc. Prof. 1972, Asst. Lib. Service 1972, Assoc. Lib. 1974–84; Fellow, World Acad. Art & Sci.; Trustee, Pub. Affairs Info. Service New York; Hon. Chief Librarian, Beijing Agricultural Univ.; Pres., Assn. of Rsch. Libraries 1993–94; author: 'Organising the Propaganda Instrument: The British Experience' 1975; co-author: 'Conflict Over Communications Policy: A Study of Federal-Provincial Relations and Public Policy' 1980; 'The Best Gift: A Record of the Carnegie Libraries in Ontario' 1984; recreations: photography, communications technology, microcomputers; Home: 7 Maplewood Dr., Guelph, Ont. N1G 1L9; Office: Guelph, Ont. N1G 2W1.

**BLACK, Joseph Laurence,** E.D., LL.D.; company president; b. Middle Sackville, N.B. 28 May 1900; s. Frank B. and Eleanor L. (Wood) B.; e. Sackville, N.B. Public Schs.; Upper Canada Coll., Toronto, Ont. (1917–18); Royal Mil. Coll., Kingston, Ont. (Grad. 1921); m. Gwendolyn, d. Nathaniel McDonald, Thedford, Ont., 1935; children: Joseph Laurence, jr., Janet McDonald, John Donald; PRESIDENT, J.L. BLACK & SONS LTD. (Rentals, Investments, Estbd. 1847); Dir., served in N.P.-A.M., 1921–39; 2nd World War with Candn. Active Army, 1940–45; Conservative; Protestant; recreations: golf, fishing; Clubs: Sackville Country; Aesculapius Fishing; R.M.C. of Canada; Home: Middle Sackville, N.B.; Office: P.O. Box 68, Sackville, N.B. E0A 3C0.

**BLACK, Joseph Laurence, Jr.,** M.A., Ph.D., F.R.S.A.; university professor; b. Middle Sackville, N.B. 16 Jan. 1937; s. Joseph Laurence and Gwendolyn (Macdonald) B.; e. Mt. Allison Univ., B.A. 1958; Boston Univ., M.A. 1962; McGill Univ., Ph.D. 1968; m. Janice, d. J.D. and Melba Jernigan, 23 Aug. 1960; children: Joseph; Jennifer; Laura Ruth; DIR., CTR. FOR CANADIAN-SOVIET STUDIES, CARLETON UNIV. 1990– ; Teacher, Ashbury Coll. (Ottawa) 1961; Assoc. Prof., St. Joseph Teachers Coll. (Montreal) 1964; Prof., Laurentian Univ. 1968; joined present univ. as Prof. 1976; Dir., Inst. Soviet & East European Studies, Carleton Univ. 1982–90; author 'Origins of the Cold War: A Handbook' 1972; 'Essays on Karamzin' 1975; 'Nicholas Karamzin and Russian Society in 19th Century' 1975; 'Citizens for the Fatherland: Russian Education in 18th Century' 1979; 'G.-F. Müller and the Imperial Russan Academy of Sciences, 1725–1783' 1986; 'Origins of the Cold War: Critically Annotated Bibliography' 1986; 'Sisyphus and Poland: Observations on Martial Law' 1986; 'USSR Documents Annual' 1987, 1988, 1989, 1990 (2 vols.), 1991 (2 vols.), 1992 (2 vols.); 'Nearly Neighbours: Canada and the Soviet Union' 1989; 'G.-F. Müller and Siberia' 1989; 'Into the Dustbin of History. The USSR from Coup to Commonwealth, 1991' 1993; Vice-Pres., Cdn. Assn. Slavists 1984–86; Club: Rideau Tennis; Aesculapius Fishing; recreations: fishing; tennis; Home: 2651 Ulster Cres., Ottawa, Ont. K1V 8J5; Office: History Dept., Carleton Univ., Ottawa, Ont. K1S 5B6.

**BLACK, Linda Hunt,** LL.M.; public servant; b. St. John's, Nfld.; d. Douglas and D. Elizabeth (Pearce) Hunt; e. Candn. Jr. Coll., Lausanne, Switz.; Meml. Univ. of Nfld.; Dalhousie Univ., LL.B. 1975; Univ. of Ottawa, LL.M. 1982; m. Douglas Black 1977; children: Sarah, Ian; ASST. DEP. MIN., LABOUR, DEPT. OF EMPLOYMENT & LABOUR RELNS., GOVT. OF NFLD. & LABRADOR 1988– ; Legislative Couns. 1976–86; Solicitor 1986–88; Mem., Nfld. Law Reform Comn. 1982–90; Office: P.O. Box 8700, St. John's, Nfld. A1B 4J6.

**BLACK, Malcolm Charles Lamont;** stage director; producer; writer; teacher; actor; b. Liverpool, England 13 May 1928; s. Kenneth Lamont and Althea Joan (Childs) B.; e. Bryanston Sch. 1946; Old Vic Theatre Sch. 1950; m. 1stly Diane Forhan 1955 and 2ndly the late Charla Doherty 1967; children: Duncan Lamont, Trevor; Artistic Dir., Theatre Plus 1985–89; Production Staff BBC 1952–56; Res. Dir. & Mgr., Crest Theatre 1957–59; Admin., Am. Shakespeare Fest. Acad. 1959–61; Art. Dir., Vancouver Playhouse 1964–67; Drama Prof., Univ. of Washington 1968–70; City Univ. of N.Y. 1970–74; Theatre Prof., York Univ. 1974–78; Art Dir., Theatre N.B. 1978–84; Stage Dir., Plays, Musicals & Operas, var. other theatres in Can. & U.S.; T.V. Dir. for 20th Century Fox; Guest Dir., Juilliard Sch.; Yale Shakespeare Inst.; Nat. Theatre Sch. of Can., etc.; dir. of some 200 prodns.; Candn. Drama Award 1967; Silver Jubilee Medal 1978; Can. Counc. Sr. Arts Award 1978; Chrmn., Theatre Training in Canada Ctte., Can. Counc. & author of anglophone sect. of Report 1977; Mem., Arts Adv. Panel, Theatre Sect., Can. Counc. 1978; Candn. Actors' Equity Assn; ACTRA; Soc. of Stage Dir. & Choreographers; author: 'From First Reading to First Night' 1976 and num. articles & original material and adaptations for T.V.; caricatures; recreations: ornithology, dog racing, drawing; Home: 251 Boston Ave., Toronto, Ont. M4M 2V1.

**BLACK, Murray B.;** real estate executive; b. Montreal, Que. 5 Nov. 1935; s. Jack and Ethel Beatrice (Fitleberg) B.; e. Baron Byng High Sch. Montreal; m. Lila d. Joseph Hersh and Minnie Buium 3 June 1956; children: Cynthia, Shari, Peter; DIR. & OFFICER, PLACE BONAVENTURE INC.; Owner and Dir., Century Investments; Pres. & Dir.: Murray Black Convention Entertainment Inc.; Mister Mini Post Inc.; Home: 1417 Elizabeth Blvd., Chomedey, Laval, Que. H7W 3K1; Office: P.O. Box 1000, Place Bonaventure, Montreal, Que. H5A 1G1.

**BLACK, Naomi,** A.B., M.A., Ph.D.; professor of political science; b. Newcastle-upon-Tyne, England 13 Feb. 1935; d. Max and Michal (Landsberg) B.; e. Cornell Univ. A.B. (with distinction & High Hon. in Govt.) 1955; Yale Univ. M.A. 1957, Ph.D. 1964; m. S.P. s. Dorothy and Harry Rosenbaum 23 May 1958; children: Samuel Leonard, Susanna Eve; PROF., DEPT. OF POLITICAL SCIENCE, YORK UNIV. 1985– ; Instr. in

Pol. Sci., Brown Univ. (Providence R.I.) 1963–64; Instr. in Govt., Indiana Univ. 1964–65; Asst. Prof., present univ. 1965–71; Assoc. Prof. 1971–84; author: 'Social Feminism' 1989; co-author: 'Canadian Women: A History' 1988; editor: 'Readings on the International Political System' 1970, 'My Mother the Judge' 1981, 'Women and World Change: Equity Issues in Development' 1981; Office: 4700 Keele St., North York, Ont. M3J 1P3.

**BLACK, Sam,** D.Litt., R.C.A., R.S.W.; artist; educator; b. Ardrossan, Scot. 5 June 1913; e. Ardrossan Acad.; Glasgow Sch. of Art; Jordanhill Coll. of Educ. Glasgow grad. D.A. (Glas), A.T.D. (Lon) 1936; m. Elizabeth Morton Howie May 1941; four d.; PROF. EMERITUS EDUC., UNIV. OF B.C. 1978– ; teacher elem. and secondary sch. Scot.; after war service His Majesty's Inspr. of Schs. Eng.; Prince. Lectr. in Art, Jordanhill Training Coll. Glasgow 1949–58; Prof. of Fine Arts and Art Educ. Univ. of B.C. 1958–78; Commonwealth Visiting Fellow to Australia 1963; has held many solo exhns.; rep. in various pub., corporate and private colls. incl. Imp. War Museum (London), Can. Council Art Bank, Nat. Gallery Can., B.C. Collection, Royal Library Collection, Windsor Castle and other colls. Can., Europe, Australia, Japan, Brazil; work selected for Permanent Coll., Urawa Woodcut Prints Assn., Japan 1989; author and illustrator 'China Sketchbook' 1976; several illustrated travel articles and numerous articles in prof. journs.; contrib. to various publs. incl. UNESCO's 'Art and Education'; 'Thought' 1961; served with Royal Scots Fusiliers 1939–45, Camouflage Offr. 1st Brit. Corps Normandy, rank Maj.; Mentioned-in-Despatches, Oak Leaf; rec'd Belgian Medal Civile 2 Class for bravery; recipient Candn. Centennial Medal 1967; Univ. of B.C. Master Teacher Award 1970; Hon. Life mem. Univ. of B.C. Alumni 1980; Members' Honour Award (for painting 'Me and My Spanish Straw Hat') 57th Annual exhbn. Candn. Soc. of Painters in Watercolour (CSPW) 1983; Honour Award (for painting 'Church at Castro Marin') 60th Annual open exhbn. CSPW 1985; Honour Award and the A.J. Casson Medal (for the painting 'Encroaching Flowers') 67th Annual open juried exhbn. CSPW 1992; prints and paintings inspired music entitled 'Sam Black sketches' composed and conducted by Stewart Grant, Lethbridge Symphony Orch. 1989; invited to design the Vancouver City Street Banners for summer 1990; Painting 'Old Pals' selected for the C.S.P. W/C Diamond Jubilee Collection presented to Her Majesty Queen Elizabeth II for the Royal Collection of Drawings & Watercolours at Windsor Castle; Award of Merit (for video film 'Sam Black Surface Flow,' produced by Bernie Motut) AMTEC Awards 1984; D.Litt. (hon. causa), Univ. of B.C. 1990; Hon. mem., Candn. Soc. for Educ. Art (Past Pres.); Founding mem. Internat. Soc. for Educ. Art (Past Vice Pres.); mem. Roy. Can. Acad. Arts.; Royal Scot Soc. Painters in Watercolour; Candn. Soc. Painters in Watercolour; Print & Drawing Council Can.; Address: The Shieling, Cardena Rd., Bowen Island, B.C. V0N 1G0.

**BLACK, Stan A.;** transportation executive; b. Ottawa, Ont. 27 Aug. 1937; e. Toronto, Ont. Sr. Matric. 1955; Univ. of Toronto, McMaster Univ. and Laurentian Univ. R.I.A. 1960; Bishop's Univ. CN Staff Training Coll. 1971; Univ. of Alta. Principles of Econ. 1974–75; m. Grace E. 31 May 1958; 2 children; PRES., ALGOMA CENTRAL RAILWAY 1990– ; Gen. Mgr. Rail Div. 1976–78; Vice Pres. Rail 1978–90; joined Canadian National Railways 1956–76 serving in Gen. Mgmt., Transport., Railway Planning, Data Systems and Railway Acctg. (Alta., Man., Que. and Ont.); Mem., Operating Comte., Railway Assn. Can.; Dir., Algoma Central Corp.; Mem., Sault Ste. Marie and District Chamber Comm. (Past Pres.); Sault Ste. Marie & 49th Field Regiment Historical Soc.; Senator, 49th Field Regiment, RCA; Clubs: Candn. Railway; Toronto Railway; Home: 25 Varsity Ave., Sault Ste. Marie, Ont. P6A 5T9; Office: P.O. Box 7000, 289 Bay St., Sault Ste. Marie, Ont. P6A 5P6.

**BLACK, W. David,** B.A., LL.B.; lawyer; b. Prince George, B.C. 1 July 1941; s. Wesley Drewett and Helen McKay (Loutit) B.; e. Victoria High 1959; Univ. of B.C., B.A. 1963, LL.B. 1966; m. Georgia L. d. Ormond and Gene Harris 12 June 1964; children: Katherine, Alison; PARTNER, DUMOULIN BLACK 1968– ; Dir., Viceroy Resource Corp.; Dir., B.C. Cancer Found.; Past Chrmn., York House Sch., Vancouver; recreations: skiing, golf, tennis, fishing; clubs: Vancouver, Shaughnessy Golf & Country, Vancouver Lawn Tennis & Badminton, Pennask Lake Fishing & Game; Home: 1509 Dunbar St., Vancouver, B.C. V6R 3L6; Office: 10th floor, 595 Howe St., Vancouver, B.C. V6C 2T5.

**BLACK, W. Gordon,** C.A.; business executive; b. Winnipeg, Man. 9 Aug. 1927; s. William Fotheringham and Mary Teresa (Douglas) B.; e. Univ. of Manitoba, C.A. 1949; children: Sandra, Perelandra, Andra-Lee, Gordon; DIR., THE CSL GROUP INC. 1988– ; Sr. Accountant, William Gray & Co. Winnipeg 1944–50; Peat, Marwick, Mitchell, Winnipeg-Montreal 1951–54; Treas., Kingsway Transports Montreal 1955–60; Sec.-Treas., Comptrollr, Vice-Pres., Finan., Sr. Vice-Pres., Canada Steamship Lines Montreal 1961–81; Sr. Vice-Pres. & Dir., present firm 1981–88; Deputy Chrmn. 1988–92; Chrmn. & Dir., Candn. Shipowners Mutual Assn.; Standard Compensation Act Liability Assn.; Dir., Canada Steamship Lines Inc.; Standard Protective & Indemnity Assn.; Mem., The Inst. of C.A.s of Manitoba 1949; of Quebec 1964; Financial Extves. Inst. Montreal 1975; Assn. for Candn. Pension Fund Management 1976; Office: 759 Victoria Square, Montreal, Que. H2Y 2K3.

**BLACKBOURN, Anthony,** B.Sc., M.A., Ph.D.; educator; b. London, Eng. 6 June 1938; s. George Henry and Edith Margaret Grace B.; e. London Sch. of Econ. B.Sc. 1959; Univ. of Ga. M.A. 1961; Univ. of Toronto Ph.D. 1968; m. Senta d. Hans and Anna Kreutzinger 8 Apl. 1969; children: Barbara, Veronica, Karen; PROFESSOR, NIPISSING UNIVERSITY 1990– ; Lectr. and Prof. Univ. of Windsor 1963–83; Pres. Nipissing Univ. Coll. 1983–90; Chrmn. Nipissing N. Devel. Council 1988–90, Nipissing E. Community Opportunities 1986–88; co-author 'Industrial Geography of Canada' 1984; Pres. Ont. Div. Candn. Assn. Geogs. 1979–80; recreations: skiing, cycling, windsurfing; Home: 173 Campbell Ave., North Bay, Ont. P1A 1W2.

**BLACKBURN, James Lawrence,** B.S.P., M.S., Pharm.D.; educator; b. Noranda, Que. 2 Feb. 1939; s. Joseph Eric and Hazel Anna B.; e. Univ. of Sask. B.S.P., 1960; Univ. of Iowa M.S. 1965; Univ. of Minn. Pharm.D. 1973; m. Shirley d. Fred and Margaret Bearman 9 Nov. 1963; children: James Ross, Laurie Ann, David Frederick; DEAN OF PHARMACY, UNIV. OF SASK. 1982– , Prof. of Pharm. 1977– ; Pharm. Apprentice Univ. Hosp. Saskatoon 1960–61; Asst. Dir. of Pharm. Regina Grey Nun's Hosp. 1961–63, Dir. 1963–68; Asst. Prof. of Pharm. present Univ. 1968, Assoc. Prof. 1971, Head, Sec. Prof. Practice Coll. of Pharm. 1980–82; Project Dir. Sask. Dial Access Drug Information Service; Chrmn., Comte. on Drug Utilization, Sask. Health 1983–91; Dir. and Vice Chrmn. Sask. Cancer Foundation 1979–89; Chrmn. of the Bd., Oliver Lodge Sr. Citizens Home Saskatoon 1981–87; Pres., Assn. of Deans of Pharmacy of Can. 1984–85; recipient Candn. Soc. Hosp. Pharms. Mead Johnson Award 1973; Coll. of Med. Continuing Educ. Award of Merit 1981; Candn. Soc. Hosp. Pharm. J.L. Summers Achievement Award 1989; Mem. Candn. Soc. Hosp. Pharms. (Pres. 1971–72); Candn. Pharm. Assn. (Bd. Mem. 1978–80); Sask. Pharm. Assn. (Council Mem. 1982– ;); Club: Saskatoon Nutana Rotary (Bd. Mem. 1982–84); Home: 2609 Eastview, Saskatoon, Sask. S7J 3G7; Office: Saskatoon, Sask. S7N 0W0.

**BLACKBURN, James Robert,** B.Sc., M.A., Ph.D.; university professor; b. Toronto, Ont. 4 March 1958; s. Walter William and Grete (Torsting) B.; e. McGill Univ. B.Sc. 1983; Univ. of B.C. M.A. 1985, Ph.D. 1989; m. Linda d. Melvin and Ursula Burrill 23 Dec. 1989; ASSISTANT PROFESSOR OF PSYCHOLOGY, MCMASTER UNIV. 1990– ; postdoctoral research fellow, Nat. Inst. of Mental Health, Lab. of Neuropsychology 1989–90; Mem., Soc. for Neuroscience; Soc. for the Study of Ingestive Behaviour; recreations: dance, literature; Home: 83 Arnold Ave., Hamilton, Ont.; Office: Hamilton, Ont. L8S 4L8.

**BLACKBURN, Robert Harold,** M.A., B.L.S., M.S., LL.D.; librarian (retired); editor; b. Vegreville, Alta. 3 Feb. 1919; s. John H. and Palma G. (Olson) B.; e. Univ. of Alberta, M.A. 1941; Univ. of Toronto, B.L.S. 1942; Columbia Univ., M.S. 1948; Univ. of Waterloo, LL.D. 1965; McGill Univ., LL.D. 1986; m. F. Patricia, d. H.A. Gibson, M.D., Calgary, Alta., 31 Dec. 1942; children: Robert G., Karen M., John H.; m. Verna Morgan 25 Sept. 1993; LIBRARIAN EMERITUS, UNIVERSITY OF TORONTO 1985– ; RCAF navigator & instructor 1942–45; Gen. Asst., Calgary Pub. Library, 1945–46; Asst. Librarian, Univ. of Toronto, 1947–54; Chief Librarian, Univ. Of Toronto 1954–81; Editor of Nfld. Supplement to 'Encyclopedia of Canada' 1949; 'Joint Catalogue of Serials in Toronto Libraries' 1953; compiler: 'Patricia Gibson Blackburn, Her Memoirs and Her Ancestry in the Families Chalmers, Edwards, Godwin, Gibson' 1992; author: 'Evolution of the Heart, A History of the University of Toronto Library up to 1981' 1989; author of various prof. articles, poems and short stories; mem., Candn. Library Assn. (Pres. 1958–59); Pres. (1963–64) Candn. Assn. of Coll. & Univ. Libs.; Bd. mem. (1965–67), Assn. of Research Libs.; Bd. Chrmn. (1967), Center for Research Libs.; Dir., Am. Lib. Assn. and Council, Assn. of Coll. & Research Libs. 1967–71; mem. Mass. Inst. of Tech. Bd. of Lib. Visitors 1970–73; Bd. mem. Assn. of Research Libs. 1971–73; mem. UBC Library Friends Adv. Council 1989–91; Consultant for Can. to 'Colliers Encyclopedia' 1950–91; Sec.-Treas., National Alliance of Covenanting Congregations; Protestant; Home: 5300 Drenkelly Court, Streetsville, Ont. L5M 2H4.

**BLACKMERE, Peter Gordon,** B.A., C.A.; chartered accountant; b. Hamilton, Ont. 10 May 1946; s. Francis A. Barber; e. Wilfrid Laurier Univ. B.A. (Hons.) 1972; C.A. 1974; m. Carol d. Lorne and Ruth Mashinter 22 May 1972; children: Wayne Allan, Christopher James; DIRECTOR OF FINANCE, PICKER INTERNATIONAL CANADA INC. 1987– ; joined Coopers & Lybrand 1972; Mgr. 1976–79; Controller, Kitchener Div., Rogers Cablesystems Inc. 1979–81; Chief Internal Auditor 1981–85; Controller, US Opns. 1985–87; Home: 150 Little Court, Bolton, Ont. L7E 3T8; Office: 7956 Torbram Rd., Brampton, Ont. L6T 5A2.

**BLACKMORE, George D.;** paper industry executive; b. Ballycastle, N. Ireland 8 June 1935; s. Samuel Cecil and Sarah Jane (McCaughan) B.; e. Ballycastle H.S.; Belfast College of Art & Technology (majored in architecture); m. Margaret d. Alex and Edith May 14 March 1959; children: Mark Andrew, Jane Leslie, Adam George; VICE PRESIDENT & GENERAL MANAGER, DOMTAR SPECIALTY FINE PAPERS DIV. 1991– ; emigrated to Canada 1959; joined Sales/Mktg. Dept., Domtar Inc. 1961; Reg. Sales Mgr., Western Canada, Domtar Corrugated Containers Div. 1978–81; Gen. Mgr., Western Canada 1981–85; Vice Pres. & Gen. Mgr., Domtar Roofing, Fibreboard & Insulating Div. 1985–87; Domtar Corrugated Containers Div. 1987–91; Dir., Paperboard Packaging Environ. Council; Ont. Pulp & Paper Industry Labour-Mngt. Ctte.; Schiffen Haus (Canada) Ltd.; Candn. Corrugated Case Assn.; Jellco Packaging Ltd.; recreations: golf, tennis, hiking; clubs: Cornwall Golf & Country; Home: R.R. 1, Box 314, Williamstown, Ont. K0C 2J0; Office: 800 Second St. W., P.O. Box 40, Cornwall, Ont. K6H 5S3.

**BLACKSHAW, Robert A.,** B.Sc.; office automation executive; b. Montreal, Que. 24 May 1947; s. Wesley Daines and Gisele Louise (Dion) B.; e. Sir George Williams Univ. B.Sc. 1971; m. Kelly E. d. Robert and Joyce Campbell 13 Feb. 1982; children: Courtney Lynn, Wesley Buchanan; CHRMN., CHIEF EXTVE. OFFR. & CO-FOUNDER, KEYWORD OFFICE TECHNOL. 1980– ; 1968–77: Systems Software Analyst, United Aircraft of Can. Ltd.; Computer Systems Analyst, Air Can.; Prod. Planning Dir., Multiple Access Div. of Can. Systems Group; Co-founder & Pres., RND Investments 1977–80; recreations: skiing, golf, squash; clubs: Glencoe, Pinebrook Golf & Country; Home: 11 Stradbrooke Rise SW, Calgary, Alta. T3H 1T8; Office: 2816 11th St NE, Calgary, Alta. T2E 7S7.

**BLACKSTONE, Mary A.,** B.A., M.A., Ph.D.; university professor and administrator; b. Ellsworth, Maine 5 May 1949; d. Albert Henry and Hazel Rae (Colpitts) B.; e. Univ. of Maine B.A. (highest hons.) 1971; Univ. of N.B. M.A. 1973, Ph.D. 1978; m. Cameron s. Howe and May Louis 16 May 1981; DEAN OF FINE ARTS, UNIV. OF REGINA 1990– ; Postdoctoral Fellow and Researcher, Records of Early English Drama 1978–81; Lecturer, English, Erindale Coll., Univ. of Toronto 1979–81; Univ. of Regina 1982–83, 1986–87; Asst. Prof., English, Wash. & Jefferson Coll. 1981–82; Univ. of Regina 1983–86; Drama, Univ. of Alta. 1987–90; Co-ord., Grad. Studies in Drama, Univ. of Alta. 1987–90; Assoc. Prof., Theatre, Univ. of Regina 1990– ; Chair, Sask. Arts Edn. Conf., '94 Planning Ctte. 1993– ; Sask. Film/Video Profl. Devel. Co-ord. Ctte. 1992– ; Chair, Candn. Assn. of Fine Arts Deans 1993– ; Maine/N.B. Exchange Scholarship 1969–70; Canada Council Doctoral Fellowships 1974–76; REED Postdoct. Fellowship, Univ. of Toronto 1978–79; holder of SSHRC & NEH grants; Mem., Bd. of Trustees, MacKenzie Art Gall. 1990– ;(Personnel Ctte. 1990–93); Regina Symphony Orch. 1991– ;(Sec. Bd. of Trustes & Extve. Ctte. 1992– ; Chair, Program Ctte. 1992– ;); other past extve. positions; Mem., Am. Soc. for Theatre Research; Shakespeare Assn. of Am.; Internat. Shakespeare Assn.; Poculi Ludique Societas; Malone Soc.; Soc. Internat. pour l'Etude du Théâtre Medieval; Alta. Conf. on Theatre; Candn. Assn. of Fine Arts Deans; Candn. Conf. on the Arts; Sask. Writers Guild; Sask. Playwrights Ctr.; Assn. of Cultural Extves.; Literary Managers and Dramaturgs of Am.; Internat. Fed. for Theatre Rsch.;

author: 'Robin Hood and the Friar' 1981, one book chapter and contbn. to REED newsletter; dramaturg: 'Dancing in Poppies' 1993, 'Beauty and the Beast' 1993; vocal soloist; recreations: tennis, gardening, piano; Office: Regina, Sask. S4S 0A2.

**BLACKWELL, Rt. Rev. Douglas Charles,** D.D.; bishop; b. Toronto, Ont. 3 June 1938; e. Northern S.S.; Wycliffe Coll., Univ. of Toronto grad. 1964, D.D. (honoris causa) 1990; m. Sandra Dianne Griffiths 1963; children: Deborah, Kathryn, Mark; REGIONAL BISHOP OF TRENT-DURHAM 1988– ; Asst. Curate, St. Stephen's Ch., Diocese of Calgary, 1964–66; Cochrane Mission 1966–68; Incumbent, St. Paul's Ch. North Battleford, Diocese of Saskatoon 1968–73; Asst. Dir., Aurora Conf. Ctr., Diocese of Toronto 1973–77; Extve. Asst. to Archbishop of Toronto 1977–88; Diocesan Dir. of Communications 1986–88; appt. Archdeacon of York 1987; elected by Electoral Synod of Diocese of Toronto 1 June 1988 & consecreated Bishop in the Church of God 15 Sept. 1988; Mem., Whitby Homes Corp.; Bd. of Trustees, Wycliffe College; 5 yrs on Civic Awards Ctte. of Toronto; recipient Mayor's Civic Award; Home: 63 Glen Dhu Dr., Whitby, Ont. L1R 1K3; Office: 300 Dundas St. W., Whitby, Ont. L1N 2M5.

**BLACKWELL, John Henry,** E.D., M.Sc., Ph.D.; educator; b. Melbourne, Australia 9 July 1921; s. Matthew Drummond and Vera Isabel Marion (Lillies) B.; e. Univ. of Melbourne B.Sc. 1941; Univ. of W. Ont. M.Sc. 1947, Ph.D. 1952; m. Betty Stanmore d. late Thomas Herbert Smith 19 Apr. 1947; children: Stephen D., J. Gerald, Patricia F.M. (Morden), Thomas M.; PROF. EMERITUS OF APPLIED MATH., UNIV. OF WESTERN ONT. 1986– ; Instr., Asst. Prof. Assoc. Prof., Prof., Dept. of Physics 1947–1960; Prof. Dept. of Math. 1960–67; Prof. and Chrmn. of Applied Math. 1967–76, Prof. of Applied Math. and Extve. Asst. to Pres. (Planning) 1976–80; Prof. of Applied Math., Univ. of W. Ont. 1981–86; Visiting Fellow, Australian Nat. Univ. Canberra 1955–56; UK Commonwealth Fellow, Oxford Univ. 1964–65; served with Citizen Mil. Forces (Inf.) Australia 1939–42, Australian Imp. Force (RAEME) 1942–46 (Australia, UK and N.W. Europe), rank Capt.; Candn. Offrs. Training Corps 1958–67, rank Lt. Col.; author various articles heat transfer, magnetohydrodynamics, microwave spectroscopy in Candn. and foreign scient. & engn. journs.; Fellow, Inst. Math. & its Applications; Fellow, Candn. Soc. Mech. Engrs. (Past Vice Pres.); Candn. Applied Math. Soc.; Engn. Inst. Can.; Royal Candn. Legion; P. Conservative; Anglican; recreations: golf, photography; Clubs: London Hunt & Country; Home: 2 Runnymede Cres., London, Ont. N6G 1Z8.

**BLACKWOOD, Allister Clark,** M.Sc., Ph.D., F.R.S.C.; microbiologist; educator; b. Calgary, Alta. 22 Nov. 1915; s. Allister Chester and Bessie Emerson (Saunders) B.; e. Univ. of Alta. B.Sc. 1942, M.Sc. 1944; Univ. of Wis. Ph.D. 1949; m. Mildred d. Jack Marsh, Drumheller, Alta. 1 May 1943; children: Alan Clark, Marsha Ellen, Susan Mildred; PROF. EMERITUS, DEPT. MICROBIOL., FAC. OF AGRIC., MACDONALD COLL., MCGILL UNIV. 1981– , Prof. of Microbiology there 1957–81, Chrmn. of Dept. 1957–68, Dean of Faculty and Vice Princ. of Coll. 1972–77; joined Div. of Applied Biol. Nat. Research Council, Ottawa 1944–46, Prairie Regional Lab. Saskatoon 1948–57; holds US Patent Production of Glycerol by Fermentation; rec'd Centennial Medal 1967; Silver Jubilee Medal, 1977; author or co-author numerous articles, reviews, book chapters; Hon. mem. Que. Soc. de Microbiologie (Pres. 1962–63); Hon. mem. Candn. Soc. Microbiol. (Pres. 1964–65); Am. Soc. Microbiol.; Assn. Faculties Agric. Can. (Pres. 1975–76); Fellow, Royal Soc. of Can.; Kappa Sigma; Anglican; recreations: curling, swimming; Home: 466 Hemsworth Rd., Qualicum Beach, B.C. V9K 1B6.

**BLACKWOOD, David Lloyd,** R.C.A., D.Litt., LL.D.; artist; b. Wesleyville, Nfld. 7 Nov. 1941; s. Capt. Edward and Molly (Glover) B.; e. Wesleyville Mem. High Sch. 1959; Ont. Coll. of Art Toronto (Govt. Nfld. Centennial Scholarship) Hon. Grad. Drawing & Painting 1963, rec'd Travelling Scholarship to visit maj. Am. Colls. Washington and N.Y., grad. work Painter-Printmaker 1963–64; m. Anita Elizabeth d. Adrian Bonar, Toronto, Ont. Sept. 1970; one s. David Bonar; Assoc., Ont. College of Art, 1963; Artist-in-Residence Erindale Coll. Univ. of Toronto 1969–75; Art Master, Trinity Coll. Sch. Port Hope, Ont. 1963–88; rep. in pub. and private colls. incl. Nat. Gallery Can., Nat. Gallery Australia, Montreal Museum Fine Arts, Art Gallery Ont., Vancouver Art Gall., Edmonton Art Gall., Uffizi, Florence, various Candn. and USA univs. and business firms, private coll. Queen Elizabeth; maj. exhns. incl. Univ. of Me. 1980, Blackwood Prints 1967–80 Milan, Italy 1980 also Bologna, Venice and Rome, Retrospective Canada House London 1986; Dir., Sault Coll. Applied Arts; Candn. Prison Arts Foundation; Trustee, Art Gallery of Ont.; Patron, Candn. Outward Bound Wilderness Sch.; Patron, Nat. Screen Inst. Can.; co-author 'Wake of the Great Sealers' 1974; subject of NFB film Blackwood 1974 (rec'd 10 internat. film awards incl. Oscar nomination); subject of book 'Art of David Blackwood' by William Gough; maj. awards incl. Purchase Award Biennial Exhn. Nat. Gallery Can. 1964; Purchase Award Nat. Gallery Australia 1967; Ingres Medal Govt. France 1963; Internat. Graphics '71 Award Montreal Museum Fine Arts; First Internat. Norweigian Biennial Prints Award 1972; Biennale Internat. de L'estampe Paris 1973; 8th Burnaby Internat. Biennial 1975; Hon. Academician with Gold Medal, Italian Acad. Fine Arts 1980; Hon. Life Mem., Art Gall. of Ont. 1988; el. mem. Royal Candn. Acad. 1975 (Vice Pres.); mem. Ont. Soc. Artists; Print & Drawing Council Can.; Candn. Soc. Painters Water Colour; recreations: hist. research related to Nfld., collecting Candn. art & antiques, reading, writing, photography, music; Address: 22 King St., Port Hope, Ont. L1A 2R5.

**BLADES, Ann;** artist; illustrator; b. Vancouver, B.C. 16 Nov. 1947; d. Arthur Hazelton and Dorothy (Planche) Sager; e. Crofton House School, Vancouver; Univ. of B.C., Teaching Cert. 1967; B.C. Inst. of Tech., R.N. 1974; m. David Morrison; elem. sch. teacher 1967–71; nurse (part-time) 1974–80; illustrator of children's books since 1968; artist (Bau-Xi Gallery) since 1982; author and illustrator: 'Mary of Mile 18' 1971 (book), 1981 (film); 'A Boy of Taché' 1973; 'The Cottage at Crescent Beach' 1977; 'By the Sea: An Alphabet Book' 1985; 'The Seasons Boardbooks' 1989; illustrator: 'Jacques the Woodcutter' 1977; 'A Salmon for Simon' 1978; 'Six Darn Cows' 1979; 'Anna's Pet' 1980; 'Pettranella' 1980; 'A Candle for Christmas' 1986; 'Ida and the Wool Smugglers' 1987; 'The Singing Basket' 1990; 'A Dog Came, Too' 1992; 'A Ride for Martha' 1993; Candn. Assn. of Children's Libs. Book of the Year Award 1972; Can. Counc. Children's Lit. Award for Illustration 1979; Candn. Assn. of Children's Libs. Amelia Frances Howard-Gibbon Award 1979; Elizabeth Mrazik-Cleaver Candn. Picture Book Award 1986; Candn. Nominee, Hans Christian Andersen Award for illustration 1987; recreations: garage sales, gardening; Address: 2701 Crescent Dr., Surrey, B.C. V4A 3J9.

**BLADES, D. Nolan;** petroleum executive; b. Camrose, Alta. 6 Aug. 1942; e. Univ. of Alta. B.Sc. 1964; m. Carol; children: Ryan, Meghan; PRESIDENT AND C.E.O., PURSUIT RESOURCES INC. 1993– ; ERCB 1964–74; Ashland Oil Canada 1974–78; Engn. Mgr., Kaiser Oil Ltd. 1979–80; Oakwood Petroleums Ltd. 1980–83; Sr. V.P. & V.P. Prod. & Opns. 1983–84; Sr. V.P. 1984–85; Extve. Vice Pres. 1985–89; Extve. Vice Pres., Chauvco Resources Ltd. 1989–92; Pres. & C.O.O. 1992–93; Dir., Pursuit Resources Inc.; Dir., United Way of Calgary; mem., Candn. Inst. of Mining & Metallurgy; Soc. of Petroleum Engrs.; Assn. of Profl. Engrs., Geologists & Geophysicists of Alta.; recreations: skiing, hiking; Home: 373 Wildwood Dr. S.W., Calgary, Alta. T3C 3E4; Office: 475, 441 – 5th Ave. S.W., Calgary, Alta. T2P 2V1.

**BLAIKIE, William Alexander,** B.A., M.Div.; politician; clergyman; b. Winnipeg Man. 19 June 1951; s. Robert Nisbet and Kathleen (Taylor) B.; e. Univ. of Winnipeg B.A. Phil. & Religious Studies 1973; Toronto Sch. of Theology M.Div. 1977; m. Brenda d. William and Isobel Bihun 29 June 1973; children: Rebecca, Jessica, Daniel, Tessa; MEMBER OF PARLIAMENT FOR WINNIPEG – TRANSCONA 1993– ; (M.P. for Winnipeg, Bird's Hill 1979–88; Winnipeg - Transcona 1988, re-el. 1993); UNITED CHURCH MINISTER; Min. North End Community Ministry (an outreach proj. of United Ch.) 1977–79; el. to House of Commons 1979; Social Policy Critic for Fed. N.D.P. Caucus; re-el. 1980; Health Critic for N.D.P. 1980–84; mem. Standing Ctte. on Health, Welfare & Social Affairs 1979–84; mem. Special Parlty. Task Force on Fed.-Prov. Fiscal Arrangements; Vice-Chrmn. Special Ctte. on Parliamentary Reform 1982–83; Fed. N.D.P. Caucus Chrmn. 1983–84 and 1993– ; apptd. N.D.P. Environ. Critic 1984; mem. Spec. Comte. on Acid Rain 1984–87, Vice Chrmn. Special Ctte. on Reform of the House of Commons 1984–85; mem. Standing Ctte. on Environment & Forestry 1984–87; mem. Standing Ctte. on Private Member's Business 1986–87; N.D.P. External Affairs Critic 1987–90; mem. Standing Ctte. on External Affairs & Internat. Trade 1987–90; mem. Special Ctte. on the Peace Process in Central Am. 1988; N.D.P. Tax Policy Critic 1990– ; N.D.P. Deputy House Leader 1991– ; mem. Standing Ctte. on Finance 1990– ; N.D.P. Internat. Trade Critic 1993– ; Vice Pres., Candn. Br., Commonwealth Parlty. Assoc. 1985– ; mem. Parliamentarians for Global Action; mem., Royal Candn. Legion Transcona Br. #7; Transcona Meml. Un. Ch.; Hon. Pres. Manitoba Youth Parliament 1982–84; Hon. Patron Transcona Hist. Mus.; Club: Park City West Community; recreations: canoeing, camping, skiing, skating, swimming, playing bagpipes; Home: 82 Spring Meadow Cr., Winnipeg, Man.; Offices: #6, 1600 Regent Ave. W., Winnipeg, Man. and House of Commons, Ottawa, Ont. K1A 0A6.

**BLAIN, Lawrence Alexander,** B.A., M.A., Ph.D.; investment banker; b. North Vancouver 2 May 1947; s. Winslow Alexander and Evelyn Elizabeth (Jenkins) B.; e. Univ. of B.C. B.A. 1969; Carleton Univ. M.A. 1971; Univ. of B.C. Ph.D. 1977; m. Linda d. Michael and Joan Nutter 28 July 1979; children: Alexa Lawrie, Owen Michael; VICE-PRESIDENT & DIRECTOR, RBC DOMINION SECURITIES (formerly Pemberton Securities) 1984– ; Economist, Rsch. Dept., Bank of Canada 1975–79; Dir., Central Borrowing & Planning, Prov. Treas., Min. of Finance, Prov. of B.C. 1978–84; Vice-Chair, Pacific Reg., Investment Dealers Assn.; club: Vancouver; Home: 3256 W. 26 St., Vancouver, B.C.; Office: Suite 2100, Park Place, 666 Burrard St., Vancouver, B.C. V6C 2X8.

**BLAIR, Hon. D. Gordon,** LL.B., B.C.L.; judge; b. Regina, Sask. 23 Dec. 1919; S. Duncan and Eliza Martha (Elliott) B.; e. Regina Pub. and High Schs.; Univ. of Sask. B.A. 1939, LL.B. 1941; Oxford Univ. (Rhodes Scholar 1941) B.C.L. 1947; m. Sarah Margaret d. Charles William Milton 24 June 1946; two s. David Allen, Stephen Gordon; JUDGE, COURT OF APPEAL ONT. since 1976; called to Bar of Sask. 1942, Ont. 1952; cr. Q.C. 1975; Foreign Service Offr. Dept. External Affairs 1945–47; Partner, Francis, Woods, Gauley & Blair, Saskatoon 1948–50; Extve. Asst. to Min. of Justice 1951–52; Partner, Herridge, Tolmie, Gray, Coyne & Blair, Ottawa 1953–75; el. to H. of C. for Grenville-Carleton 1968–72; Chrmn. H. of C. Comte. on Procedure & Organ. 1968–72; Del. 25th Gen. Assembly U.N. 1970; Vice Chrmn. Ont. Comn. on El. Contributions & Expenses 1975; served as Lieut. with Irish Regt. of Can., wounded Italy 1944, Capt. A.G. Br., N.D.H.Q. 1944–45; mem. Candn. Judges Conference (Chrmn. 1983–84); Candn. Section, Internat. Comn. Jurists (Pres. 1973–76); Candn. Bar Assn.; Royal Candn. Legion; United Church; recreations: golf, reading; Clubs: Rideau; Royal Ottawa Golf; Links O'Tay Golf & Country (Perth, Ont.); Royal Candn. Mil. Inst. (Toronto, Ont.); Home: Apt. 1608, 65 Harbour Sq., Toronto, Ont. M5J 2L4; Office: Osgoode Hall, Toronto, Ont. M5H 2N5.

**BLAIR, David John,** B.S.P., M.D.; physician; b. Macklin, Sask. 7 Feb. 1943; s. Harvey and Elfreda Elizabeth (Brinson) B.; e. Univ. of Sask. B.S.P. 1966, M.D. 1971; Cert. Coll. Family Practice 1981; m. Roberta Diane d. Edgebert and Teresa Bolingbroke 4 Sept. 1967; children: Timothy David, Susan Diane; Associate, Quinsam Medical Group 1974–.; postgrad. training Vancouver Gen. Hosp. 2 yrs.; med. practice Campbell River 1973– ; mem. Active Staff Campbell River & Dist. Gen. Hosp.; mem. B.C. Med. Assn. (Area Del. 1981–85, Chrmn. Bd. Dirs. 1984–85, mem. Exec. [Hon. Secy.-Treasr.] 1985–86); mem. Counc. and Bldg. Ctte. St. Peter's (Ang.) Ch.; Club: Toastmasters Internat.

**BLAIR, Douglas Keith,** B.Com., M.B.A.; business executive; b. Toronto, Ont. 8 April 1950; s. Willis L. and Elsie E. (Clode) B.; e. Univ. of Toronto, B.Com. 1972; York Univ., M.B.A. 1975; m. Marilyn d. William B. and Isobel Waugh 21 Dec. 1984; children: Jennifer, Geoffrey, Andrew; PRES., NORIMCO DIVISION OF BATA INDUSTRIES LTD. 1992– ; Acct., Price Waterhouse 1972–74; Controller, Vice-Pres., Winnwell Ltd. 1974–79; Mktg. Mgr. then Extve. Vice-Pres., Cooper Can. Ltd. 1979–86; Pres., Candn. Thermos Products Inc. 1986–92; Dir., Bata Industries Ltd.; Shoe Manufacturers Assn. of Canada; Two/Ten Found. of Canada; Bd. of Regents, Victoria Univ.; Chancellor's Counc., Victoria Univ.; Club: Empire; Home: 331 Lytton Blvd., Toronto, Ont. M5N 1R9; Office: 445 Apple Creek Blvd., Suite 200, Markham, Ont. L3R 9X7.

**BLAIR, Michael Finley Lawrence,** B.A., M.B.A.; business executive; b. Cornwall, Ont. 6 Dec. 1945; s. James Roderick and Peggy (Britt) B.; e. Royal Mil. Coll. Can. B.A. 1968; Univ. of W. Ont. M.B.A. 1976; two s. James Robert, John Edward; CHIEF EXTVE. OFFR., ALGONQUIN MERCANTILE CORP. 1989– ; Dir., Algonquin Mercantile Corp.; Renegade Capital Corp.; Prenor Group Ltd.; Helix Circuits Inc.; served with RCAF 1964–74, Fighter Pilot, rank Flight Lt.; Assoc. McKinsey & Co. Inc. 1976–78; Vice Pres. Corporate Devel. Canadian General Electric Co. Ltd. 1978–84; Pres. The Enfield Corporation Ltd. 1984–89; recreations: tennis, hiking; Club: RMC; Home: PH 2 Bayview Tower, Ruperts Landing, Collingwood, Ont. L9Y 4T9; Office: Unit 11, 668 Millway Ave., Concord, Ont. L4K 3V2.

**BLAIS, André,** B.A., Ph.D.; university professor; b. Drummondville, Que. 24 Jan. 1947; s. Ferdinand and Simone (Chaput) B.; e. Univ. Laval., B.A. 1969; York Univ., Ph.D. 1978; m. Suzanne d. Gerard and Antoinette Lacharité 3 Aug. 1975; children: Genevieve, François-Yves, Louis, Viviane; PROF., POL. SCI., UNIV. OF MONTREAL 1989– ; Asst. Prof., Dept. of Pol. Sci., Univ. of Ottawa 1972–74; Asst. Prof., Univ. Laval 1974–75; Assoc. Fellow, Ctr. de Recherche et Devel. en Econ. 1985– ; Assoc. Ed. 'Canadian Public Policy' 1985–91; author: 'A Political Sociology of Public Aid to Industry' 1986; co-author: 'Les Elites politiques les bas-salariés, et la politique du logement à Hull' 1976; 'Letting the People Decide' 1992; editor: 'Industrial Policy' 1986; co-editor: 'The Budget Maximizing Bureaucrat' 1991; Home: 2986 Ave. de Soissons, Montréal, Qué. H4N 2K5; Office: Montréal, Qué. H3C 3J7.

**BLAIS, Gaston,** B.A.; public servant; b. Sturgeon Falls, Ont.; e. Ottawa Univ. B.A. 1965; one s.: Marc-André; DIRECTOR GENERAL, ARTS & POLICY PLANNING, DEPT. OF COMMUNICATIONS 1988– ; Regional Development Officer, Ontario Arts Council 1973; Producer/Dir., Office de la TV édu. de l'Ontario (TVO) 1979–81; Dir., Cultural Initiatives Program then Dir., Arts Policy, Dept. of Communications 1981; seconded to External Affairs 1987; Asst. Prof., Faculty of Fine Arts, York Univ. 1970–73; studied theatre at the Bristol Old Vic in England and Mime at Jacques Lecoq School in Paris; recreations: golf, skiing; Home: 35 Oak St., Aylmer, Que. J9H 5W4; Office: 300 Slater St., Room 348, Ottawa, Ont. K1A 0C8.

**BLAIS, Hon. Jean-Jacques,** Q.C., P.C., B.A., LL.B.; b. Sturgeon Falls, Ont. 27 June 1940; s. Rodolphe Gaston and Claire (Rochon) B.; e. Ecole Sacré-Coeur and Sturgeon Falls (Ont.) High Sch. 1958; Univ. of Ottawa B.A. 1961, LL.B. 1964; Osgoode Hall 1966; m. Maureen Ann d. late Edward Michael Ahearn, Ottawa, Ont. 20 May 1968; children: Stéphane, Alexandre, Marie-José; read law with Joseph Sedgwick, Q.C.; called to Bar of Ont. 1966; assoc. law practice with George Campbell Miller, Toronto and retained for firm Miller and Blais by various labour groups 1966–70; practised at Criminal Bar appearing before criminal tribunals incl. Supreme Court of Can.; became Partner Blais, McLachlan & Duchesneau-McLachlan, N. Bay 1970; apptd. Q.C. 1979; mem. Adv. Comte. on French Educ. Metrop. Toronto 1969; Cand. Toronto Bd. of Educ. 1969 (def.); el. to H. of C. 1972, re-el. 1974, 1979 and 1980; apptd. Parlty. Secy. to the Pres. of the Privy Council 1975; Postmaster Gen. of Can. and Depy. House Leader 1976; Solicitor General for Can. 1978; Min. of Supply and Services and Receiver General Can. 1980; Min. of Nat. Defence 1983–84; mem. Security & Intell. Review Comte. 1984–91; Partner, Lette, McTaggart, Blais, Martin (Ottawa law firm); Pres., The Government Business Consulting Group Inc.; Chrmn., Ottawa Life Sciences Technology Park; mem. Exec. Ctte., Bd. of Govs., Univ. of Ottawa; Amnesty Internat.; Liberal; R. Catholic; recreations: skiing; swimming; Home: 1111 River Rd., Ottawa, Ont. K1K 3W2; Office: 1000–100 Sparks St., Ottawa, Ont. K1P 5B7.

**BLAIS, Marie-Claire,** C.C. (1972); author; b. Quebec, Que. 1939; studied lit. and philos. Laval Univ.; awarded Guggenheim Fellowship 1963 and 1964; author of 'La belle Bête' 1959, (trans. into Eng. as 'Mad Shadows' 1960); 'Tête blanche' 1960 (Eng. trans. 1961); 'Le jour est noir' 1962 (trans. into Eng. as 'The Day is Dark'); 'Pays voilés' (poems) 1963 (trans. into Eng. as 'Existences' 1964); 'Une saison dans la vie d'Emmanuel' 1965 (Eng. trans. 'A Season in the Life of Emmanuel' 1966); 'Les Voyageurs Sacrés'; 'L'insoumise' 1971 (trans. into Eng. as 'The Fugitive' 1978); 'L'exécution; pièce en deux actes' (play) 1968 (trans. into Eng. as 'The Execution' 1976); 'Manuscrits de Pauline Archange' 1968 and 'Vivre, Vivre' 1969 (both trans. into Eng. as 'The Manuscripts of Pauline Archange' 1970); 'Vivre, Vivre' 1969; 'Les Apparences' 1970 (trans. into Eng. as 'Durer's Angel' 1972); 'Le Loup' (novel) 1972 (trans. into Eng. as 'The Wolf' 1974); 'Un Joualonais sa Joualonie' 1973 (trans. into Eng. as 'St. Lawrence Blues' 1974); 'Une liaison parisienne' 1976 (trans. into Eng. as 'A Literary Affair' 1978); 'L'Ocean' 1977 (trans. into Eng. as 'The Ocean' 1978); 'Les nuits de l'underground' 1978 (trans. into Eng. as 'Nights in the Underground' 1979); 'Le Sourd Dans La Ville,' 1980 (trans. into English as 'Death to the City' 1981); 'Visions d'Anna' (novel) 1982 (trans. into English 1984); 'Printemps 1981' (novel) 1984; 'Sommeil d'Hiver' (play) 1985; 'Fière' (play) 1985; 'L'Ange de la Solitude' (novel); 'l'Ile' (play; trans. by David Lobdell); 'A Garden in the Storm' (play; trans. by David Lobdell); 'Parcours d'un Ecrivains: Notes Americaines' (essay) 1993; Address: 448 Chemin Sims, Kingsbury, Qué. J0B 1X0.

**BLAIS, The Hon. Pierre,** B.A., LL.B.; politician; b. Berthier-sur-Mer, Que. 30 Dec. 1948; e. Laval Univ. B.A. 1968, LL.L. 1976; m. Chantal Fournier; children: Marie-Hélène, Pierre-François, David, Julie; Min. of Justice and President of Privy Council 1993; partner, Montmagny law practice 1976–84; Parl. Sec. to Agric. Min. 1984–86; to Deputy Prime Minister 1986–87; Solicitor General of Canada 1989–90; Min. of Consumer and Corporate Affairs 1990–93; Min. of State for Agric. 1987–93; Min. of Justice and Attorney Gen. of Canada 1990–93; Mem. Cabinet Cttes.: Priorities & Planning and Operations; Past Mem., Standing Ctte. on Agric.; Past Chrmn., P.C. MPs agric. caucus; Vice-Pres., Cons. de dével. de la Côte-du-Sud 1972; Pres., Club Richelieu-Montmagny 1981; Teacher, Laval Univ.; Univ. of Que. at Rimouski; Lectr., Cégep de La Pocatière; var. mngt. posts at reg. & munic. levels; Office: Rm. 448, Confederation Bldg., House of Commons, Ottawa, Ont. K1A 0A6.

**BLAISE, Clark Lee;** writer; b. Fargo, N.D. 10 Apr. 1940; s. Leo Romeo and Anne Marion (Vanstone) B.; e. Denison Univ. A.B. 1961; Univ. of Iowa M.F.A. 1964; Denison Univ. Hon. Ph.D. 1979; m. Bharati d. Sudhir Lal and Bina Banerjee Mukherjee 19 Sept. 1963; children: Bart Anand, Bernard Sudhir; Prof., Concordia Univ. 1966–78; York Univ. 1978–80; Skidmore Coll. 1980–81, 1982–83; Visiting Prof., Univ. of Iowa 1981–82; Writer-in-Res., David Thompson Univ. Ctr. 1983; Emory Univ. 1985; Adjunct Prof., Columbia Univ. 1986; numerous short residencies in Candn. & U.S. univs.; Can. Counc. grants; Guggenheim Fellow, Nat. Endowment for the Arts grant; mem., P.E.N.; author (short story collections): 'A North American Education' 1973; 'Tribal Justice' 1974; 'Resident Alien' 1986; (novels): 'Lunar Attractions' 1978; 'Lusts' 1983; co-author: 'Days and Nights in Calcutta' 1977; co-editor: 'Here and Now' 1977; 'Best Canadian Stories' 1978, 1979, 1980 (three sep. edns.); recreations: travel, jogging; Office: c/o The Porcupine's Quill Inc., 68 Main St., Erin, Ont. N0B 1T0.

**BLAKE, Donald Edward,** M.A., M.Phil., Ph.D.; educator; b. Blairmore, Alta. 24 May 1944; s. Andrew Gwilym and Edith Mary Myfanwy (Brown) B.; e. Univ. of Alta. B.A. 1965, M.A. 1967; Yale Univ. M.Phil. 1969, Ph.D. 1972; m. Lorna d. Ernest and Ann Krahulec 16 July 1966; two d. Erin Colleen, Arlette Elaine; PROF. OF POL. SCI. UNIV. OF B.C. 1985– , Head of Dept. 1990– ; joined present Univ. 1970, Assoc. Prof. 1977; Prin. Adv. B.C. Royal Comn. Electoral Boundaries 1987–88; Adv. Yukon Electoral Boundaries Comn. 1991; recipient Can. Council Fellowship 1975–76; SSHRC Fellowship 1981–82; Yvan Corbeil Rsch. Prize 1987; Killam Rsch. Fellowship 1988–89; author 'Two Political Worlds: Parties and Voting in British Columbia' 1985; co-author 'Grassroots Politicians: Party Activists in British Columbia' 1991; co-ed. 'Party Leadership in Canada: Experiences of the Provinces' 1991; asst. ed. Candn. Jour. Pol. Sci. 1978–81; mem. Am. Pol. Sci. Assn.; Candn. Pol. Sci. Assn. (Dir. 1975–77); recreations: photography, hiking, skiing; Home: 2918 W. 31 Ave., Vancouver, B.C. V6T 1W5; Office: Vancouver, B.C. V6T 1Z1.

**BLAKE, Mervyn Alexander Clifford;** actor; b. Dehra Dun, India 30 Nov. 1907; s. Walter Clifford and Gertrude Beatrice (Pearce) B.; e. Eggar's Grammar Sch. UK 1919; St. Joseph's Coll. North Point, Darjeeling, India 1927 (Sch. Cert.); Royal Acad. Dramatic Art London, Eng. 1930–32; m. Christine V. d. Isaac and Joan Bennett 8 Nov. 1951; children: Andrew, Bridget, Tim Davisson (step-son); first profl. appearance Embassy Theatre Swiss Cottage London 1933; toured with Eng. Classical Players 1934; understudied various roles Playhouse Theatre London Westend, Aldwych Theatre, Old Royalty Theatre London Westend 1934–35; repertory theatre UK 1935–39; appeared with Paul Robeson Westminster Theatre London during this period and with Alistair Sim Grafton Theatre London; 1936 films incl. 'Things To Come' with Raymond Massey, Ralph Richardson; 'Ghost Goes West'; 'Crackers with Nervo & Knox'; served with RASC 1940–45 N.W. Eur., rank Capt.; formed Tam 'O' Shanters to entertain forward troups during advancement Germany; joined Shakespearian Co. touring Germany (Entertainment Nat. Service Assn.) 1945–46; repertory theatre Guildford, Eng. 1946; joined H.M. Tennent's prodn. 'Antony and Cleopatra' Piccadilly Theatre London appearing with Dame Edith Evans, Anthony Quayle (understudied); joined Young Vic Co. 1947–51, toured UK annually and N.W. Eur.; joined Shakespeare Meml. Theatre Co. 1952–55 appearing with Peggy Ashcroft, Michael Redgrave, Siobhan McKenna, Margaret Leighton, Laurence Olivier, Vivien Leigh, Dirs. incl. Anthony Quayle, Sir John Gielgud; frequent radio broadcasts BBC; appeared Lyric Theatre and Comedy Theatre London Westend 1956; mem. Stratford Shakespearian Festival, Can. since 1957 (at invitation of Michael Langham); toured Can. and USA with Canadian Players 7 seasons; Festival tours incl. Chichester Festival Eng. 1964, The Hague, Utrecht, Copenhagen, Warsaw, Krakov, Moscow, Leningrad 1973; toured Australia 1974 (Perth, Adelaide, Melbourne, Sydney), USA 1986; played title role 'King Lear' S. Ill. Univ. 1965; maj. Candn. theatre appearances incl. Man. Theatre Centre 1966–68, 1974; Vancouver Playhouse 1967–68, Nat. Arts Centre Ottawa 1971, 1973, 1975; readings incl. Brock and Waterloo Univs. 1971; appearances CTV, ETV series on Shakespeare, CBC TV; 1991 season (36th in succession) with Hamlet (Gravedigger), Much Ado About Nothing (Sexton), Musical of Carousel (Dr. Seldon); 1992 season (40th anniversary of Stratford Fest.) with Tempest (Gonzalo), Romeo & Juliet and Measure for Measure; recipient Queen's Silver Jubilee Medal 1978; seat named in each of The Stratford Shakespearian Festival's 3 theatres 1979, 1987; Dora Mavor Moore Award Best Feature Performance 1987; presented with bronze bust of Shakespeare by John Neville for having played in all of Shakespeare's plays 1989; subject of biography by Astrid Bowner forthcoming; Life mem. Candn. Actors Equity Assn. (former mem. Council); Alliance Candn. Cinema, TV & Radio Artists; R.Catholic; Clubs: Stratford Festival Theatre Cricket (Founder); Royal Candn. Legion Veterans; Army, Navy & Air Force Veterans; Home: 287 Huron Rd., Sebringville, Ont. N0K 1X0.

**BLAKELY, Robert William,** B.A., LL.B.; lawyer; b. Toronto, Ont. 16 Apr. 1948; s. Herbert and Sylvia (Greenshields) B.; e. Queen's Univ., B.A. 1970, LL.B. 1973; m. Christine d. George and Anne Gardiner 5 Jan. 1974; children: Lindsay, Kristin, Carolyn; PRES. LIKRILYN INVESTMENTS LTD. 1990– ; Dir.: A Buck or Two Stores!; Eastbourne Investments Ltd. (New York) 1992– ; Merchant Private Limited; Perojean Investments; Prime Spot Media Inc.; Resource Plastics Inc.; Rewco Printing Group 1991– ; Vice-Pres., The Caring Found.; called to Ont. Bar 1975; joined Gambin & Bratty 1975; joined Raymond & Honsberger 1983; Partner, Raymond & Honsberger 1984–90; Chrmn., N. Toronto Working Ctte.; Dir., Children's Aid Soc. Found.; Lake of Bays Assn. 1989; Past Pres., Oriole Park Assn.; Ont. Bar Assn.; Candn. Bar Assn.; recreation: sports; Club: Rosedale; Office: Suite 710, One First Canadian Place, 100 King St. W., Toronto, Ont. M5X 1A6.

**BLAKELY, W. Thomas;** internationally syndicated columnist; author; b. Hamilton, Ont. 2 Oct. 1913; s. William Robert and Lydia Lucretia (Deynarde) B.; e. High Schs., Hamilton, Ont.; m. Patricia Norma, d. late Robert John Leader, 19 Oct 1956; children: Thomas Patrick; admitted to printing apprenticeship, Hamilton 'Herald' (now defunct), Sept. 1932; successively attached to Ed. and Advertising Depts. till suspension of paper in 1936; Freelance fiction writer 1936–38; Advertising Mgr. and Asst. Ed of Temiskaming 'Speaker,' New Liskeard, Ont. 1939; Asst. Advertising Mgr., Fort William 'Times-Journal' 1940–42, and after war services became Indust. Promotion Mgr.; Copywriter and Creative Dir., McKim Advertising Ltd. 1946–49; Dir. of Advertising & Pub. Relations, Yardley of London (Canada) Ltd. 1949–53; named Mgr. of Montreal Office of McConnell, Eastman & Co. Ltd. Sept. 1953, Vice-Pres. 1954, Dir. 1958; Dir., Pub. Relations, Domtar Ltd. 1967; apptd. President, Assn. of Candn. Advertisers 1970–81; served in 2nd World War with R.C.N. as Ordinary Seaman in 1942; service in mid-Atlantic convoy duty; discharged with rank of Lieut. 1945; mem. Pub. Relations Soc.; Protestant; Clubs: Naval Officers; Toronto and Montreal Press; Address: 265 Chaplin Cres., Toronto, Ont. M5P 1B1.

**BLAKENEY, Hon. Allan Emrys,** P.C., O.C., Q.C., M.A., LL.B., LL.D.; b. Bridgewater, N.S., 7 Sept. 1925; s. John Cline and Bertha May (Davies) B.; e. Bridgewater (N.S.) High Sch.; Dalhousie Univ., B.A. 1945, LL.B. 1947; Nova Scotia Rhodes Scholar 1947; Oxford Univ., B.A. 1949, M.A. 1955; m. Mary Elizabeth (Molly) Schwartz d. Dr. Hugh W. Schwartz, Halifax, N.S. (d. 1957) Sept. 1950; m. Anne Louise, d. Cyril H. Gorham, Halifax, N.S. May 1959; children: Barbara, Hugh, David, Margaret; formerly a Dir. of several Co-op. Assns.; called to the Bar of N.S. 1950, and Sask. 1951; cr. Q.C. 1961; Secy. and Solr. for Crown Corps. Prov. of Sask., 1950–55; Chairman, Sask. Securities Comm., 1955–58; in private practice, Davidson, Davidson &

Blakeney, 1958–60; Griffin, Blakeney, Beke, Koskie & Lueck, 1964–70; Min. of Educ., Sask., 1960–61; Prov. Treas. 1961–62, Min. Pub. Health, 1962–64; el. to Sask. Leg. for Regina City, 1960; re-el. for Regina W. 1964, and for Regina Centre 1967, 1971, for Regina Elphinstone 1975, 1978, 1982 and 1986; Leader of the Opposition, Prov. of Sask. 1970–71; Premier 1971–82; Leader of the Opposition 1982–87; retired from Legislature 1988; apptd. Privy Council of Canada 1982; Prof. of Constitutional Law, Osgoode Hall Law Sch., York Univ. 1988–90; Prof. of Constitutional Law, Univ. of Sask. 1990–92; Mem., Royal Comn. on Aboriginal Peoples 1991–93; Hon. Doctor of Civil Law, Mt. Allison Univ.; Hon. Doctor of Laws: Dalhousie Univ., York Univ., Univ. of Western Ont., Univ. of Regina; Officer, Order of Canada 1992; mem., Law Soc. Sask.; Cdn. Bar Assoc.; N.D.P.; Baptist; Address: 1752 Prince of Wales Ave., Saskatoon, Sask. S7K 3E5.

**BLAKLEY, Barry Raymond,** D.V.M., Ph.D.; university professor; b. Saskatoon, Sask. 3 July 1949; s. Edwin Raymond and Dorothy Joan (Hesselwood) B.; e. Univ. of Sask., B.Sc. 1971, D.V.M. 1975, M.Sc. 1977; Univ. of Cincinnati, Ph.D. 1980; m. Pat d. John and Bertha Mathinos 1 May 1982; one s. Matthew Raymond; two d. Alicia Mae, Bethany Suzanne; PROF., DEPT. OF VET. & PHYSIOL. SCIENCES, UNIV. OF SASK. 1986– ; Assoc. Prof. 1980–86; Chrmn., Grad. Toxicology Prog.; Supr., Diagnostic Toxicology Lab., Vet. Teaching Hosp.; Med. Rsch. Counc. Fellow 1975–80; mem. Candn. Vet. Med. Assn.; Sask. Vet. Med. Assn.; recreations: hockey, softball; Home: 438 Kingsmere Blvd., Saskatoon, Sask. S7J 3V2; Office: Saskatoon, Sask. S7N 0W0.

**BLAKLEY, Harold W.,** B.A.Sc.; business executive; b. Grimshaw, Alta. 1 Feb. 1923; s. Everett Thomas and Mabel (Archibald) B.; e. Grimshaw (Alta.) High Sch. 1939; Univ. of Toronto B.A.Sc. 1950; m. Bertha Florence d. Sam Brett, Toronto, Ont. 11 Sept. 1948; CHIEF EXECUTIVE OFFICER, CANADA SOUTH DEVELOPMENTS INC.; Sales Engr. Ashland Oil & Refining Co. Inc. Cleveland, Ohio 1950–52; Babcock & Wilcox Ltd. Galt, Ont. 1952–56; Gen. Mgr.-Can. Illinois Tools Ltd. Don Mills, Ont. 1956–59; Pres., Crane Canada Ltd., Montreal 1959–63; Consolidated Bakeries Ltd. Toronto 1963–64; Carling Breweries Ltd. Toronto 1964–67; Formosa Spring Brewery Ltd. Toronto 1967–71; Columbia Brewing Co. Ltd. Vancouver 1971–77; Extve. Vice Pres. and Dir., Vickers Can. Inc. 1977–78; Chrmn., Pres. and C.E.O. 1978–82; Vice Chrmn., Vickers Can. Inc. 1982–83; Pres., Tricapital Management Ltd. 1983–85; Pres., Idea Corp. 1985–86; served with RCAF 1942–45 Can. UK and Europe; Anglican; recreation: tennis, golf, hiking; Club: Vancouver; Home: 1800 Collegeway, Ste. GT04, Mississauga, Ont. L5L 5S4.

**BLANCHARD, J. Ewart,** B.Sc., M.A., Ph.D., F.R.S.C.; geophysicist; b. Truro, N.S. 22 March 1921; s. Aubrey B. and Agnes George (Blair) B.; e. Dalhousie Univ., B.Sc. 1940; Univ. of Toronto, M.A. 1947, Ph.D. 1952; m. Mary Helena Sandilands, 5 July 1958; children: Jonathan Sandilands, Megan Blair; Geol. Survey of Can., summer 1940; Asst. Forecaster, Meterol. Service, Dept. of Transport, 1940–42; Party Chief Geophys. Surveys, Conwest Exploration Ltd., summers 1946 and 1947; Geophysicist, Newmont Mining Corp., 1948–49; Lectr. in Physics, Dalhousie Univ., 1949–52; Asst. Prof. 1952–57; Assoc. Prof. 1957–64; Prof. 1964–66; Dir. Geophysics Div., N.S. Research Foundation, 1949–66, Vice Pres. 1966–68; Acting Dir., Dalhousie Inst. of Oceanography, 1964–65; Pres., Nova Scotia Research Foundation Corp. 1968–84 (mem. Bd. of Dir. 1984– ;); served with RCN 1942–45; rank Lieut.; author of numerous papers for learned journs.; Fellow Roy. Soc. of Can.; mem. Soc. Exploration Geophysicists; Am. Geophys. Union; Candn. Assn. Physicists; Can. Inst. Mining and Metall.; N.S. Inst. Science; Presbyterian; recreations: golf, tennis; Home: 6470 Coburg Rd., Halifax, N.S. B3H 2A7.

**BLANCHARD, The Hon. Mr. Justice Jacques,** B.A., L.Ped., B.Hist., L.L.L., C.R., Ph.D.(H); judge; b. Chandler, Que. 5 March 1936; s. Georges-Etienne and Cécile (Boucher) B.; e. Collége Ste. Anne B.A. 1956; Laval Univ. B.Ped. 1962, B.Hist. 1963, L.Ped. 1967; Ottawa Univ. L.L.L. 1967; Ste. Anne Univ. Ph.D. (Honoris causa) 1988; m. Nicole d. Jos. Fortin 19 Aug. 1961; children: Josée, Nathalie, Sophie, Jacques Jr.; JUDGE, SUPERIOR COURT OF QUE. 1987– ; Teacher, Que. City Schools 1962–66, 1968–70; Laval Univ. 1974–78; Office in Quebec City 1968–84; Blanchard, Gaulin & Assoc. 1979–82; Blanchard, Fontaine & Assoc. 1983–87; Mem., Assn. des Pedagogues Admin. du Qué.; Assoc. des Prof. du Qué.; Mem., Candn. Judges Conf.; Candn. Inst. for the Admin. of Justice; Bd. of Dir., Symphony Orch. of Que.; Garrison Club of Que.; Villa Bagatelle Found.; Laval Hosp. Found.; Vice-Pres., Kiwanis Club; Bd. of Dir., Air Canada 1984–87; numerous past extve. positions; Home: 1430, de Godefroy, Sillery, Que. G1T 2E4; Office: 300, boul. Jean Lesage, Rm. R-317, Quebec City, Que. G1K 8K6.

**BLANCHET, Madeleine,** md., M.Sc.; executif du gouvernement; née Québec 26 avril 1934; f. Roméo et Lucie (Samson) Blanchet; é. Laval, md.; Harvard, M.Sc.; ép. Pierre f. Bernard et Georgette Cazalis 11 août 1972; enfants: Vincent, Catherine; VICE-PRÉSIDENTE DU FORUM POUR LE PLEIN-EMPLOI 1992– ; Dir. méd. du Serv. de santé d'Hochelaga (Montréal) 1963–66; Cons. en épidémiologie à la Comn. d'enquête sur la santé et le bien-être social du Qué. 1970–71; Coord. pour le Qué. de l'enquête Nutrition-Can. 1971–72; Chef du Service des études épidémiologiques du min. des Affaires sociales du Qué. 1972–79; Présidente du conseil des affaires sociales du gouv. du Qué. 1980–92; Mem. du Conseil nat. de la statistique, Statistique Can. 1986– ; du Conseil sci. de l'Inst. de rech. en santé et sécurité au travail 1987–92; de la Soc. royale du Can. 1989– ; co-auteur: 'La périnatalité' 1973, 'Une politique québécoise en matière de nutrition' 1977; editeur: 'Objectif: Santé,' 'Dénatalité: des solutions' 1988, 'Deux Québec dans un' 1989; 'Agir Ensemble' 1990; loisirs: Ski de fond, yoga; résidence: 1264, Du Moulin, St-Nicolas (Qué.) G0S 2Z0; bureau: 1126, chemin St-Louis, Sillery, (Qué.) G1S 1E5.

**BLANCHETTE, Manon,** B.F.A., M.A.; museum curator; b. Montréal, Qué. 1 Oct. 1952; s. René and Gabrielle (Malouin) B.; e. Concordia Univ. B.F.A. 1976; Univ. of Montréal M.A. 1981; DIRECTOR OF COMMUNICATIONS AND MARKETING, MUSÉE D'ART CONTEMPORAIN DE MONTRÉAL 1983– ; Curator of Edn., Musée d'art contemp. 1977–78; Curator 1980–83; Dir., Soc. des Artistes en arts visuels 1979–80; worldwide travel for rsch. 1983–84; Univ. du Qué. at Chicoutimi 1984–85; Curator, Walter Phillips Gallery, Alta. 1985–86; Chief Curator, Musée d'Art Contemporain de Montréal 1986–91; Head of Cultural Services, Candn. Embassy, Paris 1991–92; Mem., Internat. Assn. of Art Critics; Collaborator, Magazine Vie des Arts and Vanguard; author: 'Tom Sherman' 1982, 'Ulysse Comtois,' 'Colonnes de sables,' 'Speak White' 1983, 'Resistance or Submission' 1986, 'Ken Lum' 1988, 'Blickpunkte' (a German Exhbn.) and num. articles, specialized mags.; teacher, theory of art; Prés., Soc. d'esthètique du Qué. 19..–92; Bd. mem., Les Ballets Jazz de Montréal 19..–93; Pro Musica; Orchestre Metropolitain 19..–93; Centre d'Art de St. Adèle 19..–93; Société de Musique contemporaine; Centre de Musique Canadienne; decorated Chevalier de l'Ordre des Arts et Lettres 1992; Home: 3430 Peel St., Apt. 6A, Montreal, Que. H3A 3K8; Office: 185 St. Catherine St. W., Montreal, Que. H2X 1Z8.

**BLANEY, John (Jack) Patrick,** Ed.D.; educator; b. Vancouver, B.C. 24 Feb. 1937; s. Patrick Bramhill and Helen Jane (McNaught) B.; e. Univ. of B.C. B.Ed. 1960, M.Ed. 1965; Univ. of California Ed.D. 1970; m. Shirley, d. Gilbert and Gwendolyn Fraser, 8 May 1959; children: Patrick Harvey, Erin Lea Burke; VICE-PRESIDENT FOR HARBOUR CENTRE AND EXTERNAL RELATIONS, SIMON FRASER UNIVERSITY; High Sch. teacher, Osoyoos, B.C. 1960–61; Univ. of B.C. Extension Dept.: Dir. Study-Discussion Program in the Liberal Arts 1962–63, Dir. Educ.-Extension Program 1963–66, Asst. Dir. 1966–67; Univ. of B.C. Centre for Cont. Educ.: Assoc. Dir. 1967–74; Simon Fraser Univ.: Dean of Cont. Studies 1974–84, Vice-Pres. Univ. Devel. 1981–87; Exec. and Pres. Can. Assn. for Univ. Cont. Educ. 1980–81; mem., B.C. Pub. Service Comn. on Sr. Mgmt. Training; Prov. Comn. on Univ. Progs. in Nonmetrop. Areas; consultant to univs. and Alta. Human Resources Rsch. Counc.; Gov., Vancouver Museum and Planetarium 1978–81; Dir., Vancouver Academy of Music 1984–85; Asia Pacific Festival 1984–86; Leon and Thea Koerner Foundn. 1986– ; Vancouver Bd. of Trade 1990–91; KCTS/Channel 9 Public Television 1986–91; Lambda Alpha Internat. 1989– ; Vancouver Police Board 1992– ; membership of other boards and cttes.; various external teaching assignments; mem. of American Educ. Rsch. Assn., Can. Assn. for Adult Educ., Centre for Arts, Science and Technol.; Outstanding Adult Educator Award, Pacific Assn. for Cont. Educ. 1983; Hon. Life Mem., Candn. Assn. for Univ. Cont. Educ.; Distinguished Leadership Award, President's Club, Simon Fraser Univ. 1989; Consulting Ed. and Prev. Ed.of Jour. of Can. Assn. for Univ. Cont. Educ.; author and co-author of numerous scholarly books and articles about cont. educ., mgmt. & leadership; recreations: reading, hiking; Home: 1851 West 36th Ave., Vancouver, B.C. V6M 1K6; Office: Simon Fraser University, Burnaby, B.C. V5A 1S6.

**BLANK, Harry,** Q.C., B.C.L., B.Sc.; advocate; b. Montreal, P.Q. 24 May 1925; s. Udel and Molly (Zinman) B.; e. Baron Byng High Sch., Montreal, (Grad. 1941); McGill Univ., B.Sc. 1947, B.C.L. 1950; m. 2ndly, Elaine Sloane, d. late Jacob Sloane, Boston, Mass., 18 Nov. 1967; children: David, Joyce, Gale, Caren, Andrew, Michael; called to the Bar of Que., 1950; served in 2nd World War; No. 2 Candn. Army Univ. Corp., 1943; Candn. Inf. Corps, 1944; overseas with North Shore Regt. (N.B.), 1944; wounded in action, 1945; Royal Montreal Regt., 1945; McGill C.O.T.C., 1946–50; el. to Nat. Assembly of Que. for Montreal-St. Louis, g.e. June 1960; re-el. 1962, 1966, 1970, 1973, 1976, 1981; Depy. Speaker, National Assembly 1971–76, Joint Chrmn. of Committees 1976–85; el. Extve. mem. Commonwealth Parl. Assn. representing Canadian region 1975–78, del. to Assn. conferences Australia 1970, Mauritius 1976, Ottawa 1977, Jamaica 1978, Fiji 1981, Nairobi 1983; also exec. meetings St. Lucia 1976, Sierra Leone 1977, Penang 1978; mem., Cercle de Juif Langue Française; Canadian Legion; B'Nai Brith; K. of P.; Liberal; Hebrew; recreations: flying (pte. pilots lic.), golf, fishing; Club: Montefiore; Home: 9 Redpath Row, Montreal, Que. H3G 1E6; Office: 1255 University St., Suite 1416, Montreal, P.Q. H3B 3X1.

**BLANSHARD, J. Barrie,** B.Sc., P.Eng.; business executive; b. England 7 Nov. 1930; s. William Frederick and Maud (Mayes) B.; e. Univ. of Toronto B.Sc. 1953; EXECUTIVE VICE-PRESIDENT, ST. MARY'S CEMENT CO.; Mem., Assn. of Profl. Engrs. of Ont.; Home: The 'Pinetree,' 1520 Pinetree Cres., Mississauga, Ont.; Office: 2200 Yonge St., Toronto, Ont. M4S 2C6.

**BLASER, Lorenz Paul,** B.Sc.; company executive (ret.); b. Markinch, Sask. 12 Feb. 1916; s. Paul and Barbara (Appenheimer) B.; e. Univ. of Sask., B.Sc. (Chem. Engn.); m. Marjorie Jean, d. late Herbert Orr, 4 July 1942; children: Barbara Lynn, Paula Jean, David Lorenz Paul; joined British American Oil Co.'s Calgary Refinery, 1939 and transf. to Moose Jaw Refinery as Asst. Chemist, 1941; subsequently apptd. Refinery Chemist in Moose Jaw; Resident Process Engr. at Moose Jaw, 1945; Head, Process Engn. Div., Toronto, 1949–52; Asst. Mgr., Moose Jaw Refinery, 1952–54; Chief Engr., Toronto, 1954–58; Gen. Mgr. of Mfg., 1958–63; Vice-Pres. (Mfg.) 1963–65; Vice Pres., Personnel, Trans., Crude Products Supply 1965; World Wide Coordinator of Refining, Gulf Oil Corp. 1966–67; returned to Canada as Senior Vice-Pres. 1967; Extve. Vice Pres. and Dir. 1976; Pres. Gulf Canada Products Co. 1979–81; Retired 1981; mem., Ont. Assn. Prof. Engrs.; United Church; recreations: golf, gardening; Clubs: Donalda; Granite; Home: 605 – 225 The Donway West, Don Mills, Ont. M3B 2V7.

**BLATHERWICK, Francis John,** C.St.J., C.D., M.D., F.R.C.P.(C); physician; b. Winnipeg, Man. 11 Sept. 1944; s. Francis Earl and Vicci (Skibinski) B.; e. Univ. of Alta. B.Sc. 1969, M.D. 1969 (Gold Medals in Surg. & Med.); Univ. of Toronto D.P.H. 1975 (Fraser Medal); m. Carol, M.D. d. George and Dorothy Dann 26 August 1967; three s. James Edward, David Allan, Douglas Stephen; MED. HEALTH OFFR. CITY OF VANCOUVER 1984– ; Prin. Med. Offr. Naval Reserve HMCS Discovery 1971– , rank Surg. Commdr.; Clin. Prof. Univ. of B.C. 1993– , Clin. Prof. (UBC) 1976– ; Asst. Med. Health Offr. Vancouver 1971–74; Med. Health Offr. Simon Fraser Health Unit 1975–84; served with Gov. Gen.'s Foot Guards 1961–62, RCAF 1963–69, RCAMC 1970; Prov. Comnr. (B.C.) St. John Ambulance 1987–90; author 'Aircraft on Display in Canada' 1975; 'Canadian Airline Histories' 1977; 'DeHavilland Canada – Buffalo, Dash 7, Twin Otter and ST27' 1978; 'History of Public Health in British Columbia' 1980; 'Canadian Bravery Decorations' 1983; 'Canadian Orders Decorations and Medals' 1985 (3rd ed.); 'A History of Airlines in Canada' 1989; 'Royal Canadian Air Force Honours and Awards 1920–1968' 1991; '1000 Brave Canadians' 1991; 'Royal Canadian Navy Honours and Awards 1910–1968'; 'Canadian Army Honours and Awards 1902-1968'; Hon. Mem., Candn. Inst. of Public Health Inspectors; Pres., Defence Med. Assoc. of Can. 1988–89; Vice Pres., Canada NATO Reserve Med. Offrs. Assoc. (CIOMR) 1992– ; rec'd Merit Award, Candn. Assoc. of Municipal Administrators 1988; President's Award, Candn. Public Health Assoc., B.C. Br. 1988; Commander, Order of St. John 1989; awarded Commemorative Medal for 125th Anniversary of Candn. Confederation; recreations: hockey, writing, military medals; Office: 1060 West 8th Ave., Vancouver, B.C. V6H 1C4.

**BLEACKLEY, Lachlan M.,** B.A.; executive; b. Winnipeg, Man. 17 June 1934; s. Lachlan Mackinnon and Gudrun Sigridur (Eggertson) B.; e. Univ. of W. Ont., B.A. (Hon. Bus. Admin.) 1959; m. Jael d. Camilo and Lola Escobar 29 Sept. 1983; children: Pamela, Patricia, Lachlan, Michael; Pres., C.E.O. & Dir., Northwest Digital Ltd. 1988–.; Acct. Rep., ICT (Can.) Ltd. 1959–62; Mktg. Mgr., IBM Can. Ltd. 1962–69; Pres., Cybermedix Ltd. 1970–79; Owner-Operator, Scientific Alliance Labs Calif. 1979–82; Pres., Cybermedix Health Services Ltd. 1982–87; Pres., Ont. Assn. of Med. Labs. 1984–87 (Dir. 1974–87); Pres. & Dir., Assn. des Labs. Médicaux Privés du Qué. 1986–87; Club: Royal Candn. Mil. Inst. (Toronto); Home: 68 – 4100 Salish Dr., Vancouver, B.C. V6N 3M2.

**BLENKARN, Donald A.,** Q.C., M.P., LL.B.; lawyer; former politician; b. Toronto, Ont. 17 June 1930; s. Alec Charles and Marjory May (Odell) B.; e. Runnymede Coll. Inst.; Univ. of Toronto Law Sch. LL.B. 1952; m. Marguerite d. late Harry and late Margaret Wilkinson 16 July 1955; children: Bruce, Brenda, Brian; called to Bar of B.C. 1953, Ont. 1953; cr. Q.C. 1969; formerly Sr. Partner, Blenkarn, Roche Associates; Secy.-Treas. M.A. Henry Ltd. Dundas, Ont.; Timagami Financial Services, Mississauga; Hurontario Mgmt. Services, Mississauga; el. to H. of C. for Mississauga South g.e. 1972, def. 1974, re-el. 1979, 1980, 1984, 1988; el. Chrmn. of H. of C. Standing Ctte. on Finance and Economic Affairs Nov. 1984; re-el. Chrmn., Standing Ctte. on Finance Apr. 1989, resigned Apr. 1991; Clubs: Mississauga Golf and Country; Port Credit Yacht; Credit Valley Golf and Country.

**BLEY, Paul;** pianist; composer; b. Montreal, Que. 10 Nov. 1932; s. Joseph and Betty (Marcovitch) B.; e. Que. Conserv.; McGill Sch. of Music (rec'd jr. dipl. at age 11); Juilliard Sch. of Music; began study of violin at 5 yrs., piano at 8 yrs.; played N.Y. City clubs, midwestern and Cal. coll. concerts and nightclubs in Los Angeles (incl. a group with Ornette Coleman and Don Cherry), 1954–60; toured Germany with Jimmy Guiffre 'Three,' 1960 and Japan with S. Rollins, 1963; re-formed own trio for Bard Coll. Concert, 1964; mem. Jazz Composers Guild 1964–65; Trio concerts at Museum of Modern Art and Newport Jazz Festival, 1965; 1st European tour with own trio, 1965, 2nd tour 1966; won 2nd place in Jazz & Pop Mag. Internat. Critics Poll, 1965 and 1969 (Pianists category); has recorded over 30 L.P.s 1953–72; 1st Moog Synthesizer Soloist Concert, Philharmonic Hall, N.Y. 1969; 4 European tours with Synthesizer Show, 1970–71; 6 European solo piano tours 1972–74; formed IAI Records & Videotapes 1975; toured Europe, solo piano concerts 1978, 1979; feature film 'Imagine the Sound' 1981; semi-annual European Tours 1982–94; won Prix de Jazz, Paris, France 1988; 1988 annual NYC appearances S. Basil; 1989 tour C. Haden & P. Motian; recorded 50th CD as leader 1990; 4 night Retrospective, Montreal Jazz Festival 1992; piano improvisation teacher, New England Conservatory 1992– ; solo piano tour of Israel 1993; Office: IAI Records, P.O. Box 4, 33 Lancaster St., Cherry Valley, New York 13320.

**BLICKER, Seymour,** B.A.; writer; b. Montreal, Que. 12 Feb. 1940; s. Joseph and Jennie (Forman) B.; e. Loyola Coll. of Montreal B.A. 1962; m. Susan Wanda d. Phillip and Florence Colman 13 June 1963; children: Andrea, Jason, Ari, Jamie; Sr. Fellowship, Can. Counc. 1974; Ont. Arts Counc. Award 1977; Lapitsky Found. Award; Mem., P.E.N. Internat. (Candn. Ctr.); Writers Guild of Am., West, Inc.; Dramatists Guild; ACTRA; Authors League of Am.; author: 'Blues Chased a Rabbit' 1969, 'Shmucks' 1972, 'The Last Collection' 1976 (novels); has written extensively for film & TV in the U.S. & Can., as well as for profl. stage; Stage plays including 'Up Your Alley,' and 'Never Judge A Book By Its Cover' produced in Canada, U.S.A. and Europe; Special Lecturer in Creative Writing, Concordia Univ., Montreal 1978–90; Home: 804 - 240 Oriole Parkway, Toronto, Ont. M5P 2H1.

**BLICKSTEAD, John Richard,** B.Com., M.B.A.; business executive; b. Trois Rivières, Qué. 10 Feb. 1955; e. Carleton Univ. B.Com. 1975; Univ. of Toronto M.B.A. 1976; m. Martha Lee 1980; two s. Michael, John; Exec. Vice Pres. Candn. Operations Peoples Jewellers Ltd. and Pres. Mappins Jewellers 1991– ; Dir. Cantrex Corp.; Bus. Devel. Mgr. Bell Canada 1977–79; Sr. Cons. Hickling Johnston Ltd. 1979–82; Mktg. Mgr. present Co. 1982, Mappins 1983, Mdse. Mgr. Peoples Div. 1986, Sr. Vice Pres. Mdse. & Operations 1987, Sr. Vice Pres. Can. 1990; Dir. Royal Ont. Museum Communications Ctte.; Home: 107 Woodridge Lane, Rogers, Arkansas 72756.

**BLISHEN, Bernard Russell,** M.A.; retired university professor; b. Harleston, Eng. 21 Sept. 1919; s. Henry Charles Adolphus and Lilly Anne (Shipp) B.; came to Can. 1935; e. McGill Univ., B.A. 1949, M.A. 1950; Columbia Univ. 1955–56; m. Ruth Edith, d. Ernest Popkin, 21 May 1947; children; Jennifer, Joan, Susan, Peter; Chief Institutions Sec., Dom. Bureau of Stat. 1950–56; Lect., Univ. of Brit. Columbia, 1956–60; Asst. Prof. 1961; Research Dir., Royal Comn. on Health Services, 1961–64; Assoc. Prof., Trent Univ. 1964–66; Prof. and Chrmn., Dept. of Sociology, 1966–67; Dean of Grad. Studies 1967–73; Dir., Inst. for Behavioural Research, York Univ. 1974–78; Prof., Dept. of Sociology 1974–89; Professor Emeritus and Senior Scholar; served in 2nd World War, R.C.N. 1939–45; received Columbia University Fellowship; Laidlaw Fellowship; Nuffield Travelling Fellowship; Soc. Sci. and Humanities Research Council Leave Fellowship; member, Canadian Sociol. & Anthrop. Assn. (Pres. 1977–78); co-ed. 'Canadian Society' 1964; author 'Doctors & Doctrines' 1969; 'Doctors in Canada: The Changing World of Medical Practice' 1991; co-author 'Does Money Matter' 1973; 'Stations & Callings' 1982; plus articles in learned journals; Anglican; recreation: sailing; Home: 531 Hunter St. W., Peterborough, Ont. K9H 2M9; Office: York University, Downsview, Ont. M3J 1P3.

**BLISS, Harvey John,** LL.B., Q.C.; lawyer; b. Toronto, Ont. 6 Oct. 1933; s. Henry and Ida (Hoffman) B.; e. Jarvis Coll. Inst. Toronto; Univ. of Toronto B.Com. 1955; LL.B. 1958; m. Eileen May d. Joseph Sullivan 4 Feb 1966; two d. Kimberley Anne (dec.), Deborah Leigh; PROPRIETOR, BLISS & ASSOCIATES 1973– ; called to Bar of Ont. 1960; cr. Q.C. 1978; Certified by L.S.U.C. as specialist in civil litigation; Partner, Levinter, Whitelaw, Dryden, Bliss & Hart 1965–73; mem. Nat. Council on Adm. of Justice in Can., Chrmn. 1975–78, Vice Chrmn. 1978–82; Dir. Candn. Inst. for Adm. Justice 1977–85, Vice-Pres. 1980–85; mem. Gov. Council Candn. Sec., Internat. Comn. Jurists 1974–86, Vice-Pres. 1980–81, 1983–86; Instr. in Trial Practice, Osgoode Hall Law Sch. York Univ. 1970–76; Instr. in Civil Procedure, Bar Admission Course 1962–71; mem. Candn. Bar Assn. (Nat. Council 1968–90, Nat. Exec. 1984–86, Vice Pres., Ont Br. 1986–87, Pres. 1987–88); Co. York Law Assn.; Medico-Legal Soc. Toronto; Advocates' Soc. Toronto; Assoc. des Juristes d'Expression Française de l'Ontario; Internat. Bar Assn.; Law Soc. Upper Can.; Sigma Alpha Mu (Pres. 1954–55); recreations: collecting Quimper faïence, growing bonsai, collecting wine, travel, languages; Home: 19 Chelford Rd., Don Mills, Ont. M3B 2E4; Office: 133 Richmond St. W., Suite 402, Toronto, Ont. M5H 2L3.

**BLISS, John William Michael,** Ph.D., F.R.S.C.; historian; author; b. Leamington, Ont. 18 Jan. 1941; s. Quartus and Anne Lavelle (Crow) B.; e. Kingsville Pub. Sch. and Dist. High Sch.; Univ. of Toronto B.A. 1962, M.A. 1966, Ph.D. 1972; m. Elizabeth Jane d. Robert Haslam, Harrow, Ont. 29 June 1963; children: James, Laura, Sara; PROF. OF HISTORY, UNIV. OF TORONTO; Teaching Asst. Harvard Univ. 1967–68; mem. Gov. Council Univ. of Toronto 1975–78; author 'A Living Profit: Studies in the Social History of Canadian Business 1883–1911' 1974; 'A Canadian Millionaire: The Life and Business Times of Sir Joseph Flavelle, Bart.' 1978 (F.-X. Garneau Medal and Sir John A. Macdonald Prize, Candn. Hist. Assn.; Univ. of B.C. Medal Candn. Biog.; City of Toronto Book Award; Toronto Hist. Bd. Award of Merit); 'The Discovery of Insulin' 1982 (City of Toronto Book Award; Jason Hannah Medal, Royal Soc. of Can.; Wm. H. Welch Medal, Am. Assoc. for the History of Medicine); 'Banting: A. Biography' 1984; 'Northern Enterprise: Five Centuries of Canadian Business' 1987 (National Business Book Award); 'Plague: A Story of Smallpox in Montreal' 1991; numerous scholarly and popular articles maj. Candn. journs. and newspapers (recipient National Magazine Awards, 1981, 1982); Fellow, Royal Society of Canada (el. 1984; J.B. Tyrell Medal 1988); City of Toronto Award of Merit 1990; Dir., Univ. of Toronto Press; Home: 314 Bessborough Dr., Toronto, Ont. M4G 3L1; Office: History Dept, Univ. of Toronto, Toronto, Ont. M5S 1A1.

**BLISSETT, William Frank,** M.A., Ph.D., F.R.S.C.; educator; b. East End, Sask. 11 Oct. 1921; s. Ralph Richardson and Gladys Anne (Jones) B.; e. Victoria High Sch. 1939; Victoria (B.C.) Coll. 1941; Univ. of B.C., B.A. 1943; Univ. of Toronto M.A. 1946, Ph.D. 1950; PROFESSOR EMERITUS, UNIV. OF TORONTO 1987– ; Teaching Asst., Lectr. and Instr. in Eng. Univ. of Toronto 1946–50; Assoc. Prof. of Eng. Univ. of Sask. 1950–57; Prof. 1957–60; Prof. and Head of English, Huron Coll. London, Ont. 1960–65; Prof. of English, Univ. Coll., Univ. of Toronto 1965–87; Ed. 'University of Toronto Quarterly' 1965–76; 'Reid MacCallum: Imitation and Design' 1953; 'Editing Illustrated Books' 1980; co-ed. 'A Celebration of Ben Jonson' 1972; 'The Spenser Encyclopedia' 1990; author: 'The Long Conversation: A Memoir of David Jones' 1981; various articles Shakespeare, Ben Jonson, Spenser, David Jones, lit. Wagnerism; H.B. de Groot and Alexander Leggatt, ed., 'Craft and Tradition: Essays in Honour of William Blissett' (contains a checklist of principal writings of W.B.) 1990; Hon. Fellow Huron Coll. 1966; mem. Assn. Candn. Univ. Teachers Eng.; Candn. Fed. for Humanities 1980–84; Toronto Wagner Soc.; Anglican; Home: 36 Castle Frank Rd., Apt. 212, Toronto, Ont. M4W 2Z7; Office: University College, University of Toronto; Toronto, Ont. M5S 1A1.

**BLOCK, Dr. Henry J.,** R.I.B.C., Doctorate of Humanities; investor; b. Saskatchewan 28 May 1926; s. John (Henry) and Helen M. (Sawatzky) B.; e. Real Inst. of B.C.; Hon. Doct. Trinity Univ. Western Canada; m. Laura d. Lena Watson 16 Aug. 1984; 7 children; CHAIRMAN, BRITISH GROUP LTD. 1980– ; Sales Mgr., American Motors (Canada) 1950–55; Pres., Block Bros. Industries Ltd. 1955–80; Past Mem., Real Council of B.C.; Econ. Council for the Govt. of B.C.; Dir., Campus Crusade for Christ (Canada); Leadership Ministries (Canada); international speaker; Doctorate of Humanities, Trinity Western Univ.; recreations: golf, farming; Home: 1287 – 133 A Ave., Surrey, B.C. V4A 4C4; Office: 15595 – 24 Ave., Surrey, B.C. V4A 2J4.

**BLOCK, Sheila R.,** B.A., LL.B.; lawyer; b. Toronto, Ont. 18 Oct. 1947; d. Aaron Elliott and Muriel Emilia (Cromb) Sulman; e. Univ. of Toronto 1965–68; Carleton Univ. B.A. (Hons.) 1969; Univ. of Ottawa LL.B. 1972, gold medallist; children: Emily, Mary Ellen, Daniel; PARTNER, TORY TORY DESLAURIERS & BINNINGTON; Chair, Executive Ctte. 1989–93; practising civil litgation at all levels of courts & before admin. tribunals; Faculty, Nat. Inst. for Trial Advocacy; Fellow, Am. Coll. of Trial Lawyers; Internat. Soc. of Barristers; Vice-Pres. & Dir., Trillium Found.; Mem., Law Soc. of U.C.; The Advocates' Soc.; Candn. Bar Assn.; The Private Court; Dir., Candn. Civil Liberties Assn.; Dir., Canadian Club; Office: Box 270, #3000, Toronto-Dominion Centre, Toronto, Ont. M5K 1N2.

**BLOCK, Walter Edward,** Ph.D.; economist; b. New York City, N.Y. 21 Aug. 1941; s. Abe and Ruth (Peps) B.; e. Columbia Univ. Ph.D. 1972; m. Marybeth d. Robert and Elinor Zimmer 23 May 1976; children: Matthew, Hannah; ASSOC. PROF., ECONOMICS DEPT., COLLEGE OF THE HOLY CROSS 1991– ; Instr. in Econ. Stony Brook, S.U.N.Y. 1967–68; Instr., Asst. Prof. of Econ. Rutgers Univ. 1968–71, 1975–79; Sr. Rsch. Fellow, The Fraser Inst. 1979–91; Asst. Prof. of Econ. Baruch Coll. C.U.N.Y. 1971–74; Visiting Fellow, The Fraser Inst. 1979; freelance cons. econ. Tax Found., Bus. Week Mag., Community Housing Improvement Prog., Coalition to Save New York 1974–76; N.Y. State Regents Scholar Brooklyn Coll. 1959–64; Earhart Fellow Columbia Univ. 1966–68; Rsc. Fellow Cato Inst. 1977–78, Adjunct Scholar 1982– ; Adjunct Scholar Ludwig von Mises Inst. Auburn Univ. 1983– ; editor: 'Zoning: Its Costs and Relevance' 1980; 'Rent Control: Myths and Realities' 1981; 'Discrimination, Affirmative Action and Equal Opportunity' 1982; 'Taxation: An International Perspective' 1984; 'Theology, Third World Development, and Economic Justice' 1985; 'Morality of the Market: Religious and Economic Perspectives' 1985; 'Reaction: The New Combines Investigation Act' 1986; 'Religion, Economics and Social Thought' 1986; 'Man, Economy and Liberty' 1988; 'Economics and the Environment: A Reconciliation' 1990; 'Economic Freedom: Toward a Theory of Measurement' 1991; 'Breaking the Shackles: The Economics of Deregulation' 1991; author: 'Defending the Undefendable' 1976; 'Amending the Combines Investigation Act' 1982; 'Focus on Economics and the Canadian Bishops' 1983; 'Focus on Employment Equity: A Critique of the Abella Royal Commission on Equality in Employment' 1985; 'The U.S. Bishops and their Critics: An Economic and Ethical Perspective' 1986; 'Lexicon of Economic Thought' 1988; mem., Am. Economic Assn.; Western Economic Assn.; B.C. Assn. of Professional Economists; Candn. Economic Assn.; Candn. Assn. for Business Economics; Am. Law and Economics Assn.; recreations: handball, swimming, karate; Office: Worcester MA 01610.

**BLODGETT, Edward Dickinson,** Ph.D., F.R.S.C.; university professor/writer; b. Philadelphia, U.S.A. 26 Feb. 1935; Candn. citizen; s. Edward Dickinson and Grace Boyden (Lindabury) B.; e. Amherst Coll. B.A. 1956; Univ. of Minn. M.A. 1961; Rutgers Univ. Ph.D. 1969; m. Irena Kamila (Krupičkova); children: Gunnar, Astrid, Kirstin; PROFESSOR, UNIV. OF ALTA. 1975– ; Res. Master in English, Girard Coll. 1958; T.A., Univ. of Minn. 1958–61; Instr. in French, Inst. for Am. Univ., Aix-en-Provence (France) 1962–63; Instr. in English, Gen. Lit. & Classics, Rutgers Univ. & Douglass Coll. 1963–66; Asst. & Assoc. Prof., Univ. of Alta. 1966–74, Chair, Comparative Lit. and Film Studies 1975–85 and 1991–93; Vis. Prof., Univ. de Sherbrooke 1979; Freie Univ. Berlin 1988; Assoc. Ed., 'Canadian Review of Comparative Literature' 1974– ; Ed. Bd., 'Studies in Canadian Literature'; Extve. Counc., The Calgary Inst. for the Humanities 1977–88; other past extve. posts; Delta Phi Lamda; Lamda Alpha Psi; F.R.S.C.; author: 'Take Away the Names' 1975, 'Sounding' 1977, 'Beast Gate' 1980, 'Arché/Elegies' 1983, 'Musical Offering' 1986, 'Da Capo' 1990 (poetry); 'Configuration' 1982, 'Alice Munro' 1988 (lit. criticism); num. articles, reviews, public lectures, conferences; co-translator: 'The Love Songs of the Carmina Burana' 1987; recreations: lute-playing, squash, back-packing; Home: 11424–56 Ave., Edmonton, Alta. T6H 0Y3; Office: Edmonton, Alta. T6G 2E6.

**BLOEDEL, Prentice;** lumber company executive; b. Bellingham, Wash. 13 Aug. 1900; s. Julius H. and Mina (Prentice) B.; e. Yale Univ., A.B. 1921; m. Virginia L. Merrill, 16 Aug. 1927; children; Virginia P.(Mrs. Charles B. Wright, Jr.), Eulalie M. (Mrs. Ernst Schneider); Instr. Thatcher Sch. Ojai, Cal., 1921–22; engaged in lumber business, Bellingham, 1923–28; with Bloedel, Stewart & Welch Ltd., Vancouver, B.C., 1929–51, Pres. 1942–51; Vice Chrmn., MacMillan & Bloedel Ltd., Vancouver, 1951–56, Dir., 1951–59; Dir., MacMillan, Bloedel & Powell River Ltd., 1956–65; Dir., MacMillan Bloedel Ltd., 1966–72, National Bank of Commerce (Seattle) 1956–73; The Bank of Montreal, 1951–53; Marine Bancorporation, 1963–73; mem., Adv. Comte., Toronto General Trusts Corp., 1947–63; B.C. Council of Boy Scouts (mem. 1942–47, Pres. 1947–48); made Freeman of City of Vancouver March 1971; Episcopalian; Clubs: Vancouver; University and Rainièr (Seattle, Wash.); Address: 1223 Spring St., Seattle, Washington 98104.

**BLOEMEN, Peter Jozef Marie**; consultant; b. Tilburg, The Netherlands 17 October 1930; s. Johan F. and Constantia J. (Loeff) B.; e. Gymnasium B 1949; Nijenrode, Netherlands Sch. of Bus. 1951; m. Dorine d. Eugene and Dorothea van de Weijer 2 Mar. 1957; children: Peter-Paul, Maarten, Véronique, Marie-Charlotte; various mngt. functions overseas branches, Algemene Bank Nederland N.V. (and its predecessor Nederlandsche Handel Maatschappij N.V.) 1951–69; Pres., Trucena Investments Limited 1969–89; Dir., Halifax Insur. Co.; ING Canada Corp.; Le Groupe Commerce Compagnie d'Assurance; NN Life Insur. Co. of Canada; Mem., Bd. of Gov., Appleby Coll.; Roman Catholic; recreations: art, reading, golf, sailing, skiing; clubs: The National, The Goodwood, The Toronto Golf, The Oakville; Home: 50 Walker St., Oakville, Ont. L6K 1A3; Office: P.O. Box 523, Suite 4320, Canada Trust Tower, BCE Place, 161 Bay St., Toronto, Ont. M5J 2S1.

**BLOHM, Hans-Ludwig,** C.P.A., M.P.A.; photographer; b. Rendsburg, Germany 12 Nov. 1927; s. Hans Jakob and Auguste Katharine Elise (Hansen) B.; e. Altstadter Volksschule; Christian Timm Mittelschule Rendsburg; CPA (Craftsman of Photographic Arts) 1972; MPA (Master of Photographic Arts) 1974; m. Ingeborg d. Rudolf and Kathe Ramm 2 Nov. 1956; children: Norman, Heike, Sigrid; PRIN. foto blohm – associates ltd. 1970– ; came to Can. 1956, Master Carpenter 1955 in Germany; various occupations 1956–63; carpenter 1956–58; darkroom technician and manager 1958–63; Tech., Photog. and Partner, Photo Features Ltd. 1963–66; freelance cameraman CBC 1964–66; freelance photog. since 1966; participant Expo 67, numerous Nat. Film Bd. books, publs. and audio visual progs.; Art Expo 80, New York; frequent lectr.; solo exhns. incl. Ottawa, Montréal, Toronto; solo internat. travelling exhns.: 'From Bonavista to Vancouver Island,' 'Serendipity' and 'Pebbles to Computers' for External Affairs Canada, travelling in many European countries, India, Pakistan, various S.E. Asian countries, Japan, Australia, South and Central America, U.S.A., China (1989) and Russia (1990); author 'The Beauty of Ontario,' 'The Beauty of British Columbia,' 'The Beauty of Québec,' 'The Beauty of the Maritimes' 1983–84; 'Alaska' 1985; co-author 'Eggcarton Zoo' 1986; 'Sciencescape' 1986; 'Pebbles to Computers' 1986 (also 1987 Calendar and documentary subject TV Ont.); 'Eggcarton Zoo II' fall 1989; served with German Navy 1943–45; recreations: photography, gardening; Clubs: German-Candn. Cong.; Nat. Press Club; Address: 64 Avonlea Rd., Nepean, Ont. K2G 0J5.

**BLOM, Nicolaas August,** B.A., LL.B.; solicitor; b. Wassenaar, Holland 16 Nov. 1936; s. Jan and Jacoba L.D. (Veth) B.; e. Port Moody (B.C.) High Sch. 1955; Univ. of B.C., B.A. 1959, LL.B. 1962; m. Marlene J. d. William and Vera Pearce 3 June 1967; two d. Kathleen, Nicole; ASSOCIATE COUNSEL, McCARTHY TÉTRAULT, Vancouver 1992; Dir. Pitt Polder Ltd.; called to bar of B.C. 1963; articled with law firm Ladner Downs becoming mem., Assoc. and Partner 1962–80; joined Grosvenor International Canada Limited as Gen. Mgr. 1980–85, Pres. 1985–89; Sr. Vice-Pres., Grosvenor International Holdings Ltd. 1990–91; Dir. and Vice-Pres., Urban Devel. Inst. Pacific Region 1986–89; President elect, Rotary Club of Vancouver 1993–94; mem. B.C. Bar Assn.; Club: The Vancouver; Home: 6340 Cedarhurst St., Vancouver, B.C. V6N 1J1; Office: 1300, 777 Dunsmuir St., Vancouver, B.C. V7Y 1K2.

**BLOMQVIST, Åke Gunnar,** B.Comm., Ph.D.; professor of economics; b. Norrtälje, Sweden 15 Sept. 1941; s. Stig G:son and Ingrid (Andersson) B.; e. Stockholm School of Economics B.Comm. 1964; Princeton Univ. Ph.D. 1971; m. Patricia Irene d. Arthur and Margaret Rusnell 14 Feb. 1991; children: Karen, Jennifer, Jeffrey, Meaghan, Gregory; PROFESSOR OF ECONOMICS, UNIVERSITY OF WESTERN ONTARIO 1981– ; Lecturer, U.W.O. 1968; Visiting Prof., Univ. of Ghana 1970–73; Inst. of Internat. Econ. Studies Stockholm 1979–80; Stockholm Sch. of Econ.; Applied Econ. Rsch. Centre Karachi; principal areas of teaching & research: econ. of devel. countries and econ. of health care & social policy; Consultant, CIDA, IDRC, World Bank, Govt. of Sweden, Consumer & Corp. Affairs Canada, Candn. Med. Assn., World Health Orgn., and others; has conducted rsch. & lectured in Nigeria, Ghana, Zimbabwe, Pakistan & India & several countries in Eur.; author: 'The Health Care Business' 1979, 'The Swedish Health Care System in International Perspective' 1990; editor: 'Limits to Care' forthcoming; co-author: 'Economics' 1983, '87, '90, '94; author/co-author of over 35 journal articles, reports and book chapters; recreations: reading, canoeing, fishing; Home: 80 Killarney Rd., London, Ont. N5X 2A9; Office: Econ. Dept., U.W.O., London, Ont. N6A 5C2.

**BLONDEAU, Gilles,** B.A., B.Com., F.S.A., F.I.C.A.; actuary and insurance executive; b. Quebec City, Que. 5 Oct. 1940; s. Cylien and Rose (Drolet) B.; e. Coll. des Jésuites (Garnier) 1958; Univ. Laval B.A. 1960, B.Com. 1963; Fellow Soc. of Actuaries and Cndn. Inst. of Actuaries 1967; children: Nathalie, Anabelle; CHRMN. AND C.E.O., GROUPE OPTIMUM INC. 1979– ; Chrmn., St. Lawrence Reassurance Co.; Optimum Re Insurance Co. (Texas); Vie Optimum (France); National Insurance Co.; Optimum Consultants & Actuaries; Synergie Informatique Inc.; Optimum Foncier Inc.; The British Columbia Insurance Co.; National Frontier Insurance Co.; St. Lawrence Financial Corp.; Dir., Domtar Inc.; Fonds des Professionnels; Compagnie Financière Martin-Maurel (Banque, France); joined Swiss Reinsurance Co. Zurich 1963–65; Vice Pres. Canadian Reassurance Co. Toronto 1965–69; Pres., Blondeau and Co. 1969–78; Optimum Group Inc. 1979–88; R. Catholic; Home: 3596 rue Principale, Dunham, Qué. J0E 1M0; Office: 425 ouest, boul. de Maisonneuve, Bureau 1700, Montréal, Qué. H3A 3G5.

**BLONDIN-ANDREW, Ethel D.,** M.P., B.Ed.; politician; b. Fort Norman, N.W.T. 25 Mar. 1951; d. Joseph Zaul and Mary Therese (Tatti) B.; e. Univ. of Alta. B.Ed. 1974; children: Troy, Tanya and Timothy Townsend; SECRETARY OF STATE (TRAINING & YOUTH), GOVT. OF CANADA 1993– ; M.P. FOR THE WESTERN ARCTIC 1988– ; teaching assignments: Tuktoyaktuk, Ft. Franklin, Ft. Providence 1974–81; Lang. Spec., Dept. of Edn., Yellownife 1981–84; Teacher, Univ. of Calgary & Arctic Coll. 1983; Mgr. then Acting Dir., Pub. Serv. Comn. of Can. 1984–86; Asst. Depy. Min., Culture & Commun., Yellowknife 1986–88; Bd. Mem., Arctic Inst. of N. Am.; Nat. Steering Ctte., Aboriginal Lang. Policy Devel.; Chairperson, Indigenous Lang. Dev. Rev. Ctte.; Counc., Ft. Providence Settlement Counc.; MLA award for Culture & Heritage Preservation (Elders Project) 1987; Hilroy Scholarship Award, R.C. Hill Char. Found. 1982; Govt. Serv. Award for 10 yrs. pub. serv. 1982; Outstanding Young Candn. Award 1978; Sr. Project Cons. & Proofreader: 'Nahecho Keh – Our Elders'; Home: 5105 – 53rd St., Yellowknife, N.W.T.; Office: Room 247, West Block, House of Commons, Ottawa, Ont. K1A 0A6.

**BLOOM, David Ronald,** B.Sc.Phm.; pharmacist; b. Toronto, Ont. 20 Apl. 1943; s. Samuel and Tillie B.; MacKenzie Coll. Inst. Toronto; Univ. of Toronto B.Sc.Phm. 1967; m. Molly d. Carl and Bea Rosenbloom 8 May 1966; children: Michael, Corinne; CHRMN. AND CHIEF EXEC. OFFR., SHOPPERS DRUG MART LTD. 1986– ; Dir., Shoppers Drug Mart Ltd.; Pharmaprix Ltée; Imasco Ltd.; Dir. Operations 1972, Vice Pres. Operations 1973, Exec. Vice Pres. Operations and Pres. Central Ont. & Man. Region, Pres. Top Drug Mart Ltd. 1982; Pres. & Chief Exec. Offr. Shoppers Drug Mart, Toronto 1983; Chrmn., Koffler Inst. of Pharmacy Mgmt., Univ. of Toronto; Past Chrmn. Retail Council Can.; mem., C.E.O. Organization; Candn. Jr. Chamber/Jaycees; Bd. of Dir., Mount Sinai Hosp. Toronto; Bd., Color Your World; Chrmn., Candn. Assoc. Chain Drug Stores; Ont. Pharmacists Assn.; Nat. Assn. of Chain Drug Stores (U.S.A.); Rho Pi Phi; recreations: tennis, boating, skiing; Club: Primrose; Home: Thornhill, Ont.; Office: 225 Yorkland Blvd., Willowdale, Ont. M2J 4Y7.

**BLOOM, Myer,** M.Sc., Ph.D., F.R.S.C., F.A.P.S.; physicist; educator; b. Montreal, Que. 7 Dec. 1928; s. late Israel and Leah (Ram) B.; e. Baron Byng High Sch. Montreal 1949; McGill Univ. B.Sc. 1949, M.Sc. 1950; Univ. of Ill. Ph.D. 1954; m. Margaret Patricia d. late Roy Franklin Holmes 29 May 1954; children: David, Margot; PROF. OF PHYSICS, UNIV. OF B.C. since 1963; Nat. Research Council Postdoctorate Fellow, Univ. of Leiden 1954–56; Asst. Prof. Univ. of B.C. 1957–60, Assoc. Prof. 1960–63; Visiting Prof. Harvard Univ. 1964–65; Univ. de Paris 1971–72, 1978–79, 1986; rec'd Alfred P. Sloan Fellowship 1961–65; Steacie Prize 1967; Biely Prize 1969; Candn. Assn. Phys. Gold Medal 1973; Izaak Walton Killam Mem. Scholarship 1978; Chrmn.'s Award for Career Achievement, Sci. Counc. of B.C. 1992; Fellow, Candn. Institute for Advanced Rsch. 1990– ; author numerous research and review articles on Nuclear Magnetic Resonance and its application to physics and biology; ; mem. Candn. Assn. Physicists; recreations: skiing, hiking, squash; Home: 5669 Kings Rd., Vancouver, B.C. V6T 1K9; Office: Vancouver, B.C. V6T 2A6.

**BLOOMBERG, Lawrence S.,** B.Comm., M.B.A., C.F.A.; securities/brokerage executive; b. Montreal, Que. 28 May 1942; s. Sol and Sylvia B.; e. Sir George Williams Univ., B.Comm. 1963; McGill Univ., M.B.A. 1965; C.F.A. 1970; m. Frances d. Florence and Albert Sheiner; children: Debra, Bonnie, Jonathon; PRES., C.E.O. & DIR., FIRST MARATHON INC. 1984– ; Dir., Cinram Ltd. and of several private companies; various mgmt. positions incl. Head of Rsch., Vice-Pres. & Dir., Institutional Equity Sales, Nesbitt Thomson and Co. 1965–75; Vice-Pres. & Dir., Inst. Equity Sales, Pitfield MacKay Ross 1975–79; Founding Mem., First Marathon Securities Ltd. 1979; Past Mem., Young President's Organization; Mem., XPO 1992– ; Mem., World President's Organization; Business Council on National Issues; C.D. Howe Institute; Mem. Bd. of Govs., Mount Sinai Hosp. (mem., Budget & Finance Ctte.) ; Baycrest Centre for Geriatric Care; Bd. of Trustees, Royal Ont. Museum (Chrmn., Finance Ctte.); Co-Chrmn., Toronto's 1994 United Jewish Appeal/Operation Exodus Campaign; has been involved in past United Way campaigns; Past Gov., Junior Achievement of Canada; Past Mem. Bd. of Govs., The Toronto Stock Exchange; Mem., Rector's Circle, Concordia Univ.; Founding Mem., Concordia's Faculty of Commerce and Admin. Business Advisory Ctte.; recreations: marathon running, golf; Office: The Exchange Tower, 2 First Canadian Place, Suite 3100, P.O. Box 21, Toronto, Ont. M5X 1J9.

**BLOOMFIELD, Arthur Irving,** M.A., Ph.D.; university professor; economist; b. Montreal, Que. 2 Oct. 1914 (U.S. citizen since 1945); s. Samuel and Hanna Mai (Brown) B.; e. McGill Univ., B.A. 1935, M.A. 1936; Univ. of Chicago, Ph.D. 1942; Hon. M.A., Univ. of Pennsylvania 1971; Hon. Doctor in Economics, Han Yang Univ., Seoul, Korea, 1987; m. Dorothy Reese 18 Jan. 1987; EMERITUS PROF. OF ECON., UNIV. OF PENNSYLVANIA 1985– ; (Prof. of Econ. there 1958–85); Econ., Fed. Reserve Bank of N.Y., 1942–58 (Sr. Econ. and Offr. 1953–58); Consultant to Foreign Econ. Adm. of U.S. Govt. 1944–45; Adviser to Bank of Korea and Korean Ministry of Finance 1949–50; Adviser to U.N. Korean Reconstr. Agency in Korea, 1951–52; Econ. Consultant to U.S. Govt. agencies in Vietnam, Cambodia and Laos, 1953, 1954, Korea 1956, 1960 and Congo/Zaire 1966, 1967, 1968; Consultant to Ford Foundation in Malaysia 1964; Consultant to Central Bank of Malaysia 1983; Sr. Econ. on prof. staff of Comn. on Foreign Econ. Policy of U.S. Govt., 1954; Head, U.S. Del. to Working Party of Experts on Financial Aspects of Econ. Devel. Programs in Asia and Far E., Bangkok, 1954; mem. adv. Comte. to Philippine Central Bank Comn., 1955–56; Visiting Prof. of Econ., The Johns Hopkins Univ., 1961, Princeton Univ. 1963, The City Univ. of N.Y. 1965; rec'd Allen Oliver Gold Medal and Grad. Fellowship (Econ.), McGill Univ., 1935; Pre-Doctoral Fellowship, Social Science Research Council, 1939–40; Guggenheim Fellowship 1956 (not availed of); Rockefeller Foundation Fellowship, 1957–58; Ford Foundation Faculty Research Fellowship, 1962–63; Consultant to U.S. Dept. of State, 1970–82; Visiting Prof. of

Economics, Univ. of Melbourne 1972; Observer, Annual Meeting, African Devel. Bank, Abidjan, 1979; Editorial Board, Journal of Post-Keynesian Economics; author: 'Capital Imports and the American Balance of Payments, 1934–1939' 1950; 'Banking Reform in South Korea' 1951; 'Monetary Policy under the International Gold Standard, 1880–1914' 1959; 'Speculative and Flight Movements of Capital in Postwar International Finance' 1954; 'Short-term Capital Movements under the Pre-1914 Gold Standard' 1963; 'Patterns of Fluctuation in International Investment before 1914' 1968; 'Essays in the History of International Trade Theory' 1994; other writings incl. articles in prof. journs. and in symposia; mem., Am. Econ. Assn.; Am. Assn. Univ. Profs.; Club: Cosmos (Washington, D.C.); Jewish; Home: 2362 King Place, N.W., Washington, D.C. 20007.

**BLOOMFIELD, Michael I.,** M.Sc.; wildlife biologist; environmental educator; b. Cleveland, Ohio 1 Feb. 1950; s. Daniel and Frances B.; e. Merced (Cal.) Coll. 1971; Ohio State Univ. B.Sc. 1974; Univ. of Alta. M.Sc. 1979; m. Chris d. Donald and Lola French 10 Jan. 1971; FOUNDER AND EXEC. DIR. HARMONY FOUND. OF CAN. 1985– ; Regional Wildlife Biol., Prov. Caribou Specialist Alta. 1978–83; Exec. Dir. Humane Soc. Ottawa-Carleton 1983–86; teacher, cons., advisor environmental trends and progs.; advisor/director numerous community/professional organizations; Founder: Summer Inst. Environmental Values Education; ECOmmunity - community training for sustainable development; Green Works - workplace training for the environment; recipient UN Global 500 Award presented at Earth Summit, Rio de Janeiro, Brazil 1992; recipient, 1994 Candn. Commonwealth Foundation Fellowship (to promote Commonwealth understanding); author: 'Home and Family Guide' 1989; 'Workplace Guide Practical Action for the Environment' 1991; 'Community, Workshops for the Environment' 1992; contbr. editor: 'Green Works' 1993; editor: 'A Canadian Response to the Challenge of Sustainable Development' 1988 and various profl. publs.; Exec. producer (video) 'Positive Action for the Environ' 1992; mem. Governing Council UNEP Global 500 Forum; mem. Sigma Xi Found.; Gamma Sigma Delta; recreations: cross-country skiing, bicycling, anthropology, history; B.C. Office: 209 Market Square, 560 Johnson St., Victoria, B.C. V8W 3C6; Ottawa Office: 145 Spruce St., Suite 202A, Ottawa, Ont. K1R 6P1.

**BLOUIN, Arthur G.A.,** B.A., M.A., Ph.D., C.Psych.; psychologist; b. Ottawa, Ont. 22 Nov. 1947; s. Arthur Eugene and Jean Elizabeth (McDonald) B.; e. Laurentian H.S.; Carleton Univ. B.A. (Hons.) 1974, M.A. 1976; Univ. of Ottawa Ph.D. 1980; George Washington Univ., post-doctoral fellowship 1981; m. Jane Helen d. Bernard and Mary Johnson 9 June 1979; children: Arthur, Brittany, Christopher; DIRECTOR OF PSYCHOLOGY, OTTAWA CIVIC HOSP. & ASSOC. PROF., FAC. OF MED., UNIV. OF OTTAWA 1988– ; Assoc. Dir., Lab. of Behavioral Med., Children's Hosp., Nat. Med. Ctr. (Washington) 1981–83; Psychologist, Ottawa Civic Hosp. 1983; Dir. of Research, Dept. of Psychiatry 1984; Adjunct Prof., Psychology, Carleton Univ.; Mem., Bd. of Dir., Ont. Chief Psychologists Assn. 1990–92; C-DIS Group Inc.; Ontario Mental Health Foundation Fellow 1980–81; author of over 40 sci. pubns. in psychology & psychiatry; recreations: 2nd degree black belt – taekwondo; club: Tae Eun Lee, Taekwondo School; Home: 23 Millman Court, Kanata, Ont. K2L 2P5; Office: 1053 Carling Ave., Ottawa, Ont. K1Y 4E9 and Private practice: 300 March Rd., Kanata, Ont. K2K 2E2.

**BLOUIN, Georges H.;** industrial executive; b. Giffard, Que. 17 Nov. 1933; s. Henri and Juliette (St-Pierre) B.; e. Laval Univ. B.Sc. 1956; m. Elmina d. Adelard Bouchard 29 Dec. 1957; children: Steve, Manon, Eric; PRESIDENT AND CHIEF OPER. OFFR., TIMMINCO METALS, A DIVISION OF TIMMINCO LTD. 1968– ; Cerro Corp., S. Am. 1956–66; Harvey Aluminum, W. Africa 1966–68; Dir., Internat. Magnesium Assn.; Timminco Technologies Corp.; Timminco Pty. Ltd.; mem., Que. Order of Engrs.; Am. Soc. for Metals; recreations: reading, fishing; Home: 30 Mutchmor Rd., Ottawa, Ont. K1S 1L7; Office: Haley, Ont. K0J 1Y0.

**BLOUIN, Georges Henri,** B.A., LL.B.; diplomat; b. Montreal, Que. 4 June 1921; s. Charles Henri and Hermine (Panneton) B.; e. Collège Sainte-Marie, Montreal, B.A. 1944; Univ. de Montréal, LL.B. 1948; m. Denise (dec.) d. Auguste Angers, St. Lambert, Que. 12 Feb. 1948; children: Pierre A., Micheline; Chief of Protocol of Canada 1983–85; 2nd Secy., Candn. Embassy, New Delhi, 1951–53; Consul in San Francisco, 1955–58; Counsellor, Candn. Embassy, Athens, 1961–63 and Brussels, 1963–65; Ambassador to Federal Republic of Cameroun (Yaoundé) and also accredited to Republic of Gabon, of Chad and Central African Republic, 1965–67; Min. Candn. Embassy, Washington, 1967–70; Dir. Gen. Personnel, Dept. of External Affairs, Ottawa, 1970–73; Ambassador to Spain and Morocco 1973–77; Assist. Under-Secy. of State for External Affairs 1977–79; Ambassador to the Netherlands 1979–83; R. Catholic; recreation: golf; Home: 130 Rideau Terrace, Ottawa, Ont. K1M 0Z2.

**BLOUIN, Glen,** B.A., M.For.; association executive; b. Montreal, Que. 10 Oct. 1946; s. Walter E. and Agnes (Jaffray) B.; e. Loyola H.S. 1963; Loyola College B.Comm.Arts 1968; Maritime Forest Ranger School 1976; Univ. of N.B. M.For. 1988; m. Michelle d. Paul and Annette LaBarre 1976; children: Stephanie, Phillip; EXECUTIVE DIR., CANADIAN FORESTRY ASSN. 1988– ; Asst. Nat. Advtg. Mgr., Capitol Records (Canada) 1969–71; Owner, The Cabbagetown Cobbler Toronto 1971–74; Forest Technician, N.B. Forest Extension Serv. 1977–86; Manager, Woodlot Education 1986–88; Extve. Sec., Candn. Forestry Found.; Dir., Jr. Forest Wardens; Chair, CIF Forest Edn. Working Group; Mem., Candn. Inst. of Forestry; Founding Mem. & Treasurer, EECOM Environmental Educators Network; Mem., National Forest Round Table; author: 'Weeds of the Woods: Small Trees and Shrubs of the Eastern Forest' 1st ed. 1984, 2nd ed. 1992; editor: National Woodlot Owners Forum 1988, EDUFOR 1991, ENVIROFOR 1991 (proceedings); recreations: music, photography; Home: Box 370, Mont Cascades, Cantley, Que. J0X 1L0; Office: 185 Somerset St. W., Suite 203, Ottawa, Ont. K2P 0J2.

**BLOUIN, Me Michèle,** Lic. en droit; lawyer; b. Quebec City 6 Nov. 1941; d. Jacques-Emile and Simonne (L'Heureux) B.; e. Univ. de Montréal, lic. en droit 1974; m. Jean-Guy s. Arthur Martin 11 July 1987; one d.: Daphné Cousineau Blouin; MEM., CANADIAN INTERNATIONAL TRADE TRIBUNAL 1990– ; Lawyer, Geoffrion, Prud'Homme 1975–81; Radio-Canada 1981–86; Sr. Assoc. Blouin, Gagnon Lawyers 1986–90; Mem., PEN International; Candn. Counc. of Admin. Tribunals; Bar of Quebec; author: 'Le Jardin de Cristina' 1978 (novel); 'Le Jardin de Cristina' 1978 (play); 'Du Saint-Laurent au nil' 1981 (essay); Home: 1705 – 7th Ave., Val Morin, Que. J0T 2R0; Office: 365 Laurier Ave. W., Ottawa, Ont. K1A 0G7.

**BLUE JAYS BASEBALL CLUB;** 1993 World Series Champions: Robert Alomar, Brent Andrews (assistant trainer), Bob Bailor (first base coach), Pat Borders, Scott Brow, Rob Butler, Willie Canate, Joe Carter, Tony Castillo, Galen Cisco (pitching coach), Darnell Coles, Danny Cox, Tommy Craig (trainer), Mark Eichhorn, Tony Fernandez, Jesus Figueroa (batting practice pitcher), Cito Gaston (manager), Alfredo Griffin, Juan Guzman, Rich Hacker (special assignment coach), Rickey Henderson, Pat Hentgen, Larry Hisle (batting coach), Dennis Holmberg (bullpen coach), Geoffery Horne (strength and conditioning coordinator), Randy Knorr, Al Leiter, Nick Leyva (third base coach), Paul Molitor, Jack Morris, John Olerud, Jeff Ross (clubhouse manager), Dick Schofield, Ed Sprague, Dave Stewart, Todd Stottlemyre, Gene Tenace (bench coach), Mike Timlin, Duane Ward, Turner Ward, Devon White, Eddie Zosky.

**BLUGER (NEILY), Marianne Sasha,** B.A.; poet; association executive; b. Ottawa, Ont. 28 Aug. 1945; d. Walter Vladimir and Ruth Anna (Mallory) Bluger; e. Fisher Park High Sch. 1963; McGill Univ. B.A. 1967 (Univ. Scholar); m. Samu Kim 1 June 1968; div. 1986; children: Maji Raphael, Agi Micheline; m. Larry Earle Neily 12 Jan. 1991; EXEC. SEC.-TREAS. CANDN. WRITERS' FOUND. INC. 1975– ; author (poetry) 'The Thumbless Man' 1981; 'On Nights Like This' 1984; 'Gathering Wild' 1988; 'Summer Grass' 1992; Ethel Wilson Scholar McGill 1965–67; Fed. Repub. of Germany Travelling Scholar 1965; Ont. and Can. Council Arts Grants; various hons. poetry incl. Archibald Lampman Award for Poetry 1993; Canada Council Arts B Award 1989; St. Matthias' Sunday School Superintendent 1977–80; Co-founder Christians Against Apartheid 1984; Treas. Haiku Soc. Can. 1988–91; Anglican; P. Conservative; recreations: birdwatching, gardening, darts; Club: Ottawa Field Naturalists; Home: 124 Clarendon Ave., Ottawa, Ont. K1Y 0R3; Office: P.O. Box 3071 Stn. C, Ottawa, Ont. K1Y 4J3.

**BLUME, Helmut;** musician; broadcaster; professor; b. Berlin, Germany 12 Apr. 1914; s. Dr. Gustav and Romana (Sachs) B.; m. Ljerka Putić; e. Univ. of Berlin (1932–33); Acad. of Music, Berlin, Grad. (1933–38); Toronto Conservatory of Music, (1942–43); Dean, Faculty of Music, McGill Univ. 1963–76; Prof. Emeritus; Fellow, Roy. Soc. of Arts 1976; joined Staff of the Univ. in 1946; regular contrib. to CBC programs as writer, commentator and pianist; Music Consultant, CBC Internat. Service; Pres. of Ger. Benevolent Soc. of Montreal 1980–85; co-author of 'Canada's Story in Song' 1960; author of 'Form in Music' (record-album) 1960; 'A National Music School for Canada' 1978; various short stories and numerous Candn. newspaper reviews of recitals, radio and television programs; Piano Recitalist, 1942–54; Head of German Sec., CBC Internat. Service, Montreal, 1944–46; awarded (first) for 'Music to See,' produced by Ted Pope (22nd Am. Exhn. of Educ. Radio-TV Programs, Ohio State Univ. 1958); elected Hon. Mem., Candn. University Music Soc. 1993; Lutheran; recreations: boating, swimming; Home: 20 Windsor Ave., Westmount, Que. H3Y 2L6.

**BLUMENAUER, George Henry,** B.A.Sc.; executive b. Nelson, B.C. 13 Oct. 1921; s. late Alice May (Swanell) and John Richard B.; e. Cranbrook (B.C.) High Sch.; Univ. of B.C., B.A.Sc. (Mech. Engn.); m. Margaret Emma, d. late Christian M. Nielsen, 18 Oct. 1947; three s. Richard, William, Christian; CHRMN., OTIS CANADA, INC. 1984– ; Vice Chrmn. & Dir., Mutual Life Assurance Co. of Canada; Dir., DOFASCO Inc.; Timminco Ltd.; mem. Adv. Bd., Lehndorff Canadian Properties; Works Engn. present co. 1947; Service Sales, Toronto (Ont.) District 1948; New Sales Rep. 1949; Asst. District Mgr., Toronto (Ont.) Dist. 1950, Dist. Mgr. 1953; Gen. Mgr., Operations, Hamilton, Ont. 1959; Vice-Pres. 1961; Chrmn. and Pres. 1962; Chrmn. & C.E.O. 1981; Chrmn. 1984; served during 2nd World War with R.C.E.M.E.; mem., Assn. Prof. Engrs. Ont.; Engn. Inst. Can.; Un. Church; recreations: golf, fishing, Clubs: Mississauga Golf & Country; Hamilton Golf & Country; Hamilton; Caledon Mountain Trout; York (Toronto); The Loxahatchee Club, Jupiter, Fl.; Home: 142 Claxton Dr., Oakville, Ont. L6J 4N9; Office: P.O. Box 550 (710 Dorval Dr.), Oakville, Ont. L6J 5B7.

**BLUMES, Mark W.;** merchandise executive; b. Calgary, Alta. 24 June 1943; s. Abraham Barney and Ruth (Polsky) B.; e. Southern Alta. Inst. of Tech. Merchandising Admin. 1964; m. Roslyn d. Joe and Mini Fayerman 17 Sept. 1971; children: Terri, Jeremy, Mira, Chad; FOUNDER AND CHIEF EXEC. OFFR. MARK'S WORK WEAR HOUSE LTD. 1977– ; Mgmt. Trainee Hudson Bay Co. 1964, Sr. Exec. Divisional Merchandise Mgr. 1983; recreations: tennis, skiing, golf; Home: 348 Pumphill Gdns. S.W., Calgary, Alta. T2V 4M7; Office: #30, 1035 – 64th Ave. S.E., Calgary, Alta. T2H 2J7.

**BLUMES, Morley (Moe) Allan,** C.A.; women's retail clothing executive; b. Calgary, Alta. 24 June 1943; s. Ruth B.; e. Central H.S. 1961; Univ. of Calgary 1966; divorced; children: Michael, Lauren; PRESIDENT & CHIEF EXECUTIVE OFFICER, SEIFERTS GROUP, INC. 1991– ; joined Thorne Riddell 1965; C.A. 1970; Partner 1976; Executive Vice-Pres., Mark's Work Wearhouse, Ltd. & Chief Financial Offr., Pres. & Chief Extve. Offr., Pro-Formance Automotive Ltd. 1981–91; Chief Financial Officer, Grafton Group, Ltd. 1991; Mem., Candn. Inst. of C.A.s (Mem., Acctg. Standards Ctte.); Inst. of C.A.s of Alberta; frequent public speaker/lecturer; Bd. Mem., Calgary Jewish Community (Treas. 1988); 1988 Olympic Volunteer; participated in devel. of spectator serv. training manuals & Vice Chair, spectator serv. at opening/closing ceremonies; recreations: skiing, golf, reading business journals; Address: 2034 – 21 Avenue S.W., Calgary, Alta. T2T 0N7.

**BLUMSOM, Henry Thomas;** motion picture executive (retired); b. Toronto, Ont. 5 Sept. 1921; s. Henry James and Adelaide Mae (Inwood) B.; e. Scarborough (Ont.) Coll. Inst.; m. 2ndly Mary Bowers, 24 Oct. 1981; PRESIDENT, ODEON THEATRES (CANADA) LTD. 1974–77; Accounting Dept. York Trading Ltd. 1936–40, 1945–46; Acct., Eagle Lion Films, 1946; joined present Co. Chief Acct. 1954, Asst. Treas. 1955, Treas. 1957, Secy. Treas. 1962, Dir. 1963, Vice Pres. 1972; served with RCAF as Flying Instr. 1940–45; rank Flying Offr.; Secy. Treas., Entheos Lodge Found., 1980–82; Freemason (P.D.D.G.M.); Anglican; recreations: photography, golf; Home: 303 – 410 Main St. E., Saskatoon, Sask. S7N 0B8.

**BLUMSTOCK, Robert E.,** Ph.D.; educator; b. New York City, N.Y. 5 Oct. 1934; s. Ernest and Sari (Berger) B.; e. City Coll. of N.Y. B.A. 1956; Univ. of Ore. Ph.D. 1964; m. Ruth d. Robert Singer 19 Jan. 1958; children: Judith Evelyn, Miriam Rita; ASSOC. PROF. OF SOCIOL. McMASTER UNIV.; Instr. in Sociol. Univ. of Conn. 1962–64; Asst. Prof. present Univ. 1964, Chrmn. of Sociol. 1968–71; Visiting Lectr. Karl Marx Univ. Budapest 1972; Visiting Prof., Attila Jozsef Univ., Szeged, Hungary 1990; Researcher, Candn. Centre for Folk Culture Studies, Nat. Museum of Man, Ottawa; Consultant, Nat. Film Bd.; served with U.S. Army 1957–59; ed. 'Bekevar: Working Papers on a Hungarian-Canadian Prairie Community' 1979; contributing author 'Public Opinion in European Socialist Systems' 1977; 'Survey Research and Public Attitudes in Eastern Europe and the Soviet Union' 1981; author various articles prof. journs.; SSHRCC-Hungarian Acad. of Sciences Bilateral Exchange Programme Award, 1983; mem. Adv. Bd. Hungarian Studies Review; Assoc. Ed., Sociological Analysis 1983–86; Jewish; recreation: swimming; Home: 8 Daleview Court, Hamilton Ont. L8S 3L8; Office: Hamilton, Ont. L8S 4M4.

**BLUNDELL, William Richard Charles,** B.A.Sc.; company executive; b. Montreal, Que. 13 Apr. 1927; s. Richard Charles and Did Aileen (Payne) B.; e. Univ. of Toronto, B.A.Sc. 1949; m. Monique, d. Paul Audet, Quebec, Que., 20 March 1959; children: Richard Paul, Emily Claire, Michelle Ann, Louise Chantale; Dir., Alcan Aluminium Ltd.; Amoco Canada Petroleum Co. Ltd.; Candn. Inst. for Advanced Rsch.; CP Forest Products Ltd.; Disys Corp.; Export Development Corp.; Lawson Mardon Group; The Manufacturers Life Ins. Co.; Markborough Properties; Proctor & Redfern Group; Purolator Courier Ltd.; Sceptre Investment Counsel Ltd.; Seaside Cable TV; Swiss Bank Corp. (Canada); joined Canadian General Electric 1949; apptd. Vice Pres., Finance 1968, Consumer Products, 1970, Apparatus & Heavy Machinery 1972; Pres. & C.E.O. Camco Inc. 1979; Chief Oper. Offr. General Electric Canada Inc. 1983, Pres. & C.E.O. 1984, Chrmn. & C.E.O. 1985–90; Mem., Bd. of Govs., Univ. of Toronto; Anglican; recreation: sports; Club: Granite; Toronto; Mount Royal; Home: 45 Stratheden Rd., Toronto, Ont. M4N 1E5.

**BLYTH, Graham D. (Sam),** B.A., M.A.; tour operator; educator; b. Camp Shilo, Man. 4 Feb. 1954; s. David Wilson and Rev. Patricia Blanche B.; e. Ashbury Coll. 1967; Trinity Coll. Sch. 1969; Cambridge Univ., B.A. (Hons.) 1975, M.A. 1978; The Univ. of Paris 1976; m. Rosemarie Caroline d. Thomas J. and Sonja Bata, 1 Sept. 1985; children: Francesca, Madeleine; FOUNDER AND C.E.O., BLYTH & CO. 1977– ; Chrmn., Marine Expeditions 1993– ; Dir., Elnos Corporation; Mng. Dir. Lycee Canadien en France (private sch.) 1985– ; Mng. Dir., Université Canadienne en France 1987– ; Dir., Empire Club of Can.; Dir., Cambridge Univ. Canadian Trust; Dir., Lester B. Pearson Coll.; recipient, Silver Medal of St. Jean (France); Canadian Business Excellence Award for Entrepreneurship 1987; Canadian Business Excellence Award for Marketing 1991; BTA Award 1991 Worldwide Marketing Award; Berger-Sullivan Tourism Man of the Year Award 1990; Cambridge Blue; recreations: biking, mountain climbing, anthropology; Clubs: Hawkes; YPO; Badminton and Racquet; Toronto Lawn Tennis; Home: 111 Cluny Dr., Toronto, Ont. M4W 2R5 and Place du Centenaire, 06230, St. Jean Cap Ferrat, France.

**BOADWAY, Robin William,** B.Eng., B.A., B.Phil., Ph.D.; university professor; b. Regina, Sask. 10 June 1943; s. Judson Claude and Laura Alice Adela (McWilliams) B.; e. Central Coll. Inst. (Moose Jaw) 1960; Royal Mil. Coll. B.Eng. 1964; Oxford Univ. B.A. 1966, B.Phil. 1967; Queen's Univ. Ph.D. 1973; Rhodes Scholar (Sask.) 1964; Post-doctoral fellowship, Univ. of Chicago 1976–77; m. Bernadine d. James and Patricia MacDonald 18 July 1970; children: Andrew Robin, John James; Canadian Armed Forces 1964–72 (attained rank of Major); Lectr. Royal Mil. Coll. 1969–72; Asst. Prof. of Economics, Queen's Univ. 1973; Post-doctoral fellow in Pol. Econ., Univ. of Chicago 1976–77; Assoc. Prof. of Econ. Queen's Univ. 1976; Prof. of Econ. 1980; Head, Dept. of Economics and John Deutsch Inst. for the Study of Economic Policy, Queen's Univ. 1981–86; Sir Edward Peacock Prof. of Econ. 1991– ; Cons., Dept. of Finance; Econ. Counc. of Can.; Candn. Tax Found.; Royal Comm. on the Econ. Union and Develop. Prospects for Can.; World Bank; author: 'Public Sector Economics' 1979 (co-author 2nd ed. 1984); 'Intergovernmental Transfers in Canada' 1980; co-author: 'The Impact of the Mining Industries on the Canadian Economy' 1977; 'Canadian Tax Policy' 1980 (2nd ed. 1984); 'Equalization in a Federal State' 1982; 'Welfare Economics' 1984; 'Taxation and Savings in Canada' 1988; 'Taxes on Capital Income in Canada' 1987; 'The Constitutional Division of Powers: An Economic Perspective' 1992; 'Intergovernmental Fiscal Relations in Canada' 1993; editor, Canadian Journal of Eonomics 1987– ; numerous articles in learned journals and contributions to edited volumes; Fellow, Royal Soc. of Can. 1986; recreations: jogging, cycling, tennis; Home: 203 College St., Kingston, Ont. K7L 4L9; Office: Dept. of Economics, Queen's Univ., Kingston, Ont. K7L 3N6.

**BOAG, Peter Thomas,** B.Sc., Ph.D.; university professor; b. Montreal, Que. 14 May 1952; s. Thomas Johnson and Lorna Christian (Milne) B.; e. South Kent H.S. 1970 cum laude; Queen's Univ., B.Sc. (Hons. 1st class) 1974; McGill Univ., Ph.D. (Dean's Hon. List) 1981; m. Dr. Laurene May d. Willa and Edward Ratcliffe 19 May 1984; children: Gemma Christian, Angela Elaine, Thomas Howard; ASSOC. PROF., BIOLOGY, QUEEN'S UNIV. 1989– ; Subarctic biol. rsch. 1972–74; biol. rsch., Galapagos Islands on Darwin's finches 1975–78; Lectr., Trent Univ. 1979–81; NSERC Postdoct. fellow, Univ. of Oxford 1981–83; NSERC Univ. Rsch. Fellow & Assoc. Prof., Queen's Univ. 1983–94; NSERC E.W.R. Steacie Fellow 1994–96; current rsch.: molecular & quantitative genetics of vertebrate populations; mem., Am. Ornitholog. Union (Elective Fellow); Soc. for the Study of Evolution; Cooper Ornithol. Soc.; Wilson Ornithol. Soc.; Assn. of Field Ornithol.; author of 1 book & approx. 50 sci. papers; editor: 'Darwin's Finches' 1983; Home: R.R. 1, Kingston, Ont. K7L 4V1; Office: Kingston, Ont. K7L 3N6.

**BOAG, T.J.,** M.B.Ch.B., F.R.C.P.(C); Liverpool, Eng. 11 Apr. 1922; s. John Harvey and Elizabeth (Johnson) B.; e. Merchant Taylor's Sch. Crosby, Eng. 1939; Univ. of Liverpool M.B.Ch.B. 1944; McGill Univ. Dipl. in Psychiatry 1953; Candn. Inst. of Psychoanalysis 1954–58; m. Lorna Christian d. late Herbert Stewart Milne 1 July 1950; children: Peter Thomas, Graham Stewart, Patricia Janet, Alexander Harvey; EMERITUS PROF. OF PSYCHIATRY, QUEEN'S UNIV. 1988, Prof. of Psychiatry 1967–88; Hon. Staff, Kingston Gen. Hosp.; Consultant, Hotel Dieu Hosp.; Asst. Dir. Allan Mem. Inst. 1959–61; Asst. Prof. of Psychiatry McGill Univ. and mem. Attending Staff Royal Victoria Hosp. Montreal 1953–61; Prof. of Psychiatry and Chrmn. of Dept. Univ. of Vt. 1961–67; Attending Psychiatrist and Chief of Service, Mary Fletcher Hosp., DeGoesbriand Mem. Hosp. and Med. Centre of Vt. 1961–67 also Consultant Vt. State Dept. Health and Vt. State Hosp.; joined present Univ. as Prof. and Head Dept. Psychiatry and Psychiatrist in Chief Kingston Gen. Hosp. 1967–75; Dean, Faculty of Medicine, 1975–82; Vice Principal, Health Sciences, 1983–88; served with RAMC 1944–47, rank Capt.; author 32 prof. publs.; Life Fellow, Am. Psychiatric Assn.; Royal College of Phsycians and Surgeons of Can.; Life Mem., Candn. Psychiatric Assn.; Candn. Med. Assn.; Ont. Med. Assn.; Alpha Omega Alpha; Assoc. mem. Sigma Xi; Anglican; recreations: bird watching, cross-country skiing, pottery collecting, opera, painting; Home: R.R. 2, Perth Rd., Ont. K0H 2L0.

**BOAKE, George Elliott,** B.Arch., F.R.A.I.C.; architect; b. Toronto, Ont. 7 Apr. 1927; s. George Wilfrid and Rose Mortimer (Elliott) B.; e. Univ. of Toronto Sch. 1945; Univ. of Toronto Sch. of Archit. B.Arch. 1951; m. Patricia Ann d. Kenneth and Nina Vaughan 8 Nov. 1951; children: Stephen A.E., Brian G., Ian V.; PRESIDENT, ARCHITECTS CRANG & BOAKE INC. 1984– ; formed partnership with James C. Crang 1952; major archit. commissions for ind., comml., and institutional clients across Can., U.S.A., and Gt. Brit.; completed Metro Toronto Convention Centre 1984; author 'The Unexplored Option' (a concept for a floating airport system for Toronto) 1970; firm awarded 2nd prize in Internat. Competition Tete Defense, Paris 1983; finalist in internat. competition 'Grand Buildings' Trafalgar Square London; recreations: painting, tennis; Clubs: Univ. of Toronto; Caledon Mountain Trout; Badminton & Racquet; Homes: Toronto and R.R. #1, Alliston, Ont.; Office: 85 Moatfield Dr., Don Mills, Ont. M3B 3L6.

**BOAKS, Ronald;** artist; b. Newmarket, Ont. 9 Feb. 1952; s. William Gordon and Wreatha May (Legge) B.; e. Sheridan Coll.; m. Lenore K. d. William and Verna Richards 12 May 1984; children: Amelia May, William Elliot; exhns. incl. Brantford Art Gallery, 'A' Space Toronto and Montreal Museum of Art 1976, Art Gallery of Hamilton, Kitchener Waterloo Gallery 1977, 'A Space', Univ. of Guelph 1978, Gallery Don Stewart Toronto 1982, Art Gallery Ont. Rental Gallery (Critic's Choice), Shelley Lambe Fine Art 1983, Marianne Friedland Gallery (Toronto & Naples, Fla.) 1985, 1986, 1988, 1990, 1991, Shayne Gallery Montreal 1988; rep. various nat. and internat. corporate colls.; Address: 107 Neville Park Blvd., Toronto, Ont. M4E 3P7.

**BOARETTI, Louis,** B.Comm., C.A.; financial consultant; b. Toronto, Ont. 14 Jan. 1921; s. William Joseph and Marie (Civise) B.; e. Univ. of Toronto B.Comm. (Hons.) 1948; Queen's Univ. (Hons.) C.A. 1951; m. Marjorie d. Ethel and Robert Short 1951; children: Katherine Marie, Robert William; Controller, Reichold Chemicals 1951–53; Treas., Thor Washing Machine 1953–60; Vice-Pres., Finance & Dir., Irwin Toy Limited 1960–86; Dir. 1960–91; Bd. Mem., Mississauga Library 1960–85 (Chrmn. 1 year); Life mem., Ont. C.A. 1991; recreations: golf, reading; club: Peridia Golf Club, Florida; Home: 1413 Lochlin Trail, Mississauga, Ont. L5G 3V5.

**BOAST, Keith E.,** Q.C.; financial executive; b. Kapuskasing, Ont. 10 May 1940; s. Chester Winfield and Alberta Lawrence (Manson) B.; e. Trinity College, Univ. of Toronto B.A. (Hons.) 1963; Osgoode Hall Law Sch. LL.B. 1971; called to Bar 1973; m. Dorothy d. Frank and Doris Damon 28 Dec. 1983; children: Laura, Gordon, Richard, John, Jennifer; VICE-PRESIDENT, THE TORONTO STOCK EXCHANGE 1984– ; Counsel Enforcement Branch, Ont. Securities Comn. 1973; Solicitor, Corp. Finance Br. 1975; Legal Advisor to the Comn. 1977; Vice-Chairman 1983; Office: 2 First Canadian Place, Toronto, Ont. M5X 1J2.

**BOATMAN, C.W.J. (Chris),** B.Sc.; hydro executive; b. Northern Ireland 16 Aug. 1942; s. Herbert Arthur and Teresa Bridget (Convery) B.; e. Univ. of London, B.Sc. 1963; children: James, Sarah; former Vice-Pres., Power Smart; Sr. Contracts Engr. 1967–73; Construction Mgr., Peace Canyon Generating Stn. 1973–80; Project Mgr., Peace Site C Project 1980–84; Mgr., B.C. Hydro Internat. Ltd. 1984–86; Extve. Asst. to the Chrmn. & Pres. 1986–87; Pres. & C.E.O., B.C. Power Export Corp. 1988–89; Vice Pres., Corp. & Environ. Affairs & Extve. Asst. to the Chrmn., B.C. Hydro & Power Authority 1987–..; Dir., Vancouver Rugby Union; Pres., Lions Club; recreations: golf, squash, tennis; clubs: Quilchena Golf & Country, Jericho Tennis (Bd. Mem.); Home: 3544 Point Grey Rd., Vancouver, B.C. V6R 1A8.

**BOBROW, Ella;** writer, poet, journalist; b. Nikolaiev, USSR 12 Dec. 1911; d. Johann and Adelina (Hass) Rung; e. Higher Sch. of Trade & Comm. 1930; various writing courses; 1st m. Nikolai s. Fiodor and Anna Bobrow 24 Aug. 1935; 2nd m. Leon s. Joshua and Ita Zuckert 15 Dec. 1969; children: Igor, Norah; office worker, Ukraine 1930–42; part-time librarian; mem., Friends of a Book Club; Atlanta Import-Export Co. (Germany) & writing & studying languages 1945–49; office work combined with literary activities in Canada 1950–74; Co-Editor, 'Sovremennik' 1963–76; freelance reporter, Radio Can. Internat., Russian section 1971–79; mem., Candn. Authors Assn.; The League of Candn. Poets; The Writers' Union of Can.; Internat. PEN; and several other orgns.; author: 'Irina Istomina' (Russian) 1967, (English) 1980, (German) 1983 & republished 1993; 'I Wait for a Miracle' 1970; 'Yantarny Sok' 1977; 'Autumnal Cadenza' 1985; 'The Three Brave Snowflakes, Fairy Tale' (Russian) 1961, (Eng.) 1982, (German) 1986 & reprinted 1991 & 1992; 'A King in Space' a fairy-tale (published in Russian and translated and published in German); 'Nasledie' (a monograph about the life and works of Irina Odoevzeva 'A Literary Portrait'); 'In the Gleam of Northern Lights' a 5-part poem about Canada and its people was used by Candn. composer León Zuckert for his Choreographic oratorio with the same title; three published lectures; poetry incl. in many anthologies: Washington (1966), Portugal (1990), Philadelphia (1991), Korea (1991 & 1992), Moscow (1994), New York (1994), Olympic Anthology Barcelona '92, Madras (1993); song writer; numerous book reviews & articles pub. worldwide; her poetry and critical essays were repeatedly programmed by radio stations in Moscow and Sverdlovsk; since 1991 her books are part of a display in the Literary Museum, Moscow (Emigré Literature); Home: 14 Gooch Court, Toronto, Ont. M6S 2N8.

**BOBYE, Wayne I.,** B.Comm., M.B.A., C.M.A.; oil industry executive; b. Vancouver, B.C. 6 Dec. 1947; s. Fred John and Lillian (Swenson) B.; e. Univ. of B.C. B.Comm. 1970, M.B.A. 1971; Soc. of Mngt. Accountants C.M.A. 1987; m. Marg d. Kurt and Helga Schulz 27 June 1970; children: Lori-Anne, Scott, Kathryn; VICE-PRES. FINANCE & CHIEF FINANCIAL OFFICER, TALISMAN ENERGY 1992– ; Sales Analyst / Coord., CP Air 1971–75; Dir., Market Planning, PWA 1975–79; Mgr., Corp. Planning, Husky Oil 1979–82; Mgr., Financial Planning, Canterra 1982–88; Vice-Pres. Finance & Chief Finan. Offr., Triton Canada 1989–92; Dir., Ethos Energy Inc.; Fortuna Petroleum; Junior Achievement; Lectr., Univ. of Calgary; Assoc. Mem., Chartered Inst. of Transport 1985; Treas., Calgary Petroleum Men's Fastball League; co-author of two research articles; recreations: fastball, skiing; Home: 8 Canova Rd. S.W., Calgary, Alta. T2W 2G3; Office: 2400, 855 – 2nd St. S.W., Calgary, Alta. T2P 4J9.

**BOBYN, Edward Joseph,** B.Sc., M.E.E.; retired Canadian public servant; b. Krydor, Sask. 11 Dec. 1921; s. James D. and late Katherine (Borytzki) B.; e. Univ. of Sask. B.Sc., 1944; Johns Hopkins Univ. M.E.E. 1948; m.

Helen Lydia d. late Jacob Bubniuk 11 Oct. 1945; children: James Edward, Patricia Joan, John Dennis, Diane Christine, Stephen Michael, Michèle Lynne; CONSULTANT, RESEARCH AND DEVEL. since 1983; Head, Instrumentation Sec. Candn. Armament Research & Devel. Estab. 1948, Depy. Supt. Guided Missile Wing 1950 and Supt. 1955, Supt. Systems Wing 1958–60; Chief of Systems Research, SHAPE Air Defence Tech. Centre, Holland 1960–63; Dir. Systems Evaluation RCAF HQ 1963–64; Chief Supt. Suffield Exper. Stn. Ralston, Alta. 1964–68; Dir.-Gen. Defence Research Estab. Valcartier, Que. 1968–72; Depy. Chrmn. (Scient.) Defence Research Bd. 1972–74; Chief of Research and Devel., Dept. Nat. Defence 1974–83; served with Royal Candn. Corps of Signals 1943–47, rank Lt.; mem. Scient. Comte. Nat. Reps. SHAPE Tech. Centre Holland (Candn. Nat. Rep.) 1968–83; NATO Adv. Group for Aerospace Research & Devel. (Nat. Del.) 1974–83; NATO Defence Research Group (Nat. Del.) 1975–83; Non-Atomic Mil. Research & Devel. Sub-comte. (Candn. Princ.) 1976–83; mem. Communications Research Adv. Bd., Dept. of Communications 1979–83; mem. Armed Forces Communications and Electronics Assn., Engn. Inst. Can.; Candn. Research Mang. Assn.; Assn. for Advancement of Science in Canada; Ukrainian Prof. & Businessmen's Assn.; Ottawa-Carleton Bd. of Trade; Honorary Fellow, Cdn. Aero. and Space Int.; Rotary Club Can.; Sigma Xi; Awarded Queen's Silver Jubilee Medal, 1977, Centennial Medal, 1967; Recreations: Woodworking, Fishing, Photography, Music; Home: 2218 Aster St., Ottawa, Ont. K1H 6R6.

**BOCK, Jacques,** B.S.; industrialist, lumberman; b. Montreal, P.Q. 10 Dec. 1932; s. Roland and Jeanette (Francoeur) B.; e. Universidad de Las Americas; Univ. of S. Cal., B.S. (Pub. Adm.) 1957; PRES. and GEN. MGR. BOCK & TÉTREAU INC.; Pres., Megaforex Industries Inc.; Dir., Shearer-Bock Inc.; Bock Corp. Inc.; Colbert Investments Inc.; Past Dir., Air Canada; Texaco Canada Inc.; Past Pres. Candn. Lumbermen's Assn.; Nat. Assn. of Independent Bldg. Materials' Distributors; Past Dir. N. Am. Wholesale Lumber Assn.; Que. Forestry Assn.; mem., Am. Assn. Pub. Adm.; Am. Acad. Pol. & Social Science; Newcomen Soc.; Office: 50 boul. Stinson, St-Laurent, Qué. H4N 2E7.

**BODDINGTON, George Beck,** B.A.; consultant; b. Toronto, Ont. 29 Sept. 1948; s. Dr. George David Mitchell and Elizabeth Margaret (Beck) B.; e. Univ. of Toronto Schs. 1967; Univ. of W. Ont. B.A. 1970, Dip. Journalism 1971; m. Shirley H. d. Dr. Archibald and Betty Denison 1 June 1973; children: Stephanie, Andrew; PRESIDENT, POLICY CONCEPTS INC. 1984– ; Sr. Policy Adv. to Min. of Agric. and to Min. of Health; Exec. Offr. to Min. of Energy; freelance journalist; recreations: squash, tennis, skiing, equestrian pursuits; Club: Bethany Hills Hunt; Home: R.R. 3, Port Hope, Ont.; Office: 211 Consumers Rd., Suite 205, North York, Ont. M2J 4G8.

**BODDY, Janice Patricia,** B.A., M.A., Ph.D.; university professor; b. Toronto, Ont. 11 July 1951; d. Roger Leigh and Patricia Theresa (Pougnet) Boddy; e. McGill Univ. B.A. (Hons.) 1972; Univ. of Calgary M.A. 1974; Univ. of British Columbia Ph.D. 1982; m. Ronald s. A.E.A. and Shirley P. Wright 2 June 1985; ASSOC. PROF., SOCIAL & CULTURAL ANTHROPOLOGY, UNIV. OF TORONTO 1990– ; Lectr., Univ. of Toronto 1978–79; Univ. of Man. 1979–80; Lakehead Univ. 1980–81; Univ. of Toronto 1981–82; Asst.Prof. 1982–83, 1985–90; SSHRC postdoctoral rsch. 1983–85; Instr., Ont. College of Art 1985; fieldwork in N. Sudan 1976–77, 1983–84 (cultural anthropology, gender issues); Edit. Bd., 'Anthropological Horizons'; consultant to Guggenheim and MacArthur foundations; Dir., Horizons of Friendship Devel. Orgn.; Mem., Royal Anthro. Inst.; Candn. Anthro. Soc.; Am. Anthro. Assn.; Soc. for Cultural Anthro.; Am. Ethno. Soc.; Med. Anthro. Soc.; Sudan Studies Assn.; author: 'Wombs and Alien Spirits: Women, Men and the Zar Cult in Northern Sudan' 1989 (shortlisted for Governor General's Lit. Award for Non-Fiction and for M.J. Herskovits Award, African Studies Assn. 1990); Office: 1265 Military Trail, Scarborough, Ont. M1C 1A4.

**BODDY, Trevor Duncan,** B.A., M.E.Des.(Arch.); educator; urban designer; architectural historian and critic; b. Edmonton, Alta. 7 March 1953; s. Walter Lewis and I. Joan B.; e. Ross Sheppard High Sch. Edmonton; Univ. of Alta. B.A. 1975; Univ. of Calgary M.E.Des.(Arch.) 1983; Inst. Advanced Studies in Arch. York, Eng. Historic Preservation course 1982; m. Janet d. Harold and Joan Harper 27 Dec. 1985; one d. Adair Sonya Joan; one s. Alden James; ASST. PROF. OF ARCH. CARLETON UNIV. 1987– ; arch. critic and writer variety Candn., Am. and Brit. scholarly, profl. and gen. mags. since 1978; self-employed urban design and hist. preservation cons. various arch. firms, govt. agencies and private founds. since 1980; Lectr. in Arch. Univ. of B.C. 1983–85; Visiting Prof. Univs. of Ore. and Man. 1985–87; frequent pub. lectr. arch. and urban topics univs., profl. bodies and comunity orgns.; invited participant Banff Centre Artist's Colony 1991, participant Banff Book Publishing Course 1983, Criticial Fictions Workshop 1989; recipient Can. Council Arts Grant 'B' Arch. 1980, 'A' Arch. 1988; rsch. and writing grants Alta. Culture, Sec. of State; mem. Comité Internationale des Critiques d'Arch. (one of 3 Candns.); el. Chrmn., History, Theory & Criticism Ctte. and Candn. Co-rep. to the Internat. Forum of Young Architects 1991; mem. Bd. Centretown Citizens Ottawa Corp. 1991; mem. Bd. Vancouver Centre for Dance 1984; NeWest Publishers Edmonton 1982; author 'Modern Architecture in Alberta' 1987; 'The Architecture of Douglas Cardinal' 1989 (winner Book of the Year and Best Book Design Award Alta. Publishers Assn.; finalist Best Book Arch. Criticism Pub. Worldwide during previous 3 yrs. Internat. Union of Architects World Cong. Montreal 1990); ed. 'Prairie Architecture' 1982; Hon. Mem., Bulgarian Union of Architects 1991; mem. Soc. Study Arch. Can.; Soc. Arch. Historians; ICOMOS Can.; CICA; Home: Box 48, R.R. #1, Chelsea, Que. J0X 1N0; Office: Sch. of Architecture, Carleton Univ., Ottawa, Ont. K1S 5B6.

**BODEL, Donald H.,** B.Com., C.A., F.R.I., C.R.E.; real estate consultant; b. Kingston, Ont. 25 Jan. 1938; s. James Howard and Mary Olive (Bodel) Fairbanks; e. Univ. of B.C., B.Com. 1961; C.A. 1964; Real Estate Dipl. Course 1964–67; m. Muriel Joan, d. Ronald and Muriel Gourlay, Vancouver,B.C., 22 Aug. 1964; s. Kenneth H., David R., John M.; PRESIDENT, RICHARD ELLIS, INC. 1989– ; joined Peat Marwick Mitchell & Co., Vancouver, B.C. 1961; Gen. Mgr., Dominion Management Co., Vancouver 1964; Exec. Vice-Pres., Fidelity Trust 1974; Pres. Richard Ellis Inc. 1976–83; Principal, The Lexington Co. 1983–89; mem. Bd. of Govs., Regent Coll., 1969–74 (Chrmn. 1973–74); Bd. of Trustees, Inter Varsity Christian Fellowship; Am. Soc. of Real Estate Counselors; Lambda Alpha Internat.; Protestant; Clubs: Economic Club (Chicago); Mid Day (Chicago); Home: 840 Sheridan Rd., Winnetka, Illinois 60093.

**BODENHAMER, William Turner;** manufacturing executive; b. Ty Ty, Ga. 27 Sept. 1937; s. William Turner and Miriam (Brooks) B.; e. Ga. Inst. of Technol. Atlanta 1955–59; Ga. State Univ. Grad. Sch. of Bus. 1980–82; children: William Glynn, Cheryl Elizabeth; CHRMN., PRES. & CHIEF EXTVE. OFFR., HARDING CARPETS INC. and SORELTEX INTERNATIONAL INC.; Vice Pres. & Dir., Candn. Polaris Investments Inc.; Pres. & Dir., 2759187 Canada Ltd.; Dir., CVD Capital Corp. (Vancouver, BC); Spectral Diagnostics Inc. (Etobicoke, Ont.); Hudson Bay Diecasting Ltd. (Brampton, Ont.); Provincial Papers, Inc. (Thunder Bay, Ont.); Instr. Albany (Ga.) Area Tech. Sch. 1962–64; Prin. Area Tech. Sch. Marietta, Ga. 1964–65; Sr. Cons. Kurt Salmon Associates, Atlanta 1965–66; Sales Rep. Honeywell EDP 1966–67; Vice Pres. E.T. Barwick Industries 1967–71; Pres. Venture Carpets Drummondville, Qué. 1971–75; Sr. Vice Pres. Sweetwater Carpet Corp. Ringgold, Ga. 1976–80; Pres. Harding Carpets Ltd. Mississauga 1982–85; Chrmn. & C.E.O., Coronet Carpets Inc. 1986–93; Pres. Ga. Tech. Edn. Assn. 1964; Dir. Candn. Carpet Inst. 1982–84; recreations: golf, flying; Clubs: National Golf (Woodbridge, Ont.); Loxanatchee Golf (Jupiter, FL); The Farm (Dalton, GA); Office: 1333 Eglinton Ave. E., Mississauga, Ont. L4W 2L4.

**BODILEY, Arthur Phineas,** M.B.E., F.C.I.I.; insurance executive (retired); b. Northampton, Eng., Sept. 1913; s. late Phineas Walgrave and Mary (Beeby) B.; e. Prince Henry's Grammar Sch., Otley, Eng.; m. Dod, d. late Charles Leazell 1945; two d., one s.; formerly Pres. for Can., Prudential Assurance Co. Ltd.; joined the Co., 1930, successive appts. in U.K. and Can. (past mem. Candn. Bd.); 1938–45, 2nd Middlesex Yeomanry (T.A.); Royal Signals, N. Africa, Syria, India, Burma, rank Major; awarded M.B.E. (mil.); past Pres. Can. Save the Children Fund; past Dir.: Montreal Children's Hospital Corp. and Fund; recreations: music, books, nature; Home: Saxted House, Tower Street, Emsworth, Hants., U.K.

**BODKIN, M.A. (Jill),** B.A.; financial institutions and corporate finance advisor; b. Belleville, Ont. 18 June 1943; d. J.C. Kenneth and Marie Alice (Foley) Madsen; e. Univ. of Alta. B.A. 1963; Maxwell Sch. of Pub. Affairs, Syracuse Univ. M.A. course in Pub. Adm. 1981; one child: Alicyn; PARTNER & DIRECTOR OF FINANCIAL SERVICES, ERNST & YOUNG (formerly Clarkson Gordon) 1988– ; Govt. of Can. 1965–81, Secretariat to Cabinet Ctte. on Econ. Devel.; Dep. Min. of Consumer & Corporate Affairs, B.C. 1981–86; Founding Chrmn. & C.E.O., B.C. Securities Comn. 1986–87; Extve.-in-Residence, Univ. of B.C. 1987; Chrmn., Celgar Expansion Review Panel, fed. EARP, B.C. MPRP 1990; Steering Ctte., National Forum on Post-Secondary Educ., Saskatoon 1987; Chrmn., Conf. Bd. Working Group on Trade in Financial Services 1988–91; Vice-Chrmn. & Dir., Vancouver Bd. of Trade 1988– ; mem., Fin. Services SAGIT to Candn. Min. of Trade 1988– ; mem., B.C. Science Counc. Fiscal Ctte.; Internat. Visitor U.S. Govt. to examine domestic & internat. banking issues with Bus. & Govt. leaders 1984; mem. Adv. Ctte. Faculty of Comm. Univ. of B.C. 1985–90; Trustee and Dir., Inst. for Rsch. in Public Policy 1987– ; Dir., Open Learning Foundation 1993– ; Trustee, Thai Development Rsch. Institute 1993– ; mem., Swiss-Canadian C. of C.; mem., Hong Kong-Canada Business Assoc.; Home: 2201D, 1600 Beach, Douglas House, Vancouver, B.C. V6G 1Y8; Office: P.O. Box 10101, 700 W. Georgia St., Vancouver, B.C. V7Y 1C7.

**BODSWORTH, Fred;** writer; b. Port Burwell, Ont. 11 Oct. 1918; s. Arthur John and Viola (Williams) B.; e. Port Burwell Cont. Sch.; m. Margaret Neville, d. late Joseph Banner, 8 July 1944; children: Barbara, Nancy, Neville; Reporter, St. Thomas 'Times-Journal' 1940–43; Reporter and Editor, Toronto 'Daily Star' and 'Star Weekly' 1943–46; Asst. Editor, 'Maclean's Magazine' 1947–55; author: 'Last of the Curlews' 1955; 'The Strange One' 1960; 'The Atonement of Ashley Morden' 1964; 'The Sparrow's Fall' 1966; 'The Pacific Coast' (Illustrated Natural History of Canada series); co-author 'Wilderness Canada' 1970; approx. 100 articles in 'Maclean's Mag.,' and many articles in other Candn. and Am. mags.; Past Pres., Fed. Ont. Naturalists; Dir., Natural Sci. of Can. Ltd. 1980–87; Hon. Dir., Long Point Bird Observatory 1970– ; Chrmn., Bd. of Trustees, James L. Baillie Memorial Fund for ornithological research 1975–88; recreations: bird watching, nature study; Clubs: Toronto Ornithological; Toronto Field Naturalists'; Brodie; Writers' Union of Canada; Address: 294 Beech Ave., Toronto, Ont. M4E 3J2.

**BOECKNER, Robert G.,** F.S.A., F.C.I.A.; consulting actuary; b. Toronto, Ont. 1 Oct. 1941; s. Howard and Alma (Walter) B.; e. Univ. of Toronto B.Sc. 1963; children: Mark, Laura, Catherine; PRINCIPAL, WILLIAM M. MERCER LTD. 1990– ; joined Crown Life Ins. in 1963; Sr. Vice-Pres., U.S. Ins. Operations 1983–86; Vice Pres., Imperial Life Ass. Co. and Laurentian Life Ins. Inc. 1987–90; Pres., The Laurentian/Imperial Co. 1987–90; mem. Candn. Inst. of Actuaries; Am. Acad. of Actuaries; recreations: sailing, cross-country skiing; Clubs: National; Granite; Home: 37 Marmot St., Toronto, Ont. M4S 2T4.

**BOGART, W.A.,** B.A., LL.M.; educator; b. Pembroke, Ont. 23 Feb. 1950; s. Colin Arthur and Bernice Margaret (Knott) B.; e. Univ. of Toronto B.A. 1971, LL.B. 1974; Harvard Law Sch. LL.M. 1980; m. Linda Bertoldi d. Joseph and Emily Bertoldi 9 Aug. 1975; one d. Amelia Bernice Bertoldi; PROF. OF LAW UNIV. OF WINDSOR 1984– ; law practice Fasken & Calven 1974–77; Ont. Law Reform Comn. 1977–79; Assoc. Prof. present Univ. 1980; Visiting Prof. Osgoode Hall Law Sch. 1985, Univ. of Toronto Faculty of Law 1987–88; author: 'Courts and Country' 1994; co-author: 'Civil Litigation' 4th ed. 1992; recreations: running, swimming; Office: 401 Sunset Ave., Windsor, Ont. N9B 3P4.

**BOGDANOW, George Waldemar Boegler,** Dipl.-Kfm., M.A., F.C.M.A.; professional accountant and economist; b. Lodz, Poland 3 June 1926; s. Alexander Yegorowich and Olga Boegler (Jeske) B.; e. Univ. of Munich Diplom-Kaufmann 1948; Simon Fraser Univ. M.A. (Econ.) 1970; Soc. of Mngt. Accts. of B.C. C.M.A. 1969; m. Erika Emily Therese d. Otto and Anna Th. Riese 24 Nov. 1950; children: Barbara Ruth, Thomas Carl Alexander; VICE-PRES., TREASURER & CHIEF FINANCIAL OFFR., GWIL INDUSTRIES INC. 1980– ; various extve. finan. positions 1950–67; Instructor, Simon Fraser Univ. 1967–71 (part-time 1971–76); Pres., Atlas Construction & Crane Service Ltd. 1972–73; Sr. Vice-Pres. Finance & Admin & C.F.O., Great West Steel Industry Ltd. 1971–80; Gen. Conf. Chair, 1992 Nat. Conf., The Soc. of Mngt. Accountants of Canada; part-time instructor, Inst. of C.A.s of B.C.; management consultant 1969– ; Past Dir., GWS & Shell (U.K.); GWS-Krupp Ltd. (Germany); Birtley Engineering Ltd. (U.K.); Great West Steel Indus. Ltd.; Atlas Construction & Crane Serv. Ltd. and others; Fellow, C.M.A. 1982; Life Mem., Soc. of Mngt. Assts. of B.C. 1991; Dir., Steelworkers Credit Union 1955–61; Trustee, FEI Vanc. Chap. Scholarship Fudn 1985–91; Dir., Soc. of Mngt. Accts. of Can. 1981–84 (B.C. Pres. 1983–84; Council Mem. 1967–70, 1980–85); Life Mem., Financial Extves. Inst. Vanc.; Nat. Model Railroad Assn.; Am. Philatelic Soc.; Mem., Am. Acctg. Assn.; Past Boy Scout Master; author of 8 presented/published conf. papers 1948– ; recreations: sailing, video/photo, model railroads, railfan, philately; clubs: Eagle Harbour Yacht, Hollyburn Country; Home: 1126 Hillside Rd., W. Vancouver, B.C. V7S 2G4; Office: 555 West 12th St., Ste. 650, Vancouver, B.C. V5Z 3X7.

**BOGERT, Maj.-Gen. Mortimer Patrick,** C.B.E. (1953), D.S.O. (1943); officer; b. Toronto, Ont. 17 Mar. 1908; s. Mortimer Selwyn and Georgina Maud (Crombie) B.; e. Selwyn House Sch., Montreal; Ashbury Coll., Ottawa; Roy. Mil. Coll. 1926–30; McGill Univ. 1930–31; Commissioned in Black Watch (Royal Highlanders of Canada) 1930; Royal Canadian Regiment (Permanent Force), Canada, 1932; proceeded overseas on staff of 1st Candn. Div. 1939; attended Staff Coll., Camberley, Eng., 1940; attached to Brit. Army in Middle East 1942; Commanded W. Nova Scotia Regt., Sicily and Italy 1943; awarded D.S.O. 1943; wounded 1943; served as G.S.O.1, 1st Candn. Div. (Italy) 1944; awarded O.B.E. 1944; commanded (temp.) 3rd Candn. Inf. Bde. 1944; Brig., Commndg. 2nd Candn. Inf. Bde. in Italy and Holland 1944–45; commanded 8th Candn. Inf. Bde., Candn. Occupation Force in Germany 1945–46; awarded Croix de Guerre (France) 1944; awarded Aristian Andreas (Greece) 1944; Commanded Eastern Ont. Area 1946; subsequently B.C. Area; Commdr., 25th Candn Inf. Brigade, Korea, Apl. 1952–Apl. 1953; awarded C.B.E. 1953; awarded Legion of Merit (officer, U.S.A.) 1953; Depy. Adj.-Gen. Army Hdqrs., Ottawa, 1953–54; Commandant, Candn. Army Staff Coll., Kingston, Ont., 1954–58; promoted to rank of Maj.-Gen., G.O.C. Eastern Command, Halifax, N.S., 1958; retired from Candn. Army, 1962; named by Brit. Colonial Office as one of two-man Comn. to investigate the future of Kenya's northern prov., Oct. 62; Anglican; recreations: shooting; bridge; Address: 11, Donnington Park, Donnington, Newbury, Berkshire, England RG13 2DZ.

**BOGGS, Jean Sutherland,** O.C. (1973), Ph.D., LL.D., F.R.S.C., b. Negritos, Peru 11 June 1922; d. Oliver Desmond and Humia Marguerite (Sutherland) B.; e. Alma Coll., St. Thomas, Ont., 1934–38; Trinity Coll., Univ. of Toronto, B.A. 1942; Radcliffe Coll. A.M. 1946, PhD. 1953; unm.; CHRMN. & CHIEF EXEC. OFFICER, CAN. MUSEUMS CONSTRUCTION CORP. 1982– ; Dir., Philadelphia Museum of Art 1978–82; Educ. Secy., Art Assn. of Montreal 1942–44; Asst. Prof. Skidmore Coll., N.Y. 1948–49; Asst. Prof. Mount Holyoke Coll., Mass. 1949–52; Asst. and Assoc. Prof. Univ. of Calif. 1954–62; Curator, The Art Gallery of Toronto 1962–64; apptd. Steinberg Prof. of Art Hist., Washington Univ., St. Louis 1964–66; Dir., The National Art Gallery of Canada 1966–76; Prof. of Fine Arts, Harvard Univ. 1976–79; arranged Picasso and Man. Exhn., The Art Gallery of Toronto 1964; publications: 'Portraits by Degas' 1962 and various articles on Degas; 'The National Gallery of Canada' 1971; Anglican; Address: P.O. Box 395, Stn A, Ottawa, Ont. K1N 8V4.

**BOGGS, Joan M.,** B.A., M.Sc., Ph.D.; scientist; b. Endicott, N.Y. 18 Aug. 1946; d. Norris Eugene and Emma Griffith (Bauder) Raymond; e. Reed Coll. B.A. 1968; Univ. of Toronto M.Sc. 1970, Ph.D. 1975; m. Steven A. s. Alice and Arthur B. 24 May 1968; SR. SCIENTIST HOSPITAL FOR SICK CHILDREN AND ASSOC. PROF., UNIV. OF TORONTO 1985– ; post-doctoral work, Hosp. for Sick Children 1975–78; Sr. Rsch. Assoc. 1978–80; Scientist & Asst. Prof., Dept. of Clinical Biochem., Univ. of Toronto 1980–85; Career Devel. Award, Multiple Sclerosis Soc. 1979–83; Scientist Award, MRC 1983–88; Secretary, Candn. Biochemical Soc. 1983–86; Mem., N.Y. Acad. of Sciences; Am. Soc. for Neurochem.; Biophysical Soc.; Candn. Soc. for Biochem. & Molecular Biol.; author/co-author of 70 papers in sci. journals; Assoc. Ed., 'Chem. & Physics of Lipids'; recreations: hiking, canoeing, gardening; Home: 63 Pears Ave., Toronto, ON M5R 1S9; Office: 555 University Ave., Toronto, Ont. M5G 1X8.

**BOGGS, William Brenton,** O.C., O.B.E., B.Eng., F.C.A.S.I., F.C.S.M., F.I.O.D.; company executive; b. Douglas, Arizona 18 Dec. 1918; s. William B. Boggs; (naturalized Canadian); e. McGill Univ., B.Eng. (Mech.) 1940; m. Hughene, d. A.T. Parkes, 7 Feb. 1948; children: William B., Talbot H., Mary Catherine; CHRMN., FIELD AVIATION CO., INC. 1986– ; Past Pres. and Mem. Adv. Counc., Toronto Symphony; Chrmn., Candn. Mfrs. Assn. 1982–83; Chrmn., Candn. Assn. of Data Processing Organizations 1976–77; Chrmn., Aircraft Industry Assn. of Can. 1967–68, also 1987–88; with Trans-Canada Air Lines, 1945–50; Canadair Ltd. 1950–57; joined Hawker Siddeley Canada Ltd., 1957, and subsequently Vice-Pres., Transp. Equipment; Pres., and C.E.O. de Havilland Aircraft of Can. Ltd. 1965–70; Pres. and C.E.O. Canada Systems Group 1971–82 and Chrmn. 1982–83; Chrmn., Pres. & C.E.O., de Havilland Aircraft of Can. Ltd. 1984–86; served in 2nd World War with R.C.A.F., 1940–45 as Sqdn. Ldr.; awarded O.B.E.; Officer of the Order of Canada 1987; Baptist; recreations: golf, tennis; Clubs: National; Rosedale Golf; Granite; Queen's; Hillsboro Tennis (Pompano Beach); Rideau (Ottawa); Home: 190 Roxborough Dr., Toronto, Ont. M4W 1X8.

**BOGLE, Edward (Ted) Warren,** B.Sc., M.Sc., Ph.D.; energy executive; b. Peterborough, Ont. 15 Dec. 1951; s. Roy Thomas and Doris Virginia B.; e. Queen's Univ. B.Sc. 1974, M.Sc. 1977, Ph.D. 1980; m. Nansi E. d. Eric and Evelyn Kihl 16 Oct. 1976; children: Andrew, Graham; VICE-PRESIDENT, EXPLORATION, TALISMAN ENERGY INC. 1992– ; Project Supvr., Frontier Exploration 1984–86; Co-ord., Oil & Gas Planning, Talisman Energy (BP Canada) 1986–87; Mgr., Devel. Geol. 1987–89; Devel. 1989–90; Foothills 1990–92; Dir., Fortuna Petroleum; Candn. Assn. of Petroleum Producers (B.C. Div.); Mem., AAPG, CSPG, APEGGA; Office: Suite 2400, 855 2nd St. S.W., Calgary, Alta. T2P 4J9.

**BOGLE, Hon. Robert John,** B.A., M.L.A.; politician; b. Calgary, Alta. 29 Aug. 1943; s. Robert and Phoebe Alberta (Orford) B.; e. Masinasin Sch. County of Warner; Erle Rivers High Sch., Milk River, Alta.; Mount Royal Coll. Calgary; Univ. of Lethbridge; Sir George Williams Univ.; m. Dr. Elisabeth Christine d. Dr. Hans Lewke, Calgary, Alta. 30 July 1977; children: Shannon Christine, John Hans, Lee Bernard, Julie Ann; former high sch. teacher and businessman; mem. Milk River Town Council 1969–75; el. M.L.A. for Taber-Warner prov. g.e. 1975, re-el. 1979, 82, 86, 89; Min. without Portfolio responsible for Native Affairs 1975; Min. of Social Services & Community Health, Alta. 1979–82; Min. of Utilities & Telecommunications, Alta. 1979–82; Mem., Agricult. & Rural Affairs Caucus Ctte.; Chrmn., Alta. Agriculture Rsch. Inst.; Chrmn., Irrigation Caucus Ctte.; Chrmn., Select Special Ctte. on Electoral Boundaries; Charter mem. Kinsmen Club; mem. Chamber Comm.; Businessmen's Assn.; P. Conservative; Anglican; Home: P.O. Box 515, Milk River, Alta. T0K 1M0.

**BOGUSKY, Alf,** B.F.A.; art museum director; b. Lethbridge, Alta. 16 Mar. 1947; s. Frank and Mildred (Kostelnick) B.; e. Univ. of Lethbridge B.F.A. (with distinction) 1975; EXEC. DIRECTOR, EDMONTON ART GALLERY 1992– ; Instr., Contg. Edn., Univ. of Lethbridge 1975–78; Dir., Curator, Southern Alberta Art Gallery 1979–85; Dir., Art Gallery of Windsor 1985–92; Bd. Mem., Ont. Assn. of Art Galleries 1989– ; Chrmn., Founding Ctte., Alta. Assn. of Art Galleris 1981; Sec., Candn. Art Museums Directors 1986–89; numerous lectures, jury & assessment panels, organized several profl. workshops; Dir., Windsor 2000 Reg. Econ. Diversification Ctte.; numerous other community involvements incl. United Way (Leader of the Way), multicultural council advisory; author of a number of prefaces, introductions, forewords & texts for exhib. catalogues; Home: #402 – 8220 Jasper Ave., Edmonton Alta. T5H 4B6.

**BOHM, Thomas P.,** B.A.; business executive; b. Santiago, Chile 13 Dec. 1943; s. John O. and Gertrudis C. (Hayn) B.; e. Univ. of Chile B.A. 1961; grad. Business Sch., W. Germany 1966; m. Patricia d. Earl McQuaig 21 Sept. 1990; children: Kristian, Julian, Alexander, Stephanie; VICE-PRES., PHILLIPS CABLES LTD. 1990– ; Export Area Mgr., Timberjack (Woodstock Ont.) 1967; Trade Offr., Dept. of Indus., Trade & Commerce (Ottawa) 1970; Export Mgr., present firm 1973; Mem., Export Assn.; has lived in South America, Western Europe & North America; fully fluent in several languages & cultures; recreations: golf, boating; club: Brockville Country; Home: 155 Hartley Street, Brockville, Ont. K6V 3N4; Office: 550 King St., Brockville, Ont. K6V 5W4.

**BOHNE, Harald;** publisher; b. Darmstadt, Germany 15 March 1929; s. Fritz and Anna Louisa (Landmann) B.; e. Bunsen Real Gymnasium, Heidelberg, Germany 1950; came to Can. 1954, naturalized 1960; m. Jean Marcelle Shaver 1 July 1955; Director, Univ. of Toronto Press 1977–89; Mgr. Univ. of Toronto Bookstore 1958, Business Mgr. Univ. of Toronto Press 1960; Asst. Dir. 1970, Assoc. Dir. 1975; co-author 'Publishing: The Creative Business' 1973; Ed. 'Canadian Books in Print' 1970, 1971, 1972, 1973; mem. Candn. Booksellers Assn. (Pres. 1962–64); Assn. Candn. Publishers (Pres. 1977–78; 1986–87); Assn. Candn. Univ. Presses (Pres. 1988–89); Book and Periodical Development Counc. (Chrmn. 1990–91); Co-Chair, Candn. Reprography Collective (CanCopy) 1989–92; Chair, Candn. Copyright Inst. 1992–93; Winner of Eve Orpen Award for Publishing Excellence, 1980; United Church; Address: 14 Tranby Avenue, Toronto, Ont. M5R 1N5.

**BOILARD, Hon. Jean-Guy,** B.A., LL.L.; judge; b. Lyster, Co. Megantic, Que. 15 Aug. 1937; s. Donat and Juliette (Fillion) B.; e. St. John's Coll. Co. Iberville, Que. B.A. 1957; Univ. of Montreal Law Sch. LL.L. 1960; children: François, Stéphane; JUSTICE, SUPERIOR COURT OF QUE.; called to Bar of Que. 1961; R. Catholic; recreation: vintage automobiles; Home: 1250 Ave. Leclair, Verdun, Qué. H4H 2M5; Office: Court House, Montreal, Qué.

**BOILY, The Hon. Mr. Justice Pierre;** judge; b. Sherbrooke, Que. 18 May 1939; s. Thomas Chase and Madeleine (Thibault) B.; e. St. Charles Sem., B.A. 1960; Univ. of Sherbrooke, law licence 1963; Laval Univ., D.E.S.; called to Bar 1964; m. Françoise d. Jacques and Suzanne (Marcoux) Lagassé 29 Aug. 1964; children: Jean-Charles, Patrice, Nicolas; JUDGE, SUPERIOR COURT OF QUEBEC 1983– ; Sr. Partner Boily, Fontaine, Panneton, Lagassé-Boily and McLernon; mem., Gen. Counc., Consulting Ctte. for Trust Accounts and Profl. Inspection and various other cttes., Prov. Bar of Que. (Pres., Dist. of St. Francis 1978–79); mem., Nat. Counc., Candn. Bar Assn. (Treas. Que. 1981–83); Pres. Arbitration Courts (Educ.); Appeal Ctte. Gen. and Prof. Teaching 1982–83; Centre Notre-Dame de l'Enfant 1971–76; founder, mem. and Treas., L'Ecole Plein-Soleil; mem. Admin. Ctte., St-Charles Seminary 1978–80; Pres., l'Aide à l'Educ. Borroméenne 1972–79; Administrator, la Caisse d'Etablissement de l'Estrie 1972–80; Pres., Exec. Ctte., Prov. Liberal Assn. of Sherbrooke 1980–82; Lectr./teacher, Fac. of Law, Univ. of Sherbrooke and Sch. of Profl. Formation of the Que. Bar; Counc. mem., Fac. of Law, Univ. of Sherbrooke 1972–83; recreations: tennis, skiing; Club: North Hatley Tennis; Home: 230 Howard, Sherbrooke, Que. J1J 3K7; Office: 375, King ouest, Sherbrooke, Que. J1H 6B9.

**BOIS, Pierre,** M.D., Ph.D.; medical research organization executive; b. Oka, (Cté des Deux Montagnes) Qué. 22 Mar. 1924; s. Henri C. and Germaine (Ethier) B.; e. Univ. Laval, B.A. 1948; Univ. Montréal, M.D. 1953; Inst. méd. et chir. experimentales, Univ. Montréal, Ph.D. 1957; m. Joyce Casey, 8 Sept. 1953; children: Monique, Marie, Louise; Pres., Medical Research Council of Canada 1981–91; Research Fellow in Pathology, Univ. Montréal 1957; Asst. Prof. Histology & Embryology, Univ. Ottawa 1958; Asst./Assoc. Prof. Pharm., Univ. Montréal 1960; Prof. and Head Anat., 1964, Dean, Faculty Med. 1970; author over 130 publications in the fields of experimental medicine, endocrinology, pharmacology and anatomy; Hon. Life Mem., Candn. Assn. for Laboratory Animal Sciences 1969; Mem. Royal Soc. Can. 1974; Fellow, R.C.P.S.C. 1978; Hon. Degrees: Univ. Ottawa 1982; Univ. of Manitoba 1985; Univ. of Sherbrooke 1986; Univ. McGill 1992; Univ. Western Ontario 1992; Francisco Hernandez Award, Panam. Fedn. Assns. Med. Schs. (PAFAMS) 1986; Emeritus Professor, Univ. Montréal 1987; Hon. Mem., Internat. Assoc. for Dental Rsch. 1988; Chevalier de l'Ordre National du Mérite, République française 1988; Duncan Graham Award, R.C.P.S.C. 1988; Chrmn., Bd. Trustees, G. Malcolm Brown Memorial Fund; mem. Candn. Assn. Anatomists (Pres. 1969–70); mem., Fr. and Am. Assn. Anatomists; Am. Assn. for the Advancement of Sci.; Candn. Fed. Biological Societies; Club de recherches cliniques du Québec (Secy. 1964); recreation: reading; Club: Le Cercle Universitaire d'Ottawa; Home: 6227 Saraguay W., Pierrefonds, Que. H8Y 2H9.

**BOISCLAIR, Marc-André;** company president; b. Montreal, Que. 1 Dec. 1922; e. Montreal, Que.; PRESIDENT, INVESTER INC.; served in 2nd World War with R.C.N.V.R. as Lieut.; R. Catholic; recreations: skiing, gardening, travelling; Home: 756 McEachran, Outremont, Que. H2V 3C7; Office: 4505 Cote des Neiges, Suite 2, Montreal, Que. H3V 1E7.

**BOISVERT, Donald P.J.,** M.D., Ph.D.; physician, association executive; b. Legal, Alta. 20 Dec. 1943; e. Uiv. of Alta. M.D. 1971, Ph.D. 1978; m. Linda J. Martin, B.Ed., M.B.A.; two children; EXECUTIVE DIRECTOR, CANADIAN COUNCIL ON ANIMAL CARE 1992– ; Internship 1971–73; MRC Rsch. Fellow, Univ. of Alta. 1973–76; Wellcome Surgical Rsch. Inst. Glasgow Scotland 1976–77; Resident, Univ. Hosp. Edmonton 1977–80; Rsch. Fellow, Surgery, Univ. of Alta. 1980–81; Assoc. Rsch. Prof. 1981–90; Rsch. Prof. 1990– ; Fellow, MRC 1973–77; Research Prize, Am. Acad. of Surgeons 1979, '80; Scholarship Award, Alta. Heritage Fund for Med. Rsch. 1981–86, renewal award 1986–93; recipient of several rsch. grants; lecturer; Mem., Internat. Soc. of

Cerebral Blood Flow & Metabolism; Soc. of Magnetic Resonance in Med.; Soc. for Neuroscience; Stroke Council, Am. Heart Assn.; Am. Assn. of Neuro. Surgeons; Sr. Investigator, Univ. of Alta. NMR (Nuclear Magnetic Resonance) Group 1982– ; Mem., Univ. of Alta. NMR Policy Ctte. 1983– ; External Reviewer, MRC 1983– ; Mem., Sci. Review Ctte., Alta. Heart & Stroke Found. 1984– ; Human NMR Clin. Rsch. Ctte. 1986– ; U. of A. Health Sci. Animal Welfare Ctte. 1986– ;(Chair 1990– ;); Univ. Animal Policy & Welfare Ctte. 1990– ; Referee, 'J. of Cerebral Blood Flow and Metabolism' 1985– ; Chair, Animal NMR Rsch. Ctte. 1986– ; several past ctte. positions; ; co-editor: 'Neuromethods' vol. 3 1988, 'Magnetic Resonance in Cancer' 1985; author/co-author of 51 papers and 51 abstracts; recreations: alpine skiing, golf, walking, swimming (reef snorkling), sailing, reading, painting; Address: 315 – 350 Albert Street, Ottawa, Ont. K1R 1B1.

**BOISVERT, Hon. Guy W.,** B.A., B.C.L.; superior court judge; b. Normetal, Qué. 13 Aug. 1942; s. Alfred J. and Ozélie M. (Bernard) B.; e. Univ. du Sacré-Coeur B.A. 1963; Univ. of N.B., B.C.L. 1966; m. Estelle Jean d. Onézime and Joséphine Jean 5 Aug. 1967; children: Christian, Jean-François, René; JUDGE, COURT OF QUEEN'S BENCH OF N.B. 1983– ; law practice Bathurst, N.B. 1966–83; Home: 1755 Carl Dr., Bathurst, N.B. E2A 4G8; Office: (P.O. Box 5001) Court of Queen's Bench Chambers, Bathurst, N.B. E2A 1E1.

**BOLAND, Hon. Janet Lang,** B.A.; judge; b. Kitchener, Ont. 6 Dec. 1928; d. George W. and Miriam (Geraghty) Lang; e. Kitchener, Ont.; Convent of Sacred Heart (Kenwood) Albany, N.Y.; Waterloo Coll.; Univ. of W. Ont. B.A.; Osgoode Hall Law Sch.; D.C.L. (Hon.) Wilfrid Laurier Univ. 1974, LL.D. (Hon.) 1976; m. 1 Oct. 1949; children: Michael Frederic, John Christopher, James Nicholas; JUDGE, TRIAL DIV. SUPREME COURT OF ONT. since 1976; called to Bar of Ont. 1950; cr. Q.C. 1966; began private law practice 1950; reported in Court of Appeal for Ont. Weekly Notes and Ont. Reports; mem. Panel Reform for Women Jt. Comte.; joined White, Bristol, Beck & Phipps, Toronto 1958; Partner, Lang, Mitchener, Farquharson, Cranston & Wright, Toronto 1968; apptd. Judge Co. of York 1972; R. Catholic; recreations: skiing, tennis, travel; Home: 164 Inglewood Dr., Toronto, Ont. M4T 1H8; Office: Osgoode Hall, Toronto, Ont. M5H 2N5.

**BOLDT, Keith Sheldon,** B.Ch.Mus., Hons.B.Mus.; tenor; b. Saskatoon, Sask. 13 Apr. 1963; s. Dennis C. and Margaret (Block) B.; e. Warman H.S. 1981; Candn. Mennonite Bible College B.Ch.Mus. 1984; Wilfrid Laurier Univ. Hons.B.Mus. 1988; m. Katherine d. David and Donna Ramseyer 30 June 1989; Canada Opera Piccola Victoria B.C. 1986; Candn. Opera Co. Ensemble 1988–90; Bel Canto Seminar Siena Italy 1990; L'Atelier lyrique de l'Opéra de Montréal 1990–91; Vancouver Opera Young Artists Programme 1991–92; Debut role: Alfredo in 'La Traviata' Edmonton Opera 1992; currently an opera & concert performer throughout Canada; singing teacher: Edward Zambara; scholarships: Sask. Arts Bd. Grant 1986 and 1987; Dr. Gladys Whitehead Scholarship 1987; 1st Prize, Bel Canto Vocal Comp. 1990; Edmonton Opera Guild 1992; Vancouver Opera Found. 1992; Vancouver Opera Guild 1993; Mennonite; recreations: farming, fishing, cooking; former club: 4-H; Home: Toronto, Ont.

**BOLDUC, J. Emilien,** M.Sc., B.Sc.; banker; b. Roberval, Que. 10 March 1939; s. François N. and Georgette N. (Neron) B.; e. Laval Univ. B.Sc., M.Sc. 1967; m. Gisèle d. Benoit Pigeon 11 Dec. 1976; children: Chantal, Eric; EXYVE. VICE-PRES. & CHIEF FINANCIAL OFFICER, ROYAL BANK OF CANADA 1990– ; joined Roberval branch of Royal Bank 1957 & held posts at branches in Ste. Foy, Gagnon and St. Rémi, Que. as well as Alexandria, Ont.; Credit Offr., Montreal Main Branch 1967; Asst. Mgr. St. James Branch 1968; Credit Offr., Candn. Loans, Head Office & Mgr., Mntg. Devel., Personnel 1973; Sr. Asst. Mgr. Montreal Main Br. 1976; Dep. Mgr. 1978; Vice-Pres., Eastern U.S.A. New York 1979; Mng. Dir., Banque Belge pour l'Indus. (formerly Royal Bank) Belgium 1982; Sr. Vice-Pres., World Corporate Banking U.K. 1985; Sr. Vice-Pres. & Chief Inspector 1986; Extve. Vice-Pres., Finance 1988; internal directorships; Roman Catholic; recreations: fishing, tennis; Home: 185 Tower, Beaconsfield, Que. H9W 5T3; Office: 1 Place Ville Marie, P.O. Box 6001, Montreal, Que. H3C 3A9.

**BOLDUC, Roch,** O.C., B.A., LL.L.; executive; b. St. Raphael, Que. 10 Sept. 1928; s. Edgar and Antoinette (St.-Pierre) B.; e. Laval Univ., B.A. 1948, LL.L. 1951; Univ. of Chicago, post-grad. study 1953; m. Gisele d. Joseph and Yvonne Lacroix 22 May 1954; children: Louise, Jacques, Richard, Andre; Dir., The Personal 1988– ; Rothman's Inc.; Senator 1988; Job Analyst, Govt. of Que. 1953–56; Dir., 1956–65; Civil Serv. Comnr. 1965–69; Dep. Min., Civil Serv. Dept. 1969–73; Mun. Affairs 1973–78; Chrmn., Civil Serv. Comn. 1978–82; Vice Pres., CGI Group 1983–85, 1987–88; Lectr., Univ. of Montreal 1955–60; Laval Univ. 1960–65; Concordia Univ. 1983; Tech. Adv., The World Bank in Africa; Del., var. internat. conf. 1956–86; Secy.-Gen., Govt. of Que. 1985–86; Hon. LL.D., Concordia Univ.; Vanier Medal – IPAC; Officer, Order of Canada; Mem., Nat. Defence Coll. 1973; Gov., Laval Univ.; Mem., Candn. Inst. of Pub. Admin.; author of num. articles 1964–83; recreations: skiing, golf; Clubs: Royal Québec; Home: 937 Gatineau, Ste-Foy, Que. G1V 3A2.

**BOLEN, Norm Frances,** B.A.; broadcasting executive; b. Regina, Sask. 29 Nov. 1948; s. George Peter and Irene (D'Aoust) B.; e. St. Louis College, Moose Jaw, Sask. 1967; Univ. of Sask., B.A. with distinction 1970 (gen. proficiency scholarship); m. Catherine L. d. Michael James and Mary Redmond 19 Dec. 1981; children: Michael James, Sarah Diane, David George; REGIONAL DIR., CBC ONTARIO REGION (ENGLISH) 1993– ; Field Worker, Candn. Union of Students 1969–70; Pres., Sage Commun. & Rsch. Ltd. 1973–74; Researcher, Nat. Health Grant, Univ. of Sask. 1975–76; TV Reporter & Editor, CBC Saskatoon 1976–83; Extve. & Area Prod., News & Current Affairs, CBC Regina 1983–85; Extve. Prod., 'Sunday Morning,' CBC Network Radio 1985–87; Dir. of TV, English Serv., Que. Region, CBC Montreal 1987–89; Dir., English TV Prog., CBC Ottawa 1989–93; Sess. Lectr., Sch. of Jour., Univ. of Regina 1984–85; Sess. Lectr., Carleton Univ., Ottawa School of Journalism 1993– ; CBC del., Berlin Conf. of Eur. Broadcasting Union 1985; Candn. Shop Steward 'Input 91,' Dublin, Ireland; 'Input 92', Baltimore, Maryland (Input: Internat. Public Television Screening Conf.); Candn. National Coordinator Input 1992– ; Mem., CBC/NABET Nat. Joint Ctte.; Trainer, Jamaica Broadcasting Corp. 1990– ; South Africa Education Trust, Radio & TV Workshop 1990, 1993; Contract Cons., Sec. of State 1973; Chrmn., Nat. Training Ctte., CBC TV 1989– ; Moose Jaw Optimist Club Boy of the Year 1966; Golden Sheaf Award & Sask. Cable TV Assn. Award, Yorkton Internat. Film Fest. 1982; co-winner, CBC Anik Award 1981; mem., Academy of Candn. Cinema & Television; Ottawa Heart Inst. Telethon Adv. Bd. 1989–91; Mem. Adv. Bd., Candn. Mothercraft of Ottawa-Carleton 1990– ; Mem. Journalism Adv. Bd., Algonquin Coll., Ottawa 1991– ; jury mem., Gemini Awards 1991, '92 (jury chrmn. 1992); past mem. several orgns.; Editor-in-Chief, 'The Carillon' 1968–70; 'Prairiefire' 1971–72; Contbr., 'Maclean's,' 'Wine Tidings'; recreations: cycling, swimming, wine; clubs: Candn., Ottawa Opimian Soc.; Home: 573 Roosevelt Ave., Ottawa, Ont. K2A 2A2; Office: P.O. Box 3220, Stn. 'C,' Ottawa, Ont. K1Y 1E4.

**BOLGER, Rev. Dr. Francis W.P.,** B.A., S.T.L., M.A., Ph.D.; university professor; b. Stanley Bridge, P.E.I. 8 July 1925; s. Thomas and Margaret (Walsh) B.; e. Prince of Wales College; St. Dunstan's Univ. B.A. 1947; Univ. of Montreal S.T.L. 1951; Univ. of Toronto M.A. 1956, Ph.D. 1959; PROFESSOR OF HISTORY, UNIV. OF PRINCE EDWARD ISLAND 1969– ; ordained Roman Catholic priest 10 June 1951; Diocese of Charlottetown 1951– ; Assoc. Pastor, St. Dunstan's Basilica Charlottetown 1951–53; Prof. of History, St. Dunstan's Univ. 1959–69; Chaplain, Air Force Reserve 1954–60; USSO Officer, R.C.A.F. 1960–67; award for excellence in teaching, Univ. of P.E.I. 1986–87; P.E.I. Model Educator Prize 1990; P.E.I. Rep., Historical Sites & Monuments of Canada 1966–78, 1990– ; Pres., Candn. Catholic Hist. Assn. 1964; Pres.-Gen. 1965; Chrmn., Lucy Maud Montgomery Found. Bd. 1980; Islander of the Year 1974; author: 'P.E.I. and Confederation, 1863–1873' 1964, 'The Years before Anne' 1974; co-author: 'Spirit of Place' 1982, 'Memories of the Old Home Place' 1984; editor: 'Canada's Smallest Province'1973; co-editor: 'My Dear Mr. M.: Letters of L.M. Montgomery to G.B. Macmillan' 1980; recreations: golf, swimming; Home: Stanley Bridge, P.E.I. C0A 1E0; Office: Charlottetown, P.E.I. C1A 4P3.

**BOLLEY, Andrea,** B.F.A.; artist, painter; b. Guelph, Ont. 15 Aug. 1949; d. Dr. Hildo and Laura Pia (Maurino) B.; e. Univ. of Windsor 1975; solo exhibitions: Upper Canada Brewing Co. 1993; Klonaridis Gall. Toronto 1989, '90, '91; Gallery One Toronto 1984, '85, '86; Agnes Etherington Art Ctr. Kingston 1981; Pollock Gall. Toronto 1977, '78, '80; The Art Gall. of Brant 1977; IDA Gall. York Univ. 1976; group exhibitions incl.: Triangle, New York 1991, 1992, 1993; Upper Canada Brewing Co., Toronto 1992; Magnum Books, Ottawa 1991; Mississauga Civic Ctr. Art Gall. 1990; John Schweitzer Gall. Montreal (catalogue) 1989; Klonaridis Gall. 1988; Gallery One 1984, '85, '86; Triangle N.Y. 1985 and '91, Art Gall. of Hamilton travelling exhib. (catalogue) 1981; Art Gall. of Ont. 1981; Alta. Coll. of Art Calgary (catalogue) 1980; Grapestake Gall. San Francisco 1980 and numerous others; collections: Can. Counc. Art Bank; Art Gall. of Windsor; Labatt's of Can. Ltd.; Citicorp (Canada) Ltd.; Candn. Imperial Bank of Commerce; Max Factor Ltd.; Chatelaine Magazine; J.E. Seagram Ltd.; The McGill Club; Imperial Oil; Citibank Canada; Toronto-Dominion Bank; Casey House; American Express; Guaranty Trust; Abitibi Paper; Triangle, N.Y.; The Toronto Sun; Toronto Dominion Bank; Arthur Gelgoot & Assoc., and private collections Canada, U.S.A., & Europe; subject of several newspaper & mag. articles; comn.: Yonge Street Diner 1984; teacher: Arts Sake Toronto 1982, Activity Ctr., Art Gall. of Ont. 1979, '80; awards & grants: Ont. Arts Counc. 1975, '76, '78, '79, '84, '85; Can. Counc. 1976, '80; O.S.A. Purchase Award, J.E. Seagram and Son Ltd. 1980 and several others; Office: 145 Danforth Ave., Toronto, Ont. M4K 1N2.

**BOLOTEN, Jeffrey,** B.Com., LL.B.; book publishing executive; lawyer; b. Montreal, Que. 9 Dec. 1959; s. Herbert and Shirley (Aspler) B.; e. McGill Univ. B.Com. 1982; Osgoode Hall Law Sch. Toronto LL.B. 1985; Harvard Univ. Radcliffe Publishing Course 1987; SENIOR PUBLISHER, LONGMAN U.K. LAW, TAX & FINANCE 1992– ; joined Circulation Dept. Saturday Night mag. 1987; Penguin Books Canada Ltd. 1987–91, Assoc. Pub. and Sec. Bd. Dirs.; mem. Law Soc. Upper Can.; Candn. Bar Assn.; Assn. Litteraire et Artistique Internat.; Law Soc. of England & Wales; Home: 14 Artesian Rd., Garden Flat, London W2 5AR, England.

**BOLTON, Charles Thomas,** B.S., M.S., Ph.D., F.R.S.C.; professor; b. Camp Forrest, Tenn. 15 Apr. 1943; s. Clifford Theodore and Pauline Grace (Voris) B.; e. Univ. of Ill., B.S. 1966; Univ. of Michigan, M.S. 1968, Ph.D. 1970; m. Susan d. William and Mary Challenger 3 Oct. 1986; ASSOC. DIR., DAVID DUNLAP OBSERVATORY, DEPT. OF ASTRON., UNIV. OF TORONTO 1978–88, 1989– ; post-doct. fellow, David Dunlap Observ. 1970–73; Asst. Prof., Univ. of Toronto 1970–71, Instr., Scarboro. Coll. 1971–72, Asst. Prof., Erindale Coll. 1972–73 (part-time); Asst. Prof., David Dunlap Observ. 1973–76; Assoc. Prof. 1976–80; Prof. 1980– ; co-discoverer of first black hole; Mem., Sci. Adv. Ctte., Canada-France-Hawaii Telescope Corp. 1983–85; Cons., Candn. Nat. Ctte., Comn. Internat de l'Eclairage 1975– ; Phi Kappa Phi; Royal Soc. of Canada (Secretary, Mathematics and Physical Sci. Div., Academy III 1992– ;); Internat. Astron. Union (Mem., Comn. 27, 42); Candn. Astron. Soc. (Nom. Ctte. 1981; Solar Power Satellites Ctte. 1981–85; Chrmn., Subctte. on Image Processing 1981–83; Optical Astron. 1983–85); Royal Astron. Soc. of Can. (2nd Vice-Pres., Toronto Ctr. 1981–84); Am. Astron. Soc.; Astron. Soc. of the Pacific; Sigma Xi; Univ. of Ill. Alumni Assn.; recreations: softball, weightlifting; Home: 326 Palmer Ave., Richmond Hill, Ont. L4C 1P3; Office: P.O. Box 360, Richmond Hill, Ont. L4C 4Y6.

**BOLTON, Hugh John,** B.A., C.A.; financial executive; b. Edmonton, Alta. 21 May 1938; b. John Baird and Margaret Mabel (Morrison) B.; e. Univ. of Alta. B.A. 1959; Inst. of Chartered Accts. of Alta. C.A. 1963; m. Margot d. Fred and Leance Blythe 4 Feb. 1961; children: Robert Scott, Patricia Blythe, Cydney Jane; CHRMN. AND CHIEF EXTVE. PARTNER, CHRMN. OF PARTNERSHIP BD., COOPERS & LYBRAND CANADA 1991– ; student in accounts, Willetts, Berge & Co. Edmonton 1959–63; Staff C.A. 1963–64; Partner 1964–76; Partner-in-Charge 1976–80; company merged with Coopers & Lybrand 1 March 1980; Partner-In-Charge, Edmonton Office, 1980–86; Mng. Partner, Can. Opns., Toronto 1986–88; Vice Chrmn., Nat. Opns. & Member, Extve. & Policy Cttes. 1988–91; Mem., Candn. Inst. of C.A.s 1963– ; Candn. Tax Found. (Gov. 1976–80; Mem., Extve. Ctte. 1980–82); Mem., Adv. Counc., Sch. of Business, York Univ.; Mem. Bus. Adv. Council, Univ. of Alta.; Dir. and Treas., Metro Toronto Br., Candn. Diabetes Assoc.; Dir.-at-Large, Junior Achievement of Canada; Phi Delta Theta 1958–59; recreations: gardening, photography, hunting, squash, woodworking; Clubs: Emerald Hills Golf; Toronto; Cambridge; Home: 433 Heath St. E., Toronto, Ont. M4G 1B6; Office: 145 King St. W., Toronto, Ont. M5H 1V8.

**BOLTON, James Robert,** Ph.D.; educator; b. Swift Current, Sask. 24 June 1937; s. James Linden and Mary Margaret (McFadden) B.; e. Univ. of Sask. B.A. 1958; M.A. 1960; Univ. of Cambridge Ph.D. 1963; m. Wilma Burdette, d. late William G. Hall, 26 Dec. 1959; children: Judith Louise; James Thomas; PROF., DEPT. OF CHEMISTRY, UNIV. OF WESTERN ONTARIO 1970– ; and Dir., Photochemistry Unit there 1979–85; On leave as a Sr. Rsch. Fellow with Solarchem Environmental Systems, Richmond Hill, Ont. 1991–93; Consultant to Solar Energy Research Institute (Colorado) 1978–86; Postdoctoral Fellow, Columbia Univ. 1963; Assoc. Prof. of Chem., Univ. of Minnesota 1967; Prof. 1969 (Assoc. Chrmn. of Chem. Dept. 1968–70); Sloan Research Fellow 1966–68; CIL Lecturer, Simon Fraser Univ. 1982; Van Cleave Lecturer, Univ. of Regina 1982; patentee in field; author 'Solar Cells – Canada'; co-author (with J.A. Weil and J.E. Wertz) 'Electron Paramagnetic Resonance: Theory and Examples' 1993; (with D.R. Arnold et al.) 'Photochemistry: An Introduction' 1974; co-ed. (with H.M. Swartz and D.C. Borg) 'Biological Applications of Electron Spin Resonance' 1972; ed. 'Solar Power and Fuels: Proceedings of First International Conference on Photochemical Conversion and Storage of Solar Energy' 1977 (Chrmn. of Organizing Ctte. for that conf.); author or co-author over 200 research papers, reviews, articles, book chapters, etc.; Fellow, Chem. Inst. of Can.; mem. Amer. Chem. Soc.; Inter-Amer. Photochemical Soc.; Solar Energy Soc. of Can., Inc. (past Chrmn.); Chrmn. 1980 Gordon Conf. on Magnetic Resonance in Medicine and Biology, Tilton, N.H.; Chrmn., Physical Chem. Div., Chem. Inst. of Can. 1981–83; Dir., Chemists' Affairs 1983–85; First Pres. of the newly founded Candn. Soc. for Chemistry 1985–87; Noranda Lecture Award of the Chem. Inst. of Can. 1978; Unitarian; recreation: music; Home: 92 Main St., Ayr, Ont. N0B 1E0; Office: Dept. of Chemistry, Univ. of Western Ontario, London, Ont. N6A 5B7.

**BOLTON, Richard,** M.Sc., Ph.D.; physicist; b. Montreal, Que. 16 Oct. 1939; s. Richard Ernest and Elizabeth Armour (Robertson) B.; e. Lower Can. Coll. 1957; McGill Univ., B.Sc. 1960, M.Sc. 1963; Univ. of Montreal, Ph.D. 1966; m. Sandra d. Ferns and Maryon Cassidy 19 Dec. 1964; children: Andrew, Sarah, Philip; DIR. GEN., CENTRE CANADIEN DE FUSION MAGNETIQUE 1986– ; Asst. Prof., Univ. of Montreal 1966–68; Rsch. Assoc., Culham Lab., U.K. Atomic Energy Authority 1968–73; Researcher, Hydro-Qué. Rsch. Inst. 1973–78; Project Mgr., Tokamak de Varennes Fusion Project, Hydro-Que. Rsch. Inst. 1978–86; Mem., NRC Adv. Ctte. on fusion related rsch. 1983–86; Vis. Prof., INRS-énergie (Univ. of Que.) 1979; Lectr., Univ. of Que. at Montreal 1974–78; nom. to Sci. Counc. of Canada 1987 & its Extve. Ctte. 1989; NRC Grad. Student scholarship 1961–64; Gov., Lower Can. Coll. 1986–92; mem. NRC Adv. Bd. on TRIUMF (ABOT) 1992– ; mem., Candn. Nuclear Assn. (Nat. Counc. 1984–86); Candn. Assn. of Physicists; author/co-author of approx. 20 sci. articles on plasma physics; recreations: skiing, tennis, sailing; club: Hillside Tennis; Home: 507 Argyle Ave., Westmount, Que. H3Y 3B6; Office: 1804 Montée-Ste-Julie, Varennes, Que. J3X 1S1.

**BOLTON, Richard Ernest,** B.Sc., F.R.A.I.C., R.C.A.; b. Montreal, Que. 18 March 1907; s. William Ernest and Catharine Hamilton (McClure) B.; both of Montreal, Que.; e. Westmount (Que.) High Sch.; McGill Univ.; Mass. Inst. Tech. B.Sc.(Arch) & Bronze Medal; m. Elizabeth Armour, d. late A. Armour Robertson, M.D. of Montreal, P.Q.; one d. and one s.; in private practice as a principal 1933–70; Chancellor, Coll. of Fellows, Roy. Arch. Inst. Can. 1970–73; Pres., P.Q. Assn. of Architects, 1961; served in 2nd World War; Lieut.-Commdr., R.C.N.V.R.; mem. Royal Cndn. Acad. Arts; Fellow, Royal Architectural Inst. of Canada; Hon. Fellow Heraldry Soc. of Can.; Anglican; Clubs: St. James's; Royal St. Lawrence Yacht; Home: 4501 Sherbrooke St. W., Apt. 3–A, Westmount, Que. H3Z 1E7.

**BOLUS, Malvina Marjorie,** O.C.; b. Fox Bay, Falkland Islands 4 July 1906; d. Percy Reginald, M.D., O.B.E. and Viola Constance (Felton) B.; e. Bedales, Petersfield, Hants., Eng.; Sydenham High Sch., London, Eng.; Clark's Coll. London, Eng.; came to Can. 1926; mem. H. of C. staff 1928–36, Secy. to Agnes Macphail, M.P. 1933–36, comtes. and Hansard staff sessions 1936–39; Personal Asst. to Sr. Offr. Candn. Mil. HQ London 1939–44; Secy. to Head of London Mission Office of Scient. Research & Devel. London and New York 1944–45; Asst. Ed. Candn. Geog. Soc. 1946, mem. Ed. Comte. 1950–56; Pub. Relations Hudson's Bay Co. Winnipeg 1956; Ed. 'The Beaver' mag. 1958–72; Officer, Order of Canada 1970; recipient Candn. Hist. Assn. Cert. of Merit 1961; Wash. State Hist. Soc. Robert Gray Medal 1970; Am. Assn. State & Local Hist. Award of Merit 1972; author 'Image of Canada' 1953; 'Eskimo Art' 1967; 'People and Pelts' 1972; mem. Candn. Women's Press Club 1947–72; Council Man. Hist. Soc. 1960–65; Historic Sites Adv. Bd. Man. 1958–65; Council Champlain Soc. 1971; Man. Naturalists; Geog. Soc. Man.; Victoria B.C. Natural Hist. Soc.; recreations: travel, swimming, birding, gardening; Address: 5 – 2981 Craigowan Rd., Victoria, B.C. V9B 1N2.

**BONAR, Lucian George,** B.A.Sc., M.S., Ph.D.; business executive; b. Lodz, Poland 1 June 1934; s. Henry and Janina Wierska B.; arrived in Can. 1941; e. Univ. Toronto, B.A.Sc. 1958; Univ. Calif., M.S. 1959; Cambridge Univ., Ph.D. 1962; m. Stephanie, d. Sen. T. D'Arcy and Lilian Leonard, 1 June 1963; children: Daphne Leonard; Justin Gray; CHRMN., PRES. & C.E.O., INTERNATIONAL UNP HOLDINGS LTD., Toronto; Chrmn. Supervisory Bd.: IBIS Ltd.; BIAWAR Ltd.; UNIPAK Ltd.; Dir., Marsulex Inc.; Vice-Pres., Falconbridge Ltd. 1962–70; Pres., Bonar Associates 1970–71; Sr. Vice-Pres., Nickel Div., Amax Inc. 1972–80; Pres., Cabot Mineral Resources 1980–81; Vice Pres., Falconbridge Ltd. 1981–86; Chrmn. & C.E.O., Eldorado Nuclear Limited, Ottawa 1987–88; rec'd. Athlone Fellowship 1959–61; Nat. Research Counc. Can. Special Scholarship 1961–62; mem. clubs: R.C.Y.C. (Toronto); The Toronto (Toronto); National (Toronto); Badminton and Racquet (Toronto); Oxford and Cambridge (London); Home: 10 Cadogan Gardens, London SW3 2RS, England; Office: London, England.

**BONAR, Ronald Frank,** B.A., LL.B., KCM; corporate counsel; b. Toronto, Ont. 12 Apr. 1931; e. Forest Hill Coll. Inst. Toronto 1949; Univ. of Toronto B.A. 1953; Osgoode Hall Law Sch. 1957; LL.B. 1991; m. Joyce 3 Aug. 1956; children: Andrew Ronald Russell, Carolyn Virginia Louise; DIR., VICE PRES., CORP. COUNSEL AND SECY., COLGATE-PALMOLIVE CANADA INC. 1991– ; law practice Johnston, Sheard & Johnston 1958–59; Law Dept. The Goodyear Tire and Rubber Co. of Canada Ltd. 1959–64; Gen. Counsel, Colgate-Palmolive Ltd. 1964, Vice Pres. Gen. Counsel 1968–76, Dir. and Secy. 1971–76; Dir., Secy., Vice Pres. and Corp. Counsel, CKR INC. 1976–91; mem. Candn. Cosmetic, Toiletry & Fragrance Assn. (Chrmn. 1978–79, Dir. 1973–82, Adv. Bd. 1982– , Chrmn., Regulatory Review Ctte. 1985–88); Candn. Mfrs.' Assn. (Chrmn. Leg. Comte., Dir. 1985); Soap & Detergent Assn. Can. (Pres. 1987, 1993; Chrmn. Leg. Comte., Dir. 1985– ;); Assn. Candn. Gen. Counsel (Secy-Treas. 1981–82, Vice Pres. 1991–93); Bd. Trade Metrop. Toronto; Presbyterian; Clubs: University (Toronto); Lawyers'; Ordo Constantini Magni; Office: 99 Vanderhoof Ave., Toronto, Ont. M4G 2H6.

**BOND, Courtney Claude Joseph,** B.A., D.L.S.; cartographer; writer; b. Toronto, Ont. 14 Apl. 1910; s. Charles Frederick and Blanche Agnes (Troman) B.; e. St. Mary's Coll. Halifax; St. Michael's Coll. Toronto; Carleton Univ. B.A. (Hist.) 1961; Univ. of Ottawa B.A. (Music Conc.) 1979; m. Elisabeth d. John and Maud Berton 1 Jan. 1938; two s. Timothy, Courtney Frederick; joined RCE 1932, rank Sapper; topographical mapping of Can. with Geog. Sect. Gen. Staff 1933–45; rec'd. Commission as Dominion Land Surveyor 1945; Cartographer, Hist. Sect. Gen. Staff 1945–60, rank Maj.; Historian, Nat. Capital Comn. Ottawa 1961–68; Head, Candn. Sect. Nat. Map Coll. Pub. Archives Can. 1968–71; Head, Atlas Sect. Surveys & Mapping Div. Dar es Salaam, Tanzania (CUSO) 1971–74; Cartographer, 'Canadian Geographical Journal' 1975–77; Chief Cartographer, Charnell & Assoc., Punel, Gilan, Iran (E.D.C. Project) 1977–78; recipient Cert. of Merit Candn. Hist. Assn. 1966; Le Prix Louis Taché, Institut d'histoire et récherches sur l'Outaouais 1983; author 'City on the Ottawa/Ville sur l'Outaouais' 1965; 'Surveyors of Canada 1867–1967' 1967; 'The Ottawa Country/Le Pays de l'Outaouais' 1968; 'An Iron in Many a Fire' autobiog. 1982; 'Where Rivers Meet: An Illustrated History of Ottawa' 1984; '40 Years A Sailin! A History of Sail RA' 1987; 'How About the General?: sundry writings' 1992; regular contributor to 'Glebe Report' 1986– ; co-author 'Hurling Down the Pine' 1965, 1987; ed. 'The Cat's Meow' (by Elisabeth S. Bond) 1991; 'Fifty Years a-Building' (by Josef Jaromir Hrazdira) 1991; compiled and drew maps official hists. Candn. Army First & Second World Wars, Korean War 1945–60; maps D.G.G. Kerr's 'Historical Atlas of Canada' 1961 and many works Candn. hist. 1959–71; 'Atlas of Tanzania' 1976; Chrmn. Fairhaven Cooperative Community Inc. 1961–71; Eng. Lang. Sec. Candn. Hist. Assn. 1965–71; recreations: music, PC networking, swimming; Home: 804 – 151 Bay St., Ottawa, Ont. K1R 7T2.

**BOND, David Edward,** B.A., M.A., Ph.D.; banker; b. Hamilton, Ont. 13 Apr. 1938; s. Kener Eldridge and Evelyn Lucy (Spohor) B.; e. Dartmouth Coll., B.A. cum laude 1960; Yale Univ. M.A. 1961, Ph.D. 1965; children: Peter, Kristina, Pierre Paul (Proulx), Jean Francois (Proulx), Rachel Elizabeth (Proulx); VICE PRES., PUBLIC AFFAIRS, AND CHIEF ECONOMIST, HONG KONG BANK OF CANADA 1989– ; Asst. Prof. of Econ., Univ. of W. Ont. 1964–67; Asst. & Assoc. Prof. of Econ., Univ. of B.C. 1967–71; Extve. Dir., Consumer Counc. 1972–73; Dir. Gen., Census 1973–75; Asst. Depy. Min., Intellectual Property & Corp., Consumer & Corp. Affairs 1975–81; Depy. Sec., Min. of State Econ. & Regl. Devel. 1981–82; Fed. Econ. Devel. Co-ordr., B.C. 1982–85; Pres., Candn. Assn. of Broadcasters 1985–87; Prof. des Sciences Administratives, Univ. du Québec à Hull 1988–89; Phi Beta Kappa; Woodrow Wilson Fellow 1961; co-author: 'Trade Liberalization and the Canadian Furniture Industry' 1966; 'Money and Banking' 1975; 'The Economics of the Canadian Financial System: Theory, Policy and Institutions' 2nd ed. 1982; recreations: antique collector, beekeeper; Home: 1603 - 1260 Nelson St., Vancouver, B.C. V6E 1J7; Office: 3rd Flr., Hong Kong Bank of Can., 885 W. Georgia, Vancouver, B.C. V6C 3E9.

**BOND, J. Richard,** M.S., Ph.D.; educator; b. Toronto, Ont. 15 May 1950; s. Jack Parry and Margaret (Sandham) B.; e. Univ. of Toronto, B.Sc. 1973; Cal. Inst. of Technol. M.S. 1975, Ph.D. 1979; PROF. CANDN. INST. FOR THEORETICAL ASTROPHYSICS, UNIV. OF TORONTO 1987– ; Sci., Gamma Ray Astron. JPL Pasadena 1975–76; Visiting Sci. Nuclear Theory Neils Bohr Inst. 1976–77; Rsch. Asst. Kellogg Radiation Lab Caltech 1973–78; Postdoctoral Fellow/Lectr. in Astron. Univ. of Cal. Berkeley 1978–81; Rsch. Fellow, Inst. of Astron. Cambridge Univ. 1982–83; mem. Inst. for Theoretical Physics Univ. of Cal. Santa Barbara 1984; Asst. Prof. of Physics Stanford Univ. 1981–85, Assoc. Prof. 1985–87; Assoc. Prof. present Inst. 1985–87; Acting Dir. present Inst. 1990–91; Steacie Prize 1989; Steacie Fellow 1989–91; Fellow, Candn. Inst. Advanced Rsch. 1986– ; Sloan Found. Rsch. Fellow 1985–89; Fellow, Churchill Coll. Cambridge 1982–83; Richard P. Feynman Fellow Caltech 1974–75; author over 75 articles sci. publs. astrophysics & cosmology; mem. Am. Physical Soc.; Am. Astron. Soc.; Candn. Astron. Soc.; Internat. Astron. Union; Office: Toronto, Ont. M5S 1A1.

**BOND, Ronald Bruce,** M.A., Ph.D.; educator; b. Hamilton, Ont. 15 Aug. 1946; s. Bernard Bruce and Verna Belle (Curtis) B.; e. McMaster Univ. B.A. 1968, M.A. 1969; Univ. of Toronto Ph.D. 1972; Royal Conserv. of Music Toronto A.R.C.T. (piano) 1963; Royal Candn. Coll. of Organists A.R.C.C.O. (organ) 1968; m. Shirley d. Victor and Dorothy Ross 1969; children: Jennifer, Geoffrey; DEAN OF HUMANITIES UNIV. OF CALGARY 1989– , Prof. of Eng. 1988– ; Lectr. in Eng. Univ. Coll. Univ. of Toronto 1972; Asst. Prof. of Eng. present Univ. 1973, Assoc. Prof. 1979, Asst. Dean of Humanities 1977–79, Assoc. Dean 1979–81, Head of Eng. 1985–89; ed. 'Certain Sermons or Homilies' 1987; co-ed. 'The Yale Edition of the Shorter Works of Edmund Spenser' 1989; mem. Humanities Assn. Can. (Pres. Calgary Br. 1980–81); Candn. Assn. Chairs of Eng. (Pres. 1988–89); recreations: squash, swimming; Club: Calgary Winter; Home: 314 Scimitar Bay N.W., Calgary, Alta. T3L 1L9; Office: 2500 University Dr. N.W., Calgary, Alta. T2N 1N4.

**BONDAR, Roberta Lynn,** O.C., O.Ont., M.D., Ph.D., F.R.C.P.(C); b. Sault Ste. Marie, Ont. 4 Dec. 1945; e. Univ. of Guelph B.Sc. 1968; Univ. of W. Ont. M.Sc. 1971; Univ. of Toronto Ph.D. 1974; McMaster Univ. M.D. 1977; Univ. of W. Ont. F.R.C.P.(C) 1981; D.Sc. (Hon.) Mt. Allison Univ. 1989; D.Hum.L. (Hon.) Mount St. Vincent Univ. 1990; D.Sc. (Hon.) Univ. of Guelph 1990; Fellow, Ryerson Polytechnical Inst. 1990; D.Sc. (Hon.) Lakehead Univ. 1991; D.Sc. (Hon.) Algoma Coll., Laurentian Univ. 1991; D.Sc. (Hon.) Saint Mary's Univ. 1992; D.Sc. (Hon.) McMaster Univ. 1992; LL.D. (Hon.) Univ. of Regina 1992; LL.D. (Hon.) Univ. of Calgary 1992; D.U. (Hon.) Univ. of Ottawa 1992; D.Sc. (Hon.) Univ. of Toronto 1992; D.Sc. (Hon.) McGill Univ. 1992; D.Sc. (Hon.) York Univ. 1992; D.S.L. (Hon.) Wycliffe College, Univ. of Toronto 1993; D.Sc. (Hon.) Royal Roads Military College 1993; D.Sc. (Hon.) Memorial Univ. 1993; D.Sc. (Hon.) Laval Univ. 1993; D.Sc. (Hon.) Carleton Univ. 1993; Officer, Order of Canada 1992; Order of Ontario 1993; several high sch. awards; fellowships: Ont. Grad. 1970–71, N.R.C. scholarship 1971–73, N.R.C. postdoctoral fellowship 1974, Ont. Min. of Health 1981, Med. Rsch. Counc. 1981–82, Wm. A. Vanderburgh, Sr. Travel Award 1976; ASTRONAUT, CANADIAN ASTRONAUT PROGRAM 1983–92; First Candn. woman astronaut in space 22 Jan. 1992; Prime Payload Specialist for STS-42, IML-I (First Internat. Microgravity Lab. Mission); Bd. of Dirs., Internat. Space Univ., Can. 1987–92 (ex officio); Mem. Scientific Advisory Panel, Premier's Council on Science & Technology 1988–89; Bd. of Trustees, Nat. Museum of Sci. and Tech. 1990–93; Bd. of Regents, Candn. Mobile Athlete and Sport Hosp. 1992–93; Mem., Public Advisory Cttee. on State of the Environment Reporting 1992–93; Adv. Bd., Order of Canada (Gov. Gen's. representative) 1993; Senior Advisor, Royal Commn. on Education, Prov. of Ont. 1993; Rsch. Asst., Dept. of Fisheries & Forestry 1963–68; Coach, Archery Team and Phys. Ed. Lectr., Univ. of Guelph 1966–67, Histology Tech. (part-time) Dept. of Zoology, Univ. of Guelph 1967–68; Teaching Asst., Univ. of Toronto 1970–74; Intern, Toronto Gen. Hosp. 1977–78; Resident, Univ. of W. Ont. 1978–80; Neuro-ophthalmology Fellow, Tuft's New England Med. Ctr. 1981; Toronto Western Hosp. 1981–82; Asst. Prof., McMaster Univ. 1982–84; Dir., Multiple Sclerosis Clinic, Hamilton-Wentworth Region 1982–84; Asst. Prof., Dept. of Medicine, Div. of Neurology, Ottawa Gen. Hosp., Ottawa, Ont. 1985–88; Lectr., Dept. of Nursing, Univ. of Ottawa 1985–88; Chrmn., Candn. Life Sciences Cttee. for Space Station, Nat. Rsch. Council of Canada 1985–89; Civil Aviation Medical Examiner, Health & Welfare, Canada 1986–93; Rsch. Fellow, Playfair Inst. Oculomotor Lab., Toronto Western Hosp. 1989; Life Sciences Representative, Candn. Adv. Council on the Scientific Utilization of Space Station 1986–88; Lectr., Dept. of Nat'l Defence Flight Surgeon course, Biomedical Aspects of Space Flight 1986–92; Scientific Staff, Sunnybrook Medical Centre 1988–93; Payload Specialist Candidate for the First Internat. Microgravity Lab. Shuttle Flight (IML-1) 1989–90; Prime Payload Specialist for the First Internat. Microgravity Lab. Shuttle Flight (IML-1) 1990–92; Adjunct Prof., Dept. of Biology, Univ. of New Mexico, Albuquerque, N.M. 1991–93; Distinguished Prof., Ryerson Polytechnical Institute 1992–93; Visiting Rsch. Scholar, Dept. of Neurology, Univ. of New Mexico 1993–94; Visiting Distinguished Fellow, Faculty of Health Sciences, McMaster Univ. 1993–94; Visiting Rsch. Scholar, Universities Space Rsch. Assn., Johnson Space Centre, Houston, Texas 1993–94; lectures: James S. Simpson Mem. Lectr., St. Joseph's Health Ctr. 1984; Elizabeth Bagshaw Mem. Lectr., Hamilton Acad. of Med. 1985; Aaron Brown Lectr., Phi Delta Epsilon Med. Fraternity, Univ. of Toronto 1987; Royal Coll. Lectr., Royal Coll. of Phys. and Surg. of Can. 1991–93; Snider Lectr., Erindale Coll., Univ. of Toronto 1992; Riley - Jeffs Lecture - Candn. Assn. of Dieticians 1993; Herbert and Angela Bruce Lecture, Wellesley Hosp. 1993; Royal College Lecture, Royal College of Physicians and Surgeons of Canada 1993; Harry D. Armstrong Lecture, Aerospace Medical Assn. 1993; Jasper Lecture, Candn. Assn. for Neurosciences 1993; recipient: Career Scientist Award, Prov. Min. of Health 1982–83; Spec. Achievement Award, Woman of the Year Awards 1984; Vanier Award, Jaycees 1985; Co-recipient F.W. (Casey) Baldwin Award, Candn. Aeronautics & Space Inst. 1985; Presidential Citation of Honour, Alabama Agric. and Mech. Univ. 1990; William R. Franks M.D. Award, Candn. Soc. of Aerospace Medicine 1990; Sault Ste. Marie Medal Merit 1991; MacLachlan Coll. & Prep. School, Proud to be Canadian Medal, Canada 125, Oakville, Ont. 1992; Paul Harris Recognition Award (1992) Rotary Club of Ancaster; Presidential Citation, Am. Acad. of Neurology 1992; Hubertus Strughold Award, Space Medicine Branch, Aerospace Med. Assn. 1992; NASA Space Medal 1992; Award of Merit, Univ. of W. Ont. Alumni 1992; La Personalité de l'Année 1992, La Presse; Medaille de L'Excellence, L'Association des Médecins de Langue Française du Canada 1992; President's Award, The College of Physicians and Surgeons of Ont. 1992; Alumnus of the Year, Univ. of Western Ont. 1992; Canada 125 Medal 1992; Kurt Hahn Award, Outward Bound, Canada 1993; YWCA Woman of Distinction Award, Prince Albert, Sask. 1993; Outstanding Candn., Armenian Community Centre of Toronto 1993; Alumnus of the Year, Univ. of Guelph 1993; Inductee, Hamilton Gall. of Distinction 1993; Secretary, Candn. Soc. of Aviation Med. 1984–85 (Treas. 1983–84); Hon. Life Mem., Candn. Fedn. of Univ. Women 1985; Hon. Life Mem., Girl Guides of Can. 1986; Hon. Patron, Young Scientists of Canada 1987; Hon. Life Mem., Fed. of Medical Women of Canada 1991; Hon. Patron, Candn. Federation of Business and Prof. Women's Clubs 1992; Hon. Mem., Algoma West Acad. of Med. 1992; Hon. Chairperson, Parkinson Found. of Can. 1992; Hon. Mem., The Dominion of Canada Rifle Assn. 1992; Hon. Patron, Mission Air Transp. Network 1992; Hon. Life Mem., Science North 1992; Mem. Hon. L'Assn. des Médecins de Langue Française du Canada 1992; Hon. Dir., Candn. Space & Tech. Centre, London 1993; Hon. Life Mem., Zonta Internat. 1993; Hon. Event Dir., Guelph '93, Internat. Camp, Girl Guides of Canada 1993; Hon. Dir., Save Our North Atlantic Resources 1993; Hon. Patron, The Aphasia Centre, North York, Ont. 1993; Hon. Chairperson, Candn. Coalition for Quality Daily Physical Education 1993; Hon. mem., Bootmakers of Canada (Sherlock Holmes Soc.) 1993; Extve. Council, The Lung Assn. 1993; Hon. Patron, Ont. Bushplane Heritage Centre 1993; Hon. Chair, Women's Soccer Competition, World Student Games 1993; Hon. Chair, 24-Hour Relay for Health, Chedoke-McMaster Hosp. Found. 1993; Hon. Colonel, 22 Wing, Candn. Armed Forces, Hornell Heights, Ont. 1993; Hon. Patron, Ont. Parks Assn. 1993; Hon. Chairperson, Friends of the Environment Found. 1993; mem. Amer. Acad. of Neurology; Candn. Neurological Soc.; Candn. Aeronautics & Space Inst.; Coll. of Physicians & Surgeons of Ont.; Aerospace Med. Assoc.; Candn. Soc. of Aerospace Medicine; Candn. Fed. of Univ. Women; Albuquerque Aerostat Ascension Assoc.; Am. Soc. for Gravitational & Space Biology; Fed. of Med. Women of Can.; Assn. of Space Explorers; Candn. Medical Protective Assn.; Royal Coll. of Physicians and Surgeons of Can.; Candn. Assn. of Sports Medicine; Candn. Medical Protective Assn.; author of numerous scholarly articles, papers and public presentations; Office: 1200 Main St. W., Hamilton, Ont. L8N 3Z5.

**BONETTA, Laura Paola,** B.Sc., Ph.D.; b. Cremona, Italy 2 Feb. 1963; d. Pietro Luigi and Clementina (Nolli) B.; e. Richview C.I. 1982 (English Proficiency Award); Univ. of Toronto B.Sc. (Hons.) 1987, Ph.D. 1992; ASST. BIOLOGY EDITOR, 'NATURE' (scientific journal) 1993– ; thesis and research on the role of genetics in Wilms' Tumour patients (mainly children) has received much media attention; Grad. Adv. Ctte., Dept. of Microbiol., Univ. of Toronto 1987–89; Teaching Asst., Dept. of Genetics 1990–91; McPherson Award, Univ. of Toronto, Dept. of Microbiol.; Research Fellow, Molecular Oncol. Lab., Imperial Cancer Rsch. Fund (London, England) 1992–93 (focus of study: breast cancer); author of 2 scientific articles in 'Science'; has presented papers at various internat. meetings; recreations: horseback riding, dance; Home: 51 Valecrest Dr., Toronto, Ont. M9A 4P5; Office: Nature, 4 Little Essex St., London WC2R 3LF, England.

**BONGIE, Laurence L.,** Ph.D.; educator; b. Turtleford, Sask. 15 Dec. 1929; s. Louis Basil and Madalena (Pellizzari) B.; e. Univ. of B.C., B.A. 1950; Univ. of Paris Ph.D. 1952; m. Elizabeth A. E. d. William G. Bryson 14 July 1958; one s. Christopher L.; PROF. EMERITUS OF FRENCH, UNIV. OF B.C. 1992– ; Lectr. present Univ. 1953, Instr. 1954, Asst. Prof. 1956, Assoc. Prof. 1961, Prof. and Head 1966–92; recipient Humanities Research Council Fellowship 1955–56; Can. Council Sr. Fellowship 1963–64, 1975–76; Social Sciences & Humanities Fellowship 1982–83; Killam Sr. Fellowship 1982–83; 'Officier de l'Ordre des Palmes Académiques'; Sr. Killam Research Prize 1987; author 'David Hume, Prophet of the Counter-Revolution' 1965; 'Diderot's Femme Savante' 1977; 'Condillac, Les Monades' 1980; 'The Love of a Prince: Charles Edward Stuart in France, 1745–1748' 1986; various articles; mem. French, Internat., Am. and Candn. Soc's 18th Century Studies; Founding mem. B.C. Soc. Translators & Interpreters; R. Catholic; recreations: cycling, hobby farming; Home: 4651 Simpson Ave., Vancouver, B.C. V6R 1C2; Office: Dept. of French, Univ. of B.C., Vancouver, B.C. V6T 1Z1.

**BONHAM, David H.,** B.Com., B.A., LL.M., F.C.A., Q.C.; educator; lawyer; chartered accountant; b. Calgary, Alta. 22 Aug. 1932; s. Herbert H. and Sophie (Lund) B.; e. Univ. of Sask. B.Com. 1953, B.A. 1958, LL.B. 1960; Harvard Law Sch. LL.M. 1965; m. Heather d. John H. Barclay 27 Aug. 1960; children: Scott, Warren, Andrew; PARTNER, CUNNINGHAM, SWAN, CARTY, LITTLE & BONHAM, KINGSTON, ONT. 1978– ; Faculty mem. Coll. Comm. Univ. of Sask. 1960–64; joined Queen's Univ. 1965, Vice-Prin. (Finance) 1971–77, Vice Prin. (Resources) 1984–88; Prof. of Law and Sch. of Bus., 1967–89; Prof. Emeritus, Queen's Univ.; Gov. Kingston Gen. Hosp.; Independent Chrmn., Counc., Royal Coll. of Dental Surgeons of Ont.; Chair, Providence Continuing Care Centre, Kingston; Mem., Bd. of Govs., Algoma Univ. Coll., Sault Ste. Marie, Ont.; Fellow, Inst. C.A.'s Ont. (Pres. 1980–81) and Inst. C.A.'s Sask.; Pres. Candn. Inst. C.A.'s 1988–89; Trustee, First Bapt. Ch. Kingston; recipient, Inst. C.A.'s Ont. Award of Outstanding Merit 1992; Home: 252 Avenue Rd., Kingston, Ont. K7M 1C7; Office: 259 King St. E., Kingston, Ont. K7L 4W6.

**BONHAM, Mark Stephen,** M.Sc., B.Comm., F.L.M.I.; financial executive; b. Guelph, Ont. 25 June 1959; s. Ralph and Kathleen (Riach) B.; e. Univ. of Toronto B.Comm. 1982; London Sch. of Econ. M.Sc. 1986; PRES. & CHIEF EXEC. OFFR., BPI CAPITAL MGMT. CORP. 1986– ; Investment Administrator, Can. Life Assur. Co. 1982–84; Mem., Conference Bd. of Canada, Council on Investment Issues; Pres., Alpha Delta Phi, Toronto 1981–82; recreation: mountain biking, tennis; Home: 10 Yonge St., Suite 2205, Toronto, Ont. M5R 1E4; Office: Suite 1001, 10 Bay St., Toronto, Ont. M5J 2R8.

**BONIFACHO, Bratsa;** artist; b. Belgrade Yugoslavia 1937; e. Sumatovachka Sch. of Art Belgrade 1957–59; Univ. of Belgrade 1960–65; Accad. di Belle Arti Italy, Atelier Kruger W. Germany (summer courses) 1966–68; initiated & developed 'rooftop painting' – large-scale imagery painted on outsides of bldgs. in Belgrade which attracted attention of public & media; appeared as guest on many Eur. TV & radio shows; emigrated to Can. 1973; Candn. citizen 1976; solo exhibitions: Artropolis 93; Fran Willis Gall., Victoria, B.C. 1993; Patrick Doheny Fine Art Gall., Vancouver, B.C. 1993; Richmond Art Gall, Richmond, B.C. 1993; Seattle Art Fair, Washington, U.S.A. 1993; Patrick Doheny Fine Art, Vancouver 1992; Fran Willis Gall., Victoria 1992; Heffel Gall. Limited Vancouver, B.C. 1988, '90, '91; Quan-Schieder Gall. Toronto 1989, '90; Atelier Gall. Vancouver 1987; Burnaby Art Gall., Richmond Art Gall. 1982; Contemporary Art Gall. Vancouver, B.C. 1979; Gall. Scollard, Toronto 1978; Threshold Gall., Vancouver, B.C. 1993; participated in many juried exhibs. in B.C. 1974–93; teacher: painting & drawing, Sch. of Fine Arts, Belgrade 1967–68; private tutoring 1979–87; Office: c/o Bonifacho, P.O. Box 549, Stn. A, Vancouver, B.C. V6C 2N3.

**BONIN, Bernard,** L.Sc.Com., D.Sc.Éc., F.R.S.C.; civil servant; b. Joliette, Qué. 29 Sept. 1936; s. Georges and Thérèse (Racette) B.; e. Univ. de Montréal L.Sc.Com. 1958; Univ. de Paris Dip. d'études supérieures en sciences économiques 1962, Doctorat en sciences économiques 1966; m. Andrée d. Alfred and Claire Grégoire 15 Aug. 1960; children: Brigitte, Michel; DEPUTY GOVERNOR, BANK OF CANADA 1988– ; Prof. École des hautes études commerciales 1958–74, École nationale d'adm. publique 1979–88; Asst. Dep. Min., Min. de l'immigration et Min. des affaires intergouvernementales du Qué. 1974–79; author 'L'investissement étranger à long terme au Canada' 1967; 'L'entreprise multinationale et l'état' 1984; co-author 'A propros de l'Association économique Canada-Québec' 1980; 'Innovation industrielle et analyse économique' 1988; mng. ed. 'L'actualité économique' 1966–71; Candn. Jour. Econ. 1972–74; Candn. Pub. Policy 1980–82; recreations: music, reading, sports; Home: 1204, 175 Laurier, Hull, Qué. J8X 4G3; Office: 234 Wellington St., Ottawa, Ont. K1A 0G9.

**BONISTEEL, Roy,** D.Lit., D.D., LL.D., D.Hum.Litt.(Hon. Causa); broadcaster; b. Ameliasburgh, Ont. 29 May 1930; s. Charles Benson and Florence (Hunt) B.; e. Stirling (Ont.) and Port Colborne (Ont.) High Schs.; Laurentian Univ. D.Lit. 1979; Queen's Univ. D.D. 1980; Univ. of Windsor LL.D. 1982; Mount St. Vincent Univ., D.Hum.Litt. 1983; St. Francis Xavier Univ. LL.D. 1985; Univ. of Prince Edward Island LL.D. 1987; m. Jane d. Ernest and Anis Harrison 1 March 1980; children (by previous marriage): Mandy Leigh, Steven Roy, Lesley Virginia; Host, CBC TV Man Alive 1967–89; Prop. Roy Bonisteel Communications Ltd.; Reporter, Bellevile Intelligencer 1948, Trenton Courier-Advocate 1949–50; Announcer, CJBQ Belleville 1951–52; Announcer-Program Dir. CKTB St. Catharines 1953–64; Freelance Radio Producer and Dir. Niagara Pub. Relations Bureau 1964–65; Dir. of Broadcasting (B.C.) Un. Ch. of Can. 1965–66; Nat. Radio Co-ordinator, Ang., R.C. and Un. Chs. 1967–70; Dir. Inter Pares; recipient ACTRA Awards Best Host TV 1979; Gordon Sinclair Award for Excellence in Broadcast Journalism 1985; Christian Culture Award Assumption Univ. 1982; author 'In Search of Man Alive' 1980; 'Man Alive: The Human Journey' 1983; 'There was a Time' 1990; mem. Arts for Peace; recreations: gardening, antique collecting; Home: R.R. 5, Trenton, Ont. K8V 5P8.

**BONNELL, Hon. M. Lorne,** C.M., M.D.; senator; physician; b. Hopefield, P.E.I. 4 Jan. 1923; s. Henry George Horace and Charlotte Matilda (MacEachern) B.; e. Hopefield Sch., P.E.I. 1929; West Kent Sch., Charlottetown, P.E.I. 1934; Prince of Wales Coll., Charlottetown, P.E.I. 1939–43; Dalhouse Univ., M.D. (Master Surg.) 1949; Lic, Med. Council of Can.; m. late Ruby, d. John Jardine, Freetown, P.E.I., 6 July 1949; children: Mark Lorne, Linda Florence; Phys. and Surg., Murray River and Montague, P.E.I.; mem., Med. Staff King's Co. Mem. Hosp., Montague; entered prov. politics in Fourth Dist. Kings Co. P.E.I. April 1951; el. as Private mem. until 1955, re-el. 1955 and apptd. Min. of Health; re-el. as a mem. of Opposition 1959 and 1962; re-el. 1966 and apptd. Min. Welfare and Min. Tourist Devel.; Min. Responsible for Housing 1970; resigned from Prov. politics Nov. 1971 and summoned to Senate of Can., 15 Nov. 1971; mem., Standing Senate Comte. on Social Affairs, Sci. & Tech., Fisheries, Veterans Affairs, Banking, Trade and Commerce and sub-ctte. on Employment & Training; Chrmn., Special Ctte. on the Patent Act; mem. P.E.I. Med. Assn.; Candn. Med. Assn.; Pres., Hamon Enterprises; Island Cablevision Ltd.; Freemason (P.M.); Liberal; Presbyterian; recreation: golf; Home: Murray River, P.E.I. C0A 1W0; Office: The Senate, Ottawa, Ont. K1A 0A4.

**BONNER, Hon. Michael Joseph,** B.A., LL.B.; judge; b. Ottawa, Ont. 13 Apl. 1935; s. Edmund Joseph and Leone (Weishar) B.; e. St. Malachy's Separate Sch. Ottawa; Glebe Coll. Inst. Ottawa; Queen's Univ. B.A. 1957, LL.B. 1960; m. Rosalie d. Walter and Anne Koroniak 9 June 1962; children: Kathleen Sarah, Michael Andrew; JUDGE, TAX COURT OF CAN. 1983– ; called to Bar of Ont. 1962; law practice Adv. Sect. Dept. of Justice, Ottawa 1962; Snipper, Cohen & Murray 1962–66; Tax Litigation Sect. Dept. of Justice 1966–73, Toronto Regional Office 1973–76; Stikeman, Elliott, Robarts & Bowman 1976–78; mem. Tax Review Bd. 1978; Home: 2379 Whitehaven Cres., Ottawa, Ont. K2B 5H2; Office: 200 Kent St., Ottawa, Ont. K1A 0M1.

**BONNER, Robert William,** Q.C., B.A., LL.B., C.D.; barrister and solicitor; b. Vancouver, B.C. 10 Sept. 1920; s. Benjamin York and Emma Louise (Weir) B.; e. Pub. and High Schs., Vancouver, B.C.; Univ. of British Columbia, B.A. (Econ. and Pol. Science) 1942; Univ. of B.C. (Faculty of Law) Grad. 1948; m. Barbara, d. Rodney Robinson Newman, Vancouver, B.C. 16 June 1942; children: Barbara Carolyn, Robert York, Elizabeth Louise; Dir.: Energy Supplies Allocation Board; Grace Hosp.; read law with firm Clark, Wilson, White, Clark and Maguire Vancouver, British Columbia; called to the Bar of B.C., 31 July 1948; cr. Q.C. 1 Aug. 1952; before entering B.C. Govt. practised law with the firm of Clark, Wilson, White, Clarke & Maguire, Vancouver, B.C.; following grad. joined Candn. Army in 1942; served with Seaforth Highlanders of Can. in Can., U.K., N.Africa, Sicily and Italy; wounded in action in Italy; retired from active service with rank of Major in 1945; apptd. Lieut.-Col. in Reserve Force, commanding Univ. of B.C. Contingent, C.O.T.C., 1946 till retiring in Dec. 1953; entered B.C. Govt. as Atty.-Gen. in Aug. 1952, and el. mem. for Columbia, 24 Nov. 1952; re-el. mem. for Vancouver-Point Grey, 9 June 1953, cont. as Atty.-Gen.; apptd. Min. of Educ., 19 Oct. 1953, relinquishing this portfolio 14 April 1954; re-el. in g.e. 1956 cont. as Atty.-Gen.; in addition to post of Atty.-Gen. apptd. Min. of Indust. Devel. Trade & Comm. 1957–64; re-el. in g.e. 1960 and 1963; re-el. mem. for Cariboo in by-el. Nov. 1966; retired as Atty.-Gen. May 1968; joined MacMillan Bloedel Ltd. as Sr. Vice-Pres., Adm. 1968; Exec. Vice-Pres., Adm. 1970; Vice-Chrmn. 1971, Pres. and Chief Exec. Offr. 1972, Chrmn. 1973–74; Chrmn. and Dir. British Columbia Hydro and Power Authority 1976–85; former Dir.: IBM (Canada) Ltd.; INCO; Montreal Trust Co.; mem., Candn. Bar Assn.; Law Soc. of B.C.; Vancouver Bar Assn.; Delta Upsilon; Freemason; Social Credit; Anglican; recreations: boating, photography; Clubs: Union; Vancouver; Capilano Golf & Country; Home: 5679 Newton Wynd, Vancouver, B.C. V6T 1H6; Office: 3183 – 595 Burrard St., Vancouver, B.C. V7X 1G4.

**BONNYCASTLE, Richard A.N.,** B.Comm.; investor, financial consultant; b. Winnipeg, Man. 26 Sept. 1934; s. Richard Henry G. and Mary Frances (Northwood) B.; e. Ravenscourt Sch.; Trinity Coll. Sch.; Univ. of Man., B.Comm.; FOUNDER, CAVENDISH INVESTING LTD. 1970– ; Group Rep., Great West Life Winnipeg 1956; Richardson Securities (Winnipeg, Calgary, Toronto) 1963–70; Chrmn., Cavendish Investing Ltd.; Dir., Candn. Conquest Exploration Inc.; NuGas Limited; Patheon Group Inc.; Sinteris Ltd.; Westco Restaurants Inc.; Candn. Schizophrenia Found.; Trustee: Inst. for Wetland and Waterfowl Rsch.; Fort Whyte Ctr. for Environmental Educ.; Jockey Club of Can.; Zeta Psi Assn.; recreations: golf, horse racing; clubs: St. Charles Country; Royal Candn. Yacht; Glencoe Golf & Country (Calgary); de Anza Country; Toronto Hunt; Terminal City (Vancouver); Manitoba; Victoria; Univ. Club (N.Y.); Home: Box 10, Site 14, R.R. #5, Calgary, Alta. T2P 2G6; Office: #4615, 400 – 3 Ave. S.W., Calgary, Alta. T2P 4H2.

**BONYUN, Peter A.,** B.Comm., C.A.; financial executive; b. Toronto, Ont. 30 Aug. 1947; s. Victor A. and Florence M. B.; e. Univ. of Toronto B.Comm. 1970; m. Eleanore d. Mike and Eleanore Wheeler 9 May 1970; children: Jeffrey, Ian; TREASURER, SHERRITT INC. 1987– ; joined Clarkson Gordon & Co. 1970; joined Keeble Cable Television Ltd. 1973; Financial Analyst, Sheritt Gordon Limited 1975; Manager Banking 1975; Mgr., Financial Planning 1979; Controller Manitoba Operations 1980; Asst. Treasurer 1984; Home: 21441 Twp. Rd. 522, Sherwood Park, Alta. T8E 1G1; Office: Fort Saskatchewan, Alta. T8L 2P2.

**BOONE, Geoffrey Lynn;** b. Toronto, Ont. 11 May 1935; s. Geoffrey Lynn and Martha Lillian (White) Boone; e. Trinity College Sch.; m. Elaine d. Vincent and Rita Altieri 14 July 1973; children: Philip, Mardi, Jennifer, Colin; SALES ASSOCIATE, REMAX ISLAND REALTY; Chrmn., Phoenix Fibreglass Ltd. (Oakville) 1991–..; Salesman, Dominion Securities 1954–63; Branch Mgr., Midland Secur. 1963–69; Inst. Sales, A.E. Osler 1970–72; Extve. Vice-Pres., J.B. White 1972–75; Vice-Pres., Burns Fry Limited 1976–91; Mem., President's Club, Burns Fry Limited 1983–91; Investment Dealers Assn. (Honours) 1954–56; Candn. Securities Inst., F.C.S.I. 1976; recreations: golf, tennis, sailing, skiing; Clubs: Toronto Golf, Mid Ocean (Bermuda), Ballybunion (Ireland), Coral Beach (Bermuda), Badminton & Racquet (Toronto); Royal and Ancient Golf, St. Andrews (Scotland); Office: 840 William Hilton Parkway, Hilton Head 29928 USA.

**BOONE, James Edward,** M.D., F.R.C.P.(C); physician; educator; b. Hamilton, Ont. 31 July 1927; s. Frank H. and Helen G. Boone; e. Earl Kitchener and Westdale Secondary Sch. Hamilton; Univ. of Toronto M.D. 1951; m. Joan G. d. Enna E. Dauphinee, Sarnia, Ont. 24 May 1958; children: Thomas J., Charles M., Peter D.; PROF. AND CHRMN. OF PEDIATRICS, UNIV. OF W. ONT. since 1973; Asst. Prof. of Pediatrics, Univ. of Toronto 1964, Assoc. Prof. 1967; Chrmn. Postgrad. Manpower Comte., Council Ont. Faculties of Med. 1972–79; mem. Med. Manpower Adv. Comte. Ont. 1977–79; author various publs. juvenile rheumatoid arthritis, med. manpower; Anglican; recreations: wilderness canoeing, fishing; Office: Children's Hosp. of W. Ont., 800 Commissioners Rd. E., London, Ont. N6C 2V5.

**BOONE, Laurel Blenkinsop,** Ph.D.; writer, editor; b. Yorkton Sask. 23 Mar. 1942; d. John and Patience Mattie (Baynes) Blenkinsop; e. McGill Univ., B.A. (Hons.) 1963; Univ. of Maine M.A. 1977; Univ. of N.B. Ph.D. 1981; m. Edward s. Edward F. and Ethel Mullaly 8 May 1981; children: Storer John Boone, Jacob Blenkinsop Boone, Sarah Catherine Mullaly; ACQUISITIONS EDITOR, GOOSE LANE EDITIONS 1991– ; University instructor 1974–84; writer and editor 1985– ; Ed. Bd., 'Studies in Canadian Literature' 1985–89; Assoc. Ed. 1989– ; Book Review Ed., 'Fiddlehead' 1985–90; Contrb. Ed., 'Books in Canada' 1989– ; Literary Ed., Goose Lane Editions 1989; Bd. of Dir., Goose Lane Edns.; Hon. Rsch. Assoc., Dept. of English, Univ. of N.B.; Editor: 'William Wilfred Campbell: Selected Poetry and Essays' 1987, 'The Collected Letters of Charles G.D. Roberts' 1989; recreations: music, drama; Home: 511 Mansfield St., Fredericton, N.B. E3B 3A1.

**BOOTH, Andrew Donald,** D.Sc., Ph.D., P.Eng., C.Eng. (U.K.), C.Phys.(U.K.); university president; b. East Molesey, Surrey, Eng. 11 Feb. 1918; s. Sidney Joseph, O.B.E., and Katherine Jane (Pugh) B.; e. Univ. of London, B.Sc. (1st Class hons.) 1940; Univ. of Birmingham, Ph.D. 1944; Inst. for Advanced Study, Princeton, 1947; Univ. of London, D.Sc. 1951; m. Kathleen Hylda Valerie, Ph.D., d. F. Britten, Warwickshire, Eng., 30 Aug. 1950; children: Ian Jeremy Macdonald, Amanda Jane; Chrmn. of Bd., Autonetics Research Associates since 1978; Pres., Lakehead Univ. 1972–78; Interdisciplinary Prof. of Autonetics, Case-Western Reserve Univ., Cleveland 1963–72; Scient. Adv., Internat. Computers & Tabulators Ltd. (Eng.); Dir., Wharf Engn. Labs (Eng.); Asst. Chief Engr., Morris Engines, Coventry, 1939–40; Sr. Research Scholar Brit. Rubber Producers' Assn., 1940–44; Research Phys., 1945, Nuffield Fellow, Birkbeck Coll., Univ. of London, 1946–49; Visiting (full) Prof. of Theoretical Physics, Univ. of Pittsburgh, 1949; Dir., Computer Project, Birkbeck Coll., Univ. of London, 1950–55; Univ. Reader in Computational Methods, London, 1955–62; Head, Dept. of Numerical Automation, Birkbeck Coll., 1957–62; Head, Dept. of Elect. Engn., Univ. of Sask. 1962–63; Dean, Coll. of Engn. mem., Research Comte., Marie Curie Mem. Foundation, 1957–62; mem. Council of Nat. Res. Council of Canada since 1975; awarded Hon. Fellowship, Inst. of Linguists, 1961; Hon. Dir. of Research, Birbeck Coll., 1962; author of 'Fourier Technique in X-Ray Organic Structure Analysis' 1948; 'Automatic Digital Calculators' 1st ed. 1953, 2nd ed. 1956; 'Numerical Methods' 1st ed. 1955, 2nd ed. 1956; and others; over 300 scient. papers in journs; inventor of Magnetic Storage Drum for computers; basic patents on Magneto-strictive store, multi-core magnetic storage; awarded Centennial Medal 1967; Gov., Ladbroke Sch., London, 1956–59, Eastbourne Training Coll. (Eng.); 1960–62; Fellow, Inst. Electronic and Radio Engrs.; Fellow, Brit. Inst. Electrical Engrs. (mem. Council 1955–62; Chrmn., Papers Comte., 1955–62; Chrmn., Computer Group, 1957–62; Vice Pres., 1965–67; Chrmn., Canadian Div., 1965); Chrmn., Vancouver Island Br., Engrg. Inst. of Can. 1986; Fellow, Brit. Inst. Physics; Chrmn., Vancouver Island Br., Engr. Inst. of Can.; Church of England; recreations: motoring, mountaineering, music; Club: Athenaeum (London); Hon. mem. Univ. Club of Toronto; Home: Timberlane, 5317 Sooke Rd., R.R. 1, Sooke, B.C. V0S 1N0.

**BOOTH, James K.B.,** B.Sc., P.Eng.; consultant; mining and petroleum executive; b. Eng. 18 Jan. 1922; s. John Arthur and May (Brooks) B.; e. Royal Sch. of Mines Univ. of London B.Sc., A.R.S.M. 1950; m. Margaret d. Vincent and Francis Illing Jan. 1951; children: Gillian Margaret, Jacqueline Anne, (John C.B. dec.); Partner, Derry Michener Booth & Wahl 1968–90; Dir.: James K.B. Booth Ltd.; Bar Environmental; Gold Trust; Queenston Mines Ltd.; Mining Geol. Colonial Geol. Survey Tanganyika, E. Africa 1950–53; Spl. Project Geol. Selection Trust London 1953–54; Rio Tinto Canadian Exploration 1954–64, Exploration Mgr., Vice Pres. New Projects, Toronto; Mng. Dir. Canadian Superior Exploration, Toronto 1964–68; recreation: golf; Clubs: Toronto Golf; Imperial Golf, Naples Fla.; University; Home: Apt. 1115 Fairways, 1400 Dixie Rd., Mississauga, Ont. L5E 3E1.

**BOOTH, Ronald Findlay,** B.A., LL.B.; b. Brandon, Man. 29 July 1935; s. Wilfrid Gatley and Eleanor Jean (Findlay) B.; e. Pub. Schs. Brandon and Dauphin, Man.; Univ. of Man. B.A. 1957, LL.B. 1960; m. Ruth Caroline d. Walter T. Murray 16 May 1958; children: Pamela Lynn, Jennifer Caroline, Jillian Tracy; GROUP EXTVE., CHRMN.'S OFFICE, TATE & LYLE PLC 1990– ; read law with Thompson, Shepard, Dilts, Jones & Hall, Winnipeg; called to Bar of Man. 1960, Bar of Ont. 1964; practised law with Kerr, Meighen, Haddad & Booth, Brandon, Man. 1960–64; Asst. Solr. The Steel Co. of Canada Ltd., Hamilton, Ont. 1964, Asst. Secy. and Sr. Solr. 1967–72; Secy. and Legal Counsel, RCA Ltd. Ste. Anne-de-Bellevue, Que. 1972, Vice Pres., Secy. and Gen. Counsel 1974–76; Vice Pres. and Gen. Counsel 1976–80; Extve. Vice Pres., Redpath Ind. Ltd. 1980–81; Vice Pres., Corporate Development 1981–86; Vice-Pres. & Secy. 1986–90; Zeta Psi; Anglican; recreations: tennis, sailing, skiing; Office: Sugar Quay, Lower Thames St., London EC3R 6DQ England.

**BOOTHE, Paul Michael,** B.A., Ph.D.; university professor; b. Toronto, Ont. 29 March 1954; s. Edward Joseph and Joyce Evelyn (Conlin) B.; e. Ajax H.S. 1972; Univ. of Western Ont. B.A. (Hons.) 1976; Univ. of B.C. Ph.D. 1981; m. Patricia d. Wilfred and Nancy Ripley 28 Oct. 1978; children: Katherine, Robert, Allison, Kevin; PROFESSOR, ECONOMICS DEPT., UNIV. OF ALBERTA 1992– ; Economist, Internat. Dept., Bank of Canada 1981–84; Sessional Lectr., Econ. Dept., Carleton Univ. 1982–84; Asst. & from 1986, Assoc. Prof., Econ. Dept., Univ. of Alta. 1984–91; Visiting Econ., Alberta Treasury, Edmonton 1989–90; Visiting Scholar, School of Policy Studies, Queen's Univ. 1991–92; Consultant, Bank of Canada; Govt. of Alberta; Ed. Bd., 'Can. J. of Econ.' 1986–89; Extve. Ctte., Candn. Econ. Assn. 1990–92; Assoc. Ed., 'Can. Public Policy' 1990–95; Roman Catholic, St. Agnes Parish, Edmonton; Pres., Aspen Garden Community League Edmonton 1989–91; co-author: 'A Study of the Efficiency of Foreign Exchange Markets' 1983, 'International Asset Substitutability' 1985 and journal articles; recreations: skiing, sailing; Home: 12512 39A Avenue, Edmonton, Alta. T6J 0P5; Office: Edmonton, Alta. T6G 2H4.

**BORDEN, John Harvey,** B.Sc., M.Sc., Ph.D., B.C.E., R.P.F., R.P.Bio., F.E.S.C.; university professor; b. Berkeley, Calif. 6 Feb. 1938; s. Charles Edward and Alice Victoria (Witkin) B.; e. Wash. St. Univ., B.Sc. 1963; Univ. of Calif., Berkeley, M.Sc. 1965, Ph.D. 1966; m. Edna d. Ronald and Beatrice McEachern 23 June 1962; children: Patrick Carl, Ian McEachern; PROF., CTR. FOR PEST MNGT., DEPT. OF BIOL. SCI., SIMON FRASER UNIV. 1975– ; Asst. Prof. 1966–69; Assoc. Prof. 1969–75; Prof. 1975– ; Rsch. Prof. (1981 only); Dir., Chem. Ecol. Rsch. Group 1981– ;& NSERC Sr. Industrial Rsch. Prof. 1991– ; Vis. Sci., Forestry Comn. Rsch. Lab., Farnham, Surrey, UK (1976–77); Assoc. Mem., Plant Biotechnol. Inst., NRC, Saskatoon 1985– ; Board Certified Entomol., Entomol. Soc. Am. 1971– ; Reg. Profl. Forester, Assn. of B.C. Profl. Foresters 1985– ; Reg. Profl. Biologist, Assn. of Profl. Biologists of B.C. 1988– ; Phi Beta Kappa 1963; Phi Kappa Phi 1963; Sigma Xi 1965; Nat. Sci. Found. (US) Coop. Grad. Fellowship 1964–66; C.G. Hewitt Award 1977, Fellow 1981, Gold Medal 1988, Entomol. Soc. of Can.; J.E. Bussart Mem. Award, Entomol. Soc. of Am. 1984; Gold Medal in Nat. & Appl. Sci., Sci. Counc. of B.C. 1985; Award of Excellence, Profl. Pest Mngt. Assn. of

B.C. 1986; Sci. Achievement Award, Candn. Inst. of Forestry 1986; Killam Rsch. Fellowship, Canada Counc. 1989–91; Mem., Strategic Grants Ctte., NSERC; Premier's Adv. Ctte. on Sci. & Technol., Prov. of B.C.; Citizen's Adv. Bd., B.C. Forest Alliance; author of over 240 papers, book chapters, 1 glossary & 1 bibliography; co-author: 'Insects in the Classroom' 1972; Home: 6552 Carnegie St., Burnaby, B.C. V5B 1Y3; Office: Burnaby, B.C. V5A 1S6.

**BORENSTEIN, Sylviane,** B.A., B.C.L.; lawyer; b. France 9 Feb. 1943; d. Georges and Fernande (Krosberg) Wegliszewski; e. Lycée Molière Paris; Monkland High Sch. Montreal 1959; Sir George Williams Univ. B.A. 1963; McGill Univ. B.C.L. 1966; m. C.J. Borenstein 21 June 1964 (div.); children: Richard, Lorna, Marianne, Marc; Pres. Bar of the Prov. of Que. 1990–91; called to Bar of Que. 1967; Assoc. law firm Amaron & Stead 1967–73; Dir. Legal Aid Office Outremont-Park Extension 1973– ; Vice Pres. present Bar 1989; Bd. Govs. Lord Reading Law Soc. Montreal; Co-chair, Law & Social Action Ctte., Candn. Jewish Congress; mem. Candn. Bar Assn.; Pres., Assn. d'Entraide des Avocats de Montréal; Bd. Govs., Candn. Council Christians & Jews; Women's Fedn. of A.J.C.S.; Candn. Human Rights Foundation; Council Candn. Bar Assn.; Extve. Mem., Baron de Hirsch Inst.; Hon. Pres., Auberge Transition; recreations: classical music, travel; Home: 180 Eton Cres., Hampstead, Que. H3X 3K3; Office: 154 Laurier West, Suite 230, Montreal, Que. H2T 2N7.

**BORG, Patrick L.,** B.A.; business executive; b. Toronto, Ont. 23 March 1953; e. York Univ. B.A.; Humber College Hons. Bus.; GENERAL MANAGER, TAMBRANDS CANADA 1991– ; Sales Rep. and various progressive positions, Procter & Gamble 1977–85; Nat. Sales Broker Mgr. 1986; Director of Sales, Tambrands Canada 1988; Vice-Pres., Sales 1990; Mem., Y.P.O.; G.P.M.C.; C.W.D.A.; C.I.R.A.; recreations: golf, squash, furniture restripping and repair; clubs: Beacon Hall Golf, Founder, Board of Trade; Office: Suite 600, 100 York Blvd., Richmond Hill, Ont. L4B 1J8.

**BORGESE, Elisabeth Mann,** B.A., Ph.D.; educator; b. Munich, Germany 24 April 1918; d. Thomas Paul and Katia (Pringsheim) Mann; e. Freies Gymnasium Zurich B.A. 1935; Conserv. of Music Zurich Dip. 1936; Mount St. Vincent Univ. Ph.D. h.c. 1985; m. Giuseppe Antonio s. Giuseppe and Maria Borgese 23 Nov. 1939; two d. Angelica, Dominica; PROF. OF POL. SCI. DALHOUSIE UNIV. 1979– ; Rsch. Assoc. Univ. of Chicago 1945–52; Ed., 'Common Cause' 1948–52; 'Diogenes' (UNESCO) 1952–62; 'Perspective USA' 1953–62 (Intercultural Publications Inc.); Exec. Sec. Bd. Eds., 'Encyclopaedia Britannica' 1964–66; Sr. Fellow, Center for Study Democratic Instns. 1964–78; Sr. Killam Fellow present Univ. 1978–79; Chrmn. Internat. Ocean Inst. Malta 1972– ; Chrmn. Bd. Dirs. Internat. Centre Ocean Devel. (Candn. Crown Corp.) 1986–92; mem, Bd. of Trustees, Nova Scotia Environmental Trust Fund 1990– ; recipient Cross for High Merit Govt. Austria 1983; Sasakawa Internat. Environment Prize (UN) 1987; Gold Medal, Found. for International Studies, Malta 1988; Order of Canada 1988; Order of Merit Colombia 1992; Friendship Award, China 1992; St. Francis of Assisi Internat. Environment Prize 1993; author 'To Whom It May Concern' (short stories) 1962; 'Ascent of Woman' 1964; 'The Language Barrier' 1966; 'The Ocean Regime' 1968; 'The Drama of the Oceans' 1976; 'Seafarm' 1981; 'The Mines of Neptune' 1985; 'The Future of the Oceans' 1987; Chairworm and Supershark (a book for children) 1992; 3 plays: 'Only the Pyre' 1987; 'Pieces and Pawns' (unpublished); 'Eat Your Fishballs, Tarquin' (unpublished); ed. 'Pacem in Maribus' 1972; 'Tides of Change' 1974; 'Ocean Yearbook,' 10 vols. 1980– ; 'Ocean Frontiers' 1992; mem. World Acad. Arts & Sci.; Third-World Acad. Sci.; Home: Sambro Head, Halifax, N.S.; Office: International Ocean Institute, Dalhousie Univ., 1226 Le Marchant St., Halifax, N.S. B3H 3P7.

**BORGESON, Mervin Carl;** b. 3 July 1940; s. Arne and Anne (Gabruch) B.; e. Lutheran Coll. Bible Inst. 1961–62; Camrose Luth. Coll. 1963–64; m. Kareen H. d. Harold and Clara Johnson 7 Nov. 1964; children: Katherine, Heather, Brenda; EXECUTIVE DIR., ALBERTA REAL ESTATE INSURANCE EXCHANGE, Calgary, Alta. 1990– ; United Farmers of Alta. 1964–66; General Agent, Lutheran Brotherhood Insur. (U.S.) 1966–73; Dir., Borgeson Enterprises Ltd. 1974–89; Sales Mgr., Maher Real Estate Ltd. 1975–78; Mgr. & Sales, Mattila Agencies Ltd. 1978–90; Past Pres., Candn. Real Estate Assn. 1989–90 (Chrmn. of Mngmt. Bd. 1988–89, Vice-Pres. 1987, Dir. 1985–86); Past Pres., Sask. Real Estate Assn. 1984 (Dir. 1983–82); Pres., Battleford Real Estate Bd. 1978; Pres., Brampton-Mississauga Life Underwriters Assn. 1971–72; Mem., Junior Beaver's Baseball team, N. Battleford, Sask. (Prov. of Sask. Champions 1958); recreations: baseball, golf, hockey; Home: 100 Scandia Rise N.W., Calgary, Alta. T3L 1V6; Office: 828 – 12 Ave. S.W., Calgary, Alta. T2R 0J3.

**BORINS, Edward H.,** B.A., B.Ed., M.A.; bookseller; b. Toronto, Ont. 1 Sept. 1942; s. Norman and Adeline (Fine) B.; e. Forest Hill Coll. Inst. 1960; Neuchâtel Jr. Coll. 1961; Univ. of Toronto B.A. 1965; McGill Univ. M.A. 1968; Univ. of Toronto B.Ed. 1970; m. Eva M. d. Dr. Maria Bohlig and Dr. G.K. Bohlig 5 June 1966; children: Sara Joy, David Benjamin, Daniel Alexander; Teacher, Woburn S.S. 1970–73; Mgr., David Mirvish Books on Art 1973–79; founder and co-owner of Edwards Books & Art now in five locations; Pres., Edsed Investments Limited; Consultant, Collier-Macmillan Candn. Hist. Prog. 1970–73; author: 'Canada in the Days of New France' 1971; contrib.: 'Dictionary of Canadian Biography' vol. 3, 1974; mem., Candn. Adv. Bd., Neuchâtel Jr. Coll.; National Ctte. Chrmn., The Word on the Street; recreations: collecting art and books, physical fitness; Clubs: Cambridge Club; Office: 356 Queen St. W., Toronto, Ont. M5V 2A2.

**BORINS, Sandford Fredrick,** Ph.D.; university professor; b. Toronto, Ont. 7 June 1949; s. Sidney and Beverley (Ludwig) B.; e. Harvard Coll., A.B. magna cum laude 1971; John F. Kennedy Sch. of Govt., M.P.P. 1974; Harvard Univ., Ph.D. 1976; PROF., FAC. OF MANAGEMENT, UNIV. OF TORONTO and ADJUNCT PROF., JOHN F. KENNEDY SCHOOL OF GOVERNMENT, HARVARD UNIV. 1993–94; Chair, Div. of Managment and Economics, Scarborough, Coll., Univ. of Toronto; Asst. Prof., Carleton Univ. 1975–77; Northwestern Univ. 1977–79; Asst. Prof., York Univ. 1979–82, Assoc. Prof. 1982–87, Assoc. Dean, Prof., Fac. of Admin. Studies 1985–88; Dir., Case Progr. in Candn. Public Admin. 1981–85; Consultant, various fed. and prov. agencies and U.S. Nat. Acad. of Sci.; freelance writer, 'Globe and Mail'; el. Phi Beta Kappa 1971; Jewish; mem., Inst. of Public Admin. of Can. (Nat. Extve. Ctte. 1985–87, 1989–90); author: 'The Language of the Skies' (Fr. & Eng. eds.) 1983; 'Investments in Failure' 1986; co-author: (with Allan Blakeney) 'Political Management in Canada' 1992; numerous profl. articles; received Certificate of Merit, Social Sci. Fedn. of Can. 1990; recreations: hiking, travel, skiing, running; Clubs: Harvard (Toronto); Internat. House of Japan (Tokyo); Home: 236 Elm Rd., Toronto, Ont. M5M 3T8; Office: Fac. of Mgmt., Univ. of Toronto, 246 Bloor St. W., Toronto, Ont. M5S 1V4.

**BORINS, Hon. Stephen,** B.A., LL.B.; judge; b. Toronto, Ont. 3 Oct. 1934; s. Norman, Q.C. and Adeline (Fine) B.; e. Forest Hill Coll. Inst. 1952; Univ. of Toronto B.A. 1956, LL.B. 1959; Law Soc. Upper Can. Bar Admission Course 1961; m. Elaine F., M.D., F.R.C.P.(C) d. Dr. Bernard Manace 11 July 1960; two d. Jennifer, Gwen; JUSTICE, ONTARIO COURT OF JUSTICE (GENERAL DIV.) 1990– ; Deputy Judge of the Supreme Court of the Yukon Territory 1982– ; called to Bar of Ont. 1961, Bar of Yukon 1975; Law Clk. to Chief Justice High Court of Ont. 1961–62; private law practice 1962–69; co-counsel to Royal Comn. Inquiry into Civil Rights 1966–71; Prof. of Law, Osgoode Hall Law Sch. 1969–75, Assoc. Dean 1972–75; Judge, Dist. Court of Ont. 1975–90; Dir., Candn. Judicial Seminar 1970–74; mem. Senate York Univ. 1970–74; Bencher, Law Soc. Upper Can. 1971–75; rec'd Treas.'s Medal, Law Soc. First Prize, Lawyers Club First Prize 1961; co-author 'Canadian Civil Procedure' 1973, 2nd ed. 1977; author various book chapters, articles and addresses on legal topics; Jewish; recreations: tennis, golf; Clubs: York Racquets; Office: Osgoode Hall, 130 Queen St. W., Toronto Ont. M5H 2N5.

**BORNEMISA, Adrian Charles,** L.es D., LL.D.; management consultant; b. Szentes, Hungary; s. Charles J. and Helene H. (von Adorjan) von Bornemisza; e. Univ. of Budapest LL.D. 1946; Univ. of Geneva L.es D. 1946; Inst. Internat. Studies Geneva Cert. 1947; m. Clara d. Leslie Acs 19 Apr. 1947; children: Anne-Marie, Peter Charles; PRES, ABOR CONSULTANTS INC. 1985– ; Vice Pres., Tenga Capital Corp. 1988– ; Dir.: The Great Atlantic & Pacific Tea Co.; Canvib Investment Corp., Adv. to Tengelmann Group Muelheim, W. Germany; Mem., Adv. Bd., International M.B.A. and Business and Environment Programs, York Univ.; held exec. positions John Inglis Co. Toronto; Canadian Canners Ltd., Hamilton; Procor Ltd., Toronto; General Steel Industries Inc., St. Louis; Atlas Petroleum Inc., Montreal and Nassau; Rio Tinto Zinc Corp., London, Eng.; Sr. Co-ordinator Foreign Invest., Govt. Ont.; Adv. internat. trade & invests. several Candn. firms; author various articles foreign trade & invest. Cdn. & Eur. publs.; Founding Chrmn., Hungarian-Canadian Chamber of Commerce; mem. Bd. Trade Metrop. Toronto; Anglican; recreations: tennis, skiing; Address: 1 Concorde Place, Ste. 1804, Don Mills (Toronto), Ont. M3C 3K6.

**BORRA, Ermanno F.,** Ph.D.; university professor; b. Gattinara, Italy 23 Mar. 1943; s. Paolo and Mary (Beretta) B.; e. Univ. of Turin, Dr.Phys. 1967; Univ. of W. Ont., Ph.D. 1972; m. Rosa d. Rosa and Victor Rivera; one d., Diana; one s., Alexander; PROFESSOR OF PHYSICS, UNIV. LAVAL 1982– ; Carnegie Fellow, Mt. Wilson-Palomar Obs. 1972–75; Visiting Prof., Univ. Laval 1975–77; Asst. Prof. 1977–79; Assoc. Prof. 1979–81; Visiting Scientist, Arizona Univ. 1981–82; mem., Am. Astronomical Soc.; Candn. Astronomical Soc.; Internat. Astronomical Union; recreations: skin diving, cross country skiing, hiking, bicycling; Home: 1784 Kilmarnock, Sillery, Qué. G1T 2V9; Office: Physics Dept., Univ. Laval, Québec, Qué. G1K 7P4.

**BORSCH, Roman Nickolas,** M.D., F.R.C.P.(C.), F.A.P.A.; physician; b. Brooklin, Ont. 23 Apr. 1932; s. Nickolas and Anna (Scych) B.; e. Univ. of Toronto M.D. 1957; R.C.P.S. 1965; A.B.P.N. 1966; Toronto Inst. for Psychoanalysis grad 1978; children: Anne Marie, Barbara Lynn, Linda Susan, Michael Roman; private med. practice Toronto 1966– ; Faculty, Toronto Inst. for Psychoanalysis; Internship St. Michael's Hosp. Toronto 1957–58; Psychiatric Residency St. Thomas (Ont.) Psychiatric Hosp. 1958–59, Menninger Sch. of Psychiatry Topeka Kans. 1959–62; Clin. Dir. Osawatomie (Kans.) State Hosp. 1962–64; mem. Staff C.F. Menninger Memorial Hosp. 1964–66; Extve.: Toronto Psychoanalytic Soc.; Am. Psychiatric Assoc. (Ont. District Br.); M.T.C.C. 698; Candn. Psychoanalytic Soc.; mem. Bd. Trade Metrop. Toronto; author various articles sci. journs.; recreations: flying, sports; Home: 900 Yonge St., #904, Toronto, Ont. M4W 3P5; Office: 127, 400 Walmer Rd., Toronto, Ont. M5P 2X7.

**BORSON, Roo,** B.A., M.F.A.; writer; b. Berkeley, Cal. 20 Jan. 1952; d. Harry J. and Frederica Josephine (Esterly) B.; e. Goddard Coll. Vt. B.A. 1973; Univ. of B.C. M.F.A. 1977 (MacMillan Prize for Poetry); author (poetry) 'Landfall' 1977; 'In the Smoky Light of the Fields' 1980; 'Rain' 1980; 'A Sad Device' 1981; 'The Whole Night, Coming Home' 1984 (nominated Gov. Gen's Award); co-author 'The Transparence of November/Snow' 1985; 'Intent, or the Weight of the World' 1989; recipient First Prize for Poetry CBC Lit. Competition 1982 and Third Prize 1989, also Third Prize for Personal Essay 1990; numerous readings Can. and USA; represented nat. and internat. anthols. and mags.; teacher writing workshops Univ. of B.C., Concordia Univ., Ryerson Polytechnical Inst., Upper Can. Writers' Workshop and Maritime Writers' Workshop; participated short-term writer-in-residence prog. Can. Council, served various Arts Award Juries; recipient of several O.A.C. and Canada Council writing grants; Writer-in-residence, Univ. of Western Ont. 1987–88; Concordia Univ. spring 1993; Judge, 1986 CBC Lit. Competition, also poetry competitions in several provinces; Judge, CCA Award; mem. League Candn. Poets; Writers' Union Can.; Internat. P.E.N.; 'Pain Not Bread' (poetry group); Address: TWUC, 24 Ryerson Ave., Toronto, Ont. M5T 2P3.

**BORWEIN, Bessie,** Ph.D.; professor; b. Johannesburg, S.A. 17 Mar. 1927; d. Jacob (dec.) and Mary (Zisman) Flax (dec.); e. Athlone H.S. 1943; Univ. of the Witwatersrand, B.Sc. 1947, B.Sc. (Hons.) 1948; Univ. of Western Ont., Ph.D. 1973; m. David s. Joseph (dec.) and Rachel B. (dec.) 30 June 1946; children: Jonathan, Peter, Sarah; ASSOC. PROF., ANATOMY, UNIV. OF WESTERN ONTARIO 1984–92, EMERITUS 1992– ;and ASSOC. PROF. OPHTHALMOL. 1987– , Assoc. Dean, Rsch. Medicine 1987–92, Asst. Dean, Rsch. Medicine 1992– ; Demonstrator, Univ. of the Witwatersrand and Univ. of London 1946–50; Biology Teacher, St. Leonards Sch. for Girls, Scotland, 1955–59; Instructor, Rsch. Asst., Lectr., Asst. Prof., Univ. of West. Ont. 1964–83; Women of Distinction Award, London, Ont. 1984; Bd. Mem., Madame Vanier Children's Serv. (1985–89), Rsch. Committee 1985– ; Co-Chrmn., United Way UWO Campaign 1986; Pres., London Section, Nat. Counc. Jewish Women 1968–70; Chrmn., Pollution Probe Noise Subctte. 1972–77; various community assns. & univ. cttes.; Fellow, Westminister Institute for Ethics & Human Values (London); recipient, Gordin Kaplan Award, Candn. Fed. Biol. Socs. (for public awareness of science) 1992; awarded Commemorative Medal for 125th Anniversary of Candn. Confederation; author of 15 articles & 1 book chapter; rsch. on ultra structure of the retina and especially effects of laser light on the retina; Founding Bd. Mem., Partners in Research; Bd. Mem., Alzheimer Soc. of London & Middlesex 1992– ; mem., Assoc. for Rsch. in

Vision & Ophthalmology (USA); Candn. Assoc. of Anatomists; Candn. Bioethics Soc.; Candns. for Health Rsch.; recreations: family & friends, bridge, walking, theatre, films, books, politics; Home: 1032 Brough St., London, Ont. N6A 3N4; Office: Office of Dean of Med., Rsch. Office, Med. Sci. Bldg., Univ. of West. Ont., London, Ont. N6A 5C1.

**BORWEIN, David,** Ph.D., D.Sc., F.R.S.E.; educator; b. Kaunas, Lithuania 24 March 1924; e. Univ. of Witwatersrand, S. Africa B.Sc. (Eng.) 1945, B.Sc. (Hons.) 1948; Univ. Coll. London, Eng. Ph.D. 1950, D.Sc. 1960; m. Bessie Flax 30 June 1946; children: Jonathan Michael, Peter Benjamin, Sarah Tanya; EMERITUS PROF. OF MATH., UNIV. OF WESTERN ONT. 1989– ; Lectr. in Math. St. Salvators Coll. St. Andrews Univ. Scot. 1950–63; Visiting Prof., Univ. of Western Ont. 1963–64, Prof. 1964–89, Head of Math. Dept. 1967–89; served with S. African forces 1945; author over 100 research articles math. journs.; co-ed.: Analysis, Internat. Journ. of Analysis & its Application; mem. Candn. Math. Soc. (Pres. 1985–87); Math. Assn. Am. (Assoc. Ed. Am. Math. Monthly 1981–85); Am. Math. Soc.; London Math. Soc.; recreations: swimming, tennis, bridge, reading, theatre; Home: 1032 Brough St., London, Ont. N6A 3N4; Office: Dept. of Math., Univ. of W. Ont., London, Ont. N6A 5B7.

**BORWEIN, Jonathan Michael,** M.Sc., D.Phil.; educator; b. St. Andrews, Scot. 20 May 1951; s. David and Bessie (Flax) B.; e. Univ. of W. Ont. B.Sc. 1971; Oxford Univ. (Rhodes Scholar) M.Sc. 1972, D.Phil. 1974; m. Judith Dierdre d. Fred and Helen Scott-Roots 17 Sept. 1973; three d. Rachel Laura, Naomi Simone Hannah, Tova Rebekah; SHRUM PROFESSOR OF SCIENCE, SIMON FRASER UNIV. 1993–98; Prof. of Math., Dalhousie Univ. 1984– ;(on leave 1991–93), Rsch. Fellow Dalhousie Univ. 1974, Asst. Prof 1976–80, Assoc. Prof. 1982–84; Asst. Prof. Carnegie-Mellon 1980, Assoc. Prof. 1981–82; Prof. of Math., Dept. of Combinatorics and Optimization, Univ. of Waterloo 1991–93; Sr. Killam Fellow, Dalhousie Univ. 1987–88; Coxeter-James Lectr., Candn. Math. Soc. 1987; Chrmn., NSERC Mathematics Grants Selection Ctte. 1989–91; co-author 'Pi and the A.G.M.' 1987; co-author (with E.J. Borowski) 'A Dictionary of Mathematics' 1989; co-author 'A Dictionary of Real Numbers' 1989; awarded APICS/Fraser Gold Medal for Rsch. Excellence 1988; Chauvenet Prize and Hasse Prize, Mathematical Assn. of Am. 1993; mem. Candn. Math. Soc. (Dir. 1983–87; Rsch. Ctte. 1985–88); Math. Assoc. Amer., Amer. Math. Soc.; SIAM; AAAS; CAMS; NDP; recreations: swimming, theatre, bridge; Home: 401 Craigleith Dr., Waterloo, Ont. N2L 5B5.

**BORWEIN, Peter B.,** Ph.D.; university professor; b. St. Andrews, Scotland 10 May 1953; s. David and Bessie (Flax) B.; e. Univ. of West. Ont., B.Sc. 1974; Univ. of B.C., M.Sc. 1976, Ph.D. 1979; m. Jennifer d. Murry and Jean Moore 28 Nov. 1980; children: Alexandra, Sophie, Theresa; DEPT. OF MATH AND STATS, SIMON FRASER UNIV. 1993– ; NATO postdoctoral fellow, Oxford Univ. 1979–80; Faculty Member, Dept. of Math, Statistics & Computing Sci., Dalhousie Univ. 1980–93; Assoc. Dir., Centre for Experimental and Constructive Mathematics; author of numerous sci. papers; co-author (with J. Borwein): 'P1 and the AGM: A Study in Analytic Number Theory and Computational Complexity' 1987, 'A Dictionary of Real Numbers' 1990; Office: Burnaby B.C. V5A 1S6.

**BOSA, Hon. Peter,** C.L.U.; senator; insurance executive; b. Bertiolo-Udine, Italy 2 May 1927; s. late Antonio and late Angela (Moro) B.; e. Elem. Sch. Bertiolo-Udine, Italy; Hamilton (Ont.) Mt. High Sch. 1951; C.L.U., Univ. of Toronto 1968; m. Teresa d. late Alessandro and Concetta Patullo, Boiano, Italy 20 July 1968; children: Angela, Mark; PRESIDENT, CLOVER INSURANCE BROKER LTD.; Foreman Cutting Dept. Sainthill Levine Co. Ltd. Toronto 1948–57; Life Underwriter since 1957, North American Life; Ald. Ward 3 Borough of York 1969, re-el. 1972, 1974; Special and Extve. Asst. to Min. of Citizenship & Immigration, Govt. House Leader and Postmaster Gen. 1963–65; summoned to Senate 1977; Dir. Northwestern Gen. Hosp. 1970–89; Chrmn. Candn. Consultative Council on Multiculturalism 1976–79; Senate Ctte. on Foreign Affairs & social Science & Technology; mem. Life Underwriters Assoc. of Can.; Candn. Italian Business & Prof. Assn. Toronto; Toronto Life Underwriters' Assn.; Toronto Ins. Agts. Assn.; Liberal; R. Catholic; recreations: chess, golf; Clubs: Famee Furlane; York Lions; Home: 22 Neilor Cres., Etobicoke, Ont. M9C 1K4.

**BOSC, Marc Joseph,** B.Comm., M.A.; public servant; b. St-Boniface, Man. 21 July 1960; s. Hubert and Thérèse (Dacquay) B.; e. Coll. sec. de Saint-Boniface; Carleton Univ., B.Comm. 1982, M.A. (pub. admin.) 1989; m. Peggy d. William and Ina Humphries 14 Aug. 1982; children: Caroline Margaret, Natalie Ina; ACTING DEPUTY PRINCIPAL CLERK, BOURINOT OFFICE, HOUSE OF COMMONS 1993– ; Rsch. Asst., Secretariat Offr., Office of the Min. of Employment & Immigration 1980–83; Legis. Asst. to Min. of State (Finance) 1983–84, to Min. of Nat. Revenue 1984; Procedural Clerk, Table Rsch. Branch and Committees Directorate, House of Commons 1986–90; Extve. Asst. to the Clerk of the House of Commons 1990–92; Procedural Clerk, Public Bills Office, House of Commons 1992–93; Past Pres. Bd. of Dirs., Children on the Hill Daycare Centre; Mem. Bd. of Dirs., 'La Clémentine' Daycare Centre; Pres., Parent Teacher Assn. 'École Élémentaire Gabrielle Roy'; editor: 'The Broadview Book of Canadian Parliamentary Anecdotes' 1988; club: The Millennium; Home: 2641 Colman St., Ottawa, Ont. K1V 8J7; Office: Room 1200, 151 Sparks St., House of Commons, Ottawa, Ont. K1A 0A6.

**BOSC, Paul Michel;** oenologist; b. Marengo, Algeria 17 July 1935; s. Armand Joseph and Suzanne (Galibert) B.; e. Univ. of Dijon (Burgundy) Oenologist 1954; m. Andrée Raymonde d. Pierre and Eleonore Vaquer 6 Dec. 1958; two s. Paul-André, Pierre-Jean; FOUNDER & CO-OWNER, CHATEAU DES CHARMES WINES LTD. 1978– ; Gen. Mgr. Societé Civile de Vinification Marengo, Algeria 1956; Chief Oenologist, Dir. Rsch. & Devel. Chateau Gai Wines, Niagara Falls, Ont. 1974; mem. Tech. Ctte. Grape & Wine Adjustment Prog. (rep. Wine Council Ont.); Dir. Vintners Quality Alliance; Wine Council Ont.; recreation: skiing; Club: White Oak Inn; Home: York Rd., St. Davids, Ont. L0S 1P0; Office: P.O. Box 280, St. Davids, Ont. L0S 1P0.

**BOSHER, John Francis,** B.A., Ph.D., F.R.H.S., F.R.S.C.; educator; b. Sidney, B.C. 28 May 1929; s. John Ernest and Grace (Simister) B.; e. North Saanich High Sch. 1946; Victoria Coll. B.C. 1946–48; Univ. of B.C. B.A. 1950; Univ. of Paris D.E.S. d'Histoire 1954; Univ. of London Ph.D. 1957; m. Kathryn Cecil d. Henry Deryck Berry, Mexico 28 May 1968; children: Sylvia Liane, Lise Diana (from previous marriage); Kathryn Grace, George Henry Francis; PROF. OF HIST., YORK UNIV. since 1969 and Distinguished Rsch. Prof. 1989; Administrative Offr. Civil Service Comn. Ottawa 1951–53; Asst. Lectr. King's Coll. Univ. London 1956–59; Prof. Univ. of B.C. 1959–67, Cornell Univ. 1967–69; Visiting Fellow, All Souls Coll., Oxford 1991–92; author 'The Single Duty Project' 1964; 'French Finances 1770–1795' 1970; contrib. 'New Cambridge Modern Hist.' vol. 8; ed. and contrib. 'French Government and Society 1500–1850' 1973; 'The Canada Merchants 1713–1763' 1987; 'The French Revolution' 1988; 'Men and Ships in the Canada Trade 1660–1760: A Biographical Dictionary' 1992; over 40 articles on 18th century France and Can.; guest lectr. various insts. France, U.S. and Can.; mem. Econ. Hist. Soc. (Eng.); Royal Soc. of Can. since 1976; Royal Hist. Soc. (Eng.); Soc. French Hist. Studies (U.S.); Anglican; recreations: music, gardening; Office: 4700 Keele St., North York, Ont. M3J 1P3.

**BOSLEY, Hon. John William,** P.C., M.P., B.A.; politician; b. Toronto, Ont. 4 May 1947; s. Murray Arthur William and Mary Elizabeth (Veitch) B.; e. Upper Can. Coll. Toronto; Univ. of Toronto Trinity Coll. B.A. 1968; York Univ. grad. work environmental studies & urban planning; m. Nicole Bienvenue Novak 19 Oct. 1984; Ald. City of Toronto 1974–78, mem. Exec. Comte. City and Metro 1977–78; SPEAKER, HOUSE OF COMMONS 1984–86; el. to H. of C. for Don Valley W. g.e. 1979, re-el. 1980, 1984, 1988; Parlty. Secy. to Prime Min. 1979; mem. Special Jt. Comte. on Official Langs. and Chrmn. PC Caucus Ctte. on Cultural Affairs 1981; Spokesman for External Relations in Shadow Cabinet 1983; Chrmn., Special Ctte. on the Peace Process in Central America; Chrmn., Standing Ctte. on External Affairs and Internat. Trade; prior to 1974 served in public relations counselling, real estate brokerage; mem. Nat. Council Royal Commonwealth Soc.; Anglican; P. Conservative; recreations: golf; Clubs: Rosedale Golf; University (Toronto); Office: House of Commons, Ottawa, Ont. K1A 0A6.

**BOSLEY, Murray Arthur William,** B.Comm., F.R.I.; real estate broker; b. Toronto, Ont. 7 Mar. 1915; s. William Henry, O.B.E. and Elsie M. (Crokam) B.; e. University of Toronto Schs. (1932); Trinity Coll., Univ. of Toronto, B.Com. 1936; CHRMN., W.H. BOSLEY & COMPANY LTD. General Real Estate Estbd. 1928; Past Pres., Candn. Assn. of Real Estate Bds. (1958); Past Pres., Candn. Inst. of Realtors (1960); Past Pres., Toronto Real Estate Bd. (1951 and 1952); Past Pres., Ont. Assn. of Real Estate Bds. (1954); Real Estate Advisor to Dept. of Nat. Defence, Ottawa 1939–41; Asst. to Gen. Mgr., Wartime Housing Ltd. 1941–42; Past Trustee Sunnybrook Health Centre; Past Chrmn., Lyndhurst Hospital; Past Pres. Can. Chapter Int. Real Estate Federation; mem. Toronto Advisory Comte., Salvation Army; served in 2nd World War with 12th Candn. Field Regt. Delta Upsilon; Anglican; recreations: Golf, photography; Clubs: National (Past Pres.); Badminton & Racquet; Toronto Hunt; Rosedale Golf (Past Pres.); Rotary (Past Pres.); Home: 61 St. Clair Ave. W.; Office: Yonge Corporate Centre, 4120 Yonge St., Suite #608, North York, Ont. M2P 2B8.

**BOSLEY, Raymond Sedgemore Lock,** F.R.I., C.P.M.; Ont. land economist; retired real estate broker; b. Toronto, Ont. 22 Aug. 1921; s. William Henry, founder of the firm of W. H. Bosley & Co., and Elsie M. (Crokam) B.; e. Univ. of Toronto Schs.; Northern Vocational Sch., Toronto, Ont. (special courses in Real Estate Appraisal and Property Mang.); m. Dorothy Claire, d. T.H. Dickinson, 2 June 1943; three s. Michael, Thomas, William; Chrmn., W.H. Bosley & Company Ltd., Real Estate Brokers, Estbd. 1928, Retired; Pres., Toronto Real Estate Bd. 1958; Hon. Life Mem. Toronto Real Estate Bd.; Sr. Vice Pres. and mem. of Gov. Counc., Inst. of Real Estate Management of the Nat. Assn. of Real Estate Bds., Chicago; Charter Pres., Ont. Chapter, Inst. of Real Estate Mgmt; mem. Bd. of Dirs., Abbeyfield Houses Soc. of Canada (Pres. 1989–90); Past Secy., Bldg. Owners & Managers Assn.; Past Pres. Toronto Central Branch, Can. Red Cross Soc.; Past Pres., Rotary Clubs of Toronto (1970); served in 2nd World War with R.C.N.V.R. and R.C.A., rank Lieut.; Anglican; recreations: golf, photography, boating; Clubs: Granite; Rosedale Golf; Rotary (Past Pres.); Past Pres. Rotary Laughlen Centre; Home: 3900 Yonge St., Suite 602, Toronto, Ont. M4P 3N6.

**BOTHWELL, The Right Rev. John C.,** D.D. (Ang.); retired bishop; b. Toronto, Ont. 29 June 1926; s. William Alexander and Anne (Campbell) B.; e. Runnymede Pub. Sch. 1939 and Humberside Coll. Inst. 1944 Toronto; Trinity Coll. Univ. of Toronto B.A. 1948, L.Th. 1951, B.D. 1952, D.D. 1972; Hon. D.D., Huron Coll., Univ. of W. Ont. 1988; Hon. D.D., Wycliffe Coll., Univ. of Toronto 1988; m. Joan d. Hector Cowan, 29 Dec. 1951; children: Michael, Timothy, Nancy, Douglas, Ann; Chancellor, Trinity Coll., Univ. of Toronto 1991– ; o. Deacon 29 Apr. 1951, Priest 4 May 1952; Asst. Priest St. James Cath. Toronto 1951–53; Sr. Asst. Christ Ch. Cath. Vancouver 1953–56; Rector St. Aidan's Oakville 1956–60 and St. James' Dundas, Ont. 1960–65; Canon of Christ's Ch. Cath., Hamilton, Ont. 1963; and Programme Dir. Niagara Diocese 1965–69; Extve. Dir. of Program Nat. HQ Ang. Ch. Toronto 1969–71; el. Bishop Coadjutor Niagara Diocese 1971; Bishop of Niagara 1973–91 and Metropolitan of Ontario 1985–91; retired; Exec. Mem. Hamilton Soc. Planning Council 1972–76 (Pres. 1976–78); Bd. mem., Hamilton United Way (Vice Pres. 1983, Pres. 1984) and Ontario Council for Social Development; Official Visitor Ridley Coll. St. Catharines 1973–91, St. John's Boys Sch., Elora, Ont. 1973–91 and Candn. Ch. of the Sisters of the Church 1973–91; mem. Gen. Synod and Ont. Prov. Synod Ang. Ch. of Can. 1969–93; mem. various ecumenical and inter ch. comtes. and bds.; Dir., Hamilton Fndn. 1982–86 (Vice Pres. 1983, Pres. 1984); Bd. Mem., Hamilton United Way 1980–86, Pres. 1984–86; Bd. Mem., Hamilton Soc. Planning Counc. 1974–80, Pres. 1978–80; inducted to City of Hamilton Gallery of Distinction 1993; author: 'Taking Risks and Keeping Faith' 1985; 'Keeping Faith Day By Day' 1989; 'Old Time Religion or Risky Faith?' 1993; Hon. Sr. Fellow, Renison Coll., Univ. of Waterloo 1988; Home: 838 Glenwood Ave., Burlington, Ont. L7T 2J9.

**BOTHWELL, Robert Selkirk,** Ph.D., F.R.S.C.; historian; university professor; b. Ottawa, Ont. 17 Aug. 1944; s. John Robert and Mary Pauline (Rutherford) B.; e. Ridgemont H.S.; Univ. of Toronto B.A. 1966; Harvard Univ. A.M. 1967, Ph.D. 1972; m. Gail Alexander Corbett 1993; two d.: Eleanor Myfanwy, Alice Pauline; PROF. OF HISTORY, UNIV. OF TORONTO 1981– ; Teaching Fellow, Harvard Univ. 1968–70; Lectr. 1970, Asst. Prof. 1972, Assoc. Prof. 1975 present Univ.; Assoc. Ed. & Ed. 'Canadian Historical Review' 1972–80; Woodrow Wilson Fellow 1966; recipient Corey Prize, Candn. & Am. Hist. Assns. 1980; Liberal; Sr. Fellow, Trinity Coll.; mem., Extve. Ctte., Trinity Coll. 1988–91; mem., Candn. Ctte. for the History of the Second World War; Candn. Inst. of Internat. Affairs; Bd. mem., Ont. Heritage Found. 1987–93 (Chrmn., Archaeology Ctte. 1988–92; Co-chair, History & Archaeology Ctte. 1992–93; mem., Extve. Ctte. 1988–93); Bd. mem., C.D. Howe Memorial Found. 1990– ; Mem., Bd. of Govs., Branksome Hall Sch. 1989–91; author: 'The World of Lester Pearson' 1978; 'Eldorado: Canada's National Uranium Company' 1984; 'A Short History of Ontario' 1986; 'Years of Victory' 1987; 'Nucleus' 1988; 'Loring Christie' 1988; 'Laying the Foundations' 1991; 'Canada & the United States' 1992; numerous articles & reviews in Candn., US & UK periodicals; co-author: 'C.D. Howe: A Biography' 1979; 'Canada since 1945' 1981, 2nd ed. 1989; 'The Great Brain Robbery' 1984; 'Canada 1900–1945' 1987; 'Pirouette' 1990; co-editor: 'Policy by Other Means' 1972; 'The In-Between Time' 1975; radio lectr., CJRT 1990–94; book review editor, 'Behind the Headlines' 1993– ; recreations: walking, reading; Home: 103 Farnham Ave., Toronto, Ont. M4V 1H6; Office: Trinity Coll., Toronto, Ont. M5S 1H8.

**BOTSFORD, Sara L.;** actress, producer; b. Kirkland Lake, Ont. 8 Apr. 1951; d. John Herman and Katherine Louise (Davis) B.; e. Kirkland Lake C.V.I.; York Univ.; ASSOC. PRODUCER, E.N.G. SERIES 1989– ; started at Stratford Festival 1973/74 season; worked primarily on stage in Toronto & Montreal playing leading roles from 1974–79 (The Rivals, Hamlet, Ashes The Club); moved to N.Y. city in 1979; worked on and off Broadway 1979–89; films: 'Bells' 1980, 'By Design' 1981, 'Still of the Night' 1982, 'Gunrunner' 1986, 'Deadly Eyes' 1982, 'Legal Eagles' 1987, 'Jumping Jack Flash' 1987; television includes: 'As the World Turns' 1988; E.N.G. series lead (Anne Hildebrandt) 4 seasons; Genie nom. for By Design 1982; Obie Award for Top Girls 1983 (NYC); Gemini nom. for lead actress of E.N.G. 1991, 1992; Teacher, Equity Showcase and privately; Bd. of Dir., Young Peoples Theatre 1992; Hon. Chairperson, Interval House; Office: c/o CTV, 42 Charles St. E., Toronto, Ont. M4Y 1T5.

**BOTTERELL, E. Harry,** O.C., O.B.E., M.D., M.S. (Tor.), F.R.C.S.(C), D.Sc. (Hon.), LL.D.; neurosurgeon; b. Vancouver, B.C. 28 Feb. 1906; s. John Esterbrook and Louise Ethel (Armstrong) B.; e. Ridley Coll., St. Catharines, Ont.; Univ. of Manitoba M.D. 1930; Univ. of Toronto M.S. 1936; D.Sc. (Hon.) McGill 1972; LL.D. Queen's 1973; winner Lister Prize Univ. of Toronto 1937, George Armstrong Peters Prize Univ. of Toronto 1939; m. Margaret Talbot, d. Mt. Rev. Archbishop Samuel Pritchard Matheson; children: Daphne, Jocelyn; Prof. Emeritus of Surgical Neurol. and Clinical Anatomy, Queen's Univ. since 1974; House Surg. Winnipeg Gen. Hosp. 1929, Resident in Gen. Surg. 1930; Resident Physician, Montreal Gen. Hosp. 1931; Resident Surg. Toronto Gen. Hosp. 1933; Clinical Clerk neurol. Nat. Hosp. London U.K. 1934; Research Fellow Neurophysiol. Yale Univ. 1935; Lect. in neurophysiol. and Resident Neurosurg. Lect. and Jr. Neurosurg., and Consulting Neurosurg. Toronto General Hospital 1936–40; Sr. Neurosurg. 1945–62 and Assoc. Prof. of Surg. (Neurosurg.) Univ. of Toronto, Prof. 1961–62; Dean of Med. Queen's Univ. 1962–70, Vice-Princ. Health Scs. 1968–71, Special Advisor to Princ. Health Scs. 1971–74; served in 2nd World War RCAMC overseas 1940–45, rank Lt.-Col.; Sr. Neurosurg., Christie St. Hosp. Jt. Services Neurosurg. Unit and Sunnybrook Hosp. Neurosurg. Unit D.V.A., 1945–55; Neurolog. Consultant, mem. Med. Adv. Bd. and Bd. of Govs. Lyndhurst Hosp.; One-man Ctte. Enquiry into Health Care System in Min. Correctional Services in Ont. 1971; One-man Ctte. enquiring into animal health care services Ont. Min. Agric. and Food 1974; Chrmn. Nat. Health Services Adv. Ctte. for Correctional Service Canada; Hon. Fellow, Roy. Coll. of Surgeons (Edinburgh); Hon. mem. Soc. Brit. Neurol. Surgs.; Hon. mem. Australasian Neurosurg. Assn.; Sr. mem. American Neurosurg. Assn.; Hon. mem. Can. Assn. Phys. Med. and Rehabilitation; Hon. mem., Ont. Medical Assn.; Hon. mem. Soc. de Neurochirurgie de langue Francais; Sr. mem. Soc. Neurol. Surgs.; Sr. mem. Am. Neurol. Assn.; Sr. mem. Acad. Neurol. Surg.; Sr. mem. Am. Assn. Neurol. Surgs.; Sr. mem. Cndn. Med. Assn.; F.N.G. Starr Award of Can. Med. Assn. 1977; Comm. Citation, Correctional Service Can. 1980; John Orr Award, Toronto Br., Queen's Alumni 1989; Zeta Psi; Anglican; recreation: sailing; Home: 2 Lakeshore Blvd., Kingston, Ont. K7M 4J6.

**BOTTING, Dale W.,** B.Ed., B.Sc.; association executive; b. Prince Albert, Sask. 7 June 1953; s. Walter Alfred and Mary Ann (Gere) B.; e. Univ. of Sask. B.Sc. (Biol.) & (Geog.) 1975, B.Ed. 1977; Banff Sch. Cert. Social Impact Assessment 1979; m. Geraldine d. George and Doris Graham 14 Feb. 1975; children: Quinn, Kelsey, Dylan; EXTVE. DIR., PRAIRIE REGION, CANDN. FEDN. OF IND. BUS. 1991– ; Pres., Dale Botting and Associates; Dir. W.A.B. Holdings Ltd.; during 1970's and early 1980's Environmental Mgmt. Cons. Sask. Dept. of Environment and private sector incl. Lavalin Inc. and Churchill River Bd. of Inquiry; Exec. Dir. Sask. Dept. Sci. & Technol.; Premier of Sask.'s Coordinator of Regulatory Reform 1982–84; Dir. of Resource Policy Premier's Planning Bureau and Sec. to Sask. Cabinet Ctte. on Central & Regulatory Services 1983–84; Dir., Provs. Sask. & Man., present Fedn. 1985–86, Dir., Provincial Affairs 1986–89; Dir., Environmental Partnerships, Sask. Dept. of Environment 1991–92; recipient Nat. Rsch. Council Postgrad. Scholarships 1975–76; Candn. Assn. Geogs. Award Most Distinguished Grad. Sask. 1975; D.S. Rawson Award Most Distinguished Grad. Biol. Sask. 1975; author or co-author various reports, sci. articles and environmental guidelines; recreations: family, tennis, camping, hiking; Office: #950 – 1783 Hamilton St., Regina, Sask. S4P 2B6.

**BOUCHARD, Hon. Benoît,** P.C., LL.L.; politician; b. Roberval, Que. 16 Apr. 1940; e. Laval Univ.; m. Jeannine Lavoie; three children; Principal, Coll. Notre-Dame; Polyvante; Villa étudiante de Roberval; Min. of National Health & Welfare 1991–93; Dir. Gen., Cégep at St-Félicien since 1979; mem., Féderation des Cégeps; city councillor for the Town of Roberval 1973–80; 1st el. H. of C. (Roberval) g.e. 1984; re-el. g.e. 1988; Min. of State (Transport) 1984–85; sworn to the Privy Council 1984; apptd. Secy. of State 1985; Min. of Employment & Immigration 1986–88; Min. of Transport 1988–90; Min. of Industry, Science and Technology 1990–91; P.C.; Address: 237 Ménard Ave., Roberval, Qué. G8H 1P4.

**BOUCHARD, Denis;** actor; b. Montréal, Qué. 9 Oct. 1953; s. Fernand and Jacqueline (Le Royer) B.; e. Nat. Theatre Sch., grad. 1977; acted in films 'Racing to the Bomb' 1985; 'He Shoots, He Scores' 1986; 'Les tisserands du pouvoir' 1987; 'Les Matins Infidèles' 1988; 'Jésus de Montréal' 1988; 'Rafales' 1990 (also co-author); 'Love-Moi' 1990; plays: 'Périclès' 1984; 'Les fridolinades' 1987; 'La cité interdite' 1990; 'À toi pour toujours ta Marie-Lou Sainte-Carmen-de-la-Main Damné Manon, Sacré Sandra' 1991; mem. Ligue Nationale d'Improvisation 1978–85; Lectr., Nat. Theatre Sch. 1984– ; co-author of plays 'La déprime' 1981; 'Terminal Blues' 1983; 'Raz de Marée' 1985; 'La Farce de L'Âge' 1990; 'Pare-Chocs' 1992; 'René Lévesque' 1993; Co-founder of theatre co. Le Klaxon; Address: 4696 De Grand Pré, Montréal, Qué. H2T 2H7.

**BOUCHARD, Gérard,** M.A., Ph.D., FRSC; university professor; b. Jonquière, Que. 26 Dec. 1943; s. Philippe and Alice (Simard) B.; e. Laval Univ., M.A. 1968; Univ. de Paris, Ph.D. 1971; m. Lise d. Armand and Alberta Bergeron 16 Aug. 1968; children: Catherine, Olivier; FOUNDER & DIR., SOREP 1972– ; major achievement of SOREP is devel. of computerized population register used in fields of social sci., hist., demography & human genetics; teaching appointments: Ecole des Hautes Etudes en Sci. Soc. (Paris) 1977; Laval Univ. 1988– ; mem., numerous sci. assns. & ed. bds. of jours.; FRSC 1985– ; ACFAS Prize (Que.) for interdisciplinary studies; Co-founder, Corp. de rech. et d'action sur les maladies héréditaires; author: 'Le village immobile' 1972; co-author: 'Les Saguenayens' 1983, 'Le Système SOREP de reconstitution des familles' 2 vols. 1985, 'Histoire d'un génôme' 1991; Home: 1541, Martinets, Chicoutimi, Que. G7H 5X9; Office: SOREP, 935 est rue Jacques-Cartier, Chicoutimi, Que. G7H 2B1.

**BOUCHARD, Jacques;** advertising executive; b. Montreal, Que. 29 Aug. 1930; s. Bernard and Lucienne (Leduc) B.; e. St. Laurent Coll., B.A. 1948; Univ. of Montreal, L.S.P. 1952; Heed Univ., Fla., M.A. (Educ.); m. Caroline, d. Antoine Maranda, 13 June 1969; one d. Veronique; CHRMN. EMERITUS, BCP STRATEGY-CREATIVITY INC.; commenced as Translator, Vickers & Benson Ltd., Montreal 1949; Mgr., French Advertising, James Lovick Ltd. 1955; Acct. Supv., J. Walter Thompson Co. Ltd. 1956; Advertising Mgr., La Brasserie Ltd. 1957; recreations: horseriding, billiards; Clubs: Le Publicité de Montreal; Advertising & Sales Executive; Young Presidents' Organization Inc.; American Political Consultants; Canadian; Home: Chateau de la Briche, 37340 Hommes, Indre-et-Loire, France; 3300 St. Joseph Blvd. E., Montréal, Qué. H1X 3GS; Office: 1000 Sherbrooke St. W., 20th Flr., Montréal, Qué. H3A 3G9.

**BOUCHARD, Linda,** B.A., M.M.; composer-conductor; b. Val d'Or, Que. 21 May 1957; d. Claude and Thérèse (Charron) B.; e. Bennington Coll. B.A. 1979; Manhattan Sch. of Music M.M. 1982; COMPOSER-IN-RESIDENCE, NATIONAL ARTS CENTRE ORCHESTRA, OTTAWA, CANADA 1992– ; Conductor, New Music Groups, Asst. Conductor, Children's Free Opera of N.Y. and Artistic Dir., Abandon Ensemble (N.Y.) 1979– ; Guest Conductor, Atelier de musique contemporaine, Univ. of Montreal 1990–92; composed over 50 compositions in orchestral, chamber music, vocal, opera and for dance companies; 4 composition prizes (PRO-CAN), First Prize: Indiana State Univ. Contest 1986; First Prize: Nat. Assn. of Composers (US) 1981; First Prize: Princeton Contest 1992; Residency at Camargo Found. in France, Yaddo, MacDowell Colony; recordings: ECM (Germany), RCI (Canada), CRI (USA); publisher: Doberman-Yppan (Que.), Musigraph (Montreal); Home: P.O. Box 530, Stn. C, Montreal, Que. H2L 4K4; Office: P.O. Box 1534, Stn. B, Ottawa, Ont. K1P 5W1.

**BOUCHARD, Honourable Louis-Philippe,** B.A., L.èsD.; né Amos, Qué., 28 juil. 1918, f. Dalmas et Laurette (Fortin) B.; é. Séminaire de Qué., B.A. (cum laude, médaille du lt.-gov.) 1939; Univ. Laval, L. ès D. (cum laude, médaille du lt.-gov.) 1946; Ecole des Hautes Etudes Comm., Univ. de Montréal; études en comptabilité et cours de perfectionnement en adm., en collab. avec l'Univ. d'Harvard 1961; ép. Gilberte Savoie, 26 juin 1945; enfants: Marie, Jacqueline, Guy; JUGE DE LA COUR PROVINCIALE, QUE.; Vice-prés. Comn. des transports du Qué.; sous-ministre fondateur du ministère des Institutions financières du Québec; Prés.-dir. gén., Régie de l'assurance-depôts du Qué.; Prés., Comité d'étude sur l'industrie des valeurs mobilières au Qué.; Vice-prés. honoraire, Conseil Saint-Jean de Qué.; Dir., Assn. canadienne pour santé mentale; avec le Trust Général du Canada, Dir.-gérant, succursale de Qué. 1955, Dir. Gén. adjoint de la Cie 1965; Conseiller spécial auprès de l'Executif, du Gouvernement du Québec 1968; admis au Barreau 1946; nommé C.R. 1968; catholique romaine; récréation: golf, pêche; résidence: 1321 Preston, Sillery, Qué. G1S 4L3.

**BOUCHARD, Lucien,** B.A., B.S.Sc., LL.L; politician; b. St-Coeur-de-Marie, Que. 22 Dec. 1938; s. Philippe and Alice (Simard) B.; e. Coll. de Jonquière, B.A. 1959; Univ. Laval, B.S.Sc. 1960, LL.L. 1963; called to Qué. Bar 1964; LEADER OF THE OFFICIAL OPPOSITION, GOVT. OF CANADA 1993– ; priv. law practice, Chicoutimi 1964–85; 1st Chrmn, Que. Edn. Arbitration Bd. 1970–76; Chief Couns. for Cliche Comn. Inquiry on Constrn. Indus. 1974–75; Mem., Martin Bouchard Comn. on Que. Pub. Sector's Negotiation 1978–79; Mem., Que. Bar Extve. Ctte. 1978–79; Coord., Que. Govt. negotiation with pub. sector's employees 1978–81; Dir., Société génerale de financement; Donohue Inc.; Corp. de dével. des investissements du Can. 1981–85; Candn. Ambassador to France 1985–88; elected Conservative Member of Parliament, Lac-Saint-Jean June 1988; re-elected November 1988; Secretary of State 1988–89; Min. of the Environment 1989–90; sat as Independent M.P., Lac-Saint-Jean 1990; Leader, newly formed Bloc Québecois 1990; Chrmn. & Leader, Bloc Québécois 1991– ; author: 'À visage découvert' (essay) 1992; also number of specialized articles in legal and labour relations journals; co-author: 'Martin-Bouchard Report 1977–78'; Office: Room 409-S, Centre Block, House of Commons, Ottawa, Ont. K1A 0A6.

**BOUCHARD, Micheline,** M.Sc., P.Eng.; computer consultant; b. Montreal, Que. 22 Apl. 1947; d. Henri and Claire (Larochelle) Bouchard; e. Ecole Polytechnique Univ. de Montréal B.Sc. 1969, M.Sc. 1978; m. Jean-Paul s. Gabriel and Aimée Sardin 11 Jan. 1974; children: Valérie, Frédéric; VICE PRES. MKTG. DMR GROUP INC. 1988– ; Dir. Canada Post; Corby Distilleries; Gaz Métropolitain; Uni-Média; London Insurance Group; Monsanto Canada; Eng., Transmission Lines/System Planning, Rsch. Hydro-Québec 1969–77, Asst. Vice Pres. Info. 1980–81, Asst. to Pres. & Chief Exec. Offr. 1981–83, Comm. Del. Large Accts. 1983–87; Vice Pres. Mgmt. Cons. CGI Group 1987–88; Dir. Pub. Policy Forum 1987–92; named Woman of Yr. Bus. 1981; Candn. Council Profl. Engs. (Pres. 1992–93); Order Engs. Que. (Pres. 1978–80); Montreal C. of C. (Vice Pres. 1983–87); Montreal Bd. Trade (Vice Pres. 1989–92); recreations: sailing, horseback riding; Home: 901 Des Hirondelles, St. Bruno, Que. J3V 6E4; Office: 2300, 1200 McGill College Ave., Montreal, Que. H3B 4G7.

**BOUCHARD, Paul,** B.A., L.ès D.; educator; b. Québec, Qué. 18 Apr. 1908; s. Alfred and Bernadette (Boulet) B.; e. Univ. Laval B.A. 1928, L.ès D. 1931; Wadham Coll. Oxford (Rhodes Scholar) B.C.L. 1931–34; Universidad de Zaragoza 1932; Universidad de Chile Cert. Latin Am. Studies 1943; Founder and Dir. of 'La Nation' first separatist paper publ. in Que., origin of the movement for Que. independence 1934; Independance candidate, Lotbinière Co. 1937; anti-conscription and Independance candidate in Quebec City 1940 and 1942; joined Duplessis' campaign for provincial autonomy 1945; publicist and mem., Nat. Union Central Orgn. 1946–59; Contributor, Nat. Union weekly 'Le Temps'; retired from the Nat. Union and politics at Duplessis' death 1959; Prof. of Econ. Geog. of Latin Am., Univ. Laval 1946–63; Prof. of Hist. of Latin Am., Spain & Portugal 1961–76; Invited Lectr., Latin Am. Hist., Univ. of Ponce, Puerto Rico 1962; Prof. of Hispanic Hist. for Adults & Retired People 1983–90; currently Lectr., Univ. of Laval; called to Bar of Qué. 1931; Pres. Circulo Cervantes-Camoens 1960–70; Lectr. Nat. Defence Coll. Kingston 1965–71; Organizer Laval Internat. Conf. on Latin Am. 1968, Ed. Conf. Report 1970; Laval Univ. delegate to Hispanic Internat. Confs.: Lake Couchiching, Ont. 1960; Cartagena, Colombia, 1961; Banff, Alta. 1964; Guatemala 1965; Nijmegen, Holland 1965; Georgetown, Guyana 1966; Buenos Aires 1966; Asunción, Paraguay 1966; Mexico City 1968; Quebec 1968; Salamanca, Spain 1971; Quebec 1978; Titular mem. Inst. de Cultura Hispanica, Madrid 1962; Honorary Consul du Guatemala 1959–94; ed. 'La Sociéte de Géographie de Québec 1877–1970' 1971; author numerous publs. in Fr., Eng. and Spanish; Prés. du Centre Espagnol de l'Université Laval 1960–70; Prés. de la Société de Géographie de Qué. 1960–70 et 1974–94; Prés. La Soc. des Ecrivains Canadiens Qué. sect. 1973–80, Prés. gén. of Soc. 1979–81; Prés., La Fond. Paul Bouchard pour les sciences de la Terre, de l'Homme et de la Nature 1984; Founder and Dean, Que. Assoc. of Hon. Consuls 1983; l'Ordre du Mérite, La Société St-Jean Baptiste de Québec 1974; Life Mem., Friends of the Bodleian Library, Oxford 1985; mem. Internat. Assn. Hispanists; Candn. Hist. Soc.; Candn. Assn. Rhodes Scholars; Wadham Coll. Assn. Oxford; P.E.N. Club International of Montreal; Club: Québec Garrison; Address: 50 rue Aberdeen, Québec, Qué. G1R 2C7.

**BOUCHARD, Serge,** B.A., M.A., Ph.D.; writer, anthropologist, consultant; b. Montreal, Que. 27 July 1947; s. Roméo and Emilienne (Lupien) B.; e. Univ. of Montreal B.A. 1967; Laval Univ. M.A. 1972; McGill Univ. Ph.D. 1980; m. Ginette d. Emile Noël 3 Aug. 1968; one s.: Serge-Alexandre; OWNER, SERGE BOUCHARD CONSULTANT INC. 1992– ; Lecturer, Laval Uni. 1975–80 Univ. of Montreal 1980, Univ. of Que. 1988; Co-Founder, SSDCC Inc. 1980–88; Dir. of Rsch., Inst. de recherche en Santé-sécurité du travail 1988–91; Commissioner, Public Hearings on Montreal Waste Management Project 1992; Consultant in social science for 20 years; Consultant, SQ, RCMP & Candn. College of Police; writer and reader for CBC Radio; Pres., Candn. Assn. of Applied Anthropology; author: 'Le Moineau domestique' 1991 (short essays), 'Ways and Meanings in Long-Distance Trucker's Life' forthcoming (PhD thesis); editor: 'Life Story of Mathieu Mestokosho: Montagnais Hunter of Mingan' 1977, 'Journal of a Simple Missionary: Joseph-Étienne Guinard' 1980; co-author: 'From Reduction to Coexistence: A history of the relationships between Natives and Canadians from 1500 to the present' 1986; Address: 15603 Bellerive, Pointe-aux-Trembles, Montreal, Que. H1A 2B1.

**BOUCHAT, Guy Gilles,** B.Comm.; transportation executive; b. Montreal, Que. 6 April 1926; s. Jean Pierre and Irene Marie (Hardy) B.; e. Coll. Classique Ste. Croix, Sir George Williams Univ. B.Comm. 1959; m. Maureen Clarke; children: Suzanne, Louise; PRES. & CHIEF EXECUTIVE OFFICER, MONTREAL SHIPPING INC. 1991– ; Treasurer, Montreal Shipping Inc. 1968; Vice-Pres. 1978; Extve. Vice-Pres. 1986; Dir., Pres. & C.E.O., Allied Steamship Lines; Trealmont Transport Inc.; Chair, Extve. Council, Shipping Fed. of Canada; Bd. of Dir., Maritime Employers Assn.; Table de Concertation sur l'indus. Maritime de Montréal; Past Mayor, City of St Lambert; Past Chair, Council of Mayors of the South Shore; Pres., Que.-Canada Unity Movement during Que. Referendum; Past Pres., Bd. of Soc. d'Habitation du Qué.; Found Pres., St Lambert Cultural & Hist. Soc.; Founding Pres., Marsil Museum; recreations: golf; clubs: Richelieu Valley Golf & Country (Founder & Past Pres.); Home: 103 de Champagne, St Lambert, Que. J4S 1E5; Office: 360 rue Saint Jacques, Montreal, Que. H2Y 1R2.

**BOUCHER, Pierre-Yves,** B.A., LL.B., D.E.S.D.; lawyer, university executive; b. Ottawa, Ont. 2 Nov. 1942; s. Emile and Alice (Roux) B.; e. Univ. of Ottawa B.A. 1962, LL.B. 1965, D.E.S.D. 1966; Law Soc. of U.C. Bar Admission Course 1967; m. Pierrette d. Albert and Marianne Groulx 7 Feb. 1970; children: Eric, Alain; UNIVERSITY SECRETARY, UNIVERSITY OF OTTAWA 1990– ; Asst. to the Vice-Rector, Academic, Univ. of Ottawa 1967–70; Legal Counsel 1970–71; Partner, Séguin, Landriault, Patenaude & Boucher 1971–75; Legal Counsel, Univ. of Ottawa 1975–82; Assoc. Extve. Dir., Assn. of Univs. & Colleges of Can. 1982–89; Extve. Vice-Pres. 1989–90; Lecturer, Comp. Law Centre, Univ. of Ottawa 1966; Civil Law Section 1968–73 and Common Law Section 1976–91 (part-time); Univ. of Montreal Law Fac. 1972; Mem., Law Soc. of U.C. 1967– ; Candn. Assn. of Univ. Solicitors 1980– ;(Vice-Pres. 1980–81, Pres. 1981–82); Consultative Ctte. on Intellectual Property 1989– ; clubs: Le Cercle universitaire d'Ottawa; Home: 2177 Quinn Cres., Ottawa, Ont. K1H 6J5; Office: 550 Cumberland, Ottawa, Ont. K1N 6N5.

**BOUDREAU, Allan Paul,** B.Comm., LL.B.; supreme court judge; b. Concession, N.S. 13 Apr. 1943; s. Denos and Gertrude (O'Neil) B.; e. Clare Dist. H.S. 1960; Saint Mary's Univ. B.Comm. 1972 (Commerce Gold Medal; Gov. General's Medal); Dalhousie Univ. Law Sch. LL.B. 1975; m. Beth d. Red and Lynn Chisholm 30 Aug. 1969; children: Paul, Michael; JUDGE, SUPREME COURT OF NOVA SCOTIA 30 March 1990– ; Royal Bank of Can. 1960–72; private practice of law, Halifax 1975–84; Church Point 1984–90; Dir., Univ. Ste. Anne, Church Point; recreations: golf, sailing, tennis; clubs: Clare Golf & Country, Bedford Basin Yacht; Office: Box 2314, Halifax, N.S. B3J 3C8.

**BOUDREAU, Marcel,** B.A., B.Ph., M.B.A.; business executive; b. Chéticamp, N.S. 11 Oct. 1936; s. Alexandre Jean and Albertine (Jalbert) B.; e. Univ. of Ottawa, B.A., B.Ph. 1956; Univ. of Western Ont. M.B.A. 1958; m. Madeleine Isabelle 24 Aug. 1957; children: Jean, Isabelle; EXECUTIVE VICE-PRESIDENT, ROYNAT INC. 1981– ; Planning Dept., Industrial Life Insurance Co. Quebec City 1958–61; Credit Offr., Federal Business Devel. Bank 1961–63; various functions within Que. Region & Head Office, RoyNat Inc. 1963– ; Dir. 1989– ; Bd. of Dir., Heart and Stroke Found. of Que. (Past Pres.); recreations: skiing, golfing; clubs: Club Saint-Denis, Laval sur-le-Lac Golf Club, University Club; Home: 30, rue Berlioz, #314, Nuns' Island, Verdun, Que. H3E 1L3; Office: Place Montreal Trust, 1800 McGill College Ave., #1800, Montreal, Que. H3A 3J6.

**BOUDREAU, Rolland,** Q.C., B.A., LL.L.; business executive, lawyer; b. Montreal, P.Q. 12 Dec. 1932; s. Arthur and Germaine (Rolland) B.; e. Coll. Ste-Marie B.A. 1954; Univ. of Montreal LL.L. 1957; McGill Univ. 1957–58; m. Micheline d. Antonio and Berthe Gendron 17 Sept. 1960; children: Johanne, Marc; Vice Pres. Law, Canadian National Railways 1982–93, Retired; Adv. Couns., Fed. Dept. of Justice 1959–63; Solicitor, H.Q. Law Dept. CN 1963–67; St. Lawrence Reg. Law Dept, CN & E. Reg. Air Can. 1967–72; Regional Couns. 1972–77; Asst. Gen. Couns., H.Q. Law Dept., CN 1977–81; Gen. Couns. 1981–82; Dir., Canaven Limited 1979– ; Dir. & Mem., Extve. Ctte., Canaprev Inc. 1979– ; Q.C. 19 Sept. 1973; Bâtonnier, Montreal Bar Assn. 1988–89; Vice-Pres., Bd. of Dir. & Extve. Ctte. Mem., CEGEP du Vieux-Mont. 1974–78; Dir., Ecole de Tech. Sup. 1980–86; Mem., Que. Bar; Candn. Bar Assn.; Assn. of Candn. Gen. Couns. (Vice-Pres. 1990–91); recreations: golf; club: Val Morin Golf; Home: 11 O'Reilly, Apt. 1010, Ile-des-Soeurs, Qué. H3E 1T6

**BOUDREAU, Thomas J.,** B.A., B.Sc.Soc., M.A.; professor; b. Québec City, Qué. 24 March 1937; s. Alphonse Thomas and Ginette (Kirouac) B.; e. Laval Univ. B.A. 1956, B.Sc.Soc. 1958, M.A.(Econ.) 1960; Univ. of Ottawa 1961; Univ. of Montréal Doctoral Studies in Econ. 1962–64; m. Nicole d. Oscar and Jeannette Pelletier 23 Aug. 1958; children: Hélène, Thomas (dec.), François, Christian, Eric; PROFESSOR, ÉCOLE NATIONALE D'ADMINISTRATION PUBLIQUE 1991– ; joined Bank of Canada 1960–61; Econ. Adv. and Dir. Rsch. & Documentation Centre, Coll. of Phys. & Surgs. Prov. Qué. 1961–65; Dir. Rsch. & Planning Dept. Health Qué. and mem. Health Ins. Rsch. Ctte. 1965–66; Asst. Dir. Univ. Health Centre (Planning) Univ. of Sherbrooke 1966–67, Dir. Div. Social Med. & Assoc. Prof. of Med. 1967–71, Assoc. Prof. and Nat. Health Sci. 1971–75; Asst. Dep. Min. Long Range Health Planning Br. Nat. Health & Welfare Can. 1975–77; Assoc. Gen. Sec. Exec. Council & Dep. Min. of Social Devel. Qué. 1977–80, Dep. Min. of Labour, Manpower & Income Security Qué. 1980–82, Assoc. Gen. Sec. Exec. Council & Sec. Priority Ctte. Qué. Govt. 1982–84; Dep. Min. of Edn. Que. 1984–91; Cons. Comn. Inquiry Health & Social Welfare (Castonguay Comn.) 1967–69; Chrmn. Ctte. Hosp. Manpower Qué. 1969–73 and Ctte. Nurse Practitioners Can. 1971–72; Chrmn. Comité d'étude de la Main-d'oeuvre des Caisses populaires du Qué. 1973–75; Vice Chrmn. Ctte. Health Ind. Econ. Council Can. 1973, Chrmn. 1974; Chrmn. Ctte. Concept Position Qué. Hosps. 1972–74; Dir., Musée du Québec 1991– ; Dir. Radio-Québec 1984–89; Dir. Gen. E. Twps. Health Services Planning Ctte. 1968–71; dir. various health instns.; served with RCN (R), rank Lt.; recipient Can. Council Scholarship 1958–59, 1959–60; Nat. Health & Welfare Can. Nat. Health Sci. Award 1971–74; Hon. Life Mem., Candn. Educ. Assoc.; Assoc. des Directeurs Généraux des Commissions scolaires du Qué.; recipient, Georges-Henri Levesque Medal, Laval Univ. 1993; author or co-author various health services, education and public administration publs.; recreations: tennis, bicycling, sailing, reading; Club: Garrison; Home: 1370, rue Pasteur, Sillery, Qué. G1T 2B9; Office: 945 Ave. Wolfe, Sainte-Foy, Qué. G1V 3J9.

**BOUDRIA, Don,** M.P.; politician; b. Hull, Que. 30 Aug. 1949; s. Roy and Jacqueline (Lavergne) B.; e. Cumberland & Embrun Separate Sch.; Eastview High Sch.; Univ. of Toronto, Woodsworth Coll. and Univ. of Waterloo; m. MaryAnn d. Harold Morris 28 Aug. 1971; children: Daniel, Julie; MEMBER OF PARLIAMENT FOR GLENGARRY-PRESCOTT-RUSSELL, HOUSE OF COMMONS 1984– ;and APPTD. DEPUTY GOVERNMENT WHIP 1993– ; entered Fed. Govt. 1966; Chief Purchasing Agt., Fed. Govt. until 1981; el. Counc. of Cumberland Twp. 1976, 1978, 1980; el. to Ont. Legis. Assembly, M.P.P. for Prescott-Russell 1981; Opposition Critic of Govt. Services 1981–82; Comm. & Soc. Services 1982–83; Consumer & Comml. Relations 1983–84; el. to H. of C. for Glengarry-Prescott-Russell 1984, re-el. 1988, 1993; Federal Supply & Services Critic, Official Opposition and mem. Standing Ctte. on Agric. 1984; Depy. Chrmn. Ont. Liberal Caucus 1984; Chrmn., Ont. Liberal Caucus 1985–87; Public Works Critic 1985; Govt. Operations Critic 1987; apptd. Canada Post and Govt. Operations Critic 1988, Depy. Opposition Whip 1989; Asst. House Leader for the Official Opposition 1990–93 and Govt. Operations critic; past mem. Cumberland Twp. Recreational Ctte.; founding Vice-Pres. Sarsfield Optimist Club; founding Pres. Cumberland Twp. Housing Corp.; founding Pres. Ont. Section of l'Assn. internat. des parlementaires de langue française; Home: 3455 Dessaint Cres., Sarsfield, Ont. K0A 3E0; Office: Rm. 353, West Block, House of Commons, Ottawa, Ont. K1A 0A6.

**BOUEY, Gerald Keith,** C.C., B.A., LL.D.; retired banker, consultant; b. Axford, Sask. 2 Apr. 1920; s. John Alexander and Inez Amanda (Hathaway) B.; e. Trossachs (Sask.) High Sch.; Queen's Univ., B.A. (Hons.) 1948; Queen's Univ., LL.D.; m. Anne Margaret, d. William Acheson Ferguson and Margaret Martin (Nicol), 8 Aug. 1945; children: Kathryn Anne, Robert Gerald; joined Royal Bank of Canada 1936–41; joined Bank of Canada 1948; Chief Research Dept., 1962; Adviser 1965; Depy. Gov. 1969, Sr. Depy. Gov. 1972; Gov. and Dir. 1973–87; Dir., Federal Business Development Bank 1975–87; Canada Deposit Ins. Corp. 1973–87; Export Development Corp. 1973–86; Manufacturers Life Ins. Co. 1988–91; Investment Dealers Assoc. of Can. 1988– ; Ottawa Civic Hospital Found. 1988– ; Mem. Trilateral Comn. (Candn. Group); Chairperson, Ont. Teachers' Pension Plan Bd. 1990– ; served with RCAF 1941–45; United Church; recreations: golf, cross country skiing; Clubs: Royal Ottawa Golf; Rideau; Home: 79 Kamloops Ave., Ottawa, Ont. K1V 7C8.

**BOUGAIN, Pierre A.;** hotel executive; b. Lyon, France; e. Acad. Culinaire de France; Vice-Pres. & Gen. Mgr., Royal York Hotel, CP Hotels & Resorts, Toronto 1989–.; various positions with Hilton Canada since 1958 incl. Toronto, Puerto Rico, Martinique, Montreal Aeroport Hilton and The Queen Elizabeth; Fellow, Hostelry Inst.; Certified Hotel Administrator; mem., Chevalier Comité Nat. Vins de France, Chev. De Sancerre, Acad. Culinaire de France; Sommeliers du Tastevin; Maître de Table Chaine des Rôtisseurs; recreation: golf; Clubs: Lambton Golf; Kanawaki Golf.

**BOUGIE, Jacques,** LL.L., D.S.A.; business executive; b. Montreal, Que. 6 July 1947; s. Gérard and Jacqueline (Provost) B.; e. Univ. de Montréal LL.L. 1973; École des Hautes Études Commerciales D.S.A. 1979; m. Anne-Marie d. Dr. Antonio and Consuelo (St-Aubin) Sabetta 21 June 1969; children: Caroline, Jean-Marc; PRES. & CHIEF EXTVE. OFFR., ALCAN ALUMINIUM LTD. 1993– ; Sales rep., Burroughs Bus. Machines Ltd. 1966–69; Sec. Gen. & Indus. Rel. Mgr., Comm. Scolaire Rég. de Chambly 1973–76; Dir. Gén., Soc. Québécoise d'information juridique 1976–79; joined Alcan Aluminium April 1979; Works Mgr., Beauharnois Works, Alcan Smelters and Chemicals June 1979; Dir. of Devel., Manitoba, Aluminium Co. of Can. (Winnipeg) 1981; Asst. Vice-Pres., Planning & Admin., N. Am. & Carib. (Montreal) 1982; Vice-Pres., Planning & Admin., Alcan Can. Prod. (Toronto) 1984; Pres., Alcan Extrusions 1985; Pres., Alcan Enterprises - North Am. (Montréal) 1988–89; Pres., C.O.O. & Dir., Alcan Aluminium Ltd. 1989–93; Mem. of Bd. of Dirs., Royal Bank of Canada; BCE Mobile Communications Inc.; Bell Canada; Conf. Bd. of Can.; Mem., Econ. Counc. of Can. 1987–90; Que. Bar Assn.; Club: Granite (Toronto); Office: 1188 Sherbrooke St. W., Montréal, Qué. H3A 3G2.

**BOULANGER, Guy,** B.A., L.Sc.A., F.C.A.; né à Québec le 16 avril 1943; f. Maurice et Germaine (Couët) B.; é. Univ. Laval B.A. 1965, L.ès Sc. (adm. 1968, comptables 1969); ép. Suzanne f. François et Yvette Lemieux le 17 juin 1967; enfants: Stéphane, Patrick, François; Associé chez Caron Bélanger Ernst & Young; Président de la Chambre de commerce du Québec métro; Prés. du conseil d'administration de la Société du Port de Québec; de l'Orchestre symphonique de Québec; de la campagne souscription de Centraide pour 1988; Halte Champêtre 1978–80; Assn. Marie Perreault 1985; membre de la Fondation de l'Hôpital Laval; Fondation Rousseau-Falardeau; administrateur de la Société pour les enfants handicapés du Québec; Fellow de l'Ordre des comptables agréés du Qué.; Club: Cercle de la Garnison de Québec (prés.); Royal Québec Golf; Adresse: 995, avenue des Braves, Québec, Qué. G1S 3C7.

**BOULANGER, Pierre de G.,** B.A., M.B.A.; banker; b. Montreal, Que. 13 Apr. 1942; e. McGill Univ. B.A. 1965; Univ. of Western Ont. M.B.A. 1967; m. Dawn; 2 children; SENIOR VICE-PRESIDENT, CREDIT DIV., THE TORONTO-DOMINION BANK 1988– ; Toronto Div., Toronto-Dominion Bank 1967; Asst. Mgr., Montreal 1969; Supvr., Profit Planning, E. Div. 1970; Credit, E. Div. 1971; Mgr., Comm. Devel., Que. & Atlantic Prov. Div. 1973; Superintendent, Credit, Que. Div. 1977; Asst. Gen. Mgr. & Sr. Agent, N.Y. agency 1980; Gen. Mgr. & Mgr., N.Y. branch 1982; Vice-Pres., US Div. 1984; Dir., T-D Holdings (USA) Inc.; T-D (Texas) Inc.; Alternative Dir., T-D Australia Limited; clubs: Royal Candn. Yacht, Toronto Rotary Club; Office: P.O. Box 1, Toronto-Dominion Ctr., Toronto, Ont. M5K 1A2.

**BOULET, Lionel,** O.C., B.A., M.Sc., D.Sc., D.Gén.; utilities executive; b. Québec City, Qué. 29 July 1919; e. Univ. Laval, B.A. 1938, B.Sc. (elect. engn.) 1944, D.Sc. 1972; Illinois, M.Sc. 1947; doctoral courses 1948; Sir George Williams Univ., D.Sc. 1968; Univ. Ottawa, D.Gén. 1971; Fellow Eng. Inst. of Canada 1973; D.Sc. (hon. causa) Laval 1972, McGill 1977; m. Ruth Milette; children: Christiane, Geneviève, Jean-François, Isabelle; with Boulet & Boulet, C.As. 1938–40; Student Engr., Saguenay Power Co., Ile Maligne, 1941; Jr. Acct., Boulet & Boulet 1942; Student Engr., R.C.A. Victor Co. 1943; Jr. Engr. 1944; Lab. Asst., Univ. Laval 1945; Champaign Research Asst., Univ. Illinois 1946, Assoc. 1947; Lectr., Elect. Engn., Univ. Laval 1948; helped estb. Research Lab., R.C.A. Victor Co. 1948–50; Asst. Prof., Elect. Engn., Univ. Laval 1950, Prof. 1953; Research Consultant, C.A.R.D.E. 1950–53; Head of Dept. and Research Lab. 1954; taught Operations-Research math. to econ. and business adm. profs.; joined Hydro-Québec as Consultant 1964; Tech. Adv. to Gen. Mgr. 1965; Dir., Rsch. Inst. 1967; Pres., F.D.S.T. 1984–86; Prés. Conseil Lalonde, Girouard, Letendre 1985–88; Dir. by interim, Inst. Armand-Frappier 1988; awarded: Prince of Wales Decoration; Corp. Prof. Engrs. Qué. Prize and Engn. Inst. Can. Prize 1943; Inst. Elect. & Electronic Engrs. Prize 1944 (Montreal Sec. Award 1943); Canada Medal 1967; Archambault Medal 1970; Pres., Ext. Adv. Bd., Faculty of Science, Laval Univ.; Pres. Conseil de la Politique scientifique du Québec; Past Chrmn., Qué. Sec., Am. Inst. Elect. Engn.; Chrmn., Univ. Prof. Sec., Candn. Elect. Assn.; Comte. on Research, Corp. Prof. Engrs. Qué.; Pres. Int. Electric Res. Exch. 1976; Sigma Xi; Officer, Order of Canada; R. Catholic; Home: 755 Muir, App. 201, St. Laurent, Qué. H4L 5G9.

**BOULET, Roger H.,** B.F.A. (Hons.); art gallery administrator; curator; b. St.-Boniface, Man. 15 Feb. 1944; s. Henri Elzear and Jeanne B.; e. Coll. de St.-Boniface; Univ. of Man., B.F.A. (Hons.) 1970; Dir./Cur., Art Gallery of the South, Okanagan 1993– ; Dir., Art Gallery of Greater Victoria 1975–80; Dir./Cur., Burnaby Art Gall. 1981–87; Dir., The Edmonton Art Gall. 1987–91; Can. Counc. Grant 1970; author (partial list): 'F.M. Bell-Smith (1846–1923)' 1978, 'The Tranquility and the Turbulence' 1982, 'The Silent Thunder' 1982, 'The Canadian Earth' 1982; recreations: music.

**BOULTBEE, John A.,** B.Com., C.A.; business executive; publisher; b. Toronto, Ont. 4 July 1943; s. Thomas Edward and Helene Marion (Pattison) B.; e. Univ. of Toronto B.Com. 1967; C.A. Ont. 1970; m. Sharon d. Owen and Roberta Whitby 28 Dec. 1985; children: Paul, Leslie, Michael; VICE PRES. AND CHIEF FINANCIAL OFFR., DIR. HOLLINGER INC. and ARGUS CORP. LTD. 1986– ; Dir. Gordon Investment Corp.; Key Publishers Co. Ltd.; Consolidated Enfield Corporation; The Financial Post Co.; joined McDonald Currie & Co. 1967; Mgr. Coopers & Lybrand 1973, Partner 1977, Partner-in-Charge Toronto Tax Group 1985; apptd. Publisher, Saturday Night Magazine Inc. 1988, Pres. 1989; recreations: bicycling, skiing, tennis, squash; Club: The Boulevard; Home: 63 Valecrest Dr., Etobicoke, Ont. M9A 4P5; Office: 10 Toronto St., Toronto, Ont. M5C 2B7.

**BOUMA-PYPER, Marilyn Minke,** BPE; graphic designer; b. Meaford, Ont. 7 June 1955; d. Frank (Feike) and Tina (Tjitska) (Abma) Bouma; e. West Hill S.S., Owen Sound 1973 (Hons.); McMaster Univ., 3 yrs.; York Univ., B.P.E. 1977; Senate scholarship 1974; m. Ian Donald s. Martha Evelyn and the late Colonel D.G. Pyper, M.C. 17 Sept. 1983; one d.: Rosalind Martina Pyper; foster child: Marcos Octavio Suchite (Guatemala); DESIGNER, ART GALLERY OF ONT. 1980–93; Richardson, Bond and Wright Printing Co. 1978; Jr. Designer, Partners in Print 1978–80; Design awards from Ont. Assn. of Art Galleries, Alcuin Soc., Studio Magazine, Advertising & Design Club of Canada, Applied Arts; West Hill S.S. Athletic Award plus award for best contrib. student; mem., Advertising & Design Club of Canada; The Soc. of Graphic Designers of Canada; The Am. Inst. of Graphic Arts; St. Crispins Daycare; First Christian Reformed Ch.; exhibits: Nathan Philips Sq. Outdoor Exhib.; Trinity Coll.; Harbourfront; Round-up, Art Gall. of Ont.; recreations: avid runner, swimmer, acting; clubs: Kew Beach Tennis; Home: 127 Heale Ave., Scarborough, Ont. M1N 3Y2; Office: 317 Dundas St. W., Toronto, Ont. M5T 1G4.

**BOURAOUI, Hédi,** M.A., Ph.D.; university professor; writer; b. Sfax, Tunisia 16 July 1932; e. Univ. de Toulouse Licence es Lettres (Engl. Lit.) 1958; Indiana Univ. M.A. (Engl. and Am. Lit) 1960; Cornell Univ. Ph.D. (Romance Studies) 1966; HEAD, FRENCH STUDIES, YORK UNIV. 1993– ; Assoc. Prof. of French, York Univ. 1968, Acting Admin. Coordr. of Linguistics & Lang. Training Div. 1969, Grad. Fac. Eng. Dept. 1969, Chrmn. Lang and Culture Ctte. 1971, Prof. French and Comparative Lit. 1973; Master, Stong College, York Univ. 1978–88; recipient hon. title of University Professor 1984; Médaille Cyrille et Méthode, 1300e Anniversaire de l'Etat bulgare 1982; Médaille d'Argent, Poèsiades, Inst. Académique de Paris 1982; Prix France-Canada, Fondation Michel-Ange 1984; Prix Montaigne, Fond. Michel-Ange 1985; Grand Prix International de Poésie de la 11ème Biennale Azuréenne de Cannes 1987; Prés. d'Honneur 'Expression '89 Haute Bretagne', Rennes, France; Correspondant au Canada, 'Nouvel Art du Français'; Docteur (hon. causa), World Congress of Poets, Bangkok, Thailand 1988; Vice Prés. Assoc. des Auteurs de l'Ontario 1992; author poetry 'Musocktail' 1966; 'Tremblé' 1969; 'Eclate Module' 1972; 'Vésuviade' 1976; 'Sans Frontières/Without Boundaries' 1979; 'Haituvois suivi de Antillades' 1980; 'Tales of Heritage' 1981; 'Vers et l'Envers' 1982; 'Ignescent' 1982; 'Echosmos' 1986; 'Tales of Heritage II' 1986; 'Investiture' 1984; drame poétique 'Immensément Croisés' 1969; essais: 'Créaculture I' 1971; 'Créaculture II' 1971; 'Structure intentionelle du "Grand Meaulnes": vers le poème romancé' 1976; (ed.) 'The Canadian Alternative' 1980; 'The Critical Strategy' 1983; texte d'apprentissage de langue 'Parole et action' 1971; 'Robert Champigny: poète et philosophe' 1987; nouvelle 'Seul' 1984; 'L'Icônaison' (novel) 1985; 'Reflet Pluriel' 1986; 'Emergent les branches' 1986; 'Arc-en Terre' (poetry) 1991; 'Emigressence' (poetry) 1992; 'Bangkok Blues' (novel) 1993; Pres.: Maghreb Studies Assn., London, Engl. 1984; African Lit. Assn. 1983; Candn. Soc. for Comparative Study of Civilizations 1980–83; Corr. for Sinbad, Morocco 1983; mem. Planning Ctte. for the celebration of Ont. Bicentennial 1983; Adv. Bd. on Multiculturalism 1980; Fellow, Candn. Internat. Acad. of the Humanities and Social Sciences 1979; Home: 2911 Bayview Ave., Apt. 214J, Willowdale, Ont. M2K 1E8; Office: c/o French Studies, 324 Stong College, York University, 4700 Keele St., North York, Ont. M3J 1P3.

**BOURASSA, Robert,** M.N.A., M.A.; lawyer; politician; b. 14 July 1933; e. Jean-de-Brébeuf Coll. (Arts) 1953; Univ. de Montréal (Law; Gov. Gen. Medal) 1956; Oxford Univ. M.A. (Politics, Philos. & Econ.) 1959; Harvard Univ. M.A. (Internat. Tax and Corp. Law) 1960; m. Andrée, d. late Edouard Simard, Sorel, Qué.; children: François, Michelle; grandchildren: Mathieu, Simon; Premier, Province of Québec 1970–76 and 1985–94; joined Fed. Civil Service 1960 as a Fiscal Advisor in Nat. Revenue Dept.; Lectr. on Econ. and Public Finance, Univ. of Ottawa; apptd. Secy. and Research Dir. for Bélanger Comn. on Taxation, Qué. 1963–65; first el. to Qué. Nat. Assembly for Mercier, g.e. 1966; served as Opposition Financial Critic; chosen Leader of Qué. Liberal Party 17 Jan. 1970; sworn in as Prime Min. of Qué. and Min. of Finance 12 May 1970, assumed Portfolios of Finance till Oct. 1970, and of Intergovernmental Affairs Feb. 1971–Feb. 1972; re-el. Oct. 1973; withdrew from active politics 1976; taught and conducted research at Inst. d'études européennes in Brussels, and Inst. européen d'adm. des affaires (INSEAD) in Fontainebleau; Prof., Center of Advanced Internat. Studies, John Hopkins Univ., Washington 1978; Prof. Laval and Montréal univ. 1979; Visiting Prof., Univ. of Southern California, Los Angeles 1981; Visiting Prof., Yale Univ., New Haven 1982; re-el. Leader of Québec Liberal Party 15 Oct. 1983; sworn in as Leader of Official Opposition 14 June 1985; el. M.N.A. for Bertrand 1985; sworn in as Prime Minister of Qué. Dec. 1985; el. M.N.A. for St. Laurent Jan. 1986; re-el. Sept. 1989; author: 'Bourassa/Québec!' 1970; 'La Baie James' 1973; 'James Bay' 1973; 'Les années Bourassa: l'intégrale des entretiens Bourassa – St-Pierre' 1977; 'Deux fois la Baie James' 1981; 'Power from the North' 1985; 'L'Energie du Nord: la force du Québec' 1985; 'Le défi technologique' 1985; Office: 885 Grande-Allée E., Bldg. J, 3rd flr., Québec, Qué. G1A 1A2.

**BOURASSA, Robert Michel,** B.Sc., LL.B.; judge; b. Shawinigan, Qué. 2 Aug. 1944; s. Michel Robert and Winnifred Theresa (Blair) B.; e. St. Francis Xavier Univ. B.Sc. 1965; Queen's Univ. LL.B. 1970; m. Ellen d. John and Margaret O'Meara 17 June 1972; children: Christopher, Simone; TERRITORIAL COURT JUDGE N.W.T. 1981– ; Depy. Judge, Yukon Territory 1985– ; private law practice 1972–81; Teaching Master St. Lawrence Coll. 1976–78; Pres. Civet Helicopters Ltd. 1976–79; Depy. Reeve Portland Twp. 1976–80; contrib. Law Reform Comn.; participant various ednl. confs. environmental law; Secy., Prov. Judges Assn. 1982; Secy., Candn. Assn. Prov. Court Judges; Bd. of Dirs., Northern Justice Soc.; Field Placement Supervisor, Simon Fraser Univ. Sch. of Criminology; Chrmn., NWT Judge's Assoc.; recreations: sailing, flying, boat building, writing; Clubs: Lions; NRHQ Mess; Home: Yellowknife, N.W.T. X1A 1X2; Office: P.O. Box 550, Court House, Yellowknife, N.W.T. X1A 2N4.

**BOURBEAU, Jean-Louis,** B.A., B.Sc., F.C.I.A.; actuary; executive; b. St-Félix de Kingsey, Qué. 24 June 1934; s. Omer and Yvette (Lebel) B.; e. Coll. Ste-Croix, Montréal B.A. 1956; Univ. de Montréal B.Sc. 1958; Fellow Canadian Institute of Actuaries; m. Suzanne d. Denis and Thérèse Montpetit 2 July 1960; children: Pierre, Marie-Hélène; CHRMN. & C.E.O., WILLIAM M. MERCER LIMITED 1987– ; Extve. Vice Pres. & Dir., William M. Mercer Companies, Inc. (New York); Dir., Mercer Consulting Group Inc.; Actuarial Asst. Alliance Mutual Life, Montréal 1958–64, Dir. of Adm. 1964–70, Dir. of Group Mktg. 1970–78; Consultant, present Co. Montréal 1979, Vice Pres. 1980, Head of Office and Dir. Montréal 1981, Head of Can. E. and Dir. Toronto 1984; Bd. of Dir., Toronto Symphony; mem. Assn. Candn. Pension Mgmt.; Candn. Pension Conf.; Bus. Council Nat. Issues; Soc. of Actuaries; Candn. Inst. of Internat. Affairs; Internat. Assn. Actuaries (Council); recreations: music, theatre; Clubs: St-Denis (Montréal); Toronto; Empire (Toronto); Canadian Club (Toronto); Le Cercle Canadien, Past Pres. (Toronto); Home: 90 Forest Hill Rd., Toronto, Ont. M4V 2L5; Office: BCE Place, 161 Bay St., P.O. Box 501, Toronto, Ont. M5J 2S5.

**BOURDEAU, Yvan J.P.,** B.A., B.B.A., M.B.A.; banker; b. Montreal, Que. 12 June 1948; s. Jean-Guy Albert and Lucie (Choquette) B.; e. Coll. St. Ignace, B.A. 1968; Hautes Etudes Commerciales, B.B.A. 1971; Univ. of B.C., M.B.A. 1972; m. Hiroko d. Takuo Inagawa Nov. 1976; children: Monique Maya, Katherine Yuki; EXECUTIVE VICE-PRES. & TREAS., BANK OF MONTREAL 1988– ; Econ. Teacher, Bois de Boulogne 1970; Bank Rep., Japan, Bank of Montreal 1973–76; Dep. Mgr., Singapore Br. 1976; Mgr., Loan Synd., Asia & Pacific Div. 1977; Vice-Pres. & Mgr., Seoul Br. 1980; Vice-Pres. & Dist. Extve., Tokyo Br. 1985; Sr. Vice-Pres. & Mgr. 1986; recreations: tennis, sailing; clubs: Granite, Tanglin; Office: First Canadian Place, 17th floor, P.O. Box 1, Toronto, Ont. M5X 1A1.

**BOURGAULT, Lise,** M.P.; politician; b. St-Pamphile, Qué. 5 June 1950; e. St-Pamphile elem. sch.; Coll. Bellechasse St-Damien; Ahuntsic Coll. Dip. in Adm.; Laval Univ. B.A. course in Adm.; el. to H. of C. for Argenteuil-Papineau 1984; served as mem. Standing Cttes. on Transport, Miscellaneous Estimates and Agric.; apptd. to Special Ctte. on Reform of H. of C.; Parlty. Secy. to the Min. of Consumer & Corp. Affairs 1987–88; Parlty Secy. to the Min. of National Health & Welfare 1988–91; Parlty Secy. to Min. of Supply & Services 1991–92; former Founding Pres. L'Association des propriétaires de logements locatifs du Qué.; Mng. Dir. L'Association des propriétaires d'Immeubles du Qué.; Adm. Les Immeubles Terram Inc.; Adm. Sec. ESSO Home Comfort Centre; frequent guest speaker implication legis. rental sector; guest several open-line radio progs. tenant/landlord problems; author various articles; mem. Montréal C. of C.; Qué. Businessmen's & Businesswomen's

Assn.; Sec. L'Association du Qué. pour les déficients mentaux; Home: 5–629 Inter Quartier, Lachute, Qué.; Office: 129 West Block, House of Commons, Ottawa, Ont. K1A 0A6.

**BOURGAULT, Pierre L.,** B.A., B.Sc., Ph.D., F.C.I.C.; P.Eng.; electrochemist; b. St. Brieux, Sask. 5 July 1928; s. Georges and Louise (Boissière); e. Coll. Mathieu (Lib. Arts) B.A. 1950; Univ. of Sask., Engn. 1951; Univ. of Ottawa B.Sc. 1953, Ph.D. (summa cum laude) 1961; m. Denise, d. Elzéar and Annette Tremblay, Ottawa, Ont., Aug. 1957; children: Bernard, Robert, Adèle, Jérôme, Louise; President, Chinook Phi-Beta Corp. 1988–..; with Johnson, Matthey and Mallory, Toronto in various positions leading to Div. Mgr. 1960–69; Science Advisor, Science Council of Can., Ottawa 1969–71; apptd. Dean of Engn., Univ. of Sherbrooke 1971–72; Asst. Secy. (Policy) Min. State for Science and Technol. 1972–75, Asst. Deputy Min., Energy, Mines and Resources 1975–80; Vice-Rector (Admin.) Univ. of Ottawa 1980–88; mem. Extve. Comte., Canadian Club of Ottawa; mem. Bd. and Audit Comte., BEST Energy Systems Inc.; Dir. and Chrmn. Extve. Comte., Ottawa Health Sciences Centre; former Dir. Ottawa/Brennan Inc.; former Dir., mem. Extve. Comte. and Vice Pres., World University Service of Can.; former Gov., Univ. of Ottawa; mem.: Candn. Accreditation Board, Counc. of Profl. Engrs.; Nat. Design Council of Canada; Standards Council of Canada; Assn. Prof. Engrs. Ont.; Candn. Research Mgmt. Assn.; author 'Innovation and the Structure of Canadian Industry'; also numerous articles in prof. and learned journals; holds various patents for batteries, capacitors and other electrochemical devices; R. Catholic; Home: 2003 Boake St., Orleans, Ont. K4A 3K1.

**BOURGEAU, Pierre G.,** B.A. Pol. Sc., LL.B., P. Adm., Adm. A., F.I.C.B., F.C.I.S.; barrister and solicitor; banker; executive; b. Ont. 21 Jan. 1939; s. Gérard Roger and Colombe (Handy) B.; e. Guigues, Brébeuf and Académie de La Salle, Ottawa; Univ. of Ottawa B.A. Pol. Sc. 1961, LL.B. 1965; Post-Graduate Studies (Doctorate Course-Civil Law) Univ. of Ottawa 1965–66; Osgoode Hall Bar Admission Course 1967–68; called to Bar of Ont. 1968; m. Nicole d. Jacques de Terwangne, Hudson, Que., 21 July 1973; one s. Pierre-Daniel; EXTVE. DIR. (interim), CONSTANCE-LETHBRIDGE REHABILITATION CTR. 1991– ; Gen. Counsel, Lavalin Group 1989–91; mem. Candn. Dipl. Corps, Dept. External Affairs 1968–70, Legal Advisor UN Session 1969, to Dept. Secy. of State on behalf of Fed. Dept. of Justice 1970–72; Legal Advisor Canadair Ltd. Montreal 1972–74; joined Churchill Falls (Labrador) Corp. Ltd. as Gen. Counsel and Secy. 1974; Vice Pres., Legal, and Gen. Counsel and Sec. 1975–79; Secretary, Twin Falls Power Corp. 1974–78; Vice Pres. (Legal) 1978–79; Gen. Counsel and Secy., Celanese Canada Inc. 1979–85 (Dir. 1982–84); Sr. Asst. Secy. Bank of Montreal 1985–86; Secy. 1986–89; Chrmn. & Pres., Constance-Lethbridge Rehabilitation Centre 1981–91; Dir., Lethbridge Found.; Dir., Constance-Lethbridge; Candn. Rehabilitation Council for the Disabled; Parkinson's Found.; mem. Law Soc. Upper Can.; Bar of Ont.; Bar of Que.; Candn. Bar Assn.; Inst. of Candn. Bankers; Inst. Chartered Secretaries and Administrators; Am. Soc. of Corporate Secretaries, Inc.; La Corporation Professionnelle des Administrateurs Agréés du Québec; R. Catholic; recreation: travel, swimming; Club: St. James's; St. Denis; Home: 615 Lazard Ave., Town of Mount Royal, Que. H3R 1P6.

**BOURGEAULT, Guy,** L.PH., D.TH.; university professor; b. Montréal, P.Q. 4 May 1933; s. Henri and Lucienne (Charron) B.; e. Montréal and Rome 1969; PROF. TIT., FAC. OF EDUC.; COLLAB., CENTRE DE RECHERCHE EN DROIT PUBLIC, UNIV. MONTREAL 1969– ; Edit. 'Relations' 1969–76; Mem. Univ. Counc. 1976–85; Dean, Fac. of Continuing Educ. 1977–85; author 'Décalogue et morale chrétienne' 1970; co-author 'La société québécoise face à l'avortement' 1973; 'Mariage: rêve, réalité' 1975; 'Pour une démocratisation de l'éducation des adultes' 1981; 'Education des adultes et éducation permanente dans les universités québécoises: émergences et convergences' 1982; 'Université et collectivités: vers de nouveaux rapports' 1983; author 'L'environnement: enjeux éthiques et politiques' 1984; 'Jalons pour une éthique de la prévention' 1985; 'Formation des Adultes et Ethique' 1987; 'Une éthique de la responsabilité: perspective, repères, jalons' 1990; 'L'Ethique et le droit face aux nouvelles technologies biomédicales' 1990; 'Démocratisation de l'école, recherche de l'excellence, pratiques de pédagogie différenciée: réflexions sur la problématique de l'égalité en éducation' 1994; mem. ACEEA (Assn. candnne. pour l'étude de l'éducation des adultes); ICEA (Inst. candn. d'éducation des adultes); Société canadienne de bioéthique; Pres., Conseil de presse du Québec; Office: Université de Montréal, C.P. 6128, Succursale A, Montréal, Qué. H3C 3J7.

**BOURGIE, Marc,** C.M.; business executive; b. Verdun, Que. 23 July 1926; s. Albert and Florida (Vervais dit St-Amour) B.; e. Acad. St-Léon de Westmount; Coll. Mont St-Louis; Univ. de Montréal; m. Claire d. Albert Sabourin 31 Aug. 1950; children: Mrs Claude Bourgie Bovet, l.l.l. and Pierre Bourgie; CHAIRMAN OF THE BOARD, URGEL BOURGIE LIMITÉE; Extve. Mem., Nat. Bank of Canada; Chrmn., Bellemont Ltd.; Administrator, Industrielle-Alliance Ltd.; Mem., Order of Canada; 125th Anniversary of Confederation Medal; La Confrèrie des Chevaliers du Tastevin, Dijon France; Chevalier de l'Ordre Equestre du Saint-Sépulcre de Jérusalem; Gov., Univ. de Montréal; Mem. of Corp., Notre-Dame Hosp.; Chrmn., Ctr. de Santé St-Henri; recreations: golf; Clubs: Laval-sur-le-Lac Golf; Mount-Royal; St-Denis; Home: 3, chemin Ile Roussin, Laval-sur-le-Lac, Qué. H7R 1B2; Office: 2630 West, Notre-Dame St., Montréal, Qué. H3N 1N8.

**BOURGIE, Pierre,** B.Comm.; business executive; b. Montreal, Que. 22 Oct. 1956; s. Marc and Claire (Sabourin) B.; e. Ottawa Univ. B.Comm.; PRESIDENT, URGEL BOURGIE LIMITÉE; Dir., Banque Laurentienne; Le Devoir; Gaz Métropolitain; Groupe Val Royal; Urgel Bourgie Ltée.; Parc Commémoratif de Montréal Inc.; Société financière Bourgie; Lépine-Cloutier Ltée.; clubs: YPO, St-Denis, Laval-sur-le-lac; Home: 1951, rue Baile, Montréal, Qué. H3H 1P6; Office: 2630, Notre-Dame ouest, Montréal, Qué. H3J 1N8.

**BOURHIS, Richard Y.,** B.Sc., Ph.D., F.CPA; university professor; b. Montreal, Que. 14 Aug. 1950; s. Roland Y. and Gisele M. (Major) B.; e. McGill Univ., B.Sc. 1971; Univ. of Bristol, UK Ph.D. 1977; m. Louise d. Eva and Lorenzo Emond 18 May 1980; children: Chantal, François-Xavier; PROF., DEP. DE PSYCHOLOGIE, UNIV. DU QUE. A MONTREAL 1988– ; Rsch. Assoc., Univ. of Bristol 1975–77; Asst. Prof., Dept. of Psych., McGill Univ. 1977–78; McMaster Univ. 1978–83; Assoc. Prof. 1983–88; Cons., Comnr. of Official Languages, Can. 1983– ; Cons., Basque Language Secretariat, Spain 1989– ; Ed. Bd. Mem., 'The European Journal of Social Psychology' 1983–91; 'Journal of Language and Social Psychology' 1982– ; specialist in issues related to language planning, cross cultural communication, prejudice, discrimination and intergroup conflict; Ed. cons. for numerous N. Am & Eur. Psych. jours.; elected Fellow, Candn. Psych. Assn. 1988; Mem., Candn. Psych. Assn.; Internat. Communication Assn.; La Société québécoise pour la rech. en psych.; Soc. for experimental social psychology; Fgn. Affiliate, Eur. Assn. of experimental Soc. Psych.; author of over 60 sci. papers in N. Am & Eur. jours.; editor: 'Conflict and language planning in Quebec' 1984; recreations: antiquarian prints; Home: 3844 Avenue Old Orchard, N.D.G. Montréal, Québ. H4A 3B1; Office: C.P. 8888, Succ. A, Montréal, Qué. H3C 3P8.

**BOURKE, Douglas T.,** B.Eng.; executive; b. Montreal, Que. 9 Aug. 1925; s. George Wesley and Beatrice Minerva (Mitchell) B.; e. Westmount (Que.) High Sch.; McGill Univ., B.Eng. 1949; Mang. Training Course, Univ. of Western Ont. 1966; Advanced Mang. Program, Harvard Univ. 1971; m. Sheila Ross, d. late William Adams Ramsay, 1 March 1950; children: Andrew Thomas, Jane Cynthia, Diana Ramsay; with Drummond McCall Inc. 1951–1981 (Pres. and Dir. 1972–1981); Dir., GBC North Am. Growth Fund; served in 2nd World War, R.C.A.F., Pilot Offr. – Flight Engr., 1943–45; Past Pres., McGill Grad. Soc.; Candn. Steel Service Centre Inst.; Past Chrmn., Study Corp.; Montreal Gen. Hospital Corp. and Centre; Gov. & Chrmn., Montreal Gen. Hosp. Found.; Gov., McGill Univ.; Delta Upsilon; United Church; recreations: tennis, golf, skiing; Clubs: University; Montreal Indoor Tennis; Mount Bruno Country; Belleair Country; Address: 1 Wood Ave., Westmount, Que. H3Z 3C5.

**BOURKE, George Mitchell;** investment consultant; b. Montreal, Que. 8 Feb. 1923; s. George Wesley and Beatrice Minerva (Mitchell) B.; e. Westmount High Sch., 1940; Roy. Mil. Coll., grad. 1942; McGill Univ., B.Eng., 1948; m. Camille, d. Arthur Dion, 20 Nov. 1982; children: Steven Mitchell, Michael George, Julia Elizabeth; CHRMN. & DIR., BOLTON TREMBLAY INC.; joined Investment Dept., Sun Life Assnce. Co. of Can., 1948; promoted Asst. Treas., 1957; Assoc. Treas., 1960; Secy.-Treas., Cornwall Street Rly., Light & Power Co. Ltd., 1951–61; Dir., 1961; joined present Co., Oct. 1961; mem., Montreal Inst. Invest. Analysts; Alderman, City of Dorval, 1958–60; served overseas during second World War with Roy. Candn. Arty. in Eng., France, Belgium and Holland, 1942–45; discharged with rank of Capt.; Unitarian; recreation: photography; Home: 3460 Redpath St., Apt 105, Montreal, Que. H3G 2G3; Office: 1100 University St., Montreal, Que. H3B 4K5.

**BOURKE, Richard David,** M. Arch., O.A.Q., R.C.A., F.R.A.I.C.; architect, university administrator; b. Montreal, Que. 22 Oct. 1931; s. late George Wesley and late Beatrice (Mitchell) B.; e. Westmount (Que.) High Sch. 1948; McGill Univ. B. Arch. 1954; Harvard Univ. M. Arch. 1959; m. Judith Margaret (deceased), d. late George Selwyn Veith 19 Mar. 1955; children: Meredith Margaret, Thomas David; m. 2ndly Marlene, d. late Michael Greenberg, 13 May 1982; SECRETARY-GENERAL, McGILL UNIV. 1981– ; joined J.B. Parkin Architects Toronto 1955–58; Dobush, Stewart, Bourke, Montreal 1960–65; Dobush, Stewart, Bourke, Longpre, Marchand, Goudreau 1965–72; Extve. Asst. to Princ. McGill Univ. 1972, Dir. Devel. & Commun. 1975; Dir. Univ. Relations 1980; Pres., Univ. Club Montreal 1984–85; Dir. Miss Edgar's and Miss Cramp's Sch. Montreal 1972–75; Dir., Dawson Coll., Montreal 1988–91; Dir., McCord Museum, Montreal 1981– ; Council mem. O.A.Q. 1964–66; Vie des Arts 1985–90; Société des Musées de Sciences Naturelles de Montréal 1992– ; United Church; recreations: sailing, skiing, tennis; Clubs: University; Hillside Tennis; Home: 28 Place Richelieu, Montreal, Que. H3G 1E8; Office: 845 Sherbrooke St. W., Montreal, Que. H3A 2T5.

**BOURKE, Thomas John,** B.Sc.; publisher; b. Chesterville, Ont. 21 Feb. 1937; s. Thomas John B.; e. Mich. Technol. Univ. B.Sc. 1961; m. Melodie Ann d. late Arthur J. Booth 24 Aug. 1963; three d. Gillian, Jacqueline, Jennifer; PRESIDENT & C.E.O., TELE-DIRECT (PUBLICATIONS) INC. 1981– ; PRES. & C.E.O., TELE-DIRECT (SERVICES) INC. 1985– ; Dir., Sanford Evans Communications Ltd., Winnipeg; Edward H. O'Brien Pty. Ltd., Australia; National Telephone Directory, N.J.; Penn-Del Directory Corp. Penn.; Al Wahda Express, Dubai; Falcon Publishing, Bahrain; Telemap Limited, U.K.; started career as Marketing Rep. Bell Canada 1961, Directory Dept. 1968, Div. Directory Production Mgr. 1970; Vice Pres. Production, Tele-Direct Ltd. 1971, Vice Pres. Marketing 1972, Operating Vice Pres. 1973; R. Catholic; recreations: golf, tennis, squash; Clubs: Montréal Badminton & Squash Club; Royal Montreal Golf; St. James's; Weston Golf & Country (Ont.); Montreal Board of Trade; Toronto Board of Trade; Canadian Club; Home: 45 Lakeshore Rd., Ste. #420, Pointe-Claire, Qué. H9S 4H3; Office: 1600 boul. René-Lévesque ouest, Ste. #1850, Montréal, Qué. H3H 1P9.

**BOURNE, Charles B.,** B.A., LL.M., S.J.D., LL.D. (hon. causa), F.R.S.C.; educator; b. Barbados 19 Feb. 1921; s. Beresford and Lilian May (Ward) B.; e. The Lodge Sch. Barbados 1938; Univ. of Toronto B.A. 1945; St. John's Coll. Cambridge LL.M. 1947; Harvard Law Sch. S.J.D. 1970; m. Barbara d. Glenville and Dorothy Farmer 20 Aug. 1949; children: Frances, Peter, Angela; PROF. EMERITUS, UNIV. OF B.C. 1986– , Prof. of Law 1957–86, Adv. to the Pres. 1975–86; called to the Bars of England by the Middle Temple 1947, Barbados 1949, B.C. 1957; Asst. Prof. Univ. of Sask. 1947–50; Assoc. Prof. present Univ. 1950–57; Acad.-in-Residence Legal Bureau Dept. of External Affairs Ottawa 1971–72; Hon. Solicitor and mem. Bd. of Govs. Vancouver Sch. of Theol. 1971–80; Mem., Permanent Court of Arbitration, The Hague 1978–84; author numerous articles legal journs.; Ed.-in-Chief 'Canadian Yearbook of International Law' 1962–93; mem. Candn. Br. Internat. Law Assn. (Pres. 1961–64); Candn. Council on Internat. Law (Pres. 1978–80); Candn. Bar Assn. 1947–86; awarded The John E. Read Medal in Internat. Law 1986; Chrmn., Internat. Law Assn. Ctte. on Internat. Water Resources Law 1990– ; recreations: reading, walking, gardening, croquet; Home: 1576 Newton Cres., Vancouver, B.C. V6T 1W7; Office: 1822 East Mall, Vancouver, B.C. V6T 1Z1.

**BOURNE, Larry Stuart,** M.A., Ph.D., F.R.S.C.; educator; b. London, Ont. 24 Dec. 1939; s. Stuart Howard and Florence Evaline (Adams) B.; e. Univ. of W. Ont. B.A. 1961; Univ. of Alta. M.A. 1963; Univ. of Chicago Ph.D. 1966; m. Paula T. d. J.A. O'Neill, Liverpool, Eng. 14 Aug. 1967; children: David S. A., Alexandra L. E.; PROF. OF GEOGRAPHY AND PLANNING, UNIV. OF TORONTO since 1973 and Dir. Centre for Urban and Community Studies 1972–84; Post-doctoral Fellow, Centre for Urban Studies, Univ. of Chicago 1965–66; Asst. Prof. of Geog. present Univ. 1966, Assoc. Prof. 1969, Assoc. Dir. Centre for Urban and Community Studies 1969; Visiting Prof. London Sch. of Econ. 1972–73; Centre for Environmental Studies, London 1978–79; Meiji Univ., Tokyo 1991; Consultant and Advisor to various levels govt.; mem. numerous internat. research and policy groups incl. Internat. Inst. for Applied Systems Analysis (Austria), Chrmn., Internat. Geog. Union Comn. on Urban Systems and Urban Development 1984–92; author 'Private Redevelopment of the Central City' 1967; 'Urban Systems: Strategies for Regulation' 1975; 'The Geography of Housing' 1981; Ed. 'Internal Structure of City' 1971, 2nd ed. 1982; co-ed. 'Urban Systems Development in Central Canada' 1972; 'The Form of Cities in Central Canada' 1973; 'Urban Futures for Central Canada' 1974; co-ed., 'Systems of Cities' 1978; 'Urban Housing Markets' 1979; 'Urbanization and Settlement Systems' 1984; 'Progress in Settlement Systems Geography' 1986; 'Urban Systems in Transition' 1986; 'The Changing Geography of Urban Systems' 1989; 'Urbanization and Urban Development' 1991; 'The Changing Social Geography of Canadian Cities' 1993; author numerous journ. articles, reports and papers; rec'd Can. Council Research Fellowship 1972–73; SSHRCC Leave Fellowships 1978–79 and 1984–85; Honours Awards from the Candn. Assoc. of Geographers and the Assoc. of Am. Geographers 1985; Award for Service, Ont. Div., Can. Assoc. of Geographers 1989; Fellow, Royal Soc. of Can.; Pres., Can. Assn. of Geographers 1993–94; mem. Int'l. and Cdn. Regional Science Assn.; Candn. Assn. Geographers; Assn. Am. Geographers; Urban Studies; Candn. Assn. Univ. Teachers; Delta Upsilon; Lambda Alpha; recreations: tennis, basketball, hockey; Home: 26 Anderson Ave., Toronto, Ont. M5P 1H4; Office: 100 St. George St., Toronto, Ont. M5S 1A1.

**BOURNE, Lesley-Anne,** B.A., M.F.A.; university professor, poet; b. North Bay, Ont. 9 Sept. 1964; d. John Frederick and Eva Ilene (Nichol) B.; e. York Univ. B.A. (Hons.) 1987; Univ. of B.C. M.F.A. 1989; m. Richard s. Gloria and Harvey Lemm 6 Sept. 1991; UNIVERSITY LECTURER, UNIV. OF P.E.I. 1991– ; participant, Summer Writing Program, The Banff Centre for the Arts 1985–87; Writing Studio 1990; Coordinator, The Teaching Centre, Univ. of P.E.I. 1990–93; Banff Centre's Bliss Carman Poetry Award 1986; Air Nova Poetry Award 1990; Finalist, Gerald Lampert Award for Best First Book of Poetry; Coles Prize for Short Fiction; Carl Sentrer Short Fiction Award; Mem., League of Canadian Poets; P.E.I. Writers' Guild; P.E.I. Council of the Art; author (poetry): 'The Story of Pears' 1990; 'Skinny Girls' 1993; Home: 186 King St., Charlottetown, P.E.I. C1A 1C1; Office: Dalton 407, Univ. of P.E.I., Charlottetown, P.E.I. C1A 4P3.

**BOURNE, Robert Porter (Robin),** C.D., B.A.; b. Tunbridge Wells, Kent, U.K. 5 Aug. 1930; s. late Kenneth Morrison Bourne; e. Ridley Coll. St. Catharines, Ont. 1948; Royal Mil. Coll. of Can. 1952; Univ. of W. Ont. B.A. 1954; Carleton Univ. 1979–80; m. late Patricia d. late Donald Robert Agnew; children: Mark Kenneth, Anne Susan Blossom, John Frederick, Peter David Anthony; m. Candice Lee Munro; one child: Kate Marion Robin; comnd. Lt., R.C.A. 1952; served Korean War 1952–53, Germany, 1955–57, Cyprus (U.N.) 1967–68, seconded to Privy Council Office, 1968–71; seconded to Dept. Solr. Gen., 1971; retired as Col. 1972; Asst. Depy. Min. - Police and Security, Dept. Solr. Gen. Can. 1972–79; Asst. Depy. Min., Police Serv., B.C. Min. of Attorney Gen. 1981–89; Hon. Col., 5 (B.C.) Field Regiment, Royal Candn. Artillery 1992; Mem., Bd. of Trustees, Art Gall. of Gter. Victoria; Mem., Royal Military Coll. Club of Can.; Royal United Services Inst. of Vancouver Island; Life Mem., Candn. Assoc. of Chiefs of Police; Anglican; recreations: squash, canoeing, hiking, gardening; Home: 4025 White Rock St., Victoria, B.C. V8Y 4M4.

**BOURNS, Arthur Newcombe,** O.C., B.Sc., Ph.D., D.Sc., L.L.D., F.R.S.C., F.C.I.C.; chemist; b. Petitcodiac, N.B., 8 Dec. 1919; s. Evans Clement and Kathleen (Jones) B.; e. Acadia Univ., B.Sc. 1941, D.Sc. 1968; McGill Univ., Ph.D. 1944; McGill Univ. D.Sc. 1977; Brock U. L.L.D. 1980; Univ. of N.B., D.Sc. 1981; McMaster Univ., D.Sc. 1981; m. Marion Harriet, d. William S. Blakney, Petitcodiac, N.B., 23 June 1943; children: Mrs. Barbara Brown, Mrs. Susan Milne, Robert Evans, Brian Hugh; PROFESSOR EMERITUS OF CHEMISTRY, MCMASTER UNIV. 1980– ; Research Chem., Research Labs., Dominion Rubber Co. Ltd., 1944–45; Lectr., Acadia Univ. 1945–46; Asst. Prof. of Chem., Univ. of Sask. 1946–47 and McMaster Univ. 1947–49; Assoc. Prof., McMaster Univ. 1949–53; Prof. 1953; Dean, Faculty of Grad. Studies 1957–61; Chrmn., Dept. of Chem. 1965–67; Vice-Pres., Science and Engn. Div. 1967–72; Acting Pres. 1970; Pres. 1972–80; Chrmn., Internat. Advisory Panel, Chinese Provincial Univ. Development Project 1985–92; Nuffield Travelling Fellowship in Sciences, Univ. Coll., of London, Eng. 1955–56; memberships: Ancaster Pub. Sch. Bd. 1963–64; Comte. on Univ. Affairs, Prov. of Ont. 1964–69; Nat. Research Council of Can. (mem.: Council, Extve. Comte., Co-Chrmn. 1971 and Chrmn. 1972–75, Comte. on Grants and Scholarships); Royal Botanical Gdns. (mem. Bd. and Vice-Chrmn. 1972–80); Assn. Univs. and Colls. Can. (mem. Bd. Dirs. 1974–77); Natural Sciences and Engineering Research Council (mem.: Council and Extve. Comte. 1978–85, Comte. on Strategic Grants 1978–83, Univ.-Ind. Interface Adv. Comte. 1979–83, Chrmn. Comte. on Grants and Scholarships 1978–83, Visiting Rsch. Offr. 1983–84); Candn. Inst. for Advanced Research (mem. Rsch. Counc. 1983–89); Vice-Chrmn., Royal Soc. of Can. Comte. on Univ. Rsch. 1989–90; Council of Ont. Univs. (mem. Council 1972–80 and Vice-Chrmn. 1976–78); Candn. Bureau Internat. Educ. (Pres. and Chrmn. Extve. Comte. 1973–76); McMaster Univ. Medical Centre (mem., Bd. Trustees, Extve. Comte. 1972–79); Chedoke-McMaster Hosp. (mem. Bd. Trustees, Extve. Comm. 1979–80); Bd. of Gov., Mohawk Coll. of Applied Arts & Technol. 1975–82; Ed. Bd. 'Science Forum' 1967–73; Dir. Slater Steel Co., 1975–80; Vice-Chrmn. 1959–60 and Chrmn. 1961–62 Gordon Research Conf. on Chem and Physics of Isotopes; Brit. Council Lect. 1963; awarded Montreal Medal, Chem. Inst. of Can. 1976; Hon. Prof., Jiangxi Univ. P.R.C. 1989– ; writings incl. numerous research publs. in field of phys. organic chem. for various prof. journs.; recreations: travel; Address: 2407 Woodword Ave., Unit 10, Burlington, Ont. L7R 1V2.

**BOURNS, Charles David,** B.Com.; banker; b. Vancouver, B.C. 30 Aug. 1932; s. Thomas Watters and Allace Ruth (Stevens) B.; e. Magee High Sch. Vancouver 1951; Univ. of B.C. B.Com. 1956; m. K. Mary d. Samuel G. and Winifred Lee 18 May 1956; children: Kathleen, Kevin, Megan; ASST. GEN. MGR. CAPITAL FUNDING, BANK OF NOVA SCOTIA 1987– ; Indust. Engr. Du Pont of Canada Ltd. Kingston, Ont. 1956–60; Sr. Financial Analyst H.O. Ford Motor Co. of Canada 1960, Mgr. Cost Analysis Oakville Div. 1961, Mgr. Operations Analysis Windsor Div. 1962–65; Mgr. Corporate Accounting Burns Foods Ltd. Calgary 1965–66; Div. Controller Columbia Cellulose Ltd. Prince Rupert, B.C. 1966–68; Supvr. Financial Planning & Analysis Royal Bank of Canada Montreal 1968–74; Administrator Subsidiary Co's present Bank 1974–80; Asst. Gen. Mgr. Finance & Admn. 1980–83; Asst. Gen. Mgr., Mgt. & Fin. Information Syst. 1983–87; Anglican; recreations: golf, fishing; Club: York Downs Golf & Country; Arbutus Ridge Golf & Country; Office: 44 King St. W., Toronto, Ont. M5H 1H1.

**BOURQUE, Andre Pierre;** executive; auto racer; b. Ottawa, Ont. 7 Oct. 1958; s. Henri Pierre and Barbara Joan (McNeil) B.; e. Coll. St-Alexandre; Univ. of Ottawa Business Adm.; VICE-PRESIDENT, BOURQUE PIERRE & FILS LTD.; Dir. & Co-Founder Lively Arts Market Builders 1981–83; participant in 1989 British F3000 Championship; mem. Junior International Club of New York; Princess Grace Foundation; Tibet House (N.Y.); Federation Internat. de l'Automobile Paris; Sports Car Club of America; ASN FIA Canada; R. Catholic; recreations: reading, travel, the arts; Home: 40 Boteler, Ottawa, Ont. K1N 9C8; Office: 301–401 King Edward Ave., Ottawa, Ont. K1N 9C9.

**BOURQUE, Ronald J.G.,** B.Comm., M.A., F.C.G.A.; educator and administrator; b. 22 April 1943; e. St. Francis Xavier Univ. B.Comm. 1966; Rider College M.A. 1976; C.G.A. 1983; m. Katharine Toner 21 June 1969; children: Daniel, Michel; CHAIR, DIVISION OF ACCOUNTING, UNIV. OF MONCTON 1985– ; Instructor, N.B. Inst. of Technology 1970, 1972–73; contract with Comn. for Tech. Edn. & Vocational Training, Lusaka, Zambia 1971–72; Instructor, Univ. of N.B. 1973–76; secondment to UNB-CIDA project, Kenya Technical Teachers College; invited by World Bank to prepare report on Madagascar Project 'Accounting and Audit Training' 1980; Bus. Edn. Section, Vocational Edn. Div., Fac. of Edn., UNB; Assoc. Prof., Lee & Martin & L & M EDP Services while on sabbatical leave 1983–84; Mem., New Brunswick Economic Council; Moncton Volunteer Centre; Life Mem., Certified Gen. Accountants' Assn. of Canada (President 1992–93); C.G.A. Canada Fellowship 1990; Home: 22 Portledge Ave., Moncton, N.B. E1C 5S4; Office: Moncton, N.B. E1A 3E9.

**BOUSFIELD, Gerald Arthur Harvey,** B.A., M.A.; editor, writer; b. Peterborough, Ont. 29 Sept. 1943; s. Gerald Edmund Wheeler and Dorothy Phyllis (Starr) B.; e. R.H. King C.I.; Univ. Coll., Univ. of Toronto B.A. 1966, M.A. 1969; EDITOR, MONARCHY CANADA 1975– ; Founding Mem., Monarchist League of Canada 1970; Toronto Chair 1977–80; Dir. & Vice-Chair 1977; Life Mem. 1985; media commentator and lecturer; Gov., The Riverdale Hosp. 1989– ; Life Mem., Kilkenny Archaeol. Soc. 1983; Friends of St. David's Cathedral 1985; Anglican-Catholic; co-author: 'Lives of the Princesses of Wales' 1983, 'Royal Spring' 1989, 'Royal Observations: Canadians and Royalty' 1991, 'Canada's King and Queens' 1993; co-editor: 'Loyalist Vignettes and Sketches' 1984; contbr.: 'Loyal She Remains: A Pictorial History of Ontario' 1984, 'Canada: from sea unto sea' 1986, 'Allegiance: The Ontario Story' 1991; correspondent, Berkswell's annual 'Royal Year' 1982– ; rsch. asst. to Esther Fraser for 'Wheeler' 1978; Queen's Commemorative Medal for the 125th Anniversary of Confederation 1992; clubs: Royal Overseas League; Home: 24 The Links Rd., No. 321, Willowdale, Ont. M2P 1T6; Office: 3050 Yonge St., Suite 206, Toronto, Ont. M4N 2K4.

**BOUTHILLETTE, Roland,** B.A.Sc., M.Sc., Eng.; educator; b. Montréal, Qué. 3 Nov. 1922; s. late Adélard and late Rébecca (Jobin) B.; e. Coll. Mont Saint-Louis; Univ. de Montréal, Ecole Polytech. B.A.Sc. (Mech. & Elect. Eng.) 1946; Ill. Inst. of Tech. M.Sc. (Mech. Eng.) 1948; m. Françoise B. d. late Egilles Lord, Montréal 1949; four d. Chantal, France, Elise, Lucie; Pres. and Principal, La Corporation de l'Ecole Polytechnique de Montréal 1984–89; Co-founder & Chrmn., Bouthillette, Parizeau & Assoc., Consulting engineers 1956– ; Dir., Fondation de l'Hôpital du Sacré-Coeur; Asst. and Assoc. Prof. present inst. 1948–58; Pres. Assn. des Diplômés de Polytechnique 1972; mem. Order Engs. Qué.; Assn. Cons. Engs. Qué.; Assn. Cons. Engs. Can.; Am. Soc. Heating, Refrigerating & Air Conditioning Engs.; The Candn. Acad. of Engr. 1989; Chambre de Comm. de Montréal; recreations: golf, fishing; Clubs: Islesmere Golf; Saint-Denis; Home: 1001 Place Mont-Royal, Montreal, Que. H3A 1P2.

**BOUTIN, Robert P.,** B.A.; retail executive; b. Montreal, Que. 18 March 1947; s. Ulysse C. and Mildred M. (Craig) B.; e. McGill Univ. B.A. 1969; m. Micheline d. Maria and Robert Vallet 8 Nov. 1969; children: Michel, Annick; progressed from Management Trainee to General Manager 'The Bay' Quebec Operations 1969–83; Extve. Vice-Pres., Lise Watier Cosmetics 1983–85; President, Chas. Ogilvy 1985–87 (relaunched Ogilvy as a major fashion & home fashion speciality dept. store); Vice-Pres., Merchandising & Marketing, Birks Canada 1987–93; Home: 406 Pine Ave. W., Apt. 71, Montreal, Que. H2W 1S2.

**BOUTIN, Roland,** c.m.a., f.l.m.i., f.c.m.a.; employee benefits consultant; b. Tadoussac, Que. 12 Nov. 1930; s. Joseph Onésime and Marie (Lévesque) B.; e. Acad. de Qué. 1948; Laval Univ.; Soc. of Mngt. Accts., c.m.a. 1953; Life Office Mngt. Assn. Inst., f.l.m.i. 1963; m. Denise d. Cécile and Sylvio Racette 1 July 1957; children: Sophie, Nicolas; PRINCIPAL., WILLIAM M. MERCER LTD. 1987– ; var. mngt. posts incl. Dir. of personnel, La Laurentienne 1950–65; Régie des rentes du Qué. 1966–81 (incl. special assignment to Great Brit. & Switz. to study priv. pension system & applicable legislation); Employee Benefits Cons. (Head, Quebec City office), William M. Mercer Ltd. 1981–87; Pres., Candn. Pension Conf. 1988–89; Co-founder & former pres., Ctr. d'études et de form. sur les avantages sociaux; Fellow, Soc. of Mngt. Accts. of Can.; Mem., Hop. St-Sacrement Found.; Roman Catholic; Mem., Soc. of Mngt. Accts. of Que. & Can.; C. de C. et d'indus. du Qué. métro.; co-author of 3 reports; recreations: symphony orchestra, opera, travel, reading, skiing; club: Quebec Garrison; Home: 6150, ave. Beaumont, Charlesbourg, Que. G1H 4K1; Office: 1175, rue Lavigerie, bur. 480, Sainte-Foy, Que. G1V 4P1.

**BOUTON, Charles Pierre,** D.E.S., D. ès L.; b. Paris, France 17 Feb. 1926; s. Pierre Alexandre and Madeleine Augustine (Guillot) B.; e. Baccalauréat (1st and 2nd) Paris, France 1943–44; Univ. de Paris (Sorbonne) Lic. ès Lettres 1947, Dipl. d'Etudes supérieures 1949, D. ès L. 1969; m. Eliane Pierrette, d. late Pierre Ernest Poulet, 3 Aug. 1946; children: Jean-Francois Pierre, Denys Pierre Gérard; Prof. of French & Linguistics, Simon Fraser Univ. 1971–91, retired; Professor emeritus; Prof. French Lit. and Lang., Educ. Nat., France 1947; Asst. Lectr. in French, Dundee Univ. Coll., Scot. 1951; Alliance Française, Ecole pratique de Paris 1952–67 (Prof. 1952, Asst. Dir. de l'Ecole and Séminaire de pédagogie, ling. et psycholing. 1958); Prof. French and Ling., Converse Coll., Spartanburg, S.C. 1967; Prof., present Univ. 1971; (Chrmn. Modern Langs. Dept. there Sept. 1973–78); author of 'Les Grammaires françaises de Claude Mauger' 1972; 'L'Acquisition d'une langue étrangère' 1974; 'Le développement du langage' 1976; 'La signification' 1979; 'La linguistique appliquée' 1979; 'Les Mécanismes d'Acquisition du français langue étrangère' 1969; 'La Neurolinguistique' 1984; 'Le Discours Physique du Langage' 1984; Edit. 'Le Misanthrope' 1962;

'Madame Bovary' 1969; 'La Démocratie en Amérique' 1973; Co-author 'Des Machines et des Hommes' 1964; 'La Langue de l'Automobile' 1966; 'Regardons, Ecoutons, Parlons' 1968; 'Glossaire de français scientifique' 1970; also articles in various prof. mags. and journs.; el. Chevalier, La Confrérie des Chevaliers du Tastevin (1974); Palmes académiques 1991; mem. Assn. française de ling. appliquée; Candn. Assn. Univ. Teachers; Ling. Assn. B.C.; R. Catholic; Home: 952 Roche Point Dr., North Vancouver, B.C. V7H 2T7.

**BOVILLE, Byron Walter,** B.A., M.Sc., Ph.D.; university professor; b. Ottawa, Ont. 14 Dec. 1920; e. Univ. of Toronto, B.A. 1942; McGill Univ., M.Sc., Ph.D. 1961; m. Flora Milne 13 May 1989; children: Byron, Jo-Anne, Susan, and Fred, Kevin, Doug Jamieson; ADJUNCT PROF., DEPT. OF EARTH & ATMOS. SCIENCE, YORK UNIV. 1982– ;(Chair 1986–88); Meteorologist, Meteor. Serv. of Can. 1942–56; Prof., McGill Univ. 1957–72; Chrmn., Dept. of Meteor. 1967–70; Rsch. Dir., Atmospheric Environ. Serv. & First Dir., Candn. Climate Ctr. 1972–79; organized World Climate Prog., WMO Geneva 1980–82; Cons. to UNEP on ozone layer; Fellow, Am. Meteor. Soc.; recipient, Patterson Medal; awarded, Massey Medal 1990 (Royal Candn. Geog. Soc.); Life Mem., Candn. Meteor. & Oceanographic Soc. (several extve. offices); Sigma Xi; The Sci. Rsch. Soc.; author of several sci. pubs.; active teacher & researcher on dynamic meteor., climate & the ozone layer worldwide; recreations: golf, skiing, curling; club: Trehaven Golf (Match Play Title 1987); Home: R.R. 1, Hawkestone, Ont. L0K 1T0; Office: 4700 Keele St., North York, Ont. M3J 1P3.

**BOW, Malcolm Norman;** diplomat (retired); b. Regina, Sask. 30 Sept. 1918; s. Dr. Malcolm Ross and Norma (Wallace) B.; e. Garneau Public and High Schs., Edmonton, Alta.; Univ. of Alta. (1938–40); Univ. of Brit. Columbia (1947–48); Acad. of Internat. Law, The Hague, Netherlands, 1948; m. Betty Rundle, d. Bertram R. Roberts, Shoreham-by-Sea, Sussex, Eng., 6 March 1945; children: Paul (deceased), Jane, Michael, Neil; Vancouver 'Daily Province,' 1946–49; joined Dept. of External Affairs, Ottawa, 1949; Vice Consul, New York, 1950–53; Ottawa 1953–56; First Secy., Candn. Embassy, Madrid, 1956–58 and Chargé d'Affaires a.i. there 1958–59; Ottawa, 1959–60; Counsellor and Chargé d'Affaires, Candn. Embassy, Havana, Cuba, 1961; Special Asst. to Secy. of State for External Affairs, Ottawa, 1962–64; Ambassador to Czechoslovakia (1964–68) (concurrently to Hungary 1965–68); apptd. Dir. Arms Control and Disarmament Div., Dept. External Affairs, Dec. 1968, Dir. of Latin Am. Div. March 1971; apptd. Ambassador to Cuba, 1973–75 (and concurrently to Haiti 1975); Dir.-Gen. of Security and Intelligence, Ottawa 1975–76; served in 2nd World War; Candn. Army, 1940, Calgary Highlanders, Eng., Lieut.; British Army, Burma, Capt.; Candn. Army Pacific Force, Major, 1946; recreations: golf, travel, research, writing; Home: 2514 Shoreacres Road, (P.O. Box 2475), Sidney, B.C. V8L 3Y3.

**BOWDEN, E. Stuart,** B.Sc., M.Sc., M.B.A., C.A., N.P.; executive; b. Montreal, Que 10 May 1954; s. Albert Earl and Agnes B.; e. Univ. of Toronto B.Sc. (Hons.) 1977, M.Sc. 1979; York Univ. M.B.A. 1981; C.A. 1983; m. Shelley M. d. James and Marie Hornell 3 July 1981; children: Andrew Robert, Katherine Anne; VICE-PRES. OF FINANCE & ADMIN., SAS INSTITUTE (CANADA) INC. 1988– ; Auditor, Clarkson Gordon; Manager / Sr. Consultant, Woods Gordon / The Clarkson Co. 1980–86; Vice-Pres. Finance, Neo-Visuals Inc. 1986–88; specialty: general mng., new venture start-up, finance; Mem., Information Technology Assn. of Canada (Chrmn., Taxation & Finance Ctte.; Software Sector Ctte., Prov. of Ont.; Ctte. for Software); Medical Research Council of Canada Scholar 1977; Chief Financial Offr., Scarborough East Prov. P.C. Assn.; Mem., Institute of Chartered Accountants; Alpha Delta Phi Frat.; recreations: golf, badminton; Home: 42 Regency Square, Scarborough, Ont. M1E 1N3; Office: BCE Place, 181 Bay St., Suite 2220, P.O. Box 819, Toronto, Ont. M5J 2T3.

**BOWDEN, John W.,** B.Sc., M.B.A.; banker; b. Edmonton, Alta. 1 June 1948; e. Carleton Univ. B.Sc. 1970; Queen's Univ. M.B.A. 1972; m.; 5 children; EXECUTIVE VICE-PRES., CANADIAN IMPERIAL BANK OF COMMERCE 1986– ; var. branch positions, Ont., CIBC 1972–80; Vice-Pres., Corp. Banking Div. 1981–83; Sr. Vice-pres., Corp. & Merchant Banking 1983–86; Office: Commerce Court W., Toronto, Ont. M5L 1A2.

**BOWDER, Donald,** F.C.A.; bank executive b. England 4 March 1935; s. William Henry and Mabel (Linford) B.; e. Woodhouse Grove School 1952; m. Marian d. Arnold and Alice Busfield 22 July 1958; children: Jennifer, Robert, Sarah; SENIOR VICE-PRESIDENT AND CHIEF ACCOUNTANT, CANADIAN IMPERIAL BANK OF COMMERCE; Partner, U.K. Chartered Accountants 1958–66; Chief Accountant, U.K. Building Soc. 1966–69; various financial positions, CIBC Toronto 1969– ; Fellow, Inst. of C.A.'s in England & Wales (FCA) 1957; recreations: tennis, squash, golf; clubs: The Oakville; Home: The Granary, No. 301, Oakville, Ont. L6J 6M9; Office: Commerce Court North, 5th floor, Toronto, ont. M5L 1A2.

**BOWDRING, Paul Edward,** B.A., B.Ed.; writer; editor; educator; b. Bell Island, Nfld. 24 March 1946; e. Meml. Univ. of Nfld. B.A., B.Ed. 1970; ENGLISH INSTR., CABOT COLLEGE 1975– ; recipient First Prize Fiction 1980, 1985 Nfld. & Labrador Arts & Letters Competition; Can. Council Grant 1991; Nfld. & Labrador Arts Council Grant 1991; St. John's City Council Arts Grant 1993; author 'The Roncesvalles Pass' novel 1989; co-ed. and co-pub. 'TickleAce' lit. mag. 1979–87; Founding mem. Writers' Alliance Nfld. & Labrador 1987 (Exec. mem., Chair Readings Ctte. 1989–90); recreations: reading, music, films, travel, tennis, bicycling, walking; Home: 11 Stoneyhouse St., St. John's, Nfld. A1B 2T5; Office: Academic Dept., Cabot College, P.O. Box 1693, St. John's, Nfld. A1C 5P7.

**BOWEN, Gail Dianne Bartholomew,** B.A., M.A.; writer, university professor; b. Toronto, Ont. 22 Sept. 1942; d. Albert Benjamin and Doris Mary (Miller) Bartholomew; e. Univ. of Toronto B.A. 1964; Univ. of Waterloo M.A. 1975; Univ. of Sask., grad. work in Can-Lit 1976–79; m. Ted s. Hazel and Edwin B. 31 Aug. 1968; children: Hildy Wren, Max Benjamin, Nathaniel Peter; PROF., UNIV. OF REGINA, SASKATCHEWAN INDIAN FEDERATED COLLEGE; University teaching at variously Univ. of Saskatchewan, Gabriel Dumont Inst. & present univ. 1976– ; regular Arts Columnist, CBC Radio Sask. 1991– ; frequent speaker at schools, libraries & arts insts.; nominated Books in Canada/W.H. Smith First Novel Award 1990 for 'Deadly Appearances'; Anglican; Mem., Sask. Writers Guild; Crime Writers of Canada; YWCA; ACTRA; author: 'Deadly Appearances' 1990, 'Murder at the Mendel' 1991, 'The Wandering Soul Murders' 1992 (novels); co-author: '1919 The Love Letters of George and Adelaide' 1987 (novella); 'Dancing In Poppies' (adaption of '1919' into play); 'Beauty and the Beast' (play); recreations: aerobics, Church School teacher 1973–91; Home: 2836 Retallack St., Regina, Sask. S4S 1S7; Office: CW 210, SIFC, U. of Regina, Regina, Sask. S4S 0A2.

**BOWEN, Lynne Elizabeth,** B.Sc., R.N., M.A.; historian; b. Indian Head, Sask. 22 Aug. 1940; d. Desmond and Isobel (Boyd) Crossley; e. Univ. of Alta. B.Sc., R.N. 1963; Univ. of Victoria M.A. 1980; m. Richard Allan s. Edwin and Florence Bowen 25 Aug. 1962; children: Michael, Andrew, Elizabeth; nurse, Victorian Order of Nurses 1963–64; taught as guest lecturer, sessional college lecturer 1980– ; Maclean Hunter Lectr., Univ. of B.C. 1992– ; author 'Boss Whistle' 1982; 'Three Dollar Dreams' 1987; 'Muddling Through' 1992; Eaton's B.C. Book Award 1983; Candn. Hist. Assn. Regional Certificate of Merit 1983 and 1992; B.C. Lieut.-Gov.'s Award for Writing Hist. 1987; Hubert Evans Non-Fiction Prize, B.C. Book Awards 1992; mem. Writer's Union of Can.; B.C. Fedn. of Writers; Nanaimo Harbourfront Centre Soc. (Bd. of Dirs.); Nanaimo Hist. Soc.; Internat. P.E.N.; recreations: sailing, skiing, reading; Address: 4982 Fillinger Cres., Nanaimo, B.C. V9V 1J1.

**BOWEN, Walter M.,** B.A., LL.B., Q.C.; lawyer; b. Trenton, Ont. 2 July 1934; s. Walter Melsop and Helen Irene (Patrick) B.; e. Univ. of Toronto Hons. B.A. 1957, LL.B. 1960; m. Elizabeth S. d. St. Clair Balfour 2 July 1970; children: Arabella Claire Southam, Staunton St. Clair Melsop; LAWYER, CASSELS, BROCK & BLACKWELL 1977– ; Dir., Southam Inc. (Chrmn., Pension Ctte.), director of other companies; called to the Bar 1962; cr. Q.C. 1974; practice in corp. law with emphasis on acquisitions and divestitures; co-author: 'Purchase and Sale of a Business' 1982; Clubs: York; Toronto; Badminton and Racquet; Toronto Golf; Home: 25 Chestnut Park Rd., Toronto, Ont. M4W 1W4; Office: 40 King St. W., Suite 2100, Toronto, Ont. M5H 1B5.

**BOWERING, George Harry,** M.A.; poet and fiction writer; b. Okanagan Falls, B.C. 1 Dec. 1936; s. Ewart Harry and Pearl Patricia (Brinson) B.; e. S. Okanagan High Sch., Oliver, B.C.; Victoria (B.C.) Coll.; Univ. of Brit. Columbia, B.A. 1960, M.A. 1963; Univ. of Western Ontario; m. Angela Maya, d. E.H. Luoma, Courtenay, B.C., 14 Dec. 1963; Vice-Pres., The Nihilist Party of Can. (London); former L.A.C. in R.C.A.F. (photographer); author: 'Sticks & Stones' 1963; 'Points on the Grid' 1964; 'The Man in Yellow Boots' 1965; 'The Silver Wire' 1966; 'Mirror on the Floor' 1967; 'Baseball' 1967; 'Rocky Mountain Foot' 1969; 'Two Police Poems' 1969; 'The Gangs of Kosmos' 1969; 'Sitting in Mexico' 1970; 'Al Purdy' 1970; 'George, Vancouver' 1970; 'Genève' 1971; 'The Story So Far' 1970; 'Touch: Selected Poems' 1971; 'Autobiology' 1972; 'Fiddler's Night' (novel) 1972; 'In the Flesh' 1974; 'Curious' 1974; 'Flycatcher and Other Stories' 1974; 'At War with the U.S.' 1975; 'Allophanes' 1976; 'The Concrete Island' 1977; 'A Short Sad Book' 1977; 'Poem & Other Baseballs' 1977; 'Protective Footwear' (stories) 1978; 'Concentric Circles' 1978; 'Another Mouth' 1979; 'Three Vancouver Writers' 1979; 'Burning Water' (Novel) 1980; (ed.) 'Fiction of Contemporary Canada' (Stories) 1980; 'Particular Accidents' (poetry) 1980; (ed.) 'Great Canadian Sports Stories' 1979; 'West Window' (poetry) 1982; 'A Way With Words' (essays) 1982; 'Smoking Mirror' (poems) 1982; 'Ear Reach' (poems) 1982; 'An eaux troubles' (récit) 1982; 'The Mask in Place' (essays) 1982; 'A Place to Die' (stories) 1983; 'Kerrisdale Elegies' 1984; 'Craft Slices' (essays) 1985; (ed.) 'Sheila Watson and "The Double Hook"' (essays) 1985; 'Seventy-One Poems For People' (poetry) 1985; 'Delayed Mercy' (poems) 1986; 'Caprice' (novel) 1987; 'Errata' (literary theory) 1988; 'Imaginary Hand' (essays) 1988; 'Sticks & Stones' (poetry), new ed. 1989; 'Harry's Fragments' (novel) 1990; (ed.) 'Taking the Field' (stories) 1990; 'Urban Snow' (poetry) 1992; (ed.) 'Likely Stories' 1992; 'George Bowering Selected Poems: 1961–92' (poetry) 1993; 'The Moustache' (memoir) 1993; Gov. Gen. Award for Poetry, 1969; Can. Council Sr. Arts Awards 1971, 1977, 1991; Gov. Gen. Award for Fiction 1980; Winner, bpNichol Chapbook prize 1991, 1992; Romantic Anarchic Left; Religion: Protestant Agnostic; recreation: softball; Address: 2499 W. 37 Ave., Vancouver, B.C. V6M 1P4.

**BOWERING, Marilyn Ruthe,** M.A.; author; b. Winnipeg, Man. 13 Apr. 1949; d. Herbert James and Elnora May (Grist) B.; e. Univ. of Victoria B.A. 1971, M.A. 1973; Univ. of B.C. 1968–69; author 'Love As It Is' (poetry) 1993; 'Calling All the World' (poetry) 1989; 'To All Appearances a Lady' (novel) 1989; 'Anyone Can See I Love You' (poetry) 1987; 'Grandfather Was A Soldier' (poetry) 1987; 'The Sunday before Winter: New and Selected Poems' 1984; 'Giving Back Diamonds' (poetry) 1982; 'Sleeping with Lambs' (poetry) 1980; 'The Visitors Have All Returned' (fiction) 1979; 'The Killing Room' (poetry) 1977; 'One Who Became Lost' (poetry) 1976; 'The Liberation of Newfoundland' (poetry) 1973; 'Grandfather Was A Soldier' (radio drama, BBC) 1983; 'Anyone Can See I Love You, Marilyn Monroe' (radio drama, BBC) 1986; 'Laika and Folchakov' (radio drama, CBC) 1987; 'A Cold Departure' (radio drama, CBC) 1989; rec'd Nat. Mag. Award Poetry 1978, 1989; Lectr. in Creative Writing, Univ. of Victoria 1978–80, 1982–86, 1993, 1994; Ed. and Writer gregson/graham 1978–80; rep. in journs. and anthols.; mem. Writers' Union Can.; Address: c/o 3777 Jennifer Rd., Victoria, B.C. V8P 3X1.

**BOWERING, William David Samuel,** B.A., M.Sc., Ph.D., D.Sc.; university administrator; b. Vancouver, B.C. 16 Aug. 1932; s. Ebbie William and Marguerite Marie (Marshall) B.; e. Univ. of B.C. B.A. (Hons.) 1954, M.Sc. 1956); McGill Univ. Ph.D. 1960; Cambridge Univ. Ph.D. 1964; m. Patricia d. Bradford and Estelle Walsh 4 Oct. 1958; children: Andrew, Carolyn, Paul; PRESIDENT, OKANAGAN UNIVERSITY COLLEGE; Research Chemist, CIL 1961–65; Columbia Cellulose Ltd. 1965–69; College Prof., Asst. Dean, Dean, Vice-Pres., Pres., Okanagan Univ. College 1969– ; Mem., Central Okanagan Econ. Devel. Comn.; Okanagan Univ. College Faculty Assn. 1969–71; Trustee, Nat. Museum of Sci. & Tech.; Science Council of Canada 1991–92; Okanagan Symphony Soc. 1969–77; Kelowna Econ. Recovery Envir. Devel. Assn.; Applied Sci. Technologists & Technicians of B.C. (Hon. Mem.); Ritsumeikan Univ., Kyoto, Japan Hon. D.Sc. 1993; recreations: walking, boating, skiing; clubs: Kelowna Yacht; Home: 985 Augusta Court, Kelowna, B.C. V1Y 7T8; Office: 3333 College Way, Kelowna, B.C. V1V 1V7.

**BOWERS, Gerald C.,** B.A.; hydro executive; b. Montreal, Que. 12 May 1950; s. Clarke and Rachel (Fleming) B.; e. Memorial Univ. of Newfoundland B.A. (Econ.) 1974; m. Heather d. Peter and Audrey Walters 19 July 1975; children: Amy, Ross, Mark/ ASSISTANT TREASURER, NEWFOUNDLAND AND LABRADOR HYDRO 1986– ; Math Teacher, Henry Gordon Academy 1971–72; Staff Economist, Conference Board of Canada 1974–77; Sr. Engineering economist, Bell Canada 1977–80; Supervisor of Rates, Newfoundland & Labrador Hydro 1980–86; Dir., Boy Scouts, Older Boys Parliament of Quebec; Kideny Foundation of Canada

(NF Branch); Church Warden, St. Mark's Anglican Church St. John's; recreations: sailing; club: Terra Nova Sailing; Home 34 Eastmeadows Cres., St. John's, Nfld.; Office: P.O. Box 12400, St. John's, Nfld. A1B 4K7.

**BOWEY, James Lorne,** M.A.; professor; strategy consultant; b. Galt, Ont. 14 Oct. 1953; s. Lorne Henry and Lily Kemp (Rintoul) B.; e. Galt C.I. 1970; Mohawk Coll. of Applied Arts, dipl., Bus. Admin. 1975; Univ. of Lancaster, M.A. 1977; children: Kristen Ernesaks, Michael Lorne; PROFESSOR OF INTERNATIONAL BUSINESS, BISHOPS UNIV.; Pres., Bowey & Assoc. Inc. 1979– ; Mktg. Controller, Denny Stewart Shoes, Savage Shoes Inc. 1977–79; Sr. Partner, Santana Inc. 1980–84 (when it was bought by Warrington Inc.); Dir., Warrington Inc. 1984–87; Footwear & Leather Inst. of Can. 1982–88 (Chrmn., 1984–87); recreations: hockey, golf, skiing, squash; Home: 285 Vimy St. N., Sherbrooke, Que. J1J 3M6; Office: Bishop's Univ., Lennoxville, Que.

**BOWIE, Douglas Murray,** B.Sc.; writer; b. Kingston, Ont. 11 Feb. 1944; s. Murray Richardson and Catharine Elizabeth (Kidd) B.; e. Glebe Coll. Inst. Ottawa; Queen's Univ.; Carleton Univ., B.Sc. 1965; m. Joan d. John R. and Jane Dacey 23 Oct. 1971; one d. Alison; author over 30 films and TV dramas incl. 'Who Was the Lone Ranger' 1967; 'Amnesty' 1968; 'You and Me' 1971; 'Gunplay' 1971; 'U-Turn' 1973; 'Bargain Basement' 1974; 'The Man Who Wanted To Be Happy' 1975; 'A Gun, A Grand, A Girl' 1976; 'Scoop' 1977; 'The War Is Over' 1977; 'The Newcomers (The Italians) 1978; 'Empire, Inc.' TV mini-series 1983 broadcast 61 countries (4 ACTRA Awards incl. Best Writer TV Drama 1984); 'Love and Larceny' 1985 (Gemini Award Best TV movie 1986); 'The Boy in Blue' 1986; "Chasing Rainbows" 14 hour mini-series broadcast 1988; 'Obsessed' (Best Canadian Film, Montreal Film Festival 1988); 'Grand Larceny' 1991; 'The Noble Pursuit' (stage play) premiered 1991; co-editor: 'Best Canadian Screenplays' 1992; mem. ACTRA; Acad. Candn. Cinema; recreations: tennis, skiing, golf; Address: 414 Albert St., Kingston, Ont. K7L 3W3.

**BOWIE, Peter Guy,** B.Com., M.B.A., F.C.A.; chartered accountant; b. Ottawa, Ont. 16 June 1946; s. Thomas G. and Harriet J. (Plaxton) B.; e. St. Mary's Univ. B.Com. 1969; Univ. of Ottawa M.B.A. 1976, C.A. 1978; Advanced Management Program, Harvard 1993; m. Judith d. Robert and Elizabeth MacDonald 31 Aug. 1968; children: Kimberly, Shannon, Michelle, Alexis, Gregory; PARTNER, DELOITTE & TOUCHE 1983– ; Group Managing Partner; served Financial Mgmt. Northern Telecom; Microsystems International; Past Chrmn. and Dir. Ottawa-Carleton Econ. Devel. Corp.; Dir. Ottawa-Carleton Rsch. Inst.; Co-Chair, Univ. of Ottawa Vision Campaign; mem. Inst. C.A.'s Ont.; recreations: sailing, skiing; Clubs: Rideau; Country; Office: Royal Bank Centre, 90 Sparks St., Ottawa, Ont. K1P 5B4.

**BOWKER, Kenneth Wilkinson,** P.Eng., C.Eng., M.I.Mech.E.; air pollution equipment executive; b. England, U.K. 8 Jan. 1944; s. Leslie Wilkinson and Freda (Bellis) B.; e. P.Eng., M.I.Mech.E., Chartered Eng. H.N.C. plus part I & II of I.Mech.E. exams (B.Eng. equivalent), U.K. 1972; m. Kathleen d. Thomas and Ella Ellis 31 Dec. 1969; children: Carl Wilkinson, Karina Jane, Alison; EXTVE. VICE PRES., FLAKT CANADA LTD. 1990– ; Operations, Commissioning, Project Management, Gas Turbine Develop., Nuclear Reactor Operation, Central Electricity Generating Bd., U.K. 1960–74; Project Mgr., Combustion Engr. 1974–77; Dir., Service, Combustion Engr. 1977–82; Dir., Prod. & Cost Reduction, Combustion Engr. 1982–83; Vice-Pres., Power Systems Services, Combustion Engr. 1983–85; Vice-Pres., Opns., Combustion Engr. 1985–88; Pres., C.E. Vidaplate 1985–87; Pres. & Dir., Kone Wood Ltd. 1988–90; Dir., Kone Wood Internat. 1988–90; author/co-author, several tech. papers; Tutor, degree level course on power plant design/opn.; recreations: golf, squash, tennis, skiing; clubs: var. memberships; Home: 520 Minto Place, Rockcliffe, Ont. K1M 0A8.

**BOWKER, Wilbur Fee,** O.C., Q.C., LL.M., LL.D.; retired university professor; b. Ponoka, Alta. 18 Feb. 1910; s. George Elwyn and Ida Ethel (Pritchard) B.; e. Ponoka High Sch.; Univ. of Alta. B.A. 1930, LL.B. 1932, LL.D. 1972; Univ. of Minn. LL.M. 1953; Sterling Fellow Yale Law Sch. 1952–53; m. Marjorie d. Frank and Mary Montgomery 12 Oct. 1940; children: Blair, Lorna Pennie, Keith; law practice Edmonton 1932–42; served with Candn. Army 1942–45, rank Capt.; Prof. of Law Univ. of Alta. 1945–75, Dean of Law 1948–68; Dir. Alta. Law Reform Inst. 1968–75; mem. Uniform Law Conf. 1952–75, Pres. 1965; Pres. Candn. Assn. Law Teachers 1956, mem. since 1947; mem. Rsch. Ctte. Alta. Cancer Bd.

1975–84, Chrmn. 1980–84; Chrmn. Adv. Ctte. Dependent Adults Act 1982–85; Chrmn. Alta. Judicial Council 1988– ; Mem., Provincial Archives Advisory Board 1991– ; cr. K.C. 1951; Hon. Bencher Law Soc. Alta. 1976; Hon. Prof. of Law Univ. Calgary 1977; Hon. mem. Candn. Bar Assn. 1979, recipient Pres's Award 1989; Justice Medal Candn. Inst. Adm. Justice 1989; O.C. 1990; Atty.-Gen.'s Bldg. Edmonton named Bowker Bldg. 1981; Alta Chapter Phi Delta Phi named Bowker Inn 1985; Wilbur Bowker Visiting Professorship in Law Univ. Alta. estbd. by former students 1989; author 'Consolidation of Fifty Years of Legal Writings 1938–1988' 1989; mem. Rotary Edmonton; Freemason; Delta Kappa Epsilon; United Church; recreations: camping, travel; Home: 10925 – 85 Ave., Edmonton, Alta. T6G 0W3; Office: 402 Law Centre, Univ. of Alberta, Edmonton, Alta. T6G 2H5.

**BOWLBY, Bradford Hugh Blaikie,** Q.C., M.A., LL.B.; b. Toronto, Ont. 20 June 1916; s. Allington Tupper, Q.C. and Mary (Blaikie) B.; e. Univ. Toronto Schs.; Trinity Coll., Univ. Toronto B.A. 1938, M.A. 1939; m. Anne Elizabeth, d. William Otter Morris, 18 Sept. 1948; children: David Bradford Tupper, Margaret Jane, Sarah Elizabeth; PARTNER, BOWLBY & BOWLBY; Chrmn., Assessment Review Court 1976–85; Fed. Organizer, P.Cons. Party 1965; Chrmn., Inter Church Comte. on Legal Affairs; read law with Bowlby, Macdonald & Co., Toronto, Ont.; called to Bar of Ont. 1942; cr. Q.C. 1954; mem., Co. York Law Assn.; Toronto Central P.C. Assn. (Pres. 1955); Pres. St. Paul's P.C. Assn. 1963; P. Cons.; Anglican; recreations: curling, boating; Clubs: R.C.Y.C.; Toronto Cricket, Skating & Curling; Albany; Home: 8 Fairmeadow Ave., Willowdale, Ont. M2P 1W5; Office: 330 Bay St., Toronto, Ont. M5H 2S8.

**BOWLER, Harry,** C.A., A.C.I.S., P.Admin.; b. Edinburgh, Scot. 14 June 1925; s. Harry and Mary (Harper) B.; e. The James Clark Sch. Edinburgh; Skerry's Coll. Edinburgh; m. Helen d. George and Francis Darling 21 July 1950; children: Elspeth, Bruce, Scott; Pres. and Dir., Budd Canada Inc. 1986–91, retired, Treas. and Controller, Inco Ltd. New York 1969–73; Vice Pres. Finance Bell Canada 1973–80; Northumberland Consultants 1980–86; mem. Inst. C. A.'s Ont.; Inst. Chart. Secs. & Adms.; Financial Execs. Inst.; Rotary; United Ch.; recreation: gardening; Home: Box 87, Cobourg, Ont. K9A 4K2.

**BOWMAN, Clement Willis,** C.M., B.A.Sc., M.A.Sc., Ph.D.; engineering/science executive; b. Toronto, Ont. 7 Jan. 1930; s. Clement Willis and Emily (Stockley) B.; e. Univ. of Toronto B.A.Sc. 1952, M.A.Sc. 1958, Ph.D. 1961; m. Marjorie d. Albert and Laura Greer 1954; children: Elizabeth Ann, John Clement; TECHNOLOGY CONSULTANT, CLEMENT W. BOWMAN CONSULTING INC.; Plant & Rsch. Engr., C.I.L./DuPont of Can. 1952–57; Rsch. Engr., Imperial Oil Enterprises 1960–62; Rsch. Mgr., Syncrude Can. 1963–69; Chem. Rsch. Mgr., Imperial Oil Enterprises 1969–71; Petrol. Rsch. Mgr. 1971–75; Chrmn. & Chief Extve. Offr., Alta. Oil Sand Technol. & Rsch. Authy. 1975–84; Vice-Pres., Rsch. Dept., Esso Petrol. Can. 1984–86; Bd. Mem., Candn. Assn. for the World Petrol. Cong. 1985–87; Alta. Rsch. Council 1978–91 (Pres. 1987–91); Counc. Mem., Nat. Rsch. Counc. of Can. 1986–89; several former assn. extve. posts; recipient, 25 year 'Meritorious Serv. Medal' Univ. of Toronto Alumni Assn. 1977; Queen's Jubilee Medal 1977; Karl A. Clark Distinguished Service Award 1989; Centennial APEGGA Award 1989; Candn. Rsch. Mgmt. Assoc. Medalist 1991; Alta. Sci. and Technology Leadership Award 1991; Alberta Achievement Award 1991; R.S. Jane Memorial Lecture Award (CSChE) 1993; Hon. Fellow, Chem. Inst. of Canada 1993; Member of the Order of Canada 1994; Mem., Assn. of Profl. Engrs. of Ont.; Assn. of Profl. Engrs., Geol. & Geophys. of Alta.; Chem. Inst. of Can.; Candn. Soc. for Chem. Engrs.; Candn. Rsch. Mngt. Assn. (Vice-Chrmn. 1988, Chrmn. 1989); Fellow, Candn. Acad. of Engrg.; author/co-author of 25 articles/papers; holder of 13 patents; recreations: skiing, jogging; Address: 2112 Huron Shores Dr., R.R. #5, Sarnia, Ont. N7T 7H6.

**BOWMAN, Jon;** travel executive; b. Saint John, N.B. 8 Jan. 1940; s. Geoffrey W.B. and Barbara (Nagle) E.; e. Acadia Acad.; Acadia Univ.; m. Marion d. Jim and Dorothy Besse (now Mrs. Alexander Fisher); children: Janice, Scott, Karena; REGIONAL MANAGER, HARVEY'S TRAVEL LTD. 1979– ; Pres., Alliance of Candn. Travel Assns. 1985–86; mem., Moncton Lodge No. 229; BPO Elks of Can.; recreations: walking, sailing; Moncton Rotary; Clubs: River Gyro; Moncton Press; Home: 369 Callowhill Rd., Riverview, N.B. E1B 4N3; Office: 12 Cameron St., Box 1145, Moncton, N.B. E1C 8P6.

**BOWN, Herbert Gideon,** O.C., M.Eng., P.Eng.; consultant; b. Badger's Quay, Nfld. 22 Feb. 1943; s. Herbert Spenser and Gwendolyn (Barefoot) B.; e. Badger's Quay Sch. High Sch. Dip. 1959; Memorial Univ. of Nfld. Dip. Engr. 1962; Tech. Univ. of Nova Scotia B.Eng. 1964; M.Eng. 1966; Grad. Studies (Systems Engrg./Psych.) Carleton Univ. 1974–76; m. Maureen Elizabeth Woodrow; children: Stephen, Michael, David; PRESIDENT, C.E.O. AND FOUNDER, IDON CORPORATION 1983– ; PRESIDENT & C.E.O. OF SOFTVIEW CORP. 1986– ; Adjunct Prof., Computer Science, Memorial Univ. of Nfld.; Pres. & C.E.O., Idon Atlantic Inc. 1989– ; conducted R & D. and CAD and computer graphics in support of Candn. Space Prog., Def. Rsch. Telecommunications Est. 1966–69; with Dept. of Communications Rsch. Ctr., Govt. of Can. as Dir., Dir. Gen. of Info. and Tech.; Project and Prog. Mgr. Image Communications; and with Communications Rsch. Ctr. 1969–81; Vice-Pres. Corp. Devel., Vice-Pres. Sales & Mktg. NORPAK Corp., Kanata, Ont. 1981–83; Gov. Internat. Counc. for Computer Communications; Bd. of Dir., Candn. Ctr. for Marine Communications (CCMC); Candn. Advanced Technology Assoc. (CATA); Hon. mem. CBC Adv. Ctte. on Sci. and Tech.; author several technical publs.; mem. Assn. of Profl. Engrs. of Ont.; Inst. of Electrical and Electronics Engrs.; recipient Order of Can. 1984; Profl. Engr.'s Gold Medal 1983; Publ. Service Merit Award 1980; co-recipient Touche, Ross New Perspective Award 1981; recreations: sailing, skating; Home: 80 Waverley St., Ottawa, Ont. K2P 0V2.

**BOYANOWSKY, Ehor Orest,** B.A., M.S., Ph.D.; university professor; b. Toronto, Ont. 9 June 1943; s. Dmitro and Katerina (Choma) B.; e. Univ. of Western Ontario B.A. (Hon.) 1966; Univ. of Wisconsin M.S. 1968, Ph.D. 1971; 2nd m. Vicky d. James and Isobel Mulholland 1 Dec. 1986; children: Alexei James; Jennifer, Thea (previous marriage); PROFESSOR, SCHOOL OF CRIMINOLOGY, SIMON FRASER UNIV. 1975– ; Dalhousie Univ. 1971–74; Visiting Prof., Univ. of B.C. 1974–75; London Sch. of Econ. 1980; Vice-Pres., SFU Fac. Assn. 1982–83; Pres. 1983–84; Pres., Confed. of Fac. Assns. of B.C. (CUFABC) 1985; Mem., Univ. Senate 1985–87; Vice Pres., CUFABC 1993–94; Pres. CUFABC 1993–94; Cons. to NRC, SSHRCC, MRC, Harry Guggenheim Found. & several profl. journals; Univ. of W. Ont. Gold Key 1966; fellowships: Prov. of Ont. 1966, Can. Counc. 1969–70, SSHRCC Leave 1980; Vice-Pres., Steelhead Soc. of B.C. 1986–89; Pres. 1990–92; Mem., Can. & Am. Psych. Assns.; Fellow, Internat. Soc. for Rsch. on Aggression; author of 30 profl. articles & monographs in crim. & psych. and 28 freelance articles on outdoors & river conservation; recreations: fly-fishing, writing, photography; club: Totem Fly Fishers; Home: 8089 Pasco Rd., W. Vancouver, B.C. V7W 2T5; Office: Burnaby, B.C. V5A 1S6.

**BOYCHUK, Ernest Carl,** LL.B.; judge; b. Saskatoon, Sask. 29 Mar. 1934; s. John and Anna B.; e. Univ. of Sask. B.A. 1956, LL.B. 1958; m. Linda Elizabeth July 1983; children: Christopher, Daryl, Philip, Terrance, Marianne; ASSOC. CHIEF JUDGE, PROV. COURT OF SASK. 1982– ; articled Rees, Shmigelsky, Schmeiser 1958; Partner 1960; City Prosecutor, Saskatoon 1963; Asst. City Solicitor 1965; Judge, Prov. Court of Sask. 1967; Ombudsman, Prov. of Sask. 1973; apptd. Q.C. 1976; Chief Judge, Prov. Court of Sask. 1976; Chrmn., Sask. Pub. Sector, Price & Compens. Bd. 1976; Sask. Pub. Utilities Review Comn. 1982; Chrmn., Provincial Store Hours Inquiry 1992– ; Extve. & Commdg. Offr., H.M.C.S. Unicorn, rank Comdr.; Hon. Aide de Campe, Gov. Gen. Vanier; Mitchner; Lt. Gov. Worobetz; Candn. Forces Decoration; Centennial Medal; Silver Jubilee Medal; Sea Cadet Scholarship; Nat. Defense Telescope; Best Class Leader of the Empire Award; Cadet Tatoo Award; Pres., Vice-Pres. & Sr. Stick, Coll. of Law; Pres., Jr. & Internat. Optimist Club; Dir., John Howard Soc.; Candn. Found. fo Ukrainian Studies; Hockey Comnr., Saskatoon & Regina; Adv. Bd., Campion Coll., Univ. of Regina; mem., Internat. Platform Assn.; Sask. Bar Assn.; Candn. Bar Assn.; Internat. Bar Assn.; Ombudsman Ctte.; Ombudsman Adv. & Acad. Adv. Bds.; Pres., Ukrainian Canadian Business & Professional Club, Saskatoon 1990–93; author 'Saskatchewan Ombudsman Reports' 1973, 1974, 1975; Home: 321 Avenue L North, Saskatoon, Sask. S7L 2P5.

**BOYD, David William,** B.Sc., M.A., Ph.D., F.R.S.C.; educator; b. Toronto, Ont. 17 Sept. 1941; s. Glenn Kelvin and Rachael Cecilia (Garvock) B.; e. Carleton Univ. B.Sc. 1963; Univ. of Toronto M.A. 1964, Ph.D. 1966; m. Mary Margaret d. John and Estelle Shields 26 Sept. 1964; children: Deborah, Paul, Kathryn; PROF. OF MATH., UNIV. OF B.C. 1974– ; Head of Dept. 1986–89; Asst. Prof. of Math., Univ. of Alta. 1966–67; Asst.

Prof. of Math. Cal. Inst. of Technol. 1967–70, Assoc. Prof. 1970–71; Assoc. Prof. of Math. present Univ. 1971–74; Visiting Prof. Univ. of Paris 1981; E.W.R. Steacie Prize for Sci. 1978; mem. Math. Assn. Am.; Am. Math. Soc.; Candn. Math. Soc. (mem. Council 1973–75, Vice Pres. 1979–81); recreations: music, hiking, cycling; Office: Vancouver, B.C. V6T 1Z2.

**BOYD, James Henderson,** R.C.A., F.I.A.L.; artist; b. Ottawa, Ont. 16 Dec. 1928; s. William Abercrombie and Mary (Henderson) B.; e. Ottawa Tech. High Sch.; Art Students League N.Y.; Nat. Acad. N.Y.; Contemporaries Workshop N.Y.; Vignette Engraver Canadian Bank Note 1946–52; free-lance CBC; Resident Artist Univ. of W. Ont. 1967–69, mem. Senate Hon. Degree Comte. 1968–69, Chrmn. Art Acquisitions Ctte. and Curator Art Coll,; Head of Printmaking, Ont. Coll. of Art 1970–71, Faculty 1971–73; part-time lectr. Univ. of Ottawa 1973–89; Condordia Univ. 1976–77; rec'd First Prize 1st Nat. Print Show Vancouver; 'Venezuela Prize,' Chile Biennale 1965; executed murals: J.W.I. Industries; Schoeler and Heaton, Archs.; Ext. of Univ. of Ottawa, Macdonald Bldg; carved doors Campbellton Lib.; Maritime Museum, Summerside, P.E.I.; PSAC Bldg. Ottawa; Entr. Sculpture, Cdn. Pav., EXPO '70, Japan; rep. in various perm. colls. incl. Nat. Gallery Can.; Museum of Modern Art N.Y.; Victoria & Albert Museum; Lugano Art Gallery; Art Gallery Ont.; Nat. Art Gallery S. Africa; Museum of Contemporary Art, Skopje, Yugoslavia; exhbns.: 18th Int. Biennial of Graphic Art, Ljubljana, Yugoslavia; Int. Biennial of Humour & Satire, Gabrovo, Bulgaria 1989; mem. Accademia Italia delle Arti & del Lavoro (with Gold Medal); Statue of Victory, (World Culture Prize) Italy 1984; Premio Milano 1988; Candn. Artists Representation (Spokesperson, Local Rep. Ottawa 1978; Vice Spokesperson Ont. 1974–75; Chief Steward, CUEW, local 10, Univ. of Ottawa 1990–91); Extve., Part-time Professors, Univ. of Ottawa 1992; Candn. High Commissioner for House of Boyd Soc.; Home: Matawatchan, Ont.; Mailing Address: P.O. Box 2400, Stn. D., Ottawa, Ont. K1P 5W5.

**BOYD, Liona,** B.Mus., C.M., O.O., LL.D.; musician; composer; classical guitarist; b. London, Eng.; d. John Haig and Eileen (Hancock) B.; came to Can. 1957; e. Kipling Coll. Inst. 1967; Univ. of Toronto B.Mus. 1972; Eli Kassner Guitar Acad.; m. John B. Simon, California 1992; studied with Alexandre Lagoya; internat. concert artist and T.V. personality; performed concerts in North, South & Central America, Japan, China, Europe, India, Nepal, Cuba, Jamaica, Britain, Singapore, Hong Kong, Indonesia, Thailand, Malasia, Mexico, Egypt, New Zealand and Turkey; 19 long playing records (with CBS/Sony & A&M Records): 'The Guitar'; 'Artistry of Liona Boyd'; 'Miniatures for Guitar'; 'The First Lady of the Guitar'; 'The First Nashville Guitar Quartet' (with Chet Atkins); 'Liona Boyd with Andrew Davis conducting Eng. Chamber Orchestra'; 'Spanish Fantasy'; 'A Guitar for Christmas'; 'Virtuoso'; 'Live in Tokyo'; 'The Best of Liona Boyd'; 'The Romantic Guitar of Liona Boyd'; 'Persona'; 'Encore'; 'Highlights'; 'Paddle to the Sea'; 'Christmas Dreams'; 'Dancing on the Edge'; 'My Own Favourites'; 2 gold records, 1 platinum record; music books: 'Liona Boyd First Lady of the Guitar'; 'Miniatures for Guitar'; 'A Guitar for Christmas'; 'Folk songs from around the World'; 'Meet Liona on the Guitar'; 'Favourite Solos'; many compositions incl. 'Concerto Baroquissimo' and 'My Land of Hiawatha'; TV performances incl. CBC Superspecial 'Liona' 1978, Documentary 'First Lady of the Guitar'; as well as numerous appearances on television talk shows (incl. the 'Tonight Show'), variety shows, and Boston Pops; has performed privately for Ronald Reagan, Margaret Thatcher, Queen Elizabeth II of England, King and Queen of Spain, Fidel Castro, and President of Mexico; Summit Conf. at Montebello; opening act for Gordon Lightfoot 1978 and Tracy Chapman 1989; compositions and arrangements sound track to CBC TV Drama 1979; premiered 'Concerto of the Andes' by Richard Fortin, Costa Rica 1990; rec'd Juno Award 4 times; Vanier Award 1979; Member, Order of Canada 19..; Order of Ont. 1991; Winner of Poll, 'Guitar Player Mag.' U.S., Best classical guitarist 1985, 86, 87, 88; inducted into the Guitar Player Hall of Fame 1993; performed on Royal Command Gala performance, Edinburgh, July 1985; LL.D. (h.c.) Univ. of Lethbridge 1982, Brock Univ. 1990, Simon Fraser Univ. 1991; Hon. Mayor of San Antonio, Texas; mem. Am. Fed. Musicians; Address: c/o SOCAN, 41 Vallebrook Dr., Toronto, Ont. M3B 2S6.

**BOYD, Michael Manford,** B.A., M.B.A.; investment banker; b. London, Ont. 15 Aug. 1951; s. Manford William and the late Janice Elaine (Kolfage) B.; e. Univ. of W. Ont., B.A. 1974, M.B.A. 1976; m. Shelagh; children: Conan A., Amanda D., Kathleen N., Hannah J.; Senior Vice-Pres., Syndication Marleau, Lemire Securities Inc.; Pres. Junior Industrial Finance Corp. 1990–92; former Pres. and Dir. BG Acorn Management Ltd. 1983–88; Dir. Epic Data Inc.; Invest. Analyst, Bank of Montreal 1976–77; Invest. Offr. RoyNat Inc. 1977–78; Invest Mgr. Toronto Dominion Bank, TD Capital Group 1978–80; Vice Pres. Citibank Canada 1980–83; Past Dir. Assn. Candn. Venture Capital Co's; recreations: riding, orchid grower, pigeon fancier; Club: Eglinton and Caledon Hunt; Home: 12 Country Club Dr., Etobicoke, Ont. M9A 3J4.

**BOYD, Neil Thomas,** LL.B., LL.M.; university professor; b. Deep River, Ont. 30 Oct. 1951; s. Alan William and Betty Margaret B.; e. Univ. of W. Ont., B.A. 1974; Osgoode Hall Law Sch., LL.B. 1977, LL.M. 1979; m. Isabel d. Ted and Stella Hocking 29 Dec. 1980; one s. Christopher; Dir., Criminology Research Centre, Simon Fraser Univ. 1986–87, 1988–89; Dir., Sch. of Criminology, Simon Fraser Univ. 1987–88; research consultant, Min. of Justice & Solicitor-Gen. (Can.), Statistics Can.; Osgoode Hall Law Sch. Competition Fellowship 1977; mem., Amnesty Internat.; Candn. Civil Liberties Assn.; Oxfam Can.; author 'High Society: Legal and Illegal Drugs in Canada' 1991; 'The Last Dance: Murder in Canada' 1988; ed./author 'The Social Dimensions of Law' 1986; Extve. Prod. (educational television documentaries): 'Pleasure and Pain: Drug Use and Abuse' 1986; 'The Last Dance' 1989; recreations: running, tennis; Home: Mt. Gardner, Bowen Island, B.C. V0N 1G0; Office: Burnaby, B.C. V5A 1S6.

**BOYD, The Hon. Phyllis Marion,** M.P.P., B.A.; politician; b. Toronto, Ont. 26 Mar. 1946; d. Archibald Clinton and Dorothy Cora (Merrill) Watt; e. York Univ. B.A. (Hons.) 1968; m. Terry M. s. Irving and Marian B. 10 Sept. 1966; child: Christina Nicole; ATTORNEY-GENERAL AND MINISTER OF WOMEN'S ISSUES, PROV. OF ONT. 1993– ; Extve. Asst. to Pres., York Univ. 1971–73; York Univ. Fac. Assn. 1974–77; Admin., Kaleidoscope Presch. Res. Ctr. 1977–81; Admin. Asst., Profl. & Mng. Assn., UWO 1982–84; Extve. Dir., London Battered Women's Advocacy Clinic 1984–90; Pres., London Status of Women Action Group 1982–84 & 1986–87; Bd. Mem., Thames Valley Addiction Assessment & Ref. Ctr. 1987–90; Mem. & Sec., London Daycare Adv. Ctte. 1986–90; Bd. of Dir., London Cross Cult. Learner Ctr. 1985–90; London Coord. Ctte. on Family Violence 1984–90; Min. of Educ., Ont. 1990–91; Min. of Community and Social Services, Ont., with Responsibility for Women's Issues 1991–93; Outstanding Young Londoner 1986; Mary Campbell Community Service Award 1990; John Robinson Award 1990; author: 'Report on the Impact of Provincial Initiatives on Wife Assault in the London-Middlesex Area' 1989 and a 1985 Handbook for Counsellors & Advocates of Battered Women; editor: 'Report on the Fourth Nat. Conf. on Women in Coll. & Univ. in Canada' 1974; Offices: 637 Dundas St. E., Centretown Mall, London, Ont. N5W 2Z1 (const.); 11th Floor, 720 Bay St., Toronto, Ont. M5G 2K1.

**BOYD, Robert Edward,** C.A.; financial executive; b. Moose Jaw, Sask. 20 Feb. 1939; s. the late John Robert and late Irene Weltha (Bandle) B.; C.A. 1971; m. Faye d. Dick Reid 15 July 1965; EXTVE. VICE PRES. FINANCE AND CHIEF FINANCIAL OFFR., THE OSHAWA GROUP LIMITED 1991– ; various sr. financial positions Gulf Canada Ltd. Calgary/Toronto, Gulf Mineral Resources Toronto, Gulf Oil Corp. Pittsburgh 1956–85; Chief Financial Offr., Oxford Development Group Ltd. Toronto 1985–89; Chief Financial Offr., Jannock Ltd. 1990–91; mem. Council Financial Execs. Conf. Bd. Can.; Ottawa Liason Ctte., Candn. Chamber of Comm.; Financial Execs. Inst.; Candn. Inst. of Chartered Accountants; recreations: squash, tennis, skiing; Club: Oakville; Home: 180 Maple Grove Dr., Oakville, Ont. L6J 4V1; Office: 302 The East Mall, Etobicoke, Ont. M9B 6B8.

**BOYD, Winnett,** B.A.Sc., P.Eng.; b. Prestatyn, N. Wales, 17 Oct. 1916; s. Winnett Wornibe (Cndn.) and Marjorie Sterne (St. George) B. (Am.); came to Can. 1917; e. Trinity Coll. Sch., Port Hope, Ont.; Somers Coll., Bermuda; Jarvis Coll. Inst., Toronto, Ont.; Univ. of Toronto, B.A.Sc., 1939 (1st of 166, sev. scholarships); Mass. Inst. Tech. post grad. studies (on scholarship); m. Jean Winnifred Ransom, d. Mrs. N. C. Sutherland, Town of Mount Royal, Que., 30 May 1942; two d., Wendy Susan Lee Lloyd, Pamela Ann Boyd; PRESIDENT, WINNETT BOYD LTD. 1981– ;and BMG Cycles Inc. 1986– ; Teaching Asst., Mass. Inst. Tech., 1939–40; Jr. Engr., Demerara Bauxite Co., Brit. Guiana, 1940–41; Engr., Aluminum Co. of Canada Ltd., Montreal, 1941–42; Shawinigan Falls, P.Q., 1942–43; with Nat. Research Council, 1943–44, studying jet engines in England; with Turbo Research Ltd., 1944–46 (i/c Engine Design Sec., 1945–46); joined A. V. Roe Can. Ltd., Gas Turbine Engn. Divn., 1946–50; Chief Designer, 1946–48; Asst. Chief Engr. and Chief Designer, 1948–50; Sr. Partner, Winnett Boyd Associates, Pres., Winnett Boyd Ltd., 1951–59; Pres., Arthur D. Little of Can. Ltd. 1959–81; 1951–57, Chief Mech. Engr., in charge NRU reactor design for the C. D. Howe Co. Ltd.; during period of employment with Turbo Research Ltd., and A. V. Roe Can. Ltd., undertook and completed design of Canada's first jet engine the 'Chinook,' and later the 'Orenda'; since April 1956 conceived, designed and promoted the Daniels-Boyd Nuclear Steam Generator (world rights acquired by Arthur D. Little Inc.); mem., Assn. of Prof. Engrs. Ont.; joined R.C.N.V.R., Sept. 1943 as Sub. Lieut. (E), and seconded to Nat. Research Council, Nov. 1943 to engage in jet engine work in Eng.; attended 2 Pugwash Confs; found. mem. Cdn. Assoc. for Club of Rome; def. PC cand. for York-Scarborough, g.e. Oct. 1972; founded BMG Publishing Limited 1974; currently promoting his patented back-pedalling brake for multi-speed bicycles; awarded U. of T. Engineering Alumni Medal in 1948 at age 31 (youngest recipient ever) for his jet engine work; inducted into U. of T. Engineering Alumni Hall of Distinction in 1981; Anglican; recreations: skiing, swimming, cycling; Clubs: Toronto; Montreal Badminton & Squash; Home: 107 Victoria Place, R.R. No. 1, Bobcaygeon, Ont. K0M 1A0; Office: Flexmaster Bldg., 20 West Pearce St., Richmond Hill, Ont. L4B 1E3.

**BOYER, James Patrick,** Q.C., B.A., M.A.; LL.B.; writer; lawyer; b. Bracebridge, Ont. 1945; s. Robert James and Patricia M. B.; e. Carleton Univ., B.A. (Hons.); Univ. of Toronto, M.A., LL.B.; studied French Candn. Lit., Univ. de Montreal; Internat. Law, Acad. of Internat. Court of Justice, The Hague; m. Corinne Mudde 15 Aug. 1970; el. to H. of C. for Etobicoke-Lakeshore g.e. 1984; re-el. g.e. 1988; lawyer, Fraser & Beatty until 1989; Parliamentary Sec. to the Sec. of State for External Affairs 1989–91; Parliamentary Sec. to Min. of National Defense 1991–93; Chrmn., Parlty. Ctte. on Equality Rights & Parlty. Ctte. on Status of Disabled Persons; Extve. Dir., Fed. Task Force on Conflict of Interest 1983–84; Extve. Asst. to former Ont. Attorney Gen. A. Wishart; has served on several standing cttes.; Chrmn., PC Caucus Ctte. on Redistrib. & Election Law; Mem., Ont. & N.W.T. bars; Candn. Civil Liberties Assn.; Amnesty Internat.; The Churchill Soc.; Nature Conservancy of Can.; Candn. Inst. of Internat. Affairs; Arctic Inst. of N. Am.; Candn. Counc. on Internat. Law; Writers' Union of Can.; author: 'Political Rights' 1981, 'Lawmaking by the People' 1982, 'Money and Message' 1983, 'Election Law in Canada' 1987, 'Local Elections in Canada' 1988; 'The People's Mandate' 1992; 'Direct Democracy in Canada' 1993; 'Hands-On Democracy' 1993; as well as weekly newspaper column & articles; specialist in election law and democratic procedures; Residence: 'Mimico' 2583 Lakeshore Blvd. W., Etobicoke, Ont. M8V 1G3.

**BOYER, William S.,** B.A., B.Ed.; headmaster; b. Toronto, Ont. 16 July 1952; s. Edgar Alexander and Margaret Kathleen (Hedge) B.; e. Univ. of Toronto B.A. 1976, B.Ed. 1977; m. T. Colleen d. Paul and Lorraine Buckley 16 Oct. 1976; children: Justin Alexander, Sean James; HEADMASTER, TORONTO FRENCH SCHOOL 1992– ; Teacher, Crescent School 1977–89; Head, French Dept. 1980–89; Dir. of Admissions 1987–89; Headmaster, Neuchâtel Jr. College Switz. 1989–92; summers: Teacher, North York Bd. of Edn. 1984, Cours d'été à Nice 1980, '81; Principal, Summer French Program, St. Pierre et Miquelon and Villefranche, France 1981, '82, 85; Martinique 1986, '87; Dir. Summer Lang. Prog., Blyth & Co. 1988; Principal, Neuchâtel Jr. Coll. 1991; Dir., Canada-Swiss Assn. 1991–92; Neuchâtel Internat. Club 1991–92; recreations: reading, sports, travel; Home: 294 Lawrence Ave. E., Toronto, Ont. M4N 1T7; Office: 318 Lawrence Ave. E., Toronto, Ont. M4N 1T7.

**BOYLE, Christine Lesley Maureen,** LL.M.; educator; b. Lisburn, N. Ireland 10 Mar. 1949; d. James Leslie and Norah (Duff) B.; e. Queens Univ. Belfast LL.B. 1971; Queen's Univ. Kingston LL.M. 1972; m. Thomas H. s. Helen and Donald Kemsley 16 May 1985; PROF. OF LAW, UNIV. OF B.C. 1992– ; Barrister-at-Law Inn of Court of N. Ireland 1973; called to Bar of N.S. 1984; Lectr. in Law Queens Univ. Belfast 1972–73, Visiting Lectr. 1978–79; Lectr. in Law Univ. of W. Indies 1973–75; Asst. and Assoc. Prof. of Law Univ. of Windsor 1975–81; Prof. of Law, Dalhousie Univ. 1981–92; Walter S. Owen Visiting Prof., Univ. of B.C. 1990–92; author 'Sexual Assault' 1984; co-ed. 'Contracts, Cases and Commentaries' 4th ed. 1989; recreations: reading, gardening; Home: 1593 Larch St., Vancouver, B.C. V6K 3N6.

**BOYLE, Harry J.,** O.C. (1977); D.Litt.; executive and writer; b. St. Augustine, Ont. 7 Oct. 1915; s. William A. and Mary Madeleine (Leddy) B.; e. Wingham (Ont.) High Sch.; St. Jerome's Coll., Kitchener, Ont.; m. Marion, d. Michael McCaffrey, 3 Jan. 1937; children: Patricia, Michael; publisher of small mag. 1934; subsequently freelance writer and newspaper stringer in W. Ont., especially for 'The London Free Press' and 'The Toronto Globe and Mail'; Radio Stn. CKNX, Wingham, Ont., 1936–41; 'The Stratford Beacon-Herald,' 1941–42; joined CBC as Farm Commentator, 1942; became Supvr., Farm Broadcasts, Program Dir., Trans-Can. Network and Radio Network Supvr. of Features; Dir., Nat. Farm Radio Forum, 1942–46; Visiting Fellow, Inst. of Candn. Studies, Carleton Univ. 1968–69; mem. Faculty, Banff Sch. of Fine Arts; radio credits incl.: 'CBC Wednesday Night,' 'Assignment' and 'Project' series; weekly columnist 'The Toronto Telegram' 1957–68; Vice-chrmn. 1968–76, Chrmn., C.R.T.C. Comm. 1976–77; Columnist, Montreal Star 1978; mem. Ont. Arts. Council, 1979–82; wrote no. of radio plays incl. 'Strike' and 'The Macdonalds of Oak Valley'; also stage play 'The Inheritance' produced by Museum Theatre, Toronto, 1950; author of 'Mostly in Clover' (essays) 1961; 'Homebrew and Patches' (essays) 1963 (winner of Leacock Medal for Humour); 'A Summer Burning' (novel) 1964; 'With a Pinch of Sin' (novel) 1966; 'Straws in the Wind' (essays) 1969; 'The Great Canadian Novel' 1972; 'Memories of a Catholic Boyhood' (novel) 1973; 'The Luck of the Irish' (novel) 1975; John Drainie Award by Assn. Candn. Television and Radio Artists for his contrib. to broadcasting, 1970; winner, Leacock Medal for Humour 1975; Hon. D.Litt. Trent Univ. 1974 and Hon. Fellow of Lady Eaton Coll. there; Hon. L.L.D. (Concordia Univ.) 1978; named to Candn. Newspaper Hall of Fame 1979; Jack Chisholm Award, Candn. Film & TV Dir. Ass., 1980; The Rogers Award for Distinguished Service to Broadcasting 1983; Award from the Assn. for the Study of Candn. Radio and Televison 1986; mem., Writers' Union; R. Catholic; Club: Arts & Letters; Home: 12 Georgian Crt., Toronto, Ont. M4P 2J8.

**BOYLE, J. Allan;** banker; b. Orillia, Ont. 10 May 1916; s. Mr. and Mrs. W. J. Boyle; e. Orillia (Ont.) Coll. Inst.; Univ. of W. Ont., Mang. Training Course; Hon. Dir., Coscan Development Corp.; Retired Pres., Toronto-Dominion Bank; joined the Toronto-Dominion Bank, Orillia, Ont. 1934, serving subsequently at Toronto and N.Y., Special Rep. N.Y. 1956, Agent N.Y. 1964, Asst. Gen. Mgr. H.O. Internat. Div. 1966; Gen. Mgr. Adm. 1968, Depy. Chief Gen. Mgr. 1968; Exec. Vice-Pres. and Chief Gen. Mgr. 1972; Pres. 1978 (now retired); served with R.C.A.F. 1940–45; Cndn. Bankers' Assn. (Pres. 1974–75); Past Pres. Can. Club of Toronto; Toronto Redevelopment Adv. Council; recreations: golf, curling, bridge; Clubs: Thornhill Country; Granite; York; Toronto; Sara Bay Country, (Sarasota, Fla.); Office: Toronto-Dominion Centre, Toronto, Ont. M5K 1A2.

**BOYLE, John B.;** artist; b. London, Ont. 1941; e. self-taught; solo exhibitions incl.: Nancy Poole's Studio 1972–76, 77, 78, 81, 83, 84, 85, 89 & 91, London Reg. Gall. retrospective 1991, Susan Whitney Gall. Regina 1986, Tom Thomson Mem. Gall. 1983, Latcham Gall. 1982, Saidye Bronfman Ctr. 1977, London Reg. Gall. 1974, Rodman Hall Arts Ctr. St. Catharines 1971, 20/20 Gall. 1967; group exhibitions incl.: Univ. of Waterloo Gall. 1991, 'Political Landscapes' Tom Thomson Gall. Owen Sound 1989, McIntosh Pub. Gall. 1989, Nancy Poole's Studio, 'About Faces' 1988, Art Space Peterborough 1986, Edge and Image, Concordia Univ. 1984, London Reg. Gall. 1984 and numerous others; internat. exhibitions incl.: toured Europe with 13 other artists 4 pub. galls. in Belgium 1985–86 and Pavillon des Arts, Paris (hard cover catalogue 'Human Touch'), Mus. of Contemporary Art, Mons, Belgium 1979, 'Rural Consciousness,' circulated London, N.Y., Paris 1978–79, 'Canada Trajectoires' Musée d'Art Moderne Paris 1973, 3-man show, Blansko, Czech. 1971; grants & awards incl.: Canada Council 'A' Grant 1987, Suncor Comn. 1984, Ont. CAD/CAM comn. 1983, 'New Queen St. Subway Mural' comn. 1980; collections: Canada Council Art Bank, Nat. Gall. of Can., Art Gall. of Ont., Montreal Mus. of Fine Arts, London Reg. Art Gall., U.W.O., Corp. of the City of Toronto, Clarkson Gordon Coll., Tom Thomson Mem. Art Gall., Rodman Hall Arts Ctr., CIL Coll., Brock Univ., Norcen Coll. Dalhousie Univ. Coll., Confed. Gall. P.E.I., E. York Bd. of Edn., Beaverbrook Art Gall., Woodstock Public Gall.; subject of several reviews & articles; Office: c/o Nancy Poole's Studio, 16 Hazelton Ave., Toronto, Ont. M5R 2E2.

**BOYLE, Joseph,** B.A., Ph.D.; university professor; b. Philadelphia, Pa. 30 July 1942; s. Joseph M. and Marion T. (Siegfried) B.; e. La Salle Univ. B.A. 1965; Georgetown Univ. Ph.D. 1970; postdoctoral studies, Brown Univ. 1975–76; m. Barbara E. d. Andrew and Mary Anne Dean 4 June 1966; children: Marion, Thomas, Deirdre, Mary Anne; PRINCIPAL, ST. MICHAEL'S COLLEGE, UNIV. OF TORONTO 1991– ; Asst. Prof. of Philosophy, St. Fidelis Coll. 1968–70; Aquinas Coll. 1970–76; Univ. of St. Thomas 1976–81; Assoc. Prof. 1981–86; Prof. of Philos., St. Michael's College, Univ. of Toronto 1986– ; Edit. Bd. Mem., 'Am. Cath. Philos. Q.,' 'Am. J. of Jurisprudence,' 'Linacre Q.'; Book Review Ed., 'Linacre Q.'; Cons., The Pope John Center; Pres., Am. Cath. Philos. Assn. 1989; co-author: 'Free Choice' 1976, 'Life and Death with Liberty and Justice' 1979, 'Catholic Sexual Ethics' 1985, 'Nuclear Deterrence, Morality and Realism' 1987; author of over 50 scholarly articles; Home: 126 Barton Ave., Toronto, Ont. M6G 1P9; Office: 81 St. Mary St., Toronto, Ont. M5S 1J4.

**BOYLE, Leonard Eugene,** O.C., O.P., S.T.M., D.Phil.; priest; b. Donegal, Ireland 13 Nov. 1923; s. Owen and Margaret (Walsh) B.; e. var. schs. in Ireland; Oxford Univ. D.Phil. 1956; Dominican Order S.T.M. 1982; PREFECT, VATICAN LIBRARY 1984– ; joined Dominican Order 1943; o. priest 1949; Prof., Hist. of Theology, Univ. of St. Thomas, Rome 1956–61; Prof., Palaeography and Diplomatics, Pontifical Inst. of Medieval Studies, Toronto 1961–84; Fellow, Roy. Hist. Soc. London 1963; Fellow, Medieval Acad. of Am. 1980; Pres., Comité international de paléographie 1985– ; Pres., Fédération internationale des Instituts d'études médiévales 1988– ; corresponding Fellow, British Acad. 1988; Gen. Ed.: 'Calendar of Papal Registers Relative to Great Britain and Ireland' 1970– ; author: 'A Survey of the Vatican Archives' 1972; 'The Community of SS. Sisto and Clemente' 1977; 'Pastoral Care, Clerical Education and Canon Law, 1200–1400' 1981; 'Medieval Latin Palaeography: A Bibliographical Introduction' 1984; Officer, Order of Canada 1987; Home: Biblioteca Apostolica Vaticana, Vatican City, 00120 Italy.

**BOYLE, Willard Sterling,** M.Sc., Ph.D., F.A.P.S.; physicist; association executive; b. Amherst, N.S. 9 Aug. 1924; s. Ernest Sterling and Bernice Teresa (Dewar) B.; e. Lower Can. Coll. 1942; McGill Univ. B.Sc. 1947, M.Sc. 1948, Ph.D. (Physics) 1950; m. Aileen Elizabeth d. Alfred Leslie Joyce 15 June 1946; children: Robert, Cynthia, David, Pamela; Asst. Prof. Royal Mil. Coll. Kingston 1951–53; mem. Tech. Staff Bell Labs 1953–62; Dir. Space Science Centre Bell Communications 1962–64; Dir. and Extve. Dir. Semicontor & Integrated Circuit Devel. Bell Labs 1964–74, Extve. Dir. Research on Lightwave Communication, Quantum Electronics, Digital Electronics 1974–79; Consultant to govt. and industry on mang. science and technol. in affiliation with Atlantic Research Associates 1979; served with RCNVR 1942–46, Fleet Air Arm, Pilot Operations with RN, rank Lt.; author over 40 tech. papers electronics, solid state physics, plasma physics; holds 16 patents incl. Fundamental Patents on Charge Coupled Devices and Semi Conductor Junction Laser; recipient Ballantine Medal Franklin Inst.; Morris Liebman Award Inst. Elect. & Electronic Engrs.; LL.D. (Hon.) Dalhousie Univ. 1984; el. to Nat. Acad. Engn. 1973; Fellow, Inst. Elect. & Electronic Engrs.; mem. Am. Assn. Advanc. Science; Royal Candn. Legion; recreation: sailing; Address: P.O. Box 180, Wallace, N.S. B0K 1Y0.

**BOYLE, William John Sydney,** M.A.; cultural executive; b. Toronto, Ont. 10 May 1948; s. John Allan and Doris Sydney (Mullett) B.; e. York Univ. B.A. 1969, M.A. 1971; GEN. MGR. AND C.E.O., HARBOURFRONT CENTRE 1991– ; Dir., Public Programmes, Harbourfront 1986– , Dir., The Power Plant Gall. 1987–89; Founding Exec. Dir. Visual Arts Ont. 1974–83; Exec., 10th Internat. Sculpture Conf. 1976–78; Visual Arts Co-ordr. C-I-L Inc. 1982–83; Bd. mem. Toronto Sculpture Garden 1983–89; Chrmn. Internat. Exposure Candn. Artists Nat. Conf. 1983; Dir., The Art Gallery at Harbourfront 1983–87; Mgr. Visual Art Harbourfront Corp. 1983–87; mem. Arts Adm. Adv. Counc. Univ. of Waterloo 1984– ; Hosp. for Sick Children Fundraising Ctte.; Chrmn. The Cultural Imperative nat. arts conf. 1985; ed. 'Art in Architecture: Art for the Built Environment' 1982; 'Visual Arts Handbook' 1978, 2nd ed. 1982; 'The Facts of Art' 1982; 'Index of Ontario Artists' 1976; 'Artviews Magazine' 1977–84; 'Artist's Guide for Native Communities' 1980; 'Toronto Art and Artist's Guide' 1983; 'Gallery Annual' 1985; 'Cityforms' guide to pub. art 1978; various gallery exhn. catalogues 1983–89; numerous articles; Pres. Assn. Cultural Execs. 1983–84, Bd. mem. 1979–84; Bd. mem. Ont. Assn. Art Galleries 1980–83; Bd. mem. Internat. Readings at Harbourfront 1986– , Bd. mem., The Power Plant 1987– ; Mem., Public Art Policy Adv. Ctte., Metropolitan Toronto 1988– ; Bd. mem., Internat. Sculpture Source, Washington, D.C. 1987–88; Home: 428 Sumach St., Toronto, Ont. M4X 1V5; Office: 410 Queen's Quay W., Toronto, Ont. M5V 1A2.

**BOZINOFF, Lorne,** B.Com., M.B.A., M.Ed., M.A., M.Sc., M.I.R., Ph.D., C.M.C.; market and public opinion executive; b. Toronto, Ont. 14 Sept. 1953; s. Chris and Mary (Pavloff) B.; e. Univ. of Toronto B.Com. 1976, M.B.A. 1977, Ph.D. 1980, M.Ed. 1982, M.A. 1983, M.Sc. 1985, M.I.R. 1989; m. Cynthia Mikan; SR. VICE PRES. GALLUP CANADA INC. 1987– ; part-time lectr. Univ. of Toronto; Prof. of Mktg. Pa. State Univ. 1981–82; Mktg. Rsch. Mgr. Bell Canada 1982–85; Sr. Cons. Coopers and Lybrand 1985–87; co-author 'The Gallup Report' publ. twice weekly in major Candn. newspapers; author over 50 articles on public opinion and marketing rsch.; frequent radio and television commentator; has contributed chapters to 'Services in Canada' 1989; 'Social Research Methods Applied' 1991; mem. Am. Assn. Pub. Opnion Rsch.; Am. Mktg. Assn.; Assn. for Consumer Rsch.; Candn. Pol. Sci. Assn.; Inst. of Certified Mngmt. Consultants of Ont.; Profl. Mktg. Rsch. Soc.; recreation: travel, sailing; Home: 266 Rusholme Rd., Toronto, Ont. M6H 2Y8; Office: 10F, 180 Bloor St. W., Toronto, Ont. M5S 2V6.

**BRACCO, Hon. John D.,** B.Ed., LL.B., D.D. (Hon.); judge; b. Edmonton, Alta. 31 March 1925; s. William and Annie (Semenchuk) B.; e. pub. and high schs. Edmonton and Redwater, Alta.; Univ. of Alta. B.Ed. 1949, LL.B. 1956; m. Laura d. Adam and Hilma Louhela 23 Aug. 1952; children: Helmi, Darryl, Carole, Katrysha; JUSTICE OF COURT OF APPEAL OF ALTA. 1987– ; reg'd seed crop insp. and field worker econ. surveys prior to univ.; high sch. teacher, Strathmore 1949–52, Edmonton Pub. Sch. Bd. 1952–53; law practice Edmonton and Redwater 1957–75; sessional instr. in comm. law R.I.A. 1965–68; Judge, Court of Queen's Bench of Alta. 1975–87; conciliator and mediator collective agreements disputes field of pub. edn., colls. & univs.; collective agreement negotiator pub. sch. bds. & community colls.; Trustee and Chrmn. Edmonton Pub. Sch. Bd. 1964–71; mem. Senate Univ. of Alta. 1955–56, 1966–73; Chrmn. Senate St. Stephen's Coll. 1976–85, mem. Senate 1966–85; recipient Mothersill Scholarship 1956; Hugill Cup (debating) 1948; D.D. (h.c.), St. Stephens Coll. 1987; mem. Edmonton C. of C. (Edn. Ctte.); Alta. Fedn. Home & Sch. Assn. (Pres. & mem. Exec.); Prov. Vice Pres. Alta. Sch. Trustees Assn. 1965–69; United Church; recreations: cross country skiing; Home: (P.O. Box 2550) Canmore, Alta. T0L 0M0; Office: 530 – 7th Ave. S.W., Calgary, Alta. T2P 0Y3.

**BRACKEN, Harry McFarland,** M.A., Ph.D.; professor, retired; b. Yonkers, N.Y. 12 March 1926; came to Can. 1966; Candn. citizen; s. Harry S. and Grace (McFarland) B.; e. Trinity Coll., Hartford B.A. 1949; Johns Hopkins Univ. M.A. 1954; Univ. of Iowa Ph.D. 1956; m. Eva Maria Laufkotter 24 Dec. 1949 (div.); children: Christopher, Timothy; m. 2ndly Elly van Gelderen 19 June 1985; Prof. of Philosophy, McGill Univ. 1966–91; Instr., Univ. of Iowa 1955–57, Asst. Prof. 1957–61; Assoc. Prof. Univ. of Minnesota (Mpls.) 1961–63; Prof. Arizona State Univ. 1963–66; Prof. Phil. Univ. of Calif. (San Diego) 1970; Visiting Prof. of Phil., Trinity Coll., Dublin, and of Metaphysics, Univ. Coll., Dublin 1972–73, 1979–80; adjunct mem., Phil. Dept., Erasmus Univ., Rotterdam 1988–90 and Rijksuniversiteit Groningen 1990; served with U.S. Navy, Pacific theatre, 1943–46; author of 'The Early Reception of Berkeley's Immaterialism: 1710–1733' 1959 (rev. 1965); 'Berkeley' 1974; 'Mind and Language: Essays on Descartes and Chomsky' 1984; 'Freedom of Speech: Words Are Not Deeds' 1994; other writings incl. articles on seventeenth and eighteenth century philosophers (Descartes, Malebranche, Bayle, Locke, Hume, Reid), the philosophy of Noam Chomsky, the history of freedom of speech from Bayle to the present with special attention to Am. and Candn. jurisprudence; Ed. Consultant, Berkeley Newsletter; rec'd. Acad. Freedom Award, Arizona Civil Liberties Union, 1966; J.K. Segal Found. for Jewish Culture, Educ. Award, 1972; mem., Am. and Candn. Philosophical Assn.; Home: G. Borgesiuslaan 125, 9722 RE Groningen, The Netherlands.

**BRADFIELD, Michael,** Ph.D.; university professor; b. Niagara Falls, Ont. 11 June 1942; s. Kenneth and Catherine (Mehlenbacher) B.; e. McMaster Univ., B.Comm. 1964; Brown Univ., Ph.D. 1971; m. Suellen d. Kenneth and Violet Fraser 29 June 1968; children: Sarah, Nancy, Kate; PROF., ECON. DEPT., DALHOUSIE UNIV. 1968– ; Vis. Asst. Prof., Simon Fraser Univ. 1974–75; Vis. Scholar, Univ. of Virginia 1981–82; Cons., N.S. Med. Assn.; Dept. of Communications, Govts. of B.C. & Can.; Atlantic Devel. Counc.; N.S. Dept. of Devel.; Can. West Found.; author: '7th Annual Review, Atlantic Provinces Economic Council' 1973, 'Regional Economics: Analysis and Policy in Canada' 1988; 'Long Run Equilibrium Under Pure Monopsony' Candn. Journal of Economics; co-author: 'Major Investments in the Atlantic Provinces, 1983 to 1985' 1983; 'Economic Development - Policies/Atlantic Possibilities'; recreations: squash, canoeing, tennis; Home: 6324 Cornwall St., Halifax, N.S. B3H 2J1; Office: Halifax, N.S. B3H 3J5.

**BRADFORD, Robert William,** C.M.; aviation artist; museum director (retired); b. Toronto, Ont. 17 Dec. 1923; s. Cecil Leopold and Grace (Clarke) B.; e. Weston Tech. Sch.; War Emergency Training Plan, Sci. Math., Eng. 1942; m. Ruth d. Frank and Dorothy Hathway 26 June 1948; children: John Robert, Kathryn Anne, Carolyn Elizabeth; Artist; Dir. Nat. Aviation Museum 1988–89; Illus. A.V. Roe Canada Ltd. 1949–53; Illus. The De Havilland Aircraft of Canada Ltd. 1953; Chief Illus. 1956–66; Asst. Curator present Museum 1966, Curator 1967–81, Assoc. Dir. 1984–88; Acting Dir. Nat. Museum of Sci. & Technol. 1982–83; served with RCAF 1942–45, Pilot; rep. art coll.: War Art Coll., Candn. War Museum; Nat. Aviation Museum; Aviation Hall of Fame Edmonton; Billy Bishop Heritage Owen Sound and various corporate and private colls.; author 'Airborne' 1983; designed and produced 16 paintings for Canada Post stamps; Am. Aviation Hist. Soc. Artists Award 1974; Fédn. Aéronautique Internat. Paul Tissandier Award Artistic & Curatorial Achievement in Aviation 1982; Publ. Service Award of Merit 1988; Member of the Order of Canada 1989; awarded Commemorative Medal for the 125th Anniversary of the Confederation of Canada 1992; Patron, Candn. Aviation Hist. Soc.; Home: R.R. 2, Kinburn, Ont. K0A 2H0.

**BRADFORD, William Elwood,** B.Com., F.C.G.A.; b. Montreal, Que. 14 Oct. 1933; s. Elwood J. and Jessie (Murray) B.; e. Concordia Univ. Montreal B.Com. 1960; Cert. Gen. Acct. 1960; m. Dolores d. late J.A. MacDonnell 6 Nov. 1954; children: Michael, Gary, Sandra, Maureen, Laurie, Joseph, Janet; DEPUTY CHRMN., CHIEF EXTVE. OFFR. AND DIR. NORTH AMERICAN LIFE ASSURANCE CO. 1993– ; Dir., Poco Petroleums Ltd.; Rio Algom Ltd.; joined Northern Electric Co. Ltd. 1950–59; Canada Iron Foundries Ltd. 1959–62; Asst. Controller, Reynolds Extrusion Co. Ltd. 1962–66; Vice Pres. and Controller, Churchill Falls (Labrador) Corp. Ltd. 1967–70; Vice Pres. and Sr. Financial Offr., Brinco Group of Co's 1970–74; Extve. Vice Pres. Finance, Bank of Montreal 1975, Extve. Vice Pres. Finance and Adm. 1976, Extve. Vice Pres. and Depy. Gen. Mgr. Domestic Banking 1978, Extve. Vice Pres. and Gen. Mgr. Domestic Banking 1979, Extve. Vice Pres. and Chief Gen. Mgr. 1980, Pres. 1981, Depy. Chrmn. 1983; Pres., C.E.O. & Dir., North Am. Life Assurance Co. 1987–93; Vice-Chrmn., Life Office Mgmt. Assoc. (LOMA); mem. Cert. Gen. Accts. Assn. Ont.; Financial Extves. Inst.; R. Catholic; recreations: tennis, squash, golf, skiing, hunting, fishing; Clubs: Mount Royal (Montreal); Cambridge; Lambton Golf & Country (Dir.); The Toronto; Home: 1333 Watersedge Rd., Mississauga, Ont. L5J 1A3; Office: 5650 Yonge St., Toronto, Ont. M2M 4G4.

**BRADLEY, William W.,** B.A., LL.B.; judge; b. Kincardine, Ont. 9 May 1942; s. William K. and Ethel (Fitzgerald) B.; e. Univ. of W. Ont., B.A. 1965, LL.B. 1968; m. Carol A. Bradley (née Wauchope); children: Julia, Melissa, Ian; JUDGE, PROV. CT. (FAMILY DIV.), JUDICIAL DIST. OF YORK REGION 1984– ; called to Ont. Bar 1970; Partner, Bradley & Wolder, Ft. Frances, Ont. 1970–80; Prov. Judge, Criminal & Family Divs., Dist. of Kenora 1980–84; Home: 286 Plymouth Trail, Newmarket, Ont. L3Y 6G7; Office: 50 Eagle St. W., Newmarket, Ont. L3Y 6B1.

**BRADLEY, Bettie;** editor; b. Toronto, Ont. 21 May 1933; d. Henry Ralph and Jane (Balmer) Blight; e. New York Sch. Interior Design; divorced; children: John Deacon, Jayne Rebecca, Meghan Balmer; VICE PRES., FAMILY COMMUNICATIONS INC. 1984– ; Founder, YOU mag. 1982– ; Host 'The New You' TV prog.; author 'The New You' 1985; former columnist The Toronto Telegram; former Vice Pres. Bradley-Vale Advertising Ltd.; mem. Candn. Cosmetic Toiletries & Fragrances Assn.; Candn. Cosmetic Careers Assn.; recreations: tennis, golf; Club: Mississauga Golf & Country; Home: Suite 1011, 1300 Bloor St., Mississauga, Ont. L4Y 3Z2; Office: 37 Hanna Ave., Toronto, Ont. M6K 1X1.

**BRADLEY, David Henry,** B.A., M.A.; association executive; b. Toronto, Ont. 26 Feb. 1958; s. Warren Calvin and Jean (Owcharuk) B.; e. Thomas L. Kennedy S.S. 1976; Univ. of Toronto B.A. 1980; Queen's Univ. M.A. 1982; m. Heather Bowden 15 Oct. 1983; PRESIDENT, ONTARIO TRUCKING ASSOCIATION 1991– ; Consultant, Touche Ross & Partners 1982–84; Financial Markets Economist, Bank of N.S. 1984–85; Dir. of Economics, Ontario Trucking Assn. 1985; Vice-Pres. & General Manager 1989; Former Economics Instr. for Cert. Management Accounts Program; Vice-Chrmn., Better Roads Coalition; Former Vice-Chrmn., Employers Council on Workers' Compensation; Mem., Candn. Transp. Research Forum; Metro. Toronto Bd. of Trade; Christ Church United, Mississauga; recreations: hockey, fishing, reading, golf; Office: 555 Dixon Road, Rexdale, Ont. M9W 1H8.

**BRADLEY, (Thomas) Douglas,** B.A., M.D., F.R.C.P.(C); physician; b. Vegreville, Alta. 7 Sept. 1951; s. Thomas Allan Maclennan and Barbara Adelaide (Belcher) B.; e. Ross Sheppard Composite High Sch. Edmonton 1969; Univ. of Alta. B.A. 1973, M.D. 1978; m. Grace d. Edwin and Anita Chau 9 Aug. 1980; two d., Helen Barbara, Sarah Anne; STAFF PHYS. TORONTO GEN. HOSP. 1985– ; Assoc. Prof. of Med. Univ. of Toronto; Dir. Sleep Rsch. Lab. Queen Elizabeth Hosp.; Dir. Sleep Lab. Toronto Hosp. (General Div.); internship and residency in Internal Med. Univ. of Toronto 1978–81; residency in Respiratory Med. 1981–83; Fellow, Candn. Thoracic Soc. 1983–84; Fellow, Med. Rsch. Council Can. 1984–85; rsch. training in Sleep Apnea Syndromes Univ. of Toronto 1982–86 and in Respiratory Muscle Physiol. & Sensation McGill Univ. 1984–85; recipient First Prize Toronto Gen. Hosp. Residency Rsch. Competition 1982–83, 1983–84; Career Scientist Award, Ont. Min. of Health 1988–93; winner, Univ. of Toronto Dept. of Medicine's Rsch. Award 1992; Connaught Found., Ont. Thoracic Soc., Medical Rsch. Council of Can. and Ont. Min. of Health rsch. grants; author or co-author various med. articles; recreations: hiking, canoeing; Home: 209 Walmer Rd., Toronto, Ont. M5R 3P7; Office: 212, 10 EN, 200 Elizabeth St., Toronto, Ont. M5G 2C4.

**BRADLEY, Fred D.,** M.L.A.; politician; b. Blairmore, Alta. 17 Sept. 1949; s. James Clarke and Thelma Elin (Pinkney) B.; e. Isabelle Sellon High Sch. Blairmore; Univ. of Alta.; CHRMN. ALTA. RSCH. COUNCIL 1986– ; Vice Pres. F.M. Thompson Co. Ltd.; el. M.L.A. for Pincher Creek-Crowsnest 1975, re-el. since; mem. Kananaskis Citizens' Adv. Ctte. 1978–82; mem. and latterly Chrmn. Alta. Environmental Rsch. Trust 1975–79; Dir. Syncrude Canada Ltd. 1979–82; Min. of Environment, Alta. 1982–86; mem. Hillcrest Miners' Lit. & Athletic Assn.; Freemason; Elks; Zeta Psi; Anglican; P. Conservative; Home: P.O. Box 390, Blairmore, Alta. T0K 0E0.

**BRADLEY, Michael Anderson;** see DE SACVILLE, Michael Anderson.

**BRADLEY, Richard Alan,** M.A.; educator; b. Portland, Dorset, Eng., 6 Oct. 1925; s. Reginald Livingstone and Phyllis Mary (Richardson) B.; e. Milner Court, Kent, Eng.; Marlborough Coll. (Wiltshire, Eng.); Trinity Coll., Univ. of Oxford, M.A.; m. Mary Anne Vicary, 23 Nov. 1971; one s., two ds. (of former marriage); Asst. Master, Dulwich Coll., London, Eng. 1949; Asst. Master and Head Hist. Dept., Tonbridge Sch., Kent, Eng. 1950–66; Head Master, St. Edward's Sch., Oxford, Eng. 1966–71; Head Master, Ridley Coll., St. Catharines, Ont. 1971–81; Head Master, The Rivers School, Weston, Mass. 1981–91; Project Dir., Nat. Assoc. of Independent Schs. U.S.A. 1991; Pres., English-Speaking Union (Boston Br.) 1992; served in 2nd World War with Royal Marines 1943–46; Comnd. and served in India and Java with 34th Amphibian Support Regt.; Anglican; recreations: sports, drama, mountaineering; Clubs: Vincent's (Oxford, Eng.); Public Schools (London, Eng.); Oxford and Bermondsey (U.K.); Address: 10 Carver Hill, South Natick, Mass. 01760.

**BRADLEY, Robert Emmett,** B.Sc., B.A., M.Sc., Ph.D.; mathematician; b. Montreal, Que. 17 Sept. 1957; s. Robert Emmett Charles and Rosemary Joan (Gallagher) B.; e. Concordia Univ. B.Sc. (Gov.-Gen.'s Award), 1979; Oxford Univ. B.A. (Rhodes Scholar) 1981; Univ. of Toronto M.Sc. 1984, Ph.D. 1989; ASST. PROF. OF MATH., ADELPHI UNIV. 1991– ; Defence Research Asst., Dept. of National Defence 1979; Technical Programmer, Cycare Systems Canada Ltd. 1981–83; Lectr. and Teaching Asst., Dept. of Math., Univ. of Toronto 1983–89; Visiting Asst. Prof. of Math, Northwestern Univ. 1989–91; Dir., Univ. of Toronto Community Radio Inc. (CIUT-FM), Sec. 1985–86; Chrmn. 1986–87; co-founder, St. James' Gate Soc., Oxford; recreations: music, brewing, painting; Home: 73 Argyle Rd., Stewart Manor, New York 11530; Office: Dept. of Math. & Computer Sci., Adelphi Univ., Garden City, New York 11530.

**BRADLEY, Ronald James,** B.A.; association executive; b. Hamilton, Ont. 1 Feb. 1950; s. Allan and Betty Helen (Murrell) B.; e. Univ. of W. Ont., B.A. 1975; m. Sandra d. Edward and Joan Deschaine 28 Sept. 1974; two s. Owen, Tristan; National Exec. Dir., Candn. Diabetes Assn. 1986–89; Exec. Dir. S.W. Ont. Candn. Youth Hostel Assn. 1975–77; Field Worker Hamilton-Niagara Dist. Candn. Cancer Soc. 1977–80; Dist. Dir. Metrop. Toronto Dist. 1980–86; mem. Inst. Assn. Execs.; Nat. Voluntary Orgns.; Nat. Voluntary Health Orgns.; Bd. Trade Metrop. Toronto; Home: 3168 Longmeadow Rd., Burlington, Ont. L7M 2J5.

**BRADLEY, Winston Patrick;** trust company executive; b. Oshawa, Ont. 18 March 1934; s. Charles and Catherine Adliza (Sutton) B.; e. Oshawa Coll. & Vocational Inst. 1952; Appraisal Inst. Can. 1965; Bd. Trade Metrop. Toronto Mgmt. Acctg. Dipl. 1966; L'Institut de Langues Modernes Saint John, N.B. Dipl. 1973; m. Sybil d. John and Jean Cochrane 29 July 1957; children: Kelly, Patrick, Sean; REGIONAL VICE PRES., ATLANTIC CANADA, CONFEDERATION TRUST CO. 1988– ; Dir., Homes for Independent Living; Mortgage Clk. Royal Trust 1963, Br. Mgr. 1968, Div. Mgr. Mortgage 1975–78; Asst. Gen. Mgr. Continental Bank 1978–81; Vice Pres. Lending Central Trust 1981, Sr. Vice Pres. Lending 1982, Vice Pres., Head Office Branch 1984–87; mem. Trust Co's Inst. (Mortgage Services Curriculum Comte.); Assoc. mem. Conf. Bd. Can.; Dir., Halifax Downtown Business Corp.; Founding Chrmn., Downtown 'Business Improvement District' Commn. (BID); Pres., Halifax Chapt. Candn. Cancer Soc. & mem. National Bequests Ctte.; Assoc. mem., Treasury Mgmt. Assoc. of Can.; mem. St. Mary's Univ. Varsity Club; Bd. of Trade; Charitable Irish Soc.; Candn. Martyrs' Parish Halifax; mem., St. Mary's Lawn Bowling; Halifax Homeowners Assoc.; co-author Mortgage Services Training Manuals; hockey coach CAHA Level III; Club: Halifax Curling; Home: 5747 Atlantic St., Halifax, N.S. B3H 1H1; Office: 1949 Upper Water St., Ste. 215, Halifax, N.S. B3J 3N3.

**BRADLOW, John,** M.B.A.; merchant banker; b. Johannesburg, South Africa 10 Aug. 1943; e. Univ. of Witwatersrand, B. Comm.; Harvard, M.B.A.; m. Brenda Merle 14 June 1969; children: Richard and Michael; PARTNER, PRIVATE EQUITY MANAGEMENT CORP.; Dir.: First City Trustco Inc.; Westar Group Ltd.; Marsulex Inc.; Am. Eagle Petroleums Ltd.; Fabrene Inc.; former Pres., First City Capital Markets (Canada) Ltd.; mem. Inst. of Chartered Accountants of Ont.; Office: 151 Yonge St., 185h Flr., Toronto, Ont. M5C 2W7.

**BRADSHAW, Jean Ellen (Jinnie),** B.A.; transportation executive; b. Toronto, Ont. 31 Oct. 1942; d. John Seymour and Wilhelmina Jean (Hutchinson) Jory; Univ. of W. Ont., B.A. 1965; Univ. of Toronto Secondary Sch. Teaching Cert. 1967; m. James William s. Earl James and Margaret Adelaide Bradshaw 27 Dec. 1980; step-children: Tracey Ann, Gregory James; PAST PRES., MISSION AIR TRANSPORTATION NETWORK 1992– ; Secondary Sch. Teacher 1965–73; Mktg. Mgr. Air Canada 1973–84; Co-Founder and Pres., MATN 1984–91; First Vice-Pres., Candn. Women's Breast Cancer Found. 1987–89; mem., Fashion Show Ctte., Candn. Cancer Soc. 1987–90; Dir.: Princess Margaret, The Cancer Hosp. 1992– ;(Council mem. 1990–92); Women's College Hosp. 1992– ; mem., Timothy Eaton Meml. Ch.; recreations: skiing, tennis, travel; Clubs: Caledon Ski; Granite; Lyford Cay; Home: 68 Cheltenham Ave., Toronto, Ont. M4N 1P7; Country: R.R. #2, Hillsburg, Ont. N0B 1Z0; Office: 200, 10 Alcorn Ave., Toronto, Ont. M4V 3B1.

**BRADSHAW, Marian Hahn;** publisher; b. Toronto, Ont. 5 July 1922; d. James E. and Dorothy (McLagan) Hahn; e. Bishop Strachan Sch.; St. Genevieve Sch.; m. John s. Cecil and Jane B. 24 Mar. 1968; children: Bruce, David, John, Peter Adams; Publisher, Canadian Collector 1966–87; Antiques Ed., 'Ontario Homes & Living'; Founding Ed., 'Canadian Collector' 1966– , Publisher, 1985–87; extensive lecturing Can. & U.S.; Founding mem., Royal Ont. Mus. Women's Ctte. 1960; Founder, Candn. Antique Dealers Assn. 1967; Consultant, Macdonald Stewart Found.; mem. Bd., Royal Ont. Mus.; G.R. Gardiner Mus.; Grange Ctte.; Art Gall. of Ont. (Dir.); Chateau Dufresne; Montreal Mus. of Decorative Arts; Lake St. Louis Hist. Soc.; served with distinction, Candn. Red Cross Corps, W.W. II; recipient Award of Merit, Toronto Hist. Bd. 1980; Volunteer Service Award, Min. of Citizenship & Culture 1985; past mem. Bd., Ont. Heritage Found.; Toronto Hist. Bd.; Candn. Soc. of Decorative Arts; Jr. League of Toronto; Garden Club of Toronto; mem., Eng. Ceramic Circle; Assn. for Preserv. & Tech.; Wedgwood Soc.; Candn. Mus. Assn.; Friends of Mus.; Furniture Hist. Assn.; Am. Ceramic

Circle; author & orgnr., several symposiums & seminars; author (intro.): 'Prized Possessions from Private Homes' 19..; recreation: flower arranging.

**BRADSHAW, Marvin Robert,** B.Sc.; natural gas industry executive; b. Phoenix, Ariz. 20 July 1943; s. Hall and Mary (Duncan) B.; e. Univ. of Ariz. B.Sc. (Aerospace Engr.) 1967; m. Maureen d. Jim and Jane Ferguson 22 July 1978; children: Jesson, James, Alexandra; DIV. VICE-PRES., PAN-ALBERTA GAS LTD. 1987– ;and PRES. & CHIEF OPERATING OFFR., NATGAS CANADA INC. 1992– ; commissioned as reserve offr., U.S. Army Artillery 1967; 2 yrs. active military service; rec'd var. military decorations; Proj. Engr. & Exec. Asst. to Chrmn., Newbery Energy Corp. 1969; Vice-Pres. & Gen. Mgr. of subsidiary in West Texas 1970; exec. position with Candn. subsidiary 1975; joined Pan-Alberta Gas Ltd. as Mkt. Devel. Coord. 1978; apptd. Dir. of Mktg. 1981; Vice-Pres., Mktg. 1986; Div. Vice-Pres. 1987; Pres. & C.O.O., NatGas Canada Inc. 1992; awarded Candn. Gas Assn. Distinguished Service Mktg. Award 1988; mem. Pacific Coast Gas Assn. (Chrmn. 1988–89); Candn. Gas Assn.; Am. Gas Assn.; Midwest Gas Assn.; Calgary Ch. of Comm.; Heritage Pk. Soc.; Advisory Bd., Variety Club of Southern Alta.; The Smithsonian Assocs.; Master Mason, Scottish Rite of Freemasonry; recreations: fishing, hunting, golfing; Clubs: Calgary Petroleum; Calgary Profl.; Silver Springs Golf & Country; Home: 307 Dalcastle Mews N.W., Calgary, Alta. T3A 2P1; Office: #500 – 707 8th Ave. S.W., Calgary, Alta. T2P 3V3.

**BRADY, John Mary,** B.A., B.Ed., M.Ed.; teacher; b. Dublin, Ireland 10 July 1955; s. Christopher and Mary (Carroll) B.; e. Oatlands Coll., Dublin 1972; Trinity Coll., Dublin, B.A. 1980; Univ. of Toronto, B.Ed. 1981, M.Ed. 1985; m. Johanna d. Anton and Elfriede Wagner 1 Aug. 1981; children: Julia, Michael; TEACHER, YORK REGION R.C. SEPARATE SCH. BD. 1988– ; Bank of Ireland 1972–75; R.C.M.P., Yellowknife, N.W.T. 1975–76; Sch. Dist. 88, Terrace, B.C. 1981–84; TV Ont. 1985–86; convenor/orgn., Candn. branch Trinity Coll. Dublin Grad. Assn.; author: 'A Stone of the Heart' 1988, 'Unholy Ground' 1989, 'Kaddish in Dublin' 1990, 'All Souls' 1993 (novels); work in progress 'The Good Life' forthcoming; recipient Arthur Ellis Award (Crime Writers of Canada) 1989; recreations: swimming, walking, talking; Office: c/o HarperCollins Publishers, Hazelton Lanes, Suite 2900, 55 Avenue Rd., Toronto, Ont. M5R 3L2.

**BRAGG, David K.,** B.A.Sc., C.A.; food distribution executive; b. Guelph, Ont. 8 Sept. 1948; s. Kenneth K. and Catherine L. (Keller) B.; e. Streetsville H.S. 1967; Univ. of Toronto B.A.Sc. 1971; York Univ.; m. Patricia d. Stanley and Gladys Lancaster 25 June 1971; children: Sarah, Michael; SENIOR VICE-PRESIDENT, LOBLAW COMPANIES LIMITED; CUSO in Jamaica 1971–73; Clarkson Gordon Toronto 1973–78; Arthur Young, New Zealand 1978–79; Clarkson Gordon Toronto 1979–83; Controller, Loblaw Companies Limited 1983; Vice-Pres.; Home: 242 Evelyn Ave., Toronto, Ont. M6P 2Z9; Office: 22 St. Clair Ave. E., Toronto, Ont. M4T 2S8.

**BRAHIMCHA, Edgard,** B.Sc.; business executive; b. Cairo, Egypt 26 June 1933; s. John F. and Jeannette S. (Khayat) B.; e. Univ. St-Joseph Beirut Lebanon Bacc. Sciences 1951; m. Thérèse d. Elias and Rafia Haddad 8 Oct. 1966; children: Myriam, Pia, Fadi; REGIONAL VICE-PRES., MARKETING, MIRON INC. 1982– ; VICE-PRES. & GEN. DIR., MIRON CEMENT, div. of ESSROC Canada Inc. 1989– ; Assoc., F.J. Brahimcha & Co. Syria 1952–59; Gen. Mgr., Lebanese Finance Co. Beirut 1959–66; A.C. Assouad Tanning Co. Ethiopia 1966–75; Vice Pres. & Gen. Mgr., A. & C. Assouad Can. Ltée. 1976–80; Pres./Owner, Brexco Inc. 1980–82; Mem., La C. de C. de Montréal; Le Bureau de C. de Montreal; C. de C. du Québec; recreations: travelling, nordic skiing, reading; Home: 2435 Pérodeau, Sillery, Qué. G1T 2J4; Office: 3700 Notre-Dame est, Montréal, Qué. H1W 2J8.

**BRAID, E. Arthur,** C.M., LL.B., LL.M., Q.C.; university professor; b. Winnipeg, Man. 21 Aug. 1934; s. William Gordon and Myrtle (Seel) B.; e. Univ. of Manitoba LL.B. 1960; Univ. of London, London Sch. of Econ. & Pol. Sci. LL.M. 1967; m. Judith d. William and Irene Pollard 29 Dec. 1961; children: Sondra, Kyle, Lianne; PROF., FACULTY OF LAW, UNIV. OF MANITOBA 1964– ; Lawyer, Newman, MacLean & Assoc. 1956–64; Counsel, I.L. Jessiman & Assoc. 1977–80; Pitblado & Hoskin 1980–91; Assoc. Editor, Western Weekly Reports 1966– ; lecturer, Banff Sch. of Advanced Management 1969–93; Sessional Lecturer, Fac. of Mngt., Univ. of Man. 1964– ; Dean, Faculty of Law, Univ. of Man. 1994– ; Mem., Order of Canada 1992; Gov. Gen. 125 Anniversary Medal 1993; Mem., Senate, Univ. of Man. 1969– ; Mem., Bd. of Gov., Univ. of Man. 1978–89, 1990– ; Bd. Mem., Cdn. Paraplegic Assn. 1969– ;(Pres. 1990–92); Bd. Mem., Man. Paraplegic Assn. 1969– ;(Pres. 1969–76); Man. Paraplegic Fdn. 1980– ;(Vice-Pres.); Chancellor, Anglican Diocese of Rupert's Land 1992– ; Mem., Man. & Cdn. Bar assns.; Law Soc. of Man. 1956– ; Assn. of Cdn. Law Teachers 1964– ; extensive charitable work; Home: 3602 Vialoux Dr., Winnipeg, Man. R3R 0A4; Office: Faculty of Law, Univ. of Manitoba, Winnipeg, Man. R3T 2N2.

**BRAID, Katharine F.,** B.A., M.A., LL.B.; transportation executive; b. New Haven, U.S.A. 1 Nov. 1946; d. William and Pauline (Coffin (Woodman) Ford; e. Bryn Mawr College B.A. 1967; Sorbonne M.A. 1968; Univ. of Toronto LL.B. 1972; m. Robert L. s. Quentin and Nora Shirriff 1982; children: Ford and Paul Shirriff; EXECUTIVE VICE-PRESIDENT, CP RAIL SYSTEM 1993– ; Legal Offr., Dept. of Justice (Canada) 1974–78; Litigation Lawyer, Toronto Reg. Office Law Dept., Candn. Pacific 1978–84; Toronto Regional Counsel 1984–87; Asst. Vice-Pres., Law 1987–89; Vice-Pres., Candn. Pacific Legal Services 1989–93; Sr. Vice-Pres., Legal Services & Strategy Development, CP Rail System 1993; Dir., Delaware and Hudson Railway Co., Inc.; Napierville Junction Railway Co.; CP Technologies; Adv. Bd., Canada-U.S. Law Inst.; Advisory Bd., Candn. Corporate Counsel; Office: 40 University Ave., Suite 918, Toronto, Ont. M5J 1T1.

**BRAIDE, David Ian William,** B.A., M.A.; institute chairman; b. Liverpool, Engl. 1928; e. Univ. Sch., Victoria, B.C.; Trinity Coll. Sch., Port Hope, Ont.; Univ. of B.C.; Univ. of Toronto; B.A., Econ. & Pol. Sci.; M.A., Econ.; m. Janet Harbron 1949; children: Robbie David, Martha Janet, Mary Jane Davida; CHRMN., CANDN. INST. FOR INTERNATIONAL PEACE AND SECURITY 1989– ; Econ. Asst. C-I-L Montreal 1949, Econ. Studies Mgr. 1956, Control Mgr. Explosives Div. 1961, Gen. Mgr. Fabrikoid Div. 1964, Exec. Asst. to Sr. Vice-Pres. 1966; Vice-Pres. C-I-L. Inc. Montreal 1968; ICI North Am. Ltd. New York, N.Y. 1971; C-I-L Inc. Montreal 1972; C-I-L Inc. Toronto 1975; Vice Pres. & Dir. C-I-L Inc. Montreal 1978–85; Sr. Vice Pres. C-I-L Inc. Toronto 1980; Vice Chrmn. C-I-L Inc. 1984–85; Pres., The Niagara Inst. 1986–88; Chrmn. Candn. Chamber of Comm. 1978–79 (Vice-Pres. 1976–78; Vice-Chrmn. Exec. Counc. 1972–74); Dir.-at-Large and Chrmn. Legislative Action Ctte., Soc. of the Plastics Industry 1977–79; mem. Bd. of Dir. Montreal Museum of Fine Arts 1979–81 (Hon. Trustee 1981– ;); mem. Bd. of Dir. Metrop. Montreal YMCA 1972–80; Pres. Candn. Counc. Internat. Chamber of Commerce 1981–84; First Vice-Chrmn. Internat. Bus. Counc. of Can. 1984; mem. of Exec. Ctte., Candn.-Am. Ctte. 1980–88; Chrmn. Task Force on Canada-U.S. Trade Policy 1985; mem. Bd. of Dir. and Depy. Chrmn., St. Michael's Hosp. 1976–79, 1981– ; mem., Bd. of Dir., Niagara Inst. 1986– ; mem., Bd. of Dir., Candn. Inst. for Internat. Peace and Security 1986– ; recreations: gardening, photography, sailing.

**BRAIDWOOD, Hon. Thomas Reid,** B.A., LL.B.; judge; b. Vancouver, B.C. 29 Dec. 1930; s. Frank and Lillian (Esplan) B.; e. Univ. of B.C. B.A. 1953, LL.B. 1956; m. Anne d. Lars Johnson 4 Aug. 1956; children: Tom, Kim, Mark; JUDGE, SUPREME COURT OF B.C. 1990– ; called to Bar of B.C. 1957; cr. Q.C. 1970; Founder and Partner Braidwood, Nuttal MacKenzie 1963; guest lectr. Univ. of B.C.; assoc. continuing legal edn.; mem. Am. Coll. Trial Lawyers; Bencher of Law Society of B.C. 1973–74, 1980–84; recreations: tennis, skiing, yachting; Clubs: West Vancouver Yacht; Hollyburn Country; Office: 800 Smithe St., Vancouver, B.C. V6Z 2E1.

**BRAIT, A.A.,** C.M., B.A.Sc., P.Eng.; telecommunications executive; b. Cooksville, Ont. 12 Dec. 1924; s. Otto and Adele B.; e. Port Credit (Ont.) High Sch.; Univ. of Toronto, B.A.Sc. 1946; m. Margaret Rebecca, d. Samuel Norris, 2 Sept. 1950; one s., Richard; CHRMN., NEWTEL ENTERPRISES LTD. 1985– ; joined Bell Canada in Toronto, 1946; held a variety of engn. positions with Bell until apptd. Chief Engr., Avalon Tel. Co., St. John's, Nfld., 1964; returned to Bell in 1966 and held several exec. positions in Montreal and Ottawa before returning to Nfld. in 1970; Chrmn., Newfoundland Tel. Co. Ltd. 1970–91; Past Chrmn., Economic Counc. of Nfld. and Labrador; Chrmn., ICOMM; Dir., Fishery Products Int'l.; Member of the Order of Canada 1994; mem., Assn. Prof. Engrs. Nfld.; Assn. Prof. Engrs. Ont.; St. John's Bd. Trade; Candn. Chamber Comm.; Past Pres., Atlantic Provs. Econ. Council; Anglican; recreation: golf; fishing; Clubs: Bally Haly Golf; Murray's Pond; Rotary; Home: 21 Rennie's Mill Rd., St. John's, Nfld. A1C 3P9; Office: Ft. William Bldg., 6th Floor, St. John's, Nfld. A1C 5H6.

**BRAITHWAITE, J. Lorne,** B.Com., M.B.A., I.D.A.; executive; b. Dewberry, Alta. 16 July 1941; s. Joseph and Olga (Prill) B.; e. Univ. of Alta. B.Com. 1963; Univ. of W. Ont. M.B.A. 1969; Calgary, Alta. I.D.A. 1970; m. Josie d. Mary and Harry Bey 13 Feb. 1962; children: Todd, Jodi, Troy, Travis; PRES. AND CHIEF EXEC. OFFR. CAMBRIDGE SHOPPING CENTRES LIMITED 1978– ; Dir. (inside Cambridge), Cambridge Leaseholds Limited; Cambridge Shopping Centres Limited; Cambridge Western Leaseholds Limited; (outside Cambridge) C.I.P.R.E.C. (Cdn. Inst. of Public Real Estate Cos.); Interprovincial Pipe Line Inc.; Jannock Limited; Bd. of Govs., Metro Toronto and York Region, Jr. Achievement; OMERS Realty Corp.; Wage Adm., Sales Mgr., Asst. Mgr. T. Eaton Co. Ltd., Winnipeg, Calgary and Vancouver 1963–67; Project Mgr. ATCO Industries Calgary 1969, Sales Mgr. 1969–70, Vice Pres. Mktg. 1970–71; Sales & Merchandise Mgr. T. Eaton Co. Ltd., Edmonton 1971–74; Project Mgr. Oxford Development Group Edmonton 1974–76, Sr. Vice Pres. Devel. Calgary 1976–78; Pres. & C.E.O., Cambridge Shopping Centres Ltd. 1978 to present; Mem., XPO and World Presidents' Orgn.; recreations: squash, hockey, golf; Clubs: Bayview Golf & Country; Goodwood; Toronto; Fitness Inst.; Home: 15 Daffodil Ave., Thornhill, Ont. L3T 1N2; Office: 95 Wellington St. W., Ste. 600, Toronto, Ont. M5J 2R2.

**BRAITHWAITE, Leonard,** Q.C., B.Com., M.B.A.; b. Toronto, Ont. 23 Oct. 1923; s. Reginald and Wilhelmina (Cox) B.; e. Harbord Coll. Inst., Toronto; Univ. of Toronto, B.Com. 1950; Harvard Univ., M.B.A. 1952, LL.B. 1958; Osgoode Hall Law Sch.; two s., Roger John Austin, David Leonard; read law with the late H.L. Rowntree, Q.C. and H.G. Chappell, Q.C.; called to Bar of Ont. 1958; cr. Q.C. 1971; served in Can. and Overseas with RCAF during World War II; el. to Bd. of Educ. for Twp. of Etobicoke 1960 and served on various comtes, incl. Adv. Vocational Comte.; served on Etobicoke Planning Bd. for 2 yrs.; el. to Council of Twp. of Etobicoke for Ward 4 in 1962; el. M.P.P. in prov. g.e. 1963 (first Negro el. to Parl. in Can.); Bd. of Control for Etobicoke and Metro Toronto Council 1982; mem. Bd. of Govs., Etobicoke Gen. Hosp. and West Park Hosp.; Past Pres., Royal York Garden's Community Assn.; Lectr., Inst. of Business Adm., Univ. of Toronto, 1953–54; sponsor of boys' and girls' sports teams; mem., Candn. Bar Assn.; Co. York Law Assn.; Advocates' Soc.; Criminal Lawyers' Ass.; Metro. Toronto Bd. of Trade; Phi Delta Phi; Liberal; Anglican; recreations: outdoor sports, reading; Clubs: Harvard Business; Kiwanis; Office: Richview Square, 250 Wincott Dr., Etobicoke, Ont. M9R 2R5.

**BRAITSTEIN, Marcel,** R.C.A.; sculptor; educator; b. Belgium 11 July 1935; s. Arthur and Paula (Eckstein) B.; e. Ecole des Beaux-Arts de Montréal 1953–59; Instituto Allende, San Miguel de Allende, Mexico 1959–60; m. Dianne Carol (dec'd 2 June 1993) d. William Farrar 2 Oct. 1965; two d. Paula, Lara; PROF. OF FINE ARTS, UNIV. DU QUE. 1969– , U.Q.A.M.; Visiting Prof. Mt. Allison Univ. Sackville, N.B. 1973–75; one-man exhns.: Galerie Ptah Brussels 1960; Galerie Agnès Lefort Montreal 1961, 1963, 1965; Galeria Jacobo Glantz Mexico 1961; Montreal Museum of Fine Arts 1963; Whitney Gallery Montreal 1970; Galerie Entremonde Paris 1970; Romi Goldmuntz Centrum Antwerp 1971; Gallery 93 Ottawa 1972; Owens Art Gallery Sackville, N.B. 1973; Confederation Centre Art Gallery P.E.I. 1974; Univ. de Moncton 1975; Univ. du Qué. 1979; Galerie Les 2B, Montréal 1983; Regional Museum of Vaudreuil-Soulanges 1988; Bishops Univ. 1990; rep. in group exhns. Can., USA, Mexico and Europe since 1957; rep. pub. colls. Montreal Museum of Fine Arts, Art Gallery Ont., Winnipeg Art Gallery, Confederation Centre P.E.I.; recreations: sailing, cross-country skiing, reading; Home: 61 Macaulay Lane, Hudson Heights, Que. J0P 1J0; Office: P.O. Box 8888, Stn. A, Montreal, Que. H3C 3P8.

**BRAMAN, Dennis Richard,** B.Sc., M.Sc., Ph.D.; museum curator; b. Oyen, Alta. 12 Nov. 1947; s. Russell Leon and Mary Gertrud (Coates) B.; e. Southern Alta. Inst. of Technology 1968; Univ. of Calgary B.Sc. (Hons.) 1974, M.Sc. 1976; Colorado School of Mines; Univ. of Calgary Ph.D. 1981; m. Lena d. Stina and Tage Suneby 29 Dec. 1981; children: Nathan Craig, Ryan Nicholas; CURATOR OF PALAEOBOTANY, ROYAL TYRRELL MUSEUM 1983– ; Research Asst., Univ. of Calgary 1976–77; Teacher, Mount Royal College 1977; Teaching Asst., Univ. of Calgary 1980–82; Lectr. 1982; Research Assoc. & Curator, Geol. Survey of Canada 1981–83; Mem., Alta. Palaeontological Adv. Ctte. 1990– ; Acting Asst. Dir., Research & Collections,

Royal Tyrrell Museum 1991– ; Mem., Candn. Soc. of Petroleum Geologists; Am. Assn. of Petroleum Geol.; Am. Assn. of Stratigraphic Palynologists; Candn. Assn. of Palynol.; Internat. Fed. of Palynol. Soc.; author/co-author of 17 sci. papers; compiler/editor: 8 regional or local field guides; recreations: curling, bird watching, model trains, mystery novels; Home: 404 – 14th Street S.E., Drumheller, Alta. T0J 0Y5; Office: P.O. Box 7500, Drumheller, Alta. T0J 0Y0.

**BRAMWELL, Rollo;** paper industry executive; b. Norwich, England 17 June 1948; s. Roy and Mary (Smith) B.; e. Business Admin. & Mktg., Oxford Polytechnic, Aston Univ. (UK), Univ. of Western Ont., Columbia Univ., Univ. of Maine; m. Chauncey d. Tom and Edith Fitzsimmons 26 May 1973; children: Graydon, Alison; PRES. & CHIEF EXTVE. OFFR., PERKINS PAPERS LTD. 1989– ; Mngt. Trainee, Harrods (UK) 1966–68; Product Mgr., Brooke Bond Foods (Can.) 1971–74; joined present firm 1974; Vice-Pres. Mktg. Sales, Consumer Prod. Div. 1978–79; Vice-Pres., Mfg. 1979–81; Vice-Pres. & Gen. Mgr., Consumer Prod. Div. 1981–83; Vice-Pres., Mktg. & Sales 1983–89; Dir. 1983– ; Bd. Mem., Institut de Réadaptation de Montréal ('Montreal Rehab.'); Bd. of Dirs., Candn. Pulp & Paper Assn.; Chrmn., Environmental Choice Program Cttee., Candn. Pulp & Paper Assn.; Bd. Mem., Braeside Golf Club; awarded Commemorative Medal for 125th Anniversary of Candn. Confederation; Office: 2345 Autoroute des Laurentides, Laval, Que. H7S 1Z7.

**BRAND, John Charles Drury,** Ph.D., D.Sc.; chemist; educator; b. Durban, S. Africa 21 May 1921; s. Andrew Nevill and Helen Mabel (Drury) B.; e. Michaelhouse, Balgowan, Natal, S.Africa; Univ. of London B.Sc. 1941, M.Sc. 1943, Ph.D. 1946, D.Sc. 1956; m. Evelyn Grace d. late Bertram Leonard Meek 25 Sept. 1943; one s. David Andrew; PROF. OF CHEM. UNIV. OF W. ONT. since 1969; Sr. Lectr. Univ. of Glasgow 1947–64; Prof. Vanderbilt Univ. 1964–69; co-author 'Molecular Structure' 1959, 2nd ed. 1974; 'Applications of Spectroscopy' 1965; scient. papers various journs.; Chem. Inst. of Can. medal 1987; mem. Candn. Assn. Physicists; Candn. Inst. Chem.; Royal Soc. Can.; Home: Box 2068, Bayfield, Ont. N0M 1G0; Office: London, Ont. N6A 5B7.

**BRAND, Oscar,** B.A.; writer; composer; entertainer; b. Winnipeg, Man. 7 Feb. 1920; s. I.Z. and Beatrice (Shulman) B.; e. Brooklyn Coll. of Coll. of City of N.Y., B.A. (Psychol.); m. Karen Grossman; children: Jeannie, Eric, James, Jordan; Pres., Gypsy Hill Music; mem. Creative Bd. Sesame Street; Curator, Songwriters Hall of Fame; Critic, CBC 'Playdate'; Host, NPR's 'Voices' and 'Sunday'; Host, 'Let's Sing Out' CBC, CTV; mem. Faculty, Hofstra Univ., N.Y. and New Sch., N.Y.; music consultant to Bill Moyers '20th Century' PBS-TV Series 1984; author of 10 published books incl.: 'Singing Holidays'; 'The Ballad Mongers'; 'Bawdy Song Book'; 'Songs of 76'; 'Party Songs' 1985; has recorded 80 L.P.s and written 76 documentary and indust. films (rec'd Venice, Edinburgh and Cannes Festival awards, Golden Reel, Scholastic, Freedoms Foundation, Peabody, Ohio State and Emmy Awards); creator of score for: 'In White America'; 'How To Steal An Election'; 'The Joyful Noise'; 'The Education of Hyman Kaplan'; presently composing score and writing lyrics for musical 'Thunder Bay'; compositions incl.: 'Something to Sing About'; 'When I First Came to This Land'; 'A Guy is a Guy'; songs for films incl.: 'The Fox' 1967; 'Sybil' 1972; 'The Long Riders' 1983; 'Ironweed' 1988; served with US Army as Psychol., 1942–45; rec'd Unit Award; Legion of Merit; Laureate (Pol. Sci.) Univ. of Fairfield 1972; Hon. mem., Radio Pioneers of Am. 1986; Hon. Ph.D., Univ. of Winnipeg 1987; Co-ordinator of Folk Music for N.Y. Mun. Stn.; Trustee, Newport Festival Foundation; mem., N.Y. State Folklore Assn.; Dramatists Guild; ACTRA; SAG; Address: 141 Baker Hill, Great Neck, NY 11023.

**BRANDEN, Victoria,** M.A.; writer; b. Clinton, Ont.; d. Albert Edward and Mary Elizabeth (Dillon) Fremlin; e. Univ of Alta. B.A. 1950; Univ. of Toronto M.A. 1963; m. Richard Branden 9 Feb. 1952; one s. Miles Geoffrey; served publishing and journalism fields and taught 15 yrs. various schs. and colls.; freelance writer articles and short stories various mags., CBC (some adapted as plays), anthols.; contrb. TV series 1970's and episode Yorkshire TV series 'World of Strange Powers'; regular columnist 'National Independent,' 'Humanist in Canada,' 'Farmworker'; recipient Can. Council Award grad. study 1963; 'B' Award for writing 1980; Cummings Fellowship Grad. Study Trinity Coll. 1951; Candn. Women's Press Club Award for Comedy (mini-series half-hour plays) 1967; Hamilton Candn. Club Service to Lit. Award 1981; Environmentalist of the Year Award 1992; author 'Mrs. Job' novel 1979; 'Understanding Ghosts' non-fiction 1980; 'Flitterin' Judas' novel 1985; 'In Defence of Plain English: The Decline and Fall of Literacy in Canada' non-fiction 1992; 'Give Up the Ghost' non-fiction 1992; 'The Fish Prince' children's book, forthcoming; Atheist; NDP; recreations: swimming, riding, skiing, skating; Clubs: Hamilton-Burlington Humanists; Address: P.O. Box 581, 65 Wellington St., Waterdown, Ont. L0R 2H0.

**BRANDON, Robert Joseph,** B.Sc., P.Eng.; engineer; b. London, U.K. 24 Dec. 1948; s. Robin Joseph and Patricia Mary (Le Brasseur) B.; e. Univ. of Southampton, B.Sc. 1972; m. Laura d. Prof. Gerald and Mary Graham 21 Sept. 1974; children: Robert, Amy, John Francis; VICE PRES., AES CANADA INC. 1993– ; Project Engr., Rolls-Royce (B.E.D.) 1972–76; Assoc. Engr., Ont. Rsch. Found. 1976–79; Inst. of Man & Resources 1974–82; Partner, IEA Cons. Group Ltd. 1982–85; Gen. Mgr., P.E.I. Energy Corp. 1985–93; Pres., Candn. District Energy Assn.; Secy./Treas., Candn. Wind Energy Assn.; recreations: sailing, travel; Home: 13 Rupert St., Ottawa, Ont. K1S 3S2; Office: 253 Ontario St., Kingston, Ont. K7L 2Z4.

**BRANDOW, Judith Michael (Judy);** journalist; b. Hamilton, Ont.; d. Clare Lorne and Ora Maud (Johnson) B.; e. Grantham High Sch. St. Catharines, Ont.; MAGAZINE CONSULTANT AND FREELANCE WRITER and PRES., SANIPOUCH PRODUCTS INC.; Reporter, St. Catharines Standard 1963–68; Reporter and Asst. City Ed. (Women) Toronto Telegram 1968–71; Women's Ed. The Hamilton Spectator 1971–73; journalism teacher Ryerson Polytech. Inst. 1973–74; Family Ed. Toronto Star 1974–77; Ed.-in-Chief, Canadian Living Magazine 1977–88; Columnist, Toronto Sun 1989–93; Project development dir. for Participaction 1990–91; Chair, Metro Toronto Convention Centre; recreations: skiing, sailing, tennis, antiques, cooking; Clubs: W. Toronto Toastmasters; Home: 227 Lakeshore Dr., Toronto, Ont. M8V 2A7.

**BRANDT, Andrew (Andy) S.;** government agency executive; b. London, Ont. 11 June 1938; s. Andrew and Katherine (Matz) B.; e. St. Peter's Grade Sch. and Cath. Central High Sch. London; Univ. of Waterloo, Economics Course; m. Patricia d. Lorne St. Clair 2 July 1962; two d. Sherri, Lori; CHRMN. & C.E.O., LIQUOR CONTROL BD. OF ONT. 1991– ; Ald. City of Sarnia 1971–75, Mayor 1975–81; el. to Ont. Leg. as M.P.P. for Sarnia 1981; Parlty. Asst. to Min. of Labour 1981–83; Min. of the Environment, Ont. 1983–85; Min. of Industry & Trade, Ont. 1985; Leader of the Ont. Progressive Conservative Party 1987–90; Dir., Counc. for Candn. Unity; Chrmn. of the Bd. of Dirs., Lambton College Foundation; Hon. Patron, Lambton County Branch of the Candn. Mental Health Assn.; Former Vice Pres. and Dir. Assn. Muns. Ont.; recipient, Paul Harris Award for outstanding community service, Rotary Club; Past Chrmn. Sarnia Un. Appeal; Officer of the Ordre du Mérite Agricole, Govt. of France; Life mem. Am. Fedn. Musicians; Hon. mem. 'C' Sqdn. First Hussars Armoured Regt. Candn. Armed Forces; RCAF Assn.; Naval Assn.; mem. Sarnia & Dist. Chamber of Comm.; invited speaker numerous confs., seminars and meetings; recreations: music, sports, humour, political philosophy; Club: Sarnia Kiwanis (Past Pres.); Office: 55 Lakeshore Blvd., Toronto, Ont. M5E 1A4.

**BRANDT, Caryl M.V.;** film executive; b. Swan Lake, Man. 15 March 1949; d. George and Yvette Marie Emilienne (Hutlet) B.; e. N. Alta. Inst. Technol. Radio and TV Arts 1969; m. Lawrence Albin Marshall s. Albert and Anne Malazdrewich 3 May 1980; children: Rochelle, Darryl; Exec. Dir., Nat. Screen Inst.-Can. 1988–90; Vice Pres., Project Devel. & Promotion Alberta Motion Picture Development Corp. 1985–87; Exec. Producer Current Affairs CBC Edmonton 1982–85; Producer/Dir. 'Points West' weekly documentaries CBC Winnipeg 1979–82; freelance producer/dir. specials, commercials, ednl. progs. and prodn. mgr. features, commercials 1974–82; recipient 1977 Alta. Motion Picture Inds. Assn. Best of Festival 'The Grand Opening'; Candn. Film & TV Assn. and CanPro Best Sports Special 'Challenge for '78' 1978; Yorkton Festival Merit Award 1981 and Best Documentary under 30 mins. 'Prairie Women' 1987; Prix Anik Best Regional Info. Series 1982; Home: P.O. 1709, Canmore, Alta. T0L 0M0.

**BRANDT, Diana Ruth,** M.A., Ph.D.; writer; editor; educator; b. Winkler, Man. 31 Jan. 1952; d. Henry J. and Mary (Zacharias) Janzen; e. Univ. of Man. B.A. (Hons.) 1975; Univ. of Toronto M.A. 1976; Univ. of Man. Ph.D. 1993 (Patrick Mary Plunkett Scholarship, Drummond Scholarship in Candn. Studies); children: Lisa, Alison; Lectr. in Eng., Univ. of Winnipeg 1986– ; author 'questions i asked my mother' 1987; 'Agnes in the sky' 1990; 'mother, not mother' 1992; 'Wild Mother Dancing' 1993; poetry ed. 'Prairie Fire'; former co-ed. 'Contemporary Verse 2'; former fiction ed. 'HERizons'; recipient Lampert Meml. Award 1987; nominated Gov. Gen.'s Award poetry 1987, Commonwealth Poetry Prize 1988; recipient McNally Robinson Award for Manitoba Book of the Year 1990; nominated Pat Lowther Award 1992; mem. League Candn. Poets (Man. Regional Rep. 1987–90; 2nd Vice Pres. 1990–91); Man. Writers Guild; TWUC; P.E.N. (Manitoba Regional Rep. 1992– ;); Home: 932 Jessie Ave., Winnipeg, Man. R3M 1A9; Office: Univ. of Winnipeg, Winnipeg, Man.

**BRASS, Lorne;** actor; director; b. Ottawa, Ont. 26 March 1959; s. Allan Edward and Rose E. (Rubenzahl) B.; one d. Ariane-Eva-Paré; Resident, Candn. Centre for Advanced Film Studies Toronto; Part-Time Prof. of Drama Concordia Univ. Montreal; Theatre Dir./Creator Carbone 14 Montreal 1980–87; Co-Dir. 'Chagall' Museum of Fine Arts; 'Metropolis' (docu-fiction); actor 'Un Zoo La Nuit/Night Zoo' 1987; Dir. Commercials Ciupka Films Montreal; recipient Critics Award Best Dir. 1984–85; Coq Bronze Award 1989; Award for 'Artistic Excellence' 1989; toured various theatre prodns. Can., USA, Israel, Eur.; poetry publ. various lit. jours.; recreations: reading, Aikido, skiing, fly-fishing, travel; Home: 5279 Waverly, Montreal, Que. H2T 2X6.

**BRASSARD, Jean-Luc;** athlete; s. Jean and Jeanne d'Arc Ouellette Brassard; MEMBER, CANADIAN SKI ASSOCIATION - FREESTYLE; Gold Medal, Men's Moguls, 1994 Olympics, Lillehammer, Norway; Home: Grande-Ile, Que.; Office: c/o Freestyle Ski, 1600 James Naismith Dr., Gloucester, Ont. K1B 5N4.

**BRASSARD, Jean-Marie,** Q.C., B.A., LL.L.; juge; né Montréal, Qué. 3 nov. 1921; f. Amédée et Estelle (Beauchamp) B.; é. Coll. de l'Assomption, B.A. 1943, Univ. de Montréal, LL.L. 1946; Univ. Western, Dipl. en Anglais 1946; ép. Madeleine f. Albert et Yvonne Martial 30 déc. 1950; enfants: Louise, Suzanne, Pierre; JUGE, COUR SUPERIEURE DU QUEBEC 1981– ; admis au Barreau du Qué. 1946; nommé C.R. 1964; Assoc., Brassard et Fabien 1947–56; Brassard, Hamel et Brûlé 1957–61; Brassard, Hamel, Belisle & Lefebvre 1962–65; Martel, Brassard, Deschamps & Paiement 1965–68; Pinard, Martel, Brassard, Deschamps & Cantin 1968–70; Martel, Brassard & Cantin 1970–81; Prés. des Comités de discipline du Barreau, des Archits., des Méds., des Chims., des Psychols. et des Notaires; Prés., Club des Francs de Montréal; Club Optimiste St-Laurent: Club Richelieu St-Laurent; Mem., Com. Cathol. du Cons. Sup. de l'Edn. 1974; Clubs: Vallée du Richelieu Golf; Ile des Soeurs Tennis; résidence: 11, 778 Tracy, Montréal, Qué.; bureau: Ch. 16.36, Palais de Justice, 1 est, Notre-Dame, Montréal, Qué. H2Y 1B6.

**BRATTON, Robert Dickson,** M.Sc., Ph.D.; educator; b. Winnipeg, Man. 26 May 1935; s. Arnold Robert and Isabel (Dickson) B.; e. Univ. of Man. 1953–55; Sporthochschule Koln, Germany 1957–58; George Williams Coll. Chicago B.Sc. 1959; Univ. of Cal. Los Angeles M.Sc. 1961; Univ. of Ill. Ph.D. 1970; m. Marilyn d. Claude and Electa Durham 20 Aug. 1960; children: Gregory Robert, Rodney Allen, Tanice Marilyn (dec.); Prof. of Physical Edn. Univ. of Calgary 1976–.., retired; Phys. Recreation Dir. Chicago Boys Club and Bethlehem Community Centre 1955–59; Sci. and Phys. Edn. Teacher Elmwood High Sch. Winnipeg 1959–60; Instr. in Phys. Edn. present Univ. 1961, currently Asst. Dean (Grad. Prog.); recipient Centennial Award 1967; Govt. Alta. Service Award 1974 and Achievement Award 1976; author 'Power Volleyball for Player, Teacher and Coach' 1968; 'Canadian Volleyball, A History to 1967' 1972; '300 Plus Volleyball Drills and Ideas' 1974; 'Volleyball Team Tactics and Training' 1984; co-author 'Basic Volleyball Skills and Concepts' 1980; '400 Plus Volleyball Drills and Ideas' 1985; 'Volleyball Skills and Game Concepts: Beginner to Advanced' 1986; 'Government Involvement in Physical Education, Sport and Recreation' 1982, revised 1983; Chrmn. Ed. Bd. 15 monographs 'Sociology of Sport' 1978–79; mem. extve. Alta. and Candn. Volleyball Assns. 1961–87; recreations: skiing, cycling, travel, curling; Home: 3208 Exshaw Rd. N.W., Calgary, Alta. T2M 4E9.

**BRATTY, Rudolph Peter,** Q.C.; lawyer; real estate developer; b. Toronto, Ont. 30 March 1932; s. Donato Valentino and Rina (Olivero) B.; e. Forest Hill Coll. Inst. 1950; Univ. of Toronto B.A. 1953; Osgoode Hall Law Sch. 1957; m. Catherine d. Malcolm and Ann Sinclair 16 May 1964; children: Matthew, Mark, Christopher, Michael, Jennifer; SR. PARTNER, BRATTY AND PARTNERS; Dir. Canada Trust Co.; Toronto Sun Publishing Co.; The Financial Post; Lake Ontario Cement

Ltd.; Cineplex-Odeon Corp.; Petro-Canada; Leisure World Nursing Homes Ltd.; Ruland Realty Ltd.; Erin Mills Developments Corp.; Consolidated H.C.I. Holdings Ltd.; Brampton Brick Ltd.; cr. Q.C. 1970; mem. Governing Council Univ. of Toronto; Dir. St. Michael's Hosp.; Ont. Crippled Children's Centre; Candn. Opera Co.; Un. Way; Big Bros. Metrop. Toronto; Italian Candn. Benevolent Corp.; McDonald's House; Candn. Counc. of Christians and Jews; Adv. Counc. Banting & Best Inst.; Adv. Counc. Centre for Neurodegenerative Diseases; Knight of the Sovereign Order of Malta; recreations: sports, politics, reading; Clubs: St. George Golf; Bayview Golf; York Racquets; Craigleith Ski; Home: 61 Edenvale Cres., Islington, Ont. M9A 4A5; Office: 4950 Yonge St., Suite 2000, North York, Ont. M2N 6K1.

**BRAULT, Marc André,** B.A., L.LL.; federal civil servant; b. Montréal, Qué. 25 Apr. 1943; s. Marcel and Madeleine (Lalonde) B.; e. Coll. St. Charles Garnier B.A. 1963; Laval Univ. LL.L. 1966; m. Danièle d. Jean-Louis and Marguerite Lemieux 4 March 1967; children: Simon, Nadia; CANADIAN AMBASSADOR TO SOUTH AFRICA 1993– ; Asst. Trade Comnr. Ottawa 1966, Second Sec. (Comm.) Tel-Aviv 1967, Trade Comnr. Johannesburg 1969, Dir. (Personnel) Ottawa 1973, Econ. Counsellor Paris 1976; Dir.-Trade (Africa) Dept. Ind. Trade & Comm. 1981; Dir. Gen.-Africa Dept. External Affairs 1983; Asst. Dep. Min. (Africa & Middle E.) Dept. of External Affairs 1985–88; Ambassador of Canada to Egypt 1988–90; Min. (Econ.) and Depy. Head of Mission, Canadian Embassy to the USA 1990–93; Office: Canadian Embassy, P.O. Box 26006, Arcadia, Pretoria 0007, South Africa.

**BRAULT, Michel;** film director; b. Montreal, Que. 25 June 1928; s. Paul Henri and Celine (Marchand) B.; e. Seminaire de St-Jean; Coll. Stanislas; Univ. de Montréal; m. Marie-Marthe Tardif; children: Nathalie, Anouk, Sylvain; Partner, Nanouk Films 1965– ; filmbiog. incls. Dir./Cameraman 'Les Raquetteurs' 1958; 'Pour la Suite du Monde' 1963; Dir. 'Entre la Mer et l'Eau Douce' 1967; 'Les Ordres' 1974; 'L'Emprise' 1988; 'Les Noces de Papier' 1989; 'Shabbat Shal' 1992; Dir./Producer 'A Freedom to Move' (filmed in Omnimax) 1985; Cinematog. 'Mon Oncle Antoine' 1971, 'Kamouraska' 1972, both dir. by Claude Jutra; 'Le Temps d'une Chasse' 1972 (dir. Francis Mankiewicz); 'Threshold' 1980, 'Louisiana' 1983, 'No Mercy' 1986, 'Dead Man Out' 1988 (Dir. Dick Pearce); 'The Great Land of Small' 1987 (Dir. Vojtech Jasny); recipient 6 Genie Awards; Prix de la Mise en Scène (Cannes); mem. Assn. des Réalisateurs et Réalisatrices du Qué.; Address: 1168 Richelieu Beloeil, Quebec City, Que. J3G 4R3.

**BRAUN, Aurel,** M.A., Ph.D.; b. Romania 18 Oct. 1947; s. Robert and Szerena (Farkas) B.; e. Univ. of Toronto M.A. 1973; London Sch. of Econ. Ph.D. 1976; m. Julianna d. Leslie and Erika Borsa 26 June 1980; two s. Daniel Michael, David Alexander; PROF. OF POL. SCI. UNIV. OF TORONTO 1988– , Rsch. Assoc. Centre for Russian & E. Eur. Studies and Centre for Internat. Studies; Asst. Prof. of Politics Queen's Unv./Royal Mil. Coll. 1976–77; Asst. Prof. of Pol. Sci. Univ. of W. Ont. 1977–80; Visiting Scholar Hoover Instn. Stanford Univ. summers 1981, 1983; Assoc. Prof. of Pol. Sci. present Univ. 1980–88; frequent contbr. TV and radio progs.; lectr. Nat. Defence Coll.; IBM Exec. Mgmt. Prog. N.Y.; recipient PECSU Award teaching excellence 1982–83; Dir. Hungarian Rsch. Inst. Can.; author 'Romanian Foreign Policy Since 1965: The Political and Military Rights of Autonomy' 1978; 'Small State Security in the Balkans' 1983; 'Ceausescu: The Problems of Power' (monograph) 1980; ed. and contbr. 'The Middle East in Global Strategy' 1987; 'The Soviet-East European Relationship in the Gorbachev Era: The Prospects for Adaption' 1990; 'The Warsaw Pact: The End of an Era' forthcoming; mem. Candn. Pol. Sci. Assn.; Am. Assn. Advanc. Slavic Studies; Soc. Romanian Studies; Candn. Profs. for Peace in Middle E. (Vice Chrmn. 1984–89); recreations: music, gardening, bicycling, travel; Home: 749 Briar Hill Ave., Toronto, Ont. M6B 1L7; Office: Toronto, Ont. M5S 1A1.

**BRAUN, Martin Gerald,** B.A., M.B.A., C.F.A.; investment counsellor; b. Montreal, Que. 11 Sept. 1953; s. Peter and Miriam (Grunfeld) B.; e. Wagar H.S. 1970; McGill Univ. B.A. 1975; Univ. of Western Ont. M.B.A. 1981; m. Reesa d. Allen and Ruth Slayen 6 May 1983; children: Adam, Alyssa; PORTFOLIO MANAGER & PARTNER, GLUSKIN SHEFF & ASSOC. 1992– ; Securities Analyst, Richardson Greenshields 1981–85; Vice-Pres., Investments, Beacon Capital 1985–87; Securities Analyst, Vice-Pres., Richardson Greenshields 1987–88; Analyst, Gluskin Sheff & Assoc. 1988–92; Chartered Financial Analyst Designation; B'nai B'rith of Canada; recreation: travel; Home: 40 Dundurn Cres., Thornhill, Ont. L4J 6Y9; Office: Suite 2014, 20 Queen St. W., Toronto, Ont. M5E 3R3.

**BRAUNSTEIN, Jeff;** actor, director; b. Cairo, Egypt 22 May 1946; s. Harry and Riquette (Cadranel) B.; e. primary edn. var. schools around world; H.S., London, Engl. 1962; Chiswick Drama Sch. 1963–65; m. Maja d. Pall and Harpa Ardal 18 Sept. 1971; children: Paul, Inga; PRES., CANADIAN ACTORS EQUITY COUN. 1988– ; elected to Equity Counc. 1980; Treas. 4 yrs.; Vice-Pres. 3 yrs.; has worked extensively as an actor & dir. in theatres, film & TV across Can., U.S. & U.K.; emigrated to Can. 1969; Founder & Pres., Asterix Prodns.; Bd. Mem., 'Arts & the Cities'; club: Waterfront; Home: 5 Withrow Ave., Toronto, Ont. M4K 1C8; Office: 100W – 250 The Esplanade, Toronto, Ont. M5A 1J2.

**BRAVERMAN, Doreen,** B.Ed., M.B.A., F.B.A.; business executive; e. Univ. of B.C., B.Ed.; Candn. Sch. of Mgmt., M.B.A., F.B.A.; MANAGING DIR. & SECY., BRAVERMAN GROUP OF COS.; Secy., Braverman Holdings Ltd.; J. Braverman Inc.; Pres., The Flag Shop Inc.; The Vancouver Flag Shop Inc.; Atlas Textile Print Ltd.; 399560 Alberta Ltd.; Partner, The Flag Shop, Victoria, B.C.; Ed., 'The Flag & Banner' newspaper; Dir., Candn. Labour Market & Productivity Centre; Amer. Assoc. Textile Chemists & Colorists; Mem. & Past Pres., North Am. Vexillological Assoc.; Founder & Mem., Candn. Flag Assoc.; Delta Zeta Alumn.; Mem., Kitsilano Chamber of Comm.; Mentor, Step Up for Women, FBDB; Mem., Vancouver Extves. Assn.; Zone Capt., Salvation Army Appeal; Club: Vancouver Lawn Tennis & Badminton; Home: 4414 Yew St., Vancouver, B.C. V6L 3C8; Office: 1755 W. 4th Ave., Vancouver, B.C. V6J 1M2.

**BRAWN, Robert Gerald,** B.Sc., P.Eng.; petroleum executive; b. Calgary, Alta. 24 Sept. 1936; s. Gerald and Daisy (Mamini) B.; e. Pub. and High Schs. Calgary; Univ. of Alta. B.Sc. (Chem. Eng.) 1958; m. Carole d. Oliver Stevens, Calgary, Alta. 19 July 1958; children: Sheryl, Dean, Kelly, Patti; CHAIRMAN AND DIR., DANJOLYN RESOURCES LTD.; Pres. & Dir., Danoil Energy Ltd.; Dir., EDO Canada Ltd.; Forzani Group Ltd.; Trafina Energy Inc.; The Churchill Corp.; Chem./Drilling Engr., Mobil Oil of Canada 1958–60; Engr. and Mgr. International Drilling Fluids 1960–65; Pres. S & L Refineries Ltd. 1965–70; Pres. Turbo Resources Ltd. 1970–82; Pres. Bankeno Mines Ltd. & Merland Explorations Ltd. 1982–84; Pres. OMV (Canada) Ltd. 1987–90; Danjolyn Resources Ltd. 1976– ; Chrmn., Calgary Economic Development Authority 1991– ; Past Dir.: Candn. Chamber of Commerce 1983–87; OCO '88 1985–89; Past Pres.: Calgary Chamber of Commerce 1984; Springbank Community Assn. 1975; Independent Petroleum Assn. of Can. 1981; Young Presidents Orgn. (Alta.) 1976–77; Calgary Winter Festival Foundation 1989–91; mem. Assn. Prof. Engrs. Alta.; World Presidents' Organization; Univ. of Calgary Presidents Club; Fraternity Phi Delta Theta; P. Conservative; Anglican; recreations: hockey, skiing; Clubs: Calgary Petroleum; Rotary S. Calgary; Redwood Meadows Golf & Country; Home: P.O. Box 4, Site 8, S.S. 3, Calgary, Alta. T3C 3N9; Office: #500, 505 – 3rd St. S.W., Calgary, Alta. T2P 3E6.

**BRAY, Allan Orvil;** public servant; b. Camrose, Alta. 18 Nov. 1935; s. Barnt Orvil and Anne Bernice (Watson) B.; e. Univ. of Alta.; m.; one d.; SUPERINTENDENT & CHIEF OPERATING OFFICER, ALBERTA TREASURY BRANCHES 1985– ; Mem., Fort Edmonton Found.; The Bishop's Men (Anglican); The Sir Winston Churchill Soc.; Clubs: Edmonton; Centre; Edmonton Petroleum; Office: ATB Plaza, Suite 1200, 9925 – 109 St., Edmonton, Alta. T5K 2J8.

**BRAYBROOKE, David,** M.A., Ph.D., F.R.S.C.; philosopher; educator; b. Hackettstown, N.J. 18 Oct. 1924 (naturalized citizen of Canada since 1973); s. Walter Leonard and Netta Rose (Foyle) B.; e. Hobart Coll. 1941–43; New Sch. for Social Research 1942; Downing Coll. Cambridge 1945; Columbia Univ. 1946; Harvard Univ. B.A. 1948; Cornell Univ. M.A. 1951, Ph.D. 1953; Am. Council Learned Soc's Fellow, New Coll. Oxford 1952–53, Rockefeller Foundation Grantee, Oxford 1959–60; m. Alice Boyd Noble 31 Dec. 1948; div. 1982; children: Nicholas, Geoffrey, Elizabeth Page; m. 2ndly Margaret Eva Odell, 1 July 1984 (separated 1989); CENTENNIAL COMN. PROF. OF GOVT. AND PHILOS., UNIV. OF TEXAS at Austin 1990– ; Instr. in Hist. and Lit. Hobart and William Smith Colls. Geneva, N.Y. 1948–50; Teaching Fellow in Econ. Cornell Univ. 1950–52; Instr. in Philos. Univ. of Mich. 1953–54; Bowdoin Coll. Brunswick, Me. 1954–56; Asst. Prof. of Philos. Yale Univ. 1956–63; Assoc. Prof. of Philos. and Politics, Dalhousie Univ. 1963–65, Prof. 1965–88, McCulloch Prof. of Philos. and Politics 1988–90, Emeritus 1990– ; Dean of Liberal Arts, Bridgeport (Conn.) Engn. Inst. (part-time) 1961–63; Visiting Prof. of Philos. Univ. of Pittsburgh 1965, 1966; Univ. of Toronto 1966–67; Bowling Green State Univ., Ohio 1982; Univ. of Waterloo 1985; Visiting Prof. of Pol. Science Univ. of Minn. 1971; Univ. of Calif., Irvine 1980; Univ. of Chicago 1984; Visiting Prof., Murphy Inst. of Pol. Economy, Tulane Univ. 1988; recipient Guggenheim Fellowship 1962–63; Leave Fellowship Social Sciences & Humanities Research Council Can. 1978–79, 1985–86; Visiting Fellow, Wolfson Coll., Cambridge 1985–86; Cecil H. and Ida Green Visiting Prof., Univ. of B.C., Oct. 1986; John Milton Scott Visiting Prof. of Philos., Queen's Univ. Oct. 1988; mem. Acad. Adv. Panel Can. Council Ottawa 1968–71; Council for Philos. Studies 1974–79; Ed. monograph series 'Philosophy in Canada' 1973–78; mem. adjudicating ctte. for philosophy etc., SSHRCC 1987–89, Chair 1989; mem. various journ. ed. bds.; Chrmn. Guilford (Conn.) Town Democratic Ctte. 1961–62; Cand. for Ald. Halifax 1974; mem. Bd. Educ. Guilford (Conn.) 1957–59; Dir. N.S. Civil Liberties Assn. 1976– ; author 'Three Tests for Democracy: Personal Rights; Human Welfare; Collective Preference' 1968; 'Traffic Congestion Goes Through the Issue-Machine' 1974; 'Philosophy of Social Science' 1987; 'Meeting Needs' 1987; author and ed., 'Philosophical Problems of the Social Sciences' 1965; 'Ethics in the World of Business' 1983; co-author (with C.E. Lindblom) 'A Strategy of Decision: Policy Evaluation as a Social Process' 1963; numerous articles prof. journs. and colls.; served with Army of the U.S. 1943–46, Corps of Engrs., Signal Corps, Code Clk. European Theatre; mem. Phi Beta Kappa; Am. Philos. Assn. (Extve. Ctte. E. Div. 1976–79); Am. Pol. Science Assn. (Vice Pres. 1981–82); Am. Soc. Pol. & Legal Philos.; Candn. Assn. Univ. Teachers (Vice Pres. 1974–75, Pres. 1975–76); Candn. Peace Research & Educ. Assn.; Candn. Philos. Assn. (Pres. 1971–72); Candn. Pol. Science Assn.; recreations: reading, music, walking, swimming; Club: Waegwoltic; Homes: 1 Prince St., #510, Dartmouth, N.S. B2Y 4L3 and 1500 Scenic Dr., #300, Austin, TX 78703; Offices: (Dalhousie Univ., Philos.), Halifax, N.S. B3H 3J5; (Univ. of Texas, Govt.), Austin, TX 78712-1087.

**BRAYFORD, William Barrie,** B.E.Sc., C.A.; business executive; b. Toronto, Ont. 17 Apr. 1947; s. Leslie O. and Marion S. (Campsall) B.; e. Univ. of W. Ont. B.E.Sc. 1969; C.A. (Ont.) 1972; m. Katharine d. Charles and Meryl Kirkness 26 Aug. 1977; two d. Megan Elizabeth, Katharine Jane; CHIEF FINANCIAL OFFICER, MILLER PAVING LIMITED, Markham, Ont.; Partner, Doane Raymond, Chartered Accountants (by merger from Brayford & Co./Pannell Kerr MacGillivray) 1979, retired; Dir. and Founder, Golden Terrace Resources 1987– , estbd. co. 1983 served as Pres. and Sec.-Treas. until 1987; Past Dir. and Vice Chrmn., Northern Ont. Development Corp.; Past Dir., Innovation Ont. Corp.; Past Secy. Treas., Northern Opportunities Inc.; C.A., Clarkson Gordon & Co. London, Ont. 1972; Arthur Young & Co., Charles Kempe & Co. Hamilton, Bermuda 1976–79; former Comnr. Ont. Northland Transp. Comn. 1986; Dir., Fed. Lib. Assoc.; Chief Financial Officer & Dir., Ont. Lib. Assoc. (Past Pres.); recreations: boating, skiing; Club: Engineering (Toronto); Home: 554 Village Parkway, Unionville, Ont. L3R 4K8; Office: 505 Miller Ave., Markham Industrial Park, Markham, Ont. L3R 9R8.

**BRAZEAU, Paul Ernest,** Ph.D.; neuroendocrinologist; b. Sherbrooke, Que. 26 July 1943; s. Paul Emile and Cécile (Bégin) B.; e. Univ. of Sherbrooke, Fac. of Sci., Ph.D. 1971; Fac. of Med., post-doct. training 1971–74; Dr. R. Guillemin's Lab., Salk Inst. for Biol. Rsch. (Calif.); children: Elaine, Sophie; DIR., LAB OF NEUROENDOCRINOLOGY, NOTRE-DAME HOSP. 1983– ; Rsch. Asst., Pediatrics, Univ. of Sherbrooke 1970–71; Salk Inst. 1971–74; Rsch. Assoc., Exp. Med., McGill Univ. 1974–78; Assoc. Mem. of Physiol. 1977–78; Sr. Rsch. Assoc., Salk Inst. 1978–83; Rsch. Prof., Med. & Accred. Prof. of Nutr. & of Physiol., Univ. of Montreal 1984– ; The Pimstone Prize, IInd Internat. Symp. on Somatostatin, Serono Found. (Germany) 1981; Mem., Candn. Soc. of Endocrin. & Metabol. 1972– ; Am. Endocrine Soc. 1975– ; Candn. Soc. of Clin. Investigation 1976–78; Counc. Mem., 'Medical Research Council of Quebec' 1978– ; Assoc. Ed., 'Canadian Journal of Physiology and Pharmaco.' 1976–78; author of 181 pubs. & 122 abstracts 1969– ; Home: 12460 Odette Oligny, Cartierville, Qué. H4J 9Z7; Office: 1560 E. Sherbrooke St., Montreal, Qué. H2L 4M1.

**BREBNER, Dann Antony,** B.A., M.B.A., C.F.A.; investment counsel; b. Montreal, Que. 23 June 1945; s.

Frederic Rous and Doreen Elizabeth (Dann) B.; e. Queen's Univ., B.A. 1966; Univ. of W. Ont., M.B.A. 1968; Univ. of Virginia, C.F.A. 1976; m. Mary d. Sidney and Margaret Robinson 18 Dec. 1971; children: David, Robin, Katy; PARTNER, LAKETON INVESTMENT MGMT. 1979– ; Venture Capital 1969–74; Johnston MacBrien Ltd. 1974–79; Dir., Insertek Electronics; Laketon Investment Mgmt. Ltd.; BPM Consulting Ltd.; Enterprise Canada Management Ltd.; Lakefield Arms Ltd.; Past Chrmn., P.C. Ont. Fund; Mem., Toronto Soc. of Finan. Anlaysts; recreations: curling, skiing, golf; Clubs: Toronto Golf Club; Toronto Cricket; Skating & Curling; The Fitness Inst.; Home: 24 Dunbar Rd., Toronto, Ont.; Office: PO Box 31, Royal Bank Plaza, Toronto, Ont. M5J 2J1.

**BRECHER, Michael,** B.A., M.A., Ph.D.; F.R.S.C. university professor; b. Montreal, Que. 14 March 1925; s. Nathan and Gisela (Hopmeyer) B.; e. Strathcona Acad., Outremont, Que.; McGill Univ., B.A. (1st Class Hons. and Allan Oliver Gold Medal Econ. and Pol. Science) 1946; Yale Univ., M.A. (Internat. Relations) 1948, Ph.D. (Internat. Relations) 1953; m. Eva, d. His Eminence, Chief Rabbi Nissim Danon of Palestine, 7 Dec. 1950; children: Leora, Diana Rose, Seegla; ANGUS PROF. OF ECONOMICS AND POLITICAL SCIENCE, McGILL UNIV. 1993– ; Lectr. there 1952–54; Asst. Prof. 1954–58; Assoc. Prof. 1958–63; Prof. since 1963; Publications: 'The Struggle for Kashmir' 1953; 'Nehru: A political biography' 1959 (abridged ed. 1961; transl. into Hindi, German, Italian, Japanese); 'The New States of Asia' 1963; 'Succession in India: A Study in Decision-Making' 1966; India and World Politics' 1968; 'Political Leadership in India: An Analysis of Elite Attitudes' 1969; 'The Foreign Policy System of Israel: Setting, Images, Process' 1972; 'Decisions in Israel's Foreign Policy' 1974; 'Israel, the Korean War and China' 1974; 'Studies in Crisis Behavior' 1979; 'Decisions in Crisis' 1980; 'Crisis and Change in World Politics' 1986; 'Crises in the Twentieth Century: Vol. 1, Handbook of International Crises; Vol.2, Handbook of Foreign Policy Crises' 1988; 'Crisis, Conflict and Instability' 1989; 'Crises in World Politics' 1993; more than 75 articles in scholarly journals; Visiting Prof. of Pol. Sci., Univ. of Chicago 1963, Univ. of California, Berkeley 1979, Stanford Univ. 1980; Visiting Prof. of Internat. Relations, the Hebrew Univ., Jerusalem 1970–75; awarded the Watumull Prize by Am. Hist. Assn. for 'Nehru' biography, 1960; Woodrow Wilson Foundation Award of Am. Pol. Science Assn. for 'Foreign Policy System of Israel' 1973; Nuffield Foundation Travelling Fellowship 1955–56; Rockefeller Foundation Travelling Fellowship 1964–65; John Simon Guggenheim Fellowship 1965–66; Canada Council Killam Awards (rsch. fellowships) 1970–74 and 1976–79; founder, Shastri Indo-Can. Inst. 1968 (Pres. 1969, 1970); Dir., Int. Crisis Behaviour Project 1975– ; Fieldhouse Award for Distinguished Teaching, McGill Univ. 1986; mem., World Assn. of Internat. Rels.; Internat., Am. Candn., Israeli Pol. Science Assns.; Internat. Studies Assn.; Brit. Internat. Studies Assn.; Jewish; Address: 855 Sherbrooke St. W., Montreal, Qué. H3A 2T7.

**BRÉGENT, Michel-Georges Auguste Joseph;** composer; b. Montreal, Que. 28 Jan. 1948; s. Raymond and Annette (Nadeau) B.; e. Conserv. de mus. de la prov. du Qué., licence; divorced; one d.: Dominique Petrowska; major commissions: Montreal Symph. Orch.; Soc. de Mus. Contemporaine du Qué.; L'Orch. des Jeunes du Qué.; Soc. Radio Can.; The Candn. Opera Co., etc.; Jury Mem., Can. Counc. for the Arts; Min. of Cultural Affairs, Prov. of Qué.; Mem. (Sec., then Vice-Pres.), Candn. League of Composers; Candn. Mus. Ctr. (Admin. Bd., Nat. & Reg.); The Performing Rights Orgn.; First mention & special prize, Italia Prize 1985 (internat. comp. of broadcasters, for I.B.C.); Vice-Pres., 'Les Ami(e)s de Claude Vivier'; Artistic Ctte., S.M.C.Q.; recreations: listening to music, body building; Home: 5304 avenue du Parc, App. E, Montreal, Que. H2V 4G7.

**BREGMAN, Michael,** B.Sc., M.B.A.; business executive; b. Toronto, Ont. 17 June 1954; s. Louis and Yetta (Perlman) B.; e. Wharton Sch. Univ. of Pa., B.Sc. 1975; Harvard Univ., M.B.A. 1977; m. Barbara d. Erwin and Hilda Greenberg 7 May 1978; children: Jacob, Marci, Sarah, Carolyn; FOUNDER, CHRMN. AND CHIEF EXEC. OFFR. mmmuffins, Ltd. 1979– ; Chrmn. & C.E.O., Second Cup Coffee Co. Ltd.; Dir. Corporate Devel. Loblaws Ltd. 1977–79; Bd. of Dirs. Extve. Ctte., Mt. Sinai Hosp.; Clairvest Group Inc.; White Rose Crafts & Nursery Ltd.; mem. Young Pres. Orgn.; Harvard Bus. Sch. Club Toronto; recreation: athletics; Office: 3300 Bloor St. W., 9th Flr., Center Tower, Box 54, Etobicoke, Ont. M8X 2X3.

**BREHAUT, Charles Henry,** B.Sc., M.B.A.; mining executive; b. Copper Mountain, B.C. 23 Apr. 1938; s. Cecil Henry and Joan (Pack) B.; e. Queen's Univ., B.Sc. 1959; Univ. of B.C., M.B.A. 1965; m. Jennie d. Frank and Mary Palycia 5 Nov. 1966; children: Paul, Glen; SR. VICE PRES., ENVIRONMENT, PLACER DOME INC. 1991– ; Pres., C.E.O. & Dir., Equity Silver Mines Ltd.; Dir., Gibraltar Mines Ltd.; Asst. to Pres., Falconbridge Limited 1969–75; Mgr., Mine Evaluations, Noranda Mines Limited 1976–78; Vice-Pres., Opns., Dome Mines Limited 1978–83; Pres. & C.O.O., Dome Mines Ltd. 1983–87; Sr. Vice-Pres., Candn. Operations, Gold Mining Group, Placer Dome Inc. 1987–91; Past Pres. Award for Contrib. to Mining at an Early Age, Candn. Inst. of Mining; Fellowship Award, Candn. Inst. of Mining 1989; Mem., Premier's Counc. of Ont.; Dir., Ont. Mining Assn.; Mining Assn. of Can.; Internat. Counc. on Metals and the Environment (ICME); Mem., Assn. of Prof. Engrs. of Ont.; Cdn. Inst. of Mining & Metallurgy; Clubs: Ontario; Engineers; Home: 26 Pinehurst Cres., Islington, Ont. M9A 3A5; Office: P.O. Box 350, Suite 2422, Royal Trust Tower, T-D Centre, Toronto, Ont. M5K 1N3.

**BREHN, Ralph A.,** B. Com.; executive, retired; b. Lachine, Que. 6 Feb. 1931; s. Charles George and Ariella (Godard) B.; e. Sir George Williams Univ. B.Com. 1963; Exec. Devel. Inst.; m. Pierrette d. Gerard and Germaine Girard 14 Sept. 1957; children: Linda, Thomas; Former Pres., Ralph A. Brehn Inc.; Dir., Hunter Douglas Canada Inc.; Plastibec Ltée (both 1989); Vice Pres. Mfg. and Eng., Dir. Tappan-Gurney Ltd. 1960; Vice Pres. Mfg. and Eng., Dir. Hunter Douglas Canada Ltd. 1971; Pres. Hunter Douglas Building Materials and Exec. Vice Pres., Dir. Hunter Douglas Canada Ltd. 1976; Exec. Vice Pres. and Gen. Mgr. Hunter Douglas Inc. Durham, N.C. 1979; Regional Mgr. MacMillan Bloedel Building Materials, Toronto 1980; Pres. & Dir., Hunter Douglas Canada Ltd. 1982–89; former Pres., Home Development Corp.; former Lectr. in Labour Relations McGill Univ. Mgmt. Inst.; Past Pres. and Dir. Exec. Devel. Inst.; recreations: golf, sailing, skiing, organ music, reading, travel; Club: Mountain Acres Golf & Country; Home: 4410 Paiement, Ste. Agathe Nord, Lantier, Que. J0T 1V0.

**BREITBACH, Norbert Wilhelm Maria,** LL.M.; financial executive; b. Frankfurt/Main, Germany 30 Dec. 1945; s. Dr. Johannes and Elfriede (Hillenbrand) B.; e. Univ. of Freiburg; U niv. of Frankfurt Master of Law 1973; m. Xenia d. Edith and Branco Malinovic 5 Sept. 1975; one d.: Caroline; EXECUTIVE VICE-PRES., FINANCE, SCHENKER OF CANADA 1981– ; Asst. to Dir. of Finance, Schenker Germany 1973–81; Dir., German School (Montreal); recreations: golf, skiing; Home: 119 Kirkland Blvd., Kirkland, Que. H9J 1N8.

**BREITHAUPT, James Roos,** K.St.J., C.D., N.N., G.C.P.R., K.C.L.J., K.C.C.M., C.M.L.J., Q.C., B.A., M.A., LL.B.; lawyer; b. Kitchener, Ont. 7 Sept. 1934; s. the late Maj. Rudolph Anthes, M.B.E., E.D., B.A. and Marion Elizabeth (Roos) B.; e. Univ. of Western Ont. B.A.; Univ. of Toronto M.A., Osgoode Hall LL.B.; cr. Q.C. 1975; m. Jane Adamson (M.A., B.Ed.), d. Deryck and Iva A. 26 Oct. 1974; children: Jennifer Jane, Martha Anne; CHAIRMAN COMMERCIAL REGISTRATION APPEAL TRIBUNAL 1989– ; Chrmn., Ontario Law Reform Comn. 1984–89; Chrmn., Law Reform Conf. of Can. 1987–88; lawyer in Kitchener since 1962; teacher Wilfrid Laurier Univ. 1962–67, 1978–81; el. to Ont. Legis. 1967; re-el. 1971, 1975, 1977, 1981; Liberal Critic for Treasury, Revenue, Consumer & Comml. Rlns., Atty. Gen.; Chrmn. Pub. Accts. Ctte. 1968–73; Select Ctte. on Comp. Law during Ins. Ind. series volumes on Automobile Ins., Gen. Ins., Life Ins., Accident & Sickness Ins. 1977–81; House Leader for Opposition 1973–78; Lieut. Col. & C.O., Highland Fusiliers of Can.; Militia Offr. 1952–78; Gov. WLU & Waterloo Lutheran Seminary 1969–78; Vice-Chrmn. K.W. Symphony Orch. Assn.; Candn. Inst. of Internat. Affairs; Sunbeam Home; YMCA; Red Cross; K-W Overseas Aid; Vice Chancellor, Order of St. Lazarus in Can.; mem. Priory Chapter for Can., Order of St. John since 1981; Pres., St. John Ambulance (Ont. Counc.) 1989–91; Niadh Nask; Internat. Constantinian Order; Kappa Alpha Soc.; Phi Delta Phi Legal Frat.; Nat. Counc. Boy Scouts of Can.; Lutheran; Clubs: K-W Naval Vet., Br. 50 and Br. 412 (Polish), Roy. Candn. Legion; Roy. Candn. Military Inst.; Concordia; Home: 95 - 121 University Ave. E., Waterloo, Ont. N2J 4J1; Office: 1 St. Clair Ave. W., 12th Flr., Toronto, Ont. M4V 1K6.

**BREITHAUPT, John Duncan,** B.A.Sc.; retired steel company executive; b. Peterborough, Ont. 31 July 1927; s. John Edward and Elspeth G. (Mavor) B.; e. Brown Sch. and Univ. of Toronto Schs. 1945; Univ. of Toronto B.A.Sc. 1949; Univ. of W. Ont. Mang. Training Course 1968; m. Margaret Isabel d. late George Dealtry Woodcock 31 Dec. 1949; children: Mary, Catharine, George, Barbara, James, Jill; GEN. MGR. CORPORATE PLANNING, STELCO INC. since 1978; Dir., Shaw Industries Ltd.; Torcad Ltd.; D.C. Chrome Ltd.; Dist. Sales Mgr. Page Hersey Tubes Ltd. Calgary 1960; Plate Sales Mgr. Steel Co. of Canada Ltd. 1965, Asst. Gen. Sales Mgr. 1972, Gen. Sales Mgr. 1975; Dir. Hamilton Chamber Comm.; Extve. Comte. Hamilton & Dist. Candn. Mfgrs. Assn.; mem. Assn. Prof. Engrs. Prov. Ont.; Phi Delta Theta; P. Conservative; Anglican; Clubs: Hamilton; Engineers (Toronto); Burlington Golf & Country; Home: 592 Deborah Cresc., Burlington, Ont. L7T 2N1.

**BREITHAUPT, Robert W.,** B.Sc., M.Sc., Ph.D.; research executive; b. Kitchener, Ont. 19 Aug. 1937; s. Fred A. and France M. (Bean) B.; e. Queen's Univ. B.Sc. (Hons.) 1960, M.Sc. 1962; Univ. of London (U.K.) Ph.D. 1965; Commonwealth Scholar 1962–65; m. Nola d. Albert and Virginia Juraitis; VICE-PRESIDENT TECHNOLOGY & PROGRAMS, VISTAR TELECOMMUNICATIONS INC. 1993– ; Research Officer, NRC antenna R&D 1965–69; Microwave Project Leader, Space Electronics, Communications reserach Centre (DOC) 1969–74; Dir. 1975–79; Dir., Space Programs & MSAT, DOC H.Q. 1979–85; Director General 1986; CRC DG Communications Technologies 1988–92; Interim President, CRC 1992; Mem., Advisory Bd., NRC Inst. of Information Technologies 1991– ; various public service merit awards; Outstanding Achievement Award (Public Serv.) 1991; Edit. Bd., Electronic Letters; recreations: sailing, woodworking; Home: 36 Melgund Ave., Ottawa, Ont. K1S 2S2; Office: Ste. 1410, 427 Laurier Ave. W., Ottawa, Ont. K1G 3J4.

**BREMNER, Ronald Samuel,** B.A.; television executive; b. Hamilton, Ont. 15 Sept. 1947; s. Samuel L. and Gertrude C. (Uravitch) B.; e. Hillfield Coll. Hamilton 1967; Univ. of Guelph B.A. 1971; m. Suzanne d. William and Doris Anderson 17 Nov. 1972; two s. Mark, Scott; PRES. AND CHIEF EXEC. OFFR. BRITISH COLUMBIA TELEVISION 1990– ; Retail Sales Rep. CKNW/CFM Radio Vancouver 1974, Gen. Sales Mgr. 1979, Vice Pres. & Dir. of Sales 1982, Vice Pres. & Gen. Mgr. 1986, Pres. & Gen. Mgr. 1989–90; Dir. Vancouver Better Bus. Bureau; Co-Chrmn. Royal Columbian Hosp. 75th Anniversary Campaign; Gov. Shawnigan Lake Sch.; mem. Police Bd. New Westminster, B.C.; recreation: golf; Clubs: Vancouver Golf; Westminster; Home: 19 Elsdon Bay, Port Moody, B.C. V3H 3Z2; Office: P.O. Box 4700, Vancouver, B.C. V6B 4A3.

**BRENNAN, Joseph Aloysius (Al),** B.Sc.F.; b. St. John's Nfld. 1 Oct. 1937; s. William Joseph and Ellen M. (MacDonald) B.; e. Univ. of N.B. B.Sc.F. 1960, Grad. Studies 1969–70; Reg'd Profl. Forester 1986; Nat. Defence Coll. Kingston n.d.c. 1985–86; m. Bernice d. John and Monica McCrowe 1963; children: Colleen, Paul, Nancy, Maureen; VICE PRESIDENT, PROFORMA FORESTRY CONSULTANTS 1993– ; Regional Forester, Corner Brook and St. John's, Nfld. 1960–65; Instr. Coll. of Trades & Tech. St. John's 1966–67; Dir. Forest Mgmt. Nfld. 1967–73; Asst. Dep. Min. Forestry, Nfld. 1973–78; Asst. Dep. Min. Alta. Forest Service 1978–85; Exec. Offr., Forest Ind. Devel. Div. Forestry, Lands & Wildlife, Alta. 1986–93; mem. Candn. Inst. Forestry; Alta. Forestry Assn. (Pres. 1983–85); recreations: outdoor activities, hunting, fishing, golf; Home: 4112 – 120 St., Edmonton, Alta. T6J 1Y1; Office: 10160 – 112 St., Edmonton, Alta. T5K 2L6.

**BRENNAN, Robert Bryan,** C.A.; utilities executive; b. St. Boniface, Man. 14 Jan. 1941; s. Walter R. and Olive Margaret (Threlfall) B.; e. C.A. 1966; Univ. of Man. Bus. Mgmt. 1971; m. Jackie Reico 18 July 1964; two d. Bonnie, Bobbi; PRES. AND CHIEF EXEC. OFFR. MANITOBA HYDRO 1990– ; Internal Auditor present Co. 1964, Chief Internal Auditor 1968, Mgr. Corporate Acctg. 1974, Mgr. Corporate Acctg. and Financial Planning 1977, Div. Mgr. Financial Services 1984, Corporate Controller 1986, Vice Pres. Finance & Admin. and Chief Financial Offr. 1987, Sr. Vice Pres. Finance and Chief Financial Offr. 1989–90; Dir.: Manitoba Electrical League; Power Smart Inc.; Candn. Elect. Assn.; Conf. Bd. of Can.; mem. Inst. C.A.'s Man.; Winnipeg C. of C.; Inst. Pub. Adm. Can.; Home: 50 Barker Blvd., Winnipeg, Man. R3R 2E1; Office: P.O. Box 815, 820 Taylor Ave., Winnipeg, Man. R3C 2P4.

**BRENNAN, W. John,** B.Comm., M.B.A., Ph.D.; university administrator; b. Montreal, Que. 11 Feb. 1942; e. Loyola Coll. B.Comm. 1962; Univ. of Michigan M.B.A. 1965, Ph.D. 1972; m. Beverley Davis; children: Leigh Ann, Colleen, Michael; DEAN, COLLEGE OF COMMERCE, UNIV. OF SASKATCHEWAN 1981– ; Audit Staff, Touche Ross 1962–65; Sec., Internat. Acctg. Standards Ctte. (London, England) 1975–77; Fac. Mem.,

Dept. of Acctg., present univ. 1967–81; Dept. Head 1979–81; Visiting Prof., Waseda Univ. (Tokyo, Japan) 1987; Dir., SaskOil & Gas Corp. 1986– ; Banff Sch. of Advanced Mngt. Bd. 1981– ; Inst. of Candn. Bankers 1985– ; Pres., Inst. for Saskatchewan Enterprise 1992–93; Mem., Candn. Acad. Acctg. Assn.; Internat. Assn. of Acctg. Edn. & Rsch.; Am. Acctg. Assn. (Internat. Section); Candn. Fed. of Deans of Mngt. & Admin. Studies; Candn. Inst. of C.A.s; Inst. of C.A.s of Sask.; Sask. C. of C. (Pres. 1991–92); Saskatoon Bd. of Trade; Rotary Club of Sask.; Jr. Achievement of Sask.; Candn. Club of Sask.; Candn. Counc. on Native Business; govt. appointments: Rafferty-Alameda Bd. of Inquiry 1987–88; Sask. Human Resource Assessment & Planning Ctte.; Adv. Counc., Mngt. Ctte., Can./Sask. Subsidiary Agreement on Advanced Technol.; Audit Ctte. of the Prov. of Sask.; recreations: golf; Home: 401 Copland Crescent, Saskatoon, Sask. S7H 2Z4; Office: Rm. 184, Commerce Bldg., Saskatoon, Sask. S7N 0W0.

**BRENNEMAN, Ronald A.,** B.A.Sc., M.Sc.; oil industry executive; b. London, Ont.; e. Univ. of Toronto B.A.Sc. 1968; Univ. of Manchester M.Sc. 1969; PRESIDENT, IMPERIAL OIL LIMITED 1992– ; various positions, engineering and planning assignments, Imperial Oil Limited 1969–77; Operations Mgr. (Strathcona) 1977; managerial positions in exploration & production (Calgary) 1978–83; moved to corp. H.Q., Exxon Corp. N.Y. 1983–86; Vice-Pres. & Gen. Mgr., Production Dept. (Calgary) 1986; Vice-Pres. 1989 (oversaw corp. merger between Imperial & Texaco Canada Inc.); Sr. Vice-Pres. & Chief Finan. Offr. 1989–92; Bd. of Trustees, United Way of Greater Toronto; Hospital for Sick Children; has been active in the Candn. Petroleum Assn., the Canada Safety Council, the United Way of Calgary, and was campaign chairman of Hillcrest Hospital Renewal Fund; Office: 111 St. Clair Ave. W., Toronto, Ont. M5W 1K3.

**BRENNER, Reuven Robert,** B.Sc., M.A., Ph.D.; consultant; b. Roumania 4 Jan. 1947; s. Jacob and Gladys (Sandor) B.; e. Hebrew Univ. Jerusalem B.Sc. 1972, M.A. 1974, Ph.D. 1978; m. Gabrielle A. d. Ewa and Michel 21 Oct. 1973; two s. Adi Emanuel, David Benjamin; REPAP CHAIR IN ECON. SCH. OF MGMT. McGILL UNIV. 1991– ; Assoc. Fellow CRDE Univ. de Montréal; previously Prof. Univ. de Montréal; Visiting Prof. N.Y. Univ. and Univ. of Chicago; served Israeli Army; Bank of Israel; Hebrew Univ.; guest lectr. maj. U.S. univs.; mem. del. Hoover Inst. Stanford Univ. participating confs. Eur., Mexico, USSR; cons. various corporate and govt. orgns. incl. McDonald and Bélanger Campeau Comns.; former Fulbright Fellow; recipient Killam Fellowship 1991–93; 2 books named outstanding Acad. Books pub. U.S. 1985, 1987; author 'History – The Human Gamble' 1983, transl. Spanish 1989; 'Betting on Ideas' 1985; 'Rivalry' 1987; 'Gambling and Speculation' 1990, transl. French; ed. 'Educating Economists' 1991; 'Labyrinths of Prosperity' 1994; mem. Am. Econ. Assn.; Candn. Law & Econ. Soc.; Candn. Econ. Assn.; Royal Econ. Soc.; recreations: opera, concerts, tennis; Home: 4570 Circle Rd., Montreal, Que. H3W 1Y7; Office: 1001 Sherbrooke St. W., Montreal, Que. H3A 1G5.

**BRENT, Donald William Calder,** B.A.; b. Toronto, Ont. 14 Sept. 1924; s. Reginald William and Ethel Mary (Calder) B.; e. Univ. of W. Ont. B.A. (Econ. & Pol. Sci.) 1950, Dip. in Business Adm. 1951; m. Joan d. Alan and Marion Taggart 16 Oct. 1954; children: Kathryn Janet, Alastair William Calder, Martha Anne; Chrmn., Amtelecom Group Inc.; Manitoulin Island Telephone Co. Ltd.; AGI Cablevision Inc.; Coldwater Communications Inc.; Chrmn. & Dir., Clearview Cable TV Inc.; joined A.E. Ames & Co. Ltd. 1951; Isard, Robertson & Co. Ltd. 1955, Dir. 1959, subsequently Isard, Robertson, Easson Co. Ltd., Dir. 1962, Vice Pres. 1970; joined Midland Doherty Ltd. 1976; retired 1987; Fellow, Financial Analysts Soc.; served with RCAF 1942–46, Overseas 1944–46; Gov. Candn. Corps Commissionaires London Div.; mem. Royal Candn. Legion; RCAF Assn.; Bomber Command Assn. (UK); United Church; P. Conservative; Home: 178 Wychwood Park Dr., London, Ont. N6G 1R9; Office: 18 Sydenham St. E., Aylmer, Ont. N5H 3E7.

**BRENZEL, Lawrence Aubrey;** financial executive; b. 23 June 1927; m. Sally Barbara Greisman June 1950; children: Henry Samuel, Elizabeth Gay, Alison Mary, James Mehr, Peter Mehr, Stephanie Jane Mehr; PRESIDENT, LAWRENCE A. BRENZEL LIMITED 1950– ; various management positions Lady Ellis Shops Limited, Alltex Industries Limited, Elco Limited, Buckingham Mills Limited, Wisener & Partners Co. Ltd.; Wisener & Assoc. Inc. 1950–75; ; Pres., L.A. Brenzel Securities Inc. 1975– ; Vice-Pres. & Dir., Park Indus-

tries 1987– ; numerous past community executive positions; Mem., Financial Services Group, United Jewish Welfare Fund 1960– ;(Mem., Toronto Div. 1965– ;); Life Gov., Shaw Festival Theatre Foundation 1985– ; Trustee, Ont. Coll. of Art Found. 1987– ; National Arts Ctr. 1992– ; clubs: Albany, National, Primrose, Wall St., Queens; Home: 27 Lynwood Ave., Toronto, Ont. M4V 1K3; Office: 33 Harbour Sq., Ste. 817, Toronto, Ont. M5J 2G2.

**BRESLIN, Mark,** B.A.; comedy entrepreneur; b. Toronto, Ont. 2 May 1952; s. Ruben and Matilda (Shore) B.; e. York Univ., B.A. 1974; PRES., YUK-YUK'S INC. 1978– ; Dir., Theatre & Music, Harbourfront 1974; Pres., Funny Business Prodns. Inc.; Producer, 'The Late Show' starring Joan Rivers, FOX TV 1986–88; Office: 1280 Bay St., 2nd Floor, Toronto, Ont. M5R 3L1.

**BRETON, Albert,** B.A., Ph.D., LL.D., O.C. (1984), F.R.S.C. (1976); economist; b. Montmartre, Sask., 12 June 1929; s. Albéric T. and Jeanne (Nadeau) B.; e. Coll. de S. Boniface, Univ. of Man. B.A. 1951; Columbia Univ. Ph.D. (Econ.) 1965; LL.D. Coll. de S. Boniface, Univ. du Manitoba; m. Margot, d. Gilbert Fournier, Montréal, Qué.; children: Catherine, Natalie, Françoise, Robert; PROF. OF ECONOMICS, UNIV. OF TORONTO since 1970; Asst. Prof. of Econ. Univ. de Montréal 1957–65; Dir. of Research, The Social Research Group, Montreal 1956–65; Visiting Assoc. Prof. Carleton Univ. 1964–65; Professeur invité, Université Catholique de Louvain (Belgique) 1968–69; Lectr. in Econ. 1966–67 and Reader in Econ. 1967–69 London Sch. of Econ.; Visiting Prof. of Candn. Studies Harvard Univ. 1969–70; Professeur Invité, Université de Paris I, Panthéon-Sorbonne et Institut d'Etudes Politiques de Paris 1990; awarded Candn. Social Science Research Council Grant 1955–56; Can. Council Grant 1959–60; Guest of the Inst., Mass. Inst. of Technol. 1959–60; Post-Doctoral Fellow, Univ. of Chicago 1965–66; co-recipient Can. Council Killam Sr. Research Scholarship 1972, 1974; Connaught Sr. Research Fellowship 1986–87; Vice-Chrmn., Fed. Cultural Policy Review Comm.; Gov., National Theatre Sch. of Can. 1981–84; Commr., Royal Commn. on the Economic Union and Develop. Prospects for Canada; Pres., Candn. Economics Assoc. 1988–89; author 'The Economic Theory of Representative Government' 1974; co-author (with A.D. Scott) 'The Economic Constitution of Federal States' 1978, 'The Design of Federation' 1980; (with R. Breton) 'Why Disunity' 1980; (with R. Wintrobe) 'The Logic of Bureaucratic Conduct' 1982; author or co-author numerous articles in various journs.; Home: 160 Rosedale Hts. Dr., Toronto, Ont. M4T 1C8.

**BRETON, Raymond Jules,** M.A., Ph.D.; educator; b. Montmartre, Sask. 19 Aug. 1931; s. Albéric T. and Jeanne (Nadeau) B.; e. St. Boniface Coll.; Univ. of Man. B.A. 1952; Univ. of Chicago M.A. 1958; Johns Hopkins Univ. Ph.D. 1961; m. Lily Thérèse d. Alexandre Laliberté, Cap-de-la-Madeleine, Qué. 20 Aug. 1955; children: Marc, Michèle, Suzanne, Lorraine, Daniel; PROF. OF SOCIOL., UNIV. OF TORONTO; Dir., Grad. Studies in Sociology 1981–85; Program Dir. Inst. for Research on Pub. Policy 1976–81; Research Dir. The Social Research Group, Montreal 1957–64; mem. Comte. on Aid to Publs. Social Science Research Council 1969–72; Can. Council Acad. Panel 1970–72, Chrmn. Consultative Group on Social Surveys 1973–75, mem. Univ. of Toronto Task Force on Council's Comn. on Grad. Studies in Humanities and Social Sciences 1974; mem. ad hoc Comte. on Research, Ont. Econ. Council 1976–77; Chrmn., Candn. Ethnic Studies Adv. Ctte., Dept. of the Sec. of State, Ottawa 1987–90; rec'd Samuel S. Fels Fellowship 1960–61; Can. Council Leave Fellowship 1972–73 and 1981–82; Sr. Rsch. Fellow, Statistics Can. 1987–88, 1989–90; Sr. Connaught Fellowship in the Social Sciences 1988–89; author 'Academic and Social Factors in Career Decision-Making: A Study of Canadian Secondary School Students' 1972; 'The Governance of Ethnic Communities: Politcal Structures and Processes in Canada' 1991; 'Why Meech Failed: Lessons in Canadian Constitutionmaking' 1992; Co-author 'The Social Impact of Changes in Population Size and Composition: An Analysis of Reactions to Patterns of Immigration' 1974; 'Cultural Boundaries and the Cohesion of Canada', 1980; 'Why Disunity: An Analysis of Linguistic and Regional Cleavages in Canada' 1980; 'La Langue de Travail au Québec'; Editor 'Aspects of Canadian Society' 1974; 'The Quebec and Acadian Diaspora in North America' 1982; 'Ethnic Identity and Equality: Varieties of Experience in a Canadian City' 1990; 'Canadian Review of Sociology and Anthropology' 1973–76; mem. or past mem. various ed. bds.; author various articles immigrant integration, interethnic relations, language policies, etc.; mem. Royal Soc.

Can.; Candn. Sociol. & Anthrop. Assn. (Extve. Comte. 1970–72); Internat. Sociol. Assn. (Vice Pres., Rsch. Ctte. on Ethnic and Racial Minorities 1982–86); Candn. Ethnic Studies Assn. (Extve. Comte. 1973–77); Am. Sociol. Assn.; R. Catholic; Home: 70 Sheldrake Blvd., Toronto, Ont. M4P 2B4; Office: 203 College St., 5th Flr., Toronto, Ont. M5T 1P9.

**BREWER, Douglas G.,** B.A., Ph.D., F.C.I.C.; educator; b. Toronto, Ont. 22 Dec. 1935; s. George W. and Lois E. (Buck) B.; e. Balmy Beach Pub. Sch. 1949; Univ. of Toronto Schs. 1954; Univ. of Toronto B.A. 1958 (Victoria Coll.), Ph.D. 1961; m. Marilyn J. d. John and Mary Dodd 9 Sept. 1961; children: Sharon Elizabeth, Dyanne Patricia; PROF. OF CHEM., UNIV. OF N.B. 1972– ; Asst. Prof. 1961, Assoc. Prof. 1966, Prof. and Chrmn. of Chem. 1972, Acting Dean of Science 1975, Dean of Science 1977–86, Acting Vice-Pres. (Academic) July-Dec. 1985; Chrmn., Dept. of Chemistry Univ. of N.B. 1987–1992; Dir. Candn. Turfgrass Research Foundation 1984–86; author or co-author numerous articles prof. journs.; Pres. Royal Candn. Golf Assn. 1986–87; Pres., Candn. Golf Found. 1984–86; Candn. rep. and mem. Admin. Ctte., World Amateur Golf Council 1988–92; recreations: golf, fishing, hunting; Club: Fredericton Golf and Curling; Home: 12 Riverview Court, Fredericton, N.B. E3B 5Y7; Office: Fredericton, N.B. E3B 5A3.

**BREWER, Jane;** mayor; b. Toronto, Ont. 15 Apr. 1924; d. John Alexander and Clara Wilhelmina Davison; e. Preston H.S. 1940; MAYOR, THE CORP. OF THE CITY OF CAMBRIDGE 1988– ; Alderman, City of Cambridge 1979–88; Councillor, Reg. Mun. of Waterloo 1983– ; Extve. Counc., Lutheran World Fedn.; Mem., Court of Adjudication, Evangelical Lutheran Ch. in Can.; Past Chrmn., Bd. of Gov., Conestoga Coll.; Past Regent, Preston I.O.D.E.; Mem., Corp. of Cambridge Meml. Hosp.; Past Pres., St Peters Lutheran Ch.; Past Vice-Chrmn., Synod Counc., E. Can. Synod; Past Chrmn., Office of Finance and Mngt., Evangelical Lutheran Ch. in Can.; Hon. Chrmn., United Way; Home: 105 Pheasant Ave., Cambridge, Ont. N3H 2L8; Office: 73 Water St., North, Cambridge, Ont. N1R 5W8

**BREWSTER, Donald Burgess,** Ph.D.; computer systems executive; b. Leeds, Eng. 17 Nov. 1931; s. John Duncan and Jessie Mathieson (Ross) B.; e. Ripon (Eng.) Grammar Sch. 1950; Leeds Univ. B.Sc. 1954, Ph.D. 1958; Harvard Grad. Sch. of Business 1968; Oxford Centre for Mang. Studies 1978; one d. Claire; PRES., PROFIGARD INC. since 1982; Plant Supvr. Texaco Trinidad Inc. 1958–60; Sr. Devel. Engr. Dupont of Canada 1960–61; Adv. Systems Engr. IBM Canada 1961–64; Research Dir. Westvaco Corp. 1964–69; Vice Pres., SDK & H Ltd. (consultants) 1969–71; Task Force Mgr., Marketing Mgr., Mang. Dir. S. Pacific, Marketing Dir. Europe, Measurex Corp. 1971–77; Corp. Tech. Dir., Kruger Inc., 1978–81; technical editor and author 'Pulp & Paper Mill-wide Process Control Systems' 1993; contributor 'Paper Making Systems and Their Control' 1970; over 50 publs. and patents; mem. Candn. Pulp & Paper Assn.; Fellow, Tech. Assn. Pulp & Paper Indust.; recreations: classical music, tennis, cross-country skiing, travel; Club: Trafalgar Tennis; Home: 3621 University St., Apt. 9, Montreal, Que. H3A 2B3; Office: 1425 René-Lévesque Blvd. W., Suite 505, Montréal, Qué. H3G 1T7.

**BREWSTER, Elizabeth Winifred,** A.M., B.L.S., Ph.D., D.Lit.; poet; novelist; educator; b. Chipman, N.B. 26 Aug. 1922; d. Frederick John and Ethel May (Day) B.; e. Sussex (N.B.) High Sch. 1942; Univ. of N.B., B.A. 1946, D.Lit. 1982; Radcliffe Coll. A.M. 1947; Kings Coll. Univ. of London 1949–50; Univ. of Toronto B.L.S. 1953; Ind. Univ. Ph.D. 1962; PROFESSOR EMERITUS, UNIV. OF SASK. 1990– , Prof. of English 1980–90; served various libs. incl. Queen's Univ., Carleton Univ., Ind. Univ.; Mount Allison, N.B. Legislative, Univ. of Alta.; teacher Victoria Univ. B.C. 1960–61; joined present Univ. 1972; author 'East Coast' (poems) 1951; 'Lillooet' (poem) 1954; 'Roads' (poems) 1957; 'Passage of Summer' (poems) 1969; 'Sunrise North' (poems) 1972; 'In Search of Eros' (poems) 1974; 'The Sisters' (novel) 1974; 'Sometimes I Think of Moving' (poems) 1977; 'It's Easy to Fall on the Ice' (stories) 1977; 'The Way Home' (poems) 1982; 'Digging In' (poems) 1982; 'Junction' (novel) 1982; 'A House Full of Women' (stories) 1983; 'Selected Poems, 1944–1984' (2 vols.) 1985; 'Visitations' (stories) 1987; 'Entertaining Angels' (poems) 1988; 'Spring Again' (poems) 1990; 'The Invention of Truth' (stories and essays) 1991; 'Wheel of Change' (poems) 1993; recipient E.J. Pratt Gold Medal and Prize Univ. of Toronto 1953; Univ. of W. Ont. Pres.'s Medal and Award for Poetry 1979; Can. Council Sr. Artists Awards Poetry 1971–72, 1976, 1978–79, 1985–86; CBC Award for Poetry 1991; mem. League Candn. Poets;

Writers Union Can.; Sask. Writers Guild; Assn. Candn. Univ. Teachers Eng.; Assn. Candn. & Que. Lit.; Candn. Assn. Commonwealth Lit. & Lang. Studies; PEN Internat.; Home: 206 Colony Square, 910-9th St. E., Saskatoon, Sask. S7H 0N1; Office: Saskatoon, Sask. S7N 0W0.

**BREYFOGLE, Peter Nicholas,** B.Eng., M.B.A.; executive; b. Barcelona, Spain 24 Sept. 1935; s. Robert Joshua and Elsie (McLaughlin) B.; e. Winchester Coll., Eng., 1949–54; Cambridge Univ., B.Eng. 1957; Harvard Univ., M.B.A. 1959; came to Can. 1936; m. Josephine Mary, d. B.A. King, Dorset, Eng., 11 Dec. 1965; one s. Nicholas Brenton; MANAGING PARTNER & DIR., INVESTCAN FINANCIAL CORP.; Senior Vice-Pres., Finance and Admin. Dome Petroleum Ltd. 1978–82; joined Massey-Ferguson as Financial Analyst, Toronto, Ontario, 1959; Plans and Controls Coordinator, Massey-Ferguson Export, Coventry, Eng. 1961; Gen. Financial Analysts Mgr., Massey-Ferguson Ltd., Toronto 1964; Comptroller, MF Inc./MF Industries, Toronto and Des Moines 1965; Comptroller, Massey-Ferguson Ltd., Toronto 1969; Vice Pres., Corp. Operations 1972; Exec. Vice-Pres., Europe 1975–78; Financial Consultant 1982–83; mem. Financial Executives Inst.; Anglican; recreations: golf, squash, sailing, tennis, bridge; Clubs: Royal Canadian Yacht; Toronto Golf; Caledon Ski; Leander; Home: 1 Highland Gardens, Toronto, Ont. M4W 2A1; Office: Royal Bank Plaza, North Tower, Suite 1525, P.O. Box 75, Toronto, Ont. M5J 2J2.

**BRICKMAN, James R.A.,** B.A.; brewery executive; b. Waterloo, Ont. 18 Dec. 1952; s. Joseph and Janet Christine (McNally) B.; e. St. Andrews Coll. Aurora 1971; Candn. Jr. Coll. Lusanne, Switzerland 1972; York Univ. B.A. 1975; m. Lesley Louise d. William and Elizabeth Claridge 5 May 1990; two d. Janet Louise, Jamie Elizabeth; PRES. AND FOUNDER BRICK BREWING CO. LTD. 1984– ; joined Baker-Lovick Ad Agency 1975; estbd. Brick Promotions 1976; recipient Jr. Achievement Award; Spirit of Jr. Achievement Award 1985; Dir. Brewers Assn. Can.; Brewers of Ont.; Club: Westmount Golf & Country; Home: Waterloo, Ont.; Office: 181 King St. S., Waterloo, Ont. N2J 1P7.

**BRIDGER, William Aitken,** M.Sc., Ph.D., F.R.S.C.; educator; b. Winnipeg, Man. 31 May 1941; s. William Aitken and Vera Elsie (Gibson) B.; e. Univ. of Man. B.Sc. 1962, M.Sc. 1963, Ph.D. 1966; m. Irene d. Nicholas and Theresa Fecycz 20 Jan. 1983; children: Andrea, Eric, Keith, Jocelyn; ASSOC. VICE-PRES. (RESEARCH), UNIV. OF ALTA. 1993– , Prof. of Biochem. 1977– , Chair, Dept. of Biochem. 1987–93; Rsch. Fellow Inst. for Cancer Rsch. Philadelphia 1965; Med. Rsch. Council Fellow Univ. of Cal. Los Angeles 1966–67; joined present Univ. 1967; Visiting Prof. The Rockefeller Univ. N.Y. 1984–85; co-author 'Cell ATP' 1983; numerous rsch. papers, book chapters; mem. Candn. Biochem. Soc. (Sec. 1974–80, Pres. 1984–85); Candn. Fedn. Biol. Socs. (Bd. mem. 1974–80, 1984–86, 1990–93); Home: 969 Ogilvie Blvd., Edmonton, Alta. T6R 1K8; Office: Edmonton, Alta. T6G 2H7.

**BRIDGES, Geoffrey Charles Thomas;** airline executive; b. London, Eng. 19 Feb. 1933; s. Charles George and Martha Jane (Ferguson) B.; e. Latymer Upper Sch.; Balliol Coll. Oxford; m. Cluaran d. Andrew and Ethel Baynes 9 July 1957; children: Roger, Guy, Tracy; Vice Pres. Cargo, Air Canada 1989–..; mem. Adv. Bd. Air Cargo Inc.; served British Airways Africa, Australia, Can. Eur., Middle E. & UK various sr. positions Passenger, Cargo & Customer Service, Mng. Dir. Cargo 1983–89; named Freeman City of London; Fellow, Chart. Inst. Transport; Chrmn. Internat. Air Transport Assn. Cargo Ctte.; Home: 1509 Sherbrooke St. W., Montréal, Qué. H3G 1M1.

**BRIERLEY, J.E.C.,** B.A., B.C.L., Dr.de l'U. (Paris), LL.D. (Dickinson); educator; b. Montreal, Que. 5 March 1936; s. James G., Q.C. and M. W. (McLean) B.; e. Bishop's Univ. B.A. 1956; McGill Univ. B.C.L. 1959; Univ. de Paris Dr.de l'U. 1964; Dickinson LL.D. 1985; m. Jane d. W. O. and U. M. Bartlett 29 July 1960; children: Sarah, Timothy; SIR WILLIAM MACDONALD PROF., FAC. OF LAW, McGILL UNIV. 1979– ; called to Bar of Que. 1960; Prof. of Law present Univ. 1964– , Dean of Law 1974–84; author or co-author various publs. Que. and Cndn. law; mem., Internat. Acad. of Comparative Law; Internat. Acad. of Estate & Trust Law; Clubs: Faculty; University; Brome Lake Boating; Office: 3644 Peel St., Montreal, Que. H3A 1W9.

**BRIGGS, Geoffrey Hugh,** M.A.; retired librarian; b. Leeds, Eng. 14 Apr. 1926; s. Harry and Charlotte Irene (Black) B.; e. King's Sch. Rochester, Eng. (King's Scholar); St. John's Coll. Cambridge Univ. B.A. 1947, M.A. 1949 (Choral Scholar); Univ. Coll. London Dipl. Archives and Dipl. Librarianship 1949; m. Judith Mary d. Frederick A. de la Mare, Hamilton, N.Z. 6 Dec. 1950; two s. Nicholas, Peter; Asst. Librarian, London Univ. 1949–54; Depy. Librarian, Victoria Univ. of Wellington, N.Z. 1954–67; Univ. of Calgary 1967–69; Univ. Librarian, Carleton Univ. 1969–91; mem. Candn. Assn. Research Libs. (Pres. 1979–80); recreations: music, fishing; Home: 10 Caroline Ave., Belair, South Australia 5052.

**BRIGHT, David,** B.A., M.A.; doctoral student; b. Emsworth, Hampshire, England 4 Sept. 1963; s. Leslie Anthony William and Margaret Jeanne (Wright) B.; e. Beechen Cliff Sch. 1982; Univ. of Birmingham B.A. (Special Hons.) 1987, Univ. of Calgary M.A. 1990; Insurance Clerk, NatWest Insurance Serv., Bristol, England 1982–84; Circulation Mgr., Pickwick Press, Cheltenham, England 1988; Church of England; Socialist; Academic Dir., Grad. Students' Assn., Univ. of Calgary 1990–91; Pres. 1991–92; editor: 'The Matrix' (Univ. of Calgary grad. journal); co-editor: 'Canadian Labour History: Selected Readings' 1994; author of one journal article; recreations: squash, soccer, blues guitar; Home: #1 – 2740 Brentwood Blvd., Calgary, Alta. T2L 1V4; Office: Dept. of History, Univ. of Calgary, Calgary, Alta. T2N 1N4.

**BRIGHT, Heather M.,** B.A., C.F.P.; financial planner; b. Plymouth, England; e. McMaster Univ. B.A. (Hons.) 1983; divorced; children: Gabrielle, Katherine; FINANCIAL PLANNER, BRIGHT & ASSOCIATES 1993– ; Homemaker / Volunteer / Student 1968–85; Manager of Human Resources, Sternson Limited 1985–87; Pres., Money Concepts (Brantford) 1988–93; President, Brantford Regional Chamber of Commerce (1993); Office: 156 Brant Ave., Brantford, Ont. N3T 3H7.

**BRIGHT, John Camsell (Cam);** computer executive; b. Winnipeg, Man. 31 Oct. 1938; s. John H. and Pauline M. (Forbes) B.; e. Kelvin High Sch. 1955; St. John's Coll. Winnipeg 1956; Univ. of Man. 1957–58; Am. Mgmt. Assn. course 1968; m. Janet d. Gavin and Anne Lawson 18 March 1961; children: Lindsay, Douglas, Steven; VICE PRES. OPERATIONS AMDAHL CANADA LTD. 1986– ; Dir., Amdahl Canada Ltd. 1992– ; Data Processing The Great West Life Assurance 1958–64; EDP Mgr. Eatons W. Div. Winnipeg 1964–68 & Eatons Nat. Toronto 1968–71, Dir. Eatons Tax Services 1970–71, Eatons Co. Adm. Services Mgr. Toronto 1971–72, Vice Pres. Operations, Vice Pres. Processing Services Group, Sr. Vice Pres. Canada Systems Group 1972–86; Dir. Multiple Financial Services 1983–86; mem. Friends of Seneca, Seneca Coll. 1987–88; active Un. Way Winnipeg, Toronto, Mississauga; mem. Bd. Trade Metrop. Toronto; recreations: fitness, gardening, tennis; Clubs: Adelaide; Ont. Racquet; Mississauga Golf & Country; Home: 1332 Prince Albert Court, Mississauga, Ont. L5H 3S1; Office: 5F, 1 First Canadian Pl., Toronto, Ont. M5X 1A4.

**BRILLINGER, David Ross,** M.A., Ph.D., F.R.S.C.; educator; b. Toronto, Ont. 27 Oct. 1937; s. Austin Carlyle and Winnifred Elsie (Simpson) B.; e. Univ. of Toronto Schs. 1955; Univ. of Toronto B.A. 1959; Princeton Univ. M.A. 1960, Ph.D. 1961; m. Lorie d. Frederick and Priscilla Silber 17 Dec. 1961; two s. Jef Austin, Matthew David; PROF. OF STATS., UNIV. OF CAL. BERKELEY 1969– ; Chrmn. of Stats. 1979–81; Lectr. in Math., Princeton Univ. and mem. Tech. Staff Bell Laboratories 1962–64; Lectr. becoming Reader in Stats. London Sch. of Econ. 1964–70; Woodrow Wilson Fellow 1959; Bell Telephone Labs. Fellow 1960; Soc. Sci. Rsch. Council Postdoctoral Fellow 1961; Miller Prof. 1973; Guggenheim Fellow 1975–76, 1982–83; recipient R.A. Fisher Award 1991; Gold Medal, Candn. Statistical Soc. 1992; Pres.-Elect., Institute of Mathematical Statistics 1993; author 'Time Series: Data Analysis and Theory' 1975; ed. 'Collected Works of J.W. Tukey' Vols. 1 and 2 1984; 'International Statistical Review' 1987–91; co-ed. 'Handbook of Statistics' Vol. 3 1983; 'Directions in Time Series' 1980; Fellow, Am. Acad. of Arts and Sciences; Am. Stat. Assn.; Am. Assn. Advanc. Sci.; Inst. Math. Stats.; Mem., Internat. Stat. Inst.; Stat. Soc. Canada; Royal Stat. Soc.; Seismol. Assn. Am.; Bernoulli Soc.; Candn. Math. Soc.; Office: Statistics Dept., Univ. of Calif., Berkeley, CA 94720.

**BRIMACOMBE, James Keith,** O.C., Ph.D., D.I.C., D.Sc.(Eng.), F.R.S.C., F.C.A.E., F.T.M.S., F.C.I.M., P.Eng.; educator; b. Windsor, N.S. 7 Dec. 1943; s. Geoffrey Alan and Mary Jean B.; e. Delbrook High Sch. N. Vancouver 1961; Univ. of B.C., B.A.Sc. 1966; Imp. Coll. Sci. & Technol. Univ. of London Ph.D., D.I.C. 1970, D.Sc.(Eng.) 1986; m. Margaret d. John and Elaine Rutter 7 Feb. 1970; two d. Kathryn Margaret, Jane Margaret; ALCAN CHAIR IN MATERIALS PROCESS ENG., DIR. AND FOUNDER CENTRE FOR METALL. PROCESS ENG. UNIV. OF B.C. 1985– , Asst. Prof. 1970, Prof. 1979, Stelco/NSERC Chair 1985–91; Dir., Ont. Ctr. for Materials Rsch. 1990–92; The Minerals, Metals and Materials Soc. 1990–95; The Iron and Steel Soc. 1990–95; Cons. to numerous Candn., U.S. and Overseas metall. co's; recipient numerous acad. and profl. awards & distinctions incl.: Champion H. Mathewson Gold Medal, Metall. Soc. AIME 1980; E.W.R. Steacie Fellowship, NSERC 1980–82; B.C. Sci. & Eng. Gold Medal 1985; Ernest C. Manning Prin. Award 1987; Alcan Award, Metall. Soc. CIM 1988; Extractive Metall. Lectr., TMS 1989; Izaak Walton Killam Memorial Prize for Engr., Can. Counc. 1989; Bell Canada Forum Award, Corporate-Higher Education Forum 1989; Officer, The Order of Canada 1989; Commemorative Medal, 125th Anniversary of Candn. Confedn. 1992; Howe Memorial Lectr., Iron and Steel Soc. of AIME 1993; co-author: 'Continuous Casting' Vol. II 1984; 'The Mathematical and Physical Modeling of Primary Metals Processing Operations' 1988; author or co-author over 200 sci./tech. papers; Distinguished mem. Iron & Steel Soc. (1987); The Minerals Metals and Materials Soc. (Chrmn., Extraction and Processing Div. 1988–92, Pres. 1993); mem. Assn. Profl. Engs. Prov. B.C.; Candn. Inst. Mining & Metall. (Pres. Metall. Soc. 1985–86); Inst. of Materials; ASM Internat.; Iron & Steel Inst. Japan; Sigma XI; Sigma Tau Chi; recreations: jogging, travel, photography, music; Home: 2746 West 30th Ave., Vancouver, B.C. V6L 1Y9; Office: The Centre for Metallurgical Process Engineering, Univ. of B.C., Vancouver, B.C. V6T 1Z4.

**BRIMELOW, Peter,** B.A., M.B.A.; journalist; b. Warrington, Lancashire, England 13 Oct. 1947; s. Frank Sanderson and Bessie (Knox) B.; e. Univ. of Sussex, B.A. (Hons.) 1970; Stanford Univ. Grad. Sch. of Bus., M.B.A. 1972; m. Margaret Alice d. Frederick James and Mary Laws 20 Sept. 1980; one son: Alexander James Frank; SENIOR EDITOR, 'FORBES' MAG. (NY) 1986– ;and CONTRIBUTING EDITOR, 'NATIONAL REVIEW' 1993– ; Columnist, 'Times' of London 1986–90; 'Financial Post' 1978–80 and 1988–90; Security Analyst, Richardson Securities of Can. 1972–73; Asst. Ed., 'Financial Post' 1973–76; Bus. Ed., 'Maclean's Magazine' 1976–78; Contbr. Ed./Columnist, 'Financial Post' 1978–80; Econ. Couns., U.S. Senator Orrin G. Hatch 1979–81; Assoc. Ed., 'Barron's' mag. 1981–83; 'Fortune' mag. 1983–84; Contbr. Ed., 'Barron's' 1984–86; Columnist, 'Toronto Sun' 1980–82; Columnist/Contbr. Ed., 'Chief Executive Magazine' 1984–86; 'Influence Magazine' 1985–88; Visiting Assoc., Americas Soc./Candn. Div. 1987–88; Toronto Press Club/Royal Bank Nat. Bus. Writing Award 1976; Citations 1977, 1978; Gerald Loeb Award 1990; Episcopalian; Mem., Philadelphia Soc.; author: 'The Wall Street Gurus: How You Can Profit from Investment Newsletters' 1986, 'The Patriot Game: Canada and the Canadian Question Revisited' 1986; Office: 60 Fifth Ave., New York, NY 10011.

**BRIMLEY, C. Charles,** M.Sc., B.Ed.; association executive; b. Sarnia, Ont. 27 Jan. 1952; s. Charles Dunn and Isabella Pearl (Carter) B.; e. Univ. of W. Ont. B.Sc. 1975, M.Sc. 1977, B.Ed. 1978; cert. as Applied Science Technol. 1985; two d. Angélique, Jacqueline; EXEC. DIR. CANDN. COUNCIL OF TECHNICIANS & TECHNOLS. 1984– ; Teaching Master Biol. Sci's St. Lawrence Coll. Applied Arts & Technol. Brockville, Ont. 1978–80; mem. Faculty Internat. Baccalaureate Prog. in Biol./Chem. Lester B. Pearson Coll. of Pacific, Victoria 1980–81; Asst. Nat. Coordinator Health & Community Services, Candn. Red Cross Soc. HQ Toronto 1981–82 and of Safety Services (First Aid) 1982–84; mem., Eng. Human Resources Bd. Candn. Council Profl. Engs. Ottawa; Life-mem., Ont. Assn. Cert. Eng. Technicians & Technols.; Candn. Advanced Technol. Assn.; Candn. Eng. Human Resources Bd.; mem., Steering Ctte. studying human resources for Consulting Engineering Industry; mem., Ctte. on National Standards for Technologists; mem., Candn. Soc. Assn. Execs.; author, ed. various Red Cross publs.; recreations: outdoor sports, percussionist; Home: 9, 2610 Draper Ave., Ottawa, Ont. K2H 8X8; Office: 285 McLeod St., Ottawa, Ont. K2P 1A1.

**BRIN, Marcel,** M.B.A.; business executive; b. Granby, Que. 19 Aug. 1947; s. Robert and Jacqueline (Savoix) B.; e. Ecole H.E.C., Univ. of Montreal, M.A. 1970, M.B.A. 1977; m. Aline d. Oliver and Gabrielle Moreau 20 Sept. 1974; children: Isabelle, Catherine, Geneviève, Jean; PRES. & GEN. MGR., OPTO-PLUS INC. 1993– ; Prog. Analyst, IBM Can. 1970; Gen. Mgr., Chrysler dealership 1972–75; Sr. Analyst, Royal Bank 1978–80; Extve. Vice-Pres. & Gen. Mgr., Pilon Office Supplies 1980–83;

Gen. Mgr., Services Optometriques 1983–87; Extve. Vice-Pres. & Gen. Mgr., Sodisco Inc. 1987–88; Pres. & Gen. Mgr., Sopa Inc. 1989–93; Pres., Que. MBA Assn. 1980–81; HEC School's Grad. Assn. 1986–87; recreations: jogging, swimming; club: Que. MBA Assn.; Home: 235 Desaulniers, St. Lambert, Qué. J4P 1M5; Office: 133 de la Commune West, Suite 401, Montreal, Que. H2Y 2C7.

**BRINGHURST, Robert,** B.A., M.F.A.; poet; b. Los Angeles, Cal. 16 Oct. 1946; s. George Heber and Marion Jeanette (Large) B.; e. Mass. Inst. Technol.; Univ. of Utah; Ind. Univ. B.A. 1973; Univ. of B.C. M.F.A. (Writing) 1975; one d. Piper Laramie; author (poetry) 'The Shipwright's Log' 1972; 'Cadastre' 1973; 'Deuteronomy' 1974; 'Eight Objects' 1975; 'Bergschrund' 1975; 'Jacob Singing' 1978; 'The Stonecutter's Horses' 1979; 'Tzuhalem's Mountain' 1982; 'The Beauty of the Weapons; Selected Poems 1972–82' 1982, US ed. 1985, Portuguese ed. 1994; 'Tending the Fire' 1985; 'The Blue Roofs of Japan' 1986; 'Pieces of Map, Pieces of Music' 1986, U.S. ed. 1987; 'Conversations with a Toad' 1987; (hist. & criticism) 'Ocean/Paper/Stone' 1984; 'Shovels, Shoes and the Slow Rotation of Letters' 1986; 'Visions: Contemporary Art in Canada' (co-ed.) 1983; 'Part of the Land, Part of the Water: A History of the Yukon Indians' (co-author) 1987; 'The Black Canoe' 1991, 2nd ed. 1992; 'The Elements of Typographic Style' 1992; (narrative prose) 'The Raven Steals the Light' (co-author) 1984, Japanese ed. 1986, French ed. 1989; (stage prodns. and works for multiple voices) 'Jacob Singing' Kaleidoscope Theatre, Victoria 1984; 'The Blue Roofs of Japan: A Score for Interpenetrating Voices' toured USA and Can. 1985–86, CBC Radio 1986; 'New World Suite' Vancouver Internat. Writers Festival 1990; Retrospective exhibition: 'The Poet & Typography of Robert Bringhurst,' Clark Library, UCLA, Los Angeles 1993; Visiting Lectr. in Creative Writing Univ. of B.C. 1975–77 and in Eng. 1979–80; Poet-in-Residence, Sch. of Fine Arts Banff Centre 1983; taught writing workshops sponsored by Ojibwa & Cree Cultural Centre N. Ont. 1985–86; lectr. on Candn. art & lit. univs. Australia, Japan, N.Z., Fiji 1985, Austria 1988, Spain, Germany, Portugal, Italy, UK, Ireland, 1989–90; lectr. on design hist. and hist. of literacy Simon Fraser Univ. 1983–84; cons. ed. and typographer various publishing houses Can., USA, Australia 1978–86; Writer-in-Residence Univ. of Winnipeg 1986; Univ. of Edinburgh 1989–90; Ashley Lectr., Trent Univ. 1994; Gen. Ed. Kanchenjunga Press, San Francisco and Vancouver 1973–79; Contbg. Ed. 'Fine Print' mag. San Francisco 1985–90; recipient Can. Council Arts Grants and Sr. Arts Grants 1975, 1980, 1984, 1986, 1993; CBC Poetry Prize 1985; Alcuin Soc. Design Awards 1984, 1985, 1993; Guggenheim Fellowship 1987; Canada/Scotland Exchange Writer 1989–90; mem. Writer's Union Can. (Nat. Council 1985–87); various environmental orgns.; Address: P.O. Box 280, Bowen Island, B.C. V0N 1G0.

**BRINKMAN, George L.,** B.S., Ex.M., Ph.D.; university professor; b. Minneapolis, Minn. 3 Oct. 1942; s. Loris B. and Aline C. (Slyfield) B.; e. Washington State Univ., B.S. 1964, Ex.M. 1965; Michigan State Univ. Ph.D. 1969; m. Elizabeth d. Floyd and Elizabeth Neal 30 Jan. 1965; children: Lori, Diane, Deborah; CHAIR, DEPT. OF AGRIC. ECON. & BUS., UNIV. OF GUELPH 1991– , PROF. 1981– , Acting Chair 1990–91; Asst. Prof., Dept. of Econ., Kansas State Univ. 1969–73; Assoc. Prof., Sch. of Ag. Econ. & Extension Ed., Univ. of Guelph 1973–80; Vis. Prof., Food & Resource Econ. Dept., Univ. of Florida 1980–81; Partner, Intercambio Ltd.; Cons., Agric. Can.; Statistics Can.; Auditor Gen. of Can.; Agric. Counc. of Ont.; Econ. Counc. of Can.; Candn. Min. of State for Econ. & Reg. Devel.; N. Atlantic Fisheries Task Force; USAID; Best Article Award, 'Canadian Journal of Agricultural Economics' 1978; mem., Candn. Agric. Econ. & Farm Mngt. Soc. (Pres. 1982); Agric. Inst. of Can. (Nat. Counc. 1984–86); Am. Agric. Econ. Assn.; Community Devel. Soc.; author: 'The Agricultural Finance Problem in Perspective' 1986; co-author: 'Micropolitan Development' 1976; editor: 'The Development of Rural America' 1974; recreation: fishing; Home: 14 Hickory St., Guelph, Ont.; Office: Guelph, Ont. N1G 2W1.

**BRION, Christopher Edward,** B.Sc., Ph.D., F.R.S.C., F.C.I.C.; educator; b. Ruislip, UK 5 May 1937; s. Joseph Richard and Bessie May (Carter) B.; e. Univ. of Bristol B.Sc. 1958, Ph.D. 1961; m. Elizabeth d. Reginald and Kathleen Rogers 15 Apl. 1961; children: Catherine Mary, Peter Martin, Susan Rosemary; PROF. OF CHEMISTRY, UNIV. OF B.C. 1976– ; Postdoctoral Fellow in Chem. present Univ. 1961, Asst. Prof. 1964, Assoc. Prof. 1969; Visiting Prof.: Flinders Univ. of S. Australia 1978–79; Fed. Univ. of Rio de Janeiro 1982; Kuwait Univ. 1985; Chinese Acad. of Sci's 1985; Tokyo Inst. of Technol. 1986; Inst. for Molecular Science, Okazaki, Japan 1990; recipient NRC Sr. Rsch. Fellowship 1969; Noranda Award Chem. Inst. Can. 1977; Fellow, Chemical Inst. of Can. 1978; John Simon Guggenheim Meml. Fellow 1978; Herzberg Award Spectroscopy Soc. Can. 1983; Jacob Biely Faculty Rsch. Prize Univ. of B.C. 1984; Can. Council Killam Rsch. Fellow 1984–86; Fellow, Royal Soc. of Can. 1987; Univ. of B.C. Killam Rsch. Prize 1987; Izaak Walton Killam Memorial Senior Fellowship, U.B.C. 1990; John C. Polanyi Award in Chemical Physics, Candn. Soc. for Chemistry 1993; author over 240 publs. sci. jours. and books; mem. Chemical Inst. of Can.; Candn. Assn. Physicists; Spectroscopy Soc. Can.; Am. Chem. Soc.; Home: #219 – 2200 Highbury St., Vancouver, B.C. V6R 4N8; Office: 2036 Main Mall, Vancouver, B.C. V6T 1Z1.

**BRISCOE, Robert,** B.Sc., M.B.A.; manufacturer; b. Montreal, Que. 20 Dec. 1941; s. John Richard and Anna Pearl (Pitcher) B.; e. Chambly Co. High Sch. St. Lambert, Que. 1960; Sir George Williams Univ. B.Sc. 1967, M.B.A. 1973; m. Marielle Raymonde, d. Jacques Rousseau, 28 Oct. 1961; children: Lorraine, Tracey, Susan, Robert Glen; PRES., ALIMPLUS DISTRIBUTION INC.; Pres., Macco Organiques Inc.; Chrmn., Lallemand Inc.; Dir., IEC Holden; Technilab; recreations: golf, skiing, fishing; Clubs: St-Denis; Mount Bruno C.C.; Brome Lake Boating; Knowlton Golf; Home: 4175 Ste-Catherine West, Apt. 504, Westmount, Que.; Office: 8180 Côte de Liesse Rd., St. Laurent, Qué. H4T 1G8.

**BRISEBOIS, Marcel,** O.C., B.A., L.Th., L.LL.; directeur de musée; né Valleyfield, B.A. 1954; Grand Séminaire de Montréal, L.Th. 1968; La Sorbonne Paris, L.LL. 1967; DIRECTEUR, MUSEE D'ART CONTEMPORAIN DE MONTREAL 1985– ; professeur, Coll. de Valleyfield 1958–61, professeur responsable de département 1968–71, adjoint au directeur des services pédagogiques 1971–79, Secrétaire général 1979–85; animateur-interviewer Radio-Canada, Montréal 1960; Legion d'Honneur 1989; Ordre du Canada 1990; Ordre de Malte 1992; récreations: natation, bicyclette, lecture, musées et galeries; Adresse: 209 Montcalm, Valleyfield, Qué. J6T 2E3; Bureau: 185, rue Sainte-Catherine Ouest, Montréal, Qué. H2X 1Z8.

**BRISKIN, Linda,** M.A., Ph.D.; educator; b. Montréal, Qué. 17 June 1949; d. Bernard and Anne (Gasco) B.; e. McGill Univ. B.A. 1970, Teaching Cert. 1971; York Univ. M.A. 1977, Ph.D. 1986; ASSOC. PROF. OF SOCIAL SCIENCES, YORK UNIV. 1991– , Asst. Prof. 1986; Teacher, Prot. Sch. Bd. Greater Montréal 1971–75; Teaching Master, Sheridan Coll. 1978–86, Dir. Centre for Women 1980–82; Status of Women Ctte., Ont. Confed. of Univ. Fac. Assocs. 1990–92; Bd. of Dir. Opportunity for Advancement 1987–89; Can. Council Fellow 1975–76; Social Sci. & Humanities Rsch. Council Fellow 1977–78, 1983–84; Ont. Arts Council Writer Stimulation Grant 1977, 1982, 1985; producer/director: 'Rising Up Strong: Women in the '80s' (video documentary) 1981, updated 1992; co-author: 'The Day the Fairies Went on Strike' (juvenile) 1982 ('Quand les fées font la grève' trans. 1986); 'Feminist Organizing for Change: The Contemporary Women's Movement in Canada' 1988; co-editor: 'Union Sisters: Women in the Labour Movement' 1983; 'Feminist Pedagogy: Teaching and Learning Liberation' 1990; 'Women Challenging Unions: Feminism, Democracy, Militancy' 1993; numerous articles; Office: 4700 Keele St., North York, Ont. M3J 1P3.

**BRISSON, Germain J.,** M.Sc., Ph.D.; professor; b. St-Jacques, Que. 12 Apr. 1920; s. Antonio and Clara (Gaudet) B.; e. Univ. of Montreal B.A. 1942; Laval Univ. B.Sc. (Agric.) 1946; McGill Univ. M.Sc. (Animal Nutrition) 1948; Ohio State Univ. Ph.D. 1950; m. Yvette d. Laurent Dalpé, Ste-Marie Salomée, Qué. 7 July 1948; 5 children; Prof. of Nutrition Dept. Animal Sciences Univ. Laval 1962–87, Dir. Program de doctorat en nutrition 1977–87; Dir. Centre de recherche en nutrition 1968–78; author 'Lipids in Human Nutrition' 1982; over 110 articles various aspects nutrition; recipient Golden Award Candn. Feed Industry Assn. 1979; Mérite Agronomique, Commandeur de l'Ordre du Mérite Agronomique de l'Ordre des Agronomes du Qué. 1982; Certificate of Merit, Can. Soc. Animal Sci. 1982; Prix Léo-Pariseau, ACFAS 1983; Prix LHermite, Acad. Nationale de Médecine, Paris 1983; Prix Mérite Henri L. Bernard 1985; Fellow, Agriculture Inst. Can.; Prix du Québec 1988, Marie-Victorin; Prof. Emeritus 1990; mem. Am. Dairy Science Assn.; Am. Soc. Animal Sci.; Can. Soc. Animal Sci.; Ordre des agronomes; Am. Inst. Nutrition; R. Catholic; Home: 1084 de Nouë, Ste-Foy, Qué. G1W 4L3; Office: Pavillon Comtois, Québec City, Qué. G1K 7P4.

**BRITT, John Richard,** M.Eng.; mining executive; b. Montreal, Que. 13 Feb. 1949; s. J. Theodore and Margaret (Ambler) B.; e. McGill Univ. B.Eng. 1971, M.Eng. 1973; m. Diana d. John and Anne Thomas 1 July 1972; children: Christopher, Alison; CORPORATE DIR. OF MKTG. CURRAGH INC. 1992– ; Mgr. Corporate Planning/Mktg. Gulf Minerals Canada Ltd. 1975–82; Project Mgr. Corporate Devel. Gulf Canada Ltd. 1982–83; Vice Pres. Internat. Mktg. Luscar Ltd. 1983–89; Dir. of Mktg. Denison Mines Ltd. 1989, Vice Pres. Mktg. 1990–92; mem. Candn. Nuclear Assn.; Assn. Profl. Engs. Prov. Ont.; Club: Ontario; Office: Ste. 1900, 95 Wellington St. W., Toronto, Ont. M5J 2N7.

**BRITTAIN, William Bruce,** D.F.C., B.Sc.; Canadian public service (ret'd); b. Truro, N.S. 10 Feb. 1922; s. late William Harold and Mary Macdonald (Cruickshank) B.; e. Macdonald Coll, McGill Univ., Teaching Cert. 1941. B.Sc. and High Sch. Teaching Dipl. 1949; m. Catherine Ewing, d. late John W. Wood, 22 June 1946; children: Elizabeth Ewing, Catherine Bonney, William Harold Bruce; joined Dept. of Agric., Ottawa, as Asst. Dir. of Personnel, 1949–50; apptd. Chief, Adm. Div., Science Service, 1950–54; National Health and Welfare Asst. Dir., Indian Health Service, 1954–62; Assoc. Dir., Medical Services, 1962–65; Dir.-Gen., Adm. 1965; Treasury Bd., Management Improvement Br. 1969–70; Asst. Dep.-Min. Veterans Affairs 1970, Depy. Min. 1975–85; R.C.A.F. 1941–45; AC2 to Squadron Leader; Flying Instr., Training Command; Bomber Command – 6 (Candn.) Group, U.K.; P.O.W. Denmark, Germany; awarded D.F.C.; former Pres. Can. Inst. Pub. Adm. 1980–81; Past Pres., Friends of the Candn. War Museum; Vice Chair, Bd. of Dirs., The Perley Hosp.; United Church; Home: 10 Chinook Cr., Nepean, Ont. K2H 7E1.

**BRITTON, William Leonard,** B.A., LL.B., Q.C.; b. Kirkland Lake, Ont. 15 Dec. 1934; s. Leonard William and Jeanne (LaFleche) B.; e. Univ. of W. Ont. Hons. B.A. 1958; Univ. of B.C. LL.B. 1962; m. Linda Susan d. Don Menzies, Kamloops, B.C., 26 Dec. 1960; children: Christopher, Angela, Daniel, Jane; CHRMN. & NATIONAL MANAGING PARTNER, BENNETT JONES VERCHERE (law firm); Dir., ATCO Ltd.; Canadian Utilities Limited; North American Life Assurance Co.; Denver Bronco Football Club; Alberta Power Ltd.; ATCO Enterprises Ltd.; ATCOR Ltd.; Thames Power Ltd.; Easton United Holdings Ltd.; read law with Chambers, Might & Co.; called to Bar of Alta. 1963; mem. Cdn. Bar Assn.; Law Soc. of Alta.; recreations: squash, skiing; Clubs: Calgary Petroleum (former Dir.); Calgary Golf & C.C.; Home: 408 Wilderness Pl. S.E., Calgary, Alta. T2J 2G5; Office: 4500 Bankers Hall E., 855 – 2nd St. S.W., Calgary, Alta. T2P 4K7.

**BROADBENT, The Hon. J. Edward,** O.C., M.A., Ph.D., LL.D., P.C.; b. Oshawa, Ont. 21 March 1936; s. Percy Edward and Mary Anastasia (Welsh) B., Tweed, Ont.; e. Univ. of Toronto, B.A. (Philos.) grad. 1st, M.A. (Philos. of Law), Ph.D. (Pol. Science); London Sch. of Econ., post-grad. work; m. Lucille Allen, 29 Oct. 1971; children: Paul Charles, Christine Elizabeth; PRES., INTERNATIONAL CENTRE FOR HUMAN RIGHTS & DEMOCRATIC DEVELOPMENT, Jan. 1990; Prof. of Pol. Science, York Univ. 1965–68; el. to H. of C. for Oshawa-Whitby g.e. 1968; re-el. 1972, 1974, 1979, 1980, 1984 and 1988; el. Chrmn., Fed. Caucus 1972; el. Leader of N.D.P. 1975; Leader, New Democratic Party 1975–89; resigned from leadership of N.D.P. 1989; resigned seat 1989; Vice-Pres., Socialist International 1978–89; sworn into the Privy Council, 17 April 1982; served with RCAF; rank Pilot Offr.; two Univ. of Toronto Open Fellowships and two Canada Council Scholarships for post-graduate study in Canada and England; LL.D. (hon. causa) Dalhousie Univ. 1990; York Univ. 1991; D.Litt.S., Trinity Coll., Univ. of Toronto 1990; author, 'The Liberal Rip-Off' 1970; Officer of the Order of Canada 1993; Dir., Candn. Civil Liberties Assn.; Public Policy Forum; mem. Candn. Pol. Science Assn.; Office: 63 rue de Brésoles, Montréal, Qué. H2Y 1V7.

**BROADBENT, Richard Alan,** B.A.; foundation executive, corporate director; b. Toronto, Ont. 20 July 1945; s. Joseph Alan and Marjorie Jean (McEachern) B.; e. Prince of Wales Sch.; Univ. of B.C. B.A. 1968; Queen's Univ.; m. Judy d. George and Ann Gardiner 3 Nov. 1979; children: Samuel Alan, Matthew Joseph; CHRMN. & DIR., FAIRWATER CAPITAL CORP.; Pres., The Maytree Found.; Dir. of Information, The Rubber Assn. of Can. 1973–77; Pres. 1977–81; Dir., Scott's Hosp. Inc.; Chrmn., Scott's Hospitality Foundation; Chrmn., Caledon Inst. of Social Policy; Chrmn., The Investors' Circle; recreations: tennis; clubs: Queen's; Toronto Lawn Tennis; Home: 69 Lynwood

Ave., Toronto, Ont. M4V 1K5; Office: P.O. Box 82, 1 Dundas St. W., Toronto, Ont. M5G 1Z3.

**BROADFOOT, Barry Samuel,** B.A.; writer; b. Winnipeg, Man. 21 Jan. 1926; s. Samuel James and Sylvia Marie (Scoular) B.; e. Univ. of Man. B.A. 1949; children: Susan Elaine, Ross Archer; m. 2ndly Lori (Wilcock) Classon, 1984; served newspaper and wire services 29 yrs. as photo ed., sports ed., night city ed., city ed., news ed., travel ed., book ed., mag. ed., roving corr., columnist; commentator 13 part TV series Alta.'s Pioneers; author 'Ten Lost Years' 1973; 'Six War Years' 1975; 'The Pioneer Years' 1976; 'Years of Sorrow, Years of Shame' 1977; 'My Own Years' 1983; 'The Veterans' Years' 1985; 'The Immigrant Years' 1986; 'Next-Year Country' 1988; 'Ordinary Russians' 1989; 5 books travel in Can.; popular mag. articles, special assignments Candn. newspapers, Am. and Eng. mags.; rep. in anthologies; served with Candn. Infantry Corps 1943–45; recreations: fishing, boating, hiking, world travel, reading and correspondence; Address: 3996 Morningside Rd., Nanaimo, B.C. V9T 1N5.

**BROADFOOT, Dave,** O.C., C.S.P.; comedian, actor, director, producer, writer; b. North Vancouver, B.C. 5 Dec. 1925; s. Percy and Beatrice (Chappell) B.; e. Ridgeway Jr. H.S. 1943; Athabasca Univ. Hon. Doctorate; m. Diane d. Gerard and Lucienne Simard 13 Jan. 1967; one d.: Valérie; enlisted Merchant Navy 1943; retired as Marine Engr. 1947; joined family clothing business 1947 and later Woodwards Dept. Stores; joined North Vancouver Community Players 1947 where he began to develop his 'stand-up' comedy act; first profl. engagement, Sirrocco (Victoria, B.C.) 1952; moved to Toronto 7 Sept. 1952 (the day TV broadcasting began in that city); TV debut 'The Big Revue' 1952; Featured Comedian & Writer, 'Spring Thaw' 10 years; appeared on 'Ed Sullivan Show' 1955; 'Comedian of the Year' 1959 (a year in which he prod. & performed over 90 radio & TV sketches); appeared in 'Clap Hands' London, Eng. 1962; command performance for Her Majesty Queen Elizabeth II & Prince Philip, Confed. Ctr. Charlottetown 1964; headed up variety shows for Canada's armed forces in Japan, Korea, the Gaza Strip, Cyrpus, Golan Heights & Germany 1953, '55, '59, '74, '82; productions incl. 'Well Rehearsed Ad Libs,' 'Canada Goose,' 'Squeeze,' 'Take a Beaver to Lunch,' 'Dave Broadfoot Comedy Special,' 'Tien toi bien après les oreilles à Papa'; Member, 'Royal Canadian Air Farce' 1973–88 (show won 13 nat. awards); released recording 'Wall to Wall Broadfoot' 1974 (Juno Award); honoured at RCMP H.Q. 1977; performed before Pres. Reagan 1981, Her Majesty Queen Elizabeth 1982 (both Nat. Arts Ctr.); 1st profl. comedian to appear at Candn. Embassy Washington, D.C. 1982; speciality is contemporary satire; currently averages over 100 convention appearances a year as well as numerous presentations of his one man stage show 'Dave Broadfoot's Comedy Crusade'; 13 ACTRA awards for writing & performing in Radio & TV; Cert. Speaking Profl. Award (US); Queen Elizabeth Silver Jubilee Medal; Hon. Staff Sgt. R.C.M.P.; Officer, Order of Canada; Mem., Alliance of Candn. Cinema TV and Radio Artists; Nat. Speakers Assn.; Candn. Actors Equity Assn.; Candn. Merchant Navy Assn.; author: 'Sex and Security' 1974; Address: 7 Hillholm Rd., Toronto, Ont. M5P 1M1.

**BROADFOOT, Ken H.G.,** B.Comm.; public servant; b. Calgary, Alta. 15 Mar. 1937; s. E. Maurice and Mauree (McFaul) B.; e. Univ. of Alta., B.Comm. 1958; m. Patricia d. Charles and Myrtle Lomas 11 Sept. 1957; children: Michael, Douglas, Sheila; Deputy Min., Alta. Technol., Rsch. & Telecommunications 1986–..; var. mngt. positions, Imperial Oil 1958–73; Dir., Dept. of Industry & Commerce, Alta. Govt. 1973–76; Asst. Dep. Min., Alta. Bus. Devel. & Tourism 1976–79; Devel. & Trade Div., Alta. Econ. Devel. 1979–86; Alta. Govt. Telephones Comn.; recreations: golf, skiing, jogging; Club: Edmonton Country (Pres.); Home: 12712 – 39 Ave., Edmonton, Alta. T6J 0N4.

**BROADHURST, William H.,** B.Com., F.C.A.; chartered accountant; b. Montréal, Qué. 2 Feb. 1929; s. late Thomas and late Mary Agnes (Shea) B.; e. St. Michael's Coll. Sch.; Univ. of Toronto B.Com. 1951; C.A. Ont. 1954; m. Arden Patricia d. James Howard Spence 15 Sept. 1962; children: Thomas, David, Laurence, Jeremy, Karen, Deborah, Joanna, Maura; Partner, Price Waterhouse 1965–91, mem. Exec. Ctte. 1975–90, Partner-in-Charge Toronto Office 1977–1985; Chrmn. and Sr. Partner 1985–90; Past Pres. St. Michael's Coll. Alumni Assn.; Dir. Univ. of Toronto Alumni Assn. 1963–66, Dir. and mem. Exec. Ctte. Varsity Fund 1966–74, Chrmn. 1972–74, mem. Senate Univ. of Toronto 1971–72, Governing Council 1972–80, 1983–86, Vice Chrmn. of Council 1978–80; Mem., Ont. Counc. on Univ. Affairs 1986– ; Public Gov., Toronto Stock Exchange 1991– ; Mem., Ont. Press Council 1993– ; Dir. Toronto Symphony 1980– , Treas. and Chrmn. Finance Ctte. 1983–89, Pres. 1991–92; mem. Adv. Bd. St. Michael's Choir Sch. 1983–87; Chrmn. ShareLife Adv. Bd. 1985–86; mem. Bd. Toronto French School 1986–89; mem. Inst. C.A.'s Ont. (Council 1969–77, Pres. 1976–77); Bd. Govs. Candn. Inst. C.A.'s 1974–77; Pres. Pub. Accts. Council Prov. Ont. 1984–85; Vice Pres. Candn. Acad. Acctg. Assn. 1982–84; R. Catholic; recreations: curling, swimming; Clubs; Granite; National (Pres. 1979); Home: 42 Garfield Ave., Toronto, Ont. M4T 1E9.

**BROCHU, Robert A.,** B.A., F.S.A., F.C.I.A.; management consulting executive; b. Halifax-Sud, Que. 9 Mar. 1939; e. Laval Univ. B.A. 1962; m. Liliane L. Roy 2 June 1962; children: Nathalie, Pierre, Charles; EXEC. VICE PRES., WILLIAM M. MERCER COMPANIES, INC. N.Y. 1987; Dir., William M. Mercer Ltd. (Canada); William M. Mercer, Companies, Inc.; William M. Mercer, Incorporated (U.S.); William M. Mercer Fraser Limited (UK); Asst. Actuary, Equitable Life Assurance Soc. N.Y. 1962; Asst. Gen. Mgr. Operations Que. Health Ins. Board 1969; Sr. Consultant, William M. Mercer Ltd. 1972, Dir. 1977, Exec. Vice Pres. Operations 1980, Pres. 1982; Exec. Vice Pres. William M. Mercer-Meidinger, Inc. (U.S.) 1984; Fellow, Cndn. Inst. of Actuaries; Soc. of Actuaries; mem. Am. Acad. Actuaries; Internat. Assn. Consulting Actuaries; Cdn. Inst. Int'l. Affairs; Clubs: St. James (Montreal); National (Toronto); Canadian (N.Y.); Home: 655 Park Ave., New York, N.Y. 10021.

**BROCK, Rear Admiral Jeffry Vanstone,** D.S.O., D.S.C., C.D.; R.C.N. (retired); b. Vancouver, B.C. 29 Aug. 1913; s. late Capt. Eustace Alexander B. and Margaret Phoebe (Jukes) B.; e. St. John's Coll. Sch., Winnipeg, Man.; Univ. of Manitoba; m. Patricia Elizabeth, d. late John Henry Folkes, 11 March 1950; children: Jeffrey Patrick Alexander, Constance Alexandra (Mrs. P.R. McCurdy), Wm. Ranulf Augustus D'Aguilar; began career with business associations with Great West Life Assnce. Co. and Cockfield, Brown & Co. of which he was W. Mgr.; 1st Lieut., Winnipeg Div., R.C.N.V.R. 1934; in Command Vancouver Div. 1936; Staff Signals Offr. to Flag Offr. Pac. Coast, 1939; on loan service with Royal Navy, Mar. 1940; and until Nov. 1944 served afloat in N. Atlantic, W. Africa, N. Africa, Italy and E. Mediterranean, and during this period held appts. in Command of HMS 'Kirkella,' HMS 'Rununculus,' HMS 'Stonecrop,' HMS 'Bazely,' and as spare Escort Commander W. Approaches; Mentioned in Despatches; D.S.C.; promoted Commdr.; Nov. 1944–July 1945, Sr. Offr., 6th Candn. Escort Group; 1945–47, Sr. Offr., W. Naval Reserve Divns., in Command HMCS 'Ontario,' R.C.A.F. Staff Coll.; Dir. of Naval Plans, Ottawa, 1948–50; May 1950, apptd. Capt. (D) West Coast Candn. Destroyer Flotilla; departed for Far East and Korean War as Commdr., Candn. Destroyers Far East; Mentioned in Despatches; D.S.O.; U.S. Legion of Merit (Offr.); returned to Can. July 1951 on appt. as Naval mem. of Dir. Staff, Nat. Defence Coll. of Can.; Naval Member, Candn. Jt. Staff, London, Eng., and Naval Adviser to the High Commr. for Can., 1953–57; apptd. Sr. Candn. Offr. Afloat (Atlantic), June 1957; Asst. Chief of the Naval Staff (Air & Warfare) and mem. of the Naval Bd., 1958; promoted Rear Adm. and apptd. Vice Chief of Naval Staff July 1961 and mem. of Can. U.S. Permanent Jt. Bd. on Defence; apptd. Flag Offr. Atlantic Coast and Maritime Commdr. Atlantic, July 1963; retired June 1965; P. Conservative cand. for Nanaimo, Cowichan and The Islands, g.e. 1968; author: 'The Dark Broad Seas' 1981; 'The Thunder and The Sunshine' 1982; 'Builders Bay' 1992; 'Accounting for Angela' 1992; Anglican; recreations: fishing, sailing, travel; Home: Westport, Ont. K0G 1X0.

**BROCK, William T.,** B.Sc.A., B.A.Sc., M.B.A., F.I.C.B.; banker; b. Stratford, Ont. 18 Nov. 1936; s. Russell Franklin and Marion Ruth (Morley) B.; e. Ont. Agric. Coll. Guelph, B.Sc.A. 1958; Univ. of Toronto, B.A.Sc. (Mech. Eng.) 1959; Univ. of W. Ont., M.B.A. 1963; Queen's Univ., F.I.C.B. 1964; m. Mary Anne King 5 Oct. 1962; children: Jeffrey, Karen; VICE CHRMN. CREDIT, THE TORONTO-DOMINION BANK 1992– ; Supr. Agric. Dept., Toronto-Dominion Bank 1964, First Asst. Mgr. Br. Montréal 1966; Asst. Gen. Mgr. Midland and International Banks Ltd. (on secondment) 1968–70, London, Eng.; Asst. Gen. Mgr. & Sr. Rep. Far E., Hong Kong 1970, Vice Pres. & Gen. Mgr. Asia & Australasia Div. Singapore 1972, Vice Pres. & Gen. Mgr. Eur., Middle E. & Africa Div. London, Eng. 1976, Sr. Vice Pres. Internat. Banking, Group H.O. 1980, Exec. Vice Pres. of Group 1981, Exec. Vice Pres. N. Am. Credit 1984; Exec. Vice Pres. Credit Div. 1986; Vice Chrmn., Credit 1992– ; Dir. Dover Industries Ltd.; Chrmn., Bd. of Govs., Univ. of Guelph; Clubs: National; York; Home: Suite 904, 150 Heath St. W., Toronto, Ont. M4V 2Y4; Office: P.O. Box 1, Toronto Dominion Centre, Toronto, Ont. M5K 1A2.

**BROCKLEBANK, Robert A.,** B.A.Sc., P.Eng.; business executive; b. Toronto, Ont. 23 July 1930; s. Alexander and Elva (Reilly) B.; e. Univ. of Toronto B.A.Sc. (Hons.) 1952; m. M. Paula d. Isaac and Marie Irving 18 Jan. 1975; children: Jeffrey, Lisa; PRES., THE MCELHANNEY GROUP LTD. 1969– ; Project Engr. then Chief Engr., Hunting Survey Corp. Ltd. 1952–63; Gen. Mgr., The McElhanney Group Ltd. 1964–69; Pres., Assn. of Consulting Engrs. of Can. 1986–87 (Dir. 1982–87); Past Chrmn., Candn. Assn. of Aerial Surveyors; Past Pres., Cons. Engrs. of B.C.; Bd. Chrmn., Vancouver Community Coll. 1990–92 (Dir. 1988–92); Hon. Dir., VCC Foundation 1993– ; author of 20 pub. tech. papers; clubs: Arbutus, Engineers; Home: 1419 West 47th Ave., Vancouver, B.C. V6M 2L9.

**BRODEUR, Alphonse William;** company president; b. Montreal, Que. 15 April 1931; s. Alphonse T. and Nora (Hope) B.; e. High Sch., Montreal; Trinity College Sch., Port Hope, Ont.; McGill Univ., B.Com. 1953; m. Heather Ruth, d. late Grand Gordon, 3 March 1962; three s.; PRESIDENT, CASSIDY'S LTD. since 1968; Dir., Round Agencies Ltd.; Equipment Finance Corp. Ltd.; Standard Cottons Ltd.; joined Co. 1953; apptd. Office Mgr., 1956; Sales Mgr., Toronto, 1957; Asst. Gen. Mgr., 1962; Gen. Mgr., 1964; awarded Centennial Medal, 1967; mem. Montreal Bd. Trade; Candn. Restaurant Assn.; Quebec Hotel & Suppliers Assn.; Anglican; recreations: squash, golf, curling, gardening; Clubs: Royal Montreal Golf; Badminton & Squash; Home: 33 Whitney Ave., Toronto, Ont. M4W 2A7; Office: 95 Eastside Dr., Toronto, Ont. M8Z 5S5.

**BRODEUR, Claude,** M.A., Ph.D.; educator; b. Holyoke, Mass. 29 May 1931; s. Claude and Leonie (Drapeau) B.; e. Fordham Univ. B.A. 1954, M.A. 1956; Univ. of Toronto M.A. 1957, Ph.D. 1967; ASSOC. PROF. FACULTY OF EDN. UNIV. OF TORONTO 1968– , Chrmn. Dept. Ednl. Psychol. 1984–92, mem. Univ. Gov. Council 1987–93; Instr. in Ethics Victoria Coll. present Univ. 1960, Lectr. in Philos. 1961–62, Assoc. Victoria Coll. 1977–78; Adm. Asst. & Founder Dept. Student Affairs Univ. of Waterloo 1962, Lectr. in Philos. 1962–65; Instr. in Social Sci. Ryerson Polytech. Inst. Toronto 1966–68; Adjunct Prof. and mem. Planning Ctte. Brookdale Community Coll. Lincroft, N.J. 1973–74; recipient Commendation Award 1972 and Cert. of Merit 1984 Concept Therapy Inst. San Antonio, Tex.; Co-founder Prime Mentors of Can., Dir. and Vice Pres. 1987– ; Secy., Bd. of Dir. 1992– ; mem. Ont. Govt. Rent Review Adv. Ctte.; mem. various ed. bds.; mem. Am. Psychol. Assn.; Candn. Psychol. Assn.; Ont. Soc. Clin. Hypnosis (Dir. and Treas. 1988–90; Pres.-Elect 1993–94); Chrmn., Bd. of Trustees, Stanley Kushner Memorial Fund (Ont. Soc. Clin. Hypnosis) 1992– ; Phi Delta Kappa; recreation: golf; Club: Faculty Club, Univ. of Toronto; Office: 502 - 131 Bloor St. W., Toronto, Ont. M5S 1S3.

**BRODEUR, Hélène,** B.A.; writer; b. Val-Racine, Que. 13 July 1923; s. Joseph and Marie-Ange (Turcotte) B.; e. St. Mary's Acad.; Ottawa Normal Sch., Teacher's Cert. 1940; Univ. of Ottawa B.A. 1946; 1st m. Robert s. Albert and Eva (Blais) Nantais 26 Aug. 1947; divorced 1969; children: Pierre, Giselle, Leo, Jean, Sylvie; 2nd m. Normand St. James 30 May 1974; Primary School Teacher 1941–43; H.S. Teacher 1946–47; Information Offr. 1963; retired as Dir. of Communications, Treasury Board 1978; author: 'La quête d'Alexandre' 1981 (Prix Champlain), 'Entre l'aube et le jour' 1983 (Prix du Nouvel-Ont., Prix du Droit), 'Les routes incertaines' 1986 (historical novels in French); 'Alexandre' 1983, 'Rose-Delima' 1987, 'The Honourable Donald' 1990 (historical novels in English); 'Les Ontariens' 1983 (TV script); recreations: gardening; club: Press Club of Ottawa; Office: P.O. Box 1018, Manotick, Ont. K4M 1A8.

**BRODHEAD, Tim,** B.A.; agency executive; b. Montreal, Que. 16 Apl. 1943; s. Edgar R. and Pamela J. (Browne) B.; e. Univ. de Poitiers; McGill Univ. B.A. 1964; Univ. of Ibadan, Nigeria; VICE PRES. & CHIEF OPERATING OFFR., THE J.W. McCONNELL FAMILY FOUNDATION 1992– ; Lectr. in Pol. Sci. Univ. of Ife, Nigeria 1965–68; Dir. W. Africa CUSO 1969–73; Exec. Dir. Euro Action Accord, London, UK 1973–77 and Inter Pares, Ottawa 1977–84; Rsch. Assoc. North South Inst. 1985–86; Exec. Dir., Candn. Council for Internat. Coop. 1987–92; Board mem., Calmeadow Found. Toronto; Rural Advanc. Fund Internat. Amsterdam; North-South Institute; CIVICUS; Co-Chrmn., Partners for Children Fund; co-author: 'Bridges of Hope?' 1988; Office: 1130 Sherbrooke St. W., Montreal, Que. H3A 2M8.

**BRODIE, Don Edward,** M.Sc., Ph.D.; educator; b. Can. 8 Sept. 1929; s. Frank and Matilda Ann (Broadbent) B.; e. Toronto Normal Sch. Elem. Teaching Cert. 1949; McMaster Univ. B.Sc. 1955, M.Sc. 1956, Type A Math. & Physics Specialist Cert. 1957, Ph.D. 1961; m. Naureen Elizabeth d. Thomas Earl and Edith May Petch 27 Aug. 1955; children: Trevor Thomas, Heather Ann, Tracy Lynn; PROF. OF PHYSICS, UNIV. OF WATERLOO 1965– , Dean of Science 1982–90; elem. sch. teacher Franklin Twp. 1948–51; high sch. teacher of Physics Toronto 1957–58; Lectr. in Physics present Univ. 1958–59, Asst. Prof. 1961, Assoc. Prof. 1965, Acting Chrmn. of Physics 1974–75; Visiting Research Scient. IBM Yorktown Hts. 1962; Consultant: Ontario Hydro & AECL Power Projects 1966–67; Ministry of State for Science & Technol. 1972; ARCO Ventures Co. Los Angeles 1980–82; Silonex Inc., Montreal 1986–88; Litton Systems Canada Ltd., Rexdale 1986–87; CME Telemetrix, Waterloo 1988; Electrohome Ltd., Kitchener 1988–90; Mem., Bd. of Dirs., Ont. Centre for Materials Rsch. 1988–90; Dir. Guelph-Waterloo Program Grad. Work Physics 1980–81; NRC Grant Selection Comte. on Publs. 1972–76, Chrmn. 1975–76; named Dean's Honour Roll 1955; recipient NRCC Bursary 1956, Studentship 1960; Dupont of Canada Scholarship 1956–57; Woodrow Wilson Mem. Fellowship 1959; co-inventor Candn. Patent Reactive Plating Method and Product; author numerous publs.; Vice Chrmn. Div. Solid State Physics 1972–73; Chrmn. Div. Condensed Matter Physics 1973–74; mem. NSERC Energy Panel for Strategic Grants Program 1982–85; recreations: cross-country skiing, fishing, woodworking; Home: 741 Wideman Rd., Waterloo, Ont. N2J 3Z4; Office: Univ. of Waterloo, Waterloo, Ont. N2L 3G1.

**BRODIE, Robert Gordon,** B.A.Sc., M.B.A.; real estate investor; b. Vancouver, B.C. 22 July 1931; s. Malcolm Gordon and Jessie Mildred (Hall) B.; e. Univ. of B.C., B.A.Sc. 1953; Harvard Bus. Sch., M.B.A. 1958; m. Suzanne d. Percy and Edith Lewis 29 June 1956; children: Taryn, Dallas, Fiona; CHRMN., PRES. & C.E.O., CARDIFF ESTATES LTD.; Founder, Merit Oil Co. Ltd. 1959; Norgal Investments Ltd. 1959; sold Merit Oil to Petro Can. 1981; Pres., Chrmn. & C.E.O., Turbo Resources Ltd. 1986–90; Dir., B.C. Gas Inc.; Trans Mountain Pipe Lines Ltd.; Pres., Vancouver Symphony Soc. 1972–74; Commodore, Royal Vanc. Yacht Club 1977–79; Gov., Olympic Trust of Can. 1978– ; Trustee, B.C. Sports Hall of Fame & Museum 1980–88; Chrmn., B.C. Auto. Assn. 1988–90; Pres., Vanc. Art Gallery 1983–85; Pres., Candn. Auto. Assn. 1985–87; elected Commander, Order of St. John 1993; recreations: skiing, power boat cruising; Clubs: Vancouver Club; Royal Vancouver Yacht; Shaughnessy Golf & Country; Home: 1570 West 35th Ave., Vancouver, B.C. V6M 1H2; Office: Ste. 3050 – 700 W. Georgia St., P.O. Box 10030, Pacific Centre, Vancouver, B.C. V7Y 1A1.

**BRODIE, William Woollcombe (Bill);** production designer/art director; b. Ottawa, Ont. 24 Aug. 1931; s. William H. (Steve) and Maithol H. (Woollcombe) B.; e. Browns Sch.; Oakwood Coll. Inst.; m. 1stly Leah N. Griffiths Nov. 1950 (dissolved Feb. 1962); children: Matthew, Catherine, Simon; m. 2ndly Ann d. James and Joan Pritchard 1 Feb. 1964; PRES., OTISART INC. 1983– ; Art Dir., numerous films & TV shows 1953– ; 'Barry Lyndon' 1974; 'Joseph Andrews' 1976; Supr. Art Dir., 'Superman I' 1977–79; Prod. Designer, 'Silence of the North' 1979–80; 'The Grey Fox' 1980; 'Draw' 1983; 'One Magic Christmas' 1985; 'Dead of Winter' 1986; 'Short Circuit II' 1987; 'The Little Kidnappers' 1989; 'Body Parts' 1990; Genie Award Winner, 'Grey Fox' 1983; Genie Award Nomination, 'One Magic Christmas' 1986; 'Draw' 1985; 'Silence of the North' 1982; Bd. of Dir., Acad. of Candn. Cinema & TV 1983– ; Mem., Directors Guild of Can. 1977– ; Assn. of Cinematographers & TV Tech. ( U.K.) 1956– ; Writer, Dir., Co-Prod., 'Terry Whitmore for Example' 1968–69 which was invited to show at Dir. Fortnight, Cannes Film Festival, San Francisco Film Festival, and Pesaro Film Festival 1969 and recd. Quality Award, Swedish Film. Inst. 1969; recreations: dog loving, sketching, sculpting, enthusiastic resident of Toronto's beaches; Address: 18 Nursewood Rd., Toronto, Ont. M4E 3R8.

**BRODSKY, Lynn Myer,** B.Sc., M.Sc., Ph.D., B.Ed.; secondary school biology teacher; b. Ottawa, Ont. 23 June 1958; d. Myer Michael and Therese Anita (de la Salle) B.; e. Carleton Univ., B.Sc. (Hons.) 1980, M.Sc. 1982; Queen's Univ., Ph.D. 1986; Univ. of West. Ont., B.Ed. 1989; m. Michael R. s. James and Vera Leslie 4 Sept. 1980; SCIENCE TEACHER, UPPER CANADA COLLEGE 1992– ; NSERC Scholar 1984–86; NSERC Postdoct. Fellow 1986–88; Secondary Sch. Biol. Teacher, London Central S.S. 1989–92; Rsch. funding from World Wildlife Fund; Candn. Wildlife Serv.; Queen's Univ.; Nat. Sportsman's Fund; mem., Toronto Humane Soc.; Greenpeace; World Wildlife Fund; Candn. Kennel Club; author of 12 scientific articles; recreations: canoeing, hiking, roses, watching birds; Home and Office: Upper Canada College, 200 Lonsdale Rd., Toronto, Ont. M4V 1W6.

**BROMKE, Adam,** M.A., Ph.D.; university professor; b. Warsaw, Poland 11 July 1928; came to Can. 1950; s. Waclaw and Romualda (Beckmann) B.; e. St. Andrews Univ. M.A. 1950; Univ. of Montreal Ph.D. 1953; McGill Univ. Ph.D. 1964; m. Ewa Boniecka d. Zytomirska 29 Dec. 1986; grown sons from previous marriage: PROF. OF HUMANITIES, THE POLISH ACADEMY OF SCIENCES, WARSAW 1990– ; Lectr. Univ. of Ottawa 1952–53; Lectr. Univ. of Montreal 1952–54; Ed.-in-Chief, Polish Overseas Proj., Free Europe Comte., N.Y. 1955–57; Conference leader and Lectr. McGill Univ. 1957–60; Rsch. Fellow, Russian Rsch. Centre, Harvard Univ. 1960–62; at Carleton Univ. as Asst. Prof., 1962; Chrmn. Soviet and European Studies 1963–66; Assoc. Prof. 1964; Prof. 1967; Chrmn. of Dept. 1968–71; Prof. of Pol. Sci., McMaster Univ. 1973–89; Chrmn. of Dept. 1973–79; Prof. Emeritus 1988; Man. Ed., 'Candn. Slavonic Papers' 1963–66; columnist 'The Toronto Star' 1986–87; served with Polish Underground Army 1944–45; Polish Forces under Britain's Comm. 1945–47 (Germany, Italy, U.K.); discharged as Offr.-in-Comn.; twice awarded Polish Army Medal; Cross of the Polish Underground; Cross of the Warsaw uprising; author of 'The Labour Relations Board in Ontario' 1961; 'Poland's Politics: Idealism vs. Realism' 1967; 'Poland: The Last Decade' 1981; 'Poland: The Protracted Crisis' 1983; 'Eastern Europe in the Aftermath of Solidarity' 1985; 'The Meaning and Uses of Polish History' 1987; 'East-West Relations in the 1980s'; Ed.: 'Poland's Protracted Crisis' 1983; 'The Communist States at the Crossroads' 1967; 'The Communist States and the West' 1967; 'The Communist States in Disarray, 1965–1971' 1972 (Polish trans. 1973); 'Gierek's Poland' 1973; 'The Communist States in the Era of Detente, 1971–1977' 1978; papers on intl. politics and Eastern Europe in several professional jnls. and N.A. newspapers; mem., Candn. Assn. of Slavists (Vice Pres. 1966–68, Pres. 1968–69); Candn. Political Assn.; Am. Assn. for the Advancement of Slavic Studies; Intl. Political Science Assn.; Intl. Comte. for Soviet and European Studies (Pres. 1974–80); awarded the Polish Order of Merit, Commander Rank 1988; R. Catholic; recreations: serious reading, light music; Residence: Bernardynska 22/26, 02–904 Warszawa, Poland.

**BROMLEY, David Allan,** B.Sc., M.Sc., M.A., M.S., Ph.D., D.Sc., D.Eng.Tech., Sc.D., F.A.P.S., F.A.A.A.S., F.R.S.A. (London), Dr. Nat. Phil. (Frankfurt); Dr. d'Etat, Science (Strasbourg); Dr. Sc.(Queen's); Litt. D. (U. of Bridgeport); Sc.D. (U. of Notre Dame); D.Sc. (U. of Witwatersrand); Dottore-Science (U. of Padua); Hu.L.D. (Univ. of New Haven); D.Sc. (Trinity Coll.); physicist; university professor; b. Westmeath, Ont. 4 May 1926; s. Milton Escort and Susan Anne (Anderson) B.; e. Queen's Univ., B.Sc. (Engn. Physics) 1948, M.Sc. (Physics) 1949; Univ. of Rochester, M.S. 1950 Ph.D. (Nuclear Physics) 1952; Yale Univ., M.A. 1961; m. Patricia Jane, d. Thomas Patrick Brassor, Kingston, Ont., 30 Aug. 1949; children: David John, Karen Lynn; Asst. to Pres. George Bush for Science and Technology; Dir., White House Office of Science and Technology Policy; Chrmn., President's Counc. of Sci. & Technol. Advisers; currently on indefinite leave from the Henry Ford II Professorship at Yale; Henry Ford II Prof. of Physics, Yale Univ. since 1972 and Chrmn. of Dept. 1970–77; Dir., A.W. Wright Nuclear Structure Lab. 1962–89; Operating Engr., Ont. Hydro Elect., 1946; Demonst., Queen's Univ., 1947; Jr. Research Offr., NRC (Can.) 1948; Univ. of Rochester, Instr. 1952–54, Asst. Prof. 1954–55; Atomic Energy of Canada Ltd. 1955–60 (Assoc. Research Offr., 1955–56; Sr. Research Offr., 1957–60; Sec. Head, Accelerators, 1958–60); Assoc. Prof. of Physics, Yale Univ., 1960–61 and Assoc. Dir. Heavy Ion Accelerator Lab.; with J.M. McKenzie devel. first room temp. semiconductor nuclear detectors and first used these in nuclear research; with E. Almqvist first used light helium istopes as projectiles in nuclear research; discovered first nuclear molecules; with H.W. Fulbright designed and built first variable energy cyclotron; with Chalk River and High Voltage Engn. staff devel. first tandem accelerator and first Emperor tandem accelerator respectively; with J. Birnbaum (IBM) devel. first completely integrated computer based nuclear data acquisition system; pioneered in use of heavy ion beams in precision study of nuclear phenomena; Dir., UNC Inc. 1967–89; United Illuminating Co. 1972–89; Union Trust Co. 1975–89; Northeast Bancorp Inc. 1975–89; Chronar 1984–85; Barnes Engineering Co. 1981–85; Oak Ridge Assn of Univs. 1968–72; Southeastern Universities Rsch. Assn. 1982–89; Univ. of Bridgeport 1979–86; Associate Ed., McGraw Hill Book Co. 1970–89; Consulting Ed. Nuclear Instruments and Methods; American Scientist; Annals of Physics; Il Nuovo Cimento; Nuclear Science Applications; Science, Technology and the Humanities; Journal of Physics; Technology in Society; Consultant, Brookhaven, Los Alamos, Argonne, Oak Ridge Nat. Labs., Bell Telephone Labs., IBM Corp., High Voltage Engn., Gen. Telephone and Electronics Co.; awarded Gov. Gen. of Canada Medal 1948, Queen's Univ. Medal 1948, Distinguished Public Service Medal, Center for The Study of the Presidency 1992, Carey Medal AAAS 1993, Shell Fellowship 1949, NRC (USA) Fellowship 1952, Guggenheim Memorial Fellowship 1977; Humboldt Prize 1978, 1982 and 1984; Distinguished Alumnus Award, Univ. of Rochester 1985; U.S. National Medal of Science 1988; Louis Pasteur Medal, Univ. of Strasbourg 1991; Executive of the Year Award, R&D Magazine 1992; D.Sc.: Renssdaer Polytechnic; Polytechnic Univ. of N.Y.; Ohio State Univ. Fordham Univ.; Coll. of William and Mary; Northwestern Univ.; Lehigh Univ.; D.Eng.Tech., Wentworth Inst. of Technol.; Sc.D., Illinois Inst. of Technol.; Univ. of Mass.; State Univ. of N.Y.; Colorado Sch. of Mines, Drexel Univ.; Chrmn. U.S. Nat. Comte., Internat. Union of Pure and Applied Physics; Pres. Int'l. Union of Pure and Applied Physics; Chrmn., Nat. Physics Survey Comte., Nat. Acad. Sciences; Chrmn., Office of Physical Scs., N.R.C.; mem. Candn. Assn. of Physicists; Conn. Acad. Science & Engn.; U.S. Nat. Acad. of Sci.; Fellow, Brantford Coll., Yale Univ.; Am. Acad. Arts & Sciences; Am. Assn. Advanc. Science (Chrmn. Physics Sect. 1977); Pres., Am. Assn. Advancment of Sci. 1979, Chrmn. 1982; mem., Adv. Bd. Inst. for Nuclear Power Ops. 1981–83; Electric Power Research Inst. 1982–86; mem. Counc. on Foreign Relations; mem., Extve. Bd. International Counc. of Scientific Unions; Benjamin Franklin Fellow, Royal Soc. of Arts (London); mem. at Large, Nat. Research Council (Chrmn. Comte. on Nuclear Science NAS-NRC) 1963–78; mem., Naval Sc. Bd. NAS-NRC 1973–78; High Energy Physics Adv. Panel, ERDA 1972–78; Nuclear Sci. Adv. Comm. US-DOE/NSF 1979–85; Jt. U.S.-U.S.S.R. Working Group on Science Policy and on Research on Fundamental Properties of Matter; Chrmn., CSCPRC formal U.S. nuclear science delegation to Peoples Republic of China 1979; Chrmn., Gandhi-Reagan Blue Ribbon Panel on Indo-US Cooperation in Science and Technology; Chrmn., Sarney-Reagan Blue Ribbon; Panel on Brazil-US Cooperation in Science and Technology; Mem., White House Science Council 1981–89; Mem., U.S. National Science Bd. 1988–1989, 1993–95; Extve. Comte. and U.S. Nat. Comte., Internat. Council of Scientific Unions; Chrmn., Jr. Faculty Fellowship Ctte., David and Lucile Packard Found. 1988– ; co-author of 'Proceedings of the Kingston Conference' 1960, and 'Perspectives in Physics' 1969; 'Physics in Perspective' 1972–73; author of over 450 publ. in scient. and tech. lit.; 'Large Electrostatic Accelerators' 1976; 'Detectors in Nuclear Science' 1978; 'Nuclear Science in China' 1980; 'Heavy Ion Science' 8 vols., 1984; Sigma Xi; Presbyterian; recreations: archeology, music, photography; golf; Clubs: Mory's (New Haven); Army and Navy (Washington, D.C.); Office: Office of Sci. and Technol. Policy, Extve. Office of The Pres., The White House, Washington, DC 20500.

**BRONCZEK, David J.,** B.A.; transportation executive; b. Ohio 22 June 1954; s. Walter John B.; e. Kent State Univ. B.A. 1976; m. Judy d. Joseph and Mildred Anton June 1977; children: Matthew, Sarah, Jennifer; VICE-PRESIDENT & GENERAL MANAGER, FEDERAL EXPRESS CANADA LTD.; Senior Manager, Federal Express Corp., Los Angeles; Managing Director, Liberty District; Dir., Economic Advisory Council (Mississauga); Conference Board of Canada; Toronto Board of Trade; Managing Director of the Year 1986 Federal Express Corp.; Vice President of the Year 1988 Federal Express Corp.; recreations: sailing, golfing, travel; clubs: Toronto Board of Trade; Home: 1736 Sir Monty's Dr., Mississauga, Ont. L5N 1A5; Office: 50 Burnhamthorpe Rd. W., Suite 1201, Mississauga, Ont. L5B 3C2.

**BRONFMAN, Charles Rosner;** O.C.; industrialist; b. Montreal, Que. 27 June 1931; s. Saidye (Rosner) and late Samuel B.; e. Selwyn House Sch. Montreal; Trinity Coll. Port Hope, Ont.; McGill Univ.; m. Andrea Morrison 1982; two children: Stephen Rosner, Ellen Jane; CO-CHRMN., CHRMN. EXEC. CTTE., THE SEAGRAM COMPANY LTD.; Chrmn., CRB Foundation; Claridge Israel Inc.; Dir., E.I. du Pont de Nemours & Company; Power Corp. of Can.; joined Seagram Co.

Ltd. 1951; Vice-Pres. and Dir. 1958; Exec. Vice-Pres. 1971; Chrmn. Exec. Com. 1975; Deputy Chrmn. 1979; Co-Chrmn. 1986; Hon. Chrmn., Can.-Israel Securities Ltd.; Hon. Pres., United Israel Appeal of Can.; Past Pres., Allied Jewish Community Services of Montreal; Dir. Can. Council of Christians & Jews; mem. Montreal Bd. Trade; Shaar Hashomayim Cong., Westmount; Clubs: Montefiore; Mount Royal; Saint-Denis; Elm Ridge Golf & Country; Palm Beach Country; Office: 1430 Peel Street, Montreal, Que. H3A 1S9.

**BRONFMAN, Edgar M.,** B.A.; industrialist; b. Montreal, Que. 20 June 1929; s. Saidye (Rosner) and the late Samuel B.; e. Trinity Coll. Sch. Port Hope, Ont.; McGill Univ., B.A. 1951; CHRMN. & C.E.O., THE SEAGRAM COMPANY LTD. 1975– ; Dir., E.I. duPont de Nemours & Co.; Pres., World Jewish Congress; Trustee and Chrmn., Anti-Defamation League of B'nai B'rith New York Appeal; Pres. Samuel Bronfman Foundation; Dir. Int'l. Executive Service Corps; Am Technion Soc.; Citizens Ctte. for N.Y.C.; Dir., U.S.-U.S.S.R. Trade and Economic Counc., Inc.; Weizmann Inst. of Science; mem., Union of Am. Hebrew Congregations (bd. of delegates); Sch. of Internat. and Public Affairs, Internat. Adv. Bd., Columbia Univ. (chrmn. of planning ctte.); mem. Am. Jewish Committee (exec. ctte.); Am. Jewish Congress; Am. Cancer Soc., N.Y.C. Div.; B'Nai B'rith Int'l.; Business Ctte. for the Arts, Inc.; Center for Inter-Am. Relations, Inc.; Ctte. for Economic Development; Council or Foreign Relations; Foreign Policy Assn.; Hundred Year Assn. of N.Y.; Nat. Urban League (Finance Ctte.); United Jewish Appeal/Federation of Jewish Philanthropies; Office: 375 Park Ave., New York, N.Y. 10152.

**BRONFMAN, Edward M.,** B.Sc.; executive; b. Montreal, Que. 1 Nov. 1927; s. Allan and Lucy (Bilsky) B.; e. Selwyn House; Bishop's Coll. Sch.; Babson Coll. (Mass.), B.Sc. (Business Adm.) 1950; children: Paul Arthur, David Eric, Brian Anthony; PRES., BRONCORP INC. and DEPY. CHRMN. BD., EDPER ENTERPRISES LTD.; Dir., Hees International Bancorp Inc.; Ranger Oil Ltd.; Astral Communications Inc.; Brascan Ltd.; Carena Developments Limited; Nat. Co-Chairperson, Candn. Council for Christians and Jews; Mem. Bd. of Dirs., Candn. Council for Aboriginal Business; Candn. Psychiatric Rsch. Foundation; Candn. Centre for Global Security; Candn. Found. for AIDS Rsch. (CanFAR); Hon. Chrmn., Nat. Mental Health Fund; Mem. Bd. of Govs., Hebrew Univ. of Jerusalem; recreations: skiing, running; Office: BCE Place, P.O. Box 778, Toronto, Ont. M5J 2T3.

**BRONFMAN, Paul,** B.A.; film production executive; b. Montreal, Que. 28 May 1957; s. Edward M. and Beverly (Chertkow) B.; e. St. Georges H.S.; Concordia Univ.; Univ. of Toronto, B.A. (Comm.) 1983; m. Judy 29 June 1980; children: Alexandra, Jonathan, Andrew; OWNER, COMWEB CORP. 1988– ; Owner, Music Machine Mobile Disco 1973–75; Asst. Prod. Mgr., Donald k Donald Prodns. 1976–77; Sound & Studio Co-ord., Pathé Sound 1978–80; Prod. Admin., Astral Film Prodns. 1983; Dir., Advtg. & Promo., First Choice/Super Channel 1984–85; Vice-Pres. Sales & Mktg., Bellevue Home Entertainment 1985–86; Vice-Pres., Business Devel., Astral Film Enterprises 1986–88; Address: 1200 Bay St., Ste. 703, Toronto, Ont. M5R 2A5.

**BRONFMAN, Peter Frederick,** B.A.; business executive; b. Montreal, Que. 2 Oct. 1929; s. Allan and Lucy (Bilsky) B.; e. Lawrenceville Sch., N.J.; Yale Univ., B.A. 1952; m. Diane Feldman, 8 Dec. 1953 (div.); m. 2ndly, Theodora Reitsma, 4 Feb. 1976 (div.); m. 3rdly Lynda Hamilton 19 Apr. 1985; children: Linda, Bruce, Brenda; CHAIRMAN, EDPER INVESTMENTS LIMITED and CHAIRMAN, EDPER ENTERPRISES LIMITED; Dir., Brascan Limited; Trilon Financial Corp.; Trizec Corp. Ltd.; Carena Developments Ltd.; John Labatt Ltd.; Hees International Bancorp. Inc.; Hollinger Inc.; Noranda Inc.; The Toronto Blue Jays Baseball Club; Hon. Dir., Doctors Hosp.; Mem. Adv. Counc., Barbra Schlifer Commemorative Clinic; St. Stephens Community House; Dancer Transition Centre; recreations: tennis, swimming; Club: York Racquets; Office: BCE Place, 181 Bay St., P.O. Box 778, Toronto, Ont. M5J 2T3.

**BROOK, Adrian Gibbs,** Ph.D., F.C.I.C., F.R.S.C.; university professor; b. Toronto, Ont. 21 May 1924; s. Frank Adrian and Beatrice Maud (Wellington) B.; e. Lawrence Park Coll. Inst., Toronto, Ont.; Univ. of Toronto, B.A. 1947, Ph.D. 1950; m. Margaret Ellen, d. Samuel E. Dunn, Ottawa, Ont., 18 Dec. 1954; children: Michael Adrian, Katherine Mary, David Lindsay; UNIVERSITY PROFESSOR EMERITUS, Prof. of Chemistry, Univ. of Toronto 1962–89 and Chrmn. of Dept. 1971–74; Lectr. in Chem., Univ. of Sask., 1950–51; Nuffield Foundation Fellow in Chem., Imp. Coll. of Science & Tech., London, Eng., 1951–52; Post-doctoral Fellow, Iowa State Univ., 1952–53; Lectr., Univ. of Toronto, 1953–56, Asst. Prof., 1956–59, Assoc. Prof., 1959–62, Assoc. Chrmn. of Dept. 1968–69, Acting Chrmn. 1969–71; awarded Regents Gold Medal in Physics and Chem., 1947; Kipping Award in Organsilicon Chem. (Am. Chem. Soc.) 1973; CIC Medal 1985 (Chemical Inst. of Canada); University Professor (Univ. of Toronto) 1987; author of over 130 articles in scient. and prof. journs.; mem. Am. Chem. Soc.; Chem. Inst. of Canada; served in 2nd World War with R.C.N.V.R., 1943–45; United Church; recreations: computing, windsurfing; Home: 79 Glenview Ave., Toronto, Ont. M4R 1P7.

**BROOK, Timothy James,** B.A., A.M., Ph.D.; university professor; b. Toronto, Ont. 6 Jan. 1951; s. John Frederick and Barbara Ada (MacLatchy) B.; e. Univ. of Toronto B.A. 1973; Harvard Univ. A.M. 1977, Ph.D. 1984; spouse: Fay d. Al and Bette Sims; children: Vanessa (Galt), Katherine, Taylor, Jonah; ASSOCIATE PROF. OF HISTORY, UNIV. OF TORONTO 1991– ; MacTaggart Fellow, Dept. of History, Univ. of Alberta 1984–86; Asst. Prof., Dept. of History, Univ. of Toronto 1986–91; Assoc. Dir., Univ. of Toronto/York Univ. Joint Ctr. for Asia Pacific Studies; has spent 3 years in China & 2 years in Japan; speaks & reads Chinese & Japanese; Mem., Candn. Asian Studies Assn.; Amnesty Internat.; author: 'Geographical Sources of Ming-Qing History' 1988, 'Quelling the People' 1992; 'Praying for Power' 1993; editor: 'The Asiatic Mode of Production in China' 1989; co-editor: 'National Policy and Local Power' 1989; recreations: music, poetry, travel; Home: 647 Carlaw Ave., Toronto, Ont. M4K 3K6; Office: Toronto, Ont. M5S 1A1.

**BROOKE, Ralph Ian,** B.Ch.D., L.D.S., M.R.C.S., L.R.C.P., F.D.S.R.C.S., F.R.C.D.(C.), F.I.C.D.; educator; b. Leeds, Eng. 25 Apr. 1934; s. Michael and Jeanette (Cohen) B.; e. Leeds Grammar Sch. 1951; Leeds Univ. B.Ch.D. 1957; m. Lorna d. George and Ethel Shields 21 Apr. 1963; two s. Michael, Andrew; VICE-PROVOST, HEALTH SCIENCES 1987– ; DEAN OF DENTISTRY, UNIV. OF W. ONT. 1982– , Prof. of Oral Med. 1972– ; House Surg., Leeds Dental Hosp./St. Georges Hosp. London 1957–58, Leeds Gen. Infirmary/Chapel Allerton Hosp. Leeds 1963–64; Lectr. in Clin. Dental Surg. Leeds Univ. 1964, Sr. Lectr. 1969; Consultant, Dental Surgs. Un. Leeds Hosps. 1969–72; Prof. and Chrmn. of Oral Med. present Univ. 1972–82; Chief of Dentistry, Univ. Hosp. London, Ont. 1972–92; co-author 'Diseases of the Jaws of Interest to Dentists' 1973; 'Cancer Medicine' 1974, 2nd ed. 1981; Past Pres. Candn. Acad. Oral Pathol. 1978–79; Past Pres., Assoc. of Candn. Faculties of Dentistry; Pres., Candn. Acad. of Oral Med.; Chrmn., Candn. Commn. on Dental Accreditation; Office: Dental Sciences Bldg., Univ. of W. Ont., London, Ont. N6A 3K7.

**BROOKE, Stephen James,** M.A., D.Phil.; historian; b. Deep River, Ont. 16 June 1960; s. John and Mary (Clark) B.; e. Halifax W. High Sch. 1978; Univ. of King's Coll. B.A. 1982; McGill Univ. M.A. 1984 (Social Sci. & Humanities Rsch. Council Can. Scholar 1983); Queen's Coll. Oxford D.Phil. 1988 (Commonwealth Scholar 1984–86, Overseas Rsch. Award 1986, Rsch. Fellow in Modern Hist. 1986–89); CARNEGIE PROF. OF HIST. UNIV. OF KING'S COLL. AND ASSOC. PROF. OF HIST. DALHOUSIE UNIV. 1989– ; author 'Labour's War: the British Labour Party During the Second World War' 1992; R. Catholic; Office: Dalhousie Univ., Halifax, N.S. B3H 3J5.

**BROOKING, Ruth Patricia,** B.A., B.L.S.; retired librarian; b. West Whitby Twp., Ont.; d. Ernest Covini and Hazel Olive (Hutchings) B.; e. Brooklin Continuation Sch. 1945; Oshawa Coll. & Vocational Inst. 1946; Queen's Univ. B.A. 1958; Univ. of Toronto B.L.S. 1962; Chief Executive Officer, Oshawa Public Library 1974–93, Retired; Head of Tech. Services present Lib. 1962, Head of Adult Services 1964, Asst. Chief Librarian 1967, Acting Chief Librarian 1973; mem. Candn. Lib. Assn.; Ont. Lib. Assn.; Pine Ridge Cable TV Programming Adv. Bd.; Y.W.C.A. Advisory Bd.; United Church; recreations: farming, skiing, bicycling, swimming, reading; Club: Canadian (Past Pres., Candn. Club of Durham Region); Rotary (Oshawa); Home: R.R. 1, Whitby, Ont. L1N 5R5.

**BROOKS, Bonnie;** fashion executive; d. Gordon E. and Rose E. Brooks; Pres., Town & Country Stores (Div. of Dylex) 1990–..; Fairweather 1973–81; Marketing Mgr., Holt Renfrew 1981–83; Vice Pres., Mktg. & Sales 1983–87; Exec. Vice Pres., Merchandising 1987–90; Dir., Cdn. Advertising Foundation; 'NRMA' Sales Promotion; Fashion Group Internat. Inc.; 'Women Who Make a Difference' award Toronto 1989; Home: 7 Wychwood Park, Toronto, Ont. M6G 2V5.

**BROOKS, Frank Leonard;** artist; b. London, Eng. 7 Nov. 1911; s. Herbert Henry and Ellen (Barnard) B; came to Can. 1912; e. Pub. and High Schs., North Bay, Ont.; Central Tech. Sch. and Ont. Coll. of Art, Toronto, Ont.; travelled and studied in Eng., France and Spain 1932–34; Ont. Teachers' Training Coll., Hamilton, Ont.; Escuela Universitaria de Bellas Artes, San Miguel de Allende, Mexico, lithography and fresco, 1947; m. Reva, d. M. Silverman, Toronto, Ont., 18 Oct. 1935; has exhibited throughout Can., also in Eng. and N.Y.; paintings in collection of Nat. Gallery, Ottawa, Art Gallery of Ontario, Museum of Modern Art, Mexico, Palacio de Bellas Artes, Mexico, D.F. (Exhibition of Paintings and Tapestries 1976), S. J. Zacks Coll., Toronto and Art Gallery, London, Ont., Worcester Art Museum (US); Carpenter Gallery, Dartmouth Coll., N.H., Ohio Univ., as well as in many private collections; Exhibitions at Ohio Univ., Athens, Ohio; Dartmouth Coll.; Santa Barbara Museum of Art; Lucien Labaudt Art Gallery, San Francisco; Witte Museum, San Antonio; appointed Teacher of Art, N. Vocational School, Toronto, Ont. 1937; served in World War 1943–45 with R.C.N.V.R. as Lieut.; Official War Artist 1944; mem. Roy. Candn. Acad. of Arts; author: (books) 'Watercolor ... A Challenge' 1957; 'Oil Painting Traditional and New' 1959; 'Wash Drawing' and 'Casein' 1961; 'Painting and Understanding Abstract Art' 1964; 'Painter's Workshop' 1969; established Leonard and Reva Brooks Foundation, Queen's Univ., Kingston 1992; Home: Calle de la Quinta No. 10 (Guadiana) Box 84, San Miguel de Allende, Gto., 37700 Mexico.

**BROOKS, Frederick Dane,** A.A., B.A., M.Ed., ED.S.; educational systems psychologist; b. Brooklyn, N.Y. 5 Feb. 1948; s. Gene and Norma B.; e. Univ. of West Florida B.A. 1971; Kent State Univ. M.Ed. 1975, ED.S. 1976; children: Thane, Justin, Kevin, Dana; PRES., BUSINESS INFORMATION EXCHANGE (BIE INTERNATIONAL) 1993– ;and PRES. & CHIEF EXTVE. OFFR., EdUpsych inc. 1990– ; Assoc. Prof., Univ. of Manitoba 1976–78; School Psychol., Min. of Edn. Manitoba 1976–77; Reg. Coord. Child Devel. Support Serv. 1976–78; Sr. Prog. Dir., Cochrane Temiskaming Resource Ctr. 1978–80; Extve. Dir., Velleman Nonprofit Housing Corp. Toronto 1989; Plainfield Childrens Home 1980–90; Velleman Found. 1983– ; Pres., MBA Devel. Internat. Inc. 1989– ; Extve. Mem., Candn. Coll. of Health Extves.; Ont. Psychol. Assn. (Assoc. Mem. 1980); Western Can. Admin. Counc. 1977–79; Extve. Mem., Counc. for Exceptional Children 1977–81; Adv. Mem. & Past Chrmn., Loyalist Coll. DSW Prog. 1983–87; Fac. Advr., Candn. Sch. of Mngt. 1978, 79, 84, 85; Extve. Mem., Internat. Health Econ. & Mngt. Inst. 1989– ; Quinte Area Coord., Share the Flame Olympic Torch Relay 1987; Man in Motion Rick Hansen World Tour 1987; Cert. of Merit, Govt. of Can. Community Contbn. 1988; Extve. of the Year Award, Profl. Sec. Internat. 1984; Municipal Couns., Corp. of Twp. of Sidney 1988– ; V.P., Belleville & Dist. C. of C. 1986–88; Barker, Tent 28 Variety Club of Ont. 1988, 89, 90; author of articles and guest speaker-presentor; recreations: Peter Puck Sr. Hockey, weight lifter, alpine intermed. skier; club: Stirling Fast Ball; Office: P.O. Box 20004, Belleville, Ont. K8N 5V1.

**BROOKS, Leonard James, Jr.,** B.Com., M.B.A., F.C.A.; educator; university administrator; b. Toronto, Ont. 7 Feb. 1944; s. Leonard James and Dorathy Maud (Currie) B.; e. Univ. of Toronto B.Com. 1966, M.B.A. 1967; C.A. 1970; F.C.A. 1982; m. Jean Marilyn d. John and Aida McPherson 1966; children: Catherine Anne, Leonard James III, Heather Lindsay, John Alexander; PROF. OF ACCTG. AND BUSINESS ETHICS, UNIV. OF TORONTO, 1987– ; joined Univ. of Toronto 1974; Assoc. Dean of Social Sci's 1980–88; Vice Prin. Adm. Erindale Campus, Univ. of Toronto 1982–88; joined Touche Ross & Co. 1967–74 becoming Audit Mgr. and Dir. of Manpower; Dir. Candn. Centre for Ethics & Corporate Policy; Ed. 'The Corporate Ethics Monitor'; Mem., Ed. Bd. 'The Journal of Business Ethics'; author 'Canadian Corporate Social Performance' 1986 (nominated Nat. Bus. Book Award); numerous articles acad. and profl. jours.; Mem., Interprovl. Bd. Examiners Candn. Inst. C.A.'s 1976–78, Chrmn. 1978–80; Chrmn. Syllabus Ctte. 1981–86; Pres. Candn. Acad. Acctg. Assn. 1985–86, Dir. 1980–87; United Church; recreations: fishing, team sports, tennis, golf; Club: Tecumseh Tennis; Home: 791 Terlin Blvd., Mississauga, Ont. L5H 1T1; Office: Erindale Campus, Mississauga Ont. L5L 1C6 and Faculty of Management Studies, 246 Bloor St. W., Toronto, Ont. M5S 1V4.

**BROOKS, Michael (Jake) Jan,** M.A., M.B.A.; non-profit management specialist, association executive; b. Grand Junction, Colo. 8 Dec. 1956; s. David Barry and Toby Judith (Haftka) B.; e. Carleton Univ. M.A. 1979; York Univ. M.B.A. 1984; EXECUTIVE DIRECTOR, INDEPENDENT POWER PRODUCERS' SOCIETY OF ONT. 1990– ; Action Research; Ont. Environment Network; Energy Mines and Resources Canada; Synergistics Consulting; Algonquin College; Ottawa Co-op Garage; Ten Days for World Devel; Main Writer & Prod. Mgr., Ont. Credit Union Central Newsletter 1987, '88; Pollution Probe Found. 1980s; Co-founder, Independent Power Prod. Soc. of Ont. 1986; Sec., Robert Owen Found.; Editor: 'IPPSO FACTO' & Ottawa Co-op. Dir. 1980; Office: 163 Eastbourne Ave., Toronto, Ont. M5P 2G5.

**BROOKS, Reva;** photographer; b. Toronto, Ont. 10 May 1913; d. Morris and Jennie (Klein) Silverman; e. Dovercourt Pub. Sch., Central High Sch. of Comm., Central Tech. Sch., Toronto; Univ. of Toronto night courses; m. Frank Leonard Brooks 18 Oct. 1935; Exhns.: Toronto, London, Montreal, Vancouver galleries; Santa Barbara Museum of Art; Anglo-Mexican Inst. Mexico; Witte Museum, San Antonio, Texas; Museum of Modern Art N.Y.; Dartmouth Coll.; Group Show Creative Photography 1956; Salon Internat. du Portrait Photographique, Bibliothèque Nationale, Paris 1961; Grands Photographes de Notre Temps, Versailles 1962; Expo Montreal 1967; Palacio de Bellas Artes Mexico 1970; Centro Cultural Instituto Nacional de Bellas Artes, San Miguel de Allende, Mexico; Casa de Cultura Aguascalientes, Mexico; Universidad de Guanajuato; Travelling Exhn. USA 1971; Royal Ont. Museum 1972; rep. in coll.: Bibliothèque Nationale Paris; Museum of Modern Art N.Y.; Instituto Nacional de Bellas Artes Mexico; David Alfaro Siqueiros Mexico; Rufino Tamayo Mexico; Rico Lebrun Los Angeles; John Huston Ireland; MacKinley Helm Coll. Santa Barbara; Ansel Adams Carmel; Ayala & Samuel J. Zacks Toronto; Helen Hayes N.Y.; Kate Simon N.Y.; Henry Miller Calif.; Freeman Tovell Ottawa and other Candn. Mexican Am. and European artists and collectors; various publs. of works; contrib. 'Enciclopedia del Sapere' Milan; Nat. Univ. of Mexico 1974; San Francisco Museum of Modern Art 1975 and Travelling Exhn. 1976; Nat. Film Bd. Can. 1975; Catalogue 'Photography 75'; established Leonard and Reva Brooks Foundation, Queen's Univ., Kingston 1992; Home: Calle de la Quinta No. 10 (Guadiana), P.O. Box 84, San Miguel de Allende, Gto., 37700 Mexico.

**BROOKS, Robert Leslie,** B.Sc., M.B.A.; banker; b. Kelvington, Sask. 2 June 1944; e. Univ. of Man. B.Sc. 1965; Univ. of W. Ont. M.B.A. 1968; m. Brenda Mary 28 Dec. 1968; children: Derek, Keith and Ian; EXTVE. VICE-PRES., INVESTMENT BANKING, THE BANK OF NOVA SCOTIA 1986– ; Vice Pres. & Dir., Scotia Mortgage Corp.; Dir., ScotiaMcLeod Inc.; ScotiaMcLeod (Hong Kong) Inc.; Scotia Investment Mngmt. Ltd.; Scotia Realty Ltd.; The Bank of Nova Scotia Properties Inc.; Scotia Securities; Mem., Financial Extves. Inst.; Systems Comptroller present Bank 1971, Supvr. Systems Planning 1972, Chief Acct. 1973, Comptroller & Chief Acct. 1977; Gen. Mgr. Finance & Admn. 1980; Sr. Vice-Pres., Mgmt. & Finanical Information Systems 1983; Extve. Vice Pres. & Gen. Mgr., Finance & Admin. 1985; Clubs: Empire (Past Pres.); National; Home: 2061 Lakeshore Rd. E., Oakville, Ont. L6J 1M4; Office: 6th Flr., Scotia Plaza, 44 King St. W., Toronto, Ont. M5H 1H1.

**BROOKS, Ronald James,** B.Sc., M.Sc., Ph.D.; university professor; b. Toronto, Ont. 16 Apr. 1941; s. Thomas Eric and Betty Lilian (McCullough) B.; e. Univ. of Toronto B.Sc. 1963, M.Sc. 1966; Univ. of Illinois Ph.D. 1970; m. Gladys d. Edward and Katharine Stephenson 26 Sept. 1985; children: Hilary Ann, Jennifer Lyn, Payton Walker; PROFESSOR, DEPT. OF ZOOLOGY, UNIV. OF GUELPH 1970– ; DistinguishedProf. Teaching Award 1989; Dir., Wildlife Research Station Algonguin Park; Mem., Animal Behaviour Soc.; Am. Soc. of Mammalogists; Sigma XI; Am. Soc. of Naturalists; Am. Soc. of Ichthyologists & Herpetologists; Internat. Union for Conservation of Nature; Species Survival Comm.; recreations: boxing, research; Home: RR 1, Orton, Ont. L0N 1N0; Office: Guelph, Ont. N1G 2W1.

**BROOKS, Vernon Bernard,** M.Sc., Ph.D.; neuroscientist; educator; author; b. Berlin, Germany 10 May 1923; s. Martin and Margarete (Hahlo) B.; e. Univ. of Toronto B.A. 1946, Ph.D. 1952; Univ. of Chicago M.Sc. 1948; m. Nancy Fraser 29 June 1950; children: Martin Fraser, Janet Mary, Nora Vivian; PROFESSOR EMERITUS, UNIV. OF WESTERN ONT. 1988; Lectr. in Physiol. McGill Univ. 1950–52, Asst. Prof. 1952–56; Visiting Fellow in Physiol. Australian Nat. Univ. 1954–55; Asst. Prof. Rockefeller Univ. 1956–60, Assoc. Prof. 1960–64; Prof. of Physiol. New York Med. Coll. 1964–71, Chrmn. of Physiol. 1964–69; Prof. of Physiol. Univ. of W. Ont. 1971–88, Chrmn. of Physiol. 1971–76; author over 100 publs.; ed.: 'Motor Control' 1981; (Vol 2 of Section I, 'Handbook of Physiology,' Am. Physiol. Soc.); author: 'The Neural Basis of Motor Control' 1986; mem. Ed. Bds. various scient. journs.; mem. Am. Physiol. Soc.; Candn. Physiol. Soc.; Internat. Brain Research Organ.; Soc. Neuroscience; Unitarian; recreations: reading, writing, cottage; Home: 99 Euclid Ave., London, Ont. N6C 1C3; Office: London, Ont. N6A 5C1.

**BROOKS-HILL, Frederick Bancroft,** B.Com.; retired executive; b. South Mountain, Ont. 14 Apr. 1909; s. Frederick and Harriet Elizabeth (Bancroft) B-H.; e. Newington, Ont. Pub. Sch. 1913; Clinton St. Pub. Sch. Toronto 1918; Univ. of Toronto Schs. 1926; Univ. of Toronto B.Com. 1930; m. Helen d. James and Mary Mason 9 Sept. 1939; children: Heather, Frederick J., Robin William, Gillian; Dir. Finlayson Enterprises Ltd.; joined Actuarial Dept. Confederation Life Assn. 1930, Invest. Area 1935–39, 1945 becoming Invest. Analyst, Mgr. Bond Dept., Invest. Vice Pres. U.S.A. and Caribbean, Invest. Vice Pres. Can., retired 1973; mem. Finance Comte., Nat. Office Candn. Bible Soc.; Invest. Comte. Toronto Ang. Synod; Toronto Soc. Financial Analysts 1949–51; served with RCNVR 1939–45, rank Cdr.; recreations: golf; Clubs: Stony Lake Yacht; Oakville Golf; Royal Candn. Mil. Inst.; Springdale Hall (S.C.); Office: 41 Second St., Oakville, Ont. L6J 3T1.

**BROPHEY, Peter M.,** B.Com., C.A.; public affairs consultant; b. Montréal, Qué. 5 Oct. 1928; s. Harold Millar and Madelaine Margaret (Cameron) B.; e. McGill Univ. B.Com. 1949; Qué. Order C.A.'s 1952; Ont. Inst. C.A.'s 1970; m. Helena d. Ernest and Eva Burrows 22 Sept. 1951; children: Susan, Jean, Tina; Vice Pres., Corporate Affairs, Xerox Canada Inc. 1974–89, Dir. 1974–92; Deloitte Haskins & Sells, Montréal 1949–54; Johnson & Johnson Ltd. 1954–70, Vice Pres. Finance and Dir.; lectr. evening Accountancy courses McGill Univ. 1956–60; Vice Chrmn., CJRT-FM Inc. 1985–91; Pres., Ont. C. of C. 1988; Chrmn. Candn. Bus. Equipment Mfrs. Assn. 1978–79; Pres. Inst. Pol. Involvement 1982–84; Chrmn. Inst. Donations & Pub. Affairs Rsch. 1980–83; Mem., Economic Counc. of Can. 1989–92; Address: 33 White Bark Way, R.R. 1, Belwood, Ont. N0B 1J0.

**BROPHY, John J.,** B.Sc., C.F.A., F.S.A., F.C.I.A.; actuary; b. Belfast, N. Ireland 28 Nov. 1949; s. James and Mary (Glass) B.; e. Queen's Univ. Belfast B.Sc. 1973; m. Barbara Ellen d. John and Gladys Bonnell 13 Jan. 1986; PARTNER, PEAT MARWICK THORNE ACTUARIAL & BENEFITS INC. 1988– ; joined Dominion Life Assurance Co. 1976–85, Pension Mktg. Offr.; Peat Marwick 1985; co-author 'Pensions and Retirement Planning' 1985; 'Pensions and Retirement Planning: New Rules and Strategies' 1987; 'Pensions and Retirement Income Planning 1990–1991: New Tax Rules and Strategies' 1991; 'Pensions and Retirement Income Planning' 1993; Former Dir. Assn. Candn. Pension Mgmt.; Chrmn., Candn. Institute of Actuaries' Ctte. on Investment Practice 1993– ; mem. Candn. Compensation Assn.; Toronto Soc. Financial Analysts; recreations: golf, racquetball; Club: Hidden Lake Golf & Country; Home: 5300 Cedar Springs Rd., RR3, Campbellville, Ont. L0P 1B0; Office: P.O. Box 31 Commerce Court W., Toronto, Ont. M5L 1B2.

**BROSSARD, Hon. André,** B.A., LL.L., J.C.A.; judge; b. Montreal, Que. 10 Jan. 1937; s. Hon. Roger and Simone (Blais) B.; e. Coll. Ste. Marie, Montreal B.A. 1956; Univ. of Montreal, Fac. of Law LL.L. 1959; m. Ginette d. Antoine and Gisèle Bruneau 11 Feb. 1961; children: Alain, Christian, Thierry; JUDGE, APPEAL COURT OF QUEBEC 1989– ; Partner Stikeman and Elliot, Montreal 1968–78; Batonnier, Bar of Prov. of Que. 1976–77; Partner Desjardins, Ducharme & Assoc., Montreal 1978–83; Judge, Superior Court of Que. 1982–89; Nat. Exec. Candn. Bar Assn. 1978–80 (Pres. Que. Br. 1981–82); Pres., Candn. Judges Conference 1993–94; mem. Candn. Inst. for the Admin. of Justice; Prize, Bar of Paris (first at Que. Bar admission exams) 1960; Office: 1 est, Notre Dame, Montreal, Que. H2Y 1B6.

**BROSSARD, Nicole;** poet; novelist; b. Montréal, Qué. 27 Nov. 1943; d. Guillaume and Marguerite (Matte) B.; one d. Julie Brossard-Soublière; Co-founder and Dir. 'La Barre du Jour' (lit. mag.) 1965–75; 'Les Têtes de Pioche' (feminist newspaper) 1976–79; 'La Nouvelle Barre du Jour' 1977–79; Co-dir. (NFB film) 'Some American Feminists' 1976; Founder/éditrice, L'intégrale (feminist press) 1982; Visiting Prof. Queen's Univ. 1983–84; Short-Term Fellow, Princeton Univ. 1991; author (poetry): 'Aube à la saison in Trois' 1965; 'Mordre en sa chair' 1966; 'L'écho bouge beau' 1968; 'Suite logique' 1970; 'Le centre blanc' 1970; 'Mécanique jongleuse' 1974; 'La partie pour le tout' 1975; 'Le Centre blanc' 1978; 'Amantes' 1980; 'Double Impression' 1984; 'L'aviva' 1985; 'Domaine d'écriture' 1985; 'A tout regard' 1989; 'Installations' 1989; 'Langues obscures' 1992; (novels): 'Un livre' 1970; 'Sold-out' 1973; 'French Kiss' 1974; 'L'amèr' 1977; 'Le sens apparent' 1980; 'Picture Theory' 1982; 'Le Désert Mauve' 1987; (prose): 'La nuit verte du Parc Labyrinthe' 1992; (essay): 'La lettre aérienne' 1985; (translations): 'A Book' 1976; 'Turn of a Pang' 1976; 'Daydream Mechanics' 1980; 'These Our Mothers' 1983; 'French Kiss' 1986; 'Lovhers' 1986; 'Sous la langue/Under tongue' (edition bilingue) 1987; 'The Aerial Letter' 1988; 'Surfaces of Sense' 1989; 'Die Malvenfarbene Wüste' 1989; 'La Lettera Aerea' 1990; 'Mauve Desert' 1990; 'Picture Theory' 1991; 'Green Night of Labyrinth Park,' édition trilingue (French, English & Spanish) 1992; co-author, (with Lisette Girouard) 'Anthologie de la poésie des femmes au Québec' 1991; recipient: Gov. Gen.'s Award Poetry 1974, 1984; Grand Prix de la Fondation des Forges 1989; Prix Athanase-David 1991; Harbourfront Festival Prize 1991; Doctorat (hon. causa) Univ. of Western Ont. 1991; membre de l'Académie des lettres du Québec 1993; Vice Pres. Union des écrivains québécois 1983–85, Dir. 1977–79; Address: 34 ave. Robert, Outremont, Qué. H3S 2P2.

**BROSSEAU, (Joseph Charles Edmond) Lucien,** B.Sc., D.M.G., A.D., F.A.I.M., F.F.A.F., F.I.B.A., F.Adm.A.; insurance executive; b. Montreal, P.Q. 28 Jan. 1920; s. Rosario and Zelia (Dufour) B.; e. Sch. Mont St-Louis B.Sc. 1940; Univ. Laval D.M.G. 1946; Univ. d'Edinbourg, Scotland A.D. 1951; m. Gilberte 14 July 1940; children: Michel, Micheline, Lesley; PRES. & C.E.O., LA SURVIVANCE 1976– ; Bd. Chrmn. and Pres., Extve. Comm., Les Clairvoyants 1988– ; with Les Prévoyants du Canada 1944–48; Actuary, La Solidarite Ins. Co., Que. City 1951–59; Lectr., Univ. Laval 1954–55; joined current firm 1959 as Dir. Gen.; V.P. & Dir. Gen. 1968, Pres. 1976; Pres., Hôtel-Dieu de St-Hyacinthe 1972–91; Candn. Life and Health Ins. Assn. 1978–82 (mem. Public Relations Comte.); Prés., Comité des Affaires Régionales du Qué. 1980–84; (Nat. Extve. 1981–83); Extve. Comte., Centre des Dirigeants d'Entreprises 1975–77; Bd. du Conseil d'Expansion Economique 1978–83; recipient Can. Silver Jubilee Medal 1978; Fellow, President's Counc., Amer. Inst. of Mgmt.; Fellow, Corp. Prof. des Administrateurs Agrées du Qué. 1989; Pres., Corp. Prof. des Administrateurs Agréés du Qué. 1973–75; recipient 'merite C.I.Q.' (Conseil Interprofessionnel du Québec) 1991; Prés., Chambre de Comm. de St-Hyacinthe 1963–65; Gov., Univ. Laval (Chaire en Assurance) 1981; mem. & Hon. Pres., Club des Actuaires de Montreal; Fellow, Financial Analyst Fed.; author numerous articles in profl. journals; frequent speaker at conferences, including Internat. Biographical Conference and Silver Jubilee of Queen Elizabeth II, 1977; Fellow, International Biographical Assn., Cambridge, England 1977; Home: 2580, St-Pierre ouest, St-Hyacinthe, Qué. J2T 4R9; Office: C.P. 10,000, St-Hyacinthe, Qué. J2S 7C8.

**BROSZ, Helmut Gunter,** B.A.Sc., D.B.A., P.Eng.; consulting forensic engineer; b. Vienna, Austria 21 Dec. 1942; e. Univ. of Toronto B.A.Sc. 966, D.B.A. 1970; m. Elizabeth Jean; PRESIDENT & CHIEF EXECUTIVE OFFICER, BROSZ AND ASSOCIATES 1970– ; Fellow, American Academy of Forensic Sciences; Chair, Engineering Section, Candn. Soc. of Forensic Sciences; Mem., I.E.E.E.; Internat. Electrical Testing Assn.; Assn. of Profl. Engrs.; Candn. Electrical Assn.; Candn. Hospital Engr. Soc.; Internat. Assn. of Arson Investigators Inc.; author of several technical papers, articles & maintenance specificatons; has presented courses and instruction at var. institutions; Expert Witnessing; Office: 64 Bullock Drive, Markham, Ont. L3P 3P2.

**BROTT, Alexander,** O.C., Mus.D., F.R.S.A., LL.D., Kt. of M., GCMSS; conductor, composer, violinist; professor; b. Montreal, Que., 14 March 1915; s. Samuel and Annie (Fuchsman) B.; e. McGill Univ.; Julliard Sch. of Music, New York; Univ. of Chicago, D.Mus.; Hon. LL.D. Queen's Univ. 1973; D. Mus (honoris causa) McGill Univ., 1980; m. Charlotte, d. Walter Goetsel, Montreal, P.Q., 11 Apr. 1943; two s. Boris, Denis; FOUNDER AND MUSICAL DIR., McGILL CHAMBER ORCHESTRA 1939– ; solo violinist and asst. conductor, Orchestre symphonique de Montréal and Prof. of Music, McGill Univ., Conductor in Residence (and former Chrmn. of the Dept.) 1939–80; former Artistic Dir., Montreal 'Pops' Concerts Inc.; Kingston 'Pops' Concerts; Founder-Conductor 'Les Jeunes Virtuoses de Montreal' 1986; was responsible for commissioning Candn. and Québec works for the McGill Chamber Orch. (asst. by the Lapitsky Found. and the Can.

Counc.); compositions incl.: 'Martlet's Muse' commissioned by McGill Grad. Soc. (symphonic work based on McGill tunes); 'Centennial Celebration'; 'La Corriveau' (ballet); 'Pristine Prisms in Polychrome'; 'Paraphrase in Polyphony' 1967; 'Spasms for Six,' 'Accent' 1971; 'Circle, Triangel for Squares'; 'My Mother - My Memorial'; 'Cupid's Quandary' (with strings, solo violin, solo percussion); Symphonic works: 'From Sea to Sea'; 'Concordia'; 'Oracle'; 'Fancy & Folly'; 'Royal Tribute'; 'Analogy in Anagram'; 'Spheres in Orbit'; 'War & Peace'; 'Prelude to Oblivion'; 'Violin Concerto'; 'Arabesque for Cello and Orchestra'; String Orchestra: 'Lullaby & Procession of the Toys'; 'Ritual'; 'Dirge'; 'Three Astral Visions'; A Capella Choir: 'Canada Case History'; 'Israel'; 'The Emperor's New Clothes' 1971; 'The Young Prometheus' 1971; and a number of chamber works; Compositions incl. over 50 symphonic works, chamber works and works for solo instruments; toured U.S.S.R. (1966), Switzerland, Mexico (Cervantino Internat. Festival), Belgium, France, Poland, Hungary, Czechoslovakia, U.S., S. America: Columbia, Chile and Argentina; Can. with McGill Chamber Orchestra; commissioned by C.B.C. to research and orchestrate unpub. works of Beethoven, two of which ('The Young Prometheus' and '7 Minuets 6 Canons') rec'd world premiers in Can.; commissioned by C.B.C. to arrange for strings the music of Scarlatti and Schumann; presently arranging Tchaikovsky songs for strings in commemoration of 'Tchaikovsky Year'; Conductor and Mus. Dir. Kingston Symphony Orch. 1965–80; apptd. Musical Dir. Emeritus 1981; anthology of his music, on seven records, released by Radio-Canada 1985; 'Violin Concerto,' 'Arabesque' and 'Astral Visions' released on CD 1993; Hon. Mem. Zoltan Kodaly Acad. and Inst.; Fellow, London Royal Soc. of Arts since 1960; invested 'Chevaliers de Malta' 1985 in recognition of most appreciated professional and artistic activity; Knight of Malta of the Order of St. John of Jerusalem; Chevalier de l'Ordre Souverain de la Milice 1990; Awards: two Olympic Medals for compositions (London and Helsinki); Sir Arnold Bax Gold Medal; Lord Strathcona Scholarship; Elizabeth Sprague Cooledge Award (twice); Loeb Mem. Award (twice); CPAC Award (thrice); Candn. Music Council Medal for contribution to music in Can. 1976; Queen's Anniversary Silver Jubilee Medal 1978; Medal of Order of Can. 1979; America Community Distinction 1986; Order of Quebec 1988; Diploma of Distinction, Candn. Assoc. of Orchestras 1990; Merit for Life (GCMSS) 1990; Commemorative Medal, 125th Anniversary of Candn. Confedn. 1992; elected Great Montrealer 1993; mem., Composers Authors & Publishers Assn.; Musicians Guild of Montreal; Home: 5459 Earnscliffe, Montreal, Que. H3X 2P8.

**BROTT, Boris,** O.C., LL.D.; music director and conductor; b. Montreal, Que. 14 March 1944; s. Alexander and Lotte (Goetzel) B.; e. Conservatoire de Musique, Montreal; McGill Univ.; studied conducting with Pierre Monteux, Igor Markevitch, Leonard Bernstein and Alexander Brott; CONDUCTOR, ARTISTIC DIR., VENTURA COUNTY SYMPHONY (Ventura, Calif. USA) 1992– ; Co-Conductor, McGill Chamber Orchestra, Montreal, Que. 1989– ; Artistic Dir., Brott Music Festival, Hamilton, Ont. 1988– ; Pres., Great Music Canada 1977– ; made debut as violinist with Montreal Symphony 1949; founded Philharmonic Youth Orchestra of Montreal 1959; Asst. Conductor, Toronto Symphony 1963–65; Principal Conductor, Northern Sinfonia, Eng. 1964–68; Asst. Conductor, N.Y. Philharmonic 1968–69; Music Dir. and Conductor, The Hamilton Philharmonic 1969–90; Music Dir. and Conductor, Lakehead Symphony 1968–72, Regina Symphony 1971–72; Principal Conductor, BBC Welsh Symphony Orchestra 1972–79; Principal Conductor, CBC Winnipeg Orchestra 1976–83; Artistic Advisor, Symphony Nova Scotia 1981–86; Artistic Dir., Ontario Place Pops 1983–91; Artistic Dir., Stratford Summer Music Festival 1983–84; has guest conducted all major orchestras in Can.; BBC Symphony Orchestras in Glasgow, Manchester, London and Cardiff; The Philharmonia; Royal Philharmonic; Liverpool Philharmonic; L'Orchestre des Concerts Colonne, Paris; RIA, Rome and Milan; RIAS Berlin; Berlin Philharmonic; Los Angeles Philharmonic; Chautauqua Symphony; Orquesta Sinfonica de El Salvador, del Estado de Mexico; Jerusalem Symphony; Nat. Symp. of Mexico; Mexico Philharmonic; has recorded for Mace Studios and Canadian Talent Library; awarded Pan American Conductors' Prize 1958; International Conductor's Competition, Liverpool, England; Gold Medal, Dimitri Mitropoulos Internat. Conductors' Competition, N.Y. City 1968; Jr. Chamber of Commerce Award 'One of Canada's Ten Outstanding Young Mem for 1969'; Jr. Chamber of Commerce Award 'One of Canada's Five Outstanding Young Men of 1973'; B.M.I. Award for Innovating Programming 1983, 1985; American Music Award, N.Y. City, New York 1986; Officer of the Order of Canada Award 1987; el. Nat. Pres., Jeunesse Musicales 1987; Hon. LL.D., McMaster Univ. 1988; Knight of Malta 1990; writer-host-conductor of numerous TV and Radio shows incl. 'Music from Bach to Rock' (Ohio State Award Winner), 'Music – Why Bother?,' 'Hear Out' (Ohio State Award Winner), 'Brott to You,' 'Brott Backstage,' also featured on numerous CBC-TV specials incl. Musicamera, Glenn Gould Series 'Music in our Time' and 'Boris and Those Magnificient Music Machines'; Music dir., series of syndicated TV programmes, 'The Palace'; music dir. and conductor of 'Great Artists in Concert' TV series; Hon. Chrmn. Christmas Seal Campaign 1980–82; Office: 301 Bay St. South, Hamilton, Ont.

**BROTT, Denis;** cellist; b. Montreal, Que. 9 Dec. 1950; e. Conservatoire de Musique Montreal 1959–67; Juilliard School 1964–68; Indiana Univ. 1968–71; Univ. of S. Calif. 1971–75; m. Julie; children: Talia, Aleta, Vanessa, Joshua; PROFESSOR OF CELLO AND CHAMBER MUSIC, CONSERVATOIRE DE MUSIQUE DE MONTREAL; Principal Cellist, McGill Chamber Orch. 1989– ; recognized as one of Canada's finest & most distiguished performing artists; discography includes 20 chamber music recordings incl. the complete string quartets of Beethoven with the Orford String Quartet and 'Homage to Piatigorsky' a solo CD paying tribute to his mentor; 2 Juno Awards; Knight of Merit, Order of the Sovereign Military Order of Saint John of Jerusalem; Grand Prix du Disque; numerous other awards; career was launched with performance in Munich Internat. Cello Competition; N.Y. Affiliate Artist Award; Young Musician's Found. Debut Award; Merriweather Post Competition; Montreal Symphony Orch. Competition; has performed at numerous Festivals incl. Festival of the Sound in Parry Sound, Ont. (Artistic Dir. 1991); Fac., Music Academy of West Santa Barbara, Calif. & performed chamber music at festivals in Hampden-Sydney, Virginia and Sitka, Alaska; Jury, Evian International String Quartet Competition France 1993; concertizes as recitalist, chamber artist & soloist with orch.; Instrument Bank, Canada Council loaned Mr. Brott an exceptional 1706 Tecchler cello for his exclusive use for the duration of his career in recognition of his artistry; extensive discography; Address: Box 594, Victoria Station, Westmount, Que. H3Z 2Y6.

**BROTTO, Paul E.,** B.Sc., M.B.A.; transportation executive; b. Italy 16 July 1951; e. McGill Univ. B.Sc. 1972, M.B.A. 1977; m. Kathleen; children: Theresa, Melissa, Christina; VICE-PRESIDENT, FINANCIAL PLANNING & CONTROLLER, AIR CANADA 1993– ; joined Passenger Marketing / Forecasting Dept. of Air Canada 1972 and progressed through various functions incl. Sr. Manager Marketing Planning, Sales Mngt. & Devel. Director; Dir., Financial Evaluations 1983; Sr. Dir., Financial Planning 1984; Market Devel., South and Charters 1985; Pres. & Chief Extve. Officer, Air Canada Vacations 1986; Vice-Pres., Passenger Mktg. 1991; Candn. rep. to H.R.H. Duke of Edinburgh Commonwealth Study Conf. Australia 1986; Mem., Montreal Chamber of Commerce; Bd. of Dir., Touram Inc. (Air Canada Vacations); Bd. of Dirs., The Gemini Group; Office: Air Canada Centre 278, P.O. Box 14,000, Postal Station Saint-Laurent, Montreal, Que. H4Y 1H4.

**BROUGH, John Albert,** B.A., C.A.; financial executive; b. Kirkland Lake, Ont. 6 Dec. 1946; s. Albert and Maggie (Cunliffe) B.; e. Kirkland Lake C. & V.I. 1964; Univ. of Toronto B.A. 1968; Peat Marwick Thorne C.A. 1973; m. Lesley d. George and Aurel Wallace 14 Aug. 1971; children: Geoffrey, Andrew, Allison; SENIOR VICE PRESIDENT & CHIEF FINANCIAL OFFICER, MARKBOROUGH PROPERTIES INC.; joined Markborough Properties 1974 and proceeded through the ranks as Asst. Controller, Controller, Director – Financial Planning, Treasurer, Vice-Pres., Finance to present position; Mem., Candn. Inst. of C.A.s; Ont. Inst. of C.A.s; recreations: golf, theatre, tennis; clubs: Granite, Summit Golf; Home: 84 Golfdale Rd., Toronto, Ont. M4N 2B7; Office: 1 Dundas St. W., Ste. 2800, Toronto, Ont. M5G 2J2.

**BROUGHTON, Roger James,** M.D.,C.M., Ph.D., F.R.C.P.(C); medical researcher; b. Montreal, Que. 25 Sept. 1936; s. James William and Edith Olwen (Edwards) B.; e. Queen's Univ. M.D.,C.M. 1960; McGill Univ. Ph.D. 1967; m. Wendy d. William and Doreen Buchanan 1987; children: Lynn, Michael, Katherine; PROF. OF MED. (NEUROL.) AND PSYCHOL. UNIV. OF OTTAWA 1976– ; interned Univ. Hosp. Saskatoon 1960–61; rsch. epilepsy and sleep with Prof. Henri Gastaut, Marseilles, France 1962–64; Rsch. Fellow Montreal Neurol. Inst. McGill Univ. 1964–65, Asst. Prof. of Neurol. and Neurosurgery 1965–68; Assoc. Prof. of Med. (Neurol.), Pharmacol. and Psychol. present Univ. 1968–76; Expert, World Health Orgn. 1967–73; mem. Sci. Adv. Ctte. Center for Narcolepsy Stanford Univ. 1982– ; Career Investig. Med. Rsch. Council Can. 1968– ; co-author 'WHO Dictionary of Epilepsy' 1971; 'Epileptic Seizures' 1972; ed. 'Acquisition of Bioelectrical Data' 1976; 'Narcolepsy and the Hypersomnias' (B.Roth) 1980; 'Henri Gastaut and the Marseilles School's Contribution to the Neurosciences' 1982; co-ed. 'Sleep and Alertness' 1989; co-ed. 'Medical home monitoring' 1990; 'Sleep, Arousal and Performance' 1991; cons. ed. numerous sci. jours.; author 180 sci. articles, numerous book chapters; holds 3 patents Can. and U.S.; Hon. mem. Brazilian Acad. Neurols.; Latin Am. Sleep Soc.; Czechoslovakian Med. Soc.; Cuban Neurosci's Soc.; Western EEG Soc.; mem. Sleep Rsch. Soc. (Pres. 1972–75); E. Assn. Electroencephalographers (Pres. 1979–80); Candn. Sleep Soc. (Founding Pres. 1986–88); recreations: skiing, sailing, tennis, amateur radio, painting; Clubs: Britannia Yacht; Ottawa West Tennis; Home: 2824 Grandeur Ave., Ottawa, Ont. K2B 6Y9; Office: Ottawa Gen. Hosp. 501 Smyth Rd., Ottawa, Ont. K1H 8L6.

**BROUILLETTE, Yves,** B.Sc., F.C.A.S., F.C.I.A.; insurance executive; b. Ste-Geneviève de Batiscan 2 May 1951; s. Wallace and Mariette (Jacob) B.; e. Laval Univ. B.Sc. 1972; F.C.A.S. (New York) 1975 (1st Quebecer to obtain full membership in this society); F.C.I.A. 1987; Harvard Bus. Sch., adv. mngt. prog.; m. Dominique d. Paul-Emile and Yvette Savard 30 Dec. 1972; children: Benoit, Luc, Catherine; PRES. & CHIEF EXTVE. OFFR., ING CANADA & THE COMMERCE GROUP INSUR. CO. 1990– ; Rsch. Asst., Que. Govt. Study Ctte. on Auto. Insur. (Gauvin Ctte.) 1972–74; joined present firm 1974; Actuary 1974–78; Vice-Pres. & Actuary 1978–84; Extve. Vice-Pres., Personal Lines 1984–90; Dir., ING Canada; Commerce Group Insur. Co.; Mem., IBC, Qué. Ctte.; Dir., Underwriters Adjustment Bureau Ltd.; recreations: badminton, skiing, tennis; club: St-Denis; Home: 780 Tellier St., Saint-Hyacinthe, Que. J2S 6N1; Office: 2450 Girouard St. W., Saint-Hyacinthe, Que. J2S 3B3.

**BROUSSEAU, André,** B.A., B.Ped., L.Ped.Lettres, Schol.Ph.D.; university administrator; b. Maskinongé, Qué. 27 Aug. 1938; s. Aiméo and Aline (Lemyre) B.; e. Laval Univ. B.A. 1960, B.Ped. 1962; Univ. of Montreal L.Ped.-Lettres 1970; Univ. of Ottawa Schol. Ph.D. 1967; VICE-RECTOR & SECRETARY GENERAL, UNIV. OF QUEBEC AT TROIS RIVIERES 1989– ; Sec. of Planning Ctte. to create a new univ. 1968–69 (Business Admin. Dept. Head 1968–69), present univ.; Vice-rector, Communications 1970–75; Vice-rector & Secretary Gen. 1975–80; Sec. General 1980–89; Pres., Candn. Univ. Sec. Gen.'s Assn. 1979–82, 1986–88; Internat. Group of French Univ. Sec. Gen. 1987–89; Bd. Mem., Laflèche College Trois-Rivières 1991– ; Extve. Vice-Pres., Fond. C.E.U. de Trois-Rivières 1970– ; Bd. Mem., Union Québécoise, General Insur. Co. 1985– ; Canassurance, Gen. Insur. Co. 1988– ; Cogeco Radio & Television 1989– ; Health Insur. Agency 1985–88; Chrmn., Public Edn. Ctte., Quebec Heart Found. 1977–80; Mem., Tribune for executive pension plan, Que. Treas. Bd. 1988– ; Man of the Year, Hebdo Journal of Greater Trois-Rivières 1985; Best Achievement, Reg. Council of Health & Social Serv. 1990; Hon. Offr., Ste-Marie Hosp. 1991; Prix du Conseil des Hôpitaux de Montréal 1992; Bd. Chrmn., Candn. Hospital Assn. 1991–92, Bd. Dir. 1986– ; Bd. Chrmn., Que. Hosp. Assn. 1982–86; Bd. Chrmn., Ste-Marie Hosp. 1978–88; Bd. Mem., Douglas Rsch. Ctr. 1983–87; Gov., Ste-Marie Found. 1990– ; Chrmn., Municipal Comn., Cultural Centre, Trois-Rivières 1968–70; Mem., Trois-Rivières C. of C.; Assn. litt. et artistique internat.; Del., Am. Hosp. Assn.'s House of Delegates 1991– ; Am. Hosp. Assn.'s Congress of Trustees Alternate 1991– ; host & editor of radio & TV edn. programs; Bd. Mem., Radio Trois-Rivières Inc. CHLN (Telemedia) 1969–70; Chief Instr., Royal Candn. Air Force 1957–60; author & writer of many briefs & studies on univ. teaching & rsch.; recreations: skiing, swimming; Home: 1835, Place Georges-Lambert, Trois-Rivières, Qué. G8Y 2K2; Office: 3351, boul. Des Forges, Trois-Rivières, Qué. G9A 5H7.

**BROWES, The Hon. Pauline,** B.A., P.C.; politician; b. Harwood, Ont. 7 May 1938; d. Robert Earle and Clara Phyllis (Sandercock) Drope; e. Toronto Teachers' College; York Univ. B.A. 1979; m. Dr. George Harold s. Marjorie and Jack B. 2 Sept. 1961; children: Tammy, Janet, Jeffrey; Minister of Indian Affairs & Northern Development, House of Commons 1993; 1st elected M.P. for Scarborough Centre g.e. 1984; re-elected g.e. 1988; Parly. Sec. to Min. of Environment 1986–88; Parly. Sec. to Secretary of State for Canada & Min. of State (Multiculturalism & Citizenship) 1989–91; Min.

of State (Environment) 1991–93; Min. of State for Employment & Immigration 1993; Min. of Indian Affairs and Northern Development 1993; Teacher, Scarborough Bd. of Education prior to 1975; Mem., Practitioner Review Ctte., Min. of Health, Ont. 1975–81; Mem. & Former Chair, Scarborough Bd. of Health 1979–84; Mem., Metropolitan Toronto Housing Authy. 1980–81; Appeal Ctte., Residential Tenancy Comn. of Ont. 1981–84; P.C.; Anglican; clubs: Albany, Rideau, Scarborough Golf & Country; Riding Office: 2163 Lawrence Ave. E., Scarborough, Ont. M1P 2P5.

**BROWN, Hon. A. Garnet,** former M.L.A.; politician; food broker; b. Halifax, N.S. 22 May 1930; s. Alexander Garnet and Margaret B.; e. Halifax, N.S. m. Elizabeth Anne, d. Earl Lowe, Sheet Harbour, N.S., 22 Aug. 1953; children: Karen, Robert, James, Jacqueline; PRES., A.G. BROWN INTERNATIONAL LTD. 1992– ; Pres., A.G. Brown & Son Ltd.; A.G. Brown & Son 'Seafood Division'; Brown Brokerage Ltd.; D & G Leasing; Brown Brokerage Real Estate; former Dir. Investors Group; Dartmouth Cable T.V.; Past Pres. Candn. Food Brokers; served as campaign mgr. for former Premier of N.S. fed. g.e. 1965, prov. el. 1967 and prov. leadership Lib. Party 1966; Pres. N.S. Lib. Assn. 1968–71; el. M.L.A. for Halifax-E. Shore 1969; re-el. 1970, 1974; apptd. Min. of Highways and of Pub. Works 1970; Min. of Tourism 1971; Prov. Secy. & Min. of Recreation 1975; has rec'd numerous awards during govt. service; Gov., Mount St. Vincent Univ.; led N.S. del. to Munich in successful bid to bring first World Canoe Championships to Dartmouth, N.S. 1978; has served as Exte. mem. Dir. and participant in many prof. and community organs. incl. Nat. Dir. Duke of Edinburgh Awards; Past Pres. N.S. Food Brokers' Assn.; Halifax Ad & Sales Club; former Nat. Dir. Candn. Roads & Transport. Assn.; el. Pres. 1975–76, Candn. Food Brokers' Assn.; mem. N.S. Hall of Fame; mem. Halifax Bd. Trade; Young Pres' Internat.; Liberal; R. Catholic; recreations: golf, bridge, swimming; Clubs: The Halifax; Ashburn Golf & Country; Saraguay; Oakfield Golf & Country; Home: 7061 Fielding Ave., Halifax, N.S. B3K 5L8.

**BROWN, Alan Charles MacKenzie,** B.A.Sc., M.A.T.; b. Vancouver, B.C. 3 July 1937; s. Ralph MacLachlan and Margaret James (Rankin) B.; e. Univ. of B.C., B.A.Sc. 1959; Brown Univ. M.A.T. 1968; m. Alix d. Harold and Margaret Husband 29 Dec. 1962; children: Lindsay, Julie, Alison; Headmaster, St. George's School 1971–89; Teacher, Wandsworth Sch. London, Eng. 1959–60; Malay Coll. Malaysia 1961; Head of Sci. Shawnigan Lake Sch. 1963–68; Comnr. Forensic Psychiatric Services Comn. 1979–84; Dir. Open Learning Inst. 1978–85; Clubs: Vancouver; Vancouver Lawn Tennis & Badminton; Home: 1646 Laurier Ave., Vancouver, B.C. V6J 2V4.

**BROWN, Alice J.,** R.N.; co-operative director and consultant; b. Oklahoma City 23 March 1938; d. Theodore R. and Mattie A. (Abston) Taylor; e. Univ. of Oklahoma School of Nursing R.N. 1959; m. Bert s. James and Jean Brown 16 Sept. 1965; one d.: Angela, Susan; DIRECTOR, CALGARY CO-OP. ASSN. 1982– ;AND FEDERATED CO-OPERATIVES LTD. 1987– ; Nursing Supervisor 1959–68; Farmer 1968–92; Volunteer, Calgary Co-op. 1977–82; Corp. Secretary 5 years; Mem., Candn. Advisory Council, Status of Women 1989–92; Advisory Ctte., CBC 1987–90; Pres., First Alta. Farm Women's Conf. 1986; Mem., Alta. AADC Review Ctte. 1986–87; Corp. Sec.-Treas., Brownhill Farms Ltd.; Corp. Sec.-Treas., Canada West Foundation 1991– ; Home: Box 21, Kathryn, Alta. T0M 1E0.

**BROWN, Allan Gordon,** B.A., M.A.; writer; editor; b. Victoria, B.C. 8 Aug. 1934; s. Clarence Sandwith and Constance Doris (Meads) B.; e. Brentwood Coll.; University Sch.; Univ. of B.C., B.A. (Hons.) 1969, M.A. 1970; m. Patricia d. Thomas and Mary Salt 15 May 1970; Teaching Master, Saint Lawrence Coll. Saint-Laurent 1983–92; Lit. Ed., 'Quarry' magazine 1982–84; Co-editor, Quarry Press 1982–84; Writer-in-Res., Kapuskasing Public Library 1987–88; Assoc. Mem., Freelance Eds. Assn. of Can.; Mem., The Federation of B.C. Writers; Mem., Powell River Community Arts Council; author: 'Figures of Earth' 1979, 'By Green Mountain' 1980, 'Locatives' 1982, 'This Stranger Wood' 1982, 'Winter Journey' 1984, 'The Almond Tree' 1985, 'The Burden of Jonah ben Amittai' 1991; 'Forgetting' 1991 (books & poetry collections); poetry published in Candn. journals since 1962; critical articles pub. Candn. jours. & newspapers 1975– ; Home: 6963 Egmont St., Powell River, B.C. V8A 1T7.

**BROWN, Anthony William Aldridge,** M.B.E., B.Sc.F., M.A., Ph.D. F.R.S.C.; b. Horley, Surrey, Eng. 18 Nov. 1911; s. William and May (English) B.; e. Winchester Coll. Eng., 1925–29; Univ. of Toronto, B.Sc.F. 1933; M.A. 1934; Ph.D. (Biochem.) 1936; London Sch. of Hygiene and Tropical Med., 1936–37; m. Jocelyn, d. Norman Evill, Hampstead, London, Eng. 11 June 1938; children: Hilary, Virginia, Kathryn; JOHN A. HANNAH DISTINGUISHED PROFESSOR EMERITUS, MICHIGAN STATE UNIV. 19.. and COPY EDITOR, BIOSCIENCE EDIPRINT, GENEVA 1983– ; Sessional Lectr. in Entom., Macdonald Coll., McGill Univ. 1937–38; Asst. Entom., Dom. Dept. of Agric., i/c Candn. Forest Insect Survey 1938–42; Ed. 'The Canadian Field-Naturalist' 1940–42; served in 2nd World War 1942–45; Maj., Directorate of Chemical Warfare; awarded M.B.E.; appt. Head, Entom. Sect., Experimental Station, Suffield, of Defence Research Bd., 1945–47; Prof. and Head, Dept. of Zool., Univ. W. Ont. 1947–69; Head, Vector Ecology Sect., World Health Organization, Geneva 1969–73; Dir., Pesticide Rsch. Center, Mich. State Univ. 1973–76; Occasional Consultant, World Health Organ. 1976–82; formerly Assoc. Comte. mem., Defence Research Bd., U.S. Nat. Research Council, World Health Organ.; Special Consultant, U.S. Pub. Health Service; Biologist, World Health Organ. 1956–58 (special leave of absence); mem., Edit. Bd., 'Annual Review of Entomology'; Research Fellowship of Royal Soc. of Can. in the Biol. Sciences, 1936–37; awarded Entomol. Soc. Can. Gold Medal for Achievement, 1963; Pres.: Entomol. Soc. Can. 1962; Am. Mosquito Control Assn., 1965; Entomol. Soc. Am., 1967; Candn Soc. Zool. 1968; Hon. mem.: Entom. Soc. Ont.; Entom. Soc. Am.; Fellow, Royal Society of Canada (Acad. Science); author: 'Insect Control by Chemicals,' 1951; 'Insecticide Resistance in Arthropods,' 1958; 'Ecology of Pesticides' 1978; co-author: 'Entomology Medical & Veterinary,' 1954; many scient. papers for tech. journs.; Kappa Alpha; Anglican; Address: Chemin du Vallon, 1261 Genolier, Switzerland.

**BROWN, Arnold,** O.C. (1981), D.D., L.H.D.; Salvation Army officer; b. London, Eng. 13 Dec. 1913; s. Arnold Rees and Annie (Horrocks) B.; came to Canada 1923; e. Belleville (Ont.) Coll. Inst.; Trinity Coll. of Music; L.H.D. Asbury Coll. 1972; D.D. Olivet Coll., 1981; m. Jean Catherine, d. late James Barclay, 15 Sept. 1939; children: Heather Jean, Beverley Ann; Comnd. Salvation Army Offr. 1935, i.c. Salvation Army work, Bowmanville, Ont. 1935, Asst. Ed. 'The War Cry' (Can.) 1936, Nat. Information Offr. (inaugurating Salvation Army Radio & TV work) 1946, Nat. Youth Offr. 1962, Dir. Internat. Public Relations, Salvation Army London, Eng. 1964, Chief of Staff. Internat. Salvation Army, London, Eng. 1969–1974; Territorial Commdr. – Can. and Bermuda, Toronto, Ont. 1974–77; General 1977–81; author of 'What Hath God Wrought?' 1952; 'The Gate and the Light' 1983; 'Fighting for His Glory' 1987; 'YIN-the Mountain the Wind Blew Here' 1988; 'With Christ at the Table' 1991; also numerous articles in mags. and journs.; made Freeman of City of London (Eng.) 1978; Offr. of Order of Can. 1981; Protestant; recreations: reading, writing, music; Clubs: Rotary (Past Pres. and hon. mem., London, Eng. Br. 1970–71; hon. mem., Downtown Toronto); Home: 1200 Don Mills Rd., Suite 416, Don Mills, Ont. M3B 3N8.

**BROWN, The Rt. Rev. Arthur Durrant,** B.A., L.Th., D.D.; Anglican bishop; b. Guelph, Ont. 7 Mar. 1926; s. Edward Sutherland and Laura Agnes (Durrant) B.; e. Kitchener Coll. Inst.; Univ. of W. Ont. B.A. 1949; Huron Coll. L.Th. 1949, D.D. 1979; Wycliffe Coll. D.D. 1980; m. Norma Inez d. Leslie and Inez Rafuse 11 June 1949; children: Joanne, Judith, Carolyn; grandchild: Sarah; BISHOP OF YORK-SCARBOROUGH, SUFFRAGAN BISHOP OF ANGLICAN DIOCESE OF TORONTO 1981– ; o. Deacon 1949; Priest 1950; Rector, Paisley Pinkerton Cargill 1948–50; Glanworth & St. Stephen's Ch. 1950–53; St. John's Ch. 1953–63; St. Michael & All Angels 1963–80; Rural Dean of Essex 1960–62; mem., Corp. of Huron Coll. 1961– ; Canon, St. James Cathedral 1973; Archdeacon of York, Dioc. of Toronto 1974–80; Broadcaster 'Moments of Meditation' CFRB 1964–85; Columnist, Toronto 'Sunday Sun' 1974–86; mem. Jud. Counc., Prov. of Ont. 1979–85; Chrmn. Candn. Friends to West Indian Christians (Ont.) 1982– ; Chrmn. Pension Ctte., Anglican Ch. of Can. 1983– ; Hon. Chrmn., Candn. Found. on Compulsive Gambling (Ont.) 1983– , Humanitarian Award 1990; mem. Adv. Ctte., Ontario Homes for The Aging, 1985– ; mem., Ont. Press Council 1986–87; Chrmn., 1984 Royal Visit Children's Fund 1984; Patron and Mem., Adv. Ctte., Candn. Diabetes Assn. (Annual Fund Raising Campaign) 1984– ; Home: 5 Gossamer Ave., Willowdale, Ont. M2M 2X1; Office: 3333 Finch Ave. E., Agincourt, Ont. M1W 2R9.

**BROWN, Barry D.,** Q.C., LL.B.; lawyer; b. St. Mary's Ont. 13 Jan. 1933; s. J. Clifton and Madeleine O. (Johnston) B.; e. St. Mary's & Dist. High Sch.; Univ. of Toronto; Osgoode Hall Law Sch., LL.B. 1962; m. Barbara A. d. George and Nina McTavish 23 June 1984; children: Christopher Dean, Melinda L. Davidson; SR. PARTNER, BENSON, PERCIVAL, BROWN & WALSH 1970–90; called to Bar of Ont. 1964; cr. Q.C. 1975; mem. Co. of York Law Assn. (Past Pres.); Advocates' Soc. Ont. (Past Dir.); Law Soc. Upper Can.; Candn. Bar Assn.; Medical/Legal Soc.; Internat. Assn. Defence Counsel; Past Area Ctte. Chrmn., Ont. Legal Aid Plan; Bd. of Dirs., Defense Rsch. Inst.; Clubs: Lawyers'; Cambridge; Royal Candn. Mil. Inst.; Home: 1324 Clarkson Rd. N., Mississauga, Ont. L5J 2W5; Office: 800, 250 Dundas St. W., Toronto, Ont. M5T 2Z6.

**BROWN, Covell Dorn,** B.A., M.B.A.; consultant; b. Longview, Wash. 17 Oct. 1937; s. Hugh Dorn and Edythe C. (Kenny) B.; e. Green Mountain Grade Sch. Woodland, Wash.; Anchorage (Alaska) High Sch.; Univ. of Cal. Santa Barbara B.A. 1960; Harvard Univ. M.B.A. 1962; Columbia Univ. grad. studies Mgmt. Systems and Law 1963; m. Mary d. Barry and Joan Montgomery 26 Jan. 1968; children: Tracey Annette, Winsome Sarah Montgomery, Victoria Rachael Montgomery, Nicholas Covell Montgomery; CHRMN. AND C.E.O., VERITAS CONSULTANTS CORP. 1971– ; joined Arthur Young & Co. New York City 1962–66, Sr. Acct.; Harbridge House, Boston 1966–71, Mgmt. Cons. stationed Boston, Dublin, Ireland, Toronto, Gen. Mgr. Toronto Office 1969–71; First Vice Pres., Secy. Treas., Internat. Mgmt. Development (IMD); Past Chrmn. Harvard Bus. Sch. Club Toronto; Past Candn. Area Chrmn. Harvard Sch. Bus. Alumni Assn.; former mem. Bd. Metro Toronto YMCA; recreations: family, sailing, skiing, upland & waterfowl shooting, wine collecting, arts; Clubs: The York; RCYC; Caledon Ski; York Skeet; Harvard (N.Y.C. & Boston); Home: 67 Chestnut Park, Toronto, Ont. M4W 1W7; Office: 14 Dundonald, Toronto, Ont. M4Y 1K2.

**BROWN, Daniel John,** B.Sc., M.A., A.M., Ph.D.; university professor; b. New Westminster, B.C. 7 Aug. 1941; s. J. Douglas and Marguerita M. (Williamson) B.; e. Univ. of B.C. B.Sc. 1963, M.A. 1968; Univ. of Chicago A.M. 1971, Ph.D. 1972; m. Marnie d. Edwin and Edna Mountain 26 Aug. 1967; children: Trevor, Leanne; ASSOC. PROF., EDUCATIONAL ADMINISTRATION, UNIV. OF B.C. 1977– ; Asst. Prof., State Univ. of New York at Buffalo 1971–77; academic interests: decentralization, voluntarism, & enterprise in edn.; author: 'Decentralization and School-based Management' 1990, 'Decentralization: The Administrator's Guidebook to School District Change' 1991; 'Schools With Heart: Voluntarism and Public Education' 1994; Office: Vancouver, B.C. V6T 1Z4.

**BROWN, David Andrew,** C.A.; business executive; b. Montreal, Que. 21 May 1939; e. McGill Univ. C.A. 1962; m.; 3 children; VICE-PRESIDENT, ADMIN. CORPORATE SECRETARY, GLAXO CANADA INC. 1986– ; Auditor, Peat Marwick, Mitchell & Co. 1962–65; Sec.-Treas., Abbott Labs. Ltd. 1965–75; Compt., Bank of Montreal 1975–77; Vice-Pres., Finance, Harold P. Cowan Co. Ltd. 1978–86; Mem., Pharmaceutical Mfrs. Assn. of Can.; Am. Mngt. Assn. (Fin. Adv. Bd., Candn. Mngt. Centre); Mississauga Economic Development Advisory Board; Office: 7333 Mississauga Road N., Mississauga, ON L5N 6L4.

**BROWN, Derek,** B.Comm., LL.B.; investment banker; b. Saint John, N.B. 13 May 1945; s. George Albert and Eileen (Brock) B.; w. Rothesay C.S. 1962; Dalhousie Univ. B.Comm. 1966, LL.B. 1969; m. Margaret Ann d. Florence and W. Ernest Burstall 13 Dec. 1975; one s.: George William; VICE-PRESIDENT AND DIRECTOR, RBC DOMINION SECURITIES INC. 1976– ; Extve. Asst. to the President, CTV Television Network Ltd. 1969–71; joined present firm 1971; Dir. 1978; Resident Director, Alberta 1979–84; Dir., RBC Dominion Securities Limited 1988– ; Dir., RBC Dominion Securities Found. 1978– ; Chrmn. 1989– ; Bd. Mem., Calgary General Hosp. 1981–84; Toronto Western Hosp. 1984–86; Toronto Gen. Hosp. 1986–88; Anglican Ch. of Can.; P.C.; Phi Delta Theta; Lt. (retd), Royal Candn. Naval Reserve; Mem., Naval Officers Assn. of Can.; Royal Alta. United Services Inst.; UNTD Assn. of U.C.; Sir Winston Churchill Soc. for the Advancement of Parlty. Democracy; Candn. Institute of Chartered Business Valuators; recreations: golf, skiing, sailing; clubs: Pinebrook Golf & Country, Calgary Golf & Country, Ranchmens, Albany of Toronto, Lambton Golf & Country, Halifax, Royal Nova Scotia Yacht Squadron, Chester Golf, Chester Yacht; Home: 48 St. Andrew's Gardens, Toronto, Ont. M4W 2E1; Office: P.O. Box 21, Commerce Court S., Toronto, Ont. M5L 1A7.

**BROWN, Donald I.,** CIB; insurance broker; b. Montreal, Que. 19 Dec. 1931; s. late Charles Arrol and Estelle (Lynch) B.; e. Loyola of Montreal; Sir George Williams Univ. comm.; m. Brenda McMillan 15 Nov. 1991; children: Karen, Deborah, Stephen; HONORARY CHRMN., JOHNSON & HIGGINS LTD. since 1993; Dir. Dupuis Parizeau Tremblay Inc.; Foster Higgins; Sibson & Co.; joined Johnson & Higgins (Canada) Ltd. 1950, Mgr. Production Dept. 1963; joined E. A. Whitehead as Partner 1965, Vice Pres. and Dir. 1966. Vice Pres. and Dir.-Ont. 1970; Vice Pres. and Dir. Tomenson Saunders Whitehead Ltd. 1973, Exec. Vice Pres. and Dir. 1975 and Dir. Tomenson Alexander Ltd. 1975; Chrmn., Pres., C.E.O. & Dir., Johnson & Higgins Ltd. 1975–93; Past Pres. Montreal Central Lions Club; Inter Service Club Council; Pres., Bd. Trade Metrop. Toronto 1993–94; recreations: golf, curling, travel; Clubs: Toronto Club; Mount Royal (Montreal); Royal Montreal Golf; St. George's Golf & Country (past Dir.); Toronto Golf; Cambridge; Bd. of Trade, Metro. Toronto; Home: 30 Elgin Ave., Toronto, Ont. M5R 1G6; Office: Scotia Plaza, P.O. Box 1010, 40 King St. W., Toronto, Ont. M5H 3Y2.

**BROWN, Donald Robert,** Q.C., LL.B.; b. New Glasgow, N.S. 10 Sept. 1945; s. Norman Douglas and Margaret Jessie (Miller) B.; e. Mt. Allison Univ., Dalhousie Univ. Law Sch., LL.B. 1968; Duke Univ. AMP; VICE PRES., GEN. COUNS. & SECY., SUNCOR INC. 1988– ; DIR. & SECY., SUNOCO INC. 1989– ; Barrister & Solicitor, Blake, Cassels & Graydon 1970–78; Gen. Solic. & Asst. Sec., Shell Can. Ltd. 1978–79; Gen. Couns., The Bank of Nova Scotia 1979–84; Vice Pres. & Gen. Couns., Traders Group Ltd., Guaranty Trustco Ltd. & Guaranty Trust Co. of Can. 1984–88; Q.C. 1983; Mem., Law Soc. of Upper Can.; N.S. Barristers Soc.; Candn. Bar Assn.; Internat. Bar Assn.; Am. Corp. Couns. Assn.; Inst. of Corp. Dirs. in Can.; recreations: tennis, golf; Clubs: Granite; National; Devil's Pulpit Golf Assoc.; Home: 378 St. Clements Ave., Toronto, Ont. M5N 1M1; Office: 36 York Mills Rd., North York, Ont. M2P 2C5.

**BROWN, Downie;** manufacturer; b. Glasgow, Scot. 17 June 1943; s. Robert and Helen Margaret (Marshall) B.; e. Hutcheson's Boys Grammar Sch. Glasgow 1952–60; Inst. C.A.'s Scot. Apprentice 1960–65, mem. 1965; Glasgow Univ. 1962–64; m. Moya d. George McAuley, N. Ireland, 3 Oct. 1975; children: Matthew Robert McAuley; Kirsty Margaret; FINANCE DIR., RTZ PILLAR LTD.; Dir., Indal Ltd.; Divisional Controller, Pillar Engineering 1968–72; Extve. I.M.G., mng. sports personalities and entertainment celebrities 1972; held various accounting & mgmt. positions Indal Ltd. 1973–86; Financial Dir., Pillar Building Products Ltd. 1986–90; joined present co. 1990; served as Capt. Scot. and Brit. Internat. Swim Teams, competed in World University Games 1963, Commonwealth Games 1966, 1970 and World Masters Games 1985; mem. Inst. C.A.'s Scot.; Protestant; recreations: golf, squash, tennis, swimming, reading, music; Home: Shepherds Close, Byways, Gravel Path, Berkhamsted, Herts, UK HP4 2PJ; Office: Cleveland House, 19 St. James's Square, London SW1Y 4JG England

**BROWN, Maj. Gen. George Grenville,** C.D. (and 3 Bars); retired army officer; b. Saskatoon, Sask. 17 June 1922; s. late Arthur Richardson, B.Sc., LL.D. and Marie Pauline (Grambo) B.; e. Pub. and High Schs., Lloydminster and Regina, Sask., 1940; Royal Mil. Coll., 1940–42 mq; Staff Coll. Camberley Eng., 1956 psc; Assoc. Inf. Offrs. Advanced Course USA, 1952; Nat. Defence Coll., 1968–69 NDC; m. Constance Helen Bridgman (d. 1971) 27 Oct. 1946; children: Shaun Richardson Grenville, Shelley Jean Marie, Patrick Arthur Raymond; 2ndly, Pauline Hazel Boismenu, April 1972; one. s Steven John; comnd. and posted overseas 1942; joined Loyal Edmonton Regiment, Italy, 1943; wounded in Battle of Naviglio Canal 1944; served as operations officer Holland 1945; returned to Canada to join Pacific Force 1945; joined PPCLI Regular Army 1946; served in W. Can. in various Reg. and Staff Appts. until promoted Maj. 1952 and co. commdr. 2 PPCLI Calgary and Germany 1953–55; Bgde. Maj. 1st Candn. Inf. Bgde. Group, 1957–60; GSO 2 1st Brit. Div., Army on Rhine, 1960–62; promoted Lt. Col. 1962 and C.O. 1st PPCLI Victoria (named Hon. Citizen 1963); Germany 1963–65, returned to Can. to assist in formation of Mobile Command and restructuring Infantry on unification of Forces; Col. 1966 and apptd. Chief of Inf., HQ Mobile Command; Dir. of Equipment Requirements (Land Forces), CFHQ, 1969; Brig. Gen. and Chief of Staff Operations, Mobile Command, 1970–72; responsible for overall planning deployment and operations of army during 'October Crisis' Oct. 1970; 1 Combat Group & Can. Forces Base, Calgary 1972–74; promoted Maj. Gen.

Aug. 1974 and apptd. Chief Land Operation NDHQ Ottawa; Depy-Commdr. Mobile Command 1975; Army mem. permanent Joint Bd. on Defence (Can./U.S.); head of delegation to quadripartite agreement for Standardization, and to Chief of Staff Com. Organ. of Amer. States 1974–77; made Honorary Indian Chief 'We Cha Ano Nicha' ('Defender') 1964; awarded Centennial Medal 1967; Queen's Jubilee Medal 1978; admitted to Order of St. John 1976; apptd. Col. of the Regt. PPCLI 1977 (retired 1983); joined Alberta Energy Co. 1978; retired 1987; mem., Royal Mil. Coll. Club of Can.; Loyal Edmonton Regt. Assn.; Vice-Patron, PPCLI Regt'al Assn.; Camberley Staff Coll. Grad. Assn.; Royal Alberta United Services Inst.; Patron, Calgary Military Museum Soc.; Club: Ranchmen's; recreations: skiing, gardening; Home: 844 Oakside Circle S.W., Calgary, Alta. T2V 4P7.

**BROWN, Gerald Daniel;** executive; b. Windsor, Ont. 3 Apr. 1929; s. late Gerald M.B. and Wiltrude (Dunwoody); e. Pub. and High Schs., Toronto, Ont.; m. Valerie. d. late William McKay, May 1949; children: Drew, Victoria, Deborah, Michael; Chrmn. and C.E.O., Pir Communications Inc. 1979–.; Chairman, PIR Advertising Ltd.; Dir., Sunnybrook Medical Centre; Chrmn. Canada News-Wire Ltd.; served as Editor of Canadian daily, weekly and business pubs. and as Pub. Relations Consultant till joining present Co. in 1952 as Acct. Extve.; el. a Dir., 1955; apptd. Vice-Pres. and Mang. Dir., 1958; Pres., Public and Ind. Relations Ltd.; mem., Candn. Public Relations Soc.; Inst. of Public Relations; Internat. Public Relations Assoc.; Public Relations Soc. of Am.; Candn. Chamber Comm.; Gov., Frontier Coll.; Anglican; recreations: charitable activities, outdoor sports; Clubs: Granite; Empire; Devil's Glen Country; Home: 90 Ardwold Gate, Toronto, Ont. M5R 2W2.

**BROWN, Gregory M.,** B.A., M.D., Ph.D., F.R.C.P.(C); educator; b. Toronto, Ont. 27 March 1934; s. Norbert Joseph and Nellie Shaw (Diack), M.D., Brown; e. Univ. of Toronto B.A. 1955, M.D. 1959; Univ. of Rochester Ph.D. 1971; m. Audrey C. d. Harvey and Christina Shute 18 June 1960; children: Jacqueline Anne Embleton, David Michael, Mary Catherine, Paul Douglas, Barbara Suzanne French, Joyce Christina, Patricia Elizabeth, Anne Marie; DIR. OF RSCH., CLARKE INST. OF PSYCHIATRY AND PROF. DEPTS. OF PSYCHIATRY AND PHYSIOLOGY, UNIV. OF TORONTO 1990– ; Prof. Emeritus of Biomedical Sciences, McMaster Univ. and Prof. Emeritus of Psychiatry 1977– ; Chrmn. of Neurosciences 1977–87; Pres. CIDtech Research Inc.; Asst. Prof., Assoc. Prof. and Prof. of Psychiatry Univ. of Toronto 1969–77; recipient John Dewan Award Ont. Mental Health Found. 1980; Heinz Lehmann Award, Candn. Coll. Psychoneuropharmacol. 1983; MRC Visiting Sci. Award 1984–85; ed. 'Neuroendocrinology and Psychiatric Disorder' 1984; 'The Pineal Gland. Endocrine Aspects' 1985; 'Clinical Neuroendocrinology' 1988; mem. various ed. bds.; mem. Am. & Candn. Med. & Psychiatric Assns.; Endocrine Soc.; Am. Psychosomatic Soc.; Internat. Soc. Psychoneuroendocrinol.; Candn. Coll. Neuropsychopharmacol.; recreation: singing (opera & musical comedies); Home: 1382 Crestdale Rd., Mississauga, Ont. L5H 1X7; Office: 250 College St., Toronto, Ont. M5T 1R8.

**BROWN, Henry Laing,** LL.B.; lawyer; b. Hamilton, Ont. 10 Mar. 1948; s. Langford Arnold and Doris Marie (Wilker) B.; e. Westdale S.S.; Hamilton C.I.; Univ. of West. Ont., 1967–69; Univ. of B.C., LL.B. 1972; m. Kathleen d. Ernest and Mary Curling 18 May 1973; children: Kalan, Maryn, Casson; PARTNER, RUSSELL & DuMOULIN 1980– ; called to B.C. Bar 1973; articled & assoc. with Russell & DuMoulin 1972–80; Lectr., Cont. Legal Edn. of B.C.; The Candn. Inst.; Univ. of B.C. (part-time); Simon Fraser Univ. Continuing Studies; Profl. Legal Training Prog.; Past Dir. & Treas., The Lawyers Inn; Past Pres. and Trustee, The Vancouver Art Gall. Assn.; Trustee, Vancouver Inst. for the Visual Arts; Past Pres., Contemporary Art Soc. of Vanc.; Past Dir., The Contemporary Art Gall.; Mem., Candn. Bar Assn.; recreations: collecting & studying contemporary art, tennis, squash, golf; Club: Hollyburn Country; Home: 1057 Blue Grouse Way, N. Vancouver, B.C. V7R 4N7; Office: 1500 – 1075 West Georgia St., Vancouver, B.C. V6E 3G2.

**BROWN, Ian Peter Bennett,** B.A.; writer; broadcaster; b. Lachine, Que. 4 Feb. 1954; s. Peter Henry and Cicely Hilda (Betts) B.; e. Selwyn House Westmount, Que.; Trinity Coll. Sch. Port Hope; Trinity Coll. Univ. of Toronto B.A. 1976; Harvard Univ. Dip. 1976; m. Johanna d. Robert and Joanne Schneller 9 Sept. 1989; currently freelance writer and broadcaster Los Angeles; staff writer The Financial Post 1976–78; Assoc. Bus. Ed.

Maclean's mag. 1978–79; freelance writer and broadcaster 1979–84; Feature Writer The Globe and Mail 1984–88; Host 'Later The Same Day' CBC Radio 1989–90; Instr. in Writing Radcliffe Publishing Procedures Course Harvard Univ. 1981–88; Sr. Ed. BGMRW Holdings Inc. (publishers); regular panelist 'Morningside' CBC Radio 1988–93; recipient Nat. Newspaper Award 1984; Nat. Mag. Award 1978, 1987, 1991, 1992; Nat. Bus. Book Award 1990; author: 'Freewheeling' 1989; 'Man Overhead' 1993; mem. Candn. Parks & Wilderness Soc.; recreations: reading, skiing, mountaineering; Club: The Dog; Home: 87 Gore Vale Ave., Toronto, Ont. M6J 2R5 and 8400 West 4th St., Los Angeles, CA 90048.

**BROWN, Jack Ernest,** B.A., B.L.S., M.A., LL.D.; librarian; b. Edmonton Alta. 1 Mar. 1914; s. Ernest William and Maud Alice (Jarman) B.; e. Univ. of Alta., B.A. 1938; McGill Univ. B.L.S. 1939; Univ. of Chicago M.A. 1940; L.L.D. Univ. Waterloo 1965, McMaster Univ. 1978; m. Estelle A., d. late Frank Coles, 26 Dec. 1944; children: Frances, Keith; Science Information Consultant 1982–89; Prof., Grad Sch. Library Sci., McGill Univ. 1977–82; Dir. Can. Inst. Scientific and Tech. Information, NRC 1974–77; (Nat. Science Librarian 1957–74); Reference Librarian, Edmonton Public Library 1940–42; Library Assistant, New York Public Library, Science and Tech. Div., 1942–57 (Asst. Librarian, Brown Univ., Providence, R.I. 1946–47); sometime Visiting Lectr., McGill Univ. Lib. Sch.; Toronto Univ. Lib., Sch.; Ottawa Univ. Lib Sch.; mem., Candn. Lib. Assn. (Councillor 1961–64); Assn. of Coll. & Research Libs. (Dir. 1961–64); Nat. Research Council Assoc. Comte. on Scient. Information (Secy.); Candn. Nat. Comte. for Internat. Fed. for Documentation (Secy.); Internat. Fed. for Documentation (Vice Pres., 1965–67); mem. OECD Information Policy Group; NRC Adv. Bd. on Scient. & Tech. Information; Can. Assoc. Information Science; Can. Library Assn.; Special Libs. Assn.; Candn. Library Assn. Outstanding Service to Librarianship Award, 1979; Libraries & Inf. Services, Award for Special Librarianship in Can., 1979; Anglican; recreations: music, gardening; Home: 417 Meadow Dr., Ottawa, Ont. K1K 0M3.

**BROWN, James Eedy,** B.A.; writer; b. Brantford, Ont. 3 Nov. 1945; s. James E. and Helen Elizabeth (Eedy) B.; e. Sir Wilfred Laurier Univ. B.A. 1968; M. Lorna d. Lars and Agnes Strom 28 Feb. 1972; children: Jean-Pierre, Alexandre, Elizabeth; Lectr. in Communications Fanshaw Coll. 1972–74; writer; researcher Nat. Film Bd. 1974–77; Lectr. in Eng. Writing Concordia Univ. 1980–85; Entertainment Ed. Pulse News CFCF-TV Montréal 1980–86; Film Producer, Head of Feature Film Devel. Telescene Prodns. Montréal 1988; Extve. Vice Pres., Telescene Film Group, Montréal 1989; author, 'The Lively Spirits of Provence' 1974; 'Stepping Stones' 1975; 'So Free We Seem' 1976; 'Shrewsbury' 1977; 'Super-Bike' 1982; writer/prod., feature films 'Keeping Track' 1985; prod., 'Obsessed' 1986; 'Kurwenal' 1987; 'Malarek' 1988; 'A Cry in the Night'; writer, 'The Brylcreem Boys' 1989; Extve. Prod., 'Une Histoire Inventée' 1990; TV Series 'Urban Angel' CBC 1990; 'Urban Angel' CBC and CBS 1991; 'Salt on Your Skin'; United Church; recreation: auto sports; Club: Vintage Automobile Racing Assn.; Home: 2 Knivet Rd., London SW6 1JH England; Office: Studio 8, 125 Moore Park Rd., London SW6 4PS England.

**BROWN, Jennifer Stacey Harcourt,** A.M., Ph.D.; educator; b. Providence, R.I. 30 Dec. 1940; d. the late Harcourt and Dorothy Elizabeth (Stacey) Brown; e. Brown Univ. A.B. 1962; Harvard Univ. A.M. 1963; Univ. of Chicago Ph.D. 1976; m. Wilson B. s. Wilson R. and Doris Brown 8 June 1963; one. s Matthew Harcourt; PROF. OF HIST. UNIV. OF WINNIPEG 1988– ; (Assoc. Prof. 1982–88), Gen. Ed. Rupert's Land Rsch. Centre 1984– ; Asst. Prof. Colby Coll. Waterville, Me., Northern Ill. Univ., Ind. Univ. 1966–82; Visiting Distinguished Prof. of Candn. Studies Univ. of Alta. 1982; Rsch. Fellow Newberry Lib. Chicago 1982; Publs. Ed. Middle Am. Rsch. Inst. Tulane Univ. 1975–82; mem. Gov. Council Man. Hist. Soc. 1985–87; Dir. Man. Record Soc.; mem. Council, Champlain Soc. 1986– ; Councillor, Am. Soc. Ethnohist. 1984–86; mem. Adv. Counc., Candn. Historical Review 1991–94; Pres., Am. Soc. Ethnohist. 1989–90; Hist. Cons. Nat. Film Bd. series 'Daughters of the Country' 1984–86; Woodrow Wilson Fellow 1962–63; author 'Strangers in Blood: Fur Trade Company Families in Indian Country' 1980 (Hon. Mention Sir John A. Macdonald Prize); co-ed. 'The New Peoples: Being and Becoming Metis in North America' 1985; co-author 'The Orders of the Dreamed: George Nelson on Cree and Northern Ojibwa Religion and Myth' 1988; ed. 'The Ojibwa of Berens River, Manitoba: Ethnography into History' 1992 by A. Irving

Hallowell; numerous articles, conf. papers ethnohist; contr. 'Dictionary of Canadian Biography,' 'Canadian Encyclopedia'; Phi Beta Kappa Honor Soc.; recreation: summer cottage; Home: 336 Kingsway Ave., Winnipeg, Man. R3M 0H5; Office: 515 Portage Ave., Winnipeg, Man. R3B 2E9.

**BROWN, Jerome V.,** Ph.D., M.S.L.; university professor; b. New York City, NY 4 Sept. 1936; s. George Vincent and Nora Mary (Lyons) B.; e. Iona Co., New Rochelle, N.Y., B.A. 1958; Univ. of Toronto M.A. 1960, Ph.D. 1969; Pontifical Inst. of Mediaeval Studies M.S.L. (Licentiate in Med. Studies) 1973; m. Esther d. Joseph and Giovanna Vella 27 June 1964; children: Terence, James, John Paul; Lectr., Assist. Prof., Assoc. Prof., Prof. of Philosophy, first at Assumption Univ., then at the Univ. of Windsor, since 1961; Dean of the Faculty of Arts 1981–85; Visiting Lectr., Catholic Univ. of Leuven, Belgium 1975; Mem., Editorial Comn., 'Opera Omnia' of Henry of Ghent; author of numerous articles in scholarly journals; mem., Société International Pour L'Etude De La Philosophie Médiévale; Candn. Studies Assn.; Pres. & Dir., Windsor Teachers Credit Union 1970–72, Dir. 1963–74; Woodrow Wilson Fell. 1958; Univ. of Toronto Open Fellowships 1959, 1962; Can. Council Fell. 1960, 1961, 1967; Can. Coun. Summer Research Grants 1971, 1973; Dept. of External Affairs Travel Fell. 1975, 1977; S.S.H.R.C. Travel Grant 1977; S.S.H.R.C. International Consultation Grants 1981, 1986, 1987; S.S.H.R.C. Research Grant 1982, 1983, 1990, 1991; Roman Catholic; Home: 261 Esdras Pl., Windsor, Ont. N8S 2M4; Office: University of Windsor, Windsor, Ont. N9B 3P4.

**BROWN, Kenneth Charles,** B.A.; diplomat; b. Ann Arbor, Mich. 13 Feb. 1925 (came to Can. 1925); s. late Prof. George Williams and Vera Beatrice (Kenny) B.; e. Univ. of Toronto. B.A. 1945; Oxford Univ. (Rhodes Scholar), B.A. 1948; m. Ruth Louise, d. Earl Johnston, Sarnia, Ont., 3 July 1948; children: David, Deborah, Christopher, Andrew; joined Dept. of External Affairs in London, Eng., July 1948; Ottawa Dec. 1948; Second Secy., Havana 1951; Ottawa 1954; Second Secy., Berne 1957; First Secy. 1959; Ottawa 1960; Counsellor, Washington 1963; Ottawa 1967; Ambassador to Cuba and Haiti 1970; Ottawa 1973; Ambassador to Sweden 1976; Chrmn., Refugee Status Advisory Comte., Can. Employment and Immigration Commission Ottawa 1980; Co-ordinator, Access to Information and Privacy, Dept. of External Affairs 1982; Sr. Policy Adv., Treasury Bd. Staff 1987; retired 1988; served with Candn. Army in N.W. Europe 1944–46; rank Sgt. on discharge; Un. Church; recreations: skiing, canoeing, bridge, tennis; Home: 285 Mariposa Ave., Ottawa, Ont. K1M 0T4.

**BROWN, Logan Rae,** B.A.; industrialist; b. Guelph, Ont. 6 Aug. 1927; s. C.H. Sherman and Vera Irene (Rae) B.; e. Pub. Sch. and London (Ont.) Central Coll. Inst.; Univ. of W. Ont., Sch. of Business, Hon. B.A. 1950; m. Betty Catherine, d. Sam McMahon, Toronto, Ont., 7 July 1951; children: Jordan, Christopher, Sandra; CHRMN., ROBIN HOOD MULTIFOODS INC. 1970– ; Vice-Pres., International Multifoods, Minneapolis, Minn. 1971–89; began career as Sales Rep., Lever Brothers Ltd. 1950; Marketing Research Dept. 1950; Brand Mgr. 1952; New Products Mgr. 1955; Marketing Mgr. 1957; joined Libby, McNeill & Libby of Canada Ltd. as Dir.-Marketing 1960; Pres. and Mang. Dir. 1964; Vice-Pres., International, Libby, McNeill & Libby, Chicago 1966–69; Pres. present firm 1969, C.E.O. 1970–89; with C.O.T.C., sch. of Inf., Camp Borden, 1946–50; qualified as Lt.; Past Offr., Elgin Regt., St. Thomas, Ont.; Candn. Intelligence Corps, Toronto, qualified as Capt.; Nat. Dir., Am. Marketing Assn. 1958–60, (Past Pres. Toronto Chapter 1955–56); mem. Ed. Review Bd., 'Marketing in Canada' (1958); Chrmn. (1974) Grocery Products Mfrs. of Can.; mem. Adv. Council Banff Sch. Fine Arts 1971; Dir. The Council for Canadian Unity; Chrmn. (1973) Food & Beverage Industry Comte., Outlook Conf.; mem. Candn. Mil. Intelligence Assn.; 2nd Vice-Pres. and Chrmn. 1976 Building Fund Campaign, Montreal YMCA; mem., Bd. Gov., North York Gen. Hosp.; mem., Adv. Council, Fred C. Manning Sch. of Business, Acadia Univ. 1980; Adv. Bd., Liberty Mutual 1978; Extve. Comte., National Inst. of Nutrition; Gov., Nat. Theatre Sch. of Can. 1985–88; Vice Pres. of Equity Showcase Theatre; awarded Knight of the Golden Pencil, Food Industry Assoc. of Can. 1989; Zeta Psi; Protestant; recreation: golf; Clubs: Granite; St. James's; Royal Montreal Golf; Toronto Badminton & Racquet; Toronto Hunt; Rosedale Golf; The Club (Pelican Bay, Naples, Florida); Home: 15 Glenallan Rd. Toronto, Ont. M4N 1G6; Office: 60 Columbia Way, Markham, Ont. L3R 0C9.

**BROWN, Lyal Douglas;** writer; b. Medicine Hat, Alta. 1 Nov. 1929; s. Oliver Cromwell and Ena Duncan (Beattie) B.; e. Crescent Heights C.I. 1948; Montana State Univ. 1948–49; Univ. of B.C. 1949–50; m. Barbara d. Frank and Genevieve Wyatt 27 June 1952; children: Heather, Gordon, Kirk, Sharyl; priv. radio announcer 1950–52; Writer, Dir. Info. Serv., Extve. Asst. to Gen. Mgr., CBC 1952–60; freelance writer/broadcaster (TV, radio, film documentaries, 70 TV plays, 6 radio plays) 1960– ; Host/writer, 'Eye to Eye' 1962–63; 'Sunday Supplement' 1970–73; teleplays incl. 'Angel Against the Night' 1974, 'The Albertans' 1979, 'Ritter's Cove' (series, co-written with Barbara Brown) 1980, 'Beachcombers' (story ed.) 1986; 'Body Clock' (stage play written with Heather Brown) 1989; Pres., L. Douglas Brown Ltd. 1970– ; Bd. of Dir., Tegra Enterprises 1984–87; Mem., ACTRA (Toronto Br. Counc. 1976); Vice-Pres., ACTRA Writers Counc. (Vanc.) 1985; recreations: painting, music; Home/Office: 14864 – 17th Ave., Surrey, B.C. V4A 6V4.

**BROWN, M. Grant,** P.Eng., M.B.A.; merchant banker; b. Montreal, Que. 2 July 1949; s. George Grant and Edna Nancy (Key) B.; e. McGill Univ., B.Eng. 1971; McMaster Univ., M.B.A. 1979; licensed private pilot 1991; m. Janis d. Percy and Helen Coxon 1 Sept. 1973; children: Taylor Jason, Jordan Andrew, Schenley Kyra; VICE CHAIRMAN, CANDN. CORP. FUNDING LTD.; Design Engr. then Mgr., Bus. Devel., Cambrian Engineering, Div. of Agra Industries 1971–78; Founder, Wyemet Indus. Inc. 1978–81; Assoc., Vengrowth Capital Funds 1982–84; Vice-Pres., Candn. Corp. Funding Ltd. 1984; Partner & Sr. Vice-Pres. 1985; Extve. Vice Pres. 1986; Vice Chrmn., CCFL Mezzanine Partners of Canada Ltd.; Pres., Canadian Pension Capital Corp.; Dir., BMG Canada Limited; Adpak Internat. Ltd.; Premier Propane Inc.; Mark Anthony Group Ltd.; Vancouver Wharves Ltd.; Oakville Trafalgar Mem. Hosp.; Clubs: Muskoka Lakes Golf and Country; Osler Ski, Fitness Inst., Oakville Golf; Home: 341 Acacia Court, Oakville, Ont. L6J 6K5; Office: 70 University Ave., Ste. 1450, Toronto, Ont. M5J 2M4.

**BROWN, Malcolm Clarence,** M.A., Ph.D.; educator; economist; b. Saint John, N.B. 15 June 1941; s. Clarence M. and Marion B.; e. Dalhousie Univ. B.A. 1963; Queen's Univ. M.A. 1965; Cornell Univ. M.A. 1968, Ph.D. 1969; married; children: Tiffany Lynne, Robert Malcolm, Christopher Keogh; PROF. OF ECON., UNIV. OF CALGARY 1981– ; Instr. Univ. of Sask. 1964–66, Cornell Univ. summer 1969; Asst. Prof. present Univ. 1969, Assoc. Prof. 1973, Adm. Asst. in Econ. 1970–73, Killam Resident Fellow 1980; Visiting Prof. of Econ., Victoria Univ. of Wellington, N.Z. 1975; Visiting Fellow, Centre Rsch. Fed. Financial Relations, Australian Nat. Univ., Canberra 1976; Jt. Visiting Fellow, Health Econ. Rsch. Unit & Centre Rsch. Fed. Financial Relations 1983–84; Visitng Fellow, National Ctr. for Epidemiology and Population Health, Australian Nat. Univ. 1990; Visiting Fellow, NHMRC National Ctr. for Health Program Evaluation, Monash and Melbourne Univs. Australia 1990–91; recipient various comns., Social Sci.'s & Humanities Rsch. Council and Can. Council Felowships & Grants, Prov. Ont. Grad. Fellowship; author 'Caring for Profit: Economic Dimensions of Canada's Health Industry' 1987; 'Health Economics and Policy: Problems and Prescriptions' 1991; and numerous publs., papers, reviews re health economics and intergovernmental fiscal relations; mem. Candn. Econ. Assn.; Candn. Health Econ. Rsch. Assn.; Am. Econ. Assn.; recreations: golf, squash, swimming, canoeing; Home: 3851 Point McKay Rd., Calgary, Alta. T3B 4V7; Office: Calgary, Alta. T2N 1N4.

**BROWN, Martin John Kingston,** B.Sc., F.I.A., F.C.I.A.; consulting actuary; b. London, Eng. 1 March 1946; s. Sydney John and Vivian Florence (Kingston) B.; e. Stationers' Company Sch. London 1964; Univ. of Leeds B.Sc. 1967; m. Lynn d. Kenneth and June Bentham 27 Feb. 1971; children: Philip Alexander, Samantha Kate, James Richard, Caroline Louise; CONSULTING ACTUARY, THE WYATT CO. 1991– ; joined Legal and General Assurance Society Ltd. as trainee actuary London, Eng. 1967; immigrated to Can. 1975 and joined Charles A. Kench & Associates Ltd. as Consulting Actuary; Partner and Chief Actuary Bates, Thouard, Tierney & Brown 1978, merged with The Wyatt Co. in 1983 and continued as Consulting Actuary and mem. Mgmt. Ctte.; Sr. Partner, mem. Mgmt. Ctte. and Dir., Sobeco Group Inc. 1989–91; returned to the Wyatt Co. 1991; mem. Ont. Regional Council Candn. Pension Conf. 1985–87; mem. Candn. Inst. Actuaries Ctte. Pension Plan Financial Reporting; recreations: family activities, home improvement, swimming; Home: 520 MacDonald Rd., Oakville, Ont. L6J 2B9; Office: Ste. 1100, One Queen St. E., Toronto, Ont. M5C 2Y4.

**BROWN, Mel M.,** B.A.Sc.; electrical manufacturer; b. Dauphin, Man. 1 March 1928; s. William Freeman and Edith Mary Margaret (Flavelle); e. Univ. of B.C. B.A.Sc. 1950; m. Joan d. Laura and Charles Foster 26 April 1952; children: Ron, Steve; PRESIDENT & CHIEF EXECUTIVE. OFFICER, SQUARE D CANADA 1986– ; Sales assignments in four provinces, Canadian General Electric; Business Mngt. in Peterborough; Mgr., Marketing & Sales, Industrial Apparatus Business 1978–86; recreations: curling, golf, plate collecting, reading; Home: 14 Mullen Place, Georgetown, Ont. L7G 2R9; Office: 6675 Rexwood Rd., Mississauga, Ont. L4V 1V1.

**BROWN, Michael Gary,** B.A., M.A., M.H.L., Ph.D., D.H.L. (Hon.); university professor; b. Scranton, Pa. 31 March 1938; s. Albert Joseph and Eunice (Levy) B.; e. Harvard Coll., B.A. 1960; Columbia Univ., M.A. 1963; Jewish Theological Seminary, M.H.L. 1966, rabbi 1968; State Univ. of N.Y. at Buffalo, Ph.D. 1976; m. Francine d. Benjamin and Barbara Nison 2 Sept. 1968; children: Joshua, Matthew, Abigail; ASSOC. PROF. OF HUMANITIES & HEBREW, YORK UNIV. 1968– ; Chair of Candn. Studies, Vis. Assoc. Prof., Inst. of Contemporary Jewry, Hebrew Univ., Jerusalem 1980–82; Vis. Assoc. Prof., Hist., Univ. of Toronto 1983–84; Vis. Assoc. Prof., Hist., Univ. of Calif. at San Diego 1985, 1988; Co-ord., Prog. in Jewish Teacher Education, Facs. of Arts and Edn., York Univ. 1982–89; Dir., Nat. Leadership Training Inst., Camp Ramah, 1975–80; Fellow, Am.-Holy Land Study Proj. 1985–87; Co-Chrmn., Education Ctte. and Dir., Assoc. Hebrew Schs.; Chrmn., Candn. Seminar on Zionist Thought; Co-Chrmn., Can. Ctte., Internat. Center for the Univ. Teaching of Jewish Civilization; mem., Assn. for Jewish Studies; Rabbinical Assembly; Toronto Bd. of Rabbis; recipient, D.H.L. (Hon.), Jewish Theological Seminary 1994; author: 'Jew or Juif? Jews, French Canadians, and Anglo-Canadians, 1759–1914' 1987; editor: 'Aspects of Antisemitism: Contexts and Curricula' 1994; Home: 293 Chaplin Cres., Toronto, Ont. M5P 1B1; Office: Vanier 250, York Univ., 4700 Keele St., North York, Ont. M3J 1P3.

**BROWN, Michael J.,** B.A.; executive; b. Vancouver, B.C. 12 Apr. 1939; s. William Thomas and Daphne Georgina (Jackson) B.; e. Univ. of B.C., B.A. 1960 (Gov. Gen.'s Silver Medal); Oxford Univ. (Rhodes Scholar) B.A. 1962; m. Ena J. 1983; children: Maura J., Meghan G., Hilary A.; PRESIDENT AND CO-FOUNDER, VENTURES WEST MANAGEMENT INC. 1983– ; Pres., Ventures West Technologies Ltd.; mem., National Biotechnology Advisory Ctte.; Task Force on Atmospheric Change (City of Vancouver) 1990; Science Council of B.C.; Dir., MacDonald Dettwiler & Associates Ltd.; Ballard Power Systems Inc.; Ballard Battery Systems Inc.; Mobile Computing Corp.; Canguard Pharma Inc.; joined Odlum Brown & T.B. Read Ltd. 1962–68, Partner and Dir. 1965–68; Co-Founder and Pres. Brown Farris & Jefferson Ltd. 1968–72; Co-Founder and Pres., Ventures West Capital Ltd. 1973–84; Chrmn., MDI International Mobile Data Inc. 1978–88; Dir., Wardair Inc. 1967–68, 1985–89; mem. Financial Analysts Soc.; recreations: golf, carpentry; Club: Vancouver; Home: 1220 Nepal Cres., West Vancouver, B.C. V7T 2H3; Office: 250, 375 Water St., Vancouver B.C. V6B 5C6.

**BROWN, Murray Thompson;** retired broadcasting executive; b. Kitchener, Ont. 2 June 1917; s. Ira Sylvester and Isabel Ada (Thompson) B.; e. Amherstburg, (Ont.) High Sch. (1930–35); Parkdale Coll. Inst., Toronto, Ont., 1935–36; Univ. of Western Ont. (Management Training), Aug.-Sept. 1948; m. Clarice Victoria, d. Russell Gibson, Montreal, P.Q., 10 Apl. 1948; children: Judith Belle, Murray Craig; Dir., The Blackburn Group Inc.; Pres., Central Can. Broadcasters Assn., 1952; began as Clerk, Confed. Life Assn., Toronto. Ont., 1936–37; joined Burt Business Forms Ltd. (now Moore Business Forms Ltd.), 1937; held various stat. and sales positions, 1937–45; apptd. Announcer and Writer for CFPL, 1945; Commercial Mgr., 1946–49; apptd. Stn. Mgr. 1949, Gen. Mgr. 1955, Pres. 1968; retired 1984; Pres., Candn. Assn. of Broadcasters, 1960; Chrmn. (1974–75) Candn Advertising Adv. Bd.; Campaign Chrmn. London Un. Way (1973); inducted into Candn. Assn. of Broadcasters Hall of Fame 1992; United Church; recreations: golf, tennis; Clubs: London; London Hunt & Country (Pres. 1976); Home: 139 Wychwood Place, London, Ont. N6G 1S7.

**BROWN, Nancy Jones,** B.A., M.S.W., A.C.S.W., C.S.W., N.A.S.W.; diplomate in clinical social worker; b. Pittsburgh, Pa. 27 Jan. 1943; d. Oliver Woodford and Alma (Wesley) J.; e. Mt. Holyoke Coll. B.A. 1965; Smith Coll. M.S.W. 1967; m. George Dixon B. 20 May

1972; children: George Oliver Robinson, Janice Marileine; EXTVE. DIR., HALTON FAMILY SERVICES 1976– ; Caseworker, Child & Family Serv., Norfolk, Va. 1967–68; Sch. Social Worker, Spec. Serv. Project, Middletown (R.I.) Sch. System 1969; Sr. Psychiat. Social Worker, Newport Co. Mental Health Clinic 1969–72; Sch. Soc. Worker (Mich.) 1972–73; Staff Social Worker, Child Evaluation and Treatment Ctr., Barnert Hosp. (N.J.) 1973–74; Sr. Social Worker, Community Ctr. for Mental Health (N.J.) 1974–75; Unit Supvr., Catholic Children's Aid Soc. of Metro. Toronto 1975–76; Mem., Nat. Assn. of Social Workers; Acad. Cert. Social Workers; Ont. Coll. Cert. Social Workers; Home: 129 All Saint Cres., Oakville, Ont. L6J 5Y6; Office: 235 Lakeshore Rd. E., Oakville, Ont. L6J 5C1.

**BROWN, Patrick John,** M.A.; foreign correspondent; b. Birmingham, UK 22 June 1947; s. Harry and Iris Mary (Patten) B.; e. King Edwards Sch. Birmingham; Downing Coll. Cambridge B.A. 1969, M.A. 1971; m. Nguyen Thi Oanh 1974; two d. Jesse Tri Minh, Dominque Tri Chau; London Correspondent, CBC Radio News 1980–..; Fisheries Offr. Sierra Leone 1965–66; Systems Analyst, London 1969–70; Freelance writer Montréal 1971–74; Ed. Radio Can. Internat. 1974–76; Reporter CBC Montréal 1976–80; co-author 'Winners Losers' 1976; Clubs: C & S; Prince of Wales; Office: c/o CBC National Radio News, Rm. 3A137, Box 500, Stn A, Toronto, Ont. M5W 1E6.

**BROWN, Peter Maclachlan;** investment executive; b. Vancouver, B.C. 15 Dec. 1941; s. Ralph B.; e. Shawinigan Lake Private Sch.; St. George's Private Sch.; Univ. of B.C.; m. Joanne; children: Jamie, Jason; CHAIRMAN & C.E.O., CANACCORD CAPITAL CORPORATION 1968– ; Past Vice-Chrmn. of Bd. (and Chrmn. Fin. Ctte.) Expo '86; Past Chrmn. Univ. of B.C.; Past Chrmn.: B.C. Place Corp.; B.C. Development Corp.; Past Dir.: Breakwater Resources Ltd.; Corona Corp.; Prime Capital; Internat. Cable Casting; Past Trustee, Vancouver Art Gallery; Trustee and Gov., St. George's Private Sch.; Past Gov., Atlantic Inst. for Internat. Affairs; Past Chrmn., Vancouver Stock Exchange; Mem. National Exec. Ctte., Investment Dealers' Assn. of Can.; Past Chrmn., Audit Ctte., Univ. of B.C.; Past Dir., Asamerica Inc.; recipient Businessman of the Year Award, Chamber of Commerce 1981; mem. Young Pres.'s Orgn.; Chief Extve. Organization; Clubs: Vancouver Lawn & Tennis; Faculty (Univ. of B.C.); Club: Shaughnessy Golf & County; Home: 4833 Belmont Ave., Vancouver, B.C. V6T 1A9; Office: Box 10337, Pacific Centre, 700 W. Georgia St., Vancouver, B.C. V7Y 1H2.

**BROWN, R. Don;** tobacco industry executive; b. Winnipeg, Man. 9 June 1940; e. Bedford Rd. Collegiate; Candn. Services College Royal Roads; Univ. of Manitoba; m. Deanna; two daughters; CHAIRMAN, PRES. & CHIEF EXTVE. OFFR., IMPERIAL TOBACCO LTD. 1993– ; joined present firm as Sales Rep. 1963; Regional Sales Mgr. B.C. 1981; Nat. Sales Dir. 1984; Vice-Pres. Marketing 1985; Pres. & Chief Op. Offr. 1991; Bd. of Dir., IMASCO 1993; Office: 3810 Saint Antoine St., Montreal, Qué. H4C 1B5.

**BROWN, R. James,** B.Comm., C.A.; financial executive; e. Univ. of Calgary B.Comm. 1973, C.A. 1976; MANAGER, EXPLORATION FINANCE & ADMINISTRATION, WASCANA ENERGY INC. 1993– ; Vice-Pres., Finance & Admin., Thomson-Jensen Energy 1984–87; Treas., Saskatchewan Oil & Gas Corp. 1987–92; Vice-Pres. Finance, Wes Cana Energy Marketing Inc. 1992–93; Mem., Financial Executives Institute; Office: 2600, 205 – 5th Ave. S.W., Calgary, Alta. T2P 2V7.

**BROWN, Richard George Bolney,** M.A., D.Phil.; research ornithologist; b. Wolverhampton, U.K. 15 Sept. 1935; s. George Bolney and Nora (Taylor) B.; e. Downside Sch. 1949–53; New Coll., Oxford 1953–57; Oxford Univ. B.A. (Hons.) 1957, D.Phil. 1962; RSCH. SCIENTIST, CANDN. WILDLIFE SERVICE 1967– ; Post-doct. rsch., Dept. of Zool., Oxford 1962–65; Rsch. Assoc., Dept. of Psych., Dalhousie Univ. 1965–67; Mem. Ed. Bd., 'Canadian Journal of Zoology' 1985–91; Elective Mem., Am. Ornithol. Union 1978; Candn. Sportsmen's Shows/Outdoor Writers of Canada Outdoor Writing Award (Books) 1983); Candn. Sci. Writers' Assn. Sci. Journalism Award 1984; Mem., Brit. & Am. Ornithol. Unions; author: 'Voyage of the Iceberg' 1983, 'Revised Atlas of Eastern Canadian Seabirds' 1986; co-author: 'Atlas of Eastern Canadian Seabirds' 1975; editor/transl.: Finn Salomonsen's 'Fuglene på Grønland' ('The Seabirds of Greenland'); recreations: books, wine, birdwatching, oceanographic cruises; Home: 45 Vimy Ave., Halifax, N.S. B3M 4C5; Office: CWS, Bedford Inst. of Oceanography, P.O. Box 1006, Dartmouth, N.S. B2Y 4A2.

**BROWN, Robert C.,** M.Sc., Ph.D.; educator; b. John Day, Ore. 21 Feb. 1938; s. Arthur Robert and Gladys (Ellen) B.; e. Ore. State Univ. B.Sc. 1960, M.Sc. 1962 (Resources Mang.); Mich. State Univ. Ph.D. 1967 (Geog.); m. Sylvia J. Currie; children: Robert C. Jr., William Douglas, Rebecca Lynn; DEAN OF ARTS, SIMON FRASER UNIV. 1978– , Assoc. Prof. of Geog. 1971– ; served with U.S. Army Arty. 1962–65, rank Capt.; Asst. Prof. Okla. State Univ. 1965–67; Asst. Prof. present Univ. 1967, Dean of Interdisciplinary Studies 1972–77; mem. Candn. Assn. Geogs.; Candn. Regional Science Assn.; Am. Assn. Geogs.; W. Regional Science Assn.; recreations: golf, skiing, fishing; Club: Pitt Meadows Golf; Home: 19519 115 A. Ave., Pittmeadows, B.C. V3Y 1R5; Office: Dean of Arts, Simon Fraser Univ., Burnaby, B.C. V5A 1S6.

**BROWN, Robert Craig,** M.A., Ph.D., F.R.S.C.; educator; b. Rochester, N.Y. 14 Oct. 1935; s. Ralph Nelson Jennings and Marion F. (Black) B.; e. Livonia (N.Y.) Central Sch. 1953; Univ. of Rochester B.A. 1957; Univ. of Toronto M.A. 1958. Ph.D. 1962; m. Gail d. John Detgen, Haworth, N.J. 21 May 1960; children: Bradley Bower, Brenda Berkeley, Brian Blair; PROF. OF HISTORY, UNIV. OF TORONTO since 1970; Asst. Prof. of Hist. Univ. of Calgary 1961–64; present Univ. 1964, Assoc. Prof. 1966, Dir. of Grad. Studies 1972–73, Assoc. Chrmn. Dept. Hist. 1974–77; Assoc. Dean, Sch. of Grad. Studies 1981–85, Acting Dean 1985, Vice Dean, Fac. of Arts and Science 1987–92; Chrmn. Dept. History 1992– ; Pres., Academy II, Royal Soc. of Can. 1991– ; (Vice Pres. 1988–91); Sr. Fellow, Massey Coll. 1987– ; rec'd various Can. Council Fellowships; Izaak Walton Killam Sr. Research Scholarship; S.S.H.R.C. leave grant; author 'Canada's National Policy 1883–1900' 1964; 'Robert Laird Borden: A Biography' Vol. 1 1975, Vol. 2 1980; co-author 'Canada Views the United States' 1966; 'Confederation to 1949' 1966; 'The Canadians 1867–1967' 1967; 'Canada 1896–1921' 1974; 'Twentieth Century Canada' 1983; 'Nation: Canada Since Confederation' 1990; ed. 'The Illustrated History of Canada' 1987; 'Histoire Générale du Canada' 1988; author various articles, essays and reviews; mem. Candn. Hist Assn. (Council 1964–67, 1978–82, Vice-Pres. 1978–79, Pres. 1979–80); Am. Hist. Assn.; Research Counc. 1982–85, Candn. Inst. for Advanced Research; United Church; Home: 175 Glenview Ave., Toronto, Ont. M4R 1R4.

**BROWN, Robert Douglas,** B.Com., M.A., F.C.A.; b. Stratford, Ont. 3 Aug. 1934; s. late Ernest William and Mary Ellen (Keil) B.; e. Pub. and Secondary Schs., Stratford, Ottawa and Toronto, Ont.; Parkdale Coll. Inst., Toronto 1952; Univ. Coll., Univ. of Toronto, B.Com. 1956; Univ. of Chicago, Div. of Social Sciences, M.A. (Econ.) 1957; C.A.(Gold Medal, Ont. Inst. and Silver Medal Award, Candn. Inst. Chart. Accts.) 1960; m. Wendy Frances, d. late Frank Day, 23 Dec. 1961; children: Michelle Mary Lorraine, Robert Carleton; CHAIRMAN & SENIOR PARTNER, PRICE WATERHOUSE 1990– ; admitted to Partnership 1966, Sr. Tax Partner 1968–85, Vice Chrmn. 1985–90, mem. Policy Bd. 1976– ; Extve. Partner – Tax, Price Waterhouse International 1974–79; Gov., Candn. Tax Found. 1985– , Vice Chrmn. 1989–91 and Chrmn. 1991–92; Chrmn., Toronto French Sch. 1980–82, Dir. 1974– ; Mem., Adv. Ctte., Sch. of Bus. Admin., Univ. of Western Ont.; Mem., Ont. Bus. Adv. Counc. 1990– ; Mem., Bus. Counc. on Nat. Issues 1990– ; former tax advisor; Lectr., then Asst. Prof. (part-time) Dept. of Pol. Economy, Univ. of Toronto 1962–72; Special Lect., Advanced Tax, Osgoode Hall Law Sch. 1972–77; served as tax consultant to various govts.; Inst. Chart. Accts. Ont.; Candn. Inst. Chart. Accts. (Chrmn. Tax Course Study Group 1973–75; Chrmn. Taxation Comte. 1971–73); Candn. Br., Internat. Fiscal Assn.; (Candn. Speaker at World Congresses 1971 and 1982); Mem., Adv. Comm. to Min. of Finance 1987; Chrmn. Task Force on Resources of Canada West Found., 1975–77; Mem., Comte. on Inflation and the Taxation of Personal Investment Income (Lortie Commission), 1982; Mem., Energy Options Task Force, Fed. Dept. of Energy, Mines and Resources 1987–88; author numerous articles on taxation and other subjects in leading newspapers, mags. and professional journals; speaker at prof. and indust. conferences; recreations: swimming, reading; Clubs: National; Granite; Cambridge; Home: 164 St. Leonard's Ave., Toronto, Ont. M4N 1K7; Office: P.O. Box 190, 1 First Canadian Place, Toronto. Ont. M5X 1H7.

**BROWN, Robert E.;** financial services executive; b. London, Ont. 5 May 1939; s. Robert M. and May (Crane) B.; e. high sch. grad.; Univ. of West. Ont., Mgmt. Training Course 1973; Queen's Univ., Extve. Devel. 1983; m. Faith d. Arthur and Olive Lehman 30 Apr. 1960; children: Mark, Trish, Andrew, Joanne; PRES., IMPERIAL LIFE ASSURANCE CO. 1991– ; Vice Chrmn., Pres. & C.E.O., Laurentian Financial Services Inc. and Chrmn., Pres. & C.E.O., Laurentian Funds Mgmt. Inc. 1988– ; Dir. of Group Ins., London Life Ins. Co. 1959–84; Vice Pres., Group Mktg., Imperial Life Assur. Co. of Can. 1984–86; Pres. & C.E.O., Eaton Trust Co. 1986–87; Pres. & C.E.O., Eaton Funds Mgmt. Ltd. 1986–88; Pres. & C.O.O., Eaton Life Assur. Co. 1986–87; Pres. & C.E.O., Laurentian Financial Services Inc. 1986–88; Vice Pres., Mktg., The Laurentian Group Corp. 1986–88; Extve. Vice Pres., Financial Services 1988–91; Dir., Laurentian Funds Mgmt. Inc.; Laurentian Fin. Serv. Inc.; The Laurentian/Imperial Co.; Laurentian Asia Ltd.; Laurentian Technology Inc.; Clubs: London Hunt & Country; Home: 73 Widdicombe Hill Blvd., PH6, Etobicoke, Ont. M9R 4B3; Office: 310 Front St. W., 2nd Flr., Toronto, Ont. M5V 3B8.

**BROWN, Robert Leigh,** F.C.I.A., F.S.A., A.C.A.S.; professor; consulting actuary; b. Lindsay, Ont. 25 Feb. 1949; s. LeRoy George and Aili T. (Forbom) B.; e. Univ. of Waterloo, B.Math. (Hons.) 1971; m. Andrea I. d. Alton and Judith Langille 20 May 1972; children: James R., Allison J.; ASSOC. PROF., UNIV. OF WATERLOO 1971– ; F.S.A. 1976; F.C.I.A. 1977; A.C.A.S.1980; tenured 1984; Pres., Candn. Inst. of Actuaries 1990–91; Counc., City of Waterloo 1988–94; author: 'Economic Security in an Aging Population' 1991; 'Introduction of the Mathematics of Demography' 1991, 2nd ed. 1993; 'Introduction to Ratemaking and Loss Reserving for Property Casualty Insurance' 1993; co-author: 'Mathematics of Finance' 1979, 1984, 1988, 1993 4th ed.; 'Contemporary Mathematics of Finance' 1984; recreation: running (2:30 marathon); Home: 189 Castlegate Cres., Waterloo, Ont. N2L 5V1; Office: Dept. of Statistics & Actuarial Sci., Univ. of Waterloo, Waterloo, Ont. N2L 3G1.

**BROWN, Ronald C.,** Q.C., B.A.; barrister and solicitor; b. Sarnia, Ont. 12 June 1929; s. Jacob Laverne and Hilda (Spittlehouse) B.; e. Public Schs.,Stratford, Windsor and Hamilton, Ont., High Sch., Hamilton, Ont.; McMaster Univ., B.A. 1952; Osgoode Hall Law Sch.; m. Mary, d. Charles W. Bowyer, 28 Aug. 1954; children: Christine, Robert, Ian; PARTNER, BLAKE CASSELS & GRAYDON; Dir., The National Life Assurance Co. of Can.; Fuji Bank Canada; read law with present firm; called to Bar of Ont. 1956; mem. Candn. Bar Assn.; Un. Church; recreation: golf; Clubs: Donalda; National; Home: 62 Airdrie Rd., Leaside, Ont. M4G 1M2; Office: Box 25, Commerce Court W., Toronto, Ont. M5L 1A9.

**BROWN, Ronald Franklyn,** M.A.; freelance writer, photographer; town planner; b. Kingston, Ont. 28 Apl. 1945; s. Arnold Robert Henry and Ethel Millicent (Millard) B.; e. Univ. of Toronto B.A. 1966; Univ. of Waterloo M.A. 1968; m. Bebe d. Mohamed K. Baksh 13 Oct. 1973; children: Jeri Aliya, Ria Nadira; Special Planning Adv. to Govts. of Trinidad/Tobago and Guyana 1969–71; Urban Designer Guyana's Interior Land Resettlement Scheme; Regional Planner Rural S. Ont. 1971–74; Recreational Planner Rideau Trent Severn Waterway 1975–80; Revitalization Specialist remote communities N. Ont.; Adv. to Govts. Can. and Ont. on Can.'s Historic Railway Stns.; lectr., writer and photographer ghost towns, ry. stns., backroad exploring and hist. landscapes; author and photog. 'Ghost Towns of Ontario' 2 vols. 1979, 1982 and 'Field Guide' 1990; 'Saving Rural Ontario' 1981; 'Back Roads of Ontario' 1984; 'Ghost Towns of Canada' 1987; '50 Unusual Things To See In Ontario' 1989; 'The Train Doesn't Stop Here Anymore' 1991; frequent contbr. to Candn. geog. and heritage mags.; mem. Metro Central YMCA; Candn. Book & Periodical Devel. Council (Dir. 1988– ;); Candn. Inst. Planners; Writers Union Can.; recreation: wilderness camping & canoeing; Home: 40 Marilyn Cres. Toronto, Ont. M4B 3C6.

**BROWN, Rosemary,** M.L.A., B.A., M.S.W.; b. Jamaica, B.W.I. 17 June 1930; d. Ralph and Enid (James) Wedderburn; e. Wolmer's Sch. for Girls, Jamaica; Mcgill Univ., B.A. 1955; Univ. of B.C., M.S.W. 1964; St. Vincent Univ., Halifax, D.H.L. 1981; m. William T., s. William B., 12 Aug. 1955; children: Cleta Denise, William Garrison, Jonathan Llewelyn; Founding mem.-trainer, Volunteers for Vancouver Crises Intervention and Suicide Prevention Centre; Social Worker, Children's Aid Soc. of B.C.; Montreal Children's Hosp.; Vancouver Neurol. Soc.; Counsellor, Simon Fraser Univ. since 1969; Ombudswoman, Status of Women Council B.C. 1970–72; el. to B.C. Leg. 1972 (becoming 1st ever Black woman to hold elected office in any Candn. Parlt.); re-el. 1975, 1979, 1983; Adv. Council, Sch. of Social Work, Univ. of B.C. 1974; U.N. Human

Rights Fellowship 1973; Black Award, Nat. Black Coalition of Can. 1974; mem. Status of Women Council of B.C.; Council of Continuing Educ., Univ. of B.C.; N.D.P.; recreations: reading, weaving; Clubs: University Women's; National Black Coalition of Canada; Office: c/o Random House, 33 Yonge St., Suite 210, Toronto, Ont. M5E 1G4.

**BROWN, Ruth Louise,** B.A., M.S.W.; social worker; b. Sunkist, Sask. 23 Sept. 1922; d. Earl and Isabel (Fowler) Johnston; e. Univ. of Toronto B.A. (Hons.) 1945, M.S.W. 1947; Univ. of Stockholm, Dipl. 1980; m. Kenneth Charles s. George and Vera B. 1948; children: David, Deborah, Christopher, Andrew; PRESIDENT, NATIONAL COUNCIL OF WOMEN OF CANADA 1992– ; Supervisor, Children's Aid Soc. of Ottawa-Carleton 1968–70, 1982–87; Co-ord. of Volunteers 1974–76, 1980–82; Pres., Council of Women of Ottawa & Area 1987–90; Nat. Convener, Child & Family, Nat. Council of Women of Canada 1990–92; Vice-Pres. 1991–92; accompanied husband on five fgn. service postings: Havana Cuba 1951–54, 1970–73, Berne Switz. 1957–60, Washington 1963–67, Stockholm Sweden 1976–80; Pres., Fgn. Serv. Community Assn. 1980–82; Mem., Candn. Assn. of Social Workers; Ont. Assn. of Profl. Social Workers; Un. Ch. of Can.; recreations: skiing, canoeing, bridge; Home: 285 Mariposa Ave., Ottawa, Ont. K1M 0T4; Office: 270 MacLaren St., Ottawa, Ont. K2P 0M3.

**BROWN, Shirley Ann,** B.I.D., M.A., Ph.D.; university professor of art history; b. Halifax, N.S. 24 Aug. 1943; s. Herman W. and Margaret M. (Bonn) B.; e. Univ. of Manitoba B.I.D. 1965; Ohio State Univ. M.A. 1967; Cornell Univ. Ph.D. 1977; m. Michael W. Herren 13 April 1975; children: Sarah, Michael; ASSOCIATE PROF. OF ART HISTORY, ATKINSON COLLEGE, YORK UNIV. 1981– ; Asst. Prof., Univ. of Miami 1967–72; Visiting Lectr., Florida Atlantic Univ. 1972, '73; Asst. Prof. of Art History, York Univ. 1975–81; Dir. of Graduate Art History 1982–86, 1992– ; Founder-Dir., Registry of Stained Glass Windows in Canada 1986– ; Mem., Universities' Art Assn. of Canada; Architectural Conservancy of Ont.; author: 'The Bayeux Tapestry: History & Bibliography' 1988 and 8 journal articles; Office: 4700 Keele St., North York, Ont. M3J 1P3.

**BROWN, Stephanie Arehart,** B.F.A., M.A.; antique jewelry dealer, animal protection volunteer; b. Mansfield, Ohio 10 Jan. 1945; d. Derl Leiter and Alethea Barnett (Hostetler) Arehart; e. Ohio Univ. B.F.A. 1967, M.A. 1969; m. Kenneth R. s. Winifred and James B. 20 June 1970; children: Lia Michelle, Melanie Nicole; OWNER, STEPHANIE BROWN JEWELRY; Pres., Candn. Fed. of Humane Societies 1989–92; Vice-Pres. 1978–89; Chair, Sealing Ctte. 1980–91; Experimental Animals Ctte. 1983–93; Co-chair, Marine Mammals Ctte. 1992–93; Pres., Toronto Humane Soc. 1974–78; Mem., Dept. of Fisheries & Oceans' Adv. Team on Harbour Porpoise Halifax 1991–93; Councillor, Candn. Council on Animal Care Ottawa 1982–93; Secy.-Treasr. 1993; Mem., Bd. of Dir., The Joseph F. Morgan Rsch. Found. 1990–93; Chair, Adv. Bd., Univ. of Guelph, Ctr. for the Study of Animal Welfare 1992–93; Animal Care Ctte., Hosp. for Sick Children 1982–85; Toronto Western Hosp. 1985–88; The Working Group on Animals Med. Rsch. Council of Canada 1985–89; organized & chaired, Symposia on the seal hunt 1982, reducing animals used in toxicity testing 1987, whales in captivity 1990; Co-Founder, Candn. Coalition for the Protection of Whales 1990; Editor: 'Caring for Animals' newsletter 1984–93, 'Whale Kind' newsletter 1992–93; author, various documents & articles 1984–93; awarded Commemorative Medal for 125th Anniversary of Candn. Confederation 1993; recreations: cycling, gardening; Address: 117 Cottingham St., Toronto, Ont. M4V 1B9.

**BROWN, Thomas Campion,** M.D., F.C.A.P., F.R.C.P.C.; retired physician; b. Winnipeg, Man. 27 March 1920; s. Frank Herbert, C.B.E. and Elizabeth (McIlroy) B.; e. Univ. of Toronto Schs.; Univ. of Toronto, M.D. 1943; m. Joye Louise, d. Vorwerk Ernst, Waterloo, Ont., 23 Aug. 1943; children: Sheila Joye (Mrs. R. K. Munro), Lynda C. E. (Mrs. M. Tanaka), Thomas C.; PATHOLOGIST (HONORARY), PRINCESS MARGARET HOSP.; PROFESSOR EMERITUS, DEPT. OF PATHOLOGY, FACULTY OF MEDICINE UNIV. OF TORONTO; served with R.C.A.M.C. during 2nd World War, rank Maj.; recipient Candn. Centennial Medal 1967; Queen's Silver Jubilee Medal 1977; mem., Acad. of Med., Toronto (Past Pres.); Ont. Med. Assn.; Candn. Med. Assn.; Ont. Assn. Pathols.; Candn. Assn Pathols.; Medico-Legal Soc. Toronto; Am. Soc. Clin. Pathols.; Coll. Am. Pathols.; Internat. Acad. Pathol.; Nu Sigma Nu; Presbyterian; Clubs: York Downs Golf & Country; University; Aesculapian; Home: 38 Glengrove Ave. W., Toronto, Ont. M4R 1N6.

**BROWN, Wallace,** M.A., Ph.D., F.R.Hist.Soc.; university professor/writer/broadcaster; b. Edmonton, Alta. 20 Nov. 1933; s. Alexander Binnie and Mary MacFarlane (Wallace) Brown; e. Heath Grammar Sch., 1949–52; Oxford Univ., B.A., M.A. 1957; Univ. of Calif., Berkeley, Ph.D. 1964; m. Paula L. d. Paul and Phyllis Bollinger 28 Apr. 1971; children: Catherine, Alexander, Paul, Emily; PROF., DEPT. OF HIST., UNIV. OF NEW BRUNSWICK 1967– ; Sergeant, R.A.E.C., Brit. Army 1952–54; Tutor, Univ. Tutorial Coll., London 1957–58; Asst. Prof., Univ. of Alta. 1963–64; Brown Univ. 1964–67; elected fellow, Royal Hist. Soc. 1986; Hon. Vice-Pres., The United Empire Loyalists Assn. of Can.; Mem., Ed. Bd., 'Anglican and Episcopal History'; Pres., Fredericton Soc. of St. Andrew 1977–79; author: 'The King's Friends' 1961, 'The Good Americans' 1969; co-author: 'Victorious in Defeat' 1984; editor: 'The American Revolution in Context' 1984, 'The Nova Scotia Records of the U.S.P.G.' 1985; recreations: scotch whisky, cooking; club: The Second of January; Home: 278 Northumberland St., Fredericton, N.B. E3B 3J7; Office: Fredericton, N.B. E3B 5A3.

**BROWN, William Thomas,** M.B.E., E.D., M.A.; retired investment dealer; b. Vancouver, B.C. 10 May 1912; s. Albert Malcolm and Edith Elizabeth (Wootton) B.; e. Univ. of Brit. Columbia B.A. 1932; Oxford Univ., B.A. 1934, M.A. 1937; m. late Daphne Georgina, d. Philip H. Jackson, Fordingbridge, Hants., Eng., 29 Dec. 1937; children: Michael Jack, Peter Thomas, Jane Daphne (Mrs. Gordon S. Ball); HON. CHAIRMAN, ODLUM BROWN LTD.; Hon. Dir., Vancouver Foundation; Hon. Dir. Nature Trust of B.C.; Dir., Chris Spencer Foundation; former Dir.: B.C. Telephone Co.; Bank of British Columbia; Fidelity Life Assurance Co.; Wardair International Ltd.; Century Insurance Co.; Chairman, Public Library Bd., City of Vancouver (1960–61); Pres. Men's Candn. Club of Vancouver, 1950–51; Greater Vancouver Dist. Boys Scouts Assn. (1952); Pres. (1966–67) Investment Dealers Assn. of Can.; apptd. a mem., Royal Comm. on Banking & Finance (Fed.) Oct. 1961; with Odlum Brown Co. 1935–39; served in 2nd World War; with Irish Fusiliers (Vancouver Regt.) 1939–44; Staff Hdqrs., Candn. Army and then Essex Scottish Regt.; wounded in Normandy, Aug. 1944 awarded M.B.E.; retired from Army with rank of Lieut.-Col.; Psi Upsilon; P. Conservative; Anglican; Club: Vancouver; Home: 311 Shaughnessy Pl., 4900 Cartier St., Vancouver, B.C. V6M 4H2.

**BROWNE, Dennis Brian,** B.Com., LL.B.; diplomat; b. Winnipeg, Man. 27 May 1940; s. Samuel and Kathlyn Mary (Holland) B.; e. Lester Pearson High Sch. New Westminster, B.C.; Univ. of B.C., B.Com. 1964, LL.B. 1965; m. Normanna d. Norman and Christina MacRitchie 1963; children: Christina, Jennifer; DIRECTOR GENERAL, TRADE COMPETITIVENESS BUREAU, DEPT. OF EXTERNAL AFFAIRS, CAN. 1991– ; joined Trade Comnr. Service 1965, Comm. Sec. Oslo 1966, London 1969, Canberra 1971, Comm. Counsellor Moscow 1974; Chief Commodity Arrangements Div. Dept. Ind., Trade & Comm. Ottawa 1976, Comm. Counsellor Washington 1979; Dir. Commodities, Resources & Agric. Trade Policy, Dept. of External Affairs Ottawa 1981, Dir. Gen. Agric. Fish & Food Products Bureau Ottawa 1983; Chrmn. OECD High Level Group on Commodities 1981–82, Jt. Working Party on Agric. & Trade 1983–87; Candn. Ambassador to Sweden 1988–91; Address: 125 Sussex Dr., Ottawa, Ont. K1A 0G2.

**BROWNE, Hon. Edward Rowan (Ted),** H.B.A., LL.B.; judge; b. London, Ont. 19 May 1933; s. Thomas Alexander and Norma Charlotte (Summers) B.; e. Univ. of W. Ont. H.B.A. 1958; Osgoode Hall Law Sch. LL.B. 1961 (Admiralty Law Prize 1961); m. S. Gail d. Douglas S. and Sheila Forster 25 June 1960; three d. Laura Gail, Sarah Evelyn, Martha Louise; JUDGE, ONT. COURT OF JUSTICE GEN. DIV. 1990– ; law practice Purcell, Downey, Deane & Browne; Giffen & Pensa 1963–66; sole practioner 1966–67; Partner, Browne, Burgard, Robinson, Venutti 1967–82; part-time Asst. Crown Atty. 1966–82; Instr. in Estate Planning Bar Admission Course London, Ont. 1974; Master, Supreme Court of Ont. at London and Dep. Registrar in Bankruptcy 1982; cr. Q.C. 1974; Chrmn. Un. Way Greater London 1983–85, Dir. 1974–86; Regional Vice Pres. Un. Ways of Ont. 1984–85; Dir. Un. Way Can. 1986–89; Solr. War Meml. Childrens Hosp. to 1982; Council mem. Twp. of London 1980–82; P. Cons. Cand. for London N. g.e. 1981; Dir. W. Ont. Conserv. of Music 1987– ; Chrmn. Bd. Stewards Metrop. Un. Ch. 1988–90; recreation: sailing; Home: 30 Northcrest Dr., RR2, London, Ont. N5X 3V8; Office: Court House, 80 Dundas St. E., P.O. Box 5600, London, Ont. N6A 2P3.

**BROWNE, Robert Geoffrey,** B.A.; investment banking executive; b. Toronto, Ont. 21 July 1953; s. Robert Abraham and Kathleen Emma (Nettlefield) B.; e. Ridley Coll.; Univ. of W. Ont. B.A. (Econ) 1976; m. Nancy d. Barry and Janet Humphreys 28 Sept. 1979; children: Robert Edward, Lauren Kathleen; MNG. DIR., CIBC WOOD GUNDY CAPITAL 1989– ; Assoc. Dir., CIBC Ltd. (U.K.) 1979–80; Asst. Gen. Mgr., Treasury, Canadian Imperial Bank of Commerce Head Office 1980–83; Vice-Pres. Merchant Banking, Toronto 1983–86; Sr. Vice-Pres., Investment Bank 1986–88; Dir., Wood Gundy Inc. 1988– ; CIBC Wood Gundy Capital Corp.; CIBC Wood Gundy Ventures Inc.; Dir., PSP Acquisition Inc.; Altamira Capital Corp.; Pelmorex Broadcasting Inc.; Profl. Sports Pubns. Inc.; 890269 Ontario Inc.; St. Clair Group Investments Inc.; Candn. Mezzanine Fund; Miralta Capital Corp.; recreations: golf, tennis, skiing, squash; clubs: Toronto Golf, Badminton & Racquet, Muskoka Lakes Golf & Country, Toronto Club, Holimont Ski; Home: 294 Dawlish Ave., Toronto, Ont. M4N 1J5; Office: P.O. Box 500, B.C.E. Pl., Toronto, Ont. M5J 2S8.

**BROWNE, Stephen Bruce,** B.A., M.A.; investment executive; b. London, Ont. 4 May 1949; s. James David and Edith Mary (Phillips) B.; e. Univ. of West. Ont., B.A. (Hons.) 1971; Carleton Univ., M.A. 1976; m. Leslie d. John and Grace Farrell 9 Oct. 1971; children: James, Sarah; PRESIDENT AND C.E.O., MUTUAL ASSET MANAGEMENT LTD. 1993– ; Economist, Dept. of Finan., Govt. of Can. 1971–76; Chief, Short-Term Econ. Forecasting 1977–78; Sr. Econ., Monetary & Finan. Analysis, Bank of Montreal 1979–80; Sec., Funds Mngt. Ctte. 1980–81; Chief Econ., Sun Life Assur. Co. of Can. 1981–84; Vice-Pres., Investments 1984–89; C.E.O. and Dir., Canadian Enterprise Development Corp. Ltd. 1987–89; Sr. Vice-Pres. & Chief Investment Offr., Bank of Montreal Investment Mngt. Ltd. 1989–92; recreations: motorcycle sport/touring; club: Cambridge; Home: 3383 Sawmill Valley Dr., Mississauga, Ont. L5L 2Z8; Office: 227 King St. S., Waterloo, Ont. N2J 4C5.

**BROWNLEE, Kenneth Wayne,** B.Com., F.C.A.; public accountant; b. Pembroke, Ont. 22 Oct. 1944; s. Ken and Doris (Hunt) B.; e. pub. and high schs. Ottawa 1962; Carleton Univ. B.Com. 1965; C.A. 1968; m. Ruth Elaine Helson May 1966; children: Christine Ruth, Laura Ann, Kimberley Lynn; VICE CHRMN. HUMAN RESOURCES PEAT MARWICK THORNE 1989– ; articled with Peat Marwick Mitchell & Co. Ottawa 1965–68, Mgr. 1970, Sr. Mgr. Nat. Office Toronto 1972–74, Partner Ottawa 1974–82, Mng. Partner London 1982–89; recreations: golf, tennis, boating; Clubs: London; London Hunt & Country; Home: 63 Wimbledon Court, London, Ont. N6C 5C9 and 2612, 33 Harbour Sq., Toronto, Ont. M5J 2G2; Office: 5400, 40 King St. W., Toronto, Ont. M5H 3Y2.

**BROWNRIDGE, Hon. Russell Lawrence;** judge; b. Saskatoon, Sask. 23 Nov. 1914; s. Alvin Arthur and Ethel Anna (Bates) B.; e. Univ. of Sask. (Arts 1937); Law, 1939; m. Mary Esther, d. Robert Roycroft, 4 July 1942; two s. Robert Alvin, James Russell; JUSTICE, COURT OF APPEAL, SASK., Oct. 1961, retired 1988; read law with J.G. Diefenbaker, Q.C.; called to the Bar of Sask. 1940; cr. Q.C. 1951; entered the firm of Ross, Gilmour & Brownridge, 1941 and successor firm Gilmour & Brownridge, 1943–47 practising alone 1947–58 when organ. firm of Brownridge & Schollie (1958–59); Justice, Court of Queen's Bench, Sask., 1959–61; served for five years as Alderman, City of Moose Jaw; Past Pres. of Canadian Club, Family Services Assn.; Past Lt.-Gov., Kiwanis Club and many other civic organs.; National Pres., Candn. Red Cross Soc.; Chrmn. Regina Chapter, Candn. Council of Christians & Jews; mem. Bd. of Govs., Regina Orchestral Soc.; Chrmn., Sask. Electoral Boundaries Comn.; mem., Candn. Bar Assn.; Elder St. Andrew's United Church; Moose Jaw & Lakeview United Church, Regina; Freemason; recreations: golf, swimming, curling; Home: 90 Academy Park Rd., Regina, Sask. S4S 4T7.

**BRUCE, Erika v.C.;** senior government executive; b. Vienna, Austria 16 Mar. 1937; d. Ernst and Margarethe (v. Zinner) Goetz; e. Vienna, Austria; Vienna Sch. of Econ. & Bus. Adm. Dip. 1958, Doctorate in Pol. Econ. & Bus. Adm. 1960; Sorbonne; Waterloo Lutheran Univ. M.A. (Archaeol.) 1972; m. Geoffrey F. Bruce 19 Sept. 1972; DIR. OF INFORMATION AND PRESS, NORTH ATLANTIC TREATY ORGN. (NATO), Brussels; held various positions S.A. des Automobiles Peugeot Madrid and Paris 1959–61; Ed. Paul Zsolnay/Heinemann Publishers Vienna 1962–66; Corr. for Cultural Affairs, Munich 1966–67; Exec. Offr. Humanities & Social Sci's Div. Can. Council 1968–72, Ottawa Dir. Killam Prog. 1972–73; Prog. Dir. The Tinker Found., Inc. 1974–78, New York; Coordinator of Official Langs., The Senate of Can. 1982–83, Ctte. Offr. 1983–84; Dir. Gen. Prog. Br., Social Sciences & Humanities Rsch. Council 1984–87; archaeol. rsch. activities incl. Israel and Turkey 1971–76; author various articles; transl. novels, essays & tech. documentation 1963–68; mem. Inst. Gen. Mgmt.; Planning Forum Ottawa (Internat. Soc. Planning & Strategic Mgmt.); Centre for European Policy Studies, Brussels; Château Ste. Anne; recreation: reading; Home: 19 Ave. Jeanne, 1050 Brussels, Belgium; Office: NATO, Brussels, Belgium.

**BRUCE, Geoffrey F.,** M.A.; retired diplomat; b. Kingston, Ont. 30 June 1925; s. Dr. Everend Lester and Mary B.; e. Queen's Univ. B.A. 1947, grad. work 1948 Columbia Univ., M.A. 1952; New Sch. for Social Research 1948–49; Nat. Defence Coll. 1970–71; m. Dr. Erika von Conta, 19 Sept. 1972; children: David, Ian, Karen; Ambassador of Canada to Portugal 1987–90; Candn. Embassy Tel Aviv 1955–57; Candn. High Comn. Colombo, Sri Lanka 1960–63; Candn. Embassy Vienna, Austria and Candn. Mission to Internat. Atomic Energy. Agency, Vienna, 1963–67; Dir., Science and Environmental Relations, Dept. External Affairs, Ottawa 1971–73; Min. and Depy. Perm. Rep to United Nations, and Candn. Rep. to Econ. and Social Council UN, New York 1973–77; Adjunct Prof. Pol. Sci., Winthrop College, Rock Hill, South Carolina 1976–1978; Fellow, Harvard Univ. Center for Intern. Affairs 1977–78; Chrmn. U.N. Commission on Transnational Corporations 1978; High Commr. for Can. to Kenya and concurrently to Uganda 1978–1982; Permanent Rep. of Canada to U.N. Environment Program and to U.N. Commission for Human Settlements 1978–82; Vice-Pres., Policy, Candn. Internat. Development Agency 1982–84; Vice Pres., Business Cooperation Br., CIDA 1984–87; Commnd. 2nd Lt. Candn. Army Reserve; mem. Prof. Assn. Foreign Service Offrs.; recreations: theatre, music, visual arts, travel, swimming, tennis; Home: Ave. Jeanne 19, Brussels 1050 Belgium.

**BRUCE, George Stewart Wallace;** consulting geologist; b. Anstruther, Scotland 7 May 1925; s. Lawrence and Georgina (Stewart) B.; e. Univ. Toronto, B.A.Sc. 1947; M.A.Sc. 1953; m. Madge Helen, d. Bruce and Malvina MacPhail, 23 Apr. 1955; children: Robert Wallace; Nancy Jean; PRES., G.S.W. BRUCE & ASSOCIATES INC.; Fellow, Geological Assn. Can.; mem. Assn. Prof. Engineers Ont. and Man.; Soc. of Economic Geologists; Clubs: The Albany Club; The Ontario Club; Home: 11 Collingsbrook Blvd., Agincourt, Ont. M1W 1L5.

**BRUCE, (William) Harry,** B.A.; editor; author; freelance journalist; b. Toronto, Ont. 8 July 1934; s. Charles Tory and Agnes (King) B.; e. Brown Pub. Sch. and Oakwood Coll. Inst. Toronto; Mount Allison Univ. B.A. 1955; London Sch. of Econ. 1956–57; Massey Coll. Univ. of Toronto 1969–70; D.C.L. (hon. causa) Univ. of King's Coll., Halifax 1985; LL.D. (hon. causa), Univ. St. Francis Xavier, Antigonish, N.S. 1991; m. Penny d. Clifford A. Meadows 10 Sept. 1955; children: Alexander, Annabel, Max; PRESIDENT, EAST COAST EDITORIAL LTD.; Reporter, 'The Ottawa Journal' 1955–59; mem. Parlty. Press Gallery 1958–59; Reporter, 'The Globe and Mail' 1959–61; Asst. Ed., 'Maclean's' mag. 1961–64; Mang. Ed. 'Saturday Night' mag. 1964–65; Mang. Ed., 'The Canadian Magazine' 1965–66; Assoc. Ed. and Featured Columnist, 'The Star Weekly' 1967–68; Columnist, 'The Toronto Daily Star' 1968–69; Reports and Reviews Ed., Columnist, 'Maclean's' 1970–71; Extve. Ed., Nova Scotia Light and Power Co. Ltd. 1971; TV Talk-Show Host 'Gazette' CBC Halifax 1972; freelance writer 1973–79; Editor, 'Atlantic Insight' 1979–80, Extve. Ed. 1981; Editor, 'Atlantic Salmon Journal' 1991; Editor-in-Chief, Atlantic Salmon Federation 1992– ; mem. Founding Bd., Writers' Fed. of N.S.; rec'd ACTRA 'Nellie' for 'Word from an Ambassador of Dreams' (best radio drama) 1977; winner first annual Evelyn Richardson Mem. Lit. Award for 'Lifeline,' best non-fiction book by a Nova Scotian 1978; Brascan Award for Culture, National Mag. Awards 1981; top prize for mag. writing, Atlantic Journalism Awards 1983, 1984, 1986, 1992, 1993; Toronto-Dominion Bank Award for Humour, National Mag. Awards 1983; runner-up, first National Business Book Award for 'The Man and the Empire: Frank Sobey' 1986; winner first annual City of Dartmouth Book Award, and first annual Booksellers' Choice Award, Atlantic Provinces Booksellers' Assoc. for 'Down Home: Notes of a Maritime Son' 1989; author 'The Short Happy Walks of Max MacPherson' 1968; 'Nova Scotia' 1975; 'Lifeline' 1977; 'R.A.: The Story of R.A. Jodrey, Entrepreneur' 1979; 'A Basket of Apples: Recollections of Historic Nova Scotia' 1982; 'Each Moment as it Flies' 1984; 'The Gulf of St. Lawrence' 1984; 'The Man and the Empire: Frank Sobey' 1985; 'Movin' East' 1985; 'Down Home: Notes of a Maritime Son' 1988; 'Maud: The Life of L.M. Montgomery' 1992; commentary, short articles in several anthols., numerous essays, reviews and columns in maj. Candn. newspapers and mags.; recreations: angling, sailing, swimming, walking; Home: General Delivery, St. Andrews, N.B. E0G 2X0.

**BRUCE, Iain Anthony Fyvie,** M.A., Ph.D.; educator; b. Edinburgh, Scot. 1 June 1937; s. Frederick Fyvie and Betty (Davidson) B.; e. Gonville and Caius Coll. Cambridge B.A. 1958, M.A. 1962; Univ. of Sheffield Dipl. Ed. 1959, Ph.D. 1963; m. Pamela d. James and Alice Pilling 9 Apr. 1960; children: Helen Elizabeth, Peter Anthony; PROF. OF CLASSICS AND HIST., MEMORIAL UNIV. OF NFLD. 1974– ; Dean of Arts there 1974–83; Asst. Master, Worthing High Sch., Eng. 1959–63; Asst. Prof. of Classics present Univ. 1963, Assoc. Prof. 1968; mem., Nfld. and Labrador Panel of Labour Arbitration Bd. Chairmen 1977– ; author 'An Historical Commentary on the Hellenica Oxyrhynchia' 1967; mem. ed. bd. Phoenix 1972–74, 1979–81; mem. Council, Classical Assn. Can. 1966–68, 1969–71, 1988–90; Home: 26 Johnson Cres., St. John's, Nfld. A1B 2J4; Office: St. John's, Nfld. A1C 5S7.

**BRUCE, James D.;** newspaper editor; b. Nashwaak Bridge, N.B. 10 Oct. 1941; m. Nancy Begin of Windsor, N.S. 1964; children: James Jr., Robert; EDITOR, THE WINDSOR STAR 1992– ; Reporter, Halifax Herald 1962–64; joined Windsor Star as Reporter, then Asst. Telegraph Ed., Telegraph Ed., and left as Asst. Metro Ed. 1964–69; Asst. Nat. Ed., Toronto Star 1969–70; returned to Windsor Star as Asst. City Ed., then City Ed., News Ed., Asst. Mng. Ed., Acting Mng. Ed., and lastly Mng. Ed. 1970–92; Part-time Instr., Journalism, St. Clair College 1982–83; Mem., Press Club of Windsor (Past Pres.); Edit. Ctte., Candn. Daily Newspaper Assn.; Western Ont. Newspaper Awards; Home: 9539 Midfield Cres., Windsor, Ont. N8R 1W9; Office: 167 Ferry St., Windsor, Ont. N9A 4M5.

**BRUCE, Phyllis Louise,** M.A.; editor; b. Ottawa, Ont. 16 May 1939; d. Victor Noble and Manada (Fredenburgh) b.; e. Glebe Coll. Inst. Ottawa 1957; Carleton Univ. B.A. 1961; Univ. of Toronto M.A. 1967; Ont. Coll. of Edn. Secondary Sch. Teaching Cert. 1964; PUBLISHER, PHYLLIS BRUCE BOOKS, an imprint of HarperCollins Publishers Ltd. 1992– ; Teacher of Eng. Glebe Coll. Inst. Ottawa, Lawrence Park Coll. Inst. Toronto; Lectr. in Eng./Candn. Studies, Vancouver Community Coll., Langara Coll. 1974–77; Ednl. Ed. Thomas Nelson (Canada), Van Nostrand Reinhold, Copp Clark 1967–74; Exec. Ed., Publisher, Van Nostrand Reinhold 1977–83; Exec. Ed., Key Porter Books 1983, Vice Pres. & Editor-in-Chief 1987–92; co-ed. 'Fifteen Canadian Poets' poetry anthol. 1970; 'Fifteen Canadian Poets Plus Five' 1980; mem. ed. bd. The Canadian Forum 1970–78; Pres. Book Publishers Profl. Assn. 1981–83; Home: 404 – 50 Prince Arthur Ave., Toronto, Ont. M5R 1B5; Office: HarperCollins Canada, Ste. 2900, 55 Avenue Rd., Toronto, Ont. M5R 3L2.

**BRUCE, William Robert,** M.Sc., Ph.D., M.D., F.R.S.C., F.R.C.P.S.; physician in research; b. Hamheung, Korea 26 May 1929; s. George Findlay and Ellen (Tate) B.; e. Univ. of Alta., B.Sc. (Chem.) 1950; Univ. of Sask., Ph.D. (Physics) 1956; Univ. of Chicago, M.D. 1958; Lic., Med. Council of Can.; m. Willa Margaret, d. William Graham MacFarlane, June 1957; children: Graham, Lynda, Kevin; SENIOR SCIENTIST, ONTARIO CANCER INST.; Prof., Dept. of Med. Biophysics, Univ. of Toronto, since 1966; joined present Univ. Dept. as Lectr., 1959–60; Asst. Prof. 1960–64; Assoc. Prof. 1964–66; joined Physics Div. of Ont. Cancer Inst., 1959; awarded Medal for Med., Royal Coll. Phys. and Surgs. Can., 1968; McLaughlin Gold Medal 1980; Dir., Am. Assn. Cancer Research; United Church; Home: 4 Marshfield Court, Don Mills, Ont. M3C 3E3.

**BRUCK, Peter A.,** M.A., Ph.D., Dr.jur.; educator; b. Vienna, Austria 8 Oct. 1950; s. Hans Georg and Elisabeth Charlotte (Khol) B.; e. Humanist Gymnasium Vienna 1968; Univ. of Vienna Dr.jur. 1973; Univ. of Iowa M.A. 1975; McGill Univ. Ph.D. 1984; m. Hania d. Eugeniusz and Irena Fedorowicz 1 Sept. 1978; children: Julia, Cyprian, Cecilia, Emilia; PROF. AND HEAD, INTERNAT. RSCH. PROGRAMME ECONOMY & FUTURE OF PRINT MEDIA, UNIV. OF SALZBURG, AUSTRIA 1991– ; Cons. Organizational Devel. and Pol. Edn. Union and Adult Edn. Orgns. Switzerland, Austria and Germany 1973–75; journalistic work various Eur. broadcasters and CBC-Internat. 1977– ; rsch. work communication policy for govt. depts. and media orgns. 1982– ; Prof. & Dir., Centre for Communication, Culture & Society, Carleton Univ. 1985–89; author, ed. various publs.; recipient Austrian Fulbright Scholarship in Social Sci's 1975; mem. Candn. Communications Assn. (Conf. Chrmn. 1986); Internat. Assn. Mass Communication Rsch.; Internat. Communication Assn.; Union Democratic Communication; Am. Sociol. Assn.; Office: Ottawa, Ont. K1S 5B6.

**BRUDNER, Alan S.,** B.A., M.A., Ph.D., LL.B.; university professor; b. Toronto, Ont. 6 Nov. 1943; s. Isadore and Lillian (Penner) B.; e. Univ. of Toronto B.A. (Hons.) 1966, M.A. 1968, Ph.D. 1976, LL.B. 1983; m. Susan d. Louis and Anne Zimmerman 3 Sept. 1972; children: Jennifer, Avi; ASSOC. PROF., FACULTY OF LAW & DEPT. OF POL. SCIENCE, UNIV. OF TORONTO 1988– ; Visiting Asst. Prof., Concordia Univ. 1979–80; Asst. Prof., Carleton Univ. 1983–84; Univ. of Toronto 1984–88; Panelist, Legal Aid Ctte. for Test Cases & Group Applications 1988– ; Human Subjects Ethical Review Ctte., Univ. of Toronto 1984– ; Consultant, Ont. Law Reform Comn. 1984; on Strict Penal Liability 1988; Jacob Burke Scholar-in-Residence, Cardozo Law School, Yeshiva Univ. 1990; author: 'The Unity of the Common Law: Studies in Hegelian Jurisprudence' and several research articles; Editorial Bd., 'University of Toronto Law Journal' 1992– ; Consulting editor, 'Canadian Journal of Law and Jurisprudence' 1993– ; Book Review Ed., 'University of Toronto Law Journal' 1987–92; Co-editor, 'University of Toronto Faculty of Law Review' 1982–83; recreations: fiction, baseball; Home: 63 Ridge Hill Dr., Toronto, Ont.; Office: Toronto, Ont. M5S 1A1.

**BRUEMMER, Fred,** O.C. (1983), R.C.A.; author; photographer; b. Riga, Latvia 26 June 1929; came to Can. 1950; m. Maud van den Berg 31 March 1962; two s.; author 'The Long Hunt' 1969; 'Seasons of the Eskimo' 1971; 'Encounters with Arctic Animals' 1972; 'The Arctic' 1974; 'The Life of the Harp Seal' 1977; 'Children of the North' 1979; 'Bear River' 1980; 'The Arctic World' 1985; 'Arctic Animals' 1986; 'Seasons of the Seal' 1988; 'World of the Polar Bear' 1989; 'The Narwhal' 1993; various articles Am., Candn. and European mags. in Eng., French and German; rec'd Queen's Silver Jubilee Medal 1977; Order of Canada 1983; Sandford Fleming Medal, Royal Candn. Inst. 1989; Dr. Lit., h.c. Univ. of New Brunswick 1989; Fellow, Arctic Inst. of N.Am. 1990; Protestant; Address: 2 Strathearn South, Montreal West, Que. H4X 1X4.

**BRUK, John,** B.Com., LL.B.; lawyer; b. Blato, Yugoslavia 5 March 1930; s. Kuzma Bosnic and Jelica (Kalogjera) B.; e. Univ. of B.C. B.Com. 1957, LL.B. 1958; m. Carol (dec.); m. 2ndly, Helen 29 Sept. 1992; children: Mark, Ian, Bruce, Steven; 1988– ; Chrmn., PRESIDENT, TRILON PACIFIC CORP. First Property and Casualty Corp.; Vancity Insurance Services Ltd.; Depy. Chrmn., China Investment & Development Co. Ltd.; Trilon Bancorp Inc.; Dir., Weldwood of Canada Ltd.; Founding Chrmn., Asia Pacific Found. of Canada; Lectr. Univ. of Wash. 1957–58; articling student Lawrence & Shaw, Vancouver 1959–60; called to Bar of B.C. 1960; Partner, Nemetz, Austin, Christie & Bruk, Vancouver 1960–63; Lawrence & Shaw 1963–74; Chrmn. of Bd. Dynasty Explorations Ltd. Vancouver 1974–75; Pres. and C.E.O. Cyprus Anvil Mining Corp. 1975–82; Chrmn. Asia Pacific Found. of Canada 1983–87; mem. Candn. Bar Assn.; Law Soc. B.C.; Internat. Counc., Asia Soc.; Assoc. Mem., Inst. of Fiscal & Monetary Policy, Ministry of Finance and the Found. for Advance Information and Research, Japan; R. Catholic; recreations: reading, music; Clubs: Vancouver; Capilano Golf & Country; Home: #302 – 738 Broughton St., Vancouver, B.C. V6G 3A7; Office: #1273 – 595 Burrard St., Vancouver, B.C. V7X 1J1.

**BRULEY, Kenneth J.,** F.C.A.; chartered accountant; b. Port Arthur, Ont. e. Lakehead Univ.; Michigan Tech. Univ.; C.A. Thunder Bay 1967; m. Linda 27 Feb. 1965; children: Denise, Brian; OFFICE MANAGING PARTNER, ERNST & YOUNG, THUNDER BAY 1978– ; Clarkson Gordon Toronto 1971; Partner 1973; transferred to St. John's, Nfld. to open Clarkson Gordon office 1973; Manager 1973–78; Past Pres., Thunder Bay C. of C.; Pres., Rotary Club of Thunder Bay; Dir., Thunder Bay Ventures Community Futures Ctte.; Treas., Thunder Bay Airport Privatization Ctte.; awarded FCA 1984; Office: P.O. Box 3475, 215 Red River Rd., Thunder Bay, Ont. P7B 5J9.

**BRULOTTE, Raymond,** B.A., M.A.; professeur d'université; né. Arthabaska, Qué. 16 sept. 1951; f. Anselme f. Gisèle (Vallières) B.; é. Univ. du Qué. à Trois-Rivières B.A. 1974; Univ. Laval M.A. 1982; scolarité de doctorat;

ép. Lucie Rompré; PROFESSEUR D'ÉCONOMIE, TÉLé-UNIVERSITÉ 1978– ; Journaliste, 'Le Nouvelliste' 1972–74; Économiste, Conseil de la Coopération du Québec 1974–78; Consultant, Conseil executif, Gouv. du Qué.; Administrateur, Caisse Desjardins de Sillery 1991–94; Membre du Conseil d'admin. et du com. exécutif, Télé-Université 1991–94; mem., Assn. des économistes québécois; auteur: 'Vie économique québécoise' 1979, 'Initiation à la coopération' 1988, 'La municipalité' 1981, 'Coopératives de travailleurs' 1990 et divers articles dans des revues scientifiques et mags.; loisirs: bicyclette, natation; clubs: Cyclorizon, Maîtres nageurs de Ste-Foy; rés.: 1279, ave De Villars, Sillery, Qué. G1T 2C1; bureau: 2600, boul. Laurier, 7e étage, Ste-Foy, Qué. G1V 4V9.

**BRUN, Henri,** B.A., B.Ph., L.èsL., LL.L., D.E.S., LL.D.; university professor, lawyer; b. Quebec, Que. 11 April 1939; e. Laval Univ. B.A., B.Ph., L.èsL., LL.L., D.E.S.(Paris), LL.D.; m. Gaétane Giguère 29June 1963; children: Pierre, Louis, Bernard; PROFESSOR LAW, LAVAL UNIV. 1967– ; Member of the Bar, Prov. of Qué. 1963; Extve. Vice-Dean, Fac. of Law, Laval Univ. 1972, 1973, 1987, 1988; Dean 1988–89; Editor, 'Les Cahiers de Droit' 1981–91; Dir., Constitutional Branch, Dept. of Justice, Govt. of Que. 1978–82; author: 'Le formation des institutions parlementaires du Québec' 1970, 'Le territoire du Québec' 1974, 'Droit constitutionnel' 1990, 'Chartes des droits' 6th ed. 1993; Office: Quebec, Que. G1K 7P4.

**BRUNEAU, Angus Andrew,** O.C., P.Eng., B.A.Sc., D.I.C., Ph.D., D.Eng. (hon. causa); executive; b. Toronto, Ont. 12 Dec. 1935; s. Earl Angus and Lois McClung (Gordon) B.; e. Univ. of Toronto B.A.Sc. 1958; Imp. Coll. London D.I.C. 1962; Univ. of London Ph.D. 1962; m. Jean d. James and Laura McInnis 16 May 1959; three s. Peter, Ian, Stephen; CHRMN., PRES. & C.E.O., FORTIS INC. 1988– ; CHRMN., NEWFOUNDLAND POWER 1990– ; Chrmn.: Air Nova 1988– ; Unitel-Newfoundland Ltd.; Fortis Trust; Fortis Properties; Dir.: Maritime Electric Co. Ltd. 1990– ; The SNC Group Inc. 1991– ; Lectr. in Math. Univ. of Waterloo 1958–59; Lectr. in Materials Science Queen Mary's Col. and Imp. Coll. London 1960–62; Lectr. and Research Materials Engn., Materials Sci. Group Leader Univ. of Waterloo 1962–68, Dir. of Gen. Engn. 1966–68; Prof. and Founding Dean of Engn. and Applied Sci., Mem. Univ. of Nfld. 1968–73, Vice Pres. Prof. Schs. and Community Services 1974–78; Dir. Churchill Falls (Labrador) Corp. 1974–78; Chrmn. Bd. Govs. Nfld. Oceans Research and Development Corp. 1974–80; Dir. Newfoundland and Labrador Hydro 1976–86; Lower Churchill Development Corp. 1978–86; Pres., Bruneau Resources Management Ltd. 1979–86; Pres. and Dir. Terra Nova Peat Ltd. 1981–86; Dir. and Vice-Pres., Southside Hills Corp. Ltd. 1980–86; Atlantic Provs. Economic Counc. 1983–87; C.E.O., Newfoundland Light and Power Co. Ltd. 1986–90; Chair, Federal Private Sector Challenge Group 1990– ; mem., National Adv. Panel on Advanced Industrial Materials 1990– ; mem. Sci. Council Can. 1971–77; Natural Sciences & Engn. Research Counc. 1978–83; Chrmn. Bd. Govs. Centre for Cold Ocean Resources Engn. 1973–85; Chrmn. St. David's Group Homes 1979–84; Chrmn. various bds. and comtes. Nat. Research Council 1972–82; mem. Council, Candn. Inst. Advanced Research 1982–87; Mem. Ocean Industry Development Office 1982–86; Bank of Montreal Bus. Adv. Bd. 1983–85; Task Force on Federal Policies and Programs for Technology Development (MOSST) 1983–84; Mem., Energy Options Adv. Bd. 1987–88; Chrmn., Nat. Marine Counc. 1988–90; Mem., Policy Ctte., Candn. Constitution and Political Reform Task Force, BCNI; co-ed. 'Arctic Systems' 1977; author numerous reports and papers; Officer, Order of Canada 1983; mem. Assn. Prof. Engrs. Nfld. (rec'd Award of Merit); Fellow, Candn. Acad. of Engn. (Gold Medal Recipient 1988); Julian C. Smith Award, E.I.C. 1992; Fellow, Engn. Inst. Can.; Presbyterian; recreations: gardening, woodworking, photography, squash; Clubs: Crow's Nest; Cabot; University (Toronto); Home: 53 Tupper St., St. John's, Nfld. A1A 2T6; Office: PO Box 8837, St. John's, Nfld. A1B 3T2.

**BRUNEAU, Claude,** C.M., LL.L., M.B.A.; executive; b. Montreal, Que. 7 Sept. 1931; e. Coll. Ste-Marie, Montreal B.A. 1951; Univ. de Montréal LL.L. 1954; Univ. of W. Ont. M.B.A. 1959; PRES., SANPALO INVESTMENTS CORP. 1989– ; Dir., Baca Resources Ltd.; Boulanger Inc.; Canada World Youth; Key Porter Books Ltd.; Maison Cousin Inc.; Audit Ctte., The Montreal Mus. of Fine Arts; Nestlé Enterprises Limited Adv. Bd.; Pallas Invest S.A.; LGS Group Inc.; The Verdun Hospital Found.; Univ. of Western Ont. Business Sch.'s Adv. Ctte.; Women in Mgmt. Rsch. Program Adv. Ctte.; mem. Que. Bar Assn.; Clubs: C.D. Howe Inst.; The Metropolitan (NY); Mount Bruno Country; The Mount Royal; The York; Office: 751 Victoria Square, Montreal, Que. H2Y 2J3.

**BRUNEAU, Marc Y.,** B.Com., L.Sc.Com., F.C.A.; b. St. Damase, Que. 28 May 1935; s. J. Roméo and Fabiola (Beauregard) B.; e. St. Charles Garnier Sch.; St. Stanislas High Sch. 1957; Hautes Etudes Commerciales Univ. of Montreal B.Com. 1956, L.Sc.Com. 1957; C.A. 1958; m. Claire Lussier d. Roméo Lussier 10 June 1967; one s. Marc G.; PARTNER & MEMBER OF THE MGMNT. CTTE., RAYMOND, CHABOT, MARTIN, PARÉ; Sr. to Mgr. McDonald, Currie (Coopers & Lybrand) & Co. 1958–62; Advisory Counc., Candn. Heart Foundation; Que. Heart Foundation; Dir. & Extve. Mem., Montreal Heart Inst. Research Fund; Dir., Royal Candn. Mint; Dir., P.C. Canada Fund; mem. Chart. Inst. C.A.'s; Chambre de Comm. de Montréal; R. Catholic; Clubs: Laval-sur-le-Lac (Past Pres.); St-Denis (Past Pres.); Home: 1274 Mont-Royal Blvd., Outremont, Que. H2V 2H8; Office: National Bank Tower, Suite 1900, 600 de la Gauchetiere St. W., Montreal, Que. H3B 4L8.

**BRUNEAU, William Arthur,** B.A., B.Ed., M.A., Ph.D.; university professor; b. Frontier, Sask. 5 March 1944; s. Arthur and Eva Harriet (Armstrong) B.; e. Univ. of Saskatchewqan B.A. 1964, B.Ed. 1966, M.A.(Ed.) 1968; Univ. of Toronto Ph.D. 1977; m. Sandra d. Elgin and Marguerite Steen 10 Oct. 1964; children: Jon William, Rochelle Andrea; PROFESSOR, UNIV. OF B.C. 1971– ; High School Teacher, Calgary, Alta. 1965–67; Mem. & Extve. Offr., Candn. Soc. for the Study of Higher Edn.; Candn. Assn. of Found. of Edn.; Soc. for French Hist. Studies (Life Mem.); Internat. Standing Ctte. for the Hist. of Edn. (Europe); Candn. Soc. for the Study of Higher Edn.; Candn. Hist. of Edn. Assn.; Candn. Assn. of Learned Journals; elected Trustee, Vancouver School Bd. 1990–93; Pres., Univ. of B.C. Faculty Assn. 1992–94; Jury Mem., Pub. Subsidy Ctte., Prog. of Aid to Scholarly Pubn., Social Sci. Fed. of Canada; Doctoral Fellowships Ctte., SSHRCC; Editor-in-Chief, 'Canadian Journal of Education/Revue canadienne de l'éducation' 1987–92; Mem., N.D.P. 1962– ; Pres., Vanc.-Point Grey N.D.P. Constituency Assn. (1981); author: 'A Matter of Identities: The UBC Faculty Association, 1920–1990' and 45 articles, reviews & monographs; recreations: music; Home: 3817 W. 16th Ave., Vancouver, B.C. V6R 3C6; Office: 2125 Main Mall, Vancouver, B.C. V6T 1Z4.

**BRUNEL, Louis,** B.A., L.Sc.Com.; executive; b. Montreal, Que. 21 June 1941; s. Donat and Maria (Perron) B.; e. Coll. des Eudistes Montréal B.A. 1962; Ecole des Hautes Etudes Commerciales L.Sc.Com. 1965; m. Carole d. Henri Pérusse, Ste-Foy, Que. 10 May 1975; children: Marie-Hélène, Jean-Lou, Ludovic, Rosalie; VICE PRES., CORP. DEVELOPMENT, LE GROUPE VIDEOTRON LTEE 1988– ; Vice Chrmn., Videotron Communication Ltd.; Dir., Videotron Corp. Ltd., Videotron Investment (UK) Ltd.; Videotron Management (UK) Ltd.; Videotron West Side Ltd.; La compagnie d'assurances L'Union québécoise; Canassurance, compagnie d'assurance; Seteca S.A. (Spain); Gouverneur, Blue Cross Quebec; Data Processing Machine Operator, Les Pharmacies Universelles, Limitée 1958, Analyst Programmer 1962, Chief Acct. 1964–66; Asst. to Dir. Adm. Computer Center Univ. of Montreal 1966, Dir. of Center 1967–69; Dir. of Computer Center, Quebecair 1969; Dir. Computer Systems Devel. Univ. of Que. 1969, Asst. Vice Pres. Communications 1970; Vice-Pres. Communications and Dir., 1971–79; Chrmn. and Gen. Dir., Ecole Nat. d'Administration Publique 1979–81; Vice-Pres. & Gen. Dir., Cablevision Nationale Ltée 1981–83; Dir. Télé-Université 1973–76; Pres. & C.E.O., Groupe Pharmaceutique Focus Inc. 1983–87; Mng. Dir., Les Ordinateurs Hypocrat Inc. 1987; mem. Assoc. Comte. Instructional Technol. Nat. Rsch. Council Can. 1976–79; Chrmn. Le Presses de l'Univ. du Qué. 1975–79; rec'd Prix du Journalisme Scientifique du Canada 1975; Merite HEC 1986; author 'Telecommunications: Des Machines et Des Hommes' 1978; co-author 'University at Home' 1977; numerous articles and lectures on computers, satellites, information, telecommunications, cable and innovation; R. Catholic; recreations: tennis, reading, painting, camping; Home: 196 Pierre Foretier, Ile Bizard, Que. H9C 2B1; Office: 2000 Berri St., Montreal, Que. H2L 4V7.

**BRUNELLE, Dorval,** B.A., LL.B., Doct. 3e cycle; university professor; b. Montréal, Qué. 8 Sept. 1941; s. Jean and Marielle (Dorval) B.; e. Coll. Stanislas, B.A. 1959; Univ. de Montréal, LL.B. 1962; Ecole pratique des Hautes Etudes, Paris, doct. 3e cycle 1973; m. Marina d. Ileana and Lucien Greciano 29 Oct. 1971; one d.: Daphné; PROF., DEPT. OF SOCIOLOGY, UNIV. DU QUE. A MONTRÉAL 1970– ; (Chrmn., Dept. of Sociology 1988–92); Extve. Sec. to Min. of Munic. Affiars (Qué.) Hon. Pierre Laporte 1964–66; Journalist, Radio Can. 1967–68; author: 'Le Code civil et les rapports de classes' 1975, 'La Désillusion tranquille' 1978, 'La Raison du capital' 1980, 'L'Etat solide. Sociologie du fédéralisme au Canada et au Québec' 1982, 'Socialisme, étatisme et démocratie' 1983, 'Les trois colombes' 1985; 'Le libre-échange par défaut' (co-author C. Deblock) 1988, 'L'Ere des libéraux. Le Pouvoir fédéral de 1963 à 1984' (co-author Y. Bélanger et alii) 1989; club: The Mount Royal Tennis; Home: Montreal, Qué.; Office: C.P. 8888, Succ. A., Montréal, Qué. H3C 3P8.

**BRUNELLE, Hon. Rene;** b. Penetanguishene, Ont. 22 Jan. 1920; s. Pierre and Ida (Beaupre) B.; e. High Sch., Timmins, Ont.; Ottawa (Ont.) Normal Sch.; Khaki Univ., London Eng.; Univ. of Toronto; Laurentian Univ. LL.D. 1978; m. Andree Hebert, Nov. 1956; children: Louis, Suzanne, Pierre, Kelly; Dir. Northern Telephone Co.; 1st el. to Ont. Leg., by-el. May 1958; re-el. since; apptd. Min. Lands and Forests, Nov. 1966, Min. Mines, Nov. 1967; apptd. Chrmn., Ont. Parks Integration Bd., March 1968; formerly Chrmn., Select Comte. of Leg. on Mining; Min. of Social & Family Services, Ont. 172; Prov. Sec. for Resources Develop. 1977–81; enlisted in R.C.A. 1942; Comnd. 2/Lt. 1943; Overseas 1944, serving as Canloan Offr. with Monmouthshire Regt. till discharge 1946; Tourist Operator, Remi Lake, Moonbeam, Ont.; P. Conservative; R. Catholic; K. of C.; recreations: hunting, fishing, canoeing, skiing; Home: Moonbeam, Ont. P0L 1V0.

**BRUNET, Pierre,** F.C.A.; investment dealer; b. Montréal, Que. 3 March 1939; s. Paul E. and Liliane (Brisson) B.; e. Coll. Olier, classical studies, 1951–59; Univ. of Montreal (HEC). C.A. degree 1964; m. Louise, d. Adolphe Simard, 17 June 1961; children: Lucie, Isabelle, Philippe, Bernard; PRES. & CHIEF EXECUTIVE OFFICER, LÉVESQUE BEAUBIEN GEOFFRION INC. 1970– ; commenced as C.A., Samson, Bélair & Associés, Chart. Accts. 1959–64; Treas. and Dir., Morgan, Ostiguy & Hudon Inc. 1964–70; Chrmn., Investment Dealers Assn. of Can. 1984–85; Dir. Industrial-Alliance Life Insurance Co.; Groupe Transcontinental G.T.C. Ltée; (Pres.) Montreal Symphony Orchestra; Candn. Center for Architecture; Former Pres. (1982–83) Montreal Chamber of Commerce; Former Chrmn., Financial Administrators section, Invest. Dealers Assn. of Can. 1984–85; Montreal Chamber of Comm. 1983–84; National Contingency Fund 1972; Que. Inst. of Chartered Accountants 1978–79; Chrmn. Montreal Stock Exchange 1974–75 (Gov. 1972); R. Catholic; recreations: swimming, skiing, tennis; Clubs: Club Saint-Denis; Mount-Royal; St. James's; Hermitage; Home: 1321 Sherbrooke St. W., Apt. F-61, Montreal, Que. H3G 1J4; Office: 155 Metcalfe St., 5th Floor, Montreal, Que. H3B 4S9.

**BRUNSEK, Judy Irene,** B.A.; publisher; b. Toronto, Ont. 13 Sept. 1958; d. Stanislav and Zinka (Jerancic) B.; e. Loretto Coll. Sch., 1977 (1st in class); St. Michael's Coll., Univ. of Toronto, B.A. (Hons.) 1981; m. Michael C. De La Haye 9 May 1992; VICE PRES. MKTG. AND SALES, HARPERCOLLINS*CANADA*LTD. 1991– ;and Mem. of Bd.; Publicity Co-ordinator, Prentice-Hall Canada Inc. 1981–85; Publicity Dir., McClelland & Stewart 1985–88; Publisher, Quill & Quire 1988–91; Lectr., The Banff Publishing Workshop, Banff Sch. of Fine Arts; Roman Cath.; Mem., Book Promoters Assn. of Can. (Founding Pres. 1988–89; Past Pres. 1989–90); Book Publishers Profl. Assn. (Pres. 1988–89); Home: 222 Glenholme Ave., Toronto, Ont. M6E 3C4; Office: 55 Avenue Rd., Ste. 2900, Hazelton Lanes, Toronto, Ont. M5R 3L2.

**BRUTON, Leonard Thomas,** B.Sc., M.Eng., Ph.D., F.I.E.E.E.; educator; engineer; b. London, Eng. 9 Sept. 1942; s. Archibald Stanley and Marie Florence (Lancashire) B.; e. Willesden Grammar Sch. 1961; Univ. of London B.Sc. 1964; Carleton Univ. M.Eng. 1967; Univ. of Newcastle Upon Tyne Ph.D. 1970; m. Avis d. Frank and Lily Makin 22 Aug. 1964; children: Alexander, Michelle, Nicole, Adrian; PROFESSOR OF ELECTRICAL AND COMPUTER ENGINEERING, UNIV. OF CALGARY 1985– ; mem. Scient. Staff Circuit Design Bell Northern Research Ltd. Ottawa 1964–67; Lectr. in Elect. Eng. Univ. of Newcastle Upon Tyne 1967–70; Asst., Assoc. and Full Prof. of Elect. Eng. Univ. of Calgary 1970–83, Head of Elect. Eng. 1977–81; Dean of Eng., Univ. of Victoria 1983–85; Cons. in signal processing and microelectronics; recipient Am. Soc. of Edn. Pacific N.W. Sect. Teaching Award 1977; Manning Principal Award for Innovation 1991; Alberta Science and Technology Award for Innovation in Science 1992; author 'RC-Active Filters: Theory and Design' 1980; recreations: squash, photography, tennis; Home: 388

Capri Cres. N.W., Calgary, Alta. T2L 1B2; Office: 2500 University Dr. N.W., Calgary, Alta. T2N 1N4.

**BRUYÈRE, Christian;** screenwriter/filmmaker; b. Paris, France 27 Feb. 1944; s. Jacques and Anne (Avakian) B.; e. USC Film Sch., Los Angeles; m. Rosalia d. Lyle and Mary Dean 24 May 1987; children: Yarrow, Karen, Stephen; Writer: various episodes of 'Beachcombers' & 'Danger Bay'; Writer/Producer: 'Walls' (feature film) 1984, 'Dads and Kids' (Genie Award winner 1987 for Best Documentary; 1985 Golden Sheaf Award, Yorkton Fest.; Blue Ribbon, Am. Film Fest.); Writer/Director/Producer: 'Shelley' (feature film in Cannes 1987); 'New Happiness' (TV documentary) 1993; Co-Writer/Director/Producer: 'Rape: Face to Face' 1984 (Blue Ribbon, Am. Film Fest.); Producer: 'Kootenai Brown' (feature film) 1991; 'Cadillac Girls' (feature film) 1992; Extve. Producer: 'Blockade' (feature documentary) 1993; Pres., B.C. Film Indus. Assn. 1987–89; Screenplay writing instr., Creative Writing Dept., Univ. of B.C.; B.C. Extve., Candn. Film & TV Assn. 1987–88; ACRMPIA, Alliance of Candn. Regional Motion Picture Indus. Assn.; author: 'In Harmony with Nature' 1975, 'Country Comforts' 1976 (tech. & sociological); 'Walls' 1979 (pub. theatrical play); 'Selling It' 1987 (film indus. mktg. manual); recreations: baseball, volleyball, etc.; Home: 3206 W. 12th Ave., Vancouver, B.C. V6K 2R9; Office: 204 – 111 Water St., Vancouver, B.C. V6B 1A7.

**BRYANS, Alexander McKelvey,** M.D., M.Ed., F.R.C.P. (C); physician, retired; b. Toronto, Ont. 16 Sept. 1921; s. Dr. Fred Thomas and Barbara (McKelvey) B.; e. Univ. of Toronto Schs. (1932–39); Univ. of Toronto, M.D. 1944; Mich. State Univ. M.Ed. 1971; m. Elaine, d. S.G. Fildes, Town of Mount Royal, P.Q. 30 May 1954; children: John Alexander, Susan Gail, Mary Catherine; PROFESSOR EMERITUS OF PAEDIATRICS, QUEEN'S UNIV.; Prof. of Paediatrics, Queen's Univ., since 1959; served in R.C.A.M.C., 1942–46; Fellow, Royal College of Physicians and Surgeons of Canada; Fellow, Am. Acad. Pediatrics; mem., Candn. Med. Assn.; Ont. Med. Assn., Candn. Paediatric Soc.; Past Pres., Physicians for Global Survival / Canada; United Church; recreations: skiing, camping; Address: 31 Lakeland Points Dr., Kingston, Ont. K7M 4E8.

**BRYANS, Davis;** association executive; PRESIDENT, ONTARIO BEEKEEPERS' ASSOCIATION; Address: Bayfield, Ont. N0M 1G0.

**BRYANT, Christopher Hayden;** college president; b. Halifax, N.S. 25 Jan. 1944; s. William Hayden and Norah Page (Richardson) B.; e. Lower Can. Coll. 1961; McGill Univ., B.A. (Hons.) 1965; Harvard Univ., MAT 1968; m. Sybil d. Horace and Petronella Hutchinson 20 May 1972; children: Jeffrey Hayden, Peter Hutchinson, Jacqueline Moale; PRESIDENT, HOLLAND COLLEGE 1992– ; Dir., Internat. Programs, Fed. of Cdn. Municipalities 1990–92; Field Staff Offr. (Jamaica), CUSO 1969–73; Reg. Dir. (Caribbean-Barbados) 1973–74; Dir., Human Resources Div. (Ottawa) 1973–77; Regional Field Offr. (Papua New Guinea) 1977–83; Extve. Dir., CUSO 1983–90; Anglican; Home: 93 Bardin Ct., West Royalty, P.E.I. C1E 1L9; Office: 285 Kent St., Charlottetown, P.E.I. C1A 1P4.

**BRYANT, Thomas Alex,** Ph.D.; executive; consultant; b. The Pas, Man. 24 Aug. 1953; s. Joseph Edward and Mary A. (Harrington) B.; e. St. Andrew's Coll. Aurora, Ont.; Carleton Univ. B.A. 1973, Hons. 1974; Mass. Inst. Technol. S.M. 1977, Ph.D. 1982; postgrad. studies Harvard, Univ. of Mich.; m. Robin d. Willard and Marjorie Reenstra 10 May 1980; children: David Harrington, Michelle Alixanne, Christine Tamara; ASSOC. PROF., MGMNT. & MARKETING, FACULTY OF BUSINESS, BROCK UNIVERSITY and DIR., BURGOYNE CENTRE FOR ENTREPRENEURSHIP 1993– ; Founder and Pres., Brystra Consultants, Regina/Waterloo 1984– ; Chrmn., Pres. and Chief Exec. Offr. Professional Electronic Services Inc. Regina 1987– ; Rsch. Staff Harvard Univ. 1980–81; Peat Marwick & Partners Ottawa 1982–84; Co-Founder, Pres. and Chief Exec. Offr. Taycor Management Corp. Regina 1986–89; Pres., Candn. Centre for Creative Technol. 1989–91; Exec. Dir. Shad Valley Prog. 1989–91; former lectr. Univ. of Regina Faculty of Adm.; Adjunct Prof., Mgmt. Scis., Univ. of Waterloo 1990– ; Can. Council Doctoral Fellow 1975–78; author numerous consulting and rsch. reports; mem. Candn. Evaluation Soc.; Am. Mktg. Assn.; Candn. Water Resources Assn.; Soc. Mfg. Engs.; The Planning Forum; recreations: rugby, flying, canoeing; Clubs: Waterloo-Wellington Flying; Home: 519 Clair Creek Blvd., Waterloo, Ont. N2T 1S1; Offices: Taro Hall 316, Brock Univ., St. Catharines, Ont. L2S 3A1 and P.O. Box 125, Waterloo, Ont. N2J 3Z9.

**BRYDEN, John Herbert,** B.A., M.Phil.; politician; author; b. Dundas, Ont. 15 July 1943; s. Thomas Hazell and Ruth Margarite (Arthur) B.; e. Dundas Dist. H.S.; McMaster Univ., B.A. (Hons.) 1966; Univ. of Leeds, M.Phil. 1968; m. Catherine d. Herbert S. and Kathleen Armstrong 26 Aug. 1967; children: Andrew, Cathleen, Deirdre; LIBERAL M.P. HAMILTON-WENTWORTH 1993– ; copy editor, Univ. of Toronto Press 1968–69; Reporter, features writer, art critic, city ed., The Hamilton Spectator 1969–77; copy ed., science page ed., The Globe and Mail 1977–79; insight ed., senior ed., finan. ed., mag. ed., The Toronto Star 1979–89; United Church; author: 'Deadly Allies: Canada's Secret War, 1937–1947' 1989; 'Best-Kept Secret: Canadian Secret Intelligence in the Second World War' 1993; Home: 83 Lynden Rd., Lynden, Ont. L0R 1T0.

**BRYDEN, Ronald,** M.A.; educator; b. Trinidad 6 Dec. 1927; s. William Francis and Flossie Lee (Samuel) B.; e. Ridley Coll. St. Catharines, Ont. 1945; Univ. of Toronto B.A. 1950; Cambridge Univ. B.A. 1953; m. Patricia Bowen-Davis d. Philip and Esther Vos 1963, dissolved 1986; children: Diana Elizabeth, Pier Katharine, Matthew David; Prof. of Drama, Univ. of Toronto 1979–93; and Dir. Grad. Centre for Study of Drama 1981–85, 1986–91; joined BBC News Service 1956–60; Lit. Ed. 'Spectator' London 1961–63; Ed. 'Town Magazine' London 1963–64; Theatre Critic 'New Statesman' 1964–66, 'Observer' 1966–71, London; Play Adviser, Royal Shakespeare Co. 1971–75; Visiting Prof. present Univ. 1976–79; Gov. Stratford Festival 1978–84; Bd. Mem., Canadian Stage Co., Toronto 1987–89; Literary Advisor, Shaw Festival 1992– ; Ed. Bd. 'Modern Drama' 1979– ; Ed. Bd. 'Theatre History in Canada 1980– ; author 'The Unfinished Hero and Other Essays' 1969; ed. 'Whittaker's Theatre' 1985; recreation: travel; Home: 12 Oriole Cres., Toronto, Ont. M5P 1L5; Office: Graduate Centre for Study of Drama, Univ. of Toronto, Koffler Centre, 214 College St., Toronto, Ont. M5T 2Z9.

**BRYDEN, William MacDonald,** Q.C., B.A.; barrister and solicitor; b. Welland, Ont. 27 July 1926; s. Russell James and Letitia Lillian (Morrison) B.; e. McMaster Univ. B.A. 1947; Osgoode Hall; called to Bar 1950; m. Margaret Patton, d. Robert and Anne Morton 30 Apr. 1955; children: Catherine, Russell, Barbara, Robert, John; PARTNER, OSLER, HOSKIN & HARCOURT 1956– ; Dir. Bethlehem Steel (Canada) Ltd.; The Borden Co. Ltd.; Ethyl Canada Inc.; Kawneer Co. Canada Ltd.; KG Land Corp.; Amax Gold Canada Ltd.; Amax Securities Canada Ltd.; Regin Properties Ltd.; Krug Properties; Sybron Chemicals Canada Ltd.; Wella Can. Ltd.; Zanella Canada Inc.; read law with present firm 1948; called to the Bar 1950; practised law with same firm 1950–55; created Queen's Counsel 1964; mem. Law Soc. of Upper Can.; Candn. Bar Assn.; Candn. Tax Foundation; County of York Bar Assn.; Dir. Candn. Nat. Exhbn.; Ont. Shorthorn Club; Glenview Presbyt. Church, Toronto; recreations: golf; hockey; tennis; Clubs: Albany (Dir.; past Pres.); Badminton and Racquet; Toronto Golf; Adelaide; Home: R.R. 1, Orangeville, Ont. L9W 2Y8; Office: P.O. Box 50, First Canadian Place, Toronto, Ont. M5X 1B8.

**BRYDON, Diana,** B.A., M.A., Ph.D.; university professor; b. Hamilton, Ont. 27 Oct. 1950; d. Norman James and Catherine Marie (Inch) Maxwell; e. Univ. of Toronto B.A. 1972, M.A. 1973; Australian Nat. Univ. Ph.D. 1977; m. William H. s. William and Elizabeth B. 30 June 1971; PROFESSOR, UNIV. OF GUELPH 1992– ; Asst. Prof., Univ. of B.C. 1979; Assoc. Prof. 1987; Univ. of Guelph 1989; Administrator & Internat. Judge, Commonwealth Writers Prize 1991, '92; Chair, Regional Judging Panel for Canada & the Caribbean, Commonwealth Writers Prize 1989, '90; Judge, Canada-Australia Lit. Award, Canada Council 1991; Dillon's Commonwealth Poetry Prize 1988; E.J. Pratt Award, Lincoln G. Hutton Award, Victoria Coll. 1971; Ont. Grad. Scholarship 1972; Commonwealth Scholarship 1973–76; George Drew Meml. Trust Fund Award 1982; SSHRCC Leave Grant 1984–85; Univ. of Guelph Fac. Assn., Prof. Teaching Award, Coll. of Arts 1992; SSHRC Research Grant 1992–95; Pres., Candn. Assn. for Commonwealth Literature and Language Studies 1989–92; author: 'Christina Stead' 1987; co-author: 'Decolonising Fictions' 1993; editor: 'World Literature Written in English' 1989– ; editorial board mem., 'Ariel,' 'Australian and New Zealand Studies in Canada,' 'English Studies in Canada,' 'Essays in Canadian Writing,' 'Kunapipi,' 'Span,' 'Studies in Canadian Literature,' 'Westerly'; Home: Box 8, R.R. #4, Rockwood, Ont. N0B 2K0; Office: Guelph, Ont. N1G 2W1.

**BRYDONE, J. Eleanor;** interior designer; b. Ontario, Canada; d. Joseph and Ethel Sarah (Roe) B.; e. Ont. Coll. of Art, F.O.C.A. (Hon.) 1959–63; Hon. Fellow, OCA 1989; m. Robert Hagarty 17 Dec. 1970; PRES., RICE BRYDONE LIMITED 1971– ; Design Dir., A.D. Pollard & Assoc. 1963–71; American Soc. of Interior Designers (ASID): Past Pres., N.Y. Canada East Chapter, 1987–89; National Communications Chair 1989–91; National Dir., District 20 1991–92; National Task Force Chair, Marketing 1991–93; Toronto Region Co-Chair, ASID 1993– ; Fellow, ASID 1993– ; Juror, Inst. of Business Designers (IBD)/Interior Design Magazine 1990 Contract Design Competition; Product Exhibitor Advisor, Annual Internat. Interior Design Exposition 1990–93; Adv. Bd. Mem., A & D Business Magazine 1988–91; Contract Magazine 1986–90; Mem., Design Counc., Steelcase Inc. 1990–95; Awards for Excellence: in Barrier-Free Design, Rogers Cablesystems Inc. 1990; in Hotel Design, SkyDome Hotel 1990; in Corp. Office Design, Metro Hall for the Municipality of Metro. Toronto 1993; in Extve. Office Design, Canada Trust 1991; in Gen. Office Design, Rice Brydone Limited 1991 and Saatchi & Saatchi 1992; IBD Award, USA, Tech. & Creative Solutions, McKim Baker Lovick/BBDO 1993; Historical Restoration, 320 Bay St. 1992; Financial Post Design Effectiveness Awards, Blake, Cassels & Graydon 1993; Mem., representing Ont. C. of C., Premier of Ontario's Task Force on Investment in Ont.; Mem. of Jury, Toronto Arts Awards 1993; Regional Presidential Citation ASID 1990; National Presidential Citation, ASID 1990; Presidential Citation for chairing Am. Soc. of Interior Designers Nat. Conf. held in Toronto 1987; Juror, ASID Human Environ. Award 1989; Steering Ctte. for Premier's Amethyst Award on barrier-free design, Ont. Office for Disabled Persons; Chairperson, resp. for renovation & refurbishing of Casey House, Toronto's first AIDS hospice; Mem., Assn. of Registered Interior Designers of Ont. (ARIDO); Profl. Mem., Interior Designers Canada (IDC); Mem., Inst. of Business Designers; co-author: 'Organization and Design: The Double Discipline' 1983; recreations: classical pianist, opera, baseball fan, biking; Home: 827 Millwood Rd., Toronto, Ont.; Office: 553 Richmond St. W., Toronto, Ont. M5V 1Y6.

**BRYM, Robert Joseph,** M.A., Ph.D.; educator; b. Saint John, N.B. 16 Aug. 1951; s. Albert and Sophie Miriam (Shulman) B.; e. Saint John High Sch. 1969; Dalhousie Univ. B.A. 1972, M.A. 1973; Hebrew Univ. of Jerusalem; Univ. of Toronto Ph.D. 1976; m. Rhonda d. John and Betty Lenton 27 Aug. 1987; children: Shira, Talia, Ariella; PROF. OF SOCIOL., UNIV. OF TORONTO 1984– ; Asst. Prof. Meml. Univ. of Nfld. 1976–78; Asst. Prof. present Univ. 1978, Assoc. Prof. 1980; Pacey Lectr. Univ. of N.B. 1991; author 'The Jewish Intelligentsia and Russian Marxism: A Sociological Study of Intellectual Radicalism and Ideological Divergence' 1978; 'Intellectuals and Politics' 1980; 'The Jews of Moscow, Kiev and Minsk: Identity, Antisemitism, Emigration' 1994; co-author 'Soviet-Jewish Emigration and Soviet Nationality Policy' 1983, Italian ed. 1985; 'From Culture to Power: The Sociology of English Canada' 1989; 'The Social Condition of Humanity' Candn. ed. 1991; ed. 'The Structure of the Canadian Capitalist Class' 1985; 'Regionalism in Canada' 1986; co-ed. 'Underdevelopment and Social Movements in Atlantic Canada' 1979; 'The Capitalist Class: An International Study' 1989; 'Soviet-Jewish Emigration and Resettlement in the 1990s' 1991; 'The Jews in Canada' 1993; Sociol. Ed. Candn. Review Sociol. & Anthrop. 1986–89; Assoc. Ed. Candn. Jour. of Sociol. 1980–86, 1989– ; Ed. Sage Studies in International Sociology 1990– ; Contbg. Ed. Viewpoints: Candn. Jewish Quarterly 1984– ; Advisory Bd. Mem., International Sociology; Ed., Current Sociology 1993– ; mem. Candn. Sociol. & Anthrop. Assn.; Internat. Sociol. Assn.; Am. Assn. for the Advancement of Slavic Studies; Candn. Friends of Peace Now (Exec. 1983–92); National Mem., Ctr. for Refugee Studies, York Univ.; Home: 70 Chaplin Cres., Toronto, Ont. M5P 1A3; Office: 5F, 203 College St., Toronto, Ont. M5T 1P9.

**BRYNELSEN, Bernard Orlando,** B.A.Sc.; mining engineer; b. Vancouver, B.C. 22 Aug. 1911; s. John and Anna (Knutsen) B.; e. Pub. and High Schs., Vancouver; Univ. of British Columbia, B.A.Sc. 1935; one yr. Geol. post-grad. work 1936; m. Eileen Manning, d. William R. Simon, Portland, Ore., 15 May 1937; one d., Karen Lorene MacGregor; Chrmn., Brenda Mines Ltd.; Forester Resources Ltd.; Chrmn., Seine River Resources Inc.; Weaco Resources Ltd.; Dir., ViceRoy Resources Corp.; and several minor mining companies; began as Field Engr., Inca Mining Corp. 1932; joined Polaris Taku Mining Co. as Mine Supt. 1936–42; Mgr., Consolidated Nicola Goldfields 1942–43; Constr. Supt., Keyes Constr. Co. 1943–45; Mgr. for B.C. with Que. Gold Mining Corp. 1945–48; West. Mgr., Noranda Exploration Co. 1948–retirement; recipient, Order of B.C.

1991; mem. Prof. Engrs. of B.C.; Candn. Inst. of Mining & Metall.; Assoc., Inst. of Mining Engrs.; Sigma Phi Delta; United Ch.; recreations: Yachting, fishing; Clubs: Royal Vancouver Yacht; Capilano Golf & Country; Terminal City; Vancouver; Home: 1962 Knox Road, University Hill, Vancouver, B.C. V6T 1S6.

**BRYSON, Neil A.,** B.Sc., M.B.A., P.Eng.; manufacturing executive; b. USA 11 July 1929; s. Akbar C. and Bethine M. (Smith) B.; e. Univ. of Sask., B.Sc. 1950; Univ. of Toronto, M.B.A. 1956; m. Olga 1953; children: Scott, Grant; PRES. & DIR., BRINKS CANADA 1990– ; Dir., Brinks Home Security; Vice-Pres., Westinghouse Canada Inc. 1977–90; Gen. Mgr., Internat. Opns.; Westinghouse Electric Corp. 1981–83; Pres., Transelectrix Technol. Inc. 1987–90; Chrmn., Toffet Investments; Pres., Wentworth Mould & Die 1990–92; Dir., Burlington Air Express; Home: 554 Deborah Cres., Burlington, Ont. L7T 2N1.

**BRZUSTOWSKI, Thomas Anthony,** B.A.Sc., A.M., Ph.D., P.Eng.; educator; b. Warsaw, Poland 4 Apr. 1937; s. Jerzy Michal and Helena (Bielicka) B.; e. N. Toronto Coll. Inst. 1954; Univ. of Toronto B.A.Sc.(Engn. Physics) 1958; Princeton Univ. A.M. 1960, Ph.D. (Aeronautical Engn.) 1963; m. Louise Marguerite d. John A. Burke, Montreal, Que. 4 Apr. 1964; three s. John Michael, Marc-André, Paul Thomas; DEPUTY MIN., THE PREMIER'S COUNC. ON ECONOMIC RENEWAL 1991– ;and THE PREMIER'S COUNCIL ON HEALTH, WELL-BEING AND SOCIAL JUSTICE 1993– ; Depy. Min. of Colleges and Universities for Ont. 1987–91; Provost & C.O.O., Univ. of Waterloo June-Oct. 1987 and teacher of Mech. Engn. there since 1962, Vice-Pres. Acad., 1975–87; Principal Consultant to Energetex Engineering 1981–87; rec'd various scholarships 1954–58 (Wallberg, APEO, McKee-Gilchrist, Avro Aircraft); Air Reduction Fellowship 1958–60; Ford Foundation Residency in Engn. Practice 1970–71; Angus Medal, Eng. Inst. of Can. 1976, 1978 and 1982; mem. Bd. of Govs. Univ. of Waterloo 1973–77; Bd. Dirs., Stratford Shakespearean Festival 1980–83; Kitchener-Waterloo Philharmonic Choir 1976–83; Chrmn., Comte. of V-P's Academic, Counc. of Ont. Univs. 1982–85; mem. Adv. Counc. for Mech. and Aerospace Engn., Princeton Univ. 1981–87 (Chrmn. 1983–87); Chmrn., Adv. Comte. on Energy, National Rsch. Counc. of Can. 1984–85; mem. Ont. Counc. Univ. Affairs 1987; Fellow, Eng. Inst. of Can.; Candn. Soc. Mech. Eng.; mem. Assn. Prof. Engrs. Prov. Ont.; R. Catholic; recreations: tennis, squash, hiking, skiing, photography; Home: 5383 Drenkelly Court, Streetsville, Ont. L5M 2H9; Office: 1 Dundas St. W., 25th Flr., Toronto, Ont. M7A 1Y7.

**BUCHANAN, Allan R.,** B.A.Sc., P.Eng.; business executive; b. Toronto, Ont. 7 Dec. 1928; s. William Benjamin and Alma Florence (Henderson) B.; e. Humberside Coll. Inst. 1948; Univ. of Toronto B.A.Sc. 1952; m. Margaret d. Fred and Mabel Proctor 3 May 1952; children: Brenda, Peter, Tina, Trudy; PRESIDENT, BUCHANAN CONSULTING 1982– ; Dir.: Norpac Corp.; Carp Systems International; Infographic Systems; joined Standard Oil (N.J.) Aruba 1952–55; Atomic Energy of Canada Ltd. Chalk River 1955–57; Vice Pres. and Gen. Mgr. Renfrew Aircraft & Engineering Ltd. Renfrew, Ont. 1957–62; Vice Pres. Operations and Asst. Gen. Mgr. Computing Devices of Canada Ltd. Ottawa 1962–69; Acting Gen. Mgr. Leigh Instruments Ltd. Carleton Place, Ont. 1969–71; Founding Pres., Pres. and C.E.O. Lumonics Inc. 1971–79, Chrmn. 1979–84; recreations: sports, photography; Club: Seabee Fish & Game; Address: 231 Grandview Rd., Nepean, Ont. K2H 8B9.

**BUCHANAN, Hon. Elmer,** B.A., M.P.P.; politician; b. Havelock, Ont. 26 Dec. 1946; s. Alex P. and Jean A. (Stevenson) B.; e. Queen's Univ. B.A. 1972; m. Gesina; children: Todd, Paul; MIN. OF AGRICULTURE, GOVT. OF ONTARIO 1993– ; first elected to Ont. Leg. (Hastings-Peterborough) g.e. 1990; Min. of Agriculture and Food 1990–93; formerly high school vice-principal; volunteer community service worker; NDP; Office: 801 Bay St., 11th Flr., Toronto, Ont. M7A 2B2.

**BUCHANAN, Hon. J. Judd,** P.C., B.A.(Econ.), M.B.A.; executive; b. Edmonton, Alta. 25 July 1929; s. the late Chief Judge Nelles Victor and late Helen (de Silva) B.; e. Univ. of Alta. B.A.(Econ.) 1953; Univ. of W. Ont. M.B.A. 1955; m. Kay Eleena d. late Harry Ezra and late Gerda (Wolff) Balfour 3 May 1952; children: Duncan Grant, Gregg Balfour, James Harry; PRES., RUNDLE INVESTMENTS LTD. 1987– ; Chrmn., Silver Star Mountain Resorts Ltd.; Chrmn., Ensign Chrysler Plymouth Ltd.; Dir. Laurentian Financial Services Inc.; Agent, London Life Insurance Co. 1957–74; mem. Bd. of Educ., London, Ont. 1966–68; M.P. for London West 1968–80; Chrmn. Ontario Liberal Caucus; Parlty. Secy., Min. of Indian Affairs and Northern Develop. 1970; Parlty. Secy., Min. of Finance 1972; Min. of Indian Affairs and Northern Develop. 1974; Min. of Public Works and Min. of State for Sci. and Tech. 1976; Pres., Treasury Bd. 1978; Defence Critic for the Opposition 1979; Chrmn. & Dir., CNG Fuel Systems 1980–87; Liberal; Chrmn., Greater Victoria Hospital Soc.; United Church; recreations: skiing, kayaking, sailing; Home: 2955 Seaview Rd., Victoria, B.C. V8N 1L2.

**BUCHANAN, Hon. John MacLennan,** P.C., Q.C., M.L.A., B.Sc., LL.B., D.Eng., LL.D., D.C.L., D.Pol.Sc.; politician; b. Sydney, N.S. 22 Apr. 1931; s. Murdoch William and Flora Isabel (Campbell) B.; e. Sydney Acad.; Mount Allison Univ. B.Sc.; Dalhousie Univ. LL.B.; D. Eng. (hon.) Tech. Univ. of N.S. 1979; D.C.L. (hon.) Mount Allison Univ. 1980; LL.D. (hon.), St. Mary's Univ. 1981; LL.D. St. Francis Xavier Univ. 1986; D.Pol.Sc., Univ. Ste. Anne 1989; m. Mavis Olive Charlotte d. Daniel Forsyth and Gertrude Barr, Bear River, N.S. 1 Sept 1954; children: Murdoch William, Travis Campbell, Nichola Ann, Natalie Flora, Natasha Heather; Premier of N.S., Pres. of Extve. Council and Chrmn. of Policy Bd. 1978–90; cr. Q.C. 1972; el. M.L.A. for Halifax Atlantic prov. g.e. 1967, re-el. since; Min. of Pub. Works and Min. of Fisheries 1969; Leader of P. Cons. Party N.S. 1971; Min. of Finance 1978–79; appointed to Privy Council 1982; Apptd. to the Senate 1990; Dir., Buchanan Soc. of Glasgow, Scotland; Freemason; P. Conservative; United Church; Clubs: City; Lions; Address: 3 Leiblin Dr., Halifax, N.S. B3R 1N2.

**BUCHANAN, William Gavin,** L.V.O., F.R.S.A.; transportation consultant; b. London, Ont. 8 June 1921; s. Edward Victor and Faith Chisholm (Turnbull) B.; e. St. George's Pub. Sch., London, Ont.; St. Andrew's Coll., Aurora, Ont.; Oxford Univ.; m. 1st Diana, d. Sir Hugo Cunliffe-Owen, 1947; 2ndly, Elizabeth F., d. D.H. Currer Briggs, Leeds, Yorkshire, 17 Oct. 1955; children: Gray, James, Victoria, Elizabeth; CHRMN., BRITISH RAILWAYS BOARD ADVISORY GROUP ON DISABILITY 1981– ; Patron, Lester B. Pearson College of the Pacific; mem. Adv. Panel on Disability, U.K. Dept. of Transport; mem. Counc., Handicapped Anglers Trust; Pres., Assn. for Spinal Injuries Rsch. & Rehab.; Patron, Internat. Spinal Rsch. Trust; served in WW II with RCA; 1st Candn. Div. Sicily, Italy; A.D.C. to Lt.-Gov. of Ont. 1947–52; Trade Advisor, Dept. of Trade & Indust. Ont., 1948–49; Maclean-Hunter Publishing Co., Toronto, 1949–57; Mgr. for E. Can., The Financial Post, Montreal, 1957–67; joined Candn. Nat. Railways as Asst. to the Pres. 1967; Gen. Mgr. 1968–78; Vice Pres., Europe 1978–81; Sch. Commr., City of Westmount, Que. 1961–63; Bd. of Govs., Selwyn House Sch., Montreal, 1963–68; Vice Chrmn., Candn. Univ. Service Overseas; 1966–67; Nat. Chrmn. for Can., Royal Commonwealth Soc., 1966–67; Depy. Chrmn., Central Council Royal Commonwealth Soc., London Eng. 1973 (Vice-Pres. 1977– ;); mem. Candn. Del. to NATO Planning Bd. for Ocean Shipping 1970–71; mem., Internat. Cargo Handling Co-ordination Assn. (Extve. Comte. 1970); Pres., Can.-UK Chamber Comm., London, Eng. 1971–72; Exec. Council Canada Club, London England, 1975–78; Chrmn., N. Amer. Comm., London Cham. of Comm. and Ind. 1978–81; Chrmn. Maple Leaf Club, London England, 1979–80; Chrmn., Prince of Wales Advisory Group on Disability 1984–91; Freeman, City of London; el. Fellow, Royal Soc. of Arts 1990; apptd. Lt., Royal Victorian Order, 1993; recreation: fly fishing; Club: Inst. of Directors (London, Eng.); Home: Black Ven Farm, Nutley, Sussex, England TN22 3EH.

**BUCHANAN, William Wills,** F.C.A.; association executive; b. Glasgow, Scot. 20 Aug. 1930; s. David and Lily Maud (Mitchell) B.; e. Glasgow Acad.; Gresham House (Kilmarnock & Beith, Scot.) 1948; m. Zora d. Stevan and Margaret George 15 Jan. 1955; four d. Fiona, Elizabeth, Sheila, Wendy; SR. VICE PRES., STUDIES & STANDARDS, CANDN. INST. OF C.A.'S 1985– ; joined Grahams, Rintoul, Hay, Bell & Co., Glasgow 1948–54; Peat, Marwick, Mitchell & Co., 1954–85, served in Vancouver, London, Ont., Winnipeg, Toronto, el. Partner 1960, Dir. of Audit Toronto Office 1975–85; Chrmn. CICA Acctg. Standards Ctte. 1974; Accts. Internat. Study Group 1974–77; Dir. and Past Chrmn., Scarborough Grace Hosp.; Mem. Adv. Bd., Performing Arts Lodges of Can.; Mem. and Past Chrmn. Adv. Bd. Salvation Army Metrop. Toronto; Past Chrmn., Pres. and Dir. CentreStage Co. Toronto, Man. Theatre Centre Winnipeg; Past Chrmn. Balmoral Hall Sch. for Girls, Winnipeg; Past Chrmn. and Pres. Un. Way of Winnipeg; mem. CICA, ICAO and Inst. C.A.'s Scot.; Am. Acctg. Assn.; Candn. Acad. Acctg. Assn.; Bd. Trade Metrop. Toronto; Rosedale United Church; recreations: travel, fitness, philately; Clubs: National; RCYC; Cambridge; Home: 57 Sherwood Ave., Toronto, Ont. M4P 2A6; Office: 277 Wellington St. W., Toronto, Ont. M5V 3H2.

**BUCHWALD, Harold,** C.M., Q.C., B.A., LL.M.; b. Winnipeg, Man. 22 Feb. 1928; s. Frank and Bessie (Portigal) B.; e. Queenston Pub. Sch., Robert H. Smith Jr. High Sch. and Kelvin High Sch., Winnipeg, 1944; Univ. of Man., B.A. 1948, LL.B. 1952, LL.M. 1957; m. Darlene Joy, d. Joseph Besbeck, Los Angeles, Cal., 5 June 1960; children: Jeffrey Joshua, Richard Dan; PARTNER, BUCHWALD, ASPER, GALLAGHER, HENTELEFF since 1970; Dir., Metropolitan Properties Corp.; CHUM (Man.) Ltd.; Chrmn. Winnipeg Adv. Bd., Montreal Trust Co.; called to Bar of Man. 1952; cr. Q.C. 1966; Lectr. on Co. Law, Man. Law Sch., 1957–61; Sessional Lectr. on Consumer Protection, Faculty of Law, Univ. of Man. 1969–78; First James L. Lewtas Visiting Professor, Osgoode Hall Law School, York Univ., Toronto 1977; Visiting Research Fellow, Inst. for Legisl. Research and Comparative Law, Hebrew Univ. of Jerusalem 1978; Hon. Fellow of the Hebrew Univ.; Special Counsel to Man. Govt. on Consumer Protection Matters, 1965–70; Bd. Chrmn., Candn. Scholarship Trust Found. 1986–88; Bd. Chrmn., Candn. Scholarship Trust Consultants, Inc. 1988–90; Chrmn., Candn. Consumer Council 1971–73; Pres., Jewish Found. of Man. 1987–91; Pres., Candn. Club of Winnipeg 1990–91; Extve. mem., Winnipeg 2000 Leaders Ctte. 1990– ; Bd. mem and Chrmn. Ethics Ctte., Winnipeg Health Sciences Centre 1989– ; Chrmn. Host Ctte., 7th Internat. Winter Cities Winnipeg 1996; Nat. Chrmn., Can.-Israel Comte. 1979–83; Pres., Winnipeg Symphony Orchestra 1984–86; mem., Nat. Bd., Candn. Council of Christians and Jews 1982–91; Bd. Chrmn., Winnipeg Health Sciences Centre Found. 1989–92; Gen. Campaign Chrmn., Combined Jewish Appeal of Winnipeg 1980; Pres. Law Society of Manitoba 1975–76; Gov. Canadian Tax Foundation 1973–76; mem. Bd. of Govs., Hebrew Univ. of Jerusalem; Pres., Winnipeg Chapter, Candn. Friends of Hebrew Univ. 1969–77, Hon. Pres. 1993– ; Chrmn., Adv. Bd., B'nai Brith Hillel Foundation, Univ. of Man., 1953–56; Chrmn., B'nai Brith Camp Bd., 1960–63; Pres. 1974–76 and Gov., YMHA Community Centre, Winnipeg; Dir., Winnipeg Football Club 1966–70; Dir., Winnipeg Symphony Orchestra 1966–68 (Hon. Solr. 1967–68); Dir., Rainbow Stage, Inc. 1966–68; author 'Administration & the Carter Report' 1967; co-author 'Farmers & the White Paper on Tax Reform' 1970; author of weekly column 'The Tax Corner,' Toronto 'Globe & Mail Report on Business' 1966–68; Contrib. Ed., Can. Business Law Journ.; other writings incl. articles and papers for various publs.; mem. Law Soc. Man. (Pres. 1975–76; Life Bencher); Man. Bar. Assn. (Pres. 1970–71); Candn. Bar Assn. (Nat. Chrmn., Taxation Sec. 1970–71 and Pub. Relations Comte. 1965–67); Nat. Jt. Comte. of Candn. Bar Assn. & Candn. Inst. C.A.'s on Tax Matters (Co-Chrmn. 1970–71); Sigma Alpha Mu (Pres. Sigma Xi 1947–48; Regional Gov. 1956–58); Freemason; Jewish; recreations: golf, cross-country skiing, spectator sports; Home: 411 Park Blvd. N., Winnipeg, Man. R3P 0H1; Office: 2500 – 360 Main St., Winnipeg, Man. R3C 4H6.

**BUCHWALD, Manuel,** O.C., A.B., Ph.D.; scientist/university professor; b. Lima, Peru 7 June 1940; s. Theo and Eva (Schneider) B.; e. Franklin D. Roosevelt H.S. 1957; Dartmouth Coll., A.B. 1972; Brandeis Univ., Ph.D. 1967; m. Cheryl d. Ralph and Isabelle Cowan 7 Sept 1985; SENIOR SCIENTIST, RESEARCH INSTITUTE, HOSP. FOR SICK CHILDREN 1970– , Associate Dir. 1982–91; PROF., UNIV. OF TORONTO 1986– ; Staff Geneticist, H.S.C. 1971– ; Asst. Prof., Univ. of Toronto 1973–77; Assoc. Prof. 1977–86; Acting Dir. 1986–87; Vis. Sci., Univ. of Calif. 1978–79; Inst. Pasteur, Paris, France 1993; Mem., Premier's Counc. on Health, Well-being and Social Justice, Prov. of Ont. 1991– ; Chrmn. & Mem., Rsch. Adv. Ctte., Candn. Cystic Fibrosis Found. 1985–91; Panel on Awards to For. Nats., Candn. Min. of External Affairs 1982–85; Officer, Order of Canada 1991; Commemorative Medal, 125th Anniversary of Candn. Confedn. 1992; Fanconi Anemia Award of Merit 1992; Phi Beta Kappa 1961; A.B. summa cum laude 1962; 10–year serv. pin, Ont. Min. of Citizenship & Culture 1990; Bd. Mem., Toronto East End Literacy 1980–91 (Pres. 1981–87; Treas. 1989–90); Sec., Ctr. for Spanish Speaking Peoples 1976–78; Chrmn., Subctte. on Restoration of Ravine Lands, City of Toronto 1972–74; Mem., Candn. Genetics Soc.; Am. Soc. of Human Genetics; author & co-author of over 100 sci. papers; co-author: 'Foxes and Watercress' 1972; recreations: thoroughbred racing; Home: 15 Dearbourne Ave., Toronto, Ont. M4K 1M6; Office: 555 University Ave., Toronto, Ont. M5G 1X8.

**BUCK, Carol,** M.D., Ph.D., D.P.H., F.A.C.E., F.R.S.C., LL.D.; professor emerita; b. London, Ont. 2 Apr. 1925; d. Albert Henry and Evelyn Florence (Parsons) Whitlow; e. Univ. of W. Ont., M.D. 1947, Ph.D. 1950; London Sch. of Hygiene & Tropical Med., D.P.H. 1951; Dalhousie Univ., LL.D.; m. Robert Crawforth Buck, 1946; two d., Lucy Anne, Effie Louise; PROFESSOR EMERITA 1990– ; Prof., Dept. of Epidemiology & Biostatistics, Univ. of W. Ont. 1978–90; Rockefeller Fellow, Dept. of Epidemiol. and Med. Stat., London Sch. of Hygiene and Tropical Med., 1951–52; Asst. Prof., Dept. of Psychiatry and Preventive Med., Univ. of W. Ont., 1952–56; Assoc. Prof. 1956–62; Prof. of Preventive Med. 1962–66; Prof. & Chrmn., Dept. of Community Medicine 1967–72; Prof. and Chrmn., Dept. of Epidemiol. & Prev. Medicine 1972–77; mem. Science Council of Can., 1970–73; mem., Candn. Pub. Health Assn.; Canadian Assn. Teachers of Soc. and Preventive Med.; Society for Epidemiologic Research; Pres., Internat. Epidemiol. Assn. 1981–84; Club: University; Home: 181 Elmwood Ave., London, Ont. N6C 1K1.

**BUCK, Robert John,** B.A., M.A., Ph.D.; emeritus professor; b. Vermilion, Alta. 5 July 1926; s. Frank Jackson and Katherine Elizabeth (MacKinnon) B.; e. Univ. of Alberta B.A. 1949; Univ. of Kentucky M.A. 1950; Univ. of Cincinnati Ph.D. 1956; m. Helen d. Sideris Vasiliou 31 July 1955; children: George H., Zoe E.; PROF. EMERITUS OF CLASSICS, UNIVERSITY OF ALBERTA 1991– ; Asst. Prof. Univ. of Kentucky 1955–60; Assoc. Prof. Univ. of Alberta 1960–66; Prof. of Classics 1966–91; Head of Dept. of Classics 1964–72; served with RCAF 1944–45; author 'History of Boeotia' 1979; 30 articles and monographs on topics in Greek Hist., Greek and Roman archaeology; Fellow of the Candn. Inst. in Rome 1976; mem., Managing Comte. Am. Sch. of Classical Studies, Athens 1961–83; Bd. of Dir. Candn. Mediterranean Inst. 1979–85, Vice Pres. (Greece) 1982–85; Past Vice Pres. Candn. Archaeological Inst. at Athens 1973–79; of Classical Assn. of Can. 1970–73 (Pres. 1986–88); Kappa Sigma; N.D.P.; Anglican; Clubs: Faculty, Univ. of Alta.; recreations: skiing, model railroading; Home: 11752 University Ave., Edmonton, Alta. T6G 1Z5; Office: University of Alberta, Edmonton, Alta. T6G 2E5.

**BUCKAWAY, Catherine Margaret;** writer; b. North Battleford, Sask. 7 July 1919; d. Alfred Edward and Margaret (Hall) Wyatt; m. 1 Apl. 1941; widow; two d. Scarlett Anne Block, Judith Mae Rioch; author 'The Prairie Rose Story' hist. 1960; 'Strangely the Birds Have Come' 1973; 'Air 17' 1973; 'Bryte' 19..; 'The Silver Cuckoo' 1974; 'The Lavender Nightingale' 1978; 'Alfred, The Dragon Who Lost His Flame' 1982; 'Charlotte' hist. 1976; 'Waiting for George' 1985; 'Blue Windows' 1988; 'Stardust Chapbook' 1989; 'Riding Into Morning' 1989; 'The Sudden Forgiveness' (chapbook) 1990; 'Dinosaurs Have Feelings Too' (chapbook) 1991; recipient First California Bank & Yuku Haru Award First Place Can., USA and Japan for Haiku 1978; Can. Council Grant Asian Lit. 1971; Carling Community Arts Found. 1972; Grant Japanese Poet Culture; 2 Sask. Arts Bd. Grants Asia Lit. 1973, 1979; Kinsman Found. Grant 1985; Don McIntosh Award 1985; 3,547 poems published to date 1993; work published in 50 countries; rep. Univ. of Sask. Archives, Museum of Haiku Lit. Tokyo (250 Haiku), Glenbow Found. and other book colls.; mem. League Candn. Poets; Sask. Writers Guild; Address: Porteous Lodge, 833 Avenue PN, Saskatoon, Sask. S7L 2W5.

**BUCKEE, James W.,** B.Sc., D.Phil.; petroleum executive; b. Winchester, England 24 March 1946; s. Edgar and Margaret Amy (Thomas) B.; e. Univ. of Western Australia B.Sc. (Hons.) 1967; Oxford Univ. D.Phil. 1970; m. Susan d. Brigadier Dennis and Jill O'Flaherty 3 Sept. 1971; children: Clare, Fiona, Caroline, Alice; PRESIDENT & CHIEF EXECUTIVE OFFICER, TALISMAN ENERGY INC. 1991– ; Chief Reservoir Engineer, BP Exploration 1983–87; Operations Manager with Brit. Petroleum in Norway 1987–88; Vice-Pres., Development Programs, BP Alaska 1988–89; Manager, Planning, BP Exploration, London 1989–91; Home: 240 – 40th Ave. S.W., Calgary, Alta. T2S 0X3; Office: Suite 2400 – 855 2nd St. S.W., Calgary, Alta. T2P 4J9.

**BUCKINGHAM, Robin,** B.A.; insurance executive; b. Toronto; e. Laurentian Univ. B.A. 1978; SENIOR VICE PRESIDENT, HUMAN RESOURCES, THE CUMIS GROUP LIMITED 1993– ; Vice President, Personnel Administation, National Life Assurance co. of Canada 1981–93; Bd. of Dir., Life Insurance Inst. of Canada 1989; Office: 151 North Service Rd., Burlington, Ont. L7R 4C2.

**BUCKLAND, Charles Smillie,** B.Com.; electrical manufacturing executive; b. Sherbrooke, Que. 3 March 1934; s. Charles Percy and Clara Louise (Smillie) B.; e. Sir George Williams Univ. B.Com. 1961; m. Jane d. David and Dorothy Turnbull 20 June 1962; two s. Brett, Darin; PRES., HOLOPHANE CANADA INC. 1981– ; Dist. Sales Mgr. Holophane Div. present Co. 1972, Nat. Sales Mgr. 1973, Pres. 1981; Dir. Rosseau Lake Coll. 1982–87; Dir. P.R.M. Associates; Dir. 397222 Ontario Ltd.; Dir. 498070 Alberta Ltd.; Dir. Elect. & Electronic Mfg. Assn.; mem. Illuminating Eng. Soc.; Protestant; recreations: flying, tennis, golf, squash, skiing; Clubs: Brampton Golf; Mississauga Golf & Country; Home: 49 Pinewood Trail, Mississauga, Ont. L5G 2L2; Office: 1620 Steeles Ave., Brampton, Ont. L6T 1A5.

**BUCKLAND, George Russell,** B.A.; business executive; b. Ottawa, Ont. 4 March 1940; s. George Henry and Mollie Elizabeth (Russell) B.; e. Carleton Univ. B.A. 1963; Univ. of Ottawa 1964; Univ. of Western Ont. mngt. training course 1981; m. Sonja d. Axel and Margaret Pedersen 21 Dec. 1963; children: Erik, Krista, Karin; MANAGING PARTNER, BEDFORD CONSULTING GROUP 1988– ; Asst. Vice-Pres. & Manager, Human Resources, Falconbridge Ltd. 1970–82; Vice-Pres., Kidd Creek Mines Ltd. 1984–86; Vice Pres., Saint John Shipbuilding Ltd. 1986–87; Vice Pres., Curragh Resources 1987–88; Mem., CIMM, AIME, IACPR; awarded Hogan Medal, Carleton Univ. 1963; Pres. Sudbury YMCA 1976–80; recreations: golf, squash, sailing; clubs: Royal Candn. Yacht; Home: 1351 Falgarwood Dr., Oakville, Ont. L6H 2P4; Office: Suite 305, 162 Cumberland St., Toronto, Ont. M5R 3N5.

**BUCKLEY, Helen Lawrence,** B.A.; economist, writer; b. Winnipeg, Man. 3 Feb. 1923; d. David Campbell and Mildred Helen (Kelly) Aikenhead; e. Univ. of Man. B.A. 1943; Univ. of Sask. B.A. (Hons.) 1946; m. Kenneth s. Helen and Jesse Buckley 1945; children: Margaret (Marg), Ruth, Carol; FREELANCE CONSULTING ECONOMIST 1982– ; Jr. Econ., Wartime Prices Bd. 1943–45; Economist, Ctr. for Community Studies Sask. 1962–67; Statistics Canada, Chief Rsch. Labour Div. 1967–72; Dept. of Manpower & Immigration, Chief Rsch. Div. 1972–77; Analyst, Reg. Div., Dept. of Finance 1977–82; Writer (rsch. & writing on Indian policy) 1988–92; Mem., National Council of Women (Economics Chair 1993–94); author: 'From Wooden Ploughs to Welfare: Why Indian Policy Failed in the Prairie Provinces' 1992, 'Trapping & Fishing in Northern Saskatchewan' 1962 and numerous fed. govt. studies; co-author: 'Economics for Canadians' 1960, 'The Indians and Metis of Northern Saskatchewan' 1963, 'Canadian Policies for Rural Adjustment' 1967; recreations: walking, travel, gardening; Address: 3 Leonard Ave., Ottawa, Ont. K1S 4T6.

**BUCKLEY, Jerome Hamilton,** A.M., Ph.D. university professor; literary historian; b. Toronto, Ont. 30 Aug. 1917; s. late James Ora and Madeline Isabelle (Morgan) B.; e. Victoria Coll., Univ. of Toronto, B.A. 1939; Harvard Univ., A.M. 1940, Ph.D. 1942; m. Elizabeth Jane, d. late John Alexander Adams, 19 June 1943; children: Nicholas, Victoria, Eleanor; GURNEY PROF. OF ENG. LIT. EMERITUS, HARVARD UNIV. 1987– ; Instr. to Prof. of Eng., Univ. of Wisc., 1942–54; Prof. of Eng., Columbia Univ., 1954–61; Prof. of English, Harvard Univ. 1961–75; Gurney Prof. of Eng. Lit., Harvard Univ. 1975–87; Guggenheim Fellow 1946–47 and 1964; rec'd Christian Gaus Award 1952; Am. Philos. Soc. Grant 1956; Neesima Lectr., Doshisha Univ. (Kyoto, Japan) 1989; author: 'William Ernest Henley' 1945; 'The Victorian Temper' 1st publ. 1951; 'Tennyson: The Growth of A Poet' 1st publ. 1960; 'The Triumph of Time' 1966; Ed.: 'Poetry of the Victorian Period' 1965; 'Poems of Tennyson' 1959; 'Masters of British Literature' 1962; 'The Pre-Raphaelites' 1968; 'Victorian Poets and Prose Writers' (bibliog.) 1977; 'David Copperfield' 1990; author 'Season of Youth: From Dickens to Golding' 1974; Ed. 'The Worlds of Victorian Fiction' 1975; author 'The Turning Key: Autobiography and the Subjective Impulse' 1984; mem., Modern Lang. Assn. (Ed. Bd. 1963–68); American Academy of Arts and Sciences; Tennyson Soc. (Vice Pres.); Internat. Assn. Univ. Profs. Eng.; Browning Soc.; Fellow, Huntington Library 1978; mem. Chancellor's Counc., Victoria Univ., Toronto 1984– ; Hon. mem., Phi Beta Kappa 1987; Democratic; Anglican; recreation: travel; Home: 191 Common St., Belmont, Mass. 02178; Office: Widener Library 245, Cambridge, Mass. 02138.

**BUCKLEY, John O.,** B.Comm., C.A.; financial executive; b. 1946; e. Mount Allison Univ. B.Comm. 1969; m.; 3 children; PARTNER, BUCKLEY & NIXON 1974– ; articled with Thorne Riddell, C.A. 1971; Chief Accountant, Baxter Dairies (1961) Ltd.; 1972–73; Office: P.O. Box 1319, Sussex, N.B. E0E 1P0.

**BUCKLEY, Peter Cregan;** news editor; b. Montreal, Que. 25 Oct. 1933; s. George Edward and Ada Elizabeth (Tylee) B.; e. Thomas D'Arcy McGee H.S. 1950; Univ. of Toronto, Southam Fellow 1969–70; Georgetown Univ., advanced French 1973–74; SUPERVISING EDITOR, THE CANADIAN PRESS 1989– ; Messenger, Canadian Press (Montreal) June 1950; Edit. staff mem. Oct. 1950; Que. 1954–56; Vancouver 1956–60; Toronto 1960–65 (excl. 12 mos. spent in Congo and Cyprus); London, Engl. 1965–67; Moscow 1967–69; Washington 1970–75; Depy. Bureau Chief, Montreal 1975–79; General News Editor, Toronto 1979–89; Editor, CP Stylebook 1992; foreign reporting citation, Natl. Newspaper Awards 1987; Lectr., Concordia Univ. 1976–77; R. Catholic; mem., Candn. War Correspondents Assn.; recreations: skiing, walking; Home: 390 Wellesley St. E., #1, Toronto, Ont. M4X 1H6; Office: 36 King St. E., Toronto, Ont. M5C 2L9.

**BUCKLEY, William Peter,** B.A.Sc., M.B.A., A.M.P.; business executive; b. Montreal, Que. 30 Nov. 1948; s. William Barron and Mary Phyllis (O'Gorman) B.; e. Univ. of Toronto, B.A.Sc. 1971; York Univ., M.B.A. 1981; Harvard Bus. Sch., A.M.P. 1986; m. Anne d. James and Jessie MacDougall 4 Aug. 1978; one d.: Laura Anne; PRES., BURNDY CANADA INC. (resp. for Canada & Australia) 1989– ; Engineering trainee, present firm 1971; Sales Mgr., Electronics Div. 1974; Gen. Mgr., Elect. Div. 1979; Vice-Pres. & Gen. Mgr. 1985; Former Candn. Champion Sailing, Catamaran Div.; Former Candn. Champion & Bronze Medallist, Bicycle Racing; Ont. team mem. for both sports; mem., Assn. of Profl. Engrs. of Ont.; The Harvard Club; Toronto Bd. of Trade; The Toronto Electric Club; Mem. Bd., Electrical & Electronics Mfg. Assn. of Can. (EEMAC); Mem. Bd., Candn. Electrical Distributors Assn. (CEDA); recreations: sailing, skiing; club: The Peaks; Home 2 Red Oaks Cr., Toronto, Ont. M4G 1A5; Office: 1530 Birchmount Rd., Scarborough, Ont. M1P 2G9.

**BUCKWOLD, Hon. Sidney,** B.Com.; senator; wholesaler; b. Winnipeg, Man. 3 Nov. 1916; s. Harry and Dorothy (Freedman) B.; e. McGill Univ., B.Com. 1936; LL.D (Honoris causa) Univ. of Sask. 1982; m. Clarice, d. Samuel Rabinovitch, 17 Sept. 1939; children: Jay Murray, Judith Miriam, Linda Ruth; Pres. and Gen. Mgr., Buckwold's Ltd. (joined Co. in 1936); Chrmn., Senate Banking, Trade and Commerce Ctte.; served in 2nd World War, R.C.A.S.C. 1942–45; Hon. Col. North Sask. Reg. 1972–88; Mayor of Saskatoon, Sask. 1958–63 and 1967–71; summoned to Senate of Can., Nov. 1971; Freemason; Jewish; Liberal; recreation: golf; Clubs: Saskatoon; Riverside Golf & Country; Home: 1101 - 730 Spadina Cres. E., Saskatoon, Sask. S7K 4H7; Offices: 75 - 24th St., Saskatoon, Sask. S7K 0K3.

**BUDD, John S.,** B.Comm., F.C.A.; chartered accountant; b. Toronto, Ont. 8 July 1945; e. Univ. of Toronto B.Comm. 1967; m. Susan Anne Dundas; children: Michael, Steven, Christopher; PARTNER, DELOITTE & TOUCHE 1979– ; tax specialist since 1970; frequent lecturer at tax courses, seminars & conferences; Mem., Toronto Estate Planning Council 1979– ; Ont. Inst. of C.A.s; C.A. 1970; F.C.A. 1991; author: 'Second Property Strategies – Take Advantage of the $100,000 Tax Exemption While You Can' 1992; co-author and instructor of several CICA tax courses; co-editor: 'Goodman on Estate Planning' and 'Canadian Guide to Personal Financial Management' 1993; Office: 181 Bay St., Ste. 1400, Toronto, Ont. M5J 2V1.

**BUDD, Ruth June;** musician; b. Winnipeg, Man. 20 June 1924; e. high sch. Winnipeg; B.C. Sch. of Pharmacy & Sci.; Toronto Conserv. of Music; Univ. of Toronto Fac. of Music; children: Gillian, Kevin; studied mandolin at 6 yrs., violin and piano; played string bass in high sch. orchestra, continued playing and studying bass in Vancouver joining Vancouver Jr. Symphony and subsequently Vancouver Symphony; toured from Vancouver to Winnipeg with all-girl band; joined Toronto Symphony Orchestra as first woman bass player 1947; mem. Symphony Six 1952; mem. CBC Symphony 10 yrs., Stratford Festival Orchestra 10 yrs.; Princ. Bass with Halifax Symphony Orchestra; invited to return to the Toronto Symphony 1964, retired 1989; Asst. Princ. Bass, Okanagan Symphony 1991–92; Vancouver Opera Company 1992 and 1993; numerous cross-country childrens concerts in groups and as soloist; solo bassist, Hart House Orch. (Boyd Neal, conductor); named Woman of Distinction (Arts Category) 1983 by YWCA (Toronto); founding Chrmn. Organ. of Candn. Symphony Musicians (OCSM); mem. Performing Artists for Nuclear Disarmament; Founder, Toronto Senior

Strings 1993; Home: 407 St. Clair Ave. E., Toronto, Ont. M4T 1P6.

**BUDDLE, Harold William (Harry),** C.A., M.B.A.; banker; b. Hamilton, Ont. 25 July 1940; s. Frederick and Ena Buddle; e. C.A. Ont. 1964; Simon Fraser Univ. M.B.A. 1987; m. Judy d. Rose and Leon Hudecki 31 Aug. 1963; children: Peter, Kathleen, Paul, Matthew, Andrew, Stephanie, Michael, Christina, Sarah; CHIEF EXECUTIVE OFFICER, CAPITAL CITY SAVINGS 1987– ; Dir., Ethical Funds Inc.; Ethical Funds Investment Services Inc.; Co-op Press Ltd.; article C.A., MacGillivray & Co., Grier Dyer & Co. 1959–64; Mgr., Del Monte Corp., Nabisco 1964–69; Sperry Univac, Unisys Corp. 1969–78; Vice Pres., B.C. Central Credit Union 1978–83; Credit Union Deposit Insur. Corp. of B.C. 1985–87; Mem. Adv. Counc., Economic Development Edmonton; Chrmn., Cudata Adv. Ctte., Credit Union Central, Alberta; Dir., Newman Coll. and St. Joseph's Seminary Found.; recreations: flying, jogging; clubs: Derrick Golf; Edmonton Downtown Rotary; Edmonton; Edmonton Alberta; Office: 8723 – 82 Avenue, Edmonton, Alta. T6C 0Y9.

**BUDOVITCH, Judith Chernin,** B.A., B.Ed., LL.B.; lawyer; b. Sydney, N.S. 9 Sept. 1947; d. Mendle and Etta (Gaum) Chernin; e. Dalhousie Univ. B.A. 1969; Univ. of N.B. B.Ed. 1970, LL.B. 1975; m. Arnold Richard s. Frank and Daisy Budovitch 29 June 1969; two s. Eric Louis, Paul Ross; LEGAL ADM. RESIDENTIAL TENANCIES PROG. DEPT. OF JUSTICE N.B. 1983– , Adm. Rent Review Act; law practice and Lectr. in Comm. Law, Ludlow Hall Law Sch., Univ. of N.B. 1975–81; mem. Pay Equity Ctte., Prov. N.B.; Chrmn. Bd. Govs., Beaverbrook Art Gallery; mem. Bd. of Govs., Mount St. Vincent Univ., Halifax, N.S.; mem. Alumni Council Univ. of N.B.; Hon. mem. Delta Theta Phi 1985; Dir. Atlantic Jewish Council; Un. Israel Appeal Can.; Past Dir. Fredericton Found.; Fredericton YM-YWCA; Home: 28 Alexandra St., Fredericton, N.B. E3B 1Y4; Office: 300 St. Mary's St., Fredericton, N.B. E3B 5H1.

**BUDRA, Paul Vincent,** B.A., M.A., Ph.D.; university professor; b. Toronto, Ont. 3 July 1957; s. Victor John and Gay Ingrid (Laurinavicius) B.; e. Riverdale C.I. 1975; Univ. of Toronto B.A. 1979, M.A. 1980, Ph.D. 1987; m. Karen d. Rolf and Marlene Yri 4 Aug. 1984; two s.: John Christian, Max David; ASST. PROF., DEPT. OF ENGLISH, SIMON FRASER UNIV. 1989– ; Communications Instr., Humber College 1985–86; Teaching Master, English & Media Studies, Centennial Coll. 1987–89; Lectr., English, Univ. of Toronto 1987–89; extensive freelance journalism; some screenwriting (film & TV); has worked as a professional comedian; Sr. Fellow, Ctr. for Reformation & Renaissance Studies, Univ. of Toronto 1987–88; author of trade journal & academic articles as well as conf. papers; received considerable media attention over public lecture entitled: 'Submission Hold: The Sexual Politics of Professional Wrestling'; recreations: popular culture, cooking, guitar; Home: 1891 Duchess Ave., West Vancouver, B.C. V7V 1R2; Office: Burnaby, B.C. V5A 1S6.

**BUDREVICS, Alexander,** F.C.S.L.A., F.A.S.L.A.; landscape architect; b. Riga, Latvia 3 Jan. 1925; s. Alfreds and Adele (Martinovs) b.; e. State Horticultural Sch. 1944; St. Alban's Sch. of Art 1949; London Coll. of Art 1951; m. Milija d. Roberts Vite 8 April 1948; children: Valdis, Dace, Arnis; PRES., ALEXANDER BUDREVICS & ASSOC. LTD. 1965– ; prac. landscape archit., Latvia, Germany, Belgium, England; emigrated to Can. 1952, worked as landscape archit., var. firms; designed over 3000 projects incl. Nat. Home Show 1958– , CNE horticult. shows and Century Square; num. awards for design excellence; Partner, Golf Course Devel. Assoc.; Fellow, Candn. and Am. Socs. of Landscape Archits.; Am. Inst. of Landscape Archits. (Past Pres.); Life Mem., Candn. Soc. of Landscape Archits; Trustee, Helen M. Kippax Meml. Scholarship Fund; Pres., Candn. Latvian Bus. & Profl. Assn. 1971– ; Chrmn., Extve. Bd., Latvian Boy Scouts Assn. 1982– ; Pres., Latvian National Fedn. Gen. Assembly in Can.; Past Pres., 'Kristus Darzs' Home for the Aged; Past Pres. of num. assns.; author: num. profl. articles; recreations: gardening, travel, golf; Clubs: Bd. of Trade; The Empire Club of Can.; Home: 123 Overland Dr., Don Mills, Ont. M3C 2C7; Office: Two Park Centre, 895 Don Mills Rd., Suite 808, Don Mills, Ont. M3C 1W3.

**BUELL, Thomas Allan,** B.Sc.F.; executive; b. Toronto, Ont. 14 Nov. 1931; s. Allan F. and Jessie L. (Stayner) B.; e. Univ. of Toronto B.Sc.F. 1956; m. Phyllis Lee 27 Aug. 1955; children: Elizabeth, Christopher, Michael, Robert; CHRMN., WELDWOOD OF CANADA LTD. 1979– ; Dir., Placer Dome Inc.; B.C. Gas Inc.; Swiss Bank Corp. (Can.); Mayne Nickless Canada Inc.; Lafarge Corporation; joined Kimberley Clark Corp. 1956–61; Mng. Dir. Hardply Corp. Ltd. 1961–64; Mgr. Ash St. Plant present Co. 1964; Gen. Mgr. W. Coast Mfg. 1968, Vice Pres. Mfg. 1971, Dir. 1974, Pres. & C.E.O. 1975–92, Chrmn. 1979– ; Chrmn., Candn. Forest Industries Council; Co-Chrmn., Western Wood Products Forum; Mem., Forest Sector Advisory Council (Adv. Ctte. to Fed. Govt.); Dir., Kaiser Youth Foundation; Mem. Citizens Bd., Forest Alliance of B.C.; Mem., Adv. Counc., Fac. of Comm. & Bus. Admin., Univ. of B.C.; Chrmn., Dean's Adv. Council, Faculty of Forestry, Univ. of B.C.; Chrmn., Wildlife Habitat Canada; recreations: sailing, fishing; Clubs: Royal Vancouver Yacht; Vancouver; Home: 486 Tsawwassen Beach Rd., Delta, B.C. V4M 2J2; Office: PO Box 2179, 1055 W. Hastings St., Vancouver, B.C. V6B 3V8.

**BUFFIE, Margaret,** B.F.A.; writer; b. Winnipeg, Man. 29 March 1945; d. Ernest William John and the late Evelyn Elizabeth (Leach) B.; e. various Winnipeg pub. and high schs.; Univ. of Man. B.F.A. 1967, Cert. of Edn. 1976; m. James s. James and Barbara Macfarlane 9 Aug. 1968; one d. Christine Anne; Illustrator, Hudsons Bay Co. 1968–70; Drawing & Painting Instr. Winnipeg Art Gallery, Adult Instr. Winter Progs. 1974–75; High Sch. Art Instr. River East Sch. Div. 1976–77; freelance illustrator and painter to 1985; Univ. of Winnipeg, Cont. Ed. Instr., Creative Writing 1993; author: 'Who Is Frances Rain' young adult novel 1987; 'The Guardian Circle' young adult novel 1989; 'My Mother's Ghost' young adult novel 1992; recipient Young Adult Candn. Book Award 1988; First Runner-up Candn. Lib. Assn. Book of Yr. Award 1988; shortlisted Ruth Schwartz Children's Book Award 1988–89, 1993–94; Notable Candn. Fiction List 1989, 1993; ALA Best Books of the Year List 1990; Internat. Youth Library Notable Young Adult Book 1991; chosen Candn. Children's Book Centre's Our Choice/Your Choice 1988–93 Catalogues; nominated for Gov. Gen.'s Award 1992; The Candn. Lib. Assn. Book of the Year 1993; Mr. Christie's Book Award 1993; Manitoba Book of the Year 1993; Ont. Arts Council Grant 1987, 1989, 1990, 1993; mem. Candn. Authors Assn.; Candn. Soc. Children's Authors, Illustrators & Performers; Candn. Children's Book Centre; Man. Writers Guild; Writers Union of Can.; IBBY (Internat. Bd. on Books for Young People - Canada); recreations: canoeing, birding, reading, cooking; Home: 165 Grandview St., Winnipeg, Man. R2G 0L4.

**BUGG, William John Franklin,** M.D., C.R.C.S.(C)., M.H.A.; b. Wingham, Ont. 25 Jan. 1912; s. James Herbert and Margaret Nielen (Galbraith) B.; e. Central Coll. Inst. London, Ont. 1932; Univ. of W. Ont. M.D. 1938; Candn. Hosp. Assn. Mang. Course 1954; Inter Agency Inst. for Hosp. Adms. Washington 1964; m. Blanche Mary d. Donat Godin 16 June 1942; children: Judith, William, James, Stephen; Hosp. Director, Westminster Hosp. D.V.A. London 1966–74; former Asst. to Asst. Depy. Min. Veterans Affairs Ottawa; mem. Senate, Univ. of W. Ont. 1968–71; served with R.C.A.M.C. Can. and Overseas World War II, rank Capt.; rec'd Centennial Medal 1967; Candn. Red Cross Citation; Chrmn. and Founding mem. London & Dist. Health Assn.; mem. Royal Candn. Legion (Extve.); recreations: hunting, fishing, amateur radio; Address: R.R. 1, Morpeth, Ont. N0P 1X0.

**BUHASZ, Laszlo Janos Sebastian,** B.A.; journalist; b. Budapest, Hungary 27 March 1949; s. Leslie and Julianna (Terhes) B.; e. Univ. of Calgary, B.A. 1970; Univ. of W. Ont., Dip. in Journalism 1971; m. Suzanne d. Erle and Marjorie Dyer 23 Aug. 1986; children: Angela Marie, Jason Sebastian; TRAVEL EDITOR, THE GLOBE & MAIL 1991– , Exec. Ed. 1987–91; Reporter, The Albertan 1971–73; Bus. Ed. 1973–74; Managing Ed. 1974–79; Sr. Ed., Globe & Mail 1979–81; Asst. Managing Ed. 1981–83; Asst. Ed. 1983–87; mem. Adv. Bd. & Instr., Mt. Royal Coll. Journalism Sch. 1977–78; mem. Ed. Ctte., Candn. Daily Newspaper Pubs. Assn.; Assoc. Press Managing Eds. 1983; mem. Ont. Press Counc. 1986–91; Commonwealth Journalists Assn.; recreations: swimming, squash, badminton; Home: R.R. #1, Oro Stn., Ont. L0L 2E0; Office: 444 Front St. W., Toronto, Ont. M5V 2S9.

**BUHLER, Alfred P.,** B.A.; financial executive; b. Palo Alto, Calif. 27 May 1940; s. Jacob A. and Mildred (Renfrow) B.; e. Marguerite L. 28 May 1965; e. Calif. State Univ. B.A. 1963; moved to Canada 1991; PRESIDENT & CHIEF EXECUTIVE OFFICER, BANK OF AMERICA CANADA 1992– ; various assignments in Argentina, Bolivia, Dominican Rep., Guatemala, Miami, Panama, Paraguay, Peru, Philippines, St. Croix, Venezuela, Bank of America 1965–86; Head of Division Credit Admin., Europe, Middle East & Africa, London 1986–87; Country Credit Mgr., Madrid, Spain, 1987–91; Sr. Credit Officer, Bank of America Canada Toronto 1991–92; Dir., Bank of America Canada Leasing Corp.; Bank of America Canada Securities Corp.; Bank of America Canada; Mem., Candn. American Ctte.; The Candn. Council for the Americas; recreations: golfing, hiking, art history; clubs: The National, The National Golf; languages: English, Spanish; Office: 4 King St. W., 18th Floor, Toronto, Ont. M5H 1B6.

**BUHR, Glenn A.,** B. Mus., M. Mus., A.Mus.D.; composer; b. Winnipeg, Man. 18 Dc. 1954; s. Glen D. and Glenda P. (Hamm) B.; e. Univ. of Man., B.Mus. 1979; Univ. of B.C., M.Mus. 1981; Univ. of Mich., A.Mus.D. 1984; m. Bonnie d. James and Kathleen Highlands 16 Feb. 1974; children; Jennifer, Erin, Stephen, Nicholas; ASSOC. PROF., MUSIC COMP., WILFRID LAURIER UNIV. 1984– ; Composer-in-Residence, Winnipeg Symphony Orch. 1990– ; recent perfs.: 'Ecstasy' St. Louis Symphony 1989; Double concerto, Toronto Symphony Orch. 1992; Trumpet concerto, Montreal Symphony Orch. 1992; Piano concerto, Louis Lortie and the Winnipeg Symphony Orch. 1992; Recordings: Glenn Buhr, Songs; Akasha - orchestral works; Pro Loco Corciano Comp. Prize 1985; 1st Prize Am. Harp Assoc. 1986; Mem. & Assoc. Comp., Candn. Music Ctr.; composer: 'Lure of the Fallen Seraphim' for orchestra 1987; 'The Cycle for Spring' for choir and orchestra 1988; Home: 75 King's Dr., Winnipeg, Man. R3T 3E7; Office: Winnipeg Symphony Orch., Rm. 101, 55 Main St., Winnipeg, Man. R3B 1C3.

**BUIK, William A.,** M.A., C.F.A.; investment executive, retired; b. Toronto, Ont. 1 Jan. 1930; e. Univ. of Toronto B.A. 1950, M.A. 1958; Chart. Financial Analyst 1968; m. Elizabeth Ann (Creighton) 10 June 1961; children: Catharine Ann, Sandra Helen; Vice-Chrmn., Jones Heward Investment Management Inc.; Dir. Burns Fry Ltd.; joined present co. 1964; St. James-Bond Ch.; Nepal School Projects; Club: Osler Bluffs Ski; Home: 78A Lowther Ave., Toronto, Ont. M5R 1C8; Office: 145 King St. W., Toronto, Ont. M5H 3Z9.

**BUI-QUANG, Hung,** M.Eng., M.B.A.; engineering executive; b. Vietnam 6 Jan. 1948; s. Trach and Xuan Nguyen (Vo. Thi) B.; e. Univ. of Montreal, B.A. 1970, M.A.(Chem.) 1973; McGill Univ. dipl. of mngt. 1977, M.B.A. 1980; m. Mrs. Huong Do 3 Aug. 1974; 1 son and 1 daughter; PRESIDENT, CONSULGAZ INC. (GAZ METROPOLITAIN INC. SUBS.) 1988– ; Chrmn. of the Bd., Industries Dettson; Multi-Ind Inc.; Pres. & Chrmn. of the Bd., NGTC; joined Gaz Métropolitan 1974; worked in Planning & Mktg. depts.; Gen. Dir., Mktg. 1981; Assoc. Vice-Pres., Mktg. & Rates 1982; Vice-Pres., Mktg. & Technol. 1985; Vice-Pres., Sales, Western Zone & Technol. 1986; Vice-Pres., Sales, Major Indus. & Technol. 1987; Vice-Pres., Corporate Affairs & Mktg. 1988–91; Vice-Pres., Marketing and Sales 1991; Dir., Canadian Gas Research Inst.; Mem., Ordre des ingénieurs du Qué.; Office: 1717, rue du Havre, Montréal, Qué. H2K 2X3.

**BUISSON, Gabriel;** industrialist; b. Shawinigan, Que. 29 June 1927; s. Rosario and Rose (Martin) B.; e. Immaculée Conception and Shawinigan (Que.) Tech. Sch.; Internat. Correspondence Schs. Inc., Dipl. in Chem. Engn.; m. Pauline, d. Patrick Arseneault, 19 Nov. 1949; children: Claude, Serge, Josette, André; PRESIDENT AND C.E.O. LAURENTIDE CHEMICALS INC.; Pres., 81735 Canada Ltée; Soc. de Gestion Cascade Ltée; Laurentide Chemicals, Atlantic Div. Ltd.; Peinture Nationale Ltée; Past Vice Pres., Shawinigan Sr. Chamber Comm.; mem., Candn. Mfrs. Assn.; Past Dir., Centre des Dirigeants D'Entre prise; R. Catholic; recreations: golf, fishing, reading; Club: Club de Golf Shawinigan-Sud Inc. (Founder, sole shareholder, Pres.); Home: 90 Terrasse Cascade, Shawinigan-Sud, Que. G9P 2V3; Office: 4660 – 12th Ave., Shawinigan-Sud, Que. G9N 6V2.

**BUITENHUIS, Peter Martinus,** B.A., Ph.D.; university professor emeritus; writer; b. London, Eng. 8 Dec. 1925; came to Can. 1959; s. John A. and Irene (Cotton) B.; e. Brentwood Sch., Essex, Eng.; Jesus Coll. Oxford, Eng., B.A. 1949, M.A. 1954; Yale Univ. Ph.D. 1955; m. Marguerite Ann d. Ross Stephenson 11 Dec. 1977; children: Juliana Polley, Adrian Peter Ross, (and by previous marriages) Paul Jason, Penelope Anne, Pym Susan, Beatrix Cameron, Hugo Donald; PROF. EMERITUS OF ENGLISH, SIMON FRASER UNIV. 1975– ;(Chrmn. of Dept. 1975–81); Instr. Univ. of Oklahoma, 1949–51; Instr. Am. Studies Yale Univ. 1954–59; Asst. and Assoc. Prof. Vict. Coll. Univ. of Toronto, 1959–66; Visiting Prof. Univ. of Calif., Berkeley, 1966–67; Prof. McGill Univ., 1967–75; Visiting Prof. and Lectr. Macalester College, Minn., 1961–

62; Wesleyan Univ. Middletown, Conn., 1958; State Univ. of Buffalo, N.Y., 1964; Berlin, Wurzburg, Kiel, Hamburg, Manchester; served with Royal Navy, 1943–46, rank Sub. Lt.; France and Germany Star, 1939–45 Star; author 'Hugh MacLennan' 1968; 'Viewpoints on Henry James's Portrait of a Lady' 1968; Ed. 'Selected Poems of E.J. Pratt' 1969; 'The Grasping Imagination: The American Writings of Henry James' 1970; 'The Canadian Imagination' (contrib. to) 1978; 'The Stoic Strain in American Literature' (contrib. to) 1979; 'The Restless Analyst: Essays by Henry James' 1980; 'The Great War of Words: British, American and Canadian Propaganda and Fiction 1914–1933' 1987; Ed. (with Ira Nadel) 'George Orwell: A Reassessment' 1989; 'The House of the Seven Gables: Severing Family and Colonial Ties' 1991; essays on Saul Bellow, Stephen Crane, Arnold Bennett, H.L. Mencken, Mary McCarthy, J.D. Salinger, Propaganda of the Great War; regular reviewer for the 'Globe and Mail'; mem., Assn. for Can. Studies; Am. Studies Assn.; Br. Assn. for Am. Studies; Candn. Assn. for Am. Studies (Pres. 1968–70); Candn. Assn. of University Teachers; Candn. Assn. for Chrmn. of English (Pres. 1978–79); Candn. Council Fellow, 1963–64; Am. Council of Learned Societies Fellow, 1972–73; SSHRC Leave Fellowship, 1982–83; SSHRC Rsch. Grant 1991–94; recreations: skiing, sailing, squash, jogging; Home: 7019 Marine Dr., W. Vancouver, B.C. V7W 2T4; Office: Burnaby, B.C. V5A 1S6.

**BUJOLD, Geneviève;** actress; b. Montreal, Que. 1 July 1942; d. Firmin and Laurette (Cavanaugh) B.; e. Hochelga Convent for 12 years; Conserv. of Dramatic Arts. Montreal, 3 yrs; m. Paul Almond (div.) 18 Mar. 1967; one s. Matthew James; rec'd Susanne Bianchetti Award, Paris, for 'La Guerre est Fini' 1966; Emmy nomination for 'Saint Joan' 1967; Best Actress Award, Carthagenia Film Festival; winner of ETROG for best actress 'Isabel' 1968; Hollywood Golden Globe Award and Acad. Award nomination for 'Anne of the Thousand Days' 1969; winner of ETROG for best actress 1970; Earle Grey Award (ACTRA) 'for most outstanding performer in Canada' 1972; Films include: 'Act of the Heart'; 'Journey'; 'King of Hearts'; 'The Thief'; 'Alex and the Gypsy'; 'Kamouraska'; 'Obsession'; 'Murder by Decree'; 'Coma'; mem., ACTRA; Union des Artistes.

**BULL, Fruji Elizabeth,** B.J.; association executive; b. Budapest, Hungary 11 Nov. 1943; d. Stephen Alexander and Charlotte Elizabeth (Zimnic) C.; e. Lisgar Coll. 1962; Carleton Univ., B.J. 1968; m. John J. s. Fredrick and Marjorie Bull 24 Oct. 1964; children: Jeoffrey Steven, Stephen William; PRES., CANDN. ASSN. OF DATA, PROFL. SERVICES SOFTWARE ORGANIZATIONS 1988–..; freelance writer 1970–72; researcher, H. of C., Minister's Office 1972–74; Public Servant, Sec. of State 1974–76; Public Serv. Comn. & Indus., Trade & Comm. 1976–82; Mgr./Acting Dir., Marine, Urban & Rail, Reg. Indus. Expansion 1982–86; Dir., Indus. Analysis & Liaision, Trade Negotiations Office 1986–88; Dir., CrimeStoppers, Ottawa; Fund raiser, Civic Hosp. Found.; recreations: tennis, skiing, bridge, chess; Home: 65 Pond St., Ottawa, Ont. K1L 8J1.

**BULL, Roger Anthony,** B.A.; diplomat; b. New York, N.Y. 7 July 1931; s. William Frederick and Marjorie Ruth (Eoll) B.; e. Kings Prep Auckland, N.Z.; Primary Schs. Can.; Tacoma Park Jr. High, Silverspring, MD.; Lisgar Coll. Inst. Ottawa; Univ. of Toronto, B.A. 1954; Oxford Univ. (Rhodes Scholar); m. Thérèse Marie Rickman d. John and Elizabeth Doyle 17 July 1984; children: Adam, Philip, Nicholas Bull; Angela, Genevieve & Sean Rickman; EXTVE. DIR., PACIFIC NORTHWEST ECONOMIC REGION (PNWER), an assoc. of Candn. and Am. state and province legislators; joined Trade Comnr. Service Can. 1957 serving Detroit, Leopoldville, Bogota, Ottawa, Moscow and Dublin; Dir. Comm. Policy Div. External Affairs 1971–74; Min. Rome 1974–78; Mgr. Intergovt'al Affairs AECL 1978–79; Chief Inspr. Foreign Operations ICER 1979–81; Asst. Under Sec. USA, Office Trade Devel. External Affairs 1981–83; Coordinator Davos Task Force 1983–84; Candn. High Comnr. to Botswana & Zimbabwe, Ambassador to Angola & Mozambique 1984–89; Consul General, Seattle, Washington, U.S.A. 1990–93; Rapporteur World Food Council 1977–79; Dep. Head Candn. Del. to S. African Devel. Coordination Conf. Ministerial Meetings Mbabane 1985, Harare 1986, Gaborone 1987, Luanda 1989; Candn. Rep. 20th Anniversary Botswana Independence 1986; Depy. Head Candn. Del. to Commonwealth Law Mins. Meeting Harare 1986; Chrmn. St. Georges English Sch. Rome 1977–78; mem., Adv. Bd., World Trade Club, Seattle 1993– ; mem., Vancouver Bd. of Trade; Seattle Chamb. of Comm.; mem., Candn. Assn. Rhodes Scholars; Anglican; recreations: sailing, reading, travel; Clubs: Circolo Della Vela Di Roma; Rainier; Seattle Yacht; Sudden Valley Golf; Home: 4903 Woodlawn Ave. N., Seattle, Washington 98103, U.S.A.

**BULLER, Herman,** B.A., B.Ed., B.C.L.; author; teacher; b. Montreal, Que. 30 April 1923; s. Joseph and Lily (Fruchter) B.; e. Strathcona Acad., Montreal, 1939; Sir George Williams Univ., B.A. 1943; Univ. of Toronto, B.Ed. 1970; McGill Univ., B.C.L. 1946; Univ. of Toronto, Ont. Coll. Educ., Perm. High Sch. Cert. 1957; m. Adele Eve, d. Adolph Gottlieb, Toronto, Ont. 11 June 1946; presently teaching econ. hist. and theory for N. York Bd. of Educ.; previously taught Eng. lit. and creative writing; served with C.O.T.C., Sir George Williams Univ. and McGill Univ.; author 'One Man Alone' 1963 (Canadiana Award 1963); 'Quebec in Revolt' 1965 (paperback ed. 1966); 'The Revolt of the French Canadian Youth' 1966; 'This My Land' (novel) 1968; 'Days of Rage' (novel) 1974; 'Tania: The Liberation of Patty Hearst' (play) 1975; critical reviews have appeared in 'The Telegram,' Toronto, 'The Montreal Star,' 'La Presse,' Montreal, 'Toronto Daily Star,' etc.; has written several short stories; mem., Ont. Secondary Sch. Teachers Fed.; Candn. Authors Assn.; Hebrew; Address: 9 Kingsbridge Court, Willowdale, Ont. M2R 1L6.

**BULLIVANT, John Geoffrey;** business executive; b. Manchester, England 25 June 1931; s. John Norman and Dorothy (Williamson) B.; e. St. Bees P.S.; Manchester Inst. of Tech.; Manchester Univ.; M. Jean d. Harry and Elizabeth Wood 9 June 1956; children: Jennifer Wendy, Jane Melanie, Jonathon Roger; EXTVE. VICE-PRES., STERLING LTD.; Indus. Engr., Northern Electric 1956– ; Vice-Pres., Sterling Varnish Co. of Can. 1968– ; Pres., St. Catharines Gen. Hosp. Found.; Dir., St. Cath. C. of C.; St. Cath. Rotary Club; Rolls Royce Owners Club; Sr. Lay Reader, St. Thomas Ch.; Mem., Engr. Inst. of Can.; Inst. of Electronic & Electrical Engrs.; Soc. of Mfg. Engrs.; recreations: golf, running, antique cars; Clubs: St. Catharines; St. Catharines Golf & Country; Home: 10 Thairs Ave., St. Catharines, Ont. L2R 6P1; Office: P.O. Box 554, St. Catharines, Ont. L2R 6X1.

**BULLOCH, John F.D.,** B.A.Sc., M.B.A.; association executive; b. Toronto, Ont. 24 Aug. 1933; e. Univ. of Toronto, grad. (Engn. and Business) 1956, M.B.A. 1964; m. Mary Helen, 1955; 2 children; PRES. & FOUNDER, CANADIAN FEDERATION OF INDEPENDENT BUSINESS 1971– ; joined Imperial Oil 1957; Mgr., Baier Fuels Ltd., Kitchener, Ont. 1959–63; student, Univ. of Toronto 1963–64; Lectr., Ryerson Polytechnical Inst. 1964–69; Pres. and Founder, Candn. Council for Fair Taxation 1970; Mem. Steering Ctte., Internat. Small Business Congress; mem. Assn. of Profl. Engrs. of Ont.; awarded Fellowship, Ryerson Polytechnical Inst. 1981; recipient: Distinguished Business Alumni Award, Univ. of Toronto 1987; Wilford L. White Fellowship, Internat. Counc. for Small Bus., for leadership and commitment to small business throughout the world; recreations: tennis, sailing, summer cottage; Home: Willowdale, Ont.; Office: 4141 Yonge St., Willowdale, Ont. M2P 2A6.

**BULLOCK, Roger Clare;** foundation executive; b. Stratford, Ont. 1 Feb. 1958; s. L. Clare and Shirley I. (Armstrong) B.; e. Waterford Dist. H.S. S.S.G.D. 1976; Humber College of Applied Arts & Technol., funeral serv. dipl.; GENERAL MANAGER, CANADIAN FOUNDATION FOR AIDS RESEARCH; Ont. Funeral Directors licence 1978– ; Home: 3970 Victoria Rd., Crystal Beach, Ont. L0S 1B0; Office: 120 Bloor St. E., 1st Floor, Toronto, Ont. M4W 1B8.

**BULMAN, W. John A.;** printing executive; b. Winnipeg, Man. 23 March 1929; m. Laureen Joy Tucker; children: Robert, Michael, Philip; CHRMN. & PRES., THE BULMAN GROUP LIMITED; Past Chrmn., Man. Telephone System; Dir. & Vice-Pres., Wawanesa Mutual Insur. Co.; Wawanesa Mutual Life Co.; Dir., Ancast Indus. Ltd.; Guaranty Trust Co. of Can.; Guaranty Trustco Limited; Traders Group Limited; Dir., Bally Canada Inc.; Mem., Man.-Sask. Div., Candn. Mfg. Assn. (Chrmn. 1971–74, Pres., Nat. Bd. of Dir. 1979–80); Nat. Assn. of Printers & Lithographers 1967– ; (Chrmn. 1974–76 & Past Dir.); Dir., Graphic Arts Tech. Found. 1972–79 (Soc. of Fellows 1983); Man. Inst. of Mgmt. Inc. 1965– ; (Chrmn. 1969–72, Fellow 1972); Royal Candn. Geog. Soc. (Fellow 1977); Founding Mem., Candn. Inst. of Mgmt. (Man. div.) 1963– ; (Pres. 1968–69, granted P.Mgr. 1975); Past Trustee, Graphic Communications Internat. Union-Supplemental Retirement & Disability Fund 1975–86; Past Mem., Bd. of Govs. Winnipeg Art Gallery (Pres. 1971–74); Pres., United Way of Winnipeg 1981–82; Mem. & Past Chrmn., Bd. of Regents, Univ. of Winnipeg 1977–79; Chancellor, Univ. of Winnipeg 1984– ; Univ. of Winnipeg, Hon. LL.D. 1983; Chrmn., Health Sci. Ctr.; Past Chrmn., Tech. & Vocl. Training Adv. Ctte. 1967–69; Mem., Crescent Fort Rouge Ch. (Past Chrmn., Ctte. of Stewards & Chrmn. of Offical Bd. 1977–78; recreations: swimming, scuba diving, sailing; Home: 761 Queenston St., Winnipeg, Man. R3N 0X8; Office: 61 Gertie St., Winnipeg, Man. R3A 0B2.

**BULMER, Ronald W.,** B.Sc.; association executive; b. Renfrew, Ont. 30 Nov. 1942; s. Willard and Irene (Thompson) B.; e. Cornell Univ., B.Sc. 1967; m. Judith d. Thelma and Jack Nasby 18 Sept. 1966; children: Michael, Kathryn, Lori; PRES., FISHERIES COUNC. OF CAN. 1983– ; Prod. Mgr., Can. Packers Ltd. 1967; Acct. Extve., Cunningham & Walsh Advtg. Inc. 1968; Brand Mgr., Liggett & Myers Inc. 1969–70; Sr. Prod. Mgr., Gen. Foods Ltd. 1971–72; Vice-Pres., Mktg., Benson & Hedges (Can.) Ltd. 1972–78; Pres., Candn. Assn. of Fish Exporters 1978–83; Candn. Assn. of Fish Exporters; North Atlantic Sea Food Assn.; Seafood Advisory Counc.; Mem., Can. Japan Bus. Counc.; recreations: golf, skiing, hunting; Club: Carlton Golf & Yacht; Home: 6536 Temagami Court, Manotick, Ont.; Office: 806–141 Laurier Ave. W., Ottawa, Ont. K1P 5J3.

**BUMSTEAD, R. Glenn,** Q.C., B.A., LL.B.; b. Meaford, Ont. 20 Oct. 1938; s. David L. and Margaret S. (Miller) B.; e. Meaford (Ont.) High Sch.; Univ. of Alta. B.A. 1965; Osgoode Hall Law Sch. LL.B. 1968; m. Rosemary June 1986; children: John G., Andrea M., Julia D.; SR. VICE PRES., GEN. COUNSEL AND SECY. THE TORONTO-DOMINION BANK 1981– ; and Vice Pres. & Dir., The Pension Fund Society of The Toronto-Dominion Bank; Dir., Deputy Chrmn., TD Reinsurance (Barbados) Inc.; Dir., TD Mortgage Corporation; TD Pacific Mortgage Corporation; Pacific Centre Limited; Pacific Centre North Limited; Toronto-Dominion Centre Limited; Toronto-Dominion Centre West Limited; Toronto-Dominion Realty Co. Limited; Toronto Dominion Place Limited; Terbert Investment Properties Limited; Beaufort Sea Programme Limited; T.E.C. Hotels Limited; T.E.C. Operations Ltd.; Toronto-Dominion Real Estate Inc.; Dir., Secy. & Mng. Dir. Legal Affairs, Toronto Dominion Securities Inc.; Dir. and Asst. Sec., Pendom Limited; Dir. & Sec. Penoce Limited; Penlim Investments Limited; Partner, Bantor Co.; read law with Thomson, Rogers; called to Bar of Ont. 1970; law practice Thomson, Rogers 1970–72; Gen. Counsel and Asst. Secy. General Motors of Canada Ltd. 1972–76; served with RCAF 1957–63; mem. Candn. Bar Assn.; York Co. Law Assn.; Law Soc. of Upper Can.; Internat. Bar Assn.; The Institute of Corporate Directors; Office: Toronto-Dominion Centre, Toronto, Ont. M5K 1A2.

**BUMSTED, John Michael,** Ph.D., F.R.H.S.; educator; b. White Plains, N.Y. 12 Dec. 1938; s. John Francis and Mary Agnes B.; e. Tufts Coll. B.A. 1959; Brown Univ. Ph.D. 1965; m. Wendy d. Maldwyn and Eleanor Williams 2 May 1983; children: Jonathan, Carla, Hannah, Siân, Michael; PROF. OF HIST. ST. JOHN'S COLL. UNIV. OF MAN. 1980– ; Instr. Tufts Univ. 1963–65; Asst. Prof. Simon Fraser Univ. 1965–67, Assoc. Prof. 1969–75, Prof. 1975–80; Asst. Prof. McMaster Univ. 1967–69; W.P. Bell Visiting Chair in Maritime Studies Mount Allison Univ. 1985–86; author 'Henry Alline 1748–1784' 1971, reprinted 1984; 'The People's Clearance: Scottish Emigration to British North America 1770–1815' 1982; 'Land, Settlement and Politics in 18th Century P.E.I.' 1987 (winner J.W. Dafoe Book Prize 1987); ed. 'The Collected Writings of Lord Selkirk' 2 vols. 1984, 1988; co-ed. 'An Account of a Voyage to the North West Coast of America in 1785 and 1786 by Ensign Walker of The Bombay Army' 1982; 'The Peoples of Canada: A History' (2 vols., 1992, 1993); Ed., Selkirk Papers; mem. Exec. Centre d'Etude Quebec; Fellow, Pilgrim Soc.; Anglican; recreation:gardening; Home: 202 Elm St., Winnipeg, Man. R3M 3P2; Office: Winnipeg, Man. R3T 2N2.

**BUNDY, Robert G.,** B.Comm.; commissioner; b. Toronto, Ont. 25 Jan. 1923; s. Harry and Clara B.; e. Duke of Connaught Pub. Sch.; Riverdale Collegiate Inst.; Univ. of Toronto, Victoria Coll. B.Comm. 1947; m. Waltraud d. Karl and Anna Gundlach 7 Dec. 1956; children: Karl Sunter, Claire-Anne, Harry Brock, Stuart George, Derek Robert; Commissioner, Parks and Property Dept., Mun. of Metro. Toronto 1977–..; Vice-Pres. Bundy Construction Ltd. 1948–58; Gen. Mgr. Parking Authority of Toronto and mem. City of Toronto Treas. Bd. 1958–74; Pres. and Gen. Mgr. Revenue Control Systems Ltd. 1974–77; Candn. Naval Offr., loaned to Royal Navy; served in aircraft carrier with Home Fleet out of Scapa Flow; served in Combined Operations with Indian Army in S.E. Asia; awarded Canadian Centennial Medal 1967; past Pres. Internat. Mun. Parking Cong.; Hon. Life mem. Ontario Traffic Conf.; past Sub.-Ctte.

Chrmn. Transp. Rsch. Bd., Nat. Rsch. Counc., Nat. Acad. of Sciences & Engrg., Washington, D.C.; past Nat. Pres. Naval Offr.'s Assn. of Can.; mem. Bd. of Mgmt., Navy League of Can., Ont. Div.; past Pres. Toronto Brigantine Inc.; mem. French Chamber of Comm. in Can.; German Candn. Bus. and Profl. Assn. Inc.; Hon. Life Mem. German Candn. Club Harmonie; Candn. rep., Rsch. Grp. UT5 Orgn. for Econ. Co-operation and Devel.; Depy. Chrmn. Joint U.S.-Can. Naval Offr.'s Liaison Ctte.; Dir.: Royal Agricultural Winter Fair; Civic Garden Centre Found.; Gov.: Hockey Hall of Fame.; Can. Sports Hall of Fame (Chrmn.); Anglican; Club: The Toronto Hunt (Past Pres.); Home: 88 Pine Cres., Toronto, Ont. M4E 1L4.

**BUNGE, Mario Augusto,** Ph.D., LL.D.; educator; author; b. Buenos Aires, Argentina 21 Sept. 1919; s. Augusto and Maria (Müser) B.; e. Universidad Nacional de La Plata Ph.D. 1952; Simon Fraser Univ. LL.D. 1981; m. Marta Irene d. Ricardo Cavallo, Buenos Aires 5 Feb. 1959; children: Carlos F., Mario A.J. (by first marriage); Eric R., Silvia A.; FROTHINGHAM PROF. OF LOGIC & METAPHYSICS, McGILL UNIV. 1981– ; Teaching Asst. in Exper. Physics Universidad Nacional de La Plata 1943, Prof. of Theoretical Physics 1956–59; Teaching Asst. in Math. Physics Universidad Nacional de Buenos Aires 1946–52, Prof. of Theoretical Physics 1956–58, Prof. of Philos. 1957–62; Visiting Prof. Univ. of Pa. 1960–61, Univ. of Texas 1963, Temple Univ. 1963–64, Univ. of Del. 1964–65, Universität Freiburg 1965–66, Aarhus Univ. 1972, ETH Zurich 1973, Universidad Nacional Autónoma de México 1975–76; Université de Genève 1986–87; Prof. of Philos., present Univ. 1966–81; Fellow, Alexander von Humboldt Stiftung 1965–66, John Simon Guggenheim Foundation 1972–73; Prince of Asturias Prize in Humanities and Communication 1982; author 'Temas de educación popular' 1943; 'Causality' 1959 (translated into 7 languages); 'Metascientific Queries' 1959; 'Etica y ciencia' 1960; 'Cinemática del electrón relativista' 1960; 'Intuition and Science' 1962 (transl. into 2 languages); 'The Myth of Simplicity' 1963; 'Scientific Research' 2 vols. 1967; 'Foundations of Physics' 1967; 'Teoría y realidad' 1972; 'Philosophy of Physics' 1973 (transl. into 5 languages); 'Method, Model and Matter' 1973; 'Sense and Reference' 1974; 'Interpretation and Truth' 1974; 'The Furniture of the World' 1977; 'A World of Systems' 1979; 'Epistemología' 1980; 'The Mind-Body Problem' 1980; 'Ciencia y desarrollo' 1980; 'Scientific Materialism' 1981; 'Economía y filosofía' 1982; 'Exploring the World' 1983; 'Understanding the World' 1983; 'Lingüística y filosofía' 1983; 'Controversias en física' 1983; 'Philosophy of Science & Technology' 1985; 'Seudociencia e ideología' 1985; 'Racionalidad y realismo' 1986; 'Razón e intuición' 1986; 'Philosophy of Psychology' (with Rubén Ardila) 1987; 'Vistas y entrevistas' 1987; 'Ethics' 1989; 'Mente y sociedad' 1989; over 400 scholarly articles; Founder and later Headmaster, Universidad Obrera Argentina, Buenos Aires 1938–43; mem. Asociación Física Argentina; Agrupación Rioplatense de Lógica y Filosofía Científica (Past Pres.); Asociación Mexicana de Epistemología (Past Pres.); Inst. Internat. de Philosophie; Académie Internationale de Philosophie des Sciences; Amer. Assn. Advancement of Sci.; Royal Soc. of Canada; Soc. Exact Philos.; Candn. Philos. Assn.; Candn. Soc. Hist. & Philos. Science; Brit. Soc. Philos. Science; Fedération Internat. de Sociétés de Philosophie; Ed. 7 collective works; gen. ed. book series 'Studies in the Foundations and Philosophy of Science,' 'Library of Exact Philosophy,' 'Episteme,' 'Foundations and Philosophy of Science and Technology'; biog. 'Scientific Philosophy Today: Essays in Honor of Mario Bunge' 1982; 'Encuentros con Mario Bunge' 1989; 'Studies on Mario Bunge's Treatise' 1990; 'Entretiens avec Mario Bunge' 1993; Liberal; recreations: reading, music, walking, swimming; Home: 29 Bellevue Ave., Westmount, Que. H3Y 1G4; Office: 3479 Peel St., Montreal, Que. H3A 1W7.

**BUNTING, Christopher Henry,** B.A.; public relations executive; b. Ottawa, Ont. 23 May 1951; s. Christopher William and Eileen Florence (Williamson) B.; e. Carleton Univ., B.A. (Pol. Sci.) 1973, Hons. B.A. (Commun.) 1983; CHRMN. & C.E.O., CONTINENTAL PIR COMMUNICATIONS 1990– ; various positions, Govt. of Can. 1975–83; Mng. Dir., Continental Golin/Harris Ottawa Bur. 1985; Extve. Vice Pres., Continental Golin/Harris Communications Inc. 1986–89, Chrmn. & C.E.O. 1989–90; elected 1st Candn. Chrmn., Bd. of Internat. Assn. of Bus. Communicators (IABC) 1985–86; 1987 Communicator of the Year, Nat. Br., IABC; Fellow, IABC 1992; Mem., Bd. of Dirs., Golin/Harris Communications Inc.; Mem., National Practice Bd., Shandwick N. Am.; Pres., CANFAR; Mem., Bd. of Dirs., Clarke Institute Foundation; named Associate, Carleton Univ. 1988; Anglican; Mem., Internat. Public Relns. Assn.; Candn. Public Relns. Soc.; Internat. Assn. of Business Communicators; Public Affairs Assn. of Can.; recreations: swimming, boating, skiing; Club: Royal Candn. Yacht; Nat. Press Club of Can.; Home: 190 St. George St., Toronto, Ont.; Office: 10th Flr., 415 Yonge St., Toronto, Ont. M5B 2E7.

**BUNTING John Pearce,** B.Comm.; b. Toronto, Ont. 6 Sept. 1929; s. Alfred and Harriet Lee B.; e. Appleby Coll., Oakville; McGill Univ., B.Comm., 1952; m. Stephanie Keeley, 26 Sept. 1977; children: Mark Alfred, Elsa Brenda, Harriet Elizabeth, Alexandra Keeley, Charles Pearce; PRES. & C.E.O., THE TORONTO STOCK EXCHANGE 1977– ; Dir., Canadian General-Tower Ltd.; Dir./Past Pres., St. John's Hosp. 1983–86; Pres., St. Patrick's Benevolent Soc.; Past Chrmn., Appleby Coll.; Pres. Ticker Club 1976–77; Pres., Fed. Internat. des Bourses de Valeurs 1983–84; with McLeod, Young & Weir, 1952–55; joined Alfred Bunting & Co. Ltd. 1955 (apptd. Pres. 1967); Anglican; Kappa Alpha; recreations: tennis, windsurfing, skiing; Clubs: Osler Bluff Ski; Home: 18 Arkendo Dr., Oakville, Ont. L6J 5T9; Office: Exchange Tower, 2 First Canadian Place, Toronto, Ont. M5X 1J2.

**BUNZE, George Joseph,** C.M.A.; professional accountant; b. Markt Oberdorf, Germany 7 Aug. 1943; s. Gebhard Seelos and Charlotte Ilse Bunze; e. McGill Univ. C.M.A. 1968; m. Kathleen d. Felix and Vivian Jean 24 July 1965; children: Deborah-Jean, Stefanie Barbara, Richard Mark; EXTVE. VICE-PRES. FINANCE, CHIEF FINAN. OFFR. & DIR., KRUGER INC. 1993– ; Comptroller's Dept., ITT Canada Ltd. 1962–65; Internal Auditor & Acct., Kruger Inc. 1965–69; Supvr., Acctg. Serv. 1969–74; Mgr., Corp. Acctg. & Insur. 1974–76; Asst. Corp. Comptroller 1976–79; Corp. Comptroller (Offr.) 1979–82; Vice-Pres., Corp. Comp. & Treas. 1982–85; Sr. Vice Pres., Treasurer and Chief Finan. Offr. 1985–92; Dir., Corner Brook Pulp & Paper Co. Ltd.; Manistique Papers Inc.; Kruger Inc.; Mem., Tax Extves. Inst.; Finan. Extves. Inst.; Soc. of Cert. Mngt. Accts. of Canada; Candn. Pulp & Paper Assn. Financial Officers Ctte. (Past Chrmn., Tax Adv. Ctte.); Montreal Bd. of Trade; recreations: skiing, reading, biking; clubs: Saint James, West Island Tennis; Home: 351 Penn Rd., Beaconsfield, Montreal, Que. H9W 1B5; Office: 3285 Bedford Rd., Montreal, Que. H3S 1G5.

**BURBIDGE, Frederick Stewart,** B.A., LL.B.; retired corporate director; b. Winnipeg, Man. 30 Sept. 1918; s. Frederick Maxwell and Susan Mary (Stewart) B.; e. Ravenscourt Sch. Winnipeg; Univ. of Manitoba, B.A. 1939; Man. Law Sch., LL.B. 1946; m. Cynthia Adams Bennest, 27 April 1942; children: John Bennest, George Frederick; former Dir., Canadian Pacific Ltd.; C.I.L. Inc.; Marathon Realty Co. Ltd.; Soo Line Railroad Co.; Bank of Montreal (mem. Exec. Comm.); Pan Canadian Petroleum Ltd.; AMCA Internat. Ltd.; ICI American Holdings Inc.; called to Bar of Man. 1946; entered Candn. Pacific Law Dept., Winnipeg 1947 as Asst. Solr.; served in various capacities within CP Rail and CP Limited; Pres. 1972; Chrmn. & CEO 1981–85; Chrmn. 1985–86; Gov. Emeritus, McGill Univ.; R.C.N. 1941–45, rank Lt.; Club: Mount Royal; Office: Ste. 800, Place du Canada, PO Box 6042, Stn. 'A,' Montreal, Que. H3C 3E4.

**BURBIDGE, Nicolas William Russell,** F.C.I.S., P.Adm.; trust company executive; b. Guildford, England 21 Jan. 1946; s. Shirley William Russell and Marjorie Anne (Brown) Choules; e. Fullbrook School (U.K.) 1962; Kingston College; Balham & Tooting Coll. of Commerce; Farnborough Tech. College 1963–67; O.N.C. Bus. Studies; Inst. of Chartered Secretaries, grad. 1969; m. Myfanwy d. John and Morfydd Gibson 24 June 1967; children: Gavin Nicolas, Meredith Jane, Jeremy Michael (dec.); Managing Partner & Corporate Secretary, Royal Trust 1987–93; Molsons Brewery 1967–69; Asst. Sec., Northern Telecom 1969–74; Brinco Limited 1974–75; Royal Trust 1975–87; Mem., Internat. Professional Standards Ctte., Inst. of Chartered Secretaries & Administrators; Past Chair, Ont. Br., Inst. of Chartered Secretaries & Administrators; Mem., Ed. Bd., Nat. Investor Relations Inst.; Hon. Treas., The Japan Soc.; Co-chaired Town of Oakville Task Force which implemented Municipal Arts Policy (one of 1st in Ont.); Former Pres., Oakville Arts Council; Former Chair, Oakville Ctr. for the Performing Arts; Past Pres., Oakville Symphony; Anglican; Former People's Warden & Former Treas., Trinity Church (St. Bruno, Que.) 1970–74; recreations: choral (chamber) music (member, The John Laing Singers, Hamilton, Ont.); Home: 119 Walby Dr., Oakville, Ont. L6L 4C9; Office: Suite 300, Royal Trust Tower, Toronto, Ont. M5W 1P9.

**BURBRIDGE, Kenneth Joseph,** M.A., B.C.L., Ph.D.; b. Bathurst, N.B. 2 July 1911; s. Harry Joseph and Elizabeth (Foley) B.; e. St. Thomas Univ.; St. Francis Xavier Univ., B.A. (1935) and M.A. (1936); Univ. of New Brunswick, B.C.L. (1939); Univ. of Ottawa, Ph.D. (1942); m. Marion Catherine Smith, 20 Nov. 1943; children; John Kenneth, Sheila Marie; engaged in private practice of law at Saint John, N.B. 1939–41; various positions in pub. service of Can. incl. Legal Counsel, Dept. of Munitions & Supply. Ottawa, 1941–43; Chief Legal Adv. to Nat. Selective Service, (Mobilization), Dept. of Labour, Ottawa, 1943–44; Legal Adv. to Unemployment Ins. Comn., Ottawa, 1945; Counsellor to Secy. of State and Dir., War Claims Branch, Dept. Secy. of State, Ottawa, 1945–47; Legal Adviser, Dept. of External Affairs, Ottawa and Counsel for Can. before Internat. Joint Comn. 1948–54; del. to Inter-Allied Reparations Agency, Brussels, 1947; Candn. Adv. to Allied Conf. on Enemy Property, London, 1947; Candn. del. to Allied Conf. on German Indust. Property Rights, Neuchatel; Candn. Observer at Council of Europe, Strasbourg; Special Adv. to Candn. dels. to UNS., 1952–53; Candn. Depy. Permanent Rep. to N. Atlantic Council (NATO) and Organ. for European Economic Cooperation (O.E.E.C.) Paris, 1954–57; Candn. del. to Columbo Plan Conf., Seattle, 1958; Candn. Del., Inter-govtl. Maritime Consultative Organ. and Econ. Comn. for Europe Conf. on Internat. Combined Transport, London, Eng. and on Internat. Shipping Leg., Geneva, 1970; Candn. Del to Internat. Conf. on Unlawful Interference with Civil Aviation 1971; Consul Gen. of Can., Seattle 1957–62; High Commr. to N.Z. 1963–67; Dir., U.S.A. Div., Dept. External Affairs 1968–70; Exec. Dir., Intern. Transport Policy, Can. Transport Commission, Ottawa 1971–78; Can. del. to Gen. Assemblies of Intern. Civil Aviation Organization (ICAO) 1974, 1977; Administrator, Maritime Pollution Claims Fund, Ottawa 1979–84; Can. del. to UNCTAD Conferences on international multi-modal transport, Geneva, 1972–77; recreations: oil painting, golf; Club: Royal Ottawa Golf; Home: 930 Sadler Cres., Ottawa, Ont. K2B 5H7.

**BURCHELL, Howard B.,** M.D., Ph.D.; cardiologist; b. Athens, Ont. 28 Nov. 1907; s. James Edward and Edith (Milligan) B.; e. Univ. of Toronto, M.D. 1932; Univ. of Minn., Ph.D., 1939; m. Margaret, d. Dr. Henry Helmolz, 14 Aug. 1942; children: Susan (Dr. S. Profeta); Judith (Mrs. J.E. Bush); Cynthia (Mrs. R. Patterson); Rebecca (Mrs. H. Wilbur); Consultant, Mayo Clinic, Rochester, Minn. 1946–67; Prof. of Med., Univ. of Minn. 1968–75 Sr. Cardiol., Univ. Unit Northwestern Hosp. 1975–78; frequent visiting Prof., Stanford U., C.A.; various guest lectureships including New York, Boston, Tel Aviv, London (Eng.), Edinburgh, Dundee, Leyden, London (Ont.), Dayton and Houston; served with U.S. Air Force 1942–46; co-author: 'Congenital Heart Disease'; Ed., 'Circulation' (1965–70) (Am. Heart Assn. Journ.); other writings incl. various articles pertaining to pathol. and physiol. of circulation; mem., Assn. Am. Phys.; Am. Physiol. Soc.; Candn. Cardiovascular Soc.; Am. Heart Assn. (Past Chrmn., Research Comte.); Alpha Omega Alpha; Sigma Xi; Independent; Universalist; recreations: history of medicine, libraries; Home: 260 Woodlawn Ave., St. Paul, Minn. 55105.

**BURDEN, Rev. Karl N.,** B.A., M.Div., Th.M., M.Ed., I.C.A.D.C.; national charitable organization executive; b. Hamilton, Ont. 3 July 1937; s. Thomas Edwin and Marion Dorothy (Smith) B.; e. McMaster Univ. B.A. 1960; Univ. of Toronto, Victoria Univ. M.Div. 1963, Th.M. 1971, OISE B.Ed. 1976, M.Ed. 1982; Internat. Certified Alcohol & Drug Counsellor (C.A.D.C.) 1991; m. Grace d. G. Stanley and Irma E. Boulter 7 July 1961; children: Mark, Janice; EXEC. DIR., CONCERNS, Canada 1979– ; served in Un. Ch. of Can. pastorates rural Sask., Oakville and Scarborough 1963–75; Elem. Teacher, Scarborough Bd. of Edn. 1976; Special Edn. Teacher, North York Bd. of Edn. 1976–77; Secondary Sch. Teacher, York Co. Bd. Edn. 1977–79; Founding mem. Drug Edn. Co-ordinating Council; mem. Ont. Council on Smoking & Health; Ont. Multi Faith Task Force on Substance Abuse; Ont. Drug Awareness Week Partnership; Internat. Council Alcohol & Addictions; Min.-in-Assn. Thornhill Un. Ch.; author: 'An Overview of Youth-Oriented Prevention Programmes in Five European Countries' and several papers presented at conferences of Internat. Congress on Alcohol and Addictions 1988–92; recreations: organ, cross-country skiing, hiking, photography; Office: 200, 11 Progress Ave., Scarborough, Ont. M1P 4S7.

**BUREAU, André,** O.C., LL.L.; communications executive; b. Trois-Rivières, Que. 10 Oct. 1935; s. Jean-Marie and Laurence (Ferron) B.; e. Classical Education, Séminaire de Trois-Rivières; Laval Univ. LL.L. (cum laude) 1958; Univ. de Paris 1960; m. Thérèse Quessy 31 Aug. 1959; children: Yves-André, Jean, Bernard; VICE-CHRMN., PRES. & C.E.O., ASTRAL BROADCAST-

ING GROUP INC.; VICE-CHRMN., ASTRAL COMMUNICATIONS INC. and ASTRAL COMMUNICATIONS INTERNATIONAL; Counsel, Heenan Blaikie, Lawyers; lawyer, Trois-Rivières 1960–68; Exec. Vice-Pres., La Presse, Montreal 1968–72; lawyer 1973–76; Extve. Vice-Pres., Télémédia Communications Ltée, Montreal 1976–80, Pres. 1980–81; Pres., Telemedia Ventures 1981–82; Pres. and C.E.O., Candn. Satellite Communications Inc. 1982–83; Chrmn., Candn. Radio-Television and Telecommunications Comn. (CTRC) Ottawa 1983–89; Officer, Order of Canada 1994; Home: 1670 Markham, Town of Mount-Royal, Que. H3P 3B2; Offices: Maison Astral, Ste. 200, 2100 Ste-Catherine St. W., Montreal, Que. H3H 2T3 and Heenan Blaikie, 1250 René Lévesque W., Bureau 2500, Montreal, Que. H3B 4Y1.

**BURFIELD, M. Jane Petersen,** B.A.; business executive; b. Toronto, Ont. 15 Oct. 1948; d. Niels Forrester and Margaret Bettina (Bauckham) Petersen; e. Bishop Strachan Sch. Toronto 1967; York Univ. B.A. 1971; St. Godrics Coll. London, Eng. 1972; m. Mark s. Harvey and Loretta Burfield 16 May 1975; three d. Miranda, Jennifer, Katharine; Dir. and Sec. Treas. Inventures Capital; Asst. Ed. Candn. Real Estate Assn. 1972–76; apptd. Bd. Dirs. Investors Finance Corp. 1971 becoming Sec.-Treas., currently Vice Pres.; apptd. to Bd. and later Audit Ctte. Commercial Financial Corp. Ltd. 1984, Wellington Trust Co. 1985; Pres. Griffund Holdings 1985–90; taught Communications Humber Coll. Toronto; Dir. Etobicoke YMCA 1980–81; mem. Mgmt. Ctte. YMCA Geneva Park; mem. Jr. League Toronto; YMCA Can.; Anglican; recreations: sailing, reading, bridge; Club: Granite; Home: 447 Glencairn Ave., Toronto, Ont. M5N 1V4; Office: 500, 95 King St. E., Toronto, Ont. M5C 1G4.

**BURFORD MASON, Roger,** B.A., Ph.D.; writer, editor; b. Mildenhall, England 19 Nov. 1943; s. Frederick John and Hazel Marion (Wells) Mason; e. Hamond's Sch. (U.K.); Hatfield Polytechnic B.A. (Hons.) 1981; Loughborough Univ. Ph.D. 1987; Cambridge Inst. of Edn., dipl. in edn. mngt. 1988; m. Aileen d. T.A. and E.M. Reilly 19 Feb. 1966; one s.: Oliver; EDITOR/PUBLISHER, THE DANFORTH REPORT 1993– ; taught high school, community college, teacher training (U.K.); Editor & Pub., 'Albion' 1977–88; Co-Founder, Editor & Publisher, 'Grand Piano' 1983–88; immigrated to Canada April 1988; Assoc. Ed., 'Toronto's Midtown Voice' 1989–92; Editor, Thornhill Publications 1989–93; Mng. Ed., 'Canadian Notes & Queries' 1990– ; frequent contbr., 'Globe & Mail,' 'Toronto Star,' 'Dalhousie Review,' 'Books in Canada,' etc.; author: 'Up at the Big House' 1982, 'The Private Press in Hertfordshire' 1986, 'Tillfield for the Cup' 1987, 'Keep on Running' 1988, 'Telling the Bees' 1990, 'The Turning Tide' 1990, 'Colourful Canada' 1992, 'The Beaver Picture & Other Stories' 1992; U.S. Information Serv. Travel Bursary 1984; British Council Award for Travel/Writing in Ont. 1986; Ont. Arts Council Writer's Award 1988, 1989, 1991, 1992, 1993; recreations: jazz, fishing, travel; Home: 240 Seaton St., Toronto, Ont. M5A 2T4.

**BURGE, John David Bryson,** B.Mus., M.Mus., D.M.A., A.R.C.T.; university professor / composer; b. Dryden, Ont. 2 Jan. 1961; s. David Roy and Mary Elizabeth (Briscoe) B.; e. Assoc., Royal Conservatory of Music 1979; Univ. of Toronto B.Mus. 1983, M.Mus. 1984; Univ. of B.C. D.M.A. 1989; m. Nancy Frances d. David and Margaret Gilchrist 4 June 1982; children: Ian David, Eric Robertson; ASST. PROF., SCHOOL OF MUSIC, QUEEN'S UNIV. 1987– ; studied composition with John Beckwith, Walter Buczynski, John Hawkins and Stephen Chatman; has written music for a wide variety of mediums, incl. many choral works performed by the Elmer Iseler Singers, Vancouver's Cantata Singers, the Phoenix Chamber Choir, the BBC Singers & num. other choirs; composition awards incl. five awards in the Performing Rights Orgn. of Canada Young Composers Competition 1985–88; 'Concerto for Piano and Orchestra' was commissioned and premiered by the Kingston Symphony, Glen Fast, Conductor and Brian Finley, soloist 11 March 1992; 'Thank You God: A Children's Prayer Cycle' was commissioned and premiered by the Glen Ellyn Children's Chorus, Sandra Prodan, Conductor 1993; Music published by Jaymar Publishers, London, Ont.; Mem., Candn. Music Centre; Candn. League of Composers; Candn. Univ. Music Soc.; Soc. of Candn. Composers Authors & Music Publishers; recreations: squash, windsurfing, bridge; Home: 35 Chartwell Cres., Kingston, Ont. K7K 6M6; Office: Kingston, Ont. K7L 3N6.

**BURGENER, Peter,** B.Arch.; architect; b. Toronto, Ont. 18 May 1950; s. John E. and Elinor R. (O'Neill) B.; e. Michael Power High Sch. Islington, Ont.; Univ. of Toronto B.Arch. 1975; m. M. Jocelyn d. Kenneth and Patricia Rivers 6 May 1972; children: Samantha Elizabeth, Matthew Sean, John Christian, David Peter; PARTNER, BURGENER LACHAPELLE KILPATRICK ARCHITECTS 1993– ; Dir., TownFrame Urban Design Group; Matrix Landscape Architecture; served arch. positions Ont., Sask. and Alta. 1975–78; commenced practice as Peter Burgener Arch. 1978, subsequently Burgener Gallant Archs. 1978–79, Burgener Gallant Lachapelle Archs. 1979–82, Burgener Lachapelle Archs. 1982–89, Burgener Lachapelle Kilpatrick Archs. 1989–90; Partner, The Webb Zerafa Menkès Housden Partnership 1990–92; Partner BLK/WZMH Archs. 1990–93; Dir. CBL Design Group 1986–93; Domus Design Group 1988–93; recipient ICSC Nat. Design Award 1985; Alta. Planning Award 1986; mem. Gov. Council & Extve. Ctte., Univ. of Toronto, Past Pres. Alumni Assn. Calgary; Vice-Chrmn., Calgary Dist Hosp. Group Bd. 1989–93; Dir. 500 Club S. Alta.; mem. Calgary Planning Comn. 1987–89; Calgary Devel. Appeal Bd. 1983–87; Chrmn. Candn. Council Christian & Jews W. Regional Bd. 1983–85; mem. Internat. Council Shopping Centres; Ednl. Facility Planning Inst.; Calgary Real Estate Forum; Bldg. Code Review Ctte. City of Calgary; Chancellor's Club Univ. of Calgary; Calgary Centre P.C. Assn. Bd. Dirs.; Winston Churchill Soc.; Royal Arch. Inst. Can.; Prov. Arch. Assn. Alta., B.C. & Ont.; R. Catholic; recreations: travel, cycling, sailing; Club: Glencoe (Calgary); Home: 502 Scarboro Ave. S.W., Calgary, Alta. T3C 2H6; Office: 600, 550 6th Ave. S.W., Calgary, Alta. T2P 0S2.

**BURGESS, Bernard Whittaker,** M.Sc.; retired pulp and paper executive; b. Ottawa, Ont. 7 Jan. 1921; s. Cecil and Violet (Hervey) B.; e. Hopewell Ave. Sch., Ottawa; Glebe Coll. Inst., Ottawa; Ottawa Tech. High Sch.; Queen's Univ., B.Sc. 1944, M.Sc. 1946; m. Evelyn Pearl, d. Richard Stethem, 25 May 1946; children: Brian Stethem, John Bernard Scott, Kathryn Ann (Mrs. Douglas Lamb), Mary Elizabeth (Mrs. John Roy); Commenced as Sr. Chemist, The E.B. Eddy Co., Hull, Que. 1945; Tech. Asst., Tech. Sec., Candn. Pulp and Paper Assn., Montreal 1946; joined Pulp and Paper Rsch. Inst. of Can. as Asst. to Pres., 1952, Secy. and Business Mgr. 1955, Vice-Pres. Adm. 1967, Exec. Vice-Pres. 1971, Dir. 1977, C.O.O. 1978, Pres. & C.E.O. 1979, Depy. Chrmn. 1986–92; Alderman, Village of Senneville, Que. 1961–67 and Mayor 1967–75; Councillor, Montreal Urban Community 1970–75; mem. Tech. Sec., Candn. Pulp and Paper Assn.; Tech. Assn. Pulp and Paper Industry; Chem. Inst. Can.; Assn. Prof. Engrs. Ont.; mem. Adv. Council on Engn., Queen's Univ. 1968–75; Chrmn. 1973–74; mem. Council, Queen's Univ. 1975– ; Trustee, Queen's Univ. 1980–92 (mem. Exec. Comte. 1981– ;); Chrmn. Communications Comte. 1982; mem. Finance Comte. 1983–92; Investment Comte. 1984– ;); Dir.: Tembec Inc.; Gov., Kingston General Hosp. 1992– ; Gov., Brockville General Hosp. 1993– ; Trustee, St. Vincent de Paul Hosp., Brockville 1986–92; Church of England; recreations: skiing, golf, woodworking; Clubs: Forest and Stream; Brockville Country; Home: 427 Hillcrest Rd., Elizabethtown, Ont. K6V 7C3.

**BURGESS, Ellen Diane,** MD, FRCPC, FACP; university professor; b. Winnipeg, Man. 9 Nov. 1953; d. Fred Owen and Norma Louise (Hansher) B.; e. Univ. of Manitoba M.D. 1976; post grad. edn. at Univ. of Man. 1976–79, Univ. of Washington 1979–81, Univ. of Alta. 1981–82; m. Kenneth s. Dr. Eric and Louise Larking 17 May 1986; children: Ian Katherine; ASSOC. PROF., FAC. OF MEDICINE, UNIV. OF CALGARY 1989– ; Asst. Prof., present univ. 1982–89; Asst. Dean, Admission & Student Affairs 1986–88; Dir., Nephrology Edn. Prog. 1988– ; Pres., Healthwest Consultants, Inc. 1991– ; Dir., Peritoneal Dialysis Prog., Foothills Hosp.; FRCPC 1982 (internal medicine), 1983 (nephrology); FACP 1986; Bd. of Dir., University Day Care Soc. 1988–90; Bd. Mem., Candn. Hypertension Soc. 1990– ; Mem., Am. & Internat. societies of Nephrol.; Internat. & Am. societies of Hypertension; Am. Fed. of Clinical Rsch.; author of 50 sci. papers, 70 sci. abstracts & 3 book chapters; recreations: swimming, cycling; Office: 1403 – 29th St., Calgary, Alta. T2N 2T9.

**BURGESS, John Herbert,** C.M., B.Sc., M.D.; physician; educator; b. Montreal, Que. 24 May 1933; s. John Frederick Burgess; e. Lower Can. Coll. Montreal 1951; McGill Univ. B.Sc. 1954, M.D., C.M. 1958; Univ. of Birmingham Research Fellow 1960–62; Univ. of Calif. San Francisco Research Fellow 1964–66; m. Andrea Clouston d. Andrew Scott Rutherford, Westmount, Que. 30 May 1958; children: Willa, Cynthia, Lynn, John; DIR., DIV. OF CARDIOLOGY, MONTREAL GEN. HOSP. 1973– ; Prof. of Med. McGill Univ. 1975– ; (Chrmn. Cardiol. Training there 1974–84); Consulting Cardiol. Douglas Hosp., Barrie Mem. Hosp., Huntingdon Gen. Hosp., Baffin Regional Hosp.; Dir. Cardiorespiratory Lab. present Hosp. 1968–73; Asst. Prof. of Med. McGill Univ. 1966, Assoc. Prof. 1969–75; Examiner, Royal Coll. Phys. & Surgs. Can. 1970–85 (Mem. Council); Chrmn., Com. on Examinations 1982–88, Vice Pres. (Medicine) 1988–90, Pres.-elect 1989–90, Pres. 1990–92, Past Pres. 1992–93; Chrmn., McLaughlin Test Comte. Internal Med. 1978–81; Test Comte. in Med., Med. Council Can. 1978–81; recipient Wood Gold Medal 1958; Nuffield Travelling Fellowship in Med. 1960–62; R. Samuel McLaughlin Fellowship 1964–66; Med. Research Council Can. Scholarship 1966–71; Charles O. Monat Associateship 1971–74; author various research articles; editor 'International Abstracts in Cardiology'; mem. Candn. Heart Foundation (Vice Chrmn. Scient. Review Comte. 1980–83); Am. Coll. Phys. (Gov. for Que. 1979–83); Montreal Cardiac Soc. (Pres. 1978–80); Lafleur Reporting Soc. (Pres. 1977–78); Candn. Cardiovascular Soc.; Candn. Soc. Clin. Investigation; Am. Physiol. Soc.; Am. Assn. Advanc. Science; Am. Heart Assn.; Am. Coll. Cardiol.; N.Y. Acad. Sciences; Alpha Omega Alpha; Member, Order of Canada; Fellow (Hon.), Coll. of Physicians of South Africa; Fellow (Hon.), Royal Australasian Coll. of Physicians; Fellow, Royal College of Physicians of Edinburgh; recreations: cross-country skiing; Home: 639 Murray Hill, Westmount, Que. H3Y 2W8; Office: 1650 Cedar Ave., Montreal, Que. H3G 1A4.

**BURGESS, Rachel Lillian,** C.M., B.S., PH.D.; psychologist; teacher; consultant; counselor; hypnotist; b. Grand Falls, N.B. 9 Nov. 1935; d. Joseph I. and Aurolie (Leclerc) Cormier; e. Grand Falls, N.B. Pub. Sch.; Nursing Sch. Montreal 1951–52; Univ. of Me. Bachelor in Psychol. 1971, Master in Emotionally Disturbed 1974, B.S. 1975, Teacher's Licence 1976, Master's Degree in Counselling 1979; Hon. degree: Doctor of Laws (Ph.D.) U. of St. Thomas 1980; C.A.S. degree (Cert. of Advanced Studies in Counselling) Univ. of Maine at Orono, Maine 1986; m. Lee A. Burgess, Grand Falls, N.B. 4 Sept. 1956; children: Jimmy, Leah, Donna, Carl, Alison; Past Princ. and Dir., Burgess Center for Handicapped, founder of sch. and sheltered workshop, teacher and counselor; private Counsellor practice 1987; Hypnotist; rec'd Record Achievement, Univ. of Me. 1971; Vanier Award 1971; Order of Canada, 1978; Model Educator, N.B. 1989; Member of Order Souverain et Militaire de la Milice du Saint Sepulcre 1989; Dame Commandeur, Confederation of Chivalry, Sydney, Australia; Member, Merit for Life, Sydney, Australia 1989; mem. Literacy Assn.; Mental Assn.; Psychol. Assn.; Mentally Retarded Assn.; Teachers' Assn. (Dir.); Counselors' Assn.; Hon. Pres., Assoc. Jeunesse-Education, Moncton, N.B.; listed in Community Leaders of the World; International Directory of Distinguished Leadership et al.; awarded Commemorative Medal for 125th Anniversary of Candn. Confederation 1993; R. Catholic; recreations: skiing, guitar, reading, thinking, meditation, philosophy; Address: 219 St. Georges St., Grand Falls, N.B. E3Y 1C3.

**BURGESS, Robert K.,** B.Comm.; research executive; b. Toronto, Ont. 29 Aug. 1957; s. Kenneth Elwood and Jessie May (Burleigh) B.; e. McMaster Univ. B.Comm. 1979; PRESIDENT, CHIEF EXECUTIVE OFFICER, CHIEF OPERATING OFFICER & DIR., ALIAS RESEARCH INC. 1992– ; Honeywell Information Systems & Digital Equipment 1979–84; joined Silicon Graphics Inc. as Sales Rep. 1984; progressed as Branch Manager, Regional Manager, President, SGI Canada and Vice-Pres., Applications until 1991; Pres. & C.O.O., Alias Research Inc. 1991; Bd. Dir., Alias Research Inc.; Mem., Young President's Orgn.; recreations: television, hockey, golf, charity; Office: 110 Richmond St. E., Toronto, Ont. M5C 1P1.

**BURGHAM, Ian,** B.A., M.Litt.; publisher; b. Auckland, N.Z. 1 Aug. 1950; s. Allen Russell and Barbara Jean (Wallace) B.; e. Queen's Univ. Kingston B.A. 1973; Univ. of Edinburgh M.Litt. 1980; m. Catherine d. Allen and Mary West 27 Aug. 1971; PUBLISHER AND PRES. GROSVENOR HOUSE PRESS INC. 1982– ; Dir., Pegasus Healthcare Internat.; joined Canongate Publishing Co. Edinburgh 1977–80; Publishing Mgr. MacDonald Publishers (Edinburgh) Ltd. 1980–82; recreations: music, canoeing, cross-country skiing, sailing; Office: 2 Pardee Ave., Ste. 203, Toronto, Ont. M6K 3H5.

**BURGHARDT, John Bradford, Jr.,** B.A.; advertising executive; b. Englewood, N.J. 13 Sept. 1939; s. John Bradford (dec.) and Ruth Kathryn (Hay) B.; e. Williams Coll. Williamstown, Mass. B.A. 1961; m. Nancy-Lane d. Philip and Anne Rogers 21 Oct. 1967; two d. Lissa, Rebecca; PRES. BURGHARDT WOLOWICH CRUNKHORN KIBBLE INC. 1985– ; Dir. Video Research &

Development Corp. Boston; Copywriter, Copy Supr. Young & Rubicam, New York 1961, Head Copy Dept. Young & Rubicam Italia, Milan 1970, Vice Pres.-Creative Dir. Young & Rubicam Canada, Toronto 1971–74; Pres. John Burghardt Creative Services, Toronto 1974–85; Chrmn. Bessie Awards for excellence in TV Advt. 1987; mem. Communications Ctte. Toronto/Ont. Olympic Council; author various films for pre-revolutionary Iranian govt. incl. 'The Presence of Persia' 1977; 'The Art of the Book' 1977; creator-writer 'Freedom to Speak' (12–part TV series PBS) 1982; creator & producer, stereo album on the environment, 'Earth, Air & Water'; mem., SOCAN (Soc. of Composers, Authors, & Music Publishers of Can.); other films, mag. articles; recreations: golf, tennis, skiing; Club: St. George's Golf & Country; Home: 62 Lyall Ave., Toronto, Ont. M4E 1W3; Office: 510 King St. E., Toronto, Ont. M5A 1M1.

**BURGIS, Grover Cornelius,** B.Sc., M.L.I.S.; librarian; b. Toronto, Ont. 20 Apr. 1933; s. Sinclair Grover and Gladys (Arnold) B.; e. Markham (Ont.) High Sch. 1953; Wheaton Coll. B.Sc. 1956; Univ. of Toronto Sch. Grad. Studies Mktg. Rsch. Course 1957–58; Univ. of Pittsburgh Grad. Sch. Lib. & Info. Sci's M.L.I.S. 1967, Ph.D. student 1973–75; Mass. Inst. of Technol. Info. Mgmt. Technol. 1968; Mgmt. Work Conf. Interpersonal Competence Harrisburg, Va. 1981; Team Bldg. & Process Cons. Chicago 1982; DIR., CITY OF BRAMPTON PUBLIC LIBRARY AND ART GALLERY 1983– ; Ind. & Agric. Chem. Sales Rep. Shell Oil Co. of Canada Ltd. 1956–59; Mktg. Field Rep. ERCO Industries 1959–61; Owner and Mgr. Nite and Day Laundromat, Toronto 1960–62; Mktg. Field Rep. A.C. Nielsen Co. of Canada Ltd. 1961–64; Rsch. and Liaison Offr. Royal Comn. Bilingualism & Biculturalism 1964–66; Info. Analyst Knowledge Availability Systems Centre Univ. of Pittsburgh 1966–67; Head, Tech. Services Univ. of Sask. 1967–70; Dir. Rsch. & Planning Br. Nat. Lib. of Can. Ottawa 1970–73; Extve. Dir. Captain Library Services Inc. N.J. 1975–76; Chief Lib. Thunder Bay Pub. Lib. 1976–83; Bd. mem. Magnus Theatre Northwest 1982–83; Founding Bd. Mem., Brampton Symphony Orchestra; Benefactor: Nat. Exhn. Centre & Centre Indian Art; Thunder Bay Community Auditorium; Eleanor Drury Children's Theatre; Cambrian Players; mem., Art Gallery of Ont.; author numerous publs.; mem. Alliance Française (Princeton); Candn. Lib. Assn.; Ont. Lib. Assn.; Candn. Assn. Info. Sci's; Am. Lib. Assn.; Am. Soc. Info. Sci's; Special Libs. Asnn.; N.J. Lib. Assn.; Assn. Lib. Bds. Ont. (mem. Extve.); Chief Extves. Large Pub. Libs. Ont. (Chrmn.); Assn. of Art Galleries of Ont.; Chrmn. Liaison Comte. for Ministry of Citizenship and Culture 1983–85; Internat. Biog. Assn.; Beta Phi Mu; recreations: creative writing, skiing; Clubs: Royal Canadian Yacht (Toronto); Franco American (N.Y.); Home: 16 Peel Ave., Brampton, Ont. L6W 1X2; Office: 65 Queen St. E., Brampton, Ont. L6W 3L6.

**BURHENNE, Hans Joachim,** M.D., F.R.C.P.(C), F.A.C.R.; F.F.R.R.C.I.(Hon.); educator; physician; b. Hannover, Germany 27 Dec. 1925; e. Ludw. Maximilian University Germany, 1946–51, M.D. Harvard Medical School, Training in Radiology, 1954–58; m. Linda Warren, 20 Oct. 1978 children: Mark, Antonia, Yvonne (first marriage) came to Can. 1978; PROF. OF RADIOLOGY, UNIV. OF B.C.; Head of Radiology, Vancouver Gen. Hosp. 1978–91; recipient Cannon Medal Soc. G.I. Radiologists 1982; author 'Alimentary Tract Roentgenology' 4th ed. 1989; mem. Candn. Assn. Radiols. (Hon. Treas. 1981–84); Chrmn., Section of Radio Diagnosis, Internat. Soc. of Radiology 1989– ; Office: 10th Ave. and Heather, Vancouver, B.C. V5Z 1M9.

**BURKA, Petra;** former figure skater; sports commentator; b. Amsterdam, Holland 17 Nov. 1946; d. Ellen Ruth (Danby) and Jan B.; came to Can. 1951; e. Kipling Coll. Inst., Vincent Massey Coll. Inst. and Lawrence Park Coll. Inst., Toronto, Ont.; Jr. Candn. Skating Champion 1961; Sr. Candn. Champion 1964–66; N. Am. Champion 1965; Third, Olympics, 1964; World Championships, Third 1964, First 1965, Third 1966; entered Prof. ranks 1966; Candn. Woman Athlete of the Year 1964, 1965; Lou Marsh Trophy Winner, 1965; subsequently worked in public relations capacity, Fitness & Amateur Sport Directorate, Dept. Nat. Health and Welfare, Ottawa, Ont.; researcher and production assistant on television and feature film projects; commentator for CBC and CBS (U.S.) television coverage of figure skating events; mem., Sports Hall of Fame; Anglican; Hon. Life mem., Toronto Cricket, Skating & Curling Club; Address: 13 Bushey Ave., Toronto, Ont. M6N 2R4.

**BURKA, Sylvia May;** financial executive, speedskater; b. Winnipeg, Man. 4 May 1954; d. John and Ilga (Bormann) B.; e. Gordon Bell H.S. 1972; var. univ. courses; common law spouse: W. David s. William and Catharine Hogg (9 years); FINANCIAL OFFICER & PARTNER, CANCORE BUILDING SERVICES LTD.; speedskating career spanning 15 years 1965–80 during which time she broke every prov. & nat. record as well as many track records in Eur.; Canada's Top Female Speedskater 1969–80; competed in Winter Olympic Games 1972, '76, '80; in World Overall & Sprint Championships 1970–80; Jr. World Champion Assen Holland 1973; Sr. Ladies World Champion Gjovik, Norway 1976; Sr. World Sprint Champion Alkmaar, Holland 1977; Canadian Skater of the Year 7 times; World Records in Speedskating Davos, Switz. 1973, Inzell, Germany 1976; in cycling 1000 m. Montreal 1982; competed World Cycling Championships 1980, '81, '82; Candn. Championship Medals & Records in Cycling; Best Performance in Olympic Games (4th in 1000 m) 1976; Female Athlete of the Year in Canada 1977; inducted Canada Sports Hall of Fame 1977; var. prov. awards; Order of Buffalo Hunt; Govt. House Award; recreations: nordic skiing, water-skiing, running, inline skating; Address: 1306 Queen St. E., Toronto, Ont. M4L 1C4.

**BURKE, Albert St. Croix;** public service executive; b. St. Jacques, Fortune Bay, Nfld. 3 Jan. 1940; s. Cornelius and Esther (St. Croix) B.; e. St. Boniface High Sch.; Coll. of Trade & Technol. St. John's, Nfld.; m. Ruth d. Gordon and Elizabeth Williams 19 Sept. 1964; children: Todd, Sean, Dianne, Mark; Bd. Mem., The Public Service Staff Relations Bd.; served 17 yrs. Agric. Can. Rsch. Stn., St. John's; Regional Vice Pres., Agric. Union, Pub. Service Alliance of Can. 1969, Exec. Vice Pres. of Union 1975, Nat. Pres. 1981–83; first Exec. Vice Pres. PSAC 1983, re-el. 1985, 1988–91; Life mem. & former Dir., PSAC Holdings; former mem. Adv. Ctte. Pub. Service Superannuation Act; former PSAC Rep. Jt. Consultation Ctte. Pub. Service Comn.; former Alternate to Nat. Pres. Nat. Jt. Council; Chartered mem. Lions Internat., former Dir., Vice Pres. and Pres. Kilbride Lions Club; recipient numerous honours and plaques from Agric. Union and from Community of Kilbride (served as Chrmn. Citizens Ctte. 8 yrs.); Dir. Fund Raising Campaign Ottawa Gen. Hosp.; recreations: golf, walking, fishing, bicycling, baseball; Home: 6564 Orningview St., Orleans, Ont. K1C 7H1; Office: C.D. Howe Bldg., West Tower, 240 Sparks St., (P.O. Box 1525, Stn. B) Ottawa, Ont. K1P 5V2.

**BURKE, Earla,** B.A., B.J., CFP; executive; b. Kirkland Lake, Ont. 12 Aug. 1935; d. Earl Easton and Laura Amy (Wright) b.; e. Univ. of Toronto Cert. in Bus. 1970; York Univ. B.A. 1976; Carleton Univ. B.J. 1978; Coll. for Financial Planning, Denver, Col., CFP 1987; divorced; children: Clayton, Virginia, Stacy, Cindy, Jason; PRESIDENT, MONEYSTRATEGY INC. 1983– ; Bus. Teacher, Seneca Coll. 12 yrs.; owner/mgr. assn. mgmt. firm 4 yrs.; personnel mgr. 4 yrs.; lectr. in acctg.; conducts Financial Planning seminars; private pilot's licence; naui scuba cert.; mem. Candn. Inst. Mgmt. (Dir. of Edn. 1984–86); Gov., Invest. Funds Inst. Can. 1986–92 (Chrmn. Independent Dealers 1983–88); recreations: skiing, tennis; Office: 1177 Yonge St., Ste. 110, Toronto, Ont. M4T 2Y4.

**BURKE, John Kevin Neil,** B.Eng., M.B.A.; merchant banker; b. Three Rivers, Que. 8 Jan. 1941; s. John William and Elva Beatrice (McNeil) B.; e. Three Rivers H.S. 1958; McGill Univ. B.Eng. 1963; Univ. of Western ONt. M.B.A. 1968; m. Beverley Beaudin d. Victoria and Bruce Hunter 4 July 1964; children: Victoria, Carolyn, Neil; DIRECTOR & FOUNDING SHAREHOLDER, LANCASTER FINANCIAL INC. 1986– ; Senior Investment Research Analyst, Burns Fry Ltd. 1968–73; Sr. Inst. Rep. 1973–76; Assoc. Mergers & Acquisitions 1976–80; Dir. in charge of Mergers & Acquisitions 1980–86; Royal Canadian Navy, retired as Lieutenant 1958–66; recreations: fishing, painting; club: National; Home: 40 Baby Point Cres., Toronto, Ont. M6S 2B8; Office: One First Canadian Place, Suite 5700, P.O. Box 18, Toronto, Ont. M5X 1A9.

**BURKE, Martyn;** writer, film director; e. Royal York Collegiate; McMaster Univ.; has produced & directed documentaries for CBC, CBS, PSB & TF-I in France including 'Connections' (an investigation into organized crime), 'Idi Amin,' 'Witnesses' (the war in Afghanistan) and many others; Anik Award for best CBC documentary; Genie – Canadian Film Award for best feature film screenplay; Prix Gemaux for best directing, French-language documentary; currently living in both Santa Monica, Calif. and Toronto; author: 'Laughing War' 1980, 'The Commissar's Report' 1984, 'Ivory Joe' 1991 (fiction).

**BURKE, Rebecca Ann,** B.A., M.F.A.; artist, university professor; b. Kalamazoo, Mich. 25 Oct. 1946; d. Robert Eugene and Corrine Sarah (Loy) B.; e. Western Mich. Univ. 1964–66; Univ. of Guam B.A. 1969; Ohio State Univ. M.F.A. 1972; m. John R. s. Raymond and Kathleen Burke 20 Nov. 1965; divorced; one s.: Shawn Patrick Burke; PROFESSOR, DEPT. OF FINE ARTS, MOUNT ALLISON UNIV. 1992– ; Instr., Grant MacEwan Community Coll. 1976–80; Asst. Prof., present univ. 1980; Assoc. Prof. 1984, Head, Dept. of Fine Arts 1990–93, Prof. 1992; solo exbns. incl.: Gallery Connexion, Fredericton; Mt. St. Vincent Univ. Art Gall., Halifax 1988, Confed. Ctr. Art Gall., Charlottetown 1985, Owens Art Gall. Sackville 1984, Struts Gall. Sackville 1983 and earlier exbns.; 2-person exbns. incl.: Walter Phillips Gall., The Banff Centre, Banff and Student's Union Art Gall., Univ. of Alberta 1981 and earlier exbns.; group exbns. incl.: Galerie Sans Nom, Moncton and The XXV Internat. Prix of Contemporary Art of Monte Carlo Fond. Prince Pierre De Monaco, Monte Carlo, Monaco 1991, 'Atque Ars,' The Owens Art Gall., Mt. Allison Univ. and Lachine Canal Complex Montreal 1990, Main Hall, Can. Pavilion, Expo '86 Vanc. 1986, Pauline McGibbon Cultural Ctr. Toronto 1984, The Owens Art Gall. 1981, 89, 90, 91, 92, Struts Gall. 1981, 83, 84, 85, 89, 90, 91 and numerous earlier exbns.; commissions incl.: Kinetic sculpture comn., Main Hall, Can. Pavilion, Expo '86 Vanc. 1986; recipient of several grants, awards and fellowships; cited in numerous mags., jours., books, catalogues since 1973; Mem., Struts Gall. 1980– ; (Vice-Pres. 1989–90); Candn. Artists' Rep. 1982–92, Lane Studies Inc. (Sackville) (Pres. 1981–90; Mount Allison Fac. Assn. 1980–92 (Sec. 1988–89); recreations: gardening, swimming, nordic skiing; clubs: University; Home: P.O. Box 1388, Sackville, N.B. E0A 3C0; Office: Dept. of Fine Arts, Mount Allison Univ., Sackville, N.B. E0A 3C0.

**BURKE, Ronald J.,** M.A., Ph.D.; educator; b. Winnipeg, Man. 22 Oct. 1937; s. John Stanley and Anne Katherine (Moskal) B.; e. Univ. of Man. B.A. 1960; Univ. of Mich. M.A. 1962, Ph.D. 1966; children: Sharon, Rachel, Jeff; PROF. OF ADM. STUDIES, YORK UNIV. 1972– ; Assoc. Dean, Research; Sr. Fellow, Nat. Center Mgmt. Rsch. & Devel. Sch. of Bus. Adm. Univ. of W. Ont. 1988– , Imperial Life Profl. of Orgnl. Behaviour 1988– ; Teaching Asst. Univ. of Man. 1959–60; Teaching Fellow, Univ. of Mich. 1960–62, Rsch. Asst. 1962–66; Asst. Prof. Univ. of Minn. 1966–68; Asst. Prof. present Univ. 1968, Assoc. Prof. 1969; Cons. various bus. and govt. orgns.; recipient numerous rsch. grants incl. York Univ. Ford Found. Grants 1969–72, rsch. & travel grants 1976–78; Can. Council Grants 1974–75; Imperial Oil Rsch. Grants 1974–80, 1986–88, Donner Found. Grant 1975–77; Fed. Dept. Labour Grant 1972–74; Bronfman Awards 1976–77, 1979–80; Health & Welfare Rsch. Grant & Scholar 1977–79; Social Sci. & Health Rsch. Grants 1979–80, 1986–87; Ont. Min. Labour 1982; Nat. Adv. Council Status Women 1988–89; author or co-author numerous sci. publs.; Founding Ed. Candn. Jour. Adm. Sci.; mem. Candn. Psychol. Assn.; Am. Psychol. Assn.; Acad. Mgmt.; Adm. Sci's Assn. Can.; recreations: walking, reading, gardening; Home: 252 Cortleigh Blvd., Toronto, Ont. M5N 1P7; Office: 4700 Keele St., North York, Ont. M3J 1P3.

**BURLEY, Stephen Kevin,** B.Sc., D.Phil., M.D.; physician; scientist; b. London, England 13 Nov. 1957; s. Kevin Hubert and June Peggy (Arthurton) B.; e. Sir Fredrick Banting S.S.; Univ. of Western Ont., B.Sc. (Hons.) 1980, Oxford Univ., D. Phil. 1983 (Rhodes Scholar, Ont. & Exeter); Harvard Med. Sch., M.D. magna cum laude (1987); PHYSICIAN and STRUCTURAL BIOLOGIST; Mem., Biophysical Soc.; author & co-author of sci. papers; recreations: mountaineering; Club: Alpine Club of Can.; Home: 500 East 63rd St., New York, NY 10021.

**BURMAN, Tony;** journalist; b. Montreal, Que. 13 June 1948; s. J. George and Clare Walsh B.; e. Loyola College; m. Margot Trevelyan 24 June 1977; children: Jeremy, Jacquie; EXECUTIVE PRODUCER, CBC PRIME TIME NEWS 1993– ; and AREA EXECUTIVE PRODUCER, CBC DAILY INFORMATION PROGRAMS 1993– ; Reporter, The Montreal Star 1969–72; Extve. Prod., 'Cross-Country Check-up,' CBC Radio Montreal / Contbg. Prod., 'As It Happens' / Story Editor, CBC Television 1972–75; Sr. Prod, Lineup / Assignment Ed., 'The National' CBC Toronto 1975–81; Extve. Prod., 'The National' 1980–82; European Bureau Prod., London, CBC Nat. TV News 1982–85; Sr. Documentary Producer, 'The Journal' 1986–90; Chief News Editor, CBC, National TV News 1990–93; Mng. Dir., CBC Newsworld 1992; major documentaries: 'Sudan: Children of Darkness' (Gemini Award 1990; Unda Prize Monte Carlo Fest. 1991); 'Spanish Civil War: Last Great

Cause (Gemini 1988); 'Nelson Mandela: A Profile' (Gemini nom. 1986); 'Ethiopia Revisited' 1989, 'The Reagan Years 1988, 'Air India Crash' (Best Documentary, 1987, Candn. Assn. of Journalists); Home: 375 Keewatin Ave., Toronto, Ont. M4P 2A4; Office: Box 500, Station A, Toronto, Ont. M5W 1E6.

**BURNET, Jean Robertson,** C.M., Ph.D.; educator; b. Toronto, Ont. 10 June 1920; d. John and Jemima (Sheals) Burnet; e. Strathcona Pub. Sch. and Owen Sound (Ont.) Coll. & Vocational Inst.; Univ. of Toronto Victoria Coll. B.A. 1942, M.A. 1943; Univ. of Chicago Ph.D. 1948; D.Litt., York Univ. 1985; PROFESSOR EMERITUS, YORK UNIVERSITY 1985– ; Instr. to Assoc. Prof. Univ. of Toronto 1945–67; Prof. of Sociol., Glendon Coll., York Univ. 1967–85; Visiting Lectr. Univ. of N.B. 1948–49; Chrmn. of Sociol. Glendon Coll. 1967–72, 1974–76, Co-ordinator of Candn. Studies 1973–74; Research Assoc. Royal Comn. of Bilingualism & Biculturalism 1966–69; Chrmn. Candn. Ethnic Studies Adv. Comte. Dept. Secy. of State 1973–87, mem. Ethnic Hist. Adv. Panel 1975–86; rec'd Guggenheim Fellowship 1955–56; Can. Council Fellowship 1972–73; named Learned Assoc. Univ. of Windsor 1976; author 'Next-Year Country' 1951; 'Ethnic Groups in Upper Canada' 1972; (with Howard Palmer) 'Coming Canadians: An Introduction to the History of Canada's Peoples' 1988; various book chapters, articles on ethnic relations and multiculturalism; Ed.-in-Chief 'Canadian Review of Sociology and Anthropology/La Revue Canadienne de Sociologie et d'Anthropologie' 1963–68; Ed., 'Ontario History' 1990– ; Member of the Order of Canada 1989; Outstanding Contribution Award, Candn. Sociol. and Anthrop. Assoc. 1990; Candn. Sociol. & Anthrop. Assn.; Candn. Ethnic Studies Assn.; Am. Sociol. Assn.; Home: 494 St. Clements Ave., Toronto, Ont. M5N 1M4; Office: 2275 Bayview Ave., Toronto, Ont. M4N 3M6.

**BURNETT, David Grant,** B.A., M.A., Ph.D.; curator, writer and gallery owner; b. Lincoln, Eng. 1 Oct. 1940; s. Wilfred Burnett of Fredericton, N.B.; e. Univ. of London, Birkbeck Coll. B.A. 1965, Courtauld Inst. of Art M.A. 1967, Ph.D. 1973; children: Charles, Wenham, Emma; m. 2ndly Marilyn Schiff 1983; Lectr. in Hist. of Art Univ. of Bristol 1967–70, Assoc. Prof. of Art Hist. Carleton Univ. 1970–80, Chrmn. of Dept. 1974–77, 1978–79; Curator, Contemporary Candn. Art, Art Gallery of Ont. 1980–84; exhns. and catalogues incl. 'A Tribute to Paul Klee 1879–1940' Nat. Gallery Can. 1979; 'Guido Molinari Drawings' Agnes Etherington Art Centre Kingston 1981; Robert Bourdeau and Phillip Pocock, A.G.O. 1981; 'Gershon Iskowitz' A.G.O. 1982; 'Alex Colville' A.G.O. 1983; 'Noel Harding' A.G.O. 1982; 'Oscar Cahén' A.G.O. 1983; 'Toronto Painting '84' A.G.O. 1984; 'Harold Town Retrospective' A.G.O. 1986; other catalogues: 'Guido Molinari: Quantificateur' Musée d'art contemporain Montreal 1979; 'Jeremy Smith' Mira Godard 1985; 'Jack Chambers Retrospective' London Regional Art Gall. 1988; numerous articles, reviews, papers field of art; series 5 programs on Modern Art CTV 1976–77 and 5 on Landscape Painting 1979; various radio and TV interviews; author 'Contemporary Canadian Art' (with Marilyn Schiff) 1983; 'Alex Colville' 1983; 'Town' 1986; 'Anton Cétin' 1986; 'Jeremy Smith' 1988; 'Cineplex Odeon: The First Ten Years. A Celebration of Contemporary Canadian Art' 1989; 'Masterpieces of Canadian Art from the National Gallery of Canada' 1990; Can. Council Grants 1974, 1980; served numerous comtes. Can. Council Awards to Artists; Univ. Art Assn. Can. (Secy.-Treas.); Assn. Univs. & Colls. Scholarship Bd.; A.C.A.P. Discipline Force (Chrmn. 1979–80); mem. Internat. Assn. Art Critics; recreations: music, reading, flying; Office: 201 Glengrove Ave. W., Toronto, Ont. M4R 1P4.

**BURNETT, John Thomas,** Q.C.; lawyer; b. Niagara Falls, Ont. 15 Apr. 1931; s. Fred and Sarah Duncan (Smyth) B.; e. Univ. of Toronto, B.A. 1953, LL.B. 1956; York Univ. LL.B. 1991; called to Bar of Ont. 1958 after attending Osgood Hall Law Sch.; Grad. study, McGill Univ. and Hague Acad. of Internat. Law 1969–70; children: John Stephen, Marcia Anne, Jill Elizabeth; SR. VICE-PRES. & GEN. COUNSEL, THE ROYAL BANK OF CANADA 1984– ; Founding partner, Broderick, Burnett, McLeod, Clifford, Marinelli, Amadio 1958–69; Vice-Pres., Secy. & Asst. Gen. Counsel, Northern Telecom 1974–80; Vice-Pres. & Gen. Counsel, Royal Bank of Canada 1980–84; mem., Candn. Bar Assn.; Law Soc. of Upper Can.; Que. Bar Assn.; Internat. Law Assn.; Assn. of Candn. Gen. Counsel; recreations: golf, tennis, theatre; Club: Inverugie Golf; Home: 33 Harbour Sq., #1401, Toronto, Ont. M5J 2G2; Office: Royal Bank Plaza, Toronto, Ont. M5J 2J5.

**BURNETT, Theodore F.,** B.A., LL.B.; business executive; b. Toronto, Ont. 10 Feb. 1947; s. Jack H. and Mary (Frolick) B.; e. Northview Hts. S.S. 1965; Univ. of Toronto B.A. 1968, LL.B. 1971; called to Ont. Bar 1973; m. Esther d. Rose and Sydney Roth 28 June 1972; children: Joshua, Emily, Zachary; PRES., BURNAC LEASEHOLDS INC. & BURNAC CORP. 1987– ; Solicitor, Rosenfeld Schwartz 1973–77; Principal, Burnett & Jacobson 1978–87; Sole Prop., Burnett & Jacobson, Barristers & Solicitors; Pres., Josham Farms Limited; Office: 48 St. Clair Ave. W., Suite 700, Toronto, Ont. M4V 3B6.

**BURNEY, Derek,** B.A., M.A.; executive; b. Fort William, Ont.; e. Queen's Univ. B.A., M.A.; m. Joan Peden; 4 children; CHRMN., PRES. & C.E.O., BCE TELECOM INTERNATIONAL INC. and EXTVE. VICE-PRESIDENT, INTERNATIONAL, BCE INC. 1993– ; Foreign Serv. Offr., Dept. of External Affairs 1963; Wellington, N.Z. 1965; Tokyo 1965; intensive lang. training, U.S. State Dept. Japanese Studies Ctr. Tokyo 1967–69; Counsellor for Pol. Affairs, Candn. Embassy Tokyo 1969–72; Head, Officer Assignment Section, Personnel, H.Q. 1972; Dir., Pacific & N.E. Asia Div. 1975; Sr. Dept. Asst. to Sec. of State for External Affairs & concurrently Official Spokesman for External Affairs 1976; Ambassador to the Rep. of Korea 1978; Administrator, Ottawa Summit, H.Q. 1980; Asst. Under-Sec., Bur. of Trade, Devel. & Gen. Econ. Relations 1981; Asst. Dep. Min. for U.S. Affairs 1983; Agenda Coord., Que. Summit Meeting March 1985; Assoc. Under-Sec. of State, External Affairs Sept. 1985; Chief of Staff to the Prime Minister 1987–Dec. 1988; Canadian Ambassador to the United States 1989–93; Personal Rep. of P.M. for Economic Summits in Houston 1990, London 1991, and Munich 1992; Office: 1000, rue de La Gauchetiere O., Suite 1100, Montreal, Que. H3B 4Y8.

**BURNHAM, Elizabeth (Libby),** Q.C., B.A., LL.B.; lawyer; b. Florenceville, N.B. 14 Nov. 1938; d. Harry S. and Margaret L. (McKay) B.; e. Univ. of N.B. 1957; Acadia Univ. B.A. 1960; Dalhousie Univ. LL.B. 1963; m. Mr. Justice G. Gordon Sedgwick; children: John, Anne, James; COUNSEL, BORDEN & ELLIOT, Toronto; practised Gilbert, McGloan & Gillis, Saint John 1963–67; Legal Dept., The T. Eaton Co. Limited, Toronto 1967–71; Sr. Advisor to Premier of New Brunswick 1970–87; Dir., Canadian Club of Toronto 1993– , Candn. Broadcasting Corp. 1987–93; Project Development Cttee., Human Resources, Extve. & Nominating Cttes. CBC; Dir., Wellesley Hosp. 1990– ; Planning and Development Cttee., Wellesley Hospital 1992– ; Trustee, Genesis Rsch. Found. for Womens' Health 1990–93; Dir., Queen Elizabeth Hosp. Found. 1992– ; Dir., New Brunswick Symphony Found. 1992– ; Ont. P.C. Fund 1987–91; Conservation Review Bd., Ont. Heritage Act 1987–93; Chair, WIN (support fund for P.C. women candidates) 1987–92; Committee for '94 (non-partisan group for advancement of women in political and public life); Cdn. Rep. at UN Expert Group meeting on women in public life, Vienna, Austria, May 1991; Member of the N.B. Bar 1963– ; Member of the Ontario Bar 1978– ; Apptd., Federal Queen's Counsel 1992; Home: 21 Lamport Ave., Toronto, Ont. M4W 1S7; Office: Scotia Plaza, 40 King St. W., Toronto, Ont. M5H 3Y4.

**BURNHAM-STAEHLI, Eva Gertrud;** conservator, costume and textiles; b. Bern, Switzerland 5 April 1946; d. Gottfried Johann and Gertrud (Bachofner) Staehli; e. studied textiles at Frauenschule Bern; trained in textile conservation, Abegg Stiftung, Riggisberg, Switzerland; m. Mark D. s. Harold and Dorothy (McDonald) Burnham 1 Oct. 1971; divorced 1986; CONSERVATOR, COSTUME & TEXTILES, MCCORD MUSEUM OF CANADIAN HISTORY 1991– ; Textile & Tapestry Conservator, Abegg-Stiftung & Historisches Museum (Bern, Switz.) 1967–71; Conservator, Textiles, Royal Ont. Mus. 1971–76; Chief Conservator, Textiles, Candn. Conservation Inst. 1976–91; editor of Textile Conservation newsletter 1984– ; Home: 41 Staynor St., Montreal, Que. H3Z 1V1; Office: 690 Sherbrooke St. W., Montreal, Que. H3A 1E9.

**BURNS, Darlene Catherine,** C.H.R.P.; human resources executive; b. Brockville, Ont. 21 Oct. 1952; d. Andrew John and Mildred Carrie (Antoine) McCombie; e. Brockville C.I. 1970; Queen's Univ. 1991– ; m. J. Brian s. W. Robert and Muriel Burns 6 Oct. 1978; one s.: Casey Kenneth; MANAGER, COMPENSATION AND BENEFITS, BLACK AND DECKER CANADA INCORPORATED 1987– ; Materials Planner, Buyer, Black and Decker Canada Incorporated 1976–85; Human Resource Specialist 1985–87; Cert. Human Resource Profl. Designation 1989; Cert. of Proficiency in Employee Benefits 1992; Statement of Achievement (St. Lawrence Coll.), Materials Mngt. 1985, Human Resources 1987, Extve. Mem. & Trustee, Leeds & Grenville United Way Assn. 1987–89; Pres. & Extve. Mem., St. Lawrence Valley Personnel Assn. 1989–93; recreations: golf, guitar, piano; clubs: Royal Brock Spa & Sports; Home: RR 3, Hudson Point, Brockville, Ont. K6V 5T3; Office: 100 Central Ave., Brockville, Ont. K6V 5W6.

**BURNS, H. Michael;** insurance executive; b. Toronto, Ont. 19 June 1937; s. late Charles Fowler Williams and Janet Mary (Wilson) B.; e. Trinity Coll. Sch., Port Hope; Cornell Univ., Ithaca N.Y.; m. Susan P., d. C.A. Cathers, Toronto 23 Dec. 1980; children: Charles F.M., Janet Michelle; CHRMN. & DIR., CROWN LIFE INSURANCE COMPANY and DEPY. CHRMN. & DIR., CROWNX INC.; Pres. & Treas., Kingfield Investments Ltd. (and associated subsidiary companies); Dir., Algoma Central Railway; Beutel, Goodman & Co. Ltd.; Crown Financial Management Limited; Denison Mines Limited; Derby International S.A.; Fiduciary Investment Co. (N.J.); Landmark Corp.; SJM Oil & Gas Inc.; Burns Bros. & Denton Ltd. (Burns Fry Ltd.), Toronto, Vancouver, and New York 1958–77; Vice-Pres. then Chrmn., Crown Life Insur. Co. 1971– ; Chrmn. then Pres., Crownx Inc. 1980– ; Chrmn., Crowntek Inc. 1985–87; Gov. Trinity Coll. Sch.; Chrmn. & Trustee, McMichael Canadian Collection; Gov., Olympic Trust of Canada; Trustee, Sunnybrook Health Science Ctr.; Vice-Chairperson & Dir., Candn. Found. For AIDS Research; Dir., Candn. Council of Christians and Jews; Dir., Candn. Simmental Assn.; Dir., Royal Agric. Winter Fair; Kappa Alpha; recreations: farming; Clubs: Toronto; York; Home: Kingswood, R.R. 3, King City, Ont. L0G 1K0; Office: 120 Bloor St. E., 7th Floor, Toronto, Ont. M4W 1B8.

**BURNS, Hal;** provincial civil servant; b. Collingwood, Ont. 17 July 1937; s. Harold Edward and Marie Christine (Mowat) B.; e. Ryerson Inst. Technol.; Registrar, Travel Ind. Act Ont. 1987–..; Broadcaster 1957–60, CJRH Richmond Hill, Radio Jamaica (Kingston, Jamaica) and CFGM Toronto; Travel Agency Mgr. 1960–74; Owner Hal Burns Travel Ltd. Etobicoke 1974–87; Exec. Vice-Pres. and Bd. mem. Non-Smokers Rights Assn. Can.; Founding Vice-Pres. Independent Travel Profls. Can. and Travel Agts. Action Group; Past Vice-Pres. Candn. Inst. Travel Counsellors; Past Dir. Kiwanis Kingsway; Home: 2810 - 24 Mabelle Ave., Etobicoke, Ont. M9A 4X8.

**BURNS, James William, (Jim),** O.C., B. Com., M.B.A., LL.D., C.L.J.; business executive; b. Winnipeg, Man., 27 Dec. 1929; s. late Charles William and Helen Gladys (Mackay) b.; e. Gordon Bell High Sch., Winnipeg; Univ. of Man., B. Com; Harvard Univ., M.B.A.; m. Barbara Mary, d. G. F. Copeland, 12 Aug. 1953; children: James F. C., Martha J., Alan W.; DEPUTY CHAIRMAN, POWER CORP. OF CANADA; Past Chrmn., Power Financial Corp.; Chrmn. & Dir. The Great-West Life Assurance Co.; Chrmn. Extve. Ctte. & Dir., MD Investment Services Ltd.; Dir., The Investors Group; Power Financial Corp.; IBM Canada Ltd.; Chrmn., Advisory Group, Extve. Compensation in the Public Service; Gov., Internat. Mgmt. and Develop. Inst., Washington, D.C.; Honorary Lt. Col. Queen's Own Cameron Highlanders of Canada; past Chrmn., The Conference Bd. of Canada; Hon. Chrmn., Manitoba Museum of Man and Nature; Mem., Governor's Counc., Shaw Festival; recreations: fishing, golf, hunting; Clubs: St. Charles Country; Manitoba (Winnipeg); Albany, Beacon Hall, Toronto (Toronto); Mount Royal; Mount Bruno Country (Montréal); The Landings Club, Inc. (Savannah, GA); Office: 751 Victoria Sq., Montreal, Que. H2Y 2J3.

**BURNS, Latham Cawthra,** B.A.; investment dealer; b. Toronto, Ont. 26 June 1930; s. Herbert Latham and Isobel (Cawthra) B.; e. Trinity Coll. Sch., Port Hope, Ont.; Collegiate Sch. (N.Y.); Cornell Univ., B.A.; m. Patricia-Annette, d. Paul Higgins, 1 May 1971; children: Reed Cawthra, Holton Latham, Farish Victoria, Cawthra Caroline, Ainsley Isobel; HONORARY CHAIRMAN, BURNS FRY LIMITED; Dir., Echo Bay Mines Ltd.; Slough Estates Canada Ltd.; Standard Products (Canada) Ltd.; joined present Co. 1952; Delta Kappa Epsilon; Anglican; recreations: golf, tennis; Clubs: York; The Toronto; Toronto Badminton & Racquet; Toronto Hunt; Home: 146 Warren Rd., Toronto, Ont. M4V 2S5; Office: First Canadian Place, Suite 5000, P.O. Box 150, Toronto, Ont. M5X 1H3.

**BURNS, Michael Cornelius,** B.A.; business executive; b. Regina, Sask. 18 Jan. 1939; s. Cornelius Florenz and Mabelle Evelyn (Hogg) B.; e. Univ. of Manitoba, B.A. 1960, IBM Corp. Adv. Extve. Sch. 1974; m. Bette Ann d. James and Gertrude Elizabeth Billyard 30 Sept. 1967;

children: Matthew, Joanne, Christopher; EXTVE. VICE-PRES., FINANCE & ADMIN., B.C. GAS INC. 1989– ; Pres. Sentinel Strategies Ltd. 1979–89; Chrmn. & Pres., Pilot Laboratories Corp. 1986–89; Vice-Pres., IBM Can. 1960–79 (incl. sr. extve. positions IBM World Trade Corp. & IBM Am. Far East Corp.); Chrmn., Cabinet Review Ctte. on auto ins., Prov. of Man. 1979; Gen. Mgr., Expo 86 Corp. 1981–82; Sr. Extve. in Gas Utility Corp.; Chrmn., Internat. Approval Services, Cleveland, Ohio; Dir., Fuelmaker Corp.; Inland Pacific Energy Corp.; Inland Gas & Oil; Inland Gas Marketing; Former Dir., Atomic Energy of Canada Ltd.; B.C. Trade Develop. Corp.; International Financial Centre, Vancouver; Pine Point Mines Limited; Dome Advertising (B.C.) Ltd.; Urban Transp. Devel. Corp.; Yorkshire Trust Co.; Eaton Trust; Banco National de Lavoro (BNL); Univ. of Man. Centennial Distinguished Alumnus Award 1976; Chrmn., Red Shield Appeal; Roman Catholic; Past Chrmn., B.C. Soc. Credit Funding Ltd.; B.C. Dir., PC Can. Fund; Former Dir., St. Paul's Hosp.; Candn. Counc. of Christians & Jews; Vancouver Coll.; Vancouver Symphony Soc.; Anna Wyman Dance Theatre; UBC Comm. Advy. Bd.; St. Anthony's Sch.; contbr. author to: 'Report of the Ministerial Insurance Review Committee' 1979; 'Privatization: Tactics & Techniques' 1987; 'Considerations in Privatizing a Large Crown Corporation' Fraser Inst. 1989; recreations: skiing, tennis, hunting, fishing; Clubs: Vancouver; Whistler Mountain Ski; Vancouver; Candn.; Hollyburn Country; Vancouver Bd. of Trade; Home: 996 Anderson Cres., West Vancouver, B.C. V7T 1S7; Office: 1111 W. Georgia St., Vancouver, B.C. V6E 4M4.

**BURNS, Patrick Dennis;** insurance executive; b. Toronto, Ont. 9 Aug. 1928; s. Albert Edward and Elizabeth (Murphy) B.; e. St. Michael's Coll. Sch., Toronto, 1942–46; m. June Lorraine, d. Stanley Allcock, Toronto, 10 Nov. 1951; children: Patricia Anne, Barbara Lynn; Chrmn., Pres. & C.E.O., Confederation Life Ins. Co. 1990–93, retired; joined Confederation Life Ins. Co. 1946; apptd. Mgr., Planning 1956; Data Processing Extve. 1961; Dir., Systems and Computors 1965; Asst. Vice Pres. 1967; Adm. Vice Pres., Corporate 1968; Vice Pres. and Controller 1970; Vice Pres., Group Ins. 1971; Vice Pres., Cdn. Oper. 1974; Extve. Vice-Pres. and Dir. 1980; Pres. 1982; Pres. and C.E.O. 1985, Chrmn. 1990; Fellow, Life Office Mgmt. Assn. 1950; Dir., Junior Achievement of Canada; Past Pres., Candn. Assn. of Accident & Sickness Insurers; former Dir., Life Office Management Assn.; Past Chrmn., Candn. Life & Health Insurance Assn.; Liberal; R. Catholic; recreations: golf, curling; tennis; Clubs: Donalda; National; Home: 156 Underhill Dr., Don Mills, Ont. M3A 2K5.

**BURNS, Peter Thomas,** Q.C., LL.M.; educator; lawyer; b. Dunedin, N.Z. 13 July 1938; s. Albert Peace and Elizabeth Eileen (Hyde-Harris) B.; e. King's High Sch. Dunedin 1957; Univ. of Otago (N.Z.) LL.B. 1962, LL.M. 1963; m. Charlotte d. John Geddes and Olwyn Watson 5 Dec. 1964; children: Andrew John, Victoria Anne; PROFESSOR OF LAW, UNIV. OF BRIT. COLUMBIA 1971– ; and Dean of Law 1982–91; Assoc. Counsel, Blake, Cassels and Graydon, Barr. & Sols., Vancouver 1991– ; Lectr. in Law, Otago Univ. 1964–65; Sr. Lectr. in Law Auckland Univ. 1966–68; Asst. Prof. of Law Univ. of B.C. 1968, Assoc. Prof. 1969; Comnr., Law Reform Comn. of B.C. 1986–93; Vice-Chrmn., Forestry Resources Comn. of B.C. 1989–91; Consultant to various fed. and prov. govt. depts. and law reform comns.; Mem., U.N. Ctte. of Experts on the Suppression of Torture 1987– ; Chrmn., Internat. Centre for Criminal Law Reform and Criminal Justice Policy, Vancouver 1993– ; Visiting Fellow, Centre for Socio-Legal Studies Oxford 1981, Wolfson Coll. Oxford 1981; Barrister and Solr. Supreme Courts N.Z. 1964 and B.C. 1975; author 'A Casebook in the Law of Crimes' 2nd ed. 1972; 'Criminal Injuries Compensation: Social Remedy or Political Palliative for Victims of Crime?' 1980, 2nd ed. 1991; co-author 'The Functions and Powers of Justices of the Peace and Coroners' 1968; co-ed. 'Criminal Procedure: Canadian Law and Practice' 1981; recreations: writing, travel; Club: Vancouver; Home: 6558 Beechwood St., Vancouver, B.C. V6P 5T9; Office: 1822 East Mall, Vancouver, B.C. V6T 1Y1.

**BURNS, Stephen Edward,** B.A., C.A., M.B.A.; chartered accountant; b. Toronto, Ont. 26 July 1942; s. Mort J. and Sylvia (Fishbain) B.; e. Forest Hill C.I. 1960; Univ. of Toronto B.A. 1964; Queen's Univ. C.A. 1967; York Univ. M.B.A. 1971; m. Erica d. Sydney and Shirley Mendelson 5 May 1981; children: Matthew, Simon, Lucas; PARTNER, BEALLOR, BEALLOR & BURNS 1972– ; Partner, Starkman, Kraft, Rothman, Berger & Grill 1968–72; specialist in cons. serv. to owner-managed businesses; Founding Vice-Pres., Internat. Group of Acctg. Firms; Dir., CUC Broadcasting; Secretary, Weizmann Inst. for Sci.; Treas., Starlight Found.; Mem., Candn. Inst. of C.A.s; Inst. of C.A.s of Ont.; author of mag. articles; recreations: bridge, sailing, scuba; Clubs: Island Yacht; Home: 2 Alexandra Wood, Toronto, Ont. M5N 2R9; Office: 28 Overlea Blvd., Toronto, Ont. M4H 1B6.

**BURR, Ronald C.,** M.D., C.M., F.R.C.S. (Edin.), F.R.C.S. (C.), F.A.C.R., K.St.J.; radiologist; professor emeritus; b. 1 Aug. 1904; e. Queen's Univ., M.D., C.M. 1932; Fellow, Royal Coll. of Surgeons, Edinburgh, 1935; Cert. Specialist in Diagnostic and Therapeutic Radiol., Roy. Coll. Physicians & Surg. of Can., 1943; Royal Coll. of Surgeons, Can. (ad eundem), 1947; Fellow Emeritus, Amer. Coll. of Radiology; m. Theo. Tamblyn, 20 Sept. 1934; one d., Catherine; former Director, Ontario Cancer Foundation (Kingston Clinic); and Prof. of Radiotherapy, Queen's Univ., Kingston, Ont.; Resident Interne at Kingston Gen. Hosp. 1933–34; promoted to Asst. Radiologist, 1935; became Acting Head, Dept. of Radiology, Queen's Univ., and Kingston Gen. Hosp., 1939; apptd. Dir., Ont. Inst. of Radiotherapy, which in 1947 became the Ont. Cancer Foundation (Kingston Clinic); retired 1971; served in 2nd World War 1940–45; Lieut.-Col. commanding No. 1 Field Ambulance (Reserve); mem., Mun. Bd. of Educ., 1945–48; Pres., Kingston Acad. of Med.; Fellow Emeritus, Am. Coll. of Radiology; Life mem., Candn. Assn. of Radiologists (Pres. 1955); Life Mem. Ont. Med. Assn. 1971 (Dir. 1953–55); sr. mem. Candn. Med. Assn. 1982; Kt. of Grace, St. John Ambulance 1979; Honoured by K.G.H. who named new Ronald C. Burr wing in 1977; United Church; Home: 67 Kensington Ave., Kingston, Ont. K7L 4B4.

**BURRIDGE, Kenelm Oswald Lancelot,** M.A., B.Litt., Ph.D.; educator; b. St. Julian's, Malta 31 Oct. 1922; s. William and Jane Cassar Torregiani B.; e. Dragon Sch. Oxford, Eng. 1936; Blundell's Sch. Tiverton, Devon 1939; Exeter Coll. Oxford Univ. B.A. (Jurisprudence) 1948, Dipl. in Social Anthrop. 1949, B.Litt. 1950, M.A. 1952; Australian Nat. Univ. Ph.D. 1953; m. Rosabelle Elizabeth Griffiths (d. 1971), Sept. 1950; one s. Julian Langford; m. 2ndly Anna Wytske Emslie, Aug. 1984; PROF. OF ANTHROP., UNIV. OF B.C. since 1968 and Head Anthrop. there 1974–81; Govt. Scholar Oxford Univ. 1946–50; Scholar Australian Nat. Univ. 1953 (fieldwork New Guinea); Research Fellow Univ. of Malaya 1956; Prof. and Head of Anthrop. Univ. of Baghdad 1958; Univ. Lectr. in Ethnol. Pitt Rivers Museum, Univ. of Oxford 1968, Foundation Fellow St. Cross Coll.; Visiting Lectr. Univ. of W. Australian 1967; Visiting Prof. Univ. of B.C., Prof. 1968; served with RN 1939–46 Atlantic, Mediterranean, Indian Ocean, E. Indies, specialized submaries, POW 6 months (escaped), Twice Mentioned in Despatches, rank Lt.; rec'd Can. Council Award 1970, 1971; Guggenheim Fellowship 1972–73; Visiting Fellow and Lectr. Princeton Univ. 1977; Killam Fellow, S.S.H.R.C.C. Leave Fellowship 1979–80; Emeritus 1988; author 'Mambu: A Melanesian Millennium' 1961; 'Tangu Traditions' 1969; 'New Heaven, New Earth' 1969 (Spanish transl. 1970); 'Encountering Aborigines' 1973; 'Someone, No one' 1979; 'In the Way' 1991; numerous reviews, essays incl. articles for 'Encyclopaedia Britannica,' 'The Encyclopedia of Religion' and 'Encyclopaedie de la Pleiade' on religious theoretical and ethnographic matters; Hon. Fellow, Royal Anthrop, Inst, Gt. Brit. & Ireland; Assn. Social Anthrops.; Am. Anthrop. Assn.; Candn. Sociol. & Anthrop. Assn.; Candn. Ethnol. Soc.; Royal Soc. Can.; R. Catholic; recreations: hiking, sailing, motoring; Home: 231 Prince John Way, Nanaimo, B.C. V9T 4L4; Office: 2075 Wesbrook Pl., Vancouver, B.C. V6T 1W5.

**BURRIDGE, Robert Eric,** B.Sc.E., M.S., Ph.D.; educator; university administrator; b. Plaster Rock, N.B. 29 Aug. 1931; s. Albert Charles and Bessie Anne (MacInnes) B.; e. Univ. of N.B. B.Sc.E. (Elect. Engn.) 1953; Univ. of Wisc. M.S. 1962; McGill Univ. Ph.D. 1968; m. Ardeth Elma d. late Edgar Ball 16 May 1953; children: Stephen Robert, Colin Andrew, Lori Anne; VICE PRES. (ACADEMIC) EMERITUS 1991– ; Vice Pres. (Academic), Univ. of N.B. and Prof. of Elect. Engn. 1980–91; Grad. Apprentice, British Thomson Houston Co. Rugby, Eng. 1953–55; Asst. Prof. of Elect. Engn. present Univ. 1955–63, Assoc. Prof. 1963–70, Chrmn. and Prof. of Elect. Engn. 1970–75, Dean of Engn. and Prof. 1976–80; Acad. Visitor, Imp. Coll. of Science & Technol. London, Eng. 1975–76; mem. Council, N.B. Research & Productivity Council 1976–91; recipient Beaverbrook Scholarship 1948–53; Athlone Fellowship 1953–55; Sir George Nelson Award Engn. Inst. Can. 1966; Centennial Medial, I.E.E.E. 1984; author over 20 tech. articles electric power engn.; Life mem., Assn. Prof. Engrs. Prov. N.B. (mem. Council 1980–82, 2nd Vice Pres. 1982, 1st Vice Pres. 1983, Pres. 1984); Extve. Mem., Candn. Counc. of Profl. Engrs. 1990– , Pres. Elect 1992/93, Pres. 1993/94; Engn. Inst. Can.; Candn. Engn. Accreditation Bd. 1986–89; Sr. mem. Inst. Elect. & Electronic Engrs.; Baptist; recreations: reading, skiing, history; Home: 790 Windsor St., Fredericton, N.B. E3B 4G5; Office: P.O. Box 4400, Fredericton, N.B. E3B 5A3.

**BURROUGHS, Gary Forest,** B.A., C.A.; hotelier; b. Southport, Eng. 8 Dec. 1945; s. Harry West and Edna (Berry) B.; e. Ridley Coll. St. Catharines, Ont. 1964; McMaster Univ. B.A. 1968; C.A. Ont. 1973; m. Sarah d. Dr. C. Bruce and Betty Rigg 23 June 1973; two d.: Alexandra, Josephine; PRES., OBAN INN LTD. 1975– ; Pres., T.G.B. Construction; Dir. Dayton Walther Corp.; joined Peat Marwick Mitchell & Co. 1968–73; Smiley, Scott & Ralph 1973–75; Gov. Ridley Coll.; Past Chrmn. Shaw Festival Found.; Past Pres. Niagara-on-the-Lake C. of C.; recreations: golf, tennis, skiing; Clubs: St. Catharines Tennis; Niagara-on-the-Lake Golf (Past Pres.); Toronto Golf; Badminton & Racquet (Toronto); Royal Candn. Mil. Inst. (Toronto); Home: 116 Simcoe St., Niagara-on-the-Lake, Ont. L0S 1J0; Office: 160 Front St., Niagara-on-the-Lake, Ont. L0S 1J0.

**BURRY, C. James,** B.A.Sc., S.M., P.Eng.; educator; b. Toronto, Ont. 26 Nov. 1930; s. James Alexander S. and Dorothy Alexandria (Fox) B.; e. Royal Mil. Coll. Kingston grad. 1953; Univ. of Toronto B.A.Sc. 1954; Mass. Inst. Technol. S.M. 1962; m. Winifrede d. Guy Warwick Rogers 26 Oct. 1957; children: Guy James Rogers, Donald Alexander, John Douglas; Prof. of Civil Eng. Ryerson Polytech. Inst. 1967–91; Dir. St. Mary's Cement Corp.; consulting eng. 1954–67; mem. Assn. Prof. Engs. Prov. Ont.; Pollution Control Assn. Ont. (Dir. 1975–84, Pres. 1979–80); Anglican; recreations: micro computers, military modelling; Home: #504, 70 Rosehill Ave., Toronto, Ont. M4T 2W7.

**BURTCH, Michael Allan,** B.A. (Hons.); art gallery director; b. Kingston, Ont. 3 Oct. 1949; s. Edgar Thomas and Edith Pearl (Eady) B.; e. Brandon Univ. 1972–74; Queen's Univ., B.A. (Hons.) 1977; m. Linda d. Alexander and Marion Rogers 3 June 1972; children: Sarah Ann, Michelle Elizabeth; DIR. & CURATOR, ART GALLERY OF ALGOMA 1981– ; Edn. Offr., Robert McLaughlin Gallery 1977–78; Dir. & Curator, Lindsay Art Gallery 1978–81; Instr., Sir Sanford Fleming Coll. 1979–81; Sault Coll. 1982–85; Lectr., Algoma Univ. Coll. 1984– ; Pres., Ont. Assn. of Art Galleries 1986–87; Rotary Internat. Scholarship for Study Exchange to the Philippines 1985; numerous group and solo exhibits and performances as a practising artist and musician; author of var. exhibition catalogues incl. John Howlin 1985, (with P. Grattan) David Blackwood 1985, Evan Penny 1987; curated 'Sans Demarcation' June–Oct. 1987; received Allied Arts Award (for Sault Ste. Marie Waterfront Sound Sculpture) Ont. Assoc. of Architects 1990; recreations: power boat racing, fishing, skiing; Home: 27 Retta St., Sault Ste. Marie, Ont. P6A 4B7; Office: 10 East St., Sault Ste. Marie, Ont. P6A 3C3.

**BURTON, Clifford Chickering,** B.S.; retired engineer; b. Chicago, Ill. 13 Dec. 1917; s. Clifford Eugene and Margaret Theresa (Murrell) B.; e. Calif. Inst. of Technol. B.S. 1940; m. Marcella Rogers d. Thomas S. Cole 29 Aug. 1946; one s. Dr. Thomas E.; Engr. Texaco Inc. New York 1940–48; Vice Pres. C F Braun & Co. Alhambra, Calif. 1971, Pres. and Dir. 1971–79, joined Co. 1948; Pres., Chief Extve. Offr., Dir. PCL-Braun-Simons Ltd. Calgary 1979–81; Adv. to Mgmt. PCL-Braun-Simons Ltd. 1982 (ret.); recipient Distinguished Alumni Award Calif. Inst. Technol. 1974; Clifford C. Burton Scholarship in Chem. Engn. estbd. Univ. of Calgary 1981; Fellow, Am. Inst. Chem. Engrs.; life mem. APEGGA; recreations: hiking, skiing, photography; Clubs: Sante Fe Country; California (Los Angeles); Alpine of Canada; Home: Route 4, Tano Rd., Box 222, Santa Fe, NM 87501, USA.

**BURTON, Denis Eugene Norman;** artist; teacher; illustrator; printmaker; b. Lethbridge, Alta. 6 Dec. 1933; s. Clarence Edward Frederick and Bertha Jean (Tiller) B.; e. Lethbridge Coll. Inst., 1950; Pickering Coll., Newmarket, Ont. 1952; Ont. Coll. of Art, Toronto (where rec'd R.S. McLaughlin, J.F.M. Stewart and R.C.A. scholarships) 1956; m. Diane Fern, d. Louis J. Pugen, 9 Sept. 1970; children: Varyn Erica Clare (by previous m.); Maihyet Etanya; Dir. 'New School of Art' Toronto 1971–77; founded (with R. Hedrick & J. Sime, Toronto, 1965) and was Pres. Arts' Sake Inc: 'The Institute for Visual Arts,' until Nov. 1978; One Man Retrospective Exhibition of Drawings, Lynnwood Art Centre, Simcoe, 1980; One Man Retrospective Cardigan-Milne Gallery, Wpg. 1980; apptd. Artist in Residence, Emily Carr Coll. of Art, Vancouver, 1979–80; full-time instructor, 1980–81; Retro exhibition travelled to ten major Cdn. galleries and universities 1977–79; Chrmn., Drawing & Painting Dept., Ont. Coll. of Art, 1970–71; employed as Graphic Designer, CBC, Toronto 1957–60; T.V., Film Promotion & Advertising Designer, TDF Advertising-Artists Ltd., Toronto 1963–64; has exhibited widely in leading galleries and museums throughout Can. and U.S.A.; awards incl. Walker Art Centre Biennial (3) 1958; Granby International 1959; Can. Council 1961, 1967, Sen. Awards 1969, 72, 73, 75, 76; purchase prize at Winnipeg Biennial Show 1968; works rep. in several Can. and Am. pub. and pte. Colls. incl: Walker Art Centre, Minneapolis, Metropolitan Museum of Art, N.Y., Pasadena Art Museum, Nat. Gallery, Ottawa; Montreal Museum of Fine Arts; Art Gallery of Ont. Can. Council Art Bank, etc.; commissioned murals for Mr. and Mrs. J. D. Eaton, 1962; and Edmonton Internat. Airport, 1963; designed Henry Kelsey Mem. postage stamp, 1970; has contrib. illustrations for several Can. mags. and articles to art and archaeol. journs in Can. and U.S.A.; recreation: Jazz playing (saxophone, drums).

**BURTON, Frances Dominique,** B.S., M.A., Ph.D.; university professor; b. Villecresnes, France 11 Aug. 1939; d. Emanuel (Buckenholz) and Rita Dinah (Cahen) B.; e. Oakwood H.S. 1959; Barnard Coll.; N.Y. Univ., B.S. 1960, M.A. 1962; City Univ. of N.Y., Ph.D. 1969; m. Peter s. Aubrey and Blanche Silverman 2 May 1971; children: Alexis Corinna and Leah Andrea; PROF. OF ANTHROPOLOGY, UNIV. OF TORONTO 1969– ; H.S. Teacher, Soc. Studies 1960–67; seconded from Tulane Univ. to L.S.B. Leakey of the Limuru Primate Ctr., Tigoni, Kenya doing rsch. on Cercopithecus species 1966; Rsch., Holloman Airforce Base Primate Ctr.; Delta Reg. Primate Ctr.; New England Primate Rsch. Ctr. 1967–69; Lectr., Hunter Coll., CUNY 1967–69; rsch. at Univ. of Toronto on sexuality in macaques; current: hybrids in Kowloon, Hong Kong; 1st to experimentally show that monkey females experience orgasm 1970; rsch. on lifeways of Macaca sylvanus in Gibraltar 1970–81; rsch. H.K. polyspecific associations; rsch. China Presbytis. interactive multi-media and video; Admin. Asst., Tigoni Primate Ctr. (Kenya); Cons. (TV): 'CBC, The Nature of Things'; 'Bill Burrud's Animal World'; 'Lorne Greene's New Wilderness'; 'Vancouver Zoo'; 'Metro Toronto Zoo'; Bd. of Dir., Metro Toronto Zoo 1975–77; Newmarket Montessori Sch. 1975–81; Mem., Adv. Counc., York Arts Prog.; Internat. Primatol. Soc.; Canadn. Assn. of Physical Anthropol.; Am. Assn. for the Advancement of Sci.; Amnesty Internat.; author/co-author/editor of 18 jour. articles, papers & book; recreations: raising & studying social behaviour of domestic poultry, organic gardening, skiing, squash, writing poetry; Home: 17 Baltic Ave., Toronto, Ont. M4J 1S1; Office: Div. of Soc. Sci., Scarborough Campus, 1265 Military Trail, Scarborough, Ont. M1C 1A4.

**BURTON, G. Allan,** D.S.O., C.M., E.D., O.St.J., LL.D., K.C.L.J.; retired company chairman; b. Toronto, Ont., 20 Jan. 1915; s. late Charles Luther, C.B.E., D.C.Sc., LL.D. and Ella Maud. (Leary) B.; e. Lycee Jaccard, Lauzanne, Switzerland, 1929–30; Univ. of Toronto Schs., 1926–34; Univ. of Toronto (Arch.), 1934–35; m. Audrey Caro (deceased), d. late John Roy Syer, Toronto, Ont., 12 May 1938; children: James, Gail (Mrs. John Kendall), Lynn (Mrs. David Bennett); Janice (Mrs. Janice Baker); m. Mrs. Betty Kennedy, 15 Oct. 1976; joined The Robert Simpson Co. Ltd., Toronto, 1935; appointed General Manager, Toronto store, 1951; Director, 1953; Vice-President 1957; promoted as Vice-Pres. and Mang. Dir., 1958; Pres., 1964; Chrmn. and CEO 1968–79; comnd. 2nd Lt. in the Governor-General Body Guard, January 1933; Active Militia G.G.H.G., 1933–40; Active Service with G.G.H.G. in England, Italy, Holland and Germany, 1940–45; Lt. Col. Commanding G.G.H.G., 1948–50; Hon. Lt. Col. G.G.H.G. 1965–70; awarded D.S.O. Italy 1944 and E.D. 1949; C.M. 1985; Chrmn., United Appeal Metrop. Toronto, 1961; Pres., Bd. Trade Metrop. Toronto, 1962–63; Pres., Metrop. Toronto Indust. Comn., 1967–69, and Chrmn. Bd. 1969–71; Kt. Commander of St. Lazarus of Jerusalem 1964; Bro. Offr., St. John of Jerusalem 1962; mem., Redevel. Adv. Council Metrop. Toronto (Founding Chrmn.) 1960–62; Trustee, Hosp. for Sick Children 1963–77; Hon. Trustt, Hosp. for Sick Children 1990– ; Pres., Royal Agricultural Winter Fair 1982–83; Business Adv. Council, Sch. of Business, Univ. of W. Ont. 1970–80; G.G.H.G. Assn.; former Chrmn., Halton Region Conservation Foundn.; author: 'A Store of Memories' 1986; Psi. Upsilon; Freemason; recreations: golf, painting, fishing, shooting; Clubs: Arts & Letters (Life Mem.); York; Toronto; Mount Royal (Montreal); Royal Canadian Military Inst. (Life Mem.); Hamilton Golf and Country (Ancaster, Ont.); Tamahaak (Ancaster); Canadian; Empire; Eglinton Hunt (jt. M.F.H. 1953–70); Rolling Rock (Ligonier, Pa.); Lyford Cay (Nassau, Bahamas); Ristigouche Salmon (Pres. 1987–91) Matapedia, P.Q.; The Cavalry and Guards (London, England); Home: Limestone Hall Farm, R.R. 2, Milton, Ont. L9T 2X6; and 68 Old Mill Rd., Etobicoke, Ont. M8X 1G8.

**BURTON, Ian,** B.A., M.A., Ph.D., FRSC; geographer; environmental scientist; public servant; professor; b. Derby, Eng. 24 June 1935; s. Frank and Elsie (Barnes) B.; e. Derby Sch., Univ. Birmingham B.A. 1956, M.A. 1957; Oberlin Coll. 1957–58; Univ. of Chicago Ph.D. 1962; DIR. ENVIRONMENTAL ADAPTATION, ATMOSPHERIC ENVIRONMENT SERVICE 1990– ; Fulbright Scholar 1957–61; Fellow, English Speaking Union 1957–58; Lectr., Univ. of Indiana 1960–61; Queen's Univ. 1961; Cons., Ford Found. (India) 1964–66; Prof., Dept. of Geog., Univ. of Toronto 1968–90; Adjunct Prof. 1990– ; Prof., Environ. Sci., Univ. of E. Anglia 1973; Sr. Advr., IDRC 1972–75; Dir., Inst. for Environ. Studies, Univ. of Toronto 1979–84; Sr. Connaught Fellow & Ecole des Hautes Etudes en Sci. Soc., Paris 1984–86; Science Policy Adv., Corp. Policy Group, Environment Canada 1989–90; Dir., Internat. Fed. of Insts. for Advanced Study (IFIAS) 1986–92 (Trustee 1979–84); Extve. Bd., Found. for Internat. Training (FIT) 1992– ; num. extve., comn. & cons. positions for UNESCO, Resources for the Future Inc., World Health Orgn., Man and the Biosphere Prog., UN cons. in USSR, Cdn. Transp. Comn., Royal Comn. on Ocean Ranger Marine Disaster, Ford Found. (Nigeria), Montreal Engr. Co., World Resources Inst. (Washington, D.C.), International Inst. for Sustainable Development (Winnipeg), 1970– ; Adv. Panel on Drug Risk, Candn. Public Health Assoc.; FRSC 1983– ; Fellow, World Acad. of Arts and Science 1986– ; co-author: 'The Human Ecology of Coastal Flood Hazard in Megalopolis' 1968, 'The Environment as Hazard' 1978; co-editor: 'Readings in Resource Management and Conservation' 1965, 'Environmental Risk Assessment' 1980, 'Living with Risk' 1982, 'Geography, Resources and Environment' 1986 (2 vols.); recreations: swimming, sailing, hiking, cricket; Home: 72 Coolmine Rd., Toronto Ont. M6J 3E9 and 22 Rideau Terrace, Ottawa, Ont. K1M 2A1; Office: Atmospheric Environment Service, 4905 Dufferin St., Downsview, Ont. M3H 5T4 and La Salle Acad., 373 Sussex Dr., Ottawa, Ont. K1A 0H3.

**BURWASH, Donald A.,** B.A. (Hon.), LL.B.; corporate lawyer; b. New York, N.Y. 20 May 1930; s. Adam B. and Evelyn C. B.; e. Univ. of Toronto B.A. (Hons. Pol. Sci. and Econ.) 1954; Osgoode Hall Law Sch. 1958; CORPORATE LEGAL CONSULTANT; Past Vice Pres., Sec., Gen. Counsel and Dir., Coca-Cola Ltd. 1962–91; Legal Counsel, Coca-Cola Foods Canada Inc.; Irwin Toy Ltd.; mem. Univ. of Toronto Governing Council, Audit Ctte.; Bar Admission Course Instructor, Osgoode Hall 1992– ; Past Chrmn., Student Awards Ctte. and Past Vice-Pres., Univ. of Toronto Alumni Assoc.; Bd. Stewards, Timothy Eaton Meml. Ch.; Past Vice Pres. and Secy., Assoc. of Candn. General Counsel; mem., YMCA Youth Employment Ctte.; Past Vice-Pres., Corp. Counsel Sect., Candn. Bar Assoc.; recreations: sailing, skiing, running, badminton; clubs: Badminton & Racquet (Toronto); RCYC; Address: 273 Lawrence Ave. E., Toronto, Ont. M4N 1T6.

**BURY, Brenda,** B.A.; portrait painter; b. North England; e. Univ. of Reading in Berkshire B.A. (Hons. Fine Art) 1956; portraits incl. Lord St. Oswald, Sir Philip Williams, Lord King of Wartnaby, Catherine MacMillan (Sir Harold's daughter), Lord Hailsham, Sir Alan Herbert, M.P., Sir Leonard Oughterbridge, Rt. Hon. John Diefenbaker, Hon. Maurice Duplessis, Mrs. Pierre Salinger (Washington), Duke of Lerma (Spain), Governor General and Lady Hailes (Trinidad), Sir Grantley Adams (Barbados), Lord Mountbatten of Burma 1965, Her Majesty the Queen 1969, first 19 Brit. Conservative members of the European Parliament 1979, Her Excellency Madame Jeanne Sauve 1984, The Right Honourable Mrs. Thatcher and her advisers 1985; her work has taken her to many vastly different countries & societies giving her the variety and stimulus necessary for the development of her painting; she has lived with Inuit in the Arctic and royal families in Saudi Arabia; works displayed at the Royal Academy, the Royal Soc. of Portrait Painters, Christies of London, etc.; Studio: 96A Beverley St., Toronto, Ont. M5T 1Y2.

**BURY, Charles Arthur;** newspaper editor; b. Montréal, Qué. 26 March 1946; s. William Stewart and Patricia Marion (Armstrong) B.; e. MacDonald High Sch. Ste-Anne de Bellevue, Qué. 1963; McGill Univ.; Concordia Univ.; m. Berit Elizabeth d. Andreas and Astri Lundh 27 Dec. 1971, div. 1980; children: Luke Armstrong, Rachel Astri Lundh; ED.-IN-CHIEF, SHERBROOKE RECORD 1981– ; various positions 1965–77; Journalist, Photog., Ed. Townships Sun 1977–81; contbr. CBC Radio 1980– ; newsroom cons. Fiji Sun newspaper 1987; Lectr. in Journalism Univ. de Sherbrooke 1988–92; Owner-operator Bunker Hill Stump Ranch woodlot-tree farm Ste-Catherine de Hatley 1983– ; recipient Golden Door Award Montréal 1971, 1972; Louis C. O'Neil Prize for Journalism 1983; Environmental Award Memphremagog Conservation Inc. 1988; Pres. Oeuvre de terrains de jeux Ste-Herménégilde, Qué. 1973–76; Dir. E. Twps. Citizens' Assn. 1975–79; mem. Adv. Bd. E. Twps. Tech. Inst. 1987– ; author 'The Royal Rifles of Canada in Hong Kong 1941–45' hist. 1986; co-author 'The Anglo Guide to Survival in Quebec' humour 1986; 'Anglos 2, The Sequel' humour 1989; mem. Candn. Press; Founding mem. Centre Investig. Journalism (now Candn. Assn. Journalists) 1978, Dir. 1980– , Chrmn. 1985– ; Dir. E. Twps. Press Club 1981–86; mem. Que. Outdoor Writers Assn.; Investig. Reporters & Eds.; recreations: travel, swimming, target shooting, amateur naturalist; Clubs: Champ de tir de l'Estrie; Trois Cantons Fish & Game; Home: 26 Conley St., Lennoxville, Qué. J1M 1L9; Office: 2850 Delorme St., Sherbrooke, Qué. J1K 1A1.

**BUSH, John Arthur Henry,** LL.B.; mining executive; b. Toronto, Ont. 1942; s. Arthur John and Gertrude Ruth (Barry) B.; e. Laurentian Univ.; Osgoode Hall Law Sch. LL.B. 1973; m. Kate d. Terry and Nancye Bayly; children: Keri, Jennifer; VICE PRES., GEN. COUNSEL, SEC. RIO ALGOM LIMITED 1990– ; Counsel present Co. 1975, Asst. Sec. 1981, Vice Pres., Sec. 1988; mem. Bd. Trade Metrop. Toronto; recreations: skiing, golf, rugby; Clubs: Cambridge; Holimont; Office: 2600, 120 Adelaide St. W., Toronto, Ont. M5H 1W5.

**BUSHUK, Walter,** M.Sc., Ph.D., Dr.(h.c.), F.R.S.C., F.C.I.C., F.A.I.C., F.A.A.C.C., F.C.I.F.S.T.; educator; b. Poland 2 Jan. 1929; s. Anton and Helen (Mucha) B.; e. Univ. of Man. B.Sc. 1952, M.Sc. 1953; McGill Univ. Ph.D. 1956; The Agric. Univ. Poznan, Poland Dr. (h.c.) 1989; m. Jean d. Charles and Irene Huston 25 June 1955; two s. Darrell Andrew, Donald Brent; NSERC RSCH. PROF. OF FOOD SCI. UNIV. OF MAN. 1984– ; Rsch. Sci. Grain Rsch. Lab. Candn. Grain Comn. 1953–62, Head of Wheat Sect. 1964–66; Dir. of Rsch. Ogilvie Flour Mills Ltd. Montreal 1962–64; Prof. of Plant Sci. present Univ. 1966–72, 1973–78, Head of Plant Sci. 1978–80, Assoc. Vice Pres. (Rsch.) 1980–84, Head of Food Sci. 1991– ; Dir. of Technol. Candn. Internat. Grains Inst. 1972–73; recipient W.J. Eva Award Candn. Inst. Food Sci. & Technol. 1972; C.W. Brabender Award Am. Assn. Cereal Chems. 1974, Thomas Burr Osborne Medal 1983; Medal of Merit Nat. Food Rsch. Inst. Japan 1977; Jubilee Award Univ. Man. Alumni Assn. 1978; M.P. Neumann Medal German Assn. Cereal Rsch. 1989; Univ. Medal Univ. of Helsinki 1989; author or co-author over 200 sci. and tech. articles and book chapters on end-use quality wheat & other grains; ed. 'Rye: Chemistry and Technology'; mem. Agric. Inst. Can.; Am. Assn. Cereal Chems. (Pres. 1976–77); Candn. Inst. Food Sci. & Technol.; Biomass Energy Inst.; Sigma Xi; recreations: tennis, bridge, carpentry; Club: Unicity Racquet; Home: 26 Millikin Rd., Winnipeg, Man. R3T 3V4; Office: Winnipeg, Man. R3T 2N2.

**BUSSANDRI, Claudio F.,** B.Eng., M.B.A.; business executive; b. Salsomaggiore, Italy 9 April 1947; s. Adriano and Emma Pasqualina (Boselli) B.; e. McGill Univ. B.Eng. (Hons.) 1969, M.B.A. 1976; m. Diane d. Alex and Iris McCombe 30 Aug. 1980; children: Kristen, Alexander; PRESIDENT & CHIEF OPERATING OFFICER, LANTIC SUGAR LTD. 1987– ; Mgr., Production Planning & Inventory Control, Gillette of Canada 1969–73; Project Mgr. 1973; Mgr., Operational Planning 1974; Inventory Mgr., Nabisco Brands Limited (formerly Standard Brands) 1974–75; Dir. of Distbn. 1975–76; Vice Pres., Corp. Distbn. 1976–80; Pres. & Gen. Mgr., Club Coffee Cos. 1980–84; Vice-Pres. & Gen. Mgr., Food Service Div. 1984–87; Chrmn., Grocery Products Manufacturers of Canada; Mem., Business Council on Nat. Issues; Bd. Mem., Candn. Sugar Inst.; Bd. Mem., Montreal Children Hospital Found.; Les Grands Ballets Canadiens; recreations: photography, squash, skiing, computers, reading; Home: 524 Mount Pleasant, Westmount, Que. H3Y 3H5; Office: 1 Westmount Sq., Westmount, Que. H3Z 2P9.

**BUSSIÈRES, Yvan,** B.ès A., B.Sc.A., M.B.A.; engineer; executive; b. Verchères, Qué. 8 June 1943; s. Gaston and Laurette (Pigeon) B.; e. Coll. Sainte-Marie, Montréal B.ès A. 1963; Ecole Polytechnique, Montréal B.Sc.A. 1968; Univ. de Sherbrooke M.B.A. 1973; m. Michelle d. Olivier and Marthe Dubois 11 June 1966; PRES., UNIVA INC. (formerly PROVIGO INC.) 1990– ; Chrmn., Provigo Distribution Inc.; Provigo Corp.; Chrmn., Loeb Inc.; C Corp. Inc.; Projects Eng. Kentville

Div. N.S., CP Rail 1968 and Qué. Div. 1970, Eng. Sherbrooke Div. 1970–71; Mgr. Real Estate Provigo Inc. 1974, Dir. Real Estate 1977, Vice Pres. Real Estate 1980, Vice Pres. Adm. & Treas. 1981, Vice Pres. Finance, Adm. & Treas. 1984; Exec. Vice Pres. Retail Operations, Provigo Distribution Inc. 1985, Pres. & C.O.O. 1985–89; Sr. Extve. Vice Pres. & C.O.O., Provigo Inc. 1989; Past Chrmn., Candn. Counc. of Grocery Distributors; Mem., Bd. of Dirs., Retail Counc. of Can.; Bd. of Dirs., Cercle des Chefs Mailleurs du Québec; mem., Montréal Chamber of Commerce; Jeune Chambre de commerce de Montréal; Assoc. of MBA's of Qué.; Candn. Inst. of Engrs.; Order of Engrs. of Qué.; Office: 1250 René Lévesque Blvd. W., Montréal, Qué. H3B 4X1.

**BUTALA, Sharon Annette,** B.Ed., B.A.; writer; b. Nipawin, Sask. 24 Aug. 1940; d. Achille Antoine and Margaret Amy Alexis (Graham) Le Blanc; e. Univ. of Sask. B.Ed. 1962, B.A. 1963, P.G. Dip. 1973; m. Peter s. George and Alice Butala 21 May 1976; one s. Sean Anthony Hoy; formerly Special educator; author of text of 'Harvest' Book of photographs 1992; author: 'The Fourth Archangel' novel 1992; 'Upstream' novel 1991; 'Fever' short stories 1990; 'Luna' novel 1988; 'The Gates of the Sun' novel 1986; 'Queen of the Headaches' short stories 1985; 'Country of the Heart' novel 1984; co-author 'Coming-Attractions' short stories 1983; recipient Sask. Writers' Guild Long Fiction Award 1982, Maj. Drama Award 1985, 1989; Writers' Choice Award 1986; short-listed Books in Can. Best First Novel Award 1984 and Gov. Gen.'s Literary Prize 1986; Annual Author's Award, Canadian Fiction Magazine 1988; Silver Award for Fiction, National Magazine Awards 1991; short-listed Commonwealth Writers' Prize, Canada-Caribbean Region 1991; Author's Award. Paperback Fiction, Foundation for the Advancement of Candn. Letters 1992; Gold Saskatchewan Award, Western Magazine Awards 1993; mem. Sask. Writers' Guild (Dir. 1983); PEN; T.W.U.C.; ACTRA; Address: P.O. Box 428, Eastend, Sask. S0N 0T0.

**BUTCHER, John Douglas,** B.Sc.F., C.M.A.; financial executive; b. Birmingham, England 26 Oct. 1943; s. Douglas Frederick and Joan Margaret (Paton) B.; e. Univ. of Toronto B.Sc.F. 1967; Soc. of Mngt. Accountants C.M.A. 1972; children: John, Daniel, Bryan, Robyn; CONTROLLER, COLD METAL PRODUCTS CO. LTD. 1987– ; Professional Forester, Great Lakes Paper Co. Ltd. 1967–69; Supervisor, Gen. Acctg., International Harvester 1969–70; Cost Acctg. 1970–71; var. acctg. & mfg. supervisory & mngt. positions, Stanley Works divisions 1971–87; Home: c/o P.O. Box 20068, Upper James Rd., Hamilton, Ont.; Office: 65 Imperial St., Hamilton, Ont. L8L 7V2.

**BUTEUX, Paul Edward,** B.Sc.(Econ.), Ph.D.; educator; b. London, Eng. 25 Apr. 1939; s. Edward William and Phyllis Eileen (Droy) B.; e. Sir George Monoux Grammar Sch. London; London Sch. of Econ. & Pol. Sci. B.Sc. 1961, Ph.D. 1977; PROF. OF POL. STUDIES, UNIV. OF MAN. 1984– , Dir. Prog. Strategic Studies 1986– ; Fellow, Centre Internat. Studies London Sch. of Econ. 1980–81; Sr. Assoc. mem. St. Anthony's Coll. Oxford 1985; joined present Univ. 1963; mem. Bd., Atlantic Council Can.; Candn. Inst. Strategic Studies; Dept. External Affairs Consultative Group Arms Control & Disarmament; NATO Fellow 1979; Dept. Nat. Defence Fellow 1980; Rh Inst. Award 1983; Adjunct Fellow Centre Internat. & Strategic Studies York Univ.; author: 'The Politics of Nuclear Consultation in NATO 1965–1980'; 'Strategy, Doctrine and the Politics of Alliance: Theatre Nuclear Force Modernization in NATO' 1983; numerous articles NATO, East-West relations, Internat. Pol., Defence Policy; mem. Candn. Inst. Internat. Affairs; Candn. Pol. Sci. Assn.; Internat. Inst. Strategic Studies; Royal Candn. Military Inst.; recreations: skiing, sailing; Office: Winnipeg, Man. R3T 2N2.

**BUTLER, David Gordon,** M.Sc., Ph.D., D.Sc., F.R.S.A.; university professor, endocrinologist; b. Vancouver, B.C. 5 May 1936; s. Gordon Henry and Mary Isabel (Dobson) B.; e. Lord Byng H.S. 1955; Univ. of B.C., B.Sc. 1959, M.Sc. 1961; Univ. of Sheffield, Ph.D. 1964, D.Sc. 1985; m. Marjorie d. Leonard and Dora Schofield 19 June 1965; children: Andrew Gordon, Ian Leonard; PROF. OF ZOOLOGY, UNIV. OF TORONTO 1976– ; Demonstrator, U.B.C. 1959–61; Univ. of Sheffield 1961–62; Ont. Rsch. Found. Predoct. Scholarship 1961–64; Royal Soc. Vis. Scientist, Naples Zool. Stn., Italy 1962; Asst. Prof. of Zool., present univ. 1964; Assoc. Prof. 1967; Brit. Counc. Award, Vis. Assoc. Profl., Zool., Cambridge Univ. & Christ's Coll.; F.R.S.A. 1984; Assoc., Massey Coll. 1984; Mem., Univ. Coll. 1985; Royal Soc. Sci. Exchange Award, Vis. Prof., Physiol., Cambridge Univ. & Christ's Coll. 1986; author/co-author of numerous pubs. in field of comparative vertebrate endocrinol., principally hormonal control of salt & water balance in animals; recreations: heraldry, karate, salmon fishing; club: United Ch.; Home: 105 Confederation Way, Thornhill, Ont. L3T 5R4; Office: Toronto, Ont. M5S 1A1.

**BUTLER, Edith,** B.A., L.esL., O.C.; singer, songwriter; b. Paquetville, N.B. 27 July 1942; d. Johnny and Lauretta (Godin) B.; e. Univ. of Moncton B.A.; Laval Univ. L.esL.; N.B. Univ. D.esL. Honoris Causa; Moncton Univ. D.esMus. Honoris Causa; Touring in U.S.A., Japan, Canada, France, Switz., Belgium incl. prestigous theatres such as Olympia of Paris 1970–93; 20 albums in 20 years; Pres., KAPPA Record Co.; Trictrac Pub. Co.; Superstrat Production Co.; Officer, Order of Canada; Nelly Awards; Felix Awards; Bd. Mem., Canada Council; Mem., SPACQ, SOCAN, SODRAC, UDA; musical composer of 20 albums & editor of 410 songs; recreations: walking; Home: 86 Côte Ste-Catherine, Outremont, Que. H2V 2A3; Office: c/o Lise Aubut.

**BUTLER, Geoffrey Frank,** B.A., M.B.A.; theatre manager; arts administrator; b. Rochford, Eng. 15 Apr. 1947; s. Wilfred Frank and Lillian Joan (Slater) B.; e. York Univ. B.A. 1969, M.B.A. 1977; m. Lyndia d. Marie Eberhardt 10 Apr. 1971; children: Christopher, Stephanie; ARTS MANAGEMENT CONSULTANT 1990– ; Mgr. Minkler Auditorium, Seneca Coll. 1970–74; Prog. Coordr., Algonquin Regional Library System, Parry Sound 1974–75; Mgr. Univ. of Waterloo Arts Centre 1975–79; Gen. Mgr. Kitchener-Waterloo Symphony Orch. 1978–78; Gen. Mgr. The Centre in the Square, Kitchener 1979–83; Gen. Mgr. Toronto Internat. Festival 1981–83; Extve. Dir., The Corp. of Massey Hall and Roy Thomson Hall 1983–90; Past Pres. Internat. Soc. of Performing Arts Admin.; Pres., Performing Arts Development Fund of Toronto; mem. Nat. Adv. Ctte., Univ. of Waterloo, Univ. of Waterloo Arts Admin. Prog.; occasional teacher Confederation Coll., Thunder Bay; mem. Alumni Adv. Counc., Fac. of Admin. Studies, York Univ.; recreations: walking, reading; Club: Rotary of Toronto; Office: 60 Courcelette Rd., Scarborough, Ont. M1N 2S8.

**BUTLER, Gordon Cecil,** B.A., Ph.D., F.R.S.C.; biochemist; b. Ingersoll, Ont. 4 Sept. 1913; s. Irvin and Edna M. (Harris) B.; e. Ingersoll Coll. Inst. (1926–31); Univ. of Toronto, B.A. 1935, Ph.D. 1938; Univ. of London, 1938–40; m. Jean S., d. G.D. Meeke, Hamilton, Ont., 3 July 1937; children: Judith, Stephen, Gregory, Susan; CONSULTANT, DIV. OF BIOL. SCI., NAT. RESEARCH COUNCIL OF CAN., 1978–85; Research Chemist, Chas. E. Frosst & Co. 1940–42; N.R.C. Atomic Energy Project 1945–47; Prof. of Biochem., Univ. of Toronto, 1947–57; Dir. of Biol. & Health Physics Div., Atomic Energy of Can. Ltd., 1957–65; Nat. Res. Council of Can., Dir. Radiation Biol. 1965–68; Dir. Biol. 1968–72; Dir. Biol. Sci. Div. 1972–78; Group Dir., Biol. Sci. Labs 1974–78; mem. NRCC Assoc. Comte. on Scientific Criteria for Environmental Quality Vice Chrmn. 1970–87; NRCC Assoc. Comte. on Toxicology Chrmn. 1981–87; AECB Adv. Comte. on Radiological Protection Chrmn. 1979–87; U.N. Scient. Comte. on Effects of Atomic Radiation (past Chrmn.) 1962–85; Internat. Comm. on Radiological Protection Comtes. 4 and 2, 1963–77; Sci. Comm. on Problems of Environment (Chrmn., Candn. Nat. Comm. 1978–81); Scientific Group on Methodologies for the Safety Evaluation of Chemicals, Vice Chrmn. Extve. Comte. 1980–87; Candn. Physiol. Soc.; Cdn. Biochem Soc. (past Pres.); Am. Soc. Biol. Chemists; Health Physics Soc.; Am. Assn. Advanc. Sci.; Candn. Soc. for Cell Biol.; Assn. for the Advancement of Sci. in Can.; Candn. Fed. Biol. Socs. (past Chrmn.); Roy. Soc. of Can. (Pres. Acad. of Sci. 1974–75); Scientists and Engineers for Energy and Environmental Security Inc. (mem. Bd. Dirs. 1981–82); Internat. Foundation for Sci. (Vice Pres. 1975–81; Pres. 1982–87); joined present Council as Dir., Radiation Biol. Div. 1965; served in 2nd World War in Chem. Warfare, 1942–45; retired with rank of Major; United Church; recreations; golf, carpentry; Home: 4694 West 13th Ave., Vancouver B.C. V6R 2V7.

**BUTLER, James Robert,** M.A., Ph.D.; educator; conservation scientist; b. Wheeling, W.Va. 24 Feb. 1946; s. Charles Edward and Madelyn Elizabeth (Miller) B.; e. W.Va. Univ. 1964–66; Ohio State Univ. B.A. 1968; Manhattanville Coll. N.Y. M.A. 1973; Univ. of Wash. Ph.D. 1980; PROF. OF PARKS, WILDLIFE, CONSERVATION BIOLOGY, UNIV. OF ALTA. 1988– , Founder and Assoc. Dir. Internat. Inst. Protected Areas Mgmt.; served as Chief State Naturalist State of Ky. and as environmental edn. specialist USA 1969–76; Head of Interpretation & Edn. Prov. Parks Alta. 1976–79; Full Prof. present Univ. 1987; global conserv. sci. in mgmt. & protection parks, nature reserves, threatened wildlife species; considered a world authority on parks, protected areas, the people-wildlife interface, and ecotourism; recent projects in Europe, Indonesia, Central and South America, the Carribean, Africa, and Soviet Union; Founder and Sr. Ed. 'Borealis' mag. Candn. Parks & Wilderness Soc., Vice Pres. and Dir. of Soc.; Founder and Dir. Heritage Interpretation Internat.; Pres. Peregrine Inst. Rsch. & Planning Associates; mem. Candn. Environmental Adv. Council Fed. Min. Environment; Dir. Am. Nature Study Soc.; mem. Eco-tourism Ctte. Internat. Council Bird Preservation; Chair Fed. Task Force Nat. Protected Areas Vision for Can.; frequent guest lectr., radio & TV commentator; sci. adv. numerous environmental films & publs.; co-host Wildlife Internat. TV series; recipient, Edmonton Natural Hist. Soc. Conserv. Award 1990; College Teaching Award, NACTA 1991–92; Defender of the Wilderness Award, W. Canada Wilderness Ctte. 1993; author 'Fishing Canada's Mountain Parks' 1985; author, co-author, ed. numerous profl. reports, articles, book chapters, poems; recreations: nature study & lit., birding, fly fishing, photography, antique nature prints, philately, Zen; Home: 8308 120 St., Edmonton, Alta. T6G 1X2; Office: 861 General Services Bldg., Univ. of Alberta, Edmonton, Alta. T6G 2H1.

**BUTLER, John Howard,** B.A. (Hon.), LL.B., LL.M.; lawyer; b. Kitchener, Ont. 1 Nov. 1952; s. John Howard and Miriam Rose (Shantz) B.; e. Wilfrid Laurier Univ. B.A. (Hon.) 1974; Osgoode Hall Law Sch. LL.B. 1977, LL.M. 1984; m. Jacqueline Ruth d. Pauline Gladys and John Willson Bryers 16 Sept. 1983; children: John Willson Bryers, Peter McLean; PARTNER, TORY TORY DESLAURIERS & BINNINGTON 1985– ; lawyer, present firm 1979– ; seconded to First City Capital Markets Ltd. 1987–88 and Brookfield Development Corp. 1991; Dir., Dexleigh Corp.; Home: 182 Cottingham St., Toronto, Ont. M4V 1C5; Office: P.O. Box 270, IBM Tower, Toronto, Ont. M5K 1N2.

**BUTLER, Sir Michael,** Bart., Q.C.; b. Devonport, England 22 April 1928; s. late Marjorie Brown (Woods) and late Sir Thomas Butler, Bart.; e. (came to Canada 1940) Brentwood Coll., Victoria, B.C.; Univ. of Brit. Columbia, B.A.; Osgoode Hall, Toronto, Ont. Honours Law; divorced; children: Richard Michael, Geoffrey MacLean, Patrick Colman, Thomas David; three grandsons; Partner (retired), Butler, Angus; Dir.: Teck Corp.; Elco Mining Ltd.; and other public and private companies; read law with John G. Edison, Q.C., Toronto, Ont.; called to the Bar of Ont. 1954, and to Bar of B.C. 1967; retired from active law practice 1988; Address: 634 Avalon Rd., Victoria, B.C. V8V 1N7.

**BUTLER, Richard Andrew (Rick),** B.A., M.A.; writer, producer; b. Toronto, Ont. 28 Nov. 1946; s. Richard Andrew and Dorothy Jeanette (Paulson) B.; e. Truro Sr. High 1964; Carleton Univ., B.A. 1967; Univ. of Sussex, M.A. 1971; m. Linda d. Jean-Louis and Helene Renaud 7 Oct. 1987; one s.: Richard Andrew (IV); Prof.: St. Mary's Univ. 1970–71; Memorial Univ. 1972–75; Univ. of Ottawa 1976–79; producer of 12 RCA record albums incl.: 'Billy Bishop Goes to War,' 'An Evening with Stephen Leacock,' and 'Bells and Brass' (feat. The Canadian Brass & the Peace Tower Carillon); writer/dir., CBC & NFB documentaries; since 1982 writing & producing TV drama & feature films incl. 90-min. dramas, 'Maggie & Pierre' and 'Balconville'; Roman Catholic; author: 'Quebec: The People Speak' 1978 (rsch. papers on file at Les Archives Nat. du Qué.), 'The Trudeau Decade' 1979, 'Vanishing Canada' 1980; Home: 2410 31st St., Santa Monica, Calif. 90405 and 571 Jarvis St., Toronto, Ont. M4Y 2J1.

**BUTSON, Arthur Richard Cecil,** G.C., O.M.M., C.St.J., C.D., M.A., M.D., B.Chir., FRCS (Eng.), FRCS(C), FACS; surgeon; educator; b. Hankow, China 24 Oct. 1922; s. Cecil Walter and Doris Neave (Stanton-Cook) B.; e. Leighton Park Sch.; Cambridge Univ. M.A. 1946, M.B., B.Chir. 1945, M.D. 1951; Univ. Coll. Hosp. Med. Sch. London, Eng.; m. Eileen Callon 30 June 1967; children: Sarah Louise, Caroline Frances, Andrew Richard; trained as Surg. London, Eng. and Montréal; surgery practice Hamilton, Ont. since 1953; Clin. Prof. of Surg. McMaster Univ. Med. Sch. 1970– ; participated in Falkland Islands Dependencies Survey and east coastline Antarctic peninsula (previously unmapped) 1946–48, awarded George Cross and Polar Medal; served with Candn. Militia 1956–82, rank Lt. Col.; commanded Hamilton Militia Med. Co. 1973–77, twice winning trophy for best med. co. in Can.; also served as Area Surg. Central Militia Area; Hon. Col. 23 (Hamilton) Medical Coy. 1989– ; apptd. Queen's Hon. Surg. 1977–79; recipient Queen's Silver Jubilee Medal; Bgde. Surg. to St. John Ambulance since 1973 and Past Prov. Surg. for Ont. Council; rep. Can. on Interallied Confedn. Offrs.

Med. Reserves (NATO Reserve Offrs. Orgn.) 1980–84; climbed extensively in Candn. Rockies, Baffin Island, Eur. Alps & Himalayas; Leader 1978 Candn. Hindu Kush Expdn.; author or co-author numerous med. publs.; recreations: skiing, mountain climbing; breeding Galloway beef cattle; Home: 24 Auchmar Rd., Hamilton, Ont. L9C 1C5.

**BUTTERFIELD, Christopher James Agnew,** B.Mus., M.A.; composer; b. Vancouver, B.C. 17 Nov. 1952; s. James and Sybil Edith Elizabeth (Agnew) B.; e. King's Coll. Choir Sch., Cambridge U.K.; Brentwood Coll. Mill Bay B.C.; Univ. of Victoria B.Mus. 1975; State Univ. of N.Y. at Stony Brook M.A. 1977; m. Merrie-Ellen d. James and Wendy Wilcox 26 Oct. 1990; one d.: Claire; ASST. PROF. OF COMPOSITION, SCHOOL OF MUSIC, UNIV. OF VICTORIA 1992– ; Bd. Mem., Arraymusic Toronto; Assoc. Composer, Candn. Music Centre; Assoc. Mem., Candn. League of Composers (Extve. Mem.); Mem., SOCAN; Home: 1743 Emerson St., Victoria, B.C. V8R 2C2.

**BUTTERFIELD, David H.,** F.C.S.I.; investment banker; b. Toronto, Ont. 6 Nov. 1939; s. Harry Vernon and Violet B.; e. Ryerson Polytech. University, Business Admin. 1962; Fellow, Candn. Securities Inst.; m. Paula d. Ann and Albert Ingham June 1972; children: Adam, Jonathan; SENIOR VICE-PRESIDENT & DIRECTOR, NESBITT THOMSON INC. 1976– ; Industrial Finance, Traders Group 1962–65; Stockbroker, Wills Bickle & Co. Ltd. 1965–72; Draper Dobbie & Co. 1972–75; Chair (Ont.), Candn. Forces Liaison Council; recreatons: jogging, skiing, cottaging; clubs: Georgian Peaks; Office: Sun Life Tower, Sun Life Centre,150 King St. W., Toronto, Ont. M5H 3W2.

**BUTTERFIELD, George D.B.,** B.A., LL.B.; business executive; b. Canada 5 Feb. 1939; s. Dudley St. George and Deboarah (Barbour) B.; e. Univ. of Toronto B.A. (Hons.) 1961; Rhodes Scholar Elect Bermuda 1963; Osgoode Hall Law Sch. LL.B. 1965; m. Martha d. Sidney and Margaret Robinson 12 June 1964; children: David, Nathalie; PRES., BUTTERFIELD & ROBINSON AND BUTTERFIELD & CO.; Dir., Family Trust; recreations: sports, music, movies, books; Office: 300, 70 Bond St., Toronto, Ont. M5W 1X3.

**BUTTON, Brig.-Gen. (Ret.) Ronald B.,** C.D.; retired Canadian Forces officer; b. Toronto, Ont. 16 Nov. 1928; s. Maurice B. and Gertrude G. (Green) B.; e. RCAF Air Navig. Sch. (Wings), Summerside, P.E.I. 1950; RCAF Staff Coll. (P.S.A.C.) Toronto 1965; Nat. Defence Coll. Can. (N.D.C.), Kingston 1972; m. Olive Janet d. William Thompson 11 Oct. 1952; children: Leslie Toole, Cathy McNaughton, Patty Dacey, Tracy Kamino, Sara Roy; enlisted RCAF 1948; promoted Pilot Offr. and Flying Offr. 1950; Flight Lt. 1954; Acting Sqdn. Leader 1961; Sqdn. Leader 1962; Wing Commdr. 1967; Lt. Col. 1968; Col. 1974; Brig. Gen. 1978– ; served various appts. Can. and USA 1948–67; O.C. Candn. Forces Offrs. Sch. Esquimalt 1967–68; C.O. Candn. Forces Stn. Lowther, Ont. 1968–69; Sr. Staff Offr. Air Defence Command HQ North Bay, Ont. 1969–71; Asst. Dir. NORAD Alt. Command Post Great Falls, Mont. 1972–74; Dir. Mang. Consulting Services NDHQ Ottawa 1974–76; Commdr. Candn. Forces Base Toronto 1976–78; Air Attaché and Sr. Air Liaison Offr. Washington, D.C. 1978–81; Commdr. Central Region and Commandant Candn. Forces Training System 1981–83; retired 1983; Tech. Advr., Special Senate Comte. on National Defence 1983–84; mem. Bd. Dirs., North Bay Mental Health Services Inc. 1986–90; Dir. & Vice-Chrmn. (N. Ont. Area), Ont. Prov. Ctte. (OPC) Air Cadet League of Can. 1988– ; mem., Bd. of Dirs., Candn. Mental Health Assoc. (North Bay Br.) 1988–90; Chrmn, Sponsoring Ctte., 547 (North Bay) Air Cadet Squadron 1988–90; Nat. Pres., RCAF Assoc. 1990–92 (Nat. Vice Pres. 1988–90); mem., Bd. of Dirs., Air Force Productions Ltd. 1988– ; Colonel Commandant, Cdn. Forces Training Development Br. 1990– ; Hon. Nat. Dir., Air Cadet League of Can. 1991– ; recipient Candn. Centennial Medal 1967; Queen's Silver Jubilee Medal; awarded Commemorative Medal for 125th Anniversary of Candn. Confederation; Anglican; Clubs: 406 Wing RCAF Assn.; Br. 23, Royal Candn. Legion; Pinewood Park Golf; recreations: golf, fishing, reading; Home: 268 Ivanhoe Dr., North Bay, Ont. P1A 3B8.

**BUTTRICK, John Arthur,** B.S., M.A., Ph.D.; economist; professor; b. Rutland, Vermont 12 Sept. 1919; came to Can. 1970; s. late George Arthur and Agnes (Gardner) B.; e. elem. and sec. sch. N.Y. City; Haverford Coll., Haverford, Pa., B.S. 1941; Yale Univ. M.A. 1947, Ph.D. 1950; m. 2ndly Ann Garnett d. late Kenneth Tatlow 24 July 1958; children: Peter Miller, Hilary Jacob, Michael Samuel; Prof. of Economics, York Univ. 1970–89 (retired but still teaching one course per year); Dir. Diploma Prog. 1986–89, 1992– ; Dir. of Grad. Prog. 1979–83; Instr. Yale Univ., 1948–49; Asst. Prof. Northwestern Univ., 1949–53; Assoc. and Full Prof. Univ. of Minn. 1953–73, Chrmn. 1961–63, Dir., Grad Studies 1967–69; Chief, Minn.-los Andes Project (Colombia), 1965–66; Visiting Prof. at Stanford, Harvard, Vanderbilt, Berkeley, Los Andes, Tokyo, Singapore, People's Univ., Huazhong Univ. (P.R. China) and Univ. of W. Indies; C.P.S.; U.S.A. 1941–45, assigned to Forest Services performing surveys, econ. research, etc., in various locations; author 'Economic Development' 1954 (also Indian, Japanese and Spanish eds.); 'Theories of Economic Growth' 1960 (also Spanish ed.); 'Consumer, Producer and Social Choice' 1968; 'Who Goes to University from Toronto' 1977; 'Educational Problems and Some Policy Options' 1977; 'Aid and Development' 1979; 'Economic Discrimination in Toronto' 1987; other writings incl. bk. reviews and articles relating to econ. dev. or economics of educ. in several publs. and professional jnls.; Pres. O.E.O., Minneapolis 1967–68; Chrmn., Task Force on Child Care, Ont. Govt. 1972; Natl. Task Force of Anglican Ch. on the Econ. 1975–77; ACAP and COU Cmte. on Index Nos. 1975–78; Pres., YUFA Foundation; Treas., Advocacy Centre for Elderly; competed for N.Y. Sch. Bd., Ont., 1979 (defeated); Treas., Franz Blumenfeld Fund 1987–91; Sec./Treas., Black Creek Foundn. 1987– ; Mem., Planning Adv. Ctte., City of Toronto 1989–91; mem., Am. Econ. Assn; Candn. Econ. Assn. (Ed. Bd. 1978–81); CLU, AGO; awarded Univ. Scholarship and Jr. Sterling Fellowship, Yale 1946–49; Faculty Fellowship, Fund for Advance. of Educ. 1952–53; Faculty Fellow., Ford Found., 1960–61; Fulbright Fellow. (Japan and Singapore) 1963–64; Research Fellow, Ont. Econ. Council, 1976–77; Visiting Scholar, Columbia Univ. and N.Y.U. 1983–84; Mayflower Medal; listed in Who's Who in America, American Men of Science, Who's Who in Commonwealth; Club: 39ers; recreation: woodworking; Home: 31 Henry St., Toronto, Ont. M5T 1W9; Office: 4700 Keele St., Downsview, Ont. M3J 1P3.

**BUXTON, William A.S.,** B.Mus., M.Sc.; musician; research scientist; writer; b. Edmonton, Alta. 10 March 1949; s. William Walter and Grace Margaret (Potts) B.; e. Queen's Univ. Kingston, B.Mus. 1973; Univ. of Toronto, M.Sc. 1978; Inst. of Sonology, Utrecht State Univ.; wife Elizabeth d. E.A. Russ; children: Blair, Adam, Katy; ASSOC. PROF., UNIV. OF TORONTO 1989– ; Scientific Dir., Ont. Telepresence Project 1992– ; Consulting Rsch. Scientist, Xerox Palo Alto Rsch. Center 1989– ; Lectr. Univ. of Toronto 1979–82, Rsch. Sci. 1982–87; Cons., IBM, Apple Computer, Mattel Electronics, Xerox, Pacific Bell 1984–87; Rsch. Sci. Rank Xerox EuroParc 1987–89; Consultant, Commodore Business Machines; concerts incl. radio and TV broadcasts throughout N.Am. and Eur.; co-author 'Human-Computer Interaction: A Multi-Disciplinary Approach' 1987; author over 40 articles computer music, culture & technol.; mem. various ed. bds. incl. Chrmn. 'Computer Music Journal'; Gov. Frontier Coll. 1982–97; Pres. Computer Music Assn. 1982–87; mem. Adv. Bd. ACM/SIGCHI 1985–87; recreations: horseback riding, running, skiing; Home: 83 Cairns Ave., Toronto, Ont. M4L 1X6; Office: CSRI, Univ. of Toronto, Toronto, Ont. M5S 1A4.

**BUXTON, William Joseph,** B.A., M.A., M.Sc. (Econ.), Dr.rer.pol.; educator; b. Edmonton, Alta. 8 July 1947; s. Earl William and Dorothy Lee (Cox) B.; e. public sch.: Calgary; Palo Alto, CA; Edmonton (Strathcona Composite H.S. 1962–65); Univ. of Alta. B.A. 1969; St. John's Coll. Oxford (Rhodes Scholar) B.A. 1973, M.A. 1978; London Sch. of Econ. M.Sc. (Econ.) 1974; Otto-Suhr Inst. Die Freie Universität Berlin Dr.rer.pol. 1980; PROFESSOR OF COMMUNICATION STUDIES, CONCORDIA UNIV. 1992– ; Fellow, Lonergan Univ. College and Sch. of Community and Public Affairs, Concordia Univ.; Asst. Prof. of Sociol. & Anthrop. Laurentian Univ. summer 1976; Post-Doctoral Fellow Center for Eur. Studies Harvard Univ. 1980–82; recipient McEachran Gold Medal in Psychol. Univ. of Alta. 1969; Deutsches Akademisches Austauschdienst Stipendium 1974–75; Can. Counc. Doctoral Fellowship 1975–76; Shastri Indo-Canadian Inst., Faculty Training Fellowship 1988; SSHRCC Rsch. Grant 1988–92, 1992–95; Rockefeller Archive Centre Rsch. Grant 1989, 1993; T. Glendenning Hamilton Rsch. Grant, Univ. of Manitoba 1992; Asst. Prof. of Sociology, Univ. of N.B. 1981–85, Assoc. Prof. 1985–90; Dir., Third World Studies Programme 1990; Assoc. Prof. of Communication Studies, Concordia Univ. 1990–92; Visiting Scholar: Center for European Studies, Harvard, summer 1985, fall 1987, summers 1988–90; Southern Asian Inst., Columbia Univ., spring 1988; Dept. of Sociology, Delhi Univ., spring 1989; School for Social and Economic Develop., Univ. of South Pacific, Suva, Fiji, summer 1993; East-West Institute, Honolulu, summer 1993; Visiting Prof., Dept. of Communication, Simon Fraser Univ. spring 1994; author: 'Talcott Parsons and the Capitalist Nation-State: Political Sociology as a Strategic Vocation' 1985; numerous academic articles; Vice Pres., Assn. of Univ. of N.B. Teachers 1986–87; Extve., Fredericton South NDP (provincial) Riding Assn. 1985–87; Extve., Concordia Univ. Faculty Assn. 1992–93; co-host 'Cinéfile' (Fredericton Cablevision) 1989–90; mem. Candn. Assn. Rhodes Scholars; Candn. Assn. Sociol. & Anthrop.; Internat. Sociol. Assn.; Atlantic Assn. Sociol. & Anthrop.; Am. Sociol. Assn.; Candn. Communications Assoc.; Speech Communication Assoc.; International Communications Assoc.; Internat. Assn. of Mass Communications Rsch.; Assn. canadienne française pour l'avancement des sciences (ACFAS); Assn. canadienne des sociologues et anthropologues de langue française (ACSALF); CHEIRON; Goethe Inst., Montréal; Héritage Montréal; The Candn. Centre for Architecture; NDP; recreations: basketball, cycling, photography, cooking, scuba diving; Home: 4279 Ave. Christophe-Colomb, Montréal, Qué. H2J 3G2; Office: 7141 Sherbrooke St. W., Montréal, Qué. H4B 1R6.

**BUYERS, William James Leslie,** Ph.D., F.R.S.C., F.Inst.P., F.A.P.S.; scientist; b. Aboyne, Scot. 10 Apl. 1937; s. William and Williamina Boyd (McBey) B.; e. Aberdeen Grammar Sch. 1955; Univ. of Aberdeen B.Sc. 1959, Ph.D. 1963; m. Marilyn d. Walter and Jennie Cliff 1 Oct. 1966; children: Sarah, Andrew; SENIOR SCIENTIST, AECL RESEARCH, CHALK RIVER, ONT. 1974– ; Lectr. Univ. of Aberdeen 1963–65; Nat. Rsch. Council Fellow AECL Chalk River 1965, AECL Rsch. Offr. 1966– ; Mgr. Neutron and Solid State Physics Br., AECL Research 1985–91; Sr. Visiting Fellow Oxford Univ. 1971–72; Guest Sci. Oak Ridge Nat. Lab. 1972, Riso Nat. Lab. Denmark 1975, 1984, Inst. for Theoretical Physics Santa Barbara 1980–81; Adjunct Prof. Univ. of Toronto 1986–89; Univs. of Guelph and Waterloo 1992– ; Visiting Prof., Univ. of B.C. 1993–94; recipient Rutherford Medal for Achievement in Physics Royal Soc. Can. 1986; Fellow, Am. Physical Soc.; mem. Adv. Ctte. Solid State Div. Oak Ridge Nat. Lab.; mem. Candn. Liaison Ctte. IUPAP; Secy., IUPAP Comn. on Magnetism; editor: 'Moment Formation in Solids' 1984; author or co-author over 180 sci. publs.; mem. Candn. Assn. Physicists; Dir. Cantando Singers; Home: 9 Pine Point Rd., Deep River, Ont. K0J 1P0; Office: Chalk River, Ont. K0J 1J0.

**BUZEK, Karel,** C.M.; tree farmer; b. Frenštat, Czechoslovakia 2 May 1904; s. Karel and Marie (Čapek) B.; e. Univ. of Prague, B.Comm; m. Ellen Wilson 22 Sept. 1942; children: Peter, Caroline; Interpreter, Internat. Convention of the Free Churches, Prague 1926; Foreign Languages Dept., White Star Steamship Line, Liverpool, Eng. 1927–29; moved to Canada 1930 on request of Czechoslovak Consul in Toronto to act as his deputy; Canadian citizen 1935; Organizer, Czech. Nat. Alliance in Canada (establishing 92 chapters prior to W.W. II); Dir., Candn. Clothing Collection, UNRRA Ottawa 1945; Delegate to Can. of Czech. Red Cross 1945–48; opened travel agency (Toronto) 1946; initiated 'Candn. Fund for Czech. Refugees' 1948 (the fund still receives bequests from patriots); Co-founder, T.G. Masaryk Meml. Park (Scarborough); Mem., Candn. Inst. of Fgn. Affairs; owner/operator 200 acre tree farm (a reforestation and temporary shelter project established for refugees) 1949– ; rec'd Red Cross decoration from Pres. E. Beneš, Prague 1946; Order of Canada 1985; author: 'Between East and West' 1946; co-author: 'The 1943 Yearbook' (1st book printed in Can. in Czech. and Slovak langs); mem., Candn. Inst. for Foreign Affairs; Home: Sun Valley Tree Farm, R.R. 4, Uxbridge, Ont. L0C 1K0 and 237 Wanless Ave., Toronto, Ont. M4N 1W5.

**BWINT, Derek Shway,** B.Comm., A.I.B., C.G.A.; financial executive; b. Rangoon, Burma 3 June 1941; s. U Tha Bwint and Tha Aye Sein B.; e. Rangoon Univ. B.Comm. 1961; A.I.B. (England) 1964; Certified General Accountant Alberta 1969; m. Barbara d. Bryan A. Ellis 29 July 1970; children: Graham, Ian; TREASURER, ALBERTA ENERGY COMPANY LTD. 1991– ; Manager, Financial Analysis, Sherritt 1972–76; Manager, Financial Evaluations, Alberta Energy Co. 1976–79; Dir. 1979–88; Corp. Planning 1988–91; Dir., Alta. Oil Sands Pipeline Ltd.; Syncrude Canada Ltd.; Mem., Financial Extves. Inst. of Can. (Calgary Ch.); Office: 3900, 421 – 7th Ave. S.W., Calgary, Alta. T2P 4K9.

**BYKHOVSKY, Arkadi G.,** M.B.A., M.Sc.; forest industry executive; b. 10 Nov. 1943; e. City Univ., Seattle, Wash., M.B.A. 1978; Acad. of Forestry & Wood Technol., St. Petersburg, Russia 1968; m. Halina Eva; CHRMN. & CHIEF EXECUTIVE OFFR., HUNTER

TIMBER GROUP (U.K.) 1993– ; and EXECUTIVE DIRECTOR, WICKES PLC (U.K.) 1993– ; Dir., Normerica Building Systems, Inc. (Markham, Ont.); Mng. Dir., Noranda Forest Holdings (U.K.) 1986–93; Pres., Noranda Forest Sales Inc. 1986–93; Dir., Noranda Forest Sales (U.K.) Limited 1986–93; Sr. Vice-Pres., Noranda Forest Inc. 1987–93; Pres., Norbord Industries Inc. 1988–93; Dir., Roxul (Cda.) Inc. 1988–93; Dir., Forintek Canada Corp. 1991–93; Dir. & Regional Vice-Pres., Canada/USSR Business Council 1988–93; Chrmn., Structural Bd. Assoc. 1990–93; Home: 245 Erskine Ave., Toronto, Ont. M4P 1Z6.

**BYNOE, Brian Clive,** B.A., LL.B., Q.C.; barrister and solicitor; b. Toronto, Ont. 16 Sept. 1928; s. Clive Vickers Bynoe; e. McMaster Univ. B.A. 1953; Osgoode Hall Law Sch. LL.B. 1957; m. Audrey May d. A.N.S. Jackson, Jamaica 5 Sept. 1953; children: Roberta Ann, Nora Elizabeth, Brian Clive Vickers; sole practitioner B. CLIVE BYNOE, Q.C.; Offr. and Dir. various private co's incl. Vice Pres. and Dir. Canadian Protection Services Ltd.; Dir. Shandon Associates Ltd.; called to Bar of Ont. 1957, N.W.T. 1962; cr. Q.C. 1971; Lectr. in Criminal Law & Procedure Ont. Bar Admission Course 1960–80; Lectr. Continuing Educ. Series Law Soc. Upper Can.; sometime Lectr. in Criminal Law & Procedure Fed. Law Soc's; Counsel to several Royal Comns. incl. Royal Comn. Toronto Jail & Custodial Service; former mem. Ed. Bd. Criminal Reports (Can.); author numerous articles various aspects criminal law; Bencher, Law Soc. Upper Can.; mem. Advocate Soc.; Criminal Lawyers' Assn. (Past Pres.); Candn. Bar Assn.; Co. York Law Assn.; Lawyers' Club; P. Conservative; Anglican; recreations: racquet sports, boating, swimming, hunting, fishing, shooting; Clubs: Scarborough Rod & Gun; Toronto Lawn Tennis; Home: 12 Gordon Rd., Willowdale, Ont. M2P 1E1; Office: 480 University Ave., Suite 700, Toronto, Ont. M5G 1V2.

**BYRNE, James Michael,** B.Sc., M.Sc., Ph.D.; university professor; administrator; b. Lethbridge, Alta. 26 June 1954; s. Francis Thomas and Helen Dora (Parfitt) B.; e. Univ. of Alta. B.Sc. 1978, M.Sc. 1983, Ph.D. 1990; m. Cheryl d. Henry and Sylvia Hickie 13 Aug. 1977; children: Brendan, Kalyn, Davyn, Jayme; ASST. PROFESSOR & DIRECTOR, WATER RESOURCES INST., UNIV. OF LETHBRIDGE; hydrologist & water resources rsch. sci. since 1982; special interest in water & climate issues on N. Am. great plains; Consultant; Mem., Internat. Water Resources Assn.; Dir., Canadian Water Resources Assn. 1990–93 (Dir., Alta. Branch 1989– ;); author of 40 sci. & public interest pubns.; recreations: training golden retrievers for field trial comp. in Can. & U.S.; Office: Lethbridge, Alta. T1K 3M4.

**BYRNE, Timothy C.,** M.A., Ed.D.; educator; b. Minneapolis, Minn. 15 Apl. 1907; s. John Charles and Elizabeth (Clarke) B.; e. St. Mary's High Sch. Edmonton 1924; Univ. of Alta. B.A. 1932, M.A. (History & Economics) 1937, B.Ed. 1943; Univ. of Colo. Ed.D. 1956; m. 1stly Irma Burkholder 1933 (d. 1973); children: Joan Owen, John; m. 2ndly Catherine Carson 1974; Pres. Emeritus Athabasca Univ. 1976– ; teacher Calgary Pub. Schs. 1937–42; Supt. of Schs. Dept. Educ. Alta. 1942–49, High Sch. Inspr. 1949–57; Chief Supt. of Schs. Prov. Alta. 1957–66; Depy. Min. of Educ. Alta. 1966–71; Pres. Athabasca Univ. 1971–76; Visiting Prof. of Educ. Adm. Univ. Alta. 1976–82; Candn. Rep. Commonwealth Conf. Educ. Lagos and Canberra, Educ. Comte. O.E.C.D. Paris 1966–71; Pres. Candn. Educ. Assn. 1973–74; awarded Soc. Sci. Fed. of Can. grant for the publication of 'Athabasca University, The Evolution of Distance Education' 1989; author: 'Alberta's Revolutionary Leaders' 1991; Clubs: Windermere Golf & Country; Royal Glenora; Address: 8303 – 138 St., Edmonton, Alta. T5R 0E1.

# C

**CABANA, Aldée (Mr.),** C.M., M.Sc., Ph.D.; chemist; educator; b. Beloeil, Qué. 20 July 1935; s. Germain and Marie-Ange (Laquerre) C.; e. Univ. de Montréal, B.Sc. 1958, M.Sc. 1959, Ph.D. 1962; Princeton Univ. 1961–63; m. Lise d. Lionel Couillard, St-Marc-sur-Richelieu, Qué. 28 June 1958; children: Bruno, Marianne, Louise, Yves; Recteur, Univ. de Sherbrooke 1985–93; Lectr. in Chem. present Univ. 1963, Asst. Prof. 1964, Assoc. Prof. 1967, Prof. 1971, Dean of Sciences 1978–85; Dir., Les Industries C-MAC 1992; recipient Gerhard Herzberg Award, Spectroscopy Soc. Can. 1976; Médaille Archambault, ACFAS 1983; Médaille de l'Université de Montréal 1991; Member, Order of Canada 1993; mem. Nat. Research Council Can.; Mem. of the Bd., AUCC 1991– ; author over 40 scient. papers vibrational spectroscopy; Fellow C.I.C.; mem. Order of Chems.; C.A.P.; Spectroscopy Soc. Can.; ACFAS; Sigma Xi; R. Catholic; recreations: sailing, skiing; Home: 264 Heneker, Sherbrooke, Qué. J1J 3G4.

**CADARIO, Paul Michael,** B.A.Sc., M.A.; economist; b. Toronto, Ont. 5 June 1951; s. Harry Paul and Dorothy Mary (Higgins) C.; e. Leaside High Sch., Toronto 1969; Univ. of Toronto B.A.Sc. (Civil Engn.) 1973; Rhodes Scholar (Ont. and Magdalen) 1973; Oxford Univ. B.A. 1975, M.A. 1983; CHIEF ADMINISTRATIVE OFFR., EUROPE AND CENTRAL ASIA REGION, THE WORLD BANK, WASHINGTON, D.C. 1993– ; Economist, Western Africa Regional Office 1975–87; Principal Country Officer, China and Mongolia Dept. 1987–92; Chief Institutional Development, Asia Tech. Dept. 1992–93; Alumni Mem., Gov. Council, Univ. of Toronto 1985–94, mem. Exec. Ctte. 1987–94; Dir., The Associates of the Univ. of Toronto, Inc., N.Y. 1979– ; Pres., Univ. of Toronto Alumni Assn., Washington Br. 1977– ; Chair, Benefits Review Working Group, Mem., Adv. Ctte. on Harassment, World Bank Group Staff Assoc.; Club: Canadian (Washington, D.C.); Home: 1517 T St. N.W., Washington, D.C. 20009; Office: 1818 H St. N.W., Washington, D.C. 20433.

**CADBURY, Barbara,** C.M.; family planning advocate; b. London, Eng. 1910; e. Central Foundation, Bishops Gate; m. George Cadbury; two children; Staff of League of Nations Union, London, Eng.; Secy. for Frank Wise, M.P. Eng.; Councillor, Borough of Stoke Newington, London, el. 1934; moved to Sask. 1946; FOUNDER, PLANNED PARENTHOOD TORONTO; has done extensive work in the field of family planning in the Caribbean, the United States, Asia, and Canada; worked with Margaret Sanger, Planned Parenthood, New York, 1951–54; Pres., Family Planning Assoc. of Jamaica 1955–60; Bd. Mem., Jamaica Welfare 1955–60; apptd. jointly with husband as Special Reps. of the International Planned Parenthood Fedn., travelled extensively in Asia, 1960; founded Planned Parenthood Toronto 1961; helped to found the Family Planning Fedn. of Can. 1963; became a mem. Candn. Welfare Council 1965; directed campaign aimed at amending the Candn. Criminal Code regarding contraception 1961–69, Code Reformed in 1969; planned first National Conf. on Family Planning in Can. 1971; currently lectures on family planning; Mem., Hamilton Planned Parenthood Soc.; Planned Parenthood of Toronto; has written extensively on family planning; rec'd Governor General's Persons Award 1981; Toronto YWCA Women of Distinction Award 1982; Honoured by Population & Family Planning Sect., Am. Public Health Assoc. 1982; apptd. Member of the Order of Canada 1990; recreations: children; grandchildren; wildlife; politics; Home: 345 Church St., Suite 308, Churchill Place, Oakville, Ont. L6J 7G4.

**CADBURY, George Woodall,** C.M., M.A.; b. 19 Jan. 1907; s. George and Edith Caroline (Woodall) C.; e. Leighton Park Sch. Reading; King's Coll. Cambridge M.A. 1928 (Econ. Tripos) personal pupil of J.M. Keynes; Wharton Sch. of Finance & Comm. Univ. of Pa. 1929; m. Councillor Barbara Pearce 1935; two d.; Chrmn. Emeritus Governing Body, Internat. Planned Parenthood Fedn. 1975– ; apptd. Member of the Order of Canada 1990; granted landed status, Que., worked harvest in Alta. 1928; Resident Toynbee Hall 1929–35, 1941–43; Mng. Dir. British Canners Ltd. 1929–35; Mktg. Controller to Mng. Dir. Alfred Bird & Sons Ltd. 1935–45; Nat. Fire Service, Birmingham 1939–41; West Midland Group Post War Reconstrn. & Planning, U.K. 1939–41; on loan as Dep. Dir. Material Prodn. Min. of Aircraft Prodn. and British Air Comn. (USA) 1941–45; Chrmn. Econ. Adv. & Planning Bd., Chief Ind. Exec. Prov. Saskatchewan Canada 1945–51; Sr. Dir. Tech. Assistance Adm. UN 1951–60, Dir. Operations 1951–54, Adv. to Govts. Ceylon, Burma, Indonesia, Venezuela, Jamaica & Barbados 1954–60; Dir., Central Planning Unit & Economic and Social Adv. to Govt. of Jamaica 1955–60; Chrmn. 1969–75, Vice Chrmn. and Chrmn. of Exec. 1963–69, Special Rep. 1960– , International Planned Parenthood Fedn.; Adv. to Govts. Japan, Korea, the Phillipines, Indonesia, Sri Lanka, Thailand, Burma and Singapore; Pres. (Ont.) 1961–66, Fed. Treas. 1965–71, mem. Fed. Extve. 1961–71, Rep. on Socialist International 1961–71, Life mem. 1980, New Democratic Party, Can.; Chrmn. 1972–74, 1976–78 and Pres. 1978–82 Conservation Council Ont.; Trustee, Bournville Village Trust 1928–85; Youth Hostels Trust 1931– ; Sponsor & Council mem. Minority Rights Group Internat. 1967– ; Hon. Dir. Planned Parenthood Soc. Hamilton, Ont. 1961– ; Hon. Dir., Planned Parenthood, Toronto 1961– ; Life mem., Fabian Soc. and TGWU, U.K. 1923– ; Bd. mem. League for Ind. Democracy U.S.A. 1929– ; Dir. and Patron, Douglas Coldwell Foundn., Can. 1982– ; co-author: 'When We Build Again' 1940; 'English County' 1942; 'Conurbation' 1942; 'Essays on the Left' 1971; 'A Population Policy for Canada' 1973; recreations: railway practice & history; Address: Suite 308, 345 Church. St., Oakville, Ont. L6J 7G4.

**CADEAU, Lally;** actress; b. Hamilton, Ont. 10 Jan. 1948; d. Alvin Peter and Alice Moffatt (Mitchell) C.; e. Loretto Acad. Hamilton; Stoneleigh-Prospect Hill Sch. Greenfield, Mass.; Edenhall Convent of Sacred Heart Philadelphia, Pa.; Havergal Coll. Toronto; children: Sara Brooke, Christopher Cadeau, Bennett Mitchell; profl. actress since 1974; recipient ACTRA Du Maurier Award Best Newcomer Candn. TV 'Harvest' 1981; Bijou Award Best Actress 'You've Come Along Way Katie' 1981; ACTRA Earle Grey Award Best Acting Performance TV Leading Role 'You've Come Along Way Katie' 1982; Dora Mavor Moore Award Outstanding Performance by Female in Leading Role 'Saturday, Sunday, Monday' 1986–87; various nominations radio, film and TV; mem. Disciplinary Adv. Ctte. Can. Council Theatre Dept. 1982–85; recreations: swimming, walking, reading, cooking, decorating, gardening; Office: Oscars and Abrams, 59 Berkeley St., Toronto, Ont. M5A 2W5.

**CADIEUX, Jean,** B.A. Laval 1943, L.Comm. Montreal 1946, D.Sc.Eco., Aix en Provence 1970; né L'Original, Ontario, 29 août 1923; f. Fortunat et Elvina (LaBelle) C.; ép. Françoise, f. Esdras Chamard, St. Jean Port Joli, Qué. 5 juillet 1947; enfants: Louise, Bernard, Marie, Pierre, Hélène, Chantal, Jean P.; Dir., La cie de Gestion Atlantique; mem. Conseil d'adm., Beaverbrook Art Gallery; Musée du Nouveau-Brunswick; Institut de Memramcook; Hôpital Dr. Georges-L. Dumont; Campagne Ensemble; Prés., Entraide Univ. Mondiale de Can.; Prof. invité; Faculté des sciences écon. Aix en Provence 1970–71; recteur, Univ. de Moncton 1974–79; auteur: 'Le bilinguisme au Nouveau Brunswick' 1967; 'L'Hôpital de Maria' 1970; 'Les coûts sociaux au Nouveau Brunswick' 1972; Dir., 'Revue Economique' 1963–67; 'Revue de l'Université de Moncton' 1968–69; rec'd Ordre du Mérite du Canada; mem. Assn. des Comptables Agréés; catholique; récréations: natation; golf, bridge; Club: Richelieu; Résidence: Bureau: Moncton, N.B. E1A 3E9.

**CADIEUX, Brig. Gen. (ret'd) John Paul Anthony,** C.D., B.Eng., M.Sc., M.B.A., P.Eng.; b. North Bay, Ont. 27 Oct. 1934; s. Joseph Anthony and Clare Margaret (O'Grady) C.; e. Royal Mil. Coll., Grad. Dipl. 1957; McGill Univ., B.Eng. 1958; Queen's Univ., M.Sc. 1966; Harvard Business Sch., M.B.A. 1969; PRESIDENT & C.E.O., BANFF SCH. OF ADVANCED MANAGEMENT, BANFF, ALTA. 1991– ; various positions with Candn. Armed Forces, Transport Canada; Office of Comptroller Gen. of Can.; Correctional Service of Can.; Canadair Ltd.; Bell Helicopter Textron; 7S Building Systems; Banff Sch. of Advanced Mgmt.; rec'd RCAF Pilot Wings 1957; served with 423 All-Weather (Fighter) Sqdn., 2 (Fighter) Wing, Grostenquin, France, 1958–62; Lectr., Royal Mil. Coll. 1962–65; Depy. Sqdn. Commdr., RCAF Gimli, Man. 1965–67; Commandant, 433$^{e}$ Escadrille Tactique de Combat, CFB Bagotville, Que. 1969–71; Commandant, Coll. militaire royal de Saint-Jean 1971–73; Treasury Bd. 1973–74; Dir. Gen. Recruiting, Educ. & Trg., Hdqrs. Ottawa 1974–75; Aide-de-Camp to Gov. Gen. 1971–75; Commdr., 1 Candn. Air Group (NATO), Lahr, W. Germany 1975–77; Dir. Gen. Airports & Const. Services, Ottawa 1977–80; Ass't Comptroller Gen. 1980–83; Depy. Commr. 1983–87; Vice Pres. & Gen. Mgr. 1987–88; Extve. Vice Pres. 1988–90; Extve. Vice Pres. 1990–91; mem. Assn. Prof. Engrs. Ont.; R. Catholic; Address: The Banff School of Advanced Mgmt., P.O. Box 1020, Stn. 5, Banff, Alta. T0L 0C0.

**CADIEUX, Hon. Pierre H.,** P.C., B.A., B.C.L.; politician; b. Hudson, Que. 6 April 1948; s. Antonio and Thérèse (Leduc) C.; e. Coll. de Valleyfield and McGill Univ.; Min. of State (Fitness & Amateur Sport) & Min. of State (Youth) 1991–93; Min. of Labour, 1986–89; Min. of Indian & Northern Affairs 1989–90; Solicitor General of Canada 1990–91; el. House of Commons g.e. 1984; M.P. for Vaudreuil, Que.; mem. Quebec Bar Assn.; Ont. Bar Assn.

**CADSBY, Hon. Milton A.,** B.A.; judge; b. Toronto, Ont. 15 Jan. 1924; s. Jack David and Rose (Rafelman) C.; e. Univ. of Toronto, B.A. 1946; Osgoode Hall Law Sch. 1949; m. Maxine d. Samuel and Fanny Lichtman 17 Dec. 1950; children: Charles Bram, Catherine D. Silver, Susan L. Morrisette; JUDGE, PROV. COURT OF ONT. (CRIMINAL DIV.) 1979– ; law practice 1949–79; cr. Q.C. 1966; Past Pres. Candn. Rose Soc.; recreations: tennis, riding, fishing; Home: 28 Hilltop Rd., Toronto,

Ont. M6C 3C9; Office: 444 Yonge St., Toronto, Ont. M5H 2M4.

**CADWELL, Dorothy Helen Belle,** O.C., M.A.; public servant; b. Saskatoon, Sask., 15 Jan. 1910; d. John Wesley and Nina Jeanette (Isbister) C.; e. Univ. of Manitoba, B.A. 1930; Columbia Univ., N.Y.C., M.A. 1948; high sch. teacher in Manitoba; Personnel Administrator, then Admin. Sec. with Pub. Service Comn.; Rsch. Coordinator, Royal Comn. on Status of Women; retired 1970; mem. of C.I.D.A. task force sent to Jamaica to introduce new classification system for Jamaican Pub. Service; headed City of Ottawa and Region task force to examine status of women in that pub. service and to present recommendations; recvd. City of Ottawa's Women's Award 1979; former pres. of Ottawa Bus. and Prof. Women's Club and of Zonta Club of Ottawa; mem. of Univ. Women's Club of Am.; author of 'Murder on the House' (mystery novel) 1976; religion: Presbyn.; recreations: bridge, golf; club: Ottawa Hunt and Golf Club; Home: 3822 Revelstoke Dr., Ottawa, Ont. K1V 7C4.

**CADWELL, Roy,** M.A.; retired lawyer; b. Willcocks, Sask. 8 July 1906; s. Howard and Martha (Fletcher) C.; e. Riverdale Coll., Toronto, Ont.; Univ. of Toronto, B.A., 1930, M.A. 1932; Osgoode Hall Law Sch. 1933; m. Priscilla Ward, d. the late Walter Jones, Clearwater, Florida; CHAIRMAN, LESTER B. PEARSON PEACE PARK INC. 1967– ; Dir., Cadwell Properties Ltd., Madoc-Tweed Art & Writing Centre; read law with Ludwig, Ludwig and Schuyler; called to the Bar of Ont., formed firm and practised law with Cadwell & Piper, Toronto, 1933; Asst. Registrar, Osgoode Hall 1937; Inspr. Legal Offices 1939–40; organized Cadwell Properties Ltd. as a private holding co. 1949; Legal Advisor, Candn. Truce Commrs., Vietnam, Laos and Cambodia, Dept. External Affairs 1955–56; returned to private practise 1957; retired 1958; Offrs. Training Course, Niagara-On-The-Lake, R.C.A.S.C. 2nd. Lieut. 1939; enlisted R.C.A.M.C. Lieut. 1940, Capt. 1942; organized mil. hosps. Canada and England; part time in Personnel Selection Br.; now Reserve Offr., Capt.; Service & Overseas Medals; author of 'Communism in the Modern World'; (M.A. thesis), 'The Incidence of Automobile Accidents'; 'Clearwater, A Sparkling City'; Lecturer, Dept. Univ. Extension, Univ. of Toronto 1949–52; Liberal cand., Riverdale, Toronto, 1935; Fed. Liberal cand., Hastings-Frontenac 1965; first Pres., Don Valley Conservation Assn. 1946 and helped organize Authority 1948; Chairman, Ont. Jr. Bar; mem., Toronto Lawyers Club (to retirement); Life mem., Candn. Bar Assn.; former mem., Candn. Authors' Assn., National Writers' Club, Kiwanis Club; Past-Pres., Royal Candn. Legion, Forest Hill, Toronto; Freemason; United Church; recreations: writing, art, music, people; Homes: (spring, summer, fall) R.R. 3, Tweed, Ont.; (winter) 1109 N. Betty Lane, Clearwater, Florida.

**CAHILL, Jack;** journalist-author; b. Brisbane, Aust. 7 Apr. 1926; s. John Lawrence and Nancy (O'Sullivan) C.; e. St. Joseph's Coll. 1942; m. Marie d. John and Gladys O'Brien 28 Jan. 1956; children: Anthony, Sally, Kerry, Patrick; Feature Writer, 'Toronto Star' 1978–..; reporter on various Australian newspapers 1946–57; B.C. Legis. Bur. Ch., 'Vancouver Sun' 1959–63; Ottawa Bur. Ch. 1963–65; Queen's Park Bur. Ch., 'Toronto Star' 1966–69; Nat. Ed. 1969–70; Ottawa Bur. Ch. 1970–73; Asian Bur. Ch. (Hong Kong) 1973–78; various journalism awards incl. Nat. Newspaper Award 1975 for coverage of Vietnam War & Nat. Bus. Writing Award 1979; author: 'If You Don't Like the War Switch the Damn Thing Off! – The Adventures of a Foreign Correspondent' 1980, 'Hot Box – The Story of the Mississauga Disaster' 1981, 'John Turner – The Long Run, a Biography' 1984, 'Words of War' 1987; served RAAF 1944–46; recreation: sailing; Clubs: Oakville Yacht Squadron; Foreign Correspondents' (Hong Kong); Home: 296 Mill Rd., Apt. G5, Etobicoke, Ont. M9C 4X8.

**CAHOON, Margaret Cecelia,** M.Ed., Ph.D.; educator, nurse-researcher; b. Hallowell Twp., Prince Edward Co., Ont. 5 May 1916; d. Gordon Milton and Mary Maude (Black) C.; e. Women's Coll. Hosp. Sch. for Nurses Toronto 1943; Univ. of Toronto Cert. in Pub. Health Nursing 1946; Queen's Univ. B.A. 1950; Univ. of Toronto B.Ed. 1953, M.Ed. 1960; Univ. of Mich. Ph.D. 1967; Univ. of Edinburgh Post-doctoral Fellowship (Research) 1976; PROF. EMERITUS OF NURSING, UNIV. OF TORONTO ; mem. Gov. Council of Univ. and mem. from Gov. Council to Councils of Faculties of Dentistry and Pharm. 1979–82; 1980–82 Rosenstadt Prof. of Health Research, Sunnybrook-Univ. of Toronto Nursing Project; Staff to Supvr. Prince Edward Co. Hospt. 1943–44; Pub. Health Nurse, Town of Picton 1944–45; Pub. Health Nurse, Ont. Cancer Treatment and Research Foundation, Kingston Clinic and Instr. in Community Health Nursing Kingston Gen. Hosp. Sch. of Nursing 1946–49; Fellow in Pub. Health Sch. of Hygiene Univ. of Toronto 1950–52, Assoc. in Pub. Health 1952–64, Asst. Prof. 1964–68, Assoc. Prof. of Nursing with cross-appt. to Sch. of Hygiene 1968–70; Community Health Service E. York-Leaside Health Unit 1950–68; Visiting Prof. of Nursing Univ. of Man. 1980; mem. Bd. Health Borough of E. York 1971–75, Vice Chrmn. 1973–75; rec'd Yaffe Award Candn. Cancer Soc. 1947; Centennial Award Ont. Educ. Assn. 1960; Fellowship in Gerontology Nat. Council Jewish Women 1961; World Health Organ. Award 1963; Hon. Clin. Fellow Ont. Cancer Treatment & Research Foundation 1971–72; Ont. Ministry of Health Fellowship 1975; Sesquicentennial Award Univ. of Toronto 1977; Educ. Devel. Award 1978; author-consultant (Candn. ed.) Health Science Books 4–8 1968–71; author or co-author various articles, papers, book chapters; mem. Reg'd Nurses' Assn. Ont.; Candn. Nurses' Assn.; Candn. Nurses' Foundation (Chrmn. Comte on Research in Nursing 1971–72); Ont. Pub. Health Assn. (Pres. 1963–64); Can. Pub. Health Assn. (Gov. Council 1961–64); Am. Pub. Health Assn. (Gov. Council 1979–81); Ont. Regional Council Assn. Univ. Schs. Nursing (Chrmn. Comte. on Studies 1970–75, mem. Council 1976–80); Pi Lambda Theta; P. Conservative; Presbyterian; recreations: spinning, weaving, travel, painting; Home: 363 Main St., Wellington, Ont. K0K 3L0.

**CAIGER, Charles D.,** C.G.A., C.F.A.; pension investment executive; b. Brockville, Ont. 14 June 1944; s. Frederick John Douglas and Kathleen Maud (Birt) C.; e. Gananoque Secondary Sch. 1963; C.G.A. 1976; C.F.A. 1974; m. Barbara d. James and Betty King 28 May 1966; two s. Mark, Ian; PRES. AND CHIEF EXECUTIVE OFFR. CANADIAN PACIFIC PENSION INVESTMENT MANAGEMENT 1991– ; joined Royal Trust 1965, Mgr. Invests. Vancouver 1975, Mgr.Pension Invests. Toronto Region 1978, Nat. Mgr. Invests. 1981, Asst. Vice Pres. Pension Invest. and Chrmn. Pension Invest. Ctte. 1984; Gen. Mgr. present firm 1984, Vice Pres. 1985, Exec. Vice Pres. 1987, Pres. & C.O.O. 1990; Pres. Vancouver Soc. Financial Analysts 1976–77; mem. Toronto Soc. Financial Analysts; Anglican; recreation: sailing; Club: Trident Yacht; Home: 17 Banquo Rd., Thornhill, Ont. L3T 3G9; Office: 123 Front St. W., Toronto, Ont. M5J 2M8.

**CAILLÉ, Alain,** Ph.D., F.R.S.C.; educator; b. Saint-Jean, Qué. 17 Jan. 1945; s. Jean-Paul and Hectorine (Dubois) C.; e. Univ. de Montréal B.Sc. 1967; McGill Univ. M.Sc. 1969, Ph.D. 1971; m. Francine d. Oscar Martel 30 Apl. 1966; 2 children; VICE PRES.-RSCH. UNIV. DE SHERBROOKE 1989– ; Postdoctoral Fellow Coll. de France, Paris and Faculté des sciences (Orsay) 1971–72; Prof. of Physics UQAM Montréal 1972–74 and present Univ. 1974–89; mem. Council NSERC 1987–89, 1992– , FCAR 1990– ; mem. Acad. Sci's; Candn. Assn. Physicists; membre de l'Association canadienne française pour l'avancement des sciences; Home: 1585 rue Simard, Sherbrooke, Qué. J1J 4A7; Office: Sherbrooke, Qué. J1K 2R1.

**CAILLE, André;** business executive; b. St-Luc, Qué. 11 Sept. 1943; s. Jean-Paul Caillé; e. Univ. de Montréal, B.Sc. 1965, M.Sc. 1966, Ph.D. 1968; Post-doctorate, Biophysics 1969; m. Lyse d. Robert and Lucille Senécal 14 Aug. 1982; children: Daniel, Guillaume, Marc-Vincent; PRESIDENT & CHIEF EXECUTIVE OFFICER, GAZ METROPOLITAIN, INC. 1987– ; Dir., Vermont Gas Systems Corp. Northern New England Gas Corp.; Candn. Gas Assoc.; Am. Gas Assoc.; Dir., Fed./Prov. Ctte. on St. Lawrence River 1975; Environ. Protection Serv. 1978; Depy. Min., Dept. of Environ. 1980; Sr. Vice-Pres., Admin. & Public Affairs, Gaz Métropolitain 1983; Extve. Vice-Pres. & Chief Oper. Offr. 1985; recreations: reading, theatre, tennis; Clubs: Montreal Bd. of Trade; Canadian (Montreal); C. of C. de Montréal; Home: 345 Bloomfield, Outremont, Qué. H2V 3R7; Office: 1717 du Havre, Montréal, Qué. H2K 2X3.

**CAIN, Michael Haney,** B.A., B.C.L.; former judge; b. Chicoutimi, Que. 26 March 1929; s. Murray Vincent and Anna Marie (Feeney) C.; e. St. Patrick High Sch., Arvida, Que., 1946; McGill Univ., B.A. 1950, B.C.L. 1953; m. Huguette, d. Joseph Potvin, Chicoutimi, Que., 20 Sept. 1954; children: Murray, Evelyn; PARTNER, CAIN, LAMARRE WELLS (former Justice, Superior Court of Que. 1971–72); called to Bar of Que. 1954; cr. Q.C. 1971; Founding Pres., Foundation of Univ. of Que. at Chicoutimi Inc.; Bâtonnier of Bar of Saguenay 1970–72; mem., Bar of Que. (Gen. Council 1970–71; Extve. Comte. 1970–71 and Vice Pres. of Comte. 1971); Prov. Que. Bar Assn. (Vice Pres. 1969–70; Pres. 1971); Candn. Bar Assn. (Dir., Que. Sec. 1969–72; Vice Pres., Que. Sec. 1973–74; Pres. Que. Sec. 1974–75); Candn. Inst. for Admin. of Justice; Que. Human Rights Comm. (Comr. 1975–82); mem., Am. Coll. of Trial Lawyers; Dir., Roland Saucier Inst. Found.; Vice Pres., Bar of Que. Ins. Fund; Dir., CJMT-TV Inc.; Phi Gamma Delta; R. Catholic; recreations: tennis, golf; Home: 315 Chabanel, Chicoutimi, Que. G7H 3S1; Office: 255 Racine E., Bur. 600, Chicoutimi, Que. G7H 6J6.

**CAINE, Rebecca Sarah;** singer, actor; b. Toronto, Ont. 25 Nov. 1959; d. Prof. Geoffrey Stuart and Shirley Elwyn (Jennings) Watson; e. Princeton H.S.; Guildhall School of Music, London, England; m. William Timothy Richards 21 Aug. 1993; musical theatre: Cosette in 'Les Miserables' 1985, Christine Daae in 'Phantom of the Opera' (both original London casts), Laurey in 'Oklahoma' and Eliza Doolittle in 'My Fair Lady; recordings incl. orig. Brit. cast album of 'Les Miserables' & 'Anything Goes'; opera: has worked for New Sadlers Wells Opera, The Singers Co., and The Handel Opera Soc. for which she sang the role of 'Clomiri' in 1st Brit. revival of 'Imeneo'; other roles incl.: Despina in 'Cosi fan Tutte,' Eurydice in 'Orpheus in the Underworld,' Casilda in 'The Gondoliers,' & Musetta in 'La Boheme'; sang with Glyndebourne Fest. Opera (2 seasons) covering Fiackermilli in 'Arabella' & 3 soprano roles in world premiere of 'Higglety, Pigglety, Pop!'; principal debut as Amor in 'L'Incoronazione di Poppea'; returned to Canada 1989 to star in Candn. prodn. of 'Phantom of the Opera' & recorded Candn. cast album 1990; N. Am. operatic debut: title role in 'Lulu,' Candn. Opera Co. 1991; Pamina in 'Die Zauberflöte,' Glimmerglass Opera, U.S.A. and Despina in 'Cosi Fan Tutte,' Canadian Opera Co. 1992; Marcellina in 'Fidelio' and Rosina in 'The Barber of Seville' Tulsa Opera, U.S.A. 1993; Title Role in World Premiere of 'Jezebel' music by Derek Holman, Libetto by Robertson Davies, Internat. Choral Festival (Toronto Symphony Orchestra Debut) 1993; Michaela in 'Carmen' and Pamina in 'Die Zauberflöte' Candn. Opera Company 1993; Office: c/o Canadian Opera Company, 227 Front St. E., Toronto, Ont. M5A 1E8.

**CAINE, William Paul,** B.Eng., M.B.A.; wood products executive; b. Montreal, Que. 25 July 1935; s. William Joseph and Monica Marie (Blanchard) C.; e. Strathcona Acad. 1952; McGill Univ. B.Eng. 1957; Wharton Sch. of Business & Comm. Univ. of Pa. M.B.A. 1959; m. Karin Rettkowski 18 July 1981; children: William Terence, Carolyn Janice; CHAIRMAN AND PRESIDENT, LA COMPAGNIE COMMONWEALTH PLYWOOD LTEE 1966– ; Chrmn. and Pres., Robert Bury & Co. (Canada) Ltd.; Commonwealth Plywood Inc.; Multigrade Inc.; recreations: skiing, sailing, fishing; Clubs: Montreal Amateur Athletic Assn.; Royal St. Lawrence Yacht; Office: PO Box 90, Labelle Blvd., Ste-Therese, Que. J7E 4H9.

**CAIRNS, Hugh Alan Craig,** M.A., D.Phil., F.R.S.C.; educator; b. Galt, Ont. 2 March 1930; s. late Hugh and late Lily (Crawford) C.; e. Univ. of Toronto B.A. 1953, M.A. 1957; St. Antony's Coll. Oxford Univ. D.Phil. 1963; m. Patricia Ruth d. late L. Kingsley and late Ruth (Tuplin) Grady 17 July 1958; three d. Lynn Marie, Wendy Louise, Elaine Barbara; PROF. OF POL. SCIENCE, UNIV. OF B.C. 1971– ; Instr. in Pol. Science present Univ. 1960, Asst. Prof. 1963, Assoc. Prof. 1966, Chrmn. 1973–80; Visiting Prof., Mem. Univ. of Nfld. 1970–71; Visiting Prof. of Candn. Studies Univ. of Edinburgh 1977–78; Mackenzie King Visiting Prof. of Candn. Studies Harvard Univ. 1982–83; Brenda and David McLean Chair in Candn. Studies 1993– ; Rsch. Dir. (Institutions), Royal Commn. on the Economic Union and Development Prospects for Can.; recipient Gold Medal Pol. Science & Econ. 1953; Queen's Silver Jubilee Medal 1977; Pres.'s Medal Univ. of W. Ont. (Best Scholarly Article in Social Sciences) 1977; Molson Prize of the Canada Council 1982; Canada Council Killam Research Fellowship 1989–91; author 'Prelude to Imperialism: British Reactions to Central African Society 1840–1890' 1965; co-author 'A Survey of the Contemporary Indians of Canada: Economic Political and Educational Needs and Policies' Vol. I 1966; various articles; 'Constitution, Government and Society in Canada: Selected Essays by Alan C. Cairns' 1988; 'Disruptions: Constitutional Struggles from the Charter to Meech Lake' 1991; 'Charter versus Federalism: The Dilemmas of Constitutional Reform' 1992; mem. Candn. Pol. Science Assn. (Pres. 1976–77); Internat. Pol. Science Assn. (mem. Council 1976–79); recreations: golf, theatre; Home: #2 – 5600 Dalhousie Rd., Vancouver, B.C. V6T 1W4; Office: 452, 1866 Main Mall, Vancouver, B.C. V6T 1Z1.

**CAIRNS, James,** M.B., B.Ch., B.A.O.; physician, public servant; b. Belfast, N. Ireland 2 Dec. 1944; s. Frank Gerald and Patricia Josephine (Hanna) C.; e. St. Mac

Nissi's College; Queen's Univ. of Belfast M.B., B.Ch., B.A.O.; m. Jennifer d. Sir Harold and Lady Black 3 April 1972; children: Peter, Mark, Julie; DEPUTY CHIEF CORONER FOR THE PROVINCE OF ONTARIO 1991– ; Intern, Belfast City Hosp. 1969–70; postgrad. training in Emerg. Med. & Obs. 1970–72; Royal Coll. of Obs. & Gyn., dipl. in Obstetrics 1971; emigrated to Canada in 1972; L.M.C.C. 1973; Head, Emerg. Dept., Peel Memorial Hosp. 1976–79; appointed as Coroner 1979; Local Coroner, Brampton 1979–91; expert witness in forensic medicine at all levels of court; Doctor to Candn. Nat. Cycling Team; Mem., Am. Acad. of Forensic Sci.; Ont. Coroners Assn. (Past Pres.); Candn. Soc. of Forensic Sciences; Internat. Assn. of Coroners & Medical Examiners; recreations: competition cycling and skiing; club: Cadeceus; Home: 20 Lancefield Cres., Brampton, Ont. L6S 2R2; Office: 26 Grenville St., Toronto, Ont. M7A 2G9.

**CAIRNS, John Allan,** MD, FRCP(C), FACC; physician; cardiologist; professor of medicine; b. Trail, B.C. 13 May 1943; s. William Allan and Lois Helan (McLeod) C.; e. Univ. of B.C.; Royal Victoria Hosp., McGill Univ., MD 1968; FRCP(C) 1973 (cardiology), 1974 (medicine); m. Wendy Elizabeth d. Ernest and Winnifred Mitchell 1 June 1968; children: Jennifer Ann, Susannah Daphne, Alison Mitchell; CHRMN. OF MED., MCMASTER UNIV. 1988– ; clin. & rsch. training in cardiology, Montreal; Asst. Prof. of Med., McMaster Univ. 1975; directed Intensive Care Unit, McMaster Univ. Med. Ctr.; Assoc. Prof. of Med. 1980; Co-ord., Reg. Cardiovascular Prog. 1981; Prof. of Med. 1985; Assoc. Chrmn. of Med. 1986; recreations: skiing, music, travel; Home: 323 Bay St. S., Hamilton, Ont. L8P 3J7; Office: HSC-3W10, 1200 Main St. W., Hamilton, Ont. L8N 3Z5.

**CAIRNS, John Campbell,** B.A., M.A., Ph.D.; professor emeritus; b. Windsor, Ont. 27 Apr. 1924; s. William Garroway and Mabel Elizabeth (Campbell) C.; e. Tower House and Emanuel Schs., London, Eng.; Lawrence Park Coll. Inst., Toronto, Ont.; Ridley Coll., St. Catharines, Ont.; Univ. of Toronto, B.A. 1945, M.A. 1947; Cornell Univ., Ph.D. 1951; PROFESSOR EMERITUS, UNIV. OF TORONTO; Prof. of Hist., Univ. of Toronto 1964–89; Instr., Univ. of N. Carolina (Greensboro) 1951–52; Lectr., present Univ. 1952, Asst. Prof. 1956, Assoc. Prof. 1962–64; Visiting Prof., Cornell Univ. 1962, Stanford Univ. 1968; served with R.C.A.F. 1943–45; author 'France' 1965; co-author 'The Foundations of the West' 1963; ed. 'The Nineteenth Century' 1965; 'Contemporary France' 1978; introduction to John Stuart Mill, 'Essays on French History and Historians' 1985; various articles on modern French hist., internat. hist. and aspects of historiography; mem., Am. Hist. Assn.; Soc. for French Hist. Studies; Home: 706 - 20 Avoca Ave., Toronto, Ont. M4T 2B8.

**CAIRNS, Michael R.,** B.A.; real estate executive; b. Toronto, Ont. 10 June 1958; s. Richard B. and Hazel A. (Campbell) C.; e. Univ. of Western Ont. B.A. 1980; divorced; children: David, Alexander; SENIOR VICE-PRESIDENT, LEASING & FACILITIES PLANNING, CIBC DEVELOPMENT CORP. 1989– ; Director, Office Leasing, Cadillac Fairview Corp. 1982–87; Vice-Pres., Office Leasing, Trizec Corp. 1987–89; recreations: golf, skiing, travel; clubs: Thornhill Country, Granite, Fitness Institute; Home: 41 Parkhurst Blvd., Toronto, Ont. M4G 2C8; Office: 145 King St. W., Suite 2800, Toronto, Ont. M5H 3T7.

**CAISERMAN-ROTH, Ghitta,** B.A., R.C.A.; artist; b. Montreal, Que. 2 March 1923; d. Hanane and Sarah (Wittal) Caiserman; e. Parsons Sch. of Design New York City B.A.; Ecole des Beaux-Arts Montreal 1961; m. Max W. Roth 1962; one d. Kathe; VICE-CHAIRPERSON, CANDN. COUNCIL ON THE STATUS OF THE ARTIST, COMMUNICATIONS CANADA; teaching in Montreal; has taught at Concordia Univ., Univ. de Québec, Saidye Bronfman Centre, Nova Scotia College of Art, Arts Sutton, John Abbott Coll., P.Q. etc.; simultaneous shows in Montreal in 1988: Univ. de Montréal & L'Art Français; paintings incl. in various pub., corporate and private colls. such as McMichael Conserv. Gallery Kleinberg, Montreal Museum of Fine Arts, Nat. Gallery of Can., Vancouver and Winnipeg Art Galleries, London (Ont.) Pub. Lib. & Art Museum, Beaverbrook Art Gallery, Dept. External Affairs Ottawa etc.; rec'd Canada Council Fellowship; numerous purchase prizes; Centennial Medal 1967; rec'd Can. Counc. Explorations Grant to write 'Drawing from the Model – A Sensuous Tactile Approach' 1988, book publ. 1993; co-author: (with Friedhelm Lach) 'Creativism' 1980; (with Louise Gareau-Des Bois) 'Pulsions-Pulse' 1983; (with Rhoda Cohen) 'Insights, Surprises, Discoveries' 1993; subject of book: 'Ghitta Caiserman-Roth – Drawings and Paintings' 1988; participant 'The Canadian Landscape' (travelling show) 1983; mentioned in numerous studies of Candn. art; Pres. Atelier Graphia; mem. Royal Candn. Acad. Arts (Council mem.); Soc. Candn. Artists; represented in Montreal by Dominion Gall., in Calgary by Wallace Galleries, in Ottawa by Robertson Galleries; recreations: tennis, cross-country skiing; Club: Mount Royal Tennis; Home: 3475 Jeanne Mance, Montreal, Que. H2X 2J7; Office: 300 Slater St., Rm. 338, Ottawa, Ont. K1A 0C8.

**CAJOLET, Robert J.;** entrepreneur; b. Malartic, Qué. 16 Aug. 1940; s. Charles and Rachel (Veillette) C.; e. Univ. de Montréal – HEC; Harvard Bus. Sch. OMP 6 1982; children: Robert Charles, Julie Ann; PRES. CAMELOT INFO INC. 1991– ; Vice-Chrmn., Candn. Fund for Dental Health; Credit Supr. General Electric 1963; Dentsply International, York Pa. 1963–71, rep. assignments Can. and USA; Citicorp (Medident) Toronto 1972; Mgr. Ash Temple Qué. region 1973–76; C.E.O., Totec Group 1976–90; Pres. Harvard Bus. Sch. Assn. Montréal; Candn. Dental Industry Assoc.; Vice Chrmn., Candn. Fund for Dental Educ., Ottawa; Bd. mem., Alumni Council, Harvard Univ., Boston; mem. Montréal C. of C.; recreations: skiing, wind surfing; Club: St-Denis; Home: 12 Place Cambrai, Outremont, Qué. H2V 1X5.

**CALAMAI, Peter,** B.Sc.; journalist; b. Bloomsburg, Pa. 23 June 1943; s. Henry Joseph and Jean Elizabeth (Kennedy) C.; e. McMaster Univ. B.Sc. (Physics) 1965; m. Mary Elizabeth d. Harold L. and Frances Donald 15 March 1969; JOURNALIST (EDITOR, EDITORIAL PAGES), OTTAWA CITIZEN 1990– ; Reporter, Hamilton Spectator 1966–69; Correspondent, Southam News Ottawa 1969–73; London, U.K. 1973–77; Vancouver 1977–79; Nairobi 1979–82; Ottawa 1983–87; Washington 1988–90; Southam Fellow, Massey College, Univ. of Toronto 1982–83; Max Bell Prof. of Journalism, Univ. of Regina 1985–86 (commuted between Ottawa and Regina); Nat. Newspaper Awards 1981, '84, '85; Mitchener Award for Public Service Journalism 1988 for 'Broken Words' (writer & director); author: 'Trials and Tribulations' 1985; recreations: gardening, conchology; Home: 33 Orrin Ave., Ottawa, Ont. K1Y 3X5; Office: 1101 Baxter Rd., Ottawa, Ont. K2C 3M4.

**CALDER, Col. (James) Allan,** E.D., C.D.; b. Westmount, Que. 4 June 1908; s. Robert Ernest and Florence Emmeline (Osborne) C.; e. Lower Can. Coll.; McGill Univ. 1926–29; m. Eva Jessie Doris (Monica) dec., d. H. B. Bishop, London, Eng., 10 July 1943; one d., Susan Monica; joined Imperial Tobacco Co. of Can. Ltd. 1929; Asst. Comptroller, 1935; Comptroller, 1946; Treas., 1950; el. a Dir., 1950; Vice-Pres. and Treas., 1953; retired as Dir., Extve. Vice-Pres., March 1967; served with Canadian Mil. 1930–39; served in World War 1939–45, overseas; Lt.-Col. commanding Roy. Montreal Regt. (M.G.) 1941–43, (Hon. Lieut.-Col. 1958; Hon. Col. 1965–70); Acting Col. commandg. 'A' Group, Candn. Reinforcement Units, 1943–44; Lieut.-Col. Commandg. Sask. Light Inf., Feb. to July 1944, and Acting Brig. commandg. 1st Candn. Inf. Bgde., July to Dec. 1944, in Italy; Mentioned in Despatches; Nat. Pres., Canadian Mfrs. Assn., 1954–55; Past Chairman, Inst. of Administration; Past Chrmn., Bd. of Govs., Lower Can. Coll.; Delta Upsilon; Protestant; recreations: golf, fishing; Clubs: United Services; Kanawaki Golf; Home: Apt. 1212, The Regency, 3555 Cote des Neiges Rd., Montreal, Que. H3H 1V2; Winter address: Apt. M305, Longboat Harbour, 4430 Exeter Dr., Longboat Key, Florida 34228.

**CALDER, Brendan,** B.Math.; financial company executive; b. 20 Sept. 1946; e. Univ. of Waterloo B.Math. 1969; Advanced Mgmt. Program., Harvard Univ. 1982; m. Mary Ellen, 25 June 1971; two d.: Kate, Tess; PRES. & DIR., FIRSTLINE TRUST CO.; joined Canavest House Ltd. 1969–78 becoming Gen. Mgr. and Dir.; Consultant, The Metropolitan Trust Co. 1978–80; Pres. & Dir., The Fidelity Trust Co. 1980–83; Pres. & Dir., Counsel Trust Co., Counsel Corp. 1983–88; Fellow, The Candn. Securities Inst.; Fellow, Trust Companies Inst.; Young President's Orgn.; Clubs: National; Royal Canadian Yacht; Caledon Mountain Trout; Home: 95 Alcorn Ave., Toronto, Ont.; Office: 20 Toronto St., Ste. 600, Toronto, Ont. M5C 2B8.

**CALDER, Donald Alisdair,** B.Eng., P.Eng., M.B.A.; utilities executive; b. Edinburgh, Scotland 24 Aug. 1944; s. Donald Prentiss and Marjory Roy (Gunn) C.; e. McGill Univ. B.Eng. (Civil) 1965; Univ. of B.C. M.B.A. 1981; m. Jean d. George and Helen Crichton 17 Dec. 1966; children: Sarah Jane, Andrew, Cameron, Colin; GROUP VICE-PRESIDENT (MARKETING & DEVELOPMENT) STENTOR RESOURCE CENTRE INC., Burnaby, B.C. 1993– ; Project Engineer, Shawinigan Engineering Co. Ltd. (Montreal & Vanc.) 1965–71; joined B.C. Telephone Co. 1971; Vice-Pres., Technical Support 1988; Vice-Pres., Business Planning 1991–93; Office: 3777 Kingsway, Burnaby, B.C. V5H 3Z7.

**CALDER, Frank Arthur,** D.D., O.C., L.Th., A.O.C.; b. Nass Harbour, Nass River, B.C. 3 Aug. 1915; s. Chief Arthur Na-Gua-n Calder and Lousia (Leask) C.; e. Ang. Theol. Coll., Univ. of B.C., L.Th. 1946; m. Tamaki Koshibe, 26 Feb. 1975; 1 son, Erick; served as Member Legislative Assembly (M.L.A.) in B.C. for 26 yrs, first with C.C.F.-N.D.P., then with Social Credit; first Canadian Native Indian to be elected to any Candn. Parl't. 1949; first Canadian Native Indian appointed Minister of the Crown in Canada: Minister without Portfolio, 1972–73; known for famous 'Calder Case,' a landmark decision of the Supreme Court of Canada, 1973, on the Nishga Land Claims, a decision upon which current Indian land settlements are being considered in Can.; Founder, Nishga Tribal Council, Pres. 1955–74, Research Dir. and Consultant since 1974; Honours received: inductee, Canada's First Nations Hall of Fame 1967; Pres. Emeritus, Nishga Tribal Council 1985; Aboriginal Order of Canada 1985; Officer, Order of Canada 1988; Doctor of Divinity 1989; Anglican; Home: Somerset House, 540 Dallas Rd., Suite 229, Victoria, B.C. V8V 4X9.

**CALDER, Kathryn A.;** executive; b. Toronto, Ont. 19 July 1947; d. John and Williamina (Moffat) C.; CORP. SEC., SCOTT'S HOSPITALITY INC. 1991– ; Vice-Pres. & Corp. Sec., Fairwater Capital Corp. & Sonor Investments Limited 1987– ; Dir. & Corp. Sec., Charterways Transportation Limited; Scott's Food Services Inc.; S.C. Food Services Inc.; National School Bus Service, Inc.; Scott's Management Services Inc.; Corp. Legal Sec., McCarthy & McCarthy 1964–79; Extve. Asst., Iona Devel. Corp. 1979–80; Corp. Sec., Gardiner Group of Companies (incl. Fairwater Capital & Sonor Investments Limited) 1980–87; Corp. Sec., Scott's Hospitality Found.; The Maytree Found.; The Sonor Found.; Langar Co. Limited; Percy R. Gardiner Found.; Mem., Candn. Inst. of Chartered Secs. & Admin.; clubs: Board of Trade; Home: 116 Castlefield Ave., Toronto, Ont. M4R 1G4; Office: 181 Bay St., Suite 1500, Toronto, ON M5J 2T3.

**CALDER, Kenneth John,** B.A., M.A., Ph.D.; civil servant; b. Moose Jaw, Sask. 19 Jan. 1944; s. Earle Fenwick and Mildred Jane (Remey) C.; e. Univ. of Sask. B.A. (Hons.) 1966, M.A. 1967; London Sch. of Econ. & Pol. Sci. Ph.D. 1971; m. Odile d. Jean-René and Solange Gravereaux 15 Sept. 1972; one s.: Robert Alexandre; ASSISTANT DEPUTY MINISTER, POLICY & COMMUNICATIONS, DEPT. OF NATIONAL DEFENCE 1991– ; Analyst, Operational Rsch. & Analysis Estab., DND 1971–79; Counsellor, Candn. Delegation to NATO 1979–82; Dir. of Strategic Analysis, DND 1982–87; Dir. Gen., Policy Coordination 1987–89; Policy Planning 1989–91; author: 'Britain and the Origins of the New Europe' 1976; Home: 48 Kenilworth St., Ottawa, Ont. K1Y 3Y2; Office: National Defence H.Q., MGEN George R. Pearkes Bldg., Ottawa, Ont. K1A 0K3.

**CALDER, Robert Lorin,** Ph.D.; university professor; b. Moose Jaw, Sask. 3 Apr. 1941; s. Mildred Jane Remey; e. Univ. of Sask., B.A. (Hons.) 1964, M.A. 1965; Univ. of Leeds, Ph.D. 1970; children: Alison, Kevin, Lorin; PROF. OF ENGLISH, UNIV. OF SASKATCHEWAN 1981– ; Instr. of English, present univ. 1965; Asst. Prof. 1971; Assoc. Prof. 1976; Head., Dept. of English 1979–81; Assoc. Dean (Fine Arts & Hum.), Coll. of Arts & Sci. 1981–84; Acting Head, Dept. of Music 1989–90; author: 'W. Somerset Maugham and the Quest For Freedom' 1972, 'Willie: The Life of W. Somerset Maugham' 1989 (1989 Gov.-Gen.'s Literary Award for Non-Fiction); co-author: 'Rider Pride: The Story of Canada's Best Loved Football Team' 1985; co-editor: 'Time as a Human Resource' 1991; recreations: fishing, swimming, theatre, music, cooking; Home: 1108 11th St. E., Saskatoon, Sask. S7H 0G2; Office: Dept. of English, Univ. of Saskatchewan, Saskatoon, Sask. S7N 0W0.

**CALDWELL, John Edward,** B.Com., C.A.; business executive; b. London, Ont. 8 Feb. 1950; s. Raymond B. and Marjorie E. (Doan) C.; e. Carleton Univ. B.Com. 1972; C.A. 1974; m. Laurie E. d. Charles and Joyce Bennett 16 Dec. 1977; two d. Lindsay Elizabeth, Lauren Emily; PRESIDENT AND CHIEF EXTVE. OFFR., CAE INC. 1993– ; Dir., CAE Inc.; CAE-Link Corporation; Audit Sr. Price Waterhouse 1972–75; Controller Fisons Canada Ltd. 1975–76; joined Carling O'Keefe Breweries of Canada 1976, Controller 1979, Asst. to Sr. Vice Pres.

1979, Vice Pres., Controller 1982, Sr. Vice Pres. Finance & Adm. 1985, Exec. Vice Pres. Finance 1987; joined CAE Industries Ltd. (now present Co.) 1988; Vice Pres. Finance 1990; Sr. Vice Pres. Finance and Corporate Affairs 1992; Extve. Vice Pres. 1993; mem. Ont. Inst. C.A.'s; recreation: golf; Club: Beacon Hall; Home: 71 Babcombe Dr., Thornhill, Ont. L3T 1M9; Office: 3060 Royal Bank Plaza, Toronto, Ont. M5J 2J1.

**CALDWELL, John James,** B.Sc., M.Sc., Ph.D.; university professor; b. Winnipeg, Man. 4 Aug. 1944; s. James M. and Donna C. (Sieffert) C.; e. Churchill H.S. 1960; Univ. of Man. B.Sc. 1965; Univ. of W. Ont. M.Sc. 1966; Univ. of Wisconsin Ph.D. 1970; m. Janice d. John B. and Dorothy L. Ritchie 26 Aug. 1966; children: David Justin, Devon Corinne, Garrett Evan James; PROFESSOR, YORK UNIVERSITY 1986– ; post-doct. fellow, Lowell Observatory 1970–71; Satellite Opns., NASA Goddard Space Flight Ctr. 1971–72; Rsch. Assoc., Princton Univ. 1972–77; Asst./Assoc. Prof., State Univ. of N.Y. at Stony Brook 1977–86; Dir., Space Astrophysics Lab. Inst. for Space & Terrestrial Sci. 1988– ; Visiting Prof., Rutgers Univ. 1973–77; Univ. of Hawaii 1981; NASA Hubble Space Telescope Science Working Group 1977–1991; Mem., AAAS, AAS, CAS; author of numerous sci. papers; recreations: running, sports; Home: 34 Bunty Lane, Willowdale, Ont. M2K 1W6; Office: 4700 Keele St., North York, Ont. M3J 1P3.

**CALDWELL, Patricia Eileen,** B.A., LL.B., Q.C.; barrister & solicitor; b. Yarmouth, N.S. 24 Aug. 1947; d. Dr. Robert Marsden and Myrtle Eileen (Nichols) C.; e. Yarmouth Memorial Consolidated H.S. 1965; Acadia Univ. B.A. 1968; Dalhousie Univ. LL.B. 1971; LAWYER, PINK MACDONALD HARDING; called to Bar of N.S. 1972; Q.C. 1988; Mem., Yarmouth County Barristers' Assn.; N.S. Barristers' Soc.; Candn. Bar Bassn.; Past Mem., N.S. Barristers' Soc. Council (Qualifications, Costs and Fees, Practice Assistance, Discipline Subctte. 'B' (Vice-Chair) Prov. Judicial Appointments, Q.C. Appointments cttes.; Ad Hoc Ctte., Review of Bar Soc. Services; Bd. of Gov., Acadia Univ. (Sec. to Bd. of Gov., Acadia Univ.), Bd. of Sunset Terrace; Past Mem., Bd. of Family & Children Services of Yarmouth Co.; Victorian Order of Nurses; Big Brothers & Big Sisters of Yarmouth Co.; Yarmouth Arts Reg. Centre; Acadia Alumni Assn.; S.W. Nova Transition House Assn.; recreations: golf, tennis, performing arts; clubs: Kritosophian, Yarmouth Community Corale, Yarmouth Golf & Country, Shelburne Golf & Country; Home: 379 Main St., Yarmouth, N.S. B5A 4B3; Office: P.O. Drawer 398, Yarmouth, N.S. B5A 4B3.

**CALDWELL, Thomas Scott,** B.Comm., F.C.S.I.; investment dealer; b. Toronto, Ont. 22 Aug. 1943; s. James and Phillis Cavelle (Plenty) C.; e. McGill Univ. B.Comm. (Hons.) 1965; m. Dorothy A. d. Fred A. and Dorothy M. Boylen 17 Sept. 1966; children: Brendan Thomas North, Theodore James Piers; FOUNDER, PRES. AND DIR. CALDWELL SECURITIES LTD. 1981; Pres. & Dir., Urbana Corporation; affiliated with Merrill Lynch Canada Inc. 1965–73; Burns Fry Ltd. 1975–81; Member/ Seatholder Toronto Stock Exchange; Club: Royal Canadian Yacht; Home: 42 Forest Hill Rd., Toronto, Ont. M4V 2L3; Office: 55 University Ave., Ste. 340, Toronto, Ont. M5J 2H7.

**CALDWELL, William Glen Elliot,** B.Sc., Ph.D., F.R.S.C.; university professor; b. Millport, Scotland 25 July 1932; s. William and Catherine (Elliot) C.; e. Univ. of Glasgow, B.Sc. 1954, Ph.D. 1957; m. B. Ruth d. Charles and Beatrice North 1 Aug. 1961; children: Ian Robert, Catherine Jane, Nancy Ileane; PROF. OF GEOL. AND VICE-PRES. (RESEARCH), UNIV. OF WESTERN ONT. 1988– ; Asst. Lectr., Univ. of Glasgow 1956–57; joined Univ. of Sask. as Spec. Lectr. 1957; Asst. Prof. 1958; Assoc. Prof. 1964; Prof. 1970–80; Head, Dept. of Geol. Sci. 1971–88; Dir., Div. of Life Sci. 1971–72; Chrmn., N. Am. Comn. on Stratigraphic Nomenclature 1977–78; Pres. Geol. Assn. of Can. 1980–81; Pres., Candn. Geol. Found. 1983–90; Chrmn., Nat. Adv. Bd. on Sci. Publs. 1987–92; mem., Natural Sciences and Engrg. Rsch. Council of Can. 1988– ; Vice-Pres., Internat. Union of Geological Sciences 1989–92; Vice-Pres., Candn. Geoscience Council 1993– ; has acted as cons. to var. petroleum cos.; Fellow, Geol. Soc. of Am.; Geol. Soc. (London); Geol. Assn. of Can.; mem. Paleont. Assn.; Paleont. Soc.; Geologists' Assn.; Candn. Soc. of Petroleum Geols.; Assn. of Earth Sci. Eds.; Geol. Socs. of Glasgow and Sask.; author or co-author of var. books, chapters, papers; Ed., Candn. Jour. of Earth Sci. 1982–88; Home: 7 Foxchapel Rd., London, Ont. N6G 1Z1; Office: 319 Stevenson-Lawson Bldg., London, Ont. N6A 5B8.

**CALHOUN, Ronald George;** association executive; b. Byron, Ont. 24 June 1933; s. Crawford George and Edna Jeanetta Louise (Wells) C.; e. H.B. Beal H.S. 1951; num. courses; m. M. Frances d. Bertha and James Wentzell 20 Sept. 1952; children: Lynn Marie, Stephen Lawrence, Lori Ann; EXTVE. DIR., PARTNERS IN RESEARCH 1987– ; var. posts ending as Assoc. Placement Admin., Personnel Dept., Diesel Div., General Motors of Canada Ltd. 1952–87; Finance Chrmn., 5th World Conf. on Smoking and Health 1984; held num. offices, Candn. Cancer Soc. incl. Nat. Fundraising Chrmn. 1982–85, Nat. Co-ord., Terry Fox Marathon of Hope (coined name 'Marathon of Hope'), Sr. Volunteer Co-ord., Steve Fonyo 'Journey for Lives'; Bd. Dir., Nat.; Ont. Div., Fundraising Chair, 1975–77; Bd. of Dir., Ont. Div.; Vice-Chrmn., Nat. Public Issues Ctte. 1986–89; Nat. Chrmn., Minor's Proj. Team, 1992–93; Employers' Advocacy Council, Founding Chrmn. 1985–88; Ont. Chrmn. 1992– ; Candn. Cancer Soc. awards: Cert. of Merit 1977; Nat. Hon. Life Membership 1987; Lifestyle Award from Nat. Health & Welfare, People of Can. 1978; Gen. Motors of Can. Gold Award 1980; Humanitarian Award, People of Ont. 1987; Air Canada 'Heart of Gold Award' 1988; Mem., Nat. Bd. of Dir., ALS Soc. of Can. 1982–89; Bd. of Dir., National Candn. Diabetes Assoc. 1989–91; Bd. of Dir., & former Vice Pres., Ont. Div., Candn. Diabetes Assoc., Ont. Fundraising Chrmn. 1990–92; Nat. Co-ordinator, Ken McColm's 'Incredible Journey' for Diabetes Rsch. 1991–92; Bd. of Dir., London Urban Resources Centre 1991– ; Chrmn., London Chapter, Partners in Rsch.; Bd. of Dirs., Mogenson Trust in Physiology; Mem. of Senate, The Univ. of Western Ont. 1993– ; Fed. Lib. Cand., Oxford Riding 1978; recreations: skiing, gardening, woodworking, reading; club: Masonic Order; Home: 321 Allen St., R.R. 2, Thamesford, Ont. N0M 2M0; Office: P.O. Box 192, Stn. B., London, Ont. N6A 4V6.

**CALL, Ronald Herbert,** B.Com., M.B.A.; banker; b. Vancouver, B.C. 28 May 1942; e. Univ. of B.C., B.Com. 1966; Univ. of Cal. Los Angeles M.B.A. 1967; m.; SR. VICE PRES., CORPORATE PLANNING, BANK OF MONTREAL 1986– ; Research Analyst present Bank 1968, Personal Planning Coordinator, Marketing Div. H.O. 1970, Mgr. Mktg. & Sales Master Charge Div. H.O. 1972, Special Assignment Office of Pres. 1975, Secy. Funds Mgmt. Comte. Office of Pres. 1976, Vice Pres. Corporate Planning H.O. 1977, Sr. Vice Pres. Corporate Planning 1981, Sr. Vice Pres., Sr. Consumer Mktg. Offr. Domestic Banking 1982; Sr. Vice Pres., Sr. Marketing Offr. Corporate & Govt. Banking 1985; recreations: skiing, squash, basketball; Clubs: Ontario Racquet; Adelaide; Office: Bank of Montreal, First Canadian Place, 3rd Flr. Podium, Toronto, Ont. M5X 1A1.

**CALLAGHAN, Barry,** M.A.; author; educator; publisher; b. Toronto, Ont. 5 July 1937; s. Morley Edward and Loretto Florence (Dee) C.; e. St. Michael's Coll. Sch.; Assumption Univ.; Univ. of Toronto, St. Michael's Coll. B.A. 1962, M.A. 1964; one s. Michael Paul Morley; FOUNDER AND EDITOR, 'EXILE: A LITERARY QUARTERLY' 1972– ; and EXILE EDITIONS LTD. 1976– ; Prof. of Eng. York Univ. 1966– ; Lit. Ed. Toronto Telegram 1966–71; Producer, CBC Pub. Affairs 1968–71; Co-owner, Villon Films: Documentaries 1972–79; Commentator, Candn. TV Network 1976–82; author 'The Hogg Poems and Drawings' 1978; 'The Black Queen Stories' 1982; 'As Close As We Came' 1982; 'Stone Blind Love' 1988; 'The Way The Angel Spreads Her Wings' 1989; transl. (from French of Robert Marteau) 'Atlante' 1979, 'Treatise on White and Tincture' 1980, 'Interlude' 1982; 'Eidolon' 1991; 'Fragile Moments' (from the French of Jacques Brault) 1985; (from Serbian of Miodrag Pavlovic) 'Singing at the Whirlpool' 1982, 'A Voice Locked in Stone' 1985; 'Flowers of Ice: Selected Poems of Imants Ziedonis' 1987 (from the Latvian); 'Wells of Light' (from French of Fernand Ouellette) transl. by B.C. and Ray Ellenwood 1989; ed. 'Lords of Winter and of Love: Canadian Love Poems' 1984; ed. 'Selected Poems of Frank Prewett' 1987; 'Canadian Travellers in Italy' 1989; 'Fifteen Years In Exile' 2 vols. 1992; 'Exile's Exiles' 1992; ACTRA award, Best Television Host 1983; recipient Nat. Mag. Awards 1977, 1978, 1979, 1980, 1983, 1984, 1985, 1988; Gold Medal, Pres.'s Award for Journalism Univ. of W. Ont. 1979, 1985; Canadian Periodical Publishers award for fiction 1985; Fiction Award, CBC seventh annual Literary Competition 1985; Philips Computer Systems Literary Award 1986; Ont. Arts Council 'Works in Progress' Prize 1987; Lowell Thomas Award: Best Magazine Article about United States 1987; The White Award for Journalism (U.S.) 1988; Pushcart Prize for Prose (U.S.) 1990; Home: 20 Dale Ave., Toronto, Ont. M4W 1K4.

**CALLAGHAN, Hon. Frank Woods,** B.A., LL.B.; judge; b. Toronto, Ont. 7 Jan. 1930; s. Frank Walker, Q.C. and Elizabeth (Woods) C.; e. Univ. of Toronto Schs. 1948; Univ. of Toronto B.A. 1952, LL.B. 1955; Osgoode Hall Law Sch. 1957; m. Mary Florence (Mollie) d. S. H. O'Brien, M.D., Hamilton, Ont. 8 Oct. 1955; children: Frank Stephen, Brian Patrick, Mark Joseph, John Edward; CHIEF JUSTICE OF THE ONTARIO COURT 1990–94; called to Bar of Ont. 1957; cr. Q.C. 1966; private law practice 1957–63; Dept. of Atty. Gen. Ont. 1963–70, Sr. Crown Counsel 1967, Asst. Depy. Atty. Gen. for Ont. 1968; private practice, Toronto, Counsel to Tory, Tory, DesLauriers & Binnington 1970–72; Depy. Atty. Gen. and Depy. Min. of Justice for Ont. 1972–77; Sr. Co. Court Judge Dist. of York 1977; Judge, Supreme Court of Ont. 1978; Chief Justice of the High Court, Supreme Court of Ontario 1989–90; mem. Law Soc. Upper Can.; Candn. Bar Assn.; Club: Toronto Hunt; R. Catholic; recreations: golf, sailing; Home: 50 Glengowan Rd., Toronto, Ont. M4N 1G2; Office: Osgoode Hall, Toronto, Ont. M5H 2N5.

**CALLAGHAN, J. Clair,** B.A., B.Eng., M.S., LL.D.; educator; b. Ebbsfleet, P.E.I. 21 Feb. 1933; s. Harris William Patrick and Cora (Shea) C.; e. St. Dunstan's Univ. B.A. 1953; St. Francis Xavier Univ. Dipl. Engn. 1954; N.S. Tech. Coll. B.Eng. 1956; Mass. Inst. Technol. M.S. 1963; Concordia Univ. LL.D. (h.c.) 1984; Univ. of Prince Edward Island, LL.D. (h.c.) 1987; m. Ellen Catherine (d) d. George Mullally, Souris W. P.E.I. 14 June 1958; children: Kevin, Mary Jane, Jeffrey; PRESIDENT, CABLETEC LTD. 1990– ; Prof. of Engn. St. Dunstan's Univ. 1956–58; Research Asst. Mass. Inst. Technol. 1958–60; Prof. of Engn. N.S. Tech. Coll. 1960–66; Prof. of Engn. and Chrmn. Elect. Engn. Dept. Sir George Williams Univ. 1968–70, Dean Faculty of Engn. and Prof. 1969–77; Pres., Technichal Univ. of Nova Scotia (formerly N.S. Technical Coll.) 1977–.; Consultant, Warnock Hersey, Computing Devices of Canada, Fairey Canada Ltd., Chemcell, Consultant to Canadian Internat. Devel. Agency 1975; mem. Nat. Research Council Comte. on Scholarship 1975–78 Selection (Chrmn. 1976–78); N.R.C. Adv. Bd. on Scientific & Technological Info. 1980– ; Candn. Engn. Manpower Council 1975–77, 1977–83; mem. CBC Adv. Comte. on Science & Technology, Assn. Atlantic Univs. 1977–78; Chrmn. Council Univ. Pres. of N.S. 1978–82; Chrmn. N.S. Educational Computer Network Bd. 1978–82; Dir., N.S. Research Found. 1978–80, 1980–82, 1982– ; N.S. Tidal Power Corp. 1979–81, 1981– ; Assn. Univs. & Colls. Can.; Dir., Extve. Council 1979–81; Adv. Comm. Int. Dev. Office 1978–83; mem. Council of Maritime Premiers Comte on Research & Development; N.S. Task Force on Research and Technology 1980; City of Halifax Task Force on Offshore Activities (1981); Candn. Coll. Advanced Engn. Practice; served with RCAC (Reserve) 1953–58, rank Lt.; holds Patent on Cable Tension Control; author over 20 tech. articles in prof. journs.; mem., Assn. Prof. Engrs. N.S.; Order Engrs. Que.; Am. Soc. Elect. Engrs.; Inst. Elect. & Electronic Engrs.; Fellow Engn. Inst. Can.; R. Catholic; recreations: sailing, swimming; Club: Halifax; Office: 327 Windmill Rd., Suite 203, Dartmouth, N.S. B3A 1H7.

**CALLAGHAN, Patrick Robinson,** B.Sc., M.B.A., C.A.; business executive; b. Toronto, Ont. 23 June 1948; s. William Niles and Helen Elizabeth (Donovan) C.; e. Ancaster H.S.; Univ. of Guelph B.Sc. (Hons.); McMaster Univ. M.B.A.; m. Elizabeth B. d. Donald and Monica Jones 30 May 1970; children: Matthew Augustus, Kathleen Dunlea; PRESIDENT & CHIEF OPERATING OFFICER, CHC HELICOPTER CORP. 1990– ; Computer Prog. & Systems Analysis, Honeywell Information Systems 1974–75; Clarkson Gordon C.A.s St. John's, Nfld. 1975–79 (C.A. designation 1976); Controller, Fishery Products Internat. 1979–82; Kendall / Colgate 1982–87; Russel Steel / Federal Metals 1987–88; Chief Finan. Offr., CHC Helicopter Corp. 1988–89; Vice-Pres., Finance 1989–90; Dir., CHC Helicopter Corp.; Business Acctg. Lectr., Memorial Univ.; recreations: tennis, squash, rugby; clubs: Murrays Pond Country; Home: 42 Rennies Mill Rd., St. John's, Nfld. A1C 3P8; Office: P.O. Box 5188, St. John's, Nfld. A1C 5V5.

**CALLAWAY, Fred,** C.A.; petroleum executive; b. Cochrane, Alta. 28 March 1939; s. Alfred Ernest and Miriam (Johnson) C.; e. Univ. of Alta. C.A. 1961; Banff Sch. of Advanced Mgmt.; m. Elizabeth P. 9 July 1960; two s. Patrick Boyd, Michael Dean; VICE PRES. CORPORATE, HOME OIL CO. LTD. 1990– ; articled with and Staff C.A. Clarkson Gordon 1956–63; Chief Acct. Managers Ltd. 1963–65; Hudson's Bay Oil & Gas 1965–82, Acct., Mgr. Treasury Div., Financial Analyst Corporate Planning, Mgr. Operations Acctg., Mgr. Tax Div., Mgr. Corporate Planning, Gen. Mgr. Corporate Affairs; present Co. 1982– , Vice Pres. Corporate Affairs, Vice

Pres. Internat. Operations, Vice Pres. Corporate; Dir., Private Energy Rsch. Assoc.; Heritage Park Soc.; Alternate, Minora Resources NL; mem. Inst. C.A.'s Alta.; Calgary C. of C.; recreations: golf, skiing, reading, curling; Clubs: Calgary Petroleum; Calgary Winter; Silver Springs Golf & Country; Home: 1207 Varsity Est. Dr. N.W., Calgary, Alta. T3B 4P1; Office: 1600, 324 – 8th Ave. S.W., Calgary, Alta. T2P 2Z5.

**CALLBECK, Hon. Catherine,** M.L.A., B.Comm., B.Ed.; politician; b. Central Bedeque, P.E.I. 25 July 1939; d. Ralph and Ruth (Campbell) C.; e. Mount Allison Univ. B.Comm. 1960; Dalhousie Univ. B.Ed. 1963; Syracuse Univ. post-grad. courses in bus. admin.; PREMIER OF PRINCE EDWARD ISLAND and PRESIDENT OF THE EXECUTIVE COUNCIL 1993– ; 1st el. M.L.A., P.E.I. (Fourth Dist. of Prince) 1974 and severed as Min. of Health and Social Services & Min. resp. for the Disabled; returned to family business, Callbeck's Ltd. 1978; el. M.P. for Malpeque 1988; served as official opposition critic for Consumer & Corp. Affairs; Energy, Mines & Resources; Financial Institutions; Assoc. Critic for Privatization and Regulatory Affairs; Vice-Chair, Caucus Ctte. on Sustainable Development; el. Leader, Liberal Party of P.E.I. 23 Jan. 1993; el. M.L.A. First Dist. of Queens 29 Mar. 1993; 1st woman in Canada to be elected as Premier; Former Chair, Bd. of Confederation Centre of the Arts; Former Mem., Bd. of Regents Mount Allison Univ., Bd. of Govs. Univ. of P.E.I., Maritime Provinces Higher Edn. Commission; Former Bd. Mem., Inst. for Rsch. in Public Policy; active involvement with charitable and public service groups and organizations at all levels incl. Past Dir., P.E.I. United Fund, Candn. Heart Found. (P.E.I. Div.) and Past Mem., Prov. Ctte. for Internat. Year of the Disabled; Mem., Bedeque United Church; Home: Central Bedeque, P.E.I. C0B 1G0; Office: P.O. Box 2000, Charlottetown, P.E.I. C1A 7N8.

**CALLWOOD, June (Mrs. Trent Frayne),** O.C., O.Ont., D.C.L. (1986); writer; b. Chatham, Ont. 2 June 1924; d. Harold and Gladys (Lavoie) Callwood; m. Trent Gardiner Frayne, 13 May 1944; children: Jill Callwood, Brant Homer, Jennifer Ann, Casey Robert (d. 1982); Hon. Life Dir., Candn. Civil Liberties Assn., 1988 (Vice Pres. 1965–88); Founder, Yorkville Digger House 1967; Founder, Nellie's (Pres. 1974–77, Dir. 1985–89, 1990–92); host, CBC-TV 'In Touch' 1975–78; Host, Vision TV 'National Treasures' 1991–94; Pres. Learnxs Foundation 1976–79; Vice Pres., Wards' Retreat 1990–91; judge, Governor Generals Literary Award 1984–85; judge, National Newspaper Awards 1976–83; judge, National Magazine Awards 1988–92; judge, Western Magazine Awards 1992; Chair, judges, Candn. Assn. for Community Living Media Award 1992; Exec. Comte. Writers' Development Trust 1977–81; co-chrmn. (with Gordon Fairweather) 1st annual conference of Federal Human Rights Commission 1978; Gordon Fairweather Lectr. on Human Rights, Univ. of Ottawa 1984; Falconbridge Lectr., Laurentian Univ. 1988; Atkinson Lectr., Ryerson Sch. of Journalism 1988; Margaret Laurence Lectr., Trent Univ. 1989; George M. Dunk Lectr., Univ. of Windsor 1990; Duthie Lectr., Simon Fraser Univ. 1990; Barton Lectr., Upper Canada Coll. 1992; James A. Minifee Lectr., Univ. of Regina 1993; Margaret Laurence Meml. Lectr., Writers' Union of Can. 1993; Ruth Cooperslock Lectr., Univ. of Toronto 1993; mem. extve., Candn. Council of Christians and Jews 1978–88; Chrmn., Writers' Union of Canada 1979–80; Pres., Justice for Children 1979–80; mem. Council, Amnesty International (Canada) 1979–86; Chrmn. Ian Adams Defence Comte. 1980; Founder Jessie's Centre for Teenagers (Pres. 1982–83, 1987–89); Dir., Candn. Soc. for Abolition of Death Penalty 1981; member, Adv. Comte. on Assistive Devices, Ont. Min. of Health 1981–88; Patron, National Breast Screening Study 1982–86; Trustee, Art Censorship Trust Fund 1982–85; Chair, 0–5 Ctte. City of Toronto Children's Network 1982–88; columnist, Globe & Mail 1983–89; Dir., Candn. Inst. for Admin. of Justice 1983–85; Trustee, Pro-Choice Defence Fund 1983–89; Founding Mem., Feminists Against Censorship 1984–87; Dir., Toronto Arts Awards 1984–88; Chair, Hospice Steering Ctte. 1985–87; Founder & Pres., Casey House Hospice 1987–88, Hon. Dir. 1988– ; Pres., Casey House Foundation 1992–93; Secy., P.E.N. Canada (English-speaking) 1985–87, Vice Pres. 1987–88, Dir. 1988–89, Pres. 1989–90; Pres., Maggie's, Toronto Prostitutes Community Service Project 1989–93 (Dir. 1986– ; Secy. 1993– ;); Mem., Writers to Reform the Libel Law 1991– ; Pres., Candn. Soc. for Prison Improvement 1990– ; Dir., Credit Counselling Service of Metro Toronto 1991–92; judge, Gov.-Gen.'s Literary Awards 1984–86; named B'nai B'rith Woman of the Year 1969; City of Toronto Award of Merit 1974; Member, Order of Canada 1978; Humanities Award, Candn. Council of Christians and Jews 1978; Ida Nudel Humanitarian Award 1983; named to Candn. News Hall of Fame 1984; Manitoba Order of the Buffalo Hunt 1984; Metro Toronto Family Services Assn. Award 1985; Planned Parenthood Federation of Can. Award 1985; Officer, Order of Can. 1986; Toronto YWCA Woman of Distinction 1986; Ont. Psychological Assoc. Humanitarian Award 1987; Windsor Press Club Quill Award 1987; Metropolitan Community Church of Toronto Certificate of Appreciation 1987; Gardiner Award for Citizenship (Metro Toronto) 1988; Order of Ontario 1988; Woman of the Year, Zonta Club, Charlottetown, P.E.I. 1989; Volunteer Ontario Award 1989; UDO Award, Ryerson Journalism 1989; Marlene Moore Award, Internat. Assoc. of Residential & Community Alternatives 1990; Lifetime Achievement Award, Toronto Arts Foundation 1990; Award for Public Service, Am. Orthopsychiatric Assoc. 1991; Award, Am. Psychiatric Assoc. 1991; Bob Edwards Award, Alta. Theatre Project 1991; Toronto Hadassah-WIZO Honoree 1992; City of Etobicoke Hall of Fame 1992; Child Haven, Humanitarian of the Year Award 1992; Distinguished Candn. Award, Univ. of Regina 1993; Muriel McCowan Ferguson Award 1993; Doctor of the University, Univ. of Ottawa 1987; LL.D., Memorial Univ. of Nfld. 1988; Dr. of Sacred Letters, Trinity Coll. 1988; LL.D., Univ. of Toronto 1988; LL.D., Osgoode Hall, York Univ. 1988; LL.D., Carleton Univ., Ottawa, 1988; D.Litt., Univ. of Alberta, Edmonton 1988; D.Litt., Univ. of Guelph 1989; Fellow, Ryerson Polytechnical Inst. 1990; D. Litt., Univ. of N.B. 1990; LL.D., Univ. of Prince Edward Island 1992; D.C.L., Acadia Univ. 1993; D.Litt., Mount St. Vincent Univ. 1993; LL.D., Univ. of Western Ont. 1993; Hon. High School Diplomas, Argyle Alternative High Sch., Winnipeg 1993; Bencher, Law Soc. of Upper Canada 1987–1991; Mem., Law Soc. Certification Bd. 1989– ; author 'Love, Hate, Fear and Anger' 1964; co-author (with Dr. Marion Hillard) 'A Woman Doctor Looks at Life and Love' 1957; (with Dr. Charles W. Mayo) 'Mayo: The Story of My Family and Career' 1968; (with Marvin Zuker) 'Canadian Women and the Law' 1971; (with Barbara Walters) 'How to Talk to Practically Anybody About Practically Anything' 1973; (with Dr. Judianne Densen-Gerber) 'We Mainline Dreams' 1974; 'Otto Preminger Remembers' 1975; (with Marvin Zuker) 'The Law is Not for Women' 1976; 'Naughty Nineties: Canada's Illustrated Heritage' 1978; 'Portrait of Canada' 1981; (with Helen Gahagan Douglas) 'A Full Life' 1982; 'Emma' 1983; 'Emotions' 1986; 'Twelve Weeks in Spring' 1986; 'Jim: A Life with AIDS' 1988; 'The Sleepwalker' 1990; other writings incl. mag. articles, TV and radio scripts; Home: 21 Hillcroft Dr., Islington, Ont. M9B 4X4.

**CALMAN, Robert Frederick,** B.A., M.S.; corporate executive; b. Mineola, N.Y. 14 May 1932; s. William Arthur and Ida (Albersworth) C.; e. Yale Univ. B.A. 1954; Mass. Inst. Technol. M.S. 1967; m. Susan Jean Raphael 20 June 1959 (div. 1978); children: Andrew Frederick, Camille, Matthew Alexander; m. Doris Sumerson 9 June 1979; CHRMN. AND DIR. ECHO BAY MINES LTD. 1981– ; Dir. Corp. Consulting Group Ltd.; WHYY Inc.; The Bank of New York Trust Co. of Florida N.A.; The Gold Inst.; Silver Inst. Internat.; Am. Mining Congress; joined Chase Manhattan Bank 1954, Asst. Treas. 1961, New York City; Mobil Oil Corp. N.Y.C. 1961, Treas. N.Am. Div. 1964, Treas. Internat. Div. 1968–69; Vice Pres. Finance, Treas. IU International Corp. Philadelphia 1970, Group Vice Pres. Devel. 1972, Exec. Vice Pres. 1974, Vice Chrmn. 1978–85; Lectr. New York Univ. 1968–69; author 'Linear Programming and Cash Management/Cash Alpha' 1968; Pres. and mem. Bd. Govs. Soc. Alfred P. Sloan Fellows; Dir. Alumni Fund, mem. Corp. Devel. Ctte. Mass. Inst. Technol.; served with US Army 1955–57, rank 1st Lt., Arty.; recipient E.P. Brooks Prize M.I.T. 1967; Phi Beta Kappa; Phi Gamma Delta; Presbyterian; Clubs: Racquet (Philadelphia); Union League (Philadelphia); Home: 109 Via Vizcaya, Palm Beach, FL 33480; Office: 1 Independence Pl., #2302, Philadelphia, Pa. 19106 and 10180 101 St., Edmonton, Alta. T5J 3S4.

**CALNE, Donald Brian,** D.M., F.R.C.P.(C); physician; educator; b. London, Eng. 4 May 1936; s. Joseph Robert and Eileen Hannah (Gubbay) C.; e. St. John's Coll. Oxford (Open Scholarship 1954) B.A. 1958, B.Sc. 1959, M.A. 1961, B.M. 1961, B.Ch. 1961, D.M. 1968; m. Susan d. Arthur Wigfield 9 Apr. 1965; children: Joanna Susan, Thomas Benjamin, Max Robert; BELZBERG PROF. OF MED. AND DIRECTOR NEURODEGENERATIVE DISORDERS CENTRE, UNIV. OF B.C. 1981– ; War Meml. Entrance Scholar, Guy's Hosp. Med. Sch. 1959; Rsch. Studentship Oxford Univ. Dept. Physiol. 1959; Poulton Rsch. Fellow 1961; Welcome Rsch. Fellow 1966; Cons. Neurol. Hammersmith Hosp. and Royal Postgrad. Med. Sch. London 1969–74; Clin. Dir. and Chief Exper. Therapeutics Br. NINCDS Nat. Inst. of Health 1974–81; recipient Killam Prize 1987; Germania Rossetto Internat. Award 1988; B.C. Sci. Council Gold Medal 1988; Fred Springer Award 1993; Jacob Biely Award; mem. of three and Chrmn. of one Parkinson's Disease Founds.; author over 400 papers med. and sci. jours., 3 books neurol., ed. 8 books; mem. various ed. bds.; Hon. mem. Spanish Neurol. Assn. 1987; mem. Candn. Neurol. Soc.; Am. Acad. Neurol.; Am. Neurol. Assn.; recreations: skiing, photography, reading; Home: 4235 Nautilus Close, Vancouver, B.C. V6R 4L2; Office: 2211 Wesbrook Mall, Vancouver, B.C. V6T 1W5.

**CALVÉ, Pierre,** Ph.D.; university professor; b. Maniwaki, Que. 27 Sept. 1942; s. Jean-Paul and Antoinette (Hubert) C.; e. Univ. de Montréal, B.Ped. 1964; Georgetown Univ., M.S. 1969 (fellowship 1966–69), Ph.D. 1978; single; FULL PROF., FAC. OF EDN., UNIV. OF OTTAWA 1980– ; French Teacher, Loyola Coll. H.S. 1964–66; Dept. of Linguistics, Univ. of Ottawa 1969–80; Coord., B.A. and M.Ed. prog. in 2nd language teaching 1980– ; worldwide lectr. on bilingual edn., French linguistics; Pres., Ont. Modern Language Assn. 1981–82; Vice-Pres., Candn. Assn. of App. Linguistics 1987–89; Pres., Bd. of Dir., 'Can. Modern Language Review' 1990–93; Award of excellence, Candn. Assn. of 2nd Lang. Teach. 1986; Life Mem., Ont. Mod. Lang. Teach. Assn. 1987; mem., 10 profl. assns.; author of more than 30 scholarly articles; co-author: 'Le Français International' 1972–79; editor: 'Aspects of Immersion' 1988; co-editor: 'Le français langue seconde' 1987; recreations: skiing, sailboarding, travel, bicycling; Home: 7 Reinhardt St., Hull, Que. J8Y 5V3; Office: Ottawa, Ont. K1N 6N5.

**CALVERT, Lorne Albert,** B.A., B.D., M.L.A.; politician, clergyman; b. Moose Jaw, Sask. 24 Dec. 1952; s. Albert and Beulah Awilda (Phillips) C.; e. Univ. of Regina B.A. 1973; Univ. of Saskatchewan B.D. 1976; m. Betty Anne d. Steve and Evelyn Sluzalo 25 Oct. 1975; children: David Lorne, Stephanie Anne; ASSOCIATE MINISTER OF HEALTH, GOVT. OF SASK. 1992– ; ordained United Church Minister 1976; Minister, Gravelbourg Un. Ch. 1976–79; Zion Un. Ch. 1979–86; 1st elected M.L.A. for Moose Jaw South 1986; re-elected M.L.A. for Moose Jaw Wakamow 1991; Mem., New Democratic Party; Home: 646 Keith Cres., Moose Jaw, Sask. S6H 5P9; Office: Room 345, Legislative Bldg., Regina, Sask. S4S 0B3.

**CALVERT, Thomas William,** Ph.D., P.Eng.; university professor; b. Dunaskin, Scotland 12 April 1936; s. Thomas and Barbara (Gillies) C.; e. George Watson's Coll.; Univ. Coll., London B.Sc. 1957; Wayne State Univ. MSEE 1964; Carnegie-Mellon Univ. Ph.D. 1967; m. Lorna d. Charles and Louise Griffiths 5 Sept. 1959 (div. 1991); m. Hiromi Matsui 17 Aug. 1991; children: Jason, Rachel; PROF. OF COMPUTING SCIENCE, KINESIOL. & ENGR. SCIENCE, SIMON FRASER UNIV. 1972– ; Electr. Design Engr., ICI Ltd. (U.K.) 1957–60; Instrum. Engr., Canadair Ltd. 1960–61; Lectr., West. Ont. Inst. of Technol. 1961–64; Instr., Wayne State Univ. 1964–65; Assoc. Prof., Carnegie-Mellon Univ. 1967–72; Chrmn., Biotechnol. Prog. 1969–72; Dean of Interdisciplinary Studies 1977–85; Vice-Pres., Rsch. & Information Systems 1985–90; Bd. of Govs., Simon Fraser Univ. 1993–96; Bd. of Mngt., TRIUMF 1985–88; Bd. of Dir., Discovery Found. 1988–92; Mem., Science Council of B.C. 1988–90, Pres. 1990–92; Bd. of Gov., Sci. World B.C.; Bd. of Dir., Jumpstart Performance Soc.; Mem., Assn. for Computing Machinery; I.E.E.E.; Cong. on Rsch. in Dance; Assn. of Profl. Engrs. of B.C.; co-author: 'Classification, Estimation and Pattern Recognition' 1973; author of over 60 tech./sci. papers; Home: 4612 Strathcona Rd., N. Vancouver, B.C. V7G 1G3; Office: School of Computing Science, Simon Fraser Univ., Burnaby, B.C. V5A 1S6.

**CAMERON, Hon. A.M. (Sandy),** B.Sc.; politician; businessman; b. Sherbrooke, N.S. 16 Dec. 1938; s. Alex Whitcomb, Q.C. and Mary Kathryn (MacLean) C.; e. Sherbrooke (N.S.) Elem. and St. Mary's Rural High Schs.; N.S. Agric. Coll.; McGill Univ. B.Sc. (Agric.); m. Shirley Elaine, d. late Milton and Hilda Vatcher, N. Sydney, N.S. 12 Aug. 1961; children: Moira K., Alex Whitcomb; former Leader of the Opposition, Province of Nova Scotia 1980–86; Min. of Fisheries N.S. 1973–76; and Min. of Lands & Forests N.S. 1976; Min. of Development N.S. 1976–1978; el. to N.S. House of Assembly by-el. 1973, re.-el., defeated 1984; mem. N. Brit. Soc.; Fish & Games Assn.; Liberal; United Church; Home: P.O. Box 70, Sherbrooke, N.S. B0J 3C0.

**CAMERON, Alastair Duncan,** M.B.E., B.Sc.; consulting engineer; b. Fredericton, N.B. 28 Oct. 1920; s. Adam and Dora Isabel (Davidson) C.; e. Univ. of N.B. B.Sc.

(Civil Engn.) 1942; McGill Univ. Dipl. in Mang. 1970; m. Audrey d. late H. O. Charlton 17 May 1951; children: Duncan, Harry, Sheila, Janet; SENIOR CONSULTANT, MONENCO AGRA INC. 1984– ; Dir. Maritime Electric Co. Ltd.; Chrmn. and Mang. Dir. Monenco Jamaica Ltd.; Draftsman and Design Engr. Dominion Bridge Co. Ltd. 1946–47; various assignments Montreal Engineering Co. Ltd. as Design Engr., Resident Engr. and Supervising Engr. in Civil and Constr. Depts. 1947–56; Gen. Mgr. Maritime Electric Co. Ltd. Charlottetown 1957–63, Asst. Mgr. Econ. and Valuation Div. Montreal Engineering Co. Ltd.; 1963 becoming Mgr. 1969, Vice Pres. and Mgr. Mang. Consulting Div. 1972, Vice Pres. Mang. Consulting 1975–76, Vice Pres. Utility Mang. 1976–83; served with RCA Can. UK N.W. Europe 1942–45; mem. Order Engrs. Que.; Candn. Soc. Civil Engn.; Engn. Inst. Can.; Energy Council of Can.; Anglican; recreations: sailing, skiing; Clubs: Mount Stephen; M.A.A.A.; Home: 70 Union Blvd., St. Lambert, Que. J4R 2M5; Office: 5th Floor, 2045 Stanley St., Montreal, Que. H3A 2V4.

**CAMERON, Rev. Angus de Mille,** B.A., B.D. (Unitarian); b. Sussex Corner, N.B. 9 June 1913; s. James Logan and Harriett Bernice (de Mille) C.; e. Univ. of N.B.; Acadia Univ., B.A. 1934; Univ. of Chicago 1935–37; Meadville Theol. Sch., Chicago, B.D. 1937; m. Esther Cary, d. Frank W. Horner, Montreal, 9 Nov. 1942; children: Jean, Sheila, James, Bruce; o. 1937; Min., Adams Memorial Ch., Dunkirk, N.Y., 1937–41; Ch. of the Messiah, Montreal, Que. 1941–59; First Unitarian Ch. of Philadelphia, 1963–67; served on Bd. of Govs. of Montreal Council of Social Agencies, 1942–46; Vice-Pres., Am. Unitarian Assn. (rep. Can. on Bd. of Dirs.) 1948–51; contrib. Editor of 'The Christian Register'; author of chapter in 'Voices of Liberalism 1,' 1947; recreations: tennis, music, hunting, fishing; Clubs: Montreal Indoor Tennis; Home: 'Lochiel,' Clifton Royal, N.B. E0G 1N0.

**CAMERON, Barbara Jamie,** B.A., LL.B., LL.M.; educator; b. Trail, B.C. 4 Dec. 1952; d. James Magill and Dorothy Mae (Craik) C.; e. Univ. of B.C. B.A. 1975; McGill Univ. LL.B. 1978; Columbia Univ. LL.M. 1983; m. Christopher Duff s. Malcolm and Constance Bredt 1 Sept. 1984; ASSOC. PROF. OSGOODE HALL LAW SCH. YORK UNIV. 1987– , Asst. Dean 1991–93; Dir., Centre for Public Law and Public Policy; called to Bar of B.C. 1979, Ont. 1987; Law Clk. to Rt. Hon. R.G.B. Dickson Supreme Court of Can. 1979–80; Assoc. McAlpine, Roberts & Hordo Vancouver 1980–81; Assoc. in Law Columbia Univ. 1981–82; Asst. Prof. Cornell Law Sch. 1982–83, Asst. Prof. present Law Sch. 1984–87; Ed.in-Chief Media and Communications Law Review; Co-Editor, Canada Watch; Bd. Eds. Ont. Reports; Asst. Ed. Candn. Rights Reporter; Office: 4700 Keele St., North York, Ont. M3J 1P3.

**CAMERON, Bill;** journalist; b. Vancouver, B.C. 23 Jan. 1943; s. William Maxwell and Lorna Isobel (Bingham) C.; e. Univ. of Toronto 1962–65; m. Cheryl d. Frederick and Evelyn Hawkes 20 Dec. 1980; children: Patrick, Rachel, Nicholas; ANCHOR, THE CBC EVENING NEWS, CBC-TV TORONTO 1993– ; columnist, mem. ed. bd. Toronto Star 1968–72; assoc. ed. Maclean's mag. 1972–74; writer, reporter, commentator, anchor Global TV News Toronto 1974–79; anchor, writer, commentator CITY-TV Toronto 1979–82; co-anchor, The Journal CBC-TV, journalist and interviewer 1982–93; former instr. in jour. Ryerson Polytech. Inst.; ACTRA and Gemini Award nominee for writing & commentary TV; co-author 'The Real Poverty Report' 1970; numerous articles, reviews various mags. and newspapers; Home: 91 Delaware Ave., Toronto, Ont. M6H 2S9; Office: P.O. Box 14000, Stn. A, Toronto, Ont. M5W 1A0.

**CAMERON, Christina Stuart Ross,** M.A., Ph.D.; architectural historian; b. Toronto, Ont. 15 March 1945; d. Donald Stuart Forsyth and Bertah Millar (Roy) C.; e. Univ. of Toronto B.A. 1967; Brown Univ. M.A. 1970; Laval Univ. Ph.D. 1983; m. Hugh Fraser Townsend s. Lacey and Jean Winsor 29 Dec. 1988; step-children: Christopher, Megan, Stephanie; DIR. GEN. NAT. HISTORIC SITES, CANADIAN HERITAGE 1987– ; served as arch. hist. and hist. resources mgr.; guest lectr. Concordia Univ. 1975–77; Adjunct Prof., Art Hist. Carleton Univ. 1991– ; Gov. Heritage Can. Found.; Chrmn. World Heritage Ctte.; author numerous books and articles Candn. arch. hist. incl. 'Second Empire Style in Canadian Architecture' 1980; 'Vieux-Québec: son architecture intérieure' 1986; 'Charles Baillairgé, Architect' 1989; mem. ed. bd. Jour. Candn. Art Hist.; Office: Ottawa, Ont. K1A 0H3.

**CAMERON, D. William (Bill),** M.D., FRCP(C); physician; b. Trenton, Ont. 2 Oct. 1954; s. Donald Evan and Helen Noreen (Devlin) C.; e. Queen's Univ. M.D. 1979; m. Genevieve d. Matthew and Stephanie Wolski 11 June 1983; children: Emily, Ian, Matthew; ACADEMIC PHYSICIAN & CLINICAL INVESTIGATOR, FAC. OF MED., DEPTS. OF MED., MICROBIOLOGY & IMMUNOLOGY, SCH. OF GRADUATE STUDIES & RSCH., UNIV. OF OTTAWA & OTTAWA GEN. HOSPITAL; research interest incl. epidemiology of sexually transmitted diseases and AIDS in devel. countries and AIDS clinical epidem. & treatment trials in Canada; lab. research in bacteriology relevant to AIDS supported by Health & Welfare Canada & Am. Found. for AIDS Rsch.; Dir., Ont. Region / Candn. HIV Trials Network and practices gen. infectious disease med.; Ont. Min. of Health Career Scientist; pub. in AIDS and sexually transmitted disease rsch.; many nat. & internat. academic & sci. presentations and consultations; Office: 501 Smyth Rd., Ottawa, Ont. K1H 8L6.

**CAMERON, David Robertson,** B.A., M.Sc., Ph.D.; academic and public servant; b. Vancouver, B.C. 19 Jan. 1941; s. Maxwell A. and Hazel Bathia (Robertson) C.; e. Univ. of B.C., B.A. 1963; London Sch. of Econ. M.Sc. 1966, Ph.D. 1969; m. Stephanie d. Harald and Eleanor Dahl 11 Sept. 1965; two d. Tassie, Amy; PROF. OF POL. SCI., UNIV. OF TORONTO 1990– ; Chrmn. of Pol. Studies 1970, Dean of Arts & Sci. and Assoc. Prof. of Pol. Sci. 1975–77; Dir. of Rsch. Task Force on Candn. Unity 1977–79; Adv. Fed.-Prov. Relations Office 1979, Asst. Sec. to Cabinet, Strategic & Constitutional Planning 1980–82; Asst. Under-Sec. of State Dept. Sec. State 1982–85; Vice Pres. Institutional Relations, Univ. of Toronto 1985–87; professorial leave 1985–90; Depy. Min., Intergovernmental Affairs, Govt. of Ont. 1987–89; Ont. Rep. to the Govt. of Que. and Special Adv. to the Premier on constitutional reform 1989–90; Special Constitutional Advisor to the Premier of Ont. 1991–93; author 'The Social Thought of Rousseau and Burke: A Comparative Study' 1973; 'Nationalism, Self-Determination and the Quebec Question' 1974; mem. Candn. Pol. Sci. Assn.; Soc. québecoise de science politique; Home: 362 Berkeley St., Toronto, Ont. M5A 2X7; Office: Toronto, Ont. M5S 1A1.

**CAMERON, Donald Angus;** pharmaceutical executive; b. Saskatoon, Sask. 14 Dec. 1941; s. Robert William and Margaret (Ireland) C.; e. Candn. Inst. Traffic & Transp. 1967; Univ. of Man. Mgt. 1975; m. Marilyn d. Jack Millar 2 Dec. 1961; children: Blair, Cheryl, Bonnie; PRES. LAWTONS DRUG STORES LIMITED and LAWTONS INC. 1990– ; joined CNR 1958–68; Gulf Canada Products Ltd. 1968–79; Gen. Mgr. RGO Office Equipment Ltd. 1979–80; Region Mgr. W. Can. Petro Canada Products Ltd. 1980–83; Pres. Radon Market Place Strategist Ltd. 1983–84; Petroleum Mgr. W.Can. Mac's Convenience Stores 1984, Gen. Mgr. W.Can. 1986–87, Vice Pres. W.Can. 1987–90; Chair 1818 Soc. Parent Fund Dalhousie Univ. 1991–94; Vice Chrmn. Bd. Trustees Alta. Bible Coll. 1990; mem. Bd. (Deacon) Cambrian Hts. Ch. of Christ Calgary 1990; Mem. Bd. (Deacon) First Baptist Church, Dartmouth 1992–93; Chair, Regional Corporate Campaign Metro Halifax YMCA 1992–94; Division Chrmn., Capital Campaign, Camp Hill Medical Centre 1992–94; mem. Candn. Inst. Traffic & Transp.; Candn. Assn. Chain Drug Stores (Dir.); Halifax Bd. Trade; Dartmouth C. of C.; Baptist; Home: 48 Condor Rd., Bedford, N.S. B4A 3K8; Office: 270, 236 Brownlow Centre, Dartmouth, N.S. B3B 1V5.

**CAMERON, Donald Charles,** B.Com., C.F.A.; security analyst; b. Chesterville, Ont. 22 May 1923; s. Norman Scott and Essie Mary (Dwyer) C.; e. Primary Sch., N.Y., Montreal, Chesterville; Chesterville High Sch., 1938–42; Queen's Univ., B.Com. 1946; Univ. of Virginia, Chart. Financial Analyst, 1965; m. Lyla Anne, d. Frederick William Paynter, 10 July 1948; children: Donald Alexander, Bruce William, Jean Anne; Dir., Jones Heward Fund Ltd.; joined Jones Heward & Co. Ltd. 1946; held various positions in Invest. Mang. Dept. for 2 yrs.; trans. to Research Dept.; apptd. Dir. of Research, 1958; admitted to Partnership 1959; became Dir. of Invest. Policy 1963 and in addition Vice Pres. 1965; Pres. 1966; Depy. Chrmn. 1975; Chrmn., CEO and Dir. 1981; Chrmn. and Dir. 1983; retired 1984; Past Gov., Montreal Stock Exchge.; past Dir. Investment Dealers Assn.; Past Pres. Montreal Society Financial Analysts; R. Catholic; recreations: golf, swimming, bridge; Home: R.R. #3, 1170, 15th Sideroad, King City, Ont. L0G 1K0.

**CAMERON, Donald James;** construction executive; b. Vancouver, B.C. 30 June 1942; s. Donald James and Laverne Ann (Dumaresq) C.; e. Ryerson Poly. Inst. (Archit. Tech.) 1965; m. Joanne d. Frank and Helen Oster 28 May 1966; children: Donna, David, James, John; PRES., ONT. GEN. CONTRACTORS ASSN.; Specification Writer, Abram & Ingleson 1965–69; Cost Engr., McDougall Constrn. Mgmt. Ltd. 1970–74; Project Mgr., Ellis-Don Ltd. 1975–81; Vice-Pres., Cloke Constrn. 1981–82; Pres., Cloke Construction 1982–89; Past Chrmn. & Dir., Ont. Gen. Contractors Assn.; Club: St. Andrews East Golf; Office: 6299 Airport Rd., Ste. 703, Mississauga, Ont. L4V 1N3.

**CAMERON, Donald Maxwell,** M.A.Sc.; lawyer; b. Vancouver, B.C. 14 Nov. 1953; s. Hugh Donald and Jean Alda (MacFarlane) C.; e. Univ. of Toronto B.A.Sc.(Eng. Sci) 1975, M.A.Sc.(Aerospace) 1976, LL.B. 1979; m. Jane Helen d. Burton and Shirley Avery 25 June 1976; children: James Maxwell, John Avery, Caroline Ann; PARTNER, SIM, HUGHES, DIMOCK and SIM & McBURNEY 1988– ; called to Bar of Ont. 1981; law practice Rogers, Bereskin & Parr Toronto 1981–82; Lectr., Patent and Trade Secrets Law, Fac. of Law, Univ. of Toronto, 1993– ; joined present firm 1982; Gov. and Chair, Kingsway Coll. Sch. Etobicoke; Pres. Islington Ratepayers & Residents Assn. 1986–88, 1991–92; Pres. Etobicoke Fedn. Ratepayers & Residents Assn. 1989–90, Sec. 1990–93; Exec., Etobicoke Centre Fed. P. Cons. Assn. 1982–92; co-author 'Computer Contracts,' Canadian Forms & Precedents 1993; 'EUREKA - Now What? An Introduction to Intellectual Property' 1993; asst. ed. (Can.) 'Intellectual Property Reports', Australia; Candn. ed. 'Computer Law Reporter' USA 1988–92; contbr. 'Computer Law Reporter' Can. 1986–92; awarded Commemorative Medal for 125th Anniversary of Candn. Confederation; mem. Patent & Trademark Inst. Can. (Computer Related Technol. Ctte.); Am. Intellectual Property Law Assn. (Chair Subctte. Internat. Devels., Electronics & Computer Technol. Ctte.); Computer Law Assn.; N.Y. Patent Trademark & Copyright Law Assn.; Candn. Aeronautics & Space Inst.; Am. Inst. Aeronautics & Astronautics; Licensing Execs. Soc. (Chair, Toronto Chapter); Un. Ch. (Elder); Home: 7 Thorncrest Rd., Islington, Ont. M9A 1R8; Office: 701, 330 University Ave., Toronto, Ont. M5G 1R7.

**CAMERON, Duncan,** B.A., Ph.D.; university professor; b. Victoria, B.C. 26 Apr. 1944; s. Norman Sydney and Docia Lorraine (Bennett) C.; e. Ross Sheppard Composite H.S. 1962; Univ. of Alta., B.A. 1966; Univ. de Paris I, Ph.D. 1976; PROF. OF POLITICAL SCIENCE, UNIV. OF OTTAWA 1975– ; Dept. of Fin., Govt. of Can. 1966–68; Office of the Pres., Candn. Internat. Devel. Agency 1968–69; Fin. Advr., Candn. Del. to U.N. Gen. Assembly 1967; mem., Candn. Assn. of Poli. Sci.; Soc. Qué. de sci. poli.; Pres., Candn. Centre for Policy Alternatives; Ed., Canadian Forum; author: 'Le système monétaire internationel en voie de réforme' 1977; co-author: 'Ethics and Economics' 1984; editor: 'Explorations in Canadian Economic History' 1985; 'The Free Trade Papers' 1986; 'The Free Trade Deal' 1988; co-editor: 'Canada and the New International Division of Labour' 1985; 'The *Other* Macdonald Report' 1985; 'Policies for Full Employment' 1988; 'The Facts on Free Trade' 1988; 'Constitutional Politics' 1992; 'Canada Under Free Trade' 1993; recreations: tennis; Club: Rideau Tennis and Squash; Home: 196 Cobourg St., Ottawa, Ont. K1N 8H6; Office: Ottawa, Ont. K1N 6N5.

**CAMERON, Elspeth MacGregor,** M.A., Ph.D.; author; educator; b. Toronto, Ont. 10 Jan. 1943; d. Donald Stuart Forsyth and Bertah Millar (Roy) Cameron; e. Univ. of B.C., B.A. 1964; Univ. of N.B. M.A. 1965; McGill Univ. Ph.D. 1970; m. Paul E. s. Warren Barrett and Gertrude Ells Lovejoy 15 Apr. 1977; children: Beatrix, Hugo, Henry; ASSOC. PROF., DEPT. OF ENGLISH AND CANADIAN STUDIES PROGRAM, UNIV. COLLEGE, UNIV. OF TORONTO 1990– ; Consultant, Ryerson Polytech. Inst., Social Science & Humanities Research Council Can., the Canada Council, Univ. of Toronto Press; Prof. of Eng. Concordia Univ. Montreal 1970–77; Coordinator, Candn. Lit. and Lang. Program, New College, Univ. of Toronto 1980–90; recipient Univ. of B.C. Medal for Candn. Biog. 1981; Finalist, Gov. Gen.'s Award (non-fiction) 1981; winner Fiona Mee Award for literary journalism 1982 (hon. mention 1983); winner Silver Award, The Brascan Awards for Culture 1985; winner Silver Award, The Univ. of Western Ont. President's Medal for Excellence in Magazine Articles 1985; author 'Robertson Davies' (lit. criticism) 1971; 'Hugh MacLennan: A Writer's Life' (biog.) 1981; numerous articles and reviews Candn. writers; ed. 'The Other Side of Hugh MacLennan: Selected Essays Old and New' 1978; 'Hugh MacLennan: 1982' 1982; ed. 'A Spider Danced a Cozy Jig and Other Animal Poems by Irving Layton' 1984; 'Irving Layton: A Portrait' (biog.) 1985; 'Robertson Davies: An Appreciation' 1991; mem. Assn. Candn. Studies; Assn. Candn. Univ. Teachers Eng.; ACQL; The Writers' Union; P.E.N.; Anglican,

Home: 28 Oriole Gardens, Toronto, Ont. M4V 1V7; Office: University College, 15 King's Coll. Circle, Univ. of Toronto, Toronto, Ont. M5S 1A1.

**CAMERON, Eric,** B.A.; university professor; b. Leicester, England 18 Apr. 1935; s. Alexander and Ruth (Pattison) C.; e. Durham Univ. (King's Coll., Newcastle-Upon-Tyne), B.A. 1957; Univ. of London (Courtauld Inst.), Acad. Dipl. in History of Art 1959; m. Margaret d. Arthur and Christiana Harrold 23 June 1963; children; Gregory, Edwin, Matilda; HEAD, DEPT. OF ART, UNIV. OF CALGARY 1987– ; Process paintings & theoretical speculation while teaching art hist., Univ. of Leeds 1959–69; Collective projects, video, first installations (Vanc. Art Gall., Nat. Gall., etc.), critical writings while teaching studio art, Univ. of Guelph (Chrmn., Dept. of Fine Art 1969–72) 1969–76; Newspaper Paintings & Thick Paintings (1979– ;) plus related installations & pubs. while teaching, N.S. Coll. of Art & Design (Dir., M.F.A. prog. 1976–86) 1976–87; studio art teacher; Mem., Universities Art Assn. of Can. (Pres. 1979–85); author: 'Bent Axis Approach' 1984, 'Divine Comedy' 1990; Home: 327 Hawkwood Blvd., N.W., Calgary, Alta. T3G 3G7; Office: 2500 University Dr. N.W., Calgary, Alta. T2N 1N4.

**CAMERON, Gary,** D.S.W.; educator; b. Montreal, Que. 27 March 1947; s. John Kennedy and Margaret (Edwards) C.; e. McGill Univ. B.A. 1968; Univ. of Toronto M.S.W. 1970; Columbia Univ. D.S.W. 1983; FOUNDER AND DIR. CENTRE FOR SOCIAL WELFARE STUDIES WILFRID LAURIER UNIV. 1987– , mem. Faculty of Social Work 1981– ; joined Greater Montreal Anti-Poverty Coordinating Ctte. 1970–76; Ville Marie Social Services Centre Montreal 1974–78; Bd. mem. & Organizer Montreal Chinese Community Service Centre 1975–78; Dixie Housing Corp. Lachine, Que. 1976–78; originator and project mgr. Parent Mutual Aid Orgns. Child Welfare London, Cambridge and Brantford, Ont. 1988–91; co-investigator, Better Beginnings, Better Futures Primary Prevention Demonstrator Project 1990–95; principal investigator, Family Builders Home Support Demonstration Project 1990–93; principal investigator, Multiple Site Intensive Family Prevention Services Demonstration Project; recipient Health & Welfare Can. Fellowship 1978–80; author 'Parent Mutual Aid Organizations in Child Welfare'; co-author 'The Use of Family Support in Children's Aid Societies' 1985; 'A Study of the Nutrition Habits of Children Attending Primary Schools' 1988; co-ed. 'Intervening with Assaulted Women' 1989; 'Child Maltreatment: Expanding Our Concept of Helping' 1990; Home: 476 Kingscourt Dr., Unit 20, Waterloo, Ont. N2K 3R3; Office: Waterloo, Ont. N2L 3C5.

**CAMERON, Hugh T.;** business executive; b. Wilkie, Sask. 26 July 1930; s. Norman and Elizabeth (Robinson) C.; e. Britannia High Sch. Vancouver 1948; Univ. of B.C. 1948–51; m. Bernie d. Garnett McElroy 1953; children: 4 d.; PRES. AGASSIZ RESOURCES LTD. 1984– ; Pres. Terratech Resources Inc.; Twin Gold Mines Ltd.; Trapper Resources Ltd.; Granger Resources Corp.; Wilkie East Corp.; Vice Pres. and Dir. Repadre Resources Ltd.; Dir. Wilshire Energy Resources Inc.; joined Belkin Packaging Vancouver 1951; Ace Containers Vancouver 1952–53; Crown Zellerbach 1954–62; Dir. of Sales Bathurst Containers 1962; Vice Pres. and Gen. Mgr. Brock Containers 1966–67; Pres. and Founder Cameron Containers 1968 (sold to Paperboard Industries Corp. 1982); Internat. Gov. Weismann Inst. of Sci. Rehovot, Israel; Pres. Assn. Ind. Corrugated Converters, Washington, D.C. 1976–77; recreations: golf, tennis; Club: St. George's Golf & Country.

**CAMERON, Hugh U.,** M.B., Ch.B., F.R.C.S.(C), F.A.A.O.S.; orthopaedic surgeon; b. Dundee, Scotland 16 Apr. 1945; s. Alexander and Margaret (Urquhart) C.; e. Falkirk H.S. 1962; St. Andrew's Univ., M.B.Ch.B. 1969; Cruden Med. Health Fellowship, Strath Clyde Univ. 1970–71; Residency, Univ. of Toronto, F.R.C.S.(C) 1975; Ont. Health Fellowship, London Hosp. (U.K.) 1975–76; m. Geraldine d. Robert and Lynne Moffat 1 Sept. 1984; STAFF ORTHOP. SURGEON, ORTHOPAEDIC & ARTHRITIC HOSP. 1981– ; Staff Orthop. Surg., Toronto Gen. Hosp. 1977–81; Lectr. in Surgery, Pathology and Material Sci., Univ. of Toronto 1977; Asst. Prof. of Surgery, Pathology and Metallurgy 1982, Assoc. Prof. 1991; Adjunct Prof. Mech. Engn., Univ. of Waterloo 1983; Asst. Prof. Bioengn., Univ. of Toronto 1984; Diplomate of Am. Bd. of Orthop. Surgeons 1979; Fellow, Am. Acad. of Orthop. Surg. 1982; designer, internat'lly used artificial knee 1981; hip 1984; Carnegie Summer Scholarships 1964–65; Cross Trust Scholarship 1967–69; Brit. Jr. Hammer Throw Champ. 1963; Scottish Univ. Weight Lifting Champ. 1964; mem., World Orthopaedic Concern; Am. Knee Soc.; Candn. Orthop. Assn.; Candn. Med. Assn.; author 150 sci. articles in learned journals; Asst. Ed.: 'Journal of Arthroplasty'; Assoc. Ed., 'Sports Medicine News'; author: 'Technique of Total Hip Arthroplasty'; recreations: travel, writing; Home: 57 Highland Ave., Toronto, Ont. M4W 2A2; Office: 318–43 Wellesley St. E., Toronto, Ont. M4Y 1H1.

**CAMERON, Ian Robert,** B.Sc., Ph.D.; author; educator; b. Ross-Shire, Scot. 26 July 1931; s. Duncan and Elizabeth (Mackay) C.; e. Inverness Royal Acad., Univ. of Edinburgh B.Sc. 1953, Ph.D. 1958; m. Heather d. Harold and Beatrice Colville 21 March 1957; one d. Catriona; EMERITUS PROFESSOR OF PHYSICS, UNIV. OF N.B. (SAINT JOHN) 1993– ; Prof. of Physics 1973–92; Dean of Faculty 1979–84; Sr. Scient. Offr. U.K. Atomic Energy Authority 1958–64, Princ. Scient. Offr. 1964–67; Assoc. Prof. of Physics present Univ. 1967–73; author 'Nuclear Fission Reactors' 1982; 'Quarks, Quanta and Quasars: An Exploration of the Physical Universe' 1992; recreations: climbing, skiing, music; Home: 128 Dunedin Road, East Riverside, Saint John, N.B. E2H 1P7; Office: Saint John, N.B. E2L 4L5.

**CAMERON, James Munro,** M.A., D.L.S. (Hon.); retired university professor; b. Manchester U.K. 14 Nov. 1910; s. Alan and Jane Helen (Carruthers) C.; e. Bury Grammar Sch.; Sheffield Central Secondary Sch.; Keighley Grammar Sch.; Balliol Coll., Oxford; m. Vera (d. 1985) d. Benjamin Gartside Shaw 1934; children: Bridget Mary Macmillan, Mark Alan Shaw (d. 1984); Workers Edn. Assn., E. Yorkshire 1931–32; University Coll. Southampton 1932–35; Vaughan Coll. Leicester 1935–44; Univ. of Leeds 1944–66 (Chair of Philosophy 1960); Prof. of Phil. & Master, Rutherford Coll., Univ. of Kent at Canterbury 1966–71; St. Michael's Coll., Univ. of Toronto 1971–78; Visiting Prof., Univ. of Notre Dame 1957–58; Terry Lectr., Yale Univ. 1964; Newman Lectr., Univ. of Melbourne, Australia 1968; author: 'Scrutiny of Marxism' 1948, 'The Night Battle' 1962, 'Images of Authority' 1966; 'The Music is in the Sadness' 1988, 'Nuclear Catholics and Other Essays' 1990; editor: 'Newman's Essay on Development' (1845 ed.) 1978; co-transl.: 'Max Picard: The Flight from God' 1951; Home: 360 Bloor St. E., Apt. 409, Toronto, Ont. M4W 3M3; Office: St. Michael's College, 81 St. Mary St., Toronto, Ont. M5S 1A7.

**CAMERON, Norman Edward,** Ph.D.; university professor; b. Burks Falls, Ont. 22 Nov. 1942; s. Murray and Vera Alice (Strader) C.; e. Queen's Univ., B.A. (Hons.) 1984; Univ. of West. Ont., M.A. 1965; Univ. of Michigan, Ph.D. 1971; m. Beverly d. Kenneth and Eleanor Coulter 15 June 1968; children: Ewen Coulter, Fraser Murray Coulter (Cameron); PROF., ECON. DEPT., UNIV. OF MAN. 1985– ; Asst. then Assoc. Prof. 1969–84; Acting Head & Head 1977–79; Fellow, St. John's Coll. 1979– ; Dean of Studies 1985–88; Visitor, Queen's Univ. 1975–76, Univ. of Michigan 1989–90; Contract Rsch. for Econ. Council of Can.; Health & Welfare Can.; Can. West Found.; Expert Witness on Fin. Matters, Man. & Sask. Court of Queen's Bench, Ont. Supreme Court; Extve. Counc., Candn. Econ. Assn. 1985–88; Univ. Award for excellence in teaching 1982; Univ. Outreach Award 1983; author: 'Money, Financial Markets and Economic Activity' 1984, 1991 & 3 other books, 19 articles & book chapters; co-author: 'Economics in Action' 1983; recreations: swimming, cross-country skiing, golf, reading; Home: 601 South Dr., Winnipeg, Man. R3T 0B9; Office: St. John's Coll., Univ. of Man., Winnipeg, Man. R3T 2N2.

**CAMERON, Peter Alfred Gordon,** B.Com.; company executive; b. Toronto, Ont. 1930; e. Appleby Coll., Oakville, Ont.; McGill Univ. B.Com.; m. Suzanne M. S. Noble 1955; children: Ian, Janet, Patricia; CHRMN & DIR., THE GARFIELD GROUP 1992– ; Dir., Diversey Corp.; Canada Post Corp.; Malsham Group Inc.; NN Life Insurance Co. of Can.; Mang. Trainee, Ford Motor Co. of Can. Ltd., Windsor, Ont. 1953; Asst. to Advertising Mgr., Brading's Breweries Ltd., Toronto, Ont. 1954; Sales Rep., Wm. B. Stewart & Sons Limited 1955; Assistant Advertising Manager then Product Manager, Proprietaries Division, Warner Lambert (Canada) Limited 1956; Acct. Executive, MacLaren Advertising Co. Limited 1958; Sr. Acct. Extve., Foster Advertising Ltd. 1960, Group Supv. 1962, Vice-Pres. 1965, Group Vice-Pres. 1969; Vice Pres., Candn. Industries ltd. 1970–78; Pres. and Dir., Canadian Corporate Management Co. Ltd. 1978–87; Chrmn. & Dir., Chromalox Inc. 1987–91; continuous service in Candn. Army Mil. 1948–70; retired as Lt. Col., C.O. 48th Highlanders of Can.; re-activated 1975 as Col. Commander, Montreal Military District until 1978; re-activated January 1982 SSO/Land Chief of Reserves Council, Dept. of National Defence; promoted Brig.-Gen. and SPO CAF Reserves Jan. 1985; awarded Order of Military Merit 1977; Commander of the Order of St. John; Immed. Past Chrmn., Bd. of Dirs., Sunnybrook Medical Centre Found.; Co-Chrmn., Defence Industrial Preparedness Adv. Ctte. with Min. of Nat. Defence; Immediate Past Chrmn., Task Force on Defence Policy, Bus. Counc. on National Issues; Past Chrmn., Appleby Coll.; recreations: music, squash, skiing, golf; Clubs: York (Toronto); Toronto (Toronto); Badminton and Racquet (Toronto); Toronto Golf; Royal Candn. Military Inst.; St. James's (Montreal); Office: 56 Temperance St., Suite 200, Toronto, Ont. M5H 3V5.

**CAMERON, Robert Burns,** O.C. (1970), D.S.O., LL.D., D.Eng.; industrialist; b. New Glasgow, N.S., 28 July 1919; s. Hugh Scott and Christine (Fraser) C.; e. New Glasgow (N.S.) High Sch.; Royal Mil. Coll. 1939; N.S. Tech. Coll.; LL.D., St. Mary's Univ. 1968, St. Francis Xavier 1969; D.Eng., N.S. Tech. Coll. 1969; m. Florence Anna, d. Donald Colin Campbell, 15 Jan. 1943; children: Peggy (deceased), Christine, Hugh, Elizabeth, Robert, James, Donald, Harry; Pres. Cameron Corporation Ltd.; served with R.C.E. in Eng., Italy and W. Europe, rank Maj.; Presbyterian; Office: 379 Glasgow St., New Glasgow, N.S. B2H 5C3.

**CAMERON, Robert Parke;** diplomat; b. Montreal, Que. 15 Oct. 1920; s. late Edward Parke and late Isabel MacFarlane (Fraser) C.; e. Perth (Ont.) Coll. Inst. 1938; Univ. of Toronto Univ. Coll. B.A. 1943; m. Katharine Isobel Whiteley 17 July 1948; children: Bruce Allison Fraser, Alexander Brian, Lesley Isabella; Instr. Dept. Pol. Econ. Univ. of Toronto 1946–47; joined Dept. External Affairs 1947; service abroad: Havana 1948–50, Stockholm 1955–58, Washington 1962–65, Bonn 1965–68; Dir.-Gen. Bureau of Defence and Arms Control Ottawa 1970–74, External Affairs Rep. Can.-USA Perm. Jt. Bd. Defence 1970–74, Ambassador to Yugoslavia, Roumania and Bulgaria 1974–77 with accreditation to Roumania until 1976; Diplomat in Residence, Univ. of British Columbia 1977–78; Ambassador to Poland and to the German Democratic Republic, 1978–80; Asst. Undersecy. of State, Bureau of Int. Security Policy and Arms Control Affairs 1981–83; Visiting Foreign Service Officer, Univ. of Toronto 1983–84; Retired from External Affairs 1985; mem., Candn. Inst. Internat. Affairs; served with Candn. Army 1943–45, rank Lt.; Home: 72 Kilbarry Cres., Ottawa, Ont. K1K 0H3.

**CAMERON, Silver Donald,** M.A., Ph.D.; author; b. Toronto, Ont. 21 June 1937; s. Maxwell A. and Hazel B. (Robertson) C.; e. Univ. of B.C., B.A. 1959; Univ. of Calif. M.A. 1962; Univ. of London Ph.D. 1967; m. 1stly Catherine Ann d. late Sam Cahoon 21 Aug. 1959; children: Maxwell, Ian, Leslie, Steven; m. 2ndly Marie Louise 'Lulu' d. late Arthur Terrio, D'Escousse, N.S. 17 May 1980; one s. Mark Patrick Terrio-Cameron; author 'The Education of Everett Richardson' 1977; 'Faces of Leacock' 1967; 'Conversations with Canadian Novelists' 1973; 'Seasons in the Rain' (essays) 1978; 'Dragon Lady' (novel) 1980, paperback 1981; 'The Baitchopper' (children's novel) 1982; 'Schooner: Bluenose and Bluenose II' 1984; 'Outhouses of the West' 1988; 'Wind, Whales and Whisky: A Cape Breton Voyage' 1991; 'An Illustrated History of Marine Atlantic' (co-author) 1992; 'Once Upon A Schooner' 1992; 'Sniffing the Coast: An Acadian Voyage' 1993; 'The Prophet at Tantramar' (stage play) (Ship's Company Theatre 1988); numerous articles, radio drama, reviews, short stories, TV scripts; taught at UBC, Dalhousie, UNB before becoming freelance writer and broadcaster 1971; Writer-in-Residence Coll. of Cape Breton 1978–80; Univ. of P.E.I. 1985–86; N.S. Coll. of Art and Design 1987–88; recipient, City of Dartmouth Book Award 1992; Atlantic Booksellers Choice Award 1992; four Nat. Mag. Awards; nominated ACTRA Awards (radio drama); Internat. Prix Italia Radio Drama 1980; nominated Gemini Award 1992; founding Extve. Dir., Centre Bras d'Or; Pres., Paper Tiger Enterprises Ltd.; Pres., Novara Software Inc.; mem., Writers' Union Can.; Periodical Writers' Assn. Can.; Writers Guild of Canada; Writers' Fed. N.S.; Dir., North Isle Madame Credit Union; recreations: sailing, woodwork; Club: Lennox Passage Yacht; Address: D'Escousse, N.S. B0E 1K0.

**CAMERON, Hon. Stuart John;** judge; b. Maple Creek, Sask. 15 May 1939; s. Alexander C. and Miriam Adelaide C.; e. Campion Coll. (Regina) 1957; Univ. Sask., B.A. 1961; LL.B. 1962; m. Sonia, d. Albert and Patricia Patzernuik, 24 Nov. 1962; children: Alison; Sheila; Sandi; JUSTICE, COURT OF APPEAL FOR SASK. since 1981; articled to E.J. Moss, Q.C. 1962; admitted to Sask. Bar 1963; admitted to partnership Moss, Wimmer and Cameron 1964; merged with Balfour, Moss & Co. 1967; appointed Chief of Staff to Fed. Min. Justice 1973; elected to Sask. legislature 1975; apointed Court of Queen's Bench 1980; Past Gov., Regina Gen.

Hosp.; Treas., John Howard Soc. Sask.; Chrmn., Regina Housing Authority; Pres., Regina Bar Assn.; mem. Regina, Sask. and Candn. Bar Assns.; Present Faculty mem., Sask. Bar Admin. Course; Vice-Pres., Candn. Inst. for the Admin. of Justice; Home: 3406 Rideout Bay, Regina, Sask. S4S 7C2; Office: Court House, 2425 Victoria Ave., Regina, Sask. S4P 3V7.

**CAMP, Dalton Kingsley,** O.C., B.A., M.Sc., LL.D.; b. Woodstock, N.B. 11 Sept. 1920; s. Harold and Aurilla (Sanborn) C.; e. Pub. Sch., Piedmont, Cal., U.S.A.; Horton Acad., Wolfville, N.S.; Univ. of N.B., B.A.; Columbia Univ., M.Sc.; London Sch. of Econ. (Beaverbrook Overseas Scholar); St. Thomas Univ. LL.D.; m. 1stly Linda Atkins; children: David Kingsley, Michael George Harold, Linda Gail, Constance Marilyn, Cheryl Ann; m. 2ndly Wendy Cameron; one son Christopher Jonathan Kingsley; columnist; radio & television commentator; Sr. Adv. to the Cabinet, Privy Council Office 1986–88; mem. Ont. Royal Comn. on Book Publishing 1971–72; Chrmn. Ont. Comn. on Legislature 1973–75; def. cand. to H. of C. in g.e. 1965 and 1968; Pres., Nat. P. Conservative Party Can. 1964–69; mem. Bd. Govs. Acadia Univ.; mem., Candn. Civil Liberties Assn.; Skelton-Clark Fellow, Queen's Univ., 1968–69; author of 'Gentlemen, Players and Politicians' 1970; 'Points of Departure' 1979; 'Eclectic Eel' 1981; Officer, Order of Canada 1994; Club: Albany; Home: 'Northwood,' Cambridge, Queens Co., N.B. E0E 1B0.

**CAMP, James John (J.J.),** Q.C., B.A., LL.B.; lawyer; b. Kamloops, B.C. 14 Dec. 1943; s. Walter Leslie and Marguerite Kathleen (McRae) C.; e. Univ. of Victoria B.A. 1965; Univ. of B.C. LL.B. 1969; m. Anne d. Jack and Ann Ross 2 July 1966; children: Jason D., Andrea E.; PARTNER, CAMP, CHURCH AND ASSOCS. 1993– ; Nat. Rsch. Council Ottawa 1965–66; Univ. of B.C. 1966–69; Partner, Ladner Downs 1969–93; Dir. Pub. Interest Advocacy Centre; Vancouver Acad. of Music; Pres. B.C. Br. Cdn. Bar Assn.; Pres., Cdn. Bar Assn. 1991–92 (Treas. 1989–90, Vice Pres. 1990–91); recreations: skiing, tennis, golf, squash; Clubs: Point Grey; Arbutus; Home: 2876 W. King Edward Ave., Vancouver, B.C.; Office: 4th Floor, 555 West Georgia St., Vancouver, B.C. V6B 1Z5.

**CAMP, Thomas Chasney,** Q.C., B.A., B.C.L.; lawyer; b. Sherbrooke, Que. 27 March 1931; s. David Manning and Mary Jeane (Elder) C.; e. McGill Univ. B.A. 1952, B.C.L. 1955; m. Sylvia d. Arthur and Sarah Ponder 17 Sept. 1955; children: David Manning, Geoffrey Alexander, Katherine Sarah, Peter Osborne; PARTNER, McMASTER MEIGHEN; Student, Assoc., Partner, McMaster Meighen 1955– ; Dir., Bank of Montreal Realty Inc.; Canadian Investment Fund, Ltd.; Bullock Growth Fund, Ltd.; Trustee, Bullock American Fund; Stanstead Wesleyan College; Gov., The Fraser-Hickson Inst.; The Montreal General Hosp.; recreations: skiing, sailing; clubs: University Club of Montreal, St. James's Club of Montreal, The Forest and Stream Club, Albany Club of Toronto; Home: 153 Wolseley Ave., Montreal W., Que. H4X 1V8; Office: 630 René-Lévesque Blvd. W., 7th Floor, Montreal, Qué. H3B 4H7.

**CAMPBELL, Rt. Hon. A. Kim,** P.C., Q.C., B.A., LL.B.; politician; b. Port Alberni, B.C. 10 March 1947; d. George T. Campbell and Phyllis M. (Cook) Vroom; e. Prince of Wales Secondary Sch., Vancouver, B.C.; Univ. of B.C.; Univ. of Oregon; London Sch. of Economics; elected 19th Prime Minister of Canada 25 June 1993–4 Nov. 1993; Leader, Progressive Conservative Party of Canada 13 June 1993; Trustee, Vancouver Sch. Bd. 1980–84 (Chrmn. 1983, Vice Chair 1984); Past Dir., Vancouver Youth Symphony; Past Dir., Dunbar-Point Grey-Southlands Family and Youth Assoc.; el. B.C. g.e. 1986; el. H. of C. (Vancouver Centre) g.e. 1988; apptd. Min. of State (Indian Affairs and Northern Development) and sworn to the Privy Counc. 30 Jan. 1989; Min. of Justice and Attorney Gen. of Can. 1990–93; Min. of Defence & Min. of Veterans Affairs 1993; LL.D. (hon.), Law Soc. of Upper Canada 1992; P.C.; Anglican; Home: Ottawa, Ont. K1M 1M4.

**CAMPBELL, Hon. Alexander Bradshaw,** P.C. (1967), Q.C., M.L.A., B.A., LL.B., LL.D.; b. Summerside, P.E.I. 1 Dec. 1933; s. late Hon. Thane A. and Cecilia (Bradshaw) C.; e. Dalhousie Univ., B.A. and LL.B. (1959); McGill Univ., LL.D., (hon.) 1967; Univ.of P.E.I., LL.D. (hon.) 1979; m. Marilyn, d. Melville Gilmore, Guelph, Ont., 19 Aug. 1961; children: Blair Alexander, Heather Kathryn, Graham Melville; Appt. JUSTICE, SUPREME COURT OF P.E.I., Nov. 1978; called to Bar of P.E.I., 1959; cr. Q.C., 1966; el. M.L.A. in by-el. for 5th Prince, Feb. 1965 and Leader of P.E.I. Liberal Party, Dec. 1965; Min. of Justice and Attorney Gen. 1966–69, Min. of Development 1969–72, Min. of Agric. 1972–74; Premier of P.E.I., July 1966–Sept. 1978, re-el. to fourth term Apr. 1978, resigned Sept. 1978; Apptd. mem. of Privy Counc. 1967; former Secy. Summerside Bd. of Trade and Vice Pres. Young Liberal Assn.; Liberal; Past Chrmn., Institute of Man and Resources; Pres., Summerside Y.M.C.A. 1980–91; Past Pres., Summerside Y's Men's Club; Charter Pres., Summerside and Area Historical Soc. 1983– ; Charter Pres., P.E.I. Council, The Duke of Edinburgh's Award in Canada 1984–90; United Church; recreations: gardening, skiing, golf; Home: 330 Beaver St., Summerside, P.E.I. C1N 2A3; Office: Sir Louis Henry Davies Law Courts Bldg., Charlottetown, P.E.I. C1A 8B9.

**CAMPBELL, Alexander John,** Q.C., B.A., LL.B., LL.M.; advocate; b. Truro, N.S., 4 Apl. 1904; s. Alexander John and Blanch (Tremaine) C.; e. Truro, N.S. (Primary); Ashbury Coll., Ottawa, Ont.; Dalhousie Univ., B.A. 1925, LL.B. 1927; Harvard Law Sch., LL.M. 1929; m. the late Frances Vivian, d. late Philip Weatherbe, Halifax, N.S., 11 July 1940; two d., Susan Frances, Elizabeth Jane; m. 2ndly the late Mary Claire Gordon, widow of late Grant Gordon, Q.C., Oct. 1963; COUNSEL, GASCO LELARGE GOODHUE; read law with A.J. Campbell, K.C., 1925–27; called to the Bar of N.S. 1927 and of Quebec 1930; cr. K.C. 1946; began practice with father A. J. Campbell, Q.C., in Truro, N.S.; moved to Montreal, Que., in 1929; practising with Brown, Montgomery & McMichael; with Audette & O'Brien till 1932 when assoc. with Hon. F. Philippe Brais, Q.C., till apptd. as a Puisne Judge of the Superior Court of Que., Nov. 1946; in July 1949 resigned from the Bench and resumed practice in partnership with Hon. F. P. Brais, Q.C. till 1970; Partner, Campbell Pepper Laffoley 1970–76, Counsel 1976–87; Counsel, Gasco, Lelarge Goodhue 1987– ; Bâtonnier, Bar of Montreal 1966–67, and of Que. Prov. 1966–67; mem., Bar of Montreal; Bar, Prov. of Que.; Cdn. Bar Assn.; Fellow Am. Coll. of Trial Lawyers; Liberal; Protestant; recreation: golf; Clubs: St. James's; University; Kanawaki Golf; Hermitage; Home: 3980 Cote des Neiges Road, Apt. A31, Montreal, Que.; Office: Suite 2100, 1080 Cote du Beaver Hall, Montreal, Que. H2Z 1S8.

**CAMPBELL, Alistair Matheson,** M.A., F.I.A., F.S.A., b. Strachur, Argyllshire, Scot. 3 July 1905; s. Peter and Catherine (MacRae) C.; e. Inverness Roy. Acad., Scot.; Univ. of Aberdeen, M.A. 1927; Research Scholar in Math. 1928; m. Barbara Isabel Alexander, d. late E. Greville Hampson, 2 April 1948; has one s. Michael Alexander and three ds. Catherine, Barbara, Jill; CHRMN. EMERITUS, SUN LIFE ASSURANCE CO. OF CANADA; joined present Co. in Actuarial Dept. 1928, Asst. Actuary 1934, Assoc. Actuary 1940, Actuary 1946, Assist. Gen. Mgr. & Actuary 1947; Vice-Pres. and Actuary 1950, Vice-Pres. and Chief Actuary 1954, Extve. Vice-Pres. and Dir. 1956, Pres. and Chief Extve. Offr. 1962, Chrmn. and Chief Extve. Offr. 1970, Chrmn. 1973; Chrmn. of Extve. Comte. 1978; on loan to Foreign Exchange Control Bd., Ottawa 1939–40; served with Royal Candn. Arty. 1940–45; Past Gov. (1953–55 and 1957–59) Soc. of Actuaries; Pres. (1957–58) Candn. Life Ins. Assn.; Candn. Assn. Actuaries (Pres. 1947–48); mem. Bd. Div. Trustees, Past Vice-Pres., Hon. mem. (1956) and Hon. Gov. (1975), Candn. Red Cross Soc. (Que. Div.); Past Prov. Vice-Pres. (Que.) (1962–63) and mem. Extve. Comte. (1965), Am. Life Convention; Past Dir., Life Ins. Assn. of Am. (1968–71); Clubs: University (Montreal); the Rideau (Ottawa); Address: Apt. #9, 130 Rideau Terrace, Ottawa, Ont. K1M 0Z2.

**CAMPBELL, Allan Barrie,** O.C., F.R.S.C.; retired agrologist; b. Winnipeg, Man. 28 Mar. 1923; s. Arnold Munroe and Petrina Flora (Wilson) C.; e. East Kildonan Collegiate, Winnipeg 1940; Univ. of Manitoba, B.S.A. 1944, M.Sc. 1948; Univ. of Minnesota, Ph.D. 1954; m. Mavis, d. Peter and Mabel Millar, 15 Dec. 1950; 1 d.: Patricia; former Principal Research Scientist, Agriculture Canada; a rsch. sci. (wheat breeder) with Agric. Can. at Rsch. Stn., Winnipeg 1949–1988; developed nine cultivars of hard red spring wheat adapted to the Can. prairies, which were grown on 9 million hectares in 1988; recipient, Incentive Award, Bd. of Pub. Service of Can. and Agronomy Merit Award, both in 1976; Fellow of Agric. Inst. of Can.; Hon. Life Mem., Can. Seed Growers' Assn.; Officer, Order of Canada; Honorary Doctor of Science, Univ. of Manitoba 1992; Home: 277 Wellington Cr., Apt. 902, Winnipeg, Man. R3M 3V7.

**CAMPBELL, Anne,** APR; writer; public library admin.; b. Paddockwood, Sask.; d. Joseph John and Rose (Tomlenovich) King; e. Conservatory, Univ. of Regina; Sask. School of the Arts; m. John s. Allan and Harriet C.; divorced; children: Joseph Allan, Jacqueline Anne, Jill Andrea; Mackenzie Art Gallery 1975–78; Glenbow Mus. 1978–80; Heritage Park 1980–81; Regina Public Library 1981– ; Creative Writing Instr., Univ. of Regina Extension 1989; City of Regina Writing Award 1982; Sask. Writers Guild major awards 1984, 1989; Sask. Arts Bd. Award 1990; papers deposited Univ. of Regina Lib. Archives 1987; The Writers Devel. Trust 1989–92; mem., Candn. Public Relations Soc.; Sask. Writers Guild (Dir. 1981–83); Writers Guild of Alta.; League of Candn. Poets (Dir. 1985–86); Writers Union of Canada (National Council 1993–94); author: 'No Memory of a Move' 1983, 'Death is an Anxious Mother' 1986, 'Red Earth, Yellow Stone' 1989 (poetry); 'Angel Wings All Over' 1994; inclusion in the following anthologies: 'Dancing Visions' 1985, 'A Sudden Radiance' 1987, 'Out of Place' 1990, 'Frictions II' 1993; recreations: ice skating, walking; Home: 3315 Rae St., Regina, Sask. S4S 1S5.

**CAMPBELL, Archie Gray,** LL.B., LL.M.; provincial supreme court judge; b. Montreal, Que. 13 Apr. 1942; s. Robert McAlpine and Leona (Gray) C.; e. Lambton Kingsway P.S.; Univ. of Toronto Schs.; Univ. of Toronto, Osgoode Hall Law Sch. LL.B. 1967, LL.M. 1973; JUSTICE, ONTARIO COURT OF JUSTICE (GEN. DIV.); Counsel, Crim. Appeals & Special Prosecutions, Attorney Gen. Dept. 1969–73, 1974–75; Prov. Secretariat for Justice 1973–74; Sr. Crown Counsel, Policy Div., Min. Attorney Gen. 1975–77; Judge, High Court of Justice, Supreme Court of Ont. 1987–..; Dir., Parkdale Community Legal Serv. and Assoc. Prof., Osgoode Hall Law Sch. 1977–78; Asst. Depy. Atty. Gen., Policy 1978–81; Depy. Min. of Correctional Services 1981–82; Deputy Attorney General, Ont. 1983–86; Dir., The Osgoode Soc.; Home: 154 Eastbourne Ave., Toronto, Ont. M5P 2G6.

**CAMPBELL, Arthur Grant,** B.A.; retired diplomat; b. Montreal, Que. 18 Sept. 1916; s. Donald Grant and Sophy Edith (Field) C.; e. Upper Canada Coll., Toronto, 1934; McGill Univ., B.A. 1938; Columbia Univ., Post-grad. Studies 1951; m. Carol, d. Albert Michael Wright, 6 April 1940; one s. Ian Andrew Grant; Ambassador to Norway and Iceland 1977–81; commenced as Asst. to Secy., Candn. Chamber of Comm. and Assoc. Ed. 'Canadian Business' 1938–41; UN Secretariat, Dept. Pol. and Security Council Affairs 1946–56 (UNAEC 1946, Disarmament Comn. 1952–56); Asst. Secy., UN Comn. for India and Pakistan 1948; Political Adviser, UN Rep. for India and Pakistan 1950; joined Dept. Ex. Affairs, UN Div. 1956; Counsellor, Ten Nation Conf. on Disarmament, Geneva 1960; Counsellor, New Delhi 1960; Head, Commonwealth Div., Ottawa 1963; Min.-Counsellor, Eighteen Nation Disarmament Conf., Geneva 1967; Minister, Bonn 1969; Ambassador to South Africa, and High Commissioner to Botswana, Lesotho and Swaziland; 1972; served in R.C.A. 1941–46, U.K., Central Mediterranean, N.W. Europe; Mentioned in Despatches; Psi Upsilon; United Church; recreations: skiing, music; Home: 7 Rothwell Dr., Ottawa, Ont. K1J 7G3.

**CAMPBELL, Arthur Rae,** B.Eng., P.Eng.; executive; b. Yarmouth, N.S. 5 Sept. 1942; s. James Arthur and Margaret Winnifred (Sinclair) C.; e. McGill Univ. B.Eng. 1964; m. Carol d. Jack and Anne Fargey 2 Oct. 1965; children: Andrea, Alison, Brian; PRES., C.E.O. & DIR., PROWEST SAFETY AND ENVIRONMENTAL SERVICES LTD.; Carrae Enterprises Ltd.; Dir., Petroleum Services Assn. of Canada, Petroleum Industry Training Service; previously Pres. & Dir. Bantrel Group Engineers Ltd. 1984–87; Dir. Bechtel Canada Engineers Ltd.; served Imperial Oil over 15 yrs. areas of engn., projects, refining and adm.; Mgr. of Engn. & Devel. Petro-Canada; Vice Pres. Partec Lavalin Inc.; Vice Pres. Lavalin Inc.; Vice Pres. Corp. Planning Petro-Canada; Chrmn., Adv. Ctte. on Chemical Technology, Southern Alta. Inst. of Technology; Past Chrmn., Adv. Ctte. on Project Mgmt., Univ. of Calgary; Mem., Adv. Ctte. on Science Educ. for the Prov. of Alta.; Past Mem. Counc., APEGGA (Past Chrmn., Discipline Ctte.); Mem. Extve. Ctte. for Safety Services, Petroleum Services Assoc. of Can.; mem. Am. Inst. Chem. Engrs.; APEGGA; Soc. of Petroleum Engrs.; Candn. Soc. of Safety Engineering; Air & Waste Mgmt. Assoc.; Candn. Inst. Mining & Metall.; Clubs: Glencoe; Calgary Petroleum; Rotary; Home: 3015 – 5 St. S.W., Calgary, Alta. T2S 2C3; Office: 7058-K Farrell Rd. S.W., Calgary, Alta. T2H 0T2.

**CAMPBELL, Bennett;** teacher; former politician; b. Montague, P.E.I. 27 Aug. 1943; s. Wilfred Laurier and Edith Florence (Rice) C.; e. Poplar Point Sch.; St. Dunstan's High Sch. grad. 1960; St. Dunstan's Univ. 2 yr. Teacher Educ. Program; m. Margaret Shirley, d. Joseph Chaisson, Souris, P.E.I. 1 Aug. 1970; children: Kelly Dawn, Colin, Grant, Sherry Lee, Grace; Min. of Veterans' Affairs 1982; Leader of Opposition, P.E.I. 1979–81; Chrmn. of Treasury Bd. 1976–79; el. mem. Prov. Leg. 1970, re-el. 1974, 1978, 1979; Min. of Educ. 1972–78,

Prov. Secy. and Min. of Educ. 1974–76; Premier of P.E.I. 1978–79; Chrmn. Council of Mins. of Educ. Can. 1976; Liberal; R. Catholic; recreations: golf, boating, camping; Club: Lions; Home: (Box 28) Cardigan, P.E.I. C0A 1G0.

**CAMPBELL, Bernard F.,** B.A.; civil servant; b. Sydney, N.S. 8 Nov. 1941; s. James Anthony and Mary Claire (Merchant) C.; e. Sydney Acad.; St. Francis Xavier Univ. B.A. (Hons.) 1964; m. Mary d. Patrick and Kathleen Wilson 30 Dec. 1964; children: Alexis, Ken, Kira; PRES., WESTWINDS TOURISM CONSULTANTS 1992– ; Tourism Can., (Ottawa, Boston, NY, Cincinnati) 1964–72; Dir., U.S. Mktg. 1972–76; Indus. Relns. 1976–83; Dir. Gen., Devel. 1982–86; Dep. Min., Tourism, Prov. of Alta. 1987–92; Dir., Alta. Tourism Edn. Counc.; Cdn. Rep., Pacific Asia Tourism Assn. Edn. Authy.; Dir., Candn. Hospitality Inst.; Internat. Institute of Peace Through Tourism; Guest Lectr., Simon Fraser Univ., Ryerson, Univ. Externado Bogata, Colombia; Hon. Life Mem., Candn. Fed. Chefs de Cuisine; Mem., Inst. of Public Admin. of Can.; Adv. Ctte., Candn. Culinary Inst.; author/co-author of papers & mag. articles; recreations: hiking, skiing, music; Home: 301, 11220 – 99 Avenue, Edmonton, Alta. T5R 5P3; Office: 6th fl., 10155 – 102 St., Edmonton, Alta. T5J 4L6.

**CAMPBELL, Brooke Shaw,** B.Comm., LL.B.; corporate financier; b. Vancouver, B.C. 1 Oct. 1941; s. John Anderson and Mary Millar (Strike) C.; e. Univ. of B.C. B.Comm. 1965, LL.B. 1966; m. Janet d. John and Elizabeth Barclay 23 Dec. 1967; children: Alan Shaw, Shan Elizabeth; DIRECTOR & MGR. CORPORATE FINANCE, ODLUM BROWN LIMITED 1989– ; Commercial and Corp. Lender, Bank of Montreal 1966–76; Vice-Pres. & Dir., Pemberton Securities Limited 1976–89; Dir., Pacific Corporate Trust; Whistler Alpine Villa Ltd.; Lt., Royal Cdn. Naval Reserve; recreations: rugby, tennis; clubs: Town of Mount Royal Rugby, Hollyburn Country; Home: 96 Bonnymuir Drive, West Vancouver, B.C. V7S 1L2; Office: 1800, 609 Granville St., Vancouver, B.C. V7Y 1A3.

**CAMPBELL, Bruce Dewar,** B.Com.; executive (ret.); b. St. Thomas, Ont. 11 July 1923; s. John D.; e. Pub. and High Schs., St. Thomas, Ont; Queen's Univ., B.Com. 1950; m. Barbara I., d. William Gordon Fraser, Oct. 1959; with International Business Machines Co. Ltd., Sales Div. 1950–61; Mgr., IBM Canada Ltd. Montreal 1962; Gen. Mgr., IBM Project Expo '67, 1967 Regional Mgr. Br. Adm. 1968; joined SDI Associates Ltd. as Vice-Pres. and Dir. 1969; Pres., 1970–79; Fellow, Institute of Corporate Dirs.; Baptist; recreations: golf, travel, bridge; Home: R.R. #2, Uxbridge, Ont. L9P 1R2.

**CAMPBELL, Bruce Thomas Evison,** B.A.Sc., M.Sc., Ph.D.; entrepreneur; former astronomer; b. Vancouver, B.C. 18 Feb. 1948; s. Alan Thomas Robinson and Francis Marjorie (Greenwood) C.; e. Univ. of B.C., B.A.Sc. 1971; Univ. of Toronto M.Sc. 1973, Ph.D. 1976; m. Kaye d. James and Anna Katherine Barnett 4 Sept. 1971; children: Clayton, Spencer, Kyle; PRES., BTEC ENTERPRISES LTD.; Dir. High Winds Developments Ltd., North Secretary Holdings Ltd. and Glenlyon-Norfolk Sch.; Killam Postdoctoral Fellow Univ. of B.C. 1976–78; Resident Astronomer, Can.-France-Hawaii Telescope 1979–82; Rsch. Assoc., Dominion Astrophysical Observatory 1983–87; Nat. Rsch. Counc. Can. and Centre National de la Recherche Scientifique of France Exchange Fellow 1983; Adjunct Assoc. Prof., Univ. of Victoria 1987–90; author or co-author over 40 sci. papers; co-discoverer of a supernova in a quasar galaxy (1st such discovery) 1984; discoverer of planetlike objects in orbit about nearby solar-like stars 1986; recreations: skiing, scuba diving; Clubs: North Secretary Island Rod & Racket; Home: 4537 Rithetwood Pl., Victoria, B.C. V8X 4J9.

**CAMPBELL, Clifford Ernest Michael,** B.A., A.P.R.; communications executive; b. Toronto, Ont. 21 Jan. 1953; s. Clifford Melville and Ida Margaret (Alston) C.; e. The Priory Sch., Kingston, Jamaica; Stanstead Coll. (Que.); Trent Univ. Hon. B.A.; m. Gillian d. Mebourne and Joan Elson 28 May 1977; children: Matthew, Trevor; Chairman & C.E.O., Continental Golin/Harris Communications Inc. 1985–.; Dir. Presentations Speaker Training Centre Inc.; Canadian Aircraft Leasing Co. Inc.; Continental Canada Inc.; Canada's Challenge for America's Cup; Exec. Dir. Candn. Special Olympics Inc. and The Harry E. Foster Found. 1974–77; Vice-Chrmn. Prov. Pub. Educ. Prog. on Mental Retardation 1977–79; Vice-Pres. Pub. and Ind. Relations Ltd. 1979–82; Vice-Pres. and Gen. Mgr. present firm 1982, Pres. 1983; mem. Candn. Pub. Relations Soc. (holds profl. accreditation A.P.R. from Soc.); Internat. Assn. of Bus. Communicators; R. Catholic; recreation: sailing; Club: Oakville; Home: 1128 Kent Ave., Oakville, Ont. L6H 1Z8.

**CAMPBELL, Most Rev. Colin,** B.A., B.Th., M.A., R.S.W., D.D., Litt.D.; b. Antigonish, N.S. 12 June 1931; s. Dr. Peter Smyth and Ida (Tompkins) C.; e. St.Thomas Aquinas Sch.; St. Mary's Univ. B.A. 1952; Holy Heart Semy. Halifax B.Th. 1956; Univ. of Montreal M.A. (Social Work) 1964; Univ. of S. Cal. Los Angeles Sch. of Journalism summer 1975; BISHOP OF ANTIGONISH, N.S., CANADA 1987– ; Chancellor and Chrmn. Bd. of Govs., St. Francis Xavier Univ., Antigonish; Mem. Candn. Conf. of Catholic Bishops; o. 1956; served in a number of Halifax parishes; Pastor, St. Thomas Aquinas Parish, Halifax; St. Anthony's Parish, Dartmouth and Immaculate Conception Parish, Truro; Dir. of Soc. Services, Archdiocese of Halifax; Vicar Gen. of that Diocese for 11 yrs.; Nat. Dir., Pontifical Mission Societies, English sector of Can., responsible for missionary animation and fund raising, reporting to the Congregation for the Propagation of the Faith in Rome 1983–87; has taught at Mount St. Vincent Univ., Holy Heart Semy., N.S. Teachers' Summer Sch., Maritime Sch. of Social Work at Dalhousie Univ.; former Pres. N.S. Assn. Social Workers; N.S. Family & Child Welfare Assn.; Inst. of Pastoral Training; N.S. Social Services Council; former Vice Pres., N.S. Div., Candn. Bible Soc.; Chrmn., Bd. of Govs., Saint Mary's Univ., Halifax 1977–83; has contributed to a no. of publications incl. 'The Catholic Register,' 'The Homiletic and Pastoral Review,' 'Pastoral Life' and has publ. 'Adventures of a Parish Priest' and 'One View,' the latter a coll. of his columns, written for 9 yrs., in the Halifax Chronicle-Herald and Halifax Mail-Star; columnist, Antigonish Casket, Halifax Chronicle-Herald and Halifax Mail-Star; rec'd the Centennial Medal 1967; awarded D.D. (honoris causa), Atlantic Sch. of Theology for outstanding work in Christian education and ecumenism 1983; Litt.D. (hon. causa), Saint Mary's Univ., Halifax for his work in popular writing and teaching about the Second Vatican Council, 1987.

**CAMPBELL, Colin Duncan Hunter,** B.Sc.A.; steel company executive; b. Hamilton, Ont. 9 May 1932; s. John Dundas Cumberland and Ina Margaret (Hunter) C.; e. Univ. of Toronto, B.Sc.A. 1955; 2nd m. Jean d. Alistair and Kay McColl 29 Sept. 1988; children: Robin, Tamara, Ian, Jamie, John, Susan, Annie; Vice-Pres., Operating Serv., Dofasco Inc. 1959–91, retired 1991; Demerara Bauxite Co., British Guiana (Alcan subs.) 1956–59; joined Dofasco Inc. as Project Engr. 1959, progressed through various jobs to present post; Mem., Am. Iron & Steel Inst. (Past Chrmn.); Assoc. of Iron & Steel Engrs.; Past Chrmn. & Hon. Bd. Mem., Bd. of Gov., Hillfield Strathallan Coll.; Bd. Mem., St. Peter's Hosp., Hamilton, Ont.; Bd. Mem., Skills Canada Inc.; Home: 8 Hilton St., Hamilton, Ont. L8P 3K2; Office: Box 2460, Hamilton, Ont. L8N 3J5.

**CAMPBELL, Colin Kydd,** B.Sc., S.M., Ph.D., D.Sc., F.R.S.C., F.I.E.E.E., F.E.I.C., F.R.S.A.; educator; b. St. Andrews, Fife, Scot. 3 May 1927; s. David and Jean (Hutchison) Campbell; e. Univ. of St. Andrews B.Sc. 1951, Hons. B.Sc. 1952, Ph.D. 1960; Mass. Inst. of Technol. S.M. 1953; Univ. of Dundee D.Sc. 1984; m. Vivian Gwyn, d. late Mr. and Mrs. Oliver G. Norval 17 Apr. 1954; children: Barry Norval, Gwyn Elizabeth, Ian Harris; EMERITUS PROF. OF ELECTRICAL & COMPUTER ENGINEERING, MCMASTER UNIVERSITY 1989– ; (Prof. 1979–89); Communications Engr., Foreign Office, London, Eng., British Delegation to UN, New York and Brit. Embassy, Washington, D.C. 1946–48; Electronics Design Engr. Atomic Instrument Co. Cambridge, Mass. 1954–57; Consulting Engr. A. Kusko Inc. Cambridge 1957; Asst. Prof. of Elect. Engn. present Univ. 1960, Assoc. Prof. 1963, Prof. 1967–79, Chrmn. Elect. Engn. Dept. 1965–69, Acting Chrmn. 1977, Chrmn. Operating Ctte. Inst. for Materials Rsch. 1967–68, Assoc. mem. Depts. Physics 1962–88, Engn. Physics 1968–89, Metall. & Materials Sci. 1972–89, mem. Senate 4 yrs.; recipient Caird Trust, Dundee, Scot. Travel Award 1951; Mass. Golf Scholarship, Royal & Ancient Golf Club, St. Andrews, Scot. 1952–53; Sr. Rsch. Fellowship Nat. Rsch. Counc. Can., Visiting Rsch. Prof. of Elect. Engn. Univ. of B.C. 1969–70; 'The Inventor' insignia Candn. Patents and Development Ltd. 1973; Citation Ont. Confedn. Univ. Faculty Assns. 1976; Certificates of Appreciation McMaster Univ. Student Union 1983, 1989; Thomas W. Eadie Medal Royal Soc. Can. 1983; mem. Brit. Rsch. Del. 1959 Meeting of Nobel Physics Prize Winners, Lindau, Bavaria 1959; Exchange Sci. Semiconductor Insts. Kiev and Vilnius under auspices Nat. Rsch. Counc. Can. and Acad. Sci.'s of USSR 1976; served with Royal Corps of Signals, Brit. Army active service 1944–46, Radio Communications Engr.; RCAF Primary Reserve, C.O. 201 Univ. Sqdn., rank Sqdn. Leader 1961–68; Candn. Militia, Hamilton Militia Dist., rank Maj. 1972–73; Fellow Inst. Elect. & Electronics Engrs.; Sigma Xi; Home: 160 Parkview Dr., Ancaster, Ont. L9G 1Z5.

**CAMPBELL, D. Ralph,** C.M., D.F.C. and Bar, M.A., LL.D., D.C.L., D.Sc., F.A.I.C., F.C.A.E.S.; professor emeritus; b. Foxboro, Ont. 14 Nov. 1918; s. Fred H. and Florence Pearl (Hollinger) C.; e. Univ. of Toronto, B.A. 1949; Oxford Univ., B.A. 1951, M.A. 1958; Rhodes Scholar 1949–51; m. late Muriel Joy, d. Leslie. S. and Irene Winch, 18 June 1949; children: Hugh Frederick, Catherine Anne, Elizabeth Mary; m. 2ndly, Ruth Marion, d. Wm. A. Heron, 11 Feb. 1977; commenced as Lectr., Dept. Agric. Econ., Ont. Agric. Coll. 1951 and Head of Dept. 1952–62; mem., Ont. Marketing Enquiry 1958–59; Econ. Advisor and Acting Dir. of Planning, Govt. of Jordan 1962–64; Prof. of Econ., Assoc. Dean, Faculty of Arts and Science, Univ. of Toronto 1964–68 (Chrmn., Discipline Comte. 1968–70); mem. Task Force on Agric., Govt. of Can. 1968–70; Econ. Advisor, Min. Finance and Planning, Govt. of Kenya 1970–72; Prof. of Econ., Univ. of Toronto and Principal, Scarborough Coll. 1972–76; First J.C. Snyder Lectr., Purdue Univ. 1974; Pres., Univ. of Manitoba 1976–81; Mem., Man. Health Sci's Bd. 1976–81; Comnr., Electoral Div. Boundaries, Prov. Man. 1978; Rockefeller Foundation Economic Advr., Office of Pres., Kenya 1981–84; Dir., IDO of Assoc. of Univ. and Coll. of Can. 1984–86; Mem. Counc., Univ. of Swaziland 1986–90; Mem., Internat. Adv. Ctte., Inter-American Inst. for Co-operation on Agriculture 1988–89; Member, Order of Canada; Hon. LL.D., Univ. of Guelph 1974, Univ. of Winnipeg 1977, Univ. of Manitoba 1984; Hon. D.C.L., St. Andrews College 1981; Hon. D.Sc., McGill Univ. 1980; Fellow, Agric. Inst. of Can.; Fellow, Can. Ag. Econ. Soc.; served in 2nd World War, R.C.A.F. Pilot, Flight-Lt.; awarded D.F.C. and Bar; co-author of 'Canadian Agriculture in the Seventies' 1970 and many articles in econ. and agric. econ. journs.; Agric. Inst. Can. (Pres. 1960); Candn. Agric. Econ. Soc. (Pres. 1959); recreation: woodwork restoration; Club: Guelph-Wellington; Home: 207 Dimson Ave., Guelph, Ont. N1G 3C7.

**CAMPBELL, David Aitken,** M.A., F.R.S.C.; educator; b. Killywhan, Scot. 14 Aug. 1927; s. Walter and Isabella Ferguson (Aitken) C.; e. Hamilton Acad. 1944; Glasgow Univ. M.A. 1948; Oxford Univ. B.A. 1953, M.A. 1967; m. Cynthia d. Frederick and Vera Dutton 23 Aug. 1956; children: Alison, Helen, Fiona; EMERITUS PROF. OF CLASSICS, UNIV. OF VICTORIA 1993– ; Asst. Lectr., Lectr., Sr. Lectr. Univ. of Bristol 1953–71; Visiting Asst. Prof. Univ. Coll. Univ. of Toronto 1959–60; Visiting Prof. Univ. of Texas at Austin 1969–70; Prof. of Classics, Univ. of Victoria 1971–93; Chrmn. of Classics 1972–77; author 'Greek Lyric Poetry' 1967, new ed. 1982; 'The Golden Lyre: The Themes of the Greek Lyric Poets' 1983; 'Greek Lyric' vol. 1 1982, vol. 2 1988, vol. 3 1991, vol. 4 1992, vol. 5 1993; contbr. 'The Cambridge History of Classical Literature' vol. 1 1985; mem. Am. Philol. Assn. (Ed. Bd. Monographs 1984–86); Classical Assn. Can. (Ed. Bd. 'Phoenix' 1977–79); Classical Assn. Pacific N.W. (Pres. 1975–76); Philol. Assn. Pacific Coast; Classical Assn. Candn. W. (Pres. 1986–87); Anglican; recreation: walking; Home: 6154 Patricia Bay Hwy., Victoria, B.C. V8Y 1T2.

**CAMPBELL, Dennis Bain,** C.A.; b. Vancouver, B.C. 18 Aug. 1939; s. Herbert Alexander and Joan Margarita (Finlayson) C.; e. Nepean High Sch. Ottawa 1959; C.A. 1964; m. Susan d. William and Marion Grahame 9 Aug. 1969; children: Katharine, Leslie; PARTNER, DELOITTE & TOUCHE 1989– ; C.A. John Cross & Partners Ottawa 1964–72; Mgr. Deloitte Haskins & Sells Ottawa 1972, Partner 1976–89; Chrmn. Children's Hosp. of E. Ont. Found. 1984–86, 1990–92; Club: Rideau; Home: 18 Roberta Cres., Nepean, Ont. K2J 1G6; Office: 1000, 90 Sparks St., Ottawa, Ont. K1P 5T8.

**CAMPBELL, Donald Fraser,** C.M., M.A., Ph.D.; educator; b. Sydney, N.S. 5 March 1925; s. Andrew Dominic Campbell and Pearl Bridget (Curry) C.; e. Sydney Acad. 1942; St. Francis Xavier Univ. B.A. 1945; Cath. Univ. of Am., Theol. Coll. o. Priest 1949, M.A. 1951, Ph.D. 1956; Univ. of London Inst. of Educ. 1951–52; PRESIDENT EMERITUS AND PROFESSOR EMERITUS OF PSYCHOLOGY AND EDUCATION, UNIV. COLL. OF CAPE BRETON 1993– ; Asst. Prof. of Educ., St. Francis Xavier Univ. 1949–56; Assoc. Prof. of Psychol. and Educ., St. Francis Xavier Univ. 1956–59, Prof. and Chrmn. of Psychol. and Educ., 1959–64, Dean of Arts 1961–64; Prof. of Psychology and Education, Univ. Coll. of Cape Breton 1974–93 (and Pres. 1974–83); Advisor, N.S. Dept. of Educ. 1956–64; Faculty, N.S. Summer Sch. for Teachers 1956–63; Mem., Teacher Certification Bd. of N.S. 1956–64; Pres., Antigonish Br.,

Candn. Mental Health Assoc. 1959–64; Pres., N.S. Div., Candn. Mental Health Assn. 1961–63; Chair, Conf. on Religious Education, Diocese of Antigonish 1957–63; Chrmn., Bd. of Dirs., St. Martha's Hosp., Antigonish 1963–64; Prof. of Psychol. and Educ. and Princ. of Xavier Coll., Sydney, N.S. 1964–74; Co-dir., Renewal Prog. for Priests, Diocese of Antigonish 1967–69; Pres., N.S. Miners Museum Found. 1969–70; Bd. Mem. Miners Museum Found. 1966– ; Founding Pres., Univ. Coll. of Cape Breton 1974–83; Mem., Bd. of Dirs.: Catholic Charities and Welfare Assoc., Sydney 1964–74; St. F.X. Univ. 1964–83; Art Gall. of N.S. 1977–79; Dir., Alexander Graham Bell Inst. 1977– ; Seacape Music Ltd. 1984– ; Cape Breton Regional Hosp. Foundation 1985–91; Founding Chairperson, Centre Bras d'Or 1985–88 (Bd. Mem. 1985– ;); Mem. Prov. Med. Bd. of N.S. 1988– ; Bd. Chrmn., Casket Printing and Publishing Co. 1988– ; Mem., N.S. Working Ctte. on the Constitution 1991– ; Chrmn., Joint Consultative Ctte., Cape Breton Regional Hosp. 1991– ; Chair, Alexander Graham Bell Institute of U.C.C.B. 1992– ; Registered Psychologist, N.S.; author 'Study of the Problem Solving Ability of Children' 1956; recipient Queen's Silver Jubilee Medal 1977; Member, Order of Canada 1987; Commemorative Medal, 125th Anniversary of Candn. Confedn.; mem. Candn. Psychol. Assn.; recreations: skiing, sailing, swimming; Home: 1706, 500 Kings Rd., Sydney, N.S. B1S 1B2.

**CAMPBELL, Donald G.,** F.C.A. (1973); communications executive; b. Toronto, Ont. 14 Aug. 1925; s. late James Lindsay and Margaret (Graham) C.; e. C.A. 1950; m. Audrey Irene d. late Garnet Percy Reid, 12 Aug. 1944; children: David, Reid, Marc, Scott; CHRMN., MACLEAN HUNTER LTD. 1976– ; Dir., CFCN Comm. Ltd.; Toronto-Dominion Bank; Canada Life Assurance Co.; joined Price Waterhouse 1945–50; Treas. Noma Lites Ltd. 1950–51; Secy.-Treas. Atomic Energy Can. Ltd. Chalk River 1952–57; joined present Co. 1957, Controller and Dir. 1958, Vice Pres. Finance 1960, Extve. Vice Pres. Broadcasting and Finance 1969, Pres. and Chief Extve. Offr. 1970, Chrmn. and Pres. 1976; served with RCAF 1942–45, rank Flying Offr.; Protestant; recreations: golf, skiing; Clubs: Toronto Golf; York; Home: 8 Mariners Haven, Box 4492, R.R. 3, Collingwood, Ont. L9Y 4T9

**CAMPBELL, Donald W.,** B.A.; federal civil servant; b. Drayton, Ont. 17 Dec. 1940; s. J. Wilfred and V. Isobel (Cherrey) C.; e. Waterloo Univ. Coll. B.A. 1964; AMBASSADOR TO JAPAN 1993– ; concurrently Comnr. Northern Pipeline Agency; Dir. Export Devel. Corp.; Trustee Nat. Film Bd. Can.; career foreign service assignments Ottawa, Seattle, Kingston (Jamaica), London (Eng.), Nairobi (Kenya) 1964–84; Ambassador to Repub. of Korea 1984–85; Asst. Dep. Min. USA Br.1985–89; Sr. Asst. Dep. Min. & Coord. Can. USA Free Trade Agreement 1989; Dep. Min. Internat. Trade and Assoc. Under-Sec. of State for External Affairs 1989–93; Office: c/o External Affairs, 125 Sussex Dr., Ottawa, Ont. K1A 0G2.

**CAMPBELL, Douglas Arthur,** B.B.Admin.; insurance executive; b. Truro, N.S. 5 April 1943; e. Univ. of N.B. B.B.Admin. 1973; m. Gail Giles; children: Denise, Andrew; PRES., ROYAL LePAGE MORTGAGE CO. and SR. VICE-PRES., MORTGAGES, LONDON LIFE INSURANCE CO. 1984– ; Branch Appraiser, Canada Mortgage & Housing Corp. 1966–75; Mgr., Property Investments, Standard Life Insur. Co. 1975–77; Vice-Pres., Underwriting, Insmor Mortgage Insur. Co. 1977–80; Mgr., Corp. Lending, Royal Bank of Canada 1980–84; Dir., Devan Properties Ltd.; International Care Corp. Ltd.; Mem., Appraisal Inst. of Canada; Accredited Appraiser, Canadian Inst.; Office: 255 Dufferin Ave., London, Ont. N6A 4K1.

**CAMPBELL, Douglas John,** B.Sc., Dip.Ed.; headmaster; b. Thetford Mines, Que. 16 Mar. 1947; s. Ian Cadogan and Emily Elizabeth (McNeill) C.; e. Bishop's Univ., B.Sc. 1967, Dip.Ed. 1970; m. Donna d. James and Fern Burrows 28 June 1969; children: Timothy, Robyn; BURSAR, ST. ANDREW'S COLLEGE; Teacher, Dir. of Admissions & Housemaster, Bishop's Coll. Sch. 1967–77; Headmaster, Rosseau Lake Sch. 1977–82; Dir. of Student Serv., Lakeland Coll. 1982–83; Headmaster, Shawnigan Lake School 1983–..; Pres., Independent Schools Assn. of B.C. 1986– ; Dir., Candn. Assn. of Independent Schools; recreations: sports, fishing, gardening; Office: 300 Yonge St. N., Aurora, Ont. L4G 3H7.

**CAMPBELL, Finley Alexander,** B.Sc., M.A., Ph.D., F.R.S.C.; geologist; educator; b. Kenora, Ont. 5 Jan. 1927; s. Finley McLeod and Vivian (Delve) C.; e. Kenora High Sch. 1944; Brandon Coll. Univ. of Man. B.Sc. 1950; Queen's Univ. M.A. 1956; Princeton Univ. Ph.D. 1958; m. Barbara Elizabeth d. late Dr. R. P. Cromarty, Brandon, Man. 17 Oct. 1953; children: Robert Finley, Glen David, Cheryl Ann; EMERITUS PROFESSOR OF GEOLOGY 1988– ; Dir. and Vice Chrmn. of Bd. Candn. Energy Research Inst.; Exploration and Mining Geol. 1950–58; Asst. Prof. of Geol. Univ. of Alta. 1958, Assoc. Prof. 1963–65; Prof. and Head of Geol., Univ. Calgary 1965, Vice Pres. Capital Resources 1969, Acad. Vice Pres. 1971–76, Prof. of Geol. 1976–84; Vice Pres. Priorities and Planning 1984–88; Queen's Silver Jubilee Medal; author over 40 articles geol. topics relating to econ. geol. and mineral deposits; Vice Chrmn. and Dir., Candn. Energy Rsch. Inst.; Minister's Adv. Ctte., Tyrrell Museum of Palaeontology; Councillor, Assn. of Prof. Engrs., Geologists & Geophysicists; mem. Geol. Assn. Can.; Candn. Soc. of Petroleum Geol.; Candn. Inst. of Mining and Metallurgy; Mineral. Assn. Can.; Soc. Econ. Geol.; Mineral. Soc. Am.; Fellow, Royal Soc. of Canada (Academy of Science); P. Conservative; Presbyterian; recreations: sailing, skiing, golf, music, photography; Clubs: Glenmore Yacht; Silver Springs Golf; Clearwater Bay Yacht; Home: 3408 Benton Dr. N.W., Calgary, Alta. T2L 1W8; Office: Dept. of Geology & Geophysics, Univ. of Calgary, 2500 Univ. Dr. N.W., Calgary, Alta. T2N 1N4.

**CAMPBELL, Florence Margaret,** B.A.; research institute executive; b. Calgary, Alta. 1 Mar. 1937; d. Fred and Gladys Margaret (Barker) C.; e. Univ. of Alta., B.A. 1957; VICE PRINCIPAL (ADVANCEMENT), QUEEN'S UNIV. 1993– ; var. positions incl. edn., mktg., mngt., Extve. Asst. to Pres., and short-term internat. assignments, IBM Can. Ltd. 1965–79; Vice-Pres. & Dir., National Business and Education Centre, The Conference Board of Canada 1979–93; Mem. of Adv. Bd., Ottawa Heart Inst.; Mem. of Bd., Ottawa-Carleton Learning Foundation; Mem. Bd. of Govs., Carleton Univ.; recreations: golf, skiing; Clubs: Rideau; Ottawa Hunt & Golf; Home: #12 - 55 Whitemarl Dr., Rockcliffe, Ont. K1L 8J9; Office; Kingston, Ont. K7L 3N6.

**CAMPBELL, Frederick K.,** B.Comm.; business executive; b. Edmonton, Alta. 1 Oct. 1937; s. Gordon Wray and Helen Marie (Conroy) C.; e. Univ. of Alta. B.Com. 1961; children: Shaunna, Tani; PRES., CAMPCO INTERNATIONAL CAPITAL LTD. 1980– ; Chrmn., Bd. of Dirs., Coho Resources Ltd., Calgary; Campco Ventures Ltd.; Zedcam Investors Ltd.; Shauntan Holdings Ltd.; Past Chrmn. Citadel Theatre, Gov. Bd. Dirs.; Home: Penthouse 2, 8220 Jasper Ave., Edmonton, Alta. T5H 4B6; Office: Ste. 402, 10357 – 109 St., Edmonton, Alta. T5J 1N3.

**CAMPBELL, George Thomas,** B.A., LL.B.; association executive; b. Montreal, Que. 3 Apl. 1920; e. Victoria Coll. 1945–47; Univ. of B.C., B.A. 1949, LL.B. 1953; m. Marguerite d. Ernest and Freda Parkinson 17 Oct. 1969; children: Alix, Kim; Pres., Army, Navy & Air Force Veterans in Can. 1988–90; served with Candn. Army during WWII, Can., UK, Eur., wounded in Italy 1944; law practice Vancouver 1953–66; joined Office of City Prosecutor Vancouver 1966–85 (absorbed by Provl. Min. of Atty. Gen. 1974); served in tutorial prog. law students B.C. Law Soc.; joined present Assn. 1953; active services for srs. and mem. several bds.; Clubs: Vancouver Lawn Tennis & Badminton; Arbutus; Home: 3005 West 28th Ave., Vancouver, B.C. V6L 1X4.

**CAMPBELL, Henry Cummings,** B.L.S., M.A.; librarian; b. Vancouver, B.C. 22 Apr. 1919; s. Henry and Margaret Kennedy (Cummings) C.; e. Univ. of British Columbia, B.A. 1940; Univ. of Toronto, B.L.S. 1941; Columbia Univ., M.A. (Adult Educ.) 1948; m. Sylvia Frances, d. Harold F. Woodsworth; children: Shiela Margaret, Bonnie Kathleen, Robin Woodsworth; GENERAL MGR. ESPIAL PRODUCTIONS LTD. TORONTO; Librarian, National Film Bd. of Can., 1941–43; Head, Foreign Productions there, 1943–46; Research Assoc., Inst. of Adult Educ., Teachers Coll., N.Y., 1946–48; Librarian and Archivist, United Nations, N.Y., 1948–49; Head, Bibliographical and Research Library Development, UNESCO, Paris, France, 1949–51; Head, UNESCO Clearing House for Libraries, Paris, France, 1951–56; Chief Librarian, Toronto Public Libraries, 1956–78; Pres., Federation of Canada-China Friendship Associations, Toronto 1985–88; publications: 'CINFOLINK: Directory of Information Services in China' Toronto 1993; United Church; Home: 85 Roe Ave., Toronto, Ont. M5M 2H6.

**CAMPBELL, Ian Lachlan,** B.A., M.Sc. (Econ.), F.R.S.A., F.H.S.C., F.S.A. (Scot.), F.A.C.H., C.L.J., N.N.; college principal, retired; b. Ottawa, Ont. 3 Nov. 1927; s. Dr. George. A. and Hazel (Jeffrey) C.; e. Trinity Coll. Sch., Port Hope, Ont., 1941–42; Lisgar Coll. Inst., Ottawa, 1942–46; Carleton Coll., B.A. 1951; London Sch. of Econ. and Pol. Science, M.Sc. (Econ.) and Univ. of London 1953; m. Marion Isobel d. William Wellwood, 14 July 1950; children: Heather, Diarmid, Colin, Mora; PROF. EMERITUS OF POL. SCI. AND SOCIOL. RENISON COLL., UNIV. OF WATERLOO 1992– ; (Principal and Vice-Chancellor, Renison Coll. 1977–92); Asst. Prof. of Pol. Science and Sociol., Mount Allison Univ. 1954–56; Asst. Prof. of Sociol. 1956–65; Dir. of Extension and Dir. of Pub. Relations 1963–65; Dean, Faculty of Arts and Prof. of Pol. Science and Sociol., Bishop's Univ. 1965–69; Acting Head, Dept. of Sociol. 1967–69; Dean, Sir George Williams Faculty of Arts, Concordia Univ. 1969–74; Prof. of Sociol. Sir George Williams Univ. 1972–76; Prof. of Poli. Sci., Sir George Williams 1976–77; Dean, Faculty of Arts, Sir George Williams, Concordia Univ.; Prof. of Poli. Sci. and Sociol. 1977–92; held various civic and educ. positions incl. Ald. 1958–59 and Mayor 1962, Sackville, N.B.; Pres., Bd. Trade Sackville 1961; First Pres., Atlantic Provs. Corrections Assn. 1963; mem. Acad. Council, Maritime Sch. of Social Work 1961–65; Gov., Dom. Drama Festival 1964–65; mem. ad hoc Comte. on Govt. Grants to Que. Univs. 1965–68; Chrmn., Sherbrooke Regional C.E.G.E.P. Planning Comte. 1968–69; mem. panel of Consultants to Candn. Comte. on Corrections 1966–69; Commr., Govt. of Can. Comn. of Inquiry into Non-Med. Use of Drugs 1969; Pres., Cdn. Assn. of Deans of Arts and Sci.; Gov., Univ. of Waterloo 1978–82; Pres. Heraldry Soc. of Can. 1990–92; Fellow, Royal Soc. of Arts; Fellow, Heraldry Soc. of Can.; Fellow, Am. Coll. of Heraldry; Companion, Company of Armigers (Australia); mem., Heraldry Socs. of Scotland, England, Ireland, Can., N. Zealand, and Southern Africa; Fellow, Soc. of Antiquaries, Scotland; A/Capt., 78th Fraser Highlanders; rec'd Henry Marshall Tory Award, Carleton Coll., 1951; author of publs. in heraldry sociol. field; Tory; Anglican; Home: Richmond Square 2, 1907 – 300 Regina St. N. Waterloo, Ont. N2J 4H2; Office: Renison College, Westmount Blvd., Waterloo, Ont. N2L 3G4.

**CAMPBELL, J. Brian,** B.A., B.Sc., M.A., P.Eng.; executive; b. Winnipeg, Man. 2 June 1937; s. late Hugh A. and late Marion B. (Levins) C.; e. Univ. of Man. 1954–58; Letourneau Univ., Texas B.Sc. (Indust. Engn.) 1960; Banff Sch. Advanced Mang. 1966; Brock Univ. B.A. (Hons.) Psychology 1992; Liberty Univ. M.A. (Counselling Psychology) 1994; m. Carole Marion; d. late Harry H. Pielou 24 June 1961; children: Grant I., Lynne E.; CHRMN. & PRES., J.B.C. MANAGEMENT RESOURCES LTD. 1980– ; Analyst and Mgr. Indust. Engn. Manitoba Rolling Mills (Div. Dominion Bridge Co.) 1960, Mgr. Mfg. Services 1968–74; Extve. Vice Pres. and Gen. Mgr., Candn. Bronze Co. Ltd. 1974–76, Pres. and Dir. 1976–78; Pres., Dir. & Gen. Mgr., Cae-Montupet Diecast Ltd. 1978–80; Pres. and Dir., Amcan Castings Ltd. 1983–85; Dir., Candn. Diecasters Assn. 1983–85; Ont. Center for Automotive Parts Technology 1985–89; served with RCAF Reserve 1954; Chrmn. Jt. Use Parks Comte. Transcona, Man.; Sr. mem. Am. Inst. Indust. Engn.; Chrmn., Candn. C.W.S. Group; Vice Chrmn. Materials Comte. and Adv. mem. Man. Research Council; mem. Bd. Examiners Assn. Prof. Engrs. Prov. Man.; P. Conservative; Protestant; recreations; golf; tennis, squash, camping; Address: 4 Camelot Court, St. Catharines, Ont. L2T 3R3.

**CAMPBELL, John James Ramsay,** Ph.D., F.R.S.C. (1961); professor emeritus; b. Vancouver, B.C. 29 Mar. 1918; s. Murdoch and Margaret C.; e. Univ. of B.C., B.S.A. 1939; Cornell Univ., Ph.D. 1944; m. Emily Ann Fraser, 4 Sept. 1942; four children: PROF. EMERITUS OF MICROBIOLOGY, UNIV. OF BRITISH COLUMBIA; with Science Service, Central Exper. Farm (Grad. Asst. in Bacteriol.) 1939–40; Dept. of Nat. Defence, Research Worker, 1944–46; Prof. of Dairying UBC, 1946–65; Head, Dept. Micro biology, UBC, 1965–82; Fellow, Am. Assn. for the Advance of Science; mem., Soc. of Am. Bacteriol.; Candn. Soc. Microbiol.; rec'd Harrison Prize of Royal Soc. Can. 1969; Sigma Tau Upsilon; Gamma Alpha; Sigma Xi; Phi Kappa Phi; Protestant; Home: 3949 West 37th Ave., Vancouver, B.C. V6N 2W4.

**CAMPBELL, Rt. Hon. Kim,** see **CAMPBELL, Rt. Hon. A. Kim**.

**CAMPBELL, Michael Gordon,** B.Sc.; business executive; b. Chatham, Ont. 8 Feb. 1947; s. Robert Sutherland and Eileen Mary (Hammett) C.; e. Queen's Univ., B.Sc.(Eng.) 1971; m. Carolyn d. Robert and Caroline Mainguy 29 May 1971; children: Julia, Jeffrey, Allison; PRES., FELLOWES MANUFACTURING OF CANADA LTD. 1989– ; joined Kodak Canada Ltd. 1971; Eastern Sales Mgr., Graphic Markets Div. 1977–80; Western Sales Mgr., Consumer Prod. Div. 1980–82;

Central Sales Mgr., same div. 1982–84; Vice-Pres. Sales, present firm 1984–86; Vice Pres., Office Prod. Div. 1986–87; Extve. Vice-Pres. & Gen. Mgr. 1987–89; Pres., Candn. Office Prod. Assn.; recreations: golf, skiing; Home: 89 Cook Dr., R.R. #2, Kettleby, Ont. L0G 1J0; Office: 2750 John St., Markham, Ont. L3R 2W4.

**CAMPBELL, Mona L.,** LL.D.; executive; b. Toronto, Ont. 3 Feb. 1919; d. Frederick Keenan and Edna Lillian (Mann) Morrow; e. Toronto, Ottawa, London; m. Kenneth s. Colin Alexander and Nell (Cline) C. 14 Aug. 1967; children: John Morrow, Sarah Alexandra (Band), Mary Victoria (Macrae); PRESIDENT AND DIRECTOR, DOVER INDUSTRIES LTD. 1954– ; Pres. and Dir., Movisa Securities Ltd.; Dir., Churad Properties Ltd.; National Sea Products Ltd.; Canada Development Investment Corp.; Chrmn., Bd. of Trustees, Univ. of Guelph Heritage Investment Mgmnt. Fund; Gov., Dalhousie Coll. and Univ.; Life Mem., Toronto Gen. Hosp. Auxiliary; Metro. Toronto Zoo; Founder, Royal Ont. Museum; Hon. Dir., National Ballet Sch., Toronto; Anglican; Conservative; Clubs: Rosedale Golf; Osler Bluffs Ski; The Queen's; Home: 30 Glen Edyth Place, Toronto, Ont. M4V 2W2; Office: 96 Avenue Rd., Toronto, Ont. M5R 2H3.

**CAMPBELL, Paul Finkle,** B.Sc., P.Eng., C.A.; tax specialist; b. Belleville, Ont. 4 Aug. 1941; s. Arnold Clinton and Nellie Aileen (Finkle) C.; e. Quinte S.S. 1961; Queen's Univ. B.Sc. 1965; m. Lorraine d. Burton and Elsie Cooksley 14 Feb. 1983; children: Caroline, David; HALIFAX OFFICE DIRECTOR OF TAX, ERNST & YOUNG 1990– ; obtaining C.A., Clarkson Gordon 1965–69; Consultant, Woods Gordon 1969–71; Tax Specialist, Clarkson Gordon 1972–75; Tax Partner (Halifax office, resp. for tax practice in N.S.) 1976–86; Halifax Office Managing Partner, Ernst & Young 1986–90; Bd. of Trustees, Queen's Univ.; Trustee, Halifax Metro. YMCA; N.S. Voluntary Planning; Bd. of Managers, Bethany Un. Ch.; Mem., Inst. of C.A.s (N.S., P.E.I., N.B., Ont.); Assn. of Professional Engrs. (N.S. & Ont.); co-author of a chapter, 'Income Taxation in Canada'; recreations: sailing, nordic skiing; clubs: Halifax, Royal N.S. Yacht (Past Vice Commodore); Home: 19 Downs Ave., Halifax, N.S. B3N 2Z1; Office: 13th floor, 1959 Upper Water St., Halifax, N.S. B3J 3N2.

**CAMPBELL, Peter A.T.,** B.A., M.A., Ph.D.; consultant; b. Toronto, Ont. 19 Aug. 1936; s. Thomas Lorne and Margaret Glover (Williams) C.; e. Lawrence Park Coll. Inst., Toronto 1955; Univ. of Toronto, B.A. (Pol. Economy) 1959, M.A. (Economics) 1960; London School of Economics, Ph.D. (Economics) 1963; m. Patricia Anne d. Sam and Sally Ferguson 9 Sept. 1960; children: Nicole, Maryse, Chantal, Simon; PRINCIPAL, PETER CAMPBELL & ASSOCIATES INC.; Co-Managing Partner, Barber Green Realty Group; Financial Columnist, Toronto Sunday Star 1991– ; Editor M & A, Mergers & Acquisitions in Canada 1992– ; Special Lectr., Fac. of Admin. Studies, York Univ. 1991– ; NRC, Communication Div. 1959; Bank of Can., Rsch. Dept., Ottawa 1960–61; various positions with Wood Gundy Inc. 1961–1985 most recent incl. Dir. 1971–85; Mem., Extve. Ctte. 1976–85; Head, Bus. Devel. Unit, Corp. Fin. 1977–81; Head, Real Estate Div. & Chrmn., Canmort Cons. Limited 1979–81; Head, Fixed Income function incl. Money Market, fgn. exchange, etc. 1981–83; Pres. & Chief Extve. Offr., Wood Gundy Holdings, New York 1983–85; Chrmn., Midland Doherty Limited 1986–87; Pres. & C.E.O., Midland Doherty Limited 1987–89; Spec. Lectr., York Univ. 1963–73; Univ. of Toronto 1969–74; Univ. of Guelph 1990; Campaign Advr. on Monetary Affairs to R.L. Stanfield 1968 election campaign; active mem., Humber Valley Hockey Assn. (minor league hockey) 1981–83; Contributing Editor, Financial Post 1989 and Financial Times 1991; recreations: family, friends; Clubs: Toronto Club; Cedar Springs (Burlington); Homes: 160 Frederick St., Suite 901, Toronto, Ont. M5A 4H9 and Box #8, R.R. #3, Campbellville, Ont. L0P 1B0.

**CAMPBELL, Robert Malcolm,** B.A., M.A., Ph.D.; university professor; b. Montreal, Que. 12 Sept. 1950; s. Dougald Emmanuel and Claire Berthe (Williamson) C.; e. Loyola Coll. H.S. 1967; Trent Univ. B.A. 1974; Univ. of Toronto M.A. 1976; London Sch. of Econ. Ph.D. 1980; m. Christl d. Francis and Stonny Verduyn 10 Oct 1981; children: Malcolm Adair, Lachlan Schuyler, Colin Remy, Frances Marika; PROF., DEPT. OF POL. STUDIES, TRENT UNIV. 1992– ; Staff mem., Dept. of Pol. Studies, Trent Univ. 1980–83, 1984– ; Assoc. Prof. 1986–92; Chrmn. 1985–90, 1993– ; Admin., Trent Internat. Prog. 1983–85; Acad. Advr. 1985–90; Ed. Bd. 'Journal of Canadian Studies' 1986– ; Assoc. Ed. 1987–88, 1993–94; Co-Editor 1988–90; Cons., Econ. Counc. of Can. 1988–89; SSHRC fellowships: doctoral 1977–80; post-doct. 1983–84; Mem., Candn. Pol. Sci. Assn.; Can. Ctr. for Policy Alternatives; author: 'Grand Illusions: The Politics of the Keynesian Experience in Canada, 1945–1975' 1987; 'The Full Employment Objective in Canada 1945–85' 1991; 'The Politics of the Post: The Canadian Post Office From Public Service to Privatization, 1867–1993' 1994; an afterword in 'Business Cycles in Canada' 1984, various articles in sch. jours. and book chapters; co-author: 'The Real Worlds of Canadian Politics' 1989, 2nd ed. 1991, 3rd ed. 1994; Home: 749 Bethune St., Peterborough, Ont. K9H 4A5; Office: Peterborough, Ont. K9J 7B8.

**CAMPBELL, Robert W.;** b. Valentine, Nebraska 22 Oct. 1922; s. Harry Lee and Margaret (Haley) C.; Dir., Haliburton Co.; Ranger Oil Ltd.; served in 2nd World War, Capt., 101st Airborne Div., U.S. Army; served in Europe; Roman Catholic; Home: 3819 – 10th St. S.W., Calgary, Alta. T2T 3J2; Office: 2800, 150 – 9th Ave. S.W., Calgary, Alta. T2P 3H9.

**CAMPBELL, Robert Wayne,** B.Sc., M.Sc., RPBio., O.B.C.; research scientist; b. Edmonton, Alta. 1 Oct. 1941; s. Robert Lincoln and Mildred Winnifred (Fouts) C.; e. Univ. of Victoria B.Sc. 1976; Univ. of Washington M.Sc. 1983; m. Eileen d. Emma and Jim McCammon 26 June 1969; children: David Sean, Tessa Nicole; RESEARCH SCIENTIST, WILDLIFE BR., MIN. OF ENVIRONMENT 1992– ; Interpretive Naturalist, B.C. Parks Branch 1964–69; Curator, Vertebrate Mus., Univ. of B.C. 1969–72; Curator, Ornithology, Royal B.C. Museum 1973–92; extve. positions held in B.C. Waterfowl Soc., Pacific N.W. Bird & Mammal Soc., Vanc. Nat. Hist. Soc., Western Bird-banding Assn., B.C. Fed. of Naturalists; elected Fellow Mem., Am. Ornithologists Union; Excellence in Biology award from Assoc. Prof. Biologists, B.C.; apptd. to Order of B.C. 1992; awarded Commemorative Medal for 125th Anniversary of Candn. Confederation 1993; mem., 24 profl. & amateur assns.; author of 340 sci. & popular reports, books & papers; major works incl. a 4–vol. ref. set: 'The Birds of British Columbia'; editor/reviewer for 23 profl. orgns.; recreations: soccer; club: Bays United Youth Soccer Assn.; Home: 2511 Kilgary Pl., Victoria, B.C. V8N 1J6; Office: Victoria, B.C. V8V 1X5.

**CAMPBELL, Robin Bruce,** B.P.H.E., M.S.; physical educator; b. Calgary, Alta. 4 July 1944; s. David Livingstone and Nina (Gude) C.; e. York Mills C.I. 1963; Univ. of Toronto, Sch. of Phys. & Health Edn., B.P.H.E. 1968; Indiana Univ. M.S. (Hons.) 1972; Candn. Hosp. Assoc., H.S.M. Diploma 1991; children: Jennifer, Alison; ADMINISTRATIVE DIR., TORONTO REHAB. CTR. 1991– ; Asst. Prof., Univ. of Toronto, Sch. of Phys. & Health Edn. 1976– ; Secy., Marina Lodge; Secy. to Bd. of Dirs., Toronto Rehabilitation Centre; Pres., R. Tait McKenzie Soc., Univ. of Toronto; Treas., Candn. Assoc. of Cardiac Rehabilitation; Counc. Mem., Univ. of Toronto, Sch. of Phys. & Health Edn.; Extve. Mem., Candn. Coll. of Health Service Extves.; Mem., Olympic Club of Can.; Co-ordinator, Dept. of Athletics & Recreation, Univ. of Toronto 1968–80; Gen. Mgr., Candn. Olympic Swimming Team 1980; Programme Co-ordinator, Cardiac Dept., Toronto Rehabilitation Ctr. 1981–91; recreations: jogging, swimming, skiing; Home: 35 Ames Circle, Don Mills, Ont. M3B 3B9; Office: 347 Rumsey Rd., Toronto, Ont. M4G 1R7.

**CAMPBELL, Ross,** D.S.C., B.A.; former diplomat; b. Toronto, Ont. Nov. 4 1918; s. late Helen Isabel (Harris) and William Marshall C.; e. Univ. of Toronto Schs.; Univ. of Toronto (Trinity Coll.), Faculty of Law, B.A., 1940; m. Penelope d. late Dr. Clermont Grantham-Hill, M.B.E., 6 June 1945; two children; PARTNER, INTERCON CONSULTANTS 1983– ; Dir. and Chrmn., UXB Canada (1991) Ltd.; Dir., ADOPAC Ltd.; began career Legal Div., Dept. of External Affairs 1945; Third Secy., Candn. Legation, Oslo, 1946–47; Second Secy., Copenhagen, 1947–50; European Div. Dept. of Ex. Affairs, Ottawa, 1950–52; First Secy., Candn. Embassy, Ankara, 1952–56; Head, Middle East Div., 1957–59; Special Asst. to Secy. of State for External Affairs 1959–62; Asst. Under Secy. of State for External Affairs, 1962–64; Adv., Candn. Dels. to U.N. Gen. Assemblies and Candn. Ministerial Dels. to N. Atlantic Council, 1958–64; Candn. Ambassador to Yugoslavia, 1964–67 (concurrently), Algeria 1965–67; Ambassador and Perm. Rep. to NATO (Paris May 1967, Brussels Oct. 1967–1972); Ambassador to Japan, 1972–75; (concurrently) to Rep. of Korea 1973–74; Chairman, Atomic Energy of Canada Ltd., Jan. 1976–May, 1979; Pres., Atomic Energy of Can. Internat'l, 1979; Nuclear Consultant 1980–81; Pres., Canus Technical Services 1981–83; served with R.C.N. 1940–45; awarded D.S.C. 1944; promoted to Lt. Commdr., R.C.N.(R.) (retired), 1949; mem. Naval Offrs. Assn. Can.; Delta Kappa Epsilon; Anglican Church; recreation: gardening; Home: Rivermead House, 890 Aylmer Rd., Aylmer, Que. J9H 5T8; Office: Suite 1003, 275 Slater St., Ottawa, Ont. K1P 5H9.

**CAMPBELL, Thomas,** B.A.(Sc.); b. 28 July 1934; s. Thomas Edward and Elizabeth (O'brien) C.; e. Royal Roads Mil. Coll. 1955; m.; 2 children; PARTNER, MOGFORD CAMPBELL ASSOCIATES INC.; Trustee, Health Care & Biotechnology Venture Fund; Assoc. Sec. of Cabinet 1971–76; Depy. Min. of Northern Affairs 1977–79; Depy. Min. of Health 1979–81; Depy. Treas. of Ont. and Depy. Min. of Econ. 1981–84; Chrmn. & C.E.O., Ontario Hydro 1984–88; Vice-Chrmn., World Energy Congress 1988–89; Address: 43 Sunnydale Dr., Toronto, Ont. M8Y 2J4.

**CAMPBELL, Thomas Sebastian,** B.A.; visual artist; b. London, England 24 Aug. 1951; s. Douglas and Ann (Casson) C.; e. West High, Minneapolis 1969; Camberwell Sch. of Arts & Crafts (U.K.) 1974; one s.: Lewis Liam; Master of Props, Belgrade Theatre England 1976; Theatre Set Painter for various theatres in England 1977–82; solo exhibitions: Contact Gall. Manchester 1976; Gall. Stratford 1986; Bau-Xi Gall. Toronto 1985, '86, '88, '89, '90, '92. '93, Vancouver 1991; group exhibitions: Camden Arts Ctr. London (England) 1970; South London Gall. 1974; Royal Festival Hall 1981, '82; Kitchener-Waterloo Art Gall. 1984; Bau-Xi Gall. Toronto 1988, '89; Instr., Life Drawing, Sheridan Coll. 1989–91; Painting & Drawing, Toronto Sch. of Art 1988–92; Art Forms Prize, Kitchener-Waterloo Art Gall. 1985; collections: Canada Counc. Art Bank (Ottawa); Davies Ward and Beck, Dupont Inc, Cambridge Mngt. Planning, Superior Propane, Imperial Oil (Toronto); Etobicoke Bd. of Edn.; First City (Vanc.); London Reg. Art Gall. & Art Gall. of Ontario (rental collections); private collections in Canada, U.S. & Eur.; gallery artist, Bau-Xi Gall. Toronto; Home: 53 Brunswick Ave., Toronto, Ont. M5S 2L8; Studio: 241 Dovercourt Rd., Apt. F, Toronto, Ont. M6J 3C9.

**CAMPBELL, Virginia A.,** M.Sc., Ph.D.; retired educator; b. Saint John N.B. 12 Aug. 1930; d. J. Packard and Mary Gertrude (Kierstead) C.; e. Fairville (N.B.) Superior Sch., 1944; Saint John (N.B.) High Sch., 1947; Acadia Univ., B.Sc. 1951; Pa. State Univ., M.Sc. 1959, Ph.D. 1963; Prof. of Foods & Nutrition, Acadia Univ. since 1971 (Dean 1971–82), Retired; Internship Harper Hosp., Detroit 1951; Dietitian, Hartford (Conn.) Hosp. 1952–56; Research Asst., Univ. of Pittsburgh, 1959; Instr., Pa. State Univ., 1962; Asst. Prof. in Pediatrics & Nutrition, Sch. of Medicine, Univ. of Wash., 1963; Chief Nutrition Div., Child Devel. Mental Retardation Centre 1965–71; author of various articles in prof. journs.; mem. Profl. Health Workers Sec., Candn. Diabetes Assn.; mem. Extve. and Gov. Acadia Univ. 1979–82; mem., Candn. Dietetic Assn.; N.S. Dietetic Assn.; N.S. Nutrition Council; Candn. Diabetes Assn.; Omicron Nu; Sigma Delta Epsilon; Candn. Dietetic Assn. Merit Award 1982; N.S. Dietetic Assn. Merit Award 1986; recreations: fishing, golf, curling, cycling, carpentry, painting; Home: 1033 Old Farm Lane, New Minas, N.S. B4N 4L5.

**CAMPBELL, William Clarke,** B.A.; lawyer; b. Haileybury, Ont. 3 Dec. 1918; e. Haileybury, (Ont.) High Sch.; Victoria Coll., Univ. of Toronto, B.A.; m. Kathleen Joan Jenkins, 3 July 1943; children: William Clarke, Bryan James, Kathleen Joan; HOLDEN DAY WILSON; read law with Thomas J. Day; served with R.C.N.V.R. 1943–45; Bailli Delegue du Canada, d'Honneur Confrerie de la Chaine des Rotisseurs; Clubs: Ontario Club; Eglinton Hunt; Royal Candn. Mil. Inst.; Home: Coventry Farm, Box 362, Bolton, Ont. L7E 5T3; Office: Suite 2400, Toronto-Dominion Bank Tower, Toronto, Ont. M5K 1E7.

**CAMPEAU, Jean;** financial executive; b. Montréal, Qué. 6 July 1931; e. Sainte-Marie, Saint-Ignace Coll., B.A. 1952; École des Hautes Études Comm., B.Comm. 1955; CHRMN., BANK NATIONALE DE PARIS (CANADA); Investment broker 1955–63; manufacturing executive 1963–71; Chrmn., Domtar Inc. 1990–..; Head, Gestion de la dette pub., min. des Fin. du Qué.; Asst. Dep. Min., Fin. 1977; Chrmn. & Gen. Mgr., Caisse de Dépôt et Placement du Québec 1980–90; Office: 1981 McGill College Ave., Montréal, Qué. H3A 2W8.

**CAMPEAU, Lucien,** M.ès A.; prêtre jésuite; éducateur; né Waterville, Maine 15 juillet 1914; f. Aimé et Marie-Anne (Bureau) C.; é. Courcelles, Qué. et Séminaire du Sacré-Coeur, St-Victor, Beauce, Qué.; Univ. Laval B.ès A. 1936; Univ. de Montréal M.ès A. 1940; Immaculée-Conception, Montréal licence en philosophie 1942, licence en théologie 1949; Univ. Grégorienne licence en Histoire ecclésiastique 1956, doctorat en Histoire ecclésiastique 1967; PROFESSEUR EMERITE D'HISTOIRE, UNIV. DE MONTREAL 1980; entré chez les Jésuites 1936; prof. de Théologie de l'Immaculée-Conception, Montréal 1951; Professeur d'Hist., Univ. de Montreal 1968–80; membre de l'Institutum Historicum Societatis Iesu, Rome; l'Institut d'Histoire de L'Amérique française; la Société Royale du Can.; Comité des Fondateurs de l'Eglise du Can.; Société des Dix; Académie des Sciences morales et politiques; éditeur des 'Monumenta Novae Franciae "I" La première mission d'Acadie (1602–1616)' 1967, II 'Etablissement à Québec (1616–1634)' 1979; III 'Fondation de la Mission huronne (1635–1637)' 1987; IV 'Les grandes épreuves (1638–1640)' 1989; V 'La bonne nouvelle reçue (1641–43)' 1990; 'VI 'Recherche de la paix (1644–1646)' 1992; auteur 'La première mission des Jésuites en Nouvelle-France (1611–1613) et Les commencements du Collège de Québec (1626–1670)' 1972; 'Les Cent-Associés et le peuplement de la Nouvelle-France' 1974; 'L'Evêché de Québec (1674): Aux origines du premier diocèse érigé en Amérique française' 1974; 'Les Finances publiques de la Nouvelle-France sous les Cent-Associés 1632–1665' 1975; contrib. 'Sacrae Congregationis de Propaganda Fide Memoria Rerum: 350 ans au service des missions 1622–1972' Vol. 1/2 1972; 'L'Hôtel-Dieu de Montréal 1642–1973' 1973; 'La Mission des Jésuites chez les Hurons (1634–1650)' 1986; 'Catastrophe Demographique sur les Grands Lacs 1986; plusieurs articles sur l'histoire de l'Eglise et l'histoire de la Nouvelle-France; catholique; Adresse: Maison des Jésuites, CP 130, 175 boul. des Hauteurs, St-Jérôme, Qué. J7Z 5T8.

**CAMPNEY, Alan Farnsworth,** B.Com., LL.B.; Barrister and Solicitor; b. Ottawa, Ont. 8 Oct. 1928; s. Hon. Ralph Osborne and Vera Wilhelmina (Farnsworth) C.; e. Queens Univ. B. Com. 1951; Univ. of B.C. LL.B. 1954; m. Barbara, d. Walter and Doris Irving 24 June 1954; children: Gillian; Corinne; Charlene; PRESIDENT, VANLEY AGENCIES LTD.; Chrmn., Eurotech Building Products Inc.; Primary Equities Capital Corp.; Credit Systems International Inc.; Dion Entertainment Corp.; Dir. P.W.A. Corp.; Marathon Realty Co. Ltd.; Marathon Realty Holdings Inc.; Petrodyne Inc.; International Nesmont Industrial Corp.; Gratiam Resources Inc.; Graffoto Industries Corp.; read law with Campney & Murphy 1952–53 and 1954; called to the Bar of B.C. 1955; additional training in London, England; returned to Campney and Murphy 1956–1984; Past Chrmn., Jr. Achievement of B.C.; Gov., Vancouver Bd. of Trade (past Pres.); Hon. Vice Pres., Canada Japan Soc. (past Pres.); Hon. Dir. Western Transportation Advisory Counc.; Founding & Immediate Past Chrmn. Fraser Inst.; Gov., Building Owners & Mgrs. Assn.; mem., Pacific Basin Economic Counc.; B.C. Bar Assoc.; Candn. Bar Assoc.; recreations: gardening; swimming; reading; cooking; travelling; Clubs: Vancouver; Vancouver Bd. of Trade; Home: 1975 Hosmer Ave., Vancouver, B.C. V6J 2S7.

**CAMU, Pierre,** O.C. (1976), Ph.D., L.Litt., F.R.S.C. (1966); transport executive; b. Montreal, Que. 19 Mar. 1923; s. Pierre and Jeanne (Duval) C.; e. Montreal Univ., M.A. 1947, Ph.D. (Geography) 1951, L.Litt. 1947; Post-grad. studies at Johns Hopkins Univ., 1947–49; Dr. of Geog. (hon. causa) Ottawa Univ. 1968; LL.D. (hon. causa) Univ. of Windsor 1986; m. Marie-M., d. T.R. Trudeau, 4 Nov. 1950; children: Suzanne, Marie-Hélène, Pierre; SR. CONSULTANT 1988– ; with Geog. Branch, Department of Mines & Tech. Surveys, Ottawa, 1949–56; Prof. of Econ. Geog., Laval Univ., Quebec, 1956–60; Vice-Pres., St. Lawrence Seaway Authority, 1960–65, Pres. 1965–73; Adm., Candn. Marine Transport., Min. of Transport 1970–73; Pres. (1973–77) Candn. Assn. of Broadcasters; Chrmn., CRTC 1977–79; Pres. March Shipping Co. 1979–84; Vice-Pres., Lavalin Inc. 1984–88; author of several articles dealing with trans. and econs. of transport; co-author 'Economic Geography of Canada' 1964; Chrmn., Petroleum Monitoring Agency 1988–92; R. Catholic; recreations: skiing, boating; Club: Rideau; Cercle Universitaire d'Ottawa; Office: 358 Somerset St. E., Ottawa, Ont. K1N 6W9.

**CANDLISH, Stanley M.,** B.Sc.; retired executive; b. Montreal, Que. 23 Nov. 1925; s. the late Dr. H.M. and the late Lillian (Holtby) C.; e. Alfred Joyce (Outremont) Pub. Sch. 1930–37; High Sch. of Montreal 1938–42; McGill Univ., B.Sc. 1946, Postgrad. study in Bacter. 1946–47; m. Bridget Suzanna (Naomi) d. late Daniel J. Coady, Glace Bay, N.S. 17 July 1948; one s., Ross Maiben; DIR., PROCESS PLANNING, IMPERIAL TOBACCO LTD. 1982– ; joined present Co. as Chem. 1947; Asst. Mgr. Tech. Service Lab. 1957; Asst. Mgr. Devel. & Tech. Service Lab. 1964; Mgr. Devel. & Tech. Service 1966–69; Div. Head. Mgr., Product Devel. & Tech. Services Dept. 1978–80; Mgr., Research and Develop. 1980–82; McGill C.O.T.C. 1942–47; mem., Packaging Assn. Can. (Pres. 1967–68); Liberal; Protestant; recreations: boating, boat building, gardening; Home: PO Box 117, RR #2, Arundel, Que. J0T 1A0.

**CANDLISH, Violet Elizabeth,** B.Sc.A., M.Sc., Ph.D.; agriculturalist; b. Regina, Sask. 9 July 1931; d. James Garfield and Christy Violet (MacEwen) Gardiner; e. elem. sch. Ottawa, Ont.; Luther Coll. Regina, Sask. 1948; Macdonald Coll. McGill Univ. B.Sc.A. 1952; Univ. of Man. M.Sc. 1968, Ph.D. 1970, post-doctorate 1971–72; m. John Henry Candlish 25 July 1953 (div.); children: Lucy Ellen, Patricia Jane, Jill Elizabeth, William Edwin, Christy Alice; EXTVE. DIR., BIOMASS ENERGY INSTITUTE 1986– ; and MANITOBA INST. OF AGROLOGISTS 1991– ; RESEARCH ASSOC., UNIV. OF MANITOBA; Commr., Candn. Grain Comn. 1981–86; estbd. Beth Candlish Ph.D., Research Consultant 1978; Lecturer Candn. Internat. Grains Inst.; Research Officer and mem. Winnipeg Chamber Comm.; Science Council Can.; Research Assoc. Plant Science, Univ. Man. 1972; Research Scient. Feed Grain, Grain Research Lab. Winnipeg 1973; Research Specialist, Can. Grains Council 1976; Lib. Cand. for Ft. Garry, Man. g.e. 1977; Vice Pres. (2nd) Lib. Party of Man. 1978; Field Underwriter, N.Y. Life Ins. Co.; mem. Bd. of Regents, U. of Winnipeg; Man. Inst. of Agrologists; Assn. Am. Cereal Chems.; Man. Action Comte. Status Women; Liberal; Anglican; recreations: flying, music, theatre; Club: Winnipeg Flying; Home: 452 – 20 Fort St., Winnipeg Man. R3C 4L3; Office: 1329 Niakwa Rd. E., Winnipeg, Man. R2J 3T4.

**CANDY, John Franklin;** actor; b. Toronto, Ont. 31 Oct. 1950; d. 4 March 1994; [Editor's note: When Mr Candy was first invited to participate in Canadian Who's Who he declined because he wished to protect his privacy; his biography is included (posthumously) in this edition to record his contribution to Canadian culture and to celebrate his unique sense of humour.]; appeared in num. films incl. 'Class of '44' 1973, 'Face Off,' 'It Seemed Like a Good Idea at the Time,' 'Clown Murders,' 'Find the Lady,' 'Silent Partner,' 'Lost and Found,' 'Tunnel Vision,' 'Double Negative,' '1941' 1979, 'Blues Brothers' 1980, 'Going Berserk' 1981, 'Stripes,' 'It Came from Hollywood' 1982, 'Vacation' 1983, 'Splash' 1984, 'Brewster's Millions,' 'Volunteers,' 'Summer Rental' 1985, 'Follow that Bird,' 'Little Shop of Horrors,' 'Armed and Dangerous' 1986, 'Tears Are Not Enough,' 'Planes, Trains and Automobiles' 1987, 'The Great Outdoors' 1988, 'Uncle Buck' 1989; appeared on num. TV shows, live theatre Second City Chicago, Toronto, Los Angeles; recipient Emmy Award, Acad. TV Arts & Scis. 1981, '82; Mem., Alliance Candn. Cinema, TV & Radio Artists (award 1978, '84); Screen Actors Guild; Writers Guild of Am.

**CANLETT, Gary Frederick,** B.Comm., C.F.A.; investment manager; b. Toronto, Ont. 11 July 1935; s. Frederick M. and Violet D.C. (Rennie) C.; e. Univ. of Toronto Schools 1954; Univ. of Toronto, Victoria Coll. B.Comm. 1958; C.F.A. 1968; one s.: Geoffrey J.F. Canlett; SENIOR VICE PRESIDENT, JONES HEWARD INVESTMENT MANAGEMENT 1984– ; Investment Trainee, Fraser Dingman & Co. 1958–64; Investment Mgr., Jones Heward & Co. 1964–84; Dir. 1968; Pres., J.H. Fund 1978; Chair, J.H. American Fund 1983; Dir., Burns Fry Ltd. 1984– ; Progressive Conservative; Delta Kappa Epsilon; recreations: reading, walking; Home: 2907 – 40 Pleasant Blvd., Toronto, Ont. M4T 1J9; Office: 1920 – 145 King St. W., Toronto, Ont. M5H 3Z9.

**CANNING, Graham Richard,** C.A.; financial executive; b. South Africa 26 Jan. 1946; s. Richard Henry and Eileen (Westergren) C.; e. Witwatersrand Univ.; C.A. South Africa 1971; Ont. 1976; m. Lucie d. Paul and Mary Bruneau 4 July 1981; children: Stephen, Jennifer; VICE PRES. FINANCIAL SERVICES, BRAEMAR APPAREL INC., responsible for finance, systems & admin.; Chief Financial Offr. & Dir., Marks & Spencer Canada Inc. 1986–92; Vice-Pres. & Controller, Holt Renfrew 1981–85; Controller, Braemar Div., Dylex Ltd. 1975–81; recreations: skiing, baseball, stock market; Home: 4 MacPhail Court, Unionville, Ont. L3R 0C2; Office: 637 Lakeshore Blvd. W., Toronto, Ont. M5V 1A8.

**CANNON, Lawrence,** B.A., M.B.A., M.P.P.; politician; b. Quebec City 6 Dec. 1947; s. Louis and Rosemary (Power) C.; e. Loyola Coll. B.A.; Univ. Laval M.B.A.; divorced; children: Philippe, David, Alec; MINISTER OF COMMUNICATIONS, PROVINCE OF QUEBEC 1990– ; Assoc. Private Sec., Prime Min. of Que. Robert Bourassa 1971–76; Finan. Analyst, Que. Indus. Devel. Corp. 1978–81; Pres. & Gen. Mgr. of small mfg. co. in Que. City 1981–85; councillor, town of Cap-Rouge 1979–85; 1st elected to Que. Nat. Assembly for riding of La Peltrie 1985; Parl. Asst., Min. of Fgn. Trade & Technol. Devel.; later Parl. Asst., Min. of Tourism; Comnr., Comn. on Labour & the Econ. 1986–89; reelected 25 Sept. 1989; elected vice-pres. Nat. Assembly; Office: Edifice G, 1037 de la Chevrotière, Quebec City, Que. G1R 4Y7.

**CANTIN, J. Maurice,** Q.C., B.A., LL.B.; executive; b. Québec, Qué. 25 March 1929; s. Maurice and Florence (Lapointe) C.; e. Externat Classique St-Jean Eudes Québec B.A. 1949; Laval Univ. LL.B. 1952; m. Isabelle d. Henri and Alphéna Laliberté 20 Aug. 1953; children: Isabelle, Roger; Vice Chrmn. Pub. Service Staff Relations Bd. 1978–90; Mgr. Underwriters Adjustment Bureau 1953–57; Partner, Gagnon, De Billy et al., Québec 1959–77; Exec. Dir. Candn. Bar Assn. 1977; cr. Q.C. 1968; Vice Gov. Laval Univ. Found.; mem. Bar of Qué.; Candn. Bar Assn.; Am. Bar Assn.; Found. Legal Rsch.; Candn. Inst. Adm. Justice; Clubs: Seigniory; Amici Dell Enotria; Home: 309, 2625 Regina, Ottawa, Ont. K2B 5W8.

**CANTIN, Marc,** B.A., LL.L.; lawyer; b. Lévis, Qué. 24 Nov. 1944; s. Aurèle and Pauline (Dumont) C.; e. Coll. Lévis, B.A.; Univ. Laval, LL.L.; m. Nicole, d. Marcel Nadeau, 12 Oct. 1969; child: Louis-David; PARTNER, LANGLOIS ROBERT; Partner, Thibaudeau, Lesage & Cantin 1968; Lawyer, Flynn, Rivard 1974; Lawyer, Govt. Quebec 1975; Secy., Vice-Pres. Legal Affairs, Le Groupe Videotron Ltée. 1980–88; mem. Quebec Bar Assn.; Candn. Bar Assn.; Quebec's Jr. Bar Assn. (Pres. 1974); Ste.-Julie's Landlord Assn. (Pres. 1983); recreation: golf; Home: 42 Ave. du Parc, Ste.-Julie, Qué. J0L 2S0; Office: 2800, 1002 Sherbrooke West, Montréal, Qué. H3A 3L6.

**CANTIN, Pierre Francois Roland,** M.B.B.S., M.R.C.S., L.R.C.P., L.M.C.C., C.C.F.P.(C), F.C.F.P.(C); family physician; b. Mahebourg, Mauritius 1 Aug. 1928; s. Antoine Yves and Marguerite Fernande (Regnier) C.; e. Univ. of London M.B.B.S., M.R.C.S., L.R.C.P. 1955; m. Hilary Ingrid d. Edith and Thomas Chandler 15 Dec. 1956; children: Roland Yves, Sophie Ingrid, Jacqueline Marguerite; House Surgeon & Physician, London Hosp. 1955–56; Jr. Registrar, Whitechapel Clinic 1957; Res. Med. Offr., Civil & Victoria Hosps. (Mauritius) 1957–60; Sr. Med. Offr., Princess Elizabeth Hosp. (Rodrigues) 1960–62; Sr. Res. in Gen. Prac., Misericordia Gen. Hosp. (Winnipeg) 1962; family physician 1963– ; Med. Advisor, Workers Compensation Bd. of Man.; Lectr., Univ. of Man.; Med. Examiner, Prov. of Man.; Pres., Man. Med. Assn. 1985–86; Candn. Med. Assn.; Coll. of Family Physicians of Can.; Past Rep. for Man. Med. Assn., Counc. of Community Health; Counc. of Economics, Candn. Med. Assn.; Past Pres. Man. Chap., Coll. of Family Physicians of Can.; Councillor, College of Physicians & Surgeons of Manitoba; recreations: reading, painting; tennis; swimming; Home: 3281 Pembina Hwy., Winnipeg, Man. R3V 1T7; Office: Box 268, St. Pierre, Man. R0A 1V0.

**CANTIN, Réjean,** B.Comm.; public servant; né. Québec 5 mars 1941; f. Joseph et Cécile (Drouin) C.; é. Univ. Laval B.Comm. 1963; ép. Nicole f. Gérard et Marie-Paule Turcotte 5 juin 1965; enfants: Frédéric, Caroline; SOUS-MIN., MIN. DE LA SANTE & SERV. SOCIAUX, QUE. 1986– ; Dir. des Immobil., Min. Santé & Serv. Soc., Qué. 1971–74; Dir., prog. de santé 1974–78; Sous-min. adj. 1978–82; Dir. Gén., Ctr. Hosp. Robert Giffard 1982–86; résidence: 7005, ave. Verdon, Charlesbourg, Qué. G1H 5Y8; bureau: 1125, chemin Saint-Louis, Sillery, Qué. G1S 1E7.

**CANTOR, Allan Paul,** Q.C., B.Com., LL.B.; lawyer; b. Saskatoon, Sask. 3 May 1929; s. James Maurice and Elsie Patricia (Portigal) C.; e. Univ. of Man. B.Com. 1950, LL.B. 1954; m. Gloria Sandra d. Jacob and Lily Shapiro 25 Aug. 1957; children: Stephen Joshua, Susan Barbara, Diana Ruth, David Alexander; SR. VICE-PRES. AND GEN. COUNSEL TO THE SHARED NETWORK GROUP OF COMPANIES 1993– ; called to Bar of Man. 1954; cr. Q.C. 1978; Assoc., Cantor, Matas, Simkin & Cantor 1954–67; Partner, Simkin, Cantor, Goltsman & Rosenberg 1967–81; Sr. Partner, Simkin, Gallagher 1981–93; lectr. and instr. various courses Law Soc Man., Man. Law Sch. 1978–90; Isaac Pitblado Lectr. on Purchase Agreement & Closing of Transactions 1973 (Chrmn., Isaac Pitblado Lectures 1992); Hon. mem. Nat. Council Jewish Women of Can. Winnipeg Sect. Inc.; Dir. Council for Candn. Unity 1976–85; Pres. S. Winnipeg Lib. Assn. 1968; Chrmn. Assiniboine Park Residents Adv. Group City of Winnipeg 1972–73; Pres. Estate Planning Council Winnipeg 1986–87; Dir., Manitoba Law Found. 1986–92; Pres., Loni Beach Residents Assoc. 1991– ; mem. Special Comte. Corporate Law for

Dir. Corp. Br. Dept. Consumer, Corporate & Internal Services Prov. Man., Adv. on Man. Corp. Act.; mem. Winnipeg C. of C.; Chrmn., Environment/Sustainable Develop. Ctte. 1990–93; Man. Bar Assn. (Pres. 1982–83); Candn. Bar Assn. (Nat. Extve. 1983–84; Constitution & By-Laws Comte. 1984–87, Chrmn. 1986–87; Fellowships Comte. 1987–91, Chrmn. 1989–91); Candn. Tax Foundation; Internat. Bar Assn.; Internat. Comn. Jurists (Candn. Sect.); Freemason (Master, Menorah Masonic Lodge, 1964); Jr. Grand Steward, Grand Lodge of Manitoba 1988; District Deputy Grand Master 1992–93; Shriner; recreations: sailing, skiing, curling, baseball; Clubs: Bel Acres Golf & Country (Pres. 1967); Rotary (Pres. N. Winnipeg 1983–84); The Carleton; Home: 3 Fairhaven Rd., Winnipeg, Man. R3P 2G5; Office: 330 St. Mary Ave., Ste. 620, Winnipeg, Man. R3C 3Z5.

**CANTOR, Paul;** insurance executive; b. 8 Jan. 1942; e. Univ. of Alta. B.A. 1962; Univ. of Toronto LL.B. 1968; Ryerson Polytech. Inst. F.I.C.B. 1981; m.; PRES., C.E.O. AND DIR., CONFEDERATION LIFE INSURANCE COMPANY; Dir., various subsidiaries and affiliates in the Confederation Life Group; Torstar Corp.; held various posts, World Univ. Serv. of Canada; Dept. of Finance, Govt. of Can.; Polysar Ltd.; Canadian Imperial Bank of Comm.; mem., Law Soc. of Upper Can.; Clubs: The Toronto Hunt; The York Club; YMCA; Office: One Mount Pleasant Rd., Toronto, Ont. M4Y 2Y5.

**CANVIN, D.T.,** B.S.A., M.Sc., Ph.D., F.R.S.C. (1977); university professor; b. Winnipeg, Man. 8 Nov. 1931; s. Victor T. and Maria (Clouston) C.; e. Univ. of Man., B.S.A. 1956, M.Sc. 1957; Purdue Univ., Ph.D. 1960; m. Lois Marie, d. J.E. Endersby, Winnipeg, Man., 13 July 1957; children: Steven, Paul, Sarah, Robert; PROF. OF BIOLOGY, QUEEN'S UNIV. (Head of Dept. 1980–84; Dean, Sch. of Grad. Studies and Rsch. 1984–89); writings incl. various scient. papers in fields of plant physiol.-biochem.; mem., Candn. Soc. Plant Physiols. (awarded Society Medal 1981); Am. Soc. Plant Physiols.; Am. Soc. Agron; Anglican; recreations: curling, bridge, fishing; Office: Kingston, Ont. K7L 3N6.

**CAPARROS, Ernest,** LL.D., J.C.D., F.R.S.C.; educator; b. Malaga, Spain 18 Apl. 1938; s. Antonio Ernesto and Angeles (Soriano) C.; e. Univ. of Granada B.A. 1955; Univ. of Zaragoza LL.L. 1961; Univ. of Navarra J.C.L. 1961, J.C.D. 1962; Laval Univ. D.E.S.D. 1965, LL.D. 1973; PROF. OF LAW UNIV. OF OTTAWA 1981– , mem. Sch. Grad. Studies & Rsch. 1982– ; Asst. Prof. of Law Laval Univ. 1966, Adjunct Prof. 1967, Assoc. Prof. 1970. Prof. 1970–81, Vice Dean 1971–74, 1976–77; Visiting Prof.: Univ. catholique de Louvain 1976; Univ. of Toronto 1976; Univ. de Montréal 1979–82; Univ. of Calgary 1979; Dalhousie Univ. 1979, 1981; McGill Univ. 1980, 1983; Univ. de Sherbrooke 1980, 1985; Universidad Panamericana, México 1982; Universidad de Navarra, Spain 1984– ; Universidad de Los Andes, Bogota 1986; Universidad del Norte, Barranquilla, Colombia 1986; Universidad Nacional Autónoma de México 1987; Roman Atheneum of the Holy Cross, Rome 1991; Cons.: Law Reform Comn. Can. 1971–75; Civil Code Revision Office 1975–76; mem. Legal Council Assembly of Bishops of Québec 1982–90; Judge, Ecclesiastical Appeal Tribunal Can. 1986– ; author 'Les lignes de force de l'évolution des régimes matrimoniaux en droit comparé de québécois' 1975; 'Les régimes matrimoniaux au Québec' 3e éd., 2e tirage, corrigé (Collection Bleue) 1988; co-author 'La documentation juridique' 1973; ed. 'Les Cahiers de droit' (Laval) 1965–70; 'Revue générale de droit' (Ottawa) 1983– ; 'La Collection Bleue' 1986– ; 'Mélanges Germain Brière' 1993; co-ed. 'Essays on the Civil Codes of Québec and St. Lucia' 1985; 'Code de droit canonique' 1990; 'Code of Canon Law Annotated' 1993; Founding mem., Treas. (1968–73) and Vice Pres. (1973–92) Found. for Culture and Edn. Montreal; mem. Québec Bar; Candn. Bar Assn.; Vice Pres., Assn. québécoise de droit comparé 1991– ; Canon Law Socs. Am., Can. (Pres. 1991–93), Gt. Brit. & Ireland; Internat. Canon Law Soc. (Mem. of the Bd. 1993– ;); Internat. Soc. Family Law; Knight of Magistral Grace, Order of Malta; Commemorative Medal, 12th Anniversary, Candn. Confedn.; recreations: reading, hiking; Home: 30 Goulburn Ave., Ottawa, Ont. K1N 8C8; Office: 57 Louis Pasteur St., Ottawa, Ont. K1N 6N5.

**CAPE, David E.,** P.Eng.; construction executive; b. Montreal, Que. 19 Dec. 1938; s. John M. and Mary E. (Ogilvie) C.; e. Trinity Coll. Sch. Port Hope 1957; McGill Univ. B.Eng. 1962; m. Sylvia de Heinrich 4 Nov. 1967; children: John, David Nicholas, Jill; EXEC. VICE PRES. E.G.M. CAPE & CO. LTD. 1989– ; Field Eng. present Co. 1963, Project Adm. 1965, Supt. 1972, Contracts Mgr. 1980, Vice Pres. 1981; recreations: golf, tennis, fishing; Clubs: Hillside Tennis (Montreal); Badminton & Racquet; Mad River Golf; Home: 106 Glengowan Rd., Toronto, Ont. M4N 1G4; Office: 200, 2005 Sheppard Ave. E., Willowdale, Ont. M2J 5B4.

**CAPE, Edmund A.,** B.A., LL.B.; merchant banker; b. Montreal, Que. 25 Oct. 1950; s. David George Meredith and Anne Colhoun (Duncanson) C.; e. Lower Can. Coll. 1968; Queen's Univ. B.A. (Hons.) 1973; Univ. of Toronto LL.B. 1977; m. Ann d. Elizabeth and Richard Dillon 25 June 1976; children: Anthony, David, Katherine, Hugh; EXTVE. VICE PRES. OPERATIONS, GENTRA INC. 1993– ; Corp. Lending/Bad Loan Workouts, CIBC 1979–85; Merchant Banker, Great Lakes Group Inc. 1985–89; Merchant Banker, Trilon Financial Corp. 1989–93; Dir., Regional Cablesystems Inc.; recreations: skiing, rowing, canoeing; Home: 75 Rosedale Heights Dr., Toronto, Ont. M4T 1C4; Office: 70 York St., Suite 1110, Toronto, Ont. M5J 1S9.

**CAPE, John Christopher,** B.A.; Eng.; M.E.I.C.; general contractor; b. Montreal, Que. 2 July 1937; s. John Meredith and Mary Elizabeth C.; e. Trinity Coll. Sch. Port Hope, Ont. 1955; Bishop's Univ. B.A. 1958; Univ. of Scranton, Engn. 1966; Alexander Hamilton Inst., Business Adm. 1970; m. Beverley Joyce d. Geoff Rogers; children: Jim, Geoff, Pam; PRES. & C.E.O., E.G.M. CAPE & CO. LTD. since 1990; joined present Co. 1961, Vice Pres. 1978–90; Anglican; Clubs: Badminton & Racquet; Granite; Fitness Inst.; Office: 2005 Sheppard Ave. E., Willowdale, Ont. M2J 5B4.

**CAPELLO, Gerald (Gerry),** B.A.; public servant; b. Ottawa; e. Colorado College B.A. 1957; DEPUTY MINISTER, LABOUR CANADA 1991– ; Community Programs Dir., Dept. of Recreation & Parks, City of Ottawa 1957; Supt. of Employment, E.B. Eddy Co. 1962; various positions with Treasury Board Secretariat, Revenue Canada, Customs & Excise, and Supply & Services Canada 1966–79; Asst. Dep. Min., Opns. Serv., Supply & Serv. Canada 1979; Dep. Sec., Admin. Policy Br. 1985; Dep. Sec., Personnel Policy Br., Treasury Board Secretariat 1987; Office: Ottawa, Ont. K1A 0J2.

**CAPLAN, Elinor,** M.P.P. (Oriole); b. Toronto, Ont. 20 May 1944; d. Samuel Solomon and Thelma S. (Goodman) Hershorn; e. Centennial Coll. 1973; m. Mayer Wilfred s. Jack and Lillian Caplan 6 Sept. 1963; children: David, Mark, Zane, Meredith; ONT. LIBERAL, MINISTRY OF REVENUE, TREASURY BD. & MNGMT. BD. CRITIC; Mem. Standing Ctte. on Finance & Economic Affairs; Administrator, Leader Publishing Inc. 1971–72; Pres., Elinor Caplan & Assoc. Title Searching and Conveyancing 1973; Vice-Pres., Bayview Mews Tenants Assn. 1974–76; Alderman, City of North York 1978–85, during which time also served as mem. of numerous municipal cttes. and other boards, including Royal Commission on Metro Toronto 1978, 1980; North York Refugee Assistance Ctte. 1978; N. York Inter-Agency Counc. Srs. Ctte. 1978; N. York Condominium Ctte. 1978–81; N. York Nominating Ctte. 1978–83; N. York Lesgislation Ctte. 1978; N. York Parks & Recreation Ctte. (Chrmn. 1978); N. York Inter-Agency Counc. Children's Service Ctte. 1979 (Vice-Chrmn. 1980); N. York Planning Bd. 1979–82; N. York Devel. Ctte. (Chrmn. 1979); N. York Energy Policy & Programme Devel. Ctte. (Chrmn. 1980–81); N. York Devel. & Econ. Growth Ctte. 1980–81 (Chrmn. 1980); N. York Counc./Bd. of Ed. Liaison Ctte. 1981–83 (Chrmn. 1983); N. York Parks, Rec. & Human Services Ctte. 1981, 1983–85 (Chrmn. 1985); N. York Bd. of Health 1981–84 (mem. Fin. Ctte. 1984); N. York Inter-Agency Counc. (Vice-Chrmn. 1981–82); N. York Works Ctte. 1982; Ont. Liberal Women's Perspective Advy. Ctte. (Chrmn. 1983–1985); CORE Foundation (Community Outreach in Education) 1983–85 (Dir. 1983; mem. Project Advy. Ctte. 1985); Task Force on Pediculosis (Lice) (Chrmn. 1983–84); Human Services Advy. Counc. (Chrmn. 1983–85); N. York Rapid Transit Sub-Ctte. (Chrmn. 1983–85); N. York Transportation Ctte. (Chrmn. 1983); Task Force on Parks Mandate 1984; Sub-Ctte. on Grants Policy 1984; Neighbourhood Watch Task Force 1984; Workshop Leader, Symposium on Private Violence 1985; N. York Community, Race & Ethnic Rlns. Ctte. 1985; Chrmn., Mgmt. Bd. of Cabinet and Min. of Govt. Services, Ont. 1985–86; mem., Ont. Legislature Ctte. on Economic Affairs 1986–87; Min. of Health, Govt. of Ont. 1987–90; Ontario Liberal Municipal Affairs Critic 1990–92; Chair, Standing Ctte. on Social Develop. 1990–91; Life mem., Candn. Hadassah Wizo (Past Pres., Gila Chapter); Volunteer, United Way; recreations: music, theatre, bridge; Office: Legislative Bldg., Queen's Park, Toronto, Ont. M7A 1A4.

**CAPLAN, Gerald (Gerry) Lewis,** Ph.D.; public affairs commentator/consultant; b. Toronto, Ont. 8 Mar. 1938; s. Harold and Molly C.; e. Univ. of Toronto, B.A. 1960, M.A. 1961; Univ. of London, Sch. of Oriental & Afr. Studies, Ph.D. 1977; m. Carol Phillips; d. Maureen and Bryn 26 Oct. 1985; one stepson: Dylan David; Lectr., Univ. Coll. of Rhodesia 1965–66; Assoc. Prof., Ont. Inst. for Stud. in Edn. 1967–77; Sr. Adv. to & Campaign Mgr., Ont. NDP leader, Stephen Lewis 1970–77; Dir., CUSO-Nigeria program 1977–79; Candn. Dir., CUSO 1979; Dir., City of Toronto Health Advocacy Unit 1980–82; Fed. Sec., NDP of Can. 1982–84; Nat. Campaign Mgr., NDP, Gen. Election 1984; Co-Chair, Govt. of Can., Task Force on Broadcasting Policy 1985–86; Co-chair, Royal Commission on Learning (Ont.) 1993– ; newspaper columnist, radio & tv commentator, cons.; Dir., InterPares; White Ribbon Found.; Friends of Canadian Broadcasting; author: 'The Elites of Barotseland: A Political History of Zambia's Western Provinces' 1970; 'The Dilemma of Canadian Socialism: The CCF in Ontario' 1973; 'Just Causes: Notes of an Unrepentant Socialist' 1993; and num. articles & book reviews; co-author: (with Sen. Michael Kirby and Hugh Segal) 'Election' 1989; Home: 146 Kamloops Ave., Ottawa, Ont. K1V 7C9.

**CAPLAN, Herbert,** B.A., D.D.S., F.A.C.D., F.I.C.D.; b. Montreal, Que. 3 June 1921; s. Morris and Ethel (Gerkin) C.; e. Aberdeen Sch., Montreal, Que.; Strathcona Acad., Outremont, Que.; Loyola Coll., Montreal, Que., B.A.; McGill Univ., D.D.S.; post-grad. training, Temple Univ., 1958; m. children: Melissa Alfreda; Chief, Dept. Dentistry, Reddy Memorial Hosp., Montreal, Que.; Courtesy Staff mem., Queen Elizabeth Hosp., Montreal, Que.; Gov., Coll. Dental Surgeons of Que., 1968–72; Candn. Dental Assn., 1971–72; Judge on War Mem. Comte., Candn. Dental Assn., 1964–65; Pres., Am. Acad. Dental Med., Montreal Sec., 1963–64 and alternate del. to Nat. Body, 1964; served as Lt. during 2nd World War with Candn. Inf. Corps, 1943–45; Publications: Clinical and Prof.; mem., Pierre Fauchard Academy; Candn. Dental Assn.; Am. Inst. Oral Biol.; Am. Assn. Hosp. Dental Chiefs; Chicago Dental Soc.; Fed. Dentaire Internat.; served on Extve. Bd., Mt. Royal Dental Soc.; Alpha Omega (Pres., Montreal Alumni Chapter, 1955–56; Regent, Que. and Ont., 1957–58; Nat. Comte. Chrmnships 1958–61; Internat. Treas. and Internat. Convention Rep., 1961–64; Internat. Pres.-Elect. 1964–65; Internat. Pres., 1966); mem., McGill Grads Soc. and Past Faculty Chrmn. (Dentistry) of the Alma Mater Fund, 1960–61; apptd. Consultant in Dent., Reddy Mem. Hosp. 1967; official Del. to Fed. Dentaire Internat. by Candn. Dent. Assn. 1966; apptd. Chrmn. of Scient. Program for Candn. Dental Assn. in Montreal, 1969; Fellow, Am. Coll. of Dents.; Fellow, Internat. Coll. of Dentists; mem. Loyola Alumni Assn.; Founder mem., Dental Sch., Hebrew Univ. and mem. Supporting Alumni; Hebrew; recreations: golf, photography; Clubs: Candn. Club of Montreal; Hillsdale Golf & Country; Home: 225 Olivier, PH2, Westmount, Que. H3Z 2C7.

**CAPLAN, L. David,** B.Comm., C.A.; financial and administrative executive; b. Montreal, Que. 24 May 1940; e. McGill Univ. B.Comm. 1961; C.A. 1963; PRESIDENT AND CHIEF EXEC. OFFR., PRATT & WHITNEY CANADA 1985– ; articled for Riddel, Stead & Co., C.A.'s 1961–64; joined present firm 1964; Vice-Pres. Fin. and Admin. 1976; Exec. Vice-Pres. 1980; Pres. & C.O.O. 1984; Internat. Trade Adv. Com. Business Council on National Issues, General Aviation Mfrs. Assn.; attended Harvard Internat. Sr. Mgr.'s Prog., Switzerland 1979; mem. Candn. Inst. of C.A.'s; recreations: bridge, golf; Office: 1000 Marie Victorin, Longueuil, Que. J4G 1A1.

**CAPLAN, Paula Joan,** M.A., Ph.D.; psychologist; educator; b. Springfield, MO 7 July 1947; d. Jerome Arnold and Theda Ann (Karchmer); e. Radcliffe Coll. A.B. 1969; Duke Univ. M.A. 1971, Ph.D. 1973; children: Jeremy, Emily; FULL PROF. OF APPLIED PSYCHOL., ONT. INST. FOR STUDIES IN EDUCATION 1987– ; Asst. Prof. of Psychiatry, Univ. of Toronto 1979– , Lectr. in Women's Studies 1979– ; Clin. Psychol. Internship John Umstead Hosp. Butner, NC and NC Meml. Hosp. Chapel Hill 1972–73; Postdoctoral Fellow in Neuropsychol. Rsch. Inst. Hosp. for Sick Children, Toronto 1974–76; Lectr. in Psychiatry Univ. of Toronto 1978–79; Psychol Toronto Family Court Clinic, Clarke Inst. of Psychiatry 1977–80; Asst. Prof. of Applied Psychol. present Inst. 1980–81, Assoc. Prof. of Applied Psychol. 1982–87, Assoc. Dir. Centre Women's Studies in Edn. 1984–85, Head of Centre 1985–87; Princ. Investigator, Toronto Multi-agency Child Abuse Rsch. Project 1979–83; recipient Clin. Psychol. Fellowship US Nat. Inst. Mental Health 1969–71; Predoctoral Fellowship Duke Univ. Centre Study Aging & Human Devel., US Nat. Inst. Child Devel. 1971–73; Postdoctoral Rsch. Fellowship in Neuropsychol. Hosp. for Sick Children Toronto

1974–76; Award for Coll. and Univ. Teaching, Ont. Confedn. Univ. Faculty Assns. 1984; author: 'You're Smarter Than They Make You Feel: How the Experts Intimidate Us and What We Can Do About It' 1994; 'Lifting a Ton of Feathers: A Woman's Guide to Surviving in the Academic World' 1993; 'Don't Blame Mother: Mending the Mother-Daughter Relationship' 1989; 'The Myth of Women's Masochism' 1985, revised ed. 1993; 'Between Women: Lowering the Barriers' 1981; co-author: (with Jeremy B. Caplan) 'Thinking Critically About Research on Sex and Gender' 1993; (with Marcel Kinsbourne) 'Children's Learning and Attention Problems' 1979; editor: 'Resources for Feminist Research/Documentation sur la Recherche Feministe' 1982–84, 1985, adv. bd. mem. 1986; author or co-author numerous book chapters, articles, papers; frequent keynote speaker; numerous appearances various radio and TV progs. psychol. rsch.; Woman of Distinction Award for Health/Education/Athletics, Toronto Y.W.C.A. 1986; Fellow, Division 35, Am. Psychological Assn.; Fellow, Am. Orthopsychiatric Assn.; Fellow, Candn. Psychol. Assn.; Office: 252 Bloor St. W., Toronto, Ont. M5S 1V6.

**CAPON, Rev. Canon Anthony Charles,** M.A., B.D., D.D.; retired theological college principal; b. Chislehurst, Eng. 5 Oct. 1926; s. Charles Cyril and Hilda (Leggeri) C.; e. Trinity Coll. Cambridge B.A. 1951, M.A. 1955; Oak Hill Coll. London, Eng. G.O.E. 1953; Wycliffe Coll. Toronto B.D. 1965, D.D. 1982; m. Elizabeth d. Christopher and Doris Mowll 15 Oct. 1955; children: Paul, Frances, Christopher, Michael; Princ. Montreal Diocesan Theol. Coll. Anglican Ch. of Can. 1978–91 (retired), Canon 1978; Asst. Priest St. Paul's Ch. Portman Sq. London, Eng. 1953–56; Candn. Dir. Scripture Union 1956–70; Regional Dir. Americas Scripture Union 1970–75; Dir. of Devel. Wycliffe Coll. Toronto 1975–78; Sr. Scholar Trinity Coll. Cambridge 1951; Chrmn. Heads of Ang. Colls. Can. 1988; co-author: 'The Church and the Child' 1965; Address: 5 Loradean Cres., Kingston, Ont. K7K 6X9.

**CAPONI, Dennis F.,** B.Sc., C.L.U., C.H.F.C.; insurance executive; b. Detroit, Mich. 19 Dec. 1945; s. Vincent P. and Noel D. (Hacquoil) C.; e. St. Paul High Sch. Owosso, Mich. 1963; Xavier Univ. Cincinnati B.Sc. 1967; m. Virginia A. d. Dr. Ernest A. and Margaret V. Welch 25 June 1966; children: Dennis F. Jr., Christopher Michael, Charla Noel; Pres. D.F. Caponi Insurance Agency Limited 1992–.; Sales Mgr./Br. Mgr. Canada Life Assurance Co. 1974–92; served with U.S. Army 1967–70, Army Commendation Medal; Life Ins. Rep., Life & Qualifying Mem., Million Dollar Round Table, Nat. Quality Award Winner 1970–92; Grand Challenge Campaign Winner, Vice Pres. Cup 1984; Managers Counc. 1988; Cert. Financial Planner, Candn. Inst. Financial Planning; Pres. Life Underwriters Assn. Toronto 1987; Vice Pres. American Club Toronto 1978; Treas. Civitan Club Oakville; Pres. Etobicoke Pepsi Swim Club; Sec./Treas., Life Underwriters Assn. of Canada 1987–93; C.H.F.C. 1992; recreations: golf, skiing; Club: Islington Golf; Home: 32 Robaldon Rd., Toronto, Ont. M9A 5A7.

**CAPPE, Melvin Samuel,** B.A., M.A.; public servant/economist; b. Toronto, Ont. 3 Dec. 1948; s. David and Patricia (Wise) C.; e. Wm. Lyon MacKenzie Coll. 1967; Univ. of Toronto, B.A. 1971; Univ. of West. Ont., M.A. 1972; m. Marni (Marline) d. Barbara and Richard Pliskin 14 Nov. 1971; children: Daniel, Emily; DEPY. SECY., PROGRAM BRANCH, TREASURY BOARD SECRETARIAT, GOVT. OF CAN. 1990– ; Analyst, later Chief, Treas. Bd. Secretariat, Govt. of Can. 1975–78; Sr. Econ., Dept. of Fin. 1978–81; Dep. Dir. of Investigation & Rsch., Combines Investigation Act, Consumer & Corp. Affairs 1982–86; Asst. Depy. Min., Policy, Consumer & Corp. Affairs 1986–89; Asst. Depy. Min., Corporate Affairs and Legislative Policy, Consumer & Corp. Affairs 1989–90; Sr. Asst. Secy., Treasury Board Secretariat, Govt. of Can. 1990; Home: 483 Highland Ave., Ottawa, Ont. K2A 2J5; Office: L'Esplanade Laurier, East Tower, 8th Flr., 140 O'Connor St., Ottawa, Ont. K1A 0R5.

**CAPPON, Daniel,** M.B., B.S., F.R.C.P. (Edinburgh), F.R.C.P.(C); D.PM (Engl.); physician; educator; b. London, Eng. 6 June 1921; s. Maurice and Henrietta (Trubb) C.; e. Univ. of London, M.B., B.S. 1946; FRCP (Edinburgh); DPM 1948; m. Donna Coral d. Watcil and Marjory Bolick 1 Apr. 1977; children: Emily, Daniel; by previous marriage: Ian, Bruce, Paul, Mark, Fiona; PROF. IN ENVIRONMENTAL STUDIES, YORK UNIV. 1970– ; Analytical Therapist Toronto 1950– ; Founding mem. McLuhan Inst. Univ. of Toronto; Consultant in Architecture 1962– ; (Expo 67, CN Tower); intern St. Mary's Hosp. Med. Sch. London; resident Dorset Co. Hosp. and Bath UK 1946; Royal Army Med. Corps, India service, postgrad. Maudsley Inst. of Psych. London and Guy's Hosp. 1950; Asst. Prof. of Psychiatry Univ. of Toronto 1950–69; Prof. of Psychiatry Univ. of Md. 1969–70; media commentator 1960– ; author: 'Toward Understanding Homosexuality' 1964; 'Technology and Perception' 1967; 'Eating, Loving and Dying' 1975; 'Coupling' 1983; 'Intuition' 1990; freelance writer various Toronto Jours. and mags. 1957– ; Inventor: LAPRITE (portable desk) 1990; board games, 'INTUITION' and 'GAIA' 1991; and Intuition Quotient Test (IQ2) 1992; Fellow, Am. Psych. Assn.; Candn. Psych. Assn.; mem. Brit. Med. Assn.; ACTRA; P.W.A.C. (founding); World Psych. Assn.; Anglican; P. Conservative (Cons. 1964–74); recreations: hockey, skiing, tennis, squash, cycling, horseback riding; Clubs: Toronto Tennis Cricket Skating; Georgian Peaks (Collingwood); Home: 32 York Valley Cr., North York, Ont. M2P 1A7; Office: York Univ., 4700 Keele St., North York, Ont. M3J 1P3.

**CAPRIOTTI, Pamela J.N.,** B.A.; communication and fund-raising consultant; b. Minneapolis, Minn. 6 Nov. 1952; d. Frank John and Beatrice Joy (Ahlers) C.; e. Macalester Coll. St. Paul, Minn. B.A. 1974; m. John A. s. John and Giulia Martin 1985; children: Molly Katharine, Morgan Alexandra, Madison Elizabeth, Miranda Victoria; Pres. and Chief Operating Offr., The Martin Group, Martin Worldwide 1988–.; Ed. Minn. Found. Directory 1974, Mng. Ed. of Dir. and Ill. Found. Directory 1978–81; Vice Pres. The Martin Group 1982, Pres. (Communications) 1986–88; Past Pres. Candn. Soc. Fund Raising Execs.; Chrmn. Certification Prog. Can.; Anglican; recreation: tennis; Club: The Waterfront; Home: 521 Vesta Dr., Toronto, Ont. M5P 3A9.

**CARBONNEAU, Côme,** O.C., Ing., Ph.D.; consulting geologist; b. Saint-Jean-des-Piles, Qué. 24 Nov. 1923; s. Omer and Edith (Bordeleau) C.; e. Laval Univ. B.A. 1943, B.A.Sc. 1948; Univ. of B.C., M.A.Sc. 1949; McGill Univ. Ph.D. (Geol.) 1953; m. Françoise d. Lucien Pettigrew 15 Sept. 1951; children: Hélène, Marie, Jean, Pierre, Lise, Alain; Assoc. Prof. of Geol. Ecole Polytechnique and Univ. of Montreal 1951–63; Consulting Geol., St-Lawrence Columbium, Oka area 1953–59; Extve. Vice Pres. 1963–65; Founding Pres. and Chief Extve. Offr. SOQUEM, Quebec 1965–77; Prof. of Geol. and Mineral Econ. Laval Univ. 1977–81, Chrmn. of Geol. Faculty of Sciences & Engn. 1979–81; Pres. and Chief Extve. Offr., Corporation Falconbridge Copper 1981–86; Nomination: Officer Order of Canada, 1978; recipient A. O. Dufresne Award Candn. Inst. Mining & Metall. 1978; mem. Nat. Adv. Comte. on Mining Policies 1971–75; Nat. Adv. Comte. on Mining & Metall. 1980; Pres. Assn. Canadienne-Française pour l'Avancement des Sciences 1975–76; Dir., Univ. Laval 1970–71, Pres. Assn. des Anciens 1970–71; Gov. McGill Univ. 1973–77; author various articles scient. and prof. journs.; mem. Order Engrs. Que.; Candn. Inst. Mining & Metall.; Geol. Assn. Can.; Assn. des Géologues du Qué.; recreations: reading, skiing, cycling; Home: 2540, J. Keable, Ste-Foy, Qué. G1W 1L3.

**CARDER, Paul C.,** B.A., M.B.A.; advertising executive; b. Oak Park, Ill. 27 Jan. 1941; s. Lawrence and Irene Adele (Zahler) C.; e. Univ. of Mich. B.A. 1962; Harvard Univ. Sch. of Bus. M.B.A. 1964; common-law Kathy d. Jan and Gertrude Kamping; children: Gregory and Tracy Carder, Leigh and Amanda Kamping-Carder; PRES. AND CHIEF EXEC. OFFR. DDB NEEDHAM ADVERTISING LTD. 1990– ; Acct. Exec. Ogilvy & Mather, New York 1964–65; Vice Pres. Ogilvy & Mather Canada Ltd. 1966–73; Sr. Cons. Huntley Professional & Educational Services Toronto 1974; Vice Pres., Dir. of Client Services, Doyle Dane Bernbach, Toronto 1975–77; Sr. Vice Pres., Mng. Dir. Vickers & Benson Ltd. Toronto 1978–83; Pres. & C.E.O., Carder Gray Advertising Inc. 1983–90; mem., DDB Needham U.S./Candn. Bd. of Dir.; Dir., Harvard Business School Club of Toronto; Inst. Candn. Advt.; Nat. Ballet of Can.; mem. Lib. Party Ont.; recreation: tennis; Home: 198 Cottingham St., Toronto, Ont. M4W 3T4; Office: 33 Bloor St. E., Toronto, Ont. M4V 1C5.

**CARDIFF, Keith Curtis,** F.C.A.; retired chartered accountant; b. Eston, Sask. 26 Mar. 1921; s. George Frances and Julia Maude (Hamilton) C.; e. Edmonton Normal Sch. 1940; C.A. Alta. 1952; m. Kathleen May d. Victor Stanley and Carolyn Kaufman 6 Apr. 1943; child: Evan Reece; R.C.A.F. 1943–45, trainee, qualified pilot, and flying instructor, transferred to class E of reserve in 1945 with rank of Flying Offr., Decorations, Voluntary Service, 1939–45 Star; C.A. Student 1946–52, Patriquin Johnstone & Co., Edmonton (successor firm Patriquin Duncan McClary McClary & Co.), Staff Accountant 1953, Partner, 1954–56; Part., (Edmon.) Deloitte Haskins & Sells 1956–58, Part. (Toronto) 1959–66, Managing Part. (Hamilton) 1966–78, Audit Partner 1979–83 (retired); firm name changed to Deloitte and Touche on merger in 1990 with Touche Ross; Dir., Art Gallery of Hamilton 1980–88, (& Treasr. 1984–85); Dir. Lubrizol Can. Ltd. 1983– ; Red Cross Service: Hamilton Branch Volunteer and Offr. 1967–75, Member Ont. Div. Budget Comte. 1977, Natnl. Assist. Honourary Treas. 1978, Natnl. Hon. Treas. 1979–80, Chrmn., National Extve. Comte. 1981, Pres., 1982–83, Past. Pres. 1983–85; Red Cross honours: Hamilton Branch Serv. Award 1975, National Distinguished Serv. Award 1981, Order of Red Cross Officer 1985; active in Hamilton & District C.A. Assn. 1969–74; mem., P.R. Comte., Inst. of C.A. of Ont. 1974–77, Comte. Chrmn. 1978; Can. Inst. of C.A. P.R. Comte. 1975–77; Clubs: Charter mem., Crossroads Gyro Club of Edmonton; mem. & various offices incl. Pres., Gyro Club of Toronto 1959–70; past mem., Edmonton Golf & Country; St George's Golf & Country; Toronto; mem., Burlington Golf & Country (Past Pres.); recreations: golf, photography, bird-watching; Home: 826 Forest Glen Ave., Burlington, Ont. L7T 2L2.

**CARDINAL, Douglas J.,** O.C., B.Arch., O.A.A., M.A.A.A., F.R.A.I.C., R.C.A., LL.D.; architect; b. Calgary, Alta. 7 Mar. 1934; s. Joseph Henry and Frances Margaret C.; e. Univ. of B.C. 1953–54; Univ. of Texas, B.Arch. (Hons.) 1963; children: Allannah, Nancy Sabrina, Guy Douglas, Bret Douglas, Cheryl Carolyn, Lisa Devon, Douglas Jean-Marc; formed Douglas J. Cardinal Architect 1964; inc. Douglas J. Cardinal Architect Limited 1976; opened Ottawa office 1985; frequent speaker at confs. & symposia; designed Candn. Museum of Civilization, Hull, Que.; Selected Designer/Architect, National Museum of American Indians, Washington, DC; recipient numerous awards and wide media recognition; one of N.Am.'s authorities on Computer-Aided Drafting systems in archit.; Office: 400 - 1525 Carling Ave., Ottawa, Ont. K1Z 8R9.

**CARDINAL, Peter Christopher,** C.G.A.; banker; b. Germany 14 June 1944; s. Kurt and Lotte C.; C.G.A. 1973; m. Marilyn d. David and Hazel Barton 17 Sept. 1966; children: Amanda, Tammy; SENIOR VICE-PRES., CANDN. COMMERCIAL CREDIT TORONTO REGION, THE BANK OF NOVA SCOTIA 1992– ; joined Bank of Nova Scotia, Carling & Woodroffe, Ottawa 1964; var. admin. positions in Ottawa; Acct., Calgary Main Br. 1971; Toronto Main Br. 1973; Asst. Chief Acct. 1976; Asst. Mgr. Toronto Main Br. 1978; Dep. Mgr., Montreal Main Br. 1980; Mgr. 1983; Asst. Gen. Mgr. & Dir., Credit, Toronto Suburban Region 1985; Gen. Mgr., Credit, Toronto Region 1986; Vice-Pres. & Mgr. Toronto Main Br. 1987; Dir., Candn. Hearing Soc. Found.; clubs: The National, The Toronto Bd. of Trade, St. George's Golf & Country; Home: 521 Golden Oak Dr., Oakville, Ont.; Office: 44 King St. W., Toronto, Ont. M5H 1H1.

**CARDINAL, Tantoo;** actress; b. Ft. McMurray, Alta. 20 July 1950; d. Julia C.; e. Bonnie Doon H.S. 1968; m. John s. John H. (Sr.) and Carolyn Lawlor 14 Jan. 1988; children: (his): Eric, Bryan, Elizabeth, Annie; (hers): Cheyenne, Clifford; (theirs): Riel; first acting opportunity with CBC TV on half-hour hist. drama, then several films with Alta. Native Communications Soc., trained on the job; involved with co-devel. theatre works with Native Surv. Schs. in Saskatoon & Edmonton; major milestone in career development: 'Loyalties' written by Sharon Riis & Anne Wheeler; feature films: 'Dance with Wolves'; 'Marie Anne' (introduced Tantoo as principal actor outside of native comm.); television: 'Gunsmoke' (Movie of the Week Remake); 'Campbells' guest star; NFB series Daughters of the Country's 'Place Not Our Own'; film: 'Candy Mountain' co-prod. btwn. Switz., France & Can.; nom. Best Actress, Genie Awards 1987 for 'Loyalties'; winner, Best Actress, Am. Indian Film Fest., San Francisco 1986; Alta. Motion Picture Indus. 1987; Tairo Portugal Internat. Film Fest.; Harare, Zimbabwe Internat. Film Fest.; honoured with Eagle Feather headdress at 1st Annual Pincher Creek Internat. Aboriginal Film Fest. for contribs. to image of native people in film; Pres., United Native Youth (Alta.) 1970–71; author of five 15–min. radio dramas for Alta. School Broadcasts 1978–79.

**CARDOZO, L. Andrew,** M.A.; writer; consultant; b. Karachi, Pakistan 21 March 1956; s. Leonard and Melba (Pinto) C.; e. York Univ. B.A. (Pol. Sci.) 1980; Carleton Univ. M.A. (Pub. Admin.) 1986; m. Joann d. Gordon and Germaine Garbig 8 June 1985; children: Alice Caroline, Anthony Charles; WRITER and CONSULTANT, diversity and administration issues 1991– ; Special Asst. to Min. of State for Multiculturalism 1980–83; Ottawa Dir., Ethnikos Mgmt. Cons. of Can. Ltd. 1983–86; Cons. to Stdg. Ctte. on Multiculturalism 1986; Extve. Dir., Candn. Ethnocultural Council 1986–91; has appeared before several Parlty. Cttes. to promote human rights and interests of ethnic minorities; frequent speaker at conferences and workshops; mem., English-As-A-Second-Language Support Coalition, Ottawa; Big Brother of the Yr., Ottawa & Dist. 1988; Dir., Ottawa-Carleton Immigrant Service Orgn. 1981–84; Chair, Media Monitor on Minority Concerns 1992– ; Mem. of the Bd., Ottawa YM-YWCA; mem. Big Brothers of Ottawa & Dist.; recreations: skiing, fitness; Home: 177 Percy St., Ottawa, Ont. K1R 6E6.

**CARDY, A. Gordon,** M.C., B.Com., K.L.J.; hotelier; b. Brockville, Ont. s. Roland Hastings and Jean Davidson (Gordon) C.; e. Trinity Coll., Univ. of Toronto, B.Com. (Hons.) 1941; m. Alice Elizabeth Cochrane 18 Sept. 1948; children: Barbara, Roland, Rosemary (dec.), Gordon; PRES., CARDY INVESTMENTS LIMITED 1986– ; PRES., GORBAY COMPANY LIMITED 1986– ; Gen. Mgr., Prince Edward Hotel (Windsor, Ont.) 1951–52, Sheraton Connaught Hotel (Hamilton, Ont.) 1952–54, Sheraton Brock Hotel (Niagara Falls, Ont.) 1954–55, Sheraton Hotel (Rochester, N.Y.) 1955–56, King Edward Sheraton Hotel (Toronto) 1956–68, Royal York Hotel (Toronto) 1968–71; Vice-Pres., Central Region, CP Hotels 1971–78; Dir. Cochrane Dunlop Hardware Ltd. 1972–81; Chrmn., Pres., C.E.O. & Dir., CP Hotels Ltd. 1978–86; Dir., Canadian Pacific Air Lines Ltd. 1984–86; Dir., Journey's End Corp. 1989– ; WW2 Lt., R.C.A. 1942–45; served in Europe, decorated Military Cross; Knight Grace Mil. and Hospitaller Order St. Lazarus of Jerusalem; Pres. (1973–74), Ont. Hotel & Motel Assn.; Pres. (1975) Hotel Assn. of Canada; Pres. (1969) Ont. Heart Found.; Hon. Dir. Metro Toronto Convention & Visitors Assn.; Hotelier of the Year, Commercial Travellers Assn. (1978); Gov., Ryerson Polytechnical Inst. (1978–81); Theta Delta Chi; United Church; recreations: skiing, golf, horseback riding; Clubs: Canadian (Dir. 1985–87); Royal Candn. Mil. Inst.; Bd. of Trade of Metro Toronto; Lambton Golf & Country; Home: 53 Dunvegan Rd., Toronto, Ont. M4V 2P5.

**CARELESS, James Maurice Stockford,** O.C. (1981); F.R.S.C. (1962); university professor; b. Toronto, Ont. 17 Feb. 1919; s. late William Roy Stockford and Ada Josephine (de Rees) C.; e. Univ. of Toronto Schs.; Univ. of Toronto, B.A. 1940; Harvard Univ., A.M. 1941 and Ph.D. 1950; m. Elizabeth Isabel, d. late Gordon Robinson, 31 Dec. 1941; five children; UNIVERSITY PROFESSOR EMERITUS, UNIV. OF TORONTO 1984– ; Sheldon Trav. Fellowship, Harvard Univ. 1942–43; joined Hist. Dept., Univ. of Toronto as a Lectr. 1945; Prof. of History there 1959–84 (and Chrmn. of Dept. 1959–67); Asst. to the Naval Historian, Naval Service Hdqrs., Ottawa 1943; Special Wartime Asst., Dept. of External Affairs, Ottawa 1943–45; author 'Canada: A Story of Challenge' 1953 (awarded Gov.-Gen.'s Medal, 1954); 'The Union of the Canadas' 1967; 'Brown of the Globe' (biog.) Vol. 1 (1959) and Vol. 2 (1963); 'Rise of Cities in Canada' 1978; 'Toronto to 1918' 1984; 'Frontier and Metropolis' 1989; co-author 'The Pioneers' 1969; 'Colonists and Canadiens' 1971; 'Aspects of 19th Century Ontario' 1974; 'Pre-Confederation Premiers' 1980; also numerous articles on hist. subjects in reviews and journs.; awarded Tyrrell Medal for Candn. Hist. 1962; rec'd Gov. Gen's Award for non-fiction ('Brown of the Globe') 1964; Cruickshank Medal of Ont. Hist. Soc. 1968; Senior Research Fellow, Australian National University 1978; Trustee, Ont. Science Centre 1963–73; Dir., Ont. Heritage Foundation 1975–1981; Chrmn., Ont. Hist. Studies Series since 1982; Hist. Sites & Monuments Bd. of Can. 1980–85; Multicultural Hist. Soc., 1976–88; mem. Comn. on Post-Secondary Educ. in Ont. 1968–72; mem., Candn. Hist. Assn. (Pres. 1967–68); Ont. Hist. Soc. (Pres. 1959); Order of Ontario 1987; Address: Toronto, Ont. M5S 1A1.

**CARELESS, Robert John Paget,** C.A., F.C.A. (England & Wales); chartered accountant; b. Wolverhampton, England 10 May 1947; s. Stanley James and Barbara (Kirkham) C.; e. Bromsgrove Sch. (U.K.); m. Katie d. Herbert and Marie Bayliss 1975; children: Jonathan, David; SECRETARY-TREASURER, THE ONTARIO JOCKEY CLUB 1985– ; Audit Mgr., Ernst & Young, Birmingham, England 1971–82; Toronto 1982–85; Treas., Racetracks of Can.; Treas., E.P. Taylor Equine Rsch. Fund; Sec./Treas., Race Track Security Can.; recreations: squash, skiing, golf; Home: 1286 Devon Rd., Oakville, Ont. L6J 2L8; Office: P.O. Box 156, Rexdale, Ont. M9W 5L2.

**CARELESS, Virginia Ann Stockford,** B.A., M.A.; history curator; b. Toronto, Ont. 31 May 1946; d. James Maurice Stockford and Elizabeth Isobel (Robinson) C.; e. Brown Pub. Sch., Toronto (Gen. Prof. Scholarship) 1959; North Toronto Coll. Inst. (Beta Tau Sigma Scholarship for Excellence in English, 1962) 1964; Trinity Coll., Univ. of Toronto, B.A. (Hons.) 1968; Univ. of B.C., M.A. 1974; HIST. CURATOR, ROYAL B.C. MUSEUM 1986– ; Teaching Asst., Univ. of B.C. 1968–70; Asst. Hist., Vancouver Centennial Mus. 1969; Artifacts Rschr., Nat. Mus. of Man. 1973–74; Curator of Furnishings & Interior Design, Royal B.C. Museum 1974; Freelance hist. rschr. 1975–79; Soc. Hist. Technician, Royal B.C. Museum 1979–86; jury mem., Can. Counc. Explorations Prog. 1982–85; Canadian Sch. of Ballet Scholarship 1957, 1958; Royal Conservatory of Music of Toronto Scholarship, 1961, 1964; Trinity Coll. Fellowship 1968; Ont. Grad. Fellowship 1968; Univ. of B.C. Scholarship 1970; mem., P.E.I. Museum & Heritage Assn.; SPCA; Friends of the U.B.C. Library; Friends of Trinity Lib.; Vancouver Symphony Soc.; Victoria Symphony Soc.; Hallmark Soc. of Victoria; Endometriosis Assn.; author: 'Bibliography for the Study of B.C.'s Domestic Material History' 1976; 'Responding to Fashion: The Clothing of the O'Reilly Family' 1993; 'Clue to a Culture: Food Preparation of the O'Reilly Family' 1993; co-author: 'Impression of an Age' (Exhibit catalogue) 1969; Anglican; recreations: playing the flute, singing, replications of hist. handcrafts & cooking, hiking, creative writing, genealogy; Home: Victoria, B.C. V8V 3H3; Office: 675 Belleville St., Victoria, B.C. V8V 1X4.

**CAREY, Hon. B. Patrick,** B.A., LL.B.; chief provincial judge; b. Lucky Lake, Sask. 31 May 1942; s. Leroy C. and Lois M. C.; e. Univ. of Sask., B.A. 1963, LL.B. 1966; m. Patricia d. Thomas H.C. and Constance Barclay 8 Oct. 1968; children: Michael, Gislaine, Graeme; CHIEF JUDGE, PROVINCIAL COURT FOR THE PROVINCE OF SASKATCHEWAN 1987– ; practised law in City of Saskatoon 1966–82; Chief of Staff to Min. of Justice for the Prov. of Sask. 1982–84; Provincial Court Judge, City of Saskatoon 1984–87; Office: 1815 Smith St., Regina, Sask. S4P 3V7.

**CAREY, Barbara L.,** B.A.; writer; editor; b. Ottawa, Ont. 9 Apl. 1955; d. Kenneth Morton and Rita (McCloskey) C.; e. Queen's Univ. 1974–75; Univ. of Toronto Univ. Coll. B.A. 1977; MNG. ED. 'BOOKS IN CANADA' mag. 1988– ; Copy Ed. 'Kingston Whig-Standard' 1983–84 and King West Communications (formerly Saturday Night Publs.) 1987–88; caseworker mun. social services Kingston 3 yrs.; author (poetry) 'Undressing the Dark' 1986; 'The Year in Pictures' 1989 (finalist 1990 Trillium Award and 1989 Pat Lowther Award); 'The Ground of Events' 1994; various reviews, articles newspapers and mags.; Home: 324, 219 College St., Toronto, Ont. M5T 1R1; Office: 130 Spadina Ave., Ste. 603, Toronto, Ont. M5V 2L4.

**CAREY, John J.;** insurance executive; b. Streator, Ill. 23 May 1928; s. John J. C.; e. Univ. of Notre Dame (with hons.) 1952; m. Zelma Benckendorf; children: John Jr., Ann, Daniel, Leigh; CHRMN., ALLENDALE MUTUAL INS. CO. 1988– ; various positions, Mutual Boiler & Machinery Ins. Co. 1954–59; Mgr., Middlesex Fin. Mngt. Corp. 1959–68; Pres., The Connell Co. 1968–76; Vice-Pres., Admin., Arkwright-Boston Mfrs. Mutual Ins. Co. 1976–79; Mng. Dir., FM Ins. Co. Limited, London, Eng. 1979; Sr. Vice-Pres., Admin., Allendale Mutual Ins. Co. 1979, Sr. Vice-Pres., Regional Opns. 1980, Extve. Vice-Pres. 1981, Pres. & C.O.O. 1982, Dir. 1982, Pres. & C.E.O. 1985, Chrmn., Pres. & C.E.O. 1988; Bank of Boston 1988; Dir., ESCO Electronics Corp. 1990; Chrmn., Strategic Planning Cttee., Diocese of Providence 1992– ; Mem., Catholic Charities 1986– ; Bd. of Govs., National Assn. of Independent Insurers (NAII) 1992; Home: 12166 Water Oak Dr., Estero, FL 33928; Office: Allendale Park, Johnston, RI 02919.

**CAREY, Lewis Stafford,** M.D., C.M., M.Sc., M.S., F.R.C.P., F.A.C.R.; radiologist; educator; b. Yorkton, Sask. 9 July 1925; s. Edward H. and Gladys C.; e. King Edward High Sch. Vancouver; Univ. of B.C.; Queen's Univ. M.D., C.M. 1950, M.Sc. (Med.) 1956; Univ. of Minn. M.S. 1959; m. Beverly Jane d. Dr. Wallace Baxter, Burlington, Ont. Sept. 1950; children: Richard, Mark, Susan, John, David; patient care (clin. work), teaching and research, Univ. Hosp., Univ. of W. Ont.; Chrmn., Dept. Diagnostic Radiology & Nuclear Medicine, Univ. of W. Ont. 1971–86; residency in Surg., Mayo Clinic 1953–56, in Diagnostic Radiol. 1956–58; Diplomate Am. Bd. Radiol. 1958; holds patent Devel. Mobile X-Ray Unit for Bedside Pacemaker Insertion – Visa Cart (1972); Exper. Leader, Telemed. Exper. U-6 Using CTS Satellite Hermes 1976–77; Chrmn. Northern Health Services 1973–79; co-author 'Congenital Heart Disease: Correlation Pathological Anatomy and Angio-cardiography' 2 vols. (French and Eng.) 1965; author or co-author numerous med. publs.; Fellow, Am. Coll. Radiol.; mem. Alumnae Assn. Mayo Foundation for Med. Ed. & Research; Am. Roentgen Ray Soc.; Assn. Univ. Radiols.; Candn. Assn. Radiols.; Candn. Med. Protective Assn.; Candn. Profs. Radiol.; Council on Cardio-vascular Radiol.; Minn. Radiol. Soc.; N. Am. Soc. Cardiac Radiols.; Radiol. Soc. N. Am.; Solar Energy Soc. Can.; Home: 103 Salisbury Dr., R.R. 4, Denfield, Ont. N0M 1P0.

**CAREY, Thomas J.P.,** LL.B.; lawyer; b. Cobourg, Ont. 28 Feb. 1953; s. Thomas Joseph and Mary Norma (Lynch) C.; e. Michael Power H.S. 1972 (Ont. Scholar); Univ. of Western Ont., King's Coll. 1972–74; Univ. of Windsor LL.B. 1977; m. Karen E. d. Stanley and Ann Stanley 28 May 1982; children: Julia, Alicia; ASSOCIATE, CAREY, FROUD & MCCALLUM; called to Bar of Ont. 1979; Bencher, Law Soc. of U.C. 1988–91; Teacher, Law Soc. of Can. Bar Admission Course (Criminal Law) 1991– ; Certified Specialist in Criminal Litigation, Law Soc. of U.C. 1989; Roman Catholic; Home: 148 High Park Ave., Toronto, Ont.; Office: Suite 100C, 131 Brunel Rd., Mississauga, Ont. L4Z 1X3.

**CARGO, Ronald James;** energy executive; b. Red Deer, Alta. 1943; s. Harry James C.; e. Soc. of Mgmt. Accts. of Ont., C.M.A. degree; Univ. of Colorado, Mech. Engineering; m. Lorraine d. Reuben Deering 28 July 1967; children: Kim, Tracy, Steven; PRES. AND CHIEF EXECUTIVE OFFICER, BLUE SPRINGS ENERGY LTD. 1992– ; Chrmn. of the Bd., IPAC (Independent Petroleum Assoc. of Can.) 1989; various pos., Amerada Petroleum Corp. 1962–69; Mgr., Drilling & Prodn., Candn. Worldwide Energy Limited 1969–77; Vice-Pres., Opns. 1977–80; Sr. Vice-Pres. 1980–82; Pres., C.O.O. & Dir., Triton Canada Resources Ltd. (formerly Canadian Worldwide Energy Limited) 1982–92; Mem., Soc. of Mgmt. Accts. of Can.; Soc. of Petroleum Engrs. of A.I.M.E.; recreations: Clubs: Calgary Petroleum; Bearspaw Golf & Country; Home: Aspen Dr. N.W., Box 7, Site 21, SS1, Calgary, Alta. T2M 4N3.

**CARIGNAN, Pierre,** Q.C., M.A., LL.L.; b. Lachine, Que. 21 Apr. 1922; s. Anatole and Marie-Rose (Parker) C.; e. Coll. de Montreal 1934–40; Semy. de Philos. B.A. 1942; Univ. of Montreal, LL.L. 1945; Harvard Univ., M.A. (Econ.) 1947; m. Rita, d. Donat Heroux, Verdun, Que., 26 Feb. 1949; two d.; Isabelle, Genevieve; PROFESSOR OF LAW, UNIV. OF MONTREAL (formerly Dean of Faculty there); former mem. Consultative Comte. on Bankruptcy Leg.; former Dir. Public Law Rsch. Inst., Univ. of Montreal; former mem. Restrictive Trade Practices Comn.; called to Bar of Que. 1945; cr. Q.C. 1959; Home: 4845 West Broadway, Montreal, Qué. H4V 1R5.

**CARISSE, Jean-Claude,** B.Comm., B.Soc.Sc., C.A.E.; association administrator; b. Ottawa, Ont. 11 Apr. 1943; s. André and Yvonne (Dalpé) C.; e. Ecole Brébeuf, Ottawa 1956; Acad. de-la-Salle, Ottawa 1960; Univ. of Ottawa, B.Comm. 1967; B.Soc.Sc. 1969; children: Geneviève, Isabelle; Admin., Candn. Fed. of Mayors & Municipalities 1970–73; Owner/Chief Admin., own business (multiple-assn. mngt.) 1973–80; Extve. Dir., Candn. Veterinary Med. Assn. 1981–89; Extve. Dir., Candn. Assoc. on Gerontology 1989– ; Bd. of Adv., First Ed., 'Who's Who in Veterinary Science & Medicine' 1987; mem., Candn. Soc. of Assn. Extves. 1971– ; (Pres., Ottawa chap. 1987–88; Chrmn., Nat. Cert. Counc. 1988–89); Dir., Caisse populaire St-Jean-Baptiste of Ottawa, since 1985; recreation: racquetball, Nautilus; Club: Sporthèque de Hull; Home: 51 Pelletier, Hull, Qué. J8Z 1C4; Office: 1306 Wellington St., Ste. 500, Ottawa, Ont. K1Y 3B2.

**CARISSE, Terrance (Terry) Victor;** songwriter, publisher, entertainer; b. Ottawa, Ont. 11 July 1942; s. Victor Joseph and Edna Lillian (Matthews) C.; e. elementary and high school Ottawa; m. Aija d. Vera and Jacob Skadins 15 Oct. 1976; children: Stephen, Christian, Sean; one of Canada's most honoured & awarded singer/songwriters; wrote & performed 4 songs in Candn. movie 'Rowdyman' 1972; recipient of 13 certificates of honour for outstanding contbn. to Candn. music from BMI, PROCAN, SOCAN; awards: 7 country male vocalist awards 1980, '81, '87 (RPM), '82, '84, '85, '86 (CCMA), 1983 (Country Music News); all-time favourite country male vocalist Country Music News 1988; Composer of the Year 1981, '85, '86; Candn. Music Pub. Assn. Award 1987; album of the year: 'We Could Make Beautiful Music Together' 1981, 'Closest Thing to You' 1985, 'None of the Feeling is Gone' 1987; single of the year: 'Windship' 1981; Record Producer of the Year 1985 (CCMA); Publisher of the Year (wrote & performed theme song for World Jamboree for Boy Scouts) 1984; album discography: 'Story of the Year' 1979, 'We Could Make Beautiful Music Together' 1981 (MBS), 'A

Gospel Gathering' 1982, 'Closest Thing to You' '1984, 'None of the Feeling is Gone' 1986, 'That Was a Long Time Ago' 1989 (Savannah Records); inducted into Ottawa Valley Hall of Fame 1989; appt. to Bd. of Dir. for Ottawa Valley Hall of Fame 1994; recreations: painting (artwork), reading, fishing; Home: 5588 Richmond Rd., R.R. 7, Nepean, Ont. K2H 7V2.

**CARLISLE, David Brez,** B.A., M.A., D.Phil., D.Sc.; environmental scientist; b. U.K. 12 March 1926; s. James and Phyllis (Brez) C.; e. Oxford Univ. B.A., M.A., D.Phil, D.Sc.; m. Roxane Odette d. John and Odette de Musset Connick 1969; children: Tamsin, Julia, Daloni, Alison, Damaris; SENIOR RESEARCH SCIENTIST & RESEARCH ADVISOR, ENVIRONMENT CANADA; Physiologist, Stazione Zoologia di Napoli Italy; Physiologist, Marine Lab., Plymouth U.K.; Dir. of Rsch., Ministry of Overseas Devel., U.K.; Royal Soc., Leverhulme Prof. of Physiol., Khartoum, Sudan; Visiting Prof., Czech Academy of Sciences, Prague; Prof. & Chrmn., Biology Dept., Trent Univ.; currently Visiting Prof., Univ. of Toronto; Bursar, Marine Biol. Assn., U.K.; Chrmn., Bd. of Dir., IsoTrace Lab., Univ. of Toronto; Life Mem., Soc. of Ethnomusicology; Royal Soc. of Arts; Am. Anthropol. Assn.; Royal Anthropol. Assn.; Geological Assn.; Fellow, Royal Ontario Museum, Toronto; author: 'Feeding Mechanisms in Tunicata' 1982; 'Dinosaurs, Diamonds and Things From Outer Space: The Great Extinction' 1993; and approx. 400 sci. papers & 40 monographs; co-author: 'Endocrine Control in Crustaceans' 1959, 'The Pogonophora' 1963; editor: 'The Future of Accelerator Mass Spectrometry in Canada' 1991; Assoc. Ed. 'J. of the Marine Biol. Assn.'; recreations: rowing, music; Home: P.O. Box 3473, Station C, Ottawa, Ont. K1Y 4J6; Office: Geology Dept., University of Toronto, Toronto, Ont. M5S 3B1.

**CARLISLE, John Russell,** M.D., LL.B., F.C.L.M.; physician; b. Toronto, Ont. 1 June 1945; s. John Spencer and Shirley Ruth (Hellyer) C.; e. Univ. of Toronto, M.D. 1969, LL.B. 1973; DEP. REGISTRAR, COLL. OF PHYS. & SURGS. OF ONT. 1987– ; and TREASURER, MEDICO-LEGAL SOCIETY OF TORONTO 1993– ; sessional lectr. in Law & Med., Osgoode Hall Law Sch.; attending physician, Queen Elizabeth Hosp., Toronto 1970–74; Assoc. Registrar and Dir., Med. Rev. & Profl. Assessment, Coll. of Phys. & Surgs. of Ont., 1974–1986; Pres., Candn. Coll. of Legal Med.; Past Pres., Am. Coll. of Legal Med.; Sec., Caduceus Club of Toronto; senior med. attendant & consultant, Camp Timberlane, Haliburton, Ont.; co-author 'Cases and Materials on Law and Medicine' 1985; Home: #326, 40 Oaklands Ave., Toronto, Ont. M4V 2Z3; Office: 80 College St., Toronto, Ont. M5G 2E2.

**CARLSEN, Lloyd Niels,** M.D., C.M., F.R.C.S.(C), F.A.C.S.; plastic surgeon; b. Sask. 29 Feb. 1932; s. Martin and Dora C.; e. Luther Coll. Regina (Gold Medalist), Assoc. Arts Degree 1951; Queen's Univ. M.D. 1957; 7 yrs postgrad. training Vancouver, Queen's Univ., Glasgow Univ., Mt. Vernon Plastic Surgery Centre (London, Eng.), Toronto, New York City; Certification in Plastic Surgery 1961; m. Ruth d. George and Elsie Craig 29 Apr. 1958; children: Ian, Thor, Lisa; DIR. COSMETIC SURGERY HOSP. 1971– ; Chief of Plastic Surgery Scarborough Gen. Hosp. 1966– , mem. Active Staff 1964– , Chief of Surgery 1975–78, Co-founder Burns Unit (1st in Can.) 1966; devel. The Cosmetic Surgery Hosp. Caribbean; served Care-Medico in underdevel. countries; awarded Citation of Merit in Vietnam 1973 for training Vietnamese surgeons in patient care during war; mem. first Candn. Mt. Everest Expdn.; co-author 'The Naked Face' 1979; Past Pres., Candn. Soc. for Aesthetic (Cosmetic) Plastic Surgery 1985–86; mem. Toronto Acad. Med.; Ont. Med. Assn.; Candn. Med. Assn.; Candn. Soc. Plastic Surg.; Brit. Soc. Plastic Surgs.; Am. Soc. Plastic & Reconstructive Surgs.; Am. Soc. Aesthetic Surg.; Am. Burn Assn.; Am. Soc. Hand Surg.; Internat. Soc. Aesthetic Surgs.; Internat. Soc. Burn Injuries; recreations: alpine skiing, race car driving, mountain climbing, scuba diving; Home: 60 Fairway Heights Dr., Thornhill, Ont. L3T 3A9; Office: 4650 Highway 7, Woodbridge, Ont. L4L 1S7.

**CARLSON, Donald Arthur,** P.Eng., B. Sc.; business executive; b. Edmonton, Alta. 27 Oct. 1931; s. Arthur Victor and Belle Pearl (Snider) C.; e. Oliver Sch. and Westglen High Sch. Edmonton 1950; Univ. of Alta. B.A.Sc. (Civil Engn.) 1954; Mass. Inst. Technol. postgrad. work in constr. mang.; m. Elizabeth d. Mike Manasterski 27 Dec. 1958; children: Dennis Arthur, Susan Leslie, Douglas Scott, John David; CHAIRMAN, VENCAP EQUITIES ALBERTA LTD. 1984– ; Pres., Carlson Development Corp. Ltd.; Pres., World President's Organization, Washington, D.C. 1989; Dir., Bellanca Developments Ltd.; National Trust Co.; Princeton Developments Ltd.; Trans Mountain Pipe Line Co. Ltd.; Gov., Edmonton Eskimo Football Club; Project Mgr. A.V. Carlson Construction Ltd. 1950–64; Pres., A.V. Carlson Construction Ltd. 1964–79, Chrmn. 1979–83; mem. Prof. Engrs. Prov. Alta.; Chief Executives Organization, Inc.; Society Delta Upsilon; recreations: travel, skiing, jogging, scuba; Clubs: Skal; Edmonton Petroleum; Center; Home: 2 Laurier Pl., Edmonton, Alta. T5R 5P4; Office: 1400, 9945 – 108 St., Edmonton, Alta. T5K 2G6.

**CARLSON, Quinton L.,** B.Sc., P.E.; business executive, retired; b. Mass. 7 Dec. 1920; s. John Frederick and Helga E. (Jarl) C.; e. U.S. Naval Acad.; Penn State Univ.; Northeastern Univ. B.Sc. 1943; m. June d. William and Mayme King 4 June 1945; children: Michael, Tondra, Patricia Franche; Project Mgr., for Wm. Zeckendorff, Place Ville Marie 1958; Vice-Pres., Place Victoria project; co-founded Concordia Mngt. Co. Ltd. to build Place Bonaventure World Trade Ctr.; Offr. (Chief Engr.), U.S. Navy during World II & Korean War; achieved rank of Lieut. Comdr.; Candn. citizen; recreations: golf; club: M.A.A.A. Montreal; Home: 1 Redpath Pl., Montreal, Que. H3G 1C9.

**CARLSON, Roy L.,** M.A., Ph.D.; archaeologist; anthropologist; educator; b. Bremerton, Wash., 25 June 1930; s. Peter Lincoln and Margaret Mary (Clark) C.; e. Univ. of Wash., B.A. 1952, M.A. 1955; Univ. of Ariz., Ph.D. 1961; m. Maureen Joyce, d. James Kelly, Vancouver, B.C. 13 June 1953; children: Catherine Carroll, Daniel James, Arne Kelly, Christopher Clark; PROF. DEPT. OF ARCHAEOL., SIMON FRASER UNIV. since 1971; Dir., S.F.U. Museum of Archaeology & Ethnology 1973–79, 1984–89; Chrmn., Dept. of Archaeology, S.F.U. 1971–79, 1984–89; Curator, Klamath Co. Museum, Klamath Falls, Ore. 1957–58; Teaching and Research Asst., Univ. of Ariz., 1959; Asst. Prof., Univ. of Colo. Boulder, 1961; Field Dir., Univ. of Colo. 4th Nubian Expdn., Africa, 1965; joined present Univ. as Asst. Prof. 1966, Assoc. Prof. 1967–71; author 'Basket Maker III Sites Near Durango, Colorado' 1963; 'Eighteenth Century Navajo Fortresses of the Gobernador District' 1965; 'White Mountain Red Ware' 1970; 'Teachers' Manual for Early Indian Cultures of North America' 1973; 'Indian Art Traditions of the Northwest Coast' 1983; 'The Far West' in 'Early Man in the New World' 1983; chapters in 'Handbook of North American Indians, Northwest Coast', Vol. 7, 1990; Ed. 'Current Research Reports' (Dept. of Archaeol., Simon Fraser Univ., Publ. No. 3) 1976; 'Salvage '71: Reports on Salvage Archaeology in British Columbia' 1973; 'Archaeology in British Columbia New Discoveries' 1970; mem. Candn. Archaeol. Assn.; Soc. Am. Archaeol.; Am. Indian Art Studies Assn.; Am. Assn. for the Advancement of Sci; Home: 888 Seymour Dr., Coquitlam, B.C. V3J 6V7; Office: Burnaby, B.C. V5A 1S6.

**CARMAN, Ian Douglas,** B.A.; editor; b. St. Thomas, Ont. 17 June 1927; s. Samuel James and Bertha Lyle (Appleford) c.; e. McMaster Univ. B.A. 1950; Dir. of Corporate Development, The Globe and Mail 1987–90; Reporter 1951; Asst. to Ed. The Globe Magazine 1961, Nat. Ed. 1962, Foreign Ed. 1963, Business Ed. 1966, Ed. Report on Business 1979; Extve. Ed. 1981; recipient Nat. Business Writing Award 1979; United Church; Club: Toronto Press; Home: 2502, 50 Alexander St., Toronto, Ont. M4Y 1B6.

**CARMAN, James Keith,** B.A.Sc.; retired industrial executive; b. Talbotville, Ont. 6 June 1922; s. Samuel James and Bertha Lyle (Appleford) C.; e. Burlington High Sch.; Hamilton Tech. Inst.; Univ. of Toronto B.A.Sc. (Mech. Engn.) 1950; m. Audrey d. Wilton and Edith Moore 21 Oct. 1950; children: Lynn Suzanne Rutherford, Peter James; Process Engr. Remington Rand Ltd. 1950–52; Mfg. Engr. Electronics, Westinghouse Canada Inc. 1952–55, Project Engr. 1955–56, Supvr. Mfg. Engn. 1956–59, Supt. Indust. & Mfg. Engn. 1959–61, Mgr. Mfg. Electronics 1961–66, Mgr. Electronics Div. 1966–68, Gen. Mgr. Electronics Systems & Components Group 1968–76, Vice Pres. Marketing & Tech. Services 1976, Vice Pres. Marketing & Strategic Resources 1978, Vice Pres. Strategic Resources & External Affairs 1981, Vice Pres. Strategic Planning & Corp. Affairs 1982, Vice Pres. Commercial Development 1991, Retired; Vice Chair, Mohawk College and Chair Planning Ctte.; mem. Assn. Prof. Engrs. Prov. Ont.; mem., Hamilton & Dist. Chamber of Commerce; mem., Hamilton Dist. Salvation Army Adv. Bd.; Presbyterian; Clubs: Oakville Golf; Home: 2131 Gary Cres., Burlington, Ont. L79 1T1.

**CARMAN, Robert Dicks,** B.Sc.F.; executive; former civil servant; b. Chatham, Ont. 13 July 1932; s. Ralph Sylvester and Minnie Gwendolyn (Dicks) C.; e. Barrie Dist. Collegiate Inst.; Univ. of Toronto, B.Sc.F. 1954, Gold Medal; m. Beverley Jean d. Arthur and Sarah Hills 18 Sept. 1954; children: Douglas, Donald, Barbara; PRESIDENT, NAMRAC & ASSOCIATES LTD. 1993– ; Reforestation Soils & Site Specialist, Dept. of Lands & Forests 1954–61; Area Mgr., Kirkwood Mgmt. Unit 1961–64; Chief Silviculturalist, Northwestern Pulp & Power Co. 1964–68; Supr. of Land Use Planning, Dept. of Lands & Forests 1968–69; Supr., Planning Group, Office of the Dep. Min. 1969–71; Regional Dir., S. Ont. 1971–72; Dir., Planning & Devel., Mgmt. Bd. of Cabinet 1972–73; Exec. Dir., Progs. & Estimates 1973–77; Dep. Min., Community & Soc. Services 1978–81; Sec., Mgmt. Bd. of Cabinet 1982–85; Sec., Policy & Priorities Bd. of Cabinet 1985; Sec. of the Cabinet & Clerk of the Exec. Counc. Ont. 1985–89; Special Advisor to the Premier of Ont. 1989–90; Sr. Vice Pres., Weston Foods Ltd. 1990–93; Candn. Silver Jubilee Medal; Vanier Medal 1988; Honoree, Public Policy Forum 1989; Dir. & mem. of Exec. Ctte., Niagara Inst.; Univ. of Toronto Forestry Alumni Assn. (Pres. 1977–78); Inst. of Pub. Admin. of Can. (Ed. Bd. mem. 1982–85); author 'An Industrial Application of the Container Planting Technique,' Pulp & Paper Mag. of Can. 1967; co-author (with K.A. Armson) 'Manual for Forest Tree Nursery Soil Management' 1961; recreation: tree farming, skiing, canoeing; Home: 13 Sylvan Valleyway, Toronto, Ont. M5M 4M4.

**CARMICHAEL, Hugh,** B.Sc., M.A., Ph.D., F.R.S.C.; physicist; b. Farr, Sutherland, Scotland 10 Nov. 1906; s. Rev. Dugald and Agnes Macmillan (Macaulay) C.; e. Univ. of Edinburgh, B.Sc. (1st Class Hons. in Physics) 1929; Univ. of Cambridge, Ph.D. 1936, M.A. Cantab. 1939; Fellow, St. John's Coll., Cambridge, 1936–40; m. late Margaret Elizabeth May d. Thomas Forbes Maclennan 23 Oct. 1937; children: Dugald Macaulay, Margaret Lind (Mrs. Wilson Stuart), Elizabeth Agnes (Mrs. Gary Cooper), Hugh Alexander Lorne; Carnegie Research Fellow, University of Edinburgh, 1929–33; Clark Maxwell Research Scholar, Univ. of Cambridge, 1933–37; Demonst., University of Cambridge, 1937–44; Senior Principal Scient. Offr., Min. of Supply, Atomic Energy Mission to Can., 1944–50; Principal Research Offr., Head of Gen. Physics Br., Atomic Energy of Can. Ltd. 1950–71; during 2nd World War, Meteorol. Office, 1939–40 and Hankey Scheme, 1941–44; member of Wordie Expdn. to N.W. Greenland 1937, conducting first free balloon exper. to measure cosmic radiation near the geomagnetic pole up to an altitude of 18 miles; designed, for the 1964–65 Int. Quiet Sun Year, the NM-64 cosmic ray monitor, and promoted its manufacture in Can. and its installation worldwide; mem., Inter-Union Comm. on Solar-Terrestrial Physics, 1966–72; has written scient. and tech. reports and papers on cosmic radiation, space physics, solar flares, nuclear reactor control and instrumentation, fused silica micro-balance, nuclear physics, radio-active contamination control; mem. Candn. Assn. Physicists; American Geophys. Union; Protestant; recreations: sailing, golf, curling, hunting; Home: 9 Beach Ave., Deep River, Ont. K0J 1P0.

**CARMICHAEL, Hugh Alexander Lorne,** B.A., Ph.D.; university professor; b. Deep River, Ont. 18 Feb. 1953; s. Hugh and Mae (Maclennan) C.; e. Univ. of W. Ont., B.A. (Hons.) 1976 (gold medal); Stanford Univ., Ph.D. 1981; m. Susan d. Anna Mae and Robert Hara 17 May 1981; children: Rayna Nicole, Christopher Maclennan; PROF., ECON. DEPT., QUEEN'S UNIV. 1990– ; joined present univ. 1980; National Fellow, Hoover Inst., Stanford Univ. 1983; Vis. Prof., Univ. of Washington 1986; B.C. 1988; Australian Nat. Univ. 1989; Adv. Ed., 'Economics Letters' 1986–93, 'American Economic Review' 1991– ; Assoc. Ed., 'Canadian Journal of Economics' 1986–88, Managing Ed. 1993–94; several rsch. grants & a postdoct. fellowship (1981–83) from SSHRCC; rsch. interest mainly concerns the economics of labour market institutions; author of several scholarly articles; recreations: woodworking, windsurfing; Home: 374 Albert St., Kingston, Ont. K7L 3W2; Office: Kingston, Ont. K7L 3N6.

**CARMICHAEL, John B.W.;** B.A.; executive; b. Toronto, Ont. 14 Feb. 1952; e. Upper Canada College, Toronto; Univ. of Western Ontario, B.A. 1974; married with three children; PRESIDENT & DIRECTOR, CITY BUICK PONTIAC CADILLAC LTD. and EXCELEASE CORP.; Pres., Candn. Internat. Autoshow; Immediate Past Pres., Toronto Automobile Dealers' Assn.; Vice Pres. & Dir., Wocar Holdings Ltd.; DTE Industries Ltd.; Huntington Stud Farm Inc.; Bd. of Governors, Bishop Strachan School; recreations: golf, tennis, skiing; Office: 1900 Victoria Park Ave., Scarborough, Ont. M1R 1T6.

**CARMICHAEL, Robert-Ralph,** B.A.; artist; b. Sault Ste. Marie, Ont. 20 Dec. 1937; s. Robert Garfield and

Lila Margaret C.; e. Sault Coll. Inst. 1954; Ont. Coll. of Art A.O.C.A. (Drawing & Painting) 1959; Carleton Univ. B.A. 1964; m. Gwendolene d. Russell and Margaret Keatley 28 Aug. 1964; exhns. incl. Winnipeg Art Gallery 1972, Edmonton Art Gallery 1974, Agnes Etherington Art Gallery Kingston 1978, Tom Thomson Gallery Owen Sound 1985, Ont. Place Toronto 1986; coins minted by the Royal Candn. Mint incl. The Loon Dollar 1987, The Blacksmith Dollar (commemorative) 1988, The Bowhead Whale 100 Dollar gold coin 1988, The Lancaster 20 Dollar (commemorative) 1990; medallion, Inco, Sudbury to commemorate opening of new plant by Prince of Wales 1991; The Fairchild 71C 20 Dollar (commemorative) 1993; The Lockheed 14 20 Dollar (commemorative) 1993; rep. various pub., private & corporate colls.; author and illus. 'The Seed-Pod Book of Joy' 1974; recreations: snow shoeing, canoeing; Address: R.R.1, Echo Bay, Ont. P0S 1C0.

**CARNEGIE, James Gordon,** OStJ, KCLJ, KMLJ; association executive; b. Toronto, Ont. 22 Oct. 1934; s. Fredrick Thomas 'Andy' and Helen Webber (Bawden) C.; e. Upper Can. Coll.; Forest Hill C.I.; m. Gail Elizabeth d. Ernest P. and Olga Jarvis 25 June 1955; children: Elizabeth Anne, Martha Jane, Christopher James; EXTVE. DIR., THE ONTARIO CHAMBER OF COMMERCE 1972– ; Investment Dealer 1954–72 (Chrmn., Tor. Bond Traders Assn. 1967); Extve. Dir., Ont. Bus. Adv. Counc. 1979– ; Ont. Computerized Investment Network 1986–88; Pres. & Chief Op. Offr., Can. Opportunities Investment Network 1988– ; Mem., Bd. of Ref., Can. Unemployment Comn.; Ont. C. of C. Extves.; C. of C. Extves. of Can.; Inst. of Corp. Dir.; 'Gardiner Award' 1987 (Metro Tor Citizen of the Year); 'Top Achiever' Toronto Sun 1986; Ont. Auxiliary Police Medal 1986, Bar 1987; Paul Harris Fellow 1992; awarded Commemorative Medal for 125th Anniversary of Candn. Confederation 1993; Vice Chrmn., Metro Toronto Br., St. John Ambulance; Depy. Chief (Commndg.) Metro Toronto Aux. Police; Mem., Internat. Assn. of Chiefs of Police; Ont. Assn. of Chiefs of Police; Bd. of Trade of Metro. Toronto; Life Mem., Toronto Br., St. John Ambulance; numerous distinctions & awards; recreations: police badge collecting, model soldier painting & collecting; club: Royal Candn. Military Inst.; Home: 45 Wynford Hts. Cres., Toronto, Ont. M3C 1L2; Office: Ste. 501, 2345 Yonge St., Toronto, Ont. M4P 2E5.

**CARNES, Kenneth Duncan,** M.A.; marketing executive; b. Victoria, B.C. 25 Oct. 1947; s. William George and Mary Alphonsine (Boulet) C.; e. Univ. of Victoria B.A. 1973; Keio Univ. Tokyo M.A. 1976; m. Debbie d. Art and Shirley Warrener 16 May 1981; children: Cole Duncan, Lindsay Anne, Kimberly Janet; VICE PRES. MKTG. FORDING COAL LTD. 1983– ; Asst. Mgr. Mitsui & Co. Canada 1976–80; Mgr. Mktg. present Co. 1980, Gen. Mgr. Mktg. 1981; Dir., Candn. Carbonization Rsch. Assn.; Office: 200, 205 9th Ave. S.E., Calgary, Alta. T2G 0R4.

**CARNEY, Hon. Patricia,** P.C., B.A., M.A.; senator; economist; regional planner; b. Shanghai, China 26 May 1935; d. James and Dora (Sanders) C.; e. Univ. of B.C. B.A., M.A.; div.; children: John Patrick Dickson, Jane Reid; apptd. to the SENATE OF CANADA 1990; Adjunct Prof., Univ. of B.C.; former economic journalist; former mem., Economic Counc. of Can.; estbd. Gemini North Ltd. 1970 (consulting firm specializing in socio-economic impact studies); el. to H. of C. for Vancouver Centre 1980; served as Opposition Critic for Secy. of State, Min. of State for Finance, Min. of Finance; re-el. 1984; Min. of Energy, Mines and Resources 1984–86; Min. for International Trade, also responsible for Can.-U.S. trade negotiations 1986–88; Pres. of the Treasury Bd., Apr. to Oct. 1988; Chrmn. of Cabinet Ctte. on Trade; mem. Candn. Inst. of Planners; Assn. of Profl. Economists of B.C.; Honorary Fellow, Royal Architectural Institute of Canada 1989; LL.D. (hon. causa), Univ. of B.C. 1990; Offices: The Senate of Canada, Ottawa, Ont. K1A 0A4.

**CARON, H. Marcel,** F.C.A.; docteur hon. causa (Univ. de Montreal); O.C.; Fellow comptable agréé; né Montréal, Qué. 16 sept. 1919; f. Henri et Eva (Mercure) C.; é. Coll. Mt. St-Louis et Ecole des H.E.C., Montréal; ép. Madeleine, f. Henri Dussault, 26 nov. 1949; enfants: Pierre, Michèle, Marie, François, Robert; Président, Comité executif de La Presse Ltée et Les Publications JTC Inc.; Directeur, Gentec Inc., Societé d'Assurance-depots du Canada, Associe Exe., Clarkson Gordon 1949–84; Assoc. Woods, Gordon 1957–84; Caron Bélanger Dallaire Gagnon & Associés 1975–84; ancien président, Ordre des Comptables Agréés du Qué., Chambre de Commerce du District de Montréal, Club Laval-sur-le-Lac, Assoc. Can. d'Etudes Fiscales, Revue Commerce, Opéra du Québec; Comité Canada, Comté consultatif du Min. du Revenu du Qué., Inst. Can. des Comptables Agréés; Fiduciaire Eglise Notre Dame de Montréal; Tres. Fond. Jules et Paul-Emile Léger; Prés. hon. chaire sciences comptables H.E.C.; Loisirs: golf, voile, ski; Clubs: Laval-sur-le-Lac; St-Denis; St. James's; Résidence: 115 Chemin Côte Ste-Catherine, Outremont, Qué. H2V 4R3; Bureau: 2410 – 1 Place Ville-Marie, Montréal, Qué. H3B 3M9.

**CARON, Michel,** L.Sc.C., M.A.; Canadian public servant; b. Montréal, Qué. 3 March 1937; s. Edmond and Therèse (Lussier) C.; e. Jean-de-Brébeuf Coll. Montréal B.A. 1957; Ecole des Hautes Etudes Commerciales Montréal L.Sc.C. 1960; Queen's Univ. M.A. 1962; m. Claire d. Jean-Marie and Gabrielle Hélie 8 Sept. 1962; children: Françoise, Alain, Anne-Marie, Gabrielle; ASSOC. DEP. MIN. OF FINANCE, CAN. 1987– ; joined present Dept. 1962, becoming Asst. Dir. Fiscal Policy Div. 1971–73; Adv. Dept. Finance, Qué. 1973–74, Asst. Sec. Prog. Br. Treasury Bd. 1974–77, Dep. Min. of Finance, Qué. 1977–82; Exec. Vice Pres. Finance & Resources, Hydro-Québec 1982–86; Sr. Asst. Dep. Min. present Dept. 1986; Home: 60 Frank St., Ottawa, Ont. K2P 0X2; Office: 140 O'Connor St., Ottawa, Ont. K1A 0G5.

**CARON, Raymond,** Q.C.; b. Montreal, Que. 27 Sept. 1906; s. late Adolphe Louis and late Agnes (Dulude) C.; e. High Sch. of Montreal, 1924; McGill Univ., B.A. 1928, B.C.L. 1931; m. Brenda Beryl, d. late Charles Spurr Harding, Montreal, 21 May 1932; children: Trevor Harding, Daphne Lorraine (Mrs. L.W. Shick), Derek Raymond, Melodie Molson (Mrs. H.B. Yates); Counsel, McCarthy Tétrault (formerly Clarkson Tetrault) 1965–92 (now retired); read law with Mitchell, Ralston, Kearney & Duquet; called to Bar of Que. 1931; cr. Q.C. 1959; in practice with Mitchell, Ralston, Kearney & Duquet 1931–33; private practice 1933–36; Caron & Gillean 1936–41; Defence Industries Ltd. 1941–46; Caron & McKay and later Caron, McKay & Trépanier, 1946–65; specialist in labour law; internat. lectr., exhibitor and judge for photographic salons in Can. and U.S.; Past Pres., Royal Automobile Club of Can.; Montreal Parks & Playgrounds Assn.; Westmount Mun. Assn.; Montreal Track & Field Club; Montreal Camera Club; Montreal Clean-up Campaign; mem., Bar of Montreal; Montreal Museum of Fine Arts; Fellow, Photographic Soc. Am.; Assoc., Royal Photographic Soc. Gt. Brit.; recreations: photography, music; Clubs: The Hermitage; Address: Place Kensington, 4430 Ste. Catherine St. W., Apt. 608, Westmount, Que. H3Z 3E4.

**CARON, Richard J.,** B.M., M.M., Ph.D.; university professor; b. Montreal, Que. 23 Aug. 1954; s. Jean Marcel and Mildred Elaine (Hutchings) C.; e. Univ. of Waterloo B.M. 1977, M.M. 1979, Ph.D. 1983; m. Wendy d. Wycliffe and Vera Smith 1 May 1976; children: Julie, Matthew; ASSOC. PROF. & HEAD, DEPT. OF MATH. & STATS., UNIV. OF WINDSOR 1991– ; Asst. Prof. present univ. 1983–87; Assoc. Prof. 1987– ; First Degree Black Belt in Judo 1975; co-author of numerous research papers in professional journals; clubs: Furukawa Judo Club (Dir. & Instructor); Home: 3661 Charlevoix Ave., Windsor, Ont.; Office: Windsor, Ont. N9B 3P4.

**CARPENTER, David C.,** B.A., B.Ed., M.A., Ph.D.; writer; b. Edmonton, Alta. 28 Oct. 1941; s. Paul Hamilton and Margerie Eunice (Parkin) C.; e. Univ. of Oregon M.A. 1967; Univ. of Alta. Ph.D. 1973; Univ. of Man., post-doct. 1973–75; author: 'Wild Rose Country' 1976 (anthol.); 'The Forest' 1977 (transl.); 'Fishing in the West' 1983 (how-to); 'Jewels' 1985, 'Jokes for the Apocalypse' 1985, 'God's Bedfellows' 1988 (fiction); num. articles & poetry 1970– ; H.S. Teacher, Edmonton 1964–69; English teacher, Univ. of Sask. 1975–82; split appt. 1982– ; has also taught English at Stony Mt. Penitentiary & Univ. of Brandon; 1st prize, Candn. Novella Contest, sponsored by 'Descant Mag.' for 'The Ketzer' 1988; recreations: fly fishing, banjo playing.

**CARPENTER, Helen M.,** B.S., M.P.H., Ed.D.; educationalist; b. Montreal, P.Q. 29 March 1912; d. Robert George and Janet Maude (Brown) C.; ed. Univ. of Toronto (Nursing Dipl.) 1933; Teachers Coll., Columbia Univ., B.S. 1943, Ed.D. 1965; Johns Hopkins Sch. of Hygiene and Pub. Health, M.P.H. 1945; Outpost Service, Ont. Red Cross Hosp., 1933–34; Staff, V.O.N., Hamilton and Staff Supv., Asst. Dir., V.O.N. Toronto, 1934–42; Consultant in Pub. Health Nursing, Prov. Dept. of Health (B.C.), 1943–44; Dir., Public Health Nursing East York-Leaside Health Unit, 1945–48; Asst. Prof., Univ. of Toronto Sch. of Nursing, 1948–62, Dean, Faculty of Nursing, 1962–72, Chrmn., Grad. Dept., 1970–76, Prof. 1962–77; retired June 1977; Prof. Emeritus 1977– ; Rockefeller Foundation Fellowship (Grad. study), 1944; Cdn. Red Cross Scholarship, 1959; mem., Metro Toronto District Health Council 1980–85; Bd., Home Care Prog. for Metro Toronto 1983–87; Candn. Nurses' Assn. (Pres. 1960–62); Reg'd. Nurses Assn. Ont.; Internat. Council of Nurses (Educ. Ctte.); Vice-Pres., Cdn. Red Cross Society; Protestant; Home: Apt. 1208, 77 St. Clair Ave. E., Toronto, Ont. M4T 1M5.

**CARPENTER, Kenneth Erwin,** M.A.; university professor/art critic; b. Cabri, Sask. 5 Mar. 1939; s. Erwin Elgin and Lea (Kanuit) Kreutzweiser; e. Univ. of Toronto, B.A. 1961; Univ. of Calif. at Berkeley, M.A. 1966; m. Carole d. John and Margaret Henderson 18 Dec. 1976; children: Geoffrey John, Carolyn Margaret-Lea; PROF., DEPT. OF VISUAL ARTS, YORK UNIV.; joined Faculty, York Univ. 1964; Vis. Instr. and/or Juror, Banff Sch. of Fine Arts; Ryerson Polytechnic; Concordia Univ.; Ont. Conf. of Univ. Fac. Assns. Teaching Award 1976; Guest Critic, Emma Lake Artists' Workshop 1977; mem., Univ. Art Assn. of Can.; Internat. Assn. of Art Critics; Native Art Studies Assn. of Can.; Coll. Art Assn. of Am.; author of three exhibition catalogues 1981, 82, 92, and over 50 articles; Office: Dept. of Visual Arts, York Univ., 4700 Keele St., Downsview, Ont. M3J 1P3.

**CARPINI, Alexander J.,** D.B.A.; insurance executive; b. Montreal, Que. 14 Jan. 1951; s. Alfred Alexander and Helen Anne (Lapenna) C.; e. Univ. of Montreal D.B.A. (Double Hons. English/History) 1974; m. Maria d. Vincenzo and Guisepina Broccoli 5 Sept. 1977; children: Vincent, Nadia, Joseph; MANAGING PARTNER, GREATER MONTREAL MARKETING CENTRE, EQUINOX FINANCIAL SERVICES 1993– ; Rep., Sun Life Canada 1978; Sales Mgr. 1981; Sr. Sales Manager 1983; Branch Mgr. (Westmount), Standard Life 1988; Supt. of Agencies (Canada), Confederation Life 1991; Regional Manager (Greater Montreal) 1993; Dir., Life Ins. Managers Assn. of Can. 1988–91; L'ADAC; Master Kinsmen, National Winner Speakers Trophy; Bd. of Gov., Concordia Univ.; Bd. of Dir., Loyola College; Lakeshore Baseball Assn.; Cardinal Leger Found.; Deputy Gov., Kinsmen; Pres., Lakeshore Baseball Assn.; Loyola Alumni Assn.; Sec., Concordia Alumni Assn.; recreations: golf, skiing, hockey, baseball; clubs: Kinsmen, Whitlock; Home: 53 Wilder Penfield, Kirkland, Que. H9J 2W5; Office: 510 – 4150 St. Catherine St. W., Westmount, Que. H3Z 2X7.

**CARR, David William,** B.A., B.S.A., M.Sc., Ph.D.; publisher; consulting economist; b. Leney, Sask. 9 Dec. 1911; s. Samuel Henry and Lillian (Moore) C.; e. Univ. of Saskatchewan, B.A., B.S.A. 1948; Univ. of Wisconsin, M.Sc. 1949; Harvard Univ., Ph.D. 1953; m. Frances Eleanor, d. Chauncey Wayne Close, Cut Knife, Sask., 10 Nov. 1939; children: Glenna Lea, Candace Gail, Gertrude Lillian (d.), Frances Lynn; PROPRIETOR, HUMAN PROGRESS PRESS 1982– ; Publisher, 'Carr's Report For Executives' 1975–76; Pres., D.W. Carr & Assoc. 1959–81 (provided consulting and policy analysis studies to Fed. Depts. of Transport, N. Affairs, Reg. Econ. Expansion, St. Lawrence Seaway, Emerg. Measures, Farm Credit Corp., Atlantic Develop. Bd.; Fed. Royal Commns. on Price Spreads, Transp., Banking and Finance; prov. Commns. on Manitoba's Econ. Future, rural credit in Nfld., meat packing in Ont. & Sask., pipeline policy in Yukon Terr.; adviser to Resources for Tomorrow Conf., Air Industries Assn., African Develop. Bank (1969); Dir. numerous other economic research projects; served in 2nd World War with R.C.A.F., 1940–45, rank on discharge Flying Offr.; author 'Recovering Canada's Nationhood' 1971; 'The Ebb of Affluence' 1983; 'A Godsend for Canada' 1990; mem., Am. Econ. Assn.; Am. Men of Science; United Church; Address: 45 Hazelwood Ave., Toronto, Ont. M4J 1K4.

**CARR, Donald,** Q.C., D. Hum.Lett.; barrister and solicitor; b. Leeds, Eng. 23 June 1928; s. Harry and Florence (Goldberg) C.; e. Corinth Coll. Cheltenham, Eng.; Cheltenham Grammar Sch.; Osgoode Hall Law Sch. grad. 1951; Yeshiva Univ. D.Hum.Lett. 1983 (Hon. causa); York Univ. LL.B. 1991; m. 1stly Annette (d.) d. Harry and Pearl Eisen; m. 2ndly Judith d. Jack and Sarah Leve 8 Jan. 1977; children: Aaron, Jonathan, Alan, Gary, Adam, Elizabeth; SR. PARTNER, GOODMAN AND CARR 1965– ; called to Bar of Ont. 1951; cr. Q.C. 1964; Pres. & Dir., Candn. Jewish News; Dir., McDonald's Restaurants of Canada Ltd.; The Oshawa Group Ltd.; Pennington's Stores Ltd.; Trustee, Roycom-Summit Realty Funds; Vice Chrmn., Canada-Israel Ctte.; Gov. Univ. of Haifa; mem. Internat. Council Beth Hatefutsoth (Museum of Diaspora) Tel Aviv; mem. Bd. Lands of the Bible Archaeol. Foundation Toronto; Hon. Counsel, Cdn. Friends Haifa Univ.; United Israel Appeal of Canada Inc.; Past-Chrmn. Nat. Budgeting Conf. Cdn. Jewry; Past Pres., United Jewish Welfare Fund of

Toronto; Community Hebrew Acad. Toronto; Reading Law Club Toronto; Home: 114 Kilbarry Rd., Toronto, Ont. M5P 1L1; Office: 2300, 200 King St. W., Toronto, Ont. M5H 3W5.

**CARR, Ernest Patterson Cameron;** retired executive; b. Ottawa, Ont. 11 Aug. 1913; s. late Albert Ernest and Florence Beatrice Cameron (Wood) C.; e. Dewson St. Pub. Sch. and Central Tech. Sch. (Scholarship 1st and 2nd yrs.), Toronto, Ont.; m. Annie Phyllis, d. late Robert Harvey Nixon. Clarkson, Ont., 19 May 1939; children: John Cameron, Elizabeth Margaret Cameron (Keddie), Joanne Cameron (Losos); began business career in 1929 with T. Eaton Co. Ltd., Toronto, and held various posts with them till 1935 when he joined Howell Warehouse Co. Ltd. as Asst. to the Vice-Pres.; retired as Chrmn. after 50 years' service 1985; Past Pres., Candn. Warehousemen's Assn.; Candn. Industrial Traffic League; Past Pres., Candn. Importers & Traders Assn.; United Church; Clubs: Granite; Empire; Board of Trade; Rotary; Rosedale Golf; Home: 1 Concorde Place, Ste. 801, Don Mills, Ont. M3C 3K6.

**CARR, G. Douglas,** B.Sc., C.A.; b. Toronto, Ont. 21 Aug. 1944; s. G. Kenneth and Frances V. (Edds) C.; e. Upper Can. Coll. 1962; Queen's Univ. B.Sc. 1966; C.A. 1969; PARTNER-IN-CHARGE, TREASURY RISK MANAGEMENT PRACTICE, PEAT MARWICK THORNE 1993– , mem. Exec. Ctte. 1980–86; Mgmt. Cons. present firm 1969–71, Insolvency Practice & Trustee in Bankruptcy 1971–73, Partner Toronto Office 1973–80, Mng. Partner Edmonton Office 1980–85; Partner in Charge, Toronto Audit Practice 1985–88; Partner, National Office 1988–93; Bd. of Govs., Upper Canada College; Dir., Heart and Stroke Found. of Can.; Dir., Classical Cabaret; Past Dir.: Edmonton Symphony Orch., Toronto Symphony Orch., Alta. Heart Found., Ont. Heart Fund, Boy Scouts Alta.; Candn. Inst. C.A.'s Honours List 1969; mem. Inst. C.A.'s Ont.; Alta. Inst. C.A.'s; Office: Commerce Court West, Toronto, Ont. M5L 1B2.

**CARR, Glenna,** B.A.; executive; b. Saskatoon, Sask. 19 Oct. 1945; d. Dr. David William and Frances Eleanor (Close) C.; e. Ridgemont H.S. Ottawa Jr. Matric.; Neuchatel Coll. Switzerland Sr. Matric. 1964; Trinity Coll., Univ. of Toronto Hons. B.A. 1968; m. Alan Gordon; children: Bruce, Catherine, Ian; VICE-PRES., CORPORATE AFFAIRS, LAIDLAW INC. 1992– ; Dir., Ault Foods; previously operated own bus. in edn. media rsch., incl. publishing and edn. media, TV Ont.; apptd. Policy Analyst in Min. of Coll. and Univ. 1973; first Mgr. of an affirmative action prog., Ont. Govt. Min. of Treas., Econ. and Intergovernmental Affairs 1974; Human Resources Coordr., Min. of Treas., Econ. and Intergovernmental Affairs 1976; Mgr. then Dir. of subsidy and job creation prog. in Municipal Affairs and Housing to Dir. of Municipal Fin. Policy Br.; Exec. Dir., Ontario Women's Directorate, Govt. of Ont. 1983–86; Asst. Depy. Min., Skills Training Div., Min. of Skills Development 1986–87; Depy. Min., Min. of Skills Development, Ont. Govt. 1987–89; Depy. Min., Min. of Consumer and Commercial Relations, Ont. Govt. 1989–91; Chair, Civil Service Commission and Secy., Management Bd. of Cabinet 1990–92; Bd. of Govs., Wilfred Laurier Univ.; mem. of other boards; Office: North Service Rd., Burlington, Ont. L7R 3Y8.

**CARR, Ian;** pathologist; b. Goole Yorks, U.K. 25 Apr. 1932; e. Univ. of Glasgow M.B.Ch.B. 1955, Ph.D. 1960; Univ. of Sheffield M.D. 1973; m. Jean McNeil 1960; 4 children; PROF. OF PATHOLOGY, UNIV. OF MANITOBA; Ed., Manitoba Medicine; Pathologist Univ. of Glasgow, New South Wales, Sheffield and Saskatchewan 1956–82; author 'Biological Defence Mechanisms' 1972; 'The Macrophage' 1973; co-author 'Lymphoreticular Disease' 1977 (2nd ed. 1984); Ed. 'The Reticuloendothelial System Vol. 1' 1980; past Pres. Physicians for Social Responsibility Can.; Home: 186 Lyndale Dr., Winnipeg, Man. R2H 1K3; Office: Dept. of Pathology, Univ. of Manitoba, 770 Bannatyne Ave., Winnipeg. Man. R3E 0W3.

**CARR, Jack Leslie,** B.Com., M.A., Ph.D.; educator; b. Toronto, Ont. 9 Aug. 1944; s. Meyer and Marion (Pinkus) C.; e. Univ. of Toronto B.Com. 1965; Univ. of Chicago M.A. 1968, Ph.D. 1971; m. Honey d. Chaim and Bella Feldman 27 Dec. 1965; children: Elana, Adam, David; PROF. OF ECON. UNIV. OF TORONTO 1978– , Rsch. Assoc. Inst. for Policy Analysis 1968– ; Asst. Prof. of Econ. present Univ. 1968–73, Assoc. Prof. 1973–78, Assoc. Chrmn. and Dir. of Grad. Studies Dept. Econ. 1983–85; Acting Chrmn., 1987–88; Visiting Prof. of Econ. Univ. of Cal. Los Angeles 1975–76; cons. to ind. and govt.; lectr. various orgns.; numerous appearances TV and Radio; Hon. Woodrow Wilson Fellow 1965; Lily Honor Fellowship 1965–68; Can. Council Leave Fellowship 1975; SSHRC Leave Fellowship 1982; SSHRC Rsch. Grant 1987; author 'The Structure of a National Financial Facility for the Canadian Credit Union System' 1976; 'Wage and Price Controls: Panacea for Inflation or Prescription for Disaster' 1976; 'The Money Supply and Monetary Policy' 1978; co-author 'Cents and Nonsense: The Economics of Canadian Policy Issues' 1972; 'The Macroeconomic Effects of an Arctic Gas Pipeline on the Canadian Economy' 1975; 'Liability Rules and Insurance Markets' 1981; 'Tax-Based Income Policies: A Cure for Inflation' 1982; 'The Day Care Dilemma' 1987; mem. Candn. Econ. Assn.; Am. Econ. Assn.; Candn. Profs. for Peace in Middle E.; Jewish; Home: 163 Banbury Rd., Don Mills, Ont. M3B 2L7; Office: Toronto, Ont. M5S 1A1.

**CARR, The Hon. Mr. Justice Robert,** LL.B., LL.M.; judge; b. Winnipeg, Man. 22 July 1947; s. David and Esther (Golden) C.; e. Univ. of Man., LL.B. 1971; Harvard Univ., LL.M. 1972; m. Shawn d. Leonard and Rowena Greenberg 1 May 1975; children: Jill, David; JUDGE, COURT OF QUEEN'S BENCH, PROV. OF MAN. 1983– ; priv. practice 1973–83; Sr. Partner, Taylor, Brazzell, McCaffrey 1979–83; Lectr., Man. Law Sch. 1974–83; Course Head, Bar Adm. Course 1978–83; Student Founder & Dir., Univ. Legal Aid Ctr. 1968–71; Bencher, Law Soc. of Man. 1980–83; Fed. Govt. Grant for Constitutional Law Rsch. 1970; Past Chrmn., Man. Br. of Young Lawyers Section of Candn. Bar; Former Dir., Klinic; Bd. Mem., Winnipeg Jewish Community Counc. 1986– ; Bd. Mem., Man. Paraplegia Found. 1989– ; author 'Report to Attorney General of Manitoba on Family Law' 1982, 'Casebook on Family Law' 1981–82; Chrmn., Pitblado Lecture Series 1979–80; Office: 226 Law Courts, Winnipeg, Man. R3C 0V8.

**CARR, Roy A.,** B.A.Sc.; executive; b. Toronto, Ont. 21 Aug. 1929; s. Arthur Edwin and Ruth Adelaide (Milligan) C.; e. E. York Coll. Inst. 1948; Univ. of Toronto B.A.Sc. 1952; m. Elizabeth Ann d. Melville and Marguerite Gladman 23 Aug. 1958; one s. Robert Arthur; PRES. POS PILOT PLANT CORP. 1984– ; joined Procter & Gamble Co. 1952–66, Product Devel. Supr., Plant Chem. Eng.; Anderson Clayton Foods (Texas) 1966–72, Process Eng. Head, Plant Mgr.; Hunt Wesson Foods (Calif.) 1972–78, Oils Lab. Mgr., Assoc. Rsch. Dir., recipient Highest Merit Award; Canbra Foods (Lethbridge) 1978–86, Vice Pres. Operations; Past Pres., Am. Oil Chems. Soc. (Past Pres. Candn. Sect.); Chair, Governing Bd., Ag-West Biotech 1990–93; Pres., Internat. Oil Mill Superintendants Assoc. 1991–92; Vice-Chair, Internat. Ctr. for Agriculture, Science and Technology 1991–93; Mem. Internat. Food Technols.; Internat. Oil Millers Soc.; Internat. Union of Pure and Applied Chemists; recreations: sports, reading; Home: 302 Bate Cres., Saskatoon, Sask. S7H 3A5; Office: 118 Veterinary Rd., Saskatoon, Sask. S7N 2R4.

**CARR, Shirley G.E.;** labour union president; b. Niagara Falls, Ont.; d. John James and Mary Geraldine (Wilson) Boutilier; e. Stamford Coll. V.I.; Niagara Coll. of Appl. Arts & Technol.; m. W. Bruce s. Walter and Frances C. 29 May 1948; one s. Larry Bruce; Pres., Candn. Labour Congress 1986–92; var. posts, local, prov. & nat. levels, Candn. Union of Public Employees 1960–74; Extve. Vice-Pres., Candn. Labour Cong. 1974–84; Sec.-Treas. 1984–86; formerly: Vice-Pres., Internat. Confed. of Free Trade Unions; Chair, Commonwelath Trade Union Counc.; Bd. of Gov., Labour Coll. of Can.; Co-Chair., Candn. Labour Market & Prod. Ctr.; Counc. mem., Amnesty International; Mem. and Vice-Chairperson, Governing Body, Internat. Labour Orgn. (ILO) 1991; Chair, Workers Group of the Governing Body, ILO 1991; Officer, Order of Can. 1980; Centennial Medal 1980; Hon. LL.D., Brock Univ. 1981; D.C.L., Acadia Univ. 1984; Hon. Fellow, Ryerson Polytech. Inst. 1987; LL.D. (Hon.), McMaster Univ. 1988; Hon. Doctorate, Univ. of Western Ont. 1988; first woman elected as Leader of a Nat. Labour Body (elected unanimously); recreations: reading, embroidery; Office: c/o 2841 Riverside Dr., Ottawa, Ont. K1V 3X7.

**CARRADINE, William J.,** B.A., M.B.A.; civil service executive; b. Smooth Rock Falls, Ont. 21 Jan. 1929; s. Dennis Charles and Elsie (Darby) C.; e. Univ. of W. Ont., B.A. (Journalism) 1951, M.B.A. 1954; m. Jacqueline Ann, d. E. Allen Millsap, London, Ont., 22 Jan. 1955; children: Susan, Catherine, Christopher; DIRECTOR, BUSINESS DEVELOPMENT, GOVT. OF ONT., London, Eng. 1991; Brand Mgr., Procter and Gamble of Can. 1955–57; Mktg. Mgr., Central Am., S. Am. and Caribbean countries, Internat. Div., Procter & Gamble, Geneva 1957–60; Brand Promotion Mgr., Procter & Gamble, Brussels, Benelux 1960–66; Mktg. Mgr., Procter and Gamble, Suisse 1966–68; Vice Pres. & Gen. Mgr., London Free Press 1968–72; Vice Pres., Southam Inc., Toronto 1972; Sr. Vice Pres., Southam Inc. 1980; Sr. Vice Pres., Southam Newspaper Grp. 1983; Sr. Vice Pres., Corp. Planning, Southam Inc. 1986; lent by Southam Inc. to Govt. of Ont. as Dir., Business Devel., Paris, France 1989; Govt. of Ont., London UK 1991; Founder & Chrmn., Newspaper Mktg. Bur., Can.; past dir., Nat. Ballet of Can.; Toronto Symphony; Candn. Extve. Service Orgn.; Candn. Daily Newspaper Publishers Assoc.; Newspaper Advertising Bur. (U.S.); past Chrmn., Candn. Sect., Commonwealth Press Union; Adv. Ctte., Sch. of Journalism, Univ. of Western Ont.; Merit Award, Univ. of Western Ont.; Pres., Kappa Alpha Soc.; recreations: tennis, squash, hiking, sailing; Clubs: Royal Candn. Yacht; Badminton and Racquet (Toronto); Home: Apt. 8, Claridge House, 32 Davies St., London, England W1Y 1LG.

**CARR-HARRIS, Ian Redford,** B.A., B.L.S., A.O.C.A.; artist; b. Victoria, B.C. 12 Aug. 1941; S. Gordon Grant Macdonnell and Rosamond (Green) C-H; e. Osgoode St. Pub. Sch. Ottawa 1952; Ashbury Coll. Ottawa 1959; Queen's Univ. B.A. 1963; Univ. of Toronto Sch. of Lib. Science B.L.S. 1964; Ont. Coll. of Art A.O.C.A. 1971; m. 1966; one d. Lise Renée; Full-time instructor, Ont. Coll. of Art; solo exhns. incl. A Space Gallery Toronto 1971; Yajama/Galerie, Montreal, 1981; Dalhousie Art Gallery, Halifax, N.S. 1982; 49th Parallel Gallery, N.Y. 1983; Carmen Lamanna Gallery, Toronto 1973, 1975, 1977, 1979 (2), 1981, 1984, 1985, 1986, 1987, 1988, 1991; Art Gall. of Ont. 1988; Susan Hobbs Gall. 1993; rep. in maj. group exhns. Can., USA, Europe since 1973 incl. Paris Biennale 1975, Venice Biennale 1984, Aurora Borealis, Montreal 1985, Documenta, Germany 1987; Biennial, National Gallery of Can. 1989; Sydney Biennale 1990; rec'd Can. Council 'A' Grant 1990; Works in the collections of the National Gallery, The Art Gallery of Ontario, The Canada Council Art Bank; Home: 68 Broadview Ave., 4th Floor, Toronto, Ont. M4M 2E6; Office: Ontario College of Art, 100 McCaul St., Toronto, Ont. M5T 1W1 and c/o The Susan Hobbs Gall., 137 Tecumseth St., Toronto, Ont. M5V 2E4.

**CARRICK, Donald,** O.B.E., Q.C., B.A., LL.B.; b. Port Arthur, Ont. 18 Sept. 1906; s. John James and Mary Jane (Day) C.; e. N. Ward Pub. Sch., Port Arthur, Ont.; St. Andrews Coll., Toronto, Ont., 1918–24; Univ. of Toronto, B.A. 1928; Harvard Law Sch., LL.B. 1931; Osgoode Hall, Toronto, Ont. 1934; m. Elizabeth Frazee, d. late Gerald Bunker, 1 June 1934; children: George Manton, Ellen Grover; Counsel, Carrick, O'Connor, Coutts & Crane until retired 1967; read law with the late James Bain and late Peter White, Toronto, Ont.; called to the Bar of Ont., Sept. 1934; mem. of firm of Slaght, Ferguson & Carrick, 1934–41; practised alone, 1945–49; appt. Queen's Counsel, 22 Dec. 1955; with N.P.A.M. 1940–41; served in 2nd World War, 1941–45; on active service with 12th Field Regt., R.C.A., 1941; trans. to Office of Judge Advocate Gen. in Feb. 1942 till Sept. 1945 and stationed in U.K. and Italy; Mentioned in Despatches; el. to H. of C. for Trinity (Toronto), Nov. 1954–June 1957; life mem., Law Soc. of Upper Can.; Psi Upsilon; Liberal; United Church; recreation: golf; Clubs: Rotary; Rosedale Golf (Life Mem.); Scarboro Golf (Life mem.); Home: 329 Lytton Blvd., Toronto, Ont. M5N 1R9.

**CARRIER, Claude,** B.Sc.Adm.; communication-marketing executive; b. Quebec City, Que. 28 Dec. 1956; s. Marc and Paule (Bruneau) C.; e. Univ. Laval B.Sc.Adm. 1979; m. Marie-Andrée d. Guy and Thérèse Couture 11 July 1981; one d.: Frédérique; VICE-PRESIDENT, CLIENT SERVICES, COSSETTE COMMUNICATION-MKTG. 1991– ; Mktg. Mgr., Provigo Inc. 1979–82; Group Account Dir., Cossette-Communication Mktg. 1982–89; Planning Dir. 1989–90; General Manager, Blitz (subs. of Cossette) 1990–91; Dir., Le Théâtre français de Toronto; Mem., Cercle canadien de Toronto; Home: 62 St-Ives Cres., Toronto, Ont. M4N 3B2; Office: 931 Yonge St., Toronto, Ont. M4W 2H2.

**CARRIER, Denis,** M.Comm., D. de l'Un. (Paris); éducateur; né Windsor, Qué. 6 avril 1938; f. Arthur et Germaine (Desloges) C.; é. Univ. de Sherbrooke, M. Comm. 1959; Inst. d'Études politiques (Univ. de Paris) Dipl. Sc. pol. 1961, D. de l'Un. (Paris) 1966; ép. Lise Thibault; enfants: Luc, Julie, Marc; PROF. DE SC. ECON. ET DE SC. POLITIQUE, UNIV. D'OTTAWA depuis 1962 et Vice-Recteur, adjoint (Enseignement et Recherche) depuis 1980; Chargé de cours 1962, Prof. adjoint 1966, Prof. agrégé 1969; Dir. des études (Faculté des Sciences sociales) 1965, Secrétaire 1967, Administrateur 1969; Prés. de Comm. de révision des structures d'enseignement et de recherche de l'Univ. d'Ottawa 1972–74; Doyen de la Faculté des sciences sociales 1970–81;

Doyen de la Faculté des sciences de la santé 1989–90; Doyen de la Faculté d'éducation 1991– ; auteur de 'La stratégie des négociations collectives' 1967; également principal auteur d' 'Une stratégie pour le changement/A Strategy for Change' (1974) et de plusieurs autres articles et rapports dont 'L'Université d'Ottawa et la francophonie ontarienne' (1985); (with F.A. van Vught) 'Governmental Regulation and Curriculum Innovation in France' 1989; aussi arbitre de griefs depuis 1971; résidence: 45 rue Brady, Hull, Qué. J8Y 5L5.

**CARRIER, Marcel R.;** business information executive; b. Quebec 3 Dec. 1942; s. Gérard and Irène (Massé) C.; m. Jacqueline Turcotte; children: Josée, Chantal, Daniel, Marc; PRES., NCR CANADA LTD 1989– ; joined NCR, Sherbrooke, Que. 1960; progressed through various admin. sales & sales mngt. positions within prov. until 1983; Vice-Pres., Commercial, Indus., Med., Edn., Govt. (CI-MEG) Systems Mktg. 1983; Mng. Dir., NCR Malaysia, Brunei and Sri Lanka 1986; Mem., Conference Bd. of Canada; Ont. Business Adv. Counc.; Vice Chrmn., I.T.A.C.; Bd. of Govs., Junior Achievement of Peel; Office: 320 Front St. W., Toronto, Ont. M5V 3C4.

**CARRIERE, Berthold;** composer/musical director; b. Ottawa, Ont. 27 Feb. 1940; s. Rolland and Berthe (Paradis) C.; e. Univ. de Montréal B.Mus. 1966; Univ. of West. Ont. M.Mus. 1973; m. Nancy d. Joseph and Helen Carpenter 17 May 1969; Mus. Dir., Banff Sch. of Fine Arts 1968–72; Res. Mus. Dir., Theatre London 1972–74, Dir. of Mus. 1976–77; Dir. of Mus., Stratford Shakespearean Fest. 1976–83, 1985– ; Mus. Dir., Talk of Toronto 1980–82; Man of the Year, City of Ottawa 1967; Conductor/Arranger, Dominion Day Celeb. in presence of H.M. The Queen & H.R.H. The Duke of Edinburgh 1967; Assoc. Dir., Theatre London 1976; Guthrie Award, Stratford Shakespearean Fest. 1976; Dora Mavor Moore Mus. Dir. Award 1981, 1982, 1987; Cert. of Excellence, 6th Annual Broadcast Designers Assn. comp. 1986; Home: Box 1273, St. Mary's, Ont. N0M 2V0; Office: Stratford Fest., Box 520, Stratford, Ont. N5A 6V2.

**CARRIÈRE, Serge,** M.D. C.S.P.Q., F.R.C.P.(C); physiologist; physician; educator; b. Montreal, Que. 21 July 1934; s. Virgile and Angelina (Malouin) C.; e. Univ. of Montreal, B.A. 1954, M.D. 1959; m. Irène Lafond Dec. 1976; children: Sylvie, Brigitte, Alain, François; DEAN, MEDICAL SCH., UNIV. OF MONTREAL 1989– ; Intern, Notre-Dame Hosp., Montreal 1958–59; Resident, internal med. 1959–62; Instr., physiol., Harvard Med. Sch. 1962–64; practiced med. specializing in nephrology, Montreal 1964– ; Asst. Prof., Dept. of Med., Univ. of Montreal 1964–70; Assoc. Prof. 1970–74; Prof. 1974–80; Chrmn., Dept. of Physiol. 1980–86; Chrmn., Dept. of Med. 1986–88; Dean, Fac. of Med. 1989– ; mem. staff Maisonneuve-Rosemont Hosp.; Med. Rsch. Counc. Can. Fellow 1962–64; Scholar 1965–70; Assoc. 1971–80; mem. Candn. Soc. Physiol.; Am. Soc. Physiol.; Internat. Soc. Physiol.; Am. Soc. Nephrology; Candn. Soc. Nephrology; Am. Soc. Clin. Investigation; Candn. Soc. Clin. Investigation; mem. of counc. & exec., Med. Rsch. Counc. of Can. 1981–84; Pres., Fonds de la Recherche en Santé du Qué. 1983–88; contbr. of numerous articles on rsch. in physiol. & nephrology to sci. & med. jours.; Home: 40, du Chêne, Vaudreuil sur le Lac, Qué. J7V 5V5; Office: 2900 Edouard-Montpetit, Montreal, Qué. H3C 3J7.

**CARRIGAN, David Owen,** B.A., M.A., Ph.D.; university professor; b. New Glasgow, N.S. 30 Nov. 1933; s. Ronald and Marion Constance (Hoare) C.; e. New Glasgow (N.S.) High Sch., 1951; St. Francis Xavier Univ., B.A. 1954; Boston Univ., M.A. 1955; Univ. of Maine, Ph.D. 1966; m. Florence Catherine, d. Ronald L. Nicholson, Sydney, N.S., 1958; children: Nancy, Janet, David, Glen, Sharon, Douglas; PROFESSOR OF HISTORY, ST. MARY'S UNIV. since 1979; Asst. Prof. of Hist., Xavier Coll., St. Francis Xavier Univ., 1957–61; Assoc. Prof. and Chrmn of the Dept. 1961–67; Assoc. Prof. of Hist., Wilfrid Laurier University, 1967–68; Principal and Dean of Arts, King's Coll., Univ. of W. Ont., 1968–71; Pres., St. Mary's Univ. 1971–79; mem., Can. Council 1977–83; Council of Trustees, Inst. for Research on Public Policy 1977–83; Chrmn., Commn. on Foreign Student Policy in Canada, 1981; mem. Bd. of Dirs., Cdn. Assoc. for Treatment and Study of Families, 1984; author, 'Canadian Party Platforms 1867–1968,' 1968; 'Crime and Punishment in Canada, A History' 1991; also articles for various journs.; mem., Am. Hist. Assn.; Phi Kappa Phi; Address: Halifax, N.S. B3H 3C3.

**CARRINGTON, John W.,** B.A.Sc.; mining consultant; b. Fort William, Ont. 6 May 1913; s. Charles Kemp and Mary Dorothea (Shackleton) C.; e. Univ. of Toronto, B.A.Sc. (Mining Engn.) 1934; m. Clara Malcolm (dec.), d. late Alex Gray, 30 April 1938; m. 2ndly, Alice M. Reid, 25 Oct. 1986; children: Mary Catherine, Molly Malcolm (dec.), John Kemp; Retired editor, The Northern Miner; served in 2nd World War, Lieut., R.C.N.V.R. 1942–45; mem. Cdn. Inst. Mining & Metall.; Am. Inst. Mining, Metall. & Petroleum Engrs.; Assn. Prof. Engrs. Ont.; Anglican; Clubs: Engrs. (Past Pres.); R.C.Y.C.; Home: 85 Plymbridge Rd., Willowdale, Ont. M2P 1A2.

**CARROLL, Anne Collins;** business executive; b. Pembroke, Ont. 16 March 1949; d. Kenneth Wright and Beulah Nairn (Dougherty) Collins; e. Pembroke Coll. Inst. and Champlain Secondary Sch. 1966; Algonquin Coll.; Carleton Univ. mgmt. courses; Ont. Centre for Microelectronics Tech. Courses; Cadnetix (1985) Computer Aided Design Course Cert.; two d. Rebecca Anne, Susan Alesha; PRES. AND DIR. PriCON CORP. 1987– ; Pres. and Chief Exec. Offr. PriCon Electronics Inc. 1988– ; Dir., Eyecan Corp. 1992– ; joined Nat. Lib. Can. 1967–69; Dept. of Finance and Treasury Bd. 1969–73; Mgr. Kanata Chiropractic Centre 1980–83; Bryant Electropac Ltd. and PriCon Corp. 1983–93, Mgr. of latter Corp. 1985; Marketing Dir., Dy-4 Systems Inc. 1985–88; mem.: Exec. Fed. P. Cons. Party Lanark Carleton 1982– ; Mem. Advisory Ctte., Heritage College; Mem.: Candn. Institute of Marketing Management of Ontario (CIMMO); Ottawa-Carlton Economic Development Corp. (OEDC); International Institute of Environ. Studies (IES); Board of Trade; World Trade; Exec. Candn. Chiropractic Assn. 1982; recreations: skiing, tennis; Home: 50 Rutherford Way, Kanata, Ont. K2K 1N4; Office: 404 - 301 Moody Dr., Nepean, Ont. K2H 9C4.

**CARROLL, Donald Kevin,** Q.C., B.A., LL.B.; barrister; b. Saint John, N.B. 21 Jan. 1944; s. Donald Joseph and Imelda Marie (Daley) C.; e. St. Mary's Univ. Halifax B.A. 1965; Dalhousie Univ. LL.B. 1968; m. M. Aileen d. Edmund C. and Nora A. O'Leary 11 Nov. 1968; children: Joanna Aileen, Daniel Kevin O'Leary; PRIN., D. KEVIN CARROLL, Q.C. 1973– ; served with RCA and Office of the Judge Advocate Gen. Candn. Armed Forces 1962–70, rank Capt.; called to Bar of Ont. 1970; cr. Q.C. 1981; law practice Messrs. Thomson, Rogers, Toronto 1970–73; mem. Defence Rsch. Inst. 1976– ; Internat. Assoc. of Def. Counsel; Lectr., Candn. Bar Assn. (Ont.), Advocates Soc., Law Soc. Upper Can., Georgian Coll. of Applied Arts & Technol.; Founding Dir. Big Sister Assn. Barrie 1975–77; Dir. Barrie Assn. Safety Edn.; mem. Candn. Bar Assn. (Nat. Council– , Exec. (Ont.) 1984– , Pres. (Ont.) 1993–94); Advocates Soc.; Simcoe Co. Law Assn.; R. Catholic; recreations: tennis, skiing, sailing; Clubs: Royal Candn. Mil. Inst.; Barrie Yacht; Barrie Racquets; Home: 4 Shoreview Dr., Barrie, Ont. L4M 1G1; Office: Carroll, Heyd, P.O. Box 548, 89 Collier St., Barrie, Ont. L4M 4T7.

**CARROLL, Francis Martin,** B.A., M.A., Ph.D.; professor of history; b. Cloquet, Minnesota 31 Jan. 1938; s. Martin Francis and Virginia Carol (Johnson) C.; e. Cloquet H.S. 1956; Carleton College B.A. 1960; Univ. of Minn. M.A. 1962; Trinity College Dublin Ph.D. 1970; m. Janet d. Wallace and Margaret Foster 24 Aug. 1963; one s.: Charles Murray Howard; PROFESSOR OF HISTORY, UNIV. OF MANITOBA 1969– ; Fellow, St. John's College 1969– ; Kalamazoo College 1967–68; South Dakota State Univ. 1962–64; Dean of Studies, St. John's College 1976–78; Acting Warden 1985–86; Chair of Assembly 1989–90; Assoc. Head., Dept. of History, Univ. of Man. 1982–84; F.O. Butler Lecturer, S. Dakota State Univ. Dec. 1988; Mary Ball Washington Prof. of Am. Hist., Univ. Coll. Dublin 1984–85; Visiting Scholar in Internat. Law, Columbia Univ. Law Sch. 1980; Mem., Am. Conf. for Irish Studies; Am. Hist. Assn.; Candn. Assn. for Irish Studies; Forest History Soc.; Orgn. of Am. Historians; author: 'The WPA Guide to the Minnesota Arrowhead Country' (introduction) 1989, 'Crossroads in Time' 1987, 'American Opinion and the Irish Question, 1910–23' 1978; co-author: 'The Fires of Autumn' 1990; editor: 'The American Commission on Irish Independence, 1919' 1985; recreations: sailing; clubs: Univ. of Man. Faculty; Home: 601 Wardlaw Ave., Winnipeg, Man. R3L 0M3; Office: St. John's Coll., Univ. of Man., Winnipeg, Man. R3T 2M5.

**CARROLL, John C.,** B.A., M.B.A.; brewery executive; b. Toronto, Ont. 8 Dec. 1933; s. Joseph Claremont and Elizabeth (MacPherson) C.; e. Univ. of W. Ont. B.A. 1956; Univ. of Toronto M.B.A. 1962; m. Barbara d. George and Marion Dunbar 6 Oct. 1956; three d. Jennifer Marion Lowden, Susan Elizabeth Whitehurst, Lisa Barbara; HONORARY DIRECTOR, CANADA, MOLSON BREWERIES 1989– ; joined Dow Chemical 1956–60; Procter & Gamble Inc. 1960–66; Warner-Lambert, Can. 1966–79, Pres. Consumer Products Group; Warner-Lambert, USA 1980–86, Pres. Am. Chicle Group and Vice Pres. of Co. 1984–86; joined Molson Breweries of Canada Ltd. 1986; Dir., Laurentian General; Quaker Oats of Can.; mem. Rosedale Un. Ch.; recreations: tennis; Clubs: Granite; Royal Candn. Yacht; Naples (Fla.) Bath & Tennis; Country Club of Naples; NYU (N.Y.) University; Home: 174 Douglas Dr., Toronto, Ont. M4W 2B7; Office: 175 Bloor St. E., Toronto, Ont. M4W 3S4.

**CARROLL, Joy;** journalist; author; b. Melfort, Sask. 8 July 1924; d. John Robert and Elsie (Lee) Holroyd; e. Melfort (Sask.) High Sch. Sr. Matric. 1943; Business Course 1944; Royal Conserv. of Music; m. John Alexander Carroll 17 May 1952; children: Anne Elizabeth, Barbara Evelyn, Scott Alexander, Angus John Gregory; sometime Women's Ed. Prince Albert Daily Herald; News writer C.B.C.; Script writer, Claire Wallace; Feature Ed. New World Mag.; Extve. Ed. National Home Monthly; Candn. Ed. Better Living (N.Y.); Ed. Harlequin Books; Travel Ed. Chatelaine Mag.; author of 'Canadian Etiquette' (with Claire Wallace); 'Night of Terror'; 'Murdered Mistress'; 'God & Mrs. Sullivan'; 'Weekend'; 'The Restless Lovers'; 'The Moth'; 'Soul's End'; 'Five over Eden'; 'Pioneer days 1840–1860'; 'Proud Blood'; 'Pride's Court'; 'Murder Most Fashionable' 1984; also numerous articles and short stories in various Candn. and Am. newspapers, mags. and journs.; portrait painted by Harold Town 1948; Anglican; recreations: music, swimming.

**CARROLL, Kenneth Kitchener,** Ph.D., F.C.I.C., F.R.S.C.; university professor; b. Carrolls, N.B., 9 Mar. 1923; s. Lawrence and Sarah Della (Estey) C.; e. Univ. of New Brunswick, B.Sc. 1943, M.Sc. 1946; Univ. of Toronto, M.A. 1946; Univ. of W. Ont., Ph.D. 1949; post-doctoral studies Univ. of Western Ontario 1949–52, Cambridge Univ. 1952–54; m. Margaret, d. George and Mabel Ronson, 26 Aug. 1950; children: Douglas, Stephen, James; DIR., CENTRE FOR HUMAN NUTRITION 1990– ; Asst. Prof. to Prof. and Acting Head, Dept. of Med. Rsch. 1954–68, Prof. Dept. of Biochemistry 1968–88, Prof. Emeritus 1988– ; career investigator, Med. Rsch. Counc. of Can. 1963–; Chem. Inst. of Can., councillor, 1963–66; Can. Soc. for Nutritional Sciences: Sec. 1965–67, Pres. 1978–79; Hon. Sec., Can. Fedn. of Biol. Socs. 1967–71; Chrmn., Ctte. on Nutrition and Cancer, Internat. Union of Nutritional Sciences 1979–89; Pres., Can. Atherosclerosis Soc. 1989–91; numerous similar affiliations; recipient Earle Willard McHenry Award, Candn. Soc. for Nutritional Sciences 1987; Fellow, Am. Inst. Nutr. 1992; D.Sc., Univ. of New Brunswick 1993; author of sci. publs., incl. review articles and book chapters, on lipid metabolism and nutrition in relation to heart disease and cancer; assoc. ed.: Can. Jour. of Biochem. 1969–71, Lipids 1969–80, Nutrition and Cancer 1978– , Drug-nutrient Interactions 1981–88, Atherosclerosis 1984–89; recreations: curling, sailing; Home: 561 St. George St., London, Ont. N6A 3B9; Office: Dept. of Biochemistry, Univ. of W. Ontario, London, Ont. N6A 5C1.

**CARROLL, Paul Aylward,** B.A., LL.B., Q.C.; lawyer; b. Toronto, Ont. 31 Mar. 1941; s. Edward Austin and Mona Gertrude (Dreyer) C.: e. De La Salle 'Oaklands' 1959; Univ. of Toronto, B.A. 1962; Osgoode Hall Law Sch., LL.B. 1965; m. Catharine d. George and Theresa Richardson 10 Aug. 1963; children: Peter, Michael, AnnMarie; PARTNER, SMITH, LYONS, TORRANCE, STEVENSON & MAYER 1973– ; joined firm 1965; Dir., Dundee Bancorp Inc.; Dundee International Limited; Juno Limited; Nelson Trade & Finance Limited; NHI Nelson Holdings Internat. Ltd.; Targa Internat. Corp.; Zemex Corp.; Mem., Candn. Bar Assn.; Candn. Tax Found.; Internat. Bar Assn.; Internat. Counc. of Shopping Ctrs.; recreations: golf, skiing, tennis; Clubs: National, Cambridge; The Canadian Club, Toronto; Office: Ste. 6200, Scotia Plaza, 40 King St. W., Toronto, Ont. M5H 3Z7.

**CARROLL, Timothy Edward,** M.B.A.; university professor/politician; b. Charlottetown, P.E.I. 17 Jan. 1951; s. Claude Joseph and Mary Eileen (Dooley) C.; e. Charlottetown Rural H.S. 1969; Univ. of P.E.I., B.A. 1973; Univ. of Sask. M.B.A. 1974; m. Kathy d. Lawson and Eileen Jenkins 28 Nov. 1977; children: Melissa, Esther, Patrick Joseph (P.J.), Daniel; Min. of Agric., Prov. of P.E.I. 1986–89; mngt. positions with Ont. Vegetable Growers' Mktg. Bd., Alta. Agric. Products Mktg. Counc. & P.E.I. Market Devel. Ctr.; Comnr., Royal Comn. of Inquiry into Mktg. Practices for Potatoes in Eastern Can.; Asst. Prof., St. Francis Xavier Univ.; Sch. of Bus. Admin., Univ. of P.E.I. 1982–86; elected M.L.A. for Fifth Queens 1986, 1989, 1993; Cert. Assn. Extve.; Past Mem., Diocesan Ctte. on Christian Unity; Premiere Toastmasters of Charlottetown; Mem., St. Pius X Ch.;

author of pub. cases & rsch. papers; Home: 11 MacArthur Dr., Sherwood, P.E.I. C1A 6N2.

**CARROTHERS, Alfred William Rooke,** S.J.D., LL.D.; professor of law; b. Saskatoon, Sask. 1 June 1924; s. William Alexander and Agnes Elizabeth (Godber) C.; e. Univ. of Brit. Columbia, B.A. 1947, LL.B. 1948; Harvard Law Sch., LL.M. 1951; S.J.D. 1966; LL.D., Univ. of Sask. 1974, McMaster 1975, Calgary 1976; Order St. Lazarus of Jerusalem; Fellow, Candn. Inst. for Conflict Resolution; m. Margaret Jane, d. Col. Macgregor Macintosh, 1 July 1961; two s. Matthew, Jonathan; one d. Alexandra; Prof. Emeritus, Common Law Section, Faculty of Law, Univ. of Ottawa 1989– ; (Dean of Section 1981–83); called to the Bar of B.C. 1948, Ont. 1965, Alberta 1969; Lectr., Univ. of B.C. 1948–50; Asst. Prof., Dalhousie Univ. 1951–52; Asst. Prof., Univ. of B.C. 1952–55, Assoc. Prof. 1955–60; Dir., Inst. Indus. Rlns. 1960–62; Prof. 1960–64; Dean and Prof. of Law, Univ. of W. Ont. 1964–68; Pres., Univ. of Calgary 1969–74; Pres., Inst. for Rsch. on Public Policy 1974–77; author: 'The Labour Injunction in British Columbia' 1956; 'Labour Arbitration in Canada' 1961; 'Collective Bargaining Law in Canada' 1965 (2nd ed. 1986 with E.E. Palmer and W.B. Rayner); mem., Cdn. Assn. Univ. Teachers (Past Pres.); Assn. of Univs. & Colls. of Can. (Past Pres.); Cdn. Assn. Law Teachers (Past Pres.); Protestant; Club: Vancouver (Vancouver, B.C.); Address: 7034 Tamarin Place, Brentwood Bay, B.C. V0S 1A0.

**CARROTHERS, Hon. (Alexander) Brian (Beatty),** B.A., LL.B.; judge; b. Saskatoon, Sask. 18 Jan. 1923; s. late William Alexander and late Agnes Elizabeth (Godber) C.; e. Univ. Hill Sch.; Univ. of B.C. B.A., LL.B.; m. 1st late Jean Elizabeth d. late Clifford O. Foss 4 March 1950; children: Douglas Alexander, Robert Brian, Linda Jean; m. 2nd Sheila Arnold d. late James and Annie (Proctor) Couper 27 Dec. 1982; JUSTICE OF APPEAL, COURT OF APPEAL FOR B.C. AND JUDGE, COURT OF APPEAL FOR YUKON TERRITORY since 1973; called to Bar of B.C. 1949; cr. Q.C. 1967; law practice Davis & Co. 1949–56; Douglas, Symes and Brissenden 1956–73; served with Candn. Army UK N.W. Europe (wounded Normandy beachhead), rank Capt.; Life Bencher and Treas. (1972–73) Law Soc. B.C.; former Chrmn. Nat. Sec. and Prov. Br. Pres. (1966–67) Candn. Bar Assn.; Founding Dir. and sometime Pres. B.C. Med. Services Foundation; Life Fellow and sometime Pres. Foundation for Legal Research; West Vancouver Presbyterian Church; Zeta Psi; Club: Vancouver; Home: 1101 Waterford House, 1972 Bellevue Ave., W. Vancouver, B.C. V7V 1B5; Office: The Law Courts, 800 Smithe St., Vancouver, B.C. V6Z 2E1.

**CARROTHERS, Douglas Alexander,** B.A., LL.B., M.B.A.; lawyer / politician; b. North Vancovuer, B.C. 21 Nov. 1950; s. The Hon. Alexander Brian Beatty and the late Jean Elizabeth (Foss) C.; e. Hillside Secondary; York Univ., B.A. 1973; Osgoode Hall Law Sch., LL.B. 1977; York Univ., M.B.A. 1979; m. Marie-Elle d. Domenico and Jeanne Verdone 22 June 1973; one s.: Marc-William Alexander; ASST. VICE PRES. AND DIR., GOVT. AFFAIRS, CONFEDERATION LIFE INSUR. CO. 1990– ; M.P.P., Ontario Legislature 1987–90; called to Ont. Bar 1980; Asst. Couns., Confederation Life Insur. Co. 1980–83; Assoc. Couns. 1983–85; Asst. Vice-Pres. & Couns. 1985–87; Chrmn., Select Ctte. on Energy 1988–89; SouthWest Caucus (Prov. Liberal Caucus) 1988–89; Mem., Standing Ctte. on Public Accts. 1987–88; on Ombudsman 1987–90; on Soc. Devel. 1988–89; on Finance and Economic Affairs 1989–90; Parliamentary Asst. to Min. of Industry Trade and Technology & Chair, Parliamentary Assts. Ctte. for Small Business, Small Business Advocate 1989–90; Dir., Confed. Finan. Serv. Limited 1986–87; Pres., Halton Fed. Liberal Assn. 1986; Vice-Pres., Toronto & Dist. Lib. Assn. 1985–86; Chrmn. and Dir., Oakville Family Y. 1991– ; mem., Un. Ch.; Liberal; Law Soc. of U.C.; recreations: reading, gardening; Clubs: Oakville; Canadian Club of Oakville; Home: 202 Dunwoody Dr., Oakville, Ont. L6J 4G4.

**CARROTHERS, Gerald A.P.,** M.Arch., M.C.P., Ph.D.: Educator; b. Saskatoon, Sask. 1 July 1925; s. late William Alexander and late Agnes Elizabeth (Godber) C.; e. Univ. Hill Sch. Vancouver, B.C. 1943; Univ. of Man. B.Arch. 1948, M.Arch. 1951; Harvard Univ. M.C.P. 1953; Mass. Inst. of Technol. Ph.D. 1959; PROF. IN ENVIRONMENTAL STUDIES, YORK UNIV. since 1968; Lectr. and Research Planner, Univ. of Man. 1948–53; Research Asst. Mass. Inst. of Technol. 1953–56; Asst. Prof. Univ. of Toronto 1956–60; Assoc. Prof. and Prof. Univ. of Pa. 1960–67, Chrmn. Dept. City & Regional Planning 1961–65, Founding Dir. Inst. Environmental Studies 1965–67; Educ. Advisor, Central Mortgage and Housing Corp. Ottawa 1966–77; Founding Dean Faculty of Environmental Studies York Univ. 1968–76; Interim Dir., U. Of Toronto/York U. Joint Program in Trans. 1976–78; Visiting Professor, University of Nairobi, Kenya, 1978–80; Registrar, Ont. Professional Planners Institute 1990–92; Consultant advisor to various educ. prof. govt. and other pub. bodies in Can., U.S. and overseas; co-author 'Methods of Regional Analysis' 1960; Founding Ed. 'Plan Canada' 1959; 'Papers and Proceedings of the Regional Science Association' 1955–62; Fellow, World Acad. of Art & Science; Fellow Royal Arch. Inst. Can.; mem., Ont. Assn. Archs.; Candn. Inst. Planners; Am. Inst. Of Certified Planners; Ont. Prof. Planners Inst.; Regional Science Assn. (Pres. 1970–71); Home: 24 Bertmount Ave., Toronto, Ont. M4M 2X9; Office: York Univ., 4700 Keele St., Downsview, Ont. M3J 1P3.

**CARRUTHERS, Christopher Calvert,** B.Sc., M.D., M.B.A., F.R.C.S.(C); orthopaedic surgeon; b. Sarnia, Ont. 5 Apr. 1943; s. Walter Bethune and Edna Mae C.; e. Carleton Univ., B.Sc. 1964; Univ. of Ottawa, M.D. 1968; Concordia Univ., M.B.A. 1992; m. Donna d. William and Louise Nixon 1969; children: Lisanne, Allison, Kenneth; VICE PRES., MEDICAL AFFAIRS, OTTAWA CIVIC HOSP. 1991– , Acting Pres. & C.E.O. 1992–93; Clin. Asst. Prof. of Surg. Univ. of Ottawa; mem. Staff, Div. Orthopaedics present Hosp. 1973, Chief of Med. Staff 1986–91; Dir. Carruthers Found. Sarnia; Ashbury College, Ottawa; Past Dir., Ottawa Civic Hosp. Found.; Ottawa Civic Hosp.; Candn. Orthopaedic Found.; Ottawa Flying Club; Surveyor Candn. Council on Health Facilities Accreditation; mem. Ont. Med. Assn.; Candn. Med. Assn.; Candn. Orthopaedic Assn.; Am. Acad. Orthopaedic Surg.; Am. Coll. of Physician Extves.; Coll. of Candn. Health Extves.; recreations: flying, skiing; Home: 3540 Paul Anka Dr., Ottawa, Ont. K1V 9K8; Office: 1053 Carling Ave., Ottawa, Ont. K1Y 4E9.

**CARRUTHERS, Hon. Douglas Henry,** B.A.; judge; b. Toronto, Ont. 17 Apr. 1930; s. David Norman and Elsie Clara (Le Poidevin) C.; e. Univ. of Toronto B.A. 1951; Osgoode Hall Law Sch. LL.B. 1955; m. Barbara Janet d. Norman and Irene Clarke 1955; two s. David Clarke, James Douglas; JUSTICE, ONTARIO COURT OF JUSTICE (GEN. DIV.); called to Bar of Ont. 1955; cr. Q.C. 1968; law practice 1955–77; Judge Trial Div., The Supreme Court of Ont. 1977–..; Pres. Cdn. Inst. Advanced Legal Studies; mem. Cdn. Bar Assn.; Lawyers Club Toronto; Advocates' Soc. Prov. Ont.; recreations: tennis, skiing; Clubs: Boulevard; University; Georgian Peaks Ski; Home: 44 Belvedere Blvd., Toronto, Ont. M8X 1K2; Office: 130 Queen St. W., Toronto, Ont. M5H 2N5.

**CARRUTHERS, Norman Harry,** B.Sc., B.Ed., LL.B; judge; b. Augustine Cove, P.E.I. 25 October 1935; s. Lorne Cameron Hannah and Jean Rachael (Webster); e. Augustine Cove P.S.; Prince of Wales Coll. 1954; Mt. Allison Univ., B.Sc. 1956, B.Ed. 1961; Dalhousie Law Sch., LL.B. 1967; m. Diana d. Gordon and Anna Rodd, 11 July 1970; children: Susan Esther, Karen Isabel, John Norman; CHIEF JUSTICE OF THE SUPREME COURT, PROV. OF PRINCE EDWARD ISLAND 1985– ; CIL Calgary 1956–58; CIL Edmonton 1958–59; teacher, Chestermere Lake and Calgary, Alta. 1961–64; articles to Bell & Foster 1967; practiced law with Foster, MacDonald & Carruthers 1968–80; mem., Law Soc. of P.E.I. 1968–80; Chief Judge, Provincial Court 1980–85; Candn. Bar Assoc.; Sec. & Chrmn., P.E.I. Law Found.; Vice-Pres., P.E.I. Law Soc. 1979–80; won Smith Shield Competition Dalhousie Law Sch. 1967; Trustee, Forum for Young Canadians; mem., Spring Park United Church; Past Pres. Summerside Y's Men's Club 1984–85; Past Pres., Charlottetown Kiwanis Club; mem., Candn. Assoc. of Prov. Court Judges 1980–85; Candn. Judicial Coun. 1985– ; Candn. Inst. for the Admin. of Justice; Rotary Club of Charlottetown Royalty; Candn. Judges Conf.; Home: 16 Trafalgar St., Charlottetown, P.E.I. C1A 3Z1; Office: P.O. Box 2000, Charlottetown, P.E.I. C1A 7N8.

**CARRUTHERS, S. George,** MD, FRCPC, FACP, FRCP, FCP; professor of medicine; b. Londonderry, N. Ireland 18 Sept. 1945; s. Moses and Alice McKeague (Nicholl) C.; e. Foyle Coll.; Queen's Univ. (Belfast), M.B., B.Ch., B.A.O. 1969, M.D. 1975; F.A.C.P., F.R.C.P. (Lond.); m. Gillian d. Norman and Margaret Devon 4 Oct. 1969; children: Alison, David, Bruce, Michael; CARNEGIE & ROCKEFELLER PROF. AND HEAD, DEPT. OF MED., DALHOUSIE UNIV. 1988– ; Intern, Royal Victoria Hosp., Belfast 1969–70; various positions, Queen's Univ., Belfast 1970–75; Fogarty Internat. Fellow of U.S. Nat. Inst. of Health, Kansas Univ. Med. Ctr. 1975–77; Depts. of Med. & Pharm. & Toxicol., Univ. Hospital, Univ. of West. Ont. 1977–88; Mem., Drug Quality & Therapeutics Ctte., Ont. Min. of Health 1982–86; Chrmn. 1986–88; Piafsky Young Investig. Award of Candn. Soc. of Clin. Pharm. 1982; Senate, Univ. of West. Ont. 1984–86; Budget & Fin. Ctte. 1986–88; Pres., Candn. Soc. for Clin. Pharm. 1984–86; Pres., Candn. Hypertension Soc. 1990–91; Vice Pres., Am. Soc. for Clinical Pharmacology and Therapeutics 1991–92; Head, Dept. of Med., Victoria Gen. Hosp. 1988–91; Pres., Med. Staff, Victoria Gen. Hosp. 1992–93; Mem., Bd. of Commissioners, Victoria General Hosp. 1992–93; co-author: 'Handbook of Clinical Pharmacology' 1978, 1983; over 100 scientific papers; Un. Ch. of Can.; Fellow, Am. College of Clinical Pharmacology; recreations: reading, travel; Home: 15 Woodbank Terrace, Halifax, N.S. B3M 3K4; Office: Ste. 442 Bethune, Victoria General Hosp., Halifax, N.S. B3H 2Y9.

**CARRYER, Richard John Peter,** B.Eng.; engineer; b. Guildford, Surrey, England 30 Oct. 1950; s. Peter and Barbara (Mason) C.; e. Sir George Williams Univ., B.Eng. (Hons.) 1972; m. Jennifer 1975; VICE-PRES., ASEA BROWN BOVERI 1989– ; started career with Candn. Gen. Electric 1972–76; worked on Manitoba Hydro's HVDC Project 1976–79; Alberta Power's HVDC Interconnection with Sask. 1979–81; Mngr. of Mktg. & Engr., BBC Brown Boveri 1981–86; Vice-Pres., West. Can. 1986; Vice-Pres. & Gen. Mgr., Asea Brown Boveri 1988; Dir., Cdn. Nuclear Assn.; Mem., O.E.Q., A.P.E.O., A.P.E.G.G.A., C.E.A., I.E.E.E., Bd. of Trade (Mississauga, Toronto); Home: 2271 Bethnal Green Rd., Oakville, Ont. L6J 5J8.

**CARSE, Margaret Ruth Pringle,** C.M., A.R.A.D., A.T.C., LL.D.; dance educator; b. Edmonton, Alta. 7 Dec. 1916; d. William Allison and Margaret Ruth (Cranston); e. Strathcona H.S. and numerous schools of dance in Canada, U.S.A., U.K. and Denmark; Extve. Dir., Alberta Ballet School, 1984–89; ARAD Advanced Teachers Cert.; Founder, Alta. Ballet Co.; Founder and Principal, Alta. Ballet Sch. 1971–83; Co-Dir., 'Dance Session' Univ. of Alta.; Originator, Credit Prog. H.S. Performing Arts Prog.; Dancer, Civic Opera Prod.; Volkoff Candn. Ballet; Candn. Ballet Festivals; and numerous other productions; teacher (55 years exp.), Kinney Sch. of Dancing; Volkoff Sch. of Dancing; Candn. School of Ballet; Banff Sch. of Fine Arts, Muriel Taylor Sch. of Dancing; Alta. Ballet Sch.; Grant McEwan Coll., Teachers' Training Program; numerous choreographies for productions across Canada; lecturer, elementary and high schools in Alta.; Children's Examiner, Royal Academy of Dancing 1964–72; Life mem., Bd. of Dir., Alta. Ballet Co. & School; Advisory Bd., Mt. Royal College School of Dance; Queen's Silver Jubilee Medal 1977; Grace Bosustow Award, Royal Acad. of Dancing, London, England 1979; YWCA Tribute to Women (Arts) 1982; Sir Frederick Haultain Award 1983; inducted into the Cultural Hall of Fame (Edmonton) 1987; Dance in Canada Award 1990; honored by Edmonton Hist. Bd. & City of Edmonton 1990; Life Mem., Royal Acad. of Dancing 1991; Hon. LL.D., Univ. of Alta. 1991; Member, Order of Canada 1992; Adjudicator, Grants for Dance, Alta. Culture; Festivals in Saskatoon & Victoria; Festivals & Grants (Ukrainian), Edmonton; Panel mem., Expanding Arts 1971; Dance in Canada 1980, 1981; Cultural Ctte., Convention Ctr., Edmonton 1975; Planning Ctte., Mt. Royal College Sch. of Dance 1984; Chair, Cultural Hall of Fame Ctte., City of Edmonton Awards 1989; Adv. Bd., Dance Dept., Grant McEwan Coll. 1990; recreations: art, sculpture, pottery, handicrafts, politics, hockey, football; Home: #2502 Macdonald Place, 9925 Jasper Ave., Edmonton, Alta. T5J 2X4.

**CARSON, Alan Scott,** B.Comm., B.Ed., M.A., Ph.D.; university dean; b. St. Catharines, Ont. 28 Aug. 1949; s. G. Fraser and Shirley E. (Elliot) C.; e. Mount Allison Univ. B.Comm. 1971; Dalhousie Univ. B.Ed. 1973, M.A. 1974; Univ. of London Ph.D. 1980; m. Miriam d. Daniel and Katherine Matheson 8 May 1971; children: Brant Richmond, Jennifer Tamara; DEAN, THE FRANK H. SOBEY FACULTY OF COMMERCE and PROFESSOR OF MANAGEMENT, SAINT MARY'S UNIV. 1993– ; Asst. Prof. of Edn. Univ. of Alta. 1978–81, Queen's Univ. 1982–84; Acct. Mgr. Corporate Banking Mercantile Bank of Canada Edmonton and Hamilton 1981–82, 1984–85; Asst. Vice Pres. Corporate Banking Chemical Bank of Canada Toronto 1985–87; Vice Pres. Food Retail & Consumer Products Group Corporate Bank, Canadian Imperial Bank of Commerce 1987–91; Vice Pres., Head of Corporate Finance Div., Corporate Bank, CIBC 1991–93; instructor part-time, Faculty of Management, Univ. of Toronto 1993; recipient Can. Council Doctoral Fellowship 1974–78; lectr. corporate finance; various profl. confs.; author numerous publs.; recreations: skiing, tennis, golf; Clubs: National Club; Halifax Club; Waegwoltic Club; Home:

1925 Parkwood Terrace, Halifax, N.S.; Office: Saint Mary's Univ., Robie St., Halifax, N.S. B3H 3C3.

**CARSON, Hon. Carol,** B.A., B.Ed.; politician, educator; b. Nipawin, Sask. 5 Sept. 1945; d. George and Irene McNamar (Plageman); e. Univ. of Sask. B.A. 1965; B.Ed. 1967; m. Grant C. 18 June 1965; children: Paul, Les, Mark, Shannon, Glen; MINISTER OF MUNICIPAL GOVERNMENT, GOVT. OF SASKATCHEWAN; Teacher until 1973; 1st elected to Sask. Legislature as MLA for Melfort 21 Oct. 1991; Mayor & Councillor, City of Melfort 1985–91; Chair, Sask. Urban Municipalities Assn. Standing Ctte. on Health, the Environment & Policing Serv.; Bd. of Dir. 2 terms; Pres., Melfort & Dist. Donor's Choice 1983–85; Dir. on various local boards incl. Melfort-Kinistino Rural Devel. Corp.; Melfort Union Hospital Bd.; Melfort Parks & Rec. Bd.; Melfort Plus Indus. Bd.; Founder & Dir., Melfort's Post Secondary Edn. Ctte.; N.D.P.; United Ch.; Home: Box 1600, Melfort, Sask. S0E 1A0; Office: Room 303, Legislative Bldg., Regina, Sask. S4S 0B3.

**CARSON, Edward John,** B.A., M.A.; book publisher; b. Winnipeg, Man. 28 Sept. 1948; s. Roy Woodrow and Lillian Alice (Clemens) C.; e. Univ. of Toronto, B.A. (Hons.) 1976; York Univ., M.A. 1977; Univ. of Toronto, 1977–79; m. Joyce d. Gordon Tooze and Violet Denton 31 Oct. 1952; children: Lindsay Alissa Hannah, Mathew Edward; PRES. & C.E.O., HARPERCOLLINS CANADA LTD. 1993– ; Lectr., Ryerson Polytechnical Inst., Continuing Studies 1991– ; Program Co-Dir., Banff Publishing Workshop 1989–90; Profl. Develop. Coordinator, Book Publishers' Profl. Assoc. 1988–90; Bd. of Dirs., Trade Group, Candn. Book Publishers Counc. 1989–91; Bd. of Dirs., PEN Canada 1990– ; Pub., Stoddart/Gen. Pub. 1980–85; Lectr., Univ. of Toronto 1978–79; Vice-Pres., Publishing, Random House of Can. 1986–91; Exec. Vice-Pres., HarperCollins Canada Ltd. 1991–93; E.J. Pratt Award for Poetry 1973, 1976; St. Michael's Coll. English Award 1976; editor: 'Rune'; author: 'Scenes' 1977; Office: 1995 Markham Rd., Scarborough, Ont. M1B 5M8.

**CARSON, John Jarvis,** O.C. (1976), M.A., LL.D., D.U., D. Lett.; educator; b. Vancouver, B.C. 11 Oct. 1919; e. Univ. of B.C. B.A. 1943; Univ. of Toronto M.A. (Psychol.) 1948; York Univ. LL.D. 1972; Univ. of Ottawa D.U. 1975; Univ. of Sri Jayawardenepura (Sri Lanka) D.Lett.; widower; children: Elizabeth, John, Faith, Deborah, Daniel, Katharine; ADJUNCT PROF., FAC. OF ADMIN., UNIV. OF OTTAWA 1985– ; (and Dean of Fac. of Admin. 1976–81); Sr. Personnel Consultant J.D. Woods & Gordon Ltd. Toronto 1946–52; Mgr. of Manpower Planning & Devel. Ont. Hydro 1952–54, Dir. Employee Relations 1954–56; Dir. Indust. Relations B.C. Electric, Vancouver 1956, Vice Pres. Indust. Relations 1958, Vice Pres. and Asst. to Pres. 1960–61; Dir. of Manpower Project Royal Comm. on Govt. Organ. Ottawa 1961–62; Mgr. Staff Services B.C. Hydro & Power Authority, Vancouver 1962–64; Special Advisor on Personnel to Secy. of Treasury Bd. Can. Ottawa 1964–65; Chrmn. Pub. Service Comn. of Can. 1965–76; Past Pres. Children's Foundation of B.C.; Narcotic Addiction Foundation B.C.; Nat. Council YMCA's Can.; Prov. Commr. St. John Ambulance Bgde. B.C.; Hon. Vice Chrmn. (and past Chrmn.) Candn. University Services Overseas (CUSO); Cercle Universitaire; named Commdr. Order St. John Jerusalem; rec'd Alumni Merit Award Univ. of B.C. 1968; Order of Can. 1976; Hon. Life Mem.: Nat. Council YMCA's Can. (Past Chrmn.); Candn. Public Personnel Mgmt. Assn.; Indust. Relations Mgmt. Assn. of B.C.; Companion, Candn. YMCA Fellowship of Honour; Candn. Criminal Justice Assoc. (CCJA); mem., B.C. Psychol. Assn.; Candn. Psychol. Assn.; Internat. Personnel Mgmt. Assn.; Inst. of Public Admin. of Can.; Candn. Fed. of Deans of Mgmt.; Home: #1105 – 333 Chapel St., Ottawa, Ont. K1N 8Y8.

**CARSON, Maclem K.;** retired labour mediator; b. Belleville, Ont. 24 July 1925; s. William John and Dora Elsie (Kennedy) C.; e. Belleville Coll. Inst. m. Shirley d. Embury and Lula Adams 28 Aug. 1946; two d. Connie-Lou, Elizabeth; Ind. Relations Cons. Mediation & Conciliation Br. Labour Can. 1975–90; Clk. CNR 1943–56; Organizer, Negotiator Candn. Brotherhood Rlwy., Transp. & Gen. Workers Union 1957–64, Dir. of Organizing & Servicing 1964–69, Nat. Vice Pres. 1970–71; Conciliation Offr. Labour Can. 1972–75; acted as mediator resolving disputes in the railway, airline, postal and water transportation industries; responsible for the unionization and negotiation of labour contracts covering St. Lawrence Seaway Authority employees and seafarers employed on the Great Lakes and West Coast of Canada; Head, Candn. (Transportation) Delegation, Internat. Labour Orgn., Geneva, Switzerland 1980; mem. Profl. Devel. Ctte. Assn. Labour Relations Agencies; Soc. of Professionals in Dispute Resolution; Freemason; Presbyterian; recreations: golf, bridge, fishing; Home: P.O. Box 69, Tweed, Ont. K0K 3J0 and (Winter) 7 Hague Blvd., Bradenton, Fla. 34207.

**CARSTAIRS, Sharon,** B.A., M.A.T., M.L.A.; politician; b. Halifax, N.S. 26 Apr. 1942; d. (Senator) Harold Joseph and Vivian Alma (Martel) Connolly; e. Dalhousie Univ., B.A. 1962; Smith Coll. (U.S.), M.A.T. 1963; m. John Esdale s. Charles John and Dorothy C. 6 Aug. 1966; children: Cathi, Jennie; M.L.A. for River Heights 1986– ; teacher, Dana Hall Sch. for Girls 1963–65; Calgary Sep. School Bd. 1965–71; scriptwriter and narrator, Calgary and Region Educ. TV 1967–69; Chrmn., Bd. of Referees, Unemployment Insur. Comm. 1973–77; teacher 1978–84; 1st woman pres., Liberal Party in Alta. 1976–77; 1st woman leader, Liberal Party in Man.; Leader, The Liberal Party in Manitoba 1984–92; Leader of the Official Opposition, Manitoba Apr. 26, 1988–90; pol. exp. 1948–84: N.S.: campaign worker, exec. mem. University Club, nat. exec. mem. Univ. Liberals; Alta.: poll captain fed. elections, exec. mem. Alta. Women's Assn., sec., Pres. Liberal Party in Alta., Calgary Reg. Vice-Pres., Fed. Campaign Ctte. Mem., Prov. candidate, mem. Nat. Exec.; Man: prov. election office mgr., co-chrmn. Donors' Dinner, Fed. Campaign Ctte. Mem.; recreation: swimming; Home: 1 – 525 Wellington Cres., Winnipeg, Man. R3M 0A1.

**CARSWELL, Allan Ian,** B.A.Sc., M.A., Ph.D., FRSC; physicist; b. Toronto, Ont. 4 Oct. 1933; s. Duncan and Margaret (MacAskill) C.; e. Univ. of Toronto, B.A.Sc. 1956; M.A. 1957, Ph.D. 1960; m. Helen d. Helen and Alexander Aird 2 June 1956; children: Donald, Ruth, Diane; PROF. OF PHYSICS, YORK UNIV. 1968– ; NRC post-doct. fellow, Univ. of Amsterdam 1960–61; Lab. Dir., RCA Victor Rsch. Labs. 1961–68; Founder & Pres., Optech Inc. 1974– ; Mem. & Chrmn., Nat. Sci. & Eng. Rsch. Counc. Phys. Ctte., Ottawa 1977–81; Phys. & Astron. Adv. Ctte. 1984–89; Pres., Candn. Assn. of Phys. 1985–86; Chrmn., Am. Meteorol. Assn. Ctte. on Laser Atmospheric Studies 1984–86; Mem., Profl. Engrs. of Ont.; Am. Optical Soc.; Fellow, Royal Society of Can. 1984; Candn. Inst. of Aeronautics & Space 1982; author & co-author of over 100 pubns.; recreations: skiing, boating; Home: 17 Valloncliffe Rd., Thornhill, Ont. L3T 2W6; Office: 4700 Keele St., North York, Ont. M3J 1P3.

**CARTER, Most Rev. Alexander,** O.C., B.A., L.Th., J.C.L., LL.D. (R.C.); bishop; b. Montreal, Que. 16 Apr. 1909; s. Thomas J. and Mary (Kelty) C.; e. St. Patrick's Sch. (Grad. 1924); College de Montréal (Grad. 1930); Semy. of Philosophy, B.A. 1932; Grand Semy. of Theol., L.Th. 1936; Appolinaris Law Sch., Rome, J.C.L. 1939; Laurentian Univ., LL.D. (hon. causa) 1962; Bishop of Sault Ste. Marie 1958–85; Chancellor, Univ. of Sudbury; Vice-Chancellor, Montreal, 1940–46; Chancellor, Winnipeg, 1946–47; Vice-officials Matrimonial Tribunal, Montreal, 1948–53; Parish Priest, Holy Family, Montreal, 1953–57; Pres., Candn. Catholic Conf. of Bishops 1967–69; mem. Secretariat for Non-Believers 1967–73; mem. Vanier Inst. of the Family; National Dir., Pontifical Mission-Aid Societies for Can. 1971–77; Pres., Ont. Catholic Conf. of Bishops 1977–81; Chrmn. CCCB Episcopal Comn. for the Laity 1978–83; Publication: 'Answers'; Officer of the Order of Canada 1989; Address: 250 Silver Lady Lane, R.R. 3, North Bay, Ont. P1B 8G4.

**CARTER, The Hon. Mr. Justice Archibald McGilvery;** Q.C.; federal judge; b. Orillia, Ont. 23 Apr. 1919; s. Archibald Thomas and Nelle Winnifred (McGilvery); e. Orillia Coll. Inst. 1936; Victoria Coll., Univ. of Toronto 1940; Osgoode Hall Law Sch. 1943; m. Yaroslawa d. Andrew and Helen Worobetz 17 Sept. 1943; children: Randy Carolyn, Kim Maxine, Blair McGilvery; JUSTICE, ONTARIO COURT OF JUSTICE (GEN. DIV.) 1990– ; Artillery Captain, Candn. Armed Forces 1943–46; law practice, Orillia, Ont. 1946–62; County & District Court Judge 1962–90; Pres., Ont. Co. Court Judges Assn. 1974–75 (Extve. Mem. 1967–82); Q.C. 1954; Govt. of Can. Centennial Medal 1967; Orillia Citizen of the Year 1960; Chrmn., Bd. of Trustees, St. Paul's Un. Ch. 1948–69; Board of Elders 1962–69; Founder & Chrmn., Orillia Comm. Centre; Pres., Orillia Y's Men's Club 1952–53; Orillia YMCA 1964; Orillia P.C. Assn. 1951–62; Simcoe E. P.C. Assn. 1960–61; Chrmn., Orillia, Barrie & Innisfil Pol. Commissions 1966–73; recreations: golf, curling, swimming, walking, piano and organ playing; Clubs: Phi Gamma Delta, Univ. of Toronto 'T-holders' Assoc.; Couchiching Country, Orillia Curling; Home: 358 Old Muskoka Rd., Orillia, Ont. L3V 4G4; Office: 114 Worsley St., Barrie, Ont. L4M 1M1.

**CARTER, Colin Andre,** B.A., M.Sc., M.A., Ph.D.; professor; b. Grande Prairie, Alta. 30 Jan. 1954; s. John Adley and Amy Janet (Flaten) C.; e. Univ. of Alta., B.A. 1974, M.Sc. 1976, Univ. of Calif., M.A. 1978, Ph.D. 1980; m. Noreen d. Patrick and Maureen Roche 12 July 1981; PROF., UNIV. OF CALIFORNIA AT DAVIS 1986– ; Prof., Univ. of Man. 1980–86; author; contbr. to journs. & book chapters; co-author: 'Grain Export Cartels' 1981; 'China's Grain Trade' 1988; 'Futures and Options Markets' 1990; Cons., Candn. Internat. Devel. Agency; Agric. Can.; Dept. of Fin.; Kellogg Internat. Fellow in Food Systems 1986–89; Am. Agric. Econ. Assn. Award for 'Quality of Rsch.' 1981; Office: Univ. of Calif., Davis, Calif. 95616.

**CARTER, Hon. David John,** M.L.A., D.D.; politician; b. Moose Jaw, Sask. 6 Apl. 1934; s. Wilfred John (Archdeacon) and Mabel (Sheward) C.; e. Univ. of Man. B.A. 1958; St. John's Coll. Winnipeg L.Th. 1961, D.D. 1968; Ang. Theol. Coll., Univ. of B.C., Bachelor Sacred Theol. 1968; Speaker of the Legislative Assembly of Alta. 1986–93; Chaplain, Univ. of Calgary, S. Alta. Inst. of Technol. and Mount Royal Coll. 1965–69; also served as Rector, Cathedral Ch. of the Redeemer, Calgary; Dean, Ang. Diocese of Calgary 1969–79; Diocesan Archivist 1966–88; el. M.L.A. for Calgary-Millican 1979, re-el. as mem. for Calgary-Egmont 1982, 1986, 1989; re-el. as Speaker 1989; Founding Chrmn., Alta. govt.'s Social Care Facilities Review Ctte. and Special Adv. to Min. of Edn. on Urban Native Education 1979–86; mem. Calgary Caucus since 1979; mem. special ctte. Candn. Senate Reform; Dep. Chrmn. Legis. Offices Ctte. and Chrmn. Cttes. Search & Select prov. Ombudsman, Auditor Gen. and Chief Electoral Offr. 1982–86; mem. Senate, Univ. of Calgary 1971–77; served NOVA (Alta. Corp.) 1982–86; Dir. Calgary Canucks Jr. Hockey Team; Trinity Place Found., Alta. (housing for srs.); Calgary Exhn. & Stampede 1986–90; Pres. Alta. Br., Commonwealth Parlty. Assn.; Past Pres., Extve. Ctte., Candn. Region, Commonwealth Parlty. Assoc. (Chrmn., Second Commonwealth Parliamentary Seminar 1990); Hon. Chrmn. Lupus Erythematosus Soc. Alta.; author 'Calgary's Anglican Cathedral' 1973; 'Samuel Trivett – Missionary with the Blood Indians'; 'Prairie Profiles' 1977; 'Reflections' 1979; 'Behind Canadian Barbed Wire' 1980; Address: Box 39, Elkwater, Alta. T0J 1C0.

**CARTER, Donald Douglas,** B.A., LL.B., B.C.L.; educator; b. Picton, Ont. 10 Oct. 1942; s. Colin and Margaret Christina (McNab) C.; e. Queen's Univ. B.A. 1963, LL.B. 1966; Oxford Univ. B.C.L. 1968; m. Catherine d. John and Winnifred Best 23 July 1966; two s. Ian Michael, Colin John; PROF. OF LAW 1975– ; and DEAN OF LAW, QUEEN'S UNIV. 1993– , mem. Faculty since 1968; called to Ontario Bar 1970; Adjudicator, Ont. Pub. Service Labour Relations Tribunal 1973–75; Chrmn. Ont. Labour Relations Bd. 1976–79; Visiting Scholar, Monash Univ. Australia 1984–85; Dir. Ind. Relations Centre/Sch. of Ind. Relations, Queen's Univ. 1985–90; labour arbitrator; co-author 'Labour Law and Industrial Relations in Canada' 4th ed. 1993; contbr. 'Labour Law: Cases, Materials and Commentary' 5th ed. 1991; Assoc. Ed. 'Labour Arbitration Cases'; Pres., Candn. Ind. Relations Assn. 1991–92; Moderator, Chalmers Un. Ch. 1986–89; recreations: skiing, tennis; Home: 42 Clergy St. E., Kingston, Ont. K7L 3H8; Office: Kingston, Ont. K7L 3N6.

**CARTER, Donald S.,** B.Comm., M.B.A., C.F.A.; banker; b. Montreal, Que.; e. Concordia Univ. B.Comm. 1971; Univ. of Michigan M.B.A. 1972; C.F.A. 1990; m. Merryn; children: Michael, Andrew, Hillary; SENIOR VICE PRESDIENT, SENIOR MARKETING OFFICER & MEMBER, BOARD OF DIRECTORS, BANK OF AMERICA, CANADA, TORONTO 1991– ;– ;Citibank Canada (Toronto & Calgary) 1974–78; Project Finance, Marketing, Credit, Acct. Mngt., Bank of Montreal, Corp. Banking 1978–91; recreations: golf, tennis, photography; clubs: Boulevard; Home: 22 Crendon Dr., Etobicoke, Ont. M5C 3G4; Office: 18th fl., 4 King St. W., Toronto, Ont. M5H 1B6.

**CARTER, His Eminence G. Emmett,** C.C., L.Th., M.A., LL.D., D.D., D.H.L., Ph.D.; Cardinal (R.C.); b. Montreal, Que. 1 March 1912; s. Thomas Joseph and Mary (Kelty) C.; e. St. Patrick's Boy's Sch., Montreal; Montreal Coll.: Univ. of Montreal, B.A. 1933, B.Th. 1936, M.A. 1940, Ph.D. 1947; D.H.L., Duquesne Univ. 1962; LL.D., Univ. of W. Ont., LL.D. (hon.) Concordia Univ. 1976, Univ. 1976, Univ. of Windsor 1977; D.D. (hon.) Huron Coll., Univ. of W. Ont. 1978; D. Litt., St. Mary's University, Halifax, 1980; LL.D. McGill Univ., Montreal, 1980; LL.D. Notre Dame Univ., 1981; Elevated to Sacred College of Cardinals, June 1979; app'ted Mem. Secretariate for Non-Christians and Secretariate for Christian unity 1979; ARCHBISHOP EMERITUS

OF TORONTO 1990; o. Priest 1937; Supv., Montreal Cath. Sch. Comn., 1937–39; Founder and Principal, The St. Joseph Teachers Coll.; Charter mem. and first Pres., Thomas More Inst. for Adult Educ., 1945; Eng. Commr. of the Montreal Cath. Sch. Comn., 1948–61; Rector, St. Lawrence Coll., Quebec, 1961; Chaplain, Newman Club of McGill Univ., 1941–56; three terms as Nat. Chaplain, Candn. Fed. of Newman Clubs; elevated Hon. Canon of the Basilica of Our Lady Queen of the World, Montreal, 1953; Commdr. of Order of Scholastic Merit of Que., 1958; Conventual Chaplain, Kts. of Malta, 1960; Titular Bishop of Altiburo, 1961 (consecrated 2 Feb. 1962); Auxiliary Bishop of London, 1962–64; Bishop of London, 1964–68; apptd. Chancellor. Assumption Univ., 1964; apptd. by Pope Paul VI Candn. Rep. at Consilium for Liturgy, Rome, 1966; Archbishop of Toronto 1978–90; Chrmn., Candn. Liturg. Comm. (Eng. Sector) and Pres., Office of Liturgy (Eng. Sector) C.C.C.B. 1966; Vice-Pres., Doctrine and Faith Dept. C.C.C.B. 1969; C.C.O. 1971–73; C.C.C.B. 1973–75; Pres., C.C.C.B. 1975–77; mem., Sacred Cong. for Divine Worship 1970; Perm. Council of the Synod, 1977–83; Chrmn., Internat. Comte. for Eng. in the Liturgy 1971; Publications: 'Catholic Public Schools of Quebec' 1957: 'Psychology and the Cross' 1959; 'The Modern Challenge to Religious Education' 1961; 'A Shepherd Speaks' 1982; apptd. Companion, Order of Can. 1983; Address: 355 Church St., Toronto, Ont. M5B 1Z8.

**CARTER, George Ian,** B.Arch., MAIBC, MRAIC, ARIBA; architect; b. Woodford, Essex, Eng. 23 Sept. 1942; s. George Leslie and Phillis Mary (French) C.; e. Kelvinside Acad. Glasgow; McIntosh Sch. of Arch. Glasgow Univ. B.Arch. 1968; m. Mary Ann d. Foster and Mynnette Sheller 18 March 1981; children: Emma, Steven, Holly; PARTNER, WAISMAN DEWAR GROUT CARTER since 1983, Dir. of Design 1986– ; after grad. served private and pub. offices Scot.; designed universities, hospitals and oil processing plants, W. Africa (travelled extensively throughout Nigeria, Dahomey, Ghana, Sierra Leone and Liberia) 1972–74; came to B.C. 1974; designed hosps., office and rsch. bldgs.; left own practice to become a partner in present firm 1983; Dir. of Planning and Design Expo'86; projects incl. hospitals, prisons, mixed development, research bldgs., theme parks, naval facility; design awards incl. Discovery Parks, New Westminster Hotel, First Capital Place Office Bldg., Burnaby Gen. Hosp. and Children's/Grace Hospitals; mem. Project Mgmt. Inst.; Vancouver Board of Trade; American Planning Assn.; Urban Devel. Inst. Vancouver; Arch. Inst. B.C.; Royal Arch. Inst. Can. (Committee Chrmn.); Royal Arch. Inst. Brit. Archs.; Candn. Fedn. Artists; recipient Design Awards B.C. 1981, 1988, 1989; Writer; Adjunct Prof., Univ. of British Columbia; guest lectr.; Presbyterian; recreations: architecture, painting, photography, design, reading; Clubs: Olympic Athletic; Vancouver Rotary; Canadian; Home: 3854 S.W. Marine Dr., Vancouver, B.C. V6N 3Z9; Office: 1505 West, 2nd Ave., Vancouver, B.C. V6H 3Y4.

**CARTER, Gordon Raymond,** P.Mgr.; professional manager; b. Portlock, Ont. 1 Mar. 1924; s. Raymond and Irene Susan (Buck) C.; e. Queen's Univ., Mun. Clerks & Finan. Offr. course; m. Dorothy Elizabeth d. James and Dorothy Hamilton 15 Dec. 1948; children: Neil Raymond, Nola Jane, Wendy Susan, Karen Lee, Dorothy Gail, Lisa Colleen; CHRMN. OF BD., ADANAC MANAGEMENT LTD. 1977– ; Forest Insect Ranger, Dept. of Agric., N. Ont. 1946–51; Owner/Op., Grocery, Meat Market & Restaurant, Desbarats, Ont. 1951–61; Law Clerk, Peterson & Peterson 1961–71; Admin., Dept. of Legal Serv., Govt. of NWT 1971–75; seconded as Chief of Mun. Affairs, Dept. of Local Govt., GNWT 1975–76; Sec./Treas. & Bus. Admin., YK Sch. Dist. #1 1976–77; Extve. Mgr., NWT Law Found.; C.E.S.O. Volunteer Advisor; Accredited Assoc. Mem., Inst. of Law Clerks of Ont. to 1971; Chrmn., NWT Public Util. Bd. 1977–82; NWT Highway Transport Bd. 1971–82; Extve. Mem., Candn. Assn. of Motor Transport Admin. 1976–81 (Pres. 1979–80); Mem. ,Alta. Arbitration & Mediation Soc.; Arbitration Inst. of Can.; Address: P.O. Box 2594, Yellowknife, N.W.T. X1A 2P9.

**CARTER, Harriet Estelle,** R.C.A.; artist (prof. name Harriet Manore Carter); b. Grand Bend, Ont. 22 March 1929; d. late Lloyd Avery and late Clarissa (Hamilton) Manore; e. H. B. Beal Tech. & Comm. High Sch. London, Ont. 1948; Dundas Valley Sch. of Fine Art 1967–68; m. John G. Carter 20 Jan. 1951; children: Mrs. Lynn Anne Powell, Brian John, Scott Lloyd; prof. painter since 1969; comm. designer for glass co. 1948–51; exhns. incl. Nat. Acad. Gallery N.Y. City 1972; Harbour Front Toronto 1975; Art Gallery of Ont. 1975–76; Tokyo, Hiroshima, Nagoya 1976, also Montreal, Toronto and Calgary; Equinox, B.C. 1977; exhn. and seminar Sarnia Pub. Gallery 1977; solo exhns. Nancy Poole's Studio 1972, 1974, 1976, 1977, 1980, 1983; group exhns. W. End Gallery Edmonton 1980; 'Cloud Flowers: Rhododendrons East and West' 1981 (on tour until 1983); (watercolours) Ring House Gallery, Univ. of Alta.; rep. in various private and pub. colls. incl. Royal Collection of Drawings & Watercolours, Windsor Castle; Lt. Gov.'s Coll. (Queen's Park); Can. Council Art Bank; Hart House; Art Gall. of Brant; Sarnia Public Lib. & Art Museum; London Regional Art Gall.; London Bd. of Educ.; Lincon Bd. of Educ.; Reed Paper Co.; Norcen Energy Resources (2 paintings); Imperial Oil; C.S.P.W.C. Diamond Jubilee Collection presented to her Majesty Queen Elizabeth II for the Royal Collection of Drawings and Watercolours at Windsor Castle; Caledon Capital Corporation Collection; third runner-up Canada Mint energy coin design competition 1981; mem. Cdn. Soc. Painters in Water Colours; Ont. Soc. Artists; Royal Cdn. Acad.; Liberal; Anglican; recreations: wild-flowers, exploring small towns and villages, auctions; Home: 78 MacLennan Ave., Hamilton, Ont. L8V 1X6; Office: Nancy Pooles Studio, 16 Hazelton Ave., Toronto, Ont.

**CARTER, Harry Havilland,** M.A.; retired diplomat; b. Toronto, Ont. 4 Jan. 1918: s. Basil Brooke and Mary Isobel (Casey) C.; e. Lakefield Prep. Sch. (1929–32); Upper Canada Coll. (1932–34); Univ. of Toronto, B.A. (Pol. Science and Econs.) 1938, M.A. 1940; m. Pamela Christine, d. Stephen W. Price, 4 Dec. 1948: two d. Vivien P. (Mrs. Michael Young), Valerie I. (Mrs. William Sharkey); joined Dept. of External Affairs after war service: has served in Wash., The Hague, New York and New Delhi; apptd. Head of U.S.A. Div., Jan. 1961; subsequently Ambassador to Finland then to S. Africa; later Dir. Historical Division; retired from External Affairs Aug. 1983; served in 2nd World War; enlisted as Gunner. 1940, Commnd. Aug. 1940; served with 1st Field Regt., R.C.H.A. 3rd Medium Regt., R.C.A.; discharged with rank of Capt., 1945; Kappa Alpha; Anglican; recreations: photography, reading, music; Home: Unit 17, 174 Dufferin Rd., Ottawa, Ont. K1M 2A6.

**CARTER, Hugh Munro,** B.A.Sc.; business owner; b. London, Ont. 20 Aug. 1918; s. Robert Stewart and Evelyn Blanche (Munro) C.; e. Univ. of B.C., B.A.Sc. (Chem. Engr.); Dartmouth Coll.; Dip. in Mgmt., Am. Mgmt. Assn.; m. Mona Kathleen d. Thomas and Harriet Yielding 27 Dec. 1941; children: Jan Kathleen, Kim Thomas Robert, Bryant Munro, Lee Hugh; PRES., CARTER & CARTER 1991– ; Vice Pres., Intra Forest Hill Travel Ltd. 1990– ; Sales Mgr., Domtar 1950–53; Sales Mgr., Sharples England 1953–57; Managing Dir. 1957–62; Mktg. Dir., Pennwalt U.K. 1962–68; Managing Dir. 1968–76; Pres., Hosp. & Kitchen Eqt. Ltd. 1976–85; Shareholder & Pres., Seeworld Travel Service 1985–90; recreations: many; Clubs: Ontario Club (Past Pres.); East India Club (London, Eng.); Home: 2255 Bethnal Green, Oakville, Ont. L6J 5J8; Office: 277 Lakeshore Rd. E., Suite 211, Oakville, Ont. L6J 1H9.

**CARTER, John Hall,** B.A., D.H.A., F.A.C.H.A., Dr.Admin. (h.c.); hospital administrator; b. Toronto, Ont. 6 Apr. 1935; s. Edward Acres and Florence Elizabeth (Jordan) C.; e. Univ. of Western Ont. Hons. Bus. Admin. 1959; Univ. of Toronto Dip. in Hosp. Admin. 1962; m. Beverley d. Wilbur and Helen Fox 13 Aug. 1960; children: Kelly, Jeffrey; PRESIDENT AND CHIEF EXEC. OFFR., THE GREATER NIAGARA GENERAL HOSPITAL; previously with mktg. and sales Proctor and Gamble Co. Ltd.; Exec. Dir. Victoria Gen. Hosp.; Sr. Vice-Pres. Operations Can. Extendicare Ltd.; Pres. Extendicare Devel. and Mgmt. Ltd.; Past Chrmn. Ont. Blue Cross; Past Mem., Premier's Counc. on Health Strategy; Past Chrmn., Candn. Counc. on Health Facilities Accreditation; author various articles; past Pres. Candn. Coll. of Health Service Execs.; Past Chrmn. Ont. Hosp. Assn.; recipient Bicentennial Medal for Community Services; recreations: golf, skiing; Home: 6993 Thoroldstone Rd., Niagara Falls, Ont. L2J 1B5; Office: P.O. Box 1018, 5546 Portage Rd. S., Niagara Falls, Ont. L2E 6X2.

**CARTER, Madame Justice Mary Yvonne,** B.A., LL.B.; judge; b. Cromer, Man. 11 Oct. 1923; d. William George and Jean May (Marshall) Munn; e. Nutana High Sch. Saskatoon 1941; Univ. of Sask. B.A. 1944, LL.B. 1947; m. Roger Colenso Carter 14 June 1947; children: Stephen, Sarah, Martha, Michael, Mark, Adam; COURT OF QUEEN'S BENCH since July, 1981; Local Judge, Court of Queen's Bench and Judge of Unified Family Court since 1978; called to Bar of Sask. 1948; practiced law in partnership with spouse 1948–53; Part-time Magistrate and Judge of Magistrate's Court 1960–72; Judge of Magistrate's Court 1972–78; Anglican; recreations: gardening, cooking, bird watcher; Home: 420 Cumberland Ave. S., Saskatoon, Sask. S7H 2L4; Office: Unified Family Court, 9th Floor, Canterbury Place, 224 4th Ave. S., Saskatoon, Sask. S7K 5M5.

**CARTER, Richard,** B.A., M.A., Ph.D.; financial executive; b. Ste-Foy, Que. 16 Oct. 1952; s. Noël and Thérèse (Morissette) C.; e. Univ. Laval B.A. 1975, M.A. 1978; Virginia Polytechnic Inst. Ph.D. 1981; m. Johanne d. Auguste and Thérèse (Jobin) Fleury 21 June 1975; children: Frédéric, Valérie; SENIOR VICE-PRESIDENT PRODUCT MANAGEMENT, NATIONAL BANK OF CANADA since 1992, Sr. Vice-Pres., Finance & Chief Economist 1990–91, Vice-Pres. & Chief Economist 1988–90; Prof. of Economics, Laval Univ. and Univ. of Quebec 1982–88; Home: 1821 Marie Dubois, Carignan, Que. J3L 3P9; Office: 600 rue de la Gauchetière, 12th fl., Montreal, Que. H3B 4L2.

**CARTHY, James Joseph,** B.A.; judge; b. Toronto, Ont. 8 May 1933; s. James Weatherly and Norma Elizabeth (Bloomer) C.; e. St. Catharines Coll.; Univ. of Toronto, B.A. 19..; Osgoode Hall Law School 1958 (honors); m. Anne d. Jim and Frances McGrath 30 July 1960; children: Linda, David, Susan, John; JUDGE, COURT OF APPEAL FOR ONTARIO 1988– ; Litigation Couns., Weir & Foulds 1958–88, Partner 1963–88; Bencher, Law Soc. of U.C. 1974–88 (Chrmn. of var. cttes.); Mem.; Rules Ctte. under Judicature Act 1968–75; Dir., Mooredalehouse 1976–78; Rosedale Tennis Club 1978–84; United Ch.; Mem., Advocates Soc.; Am. Coll. of Trial Lawyers; Candn. Bar Assn.; author & editor: 'Ontario Annual Practice' 1964– ; recreations: tennis, scuba, stained glass, wood carving; Clubs: var. tennis; Home: 8 Hawthorne Ave., Toronto, Ont. M4W 2Z2; Office: Osgoode Hall, 130 Queen St. W., Toronto, Ont. M5H 2N5.

**CARTIER, Benoit,** B.A., LL.B.; corporate executive; b. Montreal, Que. 25 Sept. 1946; s. Paul Henri and Atala (Jean) C.; e. Laval Univ. (Coll. Classique de Thetford Mines) B.A. 1965; Laval Univ. LL.B. 1968; m. Louise d. Jean-Marc and Jeanne-d'Arc Labbé 20 June 1970; children: Paul, André, Charles; President, Société Nationale de l'Amiante 1986–..; Attorney, Internat. Law Dept., United States Steel Corp. 1970; Attorney & Asst. Sec., Iron Ore Mining, Quebec Cartier Mining Inc. 1971; General Counsel, Rayonnier Quebec, Div. of ITT Industries of Canada Ltd. 1977; Ceram-SNA Inc.; Mem., Quebec Bar; Candn. Bar Assn.; recreations: sailing, skiing; Home: 1206 Coleraine Ave., Thetford Mines, Que. G6G 3L1.

**CARTIER, Céline;** Administrateur; né Lacolle, Qué. 10 mai 1930; f. Henri et Marie-Reine (Boudreau) Robitaille; é. Univ. de Montréal, Diplôme supérieur pédagogie 1948, Certificats en litt. et ling. 1952; Ecole de bibliothécaires-docum. Paris, Diplôme 1962; Ecole nationale d'adm. publique, Qué. Maîtrise en adm. publique 1976; Univ. de Montréal, Maîtrise en bibliothéconomie 1982; ép. Georges Cartier 29 novembre 1952; enfants: Nathalie, Guillaume; CONSULTANT: CRC CONSEIL 1989– ; Dir. de la Bibliothèque centrale, Commission des écoles catholiques de Montréal 1964–73; Dir. des collections spéciales Univ. du Qué., Montréal 1973–76, Dir. des bibliothèques de secteurs 1976–77; Chef de la Bibliothèque générale, Univ. Laval 1977–78; Dir. Gen. des Bibliothèques, Univ. Laval 1978–88; auteur 'Cours de français' 1958; 'Recontre sur la bibliothéconomie québécoise' 1975; 'Le plan directeur pluri-annuel: un instrument-efficace pour la gestion des bibliothèques' 1986; textes radiophoniques a' Radio-Can., confs., articles, contrib. aux revues professionnelles dans les sciences de l'information; récreations: cello, reading, skiing, sailing; Adresse: 750 Place Fortier, #701, Ville-Saint-Laurent, Qué. H4L 5C1.

**CARTY, Arthur J.,** B.Sc., Ph.D., D.Sc., F.R.S.C.; university professor & administrator; b. Rowlands Gill Co. Durham, U.K. 12 Sept. 1940; s. George M. and Evelyn C.; e. Univ. of Nottingham, B.Sc. 1962, Ph.D. 1965; m. Hélène Cloutier 3 Sept. 1967; children: Richard, Stephane, Roxanne; DEAN OF RESEARCH, UNIV. OF WATERLOO 1989– ; Asst. Prof. Chem., Memorial Univ. of Nfld. 1965–67; Univ. of Waterloo 1967–69; Assoc. Prof. Chem. 1969–75; Prof. Chem. 1975; Dir., Guelph-Waterloo Ctr. for Grad. Work in Chem. 1975–79; Chrmn., Dept. of Chem. 1983–89; Chrmn., Chem. Grants Selection Ctte., NSERC 1980–81; Group Chrmn. 1982–84; Doctorat Honoris Causa, L'Univ. de Rennes, France 1986; Alcan Award, Chem. Inst. of Can. 1984; F.R.S.C. 1989; Vice-Pres., Candn. Soc. for Chem. 1989; Pres., Candn. Soc. for Chem. 1990–91; Chrmn., Roy. Soc. Can. Public Awareness of Science Ctte. 1990–93; Mem., Adv. Bd., Steacie Institute of Molecular Sciences, NRC; Mem. Bd. of Dirs., Waterloo Centre for Groundwater Rsch.; Ont. Centre for Materials Rsch.; Candn.

Industrial Innovation Ctr.; Field's Institute for Rsch. in Mathematical Sciences; Mgmnt. Bd., Institute for Chemical Science and Technology; Mem., Waterloo Economic Development Ctte.; Mem., Intelligent Manufacturing Systems (IMS), Internat. Intellectual Property Ctte.; Mem., Rsch. Advisory Ctte., Royal Victoria Hosp., London; Mem., Targeted Rsch. Ctte., Natural Sciences & Engineering Rsch. Council of Canada; Mem., Am. Chem. Soc.; Candn. Inst. of Chem.; Home: 73 McDougall Rd., Waterloo, Ont. N2L 2W4; Office: Waterloo, Ont. N2L 3G1.

**CARTY, Michael W.,** B.Comm., LL.B., Q.C.; lawyer, health executive; b. Kingston, Ont. 13 April 1932; s. John Joseph and Beatrice (Murphy) C.; e. Regiopolis Coll.; Queen's Univ. B.Comm. 1956; Dalhousie Univ. LL.B. 1959; Osgoode Hall Bar Admission 1961; m. Judith d. Victor Sydney and Winefride Bennett 25 June 1960; children: Christopher, Peter (dec.), Richard, Terence, Anthony, Anne, Shane; SR. PARTNER, CUNNINGHAM, SWAN, CARTY, LITTLE & BONHAM 1981– ;& EXTVE. VICE-PRES., RELIGIOUS HOSP. OF ST. JOSEPH HEALTH SYSTEM 1985– ; called to Ont. Bar 1961; Jr. Counsel, Royal Comn. on Crime 1961–63; joined present law firm 1963; Chair, Cath. Health Assn. of Can.; Providence Cont. Care Ctr.; Hotel Dieu Hosp. St. Catharines; Past Chair, Joint Liaison Cttes., Queen's Univ. & affil. hosps.; Pres., Cath. Edn. Found. of Ont.; Dir., Jeanne Mance Found.; The Davies Charitable Found.; Past Trustee, Queen's Univ.; Mem., Queen's Univ. Council; Past Chair, Hotel Dieu Hosp. Kingston; Pro Pontifice et Ecclesia (Papal) Award; Q.C.; Award of Honour, Frontenac, Lennox & Addington Sep. Sch. Bd.; Mem., Admin. Bd., R.C. Episcopal Corp., Archdiocese of Kingston; Presentor, Ont. Hosp. Assn.; Cath. Hosp. Assn. of Ont.; recreations: hobby farming (Highland cattle); clubs: Cataraqui Golf & Country; Home: 32 Kensington Ave., Kingston, Ont. K7L 4B5; Office: P.O. Box 460, 259 King St. E., Kingston, Ont. K7L 4W5.

**CARTY, Roland Kenneth,** Ph.D.; professor; b. Quebec City, Que. 8 Sept. 1944; s. Roland Kenneth and Catherine Elizabeth (Matheson) C.; e. Univ. of N.B., B.Sc.F. 1966; Oxford Univ. (Jesus Coll.) B.A., M.A. 1968; Queen's Univ. Ph.D. 1976; Rhodes Scholar (N.B. and Jesus) 1966; m. Elaine d. Maynard and Elizabeth McEwan 14 Dec. 1968; children: Roland Kenneth, Andrew McEwan, Leslie McEwan; PROFESSOR OF POLITICAL SCIENCE, UNIV. OF BRITISH COLUMBIA 1974– ; joint appt. Dept. of Soc. Sciences, St. Thomas Univ. and Dept. of Pol. Sci., Univ. of N.B. 1968–70; visiting scholar, Dept. of Pol. Sci., Univ. of Minn. 1980–81; Univ. of Western Australia 1988; Life Pres., Class of 1966, Univ. of N.B.; mem. United Ch.; mem. Candn. Pol. Sci. Assn. (Prog. Chair 1983); author: 'Party and Parish Pump' 1981 (Irish ed.: 'Electoral Politics in Ireland' 1983); 'Grassroots Politicians' 1991; recreations: skiing, reading; Home: 4422 West 6th Ave., Vancouver, B.C. V6R 1V3; Office: Vancouver, B.C. V6T 1Z1.

**CARVER, David H.,** A.B., M.D.; physician, educator; b. Boston, Mass. 18 Apr. 1930; s. late Elias and late Charlotte (Jaffe) C.; e. Harvard Univ. A.B.; Duke Univ. M.D.; m. Patricia Jo d. late Israel Nair and Fritzi Nair 2 Aug. 1963; children: Randolph Nair, Rebecca Lynn, Leslie Allison; PROF. & CHRMN., DEPT. OF PEDIATRICS, ROBERT WOOD JOHNSON MEDICAL SCHOOL 1988– ; Intern (Med.) Johns Hopkins 1955–56; Research Fellow (Pediatrics), Western Reserve 1956–58; Jr. Resident, Children's Hosp. Boston 1958–59, Sr. Resident 1959–60, Chief Resident 1960–61; Research Fellow (Pediatrics) Harvard 1961–63; Asst. Prof. of Pediatrics and Microbiol. Albert Einstein 1963–66; Assoc. Prof. of Pediatrics, Johns Hopkins 1966–73, Assoc. Prof. of Microbiol. 1966–76, Prof. of Pediatrics 1973–76; Prof. and Chrmn. of Pediatrics, Univ. of Toronto 1976–86, Prof. of Pediatrics 1976–88; Phys.-in-Chief, Hosp. for Sick Children 1976–86; served with USPHS Epidemic Intelligence Service 1956–58; rec'd Schaffer Award for Teaching, Johns Hopkins 1973; Bain Award for Teaching, Hosp. Sick Children 1978; mem. Ed. Bd. Pediatrics 1972–78; Comte. on Infectious Diseases Am. Acad. Pediatrics 1973–79; Study Sec. USPHS Center for Disease Control 1971–73; Prov. Research Grants Review Comte. Ont. Ministry of Health 1977–83 (Chrmn. 1981–83); author various articles research virology and infectious diseases; mem. Soc. Pediatric Research; Am. Pediatric Soc.; Am. Acad. Pediatrics; Infectious Disease Soc. Am.; Candn. Pediatric Soc.; Candn. Infectious Disease Soc.; Am. Soc. Microbiol.; Am. Soc. for Virology; Am. Assn. Advanc. Science; Jewish; Office: Robert Wood Johnson Med. Sch., One Robert Wood Johnson Place, New Brunswick, N.J., U.S.A.

**CARVER, Humphrey Stephen Mumford,** C.M., LL.D., D.Eng.; b. Birmingham, Eng. 29 Nov. 1902; s. Frank and Annie J. H. (Creswell) C.; e. Rugby Sch. Eng. 1921; Corpus Christi Coll. Oxford Univ. 1924; Sch. of Arch. London, Eng. A.R.I.B.A.; Queen's Univ. LL.D. 1979; Technical Univ. of N.S. D.Eng. 1983; Univ. of Guelph LL.D. 1987; Univ. of Waterloo, Dr. Environmental Studies (Hon.) 1989; came to Can. 1930; m. 1stly Mary Robertson (dec.) d. Rev. Dr. Charles W. Gordon Sept. 1933; one s. Peter Gordon King; m. 2ndly Anne Harley d. Hon. Mr. Justice George Sedgewick Nov. 1951; two d. Deborah Anne, Jane Mary Creswell; Partner, Borgstrom & Carver, Landscape Archs. & Town Planners 1931–37; Lectr. Sch. of Arch. Univ. of Toronto 1938–41, Research Assoc. Sch. of Social Work 1946–48; Chrmn. Research Comte. Central Mortgage & Housing Corp. 1948–55, Chrmn. Adv. Group 1955–67; served with Candn. Army NDHQ Ottawa 1942–45, rank Maj.; Member, Order of Canada 1988; author 'Cities in the Suburbs' 1962; 'Compassionate Landscape' 1975; 'The Cultural Landscape of Rockcliffe Park Village' 1986; numerous articles on city and community planning, urbanization, housing; Fellow and former Pres. Candn. Inst. Planners; Hon. mem. Candn. Soc. Landscape Archs.; NDP; recreation: watercolour painting; Club: Arts & Letters (Toronto); Home: 421 Lansdowne Rd. N., Ottawa, Ont. K1M 0X8.

**CASE, Arthur David,** Q.C., B.A., LL.B.; executive; b. Saint John, N.B. 11 Oct. 1938; s. William Arthur Scammell and Edna May (Carrick) C.; e. Univ. of N.B. B.A. 1960; Dalhousie Univ. LL.B. 1963; m. Margaret F. d. Ian and Elinor Cameron 6 June 1964; three d. Jennifer, Gillian, Ann; VICE PRES. LAW & CORPORATE AFFAIRS, SEC. BRUNCOR INC. 1989– ; Chrmn. Bruncor Leasing; Dir. Chancellor Corp.; N1 Cable TV Ltd.; Sec. The New Brunswick Telephone Co. Ltd.; Assoc. Carter, Taylor & Ryan Saint John 1963–66; Partner, Clark, Drummie & Co. or predecessor firms Saint John 1966–88; Chrmn. N.B. Adv. Bd. Montreal Trust 1988–91; Dir. Candn. C. of C. 1982–91 (Exec. Ctte. 1983–91, Chrmn. Exec. Ctte. 1984–85); Pres. Saint John Bd. Trade 1974–75; former mem. N.B. Ind. Devel. Bd.; Chrmn. Aitken Bicentennial Exhn. Centre; former Dir. & Campaign Vice Chrmn. Un. Way Greater Saint John ; mem. Bd. Govs. Saint John YM-YWCA & Junior Achievement Saint John Inc.; co-comnr. & co-author MacLauchlan Comn. Report Judges' Salaries N.B.; Chrmn. Ctte. & co-author N.B. Law Soc. Report Reform Co. Law N.B.; cr. Q.C. 1985; mem. Internat. Bar Assn.; Am. Bar Assn.; Candn. Bar Assn. (Past mem. Council); N.B. Law Soc. (Pres. 1987–89); N.B. Inst. C.A.'s (Council 1990–93); St. George's Soc.; recreations: skiing, sailing, golf; Clubs: Union; Riverside Golf & Country; Royal Kennebeccasis Yacht; Home: P.O. Box 165, Rothesay, N.B. E0G 2W0; Office: P.O. Box 5030, Saint John, N.B. E2L 4L4.

**CASE, Frederick Ivor,** M.A., D.de l'Un.; educator; b. Georgetown, Guyana 19 Sept. 1939; s. Edward Archibald and Honora Candace (Sealey) C.; e. De La Salle Coll. of Edn. Manchester, Eng. Teachers' Cert. 1960; Univ. of Hull B.A. 1965; Univ. of Leicester M.A. 1968; Univ. de Lille D.de l'Un. 1970; children: Marcel, Jean-Louis, Marc, Miriam, Daniel; PRINCIPAL OF NEW COLLEGE 1991– ; PROF. OF FRENCH, UNIV. OF TORONTO 1980– , Chrmn. of French 1985–90; sch. teacher Eng. and France 1960–68; Lectr. in French present Univ. 1968, Asst. Prof. 1970, Assoc. Prof. 1974, Assoc. Chair Grad. Studies French 1984–85, Co-ordinator African Studies Prog. 1978–80; Prés., Assoc. des Dirs. des Départements d'Études Françaises des Universités et Collèges du Canada 1989–1990; Publisher, Terebi Publications, Toronto; author 'Aimé Césaire; Bibliographie' 1973; 'La Cité Idéale dans Travail d'Emile Zola' 1974; 'Racism and National Consciousness' 1979; 'The Crisis of Identity: Studies in the Guadeloupean and Martiniquan Novel' 1985; recreation: Aikido; Office: New College, Univ. of Toronto, Toronto, Ont. M5S 1A1.

**CASE, R. Wayne,** B.B.A.; motion picture executive; b. Natchez, Miss. 23 Jan. 1937; s. Rudolph W. and Pearlie E. (Smith) C.; e. Natchez pub. and high schs.; Tulane Univ. of La. B.B.A. 1959; Univ. of S. Cal. film studies; Sr. Vice Pres., Astral Films 1989–91; joined Columbia Pictures 13 yrs. serving various positions Seattle, San Francisco, Los Angeles and Toronto (Gen. Mgr. of Can.); Twentieth Century Fox 5 yrs. Gen. Mgr. Can.; Buena Vista Distribution Inc. 3 yrs. Gen. Mgr. Can.; mem. Candn. Picture Pioneers; recreations: films, television, attending USC football games; Home: 1424 N. Crescent Hts. Blvd., Unit 79, West Hollywood, Cal. 90046.

**CASEY, Daniel Gerard,** B.A.Sc., M.B.A., P.Eng.; business executive; b. Ottawa, Ont. 15 June 1955; s. John Thomas and Madeleine Claire (Soublière) C.; e. St. Joseph's High Sch. Ottawa 1972; Univ. of Ottawa B.A.Sc. 1977, M.B.A. 1983; m. Sandra d. Bob and Phyllis Mowat 9 Aug. 1980; children: John, Andrea; PRES., ABB FLAKT ROSS INC. 1987– ; Supply and Services Can. 1977–80, Head Project Mgmt. Sect.; Flakt Canada Ltd. Ottawa 1980–85, Project Mgr.; ABB Flakt Ventilation & Refrigeration Inc., Lasalle, Que. 1986– , Pres.; Home: 5 Gervais, Kirkland, Que. H9H 1A5; Office: 304 St. Patrick, Lasalle, Que. H8N 2H1.

**CASGRAIN, André P.,** B.A., B.C.L., Q.C.; attorney at law; b. Rimouski, Que. 5 Nov. 1924; s. Perreault and Lydia (Prince) C. e: St. Dunstan's H.S.; Laval Univ. B.A. 1945; McGill Univ. B.C.L. 1950; m. Jacqueline d. Charles and Jeanne (Lévesque) Théberge 11 Sept. 1954; children: Charles Perreault, Philippe Baby; SENIOR PARTNER, CASGRAIN, BLANCHET, GAGNON, DESROSIERS AND ASSOCIATES 1975– ; admitted to Que. Bar 1950; entered practice of law with Casgrain & Tessier 1950; Mem., Que. Conf. of Arbitrators in matters relating to Labour Relns.; Fellow, Am. Coll. of Trial Lawyers; Mem., Candn. & Que. Bar assns. 1950– ; Bd. Chair, Univ. du Qué. à Rimouski 1991–94; has held directorships from time to time in various social & non-profit orgns. in Lower St.-Lawrence area, Prov. of Que.; Address: 2 St. Germain est, Bureau 400, Edifice Trust Général, C.P. 580, Rimouski, Que. G5L 7C6.

**CASHMAN, The Hon. Mr. Justice Leslie Frederick,** LL.B.; judge; b. Toronto, Ont. 18 Oct. 1920; s. late Frederick George and Elizabeth Ellen (Cooper) C.; e. Northwestern Univ. 1940–41; Univ. of B.C. LL.B. 1949; m. Edna May d. late Frederick Newman 7 Oct. 1944; children: Frederick George, Leslie Ellen Scherileese; JUSTICE, SUPREME COURT OF B.C. 1990– ; called to Bar of B.C. 1949; law practice Cashman & Currie, Quesnel, B.C. 1949–58; G. Roy Long & Co. Vancouver 1958–63; Cashman, Hope & Heinrich, Prince George, B.C. 1963–71; Judge, Co. Court of Vancouver Island 1971–90; served with Candn. Intelligence Corps Can., UK and N.W. Europe 1942–46; rec'd Medal of Merit Boy Scouts Can.; Delta Upsilon; Anglican; recreations: yachting, golf; Home: 2441 Cosgrove Cres., Nanaimo, B.C. V9S 39N; Office: Court House, 35 Front St., Nanaimo, B.C. V9R 5J1.

**CASIRO, Oscar,** M.D., FRCP(C); physician, university professor; b. Buenos Aires, Argentina 9 April 1950; s. Israel and Clara (Ziperfal) C.; e. Univ. of Buenos Aires M.D. 1974; Children's Hosp. of Winnipeg FRCP(C) 1984 (Ped.), 1985 (Neonatologist); m. Malca d. Don Koven 23 May 1980; children: Raimey, Jessica, Mathew, Naomi; ASSOC. PROF., PEDIATRICS, UNIV. OF WINNIPEG 1990– ; immigrated to Canada 1980; Asst. Prof., Ped., Univ. of Winnipeg 1985; Dir., Newborn Follow-up Program; Chair, Child Health Ctte., Manitoba Med. Assn.; consultant for several rsch. printing agencies in Canada; Edit. Bd., Family Communications Inc.; Children's Hosp. of Winnipeg Rsch. Found. Award 1983; Sidney Israels Fellowship (rsch.) 1984; member of several hosp. & univ. cttes.; research focus: long-term outcome of very premature infants; effects on the fetus of alcohol & drug abuse; Mem., Candn. Ped. Soc.; Man. Ped. Soc.; Man. Med. Assn.; Candn. Med. Assn.; author of sci. articles, abstracts, etc.; recreations: swimming, walking, cycling; Home: 520 Laidlaw Blvd., Winnipeg, MB R3P 0K9; Office: 840 Sherbrook St., CK 261, Winnipeg, Man. R3A 1S1.

**CASKEY, James Robert,** Q.C., B.A., LL.B.; barrister, solicitor, notary public; b. Toronto, Ont. 20 Oct. 1936; s. Carl Way and Helen Jessie (Bull) Caskey; e. Weston Collegiate & Voc. Sch. 1955; Victoria Coll., Univ. of Toronto B.A. 1958; Osgoode Hall Law Sch. LL.B. 1961; m. Janet d. Ross and Emily Latham 18 May 1963; children: Andrea, Susan, Jane, Sarah; SENIOR PARTNER, CIVIL LITIGATION, SISKIND, CROMARTY, IVEY & DOWLER; called to Bar of Ont. 1963; Q.C. 1979; Special Lectr., Trial Process, Univ. of W. Ont. Law Sch. 1972–82; Sr. Instr., Civil Procedure, Bar Admission Course, Law Soc. of U.C. 1977–87; Pres., Middlesex Law Assn. 1979; Mem., The Advocates' Soc.; Defence Rsch. Inst.; Chancellor, Anglican Diocese of Huron 1983–90; Chancellor Emeritus 1990; Chrmn., Bd. of Dir., Victoria Hosp. Corp. 1991–92; Mem., St. James Westminster Church Found.; author 'Professional Liability of Insurance Brokers'; recreations: golf, tennis, skiing, sailing; clubs: London, London Hunt, Lake of Bays Tennis; Home: 429 Averill Cres., London, Ont. N6C 2R8; Office: 680 Waterloo St., London, Ont. N6A 3V8.

**CASSADAY, John M.,** B.A., M.B.A.; television executive; b. Hamilton, Ont. 28 March 1953; s. Terrence Michael and Kathleen Theresa (Doyle) C.; e. Univ. of W. Ont. B.A.; Univ. of Toronto M.B.A. (Dean's List); m. Mary d. Burns and Vida Bedard Sept. 1975; children: Jake, Kate, Jesse; PRES., CHIEF EXEC. OFFR. AND DIR. CTV TELEVISION NETWORK LTD. 1990– ; Dir. Toronto Economic Development Corp.; mem. Adv. Bd. Candn. Dirs. Nestle Enterprises Ltd.; joined RJR Macdonald Inc. 1974–77; General Foods Corp. 1977–84; Sr. Vice Pres. Sales & Mktg. Campbell Soup Co. Ltd. Toronto 1984, Exec. Vice Pres. & Chief Operating Offr. 1987, Pres. 1988–89; Pres. & Chief Exec. Offr. Campbell Foods U.K., Vice Pres. Campbell Soup Co. 1989–90; mem. Dean's Adv. Council Univ. of Toronto Bus. Sch.; Bd. Govs. YMCA Metrop. Toronto; mem. Candn. Assn. Broadcasters (Bd.); YPO; R. Catholic; recreations: squash, tennis, golf; Clubs: Granite; Donalda; Office: 42 Charles St. E., Toronto, Ont. M4Y 1T5.

**CASSELMAN, Barbie,** B.A.A., FnCFS; nutritionist, author; b. 5 Feb. 1956; e. H.S. Hons. diploma 1975; Ryerson Polytechnical Inst. B.A.A. 1979; PRESIDENT, CASSELMAN & CO. INC. 1990– ; (corporate nutrition, food product development) and NUTRITION CONSULTANT, BARBIE CASSELMAN INC. 1985– ; (Inc. 1987); Nutrition Advisor (Volunteer), Lorimer Lodge 1977–78; Dietary Aid, North York Gen. Hosp. 1978; Supervisor & Counsellor, Weight Loss Clinic 1979–85; Consultant, Texaco Canada 1985; joint lipid program with Dr. Josephine Bird 1985–88; Nutrition Consultant, The Elmwood, Cambridge and Adelaide health clubs 1985–91; Assoc., Medcan (Inc.) 1985– ; created Alternative Cuisine menu & recipes, King Edward Hotel and 'Nutrifit' menu, Rothman's Corp. 1986; Nutrition Advr., Financial Post 'Inside Sports' 1989–91; Developed 'Barbie Casselman' line of Spa Cuisine 1990–92; Cons., Loblaw Internat. Merchants 'Too Good to be True' products 1991–93; Invited speaker, Empire Club of Canada 1992; Candn. Dental Assn. 1993 annual meeting; lecturer to academic, corp. & charitable institutions; media spokesperson; author: 'Barbie Casselman's Good-For-You Cooking: A Healthy Eating Guide' 1993; Address: National Bank Bldg., 150 York St., Suite 1500, Toronto, Ont. M5H 3S5.

**CASSELS, Derek;** editor; b. Edinburgh, Scotland 7 Feb. 1933; s. Thomas and Jean (Leckie) C.; e. Royal H.S. of Edinburgh; m. 2ndly Caroline d. Victor and Mary (Munro) Gray, May 1990; children (1st marriage): Mark, Martin Thomas; (2nd marriage): Alexandra; EDITOR, THE MEDICAL POST 1978– ; mem., start-up staff, The Medical Post 1965; writer/editor, various Brit. newspapers incl. The Daily Mail, The Daily Herald, The Sunday Mirror, The Sunday Mail (Glasgow); Kenneth R. Wilson Awards for Editorials 1967, 1981, 1983, 1984, 1985, 1991, 1992; Jesse H. Neal Award for Editorial Writing, American Business Press 1987, 1991; Cdn. Nat. Magazine Award 1991; mission: to propagate the notion that to be a serious journalist you don't have to be a solemn one; recreations: swimming, being walked by dog; Office: 777 Bay St., Toronto, Ont. M5G 1Z1.

**CASSIDY, Donald Nelson;** consultant; executive; b. Ottawa, Ont.; s. late Robert George and Emily Louisa (Haffey) C.; e. elem. and high schs. Ottawa; Candn. Police Coll. 1954; m. late Verlie d. Josiah and Louise Nixon 27 Oct. 1945; one s. Donald Nixon; Consultant on policing and law enforcement; joined Gov. Gen. Foot Guards, RCMP 1938–61; Pub. Service of Can. 1961–67; Dir. Gen. Ports Can. Police 1967–84; Founder and First Pres. Internat. Assn. Airport & Seaport Police 1968–70; Pres. Ottawa Div. RCMP Veterans' Assn. 1963–65, Dom. Pres. 1965–67; Asst. Sec.-Treas. and Sec.-Treas., Candn. Assn. of Chiefs of Police 1965–71, 1981–83, Exec. Dir. 1984–90; Vice Pres., National Operation Go Home 1992– ; recipient RCMP Long Service Medal; Centennial Medal; Queen's Silver Jubilee Medal; Police Exemplary Service Medal; author numerous law enforcement articles; mem. YMCA; recreation: reading; Home: 606 Bathurst Ave., Ottawa, Ont. K1G 0X8.

**CASSIDY, Michael Morris,** B.A., M.B.A.; journalist and politician; b. Victoria, B.C. 10 May 1937; s. Harry Morris and Beatrice (Pearce) C.; e. Univ. of Toronto Schs.; Petit Seminaire de Québec; Univ. of Toronto Trinity Coll. B.A. 1958; London Sch. of Econ. 1959–61; York Univ. M.B.A. 1982–84; m. Maureen Kathleen d. Rev. Wilfred Waddington, London, Eng. 25 March 1961; children: Benedict, Adam, Matthew; PRES., THE GINGER GROUP CONSULTANTS 1989– ; M.P. for Ottawa-Centre, 1984–88; N.D.P. Finance critic, 1986–88; Ed. The Varsity Univ. of Toronto 1957–58; reporter Vancouver Sun, Cdn. Press, The Statist (Eng.), Birmingham Post (Eng.); Reporter, Financial Times of Canada 1964–70; Ottawa Bureau Chief 1966–70; Prof. Sch. of Journalism Carleton Univ. Ottawa 1970–71; Ald. City of Ottawa 1970–72; first el. to Ont. Leg. g.e. 1971, re-el. 1975, 1977, 1981; Leader Ontario N.D.P., Feb. 1978–Feb. 1982; Unitarian; recreations: cross-country skiing, rural construction; Home: 301 First Ave., Ottawa, Ont. K1S 2G7.

**CASSIS, Awny Fayez,** B.A. Hons., D.P.E., Ph.D.; university professor; b. Tahta, Egypt 23 Aug. 1934; s. Fayez Thomas and Marie Louise C.; e. Ain Shams Univ. (Cairo), B.A. Hons. 1954; D.P.E. 1955; Trinity Coll., Univ. Dublin, Ph.D. 1960; m. Hilda, d. Henry and Bridie Johnston, 3 Sept. 1961; children: Irene Marie, Jehan Brigitte, Marie Louise, Nevine Muriel; PROF. OF ENGLISH, UNIV. OF LETHBRIDGE 1977– ; Lectr., Teachers' Training Coll. (Egypt) 1961; Lectr., Faculty Arts, Ain Shams Univ. (Cairo) 1964; joined present univ. as Asst. Prof. 1968; Assoc. Prof. 1969; Prof. 1977; Dean, Arts & Science 1980–85; author 'The Twentieth Century English Novel: An Annotated Bibliography of Criticism' 1977; 'Graham Greene: An Annotated Bibliography of Criticism' 1981; Bd. Trustees, St. Michael's Hosp. (Lethbridge); Roman Catholic; Home: 7 King's Place South, Lethbridge, Alta. T1K 5G9; Office: Univ. of Lethbridge, 4401 University Dr., Lethbridge, Alta. T1K 3M4.

**CASTALDI, Joseph S.,** C.R.A., A.S.A.; real estate broker; b. Malta 23 July 1936; s. Evaristo and Catherine Christina C.; e. Primary Sch., Malta; St. Aloyiusos Coll., Ryerson Coll., Malta; York Univ., Toronto; m. Virginia Vivian d. Anthony Farrugia 5 May 1957; children: Joseph Anthony, Patrick Henry, Michelle Allisston; REAL ESTATE BROKER, REMAX WEST REALTY INC.; entered R.E. business 1958 as salesperson, becoming Broker 1966; Accredited Cert. Residential Appraisor; Sr. Appraisor, Am. Soc. of Appraisors 1970; Pres. and Chapter Dir., Toronto Real Estate Bd. 1977–85, Pres. 1985– ; mem. Rate Payers of Ryde Twp. Muskoka; Sec. Gravenhurst Area Lakes Assn.; Pres. Riley Lake Assn. 1982–84; hockey team sponsor; recreations: fishing, carpentry, sports; Club: Melita Soccer; Address: 96 Rexdale Blvd., Rexdale, Ont. M9W 1N7.

**CASTEL, Jean Gabriel,** O.C., O.O., Q.C., B.Sc.; e. J.D. Univ. of Mich.; Harvard Univ., S.J.D.; Lic. en droit (Paris); Dipl., Inst. de Droit Comparé (Paris); Fullbright Scholar, 1950; Commonwealth Scholar, 1962; Killam Fellow, 1985; Cox Fellow, 1989; Docteur honoris causa (Aix-Marseille); Fellow, Royal Soc. of Canada; Assoc. Mem., Int'l. Acad. of Comparative Law; Assoc. Mem., Académie du Var; Distinguished Research Professor of Law, Osgoode Hall Law Sch., York Univ.; International Arbitrator; Barrister and Solicitor; Member of Roster of Canadians under Canada-U.S. Trade Agreement; Legal Research Asst., Un. Nations, Dept. of Econ. Affairs, 1952; sometime with Dewey, Ballantine, Busby, Palmer & Wood, New York City, 1953; Asst. Prof. of Law, McGill Univ., 1954–55, Assoc. Prof. 1955–59; Secy. of the Faculty 1957–59; Visiting Prof. of Comparative Law, Laval Univ. 1959–65; Univs. Montreal 1965, 1977, Mexico 1963, Lisbon 1964, Nice 1968, Toronto 1974, Puerto Rico 1973, McGill 1978–80, Ottawa 1979–80, Auckland 1980–81, Paris I and II (Sorbonne) 1981, Moncton 1983, Aix 1984–92, Kobe 1985; Lectures, Hague Acad. Internat. Law 1965, 1983; mem. Bd. of Eds., Cdn. Yearbook of Int'l. Law; Editor, 'Canadian Bar Review' 1957–83; Faculty Advisor to McGill Law Journ. 1954–59; Publications: 'Foreign Judgments: A Comparative Study' 1957; 'Canadian-American Private International Law' 1960; 'Cases, Notes and Materials on Conflict of Laws' 1961, and subsequent eds. 1968–1988; 'The Civil Law System of the Province of Quebec' 1962; 'International Law as Interpreted and Applied in Canada' 1965 and subsequent eds.; 'Canadian Conflict of Laws' 2 Vols. 1975–78 2nd ed. 1986; 'Droit international privé québecois' 1980; 'Canadian Criminal Law: International and Transnational Aspects' 1981; 'International Business Transactions and Economic Relations' 1986; 'Extraterritoriality in International Trade' 1988; 'Canadian Law and Practice of International Trade' 1991; Secy-Gen. Cdn. Assn. of Comparative Law 1960–65, Pres. 1971–74; mem. Council, Cdn. Bar Assn. (ex-officio 1957–84); Internat. Law Assn.; Office Revision Civil Code (Québec) 1965–75; Academic in residence, Dept. of External Affairs 1980; French Resistance 1943–45; Chevalier Légion d'Honneur, Ordre national du Mérite and Palmes Académiques; Address: Osgoode Hall, York Univ., Toronto, Ont. M5H 2N6.

**CASTELLANO, Marlene Brant,** B.A., M.S.W., LL.D.; professor and research director; b. Tyendinaga Mohawk Territory 18 Oct. 1935; d. Hubert (Bert) and Pearl (Hill) Brant; e. Queen's Univ. B.A. 1955; Univ. of Toronto B.S.W. 1956, M.S.W. 1959; m. Vincent G. s. Gaspare and Anna C. 26 Nov. 1960; children: Vincent, Gregory, Daniel, Steven; CO-DIRECTOR OF RESEARCH, ROYAL COMMISSION ON ABORIGINAL PEOPLES 1992– ; Social worker in child & family services in Belleville, Winnipeg & Toronto 1956–69; Prof., Dept. of Native Studies, Trent Univ. 1973– ; (on leave to Royal Comn. at present); Chair 1978–80, 1983–84, 1989–91; Assoc. Prof., Fac. of Edn., Queen's Univ. 1989–92; Bd. Mem., Anigawncigig Inst. 1983–91 (Chair 1983–86, 1987–91); Co-Chair, Native Edn. Council, Queen's-Trent Native Edn. Prog. 1989–91; Mem. Bd. of Govs., Queen's Univ. 1992– ; Mem. Adv. Bd., Royal Society of Canada 1992– ; Mem., Candn. Indian/Native Studies Assn.; Consultant to native orgns. & communities, fed. & prov. govt. agencies on native social devel.; contbr. to learned journals & confs. & popular dialogue on native culture & devel.; Hon. LL.D. Queen's Univ. awarded at Sesquicentennial Convocation 1991; Hon. LL.D. St. Thomas Univ. 1992; Mem., Wolf Clan, Mohawks of the Bay of Quinte; All Saint's Anglican Church, Tyendinaga; recreations: cooking, swimming; Home: Box 87, Shanonville, Ont. K0K 3A0; Office: P.O. Box 1993, Station B, Ottawa, Ont. K1P 1B2.

**CASTELLUCCI, Vincent F.,** Ph.D.; scientist; b. Montreal, Que. 26 July 1940; s. Vincenzo Danielle and Evangéline (Cardinal) C.; e. Univ. Laval, B.A. 1960, B.Sc. 1964; Washington Univ., Ph.D. 1968; m. Lise M. d. Marie-Louis and Jeanne (Simard) Bernier 12 June 1965; children: Christine J., Laurent F.; DIR., LAB. OF NEUROBIOL. & BEHAVIOR, CLIN. RSCH. INST. OF MONTREAL & PROF., DEPT. OF MED., UNIV. DE MONTREAL 1988– ; Rsch. Assoc., N.Y. Univ. Sch. of Med. 1971–73; Asst. Prof., Dept. Physiol. 1973–75; Assoc. Prof., Ctr. for Neurobiol. & Behav., Dept. of Psych., Columbia Univ. 1976–87; Mem., Ctr. de Rech. & Sci. Neurol., Univ. Montréal 1988– ; Prix M. Vachon (Univ. Laval) 1964; Eliot Award (Washington Univ.) 1968; Assoc. Mem., Sigma Xi 1968; Mem., Am. Assn. for the Adv. of Sci. 1972– ; Soc. for Neurosci. 1973– ; Am. Physiol. Soc. 1974– ; Am. Soc. for Zool. 1975– ; Assoc. canadienne-française pour l'avancement des sciences 1988; Candn. Assoc. for Neuroscience 1990; Peripatetic Club 1990; Home: 4800 W. de Maisonneuve, Westmount, Que. H3Z 1M2; Office: 110 Pine Ave. W., Montreal, Que. H2W 1R7.

**CASTLE, G.S. Peter,** Ph.D., M.Sc., BESc., DIC, P.Eng., FIEEE; professor of electrical engineering; b. Belfast, N. Ireland 30 May 1939; s. George Ernest and Letitia (Dunlop) C.; e. Univ. of West. Ont., BESc. 1961; Univ. of London, MSc. 1963; Imperial Coll., DIC 1963; Univ. of West. Ont., Ph.D. 1969; m. Judith d. Gordon and Olive Bartram 2 Sept. 1961; children: Brenda, Amy, Timothy; PROF., ELECTRICAL ENGINEERING, THE UNIV. OF WEST. ONT. 1969– ; rsch. interests: indus. application of electrostatic forces, precipitation, painting and electrophotography; previous indus. experience: Ont. Hydro, Toronto & Northern Electric Co.; Dir., Elstat Ltd.; author/co-author of over 100 articles in the field of applied electrostatics; holder of seven patents; Home: 6 Brentwood Pl., London, Ont.; Office: London, Ont. N6A 5B9.

**CASTONGUAY, Hon. Claude,** C.C., D.C.L., F.S.A., F.C.I.A.; actuary; b. Quebec, Que. 8 May 1929; s. Emile and Jeanne (Gauvin) C.; e. Académie de Qué. 1948; Laval Univ. 1948–50; Univ. of Man. 1950–51; D.C.L. Bishop's 1972; LL.D. McGill 1974, Toronto 1975; D. de l'Univ. Sherbrooke 1975; LL.D. Univ. Manitoba 1980; Laurentian Univ. 1987; Hon. Doctorate in Bus. Admin., Univ. Laval 1988; LL.D. (Hon.) Concordia Univ. 1989; Hon. Doctorate in Admin. Sci. Royal Military Coll. of Saint Jean 1990; LL.D. (Hon.) Univ. of Western Ont. 1990; m. Mimi Fauteux 22 Sept. 1956; children: Monique, Joanne, Philippe; CHRMN., LAURENTIAN BANK OF CANADA; Bd. Chrmn., Laurentian Trust of Canada; Laurentian Capital Corp.; Dir., Boreal Insurance Inc.; Laurentian Group Corp.; Laurentian Financial Inc.; Eaton's of Canada Ltd.; Corporation Financière Télésystème; Unimedia Inc.; Canadian Airlines International Ltd.; Musée d'Art Contemporain de Montréal; Assoc. Actuary Industrial Life Insurance 1951–55; Chargé de cours (Lectr.), Actuarial Dept. Laval Univ. 1951–55, Prof. Agrégé (Assoc. Prof.), 1955–57; Actuary, The Laurentian Mutual Life Assurance Co. 1955–58; Managing Dir. and Actuary, The Provident Assurance Co. 1958–62; Consulting Actuary and Partner Castonguay, Pouliot, Guérard & Associates Inc. 1962–70, 1973–77; Chrmn. Royal Comn. Inquiry Health & Social Welfare 1966–70; el. mem. Que. Nat. Assembly for Louis Hébert 1970–73, Min. of Health and Min. of Family & Social Welfare 1970–71, Min. of Social Affairs 1971–73; Mem., Bd. of Dir., Caisse de dépôt et placement du Québec 1973–78; mem. Steering Ctte. Fed.-Prov. Jt. Review Candn. Social Security System 1973–75; Pres. Govt. Que. Task Force Urbanization

1974–76; Pres. Task Force on Minimum Wages and Work Conditions 1974; mem. Fed. Anti-inflation Bd. 1975–76; Mem., Trilateral Comn. 1978–84; Pres., Candn. Inst. of Actuaries 1978; Pres., Qué.-Can. Pre-Referendum Ctte. 1978; Bd. Chrmn., Le Centre Hospitalier de l'Univ. Laval 1979–81; Bd. Mem., Inst. for Research on Public Policy 1980–85; Mem., Candn. Industrial Renewal Bd. (CIRB) 1981–86; Vice Chrmn. Credit Foncier 1979–84 and Chrmn. 1984–86; Mem., Adv. Ctte. on Privatization for Que. Govt. 1986; Chancellor, Univ. of Montreal 1986–90; Member, Senate of Canada 1990–92; served with RCNVR 1947–50, rank Sub-Lt.; Fellow, Cdn. Inst. Actuaries; Fellow, Soc. of Actuaries; Companion of the Order of Canada 1974; Medal of Laval Univ. Alumnae Assn. 1983; George Findley Stephen Award, Can. Hospital Assn. 1984; McGill Management Achievement Award, McGill Univ. 1986; Officer, Ordre National du Québec 1991; recreations: skiing, reading, painting, fishing; Clubs: Hermitage (Magog); University Club (Montreal); Home: 50 Berlioz, Ile des Soeurs, Verdun, Que. H3E 1M2; Office: 1981 McGill College Ave., Montréal, Qué. H3A 3K3.

**CASTONGUAY-THIBAUDEAU, Marie France,** M.ScN., D.H.C.; university professor; b. Causapscal, P.Q. 15 May 1931; d. Charles R. and Rose Alba (Bellefeuille) Castonguay; e. McGill Univ., B.N. 1963; Yale Univ., M.ScN. 1967; m. Louis, s. Rosaire and Lucienne Thibaudeau, 25 Jan. 1969; child: Pierre; PROFESSOR, UNIV. MONTRÉAL 1982– ; co-author (with N. Marchak) 'L'enseignement au malade' 1974; co-ed. (with R. MacKay) 'La recherche infirmière au service de la pratique (actes du 7e colloque national sur la recherche infirmière)' 1981; P.H.N., Service medico-social, Hopital Ste-Justine (Montreal) 1953–57; P.H.N., Ottawa City Health Dept. 1960–62; Supervisor, Northwestern Health Unit, Kenora, Ont. 1963–65; joined present univ. as Lectr. 1967; Asst. Prof. 1969; Assoc. Prof., Asst. Dean Research and Grad. Studies 1975; Dean, Sciences Infirmieres 1981–93; Professor 1982; mem. ed. bd., 'Santé mentale au Québec'; 'Family Systems Medicine Journal' (New York); GIRAME (Groupe interdisciplinaire de recherche en anthropologie médicale et ethnopsychiatrie); mem., Cdn. Assn. Univ. Schs. Nursing; Candn. Public Health Assn.; Amer. Public Health Assn.; Assn. canadienne-française pour l'avancement des sciences (ACFAS); Institut Vanier de la Famille; Conseil Canadien de developpement social; Candn. Soc. for Internat. Health; Mem. Publication Ctte., Assn. of Community Health Nursing Educators; mem. Bd., Centre de santé mentale communautaire de Montréal; Adm. Board of Centre Hosp. Côte des Neiges; Dir., development project in Senegal, funded by Candn. Internat. Development Agency; Sovereign Military Order of St. John of Jerusalem; recipient, D.H.C. (honoris causa) Univ. du Québec, Trois-Rivieres; Home: 1245 O'Brien, St-Laurent, P.Q. H4L 3W1; Office: Faculté des Sciences Infirmières, Univ. de Montréal C.P. 6128, Succursale A, Montréal, Qué. H3C 3J7.

**CASTRILLI, Annamarie Paola,** B.A., M.A., LL.B., Ph.D.; university governor, lawyer; b. Naples, Italy 31 Aug. 1948; d. Adolfo Luigi and Rosa Fausta (Abete) C.; e. Loretto College 1965; Univ. of Toronto B.A. (Hons.) 1969, M.A. 1970, Ph.D. 1977; Osgoode Hall, York Univ. LL.B. 1983; called to Bar of Ont. 1985; m. David s. Donald and Sybil (Ford-Smith) Carmichael 6 Sept. 1971; children: Alexander, Evan, Stefanie (Castrilli Carmichael); CHAIR, GOVERNING COUNCIL, UNIV. OF TORONTO 1993– ; private practice 1990– ; Assoc. Lawyer, Houser, Henry, Loudon & Syron 1985–89; Harries, Houser 1985; Mem., Ontario Premier's Adv. Group on the Constitution 1992– ; Vice-Chair, City of Toronto Inquiry into Crime 1991; Mem., Nat. Cong. of Italian Canadians 1990– ;and of numerous cttes. of the Congress 1978– ;(Nat. Pres. 1988–90); Chair, Nat. Redress Inquiry, Nat. Cong. of Italian Canadians 1990– (former extve. positions); Mem., Gov. Council, Univ. of Toronto 1987– ;(Vice-Chair 1989–93); Trustee, Sunnybrook Health Sci. Ctr. 1993– ; Dir., R.O.M. 1993– ; Gov., YMCA 1992– ; Chair, Candn. Ctr. for Italian Culture & Edn. 1991– ; Dir., Candn.-Italian Med. Assistance Fund 1988– ; Mem., Canada 21 1993– ; Candn. Bar Assn. 1981– ; Founding Mem., Italian-Candn. Women's Alliance 1976– ;(Vice-Pres. 1977–79); past mem. (extve.) of a number of orgns.; former lecturer & tutor, Univ. of Toronto; Prov. of Ont. Grad. Fellowships; Teaching Fellowships, Univ. of Toronto; Canada Council Rsch. Scholarship; Prov. of Ont. Volunteer Serv. Award; Toronto Sun Women on the Move Award; Peel Multicultural Council Constitutional Affairs Award; Candn.-Italian Bus. & Profl. Assn. Candn. Affairs and Canadianism award; Fed. of Italian-Candn. Seniors Achievement Award; Canada 125 Medal; Nat. Cong. of Italian Canadians, Order of Merit; author of num. journal articles, reports, briefs & newsletters; recreations: music, theatre, nordic skiing, hiking, baseball; Home: 61 Oak Ave., Richmond Hill, Ont. L4C 6R5; Office: Toronto, Ont. M5S 1A1.

**CATALLI-SONIER, Loredana,** B.Sc.N., LL.B.; lawyer, public servant; b. Italy 7 Aug. 1952; d. Giuseppe and Maria (Tittarelli) Catalli; e. Univ. de Moncton B.Sc.N. 1973; Univ. of LL.B. 1982; children: Matthew, Christina; CLERK OF THE LEGISLATIVE ASSEMBLY OF N.B. appointed 30 Nov. 1993; clerk assistant of the Legis. Assembly of N.B. 1985–93; practised law 1982–84; Mem., Canadian Bar Assn.; Nurses Assn. of N.B.; Cdn. Nurses Assn.; Law Society of N.B.; Home: 53 Shaw Lane, Fredericton, N.B. E3C 1H7; Office: P.O. Box 6000, Fredericton, N.B. E3B 5H1.

**CATLEY-CARLSON, Margaret,** B.A.; Canadian and international public servant; b. Regina, Sask. 6 Oct. 1942; d. George Lorne (Lloyd) and Helen Margaret (Hughes) Catley; e. Univ. of B.C., B.A. 1966; Univ. of the W. Indies postgrad. cert. 1970; LL.D. (h.c.) Univ. of Regina 1985; Litt.D. (h.c.) Saint Mary's Univ. 1985; Concordia Univ. 1989; Mt. Saint Vincent Univ. 1990; m. Stanley Frederick s. Alfred and Christine Carlson 30 Oct. 1970; PRESIDENT, POPULATION COUNCIL 1993– ; joined Dept. External Affairs, Can. 1966, assignments Colombo 1968, London 1975, Asst. Under-Secy. 1981; Vice Pres. (Multilateral) Candn. Internat. Development Agency 1978, Sr. Vice Pres./Acting Pres. 1979–80; Asst. Secy.-Gen. UN and Depy. Extve. Dir. (Operations) UNICEF 1981; Pres., CIDA 1983–89; Depy. Min., Health & Welfare 1989–92; recreations: skiing, gardening; Office: 1 Dag Hammarskjold Plaza, New York, N.Y. 10017.

**CATTANACH, Hon. A(ngus) Alexander;** retired judge; b. Winnipeg, Man. 26 July 1909; s. Angus Archibald and Jennie Elizabeth (Young) C.; e. Public and High Schs., Winnipeg, Man.; Univ. of Manitoba, B.A., 1929; Univ. of Sask., LL.B., 1932; m. Verena Margaret, d. James W. Miller, Carleton Place, Ont., 29 Oct. 1944; one d. Heather Edmonde; joined Dept. of Secy. of State 1936; successively served as Director, Companies Division, Asst. Under Secy. of State and Acting Under Secy. of State 1961–62; apptd. Puisne Judge of the Exchequer Court of Canada 1962; apptd. to Court Martial Appeal Court 1962; apptd. to Federal Court of Canada 1971; retired 1984; called to the Bar of Sask. 1934; cr. Q.C. (Dom.) 1952; served in 2nd World War with R.C.A.F. 1940–45, rank Wing Commdr.; Judge Advocat, War Crimes Trials, Aurich, Germany 1945–46; Life mem., Clan Macpherson Assn.; United Church; Clubs: Rideau; Home: 753 Island Park Drive, Ottawa, Ont. K1Y 0B9.

**CATTINI, Peter Andrew Bartolomeo,** B.Sc., Ph.D.; university professor; b. London, England 31 July 1958; s. Peter John and Iolanda Lydia Maria (Pedrotti) C.; e. Rutlish Sch. (U.K.) 1976; Univ. of London, King's College B.Sc. (Hons.) 1979, Ph.D. 1983; m. Elissavet d. Spyridon and Dimitra Kardami 10 Dec. 1983; children: Melissa Iolanda, Alexander Peter; ASSOC. PROF., PHYSIOLOGY, UNIV. OF MANITOBA 1992– ; NATO postdoctoral fellowship, Univ. of Calif. at San Francisco (1st to demonstrate pituitary-specific prod. using human growth hormone gene & method of transient gene transfer); Asst. Prof., Univ. of Wininpeg 1987; MRCC scholarship 1987; recipient of funding for research from MRCC, Man. Health Rsch. Council, Sellers Found., Heart & Stroke Found. & London Life Insur. Co.; Canadian citizen 1993; Rh Award for outstanding contbns. to scholarship & rsch. in the health sciences; 1st recipient London Life Award in Med. Sci.; Basic Sci. Career Devel. Award, Man. Med. Serv. Found. 1993–96; Mem., Endocrine Soc. 1987– ; Am. Soc. for Cell Biology 1990– ; author/co-author num. sci. pubns. & peer-reviewed articles for journals & funding agencies worldwide; Edit. Bd. Mem., 'Molecular and Cellular Biochemistry'; Home: Winnipeg, Man.; Office: 770 Bannatyne Ave., Winnipeg, Man. R3E 0W3.

**CATTO, Rev. Charles,** C.M., B.A., M.Div.; b. Toronto, Ont. 7 June 1929; s. Charles Edward and Marion (Haddow) C.; e. Ryerson Pub. Sch. London, Ont. 1938; Blythwood Pub. Sch. Toronto 1940; Univ. of Toronto Schs. 1946; Univ. of Toronto B.A. 1951, M.Div. 1955 (Emmanuel Coll.); m. Barbara Jean d. late Albert F. Loveys 25 Sept. 1954; children: Charles Daniel, Linda Jean, Wanda Marie, Roderick; EXTVE. DIR., FRONTIERS FOUNDATION since 1968; Dir., Keekandahsowin; Missy. with Cree Indians, God's Lake, Man. 1954–57; Missy. Bd. of World Mission, Un. Ch. Can. under Un. Ch. of Zambia 1957–62; Min. of Hampton Charge 1963–68; founded Operation Beaver under Candn. Council Chs. 1963; Operation Causepeace 1968; produced two LP albums 'Zambezi Valley Songs,' 'The Third World Sings'; Order of Can. 1979; Guest of Honour, Native Council of Can. Banquet, 1981; Aboriginal Order of Canada 1985; mem. Un. Ch. Can. Comte. on Internat. Affairs 1963–79; cross-country speaker, sponsored by Assoc. of Candn. Clubs 1986–87; Senator, Victoria Univ. 1990; NDP; United Church; recreations: skating, model building, banjo playing, table tennis; Home: 712 Kingfisher Dr., Pickering, Ont. L1W 1X5; Office: 2615 Danforth Ave., Toronto, Ont. M4C 1L6.

**CATY, J. Charles,** B.Com.; association executive; b. Holtyre, Ont. 28 Sept. 1940; s. J.J. and Alice (Guilbault); e. McGill Univ. B. Com.; m. Sallie d. A. Scott Mackay, 5 Sept. 1964; children: Julie, Nicole, Charles; PRESIDENT AND CHIEF EXECUTIVE OFFICER, INVESTMENT DEALERS ASSOCIATION OF CANADA; Vice-Pres. & Dir., W.C. Pitfield & Co. Ltd. 1963–84; RBC Dominion Securities Inc. 1984–91; Chrmn., The Toronto Stock Exchange 1989–91; Vice-Chrmn., The Canadian Depository for Securities Limited 1987–90; Dir.: Bruncor Inc.; Cabano Transportation Group Inc.; The General Accident Assurance Company of Canada; Participaction; Chrmn., Appleby Coll.; Roman Catholic; Clubs: Caledon Ski; The Goodwood Club; Mississauga Golf & Country; Blue Top Hunt; Home: 10 Ennisclare Dr. West, Oakville, Ont. L6J 4N2; Office: 121 King St. W., Suite 1600, Toronto, Ont. M5H 3T9.

**CATZMAN, Frederick Murray,** B.A., LL.B., Q.C., L.S.M.; Queen's Counsel; b. Toronto, Ont. 1 Jan. 1907; s. Oscar and Pauline (Shapiro) C.; e. Univ. of Toronto, B.A. 1926; Osgoode Hall Law Sch., Barrister-at-law with silver medal 1929; m. Irene d. Tom and Pauline Meyers 28 June 1934; one s. Marvin A., Justice of the Ontario Court of Appeal; COUNSEL, DIAMOND, FAIRBAIRN 1988– ; Lawyer, Catzman & Wahl 1929–87; Vice-Chrmn., Candn. Bar Assn. (Ont. Comml. Law Section) 1949–50; Chrmn., Personal Property Security Act of Ont. Ctte. 1960–74; Adv. Ctte., Min. of Consumer & Comml. Relns. of Ont. 1974–90; Lectr., York Univ.; Candn. Bar Assn.; Am. Bar Assn. & num. cont. edn. progs.; Guest Lectr., McGill Univ.; Q.C. 1950; Law Soc. of U.C. Medal 1986; Life Mem., Law Soc. of U.C. 1979– ; Life Fellow, Found. for Legal Rsch. 1979– ; Gov., B'nai Brith 1940–42; Founder & Vice-Pres., Beth Tzedec Congn. 1953– ; Nat. Chrmn., Community Relns. Ctte., Candn. Jewish Congress 1954–55; Columnist, Candn. Jewish News 1985– ; author: 'Bulk Sales Act of Ontario'; co-author: 'Personal Property Security Law of Ontario' 1976; 'The Personal Property Security Act' 1989; recreation: golf; Club: Primrose; Home: 5 Forest Ridge Dr., Toronto, Ont. M6B 1G9; Office: 393 University Ave., Toronto, Ont. M5G 1E6.

**CATZMAN, Marvin Adrian;** judge; b. Toronto, Ont. 1 Sept. 1938; s. Fred M., Q.C., L.S.M. and Irene (Meyers) C.; e. Univ. of Toronto B.A. (Gold Medal Sociol.) 1959, LL.B. (Dean's Key) 1962; Law Soc. Upper Can. (Treas.'s Medal for Highest Standing) 1964; m. Lynn Kaplan, Vancouver, B.C. 20 Aug. 1972; children: Penny, Julie, David; JUDGE, SUPREME CRT. OF ONTARIO, HIGH COURT OF JUSTICE, July 1981; COURT OF APPEAL, Sept. 1988; called to Bar of Ont. 1964; cr. Q.C. 1976; Law Clk. to Chief Justice High Court, Supreme Court of Ont. 1964–65; practised law with Catzman & Wahl, Toronto 1965–81; Lectr. in Bankruptcy and Insolvency Osgoode Hall Law Sch. 1974–75; Course Adm. and Lectr. Principles of Business Law Course York Univ. 1967–81; Lectr. Civil Procedure Sec. Bar Admission Course Law Soc. Upper Can. 1966–76; mem. Supreme Court of Ont. Rules Comte. 1975–81 and 1983–90; mem. Civil Rules Comte. 1990– ; Secy. Adv. Comte. Ont. Personal Property Security Act 1976–81; el. Bencher, Law Soc. Upper Can. 1979–81; Law Soc. Upper Can. Special Lectures Series Lectr. Torts 1973, Contracts 1975, Employment Law 1976, Professions 1977, Creditor and Debtor 1988; Chrmn. Series on Estate Planning & Adm. 1980, Remedies 1981; mem. Senate Univ. of Toronto 1968–72; Jewish; Office: Judges' Chambers, Osgoode Hall, Toronto, Ont. M5H 2N5.

**CAVAN, Susan G.,** B.A., LL.B.; entertainment executive & producer; b. Toronto, Ont. 8 June; d. Albert and Joyce (Heslam) C.; e. Queen's Univ. LL.B. 1976; CO-CHRMN. & C.E.O., ACCENT ENTERTAINMENT CORP. 1989– ; called to Bar of Ont. 1978; practiced entertainment law with Roberts and Drabinsky until 1980; Vice-Pres., Bus. Affairs, Cineplex Corp.; Gen. Counsel, ICC Internat. Cinema Corp. 1982; Exec. Producer, 'The Bay Boy'; Partner and Sr. Vice-Pres. Bus. & Legal Affairs Alliance Entertainment 1985, Partner & Pres., Alliance 1987; Extve. Prod. 'Bordertown'; Extve. Prod./Prod. feature films and television movies incl. 'Wisecracks,' 'South of Wawa,' 'Material World,' 'Mrs. Arris Goes to Paris,' 'Mesmer and A Sudden Darkness'; mem. Law Soc. Upper Can.; Toronto Women in Film;

Office: 207 - 209 Adelaide St. E., Suite 300, Toronto, Ont. M5A 1M8.

**CAVE, William Thompson,** B.Sc., D.Phil.; retired physical chemist; b. Winnipeg, Man. 8 June 1917; s. William and Mary Amelia (Thompson) C.; e. Univ. of Man. B.Sc. (Hons.) 1939; Rhodes Scholar; Oxford Univ. D.Phil. 1948; m. Dorothy d. Frederick and Julia Cleary 27 Sept. 1941; children: William T. Jr., Mary Frances; Tech. Liaison, Inspection Bd. U.K. & Can. 1940–44; Rsch. Chem., Shawinigan Chem. 1945–50; var. positions retiring as Dir. of Nuclear Operations and Research, Monsanto Rsch. Corp. 1951–82; Teacher, Univ. of Dayton 1959–60; Capt., Champ. Soccer Team, Univ. of Man.; Ice Hockey, Oxford; Rower, St. John's Coll.; Anglican Communion (Past Vestryman); Fellow, Am. Assn. for the Adv. of Sci.; mem., Am. Chem. Soc.; Soc. for Applied Spectroscopy (Local Pres. 1963–65); NY Acad. of Sci.; author of seven patents, 18 publ. articles & two book chapters; recreations: reading, music, curling; Address: 7021 Sulky Lane, Rockville, MD 20852.

**CAVELTI, Peter Christian;** financial executive; b. Switzerland 10 Apr. 1948; s. Jack Ulrich & Elisabeth (Curschellas) C.; e. Sch. of Commerce, St. Gallen, Comm. & Languages; Univ. of Cape Town, Fin. & Investment Bnkg.; PRES. & C.E.O., CAVELTI CAPITAL MANAGEMENT LTD. 1985– ; various mgmt. training positions with major banks in Switzerland, S. Africa, the Far East and the U.S.; Vice-Pres., Deak Canada Ltd. 1972–76; Vice-Pres., Guardian Trust Co. 1976–79; Sr. Vice-Pres. & Dir. 1979–82; Pres. & C.E.O. 1982–85; Dir., BGR Precious Metals Inc.; Blanchard Precious Metals Fund; Blanchard Strategic Growth Fund; Cavelti Capital Management Ltd.; author: 'How to Invest in Gold' 1979; 'Gold, Silver & Strategic Metals' 1983; 'New Profits in Gold, Silver & Strategic Metals' 1984; ed. pub.; 'Market Report'; recreations: skiing, climbing, hiking, tennis, sailing, music, painting; Office: 4100 Yonge St., Suite 604, Willowdale, Ont. M2P 2B6.

**CAVERS, Hon. Harry Peter;** retired judge; b. St. Catharines, Ont. 27 Dec. 1909; s. Harry A. and Laura Mabel (Lyons) C.; e. Univ. of Toronto; Osgoode Hall, 1935; m. Dorothy Alma, d. Hon. Frank L. Bastedo, Q.C., Regina, Sask., 18 Mar. 1944; one d. Dorothy Anne (Mrs. John L. Carruthers); JUDGE, CO. COURT OF ONTARIO; read law with late J.J. Bench, K.C.; called to the Bar of Ont. 1935; cr. Q.C. 1961; in partnership with late Hon. J.J. Bench, K.C. (Bench & Cavers) 1935–42; Partner, Cavers, Chown, Cairns & Hicks, St. Catharines, Ont. 1950–64; served in 2nd World War 1942–45; Lt. R.C.N.V.R.; 1st el. to H. of C. for Lincoln, g.e. 1949; re-el. g.e. 1953; def. g.e. 1957 and 1958; mem., Lincoln Co. Law Assn. (Past Pres. 1961; Hon. Life Mem. 1985) 1935–64; Candn. Bar Assn. (mem. Council 1961, 62, 63); Secy.-Treas., Co. & Dist. Judges' Assn. of Ont. 1970–74; Delegate, Commonwealth Party. Conf., Nairobi 1954, Jamaica 1956; Freemason; United Church; Clubs: St. Catharines Kiwanis (Past Pres. 1961); University Club of Toronto; St Catharines Club; Home: 207–16 Towering Heights Blvd., St. Catharines, Ont. L2T 3G9.

**CAWKER, Ruth Grace,** B.A., B.Arch.; architect; b. Edmonton, Alta. 7 Jan. 1953; d. Edgar Andrews and Marjorie Ethel (Graham) C.; e. Glendon Coll. York Univ. B.A. 1974; Univ. of Toronto B.Arch. 1980; m. Marc s. Francis and Gaby Baraness 28 Sept. 1985; one s. Julien Edgar Francis Baraness; Principal, Ruth Cawker Architect 1986–..; Chief Architect, Candn. Imperial Bank of Commerce Development Corp. 1992– ; Dir. Bureau of Arch. & Urbanism; Sharon Temple Museum Soc.; Assoc. Barton Myers Associates 1980–86; Architect, Ont. Assoc. of Architects Headquarters Bldg. 1992; Curator 'Viewpoints: 100 Years of Architecture in Ontario' 1989; Curator and Ed. 'Toronto Modern: Architecture 1945–65,' 'Toronto: Le Nouveau Nouveau Monde' 1987; co-author 'Canadian Fiction: An Annotated Bibliography' (reference) 1976; 'Contemporary Canadian Architecture: The Mainstream and Beyond' (arch. criticism) 1982, paperback 1988; co-ed. 'Building With Words' (arch. criticism) 1981; contbr. 'Storm Warning 2' (poetry) 1976; Home: 372 Brunswick Ave., Toronto, Ont. M5R 2Y9.

**CAYA, Marcel,** L.ès L., M.A., Ph.D.; historian; archivist; administrator; b. Montréal, Qué. 25 Feb. 1947; s. Jean E. and Anna (Chauvette) C.; e. Séminaire St. Antoine Trois Rivières 1965; Séminaire de Philosophie Montréal B.A. 1967; Univ. de Sherbrooke L.ès L. 1969; Carleton Univ. M.A. 1970; York Univ. Ph.D. 1981; m. Thérèse d. Paul and Juliette Bussières 11 July 1970; children: Philippe, Mathieu, Marjolaine; UNIV. ARCHIVIST, McGILL UNIV. 1977– ; Lectr. in Archives, McGill Sch. Lib. & Info. Sci's 1977– ; Archivist, Pub. Archives Can. 1970–71; Rsch. Assoc. Comn. on Candn. Studies 1973–74; Lectr. in Hist. & Archives, Univ. du Qué. à Montréal 1982–85; mem. Social Sci's & Humanities Rsch. Council Can. Consultative Group Archives 1978–80, 1983–84; Dir. Gen. McCord Museum of Candn. Hist. 1984–88; Dir., Québec Museums and Heritage Development, Dept. of Communications 1990; Dir. Gen., Corporate Policy Br., Secy. of State 1990–91; Archival Cons. Candn. Centre for Arch.; co-author 'Archives in Canada' 1980; editor 'Canadian Archives in 1992' 1992; mem. Assn. des archivistes du Qué. (prés. 1985–86); Institut d'histoire de l'Amérique française (sec. 1979–83); Assn. Candn. Archivists; Sect. Profl. Assn. Internat. Council Archives (Vice Chrmn. 1985–88, Chrmn. 1988– ;); Nat. Archival Appraisal Bd. (Nat. Chrmn. 1983–85, 1992– ; Qué. Regional Dir. 1979–88); R. Catholic; recreation: golf, tennis; Home: 50 – 14th St., Roxboro, Qué. H8Y 1M7; Office: 3459 McTavish St., Rm. MS-60, Montréal, Qué. H3A 1Y1.

**CECIL-COCKWELL, Wendy Marion,** B.A.; b. Stratford, Ont. 20 Nov. 1948; d. Laurence Leslie and Marion Yvonne (Seymour) Cecil; e. Univ. of Toronto B.A. 1971; York Univ. Extve. Mgmt. Prog. 1977; three children: Tess, Malcolm, Gareth; Chrmn., Sanford Investments Ltd.; Asst. Mgr. Pub. Info. Toronto Stock Exchange 1972–74; Dir. Pub. Affairs and other mgmt. positions, Brascan Ltd. 1974–81; Vice Pres. Business Development, Brascan Ltd. 1981–87; Vice Pres., Edper Enterprises 1986–87; Vice-Chrmn., Presidents' Ctte., Univ of Toronto; Dir., The Fraser Inst.; Gov., Olympic Trust of Canada; Dir., St. Michael's Hosp. Found.; mem. Adv. Counc. Barbara Schlifer Commemorative Clinic; Adv. Counc. Dancer Transition Centre; winner various distance races Track & Field incl. Toronto Marathon, New Orleans Marathon, Sao Paulo, Brazil 10K; Gold Medalist Candn. Championship Master's Cross Country Race 1984; Silver Medalist Ont. Masters Indoor Track & Field Championships 3000 metres 1985; World Masters Track & Field Championships Rome, Italy, 10K, 5K and Cross Country 1985.

**CEDRASCHI, Tullio,** M.B.A.; investment executive; b. Zurich, Switzerland 4 Oct. 1938; e. Coll. of Technol. Zurich Civil Engn. degree 1960; McGill Univ. M.B.A. 1968; PRES. AND C.E.O., CN INVESTMENT DIV. 1977– ; Dir., Cambridge Shopping Centres Ltd.; Hollinger Inc.; Markborough Properties Inc.; S.G. Warburg Group plc; Gov., Nat. Theatre Sch. of Can.; McGill Univ.; Civil Engr., Conrad Zschokke, S.A. Zurich 1960–61; Bureau d'Études Quoniam Paris 1961–63; BBR Switzerland and Can. 1963–65; R.R. Nicolet & Associates Montreal 1965–66; with CN Investment Div. since 1968, apptd. Gen. Mgr. 1973, Pres. & C.E.O. 1977; mem. Assoc. for Investment Mgmt. & Rsch.; Swiss-Candn. Chamber Comm.; recreations: tennis, skiing; Clubs: C.D. Howe HIPAC; M.A.A.A.; University Club (Montreal); Home: 2600 Pierre-Dupuy, Apt. 517, Montreal, Qué. H3C 3R6; Office: P.O. Box 11002, Montreal, Qué. H3C 4T2.

**CEJ, Raymond Paul,** B.Eng., M.Sc., P.Eng.; oil and gas executive; b. Prince Albert, Sask. 25 Nov. 1942; s. Paul and Jean (Fecyk) C.; e. Royal Military Coll., B.Eng. 1964; Calif. Inst. of Technol. M.Sc. 1965; m. Margot d. John and Marjorie Ryan; children: Ryan, Martin, Jeffrey; SENIOR OPERATING OFFR. - RESOURCES, SHELL CANADA LIMITED; Captain, Royal Candn. Navy 1964–69 (Armament Rsch. 1965–66); Asst. Prof. of Chem., Royal Roads Military Coll. 1967–68, 1968–69; joined Shell Canada 1969; positions held: Gas Engr., Waterton Gas Plant; Project Mgr., Supt.-Jumping; Mgr., Shell Resources; Gen. Mgr., Information & Computing; Vice-Pres. Devel.; Vice-Pres. Logistics, Mfr. & Trading, Shell Canada Products Ltd.; Home: 331 Parkview Cres. S.E., Calgary, Alta. T2J 4N8; Office: 400 – 4th Ave. S.W., Calgary, Alta. T2P 0J5.

**CELESTE, Lino J.,** B.Sc.EE; communications executive; b. Minto, N.B. 6 Oct. 1937; s. Ovidio and Rose (Corbin) C.; e. Univ. of N.B., B.Sc.EE 1960; m. Joan d. Genevieve and Roy Coholan 8 Aug. 1959; children: Christopher, Terrance; PRES. & CHIEF EXECUTIVE OFFR., N.B. TELEPHONE CO. 1986– ; Dir., Atomic Energy Can. Ltd.; Bruncor Inc.; Datacor Atlantic Inc.; Eastern Telephone and Telegraph Co.; Incutech Brunswick Inc.; Telesat Canada; var. positions, Engr. Dept., N.B. Tel 1960–69; Fed.-Prov. Devel. Agency 1970–71; J.D. Irving Ltd. 1971–74; Dir., Human Resources, N.B. Tel 1974–81; Vice-Pres. 1982–86; Past Pres., St. John Bd. of Trade; recreations: hunting, fishing, woodworking; Clubs: Riverside Country; Home: 210 Bedell Ave., Saint John, N.B. E2K 4J6; Office: P.O. Box 1430, St. John, N.B. E2L 4K2.

**CELLA, Frank;** food industry executive; b. Philadelphia, Pa.; e. Wharton School, Univ. of Pennsylvania; IMEDE Internat. Mngt. Sch. (Lausanne, Switz.) 1978; CHAIRMAN AND CHIEF EXECUTIVE OFFICER, NESTLÉ CANADA INC. 1992– ; tour of duty U.S. Army early 1960s; Sales Rep., Nestlé U.S. 1963; Product Mgr. 1968–71 (introduced Taster's Choice freeze-dried coffee to U.S. market); Mktg. Mgr. 1972–76; Vice-Pres., Sales & Mktg., Nestlé (Canada) Ltd. 1976; Pres., Nestlé 1981; Pres., Goodhost Foods 1984; Extve. Vice-Pres., Nestlé Enterprises Limited 1985; Chief Op. Offr. 1988; Chair, Grocery Prod. Mfrs. of Canda (GPMC) 1987; GPMC Task Force on Trade Policy during 1989 U.S.-Can. Free Trade talks; Sr. Vice-Pres., Carnation Co. 1989; Sr. Vice-Prs., Nestlé U.S.A. 1990; Pres. & Chief Op. Offr., Nestlé Enterprises 1991; Office: 1185 Eglinton Ave. E., Don Mills, Ont. M3C 3C7.

**CERCONE, Nicholas Joseph (Nick),** B.S., M.S., Ph.D.; university professor administrator; b. Pittsburgh, Penn. 18 Dec. 1946; e. Univ. of Steubenville B.S. 1968; Ohio State Univ. M.S. 1970; Univ. of Alta. Ph.D. 1975; ASSOCIATE VICE-PREISDENT (RESEARCH), UNIV. OF REGINA 1993– ; Programmer, IBM Corp. 1969–70; Lecturer, Ohio State Univ. 1970–71; Instructor, IBM Corp. 1971–72; Asst. Prof., Old Dominion Univ. 1975–76; Simon Fraser Univ. 1976–80; Visiting Assoc. Prof., Rensselaer Polytechnic Inst. 1980; Assoc. Prof. & Chair, Computing Science, Simon Fraser Univ. 1980–85; Prof., Computing Science, Simon Fraser Univ. 1985–93; Visiting Prof., Univ. of Victoria 1986–87; Dir., Centre for Systems Sci., Simon Fraser Univ. 1987–93; Assoc. Mem., Linguistics 1988–93; Mem., IEEE, ACM, ACL, ALLC, AAAI, CSCSI/SCEIO, CSFGR/SCRSCG, CACS/AIC, TCDE, RPS; recipient of several grants and awards; extensive public speaker; member & past member of several univ. & govt. cttes.; editor: 'Computational Linguistics' 1983; co-editor: 'The Knowledge Frontier' 1987, 'Computational Intelligence, III' 1991, 24 journal articles, 13 book chapters, 44 pub. conf. proceedings, several popular articles and technical reports; Co-editor, 'Computational Intelligence' 1992– ; Guest editor of five journals; Home: 910 West 22nd Ave., Vancouver, B.C. V5Z 2A1; Office: Regina, Sask. S4S 0A2.

**CERMAK, Josef Rudolf Cenek,** Q.C.; LL.B.; lawyer; b. Skury, Czechoslovakia 15 Nov. 1924; s. Rudolf and Rosalie (Zahalkova) C.; e. Latin Sch. Slany 1943; Charles Univ. Prague Faculty of Law JUC 1948; Univ. of Toronto, Univ. Coll., Faculty of Law LL.B. 1958; PARTNER, SMITH, LYONS, TORRANCE, STEVENSON & MAYER 1967– ; Dir. Wright Line of Canada Ltd.; Carleton Homes Ltd.; Carleton Homes (1981) Ltd.; Galahad Investments Ltd.; Lecadon International Ltd.; Lecadon Realty Ventures Ltd.; D. W. Naylor Realty Ventures Ltd.; Belfield Steel Warhouse Ltd.; called to Bar of Ont. 1960; cr. Q.C. 1975; mem. Borden, Elliot, Kelley & Palmer, Toronto 1960–61; mem. present firm 1962; mem. (actor) Nove Divadlo, Toronto; appearances with Snizek Theatre, New York and CBC Radio; author 'Going Home' (novel); 'Pokorne Navraty (poems in Czech.) 1955; 'My Toronto' (poem) 1984; Chrmn. Ed. Bd. Toronto Czech weekly 'Nase Hlasy' 1960–68; Ed. 'Zpravy News' 1965–67; contrib. various Czech. newspapers Can. and U.S.A.; recipient Panhellenic Prize (Highest Standing in Eng.); Epstein Award (Creative Writing) Univ. Coll. Univ. of Toronto; Dir. 68 Publishers Inc., Cdn. Ethnic Heritage Foundation, Cdn. Fund for Czechoslovak Refugees; Pro Arte Orchestra Soc.; mem. Cdn. Bar Assn.; Ont. Bar Assn.; Czechoslovak Soc. Arts. & Sciences Am. (Pres. Toronto Chapter 1970–79); Czechoslovak Nat. Assn. Can. (mem. Exec. 1958–70); Pro Arte Orchestra Assn. (mem. Exec. 1959–64); Sokol Gymnastic Assn.; Host, Czechoslovak TV Program 'The Window,' Toronto; recreations: tennis, skiing, reading, acting; Clubs: Lawyers'; Home: 130 Jameson Ave., Apt. 606, Toronto, Ont. Office: P.O. Box 420 Exchange Tower, 2 First Canadian Place, Toronto, Ont. M5X 1J3.

**ČERNÝ, Petr,** B.Sc.(Hons.), M.Sc., Ph.D., DR.H.C., F.R.S.C.; university professor; b. Brno, Czech. 8 Jan. 1934; s. František and Věra (Morávková) Č.; e. Univ. of Brno B.Sc. (Hons.) 1956; Univ. of J.E. Purkyne M.Sc. 1965; Czech. Acad. of Sciences Ph.D. 1966; m. Ivanka d. Robert and Marie Kamenská 1 April 1966; children: Miroslav Kotisa, Susan Gibson; PROFESSOR, GEOLOGICAL SCIENCES, UNIV. OF MANITOBA 1980– ; Mineralogist-Petrologist, Geol. Expl., Brno, Czech. 1956–62; Rsch. Offr., Moravian Mus. 1962–64; Rsch. Sci., Geol. Inst. Czech. Acad. of Sci. (Prague) 1964–68; postdoctoral fellow, Univ. of Man. 1968–71; Asst. Prof. 1971–74; Assoc. Prof. 1974–80; Grant Selection Ctte., NSERC-DEMR 1988–91; NSERC Interdisciplinary 1992–93; External Mem., Rsch. Council, Geol. Inst.

Acad. Sci. (Czech.) 1993– ; Cons., Selco Can. 1979; Tantalum Mining Corp. 1980–82; LKAB Prospektering Stockholm 1983–85; Minerex Vienna 1985–88; Dir., Microbeam Lab.; R.B. Ferguson Mus. of Mineralogy; Life Fellow, Min. Soc. of Am. 1973– ; Rh Inst. Award 1981; Médaille A.H. Dumont 1981; MAC Past Pres. Medal 1984; Univ. of Helsinki Medal 1985; Sigma Xi Award 1990; Bořický Medal 1991; Gold Medal and Doctor honoris causa, Masaryk Univ. 1991; Fellow, Royal Soc. of Can. 1991; GAC Logan Medal 1993; Acad. Sci. Czech Rep. F. Pošepný Gold Plaque 1993; Österr. Mineral. Gesell. Friedrich-Becke Medal 1994; Mem., Min. Assn. of Can. (Sec. 1976); Min. Soc. of Am. (Awards Ctte. 1986–87); Founder & Co-chair, Joint MAC-MSA Special Interest Group in Granitic Pegmatites 1991– ; Geol. Assn. of Can.; Am. Geophys. Inst.; Materials Rsch. Soc.; Deutsche Min. Gesellschaft; Geol. Föreningen Stockholm; Soc. de Géol. Appliqué; editor and co-author: 'Granitic Pegmatites in Science and Industry' 1982; co-editor and co-author: 'Lanthanides, Tantalum and Niobium'; Assoc. Ed., 'Canadian Mineralogist' 1984–92; Special Ed., 'Mineralogy and Petrology' 1992–94; Edit. Bd. Mem., 'J. of the Czech. Geol. Soc.' 1993– ; author of 168 sci. papers, 20 book contbns.; recreations: music, photography, hunting, fishing; clubs: Winnipeg Game & Fish Assn., Safari Internat., Nat. Sporting Fraternity, Ruffed Grouse Soc., Found. for N. Am. Wild Sheep, Loyal Order of Dedicated Grouse Hunters; Home: 615 Townsend Ave., Winnipeg, Man. R3T 2V3; Office: Winnipeg, Man. R3T 2N2.

**CETÍN, Anton;** painter, printmaker; b. Bojana, Croatia 18 Sept. 1936; s. Tomo and Terezija (Grcic) C.; e. Sch. Appl. Arts, Zagreb, Dept. of Painting dipl. 1959; Acad. of Fine Arts, Zagreb, Dept. of Printingmaking masters dipl. 1964; m. Milka d. Kazimir and Kata Katalenic 16 Dec. 1962; one d.: Dawn Antonia; painter, printmaker, illustrator, Paris, France 1966–68; emigrated to Can. 1968; Candn. citizen 1973; has had over 60 one-man shows worldwide, most recent: Museo del Chopo, México, D.F., México 1993; Gallery 7, Hong Kong 1993; Sony Plaza Art Gall., Tokyo, Japan 1991; Oberhausmuseum, Passau, Germany 1990; Nat. & Univ. Libr., Zagreb 1988; Beverly Gordon Gall., Dallas 1987; Mus. of Arts & Crafts, Zagreb 1986; Art Gallery of Hamilton 1978; over 140 group exhib., most recent: Art Asia '93, Hong Kong; 'Artists' Books: Made in Canada VI' Nat. Lib. of Can. 1990; Biennial of Contmp. Art 'Antonio Canova' Crespano del Grappa, Italy 1988; Int. Exhibit of Miniature Art, Del Bello Gall., Toronto 1986, '87, '89, '90; Brazil 1985; Spain 1983; Korea 1982, 1984; worldwide collections include: nat. libraries: France, Croatia, Canada; U.N. Japan; Vatican Italy; Mus. of Arts & Crafts, Museum & Gallery Center, Zagreb; Candn. Cult. Ctr. France; Oberhausmuseum, Passau, Germany; Embragel, Cabo Frio, Brazil; Univ. of Michigan, Dearborn, Princeton Univ. USA: Ont. Collection, Toronto, Art Gall. of Hamilton and numerous others; listed in Who's Who in Am. Art; Men of Achievement IBC England; Encyclopedia of Fine Arts, Croatia; extensive profl. listings; several awards abroad and in Canada; Artist of the Year, Candn. Croatian Artists Soc. 1986; audience with Pope John Paul II, Rome 1989; author: 'Eve and the Moon' (poetry) 1975; co-author: 'Amerika Croatan America' (poems & graphics) 1988; subject: 'Cetín, 1955–86' (deluxe monograph by David Burnett) 1986; A documentary film 'Two Sides of a Shadow': The Life & Art of Anton Cetín, by V-Art Productions Ltd., Toronto 1993; Home: 5 Greystone Walk Dr., PH3, Scarborough, Ont. M1K 5J5; Studio: 37 Hanna Ave., 13A, Toronto, Ont. M6K 1W9.

**CHABOT, Rev. Sister Marie-Emmanuel,** O.C., D.Ph., LL.D., o.s.u.; nonne; écrivain; née Ste-Claire-Dorchester, Qué. 19 novembre 1908; f. Docteur Joseph-Arthur-Noé et Annie (Lagueux) C. é. Coll. de Sillery 1927; Univ. of W. Ont. B.A. 1930; Univ. d'Ottawa D.Ph. 1947; Univ. Laval D.Ph. 1957, LL.D. 1984; Entrée chez les Ursulines 1931; Professeur d'anglais, de latin, de français; Directrice des études; Supérieure des Ursulines de Québec 1970–74, de Roberval 1974–78, de Stanstead 1978–82; écrivain 'Publications sur Marie de l'Incarnation'; 'Histoire des Ursulines de Stanstead'; Articles de revues; Annaliste du Monastère des Ursulines de Québec; éd. 'Marie de l'Incarnation d'après ses letttres' 1947; 'Elles on tout donné' 1984; 'Dis-moi ton nom' 1989; Adresse: Monastère des Ursulines, 2 rue de Parloir, Québec City, Qué. G1R 4M5.

**CHADDERTON, Hugh Clifford,** O.C., O.Ont., D.C.L., LL.D., CAE, O.St.J.; association executive; b. Fort William, Ont. 9 May 1919; s. William Clifford and Gladys Muriel (Blackburn) C.; e. Kelvin High Sch. Winnipeg Sr. Matric.; Univ. of Man. 1 yr.; Acadia Univ. D.C.L. 1990; m. 4 Oct. 1940; m. Nina d. Alexie and Elvira Agapitova 24 May 1985; two s. William, Brian; CHIEF EXEC. OFFR. THE WAR AMPUTATIONS OF CAN. 1965– ; News Ed. (part-time) Candn. Press 1939–40; served with Royal Winnipeg Rifles, Candn. Inf. Corps 1940–45, rank Capt.; Exec. Asst. Dep. Min. of Labour Ottawa 1945–48; Nat. Sec. Army Benevolent Fund, Mgr. Candn. Army Financial Welfare Prog. 1948–65; served as Exec. Dir. Ctte. Study Orgn. & Work Candn. Pension Comn.; Chrmn. & Hon. Sec.-Gen. Nat. Council Veteran Orgns.; devel. Key Tag Service, Address Label Service, CHAMP Prog.; active various veteran orgns.; Chrmn. Nat. Council Veteran Assns. Can.; mem. Exec. Bd. Internat. Soc. Prosthetics & Orthotics (HQ Denmark); Candn. mem. World Veteran Fedn. (HQ Paris); Patron Hong Kong Veterans' Assn.; Vice Pres. Candn. Nat. Soc. Prosthetics & Orthotics; Life mem. Dom. Command Can. Royal Candn. Legion; Hon. Life mem. Army, Navy & Air Force Veterans Can.; Hon. Pres. Sir Arthur Pearson Assn. for War Blinded; Hon. Vice Pres. Candn. Corps Assn.; mem. Perley & Rideau Veterans' Home Found.; Adv. Ctte. Prosthetics George Brown Coll. Toronto and Sunnybrook Hosp. (Univ. Toronto); Adv. Bd., Amputee Coalition of Am.; recipient Keith Armstrong Award Candn. Rehab. Council Disabled 1984; Royal Bank Award Candn. Achievement 1988; Medal of Honour Candn. Med. Assn. 1990; Order of Ont. 1990; Pinnacle Award Candn. Soc. Assn. Execs. 1991; Univ. of Winnipeg LL.D. (honoris causa) 1992; author various publs.; recreations: golf, skiing, sailing; Clubs: Fort Myers Beach Sailing; Amberwood Golf & Country; Home: 40 Kettering Private, Ottawa, Ont. K1V 0X8; Office: 2827 Riverside Dr., Ottawa, Ont. K1V 0C4.

**CHADWICK, Bruce Allen,** H.B.A.; advertising executive; b. Hamilton, Ont. 16 Nov. 1937; s. Allen Edmund and Elsie Amy (Rawlinson) C.; e. Univ. of W. Ont. H.B.A. 1960 (Award of Merit 1960); m. Betty Jane d. William and Ellen Boyer 24 Sept. 1960; children: Cameron MacRae, Jennifer Ann; C.E.O., KELLEY ADVERTISING INC. 1986– ; Dir.: Bozell Jacobs & Partners Inc. 1975–84; Interact Communications Inc. 1980–84; Publicité Thibault Kelley Inc. 1980–85; DirectArt Inc. 1980–92; Mid-Main Properties Ltd. 1983–85; The Service Letter Shop Inc. 1984–91; Acct. Exec. present co. 1960, Acct. Supr. 1968, Vice Pres. 1972, Dir. 1973, Pres. & Dir. 1974–86; mem. Communication Arts Adv. Ctte. Mohawk Coll. 1972–77, Chrmn. Advertising Adv. Ctte. 1973–77; Communications Dir. Un. Way Burlington & Hamilton-Wentworth 1982; Chrmn. Inst. Candn. Advertising 1984–86, Dir. 1975, Treas. 1979–80, 2nd Vice Chrmn. 1981, 1st Vice Chrmn. 1982–83; Pres. Candn. Ind. Advertisers 1969–70; mem. Candn. Advertisers Bd. Children's Sect. 1977–79; Vice Chrmn. CAAB-CAB Comparative Advertising Ctte. 1981–82; Dir. and mem. Exec. Ctte. Candn. Advertising Found. 1982–83; Trustee Nat. Advertising Benevolent Soc. Can. 1985–87; Dir. Hamilton/Burlington YMCA 1968–81, Exec. Ctte. 1972–81, Vice Pres. 1977–79, Pres. 1979–80, Hon. Adv. Bd. 1981, Endowment Fund Trustee 1987; Dir. Rotary Hamilton 1978–79; Dir. Art Gall. of Hamilton 1984–88; Business Adv. Ctte, McMaster Univ. 1987; Chrmn., Michael G. DeGroot School of Business 1992–93; Public Relations Ctte., Chedoke-McMaster Hosps. 1988; Dir., Hamilton Found. 1986–87; Bd. of Dirs. 1990, Vice-Chrmn. The Chedoke-McMaster Hosps. Found. 1992– ; mem. Hamilton C. of C.; recreations: skiing, sailing, squash; Clubs: Caledon Ski; Hamilton; Burlington Sailing & Boating (Sec. 1975–76, Commodore 1977); Home: 169 Oaklands Park Court, Burlington, Ont. L7T 4G9; Office: (PO Box 2250) F3 Park Place, 1 Hughson St. N., Hamilton, Ont. L8N 3E5.

**CHADWICK, James Barton,** Q.C., LL.B.; barrister; b. Toronto, Ont. 28 Oct. 1936; s. James Kent and Helen T. (O'Connor) C.; e. St. Francis Xavier Univ. B.A. 1959; Univ. of Ottawa LL.B. 1962; m. Julie V. Hayes 25 Aug. 1962; children: Thomas K., Robert J., Kevin, Laura; APPTD. TO THE HIGH COURT OF JUSTICE FOR ONT. 1988– ; apptd. to the Ontario Court of Justice, General Division 1990– ; former Partner, Burke-Robertson, Chadwick & Ritchie, Ottawa; Part-time Prof., Univ. of Ottawa Law Sch.; called to Bar of Ont. 1964; cr. Q.C. 1977; Bencher, Law Soc. Upper Can. 1975–88; Fellow, Am. Trial Lawyers Assn.; mem. Advocates Soc.; Internat. Bar Assn.; Candn. Bar Assn.; R. Catholic; Club: Rideau; Home: 91 Beaver Ridge, Nepean, Ont. K2E 6E5; Office: Court House, 161 Elgin St., Ottawa, Ont. K2P 2K1.

**CHADWICK-JONES, John Knighton,** M.A., Ph.D., D.Sc.; university professor; b. Swansea, Wales 26 July 1928; s. Thomas and Rachel (Thomas) C.-J.; e. St. Edmund Hall, Oxford Univ., B.A., M.A. 1955; Univ. of Wales, Ph.D. 1960, D.Sc. 1981; m. Dr. Araceli Carceller d. Enrique and Teresa 1965; children: Diane, John, Andrew; PROF. OF PSYCH., SAINT MARY'S UNIV. 1974– ; Montague Burton Rsch. Studentship, Univ. Coll., Cardiff 1955–57; Sci. Staff, Nat. Inst. of Ind. Psych., London 1957–60; Lectr., Univ. Coll., Cardiff 1960–66; Sr. Lectr. 1966–67; Reader in Soc. Psych. and Head, Dept. of Psych., Flinders Univ. of S. Australia 1967–68; Dir., Occupational Psych. Rsch. Unit, Univ. College, Cardiff 1968–74; Assoc. Fellow, Darwin Coll., Cambridge Univ. 1980–81; Vis. Fellow, Clare Hall, Cambridge Univ. 1982–83; Vis. Fellow, Wolfson Coll., Cambridge Univ. 1984–85; Vis. Fellow, Wolfson Coll., Oxford Univ. 1988–89; Vis. Fellow, St. Edmund's Coll., Cambridge Univ. 1990–91; Dir., Cambridge Canadian Trust 1988– ; Fellow, Candn. Psych. Assn.; Am. Psych. Assn.; Brit. Psych. Soc.; Mem., Bd. of Govs., Saint Mary's Univ. 1975–78, 1991–92; author 'Automation and Behaviour: A Social Psychological Study' 1969; 'Social Exchange Theory: Its Structure and Influence in Social Psychology' 1976; 'Absenteeism in the Canadian Context' 1980; co-author: 'Brain, Environment and Social Psychology' 1979; 'Social Psychology of Absenteeism' 1982; Club: Cymmrodorion; Home: 1105 Belmont-on-the-Arm, Halifax, N.S. B3H 1J2; Office: Saint Mary's Univ., Halifax, N.S. B3H 3C3.

**CHAGNON, André;** business executive; b. Montreal, Que. 17 March 1928; e. Ecole Technique de Montréal 1945–49; Ecole des hautes études commerciales 1955–60; m. Lucie Dolan; children: Johanne, Claude, Christian, Elaine, Isabelle; CHAIRMAN & CHIEF EXECUTIVE OFFICER, LE GROUPE VIDÉOTRON LTÉE; Technician, City of Montreal Electric Serv. Comn. 1951–54; founded electrical div. of G.M. Gest Ltd. 1954; Pres., E.R. Chagnon Ltée, electrical contractor 1957–66; created div. specializing in cable TV 1964; sold assets in construction firm & began working exclusively on cable TV 1966; Pres., Vidéotron Ltée 1967; Le Groupe Vidéotron Ltée subs. incl. Vidéotron Ltée and Télé-Métropole Inc.; European Bd. Mem., subs. of Le Groupe Vidéotron; Le Groupe Vidéotron won the 'Mercure' Enterprise of the Year, Qué. C. of C. & the 'Mercure' Innovation for the Videoway terminal June 1991; recipient, Canada Award for Business Excellence - Innovation 1991; ACRTF Grand Prize for Broadcasting & Extraordinary Contbn. as a Builder of French-language Radio & TV Sept. 1989; Grand Lauréat des Prix de Communication, Que. Min. of Comm. 1983; Man of the Month, 'Commerce' mag. Nov. 1983; Gov., Programme Portage Inc. (drug & alcohol rehab. centre); Chrmn., Leucan 1988; Opération Enfant Soleil 1990; Bd. Mem., Fond. de la Faune du Qué.; Office: 2000 Berri St., Montreal, Que. H2L 4V7.

**CHAKI, Yehuda Leon;** artist; b. Athens, Greece 11 Dec. 1938; s. Ben-Zion and Flora (Peres) Sciaky; e. Atelier Joseph Schwartzman, Tel-Aviv, Israel 1955; Avni Academy, Tel-Aviv 1960; École des beaux-arts, Paris, France; m. Grace d. Fannie and William Aronoff 10 Sept. 1963; children: Lisa, Adam; since 1962 has had over 55 one-man shows in Belgium, Norway, Israel, Japan, Boston, N.Y., Ottawa, Que. City, Vancouver, Montreal & Toronto; has participated in close to 200 group shows throughout Israel, Eur., the U.S. & Can.; represented in museums, public & corp. collections worldwide; represented in Can. by Galerie Dresdnere (Toronto) for past 25 yrs; in Que. by Galerie Madeleine Lacerte; in Montreal by Gal. Waddington-Gorce; in Ottawa by Robertson Galleries; in Vanc. by Buschlen-Mowatt; Head of Painting & Drawing, Dept. of Fine Arts, Saidye Bronfman Ctr., Montreal for 25 yrs. until 1985; Home: 435 Elm Ave., Westmount, Que. H3Y 3H9.

**CHALMERS, David Bay,** B.A.; petroleum executive; b. Denver, Colo. 17 Nov. 1924; s. David Twiggs Chalmers (dec.) and Dorrit (Bay) Chalmers (dec.); e. Public High Schs., Denver, Colo.; Dartmouth Coll., Hanover, N.H., B.A. 1947; one s. David B. Chalmers Jr.; PRES., CORAL PETROLEUM, INC. since 1973; Chrmn. of Bd. Coral Petroleum Inc., Coral Petroleum (Canada) Inc., Coral Petrofenix, Inc.; Coral Petroleum Corp.; joined Bay Petroleum Corp., Denver 1947, Landman Oklahoma City 1951, Mgr. Crude Oil Purchases 1954; Mgr. Crude Oil Purchases and Sales, Tennessee Gas Transmission (now Tenneco) 1955, Vice-Pres. 1961; Vice-Pres., Occidental Petroleum Corp. 1967 then Pres. and Mang. Dir., Jefferson Lake Petrochemicals of Canada Ltd.; Pres. of Canadian Occidental Petroleum, Ltd. and Offr. and Dir. Cansulex Limited and Petrogas Processing, Ltd. and of various affiliates and subsidiaries 1971–73; served in 2nd World War, Lieut. U.S. Marine Corps 1943–45, in Korean War 1949–50 as First Lieut.; former mem. Board of Governors, Canadian Petroleum Association; National Petroleum Refiners Association; mem., American Petroleum Institute; Texas Indep. Petroleum & Royalty Owners Assn.; Epis.; recreation: golf, tennis;

Clubs: Denver Country; Lakeside Country (Houston); Houston Petroleum; Lochinvar Golf (Houston); Wailae (Honolulu); Home: 5600 San Felipe, No. 4, Houston, Texas; Office: 600 Travis, Ste. 6120, Houston, Texas, 77002.

**CHALONER, Richard F.,** B.A., LL.B., Q.C.; lawyer, retired; b. Burlington, Ont. 5 Nov. 1933; s. Alfred M. and Kate L.C.; e. Burlington Dist. H.S. 1953; McMaster Univ., B.A. 1956; Univ. of Toronto, LL.B. 1959; Osgoode Hall, Bar Adm. Course 1961; Q.C. 1972; m. Norah Rae d. Walter and Thelma McCleary 29 Dec. 1961; children: Peter, David; Dep. Atty. Gen., Prov. of Ontario 1986–..; called to Ont. Bar 1961; Assoc., McMillan, Binch & Co. 1961–62; priv. prac., Wilson & Chaloner 1962–63; Asst. Crown Atty., Simcoe Co. 1963; Wellington Co. 1966; Crown Atty. 1967; Sec.-Tres., Ont. Crown Attys. Assn. 1968–73 (Pres. 1980); Regl. Crown Atty., Cos. of Wellington, Waterloo, Halton, Peel, Huron, Bruce & Grey 1976; Dir. of Crown Attys., Prov. of Ont. 1983; Asst. Dep. Atty. Gen., Criminal Law 1985; Big Brothers Assn. of Guelph & Wellington Co. (Charter Pres. & founder 1968–71, Mem. & Ctte. Chrmn. 1971–85; Hon. Pres. 1985); Guelph United Appeal 1968–71; Big Brothers of Canada (Dir. & Extve. Ctte.) 1973–75; recreations: amateur photography, hiking, camping, painting, cycling; Address: 100 Maple St., Guelph, Ont. N1G 2G2.

**CHAMBERLAIN, Clive Gordon,** M.D., FRCP(C); physician; b. Toronto, Ont. 28 Sept. 1935; s. Kenneth William and Leone Mabel (Everist) C.; e. Runnymede P.S. 1949; Etobicoke C.I. 1955; Univ. of Toronto, M.D. 1961, FRCP(C) 1967; m. Mary d. George and Margaret Saunderson 8 June 1963; children: Adam, Susan, Martha, Matthew; CLINICAL DIRECTOR AND PSYCHIATRIST-IN-CHIEF, QUEEN STREET MENTAL HEALTH CENTRE 1994– ; post-grad. training in Toronto & Britain (R.S. McLaughlin Trav. Fellow 1966–67); Dir., Res. Treatment Unit, C.M. Hincks Treatment Ctr. 1967–71; Family Court Clinic, Clarke Inst. of Psych. 1971–77; Extve. Dir., Prog. Policy, Children's Serv., Govt. of Ont. 1977–80; Dir., Thistletown Regnl. Ctr. 1980–82; Psych. in Chief 1982– ; Assoc. Prof., Dept. of Psych., Univ. of Toronto 1973– ; Psychiatrist-in-Chief, Thistletown & George Hull Ctrs. 1986–94; Cons., Clarke Inst. of Psych.; Hon. Cons., Hosp. for Sick Children; Home: 241 Rosedale Heights Dr., Toronto, Ont. M4T 1C7; Office: 1001 Queen St. W., Toronto, Ont. M6J 1H4.

**CHAMBERLAND, Jacques,** B.A., LL.L.; b. Montréal, Qué. 3 Nov. 1948; s. Louis-Philippe and Alexina (Deslauriers) C.; e. Coll. de Saint-Laurent B.A. 1968; Univ. de Montréal LL.L. 1971; m. Christiane d. Wilfrid and Blanche Boileau 23 Dec. 1972; children: Simon, Julien, Marie-Christine; JUDGE, COURT OF APPEAL OF QUEBEC 1993– ; Sessional Lectr. Concordia Univ. 1976–78, McGill Univ. 1978–81; Lawyer, Partner, Lavery, O'Brien, Montréal 1972–88; Deputy Minister of Justice, Que. 1988–93; recipient Lomer Gouin Award 1969; Lord Reading Soc. Award 1970; Pres. Fondation des Jeux du Qué. 1986–88; recreations: golf, hockey, tennis; Club: Le Club de golf Laval-sur-le-Lac; Home: 561 Côte Ste-Catherine, Outremont, Qué. H2V 2C2; Office: 1 rue Notre-Dame est, Bureau 12.71, Montreal, Que. H2Y 1B6.

**CHAMBERS, Edward James,** B.Comm., B.A., M.A., Ph.D.; university professor; b. Vancouver, B.C. 18 Apr. 1925; s. James and Anne Christina (Bannan) C.; e. Univ. of B.C., B.Comm. 1945, B.A. 1946, M.A. 1947; Univ. of Nebraska, Ph.D. 1953; m. A. Elizabeth d. Robert C. and Ellen Ross 7 Oct. 1945; children: Neil, Paul, Scott, Anne, Justine; PROF. OF ECONOMIC ANALYSIS, FAC. OF BUS., UNIV. OF ALBERTA 1968– ; Extve. Dir., Western Ctr. for Econ. Rsch. 1988– ; Extve. Dir., Ctr. for Internat. Business Studies 1992– ; Lectr., Whitman Coll. 1947–51; Economist, Dept. of Trade & Comm., Govt. of Can. 1953–55; Prudential Insur. Co. 1955–56; Assoc. Prof. & Dir., Bur. of Bus. & Econ. Rsch., Sch. of Bus., Univ. of Montana 1956–60; Prof., Bus. Econ., Sch. of Bus., Univ. of Washington 1960–68; Dean, present fac. 1968–76; Soc. Sci. Rsch. Fellow 1952–53; Ford Found. Rsch. Fellow in Bus. 1964–65; McCalla Rsch. Prof. 1984–85; Pres., Alta. Found. for Econ. Edn. 1978–85; Dir. 1985– ; Pres., Puget Sound Unitarian Counc. 1965–68; Edmonds Unitarian Ch. 1964–65; Beta Pheta Pi; author: 'Economic Fluctuations and Forecasting' 1961, 'National Income Analysis and Forecasting' 1975; recreations: walking, hiking, golf; club: Edmonton Country; Home: 11632 Edinbor Rd., Edmonton, Alta. T6G 1Z8; Office: Edmonton, Alta. T6G 2R6.

**CHAMBERS, J.K. (Jack),** B.A., M.A., Ph.D.; university professor / Jazz critic; b. Grimsby, Ont. 12 July 1938; s. Royce Book and Constance Rose (Shirfield) C.; e. Univ. of Windsor, B.A. 1961; Queen's Univ., M.A. 1963; Univ. of Alta., Ph.D. 1970; m. Susan E. d. Willard and Viola L'Heureux 9 Sept. 1961; children: Christopher, Alison, Jennifer; PROF., DEPT. OF LINGUISTICS, UNIV. OF TORONTO 1982– , Chair 1986–90; Secondary Sch. Teacher, London (Ont.) Bd. of Ed. 1963–64; Teacher & Head of English, East Elgin Bd. of Ed. 1964–67; Asst. Prof., Linguistics, Univ. of Toronto 1970–75; Assoc. Prof. 1975–82; Vis. Fellow, Univ. of Reading (Eng.), 1976–77, 1983–84, 1990–91; jazz reviews & articles 'Coda' magazine 1972–78; Globe and Mail 1972– ; cons. for name generation, var. advtg. firms; expert witness, var. firms on linguistic issues, esp. Trade Mark Law, obscenity trials, native land claims; Pres., Ont. Ling. Circle 1975–76; Ed., 'Canadian Journal of Linguistics' 1979–84; Adjudicator, ALCAN Comp., Montreal Internat. Jazz Fest. 1989; Ed. Bds., 'American Speech,' 'International Journal of American Linguistics'; author: 'Milestones: The Music and Times of Miles Davis' 2 vols., 1983, 1985; co-author: 'A Very Small Rebellion' 1977; 'Dialectology' 1980; co-editor: 'Dialects of English' 1991; pronunciation editor: 'Canadian Dictionary for Children' 1979; 'Canadian Dictionary for Schools' 1981; editor: 'Canadian English' 1975, 'The Languages of Canada' 1979 and author of hundreds of articles & reviews on Canadian English, English dialects, language, jazz & other topics; recreations: squash, Gothic architecture; Home: 57 Castle Knock Rd., Toronto, Ont. M5N 2J6; Office: Univ. of Toronto, Toronto, Ont. M5S 1A1.

**CHAMBERS, Thomas Frederick,** B.A., M.Sc.; college professor; b. Hamilton, Ont. 5 Nov. 1940; s. Harold Joseph Ashbridge and Madeline Agnes Detlor (Milne) C.; e. Acadia Univ. B.A. 1964; The London Sch. of Econ. & Pol. Sci. M.Sc. 1965; m. Heather d. George (Mac) and Marion Young 8 Aug. 1970; children: David M.A., Christopher T.Y., Robert F.W.; PROFESSOR, CANADORE COLLEGE OF APPLIED ARTS & TECHNOLOGY 1970– ; Trust Administrator, The National Trust Co. Ltd. 1966–68; History Teacher, Port Perry H.S. 1969–70; Pres. & Dir., Cybernetics Ltd.; current affairs consultant; Mem. Candn. Assn. for Econ. Edn.; Pres., North Bay and Area Museum 1980–82; Warden, Ch. of St. John the Divine 1983–88; author: 'Canada: Can It Be Governed' (textbook) forthcoming; recreations: writing, aerobics, nordic skiing, jogging; clubs: North Bay Nordic Ski, North Bay YMCA; Home: 328 Pearce St., North Bay, Ont. P1C 1L1; Office: P.O. Box 5001, North Bay, Ont. P1B 8K9.

**CHAMBERS, Thomas Glen,** B.A., real estate executive; b. Hamilton, Ont. 31 July 1928; s. Stewart and Isabell (Glen) C.; e. Westdale Coll. Inst. 1946; McMaster Univ., B.A. 1950; m. Barbara d. David and Mary Lindsay 17 Oct. 1953; children: Sheila Mary, Jennifer Lynne, Stewart Glen; PRES. CHAMBERS & CO. LTD. (1911); Founder and Pres. Chambers Group Ltd. 1972– ; Past Pres. Hamilton Real Estate Bd. 1961 (Hon. Life mem.); Ont. Real Estate Assn. 1973 (Hon. Life mem.); Past Dir. Candn. Real Estate Assn. 1977–78; Past Chrmn., Bd. of Govs., McMaster Univ.; Past Gov. Hamilton Civic Hosps.; Past Chrmn. Central Presb. Ch.; recreations: golf, fishing, travel; Clubs: Hamilton Golf & Country (Past Pres.); Caughnawana Fishing & Hunting (Dir.); Hamilton (Vice Chair); Home: 1488 Mineral Springs Rd., R.R. 3, Dundas, Ont. L9H 5E3; Office: P.O. Box 895, Station A, Hamilton, Ont. L8N 3P6.

**CHAMPAGNE, Gilles;** transportation executive; b. Montreal, Que. 4 Feb. 1940; s. Noel Joseph and Rita Mary (Robillard) C.; e. Montreal High Sch. 1959; Montreal Univ. études commerciales, Bus. Admin.; m. Ginette d. Rene Demers 25 Aug. 1962; children: Chantal, Benoit; PRESIDENT AND C.E.O., OCEANEX LIMITED PARTNERSHIP 1990– ; joined Clarke Transport Canada's Montreal Marine Terminal, filled various positions in Operations, Traffic and Tariffs, incl.: Asst. Mgr. Nfld. Services 1968; Sales Mgr. Marine Candn. Services, Groupage & Road Transport 1970; Asst. Sr. Vice-Pres. Multimodal Services 1974; Sr. Develop. Offr., Transportation Div., Crosbie Enterprises 1977; Gen. Mgr. Container Liner Services 1978; formed own cons. service 1980; joined the Harvey Group as Exec. Vice-Pres., Harvey's Container Transport (AFL) 1981; Pres. & C.E.O., Ace-Atlantic Container Express Inc. 1982–90; Pres., the St. Lawrence Gulf Devel. Assn.; Dir.: The Maritime Employers' Assoc.; Candn. Shipowners' Assn.; Quebec Shipowners' Assn.; Shipowners' Mutual Insurance Assn.; has participated in many seminars in Can. and U.S.; recreations: reading, swimming, golf, skiing; Home: 16 Place Chatenois, Lorraine, Que. J6Z 4K3; Office: 600 René-Lévesque Blvd. West, Ste. 901, Montreal, Que. H3B 1N4.

**CHAMPAGNE, Guy B.,** B.E., M.B.A.; executive; b. Lachine, Qué. 16 Dec. 1928; s. Albert and Eva (Meloche) C.; e. Coll. Mont Saint-Louis 1949; McGill Univ. B.E. (Civil) 1953, M.B.A. 1960; Harvard Univ. Sr. Mgmt. Prog. 1978; m. B.F. d. Charles Allaway 2 Oct. 1954; two s. Mark, Philip; PRES., CHIEF EXEC. OFFR. AND DIR. EXELTOR INC. 1980– ; Dir. Ingersoll-Rand Canada Inc. 1973–87; Pres. and Dir. Harrington Div. 1970–80; Dir. MBS Bearings Service Inc. 1980– ; Torrington do Brasil Ind. e Com. S.A. 1966–80; joined Torrington/Canada 1953, opened Montréal Regional Office and served as Dist. Mgr. 1954–62, Bearings Sales Cons. Paris, France 1962, estbd. Torrington France SARL and opened Paris Office 1963 serving as Mng. Dir. 1963–64; Asst. Gen. Mgr. Candn. Corp. Bedford, Qué. 1964, Gen. Mgr. 1965, Pres., Gen. Mgr. and Dir. 1966–80; also served as Mng. Dir. Torrington International; with the mgmt. group, structured a mgmt. buy-out of the worldwide operations of the knitting needle div. of Torrington/Ingersoll-Rand, now Exeltor Inc. 1980; mem. Task Force Can.-USA Trade Policy 1985; Chairperson Ind., Marine & Rail products SAGIT Ctte. for Can./USA Free Trade Negotiations; Mem., SAGIT for Industrial & Transportation Equipment 1988– ; Founding Dir. and Vice Chrmn. Candn.-E. Eur. Trade Council 1985– ; Gov. Qué. Hosp. Assn. 1972–86; Dir., Candn. Mfrs. Assoc. 1988; mem., Inst. of Corp. Dirs. in Can.; Candn. Export Assn. (Pres. of Que. Chapt., Dir. of Nat. Bd. 1986– ; & Chrmn. of Nat. Bd. 1990); Candn. C. of C.; Eng. Inst. Can.; Corp. des Ingénieurs du Qué.; recreations: tennis, skiing, golf, reading; Clubs: St. James's (Montréal); Cowansville (Qué.) Country; Home: 21 Victoria Ave., Bedford, Qué. J0J 1A0; Office: (P.O. Box 1500) 110 River St., Bedford, Qué. J0J 1A0.

**CHAMPAGNE, Yves,** C.A.; financial executive; b. Montreal, Que. 26 Feb. 1952; s. Roger and Gabrielle (Jacques) C.; e. Hautes Etudes Commercials 1975; C.A. 1977; m. Lorraine d. Luigi and Fernande Pizzolongo; children: Julie, Genevieve, Véronique; VICE-PRESIDENT, FINANCE & ADMINISTRATION, MULTI-MARQUES INC. 1990– ; Staff, Clarkson Gordon 1975–79; Manager 1979–81; Internal Auditor, Unipain Inc. 1981–84; Corporate Controller, Multi-Marques Inc. 1984–90; Office: 1600 boul. Henri-Bourassa O., Montreal, Que. H3M 3E2.

**CHAN, Alfred K.T.,** B.Sc., M.Eng.; executive; b. China 23 Oct. 1947; s. Bon Liong and Sau Tak (Ngor) Tan; e. McGill Univ. B.Sc. 1970, M.Eng. 1972; m. Yuen Pik d. S.K. Liu 1973; children: Victoria Teresa Zee-Ming, Anthony Paul John-Ming; BOARD CHRMN., ETAC SALES LTD. (Founder, Pres., C.E.O. & Dir. 1975–..); Founder and Dir. Karwell Trading Co. Ltd. Montréal 1972– ; Sec.-Treas. and Dir. Maplex Management and Holdings Ltd., Burlington, Ont. 1987– ; Sec.-Treas. and Dir. Consolidated Five Stars Resources Ltd., Calgary 1988– ; Office: 20 Bertrand Ave., Scarborough, Ont. M1L 2P4.

**CHAN, Lewis Tan Thoo,** B.Sc., LL.B.; lawyer; b. Hong Kong 19 Aug. 1955; s. Kwong Hon and Chung Ting (Hom) C.; e. McGill Univ., B.Sc. 1978 (grad. with distinction); Univ. of Ottawa, LL.B. 1981; m. Karen d. Woo Hing and Moon Tong (Young) Chan 23 May 1978; one s. Patrick Lewis; LAWYER, GOSS, CHAN 1983– ; Computer Analyst/Programmer, Bank of Montreal 1976–78; called to Ont. Bar 1983; Mem., City of Ottawa Ctte. of Adjustment 1985–87; former Que. Jr. Table Tennis Champion; former Que. Men's Doubles Table Tennis Champion; Pres., Candn. Ethnocultural Counc. 1988–92 (Sec. 1986–88) (appeared before num. Parlty. & other cttes.; quoted in media on a regular basis); Nat. Vice-Pres., Chinese Candn. Nat. Counc. 1984–92, Nat. Dir. 1992–93 (Ottawa Chap. Pres. 1981–83); Mem., Adv. Panel on Chinese Students in Canada (Govt. of Canada appointment) 1989–93; Mem., Adv. Ctte. on Visible Minorities to the City of Ottawa 1982–86; Mem., Ont. Cabinet Round Table on Anti-Racism 1993– ; Mem., Liquor Licence Bd. of Ont. 1989–92; Candn. Bar Assn.; Vice-Pres., Ottawa Chinese Bus. Assn. 1984–88; recreations: tennis, skiing, table tennis; clubs: Rideau Tennis and Squash Club; Candn. Table Tennis Assn.; Home: PH4 – 969 River Rd., Ottawa, Ont. K1K 3V3; Office: 211 Pretoria Ave., Ottawa, Ont. K1S 1X1.

**CHAN, Raymond T.,** B.Comm., C.A.; financial executive; b. Hong Kong 2 Nov. 1955; e. Univ. of Saskatchewan B.Comm. 1977; Alberta Inst. C.A. 1979; m. Sylvia Fung 1977; children: Cynthia, Melinda, Byron; VICE-PRESIDENT, FINANCE AND SECRETARY, TARRAGON OIL AND GAS LIMITED 1990– ; Accountant, Peat Marwick Mitchell & Co. 1977–81; Controller, Northstar Resources Ltd. 1981–82; Treas., Controller & Chief Finan. Offr., Gane Energy Corp. Ltd. 1982–84;

Vice-Pres., Finance & Controller, Am. Egale Petroleums Ltd. 1984–90; Office: 500 – 4th Ave. S.W., Ste. 2500, Calgary, Alta. T2P 2V6.

**CHANASYK, Victor,** B.Sc. (Ag), B.S. (L.A.), M.L.A.; professor; b. Vegreville, Alta. 15 Oct. 1926; s. Nicholas and Xenia (Tymchuk) C.; e. Olds Sch. of Agriculture and Univ. of Alta., B.Sc. (Ag) 1949; Univ. of Cal. (Berkeley) B.S.(L.A.) 1957; Harvard Univ. M.L.A. 1958; m. Lillian Iris d. William Nicholas Pidruchney, 14 July 1955; ADJUNCT PROF., SCH. OF LANDSCAPE ARCH., UNIV. OF GUELPH 1992–95 (Dir. of Sch. 1964–75, Prof. 1975–92, Retired 1992); horticulturist, Can. Exper. Stn., Beaverlodge, Alta. 1949–55; Commr., Mun. Art Comm., Seattle, Wash., 1959–61; landscape arch. and urban planner, Puget Planners, Inc., Seattle, 1958–61; landscape arch. and site planner, Skidmore, Owings & Merrill, San Francisco, 1961; Prof. of Landscape Arch., Dept. of Horticulture, Univ. of Guelph, 1962–64; mem. adv. ctte., Ryerson Inst. of Tech. (1968) and Humber Coll. of Applied Arts (1967); Princ., Victor Chanasyk Assoc. 1969– ; author: articles in govt. and learned publs.; mem. Ed. Bd. 'Water, Air and Soil Pollution: An International Journal of Environmental Pollution' 1970; developed first B.L.A. program in landscape arch. in Can.; planned Forillon Nat. Park, Que.; co-recipient Nat. Mfg. Design Award of Can. 1965; recipient Centennial Medal 1967; Can. Council Research Grant 1970; Life Fellow, Roy. Soc. of Arts 1972; Fellow, Cdn. Soc. of Landscape Arch. 1973; recipient Distinguished Achievement Award, Ont. Assn. of Landscape Archs. 1983; Mem. Emeritus, Ont. Assn. of Landscape Archs. 1992; mem. Cdn. Soc. of Landscape Arch. (Exec. Counc. 1965; Chrmn. Ctte. on Educ. 1975; Nat. Accreditation Counc. 1980–81; Educ. Ctte. 1980; Gov. 1981–83); Pres., Wash. Soc. of Landscape Arch. 1959–61; Ont. Assn. of Landscape Arch. (Extve. Council 1980–81, 1983–84; Pres. 1965, 1981–83); mem. Plant Improvement Prog., Royal Botanical Garden 1983– ; Ukrainian Orthodox; recreation: horticulture, conservation, bonsai; Home: 64 Woodside Rd., Guelph, Ont. N1G 2H2.

**CHANCE, Graham Wilfrid,** M.B., FRCP(Lond), FRCP(C); university professor; b. Birmingham, England 9 May 1933; s. Wilfrid Joseph and Edith Amelia C.; e. Handsworth Grammar Sch.; Univ. of Birmingham, M.B.Ch.B. 1956; Dipl. of Child Health, London 1960; FRCP(Lond) 1978; FRCP(C) 1973; med. & paed. residencies undertaken in Dept. of Paed., Univ. of Birmingham, Birmingham Children's Hosp. (U.K.) 1959–67; m. Mary E. d. David and Elizabeth Lewis 1961; children: Valerie Mary, Andrea Jane, Christine Anne; PROF., DEPT. OF PAED. & OBSTETRICS & GYNAECOLOGY, UNIV. OF WEST. ONT. 1979– ; Chrmn., Div. of Neonatal-Perinatal Med. 1990– ; Dir. of Nurseries, St. Joseph's Health Ctr. 1979–90; Dir., Regional Perinatal Outreach Prog., S.W. Ont. 1979– ; Fellow, Westminster Inst. of Ethics and Human Values; served with 2nd/2nd Goorkhas (The Sirmoor Rifles) Malaysia 1957–59; Sr. Lectr., Paed., Univ. of Birmingham 1967–70; Assoc. Prof., Paed., Univ. of Toronto 1970–78; Prof. 1978–79; Martha May Elliot Forum Lectr., Am. Public Health Assn. 1982; John T. Law Meml. Lectr., Candn. Inst. of Child Health 1988; mem., Anglican Ch. of Can.; Vice-Chrmn., Candn. Institute of Child Health 1992– ; Chrmn., Candn. Coalition for the Prevention of Devel. Disability; Fellow, Candn. Paed. Soc. (ctte. mem.); Mem., Soc. for Paed. Rsch.; Am. Paed. Soc.; Adv. Panel on Neonatology, Internat. Paed. Assn. 1987–90; Royal Coll. of Phys. & Surg. of Can., Specialty Ctte. in Neonatal-Perinatal Med. (Chrmn. 1982–88); Examiner in Paed. 1979–84; co-editor: 'Perinatal Medicine: Basic Science Underlying Clinical Practice' 1976; author/co-author of numerous med. articles, book chapters & reports; recreations: gardening, classical music; clubs: The Sirmoor Club, London, England; Home: 238 Hunt Club Dr., London, Ont. N6H 3Z1; Office: St. Joseph's Health Ctr., 268 Grosvenor St., London, Ont. N6A 4V2.

**CHANDLER, Mark Edward,** M.A., B.A.; banking executive; b. Toronto, On. 7 Sept. 1960; s. James Frederick and Brenda May (Knight) C.; e. Univ. of Western Ont. B.A. (Hons.) 1983; Queen's Univ. M.A. 1987; m. Teresa d. Thomas and Margaret Courchene 23 Sept. 1988; children: Eric James, Owen Joseph; ASSISTANT CHIEF ECONOMIST, ROYAL BANK OF CAN. 1989– ; Economist, Bank of Montreal 1984–87; Economic Cons., Coopers & Lybrand 1988; Home: 44 Clappison Blvd., West Hill, Ont. M1C 2G7; Office: 200 Bay St., 16th Floor, S. Tower, Toronto, Ont. M5J 2J5.

**CHANG, Thomas Ming Swi,** O.C., B.Sc., M.D., C.M., Ph.D., F.R.C.P.(C.); medical scientist; physician; biotechnologist; educator; b. China 8 Apr. 1933; s. Henry and Frances (Lim) C.; came to Can. 1953; e. McGill Univ. B.Sc. 1957; M.D., C.M. 1961; Ph.D. 1965; F.R.C.P.(C.) 1972; m. Lancy Yuit Lan Yan 21 June 1958; children: Harvey, Victor, Christine, Sandra; PROFESSOR OF PHYSIOLOGY 1972– , MEDICINE 1975– ; AND BIOMEDICAL ENGINEERING 1990– , MCGILL UNIVERSITY; DIR., ARTIFICIAL CELLS AND ORGANS RESEARCH CENTRE there 1979– ; Career Investigator, Med. Research Council of Can. 1968– ; Prof. of Medicine, RVH Univ. Clinic, Royal Victoria Hosp.; Hon. Staff, Montreal Chinese Hosp.; Assoc. of Chemistry, McGill Univ.; Assoc. of Chemical Engr., McGill Univ.; Hon. Prof., Nankai Univ., Tianjin, China 1983– ; Rotating Internship, Montreal Gen Hosp. 1961–62; Medical Research Council of Can. Fellow, Depts. of Chemistry and Physiology, McGill Univ. 1962–65; Lectr. in Physiology 1965–66; M.R.C. Research Scholar 1965–68; Asst. Prof. of Physiology 1966–69; Assoc. Prof. 1969–72; Prof. 1972; Asst. Prof. of Med. 1972–75; Prof. 1975; Dir. Artificial Organs Research Unit 1975–79; Consultant, Montreal Children's Hosp. 1980–93; Ed.-in-chief, Internat. Journal of Artificial Cells, Blood Substitutes and Immobilization Biotechnology 1987– ; mem. Ed. Bd. of various profl. journals; serves and has served on numerous profl. comtes., advisory bds., etc. including: Internat. Soc. for Artifical Cells, Blood Substitutes and Immobilization Biotechnology (Hon. Pres. 1990– ;); Int'l. Soc. for Artificial Organs (Counc. mem. 1977–82, Bd. of Trustees 1982–87, 1989–93, Pres. 1991 World Congress, Pres.-elect 1991–93, Pres. 1993–95); Officer of the Order of Canada; invited Lectr. and Visiting Professor world-wide; Inventor of Artificial Cells; author of books: 'Artificial Cells' 1972; 'Lecture Series on Artificial Cells' 1981; ed. 'Biomedical Applications of Immobilized Enzymes and Proteins' 1977; 'Artificial Kidney, Artificial Liver and Artificial Cells' 1978; co-ed. (with S. Sideman) 'Hemoperfusion: I Artificial Kidney and Liver Support and Detoxification' 1980; 'Hemoperfusion: II Devices and Clinical Applications' 1980; (with V. Bonomini) 'Hemoperfusion' 1981; (with E. Piskin) 'Past, Present and Future of Artificial Organs' 1983; 'Microencapsulation and Artificial Cells' 1984; 'Hemoperfusion and Artificial Organs' 1985; (with R. Geyer) 'Blood Substitutes' 1988; 'Blood Substitutes and Oxygen Carriers' 1992; author or co-author over 360 articles on topics related to artificial cells and organs, blood substitutes, kidney and liver support, immobilised enzymes and cells, microencapsulation, blood substitutes and biotechnology; profl. assns. include: Pres. and Chrmn. Organizing Comte., Fifth Internat. Symposium on 'Microencapsulation, including artificial cells' (Montreal 1983); Hon. Pres., Internat. Symposia of Hemoperfusion, Sorbents & Immobilized Bioreactants (Ankara 1982, Mexico 1985, Kiev 1986, Rostock 1988, Tokyo 1989, Rome 1990); Pres., 3rd Internat. Symposium on Blood Substitutes 1987; Pres., 8th Internat. Congress on Artificial Organs 1991; Pres., 4th Internat. Symposium on Blood Substitutes 1991; Co-Chrmn., 5th Internat. Symposium on Blood Substitutes 1993; Honorary Pres., XI World Congress, Int. Soc. for Artificial Cells, Blood Substitutes and Immobilisation Biotechnology; Protestant; recreations: classical music, tennis, weight-training, microcomputer, project controls, management approaches; Office: Artificial Cells and Organs Research Centre, McGill University, 3655 Drummond St., Montreal, Qué. H3G 1Y6.

**CHANG, Yunshik,** B.A., M.A., Ph.D.; university professor; b. Inchon, Korea; s. Taeyong and Soonee (Kim) C.; e. Seoul National Univ. B.A. 1958; Univ. of B.C. M.A. 1961; Princeton Univ. Ph.D. 1967; s. Sungbon d. Sukpyo and Insun Hong 5 Sept. 1971; children: Heeyon, Heejune; PROF., DEPT. OF ANTHROPOLOGY & SOCIOLOGY, UNIV. OF B.C. 1980– ; Instructor II, Univ. of B.C. 1964; Asst. Prof. 1966; Assoc. Prof. 1971; Prof. 1980; author: 'A Study of the Korean Population: 1966' 1974, 'The Population of Korea' 1974, 'Society in Transition with Special Reference to Korea' 1982; editor: Population Change in the Pacific Region' 1977; 'Korea: A Decade of Development' 1980; 'Society in Transition: With Special Reference to Korea' 1982; recreations: hiking, swimming, gardening; Home: 3363 West 37th Ave., Vancouver, B.C. V6N 2V5; Office: 6303 N.W. Marine Dr., Vancouver, B.C. V6T 1Z1.

**CHANT, Dixon S.,** F.C.A., company executive; b. Toronto, Ont.; s. Christopher William and Minnie Jane (Butler) C.; e. Pickering Coll., Newmarket, Ont.; Inst. of Chart. Accts. Ont., F.C.A.; m. Marion K., d. Roderick K. Macnaughton, Gananoque, 13 June 1942; s. Murray James; DEPY. CHRMN., HOLLINGER INC.; Depy. Chrmn. & Dir., The Ravelston Corp. Ltd.; Valley Cable TV Inc.; Vice-Chrmn., Am. Publishing Co.; Chrmn. of Bd. & C.E.O., Argcen Inc.; Versa Services Ltd.; Pres., Argus Corp. Ltd.; Sugra Ltd.; Chrmn. & Pres., Domgroup Ltd.; Extve. Vice Pres. & Dir., Saturday Night Magazine Inc.; Extve. Vice Pres., Unimedia Inc.; Dir., Sterling Newspapers Ltd.; Cayman Free Press Ltd.; Jerusalem Post Publications Ltd.; Palestine Post; Western Dominion Investment Co. Ltd.; Mem., Bd. of Govs., Pickering Coll.; United Church; recreations: golf, photography; Clubs: Granite (Past Pres.); Rosedale Golf; Toronto Board of Trade; Canadian; Toronto; Empire; Muskoka Lakes Golf & Country (Past Pres.); Royal & Ancient Golf C. of St. Andrews, Fife; Residences: 167 Coldstream Ave., Toronto, Ont. M5N 1X7; P.O. Box 212, Port Carling, Ont. P0B 1J0 (summer); Office: 10 Toronto St., Toronto, Ont. M5C 2B7.

**CHANT, Donald,** O.C., M.A., Ph.D., LL.D. (Hon.), F.R.E.S., F.R.S.C., F.E.S.C.; educator; b. Toronto, Ont., 30 Sept. 1928; s. the late Sperrin Noah Fulton and the late Nellie Irene (Cooper) C.; e. Univ. of Brit. Columbia, B.A. (Hons.) 1950, M.A. 1952; Univ. of London, Ph.D. 1956; Dalhousie Univ., LL.D. (hon.) 1976; Trent Univ., LL.D. (hon.) 1983; divorced; children: Jonathon, Patrick, Jeffrey, Timothy; m. K.M. Hanes, 1975; CHRMN., ONT. WASTE MANAGEMENT CORP. 1980– ; Prof. of Zoology, Univ. of Toronto 1967– ; Chrmn., Pollution Probe Foundation 1969–80; Chrmn., Candn. Environmental Advisory Council 1978–81; Chrmn., Scientific Advisory Ctte. and elected Chrmn. of Bd. of Dirs., World Wildlife Fund (Can.) 1993; Chrmn., Cdn. Ctte. of Univ. Biol. Chrmn.; Research Offr., Can. Dept. Agric. 1950; Dir., Research Lab., Can. Dept. Agric., Vineland, Ont. 1960; Chrmn., Dept. of Biol. Control, Univ. of Cal., Riverside, Cal. 1964; Chrmn., Dept. of Zool., Univ. of Toronto 1967–75, Vice-Pres. and Provost 1975–80; Dir., Joint Study Centre for Toxicology, Univs. of Toronto and Guelph 1980–82; mem., Cdn. Soc. of Zools. (Pres.); Canadian Entomol. Soc.; Ont. Environmental Assessment Bd.; author: 'Pollution Probe' 1970; 'This Good Good Earth' 1971; co-author of several other prof. books and author of over 100 prof. research publs.; rec'd. Univ. Brit. Columbia Alumni Award 1970; White Owl Conservation Award 1972; Univ. of Toronto Alumni Faculty Award 1980; apptd. Officer, Order of Canada 1988; recreations: reading, fishing, camping; Home: R.R. 2, Madoc, Ont. K0K 2K0; Office: 11th Floor, 2 Bloor St. W., Toronto, Ont. M4W 3E2.

**CHAPLIN, John Edwin;** association executive; b. London, Eng. 23 Jan. 1937; s. Horace Edwin and Elizabeth Jean (Hayes) C.; e. Dr. Challoner's Grammar Sch. Amersham, Eng. 1955; Univ. of Birmingham/General Electric Co. Ltd. Jt. Elect. Engn. Dip. 1958; Inst. of Practitioners in Advertising (UK) MIPA 1974; Communications, Advertising & Mktg. (UK) M.Cam 1974; m. Laraine d. Raymond and Kathleen Stross 23 Feb. 1974; children: Andrew, Gilly, Jonathan; PRES., PMB PRINT MEASUREMENT BUREAU 1983– ; Sole Owner, Media Research Plus; UK: Acct. Exec. Lintas Ltd. 1959–62; Mktg. Exec. The Thomson Organization Ltd. 1963–64; Media Rsch. Mgr. Royds Ltd. 1965–68; Dir. of Media Rsch. Dorland Advertising Ltd. 1969–72; Group Planning Dir. Leo Burnett Ltd. 1972–74; Bd. Dir./Media Dir. David Maculay Advertising Ltd. 1974–75; Can.: Vice Pres./Dir. Media Services Foster Advertising Ltd. 1975–77; Gen. Mgr./Project Dir. present Bureau 1978–82; Pres.: Media Rsch. Group UK 1973, 1974; Broadcast Rsch. Counc. Can. 1979–80; Dir. Candn. Advt. Rsch. Found. 1986– , Chrmn. 1993– ; author: 'A Review of Research into Viewing Behaviour during Commercial Breaks and the Effects of Television Clutter' 1978; 'How to Think about Television Commercial Wearout' 1980; mem., Prof. Market Rsch. Soc.; Am. Mktg. Assn.; Mem. Ed. Bd., Candn. Journ. Mktg. Rsch.; Conservative; recreations: tennis, photography; Home: 14 Norton Place, Church St., Woodbridge, Ont.; Office: 1502, 77 Bloor St. W., Toronto, Ont. M5S 1M2.

**CHAPMAN, Christopher Martin,** C.M., R.C.A.; film maker; b. Toronto, Ont. 25 Jan. 1927; s. Alfred Hirschfelder and Doris Helen (Dennison) C.; e. Northern Vocational Sch. Toronto; m. 1stly Aljean Pert (d.); m. 2ndly Barbara Glen d. Gerhard Kennedy; one s. Julian Christopher; PROP., CHRISTOPHER CHAPMAN LTD. 1965– ; served 6 yrs. in advertising agency prior to 1951; films incl. 'The Seasons' (Cdn. Film of Yr. Award 1954, medal from Salerno); 'A Place to Stand' (Etrog Cdn. Film of Yr., 2 Hollywood nominations, Acad. Award Oscar); 'Loring and Wyle'; 'Quetico'; 'The Persistent Seed'; 'Canada'; 'Festival' (Expo 70 Osaka); 'Impressions 1670–1970' (tercentenary Hudson's Bay Co.); 'Volcano' (70 mm Imax); 'The Happy Time' (created film component); 'Toronto the Good' (multi-media 35 mm film and slide presentation); 'A Sense of Humus' (rec'd recognition from Techfilm, Czechoslovakia); 'Rome With Anthony Burgess' (dir., filmed, ed. for Nielsen Ferns Internat.); 'Saskatchewan Land Alive' (Sask.'s Diamond Jubilee 1980); 'Kelly' (feature film) (Famous Players Film Corp., dir.); 'Wilderness' (dir., filmed, ed. 3D 70mm for Science North, Sudbury); U.S.

Pavilion film Expo 86 (70 mm multi-image); 3D Space Film, Chicago Museum of Science and Industry; 'Au Pays du Vent Leger' (3D-70mm for Parc Asterix, Paris, France); solo photographic exhbn., Robert McLaughlin Gall., Oshawa; Latcham Gallery; Major mural photographic exhbn., Royal Candn. Academy of Arts (RCA) at John B. Aird Gallery, Toronto; recipient over 35 Candn. and internat. recognitions; rec'd Ont. Film Inst. Award; R.C.A. Medal for distinguished contrib. to art of film; Centennial Medal 1967; Queen's Silver Jubilee Medal 1977; Member of the Order of Canada 1987; Commemorative Medal, 125th Anniversary of Candn. Confedn.; Hon. Pres., Candn. Cine Amateurs; Toronto Film Soc.; Centre Past Pres., Candn. Centre for Advanced Film Studies; Past-Pres., Royal Candn. Acad. Arts; Past Pres., Dirs. Guild Can.; mem. Candn. Soc. Cinematographers; Candn. Soc. Eds.; Co-founder and Pres., Land Fellowship; Uxbridge Celebration of the Arts, Artistic Past Dir. for Film; Home and Studio: R.R. 3, Uxbridge, Ont. L9P 1R3.

**CHAPMAN, Gerald Robert,** B.Sc., Ph.D.; educator; b. Hackney, Eng. 1 Dec. 1943; s. William John and Ivy Alice (Mould) C.; e. Church Rd. Primary Sch. and Leyton Co. High Sch. London, Eng. 1962; Univ. of Liverpool B.Sc. 1965, Ph.D. 1969; m. Jean d. Ben and Ada Gibson 2 July 1966; children: Nicola Helen, Peter William; PROF. OF MATH. AND STATS., UNIV. OF GUELPH 1989– ; Founding Partner and Chief Exec. Offr. Deduction and Inference (math. & stats. cons.); Dir. and Secy.-Treas. Maximus Inc.; joined present Univ. 1969, Co-Founder 1985 and Clinic Co-ord. Math. and Stats. Clinic 1987–92; recipient Couch Trophy and UK State Scholarship 1962; Ronald Hudson Prize for Geom. 1965; Distinguished Prof., Coll. of Physical and Engineering Sci., Univ. of Guelph 1991; author numerous papers pure and applied math.; mem. Candn. Math. Soc.; Candn. Applied Math. Soc.; Soc. Ind. & Applied Math.; Operations Rsch. Soc. Am.; recreations: walking, gardening, winemaking; Club: Chateau Schoch Wine Collective; Home: 56 Old Colony Trail, Guelph, Ont. N1G 4A9; Office: Guelph, Ont. N1G 2W1.

**CHAPMAN, Kenneth Ross,** M.D., M.Sc., FRCPC, FACP, FCCP; physician, university professor; b. Montreal, Que. 3 July 1953; s. Harold Frank and Helen Frances (Emberly) C.; e. Trinity Coll., Univ. of Toronto 1971–73; Fac. of Med., Univ. of Toronto M.D. 1973–77; Sch. of Grad. Studies, Inst. of Med. Sci., U. of T. M.Sc. 1983; m. Jane Carol d. Isabel and Louis Campbell 30 Dec. 1981; children: Joshua Kenneth, Gregory Campbell; DIR., THE ASTHMA CENTRE OF THE TORONTO HOSPITAL 1992– ; Asst. Prof. of Med., Case Western Reserve Univ. 1984–86; Fac. of Med., Univ. of Toronto 1986–92; Assoc. Prof. of Medicine, Univ. of Toronto 1992– ; Acting Dir., The Asthma Centre of the Toronto Hosp. 1991–92; Co-Chrmn., Collaborative Respiratory Rsch. Prog. 1990– ; Dir., Pulmonary Function Lab., Toronto Hosp., Western Site 1991– ; Civil Aviation Med. Examiner 1989– ; Med. Advr., Assistive Devices Prog., Ont. Min. of Health 1988– ; FACP 1984; Dr. H. Beatty Scholarship 1985–86; Fellow, Med. Rsch. Counc. of Can. 1982–85; Burnside Memorial Scholarship, Trinity Coll. 1971–73; Mem. & Fellow, Am. Coll. of Physicians 1979– ; Mem., Am. Physiol. Soc. 1982– ; Am. Thoracic Soc. 1979– ; Chrmn., Ed. Bd., 'Respirology' 1990– ; Ed. Bd., 'Lung and Respiration' 1991– ; recreations: running, squash, aviation; club: Mayfair Lakeshore Racquet; Home: 83 Balsam Ave., Toronto, Ont. M4E 3B8; Office: Suite 4-011 ECW, 399 Bathurst St., Toronto, Ont. M5T 2S8.

**CHAPMAN, Ross Alexander,** B.S.A., M.Sc., Ph.D., D.Sc., F.C.I.C.; government administrator; b. Oak Lake, Man. 10 Dec. 1913; s. Frank Richards and Helen Elizabeth (Ross) C.; e. Galt Coll. Inst. (Ont.), 1933; Ont. Agric. Coll., B.S.A. 1940; Macdonald Coll., McGill Univ., M.Sc. 1941, Ph.D. 1944; Univ. of Guelph, D.Sc. 1971; m. Jean McBain Currie, 7 July 1942; children: Karen Bickell, Grierson Currie PRIVATE CONSULTANT TO INTERNATIONAL AND GOVERNMENT AGENCIES on food and drug control since 1974; Asst. Prof. of Chem., Macdonald Coll., McGill Univ., 1944–48; Chief, Food Chem. Div., Food & Drug Directorate, 1948–55 and 1957–58; Dir., Research Labs., 1958–63; Asst. Dir.-Gen. (Foods), 1963–65; Asst. Depy. Min. (Food and Drugs), 1965–71; Special Adviser to Depy. Min. (Health) 1971–72; Dir.-Gen., Internat. Health Services 1972–73; Scientist, Food additives, WHO, Geneva, 1955–57; apptd. mem. Panel of Experts on Food Additives, WHO, 1958; mem. Expert Comte. on Food Additives, Rome, 1959; mem. Candn. Del. to Conf. on Food Standards, Geneva, 1962; Codex Alimentarius Comn., Head Candn. Del., Rome, 1963 and mem. Candn. Del., Geneva, 1964; Chrmn., Codex Comn. on Food Labelling, Ottawa, 1965 and 1966; mem. Panel on Food Safety, White House Conf. on Food, Nutrition & Health, 1969; Head, Candn. Del., U.N. Comn. on Narcotic Drugs Special Sessions, 1970 and to 24th regular session, 1971; Alternate rep. and Acting Head. Candn. Del. to U.N. Conf. to Adopt Protocol on Psychotropic Substances, Vienna, 1971; consultant, to World Health Organization, Geneva 1974–75; to South Pacific Comn. Noumea, New Caledonia 1975–76; to Pan Amer. Health Organization, Washington, D.C. 1977–78; to Drug Abuse Policy, White House, Washington, D.C. 1978; to Saudi Arabia, 1979; to Trinidad and Tobago and to Brazil, 1980; Pres., Senior Citizens Council of Ottawa-Carleton 1991–93; rec'd. Internat. Award, Inst. Food Technols., U.S.A., 1959; William J. Eva Award, Candn. Inst. Food Technol., 1969; Hon. D.Sc., Univ. of Guelph, 1971; Underwood-Prescott Mem. Lectureship 1972; mem., Internat. Narcotic Control Bd. 1973–76; author of over 30 scient. publs.; Fellow, Assn. Official Analytical Chems.; recreations: golf, skiing; Home: 655 Richmond Rd., Unit 48, Ottawa, Ont. K2A 3Y3.

**CHAPMAN, Stuart Leslie;** advertising executive; b. Toronto, Ont. 22 Dec. 1933; s. William and Evelyn Hamilton (Webber) C.; e. Parkdale and Humberside Coll. Insts. Toronto; m. Thelma d. Fred and Beatrice Goddard 4 Oct. 1957; children: Kimberly Pyper, Sandra Ferguson, Wendy Moore, Douglas; FOUNDING PARTNER, CHAPMAN MORRIS ADVERTISING LTD. 1966– ; previously in banking and automobile sales; former Sec. Toronto Jr. Bd. Trade; joined Toronto Globe & Mail, Advt. 1958; former Dir. of Advt. Studebaker of Canada Ltd.; former Teacher of Advt. Sheridan Coll., Oakville; Past Dir. and Treas. Inst. Candn. Advt.; Past Pres. Candn. Ind. Advertisers; Charter Pres. Brampton Jaycees; Past Internat. Pres. Studebaker Drivers Club Inc.; Past Pres. Burlington Central Lions Club; Chrmn. City of Burlington Ctte. Adjustment; Past Chrmn., Fed. Govt. Local Adv. Council/Employment; Chrmn., Crime Stoppers of Halton Region; former Vice Pres. Brampton Un. Appeal; former Advt. Chrmn. Hamilton & Dist. Un. Appeal; Past Pres. Burlington P. Cons. Fed. Riding Assn.; Burlington Lions-Optimist Minor Hockey Assn.; former mem. Brampton Recreation Comn.; Assoc. Offr. Royal Hamilton Light Inf.; author: 'Requiem to a Pioneer' 1986; recreations: tennis, skiing, antique cars; Club: Burlington Racquets; Home: 4124 Celia Court, Burlington, Ont. L7L 5L9; Office: 310, 2349 Fairview St., Burlington, Ont. L7R 2E3.

**CHAPMAN, Tony,** B.Comm.; entrepreneur; b. Montreal, Que. 30 June 1956; s. Bryson Elmor and Mae (Bellevance) C.; e. Concordia Univ. B.Comm. 1979; m. Ann Horton 7 June 1984; children: Alexandra, Michaella; FOUNDER & PRESIDENT, CAPITAL C 1992– ; owned advertising agency while attending school 1977–79; worked for Mktg. & Promotion Group 1979–82; Co-Founder & Pres., Communique (Canada's largest communication agency) 1982–92; motivational speaker; competitive sales strategist & marketing cons. to Canada's largest corps.; Former Dir., Technicomp; Mem., Young Pres. Orgn. (Extve. Ctte. 1991, '92; Candn. Univ. 1988, '90); author: 'Selling Solutions Not Stuff' recreations: tennis, golf; clubs: Mayfair; Home: 66 Wrenwood Court, Unionville, Ont. L3A 6H4; Office: 256 Adelaide St. E., Toronto, Ont. M5A 1N1.

**CHAPMAN, Wayne R.,** Q.C., B.C.L.; lawyer; b. Moncton, N.B. 29 Mar. 1943; s. Rae E. and Kathleen M. (McLeod) C.; e. Saint John H.S. 1961; Univ. of N.B. B.C.L. 1967; m. Carol P. d. M. Gerald and Roberta Teed 17 Aug. 1967; one d.: Chere; PARTNER, STEWART, McKELVEY, STIRLING, SCALES (formerly McKelvey Mcaulay Machum & Fairweather) 1970– ; admitted to Bar 1967; joined present firm 1967; Q.C. 1985; specializes in commercial litigation with particular emphasis on construction law; actively involved in health law field; Pres., Candn. Bar Assn. 1990–91; Lectr., Univ. of N.B., Bar Admission Course 1972–79; Mem., Saint John Bd. of Trade; Saint John Law Soc.; Internat. Bar Assn.; Am. Trial Lawyers Assn.; Candn. Maritime Law Assn.; Law Soc. of N.B.; clubs: Union, Rothesay tennis, YM-YWCA; Home: P.O. Box 515, Rothesay, N.B. E0G 2W0; Office: Bux 7289, Stn. A., Saint John, N.B. E2L 4S6.

**CHAPNIK, The Honourable Madam Justice Sandra,** B.A., LL.B.; judge; b. Toronto, Ont. 13 Jan. 1941; d. Saul (dec.) and Ada (Bender) Goodman; e. Forest Hill Collegiate 1959; Univ. of Toronto B.A. 1962; Ont. College of Education, S.S. Teacher's Degree 1963; Osgoode Hall Law Sch. 1976; called to Ont. Bar 1978; m. Dr. Jerry s. the late Lily and Hyman C. 19 June 1962; children: Brian, Randi, Victor, Jason; JUDGE, ONTARIO COURT OF JUSTICE, GENERAL DIVISION 1991– ; Secondary School Teacher 1963–70; Barrister & Solicitor 1978–91; Bar Admission Court Lectr. 1989, '90, '91; Bd. Mem., Osgoode Hall Law Sch. Alumni Assn. 1986– ; Nat. Extve., Candn. Bar Assn. 1990–91; Ont. Extve., 1987–89; Award of Distinguished Service, Candn. Bar Assn. (Ont.) 1990; Award of Distinction 1989; President's Award, Women's Law Assn. 1990; Bd. of Gov., Baycrest Ctr. for Geriatric Care; Bd. of Dir., Holy Blossom Temple; author of one journal article; Home: 17 Nomad Cres., Don Mills, Ont. M3G 1S5; Office: The Court House, 361 University Ave., Toronto, Ont. M5G 1T3.

**CHAPPELL, Duncan,** LL.B., Ph.D.; professor; b. Blandford, Dorset, Eng. 1 Aug. 1939; s. Francis Roy and Dorothy Margaret (Lardner) C.; e. Hobart H.S. 1955; Univ. of Tasmania, B.A. LL.B. (Hons.) 1962; Univ. of Cambridge, Ph.D. 1965; m. Rhonda d. Walter and Edna Moore 10 Apr. 1981; children: Hamish Alastair, Kirstin Fenn; DIR., AUSTRALIAN INST. OF CRIMINOLOGY, Canberra, Australia 1987– ; on leave of absence as Adjunct Prof., Sch. of Criminol., Simon Fraser Univ.; Lectr. then Sr. Lectr., Univ. of Sydney 1965–71; Assoc. Prof., Crim. Justice, State Univ. of N.Y. at Albany 1971–73; Dir., Law & Justice Study Ctr., Battelle Meml. Inst. & Adjunct Assoc. Sociol. Prof., Univ. of Washington 1973–77; Comnr., Australian Law Reform. Comn. 1978–79; Prof., Sch. of Criminol., Simon Fraser Univ. 1980– , Chair 1982–84; Vis. Prof., John Jay Coll. of Crim. Justice 1969–70; La Trobe Univ. 1977–78; Vis. Fellow, Aust. Nat. Police Rsch. Unit 1985; Cons., U.S. Dept. of Justice 1974–76; Law Found. of N.S.W. 1984– ; Adv., Candn. Min. of Justice 1983; Candn. Sentencing Comn. 1985; British Commonwealth Scholar 1962–65; Harkness Fellow 1969; Extve. Ctte. Mem., Am. Soc. of Criminol. 1976–78, 1983–84; Mem., Aust. Acad. of Forensic Sci.; Aust. & N.Z. Soc. of Criminol.; Nat. Orgn. for Victim Assistance (Extve. Bd. 1976–77); World Soc. of Victimol.; Assn. for Candn. Studies; Chrmn., Nat. Ctte. on Violence 1989; Co-Chrmn., Commonwealth Observer Mission to South Africa 1992–93; co-author: 'The Police and the Public in Australia and New Zealand' 1969; 'The Police Use of Deadly Force: Canadian Perspectives' 1985; co-editor: 'The Australian Criminal Justice System' 1972, 1977, 1986, 1993; 'Violence and Criminal Justice' 1975; 'Issues in Criminal Justice Planning' 1975; 'Forcible Rape' 1977, 1978; 'Australian Policing: Contemporary Issues' 1988; 'From Sawdust to Toxic Blobs: A Consideration of Sanctioning Strategies to Combat Pollution in Canada' 1987; 'Australian Violence: Contemporary Perspectives' 1991; Office: 4 Marcus Clarke St., Canberra, ACT, GPO Box 2944, Canberra ACT 2601.

**CHAPUT-ROLLAND, Mme Solange,** O.C. (1975); écrivaine; née Montréal, Qué. 14 mai 1919; f. Emile et Rosalie (Loranger) Chaput; é. Couvent d'Outremont (Qué.); Univ. Sorbonne 1939–40; ép. André Rolland 12 mars 1941; enfants: Suzanne Monange, Claude P.; élue deputé libéral du comté de Prévost à l'assemblie Nationale, Novembre 1979; auteurée 'Dear Enemies' (avec Gwethalyn Graham); 'Mon pays Québec ou le Canada'; 'Québec année Zéro'; 'Une ou deux Sociétés Juste'; 'la Seconde conquête'; 'Les Heures Sauvages'; 'Watergate'; 'Les Maudits Journalistes'; 'Lettres ouvertes à treize personnalités politiques'; 'Une cuisine toute simple' (avec Suzanne Monange); 'Face-to-Face' (avec Gertrude Laing); 'De l'unité à la réalité'; 'Le Mystère Québec'; éditorialiste; journaliste; écrivain politique; modérateur des radio et télévision; mem. de la Commission Pepin-Robarts sur l'unité Canadienne; Conseil de l'Université de Montréal; Cercle des Femmes journalistes; l'Union des Artistes; Comn. sur la capitale nationale 1975; reçu Prix Mem. Award 1971–73 pour ses éditoriaux; Don MacArthur Award 1975 pour ses reportages radiophoniques sur la guerre en Israel; doctorate honorifique en droit, Univ. Queen's 1984.

**CHARBONNEAU, Bernard Pierre,** B.Sc., M.Sc.; air force officer and public servant; aeronautical engineer; b. Montreal, Que. 6 Dec. 1929; s. Philippe and Germaine (Bernard) C.; e. RCAF Dip. Aeronautical Engrg. 1950; Univ. of Montreal B.Sc. Mech.-Elec. Engrg. 1953; Univ. of Michigan M.Sc. Instrumentation Engrg. 1959; children: Pierre, Julie; PRESIDENT, DOBERN CONSULTANTS LTD. 1989– ; Pres. & Chief Oper. Offr., Versatile Vickers Inc. 1984–85; Group Vice-Pres., Marine & Industrial Operations, Versatile Corp. 1985–87; Vice-Pres., Defence Projects, Lavalin Inc. 1987–89; with RCAF 12 yrs. as aeronautical engr.; subsequently joined public service, rising to level of Asst. Depy. Min., Dept. of Supply and Services; other appts. incl.: Dir. Gen. Marine & Industrial Machinery, Dir. Gen. Que. Region, Dir. Gen. Electronics and Data Processing; Nat. Dir. Mgmt. Info. Systems, C.B.C.; Defence Production Attaché, Candn. Embassy, Paris; Dir.: Datatech Systems Ltd.; Past Pres., Candn. Chapter, American Defense Preparedness Assn.; Past Dir. Crown Assets Disposal Corp.;

mem. Assn. of Profl. Engrs. of Ont.; Montreal Beaver Club; recreations: skiing, golf, flying; Club: Rideau (Ottawa); Home: 92E boul. Lac de la Sucrerie, Vendée, Qué. J0T 2T0.

**CHARBONNEAU, Hon. Guy,** B.A.; C.I.B.; C.L.J.; insurance executive; b. Trois-Rivières, Que. 21 June 1922; s. Charles F. and Marie-Rose (Lajoie) C.; e. Primary Schs.; Trois Rivières, Que.; Coll. Jean-de-Brebeuf; Univ. of Montreal, B.A. 1941; McGill Univ., Economics, 1941–42; m. Yolande Bourguignon, 29 Sept. 1972; CHRMN., PRATTE-MORRISSETTE LTEE.; Vice-Chrmn. Adv. Bd., Marsh & McLennan Ltd.; Mem. Bd. of Dirs., VS Services Ltd.; Thomson-CSF Systems Inc.; Pratte-Morrissette Ltée.; Socanav Ltée.; Quebecor Inc.; apptd. Mem. of Senate of Can. 1979; Speaker of the Senate 1984–93; commissioned 1942; joined Les Fusilliers Mont-Royal; Army Intelligence Course, Staff Coll., Kingston, Ont.; promoted Capt. overseas in 1944 and Air Liaison Offr. with French Wing of TAF in N.W. European campaign; mem. Montreal Bd. of Trade; Chambre de commerce de Montréal; Cdn. & Que. Ins. Agents & Brokers Assn.; Comdr., Military and Hospitalier Order of St. Lazarus of Jerusalem; recreations: bridge, golf, theatre arts; Clubs: Laval-sur-le-Lac; Mt. Royal; Home: 2 Westmount Square, Apt. 16–D, Westmount, P.Q. H3Z 2S4; Office: 4150 St. Catherine St. W., Suite 490, Westmount, Que. H3Z 2W8.

**CHARBONNEAU, Hubert,** M.A., Dr.de l'U.(Paris); éducateur; né Montréal, Qué. 2 sept. 1936; f. Léonel et Jeanne (Durand) C.; é. Univ. de Montréal M.A. 1958; Univ. de Paris Diplôme de démographie générale 1960, Dr.de l'U. 1969; ép. Marie-Christiane f. Frédéric et Yvonne Hellot, Clamart, France 4 nov. 1961; enfant: Blandine; Professeur Titulaire, Univ. de Montréal depuis 1976, Professeur depuis 1962; Professeur invité Universidade federale do Parana, Brésil 1978, 1980, 1983; Boursier Killam 1974–77; auteur 'Tourouvre-au-Perche aux XVIIe et XVIIIe siècles: Etude de démographie historique' 1970; 'Vie et mort de nos ancêtres: Etude démographique' 1975; co-éditeur 'Répertoire des actes de baptême, mariage, sépulture et des recensements du Québec ancien' 1980–90 (47 vol.); en collaboration 'Naissance d'une Population: Les Français établis au Canada au XVII$^{e}$ siècle' 1987; membre Société Royale du Can.; Union internationale pour l'étude scientifique de la population; Assn. des démographes du Qué. (prés.-fondateur 1971); Associacão Brasileira de estudos populacionais; Adresse: 19 ave. Robert, Outremont, Qué. H3S 2P1.

**CHARBONNEAU, Pierre W.,** B.A., M.Com.; banker; b. Montreal, Que. 11 Sept. 1944; s. Robert and Rollande B. (Brillon) C.; e. Univ. de Montréal B.A. 1964; Ecole des Hautes Etudes Commerciales M.Com. 1967; Fellow, Inst. Candn. Bankers 1968, Toronto; m. Francine d. Louis G. Bouchard 18 Aug. 1973; children: Yves, Elise; Senior Vice-Pres., Finance, & Chief Financial Officer, Federal Business Development Bank 1989–..; Dir.: Canadian Pencrown Resources Ltd.; joined Toronto Dominion Bank 1967, Money Market Rep. and Cash Mgr. 1971; Fédération du Québec des Caisses Populaires Desjardins, Financial Adv. and Money Market Mgr. 1975; Toronto Dominion Bank, Mgr. Money Market E. Can. 1977, Asst. Mgr. Credit and Supvr. Credit 1978, Mgr. Comm. Devel. & Special Project E. Can. 1979; Asst. Vice Pres. and Treas. present Bank 1981; Vice-Pres. & Treas. 1982–86; Sr. Vice Pres., Finance 1986–89; recreations: squash, tennis, skiing, golf; Clubs: M.A.A.A.; St-Denis; The Country Club (Montreal); Home: 267 Ave. des Vosges, St. Lambert, Qué. J4S 1M1.

**CHARBONNEAU, Yvon,** B.A., L.Ped., M.A.; né Mont-St-Michel, Qué. 11 juillet 1940; f. Leopold et Yvonne (Beauchamp) C.; é. Univ. Laval B.A. 1959, M.A. (science politique) 1980; Univ. de Montréal L.Ped. 1961, M.A. litt. française 1968; PRÉSIDENT, CABINET D'AFFAIRES PUBLIQUES, PREMIER; professeur de français et humanités 1961–69; enseignant-coopérant en Tunisie 1965–67; Prés. Centrale de l'Enseignement du Québec (C.E.Q.) 1970–78 et 1982–88; Pres., Commission d'enquête sur déchets dangereux (BAPE, MENVIQ) 1989–90; Vice Prés., Relations Publiques Environnement, SNC Lavalin 1990–92; Adresse: 1504, 7075 Bl. Gouin est, Montréal, Qué. H1E 5A8.

**CHARD, Rodney D.,** B.Sc.; management consultant; b. Wallasey, Eng. 13 July 1942; s. Robert and Alma C.; e. Westminster C. Sc. Eng. 1960; Hull Univ. Eng. B.Sc. 1963; McGill Univ. Dip. Bus. Adm. 1973; m. Penelope d. Geoffrey and Gay Steel 27 July 1986; two s. Philip, Christopher; PRES., CHARD CONSULTING LTD. Toronto 1991– ; Scientist, National Coal Board, Eng. 1963–65; Ops. Res. Mgr. Esso Petroleum, Eng. 1966–68; Systems Mgr. Bank of Montreal 1969–79, Vice Pres. 1980–82; Vice Pres. Canadian Imperial Bank of Commerce 1983, Sr. Vice Pres. 1986, Exec. Vice Pres. 1988–91; Former Dep. Chrmn. CIBC Mortgage Corp.; Adv. Bank Adm. Inst. (US); Dir. Candn. Payments Assn.; Club: Granite; Home: 125 Baby Point Rd., Toronto, Ont. M6S 2G7.

**CHAREST, Hon. Jean J.,** P.C., M.P., LL.B.; politician; b. Sherbrooke, Qué. 24 June 1958; e. Univ. de Sherbrooke LL.B. 1980; m. Michèle Dionne 21 June 1980; 3 children: Amélie, Antoine, Alexandra; M.P. FOR SHERBROOKE and INTERIM LEADER, PROGRESSIVE CONSERVATIVE PARTY OF CANADA 1993– ; mem. Sherbrooke Legal Aid Office (Criminal Sect.) 1981; Assoc. Beauchemin, Dussault & Charest 1981–84; el. to H. of C. for Sherbrooke 1984; Asst. Depy. Speaker, H. of C. 1984; Min. of State (Youth) 1986–90; Min. of State (Fitness and Amateur Sport) 1988–90; Dep. Gov. Leader in the H. of C. 1989–90; Min. of the Environment 1991–93; Deputy Prime Minister, Min. of Industry, Sci. & Technol. & of Consumer & Corp. Affairs, Min.-Designate, Industry & Science 1993 and Minister responsible for Federal Office Regional Development Québec; Chrmn., Special Ctte. to study the proposed companion resolution to the Meech Lake Accord 1990; mem. Cabinet Cttes. on Priorities and Planning, Economic and Trade Policy; mem. Qué. Bar Assn.; Candn. Bar Assn.; P. Conservative; recreations: skiing, sailing; Office: House of Commons, Ottawa, Ont. K1A 0A6.

**CHARETTE, Luc A.,** B.A., B.Ed., B.A.V.; art gallery director; artist; b. Edmundston, N.B. 19 Aug. 1952; s. Adelard and Jeanet (Pelletier) C.; e. Univ. de Moncton B.A. 1976, B.Ed. 1979, B.A.V. 1985; one s. Christian; DIR. UNIV. DE MONCTON ART GALLERY 1988– ; Asst. Curator Madawaska Museum 1980–87; profl. visual artist since 1975 working mainly in multi media installations; rep. various exhns. Atl. Can. & Que. since 1979; served many regional and nat. juries promotion and advanc. Fine Arts in Can.; cons. visual arts field; seminars visual arts appreciation; author various reviews, papers Acadian Artists French cultural mags.; mem. Candn. Artists Representation; Founding mem. Assn. Artists of Artist-run Centers N.B.; Assn. Internationale pour le développement des industries culturelles dans l'espace francophone; Past Pres., Acadian Professional Artist Assoc.; Mem., N.B. Art Counc. (adv. council for NB govt.); Address: Edifice Clément Cormier, Univ. de Moncton, Moncton, N.B. E1A 3E9.

**CHARLEBOIS, J.C. Yvon,** B.Comm.; retired senior public servant; b. Ottawa, Ont. 12 March 1938; s. Emile Mark and Madeleine (Deslauriers) C.; Ottawa Univ., Carleton Univ., St. Patrick's Coll., B.Comm. 1968; m. Carole d. Emile and Marjory Brousseau 2 May 1959; children: Daniel, Denise, Jo-Anne, André, Natalie; ASSOCIATE, INSTITUTE ON GOVERNANCE; began career in Public Service in Dept. of Nat. Defence 1954; joined Treasury Board 1961; Spec. Asst., Min. of Nat. Revenue & the Pres. of the Treasury Bd. 1965; Unemployment Insur. Comn. 1970; first Extve. Sec./Extve. Dir., Benefits Prog./Insur./Quebec Region, Can. Employment & Immigration Comn. 1977–88; Asst. Dep. Min., Customs Operations Br., Revenue Can. 1988–90; Visiting Asst. Depy. Min., Public Service 2000 Secretariat, Privy Council Office 1990–92; Mem. of the Bd., Chrmn. of the Extve. Ctte., Commission Scolaire Outaouais-Hull 1972–75; recreation: tennis, skiing; Clubs: Le Club Mont Tremblant; Le Country Club Aylmer; Home: 146 Champêtre, Aylmer, Qué. J9H 6W4; Office: 68 Chamberlain Ave., Ottawa, Ont. K1S 1V9.

**CHARLEBOIS, Maurice;** steel industry executive; b. L'Orignal, Ont. 3 Oct. 1930; s. Ernest and Beatrice (Dubois) C.; e. Sir George Williams Coll.; McDonald Coll.; m. Jacqueline Luce d. Armand Bertrand 27 Dec. 1952; children: Lise, Daniel, Andre, Denis, Jean; 8 grandchildren; PRES., M. & J. CONSULTANTS LTD. 1989– ; Constr. worker, E.G.M. Cape Co. 1950; joined Dominion Bridge Co. 1951; Constr. Proj. Supt. 1954–70; Mgr. of Constr., Frankel Steel 1970; Vice-Pres., Constr. 1974; Extve. Vice-Pres., Frankel Steel Constr. Serv. 1976; Vice-Pres., Mfg. & Constr. 1978; Group Vice-Pres., Mfg., Can. & U.S. 1986; Pres. & C.O.O., Frankel Steel Ltd. 1986–88; Vice-Pres., Marshall Steel Ltd. 1988–89; Bd. of Dir., Candn. Inst. of Steel Constr.; Bd. of Gov., Steel Struc. Edn. Found.; Dir., Ont. Erectors Assn. Inc.; recreations: golf, tennis; clubs: Palm-Aire Golf & Country; North Halton Golf & Country; Address: 8 Erinwood Dr., Erin, Ont. N0B 1T0 and 5651 Country Lakes Dr., Sarasota, Florida 34243 U.S.A.

**CHARLES, The Hon. Maurice Alexander,** LL.B.; judge; b. Georgetown, Guyana 6 Aug. 1920; s. James Alexander and Mabel Rosamund (Thorne) C.; e. Law Soc. of Engl., Solicitor; Univ. of London, Engl. LL.B. 1952; Gray's Inn, London, Engl. Barrister at Law; Law Soc. of Upper Can., Barrister at Law and Solicitor 1969; m. Dr. Winifred Mary d. David and Winifred Clarice van der Ross 2 Sept. 1983; children: Dr. Richard, Lorraine Elise, Maureen Alexandra; PROVINCIAL COURT JUDGE CRIMINAL DIV. 1969– ; practised as a Solicitor 1945–49; apptd. Magistrate, Her Maj. Overseas Judicial Services, Guyana 1949; trans. to Ghana as Magistrate 1956; Sr. Magistrate 1957; Judge, Supreme Ct. of Ghana 1959; ret. as most Sr. High Ct. Judge of Ghana 1967; came to Can. 1967; apptd. Prov. Judge 1969; Chrmn. Educ. Ctte. of Prov. Judges; mem. Exec., Prov. Judges Assn.; recreations: tennis, bridge; Club: Provincial Judges Assn.; Home: 28 Mellowood Dr., Toronto, Ont.; Office: 60 Queen St. W., Toronto, Ont. M5H 2M4.

**CHARLES, Ronald Downing,** B.Sc.A., M.B.A.; executive recruitment consultant; b. Vancouver, B.C. 24 June 1945; s. Eric Downing and Barbara Gordon (Selwood) C.; e. Univ. of B.C., B.Sc.A. 1969; Univ. of W. Ont. M.B.A. 1971; m. Kristina 9 Sept. 1970; two s. Christopher, Matthew; PARTNER & DIR., THE CALDWELL PARTNERS INTERNATIONAL 1987– ; Mkt. Rsch. Analyst Canadian Breweries and Jr. Product Mgr. Facelle Ltd. prior 1972; Acct. Exec., Dist. Mgr., Central Regional Mgr., Gen. Mgr. Xerox Learning Systems Inc. 1972–82; Dir. of Mktg. and Sr. Prin. Hay Management Consultants 1982–84; Vice-Pres., Mktg. & Bus. Devel. The Hume Group Inc. (Publishing Div.) 1984–87; recipient Investors Syndicate Inc. Bursary 1969; Nabob Foods Ltd. and B.C. Govt. Scholarships; recreations: riding, skiing, tennis; Club: Parkview; Home: 40 Havenbrook Blvd., Willowdale, Ont. M2J 1A5; Office: 64 Prince Arthur Ave., Toronto, Ont. M5R 1B4.

**CHARLES, William Bruce,** M.D., F.R.C.P.(C) (1946); F.A.C.P. (1967); physician; b. Toronto, Ont. 23 Nov. 1913; e. Univ. of Toronto, M.D. 1938; Diplomate, Am. Bd. of Internal Med., 1948; Consultant Staff, Toronto East Gen. Hosp.; Emeritus Assoc. Prof., Dept. of Med., Univ. of Toronto; served in 2nd World War, 1941–46; Major, No. 2 Candn. Gen. Hosp., Eng. and N.W. Europe; United Church; Home: 115 Rochester Ave., Toronto, Ont. M4N 1N9.

**CHARLES, William H.R.,** B.A., LL.M.; educator; b. Montreal, Que. 3 Sept. 1927; s. William Arthur and Phyllis (Beck) C.; e. Sir George Williams Univ. B.A. 1949; Dalhousie Univ. LL.B. 1958; Harvard Law Sch. LL.M. 1960; Univ. of Mich. LL.M. 1968; m. Dorine d. Ray and Marguerite Clark 1958; children: Susan, Timothy, Catherine, Christopher; WELDON PROFESSOR OF LAW, DALHOUSIE UNIVERSITY 1968– ; called to Bar of Alta. 1959; apptd. Q.C. 1983; Asst. Prof. of Law present Univ. 1960, Assoc. Prof. 1964, Prof. 1968, Secy. of Faculty 1963–65, Assoc. Dean 1978–79, Dean of Law 1979–85; recipient Ford Foundation Teaching Scholarship 1959; mem. N.S. Law Reform Comn.; Uniform Law Conf. Can.; Bar of N.S., Bar of Alta.; Trustee, N.S. Law Foundation Scholarship Comte.; Dalhousie Law Sch. Foundation; author 'Handbook on Assessment of Damages' 1982; contrib. 'Water Law in the Atlantic Provinces' 1968; recreations: hockey, skating, flying; Home: 1735 Beech St., Halifax, N.S. B3H 4B7; Office: Weldon Law Bldg., University Ave., Halifax, N.S. B3H 3J5.

**CHARLICK, Douglas John,** B.A., C.A.; chartered accountant; b. London, Eng. 9 July 1948; s. Frederick and Eileen Veronica (Wallace) C.; e. Cray Valley Sch. Sidcup, Kent; Univ. of Leeds Sch. of Econ. Studies B.A. 1969; m. Linda d. George Edward and Gladys Elizabeth Birch 28 Dec. 1974; children: Andrew John, Laura Elizabeth, James Douglas; PARTNER, CORPORATE FINANCE GROUP, KPMG PEAT MARWICK, London, Eng. 1990– ; articled with Peat Marwick, London, Eng. 1969–72, trans. to Nassau, Bahamas office 1972–75, joined Toronto office as mem. Bus. Investigations Practice 1975, Partner 1980, Partner-in-Charge Bus. Investigations Practice Hamilton 1983–86; Partner, Corporate Finance Group, KPMG Peat Marwick Thorne, Toronto, 1986–90; author various articles; Pres. Ont. Insolvency Assn. 1985–86; Dir. Candn. Insolvency Assn. 1984–86; Fellow, Inst. C.A.'s Eng. & Wales; mem. Inst. C.A.'s Ont. mem. Candn. Assoc. for Corp. Growth; recreations: travel, reading, sports; Home: 4 Amblecote, Fairacres, Cobham, Surrey, England KT11 2JP; Office: 8 Salisbury Square, London, England EC4Y 8BB.

**CHARLTON, Brian Albert,** M.P.P.; politician; b. Hamilton, Ont. 22 May 1947; s. John and Jean Isabel (Smith) C.; e. Hill Park S.S.; Queen's Univ., Property Assessment; m. Christine d. Rolf and Marianne Happel

16 May 1992; one d.: Jennifer; GOVERNMENT HOUSE LEADER & CHAIR OF MANAGEMENT BOARD OF CABINET, GOVT. OF ONT. 1993– ; Property Assessor, Ont. Govt. (Pres. of Local 222 OPSEU) 1968–77; 1st elected as M.P.P. for Hamilton Mountain 1977; Opposition Critic for Energy, Envir. & Revenue 1977–90; Parly. Asst. to Min. of Energy 1990; Min. of Financial Institutions 1991; also Min. of Energy 1992; Mem., New Democratic Party 1961– ; recreation: golf; Office: 12th fl., Ferguson Block, 77 Wellesley St. W., Toronto, Ont. M7A 1N3; alternate address: Govt. House Leader's Office, Room 381, Main Legislative Bldg., Queen's Park, Toronto, Ont. M7A 1A1.

**CHARLWOOD, U. Gary;** travel and realty franchising executive; b. Schoeningen, W. Germany 25 Dec. 1941; s. Albert and Ruth Ingeborg (Waltraud) C.; e. Selhurst Sch.; Heath Clark (hons.); Southampton Univ.; Am. Mngt. Pres. Assoc., grad.; children: Christopher, Martin; FOUNDER, CHRMN. OF THE BOARD & C.E.O., UNIGLOBE TRAVEL (INTERNAT.) INC. 1979– ; & CHRMN. OF THE BD. & C.E.O. CENTURY 21 CAN. 1974– ; tour guide in Austria; emigrated to Can. 1966; Sales Mgr., Independent travel agency; Passenger Agent, Western Airlines; middle mngt. post 1970; Dir., Consumer Affairs, Candn. Pacific Airlines; 50% Owner, Hunt Realty Ltd. 1972; Chrmn. & Chief Extve. Offr., Charlwood Pacific Group Canada's largest operator of franchises with 1200 outlets, 12,000 support staff; Dir./Cons., Widers Cider Ltd.; Outstanding Contrib. to Franchising award, Internat. Franchise Assn.; 1991 Entrepreneur of the Year Award, Internat. Franchise Assn.; '1993 Mktg. Exec. of the Year,' Sales & Mktg. Execs. of Vancouver; Dir., Univ. of B.C. Scholarship Found.; Charlwood Scholarship Fund, Dept. of Comm. & Real Estate; Dir., Council for Candn. Unity; Mem., ASTA, ACTA, IFA, CFA, Candn. Real Estate Assn.; Nat. Assn. of Realtors; Vanc. Bd. of Trade; German/Can. Bus. Assn.; Can./German C. of Industry & C.; German Fellowship Fund; Sovereign Order of St. John of Jerusalem, Grand Priory of Am.; Am. Mngt. Assn., Pres. Div.; recreations: marathon running, linguist, tennis, mountain climbing, reading, percussion instruments; club: Hollyburn Country; Office: 1199 W. Pender St., #900, Vancouver, B.C. V6E 2R1.

**CHARPENTIER, Fulgence,** M.B.E. (1944), C.M. (1978); b. Ste. Anne de Prescott, Ont. 29 June 1897; e. Classical Coll., Joliette, P.Q.; Laval Univ., B.A. 1917; Osgoode Hall, Toronto, 1919; m. Louise Dionne, 1934; joined Department of External Affairs, 1947; Adviser, UNO Conference, Paris, 1948; Candn. Delegate, UNESCO Fourth Session, Paris, 1949; Information Officer, Canadian Embassy, Paris, 1948–53; Adviser, UNO Conf., Paris, 1951; Del., 8th UNESCO Conf., Montevideo, 1954; Chargé d'Affaires, Candn. Embassy, Uruguay, 1953–56; Brazil, 1956–57 and at Haiti, 1957–60; Ambassador to Cameroun, Gabon, Chad, Congo (Brazzaville) and Central African Republic 1962–1965; apptd. Asst. to the Commr.-Gen. Candn. World Exhn., Montreal 1967; apptd. Asst. Editor-in-Chief 'Le Droit' 1968; Pres., L'Alliance Française; formerly Parlty. Corr., 'Le Droit' Ottawa; later with 'La Presse' Montreal; mem., Parlty. Press Gallery (Pres. 1926); Private Secy., Hon. Fernand Rinfret 1926–30; Chief French Journals, H. of C. 1936–47; apptd. Chief Press Censor 1940; Asst. Dir. of Censorship 1943, Dir. 1944–45; Alderman, Ottawa 1929–30; Controller there 1931–35; defeated cand. for Mayor 1935; served in World War with C.E.F. 1918; author 'Le Mirage Américain' 1934; 'Les Patriotes' (drama) 1938; editorialist, 'Le Droit' Ottawa; Bailli national Confrérie Chaîne des Rôtisseurs; awarded Confederation Medal and several foreign orders; King's Coronation Medal; R. Catholic; Home: 42 Southern Drive, Ottawa, Ont. K1S 0P6; Office: Le Droit, 47 Clarence St., Ottawa, Ont. K1N 9K1.

**CHARRON, André,** C.M., Q.C., B.A., LL.L.; b. Montreal, Que. 10 Dec. 1923; s. Dr. Ernest, D.D.S., D.S.C., LL.L. and Antoinette (Champagne) C.; e. Collège de Montréal, 1936–42; Collège Ste-Marie, B.A. 1942–44; Univ. of Montréal, LL.L. 1944–47; Q.C. 1964; m. Louise d. Berthold Mongeau 14 June 1956; children: André, Caroline, Guy-Philippe, Fannie; Vice Chrmn. of the Bd.: Industrial-Alliance Life Ins. Co.; The North West Life Assurance Co. of Can.; Dir.: Bell Canada; Talvest Management Fund Inc.; T.A.L. Investment Counsel Ltd.; Eagle Lumber Co. Ltd.; Lallemand Inc.; I.S.T. Group Inc.; The National Life Assurance Co. of Can.; Industrial-Alliance Life Mngmt. Corp.; Past Chrmn.: National Ctte., Investment Dealers Assn. of Can.; Governing Ctte., Montreal Stock Exchange; Legal firms: Brais, Campbell & Assocs. 1947–48; André Charron 1948–58; Charron & Mercier 1958–63; Mem. of the Order of Canada 1983; Doctorate Honoris Causa, Univ. du Québec à Montréal; R. Catholic; Clubs: Mount Royal; Mount Bruno Golf; St.-Denis; Home: 2333 Sherbrooke St. W., Apt. #1003, Montréal, Qué. H3H 2T6; Office: 2000 McGill Coll. Ave., Suite 2300, Montréal, Qué. H3A 3J1.

**CHARRON, Guy,** B.A., C.A.; chartered accountant; b. St.-Jerome, Que. 13 July 1956; s. Gerard and Laurette C.; e. Univ. of Sherbrooke B.A. 1979; C.A. 1982; m. Luce Charbonneau 20 Dec. 1979; children: Mathieu, Alexandre; PRESIDENT & CHIEF OPERATING OFFICER, LES BOUTIQUES SAN FRANCISCO INC. 1992– ; various positions ending as Dir. Samson Belair Deloitte Touche (Audit Dept.) 1979–87; Asst. to the Pres., Les Boutiques San Francisco Inc. 1988–89; Extve. Vice-Pres. 1990–91; Dir., Les Boutiques San Francisco Inc. (Public Cie); Les Boutiques Victoire Delage, Inc.; Les Boutiques West Coast Inc.; Taboo Design (1989) Inc.; Les Boutiques Les Ailes de la Mode Inc.; Vice-Pres. Finance, Assn. of Grads in Admin., Univ. of Sherbrooke; Chair, Omer De Serres; recreations: golfing, sking; Home: 2775 Place des Tourterelles, Laval, Que. H7Z 3V1; Office: 50 De Lauzon St., Boucherville, Que. J4B 1E6.

**CHARRON, Hon. Madam Justice Louise,** B.A., LL.B.; judge; b. Sturgeon Falls, Ont. 2 Mar. 1951; d. Lucien and Jeanne (Sauvé) C.; e. primary & secondary edn. in Sturgeon Falls; Carleton Univ., B.A. 1972; Univ. of Ottawa, LL.B. 1975; m. William s. William and Agnes Blake 31 Dec. 1984; one s.: Gabriel Poliquin; two stepsons: Michael and Steven Blake; JUDGE OF THE ONTARIO COURT OF JUSTICE (GEN. DIV.) 1990– ; called to Ont. Bar 1977; private law practice, Lalonde & Chartrand 1977–80; Asst. Crown Attorney, Judicial Dist. of Ottawa-Carleton 1980–85; Asst. Prof., Fac. of Law, Univ. of Ottawa 1985–88; District Court Judge & Local Judge of the High Court of Ont. 1988–90; Justice of the Ont. Court of Justice (Gen. Div.) 1990– ; mem., Assn. des juristes d'expression française de l'Ont.; co-author: 'Canadian Criminal Jury Trials' 1989; Office: 161 Elgin St., Ottawa, Ont. K2P 2K1.

**CHARTIER, Marcel,** B.A., LL.L.; lawyer, commission executive; b. Becancour, Que. 29 Oct. 1930; s. Donat and Annette (Verville) C.; e. Laval Univ. B.A. 1951, LL.L. 1957; Que. Bar Exam 1958; m. Marielle d. Hortense and Léon Méthot 30 May 1959; children: Suzanne, Marie, Eric, Lucie; COMNR., CANDN. PENSION COMN. 1985– ; general law practice in civil & crim. law, transp., labour arbitration, Trois-Rivières 1959–85; Mem., Candn. Bar Assn. (Ctte. for Appts. of Federal Judges 1985–86); Pres., Trois-Rivières Dist. Bar 1976–77; Mem., Gen. Counc., Prov. of Que. Bar several years; Mem., Que. Essential Serv. Counc.; Que. Tourism Counc. 1974–76; Conf. of Arbitrators of Que.; Arbitrator (Labour Law) 1966– ; Coroner 1966–70; Vice-Pres., Nat. Y.P.C. 1957–58; recreations: navigation, antique cars, cabinet work; clubs: W.B.C.C.I., Antique Cars of Que.; Marina de Trois-Rivières; Home: 55 Stratford Rd., Southport, P.E.I. C1A 7B9; Office: 161 Grafton St., P.O. Box 9900, Charlottetown, P.E.I. C1A 8V6.

**CHARTRAND, Alain;** réalisateur (cinéma et télévision); né. Montréal, Qué. 1 fév. 1946; f. Michel et Simonne (Monet-Chartrand) C.; é. Coll. de Longueuil 1963; Conservatoire de musique 1967; une f.: Marie; réalisations: 'Le Jardin d'Anna' 16 mm 80' (Prix Hydro-Qué, Festival du cinéma international en Abitibi) 1992, 'Un nuit à l'école' 16 mm 50' (Moniteur d'Or, Festival d'Umbria Fiction, Italie; Prix Rocky, Festival de Banff; Prix Qué.-Alta. innovation télévision) 1991; 'Montréal Ville ouverte' serie TV 13 x 60 1991; 'Ding et Dong, le film' 35 mm 95' (Golden Reel (Génie Award); Prix accueil du Public, Fest. de Baie-Comeau) 1990; 'Des amis pour La vie' 16 mm 80' 1988; mem., AQRRTC; Acad. du cinéma et de la TV; INIS; Cinémathèque québécoise; SACD; SCAM; SGDL; auteur: 'Le métier d'assistant réalisateur au cinéma' 1990; résidence: 205 Ch. North Hatley, Katevale, Que. J0B 1W0; bureau: Lino Productions Inc., 256 Square St-Louis, Montréal, Qué. H2X 1A3.

**CHARTRAND, Guy;** transportation executive; b. Montreal, Que. 15 Mar. 1946; s. Armand and Lucille (Biron) C.; e. Ecole Secondaire 'Le Plateau,' Montreal Dip. 1964; div.; children: Isabelle; Candidate, Election 1993, Federal Liberal Party, Longueuil Riding; Postal Clerk 1966–77; Supr. Post Office System 1977; President, Quebec Chapter, Transport 2000 Canada 1978–93 (Nat. Pres. 1980–85); Mem., Transportation Equipment Advisory Group on Internat. Trade, Dept. of External Affairs, Ottawa 1991–93; author several articles on transportation in 'Le Devoir'; Dir. Le Sommet Populaire; Pres. St. Lawrence Valley Ry. Soc. 1973–78; mem. Adv. Ctte. Via Rail Que. 1978–87; Le Groupe de Travail sur L'Avenir de L'Industrie de L'autobus au Que. 1982–84; Le Regroupement des Usagers du Transport Adapte de la C.T.C.U.M. 1980– ; Transp. Ctte., City of St. Hubert 1981–84; co-founder Post Office Employees Weeks, Candn. Postal System 1981; mem. Transp. Ctte., Montreal Citizen Movement; has worked for improvement of publ. transit and passenger rail system throughout Can. since 1978; recreation: fishing; Home: 132 Provence St., Ville Ile Perrot, Que. J7V 8S4.

**CHARTRAND, Luc;** journaliste; né Montréal, Qué. 3 septembre 1954; f. Roger et Judith (Lavoie) C.; ép. Chantal f. Wilfrid et Mariette (Gauthier) Gélineau-Poulin; une f. Sarah; journaliste indépendant de 1977 à 1982; A collaboré à différentes publications dont. 'Perspectives,' 'Châtelaine,' 'L'actualité,' 'Québec science'; De 1982 à 1986 a été journaliste au magazine radiophonique 'Aujourd'hui la science' de Radio Can.; De 1986 à 1987 a été journaliste a l'émission télévisée 'Contrechamp' de Radio Can.; journaliste indépendent de 1987 à 1989; journaliste à 'l'actualité' depuis 1989; récipiendaire de 3 prix de journalisme radiophonique (2 fois Johnson & Johnson 1984, 1985, 1 fois Bell Northern 1983) et plusiers prix en presse écrite dont trois 'prix d'Excellence' (1978, 1989 et 1990) de la Fondation des prix du magazine canadien, le prix Elanco 1981, et le prix du 'Texte politique de l'année' (1991) de l'Association Québécoise des Éditeurs de Magazines (AQEM); bourse de journalisme de la Fondation Asie-Pacifique du Can. 1987; co-auteur (avec Raymond Duchesne, Yves Gingras) 'Histoire des Sciences au Québec' 1988; Adresse: 6669 de Normanville, Montréal, Qué. H2S 2B8.

**CHARTRAND, Paul L.A.H.,** B.A., LL.B., (Hons.) LL.M.; university professor; b. St Laurent, Man. 27 July 1943; s. Aimé Joseph and Antoinette (Bouvier) C.; e. Manitoba Teachers College, Teach. Cert. 1964; Univ. of Winnipeg B.A. 1972; Queensland Univ. of Technol. (Australia) LL.B. (Hons.) 1980; Univ. of Saksatchewan LL.M. 1988; m. Diane E. d. Herbert and Leila Plowman 17 April 1977; children: Lisa, Daniel, Leila; ASSOC. PROF., DEPT. OF NATIVE STUDIES, UNIV. OF MANITOBA; Manitoba School Teacher 10 years; Law Teacher, Univ. of Queensland; Dept. Head & Asst. Prof. 1983; lectured and pub. widely on native law & policy issues; Mem., Fed. Royal Comn. on Aboriginal Peoples 1991; Consultant on aboriginal constitutional, legal & policy issues to various govt. & non-govt. agencies incl. Métis Nat. Council, Man. Métis Fed., Four Directions Council & Law Reform Comn. of Canada; Mem., Indigenous Bar Assn. (Bd. Mem. 1989–91); Candn. Bar Assn.; Candn. Indian/Native Studies Assn. 1985–90; Affiliate Mem., Man. Bar Assn.; author: 'Manitoba's Métis Settlement Scheme of 1870' 1991 and many articles; recreations: golf, ice hockey, semi-pro & amateur baseball until 1990 incl. nat. championships in Can. & Australia; pitched for Nat. Bronze Medal Sask. Team 1983; Home: 1576 Prairie St., Victoria, B.C. V8N 2L3.

**CHARUEST, Jacques Louis,** B.Ps., M.Ps.; consultant; b. Montreal, Que. 9 Sept. 1954; s. Louis Edouard and Claire (Gélineau) C.; e. Univ. de Sherbrooke B.Ps. 1977, M.Ps. 1978; m. Liliane d. Lucien and Rosa Grégoire 2 Dec. 1978; children: Etienne, Vincent, Evelyne; PRINCIPAL, WILLIAM M. MERCER LIMITED 1987– ; (areas of practice: H.R. Devel., Organ. Devel., Post-Merger Integration, Extve. Team-Bldg.); Training Offr., Téléglobe Can. 1978–80; Mgr., Manpower Planning, The CSL Group 1980–83; Mgr. & Dir., H.R. Devel., Dominion Textile 1983–87; Lectr., Univ. de Sherbrooke 1984–87; certified by Ctr. for Applications of Psychol. Type, Inc. as Myers-Briggs Analyst 1989– ; Mem., La Corp. Prof. des Psychologues du Qué.; Home: 7935, Nantes, Brossard, Que. J4Y 2E3; Office: 600 de Maisonneuve Blvd. W., Ste. 1100, Montreal, Que. H3A 3J4.

**CHARYK, Joseph Vincent,** Ph.D., LL.D.; executive; b. Canmore, Alta. 9 Sept. 1920; s. late John and Anna (Dorosh) C.; e. St. Patrick's High Sch., Lethbridge, Alta., 1938; Univ. of Alta., B.Sc. in Engineering Physics, 1942, LL.D. 1964; Cal. Inst. of Technol., M.S. 1943, Ph.D. 1946; D.Engineering (Hon.) U. Bologna, 1974; m. Edwina Elizabeth, d. late William Rhodes, Aug. 1945; children: William R., J. John, Christopher E., Diane E.; CHRMN. EMERITUS, C.S. DRAPER LABORATORY INC. 1991– ; (Dir. 1980–91, Chrmn. 1987–90); Jet Propulsion Lab., Cal. Inst. of Technol. 1943–46; Instr. in Aeronautics at Inst. 1945–46; Asst. Prof. of Aeronautics, Princeton Univ. 1946–49; Assoc. Prof. (assisting in estb. of Guggenheim Jet Propulsion Center, Forrestal Research Center of Univ.) 1949–55; Dir. Aerophysics & Chem. Lab., Missile Systems Div., Lockheed Aircraft Corp. 1955–56; Dir. of Missile Technol. Lab. and later Gen. Mgr. of Space Technol. Div., Aeronutronic Systems (subsidiary Ford Motor Co.) 1958–59; Chief Scientist, U.S. Air Force and later Asst. Secy. for Research & Devel. 1959–60; Under Secy. of Air Force 1960–63; Dir., COMSAT Corp. 1963–93; Pres. & Dir. 1963–79; Pres., C.E.O. & Dir., 1979–83; Chrmn., C.E.O. & Dir. 1983–85; rec'd Nat. Medal of Technology 1987; rec'd Arthur C. Clarke Award 1992; rec'd Distinguished Alumni Award, Univ. of Alta. 1994; Fellow, Am. Inst. Aeronautics & Astronautics; mem., Nat'l Acad. Engring; Internat. Acad. Astronautics; National Space Club; Fellow, Inst. Elect. & Electronic Engrs.; Sigma Xi; recreations: golf, tennis, photography; Clubs: Burning Tree; Chevy Chase; Metropolitan Club; Gulfstream; Home: 790 Andrews Ave. (A303), Delray Beach, FL; Office: 6560 Rock Spring Dr., Bethesda, MD 20817-1146.

**CHASTON, John G.**; investment dealer; b. Calgary, Alta. 5 March 1915; s. Leon Christopher and Mrs. (Greer) C.; e. W. Can. High Sch., Calgary; children: John Lionel, Margaret Elizabeth, Christina Leone, Martha Jane; SECY., CAPITAL WEST CORP.; Dir., Pemberton Houston Willoughby Inc.; Secy.-Treas., Pemberton & Son Vancouver Ltd. 1946, Dir. 1952, Vice Pres. 1966; Pres. Pemberton Securities Ltd. 1970, Chrmn. 1975; Hon. Chrmn., Pemberton Houston Willoughby 1984–89; served with R.C.A. and Royal Cdn. Ordnance Corps during World War II; rank Lt. on discharge; mem. Inst. C.A.'s B.C.; Anglican; recreation: golf; Clubs: Capilano Golf & Country, The Vancouver, Royal and Ancient Golf (St. Andrews); Home: 2866 Bellevue, W. Vancouver, B.C. V7J 1E8.

**CHATILLON, Claude**, B.A., L.P.H.; diplomate; né à Ottawa, 29 déc. 1917; fils William et Eugénie (Poulin) C.; é. Univ. d'Ottawa, B.A. BPH (1940), LPH (1941); m. Simone Boutin, 24 jan. 1948; enfants; Pierre-Yves, Elizabeth, Annick; Vice Consul, New York 1946; Deuxième Secrétaire, Ambassade du Canada, New Delhi, fév. 1948; Ottawa hdgrs. mars 1950; Deux. Secrétaire Paris, nov. 1953 et Premier juillet 1955; Coll. de la Défence nat., Kingston, Ont. sept. 1956; Ottawa, août 1957 (Dir. de l'Information – Min. des Affaires Extérieures); Consul, Seattle, mars 1959, Boston 1962; Conseiller, Ambassade du Can., Madrid et Rabat 1956; Ottawa sept. 1970 (Dir. des affaires consulaires); Dir. de la Politique consulaire nov. 1972; Ambassadeur au Cameroun, Gabon, R.C.A. et Tcahd, depuis sept. 1975 à juil. 1978; rep. du Ministère au Comité consultatif de Statut de Réfugié 1978– dec. 1982; Ret.; vol. armée canadienne 1942 (soldat), service officier au Royaume-Uni, Afrique du Nord, Sicile, Italie; démob. en 1943 (lieut.); mem. Assn. des anciens de l'Univ. d'Ottawa; Assn. du Royal 22e Régt.; Canadian Writers Found.; Assoc. des Auteurs de l'Ontario; publication: 'Carnets de Guerre' 1987; prix littéraire 'Le Droit' 1988; Catholique R.; intérêts particuliers: peinture, pêche, écriture.

**CHATTOE, John B.**, M.A.Sc.; information systems executive; b. Toronto, Ont. 10 Jan. 1940; s. Clive Harcourt and Margaret Nathalie (McMinn) C.; e. Univ. of Toronto B.A.Sc. 1964, M.A.Sc. 1970; m. Victoria d. George and Francis Sainsbury 12 May 1976; children: Alan, David, Catherine Tassie, Jim Tassie (dec.); PRESIDENT, INFORMATION TECHNOLOGY RESEARCH CENTRE 1992– ; Mgr. Systems Eng. Group Control Data Corp. 1970, Prog. Mgr. 1974, Dir. Ind. Systems 1976–77; Dir. Network Devel. Bell-Northern Research Ltd. 1978–80; Gen. Mgr. Data Networks Div. Northern Telecom Canada Ltd. 1980, Asst. Vice Pres. ISDN Introduction 1986, Asst. Vice Pres. Customer Sales/Mktg. Services 1987–90, Vice Pres. Mktg. 1990–91, Vice Pres. New Bus. Dev. 1991–92; recipient NRC Scholarship grad. studies 1968–69; mem. Assn. Profl. Engs. Prov. Ont.; Optimist Club Oakville; Home: 462 Carlton Dr., Oakville, Ont. L6J 5X3; Office: 2920 Matheson Blvd. E., Mississauga, Ont. L4W 4M7.

**CHATWIN, Leonard William**, B.A.; Canadian public service; retired; b. Vancouver, B.C. 22 Apr. 1913; s. late Henry William and Annie Louise (Murgatroyd) C.; e. Pub. and High Sch., Vancouver, B.C.; Univ. of British Columbia (1930–31; 1938–43) B.A.; m. Norma Isobel Young, 29 Dec. 1956; Extve. Producer, Challenge for Change Program, Nat. Film Bd., 1971–75; employed in business in Vancouver, B.C., 1932–38; in charge of visual educ. in the Extension Dept., Univ. of B.C. 1938–43; joined Nat. Film Bd. as Organizer of Indust. and Trade Union Circuits for B.C.; apptd. Regional Supervisor for B.C., 1943 and for Alta. also, 1945; trans. to Ottawa, 1947 as Co-ordinator of Candn. Distribution; apptd. Dir. of Distribution 1949; Gen. U.S.A. Rep. 1962–66, Asian Rep. 1967–69; Chief, Media Studies & Production Liaison 1969–71; recreations: hiking, travel, photography; Clubs: B.C. Mountaineering; Alpine Club of Canada; Vancouver Natural History Soc.; Nat. Assoc. for Photographic Art; North Shore Photo Soc.; Address: 6442 Imperial Ave., West Vancouver, B.C. V7W 2J6.

**CHAUSSÉ, Gilles**, M.A., Ph.D.; professeur; né Montréal, Qué. 6 juin 1931; f. Emile et Antoinette (Sylvestre) C.; é. Univ. de Montréal, M.A. 1958, Ph.D. 1973; PROFESSEUR D'HISTOIRE DE L'EGLISE, FACULTE DE THEOLOGIE, UNIV. DE MONTRÉAL 1986– ; Professeur d'histoire, Coll. Jean-de-Brébeuf Montréal 1969–85; Collaborateur à l'Institut historique de la Compagnie de Jésus à Rome; Récipiendaire du Mérite Diocésain 'Monseigneur Ignace Bourget' 1986; auteur 'Jean-Jacques Lartigue, premier évêque de Montréal' 1980; co-auteur: 'Les Ultramontains canadiens-français' 1985; 'Le Christianisme d'ici a-t-il un avenir?' 1988; 'Le Canada et la Révolution française' 1989; 'L'Image de la Révolution française au Québec, 1789–89' 1989; 'Québec, terre d'Évangile: les défis de l'évangélisation dans la culture contemporaine' 1991; 'Montréal, 1642-1992' 1992; 'Dictionnaire Biographique du Canada' tomes 4–8; mem. Société Canadienne d'Histoire de l'Eglise catholique (Président 1985–87, Président général 1988; Adresse: 3001 rue Lacombe, Montréal, Qué. H3T 1L5; Bureau: C.P. 6128, succ. A, Montréal, Qué. H3C 3J7.

**CHAYKIN, Maury**, B.F.A.; actor; b. Brooklyn, N.Y. 27 July 1949; s. Irving and Clarice (Bloomfield) C.; e. Univ. of N.Y. at Buffalo B.F.A. 1972; leading roles over 45 feature films, 100 TV projects, 50 plays; films incl.: 'Wargames,' 'Bedroom Window,' 'Mrs. Soffel,' 'Twins,' 'Breaking In, 'Stars and Bars,' 'Canada's Sweetheart: The Saga of Hal C. Banks' (ACTRA Award Best Actor 1986), 'Cold Comfort,' 'Camilla,' 'George's Island,' 'Dances with Wolves,' 'Hero,' 'Somersby'; Hero, Whale Music Mochay Productions Inc. (TV & feature film); recreations: tennis, gardening.

**CHEASLEY, C. Stephen**, B.A., B.C.L.; lawyer; b. Montreal, Que. 6 Nov. 1938; s. Clifford Henry and Eva Dorothy (Murch) C.; e. Montreal West High Sch.; McGill Univ. Montreal B.A. 1959; McGill Univ. B.C.L. 1962; m. Janet d. Colin McMichael 21 Jan. 1967; children: Elaine, Colin, Paige, Peter; PARTNER MARTINEAU WALKER 1974– ; Dir., Devencore Realties Ltd.; Devencore Inc.; D.R.S. Real Estate Advisors Ltd.; Capitex Real Estate Corp.; Braunkohle Transport Can. Inc.; joined Stagiaire Martineau Walker 1962–63; Lawyer Martineau Walker 1963–73; Partner 1974; Pres. Martineau Walker Inc. 1978–84; Managing Partner Martineau Walker 1978–84; Pres. Candn. Railroad Hist. Assn. 1971–77; Chrmn. Candn. Ry. Museum Comn. 1968–72; National Chrmn., Real Property Section, and mem. Counc., Candn. Bar Assn. 1975–76; Treas., Candn. Bar Annual Meeting Ctte. 1988; Treas., Bar of Montreal 1989–90; Mem. Gen. Counc., Bar of Quebec 1989–90; Dir. and Vice-Chrmn., Soc. du Vieux Port de Montreal 1984–91; Vice-Pres., Montreal Bd. of Trade 1982–84, Pres. 1984–85, Chrmn. 1985–86; Co-Chrmn. Dorval, Mirabel Ctte., Comte. de promotion econ. de Montreal 1981–82; Co-Chrmn. Comite de Promotion econ. de Montreal 1983–84; Co-Chrmn. McGill Coll. Area Urban Design Cons. Ctte. 1984; Co-Chrmn., Consultative Ctte. on the Old Port of Montreal 1985–86; Dir. and Chrmn., La Société du Centre de Conférences international de Montréal; Member, Groupe de Travail sur Montréal et sa région; Dir., Lakeshore Gen. Hosp.; mem. Candn. Bar Assn.; Que. Bar Assn.; Cedar Park Un. Ch.; recreations: Head Coach, Dorval Jets Bantam A Intercity Hockey Team 1987–88; Coach, Dorval Jets Atom A Intercity Hockey Team 1988–89; Clubs: Forest and Stream, Montreal; Home: 341 Berkeley Circle, Dorval, Que. H9S 1H6; Office: 3400 Stock Exchange Tower, Place Victoria, Montreal, Que. H4Z 1E9.

**CHECK, James Victor Patrick**, B.A., M.A., Ph.D.; educator; b. Calgary, Alta. 1 Apr. 1953; s. John and Victoria C.; e. Univ. of Calgary, B.A. (with Distinction) 1976; Univ. of Man., M.A. 1979, Ph.D. 1984; ASSOC. PROF. OF PSYCHOL. YORK UNIV. 1983– ; Pres., J. Check Research Consulting Ltd. 1984– ; SSHRCC Can. Rsch. Fellow 1987–88; Rsch. Asst. Univ. of Calgary 1975, Rsch. Assoc. 1976; Rsch. Assoc. Pilot Alta. Restitution Centre 1975–76; Rsch. Assoc. & Doctoral Fellow Univ. of Man. 1976–83, former mem. Senate; recipient Vineberg Rsch. Prize in Psychol. 1979; Francis F. Reeves Found. Bursary 1974; Prov. Alta. Undergrad. Scholarship 1975; one of 5 finalists Social Issues 1985 Dissertation Award Soc. Psychol. Study Social Issues; 3 doctoral and postdoctoral fellowships; 20 rsch. and travel grants; author or co-author of 28 jour. articles & book chapters, 26 abstracts & 80 papers presented at learned soc. meetings & confs. Can., USA, U.K., Mexico, Italy, Netherlands, Finland, Spain, Japan, Israel & Australia; guest speaker various univ. and community groups; mem. various jour. ed. bds.; book reviewer; mem. Candn. Psychol. Assn. (Past Chair, Sect. Criminal Justice Systems); Am. Psychol. Assn.; Internat. Soc. Study Individual Differences; Internat. Assn. Applied Psychol.; Internat. Soc. for Rsch. on Aggression; Candn. Communications Assn.; Soc. Sci. Study Sex (mem. Task Force Erotica, Pornography & Violent Pornography); Candn. Law & Soc. Assn.; Soc. Personality & Social Psychol.; recreations: scuba diving, skiing; Office: Psych. Dept., York Univ., 4700 Keele St., North York, Ont. M3J 1P3.

**CHEESBROUGH, Gordon F.**, B.A., F.C.S.I.; investment dealer; b. Montreal, Que. 8 Oct. 1952; e. Upper Can. Coll. 1971; Univ. of Toronto B.A. 1974; m. Julia Hendy; 3 children; CHAIRMAN AND CHIEF EXECUTIVE OFFR., SCOTIAMcLEOD INC.; joined McLeod Young Weir 1974, Head Corporate Trader 1976, Vice Pres. 1978, Head: Instnl. Bond Sales 1979, Domestic & Internat. Bond Sales & Trading 1983, Bond & Money Mkt. Sales & Trading Domestic & Internat. 1983, Dir. 1980; mem. Bd. of Trustees, Community Foundation for Greater Toronto; Chrmn., Annual Giving Upper Can. Coll.; mem. Bd. Govs., Upper Can. Coll.; Clubs: Toronto Cricket Skating & Curling; Badminton & Racquet; Lambton Golf Club; York Club; Office: P.O. Box 433 Toronto Dominion Centre, Toronto, Ont. M5K 1M2.

**CHEESEMAN, Basil Richard**, Q.C., B.A., LL.B.; barrister & solicitor; b. Toronto, Ont. 19 Oct. 1927; s. Norman and Ethel Victoria (Lloyd) C.; e. Univ. of Toronto B.A. (Hons.) 1949, LL.B. 1950; m. Doreen d. Adele and Salim Shaker 10 Nov. 1956; children: Vanessa, Noel, Stephen, Janine; PARTNER, McCARTHY TÉTRAULT (formerly McCarthy & McCarthy) 1971– ; called to Bar in Alberta 1951; read law and practiced as Partner, MacDonald Cheeseman Moore & Atkinson 1951–66; joined McCarthy & McCarthy 1966; Dir., Bank of America Canada; Skega Limited; Degussa Canada Limited; Tour & Andersson Limited; Trelleborg Mining Limited; Gov., Candn. Tax Foundation 1962–63; club: Toronto; Home: 12 Ormsby Crescent, Toronto, Ont. M5P 2V3; Office: Suite 4700, Toronto Dominion Bank Tower, Toronto-Dominion Centre, Toronto, Ont. M5K 1E6.

**CHEESMAN, Ralph Leslie**, C.D., M.Sc., D.I.C., Ph.D., F.G.S.; consulting geologist; b. Southborough, Tunbridge Wells, Eng., 19 Jan. 1924; s. Leslie H. S. and Ethel (Miller) C.; e. Eltham Coll., Eng., 1935–41; Imperial Coll., London Univ., B.Sc. (Hons. Geol.) 1950 (A.R.C.S.), M.Sc. (Geol.), D.I.C. 1951; Univ. of London, Ph.D. (Geol.) 1955; m. Hilda, d. Henry Hughes, St. Lucia, B.W.I., 2 Sept. 1950; two s., Christopher Ralph, Timothy Andrew; CONSULTING GEOLOGIST and MINERAL POLICY CONSULTANT; mem. of Teaching Staff, Dept. of Geol., Imp. Coll., Univ. of London, 1951–55 (also served as Librarian for Watt's Lib. of Geol., 1952–55); joined Dept. of Mineral Resources, Sask. as Sr. Geol. (Precambrian) 1955, Chief Geol. 1956–69, since when Consulting Geol.; Mgr.-Consultant, Sask. Mining Assn. 1973–91; Mineral Policy Consultant since 1991; Dir., Inst. for Saskatchewan Enterprise since 1989; Hon. Aide to Gov. Gen. 1971–74; served with R.N.V.R. (active 1942–46; Lieut., Reserve, since 1946; L.Cdr. R.C.N.R., 1962, Cdr. 1971; in command H.M.C.S. 'Unicorn' N.R. Div., Saskatoon 1971–74; H.M.C.S. Queen, N.R. Div. Regina 1975–76; Fellow Geol. Soc. London; Hon. Fellow, Coll. of Emmanuel and St. Chad; mem., Geol. Assn. (London); Geol. Soc. Am.; Candn. Inst. Mining & Metall.; Assn. Prof. Engrs. Sask.; Anglican; recreations: transportation history, philately, travel; Address: 4705 Pasqua St., Regina, Sask. S4S 6N7.

**CHEFF, Michel V.**, B.A., M.A.; director, curator; b. Ottawa, Ont. 8 July 1950; s. Gérard and Rita (Lefebvre) C.; e. Sheridan Coll. of Applied Arts Creative Arts Dipl. 1970; Univ. of Ottawa B.A. (hons.) 1974; Univ. of Montreal M.A. 1982; DIRECTOR, WINNIPEG ART GALLERY 1993– ; Instructor in Visual Arts, Ottawa Sch. of Art 1971–79 Prof. of Art Hist., Algonquin Coll. AAT 1976–79; Univ. du Qué. 1979–83; Instructor in Drawing 1979–83; Educator, Edn. Serv., Nat. Gall. of Canada 1974–84; Chief 1984–88; Chief Curator & Dir. of Curatorial Services, Musée du Québec 1988–93; Mngmt. Cons., Théâtre Ballet of Canada, Gal. L'Autre Equivoque, Cincinnatti Mus. of Art; Founding Mem. & Chair, Candn. Art Gall. Educators 1984–87; Mem., Bd. of Dir., PRO-ARTS 1985–90; Candn. Rep., Mus. Div., NAEA (US) 1985–90; Bd. Chair, Habitations Mont-Carmel, Que. 1990–91; Bd. Mem., Soc. des Musées québécois 1990–92; Pres., Candn. Mus. Assn. 1993– ; Vice-Pres. elect, Candn. Mus. Assn. 1991–93 (Chair, Pub. Ctte. 1990–92); Chair, Annual Conf., Soc. des musées qué. 1992; (ICOM) Intercom Ctte. for Mus. Mngt.; author: 'Dallaire' 1984, 1 book chapter & mus. articles; Office: 300 Memorial Blvd., Winnipeg, Man. R3C 1V1.

**CHEFFINS, Ronald Ian,** Q.C., B.A., LL.B., LL.M.; educator; b. Montreal, Que. 13 Jan. 1930; s. Albert Robert and Mona Beatrice (Denovan) C.; e. Univ. of B.C. LL.B. 1953, B.A. 1955; Yale Univ. LL.M. 1957; three s. Ian Michael, Brian Robert, Jonathan James; PROF. OF PUBLIC ADMINISTRATION AND POLITICAL SCIENCE, UNIV. OF VICTORIA 1987– ; Part-time Lectr. in Social Work Univ. of B.C. 1954–56; Assoc. Prof. of Law McGill Univ. 1960–65; Assoc. Prof. of Pol. Science Univ. of Victoria 1965, Prof. 1968, Chrmn. of Pol. Science 1967–69; Prof. of Law, Univ. of Victoria 1974–85; Justice of Appeal, British Columbia Court of Appeal 1985–87 and Yukon Territory Court of Appeal 1985–87; Vice Chrmn. and part-time Commr., Law Reform Comn. of B.C. 1983–85, 1987–92; Gov. Camosun Coll. Victoria 1983–85; author 'The Constitutional Process in Canada' 1969, 2nd ed. 1976; 'The Revised Canadian Constitution: Politics as Law 1986; apptd. Q.C. 1984; mem. Law Soc. B.C.; Candn. Bar Assn.; Pol. Science Assn.; recreations: sports, music; Club: Union; Office: Sch. of Public Admin., Univ. of Victoria, P.O. Box 1700, Victoria, B.C. V8W 2Y2.

**CHEHAB, Paul,** C.A.; real estate executive; b. 5 Dec. 1946; e. École des Hautes Études Commerciales C.A. 1971; children: Stephanie, Nicolas; SENIOR VICE-PRES., SHOPPING CENTRES, IVANHOE INC. 1991– ; Genstar Corp. 1976–87; The Edgecombe Group 1988–90; Mem., Candn. Inst. of C.A.s; Internat. Council of Shopping Centres; recreations: skiing, golf, tennis; Office: 413 St-Jacques, World Trade Centre, Montreal, Que. H2Y 3Z4.

**CHELSKY, Sidney Harold;** business executive; b. Toronto, Ont. 29 Nov. 1941; s. Jacob Aaron and Rose (Pearl) C.; e. Bathurst Heights Coll.; m. Brenda d. Alexander and Shirley Shindman 14 Feb. 1961; children: Brian, Jeffrey, Alexandra, Steven; PRESIDENT, CAREFUL HAND LAUNDRY & DRY CLEANERS LIMITED 1970– ; various positions with firm 1960–70; Assoc. Chrmn., Mt. Sinai Hosp. Rsch. Campaign; Chrmn., Dry Cleaning Panel, Better Business Bureau; Chrmn., Adv. Council, Dry Clearner & Launderers Institute (Ont.); Chrmn., Textile Laundry Branch (Ont.); Mem., Environmental Action Ctte. for Dry Cleaning Industry; Dir.: Eastern Candn. Launderers & Dry Cleaners Assoc.; IAPA; United Israel Appeal of Can.; United Jewish Appeal of Metro. Toronto; Past Vice Pres. & Past Dir., Primrose Club; Past Chrmn., Textile & Allied Industries Accident Prevention Assn. of Ont.; Past Pres., Dry Cleaners & Laundries Inst.; Laundry Branch of Ont.; Brotherhood of Shaarei Shomayin Congregation (past Gov.); Past Chrmn., Consumer Relations, Occupational Health & Safety and Legislative Ctte., DCLI; mem. Extve. Ctte., Advisory Counc. and Bd. of Govs., DCLI; mem. Extve. Ctte., Candn. Rsch. Inst.; Toronto Jewish Congress; Ont. Chrmn., Jabotinsky Inst. & Museum in Israel; Bd. Mem., Bible Lands Museum in Jerusalem; past mem., Task Force on Hazardous Chemicals for Ont.; Past Pres., Candn. Assn. of Ben Gurion Univ.; Mem., Internat. Bd., Ben Gurion Univ.; Club: Primrose; Home: 18 Tillingham Keep, Downsview, Ont. M6H 3A1; Office: 120 Tycos Rd., North York, Ont. M6B 1V9.

**CHEN, Jerome,** M.A., Ph.D., F.R.S.C.; educator; b. Chengdu, China 2 Oct. 1921; s. Chen Koda and Ma Huizhi; e. Southwest Associated Univs. China M.A. 1943; Nankai Inst. of Econ. China 1945; Univ. of London Ph.D. 1956; 1 d. Barbara Ling Chen; DISTINGUISHED RESEARCH PROF. OF HISTORY EMERITUS, YORK UNIVERSITY 1987; Jr. Lectr. Yenching Univ. Peking 1945–47; Sr. Lectr. in Hist. Univ. of Leeds 1963–71; Visiting Prof. Univ. of Kansas 1970; Australian Nat. Univ. 1971; Univ. of Adelaide 1974; Univ. of Kyoto 1978; Keio Univ. 1991; Univ. of Vienna 1992; Distinguished Research Prof. of History, York Univ. 1971–87; author 'Mao and the Chinese Revolution' 1965; 'Mao: Great Lives Observed' 1970; 'China and the West' 1979 etc.; 'The Nationalist Era in China' and 'The Highlanders of Central China' 1991; recreations: music, theatre, reading, travel; Home: 253 Bedford Rd., Toronto, Ont. M5R 2L3; Office: Downsview, Ont. M3J 1P3.

**CHENG, Nansen,** LL.D.; marketing and communications executive; b. Shanghai, China 23 March 1935; s. Kuo-Liang and Chai-Yun (Quia) Cheng; e. Shanghai Internat. Studies Univ. 1957; National Taiwan Univ., LL.B. 1961; Univ. of Neuchâtel, LL.D. 1965; Institut Européan des Hautes Etudes Internationales, France 1966 and Diplomatic Acad. of Vienna 1969, post-doctorate studies; m. Agathe d. Josaphat and Thérèse Ménard 3 Sept. 1972; two d. Nancy Elisabeth, Annick Mei-Ling; PRES., RICHELIEU ASIA INVESTMENT & CONSULTATION INC. since 1988; Consultant, international marketing, Quebec Govt. since 1989; Pres. and Vice Chrmn. Ossun International Trade & Investment Corp.; Chrmn. and Chief Exec. Offr. Paramex Corp.; Pres. Exec. Ctte. CIAC North America Inc.; Dir. Gen. Overseas Office China Chang-Jiang Energy Corp.; Special Adv. to Comm. Del. Vienna 1967–69; Prof. of Chinese Studies, Diplomatic Acad. of Vienna 1967–69; Legis. Adv. to Govt. of Can. 1970; successively Rsch. Prof. of Law, Univ. de Laval and Adv. Legis. & Internat. Relations Qué. Govt. until 1979; Exec. Vice Pres. The Ossun International Trading Corp. 1979–86; Pres. and Gen. Mgr. BCP-China Marketing & Communications Inc. 1986–87; recipient French Govt. Fellowship 1965; Eur. Econ. Community Fellowship 1966; Wiener Diplomatische Akademie Fellowship 1967; Home: 360 rue Logan, St-Lambert, Qué. J4P 1J2.

**CHENIER, Hilda Lorraine,** A.O.C.A.; interior designer; b. Toronto, Ont. 27 Oct. 1942; d. Vincent Harold and Gwendolyn Mary (Weales) McNamara; m. Robert John s. Jean Paul and Laura Audrey Chenier 26 Sept. 1964; one d.: Christienne Lorraine Eugenie; OWNER, D. CHENIER ASSOCIATES LTD. 1973–92; Jr. Designer, P.O.I. 1966–68; Project Designer, Eaton Design Group 1968–71; Sr. Proj. Des., Helen Moffett Assoc. 1971–72; Rice Brydone Assoc. 1972–76; Pres., present co. 1976–92; now with D.C.A. Design Inc.; mem.: Assn. of Registered Interior Designers of Ont. (Public Relations Dir. 1977, Secy. 1983, Vice-Pres. 1984); Am. Soc. of Interior Designers; part-time Instr., Ryerson Polytech. Inst. 1975–78; ARIDO Gold Award, Design Excellence 1984; Bronze Award 1984; ARIDO Gold and Silver Awards, Design Excellence 1985; ARIDO Bronze Award 1987 and 1990 (three projects); Co-Chairperson, O.C.A. Silent Auction 1991; Co-Chair, Zoological Soc. of Metro. Toronto Fund Raiser 'Zoo Do' 1991 & 1992; mem. Bd. of Dirs., Zoological Soc. of Metro. Toronto; Art Gall. of Ont.; Candn. Opera Co.; Soc. of Friends of Ont. Coll. of Art; Mem., Design Exchange; recreations: cross-country and alpine skiing, sailing, canoeing; Office: 110 Bond St., Main Floor, Toronto, Ont. M5B 1X8.

**CHENOWETH, Richard H.,** B.A., M.B.A.; corporate executive; b. Montreal, Que. 8 Jan. 1952; s. David MacPherson and M. Clare (Buck) C.; e. Lower Canada College 1967; United World College of the Atlantic, Wales; Trent Univ. B.A. 1972; Univ. of Western Ont. M.B.A. 1978 (Dean's Honours List); m. M. Gaylanne d. His Honour Judge Roderick and Eleanor Phelan 22 Aug. 1980; CORPORATE VICE-PRES., INTERCON SECURITY LIMITED 1988– ; Cowboy, Diamond 'S' Ranch 1969; Field Operations Supvr. / Mgr. for N.Am., Arctic, N. Atlantic & African Resource Exploration Projects, Kenting Limited 1972–76; Management Cons. in Strategic Planning, Opns. & Mngt. Audits, Peat Marwick Partners 1978–80; New Products Mgr., Harlequin Enterprises Limited 1980–81; Dir., Retail Mktg. 1981–83; Intl. Mktg. & Corp. Devel. 1983–84; New Ventures Group 1984–85; Vice-Pres. Mktg. N. Am. 1985–88; editor/publisher: 'Allpoints' newsletter; author of one book chapter; recreations: tennis, skiing, travel, books; clubs: The Queen's, The Osler Bluff Ski, The Granite; Home: Lawrence Park, Toronto, Ont.; Office: 40 Sheppard Ave. W., Toronto, Ont. M2N 6K9.

**CHEPA, Steven W.,** B.Com., C.A.; business executive; b. Hamilton, Ont. 25 Apr. 1939; s. William W. and Mary S. (Pyrch) C.; e. McMaster Univ. B.Com. 1962; Ont. Inst. C.A. 1965; one d. Christina Louise; CHRMN., PRES. & C.E.O. CHEPPA CORPORATION 1978– ; Dir., Disys Corp. 1974– ; Dir., Mytec Technologies Inc. 1993– ; Price Waterhouse 1962–65; Controller, Gen. Mgr. & Vice-Pres., Alarm Div., Chubb Industries 1966–71; Co-founder, Check Security Systems Ltd. 1972–74; Dir., Alcohol Countermeasure Systems Ltd. 1978–86; Co-Founder & Chrmn., Pres. & C.E.O., Disys Corporation (formerly Dicon Systems Ltd.) 1974–93; Dicon Systems awarded Grand Winner, Canada Export Award Programme 1984; Bd. of Govs., Holy Trinity Sch. 1989–91; Dir., Dancemakers 1983–86; mem., Ont. Inst. of C.A.s 1962– ; recreations: horses (show jumping and field hunters), skiing, diving; Office: 145 Wellington St. W., Suite 200, Toronto, Ont. M5J 1H8.

**CHERCOVER, Murray;** television executive; b. Montreal, Que. 18 Aug. 1929; s. Max M. and Betty (Pomerance) C.; e. Port Arthur, Ont., Matric.; Acad. Radio & Television Arts, Toronto, Ont.; Neighbourhood Playhouse, Sch. of Theatre, New York, N.Y.; m. Barbara Ann d. C.J. Holleran, Atlanta, Ga.; children: Hollis Denny, Sean Peter; PRESIDENT & C.E.O., CTV TELEVISION NETWORK LTD.; Pres. and Dir., Lancer Teleproductions Ltd.; Founding Dir., International Council, National Academy of Television Arts and Sciences; began career with CFPA Radio, Port Arthur, Ont. 1944–46; in radio and theatre, with New Play Soc., Toronto 1946–48; in U.S. 1948–52; Dir./Producer, Stock Co. in Kennebunkport. Me., Long Island Tent Theatre, Atlantic City Circle Theatre; Producer-Dir., of Network Television Drama for Louis G. Cowan Agency, 'Cosmopolitan Theatre'; Film Dir., returned to Canada 1952; until 1960 Drama Producer-Dir., C.B.C.; 'General Motors Presents,' Proctor & Gamble 'On Camera'; Ford Motor 'Playbill,' 'Space Command'; joined CFTO-TV, Baton Broadcasting Ltd., as Extve. Producer of all Prod. 1960; Dir., Programming, Vice Pres. Programming 1961; & Chrmn. Programming Comte., CTV Television Network 1961; Vice-Pres., Programming & Chrmn. of Programming for the Independent Television Network 1961; joined present interest as Exec. Vice Pres. and Gen. Mgr. 1966, Pres. & Chief Operating Offr. 1968; Pres. & Mng. Dir. 1969; Pres. & C.E.O. 1987; Past mem., Adv. Ctte. for Theatre Arts, The George Brown Coll. of Applied Arts & Technol.; Advisory Council for Film/TV Production Program, Humber College; mem., Cdn. Assn. of Broadcasters; Broadcast Executives Soc.; Central Can. Broadcasters Assn. (former Dir.); International Platform Assn.; Internat. Press Inst.; Roland Michener Foundation (Founding Dir.); Toronto Arts Production (former Dir.); Adv. Council, Cdn. Friends of Tel Aviv Univ.; Children's Broadcast Inst. (Founding Dir.); Ruth Hancock Scholarship Fund (Trustee); Vice-Chrmn. of Gen. Assly., Prix Italia Television Festival; recipient of Special Citation, Nat. Acad. of Television Arts and Sciences, Internat. Emmy Awards 1989; recipient Candn. Assn. of Broadcasters Gold Ribbon Distinguished Service Award 1986; Candn. Film & TV Assoc. Lifetime Achievement Award 1988; Founding Dir., The Found. for Ocean Research; Model Aeronautics Assn. of Can.; Toronto Radio Control Club; Downsview Radio Control Club; Antique and Classic Car Club; Morgan Owners Club; M.G.T. Registry; Ferrari Car Club; other Clubs: Royal Canadian Yacht; Bloor Park; Parkview; Wallace Pines; Dunfield; recreations: theatre, antiques, collection of fine art, aviation, antique and classic cars, squash, tennis, cycling, skiing, scuba diving; Home: 34 Dunbar Road, Toronto, Ont. M4W 2X6; Office: 42 Charles St. East, Toronto, Ont. M4Y 1T5.

**CHERNEY, Brian,** M.Mus., Ph.D.; composer; educator; b. Peterborough, Ont. 4 Sept. 1942; e. ARCT 1961; Univ. of Toronto B.Mus. 1964, M.Mus. 1967, Ph.D. 1974; Royal Conserv. Music Toronto piano and composition; taught theory and composition Univ. of Victoria 1971–72 and McGill Univ. 1972– ; compositions incl. 'Dans le crépuscule du souvenir' 1977–80; 'Group Portrait-With Piano' 1978; 'Adieux' for Orchestra 1980; 'Into the Distant Stillness' 1984; 'Illuminations' 1987; 'Playing for Time' 1981; 'String Trio' 1976 (tied for top position Internat. Rostrum of Composers 1979); 'River of Fire' for oboe d'amore and harp 1983 (won Jules Léger Prize for New Chamber Music 1985); Oboe Concerto 1989; 'Transfiguration' for Orchestra 1990; 'Doppelgänger' (for 2 flutes) 1991; author 'Harry Somers' 1975; Assoc., CM Centre; Address: McGill Univ. Faculty of Music, Strathcona Music Bldg., 555 Sherbrooke St. W. Montreal, Qué. H3A 1E3.

**CHERNEY, Lawrence Philip,** B.A., M.Mus.; musician, artistic director; b. Peterborough, Ont. 1 May 1946; s. Harry Oscar and Sylvia (Green) C.; e. Peterborough C.V.S. 1964; Univ. of Toronto B.A. 1969, M.Mus. 1978; former teachers: Perry Bauman, John Mack, Marc Lifschey, Ray Still, Robert Bloom; m. Linda d. Thomas and Anne Kelly 21 June 1977; children: Max Abraham, Niomi Anna; FOUNDING ARTISTIC DIRECTOR, MUSIC AT SHARON 1981– ; Principal Oboe, Nat. Ballet of Canada Orch. 1967–69; Oboe & English horn, Nat. Arts Centre Orch. 1969–72; Founding Mem., York Winds (Wind quintet; toured N. Am., Eur., Israel) 1972–82; toured, performed & recorded extensively as soloist throughout Eur., U.S., Can. & Israel since 1982; have comnd. & premiered nearly 40 works for oboe since 1984; recorded for RCA, Melbourne, Centrediscs, CBC, McGill, & Marquis; Founding Artistic Dir., Chamber Concerts Canada (sponsors of 'Musical Magic,' St. Lawrence Ctr. & 'Encounters,' Glenn Gould Studio) 1981– ; Ford Found. Grant 1966; num. Canada Council Awards 1967– ; Instructor, Oboe & Chamber Music, Univ. of Ottawa 1969–72; York Univ. 1973–77; Royal Conservatory of Music 1978–90; Fac. of Music, Univ. of Toronto 1978–80; recreations: wilderness canoeing; Home: 326 Brunswick Ave., Toronto, Ont. M5R 2Y9; Office: 156 Front St. W., Toronto, Ont. M5J 2L6.

**CHERNIACK, Hon. Saul M.,** C.M., P.C., Q.C., LL.B.; b. Winnipeg, Man. 10 Jan. 1917; s. Joseph Arthur, Q.C. and Fannie (Golden) C.; e. Peretz Folk, Machray and St. John's High Schs., Winnipeg; Univ. of Man.; LL.B. 1939 m. Sybil Claire, d. late Joseph and Mary Zeal, 10 July 1938; children: Howard D., Ph.D., Lawrie A., M.A.

LL.B.; Former Mem., Security Intelligence Review Comte. under Candn. Security Intelligence Service Act 1984–92; read law with Joseph A. Cherniack, Q.C.; called to Bar of Man. 1940; cr. Q.C. 1963; private law practice since 1940; served with Intelligence Cor., Candn. Army, during World War II; rank Capt.; mem. Winnipeg Sch. Bd. 1950–54; Councillor, Twp. of Winnipeg Beach, 1958–59; Ald., City of Winnipeg, 1959–60; Councillor, Metro Corp. Greater Winnipeg, 1960–62; M.L.A. 1962–81; Depy. Premier, Min. of Finance and Min. of Urban Affairs 1969 resigning 3 Jan. 1975; Past Nat. Vice Pres., Candn. Jewish Congress; past Pres., Winnipeg Jewish Welfare Fund; past Chrmn., Manitoba Hydro; apptd. mem. of Privy Council 1984; Member, Order of Canada 1994; mem., NDP; Jewish; Home: 333 St. John's Ave., Winnipeg, Man. R2W 1H2.

**CHERNICK, Victor,** M.D., F.A.A.P., F.R.C.P.(C); pediatrician; educator; b. Winnipeg, Man. 31 Dec. 1935; s. Jack J. and Mina (Tapper) C.; e. Univ. of Man. M.D. 1959; Johns Hopkins Hosp. 1960–64; m. Norma d. Saul Fordman, Winnipeg, Man. 19 May 1957; children: Marla, Sharon, Richard, Lisa; PROF. OF PEDIATRICS, UNIV. OF MAN. 1971– ; and Associate Dean (Research), Faculty of Medicine there 1983–86; Pediatrician-in-Chief, Health Sciences Centre 1971–79; Head, Section of Pediatric Respirology, Childrens Hosp. of Winnipeg 1979– ; Lectr. in Pediatrics, Johns Hopkins Univ. 1964, Asst. Prof. 1965–66; Asst. Prof. of Pediatrics Univ. of Man. 1966, Assoc. Prof. 1967–71; Prof. and Head, Dept. of Pediatrics 1971–79; Visiting Prof. of Pediatrics, Harvard Univ. 1976–77; Queen Elizabeth II Scientist 1967–73; Am. Men of Science 1968; Candn. Pediatric Soc. Medal for Research 1970; Hon. Citizen City of New Orleans 1974; John Stewart Mem. Lectr. Dalhousie Univ. 1976; Trustee, Queen Elizabeth II Scient. Fund; Co.-ed. 'Basic Mechanisms of Pediatric Resperatory Disease: Cellular and Integrative' 1991; Ed. 'Disorders of the Respiratory Tract in Children' 5th ed. 1990; Guest Ed. 'Onset and Control of Fetal and Neonatal Respiration' Vol. 1 1977; co-author, 'Respiratory Therapy of Newborn Infants and Children' 2nd ed. 1986; author or co-author numerous reviews, papers, abstracts and presentations; Fellow, Am. Thoracic Soc. 1962–64, Chrmn. Scient. Assembly Pediatrics 1970; mem. Soc. Pediatric Research (Council 1973–76); Cdn. Soc. Clin. Investigation; Midwest Soc. Pediatric Research (Pres. 1976–77); Am. Physiol. Soc.; N.Y. Acad. Science; Cdn. Physiol. Soc.; Am. Acad. Pediatrics (Exec. Ctte. Sec. Diseases of chest 1973–77); Dir. Cdn. Thoracic Soc. 1971–72; Secy. Internat. Cystic Fibrosis Assn. 1973–76; Perinatal Research Soc. (Counc. 1983–85); Royal Coll. Phys. & Surgs. of Can. (Counc. 1974–82); mem. Cystic Fibrosis Panel, Internat. Pediatric Assn.; mem. Ed. Bd. several prof. journs.; Office: Dept. of Pediatrics, Univ. of Manitoba, 770 Bannatyne Ave., Winnipeg, Man. R3E 0W3.

**CHERRY, Douglas William,** B.A., F.C.A.; chartered accountant; b. Saint John, N.B. 18 June 1927; s. Charles W. and Mary V. (Hunter) C.; e. St. Vincent's H.S. 1944; St. Thomas Univ. B.A. 1948; m. Helen d. Allen Bustin 20 June 1955; children: Mark, Michael, Teresa, Peter, Ann, David, Deborah, John; SR. CONSULTANT, COOPERS & LYBRAND 1988– ; C.A. N.B. 1953; N.S. 1957; Mem., Nat. Mngt. Ctte., Coopers & Lybrand 10 years; Partner Coopers & Lybrand 1961–88; Pres., N.S. Inst. of C.A.s 1967–68; Bd. of Gov., Candn. Inst. of C.A.s 1966, '67, '68; Fellow, N.S. Inst. of C.A.s 1977; Bd. of Govs., Halifax Children's Found. 2 terms; Mt. Saint Vincent Univ. 6 years; Tech. Univ. of N.S. 6 years; Mem., Pastoral Council, Archdiocese of Halifax 5 years; Catholic Cemeteries Comn.; Light of Life Charismatic Prayer Group; Internat. Council of Catholic Charismatic Renewal; club: Halifax; Home: 29 Turnmill Dr., Halifax, N.S. B3M 4G8; Office: Suite 600, 1809 Barrington St., Halifax, N.S. B3J 3K8.

**CHESTER, Lorne Edward,** B.A., LL.B., Q.C.; barrister and solicitor; b. Brampton, Ont. 23 Jan. 1947; s. Lorne Ernest and Patricia Clare (Saunders) C.; e. Oakville-Trafalgar H.S. 1965; Univ. of W. Ont., B.A. 1968; Univ. of Ottawa, LL.B. 1971; Bar Adm. Course, Osgoode Hall; called to Ont. Bar 1973; m. Patricia d. Helen and Denis Harbic 23 Aug. 1969; children: Tara, Kelly, Christie; PARTNER, MCQUARRIE, HILL, WALDEN, CHESTER, MCLEOD; joined McQuarrie, Hill, Walden, Swain and Chester 1973; Partner 1974; elected Councillor, Town of Lindsay 1976; acclaimed as Reeve 1978; Warden, Co. of Victoria 1985; Q.C. 1985; Former Mayor of Lindsay; apptd. Fed. Agent for Cos. of Haliburton & Victoria, Dept. of Justice 1985; Couns., Kawartha Haliburton Children's Aid Soc. 1974– ; Mem., Candn. Bar Assn.; Dir., Victoria-Haliburton Fed. P.C. Assn.; Assoc. Mem., The Royal Candn. Legion, Br. 67; recreations: hockey, skiing, canoeing, fishing; club: Lindsay Rockets; Home: 77 Sanderling Cres., Lindsay, Ont. K9V 4N4; Law Office: 64 Lindsay St. S., Lindsay, Ont. K9V 4S5.

**CHETAN, Ashok,** B.Comm., C.A.; financial executive; b. Guna, India 4 May 1951; s. Gian Swarup and Prakash Vati C. e.; Bangalore Univ. India B.Comm. 1969; articled with Fraser & Ross C.A. 1975; m. Tina d. Bhushan and Raj Chopra 17 June 1978; children: Anita, Devin; PRESIDENT, FINANCE & CHIEF FINAN. OFFR., THE JOHN FORSYTH COMPANY INC. 1993– ; Internal Auditor / Financial Analyst / Mgr., Analysis & Control / Divisional Controller, Northern Telecom 1974–79; Controller, SNC/FW Ltd. 1979–82; Group Controller, Western Canada 1982–86; Corp. Controller, The SNC Group Inc. 1986–89; Vice-Pres., Finance, The John Forsyth Co. Inc. 1989–90, Sr. Vice-Pres., Finance 1990–93; Past part-time teacher, Concordia Univ. (auditing); Dir., Penmans Inc.; Mem., Inst. of C.A.s of Ont.; recreations: tennis; Home: 5148 Frybrook Court, Mississauga, Ont. L5M 5A8; Office: 36 Horner Ave., Toronto, Ont. M8Z 5Y1.

**CHETWYND, Sir Arthur Ralph Talbot,** Bt., SCM (hon.), KCLJ, CMLJ; retired film producer; b. Walhachin, B.C., 28 Oct. 1913; s. the late Frances M. (Jupe) and the late Hon. William Ralph Talbot C., M.C., M.L.A.; e. Pub. and High Sch., B.C.; Vernon Prep. Sch., B.C.; m. Marjory M. M., d. late Robert Bruce Lang; children: Robin John Talbot, William Richard Talbot; CHRMN., CHETWYND PRODUCTIONS INC. and Brocton Hall Communications Ltd.; prior to 2nd World War, engaged in ranching, teaching and rehabilitation in B.C.; on staff of Univ. of Toronto, 1945–51 (Assoc., Sch. of Physical and Health Educ.; Publicity Offr., Univ. of Toronto Athletic Assn.); Field Supervisor Cdn. Red Cross Water Safety Programme, 1946–49; formed Chetwynd Films Ltd., 1950 (re-named Chetwynd Productions Inc. 1985); specialising in sponsored films for bus., indust., govt. and T.V.; production work of Co. includes educ. films on med., advertising, instructional, travel, safety, sports and other related subjects; has produced over 3,000 films and tape productions since 1950; over 100 nat. and int'l. awards; served in 2nd World War with R.C.A.F., 1943–45; Chief Instr. of Med. Reconditioning at end of war; Hon. Life Mem., Cdn. Film and T.V. Production Assn. (Past Pres.); Royal Commonwealth Soc., Toronto Br. (Chrmn. 1982–86; Life mem.); Life mem., Society of Motion Picture & Television Engns.; Past-Pres. and Life Mem., The Empire Club of Canada ; Dir., Royal Commonwealth Soc. of Toronto Foundation; The Bishop Fred Wilkinson Foundation; Candn. Friends of West Indian Christians; mem., The Monarchist League of Canada; The Churchill Society; Royal Commonwealth Society, London, Eng.; The Barbados National Trust (Life Mem.); Order of Saint Lazarus of Jerusalem; Freeman, City of London 1989; Anglican; recreations: swimming, volunteer work; Clubs: The Toronto Hunt; Albany (Toronto); Address: Apt. 3, 117 King St. E., Cobourg, Ont. K9A 1L2.

**CHEVALIER, Claude,** B.P.E., M.B.A.; business executive; b. Montreal, Que. 10 Feb. 1943 s. Leo Paul and Linda I. (Thetreault) C.; e. Longueil H.S.; Univ. of Ottawa B.P.E.; Univ. of Oregon M.B.A. Program; Harvard Univ. C.E.O. program; m. Monique d. Georgette and Elphère Roy Feb. 1976; children: Isabèle, François-Pierre; PRESIDENT & CHIEF EXECUTIVE OFFICER, DYNAMARK MANAGEMENT CORP.; Teacher, Phys. Ed., Régionale Ottawa; Officer, S.S. St.-Lawrence, Canada Steamship Line; Teacher, Univ. of Quebec at Montreal; Account Dir., Ted Bates Advtg.; Mktg. & Advtg. Dir., Bombardier; Pres. & Chief Extve. Offr., Dairy Bureau of Canada; Mem., Young President's Orgn.; Chair, Internat. Marketing Group and Mem., Permanent Comns. on Mktg. & Mngt., I.D.F. (33 countries); Bd. Mem., Hotel Dieu Hosp.; Maisonneuve Hosp.; Chair, CDC Consultant Ctte., Montreal Hunt; Dir., Centraide; Teléthon of Stars; recreations: horseback riding, skiing, golf; clubs: Montreal Hunt, Sanctuaire, St. Denis; Office: 635 Victoria, Westmount, Que. H3Y 2R8.

**CHEVALIER, The Hon. Francois,** B.A., LL.B., J.C.S.; court of appeal judge; b. Hull, Que. 29 Oct. 1918; s. Felix and Diane (Montpetit) C.; e. St. Alexandre & Mont-Laurier Colls., B.A. (cum laude) 1937; Montreal Univ., LL.B. 1940; m. Juliette d. J. Avila and Alice Molleur 22 Nov. 1941; children: Diane, Pierre, Jacques, Jean, France, Paul; apptd. DEPUTY JUDGE, APPEAL DIVISION, FEDERAL COURT OF CANADA 1994– ; priv. prac. 1940–63; Q.C. 1960; Crown Attorney 1960–63; Judge, Superior Court of Qué. 1963–84; Judge (ad hoc) Court of Appeal 1984–93; Spec. Mediator, Montreal Cath. Sch. Comn. & teachers 1964; Candn. & Am. Artist, Montreal Place des Arts 1965; City of Montreal & Transp. empls. 1966; presided 11 Maritime Casualty investigations; Chrmn., Fed. Elect. Bound. Comn. for Quebec (1972, 1975, 1986); Chrmn., Copyright Appeal Bd. of Canada since 1972; Lectr., Ottawa Univ. & var. forums & symposiums incl. World Intellectual Property Orgn., S.E. Asia; Vice-Pres., Jr. C. of C. Fed. of Que.; Pres., Ottawa-Hull Jeunesses Musicales; Outaouais Dram. Art Sch.; 1st Chrmn., Corp. of Psych. Hosp. P. Janet; Chrmn., Hull Red Feather Campaign 1972; Doctor (hon. causa), Ottawa Univ. 1991; Roman Catholic; recreations: travelling, reading; Home: 64, Desjardins St., Hull, Qué. J8Y 6B2; Office: Supreme Court of Canada Bldg., Wellington St. at Kent, Ottawa, Ont. K1A 0J1.

**CHEVALIER, Leo Charles,** C.M.; fashion designer; b. Montreal, Que. 8 Oct. 1934; s. Leo John and Mary Ellen (Whitten) C.; e. Loyolla Coll. 1948–52; Sch. Art.Design, Montreal Museum of Fine Arts 1951–53; Ecole des Beaux Arts de Montréal 1955; m. Monica Solange d. Michael A.V. Perdriel 21 June 1980; OWNER, LEO CHEVALIER INTL. LTD.; Asst. Mgr., Henry Morgan Co. 1955–59; Designer/costumer, Montreal Theatre Ballet 1958; Asst. Mgr./Display, R. Simpson Co. 1959–60; Freelance Fashion designer and Interior designer 1960–61; Mgr./Buyer Fraid's Co. 1961–63; Mgr./Buyer De St. Victor. 1963–65; Prop. Cheval Boutique 1966–68; Fashion Designer numerous cos. Ladieswear, Brodkin Ind. 1973–84; Designed/Executed costumes Mtl. Ballet Theatre 1958; Murals Bell Can. Head Off. 1965; Costumes, Théatre de Repentigny 1967; Designer of Year, Intl. Ladies' Garment Assn. 1967; Order of Can. 1979; Seal of Achievement Award, Clairol 1982; Founding mem. and past pres. Fashion Designers' Assn. of Can.; mem., Fashion Can.; Designer Development Cmte. (Past Dir.); Bd. mem. Can. Colour Council; Merrickville Century Theater; Centre de la Promotion de la Mode de Montréal; Via Design Award 1986; Air Canada in Flight & Passenger Serv. Uniforms 1987; Scouts Canada Uniforms, 1991 launch, 1988; Ritz Carlton Hotel Uniforms 1988; Interior Design Div. launched 1988; Artistic Dir., Hudson Garden Club 1989; Office: P.O. Box 1240, Station 'H,' Montreal, Qué. H3G 2N7.

**CHEVALIER, Hon. Maurice,** B.A., LL.L.; judge; b. Hull, Qué 24 Nov. 1920; s. Felix and Diane (Montpetit) C.; e. Univ. of Ottawa B.A. 1956, LL.L. 1959; m. Marie-Luce d. Achille and Razia Drouin Simon 31 Aug. 1942; children: Marthe, Hélène, Yves, André; JUDGE, QUEBEC COURT 1974– ; Chief Crown Atty. Dists. of Hull, Pontiac and W.Qué. 1969–74; Pres., Hull Bar Assoc. 1971–72; Home: 26 Lacasse St., Hull, Qué. J9A 1J9; Office: 3355 Place du Centre, 17 Laurier St., Hull, Qué. J8X 4C1.

**CHEVERIE, Wayne D.,** B.A., LL.B., M.L.A., Q.C.; politician/lawyer; b. Charlottetown, P.E.I. 19 May 1950; s. Charles and Clara (Austin) C.; e. St. Dunstan's H.S.; Univ. of P.E.I., B.A. 1971; Dalhousie Univ. LL.B. 1974; m. Terri d. William Bennett 1975; children: Jared, Joslin; PROVINCIAL TREASURER, GOVT. OF P.E.I. 1993– ; Chrmn., Management Board; also Min. resp. for Housing, Trade Negotiations, Native Affairs, Human Rights Comn., Public Utilities Comn. & Govt. House Leader; Partner, Campbell, Lea, Cheverie, Michael, McConnell & Pigot 1977–86; elected Liberal MLA 1986; Min. of Justice, Attorney Gen. & Min. of Labour, Govt. of P.E.I. 1986–89; Min. of Health & Social Services 1989–93; Min. responsible for the Elderly 1991–93; re-el. g.e. 1989; re-el. g.e. 1993; Mem., St. Pius X Ch. (lector); Past Mem., Candn. Bar Assn.; Past Counc. Mem., P.E.I. Law Soc.; Past Mem., Rules Ctte., Family Div. Supreme Court; served as Dir. Cath. Fam. Serv. Bur.; former lectr., Univ. of P.E.I.; recreations: golf, hockey; Home: 31 Hawthorne Ave., Charlottetown, P.E.I. C1A 5Y4; Office: P.O. Box 2000, Charlottetown, P.E.I. C1A 7N8.

**CHEVRETTE, Guy,** M.N.A., B.Péd.; politicien; né Saint-Côme, comté de Joliette, Qué. 10 janv. 1940; f. Adélard et Annette (Baillargeon) C.; é. Saint-Côme; Séminaires de Joliette et de Montfort à Papineauville; Univ. de Sherbrooke, Brevet 'A' et B.Péd. 1958; enfants: Eric, Charles; Leader parlementaire de l'Opposition officielle 1989– ; Député de Joliette (Parti Québécois); él. 1976, réél. 1981, 1985, 1989; occupé le poste de whip en chef du Gouvernement du Qué. 1979–82; ministre du Loisir, de la Chasse et da la Pêche 1982–84; ministre des Affaires sociales et président du Comité ministériel permanent du Développement social 1984–85; Leader parlementaire de l'Opposition officielle; mem. de la Comn. de Affaires sociales 1986–87; choisi à l'unanimité, Chef de l'Opposition officielle 1987–89; responsable des dossiers de la santé 1989–91, sécurité publique 1990–91, réforme ectorale et réforme parlementaire, 1989– , énergie et ressources, 1991; a été professeur à tous les niveaux et chargé de cours à l'Univ. du Qué. à Montreal dans le cadre du baccalauréat en admin.; de plus donné des cours sur l'organisation syndicale; Syndicaliste depuis le début de sa carrière d'enseignant; a occupé les postes de conseiller, de secrétaire-archiviste et de vice-prés. du conseil d'admin. au Syndicat de la féd. locale; élu premier vice-prés. de la Centrale de l'enseignement du Qué. 1974; nommé mem. de la Commission Cliche 1974; a été mem. de deux conseils d'admin. dans le domaine hospitalier et fut également prés. du Centre civique de Saint-Paul de Joliette; loisirs: golf, pêche; Adresse: 13 Bellefeuille, Joliette, Qué. J6E 7Y9; Bureau: l'Assemblée nationale du Québec, Qué.

**CHEVRIER, Jean-Marc,** B.A., B.Péd., Doctorat en psychologie; psychologist; publisher; b. Cheneville, St-Félix-de-Valois, Qué. 2 March 1916; s. Joseph Honoré and Olévina (Malette) C.; e. Univ. de Montréal B.A. 1938, B.Péd. 1940, Licence en Sciences pédagogiques 1942, Baccalauréat en psychologie 1943, Licence en psychologie 1945, Doctorat en psychologie 1949; École normale Jacques-Cartier High Sch. Teacher Dipl. 1939; 1st Cdn. to obtain dipl., Diplomate Amer. Bd. of Examiners in Profl. Psychol. 1955, after passing oral and written exams; post-doctoral studies: Univ. of Iowa, Hospital Sch. for Severely Handicapped Children 1953; Univ. of Cal., Berkely, Lawrence Hall of Science 1971; has followed 4-yr. didactic psychoanalysis with Mr. Théo Chentrier; m. Madeleine Bourassa 4 Jan. 1941; children: Marie-Paule, Marcel, Claudette, Madeleine, Robert; PRESIDENT AND EXEC. DIR., INST. OF PSYCHOLOGICAL RESEARCH INC. 1964– ; Exec. Dir. JMC Press Ltd. 1968– ; Founder & Chief Psychol. Guidance Bureau Ministry of Youth Que. Govt. 1947–53; Consultant, Comm. of Apprenticeship Printing Trades 1947–73; Laval & Chambly Coll. 1949–58, Hôpital Pasteur de Montréal 1953–60; Prof. Inst. Psychol. Univ. de Montréal 1951–57, Sch. of Rehabilitation Faculty of Med. 1953–57, Sch. of Educ. 1959–61; Founder and Dir. Psychol. Dept. Rehabilitation Inst. Montreal 1953–62; Dir. of Guidance Montreal Cath. Sch. Comn. 1962–64; Prof. Ecole Normale Secondaire 1962–63; Adm. and Pres. Edi-Quebec 1973–75; Dir., Treas., Vice Pres. Le Centre de Psychologie et de Pédagogie 1945–57; recipient Silver Medal Ecole Normale Jacques Cartier 1939; Bronze Medal Graphic Arts Industries Prov. Que. 1958; Graphic Arts Industries (USA) Award 1960; Stothers Exceptional Child Foundation Scholarship; Ministry Health & Social Welfare Can. Grant 1960–63; Award of the Corp., Corp. of Guidance Counsellors of Qué. 1990; Candn. Guidance and Counselling Assoc. Counselling Resources and Training Material Award 1991; Frank Clute Award for Profl. Rsch., Ont. Sch. Counsellors' Assoc. 1991; Distinction in psychometry from the psych. professors, Univ. of Montreal 1992; author numerous textbooks and psychol. tests; mem. Assn. Psychols. Prov. Que. (Past Pres.); Cdn. Psychol. Assn. (Life Mem.); Am. Psychol. Assn.; Cdn. Guidance & Counselling Assn. (Life Mem.); Ont. Psychols. Assn. (Hon. Life Mem.); Corp. of Psychologists of P. Qué.; Corp. of Guidance Counsellors of P. Qué.; Registered Psychologist in the Prov. of Ont.; Member Emeritus, Am. Bd. of Examiners in Prof. Psychol.; Assn. of Hong Kong Overseas Psychologists; Nat. Counc. on Psychological Aspects of Disability (Div. of Rehab. Psychology); Psychologists interested in Religious Issues; Science Teachers' Assoc. (Life Mem.); Union des écrivains québécois; Société québécoise des méthodes projectives; ACFAS; recreations: skiing, photography, golf; Home: 524 de Marigny, Laval-Des-Rapides, Ville de Laval, Qué. H7N 5A3; Office: 34 Fleury St. W., Montreal, Que. H3L 1S9.

**CHI, Nguyen Huu,** Ph.D., Licence en Droit; professor; b. Vietnam 1 Jan. 1936; s. Ky Huu and Dat Thi Nguyen; e. Michigan State Univ., Ph.D. 1965; Univ. de Saigon, Licence en Droit 1961; children: Lily, Vivi, Charles, Kimmy; PROF., CHRMN. & MEM. OF SENATE, CARLETON UNIV. 1972– ; Vice Pres., Public Survey and Forecasts of Canada Inc.; Prof., Nat. Inst. of Public Admin. (Saigon) 1965–66; Prov. Chief, Prov. Quang-Nam (S. Vietnam) 1966–67; Depy. Min., Prime Minister's Office, Govt. of Rep. of Vietnam 1967–68; Prof., Queen's Univ. 1968–72; Mem., Bd. of Dir., Candn. Pol. Sci. Assn. 1973–75; Sec. Treas. 1979–81; Pol. Advr., Counc. of Nat. Liberation of Haiti 1979–85; Mem., Bd. of Dir., Ottawa-Carleton Immigrants Serv. 1978–80; Van-Lang Public Housing Project 1982–83; Mem., Multi-Ethnic Counc. of Dalhousie 1984; Vice-Pres., Public Survey & Forecast, Inc.; Pres., Ottawa Public Housing Corp.; author: 'Research Methods in Social Science' 1975; numerous articles in scholarly journals; recreations: reading, music; Home: 1380 Prince of Wales Dr., Ottawa, Ont. K2C 3N5; Office: Dept. of Pol. Sci., Carleton Univ., Ottawa, Ont. K1S 5B6.

**CHIAPPETTA, Joseph A.N.,** B.A., Q.C.; barrister and solicitor; b. Toronto, Ont. 23 Mar. 1930; s. Frank and Mary (Perille) C.; e. St. Francis Elementary Sch.; St. Michael Coll. High Sch.; Univ. Toronto 1952; Osgoode Hall Law Sch. 1956; m. Florence, d. Joseph and Mary Farro, 1 July 1954; children: Cathy Swanson, Marie Newton, Lorraine, Frances; SR. PARTNER, BRATTY AND PARTNERS; Dir. National Trust Co.; National Trustco; Dir. and Secy. Tru-Wall Group Ltd.; Dir. and Pres. Nat. Investors Corp.; Dir. and Officer in several land development and building companies; began practice in 1956 in partnership Benedetto and Chiappetta, formed current partnership in 1968; cr. Q.C. 1969; mem. Candn. Counc. Christians & Jews; Candn. Bar Assn.; Gov. and Vice-Pres., Italian Candn. Charitable Found.; Clubs: Lambton Golf & Country; Columbus Centre; recreations: squash; tennis; Home: 11 Edgehill Rd., Islington, Ont. M9A 4N1; Office: 4950 Yonge St., Willowdale, Ont. M2N 6K1.

**CHIARUCCI, George M.C.,** B.Sc., C.A.; chartered accountant; b. Mondavio, Italy 5 May 1952; s. Armando and Adalgisa (Godi) C.; e. Loyola College B.Sc. (Hons.) 1974; McGill Univ., dipl. Acctg. 1977; m. Mara d. Remo and Clelia Lucchesi 3 July 1976; children: Sabrina, David Alexander; VICE-PRES. & CONTROLLER, HAMILTON SPECIALTY BAR DIV., SLATER STEELS 1992– ; Senior Staff Accountant, Clarkson Gordon & Co. 1974–78; Assoc. Vice-Pres., Opns. & Controller, Scotia Factors Ltd. 1978–82; Mgr., Finan. Planning, Dir., Marketing Control & Vice-Pres., Finan. Devel., Molson Breweries 1982–90; Vice-Pres. & Controller, Atlas Alloys 1990–92; Mem., Ont. Inst. of C.A.s; Soc. des comptables agrées du Qué.; The Planning Forum; recreations: squash, travel; clubs: Fitness Inst.; Office: 319 Sherman Ave. N., P.O. Box 2943, Hamilton, Ont. L8N 3P9.

**CHICOINE, F. Luc,** B.A., M.D.; paediatrician; b. Montreal, Que. 19 Apr. 1929; s. Henri and Lucienne (Danis) C.; e. Univ. of Montreal B.A. 1948, M.D. 1953; m. Pierrette d. late Charlemagne Legault 27 June 1957; one s. Jean-François; PROF. OF PEDIATRICS, UNIV. OF MONTREAL since 1971; Dir. Poison Control Center, Ste-Justine Hosp. 1959–87; Residency Univ. of Montreal 1953–55; Babies and Children Hosp. Western Reserve Univ. Cleveland 1955–57; Assoc. Prof. present univ. 1964, Prof. 1971, Chrmn. of Pediatrics 1974–82; co-author 'Precis de Pediatrie' 3rd ed. 1982; 'Poisons, Emergency Treatment'; 'Practical antibiotic guide in pediatrics' 1989 and 1992; mem. Royal Coll. Phys.; Am. Acad. Pediatrics; Candn. Med. Assn.; Candn. Pediatric Soc.; R. Catholic; Home: 115 Duchastel, Outremont, Que. H2V 3E9; Office: 3175 Chemin Ste-Catherine, Montreal, Que. H3T 1C5.

**CHIEH, Chung,** Ph.D.; professor of chemistry; b. Mau-Ming, China 13 March 1939; s. Kwan-Fu and Rao-Ying (Deng) C.; e. Nat. Taiwan Univ. B.Sc. 1963; Nat. Tsing Hua Univ. M.Sc. 1965; Univ. of B.C. Ph.D. 1969; m. Shiao-Yu d. Wei-ben and Ming Chiang 26 June 1966; children: Yuen-Shung, Baldwin Yuen-Hsiang; PROF., CHEM. DEPT., UNIV. OF WATERLOO 1987– ; Chem. Lectr., Vancouver City Coll. 1967–68; post-doct. fellow, Univ. of Waterloo 1969–70; Asst. Prof. 1970–78; Assoc. Prof. 1978–87; Vis. Prof., Univ. of Connecticut 1978; Nat. Tsing Hua Univ. 1988; Founding Chrmn., Chinese Cultural Ctr. 1973; Gen. Sec., 10th Internat. Conf. on Chem. Edn., (Waterloo, Aug. 1989) 1987–89; Founding Pres., Assoc. for Human Rights in China, Can. 1989; instrumental in release from house arrest of Gen. Sun Li-Jen (Taiwan) 1988; Mem., Am. Chem. Soc.; Am. Crystallographic Assn.; Chem. Soc. of Can.; author of one book, 84 sci. papers & 3 book chapters; Home: 240 Shakespeare Dr., Waterloo, Ont. N2L 2T6; Office: Waterloo, Ont. N2L 3G1.

**CHIKHANI, Aziz Youssef,** B.Sc., M.A.Sc., Ph.D.; university professor and administrator; b. Cairo, Egypt 25 Jan. 1949; s. Youssef Aziz and Susan Youssef (Samaan) C.; e. Cairo Univ. B.Sc. 1971; Univ. of Waterloo M.A.Sc. 1976, Ph.D. 1981; m. Claudia d. Charles and Margaret Morrison 28 June 1989; step-children: Christine, William; PROFESSOR, ELECTRICAL & COMPUTER ENGINEERING, ROYAL MILITARY COLLEGE 1980– ; Lecturer, Menoufia Univ. 1971–74; Consulting Engr., Inotrade 1971–74; moved to Canada 1974; Head, Dept. of Electrical & Computer Engineering, Royal Military College 1990– ; Adjunct Prof., Univ. of Waterloo; Univ. of Windsor; Chair, Profl. Engrs. of Ont. Kingston Chapter 1992– ; Sr. Mem., Inst. of Elecrical & Electronics Engrs. 1983– ; author/co-author 100 journal and conf. papers; recreations: tennis, soccer, reading, walking; Home: 1289 Acadia Dr., Kingston, ont. K7M 8R3; Office: Kingston, Ont. K7K 5L0.

**CHILCOTT, Hon. Mr. Justice W. Dan,** Q.C., LL.B.; judge; b. Ottawa, Ont. 15 May 1929; s. James Chilcott; e. Dalhousie Univ.; Dalhousie Law Sch. LL.B.; m. Jean Davidson Pyper 21 July 1962; children: Alison, Jenifer; JUSTICE, SUPREME COURT OF ONTARIO 1988 and DEPUTY JUDGE, SUPREME COURT OF THE NORTHWEST TERRITORIES; member of the PENSION APPEALS BOARD; former Partner, Binks, Chilcott & Simpson; called to Bar of N.S. 1954, Ont. 1956; cr. Q.C. 1966; Trustee, Grace General Hospital; Mem. Salvation Army Adv. Bd., Ottawa; Past Pres. & Life Dir., Central Canada Exhibition Assoc.; former Vice Chrmn., Police Comn., Ottawa; Treasurer, Law Soc. Upper Can.; Bd. Mem., Rideauwood Inst., Ottawa; Protestant; Clubs: Ottawa Hunt & Country; Cercle Universitarie; Home: 3194 Riverside Dr., Ottawa, Ont. K1V 8N7; Office: Court House, 161 Elgin, Ottawa, Ont. K2P 2K1.

**CHILD, Arthur James Edward,** O.C., B.Com., M.A., F.C.I.S. (1952), LL.D.; company executive; b. Guildford, Surrey, Eng., 19 May 1910; s. William Arthur and Helena Mary (Wilson) C.; e. Gananoque (Ont.) Pub. and High Schs.; Queen's Univ., B.Com. 1931; Harvard Business Sch. AMP, 1956; Univ. of Toronto M.A. 1960; LL.D. 1983 (Queen's); LL.D. 1984 (Toronto, Calgary); m. Mary Gordon 15 Dec. 1955; CHRMN. AND CHIEF EXTVE. OFFR., BURNS FOODS LTD. 1966– ; Chief Auditor, Canada Packers Ltd. 1938–52; Vice Pres. 1952–60; Pres., Intercontinental Packers Ltd. 1960–66; Chrmn., Ajex Enterprises Ltd.; A.R. Clarke and Co. Ltd.; Canada West Foundation; Pres. Jamar, Inc.; Dir., Imperial Windsor Group; RHW Foundation; Col. (Hon.) 5 Signal Regiment, South Africa Order of Good Hope, South Africa; author: 'Economics and Politics in U.S. Banking'; co-author: 'Internal Control' with Bradford Cadmus; International President, Inst. of Internal Auditors, 1948–49; mem., Royal Candn. Mil. Inst.; Officer, Order of Can. 1985; Col. (Hon.), Communications and Electronics Br., Cdn. Armed Forces; Clubs: University (Toronto) R.C.Y.C. (Toronto); R.C.M.I. (Toronto); Mt. Royal (Montreal); St. James's (Montreal); Saint-Denis; Vancouver; Harvard (Boston); Ranchmen's; Calgary Golf & Country; RVYC, Vancouver; Office: P.O. Box 2520, Stn. M, Calgary, Alta. T2P 3X4.

**CHILD, Donald A.,** C.D., B.A., M.P.A., Brig. Gen. C.F. (retired); retired international public servant/NATO international secretariat; b. Clair, Sask. 14 May 1924; s. Trayton Smith and Annie Donald (Sands) C.; e. Heaton Moor Coll., Cheshire, Eng.; Univ. of Sask., B.A. 1948; Queen's Univ., M.P.A. 1971; m. Hope; d. Fred and Edna McKay 5 Aug. 1949; children: Shelagh, Michelle; Dep. Dir., Civil Emergency Planning, N.A.T.O. HQ. 1980–88; Air Nav./Flying Offr., R.C.A.F. 1943–45; RCAF & Candn. Forces 1948–79: service in France, Germany, U.S., Belgium, & Can.; flying with 412, 419 and 440 squadrons; last appt. Sec. of the Staff, Supreme HQ Allied Powers in Europe; ret. as Brig. Gen.; joined N.A.T.O. in 1980; Mem., Internat. Inst. of Strategic Studies; Air Force Officers Assoc.; Candn. Inst. of Internat. Affairs; Royal United Services Inst.; Home: 2022 Ocean Cliff Pl., Surrey, B.C. V4A 5Y5.

**CHILDERS, Charles E.,** B.Sc.; mining executive; b. West Frankfort, Ill. 29 Oct. 1932; s. Joel M. and Cora E. (Choate) C.; e. Univ. of Ill., B.Sc. 1955; m. Norma d. Carl and Anna Casper 8 June 1952; children: Joel, Katrina; CHRMN., PRES. & C.E.O., POTASH CORPORATION OF SASKATCHEWAN INC. 1990– ; Duval Corp., Carlsbad, NM 1955–62; IMC 1963–77; Vice Pres., IMC, Esterhazy Opns. 1977–79; Pres., IMC Coal, Kentucky 1979–81; Vice-Pres., Potash Opns., IMC, Illinois 1981–82; Vice-Pres., Expansion & Devel. 1982–87; Pres. & C.E.O., Potash Corp. of Sask. Inc. 1987–90; Past Chrmn., Canpotex Ltd.; Past Chrmn., Potash & Phosphate Inst. & Found. for Agronomic Rsch.; Past Chrmn., Sask. Potash Prod. Assn. 1985–87; Bd. Mem., Potash and Phosphate Inst. of Can.; Mem. Candn. Operations Advisory Bd. of Allendale Mutual Insurance Co.; Bd. Mem., Battle Mountain Gold Co.; QUNO Corp.; Council Mem. and Chrmn. of Finance Ctte., Internat. Fertilizer Industry Assoc. (IFA); Past Chrmn., The Fertilizer Inst.; Vice-Chrmn., Mem., Fertilizer Industry Adv. Ctte. to the Food and Agriculture Orgn. of the UN; Mem., Am. Inst. of Mining Engrs.; Candn. Inst. of Mining, Metallurgy & Petroleum; Dir.-at-Large, Junior Achievement of Canada; Club: Riverside Country; Home: 102 Lakeshore Terrace, Saskatoon, Sask. S7J 3X6; Office: Ste. 500, PCS Tower, 122 – 1st Ave. S., Saskatoon, Sask. S7K 7G3.

**CHILDS, Ronald Frank,** Ph.D., D.Sc.; educator; university executive; b. Liss, Hants., Eng. 30 Nov. 1939; s. Walter Frank and Gwendoline May (Walters) C.; e. Bath Univ. B.Sc. 1966; Nottingham Univ. Ph.D. 1966,

D.Sc. 1984; m. Grace d. Robert and Barbara Walker 3 July 1965; children: Sarah, Michael; VICE PRES. (RSCH.) McMASTER UNIV. 1989– ; Postdoctoral Fellow in Chem. Univ. of Cal. Los Angeles 1966–68; Asst. Prof. of Chem. present Univ. 1968, Assoc. Prof. 1972–78, Chrmn. of Chem. 1982–84, Dean of Sci. 1984–89; Rsch. Leave Chem. Univ. of Alta. 1976; Dir.: Ont. Centre for Material Rsch. 1988–89; Telecommunications Rsch. Inst. Ont. 1989– ; Manufacturing Rsch. Corp. Ont. 1989– ; Mgmt. Technol. & Innovation Inst. 1989–92; Business Adv. Ctr. 1990– ; Fields Inst. for Rsch. in Mathematical Sciences 1992–93; Vice-Chair, Supercomputing Mgmt. Bd., Ont. Ctr. for Large Scale Computing 1990–91; author over 100 rsch. papers, reviews; Fellow, Chem. Soc. Can.; mem. Am. Chem. Soc.; Royal Chem. Soc.; Office: Gilmour Hall-112, 1280 Main St. W., Hamilton, Ont. L8S 4L8.

**CHING, Julia Chia-yi,** B.A., M.A., Ph.D., L.H.D., F.R.S.C.; university professor; b. Shanghai, China 15 Oct. 1934; d. William L.K. and Christina C. (Tsao); e. Coll. of New Rochelle B.A. 1958; Catholic Univ. of Amer. M.A. 1960; Australian Natl. Univ. Ph.D. 1972; m. Willard G. s. Gurdon C. and Miriam B. Oxtoby 25 July 1981; children: John Ching (adopted); stepchildren: David, Susan (Oxtoby); PROFESSOR, VICTORIA COLLEGE, UNIV. OF TORONTO 1981– ; Lecturer, Australian Nat. Univ. 1969–74; Visiting Assoc. Prof., Columbia Univ. 1974–75; Assoc. Prof., Yale Univ. 1975–78; Religion Dept., Univ. of Toronto 1978–81; cross-apptd. to East Asian Studies 1979– ; & Philosophy 1981– ; Visiting Prof., Rice Univ. 1985; Univ. of Tübingen 1987; Tsing-hua Univ. 1989; Ecole Pratique des Hautes Etudes Sorbonne 1992; Co-Pres., 33rd Internat. Congress of Asian & N. African Studies 1990; Fellow, Royal Soc. of Canada 1990– ; Hon. LHD, St. Andrew's Coll.,– ;N. Carolina 1993; Internat. Woman of the Year, Internat. Biog. Centre 1993–94; Trustee, United Bd. for Christian Higher Edn. in Asia 1978–85; Hocking-Cabot Trust 1992– ; Consultant, Chiang Ching-kuo Foudn. 1994– ; Hon. Advisor, Metro Chinese Cultural Centre Project 1994– ; Edit. Bd. Mem., 'J. of History of Ideas' 1976– ; 'Concilium' 1988– ; Book Review Ed., 'Philos. East & West' 1988– ; author: 'To Acquire Wisdom, the Way of Wang Yang-ming' 1976, 'Confucianism and Christianity' 1977 (also in German), 'Wang Yang-ming'(Chinese) 1988, 'Probing China's Soul' 1990, 'Chinese Religions' 1993; co-author: 'Christianity and Chinese Religions' 1989 (also in German, Italian, French, Chinese); editor: 'Records of Ming Scholars' 1987, 'Moral Enlightenment' 1992, 'Discovering China' 1992, 'Sages and Filial Sons' 1991; trans.: 'Philosophical Letters of Wang Yang-ming' 1972 (from Chinese), 'Pascal's Pensées' 1969 (selected from French into Chinese); recreation: animals, house plants, meditation; Office: Victoria College, University of Toronto, Toronto, Ont. M5S 1K7.

**CHIPMAN, Robert A.,** M.Eng., Ph.D.; university professor emeritus; b. Winnipeg, Man. 28 Apr. 1912; s. George F. and Emily R. (Christie) C.; e. Univ. of Manitoba, B.Sc. (E. Eng.) 1932; McGill Univ., M.Eng. 1933; Cambridge Univ., Ph.D. 1939; Harvard Univ. 1937–38; m. Lois M., d. Garnet S.L. Retallack, 29 June 1938; children: Eric George, Ralph Oliver, Julie Anne; PROF. EMERITUS OF ELECTRICAL ENGINEERING, UNIV. OF TOLEDO 1978– ; Assoc. Prof. of Elect. Engn., McGill Univ. 1947–57; Prof. of Elect. Engn., Univ. of Toledo 1957–78; Fellow, Inst. of Elect. and Electronic Engrs.; mem., Soc. for Hist. of Tech.; Sigma Xi; Protestant; recreation: travel; Home: 3547 Rushland, Toledo, Ohio 43606.

**CHIPMAN, Thomas B.;** retired executive; b. Toronto, Ont. 10 Nov. 1928; s. John Howland and Helen Eileen (Brown) C.; e. St. Andrew's Coll., Hon. Matric.; Univ. Toronto, 1st Yr. Commerce & Finance; Univ. Western Ont., Mgmt. Training Course 1959; m. Bernice, d. Lloyd and Cora Janes, 10 June 1961; Extve., Grand & Toy Ltd. 1973–91; Dir., Bryant Press Ltd.; Shanahan Carriage Co.; joined Brown Brothers Ltd. 1948 (Pres. 1962–72); mem. Wholesale Stationers Assn. (U.S.A.) (Dir. 1962–72; Pres. 1969–71); served as 2nd Lieut., 48th Highlanders of Can. (Militia) 1948–51; active service, 27th Candn. Infantry Brigade (Germany), rank, Lieut.; mem., Zeta Psi Fraternity (Univ. Toronto); recreations: fitness programs; golf; Clubs: Toronto Hunt; Badminton & Racquet; Briars Golf & Country; Rosedale Walking; Home: 21 Dale Ave., Apt. 522, Toronto, Ont. M4W 1K3.

**CHIPPINDALE, Warren,** B. Com., F.C.A.; corporate director; b. Denver, Colo. 22 March 1928; s. Alan and late Gem C.; e. Westmount (Que.) schs.; McGill Univ. B.Com. 1949, L.A. 1951; C.A. 1951; m. Jane Caverhill d. late John L. and late Doris Cameron 10 Nov. 1951; children: Alan, John, Linda Gendron, Debra Pellerin, Nancy Bulow; Chrmn. & Chief Exec. Partner, Coopers & Lybrand (Canada) 1971–86; Chrmn. Coopers & Lybrand (Internat.) 1971–74–77–80–84; Cdn. representative on Council of Int'l. Federation of Accountants 1982–85; Gov. McGill Univ.; Montreal Neurological Inst.; Founding Gov. Cdn. Comprehensive Auditing Foundation 1980; mem., Panel of Senior Advisors to Auditor General of Canada 1976–86; Business Council on National Issues 1978–86; Dir.: Boy Scouts of Can.; Alcan; Bell Canada; B.C.E. Mobile Communications Inc.; Bell Canada Enterprises; The Molson Companies; Canadian Investment Fund, Inc.; The Tremblant Club (1985) Ltd.; author 'Modern Audit Philosophy: The Practical Application' 1967; numerous prof. articles; co-ed. 'A Businessman's Guide to Current Value Accounting' 1977; 'Acquisitions and Mergers in Canada' 1970/77; Pres., McGill Grads.' Soc. 1976–77; Soc. Indust. Accts. Montreal 1957–58; recreations: skiing, tennis, golf; Clubs: Mount Royal; Mount Bruno Country; Montreal Indoor Tennis; Canadian (Montreal-Pres. 1966–67); Cypress Run; Home: Rue Cuttle, P.O. Box 89, Mont Tremblant, Que. J0T 1Z0; Office: 1170 Peel St., Suite 3000, Montreal, Que. H3B 4T2.

**CHIR-STIMPSON, Susanne,** B.A., M.A.; corporate executive; b. Montreal, Que. 7 March 1954; d. Bernard and Dora (Marks) Chir; e. Concordia Univ. B.A. 1981; York Univ. M.A. 1986; CEGEP Bourgchemin St. Hyacinthe, Textile Chem. dipl.; VICE-PRES., CORPORATE AFFAIRS, GLAXO CANADA INC. 1991– ; Parental Worker, Schering Inc. 1971–72; Printing & Textile Tech., CIBA-GEIGY 1972–76; CHIMO Editor 1976–80; Mgr., Public Relations 1980–84; Dir. Corp. Relations 1984–90; Vice-Pres., Decima Research 1990–91; advisor to President of Niagara Inst. on 'Leadership for the 21st Century'; Mem., Credit Valley Hosp. Found. Bd.; Candn. Science Writers Assn.; Inst. of Political Involvement Bd.; York Alumni; Concordia Alumni; Candn. Chem. Producers Assn. (Past Public Affairs Ctte.); Pharm. Mfrs. Assn. of Canada (Past Public Affairs Ctte.); CROP Protection Inst. of Canada (Past Public Affairs Ctte.); Candn. Public Relations Soc.; Internat. Assn. of Business Communications; inventor / copyright holder on Issues Management Model involving multi-stakeholder trend/issue identification; recreations: writing, nature, art; Home: Mississauga, Ont.; Office: 7333 Mississauga Rd., Mississauga, Ont. L5N 6L4.

**CHISHOLM, Jeffrey S.,** B.Sc.; banker; b. Erie, Pa. 20 March 1949; s. Daniel V. and Natalie H. (Hall) C.; e. Georgetown Univ. Washington, D.C. B.Sc. 1971; m. Mary Ellen d. Richard and Mary Joyce 27 May 1972; children: Matthew, Nellie, Brian; VICE CHRMN., CORPORATE AND INSTL. FINANCIAL SERVICES, BANK OF MONTREAL 1990– ; Trainee Harris Bank, Chicago 1971, Div. Adm. Money Mkt. Operations 1980, Group Exec. of Treasury 1981, Sr. Vice Pres. and Group Exec. Treasury 1982; Sr. Vice Pres. and Dep. Treas. World-wide Trading 1984, Exec. Vice Pres. and Treas. of Bank 1986; Dir. Nesbitt Thomson; Bd. mem., Financial Institutions Center, Wharton School of the Univ. of Pennsylvania; mem., Canadian-American Ctte.; mem., Adv. Ctte. Sports Celebrities Found.; Princess Margaret Hosp. Council; Extve. Ctte., Royal Winter Fair; Ctte. Mem., Toronto-Chicago Sister City Ctte.; Dir., Country Day School (King, Ont.); recreations: riding, training horses, fishing; Clubs: Toronto North York Hunt; Timberlane Tennis; Home: R.R.3, King City, Ont. L0G 1K0; Office: P.O. Box 1, 1 First Canadian Place, Toronto, Ont. M5X 1A1.

**CHISHOLM, Maj.-Gen. John Robert,** C.M.M., C.D., B.A.; aerospace executive; b. Kentville, N.S. 5 May 1936; s. John Thomas and Elsie Augusta (Pazant) C.; e. Sackville (N.B.) High Sch.; Coll. Militaire Royale de Saint-Jean, Que.; Univ. of Man. B.A. 1979; Staff Coll. Toronto 1969; m. Gwendolyn d. Roland and Juanita Berry Phinney 23 May 1956; children: Diane Elizabeth, Steven Bruce; VICE PRES. GOVT. RELATIONS, ROLLS-ROYCE INDUSTRIES CANADA INC. 1991– ; enlisted RCAF 1953, comnd. as Pilot 1957; served 432 Fighter Sqdn. Bagotville, Que. until 1963 followed by exchange tour with 111 Sqdn. RAF Wattisham, Suffolk, UK; Sr. Staff Offr. Flight Safety Air Defence Command HQ North Bay, Ont. 1966; served with 427 and 403 Tactical Helicopter Sqdns. Petawawa, Ont. and Gagetown, N.B.; C.O. 403 Sqdn. 1973; Dir. Flight Safety NDHQ Ottawa 1977; Base Commdr. CFB Comox, B.C. 1980; Dep. Commdr. 10 Tactical Air Group St. Hubert 1982; promoted Brig. Gen. and apptd. Commdr. 1984; Maj.-Gen. and Dep. Commdr. Air Command Winnipeg 1987, resigned Candn. Forces 1990; Vice Pres. Bus. Devel., Bristol Aerospace Ltd. 1990; Dir., Rolls-Royce Product Support; National Aviation Museum Soc.; mem. RCAF Assn.; recreations: golf, sailing, skiing; Clubs: Rideau, Royal Ottawa; Home: 6194 Voyageur Dr., Orleans, Ont. K1C 2W3; Office: 130 Albert St., Suite 912, Ottawa, Ont. K2P 5G4.

**CHISHOLM, Lionel Donald John,** M.D., F.R.C.S.(C); ophthalmologist; educator; b. Montréal, Qué. 9 July 1935; s. Donald Munro and Isabelle Ann (Frizzell) C.; e. Westdale Secondary Sch. Hamilton, Ont. 1953; Univ. of Toronto M.D. 1959, Postgrad. Med. Edn. 1964; m. Ann d. Andrew and Mildred Webster 12 Feb. 1960; children: Sarah Ann, John Webster; DEPY. CHRMN., PROF. OF OPHTHALMOLOGY AND DIR. RETINA-VITREOUS UNIT, DEPT. OF OPHTHALMOLOGY, WEST VIRGINIA UNIV., Morgantown, West Virginia; joined teaching staff Univ. of Toronto 1966, Prof. of Ophthalmol. 1979–93; Chrmn. Med. Adv. Ctte. 1981–83, Trustee 1979–83; Ophthalmologist-in-Chief, Toronto Western Hosp. 1979–87, Acting Ophthalmologist-in-Chief, Toronto Hospitals 1987–91; Trustee, Eye Research Inst. of Ont.; Fellow, Retina Found. and Mass. Eye & Ear Infirmary, Harvard Med. Sch. 1964–66; mem. active staff Hosp. for Sick Children 1967–93; author numerous sci. articles and book chapters; mem. Candn. Med. Assn.; Ont. Med. Assn. (Past Chrmn. Ophthalmol. Sect.); Am. Retina Soc. (Charter mem.); Schepens Internat. Soc. (Charter mem.); Candn. Ophthalmol. Soc.; Am. Acad. Ophthalmol.; Presbyterian; recreations: music, theatre, riding, sailing; Clubs: RCYC; Toronto & North York Hunt; Office: University Eye Ctr., West Virginia Univ. Health Sciences Ctr., P.O. Box 9193, Morgantown, West Virginia 26506–9193, U.S.A.

**CHISLETT, (Margaret) Anne,** B.A.; playwright; b. St. John's, Nfld. 22 Dec. 1942; d. Hunter G. and M. Margaret (Foley) C.; e. Holy Heart of Mary Reg. H.S. 1960; Mem. Univ. of Nfld., B.A. (Hons.) 1964; Univ. of B.C. (theatre); m. James G. s. Ruth and Murray Roy 1974; plays produced: 'A Summer Burning' 1977; 'The Tomorrow Box' 1980 (trans. & perf. in Japanese, Latvian & French; prod. & toured extensively in Japan); 'Quiet in the Land' 1981 (produced Circle Rep Theatre, NY 1986); 'Another Season's Promise' (with K. Roulston) 1986; 'Half a Chance' 1987; 'The Gift' (for children) 1988; 'Yankee Notions' 1990 (dates rep. 1st prod. date); widely prod. throughout Canada; has written several radio dramas for CBC; Co-founder with J. Roy, Blyth Summer Festival 1975 (Assoc. Dir. 1975–78); Chalmers Candn. Play Award 1982; Gov. Gen. Award (Drama) 1983; W.C. Good Award 1990; Mem., Playwrights Union of Can.; ACTRA; recreations: gardening; Home: P.O. Box 863, Clinton, Ont. N0M 1L0; Office: c/o R.A. Freedman Dramatic Agency Inc., 1501 Broadway, Ste. 2310, New York, NY 10036.

**CHITTY, Dennis Hubert,** M.A., D.Phil.; professor emeritus; b. Bristol, U.K. 18 Sept. 1912; s. Hubert Chitty; came to Can. 1930; e. Univ. of Toronto B.A. 1935; Oxford Univ. M.A. 1947, D.Phil. 1949; m. 1stly: Helen Marie (dec.) d. late Robert O. Stevens, St. Catharines, Ont. 4 July 1936; m. 2ndly: Sharon Anne Kendall d. late Sidney Wilfred Miller 13 Aug. 1988; children (by 1st marriage): Jane Carol, Kathleen Joanna, Stephen Gwilym; Prof. Emeritus of Zool. since 1978; Ont. Fisheries Research Lab. summers 1932–35; Small Mammal Research, Bureau of Animal Population, Oxford Univ. 1935–61 and Univ. of B.C. 1972–87; taught Hist. and Principles of Biol. Univ. of B.C. 1961–78 (Master Teacher Award 1973); held Nat. Sci. Foundation Fellowship at Smith Coll. 1968–69 (Sr. Foreign Scientist); Fry Medallist, Candn. Soc. Zool. 1988; author various scient. papers regulation numbers in natural populations animals especially small mammals; mem. Royal Soc. Can.; Candn. Soc. Zool.; Liberal; Home: 1750 Knox Rd., Vancouver, B.C. V6T 1S3; Office: Dept. of Zoology, Univ. of B.C., Vancouver, B.C. V6T 1Z4.

**CHIU, John Hung Cheung,** M.D., F.R.C.P.(C); medical doctor (radiologist); b. Hong Kong 14 May 1941; s. Paul Kaison and Ling (Chan) C.; e. Univ. of Hong Kong M.B., B.S. 1966; m. Yvonne d. Ting Sum and Chid Lee Tang 9 June 1968; one s.: Derrick; CONS. RADIOLOGIST, NORTH YORK BRANSON HOSP. 1974– ; Res., Ottawa Civic Hosp. 1969–73; Chief Res. 1972–73; Fellow, Mont. Neurol. Inst., McGill Univ. 1973–74; Acting Chief, Dept. of Med. Imag., present hosp. 1987; Chrmn., Cont. Med. Edn. 1983–87, 1989– ; Adv., Toronto Inst. of Med. Technol. 1983–87; Cons., Univ. of Toronto 1987– ; Pres., Chinese Candn. Med. Soc. 1981–82; Pres., N. York Branson Med. Soc. 1989– ; Counc. Mem., Ont. Med. Assn.; Conf. Chrmn., 5th Internat. Conf. on Health Problems related to Chinese in N. Am. 1990; Volunteer Serv. Award, Govt. of Ont. 1985; Pres., Catholic Immigr. Bur. 1991– ; Pres., Fed. of Chinese Candn. Profls. (Ont.) Edn. Found. 1985– ;

Treas., Chinese Inform. & Commun. Serv. 1989–91; Charter Mem., Knights of Columbus Good Shepherd Counc. (Chancellor 1983–85; Trustee 1987–90); Mem., Parish Counc., St. Edward's Ch. 1990– ; Life Mem., Art Gall. of Ont.; Royal Ont. Mus.; recreations: opera, classical music, art, travelling; clubs: Bayview Country, Toronto Mandarin; Home: 150 Heath St. W., Suite 201, Toronto, Ont. M4V 2Y4; Office: 555 Finch Ave. W., North York, Ont. M2R 1N5.

**CHIU, Ray Chu-Jeng,** M.D., Ph.D., FRCSC, FACS; professor of surgery; b. Tokyo, Japan 13 Mar. 1934; s. Ping-Hong and Li-Chu (Kuo) C.; e. Nat. Taiwan Univ., M.D. 1959; McGill Univ., Ph.D. 1970; m. Jane Mong-Hua d. Wen-Bing and Chu-Chi Tan 17 Apr. 1962; children; Daniel Yi-Han, Wendy Shiu-Wen; CHRMN., DIVISION OF CARDIOVASCULAR AND THORACIC SURGERY 1992– ; AND PROF. OF SURGERY, MCGILL UNIV. 1981– ; Intern. Baltimore City Hosp. 1961–62; Res. in Gen., Thoracic & Cardiovascular Surg., Downstate Med. Ctr., State Univ. of N.Y. 1962–68; Fellow & Scholar, Med. Rsch. Counc. of Can. 1968–76; Asst. Prof., McGill Univ. 1971–76, Assoc. Prof. 1976–81; Chrmn., Div. of Cardiovascular and Thoracic Surgery, McGill Univ. 1992; Sr. Surg. in Cardiovascular & Thoracic Surg., Montreal Gen. Hosp.; Dir. of Surg. Rsch., Montreal Gen. Hosp. Rsch. Inst.; Attending Surg., Royal Victoria Hosp.; Chrmn., Exam. Bd., Royal Coll. of Phys. & Surg. of Can. (Cardiovascular & Thoracic Surg.); Ed. Bd., Annals of Thoracic Surgery; Vis. Prof., Candn., U.S., U.S.S.R., European, Japanese & Chinese univs.; Mem., Am. Surgical Assn.; Am. Assn. for Thoracic Surg.; Soc. for Univ. Surg.; Am. Coll. of Surg.; Soc. Internat. de Chirurgie; Candn. Med. Assn.; author: 'Myocardial Protection in Regional & Global Ischemia' vol. 1 1981, vol. 2 1984 and 279 sci. papers & abstracts; editor: 'Biomechanical Cardiac Assist' 1986; 'Muscle tranformation for cardiac assist and repair' 1990; recreations: music, reading; Home: 61 Belvedere Circle, Montreal, Que. H3Y 1G9; Office: C9–169.1, 1650 Cedar Ave., Montreal, Que. H3G 1A4.

**CHIVERS, Tristram,** B.Sc., Ph.D., D.Sc., F.C.I.C., FRSChem. FRSCan; university professor; b. Bath, England 22 Aug. 1940; s. Robert Albany and Edith Grace (Tristram) Ch.; e. Colston's Boys Sch. Bristol, Eng. 1948–58; Univ. of Durham B.Sc. 1961, Ph.D. 1964; m. Susan d. Hugh and Margaret Campbell-Ferguson 31 Dec. 1966; children: Peter Tristram, Sally Jane; PROFESSOR OF CHEMISTRY, UNIV. OF CALGARY 1978– ; Asst. Prof. of Chem., Univ. of Calgary 1969–73; Assoc. Prof. 1973–78; Alcan Lecture Award, Candn. Soc. for Chem. 1987; Anglican; Treas., Candn. Soc. of Chem. 1990–92; Sr. Ed., 'Can. J. of Chem.' 1993– ; author of over 200 pubns. on main group inorganic chem.; recreations: choral singing, squash, cricket, hiking, nordic skiing; Home: 3919 Vardell Rd., Calgary, Alta. T3A 0C3; Office: Calgary, Alta. T2N 1N4.

**CHIZICK, Jerry L.;** food industry executive; b. Toronto, Ont. 24 Sept. 1948; s. Nathan and Fay (Katz) C.; e. electronics technologist; m. Sarah d. Joe and Leah Politzer 13 Jan. 1974; children: Jayson, Michelle; VICE-PRES. BUSINESS DEVELOPMENT, CORPORATE FOODS LIMITED and VICE-PRES. SALES AND MARKETING, DOUGH DELIGHT LIMITED (a Div. of Corporate Foods Ltd.) 1993– ; Dir., Circlet Foods Inc.; Purchasing Agent-Product Mgr., Faberge of Can.; Mktg. Mgr., Wampole Pharm.; Sales Mgr., Holway Packaging; Dir. of Mktg., Max Factor Canada; Dir. of Mktg., Corporate Foods Limited 1980–85, Vice Pres. Sales & Mktg. 1985–89, Sr. Vice Pres. 1989–93; Chrmn., Bakery Counc. of Canada; Home: 18 Savoy Cres., Thornhill, Ont. L4J 7W3; Office; 10 Four Seasons Place, Etobicoke, Ont. M9B 6H7.

**CHMIELENSKI, Andrew;** civil engineer; b. Warsaw, Poland 16 Apr. 1909; s. Jan Brug-Chmielenski and Maria (Kossowski) C.; e. Tech Univ. of Warsaw, Dipl. (Civil Engn.) 1934; m. Eileen Ann. d. Joseph Duffield, 25 July 1949; Design Engineer in Poland, 1934–39; Messrs. Braithwaite and Co., Engrs. Limited, London, Eng., 1946–48, Branch Manager in charge of Co.'s office in Syria, 1949–51; came to Canada Dec. 1951; Design Engr., The Foundation Co. of Canada Ltd., 1952–53; joined subsidiary Found. of Can. Engineering Corp. Ltd. (Fenco), 1953 as Design and Project Engr.; apptd. Div. Engr.-Marine Structures, 1957, Vice-Pres. 1960 (co-ordinated the work of the FENCO Reg. Offices), Pres. 1962, Chrmn. Bd. 1973, retired 1975; consultant since 1976; Publications: 'Modernization of a Harbour, St. John's, Nfld.'; served in 2nd World War, Polish, Middle East and Italian Campaigns, 1939–45 with Polish Army; awarded Polish Crosses (Krzyż Walecznych and Krzyż Zaslugi); mem., Corp. Prof. Engrs., Que.: Assn. Prof. Engrs., Ont.; Inst. Civil Engrs. Gt. Britain; Roman Catholic; recreation: gardening; Home: 3 Concorde Place, Apt. 1603, Don Mills, Ont. M3C 3K7.

**CHOCKALINGAM, Arun,** B.E., M.S., Ph.D.; medical researcher, university professor; b. Kandanur, India 5 July 1949; s. Subramaniam and Umayal Arunachalam; e. Univ. of Madras India B.E. 1970; Indian Inst. of Tech., Madras, India M.S. 1978; Memorial Univ. of Nfld. Ph.D. 1982; m. Shakuntala d. Meyyammai and Arunachalam 12 July 1972; one s.: Rajkumar; RESEARCH CONSULTANT, HEALTH CANADA 1991– ; Research Associate, Memorial Univ. of Nfld. 1981–86; Asst. Prof. 1986–92; Assoc. Prof. 1992–93; Pres., Candn. Coalition for High Blood Pressure Prevention & Control 1989– ; Dir., Candn. Hypertension Soc. 1985–88; Councillor, World Hypertension League 1989– ; Sec. Gen., Atlantic Cardiovascular Health Assn. 1980–92; Non-Res. Dir., Arma Hospitals Madras India; Mem., Adv. Bd., NHRDP Ctte. on Heart Health 1989–92; Mem., Internat. Adv. Bd., Victoria Declaration on Heart Health; Editor-in-Chief, Journal of Hypertension Control; Mem., Editorial Bds. of several medical journals; Reviewer of manuscripts and Rsch. Grant applications; First recipient, Dean of Graduate Studies Award for the best Ph.D. thesis, Memorial Univ. 1982; Chrmn., Candn. Stroke Surveillance System; author of several sci. pubns. in the field of cardiovascular medicine; Home: 1375 Talcy Cres., Orleans, Ont. K4A 3C4; Office: Health Canada, 6th Floor, Jeanne Mance Bldg., Tunney's Pasture, Ottawa, Ont. K1A 1B4.

**CHODOS, Peter F.,** B.Comm., C.A., M.B.A.; investment banker; b. Montreal, Que. 8 Jan. 1951; s. Abe and Margaret (Harris) C.; e. Westmount H.S. 1968; McGill Univ. B.Comm. (Hons.) 1972; Candn. Inst. of C.A.s 1974; Harvard Univ. M.B.A. 1976; m. Gene d. Samuel and Sara Granatstein 9 June 1974; children: Adam, Stephen; VICE PRES. AND DIR., DEACON BARCLAYS de ZOETE WEDD LIMITED 1992– ; Vice-Pres., Wood Gundy Limited 1976–81; Mng. Partner, Loewen, Ondaatje, McCutcheon & Company Limited 1983–92; Dir., ENSCOR Inc.; Consolidated Five Star Resources Ltd.; Office: 304 Bay St., Toronto, Ont. M5H 2P2.

**CHODOS, Philip,** B.C.L., LL.B.; lawyer; labour arbitrator; b. Montreal, Que. 29 Apr. 1948; s. Irving and Eva (Berger) C.; e. McGill Univ. B.A. 1969, B.C.L. 1972, LL.B. 1973; m. Frieda d. Schlomo and Maria Kuhnreich 19 Aug. 1973; children: Mark, Daniel; DEP. CHRMN., PUB. SERVICE STAFF RELATIONS BD. 1988– ; Labour Relations Secretariat, Privy Counc. Off. 1981–85; Sr. Couns., House of Commons 1985–88; Hebrew; Home: 4 Woodfern Ct., Nepean, Ont. K2H 8Y9.

**CHODOS, Robert Irwin,** B.Sc., M.A.; writer; editor; educator; b. Montreal, Que. 16 March 1947; s. Louis and Constance (Routtenberg) C.; e. Adath Israel Acad. Montreal 1963; McGill Univ. B.Sc. 1967; The Johns Hopkins Univ. 1967–68; Clark Univ. Worcester, Mass. M.A. 1990; m. Andrea d. Julius and Shirley Leis 26 Dec. 1977; children: Sarah, David; ed. Compass: A Jesuit Journal 1987– ; freelance book ed. 1976– ; and transl. Que. social sci. books 1980– ; briefings ed. This Magazine 1986– ; copy ed. RACAR 1987–90; Prin. and Teacher Temple Shalom Religious Sch. Kitchener, Ont. 1986– ; Dir., Candn. Magazine Publishers Assn. 1992– ; mem. ed. bd. Last Post mag. 1969–80, parlty. corr. 1971–72, 1976–77, news ed. 1972–74; rsch. cons. CBC radio and TV 1974–79; adjunct inst. in Eng. Fisher Jr. Coll. Clinton, Mass. 1983–84; instr. in jour. Conestoga Coll. Kitchener 1985; author 'Right-of-Way: Passenger Trains for Canada's Future' 1971; 'The CPR: A Century of Corporate Welfare' 1973; 'The Caribbean Connection' 1977; co-author: 'Winners, Losers: The 1976 Tory Convention' 1976; 'Your Place or Mine?' novel 1978; 'Brian Mulroney: The Boy from Baie-Comeau' 1984; 'Write All About It' 1986; 'Selling Out: Four Years of the Mulroney Government' 1988; 'The Unmaking of Canada' 1991; 'Quebec and the American Dream' 1991; 'Canada and the Global Economy' 1993; co-ed. 'Quebec: A Chronicle 1968–1972' 1972; 'Let Us Prey' 1974'; Jewish; recreations: travel, folk music; Home: P.O. Box 1311, New Hamburg, Ont. N0B 2G0; Office: 300, 10 St. Mary St., Toronto, Ont. M4Y 1P9.

**CHOI, Man-Duen,** M.Sc., Ph.D., F.R.S.C.; educator; b. Nanking, China 13 June 1945; e. The Chinese Univ. of Hong Kong B.Sc. 1967; Univ. of Toronto M.Sc. 1970, Ph.D. 1973; m. Pui-Wah Ip 6 Sept. 1972; children: Winston, Yvonne, Edmond; PROF. OF MATH. UNIV. OF TORONTO 1982– ; Lectr. in Math Univ. of Cal. Berkeley 1973–76; Asst. Prof. of Math. present Univ. 1976, Assoc. Prof. 1979; Coxeter-James Lectr. Candn. Math. Soc. 1983; Israel Halperin Prize 1980; Grantee, Natural Sci's & Eng. Rsch. Council Can. 1977– ; Candn. citizen 1976; author numerous rsch. articles math. jours.; Fellow, Acad. Sci's of Royal Soc. of Can.; mem. Am. Math. Soc.; Candn. Math. Soc.; Math. Assn. Am.; Office: Math. Dept., Univ. of Toronto, Toronto, Ont. M5S 1A1.

**CHOLETTE, Ronald H.;** business executive; b. Montreal, Que. 26 June 1934; s. Rolland and Anna (Jalbert) C.; e. Bourget Coll., 13th grade commercial; m. Micheline d. Paul Emile and Estelle Rouette 4 Feb. 1956; children: Jacques, Danielle, Louise, André; PRES., MOULURE ALEXANDRIA MOLDING; co-owner of firm established by father 1943 (purchased 1964); now largest wood moulding mfr. in Canada; 350 employees (incl. U.S. branch plant); annual sales $45 million; Catholic; recreations: golf, boating; clubs: Richelieu, Knights of Colombus; Home: Box 636, Alexandra, Ont. K0C 1A0; Office: 95 Lochiel E., Alexandria, Ont. K0C 1A0.

**CHOQUETTE, Gilbert,** B.A., B.C.L., D de l'Un.; writer; b. Montréal, Qué. 25 Nov. 1929; s. Claude and Pauline Geoffrion C.; e. Coll. Stanislas Montréal B.A. 1947; McGill Univ. B.C.L. 1950; Univ. de Paris D. de l'Université (Law) 1954; Univ. de Montréal Cert. de Langue et Litt. françaises 1971; m. Gilberte d. Jules and Madeleine Hoyau 16 Oct. 1954; three d. Marianne, Lorraine, Catherine; writer and sound track dir. Nat. Film Bd. 1954–68; French teacher Coll. Saint-Laurent Montréal 1968–78; poet and full time fiction writer since 1978; author (poetry) 'Au loin l'Espoir' 1958; 'L'Honneur de vivre' 1964; (fiction) 'L'Interrogation' 1962; 'L'Apprentissage' 1966; 'La Défaillance' 1969; 'La Mort au verger' 1975, reprinted 1988; 'Un Tourment extrême' 1979, transl. 'Wednesday's Child' 1981; 'La Flamme et la Forge' 1984 (Prix Esso 1984, Prix France-Québec 1985); 'Le Secret d'Axel' 1986; 'L'Étrangère ou Un printemps condamné' 1988; 'La Nuit yougoslave' 1989; 'Une Affaire de vol' 1990; mem. Union des Écrivains québécois; Académie des lettres du Québec; recreation: music (piano); Address: 2, 5765 Hudson Rd., Montréal, Qué. H3S 2G4.

**CHOQUETTE, Hon. Jerome,** Q.C., B.A., LL.L., Doctorate in economics; lawyer; b. Montreal, Que., 25 Jan. 1928; s. Claude and Pauline (Geoffrion) C.; e. Stanislas Coll., B.A.; McGill Univ., B.A., LL.L. 1949; Univ. of Paris, Doctorate in econ. (Jean Bertrand Nogaro Prize); Columbia Univ., Sch. of Business Adm.; called to Bar of Que. 1949; cr. Q.C. 1964; el. M.N.A. for Outremont in prov. g.e. 1966; re-el. 1970; Min. of Justice, Que. 1970–75; Mayor, City of Outremont, Que. 1983–91; Liberal; R. Catholic; recreations: golf, travel; Home: 4858, Chemin de la Côte-des-Neiges, Apt. 904, Montréal, Qué. H3V 1G8; Office: 5316 Park Ave., Suite 200, Montréal, Qué. H2V 4G7.

**CHOQUETTE, Son Honn. Marc,** B.A., LL.L.; juge; né Québec 18 fév. 1929; f. l'Hon Fernand, Juge de la Cour d'Appel de la Prov. de Qué. (à sa retraite depuis 1970) et de Dame Marguerite (Vallerand) C.; é. Séminaire de Québec; Coll. Charles Garnier; Univ. Laval; ép. Marie Galipeault, f. M. Jean-Paul Galipeault et Thérèse Michaud le 26 mai 1956; enfants: Claude, Marie, Bernard, Danièle, Philippe, Marc, Anick: JUGE A LA COUR DU QUÉBEC, CHAMBRE CRIMINELLE ET PÉNALE depuis 1988; admis au Barreau 1954; créé c.r. 1970; étude légale: DesRivières, Choquette, Rioux, Paquet, Goodwin et Vermette; il a été: Prés. de l'Assn. du Jeune Barreau de Qué., de la Jeune Chambre de Commerce de Qué.; conseiller du Barreau de Qué.; membre: du conseil génerale du Barreau de la province; du bureau de l'Assistance judiciaire et du Comité du Service de références du Barreau du Qué.; de l'Assn. du Barreau Candadien; de la Chambre de Commerce de Qué.; substitut de la couronne pour le dist. judiciare de Qué. 1960–66: avocat à la Cour municipale de Sillery 1977–80; nommé juge de la Cour des Sessions de la paix 1971; représentant du Québec et membre du Comité exécutif et secrétaire de l'Association canadienne des juges de Cours provinciales; occupé la fonction de juge coordonnateur de la Cour des Sessions de la paix pour le district d'appel du Québec 1980–86; Clubs: Kinsmen; Garnison (Québec): Golf de Cap-Rouge Inc.; Résidence: 1340 rue Leblanc, Sillery, Qué. G1T 2G7; Bureau: Cour des Sessions de la Province de Québec, Local B-16, Québec, Qué.

**CHORLEY, Desmond Mason;** writer; b. Liverpool, Eng. 21 June 1924; s. Herbert and Ada (Spink) C.; m. Edith d. Julius and Ida Leichnitz 11 Oct. 1952; children: Grant Mason, Pamela Jean; R.A.F. aircrew, Bomber Command 1943–47; wrote for daily newspapers & weekly bus. newspapers 1947–56; public relations writer 1956–60; advt. agy. vice-pres. – exec. & creative 1960–83; independent writer & ed. since 1983; contbr. of numerous articles to mags. in N. Am. & Europe, since 1949; articles, prose poems, prose pub. in anthologies; fiction pieces sold to C.B.C. and U.S. publs.; mem. Candn. Owners & Pilots Assn.; R.C.A.F. Assn.; Royal Candn. Legion; recreations: flying; swimming; Address: 83 Wishing Well Dr., Agincourt, Ont. M1T 1J2.

**CHORLTON, Ronald William,** B.Sc.F.; business executive; b. Birmingham, Eng. 13 Apr. 1925; s. William and Minerva (Cummings) C.; came to Can. 1928; e. Britannia Pub. and High Schs.; Univ. of B.C., B.Sc.F.; m. Mary, d. Harold Housden, 12 Sept. 1946 (dec. 1982); children: Michael William, Bruce Whitham, Lesley Bronwen, Jennifer Mary; m. Dixi Kathleen, d. late William B. Lambert and Mrs. H. Marpole of Montreal, 1984; CHAIRMAN & DIR., WAJAX LTD. 1977– ; Dir., Empire Company Ltd.; Credit Suisse Canada; served as Able Seaman, RCNVR 1944–45; Past Pres., Candn. Assoc. Equipment Distributors; mem., Ont. Prof. Foresters Assoc.; Candn. Inst. Forestry; Business Council on National Issues; Anglican; recreations: sailing, skiing, tennis; Clubs: Rideau (Ottawa); Mount Royal (Montreal); University (Toronto); Home: 81 Rideau Terrace, Ottawa, Ont. K1M 2A2; Office: 350 Sparks St., Ste. 900, Ottawa, Ont. K1R 7S8.

**CHORNEY, Harold Ross,** B.A., M.A., Ph.D.; university professor; b. St. Boniface, Man. 15 Aug. 1946; s. Joseph and Ethel (Zipursky) C.; e. Garden City Coll. 1963; Univ. of Man., B.A. (Hons.) 1968, M.A. 1970; London Sch. of Econ. 1970–72; Univ. of Toronto, Ph.D. 1984; m. Susannah Benady; children: Jessica, Samuel; ASSOC. PROF., PROG. IN PUBLIC POLICY & PUBLIC ADMIN., DEPT. OF POL. SCI., CONCORDIA UNIV. 1982– ; Econ. Cons., M.D.T. Socio-Econ. Cons. 1968; part-time Prof., Univ. of Man. 1972–73, 1976–78; Sr. Econ., Man. Housing & Renewal Corp. 1976–78; Prof. & Co-ord., Focus Prog., Dept. of Coll. & Univ., Govt. of Man. 1972–76; public affairs commentator, CBC, CTV 1970– ; Socio-Econ. Cons., Regina, Saskatoon, Govt. of Sask.; of Man.; of Ont.; fellowships: Woodrow Wilson 1968; John W. Dafoe 1969–70; Can. Counc. 1970–72; C.M.H.C. 1978–80; SSHRCC 1980–82; SSHRCC rsch. grant 1986–89; Mem., Candn. Pol. Sci. Assn.; East. Econ. Assn.; Assn. Econ. Pol.; Soc. de Sci.-Pol. Québécoise; Soc. for Advancement of Socio-Economics; Candn. Ctr. for Policy Alternatives; co-author: (with P. Hansen) 'Toward a Humanist Political Economy' 1992; author: 'Rediscovery Full Employment' 1993; 'A Regional Approach to Monetary and Fiscal Policy' 1992; 'Deficits - Fact or Fiction? Ontario's Public Finances and the Challenge of Full Employment' 1992; 'Dividing Up the Debt in the Case of Quebec Sovereignty' 1992; 'City of Dreams: Social Theory and the Urban Experience' 1989, 'The Deficit and Debt Management: An Alternative to Monetarism 1989; 'Regionalizing Monetary Policy, An Alternative to Monetarism: Learning from the Japanese Experience' (with Bernard Bouska) 1989; 'The Deficit and Public Policy' 1989, 'The Deficit: Hysteria and the Current Economic Crisis' 1985; recreations: golf, swimming, nordic skiing, painting; Home: Montreal, Que.; Office: 7141 Sherbrooke St. W., Montreal, Que. H4B 1R6.

**CHOUDHRY, Nanda K.,** B.A., M.Sc., Ph.D.; professor of economics; b. Bihar, India 10 Aug. 1930; s. Sudarshan Prasad and Savitri Devi C.; e. Patna Univ. India B.A. (Hons. & Distinction) 1948; Univ. of Wisconsin, M.Sc., Ph.D. 1963; m. Ushvendra Kaur d. Sohendra S. Sethee 24 May 1969; 2 sons; PROF., DEPT. OF ECONOMICS, UNIV. OF TORONTO; Asst. Prof., Univ. of Rochester 1958–61; Lectr. (Assoc. Prof.), Univ. of Buffalo 1961–62; Visiting Prof., Indian Statistical Inst. (India) 1962–63; Special Lectr., Assoc. Prof., Prof., present univ. 1963– ; Visiting Assoc. Prof., Univ. of Pennsylvania 1966–67; Visiting Prof., Delhi Sch. of Econ. (India) 1969–70, 1977–78; Life Mem., Indian Econometric Soc.; Cons., World Bank; Dept. of Finan. Ottawa; Econ. Counc. of Can.; Dept. of External Affairs; Past Pres., Candn. Assn. of South Asian Studies; Shastri Indo Candn. Inst.; author of 20 jour. articles; co-author: 'Trace Econometric Model of Canada' 1972, 'Local Impact of Foreign Trade' 1958; editor: 'Behind the North-South Dialogue,' 'Canada and South Asian Development: Trade and Aid'; co-editor: 'Readings in Economic Development' 1963; Home: 33 Parfield Dr., Willowdale, Ont. M2J 1C1; Office: Toronto, Ont. M5S 1A1.

**CHOUINARD, Marc R.,** B.Com., M.B.A.; retail executive; b. Trois Rivières, Qué. 23 May 1957; s. J. Roger and Gisele (Senechal) C.; e. Concordia Univ. B.Com. 1980; McGill Univ. M.B.A. 1982; m. Diane d. Gordon Wells 27 Dec. 1985; PRES., C.O.O. & DIR., WOODWARDS LTD. 1989– ; Mgr. Financial Analysis Via Rail Can. 1984 and Financial Planning 1985; Budget Mgr. Zellers Inc. 1986, Dir. Financial Planning & Analysis 1987, Vice Pres. and Controller 1988–89; Sr. Vice Pres. and Chief Fin. Offr. 1990–91, Extve. Vice Pres. 1992; Mem., Financial Extves.' Inst.; Retail Counc. of Can.; Internat. Retailers' Fedn.; Vancouver Bd. of Trade; Am. Mgmt. Assoc.; Club: Hollyburn Country; Office: 101 W. Hastings St., Vancouver, B.C. V6B 4G1.

**CHOUINARD, Marie;** artistic director; choreographer; dancer; b. Quebec, Que. 14 May 1955; FOUNDER, COMPAGNIE MARIE CHOUINARD (a dance company of seven or eight dancers) 1990; creation of choreography Le Sacre du printemps 1993; representations incl., 1993: National Arts Center (Ottawa), Festival Multiarte Escénico INBA'93 (Mexico), Serius Fun Festival, Lincoln Center (New York), Festival international de nouvelle danse, Salle Maisonneuve of Place des Arts (Montreal), Centre Geoges Pompidou (Paris); premiere of choereography 'Les Trous Du Ciel', Springdance Festival (Utrecht, Holland) 1991; representations incl.: 1992: Festival Internat. de Nouvelle Danse, Salle Maisonneuve of Place des Arts (Montreal); 1991: Premiere Dance Theatre (Toronto), Festival de Théâtre des Amériques (Montreal), 7th Winnipeg Dance Festival, National Arts Centre (Ottawa), Culturel Centrum Kortrijk (Belgium), Cultural Centrum Berchem (Belgium), Vooruit Kunstencentrum (Belgium), Hall Auditorium (Oberlin, Ohio, USA), Eurodanse (Mulhouse, France); Choreographer/soloist dancer & vocal artist: 1992: premiere of 'Terpsichore A Cappella,' Les Muses au Musée, Museum of Contemporary Arts (Montreal), premiere of 'This Instant and Eternity,' Sound Symposium (St. John's, Nfld.); 1990: premiere of 'An Open Letter to Terpsichore,' National Arts Centre (Ottawa); 1988: premiere of 'Biophilia,' Olympic Arts Festival (Calgary); premiere of 'Poeme D'Atmosphere,' in Immédiat Concerto, 4e Festival d'In(ter)ventions (Quebec); 1987: premiere of 'L'Apres-Midi d'un Faune,' Canada Dance Festival (Ottawa); 1986: premiere of 'S.T.A.B.' Canada back to Amsterdam Festival (Holland), premiere of 'Drive in the Dragon,' Museum of Contemporary Arts (Montreal), premiere of 'Gargouilles,' in Espèces nomades, Festival de poésie sonore (Québec); 1985: premiere of 'Table of Content' and 'Earthquake in the Heartchakra,' Holland Festival (Amsterdam, Holland); and approx. 20 performances; Representations incl.: Canada, Austria, Belgium, England, France, Holland, Israel, Japan, New Zealand, Spain, Switzerland, USA, in Festivals, Museums and Art galleries; Guest teacher: Grands Ballets Canadiens (Montreal), Theatre School of Amsterdam (Holland), Center for New Dance Development (Arnhem, Holland); Television network: 1990, special guest: J'aurais aimé vous voir danser, Madame Akarova, RTBF television, Belgium; 1982, special guest: Performance, television series with Laurie Anderson, Robert Wilson and Trisha Brown, ORF television Austria; Awards: 1988 Olympic Arts Commission, Gold medalist; 1987 Chalmers Award; 1986, Jacqueline-Lemieux Award; 1981: residency in Studio du Québec in New York; Recipient of numerous grants from Canada Arts Council, and Ministère des Affaires culturelles du Québec; Office: 3981 Boul. St-Laurent, Suite 615, Montréal, Qué. H2W 1Y5.

**CHOUINARD, L'Hon. Juge Roger,** B.A., LL.L., L.Sc.Soc.; né Kénogami, Qué. 9 février 1928; f. Donat et Elzire (Boivin) C.; é. Séminaire de Chicoutimi B.A. 1950 (cum laude); Univ. de Montréal LL.L. 1953 (cum laude; Mérite d'Argent 1954), L.Sc.Soc. 1953; ép. Maude fille de Philippe et Emma (Bergeron) Brassard le 30 novembre 1958; enfants: Renée, Line, Stéphane; JUGE, LA COUR D'APPEL 1983– ; admis au Barreau en 1954, pratiqua très activement le droit en société avec notamment Mes Toussaint McNicoll (par la suite juge à la Cour supérieure), P.E. Fortin (par la suite juge à la Cour provinciale), François Lamarre, Paul Casgrain; Claude Vaillancourt (maintenant juge à la Cour du Québec; nommé Conseiller de la Reine 1972; Juge à la Cour supérieure 1973 (Chicoutimi), Président du Comité général des juges de la Cour supérieure 1980–82 (Secrétaire 1978–79); Prés. des tribunaux d'arbitrage des enseignants du Qué. (pendant plusiers années); nommé sénateur internat. des Chambres de comm. des jeunes 1957; Procureur senior de la Couronne pour le district de Chicoutimi 1960–66; Arbitre des différends de travail dans les secteurs industriels et commerciaux; aussi conseiller en loi attitré de plusieurs corporations municipales; membre des comités provinciaux d'administration de la justice, d'aide juridique et de droit administratif; Prés. du comité de relations extérieures du Barreau du Saguenay; successivement conseiller et bâtonnier du Barreau du Saguenay; membre du Conseil général du Barreau du Québec; membre de l'Assn. du Barreau Canadien; Bureau: R-448, 300 boul. Jean Lesage, Québec City, Qué. G1K 8K6.

**CHOW, August,** B.Sc., M.Sc., FSA, FCIA, MAAA; actuary; b. Hong Kong 24 Sept. 1951; s. Yan Pui and Wai Fan (Yau) C.; e. Univ. of Wisconsin B.Sc. 1972; Univ. of Manitoba M.Sc. 1976; m. Lana d. Lap-Him and Pui-Wan Wong 21 Aug. 1976; children; Rebecca, Jacqueline, Emily PRINCIPAL, ACTUARIAL CONSULTING, WILLIAM M. MERCER LIMITED 1988– ; Manager, Actuarial, Crown Life 1976–80; Asst. Vice-Pres., Mercantile & General 1980–88; FSA 1978; FCIA 1979; MAAA 1980; Founder & Pres., Pacific Rim Actuaries' Club of Toronto 1993– ; author of award winning paper: 'Pricing and Reserving Considerations Under the New Canadian PPM and Tax Environemnt' 1992; recreations: bridge, travel; Home: 7 Dalewood Dr., Richmond Hill, Ont. L4B 3C3; Office: BCE Place, 161 Bay St., P.O. Box 501, Toronto, Ont. M5J 2S5.

**CHOWN, Frank Gordon,** B.Comm.; management consultant; b. Toronto, Ont. 26 June 1942; s. Joseph Gordon and Helen Theresa (Kearney) C.; e. St. Michael's Coll. Sch. 1959; Univ. of Toronto, B.Comm. 1964; m. Christine d. Nicholas and Rose Hersymik 5 Sept. 1966; children: Jeffrey, Julia, Lesley; Managing Dir., Towers Perrin Inc. (Canada) 1987–93, Retired; Benefits Cons., TPF & C Limited 1966; Principal 1972; Vice-Pres. 1978; Mgr., Vancouver Off. 1978; Toronto Off. 1984; Corp. Dir. 1986; recreations: golf, skiing, sailing; Clubs: York Downs Golf & Country; Granite; Home: 181 Dawlish Ave., Toronto, Ont. M4N 1H6.

**CHOYCE, Lesley Willis,** B.A., M.A.; writer; editor; publisher; university professor; b. Riverside, N.J. 21 March 1951; s. George Howard and Norma (Willis) C.; e. East Carolina Univ. (Greenville, NC) 1969–70; Livingston Coll. Rutgers Univ. (New Brunswick, NJ) B.A. 1972; Montclair State Coll. (Montclair, NJ) M.A. 1974; City Univ. of N.Y. Grad. Ctr. M.A. 1983; m. Terry d. Russell and Elaine Paul 19 Aug. 1974; two d. Sunyata Angeline, Pamela Elaine; EDITOR AND PUBLISHER, POTTERSFIELD PRESS 1979– ; PROFESSOR OF ENGLISH, DALHOUSIE UNIVERSITY; taught English at City Univ. of N.Y., Montclair State, Bloomfield Coll. and worked as rehab. couns. and journalist in U.S.A. before immigrating to Can. 1978; teacher St. Mary's Univ., Mt. St. Vincent Univ., N.S. Coll. of Art and Design, and Dalhousie Univ.; est. Eastern Shore Publishing Collective 1976; est. Wooden Anchor Press 1977; est. Pottersfield Press 1979; became Candn. citizen 1984; author 'Edible Wild Plants' 1977; 'Reinventing the Wheel' (poetry) 1980; 'Eastern Sure' (short stories) 1981; 'Fast Living' (poetry) 1982; 'Downwind' (novel) 1984; 'Billy Botzweiler's Last Dance' (short stories) 1984; 'The End of Ice' (poetry) 1985; 'Conventional Emotions' (short stories) 1986; 'The Top of the Heart' (poetry) 1986; The Dream Auditor' (science fiction) 1986; 'An Avalanche of Ocean' (non-fiction) 1987; 'December Six/The Halifax Solution' (non-fiction) 1988; 'The Second Season of Jonas MacPherson' (novel) 1989; 'Skateboard Shakedown' (novel) 1989; 'The Hungry Lizards' (novel) 1990; 'Magnificent Obsessions' (novel) 1991; 'Wrong Time, Wrong Place' (novel) 1991; 'Some Kind of Hero' (novel) 1991; 'Margin of Error' (short stories) 1992; 'Clearcut Danger' (Y/A Novel) 1992; 'The Ecstasy Manifesto' (murder mystery) 1992; 'Full Tilt' (Y/A Novel) 1993; 'Transcendental Anarchy' (autobiographical) 1993; 'Good Idea Gone Bad' (novel) 1993; Ed. 'Alternating Currents' 1977; 'Chezzetcook' 1977; 'Visions from the Edge' 1981; 'Cape Breton Collection' 1984; 'Art of Ice' 1992; East Coast corr., 'Poetry Canada Review'; ed./author numerous other books fiction, poetry; contrib. to periodicals; Ed. 'The Pottersfield Portfolio: Fiction and Poetry from Atlantic Canada' vols. 1–7 (an ongoing anthology); mem. Assn. of Candn. Publishers; Atlantic Publishers Assn.; Candn. Periodical Publishers Assn.; Literary Press Group (Exec. Rep. 1982–83); Writers Union of Canada; Writer's Fedn. of N.S. (Pres. 1989–91); Dalhousie Faculty Assn.; Grad. Fellow Queen's Coll., C.U.N.Y. 1977–78; Dartmouth Book Award 1990; first place short fiction/novel Writers Fedn. of N.S. Literary Competition 1980–81; third place Candn. SF&F Award 1982; Finalist for Stephen Leacock Medal 1987; winner, Creative Non-fiction Competition, 'Event' magazine 1990; Finalist, Anne Connor Brimer Award 1992, 1993; Firs Place, Candn. National Surfing Championship 1993; recreations: winter surfing; Address: R.R. #2, Porters Lake, N.S. B0J 2S0.

**CHRÉTIEN, The Right Hon. Joseph-Jacques Jean,** P.C., B.A., LL.L., LL.D., Q.C.; lawyer; politician; b. Shawinigan, Que., 11 Jan 1934; s. Wellie and Marie (Boisvert) C.; e. St. Joseph Semy., Trois-Rivières, Que.; Laval Univ.; Hon. degree in Law, Wilfrid Laurier Univ. 1981; Hon. Doct. of Law Laurentian Univ., Univ. of W. Ont. 1982, York Univ. 1986, Univ. of Alberta 1987 and Lakehead Univ. 1988; m. Aline Chaîné, Shawinigan,

Que., 10 Sept. 1957; children: France, Hubert, Michel; PRIME MINISTER OF CANADA 1993– ; and LEADER, LIBERAL PARTY OF CANADA 1990– ; called to Bar of Qué. 1958; first el. to H. of C. in g.e. 1963 and until 1984; re-el. 1990; apptd. Parlty. Secy. to Prime Minister Lester B. Pearson July 1965 and to Min. of Finance Jan. 1966; apptd. Min. of State attached to the Min. of Finance, 1967; Min. of Nat. Revenue Jan. 1968; Min. of Indian Affairs & Northern Development, July 1968; Pres. Treasury Bd. 1974; Min. of Industry, Trade & Commerce, 1976; Min. of Finance 1977; Min. of Justice, Atty-Gen. of Canada and Min. of State for Social Devel. 1980, also Min. responsible for constitutional negotiations; Min. of Energy, Mines & Resources 1982; Deputy Prime Minister & Sec. of State For External Affairs 1984; External Affairs Critic for Official Opposition 1984–86; resigned H. of C. 1986; Counsel of law firm, Lang Michener Lawrence & Shaw with offices in Ottawa, Toronto, Mississauga & Vancouver 1984–90 and also Sr. Advisor, Gordon Capital Corp. of Montréal; el. Leader of the Liberal Party of Canada 1990– ; and Leader of the Official Opposition Party 1990–93; el. M.P., Beauséjour, N.B. and became Leader of the Official Opposition, H. of C. 1990; re-elected Mem. of Parliament for St-Maurice Oct. 25 1993; mem. Que., Ont. and Man. Bars; Dir., Bar of Trois-Rivières, 1962–63; Liberal; R. Catholic; Office: House of Commons, Rm. 145E, 180 Wellington St., Ottawa, Ont. K1A 0A6.

**CHRETIEN, Michel,** O.C., M.D., M.Sc., D.Sc., F.A.C.P., F.R.C.P.(C), F.R.S.C.; medical rsch. institute director and chief extve. offr.; b. Baie Shawinigan, Qué. 26 March 1936; s. Willie and Marie (Boisvert) C.; e. Séminaire de Joliette B.A. 1955 (Gov. Gen. Award); Univ. de Montréal M.D. 1960; McGill Univ. M.Sc. 1962; Univ. de Liège D.Sc. 1981; m. Micheline d. Oscar and Laura Ruel 9 July 1960; children: Marie, Lyne; SCI. DIR. & C.E.O., CLINICAL RESEARCH INST. OF MONTREAL 1984– ; Dir., Lab. of Molecular Neuroendocrinology 1967– ; Physician Dept. Med. Hôtel-Dieu Hosp. Montréal 1967– , Head of Endocrinol. Sect. 1978–84; Titular of Med. Univ. de Montréal 1975– ; Prof. in Experimental Med. McGill Univ. 1967– ; Internship 1959–60 and Rsch. Fellow 1960–62 Montréal Hosps. and McGill Univ.; Resident in Med. Peter Bent Brigham Hosp. and Faculty of Med. Harvard Univ. 1962–64; Asst. Biochem. Hormone Rsch. Lab. Univ. of Cal. Berkeley 1964–67; Visiting Sci. Cambridge Univ. 1979; Lab. of Neuroendocrinol. Salk Inst. of San Diego 1980; mem. Grant Ctte., Nat. Cancer Inst. Can.; mem. Grant Comte. Med. Rsch. Council Can.; Award Comte. Conseil de la Recherche en Santé du Qué.; Past Vice-Pres., Que. Diabetes Assn.; frequent nat. and internat. guest speaker, lectr.; author or co-author numerous publs.; mem. various ed. bds.; Fundamental Rsch. Award Assn. des Médecins de Langue Française du Can. 1971; Clarke Inst. Psychiatry Toronto Award 1977; Michel Sarrazin Award Club du Recherches Cliniques du Qué. 1977; Archambault Medal Assn. Canadienne-Française pour l'Avancement de Sci's 1978; Marcel Piché Award Clin. Rsch. Inst. Montréal 1978; Faculty Scholar Josiah Macy Jr. Foundation 1979–80; Jeremiah Metzger Lectr. 1990; Fuller Albright Lectr., Peripatetic Club of United States 1992; McLaughlin Medal, Royal Soc. of Canada; Moehringer Mannheim Award, Candn. Biochemical Soc.; 150th Anniv. Medal, Univ. of Montreal; Sandoz Speaker, Candn. Soc. of Endocrinology and Metabolism; mem. Am. Fed. Clin. Rsch.; Candn. Soc. Clin. Investig. (Pres. 1977); Am. Assn. Advanc. Sci.; Club de Recherches Cliniques du Qué.; Candn. Biochem. Soc. (Pres. 1983); Endocrine Soc.; N.Y. Acad. Sci.; Candn. Soc Endocrinol. & Metabolism (Pres. 1986); Peripatetic Club; Candns. Health Rsch.; Am. Soc. Clin. Investig.; Am. Clin. & Climatol. Assn.; Home: 1404, 1 Côte Ste-Catherine, Montréal, Qué. H2V 1Z8; Office: 110 Pine Ave. W., Montréal, Qué. H2W 1R7.

**CHRÉTIEN, Raymond A.J.,** B.A., LL.L.; public servant; lawyer; b. Shawinigan, Que. 20 May 1942; s. Maurice and Cécile (Marcotte) C.; e. Sém. de Joliette B.A. 1962; Univ. Laval LL.L. 1965; admitted to Qué. Bar 1966; m. Kay Rousseau; children: Caroline, Louis-François; AMBASSADOR TO THE UNITED STATES 1994– ; Legal Affairs Div., DEA 1966–67; Third Sec., Perm. Mission to the U.N., N.Y. 1967–68; Asst. Sec., Fed./Prov. Relns. Ctte., Privy Counc. Office 1968–70; Extve. Asst. to Sec., Treasury Bd. 1970–71; to Pres., CIDA 1971–72; 1st Sec., Beirut 1972–75; 1st Sec. & Counsellor, Paris 1975–78; Ambassador to Zaïre 1978–81; Policy Dir., Indus., Investments & Competition, DEA 1981–82; Asst. Under-Sec., Mfg., Technol. & Transp., DEA 1982–83; Inspector Gen., DEA 1983–85; Ambassador to Mexico 1985–88; Associate Under-Secrectary of State for External Affairs (DEA), Federal Govt. 1988–91; Ambassador to Belgium and Luxembourg 1991–94; Order of the Aztec Eagle, Mexico; Office: 501 Pennsylvania Ave. N.W., Washington, DC 20001 USA.

**CHRISTENSEN, Ione Jean;** b. Dawson Creek, B.C. 10 Oct. 1933; d. Gordon Irwin Cameron; e. Duncan, B.C. and Whitehorse, Yukon 1953; San Mateo (Cal.) Coll. Business Adm., Assoc. Arts Degree 1955; m. Arthur Karsten Christensen 1 Feb. 1958; two s. Paul Cameron, Philip Karsten; Mgr., S.T.P.-Whitehorse, Energy, Mines and Resources 1984–89; Partner, Cameras North 1985– ; Dir., Petro Canada; Panarctic Oils Ltd. 1981–84; held clerical positions with Taylor & Drury, Yukon Electrical Co. and Govt. of Yukon 1955–62; Pay and Personnel Supvr. Govt. of Yukon 1962–65, Princ. Clk. Estimates 1965–66, Personnel Supvr. and Acting Dir. 1966–67; apptd. Justice of the Peace and Juvenile Court 1971; Small Debt Official 1974; el. Mayor of Whitehorse 1975, re-el. 1977 but resigned 1978 upon appt. as Commr.; Commr. of Yukon Terr. 1978–79; Pres., Hospitality North 1981–85; Dir., Boy Scouts of Can. Provincial Yukon B.C.-Council; The Yukon Fdn.; mem. Council for Can. Unity; Arctic Inst. of N. Amer. 1981–85; Yukon Outdoors Club; Chrmn. Yukon Placer Mining Guidelines Public Review Comte. 1983; Chrmn., Yukon Adv. Ctte. on Waste Mgmt. 1989– ; Dir., Northern Writer's Circle; mem. MacBride Museum; Anglican; recreations: photography, writing, backpacking, gardening; Home: 26 Takhini Ave., Whitehorse, Yukon Y1A 3N4.

**CHRISTENSEN, Jorgen Vibe,** LL.D.; retired executive; b. Vejle, Denmark 9 Nov. 1917; LL.D, h.c. Simon Fraser Univ. 1978; came to Can. 1946; m. Alice 1956 (dec.); Dir., The East Asiatic Co. (Canada) Inc. 1960–92; Dir., Eacom Timber Sales Ltd. 1978–93; Hon. Consul for Denmark in B.C. and Yukon 1960–70; Pres. and Dir., Tahsis Co. Ltd. 1960–1982; served with R.A. Hong Kong 1940–45; P.O.W.; Chrmn. Vancouver Gen. Hosp. 1973; B.C. Med. Centre 1973–76; Past Chrmn. Council of Forest Industs.; Business Council of B.C.; Maritime Museum; recreation: yachting; Clubs: Vancouver; Royal Vancouver Yacht; Home: 2298 McBain Ave., Vancouver, B.C. V6L 3B1.

**CHRISTENSEN, Paul S.,** C.A., C.M.A.; executive; b. Knubbelykke, Denmark 13 Apr. 1930; s. Magnus Sunke and Olga C.; e. C.A. 1965; C.M.A. 1961; Banff Sch. Advanced Mgmt. 1969; m. Hanna Jensen 13 Apr. 1952; children: Jan David, Jay Stewart, Susan Linda, Tina Maria; PRES. & DIR., CARTHY FOUNDATION; assoc. with Loram Group of Companies 38 yrs. serving as Vice Pres. Finance Loram International Ltd., Vice Pres. and Treas. Loram Co. Ltd., Vice Pres. Finance Manalta Coal Ltd. and Exec. Vice Pres. and Pres. of Loram International Ltd.; mem. Inst. C.A.'s Alta.; Soc. Mgmt. Accts.; Danish Businessmen's Assn.; recreations: golf, hunting, skiing, sailing; Clubs: Calgary Petroleum; Danish Canadian; Pinebrook Golf & Country; Ranchmen's; Office: P.O. Box 2554, Calgary, Alta. T2P 2M7.

**CHRISTENSEN, Rosemary Lorraine,** B.A., B.C.L.; b. Walton-on-Thames, Eng.; e. The Sorbonne, Paris, Cour de Civilisation Française 1959–60; McGill Univ. B.A. 1964, B.C.L. 1967; PRESIDENT AND DIR., THE SOMERVILLE HOUSE CORP.; Pres. & Dir. Somerville House Management Ltd.; Somerville House Securities Ltd.; Somerville House Resources Ltd.; Secy.-Treas. & Dir., The O.T. Mining Corp.; called to Bar of Que. 1968; Home: 603, Two Westmount Sq., Montreal, Que. H3Z 2S4; Office: 4115 Sherbrooke St. W., 6th Flr., Montreal, Que. H3Z 1K9.

**CHRISTENSON, Elvin Arnold,** F.C.A.; b. Jarrow, Alta. 18 Nov. 1918; s. Arnold and Edith (McCune) C.; m. Halina Wyka, children: Dwight, Eric, Karyn, Lynne, Marnie; Sr. Partner, Peat Marwick Thorne, retired; Regional Extve. Partner-Prairie Region 1974–1983; Internat. Liaison Partner 1969–74; founded predecessor firm Christenson. Morrison & Co. 1944; Chrmn. Comte. of Alta. Inst. Report on Role of Prov. Auditor 1974; Chrmn., Health Disciplines Board, Alta.; Alberta Health & Social Services Disciplines Ctte.; Accounting Education Foundation of Alberta (Inst. of Chartered Accountants of Alta.); inst. Rep. Adv. Council to Faculty of Business Adm. and Comm. Univ. of Alta., mem. Senate; Chrmn., Credit Union Deposit Guarantee Corp.; Chrmn. Bd. Trustees Univ. Hosp. Foundation; mem. Inst. C.A.'s Alta. (Pres. 1962–63); Pres. Candn. Inst. C.A.'s 1976–77 (Council 1962–63); rec'd Centennial Medal 1977; P. Conservative; United Church; recreations: golf, photography, cottage; Clubs: Kiwanis; Edmonton; Mayfair Golf & Country; Edmonton C.A.'s; Pacioli Dining; Edmonton Petroleum; Home: 12903 66 Ave., Edmonton, Alta. T6H 1Y6.

**CHRISTIAN, A. John,** B.Eng., Ph.D., F.I.C.E., M.C.S.C.E., C.Eng., P.Eng.; professional civil engineer/university professor; b. Stourport, Worcs., Eng. 28 April 1938; s. Thomas William and Patricia (Kelly) C.; e. St. Philip's Grammar Sch. 1956; Univ. of Sheffield, B.Eng. 1959; Univ. of Bradford, Ph.D. 1974; m. Veronica d. John and Doreen Cummins 28 Aug. 1965; children: Simon John, Neil Anthony; M. PATRICK GILLIN CHAIR IN CONSTRUCTION ENGR. & MNGT., UNIV. OF N.B. 1987– ; Civil/Struct Engr., London Transp. 1959–62; Struct. Cons. Engr., Ove Arup & Partners 1962–64; Civil Engr./Contract Mgr., Richard Costain Ltd. 1964–68; Lectr./Dir./Cons./Course Dir., Univ. of Bradford 1968–77; Prof./Prog. Chrmn., Civil Engr., Mem. Univ. of Nfld. 1977–87; apptd. to first chair in construction engr. in Can. 1987; Dir., Construction Technol. Ctr. (Atlantic); Bd. Mem., Can. Construction Rsch. Bd. (NB Chap.) Mem. CSCE Ntl. Ctte. (Construction Div.); Mem., Internat. Advisory Bd., Civil Engr. Comp.; Editorial Bd. Mem.: Internat. Journal of Construction Information Technology; AIENG; CIB-W65; author: 'Management, Machines and Methods in Civil Engineering' 1981; recreations: jogging, walking, skiing; Office: Dept. of Civil Engr., Univ. of N.B., Fredericton, N.B. E3B 5A3.

**CHRISTIAN, Timothy J.,** B.A., LL.M.; university professor & administrator / barrister & solicitor; b. Edmonton, Alta. 8 Jan. 1949; s. John Alexander and Ivy Lois (Welsh) C.; e. Univ. of Alta., B.A. (Hons.) 1973; Univ. of Cambridge, LL.B. 1976 (redesignated to LL.M. 1986); children: Timothy Elliott, Rosalind Anthea; DEAN OF LAW, UNIV. OF ALBERTA 1986– ; admitted to Law Soc. of Alta. 1977; Asst. Prof. of Law, Univ. of Alta. 1978; Assoc. Dean of Law 1983; Bd. of Dir., Candn. Civil Liberties Assn.; nat. Counc., Candn. Human Rights Found.; Hon. Bencher, Law Soc. of Alta.; Treas., Internat. Ombudsman Inst.; recreations: opera, squash; Home: 10443 – 85 Ave., Edmonton, Alta. T6E 2K2; Office: 485 Law Centre, University of Alberta, Edmonton, Alta. T6G 2H5.

**CHRISTIAN, William Edward,** B.A., M.A., Ph.D.; university professor; b. Queen Charlotte City, B.C. 24 Aug. 1945; s. William Edward and Dora Luella (Ketcheson) C.; e. Univ. of Toronto, B.A. 1966, M.A. 1967; London Sch. of Econ., Ph.D. 1970; m. Barbara d. Arthur and Mary Cotton 26 July 1969; children: Matthew St. John Kirkland, Adam Benjamin Sebastian; PROF., DEPT. OF POLITICAL STUDIES, UNIV. OF GUELPH; taught at Mt. Allison Univ. 1970–78; joined Guelph faculty 1978; Vis. Prof., Univ. of Toronto 1987–88, 1989–91; McMaster Univ., winter 1990; freelance journalism; Globe & Mail, Kitchener-Waterloo Record; consulting: TV Ontario, P. Conservative Party of Can.; Royal Comn. on Election Reform and Party Financing; Acad. Visitor, London Sch. of Econ. 1976–77, 1984–85, 1990; Dir., Windsor Access to Justice Yearbook; author 'George Grant: A Biography' 1993; co-author (with C. Campbell) 'Political Parties and Ideologies in Canada' 1974, 1983, 1990; ed.: 'Idea File of Harold Adams Innis' 1980; 'Innis on Russia' 1981; recreations: tribal carpets, wine, music, baseball; P. Conservative; Anglican; Home: 4 Wolseley Rd., Guelph, Ont. N1E 1J5; Office: Dept. of Political Studies, Univ. of Guelph, Guelph, Ont. N1G 2W1.

**CHRISTIANSON, David Bjorn,** B.A., C.F.P., R.F.P.; financial advisor; b. Portage la Prairie, Man. 3 Feb. 1956; s. John Aaron and A. Beverly C.; e. Tuxedo Shaftsbury H.S. 1974; Univ. of Man., B.A. 1983; m. Vera d. Erwin and Christine Steinberger 12 Feb. 1983; children: Sarah Christine, Taylor Bjorn; presently SR. ADVISOR, MACDONALD, SHYMKO & CO. LTD., financial advisors; Extve. Asst. to Dan MacKenzie, M.P. 1974–75; interior landscape cons., Los Angeles, CA 1978–82; Insur. Rep., North Am. Life 1983–84; Co-founder & Vice-Pres., Premier Candn. Securities Ltd. 1984, Pres. & C.E.O. 1988–91; Personal Trust Account Exec., Canada Trust 1991–92; Vice-Pres., Mem., Winnipeg C. of C.; Pres., Candn. Assn. of Finan. Planners, Man. Ch.; National Dir. of Ethics, C.A.F.P.; Bd. Mem., Winnipeg Symphony Orchestra; Past Pres., P.C. Party, Prov. Riding Assn. of Ft. Rouge, Man.; Home: 51 Lawndale Ave., Winnipeg, Man. R2H 1S7; Office: 1800 – 155 Carlton St., Winnipeg, Man. R3C 3H8.

**CHRISTIE, Innis McLeod,** B.A., LL.M.; public servant; educator; labour arbitrator; b. Amherst, N.S. 8 Nov. 1937; s. Harold Bent and Edith Alice (Atherton) C.; e. Amherst pub. and high schs.; Dalhousie Univ. B.A. 1958, LL.B. 1962; Trinity Coll. Cambridge LL.B., Dip. in Comparative Legal Studies 1964; Yale Univ. LL.M. 1969; m. Jeanne d. Gysbertus and Maria Van Eyck 28 June 1970; children: Merran, Michael, Loren; DEPUTY MINISTER OF LABOUR, PROVINCE OF

NOVA SCOTIA 1993– ; Asst. Prof. Queen's Univ. 1964–67, Assoc. Prof. 1967–69, Prof. 1969–71; Prof. of Law, Dalhousie Univ. 1971–91, Assoc. Dean of Law 1982–85, Dean of Law 1985–91; Visiting Lectr. Osgoode Hall Law Sch. 1969; Chrmn. Constrn. Ind. Panel, N.S., N.S. Labour Rlns. Bd. 1971–79, Chrmn. of Bd. 1972–79; Counsel, N.S. Labour Standards Tribunal 1972–80; mem. Anti-Inflation Appeal Tribunal 1976–80; Active Arbitrator various companies & unions incl. Can. Post 1967– ; Lansdowne Visiting Prof. of Law Univ. of Victoria 1980–81; Visiting Scholar Inst. for Comparative Labour Rlns. Univ. of Leuven, Belgium 1985; recipient Dalhousie Univ. Scholarship 1954–58; Dunn Scholarship in Law 1959–62; Carswell, Sweet & Maxwell Scholarship 1962–63; MacKenzie King Travelling Scholarship 1963–64; Can. Counc. Grant 1968–69; author 'The Liability of Strikers in the Law of Tort' 1967; 'Unfair Labour Practices' 1968; 'Judicial Review of Statutory Powers' 1971; 'Legal Writing and Research Manual' 3rd ed. 1988; 'Commissions of Inquiry' 1989; 'Labour Relations Law' 1990; 'Employment Law in Canada' 1993; mem. Amnesty Internat.; Internat. Comn. Jurists; Candn. Bar Assn.; Candn. Assn. Law Teachers; Candn. Inst. Ind. Rlns. Rsch.; Soc. Profls. in Dispute Resolution; Nat. Acad. Arbitrators; recreations: squash, bridge, golf, sailing, bird hunting; Home: 6095 Coburg Rd., Unit 802, Halifax, N.S. B3H 4K1; Office: Halifax, N.S. B3H 4H9.

**CHRISTIE, James Hamilton,** F.R.A.I.C., R.I.B.A., F.R.S.A.; Architect; b. Glasgow, Scot. 13 July 1929; s. late John Alexander and Ruby Kirk (Hamilton) C.; e. High Sch. of Glasgow, 1947; Glasgow Sch. of Arch., 1954; m. Jean Stuart Campbell, d. late James and Sarah Wallace, Glasgow, Scot. 24 June 1960; children: Sarah Hamilton, James Andrew, David Francis; FOUNDING PARTNER, BELL CHRISTIE MILTON Architects Inc., CALGARY; mem., Alta. Assn. of Architects; Pres., Manitoba Assoc. of Architects 1968; former Pres., Social Planning Counc. of Winnipeg; Address: 3815 – 15th St. S.W., Calgary, Alta. T2T 4A7.

**CHRISTIE, James Kenyon,** M.Sc., M.B.A., F.C.I.A., F.C.A.S., F.I.I.C., M.A.A.A.; insurance executive; b. Truro, N.S. 18 June 1951; s. Donald MacNichol and Mary Joyce (Kenyon) C.; e. Mount Allison Univ. B.Sc. (Hons.) 1972; McMaster Univ. M.Sc. 1974; Univ. of Toronto M.B.A. (Dean's list) 1989; m. Janice d. Beatty and Grace McCully 19 Aug. 1972; children: James Robert, Donald Scott; PRESIDENT, IAO ACTUARIAL CONSULTING 1992– ; joined Sun Alliance 1976; Dominion of Canada Gen. Insur. Co. 1978; Vice-Pres. & Chief Actuary 1986; Vice-Pres., Finance 1991; active in num. insur. industry orgns. incl. Assn. of Candn. Insurers; Insur. Bur. of Can.; Facility Assn.; Bd. of Dir., Casualty Actuarial Soc.; ERINOAK; F.C.I.A.; F.C.A.S.; F.I.I.C.; Mem., Am. Acad. of Actuaries; United Ch.; recreations: golf, bridge, squash; clubs: Credit Valley, Metro Toronto Bd. of Trade; Home: 4024 Rolling Valley Dr., Mississauga, Ont. L5L 2K8; Office: 18 King St. E., Suite 800, Toronto, Ont. M5C 1C4.

**CHRISTIE, John Melville,** M.A., F.F.A., F.C.I.A., A.S.A.; consulting actuary; b. Glasgow, Scotland 27 Aug. 1944; s. John Melville and Agnes Young Warnock (Clelland) C.; e. Hillhead H.S., Glasgow; Trinity Acad. & Daniel Stewart's Coll., Edinburgh; Peterhead Acad.; Glasgow Univ. M.A. (Hons.) 1966; m. Lesley d. John and Isobel Jack 28 June 1969; children: Gavin, Janet, Duncan, Nancy; CONSULTING ACTUARY, THE ALEXANDER CONSULTING GROUP 1990– ; Actuarial Student, Scottish Amicable Life Assur. Soc. 1966–69; Vice-Pres. & Actuary, B.J. Vincent Co. Ltd. 1969–74; Cons. Actuary, C.A. Kench & Assoc. Ltd. 1974–76; Cons. Actuary, William M. Mercer Limited 1976–89; Fellow, Fac. of Actuaries in Scotland 1969; Candn. Inst. of Actuaries 1969; Assoc. of the Soc. of Actuaries 1969; Mem., Shaughnessey Heights Un. Ch. of Can.; recreations: cross country skiing, running, dinghy sailing, triathlons; Club: Arbutus; Home: 6849 Adera St., Vancouver, B.C. V6P 5C2; Office: 5th fl., 900 Howe St., Vancouver, B.C. V6Z 2M4.

**CHRISTIE, Kathleen,** B.A., M.S.W., C.M.C.; management consultant; b. Vancouver, B.C. 1945; s. Thomas P. and Ruth M. (Gareau) Callon; e. Univ. of Toronto B.A. 1966; Carleton Univ. M.S.W. 1969; m. Glenn s. Frances and Andrew Christie; children: Alexander, Caitlin; PARTNER, MANAGEMENT CONSULTING, DELOITTE & TOUCHE; Social Work Practitioner, Children's Aid Soc. of Metro Toronto; Mem., Candn. Assn. of Women Executives (Past Pres.); YWCA of Canada (Past Bd. Mem.); Inst. of Certified Mngt. Consultants of Ont. (Past Council Mem.); Bd. Mem., Regis College; Finance Ctte. Mem., Baycrest Centre; club: Boulevard; Office: Suite 1300, 95 Wellington St. W., Toronto, Ont. M5J 2P4.

**CHRISTIE, Keith Hutton,** D.Phil.; foreign service officer; b. Vancouver, B.C. 18 Apr. 1948; s. Valentine (dec.) and Edna Flora (Hutton) (dec.) C.; e. John Oliver Secondary Sch. Vancouver 1966; Univ. of B.C. 1966–67; Univ. Coll., Univ. of Toronto B.A. 1971; Univ. Coll. Oxford (Rhodes Scholar) D.Phil. 1974; m. Liliana d. Rodrigo (dec.) and Lilia Zapata 23 Sept. 1971; children: Keith Roderick (dec.), John Andrew, Katherine Michelle; DIRECTOR, ECONOMIC AND TRADE POLICY GROUP, POLICY PLANNING STAFF, OTTAWA 1992; Lectr. in Hist. Univ. of Reading, U.K. 1974–75; Asst. Prof. of Hist. Univ. of B.C. 1975–76; joined Dept. of External Affairs becoming Third Sec. and Vice Consul Brazil 1977–78, Second Sec. and Vice Consul Brazil 1978–81; Offr. Latin Am. Div. Ottawa 1981–83; Trade Policy Offr. Gatt Affairs Div. 1983–86; First Sec. and Consul Peru and Bolivia 1986–88; Counsellor and Consul Peru and Bolivia 1988–89; Depy. Coordinator (Asia-Pacific region), Office of Multilateral Trade Negotiations, Ottawa 1989–91; Dir. Policy Coordination, and Candn. lead NAFTA negotiator for Emergency Action (Safeguards), Office of North American Free Trade Negotiations 1991–92; Lead negotiator, Canada for the North Am. Environmental Cooperation Agreement 1993; Woodrow Wilson Fellow 1971; author 'Colombia' 1975; 'Oligarcas, campesinos y política en Colombia: aspectos de la historia socio-política de la frontera antioqueña' 1986; 'Globalization and Public Policy in Canada: In Search of a Paradigm' 1993; 'Different Strokes: Regionalism and Canada's Economic Diplomacy' 1993; various articles profl. jours.; recreation: jogging; Home: 381 Dovercourt Ave., Ottawa, Ont. K2A 0S7; Office: 125 Sussex Dr., Ottawa, Ont. K1A 0G2.

**CHRISTIE, Robert (Wallace),** B.A.; actor, director; b. Toronto, Ont. 20 Sept. 1913; s. David Wallace, D.D., and Barbara Wilson (Alexander) C.; e. Public Schs.; Woodstock, Ont.; Public and Riverdale Coll. Inst., Toronto, Ont.; Victoria Coll., Univ. of Toronto, B.A. 1934; m. 1st Margot Syme, 14 Apr. 1937; 2ndly Grania Mortimer, 12 July 1958; children: Dinah Barbara, Cedar Townsend, Geraldine Fiona, Matthew Alexander, David MacIvor; with The John Holden Players, Toronto, Bala and Winnipeg, 1934–36; went to Engl. 1936 engaging in Prov. Repertory, then a London Production, 'The Zeal of Thy House,' followed by one season with Old Vic Co. 1938–39 (Buxton Festival, Waterloo Rd. and Mediterranean Tour); on declaration of war, joined Chelsea ARP Services, then left in 1940 to tour England in 'Desire under the Elms,' before enlistment; after war service returned to Toronto as Free-lance; Stratford Shakespearean Festival during its first 4 yrs., incl. Edin. Festival; 'Ti-Coq' in English at Montreal; Musical and Revue: 'Spring Thaw'; 'Sunshine Town'; 'Mother Goose'; 'Fine Frenzy'; 'Beggars' Opera'; Broadway Openings: 'Tambourlaine'; 'Love and Libel'; Vancouver Internat. Festival: 'Mary Stuart'; starred as Noah Hatch in CBC series 'Hatch's Mill,' 1967; on numerous occasions 'Sir John A. Macdonald,' etc., etc.; 1971–79 Teacher of Acting, Theatre Dept., Ryerson Polytech. Inst.; served in 2nd World War, 1940–45, enlisting in London, Eng.; with R.C.A.M.C. and R.C.A.S.C., Eng., France, Belgium, Holland, Germany; mem., Actors' Equity Assn.; Assn. Cdn. Radio & TV Artists, John Drainie Award 1984; N.D.P.; Club: Arts & Letters; Home: 42 Dale Ave., Toronto, Ont. M4W 1K6.

**CHRISTIE, Robert Burruss,** F.C.S.I.; investment dealer; b. Toronto, Ont. 8 Nov. 1925; s. William Lee and Katharine Adriance (Burruss) C.; e. Selwyn House School 1939; Bishop's Coll. Sch. 1943; McGill Univ. 1946; m. Vina d. Gordon and May Southam 10 July 1971; children (from prev. marriage): Karen Brooke, William Baxter, David Burruss, Thomas Baxter; INVESTMENT DEALER, RBC DOMINION SECURITIES 1981– ; Sergeant Flight Engineer, R.C.A.F. 1943–45; Clerk, Royal Trust Co. Montreal 1946–47; Amos, Christie & Co. Toronto 1947–50; Driller, Royalite Oil Co. Ltd. 1950–52; Vice-Pres., Dir. & A.G.M., Candn. Diamond Coring Ltd. 1952–57; Dir. of Sales, Robin-Nodwell Mfg. Ltd. 1958–67; Mgr., A.E. Ames & Co. Limited 1967–81; F.C.S.I. 1976; Lieutenant (retired); Flight Engineer's Badge; War Medal, C.V.S.M.; Chrmn., Alta. Dist., Investment Dealers Assn. 1979–80; Dir., Jr. Achievement of S. Alta. 1977–79; Alta. Stock Exchange Rep. to Toronto Stock Exchange Joint Indus. Ctte. on Public Ownership in Candn. Securities Indus. 1981; Mem. & Gov., Alta. Stock Exchange 1976–81; Mngt. Adv. Council, Fac. of Mngt., Univ. of Calgary 1977; Members' Affairs Ctte., Alta. Stock Exchange 1992; Zeta Psi Fraternity 1946; recreations: skiing, golf, fishing; clubs: Calgary Golf & Country, Calgary Petroleum, The Glencoe; Home: 1112 Sydenham Rd., Calgary, Alta. T2T 0T4; Office: 300 – 707 – 7th Ave. S.W., Calgary, Alta. T2P 3H6.

**CHRISTIE, Ven. William Douglas McLaren,** B.A. (Ang.); b. St. Johnsbury, Vermont 12 Nov. 1910; s. William Edward and Mabel (Mathewson) C.; e. Lennoxville (P.Q.) High Sch.; Bishop's Univ., B.A. (Theol.) 1935; Washington Coll. of Preachers; m. Pamela Kerrigan, d. Andrew Louis Henderson, England, 7 Sept. 1948; children: Peter Andrew, Mary Pamela; o. Deacon 1935 and Priest 1936; Curate at Bury, Que., 1935–36; Incumbent of Montage and Franktown (Diocese of Ottawa), 1936–39; Vankleek Hill, Ont., 1939–43; Rector of Renfrew, 1943–46; All Saints, Westboro, Ottawa, 1946–58; Rector of Trinity Ch., and Archdeacon of Cornwall, 1958; Diocesan Archdeacon & Dir. of Programme for Diocese of Ottawa, 1967–72; Diocesan Archdeacon & Rector of St. Bartholomew's Church, Ottawa, 1972–79; Chaplain to the Governor General, 1967–80; Rural Dean of Ottawa, 1951–57; Part-time Chaplain, R.C.A.F., 1941–43; Chaplain, Gov.-Gen. Foot Guards (5th Candn. Guards), 1947–58; Retired, June 30, 1979; Order of St. Lazarus of Jerusalem; Efficiency Decoration; Home: 20 Cleary Ave., Apt. 308, Ottawa, Ont. K2A 3Z9.

**CHRISTOFF, Thomas Anthony,** B.A., M.B.A.; property development executive; b. Toronto, Ont. 6 Jan. 1954; s. George and Rose (Winter) C.; e. Univ. of Toronto B.A. 1977, M.B.A. 1979; FOUNDER AND PRES. THE LANDFORD GROUP 1981– ; Cons. Nat. Rsch. Council Ont. Chapter Constrn. Council; mem. Univ. of W. Ont. Eng. Dept. Adv. Ctte. Studies in Constrn.; Dir. Polish Candn. Bus. Council; mem. Urban Devel. Inst.; Toronto Home Builders' Assn.; Championship Auto Racing Team (owner Indianpolis 500 race car); recreations: race car driver, scuba diving, single engine aircraft pilot, hockey; Office: 70 Leek Cres., Richmond Hill, Ont. L4B 1H1.

**CHRISTOPHER, Ken;** artist; b. Swift Current, Sask. 1942; e. Alta. Coll. of Art, Dipl. in Fine Arts; Simon Fraser Univ., Burnaby, B.C.; m. Virginia; children: Alberta, Charles, Ivar; exhibits artwork across Canada; represented in internat. collections; Address: Springstone Productions Ltd., 4423–37th St. N.W. Calgary, Alta. T2L 2J5.

**CHRISTY, James Richard;** writer; artist; b. Richmond, Va. 14 July 1945; s. Angelo Joseph and Mary Kathleen (Dolby) Christinzio; e. Springfield High Sch.; Univs. of West Chester, Cheyney and Villanova, Pa.; m. Linda Louise Hooper 2 June 1965 (dec.); 2nd m., Mary Anne Silva 23 Sept. 1986; author 'Beyond the Spectacle' essays 1974; 'Palatine Cat' poetry 1978; 'Rough Road to the North' travel 1980; 'Streethearts' novel 1981; 'Travelin Light' stories 1983; 'The Price of Power' biog. 1985; 'Flesh and Blood' reportage 1990; ed. 'The New Refugees' essays 1972; 'Letter From the Kyber Pass' essays 1993; contbr. numerous nat. and internat. jours.; sculptor – works in public and private colls.; various group and one man shows; sometime actor; Address: Box 2366, VMPO, Vancouver, B.C. V6B 3W5.

**CHU, Wilson;** artist; b. Canton 21 Jan. 1946; s. Lei Kun and Sock Han (Yu) C.; e. High School; m. Pei Ling Chu 12 Dec. 1980; one s.: Stanley; group shows: Harrison Galleries W. Vancouver 1982; one-man shows: Harrison Galleries 1990, 1992, 1993; Zantman Gallery Carmel Calif. 1990, 1992; Diana Paul Gallery Calgary 1993; recreations: soccer, swimming; Home: 4870 Northlawn Dr., Burnaby, B.C. V5C 3S3.

**CHUNG, Hung,** R.C.A.; artist; b. Canton, China 8 Feb. 1946; s. Chung Fook-kuan and Chiu Yee-wah; e. Nung Lin 1st Primary Sch. Canton 1957; Tak Ming Middle Sch. Hong Kong 1963; Chu Hai Coll. Civil Engn. 1965; Vancouver Sch. of Art (Sculpture) grad. 1973; rec'd Del Grauer memorial award 1974; Canada Council Arts Grant 1976, 82; one-man exhibitions; 'Searching for New Forms in Bamboo Structures' H.K. Arts Centre 1979; 'Infinity vs. Limit: a Non-Mathematical Dialogue of Self-Identity' Emily Carr Coll. of Art and Design 1982; organized and curated group exhibitions: 'Echoes After the Storm' Asian Centre, U.B.C. 1991; 'Transpositions' Community Arts Council of Vancouver 1992; award winning sculptures incl.: 'A Game Playing Between Lines and Planes' 1st Int'l. Sculpture Competition Autopista Del Mediterraneo Barcelona 1974; monument for s.s. 'Beaver' National Historic Park 1975; sculpture for 'Wood Sculpture Symposium of the Americas' 1977; 'Gate to the North-west Passage' a commerative sculpture for Capt. George Vancouver 1980; project sculptures incl.: 'Spring' Court House Complex, Vancouver 1981; '12 Points in a Classical Balance' National Capital Commission, Ottawa, 1981; exterior sculptures for Hong Kong Pavilion, EXPO 86; 'Steam Columns' (938

Howe St., Vancouver) 1991; stage design, H.K. City Contemporary Dance, Goh Ballet, RTHK, Asia TV-HK, 1982–86; set and site design for Asian Pacific Festival, Vancouver 1985, 87; design for 'Vancouver Award' CKVU-TV 1988; Address: 8026 Argyle St., Vancouver, B.C. V5P 3L8.

**CHURCH, Arthur F.,** P.Eng., M.B.A.; manufacturing executive; b. Woodstock, Ont. 26 Aug. 1952; s. Frederick and Miriam C. e. Univ. of Waterloo, P.Eng. 1976; McMaster Univ., M.B.A. 1984; m. Colleen d. William and Jill Wilson 26 Apr. 1975; children: Heather, Ian; PRES. & CHIEF EXTVE. OFFR., CHAMPION ROAD MACHINERY LIMITED 1988– ; Eng. Design Analyst, Timberjack Inc. 1976–79; Indus. Engr. Mgr. 1979–82; Materials Mgr. 1982–85; Vice-Pres., Engr. 1985–88; Bd. of Dirs., Construction Industry Manufacturers Assn. (CIMA) Milwaukee, WI; Mem., S.A.E., A.P.E.O.; Home: 150 St. George's Cres., Goderich, Ont. N7A 2L9; Office: Maitland Rd., P.O. Box 10, Goderich, Ont. N7A 3Y6.

**CHURCH, Douglas Hamilton,** B.Sc.;petroleum executive; b. Calgary, Alta. 5 Nov. 1932; s. William Kenneth and Eleanor (Hamilton) C.; e. Univ. of Alta. B.Sc. 1954; m. Linda Gail d. late Thomas George Potts 16 Jan. 1965; two s. Dean Allan, Craig Stuart; PRES., DOUGLAS H. CHURCH PETROLEUM CONSULTANTS LTD. 1988– ; joined Canadian Gulf Oil Co. and British American Oil Co. 1954–61; Texas Gulf Sulphur 1961–72; Can. Del Oil Ltd. 1972–81; Group Vice Pres., Operations & Production, Sulpetro Ltd. 1981–87; Pres., DegraSul Fertilizer Production Ltd. 1983–86; Pres., Sulbath Exploration Ltd. 1984–87; mem. Assn. Prof. Engrs. Alta.; Phi Delta Theta; recreation: golf; Clubs: Calgary Petroleum; Gyro; Earl Grey Golf; Address: 64 Sierra Vista Close SW, Calgary, Alta. T3H 3A3.

**CHURCH, Gerald C.;** financial executive; b. Lewisville, N.B. 11 October 1934; s. Aaron and Frances (MacPherson) C.; e. Moncton H.S.; various univ. courses 1972–78; CN Gen. Mngt. Training Program 1978; m. Yolande d. Germain and Yvette Serve 5 Sept. 1959; children: Johanne, Stefan; TREASURER, CANADIAN NATIONAL RAILWAY COMPANY 1981– ; joined CN 1951; various clerical positions 1951–63; various supervisory positions 1963–73; Leasing Mgr. 1973–75; Asst. Treas. 1975–81; Treas., The Canada Southern Railway Co.; numerous CN subsidiaries; Dir., St. Clair Tunnel Company (CN subs.); Dir., St. Clair Tunnel Construction Company (CN subs.); E.I.D. Electronic Identification Systems Ltd. 1989– ; Mem., Rotary Club of Montreal; Assn. of American Railroads (Treasury Div.); recreations: tennis, golf, reading, gardening, fishing; Home: 268 Inglewood, Pointe Claire, Que. H9R 5K9; Office: 935 de la Gauchetière St. W., 3rd fl., Montreal, Que. H3B 2M9.

**CHURCH, J. Gardner,** B.A., M.B.A.; civil servant; b. Perth, Ont. 10 Sept. 1947; s. Charles B. Gardner and Margaret Russel (Hay) C.; e. Perth Coll. 1966; Carleton Univ. B.A. 1969; York Univ. M.B.A., (P.A.) 1971; m. Linda d. Harry and Lorraine Hamilton 9 Jan. 1971; children: Anthony, Heather, Katharine; seconded to York Univ. & Waterloo Univ. 1992–95; Local Govt. Policy, Adv., Govt. of Ont. 1971–74; Mgr., Local Govt. Reform 1974–77; Extve. Sec., Waterloo Reg. Review Comn. 1977; Chrmn., Brantford-Brant Local Govt. Pilot Project 1978; Dir., Field Serv., Mun. Affairs, Govt. of Ont. 1979; Gen. Mgr., Min. of Mun. Affairs & Housing 1980–85; Asst. Dep. Min., Min. of Housing 1985–87; Dep. Min. 1987–88; Dep. Min., Office for the Greater Toronto Area, Govt. of Ont. 1988–92; Home: 12 Meadowcrest Rd., Etobicoke, Ont. M8Z 2Y2.

**CHURCH, John Kenneth,** B.Sc., P.Ag.; farmer, executive, agrologist; b. Calgary, Alta. 3 Nov. 1929; s. W.K. and Eleanor (Hamilton) C.; e. Univ. of Alberta B.Sc. 1952; m. Barbara d. Charles and Opal McKinnon 18 Oct. 1958; one s.: William John; CHAIRMAN, XL FOODS LTD.1990– ; actively involved in many phases of agriculture incl. a term as President (1973–74) of the Alberta Inst. of Agrologists, the profl. orgn. of university graduates in agric.; Vice-Pres. & Dir., McKinnon Allen & Assoc. (Western) Ltd. 1981–89; United Church; recreations: golf; Home: R.R. 2, Balzac, Alta. T0M 0E0; Office: Suite 250, 1209 – 59 Avenue S.E., Calgary, Alta. T2H 2P6.

**CHURCH, Kenneth Robert,** B.Com., C.A.; retired; b. Ottawa, Ont. 20 Mar. 1921; s. George Alexander and Ethel (Turley) C.; e. Queen's Univ. B.Com. 1942; Inst. of C.A.'s of Ont. C.A. 1948; m. Elsie May d. Late Edwin Chambers 9 Dec. 1944; children: Kenneth Edward, Thomas Robert; Comptroller, Hawker Siddeley Can. Inc. 1981–86; Auditor, Price Waterhouse 1942–50; Treas., Orenda Internat. Ltd. 1963–81; Vice-Pres. Finance, Orenda Ltd. 1966–73; Dir. of Finance, Orenda Div., Hawker Siddeley 1974–80; mem. and past Dir. of Toronto Branch, Financial Extves Inst. of Can.; past Chrmn. of Contracts and Finance Cmte., Air Industries Assn. of Canada; Anglican; Clubs: Weston Golf & Country; recreations: sailing, curling; Home: 30 Cedarland Dr., Islington, Ont. M9A 2K3.

**CHURCH, Robert Bertram,** M.Sc., Ph.D.; geneticist; educator; b. Calgary, Alta. 7 May 1937; s. Bertram Cecil and Alexa Winnifred (Black) C.; e. Crescent Hts. High Sch. Calgary 1955; Olds (Alta.) Coll. Dipl. 1956; Univ. of Alta. B.Sc. 1962, M.Sc. 1963; Univ. of Uppsala Dipl. 1961; Univ. of Edinburgh Ph.D. 1965; m. Joyce Maryanne d. Harry Brown, Lethbridge, Alta. 2 May 1958; children: Jeffrey Robert, Eileen Alexa; PROFESSOR EMERITUS, FACULTY OF MEDICINE, UNIV. OF CALGARY 1992– ; Assoc. Dean Research, Univ. of Calgary, 1981–88; Research Assoc. Univ. of Wash. 1965–67; Asst. Prof. Univ. Calgary 1967–69; Prof. and Head of Med. Biochem. & Biol., Univ. of Calgary 1969–83; Visiting Scient. Soviet Acad. Sciences 1972, Murdoch (W. Australia) Univ. 1977, Animal Reproduction Lab. Colo. State Univ. Fort Collins 1978; Klinck Lectr., Agriculture Inst. of Can. 1986–87; Dir. Highfield Stock Farms 1972–76; Dir., Alberta Livestock Transplants Ltd. 1971–76; Connaught Laboratories Ltd., Toronto, 1979–87; Dir. & Chrmn., Veterinary Infectious Disease Organization, Saskatoon 1985–90; Vice Chrmn., Biostar Inc., Saskatoon 1987– ; Dir., Bd. Mem., CIBA GEIGY Ltd. 1990– ; Mem. Bd. of Dirs., Alta. Rsch. Counc. 1989– ; Counc. Mem., Med. Rsch. Counc. of Can. 1990– ; Vice-Chrmn., Premier's Counc. Sci. and Technology (Alta.) 1990– ; Exec., Natural Sciences and Engineering Research Council of Canada, Ottawa, 1978–86; mem., Expert Ctte. Animal Genetics and Reproduction: Agriculture Canada 1975–83; Pres. Church Livestock Consultants 1972– ; Lochend Luing Ranches 1974– ; Dir. Calgary Exhn. & Stampede 1974–90 (Pres. 1988–90); Chrmn. Research and Technology Comte, Calgary Chamber of Commerce 1979–81; Research Comte., Alta. Cancer Bd., 1981–87; Dir., W. Airdrie R.E.A. 1978– ; Can. Lung Assn. 1980– ; Candn. Inst. for Advanced Research 1983–89; Trustee, Stockmans Memorial Found. 1986–89; rec'd Tribute to Biotechnology Award, Prov. of Alta. 1988; Distinction Award, Agriculture Inst. of Can. 1988; inducted into Candn. Agriculture Hall of Fame 1991; Distinguished Profl. Achievement Award, Univ. of Alta. 1990; inducted, Alberta Order of Excellence 1993; author over 100 scient. papers molecular genetics, genetic engineering and manipulation of reproduction in domestic animals; numerous articles on applied animal livestock mang.; United Church; recreations: livestock, ranching; Home: R.R.1, Airdrie, Alta. T4B 2A3; Office: 3330 Hospital Drive, NW Calgary, Alta. T2N 4N1.

**CHURCHER, Charles Stephen,** Ph.D., M.Sc.; professor; b. Aldershot, Eng. 21 Mar. 1928; s. George and Stephanie (Rasmus) C.; e. Univ. of Natal B.Sc. (Biol.), 1950, B.Sc. Hons. (Zool.) 1952, M.Sc. 1954; Oxford Univ. 1951; Univ. of Toronto Ph.D. 1957; m. Winifred d. Alec and Winifred Lindsay 4 July 1960; children: Nigel, Stephanie, Carol; RSCH. ASSOC., ROYAL ONT. MUS. 1962– ; and PROF. EMERITUS, UNIV. OF TORONTO 1993– ; Lectr., Dept. of Zool. 1957–60; Asst. Prof. 1960–65; Assoc. Prof. 1965–70; Assoc. Prof., Dept. of Anatomy 1968–78; Prof. 1978–93; Assoc. Dean, Arts & Sci. 1975–78; Assoc. Chrmn., Dept. of Zool. 1979–84; Acting Chrmn., Dept. of Urban & Regional Plng., Sch. of Grad. Studies 1980–81; Acting Dir., Mus. Studies Prog., Sch. of Grad. Studies 1983–85; Prof. 1970–93; Prof. Emeritus 1993– ; Prin. Investigator (Paleont.), N. Yukon Rsch. Proj. 1975–87; Dakhleh Oasis Proj., Egypt 1979– ; mem. Bd. of Mgmt., Metrop. Toronto Zool. Soc. 1979 (Vice-Chrmn. 1980–81, Chrmn. 1981–84); Bd. of Mgmt., Metrop. Toronto Zoo 1982–86; Mem., Candn. Counc. on Animal Care 1983–86 (Chrmn. 1984–85); Pres., Soc. of Vert. Paleont. 1990–92, (Mem.-at-Large, Counc. 1986–88; Vice-Pres. 1988–90; Past Pres. 1992–94); Fellow, Trinity Coll., Univ. of Toronto 1981; Mem., Am. Assn. for the Advancement of Sci. 1965, Fellow 1983; Mem., Geol. Assn. of Can. 1973, Fellow 1984; Dir., Goldfund Ltd. and Goldtrust Ltd. 1975–90; mem. Am. Soc. of Mammalogists, Am. Quaternary Assn.; Candn. Mus. Assn.; author of more than 150 sci. papers, book chapters, popular articles, etc.; recreations: sailing, hiking, woodwork, travel; Home: 20 Binscarth Rd., Toronto, Ont. M4W 1Y1; Office: Univ. of Toronto, Toronto, Ont. M5S 1A1 and Royal Ont. Mus., 100 Queen's Park N., Toronto, Ont. M5S 2C6.

**CHURG, Andrew Marc,** B.A., Ph.D., M.D.; b. New York, N.Y. 17 June 1946; s. Jacob and Vivian (Gelb) C.; e. Columbia Univ., B.A. 1967; Univ. of Chicago, Ph.D. 1971, M.D. 1973; PROF. OF PATHOL., UNIV. OF B.C. 1980– ; former mem. Depts. Pathol. Univ. of Chicago, Univ. of Cal.; ed. Pathol. of Occupational Lung Disease 1988; numerous articles lung disease; Home: 1229 West 7th, Vancouver, B.C. V6H 1B7; Office: 2211 Wesbrook Mall, Vancouver, B.C. V6T 1W5.

**CHUTE, Andrew Lawrence,** O.B.E., M.A., M.D., Ph.D., F.R.C.P.(C); b. Kodai Kanal, India, 31 May 1909; s. Jesse Edmund and Pearl (Smith), M.D. (decorated by King Geo. V with the 'Kaiser-i-Hind' for Distinguished Service to India) C.; e. Univ. of Toronto, B.A., M.A., M.D., 1935; Univ. of London, Ph.D., 1939; m. Helen Evans (M.D.), d. Robert Mills Reid M.D., C.M., Vegreville, Alta., 6 Oct. 1939; children: Judith (Mrs. Alden Redfield), Douglas; Dean of Medicine, Univ. of Toronto 1966–73 and Prof. of Pediatrics 1951–66; now Dean Emeritus, Professor Emeritus; served in World War 1940–45 as Lieut. with 2nd Light Field Ambulance 1940; Lieut.-Col. and O.C. No. 1 Candn. Research Lab. 1942; served in Eng., N. Africa, Italy and N.W. Europe; invested O.B.E., Military Division, for research work on tank warfare in N. Africa; Sir Arthur Sims Commonwealth Travelling Prof. 1966; mem., Candn. Diabetes Assn., Candn. Med. Assn.; Toronto Diabetes Assn.; Alpha Kappa Kappa; Alpha Omega Alpha; Address: R.R. #1, Loretto, Ont. L0G 1L0.

**CHUTTER, Sturley Donald Charles,** M. Com., C.A.E.; management consultant and association executive; b. Vancouver, B.C. 9 Aug. 1924; s. Thomas Sturley, M.C., and Clover May, R.N., (Walker) C.; m. Johanna Margaretha Helling, 1959; d. Jessica Caroline; s. Brian Andrew; e. Univ. of British Columbia, B.Com. (1st Class Hons.) 1944; Univ. of Toronto, M.Com. (1st Class Hons.) 1946; Northwestern Univ., Diploma in Trade Assn. Management (1st Class Hons.) 1954; Ottawa Bureau Chief, Revay & Ass. Ltd.; Cert. Assn. Exec. (C.A.E.); Past Pres., Ottawa Chapt., Project Management Inst.; formerly Gen. Mgr., Cdn. Construction Assn., 1954–75; Past Mem., Exec. Comm., Nat. Bldg. Code; Past Chrmn., Metric Comn. Sector Ctte. for Construction; Past Exec. Dir., Construction Ind. Dev. Council; Past Dir., Nat. Construction Industry Devel. Foundation; Past Vice Chrmn., Accreditation Brd., Can. Soc. Assn. Execs.; Past Vice-Chrmn., Nat. Capital Region Br., Community Planning Assn. of Canada; Comnd. in Cdn. Inf. Corps, Jan. 1945; demobilized with rank of Lieut., Nov. 1945; Past Pres., Dinner-Dance Club of Ottawa; Past Pres. Univ. of B.C. Alumni Assn., Ottawa Br.; Past Pres., Ottawa Chapt. and Dir., Can. Soc. Assn. Execs.; a Cdn. Del. to N.A. Apprenticeship Conf., San Diego, 1953, to ILO, Geneva, 1957, 1964 and 1971; Phi Kappa Sigma; Anglican; Clubs: Rideau; Rotary, Ottawa (Pres. 1993–94); Home: 18 Wren Road, Gloucester, Ont. K1J 7H7.

**CHWYL, Edward,** B.Sc., M.Sc., P.Eng.; oil & gas company executive; b. Andrew, Alta. 18 July 1943; s. William and Mary C.; e. Univ. of Alta. B.Sc. 1965, M.Sc. 1968; m. Mary d. Robert and Margaret Rutherford 29 Aug. 1987; children: Brian, Donna, Robert, Brendan; PRESIDENT, TARRAGON OIL AND GAS LIMITED; over 20 years of diversified executive management experience in oil & gas industry in Canada & U.S.; var. executive positions, Canada N.W. Energy Limited and its predecessor companies of Geocrude Energy Inc. & PanCana Resources Ltd., Mesa Petroleum (N.A.) Co. & Atlantic Richfield Co.; Extve. Vice-Pres. & Chief Operating Offr., Sceptre Resources Limited; Mem., P. Soc. of CIM; APEGGA; Home: 1008 Frontenac Ave. S.W., Calgary, Alta. T2T 1B3; Office: 2500, 500 Fourth Ave. S.W., Calgary, Alta. T2P 2V6.

**CIACCIA, The Hon. Giambattista (John),** B.A., LL.B.; politician; b. Ielsi, Italy 4 Mar. 1933; s. Pasquale and Angelina (Sabatino) C.; e. McGill Univ., B.A. 1953, LL.B. 1956; one s. Mark; MINISTER OF INTERNATIONAL AFFAIRS and IMMIGRATION AND CULTURAL COMMUNITIES, GOVT. OF QUEBEC 1994– ; Lawyer, Malouf and Shorteno 1957–59; Legal couns. & Real Estate Dir., Steinberg Ltd. 1959–66; Lawyer/Partner, Chait, Salomon, Gelber, Ciaccia, Reis, Bronstein & Assoc. 1967–69; Asst. Dept. Min., Indian & North. Affairs, Govt. of Can. 1971–73; Mount-Royal MNA 1973– ; Spec. Rep. for P.M. Robert Bourassa, natives of James Bay North. Que. settlement 1973–76; Extve. Mem., Que. Liberal Party 1977–84; Min. of Energy and Resources, Govt. of Que. 1985–89; Min. resp. for Native Affairs and Min. of Internat. Affairs, Govt. of Que. 1989–90; Min. of International Affairs 1989–94; Mem., Que. Bar Assn. 1957– ; Candn. Ital. Bus. & Profl. Men's Assn.; Nat. Cong. of Ital. Candns. 1978– ; recreations: sailing, swimming, reading, music; Office:

Edifice Hector-Fabre, 525, boul. René Lévesque est, 4e étage, Québec, Qué. G1R 5R9.

**CICANSKY, Victor,** B.Ed., B.A., M.F.A.; artist; university professor; b. Regina, Sask. 12 Feb. 1935; s. Frank (Francisc Czekanski) and Mary (Fluter) (Cicansky); e. Univ. of Sask. B.Ed. 1964; Univ. of Regina B.A. 1967; studied, Haystack Mountain Sch. of Art, Deere Isle, Maine 1967; Univ. of Calif., Davis M.F.A. 1970; m. Frances D. (dec'd. 1987) d. Arthur and Florence Gendron 13 Aug. 1966; children: Mea, Ryan; PROF., DEPT. OF VISUAL ARTS, UNIV. OF REGINA 1970– ; Banff Sch. of Fine Arts 1972; N.S. Coll. of Art 1973; Univ. of Calif., Davis 1988 and others; collections: Mus. of Modern Art, Tokyo Japan; Musée d'art contemporain Montreal; Mackenzie Art Gall. Regina; Lavalin Inc. Montreal; Claridge Collection Montreal; and others; comns.: The Garden Fence, CBC Regina 1983; Regina My World, Co-operators Regina 1979; The Old Working Class, Govt. of Sask. 1977; and others; exbns: 30 Ceramic Sculptors, John Natsoulas Gall. Davis CA 1990; L.A. '90, 5th Internat. Contemp. Art Fair 1990; New Art Forms, Navy Pier Chicago 1989; Time of the American Farm, Evanston Art Ctr. Evanston, Ill. 1988; True North/Far West, San Francisco State Univ. Gall. 1988; and others incl. Japan, England, France; Kingsley Annual Award, Calif. 1967; Royal Albert Award (U.K.) 1967; Can. Counc. Awards, Work & Travel 1968, 69, 71, 83, 89; Mem., Sask. Arts Bd. 1980–81; Bd. Mem., Mackenzie Art Gall. Inc. 1985–88; Wascana Arts Adv. Ctte., Wascana Ctr. Regina 1981– ; Mem., Arts Adv. Ctte., SIAST, Woodland Campus, Prince Albert, SK 1989–91; recreations: gardening, tai-chi; Home: 2313 Parliament Ave., Regina, Sask. S4S 4G5; Office: Univ. of Regina, Regina, Sask. S4S 0A2.

**CICCOLINI, Sam J.;** insurance executive; b. Pescosolido, Italy 3 July 1944; s. Pasquale and Filomena (Sarra) C.; e. Central H.S.; Ryerson; McMaster Univ. R.I.B.O.; m. Donna Maria Sarracini 6 July 1968; one s.: Michael; OWNER, MASTERS INSURANCE (FORMERLY CICCOLINI INSUR.) 1966– ; Partner, Delmor Funeral Homes Ltd. 1991– ; Partner, Sports Fantasy Inc. 1991– ; Credit Dept., Maclean Hunter Pub. 1961–63; Purchasing Agent, Delew Cather & Co. 1963–66; Partner, Finch (Union) Hardware; Trustee, Hospital for Sick Children (Chrmn., 5 review cttes., Genetics Dept.); Past Chrmn. 'AAA' Hockey League; Pres., Richmond Hill Vaughan 'AAA' Assn.; Advr. & Bd. Mem., City of Vaughan Hockey Assn. (Life member 1992); Life Mem., Richmond Hill Vaughan Kings Hockey Assn.; Bd. Mem., Ont. Hocky League (OHA); Pres., Mid Ont. JRC Hockey League; Chrmn., Review Ctte. for Salaries of Council, the Mayor & Reg. Counc., City of Vaughan; Chrmn., Country Kiddie College, Woodbridge 1991– ; Chrmn., Steering Ctte. for the formation of the New Minor Hockey Alliance of Ont.; recipient, Bicentennial Medal, Prov. of Ont.; Volunteer of the Year in Vaughan; Olymic Medal Award Winner, Celebration 1988; awarded Commemorative Medal for 125th Anniversary of Candn. Confederation; Past Pres., Toronto Earlscourt Rotary Club; Past Pres., St. Margaret Mary Ch. Council (Woodbridge); Mem., P.C. Party of Canada & Ont.; Home: 49 Firglen Ridge, Woodbridge, Ont. L4L 1N3; Office: 7501 Keele St., Concord, Ont. L4K 1Y2.

**CIESZKOWSKI, Edward D.,** B.Com., M.B.A.; executive; b. Warsaw, Poland 22 Feb. 1940; s. Alexander D. and Maria (Joswiak) C.; e. Stafford Polytechnic B.Com. 1960; Newcastle Univ. M.B.A. 1966; m. Diana Mignon d. John W. Thornley 1976; children: Duncan, Robert, Alistair, Hamish, Andrew, Konrad; C.E.O., DELISSER, ROMANOFF & HINE INC. 1988– ; Chrmn., Trimedia International Inc.; Asst. Controller, ABF Ltd. (Weston Group) UK 1965–69; Dir. ISSA Hotels Corp. W. Indies 1969–72; Mng. Dir. Grand Met Services, UK and Middle E. 1973–78; Exec. Vice Pres. and Chief Operating Offr. VS Services, Can. 1978–84; Pres. Eastwood Services Ltd. 1984–88; author 'Food For Thought' 1974; co-author 'Training For Success' 1977; Ed. 'The Cookery Manual' 1985; Fellow, Brit. Inst. Mgmt.; Internat. Culinary Inst.; recreations: antiques, watercolours; Office: 448 Sackville St., Toronto, Ont. M4X 1T4.

**CINADER, Bernhard,** O.C., Ph.D., D.Sc., F.R.S.C., F.R.S.C. (U.K.); scientist; educator; b. Vienna, Austria 30 March 1919; s. Leon and Adele (Schwarz) C.; e. Univ. of London B.Sc. 1945, Ph.D. (Biochem.) 1948, D.Sc. (Immunology) 1957; one d. Agatha; PROF. OF IMMUNOLOGY AND CLINICAL BIOCHEMISTRY 1969– ; Dir., Inst. of Immunology 1971–80; Univ. of Toronto, Mem. of the Governing Counc. 1980–89, Mem. of Honorary Degree Ctte. 1984–86, Mem. Exec. 1982–83, Mem., Academic Bd. 1989– ; Pres., Internat. Union of Immunological Societies 1969–74; Pres., Cdn. Soc. for Immunology 1966–69, 1979–81; Chrmn., National Ctte. for Immunology 1983–89; Beit Mem. Fellow 1949–53; Fellow of Immunochem., Inst. Pathol., Western Reserve Univ., Cleveland 1948–49; Princ. Scient. Offr. Dept. Exper. Pathol. Inst. Animal Physiol. Babraham Hall, Cambridge 1956–58; Enrique E. Ecker Lectr. in Exper. Pathol. 1964; Head, Subdiv. Immunochem., Div. Biol. Research, Ont. Cancer Inst. 1958–69; W.H.O. Consultant, Bombay, India 1981; Rockefeller Foundation Visiting Prof., Bangkok, Thailand 1982; mem. World Health Organ. Expert Adv. Panel on Immunology 1965– ; Chrmn. Adv. Bd., WHO-IUIS Inst. for Training & Research in Immunology, Amsterdam 1975–81; Chrmn., Candn. Fed. Biol. Societies 1976–77; Chrmn., IUIS-WHO Nomenclature Comte. 1980–83; IUIS rep. at I.C.S.U. 1980–89; Pres. 6th Int. Cong. of Immunology 1986; WHO Scientific and Technical Adv. Grp. (STAG) to Special Prog. of Rsch., Devel. and Rsch. Training in Human Reproduction, Geneva, Switzerland 1985–91; mem. Steering Ctte., Task force on Vaccines for Fertility Regulation, W.H.O., Geneva, Switzerland 1991– ; mem. of Ed. Bds: Cdn. Journ. of Biochemistry (1967–71), Immunochemistry (1965–69), Journ. of Immunological Methods (1970–74), Immunological Communications (1974– ;), Bolletino Dell' Istituto Sieroterapico Milanese (1973–86), Immunology Letters (1979– ;), Receptors (1980–84), Asian Pacific Journal of Allergy & Immunology (1983– ;); Immunology Investigation (1985– ;); Aging: Immunology and Infectious Disease (1987– ;); Contemporary Infectious Disease (1987– ;); Chrmn. Ed. Bd. Journ. Immunogenetics (1977–89); rec'd Old Student Prize Queen Mary Coll. Univ. London 1944; Jenner Mem. Studentship 1946; Société de Chimie Biologique (France) Medal 1954; Pasteur Medal, Institut Pasteur (France) 1960; Ignac Semmelweis Medal Budapest 1978; Queen's Silver Jubilee Medal 1977; Thomas W. Eadie Medal (Royal Society of Canada) 1982; Officer, Order of Canada 1985; Hardi Cinader Prize estbd., Dept. of Immunology, Univ. of Toronto (for best grad. student in Dept.) 1985; Landsteiner Medal, 6th Int. Cong. of Immunology, Toronto 1986; annual Bernhard Cinader Lectureship estbd. by the Candn. Soc. of Immunology 1986; Hon. Mem., Czechoslovak Med. Assoc. J.E. Purkyně 1988; Jan E. Purkyně Medal, Czechoslovakia 1988; Commemorative Medal, 125th Anniversary of Candn. Confedn. 1992; Pres., Royal Candn. Inst. 1989–90; Ed. 'Antibody to Enzymes – A Three-Component System' 1963; 'Antibodies to Biologically Active Molecules' 1967; 'Regulation of the Antibody Response' 1968, 2nd. ed. 1971; co-ed. 'Immunological Response of the Female Reproductive Tract' 1976; ed. 'Immunology of Receptors' 1977; co-ed 'Progress in Immunology VI' 1986; Series ed., 'Receptors in Biology and Medicine: The Language of Intercellular Communication' 1983–86; Series ed. 'Intercellular and Intracellular Communication,' Cambridge University Press, Cambridge, U.K. (1985–92); author over 300 scient. articles on immunology, oncology and gerontology; Research: Characterization of two distinct classes of immunoglobulins 1953; first report on tolerance, as a factor in determining response to a cross-reacting molecule 1955; hypothesis of tolerance-steered specificity 1960; Analysis of the effect of antibody on catalysis by biologically active molecules: evidence for 1. inhibition by steric hindrance, 2. competition between antibody molecules for overlapping sites on enzyme i.e. blocking of inhibitory activity and 3. alteration of configuration by antibody and consequent enzyme activation; Discovery of a murine allotype 1963; Discovery of murine complement defect as a consequence of experiments based on the hypothesis of tolerance-steered immune responsiveness 1963; Polyclonal and monoclonal reagents for the identification of rabbit T, B cells, polymorphonuclear leukocytes etc. 1973–; Analysis of polymorphic gerontological changes in different classes of suppressor cells and in thymus precursors 1977–; Analysis of age-related changes in isotypes, H1 histones, repair capacity, dopamine, insulin receptors and adrenoceptors 1984–; Development of strategies to alter progression of age-related changes by dietary, hormonal and pharmacological intervention as methods to analyze interdependence and/or independence of compartmentalized aging; Demonstration that age related increase in molecular output can be caused by changes in the relative proportion of cellular subpopulations; Honorary Curator and author of articles and catalogues on Cdn. Indian art incl. Contemporary Native Arts of Ontario 1973, Jacob Thomas and Sons 1975, The Birchbark Sings 1985, Manitoulin Island - The Third Layer 1985, rev. ed. 1986 and chapters in the exhbn. catalogues of the McMichael Gall. 'A Vision of Canada' 1970 and the Oklahoma Museum of Art '100 Years of Native American Art' 1978; Home: 73 Langley Ave., Toronto, Ont. M4K 1B4; Office: Med. Sci. Bldg., Univ. of Toronto, Toronto, Ont. M5S 1A8.

**CINQ-MARS, Irène,** B.èsArts, B.A.P., M.Sc.A.; vice-rectrice à l'enseignement; née Montréal, Qué. 8 janvier 1947; é. Collège Ste-Marie B.èsArts 1968; Univ. de Montréal B.A.P. 1973, M.Sc.A. 1976; Fellow, Assn. des arch. paysagistes du Qué. 1991; VICE-RECTRICE A L'ENSEIGNEMENT, UNIV. DE MOTNREAL 1993– ; Vice-doyenne aux affaires académiques, Fac. de l'aménagement, Univ. de Montréal 1985–89; Directrice, Ecole d'arch. de paysage 1989–90; Président de divers comités incl. Comité sur la persévérance (rech. sur l'attrition à l'Univ. de Montréal) 1991– ; mem., Conseil d'admin. Assn. des Arch. Paysagistes du Qué. 1991– ; Com. de coord. univ. de l'enseignement dans les centres hosp.; Comn. des études; Conf. des recteurs et des principaux des Univ. du Qué.; Conseil péd. de l'Ecole des HEC de Montréal; Sous-comn. du premier cycle, S.C.P.C., Univ. de Montréal et nombreux autres comités; num. projets de recherche; consultant, nombreux organisations; participant, divers événements scientifiques, académiques à caractère profl. et autres; auteure/co-auteure de nombreux publications scientifiques et professionnelles; Fellow, CLSA 1991; C.A. Coll. Jean-de-Brébeuf; Com. d'aménagement Hôp. Sainte-Justine; Com. des vice-recteurs acad. des univs. can.; Com. des vice-recteur acad.; Com. de liaison enseignement sup.; SWACC; mem., Comn. de l'enseignement collégial au Conseil sup. de l'Edn.; rés.: 288, McDougall, Outremont, Qué. H2V 3P2; bureau: C.P. 6128, Succ. A., Montréal, Qué. H3C 3J7.

**CIPOLLA, Charles A.,** B.A., C.A.; financial executive; b. Grotte, Italy 14 Sept. 1947; e. Wilfrid Laurier Univ. B.A. 1969; C.A. 1972; m. Jane; children: Andrea, Stephanie; VICE-PRES., FINANCE & SEC.-TREAS., ALLEN-BRADLEY DIVISION OF ROCKWELL INTERNATIONAL OF CANADA 1974– ; Peat, Marwick, Mitchell & Co., C.A.s 1969–74; Mem., Financial Extves. Inst. (Hamilton Ch.); Ont. Inst. of C.A.s; Cambridge C. of C.; Kiwanis Club of Cambridge; recreations: fishing, boating, squash; Home: 71 Deerpath Rd., Cambridge, Ont. N1T 1H6; Office: 135 Dundas St., Cambridge, Ont. N1R 5X1.

**CIRIA, Alberto,** B.A., LL.B.; university professor; b. Buenos Aires, Argentina 27 Jan. 1934; s. Nicolás and María (de Miguel) C.; e. Col. Nac. de Buenos Aires, B.A. 1952; Univ. nac. de Buenos Aires, LL.B. 1959; LSE, Brit. Counc. Scholar 1963–64; m. Raquel d. Francisco and Antonia González 18 Aug. 1966; PROF., DEPT. OF POL. SCI., SIMON FRASER UNIV. 1977– ; Assoc. Mem., Dept. of Spanish and Latin Am. Studies; translator, journalist, teaching asst., Buenos Aires; Asst. Prof., Univ. of Buenos Aires 1964–66; Vis. Rsch. Asst. Prof., Univ. of Calif. 1966; Univ. of N. Carolina 1966–67; Lectr., Rutgers Univ. 1967–68; Asst. Prof., Simon Fraser Univ. 1969–70; Assoc. Prof. 1970–77; Senator, Simon Fraser Univ. 1992–95; Candn. Correspondent, 'Revista Jurídica de Buenos Aires' 1986– ; Ed. Bd. 'Can. J. of Latin Am. & Caribbean Studies' 1980–90; Participating Ed. 'Latin Am. Perspectives' 1974– ; Small Grant, SSHRC 1990; Rsch. Grant, SSHRC 1987; Can. Counc. 1970; leave fellowships: 1975–76, 1982–83; Mem., Internat. Pol. Sci. Assn.; CALACS (Extve. Counc. 1981–84; 1990–93); Candn. Pol. Sci. Assn.; Latin Am. Studies Assn.; Candn. Assn. of Friends, LSE; SFU Fac. Assn.; Diamond Univ. Club; author: 'Treinta años de política y cultura' 1990, 'Política y cultura popular' 1983, 'Parties and Power in Modern Argentina' 1974 and others; editor: 'Nicolás Ciria,' a life history, 1978, 'Brecht' 1967 & others; recreations: cinema, theatre, music; Home: 403 – 5450 Empire Dr., Burnaby, B.C. V5B 1N4; Office: Burnaby, B.C. V5A 1S6.

**CLANCY, Hon. Donald Lawrence,** B.A., B.Comm., LL.B., Q.C.; supreme court judge; b. Halifax, N.S. 28 Dec. 1932; s. Clyde Sinclair and Helene Florence (Wamboldt) C.; e. Dalhousie Univ. B.A. 1953, B.Comm. 1954, LL.B. 1956; m. Ray Fraser d. Edward and Isabella Stewart 15 Aug. 1992 children: David Arthur, Mark William; JUDGE, SUPREME COURT OF BRITISH COLUMBIA 11 OCTOBER 1991– ; private practice Dawson Creek, B.C. 1958–80; Legal Services Branch, Ministry of Attorney General B.C. 1980–91; Q.C. 1987; Office: The Law Courts, 800 Smithe St., Vancouver, B.C. V6Z 2E1.

**CLANCY, James,** B.A.; labour leader; b. Kingston, Ont. 12 March 1950; e. Carleton Univ. B.A.; PRESIDENT, NATIONAL UNION OF PUBLIC & GENERAL EMPLOYEES 1990– ; Social Welfare Field Worker 1976–84; Pres., Ont. Public Service Employees Union 1984–90; General Vice-Pres., Canadian Labour Congress 1990– ; Office: 204, 2841 Riverside Dr., Ottawa, Ont. K1V 8N4.

**CLANCY, Mary Catherine,** M.P., LL.M.; politician; b. Halifax, N.S. 13 Jan. 1948; d. Douglas Gerald and Catherine Marie (Casey) C.; e. Mount Saint Vincent Univ. Halifax B.A. 1970; Dalhousie Law Sch. LL.B. 1974; Univ. of London LL.M. 1975; Asst. Dir. Continuing Legal Edn. Univ. of B.C. 1976–77; Special Adv. to Min. Responsible for Status of Women Govt. N.S. 1977–78; private law practice 1978–88; Broadcaster CBC 1984–88; Part-time Lectr. in Family Law, Legal Status of Women, Gerontol. Mount Saint Vincent Univ. 1979–88; Part-time Lectr. in Law & Social Work Maritime Sch. of Social Work 1984–88; weekly columnist Halifax Daily News 1987–88; el. Lib. M.P. for Halifax g.e. 1988; Dir. YWCA 1987–88; Gov. Dalhousie Univ. 1987–88; Mount Saint Vincent Univ. 1987– 88, Pres. Alumnae 1985–87; Dir. Ecology Action Centre Halifax 1987–88; Dalhousie Legal Aid 1986– ; Planning Ctte. Archdiocese Halifax 1985– ; Kwacha Theatre Bd. 1983–85; Bd. Mgmt. Saint Joseph's Day Care Centre 1978–83, Pres. 1981–83; Seaweed Theatre Assn. 1980–83, Vice Chrmn. 1980–81; Bd. Mgmt. Home Guardian Angel 1978–84, Vice Chrmn. 1981–82; Chrmn. Unemployment Ins. Appeal Bd. 1981–84; Bd. mem. Atlantic Ballet Co. 1983–84; Vice Pres. Atlantic, Nat. Women's Lib. Comn. 1982–86; mem. Constnl. & Legal Affairs Ctte. Lib. Party Can. 1987– ; mem. N.S. Barristers Soc.; recreations: theatre, travel; Home: 6066 Coburg Rd., Halifax, N.S. B3H 1Z7; Office: 651 Confederation Bldg., House of Commons, Ottawa, Ont. K1A 0A6.

**CLANCY, Raymond M.;** shipping exec; b. Can. 22 Oct. 1922; s. Thomas Leo and Mary Magdalen (Myron) C.; e. St. Patrick's Hall St. John's, Nfld.; m. Catherine d. James and Mary Wall 5 Sept. 1949; children: Christopher, Janine, Barbara, Cyril, Catherine; PRESIDENT, BLUE PETER STEAMSHIPS LTD.; Pres. Transports Inc.; Southern Isle Shipping Ltd.; Northlantic Shipping Ltd.; R. Catholic; recreations: numismatics, philately, photography; Home: 3 Maypark Pl., St. John's, Nfld. A1B 2E3; Office: P.O. Box 6030, Harbour Dr., St. John's, Nfld. A1C 5X9.

**CLAPINSON, Roy F.;** company executive; b. Harrow, England 3 Feb. 1943; s. Herbert Percy and Amelia Mary (Deacon) C.; e. Minehead Grammar Sch. (U.K.) 1960; Derby Coll. of Technol., higher nat. cert. (HNC), production engineering 1966; m. Sarah d. Frank and Sarah Barton 30 Sept. 1967; children: Nicholas Paul, Christopher Neal, Jonathan Keith; PRESIDENT, ROLLS ROYCE CANADA 1991; Rolls Royce apprenticeship 1960–65; Office: 9500, Cote de Liesse, Lachine, Qué. H8T 1A2.

**CLAPPISON, John H.,** B.A., F.C.A.; chartered accountant; b. Toronto, Ont. 10 July 1946; s. John Henry and June Pauline (Henry) C.; e. Upper Can. Coll. 1965, B.A. 1968; m. Lynn S. d. Mr. Justice Samuel and Helen S. Hughes 12 July 1969; children: Sarah, Susie; MNG. PARTNER, PRICE WATERHOUSE, Toronto; joined Price Waterhouse 1968; Chrmn., Bd. of Gov., Shaw Festival Theatre Found. 1987–89; Gov. and Mem. Extve. Ctte., Roy Thomson Hall 1991; recreations: squash, golf, politics, theatre; Clubs: Badminton & Racquet Club; Toronto Golf Club; Royal and Ancient Golf Club of St. Andrews, Scotland; Toronto Club; 'Roon the Ben' Golf Soc.; Home: 5 Rolland Rd., Toronto, Ont. M4G 1V4; Office: P.O. Box 190, Ste. 3300, 1 First Canadian Place, Toronto, Ont. M5X 1H7.

**CLARE, Harvey Haig,** B.A., P. Eng.; petroleum exec.; b. Vanguard, Saks. 8 Oct. 1918; s. Frederick Alexander, D.D. and Florence Mary (Holmes) C.; e. Univ. of Sask. B.A. (Chem.) 1939; Atlantic Summer Sch. of Advanced Business Adm. 1954; m. Robyn M. d. Edward and Mary Pierce 15 June 1946; children: Marily Jean, Cathryn Wendy, Johanne Pierce; Process Op., Bahrein Petroleum Co. 1939–42; Control Chem. Mfg. Imperial Oil Ltd. Calgary 1942, Contact Engr. O.A.D. Montreal 1947, Tech. Supvr. O.A.D. 1949, Asst. Tech. Supt. 1952, Tech. Supt. 1954, Chief Process Engr. Engn. Div. Sarnia 1955, Chief Operations Engr. Engn. Div. 1956, Asst. Refinery Mgr. Montreal 1958, Mgr. Refining Coordination Div. Toronto 1963, Mgr. Planning & Invest. Logistics Toronto 1965, Environmental Protection Coordinator Toronto 1969, retired 1982; Past Pres., Poly Ores Mining Co.; Founder, Petroleum Assn. for Conserv. Candn. Environment (Pres. 1972, 1977, Dir. 1971–81); Mem., Adv. Ctte. to the Min. of the Environment for M.I.S.A. (Municipal and Industrial Strategy for (Pollution) Abatement) 1986– ; mem., Chem. Inst. Can.; Hon. mem. Conserv. Council Ont.; mem., Metro Toronto Conserv. Foundation; co-author various tech. reports on oil pollution prevention; Member, Oriole York Mills United Church; recreations: bridge, golf, curling; Club: Donalda; Address: 41 Danville Dr., Willowdale, Ont. M2P 1J2.

**CLARE, Walter;** public servant; b. Sudbury, Ont. 12 Oct. 1945; s. Albert and Gladys Berdina (French) C.; e. H.S. Belleville, Ont.; m. Patricia d. Margaret and Jack Kelly 15 Oct. 1966; children: Kelly, Jake, Luke; Superintendent of Bankruptcy, Govt. of Canada 1991; started as messenger in public service; many career opportunities in var. orgns.; Past Chrmn. of Bd. & Dir., Serenity Renewal for Families; Office of Superintendent of Bankruptcy named by Auditor Gen. as outstanding orgn. in 1989 report; author of num. articles & material written in respect to consumer bankruptcy in Can.; Home: 1856 Lorraine Ave., Ottawa, Ont. K1H 6Z8.

**CLARFIELD, Avram Mark,** M.D., C.C.F.P., C.S.P.Q., FRCPC; b. Toronto, Ont. 21 Dec. 1949; s. Morris and Ida (Sherman) C.; e. Forest Hill Coll. Inst. Toronto 1967; York Univ. B.Sc. 1971, Univ. of Toronto M.D. 1975; Candn. Coll. Family Practice Cert. 1977; Fellow, Royal Coll. of Phys. & Surg. of Can. 1983; Specialist in Geriatric Med. (CSPQ) 1987; m. Ora d. Khayyam (dec.) and Freda Paltiel 25 Dec. 1977; children: Sasha, Jonah; PROF., DEPTS. OF FAMILY MED., MED. AND THE MCGILL CENTRE FOR STUDIES IN AGING, McGILL UNIV. 1990– ; Dir., Academic Affairs, Herzog Hosp., Jerusalem, Israel 1992– ; Assoc. Dir., McGill Centre for Studies in Aging 1988–92; Asst. Dean, McGill Univ. 1989–92; Chief, Div. of Geriatric Medicine, Faculty of Med., McGill Univ. 1991–92; Chrmn. Candn. Consensus Conf. on the Assessment of Dementia, Montreal 1989; Cons. in Geriatrics, Julius Richardson Hosp., Jewish Rehab. Hosp., Maimonides Geriatric Centre and Jewish Hosp. of Hope; Cons to CLSC Côte des Neiges; recipient Upjohn Postgrad. Study Award 1979; Allied Jewish Community Service Award 1981; Osler Scholarship Candn. Med. Assn. 1982; Zittrer Community Fund Award 1982 and 1986; Munk Geriatric Award 1984; Commonwealth Sr. Med. Fellow (UK) 1986; Royal Candn. Legion Fellowship in Geriatrics 1986; author: 'In Grandfather's Room' short story 1986; various articles med. jours. and newspapers; Fellow, Am. Geriatric Soc.; mem. Candn. Med. Assn.; Candn. Gerontol. Soc.; Candn. Soc. Geriatric Med.; Jewish; recreations: music, hiking, history, travel; Office: Div. of Geriatrics, Sir Mortimer B. Davis – Jewish General Hospital, 3755 Côte Ste Catherine, Montréal, Qué. H3T 1E2.

**CLARK, Brenda;** illustrator; b. Toronto, Ont. 10 Feb. 1955; d. Leonard Edward and Joan Muriel (Allen) C.; e. Sheridan Coll. Oakville Hons. grad. Illus. Course 1977; m. Robert s. Jack and Beth Courtice 6 May 1989; one s. Robin; freelance illus. educational publications since 1977 incl. Ginn & Co., Macmillan, Gage, Prentice-Hall, Acad. Press, Holt Rinehart, Nelson, Chickadee Mag., Crabtree Publishers; first picture book: 'The Yellow Flag' 1980 P.M.A. and since 1984 Kids Can Press illus. (juvenile) 'Christopher and the Dream Dragon' 1984; 'Sadie and the Snowman' 1985; 'Franklin in the Dark' 1986; 'Big Sarah's Little Boots' 1987; 'Puddleman' 1988; 'Hurry Up, Franklin' 1989; 'Little Fingerling' 1989 (IODE Toronto Chapter Award 1989, finalist Mr. Christie Award 1989); 'Franklin Fibs' 1991; 'Franklin Is Lost' 1992; 'Franklin in Bossy' 1993; 'My Cat' 1993; 'My Dog' 1993; mem. Candn. Children's Book Centre; C.A.N.S.C.A.I.P.; C.A.P.I.C.; recreations: hiking, canoeing, camping, squash; Address: R.R. l, Nestleton, Ont. L0B 1L0.

**CLARK, C. David,** M.B.A.; publishing executive; b. Hamilton, Ont. 22 Feb. 1939; s. Charles Henry and Marguerite Sandel (Waller) C.; e. McMaster Univ. B.A. 1963; Univ. of W. Ont. M.B.A. (Dean's Honour List) 1966; m.; four children; CHAIRMAN AND PUBLISHER, THE GLOBE AND MAIL; Pres. & C.E.O., Thomas J. Lipton, Inc. 1978–83; Chrmn. of the Bd., Pres. & C.E.O., Campbell Soup Company Ltd. (Can.) 1983–92; Dir., Conf. Bd. of Can.; mem. Adv. Counc. & Mem. Extve. Ctte., Sch. of Business, Univ. of Western Ont.; mem., C. D. Howe Inst.; Young Presidents' Orgn. (YPO); XPO Inc.; CEO Inc.; World Pres.'s Orgn.; Ont. Counc., Boy Scouts of Can.; Candn. Opera Co.; John P. Robarts Rsch. Inst.; Bd. of Govs., Jr. Achievement; Outward Bound Can.; Metro Toronto and Central Ont. Y.M.C.A.; recreations: jogging, squash, tennis, skiing; Office: 444 Front St. W., Toronto, Ont. M5V 2S9.

**CLARK, Campbell McGillivray,** B.Sc., M.A., Ph.D.; educator; neuropsychologist; b. Vancouver, B.C. 13 Nov. 1949; s. late Donald McGillivray and Joan Napier (Ross) C.; e. McGill Univ. B.Sc. 1972; Univ. of B.C., M.A. 1978; Univ. of Victoria Ph.D. 1982; ASST. PROF. OF PSYCHIATRY, UNIV. OF B.C. 1984– ; Fogarty Internat. Post-Doctoral Fellow, Positron Emission Tomography Sect. Dept. Nuclear Med. Nat. Insts. Health Bethesda, Md. 1982–84; B.C. Health Care Rsch. Found. Scholar 1985–89; author 5 book chapters, 78 rsch. papers; contbg. ed. Jour. Clin. & Exper. Neuropsychol.; reviewer, MRC, Health and Welfare, Canada, Candn. Psychiatric Rsch. Found.; Nat. Insts. Health, U.S. Veterans Affairs; mem. New York Academy of Science; Internat. Neuropsychol. Soc.; International Classification Soc.; recreations: sailing, skiing; Home: 5087 Connaught Dr., Vancouver, B.C. V6M 3G2; Office: Vancouver, B.C. V6T 1W5.

**CLARK, Carolyn J.,** B.A.; human resources executive; b. Toronto, Ont. 1 Sept. 1949; d. William Norville and Jean Doreen (Henders) Fowler; e. York Univ. B.A. Sociology 1968–71; Univ. of Toronto, Sch. of Continuing Studies, Compensation Mngt. 1976–77, Labour Relns. Mngt. 1978–79; m. Darryl G. s. George and Rheena C. 19 April 1975; children: Ryan William, Stephanie Jean; VICE-PRESIDENT, HUMAN RESOURCES, CANADIAN PACIFIC HOTELS & RESORTS 1988– ; Executive Search Consultant 1972–74; Supervisor of Recruitment, Canadian Pacific Hotels & Resorts 1974–75; Mgr., Recruitment & Training 1975–76; Corp. Dir., Personnel 1976–82; Extve. Dir., Human Resources 1982–88; Council of Human Resources Extves.; Candn. Tourism Rsch. Inst.; Conference Board of Canada; Dir., Bd. of Dir., Candn. Restaurant & Foodservice Assn.; Chrmn., Advisory Ctte. Education & Training, School of Hotel & Food Admin., Univ. of Guelph; Mem., Adv. Bd., Ryerson Polytechnical Inst., Hospitality & Tourism Mngt. Program; Bd. of Dirs., Candn. Injury Prevention Found.; Vice Chrmn., Candn. Hospitality Found.; Fellow, Ont. Hostelry Institute; Mem., Human Resources Professionals Assn. of Ont.; Home: 15 Heather Road, Toronto, Ont. M4G 3G2; Office: One University Ave., Suite 1400, Toronto, Ont. M5J 2P1.

**CLARK, Rt. Hon. Charles Joseph (Joe),** P.C. M.P., M.A., LL.D. (Hon.); politician; b. High River, Alta. 5 June 1939; s. late Charles A. and Grace R. (Welch) C.; e. Univ. of Alta. B.A. 1960, M.A. 1973; Univ. of N.B. LL.D. (Hon.) 1976; Univ. of Calgary LL.D. (Hon.) 1984; Univ. of Alberta LL.D. (Hon.) 1985; m. Maureen Anne d. late John J. McTeer 30 June 1973; one d. Catherine Jane; UNITED NATIONS SPECIAL REPRESENTATIVE TO CYPRUS 1993– ; President of the Privy Council and Min. Responsible for Constitutional Affairs 1991–93; Special Asst. to Hon. Davie Fulton 1966–67; Extve. Asst. to Hon. R. L. Stanfield 1967–70; el. to H. of C. for Rocky Mountain, Alta. 1972, re-el. 1974; el. Yellowhead, Alta. 1979, 1980, 1984 and 1988; Chrmn. Prog. Cons. Caucus Comtes. on Youth 1972–74 and on Environment 1974–76; Nat. Leader, Prog. Cons. Party of Canada 1976–83; and Leader of Official Opposition H. of C. 1976–79 and 1980–83 (resigned to force a Leadership Convention, February 1983); Prime Minister of Can. 1979–80; Secy. of State for External Affairs 1984–91; careers in teaching, journalism and broadcasting; Alberta Order of Excellence, Dec. 1983; R. Catholic; recreations: cross-country skiing, tennis, travel, reading; Clubs: Hillcrest Miners' Literary & Athletic Assn.; Cercle Universitaire (Hon. mem.); Ranchmen's; Office: c/o Canadian Embassy, Tel Aviv, Israel 61063.

**CLARK, Colin Whitcomb,** Ph.D., F.R.S.C.; educator; b. Vancouver, B.C. 18 June 1931; s. George Savage and Irene (Stewart) C.; e. Magee High Sch. Vancouver 1949; Univ. of B.C., B.A. 1953; Univ. of Wash. Ph.D. (Math.) 1958; m. Janet Arlene d. James A. Davidson, Georgeville, Que. 17 Sept. 1955; children: Jennifer Kathleen, Karen Elizabeth, Graeme David; PROF. OF MATH., UNIV. OF B.C. 1970– ; Instr. in Math. Univ. of Calif. (Berkeley) 1958–60; Asst. Prof. present Univ. 1960, Assoc. Prof. 1966; Visiting Scholar, Univ. of Calif. Berkeley 1965–66; Visiting Scient., New Mexico State Univ. 1970–71 and C.S.I.R.O. Div. of Fisheries & Oceanography, Sydney, Australia 1975–76; Regents' Lectr., Univ. of Calif. Davis 1986; Visiting Prof., Cornell Univ. 1987; mem. Fisheries & Oceans (Can.) Research Adv. Council 1981–87; mem. Program Adv. Comte. Internat. Center Living Aquatic Resources Mgmt. (Manila) 1982–85; author 'Elementary Mathematical Analysis' 1981; 'Mathematical Bioeconomics; the Optimal Management of Renewable Resources' 1976; 'Bioeconomic Modelling and Fishery Management' 1985; 'Resource Economics: Notes and Problems' 1987; 'Dynamic Modeling in Behavioral Ecology' 1988; numerous articles prof. journs. on pure & applied math., resource econ., biol.; mem. Candn. Applied Math. Soc. (Pres. 1981–83); Assn. Environmental & Resource Econs. (Council 1983–84); Soc. Indust. & Applied Math.; Resource Modeling Assoc. (Pres. 1987–89); recipient Killam Sr. Research Fellow 1975–76, 1981–82; Prof. Jacob Biely Faculty Research Prize 1978; recreations: hiking, cross-country skiing, gardening; Club: North Shore Hikers; Home: 9531 Finn Rd., Richmond, B.C. V7A 2L3; Office: Vancouver, B.C. V6T 1W5.

**CLARK, David James,** C.A.; financial executive; b. Fleet, England 11 Sept. 1956; s. William Ernest and Joyce Lillian (Morgan) C.; e. King Alfred's Grammar School (England); Bristol Polytechnic, accountancy course (Hons.) 1976; Inst. of C.A.s (England & Wales) 1981; (B.C.) 1983; Candn. Securities Course (Hons.) 1984; Senior Vice-Pres. & Chief Financial Offr., Security Pacific Bank Canada 1990–92; Senior Accountant, Deloitte Haskins & Sells (London, England & Vancouver) 1976–83; Mgr., Morguard Bank 1983; Asst. Vice-Pres. 1985; Vice-Pres., Security Pacific Bank 1988; Dir., Security Pacific Leasing Canada Ltd.; Security Pacific Properties Ltd.; Texas Northern Minerals Ltd.; Past Pres., Harbour Centre Mall Merchants Assn.; Field Hockey Section, Vancouver Rowing Club; recreations: field hockey, squash, tennis; clubs: Jericho Tennis, Vancouver Rowing, Fitness World; Home: 130 West 10th Ave., Vancouver, B.C. V5Y 1R8.

**CLARK, Douglas Robert;** author, editor, instructor, coach; b. Fergus, Ont. 16 May 1952; s. N. Leslie and Mildred Jean (Campbell) C.; e. Univ. of Waterloo integrated studies 1971–2; Univ. of Windsor internat. relations (Hons.) 1977–9; m. Irene d. Ludwik and Katarine Zabielski 6 Feb. 1976; children: John, Jodi; professional writer since 1979; began as weekly community newspaper reporter winning Ontario feature writing awards 2 consecutive years & one Candn. feature writing award; articles appear in 'Saturday Night,' 'Financial Post Moneywise,' 'Equinox,' 'Maclean's' and others; Instructor, plain-languge writing course; Protestant; Founder and Charter Mem., Spankers Club (an informal group of journalists devoted topublicizing wrong doing and assigning blame); Assoc. Mem., Royal Candn. Legion; author: 'Unkindest Cut: The Torso Murder of Selina Shen' 1992 (trans. Chinese; pub. Hong Kong; in film devel.) co-author: 'Billion $$$ High: The Drug Invasion of Canada' (non-fiction) 1990; freelancer; first child to survive open-heart surgery 1957 (age 5); recreations: minor sports coach, lecturer; club: Royal Canadian Legion; Home: Box 328, North Gower, Ont. K0A 2T0; Office: Box 328, North Gower, Ont. K0A 2T0.

**CLARK, Edward Ritchie,** B.Com.; retired banker; b. Toronto, Ont. 3 Feb. 1912; s. Herbert Abraham, K.C., B.A., and Mary Laura Adeline (MacNicol) C.; e. N. Toronto and Oakwood Coll. Insts., Toronto, Ont.; Univ. of Toronto, B.Com. 1933; Fellow, Candn. Bankers' Assn.; m. Eileen, d. Rev. T. J. Campbell Crawford, M.A., W. Kilbride, Ayrshire, Scotland, 11 Oct. 1945; children: Alison, Ritchie, Rosemary, Lorna; Mem. of Senate, Presbyterian College, McGill Univ., Montreal 1989–92; Convenor, Finance Ctte. 1990–92; joined Bank of Nova Scotia in Economics Dept., 1933; employed in various brs. and depts of the Bank in Toronto and New York, 1934–42; after war service entered Credit Dept. at the Gen. Mgr.'s Office, 1946; joined Industrial Devel. Bank (Crown Corp.) as a Credit Offr., Toronto Br., 1947; trans. to Vancouver as Credit Offr. in Vancouver Br. and subsequently apptd. Asst. Supv. at that office; apptd. Supv., Winnipeg Br., 1956, Montreal, 1959; Asst. Gen. Mgr. 1962; Depy. Gen. Mgr. 1966; Gen. Mgr. 1969; Chief Gen. Mgr. 1973; Vice Pres. and Chief Gen. Mgr. of Federal Business Development Bank 1975; Exec. Vice Pres. and Chief Gen. Mgr. 1976; retired 1977; Chrmn., Admin. Council of Presbyterian Church in Can. 1982–84; author: 'The IDB: A History of Canada's Industrial Development Bank' 1985; Vice Chrmn., Extve. Ctte., Tyndale-St. Georges (Inner City Mission) Montreal 1989–91; mem., Bd. of Dirs. of St. Andrew's Presbyterian Homes Foundation, Montreal; Pension Ctte., Federal Business Development Bank; Royal Commonwealth Soc.; St. Andrew's Soc. of Montreal; served in 2nd World War with R.C.A.F., 1942–46; attached to R.A.F. Overseas, 1944–46; attained rank of Flying Offr.; commanded R.A.F. units as Radar Offr.; Presbyterian; recreations: music, photography, reading; Home: 65 Franklin Ave., Town of Mount Royal, Que. H3P 1B8.

**CLARK, The Hon. Edward William;** farmer; beef producer; politician; b. Summerside, P.E.I. 24 March 1932; s. Ivan Leroy and Maisie Laura (Miller) C.; e. Central Lot 16 Sch.; B.E.T. Cornwallis Naval Base; N.S. Agric. courses; m. Ruby d. Harry and Erma Best 21 June 1958; children: Coleen Laura, Catherine Erma, Edith Lynne; Speaker, P.E.I. Legislative Assembly 1986–93; served R.C.N. 1951–52; Farmer/Beef Prod. 1952– ; elected M.L.A., P.E.I. 1970; re-el. 1974, 1978, 1979, 1982, 1986, 1989; Min. of Agric. & Forestry 1978–79; Mem., Rural Devel. Counc.; Miscouche Royal Candn. Legion; P.E.I. Heritage Found.; 4–H Club Leader 1956–63, 1968–72; Protestant; Liberal; recreations: swimming, reading; Home: Belmont, Lot 16, Miscouche, P.E.I. C0B 1T0.

**CLARK, Eileen,** B.Sc.; association executive; b. Twechar, Scot. 8 Jan. 1924; d. Rev. Thomas James Campbell and Isabel Sharpe (Hastings) Crawford; e. Ardrossan (Scot.) Acad.; Univ. of St. Andrew's B.Sc. 1943; m. E. Ritchie Clark 11 Oct. 1945; children: Alison (Mrs. W.D. Vannah), H.C. Ritchie, Rosemary (Mrs. Clark-Beattie), Lorna; Mem., Senate, Presbyterian Coll., McGill Univ., 1982–89 (Vice Chrmn. 1986–89); Vice Pres. (Que.) and Chrmn. Internat. Rlns., Candn. Fed. of Univ. Women 1968–79, Pres. 1979–82; 4th Vice-Pres., Internat. Fed. Univ. Women 1983–86, 3rd Vice Pres. 1986–89 (mem. Counc. 1977–79); Mem., Bd. of Dirs., Virginia Gildersleeve Internat. Fund for Univ. Women 1987–90 (2nd Vice-Pres. 1981–87, 1st Vice Pres. 1993– ;); served as Radar Tech. Offr. WAAF 1943–46, rank Sec. Offr.; Chrmn. Comte. on Arts & Letters, Montreal Counc. of Women 1972–73; mem. St. Andrew's Soc. Montreal (1st Vice-Pres. 1981–83, Welfare Chrmn. 1973–81, Pres. 1983–85); Docent, McCord Museum of Candn. Hist. 1991– ; Trustee, The Mount Royal Cemetery Company 1992– ; recreations: skiing, English smocking, antique porcelain; Clubs: University Women's C. of Montreal Inc.; L'Assn. des femmes diplomées des universités; Town of Mount Royal Curling; Home: 65 Franklin Ave., Town of Mount Royal, Que. H3P 1B8.

**CLARK, Gerald,** B.Sc.; writer; b. Montréal, Qué. 3 Apl. 1918; s. Samuel and Polly (Fink) C.; e. McGill Univ. B.Sc. 1939; widower; one d. Bette Ellen; War Corr. 'The Standard' Montréal 1943–45; UN Corr. 'The Montreal Star' 1952, London Corr. 1955, Assoc. Ed. 1960, Ed. 1968–79 (when newspaper ceased publ.); author 'Impatient Giant: Red China Today' 1959; 'The Coming Explosion in Latin America' 1963; 'Canada: The Uneasy Neighbor' 1965; 'Montreal: the New Cité' 1982; frequent contbr. 'Reader's Digest'; rec'd Nat. Newspaper Award, Emmy; recreation: tennis; Clubs: University; Mount Royal Tennis; Home: 3, 440 rue Bonsecours, Montréal, Qué. H2Y 3C4; Office: Montréal, Qué.

**CLARK, Hart Duncan,** B.A.; retired Canadian public servant; b. Winnipeg, Man. 30 July 1914; s. Frederick W. and Edith A. (Sutherland) C.; e. Univ. of Man., B.A. 1935 (Gold Medal Arts Hons. Course), grad. studies and teaching fellowship in Math., 1935–37; Rhodes Scholar, Merton Coll., Oxford Univ., 1937–40 (Math.); m. Lenore Morgan, Winnipeg, Man. 12 June 1943; four s: Terence, Alan, David, John, one d: Barbara; Special Adviser, Internat. Claims for Dep. Min. of Finance 1976–92; Consultant, Pension & Insur. Benefits for Human Rights Commission; Spec. Pensions Adv., Treasury Bd., 1976–86; Lectr., Univ. of Man. 1945–46; Carleton Univ. (evening classes) 1949–51; joined Federal Public Service 1947; held various positions Dept. of Finance and Treasury Bd. incl. Dir., Pensions and Ins. Div. 1953–76; Dir. Internat. Fisheries Commissions Pension Soc. 1957–94; served in 2nd World War, Exper. Offr. in Admiralty; posted E. coast Scot. 1940–43; various bases in U.S. 1943–45; United Church; recreations; curling, golf, camping; Club: Ottawa Curling; Home: 94 Avenue Rd., Ottawa, Ont. K1S 0P2.

**CLARK, Howard Charles,** M.Sc., Ph.D., Sc.D., F.R.S.C., F.C.I.C.; educator; b. Auckland, N.Z. 4 Sept. 1929; s. Eric Crago Clark, e. Takapuna Grammar Sch. Auckland 1947; Univ. of Auckland B.Sc. 1951, M.Sc. 1952, Ph.D. 1954; Cambridge Univ. Ph.D. 1958, Sc.D. 1972; m. Isabel Joy d. late Leslie Dickson 10 Apl. 1954; children: Carolynn Joy, Kristin Elizabeth; PRESIDENT, DALHOUSIE UNIVERSITY and PROFESSOR OF CHEMISTRY since 1986; Lectr. Univ. of Auckland 1954–55; Fellow, Cambridge Univ. 1955–57; Asst. prof. to Full Prof. Univ. of B.C. 1957–65; Prof. and Head of Chem. Univ. of W. Ont. 1965–76; Vice Pres. Acad. Univ. of Guelph and Prof. of Chem. 1976–86; mem. various comtes. Nat. Research Council Can. and Council Ont. Univs.; mem., National Adv. Bd. on Science & Technology 1991– ; Dir., Corporate Higher Education Forum 1990– ; mem., Commonwealth Standing Ctte. on Student Mobility and Higher Education Cooperation 1992– ; Ed. 'Canadian Journal of Chemistry' 1974–78; mem. various ed. bds.; author or co-author over 250 articles and chapters in prof. journs.; Pres. Chem. Inst. of Can. 1983–84; Hon. D.Sc., Univ. of Victoria 1989; mem. Am. Chem. Soc.; Chem. Soc. (London); United Church; recreations: tennis, swimming, gardening; Clubs: Halifax, Saraguay; Home: 1460 Oxford St., Halifax, N.S. B3H 3Y8; Office: Dalhousie Univ., Halifax, N.S. B3H 3J5.

**CLARK, Ian Christie,** M.A.; diplomat and arts executive; b. Toronto, Ont. 17 Apr. 1930; s. the late Christie Thomas and the late Gwyneth (Shannon) C.; e. Upper Can. Coll. Toronto 1948; McGill Univ. B.A. 1953, M.A. 1958; m. Nancy Cynthia d. the late Henry Lloyd Blachford and the late Grace (Trenholme) B., Montreal, Que. Aug. 1958; children: Graeme Christie, Brenda Trenholme; PRES., NOVA SCOTIA COLL. OF ART AND DESIGN, Halifax, N.S. 1990– ; Ed. & Publs. & Reports Secy., Pulp and Paper Rsch. Inst. Can. 1956; joined Dept. External Affairs Ottawa 1958; Second Secy. and Consul Brussels 1961–64; Counsellor (Information & Cultural Affairs) Paris 1967–70; Cultural Counsellor London 1970–72; Dir. of Museums and Visual Arts, Dept. Secy. of State and Special Advisor (heritage legislation) to Secy. of State 1972–77; Chrmn. Candn. Cultural Property Export Review Bd. 1977 (Special Advisor 1978–82); Secy.-Gen., National Museums of Can. 1978–83; Ambassador and Perm. Delegate of Can. to UNESCO, Paris 1983–87; mem. Extve. Bd., UNESCO 1983–87 (Vice-Chrmn. 1985–87, Vice-Pres. 24th Gen. Conf. of UNESCO 1987); author 'Indian and Eskimo Art of Canada/Art Indien et Esquimau du Canada' 1970; various articles, papers and lectures concerning the preservation of the heritage in cultural property; since 1989–90: Pres. ICOM Foundation, Paris; mem. Candn. Ctte., World Decade for Cultural Develop.; Zeta Psi; Presbyterian; recreations: tennis, skiing, fishing, canoeing; Clubs: Five Lakes; Rockcliffe Lawn Tennis (Ottawa); Saraguay; Waegwoltic (Halifax); Residence: 6770 Jubilee Rd., #4, Halifax, N.S. B3H 2H8; Office: 5163 Duke St., Halifax, N.S. B3J 3J6.

**CLARK, Ian Douglas,** B.Sc., D.Phil., M.P.P.; Canadian public servant; b. Antrim, U.K. 15 Apr. 1946; s. Sidney and Zella Irene (Stade) C.; e. Lord Byng H.S., Vancouver 1962; Univ. of B.C., B.Sc.(hons.) 1966; Univ. of Oxford (Rhodes Scholar 1966), D.Phil. 1969; Harvard Univ., M.P.P. 1972; m. Marjorie d. George Malvern and Eleanor Constance Sweet 27 July 1968; SECRETARY OF THE TREASURY BOARD 1989– ; and COMPTROLLER GENERAL OF CANADA 1993– ; Resch. Fellow, Harvard Univ. 1969–72; Analyst, Treasury Bd. Secretariat 1972–73; Exec. Asst. to Min. of State for Urban Affairs 1973–74; Dir. and later Dir. Gen., Dept. of Regional Economic Expansion 1974–78; Dir. and later Depy. Secy. (Operations), Min. of State for Econ. Devel. 1979–82; Depy. Secy. to the Cabinet (Plans), Privy Council Office, 1982–87; Depy. Min., Consumer & Corporate Affairs, Govt. of Can. 1987–89; National Rsch. Counc. Post-Doctoral Fellowship 1969; mem. Inst. of Public Admin. of Can.; author several articles in scientific and public admin. journals; recreations: tennis, cross-country skiing; Clubs: Le Cercle Universitaire; Larrimac; Cascades; Address: L'Esplanade Laurier, 140 O'Connor St., 9th Flr. E., Ottawa, Ont. K1A 0R5.

**CLARK, Joseph Adair Porter;** executive; b. Toronto, Ont. 2 Nov. 1921; s. Joseph W. G., C.B.E., D.F.C. and Hazel (Porter) C.; e. Univ. of Toronto Schools and Univ. of Toronto; m. Patricia, d. W. G. Fraser Grant, Q.C., 28 Sept. 1946; children: Joseph, Thomas, Carolyn; CORPORATE CONSULTANT, CLARKPARTNERS; Sr. Advisor, Steers Communication Associates Inc., Ottawa; Mills, Spence & Co., Toronto, 1945; Asst. Dir. of Pub. Relations, Massey-Harris Co. Ltd., 1947; with partners formed Tisdall, Clark and Co. in 1952, from which he resigned in 1979 to head Canada News-Wire (from which he retired in 1986 as Chrmn., Pres. & C.E.O.); served with RCNVR in Atlantic Area and Europe 1940–45; awarded Centennial Medal 1967; Distinguished Public Service Award, Candn. Public Relations Soc.; C. Douglas Taylor Award 'for devoted service to the cause of the disabled' The Candn. Rehabilitation Council; mem., Toronto Rehab. Centre (Past Pres.); Founding Grp. Chrmn., Candn. Rehab. Council (Past Pres.); former Chrmn., Adv. Comte. on Rehab. to Ont. Min. of Community and Social Services; accredited mem., Candn. Pub. Relations Soc.; Hon. Life Dir., Candn. Found. for Econ. Educ.; Adv. Counc., Candn. Naval Memorial Trust; Trustee, Community Foundation for Greater Toronto; Past Chrmn., Hospice King; Advisory Council, Navy League Ontario; Freemason; Anglican; recreations: fishing, reading; Clubs: Caledon Mountain Trout; Royal Candn. Mil. Inst.; Home: Highwoods, R.R. 2, King City, Ont. L0G 1K0.

**CLARK, Kenneth Bradford;** broadcaster; b. Kentville, N.S. 14 Dec. 1940; s. Ewan Somerville and Helena M.S. (Bishop) C.; e. Queen Elizabeth High Sch.; Dalhousie Univ.; m. Sally Ann d. Charles and Marjorie Lewis 12 Sept. 1964; children: C.E. Bradford, Mary Jane, Victoria A.L.; PRES. & C.E.O., TV3 TELEVISION NETWORK, Auckland, New Zealand; Vice Pres. & Gen. Mgr. CKY Television; Bd. of Dirs., TVB Canada; Bd. of Dirs., Western Assoc. of Broadcasters; broadcast performer 1947–60; Studio Dir. & Television Prod., C.B.C. 1960–68; Advt. & Sales Mgr., Federal Textiles Ltd. 1968–71; broadcast sales & sales mgmt. positions, Atlantic Television Systems 1971–80; Gen. Mgr. & Pres., New Brunswick Broadcasting Co. Ltd. 1980–89; Past Pres., Atlantic Assn. of Broadcasters; Past Dir., Candn. Assn. of Broadcasters; Past Chrmn., Network Advisory Ctte., C.B.C.; Past Chrmn., Hospice of Saint John; Past Comnr., Tourism Advisory Comn., City of Saint John; formerly, Saint John Regional Hosp. Bd., Saint John Port Devel. Comn.; Chrmn., Saint John Port Days 1987; former Vice-Pres., Saint John Bd. of Trade; former mem., Saint John Exec. Assn.; recreations: tennis, skiing; Club: St. Charles Golf; Address: Moffat Communications Ltd., CKY Television, Polo Park, Winnipeg, Man. R3G 0L7.

**CLARK, Kenneth T.,** B.Com., F.S.A., F.C.I.A.; b. Winnipeg, Man. 15 May 1933; s. Harry and Thora S. (Thordarson) C.; e. Daniel McIntyre Coll. Inst. 1951; Univ. of Man. B.Com. 1955; CONSULTING ACTUARY, ECKLER PARTNERS LTD. 1978– ; joined Prudential Insurance Co. of America, Toronto, Newark and Boston 1955–65; Milliman & Robertson Inc. Seattle, Philadelphia, New York, Toronto 1965–78; mem. Bd. Govs. Soc. Actuaries 1977–83; Council, Candn. Inst. Actuaries 1978–88, Pres. 1986–87; Club: Granite; Home: 11, 240 Broadway Ave., Toronto, Ont. M4P 1V9; Office: 15F, 789 Don Mills Rd., Toronto, Ont. M3C 1T8.

**CLARK, Lillian,** M.D., F.R.C.P.(C)., FAAP.; retired paediatrician; b. Baltimore, Md. 24 May 1919; d. Samuel and Dora Sugarman; e. Univ. of Toronto M.D. 1941; m. John W. s. J.J. and Ada C. 29 May 1946; children: Deborah Jane, James Richard; Post-grad. studies, St. Joseph's Hosp. Toronto; Intern, Hosp. for Sick Children; Chief Med. Rsident; Medical Officer, Royal Candn. Navy; F.R.C.P.(C.) 1952; Montreal Children's Hosp.; Chief (at times), Paediatrics, Greater Niagara Gen. Hosp. 1950–78; Chief (full-time) 1978–88; Hon. Staff Mem. with Emeritus privileges; Mem., Med. Adv. Ctte.; instrumental in upgrading the neonatal nursery; Special Ctte., Niagara Dist. Health Council for Peri-natal Care 1981–88; Admissions Ctte., Retarded Children's School; Med. Adv. Ctte., Niagara Peninsula Children's Centre; Infant Stimulation Program; Paediatrician, Moose Factory Hospital on James Bay 1991; initiated up-grading of a childrens' mental health clinic, Greater Niagara Gen. Hosp.; Mem., Niagara Falls Med. Soc.; Ont. Med. Assn.; Royal Coll. of Phys. & Surg. of Can.; Candn. Med. Assn.; Alumni Assn. Hosp. for Sick Children; Candn. Paed. Soc.; Fellow, Am. Acad. of Paediatrics; Glen Sawyer Award, Ont. Med. Assn. 1989; Bd. of Gov., Brock Univ. 1990–93, 1993–96; recreations: bridge, tennis, swimming, nordic skiing, rafting (took part in a rafting trip down the Nahanni River, N.W.T. July 1993); clubs: University Women's Club (Edn. Ctte. Mem. 1992–94); Greater Niagara Big Sister Assn. (Hon. Pres. 1958–93); Address: 7071 Brookfield Ave., Niagara Falls, Ont. L2G 5R7.

**CLARK, Norman A.;** association executive; b. Provost, Alta. 10 Aug. 1933; s. Oscar Livingston and Marie Agnes (Ferry) C.; e. Provost and Crescent Hts. High Schs. (Calgary); Univ. of Alta.; m. Marie E. d. Charles and Beatrice Shea 1 Feb. 1958; joined National Cash Register Co. 1953–54, 1955–58; served with RCAF 1954–55, pilot training; National Life Assurance Co. of Canada 1958–62; Motor Vehicle Mfrs. Assn. 1962–63, 1966–93 (Pres. 1984–93, retired); Richardson Securities 1963–66; Chrmn., Candn. Automotive Repair and Service (CARS) Counc.; Dir. Candn. Automotive Inst.; mem. Candn. Soc. Assn. Execs.; Soc. Automotive Engs.; Bd. Trade Metrop. Toronto; Home: 1715, 55 Harbour Square, Toronto, Ont. M5J 2L1.

**CLARK, Robert B. (Rob),** B.Comm., C.A.; financial executive; b. Kenora, Ont. 30 Sept. 1955; s. Samuel Damase and Barbara Jane (Mealey) C.; e. Sault Ste. Marie C.I. (Ontario Scholar) 1973; Univ. of Toronto B.Comm. 1978; m. Lisa d. Ellen and Joseph McInnis 2 Oct. 1987; children: Michael, Laura; CHIEF FINANCIAL OFFICER, CUDDY INTERNATIONAL CORP. 1991– ; Coopers & Lybrand 1978–81; The Molson Companies 1981–85; Molson Breweries 1985–91; Dir., Grand Theatre London; Mem., Financial Exec. Institute; recreations: golf, music; clubs: Westhaven Golf & Country; London Club; Home: 23 Conifer Crescent, London, Ont. N6K 3V3; Office: 465 Richmond St., London, Ont. N6A 5P4.

**CLARK, Robert Douglas;** television producer; b. London, Ont. 13 July 1936; s. Robert Keith and Valerie Lea (Stidolph) C.; e. London South Coll.; Glebe Coll.; H.M.C.S. Stadacona Sch. of Electronics; m. Monthip d. Sanit and Pensom Sukree; children: Diana, Susan, Keith, Beverly, Natasha, Anika; stepchildren: Christopher, Christina, Catherine; Producer, Canadian Broadcasting Corp. 1963–91; Royal Candn. Navy 1953–63; Correspondent, Vietnam 1970; Assoc. Prof. (Videomy), Univ. of Ottawa 1973–76; Cultural Studies (Thailand) 1983–84; Documentry for CIDA 'Strategies for Partnership' 1984; has produced & directed 20 documentaries reflecting culture, traditions, political, social & econ. conditions facing poorer nations of W. Africa & S.E. Asia; Sr. TV Prod., Canthai Video Prodns.; CBC's Pres. Award 1983; ACTRA awards: Best TV Program of the Year for 'Cambodia: Tragedy in Eden' 1982, 'Land of the Mountain Elephant' 1983, 'The Golden Triangle – Canada's Heroin Connection' 1985; Outstanding Achievement Award 1983; Investigative Journalism Award for 'A Reasonable Doubt' 1987; recreations: feature writing for newspaper & periodicals; photography; researching early Candn. historical events; Address: 7 Centre St., Spencerville, Ont. K0E 1X0.

**CLARK, Robert Wilfred,** B.Ed., M.A.; diplomat; b. Yorkton, Sask. 2 Aug. 1926; s. (late) Ralph and Sadie G. (McMartin) C.; e. Univ. of Sask. B.Ed. 1949, B.A. 1950, M.A. 1956; m. Sandra d. (late) Hector and (late) Ella Vallillee 10 Dec. 1979; three s. D. Randall, Michael A., David Markus; seconded to MINISTRY OF SOLICITOR-GENERAL 1988; taught high sch. 1950–54; joined Dept. of External Affairs 1956; served in Havana, San Jose (Costa Rica), Geneva; Candn. High Commr. to Sri Lanka and Ambassador to Repub. of Maldives 1979–82; Candn. Ambassador to Pakistan 1985–88; served with RCAF and Candn. Army 1944–45; United Church; recreations: golf, curling; Home: 59 Coolspring Cres., Nepean, Ont. K2E 7M9; Office: Ottawa, Ont.

**CLARK, Roger,** B.A., M.A.; association executive; b. Middlesbrough, England 12 June 1939; s. Ronald Ernest and Gwendoline (Dally) C.; e. Hele's Grammar Sch. 1950–58; Univ. of London, King's Coll., B.A. (Hons.) 1962; McMaster Univ., M.A. 1963; children: David, Christa; SECRETARY GENERAL, AMNESTY INTERNATIONAL 1988– ; French Lang. & Lit. Instr., Univ. of Sask. 1963–67; Can. Counc. grant for rsch. in Paris 1967–69; Assoc. Prof. of French, Memorial Univ. 1969–87 (Dept. Chair 1972–86); Membership Prog. Dir., present orgn. 1987–88; Dir., Cours d'été 1971–77; mem., 2-person ctte. of inquiry into Acad. Freedom, Univ. de Moncton (Candn. Assn. of Univ. Teachers) 1984; Lifetime Offr., Compagnie des cent-assoc. francophones 1980; author of scholarly articles; recreations: birding, cycling; Home: 168 Fifth Ave., Ottawa, Ont. K1S 2M9; Office: 401 – 214 Chemin Montréal, Vanier, Ont. K1L 1A4.

**CLARK, Roy Malcolm,** MB, BS, LRCP, MRCS, D(OBST) RCOG, DMRT, FRCR, FRCPC; physician, university professor; b. London, England 22 Aug. 1930; s. George William and Florence (Martin) C.; e. Latymer's Grammar Sch.; The Royal London Hospital Medical College MB, BS, LRCP, MRCS 1954; m. Betty d. Hubert and Jenny Garment May 1954; children: Paul Malcolm, Christine Anne; STAFF RADIATION ONCOLOGIST, ONT. CANCER INST./PRINCESS MARGARET HOSP. 1966– ; House Surgeon, The Royal London Hosp. 1954; Obstetric House Surgeon, Barnet Gen. Hosp. 1955; Captain, Royal Army Med. Corps, Second-in-Command, Miltary Hosp., Bovington, Eng. 1955–58; general practice 1958–60; Registrar in Radiation Oncology, Royal Northern Hosp. London, Eng. 1960–63; Sr. Registrar in Radiation Oncology, The Royal London Hosp. 1963–66; Dir. & Chair, Med. Adv. Ctte., Candn. Breast Cancer Found.; Vice Pres., Breast Cancer Internat. Centre; Mem., Candn. Med. Assn.; Brit. Med. Assn.; Am. Soc. for Therapeutic Radiology & Oncology; Candn. Oncology Soc.; Am. Soc. for Clin. Oncology; Candn. Assn. of Radiation Oncologists; Fellow, Royal Soc. of Med.; author of num. sci. pubs. on breast cancer; recreations: tennis, swimming, ice skating, fitness, landscaping; clubs: Granite; Home: 61 Hopperton Dr., Willowdale, Ont. M2L 2S7; Office: 500 Sherbourne St., Toronto, Ont. M4X 1K9.

**CLARK, Samuel Delbert,** M.A., Ph.D., LL.D., D.Litt., F.R.S.C. (1952), O.C.; educator; b. Lloydminster, Alta. 24 Feb. 1910; s. Samuel David and Mary Alice (Curry) C.; e. Univ. of Sask., B.A. 1930, M.A. 1931; London Sch. of Econ. & Pol. Science 1932–33; McGill Univ. M.A. 1935; Univ. of Toronto, Ph.D. 1938; m. Rosemary Josephine, d. late W. E. Landry, 26 Dec. 1939; children: Ellen Margaret, Samuel David, William Edmund; Prof. of Sociology, Univ. of Toronto, 1953–76, Prof. Emeritus since 1976; Lecturer Sociology, University of Manitoba, 1937; joined Univ. of Toronto as Lect. 1938; Visiting Prof. of Sociol., Univ. of Cal. (Berkeley) 1960–61; McCulloch Prof. of Soc., Dalhousie Univ., 1972–74; Visiting Prof. of Soc., Univ. of Guelph, 1976–78; Visiting Prof. of Soc., Lakehead Univ., 1978–80; Distinguished Visiting Prof., Univ. of Tsukuba, Japan, Spring 1980; Visiting Prof. of Candn. Studies, Univ. of Edinburgh, 1980–81; author of 'The Canadian Manufacturers Assn.' 1939; 'The Social Development of Canada' 1942; 'Church and Sect in Canada' 1948; 'Movements of Political Protest in Canada 1640–1840' 1959; 'The Developing Canadian Community' 1963 (new ed. with additional chapters 1968); 'The Suburban Society' 1966; 'The Canadian Society in Historical Perspective' 1976; 'The New Urban Poor' 1978; also numerous articles in learned and prof. journs.; rec'd. Guggenheim Fellowship 1944–45; Tyrrell Medal, Royal Soc. of Can. 1960; Officer Order of Can. 1978; LL.D. Univ. of Calgary 1978, Dalhousie Univ. 1979, Univ. of W. Ont. 1984, Univ. of Man. 1985; Univ. of Toronto 1988; D. Litt. St. Mary's Univ. 1979; Lakehead Univ. 1982; mem., Candn. Pol. Science Assn. (Pres. 1958–59); Candn. Assn. of Anthropol. & Sociol. (Hon. Pres.); Am. Sociol. Assn.; Pres. (1975–76) Royal Soc. Can.; Foreign Hon. mem., Am. Acad. Arts and Sciences (1976); Liberal; Address: 61 St. Clair Ave., Apt. 302, Toronto, Ont. M4V 2Y8.

**CLARK, Lieut.-Gen. Samuel Findlay,** C.B.E., C.D.; b. Winnipeg, Man. 17 March 1909; s. James and Anne Elizabeth (Findlay) C.; e. Univ. of Manitoba, (B.Sc.) (Elect. Engn.) 1932; Univ. of Sask., B.Sc. (Mech. Engn.) 1933; Staff Coll., Camberley, 1942; Imp. Defence Coll., London, 1947; m. Blanche Leona, d. Joseph and Mrs. Hamilton Seagram, Barrie, Ont., 18 Sept. 1937; Lieut., Royal Candn. Corps of Signals, 1933; Assoc. Prof. Elect. and Mech. Engn., R.M.C., Kingston, Ont.; C.O., Lieut.-Col., 5th Canadian Armoured Divn. Signals, 1941; G.S.O. 1, Candn. Mil. Hdqrs., London, Eng., 1942; Chief Signal Offr., 2nd Candn. Corps, 1942–45; Depy. Chief, Gen. Staff, Army Hdqrs., Ottawa 1945–47; Candn. Observer, W. Union Defence Organ., 1948–49; promoted Maj. Gen. 1949, Lieut.-Gen. 1958; after 1948 prior to present appt. was successively Chrmn., Candn. Jt. Staff, London, and Candn. mem. N.A.T.O. Military Cmte. and Q.M.G., Ottawa (1951), then G.O.C. Central Command, Oakville, Ont.; Chief of the Gen. Staff, Ottawa 31 Aug. 1958–1 Oct. 1961; Chrmn. of Nat. Capital Comn., Ottawa, 1961–67; Commdr. Order of Orange-Nassau with Swords; Offr., Legion of Merit (U.S.A.); Offr., St John; mem., Royal Candn. Geog. Soc.; L.M.C.S.E.E.; Engn. Inst. Can.; Assn. Prof. Engrs. Ont.; Anglican; Address: 301–1375 Newport Ave., Victoria, B.C. V8S 5E8.

**CLARK, Stephen James,** B.A.; b. Trenton, Ont. 7 Nov. 1960; s. Melvin Floyd and Mary Catherine (Creighton) C.; e. Univ. of Waterloo B.A. 1982; children: Mitchell James, Caitlin Patricia; GENERAL MGR., THE SUNDAY ADVANTAGE 1992– ; Mayor, City of Brockville 1982–91, acclaimed 1985, re-el. 1988; Pres. Assn. Muns. Ont. 1988–89; mem. Internat. Youth Yr. Adv. Cttee. Fed. Min. of Youth 1985; Past Chrmn. Brockville Police Comn.; St. Lawrence Lodge Home for Aged; mem. National Bd. of Dirs., Federation of Candn. Municipalities 1989; Mem., Rideau Valley District Health Council 1990–92; Pres., Bd. of Brockville Career Services 1992–93; Chrmn., Brockville Riverfest Inc. 1992– ; Vice-Chrmn., Brockville Foundation 1992– ; Home: 104 - 1100 Millwood Ave., Brockville, Ont. K6V 6Z3; Office: 142B Perth St., Brockville, Ont. K6V 5E5.

**CLARK, Walter Leland (Lee) Rutherford,** B.Ed., B.A. (Hons.), M.A., Ph.D.; university administrator; retired politician; b. Davidson, Sask. 16 Dec. 1936; s. William and Enid (Stein) C.; e. Univ. of Sask. B.Ed. 1959, B.A. (Hon.) 1961; Univ. of Oregon M.A. 1963; Univ. of Alta. Ph.D. 1976; m. Barbara Woods 1959; children: Cheryl, Janine; Member of Parliament 1983–93; re-elected 1984, 1988, retired 1993; Parlty. Secy. to Min. of Environment; Hist. Teacher & Dean of Men's Res., Brandon Coll. (now Univ.) 1964–83; Registrar 1967–69; mem., Progressive Conservative Party; United Church; author: 'Brandon Politics and Politicians' 1981 (pub. by Brandon Sun as Centennial project); recreations: tennis, skiing, reading, farming, community service; Home: 11 Juniper Bay, Brandon, Man. R7B 0Y7.

**CLARKE, Alan Martin,** B.A., LL.D.; commission advisor; educator; b. Stratford, Ont. 1 Aug. 1929; s. Lorne Joseph and Emily (Edgar) C.; e. Univ. of Toronto B.A. 1957; York Univ. LL.D. (honoris causa) 1992; m. Margot Morley d. Hunter Broddy and Barbara (Stephen) 10 Oct. 1958; children: Andrew David, Beth Ann, Jeffrey Hunter; COMMUNICATIONS ADV. INTERNAT. JT. COMN. 1986– ; Sec. YMCA Toronto 1950–60, also Teacher becoming Supr. Instrs. Frontier Coll.; Sec. Planning Ctte. York Univ. 1956–58; Exec. Dir. Candn. Citizenship Council 1960–66, Candn. Centenary Council 3 yrs. and of The Co. of Young Candns. 1966–68; Pres. CRD Training Associates Ltd. 1969–70; Dir. Demonst. Project Community Devel. Algonquin Coll. 1970–71, Dir. Sch. Continuing Edn. 1971–85; Adv. to Candn. Emergency Coordinator for African Famine 1985–86; mem. Candn. Del. UNESCO Gen. Conf. Paris 1987, Chrmn. Eur. Jt. Study Meeting Impact New Technols. on Culture Rural Areas, Paris 1983, Participant Experts Meeting Eur. Jt. Studies Field of Edn. Vienna 1982; Founder and First Chrmn. Bd. Dirs. Movement for Candn. Literacy 1978; recipient Centennial Medal 1967; Norman High Award 1987; Dir. Learning Found. Ottawa-Carleton; Dir., United Nations Assocs. in Can.; contrib. author: 'Strong and Free: A Response to the War Measures Act' 1970; author and ed. various reports and publs. adult edn., pub. participation, human rights, citizenship/edn. & community devel.; Home: 525 Highcroft Ave., Ottawa, Ont. K1Z 5J3; Office: 18F, 100 Metcalfe St., Ottawa, Ont. K1P 5M1.

**CLARKE, Austin Ardinel Chesterfield;** author; b. Barbados, W.I. 26 July 1934; s. late Kenneth Trotman and Gladys Irene C.; e. St. Matthias' Boys' Sch., Combermere Sch. and Harrison Coll., Barbados; Trinity Coll. Univ. of Toronto; children: Janice Elizabeth, Loretta Anne; Member of Immigration & Refugee Bd. 1988–93; Multiculturalism Advisor to Leader of the Ont. Progressive Conservative Party 1987– ; Visiting Prof. of Eng. and Am. Studies, Yale Univ. 1968–71; Jacob Ziskind Visiting Prof. of Lit. Brandeis Univ. 1970–71; Margaret Bundy Scott Visiting Prof. of Lit. Williams Coll. 1971; Visiting Prof. of Black Studies, Duke Univ. 1972–73; Visiting Prof. of Ethnic Studies, Univ. of Texas, Austin 1973–74; Adviser to Prime Min. of Barbados 1974–76; Cultural Attaché Embassy of Barbados, Washington 1974–75; Gen. Mgr. Caribbean Broadcasting Corp. Barbados 1975–76; Writer-in-Residence, Concordia Univ. Montreal 1975–76; Writer-in-Residence, Univ. of W. Ont. 1982–83; Vice Chrmn. and mem., Ont. Film Review Bd. 1984–87; mem. Metrop. Toronto Lib. Bd. 1968; Yale Aurelis Club, Yale Univ. 1969–70; Yale Club of New Haven 1970– ; P. Cons. cand. York S. Prov. Riding 1977; Trustee, Rhode Island Sch. of Design, Providence 1969–74; Fellow, Calhoun Coll. Yale Univ. 1968–70, Morse Fellow 1968; Fellow Sch. of Letters, Ind. Univ. 1969– ; rec'd Pres.'s Medal Univ. of W. Ont. 1965 Fiction; Saturday Night-Belmont Short Story Award 1965; Can. Council Lit. Award 1967, 1972, 1974–Fiction; Casa de las Americas Lit. Prize 1980 Fiction; Toronto Arts Award for Writing/Publishing 1992; author 'The Survivors of the Crossing' 1964; 'Amongst Thistles and Thorns' 1965; 'The Meeting Point' 1967; 'Storm of Fortune' 1973; 'When He Was Free and Young and He Used to Wear Silks' 1972; 'The Bigger Light' 1975; 'The Prime Minister' 1977; 'Growing Up Stupid Under the Union Jack' 1980; 'Under the Sandbox Tree' 1981; 'When Women Rule' 1985; 'Nine Men Who Laughed' 1986; 'Proud Empires' 1986; 'In This City' 1992; 'There Are No Elders' 1993; in progress, 'An American Dutchman'; co-author 'From the Green Antilles' 1966; 'Voices, 2' 1965; '34 X Schwarze Liebe' 1968; 'Stories From Ontario' 1974; 'The Toronto Book' 1976; 'Canada In Us Now' 1976; 'Canada Writes!; 1977; 'Stories Plus' 1979; 'Toronto Short Stories' 1977; 'Social Problems' 1964; 'Many Windows' 1982; 'Confrontation' (Nos. 25–26) 1983; 'Oxford Book of Canadian Short Stories' 1986; 'Confrontation' (No. 32) 1986; 'Chelsea' (No. 46) 1987; 'Contemporary Caribbean Short Stories' 1990; 'From Ink Lake' 1990; P. Conservative; Anglican; Clubs: Onyx Lions (Toronto); Arts & Letters (Toronto); Address: 62 McGill St., Toronto, Ont. M5B 1H2; Literary Agent: Harold Oder Associates, 425 Madison Ave., New York, N.Y. 10017.

**CLARKE, Brock Francis,** Q.C., B.A., B.C.L.; b. Quebec City, P.Q. 30 Aug. 1919; s. Desmond Arthur, O.B.E. and Aline (Paradis) C.; e. Quebec City; Loyola High Sch., Montreal, Que.; Loyola Coll., B.A. (magna cum laude) 1939; McGill Univ., B.C.L. (Elizabeth Torrance Gold Medal) 1942; m. Simonne de Fonville Ethier, 14 June 1951; four s., Brian, David, Kevin, Gregory, one d. Brenda; Retired Senior Partner, Ogilvy Renault; Pres. and Dir., Brook Investments Inc.; called to the Bar of Que., 1943; on active service with R.C.N.V.R. 1943–45; discharged with rank of Lieut.; Dir., The Newman Assn. of McGill Univ.; Warden, Ascension of Our Lord Parish, Westmount; Trustee, Chateau de Ramzey; Mem. Adv. Bd., Faculty of Law, McGill Univ.; mem., Candn. Bar Assn.; Quebec Bar Assn.; Candn. Tax Foundation; Roman Catholic; Clubs: Mount Royal; St. James's; Mt. Bruno Country; Murray Bay Golf; Lac à Gravel Fishing; Home: Apt. #2104, 1 Wood Ave., Westmount, Que. H3Z 3C5; Office: Suite 606, 1000 de Maisonneuve Blvd. W., Montréal, Que. H3A 3K1.

**CLARKE, Donald Walter,** M.Sc., Ph.D.; university professor emeritus; b. Vermilion, Alta. 12 Apr. 1920; s. Harold James and Helena Leonora (Opfergelt) C.; e. Univ. of Alberta, B.Sc. 1941, M.Sc. 1943; Cal. Inst. Tech., Ph.D. 1951; m. Patricia Jean, d. H.L. Clary, San Marino, Cal., 28 Apr. 1951; children: Hugh James, Donald Clary, Catherine Emily; PROF. EMERITUS OF PHYSIOL., FAC. OF MED., UNIV. OF TORONTO 1985– ; Fellow, Trinity Coll.; joined present Univ. as Asst. Prof. in Dept. of Physiol. 1951; served in 2nd World War with R.C.N.V.R. 1943–46 Electrical Lieut.; Mentioned in Despatches; Medal of Service, City of Toronto, 1977; author of several articles in scient. journs. and semi-tech. articles in soaring publs.; mem., Candn. Physiol. Soc.; Royal Candn. Inst.; Sigma Xi; Lambda Chi Alpha; United Church; recreations: amateur radio (VE3 CHB), skating, volunteer agency work; Clubs: The Faculty, Univ. of Toronto; Arts & Letters, Toronto; Home: 108 Inglewood Dr., Toronto, Ont. M4T 1H5; Office: Medical Science Bldg., Univ. of Toronto, Toronto, Ont. M5S 1A6.

**CLARKE, Ernest George,** B.D., M.A., Ph.D.; educator; b. Varna, Ont. 16 June 1927; s. Melvin E. McK. and Eva M. (Epps) C.; e. Univ. of Toronto, Victoria Coll. B.A. 1949, Emmanuel Coll. B.D. 1952, M.A. 1953; Univ. of Chicago 1949–50; Leiden Univ. Holland Ph.D. 1962; m. Ruth G. d. Standish L. Hunt, Grand Valley, Ont. 8 Sept. 1951; children: Ernest Paul, Margaret Jean, Patricia Helen, David William; PROF. EMERITUS OF NEAR EASTERN STUDIES, VICTORIA COLL., UNIV. OF TORONTO; Ed. 'Newsletter for Targumic and Cognate Studies'; author 'The Selected Questions of Isho' Bar Nun' 1962; 'Wisdom of Solomon' 1972; 'Targum Pseudo-Jonathan of the Pentateuch: Text and Concordance' 1984; mem. Candn. Soc. Biblical Studies; Soc. Biblical Lit. (USA); Assn. Targumic Studies; Internat. Soc. Study Old Testament; Fellow, Inst. for Advanced Studies at Hebrew Univ. of Jerusalem 1985–86; Acting Principal of Victoria Coll. 1988–89; Acting Dir., Graduate Ctr. for Religious Studies 1989–90; P. Conservative; United Church; recreations: bookbinding, gourmet cooking; Club: Oriental; Home: 171 Collier St., Toronto, Ont. M4W 1M2; Office: Toronto, Ont. M5S 1K7.

**CLARKE, Francis H.,** B.Sc., Ph.D., F.R.S.C.; educator; b. Montréal, Qué. 30 July 1948; s. Herbert F. and Rita M. (Tourville) C.; e. McGill Univ. B.Sc. 1969; Univ. of Wash. Ph.D. 1973; m. Gail d. John and Jill Hart 4 Feb. 1989; two d. Julia, Danielle; DIR. CENTRE DE RECHERCHES MATHÉMATIQUES UNIV. DE MONTRÉAL and Prof. of Math. 1984– ; Asst., Assoc. and Full Prof. Univ. of B.C. 1973–84; Visiting Prof. Univ. de Paris 1974–75, Univ. of Cal. Berkeley 1979–80; Killam Fellow Can. Council 1979–81; delivered Coxeter-James lecture Candn. Math. Soc. 1980; author 'Optimization and Nonsmooth Analysis' 1983, Russian transl. 1989, reissued 1990 in the SIAM Series 'Classics in Applied Mathematics'; 'Methods of Dynamic and Nonsmooth Optimization' 1989; over 90 articles math. jours.; awarded Le Prix Urgel Archambault, ACFAS (Assoc. canadienne-française pour l'avancement des sciences) 1990; recreation: tennis; Office: Montréal, Qué. H3C 3J7.

**CLARKE, Garry Kenneth Connal,** B.Sc., M.A., Ph.D., F.R.S.C.; university professor; b. Hamilton, Ont. 6 Oct. 1941; s. Kenneth Andrew Connal and Elna Marie (Skarin) C.; e. Univ. of Alta., B.Sc. 1963; Univ. of Toronto, M.A. 1964, Ph.D. 1967; divorced; one s.: Julian; PROF. OF GEOPHYSICS, UNIV. OF B.C. 1977– ; joined present univ. 1967; an authority on physics of glaciers; sci. field work has taken him to Greenland, Ellesmere Is., the Candn. Rockies, Coast mountains & the St. Elias mountains of the Yukon Terr. & Alaska; main rsch. interest is glacier & ice sheet flow instabilities & how these might affect climate & sea level; Pres., Internat. Glaciol. Soc. 1990–93 (Vice-Pres. 1987–90); Pres., Candn. Geophysical Union 1993–95 (Vice-Pres. 1991–93); Fellow, Arctic Inst. of N. Am. 1979 (Gov. 1979); Killam Sr. Fellow 1981; Fellow, Royal Soc. of Can. 1989; Royal Astron. Soc.; Mem., Am. Geophys. Union; Mem., Soc. of Explor. Geophys.; Sci. Ed., 'Annals of Glaciology' vol. 2 1980; Assoc. Ed., 'Journal of Geophysical Research' 1989–92; author of numerous sci. articles; recreations: jazz piano, hiking, skiing; Home: 1980 McNicoll Ave., Vancouver, B.C. V6J 1A6; Office: Dept. of Geophysics and Astronomy, Univ. of B.C., Vancouver, B.C. V6T 1Z4.

**CLARKE, George Elliott,** B.A., M.A., Ph.D.; writer; b. Windsor, N.S. 12 Feb. 1960; s. William Lloyd and Geraldine Elizabeth C.; e. Queen Elizabeth H.S. 1978 (scholarship in social studies); Banff Ctr., Sch. of Fine Arts, cert. 1983 (2nd prize for poetry, Bliss Carman Award); Univ. of Waterloo B.A. (Hons.) 1984; Dalhousie Univ. M.A. 1989; Queen's Univ., Ph.D. (English) 1993; Legis. Intern, Ont. Legis. Assembly 1982–83; Editor-in-Chief & Treas., Imprint Pubs., Univ. of Waterloo 1984–85; Community Devel. Worker, Black Un. Front of N.S. 1985–86; Legis. Asst. to Howard D. McCurdy, M.P. 1987–91; Teaching Asst., English Dept., Queen's Univ. 1991–93; Asst. Adjunct Prof., Queen's Univ. 1994; Columnist, Halifax Herald Ltd. 1992– ; Weekly Columnist, 'The Daily News' (Halifax) 1988–89; Writer-in-residence, Saint Mary's Univ. 1990; Writer-in-residence, Selkirk Coll. 1991; author: 'Saltwater Spirituals and Deeper Blues' 1983, 'Whylah Falls' 1990 (poetry); ed.: 'Fire on the Water: An Anthology of Black Nova Scotian Literature' 2 vols., 1991, 1992; anthologies: 'Poets Haus' 1983, 'sad dances in a field of white' 1985, 'Other Voices' 1985, 'The Atlantic Anthology,' vol. II 1986, 'The Ecphore Anthology' 1987, 'Poets 88' 1988, 'Halifax: A Literary Portrait' 1990, 'Choice Atlantic' 1990, 'Voices: Canadian Writers of African Descent' 1992, 'Introduction to Literature: Canadian, British, American' 1988, 'Anthology of Magazine Verse & Yearbook of American Poetry' 1984, '85; African Baptist; N.D.P.; 1st prize, Adult Poetry, Writers' Fed. of N.S. 1981; Archibald Lampman Award for Poetry, Ottawa Independent Writers 1991; Ontario Arts Counc. Grant 1989; Canada Counc. Grant 1990; recreations: cinema, music; club: Writers' Fed. of N.S.; Writers' Union of Can.; League of Candn. Poets; Candn. Artists Network - Black Artists in Action; Black Cultural Soc. of Nova Scotia; Home: P.O. Box 81084, Ottawa, Ont. K1P 1B1.

**CLARKE, George F.S.,** F.S.A., F.C.I.A.; retired insurance executive; b. Govan, Sask. 1 Feb. 1921; s. late E. Francene (Wallbridge) and late J. Orville C.; e. High Sch., Govan, Sask., 1939; University of Manitoba, B.Com. (Hons.) 1950; F.S.A. 1953; F.C.I.A. 1965; m. Sheila J.M. Stewart, 18 Sept. 1945 (d. 1975): one d. Georgia; m. 2ndly, Elsa Marian McLeod, 7 May 1977; Dir. and Chrmn., Renascent Fellowship and Foundation Inc.; Dir., Life Office Mgmt. Assoc. 1979–82; Royal Trustco Ltd. 1981–85; Hon. Dir., Royal Trustco Ltd. 1985–92; Candn. Cancer Soc. 1981–84; The Toronto Western & Toronto Hosp. 1982–89; Pafco Financial Holdings Ltd. 1984–89; Mem., Bd. of Govs., Univ. of Waterloo 1983–87; Adv. Counc., Fac. of Admin. Studies, York Univ. 1984–88; with Manufacturers Life Insurance Co. 1950–67 (Group Vice-Pres. 1964–67); joined Sun Life of Canada as Actuary 1967, Vice-Pres. and Chief Actuary 1968, Sr. Vice-Pres. 1970, Extve. Vice Pres. 1972, Pres. & Dir. 1978–83; served with R.C.A.F. 1942–46, in U.K., Middle E., India, Ceylon, rank Flight Lt.; Fellow, Society of Actuaries; Fellow, Candn. Inst. of Actuaries; Clubs: Granite; Toronto; Rosedale Golf; Mad River Golf; Royal Montreal Curling (Past Pres.); Home: Ste. #604, 2900 Yonge St., Toronto, Ont. M4N 3N8.

**CLARKE, Herbert M.,** B.A., B.Sc.; senior corporate executive; b. Norris Point, Nfld. 1944; e. Mem. Univ. of Nfld. B.A., B.Sc. 1965; Univ. of Mich. Cert. in Business Mang. 1967; McGill Univ. Cert. in Business Mang. 1968; m. Nora, 28 Dec. 1967; three children; EXTVE. VICE PRES., FISHERY PRODUCTS INTERNATIONAL LIMITED 1988– ; joined H.O. Aluminum Co. of Canada, Montreal 1965–69 serving as Operations Research Analyst; co-founder Newfoundland and Labrador Computer Services Ltd. 1969 serving as Training & Recruitment Mgr. and Dir. of Systems & Programming; joined Extve. Council Office, Govt. of Nfld. & Labrador 1973 serving as Dir. of Govt. Services Policy and subsequently Dir. of Econ. & Resource Policy; apptd. Depy. Min. of Forestry & Agric. 1976; Depy. Min. of Development 1979; Clerk of the Extve. Counc. and Secy. to Cabinet, Govt. of Nfld. & Labrador 1985–88; Office: 70 O'Leary Ave., St. John's Nfld. A1C 5L1.

**CLARKE, James Young,** C.D., P.Eng.; retired association executive; b. Montreal, Que. 1 Mar. 1928; s. Edward Lawrence and Shirley Edith (MacRae) C.; e. Westmount H.S. 1945; Royal Roads Naval Coll. 1947; Royal Naval Engn. Coll. 1951; R.C.A.F. Staff Coll. 1963; m. Margaret d. Hector and Claire Perks 16 Aug. 1951; children: Lynn Margaret, Janet MacRae, Susan Patricia, James Young; Pres. & C.E.O., Canadian Maritime Industries Assn. 1987–94; Retired; Royal Candn. Navy 1947–70: various engn. positions on- and offshore 1951–63; Commanding Offr. H.M.C.S. Athabaskan 1963–64; Commander, H.M.C.S. Provider 1964–67; D.N.D. Headquarters 1967–70; Commandant, C.C.G. Coll., Candn. Coast Guard 1970–73; Extve. Asst. to Depy. Min., Transport 1973–75; Dir., TC Training Inst. 1975–79; Dir.-Gen., Fleet Systems, Canadian Coast Guard 1979–87; Dir., Marine Technology Faculty, St. Lawrence Coll.; Marine Media Ltd.; Public Service Merit Award 1979; mem., Candn. Inst. of Marine Engineering; Royal Military Coll. Ex-Cadet Club; Naval Officers Assoc. of Canada; Royal Philatelic Soc. of Canada; author: numerous technical articles pub. in various profl. journs. and magazines; recreations: tennis, skiing, fishing, swimming, philately; Clubs: Wolfe County Fish & Game; Home: 2320 Alta Vista Dr., Ottawa, Ont. K1H

7M7; Office: 801 - 100 Sparks St., Ottawa, Ont. K1P 5B7.

**CLARKE, John Puleston;** business consultant and retired banking executive; b. England 6 Aug. 1929; s. George Puleston and Gladys May (Andrews) C.; e. Taunton's Sch. (Eng.); m. Olive E.M. d. John and Jane Lyons 11 Apr. 1953; children: Sandra, Brian; Sr. Vice-Pres., Special Loans, The Royal Bank of Can. 1985–89 (retired 1989); joined Royal Bank, Victoria, B.C. 1946; Asst. Mgr., Montreal Main Br. 1960; Sr. Asst. Mgr., St. Catherine & Bleury Br. 1963; Credit Inspector, Que. Dist. Gen. Mgr.'s Dept. 1967; Asst. Supvr. 1969; Mgr., St. Catherine & Stanley Br. 1971; Dir., Retail Mktg. & Devel., H.O. 1973; Reg. Mgr., Que. Dist. 1975; Dist. Mgr., Branch Banking, Mtl. Dist. 1977; Vice-Pres., Commerc. Lending, H.O. 1978; Vice-Pres., Special Loans 1982; Mem., Toastmasters Internat. (Past Dist. Lt. Gov.); Dir., Accugraph Corp.; Gentra Inc.; recreations: golf; clubs: Summerlea Golf & Country, Mount Stephen; Home: 91 – 15th St., Roxboro, Que. H8Y 1N7.

**CLARKE, Kenneth R.,** C.A.; executive; b. Buckinghamshire, Eng. 5 Nov. 1944; s. Edward and Joan (Lewis) C.; e. St. Olaves Grammar Sch. London, Eng.; Inst. C.A.'s Eng. & Wales 1968; Candn. Inst. C.A.'s 1969; m. Judith d. Rhoda and Walter Barrett 1964; one s. Adam Quinton Harvey; DEPUTY GROUP CHRMN., FINANCIAL SERVICES EDPER-BRASCAN 1993– ; Chrmn., Royal LePage Limited 1993– ; Dir. Hees International Bancorp Inc.; London Life Insurance Co.; joined Touche Ross & Co. 1966–69, trans. from London, Eng. to Toronto 1967; National Hees Industries Ltd. 1969–71; Invest. Dealers Assn. Can. 1971–73; Merrill Lynch Canada Inc. 1974–84; Great Lakes Group Inc. 1984–89, Pres., C.E.O. & Dir., Trilon Financial Corp. 1989–92; Board, PMH Foundation; recreations: sailing, skiing, hiking; Clubs: RCYC; Toronto; Home: 1236 Queen Victoria Ave., Mississauga, Ont. L5H 3H3; Office: BCE Place, 181 Bay St., Suite 4420, P.O. Box 771, Toronto, Ont. M5J 2T3.

**CLARKE, Percy Raymond,** B.Sc., P.Eng.; retired mining executive; b. Portage La Prairie, Man. 1 Sept. 1918; s. Victor Thomas and Alice Irene (Sexsmith) C.; e. Birch Hills (Sask.) Public Sch.; Portage Coll. Inst., Portage La Prairie, Man.; Univ. of Manitoba (2nd year Arts and Science) 1938; Univ. of Alta., B.Sc. (Mining Engn.) 1948; m. Pauline Mary, d. George Jennings, 9 June 1945; children: Angela, Jean, Irene, Michael; Dir., Pamour Inc. 1981–90; Pres., Texasgulf Metals Co. 1978–81; Sr. Vice-Pres. Texasgulf Inc. 1976–81; Vice Pres., Texasgulf Inc. 1973–76; Vice Pres. & Dir. Ecstall Mining Ltd. 1969–71; Gen. Mgr. Kidd Creek Operations 1969–76; Vice Pres. and Dir., Texasgulf Canada Ltd. 1971–80; Pres. & Dir., Texasgulf Canada 1980–81; joined Cominco, Trail Smelter as Jr. Engr. 1948; Mill Supt., Highland-Bell Ltd. 1950; Research Metallurgist, Noranda Mines Ltd. 1954; Mill Supt., Heath Steele Mines 1955; concurrently Base Metal Consultant (private practice) and Sr. Engr., Atomic Energy Control Bd., Univ. of Alta. 1958; Mill Supt. Kamkotia Mines Ltd. 1961; joined present Co. as Mill Supt., Timmins, Ont. 1964; Chrmn., C.E.O. and Dir., Kidd Creek Mines Ltd. 1981–83; Dir., Kidd Creek Mines Ltd. 1983–86; served in 2nd World War, Queen's Own Cameron Highlanders of Can. 1939–45; comnd. Overseas 1941, on Dieppe Raid 1942; P.O.W. 1942–45; mem. Assn. Prof. Engrs. of Ont.; Candn. Inst. Mining & Metall.; Ont. Mining Assn. (Dir. 1969–77; Pres. 1975–76 and 1982–83; Dir. 1981–83); Mining Assn. of Can. (Dir. 1976–83); Nat'l Advisory Comte on Mining Industry 1978–84; awarded C.I.M. 'Inco Medal' in 1981 for outstanding contribution to mining industry in concentrator design and operation; Anglican; recreations: skiing, golf, camping; Home: 2095 Gatestone Ave., Oakville, Ont. L6J 2G2.

**CLARKE, Peter J.,** LL.B.; lawyer; construction executive; b. Toronto, Ont. 27 June 1943; s. John Cambrey and Gabrielle Jeanne (Carbonneau) C.; e. Univ. of Waterloo, Chem. Engr. 1965; Univ. of Toronto, LL.B. 1968; m. Carole d. John Nathan and Daisy Helena Gillies 19 Oct. 1962; children: Jeffrey, Paul, Peter; PRES., C.E.O. & DIR., DINEEN CONSTRUCTION LTD. 1981– ; Partner, Robertson, Lane, Perrett 1970–78; Pres., Robert G. Wells Ltd. 1979–80; Partner, Holden, Day, Wilson 1978– ; Pres., C.E.O. & Dir., Dineen Roads & Bridges Ltd. 1981– ; Pres. & Dir., Stewart Chevrolet Oldsmobile Ltd. 1983–85; Chrmn., C.E.O. & Dir., Baknor Industries Inc.; A.S.P. Acces Floors Ltd.; Dineen Construction (Atlantic) Inc.; Mariposa Cruise Lines Ltd.; Paragon Photographic Reproductions Ltd.; Daytech Mfg. Ltd. (Can.) and Daytech Mfg. Inc. (U.S.A.); Mult-a-Frame Corp. (U.S.A.); Dir.: Derlan Industries Ltd.; Dineen Holdings Ltd.; Glitter Bay Holdings Ltd.; mem., Chief Executives Orgn.; Empire Club; Lawyer's Club; County of York Law Assn.; Candn. Bar Assn.; recreations: tennis, golf; Clubs: Kingsway Platform Tennis; CTC Tennis; Lambton Golf & Country; Boulevard; York Old Mill Tennis; Home: 39 Kingsway Cres., Toronto, Ont. M8X 2R5; Office: 70 Disco Rd., Rexdale, Ont. M9W 1L9.

**CLARKE, Richard Morel,** B.A.Sc., M.Eng.; b. Toronto, Ont. 17 July 1931; s. Roy Percy and Jean (Morel) C.; e. Allenby Pub. Sch. and Lawrence Park Coll. Inst. Toronto 1949; Univ. of Toronto B.A.Sc. 1954 (Chem. Eng.); Yale Univ. M.Eng. 1956; Rensaeller Polytechnic, Hartford, Conn. Business Mang. 1958; m. Jacqueline June d. Jack W. Eaton, Orillia, Ont. 23 Jan. 1960; two d. Stephanie S., Wendy E.; Vice Chrmn. & Dir., Hoechst Celanese Corp. 1988–..; Chrmn. and Dir., Cleyn & Tinker Inc.; Dir., Hoechst AG, Frankfurt, West Germany; Hoechst Japan, Ltd.; Tepco, Taiwan; Hoechst Canada Inc.; Celanese Canada Inc.; Lasertechnics; Celanese Mexicana S.A.; Polyplastics Co., Ltd., Japan; Menasha Corp.; Osmonics, Inc.; Hoechst Corp.; Nat. Urban League; Celgene Corp.; World Resources Inst.; Rsch. & Devel. Engr. American Cyanamid 1954; Devel. Engr. Shell Oil Co. 1955; Vice Pres. & Gen. Mgr. Joclin Manufacturing Co. 1956–68; Devel. Mgr. Cabot, Celanese Chemical Co. 1968; Marketing Mgr. Resins, Celanese Plastics 1971, Vice Pres. & Gen. Mgr. Resins 1973; Sr. Vice Pres. Marketing Indust. & Smoking Products, Celanese Fibers Marketing Co. 1975; Extve. Vice Pres. & Gen. Mgr. Celanese Canada Ltd. 1978; Pres. and C.E.O. Celanese Canada Inc. 1978–82; Vice Pres., Celanese Corp. and Pres., Celanese Specialty Operations 1982–85; Group Vice Pres., Celanese Corp. 1985–87; Sr. Extve. Vice Pres., Hoechst Celanese Corp. 1987–88; Mem., Bd. of Trustees, Americas Soc. Inc.; Fairleigh Dickinson Univ.; Psi Upsilon; recreations: tennis, golf, skiing, photography; Clubs: Greenwich Country; Mount Royal; Carmel C.C.; Home: 63 Turkey Hill Rd. S., Westport, Conn. 06880.

**CLARKE, Hon. Roderick Dunfield,** B.A., B.C.L.; judge; b. Smiths Falls, Ont. 17 Apl. 1933; s. Vincent George and Helen Hogg (Dunfield) C.; e. St. George's Pub. Sch. and Quebec High Sch. Quebec City 1953; Univ. of N.B. B.A. 1958, B.C.L. 1961; Osgoode Hall Bar Admission Course 1966; m. Diane Dawne d. late Vernon Cooper, Rothesay, N.B. 14 Oct. 1961; children: Keltie Dawne, Fraser Aubrey Briar, Wilson Braymer; ONT. PROV. COURT JUDGE (CRIMINAL DIV.) since 1974; joined The National Trust Co. Toronto 1961–64; articled law student 1964–66; called to Bar of Ont. 1966; law practice Young & Clarke 1966–74; Dir. YM-YWCA; served on numerous bds. and comtes. prior to appt.; contrib. to various legal publs.; former Secy.-Treas. and Vice Pres. Thunder Bay Law Assn.; Mem. Candn. Bar Assoc.; Assoc. of Prov. Criminal Court Judges of Ont. (mem. Education and Sentencing Ctte. 1977–80; Chrmn. of Assoc. 1981–82; el. to Extve. Ctte. 1981; Chrmn. Law Reform Ctte. 1982–83; el. 2nd Vice Pres. of Assoc. 1982; el. 1st Vice Pres. 1983; el. Pres. 1984; Chrmn., Nominating Ctte. 1986–87); Candn. Assoc. of Prov. Court Judges (Ont. delegate 1983; Ont. voting rep. 1985–86); founding mem. & mem. Bd. of Govs., Lake Superior Sch.; guest lectr. numerous educational insts.; Commander, Order of St. Lazarus; Anglican; recreations: running, tennis, golf, boating; Home: R.R. 13 Silver Harbour, Thunder Bay, Ont. P7B 5E4; Office: 1805 East Arthur St., Thunder Bay, Ont. P7E 5N7.

**CLARKE, Roger,** B.Comm., C.A.; financial executive; b. Penticton, B.C. 27 Oct. 1946; s. Gordon A. and Jean G. (Sharpe) C.; e. Univ. of B.C. B.Comm. 1968; C.A. B.C. 1970; m. Irene Bennie 1969; children: Tanya, Heather; SR. VICE-PRES., FINANCE & INFORMATION TECHNOL., BC RAIL LTD. 1993– ; Peat Marwick Mitchell Vanc. 1968–75; BC Rail Ltd., N. Van. 1975–93; Dir., Vanc. Ch., Financial Extves. Inst.; Pres. & Dir., North Shore Charitable Fdn.; Office: P.O. Box 8770, Vancouver, B.C. V6B 4X6.

**CLARKE, Ronald Johns Kennerley,** O.S.A., B.S.A.; association executive; b. Toronto, Ont. 14 July 1945; s. Harry and Sarah (Kennerley) C.; e. Malvern Coll.,; Dan. Tech.; Univ. of Wisconsin; PRES., THE ONT. SOCIETY OF ARTISTS; Bd. Mem., Heritage Foundation; Arts Sub-Ctte., Faculty Club, Univ. of Toronto; Mem., The Ontario Soc. of Artists; The Bermuda Soc. of Artists; The Faculty Club, Univ. of Toronto; The Lago Mar Beach and Country Club, Fort Lauderdale, Florida; Homes: 32 MacLean Ave., Toronto, Ont. M4E 2Z9, 160 Balmoral Ave., Apt. 803, Toronto, Ont. M4V 1J7; Offices: Suite 203, 10 Adelaide St. E., Toronto, Ont. M5C 1J3; Univ. of Toronto, 215 Huron St., Toronto, Ont. M5S 1A1.

**CLARKE, Victor Lancelot,** B.Sc., B.E., P.Eng.; executive; b. St. John's, Nfld. 16 Dec. 1925; s. Ralph Lancelot and Ida May (Tucker) C.; e. Dalhousie Univ. B.Sc. 1945; N.S. Tech. Coll. B.E. 1947; m. Alberta d. Albert and Margaret Thain 15 May 1955; children: Jane Lydia, Ian MacDiarmid, Elizabeth Jean; Executive-in-Residence, Fac. of Admin. Studies, York Univ.; apptd. Mem., Competition Tribunal by O-I-C 1990; joined Canadian General Electric 1947, assignments U.S.A. and Eng., returning to Can. 1951; Gen. Mgr., Apparatus Sales & Service Dept. 1969, Communications Systems Dept. 1973, Construction Products Dept. 1974, Vice Pres. 1972; Vice Pres. & Corp. Extve. of Planning & Development 1976; Vice-Chrmn. Sector Task Force (Elect. Industry) Tri-Lateral Task Force 1978; Special Adviser, Royal Comn. on the Economic Union & Development Prospects for Canada 1983–85; Special Adviser (Investment), Candn. High Commission, London, Eng. 1985–87; Co-Chrmn. Gen. Mfg. Group Can.-Japan Businessmen's Co-op. Comte.; Pres. Peterborough Chamber Comm.; former Warden St. Luke's Ang. Ch. Peterborough; mem. Assn. Prof. Engrs. Prov. Ont.; Inst. of Dirs.; British Commonwealth Soc.; recreations: history, photography; Address: 278 Newton Dr., Willowdale, Ont. M2M 2P7.

**CLARKE, William Hillary;** chartered accountant; b. Toronto, Ont. 5 July 1933; s. late James Reginald and Eleanor Lerrier (Aubin) C.; e. Forest Hill Schs., Toronto; Ridley Coll., St. Catharines; St. George's Sch., Vancouver; Univ. of B.C.; C.A. 1957; F.C.A. 1982; divorced; children: Alan, Hillary, John, Elizabeth, Simon; articles Price Waterhouse 1951–56; C.A. practice 1957–61; Co-Founder & Chief Fin. Offr., Vancouver Mgmt. Ltd. & Coast Apartments Ltd. 1961– ; M.P., Vancouver Quadra 1972–84; Candidate 1984 and 1988 federal elections, defeated by Rt. Hon. John Turner; Comnr. to Review Salaries of MPs & Senators 1985; Cons./Bus. Mgr. (self-employed) 1985–92; Federal Co-ordr. Royal Visit of Their Royal Highnesses the Prince & Princess of Wales 1986; Chrmn. Standing Ctte. on Fin., Trade & Econ. Affairs 1979; Public Accts. 1980–83; Anglican; Progressive Conserv.; recreations: tennis, old cars; Clubs: Vancouver; Vancouver Lawn Tennis; Home: 801 - 6060 Balsam St., Vancouver, B.C. V6M 4C1; Office: 205 - 2025 W. 42nd Ave., Vancouver, B.C. V6M 2B5.

**CLARKSON, Adrienne,** B.A., M.A., O.C., LL.D.; writer, publisher, TV broadcaster; b. Hong Kong, 10 Feb. 1939; d. William George and Ethel May (Lam) Poy; e. Lisgar Coll. Inst., Ottawa, Ont., 1956; Univ. of Toronto, B.A. (Trinity Coll.) 1960, M.A. (Eng.) 1961; Sorbonne, 1962–64; Officer, Order of Canada 1992; Dalhousie Univ., LL.D. (hon. causa) 1988; Lakehead Univ., D.Litt. (hon. causa) 1989; Acadia Univ., LL.D. (hon. causa) 1991; Hon. Fellow, Royal Conservatory of Music 1993; EXECUTIVE PRODUCER & HOST, 'ADRIENNE CLARKSON PRESENTS,' CBC TV 1989– ; Publisher, Adrienne Clarkson Books, for McClelland and Stewart, 1988– ; CBC TV: Interviewer-host, 'Fifth Estate' 1975–82; Agent General for Ontario in France, 1982–87; Pres. and Publisher, McClelland and Stewart, 1987–88; Executive Producer and Host, 'Adrienne Clarkson's Summer Festival' CBC TV, 1988–89; Gen. Editor, 'The New Woman' series, 1970–72; author: 'A Lover More Condoling' 1968, 'Hunger Trace' 1970, 'True To You In My Fashion' 1971; rec'd Centennial Medal 1967; Commemorative Medal for 125th Anniversary of Candn. Confederation 1992; ACTRA Awards: Best TV Journalist, 1974, 1982; Gordon Sinclair Award for outspokenness and integrity in broadcasting, 1975; Best Writer, TV Documentary, 1977; Gemini Award: Best Host, Light Information, Variety or Performing Arts Program, 'Adrienne Clarkson Presents' 1993; Address: CBC TV Arts, Music, Science & Variety, P.O. Box 500, Stn. A, Toronto, Ont. M5W 1E6.

**CLARKSON, Geoffrey W.,** B.A., F.C.A.; b. Toronto, Ont. 31 Jan. 1935; s. Geoffrey Perry and Sophia Amelia (Meyers) C.; e. Upper Canada Coll.; Univ. of W. Ont., B.A. (Bus. Admin.) 1958; C.A. 1961; m. Cynthia d. Douglas and Mary Johnson 27 Sept. 1958; children: Edward, Michael, Alexandra; PARTNER, ERNST & YOUNG (formerly Clarkson Gordon) 1968– ; awarded F.C.A. 1982; Trustee and Chrmn., Hugh MacMillan Rehabilitation Centre; Chief Financial Offr., Progressive Conservative Fund of Ont.; Gov., Variety Village; Past Pres. & Dir., Rosedale Golf Club; Past Trustee, St. Clement's Sch.; Past Pres., York-Toronto Lung Assn.; Past Dir., Muskoka Lakes Golf and Country Club; Past Warden, Church of St. Clement; recreations: tennis, golf, cross-country skiing; Clubs: University; Rosedale Golf; Badminton & Racquet; Muskoka Lakes Golf & Country; Home: 25 St. Leonard's Cres., Toronto, Ont.

M4N 3A5; Office: Box 251, Ernst & Young Tower, Toronto-Dominion Centre, 222 Bay St., Toronto, Ont. M5K 1J7.

**CLARKSON, Max Boydell Elliott,** M.A.; educator, b. Lenzie, Scot. 14 Oct. 1922; s. George Elliott and Helene (Mannaberg) C.; e. Stowe Sch. Buckingham, Eng. 1939; St. Andrew's Coll. Aurora, Ont. 1940; Univ. of Toronto B.A. 1943, M.A. 1946; D.C.L., St. Mary's Univ. 1988; m. Madeleine d. Michael Earls 5 June 1948; children: Max Adam, Helene Edith; PROFESSOR EMERITUS & DIR., CENTRE FOR CORPORATE SOCIAL PERFORMANCE & ETHICS, FAC. OF MANAGEMENT, UNIV. OF TORONTO 1975– ; Dir. Eastern Utilities Ltd.; Suncor; Vice Pres. Technical Charts, Inc. 1947–50; Pres. Clarkson Press Inc. 1950–57; Pres. Graphic Controls Corp. 1957–70, Chrmn. of Bd. 1970–75; Prof. of Mang. and Dean, Fac. of Mang. present univ. 1975–80; served as Operations Offr. RCNVR 1943–45, rank Lt.; Pres. Master Printers of America 1959–61; Pres. Printing Industries of America 1962; Chrmn. Mayor's Citizens' Adv. Comte. on Community Improvement Buffalo 1964–75; Clarkson Ctr. for Human Services 1970–75; Trustee D'Youville Coll. Buffalo 1975–77; Dir., The Niagara Inst. since 1972; The Shaw Festival 1969–79; The Canadian Club 1988– ; Anglican; recreation: tennis; Clubs: Buffalo; Metropolitan (N.Y.); Naval and Military (London, Eng.); York; Queens; Toronto Lawn Tennis; Caledon; Home: 23 Dunloe Rd., Toronto, Ont. M4V 2W4.

**CLARKSON, Ross T.,** Q.C.; b. Montreal, P.Q. 29 March 1922; S. Ross and Elsie Florence (Trenholme) C.; e. Selwyn House Sch. (Montreal), 1928–36; Lower Canada Coll. (Montreal) 1936–39; Univ. of Grenoble, 1947; McGill Univ., B.A., 1942, B.C.L. (1st Class Hons.), 1948; Elizabeth Torrence Gold Medal, Civil Law; Montreal Bar Assn. Prize, Civil Law; I.M.E. Prize, Common Law; Univ. of Paris, 1948–49; children: Linda Jane, Peter Ross; PARTNER, McCARTHY, TÉTRAULT; Dir. & Vice Chrmn., Munich Reinsurance Co. of Canada; Dir. & Vice Chrmn., Munich-Canada Management Corp.; Extve. Vice Pres. & Dir., Munich Holdings Ltd.; Dir., National Trust Co.; Great Lakes Reinsurance Co.; Great Lakes Reinsurance Holdings Ltd.; Hoechst Canada, Inc.; Gov., Quebec Bar Found.; Dir. and mem., Montreal Children's Hosp.; Dir. and Secy. Montreal Children's Hosp. Foundation; Gov., Montreal General Hosp. Found.; Gov. and mem., Reddy Memorial Hosp.; Life Gov., Douglas Hosp.; mem., Zeller Family Foundation; St. Mary's Hosp. Found.; Hon. Legal Counsel, Boy Scouts of Can., Que. Provincial Council; Secy. & Mem., Bd. of Dirs., Boy Scouts of Can., Que. Provincial Council, Inc.; read law with W.B. Scott, Q.C.; called to the Bar of Quebec, 1948; cr. Q.C., 1963; joined present law firm, 1949; a Partner, 1958; lectr. in law, McGill Univ. 1959–71, and McGill Centre for Continuing Educ. 1968–70; Gov., Alliance Research and Education Inst.; mem., Adv. Counc., Alliance Quebec; Co-Chrmn., Candn. Counc. of Christians and Jews; Gouverneur de la Fondation du Barreau du Québec; mem., Candn. Bar Assn.; Candn. Tax Foundation; Internat. Comn. of Jurists; Fellow, Internat. Acad. Law and Science; mem., Selwyn Old Boys Assoc., (Dir. 1954–58, Pres. 1956–57); Alpha Delta Phi; United Church; recreations: reading, photography, swimming, music, cross-country skiing, hiking; Clubs: St. James's Club of Montreal; University; Montreal Amateur Athletic Assoc.; Hillside Tennis; Home: 220 Chester Ave., Town of Mount Royal, Que. H3R 1W3; Office: 1170 Peel St., Montreal, Que. H3B 4S8.

**CLARKSON, Stephen,** M.A., Doctorat; professor; b. 21 Oct. 1937; s. George Elliott and Alice Helene (Mannaberg) C.; e. Upper Can. Coll., Toronto, Ont. 1955; Univ. of Toronto, B.A. 1959; New Coll., Oxford, M.A. 1961 (Rhodes Scholar, Ont. 1959); Fondation Nat. de Sciences Pol., Doctorat 1964 (Woodrow Wilson Fellow 1961); m. Christina McCall, 1 Sept. 1978; three d., Ashley, Kyra, Blaise; PROF. OF POL. ECONOMY, UNIV. OF TORONTO; Policy Chrmn., Liberal Party in Ont. 1969–73; Dir., Social Planning Council Metrop. Toronto 1970–73; mem. Edit. Bd., The Canadian Forum, 1965–79; joined the Univ. as Lect., Dept. Pol. Economy 1964, Asst. Prof. 1965, Assoc. Prof. 1967; Prof., 1980; Sr. Fellow, Research Inst. on Communist Affairs, Columbia Univ. 1967–68; Sub-Lt., R.C.N.V.R.; Cand. for Mayor, City of Toronto, 1969; Dir., Maison Française de Toronto 1972; author of 'L'Analyse Soviétique des problèmes indiens de sous-développement' 1970; 'City Lib: Parties and Reform in Toronto' 1972; 'The Soviet Theory of Development: India and the Third World in Marxist-Leninist Scholarship' 1978; 'Canada and the Reagan Challenge: Crisis in the Canadian-American Relationship' 1982 (2nd ed. 1985); co-author: 'Trudeau and Our Times' 1990 (winner of Gov.-Gen.'s award for non-fiction 1990; 'Trudeau: l'homme, l'utopie, l'histoire' 1990; Ed. 'An Independent Foreign Policy for Canada?' 1968; 'Visions 2020: Fifty Canadians in Search of a Future' 1970; has contrib. chapters to 'Nationalism in Canada' 1966; 'Peace, Power and Protest' 1967; 'Living in the Seventies' 1970; 'Canadian Independence' 1972; 'The City: Attacking Modern Myths' 1972; 'The Egalitarian Option: Perspectives on Canadian Education' 1975; 'Canada at the Polls: The General Election of 1974' 1975; 'America Latina y Canada' 1975; 'Nationalism, Technology and the Future of Canada' 1976; 'Party Politics in Canada' 1979; 'Problems of Change in Urban Government' 1980; 'Canada at the Polls, 1979 and 1980' 1981; 'Canada among Nations: 1984' 1985; 'Canada at the Polls' 1984, 1988; 'The Free Trade Deal' 1988; 'Les Choix géopolitiques du Canada' 1988; 'The Federal Election of 1988' 1989; 'Trade-offs on Free Trade' 1989; 'The Free Trade Agreement of 1988' 1989; 'Federalism and Political Community' 1990; 'The New Era of Global Competition' 1991; 'Etre contemporain' 1992; created simulation technique for teaching univ. politics; Pres., Univ. League for Social Reform; Survival Found. 1973–77; mem., Candn. Pol. Science Assn. (Secy.-Treas. 1966–67); Internat. Pol. Science Assn.; Candn. Inst. Internat. Affairs; rec'd John Porter prize for best book in Candn. Soc. Sci., Candn. Sociol. and Anthrop. Assoc. 1984; recreations: gardening, carpentry; Home: 44 Rosedale Rd., Toronto, Ont. M4W 2P6.

**CLARRY, John Hamilton Cameron,** Q.C., M.B.E., E.D., C.D., B.A.; b. Calgary, Alta., 21 Sept. 1919; s. Ernest Simpson and Jean Milne (Cameron) C.; e. Forest Hill Village (Toronto) Pub. Sch.; Univ. of Toronto Schs. 1938: Univ. Coll. Univ. of Toronto B.A. 1947; Osgoode Hall Law Sch. 1950 (Silver Medal); m. Elizabeth Joy d. Gordon Kennedy, Toronto, Ont., 17 Sept. 1955; children: Susan, David, Michael; COUNSEL, McCARTHY TÉTRAULT; Dir., The Canada Life Assurance Co.; mem., Ontario Teachers' Pension Plan Bd.; called to Bar of Ont. 1950; cr. Q.C. 1963; joined Irish Regt. Can. 1937–38, COTC 1938–40, commnd. Royal Candn. Army Service Corps 1940, served overseas 1940–43, 1944–46; attended and instructed Candn. War Staff Course 1943–44, D.A.Q.M.G. First Candn. Army 1944; Royal Candn. Army Service Corps (Militia) 1946–58, C.O. 5 Column 1952–55, apptd. Hon. Lt. Col. 25 Toronto Service Bn. (Militia) 1971, Hon. Col. 1982–87; mem. Bd. Govs. Candn. Tax Foundation 1967–70 and 1974–78 (Chrmn. 1976–77); mem. Council Bd. Trade Metrop. Toronto 1975–85 (Pres. 1983–84); mem. Law Soc. Upper Can.; Candn. Bar Assn.; Offr. Order Orange Nassau with Crossed Swords; Presbyterian; Clubs: Toronto; University; Royal Candn. Mil. Inst.; Home: 45 Glen Elm Ave., Toronto, Ont. M4T 1V1; Office: Ste. 4700, Toronto Dominion Bank Tower, Toronto-Dominion Centre, Toronto, Ont. M5K 1E6.

**CLAS, André,** B.A., M.A., D.Ph.; educator; b. Laning, France 1 June 1933; s. Eugène and Erna (Ditgen) C.; e. Univ. of Strasbourg B.A. 1953; Univ. of Montreal M.A. 1960; Univ. of Tübingen D.Ph. 1967; m. Sylviane d. Florimond Canepeel; children: Sophie-Dorothée, David; PROF., DEPT. OF LINGUISTICS, UNIV. OF MONTREAL 1976– ; Ed., META (Translators' Journal) 1968– ; joined present Univ. as Lectr. 1963, appointed Asst. Prof. 1967, Assoc. Prof. 1970, Chrmn. of Dept. 1972–81; Coordinator, Réseau Lexicologie, Terminologie, Traduction de l'Université des réseaux d'expression française 1989; author 'Phonétique appliquée' 1967; 'Le français, langue des affaires' 1969; 'Guide de la correspondance' 1980; 'Richesses et particularités du français écrit au Québec' 1979, 1982; 'Sons et langage' 1983; 'Compact Wörterbuch der exakten Naturwissenschaften und der Technik Band II Deutsch-Französisch' 1991; mem., Soc. de linguistique romane; Candn. Ling. Soc.; Hon. Mem., Translator Soc. of Que.; Protestant; Home: 7405 Maynard, Montreal, Que. H3R 3B3; Office: P.O. Box 6128, Succ. A, Montreal, Que. H3C 3J7.

**CLAXTON, John B.,** Q.C., B.C.L.; b. Montreal, Que. 13 Jan. 1927; s. Brooke and Helen G. (Savage) C.; e. Roslyn Sch., Lower Can. Coll. and Westmount (Que.) High Sch., 1944; McGill Univ., B.C.L. 1950; two s. David Frederick, Edward Brooke; called to Bar of Que. 1950; cr. Q.C. 1968; PARTNER LAFLEUR BROWN 1963– ; Dir., Domco Inc.; Rothmans, Benson & Hedges Inc.; Laurentian Spring Valley Inc.; Montreal YMCA Found.; Candn. Heritage of Que.; served with Candn. Army 1945; Counsel to Royal Comn. on Can.'s Econ. Prospects (Gordon Comn.), 1955–56; Lectr., Faculty of Law, McGill Univ., 1956–68; Pres., McGill Law Grads.' Soc., 1970; Dir. Jr. Bar Assn. Montreal, 1951–54 (Secy. 1953–54); mem., Council, Montreal and Quebec Bar 1972–74; Candn. Bar Assn.; Liberal; Anglican; Clubs: University; Montreal Racket; Hillside Tennis; Red Bird Ski; Canadian; Home: 468 Mount Stephen Ave., Westmount, Qué. H3Y 2X6; Office: 3725, 1 Place Ville Marie, Montréal, Qué. H3B 3P4.

**CLAYMAN, Bruce Philip,** Ph.D.; university professor and administrator; physicist; b. New York, N.Y. 2 Sept. 1942; s. Louis and Edith (Kaufman) C.; e. Rensselaer Polytech. Inst. B.Sc. 1964; Cornell Univ. Ph.D. 1969; m. Linda d. Henry and Ann Gissel 4 Sept. 1962; one d.: Annie Claire; DEAN, GRADUATE STUDIES 1985– ; and VICE PRESIDENT RESEARCH, SIMON FRASER UNIV. 1993– ; Asst. Prof., Simon Fraser Univ. 1968–73; Assoc. Prof. 1973–80; Assoc. Dean, Grad. Studies 1976–79; Prof. 1980– ; Consultant, Xerox Corp. 1980–81; Visiting Prof., Emory Univ. 1981–82; Visiting Fellow, Cornell Univ. 1992; rsch. interests: low temp. solid-state physics, spectroscopy; Bd. of Mgmt., Triumf 1977–90, Chrmn. 1988–90; Extve. Sec., Gov. Ctte., R.H. Wright Award in Olfactory Rsch.; mem., Am. Physical Soc.; Candn. Assn. of Physics; author or co-author of over 70 physics papers in refereed journs. 1966–93; recreations: piloting light aircraft, piano, cycling; Home: 1002 Saddle St., Coquitlam, B.C. V3C 3N1; Office: Burnaby, B.C. V5A 1S6.

**CLAYTON, Alastair J.,** M.B., Ch.B., D.P.H., F.F.C.M., F.A.C.P.M., F.R.C.P.(C); medical administrator; epidemiologist; b. Glasgow, Scot. 17 Apr. 1933; s. Frank and Barbara (Wadsworth) C.; e. Strathallan Sch. Perth, Scot.; St. Andrew's Univ., Scotland B. of Med., B. of Surg. 1958; Univ. of Toronto Dip. of Pub. Health (DPH) 1968; children: Fiona, Ian; Dir. Gen., Federal Centre for AIDS 1987–90; joined Royal Candn. Air Force 1959; achieved rank of Colonel and retired 1978; Dir. of Preventive Med., Candn. Forces Med. Service 1978–79; Dir. Gen., Lab. Centre for Disease Control, Dept. of Nat. Health and Welfare 1979–87; at present seconded to the Fogarty Internat. Center, National Institutes of Health, Bethesda, Maryland; received specialty qualifications in preventive med. and community health from Can., U.S.A. and U.K.; author 30 publ. articles in med. lit. on Communicable Disease Epidemiology; Adjunct Prof. Dept. of Epidemiology and Community Med., Univ. of Ottawa; past Pres. Candn. Soc. for Tropical Med. and Internat. Health; mem. Candn. Pub. Health Assn. (Dir. 1983–84); Candn. Hosp. Infection Control Assn. (Dir. 1980–83); Bd. Mem., American Coll. of Preventive Medicine 1985–87; Sci. Adv. Ctte. Caribbean Epidemiology Centre, Port of Spain, Trinidad 1979–87; Mem. Bd. of Dirs., Internat. AIDS Soc. and N. Am. Secy. 1987–90; Mem. Steering Ctte. on Vth Internat. Conf. on AIDS 1989; Mem., Sci. Adv. Ctte., World AIDS Found.; recreations: jogging, philately; Home: 6026 Loganwood Dr., Rockville, MD 20852.

**CLAYTON, Robert Norman,** M.Sc., Ph.D., F.R.S., F.R.S.C., F.A.A.S.; educator; b. Hamilton, Ont. 20 March 1930; S. Norman and Gwenda Louise (Twist) C.; e. Queen's Univ. B.Sc. 1951, M.Sc. 1952; Cal. Inst. of Technol. Ph.D. 1955; m. Cathleen d. John and Elizabeth Shelburne 30 Jan. 1971; one d. Elizabeth; ENRICO FERMI DISTINGUISHED SERVICE PROF., UNIV. OF CHICAGO 1980– ; Asst. Prof. of Geochem. Pa. State Univ. 1956–58; Asst. Prof. of Chem. present Univ. 1958, Assoc. Prof. 1962, Prof. 1966–80; author and co-author over 150 sci. publs. various research journals; Fellow, Am. Geophys. Union; Meteoritical Soc.; Home: 5201 S. Cornell, Chicago, Ill. 60615; Office: 5640 S. Ellis, Chicago, Ill. 60637.

**CLEATHER, Edward Gordon,** B.A., C.A.; financial executive; b. St. John, N.B. 11 Dec. 1929; s. Charles Gordon and Caroline Beatrice (Fleming) C.; e. Lower Canada Coll. 1947; McGill Univ. B.A. 1951; Ont. Inst. of C.A.s C.A. 1956; m. Joan d. Graham and Margaret Allen 28 Nov. 1959; children: Graham, Carolyn; PRES., C.E.O. & DIR., MACDOUGALL, GAUTHIER, MACLAREN, CLEATHER INVESTMENTS INC. 1990– ; Student & C.A., Coopers & Lybrand 1951–57; Internal Auditor, Hawker Siddley 1957–59; Secy.-Treas., Global Investment Corp. 1959–65; Vice-Pres., Fin., Dir. & Sr. Shareholder, Jones Heward & Co. 1965–77; Pres. & Dir., Edgco Inc. 1977– ; Extve. Vice-Pres., C.O.O. & Dir., Guardian Trustco Inc. & Assoc. Cos. 1978–89; Chrm. & Dir., Guardinvest Securities Inc. 1988–89; Dir., Morgan & Dilworth Inc.; Le Groupe Forex Inc.; Pres., Queen Elizabeth Hosp. Found.; Gov., McGill Univ.; former Gov. & Public Gov., Montreal Stock Exchange; former Chrmn., Fin. Admin., Investment Dealers Assn. of Can.; former Vice-Chrmn., Candn. Depository for Securities Ltd.; Past Pres., Grad. Soc., McGill Univ.; Treas., Anglican Diocese of Montreal; Past Pres. & Dir., Youth Horizons Found.; Past Pres. & Dir., Canadian Club (Montreal); Anglican; Conservative; mem., Candn. Inst. of Internat. Affairs; Ont. Inst. of C.A.s; Que. Ordre des comptables; Psi Upsilon; Life mem., Toronto Children's Aid Soc.; recreations:

sailing, skiing, cycling, tennis, music, reading; Clubs: University (Montreal); Laurentian Lodge Ski; Toronto Cricket, Skating & Curling; Home: 3555 Côte des Neiges, Montreal, Que. H3H 1V2 and R.R. #1, Chester Basin, N.S. B0J 1K0.

**CLEGHORN, John Edward,** B.Com., C.A.; banker; b. Montreal, Que. 7 July 1941; s. the late H.W. Edward and Hazel M. (Dunham) C.; e. Westmount (Que.) High Sch. 1958; McGill Univ. B.Com. 1962; C.A. 1964; m. Pattie E. d. the late Harry L. and Eileen Hart 29 June 1963; children: Charles, Ian, Andrea; PRESIDENT AND CHIEF OPERATING OFFICER, ROYAL BANK OF CANADA 1990– ; Chrmn., Royal Trust Group of Companies; with Ernst & Young (formerly Clarkson, Gordon & Co.) Chartered Accountants 1962–64; St. Lawrence Sugar Ltd., Montreal 1964–66; Mercantile Bank of Canada (Citibank affiliate) (with assignments in New York, Montreal, Winnipeg and Vancouver) 1966–74; joined Royal Bank of Can. 1974: Asst. Gen. Mgr., Project Finance Group 1975; Depy. Gen. Mgr., Corporate Lending 1976; Vice Pres., Nat. Accounts Div. 1978; Sr. Vice Pres., Planning & Marketing Internat. Div. 1979; Sr. Vice Pres. and Gen. Mgr., B.C. 1980; Exec. Vice Pres., Internat. 1983; Pres. 1986; Pres. and C.O.O. 1990; Dir., Royal Bank of Can.; The Loram Group of Companies of Calgary; McDonald's Restaurants of Can.; The Macdonald Stewart Found.; The Public Policy Forum; Chrmn. and Dir., RoyFund Group of Mutual Funds; Chrmn., Gov. General's Candn. Study Conf.; Gov., McGill Univ.; Campaign Chrmn., McGill 21st Century Fund; D.C.L. (Hon.), Bishop's Univ. 1989; LL.D. (Hon.), Wilfrid Laurier Univ. 1991; mem., Candn. Inst. of C.A.s; Fellow, Ordre des Comptables Agréés du Qué.; Clubs: Montreal Indoor Tennis; Mount Royal; York Club; Knowlton Golf; Royal Candn. Yacht; Vancouver; Office: 1 Place Ville Marie, Box 6001, Montreal, Que. H3C 3A9.

**CLEGHORN, Robert Allen,** M.D., D.Sc., F.R.C.P.(C), F.R.C. Psych., D.Sc. (Hon.); b. Cambridge, Mass. 6 Oct. 1904; s. Allen Mackenzie and Edna Theresa (Gartshore) C.; e. Pub. and High Schs., London, Ont.; Univ. of Toronto Schs., 1921–22; Univ. of Toronto Med. Sch., M.D., 1928; Aberdeen Univ., D.Sc. 1932; m. Sheena (died 1976), d. late Sir John Marnoch, 1932; children: John Marnoch, Mhairi Jane (Santiago), Ailie Moir (Zimmermann); 2ndly Elizabeth (died 1988), d. late Prof. H.H. Newman, 1977; Jr. Interne, Toronto Gen. Hosp., 1928–29; Asst. in Physiology, Marischal Coll., Aberdeen, 1929–32; Asst. Attending Phys., Toronto Gen. Hosp., 1933–46; Dir., Therapeutics Lab., Allan Mem. Inst., Montreal 1946–64; Asst. Prof. of Psychiatry, McGill Univ., 1946–49, Assoc. Prof. 1949–60, Prof. and Chrmn. of Dept. 1964–70, now Emeritus Prof.; Special lecturer, Psychiat., U. of T. 1978; Consultant Psychiatrist, SBMC, 1978–; served in 2nd World War as Major, with R.C.A.M.C.; service in Italy and N.W. Europe with No. 1 Research Lab.; mem., Candn. Med. Assn.; Physiol. Soc.; The Endocrine Soc. (Ed. Bd. 1953); Candn. Physiol. Soc.; Am. Soc. for Clinical Investigation; Am. Physiol. Soc.; Am. Psychosomatic Soc. (Past Pres.); N.Y. Acad. of Science; Am. Assn. Advanc. Science; Royal Coll. of Psychiatrists (Founding Fellow 1971) Am. Psychiatric Assn. (Life Fellow 1979); Candn. Psychiatric Assn. (Life Member 1970); Am. Heart Assn.; Candn. Psychoanalytic Soc. (Life Member 1979); Acad. of Med., Toronto; Research Associate, Harvard Univ. 1953–54; Publications: 170; Office: Dept. of Psychiatry, Sunnybrook Med. Centre., 2075 Bayview Ave., Toronto, Ont. M4N 3M5.

**CLELAND, Noel Alfred,** B.E., P.Eng.; consulting engineer; b. Sydney, Australia 21 Dec. 1929; s. Alfred Barclay and Edna (Cox) C.; e. Univ. of Sydney B.E. 1951; m. Elonde d. John and Margery Billings 9 June 1956; one s. Glenn Allen; DIR., SPROULE ASSOCIATES LTD. 1992– ; Eng. California Standard Co. 1954–56, Hudson's Bay Oil & Gas Co. Ltd. 1957–64; Vice Pres. and Gen. Mgr. Quindar Products Ltd. 1964–66; Sr. Eng. present firm 1966, Dir. 1968, Chief Eng. 1970, Vice Pres. Eng. 1972, Pres. 1983; Lectr. in Petrol. Econ. Dept. Cont. Edn. Univ. of Calgary; author or co-author numerous tech. publs. mem. Candn. Inst. Mining & Metall. (Pres. 1981–82); Assn. Profl. Engs., Geols. & Geophycists Alta. (1986–89 Council; 1st Vice Pres. 1990–91; Pres. 1991–92); Petrol Soc. CIM (Past Nat. Chrmn.); recreations: sailing, tennis, skiing; clubs: Calgary Petroleum, Ranchmen's; Home: 1219 Belavista Cres. S.W., Calgary, Alta. T2V 2B2; Office: 900, 140 – 4th Ave. S.W., Calgary, Alta. T2P 3N3.

**CLEMENHAGEN, Carol,** M.H.A.; association executive; b. Buckingham, Que. 26 Dec. 1954; d. Darlow and Ilona Hope (Cross) C.; e. Carleton Univ. B.A. 1975; Univ. of Ottawa M.H.A. (Health Adm.) 1977; PRES. CANDN. HOSP. ASSN. 1990– ; Rsch. Offr. Dept. Community Med. Univ. of Ottawa 1977–80; Mgmt. Cons. Ottawa Gen. Hosp. 1980–84; Vice Pres. present Assn. 1984–89; recreation: horseback riding; Home: 158 King George St., Ottawa, Ont. K1K 1V3; Office: 100, 17 York St., Ottawa, Ont. K1N 9J6.

**CLEMENT, Douglas M.;** business executive; b. Waterford, Ont. 17 June 1944; s. Leslie K. and Evelyn F. (Hyndman) C.; e. Norwich H.S.; Univ. of Western Ontario; m. Marietta d. Wallace and Rachel Longworth 26 Aug. 1967; children: Christian, Paul; VICE-PRES., ECONOMIC DEVELOPMENT EDMONTON 1990– ; Marketing. Mngt., Bell Canada 1965–74; Nat. Telecommunications Mgr., London Life Insurance 1974–79; self-employed, private retail buisness 1979–84; Dir., Market Devel. (Toronto & Edmonton), Northern Telecom 1984–90; Vice-Chrmn., Bd. of Dir., Alta. Microelectronic Centre; Past Dep. Chrmn., Major Accounts, United Way; Past Vice-Pres., Mktg., Bd. of Dir., Edmonton Symphony Orch.; Adv. Bd., Fac. of Engineering, Univ. of Alta.; Mem. & Past Task Force Chrmn., Edmonton C. of C.; Dir., Edmonton Sports Found.; Adv. Ctte., Grant MacEwan College; recreations: golf, music, travel, racquetball, antique cars; clubs: Edmonton Golf & Country, Edmonton Centre; Home: 686 Romaniuk Rd., Edmonton, Alta. T6R 1A5; Office: 9797 Jasper Ave., Edmonton, Alta. T5J 1N9.

**CLEMENT, Wallace,** M.A., Ph.D., F.R.S.C.; educator; author; b. Niagara-on-the-Lake, Ont. 1 Mar. 1949; s. Harold and Marjorie C.; e. McMaster Univ. B.A. 1972; Carleton Univ. M.A. 1973, Ph.D. 1976; M. Elsie d. William and Eva Andres 14 Sept. 1968; two s. Christopher, Jeffrey; DIR., INSTITUTE OF POLITICAL ECONOMY, 1993– ; and PROF. OF SOCIOL. AND ANTHROP., CARLETON UNIV. 1984– ; Asst. Prof. of Sociol. McMaster Univ 1975–1980; Assoc. Prof. of Sociol. and Anthrop. Carleton Univ. 1980–84; Visiting Research Fellow Arbetslivscentrum, Stockholm 1984–85, 1991–92; Visiting Researcher of Sociol., Univ. of New England, Armidale, Australia; Visiting Prof., Inst. for Canadian Studies, Univ. of Augsburg, West Germany 1987, 1991; recipient Ont. Grad. Fellowship 1972–73; Can. Council Fellowship 1973–75; Social Sci's & Humanities Research. Grants 1977–78, 1982–83, 1984–85, 1987–89, 1990–93, 1993–96; el. Fellow, Royal Soc. of Can. 1991; mem. ed. bd., Studies in Political Economy, Journal of Canadian Studies, Australian-Canadian Studies; SSHRCC Leave Fellowship 1984–85; Exec., Studies in Pol. Econ. of Can.; author 'The Canadian Corporate Elite: An Analysis of Economic Power' 1975; 'Continental Corporate Power: Economic Elite Linkages Between Canada and the United States' 1977; 'Hardrock Mining: Industrial Relations and Technological Change at INCO' 1981; 'Class, Power and Property: Essays on Canadian Society' 1983; 'The Struggle to Organize: Resistance in Canada's Fisheries' 1986; 'The Challenge of Class Analysis' 1988; co-author: (with John Myles) 'Relations of Ruling' 1994 over 50 articles jours. and collections essays; ed. (with D. Drache) 'The New Practical Guide to Canadian Political Economy' 1985; ed. (with G. Williams) 'The New Canadian Political Economy' 1989; recreation: tennis; Home: 1344 South Keys Pl., Ottawa, Ont. K1V 7K2.

**CLEMENTS, Hon. Gilbert R.;** politician; b. Victoria Cross, P.E.I. 11 Sept. 1928; s. Robert and Ruth C.; e. Montague Memorial School; Mount Allison; m. Wilma Catherine MacLure 8 July 1953; children: Robert, David, Gail; MINISTER OF FINANCE AND MINISTER OF THE ENVIRONMENT, GOVT. OF PRINCE EDWARD ISLAND; first elected 1970; Minister of Municipal Affairs, Environment & Tourism, Parks & Conservation 1974–78; Opposition Critic for Finance and Energy 1979–86; Min. of Finance & Min. of Community and Cultural Affairs 1986–89; Min. of Finance & Min. of the Environment 1989– ; Mem., Hillcrest United Church; Home: 30 Riverside Dr., Montague, P.E.I. C0A 1R0; Office: P.O. Box 2000, Charlottetown, P.E.I. C1A 7N8.

**CLEMENTS, John Banks,** Q.C., B.A., LL.B.; barrister and solicitor; b. Winnipeg, Man. 23 Oct. 1925; s. late Garfield Leroy and late Florrie Ada (McKinnon) C.; e. Univ. Sch. Pasadena, Calif.; Univ. of Man. B.A. 1948; Osgoode Hall Law Sch. 1952; m. Mary Louise d. late George E. Edmonds, Q.C. 31 Jan. 1959; children: Anne Elizabeth, John Edmonds; COUNSEL, LANG MICHENER 1993– ; Dir. Chesebrough-Pond's International Ltd.; John B. Clements Ltd.; Wynn's Canada Ltd.; called to Bar of Ont. 1952; cr. Q.C. 1964; joined law firm Lash & Lash (predecessor firm) Toronto 1952; Partner, Lash, Johnston 1959–86; Partner, Lang Michener 1986–93; served with RCNVR 1945; Hon. Mem., Bd. Mang. Ont. Div., Candn. Nat. Inst. for Blind; mem. Congregational Bd., Timothy Eaton Meml. Church; mem. Candn. Bar Assn.; Co. York Bar Assn.; Law Soc. Upper Can.; Zeta Psi; United Church; recreations: tennis, music, gardening; Clubs: R.C.Y.C.; National; Granite; Home: 265 Inglewood Dr., Toronto, Ont. M4T 1J2; Office: P.O. Box 747, Ste. 2500, BCE Place, 181 Bay St., Toronto, Ont. M5J 2T7.

**CLEMMENS, Robert T.,** B.Comm., M.B.A., A.I.C.B.; banking executive; b. Toronto, Ont. 31 Aug. 1952; s. Robert G. and Doloris V. C.; e. Laurentian Univ. B.Comm. 1975; York Univ. M.B.A. 1978; m. Donna A. d. George and Christine Burski 7 May 1977; children: Catherine Michelle, Robert David; EXTVE. VICE-PRES., COMMERCIAL BANKING DIV., BARCLAYS BANK OF CANADA 1989– ; progressively sr. positions following mngt. devel. program, Candn. Imperial Bank of Commerce 1975–81; Asst. Mgr. then Mgr., Commercial Accounts, present bank 1981; Deputy Mgr., Toronto Br. 1982; Vice-Pres., Credit 1983; Gen. Mgr.'s Asst. (London, U.K.) 1986; Sr. Vice-Pres. & Chief Lending Offr. 1987; Office: 304 Bay St., Box 1, Toronto, Ont. M5H 2P2.

**CLEMMER, James Murray;** management consulting executive; b. Kitchener, Ont. 26 Feb. 1956; s. Abner and Elsie (Weber) C.; e. Listowel Dist. S.S.; m. Heather d. Doug and Thelma Gray 10 Sept. 1977; children: Christopher, Jennifer, Vanessa; FOUNDER & PRESIDENT, THE CLEMMER GROUP 1994– ; Sales Rep., Supvr., Dist. Mgr., Sales Trainer then Gen. Mgr., Culligan Water Conditioning 1974–80; Co-Founder, The Achieve Group 1981–93; Dir., Market Devel., Achieve Enterprises 1981; Vice-Pres., Mktg. 1982; Vice-Pres., East. Region 1983; Extve. Vice-Pres. 1984; giver of keynote addresses to num. assn. conventions & univs.; appearances on num. TV & radio progs. & often quoted by Candn. and Am. bus. press; co-author 'The V.I.P. Strategy' (1988 nat. bestseller); author 'Firing On All Cylinders' (Candn. & U.S. bestseller); columnist, The Globe & Mail; author of numerous articles and three books; recreations: reading, swimming, family, billiards; Address: 476 Mill Park Dr., Kitchener, Ont. N2P 1Z1.

**CLERMONT, Georges C.,** Q.C.; b. Montréal, Qué. 27 Sept. 1936; s. Georges O. and Gabrielle (Grothé) C.; e. Coll. Jean de Brébeuf 1955; Univ. de Montréal LL.B. 1961; m. Marie; children: Georges R., Anne-Marie, Jean-François; GROUP VICE PRES., CANADA POST CORP.; read law with Duranleau, Dupré & Duranleau; called to Bar of Que. 1962; law practice Stewart, Crépeault & McKenna until 1968; joined Legal Dept. Bell Canada Montreal as Solr. becoming Asst. Gen. Counsel 1974; Vice Pres., Admin., CIP Inc. 1975; Vice Pres., Diversified Businesses, CIP Inc. 1980; mem. Québec Bar; Candn. Bar Assn.; R. Catholic; recreations: farming; Clubs: Rideau; Cercle Universitaire; Home: R.R. #1, Dunrobin, Ont. K0A 1T0; Office: Sir Alex Campbell Bldg., Ottawa, Ont. K1A 0B1.

**CLERMONT, Yves W.,** B.Sc., Ph.D.; educator; b. Montreal, Que. 14 Aug. 1926; s. Rodolphe and Fernande (Primeau) C.; e. Mont-Saint-Louis (Montreal) 1945; Univ. of Montreal B.Sc. 1949; McGill Univ. Ph.D. 1953; m. Madeleine d. Albert Bonneau 30 June 1950; children: Suzanne, Martin, Stéphane; PROF. OF ANATOMY, McGILL UNIV. 1963– ; (and Chrmn. of Dept. 1975–85); Lectr. there 1953, Asst. Prof. 1956, Assoc. Prof. 1960, Prof. 1963; mem. Nat'l Bd Medical Examiners Anatomy Test Comte. (U.S.) 1979–82; mem. Grant Comtes. Med. Research Council Can. 1973–77, 1978–92; mem. Review Group (1972–76) and Adv. Group, 1976–78; Expanded Program of Research in Human Reproduction, World Health Organ. Geneva; Secy. of the Lucian Award Comte. 1980– ; mem. Ford Foundation Adv. Comte. in Reproductive Sciences 1976–79; rec'd Prix Scientifique de la Prov. de Qué. 1963; S.L. Siegler Award Am. Fertility Soc. 1966; J.C.B. Grant Award, Candn. Assoc. of Anatomists 1986; The Van Campenhout Award, Candn. Fertility and Andrology Soc. 1986; The Distinguished Andrologist Award, Am. Andrology Soc. 1988; Osler Teaching Award, Fac. of Med., McGill Univ. 1990; Serono Award, Am. Andrology Soc. 1992; Fellow, Anna Fuller Foundation USA 1954–55, Lalor Foundation USA 1962; author over 135 articles cytology, histology male reproductive organs and other systems; mem. Royal Soc. Can; Am. Assn. Anatomists (Vice Pres. 1970–73); Candn. Assn. Anatomists; R. Catholic; Home: 567 Townshend, St-Lambert, Que. J4R 1M4; Office; 3640 University St., Montreal, Que. H3A 2B2.

**CLEROUX, Richard;** journalist, writer, political commentator; b. Ottawa, Ont. 14 March 1945; s. Camille and Germaine (Lalonde) C.; e. Univ. of Ottawa; m. Arlene d. Kelly and Bea Wortsman 19 Oct. 1986; one s.:

Joel; Reporter, 'Ottawa Journal' 1965; Canadian Press, Ottawa 1967; 'Ottawa Journal' 1968; Quebec Bureau Chief, 'Montreal Gazette' 1969; 'The Globe and Mail' 1971; Montreal Bureau Chief 1974; Winnipeg Bureau Chief 1981; National Affairs Reporter 1985; Ottawa Bureau 1985; left Globe and Mail in 1990 to write books; frequent contributor to radio, TV and magazines; frequent guest lectr.; taught journalism extension program, Concordia Univ.; National Newspaper Award winner 1976; Nat. Magazine Award runner-up 1978; Founding Mem., Centre for Investigative Journalism; Mem., Candn. Assn. of Journalists; Parliamentary Press Gall.; Mr. Cleroux specializes in writing about security and intelligence issues as well as political corruption; author: 'Official Secrets: The Story Behind the Canadian Security Intelligence Service' 1990 (non-fiction); 'Pleins Feux sur les Services Secrets Canadiens' 1993 (non-fiction); Home: 34 Bellwood Ave., Ottawa, Ont. K1S 1S7; Office: Parliamentary Press Gallery, Ottawa, Ont. K1A 0A6.

**CLERY, Val (Reginald Valentine);** writer, editor, broadcaster; b. Dublin, Ireland 26 Jan 1924; s. Claude Valentine and Dora Frances (Reilly) C.; e. St. Andrew's Coll.; Kingstown Grammar Sch.; m. Susan d. Arthur and Nancy Salaman 7 Oct. 1959; children: Emma, Daniel, Louisa; Brit. Army Royal Artillery & Commandos, U.K., N. Africa, Italy, Balkans 1941–47; civil servant, tea & wool wharfinger, tel. opr., writer 1947–54; profl. puppeteer 1954–55; BBC Overseas Serv. 1955–59; Prod., CBC Radio, London 1959–65; Toronto 1965–70 (conceived 'As It Happens' format); Founding Ed., 'Books in Canada' 1971–72; Columnist (Janus), 'Quill & Quire' 1973–83; freelance journalist & author 1971– ; Columnist, 'The Toronto Star' 1984–90; Editor, 'Tableau' 1985–1986; Short Fiction Award, Irish Writing (Dublin) 1947; 'The Observer' (London) 1955; author: 'Promotion & Response' 1971, 'Canada In Colour' 1972, 'Windows' 1978, 'Doors' 1978, 'A Day In The Woods' 1978, 'Seasons of Canada' 1979, 'The Solo Chef' 1981, 'The Haunted Land' 1983 (repub. as 'Ghost Stories of Canada' 1985); 'Buon Gusto' 1987; editor: 'Canada From The Newsstands' 1978; project editor: 'Cities' 1981; co-author: 'Dragons' 1979, 'A Canadian Feast' 1981; co-transl.: 'Eskimo Diary' 1980; recreations: cooking, reading; Home & Office: 40 Huntley St., Apt. 1, Toronto, Ont. M4Y 2L1.

**CLEVER, Geraldine;** executive; b. Grimsby, Ont. 21 Dec. 1930; d. Roy Charles and Frances (Rosenthal) Hicks; e. Central High Sch. of Comm. Toronto 1949; m. Pat s. Klaus and Gertrude Schmidt-Clever 30 Aug. 1956; one s. Justin Patrick Klaus; PRESIDENT AND C.E.O., CANADIAN MANOIR INDUSTRIES LTD. 1977– ; Dir., DMO Industries; Air Heat Supplies; Secy. to Treas. Liggett Drug Co. 1949–1952; Sales Service Rep. CBC-TV 1952–54; TV Time Buyer, Cockfield, Brown Advertising 1954–59; Gen. Mgr. and Vice Pres. Syndicated Film Services Ltd. 1962; Asst. to Pres. present Co. 1968, Pres. 1976, Chrmn. 1978, Pres. & C.E.O. 1991; recreations: archeology, gardening, business; Club: Albany; Home: 7 Beaumont Rd., Toronto, Ont. M4W 1V4; Office: 2 Glengrove Ave. W., Toronto, Ont. M4R 1N4.

**CLEVER, Warren Glenn,** B.A., M.A., Ph.D.; university professor, writer, publisher; b. Champion, Alta. 10 Feb. 1918; s. Martin George and Florence (Anderson) C.; e. Univ. of Ottawa B.A. 1964, M.A. 1966, Ph.D. 1970; m. Elizabeth d. James and Catherine Hall 13 June 1942; children: David (dec.), Christine; ADJUNCT PROF., ENGLISH, UNIV. OF OTTAWA 1986– ; Candn. Army 1936–66 (from private to major), active service UK, Italy, NW Europe 1939–45; Lectr., Univ. of Ottawa 1967–70; Asst. Prof. 1970–72; Assoc. Prof. 1972–82; Prof. 1982–83; Chair, Dept. of English 1972–75; Pres., Tecumseh Press Ltd. 1972– ; Vice-Pres., Borealis Press Ltd. 1971– ; Dir., Candn. Writers Found. 1974; Vice-Pres. 1976– ; recipient Ont. & Canada Council grants; evaluator for SSHRCC; Rep. British Univ. Summer Schools 1977–83; Founder, Grad. Scholarship in Candn. Lit., English, Univ. of Ottawa; Past Mem., Am. Soc. 18th-Century Studies; Assn. Can. Univ. Teachers of English; Assn. Can. & Que. Lit.; Mem., Am. Assn. of Can. Studies; Gen. Ed., U. Ottawa Short Story Series 1971–83; Co-ord., Symposium Series 1972–83; Co-ed. 'J. of Can. Poetry' 1976–85; books: 'On E.J. Pratt'; editor: 'Selected Short Stories of Duncan Campbell Scott' 1972, 'Selected Poetry of Duncan Campbell Scott' 1974, 'E.J. Pratt,' 'Charles G.D. Roberts,' 'Hugh & Ion,' 5 volumes of poetry, 4 children's books, papers on Pope, Blackmore, Pepys, Canadian literature, children's literature, Callaghan, Leacock, Layton, Lampman, Pratt, Scott, Edwin Muir, and others; recreations: reading, travel, writing, gardening; Office: Ottawa, Ont. K1N 6N5.

**CLIFF, Ronald Laird,** C.M., B.Comm., C.A. (1954); company executive; b. Vancouver, B.C. 13 March 1929; s. Ronald Lorraine and Anna Georgina (Laird) C.; e. St. George's Sch., Vancouver, B.C. (Sr. Matric. 1946); Univ. of B.C., B.Comm. 1949; m. Ardelle F. Clark, Vancouver, B.C. (1983); children: Mrs. Diana Maughan, Mrs. Leslie Tindle, Mrs. Sheila Sharp, Ronald Laird Jr.; CHRMN., BC GAS INC.; CHRMN., SOUTHAM INC.; Chrmn., Trans Mountain Pipe Line Company Ltd.; Dir., Canfor Corp.; Royal Bank of Canada; mem., Inst. of Chartered Accountants of B.C.; Trustee, Lester B. Pearson Coll. of the Pacific; Olympic Trust of Can.; Gov., Canada's Sports Hall of Fame; mem., Adv. Counc. to Fac. of Comm. and Business Admin., Univ. of B.C.; Anglican; recreations: golf, yachting; Clubs: Capilano Golf; Shaughnessy Golf; Eldorado Golf; Thunderbird Golf; Vancouver; Royal Vancouver Yacht; Office: Ste. 3134, 1055 Dunsmuir St., Box 49273, Bentall Centre, Vancouver, B.C. V7X 1L3.

**CLIFFORD, Betsy;** ski champion; b. Ottawa, Ont. 15 Oct. 1953; d. John F. and Margaret Isabel (Phillips) C.; e. Chelsea (Que.) Prot. Sch.; Notre-Dame de Lourdes, Ottawa; Hull (Que.) High Sch.; Philemon Wright High Sch., Hull, Que.; m. Dale Harvey Higgins of Wakefield, Que. May 5, 1984; four children: Blake, Carly Anne, Jolene Marie, Roseanne Margaret; won Gold Medal in Giant Slalom, Val Gardena, Italy in World Championships 1969–70; nominated to Can.'s Sports Hall of Fame; on Candn. Nat. Ski Team for 8 yrs. (selected when 14 yrs. old); placed 2nd. in World Cup Slalom event at Badgastein, Austria and at Grindlewald, Switzerland 1969–70; won world cup slaloms at Val d'Isère, France and Schruns, Austria 1970–71; tied for first place overall world cup slalom 1971; then injured; rejoined Can. World Cup team 1973 after winning 1973 CAN-AM circuit (1st Candn.); won silver medal in Downhill, St. Moritz, Switzerland in World Championships 1973–74; nominated to Amer. Nat. Ski Hall of Fame, 1978; Candn. Ski Museum Honor Roll (Candn. Ski Hall of Fame) 1982; Greater Ottawa Sports Hall of Fame 1983; Address: Alcove, Que. J0X 1A0.

**CLIFFORD, R. James,** B.A., C.I.R., M.B.A.; entrepreneur; b. London, Ont. 7 Sept. 1935; s. Chester Barr and Laurene Gertrude (Henderson) C.; e. Queen's Univ. B.A. 1957, grad. cert. in indus. relations 1958; Simon Fraser Univ. M.B.A. 1973; m. Judith d. Ida and Ed Dekinder 16 Dec. 1988; one s. Robert James; DIRECTOR & OWNER, THE CLIFFORD GROUP LTD., INDUSTRIAL RELATIONS PRODUCTS LTD. 1973– ; and 300843 B.C. LTD. 1989– ; Personnel & Labour Relations, Ford Motor Co. 1959–65; Internat. Personnel Mgr., Polymer Corp. 1965–69; Director Personnel, Placer Devel. 1969–73; Mgr. Personnel, Alcan Aluminum 1973–76; Vice-Pres., Employers Council of B.C. 1976–80; Past Dir., Employment & Immigration Adv. Council; Occupational Training Council of B.C.; Fed./Prov. Manpower Need Ctte.; Skeen Manpower Devel. Ctte.; B.C. Minor Baseball Assn.; Alcohol & Drug Dependency Society, Interlock Project; author of several articles, handbooks, book chapters and presentations; recreations: golf, fishing, baseball, woodworking; clubs: Hazelmere Golf, Vancouver; Semiahmoo Golf; Home: 501 – 15025 Victoria Ave., White Rock, B.C. V4B 1G2; Office: Suite 1810 Oceanic Plaza, 1066 W. Hastings St., Vancouver, B.C. V6E 3X1.

**CLIFT, Dominique,** B.A.; writer; b. Montreal, Que. 9 Oct. 1929; s. John Percival and Berthe (Geoffrion) C.; e. D'Arcy McGee H.S.; McGill Univ., B.A. 1954; m. Pauline Guetta; children: Nicolas, Valerie, Isabel; journalism: CBC Internat. Serv. 1954–60; Toronto Globe and Mail 1960–62; La Presse 1962–65; Toronto Star 1965–70; Montreal Star 1970–77; Lectr. in Communications, Laval Univ. 1968, 1969; author: 'Quebec Nationalism in Crisis' 1982, 'The Secret Kingdom, Interpretations of the Canadian Character' 1989 (non-fiction); co-author (with S.M. Arnopoulos): 'The English Fact in Quebec' 1979; Home: 53 Waverley, Pointe Claire, Que. H9S 4W7.

**CLIFTON, John Terrence,** R.C.A., A.O.C.A.; industrial designer; b. Peterborough, Ont. 26 July 1933; s. late Maj. Harry Kelsey and Edna Menzie (Allin) C.; e. Ont. Coll. of Art Toronto grad. 1957 AOCA; m. Elizabeth Jane Leeson d. late Henry N. Blakeney 22 Oct. 1960; children: Scott Andrew, Leeson Alexandra, Christopher Kelsey; VICE PRES., ADVANCED MOBILITY SYSTEMS CORP., Kingston; rec'd Nat. Design Council Awards; Prof. Assn. Design Awards; Design Award Man. Design Inst.; Phi Kappa Pi; private pilot; P. Conservative; Protestant; recreations: flying, fishing, aviation history; Office: 621 Justus Dr., Kingston, Ont. K7M 4H5.

**CLIMENHAGA, John Leroy,** Ph.D.; university professor; b. Delisle, Sask. 7 Nov. 1916; s. Reuben S. and Elizabeth B. (Bert) C.; e. Univ. of Sask., B.A. (Hons.) 1945, M.A. 1949; Univ. of Michigan, Ph.D. 1960; m. M.E. Grace d. Charles and Margaret Garratt 29 Sept. 1943; children: Joan M., David J.; EMERITUS PROF. OF ASTRONOMY, UNIV. OF VICTORIA 1982– ; Physics Instr., Regina Coll. 1946–48; Instr., Asst. Prof., Assoc. Prof., Prof., Univ. of Victoria 1949–82; Head, Physics Dept. 1956–69; Dean, Faculty of Arts & Science 1969–72; Mem., Am. Astron. Soc.; Astron. Soc. of the Pacific; Royal Astron. Soc. of Can.; Internat. Astron. Union (mem., Nat. Ctte. for Can. 1967–71); Nat. Rsch. Counc. Scholarship Ctte. 1969–72; NRC Radio & Elect. Engr. Div. Adv. Bd. 1971–74; Univ. of Victoria observatory named 'Climenhaga Observatory' 1982; Internat. Astron. Union named a minor planet 'Minor Planet Climenhaga' 1986; Protestant; Mem., Candn. Bible Soc. (Pres., Victoria Br. 1986–89); author of papers in sci. journals; recreations: golf, photography; Home: 2450 Sutton Rd., Victoria, B.C. V8N 1J2; Office: Univ. of Victoria, Dept. of Physics & Astronomy, Victoria, B.C. V8W 3P6.

**CLIMO, Lindee;** artist; b. Norwood, Mass. 24 May 1948; d. Hal T. and Dorothy M. (McElroy) Lawrence; e. Univ. of Arizona; Calif. State Univ. at Chico; Chapman Coll. World Campus Afloat; naturalized Candn. citizen, living in Canada since 1970; studied to do medical illustration; bred & exhibited livestock from 1960 until beginning to paint in 1974; work generally depicts livestock or wild animals, oil on canvas and sculpture; author & illustrator: 'Chester's Barn' 1982, 'Clyde' 1986; both nominated for Amelia Francis Howard Gibbon Awards, Candn. Library Assn. 'Chester's Barn' received the award in 1983; recreations: apple orchard & animal husbandry; Home: Annapolis Valley, N.S.

**CLINKARD, John James,** M.A.; economist; banker; b. Toronto, Ont. 12 June 1944; s. James Thomas and Norah Dinah (McKeag) C.; e. Deer Park Pub. Sch. and Lawrence Park Coll. Inst. 1959; Univ. of Waterloo Renison Coll. B.A. (Hon. Economics) 1971; York Univ. M.A. 1976; m. Eleanor P. d. C.W. and Tina Seale 27 Nov. 1982; children: David James, Paul Wilson, Anne Sophia; SR. ECON. CANDN. IMPERIAL BANK OF COMMERCE 1987– ; Regional Econ. Bell Canada 1973–76; Econ. present Bank 1976, Mgr. Econ. Forecasting & Stats. 1979–86; Econ. Adv. Clayton Research Associates 1976–85; author/editor numerous C.I.B.C. publications relating to economics; frequent speaker and commentator current econ. affairs; mem. Nat. Accts. User Adv. Ctte. Stats. Can.; mem. Toronto Assn. Bus. Econ. (Past Pres. 1979–80); Bd. Trade Metrop. Toronto (Econ. Policy Ctte., Municipal Finance Ctte.); Candn. Econ. Assn.; Am. Econ. Assn.; Pres. & Dir., N. York Hts. Ratepayers Assn.; Anglican; recreations: woodworking, aerobics, skiing; Club: Toronto Athletic; Home: 15 Brooke Ave., Toronto, Ont. M5M 2J5; Office: 51F Commerce Court West, Toronto, Ont. M5L 1A2.

**CLINTON, John M.,** B.A.; advertising executive; b. Vancouver, B.C. 31 Oct. 1956; e. Queen's Univ. B.A. 1977; PRESIDENT, ENTERPRISE ADVERTISING ASSOC. LTD. 1990– ; Account Director / Management Director / Vice-Pres. & Mngt. Dir. / Vice-pres. & Dir. of Client Services, JWT 1979–90; Queen's Univ. ICBC Judge; Office: 1140 Bay St., Toronto, Ont. M5S 2Z6.

**CLISSOLD, Jack Gordon,** B.A., M.B.A.; automotive executive; b. Toronto, Ont. 30 Aug. 1939; s. Harold Arthur and Mabel (Williamson) C.; e. Univ. of Toronto, B.A. 1962; York Univ., M.B.A. 1975; m. Carol Lee d. William and Audrey Mortimer 30 June 1962; children: Paul Gregory, Peter Geoffrey, Bradley Gavin; EXTVE. VICE PRES., FORD MOTOR CREDIT CO.; joined Ford Motor Co. in 1962 as Field Mgr.; Mktg. Mgr. 1968; Asst. Regional Mgr. 1971; Regional Mgr. 1975; Gen. Mktg. Mgr. 1980; Light Truck Sales Mgr., Ford Motor Co., Detroit 1984; Vice-Pres., Sales & Mktg., Ford Motor Co. of Can. Ltd. 1986; mem. Bus. Adv. Counc., McMaster Univ.; Mktg. Ctte., Toronto Skydome Corp.; Pres. Emeritus, Counc. of Mktg. Execs., Conf. Bd. of Can.; Clubs: Burlington Golf & Country; Sawgrass Country, Ponte Vedra, Fla.; Office: The American Rd., Dearborn, MI 48121.

**CLODMAN, Sara,** B.A., M.B.A.; insurance industry executive; b. Toronto, Ont. d. Kassy and Reba (Buckstein) C.; e. Univ. of Toronto B.A. (Hons.) 1979; York Univ. M.B.A. 1988; m. Joseph Jonatan 14 Dec. 1985; ASST. VICE-PRES., PUBLIC RELATIONS & COMMUNICATIONS, SUN LIFE ASSURANCE CO. OF CANADA 1993– ; Extve. Asst. to Extve. Alderman, Anne Johnston 1978–80; Pres., Sara Clodman Cons. 1981–82; Special Advr. to Hon. David Peterson 1982–

85; Mgr., Govt. Relations, Sun Life Assur. Co. of Can. 1985–87; Dir., Govt. & Indus. Relations 1987–88; Asst. Vice-Pres., Corp. Affairs 1988–90; seconded to Candn. Life & Health Insur. Assn. as Vice-Pres., Govt. Affairs 1991–93; City Council appointee, Toronto Ctte. of Adjustment 1983– , Vice-Chair 1992– ; Vice-Chrmn., Legis. Ctte., Bd. of Trade of Metro. Toronto; Dir., The National Ballet Sch.; Mem., Mensa Soc. 1982– ; club: Wellington; Office: 12th flr., 225 King St. W., Toronto, Ont. M5V 3C5.

**CLOTHIER, Robert Allan,** D.F.C.; actor; sculptor; b. Prince Rupert, B.C. 22 Oct. 1921; s. Robert LeRoy and Patty Margaret (Harding) C.; e. Vernon (B.C.) Prep. Sch.; St. Georges Sch. Vancouver 1940; Univ. of B.C. 2 yrs. Arch.; studied Theatre in Eng. 1948; Royal Acad. Dramatic Arts, London 1949; Central Sch. of Arts, Sculpture 1953; studied Sculpture under Robert Adams, London 1953; m. Shirley Broderick (actress); d. William and Gladys Broderick 29 Oct. 1957; children: John George, Jessica Anne; joined RCAF 1940, Bomber Pilot 1941–44, comnd. 1942, invalided out as result of crash 1944, awarded D.F.C. 1943; profl. actor Rep. & Touring Co's Eng. 1950–54; actor, sculptor Can. 1954– ; starred as 'Relic' CBC 'The Beachcombers' 1971– ; recipient Sculpture Purchase Prize Univ. of B.C. 1956; ACTRA Award (Nellie) Best Actor Series 1977; Gemini Award Best Actor Series 1986; Life mem. ACTRA; mem. Candn. Actors' Equity; mem. Sculptor's Soc. of Can.; recreations: skiing, swimming, design & mfr. furniture, pewter ware; Address: 1395 Ridgewood Dr., North Vancouver, B.C. V7R 1J4.

**CLOUSTON, Robert Allan Ross,** B.Sc., M.B.A.; business executive; b. Montreal, Que. 1 Nov. 1945; s. Ross Neal and Brenda Elizabeth (Kerson) C.; e. McGill Univ. B.Sc. 1968; Univ. of Western Ont. M.B.A. 1972; m. Geraldine d. George and Norberta Dunlap 22 Aug. 1970; children: Shannon, Matthew, Allison, Christian; PRESIDENT AND GENERAL MANAGER, WARNER-LAMBERT CANADA INC. 1992– ; various product management & advertising positions, General Foods, McCann-Erickson Canada 1972–75; Product Mgr., Listerine, Warner Lambert Can. 1975; progressively higher positions at head office in New Jersey 1976–86; Vice-Pres., Mktg. of Confections 1986; Bd. Mem., Non-Prescription Drug Mfrs. of Can.; one of '100 Best and Brightest Young Clients in Advertising in US,' Ad Age mag. 1986; Adv. Council Mem., Queen's Univ. Sch. of Bus.; recreations: skiing, tae kwon do; clubs: Canadian Ski Instructors Alliance; Office: 2200 Eglinton Ave. E., Scarborough, Ont. M1L 2N3.

**CLOUTIER, Cécile,** B.A., L.ès L., D.E.S., M.A., M.Ph., M.Th., D.U.P., D.Ps.; professor; writer; b. Québec, Qué. 13 June 1930; d. Adrien and Maria (de Lantagne) C.; e. Coll. de Sillery; B.A. 1951; Univ. Laval, L.ès L. 1953, Diplôme d'Études Supérieures 1954; Univ. de Paris Doctorat en Esthétique 1962; McMaster Univ., M.A. (Philo.) 1978; Univ. of Toronto, M.A. (Theol.) 1981; Univ. de Tours, Doctorat en Psychologie 1983; m. Jerzy s. Roman and Antonina Wojciechowski 26 Dec. 1966; two d. Marie-Bérénice, Ève-Moïra; PROFESSEUR D'ESTHÉTIQUE ET DE LITTÉRATURE FRANÇAISE ET QUÉBÉCOISE, DÉPARTEMENT D'ÉTUDES FRANÇAISES, UNIV. OF TORONTO 1964– ; Professeur de grec, de latin et de Littérature française à Québec 1953–58; Professeur de Littérature française et québécoise, Univ. d'Ottawa 1958–64; recipient Gov. Gen.'s Award Poetry 1986; La Société des Écrivains de France Silver Medal 1960; Centennial Medal 1967; Rsch. Award Univ. Toronto 1987; Founder & Dir. Centre de Recherche en Poésie québécoise Univ. Toronto 1985; Visiting Prof. Queen's Univ. 1981; Founder, La Société canadienne d'Esthétique; Vice Prés. de L'Association des Docteurs des Universités de France; author 'Mains de sable' 1960; 'Cuivre et soies' 1964; 'Cannelles et craies' 1969; 'Paupières' 1970; 'Câblogrammes' 1972; 'Chaleuils' 1979; 'Près' 1983; 'La Girafe' (conte) 1984; 'L'Échangeur' (poèmes) 1985; 'L'Écouté' 1986; 'Lampées' 1990; 'Périhélie' 1990; 'Ancres d'Encre' 1993; co-author 'Opuscula Aesthetica Nostra' (essais) 1984; 'Solitude Rompue' 1986; poèmes traduits: 'Springtime of Spoken Words' 1979; anthologie de poésie québécoise contemporaine en traduction ukrainienne 1968; mem. PEN Club de France; La Société des gens de lettres de Paris; L'Association des écrivains de langue française; L'Union des écrivains québécois; La Société des écrivains; recreation: lecture; Home: 44 Farm Greenway, Don Mills, Ont. M3A 3M2; Office: 7 King's College Circle, Toronto, Ont. M5S 1A1.

**CLOUTIER, Edward,** B.A., B.Ed.; computer executive; b. Sault Ste. Marie, Ont. 13 June 1956; s. Edward Joseph and Eunice Margaret (Miles) C.; e. St. Mary's College Hons. Matric. 1975; Univ. of Waterloo B.A. (Hons.) 1979; Althouse Coll., Univ. of W. Ont. B.Ed. 1980; m. Lynn d. Murray and Pat Hayes 31 May 1980; children: Matthew, Andrew; DIRECTOR OF OPERATIONS FOR CANADA AND LATIN AMERICA, BANYAN SYSTEMS INC. 1993– ; Information Systems, Royal Insur. 1982–84; C-I-L Inc. 1984–86; joined Banyan Systems 1986 to establish Candn. operation; District Mgr. 1989; Country Mgr. 1992; Banyan's 'President's Club' of Top Achievers 5 times and 'District Mgr. of Year' 1991; Roman Catholic; Home: 3623 Loyalist Dr., Mississauga, Ont. L5L 4T9; Office: 2695 N. Sheridan Way, Ste. 160, Mississauga, Ont. L5K 2N6.

**CLOUTIER, Hon. François,** B.A., M.D., F.R.C.P.(C), F.A.P.A.; psychiatrist, psychoanalyst; b. Quebec, Que. 4 Apr. 1922; s. Jean Baptiste and Anna Marie (Tousignant) C.; e. Laval Univ., B.A., M.D. (with high hons.); Dipl. in Ethnology, Musée de l'Homme, Paris; m. late Solange Hollinger, M.A., M.D., 1953; two d. Sophie, Nathalie; m. secondly Hélène Daigneault; after grad. went to Europe (France) to specialize in psychiatry and was made Asst. in Neurol. and Psychiatry of Faculty of Med. of Paris; returned to Can. and began practice, becoming Chief of the Psychiatric Dept. at Notre-Dame Hosp. and a Sr. Consultant at Queen Mary Veterans' Hosp., Montreal; Dir. Gen., World Fed. for Mental Health (1962–66) (London and Geneva); el. to Que. Nat. Assembly for Ahunsic in g.e. April 1970; apptd. Min. of Cultural Affairs, 1970; Min. of Educ. 1972–76; Min. Intergovt. Affairs 1976; Delegate gen. of Que. Govt. in France 1976; resigned on advent of P.Q. to power; resumed med. career in France and became Chief of Dept., Psychosomatic Med., Inst. psychiatrique Larochefoucauld, Paris; retired 1990; began a new career as a sculptor; Publications incl. 'Un psychiatre vous parle' 1954; 'L'homme et son milieu' 1958, 'La Santé Mentale' 1966; 'Le Mariage Réussi' 1967; about 25 scient. papers; and a book of political memoirs: 'L'Enjeu' 1977; Liberal; R. Catholic; recreation: horseback riding; Address: 9 Rue Perronet 75007 Paris, France.

**CLOUTIER, Gilles G.,** C.C., B.A., B.Sc.A., M.Sc., Ph.D, D. Sc. (hon.), F.R.S.C..; physicist; b. Quebec City, Que., 27 June 1928; e. Univ. Laval, B.A. 1949, B.Sc.A (Physics) 1953; McGill Univ., M.Sc. (Physics) 1956, Ph.D. (Physics) 1959; Honorary Doctorates: Univ. de Montréal 1982, Univ. of Alta. 1983, McGill Univ. 1986, Univ. de Lyon II, France 1987, Univ. of Toronto 1991; m. Colette Michaud; children: Hélène, Suzanne, Pierre, Benoît, Nathalie; CONSULTANT; Sr. Scient., RCA Victor Co. Rsch. Labs 1959; Prof. of Physics, Univ. de Montréal 1963–1968; Hydro-Québec Inst. of Research 1968–78 as Scient. Dir., Basic Sciences Lab., Dir. of Rsch., Asst. Dir. of Inst.; Pres. Alta. Rsch. Council 1978–83; Extve. Vice-Pres, Technol. & Internat. Affairs, Hydro-Québec 1983–85; Rector, Univ. de Montreal 1985–93; Fellow, Royal Soc. of Can. 1976; Officer, Order of Canada 1981, Companion 1994; Order of Québec 1989; Chevalier de la Légion d'Honneur 1991; mem., Candn. Assn. Physicists (Pres. 1971–72); Am. Phys. Soc.; Inst. Elect. & Electronics Engrs.; Order of Engrs. of the Province of Québec; mem., National Research Council 1973–76; Bd. mem., Université de Montréal 1976–80 and 1983–85; Pres., Conf. of Rectors and Principals of Que. Univs. 1987–89; Mem., Bd. of Assoc., Univs. & Colls. of Can. 1986–89; Corporate-Higher Educ. Forum 1987–93, Chrmn. 1992; Vice Pres., Assoc. des Universités partiellement ou entièrement de langue française (AUPELF) 1987–90; Bd. Mem., Chamber of Comm., Greater Montreal 1989–93; Mem., Bd. of Trustees, Manning Awards 1989– ; Mem. Bd. of Dirs., Centre d'initiative technologique de Montréal (CITEC) 1985–93; Asia Pacific Found. of Canada 1990– ; Bechtel Canada; Gentec Inc.; Home: 4500 Promenade Paton, Apt. 1208, Laval, Que. H7W 4Y6; Office: 2910 Boul. Edouard-Montpetit, Bureau 6, Montréal, Que. H3C 3J7.

**CLOUTIER, Robert,** B.Sc.E.E., B.Sc.Adm.E.; engineer; b. Trois Rivières, Que. 7 Jan. 1938; s. Charles-Auguste and Hilda (Nobert) C.; e. Tri-State Univ. (Angola, Ind.) B.Sc.E.E. 1961, B.Sc.Adm.E. 1962; m. Carmen d. Lucien and Yvonne Lampron 11 Sept. 1961; children: Robert Jr., Diane; SR. VICE PRES., ASST. TO THE PRES., PIRELLI CABLES INC. 1988– ; Engr. in training and Distbn. Engr. Shawinigan Water and Power 1962–63; Sales Engr. A.B. Chance Co. of Can. 1963–66, Regional Sales Mgr. 1966–71; Regional Sales Mgr. present co. 1971, Asst. Mktg. Mgr. 1971–78, Mgr. High Voltage Cable Systems 1978–83, Mktg. Mgr. 1983–84; Vice Pres., Gen. Mgr. & Dir. 1984–87; mem., Montreal Bd. of Trade; Chambers of Comm. of Que. & Can.; Chambre de Comm. Italienne; Conf. Bd. of Can.; Egypt-Can. Business Coun.; Electrical Club of Toronto; Electrical and Electronic Mfrs. Assoc. of Can.; Candn. Mfrs. Assoc.; A.M.E.E.E.Q.; Candn. Electrical Assoc.; Power Engr. Soc.; I.E.E.E.; Candn. Pulp and Paper Assn.; Candn. Inst. of Mining and Metallurgy; Candn. Copper and Brass Devel. Assn.; Ind. Mktg. Rsch. Assn. of Can.; Club d'Electricité de Montréal; Comml. Travellers Assn.; Arab-Canada Business Counc.; Candn. Standards Assn.; recreation: gardening and reading; Club: St-Denis, Montreal; Home: 754 Thibault, Ste. Therese, Que. J7E 4B8; Office: 425 St-Louis, St. Jean-sur-Richelieu, Que. J3B 1Y6.

**CLOUTIER, Robert P.,** B.Ed.; business executive; b. Ottawa, Ont. 19 July 1951; s. Leopold and Gabrielle (Bergevin) C.; e. St. Jean-sur-Richilieu Coll., Dec.Soc.Sci. 1971; Sherbrooke Univ., B.Ed. 1974; children: Mylene, Jean-François, David; PRES. & CHIEF EXTVE. OFFR., GESTION MONTEMURRO 1986– ; Gen. Mgr., Pembroke Food Liner 1974–77; Dir., Retail Opns., M. Loeb 1977–80; Devel. Hudon-Deaudelin 1980–82; Vice-Pres., Mktg. Metro-Richelieu 1982–86; Pres. & Chrmn., Delicana; Pres. CCGD (Quebec); Mem., Reg. Cons. Ctte., Nat. Bank; recreations: skiing, golf; Home: 11 Helene, Rouyn-Noranda, Qué. J9X 6E8; Office: 333 Montemurro Ave., Rouyn-Noranda, Qué. J9X 5E1.

**CLUETT, Frank,** B.A., M.A., M.Div.; theological college principal; b. Belleoram, Nfld. 6 Apr. 1934; s. Abner M. and Tryphena M. (Harding) C.; e. Belleoram H.S.; Queen's Coll., St. John's, Nfld. L.Th. 1959; Mem. Univ. of Nfld., B.A. 1968; McMaster Univ. M.A. 1971; Univ. of Toronto 1983, 1984; m. Matilda d. Eliol and Rosanna Combden 5 July 1962; one s.: Frank Donald; PROVOST, QUEEN'S COLL. 1979– ; employee, Candn. Imperial Bank of Comm. 1950–55; Rector, Anglican Parish of Greenspond, Nfld. 1959–65; Parish of Buchans, Nfld. 1965–68; Asst., Church of the Ascension, Hamilton, Ont. 1969–71; Assoc. Priest, The Parish of Corner Brook, Nfld. 1971–79; Chrmn., Anglican Sch. Bds. of Greenspond 1959–65; of Indian Bay 1960–64; Amalgamated Sch. Bd. of Buchans 1066–68; Teacher, evening course, Mem. Univ. in Corner Brook 1972–75 and summer session, St. John's 1980–85; Sec., Church Comn. on 'Future Role of Queen's Coll.' 1979–82; Mem., var. cttes. The Diocese of W. Nfld. 1976–79; The Diocese of E. Nfld. & Labrador 1980–88; Assoc. Ed. 'The Newfoundland Churchman' 1976–79; apptd. Canon, The Newfoundland Cathedral 1990; recreations: walking, swimming, coin and stamp collecting; Home: 7 Portland Pl., St. John's, Nfld. A1E 5P2; Office: Queen's College, St. John's, Nfld. A1B 3R6.

**CLUTE, Kenneth Fleury,** B.A., M.D., F.R.C.P.(C); paediatrician; b. Toronto, Ont. 19 Dec. 1918; s. Arthur Roger, Q.C. and Laurine Adele (Fleury) C.; e. Univ. of Toronto Schs., grad. 1936; Univ. of Toronto, B.A. in Classics (with 1st Class Hons. and gold medal) 1940; Univ. of Toronto, M.D. (with Hons. and gold medal) 1945; m. Roberta Jessie, d. late George Brodie, Quebec, P.Q., 24 Sept. 1955; children: Alistair Kenneth, Thomas Brodie, Geoffrey Arthur; PROF. EMERITUS, COMMUNITY HEALTH LAW, DEPT. OF HEALTH ADMIN., FACULTY OF MEDICINE, UNIV. OF TORONTO 1984– ; Jr. Interne, Toronto Gen. Hosp. 1945–46; Fellow in Surg., Hosp. for Sick Children, Toronto 1946–47; Grey Nuns' Hosp., Regina and Regina Gen. Hosp., Res. in Path. 1947–48; Sr. Interne in Paediatrics, Children's Mem. Hosp., Montreal 1948–49; Asst. Res. in Paed. 1949–50; Asst. Psychiatrist in Children's Psych. Clinic, Johns Hopkins Hosp., Baltimore 1950–51; Physician in Med. Care Clinic there and Fellow in Pediatrics, Johns Hopkins Univ. 1951–52; Rsch. Assoc. in Legal Med. and Paed., Univ. of Maryland 1952–53; in private practice of paediatrics, Toronto and mem. of Staff, Hosp. for Sick Children 1953–55; Dir. of Survey of Gen. Practice of Can., Dir. of Field Studies, Dept. of Pub. Health, Sch. of Hygiene, Univ. of Toronto 1956–61; Rsch. Secy., Candn. Assn. for Retarded Children 1962–64; Assoc. Prof. of Med. Care 1962–66 (and Albert G. Milbank Fellow in Law and Pub. Health 1964–68) Dept. of Pub. Health, Sch. of Hygiene, Univ. of Toronto; Prof. of Community Health Law, Dept. of Health Admin., Sch. of Hygiene 1966–74, Fac. of Medicine 1975–84, Univ. of Toronto; author of: 'The General Practitioner: A Study of Medical Education and Practice in Ontario and Nova Scotia' 1963; served during 2nd World War with R.C.A.M.C, 1943–46; mem., Ont. Med. Assn.; Candn. Med. Assn.; Roy. Coll. Phys. & Surg. Can.; Acad. of Med., Toronto; Nu Sigma Nu; Alpha Omega Alpha; Royal Astronomical Soc. of Can.; Anglican; recreations: reading, music, gardening, astronomy, boating; Home: 48 Castle Frank Rd., Toronto, Ont. M4W 2Z6.

**COAMBS, Robert Brian,** B.A., M.A., Ph.D.; scientist; b. Edmonton, Alta. 1 Jan. 1951; s. Robly Vernon and Muriel Flora Joanna (McRae) C.; e. Simon Fraser Univ. B.A. (Hons.) 1977, M.A. 1980; Univ. of Toronto Ph.D.

1987; separated; one d.: Christina Allison; SCIENTIST, ADDICTION RESEARCH FOUNDATION and ASST. PROF., DEPT. OF PREVENTIVE MEDICINE AND BIOSTATISTICS, FACULTY OF MEDICINE, UNIV. OF TORONTO 1992– ; has dedicated most of his training & profl. work to the field of addictions; has contribution to field through clinical work with addicts as well as teaching & rsch.; main rsch. contbns. incl. new animal models of opiate addiction, the effects of the valium group of drugs on cognition & behav. epidemiology of smoking; author of the random-walk model of addiction, a computer-based simulation system which permits the study & prediction of patterns of drug use within populations; teaches undergrad. psych., Univ. of Toronto; Consultant to fed. govt., the Marion Merrell Dow, Syntex, & Upjohn pharm. cos.; num. grad. & post grad. awards relating to academic achievement; has given num. invited addresses & conf. presentations; appears frequently on TV, radio & newspaper interviews; author of several scholarly articles; recreations: jogging, skiing, travel; Home: 30 Charles St. W., Apt. 1917, Toronto, Ont. M4Y 1R5; Office: 33 Russell St., Toronto, Ont. M5S 2S1.

**COBBETT, Stuart H. (Kip),** B.A., B.C.L.; lawyer; b. Montreal, Que. 3 June 1948; s. Stuart Ashton and Adrienne Edythe (Hanson) C.; e. McGill Univ. B.A. 1969, 1972; m. Jill d. Ronald and Mary Rankin 7 Sept. 1973; children: Alexander, William, Anne; COUNSEL, STIKEMAN, ELLIOTT 1992– ; Partner, Heenan Blaikie Mtl. 1974–85; Sr. Vice-Pres. Astral Communications Inc. and Pres., Astral Film Enterprises Inc. 1985–92; Dir., Astral Communications Inc.; Formula Growth Ltd.; McCord Street Sites Inc.; Lectr., Banking & Bills of Exchange, McGill Law Fac. 1976–84; Dir., Bishop's Coll. Sch. (Chair 1988–91); recreations: skiing, golf, tennis; clubs: University Club, Mtl., Mount Bruno Country; Office: Ste. 3900, 1155 boul. René-Lévesque O., Montreal, P.Q. H3B 3V2.

**COBBOLD, Richard Southwell Chevallier,** M.Sc., Ph.D., F.R.S.C.; educator; b. Worcester, Eng. 10 Dec. 1931; s. late Reynold Chevallier and Betty Joyce (Lindner) C.; e. Imp. Coll. of Science & Technol. Univ. of London A.R.C.S., B.Sc. 1956; Univ. of Sask. M.Sc. 1961, Ph.D. 1965; m. Margaret Mary d. late Henry St. Aubyn, Redditch, Eng. Aug. 1963; children: Adrian C., David C., Christopher M.; PROF. INST. OF BIO MED. ENGN., UNIV. OF TORONTO 1970–; Asst. Exper. Offr. Ministry of Supply U.K. 1949–53; Scient. Offr. Defence Research Bd. Can. Ottawa 1956–59; Lectr. to Assoc. Prof. of Elect. Engn. Univ. of Sask. 1960–66; Assoc. Prof. Inst. Biomed. Engn. present Univ. 1966, Prof. 1970, Dir. Inst. Biomed. Engn. 1974–83; co-recipient Premium Award Pub. Papers Inst. Elect. Engrs. 1965; author 'Theory and Application of Field-Effect Transistors' 1970, Russian ed. 1975, Polish ed. 1975; 'Transducers for Biomedical Measurements: Principles and Applications' 1974, Chinese ed. 1984; Ed. Bds.: Ultrasound in Medicine & Biology 1979– ; Journal of Biomedical Engineering 1979– ; Sensors & Actuators 1980– ; Automedica 1983– ; Medical & Biological Engineering & Computing 1987– ; Physiological Measurement 1994– ; book chapters, research papers semiconductor devices and biomed. engn. measurements; mem. Inst. Elect. & Electronic Engrs.; Candn. Med. & Biol. Engn. Soc. (Vice Pres. 1970–74); R. Catholic; recreations: tennis; Club: North Toronto Tennis; Home: 116 Ridley Blvd., Toronto, Ont. M5M 3L9; Office: Toronto, Ont. M5S 1A4.

**COBDEN, Michael,** B.A., B.Ed.; university administrator; journalist; b. Johannesburg, S. Africa 18 March 1940; s. Harry and Sara Marsh (Davidson) C.; e. Kingswood Coll. S. Africa 1957; Univ. of S. Africa B.A. 1972; Univ. of Toronto B.Ed. 1974; m. Jane d. Thomas and Helen Morley 1976; two s. Josh, Joey; DIR. SCH. OF JOURNALISM, UNIV. OF KING'S COLL. 1988– ; Journalist, Rand Daily Mail, Johannesburg and London 1960–68; Toronto Star 1968–74; Whig-Standard, Kingston 1979–88; Southam Fellow Univ. of Toronto 1985–86; Home: 6220 Cedar St., Halifax, N.S. B3H 2J9; Office: Halifax, N.S. B3H 2A1.

**COCHRAN, J.F.,** M.A.Sc., Ph.D.; educator; b. Saskatoon, Sask. 29 Jan. 1930; s. John Alexander and Frances Edith (Latham) C.; e. University of British Columbia, B.A.Sc. (Engn. Physics) 1950; M.A.Sc. (Engn. Physics) 1951; University of Illinois, Ph.D. (Physics & Math.) 1955; m. Pieternella, d. Nicholas Neuteboom, 15 Jan. 1957; children: Stephanie Anne, Alexander John; PROF. OF PHYSICS, SIMON FRASER UNIV. 1965– ; Chrmn. of Dept. 1971–74, Dean of Sci. 1981–85; started as Research Assoc. Physics Dept., Univ. Ill. 1955–56; Asst. Prof., Mass. Inst. Technol. 1957; Prof., Simon Fraser Univ., 1965; Acting Head Dept. Physics present Univ. 1968–69; Chrmn. of Dept. 1971–74; mem. Candn. Assn. Physicists (Past Chrmn. Comte. on Physics & Society, Past Chrmn. and Past Vice-Chrmn. Solid State Div., Past Councillor for B.C. and Yukon); Am. Physical Soc.; Nat. Research Council Physics Grants Selection Comte. 1971–74; awarded NRC Postdoctoral Fellowships 1956–57; Sloan Fellowships 1957–59; Assoc. Ed., Candn. Journ. Physics 1969–73; Co-ed. (with R.R. Haering) 'Solid State Physics': Vol. 1, 'Electrons in Metals' 1968; recreation: squash; Home: 4174 Rose Cres., West Vancouver, B.C. V7V 2N8; Office: Burnaby, B.C. V5A 1S6.

**COCHRANE, Barrymore Donald,** B.Sc., P.Eng.; petroleum executive; b. Creelman, Sask. 10 July 1935; s. Samuel Henry and Rose Ellen (Apps) C.; e. Univ. of Sask. B.C. 1956; m. Patricia d. Lorne and Dorothy Quick 16 Oct. 1982; children: Brent, Lauri, Alix, Matthew, Justin, Sam; stepchildren: Andrea, David, Paula, Frank; PRES. & C.E.O., NORCEN ENERGY RESOURCES LTD. 1991– ; Dir. Progas Ltd.; Exploitation Engr. Great Plains Development 1956–58; Mgr. Banner Petroleum, Trans Canada Pipe Lines Ltd. 1958–73; Canadian Arctic Gas 1973–74; Mgr. W. Operations Northern and Central Gas 1974–76; Mgr. Corporate Planning present co. 1976, Vice Pres. Corp. Planning 1979–82, Sr. Vice Pres. 1982; mem. Candn. Inst. Mining & Metall.; Alta. Assn. Profl. Engrs., Geols. & Geophysicists; recreations: golf, racquet sports; Clubs: Glencoe; Lambton Golf & Country; Earl Grey Golf; Office: 715 – 5th Ave. S.W., Calgary, Alta. T2P 2X7.

**COCHRANE, Rev. Charles Clarke,** B.A., B.D., D.D. (Presb.); b. Belleville, Ont. 30 Nov. 1910; s. William and Margaret (McConaghy) C.; e. Orillia (Ont.) Public Sch. and Coll. Inst.; Queen's Univ., B.A. 1938; Knox Coll., Toronto (Divinity), Dipl. 1939, D.D. 1969; Emmanuel Coll., Toronto, B.D. 1944; m. Isobel Jean, d. late Rev. A.E. Cameron, 25 April 1939; children: Donald Bryden, William Alexander, Douglas Charles; Minister, Presbyterian Tri-Congregations, Toronto, Ont., 1976–79, (ret'd); Min., St. Andrew's, Geraldton, Ont., 1939–41; Knox., Georgetown, Ont., 1941–48; Melville, Westmount, Que., 1948–76; mem. of Senate, Presb. Coll., Montreal, 1949–52; mem. of Bd., 1952–58; Lectr., 1964–66; mem. Bd. Westmount Y.M.C.A., 1950–58; Montreal Council for Social Order, 1952–53, Prot. Hungarian Service Assn., 1957–59, Greater Montreal Council of Chs., 1953–60 (Pres. 1957–60); Moderator, Presbytery of Montreal, 1955 and 1965, and Clerk 1957–58; Pres., Westmount Min. Assn., 1959–60; Advisor, Montreal Christian Youth Council, 1957–60; Sr. Teacher, Relig. Instr., Westmount High Sch., 1952–66; Vice-Pres., North Am. Area Council of World Alliance of Reformed Chs., 1960, Pres. 1965; mem. Bd., Children's Service Centre; Soc. for Protection of Women and Children; Elizabeth House; a trustee of the Fund to Contest the 'Padlock Law'; author: 'Jesus of Nazareth in Word and Deed' 1979; 'The Gospel According to Genesis' 1984; 'Contending With God' 1990; occasional contrib. to relig. journs.; Que. Corr., 'The Christian Century,' Chicago, 1958–66; Address: 300 Regina St. N., Richmond One, Apt. 212, Waterloo, Ont. N2J 3B8.

**COCHRANE, Dennis H.,** M.L.A., B.A., B.Ed., M.Ed.; politician, educator; b. Moncton, N.B. 26 Oct. 1950; s. Hervey L. and Helen L. (McCoubrey) C.; e. Harrison Trimble H.S. 1968; N.B. Teacher's College 1970; Univ. of N.B. B.A. 1972; Univ. of Moncton B.Ed. 1974, M.Ed. 1981; m. Susan d. J.B. and Mary O'Keefe 8 Feb. 1988; LEADER, P.C. PARTY OF N.B. AND MEMBER OF N.B. LEGISLATIVE ASSEMBLY FOR PETITCODIAC 1991– ; School Teacher, School Principal 1970–91; elected to Moncton City Council 1977; elected Mayor of Moncton 1979; re-elected 1980; elected Councillor-at-Large, City of Moncton 1983; elected P.C., Member of Parliament for Moncton 1984; United Church of Canada; Progressive Conservative; Home: 58 Linden Cres., Moncton, N.B. E1G 2B2; Office: Legislative Assembly, P.O. Box 6000, Fredericton, N.B. E3B 5H1.

**COCHRANE, Douglas H.,** C.Econ. F.T.C.I., A.A.C.I.; financial executive; b. Moncton, N.B. 27 Oct. 1918; s. David and Blanche M. (MacKinnon) C.; e. Dunfermline, Scot. Cert. of Econ. 1939; m. Margaret G. d. Frank and Edith Weaver 14 Feb. 1945; children: Wayne Douglas, Heather Lynn; Asst. Gen. Mgr. Eastern Canada Savings & Loans Co. Halifax 1963, Gen. Mgr. 1970, Vice Pres. 1973; Vice Pres. and Dir. Central Trust Co. 1976, Sr. Vice Pres. 1979, retired 1982; served with RCAF 1940–46, rank Flight Lt.; Dir. Scotia Covenants Ltd. Toronto 1967–78; Chrmn. Bd. Dirs. Waterfront Development Corp.; Central Trust Dartmouth Adv. Bd.; Commr. Supreme Court of N.S.; Appraisal Inst. Can.; Soc. U.S. Appraisers; Fellow, Trust Companies Inst. Can.; Dir. Dartmouth Hosp. Foundation; Candn. Cancer Soc., N.S. Div.; mem., National Capital Comn., Ottawa, Ont.; named Hon. Citizen, City of Winnipeg; mem. Police Assn. N.S.; Clubs: Halifax; Saraguay; Brightwood Golf; Address: 12 Louise Ave., Dartmouth, N.S. B3A 3V6.

**COCHRANE, Ethel M.;** senator; b. Lourdes, Port-au-Port, Nfld. 23 Sept. 1937; d. Edward and Mary (Lambert) Bungay; e. Mem. Univ. of Nfld., B.A. 1974; Mem. Univ. of Nfld., B.A.(Ed.) 1982; St Francis Xavier Univ., M.Ed. 1984; m. James s. Albert and Catherine Cochrane 3 Nov. 1956; MEMBER, SENATE OF CANADA since 1986; 1st woman Senator from Nfld.; taught school for 21 years; Post Office employee for 3 yrs.; mem. Internal Econ., Budgets & Admin. Ctte.; Past Pres., Maria Regina Parish Ladies Guild; Past Pres., Boy Scouts of Can., Port au Port; Past Pres., Assn. of Girl Guides & Brownies, Port au Port; Hon. Mem., 2415 Gonzaga Cadets; mem., Salvation Army Adv. Bd., Corner Brook; Past Pres., Port au Port P.C. Assn.; Mem., Social Affairs, Science & Technology Ctte.; mem. parliamentary assn., and friendship groups; Home: P.O. Box 233, Port au Port, Nfld. A0N 1T0; Office: Centre Block, The Senate, Ottawa, Ont. K1A 0A4.

**COCHRANE, Michael George,** B.A., LL.B.; lawyer, mediator, writer; b. Toronto, Ont. 21 Sept. 1953; s. George Ernest and Rachel (O'Keefe) C.; e. Carleton Univ. B.A. 1975; Univ. of Ottawa LL.B. 1978; called to Bar of Ont. 1980; one d.: Emma Rachel; LAWYER, SCOTT & AYLEN 1992– ; Lawyer, Hamilton, Appotive 1980–85; Sr. Crown Counsel, Min. of the Attorney Gen. for Ont. 1985–92 (Chair of var. cttes.; 1st Candn. fellowship awarded 1990 for studies with Nat. Assn. of Attorneys Gen. Washington); Lectr. in Law, Univ. of Ottawa Law Sch. 1981–83; Carleton Univ, Dept. of Law 1978–83; Instr., Law Soc. of U.C. Bar Admission Course 1978–83; Gov., Candn. Inst. of Conflict Resolution; Mem., Candn. Bar Assn. of Ont.; Advocate's Soc.; author: 'Family Law in Ontario for Lawyers and Law Clerks' 1990, 'Surviving Divorce: The Everyday Guide for Canadians' 1991, 'Class Actions' 1991; editor: 'Attorneys General and New Methods of Dispute Resolution' 1990; Office: Box 194, 34th fl., Royal Trust Tower, T-D Ctr., Toronto, Ont. M5K 1H6.

**COCHRANE, William Arthur,** O.C., M.D. LL.D., F.R.C.P.(C), F.A.C.P.; medical executive; b. Toronto, Ont. 18 March 1926; s. Arthur William and Olive Mary (Workman) C.; e. Univ. of Toronto M.D. 1949; Dalhousie Univ. LL.D. 1982; University of Calgary LL.D. 1983; China Acad. Taiwan LL.D. 1977; Acadia Univ. D.Sc. (hon. causa) 1991; m. Phyllis d. George Nellis Potts 14 Sept. 1951; children: Stephen, Paul, Gillian, James; Chrmn., Connaught Laboratories Ltd. 1978–89; Chrmn. & Dir., Fluor/Daniel Canada Ltd.; Pres., W.A. Cochrane & Assoc. Inc., Calgary; Dir., Connaught Laboratories Ltd.; Janus Technologies Inc. (Edmonton); CFCN Communication, Calgary; MDS Health Ventures, Toronto; Dir., Andres Wines (Winona, Ont.); Dir., The Banff Centre (Banff, Alta.); Dir., Monsanto Canada Inc. (Mississauga, Ont.); postgrad. training Pediatric research Hosp. for Sick Children Toronto, Cincinnati Children's Research Foundation, Great Ormond St. Hosp. London, Eng. 1950–56; Prof. of Pediatrics Dalhousie Univ. 1958–67; Dean of Med. Univ. of Calgary 1967–73, Pres. of Univ. 1974–78; Depy. Min. of Health Alta., Edmonton 1973–74; Mem., National Biotechnology Advisory Ctte.; recipient Nutrition Research Award Nutrition Soc. Can. 1965; NRC Research Exchange Fellow U.S.S.R. 1969; Queen's Silver Jubilee Medal 1977; awarded Commemorative Medal for 125th Anniversary of Candn. Confederation 1992; named Hon. Med. Chief Stoney Indian Band Morley, Alta. 1973; Officer of the Order of Canada 1989; author over 70 scient. articles various prof. journs.; Pres. Candn. Pediatric Soc. 1966; Candn. Soc. Clin. Investigation 1965; mem. Candn. Med. Assn.; recreations: swimming, skiing, jogging; Clubs: Thornhill Country; Glencoe; Home: 15 – 3203 Rideau Place S.W., Calgary, Alta. T2S 2T1; Office: 2000 Trimac House, 800 – 5th Ave. S.W., Calgary, Alta. T2P 3T6.

**COCHREN, Thomas H.;** builder; b. Hamilton, Ont. 15 June 1948; s. Thomas Benedict and Marcella Jane (Armstrong) C.; e. Cathedral Boys H.S.; Mohawk Coll., Bus. Admin. (Dean's Hon. Roll, Bronze Medal) 1971; m. Elizabeth Ann d. James A. and Daisy M. (Chaplin) Warnock 6 Sept. 1975; children: Nancy, Nicole, Patti Ann, Mary Heather; PRES., THOMAS COCHREN HOMES AND TOMMAR CONSTRUCTION CO. LIMITED 1980– ; Mktg. Rep., Bell Canada 1972–75 (also Chrmn., Mktg. Employees Assn. & CTEA Bargaining Ctte. Mem.); Land Developer, Cochren Constr. Co. 1975–79; an active mem., Candn. Home Builders' Assn. at all levels (Treas. 1986–88; 1st Vice-Pres. 1988; Pres. 1989); Past Pres., Hamilton & Dist. Home Builders' Assn.; Ont. Home Build. Assn.; Dir., Ont. New

Home Warranty Prog.; Chrmn. & Treasurer, Commun. Ctte.; recreations: skiing, diving, flying; Home: 13 Cumminsville Dr., P.O. Box 7, Millgrove, Ont. L0R 1V0; Office: 50 Dundas St. E., Hamilton, Ont. L9J 1B3.

**COCKBURN, Bruce,** O.C.; singer; songwriter; guitarist; b. Ottawa, Ont. 27 May 1945; e. Berklee Coll. of Music, Boston 1964–66, theory, composition and arranging; played in several rock bands incl. the Esquires and the Children, Ottawa; soloist various coffee houses and made first appearance Mariposa Folk Festival 1967; mem. folk-rock band 'Three's A Crowd' CBC TV series 1968–69; made first cross-country tour 1972; appearances Philadelphia Folk Festival 1974, Alice Tully Hall New York 1977; toured Japan with Murray McLauchlan 1977 and as soloist 1979; tours: to Central America 1983; Australia and New Zealand 1983; Santiago, Chile 1983; LP recordings incl.: 'Bruce Cockburn' 1970; 'High Winds White Sky' 1971 (certified Gold 1986); 'Sunwheel Dance' 1972; 'Night Vision' 1973 (winner Juno Award, Best Album Graphics 1975; certified Gold 1979); 'Salt, Sun and Time' 1974; 'Joy Will Find a Way' 1975 (winner Juno Award, Best Album Graphics 1976; certified Gold 1985); 'In the Falling Dark' 1977 (certified Gold 1985); 'Circles in the Stream-Live' 1977; 'Further Adventures of' 1978; 'Dancing in the Dragon's Jaws' 1979 (certified Gold 1979; Platinum 1983); 'Humans' 1980; 'Mummy Dust' 1981; 'Inner City Front' 1981 (winner CFNY-FM U-Know Award, Best Album of Yr. 1981); 'The Trouble With Normal' 1983; 'Stealing Fire' 1984 (on U.S. Billboard charts 30 wks.; certified Gold & Platinum 1985); 'World of Wonders' 1986 (certified Gold 1986); recipient numerous other Juno Awards: Candn. Folksinger of Yr. 1971, 1972, 1973; Folk Artist of Yr. 1980, 1981; Male Vocalist of Yr. 1981; Best Male Vocalist 1982; Best Folk Artist 1982; RPM Award: Top Single Recording of Yr. 1979; CFNY-FM U-Know Award: Best Male Vocalist 1980; P.R.O. Awards: for 'Wondering Where the Lions Are' 1981; for 'Coldest Night of the Year' and 'Rumours of Glory' 1982; The William Harold Moon Award 1986; BMI Awards: for soundtrack 'Goin' Down the Road' 1971; for 'Wondering Where the Lions Are' 1981; Dutch Music Industry Edison Award for 'Wondering Where the Lions Are' 1982; USC Gold Pin, Unitarian Service Comte. 1982; Order of Canada 1983; CFNY-FM Casby Award, Top Male Vocalist 1985; Casby Awards, Top Male Vocalist, Video of the Year 1986; 'Rumours of Glory' concert film 1983, videocassette 1984; 'Waiting for a Miracle' compilation singles LP 1987; 'Big Circumstance' 1989; World Tour 1989 and 1992; D.Litt., York Univ. 1989; 'Bruce Cockburn Live' 1990; 'If a Tree Falls' SOCAN Award 1990; 'Nothing But a Burning Light' 1991 (selected best album of 1991 by A.P. Wire; certified gold); Musicians Award, Toronto Arts Awards 1991; affiliate, SOCAN; Address: c/o Jehanne Languedoc, Dir., True North Records/Finkelstein Management Co. Ltd., 151 John St., Suite 301, Toronto, Ont. M5V 2T2.

**COCKBURN, Hon. G. William N.,** Q.C., B.A., B.C.L.; judge; b. St. Stephen, N.B. 14 Feb. 1931; s. late George H.I. and Bessie L. (Dinsmore) C.; e. Univ. of N.B., B.A. 1953; B.C.L. 1955; m. Marjorie M.T., d. late M. Allan Ryan, 14 Aug. 1954; children: G. William A., Beth Susanne, Richard Blair; JUDGE, PROVINCIAL COURT OF N.B. 1983– ; Chrmn., N.B. Liquor Licensing Bd. 1983–88; called to Bar of N.B. 1955; Q.C. 1978; appt'd. Prov. Court Judge 1983; el. M.L.A. 1967; re-el. 1970, 1974, 1978; Min. of Fisheries and Environment, 1970–74; Min. of Health 1974–76; Chrmn. N.B. Electric Power Commn. 1976–82; Past Lt. Gov., O.Q.M. District Kiwanis Internat.; Past Chrmn., Bd. Trustees, Charlotte Co. Hosp.; Past Dir. St. Stephen-Milltown Assn. for Retarded Children; Freemason; (Shriner); P. Conservative; Presbyterian; recreations: golf, curling; Home: 80 Avondale Court, Fredericton, N.B. E3B 1Y3; Office: Provincial Court, P.O. Box 94, Oromocto, N.B. E2V 2G4.

**COCKBURN, Wayne D.,** B.A., F.C.S.I.; investment executive; b. Toronto, Ont. 8 Dec. 1956; s. Gordon Douglas and G. Jean (Taylor) C.; e. York Univ. B.A. 1979; m. Lynda Ann d. Ken and Verna Ross 22 Sept. 1979; children: Adam, Ian, Claire; VICE-PRESIDENT & INVESTMENT EXECUTIVE, MIDLAND WALWYN CAPITAL INC. 1991– ; Dir., Suncrest Energy Inc. 1993– ; Account Executive, Canada Life Assur. Co. 1979–81; Asst. Br. Mgr., Admin., Toronto-Dominion Bank 1981–83; Investment Executive, Dominion Securities Pitfield 1983–88; Vice-Pres. & Asst. Br. Mgr., Toronto Metroplex Office, Prudential Bache Securities Canada Ltd./Burns Fry Limited 1988–91; Financial Advisor: Imutec Corp. (formerly RML Med. Labs. Inc.) 1987– ; Myo Diagnostics Inc. 1993– ; KOLVOX Communications Inc. 1993– ; Futureline Communications Co. Ltd. 1993– ; Mem., Toronto Biotechnology Initiative 1991– ; Fellowship, Canadian Securities Inst. 1985– ; Chair, General Business, United Way Toronto 1989–91; recreations: golf, skiing, tennis, badminton, coaching junior league hockey & baseball (1988– ;); clubs: Glenway Golf & Country; Home: 951 Krista Court, Newmarket, Ont. L3Y 7E9; Office: 7030 Woodbine Ave., Ste. 700, Markham, Ont. L3R 1A2.

**COCKFIELD, David Michael,** B.A., M.B.A., C.F.A.; investment counsellor; b. Hong Kong 2 Oct. 1937; s. Richard Leonard and Stella Rose (Bingham); e. Queen's Univ. B.A. 1961; Univ. of Toronto M.B.A. 1963; m. Joanne Matthews; children: John, Elizabeth, James, Ann; PRESIDENT, COCKFIELD PORRETTI CUNNINGHAM 1979– ; Officer, Bank of Canada 1963–69; Asst. Vice-Pres., Investments, Canada Trust 1969–75; Sr. Vice-Pres., James P. Marshall 1975–79; Chair, Security Home Mortgage Inv. Corp.; Twice Dir., Toronto Soc. of Financial Analysts; Past Pres., Investment Council Assn. of Ont.; recreations: gardening, skiing; Home: 88 Balsam Ave., Toronto, Ont. M4E 3B7; Office: Suite 1500, 25 Adelaide St. E., Toronto, Ont. M5C 1Y2.

**COCKS, Alan Charles,** B.Sc., M.B.A., Ph.D.; petroleum executive; b. Clacton, Eng. 17 Sept. 1943; s. William and Daisy (Parsons) C.; e. Exeter Univ. Eng. B.Sc. 1965, Ph.D. 1968; Univ. of Houston M.B.A. 1977; m. Kathleen d. William and Evelyn Reed 23 July 1967; children: Alison, Julie, Heather; PRESIDENT & CHIEF EXTVE. OFFICER, TEXACO CANADA PETROLEUM INC. 1992– ; Rsch. Geophysicist, Texaco Inc. 1968; various managerial assignments Texaco Inc. Houston; Gen. Mgr. & Dir., Texaco Ltd. London 1983; Gen. Mgr., Texaco Latin Am./W. Africa, Coral Gables, Florida 1990; recreations: walking, boating, antique collecting; clubs: Calgary Petroleum; Home: 1232 Riverdale Ave. S.W., Calgary, Alta. T2S 0Y8; Office: Ste. 3100, 150 – 6 Ave. S.W., Calgary, Alta. T2P 4M5.

**COCKWELL, Jack Lynn;** business executive; chartered accountant; b. 12 Jan. 1941; s. William Henry and Daphne Cound C.; e. Selbourne Coll.; Univ. of Capetown 1964; post-grad. with distinction 1966; children: Linda Sue, Lorie Ann, Leslie Gail, Daphne Tessa, Malcolm Jack, Gareth William; PRES., BRASCAN LTD. 1991– ; Mgr., Touche, Ross & Co. 1959–67; Extve. Vice-Pres. & Chief Oper. Offr., Edper Investments Ltd. 1968–89; Extve. Vice-Pres. & Chief Oper. Offr., Brascan Ltd. 1979–90; Vice. Chrmn. & Dir., Hees International Bancorp Inc.; Dir., Continental Bank of Canada; Astral Bellevue Pathe Ltd.; Bramalea Ltd.; Brascade Resources Inc.; Brascan Ltd.; Brookfield Develop. Corp.; Carena Developments Inc.; Coscan Development Corp.; Edper Enterpirses Ltd.; Great Lakes Group Inc.; John Labatt Ltd.; London Life Insurance Co.; Noranda Inc.; Noranda Forest Inc.; Norcen Energy Resources Ltd.; Trilon Financial Corp.; Trizec Corporation Ltd.; Mem., Adv. Bd., The Financial Post Co. Ltd.; Office: BCE Place, 181 Bay St., Suite 4400, P.O. Box 762, Toronto, Ont. M5J 2T3.

**CODE, Charles Frederick,** B.S., M.D., Ph.D., Hon. F.R.C.S.Ed., D.S.; medical researcher and educator; b. Winnipeg, Man., 1 Feb. 1910; s. Abraham and Gertrude Casilda (Drewry) C.; e. Univ. of Man., B.S. and M.D. 1934; Univ. of Minn., Ph.D. 1940; m. Gwendolyn Irene, d. A.S. Bond, 30 Dec. 1935; three children; ACTIVE EMERITUS PROF. MEDICINE AND SURGERY UC SAN DIEGO; Assoc. Dir., Center for Ulcer Research & Educ., U.C.L.A. & V.A. Wadsworth Hosp. Center, Los Angeles 1975–80; (formerly Dir. for Med. Educ. & Research, Mayo Foundation 1966–72); Lecturer in Physiol., Univ. Coll., London and National Institute for Med. Research, London, 1936–37; joined Mayo Foundation as Fellow in Physiol. and Med., 1934–35; Asst. in Exper. Surg., 1938; Instr. in Physiol. then Asst. Prof., Med. Sch., Univ. of Minn., 1939–40; joined staff of Mayo Clinic as Consultant in Physiol. and Asst. Prof. in Physiol., Mayo Foundation, 1940; Prof. of Physiol., Mayo Foundation and Chrmn., Sec. of Physiol., Mayo Clinic and Mayo Foundation, 1942–65; during World War II conducted aviation medical research 1940–46; Visiting Prof. of Physiol., St. Thomas Med. Sch., London, Eng., 1966; Botazzi Lectr., Cong. of Italian Socs., of Exper. Biol., Physiol., Biochem. and Human Nutrition, Pavia, Italy 1970; Hon. Consultant, The London Hosp., London, Eng. 1971; rec'd Physiol. Research Prize and Gold Medal, Univ. of Man., 1930; Bayliss-Starling Mem. Scholarship, Univ. Coll., London 1936; Theobald Smith Award and Medal for Research 1938; D.Sc. (Hon.) Medical Coll., Wisconsin 1978; D.Sc. (Hon.) Univ. of Man. 1981; Hon. Fellow Royal Coll. of Surgeons, Edinburgh 1984; co-author 'An Atlas of Esophageal Motility in Health and Disease' 1958; Ed., Handbooks of Physiology of Alimentary Canal, 1964–68; mem. Ed. Bd., 'Gastroenterology'; other writings incl. over 300 original scient. publs.; discoveries incl. role of histamine in allergic reactions and gastric acid secretion; definition of Esophageal Motor Disorders; role of acid in Peptic Ulcer Disease; Motor and Elect. Activity of Bowel; Interdigestive Housekeeper of the Gastrointestinal tract; Physiological Mechanism of gastric mucosal injury and resistance; Am. Physiol. Soc. (mem. Ed. Bd. and Ed.-in-Chief of Physiol. Reviews, 1957–63; Past Chrmn., G.I. Sec.); mem., Candn. Physiol. Soc.; Physiol Soc., England; Assn. Am. Physicians; Am. Gastroenterol. Assn. (Past Pres. and mem. Gov. Bd.; Past Chrmn. G.I. Research Group and Research Comte.); Episcopalian; recreations: gardening, photography, sailing, fishing; Clubs: Faculty (UCSD); Balboa (Mazatlan, Mexico); Royal Lake of the Woods Yacht (Kenora, Ont.); Home: 14946 Rancho Real, Del Mar, CA 92014 U.S.A.; Office: Section Gastroenterology, San Diego VA Medical Center, 3350 La Jolla Village Dr., San Diego CA 92161.

**CODY-RICE, Edith Harriet,** B.Sc.N., B.A., M.A., LL.B.; lawyer; b. Regina, Sask.; d. John Walter and Evelyn Sadie (Cox) C.; e. Preston H.S. 1961; Neuchatel Jr. Coll. (Switz.) 1962; Univ. of Toronto B.Sc.N. 1966; Sorbonne (Paris) 1967; Univ. of Waterloo B.A. 1968, M.A. 1973; Univ. of Toronto LL.B. 1977; called to Ont. Bar 1979; SENIOR LEGAL COUNSEL, CBC 1991– ; Lectr., Univ. of Waterloo 1968–73; Administrator, Inter-Faculty Program Bd. 1972–73; private practitioner Toronto 1979–82; Legal Counsel, CBC 1982–91; Instr., Law Soc. of U.C. Bar Admission Course; Trade Mark Agent; Charter Extve. Mem., Ottawa Valley Book Fest.; Dir., Writer's Devel. Trust 1982–90 (Chairperson 1991–93); Jury Mem., National Newspaper Awards; Mem., Law Soc. of U.C.; Candn. Bar Assn.; recreations: literature, performing arts, plastic arts; Office: 1500 Bronson Ave., Ottawa, Ont. K1G 3J5.

**COFFEY, Charles S.;** banker; b. Woodstock, N.B. 26 Nov. 1943; s. John and Catherine (Sheridan) C.; e. Woodstock H.S. 1961; Fellow, Inst. of Canadian Bankers; Grad., Tuck Extve. Program, Amos Tuck Sch. of Bus. Admin., Dartmouth Coll. 1988; m. L. Anne d. John and Joan Connell 15 July 1972; children: Andrew J., Catherine A., Jonathan M.; SENIOR VICE-PRESIDENT, BUSINESS BANKING, ROYAL BANK OF CANADA 1993– ; has held admin. positions in various branches & depts. of present bank before being apptd. Extve. Offr. 1986; Dir., Corporation of Massey Hall and Roy Thomson Hall; Dir., Candn. Centre for Creative Technology; Dir., The Candn. Shaare Zedek Hosp. Found.; Dir. & Gov., Sunnybrook Foundation; Mem., National Council, Royal Winnipeg Ballet; Mem., Eastern Bd., Candn. Aboriginal Economic Development Bd.; Mem., Nat. Adv. Counc., IMAGINE; recreations: squash, hockey, golf; Office: Royal Bank Plaza, South Tower, 8th Floor, Toronto, Ont. M5J 2J5.

**COFFEY, Robert George,** B.Com., C.A., LIC; public accountant and auditor; b. Montreal, Que. 31 July 1934; s. Frank and Helen C.; e. McGill Univ. B.Com. 1956; m. Vivienne Macdonald 9 June 1988; children: Daniel, Diane, James; VICE CHRMN. CORPORATE FINANCE AND INDUSTRIES, KPMG PEAT MARWICK THORNE 1989– ; Audit Staff Coopers & Lybrand Montreal 1956–59; Audit Mgr. Touche Ross Toronto 1959–62; Sr. Cons. P.S. Ross & Partners 1962–64; Partner Hillis & Partners 1964–65; Chief Financial Offr., Kingsway Lumber 1965–66; Cons. to Mgr. and then Partner, Ernst & Ernst 1966–71; Audit Partner Ernst & Whinney 1971–79, Partner-in-Charge Consulting 1979–86; Exec. Partner Client Services, Thorne Ernst & Whinney 1986–89; First Examiner for Candn. Inst. Mgmt. Cons.; Dir. & Past Pres. Assn. for Corporate Growth; Pres.-elect, Candn. Turnaround Mgmt. Assn.; Lectr., McGill Univ. & Univ. of Toronto; lectr. re mergers & acquisitions; advisor to Royal Comn. on Taxation & Royal Comn. on Govt. Admin., Sask.; Sr. Project Dir. for orgn. & salary reviews for PSC of Sask.; co-author 'Purchase and Sale of a Business' 1980; 'Management Letter Writing'; 'Approach to Zero-based Budgeting'; mem. McGill Alumni Assn. (Toronto Pres. 1984); Kiwanis (Past Dir.); recreations: travel, nordic skiing, birding, theatre, cottage; Club: Lambton Golf & Country; Home: 1903 – 71 Simcoe St., Toronto, Ont. M5J 2S9; Office: P.O. Box 31, Commerce Court Postal Stn., Toronto, Ont. M5L 1B2.

**COFFIN, Rev. Richard Clifford,** B.A., M.Div., D.Min.; baptist minister; b. Boston, Mass. 19 Dec. 1936; s. Clifford Elisha and Ethel Mahetabel (McAssey) C.; e. S. Boston High Sch. 1954; Acadia Univ. Wolfville, N.S., B.A. 1966; Acadia Divinity Coll. M.Div. 1969; Am. Bapt. Semy. of the West, Covina, Cal. D.Min. 1974; m. Jean d. Mackie and Jennie MacKinnon 5 May 1965; children: Margaret, Mark; GEN. SEC.-TRES. CANDN. BAPT. FEDN. 1985– ; held pastorates Jeddor-Oyster Pond Un. Bapt. Chs. 1964–66; New Minas Bapt. Ch.

1966–70; Pastor, First Bapt. Ch. Dartmouth, N.S. 1970–76; Calgary First Bapt. Ch. 1976–78; Blythwood Rd. Bapt. Ch. Toronto 1979–85; Exec. mem. Bapt. World Alliance, Exec. mem. BWA Council; Pres. & Exec. mem., N. Am. Bapt. Fellowship; Ex Officio mem. Candn. Bapt. Overseas Mission Bd.; recreation: Old Timers hockey; Home: 532 Soudan Ave., Toronto, Ont. M4S 1X4; Office: Canadian Baptist Place, 7185 Millcreek Dr., Mississauga, Ont. L5N 5R4.

**COGGER, Hon. Michel B.,** Q.C., B.A., B.Ph. L.èsL., LL.L.; lawyer; b. Quebec City, Que. 21 Mar. 1939; s. Dalton and Léda (Labrie) C.; e. Petit Sém. de Qué. 1958; Laval Univ., B.A. 1958, B.Ph. 1958, M.A. 1961, LL.L. 1963; admitted to Que. Bar 1964; m. Erica d. Frank and Hetty de Boer Aug. 1972; children: Christine, Alexandre, Nicholas; Past Nat. Dir., Progressive Conservative Party of Can. 1967–68; Press Sec., Hon. R. Stanfield campaigns 1972, 1974; Chief Couns., Leader of Opposition 1983–84; Summoned to the Senate of Can. May, 1986; Mem., Senate Standing Ctte. on Foreign Affairs, Senate Standing Ctte. on Standing Rules and Orders and Joint-Chrmn. on the Joint Ctte. on Regulations and other Statutory Instruments; Delegate at 41st General Assembly of the United Nations, Oct. 1986; Dir., Counc. for Candn. Unity; Gov., Fond. Jean Lapointe; Gov., Sch. of Business Admin., Univ. of Sherbrooke; recreations: tennis, skiing, riding; Clubs: Knowlton Golf; Brome Lake Boating; Home: R.R. 1, Knowlton, Que. J0E 1V0; Office: 1115 Sherbrooke St. W., Suite 603, Montréal, Qué. H3A 1H3.

**COGSWELL, Fred(erick William),** C.M. (1981), B.A., M.A., Ph.D.; poet, publisher; professor emeritus; b. East Centreville, N.B. 8 Nov. 1917; s. late Florence (White) and late Walter Scott C.; e. Prov. Normal Sch. 1936; Carleton Vocational Sch. 1939; Univ. of N.B., B.A. (Hons.) 1949, M.A. 1950; Edinburgh Univ. (I.O.D.E. Scholar.) Ph.D. 1952; Hon. LL.D., St. Francis Univ. 1982; D.C.L., King's Univ. 1985; LL.D., Mount Allison Univ. 1988; m. 1stly the late Margaret, d. late John Hynes 3 July 1944; m. 2ndly Gail Fox 6 Nov. 1985; children: late Carmen Patricia, Kathleen Mary; PROFESSOR EMERITUS, UNIV. OF N.B. 1983– ; Prof. there 1952–83; Writer-in-Residence, Scottish Arts Council 1983–84; author: 'The Stunted Strong' 1954; 'The Haloed Tree' 1957; 'The Testament of Cresseid' (trans.) 1958; 'Descent from Eden' 1959; 'Lost Dimension' 1960; 'Star-People' 1968; 'Immortal Plowman' 1969; 'One Hundred Poems of Modern Quebec' (trans.) 1970 (2nd ed. 1971); 'A Second Hundred Poems of Modern Quebec' (trans.) 1971; 'In Praise of Chastity' 1971; 'Chains of Lilliput' 1971; 'The House Without a Door' 1973; 'Confrontation' (trans.) 1973; 'Light Bird of Life' 1974; 'The Poetry of Modern Quebec' (trans.) 1976; 'Against Perspective' 1977; 'A Long Apprenticeship: Collected Poems' 1980; 'Selected Poems' 1982; 'Pearls' 1983; 'The Complete Poems of Emile Nelligan' 1983; 'Charles G.D. Roberts and his Works' 1983; editor and co-author (with S. MacNutt and R. Tweedie) 'The Arts of New Brunswick' 1967; (with T.R. Lower) 'The Enchanted Land' 1968; Ed. 'Five New Brunswick Poets' 1961; 'An Atlantic Anthology' Vol. 1 1983, Vol. 2 1984; 'Meditations' 1986; 'An Edge to Life' 1987; 'Charles Mair and his Works' 1988; 'The Best Notes Merge' 1988; 'Black and White Tapestry' 1989; Ed. and Transl. (with Jo-Anne Elder) 'Unfinished Dreams: Contemporary Poetry of Acadie' 1990; 'Watching an Eagle' 1991; 'When the Right Light Shines' 1992; 'In Praise of Old Music' 1992; 'In My Own Growing' 1993; contrib. 'Literary History of Canada' 1966: 'Dictionary of Canadian Biography' Vols. IX and X; 'On Canada' 1971; 'Dictionary of Literary Biography' Vols. 60 and 88; Ed. (1952–66) 'The Fiddlehead' lit. mag. and former Ed. and Publisher, Fiddlehead Poetry Books; has contrib. poems, articles, reviews to numerous leading lit. and prof. journs.; awarded Nuffield Fellowship 1959; Can. Council Sr. Fellowship 1967; Mem., Order of Canada 1981; Exchange Writer in Residence, Canada-Scotland 1983–84; Hon. Life Mem. League Candn. Poets (First Vice-Pres. 1985–86); Hon. Life Mem., Assn. of Candn. Publishers; Humanities Assn. Can. (Ed. Assn. Bulletin 1967–72); Candn. Assn. Univ. Teachers; Assn. of Que. and Candn. Literatures; Assn. of Candn. Translators; Hon. Life Mem., New Brunswick Writers Federation (Pres. 1984–85); Protestant; N.D.P.; recreation: athletics; Club: PEN; Home: 29 Island View Dr., R.R. 4, Fredericton, N.B. E3B 4X5; Office: University of New Brunswick, Fredericton, N.B. E3B 5A3.

**COHEN, Albert Diamond,** C.M.; executive; b. Winnipeg, Man. 20 Jan. 1914; s. late Alexander and Rose (Diamond) C.; e. Winnipeg Pub. and High Schs.; LL.D. (hon. causa) Univ. of Manitoba 1987; m. Irena, d. late Ing. Eduard Kanka 6 Nov. 1953; children: Anthony Jan, James Edward, Anna Lisa; CHRMN. & C.E.O., GENDIS INC.; Chrmn. & C.E.O., Sony of Canada Ltd.; Chrmn. Extve. Comte., Metropolitan Stores of Canada Ltd.; Chrmn. & C.E.O. Saan Stores Ltd.; served with RCN 1942–45; Past Pres., Winnipeg Clinic Research Inst.; The Paul H.T. Thorlakson Research Found.; Man. Theatre Centre (1968–69, 1970–71, 1976–81); Past Commr. Metric Bd. Ottawa; recipient, International Distinguished Entrepreneur Award, Univ. of Manitoba 1983; Order of Canada 1984; Commemorative Medal, 125th Anniversary of Candn. Confedn. 1992; Hon. Chrmn., St. John's-Ravenscourt School 1984; author 'The Entrepreneurs: The Story of Gendis Inc.' (Nat. Business Book Award 1986); recreations: golf, skating; Clubs: Glendale Country; Winnipeg Winter; Manitoba; Carleton; Home: 305 Park Blvd., Tuxedo, Winnipeg, Man. R3P 0G8; Office: 1370 Sony Pl., Winnipeg, Man. R3C 3C3.

**COHEN, Allan;** international marketing and management consultant; b. New York, N.Y. 30 Mar. 1933; s. Sam and Sophie (Barkelstein) C.; e. New York Univ. 1954; m. the late Paula d. Harry and Alice Morrison; son: Steven; PRES., ALLAN COHEN & ASSOCIATES LTD. 1967– ; specializes in consulting & implementation services to retailers, distributors & mfrs. of consumer goods & services in Can. & U.S.; writer, lecturer, trainer, management consultant, entrepreneur; author of over 150 articles on retailing, distribution, manufacturing, franchising, marketing, small business in major trade mags. & newspapers; lectures worldwide with audio-visual presentations; publisher, 'Working From Home,' international monthly newsletter, directories & seminars for independent consultants, entrepreneurs & small business; Producer and Host 'Working From Home' TV show; TV appearances; recreations: tennis, boating, swimming, painting, bowling; Office: P.O. Box 1722, Hallandale, FL 33008-1722 USA.

**COHEN, Andrew H.;** entrepreneur; b. Ottawa, Ont. 13 May 1946; s. Morris and Beatrice Clare (Sohn) C.; e. Queen's Univ., Kingston, Ont.; m. Susan d. William and Marian Carter 18 May 1974; children: Alice, Sally; PRES., DPI ASSOCIATES, Communications and Social Marketing 1988– ; volunteer and staff mem. in soc. policy devel. and rsch.; el. to Ctte. of Nat. Voluntary Orgn. 1977; Exec. Dir. Candn. Counc. on Children and Youth 1977–82; Dir. Gen., Consumers' Assn. of Canada 1982–88; Chrmn. ad hoc ctte. for 1979 Internat. Yr. of the Child 1979; Chrmn. 4th Candn. Conf. on Children, Ottawa 1979; Chrmn. NVO Tax Reform Ctte. 1978– ; Vice-Chrmn. Coalition of Nat. Voluntary Ogn. 1984–86; Chrmn., Coalition of Nat. Vol. Org. 1986–90; Home: 112 Broadway, Ottawa, Ont.; Office: 200 First Ave., Ottawa, Ont. K1S 2G6.

**COHEN, Andrew Zebulon,** B.A., B.J., M.A.; journalist; b. Montreal, Que. 14 Jan. 1955; s. Edgar Horace and Ruth Goldberg C.; e. The Choate School 1973; McGill Univ. B.A. 1977; Carleton Univ. B.J. 1979, M.A. 1983; NATIONAL CORRESPONDENT, SATURDAY NIGHT MAGAZINE 1993– ; and NATIONAL AFFAIRS COLUMNIST, THE FINANCIAL POST 1993– ; General Assignment Reporter, The Ottawa Citizen 1977–80; Parl. Reporter, United Press International 1980–84; Foreign Desk, Washington, UPI 1983; Political Writer, The Financial Post 1984–87; Foreign Editor 1987–90; Senior Editor 1990–91; Foreign Affairs Columnist 1989–93; freelance writer, lecturer and broadcaster; Visiting Fellow, Cambridge Univ. 1991–93; Author's Award, Public Affairs 1990; Gold Medalist, Public Issues, 1991 Nat. Mag. Awards (NMA); President's Medal, 1991 NMA; Gold Medalist, In-Depth Reporting, 1991 NMA; Fellow, Asia Pacific Found. of Canada 1989; Mem., Clare Hall College, Cambridge Univ.; PEN Internat.; Candn. Inst. of Internat. Affairs; The Churchill Soc.; Candn. Jewish Congress; author: 'A Deal Undone: The Making and Breaking of the Meech Lake Accord' 1990 and essays, book reviews, monographs; recreations: skiing, wilderness canoeing, swimming; Home: 84 Winchester St., Toronto, Ont. M4X 1B2; Office: Suite 400, 579 Richmond St. W., Toronto, Ont. M5R 1Y6.

**COHEN, David Samuel,** B.Sc., LL.B., LL.M.; university professor; b. Ottawa, Ont.; s. Alexander Joseph and Edyce (Freeman) C.; e. McGill Univ. B.Sc. (Hons.); Univ. of Toronto LL.B. 1975; Yale Univ. LL.M. 1979; m. Gloria d. Julius and Fay Kravitz 1 June 1975; children: Arielle, Daniel; DEAN, FACULTY OF LAW, UNIV. OF VICTORIA 1994– ; Legal Rsch. Offr., Law Reform Comm. of B.C. 1977–78; Law Clerk, W.Z.B. Estey, Supreme Court of Canada 1978–79; Asst. Prof., Univ. of B.C. 1979–85, Assoc. Prof. Faculty of Law 1986–93; Osgoode Hall Law Sch. 1985; Visiting Prof., Univ. of Toronto 1986; Univ. of Florida 1990; Cons., Public Interest Advocacy Ctr. 1980–82; Law Reform Comm. of Canada 1979, 1984–90; Law Reform Comm. of Ont. 1985–87; Legal Serv. Soc. of B.C. 1982–90; Killam Rsch. Award, Univ. of B.C. 1986; Pres., Consumers Assn. of Can. 1993–94 (Vice-Pres. 1982–84); Bd. of Dir. 1992–94; Mem., Federal Envir. Choice Bd. 1989–93; Candn. Law & Soc. Assn.; Candn. Law & Econ. Assn.; author of numerous journal articles; recreations: swimming, running, bicycling; Home: Victoria, B.C.; Office: Faculty of Law, P.O. Box 2400, Victoria, B.C. V8W 3H7.

**COHEN, Dian,** C.M., B.A.; economic communications consultant; b. Winnipeg, Man.; d. Hyman and Bernice (Stern) Nusgart; e. Univ. of Toronto B.A. 1956; McGill Univ., postgrad. studies 1956–63; Univ. of Miami, independent studies 1963; children: Lisa, Nina, Tamara; OWNER, DIAN COHEN PRODUCTIONS LIMITED; T.A., McGill Univ. 1957–62; Sessional Lectr., Sir George Williams Univ. 1963–67; Rsch. Econ. & Pubns. Ed., C.D. Howe Research Inst. 1965–70; Econ. & Business Commentator, CBC 1964–85; syndicated newspaper & mag. columnist & feature writer in pubns. such as 'Canadian Business,' 'Saturday Night,' 'Vancouver Magazine,' 'Toronto Star,' 'Ottawa Citizen' and others 1968–88; Developer & Producer, 'Your Money Matters' for Royal Bank of Canada 1970; 'The Money Seminar' (personal money mngt. workshops) 1975; Co-author & co-host, 'Money, Power and Politics,' CJRT-Open College, Ryerson 1977, 1986–91; Host, 'The Income Tax Phone-In' (CJRT annual phone show) 1988– ; Author/Host, 'Growth Can be Green' (CJRT documentary) 1990; Personal Money Mngt. Columnist, Pulse News, CFCF-TV Montreal 1979–82; contbg. columnist, 'Maclean's' 1982–87; Financial Post, Benefits Canada 1989– ; Business & Econ. Ed., CTV TV 1985–91; Visiting Assoc., Americas Soc. N.Y. 1989–90; Dir., Noranda Forest Inc.; PanCanadian Petroleum; Royal Insur.; CP Ltd.; Monsanto Canada Inc.; Internat. Inst. for Sustainable Devel.; YWCA Montreal Woman of Achievement 1975; Nat. Bus. Writing Award 1978, '83; First Fellow, Ryerson Polytech. Inst. 1980; Literary Guild Designation for 'Money' 1988; Mem., Order of Canada 1993; Chrmn., Adv. Bd., Nat. YMCA Employment Init. Prog.; Dir., Public Policy Forum; Trustee, Candn. Merit Scholarship Found.; Director-at-Large, Jr. Achievement; Mem., Nat. Biotech. Adv. Ctte.; ACTRA, PWAC; author: 'Money' 1987; co-author: 'The Next Canadian Economy' 1984; 'No Small Change' 1992; 'Class Action' 1993; co-editor: 'To Save a Continent' 1990; Home: Hatley, Que.; Office: 46 Wellington St. E., Aurora, Ont. L4G 1H5.

**COHEN, Erminie Joy;** businesswoman; b. Saint John, N.B. 23 July 1926; d. Mitchell Sidney and Clara Leah (Goldfeather) Bernstein; e. Saint John H.S.; Mount Allison Univ. m. Edgar R. s. Bessie and Myer C. 5 Jan. 1948; children: Cathy Tait, Shelley and M. Lee Cohen; DIR. & SHAREHOLDER, V.P. HOFFMAN'S LTD.; Woman of the Year, State of Israel Bonds 1975; Cert. of Appreciation for disting. serv. in the community outside of politics, United Nations 1991; Trustee, Saint John Free Pub. Lib. 1981–88; 1st lay woman to serve (Sisters of Charity), St. Joseph's Hosp. 1978–84; Founding Mem., Hestia House (Shelter for Battered Women) 1980–82; Family Services Saint John Inc. 1967–80; Mem., First New Brunswick Advisory Council on the Status of Women 1977–80; Founder, Saint John Women for Pol. Action 1978; Apptd. to Candn. Advisory Council on the Status of Women 1985–88; Apptd., National Capitol Commn. 1991 and Extve. Ctte. 1992; apptd. Co-Chair, New Brunswick Referendum Ctte.; Co-Chair, Special Gifts Div., Muriel McQueen Fergusson Family Violence Rsch. Ctr., Univ. of N.B. 1992– ; N.B. LEAF Found. Nat. Endowment Campaign; Pres., Shaari Zedek Syn. (1st woman) 1990– ; Vice-Pres. (Atlantic) P.C. Party of Canada; Comnr., N.B. Comn. on Candn. Federalism; Mem., Leaders of the Way Council of the United Way of Greater Saint John 1992–93; recipient, Commemorative Medal, 125th Anniversary, Candn. Confedn.; Apptd. to the Senate of Canada 1993; several other extve. positions; mem., Royal Soc. of Can.; recreations: reading, walking, people, politics; club: Westfield Golf & Country; Home: 3 Hawthorne Ave., Saint John, N.B. E2K 3S7; Office: P.O. Box 6547, Stn. A., Saint John, N.B. E2L 4R9.

**COHEN, H. Reuben,** O.C., Q.C., D.C.L., LL.D; barrister and solicitor; b. Moncton, N.B. 11 July 1921; e. Dalhousie Univ. B.A. 1942; Dalhousie Law School LL.B. 1944; m. Louise Glustein 10 Feb. 1951; children: Debra, Natalie; Law Practice in Moncton, since 1945; Pres., Brentwood Realty Ltd.; Vice-Pres., Standard Investments Ltd.; Dir., Inter-City Products Corp.; Petro-Canada; cr. Q.C. 1968; awarded D.C.L., Univ. de Moncton 1973, Acadia Univ. 1983; LL.D., St. Thomas Univ. 1985; LL.D., Univ. of New Brunswick 1988; LL.D., Dalhousie Univ. 1988; apptd. Mem. of Order of Can. 1979; Officer of Order of Canada 1990; Chancellor, Dalhousie Univ.

1990– ; mem., Moncton Rotary (Pres. 1959–60); Moncton Barrister's Soc.; Friends of the Moncton Hosp. Found. Inc. (Pres. 1977–78); Past District Gov., Rotary Intl., District 781, 1965–66; Club: Halifax; Home: 115 Hillcrest Dr., Moncton, N.B. E1E 1W5; Office: Ste. 205, 1111 Main St., Moncton, N.B. E1C 1H3.

**COHEN, Joseph Hymen,** C.M., S.B.St.J., O.B.C., LL.D.; manufacturing executive; b. Winnipeg, Man. 3 Oct. 1921; s. late Alexander and Rose (Diamond) C.; m. Frances, d. Alex and Rose Belzberg 25 Dec. 1947; children: Lori Faith, Bruce Jeffery, Phyllis Adrian; VICE-PRES. & DIR., GENDIS INC.; SONY OF CANADA LTD.; Pres., Josco Holdings Ltd.; came to Vancouver 1945 after discharge from R.C.N.V.R. (served with Calgary Highlanders Reserve); Hon. Pres. for Life, Confratellanze Italo-Candese; Hon. Mem., Big Brothers of B.C.; Hon. Vice Pres., Boy Scouts of Can. (B.C.-Yukon Provincial Counc.); mem. (past Dir. and Hon. Advisor of Bd. for life) Y.M.C.A.; mem. Royal Commonwealth Soc.; (and past Dir.) Rotary Club of Vancouver; Life Patron, Variety Club of Vancouver; past Dir. Mens Canadian Club; past mem., Vancouver Police Board; mem. Bd., Justice Inst. of B.C.; Dir. U.B.C. Alumni Resources Council; past Dir. (and Financial Chrmn., Special Gifts Division for 13 yrs) St. Vincent's Hosp.; past Financial Chrmn. (13 yrs.) St. Vincent's Hosp.; past W. Candn. Dir., Teleglobe Can.; Hon. Chrmn. Pres.'s Council fundraising drive (and past Dir.) Vancouver Symphony Soc.; Hon. Chrmn., 1979 Conference of Chiefs of Police; Hon. Chrmn., Candn. Police Assoc. Convention 1987; Hon. Chrmn., Candn. Chiefs of Police Convention 1988; Hon. Chief of Police, Vancouver Police Dept.; Hon. Offr., RCMP Mess; Depy. Chrmn., World Police & Fire Games, Vancouver, summer 1989; Chrmn., Internat. Assn. of Women Police 31st Annual Training Conference 1993; awards: Vancouver Community Man of the Year 1971; Tree of Life Award, State of Israel Bonds 1973; Good Citizen Medal, Native Sons of B.C. 1978; Vancouver Mayor's 'Good Citizen Medal' 1978; mem. Order of Canada 1979; Hon. Mem., Candn. Assn. of Chiefs of Police 1979; Queen's Medal 1980; Freeman, City of Vancouver 1980; Joseph H. Cohen Cardiology Fund, Bd. of Trustees, Vancouver Gen. Hosp. estbd. 1981; B.C. Catholic Man of the Year 1982; Medal of Merit, Boy Scouts of Can. 1982; apptd. Comnr., Vancouver Centennial Comn. 1983; Paul Harris Fellow, Rotary Club of Vancouver; co-recipient (with his five brothers) Catherine Variety Sheridan Award, Variety Club International 1983; named 'Partner in Health,' U.B.C. Health Sciences Centre 1983; first Dir. Ronald McDonald House Soc. of B.C. 1983; first mem. of his faith to receive Knights of Columbus, Vancouver Counc. 1981 Award (in recognition of charitable deeds and services extended to community); LL.D. (Hon.), Univ. of B.C. 1986; serving Brother of the Order of St. John of Jerusalem S.B.StJ. 1993; awarded Commemorative Medal for 125th Anniversary of Candn. Confederation 1992; invested with the Order of St. John of Jerusalem, as a Serving Brother 1993; recreation; golf; Club: Richmond Country; University (Vancouver); Terminal City; Home: 1035 W. 48th Ave., Vancouver, B.C. V5Z 1K2; Office: 6951 Elmbridge Way, Richmond, B.C. V7C 5B8.

**COHEN, Leonard,** O.C., LL.D.; writer and composer; b. Montreal, Que. 1934; e. McGill Univ.; LL.D. (Hon.), Dalhousie Univ.; author of 'Let Us Compare Mythologies' (poems) 1956; 'The Spice Box of Earth' (poems) 1961; 'The Favourite Game' (novel) 1963; 'Flowers for Hitler' (poems) 1964; 'Beautiful Losers' (novel) 1966; 'Parasites of Heaven' (poems) 1966; 'Selected Poems: 1956–68' 1968; 'The Energy of Slaves' (poems) 1972; 'Death of a Lady's Man' (novel) 1978; 'Book of Mercy' 1984; 'Stranger Music: Selected Poems and Songs' 1993; composer of 'Songs of Leonard Cohen' 1967; 'Songs from a Room' 1969; 'Songs of Love and Hate 1971; 'Live Songs' 1972; 'New Skin for the old Ceremony' 1973; 'The Best of Leonard Cohen' 1975; 'Death of a Lady's Man' 1977; 'Recent Songs' 1979; 'Various Positions' 1985; 'I'm Your Man' 1987; 'The Future' 1992; Address: c/o Kelley Lynch, 419 North Larchmont Blvd., Ste. 91, Los Angeles, Calif. 90004.

**COHEN, Marjorie Griffin,** M.A., Ph.D.; economist; educator; b. Franklin, N.J. 17 Feb. 1944; d. Harry Griffin and Sylvia Hadowanetz (Stephens); e. Iowa Wesleyan Coll. B.A. 1965; N.Y. Univ. M.A. 1969; York Univ. Ph.D. 1985; children: Sam, Sophie; PROF., DEPT. OF POL. SCI. AND WOMEN'S STUDIES, SIMON FRASER UNIV. 1991– ; Ruth Wynn Woodward Endowed Prof. Simon Fraser Univ. 1989–90; Comnr. B.C. Ind. Inquiry Comn. into Fisheries 1990; Sec. Nat. Planning Assn. Washington, D.C. 1965–66; Stats. Analyst and Computer Programmer McKinsey & Co. New York 1967–68; Lectr. York Univ. 1971–82, Asst. Prof. 1984–86; Prof. Ont. Inst. for Studies in Education 1986–91; Producer and Host 'Counterparts' TV Ont. and MTV 1980–81; Dir.: Candn. Centre for Policy Alternatives 1985– ; B.C. Hydro 1992– ; Co-prin. Organizer Working Skills Centre 1977, Rexdale Microskills Centre 1984 (Dir. 1984–88); ed. bd.: Candn. Forum 1977–85; Labour/Le Travail; mem. Nat. Action Ctte. Status Women (Vice Pres. 1979–80, 1985–87, 1988–89; Treas. 1977–79); Chair, Coalition Against Free Trade 1986–89; Spokesperson Pro-Can. Network; recipient Marion Porter Prize for Feminist Rsch. 1985; York Univ. Faculty Grad. Studies Dissertation Prize 1985; Laura Jamieson Book Prize 1989; author 'Free Trade and the Future of Women's Work: Manufacturing and Service Industries' 1987; 'Women's Work, Markets and Economic Development in Nineteenth Century Ontario' 1988; Home: 2073 Larch St., Vancouver, B.C. V6K 3P5; Office: Dept. of Pol. Sci., Simon Fraser Univ., Burnaby, B.C. V5A 1S6.

**COHEN, Marshall A.,** B.A., LL.B., LL.M., LL.D.; diversified internat. corp. executive; b. New Brunswick, NJ 28 March 1935; e. Univ. of Toronto B.A. 1956; Osgoode Hall Law Sch. LL.B. 1960; York Univ. LL.M. 1963, LL.D. (Hon.) 1986; PRESIDENT & CHIEF EXTVE. OFFICER, THE MOLSON COMPANIES LIMITED 1988– ; private practice of law in Toronto spec. in taxation, commercial law & corp. finance 1960–70; Dep. Min. of Indus., Trade & Comm., Energy Mines & Resources & Finance, Govt. of Canada 1970–85; Pres., Olympia & York Enterprises Corp. 1985–88; Chair, Gulf Canada Resources Limited (part of Olympia & York Group) 1986–88; Dir., The Molson Cos. Limited; Am. Barrick Resources Corp.; Am. Internat. Group, Inc.; Groupe Val Royal Inc.; Lafarge Corp.; The Toronto-Dominion Bank; Chair, Adv. Council of the Fac. of Admin. Studies, York Univ.; Business Council on Nat. Issues (Mem. Policy Ctte.); C.D. Howe Inst. (Mem. Extve. Ctte.); York Univ. (Gov.); Advisory Councils of Baycrest Ctr. for Geriatric Care & Mt. Sinai Hosp.; Chair, Internat. Trade Adv. Ctte., Govt. of Canada; Extve. Ctte. Mem., The British-N. Am. Ctte.; Internat. Councillor, The Ctr. for Strategic & Internat. Studies; The Trilaterial Comn.; Office: 3600, 40 King St. W., Toronto, Ont. M5H 3Z5.

**COHEN, Martha Ruth,** B.A., Dip.S.W., C.M., LL.D. (Hon.); b. Calgary Alta. 14 Oct. 1920; d. late Peter and Rebecca Block; e. McDougall Sch., Central Coll. Inst., Calgary, Alta.; Univ. of Alta., Edmonton, B.A. 1940; Univ. of Toronto, Dipl. S.W. 1945; Univ. of Calgary, Hon. LL.D. 1982; m. Harry (now deceased) s. late Alexander & Rose C. 29 Dec. 1945; children: Dr. Philip Frank, Cheryl Beth, Faye Patricia, David Irving; Past Mem., Candn. Ctte. for the World Decade of Cultural Development 1989–97; Founding Pres. (and one of six prin. fund-raisers), Calgary Centre for Performing Arts 1975–85; Past Bd. Mem., Old Sun College 1974–86; Mem., Arts Festival, Calgary Winter Festival 1988–91; Past Mem., Counc. for Alta. Order of Excellence; United Fund & Dist.; Univ. of Calgary Acad. Awards Ctte.; Past Pres., Nat. Counc. of Jewish Women of Can.; Providence Creche; Assn. of Alta. Coll. Admin.; Univ. of Toronto Alumni Assn.; Past Chrmn., Mount Royal Coll.; William Roper Hull Home; Social Worker, Calgary Family Service Bureau 1947–49; Founder, Calgary Jewish Family Serv.; Life Mem., Hadassah-Wizo Orgn. of Can., Calgary Br.; Mem., Counc. for the Humanities Inst., Univ. of Calgary; Past Ctte. Mem., Calgary Winter Festival; Adv. Bd. Mem., Alta. Theatre Projects; Past Mem., Calgary City Ballet; Native Arts Found.; Bd. Mem., Pro Musica; Mem. of Senate, Theatre Calgary; Hon. Patron, Calgary Folk Arts Counc.; Alta. Debate & Speech Assoc.; Prime Min. Medal, State of Israel Bonds 1970; Order of Canada Medal 1975; Alta. Achievement Award 1975; Queen's Anniversary Medal 1977; Sesquicentennial Year Plaque, Univ. of Toronto 1977; Citizen of the Year 1979; Boy Scouts of Canada Medal 1984; Paul Harris Fellow Medal 1984; Variety Club Internat. 'Lifeliner' Medal 1984 City of Calgary, The Centennial Award of Merit 1985; Theatre named 'Martha Cohen Theatre' Calgary Centre for Performing Arts; mem., Candn. Assoc. of Soc. Workers; Club: Canyon Meadows Golf and Country; Address: PH 1701, 318 – 26 Ave. S.W., Calgary, Alta. T2S 2T9.

**COHEN, Matt(hew),** M.A.; author; translator; b. Kingston, Ont. 30 Dec. 1942; s. Morris and Beatrice (Sohn) C.; e. Fisher Park and Nepean High Schs. Ottawa 1960; Univ. of Toronto B.A. 1964, M.A. 1965, grad. studies 1966; Lectr. in Religion, McMaster Univ. 1967–68; Writer-in-Residence, Univ. of Alta. 1975–76; Visiting Prof. of Creative Writing, Univ of Victoria 1979–80; Writer-in-Residence, Univ. of Western Ontario 1981; Visiting Prof., Univ. of Bologna 1984; rec'd Sr. Can. Council Arts Award 1977, 1985; John Glassco Translation Prize 1991; author 'Korsoniloff' 1969; 'Johnny Crackle Sings' 1971; 'Columbus and the Fat Lady' 1972; 'The Disinherited' 1974; 'Wooden Hunters' 1975; 'The Colours of War' 1977; 'Night Flights, And Other Stories, New and Selected' 1978; 'The Sweet Second Summer of Kitty Malone' 1979; 'Flowers of Darkness,' 1981; 'The Expatriate: Collected Short Stories' 1982; 'Café Le Dog' (stories) 1983; 'The Spanish Doctor' 1984; 'Nadine' (novel) 1986; 'Living on Water' (stories) 1988; 'Emotional Arithmetic' (novel) 1990; 'Freud: The Paris Notebooks' (stories) 1991; 'The Bookseller' (novel) 1993; Chrmn., Writers' Union of Canada 1985–86; Address: P.O. Box 401, Verona, Ont. K0H 2W0.

**COHEN, Maxwell,** O.C. (1976), Q.C., D.C.L., LL.D.; university professor and judge; b. Winnipeg, Man. 17 Mar. 1910; s. Moses and Sarah (Wasserman) C.; e. Univ. of Manitoba, B.A. 1930, LL.B. 1934; Northwestern Univ., LL.M. 1936; Research Fellow, Harvard Law Sch. 1937–38; LL.D. Univ. of N.B.; Univ. of Man.; Univ. of Ottawa; York Univ.; Dalhousie Univ.; D.C.L. Bishop's Univ.; LL.D. Carleton Univ.; m. Isle Alexandra, d. Adolph Sternberg, Vancouver B.C.; one d. Joanne Sternberg; PROF. EMERITUS OF LAW, McGILL UNIV. since 1978; formerly Dean and Macdonald Prof. of Law; Judge, ad hoc Internat. Court of Justice 1981–85; Chrmn. Candn. Sec., Internat. Jt. Comn. (Can.-U.S.) 1974–79; Prof. of Law and Scholar-in-Residence, Univ. of Ottawa 1980– ; Dir., Inst. of Air & Space Law, 1962–65; served with Candn. Army 1942–46 (final rank of Major); Head, Dept. of Econ. and Pol. Science, Khaki Univ. of Can. in Eng. 1945–46; Past Pres. and Hon. Vice-Pres., Candn. Br., The Internat. Law Assn.; mem., Candn. Bar Assn. (former Chrmn., Constitutional and Internat. Law Section); The Bars of Manitoba and Quebec; Former Chrmn. Montreal Branch, Candn. Inst. Internat. Affairs; Hon. mem., Engn. Inst. of Can. 1977; Hon. Life mem., Can. Council Internat'l Law; Hon. Vice Pres., Am. Soc. of Internat. Law 1980– ; Ed. Bd., Cdn. Yearbook of Internat.Law; Foreign Affairs Ed., 'Saturday Night' 1957–61; mem., Candn. del. to 14th Gen. Assembly of Un. Nations 1959–60; Chrmn., Special Comte. on Hate Propaganda, Min. of Justice (Fed.) 1965–66; Special Counsel on Constitutional Law, Govt. of N.B. 1967–70; Chrmn. Roy. Comn. on Labour Leg., Nfld. 1969–72; Roy. Comn. on Collège Militaire, St. Jean 1968; Special Comte. of Inquiry into Unloading of Grain Vessels Montreal Harbour 1967–68; Pres., Que. Adv. Council on Adm. of Justice 1972–74; Chrmn. Adv. Comte. on Marine & Environmental Confs. (Law of the Sea) Depts. of Environment and of External Affairs 1971–74; Chrmn., Select Comte. on Candn. Constitution, Candn. Jewish Congress 1980–82; recipient Archambault Gold Medal, Que. Soc. Criminol. 1967; Humanitarian Award, Counc. of Christians and Jews 1969; John Read Gold Medal Can. Council Internat. Law 1979; Columbia Univ. Wolfgang Friedmann Memorial Award 1981; Distinguished Service Award, Man. Bar Assn. 1984; President's Award, Candn. Bar Assoc. 1986; author of and contrib. to books and pamphlets on Public International Law, the Law of Outer Space, Canadian Constitution and Federalism, Canada/U.S. boundary waters, Labour Law, Antitrust Law, Legal Education, Nuclear, Environmental, Arctic Concerns etc.; articles in Canadian, U.S., U.K. and international legal and social science journals and newspapers; recreation: golf; Clubs: McGill Faculty; Ottawa Univ. Faculty; Rideau (Ottawa); Montefiore (Montreal); Elm Ridge Country (Montreal); Home: 1404 – 200 Rideau Terrace, Ottawa, Ont. K1M 0Z3.

**COHEN, Michael,** M.A., F.I.A., F.C.I.A., A.S.A.; actuarial consultant; b. London, England 19 Feb. 1947; s. Morris and Rose (Harris) C.; e. Central Found. Gr. Sch. 1965; Cambridge Univ., B.A. (Hons.) 1968, M.A. (Hons.) 1969; m. Marguerite d. Max and Madeleine Cousin 9 Nov. 1968; children: Raphael, Aviva; PRINCIPAL, WILLIAM M. MERCER LTD. 1988– ; Prudential Assur. Co. (U.K.) 1968–72; Group Actuary, Montreal 1972–79; Dir.-Gen., Pension Benefits Div., Office of the Supt. of Finan. Inst., Govt. of Can. 1979–88; F.I.A., F.C.I.A.; Home: 6 Fairchild Private, Ottawa, Ont. K2C 3Y5; Office: 275 Slater St., Ste. 1100, Ottawa, Ont. K1P 5H9.

**COHEN, Morley Mitchell;** executive; b. Winnipeg, Man. 2 Jan. 1917; s. Alexander and Rose (Diamond) C.; e. St. John's Tech. Sch.; Haifa Univ., Ph.D. 1986; m. Rita Lillian Stober, 4 Nov. 1957; children: Joanne (Mrs. Barry Goldmeier); Donna Susan (Mrs. Graeme Low); CHRMN. & PRES., METROPOLITAN STORES OF CAN. LTD. since 1979; Dir., Gen. Distributors Ltd.; Pres. Saan Stores Ltd. 1954–57; Extve. Vice-Pres., Gen. Distributors Ltd. 1964–78; Vice-Pres., Gendis Inc. 1979; Pres., Metropolitan Stores Can. Ltd. 1969; rec'd. 'Man of the Year' Award, Israel Bond Organization 1972; Samuel Bronfman Medal for outstanding leadership over the years 1982; served with R.C.A.F. 1940–45; Chrmn., Combined Jewish Appeal (Montreal) 1970; Treas., United Jewish Appeal 1970–71; Treas., YMHA & YWHA (Montreal) 1971; Hon. Pres. YMHA; Dir., Montreal Bd. Trade 1973–75; Chrmn., Arthritis Soc.; Mem. Campaign Cabinet (combined Jewish Appeal) 1980; Chrmn., Capital Fund Drive (YMHA) 1980; Dir., Counc. for Candn. Unity 1983; Bd. Dirs.: Jewish Community Fund Foundation; Jewish Gen Hosp. (Montreal); Montreal Gen. Hosp. 1988; Candn. Friends of Haifa Univ. 1985– ; Chrmn., Special Div., Montreal Gen. Hosp. Fundraising 1986–87; Chrmn., Bd. of Trustees YM/YWHA 1987; Assoc. Chrmn., Capital Campaign, Montreal Museum of Fine Arts 1989; Dir., Montreal Gen. Hosp. 1988; Chief Barker, Variety Club of Quebec 1989; Founder, International Golfing Soc.; recreations: golf; tennis; bridge; Clubs: B'nai B'rith; Elmridge Golf & Country (Pres. 1974–75); Banyon Country Club, Palm Beach; Montefiore (Dir.); Home: 3468 Drummond St., P.H. 1201, Montreal, Que. H3G 1Y4; Office: P.O. Box 300, Pointe Claire, Que. H9R 4P2.

**COHEN, Morrie M.,** B.Comm., B.A.; cosmetic executive; b. Montreal, Que. 18 July 1936; e. McGill Univ., B.Comm. 1960; Concordia Univ., B.A. 1965; m. Diane Louis 9 June 1965; children: Caroline, David, Robyn; PRES., REGENT INDUSTRIES LTD. 1964– ; Pres., Caroline Cosmetics Ltd. 1971– ; Modico Industries Ltd. – public holding co. 1973– ; Modico Canada Ltd. – private investment co. 1984– ; Modico U.S. Inc. – private U.S. investment corp. 1989– ; Dir., Old Brewery Mission 1990– ; Dir., Israel Cancer Rsch.; Founder, 'Old Shoes for Poor Souls' (charity orgn.); Vice Pres. & Dir., Hebrew Free Loan; Toujour Ensemble; Auberge Shalom; recreation: tennis; Clubs: Mount Royal Tennis; Montifore; Home: 65 Forden Ave., Westmount, Que. H3Y 2Z1; Office: 3600 Rachel St. E., Montreal, Que. H1W 1A9.

**COHEN, Ronald I.,** A.B., B.C.L.; lawyer/film producer; b. Montreal, Que. 28 Oct. 1943; s. Joseph and Rhoda Patricia (Shane) C.; e. Westmount H.S. 1960; Harvard Coll. A.B. 1964; McGill Univ. B.C.L. 1968; children: Lewis Charles, Lara Elizabeth, Daniel Howard Frederick; PRESIDENT, CINÉ-CINÉ PRODUCTIONS INC. 1992– ; and CHAIR, CANADIAN BROADCAST STANDARDS COUNCIL 1993– ; Bus. Mgr., Harvard Crimson 1963–64; Cons., 'The Economist' 1964–65; Attorney 1969– ; Founder, Ctr. for Public Interest Law; Prof., McGill Univ. 1971–74; Dir., Consumers Assn. of Can.; Adv., Fed. Min. of Consumer Affairs; Founding Mem., Cons. de la Protection du Consom.; Couns., Que. Police Comn. Inquiry into Orgn. Crime 1974–77; Film producer 1977– ; Founding Chrmn., Acad. of Candn. Cin. & TV 1979–82 (Bd. Mem. & Vice-Chrmn. 1982–85; Chrmn. 1985–87; Past Chrmn., 1987–88; Treas., 1988–89; Special Adv. to the Bd. 1989– ; Dir.); Chrmn., Fed. Task Force on Film Mktg., Exhib. & Dist. 1982–84; Cons., Min. of Commun.; Pres., Ronald Cohen Film Co.; Dir., Centaur Theatre 1987–91; Banff Television Found. 1989–92 (Co-Chair, Finance Ctte. 1991–92); Mem. Bd. of Dirs., Friends of the McGill Libraries 1991– ; Friends of the National Library 1991– ; (Chair, Acquisitions Ctte.); Mem., Churchill Soc. for the Adv. of Parl. Democracy; Internat. Churchill Soc.; Producer: 'Power Play' 1978; 'Running' 1979; 'Middle Age Crazy' 1980; 'Ticket to Heaven' 1981 (winner, Best Picture, Genie Awards 1982); 'Harry Tracy' 1982; 'Draw!' 1984; 'Race for the Bomb' (6 hr. mini-series) 1985; Co-Producer 'Champagne Charlie' (4 hr. mini-series) 1987; Extve. Prod. 'Ordeal in the Arctic' 1993; 'Red Rain' 1993; author: 'Quebec Votes' 1968, 'The Regulation of Misleading Advertising in Canada' 1971, 'A Bibliography of the Works of Winston Churchill' forthcoming; co-author: 'The Constitutional Validity of A Trade Practices Law for Canada' 1975, 'Making It' 1987; recreations: water skiing, hockey, skiing, tennis; Home: 1351 Potter Dr., Manotick, Ont. K4M 1C3 and Apt. 1505, 4998 de Maisonneuve Blvd. W., Montreal, Que. H3Z 1N2.; Office: Suite 1020, Place du Canada, Montreal, Que. H3B 2M2.

**COHEN, Saul,** M.D., FCFPC, S.O.M.; physician; b. Toronto, Ont. 29 Jan. 1921; s. Sam and Fanny (Meyers) C.; e. Parkdale Coll. Inst. Toronto 1938; Univ. of toronto M.D., L.M.C.C. 1943; m. Sheila d. Arnold and Ann Abrams 10 Sept. 1944; children: Stephen Russell, Mitchell Stewart, Brenda Louise; 5 grandchildren; MEDICAL CONSULTANT, ALCOHOL & DRUG DAY CARE PROGRAM, CREDIT VALLEY HOSP., Erin Mills, Mississauga, Ont. 1988– ; served with RCAMC 1943–46, rank Capt.; Family Med. Practice Melville, Sask. 1946–54, Regina Med. Centre 1954–88; Med. Cons. to Alcohol. Rehab. Centre Regina 1959–80, Ex Officio Adv. Med. Cons. to Bd. Dirs. Sask. Alcoholism Comn.; Charter mem. teaching prog. chem. dependencies Med. Sch. Saskatoon 1972; Assoc. Clin. Prof. Dept. Family Med. Plains Health Centre 1973–78, Pres. Med. Staff 1973–74; Charter mem. est. Sask. Phys. at Risk Ctte. 1976; Chrmn. Sask. Alcohol & Drug Abuse Comn. 1981–88; Sask. Order of Merit Medal 1986; nominated as Family Phys. of Yr. Sask. 1988; naming of the Dr. Saul Cohen Outpatient Centre for Treatment of Alcohol & Drug Abuse in Melville, Sask. by Melville & Dist. Alcohol & Drug Abuse Soc. 16 Sept 1988; author 'Physician's Manual on Alcoholism' 1965 (rev. 1989); numerous med. publs.; Fellow, Coll. Family Phys. Can.; Sr. Life mem. Coll. Phys. & Surgs. Sask.; Sr. mem. Candn. Med. Assn.; mem. Coll. of Physicians & Surgeons of Ont.; recreations: golf, travel, family; Club: Hidden Lake Golf and Country (Burlington, Ont.); Home: #1 – 1725 The Chase, Erin Mills, Mississauga, Ont. L5M 4N3.

**COHEN, Sidney M.;** freelance television program creator; producer, director and production consultant; b. Montreal, Que. 9 Nov. 1947; s. Edward B. and Beatrice (Rosenthal) C.; e. Northmount 1965; ECPI 1968; m. Susan d. Max and Beatrice Rosenberg 29 May 1972; children: Jay Robert, Tracy Faye; PRES., SUPER PEOPLE PRODUCTIONS LTD. 1976– ; CFCF-TV Announcer, 1963–66; Prod., Screen Gems 1966; Pub. Relns., Expo '67; Prod./Dir., CJOH-TV 1969; CFCF-TV 1972; created, sold, prod., dir. 'The Mad Dash' 1978; 'The More We Get Together'; co-creator 'Thrill of a Lifetime'; commuted weekly to Hollywood, dir. U.S. series; prod./dir. CFTO-TV 1981; Prod./Dir. of programs covering space launch, Royal Visits, Fed. & Prov. elections, political conventions, game shows; has had at least one network series each season since 1969; Dir. CTV National News & Canada AM; launched CBC's 'Midday' (over 1100 eps.); prod./dir. 'Test Pattern' for MuchMusic; Dir./Cons. 'Business World' and 'On the Arts' for CBC Newsworld; Prod./Dir. 'Pols Minute'; Dir. 'Shirley' (pilot & eps.) CTV; Dir. Macleans/CTV Constitution Special 91; Dir. 1992 Summer Olympics Barcelona-CTV; 'Just A Minute' C.R.B. Foundation; Director 1993– ; Extve. Prod., Canada AM, CTV 1993– ; Extve. Prod., New Program Development CTV 1994– ; Dir. over 8000 TV program episodes, Can.; stand-up comedy & audience warm-ups; Guest Lectr., Cunard's Queen Elizabeth 2; Concordia Univ., Ryerson Inst.; Cons., many Cdn. and internat. prodns.; trainer, CBC; Mem., Acad. of Candn. Cinema & T.V.; recreations: travel, tennis, astronomy, aircraft; Office: 21 Windsor Court Rd., Thornhill, Ont. L3T 4Y4.

**COHNSTAEDT, Joy,** B.F.A., Post grad. Dip.Ed.; professor; b. Toronto, Ont. 15 Apr. 1943; d. Edward Bertram and Dorothy Helen Rowe; e. Certificate Prog. Regina Coll. Sch. of Art 1962; Univ. of Man. B.F.A. Visual Arts 1964; Univ. of Newcastle upon Tyne, Engl. Grad. Dip. in Edn. Art Major 1966; Saskatchewan Dept. of Edn. Profl. B. Certificate Fine Arts 1966; Univ. of Sask. post-grad rsch. Social Sci. Anthrop. 1967–73; Univ. of Manitoba Interdisciplinary Ph.D. program 1988– ; Harvard Bus. Sch. Arts Admin. Certificate 1975; m. Martin L. s. Elsie and Ludwig C. 21 Apr. 1968; children: William, John, Robert, Delores, Nicolette; CHAIR, ONTARIO COUNCIL OF UNIVERSITY AFFAIRS 1992– ; Mktg. of Visual Arts, Vincent Price Art Collection 1962; Art Gallery Librarian, Winnipeg Art Gall. 1962–64; Children's Art Class, Univ. of Man. 1963–64; Archeol. Glenbow Found. 1964; Illustrator Sask. Natural Hist. Museum and Archeol. Assn. 1964–65; Art Teacher Blaydon Grammar Sch.; Teacher West Walker Jr. Sch.; Art Drama and Film classes for children, Univ. of Newcastle-upon-Tyne 1965–66; Art Teacher Regina Coll., Balfour, Martin, Thom and Central Collegiate 1964–69; Sessional Lectr. in Anthrop. and Sessional Asst., Univ. of Sask. 1969–70; Lectr. in Arts Admin. on Cultural Resources Mgmt., Banff Centre 1973, 1976; Asst. Dir. Arts Dept. of Culture and Youth, Prov. of Sask. 1973–77; Exec. Dir. Sask. Arts Bd. 1977–82; Depy. Min. of Culture, Heritage and Recreation, Prov. of Manitoba 1982–87 (Prov. of Man. 1982–89); Bora Laskin National Fellowship in Human Rights Research 1987–88; Visiting Scholar, University Coll., Univ. of Manitoba 1987–89; Dean of Fine Arts, York Univ. 1989–92, seconded to Chair OCUA 1992–95; involved in cultural anthrop., museums, collections mgmt., edn. and community devel., literary, visual and performing arts, cultural ind. of pub., recording, film video and crafts, and telecommunications; mem. National Advisory Ctte. on Culture Statistics, Stascan; mem. Fed. Cultural Policy Review Ctte.; mem., Candn. Comn. for UNESCO; served on Candn. Del. to UNESCO Gen. Assemblies in Paris and Belgrade and to the Conf. of Commonwealth Arts Agys. in England; author various articles on culture, heritage, communications and human rights; Home: 1 Humbercrest Blvd., Toronto, Ont. M6S 4K6; Office: 700 Bay St., 7th Floor, Toronto, Ont. M5G 1Z6.

**COHON, George A.,** O.C., B.Sc., J.D., Ph.D. (Hon.); senior chairman and chairman of the executive committee; b. Chicago, Ill. 19 Apr. 1937; s. Jack A. and Carolyn (Ellis) C.; came to Can. 1968; e. Pub. and High Schs., Chicago; Drake Univ., B.Sc. 1958; Northwestern Sch. Law, Juris Doctorate in Law 1961; m. Susan, d. Abe and Ann (Liberman) Silver, 4 Sept. 1960; two s. Craig, Mark; CHRMN., PRES. AND C.E.O., McDONALD'S RESTAURANTS OF CANADA LTD 1971–92; Vice Chrmn., Moscow-McDonald's; Chrmn., Bd. of Trustees, Ontario Science Centre 1986–92; Chrmn., Bd. of Govs., Exhibition Place 1983–85; Dir., Can. Post. Corp. 1981–84; Astral Inc.; McDonald's Restaurants of Canada Limited; Quno Corp.; The Royal Bank of Canada; The Toronto Sun Publishing Corp.; Candn. Friends of Haifa Univ.; Candn. Jewish News; Hugh MacMillan Medical Centre 1977–92; York Univ.; Can. Council of Christians and Jews; Fed. against Child Abuse; Ont. Men's ORT; Can. Robert F. Kennedy Memorial; Jr. Achievement of Can.; Hon. Dir., Muscular Dystrophy Assn. of Can.; Trustee, Drake Univ.; The Nat. Counc. of the Duke of Edinburgh's Award in Can.; mem., Adv. Counc., Young People's Theatre; Funding Com., Can Hearing Soc.; Grand Council of Can. Jaycees-Central Region; Nat. Adv. Council of Can. Cystic Fibrosis Foundation; Hon. mem., Nat. Council of Boy Scouts of Can.; Gov., Can. Opera Soc.; Participation House; Mt. Sinai Hosp.; YMCA of Metro Toronto & Central Ont. Lakeshore 'Y'; Olympic Trust of Can.; Toronto Chap., Dysautonomia Foundation Inc.; Patron, Toronto French Schools; founding Patron, Ronald McDonald Houses; Founder, Ronald McDonald Children's Charities of Can.; Founding Mem., Law Development Bd., Northwestern Univ. Sch. of Law; Dir., Internat. Assn. of Children's Funds-Russia; Adv., Ont. Coll. of Art; Co-Chrmn. Metro Santa Claus Parade; Special Events Chrmn., United Way of Metro Toronto 1982; Special Gifts Chrmn., Can. Council of Christians & Jews 1981; Co-Chrmn., North York YMCA Building Fund; Nat. Campaign Chrmn., State of Israel Bond, Can.; apptd. Member, Order of Canada 1987; Officer 1993; recipient, Merit Award, Northwestern Univ. Alumni Assoc. 1987; Alumni Medal Award, N.W. Univ. Alumni Assn. 1992; McGill Univ. Mngt. Achievement Award 1992; Univ. of Alta., Candn. Bus. Leader Award 1992; Ont. Med. Assn. Centennial Award 1992; Univ. of Man., Internat. Distinguished Entrepreneur Award 1992; Canada 125 Medal 1992; Person of the Year Award, The St. George's Soc. of Toronto 1993; Israel Prime Minister's Medal; Promises of Hope Award Can. Children's Foundation; B'Nai Brith Canada 1983 Humanitarian Award; Alumni Distinguished Service Award, Drake Univ.; Univ. of Haifa, Doctorate of Philosophy (hon. causis); Civic Award of Merit, City of Toronto; Human Relations Award, Candn. Counc. of Christians & Jews 1989; practiced law with Cohon, Raizes and Regal 1961–67; Licensee, McDonald's Restaurants of Ont. 1967–71; served with U.S. Army and Air Force Reserve, 1962–68; Founder and Dir., Better Boys Foundation, Chicago; Gov., Jr. Achievement of Metro Toronto & York Region; Bd. of Overseers of Harvard College, Russian Rsch. Ctr.; Dir., York Univ.; Hon. Chair, Variety Village Sunshine Games (Toronto-Chicago Sister City Ctte.); mem. Am., Ill. and Chicago Bar Assns.; Candn. Restaurant Assn. (Past Dir.); Past mem., Young Pres. Organ.; recreations: tennis, skiing, photography; Club: York Racquets; Caledon Ski; Home: 112 Forest Hill Rd., Toronto, Ont. M4V 2L7; Office: McDonald's Place, Toronto, Ont. M3C 3L4.

**COHON, Susan Silver,** B.Sc.; community volunteer, housewife; b. Buffalo, N.Y. 23 Aug. 1938; d. Abraham and Ann (Liberman) Silver; e. Northwestern Univ. B.Sc. 1960; m. George A. s. Jack and Carolyn C. 4 Sept. 1960; children: Craig, Mark; Recipient, 1991 Gardiner Award Honouring the Citizens of the Year (Metro Toronto); Bd. Chair, Village Village Sport Training and Fitness Ctr. 1990–92; Mem., Extve. Ctte., Variety Village; Bd. Mem., Ont. College of Art (1988–Feb. 1993); Candn. Paraplegic Assn.; Auxiliary Mt. Sinai Hospital; Hugh MacMillan Med. Ctr.; Bd. Mem., Univ. of Toronto Crown Foundation; Mem., Bd. of Gov., Baycrest Centre for Geriatric Care; Miss Saigon opening for Hosp. for Sick Children; recreations: tennis, travel, bridge; clubs: York Racquets.

**COKE, William J.,** B.A.; personnel executive; b. Guelph, Ont. 14 Mar. 1924; s. Joseph and Elsie Clair (Dodds) C.; e. Queen's Univ. B.A. 1948; Post Grad. Ind. Relations 1949; m. Mary d. Worden and Harriet Edwards 3 Sept. 1949; children: Barry, Charles, Cheryl, Kathryn; PRESIDENT, WILLIAM J. COKE AND ASSOCIATES LIMITED and FRANCHISE RECRUITERS

1988– ; Dir.: State Bank of India (Can.); Candn. Patricia Exploration Ltd.; Chrmn., Sudbury Management Services; Personnel Offr. Canada Packers Ltd. 1949–50; Dir. of Personnel Shirriff's Ltd. 1950–56; Sr. Cons. Retirement Plan Services 1956–60; Agy. Mgr. Excelsior Life Ins. Co. 1960–61; Gen. Mgr. Manpower Temporary Services, Canada 1961–64; Vice-Pres. Manpower Inc. (Milwaukee, U.S.A.) 1964–67; Vice-Pres. and Gen. Mgr., Manpower Temporary Services, Canada 1967–75, Pres. & C.E.O. 1975–87; Co-founder, Dir. and Past Pres. Assn. of Candn. Franchisors (designated 'Executive of Year' 1986; Award of Merit 1991); Co-founder, Dir. and Past Pres. Fedn. of Temporary Help Services; Chrmn. Goodwill Services, Toronto 1983–84; Chrmn., Corporate Campaign Ctte., Ont. Rehab. and Work Counc. 1989–90; Chrmn. Better Bus. Bur. of Metrop. Toronto 1983–84; Bd. of Dirs., St. John Ambulance of Metro. Toronto 1991– ; (Vice Chrmn. 1992– ;); Hon. Vice Consul, Republic of Togo 1990– ; Bd. of Referees, Unemployment Insurance Comn. 1990– ; Mem., Ont. Inst. of Arbitrsation and Mediation, Franchise Panel and Employment Services Panel 1992; Advisory Bd., Corrections Canada 1993; served in 2nd World War with 1st Candn. Para. Batt., Br. 6th Airborne Div.; recreations: cottage, farm, standardbred horses; Clubs: Ontario; World Trade; Bd. of Trade of Metro Toronto; Royal Candn. Mil. Inst.; Home: R.R. 3, Holland Centre, Ont. N0H 1R0; Office: Ste. 203, 20 Holly St., Toronto, Ont. M4S 3B1.

**COKER, John Martin;** retired reinsurance executive; b. Bognor Regis, Eng. 29 Mar. 1920; s. late Maj. John Nelson, M.C., T.D. and late Hilda Muriel (Martin) C.; e. Felsted Sch.; m. Edith, d. Henry Williams, 12 June 1947; CHRMN., PRES. AND DIR., MUTOR INVESTMENTS LTD. 1988– ; with Caledonian Insurance Group 1937–58: Resident Inspector for W. Indies 1950–54; Asst. Mgr. New York 1954–56; Grp.'s Asst. Mgr. for Can. and Secy., Caledonian-Canadian Insurance Co. 1956–58; Asst. Secy., Western-British America Assurance Group 1958–61; Gen. Mgr., Global General Insurance Co. 1961–63; joined Munich Reinsurance Group, Jan. 1964; served in Munich 1964–66, London 1966–69, returned to Canada 1969; Chief Agent (Non-Life) for Canada 1975–85; Pres. & Dir., Munich Reinsurance Co. of Canada 1969–85, Vice Chrmn. and Dir. 1986–90; Pres. and Dir., Munich-Canada Mgmt. Corp. Ltd. 1974–85, Vice Chrmn. and Dir., 1986–90; Pres. and Dir., The Great Lakes Reinsurance Co. 1975, Exec. Vice Pres. and Dir., 1976–82, Dir. 1982–90; Dir., Great Lakes Reinsurance Holdings 1988–90; Exec. Vice Pres. and Dir., Munich Holdings Ltd. 1969–71, Pres. and Dir. 1972–85, Dir. 1986–91; Dir., Munich Life (ex Munich-London) Mgmt. Corp. 1969–90; A.C.I.I. 1948; Hon. Chrmn., Reinsurance Rsch. Counc. 1984–91 (Chrmn., 1981–83); Dir., Insurance Bureau of Can. 1981–83 (Alt. Dir. 1977–81); A/Major, R.E. in 14th Army, 1945; Anglican; Clubs: National; Canadian; Empire; Home: Apt. 412, One Benvenuto Place, Toronto, Ontario M4V 2L1; Office: 22nd Flr., 390 Bay St., Toronto, Ont. M5H 2Y2.

**COLAS, Emile Jules,** Q.C., B.A., B.Eng., B.C.L., M.C.L., LL.D.; lawyer; engineer; b. Montreal, Que. 3 Oct. 1923; s. Emile and Elise (Pila) C.; e. McGill Univ. B.Eng. 1946; Univ. of Ottawa B.A. 1947; McGill Univ. B.C.L. 1949, M.C.L. 1950; Univ. of Ottawa, LL.D. 1980; m. Rejane Laberge 25 Oct. 1958; children: Bernard, Hubert, François; called to the Bar of Quebec 1950; cr. Q.C. 1965; Jr. Bar of Mtl. Secy. 1953–54, Vice Pres. 1954–55, Pres. 1955–56; Bar of Mtl. Mem. of Council 1956–57, 1967–69; Belgium Inst. of Intl. and Comparative Law, corresponding mem. for Can., 1957– ; Legal Aid Bureau of the Bar of Mtl., Founder 1956, Vice Pres. 1956–66, Pres. 1966–72; as repres. Natl. Conf. on Poverty (Ottawa) 1971, Honorary Pres. 1972–73; Conf. of Commiss. on Uniformity of Legislation in Can., delegate of the Bar of P.Q.: mem., 1956–63, 1965– ; Vice Pres. 1968–69, Pres., 1969–70, Honorary Pres. 1970–71; Intl. Union of Young Lawyers, Vice Pres. as rep. of Can., 1962–68; Bar of P.Q.: mem. of Council 1967–69; Candn. Bar Assn.: mem. of Council for Que. 1961– , Vice Pres. for Que. 1971–72, Chrmn. sub-cmte. on civil justice, Chrmn. natl. cmte. on legal educ. and training; Intl. Union of Lawyers, Mem. of Council for Can., 1969– ; Chrmn., Family Law Section, Natl. Conf. on Poverty (Ott.) 1972; apptd. to Adv. Counc. on Justice of P.Q. 1973; Pres., Candn. Branch, Intl. Law Assn. 1976– ; Dir., Council on Candn. Unity 1978; Intl. Law Assn. mem. of Natl. Council, Pres. of Intl. Convention 1982 (1st time in Can.); Extve. Cmte. St-John Ambulance; Trustee, Found. for Legal Research (Pres. 1985– ;); Mem., Council, Candn. Human Rights Found.; author of several papers incl. 'Le contrôle juridictionnel du pouvoir discrétionnaire' 1949; 'Les Tribunaux du travail' 1952; 'Le Procès de divorce' 1975; 'La Troisième Voie. Une nouvelle constitution' 1978; and numerous articles in professional publs. on legal aid, civil law, arbitration and labour law; extensive mem. incl. Corp. of Engn. of Que.; Engn. Inst. of Can.; Bar of P.Q.; Candn. Bar Assn.; Chambre de Commerce Française au Canada; Welfare Assn. of the Bar of Mtl; rec'd. Edwin Botsford Busteed Scholarship, 1950; Knight of Obedience, Order of Malta; Medaille de la France libérée; Chevalier de l'Ordre des Palmes académiques; Officier de l'Ordre du Bien Public; Chevalier de la Légion d'Honneur (France); Knight of St. Gregory the Great (Holy See); Knight of Justice of the Venerable Order of St. John; Hon. Consul of Tunisia (1984– ;); R. Catholic; Home: 1 Summerhill Terrace, Montreal, Que. H3H 1B8; Office: 511 Place d'Armes, Montreal, Que. H2Y 2W7.

**COLBERT, Carole;** securities industry executive; b. Ottawa, Ont. 15 July 1943; d. Walter James and Mary Cecilia (Pelot) Gillissie; e. McGill University; m. D. Jack s. Donald and Viola C. 29 June 1985; VICE PRES. & SEC., GOODMAN & COMPANY LTD. 1991– , SEC., DYNAMIC FUND MNGT. LTD. 1979– ; and BGR PRECIOUS METALS INC. 1983– ; Corp. Sec., Beutel, Goodman & Company Ltd. 1971–90; recreations: country estate (Windcrest Farm), archery, skiing, gardening, travel; Home: 131 Chassie Court, Richmond Hill, Ont. L4C 4E8; Office: 44 Victoria St., Toronto, Ont. M5C 1Y2.

**COLBOW, Konrad,** Ph.D.; university professor; b. Bremen, Germany 23 May 1935; s. Konrad L.P. and Hilde (Weber) C.; e. McMaster Univ. B.Sc. 1959, M.Sc. 1960; Univ. of B.C. Ph.D. 1963; m. Christine d. Alfred and Marie Renner 3 Sept. 1960; children: Kevin Michael, Karen Linda; PROF., SOLID STATE AND BIOPHYSICS, SIMON FRASER UNIV. 1965– ; Researcher, Bell Telephone Laboratories, N.J. 1963–65; Alexander von Humboldt Fellow, Univs. Göttingen and Konstanz, W. Germany Jan. 1972–Apr. 1973; Pres., PROFCO Technology Ltd.; author of 85 scholarly pubns. and 8 patents; author, ed. & publisher: 'Physics of Biological Membranes' 1975; Ed.: 'R.H. Wright Lectures on Olfaction' 1986–91; recreations: chess, tennis, soccer; Home: 586 St. Andrews Pl., W. Vancouver, B.C. V7S 1V8; Office: Burnaby, B.C. V5A 1S6.

**COLDWELL, Joan,** M.A., Ph.D.; educator; b. Huddersfield, England 3 Nov. 1936; d. Arthur and Nellie (Johnson) C.; e. Greenhead H.S. 1955; Bedford Coll., Univ. of London B.A. (Hons.) 1958, M.A. (with distinction) 1960; Harvard Univ. Ph.D. 1967; PROF. OF ENGLISH, McMASTER UNIV. 1984– ; and DIR. OF WOMEN'S STUDIES 1989– ; Instr. in English & Asst. Prof. of English, Univ. of Victoria 1960–71; Assoc. Prof. of English, McMaster Univ. 1972–84; Book Page Ed., 'Victoria Daily times' 1968, 1971; freelance prod., 'Ideas,' CBC 1972; leave fellowships: Can. Counc. 1969; SSRHCC 1977, 1984; Teaching Awards (two), McMaster Univ. Students' Union 1981–82; Teaching Award, Ont. Confed. of Univ. Fac. Assocs. 1989; Woman of the Year Award, Hamilton Status of Women Ctte. 1989; Mem., Bd. of Gov., McMaster Univ. 1988–91; Mem., Internat. Shakespeare Assn.; Shakespeare Assn. of Am.; Candn. Rsch. Inst. for the Adv. of Women; Candn. Assn. for Irish Studies; editor: 'Charles Lamb on Shakespeare' 1978; 'The Poetry of Anne Wilkinson' 1990; 'The Tightrope Walker: Autobiographical Writings of Anne Wilkinson' 1992; contbr.: 'The World of W.B. Yeats' 1965, 'Oxford Companion to Canadian Literature' 1983; recreations: swimming, theatre, travel; club: The McGill; Home: 803, 100 Lakeshore Rd. E., Oakville, Ont. L6J 6M9; Office: Hamilton, Ont. L8S 4M9.

**COLE, David Stephen,** B.A.; retail executive; b. Toronto, Ont. 2 Feb. 1951; s. Jack and Esther (Kendal) C.; e. Univ. of Waterloo B.A. 1972; m. Gwen d. Harry and Brenda Whalen 17 June 1979; children: Elizabeth, Ryan, Matthew; Pres. & C.E.O., Sunys Petroleum Inc. 1992–..; Vice Pres. Mktg., Coles Book Stores Ltd. 1972–78; Dir. of Mktg., Shoppers Drug Mart (Div. of Imasco) 1978–82; Extve. Vice Pres., VCS Group 1982–85; Vice Pres. Mktg., Consumers Distributing 1985–86; Senior Vice-Pres. Mktg., Oshawa Foods 1986–91; Bd. of Dir., Toronto French School; recreations: running, skiing; clubs: Alpine Ski; Home: 58 Fifeshire Rd., Willowdale, Ont. M2L 2G8.

**COLE, Douglas Lowell,** A.B., M.A., Ph.D.; historian and university professor; b. Mason City, Washington 9 Dec. 1938; s. Irving Stephen and Harriet (Grass) C.; e. Whitman College A.B. 1960; George Washington Univ. M.A. 1962; Univ. of Washington Ph.D. 1968; m. Christine d. Sheila and Philip Mullins 17 Feb. 1987; one d.: Kate; PROF., HISTORY DEPT., SIMON FRASER UNIV. 1985– ; joined present university 1966; Chair, History Dept. 1977–80; Pres., Faculty Assn. 1986–88; Visiting Prof., Monash Univ. 1968–69; Univ. of Victoria 1970–71; Darwin College, Cambridge Univ. 1980–81; Univ. of Cologne 1982–83; Assoc. Ed., 'Canadian Review of Studies in Nationalism' 1975–81; Eaton's Book Prize 1977; Candn. Historical Assn. Regional History Award 1985; Molson's Research Prize 1986; Simon Fraser Rsch. Prof. 1990–91; Trustee, Burnaby Art Gallery 1982–84; Mem., Candn. Historical Assn. (Council Mem. 1972–75); author: 'Captured Heritage' 1985; co-author: 'From Desolation to Splendour' 1977, 'An Iron Hand Upon the People' 1991; co-editor: 'Phillips in Print' 1983, 'The Journals of George M. Dawson, 1875–1878' 1989; Home: 390 E. Kings Road, North Vancouver, B.C. V7N 1H6; Office: Burnaby, B.C. V5A 1S6.

**COLE, John Wavell,** M.A.; educator; b. Kingston-upon-Thames, Eng. 29 June 1923; s. George Wavell and Mary Laura (Maslen) C.; e. Queen Elizabeth's Grammar Sch. Kingston-upon-Thames 1940; Keble Coll. Oxford B.A., M.A. 1948; m. Penny Jane d. George Arthur and Inez Mattis 7 Dec. 1973; children: by previous marriage, Elizabeth, Jennifer, Christopher; Prof. of Classics, Univ. of Trinity Coll., Univ. of Toronto 1973–88; Asst. Master Trinity Coll. Sch. Port Hope, Ont. 1949; Lectr. in Classics present Coll. 1949, Asst. Prof. 1953, Librarian 1954–61, Assoc. Prof. 1965, Head of Classics 1972–78, Dean of Arts 1978–85, Vice Provost 1980–85; Chrmn., Dept. of Classics 1986–87; Visiting Prof. Univ. of B.C. summer session 1961, 1964, 1965, 1973; Nuffield Travelling and Research Fellow 1969; mem. Regular and Special Curriculum Comtes. Ont. Dept. Educ. during 1960's, Grade XIII Examining Comte. to 1967; recipient Queen's Silver Jubilee Medal 1977; Pres., Toronto & Dist. Cricket League 1953–60; Candn. Cricket Assn. 1967–78; Candn. Del. Internat. Cricket Conf. 1976–79; Chrmn., Friends of Presqu'ile Park 1988–93; mem. Classical Assn. Can.; Am. Ancient Historians Assn.; Candn. Wildlife Assn.; Jersey Wildlife Preservation Trust; Metrop. Toronto Zool. Soc.; Candn. Nature Fedn.; Brighton Presqu'ile Naturalist Club; Candn. Humane Socs.; Candn. Geog. Soc.; recreations: outdoor sports, ornithology, walking; Club: Marylebone Cricket; Rotary International; Home: R.R. #1, Castleton, Ont. K0K 1M0.

**COLE, Leo Joseph,** B.E., P.Eng.; power corporation executive; b. Bell Island, Nfld. 19 April 1932; s. Arthur John and Theresa Mary (Fowler) C.; e. Technical Univ. of N.S. B.E. 1957; m. Marie d. Lillian and John Sweeney 11 Sept. 1965; children: Marie, Glenn; EXTVE. VICE-PRES., NFLD. & LABRADOR HYDRO and PRESIDENT, CHURCHILL FALL'S (LABRADOR) POWER CORP. 1989– ; Electrical Engr., Dosco, Bell Island 1957–59; Dist. Design. Engr., Nfld. & Labrador Hydro 1959–65; Systems Planning Engr. 1965–68; Chief Engr. 1968–74; Mgr. of Engr. 1974–76; Dir. of Engr. 1976–79; Vice-Pres. Engineering & Constr. 1979–89; Chrmn., Twin Falls Power Corp.; Bd. Mem., Gull Island Power Co. Ltd.; Mem., Assn. of Profl. Engrs. & Geoscientists of Nfld.; Inst. of Electronics & Electrical Engrs.; recreations: swimming, skating; Home: 22 Limerick Place, St. John's, Nfld. A1B 2H3; Office: Hydro Place, P.O. Box 12,500, St. John's, Nfld. A1B 3T5.

**COLE, Ronald Denis,** B.Comm., M.B.A.; business executive; b. Saskatoon, Sask. 15 Feb. 1942; s. Norman Albert and Myrtle Rosina (Inkster) C.; e. Univ. of Sask., B.Comm. 1964; Univ. de Sherbrooke, M.B.A. 1970; m. Hazel Mary d. Frank and Marjorie Egan 22 Dec. 1971; children: Sandra, Robert, Jacqueline; Pres. & Chief Extve. Offr., Hawker Siddeley Canada Inc. 1988–..; Distrib. Analyst, Molson Breweries Ltd. 1969–70; Brand Mgr., Consortium Français de Confiseries, Paris 1971–72; Advtg. & Sales Promo. Mgr., Rank Xerox S.A. 1972–73; Br. Mgr., Paris Ctr. 1974–76; Dir. of Mktg., East. Region, Xerox Can. 1977–79; Vice-Pres., Marketing CN Express 1979–80; Pres. & C.E.O., CGTX Inc. 1980–87; Vice-Pres. Opns., present firm 1987–88; Chrmn., CGTX Inc.; Dosco Overseas Engr. Ltd.; Hollybank Engr. Co. Ltd.; The Dosco Corp.; CanCar Inc.; Kockums CanCar Corp.; recreations: golf; clubs: Royal Montreal Golf; Mississaugua Golf & Country; Home: 112 Trelawn Ave., Oakville, Ont. L6J 4R2.

**COLE, Susan Patricia Cooper,** B.Sc., Ph.D.; scientist, university professor; b. Toronto, Ont. 3 Dec. 1954; d. Arthur Renwick Cooper and Elizabeth Anne (Mott) C.; e. Lawrence Park C.I. 1971; Neuchatel Jr. Coll. Switz. 1972; Queen's Univ. B.Sc. 1976, Ph.D. 1981; m. Ralph Allen s. John and Mary Whitney 29 Dec. 1982; children: John Cameron, Anne Frances, Ellen Patricia (all Cole Whitney); CAREER SCIENTIST, ONT. CANCER TREATMENT & RESEARCH FOUND. (OCTRF), KINGSTON REG. CANCER CENTRE 1985– ; postdoctoral fellow, Nat. Insts. of Health, Bethesda, Maryland 1981; joined faculty, Queen's Univ. 1983; present rank: Assoc. Prof.; recipient of rsch. grants from OCTRF; Med. Rsch. Council of Can.; Nat. Cancer Inst. of Can.; Cancer Rsch. Soc.; Mihran and Mary Basmajian Award for Excellence in Biomed. Rsch. 1988; Merck-Frosst Award, Pharm. Soc. of Can. 1991; Office: Kingston, Ont. K7L 3N6.

**COLE, Trevor Jack;** horticulturalist; b. London, Eng. 20 Apr. 1934; s. Edward Jack and Margaret Winifred (Derham) C.; e. Ealing Grammar London 1948; Simon Langton Grammar Canterbury 1952; Royal Botanic Gardens Kew 1958–60; m. Brenda d. Herbert and Elsie Briggs 1 Oct. 1960; children: Gavin James, Andrea Jane; CURATOR, DOMINION ARBORETUM 1973– ; began hortic. career Hampton Court Palace 1954 followed by 2 yrs. with Brighton Parks Dept.; served aquatic nursery 1960 becoming mgr. gen. nursery; joined Agric. Can. 1967, adaption of native flora to cultivation followed by evaluation of alpine & perennial plants; recipient Award of Merit Internat. Lilac Soc. 1982 & 1990, Garden Writers Assn. 1986; Ont. Hortic Assn. Dist. Service Award 1985; author 'The Ontario Gardener' 1991 and numerous agric. publs. relating to home gardening; Editor-in-Chief 'Practical Guide to Gardening in Canada'; Past Pres. Ottawa Hortic. Soc.; Past Dir. Rhododendron Soc. Can., Garden Writers Assn. Am. (1984–87); Ontario Rock Garden Soc. 1985–88; Home: R.R. 2, Kinburn, Ont. K0A 2H0; Office: Bldg. 72, Central Experimental Farm, Ottawa, Ont. K1A 0C6.

**COLEMAN, Albert John,** M.A., Ph.D.; emeritus professor; b. York Co., Ont. 1918; s. Frank and Phoebe (Gerrard) C.; e. Runnymede Coll. Inst., Toronto, Ont.; Univ. Coll. of Toronto, B.A. 1939; Princeton Univ., M.A. 1942; Univ. of Toronto, Ph.D. 1943; m. Marie-Jeanne Michelle, d. Rodolphe de Haller, 23 July 1953; two s. William Frank, Michael Haller; Lectr., Math. Dept., Queen's Univ. 1943–45; Travelling Secy., World's Student Christian Fed., Geneva, 1945–49; Lectr., Asst. Prof., Assoc. Prof., Univ. of Toronto, 1949–60; Prof. and Head, Dept. of Math & Statistics, Queen's Univ. 1960–80; Hon. Prof. Shandong Univ.; Dir., Internat. Student Centre, Queen's Univ. 1965–80; Visiting Prof., Dublin Inst. for Advanced Study 1952, Jilin Univ., China 1982, Shandong Univ. 1987; author of 'The Task of the Christian in the University' 1947, and 40 mathematical articles; joint ed. series of high-school math. text-books; Pres., Ont. Math. Comn. 1960–62; Pres., Cdn. Math. Soc. 1972–74; mem., Lambeth Conference 1978; Consultant to Min. of Energy Mines and Resources, 1980; Chair., Citizen's Advisory Comte., Millhaven Penitentiary, 1977–79; Chair, Devel. Comm., Internat'l Mathematical Union, 1974–78; Anglican; recreation: music (piano); Home: 1001, 185 Ontario St., Kingston, Ont. K7L 2Y7.

**COLEMAN, D'Alton Corry,** B.A., M.B.A.; transportation executive; b. Edmonton, Alta. 19 Feb. 1936; s. James A. and Phillis D. (Rigby) Coleman; e. Univ. of Western Ont. B.A. (Psychology) 1968, M.B.A. 1970; m. Shirley M. Caruk; two children: Mitchell James, Kelly Elizabeth; VICE PRES., COMMERCIAL AFFAIRS, CP RAIL 1987–..; Industrial Sales Rep., Canadian Johns-Manville Co. 1962; Analyst, Corporate Research., Consumers Gas 1969; Sales Mgr., Chateau Cartier Wines, Div. of Labatt's Ltd. 1970; Asst. Mgr., Freight Sales, CP Rail, Toronto 1972; Asst. Gen. Mgr., Mktg. & Sales 1973; Gen. Mgr., Mktg. & Sales 1974; Gen. Mgr. Mktg., Montreal 1976; Asst. Vice Pres., Mktg. & Sales 1978; Vice Pres. Eastern Region, Toronto 1981; Officer Brother Order of St. John; mem., Canadian Railway Club; Montreal Traffic Club; Toronto Railway Club; Transportation Club of Toronto; Nat. Freight Transportation Assoc.; Counc. of Internat. Business Rsch. Centre, Conf. Bd. of Can.; mem., Counc. of Mktg. Extves., Conf. Bd. of Can.; Clubs: Mount Stephen; Montreal Amateur Athletic Assn.; Univ. of Western Ont. 'W'; Fitness Inst.; Home: 1951 Baile St., Montreal, Que. H3H 1P6.

**COLEMAN, J. Gordon,** Q.C., B.A., LL.B.; lawyer; b. Montreal, Que. 3 May 1936; s. James Gordon and Margaret Eaton C.; e. Univ. of Toronto B.A. 1958; LL.B. 1961; m. Margo d. Robert G. Rudolf 4 July 1961; children: Robert, William, Mary, David; LAWYER, TORY TORY DESLAURIERS & BINNINGTON 1963– ; apptd. by the Govt. of Can. to serve on the roster of panelists for the binational dispute settlement provisions established under Chapt 18, Can./U.S. Free Trade Agreement; Dir. Dresdner Bank Canada and several Candn. public companies; called to Bar of Ont. 1963; past Lectr., Securities Regulations, Univ. of Toronto Fac. of Law; Lectr. on Internat. Lending, Cambridge Univ. (sponsored by Candn. Inst. for Advanced Legal Studies) 1985; past Head, Corp.-Comml. Section, Law Soc. of Upper Can. Bar Admission Course; Patron, former Dir. and mem. Exec. Ctte., Nat. Ballet of Can.; mem. Ont. Securities Comn. Ctte. on Candn. takeover bid legis.; author numerous articles on mergers and acquisitions; Home: 24 Hudson Dr., Toronto, Ont. M4T 2J9; Office: Ste. 3000, Aetna Tower, Box 270, Toronto, Ont. M5K 1N2.

**COLEMAN, James Hayward,** B.B.A., LL.B.; lawyer; b. Truro, N.S. 6 June 1950; s. Gerald Patrick and Katherine Anne C.; e. Saint Francis Xavier Univ. B.B.A. 1971; Dalhousie Univ. LL.B. 1974; m. Ruth d. Theodore and Catherine Rasmussen 15 May 1971; children: Jeremy James, Megan Catherine; PARTNER, MACLEOD DIXON; Dir., Ranchmen's Resources Ltd.; Siam Trading Ltd.; Oban Petroleum Ltd.; Minver Inc.; Sec. & Dir., Total Resources (Can.) Ltd.; editor: 'O'Brien's Encyclopedia of Forms' oil & gas chap.; recreations: tennis, skiing, squash, golf; clubs: Calgary Petroleum, Glencoe, Glencoe Golf & Country; Home: 257 Eagle Ridge Dr. S.W., Calgary, Alta. T2V 2V2; Office: 3700, 400 3rd Ave. S.W., Calgary, Alta. T2P 4H2.

**COLEMAN, John Hewson,** K.M., L.H.D. (Hon.), LL.D., (Hon.); executive; b. Joggins, N.S. 22 March 1912; s. William Bartholomew and Rosalie (Comeau) C.; e. Joggins Public Sch. (Matric. 1928); LL.D. St. Francis Xavier and Saint Mary's Univs.; L.H.D. Mount St. Vincent Univ. (hon.); m. Kathryn Marguerite, d. late F. Stanley Mitchell, Dartmouth, N.S., 12 Sept. 1939; children: Gerald Francis, Kathryn Claire (Mrs. J.H. Green); PRESIDENT, J.H.C. ASSOCIATES LTD.; Chrmn., Lehndorff Corp.; Cameron Corp. Ltd.; Dir., United Group of Mutual Funds; Chrmn., Maritime Steel and Foundries Ltd.; Dir., Intnl. Minerals & Chemical Corp. (Canada) Ltd.; United Financial Management Ltd.; Standard Products (Canada) Ltd.; joined Royal Bank of Canada in Amherst, N.S., Nov. 1928; served at various brs. in N.S.; trans. to Montreal, Candn. Credit Dept., 1946; apptd. Mgr., Cornwall, Ont. 1949; Winnipeg 1954; Supvr., Sask. Brs., 1957; Gen. Inspr. 1960; Asst. Gen. Mgr., 1961; Depy. Gen. Mgr. 1964; Chief Gen. Mgr., 1964; Vice-Pres., Dir. and Chief Gen. Mgr., 1966; Extve. Vice Pres. 1968; Depy. Chrmn. and Extve. Vice Pres. 1970; Kt. of Malta; Roman Catholic; recreations: golf, bridge; Club: Lambton Golf & Country; Toronto Club; Address: 561 Avenue Rd., Suite 603–4, Toronto, Ont. M4V 2J8.

**COLEMAN, John Travers;** foundation executive; b. Vancouver, B.C. 6 June 1933; s. Herbert Travers and Mabel Isobel (Gibb) C.; m. Barbara Elizabeth d. William and Celia Brownrigg 11 May 1956; children: Lisa, Leslie, Adam, Jeffrey; PRESIDENT & CHIEF EXTVE. OFFICER, CANADIAN ADVERTISING FOUNDATION 1989– ; background in tv mgmnt., radio sales, event mgmnt., ad. agency acct. mgr., public relations, editorial writing, journalism, advtg. space sales; Montreal Manager, CTV TV Network Ltd. 1967–74; Mgr., Marketing Serv. 1974–76; Dir., Information Services 1976–80; Dir., Gov. & Indus. Liaison 1980–83; Vice-Pres., Corp. & Indus. Liaison 1983–85; Vice-Pres., Corp. Affairs & Planning 1985–87; Vice-Pres., Govt. & Indus. Affairs & Corp. Sec. 1987–89; Candn. Delegate, Internat. Advtg. Assn. (N.Y.); Dir., Candn. Advertising Congress; Former Dir., Candn. Assn. of Broadcasters; Banff TV Found.; Candn. Captioning Devel. Agency; Societal Internat.; Children's Broadcast Institute; Former Mem., Adv. Council, A.C. Nielsen Co. of Canada; Co-chair, Minister's Business Advisory Council on National Drug Strategy; DOC Communications Rsch. Adv. Bd.; Former Mem., Teaching Staff (part-time), Sch. of Radio & TV, Ryerson Polytech. Inst.; Rsch. Consultant, Royal Comn. on Electoral Reform & Party Financing; author: 'Marketing the Conserver Society' 1976, 'Alone/Together' 1978, 'Canadian Content in Television' 1982, 'Canadian Television: a Broadcaster's Perspective' Innis Foundation 1988; 'Strategic Positioning of Canadian Advertising in the 90s' 1990, 'Canadian Television's Game Scenarios for the 90's' 1991; recreations: reading, researching, stained glass; clubs: Broadcast Executives Soc.; World Futures Soc.; International Inst. Communications; Home: 44 Charles St. W., Apt. 4502, Toronto, Ont. M4W 1A5; Office: 350 Bloor St. E., Toronto, Ont. M4W 1H5.

**COLEMAN, Ronald Borden,** B.Com., LL.B.; consultant; b. Middleton, N.S. 27 Dec. 1932; s. LeBaron Ernest and Jessie May (Banks) C.; e. King's Co. Acad., N.S. 1951; Dalhousie Univ., B.Com. 1955, LL.B. 1957; two s. Ronald Gary, Paul LeBaron; Pres., Independent Petroleum Assn. of Can. 1979; called to Bar of Alta. 1958; joined Home Oil Co. as Solr. 1958; resigned as Sen. Vice-President and Gen. Counsel in 1979; Pres., Dominion Equity Resource Fund Inc.; R.B. Coleman Consulting Co.; Dir., Candn. Conquest Exploration Inc.; Maritime Life Assurance Co.; NOVA Corp. of Alberta; Landmark Corp.; Law Soc. Alta.; recreations: golf; Clubs: Calgary Petroleum; Ranchmen's; Glencoe; Earl Grey Golf; Home: 2230, 720 – 13th Ave. S.W., Calgary, Alta. T2R 1M5; Office: 1710 Bow Valley Sq. 2, 205 5 Ave. S.W., Calgary, Alta. T2P 2V7.

**COLES, Don;** educator; writer; b. Woodstock, Ont.; s. John Langdon and Alice Margaret C.; e. Univ. of Toronto Victoria Coll. B.A., M.A. 1953; Cambridge Univ. M.A. 1955; m. Heidi d. August and Gretel Gölnitz 28 Dec. 1959; children: Sarah, Luke; PROF. OF HUMANITIES & CREATIVE WRITING, YORK UNIV. 1965– ; spent scholarship yr. Florence, Italy 1955; lived in continental Eur. 10 yrs. thereafter; teacher in Humanities Div. and in Creative Writing Prog. York Univ. 1965– , Dir. of Prog. 1979–85; spent no. of yrs. in Cambridge during above period; recipient Gold Medal Nat. Mag. Awards 1985 for 'Dark Fields' group of poems pub. in 'The Canadian Forum'; winner, Governor-Gen.'s Award for English Poetry 'Forests of the Medieval World' 1993; author (poetry) 'Sometimes All Over' 1975; 'Anniversaries' 1979; 'The Prinzhorn Collection' 1982; 'Landslides' (Selected Poems 1975–1985) 1986; 'K. In Love' 1987; 'Little Bird' 1991; 'Forests of the Medieval World' 1993; rep. various anthols. incl. 'Arvon International Poetry Competition Anthology' 1987; 'The Oxford Book of Canadian Verse'. 'The Penguin Anthology of Canadian Poetry', 'The Poets of Canada', 'The New Canadian Poets'; ed. 'The Moment is All' by Ralph Gustafson; former Fiction Ed. 'The Canadian Forum', poetry reviews for above and other publs.; Poetry Ed. May Studio Writing Prog. Banff Centre for Fine Arts 1984– ; mem. P.E.N. Internat.; Writer's Union of Canada; recreation: tennis; Home: 122 Glenview Ave., Toronto, Ont. M4R 1P8; Office: 4700 Keele St., North York, Ont. M3J 1P3.

**COLHOUN, Leslie Alexander,** B.A., M.A., LL.B., LL.D.; lawyer; business consultant; b. Toronto, Ont. 24 Sept. 1920; s. James and Amelia (Alexander) C.; e. Dungannon Royal Sch. 1932–38; Trinity Coll., Dublin, B.A. (Hons. 1st Class) 1948 M.A., LL.B.; Barrister-at-Law, King's Inns, Dublin, 1949; awarded Hon. LL.D. Trinity Coll., Dublin 1984; m. Heather Elizabeth Colhoun, B.A., M.A., LL.B., d. Arthur Frederick Colhoun 4 July 1970; one s. Frederick Leslie; Dir., Penreal Advisors Ltd.; Zenon Environmental Inc.; Zenon Environmental Laboratories Inc.; Zenon Environmental Systems Inc.; joined Personal Trust Dept. National Trust Co. Ltd. 1951; Corporate Trust Dept., Trust Offr. 1952, Mgr. 1961, Asst. Vice-Pres. and Mgr. 1964, Vice-Pres. Corporate Trust, 1966, Vice-Pres., Toronto 1968, Extve. Vice Pres. 1969, Pres. 1972, Pres. and Chief Extve. Offr. 1974; Chrmn. and C.E.O., National Trust Co. Ltd. 1977–84; Vice Chrmn., National Victoria and Grey Trust Co. 1984–86; mem. Lortie Comte. on Indexed Term Deposits and Registered Shareholder Investment Plans (federal 1982); mem. Wyman Comte. on Canada Deposit Insurance Corporation (federal 1985); Past Pres., Trust Companies Assoc. of Can.; Dir., St. Patrick's Benevolent Soc. of Toronto; Chrmn., Westminster Abbey Fund in Canada; Gov., Upper Canada Coll. 1984–86; mem., Governing Counc., Univ. of Toronto 1978–84; mem., District Health Counc. of Metropolitan Toronto 1984–85; Past Pres., mem. Sr. Adv. Counc., Ont. Heart Foundation; Freemason; Presbyterian; Clubs: York; Toronto; Granite; Royal Canadian Yacht; Toronto Golf; John's Island (Vero Beach, Fla.); Home: 7 Peebles Ave., Don Mills, Ont. M3C 2N9; Office: 21 King St. E., Toronto, Ont. M5C 1B3.

**COLIN, Jean-Pierre,** D.C.S., LL.L., M.B.A.; securities executive; b. Montreal, Que. 23 Sept. 1953; s. Georges and Marguerite (Savard) C.; e. McGill Univ. D.S.C. 1972; Univ. of Ottawa LL.L. 1976; member of Quebec Bar 1977; Univ. of Western Ont. M.B.A. 1980; Cdn. Securities Course 1988; New Partners & Dir. Qualifying Exam 1984; m. Maryanne E. d. Mary and Peter Kramer 7 Sept. 1991; PRESIDENT & DIRECTOR, JP COLIN SECURITIES INC. 1992– ; corp. & comm. law practice 1972–78; Credit Offr. & Mngt. Trainee, Internat. Lending Div., Royal Bank of Can. 1979; Corp. Fin. Assoc., Corp. Fin. Dept., Richardson Greenshields of Can. Limited 1980–82; Assoc., Toronto 1982–85; Vice-Pres. 1985–87; Vice-Pres. & Dir. 1987–88; Sr. Vice-Pres. & Dir. 1988–92; Pres., Caratax Management Inc. (current); Vice-Pres. & Dir., Immo-Guide Inc.; The Montreal Exchange (Working Group on Takeover Bid Legislation 1982); Investment Dealers' Assn. of Can. (Industry Rep., Ad Hoc Ctte. on Comn. Rates 1981); Univ. of Ottawa (V.P., Debating Soc. 1975–76; Pres., Liberal Club 1975); Companion of the Order of NIM; Mem., Standing Ctte. on Mineral Tax Legis. 1987; Delegate, Liberal Party of Can., Internat. Colloquium on Federalism, W. Berlin; co-author of several articles; recreations: sailing, skiing, canoeing, bicycle-touring;

clubs: Bay Moorings Yacht; Home: 1518 Carmen Dr., Mississauga, Ont. L5G 3Z1; Office: Stuie 3110, S. Tower, P.O. Box 62, Royal Bank Plaza, Toronto, Ont. M5J 2J2.

**COLLARD, Edgar Andrew,** C.M., M.A., D.Litt., D.Lit., LL.D., F.R.S.A.; newspaper editor (emeritus); b. Montreal, Que., 6 Sept. 1911; s. Gilchrist and Florence May (Luttrell) C.; e. McGill Univ., B.A. 1935, M.A. 1937; Hon. D.Litt. 1962; Hon. D.Lit., Carleton Univ., 1981; Hon. LL.D., Concordia Univ. 1993; m. Henrietta Elizabeth, d. late Rev. George H. Forde, Cookshire, Que., 23 Aug. 1947; awarded the Certificate of Merit by Candn. Hist. Assn. for outstanding contrib. to local history, 1967; apptd. Assoc. Editor of 'The Gazette' Montreal 1944, Editor 1953–70; received National Newspaper Award for Editorial Writing, 1949, 1950, 1959, 1969; author of: 'Oldest McGill' (a hist. of McGill Univ.) 1946; 'A Tradition Lives' (a hist. of 'The Gazette') 1953; 'Canadian Yesterdays' (a collection of researches in Candn. hist.) 1955; wrote chapters on Principal Dawson and Principal Peterson in 'The McGill Story,' 1960; author of: 'Montreal Yesterdays' (a hist. of 19th century Montreal) 1962; 'Call Back Yesterday' (descriptions of old Montreal) 1965; 'The Story of Dominion Square,' 1970; 'The Art of Contentment' (anthology) 1974; 'The McGill You Knew 1920–60' 1975; 'Montreal: The Days That Are No More' 1976; 'All Our Yesterdays' 1988; 'Montreal Yesterdays' (second series) 1989; '100 More Tales from All Our Yesterdays' 1990; 'Montreal - 350 Years in Vignettes'; 'Passage to the Sea: The Story of Canada Steamship Lines' 1991; also histories of 15 other corporations and institutions; has written a column on the history of Montreal in the 'Gazette,' weekly, 1944– ; apptd. Mem. of Order of Can. 1976; donated the Collard Collection of Canadiana to the National Archives of Can.; United Church; Club: University, Montreal; Home: 400 Stewart St., Apt. 1609, Ottawa, Ont. K1N 6L2.

**COLLARD, (Henrietta) Elizabeth,** C.M., M.A., LL.D., F.R.S.A.; writer; b. Sawyerville, Que. 20 Oct. 1917; d. late Rev. George Henry and late Anna Sophia (Kingston) Forde; e. St. Helen's Sch., Dunham, Que.; Cookshire (Que.) High Sch.; Mount Allison Univ., B.A. 1939, LL.D. 1971; Univ. of Maine, M.A. 1940 (Maritime Provs. Fellow); Univ. of Toronto, Exchange Student 1937–38; m. Edgar Andrew Collard, Montreal, Que., 23 Aug. 1947; Lectr., Hist. of Ceramics, Continuing Ed. Depts., Univ. of Ottawa 1984–89, McGill Univ. 1986, 1988; Sr. Latin and Eng. Mistress, St. Helen's Sch., Dunham, Que., 1940–42; Educ. Ed. 'The Gazette,' Montreal, also frequent contrib. to 'Toronto Saturday Night,' 1942–47; Consult. on ceramics to Candn. Museum of Civilization, Ottawa; hon. Curator of Ceramics, McCord Museum, McGill Univ.; Adv. Ctte. mem., Official Residences Collections 1989–93; has served on many bds. and comtes. incl. Ladies,' Lib. and Acquisition Comtes., Montreal Museum of Fine Arts; Bd. Dirs., Montreal Children's Lib. and Greater Montreal Br. of Victorian Order Nurses (Publicity Chrmn. 10 yrs.); Member of the Order of Canada 1987; author 'Nineteenth-Century Pottery and Porcelain in Canada' 1967 (rev. 1984); 'The Potters' View of Canada: Canadian Scenes on Nineteenth-Century Earthenware' 1983; 'Victorian Pottery and Porcelain in the Canadian Home' 1984 (Canada's Visual History, vol. 64); contrib. author: 'Book of Canadian Antiques' 1974; 'English Pottery & Porcelain' 1980; 'The Canadian Encyclopedia' 1985; several volumes 'Dictionary of Canadian Biography'; also many articles and reviews for various mags. in Gt. Brit., Australia, USA and Can.; mem., Eng. Ceramic Circle; recreation: amateur herpetologist; Home: Apt. 1609, 400 Stewart St., Ottawa, Ont. K1N 6L2.

**COLLE, Michael Thomas,** B.A.; politician; b. Foggia, Italy 1 Feb. 1945; s. Francesco Paulo Antonio and Lucia (Berardinetti) C.; e. St. Michael's College School OSSHD; Carleton Univ. B.A. (Hon.) 1970; m. Sharon d. Rita and Edward Markey 20 June 1970; children: Kristen, Joshua, Bianca, Liam; COUNCILLOR, MUNICIPALITY OF METROPOLITAN TORONTO 1988– ; Educator for 18 years; City Councillor 1981, 1983; Chair, Toronto Transit Comn.; Toronto Transit Consultants Limited; Canadian Urban Transportation Assn., Transit/Environ. Task Force; Mem., Corp. Ctte. of the Environ.; Roman Catholic; Liberal; author: 'The Environmental Benefits of Public Transit' report; recreations: cycling, jogging, opera; Home: 20 Humewood Dr., Toronto, Ont. M6C 2W2; Office: 55 John St., Suite 210, Toronto, Ont. M5V 3C6.

**COLLEDGE, Raymond,** B.Sc., Ph.D.; fuel and association executive; b. Hartlepool, Eng. 20 June 1930; s. Rienzi and Ellen C.; e. Sheffield, Univ., B.Sc. 1950, Ph.D. 1954; m. Viki d. Charles and Judith Searles 1 Apr. 1972; children: Matthew, Christopher; MKTG. MGR., CELANESE CAN. INC. 1981– ; Chrmn., Candn. Oxygenated Fuels Assn. 1984– ; recreations: tennis, skiing, sailing, reading, music; Home: 302 Berkeley St., Toronto, Ont. M5A 2X5; Office: 195 The West Mall, Etobicoke, Ont. M9C 5K1.

**COLLENETTE, Hon. David M.,** P.C., M.P., B.A.; b. London, Eng. June 1946; e. York Univ. B.A. 1969; postgrad. studies Carleton Univ.; m. Penny Hossack 11 Oct. 1975; one s. Christopher; MINISTER OF NATIONAL DEFENCE & VETERANS AFFAIRS, GOVERNMENT OF CANADA 1993– ; Executive Vice-President, Mandrake Management Consultants, Toronto and Ottawa; Admin. Offr., Int. Life Ins. Co. London, Eng. 1970–72; Coordinator 41st Annual Couchiching Conf. 1972; Exec. Dir., Lib. Party of Ont. 1972–74; el. M.P. for York East g.e. 1974, def. 1979, re-el. 1980, def. 1984; Parlty. Del. NATO Brussels, UN New York, E.E.C. Strasbourg, South Am.; confs. Paris, Port-of-Spain, Thessalonika, Israel; served as Parlty. Secy. to Postmaster-Gen., Depy. Govt. House Leader; Chrmn., Toronto Fed. Lib. Caucus 1976–78; Chrmn., Standing Comte. on Energy Legis. and Vice Chrmn., External Affairs & National Defence Sub-Comte. on Canada's Rlns. with Latin Am. and Caribbean 1982–83; Min. of State for Multiculturalism 1983–84; Secretary General, Liberal Party of Canada 1985–87; Anglican; recreations: squash, swimming, classical music, theatre; Clubs: University (Toronto); National Liberal (London, U.K.); Office: House of Commons, Ottawa, Ont. K1A 0A6.

**COLLETT, T. David,** P.Eng.; electrical engineer; b. Hr. Buffett, Nfld. 26 June 1942; s. Thomas and Rita (Wareham) C.; e. St. Paul's Sch. 1959; Memorial Univ. of Nfld., engineering dipl. 1962; Technical Univ. of N.S., B.E.E. 1965; m. Iris d. Caleb and Mollie Crocker 21 Oct. 1967; children: David Jr., Mark, Jonathan; VICE-PRES., OPNS., NFLD. & LAB. HYRDO-ELECTRIC CORP. 1985– ; Electrical Engr., Nfld. & Lab. Hydro 1965–67; Teshmont Cons. Ltd. 1967–68; Terminals Design & Construction Engr., present firm 1968–73; Asst. Chief Engr. 1973–75; Mgr., System Planning 1975–79; Mgr., Engineering, Lower Churchill Devel. Corp. 1979–82; Vice-Pres., Opns. & Engr., Churchill Falls Corp. 1982–85; Dir., Twin Falls Power Corp.; Mem., Assn. of Profl. Engrs. & Geoscientists of Nfld.; Sr. Mem., IEEE (Chrmn., Nfld. & Lab. section 1991): Home: 28 Jasper St., St. Johns, Nfld. A1A 4E2; Office: Hydro Place, Box 12400, St. Johns, Nfld. A1B 4K7.

**COLLETT, Wayne N.,** B.Comm.; energy executive; b. Regina, Sask. 8 Jan. 1941; s. Herbert N. and Janet M. (Bonthron) c.; e. Univ. of B.C. B.Comm. 1963; m. Catherine d. Murdoch and Anne Maclachlan 12 Nov. 1966; children: Elisabeth, Meghan; DIRECTOR, REGULATORY AFFAIRS AND RATES, WESTCOAST ENERGY INC. 1988– ; Peat Marwick Mitchell & Co. 1963–65; Manager, Vancouver, RoyNat Inc. 1965–70; London, Ont. 1970–72; Treas. Montreal 1973–79; Treasurer, Westcoast Energy Inc. 1979–88; Mem., Candn. Inst. of C.A.s; B.C. Inst. of C.A.s; Financial Extves. Inst.; recreations: tennis, skiing; Home: 4384 Starlight Way, North Vancouver, B.C. V7N 3N9; Office: 1333 West Georgia St., Vancouver, B.C. V6E 3K9.

**COLLEY, Peter Michael,** B.A. (Hons.); playwright; screenwriter; b. Scarborough, Eng. 3 Jan. 1949; s. Thomas and Irene (Firth) C.; e. Royal Grammar Sch. High Wycombe, Eng. 1968 (awarded Victor Laudorum as top athlete of yr.); Univ. of Sheffield, B.A. (Hons.) 1971; Univ. of W. Ont., M.A. (incomplete); m. Ellen Ross d. Dr. John and Marilyn Jenkins 22 Nov. 1983; Pres., Buckingham Internat. Productions; Resident Playwright Actors' Alley Repertory Theatre, Los Angeles 1989–93; Resident Playwright Grand Theatre, London, Ont. 1973–76; instr. of playwrighting Theatre Ont. summer courses; author (plays) 'The Saga of Regin' 1971; 'The Donnellys' 1974; 'You'll Get Used to It' 1975; 'The Huron Tiger' 1978; 'I'll Be Back Before Midnight!' 1979 (author of film version titled 'Illusions' 1992); 'Heads, You Lose!' 1981; 'The Mark of Cain' 1984 (co-author of film version 1985); 'When the Reaper Calls' 1990; 'Beyond Suspicion' 1991 (winner, Petro-Canada Plays Award 1991 and 1992); co-author 'The Vaudevillians' musical 1979; mem. ACTRA Writers Guild; Playwrights Union of Can.; Writers Guild Am.; Dramatists Guild; Home: 397 Soudan Ave., Toronto, Ont. M4S 1W6; Office: 21330 Celes St., Woodland Hills, Ca. 91364 USA.

**COLLIE, Michael John,** M.A., F.R.S.A., F.R.S.C.; author; educator; b. Eastbourne, Eng., 8 Aug. 1929; s. Leslie Grant and Elizabeth (Robertson) C.; e. St. Catharine's Coll , Cambridge Univ., M.A. 1956; m. Joanne Aline, d. Dr. Paul L'Heureux, St. Boniface, Man., 20 Dec. 1960; children: Peter, Jeremy, Nicholas, Katharine, Ursula; PROF. EMERITUS 1990– ; Prof. of English, York Univ. 1965–90 (Dean of Grad. Studies 1969–73); Asst. Prof., Univ. of Manitoba, 1957; Lectr. Univ. of Exeter, 1961; Assoc. Prof., Mount Allison Univ., 1962; joined present Univ. 1965; Chrmn., Dept. of Eng., 1967–69; served with Brit. Army Intelligence Corps, 1947–49; author 'Poems' 1959; 'Skirmish with Fact' 1960; 'Laforgue' 1964; 'Jules Laforgue Derniers Vers' 1965; 'The House' 1967; 'Kerdruc Notebook' 1972; 'New Brunswick' 1974; 'George Meredith: A Bibliography' 1974; 'George Gissing: A Bibliography' 1975; 'Jules Laforgue' 1977; 'Jules Laforgue Les Complaintes' 1977; 'George Gissing: A Biography' 1977; 'The Alien Art' 1979; 'George Borrow Eccentric' 1982; 'George Borrow: A Bibliographical Study' 1984; 'George Gissing: A Bibliographical Study' 1985; 'Henry Maudsley: Victorian Psychiatrist' 1988; 'Huxley at Work' 1991; mem., Modern Lang. Assn.; Internat. Assn. Univ. Profs. Eng.; Modern Humanities Research Assn.; Bibliograph. Soc.; Bibliograph. Soc. of Am.; Assn. Candn. Univ. Teachers Eng. (Pres. 1968–69); Royal Inst. Centre for the History of Sci. and Technol.; Candn. Bibliograph. Soc.; Soc. for the Hist. of Sci.; Soc. for the Social Hist. of Med.; recreations: squash, fell-walking, chess: Office: Winters College, York University, North York, Ont. M3J 1P3.

**COLLIN, Arthur E.,** M.Sc., Ph.D.; marine scientist; b. Collingwood, Ont., 16 July 1929 s. Prof. William Edwin, F.R.S.C. and Louie Viola (Leggott) C.; e. Univ. of W. Ont., B.Sc. 1953, M.Sc. 1955; McGill Univ., Ph.D. 1962; Nat. Defence Coll., 1969–70; m. Christa, d. Herbert Dedering, Germany, June 1963: children: David, Andrew, Christiane; Vice Pres., Precarn Associates, Inc. 1989–93; Scientist, Fisheries Research Bd. of Canada, 1955; Oceanographer U.S. IGY Program 1958, Polar Cont. Shelf Project, 1959–62; Visiting Research Instr., Univ. of Wash., 1962–63; Dom. Hydrographer, Candn. Hydrog. Service 1968–71; Asst. Depy. Min., Ocean and Aquatic Sciences 1974–77; Asst. Depy. Min., Atmospheric Environment Service, Dept. of the Environment 1977–80; Assoc. Depy. Min., Dept. of Energy, Mines & Resources 1980–85; Secy., Ministry of State for Science and Technology and Chief Science Advr. to Govt. 1985–87; Lieut., RCN(R); Fellow, Arctic Inst. N. Am.; recreations: skiing, sailing; Club: Rideau; Home: 17 Madawaska Dr., Ottawa, Ont. K1S 3G5.

**COLLINGWOOD, Henry, O.C.;** general merchant; b. St. John's, Nfld. 6 May 1918; s. Thomas W. and Mary A.W. (Petley) C.; e. Prince of Wales Coll., St. John's, Nfld.; m. Maureen Victoria O'Reilly, 15 Oct. 1953; three s. and one d.; CHAIRMAN & CHIEF EXEC. OFFR., BAINE, JOHNSTON & CO. LTD. (estbd. 1780); Chrmn., Woodgate Holdings Ltd.; Corisande Holdings Ltd.; Donovans Industrial Estates Ltd.; Dir., Newfoundland Offshore Services Ltd.; H. Collingwood & Co., Ltd.; Eagle River Salmon Club; mem., Royal Trust Adv. Bd.; began with present Co., 1934; apptd. Pres. 1959; Chrmn. & C.E.O. since 1972; Knight's Cross of the Royal Order of St. Olav 1975; LL.D. (hon. causa), Memorial Univ. of Newfoundland; Officer of the Order of Canada; Anglican; recreations: golf, fishing; Clubs: Murray's Pond Fishing; Home: 1 Kings Bridge Court, St. John's, Nfld. A1C 2R1; Office: Baine, Johnston Centre, 10 Fort William Place, P.O. Box 5367, St. John's, Nfld. A1C 5W2.

**COLLINS, A.F. (Chip),** O.C., C.D., F.C.I.S., P.ADM.; retired Alberta provincial civil servant; Chrmn. & Pres., Alta. Mun. Financing Corp.; Dir., Alta. Resources Railway Corp.; Mem. Alta. Securities Comn.; Office: 12 Flr., 9925 – 109 St., Edmonton, Alta. T5J 2N6.

**COLLINS, Arthur Stewart,** D.F.C.; retired advertising executive; b. Peterborough, Ont. 4 Aug. 1920; s. Frederick and Henrietta (Stewart) C.; e. Renfrew (Ont.) Coll. Inst. 1938; Queen's Univ. 1938–40; m. Patricia Mary, d. Arnold L. Holden, Toronto, Ont. 11 Sept. 1948; children: Katherine E., Michael S., Terence A., Kevin J., Brian H.; Extve. Vice Pres. and Creative Dir., Tandy Advertising Ltd., Toronto 1946–59; Vice Pres. and Dir. of Account Services, Stanfield, Johnson & Hill Ltd., Montreal 1959–62; Vice Pres. and Mgr., Montreal Office, James Lovick Ltd. 1962–63; joined Foster Advertising Ltd. as Vice Pres., Automotive Div. 1963–69; Vice Pres., Central Div. 1969–73; Pres. 1973; Chrmn. 1978; served with RCAF 1940–46, Pilot; 400 Sqdn. Overseas; Anglican; Clubs; Albany; Royal Candn. Mil. Inst.; Home: Omemee, Ont. K0L 2W0.

**COLLINS, Desmond,** B.Sc., Ph.D.; museum curator; educator; b. Daylesford, Victoria, Australia 15 July 1938; s. Harold Frederick and Minnie Margaret (Thompson) C.; e. Univ. of W. Australia B.Sc. 1960;

State Univ. of Iowa Ph.D. 1966; m. Suzanne d. John and Dorothy Reider 8 Aug. 1964; children: Katherine, Matthew, Peter; CURATOR OF INVERTEBRATE PALAEONTOL. ROYAL ONT. MUSEUM 1968– , Head of Dept. 1968–77, 1989– ; Assoc. Prof. of Zool. Univ. of Toronto 1970– ; Resch. Assoc. in Geol. McMaster Univ. 1971–85; Tech. Offr. 3, Geol. Survey of Can. Ottawa 1964–65; Sr. Rsch. Fellow, Brit. Museum (Natural Hist.) London 1966–68; author various articles; mem. Geol. Assn. Can.; Paleontol. Soc.; Palaeontol. Assn.; Internat. Palaeontol. Assn.; Home: 26 Belvedere Blvd., Toronto, Ont. M8X 1K1; Office: 100 Queen's Park, Toronto, Ont. M5S 2C6.

**COLLINS, Glenn Wilfred,** B.Ed., M.Sc.; university registrar; b. Hare Bay, Nfld. 29 May 1948; s. Wilfred Milton and Minnie Estelle (Windsor) C.; e. Memorial Univ. of Nfld. B.Sc. 1969, B.Ed. 1977, M.Sc. 1974; m. Peggy d. William and Eileen Wells 22 Aug. 1969; children: Paula, Jonathan; REGISTRAR, MEMORIAL UNIV. OF NFLD. 1982– , Sec. to Senate; Asst. Registrar present Univ. 1970, Assoc. 1975, Dep. 1976–82; Vice Chrmn. Results Ctte. Can. Summer Games 1977; Councillor Town of Wedgewood Park 1980–85, Dep. Mayor 1985–91; Scholarships: Centenary Scholarship 1966–67, 1967–68; Dr. Wm. Blackall Scholarship 1968–69; Captain Robert A. Bartlett Science Award May 1969; NRC Award 1970–71; mem. Am. Assn. Coll. Registrars & Admissions Offrs.; Assn. Registrars Univs. & Colls. Can. (Exec. Ctte. 1988–92); AUCC Scholarship Selection Ctte. 1983–88, Chrmn. 1990; recreations: hunting, fishing, boating; Home: 5 Heather Place, Wedgewood Park, Nfld. A14 4R7; Office: Elizabeth Ave., St. John's, Nfld. A1C 5S7.

**COLLINS, John Alfred,** M.D.; obstetrician and gynecologist; educator; b. Kitchener, Ont. 2 Oct. 1936; s. John Bandel and Vera (Hannahson) C.; e. Univ. of W. Ont. M.D. 1960; m. Carole Joanne Sedwick d. Bruce West, Toronto, Ont.; children: John Bruce, Blayne Linda, Anne Catherine; PROF., DEPT. OF OBSTETRICS & GYNECOLOGY, MCMASTER UNIV. 1993– ; Clin. Research Fellow, Ont. Cancer Foundation London Clinic 1967–76; Dept. of Obstetrics & Gynecology, Univ. of W. Ont. 1967–77; Asst. Dean Undergrad. Educ. Faculty of Med. 1975–77; Prof. and Head of Obstetrics & Gynecology, Dalhousie University 1977–83; Prof. and Chrmn., Dept. of Obstetrics and Gynecology, McMaster Univ. 1983–93; author or co-author various med. papers and publs.; mem. Candn. Med. Assn.; Soc. Obstets. & Gynecols. Can.; Candn. Fertility Soc.; Am. Coll. Obstets. & Gynecols.; Am. Fertility Soc.; Royal Coll. Phys. & Surgs. Can.; Home: 261 MacNab St., Hamilton, Ont. L8P 3E2; Office: Room 3N52B, 1200 Main St. W., Hamilton, Ont. L8N 3Z5.

**COLLINS, Hon. Dr. John F.,** F.R.C.P.(E), M.H.A.; b. St. John's, Nfld. 1 June 1922; s. the late James and Margaret Collins; e. St. Bonaventure's Coll., St. John's; studies in Commercial Practices and Radio-Telegraphy; Memorial Univ. 1943–45; Univ. of Edinburgh, medicine 1945–50; m. Irene Halley; children; Irene Victoria, Mark, John, Elaine; PRES., ESTRELL CONTRACTS LTD.; Extve. Dir., Terra Nova Enterprises Ltd.; el. M.H.A. for St. John's South prov. g.e. 1975, re-el. 1979, 1982, 1985; Depy. Speaker 1975–79; Pres., Treasury Bd., 1980–85; Min. of Finance, 1979–88; Min. of Health and Depy. Premier, Nfld. 1988–89; radio operator, Gander, Labrador; worked on wartime shipping activities to U.K. and Northern Russia; Research Fellowship, Child Health, Edinburgh Univ. 1959; Research Fellowship, Ont. Heart Found., Univ. of Toronto 1961; Head, Dept. of Cardiology, Janeway Child Health Centre 1966–69; Chief, Dept. of Neonatology, Grace General Hospital, St. John's 1974–78; Nat. Chrmn., Candn. Med. Assoc., Child Health Ctte. 1965–68; Pres., Candn. Paediatric Soc. 1970–71; Past Pres., Rotary Club, St. John's; P. Conservative; Offices: (Estrell) 16 Portugal Cove Rd., St. John's, Nfld. A1B 2L6 and (Terra Nova) P.O. Box 1297, St. John's, Nfld. A1C 5N5.

**COLLINS, Brig.-Gen. John James,** O.M.M., C.D., B.A., S.M.; consultant; b. Toronto, Ont. 18 Apl. 1923; s. Edgar Guy and Margery Isabel (Mott) C.; e. Univ. of B.C. B.A. 1950; Mass. Inst. of Technol. S.M. 1958; m. E. Marie d. Joseph and Ann Hudson 25 March 1948; children: James A., David A.C., Nancy L., Carol A.; served with Brit. Merchant Navy 1938–42; RAF 1942–45; RCAF 1945–66; Candn. Forces 1966–86; Office: P.O. Box 15973 Station F, Ottawa, Ont. K2C 3S8.

**COLLINS, Malcolm Frank,** Ph.D.; educator; b. Crewe, Eng. 15 Dec. 1935; s. Bernard and Ethel (Smith) C.; e. Cambridge Univ. B.A. 1957, Ph.D. 1962; m. Eileen d. late Stanley Ray 1961; children: Adrian B., Andrew M., Gillian O.; PROF. OF PHYSICS, McMASTER UNIV. 1973– , Dir., McMaster Nuclear Reactor 1987– ; Chrmn. of Physics 1976–82; Staff Scient. Atomic Energy Estab. Harwell, Eng. 1961–69; Assoc. Prof. of Physics present Univ. 1969–73; author of 'Magnetic Critical Scattering' 1989; over 90 acad. publs. condensed matter physics, slow neutron scattering; mem. Bd. Eds. Solid State Communications 1970– ; Secy., Cdn. Inst. for Neutron Scattering 1985–92; Pres. Chess Fed. Can. 1976–77, Bd. Govs. 1972– ; mem. Cdn. Assn. Physicists (Chrmn. Condensed Matter Div. 1979–80); recreations: chess, bridge; Home: 6 Penge Court, Dundas, Ont. L9H 4R4; Office: Hamilton, Ont. L8S 4M1.

**COLLINS, Mary;** B.A.; politician; b. Vancouver, B.C. 26 Sept. 1940; d. Frederick Claude Wilkins and Isabel Margaret (Copp); e. Univ. of B.C., Queen's Univ.; children: David Fredrick, Robert Joseph, Sorcha Alexia Margaret; Min. of Health and Welfare (designate of Health) 1993; Min. for Status of Women 1990–93; e. House of Commons g.e. 1984; re-el. 1988; Assoc. Min. of Defence 1989–93; Min. of Western Economic Diversification and Min. of State for the Environment 1993.

**COLLINS, Maynard William Joseph,** B.A.; author; b. Ottawa, Ont. 18 Jan. 1946; s. William Pendrick and Yvette Marie (Delorme) C.; e. Univ. of Ottawa, B.A. cum laude 1972; m. Lois d. Earl and Glorida Mayville 19 Dec. 1966; children: Aaron, David; author: 'Norman McLaren' 1976 (film criticism), 'Hank Williams: The Show He Never Gave' 1977 (play), 1981 (feature film) 'Age of Rivers' 1985 (documentary film), 'Lightfoot: If You Could Read His Mind' 1988 (biography), 'Death on Thirty Beat' 1989 (novel), 1990 (feature film screenplay) and many others; 'Hank Williams: The Show He Never Gave' has enjoyed continued critical & public success in Can., the U.S. & Eur. for over a decade; his film & TV work has been broadcast on CBC, CTV, First Choice, Global and HBO Networks and has received awards & nominations from Can. Counc., Ont. Arts Counc., ACTRA & the Chalmers Found.; he has also worked as a cultural affairs offr. for Can. Counc., SSHRCC & AUCC; Home: 67 Queen Mary St., Ottawa, Ont. K1K 1X6.

**COLLINS, Richard H.,** B.A.; business executive; e. York Univ. B.A. 1970; m. Elizabeth Hendry; children: Whitney, Andrew; MANAGING DIRECTOR, HARDMAN COMPANIES; Jr. Acct. Extve., Cockfield Brown Advertising Agency; Acct. Extve., Spitzer Mills & Bates; Asst. to Pres., Jordon Wines; Agent, N.Y. Life Insur. Co. 1971; Agent, Manufacturers Life Insur. Co. 1972; The Hardman Insur. Agency Inc. 1975 (now President); Hardman Benefit Plan Consultants Inc. 1980; Hardman Communications Inc.; Mem., Life Underwriters' Assn. of Can. (Ethics & Practices Ctte. 1979–81); Psi Upsilon Alumni Assn.; Appleby Coll. & The Winchendon Sch. Alumni; The Royal Candn. Yacht Club; The Inst. of Corp. Dirs.; recreations: squash, skiing, yacht racing; Address: 48 Yonge St., Ste. 500, Toronto, Ont. M5E 1G6.

**COLLINS, Robert George,** M.A., Ph.D.; educator; writer; b. Danbury, Conn. 6 June 1926; s. Thomas Arthur and Sara Marie (Lowe) C.; e. Miami (Ohio) Univ. B.A. 1950, M.A. 1952; Univ. of Denver Ph.D. 1959; additional studies Rutgers Univ., Columbia Univ., Univ. of Cal.; m. May Collins 17 July 1981; Prof. of Eng., Univ. of Ottawa 1976–91; Chrmn. Grad. Eng. Studies 1976–77; prior to coming to Can. in 1968 held profl. positions USA incl. Univ. of New Hampshire, San Jose State Univ., State Univ. of N.Y. Buffalo, Cal. State Univ. Los Angeles, Colo. State Univ. and Penn. State Univ.; Chrmn. Grad. Eng. Studies Univ. of Man. 1968–74 and Ed. 'Mosaic' 1969–76; Visiting Prof. of Eng. Univ. of the Americas (Mexico City), Colgate Univ. and Univ. of Canterbury (Christchurch, N.Z.); cons. to SSHRC and Can. Council re funding scholarly projects; author or compiler over 22 books most recently 'The Hand of the Arch-Sinner: Branwell Brontë' 1993, 'E.J. Pratt' 1988, 'Tolerable Levels of Violence'(novel) 1983, 1985, 'Critical Essays on John Cheever' 1983; contbr. to many lit. mags.; Founding Ed. 'The Colorado Review' 1956–59; Co-Founder 'Thalia: A Journal of Literary Humour' Univ. of Ottawa 1977–79; mem. Modern Lang. Assn. Am.; Assn. Candn. Univ. Teachers Eng.; Brontë Soc.; Kafka Soc. Am.; Conf. Eds. Learned Jours. (Pres. 1975–77); recreations: travel, hiking, rare books; Home: 1275 Richmond Rd., #1609, Ottawa, Ont. K2B 8E3.

**COLLINS, Robert John,** B.A.; writer; b. Shamrock, Sask. 10 Sept. 1924; s. John Douglas and Floy Leona (Hartzell) C.; e. elem. and high schs. Shamrock, Sask.; Univ. of Sask.; Univ. of W. Ont. B.A. (Jour.) 1950; m. Ruth d. Fred and Mary Dillon June 1952 (divorced 1972); two d. Lesley Anne, Catherine Mary; Reporter 'London Free Press' 1950–51; Asst. Ed. 'Canadian Homes' 1951–53; Western Ed. 'Maclean's' mag. 1953–58; Ed. 'Imperial Oil Review' 1959–65; Assoc. Ed. 'Reader's Digest' Can. 1966, Roving Ed. 1976–89, Contributing Ed. 1989–92; freelance writer 1967–69, 1972–75, 1992– ; Ed. 'Toronto Life' mag. 1970–72; Adjunct Prof. of Jour. Univ. of W. Ont. 1985–89; author (juvenile fiction): 'Legend of the Devil's Lode' 1962; 'Rory's Wildcat' 1965 (repub. as 'The Mystery At The Wildcat Well' 1981); (non-fiction): 'East to Cathay' 1968; 'A Great Way To Go' 1969; 'The Medes and the Persians' 1972; 'The Age of Innocence' 1977; 'A Voice From Afar' 1977; 'Butter Down the Well' 1980; 'The Holy War of Sally Ann' 1984; 'The Long and the Short and the Tall' 1986; 'Who He? Reflections on a Writing Life' 1993; co-author: 'One Thing For Tomorrow' 1981 (non-fiction); 'The Kitchen Table Money Plan' 1992 (non-fiction); recipient 26 editing and writing awards incl. Univ. of W. Ont. Pres.'s Gold Medal 1978, Silver Medal 1979; mem. Writers' Union of Can.; Protestant; recreations: gardening, cycling, skiing; Home: 300 Airdrie Rd., Toronto, Ont. M4G 1N3.

**COLLINS, Thomas Joseph,** B.A., M.A., Ph.D.; university professor; b. London, Ont. 23 Aug. 1936; s. Joseph Benedict and Margaret Jean (Collins) C.; e. Univ. Western Ont. B.A. 1959; M.A. 1961; Indiana Univ. Ph.D. 1965; div.; children: Mark, Kristen, Brendan; m. 1985; VICE-PRES. (ACADEMIC) & PROVOST, UNIV. OF W. ONT. 1986– ; (Prof. of English there 1965– ; Chrmn. Dept. Eng. 1974–82; Dean, Faculty of Arts 1982–86); author: 'Robert Browning's Moral-Aesthetic Theory: 1833–55' 1967; editor: 'Letters from the Brownings to the Tennysons' 1971; 'Letters of Robert Browning to the Rev. J.D. Williams' 1976; co-editor (with J. Pettigrew) 'Robert Browning: The Poems' 1981; 'Robert Browning: The Plays' (with R.J. Shroyer) 1988; Gen. Ed., Victorian Authors Manuscript Facsimile Series, Garland Press; mem. Ed. Bd. 'Victorian Poetry' 1974– ; 'Victorian Studies' 1979– ; awarded $5,000 Can. Counc. Research Grant 1974; $35,000 Univ. Western Ont. Academic Devel. Fund Grant 1982; $54,000 Social Sci. & Humanities Research Counc. Grant 1983–85, Browning Computer based 'Concordance' Project; $18,000 SSHRC Grant 1987–89, An Edition of the Plays of Alfred Tennyson; editor, Browning centennial issue, 'Victorian Poetry' 1989; co-editor (with R.J. Shrayer) 'A Concordance to the Poems and Plays of Robert Browning,' 7 vols.; mem. Candn. Assn. Univ. Teachers; Modern Language Assn. (Extve. Comte., Victorian Group, 1972–75); Internat. Browning Soc. (Bd. Dirs., 1976); Comte. Chrmn. Eng. Ont. (Pres., 1979–81); Candn. Assn. Chrmn. Eng. (Pres., 1979–80); Chrmn. Council of Deans of Arts & Science of Ont. 1983–85; Club: London Pacers; recreation: marathon running and triathalon participation; Home: 249 Hyman St., London, Ont. N6A 1N6; Office: Univ. of W. Ont., London, Ont. N6A 3K7.

**COLLINS-NAKAI, Ruth Lorraine,** M.D., FRCP(C), FAAP, FACC; educator; physician; b. Pincher Creek, Alta. 27 Mar. 1949; d. Lorne Burritt and Rhonda Maynard (Boughton) Collins; e. Mathew Halton High Sch., Pincher Creek, Alta. 1966; Univ. of Alta. M.D. 1972; m. Dr. S.S. Nakai s. Gurcharin and Rajendra N. 5 Apr. 1975; children: Natasha Jasleen, Sunil Collins; ASSOC. DEAN (FACULTY AFFAIRS), FAC. OF MED., UNIV. OF ALTA. 1993– , Prof. of Paediatrics 1988– ; Internship, McGill Univ. (Montreal Gen. Hosp.) 1972–73, Paediatrics Univ. Alta. 1973–74, Paediatric Cardiol., Children's Hosp. Med. Centre, Harvard Univ., Boston 1974–76; Teaching Fellowship in Paediatrics, Univ. of Alta. 1976, Asst. Prof. of Paediatrics 1977, Assoc. Prof. 1980, named Teacher of Yr., Dept. Paediatrics 1988; Dir. Heritage Paediatric Cardiol. Prog. 1978–80 and 1982–84; Straight Found. 1987–88; Mem., Premier's Counc. on Science & Technology 1992; mem. subctte. on Future of Science & Technology in Alta. 1990– ; author or co-author over 58 abstracts, 34 papers; Fellow, Am. Acad. Paediatrics; Am. Coll. Cardiol.; Alta. Med. Assn. (Pres. 1987–88); Alta. Paediatric Soc. (Sec./Treas.); Alta. Cardiovascular Soc. (Pres. 1987); Bd. of Dirs., Candn. Med. Assoc. 1988–90; mem. Candn. Paediatric Soc.; Candn. Cardiovascular Soc. (Council 1991– , Chair Ethics Ctte. 1993– ;); Am. Coll. of Cardiology (Gov. for Prairie Provinces 1989–92; Chair, Bd. of Govs. 1992–93, Extve. 1991–94, mem. Bd. of Trustees 1994–99); Am. Heart Assoc.; Councils on Epidemiol. & Cardiovascular Disease in the Young; Commnr., Premier's Commission on Future Health Care for Albertans 1987–89; Mem., Alpha Omega Alpha Soc. 1988; Dir., Muttart Found. 1989–96, Vice Pres. 1993–94; recreations: skiing, swimming, golfing, reading; Home: 15239 – 43 Ave., Edmonton, Alta. T6H 5R3; Office: 2C3.86 Walter Mackenzie Centre, Edmonton, Alta. T6G 2R7.

**COLLINS-WILLIAMS, Cecil,** B.A., M.D., FRCPC (1950); physician; b. Toronto, Ont. 31 Dec. 1918; s. Ernest and Nellie (Hewitt) C-W.; e. Univ. of Toronto, B.A. (Victoria Coll.) 1941, M.D. 1944; post-grad. work in paediatrics and paediatric allergy in Toronto, Boston and New York, 1944–50; m. Jean, d. late William Hamilton, 30 June 1944; children: Donald James, Joan; HON. CONSULTANT, HOSP. FOR SICK CHILDREN 1984– ; Professor Emeritus of Paediatrics, Univ. of Toronto 1984– ; Consultant, Hugh MacMillan Medical Centre; private practice in Toronto 1950–86; semi-retired; joined staff of present Hosp. and Univ. of Toronto 1950; on full-time staff of Hosp. and Univ. of Toronto; Sr. Staff Physician 1968–84; Head, Allergy Div. 1952–84; served with RCN 1945–46; author 'Paediatric Allergy and Clinical Immunology (as applied to Atopic Disease): Notes and Suggested Reading for Medical Students'; also over 125 articles and papers for various med. journs. and book chapters; mem. various Ed. Bds.; Fellow, Candn. Soc. Allergy & Clin. Immunology (Past Pres.); Am. Acad. Paediatrics; Am. Acad. of Allergy and Immunology; Am. Coll. Allergists; Ont. Allergy Soc. (Past Pres.); Candn. Paed Soc.; Candn. Soc. for Immunology; Ont. Thoracic Soc.; Candn. Thoracic Soc.; Am. Thoracic Soc.; Past Pres., Asthma Soc. of Can.; Dir. and Past. Pres., Assn. for the Care of Asthma; Royal Soc. of Med.; Royal Coll. of Physicians and Surgeons of Can.; Royal Candn. Inst. (Counc. 1990–92); Sigma Xi (Pres., Toronto Chapt. 1991–92); Alpha Omega Alpha; Protestant; recreation: photography; Home: Subpenthouse Five, One Aberfoyle Cres., Etobicoke, Ont. M8X 2X8.

**COLLINSON, John Wells,** C.A.; office equipment industry executive; b. Heanor, England 15 Oct. 1939; s. Denis Wells and Gladys Eda (Hardy) C.; e. Weston Collegiate 1957; C.A. 1964; m. Deanna d. Norman and Dorothea Ridsdill 3 July 1965; children: Christine, Brian, Janice; PRESIDENT AND CHIEF EXTVE. OFFICER, SAVIN CANADA INC. 1990– ; Sales Rep. & Area Mgr., Burroughs Business Machines Can. 1962–69; Candn. Mktg. Mgr., Data Systems Div., Philips Electronics Indus. Ltd. 1969–74; Internat. Mktg. Mgr., Data Systems, N.V. Philips, The Netherlands 1975–79; Vice-Pres., Olympia Business Machines Can. Ltd. 1980–85; Pres. 1985–90; Dir., Savin Canada Inc.; Copytron Co. Ltd.; Photofax Canada Ltd.; Vice-Pres., Candn. Office Machine Dealers Assn.; Anglican; Past Pres., Kinsmen Club of Mississauga; recreations: golf, sailing; Home: 830 Hollowtree Cres., Mississauga, Ont. L4Y 2V2; Office: 1730 Aimco Blvd., Mississauga, Ont. L4W 1V1.

**COLLISON, Robert M.,** B.A. (Hons.), M.Sc. (Econ.); journalist; filmmaker; b. Selkirk, Man. 1 May 1945; s. Merlin Mozart and Johanna Lorraine (Graham) C.; e. Univ. of Man., B.A. (Hons.) 1967; London Sch. of Econ., M.Sc. 1968; doct. candidate 1972; has written for most major Candn. periodicals; writer/filmmaker, Nat. Film Bd. & CBC 1981– ; Asst. Ed., 'Saturday Night' 1975–80; freelance writer, journalist, film maker 1980–87; Editor, V and Equity magazines (Vancouver, B.C.) 1987–88; Sr. Writer, Report on Business Magazine, The Globe and Mail, Toronto 1988–89; Can. Counc. doct. fellow 1968–72; num. journalism awards incl. Petroleum Prize; author's awards; nat. mag. awards; 1984 ACTRA Award for Writing for 'Prisoners of Debt, Inside the Global Banking Crisis'; 1986 Genie Award for best documentary and 1986 Grand Prix and Prize for Best Pol. or Soc. Docum., Banff Internat. TV Fest. for 'Final Offer, Bob White and the Canadian Autoworkers Fight for Independence' and 1986 Prix Italia, the Premier Award in European Broadcasting, also for 'Final Offer...'; Winner, Magazine of the Year Award (for V magazine), Western Magazine Awards 1987; Club: The Dog, Toronto; Address: 44 St. Joseph St., Toronto, Ont. M4Y 2W4.

**COLOMBO, John Robert;** editor; writer; poet; communications consultant; b. Kitchener, Ont. 24 March 1936; s. John and Irene (Nicholson) C.; e. Kitchener-Waterloo (Ont.) Coll. 1955; Univ. Coll., Univ. of Toronto, B.A. (hons.) 1959; Univ. of Toronto Sch. Grad. Studies 1960; m. Ruth F., d. Joseph Brown, Toronto, Ont. 11 May 1959; children: Jonathan, Catherine, Theodore; some book publications since 1974: 'Colombo's Canadian Quotations' 1974; 'Colombo's Little Book of Canadian Proverbs, Graffiti, Limericks & Other Vital Matters' 1975; 'Colombo's Canadian References' 1976; 'Colombo's Concise Canadian Quotations' 1976; 'Mostly Monsters' 1977; 'The Poets of Canada' 1978; 'Colombo's Book of Canada' 1978; 'Colombo's Names and Nicknames' 1978; 'Other Canadas' 1979; 'Colombo's Book of Marvels' 1979; 'Colombo's Hollywood' 1979; 'The Canada Colouring Book' 1980; '222 Canadian Jokes' 1981; 'Blackwood's Books' 1981; 'Not to be Taken at Night' (with Michael Richardson) 1981; 'Friendly Aliens' 1981; 'Poems of the Inuit' 1981; 'Selected Poems' 1982; 'Selected Translations' 1982; 'Years of Light' 1982; 'Windigo' 1982; 'Colombo's Laws' 1982; 'Colombo's Last Words' 1982; 'Songs of the Indians' 1983; 'René Lévesque Buys Canada Savings Bonds and Other Great Canadian Graffiti' 1983; 'Colombo's 101 Canadian Places' 1983; 'Colombo's Canadiana Quiz Book' 1983; 'Learn This Poem of Mine by Heart' (Poems by George Faludy edited and largely translated) 1983; 'The Toronto Puzzle Book' 1984; 'Great Moments in Canadian History' 1984; 'Canadian Literary Landmarks' 1984; (with Michael Richardson) 'We Stand on Guard' 1985; '1001 Questions about Canada' 1986; 'Off Earth' 1987; 'Colombo's New Canadian Quotations' 1987; 'Mysterious Canada' 1988; '999 Questions about Canada' 1989; 'Extraordinary Experiences' 1989; 'Songs of the Great Land' 1989; 'Mysterious Encounters' 1990; 'Quotations from Chairman Lamport' 1990; 'Mackenzie King's Ghost' 1991; 'The Dictionary of Canadian Quotations' 1991; 'UFOs over Canada' 1991; 'Dark Visions' 1992; 'Worlds in Small' 1992; 'The Little Blue Book of UFOs' 1992; 'The Mystery of the Shaking Tent' 1993; Gen. Editor, 'The Canadian Global Almanac' 1992; 'Colombo's Quotes,' wkly. nat.-network CBC-TV series; etc.; Rep., Commonwealth Arts Festival, U.K. 1965; Guest, Writers Union, Bulgaria 1975–80; Writer-in-residence, Mohawk Coll., Hamilton, Ont. 1977; Centennial Medal 1967; adviser to Ont. Arts Council 1965–69; Can. Council 1968–70; Award of Merit, Ont. Library Assn. 1977; Best Non-Fiction Paperback Book Award, Periodical Distributors 1977; Philips Information Systems Literary Award 1985; Esteemed Knight of Mark Twain 1979; Laureate, Order of Cyril and Methodius; Assns: ACTRA; PEN; Address: 42 Dell Park Ave., Toronto, Ont. M6B 2T6.

**COLOMBO, Umberto,** Ph.D.; professor; b. Livorno Italy 20 Dec. 1927; s. Eugenio and Maria (Eminente) C.; e. Pavia Univ. Ph.D. (summa cum laude) 1950; m. Milena d. Vittorio and Viviana Piperno 5 July 1951; children: Carla, Claudia; CHRMN., ENEA (ITALIAN NATIONAL AGENCY FOR NEW TECHNOLOGY, ENERGY AND THE ENVIRONMENT) 1982– ; Dept. Head, G. Donegani Rsch. Inst. 1954–67; Dir. 1967–70; Dir., Central Rsch., Montedison 1971; Dir., Strategic Planning 1972–75; Dir. Gen., Rsch. & Devel. Div. 1976–78; Chrmn., CNEN (Italian Atomic Energy Comn.) 1979–81; ENI (Italian Hydrocarbons Trust) 1982; Honda Prize for Ecotechnology 1984; delivered inaugural triennial prestige lectr., Royal Soc. & The Fellowship of Engineering, London 1988; Pres., Eur. Sci. Found.; Aurelio Peccei Found.; Mem. & Extve. of many organizations incl. Stockholm Environment Inst.; author: 'Waes Report' 1978, 'La Speranza Tecnologica' 1979, 'Scienza e Tecnologia verso il XXI Secolo' 1988; co-author: 'Beyond the Age of Waste' 1976, 1981, 'Il Secondo Pianeta' 1982; 'Le Frontiere della Tecnologia' 1990; recreations: music, farming; club: Chemists' Club; Home: Via San Martino ai Monti, 26/bis, 00184 Rome, Italy; Office: Viale Regina Margherita 125, 00198, Rome, Italy.

**COLONNIER, Marc,** M.D., M.Sc., Ph.D.; retired educator; b. Québec, Qué. 12 May 1930; s. Jean and Enilda (Bourguignon) C.; e. Univ. of Ottawa B.A., B.Ph. 1951, M.D. 1959, M.Sc. (Anat.) 1960; Univ. Coll. London Ph.D. (Neurobiol.) 1963; m. Lise d. Arthur DeGagné, Ottawa, Ont. 14 Nov. 1959; one child, Jean; Prof. of Anatomy, Univ. Laval 1976–91, retired 1991; Asst. Prof. of Anat. Univ. of Ottawa 1963–65, Prof. and Dir. of Anat. 1969–76; Asst. Prof. of Physiol. Univ. de Montréal 1965–67, Assoc. Prof. 1967–69; rec'd Lederle Med. Award 1966–69; Charles Judson Herrick Award 1967; author various articles anat. studies parts of brain concerned with vision; mem. Royal Soc. Can.; Am. Assn. Anats; Candn. Assn. Anats; Soc. Neuroscience; Cajal Club; Address: 3555 rue Berri, app 1007, Montréal, Que. H2L 4G4.

**COLSON, Daniel William,** B.A., LL.L.; b. Montreal, Que. 5 Apr. 1947; s. Philip and Kathleen (Burke) C.; e. Loyola Coll. B.A. 1968; Laval Univ. LL.L. 1971; m. Suzanne d. Armand and Marie Lambert 21 June 1975; two s. Charles Philip, Timothy Lambert; VICE CHAIRMAN, THE TELEGRAPH plc; Dir. Hollinger Inc.; Carlton Television Ltd.; The Spectator (1828) Ltd.; Hellespont Shipping Corp.; John Fairfax Holdings Ltd.; articled with Stikeman, Elliott 1971–72; called to the Bar of Que. 1972; law practice with Stikeman Elliott 1972–92; Dir. Can. Club (London), Can.-U.K. C.of C.; mem. Candn. Bar Assn.; Que. Bar Assn.; author numerous articles various publs.; R. Catholic; recreations: tennis, squash; Home: 19 Hanover Terrace, Regent's Park, London NW1 4RJ; Office: The Telegraph plc, One Canada Square, Canary Wharf, London E14 5DT, England.

**COLTER, Gary Frederick,** F.C.A.; b. Saint John, N.B. 11 Jan. 1946; s. Edwin Royden and Ina Mary (Hill) C.; e. Univ. of W. Ont. B.A. (Hons.) 1968; C.A. 1971; Trustee in Bankruptcy 1975; m. Victoria Haviland Shipp; children: Grier Barrett, Brock Jeffrey, Ashley Lind, Julie Louise, Darrell Bradley, Carolynne Patricia, Meredith Dianna, Gavin Jamieson; PRES. & C.E.O., PEAT MARWICK LTD. 1984– ; Chrmn. and C.E.O., Peat Marwick Thorne Inc. 1989– ; Mem., Peat Marwick Extve. Ctte. 1986– ; Mem., Peat Marwick Thorne Mgmt. Ctte.; Auditing/acctg. group present firm 1968–71, Tax Dept. 1971–72, Insolvency Group 1972–74, Vice-Pres. 1974–84; Partner, Peat Marwick and Peat Marwick Consulting Group 1975; Partner, Peat Marwick Thorne 1989– ; Vice Chrmn., Financial Adv. Services, Peat Marwick Thorne 1989– ; Pres., Candn. Insolvency Practitioners Assn. 1984–85; Chrmn., Fed. Govt. Private Sector Ctte. to Review Changes to Insolvency Legislation 1985–86; recreations: travel, golf, other sports; Clubs: University; Credit Valley Golf & Country; Home: 3474 Sawmill Valley Dr., Mississauga, Ont. L5L 3A4; Office: PO Box 31, Commerce Court Postal Stn., Toronto, Ont. M5L 1B2.

**COLTER, The Hon. William Edgar Charles;** judge; b. Cayuga, Ont. 14 Sept. 1916; s. Richard S., Q.C., and Aletha M. (Birdsall) C.; e. Cayuga (Ont.) Pub. and High Schs.; Ridley Coll., St. Catharines, Ont.; Univ. of Toronto, B.A. 1937, LL.B. 1941; Osgoode Hall Law Sch., Toronto, 1940; m. Elizabeth M., d. late Reginald S. Duncan, 27 Sept. 1941; two d., Ann E., Patricia J.; SUPERNUMERARY JUSTICE, ONT. COURT OF JUSTICE, (GEN. DIV.) 1990– ; read law with City Solr., Toronto; called to Bar of Ont. 1940; cr. Q.C. 1957; practised law with Colter & Colter, Cayuga, Ont., 1940–42 and 1946–48; Macoomb, Colter & Sullivan, Welland, Ont., 1948–63; Colter & Sullivan, Welland, 1963–64; apptd. Jr. Judge, Co. Court of Middlesex, 1964, Sr. Judge 1967; Chief Judge Co. & District Courts, Ont. 1974–83; Supernumerary Judge, District Courts of Ont. 1983–90; Hon. LL.D. Univ. Western Ont. 1976; served with Candn. Army 1942–46; discharged with rank of Capt., Royal Regt. of Can., 2nd Div.; mem., Candn. Bar Assn.; York Law Assn.; Sigma Chi; Anglican; Clubs: Toronto Hunt; Lawyers; London Hunt & Country; Home: 9 Thornwood Road, Toronto, Ont. M4W 2R8; Office: Court House, 361 University Ave., Rm. 331, Toronto, Ont. M5G 1T3.

**COLVILLE, David Alexander,** C.C. (1982); artist; b. Toronto, Ont. 24 Aug. 1920; e. Amherst, N.S. schs.; Mount Allison Univ. B.F.A. 1942; Hon. Degrees: Trent Univ.; Mount Allison Univ.; Dalhousie Univ.; Simon Fraser Univ.; Univ. of Windsor; Acadia Univ.; Memorial Univ. Nfld.; Univ. of Calgary; m. Rhoda Wright 5 Aug. 1942; children: Graham Alexander, John Harrower, Charles Wright, Ann Christian; teacher Mount Allison Univ. 1946–63; Visiting Artist Univ. of Calif. Santa Cruz 1967; Berliner Kunstlerprogramm 1971; Lectr., Univ. Hong Kong 1985; solo exhns. incl.: Kestner Gesellschaft (Hannover) 1969; Marlborough (London, Eng.) 1970; Gemeent Museum (Arnhem), Kunsthalle (Duselldorf), Fischer Fine Art (London) 1977; Mira Godard Galleries (Toronto, Montreal) 1978; Art Gall. of Ont. (Toronto), Staatliche Kunsthalle (Berlin), Museum Ludwig (Cologne) 1983; Montreal Mus. Fine Arts, Dalhousie Univ., Vancouver Art Gall., Exhbn. Hall (Beijing) 1984; Univ. of Hong Kong, Teien Art Museum (Tokyo), Canada House (London) 1985; Drabinsky Gall. (Toronto) 1991; rep. in various pub., corporate and private colls. incl.: Nat. Gallery Can.; Art Gallery Ont.; Musée de Beaux Arts Montreal; N.B. Museum; Museum of Modern Art N.Y.; Sammlung Ludwig Aachen; Wallraf-Rickartz Museum Cologne; Kestner Gesellschaft Hannover; Musée Nat. d'Art Moderne Paris; Museum Boymans-van Beuningen Rotterdam; subject of 'Colville' by David Burnett 1983; served with Candn. Army 1942–46, War Artist 1944–46; Companion, Order of Canada 1982; Apptd. Privy Council 1992; Honourary Colonel, 415 Squadron, Air Command; P. Conservative; Address: (PO Box 550) 408 Main St., Wolfville, N.S. BOP 1XO.

**COLVILLE, David C.,** B.Sc., B.Eng., P.Eng.; commissioner; b. Montreal, Que. 2 March 1945; s. Robert Gault and Miriam Angelina (Cameron) C.; e. Saint Mary's Univ. B.Sc. 1968; Technical Univ. of N.S. B.Eng. 1970; m. Louise d. George and Aileen Godwin 20 July 1970; children: Danielle, Andrew; COMMISSIONER, CANADIAN RADIO-TELEVISION & TELECOMMUNICATIONS COMN. 1990– ; Systems Analyst, Toll Network Design, Manager Data Services Market Support, Bell Canada Ottawa 1970–73; Communications Consultant / Sales Mgr. Data Communications, Maritime Tel & Tel 1973–76; Senior Dir., Communications Policy, Prov. of N.S. Dept. of Transportation & Communications 1976–90; Chairman, CRTC 1 Nov. 1990–30 June 1991; Mem., Bd. of Dir., Candn. Standards Assn.; Mem., Assn. of Profl. Engrs. of N.S.; Nat. Assn. of Regulatory Utility Comnrs.; Past Chrmn., Diocesan Pastoral Council, Roman Cath. Diocesis of Halifax; recreations: sailing, skiing, restoring old sports cars (currently a 1975 Triumph TR-6); Home: 6360 Seaforth St., Halifax, N.S. B3L 1R3; Office: Ottawa, Ont. K1A 0N2.

**COMACK, Brig.-Gen. Hugh,** C.M.M., C.D.; communications executive; b. Glasgow, Scotland 12 Dec. 1920; s. Hugh and Mary (Greer) C.; m. Agnes, d. Arinbjorn and Margret Bardal, 11 Sept. 1946; children: Donald, Margret; Elizabeth; Alyson; retired Pres. & CEO, Greater Winnipeg Cablevision Ltd.; Past Chrmn., National Bd. of Govs. (and Past Chrmn., Bd. of Govs., Manitoba Lakehead Br.); Candn. Corps of Commissionaires; Past Chrmn., Candn. Cable Television Assn.; Past Chrmn., Assn. of Cable Operators of Man.; served with Candn. Army 1939–46 (Militia 1948–77); Mgr., Patriotic Salvage Corps 1946; Sales Rep., O. Mondell Ltd. 1947; joined Manitoba Telephone System 1948, various positions to commercial Area Supervisor; joined G.W.C. firm as Gen. Mgr. 1968; awarded Candn. Forces Decoration 1954; 1st Bar 1968; 2nd Bar 1977; invested Commander, Order of Military Merit 1976; past Pres., St. Andrew's Soc. of Winnipeg; mem. Queen's Own Cameron Highlanders (Adv. Bd.); Club: Manitoba; Home: 32 Valleyview Dr., Winnipeg, Man. R2Y 0R6.

**COMEAU, Bernardin Joseph,** C.M., Ph.D.; business executive; b. Comeauville, N.S. 14 Dec. 1918; s. Frederic Joseph and Leonie Marie (Saulnier) C.; e. Comeauville, N.S.; Univ. Sainte-Anne, Ph.D. 1983; m. Therese Marie Anna d. Elisée and Irene Gaudet 28 June 1947; children: Marcel R., Yvette Després, Denise Clark, Janice MacDougall; CHRMN., COMEAU'S SEA FOODS LTD. 1981– ; Pres. Comeau's Seafoods Incs. Los Angeles 1974– ; Dennis Point Fisheries Ltd. Pubnico, N.S. 1976– ; Frankland Canning Co. Ltd. Church Point, N.S. 1976– ; Comeau & Saulnier Ltd. 1980– ; Comeau Marine Railway Ltd. Meteghan, N.S. 1981– ; Clyde A. Denton Ltd. Little River, N.S. 1980– ; Sec. Abbott's Harbour Motors Ltd. Pubnico, N.S. 1982– ; Skipper Fisheries Ltd. Pubnico 1985– ; Dir. COBI Foods Inc. Port Williams, N.S. 1985– ; Pres. present Co. 1946–80; Chrmn. N.S. Fishermen Loan Bd. Halifax 1979–84; Dir. Univ. Sainte-Anne, Church Pointe, N.S. 1979–83; mem. Internat. Comn. Atlantic Fisheries; Candn. Del. Candn.-Am. Bilateral Ctte.; Dir., Fisheries Counc. of Can., Ottawa (Chrmn. 1988–89); Chart mem. Saulnierville Credit Union and Sec.-Treas. first 3 yrs.; local Cancer Soc.; First Clare C. of C.; Past Pres. Fish Packers Assn. N.S.; mem. Annapolis Valley Affiliated Bd. Trade; mem. Maritime Sr. Golf Assoc. 1988; K. of C.; recreation: golf; Club: Clare Golf & Country; Address: P.O. Box 39, Saulnierville, Digby Co., N.S. B0W 2Z0.

**COMEAU, Louis Roland,** B.Sc., B.Ed., D.C.L.; educator; ex-politician; b. Meteghan, N.S. 7 Jan. 1941; s. Désiré Joseph and Antoinette Marie (Saulnier) C.; St. Mary's Univ., Dipl. Engn. and B.Sc. 1958–62; Dalhousie Univ., B.Ed. 1963; Moncton Univ. grad. requirements for M.Sc. 1967; Sr. Univ. Admin. Course, Univ. W. Ont. 1976; Venture Founder's Corp. Bus. Program 1978; m. Clarice Marie, d. Emile Theriault, Belliveau Cove, N.S. 20 June 1964; children: Louise Anne, Jacques, Martine; PRES., C.E.O. & DIR., NOVA SCOTIA POWER CORP. 1983– ; Dir. Council for Candn. Unity; Atlantic Region Management Training Centre; Candn. Electrical Assn.; Tidal Power Corp.; Prof. of Physics and Math., College Ste. Anne 1963–65 and 1967–68; Pres. there 1971–77; 1st el. to H. of C. for S.W. Nova 1968; served on many Nat. and Internat. Parliamentary Cttes.; Candn. delegate to the UN; mem. Canada-France Comn. & Inter-Parliamentary Union; Pres. & Dir., E.M. Comeau & Sons (1977) Ltd. 1977–83; Pres. & Dir., Kingston Lumber & Building Supplies Ltd. 1981–83; mem., Canada Post Corp. Review Ctte.; mem. Conseil d'Admin., Univ. Sainte-Anne; Gov., Univ. de Moncton; mem. Clare Arts Council; Soc. Historique De La Baie Ste. Marie; Opimian Soc.; Library of Univ. Sainte-Anne named 'La Bibliotheque Louis R. Comeau' in honour of achievements at Coll. Sainte-Anne; honored by the Internat. Assoc. of Fr. Parliamentarians for 'outstanding achievement in the pursuit of good relations in the cultural, economic and social interests of Francophones throughout the world' 1980; Ed.D. (hon. causa) Univ. Ste-Anne 1986; D.C.L. (hon. causa) Acadia Univ. 1993; P. Conservative; Catholic; recreations: hockey, golf, racquetball, woodworking, gardening; Clubs: Richelieu (Dir.); Halifax; Clare Golf & Country; Waegwoltic; Address: 1731 Dunvegan Dr., Halifax, N.S. B3H 4G2.

**COMEAU, Paul-André;** political scientist; b. Montreal, Que. 9 Mar. 1940; s. Henri-Paul and Annonciade (Brousseau) C.; e. Univ. de Montréal B.A. 1961, M.A 1965; Fond. nat. des Sci. pol., Paris D.E.S. 1967; m. J. Dubois 22 July 1966; one s.: Vincent; Pres., Commission d'accès à l'information du Québec 1990– ; Editor-in-Chief, Le Devoir 1985–90; Radio & TV Corr., Brussels 1970–82, London 1982–85, Radio-Canada; Assoc. Prof. of Pol. Sci., Univ. of Ottawa 1967–70; Guest Prof., Dept. of Pol. Sci., Laval Univ. 1991– ; and Dept. of Pol. Sci., Montreal Univ. 1980 and 1987; author: 'Le Bloc Populaire' 1982; 'Institutions politiques canadiennes' 1965; Ed.: 'Un été, un enfant' 1990; Home: 4684 ave. Christophe-Colomb, Montréal, Qué. H2J 3G6.

**COMERFORD, Gary Michael,** B.A., M.B.A.; insurance executive; b. St. Catharines, Ont. 2 April 1950; s. Leo Joseph and Patricia Irene (Hunniford) C.; e. Univ. of Western Ont. B.A. 1973, M.B.A. 1975; m. Catherine d. Ed and Dorothy Dixon 27 April 1974; children: Patrick Michael, Brian Michael; VICE-PRESIDENT, AGENCY SALES FOR CANADA, SUN LIFE ASSURANCE CO. OF CANADA 1991– ; Vice-Pres., Marketing, Canada Permanent Trust 1982–86; Vice-Pres., Marketing Corp. Office, Sun Life Assur. Co. of Canada 1986–88; Individual Marketing for Canada 1988–91; Lecturer, Brock Univ. 1975–88; Pres., Catholic Children's Aid Soc. of Metropolitan Toronto 1991–93; Mem., Rotary Club of Oakville (Dir. 1985–91; Pres. 1992–93); Fundraiser, Outward Bound Wilderness School; author: 'The Canadian Doctor'; Home: 1308 Mapleridge Cres., Oakville, Ont. L6M 2G8; Office: 9th Floor, 225 King St. W., Toronto, Ont. M5H 3C5.

**COMFORT, Charles Fraser,** O.C. (1972), C.D., LL.D., R.C.A.; b. Edinburgh, Scotland, 1900; came to Can. in 1912, settling in Winnipeg; e. Winnipeg School of Art; Art Students League, New York; Kunsthistorich Instituut te Utrecht; Mt. Allison Univ., LL.D. 1958; LL.D. R.M.C. of Can., 1980; served in 2nd World War as Sr. Combat War Artist in U.K., Italy and N.W. Europe, 1943–46 (discharged with rank of Major); Dir., Dept. of Mural Painting, Ont. Coll. of Art, 1935–38; Assoc. Prof., Dept. of Art & Archaeol., Univ. of Toronto, 1938–60; Dir., Nat. Gallery of Canada, 1960–65; Pres., Roy. Candn. Acad., 1957–60; Past Pres., Can. Soc. of Painters in Water Colour; Past Pres. Candn. Group of Painters; mem., Ont. Soc. of Artists; Arts & Letters Club, Toronto; Hon. Fellow, Acad. of Med., Toronto; Ont. Coll. of Art; Hon. mem., Candn. Art Museum Dirs. Organ.; Art Dirs. of Can.; Candn. Soc. of Educ. through Art; Arts Club, Montreal; Hart House, Univ. of Toronto; awarded Queen's Jubilee Medal; Italy's 'Medaglia al Merito Culturale,' 1963; Commemorative Medal, 125th Anniversary of Candn. Confedn. 1992; Gold Medal for Painting and Allied Arts, Univ. of Alta., 1963; Royal Soc. Fellowship for study in the Netherlands, 1955–56; work embraces landscapes, portraits and non-objectives in oil and water colour, murals and stone carvings; has exhibited in Can. and abroad since 1924; rep. in major Candn. Colls.; murals include Toronto Stock Exchange 1938; Toronto-Dominion Bank, Vancouver 1951; Neurol. Div., Toronto General Hosp. 1958; Nat. Lib. and Archives Bldg., Ottawa 1967; Acad. of Medicine, Toronto 1968; Publs. include 'Canadian Painting,' Massey Report, Roy. Comn. Studies 1951; 'Artist at War' 1956; 'The Moro River and Other Observations' 1970; Address: #205, 2716 Richmond Rd., Ottawa, Ont. K2B 8M3.

**COMFORT, James Brian,** B.A.; food industry executive; b. Montreal, Que. 30 Oct. 1945; s. John Rolland and Muriel Bridget (Mundey) C.; e. Verdun Catholic H.S.; Loyola Coll. B.A. 1968; m. Carol Ann d. Gladys and Edward Bailey 3 Apr. 1964; children: Shawn, Christine, Derek; PRES., NEW ZEALAND LAMB CO. NORTH AMERICA LTD. 1989– ; Asst. Dept. Mgr. (Montreal & Winnipeg), Mgr., Branded Meats (East. Can.), then Gen. Mgr., Tender Lean Beef, Can. Packers Inc. 1965–84; Pres., Alta. Beef Processors Ltd. 1984–85; Pres., New Zealand Lamb Co. Ltd. 1986–1989; recreations: golf, racquetball; Clubs: Wyldewood Golf; Racquet and Fitness Acad.; Meadowvale Rotary; Home: 1693 Kelsey Court, Mississauga, Ont. L5L 3J8; Office: 10 Four Seasons Place, Suite 400, Etobicoke Ont. M9B 6H7.

**COMISH, Robert W.,** Q.C., LL.B.; lawyer; b. Toronto, Ont. 30 Apr. 1938; s. Eric William and Marguerite Isabell (Hawkins) C.; e. Univ. Toronto, B.A. Hons. 1957–59; studied architecture, Univ. Toronto 1959–60; Osgoode Hall Law Sch., LL.B. 1963; m. Carol Ann, d. Raymond and Violet Whittington, 16 Aug. 1963; children: Troy, Tammy, Randy; COUNSEL, SMITH, LYONS, TORRANCE, STEVENSON & MAYER; Dir., Mitsui & Co. (Can.) Ltd.; The Mitsui Canada Found.; Outokumpu Mines Ltd.; Dornier Medical Systems Ltd.; Sartorius Canada Inc.; joined present firm as Student-at-law 1963; called to the bar of Ont. 1965; successively Assoc.; Partner with present firm; mem. Candn. Bar Assn.; Metro Toronto Bd. of Trade; Clubs: Royal Canadian Yacht; Craigleith Ski; Muskadasa Tennis; Home: 294 Inglewood Dr., Toronto, Ont. M4T 1J3; Office: Suite 6200, Scotia Plaza, 40 King St. W., Toronto, Ont. M5H 3Z7.

**COMISSIONA, Sergiu;** music director, conductor; b. Bucharest, Romania 16 June 1928; e. studied violin theory & comp.; studied conducting with W. Constantin Silvestri & Edouard Lindenberg; m. Robinne Florin 1949; MUSIC DIR., VANCOUVER SYMPHONY ORCHESTRA 1991– ; profl. conducting debut, Bucharest State Opera 1946; has led more than 50 major orchestras in 25 countries on six continents incl. the Montreal, Toronto & Vancouver symphonies & the great orchestras of Boston, Philadelphia, Cleveland, London, Berlin & N.Y. to name a few; appears at prestigious festivals incl. those of Aspen & Wolftrap & conducts leading opera companies around the world incl. N.Y. City Opera where he was Music Dir. under Beverly Sills 1987–89; prolific recording career incl. more than 50 recordings on labels such as Deutch Grammophon, Vanguard, Philips.; Mus. Dir. & Chief Conductor, Helsinki Philharmonic; Chief Conductor, Orquestra Sinfonica de RTVE (Madrid's radio & TV orch.); Conductor Laureate, Baltimore Symph. Orch.; Principal Guest Conductor, Jerusalem Symph. Orch.; Doctor of Humane Letters, Loyola Coll., Baltimore 1973; Hon. doctorates: Peabody Conservatory 1971 & Johns Hopkins Univ.; Alice M. Ditson Award, Columbia Univ.; Gold Medal, City of Goteborg (1st foreigner to receive); Hon. Mem., Swedish Acad. of Music; Pres., Enesco Found.; Silvestri Soc.; Founder, Baltimore Symph. Nat. Comp. for Young Conductors; Home: 10 West 66th St., Apt. 20F, New York, N.Y. 10023; Office: c/o Vancouver Symphony Orch., 601 Smithe St., Vancouver, B.C. V6B 5G1.

**COMMON, Dianne Lynn,** M.Ed., Ph.D.; university administrator/educator; b. Winnipeg, Man. 9 Dec. 1948; d. Gordon Thomas and Lorraine Olive (Pottruff) Barnson; e. Univ. of Man. B.A. 1969, B.Ed. 1973, M.Ed. 1974; Univ. of Ottawa Ph.D. 1978; HEAD OF DEPT. OF CURRICULUM AND INSTRUCTION, THE PENNSYLVANIA STATE UNIVERSITY; Teacher and Dept. Head Kelsey Sch. Div. Man. 1970–73, Assiniboine S. Sch. Div. 1974–75; Curriculum Dir. Cooperative Curriculum Project Govt. Man. 1975–76; Asst. Prof. of Edn. and Asst. Project Dir. Univ. of Man. 1978–79, Head and Assoc. Prof. of Ednl. & Adm. Founds. 1985–87; Dean of Profl. Studies and Prof. of Education, Lakehead Univ. 1987–..; Asst. Prof. and Coordinator Grad. Prog. in Curriculum & Instrn. Simon Fraser Univ. 1979–83; Assoc. Prof. of Edn. Univ. of Lethbridge 1984–85; Visiting Prof. Univ. of Jos, Nigeria 1984; recipient Univ. of Man. Grad. Students' Assn. Award for Excellence in Teaching 1987, Outreach Award Profl./Community Service 1987; Co-ordinating Ed. Primary Social Studies, Fitzhenry and Whiteside Ltd. 1983–87; ed. Jour. Ednl. Adm. & Founds.; author various jour. publs.; mem., Professors of Curriculum, Candn. Assn. Curriculum Studies (Pres.); Candn. Assn. Study Edn.; Candn. Assn. Study Higher Edn.; World Council Curriculum Studies; Am. Ednl. Rsch. Assn.; Assn. Study Higher Edn.; recreations: skiing, canoeing, backpacking, scuba diving, photography, theatre, travel; Office: 150 Chambers Bldg., College of Education, The Pennsylvania State Univ., University Park, Pennsylvania 16802 USA.

**COMPER, F. Anthony,** B.A.; banker; b. Toronto, Ont. 24 Apr. 1945; e. Univ. of Toronto B.A. (English) 1966; PRESIDENT, CHIEF OPERATING OFFICER AND DIR., BANK OF MONTREAL 1990– ; joined the Bank 1967; held various positions 1967–78; Vice Pres., Systems Development 1978–82; Sr. Vice Pres., Personal Banking 1982; Sr. Vice Pres. and Sr. Operations Offr., Treasury Group 1982–84; Sr. Vice Pres. and Mgr. London (England) Branch 1984–86; Sr. Vice Pres. and Sr. Mktg. Offr., Corporate & Govt. Banking 1986–87; Exec. Vice Pres., Operations 1987–89; Chief Gen. Mgr. and C.O.O. 1989–90; Dir., Harris Bankcorp, Inc.; Harris Trust and Savings Bank; St. Michael's Hosp.; Nesbitt Thomson Inc.; C.D. Howe Inst.; Vice-Chrmn., Gov. Counc., Univ. of Toronto; Mem. Bd. of Govs., Stratford Shakespearean Festival Found.; Dir., Toronto Learning Partnership; Dir., The Canadian Club of Toronto; Chrmn. & Exec. Council Mem., The Candn. Bankers' Assn.; Home: 130 Carlton St., Unit 1105, Toronto, Ont. M5A 4K3; Office: First Bank Tower, First Canadian Place, Toronto, Ont. M5X 1A1.

**COMPTON, Jo Ann L.,** CMC, CHRP; executive search consultant; b. London, Ont. 19 Aug. 1943; d. William C. and Marguerite L. (Denton) Graham; e. Secord Business College, Business Admin.; Certified Management Consultant; PRES., COMPTON INTERNATIONAL EXECUTIVE SEARCH 1992– ; Personnel Manager, TVOntario 1973–75; Owner & Dir., Compton Consulting Limited 1975–78; Principal, Executive Search, Hickling-Johnston Limited 1978–84; Partner, Executive Search, The Coopers & Lybrand Consulting Group 1985–92; Vice Pres. and Dir., International Assn. of Corporate & Professional Recruiters, Inc. (IACPR); Dir. & Founding Mem., IACPR, Canada; Mem., Inst. of Cert. Management Consultants of Ont.; Human Resources Professionals Assn. of Ont.; Chair, Business Information Committee, Board of Trade; Candn. Assn. of Women Executives & Entrepreneurs; Sales & Mktg. Executives of Toronto; Bd. Mem., Multiple Sclerosis Soc. 1985–87; Canadian Museum of Photography 1985–87; recreations: tennis, theatre; club: Badminton & Racquet; Home: 1177 Yonge St., #314, Toronto, Ont. M4T 2Y4; Office: One St. Clair Ave. E., Suite 803, Toronto, Ont. M4T 2V7.

**COMPTON, Leonard Pickering,** Q.C., B.Sc., LL.B.; barrister & solicitor; b. St. Eleanor's, P.E.I. 10 July 1936; s. Ralph Edmund and Muriel H.B. (Yeo) C.; e. Dalhousie Univ. B.Sc. 1957, LL.B. 1963; Q.C. (Ont.) 1980; m. Sandra d. Roy and Doris Pugh 11 Apr. 1959; children: Scott, Shelley, Nancy, Jeffrey; LAWYER, COMPTON, SHEWCHUK, MacDONELL, ORMISTON, RICHARDT & FREGEAN; Comnr., Ontario Northland Transport. Comn.; Dir., Merle Norman Cosmetics (Can.) Limited; Chancellor, Dioc. of Keewatin, Anglican Ch. of Can.; Mem., Ont. & Candn. Bar assns.; club: Royal Lake of the Woods Yacht; Home: Box 848, Keewatin, Ont. P0X 1C0; Office: 214 Main St. S., Kenora, Ont. P9N 3X7.

**COMTOIS, Pierre,** B.Sc.Comm.; trust company executive; b. St. Gabriel, Que. 3 Oct. 1943; s. Gérard and Georgette (Baril) C.; e. Inst. of Candn. Bankers, Fellow 1968; Hautes Etudes Commerciales, B.Sc.Comm. 1973; m. Micheline d. Eddy and Rosa Sarrazin 5 March 1966; children: Eric, Catherine; Group Vice-Pres., Finance, General Trustco of Canada Inc. 1982–..; var. positions with the Provincial Bk. 1961–78; Vice-Pres., Instl. Bond Sales, Lévesque, Beaubien Inc. 1974–78; Dir., Investments, Nat. Bk. of Can. 1978–82; Dir., Auberge des Gouverneurs Inc.; Fonds des Professionnels du Québec; Candn. Arthritis Soc.; Fond. de l'Hôpital Ste. Jeanne d'Arc; Dir. & mem. Extve. Ctte., Financial Extve. Inst., Montreal Chapt.; mem. Montreal C. of C.; Montreal Bd. of Trade; La Corporation Professionnelle des Administrateurs Agréés; Le Cercle Finance-Placement; Clubs: St. James; St. Denis; Home: 1685 Lajoie Ave., Outremont, Que. H2V 1R8.

**COMTOIS, Roger,** O.C., LL.L., LL.D.; éducateur; né St-Eustache, Qué. 9 février 1921; f. Isidore et Malvina (Houde) C.; é. Coll. Bourget, Rigaud B.A. 1941; St.-Michael's Coll. Toronto 1941–42; Ecole Normale Jacques Cartier, Montréal Cert. 1943; Univ. de Montréal LL.L. 1946; Univ. d'Ottawa LL.D. 1964; m. Evelyn Michaud; enfants: Lorraine (Berthold), Marie-Andrée, Bourduas; PROFESSEUR EMERITE DE DROIT, UNIV. DE MONTREAL; Notaire, Lachute, Qué. 1946–48, Professeur à la faculté de droit, Université de Montréal, Qué. 1948–1984; auteur 'Loi du notariat annotée' 1959; 'Traité de la communauté de biens' 1965; Essai sur les donations par contrat de mariage 1968; Les libéralites, 1979; mem. Soc. Royale du Can.; Officier de l'Ordre du Canada; Dir. de la Revue du Notariat; Prés. de la Chambre des notaires 1966–69; catholique; Adresse: 4875 Mira, Montréal, Qué. H3W 2B7; Bureau: 5064, Ave. du Parc, Montréal, Qué. H2V 4G1.

**CONACHER, Desmond John,** M.A., Ph.D., F.R.S.C.; educator; b. Kingston, Ont. 27 Dec. 1918; s. late William Morison and late Madeline (Cashel) C.; e. Queen's Univ. B.A. 1941, M.A. (Classics) 1942; Univ. of Chicago Ph.D. (Greek Lang. & Lit.) 1950; Dalhousie Univ. LL.D. 1992; Univ. of Victoria D.Litt. 1993; m. Mary Kathleen d. late Bernard Smith 2 Aug. 1952; children: Hugh Anthony, Susan Mary; PROF. EMERITUS OF CLASSICS, TRINITY COLL. UNIV. OF TORONTO 1984– ; Special Lectr. in Classics, Dalhousie Univ. 1946–47; Asst. Prof. of Classics 1947, Assoc. Prof. 1952–58, Univ. of Sask.; Assoc. Prof. 1958–65, Head of Classics 1966–72, Trinity Coll., Univ. of Toronto; Chrmn. Intercoll. Dept. of Classics Univ. of Toronto 1972–75, Prof. of Classics 1965–84, Professor Emeritus 1984– ; Bonsall Visiting Prof. of Classics, Stanford Univ. spring term 1981; Continuing Mem., Sch. of Grad. Studies, Univ. of Toronto 1984–90; Sessional Appt., Dept. of Classics, Univ. of Toronto 1984–85, 1985–86, 1986–87, 1987–88; Visiting Prof. of Classics: Princeton Univ., 2nd semester 1987; Univ. of Texas at Austin, spring term 1989; Univ. of Canterbury, Christchurch, New Zealand, spring term 1993; author 'Euripidean Drama' 1967; 'Aeschylus' *Prometheus Bound*: A Literary Study,' 1980; 'Aeschylus' *Oresteia*: A Literary Commentary' 1987; 'Euripides' *Alcestis* with Introduction, Translation and Commentary' 1988; contributions to 'Sources of Dramatic Theory' vol. 1, 1991; author various articles and reviews mainly Greek Tragedy prof. journs.; Fellow, Royal Soc. of Canada (el. 1976); mem. Ed. Bd. 'Phoenix' 1968–73, 1983–86; Hon. Adv. Bd. 'University of Toronto Quarterly' 1975–82; mem., Bd. of Dir., Can., Fed. for the Humanities (1981–84); mem. Classical Assn. Can. (Council 1975–78, Hon. Pres. 1991–94); Am. Philol. Assn. (Dir. 1974–77); recreation: tennis; Home: 126 Manor Rd. E., Toronto, Ont. M4S 1P8; Office: Trinity Coll., Univ. of Toronto, Toronto, Ont. M5S 1H8.

**CONDIE, Richard Lloyd,** B.A.; filmmaker; b. Vancouver, B.C. 21 Oct. 1942; s. Richard Henry and Edith Merle (Gallagher) C.; e. Univ. of Man., B.A. 1967; m. Linda d. Edward and Helen Gervais 3 June 1967; awarded 2 Can. Counc. grants 1971, 1972 to experiment in animation; writing & animating for CBC 'Sesame Street' mid-1970s; Writer, Dir., Animator, Composer, animated films for Nat. Film Bd.; recent work on Worlds Fair film for Brisbane Expo 88 & a short in IMAX format; Candn. Pavillion for EXPO 92, Seville; currently working on High End 3D Computer Animation; films include: 'John Law and the Mississippi Bubble' 1978, 'Getting Started' 1980, 'Pigbird' 1981, 'The Big Snit' (NFB) 1985; 'Heartland' (IMAX Systems) 1987; 'The Apprentice' (NFB) 1991; 33 internat. awards incl. 2 'Genies' and an 'Oscar' nomin. 1986 for 'The Big Snit'; Mem., A.S.I.F.A.; Acad. of Motion Picture Arts & Sci.; Winnipeg Film Group; Home: 220 Campbell, Winnipeg, Man. R3N 1B5.

**CONDON, Thomas Joseph,** M.A., Ph.D.; university professor; b. New Haven, Conn. 27 July 1930; s. Edmond Francis and Helen (Heffernan) C.; e. Yale Coll. B.A. 1952; Boston Coll. M.A. 1953; Harvard Univ. Ph.D. 1962; m. Ann Kathleen d. late Joseph Gregory and Genevieve (Smith) Gorman 30 May 1962; children: Katherine, Caroline, Gregory; PROF. OF HIST., UNIV. OF NEW BRUNSWICK, SAINT JOHN CAMPUS; Teaching Fellow in Hist. and Tutor, Harvard Univ. 1959–1962; Research Asst. on Hist. Preservation and Urban Renewal Boston 1962; Asst. Prof. of Hist. Univ. of N.B. Fredericton 1962–66, Prof. of Hist. and Dean of Arts 1970–77; Acting Pres., Univ. of N.B. (Fredericton & Saint John Campuses) 1979–80; Vice Pres., (Saint John) 1977–87; Exec. Assoc. Am. Council Learned Socs. N.Y. 1966–70; Visiting Assoc. Prof. of Hist. Ind. Univ. Bloomington 1967–68; Visiting Prof. of Hist. Grad. Centre City Univ. of N.Y. 1968–69; Hon. Research Fellow Inst. of U.S. Studies Univ. of London 1975–76; served with U.S. Naval Reserve 1953–57, rank Lt.; rec'd Holland Soc. N.Y. Grant 1962, Can. Council Research Grants 1964, 1965, Henry E. Huntington Lib. Summer Fellowship 1964; recipient, The Lescarbot Award, Govt. of Canada for 'Outstanding Contributions to Community Cultural Activities' 1991; Commemorative Medal for 125th Anniversary of Candn. Confederation 1992; mem. Humanities Research Council Can. 1972–73; Maritime Provinces Higher Educ. Commn. 1982–85; Chrmn. Adv. Ctte. on Arts in N.B. 1973–75; Gov. Rothesay Coll. Sch. 1977–88 and Univ. of N.B. 1977–87, 1991– ; Chrmn. Engn. Task Force Maritime Provs. Higher Educ. Comn. 1977–78; Chrmn. and Pres., Bi-Capitol Project, Inc. 1982–91; Vice Pres., 1985 Jeux Canada Games 1981–85; Bd. of Govs., Candn. Conf. of the Arts 1988– ; has served on various other educ. bds. and cttes.; mem. N.B. Museum; Beaverbrook Art Gallery; author 'New York Beginnings: The Commercial Origins of New Netherland' 1968; various articles and reviews, papers, lectures and addresses; Ed. 'ACLS Newsletter' 1968–70; mem. Ed. Bd. 'Computers and the Humanities' 1969–70 and 'Acadiensis' 1970; mem. The Mory's Assn.; Saint John Bd. Trade; R. Catholic; recreations: squash, tennis; Club: Union; Home: 268 Princess St., Saint John, N.B. E2L 1L3; Office: P.O. Box 5050, Saint John, N.B. E2L 4L5.

**CONGER, Jay Alden,** B.A., M.B.A., D.B.A.; university professor; b. Washington, D.C. 29 July 1952; c. Clement Ellis and Lianne Hopkins C.; e. Dartmouth Coll., B.A. 1974; Univ. of Virginia, M.B.A. 1977; Harvard Univ., D.B.A. 1985; PROF. OF MNGT. IN ORGANIZATIONAL BEHAVIOR, MCGILL UNIV. 1985– ; Visiting Prof., Harvard Business Sch. 1992–93 and INSEAD 1991–92; Asst. to Dir., Consumer Protection Div., Attorney General's Office (Raleigh, NC) 1974–75; Adjunct Prof. of Mktg., Georgetown Univ. 1979–80; Mgr., Internat. Mktg., Solarex Corp. 1977–80; Assoc. Cons., Harbridge House 1982–85; Pres., Jay Conger & Assoc. 1986– ; Distinguished Teaching Award, McGill Univ.; Rufus Choate Scholar, Dartmouth Coll.; Cum Laude, Dartmouth Coll.; featured in 'The Economist,' 'Globe and Mail,' 'New York Times,' 'Wall Street Journal,' and 'San Francisco Chronicle'; author: 'The Charismatic Leader' 1989; 'Learning to Lead' 1992; co-author: 'Charismatic Leadership' 1988; recreations: cross-country skiing, swimming; Home: 1227 Blvd. Mont-Royal, Outremont, Que. H2V 2H7; Office: 1001 Sherbrooke W., Montreal, Que. H3A 1G5.

**CONIBEAR, Kenneth Wilfred,** M.A.; b. Orrville, Ont. 29 Aug. 1907; s. Lewis Gilbert and Ada Mary (Gribble) C.; e. privately taught N.W.T.; Victoria H.S. Edmonton 1927; Univ. of Alta. B.A. 1931; Oxford Univ. (Rhodes Scholar) B.A. 1934, M.A. 1962; m. Barbara Edith (dec.) d. Francis and Mildred Linke 20 Dec. 1937; m. Marilyn Luella d. Ervin and Luella Ernest 16 Dec. 1989; two s. John Ward, Peter Lewis (dec.); ASSOC. DIR., CONTINUING STUDIES, SIMON FRASER UNIV. 1988; worked and wrote, London, Eng. 1934–37; Mgr. Grey Owl's 2nd lecture tour Eng. 1937; helped parents gen. store and fur trade, Fort Smith, N.W.T. 1938–43; joined RCNVR 1943–46; operated own fish packer-tugboats, Great Slave Lake 1948–57; Exec. Sec. B.C. Hosp.'s Assn. 1958–63; part-time Tutor Simon Fraser Univ. 1965–67, Asst. in Eng. 1967–77, part-time Coordr. Fac. of Arts 1977–82, Coordr. and Lectr. Sr. Citizens Prog. 1969– ; Dist. Comnr. Boy Scouts Can. S. Surrey Dist. 1959–62; author 'Northland Footprints' 1936; 'Northward to Eden' 1938; co-author 'Husky' 1940; recreations: gardening, building; Home: 3485 Point Grey Rd., Vancouver, B.C. V6R 1A6.

**CONLOGUE, Raymond Dennis,** M.A.; theatre critic; journalist; b. Toronto, Ont. 25 June 1949; s. Raymond Bartholomew and Loretta Imelda (Harrington) C.; e. Univ. of Toronto, St. Michael's Coll. B.A. 19.., Centre for Study of Drama M.A. 19..; CULTURAL CORRESPONDENT, THE GLOBE & MAIL, Montreal 1991– ; freelance broadcaster and mag. jour. 1972–75; law sch. 1976; present newspaper 1977– , Theatre Critic 1980–91; recipient Nat. Newspaper Award 1987; recreations: travel, canoeing, scuba diving; Home: 5260 Hutchison Ave., Montreal, Que.; Office: 444 Front St. W., Toronto, Ont. M5V 2S9.

**CONN, Alan William,** M.D., B.Sc., F.R.C.P.(C); physician; educator; b. Toronto, Ont. 29 May 1925; s. Hartly Robert, M.B. and Grace Margery (Heather) C.; e. Mimico (Ont.) High Sch. 1942; Univ. of Toronto Schs. 1943; Univ. of Toronto M.D. 1948, post-grad. course in Anaesthesia 1950–52, B.Sc. (Med.) 1957; R.S. McLaughlin Fellow U.K. 1952–53; m. Marian Hamilton d. Douglas Hart, Woodstock, Ont. 2 March 1948; children: Nancy Heather, Mary Ann, Wendy Elizabeth, Heather Victoria; Prof. of Anaesthesia Univ. of Toronto 1967–88; retired 1988; Prof. Emeritus 1989; Lectr. in Anaesthesia, Hosp. for Sick Children 1953–59, Chief of Anaesthesia 1960–71, Dir. Intensive Care Unit 1971–81, Chrmn., Risk Mgmt. 1982–87; Visiting Prof. Anaesthesia Research Univ. of Texas 1982; served with R.C.A.M.C. (Reserve) 1948–52, rank Capt.; RCAF 1954–60, rank Sqdn. Leader (4005 A.M.U. Reserve); author numerous book chapters Hypothermia, Anaesthesia, Intensive Care; publs. Paediatric Anaesthesia, Paediatric Intensive Care; articles on near-drowning; Gen. Practice Chapleau, Ont. 1949–50; Fellow, Am. Coll. Anesthetists; Am. Acad. Pediatrics; mem. Acad. Med. Toronto; Candn. Med. Assn.; Ont. Med. Assn.; Candn. Anaesthetists' Soc.; Am. Soc. Anesthesiol.; Internat. Anaesthesiol. Research Soc.; Assn. Anaesthetists (U.K.); Acad. Anaesthetists; Soc. Critical Care; Candn. Standards Assn.; Nu Sigma Nu; P. Conservative; United Church; recreation: travel; Clubs: Faculty (U. of T.); University (Toronto); Home: 2615 Lake Shore Blvd. W., Toronto, Ont. M8V 1G5.

**CONNACHER, James Russell;** CHAIRMAN & CHIEF EXECUTIVE OFFICER, GORDON CAPITAL CORPORATION; Office: Toronto-Dominion Bank Tower, Box 67, Suite 5300, Toronto, Ont. M5K 1E7.

**CONNAGHAN, Charles Joseph,** M.A.; Industrial relations consultant; b. Arranmore, Co. Donegal, Republic of Ireland 14 Feb. 1932; s. John and Sarah (O'Donnell) C.; e. St. Dominic's Sch. and Morrisons Acad. for Boys, Crieff, Pertshire, Scot. 1951; Univ. of B.C. B.A. 1959, M.A. 1960; m. Erma Grace d. late Walter Edwin McGuirk 27 Dec. 1958; children; Michael John, Susan Gail, Kathryn Patricia; CHIEF COMMISSIONER, B.C. TREATY COMMISSION 1993– ; Reviewer, Review of MLA Remuneration, The B.C. Legislative Assembly 1992; Chair, B.C. Provincial Judges Compensation Advisory Ctte. 1993; Trainee MacMillan Bloedel Co. 1960–61; Mgr. Indust. Relations, Atlas Steels Ltd. Welland, Ont. 1961–66 and Anglo-Canadian Pulp & Paper Mills Ltd., Quebec City 1966–70; Pres. Construction Labour Relations Assn. of

B.C. Vancouver 1970–75; Vice Pres., Admin. Serv., Univ. of B.C. 1975–80; Pres., C.J. Connaghan & Assoc. Ltd. 1980–93; mem. Univ. of B.C. Senate 1970–75, Bd. of Govs. 1972–75; Econ. Council of Can. 1976–79; Dir., Council for Candn. Unity 1977–86 (B.C. Pres. 1982–85); Dir., Contact Canada 1978– ; Past Pres. & Dir., Canada-Japan Soc. of Vancouver; Past Pres. & Dir., Canadian Club of Vancouver; Vice-Chrmn. Bd. of Trustees, St. Vincent Hosp., Vancouver, 1980–84; Trustee, Paul's Hosp. Vancouver 1976–78; mem. St. Pauls' Hospital Found. 1986–87; mem. & Co-Chrmn., Cdn. Counc. of Christians & Jews (Pacific Region); Niagara Inst.; Chrmn., Citizens' Comte. on Taxation, Munic. of West Vancouver, 1978–79; Pres., Cdn. Club of Vancouver 1984–85; Chrmn., B.C. Round Table on the Environment & the Economy 1990–92; Chrmn., B.C. Screening Ctte. of the Marshall McLuhan Distinguished Teacher Awards; mem., Transportation Task Force, Asia Pacific Initiative Adv. Ctte. 1988–93; Mem. & Vice Pres., Nat. Council & Pres., B.C. & Yukon Council, The Duke of Edinburgh's Award in Canada; Hon. mem. Boys & Girls Clubs Vancouver; Past Exec. mem., Ind. Relations Sec. Can. Pulp & Paper Assn.; mem. Bd. of Dirs., 1984 B.C. Papal Visit; The World Wildlife Fund (Can.); prepared report on German Indust. Relations for Fed. Dept. of Labour 1976; prepared report on Japanese Industrial Relations for Fed. Dept. of Labour, 1981; author number articles indust. and labour relations fields; recipient of Queen's Jubilee Medal; Beta Theta Pi; R. Catholic; recreations: squash, tennis, fishing; Clubs: Vancouver; Hollyburn Country; Home: 4626 Woodgreen Dr., West Vancouver, B.C. V7S 2V2.

**CONNELL, George E.,** O.C., LL.D, Ph.D., F.C.I.C., F.R.S.C.; biochemist; b. Saskatoon, Sask. 20 June 1930; s. James Lorne and Mabel Gertrude (Killins) C.; e. Upper Can. Coll., Toronto; Univ. of Toronto, B.A. 1951, Ph.D. 1955; m. Sheila Harriet Horan, 27 Dec. 1955; children: James, Thomas, Caroline, Margaret; Prof., Dept. of Biochem., Univ. of Toronto (Chrmn. 1965–70); Assoc. Dean Faculty of Med. 1972–74; Vice Pres. (Research & Planning) 1974–77; Pres., Univ. of Western Ont. 1977–84; Pres., Univ. of Toronto 1984–90; appts: mem., Med. Research Council 1966–70; Dir., Candn. Arthritis and Rheumatism Soc. 1965–75; Chair, Extve. Ctte., XI Internat. Congress of Biochemistry 1979; mem., Ont. Council of Health 1978–84; mem., Counc. of Ont. Univs. 1977–90 (Chair 1981–83); mem., Bd. of Govs. Upper Canada Coll. 1982–89; Mem., Corporate-Higher Education Forum (Extve. 1983–88; Chair, Task Force on Human Resource Mgmt. and Status of Higher Educ. 1983–88); Trustee, Nat. Inst. of Nutrition 1984–90, Mem. Extve. Ctte. 1989–90; mem., Bd. of Trustees, Royal Ont. Museum 1984–90; mem., Bd. of Dirs., Southam Inc. 1985–93; Mem. Candn. Adv. Bd., Liberty Mutual Insurance Co. 1989– ; Vice Chair, Environmental Assessment Bd. of Ont. 1990–93; Chair, Nat. Round Table on the Environment and the Economy 1991– ; Chair, Technical Ctte. 207 of the Internat. Standards Organization 1993– ; Co-Chair, Leadership Council of the Whitehorse Mining Initiative 1993– ; Soc. mem.: Am. Soc. of Biol. Chem.; Candn. Biochem. Soc. (Pres. 1973–74); Candn. Soc. for Immunology; Chem. Inst. of Can. (Chair, Biochemistry Div. 1969–70); Sigma Xi, The Scientific Rsch. Soc.; writings incl. over 50 scient. articles for various journs.; Anglican; Home: 240 Walmer Rd., Toronto, Ont. M5R 3R7.

**CONNELL, (James) Peter;** b. Halifax, N.S. 23 Sept. 1926; s. late James Walter and late Kathryn Whitman (Sanders) C.; e. N.S. High Schs.; Acadia Univ.; m. Ella Catherine, d. late Murdoch Gordon MacLeod M.D. and late Ima (MacLean) MacL.; children: James, David, Bruce, Douglas, Jeffrey, Elizabeth, Barbara, Kathryn; PRESIDENT, JPEC LIMITED 1986– ; Employment Supvr. Frigidaire Products of Canada Ltd. Toronto 1950–52; Asst. Personnel Mgr. Lucas-Rotax Ltd. 1952–55; Indust. Relations Mgr. Union Carbide Canada Ltd. Belleville and Montreal 1955–60; Dir. Employee Relations Allied Chemical Canada Ltd. Montreal 1961–66; Dir. Personnel, Dept. of Nat. Revenue Customs and Excise 1966–67; Dir. Gen. Personnel, Dept. of Transport 1967–68; Depy. Secy. Treasury Bd. 1969–75; Depy. Min. of Nat. Revenue for Customs and Excise 1975–82; Chrmn., Customs Co-operation Council 1980–82; Depy. Min. of Agriculture Can. 1982–86; Consultant and Special Advisor to the Ambassador (Trade Negotiations) and Chief Negotiator for Canada, Canada/U.S. Trade Agreement 1986–88; United Church; recreations: fishing, woodworking; Home: R.R. #3, Ventnor Rd., Spencerville, Ont. K0E 1X0.

**CONNELL, Philip F.,** B.A., F.C.A.; financial executive; b. Hamilton, Ont. 20 Jan. 1924; s. Maurice Williams and Kathleen C.; e. Delta Coll. Inst. Hamilton 1942; McMaster Univ. B.A. 1946; C.A. 1950; DIR., OSHAWA GROUP LTD. since 1976; joined Clarkson Gordon & Co. 1946–57; Comptroller, Canadian Westinghouse Co. Ltd. 1957–67; Controller, Domtar Ltd. 1967–68; Vice Pres. Finance, George Weston Ltd. 1968–75; Sr. Vice Pres. Finance & Dir., Oshawa Group Ltd. 1976–91; Extve. Vice Pres. & Dir., Oshawa Group Ltd. 1991–92; mem. Financial Extves. Inst. (Past Pres. Hamilton Chapter); Ont. Inst. C.A.'s ; F.C.A. 1968; United Church; Clubs: National; Hamilton; Home: 400 Walmer Rd., Apt. 2510, Toronto, Ont. M5P 2X7; Office: 302 The East Mall, Islington, Ont. M9B 6B8.

**CONNELL, W. Ford,** M.D., C.M., F.R.C.P. (Lond.), F.R.C.P.(C), F.A.C.P., F.A.C.C., LL.D.(1973); academic clinician; b. Kingston, Ont., 24 Aug. 1906; s. Dr. Walter Thomas and Florence (Ford) C.; e. Queen's Univ. Med. Sch., Grad. 1929; Post Grad. training at Toronto Gen. Hosp. (1929–31) and at Freiburg-in-Breisgau, Manchester and London (1931–33); m. Merle Beatrice (dec.), d. the late James Bruce, Grand Valley, Ont., 16 Dec. 1933; children: James Douglas, Walter Bruce, Patricia Anne; Richardson Fellow in Med., Queen's Univ., Asst. Prof. of Med. 1934–37, Assoc. Prof. 1937–42, Prof. and Chrmn., Dept. of Medicine 1942–68, Emeritus Prof.; Dir., Heart Dept., Kingston Gen. Hosp., 1933–76, Sr. Consultant to 1986; Capt. R.C.A.M.C. (Reserve); Fellow, Am. Coll. of Cardiology (1961) and Gov. for Ont., 1962; Fellow, Am. Coll. Phys. and Gov. for Ont. 1958–63; mem., Am. Bd. of Internal Med.; Conservative; Freemason (Scot. Rite); recreations: fishing, reading, philately, writing; Home: 11 Arch St., Kingston, Ont. K7L 3L4.

**CONNELLY, Eric,** F.C.A., C.M.A., A.C.I.S.; company executive; b. Amble, Northumberland, Eng. 2 June 1910; s. Thomas and Janet (Burton) C.; e. Calgary Public and Crescent Heights High Sch.; admitted C.A., Alta., 1933; F.C.A. 1957; m. 1stly Barbara Violet Ella (dec.), d. William Toole, Calgary, Alta., 31 Mar. 1948; one s. Brian William; m. 2ndly Ada Helen Christine, d. A. de Beaufort, The Hague, Netherlands, 16 Dec. 1983; Chrmn. and Dir., Barber Engineering & Supply Co. Ltd.; Barber Engn. and Controls Ltd.; Besco Industrial Products Ltd.; B.G. Controls Ltd.; Canex Edible Oils, Ltd.; Can. Exec. Organization; Formerly: Chairman, Pembina Pipeline Ltd.; Pres. Panarctic Oils, Ltd.; Vice-Pres. and Dir. Loram Ltd.; Dir. Ashland Oil Canada Ltd.; Bankeno Mines Ltd.; Merland Explorations Ltd.; Barber Industries Ltd.; Pres., Calgary Chamber of Comm.; Alta. Tuberculosis Assn. (Dir. 1943–48; Pres. 1948); Dir., Inst. of Chartered Accts. of Alta. (Council 1948–55; Pres. 1954); Hon. Treas., Calgary Exib. and Stampede (1975–77); Dir. & Lectr. Banff Sch. of Advanced Mgmt. 1955–1962; Lectr., Austrian School Advanced Management 1970; Chrmn. Calgary United Fund Drive 1968 (Dir. 1968–72); Dir. Glenbow Museum Acquisition Soc. 1980–83; mem.: Institute of Chartered Accountants of Alberta; Chartered Inst. of Secretaries and Administrators (A.C.I.S.); Soc. of Mgmt. Accts. of Can. (C.M.A.); Newcomen Soc.; Freemason (32$ Scot Rite); Shriner; Anglican; Clubs: Ranchmen's (Pres.); Calgary Petroleum; Calgary Golf & Country; Glencoe; Rotary (Paul Harris Fellow); Mill Reef (Antigua); Wailea Golf (Hawaii); Home: Apt. 4 S., Covenant House, 222 Eagle Ridge Drive, S.W., Calgary, Alta. T2V 2V7.

**CONNELLY, Karen Marie;** writer; b. Calgary, Alta. 12 March 1969; d. Denis Byron and Jacqueline Ann (Gurling) C.; e. Western Canada H.S. 1987; single; has lived in Thailand, Spain, France, and Greece (much of her work involves these places and their people); author: 'The Small Words In My Body' 1990 (poetry; winner of Kalamalka National Poetry Comp. 1990 and Pat Lowther Award for best book of poetry pub. by a Candn. woman in 1990 1991); 'Touch the Dragon' 1992 (non-fiction, travel; winner, Gov.-General's Award for non-fiction 1993, youngest ever to win this award); 'This Brighter Prison' 1993 (travel, poetry); Writer-in-Residence, Univ. of New Brunswick (six months) 1993; currently working in Greece on fiction & poetry and may publish a book of short stories in 1994; 'Most Promising Writer Under 35,' Canadian Authors Assn. 1986; Canada Council grant for work & travel in Europe; recreations: hiking, swimming, horseback riding; Address: c/o Turnstone Press, 607 - 100 Arthur St., Winnipeg, Man. R3B 1H3.

**CONNELLY, Robert George,** P.Eng.; public servant; b. Mattawa, Ont. 27 Feb. 1948; s. Walton Robert and Esther Rae (Pratt) C.; e. Mackenzie H.S. 1965; Univ. of Waterloo 1970; m. Margaret d. Norman and Valena Trewartha 31 July 1971; children: Michael, Matthew, Elizabeth; VICE PRESIDENT, FEDERAL ENVIRONMENTAL ASSESSMENT REVIEW 1978– ; Co-op Student, Proctor & Redfern Group 1966–70; Dept. of National Health & Welfare (Winnipeg) 1970–71; Environment Canada 1971–75; United Nations Economic Comn. (Geneva) 1975–78; Part-time Cons., World Health Orgn.; Former Mem., Bd. of Dir., Ottawa Gymnastics Club; Mem., Engineering Inst. of Canada; Assn. of Profl. Engrs. of Canada; recreations: coach of various soccer, hockey teams; Home: 106 Coburn Ave., Kanata, Ont. K2L 1G3; Office: Fontaine Bldg., Hull, Qué. K1A 0H3.

**CONNELLY, Ronald Ray,** B.Com., M.B.A.; executive; b. New Liskeard, Ont. 14 Feb. 1951; s. Cecil Lloyd and Myrtle Elizabeth (Keech) C.; e. Carleton Univ. B.Com. 1973; Sir George Williams Univ. M.B.A. 1974; m. Jane d. Michael and Margaret Cronin 18 March 1978; children: Kathleen Jane, Anne Catherine, Jonathan Ray; PRES. AND FOUNDER, CONNELLY EXHIBITIONS INC. 1981– ; and PRES. AND FOUNDER, 'TECHNOLOGY IN GOVERNMENT WEEK' 1993; Pres. R. Connelly Securities Ltd.; Sec.-Treas. 356123 Ontario Ltd.; Pres. Gray Harvey Wholesale Hardware 1974–80; mem. Ottawa Assn. Exhn. Mgrs. (Pres.); Ottawa-Carleton Econ. Devel. Corp.; Ottawa-Carleton Bd. Trade; recreations: skiing, basketball; Club: Ottawa Athletic; Office: 214, 2487 Kaladar Ave., Ottawa, Ont. K1V 8B9.

**CONNER, Donald C.,** B.Comm., M.B.A.; investment counsellor; b. Manitou, Manitoba 26 July 1952; s. James Clifford and Alice Florence (Bamford) C.; e. Univ. of Man. B.Comm. (Hons.) 1974; York Univ. M.B.A. 1977; m. Debby d. Allen and Marion Shepherd 19 Oct. 1974; children: Christopher, Alanna; VICE-PRESIDENT RESP. FOR EQUITY RESEARCH AND STRATEGY, HODGSON ROBERTON LAING LTD. 1986– ; Research Analyst, Pension Fund / Capital Markets Analyst, Bank of Canada 1974–76; Pension Fund Mgr., / Asst. Pension Fund Mgr. / Fixed Income Mgr. / Suprvr. Investments, Investment Dept., Bank of N.S. 1977–86; Dir., Hodgson Roberton Laing Limited; Molson Hockey Scholarship; recreations: golf; Home: 181 Kirk Drive, Thornhill, Ont. L3T 3L7; Office: 1 Queen St. E., Suite 1920, Toronto, Ont. M5C 2Y5.

**CONNOLLY, James Ross,** B.A., M.A.; teacher, writer; b. Dawson Creek, B.C. 9 Nov. 1962; s. David Rymer and Patricia Eileen (Daniels) C.; e. Shawnigan Lake School 1980; Okanagan College; Univ. of Victoria B.A., M.A. 1988; m. Maureen d. Sandy and Preston Mott 31 March 1984; children: David Jackson, Samuel James; CHAIR, DEPARTMENT OF ENGLISH, SHAWNIGAN LAKE SCHOOL 1990– ; Part-time Sessional Lecturer, Univ. of Victoria 1986–87, 1990; Teacher, Shawnigan Lake Sch. 1986– ; Co-Dir., Archetype Communications 1990– ; author: 'Dancewater Blues' 1990 (novel), 'Rough Diamond: An Oral History of Shawnigan Lake School' (non-fiction/oral history) 1992; Home: 1975 Renfrew Rd., Shawnigan Lake, B.C. V0R 2W0.

**CONNOLLY, Peter Charles;** business executive; b. Ottawa, Ont. 25 Jan. 1942; s. Hon. John Joseph and Ida Bernadette (Jones) C.; e. universities of Montreal, Ottawa, Queen's; m. Pamela d. Walter and Mary Surtees; children: Kristen, Ryan, Trevor, Elizabeth, Aidan, Jamie; SR. VICE-PRES., CANADA MORTGAGE & HOUSING CORP. 1990– ; Extve. Asst. to ministers of Health & Welfare, Nat. Revenue, Labour, Manpower & Immigration, Consumer & Corp. Affairs, M.S.U.A., Treas. Board 1965–77, 1982–84; Sr. Extve., Public Serv. of Canada 1977–81; Extve. Vice-Pres., Lavalin Inc. 1985–87; Principal Sec., Rt. Hon. John N. Turner 1987–90; candidate, general elections of 1968 and 1972 (defeated); Dir., Children's Hosp. of E. Ont.; Roman Catholic; Liberal; Mem., Financial Extves. Institute; Assn. of Profl. Extves. in Public Service; club: Cercle Univ.; Home: 100 Rothwell Dr., Ottawa, Ont. K1J 8L9; Office: 700 Montreal Rd., Ottawa, Ont. K1A 0P7.

**CONNOR, Gerald R.;** investment executive; b. Aurora, Ill. 12 Jan. 1946; s. Roy L. and Beatrice S. (Walt) C.; e. DePauw Univ. B.A. 1968; m. Carla L., d. Carl and Min Galbrecht 17 June 1967; children: Gregory S., Trevor B., Grant M.; PRESIDENT, CONNOR, CLARK & COMPANY LTD. 1977– ; Head, Opns., DuPont Glore Forgan 1967–70; Acct. Extve. 1970–72; Baker Weeks & Co. 1972–77; Vice Chrmn., Connor, Clark & Lunn Investment Mgmt.; Dir. & Offr., 20/20 Group Financial Inc.; Dir., Brita Internat. Holdings; Canada Publishing; mem., Young Presidents' Organization (Ont. Chapter); Financial Analysts Assn.; recreations: tennis, golf, skiing, squash; Clubs: Granite; Rosedale Golf; Cambridge; Devil's Glen Country; National; Mad River Golf; Home: 19 Riverview Dr., Toronto, Ont. M4N 3C6; Office: Scotia Plaza, Box 125, 40 King St. W., Suite 5110, Toronto, Ont. M5H 3Y2.

**CONNORS, Donald E.,** B.A.; business executive; b. Gravelbourg, Sask. 14 Mar. 1945; s. Thomas Francis and Simone E. (Peltier) C.; e. Univ. of Sask., B.A. 1968; m. Bernadette d. John and Nellie Marshall Oct. 1968; one s.: Corbett Bradley; MANAGING DIR., JIM PATTISON IND. LTD.; Dir. of Opns., Acme Merchandise Distrib. 1968–75; Vice-Pres., Sales & Mktg., Neonex Leisure, U.S.A. 1976–79; Vanguard Mfg. 1980–83; Past Dir., Candn. Auto. Leasing Assn.; Candn. Recreational Vehicle Assn.; Home: 8200 Aspin Dr., Richmond, B.C. V6Y 3B8; Office: 1600 – 1055 W. Hastings St., Vancouver, B.C. V6E 2H2.

**CONOLLY, Leonard William,** B.A., M.A., Ph.D.; university professor; b. Walsall, England 13 Sept. 1941; s. John and Rona Erica Jean (Thacker) C.; e. Univ. of Wales, B.A. 1963; Ph.D. 1970; McMaster Univ., M.A. 1964; m. Barbara d. William and Mary Heap 19 Dec. 1964; children: James, Rebecca; PRESIDENT & VICE-CHANCELLOR, TRENT UNIV. 1994– ; Instr. of English, Univ. of Sask. 1965–67; Asst. Prof. of English, Univ. of Alta. 1970–74; Assoc. Prof. 1974–79; Prof. 1979–81; Supvr. in English, Jesus Coll., Cambridge 1976–77; Prof. of Drama & Chrmn. of Dept., Univ. of Guelph 1981–86; Acting Dean of Arts, Univ. of Guelph 1986–87; Acting Vice-Pres. Acad., Univ. of Guelph 1990, 1992–93; Bye-fellow, Robinson Coll., Cambridge 1981, 1991; Assoc. Vice Pres., Academic 1988–92; Bd. of Dir., Guelph Spring Fest. (Pres. 1990–93); Bd. of Dir., 'World Encyclopedia of Contemporary Theatre' (Pres. 1989–92); Mem., Assn. for Candn. Theatre Research (Pres. 1977–79); Am. Soc. for Theatre Rsch.; author: 'The Censorship of English Drama 1737–1824' 1976; co-author: 'English-Canadian Theatre' 1987; editor: 'Theatrical Touring and Founding in North America' 1982; 'Canadian Drama and the Critics' 1987; co-editor: 'English Drama and Theatre 1800–1900' 1978; 'Nineteenth Century Theatre Research' 1972–80, 'Essays in Theatre' 1982–89; 'The Oxford Companion to Canadian Theatre' 1989; 'Bernard Shaw on Stage' 1991; recreations: chess, theatre, music; Home: 499 Homewood Ave., Peterborough, Ont. K9H 2N2.

**CONRAD, The Honourable Madam Justice Carole M.,** B.A., LL.B.; justice; b. Edmonton, Alta. 30 Sept. 1943; d. Clifford S. and Marget C. (Kjos) Smallwood; e. Univ. of Alberta B.A. 1964, LL.B. 1967; m. E. Keith C.; children: Derren James, Cara Janelle, Bradley Jerome; JUSTICE OF THE COURT OF APPEAL OF ALBERTA 1992– ; Justice of the Court of Queen's Bench of Alberta, Deputy Judge of the Supreme Court of the N.W.T. and of the Yukon 1986–92; Lawyer, Gill, Conrad, Cronin et al 1967–72; Conrad, Smallwood, Wilson & Hawley (later Conrad, Blumenthal and Carruthers) 1972–84; Q.C. Jan. 1980; private practice 1984–86; Vice-Chair, Rental Control Bd. 1976–77; Office: 530 – 7th Ave. S.W., Calgary, Alta. T2P 0Y3.

**CONRAD, John Beverly Freeman;** newspaper editor, journalist; b. Kentville, N.S. 9 Nov. 1952; s. Beverly Maxwell and Cassandra Marion (Wheelock) C.; e. Kings Co. Academy; Horton Dist. H.S.; Holland College, journalism 1974, media technology 1974; m. Mary Elizabeth d. Robert and Frances Newell 4 March 1983; children: Robert, Wendy; MANAGING EDITOR, AMHERST DAILY NEWS 1982– ; Reporter-Photographer, Charlottetown Guardian & Evening Patriot 1975; Chief, Summerside Bureau 1975; Reporter-Photographer, Truro Daily News 1976; News Editor, then City Editor and lastly Acting Managing Editor 1976–81; Press Sec. to then-Liberal Opposition Leader A.M. (Sandy) Cameron 1981; Assignment Editor, 'The Citizen' (weekly) 1987– ; Founding Mem., Atlantic Press Council; Mem., Adv. Ctte., Dept. of Journalism, Holland College; Past Pres. & Campaign Chair, Amherst United Way; Home: 13 Westminster Ave., Amherst, N.S. B4H 3V1; Office: Box 280, Amherst, N.S. B4H 3Z2.

**CONRAD, Margaret Rose,** B.A., M.A., Ph.D.; university professor; b. Bridgewater, N.S. 14 Sept. 1946; d. Douglas Ralph and Gladys Lavinia (Weston) Slauenwhite; e. Acadia Univ. B.A. (Hons.) 1967; Univ. of Toronto M.A. 1968, Ph.D. 1979; divorced; PROFESSOR, DEPT. OF HISTORY, ACADIA UNIV. 1987– ; Editor, Clark, Irwin Publishing Company 1968–69; Lect., Asst. then Assoc. Prof., History, Acadia Univ. 1969–87; Adjunct Prof., History, Dalhousie Univ. 1991– ; Mem., Assn. for Candn. Studies (Extve. Ctte. 1981–83); Candn. Hist. Assn. (Council 1977–80); Candn. Research Inst. for the Advancement of Women; Candn. Women's Studies Assn.; Planter Studies Centre (Founding Mem.); Adv. Bd. Mem., 'Acadiensis,' 'Atlantis,' 'Histoire Sociale,' 'Newfoundland Studies'; Mem., Bd. of Gov., Acadia Univ. 1992–94; Adv. Bd., Nat. Archives of Can. 1989–92; N.S. Mem., Historic Sites & Monuments Bd. of Can. 1990–96; author: 'George Nowlan' 1986, 'Recording Angels' 1983; co-author: 'History of the Canadian Peoples' 2 vols 1993, 'No Place Like Home' 1988, 'Twentieth Century Canada' 1974; supervising editor: 'New England Planters in Maritime Canada' 1993; editor: 'Making Adjustment' 1991, 'They Planted Well' 1988; Home: 36 Acadia St., Wolfville, N.S. B0P 1X0; Office: Wolfville, N.S. B0P 1X0.

**CONVERSE, William Rawson Mackenzie,** B.A., M.A., Ph.D., M.L.S.; librarian; b. Sherbrooke, Que. 25 Nov. 1937; s. Augustus Mackenzie and Violet Naomi (Ward) C.; e. Bishop's Univ., B.A. 1959, M.A. 1963; Univ. of Adelaide Ph.D. 1968; Univ. of Western Ont. M.L.S. 1970; divorced; two s. David, Ben; UNIVERSITY LIBRARIAN, UNIV. OF WINNIPEG 1982– ; Humanities Librarian, Memorial Univ. of Nfld. 1970; Deputy Chief Lib. (Acad.) 1973, Acting Chief Lib. 1978, Area Lib. Arts & Humanities 1979, Univ. of Calgary; Pres., Manitoba Library Assoc. 1985–86; Convenor, Intellectual Freedom Ctte., Candn. Library Assoc. 1984–86; Pres., Candn. Library Assoc. 1987–88; Steering Ctte., WIN (Winnipeg In The Nineties); recreations: film, music, reading, travel; Home: 2003 – 11 Evergreen Pl., Winnipeg, Man. R3L 2T9; Office: 515 Portage Ave., Winnipeg, Man. R3B 2E9.

**CONWAY, Brian Evans,** Ph.D., D.I.C., D.Sc., F.R.S.C., F.R.I.C., F.C.I.C.; educator; b. London, Eng. 26 Jan. 1927; s. Arthur George and Ethel (Evans) C.; e. Imp. Coll. of Science & Technol. London B.Sc. 1946, Ph.D. 1949, D.I.C.; Univ. of London, D.Sc. 1961; m. Nina Protopopos; one child Adrian; PROF. OF CHEMISTRY, UNIV. OF OTTAWA; Consultant, Hooker Chemical Co.; Brookhaven National Lab.; Continental Group (N.Y.); Chrmn. of Chem. Univ. Ottawa 1966–69 and 1975–80; mem. Nat. Research Council Chem. Grant Comte. 1975–78; rec'd Chem. Inst. Noranda Award 1964, Medal 1976; Electrochemical Soc. Henry Linford Medal 1984; Am. Chem. Soc. Kendall Award in Surface Chemistry 1984; Electrochemical Soc. Olin Palladium Medal 1989; author 'Electrochemical Data' 1952; Titular mem. of I.U.P.A.C. Comn. on Electrochemistry 1986– ; 'Theory and Principles of Electrode Processes' 1964; 'Ionic Hydration in Chemistry and Biophysics' 1981; co-ed. 'Chemical Physics of Ionic Solutions' 1966; 'Modern Aspects of Electrochemistry' 17 vols. 1954–present; over 250 research papers scient. journs.; Home: 757 Acacia Lane, Ottawa, Ont.; Office: 10 Marie Curie St., Ottawa, Ont. K1N 6N5.

**CONWAY, Garry,** B.F.A.; association executive; b. Halifax, N.S. 1 Oct. 1948; e. Nova Scotia College of Art & Design B.F.A. 1971; an artist and advocate for visual artists' profl. development, dealing with reasonable incomes for artists, protection of rights & providing profl. information on arts practice such as copyright, income tax & contracts; Chair, Ont. Status of Artists Coalition; Treas., Artist Legal Advice Serv.; Vice Chair, Artscape; CARFAC Copyright Collective; Vice-Rep., CARFAC Extve.; Office: 183 Bathurst St., Toronto, Ont. M5T 2R7.

**CONWAY, Jill Kathryn Ker,** Ph.D.; educator; b. Australia 9 Oct. 1934; d. William Innes and Evelyn Mary (Adames) Ker; came to Canada 1964; e. Univ. of Sydney, Australia B.A. 1958; Harvard Univ. Ph.D. 1969; Hon. Degrees: LL.D., St. Thomas Univ. 1974; Mount Holyoke Coll. 1975; York Univ. 1977; Univ. of New Hampshire 1977; Westfield State College 1979; Wesleyan Univ. 1980; Queen's Univ. 1984; Univ. of Toronto 1984; McGill Univ. 1985; Notre Dame Univ. 1990; Dartmouth Univ. 1990; Litt. D., Amherst Coll. 1976; Mount St. Vincent Univ. 1980; SUNY 1986; Smith Coll. 1988; Miami Univ. 1989; Univ. of Rochester 1990; D.Ed., Westfield State Coll. 1979; Providence Coll. 1987; D.Hum.L., Univ. of Massachusetts 1981; Williams College 1982; m. John James Conway 22 Dec. 1962; VISITING SCHOLAR, M.I.T. 1985– ; Dir. Colgate-Palmolive Corp.; Arthur D. Little, Inc.; Merrill Lynch & Co., Inc., Allen Group; Nike Inc.; Lend Lease International; Lectr., Univ. of Sydney, Australia 1958–60; Teaching Fellow, Harvard Univ. 1961–63; Lectr., Univ. of Toronto 1964–68; Asst. Prof. 1968–70; Assoc. Prof. 1970–75; Vice Pres., Internal Affairs 1973–75; Pres. and Sophia Smith Prof., Smith College 1975–85; Visiting Scholar, Vis. Professor, M.I.T. 1985– ; Trustee, Coll. Retirement Equities Fund 1978–86; Dir., Center for Communication, Inc. 1978–86; Counc. for Financial Aid to Education 1980–86; Independent Sector (Washington, D.C.) 1980–86; mem. Harvard Bd. of Overseers 1976–82; Cdn. Assn. of Univ. Teachers (chaired Comte. on Status of Academic Women 1972–73); Gov., New England Medical Center, Inc.; Mt. Holyoke Coll.; author of numerous books and articles in field of history of women; R. Catholic; recreations: gardening, cooking, Baroque music; Office: 65 Commonwealth Ave., Boston, MA 02116.

**CONWAY, John Frederick,** B.A. (Hons.), M.A., Ph.D.; educator; b. Moose Jaw, Sask. 19 Nov. 1943; s. Frederick and Mary Laura (Urquhart) C.; e. Royal Roads Mil. Coll. Victoria 1961–62; Univ. of Sask. B.A. (Hons.) 1966, M.A. 1968; Simon Fraser Univ. Ph.D. 1979; Univ. of Regina Bilingual Centre 1986–87; Laval Univ. French Lang. 1987; m. Sara d. Edgar and Margaret Mahood 15 Aug. 1975; children: Liam Aneurin, Aidan Devlin, Kieran Bethune, Meara Aleksandra; PROF. OF SOCIOL., UNIV. OF REGINA 1984– ; and TRUSTEE, REGINA PUBLIC SCHOOL BOARD 1991– ; Chair, Task Force on Children in Crisis; Bd. Representative, Mayor's Task Force on Hunger; psychiatric aide Sask. Hosp. 1963; psychol. intern Sask. Penitentiary 1964–65; group worker emotionally disturbed children 1966; literacy teacher Sask. Indian reserve 1967; Special Lectr. in Sociol. present Univ. 1971, Asst. Prof. 1974, Assoc. Prof. 1979; Dept. Head 1976–81; Principal, Conway and Associates, Consultants in Social Sciences; freelance broadcaster resources, econ. and pols. CBC radio and TV; freelance jour. various newspapers; monthly columnist 'Briarpatch' mag. Regina 1984–89; Visiting Prof. of Candn. Studies, Univ. of Edinburgh 1981–82; author: 'The Recrudescence of Western Canadian Separatist Sentiment' 1982; 'The Place of the Prairie West in the Canadian Confederation' 1982; 'The West: The History of a Region in Confederation' 1983, 2nd ed. 1993; 'The Canadian Family in Crisis' 1990, 2nd ed. 1993; 'Debts to Pay: English Canada and Quebec from the Conquest to the Referendum' 1992; numerous book chapters, articles & reviews profl. jours.; intervenor, Sask. electoral boundaries case, Sask. Court of Appeal 1990 and Supreme Court of Canada 1991; labour arbitrator and social science consultant; Chair, Fac. Assoc., Univ. of Regina 1990–92 (Vice-Chair 1989–90; Extve. 1989– ;); mem., Counc., Cdn. Assoc. Univ. Teachers 1990–92; mem. Adjudication Ctte., Strategic Grants, Candn. Studies Res. Tools, SSHRC 1989–91; mem. Alliance Candn. Cinema, TV & Radio Artists (Sask. Exec. 1974–75); Candn. Sociol. & Anthrop. Assn. (Chair, Social Policy Subcommittee, 1977–79); Assn. Candn. Studies (Exec. Bd. 1988–92; Awards of Merit Ctte. 1989–91; Chair, Regional Devel. Grants Ctte. 1989–92; Writing Awards Ctte. 1992– ;); Candn. Civil Liberties Assn.; recreations: reading, travel, swimming; Home: 127 Angus Cres., Regina, Sask. S4T 6N1; Office: Regina, Sask. S4S 0A2.

**COO, (Norman) Douglas,** LL.B.; judge; b. Montreal, Que. 15 Feb. 1931; s. Hugh Douglas Coo; e. Upper Can. Coll. Toronto 1948; Univ. of Toronto Law Sch. LL.B. 1952; m. Anne Butchart Gibson 24 May 1974; one s. Christopher; MEM. GEN. DIV., ONT. COURT OF JUSTICE; called to Bars of B.C. and Ont. 1953; cr. Q.C. 1964; practiced law with Shearer and Coo 1953–73; apptd. Co. Court Judge 1973; Sr. Judge, Dist. of York 1979; Past Gen. Counsel and Dir., Candn. Diabetic Assn.; Past mem. Operating Comte. Centre for Adult Educ. Toronto; Faculty of Law Capt. Varsity Fund 1962–63; mem. Faculty of Law Alumni Assn. (Past Pres.); Co. York Law Assn.; Advocates Soc. (Past Dir. and Program Chrmn.); Lawyers' Club Toronto; Candn. Bar Assn.; Lectr. in Comm. Law, Univ. of Toronto 1956–57, Lectr. in Law (Extension) 1957–60; Anglican; recreation: travel; Clubs: Albany; Royal Candn. Yacht; Office: 361 University Ave., Toronto, Ont. M5G 1T3.

**COOK, Dennis,** B.A.; management consultant; b. Newmarket, Ont. 21 Feb. 1950; s. Francis Alvin and Audrey Mae (Manning) C.; e. York Univ. B.A. 1971; m. Wendy Elizabeth d. Kenneth and Bobby Ellis 6 Sept. 1986; PRINCIPAL, KORN/FERRY INTERNATIONAL 1992– ; Program Manager, Canada Employment & Immigration Commission 1973–77; Supervisor, Recruitment, Rio Algom Limited 1977–78; Mgr., Human Resource Devel., Cara Operations Limited 1978–84; Dir., Human Resources, General Mills Can. Inc. 1984–87; Cons., Canpro Inc. 1987–89; Cons., The Coopers & Lybrand Consulting Group 1989–92; Dir., Human Resources Profls. Assn. of Ont.; Inst. of Cert. Mngt. Cons. of Ont.; Internat. Assn. of Corp. & Profl. Recruiters; Fund-raiser, The Kidney Found. of Can.; Home: 305 Durie St., Toronto, Ont. M6S 3G2; Office: Ste. 1814, 40 King St. W., Scotia Plaza, Toronto, Ont. M5H 3Y2.

**COOK, (Margaret) Eleanor Glen,** B.A., M.A., Ph.D., F.R.S.C.; university professor; b. Toronto, Ont. 20 Jan. 1933; d. Dr. John Stanley and Winifred Archina (Macdougall) Glen; e. Jarvis & Earl Haig Coll. Inst.; University College, Univ. of Toronto B.A. (Hons.) 1954; Univ. of London 1954–55; Univ. of Toronto M.A. 1957, Ph.D. 1967; m. Ramsay s. Russell and Lillian Cook 28 May 1960; children: Margaret, Markham; PROFESSOR,

DEPT. OF ENGLISH, VICTORIA COLLEGE, UNIV. OF TORONTO 1985– ; Instr., English, Univ. of B.C. 1958–59; Editor, Univ. of Toronto Press 1960–63; Lectr. / Asst. Prof. / Assoc. Prof. (all part-time), English, Victoria College, Univ. of Toronto 1967–75; Assoc. Prof. 1975–84; Associate Dean, Fac. of Arts & Science, Univ. of Toronto 1987–90; Editorial Bd., 'Wallace Stevens Journal' 1991– ; 'Connotations' 1993– ; Adjunct Fac., Grad. Centre for Comparative Literature 1984– ; Adjunct Fac., Centre for the Study of Religion 1993– ; Mellon Fellowship Selection Ctte., area IV 1987–89; Junior Fellow, Candn. Fed. of Univ. Women 1954–55; A.S.P. Woodhouse Prize 1968; Canada Council Fellow 1977–78; Yale Univ. Visiting Fellow 1978–79; SSHRCC Fellow 1985–86; SSHRCC Research recipient 1991–94; Elected Mem., Royal Soc. of Can. 1992; Mem., Assn. of Candn. Univ. Teachers of English; Modern Language Assn.; Victorian Studies Assn. of Ont. (Extve. 1988–90); etc.; author: 'Browning's Lyrics' 1974, 'Poetry, Word-Play, and Word-War in Wallace Stevens' 1988; essays and reviews; editor: 'The Craft of History' 1973; 'Allusion' ('Univ. of Toronto Quarterly' issue) 1992; co-editor: 'Centre and Labyrinth: Essays in Honour of Northrop Frye' 1983; recreations: music, birdwatching, weeding; Home: 65 Woodlawn Ave. W., Toronto, Ont. M4V 1G6; Office: Victoria College (326 NFH), Univ. of Toronto, Toronto, Ont. M5S 1K7.

**COOK, Frederick Ahrens,** M.Sc., Ph.D.; educator; b. Chicago, Ill. 15 June 1950; s. Albert Charles and Elizabeth Kennedy (Plasman) C.; e. Univ. of Wyo. B.Sc. 1973, M.Sc. 1975; Cornell Univ. Ph.D. 1981; m. Christy d. Harry and Daleen Hansen 17 Aug. 1975; one d. Adrionna; PROF. OF GEOL. AND GEOPHYS. UNIV. OF CALGARY 1988– , Dir. Lithoprobe Seismic Processing Facility 1987– ; Exploration Geophys. Conoco 1975–77; Asst. Prof. present Univ. 1982, Assoc. Prof. 1986–88; co-author 'The Cocorp Seismic Reflection Traverse Across the Southern Appalachians' 1983; over 70 sci. articles; mem. Am. Geophys. Union; Geol. Soc. Am.; Soc. Exploration Geophys; Assn. Profl. Engs., Geols. & Geophys. Alta.; recreations: mineral collecting, hiking, music; Home: 3037 29th St. S.W., Calgary, Alta. T3E 2K9; Office: Calgary, Alta. T2N 1N4.

**COOK, George Wm.;** songwriter/singer; b. New Waterford, N.S. 8 Jan. 1918; s. William Henry and Margaret Mary (Frazer) C.; e. ISC courses, grade 12; St. John's Sch.; St. Michael's Sch.; m. Elizabeth d. Elizabeth and William McGown 29 July 1972; children: George Jr., Donna, Patsy, John; Jerry, John Arnold (stepsons); 1st song copyrighted May 1936; radio show, CJCB Sydney, NS, 'The Singing Miner' 1937; 1st recording artist, country & western from Cape Breton N.S. (Melotone label); old 78 r.p.m.'s are collectors items; remade Cattle records W. Germany; Prod., Bluenose Label Canada; 'Blue Cowboy' (vol. 111); Auctioneer, Dufferin County; Ambassador, Trad. Country Music USA 1984–86; Songwriter of the Year 1985; variety show: 'George Cook Variety Shows' (Florida); songs played on radio shows around the world; listed in Ripley's Believe It or Not (60,000 songs in last 4 yrs., 160 songs a day, 2178 songs a month, composed over 100,000 songs), in Guinness Book of World Records (world record songwriter – over 110,000 songs), and in 1990 Personalities of America; 129,100 songs written and counting; a new song a day for the next 2,339 days; words written 12,651,800 and counting; holds title for world's longest one breath yodel; awarded Certificate of Merit, Men of Achievement; Citizen Award for Arts Contributions to the City of Brampton 1991; biography: 'Man and His Music: Story of George Cook' by Elizabeth Cook 1988; 'Songbook: History of Canada in Songs' 3rd album released; served in Candn. Army 1939; Royal Candn. Navy 1942; mem., Candn. Country Music Hall of Fame; Candn. Country Music Assoc.; Am. Country Music Assoc.; Adv. Bd., Am. Biographical Inst. Inc.; British Biographical Soc.; Adv. Counc., Internat. Biographical Inst., Eng.; recreations: black belt, Jiu Jitsu, boxing (also teacher); clubs: Hatshita Judo; Home: 69 Salisbury Circle, Brampton, Ont. L6V 2Z4 or 2820 E. North St., Inverness, FL, USA 32650.

**COOK, Harry D.;** company executive; Formerly Pres. and Gen. Mgr., Abbott Laboratories Ltd.; Pres., Pharm. Mfrs. Assn. of Can. 1950–51, 1963–65; Home: 9503 Commercial St., Kentville, N.S. B4N 3G3.

**COOK, Rt. Rev. Henry George,** D.D. (Ang.); b. London, Eng. 12 Oct. 1906; s. Henry George and Ada Mary (Ovens) C.; came to Can. 1912; e. Huron Coll., London, Ont., L.Th. 1935; Univ. of W. Ont., B.A. 1935, Hon. D.D. 1948; m. Opal May (B.A.), d. Wesley Thompson, London, Ont. 4 June 1935; children: David, Peter, Barbara; mem. Anglican Gen. Synod 1944–74; served as Missy. at Fort Simpson, N.W. Terr. 1935–43; Canon, Diocese of Athabasca 1940; Sr. Curate, St. Paul's Bloor St. Ch., Toronto, Ont., 1943–44; Rector of S. Porcupine 1944–45; Archdeacon of James Bay, 1945–47; Princ., Bishop Horden Sch., Moose Factory, 1945–47; Hon. Canon, Diocese of Moosonee, 1948; Supt., Indian Sch. Adm., Can., 1948–63; Suffragan Bishop of the Arctic; 1963–66, Bishop of MacKenzie 1966–74; Co-ordinator of Hist. Programs, Govt. of N.W.T. 1974–79; served some time apprenticeship of five yrs. to the trade of toolmaking and received papers from John Morrow Co., Ingersoll, Ont.; served four years with C.O.T.C.; Hon. Canon, Cath. of Athabasca (1940); recreation: mechanical models; Address: 15 Plainfield Court, Stittsville, Ont. K2S 1B9.

**COOK, John Anthony,** B.A.; investment executive; b. Toronto, Ont. 16 Feb. 1938; s. G. Norman and Jane Smith (Murray) C.; e. Upper Can. Coll. 1956; Univ. of Toronto Trinity Coll. B.A. 1961; m. Marilyn d. Charles and Evelyn Croucher 16 June 1962; children: C. Norman, Kirsten Elizabeth; VICE PRES. AND DIR. RBC DOMINION SECURITIES INC. 1981– ; joined A.E. Ames & Co. Ltd. 1962, Vice Pres. and Dir. 1973; Pres. Ames Inc. (U.S. affiliate) 1976–79; Dir. Candn. Opera Co.; Candn. Psychiatric Rsch. Found.; Phi Delta Theta; Presbyterian; recreations: tennis, travel, music; Club: Badminton & Racquet; Home: 28 Hudson Dr., Toronto, Ont. M4T 2J9; Office: P.O. Box 21 Commerce Court S., Toronto, Ont. M5L 1A7.

**COOK, John Christopher,** M.A., Dip.Arch., OAA, OAQ, MRAIC; architect; b. Ottawa, Ont. 21 June 1953; s. James Murray and Kathlyn (Bottomley) C.; e. Atlantic Coll. Wales 1971 (Ont. Scholarship to 'The United World College of the Atlantic'); Cambridge Univ., B.A. 1976, M.A. 1978, Dip. Arch. 1980 (Clare Coll.); FOUNDING PARTNER, GRIFFITHS RANKIN COOK ARCHITECTS 1985– ; (firm participates regularly in national & internat. design competitions in which it has received numerous distinctions); Lectr. in Arch. Design, Carleton Univ. 1982– ; (Prof., Sch. of Architecture, Carleton Univ. DSA (Directed Studies Abroad Programme), 3 mo. studio, Rome, Italy 1988); joined Arthur Erickson during studies 1977–78; Murray & Murray, Griffiths & Rankin 1981, Assoc. 1983; designer new Rideau Club Ottawa (for MMGR), renovations Rideau Hall, various award winning housing projects; Ontario Assn. of Architects Award of Excellence for design of Nepean Sailing Club, Canada Wood Council Award 1990; Ontario Assn. of Architects Award of Excellence for Somerset West Health and Community Services Ctr. 1992; City of Ottawa Architectural Conservation Award 1993; Past Chrmn., Ottawa Regional Soc. of Architects (ORSA); served as judge for several housing design competitions; recreations: water sports, travel; Office: 47 Clarence St., Ste. 401, Ottawa, Ont. K1N 9K1.

**COOK, Leslie Gladstone,** M.B.E. F.C.I.C.; research chemist; b. Paris, Ont. 12 July 1914; s. late Rev. William Andrew and Maude Marion C.; e. Brantford (Ont.) Coll. Inst.; Univ. of Toronto, 1932–36 (1st Class Hons. Physics and Chem. and Gertrude Davis Exchange Fellowship); Univ. of Berlin (Kaiser Wilhelm Inst. für Chemie); Dr. of Nat. Sciences 1938; Cambridge Univ. 1938–40; m. Alfreda Mary, d. late Alfred Thomas Crutcher, 26 Dec. 1940; children: Patricia Joan, Leslie Pamela, Andrew George; PRES., L.G. COOK ASSOCS. INC. (consulting on energy sci. and technol.) since 1977; Research Chemist and Physicist, Aluminum Laboratories Ltd., Arvida, Que., Toronto and Kingston, Ont. 1939–45; National Research Council, Chalk River, Ont., 1945–52; Chemist, Atomic Energy of Can. Ltd., 1952–56; General Electric Research Lab., 1956–68 (Project Analyst, 1956–59, Mgr. Project Analysis and Program Planning Secs., 1959–68); Mgr., Program Planning and Analysis Group, Corp. Research Staff, Esso Research and Engn., 1969–77; Delegue Gen. for Policy and Planning, National Research Council, Ottawa 1968–69; United Church; recreations: music; piano; Address: 726 Loveville Rd., #A46, Hockessin, Delaware 19707.

**COOK, Lyn (Evelyn Margaret Waddell),** B.A., B.L.S.; author; b. Weston, Ont. 4 May 1918; d. Edward Frank and Emma (Crawford) C.; e. Etobicoke High Sch.; Univ. of Toronto, Univ. Coll. B.A. 1940, B.L.S. 1941; m. Robb s. Jacob and Louisa Waddell 19 Sept. 1949; children: Christopher, Deborah; Lib. Toronto Pub. Lib. 1941–42; Meteorol. Observer RCAF Women's Div. 1942–46; Children's Lib. Sudbury Pub. Lib. 1946–47; script writer, dir. and narrator 'A Doorway in Fairyland' CBC 1947–52; Creative Drama Teacher, New Play Soc. Theatre Sch. (children's classes) 1956–65; Creator story hour and drama festivals Scarborough Pub. Libs. 1962–76; 2 novels adapted for CBC-TV 1965, 1967; frequent speaker schs., libs., adult workshops & children's festivals; recipient Vicky Metcalf Award 1978; author (children's lit.) 'The Bells on Finland Street' 1950 (Swiss edn. in German); 'The Little Magic Fiddler' 1951, re-issued 1981; 'Rebel on the Trail' 1953; 'Jady and the General' 1955; 'Pegeen and the Pilgrim' 1957, Paperback 1972; 'The Road to Kip's Cove' 1961; 'Samantha's Secret Room' 1963, Paperback 1973; 'The Brownie Handbook for Canada' Girl Guide Assn. Can. 1965; 'The Secret of Willow Castle' 1966, reprinted 1984; 'The Magical Miss Mittens' 1970, Paperback 1974; 'A Treasure for Tony' 1981; 'The Hiding Place' 1990, Paperback 1994; (picture-story books) 'Toys from the Sky' 1972; 'Jolly Jean Pierre' 1973; 'If I Were All These' 1974; 'The Magic Pony' 1981; 'Sea Dreams' 1981; 'A Canadian ABC' 1990; 'The Bells on Finland Street' 1991; 'Samantha's Secret Room' 1991; mem. Candn. Soc. Children's Authors, Illustrators & Performers; Writers Union Can.; recreations: music, reading, walking, landscape painting; Home: 72 Cedarbrae Blvd., Scarborough, Ont. M1J 2K5.

**COOK, Mary;** broadcaster; writer; b. Ottawa, Ont. 10 Dec. 1932; d. Albert and Mabel Ernestine (Lapointe) Haneman; e. Carleton Place High Sch.; m. J. Wallace s. John Wallace Cook 7 June 1952; children: Richard, Mary Jane, Melinda; Vice Pres. Cook's of Carleton Place Ltd.; Pres. Wallace Enterprises (pub.); joined CBC as Commentator 1956, weekly broadcaster radio series depression yrs. Ottawa Valley; frequent guest speaker, story teller, humourist; gourmet cook; recipient 6 ACTRA Awards for Excellence in Broadcasting; author 'A Collector's Stories' 1978; 'Time To Blow Out The Lamp' 1980; 'One For Sorrow, Two For Joy' 1984; 'View From The West Hill' 1987; various newspaper and mag. articles; Life mem. IODE; Presbyterian; recreations: bridge, reading; Address: P.O. Box 158, Carleton Place, Ont. K7C 3P3.

**COOK, Michael;** playwright; educator; b. London, Eng. 14 Feb. 1933; s. George William C.; e. Nottingham Univ. Coll. of Edn. T.T.C. 1965; m. Madonna d. Michael and Mary-Francis Decker 28 Dec. 1973; children: Fergus, Perdita; served with Brit. Army 1949–61, REME and Intelligence Corps; emigrated to Can. 1966; Drama Specialist, Meml. Univ. of Nfld. (Extension) 1966–69, Lectr. in Eng. 1969–73, Asst. Prof. 1973–80, Assoc. Prof. 1980–90, Prof. 1990– ; Resident Playwright, Banff Sch. of Fine Arts 1977; Artistic Dir. St. John's Summer Festival of Arts 1970–77; Theatre and Film Critic, St. John's Evening Telegram 1966–78; Playwright in Residence, Stratford Festival 1987; author (playwright) 'Colour the Flesh the Colour of Dust' 1972; 'Jacob's Wake' 1975; 'Tiln and Other Plays' 1976; 'The Head, Guts and Soundbone Dance,' 'On the Rim of the Curve,' 'Therese's Creed' 1977; 'The Gayden Chronicles' 1979; 'The Fisherman's Revenge' 1985; 'The Great Harvest Excursion' 1986; over 50 plays for CBC Radio and TV; work transl. and performed in Sweden, Germany, Switzerland, Mexico, Poland and Hungary; also produced in USA, Ireland and UK; various articles mags. and jours.; recipient Can. Council Sr. Arts Grants 1972, 1978; Queen's Silver Jubilee Medal 1977; Govt. of Nfld. & Labrador Achievement Award 1985; Nat. Radio Award., Best Original Drama 1990; Gov. Candn, Conf. Arts 1970–77; mem. Exec. Bd. Candn. Theatre Review 1979–84; Nfld. & Labrador Arts Council 1980–82; mem. Guild of Candn. Playwriters; Playwrights Union Can. (Chrmn. 1981–82); recreations: reading, good wine, conversation; Address: 43 Shrewsbury St., Stratford, Ont. N5A 2V4.

**COOK, Peter Alan,** B.A., M.A.; economist; b. Stockton, Eng. 16 Nov. 1943; s. Kevan and Genora Ashlie; e. Univ. of Victoria B.A. 1967; Univ. of Western Ont. M.A. 1970; m. Caroline d. William and Miriam Oliver 23 June 1967; children: Margot Dianne, Daniel William Peter; PRESIDENT & CHIEF EXECUTIVE OFFICER, CITIZENS TRUST 1991– ; Research Officer, Prov. of B.C. 1967–69; Economist, Federal Finance Dept. 1970–73; Vice-Pres., Candn. Econ. Serv. Ltd. 1973–77; Chief Econ., B.C. Central Credit Untion 1977–81; Sr. Vice-Pres., Vancity Savings 1981–86; Sr. Vice-Pres. & C.F.O. 1986–91; Past Pres., Financial Extves. Inst.; Past Pres., Assn. of Profl. Econ.; Dir., Vancity Community Found.; Past Pres., Vancouver Racquets Club; Group Chair, Boy Scouts of Canada; recreations: squash, sailing, skiing; club: Vancouver Racquets; Home: 6625 Maple St., Vancouver, B.C. V6P 5P4; Office: 401, 815 W. Hastings St., Vancouver, B.C. V6C 1B4.

**COOK, Ramsay,** O.C., Ph.D., F.R.S.C. (1968); D.Litt., D.de l'Un.; university professor; b. Alameda, Sask. 28 Nov. 1931; s. George Russell and late Lillie Ellen (Young) C.; e. Pub. and High Schs., Sask. and Man.; Univ. of Man., B.A. 1954; Queen's Univ., M.A. 1955; Univ. of Toronto, Ph.D. 1960; D.Litt., Univ. of Windsor

1988; D.de l'Un., Univ. of Ottawa 1992; m. Margaret Eleanor, d. late Dr. J.S. Glen; children: Margaret Michele, Markham Glen; PROF. OF HISTORY, YORK UNIV.; Gen. Ed., 'Dictionary of Canadian Biography' 1989– ; previously Prof. of History, Univ. of Toronto; Ed., Canadian Historical Review, 1963–68; Chrmn., Candn. Inst. for Historical Microreproduction 1978–83; Visiting Prof. of Cdn. Studies, Harvard Univ., 1968–69; Bicentennial Prof. of Cdn. History, Yale Univ. 1978–79; awarded Pres.'s Medal (Univ. of W. (Ont.), Scholarly Article Category 1966, 1968; author: 'The Politics of John W. Dafoe and the Free Press' 1963; 'Canada: A Modern Study' 1964; 'Canada and the French Canadian Question' 1966; (with R.C. Brown) 'Canada 1896–1921; A Nation Transformed' 1975; Ed. 'The Dafoe-Sifton Correspondence' 1967; 'Provincial Autonomy, Minority Rights and the Compact Theory' 1969; 'The Maple Leaf Forever' 1971; 'The Regenerators: Social Criticism in Late Victorian English Canada' 1985; 'Canada, Quebec and the Uses of Nationalism' 1986; Ed. 'French Canadian Nationalism: An Anthology' 1969; (with W. Mitchinson) 'The Proper Sphere' 1977; 'The Voyages of Jacques Cartier' 1993; awarded Tyrrell Medal of Roy. Soc. Can. (for contrib. to hist. scholarship, 1975); Governor-General's Award for Non-Fiction 1985; Officer of the Order of Canada 1986; mem., Cdn. Hist. Assn. (Pres. 1983–84); recreations: theatre, music, movies, bird watching; Office: 4700 Keele St., Downsview, Ont. M3J 1P3.

**COOK, Rebecca J.,** A.B., M.A., M.P.A., J.D., LL.M.; law professor; b. Bennington, Vermont 2 Dec. 1946; d. the late John Ransom and Helen Cummings (Vanderbilt) C.; e. Columbia Univ., A.B. 1970; Tufts Univ., M.A. 1972; Harvard Univ., M.P.A. 1973; Georgetown Univ. Law Ctr., J.D. 1982; Washington D.C. Bar, Attorney 1983; Columbia Univ. Sch. of Law, LL.M. 1988; m. Bernard M. s. Rose and David Dickens; ASSOC. PROF. & DIR., INTERNAT. HUMAN RIGHTS LAW PROG., FAC. OF LAW, UNIV. OF TORONTO 1987– ; cross-appt. Fac. of Med. & Sch. of Grad. Studies; Adjunct Asst. Prof., Columbia Univ. 1987– ; Dir., Law Prog., Internat. Planned Parenthood Fed. 1973–78; Assoc., Beveridge, Fairbanks and Diamond 1980; Asst. Prof. & Staff Attorney, Columbia Univ. 1983–87 (also Dep. Dir. & Co-founder, Internat. Women's Rights Action Watch); Asst. Prof. present Univ. 1987; serves on numerous cttes. & adv. panels; SSHRCC grants 1988–91; Ford Found. Grants 1989– ; author/co-author/editor of numerous monographs, books, book chapters, briefs, articles, and papers; extensive lecturer worldwide; recreations: gardening; Home: 31 Walmer Rd., #10, Toronto, Ont. M5R 2W7; Office: Toronto, Ont. M5S 2C5.

**COOK, Stephen Arthur,** Ph.D., F.R.S.C.; educator; b. Buffalo, N.Y. 14 Dec. 1939; s. Gerhard Albert and Lura H. (Lincoln) C.; e. Univ. of Mich. B.S. 1961; Harvard Univ. S.M. (Math.) 1962, Ph.D. (Math.) 1966; m. Linda d. William and Mary Craddock 4 May 1968; two s.: Gordon; James; UNIVERSITY PROF. OF COMPUTER SCIENCE, UNIV. OF TORONTO 1985– ; Asst. Prof. of Math. & Computer Science, Univ. of Cal. Berkeley 1966–70; Assoc. Prof. of Computer Science present Univ. 1970, Prof. 1975; E.W.R. Steacie Mem. Fellow 1977–78; Killam Research Fellow 1982–83; recipient ACM Turing Award 1982; Fellow, Royal Soc. of Can. 1984– ; mem. U.S. National Acad. of Sci. 1985– ; mem. Am. Acad. of Arts and Sciences 1986– ; recreations: sailing, violin playing; Home: 6 Indian Valley Cres., Toronto, Ont. M6R 1Y6; Office: Toronto; Ont. M5S 1A4.

**COOK, William Harrison,** O.C. (1969), O.B.E., M.Sc., Ph.D., LL.D., D.Sc., F.A.I.C., F.R.S.C., F.C.I.C.; retired; b. Alnwich, Northumberland, Eng. 2 Sept. 1903; s. Peter and Jean (Maitland) C.; came to Can. 1912; e. Claresholm, Alta., Sch. of Agric. diploma; Univ. of Alta., B.Sc. 1926, M.Sc. 1928; Leland Stanford Univ., Ph.D. 1931; Univ. of Sask., LL.D. 1948; Laval Univ., D.Sc. 1963; m. Ina Helen, d. Chas. Alex Stephens, 21 Aug. 1932; children: Glenn, Gail, Nancy; Hon. Secy., Royal Soc. of Can. 1950–53, Pres. of Sec. V 1956–57, Vice-Pres. of the Soc. 1961–62 and Pres. 1962–63; Ed.-in-Chief 'Canadian Journal of Research' 1943–47; served as Rsch. Asst., Univ. of Alta. 1924–30; Jr. Research Biol., Nat. Research Labs., Ottawa 1930–35; Assoc. Rsch. Biol. 1935–41; Dir., Div. of Biosciences, Nat. Rsch. Counc. 1941–68; Extve. Dir., Nat. Rsch. Counc. 1968–69; Dir. Gen., Candn. Comn. for I.B.P. 1969–74; has contrib. over 150 scient. and tech. papers in plant biochem., food chem., refrigerated storage and transport of food, structure of lipoproteins and macromolecules; Fellow, Agric. Inst. of Can.; Charter mem., Inst. of Food Tech.; Candn. Biochem. Soc. (Vice-Pres. 1964–65; Pres. 1965–66); Pres., Biol. Council of Can. 1968–69; Trustee, Biol. Abstracts 1955–60; Gov., Univ. of Guelph 1965–71; Fellow, Am. Assn. Advanc. Science; recipient Coronation Medal 1952; Centennial Medal 1967; Elizabeth II 25th Anniv. Medal 1977; Commemorative Medal for 125th Anniversary of Candn. Confederation 1992; Phi Lambda Upsilon; Sigma Xi; United Church; Home: 201 Maple Lane, Rockcliffe, Ont. K1M 1G9.

**COOK, William Raymond,** B.Com.; executive; b. Moncton, N.B. 24 Aug. 1931; s. William Elias and Eva Marie (Bannout) C.; e. McGill Univ. B.Com. 1952; m. Rose Marie d. Joseph and Rose Bardwell 16 Jan. 1965; children: Gary, Brian, Karl, Lisa, Claudine; CHAIRMAN, RADIUS FOOTWEAR INC. and PRESIDENT, PERFECT DYEING INC.; Past Pres., Cedars Home for the Elderly; Gov., Cedars Cancer Fund; Kt. Comdr. St. Ignatius of Antioch; recreation: golf, reading, breeding & racing standardbreds; Home: 1315 Dumfries Rd., Montreal, Que. H3P 2R2; Office: 3155 J.B. Deschamps St., Montreal, Que. H8T 3E4.

**COOK-BENNETT, Gail C.A.,** M.A., Ph.D.; b. Ottawa, Ont.; d. William Harrison and Ina (Stephens) C.; m. Roy F. Bennett; one son: Christopher William Stephens Bennett; e. Rockcliffe Park Pub. Sch. 1953 and Lisgar Coll. Inst. 1958 Ottawa; Carleton Univ. B.A. (Hons.) 1962; Univ. of Mich. M.A. 1965, Ph.D. (Econ.) 1968; EXEC. VICE PRES., BENNECON LTD. MANAGEMENT CONSULTANTS 1982– ; Dir. (and Chrmn. Audit Ctte.) The Manufacturers Life Insurance Co.; The Manufacturers Life Capital Corp.; The Consumers' Gas Co. Ltd.; The Toronto-Dominion Bank; Ont. Teachers' Pension Plan; Petro-Canada; Stadium Corp. of Ont. Ltd.; Inst. for Research on Public Policy; mem., Niagara Inst. Adv. Counc.; career: Doctoral Fellow 1967–68; Asst. Prof. of Econ. Univ. of Toronto 1968–74 (Research Assoc., Centre for Urban and Community Studies 1968–72; Research Assoc., Inst. for the Quantitative Analysis of Social and Economic Policy 1969–74); Dir. of Research, C.D. Howe Research Inst. 1974–76; Exec. Vice Pres., C.D. Howe Research Inst. 1977–78; Economic consultant 1979–82 former Dir., (and Mem. Extve. Ctte.; Chair, Special Ctte.; Chair Budget Ctte.) Bank of Canada; The Campbell Soup Co. Ltd.; IDEA Corp.; Cdn. Opera Co.; Multiple Sclerosis Soc. of Can.; Inst. for Hydrogen Systems; former mem., Cdn. Group, Trilateral Comn.; Gov., Univ. of Guelph; former mem., (and mem. Extve. Comte.) Ont. Econ. Counc.; Soc. Sci. and Humanities Rsch. Counc.; Adv. Ctte., Banff Centre Sch. of Mgmt.; Selection Ctte., Ernest C. Manning Awards Found.; Ed. Bd., Cdn. Public Policy-Analyse de Politiques; Premier of Ont. Adv. Comte. on Confederation; Exec. Counc., Candn. Economics Assn.; Local Non-Property Taxation Ctte., National Tax Assn./Tax Inst. of Am.; Internat. Inst. of Public Finance; author various reports, articles book chapters reviews on pub. finance and urban econ.; Project Dir. and Ed. 'Opportunity for Choice: A Goal for Women in Canada' 1976; United Ch.; recreations: skating, skiing, tennis; Home: 40 North Drive, Etobicoke, Ont. M9A 4P9; Office: P.O. Box 59, Toronto-Dominion Centre, Toronto, Ont. M5K 1E7.

**COOKE, Hon. Dave,** M.P.P., B.S.W.; politician; b. Windsor, Ont. 1 Aug. 1952; e. John McCrae & Edith Cavell & Riverside S.S.; Univ. of Windsor B.S.W. 1975; MINISTER OF EDUCATION & TRAINING, GOVT. OF ONTARIO 1993– ; 1st elected M.P.P. Windsor-Riverside, Ont. legislature 1977; subsequently re-elected in all elections; served as NDP critic for health, treasury & housing; Official Opposition House Leader 1987–90; Minister of Housing and Minister of Municipal Affairs 1990–91; Minister of Municipal Affairs, Government House Leader 1991–93; Member of Treasury Board and Policy & Priority Board 1991– ; Former Mem., Ont. Assn. of Profl. Social Workers; Office: 900 Bay St., Mowat Block, 22nd Floor, Toronto, Ont. M7A 1L2.

**COOKE, Donald B.;** business executive; b. Toronto, Ont. 19 July 1941; s. Norman James and Elizabeth Anne (Morrison) C.; e. Riverdale Collegiate Inst.; C.A. 1964; one d. Tracey; Management Consultant, Donald Cooke & Associates 1991–94; Asst. to Vice-Pres. & Treas., McGraw Edison (Canada) Ltd. 1965–67; var. positions, Allied Towers Merchants Ltd., Shulton of Canada, Arbor Capital Resources Inc. 1967–74; Controller, Control Data Canada Ltd. 1974–77; Pres. & Gen. Mgr., GE Vehicle Management, Inc. 1980–88; Gen. Mgr., Canaplan Leasing 1991–94; Dir., Candn. Automotive Leasing Assn.; Mem., Candn. Inst. of Chartered Accts.; Home: Suite 601, 85 Skymark Dr., North York, Ont. M2H 3P2.

**COOKE, Fred,** M.A., Ph.D.; university professor; b. Darlington, U.K. 13 Oct. 1936; s. Frederick William and Mary Alice (Milner) C.; e. Bootham Sch. (U.K.); Christ's Coll., Cambridge Univ. B.A. 1960, M.A. 1964, Ph.D. 1965; m. Sylvia d. John and Florence Bonner 18 July 1987; children: Su, Heather; CWS/NSERC RESEARCH CHAIR, WILDLIFE ECOLOGY, SIMON FRASER UNIV. 1993– ; Asst. Prof. then Assoc. Prof. Queen's Univ. 1964–78, Prof. Dept. of Biology 1978–93; Dir., Churchill Northern Studies Ctr. 1977–78; Killam Rsch. Fellow 1985–87; Award for Rsch. Excellence, Queen's Univ. 1986; Brewster Award, Am. Ornithologists Union 1990; author: 'Avian Genetics' 1987; recreations: bird watching, hiking; Home: 13467 18th Ave., Surrey, B.C. V4A 6B2.

**COOKE, George L.,** B.A., M.B.A.; insurance executive; b. New Liskeard, Ont. 28 June 1953; s. Arthur H. and Florence M. (Lang) C.; e. Queen's Univ. B.A. (Hons.) 1975, M.B.A. 1977; m. Erica d. Alan and Kathleen Bruce-Robertson 28 Dec. 1985; one s.: Malcolm Arthur; PRESIDENT & CHIEF EXECUTIVE OFFICER, THE DOMINION OF CANADA GENERAL INSUR. CO. 1992– ; Price Waterhouse 1977–78; Ont. Hydro 1978–80; Ontario Energy Board, Govt. of Ont. 1980–87; Automobile Insur. Bd. 1988–89; Special Advisor to Deputy Premier & Treas. of Ont., Robert F. Nixon 1989–90; Vice-Pres., S.A. Murray Consulting Inc. 1990–92; Dir., The Dominion of Canada General Insur. Co.; E-L Financial Corp. Limited; Empire Life Insur. Co.; The Dominion Group Found.; The Facility Assn.; Policy Management Systems Canada, Ltd.; Centre for Studies of Insur. Opns.; Insurance Bureau of Canada; Insurance Crime Prevention Bureau; The Assn. of Candn. Insurers; Extve. Vice-Pres., E-L Financial Corp. Limited; recreations: golf, curling; clubs: Donalda; The University Club of Toronto; Home: 388 Manor Rd. E., Toronto, Ont. M4S 1S8; Office: 165 University Ave., Toronto, Ont. M5H 3B9.

**COOKE, Herbert Basil Sutton,** B.A., M.A., M.Sc., D.Sc. Hon. LL.D.; retired educator; geological consultant; b. Johannesburg, S. Africa 17 Oct. 1915; s. late Herbert Sutton and late Edith Mary (Sutton) C.; came to Can. Oct. 1961; e. Cambridge Univ., England B.A. 1936; M.A. 1940; Univ. of Witwatersrand, Johannesburg, M.Sc. 1940; D.Sc. 1947; m. Dorothea Winifred, d. late Col. Alfred Mahony Hughes, 23 Oct. 1943; children: Christopher John Sutton, Patrick Mahony; PROFESSOR EMERITUS, DALHOUSIE UNIVERSITY 1981– ; Geologist, Central Mining and Investment Corp., Johannesburg 1936–38; Jr. Lectr. and Lectr., Geol., Univ. of the Witwatersrand 1938–47 (interrupted by war service 1941–46); Principal Geologist and Field Adviser to Univ. of Calif. African Expedition 1947–48; independent Consulting Geologist, Johannesburg 1948–53 (dir. of several mining cos.); Sr. Lectr. and Reader, Stratigraphic Geol., Univ. of the Witwatersrand 1953–61; Chrmn., Bernard Price Inst. for Palaeontological Research 1958–61; Prof. of Geol., Dalhousie Univ. 1961–63; Dean, Faculty of Arts & Science 1963–68; Carnegie Prof. of Geol. 1968–81, Emeritus 1981– ; Geological Consultant 1981–85; Fellow, Royal Soc. of S. Africa (1948); awarded Royal Soc./Nuffield Found. Bursary 1955; Alex L. du Toit Mem. Lectr. 1957; Visiting Research Assoc., Univ. of Calif., Berkeley 1957–58; Visiting Lectr., Inst. of Vertebrate Paleontology and Paleoanthropology, Beijing, China, 1984; Canadian Centennial Medal, 1967; Dalhousie Alumni Award for Teaching Excellence 1981; Raymond Dart Lectr. 1983; author 'Science in South Africa' 1949; co-author (with G.N.G. Hamilton) 'Geology for South African Students' 1939 (5th ed. 1965); co-ed. (with B.D. Malan) 'The Contribution of C. van Riet Lowe to Prehistory in Southern Africa' 1962; (with V.J. Maglio) 'Evolution of African Mammals' 1978; more than 100 scientific papers and monographs in field of geology; Life Fellow, Royal Soc. of S. Africa; Royal Meteorological Soc.; Geological Soc. of London; Geological Soc. of S. Africa; Fellow, Geological Soc. of Amer.; Hon. Life Mem. Candn. Assn. for Physical Anthropology; Palaeontological Soc. of S. Africa; Soc. of Africanist Archaeology; Life Mem., S. African Geographical Soc. (past Pres.); S. African Archaeological Soc. (past Pres.); S. African Assn. for the Advancement of Sci. (past Vice-Pres. and past Pres.); Nova Scotian Inst. of Sci. (past Pres.); Royal Commonwealth Soc., Mainland of B.C. Br. (Pres. 1985–91); mem. of several other profl. socs.; regular broadcaster of scientific talks in S. Africa; Ed., 'South African Journal of Science' 1947–57; mem. of several subcommns. and working groups of Internat. Union of Geological Sciences; Internat. Quaternary Assn. (INQUA) Internat. Geological Correlation Prog.; Conservative; Anglican; recreations: photography, travel; Home: 2133–154th Street, White Rock, B.C. V4A 4S5.

**COOKE, Jack Kent;** diversified company executive; b. Hamilton, Ont. 25 Oct. 1912; s. Ralph Ercil and Nancy (Jacobs) C.; m. Barbara Jean Carnegie, 5 May 1934 (div.); children: Ralph Kent, John Kent; m. Jeanne Maxwell Williams, 31 Oct. 1980 (div.); m. Marlena L.V.R. Chalmers 5 May 1990; Student, Malvern Collegiate; Partner Thomson Cooke Newspapers 1937–52; Pres. Station CKEY, Toronto, Ont. 1944–61; Liberty of Canada, Ltd. 1947–61; Toronto Maple Leaf Baseball Club Ltd. 1951–64; Chrmn. Bd., Pres. Consol. Press Ltd. 1952–61; Chrmn., Jack Kent Cooke Inc. 1976– ; Chrmn., Pro-Football Inc., Washington Redskins, Nat. Football League 1960– ; Pres., Calif. Sports Inc. (Los Angeles Lakers, Nat. Basketball Assn., Los Angeles Kings, Nat. Hockey League) 1965–79; Chrmn., Chief Exec. Officer Teleprompter Corp. 1974–81; Chrmn., Cooke Properties Inc. (Chrysler and Kent Bldgs., NYC) 1966– ; Chrmn., Cooke Media Group Inc. (Daily News), Los Angeles, CA 1985– ; Chrmn., Elmendorf Farm Inc., Lexington, KY 1985– ; Trustee, Little League Foundation; Mem., National Athletic Inst. (Bd. Dirs.); Home: Far Acres, Middleburg, VA 22117.

**COOKE, Michael B.,** B.Comm., M.B.A.; business executive; b. Ottawa, Ont. 10 July 1941; s. Terence W. and Eleanor J. (Brabazon) C.; e. Univ. of Alberta B.Comm. 1966; Univ. of Western Ontario M.B.A. 1970; m. Lynn Daley 25 Oct. 1963; children: Patrick, Mark; PRESIDENT, FLEXIBLE PACKAGING GROUP, INTERNATIONAL INNOPAC INC.; Office: 1600, 1055 W. Hastings St., Vancouver, B.C. V6E 2H2.

**COOKE, Michael Stephen Paul,** B.A., M.B.A.; petroleum industry executive; b. Karuizawa, Japan 8 July 1949; s. Theodore Thomas Stanley and Joan St. George (Cameron) C.; e. Univ. of Western Ont. B.A. (Econ.) 1971, M.B.A. 1973; m. Bonnie d. Carman and Jean Pollock 12 Oct. 1974; PRESIDENT & CHIEF EXECUTIVE OFFICER, COGAS ENERGY LIMITED 1992– ; Production Planner, Graphics Prod. Div., 3M Company Ltd. 1967–69; Reg. Mgr., Corp. Banking Group, Citibank Canada 1974–76; Asst. Gen. Mgr., Corp. Banking Group, Continental Bank of Canada 1977–80; Vice-Pres., Finance & Chief Finan. Offr., Stanford Resources Limited 1981; Chrmn. & C.E.O., Paragon Petroleum Corp. 1984–93; Founder, Sole Shareholder & Pres., Mical Equities Limited (investment banking co.) 1982– ; recreations: investments, flying, travel; Home: 6920 Silverview Dr. N.W., Calgary, Alta. T3B 3K9; Office: 3440, 700 – 2nd St. S.W., Calgary, Alta. T2P 2W2.

**COOKE, Walter Rowland,** B.A.; information management executive; b. Toronto, Ont. 17 Jan. 1936; s. Rowland Francis and Jane (Morgan) C.; e. Univ. of Toronto Woodsworth Coll. B.A. 1968; m. Beverley d. William and Doris Dewhurst 2 Sept. 1961; children: Diana, Jeffrey; EXEC. VICE PRES., EQUIFAX CANADA INC.; served with US Marine Corps 1956–59, rank Sgt.; Mercantile Reporting Mgr. Dun & Bradstreet 1959–61; Mgr. Ind. Div. I.A.C. Ltd. 1961–66; Corporate Mgr. T. Eaton Acceptance 1966–77; Vice Pres. Mktg. FCA International 1977–78; Exec. Vice Pres. Toronto Credits Ltd. 1978–87; Pres., CBS Credit Bureau Services 1987–89; Dir. Candn. Diabetes Assn. 1985–90; Home: 15 Rustywood Dr., Don Mills, Ont. M3A 1R6; Office: 1008, 60 Bloor St. W., Toronto, Ont. M4W 3B8.

**COOKE, William Bruce Hamel,** C.D., B.A.Sc., M.Sc.; Ph.D., P.Eng.; university professor and administrator; b. Harriston, Ont. 10 June 1935; s. Louis Hamel and Aleen (Kirk) C.; e. R.M.C. of Can. 1956; Univ. of Toronto B.A.Sc. 1957; Royal Naval Engineering Coll. 1959; U.S. Naval Postgraduate Sch. M.Sc. 1961; Queen's Univ. Ph.D. 1972; m. Phyllis d. Gerald and Lillian Nelson, 27 Apr. 1957; children; Robert Bruce, Cheryl Lynn, James Richard; Dean of Engineering, Univ. of Regina 1979–89; R.C.N. and Candn. Armed Forces as Engineering Offr., Submarine Offr. and Faculty Mem., R.M.C. 1953–71; Assoc. Prof., Univ. of Sask. (Regina) 1971–72; Research Engineer, Sask. Power Corp. Research and Devel. Centre 1972–77, Assist. Dir., 1977–79; Special Lecturer, Univ. of Regina 1972–76, Adjunct Prof. 1978–79; mem., Engineering Inst. of Can.; Candn. Soc. for Mech. Eng.; Am. Soc. of Mech. Engineers; eight published papers & numerous research reports; Ont. Canteen Fund Scholarship 1952; Mech. Engineering Prize R.M.C. 1955 and 1956; Post-Doctoral Fellowship 1971; recreations: flying, bagpipes; Clubs: Masonic; Shrine; R.M.C. Ex-Cadets Club; Home: 4441 Acadia Dr., Regina, Sask. S4S 4T5; Office: Faculty of Engineering, University of Regina, Regina, Sask. S4S 0A2.

**COOLS, Hon. Anne Clare,** B.A.; senator; social worker; b. Barbados, British West Indies 12 August 1943; d. Lucius Unique and Rosita Gordon (Miller) C.; e. Montessori Sch. of the Ursuline Convent, Barbados; Queen's College, Barbados; Thomas D'Arcy McGee High Sch., Montreal; McGill Univ., B.A. (Soc. Sciences); m. Rolf Calhoun 22 Mar. 1986; SENATOR (Liberal), summoned to the Senate of Canada 1984; Exec. Dir., Women in Transition Inc., a United Way Mem. Agency and Social Service assisting families in crisis, since 1974; was leader and innovator in creating services to assist battered wives, families in crisis and families troubled by domestic violence; was instrumental in educating public on issue of violence in families; Field instructor: Fac. of Soc. Work, Univ. of Toronto, 1977–78; Social Services Dept., Seneca Coll., Toronto 1977–80; Ryerson Polytechnic, Toronto 1978–80; Founding Vice-Chairperson and Extve. Ctte. Mem., Metro Toronto Justice Ctte. on Spousal Abuse; Mem. Bd. of Dirs.: Pauline McGibbon Cultural Centre; Social Planning Counc. of Metro. Toronto; Mem. Adv. Counc., Family Mediation-Canada; Mem., Adv. Health Ctte., Native Counc. of Can.; Order-in-Council Appt.: Nat. Parole Bd., (Temp) 1980–84; mem. Liberal Party of Can.; Lib. cand., fed. gen. elect. 1979 and 1980 in Rosedale riding in Toronto; mem, Senate Cttes.: Standing Cttes. of Nat. Finance, Legal and Constitutional Affairs, Official Languages; Special Senate Ctte. on Bill C-21 (Amendments to the Unemployment Ins. Act); Senate Task Force on the Meech Lake Accord; Anglican; Clubs: Royal Commonwealth Soc. of Can.; Empire Club of Can.; recreations: classical music, collecting Canadiana and historical memorabilia; Office: Senate of Canada, Rm. 182-F, Centre Block, Ottawa, Ont. K1A 0A4.

**COOMBE, Rosemary J.,** B.A., LL.B., J.S.M., J.S.D.; university professor; b. Toronto, Ont. 27 May 1959; d. Norman Gerald and Barbara (Lawman) C.; e. Univ. of West. Ont., B.A. (Hons.) 1981, LL.B. (With Great Distinction) 1984; Stanford Univ., J.S.M. 1988, J.S.D. 1992; PROF. OF LAW & CRIMINOLOGY, UNIV. OF TORONTO 1988– ; Editor in Chief, Univ. of Western Ont. Law Review 1983–84; Student at Articles, Goodman & Goodman 1984–85; Vis. Prof. & Karl Loewenstein Fellow in Pol. Sci. & Juris. Amherst Coll. 1990–91; Weatherhead Fellow, Sch. of Am. Research 1993; Visiting Prof. of Legal Theory, Washington College of Law 1993–94; Editorial Bd., Political and Legal Anthropology Review; Gold Medalist & recipient, Arthur T. Little Scholarship for achieving highest overall standing in the LL.B. program; mem., Am. Anthropol. Assn.; Society for Cultural Anthropol.; Assn. for Pol. & Legal Anthropol.; Law & Soc. Assn.; author of scholarly articles; recreations: architecture, film, literature, theatre and epicurean appreciation; Home: 26 Bellwoods Ave., Toronto, Ont.; Office: 84 Queen's Park Cres., Toronto, Ont. M5S 2C5.

**COOMBS, James A.,** B.A.; communications executive; b. London, Ont. 10 Aug. 1930; s. James Andrew and Sarah Helen (Clark) C.; e. Univ. of W. Ont. B.A. (Econ. and Pol. Sci.) 1952; m. Margaret Gilberta d. Gilbert Marvin and Annie Lawton Howes Oct. 1953; children: Andrew, Karen, Donald; Pres. & C.E.O., Saskatchewan Telecommunications (SaskTel) 1986–91; joined Bell Canada 1952–76; The New Brunswick Telephone Co. Ltd. 1976–86, Vice Pres. Finance until 1982, Vice Pres. Operations 1982–86; Dir., Acklands Ltd.; Telecom Canada; Westbridge Computer Corp.; Leicester Communications Ltd.; Bd. mem., Regina Symphony; SaskTel International; Candn. Counc. of Native Business; ICOMM (Interactive Communications Complex); Communications Computer Equipment and Services, SAGIT (Sectoral Adv. Grp. on Internat. Trade); Regina Economic Development Authority Counc.; Past Pres., Jr. Achievement of Sask.; Bd. Mem., Jr. Achievement (Nat.); Sr. mem., Conference Bd. Inc.; Clubs: Wascana Country; Assiniboia.

**COON, David Charles,** B.Sc.; environmentalist; b. Toronto, Ont. 28 Oct. 1956; s. Charles J. Coon and Iris Page; e. Riverdale High Sch. Pierrefonds, Qué. 1973; Vanier Coll. St. Laurent, Qué. D.E.C. Pure & Applied Sci's 1975; McGill Univ. B.Sc. 1978; m. Janice d. Mansell and Estella Harvey 4 June 1988; POLICY DIR. CONSERV. COUNCIL OF N.B. 1985– ; Project Coord. Ecol. House Pollution Probe Found. 1980–83, Energy Researcher of Found. 1983–84; cons. Nat. Film Bd. documentary 'The Underlying Threat'; Dir., East Coast Environmental Law Assn. 1992– ; Dir., Friends of the Earth Can. 1991–92; Founding Dir. Harvest Share Co-op. 1988–93; Chair Candn. Environmental Network 1989, 1990, Mgmt. Ctte. 1988–90; Founding mem. N.B.. Environment & Devel. Group; Energy Sectoral Group Premier's Round Table Environment & Econ. 1990; mem., Agricultural Advisory Ctte. on the Environment; mem., Co-op Atlantic's Ecology Ctte.; mem. Organic Crop Improvement Assn. N.B.; author: 'The Groundwater Pollution Primer' 1987; 'Rain Without Acid: The Atlantic Solution' 1988; 'The Global Warming Primer' 1992; co-author 'Petroleum on Tap: The Legacy of Leaking Underground Storage Tanks' 1986; ed. 'The Dump Dilemma: Waste Management Alternatives for New Brunswick' 1985; Home: R.R. 6, St. Stephen, N.B. E3L 2Y3; Office: 180 St. John St., Fredericton, N.B. E3B 4A9.

**COONEY, Jane,** M.L.S.; executive; b. Montréal, Qué. 18 March 1943; d. Robert C. and Florence (Nugent) Hanson; e. Marianopolis Coll. Montréal B.A. 1963; Univ. of Toronto B.L.S. 1964, M.L.S. 1974; PRES., BOOKS FOR BUSINESS LTD.; Calgary Pub. Lib. 1964–65; McGill Univ. Redpath Lib. 1965–66; Metrop. Toronto Bus. Lib. 1966–69; Mgr. Info. Centre Candian Imperial Bank of Commerce 1969–83; mem. Faculty of Lib. & Info. Sci. Univ. of Toronto 1975–79 (Alumni Jubilee Award 1983); Vice Pres. and Dir. Bank Mktg. Assn. Chicago 1983–86; Exec. Dir., Candn. Library Assn. 1986–89; named Special Libs. Assn. Toronto Chapter Mem. of Yr. 1983; mem. Special Libs. Assn. (Dir. 1982, 1986); Am. Lib. Assn.; Candn. Lib. Assn.; Ont. Library Assn.; Am. Booksellers Assn.; Candn. Booksellers Assn. (Dir. 1993–95); Address: Street Level, 120 Adelaide St. W., Toronto, Ont. M5H 1T1.

**COONS, James Donald,** B.A.; insurance executive; b. Hamilton, Ont. 2 Feb. 1938; s. Donald Franklin and the late Margaret M. (Long) C.; e. Ridley College; Univ. of Western Ont. B.A. 1960; m. Elizabeth M. d. the late Archdeacon William F. and Dorothea B. Wallace 29 June 1962; children: Donald W., J. David, Mark M.; PRESIDENT, CHIEF EXTVE. OFFICER & FOUNDER, THE LOYALIST INSURANCE CO.; Chrmn., D.F. Coons Insur. Limited; Pres., Fairsprings Holdings Ltd.; The Loyalist Group Limited; Valleyview Holdings Ltd.; Dir., Nodco Holdings Ltd.; Overseas Underwriting Mem., Lloyd's of London; Chair, Mohawk College Insur. Edn. Ctr.; Mem., Insur. Adv. Bd., Mohawk College; Past Chair, Bd. of Dir., Hamilton Civic Hospitals Found.; Treas. & Dir., Dictionary of Hamilton Biography; Mem., The Barton Lodge AF&AM; Merton Lodge of Perfection; Rose Croix & Moore Sovereign Consistory; recreations: tennis, golf; clubs: The Hamilton, The Hamilton Golf & Country, Muskoka Lakes Golf & Country, The Royal & Ancient Golf Club of St. Andrews, The Jesters, The Honourable Co. of Freeman of the City of London; Home: 'Fairview,' 267 Sulphur Springs Rd., Ancaster, Ont. L9G 4T7; Office: 911 Golf Links Rd., Suite 106, Ancaster, Ont. L9K 1H9.

**COOPER, Allan R.;** association executive; b. Toronto, Ont. 20 Sept. 1945; s. Stanley A. and Isabelle N. (McCord) C.; e. Queen's Univ. Assessment Practice & Princs.; Ryerson Polytech. Inst. Bus. Adm.; m. Katherine E. d. Thomas and Mona Moran 28 Sept. 1984; children: Alicia, Thomas; SR. VICE PRES. & TREAS., CANDN. BANKERS' ASSN. 1990– ; Assessor City of Oshawa 1964–70; Supvr. Mun. Assessment Candn. Imperial Bank of Commerce 1970–72; joined present Assn. 1972; Dir. Exec. Ctte. Candn. Depository for Securities; Past Pres. Candn. Property Tax Assn.; former mem. Comn. on Reform Property Taxation Ont. (co-author of Report 1977); mem. Bd. Trade Metrop. Toronto; Club: Cambridge; National; Office: P.O. Box 348, Commerce Court West, Toronto, Ont. M5L 1G2.

**COOPER, Hon. Arthur Gordon,** B.Comm., B.A., B.C.L., LL.D., D.C.L.; judge (retired); b. Saint John, N.B. 11 Dec. 1908; s. George Thomas and Mary Jane Underhill (Peters) C.; e. Kings Coll. Sch., Windsor, N.S.; Dalhousie Univ., B.Com. 1931, LL.D. 1968; Oxford Univ., (Rhodes Scholar, N.S. 1932), B.A. 1934, B.C.L. 1935; m. Helen Olive Hendery, 27 Sept. 1939; three s., George Thomas Hendery, John Geoffrey, Stephen Hugh; read law with Russell McInnes, Q.C.; called to Bar of N.S. 1938; cr. Q.C. 1955; Justice, Supreme Court of N.S. (Appeal) retired 11 Dec. 1983; served with RCAF, Personnel (Legal) Br., during 2nd World War; Past Pres., Candn. Bar Assn.; LL.D., Dalhousie Univ.; D.C.L. Univ. of King's Coll., N.S.; Phi Kappa Pi; Anglican; recreation: reading; travel; Clubs: Halifax, Saraguay; Home: The Carlyle, Suite 905, 6095 Coburg Rd., Halifax, N.S. B3H 4K1.

**COOPER, Austin Morley,** Q.C., B.Com.; LL.B.; barrister; b. Toronto, Ont. 10 Feb. 1929; s. Bert and Esther (Michaelson) C.; e. Univ. of Toronto Schs. 1945; Univ. of Toronto B.Com. 1949; Osgoode Hall Law Sch. (with honours; Clara Brett Martin Scholarship recipient) 1953; children: Peter Meredith, Douglas Anthony, Paul Warren; called to Bar of Ont. 1953; cr. Q.C. 1964; law practice Toronto since 1953; Sr. Partner in Cooper, Sandler, West & Skurka; certified by the Law Soc. as a specialist in criminal litigation; Fellow, Am. Coll. of Trial Lawyers; Awarded Douglas Laidlaw Medal for Excellence in Advocacy; lectr. in wills and trusts, Osgoode Hall Law Sch. 1955–56; former lectr. and instr., Bar Admission Course, Osgoode Hall Law Sch.; counsel, Royal Comn. on Fluoridation of Ont. Water Supplies

1960; el. Bencher, Law Soc. Upper Can. 1971–87 and currently Ex-Officio Bencher; Dir., The Tarragon Theatre, Toronto; founding mem. and former Dir., Advocates' Soc.; Candn. Bar Assn. (Chrmn., Civil Liberties Sub. Sec. 1964–66); mem. Metro. Toronto Task Force on Public Violence Against Women and Children 1983–84; recipient civilian citation from Metro. Toronto Bd. of Comnrs. of Police 1984; former lectr. to Ont. Prov. Police Training Ctrs. in Toronto and Brampton; former lectr. to Breathalizer Officers' Training Course at Ont. Ctr. of Forensic Sciences in Toronto; lectr. and panelist at Candn. Bar Assoc./Law Soc. Advocacy Symposia 1982–90; former faculty mem., Intensive Trial Advocacy Course, Osgoode Hall Law Sch.; panelist and lectr. at Candn. Bar Assoc. Continuing Legal Educ. Programmes; participant in Law Soc. Special Lectrs. to the Legal Profession; Toronto Lawyers Club; County of York Law Assn.; Advocates Soc.; Criminal Lawyers Assoc.; Candn. Bar Assoc.; Pi Lambda Phi; Jewish; recreations: art appreciation, music, sailing, travel, walking; Home: Apt. 1624, 33 Harbour Sq., Toronto, Ont. M5J 2G2; Office: Suite 1900, 439 University Ave., Toronto, Ont. M5G 1Y8.

**COOPER, Barbara Acheson,** B.A., M.H.Sc.; university professor; b. Havana, Cuba 1 March 1935; d. Archibald Alexander and Freda Margaret (Butcher) Acheson; e. Havergal College 1953; Univ. of Toronto dip. physiotherapy & occupational therapy 1956; McMaster Univ. B.A. Art & Art Hist. 1975, B.A. (Hons.) Art (Painting) 1977, M.H.Sc. 1981; Univ. of Wisconsin-Milwaukee Ph.D. candidate (Regent's 8% School) 1989–91); m. William Gill s. Wallace and Florence C. 9 June 1956; children: Liane Louise, James Gill; ASSOC. PROF., HEALTH SCIENCES CENTRE, MCMASTER UNIV. 1991– ; Physiotherapist in Hamilton 1956– ; Teacher, Mohawk College 1981; McMaster Univ. 1981– ; tenured 1984; Coord., Multidiscip. Master of Health Sci. Prog. 1984–88; currently Assoc. Dean, Health Sci. & Dir., School OT/PT; research on use of colour to facilitate function of elderly people; Consultant; Tech. Advr. (invited) for project sponsored by Am. Inst. of Archs., Am. Coll. Schools of Arch. & Am. Occup. Therapists Assn. 1992– ; Art Teacher 1978–79; exhibited extensively in group, 2-person & solo exbns. 1975– ; rep. in private & corp. collections worldwide; elected Soc. Candn. Artists 1975; SSHRCC Grad. Fellowship 1989–91; CMHC Grad. Fellowship 1989 (declined); Goldwyn Howland Award Candn. OT Found. 1989; COFT Scholarship 1989; Bd. of Dir., VON 1971–73; Bd. of Dirs., Dundas Valley Sch. of Art 1972– ; (Chair, Bd. of Govs. 1980–92); Jr. League of Hamilton 1959–67; Lynwood Hall Children's Mental Health Ctr. 1979–87 (Chair 1983–85); Mohawk Coll. Art Adv. & Art Acq. 1979–92; City of Hamilton Arts Task Force 1986; Barrier-Free Design Ctte. 1991– ; Adv. Bd., McMaster Univ. Art Gall. 1991– ; (Chair, Art Acq. Ctte. 1992– ; author/co-author of num. articles in peer-reviewed journals; recreations: enjoy music and gardening; clubs: Tamahaac; Home: 87 Auchmar Rd., Hamilton, Ont. L9C 1C6; Office: Health Sciences Centre, 1 J-11, Hamilton, Ont. L8S 4L8.

**COOPER, Barbara Jean,** B.A.; association executive; b. Ingersoll, Ont. 27 Aug. 1956; d. Donald Stuart and Helen Irene (Langford) Sivyer; e. Univ. of Waterloo B.A. 1992; m. Timothy s. Joan and Win Cooper 24 Aug. 1974; children: Philip Bradley and Daryl Evan (1982), Benjamin Andrew (1990); EXECUTIVE DIRECTOR, N.B. CHORAL FEDERATION 1989– ; Founding Owner, Publications Plus 1988– ; consultant for med. office personnel; private piano teacher; Dean's Hon. List, Univ. of Waterloo; Student of the Year, Herzing Inst. 1976; Advisory Ctte., U.N.B. Summer Music Camp; Bd. of Dir. & Newsletter Ed., Parents of Multiple Births Assn. of Canada Inc. 1986–90; recreations: walking, bicycling; Office: Old Soldiers Barracks, P.O. Box 6000, Fredericton, N.B. E3B 5H1.

**COOPER, Barry M.,** B.B.A.; investment executive; b. Halifax, N.S. 5 June 1944; s. Rex H. and Marian S. (Merritt) C.; e. Univ. of N.B. B.B.A. 1966; m. Susanne d. William and Dodie Powers 2 Sept. 1967; children: Anne, Victoria, Lindsay, John; EXTVE. VICE PRES., BURNS FRY 1989– ; Investment Dept., Montreal Trust 1966–69; Fry Mills Spence 1969–74; Mgr. 1974; Dir., Bruns Fry Ltd. 1976; Extve. Ctte. Mem. 1983; Chrmn., Jones Heward Ltd.; clubs: Granite, Rosedale Golf, Beacon Hall Golf, Sankaty Head Golf, Casino Tennis; Home: 8 Plymbridge Rd., Toronto, Ont. M4N 2H5; Office: P.O. Box 150, 1 First Canadian Pl., Toronto, Ont. M5X 1H3.

**COOPER, Brian M.,** B.Sc., M.B.A.; educator; b. Toronto, Ont. 5 Apl. 1939; s. Reginald S. and Elsie V. (Griffiths) C.; e. Cornell Univ. B.Sc. 1962; Candn. Sch. Mgmt. Northland Open Univ. M.B.A. 1984; m. Midge d. Jack and Margaret Eachus 23 Nov. 1962; children: Diane, Lynne, Reginald; DEAN, GEORGE BROWN COLLEGE, SCHOOL OF HOSPITALITY and SCHOOL OF FASHION 1992– ; Owner/operator 5 Ont. restaurants Burlington 1962–73; Dir. Food & Beverage and Dir. Personnel Canadian Pacific Hotels 1972–75; Teaching Master present Coll. 1975–78, Chrmn. Sch. of Hospitality 1978–92; Dir. Ont. Hostelry Inst.; Internat. Dir. Council Hotel Restaurant & Instl. Educators 1985–86; named Tourism Ont. Man of Yr. 1975; Candn. Hospitality Found. Hospitality Man of Yr. 1987; Past Chrmn., George Brown Coll. Counc. 1990–91; rec'd Bd. of Govs. Award of Excellence for leadership within a profession 1990; Cdn. Hotel & Restaurant Magazine Achiever Award 1990; Ont. Hostelry Inst. Gold Award, Educator of Year 1992–93; Fellow, Candn. Hospitality Inst. (Pres. 1980–83); Pres. Candn. Restaurant Assn. 1974; Ont. Restaurant & Food Service Assn. 1972–73; Dir. Nat. Restaurant Assn. (USA) 1973; Hon. mem. Ont. Hotel Motel Assn.; Toronto Escoffier Soc.; World Assoc. Cooks Soc.; Candn. Fed. Chefs de Cuisine; Burlington Light Opera Soc.; author various publs.; recreation: tennis; Home: 114 Seaton St., Toronto, Ont. M5A 2T3; Office: 300 Adelaide St. E., Toronto, Ont. M5A 1N1.

**COOPER, David Richard;** insurance executive; b. Toronto, Ont. 30 June 1942; s. Harold Theodore and Martha Ellen (Hasleden) C.; e. Ryerson Polytech. Inst. Business Adm. 1965; Cert. Gen. Acct. 1970; m. Barbara d. Doug and Ruth Lowe 21 May 1966; children: Andrew, Susan, Shawn; SENIOR VICE-PRES., INSURANCE SERVICES, ROYAL BANK OF CANADA 1993– ; Pres. & Dir., Royal Brokers Ltd.; joined Royal Trust 1965, Gen. Supr. Corporate Budgets 1976, Gen. Supr. Finance 1977, Asst. Vice Pres. and Comptroller 1979, Vice Pres. Profitability Planning 1980, Sr. Vice Pres. Finance and Systems 1981, Sr. Vice Pres. Information Systems & Personal Financial Services Admin. 1984, Sr. Vice Pres. Insurance Services 1989; Dir., Boy Scouts Greater Toronto Region; recreations: tennis, skiing; Clubs: Ontario; Home: 121 Acheson Blvd., Scarborough, Ont. M1C 3C4; Office: 44 Peel Centre Dr., Brampton, Ont. L6T 4M8.

**COOPER, Edward Jay,** B.Sc., B.Comm., C.A.; financial executive; b. Hamilton, Ont. 11 May 1955; s. Donald Edward, Q.C. and Evelyn Geraldine (Dawson) C.; e. Univ. of Western Ont. B.Sc. 1977; Univ. of Windsor B.Comm. (Hons.) 1979; C.A. Ontario 1981; m. Colleen d. Lorne and Ruth Delaney 19 Oct. 1991; DIRECTOR, FINANCIAL SERVICES & COMPTROLLER, THE TORONTO HOSPITAL 1993– ; Audit Manager, Clarkson Gordon 1979–87; Senior Audit Manager, Ernst & Young 1987–90; Corporate Group Controller, Joniff Corporation 1990–93; Pres. & Chair, Bathurst Hillview Cooperative Housing Inc.; clubs: National Yacht, Adelaide, Holimont Ski; Home: 51 Vanderhoof Ave., Toronto, Ont. M4G 2H3; Office: 200 Elizabeth St., Res 3-306, Toronto, Ont. M5C 2C4.

**COOPER, Fraser Barry,** B.A., M.A., Ph.D., F.R.S.C.; professor; b. Vancouver, B.C. 3 Sept. 1943; s. Henry George and Helen Patricia (Legge) C.; e. Shawnigan Lake Sch. 1962; Univ. of B.C., B.A. 1965; Duke Univ., M.A. 1967, Ph.D. 1969; m. Denise Guichon; children: Meghan Kathleen, Brendan Michael; PROF., DEPT. OF POL. SCI., UNIV. OF CALGARY 1981– ; Instr., Duke Univ. 1967; Asst. Prof., Bishop's Univ. 1969–70; York Univ. 1970–76; Assoc. Prof. 1976–81; Vis. Asst. Prof., McGill Univ. 1970; Vis. Prof., Univ. of Munich 1992; Vis. Prof., Univ. of Erlangen-Nuremburg 1992; Mem., Candn. Pol. Sci. Assn. 1967– ; (Bd. & Extve. 1984–86); author: 'Merleau-Ponty and Marxism' 1981; 'Michel Foucault' 1984; 'The End of History' 1984; 'The Political Theory of Eric Voegelin' 1986; 'Alexander Kennedy Isbister' 1988; 'The Restoration of Political Science and the Crisis of Modernity' 1989; 'Action into Nature: An Essay on the Meaning of Technology' 1991; (with David Jay Bercuson) 'Deconfederation: Canada Without Quebec' 1991; editor: 'The Resurgence of Conservatism in Anglo-American Democracies' 1987; Editor & Transl., (with Peter Emberley) 'Faith and Political Philosophy: The Correspondence Between Leo Strauss and Eric Voegelin, 1934-1964' 1993; mem. Ed. Bd., 'The Political Science Reviewer' (scholarly journal); Fellow, Royal Society of Canada 1993; recreations: hunting, fishing, skiing, hiking; Club: Pennask Lake Fishing and Game; Home: 1114 Premier Way S.W., Calgary, Alta.; Office: Dept. of Pol. Sci., Univ. of Calgary, Calgary, Alta. T2N 1N4.

**COOPER, Frederick Douglas,** B.A., F.I.C.D.; emergency planning consultant; b. Victoria, B.C. 22 June 1933; s. Richard Hamilton and Katharine Agnes (Love) C.; e. Penticton High Sch.; Sir George Williams Univ. Montreal B.A. 1962; Pub. Service Comn. Jr. Mgmt. 1962, Middle Mgmt. 1968, Sr. Mgmt. Career Assignment Prog. 1972; m. Margaret d. Leonard and Louise Van Duzer 20 Aug. 1960; children: Diana Katharine, Michael Douglas Richard; PRINCIPAL, F.D. COOPER & ASSOCIATES PLANNING CONSULTANTS 1990– ; served with RCAF 1951–58; Adm. Offr. Rsch. Stn. Agric. Can. 1963, Adm. Offr. Animal Pathol. 1964–66, Asst. Chief Classification & Pay Div. 1966–69; Chief Compensation & Classification Div. Dept. Solr. Gen. Ottawa 1969–72; Chief Adm. Services Div. Security Br. SSC Ottawa 1972, Chief Emergency Supply Planning Div. 1973–78; Dir. Plans Analysis Br. Emergency Planning Can. 1978–79; Regional Dir. B.C. and Yukon, Emergency Preparedness Can. 1979–90; Chrmn. Fed. Inst. Classification & Pay 1968–69; Chrmn. Ind. Planning Ctte. NATO 1967–69; Cons. to Colombia Govt. Disaster Planning 1986; Adv. to Edn. Adv. Ctte. Nat. Centre for Earthquake Eng. Rsch. State Univ. of N.Y. Buffalo; Chrmn. Fed./Prov. Task Force War Planning & Concept Operations 1985; Fellow, UK Inst. Civil Defence; mem., N.Y. Academy of Science; Certificate of Merit, Dictionary of Internat. Biography, Cambridge Vol. XXII; author or co-author various publs.; Life mem. Royal Un. Services Inst. Vancouver Is. (Dir. 1986–87); Pres. 410 Wing RCAF Assn. 1977; Nepean Rate Payers Assn. 1975; recreations: sailing, trailering, rockhound; Clubs: Royal Victoria Yacht; Address: 134 Linden Ave., Victoria, B.C. V8V 4E1.

**COOPER, George T.H.,** Q.C., B.Sc., LL.B., B.C.L.; barrister & solicitor; b. Halifax, N.S. 24 June 1941; s. A. Gordon and Helen O. (Hendery) C.; e. Kings Coll. Sch.; Dalhousie Univ., B.Sc. 1962, LL.B. 1965; Oxford Univ., B.C.L. 1967; m. Cynthia (Tia) d. Dr. Joseph Frederick and Catherine (MacAskill) Griffin 23 Dec. 1969; children: J. Gordon, Jennifer H.; LAWYER, MCINNES COOPER & ROBERTSON 1967– ; (PARTNER 1975; SR. PARTNER 1985); called to N.S. Bar 1967; Q.C. 1982; M.P. for Halifax & Parl. Sec. to Min. of Justice & Attorney-Gen. of Can. 1979–80; Part-time lectr., Dalhousie Law Sch.; Mem., Bd. of Dir., Canadian National Railway Co.; Autoport Ltd.; Canac Internat. Inc.; Stora Forest Indus. Ltd.; Halifax Indus. Comn. (Chrmn. 1987–90); Dir. & Chrmn. (1992– ;), Canada-U.S. Educational Exchange Found. (the Fulbright Scholarship); Managing Trustee, Estate of late Dorothy J. Killam; Rhodes Scholar, N.S 1965; Counc. of Trustees, Inst. for Rsch. on Pub. Policy 1984–90; Bd. of Govs., Dalhousie Univ. & Univ. of Kings Coll. 1982–92; Izaak Walton Killam Hosp. for Children 1984–88; Nat. Chrmn., Dalhousie Annual Fund 1984–87; Dalhousie Alumni Assn. (Pres. 1975–76); Oxford Univ. Capital Campaign (Candn. Ctte.); St. George's Soc. of Halifax (Pres. 1985–86); Wellington Soc. of Halifax; Hon. Lt. Col., No. 33 (Halifax) Service Battalion; Candn. Bar Assn.; Internat. Bar Assoc.; N.S. Barristers' Soc. (Counc. Mem. 1975–78 and 1981–84); Anglican; Progressive Conservative; recreations: tennis, politics, broadcasting, choir singing, reading; Clubs: Halifax (Ctte. Mem. 1985–90); Home: 1036 Ridgewood Drive, Halifax, N.S. B3H 3Y4; Office: Cornwallis Place, 1601 Lower Water St., Halifax, N.S. B3J 2V1.

**COOPER, Heather J.,** R.C.A.; illustrator; graphic designer; b. Eng. 16 Mar. 1945; d. Ronald Stanley and Eileen (Bunn) C.; e. W. Tech. Sch. Toronto; PRINCIPAL, HEATHER COOPER COMMUNICATION BY DESIGN LTD. 1984– ; Designer, Hathaway Templeton, Toronto 1963–67; freelance practice Heather Cooper Co. Ltd. Toronto 1967–71; Partner: Burns, Cooper Ltd. 1971–76; Burns, Cooper, Hynes Ltd. 1976–84; Lectr.: Design 25 Conf. Harvard Sci. Centre Boston; Internat. Design Conf. Aspen 1979; Alliance Graphique Internationale Cong. Prague; Am. Inst. Graphic Arts; Ont. Coll. Art; retrospective exhn. illustrative work 'The Art of the Illustrator' Toronto 1976; retrospective book of work 'Carnaval Perpetuel' 1987; recipient gold medals: New York Soc. Illustrators 1977; Art Dirs. Club Toronto 1976, 1977, 1978 (silver awards 1983, 1984); Graphica 1976; Art Dirs. Club N.Y. 1978, Cert. of Excellence 1984; Bronze Medal Internat. Poster Bienalle 1975, 1977; Certs. of Excellence: Print Casebooks Packaging 1983; Creativity 1983, 1984, 1985; CA 1983, 1985; CA Illustration Annual 1988, 1989; Art Annual 1983; AIGA Portraits 1984; mem. Alliance Graphique Internationale; Am. Inst. Graphic Arts; Royal Acad. (Candn.); Pres., Art Dirs. Club of Toronto 1988–90; Club: McGill; P.O. Box 185, Stn. Q., Toronto, Ont. M4T 2M1.

**COOPER, Helen Cecilia Sutcliffe,** B.Sc., M.Sc.; b. Melbourne, Australia 13 Nov. 1946; d. William James and Ethel Margaret Anne (FitzGerald) Sutcliffe; e. Kingston C.&V.I. 1964; Queen's Univ., B.Sc. (Hon.) 1968;

London Sch. of Econ. & Pol. Sci., M.Sc. 1973; m. Jack s. Samuel and Marian C. 4 Sept. 1971; children: Ann Helen, Heather Jane; CHAIR, THE ONTARIO MUNICIPAL BOARD 1993– ; Product Development Supervisor, Procter and Gamble Co. Ltd., Hamilton, Ont.; CUSO volunteer, Tanzania, E. Africa (Sec. Sch. Teacher) 1969–71; Tutor/Rsch. Asst., Queen's Univ. 1975; Part-time teacher, St. Lawrence Coll. 1976; Alderman, Sydenham Ward 1980–88; Mayor, The Corp. of the City of Kingston 1988–93; Past Pres., Assn. of Municipalities of Ont.; Mem., Premier's Counc. on Health, Social Justice and Well-Being; Mem., Provincial Roundtable on Environment and Economy; Home: 55 West St., Kington, Ont. K7L 2S3; Office: City Hall, 216 Ontario St., Kingston, Ont. K7L 2Z3.

**COOPER, Jennifer Anne,** LL.B.; lawyer; b. Burnaby, B.C. 29 July 1956; d. David Allan and Catherine May (Purdon) C.; e. Univ. of Man., LL.B. 1980; m. Robert Hugh s. Hugh and Janet Morrison 25 Apl. 1981; children: Christopher, Jessica; law practice PITBLADO & HOSKIN 1991– ; law practice Newman Maclean 1980–85; Exec. Dir. Women's Health Clinic Inc. 1985–91 (mem. Bd. and Chairperson 1981–85); mem. & Chairperson, Man. Assn. Women & Law 1977–84; mem. & Interim Chairperson, Man. Adv. Council Status Women 1982–86; mem. Bd. of Govs., Univ. of Man. 1987–88; Dir., Man. Assn. of Community Health Ctres. 1987–91; Chair, Women's Service Providers Network 1990–91; Chairperson, Manitoba Gender Equality Working Group, C.B.A. 1992–93; Bd. Mem., Women's Legal Education and Action Fund Foundation 1991–93; Mem., Discipline Ctte., Law Society of Manitoba 1993– ; recreations: aerobics, squash, skiing, piano; Home: 260 Montrose St., Winnipeg, Man. R3M 3M7; Office: 1900 – 360 Main St., Winnipeg, Man. R3C 3Z3.

**COOPER, Jerry Jacob Irving,** M.D., D.Psych., F.R.C.P.(C); psychiatrist; b. Toronto, Ont. 27 June 1937; s. Samuel and Eva (Gold) C.; e. Univ. of Toronto M.D. 1962, D.Psych., F.R.C.P.(C) 1965; Harvard Med. Sch., post-grad 1965–66; m. Eleanor d. David and Faye Kirsh 1 July 1962; children: Richard, Denise, James, Ian; CHIEF OF PSYCHIATRY & DIR. OF COMMUNITY MENTAL HEALTH CTR., YORK FINCH GENERAL HOSPITAL 1968– ; Chief Res. in Psych., St. Michael's Hosp. 1966–67; Act. Dir., Psych. Dept., Correctional Serv.; Cons. to 1972; Teacher, York Univ. 1967–68; Staff Psych., Toronto Gen. Hosp. & Associate Univ. of Toronto 1968–70; Cons., Youth Clinic. Serv. 1971– ; Spec. Adv. Ctte. to North York Mayor Mel Lastman; Chrmn., num. Mayor's Adv. Cttes. & Task Forces; num. extve. ctte. posts; Stonehenge Action Ctte.; Guest Lectr., Univ. of Toronto & Osgoode Hall Law Schools; Univ. of Toronto Sch. of Crim.; Pres., Cdn. Found. of Compulsive Gambling 1983– ; (Mem., Adv. Bd., New York); Dir./Extve., Assn. of Gen. Hosp. Psych. Serv.; awarded North York Mayor's Gold Medal 1973–74; Mem., Candn. Med. Assn.; Ont. Med. Assn. Candn. & Ont. Psych. Assns.; Assn. for the Adv. of Psychotherapy; Chairman Mayor Lastman's Task Force on Elder Abuse; author of numerous articles; recreations: oil painting, sketching; Office: 2111 Finch Ave. W., Downsview, Ont. M3N 1N1.

**COOPER, Joanne S.;** association executive; b. Toronto, Ont. 18 Oct. 1938; d. Aaron and Rose Brown; e. Ryerson Poly. Inst., Library Arts; York Univ., Studies in Mgmt. Orgn. and Devel.; Ont. Inst. for Studies in Edn. (OISE) Adult Edn. Prog.; m. Gordon E. s. Bert and Esther Cooper 1 Sept. 1959; children: Matthew, Andrew, Sara; EXTVE. DIRECTOR, VOLUNTEER CENTRE OF METRO TORONTO; co-founder and Dir. Inst. for Non-Profit Orgns.; publ.: 'Money Isn't Everything' (1st and 2nd eds.); 'Organizing Your Way to Dollars'; 'Fundraising Event Report'; 'How to Manage a Non-Profit Organization'; 'On Your Own: A Directory for Young Women'; 'On Your Own: A Directory for Young Men'; 'Latchkey Kids'; 'Suddenly Single'; 'Guide to Women's Groups & Resources'; 'Getting Started'; 'Teen Power'; 'Speaking Out'; 'See You at the Fair'; 'Youth Program'; 'Volunteers from the Multicultural Community'; co-prod. 'Women's Journal' (8–part TV series); 'Rape: Once is Too Often' (3–part TV series); Social Planning Ctte., Budget & Finance Ctte., Toronto Jewish Congress; Ont. Region Extve., Candn. Jewish Congress; Mem. Bd. of Dirs.: Volunteer Ontario (Chair, Trillium Ctte.); The Concerned Kids; Community Information Ctr. of Metro. Toronto; Community Foundation of Greater Toronto, Chair Grants Ctte.; Serve Canada; Candn. Assn. of Volunteer Bureaux and Centres (CAVBC); recreations: tennis, skiing, sailing, biking; Clubs: York Racquet; Home: 95 MacLennan Ave., Toronto, Ont. M4T 2H6; Office: Suite 207, 344 Bloor St. W., Toronto, Ont. M5S 3A7.

**COOPER, Keith E.,** M.B., B.S., M.Sc., M.A., D.Sc.; educator; b. Frome, Somerset, Eng. 7 Aug. 1922; s. Allen Cooper; e. Watford (Eng.) Grammar Sch. 1940; St. Mary's Hosp. Med. Sch. London M.B., B.S. 1945; Univ. of London B.Sc. 1948, M.Sc. 1950; Oxford Univ. M.A. 1960, D.Sc. 1971; m. Eileen Mary d. late George A. Cox, Watford, Eng. 22 Aug. 1946; children: John A., Peter Charles; PROF. EMERITUS 1988– ; PROF. MED. PHYSIOL., UNIV. OF CALGARY 1969– ; Dept. of Energy & Nat. Resources 1984–87; Chair, Coal Rsch. Technical Panel 1986–89; Lectr. in Physiol. St. Mary's Hosp. Med. Sch. London 1946–48; mem. M.R.C. Unit for Research on Body Temperature Regulation, Radcliffe Infirmary, Oxford, Eng. 1950–69 (Dir. 1960–69); Fellow, St. Peter's Coll. Oxford Univ. 1961–69; mem. Defence Research Bd. Cold Climatic Panel 1970–74, Biosciences Adv. Ctte. since 1975; Head of Med. Physiol. Univ. Calgary 1969–78, Assoc. Vice Pres., 1978–79, Vice-Pres. (Research) 1979–84; mem. Internat. Union of Physiol. Sciences Comn. on Thermal Physiol. 1976–84 and Chrmn. of Comn. on Teaching of Physiol. 1976–93; Mem., Internat. Counc. of Scientific Unions Ctte. on Teaching Science 1976–93; served with RAF 1948–50, Aviation Med. Inst. Farnborough, rank Flight Lt.; former mem. Bd. Extve., Calgary Philharmonic Soc.; Bd. of Dirs., Calgary Div., Cdn. Cancer Soc.; mem. Exec. Calgary, Cdn. Paraplegic Assn. 1975–79; former Bd. Dirs., Alberta Rsch. Counc. 1979–85; Chair, Bd. Dirs., Arctic Inst. of N. America 1979–85; Chrmn. 1995 Royal Candn. Coll. of Organists Convention; co-author 'Hypothermia for Surgical Practice' 1960; book chapters and numerous articles in scient. journs. on temperature regulation, hypothermia and fever; mem. Am. Physiol. Soc.; Brit. Physiol. Soc.; Cdn. Physiol. Soc. (Vice pres. 1974–75, Pres. 1975–76); Brit. med. Research Soc.; Cdn. Soc. Clin. Research; Can. fed. Biol. Socs. (Chrmn. and Pres. 1979–80); Ed. Bd., Calgary Univ. Press 1981–85; Bd. of Dir., Candn. Plains Rsch. Centre 1978–81; Mem., Alta. Office of Coal Rsch. & Technology 1983–85; Chrmn., Univ. of Calgary Neuroscience Rsch. Group 1986–88; Referee and Mem. Granting Panels of numerous Nat. & Internat. Granting Agencies; Candn. Physiol. Soc. Sarazzin Lectr. 1986; Am. Assn. Advanc. Science; N.Y. Acad. Sciences; Sigma Xi; recreations: hiking, bird watching, skiing, sailing (former Commodore, Abbey Sailing Club, Vice-Commodore, Oxford Sailing Club), music, reading old scientific books; Home: 624 Sifton Blvd. S.W., Calgary, Alta. T2T 2K7; Office: Health Science Centre, Univ. of Calgary, 3300 Hospital Dr. N.W., Calgary, Alta. T2N 4N1.

**COOPER, Marsh A.,** M.A.Sc., D.Sc., LL.D.; executive; b. Toronto, Ont. 8 Oct. 1912; s. Frederick Webster and Gertrude (Marsh) C.; e. Univ. of Toronto, B.A.Sc., M.A.Sc.; D.Sc. (Hon.) St. Francis Xavier Univ.; LL.D. (Hon.) Laurentian Univ.; m. Doris Elsie Roos, 1942; PRESIDENT, M.A. COOPER CONSULTANTS INC.; Dir., Crownx Inc.; W.M. Keck Foundation; mem., Assn. Prof. Engrs. of Prov. of Ont.; Am. Inst. of Mining, Metall. & Petroleum Engrs.; Cdn. Inst. of Mining & Metall.; Engineering Inst. of Can.; Soc. of Econ. Geologists; Pres. & C.E.O., Falconbridge Limited 1969–80; United Ch.; Clubs: Boisclair Fish & Game; Pennask Lake Fishing & Game; The Toronto; National; York; Office: 1004, 95 Wellington St. W., Toronto, Ont. M5J 2V4.

**COOPER, Mel,** C.M., O.B.C.; broadcast executive; b. St. John's, Nfld. 10 Dec. 1932; s. Ronald Clifford and Mildred (Brophy) C.; e. St. Bonaventure's Coll. St. John's; Vancouver (B.C.) Coll. grad. 1950; Univ. of B.C. 1951; m. Grace A. d. William and Ruth Eaton 24 March 1952; children: Dean, Linda, Cindy, Shelley, Randy; PRES. AND GEN. MGR., C-FAX 1070 1974– ; PRES., SEACOAST COMMUNICATIONS GROUP INC. 1990– ; Pres. Seacoast Sound, Victoria 1979– ; Pres., CKOV and CKLZ-FM Kelowna 1988– ; Chrmn., Air B.C. Ltd.; Dir., B.C. Telephone Co.; Royal Bank of Canada; National Arts Centre Corp.; Speaker, Lectr. Nat. Speakers Bureau; Radio Announcer 1950–52; News Ed. CKWX Vancouver 1952–54; Promotions Manager, CKNW Vancouver 1954–56, Gen. Sales Mgr. 1957–68, Gen. Mgr. 1969–73; Pres. Western Broadcast Sales 1965–73; Vice Pres. Radio, Western Broadcasting 1967–73; Vice Pres. Expo 86 Vancouver; recipient 'Ambassador of Tourism' Award Prov. B.C. 1987; 'Canada Award' Inter-Cultural Assn. 1988; Member of Order of Canada 1989; Victoria Enterpriser of Excellence 1990; Order of B.C. 1992; B.C. Entrepreneur of the Year 1993; Victoria 'Business Person of the Year' 1993; Chrmn. of Bd. of Govs., 1994 Commonwealth Games Soc.; Hon. Chrmn., Boy Scouts of Greater Victoria; former Dir. Bastion Theatre Co. of B.C.; Un. Way Vancouver & Victoria; Victoria Internat. Festival; Hon. Chrmn., Kaleidoscope Theatre Building Fund; B.C. Lions Soc. Telethon, The Fannin Foundation; Pres. B.C. Assn. Broadcasters 1979; Greater Victoria C. of C. 1979; Dir. Chinatown Care Soc. 1980–83; Home: 3275 Beach Dr., Victoria, B.C. V8R 6L9; Office: 825 Broughton St., Victoria, B.C. V8W 1E5.

**COOPER, Murray Wright,** B.A., C.G.A.; telecommunications executive; b. Swastika, Ont. 6 Feb. 1932; s. Ernest Austin and Sybil Almira (Wright) C.; e. elem. sch. Swastika; secondary sch. Kirkland Lake, Ont.; Univ. of W. Ont. B.A. (Hons. Bus. Admin.) 1956; Cert. Gen. Acct. 1967; m. Joan d. William and Daisy Axcell 31 July 1954; children: Michael, Richard, Todd, Susan, David; PRESIDENT, C.E.O. & DIR., NORTHERN TELEPHONE LTD. 1983– ; Dir., T. & H. Resources; Centra Gas Ont. Inc.; Jonpol Explorations; Cane Corp.; Telecommunications Dept. Ont. Northland Railway 1956–64; Asst. Sec.-Treas. present Co. 1964; Gen. Mgr. 1966; Vice-Pres. & Gen. Mgr. 1978; Pres., Gen. Mgr. & Dir. 1981; recreations: golf, sailing, skiing, curling; Clubs: Horne Granite Curling; New Liskeard Golf; Home: 34 Niven St., Box 578, New Liskeard, Ont. P0J 1P0; Office: 25 Paget St., New Liskeard, Ont. P0J 1P0.

**COOPER, Robert G.,** B.Eng., M.Eng., M.B.A., Ph.D.; educator; b. Montréal, Qué. 18 Oct. 1943; s. Charles Frederick and Doris Marion (Gravlin) C.; e. McGill Univ. B.Eng. 1965, M.Eng. 1966; Univ. of W. Ont. M.B.A. 1968, Ph.D. 1973; m. Linda Elaine d. Douglas and Helen Wornell 24 Aug. 1968; two d. Barbara Lynn, Heather Amy; LAWSON MARDON CHAIRED PROF. OF INDUSTRIAL MARKETING & TECHNOLOGY MANAGEMENT, M. DeGROOTE SCH. OF BUSINESS, MCMASTER UNIV. 1990– , Prof. of Mktg., McMaster Univ. 1983– ; Dir. of Rsch. Ind. Innovation Centre, Waterloo 1983– ; Dir. of Mktg. Prochem Ltd. 1968–70; Asst. Prof. of Mgmt. McGill Univ. 1973–77, Assoc. Dean of Mgmt. 1978–83; author 'Winning at New Products: Accelerating the Process from Idea to Launch' 1993; 'Winning at New Products' 1986; 'Winning the New Product Game' 1976; Home: 2175 Adair Cres., Oakville, Ont. L6J 5J6.

**COPELAND, Ann;** see Furtwangler, Virginia.

**COPELAND, Frederick (Rick), Jr.,** B.A., M.B.A.; banking executive; b. Ithaca, N.Y. 2 Sept. 1941; s. Frederick C. and Caroline (Day) C.; e. Bowdoin Coll. B.A. 1964; Columbia Univ. M.B.A. 1967; m. Susan d. Richard Jordan 3 Feb. 1968; children: Timothy, Chessie; PRES. & CHIEF EXTVE. OFFR., CITIBANK CANADA, COUNTRY HEAD FOR CANADA, MNG. DIR., NORTH AMERICAN GROUP 1987– ; Corp. Finan., Citicorp 1967; N.Y. 1967–69, 1972–76; London 1969–72; Head, U.S. entry level & profl. training N.Y. 1976–78; Area Mgr., Southwest U.S. (resp. for corp. finan. business in Texas, Louisiana, Oklahoma, New Mexico & offices in Dallas & Houston) 1978–83; Country Head, Taiwan 1983–87; living in Taipei 1983–87; Office: 1900, Citibank Place, 123 Front St. W., Toronto, Ont. M5J 2M3.

**COPELAND, Kenneth B.,** B.Sc.; business executive; b. Winnipeg, Man. 4 May 1941; s. Esmonde Miles and Bertha Mary C.; e. United Coll. 1959; Univ. of Manitoba B.Sc. 1964; Harvard AMP Class 99, 1986; m. Judith Anne d. Donovan and the late Dorothy Hynes 26 Aug. 1966; children: Catherine, Sarah, Craig; PRESIDENT, DIGITAL EQUIPMENT OF CANADA LTD. 1983– ; Mfg. Orgn., IBM Canada Ltd. 1964; Salesman 1967–71; Sales Mgr. (Toronto, Hamilton, Winnipeg) 1972–79; Admin. Asst. to Chrmn., Pres. & C.E.O. 1979–81; Mgr. IBM Direct 1981–83; mem. Digital Equipment Gen. Internat. Area Mgmt. Ctte.; Mem., Bd. of Dir., Information Technology Assoc. of Can.; Mem., Internat. Trade Advisory Ctte., Fed. Govt.; Labour Mgmt. Advisory Comm., Ont. Govt.; Mem., Presidential Advisory Council of Carleton Univ.; Mem., Manitoba Internat. Business Advisory Council; Chair, Business Development, 1993 Campaign Cabinet of the United Way of Greater Toronto; Mem., Metro Internat. Caravan; Mem. Bd., St. Joseph's Health Ctr., Toronto; Mem., Bd. of Dirs., Mount Sinai Hosp. Found.; Mem., Nat. Bd.: Candn. Arts Soc.; Mem., Nat. Counc., Royal Winnipeg Ballet; Former Mem., Bd. of Govs. and Former Mem., Extve. Ctte., Univ. of Waterloo; Former Mem., Nat. Board, Jr. Achievement of Can.; recreations: arts, tennis, hobby farming, golf; Clubs: Royal Ottawa Golf and Country; University Club of Toronto; Beacon Hall (Aurora); Home: R.R. #2, Campbellcroft, Ont. L0A 1B0; Office: 505 University Ave., Toronto, Ont. M5G 2H2.

**COPES, Parzival,** C.D., B.A., M.A., Ph.D., D.Mil.Sc., Dr.Philos.; professor emeritus; b. Nakusp, B.C. 22 Jan. 1924; s. Jan Coops and Elisabeth Catharina (van Olst) C.; e. Vierde Vijfjarige H.B.S., Amsterdam, 1936–41; Univ. of B.C., B.A. 1949, M.A. 1950; London Sch. of Econ. and Pol. Science, Ph.D., 1956; Royal Roads Mil.

Coll., D.Mil.Sc. (hon. causa) 1991; Univ. of Tromsø, Dr.Philos. (hon. causa) 1993; Elected foreign member, Acad. of Natural Sciences of the Russian Federation 1992; m. Dina, d. W. P. Gussekloo, Laren, Netherlands, 1 May 1946; children: Raymond Alden, Michael Ian, Terence Franklin; DIR., INST. OF FISHERIES ANALYSIS 1980– ; PROF. DEPT. OF ECON. SIMON FRASER UNIV. 1964– ; (Head Dept. 1964–69, Chrmn. 1972–75; Dir., Centre for Cdn. Studies there 1978–85); Econ. & Stat., Dom. Bureau of Stat., Ottawa 1953–57; apptd. Assoc. Prof., Memorial Univ. and successively Head, Dept. of Econ. and Prof. 1957–64; instrumental in founding Inst. of Soc. and Econ. Research there and was 1st Director of Econ. Research; Gov., Inst. of Cdn. Bankers 1967–71; Vice Pres., Social Science Federation of Can. 1981–83; served as Chairman or member of numerous arbitration and conciliation boards; served with Netherlands Resistance Army, 1944; Cdn. Army and Brit. Mil. Govt. in Germany, 1945–46; C.O.T.C. 1947–50; Canadian Army (Militia) 1950–63; author of 'St. John's and Newfoundland: An Economic Survey' 1961; 'The Resettlement of Fishing Communities in Newfoundland' 1972; Econ. Consultant specializing in fisheries resource management; Associate, Oceans Inst. of Can.; Mem., Task Force on Fisheries, Pacific Economic Cooperation Conf.; Mem. of Counc., Pacific Regional Science Conf. Organ. (Pres./Chrmn. 1977–85); mem., Cdn. Econ. Assn. (Vice Pres. 1971–73); Cdn. Assn. Univ. Teachers; W. Regional Science Assn. (Pres. 1977–78); Cdn. Regional Science Assn. (Pres. 1983–85); Internat. Inst. of Fisheries Economics and Trade (Exec. Ctte. 1982–86); Internat. Assn. for the Study of Common Property; recreations: photography, travel; Home: 2341 Lawson Ave., W. Vancouver, B.C. V7V 2E5.

**COPITHORNE, Maurice Danby,** Q.C., B.A., LL.B.; lawyer; b. Vancouver, B.C. 3 July 1931; s. Cecil James and Margery (Hill) C.; e. Univ. of B.C., B.A. 1954, LL.B. 1955; m. Tamako Yagai Aug. 1963; two s. Dan, Asa; Associate Counsel, Ladner Downs, Barristers and Solicitors, Vancouver; Adjunct Prof. of Law, Univ. of British Columbia; called to Bar of B.C. 1956; joined Dept. of External Affairs as Foreign Service Offr. 1956 serving in various capacities Ottawa and abroad; Fellow, Centre for Internat. Affairs, Harvard Univ. 1974; Dir. Gen. Legal Bureau, Dept. External Affairs Ottawa 1975, Legal Adviser 1977; Candn. Rep. Sixth Comte., UN Gen. Assembly 1975, 1976, 1978; Candn. Ambassador to Austria, Gov. for Can., Internat. Atomic Energy Agency and Candn. Perm. Rep. to UN Indust. Devel. Organ. Vienna, 1979; Chrmn. IAEA Bd. of Governors, 1980–81; Asst. Under-Sec. for Asia and Pacific Affairs, Dept. of External Affairs 1982–83; Commissioner for Canada, Hong Kong 1983–86; Douglas McK. Brown Visiting Prof. of Law, Univ. of British Columbia 1987–88; author various articles internat. law; Pres., Vancouver Chamber Choir; Dir., Laurier Inst.; mem. Law Soc. B.C.; Candn. Council Internat. Law; Candn. Bar Assn.; Candn. Human Rights Foundation; Am. Soc. Internat. Law; Sigma Tau Chi Hon. Soc.; Address: 4316 W. 2nd Ave., Vancouver, B.C., V6R 1K3.

**COPLAND, Kenneth G.,** B.Comm.; investment banker; b. Montreal, Que. 3 Jan. 1938; s. Kenneth H. and Kathleen C. C.; e. Sir George Williams Univ. B.Comm. 1959; m. May E. d. Ernest and Elizabeth Gilbey 4 May 1960; children: Katharine, Cynthia; EXECUTIVE VICE-PRES., EXTVE. CTTE. MEM. & DIR., NESBITT THOMSON INC.; various positions ending as Vice-Pres., Investment Banking, Royal Securities Corp. Ltd. 1958–71; joined present firm 1972; Dir., Laurentian Spring Valley Water; Nesbitt Thomson Corp. Limited; Chair, Humber College Found.; clubs: Lambton Golf & Country, Belleair Country, Toronto Racquet, Montreal Badminton & Squash, Boulevard, Fitness Inst.; Office: 150 King St. W., Ste. 2100, Toronto, Ont. M5H 3W2.

**COPP, Douglas Harold,** O.C. (1971), C.C. (1980), M.D., Ph.D., LL.D., D.Sc., F.R.S.C. (1959), F.R.C.P.(C) (1974), F.R.S. (1971); physiologist; b. Toronto, Ont., 16 Jan. 1915; s. Charles Joseph and Edith M. (O'Hara) C.; e. Univ. of Toronto, B.A. 1936 and M.D. 1939; Ellen Mickle Fellow, 1939–40; Univ. of Calif., Ph.D. (Biochem.) 1943; Queens LL.D. 1970, Toronto 1970; D.Sc., Ottawa 1973, Acadia 1975, British Columbia 1980; m. Winnifred A. Thompson, 15 July 1939; children: Mary, Carolyn, Patricia; PROF. PHYSIOL., UNIV. OF B.C. (Head of Dept. 1950–80; Co-ordr. Health Services 1975–79); mem. Adv. Comn., Medical & Dental Rsch., National Rsch. Counc.; Lectr. in Biochem., University of California, 1942–43; Instr. in Physiol. there 1943–45, Asst. Prof. 1945–50; Research Associate, Radiation Lab., 1943–50; Consultant, U.S. Nat. Research Council; mem. of Advisory Comm. on Isotope Distribution, U.S.A.E.C.; mem. of Science Counc. of B.C. 1981–88; Hon. Citizen, Alert Bay, B.C.; research; biol. studies with radioactive isotopes, iron metabolism, bone metabolism, heavy metals, phosphate depletion, calcium regulation in mammals and fishes, parathyroid and ultimobranchial function, stanniocalcin and corpuscles of Stannius; discovered calcitonin; mem., Am. Physiol. Soc.; Candn. Physiol. Soc. (Past Pres.); Soc. for Exper. Biol. & Med.; Scient. Secy., 2nd Internat. Conf. on Peaceful Uses of Atomic Energy 1958; Pres., Nat. Cancer Inst. of Can. 1968–70; Faculty Assoc., Univ. of B.C. 1965–66; Acad. of Sci. and Vice Pres., Roy. Soc. of Can. 1978–81; Mem. Board, Science Council of B.C. 1987–89; Science World of B.C. 1987–92; rec'd. Gairdner Foundation Annual Award 1967; Nicolas Andry Award, Assoc. Bone and Joint Surg. 1968; Claude Bernard Lecture, Univ. Montréal 1968; Beaumont Lecture, Wayne Co. Med. Soc. 1970; Jacobaeus Mem. Lecture, Gothenbourg, Sweden 1971; Helsinki, Finland 1980; Sarrazin Lecture, Candn. Physiol. Soc. 1977; Transatlantic Lecture, The Endocrine Soc., UK 1982; Faculty of Med. Medal, Univ. of Lund, Sweden 1971; Jacob Biely Rsch. Prize, Univ. of B.C. 1971; Flavelle Medal, Royal Soc. of Can. 1972; B.C. Science and Eng. Gold Medal 1980; Steindler Award, Orthopedic Rsch. Soc. 1974; William F. Neuman Award, Am. Soc. Bone & Mineral Rsch. 1983; Internat. Prize for Advances in Therapy, Rorer Found. for Medical Sci. (Italy) 1989; Hon. Citizen, Alert Bay, B.C. 1990; Address: 4755 Belmont Ave., Vancouver, B.C. V6T 1A8.

**COPP, John Terry,** M.A.; educator; b. Ottawa, Ont. 28 Sept. 1938; s. Oswald Meredith and Constance Helen (Wilson) C.; e. West Hill High Sch.; Sir George Williams Coll. B.A. 1959; McGill Univ. M.A. 1962; m. Linda d. Leo and Elizabeth Risacher 19 March 1969; children: Monica and Reuel Dechene (step-children), Robin Finlay; PROF. OF HIST. WILFRID LAURIER UNIV. 1981– , Chrmn. of Hist. 1982– , Co-Dir., Laurier Ctr. for Military Strategic and Disarmament Studies; lectr. Un. Coll. 1961–62, Loyola Coll. and McGill Univ. 1963–70, Sir George Williams and Concordia 1970–75; Visiting Prof. Univ. of Victoria 1971–72, Univ. of Ottawa 1972–73; instr. Labour Coll. Can. 1966–77; joined present Univ. 1975; co-recipient C.P. Stacey Book Award 1990, 1992; author 'The Anatomy of Poverty: The Condition of the Working Class in Montreal 1897–1929' 1974; 'The Brigade: The Fifth Canadian Infantry Brigade 1939–45' 1992; co-author 'Maple Leaf Route' 5 vols. 1982–88; 'Battle Exhaustion: Soldiers and Psychiatrists in the Canadian Army 1939–1945' 1990; ed. 'Canadian Military History'; numerous articles and pub. lectures Candn. social, labour and mil. hist.; recreations: stickball, walking; Office: Waterloo, Ont. N2L 3C5.

**COPPER, Paul,** M.Sc., Ph.D., D.I.C.; professor; b. Surabaya, Indonesia 6 May 1940; s. Willem Johannes and Wilhelmina (Dekan) C.; e. Univ. of Sask. B.Sc. 1961, M.Sc. 1962; Imp. Coll. of Sci. & Technol. London, Eng. Ph.D., D.I.C. 1965; div.; children: Pia Camilla, Lucina Pilar; PROF. OF GEOL. LAURENTIAN UNIV. 1975– ; Postdoctoral Fellow, Queen's Univ. 1965–67; Asst. Prof. present Univ. 1967, Assoc. Prof. 1970; mem. NSERC Grant Cttees. Earth Sci's 1985–88, Solid Earth Sci's 1990–91; Sec. Candn. Geol. Found. 1984–90; recipient Exhn. of 1851 Scholarship 1962–65; Thomas Huxley Gold Medal for Rsch. 1969; author numerous sci. publs.; assoc. ed. Candn. Jour. Earth Sci's 1990– ; and other profl. jours.; mem. Geol. Assn. Can.; Geol. Soc. Am.; Palaeontol. Assn. UK; Palaentol. Soc. USA; Soc. for Reef Study USA; Home: 617 Lakepoint Court, Sudbury, Ont. P3E 4S8; Office: Sudbury, Ont. P3E 2C6.

**COPPS, Sheila Maureen,** P.C., M.P., B.A.; politician; b. Hamilton, Ont. 27 Nov. 1952; d. Victor Kennedy and Geraldine Florence (Guthro) C.; e. Univ. of W. Ont. B.A. (Hons. Engl. and French); Univ. de Rouen, France 1973; McMaster Univ. 1977; one d. Danelle Lauran; DEPUTY PRIME MINISTER and ENVIRONMENT MINISTER, GOVERNMENT OF CANADA 1993– ; Depy. Leader Liberal Party; Journalist, Ottawa Citizen 1974–76; Hamilton Spectator 1977 (pt-time 1972–74); Constituency Asst. to Leader, Lib. Party Ont. (Stuart Smith) 1977–81; M.P.P. for Hamilton Centre 1981–84; sought leadership of Ont. Liberal Party 1982 (placed 2nd); Federal Liberal Leadership Candidate, 1990; R. Catholic; Liberal; Dir. Citizen Action Group; recreations: tennis, racquetball, skiing, antiques; Office: Rm. 509-5, Centre Block, House of Commons, Ottawa, Ont. K1A 0A6.

**CORBEIL, Hon. Jean,** P.C.; politician; Minister of Transport 1991–93; el. H. of C. (Anjou-Rivière-des-Prairies) g.e. 1988; sworn to the Privy Council 1989; Min. of Labour 1989–91 and Min. of State (Transport) 1990–91; P.C.; Address: 7013 Giraud, Anjou, Qué.

**CORBER, Stephen Joel,** B.Sc., M.D., D.P.H., F.R.C.P.(C); b. Montreal, Que. 18 Nov. 1944; s. Jack and Sophie (Schwartz) C.; e. McGill Univ. B.Sc. 1965, M.D. 1969; Univ. of Liverpool D.P.H. 1974; div.; children: Samantha Kym, Amanda Yarin; MED. OFFR. OF HEALTH REGIONAL MUN. OF OTTAWA-CARLETON 1980– ; Med. Offr. Peru, Moosonee (Can.), Papua, New Guinea 1970–73; Dep. Med. Offr. of Health present Mun. 1975–80; Clin. Assoc. Prof. of Med. Univ. of Ottawa; Honorary Scientific Ed., Canadian Journal of Public Health; Home: 8 Wynford Ave., Nepean, Ont. K2G 3Z3; Office: 495 Richmond Rd., Ottawa, Ont. K2A 4A4.

**CORBETT, The Hon. Marie,** B.A., LL.B., Q.C.; judge; lawyer; b. Avondale, Nfld. 14 July 1943; d. Michael and Anne (Hennessey) C.; e. McGill Univ. B.A. 1964; Univ. of Toronto LL.B. 1968; Law Soc. of Upper Can. Bar Admission Course 1970; cr. Q.C. 1983; m. C. Alexander s. Arthur and Miriam Squires 18 June 1977; children: Darrell Corbett, Edward Arthur; JUSTICE, ONT. COURT OF JUSTICE 1990– ; Judge, District Court of Ontario 1986–90; with Legal Dept., City of Toronto 1970–72; priv. practice 1972–74; mem. Ont. Municipal Bd. 1974–77; Counsel, Roy. Comn. on the Status of Pensions 1977–80; priv. practice (pension law) 1980– ; Lectr. Humber Coll. 1973; Basic Zoning Course, City of Toronto 1983–84; mem. Ont. Status of Women Counc. 1973–74; Pres. Candn. Envir. Law Assn. 1973–74; Exec. Sec., Ont. Legal Aid Task Force 1974; Hearing Offr., Hearing Panel on Indus. Waste Mgmt. 1981–83; mem. Extve., Ont. Reg. Counc., Candn. Pension Conf. 1982–84; Pension Comn. of Ont. 1982–85 (Vice Chrmn. 1985–86); Chrmn. Envir. Assessment Advy. Ctte. 1983–86; Cocoleria Umbrella 1984–86; Lectr., Bar Admission Course 1987; Chrmn., Judges' Annuities Ctte., Candn. Judges' Conf. and Ont. Superior Court Judges Assn. 1991–93; Hon. Solicitor, The Prov. Counc. of Women; Dir., Empire Club of Can.; mem. Candn. Bar Assn. (Vice Chrmn., Pensions and Benefits Section); Women's Law Assn.; County of York Law Assn.; Women of Distinction Special Award, YWCA 1993; obtained printing of stamp of first woman judge, Helen Kinnear 1993; author: 'Regulation of Private Pensions' 1983; contrib.: 'Environment on Trial' 1974; 'Pensions Today and Tomorrow' 1984; several journal articles; recreations: golf, skiing; Clubs: Albany (Toronto); Osler Bluff Ski; Cedarhurst Golf; Office: Court House, 361 University Ave., Toronto, Ont. M5G 1T3.

**CORBETT, William Allan,** B.Com., LL.B., Q.C.; solicitor; b. Ontario, Canada 21 July 1931; s. Edward E. and Leona L. (Nicholson) C.; e. Ridley College 1949; Univ. of Toronto B.Com. 1953; Osgoode Hall Law School LL.B. (Hons.) 1957; 1st m. 1955 (wife dec. 1985); 2nd m. Jacqueline d. Aubrey Davies 15 Jan. 1988; children: David, Susan, Catherine; CHAIRMAN & PARTNER, FRASER & BEATTY; Associated with Fraser & Beatty since 1953; Q.C. 1971; Dir., Varity Corp.; Polysar Rubber Corp.; Candn. Reinsur. Co.; Candn. Reassurance Co.; New Providence Devel. Co. Limited (Chrmn.); The Lyford Cay Co. Limited; Minolta Canada; Former Chair & Bd. Dir., Lloyd's Bank Canada; Former Dir., The Dellcrest Children's Centre; The Children's Aid Soc. Found. Duke of Edinburgh Awards; Mem., Law Soc. of Upper Canada; Candn. Bar Assn.; recreations: golf, tennis; clubs: Badminton & Racquet; Toronto Golf; The Club at Pelican Bay; University Club; The Lyford Cay Club; Home: 55 Harbour Square, Apt. 2311, Toronto, Ont. M5J 2L1; Office: Box 100, 1 First Canadian Place, Toronto, Ont. M5X 1B2.

**CORBIN, Hon. J. Eymard Georges,** senator; politician; b. Grand Falls, N.B. 2 Aug. 1934; s. late Georges J. and Mariane (Bard) C.; e. Coll. of Bathurst, Bathurst, N.B.; St. Louis Coll., Edmundston, N.B.; Séminaire des Eudistes, Charlesbourg, Que.; m. Yvette Michaud, Drummond, N.B.; three d. Sylvie, Louise, Isabelle; Depy. Chrmn. Senate Sub-ctte. on Security and National Defence 1991– ; Sch. Teacher, Grand Falls 1958–59; Journalist, 'The Cataract,' Grand Falls 1959–60; Information Offr., Dept. of Youth, N.B. 1961–62; Asst. Dir. 1963–64; Journalist, 'L'Evangéline,' Moncton 1962–63; Broadcaster, (NABET) CBC, CBZ Fredericton and CBD Saint John 1964–66; Dir. of Information, Prov. Comte. for Centennial of Confederation (N.B.) 1966–67; Ed., 'Le Madawaska,' Edmundston 1967–68; el. to H. of C. in g.e. 1968; re-el. 1972, 1974, 1979, 1980 for the riding of Madawaska-Victoria; summoned to the Senate 1984; Parlty. Secy. to Min. of Fisheries and Forestry 1970, Min. of Environment 1971–72; Chrmn., Nat. Lib. Caucus 1974–75; Atlantic Provs. Lib. Caucus 1975–76; Asst. Depy. Chrmn. of Committees 1982; Depy.

Speaker, House of Commons 1984; Chrmn., Senate Liberal Caucus 1988–92; Comndr., Ordre National du Lion du Sénégal; Comndr., Ordre de la Pléïade; Liberal; The Senate of Canada, Ottawa, Ont. K1A 0A4.

**CORBO, Claude,** M.A., Ph.D.; university rector; b. Montréal, Qué. 3 Oct. 1945; s. Nicola Léopold and Mignonne (Côté) C.; e. Coll. Jean de Brébeuf B.A. 1964; Univ. de Montréal M.A. 1967, Ph.D. 1973; m. Louise d. André and Jeannette Joubert 26 July 1969; two s. Martin, Vincent; RECTOR, UNIV. DU QUÉ Â MONTRÉAL 1986– ; Prof. of Pol. Sci. present Univ. 1969, Chrmn. 1972, Vice Dean Social Sci's 1972–74, Registrar 1974–78, Dean of Faculty 1978–79, Vice Rector (without portfolio) 1979–81, Vice Rector Acad. 1981–86; Co-Chair Nat. Univs. Week 1989; Pres. Comité consultatif internat. Biodôme de Montréal 1989–92; mem. Corporate Higher Edn. Forum 1989; mem. Bd.: Coll. de Rosemont 1982–86; Coll. Jean de Brébeuf 1981–92; Cinémathèque Québécoise 1990– ; Fondation de l'UQAM 1979– ; Comité de parrainage, Forum pour l'emploi 1988– ; Théâtre du Nouveau-Monde 1992– ; Saidye Bronfman Centre 1993– ; auteur: 'Mon appartenance: Essais sur la condition québécoise' 1992; named 'Great Montrealer of Tomorrow in Education' 1983; recipient Cert. of Merit Internat. Council Candn. Studies 1990; Ordre Nat. du Mérite France 1991; Mérite et reconnaissance, Conseil Québécois pour l'enfance et la jeunesse 1991; Médaille de l'Université de Montréal 1992; awarded Prix Richard-Arès 1992; Club: St-Denis; Home: 19 Terrasse les Hautvilliers, Outremont, Qué. H2V 4P1; Office: CP 8888 Succ. A, Montréal, Qué. H3C 3P8.

**CORCORAN, Terence Dollard,** B.J.; journalist/editor; b. Montreal, Que. 6 Nov. 1942; s. John Dollard and Doris Mae (Robinson) C.; e. Father Macdonald H.S. (Hons.) 1960; Carleton Univ., B.J. 1969; BUSINESS COLUMNIST, THE GLOBE AND MAIL, 1989– ; Banking Trainee/Asst. Acct., Bank of N.S. 1960–65; Reporter, The Toronto Star 1969; Ottawa Journal 1970–71; Reporter/Bus. Ed, The Canadian Press 1972–74; Bus. Writer, The Gazette (Montreal) 1974–76; Fin. Ed. 1976–78; travel in Asia 1978–79; Assoc. Ed., Fin. Times of Can. 1978–80; Mng. Ed. 1980–82; Extve. Ed. 1983–84; Editor 1984–87; Assoc. Editor, The Financial Post 1987–89; Nat. Bus. Writing Award for Excellence in Editorial Writing 1983; for Business Reporting and Writing 1976; co-author: 'Public Money, Private Greed' 1984; Home: 8 Humber Trail, Toronto, Ont. M6S 4B9; Office: 444 Front St. W., Toronto, Ont. M5V 2S9.

**CORĊORAN, William John,** B.A., LL.B.; investment dealer; b. Toronto, Ont. 2 Apl. 1933; s. John Andrew and Aphra-Mary (Clark) C.; e. Univ. of Toronto Schs. 1951; Univ. of Toronto, Trinity Coll. B.A. 1954, LL.B. 1957; m. Mary Gertrude, d. Dr. Ray Lawson, Montreal, Que. 11 Sept. 1964; children: Heather Mary, William Terence, Michael Andrew, Martha Evans; Mng. Dir., ScotiaMcLeod Inc. 1978; Dir., Debenture & Securities Corp. of Can.; Dominion & Anglo Investment Corp. Ltd.; Candn. & Foreign Securities Co. Ltd.; Algoma Central Corp.; Ont. Pension Bd.; joined Underwriting Dept. Dominion Securities Corp. 1957; Partner, Jackman Relyea Associates 1959; Asst. to Mr. E.P. Taylor, Argus Corp. 1961; joined Algonquin Building Credits 1963, Pres. 1965; Liberal; United Church; recreations: golf, tennis; Clubs: York; Badminton & Racquet; National Club; Home: P.O. Box 241, Kleinburg, Ont. L0J 1C0.

**CORDELL, Alfred Henry,** F.C.A.; business executive; b. Montréal, Qué. 25 Aug. 1928; s. Benjamin Henry and Jeanetta (Dair) C.; e. Riverside Elem. and Comm. High Schs. Montréal; McGill Univ. C.A. 1951; m. Mary d. John and Estelle Maloney 16 Aug. 1952; children: Bruce Alfred, Robert John, Diane Mary, Joanne Patricia; Exec. Vice-Pres., 3M Canada Inc. 1988–92, Dir. 1974–92; Dir. Riker Canada Inc. 1981– ; joined McDonald, Currie & Co. Montréal 1945–59; Asst. Comptroller present Co. London, Ont. 1959, Corporate Comptroller 1965, Chief Financial Offr. 1969, Vice Pres. Mktg. & Pub. Affairs 1976; mem. Royal Comn. Pensions Ont. 1977–81; Dir. St. Joseph's Hosp. London 1983–86; mem. Pub. Relations Ctte. Candn. Inst. C.A.'s 1982–84, Pub. Affairs Ctte. 1984–87; mem. Financial Execs. Inst. Can. (Dir. 1974–81; Chrmn. Pensions Study Ctte. 1974–76; Pres. S.W. Ont. Chapter 1980–81); recreation: golf; Clubs: London Hunt & Country; University (Toronto); Home: 26 Woodgate Place, London, Ont. N6K 4A4.

**COREN, Stanley,** Ph.D.; university professor, psychologist, author; b. Philadelphia, Pa. 14 June 1942; s. Benjamin and Chesna (Gart) C.; e. Univ. of Pennsylvania A.B. 1964; Stanford Univ. Ph.D. 1968; m. E. Joan d. Jean and Oliver Shaw 26 Aug. 1990; children: Benjamin, Rebecca; PROFESSOR OF PSYCHOLOGY, UNIV. OF B.C. 1978– ; Asst. Prof., Grad. Fac., The New School for Social Rsch., New York 1968–73; Assoc. Prof., present univ. 1973–78; researcher specializing in human perception (esp. vision) and neuropsych. (esp. processes assoc. with left-handedness); has served on edit. bds. of 'J. of Experimental Psych.: Human Perception & Performance,' 'Can. J. of Psych.,' 'J. of Experiemental Psych.: General'; NSERC & MRC grants; Killam Sr. Rsch. Fellow; Fellow, Am. Psych. Assn.; Candn. Psych. Assn.; Am. Soc. of Optometry; Am. Psych. Soc.; Jewish; Mem., Psychonomic Soc.; Soc. for Behav. Med.; Sigma Xi; Nat. Assn. of Scholars; author: 'The Lefthander Syndrome: Causes and Consequences of Lefthandedness' 1992; co-author: 'Seeing is Deceiving,' 'Lateral Preferences and Human Behaviour' 1981, 'Sensation and Perception' 4th. ed. 1993; editor: 'Left-handedness' 1990; recreations: dog obedience competition; club: Vancouver Dog Obedience Training Club; Home: 3597 Quebec St., Vancouver, B.C. V5V 3K3; Office: 2136 West Mall, Vancouver, B.C. V6T 1Z4.

**CORIATY, Msgr. George M.,** C.M., L.Th., B.S., Ph.D.; b. Avaré, Saô Paolo, Brazil 1 Jan. 1933; s. Michel A. and Marie J. (Nassif) C.; e. Avaré, Brazil 1940; Frères Maristes Lebanon 1943; Séminaire St-Sauveur Lebanon L.Th. l956; Columbia Pacific University Ph.D. (Social Psychol. & Pol. Science) 1981; RECTOR, ST-SAUVEUR CATHEDRAL 1964– ; Vicar Gen. and Chancellor Melkite's Eparchy in Can.; o. Lebanon 1956; Asst. Pastor O.L. of Annunciation Boston 1957–60; Asst. Pastor St-Sauveur Ch. Montreal 1960–64; elevated Msgr. 1965; nominated Apostolic Visitor to Melkites in Can. 1972, Patriarchal Vicar l973; Decorated Member Order of Canada l982; Commemorative Medal, 125th Anniversary of Candn. Confedn. 1992; Founder-Pres. Middle E. Immigrant Aid Soc. Can. 1963; Founder-Co-Pres. 'Amitiés-Que.-Proche-Orient' 1964; Founder-Pres. 'Centre Communautaire-Bois-de-Boulogne' 1972; Founder Vancouver Mission of St-George 1974; Founder St. Ann's Mission Que. (now St. John Chrysostomos Mission, Que.) 1968; Founder O.L. of Assumption Mission Toronto (now St. Joseph Melkite Church Mission) 1966; Ad Hoc Ctte. for establ. an Immigration Ministry in Que.; Founder First Byzantine Museum in N. Am.; named First Citizen of Montreal 1973; Ed.-Founder 'Trait d'Union' Review 1964; Adv. Mem., University Scholarships of Can. 1987; mem. Musée des Beaux-Arts Montréal; Chambre de Comm. Montréal; Candn. and Am. Cath. Hist. Assns.; Am. & Candn. Mang. Assn.; Candn. Ethnic Studies Assoc. (CESA); Candn. Sociol. and Anthrop. Assoc.; Intnl. Pol. Science Assn.; Learned Societies; Candn. Canon Law Soc. 1987; Lebanese Candn. Soc.; Alumni Assoc., Columbia Pacific Univ.; Hon. Life Mem., Internat. Tennis Hall of Fame; Cmdr. of the Military and Hospitaller Order of St-Lazarus of Jerusalem; Nat. Center of Oecumenism; Assn. of the Refugees; Candn. Counc. of Multiculturalism (1973–80) and other organs.; awarded Hon. Ph.D. in Byzantine Studies, Internat. Univ. Foundation 1985; Order of Merit First Class, Egypt 1986; Mem., Society for the Law of the Eastern Churches, Ottawa 1989; Address: P.O. Box 578, Stn. C, Montreal, Que. H2L 4K4.

**CORK, Edwin Kendall,** B.Com.; executive; b. Toronto, Ont.; s. Stuart Fraser and Ella (Kendall) C.; e. Univ. of Toronto Schs.; Univ. of Toronto Victoria Coll. B.Com. 1954; m. Eve d. Sir William & Lady Slater 31 Dec. 1960; children: Sarah, John, Peter, Mary; MANAGING DIRECTOR, SENTINEL ASSOCIATES LTD., BUSINESS AND FINANCIAL CONSULTANTS; Chrmn., E-L Financial Corp. Ltd.; Dir., The Bank of Nova Scotia; United Corp.; Strongco; Univ. of Toronto Press; Gilbert Jackson & Associates 1954–59; Noranda Inc. 1959–88; Christian Science; Club: National; Address: 165 University Ave., Suite 200, Toronto, Ont. M5H 3B9.

**CORKERY, James Caldwell,** B.A.Sc., M.A.Sc.; Candn. public servant; b. East Orange, N.J. 23 June 1925; s. Kirk James and Helen May (Caldwell) C.; e. Univ. of Toronto B.A.Sc. 1948, M.A.Sc. 1950; m. Jane d. William and Margaret Woodruff 19 Sept. 1953; children: Kirk, Candace; BD. CHRMN., ROYAL CANADIAN MINT 1986– ; Plant Mgr. Candn. General Electric 1957, Mgr. Mfg. 1968–70; Regional Gen. Mgr. Can. Post 1970, Depy. Postmaster Gen. 1977, Chief Operating Offr. Can. Post Corp. 1981–82; Pres. & Master, Royal Candn. Mint 1982–86; Past Pres., Gold Inst.; Past Chrmn., Ottawa Children's Treatment Centre; Past Chrmn., Oakville-Trafalgar Hosp.; Pres., Oakville Rotary 1967; Anglican; Home: 109 Mornington St., Stratford, Ont. N5A 5G2; Office: 320 Sussex Dr., Ottawa, Ont. K1A 0G8.

**CORLETT, Michael Stuart George,** B.A.Sc.; communications executive; b. Toronto, Ont. 18 June 1942; s. George Edward and Marjorie Elizabeth (Wood) C.; e. Univ. of Waterloo, B.A.Sc. 1966; children: Stephanie, Brett; GROUP VICE-PRES. MARKETING & DEVELOPMENT, STENTOR RESOURCE CENTRE INC. 1993– , GROUP VICE-PRES., BUSINESS SALES & SERVICES, BELL CANADA 1990– ; and VICE-PRES. (BELL INFO. SYSTEMS) BELL CANADA 1987– ; Sr. Vice Pres. (Nat. Systems Group) Telecom Canada 1984– ; Plant Asst. Bell Canada St. Catharines, Ont. 1966, served various staff and managerial positions St. Catharines, Niagara Falls, Fort Erie, Toronto and Barrie; apptd. Staff Supr. Mgmt. Devel. Toronto 1971, Gen. Supr. Special Assignment acting as Asst. to Vice Pres. Operations Ont. Region 1973, Div. Repair Mgr. Toronto 1975, Asst. Vice Pres. Corporate Performance – Operations, Montréal 1976, Asst. Vice Pres. Computer Communication Systems Ottawa 1978, Gen. Mgr. Computer Communications, West 1981, Gen. Mgr. Nat. Systems 1983, Vice Pres. Nat. Systems 1984; recreation: sports; Clubs: Mississauga Golf & Country; Founders' Club; Home: 293 Rambler Court, Oakville, Ont. L6H 3A6; Office: 18F, 160 Elgin St., Ottawa, Ont. K1G 3J4.

**CORLETT, Murray Alan;** bank executive; b. Toronto, Ont. 8 June 1939; s. Murray Alexander and Doris Wanda (King) C.; e. Univ. of Toronto 1961; Johnson Grad. School of Mngt., Cornell Univ. 1978; m. Katherine Robb Aug. 1978; EXTVE. VICE-PRESIDENT, CREDIT RISK MGMT., ROYAL BANK OF CANADA 1993– ; joined Royal Bank 1961; Dir., Compensation & Employee Relations 1975; Asst. Gen. Mgr., National Accounts 1981; Vice-Pres., Midwest USA, Chicago 1982; Vice-Pres., International Div. 1984; Sr. Vice-Pres., Lending International 1988; Sr. Vice-Pres., Lending Canada 1992– ; Fellow, Inst. of Canadian Bankers; Dir., Candn. Opera Company; Office: Royal Bank Plaza, Toronto, Ont. M5J 2J5.

**CORLEY, Nora Teresa,** B.L.S., M.A.; librarian; freelance writer; bibliographer; b. Montreal, Que.; d. John Kevin and Anna Sigridur (Magnusdottir) C.; e. Trafalgar Sch. for Girls Montreal 1946; McGill Univ. B.A. 1951, B.L.S. 1952, M.A. 1961; m. John Taylor s. Rev. John M. and Annie E. Murchison 17 March 1972; Publications Officer, Assoc. of Candn. Map Libraries 1987; Asst. Lib. Law Lib. McGill Univ. 1952–54; Secy., Quebec Library Assn. 1958–59; Bulletin Editor 1963–64; Pres., Montreal Chapter, Special Libraries Assn 1964–65, Chrmn. Geog. and Map Div. S.L.A. 1969–70; Lib.-in-Charge Arctic Inst. of N. Am. Montreal 1954–72; Agency Lib. Candn. Internat. Devel. 1975; Fellow, Arctic Inst. of N. Am.; author 'Polar and Cold Regions Library Resources' 1975; 'Travel in Canada: A Guide to Information Sources' 1983; 'Resources for Native Peoples Studies' 1984; various articles and reviews prof. journs.; ed. 'The Arctic Circular' 1976–83; former mem., Candn. Lib. Assn. (Vice Chrmn. Res. Sec. 1964–65); mem., Assn. Candn. Map Libs. and Archives; Indexing and Abstracting Soc. Can.; Bibliog. Soc. Can.; co-founder Northern Libs. Colloquy; Club: University Women's (Ottawa); Address: 185 Kamloops Ave., Ottawa, Ont. K1V 7E1.

**CORMACK, J.M.,** Ph.D.; executive; b. Rossburn, Man. 14 Nov. 1934; s. John W. and Jessie M. (Nickel) C.; e. Univ. Man., B.S.A.; Univ. Nebraska, M.Sc.; Iowa State Univ., Ph.D.; m. Catherine, d. George and Beatrice Crookshank 1962; children: Ronald, Kenneth, Neil, David; PRES. & CHIEF EXEC. OFFR., AGRO COMPANY OF CANADA LTD. 1988– ; Dir. XCAN Grain Ltd. 1977–87; Western Co-operative Fertilizers Ltd. 1978–87; CSP Foods Ltd. 1978–87; Prince Rupert Grain Ltd. 1982–87; Pacific Elevators Ltd. 1978–87; Man. Inst. Mgmt. Inc.; Western Grain Elevator Assn. 1978–87; Asst. Prof. Agricultural Econ., Univ. Nebraska 1964; Sr. Economist, Man. Econ. Consultative Bd. 1967; Asst. Deputy Minister, Man. Dept. Agric. 1967; Deputy Min. 1968; joined Manitoba Pool Elevators as Asst. Gen. Mgr., Admin. 1973; Gen. Mgr., Operations 1976, Gen. Mgr. 1978, C.E.O., 1984–87; mem., Agricultural Inst. Can.; Candn. Agricultural Economics Soc.; recreations: skiing; outdoor activities; Office: 450 Bridge St., Montreal, Que. H3K 2C6.

**CORMACK, Robert George Hall,** M.A., Ph.D., F.R.S.C.; botanist; b. Cedar Rapids, Iowa 2 Feb. 1904; s. Robert Walker and Jane Leith (Beveridge) C.; e. Peterborough (Ont.) Coll. Inst. 1925; Univ. of Toronto B.A. (Univ. Coll.) 1929, M.A. 1931, Ph.D. 1934; m. Margaret Evelyn d. late Samuel Archibald Dickson, Edmonton, Alta. 5 Sept. 1939; two s. Robert Douglas Dickson, David Stewart Sifton; PROF. EMERITUS OF BOTANY, UNIV. OF ALTA. 1969– ; Class Asst. Univ. of

Toronto 1929–36; Lectr. to Prof. of Bot. Univ. Alta. 1936–69; Consultant to Alta. Forestry Dept. (Ecol. & Conserv. Studies E. Slopes Rockies) 1944–69; Consultant, MacKenzie River Gas Pipe Line Project (Ecol. Studies) 1970–71; served with Edmonton Fusiliers (R) 1940–45; rec'd Candn. citizenship 1951; author 'Wild Flowers of Alberta' 1967; 2nd printing 1977; 'Wild Flowers-Banff, Jasper, Kootenay, Yoho National Parks' 1972; numerous scient. papers and popular articles plant anat. and plant ecol.; internat. authority on devel. root hairs; Life mem. Candn. Inst. Forestry; Sigma Chi; P. Conservative; Protestant; Home: #1501, 10140 – 120 St., Edmonton, Alta. T5K 1Z8.

**CORMIE, Donald Mercer,** Q.C., B.A., LL.M.; b. Edmonton, Alta. 24 July 1922; s. George Mills and Mildred (Mercer) C.; e. Pub. and High Schs., Edmonton, Alta.; Univ. of Alta., B.A. 1944, LL.B. 1945; Harvard Univ., LL.M. 1946; m. Eivor Elisabeth, d. Einar Ekstrom, 8 June 1946; children: John Mills, Donald Robert, James Mercer, Neil Brian, Bruce George, Robert Ekstrom, Allison Barbara, Eivor Emilie; Sr. Partner, Cormie, Kennedy, Barristers 1954–87; Pres. and Dir., Collective Securities Ltd.; Sea Investors Corp. (U.S.A.); Cormie Ranch Ltd.; studied law with S. Bruce Smith; former Chief Justice of Alta.; called to Bar of Alta. 1947; cr. Q.C. 1964; Partner, Smith, Clement, Parlee & Whitaker, Edmonton, Alta. 1947–53; estbd. Cormie, Kennedy 1954; Sessional Instr., Faculty of Law and Instr., Real Estate Law, Dept. of Extension, Univ. of Alta. 1949–53; served in Merchant Marine 1943–44; mem. Candn. Bar Assn. (mem. Council 1961–81; Chrmn., Adm. Law Sec. 1963–65; Vice-Pres., Alta. 1968–69); Chrmn., Research Comm., Foundation for Legal Research; Young Presidents' Organ. Inc. (Alta. Chrmn. 1966–67; N. Pacific Area Vice-Pres. 1969–71); World Business Counc.; Chief Executives Organization Inc.; Dir., Banff Sch. Advanced Mang. 1968–71; Citadel Theatre 1968–70; Founding mem., Business Adv. Counc., Univ. of Alta. 1979–88; Founding mem., Dean's Counc. of 100, Arizona State Univ. 1983– ; Dir., The Counc. for Business & the Arts in Canada 1986–88; author of 'The Power of the Courts to Review Administrative Decisions' 1945; 'Treaty Making by Canada' 1946; 'The Nature and Necessity of Administrative Law' 1960; 'Administrative Problems of Government – Alberta' 1964; 'The Administrative Agency in 1965' 1965; United Church; recreations: hunting, sailing; Clubs: The Edmonton; Home: 5101 N. Casa Blanca, #314, Scottsdale, AZ 85253; Office: 216–21, 10405 Jasper Ave., Edmonton, Alta. T5J 3S2.

**CORMIER, Alyre H.,** C.D., B.Com., F.C.A.; management consultant; b. Memramcook (Cormier's Cove), N.B. 27 Sept. 1923; s. Damien A. and Alva Marie (Landry) C.; e. St. Joseph's Univ., B.Com. 1945; m. Andréa, d. Léon and Ida Doucet, 29 June 1953; children: Jacqueline, Michelle; MANAGEMENT CONSULTANT; Pres., Greater Moncton PROBUS Club; Secy., The Moncton Region Counc. of Churches; former Dir.: Resurgo Inc. (Moncton Downtown Revitalization Corp.); Moncton Industrial Development Ltd.; Atlantic Prov. Chamber of Commerce; former Vice-Chrmn., Atlantic Development Council (DREE); N.B. Enterprise Development Bd.; Past Pres.: Adv. Bd., R.C. Archdiocese of Moncton; Greater Moncton Chamber of Commerce; N.B. Inst. C.A.s; former mem.: District 15 Bd. Sch. Trustees; Income Tax Auditor, Revenue Canada (St. John District Office) 1945, Supervising Auditor 1953; Vice-Pres. & Comptroller, Rioux Group of Companies (Fredericton) 1963; Pres., Acadia Printing Ltd. and Publisher of former French daily 'L'Evangéline' 1967; Extve. Vice-Pres., Atlantic Holdings Ltd. 1971; Prof., Faculty Business Admin., Univ. Moncton 1975–88 (6 yrs. as Extve. Dir. of affiliated Memramcook Inst.); served Candn. Naval Reserve, retiring as Lieut.-Commander 1963; rec'd. Candn. forces decoration (C.D.) 1961; admitted mem. N.B. Inst. of C.A. 1967; el. Fellow 1987; recreations: golf; reading; Clubs: Beauséjour Curling; Moncton Garrison Officers' Mess; Address: 18 Franklyn Ave., Moncton, N.B. E1C 3L1.

**CORMIER, Bernard R.;** federal public servant; b. Moncton, N.B. 14 Sept. 1939; s. Denis A. and the late Ella M. (Landry) C.; e. Moncton schools, Coll. l'Assomption (Moncton), Univ. of Moncton; m. Stella d. Théodore and Mélanie Boudreau 28 March 1959; children: Daniel, Pierre, Monique, Marc; DEPUTY CHAIRMAN, VETERANS APPEAL BOARD (CHARLOTTETOWN) 1991– ; Officer / Aircrew Trainee, RCAF 1959; Journalist, 'The Moncton Times – Transcript' 1960–64; Public Relations, CN (Montreal) 1964–65; Air Canada (Montreal) 1965–72; Assistant Director, Public Relations, Govt. of Canada 1972–74; Deputy Dir. 1974–76; Dir. 1976–78, 1978–82; Director General 1982–87; Mem., Veterans Appeal Bd. 1987; Mem., Branch No. 1 Royal Canadian Legion; Roman Catholic; Past Mem., Moncton Press Club, The Montreal Press Club & National Press Club (Ottawa); recreations: golf, gardening, wine making, repair and assembling golf clubs; club: Rustico Golf & Country; Home: P.O. Box 2676, Charlottetown, P.E.I. C1A 8C3; Office: P.O. Box 7700, Charlottetown, P.E.I. C1A 8M9.

**CORMIER, Jean Guy;** business executive; b. Campbellton, N.B. 3 May 1941; s. Simon and Leona (Arsenault) C.; e. Bathurst Coll. B.A. 1963; McMaster Univ. 1963–64; m. Helen d. Fred and Agnes Morrison 9 Sept. 1965; children: Paul, Michel; PRES., CORMIER COMMUNICATORS INC. 1986– ; Dir., Public Affairs, Dofasco 1970–75; Vice-Pres., Public Rlns., CN 1975–79; Pres., CN Hotels & Tower 1979–81; Sr. Vice Pres., Corp. Affairs, B.C. Resources Investment Corp. 1981–86; Past Chrmn., Internat. Assn. of Bus. Communicators; accredited mem., Candn. Public Rlns. Soc.; Past Pres., The Canadian Club of Vancouver; author of numerous speeches & articles; recreation: photography; Home: 2167 McMullen Ave., Vancouver, B.C. V6L 3B3; Office: Ste. 910, 1050 West Pender St., Vancouver, B.C. V6E 2N7.

**CORN, Harvey Allan,** B.A., LL.B., B.F.A.; commissioner; b. Montreal, Que. 11 July 1932; s. Jack and Fanny (Schachter) C.; e. McGill Univ. B.A. 1953; Univ. of Montreal LL.L. 1956; Concordia Univ. B.F.A. 1984; m. Shirley d. William and Toby Moigher 20 April 1958; children: Wendy, Thomas; COMMISSIONER, CANDN. PENSION COMMISSION 1993– ; Partner, Watson Poitevin, Notaries 1965–93; Past Mem., Order of Notaries, Prov. of Que. 1957–93; Mem., L'Association D.E.A. Inc. (Dominion Extves. Assn.; Past Pres.); Past Dir., United Talmud Torahs of Montreal; Dir., Caldwell Residences; Canadian Film Development Corp. (Telefilm Canada) 1985–93 (Chair 1990–93); Home: 799 Upper Belmont, Westmount, Que. H3Y 1K5; Office: 630 René Lévesque W., Suite 2300, Montreal, Que. H3B 4T8.

**CORNEIL, Ernest Ray,** B.Sc., Ph.D., P.Eng.; educator; b. Niagara Falls, N.Y. 11 Nov. 1932; s. Ernest Ruckle and Olive Stewart (Shea) C.; e. Stamford Coll. Inst. Niagara Falls, Ont. 1951; Queen's Univ. B.Sc. 1955; Imp. Coll. Univ. of London, Ph.D. 1960; m. Betty d. Cecil and Mary Garnett 29 Sept. 1956; children: Ronald, Jo-Anne, Thomas, Douglas; PROFESSOR EMERITUS; Prof. of Mech. Eng. Queen's Univ. 1970–92, retiring Aug. 1992; joined present Univ. 1958, Head of Mech. Eng. 1978–81, Dir. Computing Centre 1963–64; full-time Cons. to Bus. Products Div. Xerox Corp. Rochester, N.Y. 1967–68; Dir. Candn. Rly. Electrification Project 1975–76; Electric Locomotive Specification Project 1982–83; Candn. Inst. Guided Ground Transp. 1975–81; cons. various firms; Ford Found. Ind. Residency 1967; mem. Assn. Profl. Engs. Prov. Ont. (Pres. 1987–88); Sons of Martha Medal 1974; ASME; ASHRAE; Home: 934 Old Front Rd., Kingston, Ont. K7M 4M1; Office: Kingston, Ont. K7L 3N6.

**CORNELISSEN, Michael Adriaan,** C.A.(S.A.), M.B.A.; financial executive; b. Durban, S. Africa 1 June 1943; s. Marinus and Koos (Van der Hoeven) C.; e. Univ. of Natal, C.A. 1965; Univ. of Capetown, M.B.A. 1970; children: 2 sons; Dir., Hees International Corp.; Audit Sup., Touche Ross and Co. 1961–69; Dir. and Vice-Pres. Fin., Rennies Consolidated Holdings Ltd. 1971–75; Vice-Pres. Edper Investments Ltd. 1976; Exec. Vice-Pres. and C.O.O. Trizec Corp. Ltd. 1977–83; Pres., C.E.O. & Dir., Royal Trustco Ltd. 1983–92; Chrmn. United Way of Greater Toronto 1984; Chrmn. Financial Div., Oakville Hosp. Funding Campaign 1986; Gen. Campaign Chrmn., Nat. Ballet Sch. of Can.; Chrmn., Bd. of Dirs., Canada's Challenge for the America's Cup; Mem. Bd. of Govs., Appleby College, Oakville; Mem. Bd. of Dirs., Toronto Symphony; Conservative; Protestant; recreations: yachting, tennis, skiing; Clubs: The Toronto; Royal Candn. Yacht; Royal Vancouver Yacht; Office: Suite 1130, 505 Burrard St., Vancouver, B.C. V7X 1R5.

**CORNELIUS, Gordon Alvin;** executive; b. Dufferin Co., Ont. 23 July 1928; s. late Alvin William and Evelyn Mary (Hillis) C.; e. high sch. Orangeville, Ont.; Univ. of W. Ont. Mgmt. Training Course 1963; Harvard Univ. Advanced Mgmt. Prog. 1977; m. Charlotte M. Sutton; CHAIRMAN, INGRAM & BELL INC. 1993– ; Dir., Venture Inns Inc.; joined present Co., 1948, Sales Rep. Victoria 1952–59, Br. Mgr. Vancouver 1964, Vice Pres. Vancouver Br. 1964–65, Vice Pres. Operations Toronto 1965–73, Vice Pres. and Gen. Mgr. I&B Div. 1973–77, Exec. Vice Pres. and Gen. Mgr. I&B Div. 1977; Pres. 1978–93; Pres. & Chrmn. of the Bd. 1986; Chrmn. of the Bd. 1993; recreation: golf; Club: Thornhill Country; Home: 23 Rainbow Creekway, Willowdale, Ont. M2K 2T9; Office: 20 Bond Ave., Don Mills, Ont. M3B 1L9.

**CORNELL, Kevin Scott;** computer software executive; b. Sarnia, Ont. 27 Sept. 1951; s. William Robert and Florence Joyce (Smith) C.; e. Ryerson Polytech. Inst. Dip. in Bus. 1974; m. Brenda d. Roy and Dorothy Parkes 7 Aug. 1971; children: Amanda Brooke, Erin, Jessica; held various sr. sales & mgmt. positions Candn. computer ind. 1974–85; Br. Mgr. Mfg. Speiry Canada 1985–86; Dir. of Mktg. Data General Canada Inc. 1986–88; Pres. Encore Computer Canada Inc. 1988–90; Vice Pres., Oracle Corp. Canada Inc. 1990–92; Home: 2214 Haygate Cres., Mississauga, Ont. L5K 1L5.

**CORNELL, Paul Grant,** E.D., M.A., Ph.D., F.R.H.S.; educator; b. Toronto, Ont. 13 Sept. 1918; s. Beaumont Sandfield and Margaret Grant (Wilson) C.; e. Lower Can. Coll., Montreal; Brampton (Ont.) High Sch.; Univ. of Toronto, B.A., M.A., Ph.D. (Hist.); m. Christina Mary, d. late John Jerome Suckling, Margate, Eng., 6 Dec. 1941; children: John Grant, Virginia Susan, Benjamin William, Jennifer Margaret; Prof. of Hist., Univ. of Waterloo 1960–85; Chrmn. Dept. of History there 1960–68; Dean, Faculty of Arts 1970–73; Acting Vice Pres. (Acad.) 1972; Hon. Archivist 1977–85; Lectr.-Prof., Dept. of Hist. Acadia Univ., 1949–60; served with N.P.A.M. Peel & Dufferin Regt. 1932–36, Lorne Scots 1936–40; Candn. Army (Active) 1940–46; C.O.T.C. Univ. of Toronto 1947–50 and Acadia Univ. 1953–56; author 'The Alignment of Political Groups in the Province of Canada' 1962; 'The Great Coalition' 1967 (repr. 1971); co-author: 'Canada: Unity in Diversity' 1967 (French transl. 1969); other writings incl. various articles in hist. journs.; Fellow, Royal Hist. Soc.; mem., Candn. Hist. Assn. (Ed. 'Report' 1953–56); Ont. Hist. Soc. (Pres. 1973–74; co-ed. 'Ontario History' 1963–78; awarded Cruickshank Medal 1978); Anglican Lay Reader; Home: 202 Laurier Place, Waterloo, Ont. N2L 1K8.

**CORNELL, Peter McCaul,** C.D., M.A., Ph.D.; economic executive; b. Fort William, Ont. 28 Nov. 1926; s. Maurice Leo and Jeanette Ethel (McCoy) C.; e. Royal Candn. Naval Coll., 1st class cert. 1945; Queen's Univ., B.A. (Hons.) 1951, M.A. 1952; Harvard Univ. Ph.D. 1956; m. Kathryn d. Jeremiah and Helena Griffin 7 Sept. 1949 (dec. 1984); children: Allison, Ellen, Peter G.; m. Judith Fagan d. Lawrence and Alline Fagan 14 Sept. 1991; step-children: Andrew, Kathryn (both Slater); Dir., Economic Council of Canada 1981–86; Royal Candn. Navy & Reserve 1943–47; Active List 1947–68; commanded various patrol craft, ships and shore establishments; Commander in Supplementary Reserve 1968– ; Rsch. Dept., Bank of Canada 1956–66; loaned to Fed. Dept. of Fin. 1964–65; Bank of Eng. Cent. Banking Course 1963; var. posns. incl. Dir., Econ. Counc. of Canada 1966–86; Teaching Fellowships, Queen's Univ. & Royal Mil. Coll. 1951–52; Harvard Univ. 1953–56; Sess. Lectr., Carleton Univ. 1958; mem., Candn. Econ. Assn.; Bd. mem., Ottawa-Carleton Counc. on Aging; recreations: skiing, fishing, golfing, swimming; Home: 20 Cherrywood Dr., Nepean, Ont. K2H 6G7.

**CORNELL, Susan Elizabeth,** B.A.; communications industry executive; b. London, Ont. 3 April 1948; d. Ward MacLaurin and Audrey Viola (Banninga) C.; e. Univ. de Grenoble, dipl. du 1er degré 1968; Univ. of West. Ont. B.A. 1971; Toronto Teacher's Coll., primary spec. cert. 1971–72; VICE PRES., REGULATORY, CORP. & NATIVE AFFAIRS, CANDN. SATELLITE COMMUNICATIONS INC. 1988– ; Primary Specialist, Toronto Bd. of Edn. 1972–74; Special Asst. to Min. of the Environment, Govt. of Can. 1974–75; to Min. of Communications 1975–79; Dir. of Communications, Candn. Cable TV Assn. 1979–80; of Public Affairs 1980–81; Vice-Pres., Public Affairs 1981–86; Vice Pres., Regulatory & Corp. Affairs present company 1986–88; Trustee, Children's Hosp. of Eastern Ont. 1984–91 (1st Vice Chair 1989–91); Founding Chair, 'Children on the Hill,' 1st day-car ctr. in fed. govt. bldg. (House of Commons) 1981; Home: 705 – 1081 Ambleside Dr., Ottawa, Ont. K2B 8C8; Office: Ste. 1000, 50 Burnhamthorpe Rd. W., Mississauga, Ont. L5B 3C2.

**CORNELL, Ward MacLaurin;** b. 1924; e. Pickering Coll. Ont.; Univ. of W. Ont.; m. Georgina Saxon; 5 children; retired; commenced as Lectr. in Eng. and Hist., Pickering Coll. 1949; Gen. Mgr. Broadcast Div. (Radio), Free Press Printing Co. 1954; Pres., Ward Cornell Ltd., Creative Projects in Communication 1967–72; a Free Lance Broadcaster of numerous T.V. and Radio programmes 1946–72; Visiting Lect. Conestoga Coll. 1968–72; Agent Gen. for Prov. Ont. in U.K. 1972–78; Gen. Mgr.-European Operations, Lenroc Internat. Ltd. since Sept. 1978–80; Ont. Dep. Provincial Secy. for Social

Dev., 1980; Deputy Min., Ont. Min. of Citizenship & Culture, 1980–82; Depy. Min., Ont. Min. of Municipal Affairs & Housing 1982–85; Depy. Min., Ont. Min. of Housing 1985–88; Home: R.R. 1, Uxbridge, Ont. L9P 1R1.

**CORNHILL, David Wallace,** B.Sc., M.B.A.; gas industry executive; b. Chatham, Ont. 16 Aug. 1953; s. John Frederick and Jean (Wallace) C.; e. Univ. of Western Ont. B.Sc. (Hons.) 1977, M.B.A. 1980; m. Megan L. d. Douglas and Nola Welliver 21 May 1983; one s.: Andrew; VICE-PRESIDENT, FINANCE & ADMINISTRATION, ALBERTA & SOUTHERN GAS CO. LTD. 1991– ; final position Sr. Advisor Financial Analysis, Gulf Canada 1980–87; Manager, Financial Analysis & Tax Planning, Alberta Natural Gas 1987–88; Manager Finance 1989–91; recreations: golf, tennis, gardening; clubs: Calgary Professional, Priddis Greens Golf & Country; Office: 2900, 240 – 4th Ave. S.W., Calgary, Alta. T2P 4L7.

**CORNWALL, John Lally,** B.A., M.Sc., Ph.D., FRSC; university professor; b. Spencer, Iowa 27 April 1928; s. Russell Morgan and Inez Clare (Lally) C.; e. H.S. (Iowa) 1946; Iowa Univ. B.A. 1950; London Sch. of Econ. M.Sc. 1952; Harvard Univ. Ph.D. 1958; m. Wendy d. Percy and Florence Gubbs 7 Nov. 1986; MCCULLOCH PROF. OF ECON., DALHOUSIE UNIV. 1988– ; Asst., Assoc. & Full Prof., Tufts Univ. 1958–70; Prof., Southern Illinois Univ. 1970–76; Dalhousie Univ. 1976–93; Fulbright Lectr., Copenhagen Sch. of Econ. 1966–67; Ford Found. Fac. Rsch. Fellowship; SSHRC Fellowship; Fulbright Fellowship; Fellow, Royal Soc. of Canada; Mem., Am. Econ. Assn.; Royal Econ. Soc.; Assn. for Evolutionary Econ.; author: 'Growth and Stability in a Mature Economy' 1972, 'Modern Capitalism' 1977, 'The Conditions for Economic Recovery' 1983, 'The Theory of Economic Breakdown' 1990, 'Economic Breakdown and Recovery' 1993; co-author: 'Economic Recovery for Canada' 1984; editor: 'After Stagflation' 1984, 'The Capitalist Economies' 1991; recreations: gardening, music; clubs: Rhododendrum Soc. of Canada; Home: 479 Purcells Cove Rd., Halifax, N.S. B3P 2P1; Office: Halifax, N.S. B3H 3J5.

**CORNWELL, L. Robin,** B.A., M.B.A.; investment banker; b. New Westminster, B.C. 13 Apl. 1946; s. John and Lilian C.; e. Lawrence Park Coll. Inst. Toronto 1965; York Univ. B.A. 1969, M.B.A. 1972; m.; 3 children; SR. PARTNER, GORDON CAPITAL CORP. 1984– ; Chrmn., Cornwell Gallery of Fine Art Ltd.; Financial Analyst, Bank & Trust Co., Analyst, Harris & Partners Ltd. 1972–74; Bank of Nova Scotia 1974–75; Pitfield, MacKay, Ross Ltd. 1975–80; Founding Partner and Dir. of Rsch. McCarthy Securities Ltd. 1980–84; Chief Adv. to Standing Ctte. on Finance, Trade & Econ. Affairs, H. of C. 1982 (Report on Bank Profits) and 1983 (Status Foreign Bank Subsidiaries in Can.); Past Chrmn. Centennial Nursery Sch. for Multi-Handicapped; Office: (P.O. Box 67) Ste. 5300, Toronto Dominion Centre, Toronto, Ont. M5K 1E7.

**CORRIGAN, Harold,** B.Comm., C.A.; consultant; b. Montreal, Que., 3 March 1927; s. Harold Willard and Dorothy M. (Cauldwell) C.; e. Westmount (Que.) High Sch.; McGill Univ., B.Com. 1950; Lic. in Acct. 1953; C.A. 1956; Centre D'Etudes Industrielles (Geneva, Switzerland) Dipl. 1959; m. Eve, d. William James Howard Ellwood, 14 June 1952; two d., Susan, Ann; with Alcan Aluminium Ltd. 1950–85; Chrmn. & Dir., Continental Bank of Can.; Dir., Sears Canada Inc.; Hewlett-Packard (Canada) Ltd.; Fuji Bank Canada; MICC Investments Ltd.; Mortgage Insurance Co. of Can.; Global Election Systems Inc.; Canadian Overseas Packaging Industries Limited; Pres. & Dir., CRM Canadian Recycled Materials Corp.; served with RCNVR 1945; Pres., Candn. Mfrs. Assn. 1975–76; Chrmn., Internat. Bus. Counc. of Can. 1986–88; mem. Inst. C.A.'s Que.; Anglican; Clubs: Badminton & Racquet; Mount Royal; Toronto; University (N.Y. City; Montreal); Home: 185 Forest Hill Rd., Toronto, Ont. M5P 2N3.

**CORRINGHAM, Robert Eric Thomas,** M.B.,B.S.; physician; b. Isleworth, Eng. 25 Feb. 1949; s. Eric Thomas and Eleanor Frances (Miles) C.; e. Mayfield Coll. Sussex, Eng. 1967; Royal Free Hosp. Sch. of Med. Univ. of London M.B.,B.S. 1973; m. Suzan d. Reginald and Ivy Sollis 19 Apr. 1975; two s. Thomas William, Richard John Edward; Vice Pres., Ont. Cancer and Rsch. Foundation; C.E.O., Northeastern Ont. Regional Cancer Centre; Assoc. Prof. (Med.), Univ. of Ottawa 1990–93; Rsch. Fellow and Sr. Registrar (Oncology) Royal Free Hosp. London, Eng. 1978–83, Sr. Registrar (Haematol.) 1983–84; mem. Active Staff (Med.) Princess Margaret Hosp. Toronto, Asst. Prof. of Med. Univ. of Toronto 1984–85; Dir., Northeastern Ont. Oncology Prog., Ont. Cancer Treatment & Rsch. Found. 1985– ; recipient Charlotte Brown Prize for Postgrad. Clin. Rsch. Royal Free Hosp. Sch. of Med. 1984.

**CORRIVEAU, André;** administrateur; né Tracy, Qué. 23 mai 1947; f. Joseph Faïda et Alberta (Cournoyer) C.; é. Coll. Martel; École des Hautes Études Commerciales D.S.A. 1975; ép. Rachel f. Donald Dubé 20 septembre 1946; enfant: Annie; DIRECTEUR GÉNÉRAL, CAISSE POPULAIRE RIVIERA 1974– ; Administrateur (Dir. et Sec.) Fédération des Caisses Populaire Desjardins de Richelieu Yamaska 1984–93; Dir. Credit Industriel Desjardins 1986–89; Trustco Desjardins 1989; 2e Vice-Pres. du Conseil et Membre de l'Exécutif, Société de Portefeuille du Groupe Desjardins Ass. Générales 1989– ; La Sécurité Compagnie d'Assurance Générale du Can. 1989– ; Assurances Générales des Caisses Desjardins Inc. 1989– ; Norgroupe Assurances Générales 1990; Prés. Centre d'Action Bénévole du Bas-Richelieu Inc.; Vice-Prés. C.A. Hotel-Dieu de Sorel; Prés., Fond. Hotel-Dieu de Sorel; mem. Chambre de Comm. Sorel Tracy Métropolitain; Corp. de Développement Économique Sorel Tracy; Assn. des Directeurs Généraux des Caisses Populaires du Québec; Club: Golf les Dunes; Bureau: 3175 boul. de la Mairie, Tracy, Qué. J3R 5M7.

**CORTER, Carl Mark,** B.A., Ph.D.; university professor; b. Lock Haven, Penn. 11 Dec. 1945; s. Harold Maxwell and Helen Elizabeth (Rickard) C.; e. Needham Broughton H.S. 1963; Davidson Coll. (N.C.) B.A. 1967; Univ. of N.C. at Chapel Hill Ph.D. 1971; m. Jan d. Patricia and Alfred Pelletier 16 April 1987; children: David, Arden (Corter), Jason, Ryan, Randall (Stiefel); CHAIR, INSTITUTE OF CHILD STUDY, UNIV. OF TORONTO 1989– ; Asst. Prof., Psych., Univ. of Toronto 1971–76; Assoc. Prof. 1976–83; Assoc. Chair 1981–85; Prof. of Psych., Erindale Coll. 1983– ; Prof. of Education, Fac. of Edn. 1989– ; Day Care Liaison Offr. 1974–78; Academic Bd. 1988–89; Dir., Laidlaw Ctr. 1992–93; Visiting Scholar, Stanford Univ. 1978–79; rsch., teaching & policy interests concern infants & young children in the context of families & the educational system; Rsch. Cons., Psychiatry, Hosp. for Sick Children 1980–86; Psychology 1975–80; Adv. Bd. Mem., Candn. Mothercraft Soc.; Clarke Institute of Psychiatry; Earlscourt Treatment Ctr.; Ryerson Univ. Dept. of Early Childhood Edn.; Mem., Am. Psych. Assn.; Candn. Psych. Assn.; Sigma Xi; co-editor: 'What Makes Exemplary Kindergarten Programs Effective' 1993, 'Manual Specialization and the Developing Brain' 1983; recreations: basketball, camping, fishing, gardening, tennis; Home: 350 Queen St. S., Streetsville, Ont. L5M 1M2; Office: 45 Walmer Rd., Toronto, Ont. M5R 2X2.

**CORY, Hon. Peter de C.,** B.A.; judge; b. Windsor, Ont. 25 Oct. 1925; s. Andrew and Mildred (Beresford Howe) C.; e. Univ. of W. Ont. B.A. 1947; Osgoode Hall grad. 1950; m. Edith, d. Claude Nash 14 September 1949; children: Christopher, Andrew, Robert; SUPREME COURT OF CANADA since 1989; Supreme Court of Ont., Trial Div., Dec. 1974–..; apptd. to Ont. Court of Appeal 1981; apptd. Supreme Court of Canada, 1 Feb. 1989; called to the Bar of Ont. 1950; cr. Q.C. 1963; served as Pilot, R.C.A.F. 6 Bomber Group 1944–48; Bencher, Law Soc. of Upper Canada 1971–74; Past Pres. Advocates Soc., York Co. Law Assn.; Past mem. Council, Candn. Bar Assn.; recreations: squash, fly fishing, skeet shooting; Club: University; Office: Supreme Court of Canada, Wellington St., Ottawa, Ont. K1A 0J1.

**COSENTINO, Frank,** B.A., B.P.E., M.A., Ph.D.; educator; b. Hamilton, Ont. 22 May 1937; s. Vincenzo and Maria Annunziata (Sisinni) C.; e. Cath. High Sch. Hamilton 1956; Univ. of W. Ont. B.A. (Hons.) 1960; Ont. Coll. Edn. summers 1962–63; McMaster Univ. B.P.E. 1967; Univ. of Alta. M.A. 1969, Ph.D. 1973; m. Sheila Ann d. Charles and Gertrude McHugh 15 Aug. 1959; children: Anthony, Mary, Teresa, Peter; PROF. OF PHYS. EDN. AND ATHLETICS YORK UNIV. 1976– ; joined Sales, Canadian Pittsburgh Inc. 1960–63; Teacher Cath. High Sch. Hamilton 1963–66; Head Football Coach Univ. of W. Ont. 1970–74 (Coach Vanier Cup Champions 1971, 1974), Asst. Prof. of Phys. Edn. 1970–75, Assoc. Prof. and Chrmn. of Dept. 1975; Chrmn., Dir. and Prof. of Phys. Edn. & Athletics York Univ. 1976–81, Head Football Coach 1978–80, 1984–87; Quarterback, Hamilton Tiger Cats 1960–66, Edmonton Eskimos 1967–68, Toronto Argonauts 1969; mem. Grey Cup Teams 1961–65; Capt. Univ. W. Ont. Mustangs 1959; writer film strip 'An Audio Visual History of Canadian Sport' 1982; author 'Canadian Football: The Grey Cup Years' 1969; 'Ned Hanlan' 1978; 'Not Bad, Eh!' prose and poetry Candn. sport 1990; 'The Renfrew Millionaires: The Valley Boys of Winter 1910' 1990; co-author 'A History of Physical Education in Canada' 1971; 'Olympic Gold'; 'Lionel Conacher' 1981; 'Winter Gold' 1987; 'A History of Physical Education' 1987; 'A Concise History of Sport in Canada' 1989; R. Catholic; recreations: squash, tennis, travel; Home: 80 Nipigon Ave., Willowdale, Ont. M2M 2W2; Office: 358 Stong College, 4700 Keele St., North York, Ont. M3J 1P3.

**COSGROVE, Hon. Paul,** LL.B.; b. Thunder Bay, Ont. 30 Dec. 1934; e. Agincourt Coll. Inst. Toronto; St. Michael's Coll. Univ. of Toronto B.A.; Queen's Univ. LL.B.; m. Frances; children: Conal, Mark, Darin, Cara; JUDGE, ONT. COURT OF JUSTICE (GEN. DIV.) 1990– ; formerly Min. of Public Works, Min. Responsible for Central Mortgage & Housing Corp. and Nat. Capital Comn.; Mayor of Scarborough and Mem., Metropolitan Toronto Counc. 1973–78; el. M.P. for York-Scarborough g.e. 1980; Min. of State (Finance) Can. 1982–83; apptd. Co-Chrmn. Special Commons and Senate Comte. on Reform of Senate 1983; cr. Q.C. 1983; County Judge, District Court of Ont. (Counties of Leeds and Grenville) 1984–90; Home: 138 James St. E., Brockville, Ont. K6V 1L2.

**COSMAN, Francene Jen,** R.N.; b. Windsor, Ont. 14 Jan. 1941; d. John Douglas and Dorothy Mae (Machel) McCarthy; e. Saint John (N.B.) Gen. Hosp. R.N. 1962; Margaret Hague Sch. Jersey City, N.J. postgrad adm. and teaching; m. David s. Arthur Cosman 25 July 1964; two d. Lara Machel, Andrea Leigh; Pres., Cricklewood Giftware Inc. 1987–90; former Pres., N.S. Advisory Council Status of Women 1982–86; nurse Saint John Gen. Hosp. 1963; Head Nurse Post-Partem Unit Grace Maternity Hosp. 1968; Chairperson Planning Ctte. Bedford (N.S.) Service Comm. 1975; Councillor Halifax Co. Counc. 1976–79; Mayor Town of Bedford 1979–82; mem. Regional Parks Ctte. 1976–78; Extve. Dir., NS Liberal Assoc. 1989–93; MLA, Bedford-Fall River 1993– ; Liberal Party Whip 1993– ; mem., Bedford Village Homeowners Assoc.; City Centre Ministry 1986–88; author various reports, briefs, articles; mem. N.S. Art Gall.; Inst. Pub. Adm. Can.; recreation: hiking, swimming, cross-country skiing; Home: 59 Bedford Hills Rd., Bedford, N.S. B4A 1J8.

**COSMAN, Leslie,** B.Sc.C.E., P.Eng.; engineer; b. Winnipeg, Man. 30 July 1930; s. Charles and Minnie (Hurtig) C.; e. Daniel McIntyre C.I. (Winnipeg, Man.) Sr. Matric. 1948; Univ. of Manitoba B.Sc. Civil Engrg. 1952; m. Hazel d. Frank and Fanny Hardin 10 Oct. 1954; children: Frank Aaron, Dr. Mitchell Abraham, Dr. David Lawrence, Dr. Marvin Samuel, Dr. Ernie; CHIEF EXEC. OFFR., GENSTAR DEVELOPMENT CO. (A DIV. OF IMASCO ENTERPRISES INC.) 1984– ; with Underwood McLellan & Assoc. Ltd. 1952–61; Resident Engr. constrn. of R.C.A.F. Stn., Cold Lake 1952–57; Asst. Mgr. and Chief Engr., Calgary 1957–61; Mgr. DelRay Engrg. Ltd. Calgary 1961–73; Vice-Pres. Keith Constrn. Co. Ltd. Calgary 1973–79; Pres. Genstar Devel. Co. (Western Div.) Calgary 1979–84; mem. Assn. of Profl. Engrs., Geologists & Geophysicists of Alta.; Candn. Soc. for Civil Engrg.; recreations: downhill skiing, bicycling; Home: 4314 Staulo Cres., Vancouver, B.C. V6N 3S2; Office: #560 – 200 Granville St., Vancouver, B.C. V6C 1S4.

**COSMAN, Robert Douglas,** B.A., LL.B.; lawyer, public servant; b. Saint John, N.B. 28 Aug. 1945; s. Colburn Elijah and Helen Loretta (Titus) C.; e. Belleisle Reg. H.S. 1959–63; Univ. of New Brunswick B.A. 1970, LL.B. 1974; m. Heather d. Thomas and Ruth Downes 22 Oct. 1966; children: Robert Bruce, Colburn Douglas; LEGISLATIVE COUNSEL AND LAW CLERK, SASKATCHEWAN LEGISLATIVE ASSEMBLY 1988– ; Legislative Counsel, N.B. Dept. of Justice 1974–77; Legis. Counsel & Law Clerk, Yukon Territorial Govt. 1977–79; Dir., Regulations Revision Project, N.B. Dept. of Justice 1979–82; Asst. Parly. Counsel, House of Commons 1982–87; Home: P.O. Box 854, Lumsden, Sask. S0G 3C0; Office: Room 225, Legislative Bldg., Regina, Sask. S4S 0B3.

**COSSETTE, André,** B.A., B.Phil., LL.L., M.S.R.C.; notaire-légiste aux Affaires législatives; né Causapscal, Qué. 26 février 1929; f. Philippe et Jeanne Marcelle (Douville) C.; é. Univ. Laval B.A. 1950, B.Phil. 1950, LL.L. 1953, Diplomé d'études supérieures en droit 1964; ép. Denise f. Émilien Rochette 29 août 1953; enfants: Denis, François, Andrée, Louis, Elise, Odile; CONSEILLER SPÉCIAL EN DROIT PRIVÉ AU MINISTÈRE DE LA JUSTICE DU QUÉBEC 1991; Notaire 1954–80; Chargé de cours à la Faculté de droit de l'Univ. Laval 1955–68; Vice-prés. Chambre des Notaires du Qué. 1969–72 et Prés. 1972–75; Vice-prés. de l'Union Internationale du Notariat Latin 1975 (Prés. de la Comn. des Thèmes et des Congrès); Vice-prés. de la Comn. de Coopération Notariale Internationale 1977–89; Membre du Comité de réforme du Code civil 1986 et coordonnateur des travaux de droit civil au même Ministère; Dir. de la Direction du Droit civil au Ministère de la Justice du Qué. 1981–91; Administrateur de La Caisse Populaire de Charlesbourg; Trophée Pierre Duquet 1989; publié au-delà d'une centaine de travaux d'ordre juridique dans diverses revues juridiques; Membre de l'Ordre Internat. des Anysetiers; Membre de la Société Royale du Canada; récréations: tennis, golf; Clubs: Royal Québec Golf; Tennis Montcalm; Adresse: 215, 75 rue est, Charlesbourg, Qué. G1H 1H4; Bureau: 1200, route de l'Eglise, Ste-Foy, Qué. G1V 4M1.

**COSSETTE, J.-Claude,** M.Ed., Ph.D.; businessman; educator; b. Québec City, Qué. 1 Dec. 1937; s. Armand and Simonne (Labrecque) C.; e. Petit Séminaire de Qué. classical studies 1958; L'Ecole des Beaux-Arts de Qué. Dipl. in Advertising Art 1962, M.Ed. 1963; Laval Univ. Cert. in Marketing 1962, Cert. in Business Adm. 1970, Ph.D. 1975; Ecole du Livre Estienne, Paris Cert. 1964; m. 1stly Claire Tremblay; children: François, Joëlle; m. 2ndly Suzanne d. Antonio Nadeau; children: Guillaume, Thierry, Anaïs; PROF. TITULAIRE 1983– , DIR. GROUPE DE RECHERCE SUR L'IMAGE FONCTIONNELLE, LAVAL UNIV. and HEAD, PROGRAMME DE COMMUNICATION GRAPHIQUE 1990– ; Pres. Nadeau-Cossette Inc.; founded Cossette & Dupuis, Graphiste Associés 1964; Cossette Associés, Graphistes Conseils Ltée 1966; Bureau d'Esthétique Appliquée de Qué. Inc. 1966; Founding Pres. and Partner, Cossette Communication Marketing 1970–82; Les Editions Riguil Internat. 1982; service Royal Candn. Ordnance Corps, rank Lt.; Lectr. on Semiological Approach of Picture Communication ten Calif. univs. and research centres 1978; Pedagogical Dir. series 26 TV programs on Advertising in Que. 1977; lectr. on advertising, communication through pictures many internat. confs., univs. and colls.; author 'Communication de Masse Consommation de Masse' 1974; 'La Comportementalité et la Segmentation des marchés' 1980; 'Les Images démaquillées' 1982; 'La Publicité en action' 1987; 'Comment faire sa publicité soi-même' 1988; 'La Créativité' 1990; 3 books of poetry; various papers, articles; recipient, Prix des Communications du Québec 1984; Gold Medal Award from Assoc. of Candn. Advertisers (ACA) 1988; mem. Société des Graphistes du Qué.; Inst. Internat. de la Communication (Founding Dir.); Assn. Internat. de Sémiotique; Internat. Communication Assn.; Candn. Assn. Applied Social Research; Candn. Communication Assn.; Assn. des Compagnons de Lure; recreations: travel, walking, reading, swimming, tennis, spiritual focusing; Office: Ecole des Arts visuels, Pavillon Casault #3422, Univ. Laval, Québec, Qué. G1K 7P4.

**COSSINS, Edwin Albert,** B.Sc., Ph.D., D.Sc., F.R.S.C.; educator; b. Romford, Essex, Eng. 28 Feb. 1937; s. Albert Joseph and Elizabeth H. (Brown) C.; e. Clark's Coll. Romford, Eng. 1953; S.E. Essex Tech. Coll. Eng. 1955; Chelsea Coll. Univ. of London B.Sc. 1958, Ph.D. (Plant Biochem.) 1961, D.Sc. 1981; m. Lucille Jeanette d. Dr. Reginald Wilson Salt, Lethbridge, Alta. 1 Sept. 1962; children: Diane Elizabeth, Carolyn Jane; PROF. OF BOTANY, UNIV. OF ALTA. 1969– ; Research Assoc. Purdue Univ. 1961–62; Asst. Prof. of Botany present Univ. 1962, Assoc. Prof. 1965, Acting Head of Botany 1965–66, Prof. 1969, Dir. Introductory Biol. Program 1974–77, McCalla Research Professor 1982–83, Assoc. Dean of Sci. 1983–88; Prof. Invité, Univ. de Geneve, Switzerland 1972–73; Chrmn. Grant Selection Comte. Cellular Biol. & Genetics, Nat. Research Council Can. 1976–77; mem. Adv. Panel Strategic Grants, Natural Sciences and Engn. Research Council Can. 1978–81; rec'd Centennial Medal 1967; co-author 'Plant Life in Anaerobic Environments' 1978; 'The Biochemistry of Plants, A Comprehensive Treatise' Vol. 2, 1980, Vol. 11, 1987; 'Folates and Pterins' Vol. I 1984; over 100 scient. publs. in nat. and internat. journs.; Assoc. Ed. 'Canadian Journal of Botany' 1969–78; Corr. Ed. 'Plant Biochemical Journal' 1974–81; Life mem. Royal Soc. Can. (Rapporteur, Plant Biol. Div. 1975–77); mem. Candn. Soc. Plant Physiols. (W. Dir. 1968–70, Secy. 1973–75, Vice Pres. 1975–76, Pres. 1976–77); Am. Soc. Plant Physiols.; Japanese Soc. Plant Physiols.; Anglican; recreations: golf, curling, cross-country skiing; Club: Derrick Golf and Winter; Faculty; Home: 99 Fairway Dr., Edmonton, Alta. T6J 2C2; Office: Edmonton, Alta. T6E 2E9.

**COSTELLO, Michael,** B.A., M.A.; public servant; b. Montreal, Que. 14 June 1950; e. Univ. of Manitoba B.A. (Hons.), M.A. 1973; DEPUTY MINISTER OF FINANCE AND CORPORATE RELATIONS, GOVT. OF B.C. 1991– ; Dep. Min. of Finance & Sec. of Treasury Board, Govt. of Saskatchewan 1983–85; Vice-Pres., Crown Investments Corp., Govt. of Sask. 1985–86; Asst. Dep. Min. of Finance, B.C. Prov. Treasury 1986–91; Office: Room 109, 617 Government Street, Victoria, B.C. V8V 1X4.

**COSTERTON, J. William,** M.A., Ph.D.; educator; b. Vernon, B.C. 21 July 1934; s. Leonard Fisher and Hilda (Watson) C.; e. Univ. of B.C. B.A. 1955, M.A. 1956; Univ. of W. Ont. Ph.D. 1960; m. Vivian I. d. Colin and Dorothy McClounie 28 June 1955; children: Diane, Sheila, Robert, Nancy; NSERC PROF. OF BIOFILM MICROBIOL. UNIV. OF CALGARY 1990– ; Pres. Microbios Ltd.; Dean of Sci. Baring Union Coll. India 1960–64; Postdoctoral Fellow Cambridge Univ. 1964–66; Asst. Prof. Macdonald Coll. McGill Univ. 1966–70; Assoc. Prof. of Microbiol. present Univ. 1970, Prof. 1974– , AOSTRA Rsch. Prof. 1986–89; corporate cons.; recipient Sir Frederick Haultain Prize Sci. 1984; Isaac Walton Killam Meml. Prize Sci. 1989; author or co-author over 650 sci. papers; mem. Am. Soc. Microbiol.; Candn. Soc. Microbiol.; Home: 3823 Brooklyn Cr. N.W., Calgary, Alta. T2L 1G9; Office: Calgary, Alta. T2N 1N4

**CÔTÉ, André C.,** B.A., LL.L., Ph.D.; university professor and administrator; b. Lévis, Qué. 6 May 1947; s. Raymond and Hortense (Gingras) C.; e. Coll. de Lévis, Laval Univ. B.A. 1966; Fac. of Law, Laval Univ. LL.L. 1969; admitted to Quebec Bar 1970; London Sch. of Econ. & Pol. Sci., Univ. of London Ph.D. 1974; divorced; children: Elise, Thomas-Louis, Marie-Noëlle; PROFESSOR OF LABOUR LAW, FAC. OF LAW, LAVAL UNIV. 1974– ; Assoc. Prof. 1980; Full Prof. 1986; Sec. of the Faculty 1978–80; Dean of the Faculty 1989–93, re-elected 1993–97; Mem., Bd. of Gov. (Rep. of the Deans) 1993–95; Vice-Pres., Conf. internat. des Fac. de droit ayant en common l'usage du français (AUPELF/UREF) 1991–95; Pres., Council of Quebec Law Deans 1992–94; Visiting Prof., Labour Law, Inst. du droit du travail et de la sécurité soc., Univ. Jean-Moulin (Lyon III) 1979, '88; Fac. of Law, Univ. de Bordeaux 1992; active labour arbitrator on an occasional basis 1974– ; Pres., Acad. Panel, SSHRC 1979–80; Mem., Courtney Ctte. 1988–89; Mem., Bd. of Trustees, Internat. Inst. for Peace & Security 1990–92; Jury Mem., Commonwealth Fellowships 1990–94; Mem., Quebec Bar 1970; Candn. Bar Assn.; Que. Assn. of Law Teachers; Candn. Assn. of Law Teachers; Internat. Soc. of Labour & Social Security; author of over 30 articles & research reports pub. in learned journals and acts of conferences at nat. & internat. level; recreations: golf, skiing, reading, music; Home: 2765, chemin Ste-Foy, apt. 402, Ste. Foy, Que. G1V 4S4; Office: Pavillon De Koninck, Cité universitaire, Ste. Foy, Que. G1K 7P4.

**CÔTE, Bernard G.,** B.Com., M.B.A.; company executive; b. Montreal, Que. 16 Aug. 1931; e. Loyola Coll. B.Com. 1954; Univ. Western Ont. M.B.A. 1956; m. Isabelle McCubbin; has two s., one d.; PRES., STANMONT INC. 1982– ; Dir., DMR Group Inc.; Korlin Plastics Ltd.; Cie d'Assnce. du Qué.; Roins Co. Ltd.; Royal Insurance; Western Insurance; National Theatre Sch.; SOGAM; Marie Selick & Associates; Office Assistance Inc.; Adia Canada Ltd.; with IBM as Marketing Rep., Data Processing Div. 1956, Marketing Mgr. 1964, Br. Mgr. 1966, Dist. Mgr. Eastern Region 1967, Vice Pres. 1969; joined Omega Investments Ltd. as Pres. 1972; joined Celanese Can. Inc., 1974, Pres., C.E.O. & Chrmn. to June 1979; PRES., B.G. Coté Consulting Ltd. to 1982; served as Lieut.; R.C.N.; Chrmn., l'Ecole de Technol. Supérieure l'Univ. Qué.; Pres., Candn. Council, Internat. Ch. of Comm.; Chrmn., Centraide Montreal (United Way); Vice Pres., Concordia Univ. Centre for Mgmt. Studies; Vice Pres., Canada World Youth; Dir., Juvenile Diabetes Research Fund; Hôpital Marie Enfant pour les Jeunes; mem., Sci. Council Can.; Candn. Econ. Policy Comte.; Conf. Bd. Can.; Chambre de Comm. Montreal (Pres. 1973); Montreal Bd. Trade; recreations: skiing, golf, tennis; Clubs: Saint James's; Mt. Royal; Mount-Bruno; Hermitage Golf & Country; Canadian (Montreal); Address: 2700 Rachel St. E., Montreal, Que. H2H 1S7.

**CÔTÉ, Ernest Adolphe,** M.B.E., B.Sc., LL.B.; retired diplomat; b. Edmonton, Alta., 12 June 1913; s. Cécile (Gagnon) and late Jean Léon C.; e. Jesuit Coll., Edmonton; Laval Univ., B.Sc.; Univ. of Alta., LL.B.; Imp. Defence Coll., 1949; m. Madeleine, d. late Charles Frémont, Quebec, Que., 16 June 1945; children: Michel, Benoît, Denyse, Lucie; read law with Simpson and Macleod, Edmonton, Alberta; called to Bar of Alta. 1939; with Dept. of External Affairs 1945–55; Asst. Depy. Min. N. Affairs and Nat. Resources 1955–63; Depy. Min. (became Dept. of Indian Affairs & N. Devel. Oct. 1966) 1963–68; Depy. Min., Dept. of Veterans' Affairs 1968; Depy. Solicitor-Gen. 1968–72; Ambassador to Finland 1972–75; served as Lieut., Royal 22nd Regt., and on staff 1939–45; discharged rank Col.; M.B.E.; Mentioned in Despatches; Dir., Hôpital de Montfort, Ottawa Hon. Mem. Candn. Friends of Finland; Roman Catholic; recreations: fishing; Home: 2 Allan Pl., Ottawa, Ont. K1S 3T1.

**CÔTÉ, The Hon. Mr. Justice Jean Édouard Léon,** B.A., LL.B., B.C.L.; justice; b. Edmonton, Alta. 14 Aug. 1940; s. Jean Gustave and Cecelia Mabel Moore (Taylor) C.; e. McGill Univ. B.A. (Hons.) 1961; Univ. of Alta. LL.B. 1964; Oxford Univ. B.C.L. 1966; m. Patricia d. Donald and Dorothy Draper 19 Dec. 1970; children: J. Roger Denis, Anne Louise Gabrielle; JUSTICE, COURT OF APPEAL OF ALBERTA and of COURT OF APPEAL FOR THE NORTHWEST TERRITORIES 1987– ; articled with W.H. Hurlburt, Q.C. 1966–67; Clerk to R. Martland J. (S.C.C.) 1967–68; called to Alta. Bar 1968; Q.C. 1984; employee, then partner, Reynolds Mirth & Côté (formerly Hurlburt Reynolds Stevenson & Agrios) 1968–87; Sess. Lectr., Fac. of Law, Univ. of Alta. 1966–71, 1987–88, 1991–93; Practitioner-in-res. 1986; Head of course, Alta. Bar Admission 1971–80; Former Mem., Law Soc. of Alta. (Library Ctte. 1976–87; Insur. Ctte. 1981–86); Alta. Assoc. Ed., 'Western Weekly Reports' 1973–87; Gold Medals, McGill Univ. & Univ. of Alta.; Viscount Bennett Scholar 1964–66; R. Catholic; author: 'An Introduction to the Law of Contract' 1974; various articles; co-author: 'Civil Procedure Guide' 1992; recreations: walking, Conan Doyle, reading, old movies; Club: Edmonton; Home: Edmonton, Alta.; Office: 1A Sir Winston Churchill Sq., Edmonton, Alta. T5J 0R2.

**CÔTÉ, Jean-Eudes,** M.S.C., C.G.A., C.M.A., M.B.A.; business executive; b. Jonquière, Que. 6 Dec. 1942; s. Bertrand and Ursule (Girard) C.; e. Laval Univ. M.S.C. 1966; C.G.A. 1967; C.M.A. 1968; Univ. of Sherbrooke M.B.A. 1978; m. Noella d. Gertrude Vaillancourt 13 Aug. 1966; PRESIDENT & CHIEF OPERATING OFFR., COMMUNICATION SERVICES GROUP and CHRMN., ZOOM INC.; Mngt. Trainee, ending as Sr./Fin. Analyst, Quebec Cartier Mining 1966–70; Contr./Gen. Mgr., Pacific Mobile Corp. 1970–76; Gen. Mgr., Trivico & Vice-Pres. Mktg. Holding Group, Sofidel 1978–80; Vice-Pres. & Gen. Mgr., Claude Neon 1980–86; Extve. Vice-Pres. (Ont., Que. & Maritimes), The Jim Pattison Sign Group 1986–87 and Pres. 1987–92; Pres., Montebello Packing, Hawkesbury, Ont. 1990; Trans Ad, Toronto, Ont. 1990; Assn. des Mfrs. d'Habit. et des Vehic. Récréatifs du Qué. 1973; Assn. des M.B.A. du Qué. 1981; recipient, Scholarship Jeunes Admin. 1976 (Que. govt.); Nat. Scholarship, C.G.A. 1976; Dir., Sign Assn. of Can.; lecturer; recreations: tennis, swimming, cycling; club: Granite; Home: 40 Grace Shantz, Kirkland, Que. H9J 3A5.

**CÔTÉ, Hon. Jean-Pierre,** P.C., O.C. (1965); retired politician; painter; b. Montréal, Qué. 9 Jan. 1926; s. Joseph Émile and Cédia (Roy) C.; e. Longueuil Coll. and Sch. of Dental Technol., Montréal, Qué.; m. Germaine, d. Charles Tremblay, Gaspé, Qué., 31 July 1948; has eight children; prior to entering politics in 1963 owned and operated a dental laboratory; Pres., Longueuil Sch. Bd., 1961–63; 1st el. to H. of C. for Longueuil, g.e. 1963 and re-el. 1965, 1968; apptd. Postmaster Gen. 18 Dec. 1965, Min. of Nat. Revenue 1968–70, returned as Postmaster Gen. 24 Sept. 1970; summoned to the Senate 1 Sept. 1972; Lieut. Gov. of Québec 1978–84; Pres. 1974–78, Liberal Party of Can. (Qué. Sec.); Candn. Rep. to I.L.O., Geneva, 1964; Home: 821 Des Colibris, Longueuil, Qué. J4G 2C2.

**CÔTÉ, Marc-Yvan;** né Sainte-Anne-des-Monts 27 mars 1947; f. Horace et Fabienne (Chenel) C.; é. U.Q.T.R. lic. en. sci. pol. et en hist.; il épouse Renée Laflamme 26 juil. 1975; enfants: Marc-Alexis, Louis-Antoine; Min. de la Santé et des services sociaux SOCIAUX (responsable de la condition des aînés, de l'Office des personnes handicapées et de la réforme électorale) 1989–93; Dép. de Matane 1973–76; Rech. à l'Assemblée nat. 1976–81; Dir. de cabinet du Whip de l'Opposition 1981–83; Élu dép. de Charlesbourg juin 1983; Leader adjoint de l'Oppos., Prés. de la Comm. d'anim. et d'org. du PLQ, Org. en chef de la campagne de M. Robert Bourassa en oct. 1983, dir. adj. de l'org. de la campagne électorale de 1985; Org. en chef pour l'Est du Québec lors de la campagne électorale de 1989; Min. des Transp., responsable du Développement régional, Gouv. du Qué. 1985–89.

**COTÉ, Michael,** B.A.; educator; b. Sarnia, Ont. 21 Apl. 1946; s. Homer Peter and Rita Mary (Dawson) C.; e. St. Patrick's High Sch. Sarnia; London Teachers' Coll. Teacher's Cert. 1965; Univ. of W. Ont. B.A. 1971, Prin's Cert. 1977; m. Elizabeth d. Malcolm and Agnes Plunkett 30 Dec. 1988; children: William Russell, Kimberly, Ernest, Shelley, Jeffrey, Jennifer; Pres., Ont. Eng.

Cath. Teachers Assn. 1990–92; taught elem. sch. Sarnia and Point Edward 10 yrs.; served as Prin. St. Joseph's, Corunna 8 yrs., St. Joseph's and St. Helen's, Sarnia 6 yrs. and 2 yrs. respectively; served 15 yrs. Exec. Lambton Unit of OECTA incl. 2 yrs. as Pres., Bd. Dirs./Council of Pres. OECTA 1979–92, served various cttes.; mem. Bd. Govs. Ont. Teachers Fedn. 1983–92; Charter mem. Cath. Prin's Council Ont.; R.Catholic; recreation: golf; Home: 37 Bushmills Sq., Scarborough, Ont. M1V 1K5; Office: 400, 65 St. Clair Ave. E., Toronto, Ont. M4T 2Y8.

**CÔTÉ, Pierre,** C.M.; exécutif; né Québec, 2 fév. 1926; f. feu Jules H. et d'Andrée (Fortier) C.; é. Académie de Québec; Ont. Agric. Coll.; enfants: Pierre, André; PRÉS. DU CONSEIL D'ADMINISTRATION, CELANESE CAN. INC.; Administrateur, CAE Industries Ltée.; Mutual Life Co. Assnce. du Canada; La Garantie Co. l'Amerique du Nord; Banque de Montréal; Canron Inc.; Bombardier Inc.; Tioxide Canada Inc.; mem. Conseil consultatif de la succursale de Québec, du Trust Royal du Canada; Prés., le Conseil du Patronat du Qué.; ex-Gouv., Bourse de Montréal; Ex-Prés., Chambre de Comm. de Qué.; La Soc. Candn. de la Croix-Rouge; Conseil Nat. de l'Industrie Laitière du Can.; Conseil de Planification et de Dével. du Qué.; L'Orchestre Symphonique de Qué.; récréations: golf, pêche, chasse; Clubs: Garnison; Golf du Lac Saint-Joseph; Mount Royal; Royal Quebec Golf; Golf Mont Bruno; Résidence: 1271 Place de Mérici, Québec, Qué. G1S 3H8.

**CÔTÉ, Pierre-F.,** Q.C., LL.B., M.S.S.; lawyer; provincial civil servant; b. Québec City, Qué. 16 July 1927; s. Georges and Géraldine (Blouin) C.; e. Coll. des Jésuites, Qué. B.A. 1952; Univ. Laval LL.B. 1956, M.S.S. 1958; m. Denyse d. C. Alfred and Gabrielle (Dion) Matte 29 Apr. 1961; one s. Claude; CHIEF ELECTORAL OFFICER, QUÉ. 1978– ; mandated by the Nat. Assembly to act as a consultant to the residents of Northern Qué. for a Referendum which took place 1 Oct. 1987; and to act as a cons. for the holding of an election on Apr. 10th 1989; Mem., Official Candn. Delegation to observe the Nov. 29th, 1987 elections in Haïti; Personal rep. of Secy. Gen. of OAS; Coordinator, Observation Mission, gen. elections, Haïti 1990; called to Bar of Qué. 1958; cr. Q.C. 1976; law practice 1958–60; Private Sec. Qué. Min. of Youth 1960; Legal Counsel Qué. Dept. of Hydraulic Resources 1960–61; Exec. Asst. Qué. Min. of Natural Resources 1961–65; Dir. Manpower Reclassification Service Qué. Dept. Labour 1965–67; Asst. Sec. and Legal Counsel Fédération des Caisses Populaires Desjardins 1967–69; City Clk. Québec, Chief Returning Offr. Mun. Els., Exec. Dir. and Chief of Protocol Mayor's Offic 1969–78; Chrmn. Standing Comn. on Reform Electoral Dists. 1978–79; mem. Comn. de la Représentation électorale 1979–83, Chrmn. 1983; Chrmn. Adv. Ctte. Electoral Legis. 1983; Vice Pres. Sports Internat. Found. (Qué.); mem. (1984), Vice Chair (1986), Steering Ctte. Council Govt'l Ethics Laws of U.S.; Recipient, Fifth Annual Cogel Award 1989; Chrmn., Cogel Internat. Fund 1991; Hon. Chrmn., 20th anniversary of Carrefour Tiers-monde & 1989 fund-raising drive; mem. Qué. Bar Assn.; Candn. Bar Assn.; Candn. El. Officials Assn.; Inst. Pub. Adm. Can.; Candn. Inst. Internat. Affairs; Finalist, Public Admin., Excellence Award, Qué. 1992; recreations: swimming, reading, music, photography, gourmet cooking; Club: Garrison; Home: 3334 Hertel St., Sainte-Foy, Qué. G1X 2J4; Office: 3460 de La Pérade St., Sainte-Foy, Qué. G1X 3Y5.

**CÔTÉ, Yvon,** CFA; insurance executive; b. Victoriaville, Que. 12 Jan. 1947; s. Robert and Jeanne (Berthiaume) C.; e. Laval Univ. Licence Sc.Admin.; Inst. of Chartered Financial Analysts CFA; m. Lise d. Georges Chamberland 23 Dec. 1972; one d.: Isabelle; VICE-PRESIDENT & GENERAL MANAGER, FINANCE AND INVESTMENTS, INDUSTRIAL-ALLIANCE LIFE INSURANCE CO. 1990– ; various executive positions in data processing, finance, investments, Industrial-Alliance Life Insurance Co. 1969–90; Bd. Mem., I.S.T. Group Inc. (major data processing co.); C. of C.; Bd. Mem., The National Life Assurance Co. of Canada; Chrmn. of the Bd., Genecan Financial Corp.; Office: 1080 St-Louis Rd., Sillery, Que. G1K 7M3.

**CÔTE-HARPER, Gisèle,** Q.C., B.A., LL.L., LL.M.; barrister, university professor; b. Quebec City 10 Dec. 1942; d. Lt. Col. Joseph-Léon, K.St-J., E.D., Q.C. and Louise (Hudon) C.; e. Laval Univ. B.A. 1962, LL.L. 1965; Harvard Law School LL.M. 1969; Bar of the Prov. of Que. 1966; Q.C. 1987; one d.: Claudia Harper; PROF. OF LAW, LAVAL UNIV. 1970–72, 1974– ; Prosecutor, Juvenile Court, Montreal 1966–68; Rsch. Dir., Royal Comn. of Inquiry into Poverty, Australia 1972–74; Que. Legal Aid Comn. 1975–85; Assoc. Dean, Law, Laval Univ. 1977–79; Que. Human Rights Comn. 1981–86; Expert, U.N. Human Rights Ctte. 1983–84; Comnr., R.C.M.P. Public Complaints Comn.; Founding Chairperson, Internat. Ctr. for Human Rights & Democratic Devel. Dir.; Inter-Am. Inst. of Human Rights, San José 1991– ; Expert for the Human Dimension Mechanism of the CSCE 1992– ; Candn. Inst. for Internat. Peace & Security 1987–90; La Soc. Radio-Qué 1987–90; Candn. Admin. of Justice; Candn. Civil Liberties Assn.; Cons., Law Reform Comn. of Can.; Teacher, Que. Bar Teaching Course; SSRHCC grants/awards 1987–88, 1980–81; In-Aid-of-Publication grants, F.C.A.C. 1982, '83, '85; Mem., Candn. Bar Assn.; Que. Bar Assn.; Candn. Law Teachers Assn.; co-rapporteur: 'International Cooperation for the Development of Human Rights and Democratic Institutions' (Govt. of Can. report) 1987; co-author: 'Principes de droit pénal général' 1981; 'Droit pénal canadien' 2nd ed. 1984, 3rd ed. 1989; co-editor: 'Righting the Balances, Canada's New-Equality Rights' 1986; recreations: golf, skiing, tennis, cinema, reading; Office: Quebec, Que. G1K 7P4.

**COTSMAN, Stephen Arnold,** B.A., M.B.A.; crown corporation executive; b. Vancouver, B.C. 21 Dec. 1948; s. Samuel and Judith Marion (Golden) C.; e. Univ. of B.C., B.A. 1970, M.B.A. 1972; m. Teresa d. Abel and Elaine Schwarzfeld 21 May 1972; three s. David, Adam, Simon; VICE PRES. FINANCE & ADMINISTRATION, CBC 1986– ; joined Dept. of Pub. Works Can. 1972–77, Sr. Analyst Dept. Indian Affairs & N. Devel. Can. 1977–80, Dep. Comptroller Financial Mgmt. 1980–83, Dir. Gen. Mgmt. Services 1983–84; Asst. Vice Pres., Treas. CBC 1984–86, Chrmn. Invest. Ctte. Pension Fund; Home: 34 Lynhurst Ave., Ottawa, Ont. K1V 9W7; Office: (P.O. Box 8478) Ottawa, Ont. K1G 3J5.

**COTT, Brian,** B.B.A.; value adding reseller, developer of communications hardware and software solutions; b. Toronto, Ont. 29 Sept. 1957; e. York Univ. B.B.A. 1979; m. Julia d. James and Sybil Murphy 17 Oct. 1986; children: Jordan, Madeleine; FOUNDER & PRES., CALL-PRO CANADA INC. 1988– ; Vice-Pres., Sales, Telecommunications Terminal Systems 1982–87; recreations: jogging, skiing, fishing; Home: 79 Cheritan Ave., Toronto, Ont. M4R 1S7; Office: 30 East Beaver Creek, Richmond Hill, Ont. L4B 1J2.

**COTTERILL, Benedict Gordon Ross;** retired executive; Wareham, Dorset, Eng. March 26, 1918; s. late Gordon Edward Ross and Mary Angela (Herbert) C.; m. Violet Lorraine d. late William H. Clark, 12 Jan. 1946; children: Stanley B. (B.A. Hon.), Paul C. (B.Sc., M.D.); Asst. to Export Mgr. Page-Hersey Tubes Ltd. 1938–43, Asst. Export Mgr. 1945–46; Export Mgr. and Secy. Sino-Canadian Development Co. 1946, Offr. Sinocan Forwarders Ltd.; Mgr. and Secy-Treas. Roy Peers Co. Ltd. 1946–52; Salesman, St. Regis Paper Co. (Canada) Ltd. 1952, W. Sales Mgr. 1953, Ont. Dist. Sales Mgr. 1957, Gen. Sales Mgr. 1962; Dir. of Marketing, Consolidated-Bathurst Packaging Ltd. Bag Division 1967; Vice-Pres. and Gen. Mgr. 1968; Vice Pres. Bag Div. and Corporate Offr. of Consolidated-Bathurst Inc. 1977–83; Dir., Sr. Vice-Pres. and Gen. Mgr., Bag Div., Consolidated-Bathurst Packaging Ltd.; served with RCAF during World War II, Pilot; Anglican; recreations: golf, fishing; Clubs: Empire (Toronto); Home: York Mills Place, 3900 Yonge St., Suite 912, Toronto, Ont. M4N 3N6.

**COTTON, Crosbie Wilson;** newspaper editor; b. Sherbrooke, Que. 29 Nov. 1950; s. Charles Edward and Violet (Crosbie) C.; e. Champlain Coll. DEC 1972; m. Monica d. James F. and Jean Cole 23 June 1984; children: James, Amy, Stephanie; MANAGING EDITOR, THE CALGARY HERALD 1990– ; Labor Reporter, Montreal Star 1975; Olympic Reporter, Calgary Herald 1980–88; Sports Columnist 1988; News Editor; work has appeared in more than 50 newspapers, mags. incl. 'Sports Illustrated'; Nat. Newspapers Award Citation 1988; Pres., Calgary Press Club 1986; Home: 1949 9th Ave., Calgary, Alta. T2N 4N3; Office: P.O. Box 2400, Stn. M., Calgary, Alta. T2P 0W8.

**COTTON, Roger,** B.Sc., M.A., LL.B., LL.M.; lawyer; b. Worchester, Mass. 24 Oct. 1944; e. Southwest Missouri State Univ. B.Sc. 1966; Univ. of Arkansas M.A. 1968; Univ. of N.B. LL.B. 1979; Osgoode Hall LL.M. 1988; m. Marcia Matsui; PARTNER, TORY TORY DESLAURIERS & BINNINGTON 1993– ; Assoc. Counsel, Royal Comn. on the Northern Environ. Ont. 1982–85; Assoc. & Partner, McCarthy Tetrault 1985–89; Partner, Baker & McKenzie 1989–91; Partner, Fasken Campbell Godfrey 1991–93; Chrmn., Ontario Hydro Environmental Advisory Ctte.; Chrmn., Environmental Law Specialty Ctte., Law Soc. of Upper Canada; Past Dir. & Chrmn., Candn. Environmental Law Assn. 1981–82; Assoc. Prof. of Environ. Law, Fac. of Environ. Studies, York Univ. 1989–91; Chrmn., Nat. Environmental Law Section, Candn. Bar Assn. 1985–87; Environ. Assessment Bar Rules Ctte. 1987; Chrmn., Candn. Bar Assn. Sustainable Devel. Ctte. 1989; Duff Rinfret Scholarship; Dir., Candn. Environ. Indus. Assn. Ont.; Past Pres., Candn. Environ. Defence Fund 1985–87; Mem., Candn. Bar Assn.; Internat. Bar Assn.; author (publications): 'Commentary on Solicitor/Client Privilege' Journal of Environmental Law and Practice 1991; 'Avenues for Citizen Participation in the Environmental Arena: Some Thoughts on the Road Ahead' Univ. of N.B. Law Journal 1992; 'The Canadian Environmental Legal Regime: A Roadmap for the Foreign Investor' San Diego Law Journal 1992; co-author: 'Preventative Lawyering & the Environmental Audit, Commercial Dispute Resolution – Alternatives to Litigation' 1989, 'Environmental Impact Assessment,' Environmental Rights in Canada 1981; Chair and Editor, 'Sustainable Development in Canada: Options for Law Reform' Candn. Bar Assn. Sustainable Development Ctte. 1990; Gen. Ed., 'Canadian Environmental Law' 2nd ed. 1992; Home: 1309 Gatehouse Dr., Mississauga, Ont. L5H 1A6; Office: Aetna Tower, Box 270, T-D Centre, Toronto, Ont. M5K 1N2.

**COTTREAU, Hon. Ernest G.,** B.A.; senator (retired); b. Wedgeport, N.S. 28 Jan. 1914; s. George and Emilie (LeBlanc) C.; e. Wedgeport Pub. Sch.; Saint Anne Coll. Church Point, N.S. B.A. 1937; postgrad. studies in French and Edn.; m. Rachael d. Melbourne and Bertha Bourque 13 July 1942; one d. Simone; summoned to the Senate of Canada 1974; retired 1989; Home: 14 Porter St., Yarmouth, N.S. B5A 2Y6.

**COUCILL, Irma Sophia;** portrait artist; b. London, Ont. 8 Aug. 1918; d. Percival Harold and Mary (Krowa) Young; e. Holy Name Separate Sch. Toronto 1929; St. Angela's Coll. London, Ont. 1929–30; St. Joseph's High Sch. and St. Joseph's Convent Coll. Toronto 1934; Eastern High Sch. Comm. Toronto; m. late Walter Jackson Coucill R.C.A. 17 June 1939; two s. John Thomas, Thomas Dean; Ed. Artist, Globe & Mail 1958–60; Toronto Star 1960– ; Maclean's Magazine 1970–72; Canadian Forum; Syndicated Artist, Toronto Star Syndicate 1960–70; portrait colls.: Candn. Hockey Hall of Fame, BCE Place Toronto (275 portraits) 1958– ; Candn. Aviation Hall of Fame (at Reynolds/Alberta Museum Wetaskiwin, AB) (130 portraits) 1974– ; Candn. Business Hall of Fame, permanent exhibit BCE Place, Toronto (275 portraits) 1978–92; Candn. Indian Hall of Fame, Woodland Indian Cultural Educational Centre, Brantford (30); Exhib. of Portraits of Fathers of Confederation (36), Bytown Museum, Ottawa 1992 (Canada 125); Candn. Press Coll. Toronto (Past Presidents, Gen. Mgrs., Broadcast News Mgrs.) and other colls.; Contributing artist, 'Junior Encyclopedia of Canada' 1990; portrait presented to Un. Way Chairmen past 25 yrs.; portraits of Prime Mins. used for comm. coins/trade dollars; 20 exhns. Fathers of Confed. portraits centennial yrs. Toronto, Montreal, Ottawa, Kitchener; exhn. 55 portraits Prime Min. Trudeau Arts & Letters Club Toronto; Portrait of Terry Fox for Terry Fox Candn. Youth Centre, Ottawa; book illustrations: 'Founders and Guardians' 2nd ed. 1982; 'The Nation Makers' 1967; 'The Journal Men' 1974; 'Stories about 125 Years at Touche, Ross' by Edgar Collard (20 illus. by Irma Coucill); portrait of Dr. Wilfred Bigelow (in Cardiovascular Museum, Toronto Hosp.); two pastel portraits of His Excellency Gov.-Gen. Edward R. Schreyer, Rideau Hall Collection, Ottawa; recreations: photography, music, etymology, poetry, gardening, painting; Address: 393 Broadway Ave., Toronto, Ont. M4P 1X5.

**COUGHLAN, Dermot G.J., F.C.C.A.;** executive; b. Banbury, Eng. 1936; e. U.K.; CHRMN. FOUNDER AND CHIEF EXEC. OFFR., DERLAN INDUSTRIES LTD. 1984– ; Dir., CCL Industries Inc., Willowdale, Ont.; Crown Life Insurance Co.; Hayes-Dana Inc.; with Alcan Industries, U.K. 1957–62; Cavenham Foods 1962–68; R.T.Z. Pillar Ltd. Engineering Group 1968–70; Indal Ltd., Can. 1970; Pres. 1973; C.E.O. 1978–83; served with RAF 1954–56; Fellow, Chartered Assn. Cert. Accts. (UK); mem., Chief Extves. Organ.; World Business Counc.; Metro. Toronto Bd. of Trade; Mem. & Chrmn., Bd. of Govs., Crescent Sch. (Chrmn., Fund Raising Ctte.); recreations: tennis, golf; Clubs: The Toronto; Beaumaris; Granite; Queens; King Valley Golf Club; The Ocean Reef (Key Largo, Fla.); Card Sound Golf Club (Key Largo, Fla.); Home: 134 Glen Road, Toronto, Ont. M4W 2W3; Office: 145 King St. E., Suite 500, Toronto, Ont. M5C 2Y7.

**COUILLARD, Pierre,** B.A., B.Sc., PhD.; né Montmagny, Qué. 19 mars 1928; f. Dr. Jean-Marie et Germaine Daigneau C.; e. Petit Seminaire de Québec; Univ. Laval, B. ès A., 1947, B. ès Sc., 1951; Univ. de Pennsylvanie, Ph.D. (Zool.), 1955; boursier du Conseil Can. des Recherches, études poursuivies à l'Univ. Libre de Bruxelles, 1955–56; ép. Hélène, f. Prof. M. Pardé, Grenoble, France, 26 déc. 1955; enfants: Philippe, Catherine, Denis; Prof Émérite, Dept. des Sciences Biol., Univ. de Montréal (Dir. du Dept. 1963–67); médaille ACFAS, Northern-Telecom pour l'Enseignement des Sciences 1986; Chevalier, Ordre de Malte 1987; mem.; Soc. de Biol. de Montréal; Assoc. des Physiols. (Paris); Soc. Biol. Cell. du Canada; Sigma Xi; Catholique; recreation: voile; résidence: 5770 Northmount, Montréal, Qué. H3S 2H5.

**COULOMBE, Gérard,** Q.C., LL.L.; lawyer; b. Sainte-Marthe, Qué. 16 Oct. 1947; s. René and Emma (Leduc) C.; e. Coll. de Salaberry B.A. 1965; Univ. of Ottawa LL.L. 1968, C.E.Sc.Pol. 1968; Balliol Coll. Oxford (Rhodes Scholar) post-grad. studies; PARTNER, DESJARDINS DUCHARME STEIN MONAST 1977– ; Dir., National Bank of Canada; Christian Dior Canada Inc.; Biodev International Inc.; Envipco Canada Inc.; Dir. & Mem. Audit Ctte., Unigesco Inc.; Dir. & Mem., Audit Ctte. and Management Resources & Corp. Ctte., Camdev Corp.; Chrmn. of Bd., Lex Mundi Ltd.; called to Bar of Qué. 1969; Tech. Cons. Revenue Can. Taxation, Tax Reform 1971–72; Special Asst. Internat. Taxation and Anti-Inflation Prog. Dept. Finance Can. 1972–77; Lectr. in Taxation Univ. of Ottawa 1971–73; Special Lectr. in Internat. Law Univ. of Sherbrooke 1973–86; mem. Faculty Qué. Bar Seminar in Comml. Law 1983–86; Gen. Rapporteur 1982 Convention Internat. Fiscal Assn.; Gov. Candn. Tax Found. 1983–87; Dir. Assn. de Planification Fiscale et Financière 1983–87; mem. Counc., Internat. Fiscal Assn. Rotterdam 1981–89; mem., Oxford Law Soc.; The Osgoode Soc.; The Internat. Tax Planning Assn.; Candn. Assn. of Rhodes Scholars; C.D. Howe Inst.; Candn. Institute of Internat. Affairs; author numerous articles various tax and business jours.; R. Catholic; recreations: reading, music, snowshoeing; Clubs: Saint-Denis; Candn. Club of Montreal; Home: 243 Chemin St-Guillaume, Ste-Marthe, Qué. J0P 1W0; Office: 2400 National Bank Tower, 600 de La Gauchetière O., Montréal, Qué. H3B 4L8.

**COULOMBE, Pierre E.,** B.Com., M.Sc.C., M.A., Ph.D.; public servant; b. Québec, Qué. 6 Dec. 1932; s. Edouard O. and Elzire (Laliberté) C.; e. Univ. Laval B.Com. 1956, M.Sc.C. 1957; Cornell Univ. Ind. & Labour Relations; Univ. of Minn. M.A. 1967; Univ. de Paris (Sorbonne) Ph.D. 1970; Nat. Defence Coll. Can. Grad. Course XLI 1988; m. Janet d. Waino and Lina Pernaa 9 Sept. 1961; two d. Anne, Liisa; ADMIN. OF STATE, SPECIAL GOVT. NEGOTIATOR FOR NATIVE AFFAIRS EXEC. COUNCIL OF QUE. 1988– ; joined Procter & Gamble and Texaco Canada 1957–59; Prof. and Adm. Univ. of Ottawa 1964–69; Head of Rsch. Team Royal Comn. Bilingualism & Biculturalism 1964–69; Post-Doctoral Fellow in Mil. Sociol. Nat. Defence Can. 1970; Dir. Task Force Bilingualism and Dir. Policies, Planning & Evaluation Official Langs. Treasury Bd. Can. 1971–76; Asst. Dir. Gen. Staffing Br. Pub. Service Comn. Can. 1976–79; Dep. Sec. Exec. Council, Govt. Qué. 1979–84, Vice Pres. Office Human Resources Govt. Qué. 1984–87; served with RCN (R) as Instr., Diving Supr. Offr. sea navig. and flying 1949–59; mem. cttes. Pub. Service Renewal Qué. 1985–87, Fed. 'Public Service 2000' 1990– ; adv. ctte. pub. adm. Univ. de Moncton 1987– ; Pres. Inst. Pub. Adm. Can. 1989–90, Past Vice Pres. & Nat. Sec., el. mem. Nat. Exec. since 1985; author various articles books, periodicals and jours.; recreations: sailing, skiing, computers' Home: 2397 rue Noury, Sillery, Qué. G1T 1N3; Office: Édifice H 2e étage, 875 Grande Allée, Québec, Qué. G1R 4Y8.

**COULTER, Donald M.,** rmc, CD, B.A.Sc., M.Eng., Ph.D., P.Eng.; university professor; b. Calgary, Alta. 24 Feb. 1935; s. Hiram Frances and Helen Alyce C.; e. Royal Roads Military College diploma 1955; Royal Military College diploma 1957, M.Eng. 1967; Univ. of B.C. B.A.Sc. 1958; Univ. of Calgary Ph.D. 1970; m. Joyce 9 Aug. 1958; children: Carol-Anne, David; PROFESSOR OF MECHANICAL ENGINEERING, ROYAL MILITARY COLLEGE OF CANADA 1970– ; Engineering Officer, RCN 1953–68; Grad. Teaching Asst., Univ. of Calgary 1968–70; Head, Dept. of Mechanical Engr., Royal Military College 1993– ; Mem., ASME, APEO; author of 27 professional articles; recreations: skiing, sailing; clubs: Canadian Ski Patrol System; Home: Cartwright Point, Box 304, Kingston, Ont. K7K 5E2; Office: Kingston, Ont. K7L 5L0.

**COULTER, Michael Arthur,** B.Sc., P.Eng.; industrialist; b. Toronto, Ont. 22 May 1943; s. Warren Raymond Helen Patricia (Aldington) C.; e. Queen's Univ. B.Sc. 1966; m. Judith Constance d. Frank P. Labey, Georgetown, Ont. 28 Aug. 1965; one s. Marcus James; MANAGING DIR., CEMCORP LTD.; Pres., Cemcorp Contracting Ltd.; Partner, Jemm Enterprises; Past Pres. Gasohol Inc.; Coulter Anodizing Ltd.; Booth-Coulter Inc.; Coulter Copper and Brass Ltd.; Assoc. mem. Master Brewers Am's; Dir. & Past Pres. Candn. Heat Exchanger and Vessel Mgrs. Assn.; mem. Am. Soc. Mech. Engrs.; Past Chrmn. CSA B51; P. Conservative; Anglican; recreations: swimming, skiing, chess, music, bridge; Club: Lambton Golf & Country; Home: 2158 Fowler Lane, Mississauga, Ont. L5K 1B8; Office: 2170 Stanfield Rd., Mississauga, Ont. L4Y 1R5.

**COULTER, Thomas Henry,** B.S., M.A.; association executive and management consultant; b. Winnipeg, Man., 21 Apr. 1911; s. David and Sarah Anne (Allen) C.; e. St. Johns Coll. Sch. Winnipeg, 1925–27; Peabody High Sch., Pittsburgh, 1927–29; Carnegie Inst. of Technol., B.S. 1933; Univ. of Chicago, M.A. 1935; m. Mary Alice, d. Robert L. Leach, 25 Nov. 1937; children: Sara Anne, Anne, Jane Allen, Thomas H. II; EXTVE. VICE-PRES., LESTER B. KNIGHT & ASSOC. (management consultants) 1981–84; Dir., Chicago-Tokyo Bank; Canadian Club of Chicago; Pres., Japan-America Soc. of Chicago; Bd. Chrmn. & Dir., Wytmar & Co. Inc. Management Cons.; Dir., Executive Service Corps of Chicago; mem. Ill. Develop. Bd.; Ill. Develop. Counc.; Invest. Analyst, Shaw & Co., Chicago, 1935–36; V.P. The Zonolite Co., Chicago, V.P. 1936–45; Booz Allen & Hamilton, Mgt. Consultants, 1945–50; el. to Partnership 1948; Pres., American Bildrok Co., Chicago, 1950–54; CEO, Chicago Assn. of Commerce and Industry, 1954–81; Hon. Trustee, Skokie Valley Community Hosp. (Pres. 1955–58 and 1966–69); Dir.: Chicago Crime Comn.; Dir., Geographic Soc. of Chicago; U.S. Olympians, Midwest Chapter; Citizenship Council Metrop. Chicago; Presidents Assoc.; Chicago Council on Foreign Relations; Better Business Bureau Metrop. Chicago; Hadley School for the Blind; mem. various civic and philanthropic organs.; Chrmn., Illinois-Japan Economic Council; Hon. Dir., Japan America Soc. of Chicago 1988– ; (Pres. 1987–88); mem., Illinois Dev. Bd.; Geographic Soc. of Chicago rec'd Alumni Citation for Pub. Service, Univ. of Chicago, 1954; Alumni Merit Award for Outstanding Prof. Achievement, Carnegie-Mellon Univ., 1956; Sports Illustrated Silver Anniversary All-Am. Award, 1957; 'Honorary Citizenship' Scroll, Winnipeg, 1959; Commdr.'s Cross of Order of Merit, Fed. Repub. of Germany, 1961; U.S. Army's Outstanding Civilian Service Medal, 1961; Kt., Order of Merit of Italian Repub., 1961; Gold Badge of Honor for Merits to Repub. of Austria, 1962; Immigrants' Service League Distinguished Achievement Award, 1963; Kt. of 1st Class, Order of Lion of Finland, 1964; Offr., Royal Order of VASA of Sweden, 1965 and Commdr. 1972; Golden Badge of Hon. for Merits to Prov. of Vienna 1971; Citizen Fellowship Award, Inst. of Medicine of Chicago, 1976; Indust. Statesman Award, U.S.-Japan Trade Council, 1976; Chevalier of the Nat. Order of Merit of The Republic of France, 1978; Third Class of the Order of the Sacred Treasure of Japan, 1979; mem. State Dept.'s Top Mang. Seminar Team, Israel 1956 and Japan 1958; Dir. Japan Am. Soc. of Chicago, Inc.; mem., Amer. Mgt. Assn.; Chicago Council on Foreign Relations, Cook County Econ. Devel. Comte.; Nat. Planning Assn.; Sales & Mktg. Extves. of Chicago (Pres. 1954–55); Nat. Sales Extves. Internat. Newcomen Soc. in N. Am.; Nat. Adv. Bd., Am. Security Council Extve. Comte., Ill. Council on Econ. Educ.; Chicago High Tech Assoc.; U.S. Chamber of Comm.; Dist. Export Council, U.S. Dept. Comm.; Chicago Hist. Soc., Field Museum of Natural hist., Art Inst. of Chicago; Vice Chrmn., Internat. House, Univ. of Chicago; Governor's Council on Health and Fitness; Nat. Adv. Council. Nat. legal Centre for the Public Interest and other business and prof. organs.; Dir., Operation Able of Chicago; Protestant; Mem., National Assn. of Business Economists; Japan America Soc. of Chicago (Pres. 1984); Clubs: Circumnavigators; Commercial; Canadian; University; Glen View; Mid-America; Candn. Club of Chicago; Home: 58 Overlook Dr., Golf, Ill. 60029.

**COULTHARD, Jean,** O.C.; university professor and composer; b. Vancouver, B.C. 10 Feb. 1908; d. Walter Livingston and Jean Blake (Robinson) C.; e. Royal College of Music L.R.S.M.; private tuition from Ralph Vaughan Williams (England) and Bernard Wagenaar, Julliard School, N.Y.; m. Don s. Walter and Lilla Adams 24 Dec. 1935; one d.: Jane Coulthard Adams (Jane Poulsson); composer of two dramatic works: 'The Devil's Fanfare' 1958, 'The Return of the Native' 1956–79; compositions: 18 orchestral; 11 solo instrument(s) with orch.; 7 solo voice(s) with orch.; 39 chamber music; 30 solo voice(s); 16 chorus; 20 piano(s); 3 choir & orchestra; 1 choir; 3 keyboard; 2 music for young people; 2 vocals; 28 discographies; some publishers: Novello & Company Ltd. (U.K.), Waterloo Music Co. Limited, Frederick Harris Music Co., Berandol Music Limited; Mem., Candn. League of Composers; Candn. Music Centre; Assn. of Candn. Women Composers; Officer, Order of Canada 1978; Freeman, City of Vancouver 1978; Honorary Doctorates at Univ. of B.C. and Concordia Univ.; recreations: walking; club: Univ. of B.C. Faculty Club; Home: 407, 2222 Bellevue Ave., West Vancouver, B.C. V7V 1C7.

**COUPAL, Bernard,** Ph.D.; research executive; b. Montreal, Que. 12 Sept. 1933; s. Eugene and Marguerite (Gagnon) C.; e. Univ. of Montreal, B.Sc. 1959, M.Sc. 1962; Univ. of Florida, Ph.D. 1965; m. Pierrette d. Gerard and Simone Archambault 25 Apr. 1959; DIR. GEN., BIOCAPITAL INC., venture fund in biotechnology 1989– ; Asst. Prof., École Polytech. 1965–67; Prof., Chem. Engr., Univ. of Sherbrooke 1967–86; Vice Pres., André Marsan & Assoc. (Lavalin) 1974–86; Dir., Biotechnol. Rsch. Inst., Nat. Rsch. Counc. of Can. 1986–89; mem., Candn. Inst. of Chem.; Order of Engineers Que.; Home: 1500 Cr. Seville, Brossard, Qué. J4X 1J4; Office: 1550, rue Metcalfe, bureau 1100, Montréal, Qué. H3A 1X6.

**COUPLAND, Robert Thomas,** Ph.D.; university professor; b. Winnipeg, Man. 24 Jan. 1920; s. Thomas John Winfred and Gertrude (Macleod) C.; e. Univ. of Manitoba, Cert. in Agric. 1938, B.S.A. 1946; Univ. of Nebraska, Ph.D. 1949; one d. Lorraine Dawn; PROF. EMERITUS OF PLANT ECOLOGY, UNIV. OF SASKATCHEWAN since 1985; served as Asst. in Range Studies, Dom. Exper. Station, Swift Current, Sask., 1941–46; i/c Dom. Forest Exper. Station, Wasagaming, Man., 1946; Grad Asst. in Botany, Univ. of Nebraska, 1946–47; Johnson Fellow in Botany, Univ. of Nebraska, 1947–48; Asst. Prof. 1948–50, Assoc. Prof. 1950–57, Prof. 1957–85 of Plant Ecology, Head of Plant Ecology 1948–82, Co-ordinator of CIDA/China Grassland Project 1983– , Univ. of Sask.; Dir. of the Matador Project (Internat. Centre for Grassland Studies) and Co-ordinator of the Grassland Theme under the Internat. Biol. Programme 1967–75; Sask. Inst. of Agrol.; Brit. Ecol. Soc.; Am. Inst. Biol. Science; Ecol. Soc. of Am.; Soc. of Range Mgmt.; Agric. Inst. of Can.; Candn. Bot. Soc.; awarded Univ. of Man. Gold Medal, 1946; Can. Centennial Medal 1967; Fellow Am. Advance. Science; Fellow Linnean Soc. (London); Fellow of the Royal Canadian Geographical Soc.; editor of three books on the natural grasslands of the world; author of several papers on natural grassland and the ecology of weedy plants; present emphasis on Chinese grasslands, land use, and the nutrient balance in world agriculture; Sigma Xi; Office: Univ. of Sask., Saskatoon, Sask. S7N 0W0.

**COUPLAND, Stuart Glen,** B.Sc., Ph.D., Order of Quapick; medical researcher, neuroscientist; b. Skegness, Lincolnshire, England 10 Apr. 1948; s. Frederick Edgar and Judith Grace Pamela (Archer) C.; e. Univ. of Alta. B.Sc. 1968; Simon Fraser Univ. Ph.D. 1979; m. Barbara Hartley d. George Loweree and Margaret Earl (Greene) G. 2 June 1984; one d.: Sarah Hartley; DIR., SENSORY PHYSIOLOGY LAB., ALTA. CHILDREN'S HOSP. 1982– ; Assoc. Prof. of Pediatrics, Clin. Neurosci. & Surg., Univ. of Calgary; Dir., QSD Software; Order of Quapick 1968; memberships incl.: Sigma Xi, Soc. for Sci. Rsch. (McGill Chap.), Acoustical Soc. of Am., ARVO, ISCEV, SPR, NYAS, AAAS, CSCN; recreations: computer programming; Home: 228 – 10A Street N.W., Calgary, Alta. T2N 1W6; Office: 1820 Richmond Rd. S.W., Calgary, Alta. T2T 5C7.

**COURCHENE, Thomas Joseph,** B.A., Ph.D., F.R.S.C.; educator; b. Wakaw, Sask. 16 Sept. 1940; s. Joseph Alfred and Genevieve Elizabeth (Malone) C.; e. Univ. of Sask. B.A. 1962; Princeton Univ. Ph.D. 1967; m. Margareta d. Dr. Joseph and Erika Strohhofer 27 June 1962; children: Robert, Teresa, John; DIR., SCH. OF POLICY STUDIES, QUEEN'S UNIV. 1988; Prof. of Econ., Univ. of W. Ont. 1965–88; Robarts Chair in Canadian Studies, York Univ. 1987–88; Chrmn. Ont. Econ. Council 1982–85; Sr. Fellow C.D. Howe Inst.; former mem. ed. bd., Fraser Inst.; author 'Money, Inflation and the Bank of Canada: An Analysis of Canadian Monetary Policy from 1970 to Early 1975' 1976; 'Money, Inflation and the Bank of Canada 1975–80' Vol. II 1982; 'No Place to Stand? Abandoning Monetary Targets: An Evaluation' 1983; 'Equalization Payments: Past, Present and Future' 1984; 'Economic Management and the Division of Powers' 1986; 'Social Policy: The Mandate for Reform' 1987; 'What Does Ontario Want?' 1989; author over 100 prof. articles and other publs.; Office: Kingston, Ont. K7L 3N6.

**COURCIER, Jérôme;** banker; b. Fontenay Le Comte, France 28 June 1960; s. Philippe and Jacqueline (Monnier) C.; e. Inst. d'études pol. de Paris 1982; m. Catherine d. Robert and Charlotte Dilhac 12 Sept. 1987; children: Tanguy, Romain; FIRST VICE-PRES. & MANAGER, EASTERN REGION, CREDIT LYONNAIS CANADA 1993– ; Account Mgr., Corporate Finance, 1984–88; Project Manager 'Espace CL' 1989; Branch Group Mgr., Retail Banking 1990–92; Office: 2000 Mansfield, 16th Floor, Montreal, Que. H3A 3A4.

**COURNOYEA, Hon. Nellie J.;** politician; b. Aklavik, N.W.T. 940; two children; PREMIER, NORTHWEST TERRITORIES 1991– ; first elected to N.W.T. Legislature g.e. 1979; re-elected 1983, 1987, 1991; Min. of Renewable Resources & Min. of Culture & Communications 1983–85; Min. of Health, Min. of Energy, Mines & Resources & Min. resp. for the Public Utilities Bd. 1987 and Min. of Public Works & Highways 1988; Min. resp. for the Workers' Compensation Bd. 1988–89; Min. resp. for N.W.T. Power Corp. 1989; Govt. Leader 1991; Office: Box 1320, Yellowknife, N.W.T. X1A 2L9.

**COURTNEY, Brian William,** B.Com.; computer software executive; b. Winnipeg, Man. 22 March 1942; s. Leo N.A. and Margaret Gertrude (Chilton) C.; e. Univ. of Man. B.Com. 1945; m. Danielle Dominique d. Serge and Josette Vignole 22 Nov. 1988; children: Graham, Todd, Thea, Sophie; Vice Chrmn. & Chief Exec. Offr., Oracle Corp. Canada Inc. 1990–92; served Xerox Corp. Canada Toronto; Rank Xerox London, Eng.; recreations: tennis, golf; Home: 155 Chartwell Rd., Oakville, Ont. L6J 3Z7.

**COURTNEY, John Childs,** B.A., M.B.A., M.A., Ph.D.; university professor; b. Regina, Sask. 4 Oct. 1936; s. Elmer John and Mary Ruby (Childs) C.; e. Univ. of Manitoba B.A. 1958; Univ. of W. Ont. M.B.A. 1960; Duke Univ. M.A. 1962, Ph.D. 1964; m. Helen d. Robert and Jessie Aikman 6 June 1959; children: Joanne Elizabeth Green, John Robert; PROFESSOR, DEPT. OF POLITICAL STUDIES, UNIV. OF SASKATCHEWAN 1974– ; Asst. Prof., Brandon Coll. 1963–65; Asst., Assoc. & Full Prof. of Pol. Sci. present Univ. 1965– ; Visiting Scholar, Nuffield Coll., Oxford Univ. 1972–73, 1979–80; Academic Visitor, Harvard Univ. 1986–87; William Lyon Mackenzie King Visiting Prof. of Candn. Studies, Harvard Univ. 1990–91; Visiting Prof. of Candn. Studies, Hebrew Univ. of Jerusalem 1992; twice el. to Extve., Candn. Pol. Sci. Assn. (Pres. 1987–88); apptd. to Social Scis. and Humanities Rsch. Counc. of Can. (SSHRCC) 1985–88, re-apptd. 1988–91; el. Vice Pres., SSHRCC 1989–91; several rsch. grants from Canada Counc. and SSHRCC; recipient, Candn. Studies Writing Award, Secy. of State's Dept.; mem., United Church; Candn. Pol. Sci. Assn.; Inst. of Public Admin. of Can.; Internat. Pol. Sci. Assn.; Am. Pol. Sci. Assn.; author: 'The Selection of National Party Leaders in Canada' 1973 and numerous articles, contributions, book reviews, testimony to parliamentary cttes. etc.; ed.: 'Voting in Canada' 1967; 'The Canadian House of Commons: Essays in Honour of Norman Ward' 1985; co-ed. 'After Meech Lake: Lessons for Tomorrow' 1991; 'Drawing Boundaries: Legislatures, Courts, and Electoral Values' 1992; English-lang. ed., Candn. Journ. of Pol. Sci. 1981–84; recreations: jogging, skiing, travelling; Club: Univ. of Saskatchewan Faculty; Home: 805 Colony St., Saskatoon, Sask. S7N 0S2; Office: Saskatoon, Sask. S7N 0W0.

**COURTOIS, Bernard André,** B.A., LL.L.; telecommunications executive; b. Montreal, Que. 28 Aug. 1945; s. Rosaire and Germaine (Vermette) C.; e. Univ. of Montreal B.A. 1965, LL.L. 1968; m. Dominique d. Claude and Jeanine Jarrige 3 May 1992; children: Charles-Philippe, Dominic, Alexandre; VICE-PRESIDENT, CORPORATE AND LEGAL AFFAIRS, BELL CANADA 1993– ; practiced law in Montreal 1969–79; in Ottawa/Hull 1979–91; fields of practice: regulatory law & litigation; Mng. Partner, Ogilvy Renault (Ottawa) 1991; Vice-Pres., Law & Regulatory Affairs, Bell Canada 1991–93; admitted to Bar of Quebec 1969; Bar of Ont. 1984; Dir., Tele-Direct (Pubns.) Inc.; Bell Sygma Telecom Solutions Inc.; Treas., Univ. of Ottawa Vision Campaign 1992– ; Mem., Candn. Bar Assn. (Chair, Nat. Section on Admin. Law 1981–83); Am. Bar Assn. (Assoc.); Opimian Soc.; Commanderie de Bordeaux à Ottawa; recreations: skiing, cycling, wine; clubs: Cercle Univ. d'Ottawa; Home: 35 Blenheim, Rockcliffe Park, Ottawa, Ont. K1L 5B6; Office: Floor 6, 105 Hôtel-de-Ville, Hull, Que. J8X 4H7.

**COURTOIS, Hon. E. Jacques,** P.C., Q.C., B.A., LL.B.; b. Montreal, P.Q., 4 July 1920; s. Edmond and Cléophée (Lefebvre) C.; e. Univ. of Montreal, B.A., LL.B.; m. Joan, d. L. L. Miller, Hudson Heights, P.Q., 23 Oct. 1943; children: Nicole, Jacques, Marc; PARTNER, STIKEMAN, ELLIOTT; Chrmn., Security Intelligence Review Ctte., Govt. of Canada; Chrmn. and Dir. UNAHL Ltd.; McGraw-Hill Ryerson Ltd.; Vice Pres. and Dir. Canada Life Assurance Co.; called to the Bar of Que., 1946; cr. Q.C. 1963; mem. Bar of Montreal; served in 2nd World War with R.C.N.V.R.; R. Catholic; Clubs: York (Toronto); Mount Royal; Whitlock; Hudson Yacht; Office: 39th Floor, 1155 Rene Levesque Blvd. W., Montréal, Qué. H3B 3V2.

**COURTRIGHT, James Milton,** B.A., B.Sc. (Hons.), P.Eng.; retired university vice-principal; b. North Bay, Ont. 16 Dec. 1914; s. Milton and Sophia (Varin) C.; e. Glebe Coll. Inst., Ottawa; Univ. of Ottawa, B.A. 1937; Queen's Univ., B.Sc. (Hons.) 1941 Pres. of the Student Body (Alma Mater Soc.) 1940–41; (rec'd Jenkins Trophy 1941; Tricolour Soc.; John Henry Newman Honour Soc.); Columbia Univ., mang. course 1957; m. Mary Nora, d. Patrick Joseph Roche and Nora O'Rourke, 16 Oct. 1943; children: Joseph W., James H., Patricia N., Stephen M., John T., Mary Ellen, Anthony S., Francis G.; retired; joined Shell Canada Ltd. as Refinery Engr., Montreal, 1941, Lubrication Engr., Toronto, 1943, Mgr. Lubricants Dept., 1945, Dist. Mgr., Niagara Peninsula, 1947, Asst. to Vice Pres. and Gen. Mgr., Vancouver, 1948; Retail Sales Mgr. 1949, Sales Mgr. 1949, Gen. Mgr., Purchasing, Toronto, 1951, E. Region Marketing Mgr., Montreal, 1958, Coordinator Pub. Relations, Toronto, 1966, Coordinator Environmental Control, 1968; Vice Principal, Devel. and Infor., Queen's Univ. 1970–79 (ret.) rep. Can. in javelin throw Olympic Games, Berlin, 1936; Pan-Am. Games, Dallas, 1937 (gold medal); Commonwealth Games, Sydney, Australia, 1938 (gold medal); Former Secy. and Hon. Life Mem., Queen's Univ. Council (former Trustee of univ.); Past Pres. Serra Club of Toronto; Past Pres., Newman Assn. Montreal; Ancien Secrétaire de la Fondation Saint-Thomas d'Aquin du Can.; author numerous papers and speeches on mang., purchasing, marketing, pub. relations and environmental control; mem. Ed. Adv. Bd., 'Chemosphere' (internat. tech. publ.) 1970–75; Gouverneur de la Chambre de Comm. Prov. de Qué. 1962–65; Council mem., Montreal Bd. Trade 1965–66; Dir., Ont. Chamber Comm. 1967–72; Vice Pres., Cath. Sch. Bd., Vancouver, 1950; Life Gov., Council for Canadian Unity; Kingston District Chamber Comm., 1972–76; Past Dir.: Olympic Club of Can.; Air Pollution Control Assn., Ont. Chapter; Past Chrmn., Oil Buyers Group, Nat. Assn. Purchasing Agts. (U.S.A.); Hon. mem. Bd., St. Mary's of the Lake Hosp., Kingston; mem., Assn. Prof. Engrs. Prov. Ont.; founding mem. Candn. Assoc. of the Club of Rome; Distinguished Service Award, Queen's Univ. 1980; Sports Hall of Fame, Univ. of Ottawa 1980; Montreal Medal, Queen's Alumni 1987; Padre Laverty Award, Queen's Univ. 1991; R. Catholic; recreations: walking, reading; Home; 431 King St. W., Kingston, Ont. K7L 2X5.

**COURVILLE, Leon,** B.A., B.Comm., M.A., Ph.D.; financial executive; b. Montreal, Que. 12 Sept. 1945; s. Coll. André Grasset B.A. 1964; Hautes Etudes Commercials B.Comm. 1967, M.A. 1968; Carnegie-Mellon Univ. Ph.D. 1972; two children; SR. EXECUTIVE VICE-PRES., CORPORATE AFFAIRS, NATIONAL BANK OF CANADA 1990– ; Professor, Hautes Etudes Commercials 1982–84; joined Nat. Bank of Canada 1984; Mem., Bd. of Dir., C.D. Howe Institute; Soc. d'Investissement Jeunesse; Musée d'Art Contemporain; La Fondation de L'Institut de Recherches Cliniques de Montréal; Mem., Investment Ctte., Fond. Societe Generale de Financement Mercure; Employee Pension Plan, Nat. Bank of Canada; Office: 600 de la Gauchetière St. W., 4th floor, Montreal, Que. H3B 4L2.

**COURVILLE, Serge,** Ph.D.; educator; university professor; director, Laboratoire de geographie historique (Univ. Laval); co-director, Centre interuniversitaire d'études québécoises (Univ. Laval and Univ. du Québec à Trois-Rivières); Fellow, Royal Soc. of Canada 1992; b. Montréal, Qué. 8 July 1943; s. Marcel and Claire (Robillard) C.; e. Coll. André Grasset, B.A. 1963; Univ. Montréal, Bc.Ped. 1964, Lic.Ped. 1967, L.E.S. 1971, M.A. (Geog.) 1973, Ph.D. (Geog.) 1979; children: Charles-Erick, Alexandra; PROF., DEPT. OF GEOGRAPHY, UNIV. LAVAL 1981– ; Researcher Celat (and Admin. Bd.) 1982–89; Teacher, Montreal Cath. Sch. Bd. 1964–71; study leave with scholarship 1971–73; Co-ord., Human Sciences Prog. 1973–79; Dir., Envir. Edn. Serv., Dept. of Envir., Qué. Govt. 1979–81; Cons., La Comn. de Toponymie du Qué.; Le Musée de la civilisation du Qué.; Pres., Ctte. for granting Qué. Univ. Rsch. Ctrs., Fonds FCAR 1986–87 (Adm. Bd. 1988–92); Mem., Candn. Assn. of Geographers; L'Inst. d'Hist. de l'Am. Française (Adm. Bd. 1986–87); Candn. Hist. Soc.; French Colonial Hist. Soc. (Adm. Bd. 1985–88); Cahiers de Géographie du Qué. (Adv. Bd. 1982–91); Histoire Sociale/Social History (Adv. Bd. 1985– ;); Chaire pour le développement de la recherche sur la culture d'expression française en Amérique du Nord, Scientific Ctte., Univ. Laval 1989–93; director: 'Rangs et villages du Québec' 1984, 'Paroisses et municipalités de la région de Montréal au XIXe siècle (1825–1861)' 1988; author: 'Entre ville et campagne. L'essor des villages dans les seigneuries du Bas-Canada' 1990 (awarded le Prix Jean-Charles Falardeau (Soc. Sci. Fedn. of Can.) 1991, the Alf Heggoy Book Prize (French Colonial Historical Soc.) 1991, and Le Prix Lionel Groulx/Les Coopérants (Fond. Lionel Groulx and Les Coopérants) 1991); co-author: 'Le Monde rural Québécois au XIXe siècle' Candn. Hist. Soc.; co-editor: 'French Colonial Historical Society Proceedings' 1985–87; numerous articles on historical geography of Lower Canada/Quebec (one of which was awarded the Guy Frégault Article Prize, Institut d'histoire de l'Amérique française 1989); Home: 276 Dublin Rd., Shannon, Qué. G0A 4N0; Office: Québec, Qué. G1K 7P4.

**COUSE, Mervyn Austin,** D.F.C., B.A.Sc.; retired consulting engineer; b. Toronto, Ont. 22 Jan. 1923; e. Univ. of Toronto B.A.Sc. 1950 (Civil Engn.); m. Agnes Anderson Mitchell; four d.; served with RCAF 1942–45, rank Flying Offr.; mem. Assn. Prof. Engrs. Prov. Ont.; recreations: curling, golf; Club: Granite; Home: 100 Ruscica Dr., Toronto, Ont. M4A 1R4.

**COUSINS, Mary Louise,** B.A.Hec., R.P.Dt.; research dietitian; b. Kingston, Ont. 15 May 1950; d. Felix Joseph and Helen Lorraine McAllister; e. Univ. of Western Ont. B.A.Hec. 1972; St. Michael's Hospital Internship; m. Russell Robert s. Russell and Lorraine C. 18 Aug. 1972; children: Sarah, Peter; CLINICAL RESEARCH SCIENTIST, ASTRA PHARMACEUTICAL 1992– ; Clinical Dietician, Mt. Sinai Hosp. 1973–75; Lipid Rsch. Clin. Dietician, Coronary Prevention Trial, St. Michael's Hosp. 1975–79; Ludwig Inst. for Cancer Rsch. 1981–91; Sr. Rsch. Coord. & Mgr., Breast Cancer Prevention Trial, Ont. Cancer Inst. 1988–92; Mem., Ont. Dietic Assn. 1973– ; Candn. Dietetic Assn. 1973– ; Toronto Home Economical Assn. 1985– ; Clincial Rsch. Soc. 1992– ; Education Award, Candn. Breast Cancer Found. 1988; Roman Catholic; author/co-author of several publications; recreations: racquet sports, boating; club: University Women's; Home: 6703 Barrisdale Dr., Mississauga, Ont. L5N 2H5; Office: 1004 Middlegate Dr., Mississauga, Ont. L4Y 1M4.

**COUTTS, Herbert Thomas,** C.M. (1974), M.A., Ph.D., LL.D.; b. Hamilton, Ont. 9 Feb. 1907; s. late Charles Alexander and late Harriet I. (Hartwell) C.; e. Georgetown, Ont.; Calgary and Claresholm, Alta.; Calgary Normal Sch.; Univ. of Toronto, B.A. 1935; Univ. of Alta., M.A. 1942; Univ. of Minn., Ph.D. 1950; LL.D., Mem. Univ. of Nfld. 1968; Univ. of Alta. 1979; m. late Clara Alberta, d. late George Simpson, 26 Dec. 1938; four s., two d.; m. Alice Polley, d. Martin Garrett, Sept. 23, 1978; Teacher, Cereal, Claresholm View, Starline, 1925–30; Princ., Stavely (Alta.) S.D., 1930–33; High Sch. Asst. and Princ., Claresholm (Alta.) S.D., 1935–43; Supt. and Inspr. of Schs., Wainwright (Alta.) Sch. Div., 1943–46; Assoc. Prof. of Educ., Univ. of Alta., 1946–50, Chrmn., Div. of Secondary Educ. there 1950–55, Prof. 1951, Dean, Faculty of Educ., 1955; presently Prof. Emeritus, Univ. of Alberta; has rec'd numerous honours for prof. contributions; co-author, numerous literary publications; Fellow, Canadian Coll. Teachers; Hon. Life mem., Canadian Educ. Assn. (Pres. 1965–66); Alta. Teachers' Assn.; Candn. College Teachers (Council 1969–75); Candn. Soc. Study Educ. (Pres. 1972–74); Phi Delta Kappa (Emeritus mem.); I.O.O.F.; United Church; recreations: walking, bridge; Club: Rotary; Home: 7327 – 118 St., #305, Edmonton, Alta. T6G 1S5.

**COUTTS, James A.,** LL.B., M.B.A.; b. High River, Alta. 16 May 1938; s. Ewart E. and Alberta (Allan) C.; e. Univ. of Alta. B.A. 1960, LL.B. 1961; Harvard Sch. of Business M.B.A. 1968; CHRMN., CIC CANADIAN INVESTMENT CAPITAL LTD.; called to Bar of Alta. 1962; practised law with McLaws & Co. Calgary, Alta. 1961–63; Secy. to Prime Min. of Can., the Right Hon. Lester B. Pearson 1963–66; Grad. Student, Harvard Univ. 1966–68; Consultant McKinsey & Co. Cleveland, Zurich and Toronto 1968–70; Partner, The Canada Consulting Group, Toronto 1970–75; Princ. Secy. to Prime Minister of Canada, the Right Hon. Pierre Elliott Trudeau, 1975–81; Mem., Adv. Counc., Ctr. of Candn. Studies, Johns Hopkins Univ.; Bd. of Trustees, Extve. Ctte., The Hosp. for Sick Children, Toronto; Gov. Counc., Ont. Coll. of Art, Toronto; Trustee, Writers' Development Trust; Trustee, Pearson Coll. of the Pacific; Ctte. Mem., Lionel Gelber Book Prize for Internat.

Affairs; Liberal; United Church of Canada; recreations: skiing, hiking; Clubs: Rideau (Ottawa); University (Toronto); York (Toronto); Toronto Hunt; Nanton Golf (Nanton, Alta.); Home: 31 Lowther Ave., Toronto, Ont. M5R 1C5; Office: Canada Trust Tower, BCE Place, 161 Bay St., Suite 3840, P.O. Box 610, Toronto, Ont. M5J 2S1.

**COUTTS, Ronald Thomson,** Ph.D., D.Sc., F.R.S.C., F.R.S.C. (U.K.); educator; b. Glasgow, Scot. 19 June 1931; s. Ronald Miller and Helen Alexanderina (Crombie) C.; e. Glasgow Univ. B.Sc. 1955, Ph.D. (Chem.) 1959; Univ. of Strathclyde D.Sc. 1976; m. Sheenah d. Henry and Jessie Black 4 Sept. 1957; children: Martin, Alan, Kathryn; PROF. OF PHARMACY (MED. CHEM.) UNIV. OF ALTA. 1968– , Distinguished University Professor 1984– ; Hon. Prof. of Psychiatry 1979– ; Pres., Xenotox Services Ltd. Edmonton; Asst. Lectr. in Pharm. Chem. Royal Coll. of Sc. & Technol. Glasgow 1956–59; Lectr. in Pharm. Chem. Sunderland Tech. Coll. Eng. 1959–63; Asst. and Assoc. Prof. of Pharm. Univ. of Sask. 1963–66; Assoc. Prof. of Pharm. (Med. Chem.) present Univ. 1966, Asst. Dean of Pharm. (Grad. Studies) 1979–83, Pres., Faculty Assn. 1978–79, mem. Bd. Govs. 1982–85; Visiting Res. Prof. Chelsea Coll. Univ. of London 1972–73; author or co-author over 290 rsch. manuscripts, reviews, textbooks, chapters, patents; recipient, Candn. Coll. Neuropsychopharm. Medal 1992; Fellow, Royal Soc. Canada; Royal Soc. Chems. (UK); Chem. Inst. Can.; Pharm. Soc. Gr. Britain; Am. Assoc. Pharmaceutical Scientists; mem., Candn. Coll. Neuropsychopharm.; Assoc. Fac. Pharm. Can.; Am. Soc. Pharmacol. Exper. Therap.; Intern. Soc. Study Xenobiotics; recreations: golf, cross-country skiing, squash, music; Club: Windermere Golf & Country; Home: 4724 – 139 St., Edmonton, Alta. T6H 3Z2; Office: Faculty of Pharmacy and Pharmaceutical Sciences, Univ. of Alta., Edmonton, Alta. T6G 2N8.

**COUTURE, Jean Georges,** M.D., F.R.C.S.(C.), F.A.C.S.; surgeon; educator; b. Québec, Qué. 1 July 1924; s. Joseph and Irène (Marcoux) C.; e. Laval Univ. M.D. 1949; Bellevue Med. Center, N.Y. Postgrad. Studies Gen. Surgery 1949–54; m. Virginia d. Joseph and Virginia (Stringfellow) Nuvolini 8 Sept. 1951; children: Micheline, Elizabeth; PROF. OF SURGERY, UNIV. LAVAL 1970– , Asst. Dean of Medicine 1975–79, Chrmn. of Surgery 1981–89; author over 40 publs. surgical oncology, med. edn. and vascular prostheses; co-ed. 'Les urgences' 1984; Pres.: Royal Coll. Phys. & Surgs. Can. 1984–86; Cand. Assn. Clin. Surgs. E. Div. 1985–86; Pres., Candn. Assoc. of Gen. Surgeons 1989–90; Pres., Candn. Council on Health Facilities Accreditation; Gov. Am. Coll. Surgs. 1980–85, mem. Exec. 1981–85; Hon. mem. French Surg. Assn.; Hon. Fellow: Coll. Surgery S. Africa; Australasian Coll. Surgs.; Hon. Fellow, Royal Coll. of Surgeons of Engl.; mem. Académie de Chirurgie de Paris; Internat. Surg. Soc.; James IV Assn. Surgs.; Internat. Surg. Group; Am. Surgical Assn.; recreations: reading, golf, skiing; Home: 18 Jardins Mérici, Apt. 123, Québec, Qué. G1S 4W1; Office: Hôpital du Saint-Sacrement, 1050 chemin Ste-Foy, Québec, Qué. G1S 4L8.

**COUTURE, Murray,** B.Comm.; business executive; b. Quebec City, Que. 29 May 1932; s. Alexandre and Simone (Gignac) C.; e. Loyola Coll., B.Comm. 1953; m. Therese d. J. Achille and Marie-Paule Joli-Coeur 8 Oct. 1955; children: Murray, Helene, Andre, Julie, Martin; BD. CHRMN. & C.E.O., SANIMAL INDUSTRIES INC.; began working with co. in 1953; in 1987 acquired Lomex and formed a partnership to create a parent co. Sanimal Industries Inc.; Pres., Candn. Renderers Assn.; 1968–69; Region I Pres. 1972–73, Chrmn. 1983–84, Nat. Renderers Assn.; recreations: golf, skiing; Office: 9900, 6th St., Montréal, Qué. H1C 1G2.

**COUVELIER, Hon. Melville Bertram;** b. Vancouver, B.C. 20 Jan. 1931; s. George Melville and Hilda Kate (Brown) C.; e. Kitsilano and King Edward High Schs. Vancouver; Western Washington Coll. Bellingham, Wash.; m. Mildred Anne d. Fran and Monica Quakenbush 22 Sept. 1949; children: Richard George, Rodney Stephen, Melissa Chantelle; Dir., B.C. Bancorp; Mem. Bd. of Govs., V.S.E.; Alderman, Mun. of Saanich 1974–75, Mayor 1978–86; el. M.L.A. for Saanich and the Islands 1986; Min. of Finance and Corporate Relations, B.C. and Pres., Treas. Bd., Prov. of B.C. 1986–91 (resigned March 1991); served Crown Zellerback Canada Ltd. 12 yrs.; owned and operated Gen. Store Coal Harbour, owned Maplewood Poultry Processors 1960–72; former Pres. Union of B.C. Muns., Dir. and Chrmn. Greater Victoria Labour Relations Assn., mem. Fedn. Candn. Muns., Pres. Assn. Vancouver Island Muns., Bd. mem. Capital Region Dist., Chrmn. Greater Victoria Econ. Devel. Comn.; Founding mem. Urban Transit Authority and mem. Victoria Transit Comn.; Founding Pres. Islands '86; Founding Dir. Hortic. Centre of Pacific; Founding mem. Victoria Technol. Found.; former Pres. B.C. Lib. Party 1972–73; Home: 7, 10025 Fifth St., Sidney, B.C. V8L 2X8.

**COUZIN, Robert,** A.B., A.M., B.C.L.; barrister and solicitor; b. Chicago, Ill. 27 Nov. 1945; s. Wilfred and Rose (Mittelman) C.; e. Princeton Univ.; Univ. of Chicago A.B. 1967, A.M. 1968; McGill Univ. B.C.L. 1972; m. Phyllis d. Charles and Ida Hymowitz 13 June 1967; children: Jennifer Megan, Stephanie Fleur; PRINCIPAL, STIKEMAN ELLIOTT (Paris, France associated office) 1993– ; Woodrow Wilson Fellow; Gold Medalist in Law, McGill Univ.; num. other awards; called to Bar of Que. 1974, Ontario 1977; Partner, Stikeman Elliott 1978–93; regular speaker, Canadian Tax Foundation & other meetings; author of num. articles, learned & otherwise; former Lecturer, McGill Univ. and Univ. of Toronto; former Gov., Candn. Tax Found.; former Pres., Candn. Br., Internat. Fiscal Assn.; former Dir., B.T. Bank of Canada; Westminer Canada Ltd.; Canada Texaco Inc.; Vice Chair, Fair Tax Comn. of Ont.; recreations: amateur harpsichordist; Home: 17 avenue de Breteuil, 75007 Paris, France.

**COVERT, George David Napier,** Q.C.; B.A., B.C.L., LL.M., M.B.A.; b. Halifax, N.S., 27 Sept. 1938; s. George Leslie and Mary Kathleen Kilgour (Napier) C.; e. Univ. New Brunswick, B.A. 1960, B.C.L. 1963; Harvard Univ., LL.M. 1965; York Univ., M.B.A. 1969; m. Eleanor Patricia (deceased), d. late Frank T. Stanfield, 14 June 1969; children: Meghan Patricia, Ian David, Brian Frank; PARTNER, STEWART MCKELVEY STIRLING SCALES; Dir., Stanfield's Ltd.; Northlake Shipping Ltd.; Baader Canada Ltd.; Camp Hill Medical Ctr.; read law with Donald A. Kerr, Q.C.; called to Bar of N.S. 1966; P. Cons.; Anglican; Home: 893 Marlborough Ave., Halifax, N.S. B3H 3G7; Office: Ste. 800, Purdy's Wharf, Tower 1, 1959 Upper Water St., P.O. Box 997, Halifax, N.S. B3J 2X2.

**COWAN, Bonnie Baker,** B.A.; editorial executive; b. Chesley, Ont. 16 Apr. 1943; d. Robert Gordon and Alice May (Black) Alexander; e. Univ. of West. Ont.; Waterloo Lutheran Univ., B.A. 1965; children: Krista Baker, Jennifer Baker-Walker, David Cowan; EDITOR-IN-CHIEF, CANADIAN LIVING MAGAZINE 1988– ; H.S. Teacher, English & Latin to 1973; Community Ed., Burlington Post 1973–77; Columnist, Toronto Star & freelance writer 1977–79; Features Editor, Food Dept. Coord., then Mng. Ed., Canadian Living magazine 1979–88; Home: 466 Merton St., Toronto, Ont. M4S 1B1; Office: 50 Holly St., Toronto, Ont. M4S 3B3.

**COWAN, Charles Gibbs,** C.D., Q.C., B.A., LL.B.; lawyer; b. Cannington, Ont. 13 Nov. 1928; s. Charles Gibbs and Jean (MacFarlane) C.; e. Upper Can. Coll. Toronto 1946; Univ. of Toronto, Trinity Coll. B.A. 1950; Osgoode Hall Law Sch. 1954; Militia Staff Course msc 1959; m. Susan Mary d. late Philip Charles Tidy 24 Sept. 1954; children: Julia Mary, James Charles Strathy, Stuart Philip Gibbs; Vice-Pres., Secy. & Dir., Hollinger Inc.; Argus Corp. Ltd.; The Ravelston Corp. Ltd.; called to Bar of Ont. 1954; cr. Q.C. 1966; served with Queen's Own Rifles of Can. (Militia) 1947–63, rank Maj.; Armiger; mem. Candn. Bar Assn.; Heraldry Soc. Can.; Anglican; Clubs: Toronto; Bd. of Trade, Metro Toronto; Home: 8 Powell Ave., Toronto, Ont. M4W 2Y7; Office: 10 Toronto St., Toronto, Ont. M5C 2B7.

**COWAN, William George,** B.A., Ph.D.; educator; b. St. Petersburg, Fla. 17 Nov. 1929; s. William George and Dorothy Johanna (Fairgrieve) C.; e. St. Petersburg High Sch. 1947; Univ. of Fla.; Univ. of N.C.; Univ. of Cal. Berkeley B.A. 1951; Univ. of Salamanca, Spain; Cornell Univ. Ph.D. 1960; m. Sarah d. Daniel and Charlotte Argall 24 Dec. 1952; children: Joel, Andrew, Laura, Daniel, Robert; PROF. OF LINGUISTICS, CARLETON UNIV. 1973– ; served with U.S. Army 1951–54; Foreign Service Inst. Beirut 1960–64; Assoc. Prof. of Linguistics, Brown Univ. 1964–71; Assoc. Prof. present Univ. 1971–73, Chrmn. of Linguistics 1973–76, 1991– ; sessional lectr. Georgetown Univ., Am. Univ. of Beirut, Univ. of Toronto, Univ. de Montréal, Univ. of Ottawa, Univ. of London, Portland State Coll.; Fels Fellowship 1959–60; author 'Workbook in Historical Reconstruction' 1970; co-author 'Source Book in Linguistics' 1986; ed. Papers of the Algonquian Conf. 1975– ; Candn. Jour. of Linguistics 1984– ; co-ed. Papers of Sapir Conf. 1986; various articles and reviews scholarly jours.; mem. Linguistic Soc. Am.; Am. Anthrop. Assn.; Candn. Linguistic Assn.; recreations: woodworking, swimming; Home: 41 Glen Ave., Ottawa, Ont. K1S 2Z6; e-mail: wcowan @ Carleton. CA; Office: Dept. of Linguistics and Applied Language Studies, Carleton Univ., Ottawa, Ont. K1S 5B6.

**COWARD, Harold George,** B.A., B.D., M.A., Ph.D; university professor; b. Calgary, Alta. 13 Dec. 1936; s. George Lincoln and Hazel Isobelle (Rogers) C.; e. Univ. Alta., B.A. 1958; B.D. 1967; M.A. 1969; McMaster Univ., Ph.D. 1973; m. Rachel, d. Hugh and Frances Maiklem 10 Sept. 1960; children: David; Kenneth; Susan; DIR., CENTRE FOR STUDIES IN RELIGION AND SOCIETY and PROF. OF HISTORY, UNIV. OF VICTORIA 1992– ; Prof., Univ. of Calgary 1973–92; Head, Dept. Religious Studies 1976; Assoc. Dean, Faculty Humanities 1977; Head, Dept. Religious Studies 1979–83; Dir., Calgary Inst. for the Humanities 1980–92; Dir., Univ. of Calgary Press 1981–83; author: 'Bhartrhari' 1976; 'Sphota Theory of Language' 1980; 'Jung and Eastern Thought' 1985; 'Pluralism: Challenge to World Religions' 1985; 'Sacred Word and Sacred Text: Scripture in the World Religions' 1988; 'Hindu Ethics: Purity, Euthanasia and Abortion' 1988; 'Derrida and Indian Philosophy' 1990; co-author: 'Psychological Epistemology' 1978; 'Humanities in Alberta' 1984; 'Philosophy of the Grammarians' 1990; 'Mantra: Hearing the Divine in India' 1991; ed. 'Mystics and Scholars' 1977; 'Revelation in Indian Thought' 1977; 'Religion and Ethnicity' 1978; 'Humanities in the Present Day' 1979; 'Scholarly Communication' 1980; 'Calgary's Growth: Bane or Boon?' 1981; 'Ethical Issues in the Allocation of Health Care Resources' 1982; 'Studies in Indian Thought' 1982; 'Religions in Contact and Change' 1983; 'The Role of the Modern Union' 1985; 'Modern Indian Responses to Religious Pluralism' 1987; 'Silence, Sacred and the Word' 1988; 'Readings in Eastern Religions' 1988; 'Hindu-Christian Dialogue' 1989; 'Privacy' 1989; 'The Future of Fossil Fuels' 1991; 'Derrida and Negative Theology' 1992; 'Reflections on Cultural Policy' 1993; 'Ethics and Climate Change: The Greenhouse Effect' 1993; 'Aging and Dying: Legal, Scientific and Religious Challenges' 1993; Pres., Candn. Soc. for the Study of Religion 1984–86; Pres., Candn. Corp. for Studies in Religion 1987–90; Pres., Shastri Indo-Candn. Inst. 1986–88; Pres., Candn. Fed. for the Humanities 1990–91; Fellow, Royal Soc. of Can.; United Church of Can.; recreations: gardening, hiking; skiing; Home: 4584 Bonnieview Pl., Victoria, B.C. V8N 3V6; Office: Centre for Studies in Religion and Society, Univ. of Victoria, Victoria, B.C. V8W 3P4.

**COWARD, Laurence E.,** F.I.A., F.C.I.A., A.S.A., F.C.A.; company executive; b. London, Eng. 20 July 1914; s. Charles E. and Eleanor (Betts) C.; e. Royal Liberty Sch., Essex, Eng.; Jesus Coll., Cambridge Univ.; Inst. of Actuaries, 1939; m. Mollie Yeulett, 1 Jan. 1949; children: Michael, Jane, Anthony, Peter; DIR. EMERITUS, WILLIAM M. MERCER LTD.; joined Brit. Civil Service, London, Eng. 1935–41; apptd. Actuary of present Co. 1949; Vice Pres. 1953; Chrmn. Pension Comn. of Ont., 1963–65; Pres., Candn. Inst. of Actuaries, 1969–70; Candn. Pension Conf., 1963–65; author of 'Mercer Handbook of Canadian Pension and Benefit Plans' (CCH); Anglican; recreations: skiing, music; Clubs: National; Alpine Ski; Home: 21 Lower Links Rd., Willowdale, Ont. M2P 1H5; Office: BCE Place, 161 Bay St., Toronto, Ont. M5J 2S5.

**COWASJEE, Saros,** M.A., Ph.D.; author; educator; b. Secundrabad, India 12 July 1931; s. Dara Cowasjee; e. St. John's Coll. Agra, India, B.A. 1951; Agra Coll. M.A. 1955; Univ. of Leeds Ph.D. 1960; PROF. OF ENGLISH, UNIV. OF REGINA 1971– ; Asst. Ed. Times of India Press, Bombay 1961–63; Instr. in Eng. present Univ. 1963; Rsch. Assoc., Univ. of California, Berkeley 1970–71; guest lectr. numerous univs. Europe, Australia, N. Am., India, Fiji, Singapore; author: 'Sean O'Casey: the Man Behind the Plays' 1963 (criticism); 'O'Casey' 1966 (criticism); 'Stories and Sketches' 1970; 'Goodbye to Elsa' 1974 (novel); ''Coolie': An Assessment' 1976 (criticism); 'So Many Freedoms: A Study of the Major Fiction of Mulk Raj Anand' 1977 (criticism); 'Nude Therapy' 1978 (short stories); 'The Last of the Maharajas' 1980 (screenplay); 'Suffer Little Children' 1982 (novel); 'Studies in Indian and Anglo-Indian Fiction' 1993 (criticism); editor: with introductions 'Private Life of an Indian Prince' 1970 (novel); 'Untouchable' 1970 (novel); 'Seven Summers' 1970 (novel); 'Coolie' 1972 (novel); 'Author to Critic: The Letters of Mulk Raj Anand' 1973 (letters); 'Hindoo Holiday' 1979 (novel, introd. only); 'Mulk Raj Anand: A Check-list' 1979 (bibliog., introd. only); 'The Big Heart' 1980 (novel); 'Modern Indian Fiction' 1981 (anthol.); 'Modern Indian Short Stories' 1982 (anthol.); 'Stories from the Raj' 1982 (anthol.); 'More Stories from the Raj and After' 1986 (anthol.); 'When the British Left' 1987 (fiction anthol.); 'The Raj and After' 1987 (fiction anthol.); 'Indigo' 1987, 1993 (novel, introd. only); 'Durbar' 1987 (novel, introd. only); 'Siri Ram – Revolutionist' 1988 (novel, introd. only); 'The Wild Sweet Witch' 1989 (novel, introd. only); 'Women Writers of the Raj: Short Fiction' 1990 (anthol.); 'The Competition Wallah' 1991 (gen. introd. only); 'Orphans of the Storm: Short Fiction on the Partitioning of India' 1994 (anthol.); 'The Best Short Stories of Flora Annie Steel' 1994; contrib. to various publs., numerous articles; Gen. Ed., Arnold Publishers' (New Delhi) 'Literature of the Raj' series, 1984– ; recipient 4 Can. Council Leave Fellowships; mem. Assn. Candn. Univ. Teachers Eng.; Candn. Assn. Commonwealth Lit. & Lang. Studies; Authors Guild India; Writers Union Can.; Cambridge Soc.; Zorastrian; recreations: driving, reading, travel; Address: Regina, Sask. S4S 0A2.

**COWELL, John Walter Frederick,** B.Sc., M.Sc., M.D., CCFP, CCBOM, FRCPC; company executive officer; b. Ottawa, Ont. 6 April 1944; s. Walter Ernest and Elsie Margaret (Shennan) C.; e. Univ. of Toronto B.Sc. 1966, M.Sc. 1967, M.D. 1970; CCFP 1972; CCBOM 1980; FRCPC 1990; m. Monika Marianne d. Heinrich and Marianne Schulte; children: Stefan, Corinne, Geoffrey; CHIEF EXECUTIVE OFFICER, ALBERTA WORKERS' COMPENSATION BOARD 1992– ; general practice of medicine & occupational health cons. to num. Toronto businesses; Med. Dir. Toronto Transit Comn. 1972–77; Company Med. Dir., Candn. General Electric 1977–79; Mgr., Health Safety & Environ. Affairs 1979; Vice-Pres., Occupation & Environ. Health & Safety, Nova Corp. 1981; Vice-Pres., Health Safety & Environment, Nova Corp. of Alberta 1988–92; Pres., Novalta Property Serv. Ltd. 1987– ; Dir., Hi Point Indus. 1989– ; Allelix Crop Technologies 1988–91; Clin. Assoc. Prof. (part-time), Univ. of Calgary 1981– ; Asst. Prof. (part-time), Univ. of Alta. 1983– ; Lectr. (part-time), Simon Fraser Univi. 1988– ; Past Pres., Occupational Med. Assn. of Can.; Past Pres., Candn. Bd. of Occupational Med.; Gov., Counc. of Gov., Candn. Ctr. for Occupational Health & Safety; Dir., MEDICHEM; Mem., Occupational Health & Safety Adv. Council, Govt. of Alta.; Specialty Ctte., Royal Coll. of Physicians & Surgeons of Can.; United Ch. of Can.; author: 'Occupational Health Services: A Practical Approach' 1989; recreations: skiing, hiking; club: University Club of Toronto; Home: 12509 – 104 Ave., Edmonton, Alta. T5N 0V6; Office: P.O. Box 2415, Edmonton, Alta. T5J 2S5.

**COWIE, Bruce Edgar;** broadcaster; b. Prince Albert, Sask. 6 Mar. 1938; s. Louis Leroy and Janet (Anderson) C.; e. Prince Albert Coll. Inst.; m. Marlene Ann d. late-Michael Lehman 28 July 1958; children: Cameron Bruce, Robert Brent, Caron Dawn; PRES. AND C.O.O., Broadcast Group, ELECTROHOME LIMITED, Kitchener, Ont.; Pres., Braeside Holdings; Pres., Braeloch Consulting Ltd.; Vice-Pres., Harvard Developments Ltd.; Pres., Cedarbrae Holdings Ltd., a US Company; Vice Pres., A.P.D., U.S. Los Angeles and New York; Dir., Western Surety Co. Ltd.; Announcer, CKOM radio, Saskatoon 1956–59; Announcer, CKCK-TV, Regina 1959–68; Gen. Mgr., Armadale Productions 1968–72; Gen. Mgr., CKCK-TV, 1972–78; V.P. and Gen. Mgr., CKCK-TV, 1978–81; Pres. & Gen. Mgr., CKCK-TV & Harvard Creative Services 1981–88; Alderman, City of Regina 1974–77; named Broadcaster of the Year 1981 by Western Assn. of Broadcasters; founding Chrmn. Can Pro (TV Program Festival); Chrmn., Television Bd., Candn. Assn. of Broadcasters; past Pres. Western Football Conference; life mem. and past Pres. Saskatchewan Roughriders Football Club; mem. Quarter Century Club, Candn. Assn. of Broadcasters; Olympic Trustee; R. Catholic; Clubs: Edmonton Petroleum; Edmonton Country; recreations: skiing, swimming, golf; Office: P.O. Box 5030, Stn. E, Edmonton, Alta. T5P 4C2.

**COWIE, James F.,** B.Comm.; petroleum executive; b. Montreal, Que. 22 July 1934; s. Andrew James and Hilda Margaret (Thomson) C.; e. Various schs. Toronto Winnipeg Vancouver Victoria; Univ. of B.C., B.Comm. 1956;Advance Mgmt. Prog., Harvard Business School, 1977; m. Helen Betty Ann d. Berne C. Pickering 26 July 1957; children: James McRae, Donald Stuart, Kathryn Ann, Heather Lynn; PRESIDENT AND DIR., JAANN RESOURCES LTD.; Dir. Citadel Assurance; joined Landman, Amoco Canada Ltd. Calgary 1959, Pure Oil Co. 1964; Contracts Mgr. Central-Del Rio Oils 1965–68; Land Mgr. and Asst. Secy. Canadian Homestead Oils 1968–72; Land Mgr. Pan Ocean Oil Ltd. 1972, Vice Pres. 1974, Pres. 1975–81; Pres., Ryerson Oil and Gas Ltd. 1981–91; Zeta Psi; recreations: golf, squash; Clubs: Calgary Petroleum; Silver Springs Golf & Country; Home: 1045 Varsity Estates Pl. N.W., Calgary, Alta. T3B 3X5.

**COWING, Walter Lishman;** publisher; b. London, Eng. 14 Feb. 1926; s. Walter and Clara Emma (Kelly) C.; e. Toronto pub. schs. and East York Coll. Inst.; m. Beverley Doreen d. Arthur James Hay, D.C.M., Toronto, Ont. 24 Aug. 1946; children: Paula Doris, Richard Walter, Glen Arthur; Pres. Canada Law Book Inc. 1968–86; Pres. Canada Law Book Holdings Ltd. 1984–89; Pres., Western Legal Publications 1984–88; Pres., Garden City Press Ltd. 1986–91; Pres., Sturdi-Bilt Wood Products Ltd. 1987–92; Pres., Walbev Holdings Ltd.; served with Candn. Inf. Regt. 1944, Argylle & Sutherland Highlanders 1945; mem. Anglican; recreations: golf, curling, scuba, boating, snowmobiling; Clubs: Bayview Country (Pres. 1977); Atlantis Golf (Atlantis, Fla.); Home: 7825 Bayview Ave., LPH05, Thornhill, Ont. L3T 7N2.

**COWPERTHWAITE, Gordon H.,** LL.D., F.C.A., F.C.M.C., F.R.S.A.; company chairman and director; foundation executive; b. London, Eng. 7 Feb. 1927; s. Arthur Charles and Emma Jane C.; e. Culford Sch. Bury St. Edmunds, Eng.; McGill Univ. LL.D. 1978; m. Jean d. John Sutton 15 Sept. 1950; three s. Philip, John, Peter; Dir., Guardian Insurance Co. of Canada; Investors Group Ltd.; Sceptre Investment Counsel Ltd.; Tridel Enterprises Ltd.; joined Peat, Marwick, Mitchell & Co. London, Eng. 1943–52 qualifying as a C.A., Partner-in-Charge Mgmt. Consulting Dept. 1954–70, Managing Partner Peat, Marwick and Partners 1967; Sr. Partner and Chief Exec. Offr. Peat, Marwick, Mitchell & Co., Peat Marwick and Partners, Peat Marwick Ltd. 1970–80, Chrmn. Exec. Ctte. 1980–83 and 1988–92; Chrmn., Candn. Comprehensive Auditing Foundation 1983–93; Chrmn., Ontario Development Corp. 1989–94; Chrmn. Queen Elizabeth Hosp.; Past Chrmn., Crescent Sch. Toronto; Past Treas. Candn. Ctte. Un. World Colls.; recipient Walter J. MacDonald Meml. Award for best article 'Canadian Chartered Accountant' 1970; awarded Queen's Silver Jubilee Medal 1977; Fellow, Inst. C.A. Ontario, England, Wales and Inst. Mgmt. Cons. Ont.; Fellow, Royal Soc. of Arts; Pres. Candn. Inst. C.A.'s 1977–78; Intnl. Fed. Accts. 1980–82; recreations: golf, farming; Clubs: Toronto; Rosedale Golf & Country; Royal Poinciana Country (Naples, Fla.); Address: 602, 30 Wellington St. E., Toronto, Ont. M5E 1S3.

**COWPLAND, Michael C.J.,** P.Eng., M.Sc., Ph.D.; engineer; b. Bexhill, Sussex, England 23 Apr. 1943; s. George W. Ronald and Marjorie Ann (Plackitt) C.; e. Imperial Coll. B.Eng. 1964; Carleton Univ. M.Sc. 1968, Ph.D. 1973, D.Eng. (Hon.) 1985; children: Paula Christine, Christine Ann; PRESIDENT, COREL SYSTEMS CORP. 1985– ; Engr. Design & Project Leader, Bell Northern Research 1964–68; Mgr., Circuit Design, Microsystems Internat. Ltd. 1969–73; Pres., C.E.O. & Co-founder, Mitel 1973–84; Chrmn. 1985–86; Dir., GEAC, CATA, United Wold College, Ottawa Heart Inst.; recreations: tennis, squash; Clubs: Rideau; Thunderbird; Ottawa Athletic; Ottawa Tennis; Queensview; Home: 343 Buena Vista, Ottawa, Ont. K1S 5K8; Office: Corel Bldg., 1600 Carling Ave., Ottawa, Ont. K1Z 7M4.

**COX, Albert Reginald,** C.M., B.A., M.D., F.R.C.P.(C), F.A.C.P., F.A.C.C.; retired; b. Victoria, B.C. 18 Apr. 1928; s. Reginald Herbert Cox; e. Victoria High Sch. 1946; Victoria Coll. 1948; Univ. of B.C. B.A. 1950, M.D. 1954; m. Margaret d. L. Douglas Dobson, St. John's, Nfld. May 1954; children: Susan M., David J., Steven F.; Vice Pres. Academic and Pro-Vice Chancellor, Memorial Univ., Nfld. 1990–91, Retired; Dean of Medicine, Memorial Univ. of Nfld. 1974–87; Vice Pres., Health Sciences & Professional Schools, Memorial Univ., Nfld. 1988–90; consulting staff Gen. Hosp. St. John's Nfld.; Consultant, Grace Gen. Hosp., St. Clare's Mercy Hosp., Janeway Child Health Centre, St. John's, Nfld.; Asst. Prof. of Med. Univ. of B.C. 1961, Assoc. prof. 1964–69; Prof. and Chrmn. of Med. present Univ. 1969–74, Asoc. Dean Clin. Affairs 1972–74; author various scient. publs. cardiol. and cardiovascular physiol.; Counc., Royal Coll. Physicians & Surgeons of Can. 1986–91 and Vice Pres. (Med.) 1990–91; Ctte. Accreditation of Candn. Med. Schs. 1985–89; Past Pres., Assn. Candn. Med. Colls.; Chrmn., Candn. Interne Matching Service 1979–84; mem. Candn. Cardiovascular Soc.; Gov. (Atlantic Region) Am. Coll. Cardiology 1988–91; Candn. Soc. Clin. Investigation; Nfld. Med. Assn.; Candn. Med. Assn.; United Church; recreations: agriculture, photography; Home: 1275 Campbell Rd. RR, Cobble Hill, B.C. V0R 1L0.

**COX, Anthony L.,** C.A.; financial executive; b. Middlesex, U.K. 1951; m. Frances; 1 child; e. Kingston Polytechnical Coll., Sch. of Bus. Studies 1969; VICE-PRES. & CHIEF FINANCIAL OFFICER, SPECTRUM MUTUAL FUND SERVICES INC. 1987– ; Deloitte & Co., London, U.K. 1970–75; Peat Marwick Mitchell Montreal 1976; Touche Ross & Co. Montreal & Toronto 1977–87; Vice-Pres. & Chief Finan. Offr., Calvin Bullock Ltd.; Dir., SLS Translation Inc.; Mem., U.K. Inst. of C.A.s; Candn. Inst. of C.A.s; Investment Funds Institute: Chrmn. Conference Ctte., Mem. Taxation Ctte.; Nat. Ballet of Canada (Major Patron); recreations: jogging, tennis, skiing, gardening; Office: 55 University Ave., 15th Floor, Toronto, Ont. M5J 2H7.

**COX, Brian,** B.A., M.A., Ph.D.; university professor; b. Liverpool, Eng. 4 Aug. 1931; s. Bertram Cyril and Vera Annice (Malabar) C.; e. Univ. of Cambridge B.A. 1952, Ph.D. 1955, M.A. 1959; m. Irene d. George and Emma Austin 27 Aug. 1955; children: Nicholas D., Matthew C.; PROFESSOR AND CHAIRMAN, CENTRE FOR NUCLEAR ENGINEERING, UNIV. OF TORONTO 1989– ; Reactor Chem. Group, U.K. Atomic Energy Authority 1955–63; Branch Head, Reactor Materials & Dir., Chemistry & Materials Div., Atomic Energy of Canada Ltd. 1963–88; Dir., Candn. Nuclear Assn.; Cons., Internat. Atomic Energy Agency (Vienna); Electric Power Rsch. Inst. (Palo Alto, Ca.); Nuclear Fuel Indus. Rsch. Group; Southern Nuclear Operating Co. (Birmingham, Al.); Smith & Nephew Richards (Memphis, Tn.); AECL; Ont. Hydro, etc.; A.B. Campbell Award, Nat. Assn. of Corrosion Engrs. 1961; W.J. Kroll Zirconium Medal 1976; W.B. Lewis Medal 1988; career devoted to understanding behaviour of materials in nuclear reactors, esp. zirconium alloys used in CANDU reactors; Mem., Canadian Nuclear Soc.; Am. Nuclear Soc.; Am. Soc. for Metals; Internat. Metal. Soc.; Edit. Bd. Mem., 'J. of Nuclear Materials'; author of over 60 journal articles, 150 technical reports and 50 presentations at sci. confs.; major lecture series given in Mexico, Argentina, Taiwan, S. Korea; recreations: cycling, nordic skiing, photography; Home: 250 Queen's Quay W., Ste. 1506, Toronto, Ont. M5J 2N2; Office: 184 College St., Toronto, Ont. M5S 1A4.

**COX, David John,** B.Sc., Ph.D., A.I., Chem.E.; scientific executive; b. Hull, England 25 Apr. 1951; e. Leeds Univ. B.Sc. 1972, Ph.D. 1975; m. Angela; children: James, Alex, Laura; VICE PRES., ADVANCED TECHNOLOGIES, ALBERTA RESEARCH COUNCIL 1990– ; Dir., Alberta Microelectronics Centre 1990– ; Precarn Assoc. Inc. 1993– ; Rsch. Fellow, Univ. of York (U.K.) 1975–78; Chief Chem., Samuel Smith's Brewery 1978–80; Principal Lectr., South Bank Polytechnic 1981–84; Coord., London Ctr. for Biotechnol. 1984–85; Head of Biotechnol., South Bank Polytechnic 1985–88; Head of Biotechnology, Alberta Rsch. Council 1988–90; Mem., NSERC Strategic Grants Panel (Biotechnology) 1991– ; Mem., Am. Soc. of Chem. Engrs.; recreations: keep-fit, do-it-yourself, modern European history; Home: 311 Bulyea Rd., Edmonton, Alta. T6R 1R8; Office: P.O. Box 8330, Edmonton, Alta. T6H 5X2.

**COX, Douglas Alfred,** C.A.; business executive; b. Toronto, Ont. 21 Sept. 1937; s. Alfred George and Nellie Charlotte (Hawkins) C.; e. Scarborough Coll. 1956; Clarkson Gordon & Co., C.A. 1962; m. Diane d. Herbert and Clara Darragh 9 Sept. 1961; children: Andrea, Jeffrey, Bryan; C.E.O., Herbalife of Canada Ltd. 1986–..; Controller, American Music Corp. 1964–67; Sr. Vice-Pres. & Dir., The Foodex Group 1967–74; Pres. & C.E.O., Unifor Resource Services Group 1974–84; Pres. & C.E.O., First Venture Capital Corp. 1984–86; Dir., Bankeno Resources Ltd.; Kane Investments Ltd.; Calgary Philharmonic Orch.; Mem., Mgmt. Adv. Counc., Univ. of Calgary; Past Chrmn.: Alta. Chapter, Young Pres. Orgn.; Fac. of Business Adv. Counc., Univ. of Alta.; Past Treas. & Dir., Edmonton Eskimo Football Club; Past Pres., Edmonton Symphony Soc.; recreations: tennis, racquetball, swimming; Clubs: Centre; Calgary Golf and Country.

**COX, John F.;** auto dealership executive; b. London, England 18 May 1932; s. George and Henrietta (Hardwick) C.; e. St. Edward's Convent Sch.; m. Johanne d. Jacqueline (Pariseault) and George MacDonald 18 Sept. 1987; children: Bradley, Stefni, Jason Ambrosi (stepson); PRESIDENT, JAGUAR ROLLS-ROYCE ON BAY 1983– ; school dropout; plumber's helper; newspaper van delivery; Merchant Navy 1948–50; Nat. Serv. (Japan & Korea Mil. Police) 1950–53; warehouse packer 1953–56; bought 1st car 1932 MG J2; emigrated to Can. 1956; Salesman, Elgin Ford; Austin Motor Co.; raced Austin Healey Sprite 1960; won Candn. Class 6 Championship 1962; Sales Mgr., Austin Motor Co. 1967; Gen. Mgr., Brit. Un. Autos.; co-funded Performance Ctr. Mississauga; co-owner, Grand Touring Automobiles 1971; early franchises were Aston Martin, Rolls-Royce & B.M.W.; opened Bay and Lada 1978; Dir., Square Ct. Invest.; Minden Assoc. Motor Cars Inc.; Regent's Park Holdings; Brafni Holdings; Ensign Motors; recreations: running, skiing, boating; Clubs: RCYC; The Cambridge Club; Home: 1A Lynwood Ave., Toronto,

Ont. M4V 1K3; Office: 740 Dupont St., Toronto, Ont. M6G 1Z6.

**COX, Lionel Audley,** M.A., Ph.D., P.Eng, F.C.S., F.C.I.C., F.A.A.A.S., F.T.A.P.P.I.; research chemist; b. Winnipeg, Man. 18 Sept. 1916; s. late Harry Audley and late May Julia (Racine) C.; e. Univ. of B.C., B.A. 1941, M.A. 1943; McGill Univ., Ph.D. 1946; m. Evelyn Juliet, d. Walter Emerson Bavis, M.D., 1 Sept. 1941; children: Victoria M. R.; C. Bruce R., David A. R.; Pres., Lionel A. Cox Inc. (Research Devel. and Innovative Consultants); Teacher, Math. and Science, Univ. Sch., Victoria, B.C., 1935–40; Lectr. in Chem., Univ. of B.C., 1943–44; Chief Chem. and Consultant, Sidney Roofing and Paper Co., Victoria, 1941–44; Research Chem., American Viscose Corp., Marcus Hook, Pa., 1946–51; Sr. Research Chem. 1951–53; Vice Pres. and Dir. of Research, Johnson & Johnson Ltd., Montreal, 1953–61; Vice Pres. and Dir. of Research and Engineering, Personal Products Ltd. (Div. of Johnson & Johnson), Milltown, N.J., 1961–65; Dir. of Research & Technology Assessment, MacMillan Bloedel Ltd. 1965–77; Pres. of Lionel A. Cox Inc. (R. & D. Consultants) 1978– ; served with C.O.T.C. 1939–43; Fellow, Am. Assn. Advanc. Science; Tech. Assn. Pulp & Paper Industry; Chem. Inst. of Can.; Emeritus Rep., Indust. Research Inst. Inc.; mem.: Bd. of Mgmt., B.C. Rsch.; Am. Chem Soc.; Candn. Rsch. Mgmt. Assn.; mem., Nat. Rsch. Counc. 1971–74 and Sci. Council Can. 1974–77; Bd. of Dirs., University Hosp. Found., Vancouver, B.C.; Sigma Xi; recreations: golf, swimming; Clubs: Shaughnessy Golf & Country; Home: 4185 Yuculta Crescent, Vancouver, B.C. V6N 4A9.

**COX, Mae,** B.Ed.; community volunteer; b. Edmonton, Alta. 31 March 1930; d. Edward and Sarah (Gander) Empey; e. Univ. of Alta., B.Ed.; m. Philip James s. Matthew and Charlotte Cox 23 July 1952; children: Helen, James, Thomas, Charles, Gordon, Edward; CO-FOUNDER & EXEC. DIR., ORGAN DONORS CAN. 1974– ; employed as Co-ordinator, N. Alta., Lions Eye Bank 1985–90; taught elem. sch. in Edmonton 1950–52; Exec. Sec., Meml. Soc. of Edmonton 1962–65, 1968–78; Founding Sec., Meml. Soc. Assn. of Can. 1971–74; Pres. 1974–75; Alta. Achievement Award for Community Service 1979; founding mem., Edmonton Bird Club 1949; author: 'Human Transplants in Canada' 1978; ed. 'A Teaching Unit on Death and Dying' 1976; 'Transplant News' 1979–83; co-ed. 'Birding Around Edmonton' (pamphlet series) 1983– ; Home: 5326 Ada Blvd., Edmonton, Alta. T5W 4N7.

**COX, William H.;** broadcaster; sales executive; b. Toronto, Ont. 9 June 1933; s. G. Allan and Dorothy F.S. (Huckle) C.; e. Jarvis Coll. Inst.; m. Linda d. J. Ronald R. & Isobel Grills 19 Apr. 1963; children: Meredith, Lindsay, Allan; PRESIDENT, GLEN-WARREN BROADCAST SALES (DIV. OF BATON BROADCASTING INC.) 1985– ; Lombard Banking (U.K.) 1954–55; Sales rep., Dominion Securities Corp. Ltd. 1955–59; Sales mgr., Radio, Radio TV Representatives Ltd. 1959–63; Gen. Sales Mgr., CFTO-TV National Sales 1963–75; Vice Pres./Gen. Mgr., Glen-Warren Broadcast Sales 1975–85; mem., Candn. Assn. of Broadcast Representatives; Candn. Broadcast Executives Soc.; mem. founders' group and Gov. Olympic Trust of Can.; Vice-Pres., Candn. Olympic Assn. 1971–77, Dir. 1981–93; former Vice-Commodore, R.C.Y.C.; Olympic Yachting Team Mgr. 1968, 1972 Olympic Games; Asst. Chef de Mission, 1984 Summer Olympic Games; former Dir., Candn. Yachting Assn.; Office: Suite 300, 2 Bloor St. W., Toronto, Ont. M4W 3L2.

**COXETER, Harold Scott Macdonald,** Ph.D., LL.D., D.Math., D.Sc., F.R.S., F.R.S.C., F.I.C.A.; research mathematician; b. London, Eng., 9 Feb. 1907; s. Harold Samuel (mem. of London firm of Coxeter & Son) and Lucy (Gee) C.; e. St. George's Sch. Harpenden, Eng.; Trinity Coll., Cambridge, B.A. 1929; Ph.D. 1931 (winner of Smith's prize); Fellow there 1931–35; Rockefeller Fndn. Fellow at Princeton 1932–33; Procter Fellow at Princeton 1934–35; LL.D.: Univ. of Alta. 1957, Trent Univ. 1973, Univ. of Toronto 1979; D. Math: Univ. of Waterloo 1969; D.Sc.: Acadia 1971, Carleton Univ. 1984, McMaster 1988; Dr.rer.nat.: Univ. of Giessen 1984; m. Hendrina Johanna, d. Leonardus Brouwer, Vlaardingen, Holland, 20 Aug. 1936; children: Edgar, Susan; came to Can. 1936; PROF. EMERITUS OF MATHEMATICS, UNIV. OF TORONTO, 1980– ; Asst. Prof. there 1936–44; Assoc. Prof. 1944–48; Prof. 1948–80; Visiting Prof. at Univ. of Notre Dame 1947; Columbia Univ. 1949; Dartmouth Coll. 1964; Florida Atlantic Univ. 1965; Univ. of Amsterdam 1966; Edinburgh 1967; East Anglia 1968; Australian National 1970; Sussex 1972; Utrecht 1976; Cal. Tech. 1977; Bologna 1978; awarded H.M. Tory Medal for outstanding contrib. to Math. Science, Roy. Soc. of Can. 1950; author 'Non-Euclidean Geometry' 1942; 'Regular Polytopes' 1948; 'The Real Projective Plane' 1949; 'Introduction to Geometry' 1961; 'Projective Geometry' 1964; 'Twelve Geometric Essays' 1968; 'Regular Complex Polytopes' 1974; co-author 'The 59 Icosahedra' 1938; 'Generators and Relations' 1957; 'Geometry Revisited' 1966; 'Zero-symmetric Graphs' 1981; revised Rouse Ball 'Mathematical Recreations and Essays' (13th ed.) 1987; assisted in editing 'M.C. Escher: Art and Science' 1986; has contributed numerous papers to various scientific journals; discovered a new regular polyhedron having six hexagonal faces at each vertex, 1926; enumerated the n-dimensional kaleidoscopes, 1933; Editor-in-Chief Candn. Journal of Math., 1949–58; Pres. Can. Math. Cong. 1965–67; Int'l Cong. Mathematicians, 1974; For. Hon. Mem., Amer. Acad. Arts & Sci.; Hon. mem., Koninklijke Nederlandse Akad. van Wetenschappen; Edin. Math. Soc.; Mathematische Gesellschaft, Hamburg; Wiskundig Genootschap; London Math. Soc.; mem. Am. Math. Soc.; Math. Assn. Am.; Candn. Math. Soc.; Liberal; Protestant; recreation: music; Home: 67 Roxborough Dr., Toronto, Ont. M4W 1X2.

**COXON, Helen Cassandra,** B.A., Dip.Arch.Cons.; conservator; b. Leicester, U.K. 8 July 1960; d. John Iley and Glenise Winifred (Smith) C.; e. Wallington H.S. for Girls 1978; Univ. of Durham B.A. 1982, Dip.Arch.Cons. 1986; m. Hugh s. Lila and John Francis Theodore Spencer 7 Sept. 1985; CONSERVATOR, ROYAL ONTARIO MUSEUM 1987– ; emigrated to Canada 1985; internship in ethnographic conservation 1985–86; works mainly on metals, textiles & ethnographic artifacts; currently involved in researching history, degradation & conservation of plastics; Mem., Un. Ch. of Can.; Internat. Inst. for Conserv. of Hist. & Artistic Works; U.K. Inst. for Conserv. of Hist. & Artistic Works; IIC Candn. Group; recreations: music, crafts, outdoors; Home: 61 Wheatfield Rd., Etobicoke, Ont. M8V 2P5; Office: Conservation Dept., Royal Ontario Museum, 100 Queen's Park, Toronto, Ont. M5S 2C6.

**COYNE, John McCreary,** D.F.C., C.StJ., Q.C., M.A.; lawyer, retired; b. Winnipeg, Man. 20 June 1919; s. Hon. James Bowes, Q.C., and Edna Margaret (Elliott) C.; e. Ravenscourt Sch., Winnipeg, Man.; Univ. of Manitoba, B.A. (Hons.) 1940; Oxford Univ., B.A. 1947, M.A. 1951; m. Margery Joan, d. late Frank G. Daniels, Montreal, Que., 19 Sept. 1952; children: Jennifer, Deborah, Barbara, John, Ryland; PARTNER (Retired), OSLER, HOSKIN & HARCOURT in Ottawa (formerly Herridge, Tolmie); called to the Bar at Lincoln's Inn, London, 1947; to the Bar of Manitoba, 1948, and of Ont. 1948; cr. Q.C. 1964; served in 2nd World War with R.C.A.F. 1942–45; Mem., Candn. roster of panelists for dispute settlement procedures under Chapter 19 of Can.-U.S. Free Trade Agreement; mem., Candn. Bar Assn.; Zeta Psi; Anglican; Clubs: Rideau; Royal Ottawa Golf; Home: 101 – 31 Durham Private Rd., Ottawa, Ont. K1M 2J1; Office: 50 O'Connor St., 15th Floor, Ottawa, Ont. K1P 6L2.

**COYNE, John Michael,** B.F.A., M.F.A.; artist/educator; b. St. Stephen, N.B. 23 May 1950; s. John Joseph and Marie Eleanor (Dennison) C.; e. St. Stephen H.S.; Mount Allison Univ. B.F.A. 1975; Univ. of Regina M.F.A. 1977; PROF. OF VISUAL ARTS, SIR WILFRED GRENFELL COLLEGE, MEMORIAL UNIV. OF NFLD. 1991– ; selected one man exhibs.: Emma Butler Gall., St. John's 1990; Memorial Univ. Art Gall. 1990; Sir Wilfred Grenfell Coll. 1987, 1989; Mira Godard Gall. 1986; Acadia Univ. Art Gall. 1983, 1984; Univ. of N.B. Art Ctr. 1984; St. Mary's Univ. Art Gall. 1983; Univ. Coll. of Cape Breton Art Gall. 1983; Owens Art Gall., Mt. Allison Univ. 1983; selected group exhibs: 'Painting the Land' Mira Godard Gall. 1991; 'Newfoundland Artists' Gallery 78, Fredericton, N.B. 1988; 'The Modern Landscape' Mira Godard Gall. 1985; Bi-Centennial Invit. Exhib., Univ. of N.B. Art Ctr. 1985; 'Images' Edmonton Art Gall. 1984; 'Annapolis Valley' Art Gall. of N.S. 1980; 'Realism in Canada' Mackenzie Gall. 1978; represented in collections: Govt. of Nfld. and Labrador; Art Gall. of N.S.; Mt. Allison Univ.; N.S. Art Bank; Univ. of Regina; St. Mary's Univ. Art Gall.; Sir Wilfred Grenfell Coll.; Husky Oil; Labatt's Breweries; Bank of N.S.; Midland-Doherty; Placer Dome, Inc.; Davies, Ward & Beck; Xerox Can.; Faskin-Colvin; Abitibi-Price; Toshiba of Canada; Air Canada; private coll.; rep. by Mira Godard Gall.; Lectr., Acadia Univ. 1977–78; Asst. Prof., Acadia Univ. 1978–84; Assoc. Prof. 1984–86; Head, Dept. of Art 1983–86; Senate 1981–84; Bd. of Gov. 1985–86; Art Gall. Adv. Bd. 1978–86; Head, Dept. of Visual Arts, Sir Wilfred Grenfell Coll., Memorial Univ. of Nfld. 1986–92; Assoc. Prof. 1986–91; Prof. 1991– ; Senate 1991–92; Govt. of Nfld. & Labrador Art Procurement Ctte., D.P.W. 1986–92; Greenshields Found. Grant 1976; Mem., Coll. Art Assn. of Am.; Visual Arts Ont.; recreations: reading, photography, travel; Home: 31 Central St., Corner Brook, Nfld.; Office: Memorial Univ. of Nfld., Corner Brook, Nfld. A2H 6P9.

**COYNE, William E.,** B.Sc., M.S., Ph.D.; business executive; b. Toronto, Ont. 3 Dec. 1936; s. John T. and Lela M. (Moran) C.; e. Univ. of Toronto B.S. 1958, M.S. 1960; Univ. of Virginia Ph.D. 1963; m. Winnie Faye d. William and Viola Sheffield 21 Sept. 1963; children: Lara E. and Bethany M.; PRES., GEN. MGR. & DIR., 3M CANADA 1990– ; Rsch. Chemist, G.D. Searle Co. 1963–68; 3M Company: Central Research Lab, 1968–70; R&D Mgr., Riker Labs. 1970–75; Tech. Dir., Surgical Products Group 1975–78; Gen. Mgr., McGhan Med., Inc. 1978–80; Gen. Mgr.-Vice Pres., Surgical Prod. Div. 1980–84; Group Vice Pres. 1984–90; Dir., Cuddy Internat. Corp.; Chrmn., London Investment in Education Council; Dir., London Health Assn., Univ. Hosp.; recreations: boating, tennis; Home: 82 Quinella Place, London, Ont. N6K 4H3; Office: P.O. Box 5757, London, Ont. N6A 4T1.

**COYTE, Peter C.,** B.A., M.A., Ph.D.; university professor; b. Plymouth, Eng. 22 Oct. 1955; s. Wilfred Geoffrey and Mary Patricia (Falvey) C.; e. Univ. of Kent B.A. (Hons.) 1977; Univ. of Western Ont. M.A. 1978, Ph.D. 1982; m. Mary C. d. William and Patricia Stafford 24 July 1981; children: Emma, James, Madeline, William; ASSOC. PROF. (WITH TENURE), HEALTH ADMIN., FAC. OF MED., UNIV. OF TORONTO 1987– ; Asst. Prof., Simon Fraser Univ. 1981–83; Assoc. Prof. (with tenure), Univ. of Alta. 1983–87; Dir., M.Sc./Ph.D. Health Admin. Prog., Univ. of Toronto 1988– ; Inst. Assoc., Policy Analysis 1990– ; Mem., Grad. Fac., Community Health 1987– ; Assoc. Sci. Staff, Otolaryngology, Mt. Sinai Hosp. 1991– ; Adjunct Prof., Communicative Disorders, Univ. of W. Ont. 1989– ; Owner,PC Coyte Cons.; Academic-in-Residence, North York Gen. Hosp. 1992; Fellow, Accrediting Comn. on Edn. for Health Serv. Admin. 1989; Bd. Mem., Flemingdon Health Ctr. 1990– ; Mem., Candn. Health Econ. Rsch. Assn.; Am. Public Health Assn.; Am. Econ. Assn.; Candn. Econ. Assn.; Candn. Law & Econ. Assn.; author of 26 research articles; recreations: sports, music, cottaging; Home: 22 Sawley Dr., Willowdale, Ont. M2K 2J1; Office: Toronto, Ont. M5S 1A8.

**COZENS, John;** musician; heraldic artist; editor; adviser on protocol; b. Tottenham, Eng. 27 Apr. 1906; s. Rev. Reginald and Mrs. C.; m. Winifred Pitman (dec.); children: Joyce Marian, John Francis, Carol Judith (dec.); Hon. Secretary, Canadian Music Council; Conductor, Civil Service Choral Society and other choral groups; mem.: Candn. Heraldry Society; Ont. Reg. Music Teachers Assn.; Assn. Candn. Choral Conductors; Ont. Choral Federation; Editor, Arranger and Composer of music publ. by U.S., Candn. and Eng. Co's; Centennial Medal 1967; Candn. Music Council medal 1976; Queen's Jubilee Medal 1977; Hon. Life Mem., Royal Sch. of Church Music, Eng. 1987; Club: Arts & Letters; Address: 188 Elmwood Ave., Willowdale, Ont. M2N 3M6.

**CRABTREE, Kaye Lynn,** R.N.; artist, art instructor; b. Peterborough, Ont. 21 Sept. 1945; d. John (Jack) William and Clara (Larry) Edna (Larson) Thornton; e. Peterborough Civic Hosp. R.N. 1966; m. David R. s. Harry and Isobel C. 14 June 1969; children: Robert Douglas, Katherine Anne, James David; worked 4 years as a registered nurse; self-taught artist (with assistance from mother, also an artist); has used many media but now paints exclusively in oils; paintings are very realistic depictions of landscapes, rustic barns, waterfalls, birds, florals & seascapes and range from miniatures to large paintings; goal is to show the beauty of nature in paintings and to others; has taught oil painting for 18 years (approx. 60 students per week ranging in age from 9–94) and has been rewarded by making many people aware of the beauty of nature; volunteer art teacher in a local seniors home for 6 years; works appear in many galleries incl. Gallery on the Lake Buckhorn, Falconer Fine Art Hamilton, Special Effects Grimsby and have been sold to many homes & offices in Canada & Eur.; mem., local art councils; participant in local art shows, judged art displays & contests; recreations: writing poetry, swimming, water sports, bridge, chess, fishing, cottage on Deer Bay in Kawartha Lakes; Address: 5310 Regional Rd., Unit 81, Beamsville, Ont. L0R 1B3.

**CRAGG, Arthur Wesley,** D.Phil.; university professor; b. Bowmanville, Ont. 18 Jan. 1941; s. Arthur Richard and Florence Gertrude (Clare) C.; e. Kitchener Waterloo Coll., Strathcona Comp. H.S. 1959; Univ. of Alta. B.A.(Hons.) 1963, M.A. 1964; Oxford Univ. B.Phil. 1966, D.Phil. 1972; Rhodes Scholar (Alta.) 1964;

I.O.D.E. Travel Scholarship 1964; m. Mary Boyd d. J.W.E. and Rena Newbery 27 Apr. 1969; children: David Andrew, Elizabeth Marie, John Paul Wesley; GEORGE R. GARDINER PROFESSOR OF BUSINESS ETHICS, FACULTY OF ADMINISTRATIVE STUDIES, YORK UNIV. 1992– ; Prof., Laurentian Univ. 1967–92, Chrmn., Joint Dept. of Phil. 1975–79, 1984–90, Dir., Law and Justice Programs 1976–87, Pres. Faculty Assn. 1976–78; mem. Counc. of Ont. Univs. 1976–77; Bd. of Dirs.: Ont. Confed. of Univ. Faculty Assns. 1977–79; Candn. Assn. of Univ. Teachers 1977–79; Ed. Bd. & Bd. of Advs. 'Interchange' 1983– ; Exec. Dir., Internat. Assn. for Phil. of Law and Soc. Phil., Candn. Sect. 1984– ; Assoc. Sec. & Sec., Candn. Phil. Assn. 1984–87; Mem., Bd. & Extve., John Howard Soc., Canada, Ontario, Sudbury 1982–90; Pres., John Howard Soc. of Can. 1988–90; Chrmn., St. Andrew's United Church Counc. 1987–89; Dir., Candn. Assn. of Rhodes Scholar 1993– ; author: 'Contemporary Moral Issues' 1983, 2nd ed. 1987, 3rd ed. 1992; 'The Practice of Punishment: Toward a Theory of Restorative Justice'; Ed.: 'Challenging the Conventional'; 'Retribution and Its Critics'; recreations: music, sailing, skiing; Home: 54 Tribbling Cres., Aurora, Ont. L4G 4W9; Office: York Univ., North York, Ont. M3J 1P3.

**CRAGG, John Gordon,** Ph.D.; educator; b. Toronto, Ont. 3 May 1937; s. Gerald Robertson and Evelyn Alice C.; e. Westmount (Que.) Jr. and Sr. High Schs. 1954; McGill Univ. B.A. 1958; Cambridge Univ. B.A. 1960; Princeton Univ. Ph.D. 1965; m. Olga d. Boris Browzin, Washington, D.C. 8 Sept. 1962; two s. Michael Ian, Philip Andrew; PROF. OF ECONOMICS, UNIV. OF B.C. 1971– ; Asst. Prof. Univ. of Chicago 1964–67; Asst. Prof. present Univ. 1967, Assoc. Prof. 1968, Head of Dept. 1976–85; Dir. of Rsch., Prices & Incomes Comn. Ottawa 1969–71; author 'Wage Changes and Labour Flows in Canada' 1973; co-author 'Expectations and the Structure of Share Prices' 1982; various articles econometrics & corp. finance prof. journs. recreations: skiing, cottaging, music; Office: 997 – 1873 East Mall, Vancouver, B.C. V6T 1Y2.

**CRAGG, Laurence Harold,** M.A., Ph.D., D.C.L., D.Sc., LL.D., F.C.I.C.; university professor and administrator; b. Lethbridge, Alta. 7 Sept. 1912; s. Rev. Harry Humphries and Louise Caroline (Howson) C.; e. Wingham High Sch.; Sarnia Collegiate & Tech. Sch.; Oshawa Collegiate and Vocational Inst.; Univ. Toronto, B.A. Hons. (gold medallist) 1934; M.A. 1935; Ph.D. 1937; Hon. degrees: D.C.L. Acadia Univ., 1963; D.Sc. Univ. of N.B. 1964, McMaster Univ. 1976, Brandon Univ. 1976; LL.D. St. Thomas Univ. 1973, Mt. Allison Univ. 1976; m. Jean Irvine, d. Rev. Frederick S. and Ethel (Irvine) Dowling, 27 Dec. 1938; children: Jean Elizabeth (Sutherland); Ronald Laurence; James Frederick; PRESIDENT EMERITUS, MOUNT ALLISON UNIV. since 1975; Teaching Asst., Univ. Toronto 1934–37; Prof. Chem., Brandon Coll. 1937–43; Lectr., Asst. Prof., Assoc. Prof., Prof. Chem., McMaster Univ. 1943–59; Chrmn. Dept. Chem. 1958–59; Visiting Lectr., Univ. Mich. Summers 1954, 1955; Vice-Pres., Prof. Chem., Univ. Alta. 1959–63; Pres.-Elect, Mt. Allison Univ. 1962–63; Pres. and Vice-Chancellor, 1963–75; part-time Lectr., McMaster Univ. 1976–79; author 35 scientific papers, various articles and reviews in sci., ed., religion; author 'Let's Look at Elders' 1954; co-author (with R.P. Graham): 'An Introduction to the Principles of Chemistry' 1958; 'The Essentials of Chemistry' 1956, 1958; (with R.P. Graham and J.V. Young): 'The Elements of Chemistry' 1959, 1961; Fellow, Chem. Inst. Can. (F.C.I.C.); rec'd. Montreal Medal (Chem. Inst. Can.) 1965; Chem. Ed. Award (C.I.C.) 1966; Centennial Medal 1967; mem. Candn. Scientific Delegation to Czechoslovakia 1966; Candn. Higher Ed. Delegation to China 1974; Defense Research Bd. Panel on Shock & Plasma Expanders, 1955–63; Alta. Research Counc. 1960–63; Nat. Research Counc. 1965–68; N.B. Research and Productivity Counc. 1963–70; Sci. Counc. Can. Comte on Support of Research in the Universities, 1967–69; Chem. Inst. Can. (Dir. Professional Affairs 1957–59, Pres. 1962–63); Assn. Univs. and Colls. Can. (Dir. 1965–67); Assn. Atlantic Univs. (Vice-Chrmn. 1973–75); Assn. Commonwealth Univs.; Chrmn. Ed. Bd. Canadian Chemical Education 1964–66; UNESCO Candn. Nat. Commission 1966– ; (Pres. 1972–78); Candn. Delegation UNESCO Gen. Conf. 1972, 1974 (Vice-Chrmn.), 1976 (Vice-Chrmn.); United Church Elder; Clerk of Session; Life Elder; delegate to various Presbyteries and Conferences; Commissioner to Gen. Counc. 1948, 1950, 1952, 1954, 1956, 1971; Delegate to World Council of Churches 1961; Chrmn., Bd. Men 1956–62; Mem. Gen. Commission on Union 1967–73; Chrmn, Standing Comte. on Sci., Tech. & Ethics 1974–80; Hamilton Public Library, Bd. mem. 1949–56, Chrmn. 1953; Dir., Family Services Hamilton-Wentworth (Vice Pres. 1983–84, Pres. 1984–86); Extve. mem., U.N. Assn. (Hamilton Region) 1981–83; Hamilton Assn. for the Advancement of Lit., Sci. & Art (Pres. 1955–56, 1980–81); Sci. Teachers Assn. Ont. (Hon. Pres. 1959); Am. Chem. Soc.; Royal Soc. Arts (Fellow 1970–78); recreations: books, music, photography; gardening; curling; Home: 3252 Robert St., Burlington, Ont. L7N 1E7.

**CRAIG, Burton MacKay,** B.Sc.A., M.Sc., Ph.D.; biochemist; b. Vermilion, Alta. 29 May 1918; s. Walter Alexander and Mary Jessie (Baillie) C.; e. Univ. of Sask. B.Sc.A. 1944, M.Sc. 1946; Univ. of Minn. Ph.D. 1950; m. Inez Gladys d. late John Kalmer Guttormson 5 July 1945; children: Wayne Keith, Cheryl Lynne; Asst. Research Offr. 1950, Assoc. Research Offr. 1954, Sr. Research Offr. 1960, Princ. Research Offr. 1968, Assoc. Dir. 1969–70; Dir., Prairie Regional Lab. 1970–83; mem. Council and Extve. Comte. Sask. Research Council 1974–83; Group Dir. Nat. Research Council 1979–83, mem. Council 1980–81; mem. Can. Agric. Research Council 1974–83; Can. Agric. Services Co-ordinating Comte. 1978–83; author over 60 scient. papers, 2 book chapters; holds 2 patents; Hon. Life mem. Agric. Inst. Can.; Agric. Grad. Assn. (Sask.); mem. Chem. Inst. Can.; Am. Oil Chem. Soc.; Candn. Inst. Food Technol. (W.J. Eva Award); Am. Assn. Advanc. Science; Candn. Rsch. Mgmt. Assn.; Sask. Order of Merit; Phi Lambda Upsilon; Sigma Xi; United Church; recreations: golf, curling; Home: 423 Lake Cres., Saskatoon, Sask. S7H 3A3.

**CRAIG, James Basil,** B.Arch., M.R.A.I.C.; retired; b. Toronto, Ont. 10 Apr. 1926; s. James Henry, B.A.Sc., F.R.A.I.C. and Grace MacFarlane (Morris) C.; e. St. Pauls Sch. for Boys, Toronto, Ont.; Univ. of Toronto Schs.; Univ. of Toronto, B.Arch. 1950; m. Lise M. Chaput 1988; four children: James Bruce, Tara Patricia, Sheila Jane, D'Arcy William; former Partner, Craig, Madill, Abram & Ingleson, Toronto 1954–63; former Partner, Craig, Kohler, Dickey and Edmundson 1963–83; former Partner, Bregman & Hamann 1984–87; Partner, Craig & Beckett Architects 1988–92; Retired 1992; has designed many schools and pub. bldgs., especially in Ont.; served with R.C.N.V.R., 1945; on active Reserve, R.C.N., 1949–55, retiring with rank of Acting Lt.; mem., Ont. Assn. Arch. (Chrmn., Toronto Society 1961–62, Ottawa Soc. 1965–67) First Vice-Pres. 1979; Royal Arch. Inst., Can.; Phi Delta Theta; recreations: sailing, photography, model-building; Club: Britannia Yacht; Kingston Yacht; Home: 162 Bradford St., Ottawa, Ont. K2B 5Z3.

**CRAIG, Rev. Canon James Hannington,** M.A., D.D. (Ang.); b. Montreal, P.Q.; s. Rev. Dr. W. W. Craig, former Dean of Ont.; e. Univ. of British Columbia, B.A. 1925; Trinity Coll., Univ. of Toronto 1928–30, B.D., M.A., D.D.; m. Dianne V. 1978; children: Myrna, John, David; taught school in Vernon, B.C. 1926–28; Dean of Residence and Lect. in Practical Theol., Huron Coll., London, Ont. and at the same time Rector of St. Luke's Ch. there 1930–35; Incumbent, St. Mary's Ch., Vancouver, B.C. and Lect. at Ang. Theol. Coll. there 1935–44, when apptd. Dean of Algoma and Rector of St. Luke's Cathedral, Sault Ste. Marie 1944–51; Dean of Calgary and Rector of Cath. Ch. of the Redeemer there 1951–53; Rector, Grace Church On-the-Hill, Toronto 1953–72; retired; Address: Cherry Park, 204 - 317 Winnipeg St., Penticton, B.C. V2A 8J9.

**CRAIG, James S.,** M.Arch.; b. Moose Jaw, Sask. 17 Dec. 1912; s. Netson Ross and Carrie E. Shand (Fraser) C.; e. Univ. of Toronto, 1929–31; Univ. of Man., B.Arch. (Gold Medal) 1934; Mass. Inst. of Tech., M.Arch. 1935; m. Marion Mollie, d. late Walter Stuart Moore, 30 Nov. 1940 (dec. 14 June 1987); m. Vivian Billingsley 9 Sept. 1989; Pres., Moorecraig Co. Limited; with W. L. Somerville, 1935–39 and W. R. L. Blackwell, 1939; Architect, Ford Motor Company of Canada, 1940–45; formed partnership Blackwell & Craig, 1945, becoming Blackwell, Craig and Zeidler, 1954; changed to Craig & Zeidler, 1956 and Craig, Zeidler and Strong, 1963; retired 1973; some major projects: Ajax & Pickering Gen. Hosp.; Whitby Gen. Hosp.; Guelph Gen. Hosp. and Nurses Residence; McMaster Univ. Health Sciences Centre; Dumont Hosp., Moncton, N.B.; Chalmers Hosp., Fredericton, N.B.; Saint John Regional Hosp.; Ontario Place; firm received Massey Medal awards, 1955, 1959, 1967; Nat. Design Awards, 1962, 1964, 1967; Ont. Masons Relations Council Awards, 1964, 1965, 1966, 1968, 1970, 1971; Canadian Architect Year Book Design Awards, 1967, 1969, 1970, 1971; Trustee, Art Gallery of Ont. and Chrmn. of Exhn. Comte. for AGO, 1970–74; Dir., Art Gallery of Peterborough 1974–79; author of several articles on hosp. design in 'Candn. Hospital'; Chrmn. Peterborough Planning Bd., 1958, 1959; Peterborough United Way Campaign 1977–78, 1978–79; mem., Roy. Inst. Br. Arch.; Royal Arch. Inst. Can.; Freemason; Delta Kappa Epsilon; Protestant; recreations: skiing, sailing; Clubs: Peterborough; Peterborough Golf & Country; Address: 21 Merino Rd., Peterborough, Ont. K9J 6M8.

**CRAIG, John A.D.,** O.B.E., E.D., B.Com., F.C.A.; chartered accountant; b. Montreal, P.Q. 30 Nov. 1907; s. John and Jeanne (Eluau) C.; e. Upper Canada Coll., Toronto, Ont.; Univ. of Toronto; m. Elizabeth Hunter, d. C.W. Rous, 7 Dec. 1937; two d.: Sheila (Mrs. David Ward), Jane; formed the firm of Snyder, Craig & Co., Chart. Accts. in 1946; served with The Royal Regt. of Can. and The 3rd Candn. Inf. Div., in 2nd World War; awarded M.B.E., and O.B.E.; Order of Orange Nassau (Netherlands) and Mentioned in Despatches; mem., Inst. Chart. Accts. Ont. (Life); Candn. Tax Foundation; Art Gallery of Toronto (Life); Royal Candn. Inst. (Life mem. and former mem. of Council); St. Andrew's Soc. (Past Pres.); Fort York Br., Candn. Legion (Past Pres.); Kappa Alpha; Presbyterian; Clubs: National; Toronto Cricket, Skating & Curling; Royal Candn. Mil. Inst.; Home: 204 Heath St. W., Toronto, Ont. M4V 1V5.

**CRAIG, Kenneth Denton,** M.A., Ph.D.; educator; b. Calgary, Alta. 21 Nov. 1937; s. William Denton and Wilhelmina (MacIntyre) C.; e. Sir George Williams Univ. B.A. 1958; Univ. of B.C. M.A. 1960; Purdue Univ. Ph.D. 1964; m. Sydney G. d. Deane and Ruth Smith 10 Apl. 1971; children: Kenneth Deane, Alexandra Grace, Daniel Smith (dec.), Christopher James; PROF. OF PSYCHOL. UNIV. OF B. C. 1963– , Dir. Grad. Prog. in Clin. Psychol. 1980–82, 1987–91; Assoc. Prof. Univ. of Calgary 1969–71; Killam Sr. Fellow 1989–90; Canada Council Killam Rsch. Fellow 1992–94; various rsch. grants psychol. pain; Nat. Adv. First Aid Candn. Red Cross Soc.; Dir. Candn. Pain Found.; ed. Candn. Jour. Behavioural Sci. 1985–89; co-ed. 'Health Enhancement, Disease Prevention and Early Intervention: Biobehavioral Perspectives' 1990; numerous rsch. articles, chapters, clin. & health psychol. publs.; Fellow, Am. Psychol. Assn.; Acad. Behavioral Medicine Rsch.; Pres., Candn. Psychol. Assn. 1986–87; B.C. Psychol. Assn. 1977; Treas. Social Sci. Fedn. Can. 1988–92; Vice-Pres. (Pres.-Elect), Candn. Pain Soc. 1991–94; recreations: running, skiing; Home: 4310 Locarno Cres., Vancouver, B.C. V6R 1G3; Office: 2136 West Mall, Vancouver, B.C. V6T 1Z4.

**CRAIG, Lloyd Menten;** b. Vancouver, B.C. 27 March 1945; e. Washington State Univ. B.A. 1968; m. Heather; children: Matthew, Gavin; PRESIDENT, CHIEF EXECUTIVE OFFICER & DIRECTOR, SURREY METRO SAVINGS CREDIT UNION 1986– ; Mercantile Bank of Canada 1970–85; Mem., Vancouver Club; recreations: skiing, jogging, tennis.

**CRAIG, R. Ross;** retired industrial executive; b. Hamilton, Ont. 18 Nov. 1915; s. Norman H. and Ethel (Maguire) C.; e. Burlington (Ont.) High Sch.; three children: Gaye, Robert, David; former Vice Chrmn., Dofasco Inc.; joined firm in Time Office and Cost Distribution, 1935; trans. to Sales and Order Dept. 1939; apptd. Vice-Pres., Tin Plate and Sheet Sales, 1951; Vice-Pres., Marketing, 1961; Dir. & Vice-Pres.-Commercial, 1964; mem., Cdn. Mfrs. Assn. (Vice-Chrmn. 1982); Anglican; recreations: philately, gardening, golf, fishing, hunting; Clubs: Hamilton Golf & Country; Tamahaac Club; Hamilton; Home: 3440 Lakeshore Rd., Burlington, Ont. L7N 1B3.

**CRAIG, Ronald George,** B.A.Sc., M.A.Sc., Ph.D.; university professor; b. Victoria, B.C. 4 July 1946; s. Thomas Liddle and Lois Anne (Silk) C.; e. Univ. of Waterloo B.A.Sc. 1969, M.A.Sc. 1971, Ph.D. 1979; m. Shirley d. Charles and Jean Reid 28 June 1969; children: Douglas Reid, Heather Elizabeth; ASSOCIATE PROFESSOR, WILFRID LAURIER UNIVERSITY 1985– ; Co-founder & Secretary-Treasurer, Volker-Craig Limited 1973–79; Asst. Prof., Wilfrid Laurier Univ. 1979–85; Assoc. Dean of Business 1988– ; Acting Dean, Sch. of Bus. & Economics 1992; Acting Vice-Pres. Finance & Admin. 1993–94; Pres., Ronald George Craig Limited; Home: R.R. 2, West Montrose, Ont. N0B 2V0; Office: Waterloo, Ont. N2L 3C5.

**CRAIK, Fergus Ian Muirden,** B.Sc., Ph.D., F.R.S.C.; educator; b. Edinburgh, Scot. 17 Apr. 1935; s. George and Frances (Crabbe) C.; e. George Watson's Boys' Coll. Edinburgh 1953; Univ. of Edinburgh B.Sc. 1960; Univ. of Liverpool Ph.D. 1965; m. Anne d. Jack and Rita Catherall 22 July 1961; children: Lindsay, Neil; PROF. OF PSYCHOL. UNIV. OF TORONTO 1975– , Chrmn. of Psychol. 1985–90; Lectr. in Psychol. Birkbeck Coll. Univ. of London 1965–71; Assoc. Prof. of Psychol. present Univ. 1971; Fellow, Center Advanced Study in Behavioral Sci's Stanford Univ. 1982–83; Killam Rsch. Fellow 1982–84; Guggenheim Fellowship 1982–83; Ont. Psychol. Found. Rsch. Award 1986; Candn. Psychol. Assn. Disting. Scientific Contribution Award 1987; Am. Psychol. Soc. William James Fellow Award 1993; ed. Jour. of Verbal Learning & Verbal Behavior 1980–84; co-ed. 'Levels of Processing in Human Memory' 1979; 'Aging and Cognitive Processes' 1982; 'Varieties of Memory and Consciousness' 1989; 'The Handbook of Aging and Cognition' 1992; Fellow, Candn. Psychol. Assn.; Am. Psychol. Assn.; Soc. Exper. Psychols.; recreations: reading, walking, music, tennis; Home: 69 Howland Ave., Toronto, Ont. M5R 3B2; Office: Toronto, Ont. M5S 1A1.

**CRAM, Phillip John,** B.Sc., Ph.D.; petroleum executive; b. Reading, Eng. 5 Feb. 1943; s. George and Joan Amy (Asher) C.; e. Imp. Coll. Univ. of London B.Sc. 1964, Ph.D. 1968; m. Rae d. Walter and Marjorie Morrison 13 May 1975; two d. Sarah, Emily; Gen. Mgr., Texaco's exploration and production operations in Angola 1992– ; Rsch. Assoc. Petroleum Recovery Inst. Calgary 1969; Rsch. Chem. Texaco Exploration Canada Ltd. Calgary 1973; various managerial assignments Texaco Inc. White Plains, N.Y. 1978–87; Asst. to Sr. Vice Pres. Texaco Canada Resources Calgary 1988; Pres. and C.E.O., Texaco Canada Petroleum Inc. 1989–92; holds several US and Candn. patents; author various tech. papers; mem. Soc. Petroleum Engs.; Anglican; recreations: hiking, tennis, skiing; Club: Glencoe; Home: 2123 – 7 Street S.W., Calgary, Alta. T2T 2X3.

**CRAMER, Eugene Casjen,** Ph.D.; university professor; b. Davis, S. Dakota 22 Nov. 1935; s. John C. and Ella Mae (Alderson) C.; e. Yankton Coll., B.Mus. (cum laude) 1957; Conservatoire Americane, Fountainebleau summer 1960; Yale Univ., M.Mus. 1964; Indiana Univ. summer 1967; Harvard Univ. summer 1968; Boston Univ., Ph.D. 1973; m. Abigail d. Robert and Julie Rosegrant 22 June 1962; children: Casjen, Nelson, Seth; Music Teacher, public schools (U.S.) 1957–61; Teacher & Dept. Chrmn., Park College (Parkville, MO) 1964–70; joined present univ. 1973; prof. 1984; Music Hist. Area Chrmn. 1976–80; Acad. Advr. 1981–84; Grad. Studies Coord. 1981–85; Head 1984–93; Classical Music Critic, 'The Calgary Albertan' 1976–80; Bd. Mem., West. Bd. of Music 1984–89; Suzuki Talent Edn. Soc. of Calgary 1986–93; Music Working Ctte., 1988 Winter Olympic Arts Fest. 1985–88; Dir., Calgary Region Arts Found. 1980–88 (Bd. Mem. 1980–82, 1984–88); Chair, Standing Ctte. of Institutional Members of Candn. Univ. Music Soc. 1989–91; Vice-Pres., Candn. Univ. Music Soc. 1991–93, President 1993– ; Candn. representative, Council of the Internat. Musicological Soc. 1992– ; author: 'Officium Hebdomadae Sanctae, Tomas Luis de Victoria' 1982, 'A Basic Skills Handbook for Music History Students' 1984 and numerous articles in schol. jours.; recreations: travelling, hiking; Home: 2712 48th Ave. N.W., Calgary, Alta. T2L 1C3; Office: Calgary, Alta. T2N 1N4.

**CRAMP, Donald Arthur,** H.B.A., M.Sc.; hospital executive; b. Meaford, Ont. 23 Dec. 1936; s. Reginald Graham and Sarah Agnus (Robinson) C.; e. Univ. of W. Ont. H.B.A. 1960; Columbia Univ. M.Sc. 1962; m. Lynda d. Lawrence and Eleanor D'Acunto 14 Feb. 1970; one s. Donald Arthur Jr.; PRES. & C.E.O., PHILADELPHIA HOSPITALS AND HIGHER EDUCATION AUTHORITY 1987– ; joined Bank of America, San Francisco 1962–64; General Motors Corp. Oshawa 1964–66; Asst. Administrator, South Nassau Communities Hosp. Oceanside, N.Y. 1966–70; Dir. Highland View Hosp. Cleveland 1970–71; Sr. Vice Pres. Cuyahoga Co. Hosp. Systems 1971–76; Exec. Dir. Univ. Hosp. Univ. of Louisville 1976–80; Asst. Vice Pres. Ohio State Univ. and Exec. Dir. Ohio State Univ. Hosps. Columbus 1980–84; Pres. & C.E.O., Univ. of Alberta Hospitals 1984–87; Guest Lectr., N.Y. Sch. of Administrative Med. Columbia Univ. 1966–70; Temple Univ. 1988; Asst. Prof. of Med. Case Western Reserve Univ. Cleveland 1970–76; Adjunct Prof. of Allied Med. Profns. Ohio State Univ. 1981–84; Bd. Mem., College of Physicians 1993– ; Bd. Mem., Pennsylvania Blue Shield; Boy Scouts of Am.; Visiting Nurses Assn. (VNA) 1987– ; Invitee to Represent Dwight D. Eisenhower, People to People Culture Exchange Prog. to Soviet Union and Repub. of China 1983, 1985; mem. Gov.'s Task Force Welfare Reform, Ky.; mem. Bd. Ohio Hosp. Assn. Columbus; Fellow, Am. Coll. Hosp. Administrators; mem., Am. Hosp. Assn. (Chrmn. Rsch. & Publs. Pub. Gen. Sect. 1971–76); Beta Theta Pi; Dir. Nat. Exchange Club 1967–70; Home: 9 Rex Court, Chestnut Hill, Philadelphia, Pa. 19118–3748; Office: 1500 Land Title Bldg., Chestnut and Broad Streets, Philadelphia, Pa. 19110–1088.

**CRANDALL, Robert Hunter,** B.Com., M.B.A., Ph.D., F.C.A.; educator; b. Halifax, N.S. 20 Jan. 1930; s. William Henry and Minnie Elizabeth (Parker) C.; e. Queen's Univ. B.Com. 1951; Univ. of Cal. Berkeley M.B.A. 1966, Ph.D. 1968; C.A. 1955; m. Frances Lou d. William John Craig 9 Oct. 1954; children: Robert Craig, Ian Edward, Heather Frances, Peter Matthew; PROF. OF BUS. QUEEN'S UNIV. 1968– ; joined Ernst & Young C.A.'s 1952–59; present Univ. 1959; Cons. Fed. and Ont. Govts., Ont. Inst. C.A.'s; Dir. Frontenac Hist. Found.; author 'Intermediate Accounting: An Analytical Approach' 1990; Pres. Adm. Sci's Assn. Can. 1974–75; Home: 210 Alwington Place, Kingston, Ont. K7L 4P8; Office: Kingston, Ont. K7L 3N6.

**CRANSTON, Toller;** skater, artist; b. Hamilton, Ont. 20 Apr. 1949; e. Kirkland Lake, Ont.; Ecole des Beaux Arts, Montreal; began skating at age of 8; won Candn. Jr. Skating Championship at age of 14 (1964); won Quebec Winter Games 1967; 1968–69 won 3rd Candn. Sr. Men's Championship; 1969 3rd Grand Prix Internat., St. Gervais France; 6th North Am.; 1970 2nd in Candn. Sr., 13th World; 1971 won 1st Candn. Sr., 2nd North Am., 11th World; 1972 won 1st Candn. Sr., 9th Olympics, 5th World (1st in free-style singles div.); 1973 won 1st Candn. Sr., 5th World, won 1st Skate Canada; 1974 won 1st Candn. Sr., Bronze Medallist, World Championships (1st in free-style singles); 1975 won 1st Candn. Sr., 4th World (1st in free-style singles); 1976 won 1st Candn. Sr., Bronze Medal in Olympics; mem. ISU winter & summer tour 1971–74; turned prof. & launched own pro ice show 1976; mem. Candn. Sports Hall of Fame; his kaleidoscopic paintings have been exhibited worldwide; author & illustrator 'A Ram on the Rampage' 1977; 'Toller' 1975; 'The Nutcracker' 1985; Address: c/o Miss Janice Warren, International Management Group, 1 St. Clair Ave. E., Suite 700, Toronto, Ont. M4T 2V7.

**CRAVEN, Anthony William;** publisher; b. Townsville, Australia 9 May 1940; s. Joseph and Norah Margaret (Mitchell) C.; e. MacQuarie Univ. B.A. 1972; MNG. DIR., HARCOURT BRACE JOVANOVICH, AUSTRALIA 1990– ; Pres., C.E.O. & Dir., Harcourt Brace Jovanovich, Canada (formerly Academic Press Canada) 1983–90; Pres., C.E.O. & Dir., Holt Rinehart & Winston of Canada, W.B. Saunders, Canada 1987–90; Partner, Wallace Hadlow & Associates Publishers 1968–72; Founder, Mng. Dir., Harcourt Brace Jovanovich Group (Australia) 1972–78; Sr. Vice-Pres., Academic Press Inc., San Diego, Cal. 1978– ; Pres. & Dir., HBJ Canada 1982–90; Dir., Academic Press Japan, HBJ Canada and HBJ Australia; Office: 108 Regatta Rd., Canada Bay, Sydney, NSW– ;2046, Australia.

**CRAVEN, John R.,** B.Comm., C.A., C.M.A.; financial executive; b. Wallaceburg, Ont. 1947; e. Univ. of Windsor B.Comm. 1970; C.A. 1972; C.M.A. 1973; m. Deborah; 6 children; VICE-PRESIDENT & COMPTROLLER, CANADA TRUST 1991– ; Sr. Vice-Pres., Finance, London Life Insur. Co. until 1991; Mem., Financial Executives Inst.; Candn. Diabetes Assn. (Dir., London & District Branch); Office: 380 Wellington at King, London, Ont. N6A 4S4.

**CRAWFORD, David Creasor,** B.Comm., F.R.I.; real estate executive; b. Winnipeg, Man. 25 June 1933; s. Horace Creasor and Helen Rea (Parr) C.; e. Univ. of Man. B.Comm. 1955; m. Delia M.J.; children: Andrew Creasor, Caroline Rea; CHRMN., CREASOR GROUP OF COMPANIES; Pres. & Dir., Creasor Crawford & Co., Realtors; Dorchester Capital Company; Oldfield Kirby and Gardner Ltd.; Scottish Investment Co. Ltd.; Société Lausanne Ltd.; Dir., Upper Canada Airways Ltd.; Pres. and Dir., A.E. LePage Western, Vancouver 1974; Pres., A.E. LePage Investment & Professional Services Co., Toronto, 1977; Chrmn. A.E. LePage Commercial Realty Co., 1980; Chrmn., Royal LePage Capital Management Services 1981–88; Gov., Creasor Crawford Charitable Foundation; Dir., The Dellcrest Children's Centre; Fellow, Real Estate Inst.; Associate, Ont. Land Economists; Toronto Real Estate Bd.; Naval Officers Assoc.; Alumni Mem., Delta Kappa Epsilon; recreations: Caribbean sailing, golf; Clubs: Granite; Vancouver; Beacon Hall Golf.

**CRAWFORD, Edward Hamon,** B.A.; executive; b. Truro, N.S. 14 Aug. 1925; s. late Edward Smith and Marie Eva (Hamon) C.; e. Ruston Acad., Havana, Cuba; St. Andrew's Coll., Aurora, Ont.; Trinity Coll., Univ. of Toronto, B.A. (Pol. Science & Econ.); m. Barbara Mary, d. late W. H. Smith, 25 June 1955; children: Douglas Edward Smith, Robert Gordon Smith; CHRMN. AND DIR., CANADA LIFE ASSURANCE CO. 1990– ; Dir., Canadian Imperial Bank of Commerce; Gulf Canada Resources Ltd.; Moore Corp. Ltd.; Bd. of Dirs., Hosp. for Sick Children Foundation; Dir., World Wildlife Fund, Canada; Chrmn., Atlantic Counc. of Can.; Chrmn., Candn. Life and Health Ins. Assn. 1980–81; joined Investment Department of present Company, 1948; Investment Rep., London, Eng., 1952–57; Asst. Treas., Home Office, 1957–63, Assoc. Treas., 1963–64, Treas., 1964–67; Vice Pres. and Treas. 1967–70; Extve. Vice Pres. 1970–73; el. a Dir. 1971; Pres. and C.E.O. 1973; Bd. Chrmn., Pres. & C.E.O. 1986; Chrmn. & C.E.O. 1988; Chrmn. of the Bd. 1990; served with R.C.A.F., 1943–45; Anglican; Clubs: Granite; York; Toronto; Toronto Golf; Home: 47 Daneswood Rd., Toronto, Ont. M4N 3J7; Office: 330 University Ave., Toronto, Ont. M5G 1R8.

**CRAWFORD, James Allen;** industrial equipment executive; b. Toronto, Ont. 30 Oct. 1931; s. Julius Sigurdson and Freda (Eyvindson) C.; e. Glebe Coll. 1950; Carleton Univ.; 1st m. Lois d. A.M. McEvoy 29 Nov. 1952; 2nd m. Helen Anne d. Geo. A. Hein 3 Aug. 1982; PRES. & C.E.O., STRONG EQUIPMENT CORP. 1986– ; var. posts ending as Que. Sales Mgr., Internat. Harvester Co. of Can. Ltd. 1952–67; Ont. Sales Mgr., Wajax Ltd. 1967; Ont. Gen. Mgr. 1971; Vice-Pres., Candn. Opns. 1975; Vice-Pres. East Opns. 1980; Pres., Pitman Mfg. 1983–84; Vice-Pres., Mktg., Strong Equipment Corp. 1985; Dir., Markham Theatre; Assoc. for Corporate Growth; Pres. & current Dir., Candn. Assn. of Equip. Distr.; Mem., Holy Trinity Anglican Ch.; Clubs: York Downs Golf; Royal Ottawa Golf; Home: 26 Dale Park Ct., Thornhill, Ont. L3T 2A2; Office: 10 Director Ct., Woodbridge, Ont. L4L 7E8.

**CRAWFORD, John Sinclair,** M.D., F.R.C.P.(C); educator; b. Toronto, Ont. 12 May 1921; s. late James Sinclair and late Irene (Vokes) C.; e. Parkdale Coll. Inst. Toronto 1939; Univ. of Toronto M.D. 1944; m. Olive Margaret d. late Thomas Albert McAulay 16 Sept. 1944; three s.; PROFESSOR EMERITUS, FACULTY OF MED., UNIV. OF TORONTO 1987– ; (Chrmn. of Dept. 1972–82; Prof. of Rehabilitation Med. 1972–87); Dir. Dept. Rehabilitation Med. Toronto Western Hosp. 1954–87, Hon. Staff Phys. Dept. Med. and Past Chrmn. Med. Adv. Comte. there; Med. Dir. Hillcrest Hosp. 1962–73; Chrmn. Med. Adv. Comte. Toronto Rehabilitation Centre 1960–70; past Chrmn. Specialty Comte. Phys. Med. & Rehabilitation, Royal Coll. Phys. & Surgs.; served with RCAMC 1943–46; author various articles prof. journs.; mem. Ont. Med. Assn.; Candn. Med. Assn.; Candn. Assn. Phys. Med. & Rehabilitation (Pres. 1959); Protestant; recreations: boating, skiing; Home: 2000 Islington Ave., Ste. 1112, Weston, Ont. M9P 3S7.

**CRAWFORD, Purdy,** Q.C., B.A., LL.B., LL.M.; b. Five Islands, N.S. 7 Nov. 1931; s. Frank and Grace (Doyle) C.; e. Mt. Allison Univ. B.A. 1952; Dalhousie Univ. LL.B. 1955; Harvard Law Sch. LL.M. 1956; m. Beatrice, d. Wilfred Corbett 19 May 1951; children: David, Suzanne, Heather, Mary, Barbara, Sarah; CHRMN. AND CHIEF EXEC. OFFR., IMASCO LTD. 1985– ; Chrmn., CT Financial Services Inc.; Dir. Imasco Ltd.; Dominion Textile Inc.; CT Financial Services Inc.; Canada Trustco Mortgage Co.; Inco Ltd.; Nova Scotia Resources Ltd.; Camco Inc.; Trinova Corp.; Conference Bd. of Can.; Mem., Business Counc. on National Issues; Mem. Bd. of Govs., McGill Univ.; called to Bar of N.S. 1956, of Ont. 1958; student with Osler Hoskin & Harcourt 1956, Assoc. Lawyer 1958, Partner 1962, Sr. Partner 1970–85; cr. Q.C. 1968; Special Lectr. Osgoode Hall Law Sch. 1964–68, Univ. of Toronto Law Sch. 1969–71, Bar Admission Course 1969–72; Co.-Secy. Atty. Gen.'s Comte. on Securities Leg. 1964–65; Chrmn. Ont. Taxation Sub-sec., Candn. Bar Assn. 1966–68; Treas. Nat. Taxation Sec. 1968–70; Past mem. various comtes. on taxation and of Bd. Govs. Candn. Tax Foundation 1970–72; Cdn. Inst. of Ch. Accts. Special Comm. to Examine Role of Auditor 1977–78; Accounting Research Adv. Bd. 1977–79; United Church; recreations: golf, skiing; Clubs: Mount Bruno Golf; Parrsboro Golf (N.S.); Mount Royal; Forest & Stream; Granite; Toronto; York Downs Golf & Country; Caledon Ski; Homes: Five Islands, N.S. (summer) Belfountain, Ont. and Westmount, Que.; Office: 600 de Maisonneuve Blvd. W., Montreal, Que. H3A 3K7.

**CRAWLEY, Alexander R. (Sandy),** M.F.A.; actor; b. Ottawa, Ont. 7 Dec. 1947; s. Frank Radford (Budge) and Judith Rosemary (Sparks) C.; e. Fisher Park H.S.; York Univ. M.F.A. 1981; twice married; children: Mariah, Jonas, Amos; PRESIDENT, ALLIANCE OF CANADIAN CINEMA, TELEVISION AND RADIO ARTISTS 1991– ; born to his field; first appeared in front of a camera at the age of two months; parallel career as musician but primarily an actor on stage and screen; became politically active in ACTRA 1989; Mem., Actor's

Equity Assn.; Am. Fed. of Musicians; Office: 2239 Yonge St., Toronto, Ont. M4S 2B5.

**CRAWSHAW, John,** B.A., M.B.A., M.A.; food industry executive; b. London, England; e. New Coll., Oxford Univ. B.A. 1972, M.A. 1978; Wharton Sch., Univ. of Pennsylvania M.B.A. 1974; PRES. & CHIEF EXTVE. OFFR., H.J. HEINZ CO. OF CANADA LTD. 1991– ; joined Heinz USA, division of H.J. Heinz Co., in Pittsburgh 1974; Office: 5650 Yonge St., 16th Floor, North York, Ont. M2M 4G3.

**CREAGHAN, Mr. Justice William Lawrence Marven;** C.D., Court of Queen's Bench; b. Newcastle, N.B. 30 May 1922; s. John Adams and Alice D. (Marven) C.; e. Moncton High Sch., 1939; St. Francis Xavier Univ.; Dalhousie Univ., LL.B. 1948; m. Thérèse A., d. late Ben LeBlanc, 2 Sept. 1950; children: Lawrence, Andrew, Valerie; read law with J. A. Creaghan, Q.C.; called to the Bar of N.B. 1948; Registrar of Probate 1952–58; former Partner, Creaghan & Creaghan; served in 2nd World War; Capt. in R.C.A. in Europe and the Mediterranean; Ald., Moncton, N.B., 1952–58; el. to H. of C. for Westmorland 1958; app'ted to County Court, 1962; R. Catholic; Office: Justice Bldg., Queen St., Fredericton, N.B. E3B 5H1.

**CREAL, K.H.M.,** M.A., S.T.B.; b. Grenfell, Sask. 4 Oct. 1927; s. Howard Hubert and Colina (Macdonald) C.; e. Univ. British Columbia, B.A. 1948; Univ. of Toronto, M.A. 1949; Trinity Coll., Toronto, Ont., S.T.B. 1953; m. Dorothy Knowles, Richmond, Va., 1952–78; children: Margaret Colina, Mary Dorothy, Elizabeth Martha; m. Leona Davis of Toronto Dec. 1979; Chair, York University Senate 1986–87; Instr. in Hist., Univ. of S. Sewanee, Tenn., 1950; Rector, St. John's Ch., Winona, Ont., 1953–55; Diocesan Missioner, Diocese of Niagara, 1955–58; Gen. Secy., Gen. Bd. of Religious Educ., Ang. Ch. of Can., 1958–65; Dir., Humanities Programs, Atkinson Coll., York Univ., 1965–66; Prof. of Humanities since 1966; Chrmn. Div. of Humanities, Faculty of Arts, 1969–74; Master of Vanier Coll. 1974–82; recreations: hockey, tennis, reading; Office: Vanier College, York University, Downsview, Ont. M3J 1P3.

**CREAN, John Gale,** B.Com.; manufacturer; b. Toronto, Ont. 4 Nov. 1910; s. Gordon Campbell and Louisa Annie Evelyn C.; e. Upper Can. Coll., 1919–28; Univ. of Toronto (Comm. and Finance), B.Com. 1932; m. Margaret Elizabeth, d. late George A. Dobbie, 2 Dec. 1939; children: John F. M., Jennie E., Susan M., Patricia L.; PRESIDENT, ROBERT CREAN & CO. LTD.; Dir., Scythes & Co.; Bus. Advisor to Candn. Govt. Delegation to UN Commission on Transnational Corporations; Dir., Candn. Council on Internat. Business; Candn. Cmte. on Multinat. Enterprises 1974–80; Candn. Business Group for Multilateral Trade Negotiations 1973–79; mem. Adv. Bd., Internat. Mgmt. and Devel. Inst., Washington, D.C.; Candn. Employer del. to Internat. Lab. Organ., Geneva 1964; Chrmn. of Council, Bishop Strachan Sch. 1953–63; mem. Extve. Comte., Trinity Coll., Univ. of Toronto 1968–74; Pres., Candn. Business and Industry Adv. Ctte. 1972–74; Past Vice Pres., Bus. and Indus. Adv. Ctte. to the OECD 1972–74; Pres., Candn. Counc., Internat. Chamb. of Comm. 1970–72, 1972–75; Pres., Internat. C. of C., Paris 1975–76; Pres., Candn. Inst. Internat. Affairs 1981–85; Duke of Edinborough's 80th Study Conference 1978–80; Founding Chrmn. of Bd., Ont. Science Centre 1964–69; Chrmn., Wilton Park Assn. of Can.; Hon. Chrmn. and Hon. Dir., Hillcrest Hosp. Found.; Vice Chrmn., Harold A. Innis Found.; Past Chrmn., Ont. Divn., Candn. Credit Men's Assn. (1948); mem., Candn. Chamber of Commerce (Pres. 1955–56); mem. of Can.-U.S. Comte. of combined Chambers of Comm. 1950–53; Chrmn., Can.-U.S. Comte., Candn. Chamber Comm. 1962; has travelled extensively throughout the world; served in Queen's Own Rifles, N.P.A.M., 1928–36; C.O.T.C., Univ. of Toronto, 1942–45; Kappa Sigma (G.M.); P. Conservative; Presbyterian; recreations: tennis, badminton, sailing; Clubs; University; Badminton & Racquet; R.C.Y.C.; Address: 625 Avenue Rd., Suite 1502, Toronto, Ont. M4V 2K7.

**CREAN, Susan Margaret,** B.A., M.A.; author; b. Toronto, Ont. 14 Feb. 1945; d. John Gale and Margaret Elizabeth (Dobbie) C.; e. Istituto della Storia dell'Arte, Univ. di Firenze 1965–66; Univ. of Toronto B.A. 1967, M.A. 1969; École du Louvre dipl. 1969–70; York Univ. doctoral prog. 1972–73; m. B. Laurie Edwards; various arts-related, broadcasting and teaching positions 1966–85; Distinguished Visitor, Univ. of Alta. Jan. 1986; Maclean-Hunter Chair in Creative Non-Fiction and Business Writing, Dept. of Creative Writing, Univ. of B.C. 1989–90; author: 'Who's Afraid of Canadian Culture?' 1976, (with Marcel Rioux) 'Deux pay pour vivre: un plaidoyer' 1980 and 'Two Nations: An Essay on the Culture and Politics of Canada and Quebec in a World of American Pre-eminence' 1982, 'Newsworthy: The Lives of Media Women' 1984, 'In the Name of the Fathers: The Story Behind Child Custody' 1988 and numerous papers, studies, articles, editorials and reviews; editor: 'Twist and Shout: A Decade of Feminist Writing in This Magazine' 1992; anthologies: 'Cultural Sovereignty' in 'The Free Trade Papers' 1986, 'Reading between the Lies' in 'The Free Trade Deal' 1988, 'Writing Along Gender Lines' in 'Language in Her Eye' 1990, 'Culture, Gender and Power' in 'Changing Focus' 1991, 'Taking the Missionary Position' in 'Racism in Canada' 1991; extensive committee work in the arts, particularly publishing; Chair, The Writers' Union of Canada 1991–92; Address: 1916 West 11th Ave., Vancouver, B.C. V6J 2C6.

**CREARY, Barbara,** LL.B.; lawyer, publisher; b. Topeka, Kansas 20 July 1948; d. Robert William and Estelle Marie (Charest) C.; e. Univ. du Qué. à Montréal LL.B. 1981; called to Que. Bar 1982; divorced; one d.: AniSara Creary-Picher; PUBLISHER & FOREIGN RIGHTS DIRECTOR, LES ÉDITIONS DE LA COURTE ÉCHELLE 1987– ; Partner, Goyette, Cossette, Creary & Lefebvre 1982–87; Mem., Bd. of Dir., Assn. for the Export of Candn. Books 1992– ; Assn. nat. des éditeurs de livres 1991– ; Public Lending Right Comn. 1990– ; Extve. Ctte., Salon du livre de Montréal 1992– ; Bd. of Dir., Groupe d'aide et d'inform. sur le harcèlement sexuel au travail 1987– ; Bd. of Dir., P.L.A.C.E. Rive-Sud Inc. 1991– ; Home: 8019 Casgrain, Montreal, Que. H2R 1Z4; Office: 5243 boul. Saint-Laurent, Montreal, Que. H2T 1S4.

**CREASOR, A. Roger,** B.Comm.; bank executive; b. Bracebridge, Ont.; e. Acadia Univ. B.Comm. 1970 (J. Wilbur Cox Cup & Gold Medal); m. Peggy Lawson Weekes; children: Roger Justin, Rachel Lee Iris; SR. VICE-PRES. & GENERAL MANAGER, METROPOLITAN TORONTO, ROYAL BANK OF CANADA 1993– ; joined Royal Bank of Can. 1962; held progressively resp. positions throughout Royal Bank in branches, Dist. & Head Office, Ontario & Quebec; Vice-Pres., Personal Lending & Credit Card Serv. 1984; Vice-Pres., Credit Card Serv. 1985; Vice-Pres., Independent Business 1987; Vice-Pres., Retail Banking, Alta. & Western N.W. Territories 1988; Sr. Vice-Pres., Retail Banking, Metro Toronto 1991; Former Dir., VISA Internat.; Hon. Treas. & Council Mem., Toronto Bd. of Trade; Vice Chair, Bd. of Admin., Bd. of Trade Country Club; Advisory Bd., Sch. of Business Admin., Acadia Univ.; recreations: golf, fishing, gardening, skiing; clubs: Aurora Highlands, Aurora, Summerlea, Montreal; Office: 20 King St., W., 11th Floor, Toronto, Ont. M5H 1C4.

**CREBER, George Edgar,** Q.C.; b. Toronto, Ont. 12 Sept. 1927; s. Thomas Edgar and Clara Bernice (Humphries) C.; e. Univ. of Toronto (Econs. and Pol. Science) 1949; Osgoode Hall Law Sch., Toronto, Ont.; m. Edythe Elizabeth, d. Frederick A. Thorne, 21 June 1952; children: Kathryn Anne, Michael George; PARTNER, FOGLER RUBINOFF, Toronto; Dir., International Dunraine Ltd.; Secy. & Dir., International Pursuit Corp.; called to the Bar of Ont. 1953; Club: St. Andrews Golf; Office: Ste. 4400, Royal Trust Tower, Toronto-Dominion Centre, Toronto, Ont. M5K 1G8.

**CREED, Frank Cyprian,** B.Sc., Ph.D.; electrical engineer; b. Windsor, Ont. 3 Apr. 1921; s. Ernest Alfred and Marjorie Cora (Shepherd) C.; e. Queen's Univ. B.Sc. 1945; Univ. of London Ph.D. (Elect. Engn.) 1952; m. Elizabeth Richmond d. Norman Stanley Case 26 March 1960; mem. (Past Chrmn.) Candn. Tech. Comte., Internat. Electro-Technical Comn. on High Voltage Testing Techniques 1958– ; High Voltage Engn. Research, Nat. Research Council Can. 1945–79; Candn. mem. CIGRE Study Comte. on High Voltage Testing 1961–79; Guest Lectr. Univ. of Toronto, Univ. of Denmark; recipient Morris E. Leeds Award Inst. Elect. & Electronic Engrs. 1981; recipient, Centennial Medal, IEEE 1984; author: 'The Generation and Measurement of High Voltage Impulses'; numerous papers impulse voltage measurement (rec'd Prize Paper Award IEEE); Fellow, IEEE; mem. Assn. Prof. Engrs. Prov. Ont.; Inst. Elect. & Electronic Engrs. (Past Dir.); Anglican; recreations: golf; Address: P.O. Box 190, Hubbards, N.S. B0J 1T0.

**CREEGGAN, Rt. Rev. Jack Burnett,** L.S.T., D.C.L. (Ang.); ret. bishop; b. Bancroft, Ont. 10 Nov. 1902; s. Alfred Henry and Mary Laura (Sheffield) C.; e. Deseronto (Ont.) Pub. and High Schs.; Queen's Univ., B.A. 1925; Bishop's Univ., L.S.T. 1927; D.C.L. 1971; m. Dorothy Jarman, d. late Alexander Thomas Embury and Hester Mary (Jarman), 30 June 1931; children: (Mrs.) Mary-Isabel Wright, A.A. Burnett; retired Bishop of The Diocese of Ontario (1974); Freemason; recreations: golf, curling; Address: 32 Ontario St., Apt. 112, Kingston, Ont. K7L 2Y1.

**CREELMAN, Lyle,** O.C. (1971), M.A., LL.D., D.Sc. (hon.); retired nursing executive; b. N.S., 14 Aug. 1908; d. late Samuel Prescott and late Laura C.; e. Vancouver Normal Sch. 1926; Univ. of B.C., B.A.Sc. (Nursing) 1936; Columbia Univ. Teachers' Coll., M.A. 1939; Univ. of N.B., LL.D. 1963; D.Sc. (hon. causa), Univ. of B.C. 1992; Elem. Sch. Teacher, Richmond, B.C., 1928–32; Dir. of Pub. Health Nursing, Metrop. Health Comte., Vancouver, B.C., 1940–44; Chief Nurse, Brit. Occupied Zone of Germany, UNRRA, 1945–46; Study of Pub. Health Nursing in Can., Candn. Pub. Health Assn., 1948–49; Nursing Consultant, World Health Organ., Geneva, 1949–54 and Chief Nursing Offr., 1954–68; rec'd Centennial Medal 1967; Queen's Jubilee Medal, 1977; Protestant; Club: University Women's; Home: #702, 1455 Duchess Ave., West Vancouver, B.C. V7T 1H7.

**CREGAN, James D.J.,** Q.C., B.A., LL.B.; b. Montmartre, Sask. 19 Apr. 1918; s. James and Noemie (Ecarnot) C.; e. Public Schs., Montmartre; Coll. Mathieu, Gravelbourg, Sask.; Univ. of Ottawa, B.A.; Dalhousie Univ. LL.B.; m. 20 Sept. 1945; children: James E. Cregan, Colleen H. Cregan; called to the Bar of N.S. 1948, Alberta 1949, N.W.T. 1951; cr. Q.C. 18 Jan. 1960; began practice with Milner & Steer 1948 and admitted to partnership 1955; retired as partner 1 Jan. 1991; Sole Practitioner since; served in 2nd World War as a Pilot with R.C.A.F. overseas; mem. Law Societies of Alta. and N.W.T.; Edmonton Bar Assn.; R.C.A.F. Assn.; Mem., Alta. Aviation Counc.; K. of C.; R. Catholic; P. Conservative; recreations: golfing; Home: 323 Westridge Rd., Edmonton, Alta. T5T 1C4; Office: 10719 – 107 Ave., Edmonton, Alta. T5H 0W6.

**CREIGHTON, D. Bruce;** newspaper executive; b. Toronto, Ont. 22 July 1956; s. J. Douglas and Marilyn J. (Chamberlain) C.; e. Univ. of Western Ont.; m. Terry d. Bill and Lee Keough 6 April 1985; children: Alexandra, Sandy; EXECUTIVE-VICE PRESIDENT, FINANCIAL POST 1992– ; Circulation Dir., Toronto Sun 1980; Gen. Mgr., Calgary Sun 1986; Vice-Pres., Circulation, Financial Post 1988; Dir., Bassett Falk Research Clinic; Anglican; recreations: tennis, golf; clubs: Lambton Golf, Mayfair Tennis; Home: 17 Anderson Ave., Toronto, Ont. M5P 1H2; Office: 333 King St. E., Toronto, Ont. M5A 4N2.

**CREIGHTON, Dale Edward,** B.A., CLU, Ch.F.C., LLIF; insurance executive; b. London, Ont. 12 June 1934; s. Bert D. and Louise S. (Hope) C.; e. Univ. of Western Ont. B.A. 1959; CLU 1964 ; Ch.F.C. 1989; LLIF 1992; m. Marion L. d. Leo and Lillian Thompson 8 Dec. 1956; children: Matthew Dale, Paul Lawrence, Lyndsey Lee; EXECUTIVE VICE-PRES., OPERATIONS, LONDON LIFE INSURANCE CO. 1989– ; Group Rep. (Toronto), London Life 1959; Mgr. 1961; Reg. Mgr. (Sudbury) 1966; Supt., Group Sales & Serv. 1968; Assoc. Dir., Mktg. & Admin. Offr. 1969; Dir., Mktg., Group Benefits Div. 1970; Assoc. Dir. of Mktg., Dist. Sales Div. 1972; Dir., Mktg. 1974; Vice-Pres. & Extve. Dir., Mktg. Orgn. 1975; Vice-Pres., Mktg. 1978; Sr. Vice-Pres., Individual Mktg. 1981; Vice-Pres., London Insur. Group 1985; Extve. Vice-Pres., Life Insur. 1989; Bd. of Dir., Life Insur. Mktg. & Rsch. Assn. (LIMRA) 1977–80; LIMRA Agency Offrs. Round Table Ctte. 1981–84 (Past Chair); Mem., Bd. of Dir., London Life Insurance Co. & London Insurance Group 1992– ; Former Mem., CLHIA-LUAC Joint Ctte. on Mktg.; Past Chair, CLHIA Sr. Mktg. Offrs. Section; Former Dir., London YM-YWCA (Past Pres. & Former Mem., Extve. Ctte.); Bd. Mem., London & Dist. Br., Candn. Diabetes Assn. (Chair 1991 Annual Appeal Campaign Ctte.); Home: 70 Doncaster Place, London, Ont. N6G 2A5; Office: 255 Dufferin Ave., London, Ont. N6A 4K1.

**CREIGHTON, James Austin,** B.Sc., M.Sc., F.S.A., F.C.I.A.; investment manager; b. Truro, N.S. 15 Jan. 1950; s. Austin MacLennan and Phyllis (Crawford) C.; e. Dalhousie Univ. B.Sc. 1967; Northeastern Univ. M.Sc. 1974; m. Deborah Joan Creighton; children: Michael, Neil, Johanna; VICE PRES. & GEN. MGR., WELLS FARGO NIKKO INVESTMENT ADVISORS CANADA LIMITED 1992– ; Mgr., Group Pensions, Maritime Life Assurance Co. 1975–80; Vice-Pres. & Dir., Group Opns. 1980–83; Vice-Pres. & Gen. Mgr., Pencorp Systems Ltd. 1983–85; Sr. Vice-Pres., Trafalgar Capital Management Corp. 1985–92 (Dir.); mem., Soc. of Actuaries; Candn. Inst. of Actuaries; recreations: sports, reading, travelling; Club: The Fitness Inst.;

Home: 2077 Hadfield Court, Burlington, Ont. L7M 3V5.

**CREIGHTON, John Douglas;** O.C.; retired newspaper publisher; b. Toronto, Ont. 27 Nov. 1928; s. Stanley Dixon and Ethel Grace (Armstrong) C.; e. Runnymede Pub. Sch.; Humberside Coll. Inst.; m. Marilyn June d. Arthur and Jean Chamberlain 20 June 1953; three s. Scott, Bruce, Donald; FOUNDER, PAPER & PEN INC. 1993– ; Dir., CAE Industries Ltd.; Colonia Life Insurance Co.; worked briefly for Canadian High News and Toronto Stock Exchange; Jr. Reporter Toronto Telegram 1948, Asst. City Ed. 1962, Sports Ed. 1965, City Ed. 1967, Mang. Ed. 1969–71; Toronto Telegram closed and with 61 employees founded and became Publisher, 'The Toronto Sun' 1971–84; Pres. & C.E.O. The Toronto Sun Publishing Corp. 1982; Chrmn. of the Bd., Pres. & C.E.O. 1990; Chrmn. and C.E.O. 1991–92, Retired; Publisher, The Houston Post 1983–84 (sold paper 1987); Chrmn., The Financial Post Company 1988; author: (memoirs) 1993; Past Pres. Big Brothers Metro Toronto; serves on the Boards of several charitable organizations; recipient Eleanor Roosevelt Humanities Award; inducted into Candn. News Hall of Fame 1988; Officer, Order of Canada; recreations: reading, travel, golf, swimming; Clubs: Lambton Golf & Country; The Toronto; The Albany; The York; Toronto Men's Press (former Pres.); Les Ambassadeurs, the Mark's Club (London, Eng.); National Press (Washington, D.C.); Office: BCE Place, Canada Trust Tower, 161 Bay St., Suite 4800, P.O. Box 528, Toronto, Ont. M5J 2S1.

**CRÉPEAU, The Hon. Mr. Justice Jean,** B.A., LL.L.; superior court judge; b. Montreal, Que. 2 June 1935; s. Alexandre and Fernande (Coulombe) C.; e. Coll. Stanislas, Univ. de Paris B.A. 1955; Univ. of Montreal LL.L. 1958; m. Hélène de Eugène and Jeannine (Vallières) Barbeau 23 May 1964; children: Marie-Joëlle, Janique; JUDGE, SUPERIOR COURT OF QUEBEC 1984– ; Dir., (Que.) Candn. Judges Conference 1991– ; practiced with Monette, Fillion & Labelle; Lajoie, Gélinas, Lajoie, Bourque & Lalonde; Deschênes, Forget & Crépeau; Deschênes, de Grandpré, Godin, Paquette, Lasnier & Alary 1966–84; mem., Candn. Bar Assn. (Chrmn. Ins. Sect. 1973; mem. Nat. Extve. 1977–79; Sec., Treas., Vice-Pres. & Pres., Que. Div. 1973–81); Que. & Montreal Bar Assn.; Auto. Ins. & Rev. of Ins. Act. Cttes.; Chrmn., Ctte. on Admin. of Civil Justice in Montreal; Pres., Discipline Ctte. for Que. Bar; Order of Physicians; Order of Nurses; recreations: tennis, golf, ski; Clubs: St-Laurent Tennis; Laval-sur-le-Lac Golf; Home: 115, Les Pins, Laval-sur-le-Lac, Que. H7R 1C8; Office: 1 Notre-Dame St. E., S. 12.53, Montreal, Que. H2Y 1B6.

**CRÉPEAU, Paul-André,** C.C., Chevalier, Ordre du mérite (France), Chevalier de mérite, Ordre de St. Jean de Jérusalem (Malte); C.R., B.A., L.Ph.(Ottawa), LL.L.(Montréal), B.C.L.(Oxon), Docteur en droit (Paris); mem. de la Soc. royale du Can. (1979); né, Gravelbourg, Sask., 20 mai 1926; fils Jean-Baptiste et Blanche (Provencher) C.; é Coll. de Gravelbourg; Univ. Ottawa, B.A., 1946; L.Ph., 1947; Univ. Montréal, LL.L., 1950 (Prix du Doyen, 1949; Prix du Lieut.-Gouv. et Prix Arthur Vallée, 1950); Univ. Oxford, B.C.L., 1952 (Bourse Rhodes); Univ. de Paris, Docteur en droit, 1955 (Prix R. Dennery); LL.D. Univ. of Ottawa 1971, York Univ. 1984; Dalhousie Univ. 1989; Strasbourg III Univ. 1990; ép. Nicole, f. Fernand Thomas et Paule Noisette, 26 juin 1959; enfants: François, Marie-Geneviève, Philippe; PROF. TITULAIRE DE DROIT, UNIV. McGILL; Wainwright Prof. of Civil Law; Dir. du Centre de recherche en droit privé et comparé du Québec 1975– ; appelé au Barreau de Montreal, 1950; Conseil de la reine, 1969; Prés. de l'Office de revision du Code civil de Québec 1965–1977; Assn. can. des prof. de Droit (prés., 1964–65); Assn. qué. des prof. de droit (prés. 1965–66); Inst. International de Droit d'Expression Française (vice-prés.); Assn. qué. pour l'étude compar. du droit, (prés., 1974–85); Assn. de Droit Internat., section de Montréal, (mem. du Conseil 1970–75); Fac. Internat, pour l'enseignement du droit comparé (Strasbourg, mem. du Conseil); Prés. Académie internationale du droit comparé 1990– ; membre étranger, Académie des sciences de Pologne; Reçu Prix du Barreau du Qué., 1962; Médaille, Fondation Edouard-Montpetit, 1988; Médaille, Barreau du Qué., 1990; Prix de l'Assn. Québécoise de droit comparé 1993; Prix du Gouverneur général parer le droit 1993; publ. 'La responsabilité civile du médecin et de l'établissement hospitalier' 1956; 'La dissertation juridique' (avec Me Jean Roy) 1958; 'Eléments d'une introduction au droit international privé comparé' 1962; 'L'Avenir du Fédéralisme canadien/The Future of Canadian Federalism' (avec le Prof. C.B. MacPherson) 1965; 'La responsabilité médicale et hospitalière: évolution récente du droit québécois' 1968; Rapport sur le Code civil du Québec (en collab.) 1978; 'Code civil/Civil Code 1866–1980' (avec J.E.C. Brierley) 1981 ('Supplément 1980–83' 1983); 'La responsabilité civile de l'établissement hospitalier en droit civil canadien' 1982; 'Dictionnaire de droit privé' (en collab.) 1985; 'Private Law Dictionary and Bilingual Lexicons' (en collab.) 1988; 'Les Codes civils – Edition critique,' éd. annuelle 1981– ; 'L'intensité de l'obligation juridique' 1989; L'affaire Daigle et la Cour suprême du Canada ou la méconnaissance de la tradition civiliate dans Mélanges Brière' 1993; nombreux articles et comptes-rendus dans plusieurs périodiques; prof. invité à maintes reprises aux. univ. de Québec, Montréal, Baton Rouge (La), Edimbourg (Ecosse), Vienne (Autriche) et Poitiers (France); Catholique; récréation: natation; jardinage (fines herbes); Résidence: 5 Place du Vésinet, Montréal, Qué. H2V 2L6.

**CRESSEY, Ancel John,** B.A., LL.B; corporate executive; b. North Battleford, Sask. 7 July 1928; s. Ancel Draper and Alice Evelyn (Booth) C.; e. Univ. of Sask. B.A. 1956, LL.B. 1957; m. Mabel d. Earle and Elizabeth Dean 2 May 1951; children: Norman, Diana, Dawn; CHRMN. OF THE BD., EDMONTON POWER 1992– ; Office: Capital Square, 10065 Jasper Ave., Edmonton, Alta. T5J 3B1.

**CRESSWELL, Peter Ross,** B.Sc., B.A.Sc.; transportation executive; b. Montreal, Que. 14 March 1935; s. Herbert Arthur and P. Ethelwynne (Carpenter) C.; e. Bishops Coll. Sch. Lennoxville, Que. 1953; Bishops Univ. B.Sc. 1955; Univ. of Toronto B.A.Sc. 1959; m. Nancy Elizabeth d. Trevor Moore, Toronto, Ont. 14 Nov. 1959; children: Robert, Tracy, Susan; PRES. & C.E.O., ALGOMA CENTRAL CORP.; Pres., Fraser Ship Repairs; Marine Consultants & Designers (Canada) Ltd.; Dir. Candn. Shipowners Assoc.; The Chamber of Maritime Commerce; Assn. Prof. Engrs. Prov. Ont.; Kappa Alpha; Anglican; recreations: golf, tennis, skiing; Clubs: Sault Ste. Marie Golf; Toronto Golf; Home: 1993 Queen St. E., Sault Ste Marie, Ont. P6A 2G8; Office: P.O. Box 7000, Sault Ste. Marie, Ont. P6A 5P6.

**CRESSY, Gordon Charles,** B.Sc., M.S.W.; executive; b. Toronto, Ont. 13 Nov. 1943; s. Joseph Vincent and Sybil Lorraine (Walker) C.; e. George Williams Coll. Chicago B.Sc. 1967; Univ. of Toronto M.S.W. 1969; m. Joanne d. Keith and Joan Campbell 29 Jan. 1983; children: Joseph, Keith, Jillian, Jennifer; FOUNDING PRESIDENT AND C.E.O., METROPOLITAN TORONTO LEARNING PARTNERSHIP 1993– ; Exec. Dir.: YMCA Port-of Spain, Trinidad 1963–64, Opportunity House 1969–72; Sch. Trustee, Toronto Bd. of Edn. 1970–76, Chrmn. 1975–76; Ald. City of Toronto and Metro Toronto 1978–82, Exec. mem. 1980–82; Project Dir. Ont. Inst. Studies in Edn. 1972–81; Pres. United Way of Greater Toronto 1982–87; Vice Pres., Development and University Relations, Univ. of Toronto 1988–93; frequent keynote speaker and cons. ednl., non profit and pub. sector groups; Vice Chrmn. LLBO 1986–87; Bd. mem., Exec. Ctte. Candn. Centre Philanthrophy 1983–88; Chrmn. Bd. Nat. Council YMCAs Can. 1973–75; Hon. Vice Pres. CUSO 1984– , Chrmn. of Bd. 1982–84; rec'd Centennial Medal 1967; Queen's Silver Jubilee Medal 1977; Gardiner Award 1988; Urban Alliance Race Relations Award 1990; Kappa Delta Phi 1967; recreations: golf, swimming, table tennis; Club: Toronto Hunt; Home: 213 Walmer Rd., Toronto, Ont. M5R 2P7; Office: 21 King's College Circle, Toronto, Ont. M5S 1A1.

**CRESWELL, David,** B.A., LL.B.; lawyer; b. Canada 19..; s. James Anderson and Florence (Bailey) C.; e. Kapuskasing H.S.; Univ. of Toronto, B.A., LL.B. 1961; EXTVE. VICE-PRES., GENERAL COUNSEL & SECRETARY, NATIONAL LIFE ASSURANCE CO. 1989– ; mem., Candn. Bar Assn.; recreation: sports; club: Boulevard; Home: 1 Palace Pier Court, Unit 503, Etobicoke, Ont. M8V 3W9; Office: 522 University Ave., Toronto, Ont. M5G 1Y7.

**CREWSON, Delmore C.W.,** F.C.A.; chartered accountant; b. Man. 25 June 1942; e. Univ. of Man. C.A. 1967; m. Emily 1965; two s. David, Geoffrey; PARTNER, DELOITTE & TOUCHE 1989– ; former Dir. Winnipeg Business Development Corp.; The Forks Renewal Corp.; articled Touche Ross; joined Hudson's Bay Co. 1971, Asst. Treas. 1974; Partner Dunwoody & Co. 1976–89; Trustee, Museum of Man & Nature Found Fund (former Museum Bd. mem.); former Trustee: St. John's Ravenscourt Sch. Found.; Manitoba Inst. of C.A.'s Foundation Fund; Past Pres., Inst. of C.A.'s of Manitoba; former Bd. mem., Winnipeg Visitors & Convention Bureau; Candn. Inst. C.A.'s; recreation: golf; Clubs: Manitoba (Past Pres.); St. Charles Country; Winnipeg Winter; Home: 170 Victoria Cres., Winnipeg, Man. R2M 1X4; Office: 2300, 360 Main St., Winnipeg, Man. R3C 4H5.

**CRIBB, James Michael;** photographer/writer; b. Halifax, N.S. 1 May 1956; s. John James and Jeannine Marie-Paule (Prudhomme) C.; e. Father Macdonald H.S., Ville St. Laurent, Que. 1972; Fanshawe Coll., London, Ont. Reg'd. Respiratory Therapist 1977; m. Andrea J. d. Elizabeth and Desmond Clements 7 Apr. 1979; children: Jessica Lauren, Michaela Leanne; self-taught photographer spec. in marine environ.; freelance work for mags. & journals, incl. 'Equinox,' 'Outside,' 'Internat. Wildlife,' 'Nature Canada' 1978– ; author: 'Treasures of the Sea: Marine Life of the Pacific Northwest' 1983, 'Marine Life of the Caribbean' 1984, 'Subtidal Galapagos: Exploring the Waters of Darwin's Islands' 1986; Baha'i; Address: 261 Glacier View Dr., Comox, B.C. V9M 1G6.

**CRICHTON, Robert Alexander,** B.A., F.R.S.A.; editor; writer; graphic designer; media and public relations consultant; educator; b. Philadelphia, Pa. 13 Feb. 1931; s. Robert Alexander and Jean Craig (Fraser) C.; e. Univ. of West. Ont., B.A. (Hons.) 1953; m. Madge d. Mackinnon and Erla Phillips 10 Oct. 1964; PARTNER RE/MEDIA 1982– ; Reporter, The Telegram 1952–55; Fgn. Ed. 1963–67; The Vancouver Sun 1955–56; Reporter, Bureau Chief, Ed., The Globe and Mail 1956–61; Sr. Ed., Scottish Daily Express 1961–63; Cons., Brit. & Candn. govs. 1967–68; Founder & Chrmn., Applied Arts Div., Durham Coll. of Applied Arts & Technol. 1968–73; Asst. City Ed., Toronto Star 1973–74; Ed., Ontario Hydro 1974–79; Communic. Mgr., Canron Inc. 1979–82; Chief Judge, Internat. Assoc. Ch. Press comp. 1972 and many others; seminar chairman, panelist, organizer for Toronto Press Club, Candn. Pub. Relns. Soc., Internat. Assn. of Bus. Communic.; Past Vis. Lectr., Univ. of West. Ont.; Fellow, Royal Soc. of Arts, London, Eng. el. 1970; Toronto Firefighters Award (best story) 1955; Univ. of West. Ont. Publ. Key 1953; Mem., Extve. Ctte., Presbyn. Record 1975–78, 1978–81, 1982–85; Presbyn. Ch.; Scottish Nat. Party; Scottish Studies Foundation; Toronto Press Club 1951 (Dir., 1957–61, 1964–67, 1978–87; Chrmn., var. cttes.; Extve. Ctte. 1981–87, current member, professional development nominating and constitutional cttees.; Pres. 1985–86); Candn. Pub. Relns. Soc. 1968; Internat. Assn. of Bus. Commun. 1975 (Pres., Toronto chap. 1978); author num. daily & periodical articles; recreations: eclectic reading, travel, sports; Clubs: Toronto Press; Edinburgh Press; Glasgow Press; Address: 87 Douglas Cres., Toronto, Ont. M4W 2E6.

**CRICHTON, Vince,** B.Sc., M.Sc., Ph.D.; wildlife biologist; b. Chapleau, Ont. 7 Nov. 1942; s. Vincent Alfred and Dora Adelaine (Morris) C.; e. Univ. of Man. B.Sc. 1966, M.Sc. 1969; Univ. of Guelph Ph.D. 1972; m. Lenora d. Len and Eleanor Creedon 12 Aug. 1967; children: Scott Vincent, Susan Joan; MOOSE, ELK, CARIBOU BIOL. MAN. 1982– ; Pres. V. Crichton Enterprises Ltd.; Telonics Canada; E. Region Biol. Man. 1972; Prov. Moose Biol. 1978; Head of Surveys and Inventory 1980; invited by Swedish Govt. to Chair N.Am. Session Moose Mgmt. 2nd Internat. Moose Symposium 1984 (gave keynote address) and by USSR Acad. of Sci's to convene population dynamics session 3rd Symposium 1990 & co-ed. proceedings; Chair N.Am. Moose Conf. 1975, 1988; invited by Polish Govt. to present paper Internat. Union Game Biols. 1987; recipient Distinguished Moose Biol. Award 1988; author various articles sci. jours.; mem. Internat. Moose Ctte.; Wildlife Soc.; Wildlife Disease Assn.; Nat. Geog. Soc.; Candn. Geog. Soc.; Freemason; recreations: wildlife photography, hunting; Home: 104 Purdue Bay, Winnipeg, Man. R3T 3C7; Office: P.O. Box 24, 1495 St. James St., Winnipeg, Man. R3H 0W9.

**CRIDDLE, Ernest Edward,** B.Sc.; chemist; b. South Cypress, Man. 5 Nov. 1930; s. Talbot and Barbara (Coats) C.; e. Brandon Univ. B.Sc. 1953; m. Bertha d. Richard and Lois Lawton 6 May 1960; son Andrew; m. secondly Rosemary d. Leonard and Grace Legg 25 June 1974 (common-law); step-children: Penelope, Christopher, Michael, Audrey; COLD FUSION ELECTROCHEMIST, UNIV. OF OTTAWA 1989– ; Computer, Delta Explor. Co. 1952; Chemist, Oshkosh Filter & Softener Co. 1953; Defence Rsch. Establishment Ottawa 1953–58; Electrochemist 1958–82; Sci. Extve. Asst. to Chief 1982–88; Administrator, Electrochem., Sci. & Tech. Ctr., Univ. of Ottawa 1988–89; Pres., Union of Nat. Defence Employees local 614 1969–71; Crow's Nest Youth Ctr. Corp. 1968–70; Bd. Mem., Candn. Unitarian Counc. 1989–92; Chapter Pres., Ottawa Peace Child 1990; Anglican, Unitarian-Universalist; Boy Scouts Canada (Asst. Reg. Comnr. 1978–80; scoutmaster, cubmaster, beaver leader 1948–92; awards: 2 Wood Badges, Medal of Merit 1965; Bar to Medal of Merit 1984); St. John Ambulance First Aider 1948–90; Instr. 1961–71; Mem., Electrochem. Soc. (Chrmn., Candn. Section 1977); Chem. Inst. of Can.; Assn. of Chem. Prof. of Ont.; SCITEC; author of 3 reports; co-author of 16 reports; inventor 4 patents; co-inventor 4 patents; recreations: gardening, yachting; club: Britannia Yacht; Home: 172 Powell Ave., Ottawa, Ont. K1S 2A3; Office: 33 Mann Ave., Ottawa, Ont. K1N 6N5.

**CRIGHTON, Arthur Bligh,** D.M.A.; musician; educator; b. Calgary, Alta. 6 June 1917; s. Reginald James and Grace Carman (Armstrong) C.; Univ. of Toronto, L.R.C.T., Mus. Bac. 1948; Univ. of S. Cal., M.M. 1962, D.M.A. 1965; PROF. EMERITUS OF MUSIC, UNIV. OF ALBERTA 1982; Chrmn., Div. of Music Hist. and Lit. 1967–80; taught there in fields of music theory, hist. and applied music; Theory Consultant, W. Bd. of Music; Conductor, Univ. Symphony Orchestra, 1950–67; 'A Workbook for Music Analysis' 1980; served with RCAF during World War II; Bomber Pilot; P.O.W. Germany 1942–45; Active Reserve, Univ. of Alta. Sqdn., 1950–68; rank Lt. Col.; Assoc., Royal Candn. Coll. Organists (Past Chrmn., Edmonton Centre); Home: 8903–180 St., Edmonton, Alta. T5T 0Y3.

**CRIMMINS, James Edward,** M.A., Ph.D.; educator; b. Cardiff, Wales 4 Sept. 1953; s. James Stephen and Mary Rose (Yewlett) C.; e. St. Illtyds Coll. Cardiff; N.E. London (UK) Polytechnic; Univ. Coll. of Swansea B.A. 1977, M.A. 1980; Univ. of W. Ont. Ph.D. 1984; m. Johanne d. Clifford and Juliette Lapensée 10 Aug. 1984; ASSOC. PROF. OF POLITICAL THEORY 1987– ; and CHAIR, DEPT. OF POLITICAL SCIENCE, HURON COLL., UNIV. OF W. ONT. 1992– ; J.A.F. Stevenson Meml. Fellow 1982; SSHRCC Postdoctoral Fellow 1985–87; Am. Soc. Eighteenth-Century Studies Fellow 1989–90; author 'Secular Utilitarianism' 1990; ed. 'Religion, Secularization and Political Thought' 1989; various acad. articles 18th and 19th century pol. thought and Brit., Irish and Candn. politics; newspaper articles Candn., Brit., Irish and Eur. politics; mem. Brit. Politics Group (USA); Candn. Pol. Sci. Assn.; Candn. 18th Century Soc.; Internat. Soc. for Utilitarian Studies; Internat. Hobbes Assn.; recreations: soccer, tennis, golf, travel; Home: 1566 Hastings Dr., London, Ont. N5X 3C6; Office: 1349 Western Rd., London, Ont. N6G 1H3.

**CRIPPS, Shirley Anne,** M.L.A.; former politician; b. Westerose, Alta. 11 Sept. 1935; d. Joseph Robert and Mildred Agnes (Davis) Hoyle; e. Lakedell Sch.; Red Deer Composite High Sch. 1954; Univ. of Alta. Jr. Elem. Teaching Cert. 1955; m. Lorne s. Villiars and Clara Cripps 4 Oct. 1958; children: Christine Anne, Rosanne Louise, Maxine Lorraine (d.); elem. sch. teacher; family farm Winfield, Alta. since 1959; el. M.L.A. for Drayton Valley Alta. g.e. 1979; re-el. g.e. 1982, 1986; Apptd. Assoc. Min. of Agriculture 1986; served Extve., Alta. Charolais Assn., Agric. Soc.'s Alta.; Secy., Winfield & Dist. Agric. Soc.; Co. Recreation Bd. 1969–74; West Pine Lodge Sr. Citizen Assn.; mem. Hall Bd., Library Bd., Lions Ladies, 4H, Home & Sch.; Planning Comte. Winfield Recreation Complex 1991– ; Extve., Devon Leduc Hist. Soc.; Oat Producers Assoc. of Alta.; Advisory Council, Alberta Food Processors Assn.; mem., Drayton Valley Econ. Dev. Ctte.; Pembina Consortium; Address: Box 329, Winfield, Alta. T0C 2X0.

**CRIPTON, John Lawrence,** B.A.; impresario; b. Montréal, Qué. 29 Dec. 1942; s. John Alexander and Bertha (Thibert) C.; e. Univ. of Guelph B.A. (Hons.) 1970; m. Linda d. Jack and Constance Sword 11 Oct. 1980; children: Michael, Stephanie, Jennifer; PRES. GREAT WORLD ARTISTS LTD. 1980– ; Coordinator and Gen. Adm. Cultural Activities Dalhousie Univ. 1970–73; Gen. Mgr. Touring Office (first) Can. Council 1973–80; Dir. of Programming Festival Can. Ottawa 1978; Prod. and Prog. Cons. Toronto Internat. Festival 1984; Prod. Cultural Progs. Candn. Pavilion Expo '85 Tsukuba, Japan 1985; Prod. and Impresario Kirov Ballet of Leningrad N. Am. Tours 1986, '87, '89, '91, '92, '93; Prod. Kirov Ballet Internat. Tours Gt. Britain, Spain, Japan, Korea, Mexico 1993; Prod. Cultural Progs. and Special Events Canada Pavilion, Vancouver 1984–86 and World Expo '88, Brisbane Australia 1987–88; Artistic Consultant, Arts Festival Program, Calgary Winter Olympic Games 1988; Dir. of Production, Toronto International Choral Festival 1988–89; Bd. Mem., Arts Court, Ottawa 1988–91; Exec. Dir., Satra Entertainment Corp., New York 1991–92; Coproducer Cult. Progs. and Spec. Events Canada Pavilion, Seville Spain, Expo 1992 and Taejon Korea, Expo 1993; prod. numerous tours Candn. artists abroad and foreign artists in Can. incl. regular exchanges with China, Soviet Union and USA; first commercial performing arts tour from China to USA and Can. 1981; first to bring: Red Army Choir into the USA 1989, Yiddish Theatre into USSR 1991, Shumka Candn. Ukrainian Dancers to Ukraine 1990, Kiev Ballet to Canada 1991; arts cons. various workshop/seminars Edmonton, Ottawa, Toronto, Banff; author 'An Introduction to Microcomputers for Arts Managers' 1984; mem. Candn. Assn. Artists Mgrs.; recreation: film collecting; Club: Arts & Letters; Home: 227 Springfield Rd., Rockcliffe Park, Ont. K1M 0L1 and 40 Hickory Dr., New Canaan, Connecticut, 06840 U.S.A.

**CRIPTON, Michael John,** D.D.S., F.R.C.D.(C.); orthodontist; b. Montreal, Que. 29 Sept. 1934; s. John and Veronica (Tchachuk) C.; e. Westmount (Que.) Jr. and Sr. High Schs.; McGill Univ. D.D.S. 1957; Univ. of Montreal Dipl. in Orthodontics 1961; m. Nancy Carroll, d. Carvell G. Green, Florenceville, N.B. 27 Sept. 1958; children: Michael, Mary, Peter, David; orthodontic practice Moncton since 1961; Partner MacRealty Ltd.; Vice Pres. and Dir., Atlantic Stereo Ltd. (owners of C103 FM Stereo), Moncton, N.B.; dental practice Fredericton 1957–59; el. Councillor-at-Large Moncton 1971; re-el. 1973; unsuccessful cand. for Mayor 1974; Chrmn. Easter Seal Campaign Moncton 1964; Pres. Moncton Boys' Club 1964–66 (Bd. mem. 1962–70); mem. Nat. Dent. Examining Bd. Can. 1970–75; Dent. Adv. Comte. Dept. of Health N.B. 1969–71; Atlantic Prov's Rep. Candn. Fund for Dent. Educ. 1971–78; Fellowship, Royal Coll. of Dentists of Can. 1967; Int'l Coll. of Dentists 1978; Amer. Coll. of Dentists 1985; Acad. of Dentistry Internat. 1985; Pres.-Elect, Pierre Fauchard Academy (worldwide dental honor organization); recipient, Queen's Silver Jubilee Medal for Services to Dentistry; Candn. Dental Assn. Distinguished Service Award 1992; Pres., Candn. Assn. of Orthodontists 1979–80; National Bd. Mem., Boys & Girls Clubs of Can. (Chrmn. National Counc. 1984–86); Chrmn., Moncton Coliseum and AGRENA Comn. 1985–92; Bd. Mem., Moncton Youth Residences 1990– ; awarded Commemorative Medal, 125th Anniversary, Candn. Confedn. 1992; mem. Adv. Comte. Moncton Minor Hockey Assn.; Dir. Moncton Figure Skating Club; Extve. Comte. 1974 Candn. Figure Skating Championships; Vice Chrmn., Skate Canada 77, Moncton; Royal Coll. of Dentists of Can. (Pres. 1985–87); N.B. Dent. Soc. (Pres. 1981–82); Candn. Dent. Assn. (Pres. Sept. 1976–77); Am. Assn. Orthodontics; European Assn. Orthodontics; Fed. Dentaire Internationale (Nat. Treas.-Can. 1977–78); N.B. Dent. Soc. (Secy.-Treas.-Registrar 1964–67; Chrmn. Liaison Comte. N.B. Govt. 1969–71); Northeastern (US) Soc. Orthodontists (Long-range Planning Comte.); Anglican; recreation: curling, sailing, skiing; Clubs: Beaver Curling; Elks; Rotary (Pres. 1969–70); Home: 21 Alexander Ave., Moncton, N.B. E1E 1T3; Office: 567 St. George St., Moncton, N.B. E1E 2B9.

**CRISPO, John,** B. Com., Ph.D.; university professor; b. Toronto, Ont. 5 May 1933; s. Francis Herbert and Elizabeth Brock (Gillespie) C.; e. Upper Can. Coll. Toronto, 1952; Trinity Coll., Univ. of Toronto, B. Com. 1956; Mass. Inst. of Technol., Ph.D. (Indust. Econ.), 1960; m. Barbara Ann Bodkin; two d., Carol Anne, Sharon Elizabeth, 1 step-son Matthew Bodkin; PROFESSOR OF POLITICAL ECONOMY, FACULTY OF MGMT., UNIV. OF TORONTO; Assoc. of Centre for Industrial Relations; Chrmn., Ryde Industries Inc.; Teaching Assistant, Mass. Institute of Technol., 1959–60; Assistant Prof., Huron Coll., Univ. of W. Ont., 1960–61; joined present Univ. as Asst. Prof., 1961–64; Assoc. Prof. 1964–65; mem., Prime Min.'s Task Force on Labour Relations, 1967–69; Chrmn., Ont. Union-Mang. Council, 1967–74; frequent public speaker & media commentator; author: 'International Unionism: A Study in Canadian-American Relations' 1967; 'The Public Right to Know: Accountability in the Secretive Society' 1975; 'The Canadian Industrial Relations System' 1978; 'Industrial Democracy in Western Europe' 1978; 'A Mandate for Canada' 1979; 'National Consultation: Problem & Prospects' 1984; ed. 'Free Trade: The Real Story' 1988; 'Can Canada Compete?' 1989; 'Making Canada Work: Competing in the Global Economy' 1992; ed. and co-ed. of several books; other writings include articles for learned journs.; mem. Candn.-Am. Ctte.; C.D. Howe Policy Analysis Comte.; Internat. Trade Adv. Ctte.; recreations: farming; golfing; riding; skiing; Home: 1127 Mt. Pleasant Rd., Toronto, Ont. M4P 2M8; Office: Toronto, Ont. M5S 1A6.

**CRISTALL, Jeffrey G.,** B.Sc., C.A., C.B.V.; chartered accountant; b. Brandon, Man. 18 April 1956; s. Arthur Irving and Elinore (Simkin) C.; e. Brandon Univ. B.Sc. 1978; C.A. (Man. & B.C.) 1982; C.B.V. 1988; several courses; m. Patricia d. Sam and Alexandra Guick 27 July 1984; PARTNER, MEYERS NORRIS PENNY & CO. 1985– ; Student-in-accounts, Dunwoody & Co. 1978–82; Staff Accountant 1982–84; Meyers Norris Penny & Co. 1984–85; currently Mem., Mngt. Ctte. & Dir. of Mktg., Meyers Norris Penny & Co.; Officer, Meyers Norris Penny Limited; Vice-Pres., Westman C.A. Assn. 1990– ; several past extve. positions with W. Man. Child & Family Services, United Way, Brandon Univ., Brandon Univ. Alumni, Keystone Kinsmen; Chair, Bd. of Gov., Brandon Univ. 1991– ; club: Keystone Kinsmen (Founding Mem.); Home: 33 Almond Cres., Brandon, Man. R7B 0Z9; Office: 160 – 14th St., Brandon, Man. R7A 7K1.

**CRISTOFARO, Michael D.,** C.A., B.Comm.; accountant; b. Montreal, Que. 9 Sept. 1956; s. Carlo and Yolande (Chartrand) C.; e. Sir George Williams Univ. B.Comm. 1978; Concordia Univ., grad. dipl. in accountancy 1979; PARTNER, ARTHUR ANDERSEN & CO. 1990– ; joined Montreal office of present firm 1978; transferred to Toronto office 1989; extensive experience in mfg., distribn., pharm. & consumer products industries; expert witness for quantification of damages; significant expertise in quantification of insurance claims; Dir., Ont. C. of C. (Mem., Extve. Council and Econ. Policy Ctte.); Past Dir., Concordia Univ. Alumni Assn.; UNICEF Que.; current: Leadership Ctte. & Sector Chair, United Way of Peel; recreations: golf; club: Lionhead Golf & Country; Home: 1165 Giles Gate, Oakville, Ont. L6M 2S4; Office: 1200 Two Robert Speck Parkway, Mississauga, Ont. L4Z 1H8.

**CRNCICH, Tony Joseph,** B.Sc.; pharmacy executive, retired; b. Noranda, Que. 20 May 1930; s. Anton Joseph and Zora Marie C.; e. Leamington H.S. 1948; Univ. of Toronto B.Sc.Phm. 1953; m. Joanne d. Arthur and Claire Potvin 11 May 1957; children: Anne-Marie, Diane, Christine, Anthony, Katherine, Robert; DIR., BIG V PHARMACIES CO. LIMITED 1964– ; Lakeview Pharmacies (3 pharm.) 1956–64; founding Dir., Big V Pharmacies Co. Ltd. 1964– ; Treas. 1964–68; Chrmn., Pres. & C.E.O. 1968–91; Dir., Axa Home (Anglo Canada) Insurance Group; Green Shield Prepaid Serv. Inc.; London Devel. Advisory Bd. 1983–90; Pres., Essex County Pharm. Assn. 1967–69; Counc. mem., Ont. Coll. of Pharm. 1970–73; essay contest winner, Candn. Found. for the Advancement of Pharm. 1967; runnerup 1968; recreations: golf, sailing, bridge; Club: London Hunt and Country; Home: 75 Tetherwood Blvd., London, Ont. N5X 3W2.

**CROCKER, Olga Lillian Kaleta,** B.Ed., M.B.A., Ph.D.; university professor; b. High Prairie, Alta. 9 Mar. 1930; d. Theodore (Fred) and Kataryna Mary (Kolasa) Kaleta; e. High Prairie H.S. 1948; Univ. of Alta., B.Ed. 1953, M.B.A. 1974; Univ. of N. Dakota, courses towards M.Ed.; Univ. of Wash., Ph.D. 1977; m. Leo B. s. Lois and Leo D. C. 12 Apr. 1952; children: Terence Lee, Kevin Barry, Nathan Bryce; PROF., FAC. OF BUS. ADMIN., UNIV. OF WINDSOR 1976– ; H.S. Teacher, Edmonton 1956–74; Rsch. Assoc., Govt. of Alta. 1974; Rsch. Assoc. T.A., Univ. of Wash. 1974–76; Dir./Instr. 1974–76; Chair, Grad. Ctte., Fac. of Bus., Univ. of Windsor 1977–80; Area Head 1979–82; Adjunct Prof. & Adv., Central Michigan Univ. 1978– ; Systems Expert, UN Devel. Prog. (Afghanistan) 1964–67; Extve. Dir., Edn. Skills Process 1986– ; Equal Pay Rsch. Inst., Univ. of Windsor 1986–88; Pres., Ctr. for Workplace Dynamics 1981– ; Pres., Univ. of Windsor Fac. Assn. 1981–82; worldwide conf. participant; S. Bronfman Found. Sr. Fac. Award 1978; E.J. Benson Award 1977; scholarships: Edmonton Women Teachers' 1972; Gov. of Alta. 1948; Imperial Order of the Daughters of the Empire 1948; mem., Admin. Sci. Assn. of Can.; Candn. Indus. Relns. Assn.; C. of C.; Internat. Assn. of Quality Circles; Personnel Assn. of Ont.; several current univ. cttes. & fac. assn. positions; CAUT Rep. & Coll. Bar. Ctte. 1980–83; Windsor Rep., OCUFA 1978–80; Bd. of Govs., St. Clair Coll. of Applied Arts and Technology 1982–84; Ed. Bd.: 'Canadian Public Policy' 1979–85; author: 'Experiential Exercises in Canadian Personnel Administration,' 'Incidents and Cases in Canadian Personnel Administration' (& co-author, Teacher's Manual) 1986; num. schol. articles pub.; ms & book reviewer for many jour. & pub.; co-author: 'Quality Circles: A Guide to Participation and Productivity' 1984, 'Management Concepts and Practices' (Student Manual) 1986; Univ. of Windsor 'Job Descriptions' & 'Pay Equity' projects 1987; recreations: writing, consulting, research; Home: 272 North Talbot Rd., R.R. 2, Maidstone, Ont. N0R 1K0; Office: 410 Sunset Dr., Windsor, Ont. N9B 3P4.

**CROCKER, Robert Kirby,** B.Sc., B.Ed., Ph.D.; university professor, policy advisor; b. Carbonear, Nfld. 14 Oct. 1940; s. Charles J. and Mina (Kirby) C.; e. St. Mathews School, Memorial Univ. B.Sc., B.Ed. 1966; Univ. of Alta. Ph.D. 1969; m. Janet d. Edmund and Gertrude Legge 5 May 1966; children: Diane Heather, Susan Patricia; ASSOCIATE DEPUTY MINISTER OF EDUCA-

TION, NEWFOUNDLAND 1993– ; Teacher Glovertown, Nfld. 1957–58; Fort Sask. Alta. 1967 Prof., Memorial Univ. of Newfoundland 1969– ; Dir., Inst. for Educational Rsch. & Devel. 1978–88; Consultant, Dept. of Edn., Queensland, Australia 1979; Visiting Scholar, Stanford Univ., Michigan State Univ. 1976–77; Chair, Math. Science Task Force Nfld. 1988–89; Dean, Fac. of Edn., M.U.N. 1990–93; consultant to various local, nat. & internat. edn. agencies 1973– ; CEA Whitworth Award for Contbn. to Educational Rsch. 1987; author: 'Elementary Science Curriculum Project' vols I and II 1975, 'Towards an Achieving Society' 1989; co-author: 'Science Education in Canada' vol I 1985, vol II 1987; clubs: Royal Newfoundland Yacht; Home: 8 Mabledon Place, St. John's, Nfld. A1A 3Y7; Office: West Block, Confederation Bldg., St. John's, Nfld. A1B 4J6.

**CROCKFORD, Robert David,** B.A.; business executive; b. Hamilton, Ont. 1 Apr. 1948; s. Nelson Reginald and Frances Elaine (Scroggie) C.; e. Univ. of Western Ont., B.A. (Hons.) 1970; PRES. & GEN. MGR., THE VALLEY CITY MFG. CO. LTD. 1978– ; Reg. Rep., Dominion Securities 1972–74; various posts, Valley City Mfg. Co. Ltd. 1975–78; Dir., CallNet Enterprises Inc.; Rojust Holdings Ltd.; Past Chrmn., Bus. Adv. Counc., Sch. of Bus., McMaster Univ.; Former Chrmn., Hamilton Civic Hosps.; Mem., Hamilton Dist. Health Counc.; Chrmn., Halton-Wentworth Br., Candn. Mfg. Assn.; recreations: squash, tennis, jogging; club: Hamilton Thistle; Home: 69 South St. W., Dundas, Ont. L9G 2A6; Office: 64 Hatt St., Dundas, Ont. L9H 2G3.

**CROFT, Ian D.,** C.A.; financial executive; b. Halifax, N.S. 10 June 1942; s. Ainley Milward and Margery Helen (Simmons) C.; e. Carleton Univ. B.Comm. (Hons.) 1970; C.A. 1972; m. Beth d. Clifford and Muriel Lounsbury 8 July 1967; children: Angela Gwynneth, David Jordan; SENIOR VICE-PRES. & TREAS., THE WOODBRIDGE COMPANY LIMITED 1976– ; Bank of Montreal 1961–67; Thorne Riddell 1970–76; Dir., The Woodbridge Co. Limited; Consolidated SYH Corp.; The Thomson Co. Inc.; Thomson Equitable Corp. Limited; Candn. Gen. Insur. Co.; Guarantee Insur. Co. (U.S.); Lincoln Insur. Co. (U.S.); Scottish & York Insur. Co. Ltd.; Toronto Gen. Insur.; Traders Gen. Insur.; Victoria Insur. Co. of Can.; O.I.S. Leasing Ltd.; Provinco Financing Canada Ltd.; Central Canada Insur. Service Ltd.; Candn. Insur. Shares Ltd.; Dir. & Treas., St. Clement's Sch.; Mem., Inst. of C.A.s of Ont.; The Tax Found.; Tax Extve. Inst.; recreations: skiing, Muskoka cottage boating; clubs: The Boulevard, The Bd. of Trade of Metro. Toronto; Home: 35 Edgevalley Dr., Islington, Ont. M9A 4N8; Office: 65 Queen St. W., Toronto, Ont. M5H 2M8.

**CROFTON, Patrick Dermott,** C.D.; businessman; b. Ganges, B.C. 29 May 1935; s. Dermott Kenneth and Doris Livinstone (Taylor) C.; e. Salt Spring Island Consolidated Sch.; St. Georges Sch. Vancouver 1952; Univ. Sch. Victoria 1953; Royal Roads Mil. Coll. 1956; m. Patricia d. Trevor and Margaret Williams 9 Aug. 1958; four d. Marietta, Virginia, Susanna, Tessa; CANDN. CHRMN. CAN.-U.S. PERM. JT. BD. ON DEFENCE 1989– ; Part Owner and Pres. C.Q.A.C. Manufacturing Ltd. (machine & metal parts); served with RCN 1953–71, rank Lt. Commdr.; businessman, farmer since 1971; Ald. Mun. of Saanich 1980–84; Dir. Capital Regional Bd. 1981–84; el. to H. of C. for Esquimalt-Saanich 1984–88, Chrmn. Ctte. Nat. Defence 1985–88; Hon. Dir. Camosun Coll. Found.; Trustee, McPherson Found.; Trustee, Lester B. Pearson Coll. of the Pacific; Dir.: 1994 Commonwealth Games Soc.; Victoria Rotary Club; mem. Greater Victoria C. of C.; Saanich Peninsula C. of C.; Royal Un. Services Inst.; Candn. Inst. Strategic Studies; Naval Offrs. Assn.; Anglican; P. Conservative; recreations: sports, reading, gardening; Clubs: Victoria Golf; Union; Address: 4010 Prospect Lake Rd., R.R.7, Victoria, B.C. V8X 3X3.

**CROIZIER, Ralph Charles,** M.A., Ph.D.; educator; b. Vancouver, B.C. 8 Nov. 1935; s. Charles John and Doris Maud (Price) C.; e. Univ. of B.C., B.A. 1957; Univ. of Wash. M.A. 1960; Univ. of Cal. Berkeley Ph.D. 1965; children: Stephen, Janna, Suzanne; PROF. OF HISTORY, UNIV. OF VICTORIA 1976– ; Rsch. Fellow Harvard Univ. 1965–66; Asst. to Assoc. Prof. Univ. of Rochester 1966–75; Prof. and Chrmn. of Hist. SUNY Brockport 1975–76; Dir. Centre of Pacific & Oriental Studies present univ. 1981–83; recipient Francis Troup Paine Prize, Harvard Press for best work on hist. or phils. of med. 1970; author 'Traditional Medicine in Modern China' 1968; 'Koxinga and Modern Chinese Nationalism' 1975; 'Art and Revolution in Modern China' 1988; ed. 'China's Cultural Legacy and Communism' 1970; mem. Art Gallery Greater Victoria; recreations: running, ocean kayaking; Home: 2376 Beach Dr., Victoria, B.C. V8S 2G4; Office: History Dept., Victoria, B.C. V8W 2Y2.

**CROLL, John R.,** C.A., M.B.A.; financial executive; b. Winnipeg, Man. 11 Oct. 1927; s. George and Elsie Jane (Kitching) C.; e. C.A., Manitoba & B.C. 1952; Simon Fraser Univ. M.B.A. 1972; m. Sheila d. Edward and Eileen Twentyman; children: Todd, Geoffrey, Sandra; VICE-PRES., FINAN. & CHIEF FINAN. OFFR., CRESTBROOK FOREST INDUS. LTD. 1987– ; Asst. Sec. & later Treas. & C.F.O., Placer Dev. Ltd. 1952–69; Vice-Pres. Finan. & Admin., Med. Size Natural Resource & Indus. Complexes 1969–74; Dir., Finan. Serv., MacMillan Bloedel 1974–77; Vice-Pres., Admin. 1977–79; Vice-Pres., Comptroller 1979–81; Sr. Econ. Policy Advr. to Senator Jacob Austin (then Fed. Cabinet Min.); Corp. Vice-Pres. & Sec., Canada Dev. Invest. Corp. 1983–87; Gov., Simon Fraser Univ.; Mem., Finan. Extves. Inst. Can.; Inst. of C.A.'s (B.C. & Man.); Fellow, Inst. of C.A. (B.C.); Viceroy Resources Corp.; Mem., St. Francis-in-the-Wood; author of several papers & lectures; clubs: Vancouver, Capilano Golf & Country; Home: 3984 Bayridge Ave. W., Vancouver, B.C. V7V 3J5; Office: 1200 – 1055 W. Georgia St., Vancouver, B.C. V6E 2E9.

**CROMBIE, Hon. David Edward,** P.C., M.P., B.A.; politician; b. Toronto, Ont. 24 Apr. 1936; s. Norman Davis and Vera Edith (Beamish) C.; e. Earl Haig Coll. Inst. Toronto; Univ. of W. Ont.; Univ. of Toronto B.A. 19..; m. Shirley Ann d. John Charles Bowden 28 May 1960; children: Carrie Ann, Robin, Jonathan David; Commissioner, Royal Commission on the Future of the Toronto Waterfront 1988–91; former teacher; Ald. City of Toronto 1969–72, Mayor 1973–78; el. to H. of C. for Rosedale, by-el. 1978; re-el. 1979, 84; sworn of the Privy Council and apptd. Min. of Nat. Health and Welfare 1979; Min. of Indian Affairs and Northern Development, Canada 1984–86; Sec. of State 1986–88; P. Conservative; Home: 81 Glencairn Ave., Toronto, Ont. M4R 1M7.

**CROMBIE, Glenn N.,** B.Sc.F.; educational administrator; b. Toronto, Ont. 19 Apr. 1935; e. Earl Haig S.S. 1954; Univ. of Toronto, B.Sc.F. 1959; children; Kevin, Karen, David; PRES., CAMBRIAN COLLEGE 1982– ; Mngt. Forester, Ont. Dept. of Lands & Forests, Lindsay 1961–66; Forest Rsch. Offr., Maple & Richmond Hill 1966–68; Principal, Sir Sandford Fleming Coll., Frost Campus 1968–78; Pres., Olds College 1978–82; Dir., Cambrian Found.; N.E. Ont. Equity Network; Sudbury & Dist. C. of C.; Laurentian Hosp.; Mem., Ont. Profl. Foresters Assn.; Found Pres., Kawartha Youth Inc.; Prov. & Nat. Dir., Multiple Sclerosis Soc.; Mem., Ross Mem. Hosp. Bd.; United Way Campaign Chrmn. 1988; Office: 1400 Barrydowne Rd., Sudbury, Ont. P3A 3V8.

**CROMBIE, Jonathan David;** actor; b. Toronto, Ont. 12 Oct. 1966; s. David Edward and Shirley Ann (Bowden) C.; e. John Ross Robertson P.S. 1978; Glenview Sr. Public 1978–79; Queen Elizabeth P.S. 1979–80; Lawrence Park C.I. (Hons.) 1985; McGill Univ. 1987–88; Univ. of Toronto 1988– ; Principal roles include: film: (Gilbert Blythe in 'Anne of Green Gables' 1985, Matt Morris in 'Bullies' 1985, 'Anne of Green Gables – The Sequel' 1986, Barney Roth in 'The Day They Came to Arrest the Book' 1986, Christopher in 'The Jeweller's Shop' 1988; television: Rob Valeur in 'Mount Royal' CTV 1987; Greg Clarke in 'The Killing Ground' CBC 1988; Benny Macioli in 'Café Romeo' 1990; David Terrell in 'Shattered Vows' 1992; George in 'The Good Fight' 1993; theatre: Judas Iscariot in 'Godspell' 1987; Nicholas Beckett in 'What The Butler Saw' 1989; Producer and ensemble performer in 'Mirth' 1991; mem. of comedy group 'Skippy's Rangers' 1993; mem., Candn. Actor's Equity; ACTRA; recreations: hiking, cartooning, card games, Old Broadway musical fan; Office: c/o Michael Oscars, Oscars & Abrams Assoc. Inc., 59 Berkeley St., Toronto, Ont.

**CROMBIE, Peter S.,** B.Com., M.B.A., C.A.; b. 1944; m. Sandra Crombie; two children; e. McGill Univ. B.Com. 1965, C.A. 1967; Sir George Williams Univ. (now Concordia) M.B.A. 1971; PRES.& CHIEF OPERATING OFFR., SOFTIMAGE INC. 1993– ; Riddell Stead & Co. (now Peat Marwick Thorne) 1965–71; Pratt & Whitney Aircraft of Canada Ltd. 1972–75; Vice-Pres., Insurance Operations & Controller, Canada Mortgage & Housing Corp. 1975–82; Vice-Pres., Finance, SHL Systemhouse Inc. 1982–85; Pres., Kinburn Technology Corp. 1985–87; Chrmn. & C.E.O., Accugraph Corp. 1987–89; Extve. Vice-Pres., & C.F.O., SHL Systemhouse Inc. 1989–92; Pres., Four Line Corp. 1992–93; Club: Rideau; Royal Ottawa Golf; Four Line Hunting & Fishing; Home: 30 Whitemarl Dr., Ottawa, Ont. K1L 8J6.

**CROMIE, Peter Esmond,** B.Com.; retired industrialist; b. Vancouver, B.C. 10 Dec. 1920; s. Robert James and Bernadette Grace (McFeely) C.; e. Pub. and High Schs. Vancouver; Univ. of Brit. Columbia 1939–41 and B. Com. 1946; Univ. of Toronto 1941; m. Inez Patricia, d. Henry Ferdinand Knight, 10 Dec. 1948; children: Gail Patricia, Ronald Peter, Dana James, Edward Allan, Lin Inez, Jane Bernadette; Pres. and Dir., Plato Industries Ltd.; served in Candn. Army 1943–45; rank Sgt. Intelligence Corps; Convocation Founder, Simon Fraser University; Zeta Psi; Unitarian; recreations: jogging, tennis, bodybuilding; Clubs: The Vancouver; Vancouver Lawn Tennis; Home: Suite 310, 4900 Cartier St., Vancouver, B.C. V6M 4H2.

**CRONE, John Porter,** F.C.A. (Ireland); financial consultant & company director; b. Belfast, N. Ireland 17 May 1930; s. Robert and Anna Frances (Porter) C.; e. Royal Belfast Acad. Inst. 1942–47; Belfast Coll. of Technol. A.C.A. 1952; m. Christine Evans 3 Apr. 1954; children: Judith, Michael, Jacqueline, Jennifer, Wendy; PRES. & DIR., QUINTET RESOURCES LTD.; CanWest Gas Supply Inc.; Group Vice Pres. Corporate, & Dir., Home Oil Co. Ltd. 1977–80; Extve. Vice Pres. and Dir., Scurry-Rainbow Oil Ltd. 1977–80; Pres. & Dir. Home Petroleum Corp. Houston, Texas; Treas. Home Petroleum corp. 1968–69; Comptroller Home Oil co. Ltd. 1969–72; Mang. Dir. Home Oil (UK) Ltd. 1972–75; Vice Pres. Internat. Operations Home Oil co. Ltd. 1975–77; F.C.A., Ireland; Anglican; recreations: golf, tennis, swimming, reading, bridge, Clubs: Uplands Golf; Home: 105 - 2829 Arbutus Rd., Victoria, B.C. V8N 5X5.

**CRONE, Robert Carl;** film producer; b. Toronto, Ont. 7 Aug. 1932; s. The Rev. Walter S. and Dorothy Kathleen (Fitzsimmons) C.; e. Pub. ad High Schs., Peterborough, Ont.; Peterborough Business Coll.; Bob Jones Univ., Greenville, S.C.; m. Violet May, d. Roy Sanderson, 4 Sept. 1952; one s. David Carl; Operations Mgr. of a T.V. Stn., U.S.A., 1955; C.B.C., 1956; Freelance Motion Picture Producer, 1957; Vice-Pres., Robert Crone Pictures Ltd., 1958; Pres. and Dir., Crone Holdings Ltd., 1961; Crone Films Inc., U.S.A., 1961; Pres., Chief Extve. Offr. and Dir. Film House Ltd. 1968; Awards: T.V. Workshop, N.Y.; Gold Camera Award, 1955; Ohio State Univ. Film Award, 1959; 1981 joint recipient with wife of the special Air Canada Award, and jointly received Genie from the Acad. of Candn. Cinema for their outstanding contributions to the growth of the Canadian film industry; responsible for dir. and prod. of Motion Picture and T.V. for Nat. Lib. Fed.; rec'd Centennial Medal 1967; Civilian Citation, Board Commissioners, Metropolitan Toronto Police 1969; mem., Soc. of Motion Picture & T.V. Engrs.; Candn. Prof. Photographers Assn.; Am. Cinema Labs.; Soc. of Film Makers; Life mem. Directors Guild of Can.; Can. Soc. of Cinematographers; Can. Film Editors Guild; founding mem. Can. Acad. Film and Television Arts and Sciences; mem. Can. Film and Television Assn.; Pres., Internat. Alliance Theatrical Stage Employees 669 1987–88; Liberal; Presbyterian Church; recreations: travel, reading, music, skiing, gourmet, multi engine instrument rated pilot; Clubs: Granite; Canadian; Ontario; Home: 8175 Pasco Rd., West Vancouver, B.C. V7W 2T5.

**CRONENBERG, David;** film director; Dir., 'M. Butterfly' 1993; Dir./Scr. Play., 'Naked Lunch' 1991; Dir./Co-Scr./Prod., 'Dead Ringers' 1988; Dir./Co.-Scr., 'The Fly' 1986; 'Fast Company' 1978; Dir., 'The Dead Zone' 1983; Dir./Scr. Play, 'Videodrome' 1982; 'Scanners' 1980, 'The Brood' 1979, 'Rabid' 1976, 'The Parasite Murders' 1975, 'Crimes of the Future' 1970, 'Stereo' 1969; Office: 217 Avenue Rd., Toronto, Ont. M5R 2J3.

**CRONIN, Robert Francis Patrick,** C.D., M.D., C.M., M.Sc., F.R.C.P. (Lond.), F.R.C.P.(C); physician; educator, b. London, Eng., 1 Sept. 1926; s. Archibald Joseph and Agnes Mary (Gibson) C.; e. Princeton Univ. 1943–44 and 1947–49; McGill Univ., M.D., C.M. 1953, M.Sc. 1960; m. Shirley-Gian, d. Randal Killaly Robertson, 19 June 1954; children: David Robert, Diana Christine, Daphne Gian; MEDICAL CONSULTANT TO THE AGA KHAN HEALTH SERVICES (GENEVA); CONSULTING PHYSICIAN, MONTREAL GEN. HOSP.; mem., Faculty of Medicine, McGill Univ. 1959–84, Assoc. Dean 1969–72, Dean 1972–77, Prof. of Medicine 1972–84; Consultant (cardiology) Queen Mary Veterans' and St. Anne's Hosp. 1961; Gov., Coll. of Phys. and Surg., Que. 1968; Vice Pres., Medical Research Council, Que. 1971; M.G.H. Research Inst. 1977; Dir., Can. Heart Foundation 1978; Council, Royal Coll. of Physicians & Surgeons of Canada 1979; Dir. Found. Armand Frappier 1980; Consultant, World Bank and C.I.D.A. 1980; Pres., Grad. Soc. of McGill Univ. 1978; Gov., McGill Univ. 1982; Dir., Aga Khan Univ. Hospital (Karachi) 1985; served in 2nd World War, R.C.A.F. 1944–45; Brit. Army 1945–47, rank Lt.; R.C.A.F. Auxiliary 1956–64, rank Sqdn.-Ldr.; author of numerous articles in scient. journs. primarily in field of cardiovascular physiol., Fellow; Roy. Coll. Phys., London; Club: University (Montreal); Golf de Lausanne; Home: Champ-Riond, 1815 Baugy, Montreux, Switzerland.

**CRONYN, Hugh Verschoyle,** G.M., F.R.S.A.; artist; painter; b. Vancouver, B.C. 30 Apr. 1905; s. Verschoyle Francis and Mable Margaret (Philpot) C.; e. Ridley Coll., St. Catharines, Ont.; Franz Johnson Studio, Toronto; Art Students League, N.Y.; Acad. Lhote, Paris; American Sch. of Fine Arts, Fontainbleau; m. Jean Harris, M.A. (Oxon), d. Percy Harris, 1942; two d. Anna Catharine, Janet Margaret; before the 2nd World War worked in Paris Studios, and as Freelance artist, London, Eng; subsequent to the war, Dir. of Art at the Architectural Assn. Sch. of Arch., London, Eng.; full-time Lectr. in Painting at North East Essex Sch. of Art, Colchester, Eng., also Instr. in Lithography; paintings and portrait colls. in Eng., Sweden, Canada, U.S.A., France; mural paintings C.P.S. Empress of Canada; one-man exhns.: Nancy Poole's Studio, Charles St. Gallery, Toronto; also Montreal, Victoria, B.C., Canada House, London, Minories, Colchester, Edng., and other prov. galleries; currently painting in Can., Eng., Fr., served in 2nd World War: 1939, Royal Navy Auxiliary Patrol; 1940–46; Royal Navy, Lieut.-Commdr.; George Medal; Fellow of Roy. Soc. of Arts; Addresses: CARE 47, Forsythe St., Marmora, Ont.; Studio 3, St. Peters Wharf, Hammersmith Terrace, London, England.

**CRONYN, Hume;** actor; writer; director; b. London, Ont. 18 July 1911; s. Hume Blake (distinguished financier and publicist) and Frances A. (Labatt) C.; e. Ridley Coll., St. Catharines, Ont.; McGill Univ.; N.Y. Sch. of Theatre; Mozarteum, Salzburg, Austria; Am. Acad. Dramatic Art, New York; Hon. LL.D., Univ. of W. Ont. 1974; Hon. D. Hum. Litt., Fordham Univ. 1985; Order of Canada 1988; m. Jessica Tandy (actress) 27 Sept. 1942; children: Christopher Hume, Tandy, Susan Tettemer; intended for the law, but after some amateur experience with a group of players in Montreal, Que., joined Cochran's Stock Co., Washington, D.C., and made prof. debut in 'Up Pops the Devil' 1931; later estbd. a growing reputation when appearing in 'Three Men on a Horse' (1935–36), followed by 'High Tor,' 'Room Service,' 'Boy Meets Girl'; took first leading role 'The Weak Link' 1940; entered motion pictures in 'Shadow of a Doubt' 1943; directed an Actor's Lab. Theatre prod. of 'Portrait of a Madonna' 1946, followed by 'Now I Lay Me Down To Sleep' 1949, 'Hilda Crane' 1950, 'The Egghead' 1957; with Norman Lloyd staged the initial Phoenix Theatre prod. 'Madam Will You Walk' 1953, in which he also co-starred with his wife; scored a great hit with prod. of 'The Fourposter' 1951 (won Comoedia Matinee Club's Award 1952); on tour with 'The Fourposter' 1951, 1952, 1953; inaugurated radio series 'The Marriage' for NBC (with wife) 1953; has since appeared in 'The Honeys' 1955; 'A Day by the Sea' 1955; 'The Man In The Dog Suit' 1958; 'Sunrise at Campobello' (film) 1960; 'Cleopatra' (film) 1963; portr. Polonius in Sir John Geilgud's prod. of 'Hamlet' 1964; appd. in title role of 'Richard III' 1965; played Yepihodov 'The Cherry Orchard' and the title role 'The Miser' 1963, 1965 at Tyrone Guthrie Thea., Minneapolis; 'A Delicate Balance' at Martin Beck, N.Y. 1966 and in U.S. tour 1967; Revival 'The Miser' 1968 at Mark Taper Forum, L.A.; title role of 'Hadrian VII' Stratford 1969 and National Tour 1969–70; 'The Caine Mutiny Court-Martial' Ahmanson Thea., Los Angeles 1971–72; appeared on stage in 'Promenade All' at Alvin Theatre, N.Y.C. 1972; Samuel Beckett Festival at the Forum, Lincoln Centre, N.Y.C. ('Krapp's Last Tape'; 'Happy-days'; 'Act without words I') 1972; tour 'Promenade All' 1973; 'Krapp's Last Tape' tour 1973; performed in 'Krapp's Last Tape' Toronto 1973; 'Noel Coward in Two Keys' 1974 and tour 1975; 'Concert-recital' tour of 'Many Faces of Love'(Oct.-Nov. 1974 and 1975); 'Merchant of Venice' and 'A Midsummer Night's Dream' Stratford Fest. (Ont.) 1976; 'Many Faces of Love' London, Ont. and tour 1976; co-produced with Mike Nichols and appeared in 'The Gin Game' (Pulitzer Prize 1978) with Jessica Tandy, Long Wharf Thea., New Haven, Conn. and The Golden Thea., N.Y.C. 1977–78; 'Gin Game' national tour U.S. 1978–79, and in Toronto, Canada, London, England, and U.S.S.R. 1979; co-authored (with Susan Cooper) 'Foxfire' performed Stratford Festival, Ont. 1980, at Guthrie Theatre, Minneapolis 1981, at Ethel Barrymore Theatre 1982–83 and at Ahmanson Theatre, Los Angeles 1985–86; played Everett in 'Traveller in the Dark' Loeb Drama Centre, Cambridge, Mass. 1984; 'The Petition' at Golden Theatre, N.Y.C. 1986; Films: 'Rollover' 1981; 'Garp' 1981; 'Impulse' 1983; 'Honky Tonk Freeway' 1980; additional films: 'Gaily, Gaily' 1968; 'The Arrangement' 1968; 'There Was A Crooked Man' 1969; 'Conrack' 1973; 'Parallax View' 1973; 'Cocoon' 1984; 'Batteries Not Included' 1986; 'Cocoon: The Return' 1987; made 1st appr. in TV in 'Her Master's Voice' 1939; has acted in all major dramatic television series and appeared seven times on 'Omnibus' and three times on the Ed Sullivan Show'; teleplay 'Foxfire' a Hallmark Prod. 1987; 'Day One' 1988; 'Age Old Friends' 1989; 'Broadway Bound' 1991; 'Christmas on Division Street' 1991; sometime lectr. on drama; has written a number of short stories and has collab. with Hitchcock on the screen treatment of 'Rope' and 'Under Capricorn'; co-author (with Susan Cooper) 'The Dollmaker' (teleplay); author: 'A Terrible Liar' (memoir) 1991; at request of Pres. and Mrs. Johnson, appeared with his wife at the White House in 'Hear America Speaking' 1965; was nominated for an Academy Award for performance in 'The Seventh Cross' 1944; rec'd (with his wife) Comoedia Matinee Club's Award for 'The Fourposter' 1952; rec'd the Barter Theatre Award 'for outstanding contribution to the theatre' 1961; nominated for Antoinette Perry (Tony) Award 1961; awarded Delia Austria Medal from the N.Y. Drama League for performance in 'Big Fish, Little Fish' 1961; rec'd Antoinette Perry (Tony) Award and won the 'Variety' N.Y. Drama Critics Poll for portrayal of Polonius in 'Hamlet' 1964; rec'd Am. Acad. of Dramatic Arts Ninth Annual Award for Achievement for Alumni 1964; rec'd. Herald Theater Award for Tobias in 'A Delicate Balance'; L.A. Drama Critics Circle Award for best actor in 'Caine Mutiny Court Martial' 1972; 4th Annual Straw Hat Award for Best Dir. ('Promenade All') 1972; 1972–73 Obie Award ('Krapp's Last Tape'); el. to Amer. Theatre Hall of Fame 1974; Brandeis Univ. Creative Arts Awards for distinguished achievement 1978; nominated by Drama Desk for outstanding actor and for Antoinette Perry (Tony) Award for best actor in 'The Gin Game' 1977–78; also rec. L.A. Critics' Award for performance in 'Gin Game' 1979; received 1983 Commonwealth Award for distinguished service in dramatic arts; (with Susan Cooper) Christopher Award and Writer's Guild Award for screenplay 'Dollmaker' 1985; Humanitas Award for humanizing achievement in Television 1985; nominated for Antoinette Perry (Tony) Award as Edmund in 'The Petition' 1986; recipient of Kennedy Center Honors 1986; recipient of Alley Thea Award (Houston) 1987 in recognition of significant contrib. to the theatre arts; received the Franklin Haven Sargent Award from the Am. Acad. of Dram. Arts in recognition, as a distinguished alumnus, for the quality of acting 1988; with Ms. Tandy, received tribute for 50 yrs. of television performances, Acad. of Television Arts & Sciences 1989; with Ms. Tandy, received Encore Award for extraordinary achievement in the arts, Arnold Gingrich Arts & Business Counc. 1989; received 1990 National Medal of Arts Award from the Pres. of the U.S. in special recognition of outstanding contribution to the excellence, growth, support and availability of the arts in the U.S.; received 1990 Emmy Award for lead actor performance in 'Age Old Friends' as well as 1990 ACE Award (Cable); recipient of 1991 Theatre LA Ovation Award; nominated for 1992 Emmy Award for best supporting actor in 'Broadway Bound' and for lead actor in 'Christmas on Division Street'; rec'd Emmy Award 1992 for 'Broadway Bound' as well as Golden Globe nomination for 'Broadway Bound' 1993; nominated for Candn. Olympic Boxing Team, 1932; named to Bd. Dirs., Stratford Fest. (1st actor) 1978; Address: 63–23 Carlton St., Rego Park, N.Y. 11374.

**CRONYN, James B.;** financial consultant; b. Toronto, Ont. 17 Oct. 1921; s. James K. and Isabel (Burton) C.; e. Ridley Coll., St. Catharines, Ont.; Royal Mil. Coll., Kingston; m. Valliere d. Maj. Gen. W.H.P. Elkins, C.B., C.B.E., D.S.O. & Bar and Mrs. Phyllis Elkins 20 Sept. 1947; children: Laleah Macintosh, Peter J.E., Elizabeth Topping; Financial Consultant, Touche Ross 1982–92; served 30 yrs. Cochran Murray & Co. Ltd. (now Walwyn Stodgell Cochran Murray & Co. Ltd.), final 10 yrs. as Pres. and Chrmn.; estbd. Credit Lyonaisse of Canada, Toronto serving as Vice Pres. and Dir. 1976; Merger & Acquisitions Dept. Touche Ross 1977–82; Prin., Twigg Group 1982–92; served Candn. Armed Forces (4th P.L.D.G.) 4th Candn. Recce. Regt. 1942–45 in N. Africa, Italy & N.W. Europe; rank Capt. 1945; Past Pres. V.O.N. Can., Past Pres. V.O.N. Metro Toronto Br., Bd. mem. V.O.N. (Ont.) 2 yrs.; mem. Adv. Bd. Ridley Coll.; Past Pres. R.M.C. Club Can.; Past Pres. Invest. Dealers Assn. (Ont. Dist.); Anglican; recreations: golf, fishing; Clubs: York; Toronto Golf; London; Cascade Golf & Tennis (Metis Beach, Qué.); Home: 61 Glencairn Ave., Toronto, Ont. M4R 1M7; Office: Toronto, Ont.

**CRONYN, John B.,** B.Sc.; company director; b. London, Ont. 3 Dec. 1920; s. late Verschoyle Philip and Dorothy (Bruce) C.; e. St. George's Public Sch., London, Ont.; Ridley Coll., St. Catharines, Ont.; Univ. of Toronto, B.Sc. 1947; m. Barbara Jean, d. late Noble Duff, 22 June 1946, children: Hume Duff, Marilyn Ruth, Martha Ann; Dir., Americare Corp.; Econ. Investment Trust Ltd.; Burnlea Holdings Ltd.; R.C.O. Investments Ltd.; Huron College Foundation; Robarts Rsch. Inst.; Hon. Dir., John Labatt Ltd.; The Niagara Inst.; Past Pres. London Chamber Comm., V.O.N., Boy Scouts Assn., London, Ont.; Assn. Prof Engrs. Ont.; apprentice brewer, John Labatt Ltd., Oct. 1947; completed brewmaster's course with Nat. Brewers Acad. 1949; A.M.P. Harvard 1969; apptd. Production Mgr., John Labatt Ltd. 1950, Dir. of Production 1952, Vice-Pres. in charge of Production 1956, el. a Dir. 1959, Extve. V.P. 1962; apptd. Chrmn., Ont. Gov. Productivity Improvement Project 1969; Vice Chrmn. of Bd., John Labatt Ltd. 1973; took early retirement, retaining directorship of John Labatt Ltd. 1976; served in 2nd World War; Lieut., R.C.E.; England and N. W. Europe, 1942–46; Kappa Alpha; Anglican; Clubs: London Hunt & Country; The London; The Toronto; Longboat Key; Great Lakes Cruising; Home: 21 Doncaster Ave., London, Ont. N6G 2A1.

**CROOK, Christopher John;** banking executive; b. U.K.; m. Margie; children: Nicole, Marc; CHIEF OPERATING OFFR., HONGKONG BANK OF CANADA; Office: 70 York St., Toronto, Ont. M5J 1S9.

**CROOKS, Arthur Hew Dalrymple,** B.A., M.B.A.; executive; b. Guelph, Ont. 24 Aug. 1939; s. Hew Dalrymple Crawford and Evelyn Jean Lamont (Hamilton) C.; e. Medway High Sch. Arva, Ont. 1956; Amherst (Mass.) Coll. B.A. 1961; Univ. of W. Ont. M.B.A. 1963; m. Mary Jane d. R. Archibald and Mary Fry 11 Dec. 1965; children: Hew, Claire, Morgan; PRESIDENT, A.H.D. CROOKS LTD. (Canadian Tire Associate Dealer) 1971– ; Dir., C.T.C. Dealer Holdings Ltd. 1992– ; Nat. Sales Mgr. Consumer Products Facelle Co. Ltd. 1963–70; Pres., Cox Hamilton Holdings Ltd.; Hobgoblin Holdings Ltd.; Vice Pres., Flueckiger Holdings Ltd.; Gencon Foods Ltd.; Dir., Candn. Tire Dealer Assn. 1975–79; Gov., Brentwood College School 1993– ; mem. Lethbridge Chamber Comm.; Lethbridge Symphony Assn.; Exper. Aircraft Assn. Antique Div.; recreations: flying, skiing, boating; Club: Lethbridge Flying; Home: 3602 S. Parkside Dr., Lethbridge, Alta. T1K 0E3; Office: 1240 2nd Ave. 'A' N., Lethbridge, Alta. T1H 0E4.

**CROSBIE, Allan H.T.,** B.Com., M.B.A., B.Litt.; investment executive; b. Toronto, Ont. 18 June 1941; s. Lindsay M.T. and Margaret P. (McDiarmid) C.; e. Univ. of Toronto, B.Com. 1964; Harvard Univ., M.B.A. 1967; Lincoln Coll. Oxford, B.Litt. 1968; m. Margaret A. d. John Pickens and Vestal Reeder 1969; children: John Lindsey, David Hamilton, Pierce Burrell; MANAGING PARTNER, CROSBIE & CO. INC. 1989– ; joined Wood Gundy Ltd. 1968, Vice Pres. 1973; Vice Pres. Upper Canada Resources Ltd. 1974, Pres. and Chief Exec. Offr. 1975–77; Founding Partner, Crosbie Armitage & Co. 1978–85, Sr. Vice Pres. and Dir. Merrill Lynch Canada (successor firm) 1985–87; Pres. & C.E.O., Trilon Capital Markets Inc. 1987–89; Dir., Waldec of Canada Ltd.; Glandore Investments Ltd.; Imperial Surgical Inc.; Alta-Can Telecom Inc.; The Canadian Stage Co.; recreations: squash, sailing; Clubs: Toronto; RCYC; Home: 42 Chestnut Park Rd., Toronto, Ont. M4W 1W8; Office: One First Canadian Place, 9th Floor, P.O. Box 116, Toronto, Ont. M5X 1A4.

**CROSBIE, Chesley Furneaux,** B.A. (Hons.), B.A. (Juris), LL.B.; lawyer; b. St. John's, Nfld. 12 June 1953; s. John Carnell and Jane Ellen (Furneaux) C.; e. Bishop Field Coll, 1967; St. Andrew's Coll, 1972; Queen's Univ., B.A. (Hons.) 1976; awarded Univ. Medal in Pol. Studies; Rhodes Scholar for Nfld. 1976; Balliol Coll., B.A. (Jurisprudence) 1980; Dalhousie Law Sch., LL.B. 1982; admitted to Nfld. bar 1983; m. Lois d. Robert and Betty Hoegg, 29 May 1982; three d.: Charlotte, Catherine, Rachel; PROPRIETOR, CHES CROSBIE BARRISTERS; mem., Am. Trial Lawyers Assn.; Candn. Bar Assn.; recreations: reading, films, wine, jogging; Home: 11 Chestnut Place, St. John's Nfld. A1B 2T1.

**CROSBIE, John Carnell,** P.C., Q.C., B.A, M.P.; lawyer; retired politician; b. St. John's, Nfld. 30 Jan. 1931; s. Chesley Arthur and Jessie Elizabeth (Carnell) C.; e. Bishop Field Coll., St. John's, Nfld.; St. Andrew's Coll., Aurora, Ont.; Queen's Univ., B.A. 1953 (Univ. Medal in Pol. Science); Dalhousie Univ., LL.B. 1956 (Univ. Medal in Law); Univ. of London, post-grad. work in Law (Candn. Bar Assn. Viscount Bennett Fellowship for 1957); m. Jane Ellen Audrey, d. late Dr. John H. Furneaux, 8 Sept. 1952; children: Chesley Furneaux, Michael John, Beth; COUNSEL, HALLEY, HUNT

1994– ; Dir., Canadian Helicopters Ltd. 1993– ; read law with P.J. Lewis, Q.C.; called to Bar of Newfoundland 1957; el. to St. John's City Council as Councillor, 1965, apptd. Depy. Mayor, 1966; resigned to accept appt. in Smallwood Lib. Adm. as Min. of Mun. Affairs & Housing, Nfld., July 1966; trans. to Health Portfolio, Sept. 1967; el. M.H.A. for Dist. of St. John's W. in prov. g.e. Sept. 1966; resigned from Cabinet due to policy disagreements, 14 May 1968; joined P. Conservative Party, June 1971; re-el. for St. John's W., Oct. 1971 and March 1972; apptd. Min. of Finance and Pres. of Treasury Bd. Jan. 1972–Oct. 1974; then apptd. Min. of Fisheries, Min. of Intergovernmental Affairs and Govt. House Leader until Oct. 1975, when apptd. Min. of Mines and Energy and Intergovt. Affairs; resigned Sept. 1976 to run for Parlt. and el. M.P., St. John's W. in by-el. 18 Oct. 1976; became Opposition Energy Critic and then Indust., Trade and Comm. Critic Oct. 1977; re-el. for St. John's W. May 1979, sworn into Privy Council June 4, 1979, and app'ted Min. of Finance; re-el. for St. John's W., Feb 1980 and appt. Opposition Finance Critic; subsequently named External Affairs Critic and (Sept. 1983) Finance Critic once more; re-el. M.P. for St. John's West Sept. 4, 1984 and Appt'd. Minister of Justice and Attorney-General; appt'd. Min. of Transport June 30, 1986; appt'd. Min. for International Trade Mar. 31, 1988; Min. of Fisheries & Oceans; Min. for the Atlantic Canada Opportunities Agency, 21 Apr. 1991–25 June 1993, retired; el. to Univ. Council, Queen's University, 1967; mem. Newfoundland Law Society; Canadian Bar Association; P. Conservative; United Church; recreations: reading, tennis, fishing; Home: Hogan's Pond, near St. John's, Nfld.; Offices: Scotia Centre, P.O. Box 610, 235 Water St., St. John's, Nfld. A1C 5L3.

**CROSBIE, John Shaver;** VSM, ASM, CM; business executive; author; b. Montreal, Que. 1 May 1920; s. Thomas Champion and Margaret Ruth (Shaver) C.; e. Univs. of N.B. and Toronto; m. Catherine Patricia James, 19 Nov. 1971; four s. Peter, Stephen, Andrew, Charles; one d. Kathryn; Pres., John S. Crosbie Ltd.; with Canadian Broadcasting Corp. until 1944 when apptd. Mang. Dir., Purdy Productions then Asst. Gen. Mgr., Dancer-Fitzgerald-Sample (Canada) Ltd. 1946; Gen. Mgr., Canadian Advertising Agency Ltd., Montreal 1949; subsequently with J. Walter Thompson Co., Toronto and later as a Vice-Pres., Chicago and San Francisco; Pres., Magazines Canada (The Magazine Assn. of Can.) 1967–86; served in 2nd W.W. as Offr., Can. Army; Founding-Dir., Candn.-Am. Soc. of Calif.; former Gov., The Candn. Club of New York; Past Vice-Chrmn., Un. Appeal, Toronto; former Gov., Frontier College; Past Pres., Canadian Scene; ex-Chrmn. and Dir. Can. Advertising Found.; Founding Dir. Nat'l Mag. Awards Found., National Advertising Benevolent Soc. and International Save the Pun Found.; author: 'The Pundit'; 'Crosbie's Book of Punned Haiku'; 'The Incredible Mrs. Chadwick'; 'Canada and Its Leaders'; 'Crosbie's Dictionary of Puns'; 'Crosbie's Dictionary of Riddles', etc.; Address: 30 Standish Ave., Toronto, Ont. M4W 3B1.

**CROSBY, John Alexander;** artist; b. Toronto, Ont. 16 Jan. 1925; s. Powell Sheffield and Ruby Pearl (Sedore) C.; e. North Toronto Coll.; Univ. of Toronto; no formal art training (encouraged by T.M. Shortt of R.O.M.); m. Helen d. James and Ann Brown 6 Aug. 1949; children: Peter, Paul; freelance nat. hist. illus. unitl 1951; Artist-Naturalist, Nat. Mus. of Can. 1951–66; Museologist, Parks Canada 1966–71; Artist & Exhibits, Nat. Mus. of Can. 1974–84; retired 1984; artist, illus.: 'Birds of Canada' 1966, 1986 (ten yrs. in the making and a best seller), Charles May series of children's nat. books 1968–72, 'Birds of Colorado' (sev. plates) 1955; designer: 'Polar Bear' 1953, 'Narwal' 1968 (Candn. Wildlife series stamps) 'bird series' for Candn. currency, Bank of Can. 1986; rec'd a Merit Award for outstanding contributions to the Nat. Mus. of Natural Sciences 1986; recreations: ornithology, early photography, antique clock restoration; Home: 1035 Hindley St., Ottawa, Ont. K2B 5L9.

**CROSS, Amy Willard,** B.A.; writer; b. Washington, D.C. 9 Oct. 1960; d. Eason and Diana Linnea (Johnson) C. Jr.; e. Wellesley College B.A. 1982; m. Patrick s. C. William and Mary Louise Bermingham 2 Sept. 1989; Executive Ed. & Creator, Moxie Magazine 1985–87; writes for various newspapers & magazines including The Globe and Mail, LA Weekly 1987–93; writes radio essays for CBC and Monitor Radio; Mem., PEN; author: 'The Summer House: A Tradition of Leisure' 1992; works anthologized in 'Inside Essays' 1993, 'Canadian Content' 1992, 'Matters of Fact: Short Non-Fiction' 1992; Home: 919 Mineral Springs Rd., RR 3, Dundas, Ont. L9H 5E3.

**CROSS, Edward (Ted) Bruce,** B.A.Sc., P.Eng.; chemical engineer; b. Toronto, Ont. 21 April 1936; s. Thomas Edward and Louise Robina (Craib) C.; e. University of Toronto Schools 1953; Univ. of Toronto B.A.Sc. 1957; m. Helen d. Hugh and Nesta Colquhoun 26 Oct. 1957; children: Cindra Louise, Wendy Elizabeth, Susan Ellen; ASSOCIATE DIRECTOR, TECHNOLOGY TRANSFER AND LICENSING OFFICE, UNIV. OF WATERLOO 1990– ; Rsch. Engr., Lever Brothers Limited 1957–62; Plant Engr., Hart Chemicals Limited 1962–66; Vice-Pres., Chinook Chem. Co. 1966–78; Pres. 1978–82; Extve. Dir., Waterloo Ctr. for Process Devel. 1982–90; Pres., E.B. Cross Technical Serv. Limited 1986– ; Chairman, Soc. of Chem. Indus., Candn. Section 1990–91; Pilot with 400 and 411 squadrons, R.C.A.F. Reserve 1957–66, retired (Squadron Leader); Mem., Assn. of Profl. Engrs. of Ont.; Licensing Extves. Soc.; Assn. of Univ. Technology Managers; recreations: skiing, sailing, racquet sports; clubs: National; Home: 113 Sandy Ridge Place, Waterloo, Ont. N2T 1C5; Office: Needles Hall, Univ. of Waterloo, Waterloo, Ont. N2L 3G1.

**CROSS, Loren Jay,** B.A.Sc., M.Sc., P.Eng.; real estate developer; b. Toronto, Ont. 15 Feb. 1953; s. Gordon Frederick and Margaret (McDougall) C.; e. Univ. of Toronto B.A.Sc. 1975; Columbia Univ. M.Sc. 1977; m. Devon d. Frank and Virginia Gaffney 3 June 1989; SENIOR VICE-PRES., URBAN GROUP, MARKBOROUGH PROPERTIES 1992– ; Estimator, Leader Group 1977–80; Devel. Mgr., Rostland Corp. 1980–83; Project Architect, Crang & Boake 1984–85; Gen. Mgr., Prudential of Am. 1985–89; Vice-Pres., Devel., Markborough Properties 1989–92; Mem., Candn. Olympic Team 1976, 1980, 1984 in Yachting; Office: 2800, 1 Dundas St. W., Toronto, Ont. M5G 2J2.

**CROSS, Philip Andrew,** B.A.; economic analyst; b. Ottawa, Ont. 21 Oct. 1954; s. Clarence Melvin and Alice Maude (Bawden) C.; e. Queen's Univ. B.A. (Hons.) 1976; children: Eric, Marie; CHIEF OF CURRENT ANALYSIS, STATISTICS CANADA 1980– ; writes and comments on current state of the economy; Editor, 'The Canadian Economic Observer' 1988– ; (monthy review); Office: 24-G, Coats Bldg., Ottawa, Ont. K1A 0T6.

**CROSSGROVE, Peter Alexander,** B.Com., M.B.A.; b. Sudbury, Ont. 31 Jan. 1937; s. Alexander Davidson and Marguerite Anne (Fortier); e. Concordia Univ., B. Com. 1961; Univ. of Western Ont., M.B.A. 1965; Harvard Business Sch., Sloan Fellow D.B.A. Prog.; m. Katharine d. John K. and Patricia (Macabe) McCausland 31 March 1979; children: Alex, Bonnie, Keith; CHAIRMAN & CHIEF EXTVE. OFFR., BRUSH CREEK CORPORATION; Dir., American Barrick Resources Corp.; Astro Dairies Ltd.; BII Enterprises Inc.; C.A.R.E. Canada; Eaton's of Canada Ltd.; Gentra Inc.; Lajambe Forest Products Ltd.; Mellon Bank Canada; Ontario Cancer Institute/Princess Margaret Hosp.; Premdor Inc.; Quadra Logic Technololgies Inc.; The R-M Trust Co.; Samcor Inc.; The Toronto Hosp. Found.; United Dominion Industries Ltd.; Chrmn., The Toronto Hosp. Cardiac Centre Campaign Ctte.; Past Chrmn., The Toronto Hospital Bd. of Trustees; Home: 61 Crescent Rd., Toronto, Ont. M4W 1T6; Office: 250 Yonge St., 15th Floor, Toronto, Ont. M5B 1C8.

**CROSSLAND, The Hon. Mr. Justice James;** judge; b. Toronto, Ont. 24 July 1932; s. James and Mae Yolande (Struthers) C.; e. Univ. of Toronto, Victoria Coll., B.A. 1955; Osgoode Hall Law Sch. 1959; 1stly m. Irene Richardson (dec'd. 1967); son: James; 2ndly m. Josie d. Joseph and Ida Hunt 24 Aug. 1970; son: Joseph; apptd. to ONTARIO COURT OF JUSTICE 1990– ; called to Bar 1959; Asst. Crown Attorney, Co. of York 1960; Q.C. 1972; Judge, Prov. Court of Ont., Criminal Div. 1974; Judge, District Court of Ontario 1988–90; Counc. Mem., Medico-Legal Soc. of Toronto 1972–74; mem., Ch. of England; Home: 89 Brahms Ave., Willowdale, Ont. M2H 1H5; Office: Court House, 361 University Ave., Toronto, Ont. M5G 1T3.

**CROSSMAN, Kelly Joseph,** B.A., M.A., Ph.D.; university professor; b. Regina, Sask. 30 Sept. 1953; s. Raymond Archibald and Lilian Elizabeth (Lacey) C.; e. St. Paul's H.S. 1970; Univ. of Winnipeg, B.A. (Hons.) 1974; Univ. of Toronto, M.A. 1976; Edinburgh Univ., Ph.D. 1982; ASSOC. PROF., ART HIST., CARLETON UNIV. 1988– ; Architectural Hist., Parks Can. 1976–77; Asst. Ed., 'Architectural Design' / Academy Books 1983; Post-doct. fellow, McGill Univ. 1984–85; Arch. Hist., Heritage Br., Man. Dept. of Culture & Rec. 1986–87; SSHRCC fellowship 1978–80, 1984–85; R. Catholic; author: 'Architecture in Transition from Art to Practice 1886–1906' 1987 and various articles & reviews; recreation: music; Office: Colonel By Dr., Ottawa, Ont. K1S 5B6.

**CROTIN, Gloria;** hospital administrator; b. Montréal, Qué. 24 June 1931; d. John Graham and Jean Alexandra (Pashby) Gatehouse; e. McGill Univ. B.N. 1959; Univ. of Pittsburgh M.N.Ed. (Adm.) 1968; PRES. YORK CENTRAL HOSP. 1987– ; Dir. of Nursing present Hosp. 1963, Asst. Exec. Dir. 1974, Sr. Vice Pres. 1986; Fellow, Am. Coll. Health Care Execs.; Cert. mem. Candn. Coll. Health Service Execs.; mem. Bd. of York Region, United Way; mem. Bd. Trade Metrop. Toronto; recreation: curling; Club: Richmond Hill Curling; Home 17 St. Andrews Court, Aurora, Ont. L4G 3B2; Office: 10 Trench St., Richmond Hill, Ont. L4C 4Z3.

**CROUSE, Hon. Lloyd Roseville,** P.C.; retired provincial lieutenant governor; b. Lunenburg, N.S. 19 Nov. 1918; s. Kenneth Eleazer and Mary Bertha (Lantz) C.; e. Lunenberg Co. Acad.; m. Marion Cavell, d. Lawson E. Fraser, Bridgewater, N.S., 7 Oct. 1942; children: Marilyn Diane (Mrs. Ken Williams), Stephen Lloyd; Lieutenant Governor of Nova Scotia, retired 20th Feb. 1994; before entering politics estbd. Crouse Fisheries Ltd., Viking Fisheries Limited and Atlas Fisheries Ltd.; served with R.C.A.F. as Pilot World War II; mem., Lunenburg Town Council 1950–52; mem., Lunenburg Sch. Commrs. 1950–52; Chrmn., Lutheran Youth Bd. 1950–54; Past Pres., Lunenburg Br. 23, Royal Candn. Legion; Chrmn. and Master of Ceremonies, N.S. Fisheries Exhn. 1946–56; mem. Council, Lunenburg Bd. Trade 1946–56; 1st el. to H. of C. for Queens-Lunenburg g.e. 1957, re-el. in 1958, 1962, 1963, 1965; el. in 1968 as first rep. for new 'South Shore' constit., re-el. 1972, 1974, 1979, 1980 and 1984; retired from Parliament 1988; Chrmn., Candn. Del., Commonwealth Parlty. Conf. in U.K. 1962; Del. to NATO Parlty. Conf., Paris 1963, 1964, 1966; Brussels 1967; del. to Inter Parlty. Union Conf., Paris 1971; Del. Commonwealth Parlty. Conf. 1973; Del. C.P.A. Conf., Jamaica 1978; Del. C.P.A. Conf. New Zealand 1979; Del. to 26th Commonwealth Parlty. Conf., Lusaka, Zambia 1980; Del. to 22nd Candn. Reg. Commonwealth Parlty. Conf., N.W.T. 1982; served as Leader of Commonwealth Parlty. Del. Isle of Man Oct. 1984; Chrmn. Standing Comte. on Public Accounts 1974 and 1975; Delegate to 1981 U.N. Conference at Columbo, Sri Lanka; served on House Standing Ctte. on Mgmt. and Members' Services; apptd. Sept. 1983 by Mr. Brian Mulroney, Leader of P.C. Party, as member of Shadow Cabinet, resp. for Party's Fisheries Policies for Can.; apptd. by P.M. Mulroney to Queen's Privy Counc. (in recognition of 28 yrs. of continuous service in Parliament) 10 June 1985; mem. of Bd. of Govs., Waterloo Lutheran Univ., Kitchener, Ont. 1960–69; mem. Candn. Legion; N.S. Salmon Assn.; Pres., Candn. Branch, Commonwealth Parlty. Assn. 1984, Chrmn. 1985-88; Candn. rep., Internat. Exec., Commonwealth Parlty. Assn.; Candn. Group Interparlty. Union; Candn. NATO Parlty. Assn.; Candn. Commonwealth Parlty. Assn.; Fellow, N.S. Royal Commonwealth Society; Knight of Grace, Order of Saint John of Jerusalem; Chrmn. Nova Scotia Archives 1989– ; P. Conservative; Lutheran; Clubs: Rod & Gun; Office: Government House, 1451 Barrington St., Halifax, N.S. B3J 1Z2.

**CROW, John William,** B.A.; economist; b. London, Eng. 1937; s. John Cornell and Mary Winifred (Weetch) C.; e. Parmiter's Sch., London, Eng.; Oxford Univ., B.A. 1961; m. Ruth, d. Abbo and Helen Kent, 7 Mar. 1963; children: Rebecca and Jonathan; Governor, Bank of Canada 1987–94; joined Internat. Monetary Fund as economist 1961; Chief, North American Div. 1970; joined Bank of Can. as Deputy Chief, Research Dept. 1973; Chief 1974; Adviser 1979; Depy. Gov. 1981; Sr. Depy. Gov. 1984; Home: 694 Echo Dr., Ottawa, Ont. K1S 1P3.

**CROWE, Cameron Macmillan,** B.Eng., Ph.D., F.C.I.C., P.Eng.; educator; b. Montreal, Que. 6 Oct. 1931; s. Ernest Watson and Marianne Verity (Macmillan) C.; e. Montreal West (Que.) High Sch. 1948; Royal Mil. Coll. grad. dipl. 1952; McGill Univ. B.Eng. 1953; Cambridge Univ. Ph.D 1957; m. Jean Margaret Gilbertson 15 Feb. 1969; PROF. OF CHEM. ENGN., McMASTER UNIV. 1970– ; Sr. Devel. Engr. Du Pont of Canada Ltd. 1957–59; Asst. Prof. present Univ. 1959, Assoc. Prof. 1964, Chrm. of Chem. Engn. 1971–74; Athlone Fellow 1953–55; C. D. Howe Mem. Fellow 1967–68; co-author 'Chemical Plant Simulation' 1971; Assoc. Ed. 'Canadian Journal of Chemical Engineering' 1975–81; Fellow, Chem. Inst. of Canada; Pres., Candn. Soc. Chem. Engng. 1991–92 (Vice Pres. 1990–91, Dir. 1984–87); mem. Am. Inst. Chem. Engrs.; Assn. Prof. Engrs. Prov. Ont.; Candn. Soc. Chem. Engng.; recreations: tennis, skiing; Home: 821 Glenwood Ave.,

Burlington, Ont. L7T 2J8; Office: Hamilton, Ont. L8S 4L7.

**CROWE, Rev. Frederick Ernest,** S.J., B.Sc., B.A., S.T.D., Lic. Phil., (R.C.); theologian; educator; b. Jeffries Corner, N.B., 5 July 1915; s. Jeremiah Chesley and Margaret Lucinda (Mahoney) C.; e. Sussex (N.B.) High Sch. 1930; Univ. of N.B., B.Sc. 1934; Loyola Coll., Univ. of Montreal, B.A. 1943; Gregorian Univ., Rome, S.T.D. 1953; Coll. de l'Immaculée-Conception, Montréal, Lic. Phil. 1962; D.Litt. (Hon.), St. Mary's, Halifax 1971; D.D. (Hon.), Trinity College, Toronto 1977; LL.D. (Hon.), St. Thomas, Fredericton 1982; D.D. (Hon.), Univ. of St. Michael's Coll., Toronto 1986; PROFESSOR EMERITUS, REGIS COLLEGE, TORONTO 1980– ; Teacher of Theol. there 1953, Rsch. Prof. 1975; Dir., Lonergan Rsch. Inst. 1985–91; o. Priest, Toronto 1949; S.J. 1936; Teacher, St. Mary's Coll., Halifax, N.S. 1943–46; Pres., Regis Coll. 1969–72; Visiting Prof., Gregorian Univ., Rome 1964 and 1984; author: 'A Time of Change' 1968; 'Escatologia e missione terrena in Gesù di Nazareth' 1976; 'Theology of the Christian Word: A Study in History' 1978; 'The Lonergan Enterprise' 1980; 'Old Things and New: A Strategy for Education' 1985; 'Appropriating the Lonergan Idea' 1989; 'Lonergan' 1992; Ed.: 'Spirit as Inquiry' 1964; 'Collection: Papers by Bernard Lonergan' 1967; 'A Third Collection: Papers by Bernard Lonergan' 1985; 'Collected Works of Bernard Lonergan' 1988; contrib. 'New Catholic Encyclopedia' 1967, 1974, 1979; mem. Candn. Theol. Soc.; Catholic Theol. Soc. Am.; Jesuit Philos. Assn.; John Courtney Murray Award 1977; Honoured with volume of essays by colleagues, Trinification of the World: A Festschrift in Honour of Frederick E. Crowe in Celebration of His 60th Birthday (Regis College Press, 1978); Address: Lonergan Research Inst., 10 St. Mary St., Toronto, Ont. M4Y 1P9.

**CROWE, Marshall Alexander,** B.A., LL.B.; b. Rossburn, Manitoba, 14 April 1921; s. William Johnston and Georgina (Gammon) C.; e. Daniel McIntyre Coll. Inst., Winnipeg, Man.; Univ. of Manitoba, B.A. 1943; Univ. of Ottawa, LL.B. 1992; m. Doris Mary, d. late Richard C. Scanes, 5 Dec. 1942; children: Thomas, Alison, Helen, Sheila, Abigail; PRESIDENT, M.A. CROWE CONSULTANTS, INC. since Jan. 1978; Dir., Gulf-Mark International; Pensionfund Energy Resources Ltd.; articling student-at-law, Johnston, Buchan & Dalfen; Dept. of External Affairs, 1947–61; Econ. Adviser, Candn. Imperial Bank of Commerce, 1961–67; apptd. Asst. Secy. of the Cabinet and Asst. Clerk of the P.C. Canada 1967; Depy. Secy. of the Cabinet 1969; Pres. Can. Devel. Corp. 1971, Chrmn. 1971–73; Chrmn., Nat. Energy Bd., 1973–77; served in 2nd World War with Candn. Army (Inf.); discharged with rank of Capt.; Home: Portland, Ont. K0G 1V0 and 543 Lisgar St., Ottawa, Ont. K1R 5H4; Office: 275 Slater St., Suite 1700, Ottawa, Ont. K1P 5H9.

**CROWSTON, Wallace Bruce,** B.A.Sc., S.M., M.Sc., Ph.D.; educator; b. Toronto, Ont. 28 Jan. 1934; s. Arthur William and Clara Helena (Donnelly) C.; e. Univ. of Toronto B.A.Sc. 1956; Mass. Inst. of Technol. S.M. 1958; Carnegie Mellon Univ. M.Sc. 1965, Ph.D. 1968; m. Taka Ohkubo 15 Sept. 1961; children: Kevin, Cathy, Clare; DEAN, FACULTY OF MANAGEMENT, McGILL UNIV. 1987– ; Asst. Prof. Univ. of Alta. 1960–62; Asst. Prof. Mass. Inst. of Technol. 1966, Assoc. Prof. 1969–72; Prof., Faculty of Administrative Studies, York Univ. 1972–87 and Dean 1976–84; recipient Ford Foundation Doctoral Fellowship; Club: University (Montreal); Home: 605 Lansdowne Ave., Westmount, Que. H3Y 2V7; Office: Rm. 454, Faculty of Management, 1001 Sherbrooke St. W., Montreal, Que. H3A 1G5.

**CROZIER, Douglas Noel,** C.M., M.D., FRCPC; paediatrician; b. Toronto, Ont. 23 June 1926; s. George Crozier; e. Univ. of Toronto M.D. 1952; m. Joan; two d. Susan Jane, Stephanie Louise; SR. PAEDIATRICIAN AND CHEST PHYSICIAN, HOSP. FOR SICK CHILDREN; Asst. Prof. of Paediatrics Univ. of Toronto; Chest Consultant and mem. Med. Adv. Ont. Soc. Crippled Children; internship: Toronto E. Gen. Hosp. 1952–53, Hosp. for Sick Children 1953–55, 1956; Baby's Hosp.-Presbyterian Med. Hosp. N.Y. Fellow in Paediatric Pathol. 1955–56; Sunnybrook Hosp. 1957; Med. Dir. Bloorview Children's Hosp. 1960–70; mem. Med. Adv. Candn. Cystic Fibrosis Foundation 1960–67, Chrmn. 1960–63; Dir. Cystic Fibrosis Clinic Hosp. for Sick Children 1958–78; author or co-author numerous med. articles; Member of the Order of Canada (for work in Cystic Fibrosis) 1986; United Church; recreations: skiing, tennis, golf; Clubs: Blue Mountain Golf; Devils Glen Country; Georgian Peaks Ski; Monterra Tennis, Collingwood; Office: 9 Krista Court, Collingwood, Ont. L9Y 4N9.

**CROZIER, Lorna,** B.A., M.A.; writer/teacher; b. Swift Current, Sask. 24 May 1948; d. Emerson George and Margaret Emily (Ford) C.; e. Univ. of Sask. B.A. 1969; profl. 'A' teaching cert. 1970; Univ. of Alta. M.A. 1980; ASST. PROF., DEPT. OF CREATIVE WRITING, UNIV. OF VICTORIA 1992– ; and SPECIAL LECTR., UNIV. OF SASKATCHEWAN 1986– ; H.S. Eng. Teacher, Swift Current, Sask. 1972–77; Creative Writing Teacher, Sask. Summer School of the Arts 1977–81; Writer-in-Residence, Cypress Hills Community Coll. 1980–81; Dir. of Communications, Dept. of Parks, Recreation & Culture, Govt. of Sask. 1981–83; Writer-in-Residence, Regina Public Library 1984–85; Broadcaster & Writer, CBC Radio 1986; Guest Instr., Banff Sch. of Fine Arts 1986, 1987; Visiting Prof., Univ. of Victoria, Dept. of Creative Writing 1991–92; CBC Poetry Nat. Writing Comp., 1st prize for poetry 1987; Nat. Radio Award, 1st Prize for Best Public Radio Program of 1987; Sask. Writers' Guild Poetry Ms. Award 1984, 1987; Gov. General's Nom. for Poetry 1986, 1988; Mem., Sask. Writers' Guild (Vice-Pres. 1975–77); The League of Candn. Poets (Sask. Rep. 1979–80; Chair, Membership Ctte. 1980–81); Writer-in-residence, Univ. of Toronto 1989–90; author: 'Inside Is the Sky' 1976, 'Crow's Black Joy' 1978, 'Humans and Other Beasts' 1980, 'The Weather' 1983, 'The Garden Going On Without Us' 1985, 'Angels of Silence, Angels of Flesh' 1988 (poetry); 'Inventing the Hawk' 1992 (winner of Governor General's Award for Eng. Lang. Poetry, Candn. Authors' Assn. Award for Poetry and The League of Candn. Poets' Pat Lowther Award for Poetry 1992); co-author: 'No Longer Two People' 1979; co-editor, 'A Sudden Radiance' (Saskatchewan Poetry) Coteau Books 1987; recreations: swimming, cross-country skiing; Home: R.R. 2, 1886 Cultra, Saanichton, B.C. V0S 1M0.

**CRUESS, Richard L.,** A.B., M.D., F.R.C.S.(C), F.A.C.S., F.R.S.C.; educator; b. London, Ont. 17 Dec. 1929; s. Leigh Saunders and Martha Annette (Peever) C.; e. Princeton Univ. A.B. 1951; Columbia Univ. M.D. 1955; m. Sylvia d. Alexander and Marjory Robinson 30 May 1953; children: Leigh S., Andrew C.; DEAN OF MEDICINE, McGILL UNIV. 1981– ; and Prof. of Surg.; internship and residency Royal Victoria Hosp. Montreal and New York Orthopaedic Hosp. of Columbia Presb. Med. Center 1955–62; Research Fellow Depts. Biochem. & Orthopaedics latter Hosp. 1962–63; Attending Orthopaedic Surg. Royal Victoria Hosp. 1963–68, Orthopaedic Sur.-in-Charge 1968–81, Asst. Surg.-in-Chief (Dept. Surg.) 1979–81; Surg.-in-Chief Montreal Shriners Hosp. for Crippled Children 1970–82; Hon. Consultant in Orthopaedic Surg. Queen Elizabeth Hosp.; Past Chrmn. Div. Orthopaedic Surg. McGill Univ.; mem. Med. Research Council Clin. Grants Comte. 1972–75, mem. Council 1980–83, mem. Extve. Ctte. 1983–86; Visiting Lectr. various insts. Can., U.S.A., Australia, Scot.; served with Med. Corps U.S. Naval Reserve 1957–59, rank Lt.; recipient John Armour Travelling Fellowship 1962–63; A.B.C. (Am.-Brit.-Candn.) Travelling Fellowship 1967; Steindler Award, Am. Acad. of Orthopaedic Surgeons 1984; Kt. Comdr. of Merit, Sovereign Mil. Order of St-John of Jerusalem (Knights of Malta) 1984; Chevalier de la Tastevin, Clos de Vougeot, Bourgogne, France 1986; co-ed. 'Surgery of Rheumatoid Arthritis' 1971; 'Surgical Management of Degenerative Arthritis of the Lower Extremity' 1975; 'The Musculoskeletal System: Embryology, Biochemistry and Physiology' 1982; 'Adult Orthopaedics' 1984; author or co-author numerous med. articles, abstracts; mem. various ed. bds.; Fellow, Royal Soc. of Can.; Am. Acad. Orthopaedic Surgs.; mem.: Orthopaedic Rsch. Soc.; Assn. Orthopaedic Surgs. Prov. Que. (Treas. 1971–72); McGill Osler Reporting Soc.; A.B.C. Club; Candn. Orthopaedic Assn. (Treas. 1969–71, Secy. 1971–76, Pres. 1977–78); Am. Orthopaedic Assn.; Candn. Orthopaedic Rsch. Soc. (Pres. 1971–72); Internat. Research Soc. Orthopaedics & Traumatol.; mem. d'Honneur de la Soc. Française de Chirurgie Orthopédique et Traumatique; Chief Examiner in Orthopaedic Surg. Royal Coll. Phys. & Surgs. Can. 1970–72; Pres. Am. Orthopaedic Research Soc. 1975–76; Pres., Assoc. of Candn. Medical Colleges 1987–89; recreations: fishing, skiing, photography; Club: University; Home: 526 Mount Pleasant, Montreal, Que. H3Y 3H5; Office: 3655 Drummond St., Montreal, Que. H3G 1Y6.

**CRUICKSHANK, John Douglas,** B.A.; journalist; b. Toronto, Ont. 7 Apl. 1953; s. Norman Hamish and Jean (McPherson) C.; e. Univ. of Toronto Trinity Coll. B.A. 1976; m. Jennifer d. Morris and Reene Hunter 5 May 1979; children: Simone, Noah; MANAGING EDITOR, THE GLOBE AND MAIL 1991– ; Reporter Kingston Whig-Standard 1976–78, Montreal Gazette 1978–81; Edn. Reporter present newspaper 1981, Queen's Park Bureau Chief 1983, Vancouver Bureau Chief 1985, Foreign Affairs Writer Ed. Bd. 1989; Assoc. Ed. The Globe and Mail 1990–91; author: Weekly Internat. Affairs Column, World View; Home: 11 Sulkara Court, Toronto, Ont. M4S 2G8; Office: 444 Front St. W., Toronto, Ont. M5V 2S9.

**CRUISE, James Edwin,** B.A., M.S., Ph.D.; retired museum director; b. Port Dover, Ont. 26 June 1925; s. William Edward and Annie Gertrude (Walker) C.; e. Marburg Sch. Woodhouse 1937; Port Dover (Ont.) High Sch. 1941; Simcoe (Ont.) High Sch. 1943; Univ. of Toronto B.A. 1950; Cornell Univ. M.S. 1951, Ph.D. 1954; Univ. of Guelph LL.D. (Hon.) 1982; Teaching Asst. in Gen. Bot. & Taxonomy, Cornell Univ. 1951–54; Post-doctoral Fellow and Instr. in Bot. Philadelphia Acad. of Science (Ford Foundation Fellowship) 1954–56; Asst. Prof. State Univ. of N.J. 1956, Assoc. Prof. 1958, Prof. 1960–63; Adjunct Prof. of Bot. Princeton Univ. 1959–63; Assoc. Prof. Univ. of Toronto 1963, Prof. since 1969, Curator of Phanerogamic Herbarium 1969–75, Assoc. Chrmn. 1971–72, Assoc. Dean of Arts 1972–75; Dir. Royal Ont. Musuem 1975–85; Consultant to Nat. Science Foundation, Washington, D.C. 1959–63; Participant NSF Summer Inst. for Coll. & Univ. Instrs. Vanderbilt Univ. Nashville 1962; Dir. Plant Systematice, NSF Summer Inst. Rutgers Univ. 1963; Ed. Consultant in Systematics and Exper. Taxonomy Am. Journ. of Bot., Castanea, The Am. Nat. and Am. Midland Nat. since 1963; served with RCAF 1943–46, Air Navig. and Navig. Instr., rank Flying Offr.; rec'd Queen's Silver Jubilee Medal 1977; mem. Canadian Art Museum Directors Organization, Association of Art Museum Directors, International Council of Museums; Ont. Soc. Biols. (Pres. 1967–68, 1970–71); Candn. Bot. Assn. (Secy. 1970–72); Am. Inst. Biol. Science; Bot. Soc. Am.; Am. Soc. Plant Taxonomists; Internat. Soc. Plant Taxonomists; Phi Kappa Phi; Sigma Xi; United Church; Home: R.R. #1, Port Dover, Ont. N0A 1N1.

**CRUISE, John David,** B.A.; writer; b. Victoria, B.C. 28 March 1950; s. John Thomas and Claudia Constance Barbara (Quinn) C.; e. Univ. of Alta. B.A. 1977; Alison Griffiths; children: Claudia, Quinn-Toby; Aquatics Dir. Victoria YM-YWCA 1972; Asst. Mgr. Vancouver Youth Hostel 1973; Head Coach Mill Creek Swim Club Edmonton 1975–76; Prog. Dir. Kamloops Community 'Y' 1978; Special Projects Supvr. Grant MacEwan Community Coll. Edmonton 1979; profl. writer 1980– ; co-author 'The Money Rustlers – Self Made Millionaires of the New West' 1985; 'Fleecing the Lamb – The Inside Story of the Vancouver Stock Exchange' 1987; (with Alison Griffiths) 'Lords of the Line: The Men Who Built the CPR' 1988; 'Net Worth: Exploding the Myths of Hockey' 1991; co-recipient (with Alison Griffiths) Nat. Mag. Awards Silver Medal 1986; Runner-Up Centre Investig. Jour. 1986; Royal Bank Nat. Bus. Writing Award 1987; winner (with Alison Griffiths) for 'Lords of the Line,' Book of the Year Award, The Candn. Railroad Assoc. 1989; mem., Writers Union; Periodical Writers Assn. Can. (Regional Dir. B.C. 1982–83, Nat. Treas. 1983–85); recreation: weight lifting; Address: 738 Selkirk Ave., The Gorge, Victoria, B.C. V9A 2T5.

**CRUTCHLOW, Lewis George,** B.Sc., Ph.D., P.Eng.; Ret. Candn. Public Servant; b. Saskatoon, Sask., 14 June 1921; s. James and Mary Anne (Jacobs) C.; e. Saskatoon Tech. Coll., Sr. Matric. and Indust. Cert. 1938; Univ. of Sask., B.Sc. (Elect. Engn.) 1950; Royal Military Coll., Hon. D. Eng., 1981; m. Edith Mae, d. late William James Dickson, 18 May 1943; children: Wayne Gordon, Richard James, Garry Lewis, Mary Anne; SENIOR PRINCIPAL, CFN CONSULTANTS 1983– ; joined Nat. Defence HQ, naval engn. field, 1950; served as Chief Engr., Radar Engn. Div.; trans. to staff Asst. Depy. Min. (Requirements) 1956; subsequently Dir. Gen. of Requirements (Electronic & Communications); trans. to Treasury Bd. 1968 becoming Dir., Transport. & Communication Div., Programs Br.; returned to National Defence as Asst. Depy. Min. (Materiel) 1971, retired from public service 1982; Founding Senior Principal CFN Consultants 1983; served with R.C.A.F. 1942–45 as Radar Offr.; rank Flying Offr.; mem., Engn. Inst. Can.; United Church; recreations: boating, photography; Clubs: Ottawa Hunt & Golf; Rideau; Home: 20 Avenue Rd., Ottawa, Ont. K1S 0N9.

**CRYDER, Donald Howard,** B.A.Sc., M.A.Sc., P.Eng.; manufacturing executive; b. Toronto, Ont. 3 July 1936; s. Maurice Howard and Mary (Anderson) C.; e. Univ. of Toronto, B.A.Sc. 1958, M.A.Sc. 1960; m. Willow-Anne d. Edwin and Marie Morris 14 June 1980; children: Robert, Douglas, James, Brittany-Anne, Brent William; PRES., CROUSE-HINDS ELECTRICAL CONSTRUC-

TION MATERIALS 1980– ; Project Supvr., Ont. Dept. of Highways 1958–60; Designer, Carruthers & Wallace 1961–62; Mktg. Mgr., Molson Indus. 1962–72; Vice Pres., Mktg., Smith and Stone Ltd. 1972–80; Mem., Assn. of Profl. Engrs.; Club: Mississauga Golf & Country; Home: 64 Normandale Rd., Unionville, Ont. L3R 4K3; Office: 1160 Birchmount Rd., Scarborough, Ont. M1P 2B9.

**CRYSDALE, Stewart,** M.A., Th.M., Ph.D.; university professor/minister (Emeritus); b. Vancouver, B.C. 20 May 1914; s. Charles Agnew and Mary Olivia (Stewart) C.; e. Univ. of B.C., B.A., B.Comm. 1935; Univ. of Toronto, B.D., Th.M., M.A., Ph.D. 1968; Columbia Univ. & Univ. of Calif., Berkeley, grad. studies; m. Thelma d. Brian and Estelle Holmes 1943; children: Ann Elizabeth, David Stewart; SR. SCHOLAR AND PROFESSOR EMERITUS, YORK UNIV. 1992– , Prof. 1967; Editor, B.C. Municipal News 1936–39; Asst. Ed., B.C. Miner 1939–43; Student/Min., Williams Lake, B.C. & hinterland 1943–48; Minister in charge, Williams Lake 1943–48; Min., Rutland-Oyama, B.C. 1948–52; Colborne St. Un. Ch. & Co-chair, Relig.-Labour Counc. of Can. 1952–59; Min., St. Paul's Ave. Rd. Un. Ch. & Grad. Student, Univ. of Toronto 1959–63; Assoc. Sec., Bd. of Evangelism & Soc. Serv., Un. Ch. Gen. Counc. 1964–67; Conf. on Transition from School to Work, UNESCO, Copenhagen 1973; Internat. Conf. on Educ., Geneva 1973; Delegate, Internat. Conf. on Sociology of Religion, The Hague 1973; Visiting Prof., Univ. of Bordeaux, France 1979; Visiting Prof., Uppsala Univ., Sweden, and Univ. of Reading, Engl. 1992; numerous univ. & church comns. & cttes.; consultant & rsch. dir. for first national survey of effects of beliefs on social ethics and liberal behaviour 1964, youth in transition from school to work, national survey, 1988–91 etc.; Mem., Candn. Soc. & Anthr. Assn. (Pres. 1984–85); Soc. Sci. Fed. of Can.; Ont. Soc. & Anthr. Assn.; Am. Soc. Assn.; Internat. Soc. for the Sociology of Religion and others; author: 'The Industrial Struggle and Protestant Ethics in Canada' 1961; 'Churches Where the Action Is' 1966; 'The Changing Church in Canada' 1965; (sr. author) 'Religion in Canada' 1972; (sr. author) 'Sociology Canada' 1974, 1977; 'Religion in Canadian Society' 1976; 'Families Under Stress in Eastside, a metropolitan neighbourhood' 1991; (sr. author) 'Youths' Transition to Work in Eastside' 1994; (sr. author) 'A Productive Resilient Generation?' 1994; Hon. Doctorate conferred by York Univ. 1993; recreations: jogging, squash, painting, woodcarving, travel, canoeing; Office: York Univ., 4700 Keele St., North York, Ont. M3J 1P3.

**CSATHY, Thomas I.,** B.Sc., M.Sc., P.Eng.; engineer; b. Kaposvar, Hungary 25 Jan. 1931; s. George M. and Martha K. (Michnay) C.; e. Tech. Univ. of Budapest 1949–51, 1954–56; Glasgow Univ., B.Sc. 1957–59; Queen's Univ., M.Sc. 1959–61; m. Marianna d. Leslie and Martha Haraszti 28 July 1962; children: Francis George, Marianne Martha, Nadine Catherine; PRESIDENT, T.I. CSATHY ASSOCIATES INC. 1989– ; Chrmn. and Dir., Fulcrum Technologies Inc.; The Branham Consulting Group Inc.; Vice Chrmn. and Dir., Mosaid Technologies Inc.; Rsch. Engr., Ont. Dept. of Hwys. 1961–62; var. pos. beginning as Systems Engr. Trainee & ending as Corp. Treasurer, IBM Can. Ltd. 1963–82; Pres., Burroughs Can. 1982–86; Pres., Cognos Inc. 1986–89; recreations: tennis, bridge; Clubs: Bayview Country; Champêtre; Rideau Tennis and Squash; Rockcliffe Lawn Tennis; Home: 60 MacNabb Place, Rockcliffe Park, Ont. K1L 8J4.

**CSELKO, Ernest Heinrich Jr.;** artistic, commercial illustrator; b. Budapest, Hungary 9 May 1947; s. Ernest Steven and Katherine (Steidl) C. (both dec.); e. Nelson McIntyre Collegiate; Winnipeg Tech. Voc. Inst.; m. (Max) Martha Tracy A.O.C.A. d. J.C. Ross and the late Margaret (Tracy) Waddell 26 Jan. 1991; FOUNDER & PRES., CSELKO ASSOC. INC. & MKTG. CONSULTANT & CREATIVE DIR., EYEFUL ART-WORKS; Graphic Designer/Illus., T. Eaton Co. 1967; Hudson Bay Co. 1968–69; Art Dir., James Lovick Advtg.; McConnel Advtg.; Goodis, Goldberg, Soren; Creative Dir. (Cons.), Letrafast Can. Ltd.; Art Dir., Kert Advtg. Ltd.; Pres. & Creative Dir., Communic-Ad Inc.; Co-Founder & Pres., Cselko Walters Assoc.; associated with & rep. by Gallery on the Lake, Buckhorn, Ont.; pub. by Buckhorn Fine Art Pub. in affiliation with The Hadley House Minneapolis; private tutor of graphic design/illus. to advanced illustrators for two decades centred around a unique, condensed formula of old masters 'chiaroscuro'; selected to panel of judges for C.A.P.I.C. 1991; inventor of improved technique for black & white newsprint image reproduction (for Sears Canada Inc. & Xerox); promotional advisor, designer & illus. for countless number of nat. & internat. corps. over 25 years; included in 'Best Canadian Posters of the Century' Candn. Cancer Soc.; recognized for envir. contbn., Conservation Council of Ont.; best known for projects such as: Official Calgary Stampede Poster 1985, '87; new car intros for Gen. Motors; restructuring & supervising graphic images for Sears & Xerox; Labatt's C.N.E. Air-Show Poster; refugee from Hungarian Revolution; settled in Canada 1957; learned canoeing & wilderness survival from cinematographer Bill Mason; extensive travels in the U.S., Pacific Rim, North of L. Superior (for insight to Group of Seven); paints North American 'Buckskinners' fur trade (c.1820–60) with technical advice from Candn. Internat. Muzzle Loading Team; Mem., Ont. Fed. of Anglers & Hungers (Ctte. for Restocking Kawartha Lakes); several contbns. of Conservation Edition prints to var. charitable orgns. through Buckhorn Fine Art Pub.; subject of feature editorial & front cover 'Inside Collectibles' 1993; recreations: chess, canoeing, metaphysics; Address: 82 Balaclava St., P.O. Box 672, Bobcaygeon, Ont. K0M 1A0.

**CSÖRGŐ, Miklós,** M.A., Ph.D., F.R.S.C.; b. Egerfarmos, Hungary 12 March 1932; s. Miklós and Ilona (Veres) C.; e. Univ. of Econ. Budapest B.A. 1955; McGill Univ. M.A. 1961, Ph.D. 1963; m. Anna d. István and Eszter Tóth 10 Aug. 1957; children: Adria, Lilla; PROF. OF MATH. & STATS. CARLETON UNIV. 1972– , Assoc. Prof. of Math 1971; Lectr. Univ. of Econ. Budapest 1955–56; NRC Can. Grad. Student Scholar McGill Univ. 1960–63, Asst. Prof. of Math. 1965–68, Assoc. Prof. 1968–71; Instr. and Postdoctoral Fellow in Math. Princeton Univ. 1963–65; Can. Council Fellow and Visiting Prof. Math. Inst. Univ. of Vienna 1969–70; Visiting Prof. Dept. Math., The Univ. of Utah 1990–91; Can. Council Fellow 1976–77; Killam Sr. Rsch. Scholar 1978–80; Rsch. Achievement Award 1989–90, 1992–93; Co-Dir. Lab. for Rsch. in Stats. & Probability Carleton Univ.-Univ. of Ottawa 1982– ; Prin. Lectr. Nat. Sci. Found., Conf. Bd. of Math. Sci's Regional Conf. Series Texas A & M Univ. 1981; mem. Pure & Applied Math. Grant Selection Ctte. NSERC Can. 1979–81; author 'Quantile Processes with Statistical Applications' 1983; co-author 'Strong Approximations in Probability and Statistics' 1981; 'An Asymptotic Theory for Empirical Reliability and Concentration Processes' 1986; 'Weighed Approximations in Probability and Statistics' 1993; mem. various ed. bds.; Fellow, Inst. Math. Stats.; mem. Candn. Math. Soc. (Council 1979–83); Am. Math. Soc.; Stats. Soc. Can.; Bernoulli Soc. Math. Stats. & Probability; International Stats. Inst.; recreations: reading, walking, hockey night in Can.; Home: 18 Plaza Court, Nepean, Ont. K2H 7W1; Office: Ottawa, Ont. K1S 5B6.

**CUFF, Roy John Haslett;** journalist, critic; b. Walton-on-Thames, Surrey, U.K. 13 Jan. 1949; s. Roy Nesbeth and Mary Camilla Handfield (Haslett) C.; e. Steveston Sr. Secondary; Simon Fraser Univ.; Ryerson Polytechnical Inst.; TELEVISION CRITIC, GLOBE & MAIL 1986– ; Film Critic, Entertainment Editor & Editor, The Georgia Straight 1972–77; freelance writer (Globe, Toronto Life, Quest, etc.) & film actor 1977–84; feature writer, Globe & Mail 1984–86; National Newspaper Awards for Critical Writing 1989, '90; Host, 'Cineseen,' CKVR TV 1988–90; Home: 711 - 50 Stephanie St., Toronto, Ont.; Office: 444 Front St. W., Toronto, Ont. M5V 2S9.

**CUKIERMAN, Samuel G.,** B.A., M.B.A.; communications executive; b. Brazil 28 Jan. 1949; e. McGill Univ. B.A. 1970; Univ. of Western Ont. M.B.A. 1972; m. Esther Goldberg 13 Aug. 1972; children: Jodi, Daryl; VICE-PRES., MARKETING, ROGERS CANTEL 1992– ; Lectr., Mngt. Cons., Univ. of West Indies, Trinidad (CIDA Project with U.W.O.) 1972–73; Mgr., Corp. Mktg. Rsch., Northern Telecom 1974–78; Dir., Corp. Cash Mngt., Dir., Elec. Banking & Customer Serv., Bank of Montreal 1978–87; Vice-Pres., Mktg. & Sales, Royal Trust 1987–92; part-time lectr., Dept. of Mngt. Studies, McGill Univ., Jr. Achievement; Donald B. McKaskell Award for Mktg. Excellence; Am. Mktg. Assn. Marketer of the Year Finalist 1991–92; Office: 10 York Mills Rd., Toronto, Ont. M2P 2C9.

**CULLEN, Hon. Mr. Justice Jack Sydney George Bud,** P.C., B.A., LL.B.; federal court judge; b. Creighton Mine, Ont. 20 Apr. 1927; s. Chaffey Roi and Margaret Evelyn (Leck) C.; e. Creighton Mine (Ont.) Public Sch.; Lansdowne Public Sch.; Sudbury (Ont.) High Sch; Univ. of Toronto; Osgoode Hall Law Sch.; m. Nicole Chenier; 6 children; commenced as Barrister; 1st el. to H. of C. for Sarnia-Lambton, g.e. 1968, re-el. 1972, 1974, defeated 1979, re-el. 1980; Minister of National Revenue, Can. 1975–76; Minister of Employment & Immigration, Can. 1976–79; Chrmn., Standing Comte. on Finance, Trade and Econ. Affairs; formerly Parlty. Secy. to Min. of Nat. Defence, of Energy, Mines & Resources and of Finance; 1st Pres. Sarnia Educ. Authority; Life mem. Sarnia Kinsmen Club; United Church; Home: 125 Springfield Rd., Unit #8, Ottawa, Ont. K1M 1C5.

**CULLEN, Leonard Charles;** nurseryman; b. Toronto, Ont. 5 Feb. 1925; s. George Victor and Dorothy (Bridger) C.; e. Northern Vocational Sch. 1944; m. Constance d. Albert and Daisy Adams 12 July 1947; children: Susan, Peter, Mark, Nora, Tom; CHRMN. OF THE BD., WEALL & CULLEN NURSERIES LTD. 1947– ; began working for John A. Weall 1942; bought bus. in 1947; opened first garden centre 1949; started first nursery farm 1955; opened 5 new garden centres 1960–87; opened Cullen Gardens Inc., Whitby 1980; Bd. Chrmn., Greendale Agents & Distributors Garden Supplies; Whitby Businessman of the Yr. 1982; Candn. Award for Bus. Excellence 1987; Past Pres., Candn. Nurserymen's Assn.; mem., Ont. Nursery Trade Assn.; Am. Assn. of Nurserymen; author: 'Dig About It and Dung It' (autobiography) 1983; recreations: biking, walking, gardening; Home: 2644 Midland Ave., Agincourt, Ont. L0H 1K0; Office: P.O. Box 4040, Industrial Pk., Markham, Ont. L3R 8G8.

**CULLEN, Roy John,** C.A., M.P.A., B.A.; forest industry executive; b. Montreal, Que. 30 Dec. 1944; s. Roy Paxton and Doris Lydia (McGarrety) C.; e. Bishops Univ. B.A. 1965; C.A. 1972; Univ. of Victoria, M.P.A. 1988; m. Ethne Ann Erskine 23 July 1982; one s.: Peter Robert John; OWNER & PRINCIPAL, 20/20 MANAGEMENT CONSULTING 1993– ; C.A. apprentice, Price Waterhouse & Co. 1966–69; Winspear, Higgins, Stevenson & Doane 1970–71; Audit Supvr., Arthur Young & Co., Bermuda 1971–73; Mgr., Deloitte, Haskin & Sells Johannesburg 1973–77; Ernst & Whinney Victoria & Vancouver 1977–79; Asst. Dep. Min., Fin. & Planning, B.C. Min. of Forests 1980–87; Sr. Mngt. Cons. Mgr., Deloitte & Touche 1987–90; Vice Pres., Market & Business Devel., Noranda Forest Sales 1990–93; has held many extve. posts in community orgns.; Pres., Finan. Mntg. Inst. (Victoria) 1986; Candn. College Draft Choice, Montreal Alouette Profl. Football Club 1964–65; recreations: golf, tennis, fishing; Office: 523 Merton St., Toronto, Ont. M4S 1B4.

**CULLENS, William S.,** B.Sc., P. Eng.; manufacturer; b. Stirling, Scot. 10 Jan. 1930; s. James and Elizabeth Laura (Scott) C.; e. Stirling (Scot.) High Sch.; Univ. of Glasgow B.Sc. (Civil Engn.) 1951; m. Elizabeth Stewart Brewster 18 Mar. 1953; four d.: Kim, Gail, Laura, Jane; CHRMN. AND DIR., CANRON INC. 1991– ; Project Supt. Robert McAlpine Ltd., Montreal 1955–60; Sales Eng., Dominion Structural Steel Ltd., 1960–61; Sales and Gen. Mgr., Canron Inc. 1961–70, Group Vice Pres. 1970–76; Exec. Vice-Pres. 1976–81; C.O.O. 1977–82; Dir. 1980– ; Pres. 1981–91; CEO 1982– ; Chrmn. 1991– ; Hon. Dir. and former Chrmn. Candn. Inst. Steel Constr.; former Chrmn. Candn. Welding Bureau; Dir., Ivaco Inc.; Kamyr Inc.; mem., Profl. Engrs. of Ont.; United Ch.; recreations: golf, tennis, Clubs: Toronto Golf; The Toronto; Home: 1400 Dixie Rd., Suite 203, Mississauga, Ont. L5E 3E1; Office: 100 Disco Rd., Rexdale, Ont. M5W 1M1.

**CULLER, Eugene R., Jr.;** automotive industry executive; b. Portland, Maine 6 Dec. 1938; e. Indiana University grad.; m. Anne; PRESIDENT & CHIEF EXECUTIVE OFFICER, GOODYEAR CANADA INC.; Office: 10 Four Seasons Place, Etobicoke, Ont. M9B 6G2.

**CULLIMORE, Denis Roy,** B.Sc., Ph.D., R.M.; university professor; b. Oxford, U.K. 7 April 1936; s. Percy Edward and Edith Patricia (Williams) C.; e. Southfield Grammar Sch. 1955; Univ. of Nottingham B.Sc. (Hons.) 1959, Ph.D. 1962; m. Susan d. Charles and Iris Papworth 13 May 1964; children: Jason Roy, Andrew Johnathan; PROFESSOR OF BIOLOGY, UNIV. OF REGINA 1968– ; Lecturer, Univ. of Surrey 1962–68; Dir., Regina Water Research Inst., Univ. of Regina 1975– ; Mem., SRG, FEARO review panel for HL nuclear waste disposal 1991–; Chief Executive Officer, Droycon Bioconcepts Inc. 1987– ; author: 'Survey of the Uses and Abuses of Prairie Elevators' 1983, 'Flying Rabbit of Pense' 1984, 'Practical Manual of Groundwater Microbiology' 1993; editor: 'Int. Symposium on Biofouled Aquifers' 1986; holder of five patents, three of which have been commercialized in the area of biodetection and remediation of biofouling; recreations: cartooning, humour; Home: #C, 4212 Castle Rd., Regina, Sask.; Office: TDF, 3303 Grant Rd., Regina, Sask. S4S 5H4.

**CULLINGHAM, Gordon V.,** B.A.; writer/editor; b. Tecumseth, Ont. 24 Sept. 1923; s. John Frederick and Ella Cameron (MacKay) C.; e. Bradford High Sch. 1941; Univ. of Toronto B.A. 1950; m. Janet d. Ernest and

Helen Irwin 13 Jan. 1988; two d. (by previous marriage) Maureen Louise, Alison Sarah; PAST PRES., COUNCIL OF HERITAGE ORGANIZATIONS IN OTTAWA and PARTNER, RIDEAU WATCH (automobile heritage tours on cassette); mem. Staff Candn. Inst. Internat. Affairs Toronto 1951–53; joined CBC Toronto 1953–81 serving there, Washington, D.C. and Ottawa as Producer and Prog. Supr.; Ed. 'International Perspectives' (Ottawa bimonthly jour. foreign affairs) 1982–89; mem. City of Ottawa Local Arch. Conserv. Adv. Ctte.; Exec. Hist. Soc. Ottawa; co-writer and co-producer 'Talking of the Rideau', 'Talking up the Ottawa' and 'Talking up the St. Lawrence' (also narrator) heritage cassettes; mem. Candn. Inst. Internat. Affairs; Heritage Ottawa; Historical Soc. Ottawa; Pierian Soc.; Friends of the Rideau; Candn. Canal Soc.; Candn. Centre Arch.; Candn. Study Parlt. Group; recreations: boating, touring; Club: National Press; Address: 6, 325 Clemow Ave., Ottawa, Ont. K1S 2B7.

**CULLINGWORTH, L. Ross,** B.A.Sc., M.B.A., P.Eng.; real estate development executive; b. Toronto, Ont. 26 Sept. 1939; s. Allan J. and Ethel C.; e. E. York Coll. Inst.; Univ. of Toronto B.A.Sc. (Civil Eng.) 1963; York Univ. M.B.A. 1972; m. Betty Kathleen d. Hugh Hughes 9 July 1966; children: Kevin, Lisa; President and Chief Extve. Offr., Coscan Development Corp. 1986–..; Consulting Eng. Proctor & Redfern Toronto 1963–68; Regional Mgr. George Wimpey Canada Ltd. 1968–72, present company; Mgr. Corporate Devel. present Co. 1973, Vice Pres. Finance and Secy. 1975–78, Sr. Vice Pres., Chief Financial Offr. and Secy. 1978–79, Exec. Vice-Pres., Chief Financial Officer and Sec., 1980–83; Pres. & C.O.O. 1983–85; mem., Assn. Prof. Engs. Prov. Ont.; Dir., Candn. Inst. Pub. Real Estate Co's.; Consolidated Carma Corp.; RP Found. of Can.; Clubs: Granite; National; Bayview Country; Home: 23 York Valley Cres., Willowdale, Ont. M2P 1A8.

**CULLITY, Maurice Charles,** Q.C., LL.B., B.C.L.; lawyer; b. Subiaco, W. Australia 31 July 1935; s. Maurice and Mona Mary (Paddon) C.; e. Aquinas Coll. W. Australia; Univ. of W. Australia LL.B. 1957; Oxford Univ. (Rhodes Scholar) B.C.L. 1960; m. Heather d. Frederic and Avis French 15 Apr. 1963; children: Jocelyn, Amanda, Maurice; PARTNER, DAVIES, WARD & BECK 1980– ; called to Bars of Middle Temple 1962, Supreme Court of Victoria (Aust.) 1964, Ont. 1970; cr. Q.C. 1980; el. Bencher, Law Soc. of Upper Canada 1987, re-el. 1991; Lectr. Wadham Coll. Oxford 1960–63, 1972, 1973; Sr. Lectr. Univ. of Melbourne 1963–68; Visiting Assoc. Prof. Univ. of Pa. 1967–68; Prof. Osgoode Hall Law Sch. York Univ. 1968–84 (on leave 1979–84), Part-time Lectr. 1984–85; Part-time Lectr. Univ. of Toronto 1984–93; co-author 'Taxation and Estate Planning' 1978, 3rd ed. 1992; 'Probate Practice' 3rd ed. 1981; author numerous legal articles and papers; mem. Internat. Acad. Estates & Trusts Law (Treas. 1978–82, Vice Pres. N.Am. 1982– ;); Candn. Bar Assn.; Internat. Fiscal Assn.; Candn. Tax Found.; R. Catholic; recreations: music, reading, tennis, travel; Clubs: Pomona Valley (Ont.) Tennis; Ontario (Ont.); Home: 4 Thornlea Court, Thornhill, Ont. L3T 2R3; Office: P.O. 63, 44th Flr., 1 First Canadian Place, Toronto, Ont. M5X 1B1.

**CULPEPER, Roy E.J.,** B.A., M.A., Ph.D.; economist; b. Karachi, Pakistan 8 Aug. 1947; s. Ronald and Audrey (Pinto) C.; e. Univ. of Toronto B.A. 1969, M.A. 1970, Ph.D. 1975; m. Catherine d. James and Freda Lynham 7 June 1969; children: Sarah, Emma; VICE PRES. AND RSCH. CO-ORDINATOR, NORTH-SOUTH INST. 1986– ; Sr. Rsch. Econ., Planning Secretariat of Cabinet, Govt. of Man. 1975–78; Econ., Dept. of Fin., Ottawa 1978–81; Dept. of Ext. Aff. 1981–83; Adv. to Exec. Dir., World Bk., Washington, D.C. 1983–86; mem. Am. Econ. Assn.; Secy-Treas., Candn. Assoc. for the Study of Internat. Development 1989– ; author: 'Forced Adjustment' 1987; 'The Debt Matrix' 1988; var. articles on debt, fin., devel.; recreations: swimming, running; Home: 39 Bower St., Ottawa, Ont. K1S 0K2; Office: #200 – 55 Murray St., Ottawa, Ont. K1N 5M3.

**CULVER, David Michael,** C.C., B.Sc., M.B.A.; executive; b. Winnipeg, Man. 5 December 1924; s. Albert Ferguson and Fern Elizabeth (Smith) C.; e. Selwyn House Sch., Montreal, P.Q. 1931–39; Lower Canada Coll. 1939–40; Trinity Coll. Sch., Port Hope, Ont. 1940–41; McGill Univ., B.Sc. 1947; Harvard Grad. Sch. of Bus. Admin., M.B.A. 1949; Centre d'Etudes Industrielles, Geneva, Switzerland, 1949–50; LL.D. (Hon.), McGill Univ., York Univ.; D.Sc.App. (Hon.), Univ. of Sherbrooke; m. Mary Powell, d. Ray Edwin Powell, 20 Sept. 1949; three s., Michael, Andrew, Mark; one d., Diane; CHRMN., D. CULVER & CO. INVESTMENTS INC. 1989– ; joined Alcan Aluminium Ltd. 1949; after 40 years with Alcan retired as Chrmn. & C.E.O., 1 July 1989; Hon. Chrmn., Bus. Counc. on Nat. Issues; Dir., American Express Co.; Shearson Lehman Hutton Holdings Inc.; American Cyanamid Co.; The Seagram Co., Ltd.; mem. Internat. Counc., J.P. Morgan & Co.; Gov., Joseph H. Lauder Inst. of Mgmt. & Internat. Studies, Univ. of Pennsylvania; mem., Bd. of Trustees, Lester B. Pearson Coll. of the Pacific; former Candn. Chrmn., Canada-Japan Businessmen's Co-operation Ctte. 1977–88; served in 2nd World War with Candn. Inf. Corps, 1942–45; Companion, Order of Canada; Officer, Order of Quebec; received Order of the Sacred Treasure, Grand Cordon of Japan 1987; Office: 3429 Drummond St., Montreal, Que. H3G 1X6.

**CULVER, Dennis Falconer,** F.C.A., M.B.A., LL.D.; chartered accountant; b. Okanagan Falls, B.C. 15 Feb. 1923; s. George William and Kathleen Frances (de Courcy O' Grady) C.; e. Lord Roberts Pub. Sch. and John Oliver High Sch. Vancouver 1940; Univ. of B.C. 1940–41; C.A. 1952; Simon Fraser Univ. M.B.A. 1971; m. Eleanor R. d. Thomas and Ada Wallace 22 Apr. 1950; children: Noni, Dan, Margot, Bruce, Diana, Sheila, Hugh, Susan, Ronald; Chrmn. Culver & Co. 1954–94; served with Candn. Army 1942–46; Chief Financial Offr. Vivian Engine Works Ltd. 1950–54; practicing C.A. since 1954; Co-Chrmn. US/Candn. Task Force Internat. Recognition Profl. Acctg. Designations 1981–86; Chrmn. Task Force B.C. Recycling Agencies 1979–80; Chrmn. Special Ctte. Fundraising Policies Simon Fraser Univ. 1980, Chrmn. Task Force Reorgn. Campus Day Care Centres 1981, mem. Adv. Bd. Faculty Bus. Adm. 1977–94 (Chrmn. 1982–83); rationalization day care user fees & est. initial prov. govt. funding formula 1966–68; mem. Adv. Council to Auditor Gen. B.C. 1977–94; Founding Chrmn. Acctg. Devel. Fund B.C. 1978–79; Chrmn. Coordinating Councils Insts. C.A.'s Can. 1980–81; mem. Exec. Child Care Centre/Camp Alexandra 1958–68, Chrmn. 1965–68; Co-Chrmn. Family Service Agencies Vancouver 1968; Pres. Vancouver Symphony Soc. 1986–88; Co-founder, publisher & ed. writer 'Grapevine' 1972–83; Fellow, Inst. C.A.'s B.C. (Pres. 1977–78; mem. Standards Review Bd. 1985–90; B.C., Wash. & Ore. Ctte. on Internat. Recognition of Profl. Acctg. Designations 1988–90; Discipline Ctte. 1990–94, Chair 1993/4; Pres. Candn. Inst. C.A.'s 1981–82 (Chrmn. Ed. Bd. Mgmt. Adv. Services Manual 1973–76); Founding Chrmn. W. Provs. C.A. Services Assn. 1971–73; mem. Mgmt. Ctte. Candn. Insolvency Assn. 1983–85; Charter mem. Inst. C.A.'s of Y.T. and N.W.T.; Candn. Acad. Acctg. Assn.; Candn. Tax Found.; recipient Simon Fraser Univ. Chancellor's Distinguished Service Award 1984; Outstanding Alumni Award 1985; LL.D. Simon Fraser Univ. 1992; CICA Distinguished Service Certificate 1987; Founding Chrmn. B.C. Amateur Winemakers Assn. 1971; recreations: woodworking, oenology, camping; Club: Vancouver; Home: Hollyberry Lane, Thetis Island, B.C. V0R 2Y0; Office: 2401 – 1177 W. Hastings St., Vancouver, B.C. V6E 2K3.

**CUMING, Ronald C.C.,** Q.C., B.A., LL.B., LL.M.; university professor; b. Saskatchewan 19 Aug. 1940; s. Charles D. and Margaret R. (Caswell) C.; e. Univ. of Sask. B.A. 1962, LL.B. 1963; Columbia Univ. LL.M. 1967; m. Elizabeth M. d. Elizabeth and Frank Brucker 25 April 1965; children: Lynette, Donavon; PROFESSOR OF LAW, UNIVERSITY OF SASKATCHEWAN 1972– ; Asst. Prof. of Law, Univ. of Saskatchewan 1966; Assoc. Prof. 1969; Chairperson, Law Reform Comn. of Sask. 1978–82; Technical Advisor to Internat. Inst. for Unification of Private Law, Rome Italy 1988– ; European Bank on Reconstruction and Development 1993– ; Q.C. (Sask.); co-author: 'Handbook on Saskatchewan (1987), Alberta (1993) and British Columbia (1993) Personal Property Security Acts'; Home: 38 Deborah Cres., Saskatoon, Sask. S7J 2W8; Office: Saskatoon, Sask. S7N 0W6.

**CUMMING, Bruce Gordon,** B.Sc., Ph.D.; educator; b. London, Eng. 12 Oct. 1925; s. Herbert Ernest, M.C., M.D. and Dorothea Lillian Amphlett (Trippel) C.; e. Hereford Cath. Sch. Eng. 1938; Royal Masonic Sch. Eng. 1943; Reading Univ. B.Sc. 1952; McGill Univ. Ph.D. 1956; m. Marion Margaret d. Gordon and Florence Adams 12 July 1969; Prof. of Biol. Univ. of N.B. 1974–91; served with Seaforth Highlanders and Parachute Regt. (6th Airborne Div.) 1944–47, RAFVR 1943–44, Eng., Wales, Scot., Egypt, Palestine, rank Capt., awarded King's Badge for Loyal Service; Sci. Offr. Welsh Plant Breeding Stn. Univ. of Wales 1956; Rsch. Offr. (Plant Physiol.) Sci. Service, later Rsch. Br., Agric. Can. Ottawa 1957–65; Plant Physiol. Pioneering Rsch. Lab. U.S.D.A. Beltsville, MD 1963–64; Prof. of Botany Univ. of W. Ont. 1965–71; Chrmn. and Prof. of Biol. present Univ. 1971–74; mem. Exec. Ctte. Candn. Photobiol. Group 1963–68; Candn. Nat. Ctte. for Internat. Union Biol. Sci's, Candn. Del. to Internat. Cong. Washington, B.C. 1970, Ustaoset, Norway 1973; Exec. Ctte., Candn. Ctte. Univ. Biol. Chrmn. 1972–74; Nat. Rsch. Counc. Can. Grants Selection Ctte. Plant Biol. 1975–78; Candn. Nat. Ctte. Internat. Counc. Sci. Unions 1977–82; Dir. Kindness Club Inc. 1985– ; Mem. Adv. Bd., Internat. Found. for Study and Rsch. of Environmental Factors (SREF; Wageningen, The Netherlands) 1989– ; recipient Royal Humane Soc. (UK) Award for saving boy from drowning 1950; Brit. Govt. Grant Undergrad. Studies, Worshipful Co. Goldsmiths Postgrad. Dom. Travelling Scholarship 1952–54; Prov. of Qué. Postgrad. Scholarship 1954–56; Commonwealth Univ. Interchange Travel Grant Brit. Counc. for Study at Wye Coll. Univ. of London 1979; author or co-author over 95 publs.; mem. Candn. Soc. Plant Physiols. (Vice Pres. 1968–69, Pres. 1969–70); Atlantic Fiddlehead Rsch. Orgn. (Vice Pres. 1982–84, Pres. 1984–88); Founder, Citizens Concerned About Trapping, 1983; Co-Founder, Humane Soc. of New Brunswick (formerly N.B. Animal Protection Network) 1987; mem. Bd. of Dirs., Horticulture Centre of the Pacific; mem. 1st Candn. Parachute Bn. Assn.; special involvement: provided own home and nature-preserve land (Evergreen Farm, Penniac, N.B.), as a spiritual and cultural renewal centre for native people, called The Wabanoag Medicine Lodge (Pisoniwikwam); recreations: amateur dramatics, horticulture, photography, preservation wildlife; Home: 151 Sunny Lane, Victoria, B.C. V8S 2K6.

**CUMMING, Donald Arthur,** B.Sc.; mining executive; b. Sudbury, Ont. 10 Sept. 1937; s. Arthur Knox and Iona (McCoshen) C.; e. South Dakota School of Mines & Tech. B.Sc. 1967; Haileybury School of Mines, mining technician; m. Ruth Anne d. Marie and Bill Shaver 27 April 1963; children: Donald, Donna Lynn, James, Gregory, Scott; EXTVE. VICE-PRES. OPERATIONS, RIO ALGOM LTD. 1991– ; Vice-Pres., PCA Division, Rio Algom 1985–87; Pres., Elliot Lake Div. 1987–89; Vice-Pres., Environment & Technology 1989–91; Home: 40 Somerset Cres., Richmond Hill, Ont. L4C 8N3; Office: 2600, 120 Adelaide St. W., Toronto, Ont. M5H 1W5.

**CUMMING, George Stewart,** Q.C., B.A., LL.B.; b. Vancouver, B.C., 1 May 1928; s. George and Jessie Robertson (Stewart) C.; e. Oak Bay High Sch., Victoria, B.C. 1945; Victoria Coll., Univ. of Brit. Columbia, B.A. 1950, LL.B. 1951; m. Margaret Isabella, d. Ernest Theodore Rogers, 10 Nov. 1956; children: Catherine Irene, Brian George, Hamish Arthur; JUDGE, COURT OF APPEAL OF B.C. 1989– ; read law with T.G. Norris, Q.C.; called to the Bar of B.C. 1951; cr. Q.C. Sept. 1969; former Partner, Cumming, Richards, Underhill, Fraser, Skillings; Judge, Supreme Court of B.C. 1985–89; Club: The Vancouver; Home: 7226 Blenheim St., Vancouver, B.C. Office: 800 Smithe St., Vancouver, B.C. V6Z 2E1.

**CUMMING, Lawrence Seymour,** M.A.; consultant; b. Barrie, Ont. 18 June 1941; s. Lloyd George and Edna Jane (Seymour) C.; e. Barrie Dist. Central Coll. Inst. 1960; Univ. of W.Ont. B.A. 1963; St. Francis Xavier Univ. M.A. 1973; m. Margaret d. Asher and Iris Moyston 2 Sept. 1968; children: Vanessa, Kevin Giles; CONSULTANT IN INTERNATIONAL DEVELOPMENT; Teacher, Ottawa Bd. of Edn. 1963–65, Min. of Edn. Kenya 1965–67; Field Rep. Uganda CUSO 1968–69; Dir. E., Central and S. Africa 1969–72; Asst. Dir. of Extension & Continuing Edn. Univ. of N.B. 1973–78; Nat. Sec. (C.E.O.) Oxfam-Can. 1978–88; Exec. Dir. Broadcasting for Internat. Understanding 1989–91; Dir. Candn. Council Internat. Coop. 1973–89; mem. bds. various agencies; Assoc., E.T. Jackson and Associates Ottawa; mem. Candn. Civil Liberties Assn.; Group of 78; World Federalists; United Church of Canada; recreations: music, reading, physical recreation; Home and Office: 27 Fairbairn Ave., Ottawa, Ont. K1S 1T2.

**CUMMING, Marie Novak,** B.Sc., M.B.A.; cosumer products industry executive; b. Medford, Mass. 24 Oct. 1954; d. John E. and Claire T. (Hassett) Novak; e. Boston Coll. B.Sc. (Chem.) cum laude 1976; Leonard N. Stern Sch. of Business, New York Univ. M.B.A. 1978; m. Bruce D. s. Dr. Ronald and Merle C. 27 June 1981; children: John A., Kendall E.; Vice Pres., Opns. & Admin., Mary Kay Cosmetics Ltd. 1990–93; var. supervisory, mktg., sales, finan. & planning positions, Exxon Internat. Co. (N.Y.) 1978–83; Dir., Mktg., present firm 1983–87; Vice Pres., Mktg. 1987–90; Mem., Mississauga Bd. of Trade 1988– ; (Dir. 1989– , Treas. 1991, Secy. 1992); Candn. Assn. of Women Extves. & Entrepreneurs; Candn. Fed. of Univ. Women; Special Events Ctte., United Way of Peel Region 1993– ; (Cabinet 1990–92); club: YMCA Mississauga; Home: 287 Cairncroft Rd., Oakville, Ont. L6J 4M5; Office: 5600 Ambler Dr., Mississauga, Ont. L4W 2K9.

**CUMMING, Marion Margaret,** B.A.; heritage artist; b. Toronto, Ont. 26 July 1936; d. Gordon William and Florence Margaret (Underwood) Adams; e. Principia College B.A. 1959; Univ. of W. Ont., Althouse Coll. of Edn., Ont. Teachers Cert. 1966; university art and cultural studies in France, Mexico, Italy, Canada; m. Prof. Bruce Gordon s. Dr. Herbert and Dorothea Lillian Cumming 12 July 1969; Social Worker, Children's Aid Soc., Ont. 1959; Volunteeer art therapist with retarded and emotionally disturbed children at Manicomio de Mixcoac, Mexico City 1959–61; exhibited their artwork, Mexican N. Am. Inst., Mexico City 1961; Social Sec., Argentine Embassy Ottawa 1961–64; active volunteer 1963–91: Experiment in Internat. Living (founded 1932), Candn. Correspondent (sent individuals and groups to Mexico, France & other UNESCO countries; group leader to Mexico), Community Rep.; in Charge of Art Dept., Lisgar C.I. & UNESCO-related activities 1966–69 Ottawa; draws heritage subjects in all provinces and Arctic territories 1969– ; based with husband at Evergreen Farm (280 acres near Fredericton) 1971–92 floral arrangements through Farmers Market and operated The Flower Box and Kingsley Arts & Crafts shop & cultural centre; Teacher, N.B.; Humbercrest P.S. silver scholarship grad. medal 1949; MCC Campus Citizenship Award, Univ. of the Americas 1960; Mexico City; Centennial Medal 1967; Nat. Heritage Award 1992; Bd. of Dir. & Patron, Fredericton Heritage Trust; Erindale Housing Initiatives; involved in Native Indian issues and culture; num. positions & activities in Christian Science Ch. 1969– ; Plan Internat. 1969– ; donated collection of N.B. antiques and artifacts to Kings Landing Historical Settlement; artist: 'London Heritage' 4 printings 1972–91; solo exbns: Fredericton: Landmark Gall. 1979, Univ. of N.B. (twice), York Sunbury Mus. 1985; group shows: Marlowe Gall. Canterbury 1979, Beaverbrook Gall. (McCain) Fredericton 1989; subject of a nat. CBC film 'A Heritage to Draw Upon' 1976; recreations: restoration of old structures, furnishings, artifacts; clubs: Fredericton Heritage Trust, Voice of Women, Amnesty Internat., World Federalists, Conservation Council of N.B., S.P.C.A.; Home: 151 Sunny Lane, Victoria, B.C. V8S 2K6.

**CUMMING, Thomas Alexander,** B.A.Sc., P.Eng.; b. Toronto, Ont. 14 Oct. 1937; e. Univ. of Toronto B.A.Sc. 1960; m. E. Mary 12 Mar. 1965; children: Jennifer, Allison, Katy; PRESIDENT AND CHIEF EXECUTIVE, THE ALBERTA STOCK EXCHANGE; Office: 21st Flr., 300 – 5th Ave. S.W., Calgary, Alta. T2P 3C4.

**CUMMINGS, Gordon Eric Myles,** B.Comm., M.B.A., CMA, FCMA; business executive; b. Montreal, Que. 15 Sept. 1940; s. Gordon Myles and Phyllis Myrtle (Bennel) C.; e. Concordia Univ. B.Comm. 1964; McMaster Univ. M.B.A. 1969; m. Barbara M.T. d. Mildred and David Bodin 4 Nov. 1961; children: Lesley Erica Louise, Gordon Gregory David; CHIEF EXTVE. OFFR., UNITED COOPERATIVES OF ONT. 1990– ; Dir., L.E. Shaw Ltd.; Cobi Foods Inc.; C.F. Industries, Chicago 1992– ; UCU Petroleum Inc.; various acctg. posns. CNR 1958–60; Gillete of Canada 1960–62; Continental Can 1962–68; Asst. Controller, Bundy of Canada 1968–69; Woods Gordon 1969, el. Partner (Montreal) 1974, (Toronto) 1981; Extve. Vice-Pres. & C.O.O., 1984–85, Pres., C.E.O. & Dir., National Sea Products Ltd. 1985–89; Chrmn. & Dir., Pacific Aqua Foods 1987–89; Teacher, McGill Univ. (evgs.) 1973–81; Dir. and mem. Extve. Ctte., Soc. of Mgmt. Accts. of Can., Hon. Treas. 1984–86, Vice Pres. 1986–88, Pres., 1988–89; Pres., Que. Corp. Indus. Accts. 1976–78; mem., Govt. of Canada Advisory Ctte. on Adjustment regarding Free Trade 1988–89; Dir., Izaak Walton Killam Hosp. Found. Bd., Halifax 1987–89; Junior Achievement of Canada 1987–89; National Inst. of Nutrition 1987–89; Quebec Liberal Party (Provincial) Riding President Pointe Claire, then Nelligan Riding 1977–80; recreation: golf; Clubs: Markland Woods; Ashburn Golf; Braeside Golf; Bradenton Country; Home: 1314 Cedarbrae Dr., Oakville, Ont. L6J 2G1; Office: P.O. Box 527, Stn. A., Mississauga, Ont. L5A 3A4.

**CUMMINGS, Sharon Mia,** C.H.R.P.; human resources professional; b. Ottawa, Ont. 2 Dec. 1958; d. Gordon Claude and Dora Lillian (Eaton) C.; e. South Carleton H.S.; Algonquin Coll. Cert. in Human Resources Mngt.; Univ. of Toronto Extve. Cert. in Human Resources Mngt.; RECRUITMENT OFFICER, AFRICA, INTERNAT. FEDERATION OF RED CROSS & RED CRESCENT SOCIETIES, GENEVA, SWITZ. 1994– ; Human Resources Mgr., Orcatech Inc. 1983–84; Personnel Administrator, K.G. Campbell Corp. 1985–86; Proprietor, Consulting, Bolt Human Resources 1986– ; Manager, Employee Services, The Canadian Red Cross Soc. 1987–93; Past Bd. Mem., Central Volunteer Bureau; Mem., Human Resources Profl. Assn. of Ont. (Vice-Pres., Eastern Region); Ottawa Human Resources Profl. Assn. (Past Pres.); recreations: cycling, running, skiing; clubs: Nat. Capital Runners Assn.; Home: R.R. 2, Box 579M, Woodlawn, Ont. K0A 3M0; Office: 17 ch. des Crêts, Pt. Saconnex POB 372, CH-1211, Geneva 19, Switzerland.

**CUMMINS, Joseph E.,** Ph.D.; university professor; b. Whitefish, Montana 5 Feb. 1933; s. Harold Geddes and Catherine Cynthia (Edwards) C.; e. Stadium H.S. 1951; Washington State Univ., B.S. 1955; Univ. of Wisconsin, Ph.D. 1962; m Katherina (deceased) d. Dr. Paul vonUnterrichter Sept. 1962; one d.: Lili Frances; ASST. TO ASSOC. PROF., DEPT. OF PLANT SCIENCES, UNIV. OF W. ONTARIO, 1972– ; Post-doctoral work, Univ. of Edinburgh 1962–64; McArdle Lab. for Cancer, Res., Univ. of Wisconsin 1964–66; The Karolinska Inst. Stockholm, Sweden 1969; Visiting Asst. Prof., Dept. of Radiology, Case-Western Reserve 1967; Asst. Prof., Dept. of Biology, Rutgers Univ. 1966–67; Dept of Zoology, Univ of Washington 1967–71; Mem., Ont. Min. of Environment, Pottersburg Creek Tech. Ctte.; Urban Laegue of London, The Green Umbrella Award 1985; Special Thanks Greenpeace Canada 1984; Certificate of Merit, Ont. Min. of Environment 1988; Optimist International Community Service Award 1990; Dir. Greenpeace Canada 1985–88; Dir., Londoners to Eliminate All PCBs (LEAP) 1990– ; Dir., Dept. of the Planet Earth, Washington, D.C. 1991– ; Dir., Physicians and Scientist for a Health World, Ottawa 1991– ; Mem., Candn. Genetics Soc, Am. Soc. for Cell Biolgy; Am Genetics Soc.; Soc. for Environmnet Mutagenesis; The Rachel Carson Co.; Citizens Clearinghouse for Hazardous Wastes; author of numerous sci. pubns.; Club: Shinki Ju-Jitsu Assn.; Home: 738 Wilkins St., London, Ont. N6C 4Z9; Office: Dept of Plant Sciences, Univ. of W. Ontario, London, Ont. N6A 5B7.

**CUMMINS, William Raymond,** B.Sc., Ph.D.; university professor; b. Hamilton, Ont. 9 May 1944; s. Lindsay Stewart and Margaret Gracey (McCammon) C.; e. Millgrove P.S.; Parkside H.S.; McMaster Univ. B.Sc.; Michigan State Univ. Ph.D.; Stanford Univ., post-doct. fellow; m. Eva P. d. Robert and Agnes E. Robertson 30 Sept. 1967; children: Christopher Patrick, Andrew James; PROF., DEPT. BOTANY, ERINDALE COLL., UNIV. OF TORONTO 1991– ; Grad. Teaching Asst., Michigan State Univ. 1969–70; Rsch. Asst., U.S. A.E.C. Plant Rsch. Lab., Michigan State Univ. 1967–70; Allied Chem. Found. Predoct. Fellow 1970–71; Rsch. Assoc., Stanford Univ. 1971–73; Visiting Asst. Prof., York Univ. 1973–74; Asst. Prof., present univ. 1974–79; Assoc. Prof. 1979–91; Mem., Acad. Bd., Chrmn. Academic Policy and Procedures Ctte., Univ. of Toronto; Sec., Candn. Soc. of Plant Physiol. 1991– ; Mem., Arctic Working Group, U. of T.; Am. Soc. of Plant Physiol.; Candn. Soc. for Plant Molecular Biol.; Candn. Soc. for Improvements to our System of Edn.; Assoc., Inst. for Environmental Studies, U. of T.; Candn. Botanical Assn.; Science Teachers Assn. of Ont.; editor: 'Bulletin of the Canadian Society of Plant Physiologists' 1991–93; Chrmn., Official Bd., Streetsville Un. Ch. 1993– ; Halton Presbytery Un. Ch. of Can. 1988– ; recreations: skiing, local history; Home: 12 Steen Dr., Mississauga, Ont. L5N 2V4; Office: Rm. 3042, South Bldg., Erindale College, 3359 Mississauga Rd., Mississauga, Ont. L5L 1C6.

**CUMMINS, William Watterson,** B.Sc., C.A.; financial executive; b. Vancouver, B.C. 5 May 1932; s. Francis Watterson and Margery Etta (Torrance) C.; e. Ontario Agricultural College B.S.A.; Inst. of C.A.s, C.A.; m. Lavender d. Haidee and Charles Heavener 11 Aug. 1988 (2nd m.); children: Victoria, Louise; step-children: Duncan, Maureen; Pres., McFinley Red Lake Mines Ltd.; Chartered Accountant with large internat. firm 1959–69; two years with Northgate group of companies; now officer & director of numerous public mining companies incl. McFinley Red Lake Mines Limited and Sabina Resources Limited; Corresponding Mem., The Pewter Soc. England; recreations: antiques, spec. peweter; club: Granite.

**CUNANAN, Art;** artist; b. Philippines 20 Oct. 1944; s. Crispulo and Juana (Bartolome) C.; e. Santo Thomas Univ. Fine Arts Undergrad.; m. Lutgarda d. Bienvenido and Belen San Juan 11 Feb. 1976; children: Ervan Rey, April Leilani; commercial artist Manila until 1976; emigrated to Canada 1976; introduced at Harbour Gallery (on advice from Zoltan Szabo) 1984; participant in several groups shows with well-known Candn. & Am. artists; 1st solo exbn 1988; currently a very popular artist with very successful exbns; devotes all of his time to art and also conducts workshops; Instructor, Etobicoke Bd. of Edn.; Buckhorn Sch. of Fine Arts; Southampton Art Sch.; Mem., BLD Covenant Community (Catholic); Knights of Columbus, 3rd degree council no. 9235 Bramalea, Ont.; Assoc. Mem., CSPWC, AWS; Founding Mem., Philippine Artist Group; Address: 89 Beaconsfield Ave., Brampton, Ont. L6Y 4R6.

**CUNNINGHAM, Hon. Darrel,** B.S.A., M.L.A.; farmer, politician; b. Kelvington, Sask. 23 Jan. 1948; s. Robert Mathew and Alice (Blix) C.; e. Univ. of Sask. B.S.A. 1970; m. Donna d. Lincoln and Irene Colby 23 Dec. 1972; children: Dara, Lisa; Min. of Agriculture and Food, Govt. of Saskatchewan 1991–93; Farmer 1971–91; various summer & winter part-time positions incl. both Federal & Prov. Depts. of Agriculture; Teacher, farm management classes throughout Sask. 1973–88; Past Bd. Mem., East Central Co-op; Lintlaw Credit Union.

**CUNNINGHAM, Gordon Ross,** B.A., LL.B.; b. Toronto, Ont. 15 Nov. 1944; s. Wendell Carson and Catherine Ann (Chisholm) C.; e. E. York and Lawrence Park Coll. Insts. Toronto; Univ. of Toronto, Trinity Coll. B.A. 1966, LL.B. 1969; m. Patricia Dorothy d. Ronald George and Dorothy Westheuser 22 Dec. 1966; children: Kristyn Catherine, Kaleigh Ann, James Gordon Patrick; PRES., CHIEF EXEC. OFFR. AND DIR., LONDON INSURANCE GROUP INC. and LONDON LIFE INSURANCE CO. 1989– ; Exec. Vice-Pres. & Chief Operating Offr., Trilon Financial Corp. 1984–89; Partner, Tory, Tory, DesLauriers & Binnington 1977–84; Assoc. Mem., Tory, Tory, DesLauriers & Binnington 1971–76; Depy. Chrmn. & Dir., Wellington Insurance Co.; Vice-Chrmn. & Dir., Candn. Life & Health Insurance Assn.; Pres. & Dir., Fairmoor Holdings Inc.; Bardview Inc.; Dir., China Investment Development Corp.; Fidelity Standard Insurance Co.; Great Lakes Investments Ltd.; The John P. Robarts Rsch. Institute; Junior Achievement of Canada; London Life Financial Corp.; London General Insurance Group Inc.; London Life and General Reinsurance Company Ltd.; London Reinsurance Group Inc.; LONLIFE Financial Services Ltd.; Royal LePage Mortgage Co. (Broker) Inc.; Security First Life Insurance Co.; Spraybake Canada Ltd.; The Holden Group Inc.; Meloche-Monnex Inc.; Trilon Financial Corp.; Trilon Holdings Ltd.; Trivest Insurance Network Ltd.; National Corporate Campaign Chrmn., Candn. Diabetes Assn.; mem., Upper Canada Law Society; Canadian Bar Assn.; Business Council on Nat. Issues; United Church; recreations: golf, squash, tennis, skiing; Clubs: Rosedale Golf; University; Devil's Glen Ski; London Hunt; Mad River Golf; Portmarnock Golf, Dublin; Home: Toronto, Ont.; Office: 255 Dufferin Ave., London, Ont. N6A 4K1.

**CUNNINGHAM, Gordon Rowand,** C.M.; executive; b. Duluth, Minn. 5 Aug. 1926; s. Rowand Mitchell and Beatrice (King) C.; e. Coll. of Optometry of Ont. 1949; m. Jean Lillian d. Herbert and Dorothy Tupper 28 May 1949; children: Judith A., Barbara J., Bruce G.T.; BD. CHRMN., ONT. HOSP. ASSOC. INVESTMENT MGMT. LTD.; Candn. Army 1943–46; practised optometry, Sault Ste Marie 1949–81; Pres., Ont. Hosp. Assn. 1982–91; Pres., Ont. Blue Cross 1985–86; past Dir., Healthcare Insurance Reciprocal of Can.; Bd. Chrmn., Ont. Hosp. Assoc. Investment Mgmt. Ltd. 1988– ; Vice-Chrmn., Bd. of Trustees, Bloorview Children's Hosp.; Sault Ste Marie Medal of Merit 1975; Queen's Medal 1977; Order of Canada 1982; Life Mem., Bd. of Dir., Plummer Hosp.; Past Chrmn., Ont. Cancer Treatment & Rsch. Found.; Past Mem., Ont. Cancer Inst.; Presbyterian; Hon. Mem., Ont. Assn. of Optometrists; Club: Albany; Home: 47 Normandale Rd., Markham, Ont. L3R 4J8.

**CUNNINGHAM, J. Stewart M.,** F.S.A., F.C.I.A.; retired; Pres., C.E.O. & Dir., Seaboard Life Insurance Co.; joined Friends' Provident Life Office (parent co. of Seaboard Life) London, Eng. 1952; trans. to Fidelity Life Assurance Co., Regina 1958, H.O. moved to Vancouver 1960, Actuary 1968, Vice Pres. and Actuary 1971, Pres., C.E.O. and Dir. 1973–92; Comm. Financial Institutions Comm. of B.C.; Bd. of Govs., Crofton House Sch. for Girls, Vancouver, B.C.; Mem. Greater Vancouver Adv. Bd., Salvation Army; Mem. Bd., KCTS/9, Seattle, Washington, U.S.A.; Clubs: Vancouver; Arbutus; Home: 5947 Highbury St., Vancouver, B.C., V6N 1Y9.

**CUNNINGHAM, James William,** B. Com; business consultant; b. Montreal, Que. 22 July 1922; s. James Thomas and Margery Annie (Green) C.; e. High Sch., Montreal Que. 1939; Sir George Williams Coll., B. Com. 1952; C.A. courses, McGill Univ. 1943–47; m. Sheila Dorothy, d. late Gordon Dickson Flett, 16 Oct. 1954; children: Joanne Wendy (Mrs D. Thomas), Geraldine Gail (Mrs J. Pfeiffer), Heather May, James Gordon; articled with P.S. Ross & Sons (C.A.) 1943; Acct., Power Corp. of Canada 1947, Assistant Secretary 1950; Assistant Treasurer, Shawinigan Water & Power Co.

and Asst. Secy., Southern Canada Power Co. 1958; Schering Corp. Ltd., Comptroller 1963; Secretary-Treas. 1966; Vice Pres. 1969–75; entered independent business consulting since 1975; served in 2nd World War, R.C.A.F. 1941–42; Past Candn. Chrmn., Chart. Inst. of Secys. and Administrators; founding President, Chateauguay Home-owners' Association; mem. Institute Chart. Accts.; former mem. Bd., Central Y.M.C.A.; Liberal; Baptist; recreation: golf; Home: 19 Lang Ave., Chateauguay, Que. J6J 2A7.

**CUNNINGHAM, Lynn Allison,** B.A.; magazine editor; b. Guelph, Ont. 16 Aug. 1949; d. Kenneth Malcolm and Kathryn (Smyth) C.; e. Univ. of Guelph 1967–70; Univ. of Toronto, B.A. 1974; m. Donald William Obe s. George William and Mabel Elizabeth (Willson) O. 15 Sept. 1990; FREELANCE EDITOR, INSTRUCTOR, RYERSON SCHOOL OF JOURNALISM 1992– ; Contbg. Ed., 'Toronto Life' 1974; Assoc. Ed. 1975–76; Mng. Ed. 1977–78; Adult Trade Books Ed., Greey de Pencier Books 1978–79; Mng. Ed., 'Quest' 1979–84; freelance editor, instructor, Ryerson Sch. of Jour. 1984–85, 1986–88; Sr. Ed., 'Canadian Business' 1985–86; Sr. Contbg. Ed. 1986–88; Extve. Ed., 'Toronto Life' 1988–92; Bd. Mem., Candn. Mag. Pub. Assn. 1981–84, 1988–93 (Pres. 1982–84, 1990–92); Jury Mem., Can. Counc. 1982–92; Fac. Mem., Banff Pub. Workshop (magazine course) 1982–89 (Prog. Dir. 1984–86); Mem., Advisory Ctte., Federal Task Force on Magazines 1993; Ryerson School of Journalism 1993– ; Ont. Publishing Centre 1991– ; Founding Prog. Dir., Toronto Pub. Workshop Mag. Editing Course 1985–90; Bd. Mem., Nat. Mag. Awards Found. 1983–84, 1987–89; Home: 1 Wyandot Ave., Toronto, Ont. M5J 1E6.

**CUNNINGHAM, Norman George;** retired association executive; b. Belleville, Ont. 17 June 1924; s. John and Martha Ann (Yorke) C.; e. Queen Mary Elem. Sch. and Belleville Coll. Inst. & Vocational Sch.; m. Yuoi Chen; two s. Steven, Norman Garth; Private Consulting Practice spec. in Labour Relations, Mediation & Arbitration; Dir. and mem. Exec. Ctte. Vancouver Port Corp.; served with RCN and Candn. Merchant Navy 1941–47; Seafarers Internat. Union Can. 1948–60; private cons. several shipping lines 1960–63; Mgr. Personnel & Ind. Rlns., Northland Navigation Co. 1963–66; Agreement Adm. present Assn. 1966, Vice Pres. Operations 1976, Pres. 1977, Pres. and CEO 1982–85; Chrmn., B.C. Maritime Employers Assn. 1985–87; recreations: fishing, golf; Club: Terminal City; Address: 1502 – 140 East Keith Rd., North Vancouver, B.C. V7L 4M9.

**CURATOLO, Fred;** editorial cartoonist; b. Toronto, Ont. 29 Dec. 1958; s. Gino and Lucy (Provenzano) C.; e. C.W. Jefferys Secondary Sch. 1978; m. Trudy d. Richard and Marilyn Hutchinson 7 Apr. 1978; children: Jennifer, Adam; EDITORIAL STAFF CARTOONIST, EDMONTON SUN 1989– ; Back-up Cartoonist, Toronto Sun 1983–86; Editorial Cartoonist, Brampton Guardian/Metroland Newspapers 1986–89; cartoons also pub. in other Candn. and Am. newspapers, and in collection 'Portfolio' 1985–87 and 88 collection; mem. Candn. Editorial Cartoonists Assn.; Address: 4990 – 92 Ave., Edmonton, Alta. T6B 2V4.

**CURIS, His Excellency the Most Rev. Carlo,** Apostolic Pro-Nuncio; ambassador; b. La Maddalena (Sardinia) Italy 2 Nov. 1923; s. Domenico and Ines (Toso) C.; APOSTOLIC PRO-NUNCIO IN CANADA, EMBASSY OF THE HOLY SEE 1990– ; joined Diplomatic Corps of the Holy See 1956; has rendered services successively in Uruguay, Chile, India, the United States, & Italy; apptd. Apostolic Delegate in Sri Lanka 1971; Apostolic Pro-Nuncio in Sri Lanka 1976; in Nigeria 1978–84; in Jerusalem for Israel and Jordan and Apostolic Pro-Nuncio in Cyprus 1984; Home and Office: 724 Manor Ave., Ottawa, Ont. K1M 0E3.

**CURLEY, Paul Roger,** B.Com.; executive; b. Ottawa, Ont. 28 Aug. 1942; s. Matthew and Winnifred (Smith) C.; e. Univ. of Ottawa B.Com. 1967; Univ. of Oslo grad. dipl. in Econ. 1970; PRESIDENT, ADVANCE PLANNING & COMMUNICATION; Nat. Dir., P. Cons. Party Of Can. 1979–81; business extve. Imperial Oil Ltd. 1967–72, 1974–79; Special Asst. to Hon. Robert L. Stanfield 1972–74; Nat. Treas. P. Cons. Party Can. 1977–79, Nat. Dir. 1979–81; Gov., Univ. of Ottawa; Dir., Stratford Festival; Toronto Film Festival; Past Chrmn., Writers' Development Trust of Can.; P. Conservative; R. Catholic; Clubs: Albany (Toronto); Calgary Petroleum; Cercle Universitaire d'Ottawa; Home: 17 Harper Ave., Toronto, Ont. M4T 2L1; Office: 95 St. Clair Ave. W., Suite 1605, Toronto, Ont. M4X 1N6.

**CURLOOK, Walter,** M.A.Sc., Ph.D., P. Eng., FCAE; metallurgist; mining executive; b. Coniston, Ont. 14 March 1929; s. William and Stephanie (Acker) C.; e. Sudbury (Ont.) High Sch. 1946; Univ. of Toronto B.A.Sc. 1950, M.A.Sc. 1951, Ph.D. 1953; Nuffield Research Lab., Imp. Coll. Science & Technol., Post-doctorate Fellowship 1954; Hon. D.Sc., Laurentian Univ. 1983; m. Marie Jeanne Burak 28 May 1955; children: Christine, Paul, Michael, Andrea; VICE CHRMN. (1991) & DIR., INCO LTD. 1989– ; Commnr., P.T. Inco; Dir., TVX Gold; Rsch. Metall., Inco, Copper Cliff, Ont. 1954; Supvr. Rsch. Stn. Port Colborne, Ont. 1959; Supt. of Rsch. Copper Cliff 1960; Asst. to Gen. Mgr. 1964; Dir. Technique COFIMPAC, Paris, France 1969; Gen. Mgr. Inco Oceanie 1972; Vice Pres. Adm. and Engn. Inco, Copper Cliff 1972; Vice Pres. Corporate Planning New York 1974; Sr. Vice Pres. Production, Inco Metals Co. Toronto 1977; Pres. & C.E.O., Inco Metals Co. 1980–82; Pres., Inco Gold Co. 1987–89, Chrmn. 1989–91; Exec. Vice-Pres. & Dir., Inco Ltd. 1982; Chrmn., Inco Exploration & Techn. Services Ltd. 1989; Pres., Dir.-Gen., Goro Nickel S.A. 1992– ; first Chrmn. of Bd., Cambrian Coll. Applied Arts & Technol. Sudbury; rec'd Airey Award 1979; awarded McCharles Prize, Univ. of Toronto 1987; holds patents on process metall.; author various tech. papers; Chrmn. and Dir., Continuous Mining Systems Ltd.; Past Chrmn. and Dir., Mining Assn. Can.; Past Pres., Ont. Mining Assn.; Dir., Cambrian Foundn.; Great-West Life Assur. Co.; Fellow, Candn. Acad. Engrs. 1988; Mem., Premier's Counc. for Economic Renewal 1991– ; mem. Assn. Prof. Engrs. Ont.; Candn. Inst. Mining & Metall.; Am. Inst. Mining Engrs.; Nat'l Adv. Comte on the Mining Ind.; Catholic; recreations: hockey, jogging, skiing; Clubs: Toronto Bd. of Trade; Home: 25 Cluny Dr., Toronto, Ont. M4W 2P9; Office: P.O. Box 44, Royal Trust Tower, Toronto-Dominion Centre, Toronto, Ont. M5K 1N4.

**CURNOCK, Richard St. Helier;** actor; b. London, Eng. 9 May 1922; s. George Corderoy and Olive Emma (Glanfield) C.; e. privately educated; profnly. trained at Italia Conti Acad. London, Eng. 1927–35; m. Nancy d. John and Helen Saile 18 July 1966; children: John, Helen; fisrt profl. appearance as boy actor Arts Theatre Club London 1930; appeared in 'Peter Pan' London Palladium 1934; joined Sir John Martin-Harvey's co. 1935 touring Brit. Isles; spent 1941 season with Birmingham Repertory Theatre before returning to London to star in play by Sir Beverly Baxter; appeared 'Sweet and Low' series with Hermione Gingold, London's Ambassadors Theatre 1943–48; subsequently spent 15 yrs. in London appearing in premieres incl. Dylan Thomas's 'Under Milk Wood,' musical 'Irma La Douce' and Joan Littlewood's 'Oh! What a Lovely War' (Broadway appearance 1964); performed 19 seasons Stratford Festival Can.; appeared as Svetlovidov in Chekhov's 'Swan Song', Stratford Festival 1990, marking his sixtieth year in profl. theatre; appeared as Dr. Chasuble in 'The Importance of Being Earnest' and as Teiresias in 'The Bacchae' at the Stratford Festival; numerous appearances on and off Broadway plays and musicals; CBC TV credits incl. 'The Tempest'; 'Much Ado About Nothing'; 'Street Legal'; feature film appearance 'Paradise'; 'Tech Lab' Atlantis Films 1993; recreations: boating, swimming, fishing; Address: 100 Daly Ave., Stratford, Ont. N5A 1B8.

**CURRIE, George Napier McDonald,** B.Eng., M.Sc.; b. Montreal, Que. 13 Dec. 1927; s. George Selkirk and Louisa Hope (Napier) C; e. Selwyn House Sch., Montreal, 1933–42; Trinity Coll. Sch., Port Hope, Ont., 1942–45; Royal Candn. Naval Coll. 1947; McGill Univ., B.Eng. 1951; Univ. of Toronto, M.Sc. 1953; m. Daphne Louise, d. William Grant Fisher, London, Ont., 16 Apl. 1955; children: Stephanie Louise, Gordon Andrew McDonald, Janet Hope, George Timothy Grant; PRES., GENMAC INC. 1981– ; Dir. Meridian Technologies Inc.; Guardian Capital Group Ltd.; Charles E. Napier Co., 1951–56; Urwick, Currie & Partners 1956; Pres. Urwick, Currie and Ptnrs. Ltd. 1960–73; Chrmn., Currie, Coopers & Lybrand Ltd. 1973–78; Pres. & C.E.O., F.P. Publications Ltd. 1978–80; Extve. Vice-Pres. & Dir., A.E. Ames & Co. Ltd. 1980–81; Dir., Sunnybrook Found.; Pres. (1968–69) Candn. Assn. Mang. Consultants; Fellow, Ont. Inst. Mang. Consultants; mem. Assn. Prof. Engrs. Ont.; Kappa Alpha; Protestant; recreations: skiing, fishing; tennis; Clubs: Toronto Golf; University; Toronto; Osler Bluff Ski (Collingwood, Ont.); Badminton & Racquet; Maganissippi Fish & Game; Home: 69 Bayview Ridge, Toronto, Ont. M2L 1E3.

**CURRIE, Gordon Edwin Walter,** M.B.A., C.G.A.; corporate treasurer; b. Sarnia, Ont. 30 Aug. 1952; s. Neil and Phyllis Jean (Brown) C.; e. Univ. of W. Ont. B.A. 1974; Univ. of Toronto M.B.A. 1976; C.G.A. 1982; m. Catherine Jo d. Joseph and Rose Fisher 20 Sept. 1980; one s. Jamieson; one d. Jordan; TREAS. EMCO LTD. 1989– ; Mgr. Credit & Trade Finance N. & S. Am. Polysar Ltd. 1983, Mgr. Treasury Operations 1985, Asst. Treas. 1987–88; Pres. Participation House Sarnia Region; Dir., Financial Execs. Inst., S.W. Ont. Chapter; recreations: golf, racquet sports; Club: Greenhills Country; Home: 3943 West Graham Pl., London, Ont. N0L 1S4; Office: P.O. Box 5252, London, Ont. N6A 4L6.

**CURRIE, Gordon G.,** B.A., B.Ed., O.C.; teacher; b. Semans, Sask. 20 May 1923; s. Robert and Maryanne (Pool) C.; e. Sask. & B.C.; Athol Coll. of Notre Dame (Wilcox, Sask.), B.A.; Mt. Allison Univ., B.Ed.; m. Shirley, D. Francis Clarke, 27 Feb. 1952; children: Robert; Douglas; James; Min. of Science & Technology, and Min. of Advanced Education & Manpower, Sask. 1985–86; Teacher, Regina Sch. Bd. 1947–82; Min. Education & Continuing Education, Sask. 1982–85; Chrmn. Bd. of Govs., Whitespruce Youth Drug Treatment Ctr. 1987–92; Hon. Chrmn., Sask. Read-a-thon, Multiple Sclerosis Soc. 1988 & 1989; served 20 yrs. Balfour Tech. Sch.; 4 yrs. Vice-Principal Balfour; 4 yrs. Principal Cochrane High Sch.; 7 yrs. Principal Campbell Collegiate; well known as a sports coach, in hockey, coached Balfour Tech. team to 3 prov. championships; in baseball, coached Regina Red Sox to 4 prov. championships; in football, coached Balfour Tech. to 8 prov. championships and Regina Rams for 12 years to six nat. championships; rec'd. Wascanda Kiwanis Club's Dad of the Year Award 1963; B'nai B'rith's Outstanding Sports Personality of the Year Award 1966; city of Regina named a 'Gordon Currie Field' 1974; Candn. Amateur Coach of the Year (Air Canada) 1975; Newsmaker of the Year Award (Sask. Press Club) 1976; Gordon Currie Foundation estab. 1977; inducted into Sask. Sports Hall of Fame 1978; Outstanding Services to Football in Can. Award (CFL and Candn. Football League) 1978; rec'd. Order of Canada 1979; Gordon Currie Auditorium dedicated 1982; Regina city street named 'Currie Bay'; LL.D. (Hon.) Univ. of Regina 1987; Sask. recipient, Candn. Youth Education Excellence Prize, Les Productions Québecoises Pro-Art; 'Coach of the Year Award' named in his honour, Candn. Jr. Football 1989; Home: 48 Daffodil Cres., Regina, Sask. S4S 5A3.

**CURRIE, Philip John,** M.Sc., Ph.D.; palaeontologist; b. Brampton, Ont. 13 Mar. 1949; s. Robert Samuel and Esther Marie (Cecil) C.; e. White Oaks H.S.; Univ. of Toronto, B.Sc. 1972; McGill Univ., M.Sc. 1975, Ph.D. 1981; m. Marlene d. Joseph and Barbara Bahr 14 Aug. 1971; children: Tarl, Devin, Brett; HEAD, DINOSAUR RESEARCH, ROYAL TYRRELL MUS. OF PALAEONTOLOGY 1989– ; Curator of Palaeontol., Prov. Mus. of Alta. 1976–81; Vice-Chrmn., Planning Ctte., Tyrrell Mus. of Palaeontol. 1981–82; Asst. Dir., Tyrrell Mus. of Palaeontol. 1982–89; Adjunct Prof., Univ. of Calgary; Trustee, The Dinosaur Trust 1986– ; Expert Examiner, Candn. Cultural Property Import & Export Act 1977– ; Co-Chrmn., Dinosaur Systematics Symposium 1986; Chrmn., 4th Symp., Mesozoic Terrestrial Ecosystems 1987; Chrmn., 48th Annual Meeting, Soc. of Vertebrate Paleontology; Sci. Co-ord., Alta. section, Canada-China Dinosaur Project; extensive lecturing & speaking engagements worldwide; media work includes CBC (Nature of Things & others), BBC, PBS & Japan (NHK) TV; recipient, Sir Frederick Haultain Award (for significant contributions to science in Alta.) 1988; Mem., Soc. of Vertebrate Paleontol. (Prog. Dir. 1985–87); Alta. Mus. Assn.; Candn. Mus. Assn.; Alta. Paleontol. Soc.; Alta. Paleontol. Adv. Ctte. (Sec. 1977–89); Candn. Soc. Petroleum Geol.; Paleontol. Soc.; Internat. Living Fossil Soc.; author of 45 sci. papers & 40 popular pubns.; recreations: swimming, hiking, reading; Home: 1201, 2nd Ave. W., Drumheller, Alta. T0J 0Y2; Office: Box 7500, Drumheller, Alta. T0J 0Y0.

**CURRIE, Richard James,** B.Eng., M.B.A.; executive; b. Saint John, N.B. 4 Oct. 1937; s. Hugh O'Donnell and Agnes Coltart (Johnstone) C.; e. Tech. Univ. N.S., B.Eng. (Chem.) 1960; Harvard Univ., M.B.A. 1970; children: Jennifer Lee; Bryn Margaret; Elizabeth Gay; m. Elizabeth Royle 1990; PRES., LOBLAW COS. LTD. since 1976; Dir., Loblaw Cos. Ltd.; George Weston Ltd.; Imperial Oil Ltd.; Chrmn., Food Marketing Inst. (Washington, D.C.); Chrmn., Adv. Bd., Sch. of Business Admin., Univ. of Western Ont.; Process Engineer, Atlantic Sugar Refineries, 1960; Refining Superintendent, 1963–68; Sen. Assoc., McKinsey & Co. 1970; joined present firm as Vice-Pres. 1972; Extve. Vice-Pres. 1974; clubs: York; Rosedale Golf; recreations: golf; skiing; Home: 291 Russell Hill Rd., Toronto, Ont. M4V 2T5; Office: 22 St. Clair Ave. E., Ste. 1901, Toronto, Ont. M4T 2S7.

**CURRY, Gwen J.,** B.F.A., M.F.A.; university professor, artist; b. Victoria, B.C. 25 May 1950; d. Francis Ronald and Lily Miriam (Erikson) C.; e. Univ. of Victoria B.F.A. 1974; Arizona State Univ. M.F.A. 1978; m. James Garry s. Florence and James McKevitt June 1971; PROF., VISUAL ARTS DEPT., UNIV. OF VICTORIA 1978– ; teaches drawing & printmaking; art work incl. drawing, printmaking & mixed media; rep. by Equinox Gall. Vancouver; has had 13 one-person exhibits & particpated in over 50 group exhibits; exhib. internat. in Yugoslavia, England, Germany & the U.S.; rep. in 11 public collections incl. the Can. Counc. Art Bank & many priv. collections; Mem., Candn. Artists' Rep.; Bd. Mem., Open Space Gall. 1990–93; Home: 6807 Jedora Dr., R.R. #1, Brentwood Bay, B.C. V0S 1A0; Office: P.O. Box 1700, Victoria, B.C. V8W 2Y2.

**CURRY, Susan Guest;** volunteer; b. Winnipeg, Man. 3 May 1947; d. Wilbur Cox and Dorothy Margaret (Graham) Guest; e. Balmoral Hall Sch. 1965; Univ. of Man. Bachelor of Interior Design 1971; m. Peter D. s. D. Steele and Bertha Curry 28 Oct. 1972; children: Tara, Peter-Brent; Pres. Volunteer Ctte. Montréal Museum of Fine Arts 1991–93, Chair Museum Ball 1980, 1986, Vice Pres. Fundraising Ctte. 1975–88; Interior Designer MMDR Partners 1972–74; Chair Cystic Fibrosis Ball 1985; mem. Can. Council; Dir. Montreal Chest Hosp. Found.; Royal Winnipeg Ballet; Address: 3117 Daulac Rd., Montréal, Qué. H3Y 2A1.

**CURTIS, Charles Edward,** F.C.A.; b. Winnipeg, Man. 28 July 1931; s. Samuel and May (Goodison) C.; e. Prince Edward Sch.; E. Kildonan Coll. Inst.; Univ. of Man. C.A. 1955; m. Hilda Marion d. late Jack F. Simpson 30 Oct. 1954; one d. Nancy Maude; DEPY. MIN. DEPT. OF FINANCE MAN. 1976– ; Past C.E.O., Manitoba Energy Authority; Acting C.E.O., MTX (a subsidiary of Manitoba Telephone System); Bd. mem., Manitoba Hydro-Electric Bd.; mem. Superannuation Bd. Investment Ctte.; Teachers Retirement Invest. Fund; Workers Compensation Bd. Invest. Fund; Acting Clk. Extve. Council; joined Dunwoody & Co. 1949–54; Dept. of Nat. Revenue Income Tax Div. 1954–67, Chief Assessor N.B. Div.; Dept. of Finance Man. since 1967, Asst. Depy. Min. Budget, Accounting, Finance & Adm.; Past Chrmn. Group Comte. Cubs & Scouts Fort Garry; Past mem. and Chrmn. Bd. of Stewards Fort Garry Un. Ch.; Pres. Inst. C.A.'s Man. 1975–76; Fellow, Candn. Inst. of C.A.'s (past chrmn. Public Sector Accounting and Audit Standards Ctte.); United Church; recreations: badminton, tennis, swimming; Clubs: Manitoba; Winter Club (Winnipeg Bd. of Govs. 1974–79); Winnipeg Rotary (Hon. Treas.); Home: 596 South Dr., Winnipeg, Man. R3T 0B1; Office: Room 109, Legislative Bldg., Winnipeg, Man. R3C 0V8.

**CURTIS, Donald J.,** B.A.; advertising executive; b. Toronto, Ont. 1 Feb. 1941; s. James Abbott and Jesse Beatrice (Calhoun) C.; e. Leaside High Sch. 1959; Univ. of Toronto B.A. 1964; m. Dianne Louise Davies 7 Sept. 1963; two s. Gregory James, Daniel Gordon; Managing Dir., Goodgoll Curtis Inc. 1990– ; joined Stanfield, Johnson & Hill, Advt. 1964–68; Foote, Cone & Belding 1968–72; Vickers & Benson 1972–89; Exec. Vice Pres., Mng. Dir. Metrop. Toronto Convention & Visitors Assn., Vice Pres. Mktg. 1989; Sr. Vice Pres., Saffer Advertising Inc. 1989; Trustee Ont. Sci. Centre 1987–93; Home: 25 Tanager Ave., Toronto, Ont. M4G 3P9.

**CURTIS, Donald William Sr.;** hotel executive; b. Dover Ohio 11 March; s. Michael O'Connor and Gertrude (Schneider) C.; e. Miami (of Ohio) Univ.; Texas A & M Coll.; Univ. of Md. (Foreign Lang. Inst.); Salzburg, Austria; m. Jill Evolin, d. Col. Kennard S. Vandergrift, 6 Apr. 1957; children: Donald William Jr., David Bruce, Jill Evolin; Gen. Mgr., U.S. Govt. Recreational Centre, Berchtesgaden, Germany 1947–58; Foreign Dir. and Asst. to Pres., Steigenberger Hotel Corp., Germany 1958–62; Gen. Mgr. & Shareholder, Hotel Corp., Switzerland 1962–64; Vice Pres.-Internat. Div., Hotel Corp. of America, London, Eng. 1964–67; Pres. and Extve. Dir., Johannesburg Hotel President and Development Co., S. Africa 1967–69; Dir. Arwa South Africa (Pty) Hosiery Mfrs. Johannesburg 1967–69; Dir., Fridays Child, Toronto 1992– ; Sr. Extve. Vice Pres., Club Mediterranée, France 1969–71; Advr. to Baron Edmond de Rothschild (Hotels) Paris 1969–71; Chrmn., Pres. and C.E.O., Canadian Pacific Hotels 1972–78; Pres., C.O.O. and Dir., Skyline Hotels Ltd. 1978–80; Chrmn., Pres. and C.E.O., Canadian Hotels Internat. and Managing Dir. Alder Place Hotel 1980–86 (and Managing Dir., Ramada Hotels 1980–82); Managing Dir., Choice Hotels International Canada 1987– ; served with U.S. Army in Europe 1944–48; Consultant: Hotel Sch., Bad Reichenhall, Bavaria; USAF, Wiesbaden (Club Mang.); US Embassy Bonn (Labor Mang.); Honoured by Oberbergurmeister of Bad Reichenhall and Landrat of Landkreis; recipient: Gold Medal for Outstanding Hotel Mgr. of Yr., Germany 1953; 4 Gold Medals Hunting; All-round Trophy Competition Germany 1957; awarded title Hon. Chef by Candn. Fed. of Chefs de Cuisine 1976; Gold Medal Award, Comte. of European Excellence 1976; mem., Confrerie des Chevaliers du Tastevin, Dijon, France; Commanderie de Bordeaux, Toronto; Delta Tau Delta; Anglican; recreations: travel, hunting, fishing, reading; Home: 37 Edenbridge Dr., Islington, Ont. M9A 3E8; Office: 5090 Explorer Dr., 6th Floor, Mississauga, Ont. L4W 4T9.

**CURTIS, George Frederick,** Q.C., B.A., LL.B., B.C.L., D.C.L., LL.D., Order of the Coif. Law Soc. Award; retired; b. Stogumber, Somerset, Eng., Sept. 1906; s. William George and Florence Giles (Thorne) C.; came to Can. 1913; e. Univ. of Sask., LL.B. 1927; Oxford Univ., B.A. 1930; B.C.L. 1931; m. Doris Gwendolyn, d. Judge J. Willis Margeson, Bridgewater, N.S., 15 May 1940; children: John, Joan, Robert, Peter; Prof. of Law and Dean of the Faculty, Univ. of Brit. Columbia, 1945–71; read law with N.R. Craig, K.C., Moose Jaw, Sask.; P.H. Gordon, K.C., Regina, Sask.; called to Bar of Sask., 1931; N.S. 1944; B.C. 1948; practised his prof. with Gordon & Gordon, Regina, 1931–33; Govt. of Saskatchewan 1933–34; Assoc. Prof. of Law, Dalhousie Law Sch., 1934–38; Russell Prof. of Law there 1938–44; Viscount Bennett Prof. of Law there 1944–45; mem., MacQuarrie Comn. on Combines Leg., 1950–52; Advisor, Govt. of Can. on Law of Sea 1952–63; Visiting Prof., Harvard Law Sch., 1955–56; A.N.U. 1965; London 1971–72; Calgary 1978; Prof. of Law, 1971–77, Adjunct Prof. 1978–86; Pres., Assn. of Candn. Law Teachers, 1951–52; Chrmn., Halifax Br., Candn. Inst. of Internat. Affairs, 1937–39 and Vancouver Men's Br., 1950–52; Pres., Halifax Candn. Club, 1939–40.; Dir., Halifax Y.M.C.A., 1937–43, Regina 1932–34, Vancouver 1948; Halifax Sch. for the Deaf 1943–45; Chrmn., Candn. Commonwealth Scholarship Comte., 1959–71; Del., U.N. Conf. Law of the Sea, Geneva, 1958, 1960; Commonwealth Educ. Conf., London, Oxford, 1959, New Delhi 1962, Ottawa, 1964, Canberra, 1970; Dir. Candn. Foundation for Legal Research, 1960–71; Gov., Crofton House Sch. 1960–71; Koerner Foundation 1957–71; mem., Candn. Bar Assn.; Anglican; recreation: camping; Clubs: Faculty; Vancouver; Home: 1808 Allison Rd., University Hill, Vancouver, B.C. V6T 1S9.

**CURTIS, Norman;** insurance executive; b. Hull, Eng. 15 Nov. 1927; s. Harry C.; e. Hull (Eng.) Grammar Sch. 1946; Univ. Coll. Hull 1946–47; London Business Sch. 1974; m. Patricia Mary d. late Harold Jessop Nall 22 Oct. 1951; children: Simon Rolf, Alison Judith; CHRMN., GUARDIAN INSURANCE CO. OF CANADA since 1988; Chrmn., GRE Financial Ltd.; Dir., Canadian Group Underwriters; joined Royal Exchange Assurance, London, Eng. 1950–56, Vancouver 1957–65, Br. Mgr. Toronto 1966–69; Marketing & Planning Mgr. Guardian Royal Exchange Group (subsequently present co.) 1969–74, Vice Pres. 1974, Sr. Vice Pres. 1976; Extve. Vice Pres. 1977–80; Pres. 1980–88; UK Nat. Service (Army) 1948–50; Fellow, Ins. Inst. Can.; P. Conservative; Anglican; recreations: travel, music, reading (European hist.); Club: Albany; Home: 55 Harbour Square, Suite 3313, Toronto, Ont. M5J 2L1; Office: Guardian of Canada Tower, 181 University Ave., Toronto, Ont. M5H 3M7.

**CURWOOD, Bruce B.,** B.Comm., M.B.A., CCM, FCIS, P.Adm.; financial executive; b. Montreal, Que. 4 Aug. 1951; s. Robert H. and Helen N. (James) C.; e. Univ. of Toronto B.Comm. 1980; York Univ. M.B.A. 1986; m. Valerie d. Jack and Florence Hadden June 1982; one child: Lindsay A.; TREASURER, UNIV. OF TORONTO 1991– ; Supvr., Treas., ITT Canada Limited 1981–85; Treas., Ball Packaging Products Can. Inc. 1985–90; Nat. Dir., Inst. of Chartered Secretaries & Administrators (ICSA) (Ont. Vice Chair; Ed. Ctte. Mem.); Pension Investment Assn. of Can. (Sub-ctte. Mem. on Indus. Practices); Candn. Assn. of Univ. Bus. Offrs. (Investment Ctte. Associate); Treas. Mngt. Assn. (Perm. Cert. Cash Mgr.); ICSA Gold Medal Recipient 1990; Ont. Touch Player of the Year 1990; Touch Football Player of the Year 1977; Council of Ont. Universities (Pension Ctte. Mem.); recreations: fitness; clubs: Hart House; Home: 18 Fairmar Ave., Etobicoke, Ont. M8Y 2C8; Office: 215 Huron St., 3rd floor, Toronto, Ont. M5S 1A2.

**CUSHMAN, Robert,** M.A.; journalist, broadcaster, theatre worker; b. London, England 7 Nov. 1943; s. Harry and Diana (Sowman) C.; e. Latymer Upper School London 1962; Clare College, Cambridge Univ. M.A. 1966; m. Arlene d. Max and Ida Gould 1975; three children; COURSE DIR., AESTHETICS AND CRITICISM, YORK UNIV. 1992–93; General Trainee & later Producer, British Broadcasting Corp. 1966–70; Theatre Critic, 'The Observer' London 1973–84; Tutorial Leader, Theatre Studies, York Univ. 1991–92; much freelance work in journalism incl. the 'Globe and Mail,' 'Saturday Night,' 'New York Times' & many British pubns.; broadcasting work incl. Writer/Host, 'Songbook' (CBC), 'Book, Music and Lyrics,' 'Sweet and Low-Down,' 'First Night Impressions,' 'In Search of Alec Wilder,' etc. (BBC), 'Two on the Town'; theatre work incl. devising & perf. in 'Nashville, N.Y.'; Dir., 'Marry Me a Little'; devising & dir., 'Look to the Rainbow'; devising, dir., perf. in many other plays and revues on stage (London & the Brit. regions) & radio (BBC); has lived in Canada since 1987 and continues to work in both countries; Nathan Cohen Award for Excellence in Theatre Criticism 1990, 1991; author: 'The National Theatre, A Pictorial Record' 1971, 'Vivat Rex' (Shakespeare's History Plays) 1977.

**CUSSON, Paul,** D.M.V.; veterinarian, veterinary executive; b. St-Hyacinthe, Que. 23 June 1936; s. J. Laval and Violette (Vandal) C.; e. Univ. of Montreal D.M.V. 1962; m. Monique d. Gérard Vanier 26 May 1962; children: Luc, Guy, Simon; GENERAL MANAGER, C.D.M.V. INC. 1986– ; Veterarinarian (large animals), private practice 1962–82; Admin. Mgr., C.D.M.V. inc. 1982–86; Vice-Pres., Parco Internat. 1990–91; Mem., Bd. of Dir., Univ. of Montreal 1991– ; Adm., 'La Fondation Régina DeVos' 1982– ; Pres., Centennial Fund, Fac. of Veterinary Med., Univ. of Montreal 1986–90; Mem., Am. Assn. of Bovine Practitioners' 1982– ; Ass. Med. Vet. Praticiens Québec 1982– ; Ass. Med. Vet. Equin. 1982– ; Ass. Vet., Industrie animale 1982– ; Corp. of the Veterinarians of the Prov. of Que. 1962– ; Ass. can. Vet. 1962– ; recreations: fishing, golf; Home: 3815 Laurier Blvd., St-Hyacinthe, Que. J2S 3T8; office: 2999 Choquette Blvd., St-Hyacinthe, Que. J2S 7C2.

**CUTLER, May Ebbitt,** B.A., M.A., M.S.; book publisher; b. Montreal, Que. 4 Sept. 1923; d. William Henry and Frances (Farrelly) Ebbitt; e. McGill Univ., B.A. 1945, M.A. 1951; Columbia Univ., M.S. (Journalism) 1946; m. Philip s. Issie Cutler 17 Jan. 1952; children: Keir, Adam, Michael, Roger; FOUNDER & PRES., TUNDRA BOOKS 1967– ; Mayor, Westmount, Que. 1987–91; Ed., Candn. Press, Montreal and New York bureaux 1945–46; worked for U.N. Info. Dept. 1946–47; reporter/columnist, Montreal Herald 1947–48; feature and magazine writer, The Standard (Montreal) 1948–51; taught in Eng. Dept., McGill Univ. 1948–51; set up 3–year extension prog. in journalism at McGill Univ. 1951–54; First Prize, Centennial Lit. Awards 1967; Eve Orpen Award for Pub. Excellence 1987; Claude Aubrey Award for distinguished contributions to children's literature, Candn. sect., IBBY 1988; Boston Globe Literary Press Award 1988; author 'The Last Noble Savage' 1967; recreations: theatre, opera, music; Office: Tundra Books, 345 Victoria Ave., Westmount, Que. H3Z 2N2.

**CYBULSKI, John M.,** B.Sc., M.B.A.; executive; b. Poland 2 Aug. 1936; s. Henry and Czeslawa (Florianowicz) C.; e. Mech. Trade Sch. Warsaw, Dipl. 1951; Mech. Tech. Coll. Warsaw, Dipl. Technol. 1955; Sir George Williams Univ. B.Sc. 1966; McGill Univ. Grad. Dipl. in Mang. 1974, M.B.A. 1978; m. Susan d. Aladar Marton, Montreal, Que. 7 May 1966; SR. VICE PRES., AEROSPACE OPERATIONS, COLTEC INDUSTRIES INC, New York, N.Y. 1991– ; responsible for Menasco Aerospace, Oakville, Ont.; Menasco Aerosystems, Euless, TX; Menasco Overhaul, Burbank CA; Chandler Evans Control Systems, West Hartford, CT; Delavan Gas Turbine Products, W. Des Moines IA; Lewis Electronic Instrumentation, Naugatuck, CT; Walbar Inc., Peabody, MA and Tempe, AZ; Walbar Canada, Mississauga, Ont.; Group Pres., Colt Industries Inc. 1989–91 responsible for Menasco Aerospace, Oakville, Ont. and Menasco Aerosystems, U.S.A.; Chrmn., Menasco Aerospace Ltd., Oakville, Ont. 1984– ; joined RCA Victor Co. Montreal 1960–65 holding various technical positions; Sr. Indust. Engr., Canadian Marconi Co. Ltd., Town of Mount Royal 1965, Procurement Mgr. 1969–74; Mgr. Purchasing & Traffic, Dominion Engineering Works Ltd., Lachine, Que. 1974, Mgr. Quality Assurance 1976, Mgr. Production Planning & Control 1978; Vice Pres. and Gen. Mgr., Rail & Diesel Div., Bombardier Inc. 1978–81; Pres., Heroux Inc., Div. of Bombardier Inc. 1982; Extve. Vice Pres. present firm 1982–84; mem. Candn. Soc. Mech. Engrs.; Dir., Aerospace Industries Assoc. of Can.; McGill Grad. Soc.; recreations: sailing, skiing, travel, classical music; Home: 10 Westhaven Lane, White Plains, N.Y. 10605; Office: 430 Park Ave., New York, N.Y. 10022.

**CYNADER, Max Sigmund,** B.Sc., Ph.D.; educator; research scientist; b. Berlin, Germany 24 Feb. 1947; s. Samuel and Maria (Kraushar) C.; e. McGill Univ. B.Sc.

1967; Mass. Inst. Technol. Ph. D. 1972; Max-Planck Inst. Munich postdoctoral studies Neocortex 1972–73; PROF. & DIR. OF RSCH., DEPT. OF OPHTHALMOLOGY (also Prof. of Psychol. & Physiol.), UNIV. OF B.C. 1988– ; Asst. Prof. of Psychol. 1973, Assoc. Prof. 1977, Prof. of Psychol. 1981; Assoc. Prof. of Physiology 1979, Prof. of Physiol. 1984; Killam Rsch. Prof., Dalhousie Univ. 1984–88; awarded Killam Rsch. Prize 1989; cons. U.S. Air Force Aerospace Med.; cons. and expert testimony hwy. safety & traffic accidents; Adv. & Review Cttes.: MRC of Canada; NSERC of Can.; Human Frontier Science Program (Japan); Alta. Heritage Fund for Med. Rsch.; rsch. grants Med. Rsch. Council Can., Natural Sci. & Engn. Rsch. Council Can., Networks of Centres of Excellence: Neural Regeneration and Functional Recovery, Inst. for Robotics and Intelligent Systems, Human Frontier Science Program, Nat. Eye Insts. (USA), Suncor Inc.; rsch. contract Defence & Civil Inst. Environmental Med.; E.W.R. Steacie Fellowship Natural Sci. & Engn. Rsch. Council 1979; semifinalist Candn. Astronaut Prog. 1983; Assoc., Candn. Inst. Advanced Rsch. 1984, Sr. Fellow, 1986– , B.C. Fellow 1989– ; Fellow, Royal Soc. of Can. 1987– ; author over 135 sci. papers and book chapters on vision, computer vision, orgn. and develop. of cortex, amblyopia and strabismus; over 200 papers presented nat. and internat. sci. meetings; mem. various ed. bds.; mem. Soc. Neurosci.; Assn. Rsch. Vision & Ophthalmol.; Assn. Rsch. Otolaryngol.; Internat. Brain Rsch. Orgn.; Internat. Strabismol. Assn.; Candn. Physiol. Soc.; recreations: skiing, racquetball, bridge; Office: Fac. of Med., 2550 Willow St., Vancouver, B.C. V5Z 3N9.

**CYR, J.V. Raymond,** O.C., B.A.Sc.; executive; b. Montreal, Que. 11 Feb. 1934; s. Armand and Yvonne (Lagacé) C.; e. Ecole Polytech.; Univ. of Montreal B.A.Sc. 1958; Bell Labs., N.J. post-grad. studies in engn.; Nat. Defence Coll. 1972–73; m. Marie, d. Alphonse Bourdon, Montreal, Que. 1 Sept. 1956; children: Hélène, Paul-André; Chrmn., Bell Canada; BCE Ventures; Alouette Telecommunications; Telesat Canada; Dir., Northern Telecom Ltd.; Montreal Trust; Continental Airlines Inc.; BCE Mobile Communications Inc.; Spar Aerospace Ltd.; Bell Canada BCE; Bell Sygma; Dominion Textile Inc.; TransCanada PipeLines; Domtar Inc.; Air Canada; Teleglobe Inc.; joined Bell Canada as Engr. 1958, Staff Engr. Montreal 1965, Chief Engr. Québec City 1970, Vice Pres. Operations Staff E. Region Montreal 1973, Vice Pres. Montreal Area 1975, Exec. Vice-Pres. Quebec Region 1975, Exec. Vice-Pres. Admin. 1979, Pres. 1983–85; Chrmn., Pres. & C.E.O. 1985–87; Pres., BCE 1987–88; Chrmn., Bell Canada 1987–89 and Pres. & C.E.O., BCE 1988–89; Chrmn., Pres. & C.E.O., BCE 1989–90; Chrmn. & C.E.O., BCE 1990–92; Chrmn., BCE 1992–93; Chrmn., BCE Candn. Telecom Grp. 1992–93; Chrmn., Montreal Trust 1989–90; Chrmn., TransCanadaPipeLine 1989–92; Chrmn., Centre of Initiative for Technology (Citec), Montreal; Chrmn. of Assoc. Gov., Univ. of Montreal; mem., Ecole polytechnique de Montréal; Past Chrmn., Jr. Achievement Can.; mem.: Que. Corp. of Engrs.; Corporation de l'Opéra de Montréal; recipient Candn. Engrs. Gold Medal Award 1987; awarded Ordre du Mérite des Diplomés, Univ. of Montréal 1988; Officer of the Order of Canada; LL.D. (Hon.), Concordia Univ. 1988; Laureate of the Prix des Communications du Québec (granted by the Ministère des Communications du Qué.) 1990; Mgmt. Achievement Award, McGill Univ. 1991; named in his honour: a Chair in the Mgmt. of Technology, École Polytechnique; Great Montrealers Award 1991; rec'd Commemorative Medal, 125th Anniversary of Candn. Confedn. 1992; R. Catholic; recreations: golf, swimming; Clubs: St-Denis; Mount Royal; Founders; Islemere; Mont Bruno; St. James; Home: 12375 Poutrincourt, Montreal, Qué.; Office: 1000 Gauchetière ouest, Suite 3700, Montréal, Qué. H3B 4Y7.

**CZUBAK, George T.,** B.A.Sc., C.M.A., P.Eng., M.B.A.; financial executive; b. Toronto, Ont. 28 June 1950; s. Ted and Maria (Mikolajczyk) C.; e. Univ. of Toronto B.A.Sc. 1972, M.B.A. 1974; C.M.A. 1979; m. Danuta d. Alexandra and Stan Wujec 24 May 1975; children: Mariya, Danika, Mikala; VICE-PRES. AND CHIEF FINANCIAL OFFR., BELL SYGMA 1993– ; Financial Analyst, Texaco 1974; Co-ord., Treasury Opns., Mgr. Cost Analysis, Mgr. Performance Analysis, Suncor 1975; Mgr. Budgets & Performance Reporting, Gulf 1982; Corp. Controller, Canada Systems Group 1986; Treasurer & Vice Pres., Finance, Stone & Webster 1989; Vice-Pres. Finance, Rhône-Poulenc 1992; Mem., Assn. of Profl. Engrs. of Ont.; Soc. of Mngt. Accts. of Ont.; Financial Extves. Institute; Advisor, Sea Scouts; recreations: squash, sailing; Home: 48 Wilgar Rd., Etobicoke, Ont. M8X 1J5.

# D

**DABBIKEH, Peter N.,** B.Sc., M.B.A., C.A.; financial executive; b. 18 Sept. 1946; e. London Sch. of Econ. B.Sc. 1970; York Univ. Toronto M.B.A. 1973; C.A. 1983; m. Carol King 1971; EXEC. VICE PRES., CHIEF OPERATING OFFR. AND DIR., LAURENTIAN FUNDS MANAGEMENT INC. 1989– ; Laurentian Mutual Funds; Exec. Vice Pres. Laurentian Financial Services Inc. 1989– ; Vice Pres., The Imperial Life Assurance Co. of Can. 1990– ; joined Bank of Nova Scotia 1970–81; Ernst & Whinney, C.A.'s 1981–86; Laurentian Financial Services: Corp. Controller 1986; Chief Financial Offr. 1987–90; co-author 'Franchising in Canada' 1986; Dir., Investment Funds Inst. of Can.; mem. Toronto Assn. Bus. Econs.; Candn. Tax Found.; Candn. Inst. C.A.'s; Office: 95 St. Clair Ave. W., Toronto, Ont. M4V 1N7.

**DABYDEEN, Cyril,** M.A., M.P.A.; writer; b. Guyana, S. Am. 15 Oct. 1945; s. Abel and Hilda (Oudit) D.; e. St. Patrick's Ang. Sch. Rose Hall, Guyana; Lakehead Univ., B.A. 1973; Queen's Univ., M.A. 1974, M.P.A. 1975; author: (poetry) 'Distances' 1977; 'Goatsong' 1977; 'Heart's Frame' 1979; 'This Planet Earth' 1980; 'Elephants Make Good Stepladders' 1982; 'Islands Lovelier Than A Vision' 1986; 'Coastland: Selected Poems' 1989; 'Discussing Columbus' 1994; 'Stoning the Wind' 1994; (fiction) 'Still Close to the Island' 1980; 'The Wizard Swami' 1989; 'Dark Swirl' 1989; 'To Monkey Jungle' 1988; ed. 'A Shapely Fire: Changing the Literary Landscape' 1987; 'Another Way to Dance: Asian-Canadian Poetry' 1990; 'Jogging in Havana' 1992; 'Berbice Crossing' 1994; 'Sometimes Hard' 1994; Teacher, St. Patrick's Ang. Sch. Guyana 1962–70; Algonquin Coll. Ottawa 1975–81; Univ. of Ottawa 1982–83, 1987–92; Co-ordinator Mayor's Race Relations Ctte. Ottawa 1984–89; Race Relations Manager, Federal Govt. and Federation of Candn. Municipalities 1989–93; Poet Laureate City of Ottawa 1984–87; recipient Can. Council, Ont. Arts Council, Multiculturalism, External Affairs & Ottawa-Carleton Awards for writing & ed.; Okanagan Fiction Prize 1982; Louise Plumb Poetry Prize 1978; Sandbach Parker Gold Medal for Poetry; A.J. Seymour Lyric Poetry Prize; Certificate of Merit, Govt. of Can. 1988; mem., Candn. Assn. Commonwealth Lang. & Lit. Studies; Address: 106 Blackburn, Ottawa, Ont. K1N 8A7.

**DACCORD, J.E.,** B.Eng., P.Eng., M.Sc., F.M.C.; executive; b. Montréal, Qué.; e. McGill Univ. B.Eng. (Civil) 1953; Mass. Inst. of Technol. (Sloan Fellow) M.Sc. (Mgmt.) 1967; m. Joan; children: Joyce, Bruce, Ruth, Philip; CHRMN., THE IDEAL METALS GROUP 1985– ; Chrmn., World Vision Canada; Dir., Ideal Metal Inc.; Fonorola Inc.; Williams & Wilson Ltd.; Kom Internat.; Nat'l. Assoc. of Aluminum Distributors; World Vision Internat.; Currie, Coopers & Lybrand 1963–85, Pres. and Mng. Partner 11 yrs.; Canron Ltd. 1953–63, various positions; Clubs: St. James's (Dir.); Beaconsfield Golf; Canadian (Pres., Montréal); Office: 3399 Francis-Hughes, Laval, Que. H7L 5A5.

**DACEY, John Robert,** M.Sc., Ph.D., D.Sc., F.C.I.C., M.B.E., C.M.; educator; chemist; b. Eng. 28 Apr. 1914; s. Harry and Arabella (Wilson) D.; e. Dalhousie Univ. B.Sc. 1936, M.Sc. 1938; McGill Univ. Ph.D. 1940; D.Sc. (hon. causa): Royal Mil. Coll. 1982; Queen's Univ. 1986; m. late Jane Dean Campbell 1940; children: John W.H., Joan E. (Mrs. D.M. Bowie), Diane (Mrs. W.G. Sprules); PROFESSOR EMERITUS, ROYAL MILITARY COLL. OF CANADA; former Principal, R.M.C.; Scientific Consultant; served with Candn. Army 1940–47, rank Maj.; author over 50 scient. papers; mem. Am. Chem. Soc.; mem. Order of Canada; Sigma Xi; R.M.C. Club of Can.; Anglican; Office: Royal Military College, Kingston, Ont. K7K 5L0.

**DACKOW, Orest Taras,** B.Comm. Honours, F.S.A., F.C.I.A., M.A.A.A.; insurance executive; b. Wynyard, Sask. 17 Sept. 1936; e. Wynyard Comp. H.S. 1954; Univ. of Manitoba B.Comm. (Hons.) 1958; m. Florence; 3 children; PRES. & DIR., GREAT-WEST LIFE ASSURANCE CO. 1990– ; joined present firm 1958; Assoc. Actuary 1968; Vice-Pres., Individual Opns. 1976; Sr. Vice-Pres., U.S. 1979; Extve. Vice-Pres. & Chief Operating Offr., U.S. 1983; Extve. Vice-Pres., Corp. Finan. & Control 1988; Pres. & Dir., The Great-West Life Assurance Co. 1990– ; Pres., C.E.O. & Dir., Great-West Lifeco Inc. 1992– ; Bd. Mem., Winnipeg Metro YMCA 1971–80 (Pres. 1979–80); Denver Metro YMCA 1981–84; Nat. Jewish Ctr. for Immunology & Respiratory Med. 1985– ; Colorado Alliance of Business 1986–87; Health Sci. Ctr. Rsch. Found. 1990– ; Instrumental Diagnostics Development Office 1992– ; Office: P.O. Box 6000, Winnipeg, Man. R3C 3A5.

**DACKS, Gurston,** B.A., Ph.D.; university professor; b. Toronto, Ont. 24 Apr. 1945; s. Samuel and Ethel Teresa (Pugen) D.; e. Forest Hill Coll. 1963; Univ. of Toronto, B.A. 1967; Princeton Univ., Ph.D. 1975; m. Barbara Jekel 10 Nov. 1968; children: Joel Bryan, Andrew Mark; ASSOC. DEAN OF ARTS 1990– ; PROF., DEPT. OF POL. SCI., UNIV. OF ALTA. 1985– ; Asst. Prof. of Pol. Sci., 1971–78; Assoc. Prof. 1978–85; Chrmn., Candn. Studies 1974–76, 1984–85; Vis. Prof. of Candn. Studies, Japan 1982; Adjunct Rsch. Prof., Candn. Circumpolar Inst.; Mem., Candn. Pol. Sci. Assn/ Inst. of Public Admin. of Can.; Candn. Studies Assn.; author: 'A Choice of Futures' 1981 and articles on pol. & constitutional devel. & aboriginal claims in the Candn. north; Ed., 'Devolution and Constitutional Development in the Canadian North' 1990; Sr. Ed.: 'Northern Communities: The Prospects for Empowerment' 1988; reviewer, var. acad. journals; recreations: canoeing, reading; Home: 9667 87th Ave., Edmonton, Alta. T6C 1K5; Office: Edmonton, Alta. T6G 2H4.

**DADSON, Douglas French,** B.A., B.Ed.; educator; b. Toronto, Ont. 1 May 1913; s. Alexander Turnbull and Eva Stewart (Grafftey) D.; e. Univ. of Toronto Schs., 1931; Univ. of Toronto, B.A. 1935; Ont. Coll. of Educ., B.Ed. 1955; m. Patricia Grace, d. Charles Adamson, 22 Aug. 1942; children: Elizabeth Ann, Douglas Aleck; Dean, Fac. of Educ., Univ. of Toronto, 1963–73; Teacher, Secondary Schs., 1936–42; Instr., Univ. of Toronto Schs. 1945; Inspr., Ont. Secondary Schs. 1950; Prof., Ont. Coll. of Educ. 1954, Dean of Coll. 1963; Dean., Faculty of Educ., Univ. of Toronto 1970; served with R.C.A. 1942–44; rank Lt.; Capt., Educ. Services, 1944–45; Club: Reswick; Home: 1477 Bayview Ave., Apt. H33, Toronto, Ont. M4G 3B2.

**DAFOE, Christopher Grannis;** editor; writer; b. Winnipeg, Man. 25 July 1936; s. John Grannis and Marjorie Hall (Metcalfe) D.; e. elem. and high schs. Winnipeg; United Coll.; Stanford Univ. Dip. in Journalism 1966 (Prof. Journalism Fellowship 1966); m. Nancy d. James and Nancy Cosgrave 24 Sept. 1960; children: Christopher, Sarah, Alexander; EDITOR, THE BEAVER 1985– ; Dir., University of Manitoba Press; ed. writer, columnist Winnipeg Free Press 1955–68; columnist, critic Vancouver Sun 1968–82; freelance writing incls. CBC, Manchester Guardian, Globe and Mail, Toronto Star, Saturday Night, London Times and other publs.; author numerous plays and lit. documentaries CBC Radio; stage plays 'Two Friends' 1962, staged by Man. Theatre Centre Studio; 'The Frog Galliard' 1977, staged by New Play Centre, Vancouver E. Cultural Centre, Belfry Theatre Victoria; author 'Dancing Through Time: The First Fifty Years of the Royal Winnipeg Ballet' 1990; recipient Can. Council Awards 1968, 1973; mem. Man. Hist. Soc.; Home: 25 Purcell Ave., Winnipeg, Man. R3G 0Z9; Office: 450 Portage, Ave., Winnipeg, Man. R3C 0E7.

**DAGENAIS, Camille A.,** C.C., D.A.Sc., D.Sc., LL.D., F.E.I.C.; engineering consultant; b. Montréal, Qué. 12 Nov. 1920; s. Gilbert and Charlotte (Mitchell) D.; e. Ecole Polytech. Univ. of Montreal, B.A.Sc. 1946; Alexander Hamilton Inst., Business Adm.; École des Hautes Études Comm., Business Adm.; D.Sc. Royal Mil. Coll. of Can. 1975, Laval 1977; D.A.Sc. Sherbrooke 1975; LL.D. Toronto 1973; Eng.D. Univ. of Waterloo 1986; Doctorate, Univ. of Montreal 1987; D.Sc., McGill Univ. 1988; D.Eng. Univ. of Ottawa 1993; m. Pauline; d. Emile Falardeau, 23 Aug. 1947; children: Guy, Alain, Claude; Dir., Canadian Liquid Air Ltd.; Spar Aerospace Ltd.; Group Jean Coutu; Canam-Manac Inc.; began as Engr. radar stns. Pine Tree Line, H. J. Doran, Consultants, Montreal and subsequently Constr. Overseer Canadian Industries Ltd.; joined Surveyer, Nenniger & Chênevert as Liaison Engr. 1953, Engr. 1954, Partner 1959, Chrmn. Bd. and Gen. Mgr. 1965; Pres. 1966; apptd. Pres. SNC Enterprises Ltd. 1967; Chrmn. & C.E.O., SNC Enterprises Ltd. and Surveyer, Nenniger & Chênevert Inc. 1975–86; mem., Order of Engrs. Que. (Vice Pres. Consulting Engrs. Sec. 1966); Assn. Consulting Engrs. Can. (Pres. 1967–68; Dir., 1966–70); Candn. Soc. for Civil Engn. (Pres. 1973); Internat. Comn. on Large Dams (Vice Pres. Zone Am. 1974–77, Pres. 1982–85); Pres. Candn. Comte., Candn. Nuclear Assn. 1967–70 (Past Pres. and Dir.); Candn. Good Roads Assn. (Past Dir.); Past Dir., Corp. of Seven Wardens; Past Pres., Candn. Acad. of Engineering; Corresp. mem. Acad. Mexicana de Ingenieria; R. Catholic; recreations: hunting, fishing; Clubs: St. Denis; Mt. Royal; Home: 3495 Avenue du Musée, Apt. 401, Montreal, Qué. H3G 2C8; Office: 2 Place Félix-Martin, Montreal, Qué. H2Z 1Z3.

**DAGENAIS, Marcel G.,** M.A., Ph.D.; educator; b. Montreal, Que. 22 Feb. 1935; s. Emilien and Antoinette (Girard) D.; e. Univ. de Montréal B.A. 1952, M.A. 1958; Yale Univ. M.A. 1960, Ph.D. 1964; m. Denyse d. Charles René and Marianne Laberge 5 July 1958; children: Danielle, Michel, Jean-François; PROF. OF ECON. UNIV. DE MONTREAL 1973– ; Asst. Prof. present Univ. 1964–66, Invited Prof. 1972–73; mem. Bd. of Dir., Centre for Transp. Res. 1983–87; Invited Prof. Ecole de Hautes Etudes Commerciales 1966–67, Assoc. Prof. 1967–70, Prof. 1970–72; Invited Prof. Univ. de Genève 1969, 1987; Sir George Williams Univ. 1969–73 (part time); Univ. de Toulouse 1970; Res. Fellow, Cent. de Rech. et Dév. en Econ. 1987– ; Consultant: Société Québécoise des Transports 1993; Ass. Nat. du Qué. 1991–92; Min. des Affaires culturelles du Qué. 1990; Assn. des entrep. en cons. du Québec 1990; Via Rail 1988–89; Stats. Can. 1978–79, 1988–89; Bureau de la statistique du Qué. 1962–87; Office Auditor Gen. Can. 1981–87; Transport Can. 1980–83; Soc. d'électrolyse et de chimie Alcan Ltée 1981–83; Dyname Inc. 1973–83; TransCanada PipeLines Ltd. 1979; ministère des Affaires intergouvernementales du Qué. 1978–79; ministère des Richesses naturelles du Qué. 1975–78; Office de planification et de développement du Qué. 1976–77, 1980; ministère des Communications du Qué. 1975; F.R. Laberge et Associés 1974; Institut Internat. d'Economie Quantitative 1969–74; ministère des Affaires sociales du Qué. 1973; Banque de Montréal 1973; mem., Adv. Group Nat. Accts. Stats. Can. 1977– ; recipient, Woodrow Wilson Hon. Fellowship 1958; Société canadienne de sci. économique award 1982; Killam Rsch. Fellowship 1987–89; 'Prix du Statisticien d'expression française' (Soc. de Statistique de Paris) 1990; Prix Marcel Vincent, Ass. Can. Fr. pour L'Avan. des Sciences 1991; Fellow, J. of Econometrics 1992– ; author or co-author numerous publs.; assoc. ed. 'Journal of Econometrics' 1980– ; 'Canadian Journal of Statistics' 1980–84; mem., ed. bd. 'Advanced Studies in Theoretical and Applied Econometrics' 1982– ; (Kluwer Ac. Pub.); Société canadienne de sci. économique (Pres. 1980–81); Assn. Canadienne d'Economique (Vice Pres. 1980–82); Am. Econ. Assn.; Econometric Soc.; Am. Stat. Assn.; Candn. Stat. Assn.; Royal Soc. Can.; Conf. Res. Income & Wealth; Home: #1002, 60 Berlioz, Ile des Soeurs, Que. H3E 1M4; Office: Econ. Dept., Univ. de Montréal, C.P. 6128, Montreal, Que. H3C 3J7.

**DAGENAIS, Michel,** B.A., LL.L.; corrections executive; b. Montreal, Que. 27 June 1940; s. Paul and Juliette (L'Heureux) D.; e. Collège Stanislas; Univ. of Paris B.A. 1959; Univ. of Montreal LL.L. 1962; m. Claire d. Napoleon and Maria Courtemanche 5 Oct. 1963; children: Catherine, Sophie, Véronique, Maxime, Fanny, Guillaume; CHAIRPERSON, NATIONAL PAROLE BOARD OF CANADA; previously had private law practice; Mem., Candn. Bar Assn.; Barreau du Qué.; Am. Correctional Assn.; Am. Probation and Parole Assn.; Regional Vice-Pres., Assn. of Paroling Authorities International; Vice-Chrmn., National Joint Ctte., Candn. Assn. of Chiefs of Police and the Federal Correctional Services; Bd. of Dir., Council of Canadian Admin. Tribunals; Knight of the Order of Malta; Home: 66 Dufferin Rd., Ottawa, Ont. K1M 2A6; Office: 340 Laurier Ave. W., Ottawa, Ont. K1A 0R1.

**DAGENAIS, Yves,** C.G.A.; museum executive; b. Montreal, Que. 21 May 1938; s. Armand D. and Marguerite (Caron) D.; m. Louise d. Cécile and Alexandre Mailhot 25 June 1960; children: Sylvain, Lucie, Céline, Julie; DEPUTY DIRECTOR, NATIONAL GALLERY OF CANADA 1988– ; Dept. of Nat. Revenue (Taxation) 1955–62; Prov. Transport Enterprises 1962–80; Vice-Pres., Finan. & Admin., Murray Hill Limousine Serv. Limited 1980–82; Dir., Admin. & Finan., Montreal Mus. of Fine Arts (Acting Dir. on 2 occasions) 1982–88; Mem., Cert. Gen. Accts. Assn.; Assn. des dipl. de l'Ecole des Hautes Etudes Commerciales; Roman Catholic; recreations: golf, bridge, swimming; Home: Orleans, Ont.; Office: 380 Sussex Dr., P.O. Box 427, Stn. A., Ottawa, Ont. K1N 9N4.

**DAHL, Marilyn Olive,** O.B.C., R.N., B.Sc.N., M.A.; association executive; nurse; educator; b. Broderick, Sask. 12 Feb. 1931; d. Melferd Bernard and Bertha Olga (Anderson) Finnestad; e. Hoey (Sask.) High Sch. 1948; Victoria Hosp. Sch. of Nursing Prince Albert R.N. 1953 (general proficiency award); Univ. of B.C., B.Sc.N. 1979; Simon Fraser Univ. M.A. 1988; Univ. of B.C. Ph.D. candidate; m. Lloyd Theodore s. Helge and Jonetta Dahl 12 Sept. 1956; children: Marshall Andrew, Howard Stewart, Valerie Joan; PRES., CANADIAN DEAF AND HARD OF HEARING FORUM 1993– ; and PRES., INTERNAT. FEDERATION OF HARD OF HEARING PEOPLE (IFHOH) 1992– ; Nursing Supvr. Victoria Hosp. Prince Albert 1953–54; Swift Current Union Hosp. 1954–55; Saskatoon Univ. Hosp. 1955–56; Charge Nurse Dr. Rygiels Children's Hosp. Hamilton, Ont. 1969–71; Clin. Nurse Riverview Psychiatric Hosp. Coquitlam, B.C. 1971–77; Instr. Douglas Coll. Faculty of Nursing 1980–88; Rsch. & Cons. Hearing Health Care 1979– ; disabled consumer advocate 1980– ; Sec., Candn. Hard of Hearing Assn. 1983–84, 1st Vice Pres. 1984–85; Pres. 1985–92; mem. Steering Ctte. to form Candn. Deaf & Hard of Hearing Forum 1987–89, Vice Pres. 1989–92; Vice Pres. Internat. Fedn. Hard of Hearing (IFHOH) 1988–92; Ed., IFHOH Journ. 1990–92; writer/producer weekly children's TV prog. Medicine Hat 1967–69; author teaching video for hosps. 'Caring for the Patient Who is Hard of Hearing' 1979; various publs.; numerous nat. and internat. presentations & briefs consumer advocacy; named 'Canada's Foremost Advocate for the Hard of Hearing'; awarded Order of British Columbia 1993; Commemorative Medal for 125th Anniversary of Candn. Confederation 1993; mem. RNABC; Candn. Nurses Assn.; Alumni UBC; Alumni SFU; Can. Fed. of Univ. Women; Vancouver Bd. of Trade; Lutheran; recreations photography, sketching, hiking; Home: 1457 Morrison St., Port Coquitlam, B.C. V3C 2N6; IFHOH Office: Radegunerstrasse 10, 8045 Graz, Austria.

**DAHLIE, Hallvard,** B.A., B.Ed., M.A., Ph.D.; educator; b. Ringsaker, Norway 14 Feb. 1925; s. Christian and Elsie (Widing) D.; e. Smithers (B.C.) High Sch.; Univ. of B.C. B.A. 1950, B.Ed. 1956, M.A. 1964; Univ. of Wash. Ph.D. 1967; m. Betty d. John William and Olive McKay 4 Sept. 1950; children: Brenda Gayle, Brant Christian, Lisa, Mark William; PROF. OF ENGLISH, UNIV. OF CALGARY 1976– ; Seaman C.G.S. 'Alberni' B.C. Coast 1941–42; served with RCN 1942–43; High Sch. Teacher various B.C. schs. 1951–65; Asst. Prof. present Univ. 1967, Assoc. Prof. 1971, Head of Eng. 1974–79, Killam Resident Fellow 1982; author 'Brian Moore' 1969, 'Brian Moore' 1981; 'Alice Munro and Her Works' 1985; 'Varieties of Exile: The Canadian Experience' 1986; 'Isolation and Commitment: Frederic Philip Grove's Settlers of the Marsh' 1993; ed. 'The New Land as Literary Theme' 1978; mem. Assn. Candn. Univ. Teachers Eng.; Assn. Advanc. Scandinavian Studies in Can. (Liaison Offr. 1982– ;); recreations: skiing, canoeing, golf; Home: 3639 7A St. S.W., Calgary, Alta. T2T 2Y6; Office: 2500 University Dr. N.W., Calgary, Alta. T2N 1N4.

**DAIGNEAULT, Jean-Charles;** retired banker; b. St-Cesaire, Que. 13 Nov. 1930; s. Charlemagne and Marie-Jeanne (Yelle) D.; e. Coll. St-André de St-Cesaire; m. Lise d. Ernest and Imelda Lanoie 23 Aug. 1954; children: Michèle, Luce, Guy; DIR., BANQUE NAT. DE PARIS; 25 years with Bank of Montreal, mgr. of several branches during last 10 years; joined Banque Nat. de Paris 1971; retired as Sr. Vice-Pres. & Gen. Mgr., Que. 1989; Dir., Les Indus. Amisco Inc.; Groupe Sani-Mobile Inc.; La Soc. Candn. du Cancer, Qué.; Churchwarden, Paroisse St.-François de Sales, Longueuil, Qué.; recreations: hunting, fishing, golf; club: Country Club of Montreal; Home: 882 Laviolette, Longueuil, Que. J4J 4R3; Office: 1981 McGill College Ave., Montreal, Que. H3A 2W8.

**DAILLEY, Gordon D.,** B.A.; business executive; b. Toronto, Ont. 6 June 1941; s. Gordon Debenham and Virginia Mae (Johnston) D.; e. Univ. of N.B. B.A. 1964; m. Sara B. d. Edward and Mary Gibson 14 July 1970; children: Susan E., Timothy J.G., Jessica C.; PRES. & GENERAL MANAGER, AFRICAN LION SAFARI 1969– ; Officer, Royal Canadian Navy 1964–69; Pres., Attractions Ontario 1987, 1988; Dir., Tourism Ontario 1989, 1990; Tourism Industry Assn. of Canada 1991, 1992; The Honourable Michael Wilson's Prosperity Initiative 1992; Anglican; Mem., Royal Canadian Military Institute; recreations: skiing, skating, travelling; Home: 40 Brant Rd. N., Cambridge, Ont. N1S 2W2; Office: R.R. 1, Cambridge, Ont. N1R 5S2.

**DAINARD, James Alan,** B.A., M.A., B.L.S., Ph.D.; university professor; b. Golden, B.C. 26 May 1930; s. Courtland James and Harriet Agnes (Sanborn) D.; e. Victoria College 1949; Univ. of B.C. B.A. 1951, Teachers' Training 1952–53; M.A. 1961, B.L.S. 1962; Univ. of Alberta Ph.D. 1967; m. Norma d. Giovanni and Maria Zumello 26 May 1964; PROF., DEPT. OF FRENCH, UNIV.OF TORONTO 1989– ; Teacher, South Peace Jr.-Sr. High 1953–56; Marker, Course-writer, H.S. Correspondence Sch., Dept. of Edn., Victoria B.C. 1957–61; Reference Librarian, Metro Toronto Library 1962–63; Instr., then Asst. Prof., Romance Languages, Univ. of Alta. 1963–68; Asst. Prof., French, Univ. of Toronto 1968–72; Assoc. Prof. 1972–89; editor: 'Editing Correspondence' 1979; contbg. editor: 'Correspondance générale d'Helvétius' vols 1, 2, 3 1981– ; General Ed., 'La Correspondance de Madame de Graffigny' vols 1, 2, 3 1985– ; Home: 73 Bernard Ave., Toronto, Ont. M5R 1R6; Office: University College, Toronto, Ont. M5S 1A1.

**DAKSHINAMURTI, Krishnamurti,** M.Sc., Ph.D., F.R.S.C. (U.K.); scientist educator; b. Vellore, India 20 May 1928; s. Sattanamcheri Venkataswami Krishnamurti and Kamakshi (Sundaradekshadar); e. Univ. of Madras, B.Sc. 1946; Univ. of Rajputana, M.Sc. 1952, Ph.D. 1957; m. Ganga Bhavani, d. S. Venkataraman, Madras, India, 28 Aug. 1961; children: Shyamala Lalitha, Sowmya Sowmitri; PROF. OF BIOCHEM. AND MOLECULAR BIOL., UNIV. OF MANITOBA since 1973; Visiting Prof. Rockefeller Univ., N.Y., 1974–75; Sr. Lectr. in Biochem. Christian Med. Coll., Vellore, India, 1952; Research Assoc. in Nutritional Biochem., Univ. of Ill. 1957; Research Assoc., Mass. Inst. of Technol. 1962; Assoc. Dir. of Research, St. Joseph Hosp., Lancaster, Pa., 1963; joined present Univ. as Assoc. Prof. of Biochem. 1965; rec'd Borden Award, Nutrition Soc. Can. 1973; author of over 200 research publs. and three books; Assoc. Ed.: 'Canadian Journal of Biochemistry'; 'Neuroscience Letters'; Fellow: Roy. Soc. of Chemistry (U.K.); Candn. Coll. of Neuropsychopharmacology; Internat. Coll. of Nutrition; Am. Coll. of Nutrition; Pres., Internat. Coll. of Nutrition; mem.: Am. Soc. Biochem. & Molecular Biol.; Soc. for Neuroscience; Am. Soc. Neurochem.; Am. Inst. Nutrition; Am. Soc. for Cell Biology; Am. Diabetes Assn.; Candn. Biochem. Soc.; Biochem. Soc. (UK); Nutrition Soc. Can., Internat. Soc. Neurochem., Internat. Brain Rsch. Org.; Charter Mem.: Serotonin Club; Amer. Soc. of Hypertension; Pres., India School of Dance, Music and Theatre, Winnipeg; Hindu; Home: 934 Crestview Park Dr., Winnipeg, Man. R2Y 0V7; Office: Faculty of Medicine, Univ. of Manitoba, Winnipeg, Man. R3E 0W3.

**DALE, James,** M.A., Ph.D.; educator; b. Mussoorie, UP, India 11 July 1931; s. James Henry and Winifred Blanche (Potter) D.; e. Reed's Sch. Cobham, Surrey, Eng. 1949; Fitzwilliam Coll. Cambridge B.A. (Eng. Tripos) 1955, M.A. 1959, Ph.D. 1961; m. Patricia May Bowman 1960, div. 1976; children: Robert, Alison, D. Alexander; m. Jennifer Beck 1980; ASSOC. PROF. OF ENG. McMASTER UNIV. 1967– ; Supr. (Tutor) Cambridge Univ. 1956–59; Lectr., Asst. Prof., Univ. of Winnipeg 1959–65; Asst. Prof. Trent Univ. 1965–67; Visiting Prof.: Univ. of Toronto Grad. Dept. of Eng. 1972; Flinders Univ. of S. Australia 1981 and Sr. Rsch. Fellow Centre for Rsch. in New Lits. in Eng. 1981, Sustaining mem. since 1982; assessor SSHRC rsch. & publ. grants; supr./external examiner various postgrad. theses; recipient Tyndale Scholarship Biblical Rsch. 1955–57; Exhn. (Minor Scholarship) Fitzwilliam Coll. Cambridge 1958–59; Can. Council Rsch. Grants 1960, 1971; co-ed. 'J. Wesley: A Collection of Hymns for the People Called Methodists (1780)' 1983; contbr.: 'A Milton Encylopedia' 1978–83; 'The Contribution of Methodism to Atlantic Canada' 1992; numerous articles Charles Wesley, Commonwealth Lit. and Milton, book reviews; Life mem. Milton Soc. Am.; Candn. Soc. Renaissance Studies; Candn. Soc. Ch. Hist.; Charles Wesley Soc. (Charter mem. and Dir. 1990); mem. Exec. Candn. Assn. Commonwealth Lang. & Lit. Studies 1978–80; Anglican (lay reader); recreations: classical music, walking, reading; Club: Cambridge Union Soc.; Home: 19 Kipling Rd., Hamilton, Ont. L8S 3X2; Office: Hamilton, Ont. L8S 4L9.

**DALE, Robert Gordon,** D.S.O., D.F.C., C.D., A.D.C.; b. Toronto, Ont. 1 Nov. 1920; s. Dr. Gordon McIntyre andHelen Marjorie (Cartwright) D.; e. Univ. of Toronto Schs., 1930–39; Univ. of Toronto, Trinity Coll. 1939–40, Business Adm. Cert. Course 1946; m. Mary Austin, d. H.A. Babcock, Toronto, Ont., 3 Apr. 1948; two s.; Robert Austin, John Gordon; CHRMN. & DIR., UPPER LAKES GROUP INC.; Past Chrmn., Candn. Extve. Services Orgn.; Dir., ULS Capital Corp.; Thornmark Capital Corp.; joined Maple Leaf Mills Ltd. 1947; apptd. Plant Mgr., Toronto 1957; Gen. Prod. Mgr. 1961; Asst. to Pres. 1965; Extve. V. Pres. & Dir. 1967; Pres. and C.E.O. 1969–81; Chrmn. and C.E.O. 1981–85 (retired); joined RCAF 1940; served with RAF Bomber Command and Pathfinder Force 1941–45; retired with rank Sqdn. Leader 1945; Pres. (1972) Air Cadet League of Can. (Hon. Pres. 1983); Hon. Lt. Col., 400 Squadr. (Air Reserve) Candn. Armed Forces; Dir., Sunnybrook Medical Centre Inst.; Dir., Bloorview Childrens' Hosp. Foundn.; Chrmn., Candn. Corps of Commissionaires (Toronto and region); Aide-de-Campe to Lt. Gov. of Ontario; Past Chrmn. Extve Comte., Trinity College; mem., Bd. Trade Metrop. Toronto; Phi Kappa Pi; P. Conservative; Anglican; recreations: tennis, squash, golf, fishing; Clubs: Empire; Rosedale Golf; Badminton & Racquet; National; Royal Candn. Mil. Inst.; Home: 103 Dawlish Ave.,

Toronto, Ont. M4N 1H4; Office: 49 Jackes Ave., Toronto, Ont. M4T 1E2.

**DALE, William Scott Abell,** M.A., Ph.D., F.R.S.A.; b. Toronto, Ont. 18 Sept. 1921; s. late Ernest Abell and late Mary (Bulloch) D.; e. Univ. of Toronto Schs.; Univ. of Toronto (Trinity), B.A. 1944, M.A. 1946; Harvard Univ. (1946–48), Ph.D. 1955; Courtauld Inst., London Univ., 1948–50; m. Jane Gordon, d. late Albert T. Laidlaw, Toronto, Ont. 19 Apr. 1952; children: Michael William, John Randall, Thomas Ernest Abell; PROFESSOR EMERITUS, UNIV. OF WESTERN ONT. 1987– ; with National Gallery of Canada, 1950–57; Curator, Art Gallery of Toronto, 1957–59; Director, Vancouver Art Gallery, 1959–61; Asst. Dir., Nat. Gallery of Canada 1961–66, Acting Dir., 1965–66, Depy. Dir., 1966–67; Chairman, Fine Art (now Visual Arts) Dept., Univ. of W. Ont., 1967–75, 1985–87; Prof., Visual Arts Dept., Univ. of W. Ont. 1967–87; Res. Fellow, Dumbarton Oaks Research Library & Collection, Washington, 1956–57; served in 2nd World War with Royal Navy, Fleet Air Arm., 1944–45; author of articles and book reviews in 'Art Bulletin,' 'British Museum Yearbook,' 'Burlington Magazine,' 'Canadian Art' 'RACAR' and 'Speculum'; mem., Coll. Art. Assn. of Am.; Medieval Acad. of Am.; Royal Soc. of Arts; Internat. Center of Medieval Art; Universities Art Assn. of Can.; Address: 1517 Gloucester Rd., London, Ont. N6G 2S5.

**DALES, Samuel,** M.A., Ph.D., F.R.S.C.; educator; b. Warsaw, Poland 31 Aug. 1927; s. James and Helen (Ochs) D.; e. Tadcaster Grammar Sch. Yorks. Eng. 1943; Univ. of B.C. B.A. 1951, M.A. 1953; Univ. of Toronto Ph.D. 1957; m. late Laura Lilli Ruth d. late Emil Fischer 1952; children: Adam Charles, Pamela Ann; PROF. EMERITUS OF MICROBIOL. & IMMUNOLOGY, UNIV. OF W. ONT. 1993; Prof. 1976–93; Chrmn. 1976–80; Post-Doctoral Fellow, Nat. Cancer Inst. Can. 1957–60; Asst. Prof. The Rockefeller Univ. New York 1961–65; Assoc. Prof. OSC N.Y. Univ. 1966–69, Research Prof. 1969–76; author book chapters and over 130 scient. papers, reviews on cell-virus interactions and virus diseases; mem. Ed. Bd. 'Virology,' 'Journal of Cell Biology,' 'Virus Research'; 'Microbial Pathogenesis'; 'Journal of Virology'; 'Encyclopedia of Virology'; advisory and consultation U.S. Publ. Health Service, Medical Res. Council of Canada; mem. Fed. Socs. Exper. Biol.; Harvey Soc.; Am. Soc. Cell Biol.; The Josiah Macy Jr. Foundation Faculty Scholar 1981–82; Fellow, Royal Soc. of Can. 1989; Home: 1588 Hillside Dr., London, Ont. N6G 2P8; Office: London, Ont. N6A 5C1.

**DALFEN, Charles Marvin,** B.A., B.Phil., LL.L.; barrister and solicitor; b. Montreal, Que. 23 Feb. 1943; s. Abraham and Fay (Axelrad) D.; e. McGill Univ., B.A. 1964; Oxford Univ., B.Phil. 1966; Univ. of Ottawa, LL.L. 1969; m. Susannah d. Bernard and Alyce Cohen 27 Dec. 1966; children: Ariel Katherine, Deborah Maya; Tutor, Oxford Univ. 1965–66; Asst. then Assoc. Prof., Carleton Univ. 1967–72; Legal Advr. (Dir., Legal & Regulatory Br.), Dept. of Commun., Govt. of Can. 1970–72; Prof. of Law, Univ. of Toronto 1972–74; Dep. Min., Transport & Commun., Govt. of B.C. 1974–76; Vice-Chrmn., CRTC 1976–80; private law practice 1980– ; Broadcasting Arbitrator, Can. Elections Act 1984–89; Pres., Dalfen Assoc. Cons. Inc. 1980– ; Gov., Internat. Counc. of Computer Commun. 1973–91; Mem., Bd. of Eds., Cable TV Law & Finance (journal) 1982–93; Mem., Bd. of Dir., InterPares 1982–93; various delegations to U.N. 1969–79; author of numerous articles & reports; recreatons: nordic skiing; clubs: Country Club; Home: 472 Tillbury Ave., Ottawa, Ont. K2A 0Y7; Office: 1700 – 275 Slater St., Ottawa, Ont. K1P 5H9.

**DALGETTY, Douglas Robert,** A.I.C.B.; banker; b. Fort Frances, Ont. 22 Mar. 1941; s. Lewis Cleveland and Lillian Mae (Gross) D.; e. Fort Frances H.S.; Univ. of Man.; m. Sharon d. Peter and Marianne Reimer 8 May 1965; children: Maureen, Russell; EXTVE. VICE PRES., CANADIAN WESTERN BANK, May 1988– ; Royal Bank of Can. 1969–81; Vice Pres., Noram Devel. Corp. 1981–83; Dir. & Prin., Colchester Investments Ltd. 1981–84; Asst. Vice Pres., Commercial Lending, Western & Pacific Bank 1985; Vice Pres. 1985–86; Sr. Vice Pres. 1986–87; Extve. Vice-Pres., 1987–88; Pres., Colchester Investments Ltd.; Dir., Canadian Western Bank; Canadian Western Bank Leasing Ltd.; mem. Domestic Policy Ctte., Candn. Bankers Assoc.; mem., Hong Kong Canada Bus. Assoc.; B.C. Chamber of Comm.; Vancouver Bd. of Trade; recreations: hunting, fishing, swimming, tennis; Clubs: Terminal City; Richmond Rod & Gun; Home: 6358 Crescent Crt., Delta, B.C. V4K 4Y5; Office: 900 – Two Bentall Centre, 555 Burrard St., Vancouver, B.C. V7X 1M8.

**DALGLEISH, Donald Scott;** food industry executive; b. Smiths Falls, Ont. 28 May 1935; s. John James and Marguerite Elizabeth (Johnson) D.; e. Smiths Falls C.I. 1954; Univ. of Toronto 1968; Business Univ. of Waterloo 1965; Univ. of W. Ont. Marketing 1972; York Univ. Adv. Mktg. 1974; Harvard Univ. Mktg. Management 1991; m. Claudette d. Thomas and Jeannette Balfe 30 April 1955; children; Adrian, Hugh, Paula; PRESIDENT & GENERAL MANAGER, ALORO FOODS INC. 1980– ; Dominion Stores Ltd. 1954–55; Gamble-Robinson Ltd. 1956–58; Sales Rep., General Mills Canada Ltd. 1959; Vice-Pres. 1975–80; recruited by Fairmont Foods Ltd. to 'sell' or 'close' Aloro Foods 1980; purchased Aloro Foods 1982 & repositioned co. to a branded producer & major exporter of Aloro products; Dir. & C.E.O., Aloro Foods Inc.; Protestant; recreations: reading, bridge, golf; Home: 55 Palmer Circle, Cedar Mills, R.R. 2, Bolton, Ont. L7E 5R8; Office: 1201 Fewster Dr., Mississauga, Ont. L4W 1A2.

**DALGLISH, Keith Gordon,** B.A., F.C.A.; executive; b. Toronto, Ont. 20 Feb. 1930; s. late T. Gordon and late Kate I. (Pearson) D.; e. Univ. of Toronto Schs. 1948; Trinity Coll. Univ. of Toronto B.A. 1952; Univ. of W. Ont. Mang. Training Course 1979; m. Gail E. d. late George B. Bagwell, Q.C., Toronto, Ont. Sept. 1958; children: Tracy, Todd, Ian, Alison; SR. PARTNER, PEAT MARWICK THORNE; joined Price Waterhouse, Toronto 1953–60; Secy.-Treas. ICT (Canada) Ltd. Toronto 1960–62; Partner, Thorne Gunn Helliwell & Christenson, Toronto 1963–67; Pres. George Weston Ltd. Toronto 1968–69; Partner, Peat Marwick Thorne, Toronto 1969– ; mem. Inst. C.A.'s Ont. (Pres. 1981–82); Can. Inst. of C.A.'s (Gov. 1979–83, 91–93; Chrmn. 1993–94); Candn. Tax Foundation; recreations: golf, curling; Clubs: Toronto; Toronto Golf; Granite; Home: 65 Douglas Dr., Toronto, Ont. M4W 2B2; Office: P.O. Box 122, Scotia Plaza, 40 King St. W., Toronto, Ont. M5H 3Z2.

**DALGLISH, Peter John,** B.A., LL.B.; lawyer, advocate for street children; b. London, Ont. 20 May 1957; s. Francis William and Marianne (Frank) D.; e. Upper Can. Coll. 1969–75; Stanford Univ., B.A. 1979; Dalhousie Law Sch., LL.B. 1983; EXTVE. DIR., STREET KIDS INTERNATIONAL 1987– ; articling student, Stewart, MacKeen and Covert 1984–85; Field Worker, UN World Food Prog., El Geneina & Khartoum, Sudan 1985–86; Dir. of Emergency Unit, UNICEF Sudan 1986–87; author: '1987 UNICEF Report on Working Children, Street Children, Children in Jail, and Child Soldiers in the Middle East and North Africa'; '1992 Report for the United Nations Centre in Vienna on Violence Against Street Children'; co-author: '1992 Report on Street Youth in Papua New Guinea'; recipient, 1987 Vanier Award; 1991 Fellowship of Man Award; Bd. mem., Trails Youth Initiatives; Roman Catholic; recreations: canoeing, sailing, swimming; club: Sudan Club, Khartoum; Home: 350 Crawford St., Toronto, Ont. M6J 2V9; Office: 56 The Esplanade, Suite 202, Toronto, Ont. M5E 1A7.

**DALIBARD, Jacques René Marie Julien,** C.M., M.Sc.Arch., F.R.A.I.C.; architect; executive director; b. Le Mans, France 21 Apr. 1935; s. René Armand and Marie-Louise Josephine (Besnier) D.; e. St. Jean-de-Bethune, Versailles; Lycée du Mans, France; Univ. de Lille; Bristol Univ.; McGill Univ., B.Arch. 1964; Columbia Univ., M.Sc.Arch. 1971; m. Rina d. Pesach and Dora Barkai 16 Sept. 1979; one s. Joël-David; EXEC. DIR. THE HERITAGE CANADA FOUNDATION 1978– ; Sr. Exhibit Designer Candn. Pavilion Expo '67 1964–67; Chief Restoration Arch. & Dir. Parks Can. 1968–77; Special Adv. UNESCO cultural heritage Cyprus 1975–77; Prof. of Arch. & Dir. Historic Preservation Div. Grad. Sch. Arch. Planning & Preservation Columbia Univ. 1977–78; mem. Candn. Comn. for UNESCO; Founding mem. and Pres.: Nat. Ctte. Internat. Council Monuments & Sites (Exec. Ctte., Treas.-Gen.); Assn. Preservation Technol. (Past Pres., Founding Editor, APT Bulletin); mem. Ont. Assn. Archs.; recipient ICOMOS Warsaw Medal 1980; Médaille de la Ville de Québec 1987; D.Eng. (Hon.), Tech. Univ. of N.S. 1988; Member, Order of Canada 1991; Commemorative Medal, 125th Anniversary, Candn. Confedn.; author numerous conservation publs.; recreations: swimming, fishing, boating, golf; Home: 263 Clemow Ave., Ottawa, Ont. K1S 2B5; Office: 306 Metcalfe St., Ottawa, Ont. K2P 1S2.

**DALINDA, Tom,** B.Comm., C.A.; finance and accounting professional; b. Toronto, Ont. 30 April 1956; e. Univ. of Toronto B.Comm. 1980; C.A. 1984; m. Ausra Vaitkus 1978; children: Aurelia, Matthew, Eric; VICE-PRESIDENT, ANNUITY DIVISION, NATIONAL LIFE ASSURANCE CO. OF CAN. 1993– ; joined Peat Marwick 1980 as an accountant & attained C.A. designation, left as Sr. Accountant 1985; Div. Comptroller, National Life 1985; held various positions of increasing responsibility; most recently Vice-President & Comptroller 1989–93; Pres., Supervisory Ctte., Parama Credit Union; Home: 7 Crediton Court, Etobicoke, Ont. M9B 3B9; Office: 522 University Ave., Toronto, Ont. M5G 1Y7.

**DALLAIRE, Raymond;** industrialist; b. St-Hénédine. Qué. 16 Feb. 1932; s. late Albert and Règine (Lacasse) D.; e. St-Hénédine, (Que.) and Coll. des Marianistes, St-Anselme, Qué.; m. Rolande, d. late Clément Fortier, 12 Feb. 1966; two d. Andrée, Caroline; PRESIDENT AND DIR., P.H.-TECH INC., P.H.-TECH INTERNATIONAL INC., P.H.-TECH CORP. (U.S.), P.H.-TECH EURO S.A. (FRANCE); Pres., Raymaca Inc.; Vice Pres., Les Industries Dallaire Ltée; Former Dir., Candn. Windows & Doors Mfrs. Assn.; has served in various capacities constr. field Que., Ont. and B.C.; co-founded Dallaire Enterprises Inc. 1958, Quincaillerie Panoramique Inc. 1962, Plastique Futurama Inc. 1964; above firms merged under present name in 1971; named 'Man of the Year' by Soc. Plastics Indust. Can. 1974; rec'd The CWDMA C.P. Loewen Award 1987; holds Candn. and foreign patents window and constr. industs.; co-founder Quebec Nordiques Hockey Club; mem. Soc. Plastics Indust. Can.; Soc. Plastics Engrs. Inc.; Candn. Window and Door Mfrs. Assoc.; Comité Can.; Un. Inventors Scientists; Chambre de Comm. de Prov. Qué.; Candn. Standards Assn. (Chrmn., CSA Plastic Window Standard Ctte.); Chrmn., CGSB Sliding Doors Standard Ctte.; mem. Insul. Glass Mfrs. Assn.; Nat. Woodworkers Mfrs. Assn.; Nat. Assn. of Home Builders; R. Catholic; recreations: golf, skiing, ski-dooing, physical fitness; Home: 587 de la Falaise, Lévis, Qué. G6W 1A4; Office: 8650 de la Rive-sud Blvd., Lévis, Qué. G6V 7M5.

**DALLA-VICENZA, Mario Joseph,** C.A., C.M.A., M.B.A., F.C.M.A.; steel industry executive; b. Sudbury, Ont. 30 Oct. 1938; s. Mario V. and Cecelia (Bonaldo) D.; e. Queen's Univ. C.A. 1962; McMaster Univ. C.M.A. 1969; Lake Superior State Univ. M.B.A. 1982; Fellow, Soc. of Mngmt. Accountants of Canada 1993; m. Deanna Karen d. Lucien and Vivian Leblanc 15 July 1961; children: Janice, Peter, Mark; SR. VICE-PRES. & CHIEF FINAN. OFFR., IPSCO INC. 1988– ; C.A. pub. practice with Tessier Massicotte & Co. 1957–63; Steel Extve. ending as Gen. Mgr., Corp. Acctg., Algoma Steel Corp. Ltd. 1963–82; joined IPSCO Inc. 1983; Mem., Inst. of C.A.s (Current 2nd Vice Pres., Inst. for the Prov. of Sask.); Past Pres. Sault Ste. Marie Chap.); Soc. of Mngt. Accts. (Past Dir. & Chrmn., Nat. Audit Ctte.; Past Pres. & Counc. Mem., Sask.); clubs: Wascana Golf & Country, Assiniboia; Home: 1614 Hannon Bay, Regina, Sask. S4V 0S8; Office: P.O. Box 1670, Regina, Sask. S4P 3C7.

**DALPÉ, Jean Marc,** B.A.; comédien / auteur; né. Ottawa, Ont. 21 fév. 1957; f. Aurèle et Blanche (Nix) Dalpé; é. Université d'Ottawa, BAC.en théâtre 1976; Conservatoire d'art dramatique de Qué. 1979; Co-fondateur, Théâtre de la Vieille 17 1979; Artiste en rés. au Théâtre du Nouvel-Ont. 1981–88; Ecrivain en rés. à l'Univ. d'Ottawa 1987; Ecrivain en rés. du Festival des Francophonies, Limoges, France 1990; Prix du Nouvel-Ont. 1988; Prix du Gouverneur-General, théâtre 'Le Chien' 1989; auteur: 'Les murs de nos villages' 1979, 'Gens d'ici' 1981, 'Et d'ailleurs' 1984 (poésie); 'Le Chien' 1987 (théâtre); co-auteur: 'Hawkesbury Blues' 1982, 'Nickel' 1984 (théâtre); résidence: 5593 Hutchison St., Montréal, Qué. H2V 4B5.

**DALRYMPLE, Brian Ellsworth,** A.O.C.A.; forensic analyst; b. Toronto, Ont. 23 Sept. 1947; s. Elgin John and Jessie Marie (Becking) D.; e. Ont. Coll. of Art 1970; Sheridan Coll. (Biol. Photog.) 1980; m. Johnna Lee d. John and Betty Thompson 3 Nov. 1973; children: Stephen John, David Robert; MANAGER, FORENSIC IDENTIFICATION SERVICES, ONT. PROV. POLICE 1993– ; began work as forensic analyst 1972; initiated res. project into fingerprint detection by laser 1976, a technique now used by police depts. throughout the world; Sr. Forensic Analyst, Ont. Prov. Police 1980–93; instruct., Cdn. Police Coll., Ont. Police Coll., RCMP HQ., Sheridan Coll.; John Dondero Meml. Award 1980; Award of Merit, Inst. of Applied Sci. 1980; Foster Award 1982; Lewis Minshall Award 1984; Mem., Internat. Assn. for Identification; author various articles on fingerprint detection by laser; recreation: canoeing; Office: 90 Harbour St., Toronto, Ont. M7A 2S1.

**DALTON, Dennis Martin,** B.A., C.A.; real estate development executive; b. Barrie, Ont. 19 Jan. 1945; s. Ernest Matthew and Doris (Croft) D.; e. Univ. of Western Ont. B.A. 1967; C.A. (Ont.) 1971; m. Karen d. Gazo and Sophie Pokol 25 Mar. 1983; children: Jessica Mary, James Michael; EXTVE. VICE-PRES., SIFTON PROPERTIES LIMITED 1974– ; Johnson, Stewart, Bourne, Brown & Co. (C.A.s) 1967–72; Powertronic Equipment Ltd. (Mfgr.) 1973; Dir., Sifton Properties Limited; DDK Investments Ltd.; W-G Construction Ltd.; The Lady's a Champ Ltd.; 936461 Ont. Limited; 825086 Ont. Inc.; recreations: skiing, golf, tennis, squash; clubs: London Club; Beaver Creek Club; London Hunt and Country; London Squash Racquets; Lake of Bays Tennis; Lake of Bays Sailing; Home: 123 Tamarack Cres., London, Ont. N6K 3J6; Office: Box 5099, Terminal 'A,' London, Ont. N6A 4M8.

**DALTON, Marcia E. (Marty);** association executive; b. Pompton Lakes, N.J. 26 Nov. 1929; m. Charles H. Dalton April 1953; children: Karen Ann, Charles Scott; Pres., National Chapter of Canada IODE 1992–94; Home: London, Ont.; Office: 254, 40 Orchard View Blvd., Toronto, Ont. M4R 1B9.

**DALTON, Mary Vivian,** B.A., M.A.; university professor; b. Lake View, Harbour Main, Nfld. 11 June 1950; d. John and Ellen Joseph (Hawco) D.; e. Shamrock School; St. Joseph's School; Univ. of Toronto B.A. (Hons.) 1972; Memorial Univ. of Nfld. M.A. 1975; Univ. of Liverpool, Canada Council Doctoral Fellow; formerly married to Gordon Macdonald Rowsell; ASST. PROF., DEPT. OF ENGLISH, MEMORIAL UNIV. OF NEWFOUNDLAND 1989– ; Canada Council Fellow / Tutor, Univ. of Liverpool 1975–78; Contract Lectr., Memorial Univ. of Nfld. and freelance writer 1978–84; Lectr. in English, Memorial 1984–89; writing workshops in poetry, Writers' Alliance & Nfld. Writers' Guild; poetry readings for univs., schools, writers' orgns.; radio scripts for Nfld. CBC School Broadcasts series; Mem., Writers' Alliance of Nfld. & Lab. (Vice-Pres. 1988–89); Candn. Assn. for Irish Studies; Irish Nfld. Assn.; Resource Centre for the Arts; co-editor / co-publisher of Nfld.'s lit. mag. 'TickleAce' 1980–86; author: 'The Time of Icicles' 1989, 'Allowing the Light' 1993 (collections of poems); poems, reviews, interviews, articles in var. regional, nat. & internat. journals; recreations: gardening, swimming, yoga; Home: 15 Flavin St., St. John's, Nfld. A1C 3R8; Office: St. John's, Nfld. A1B 3X9.

**DALY, Eric,** B.A., M.B.A.; real estate executive; b. Ottawa, Ont. 13 Jan. 1948; s. Donald James and Madeleine Margaret (Thrasher) D.; e. Queen's Univ. B.A. (Hons.) 1970; York Univ. M.B.A. 1980; m. Catharine d. Ken and Marion Joyce 21 June 1984; children: Heather, Colleen, Sheelagh; VICE-PRESIDENT, INFORMATION SERVICES, ROYAL LEPAGE 1989– ; Salary Analyst, Canada Trust 1971–74; Regional Manager, Admin., Canada Housing & Mortgage Corp. 1975; Asst. Vice-Pres., Operational Planning, Canada Trust 1976–80; Area Mgr. & Mgr., Admin., Canada Trust 1980–85; Vice-Pres., Corp. Planning, Trilon Financial Corp. 1985–89; Anglican; Past Master, Bedford Masonic Lodge; active in Masonry; recreations: running, curling, motorcycling; club: Toronto Cricket; Office: 39 Wynford Dr., Don Mills, Ont. M3C 3K5.

**DALY, Kerry Joseph Eugene,** B.A., M.Sc., Ph.D.; university professor; b. Kitchener, Ont. 19 May 1955; s. Thomas L. and Marie L. (Dosman) D.; e. Carleton Univ. B.A. 1977; Univ. of Guelph M.Sc. 1982; McMaster Univ. Ph.D. 1987; m. Helen Theresa d. Stan and Leona Hudecki 21 May 1977; children: Johanna Bridget, Benjamin Stephen; PROFESSOR, DEPT. OF FAMILY STUDIES, UNIV. OF GUELPH 1987– ; co-author: 'The Adoption Alternative for Infertile Couples' (Report to Royal Comn. on New Reproductive Technologies) 1993, 'Adoption in Canada' 1993; co-editor: 'Qualitative Methods in Family Research' 1992; Home: 58 Tiffany St. W., Guelph, Ont.; Office: Guelph, Ont. N1G 2W1.

**DALY, Martin,** M.A., Ph.D.; educator; b. Toronto, Ont. 15 Nov. 1944; s. James A. and Ida (Simon) D.; e. Univ. of Toronto B.A. 1967, Ph.D. 1971; McGill Univ. M.A. 1968; PROF. OF PSYCHOL. AND BIOL. McMASTER UNIV. 1982– ; Postgrad. Fellow Nat. Rsch. Council Can. 1968–71, Postdoctoral Fellow 1971–73; Postdoctoral Fellow Sci. Rsch. Council Gt. Brit. 1973–74 Univ. of Bristol and Centre de Recherches sur les Zones Arides, Beni-Abbès, Algeria; Asst. Prof. Univ. of Cal. 1977; Assoc. Prof. present Univ. 1978; Visiting Scholar Harvard Univ. 1984–85; Fellow J.S. Guggenheim Found. 1989; Fellow Center Advanced Study Behavioral Sci's Stanford 1989–90; Treas. Internat. Soc. Behavioral Ecol. 1988–90; Pres., Human Behavior & Evolution Soc. 1991–93; co-author: 'Sex, Evolution and Behavior' 1978, 2nd ed. 1983; 'Homicide' 1988; numerous sci. jour. articles; mem. various ed. bds.; Office: Hamilton, Ont. L8S 4K1.

**DALZELL, Alexander,** B.Litt., M.A.; university professor; b. Belfast, N. Ireland 8 May 1925; s. Thomas and Jeannie Evelyn (Beattie) D.; e. Methodist Coll., Belfast; Trinity Coll., Dublin B.A. 1950, M.A. 1953, B.Litt. 1956; m. Ann d. Percy and Edna Steel 21 Aug. 1954; children: Catherine Jane, Thomas George; PROF. EMERITUS, TRINITY COLL., UNIV. OF TORONTO 1988– ; Lectr., Kings Coll., Univ. of London 1951–53; Univ. of Sheffield 1953–54; Lectr., Trinity Coll., Univ. of Toronto 1954–56; Asst. Prof. 1956–63; Assoc. Prof. 1963–68; Prof. 1968–88; Dean of Arts 1968–73; Vice Provost 1972–79; Acting Provost 1973, 1979; Hon. Fellow 1990– ; Pres., Classical Assn. of Can. 1980–82; Mem., Pub. Ctte., Am. Philological Assn. 1981–84; Ed. Bd., 'Collected Works of Erasmus'; Assoc. Ed., 'Phoenix' 1960–64; Editor 1964–71; Robson Lectr., Victoria Coll., Toronto, Oct. 1990; Contbr. (with Sir Roger Mynors & James Estes), 'Correspondence of Erasmus: Vol. 10' (Toronto) 1992; also contbr. to classical jours. and one book chapter; Home: 344 Saunders St., Fredericton, N.B. E3B 1N8.

**D'AMOURS, Alban,** M.A.; administrateur Adm.A.; né. Sainte-Françoise, Qué. 9 juillet 1940; f. Lucien et Imelda (Bouchard) D.; e. Univ. Laval M.A.; Univ. de Minnesota (études de doctorat); ép. Denise f. Yvonne et Donat Périgny; enfants: Sophie, Geneviève; INSPECTEUR ET VÉRIFICATEUR GÉNÉRAL DU MOUVEMENT DES CAISSES DESJARDINS À LA CONFÉDÉRATION DES CAISSES POPULAIRES ET D'ÉCON. DESJARDINS DU QUE. 1994– ; Prof. titulaire à l'Univ. de Sherbrooke 1969–81 (Dir. du dép. d'écon. 6 ans); Sous-ministre du Revenu du Qué. 1981–86; Sous-ministre associé à l'Energie 1986–87; Premier Vice-Prés. Planification, Communications, Marketing à la Conf. des caisses pop. et d'écon. Desjardins du Qué. 1988–90; Premier vice-prés. et chef du Développement et de la Vérification à la Conf. des caisses pop. et d'écon. Desjardins du Québec 1991–93; Mem. du Conseil d'admin. de la Caisse populaire des Fonctionnaires du Qué. 1982–87; Dir., 'L'Actualité économique' 1969–81; Prés. du syndicat des prof. de l'Univ. de Sherbrooke 1969–81; intervenant auprès de plusieurs organismes de dév. écon. rég.; siège sur différents conseils d'admin.: Grands Ballets Canadiens 1991– ; Violons du Roy (Pres.) 1991– ; Assn. des écon. du Qué. (Prés.) 1991–92; Pres. du Conseil d'admin. de la Télé-univ. 1992– ; Mem., Conseil de l'Ecole de gestion de l'UQAM 1993– ; Com. cons. de Globe 92; Inst. de rech. en pol. publique 1993– ; Inst. qué. de planification financière 1990–92; auteur de plusieurs ouvrages et articles sci. dans le domaine des pol. écon. et indus.; bureau: 100, avenue des Commandeurs, Lévis, Qué. G6V 7N5.

**DAMPIER, John Lawrence,** M.B.E., B.A.; executive; b. Strathroy, Ont. 29 Dec. 1914; s. Lawrence Henry and Edith Isabel (English) D.; e. Ridley Coll., St. Catherines, Ont., 1932; Univ. of W. Ont. B.A. 1936; m. Hilda Margaret Ingram, 17 June 1939; children: Hillarry Elizabeth (Mrs. Raymond Gamlin), Lawrence Paul, Marjorie Anne (Mrs. Kiben Williams), Helen Louise (Mrs. R.A. Wilson); Dir., B.C. Bearing Engineers Ltd.; Northwest Sports Enterprises Ltd. (Vancouver Canucks); joined Lever Bros. Ltd., Toronto, 1936–39; Sales Mgr., 1945–47; el. a Dir. 1947–50; trans. as Vice Pres., Lever Bros. Co. New York City, 1950; Vice-Pres., McCann-Erickson (Can.) Ltd., 1953–57; Asst. Publisher, Vice-Pres., Dir., The Vancouver Sun 1957–68; served with N.P.A.M., Q.O.R. of Can., 1936–39; Q.O.R. of Can., C.A. Overseas, 1939–42; HQ 3 Cdn. Inf. Div., 1942–45; M.B.E.; Order of Oranje-Nassau; Past Pres., Past Gov., Vancouver Board of Trade; Past Pres., Hon. Vice Pres., Boy Scouts of Can.; Past Pres., Patron Vancouver Public Aquarium; Past Gov., Vancouver Foundation; recreations: model railroading, boating, fishing; Club: Vancouver; Homes: 305, 5475 Vine St., Vancouver, B.C. V6M 3Z7 and Box 41 Seacrest, Nanoose Bay, B.C. V0R 2R0.

**DANBY, Frederick William,** M.D., FRCPC, DABD, FAAD; dermatologist; b. Victoria, B.C. 10 May 1943; s. Charles William E. and Margaret Lucy (Campbell) D.; e. Kingston C.V.I. 1961; Queen's Univ. M.D. 1967; m. Lynette Joan d. Maurice and Lynette Margesson 26 June 1975; children: Dawn Lynette, Claire Somerset; internship, Vanc. Gen. Hosp.; residencies in internal med., St. Francis Hosp. (Honolulu) & Hotel Dieu & Kingston Gen. Hosps.; res. in dermatol., Univ. of Toronto; Chief Res. (Derm.) Toronto Gen. Hosp. 1972–73; Cons. Staff, Kingston Gen., Hotel Dieu & St. Mary's of the Lake Hosps.; Chrmn. & Asst. Prof., Div. of Dermatol., Queen's Univ.; Past Pres., Profl. Assn. of Interns and Res. of Ont. 1972; Kingston Acad. of Med. 1985; Sec.-Treas., Candn. Dermatol. Assn. 1987–92; Mem., Candn. & Ont. Med. Assns.; recreations: windsurfing, skiing, shooting; clubs: Fort Henry Guard Club of Can.; Home: 234 Alwington Pl., Kingston, Ont. K7L 4P8; Office: 190 Wellington St., 4th Floor, Kingston, Ont. K7L 3E4.

**DANBY, Kenneth Edison;** artist; printmaker; b. Sault Ste. Marie, Ont. 6 March 1940; s. M.G. Edison and Gertrude (Buckley) D.; e. Sault Tech. & Comm. High Sch.; Sault Coll. Inst.; Ont. Coll. of Art Toronto 1958–60; children: Sean, Ryan, Noah; one-man exhns. incl.: Gallery Moos Toronto 1964, 1965, 1967–72, 1974–79, 1982–83, 1985; Galerie Godard Lefort Montreal 1966; Cologne (Germany) Kunsmarkt 1969; William Zierler Gallery New York 1972, 1973; Images Gallery Toledo, Ohio 1972; Nancy Poole Gallery London, Ont. 1972; Galerie Allen Vancouver 1975; Continental Art Agencies Vancouver 1973; Fleet Gallery Winnipeg 1973; Galerie Moos Montreal 1974; Algoma Arts Festival Sault Ste. Marie 1975; Retrospective Exhn. S. Ont. circulated by Kitchener Waterloo Art Gallery 1974–75; Candn. Consulate New York 1977; deVooght Galleries Vancouver 1977, 1980; Arras Gallery New York 1977; Wallack Galleries Ottawa 1974; 25 Years: Retrospective, MacDonald-Stewart Gall., Guelph, Ont. 1988; Gall. Moos, N.Y. 1989; rep. numerous group shows Can., USA, Europe, rep. perm. colls. Museum of Modern Art, Montreal Museum of Fine Art, Art Inst. Chicago,Nat. Gallery Can.; comns. incl. designs for Series III Olympic Coins 1976; recipient, Jessie Dow Award for best painting Montreal Exhn. Drawings & Watercolours, Nat. Gallery Can. 1964; Queen's Silver Jubilee Medal 1977; R. Tait McKenzie Chair for Sport, Nat. Sport & Recreation Centre Ottawa 1975; mem., Royal Canadian Academy; Bd. of Dirs., Canada Council 1985–91; Bd. of Trustees, Nat. Gall. of Can. 1991–94; incl. in various bibliogs.; Address: R.R. 4, Guelph, Ont. N1H 6J1.

**DANCEY, Travis Eugene,** B.A., M.D., C.M.; psychiatrist; b. Alymer (West), Ont. 22 Dec. 1905; s. Leon Eugene and Phoebe Alberta (Travis) D.; e. Aylmer Public and High Schs.; McGill Univ. (combined course), B.A. 1930, M.D., C.M. 1934, L.M.C.C. 1934; Cert. Specialist in Psychiatry, R.C.P. & S.(C) 1946, Que. C. of P. & S. 1950; m. Marjorie Janet, d. Dr. John Robertson McEwen, Huntington, Que. 17 Aug. 1935; one s. John Travis, M.D.; CONSULTING STAFF, DEPT. OF PSYCHIATRY, MONTREAL GEN. HOSP. 1990– ; Assoc. Prof. of Psychiatry, McGill Univ.; Rotating Interne, Montreal Gen. Hosp. 1934–35; Post-grad. training and Res. Psychiatrist, Verdun Prot. Hosp. 1935–42; Dist. Psychiatrist, Montreal Area 1942–44; Specialist in Psychiatry, No. 1 Neurol. Hosp., England 1944; C.O., No. 1 Candn. Exhaustion Unit, N.W. Europe, 1944 to end of war; discharged with rank of Major; Dir., Dept. of Psychiatry, Queen Mary Veterans Hosp.,and Adviser in Psychiatry to Dir. Gen. of Treatment Services, Dept. of Veterans Affairs 1945–69; private practice in psychiatry 1945–92; Mem., Bd. of Govs., Montreal Gen. Hosp.; mem., N.D.G. and Montreal West Sr. Citizens Coun. 1978– ; (mem. of Health Ctte.); mem. of Session Knox Crescent and Kensington Chs., Montreal; elected Chrmn., Residents' Council of Griffith McConnell Residence, Côte St. Luc 1994– ; Awarded Hon. Mem., Candn. Medical Soc. on Alcohol and Other Drugs 1990; Address: 5790 Parkhaven Ave., Apt. 620 & 621, Côte St. Luc, Qué. H4W 1Y1.

**DANCY, Keith Jules;** broadcasting executive; b. Toronto, Ont.; m. Jeannine Margaret (Walker); children: Robert, David, Melissa, Elizabeth, Michelle; PRES. NIAGARA BROADCASTING CORP., CJRN 710 INC.; began as High Sch. Reporter with CFRB, Toronto 1945–47; Announcer CHVC Niagara Falls, Ont. and CKDO, Oshawa, Ont. 1947; Announcer/writer with Northern Broadcasting, Kirkland Lake and Peterborough, 1948, CFNB Fredericton 1949; Announcer, Sports Dir. and Sales Mgr. at CFCF Montreal 1950–58; Mgr. CKSL London, Ont. 1959; co-founded CFOX Montreal and was Extve. Vice Pres. and Gen. Mgr. 1960–67; commentator 'Hockey Night in Canada' TV series, Montreal Canadiens 1960–67; founded CKJD Sarnia 1968; merged his interests with Rogers Broadcasting and named Pres. and Dir. 1971; purchased CJJD Hamilton 1977, CJRN Niagara Falls 1978; founded CJFT, Ft. Erie/Buffalo 1986; Niagara Broadcasting Corp. 1990; CKEY - FM 101.1 Niagara 1991; Past-Pres., Toronto Broadcast Extve. Soc.; former Rotary Club mem., London, Sarnia and Port Credit, Ont.; Past Pres., Lakeshore Rotary, Montreal, Que.; mem., CAB Quarter Century Club; recreations: tennis, swimming, boating, golf; Clubs: Long Boat Key Golf Tennis (Florida); White Oaks Tennis Club (St. Catharines); Home: Box 1620, Niagara-on-the-Lake, Ont. L0S 1J0; Office: Box 710, Niagara Falls, Ont. L2E 6X7.

**D'ANDREA, Antonio,** Dottorato in Filosofia, F.R.S.C.; b. Messina, Italy 22 Nov. 1916; s. Nunzio and Italia (Bassi) D'A.; e. High Sch. Messina 1931, Liceo

Classico Messina 1934; gained first place Concorso competition admission Scuola Normale Superiore, Pisa 1934; Univ. of Pisa, Dottorato in Filosofia 1939; EMERITUS PROF. OF ITALIAN, McGILL UNIV. 1986– ; chargé de cours Univ. of Pisa 1944–45; Visiting Prof. McGill Univ. 1949, Assoc. Prof. 1956–64, Prof. 1964–86; Emeritus Prof. 1986– ; Chrmn. of Italian 1964–76; Dir. Italian Cultural Inst. Montreal 1962–64; Pres. F.C.A.C. Que. Dept. Educ. 1971–73; Pres. Sous-comité d'évaluation Conf. des Recteurs 1976–78; Visiting Prof. of Italian Univ. of Cal. 1978; rec'd Stella della Solidarietà italiana; Grande Ufficiale, Ordine al Merito della Repubblica (Italiana); Queen's Silver Jubilee Medal; co-ed. 'Discours contre Machiavel' 1974; 'Yearbook of Italian Studies' 1971–75; author 'Il nome della storia' 1982; 'Struitture inquiete' 1993; various articles; Vice Pres., Can. Mediterranean Int.; mem. Candn. Soc. Italian Studies (Past Pres.); Assn. des Profs. d'Italien du Qué. (Past Pres.); Candn. Soc. for Renaissance Studies; Hon. Fellow, A.I.S.L.I.; Royal Soc. of Canada; Home: 66 Sunnyside Ave., Westmount, Que. H3Y 1C2; Office: Samuel Bronfman Bldg., 1001 Sherbrooke St. W., Montreal, Que. H3A 1G5.

**DANE, Nazla L.;** retired public relations consultant; b. Indian Head, Sask., 6 June 1906; d. John James and Nazla (Atolla) D.; e. Heward (Sask.) Cont. Sch.; Regina (Sask.) Coll. Inst.; Regina (Sask.) Normal Sch.; taught pub. and secondary sch. in Sask. 1925–33, during last 2 yrs. was Princ. of sch. in Cadillac; held positions in business organs. in Regina, Vancouver and then in Depts. of Munitions and Supply and Transport, Ottawa, during World War II; apptd. Dir., Educ. and Women's Divs., Candn. Life Ins. Assn. 1945–71; has been active in Candn. Pub. Relations Soc. (Toronto Branch), Women's Candn. Club, Toronto, Toronto and Area Council of Women, Inter-Club Council for Women in Pub. Affairs Toronto, Soroptimist Club Toronto, YWCA of Can.; served as mem. Bd., VON Toronto and Metro Toronto Legal Services; has been Club, Prov. and Nat. Pres., Candn. Fed. of Business & Prof. Women's Clubs (Life mem. 1966); Vice Pres. and mem. Extve., Internat. Fed. of Business & Prof. Women, 1968, Pres. 1971 (Immediate Past Pres. and U.N. Chrmn. 1974–77); received Queen Elizabeth Silver Jubilee Medal 1977; rec'd Persons Award from Gov. Gen. Jeanne Sauvé 1985; recreations: reading, writing, volunteer work, Canadiana; Address: 55 Belmont St., Toronto, Ont. M5R 1R1.

**D'ANGELO, Frank;** courier service executive; b. Toronto, Ont. 23 Nov. 1955; s. Agostino and Graziella (Napoleone) D.; e. Wilfrid Laurier Univ. 2 yrs.; York Univ. 1 yr.; m. Margaret-Anne d. James and Marie McCabe 5 Jan. 1979 (Nassau) and 4 Aug. 1979 (Toronto); children: Rina-Lee, Mathew Dean; CO-FOUNDER, PRESIDENT, CO-OWNER, THE MESSENGERS 1986– ; Personal Insur. Sales Rep., Liberty Mutual 1979–82 (top 3 out of 900+ sales reps in N. Am. 1982); Co-Founder & Vice-Pres., Downtown Express Couriers 1982–84; worked for several large nat. courier companies 1984–86; The Messengers is the only courier serv. on Bay St. serving Canada's financial heart; would like to become a member of Speakers Bureau of Right to Life; Vice-Pres., Les Massagers Montreal; Pres., Central Courier Depot Inc.; 2nd Vice-Pres., The Metro. Toronto & Area Right to Life Assn. 2 yrs. & Bd. Mem. 2 yrs.; active in raising awareness and support for unwed mothers among peers & community; Mem., Business For Life; Campaign Life Coalition; The Family Coalition Party of Ont.; Charter Mem., The Sacred Heart King Knights of Columbus 1990– ; Chair, Family Life Ctte.; recreations: reading, re-exploring youth with children and wife; Home: 221 Burton Grove, P.O. Box 2012, King City, Ont. L0G 1K0; Office: 350 Bay St., Toronto, Ont. M5H 2S6.

**DANIEL, Alan Keith;** illustrator; b. Ottawa, Ont. 12 June 1939; s. Lyman Keith and Grace Edna D.; e. McMaster Univ. 1956; Univ. of Toronto 1958; m. D. Lea d. Merle and Jean Smith 2 Feb. 1963; children: Timolin, Melissa, Jeffrey; freelance artist for over 30 years; started with jr. educational books; has created jackets for books by Anne Hebert, Pierre Berton, Farley Mowat, Chirstopher Moore, Gordon Pinsent; official posters for 1984 Olympics, the 1984, '85 Canada Day posters and many others; a series of annual report covers for Equitable Life of Can.; many historical books, children's books, a movie, a TV commercial, record jackets, etc.; included in Treasures, Candn. Children's Book Illustration prod. by The Children's Book Centre; included in show Canada at Bologna 1990; Co-winner, Toronto IODE Book Award 1993; Early Childhood News Director's Choice Award 1992; Mem., CANSCAIP; major books illustrated: 'The Magician's Trap' 1976, 'Bunnicula: A Rabbit Tale of Mystery' 1979, 'How Lazy Can You Get?' 1979, 'Flying and Swimming Creatures from the Time of the Dinosaurs' 1981, 'Les bêtes étonnantes du temps des dinosaures' 1981, 'The Baitchopper' 1982, 'In Praise of Cats' 1974, 'This Big Cat and Other Cats I've Known' 1985, 'The Orchestra' 1989, 'The Difficulty of Living on Other Planets' 1987, 'Good Families Don't' 1990, 'Return to Howliday Inn' 1992, 'The Story of Canada' 1992, 'The Grand Escape' 1993, 'Rabbit-Cadabra' 1993, 'The Bunnicula Fun Book' 1993, 'Bunnicula Esapes!' 1994; 23 Books for the Song Box pub. by the Wright Group 1990–94; recreations: canoeing, walking; Address: 59 Meadowlane Dr., Kitchener, Ont. N2N 1E8.

**DANIEL, C. William,** O.C., B.A.Sc., LL.D., P.Eng.; industrialist; b. Toronto, Ont. 17 Feb. 1925; s. late Thomas Edward and Emily Anna (Hicks) D.; e. John Ross Robertson Pub. Sch. and Lawrence Park Coll. Inst., Toronto; Univ. of Toronto, B.A.Sc. (Mining Engn.) 1947; m. Ruth Elizabeth, d. late Dr. Harry Roberts Conway, 27 Dec. 1947; children: David William, Colleen Elizabeth (Mrs. Greg Sumner), Karen Louise (Mrs. H. Terrence Kelly), Robert Conway; Dir., Wellesley Hospital Foundation; Andrés Wines Ltd.; Bank of Montreal; Bankmont Financial Corp.; Bechtel Canada Inc.; Bechtel Québec Limitée; BCE Inc.; Canfor Corp.; Mutual Life Assurance Co. of Canada; joined Royal/Dutch Shell Group of Companies as petroleum engr. in 1947; various assignments U.S., the Netherlands, Venezuela, Trinidad and Canada; apptd. Pres. & C.E.O., Shell Canada Ltd. 1974; retired 1985; mem.: Assn. Prof. Engrs. Ont.; United Church; recreations: golf, fishing, skiing; Club: Rosedale Golf; Office: c/o Bank of Montreal, 302 Bay St., 4th Flr., Toronto, Ont. M5X 1A1.

**DANIEL, John S.,** M.A., D.Sc.; educator; b. Banstead, U.K. 31 May 1942; s. John Edward and Winifred (Sagar) D.; e. Christ's Hosp. Sussex 1961; Oxford Univ. (St. Edmund Hall) B.A. 1964, M.A. 1969; Univ. of Paris D.Sc. 1969; Thorneloe Univ. A.Th. 1992; Hon. D.Litt. Deakin Univ. (Australia) 1985; Hon. D.Sc. CMR St. Jean 1988; Hon. D.Ed. CNAA (UK) 1992; Hon. LL.D. Waterloo 1993; Hon. Fellow, St. Edmund Hall, Oxford 1991; m. Kristin d. Herbert and Joyce Swanson 30 July 1966; children: Julian, Anne-Marie, Catherine; VICE CHANCELLOR, THE OPEN UNIVERSITY, U.K. 1990– ; Asst./Assoc. Prof. Ecole Polytechnique Univ. de Montréal 1969–73; Visiting Lectr., Open Univ., U.K. 1972; Dir. des études Télé-université, Univ. du Qué. 1973–77; Vice Pres. Learning Services Athabasca Univ. 1978–80; Vice-Rector, Academic, Concordia Univ. 1980–84; Pres., Laurentian Univ. 1984–90; National Defence Coll. 1989–90; Pres., Internat. Council Distance Educ. 1982–85; Candn. Soc. Study Higher Educ. 1982–83; Chair, Candn. Higher Education Rsch. Network 1985–87; Pres., Candn. Assoc. for Distance Education 1988; Mem., Council of Found., Internat. Baccalaureate 1992; Mem., Higher Education Quality Council (UK) 1993; Mem., Bd. of Trustees, Carnegie Foundation for the Advancement of Teaching 1993; recipient Distinguished Young Mem. Award Am. Soc. Metals; Officier de l'Ordre des Palmes Académiques (France); ed. 'Learning at a Distance: A World Perspective' 1982; author or co-author over 100 publs. chem., metall., communications, educ. technol.; recreation: swimming, word-processing; Home: Wednesden House, Aspley Guise, Milton Keynes MK17 8DQ; Office: The Open Univ., Milton Keynes MK7 6AA, U.K.

**DANIEL, Patrick D.,** B.Sc., M.A.Sc.; pipeline executive; b. Edmonton, Alta. 15 Aug. 1946; s. Clarence Darold and Catherine Bannerman (MacLeod) D.; e. Univ. of Alberta B.Sc. 1968; Univ. of B.C. M.A.Sc. 1970; m. Dora Lynne Mah Ming d. Jack and Song Mah Ming 18 July 1970; children: Jarrod, Paul; VICE-PRES., PLANNING, INTERPROVINCIAL PIPELINE 1988– ; Staff Engineer, Hooker Chemicals 1970–72; Mgr., Systems, Hudsons Bay Oil & Gas 1972–82; Gen. Mgr., Systems, Home Oil 1982–86; Dir., Planning, Interhome Energy 1987–88; Dir., Alta. Chamber of Resources; Mem., Van Horne Inst.; Sr. Advisory Council, Crohn's & Colitis Found. of Canada (Edmonton); Office: 3100 Bow Valley Square 2, 205 – 5th Ave. S.W., Calgary, Alta. T2P 2V7.

**DANIELS, Arthur Francis;** public servant; b. Toronto, Ont. 11 June 1944; s. Arthur F. and Florence Esther (Kay) D.; e. Univ. of W. Ont., B.A. ( Hons.) 1966; Univ. of Toronto, dip. Bus. Admin. Labour Rel. 1967; children: Spencer, Timothy, Arthur Jr., Patrick; ASST. DEPY. MIN., REGISTRATION DIVISION, MIN. OF CONSUMER & COMMERCIAL RELATIONS; Reg. Personnel Administrator, Min. of Correctional Serv. 1966–70; Mgr., Labour Rel. 1970–73; Dir. of Personnel 1973–78; Extve. Dir., 1978–82; mem. of Federal-Provincial Task Force on Victims of Crime 1982–83 (publ. 1983); Candn. Rep., Duke of Edinburgh Commonwealth Study Conf. U.K. 1983; Asst. Depy. Min., Opns., Ont. Min. of Community & Social Services 1982–86; Asst. Depy. Min., Planning, Human Resources Secretariat 1986–88; Conference Bd. of Canada, North Am. Study Tour on Quality 1993; Extve. Ctte., Inst. of Public Admin.; Dir., Operation Springboard; Vice-Chrmn., Peterborough Personnel Assn.; Bd. Mem., Ont. Assn. of Criminology & Correction; Mem., Public Personnel Assn.; Internat. Halfway House Assn.; Am. Probation Assn.; Probation Officer Assn. of Ont.; Internat. Assn. of Social Welfare; Ont. Assn. of Municipal Soc. Serv.; Students Coun. Award, King Coll., Western; Frank Neilson Award, John Howard Soc. Toronto Award of Merit; J. Howard Soc. Waterloo Achievement Award; Internat. Halfway House Assn. Award of Merit; Goodwill of Toronto Award; Chatelaine Best Companies to Work for in Canada, I.P.A.C. Award for Mgmt. Innovation; author of articles in assn. journals; recreations: cross country skiing, hiking; Home: 28 Forsyth Cres., Toronto, Ont.; Office: 4th Flr., 393 University Ave., Toronto, Ont. M5G 1E6.

**DANIELS, James Maurice,** M.A., D.Phil. F.R.S.C., C. Phys., F. Inst. P., F.R.S.A.; b. Leeds, Eng., 26 Aug. 1924; s. Bernard and Mary Mahala (Proctor) D.; e. Cross Flatts Sch., Leeds, 1929–35; Leeds (Eng.) Grammar Sch., 1935–42; Jesus Coll., Oxford Univ., B.A. 1945; M.A. 1949, D.Phil. 1952; children: Ian Nicolas James, Maurice Edward Bruce; PROFESSOR EMERITUS; PROF. OF PHYSICS, UNIV. OF TORONTO 1961–87 (Chrmn. Physics Dept. 1968–73; Chrmn. Dept. of Statistics 1983–84); Exper. Asst., Radar Research and Devel. Estab., Malvern 1944–46; Tech. Offr., I.C.I. Explosives 1946–47; Nuffield Fellow, Oxford Univ. 1951–52 and I.C.I. Fellow 1952–53; Asst. Prof., Univ. of B.C. 1953–56, Assoc. Prof. 1956–60, Prof. 1960–61; UNESCO 'Expert,' Univ. of Buenos Aires, Dec. 1958–Jan. 1959; Visiting Prof., Instituto de Fisica Bariloche, Argentina 1960–61; Visiting Prof., Low Temp. Lab., Helsinki Univ. of Technology 1974; Visiting Prof., Columbia Univ. 1978–79; Visiting Sr. Rsch. Physicist, Princeton Univ. 1984–85; Visiting Prof., École Normale Supérieure, Paris, France 1985–86; Visiting Prof., National Tsing Hua Univ., Hsinchu Taiwan 1990 and 1991–92; has served on various govt. comtes.; author 'Oriented Nuclei: Polarized Targets and Beams' 1965; other writings incl. over 80 publs. in various journs.; Alfred P. Sloan Fellow; Guggenheim Fellow; socio activo de la Asociacion Fisica Argentina; mem. Amer. Physical Soc.; Candn. Assn. of Physicists; N.Y. Acad. of Sciences; Chartered Physicist; Fellow Inst. Phys. (London); Roy. Soc. Arts (London); recreation: skiing, mountaineering; Home: 40 Cranbury Rd., Princeton Junction, N.J. 08550.

**DANIELS, Mark R.,** B.Com., Ph.D.; b. Vancouver, B.C. 15 June 1938; s. John Edgar and Mabel Emily (Hillyer) D.; e. Univ. of B.C., B.Com. 1961; Johns Hopkins Univ. Ph.D. 1965; m. Cindy Hick d. Ermanno and Maria Forza 11 Sept. 1982; children: Ryder, Gray, Aeron; PRES., CDN. LIFE & HEALTH INSURANCE ASSOC. INC. 1989– ; Econ. Policy Fellow, Brookings Inst. Washington, D.C. 1968–69; Asst. Prof. Economics, McGill Univ., Montreal 1965; Asst. Prof. Economics, Brown Univ. Providence, R.I. 1966–71; Dir., Effectiveness Evaluation Div. Treasury Bd. Secretariat 1971–73; Asst. Depy. Min. Planning & Coordination Dept. Regional Econ. Expansion 1973–79; Sr. Asst. Secy. to Cabinet Econ. Policy Privy Council Office 1979–81; Asst. Depy. Min. Econ. Programs & Govt. Finance Dept. Finance Canada 1981–82; Depy. Min. Labour Canada 1982–85; Depy. Min. Consumer & Corporate Affairs Canada 1985–87; Chrmn. & C.E.O., PAI-Public Affairs International 1987–89; Mem., Adv. Counc., Fac. of Commerce and Bus. Admin., Univ. of B.C.; Mem., Bd. of Dirs., Cdn. Native Arts Found.; Office: 1 Queen St. E., Ste. 1700, Toronto, Ont. M5C 2X9.

**DANIELS, Ronald Joel,** B.A., LL.B., LL.M.; associate professor of law; b. Toronto, Ont. 16 July 1959; s. Phillip D. and Helen Nanette (Urman) D.; e. Univ. of Toronto B.A. 1982, LL.B. 1986; Yale Univ. LL.M. 1988; m. Joanne Dana d. Larry and Ethel Rosen 23 June 1987; ASSOCIATE PROF., FAC. OF LAW, UNIV. OF TORONTO 1988– ; Rsch. Staff, Ont. Royal Comn. on Asbestos 1981–83; Editor-in-Chief, 'University of Toronto Faculty of Law Review' 1986; articling student, Tory Tory DesLauriers & Binnington 1987; Dir., Internat. Bus. & Trade Law Prog., Ont. Ctr. for Internat. Bus.; Columnist, Financial Post; mem., Toronto Stock Exchange Ctte. on Corporate Governance 1993–94; Chrmn., Ont. Government Task Force on Securities Regulation 1993–94; co-editor: 'Cases and Materials on Partnerships and Canadian Business Corporations'; author of legal articles on corporate law, securities and financial regulation; Home: 95 Wells Hill Ave.,

Toronto, Ont. M5R 3A9; Office: 84 Queen's Park Cres., Toronto, Ont. M5S 2C5.

**DANIELS, W. Douglas,** M.A.; economist; b. North Battleford, Sask. 19 Feb. 1945; s. Charles Wilfred and Ethel Bertha (Blackmore) D.; e. Univ. of Alta. B.A. 1966, M.A. 1971; m. Nancy d. Elmer and Ruth Jonson 1971; two s. Andrew, Evan; SPECIAL ADVISOR, INTERNAT. DEVEL. RSCH. CENTRE 1992– ; joined Makerere Univ. and Dept. Coop. Devel. Uganda 1966–68; Rsch. Offr. Dept. of External Affairs 1971–73; Head of Agric. Econ. Prog. present Centre 1975–79, Assoc. Dir. Planning 1979–80; Dir. Office of Planning and Evaluation 1980–92; Tech. Coordinator est. Internat. Centre for Rsch. Dry Areas, Syria 1973–76; Visiting Fellow Internat. Services for Nat. Agric. Rsch. The Hague; Pres. Soc. Internat. Devel. Ottawa 1990– ; Dir. Candn. Orgn. for Devel. through Edn. 1989– ; mem. Adv. Ctte. Candn. Jour. Devel. Studies 1987– ; Assoc. mem. Comn. Foreign Study Policy 1981; ed. 'Resource Allocation to Agricultural Research' 1982; 'Evaluation in National Agriculture Research' 1987; numerous articles acad. jours.; Office: 250 Albert St., Ottawa, Ont. K1P 6M1.

**DANIS, Marcel,** B.A., M.A., LL.B.; politician; b. 22 Oct. 1943; e. Loyola Coll. 1965; Fordham Univ.; New York; Univ. de Paris; Univ. of Montreal 1971; m. Sandra Jeffrey; two children: Caroline, Christian; Min. of Labour 1991–93; Dir., Legal Aid Office, Concordia Univ.; Prof., Law and Political Sci., Concordia Univ. 1968– ; Visiting Lectr., RCMP Coll., Ottawa 1979–84; Adviser to Premier of Que., then to Que. Min. of Industry and Comm. 1967–68; mem., Que. Bar Assoc.; Candn. Bar Assoc.; el. H. of C. (Verchères) g.e. 1984; re-el. 1988; apptd. Depy. Speaker and Chrmn. of the Cttes. of the Whole House 1984–90; Min. of State (Youth and Fitness and Amateur Sport) and Deputy Govt. House Leader 1990–91; Vice-Chrmn., Cabinet Ctte. on Human Resources, Social and Legal Affairs; Mem., Treasury Bd.; P.C.; recreations: golf, skiing.

**DANJOUX, Cyril E.,** MD, LMCC, DMRT, FRCP(C); university professor; b. Mauritius 16 Aug. 1942; s. Evan Roger and Marcelle (Battour) D.; e. Hebrew Univ., MD 1970; Univ. of Toronto, DMRT 1976; FRCP(C) 1977; m. Judith Goldman Dec. 1968; children: Ilan, Orna, Nathalie; RADIATION ONCOLOGY, TORONTO-BAYVIEW REGIONAL CANCER CENTRE, ONT. CANCER FOUND. 1991– ; Asst. Prof., Univ. of Toronto 1991– ; Cons. Staff, Sick Kids Hosp., Toronto; Active Staff, Sunnybooke Health Science Ctr.; practice interest: Lung and Paediatric Oncology; main rsch. in hyperthermia; Principal Investigator on several active clinical trials; Head, Radiation Oncol. Dept., Ottawa Regional Cancer Ctr. & Asst. Prof., Univ. of Ottawa 1977–91; Chrmn., Ottawa Reg. Cancer Ctr., Med. Adv. Ctte.; Computer Ctte.; Hyperthermia Group; mem., Candn. Med. Assn.; Candn. Oncol. Soc.; Candn. Assn. of Radiation Oncol.; Am. Soc. of Clin. Oncol.; Radiation Rsch. Soc.; Ont. Med. Assn.; N. Am. Hyperthermia Group; Candn. Assn. of Psych. Oncol.; Internat. Gynecol. Cancer Soc.; The Coll. of Phys. & Surg. of Ont.; The Royal Coll. of Phys. & Surg. of Can.; Acad. of Med.; N.Y. Acad. of Sci.; Home: 53 Franmore Circle, Thornhill, Ont. L4J 3B9; Office: 2075 Bayview Ave., North York, Ont. M4N 3M5.

**DANNER, William Edward;** retired pharmaceutical manufacturer; b. Perth, Ont. 16 Sept. 1928; s. late Helen (McNeely) and E.L. Danner; e. public school and Coll. Inst., Perth, Ont.; Univ. of B.C., B.A. 1952; former Pres., Wampole Inc. (Estbd. 1905); former Chrmn., Nonprescription Drug Mfrs. Assoc. of Can.; Clubs: Granite; XPO; Laurentian (Ottawa); Rideau (Ottawa); Links O'Tay Golf (Perth); recreations: golf, fishing, hunting, boating; Address: Box 700, Perth, Ont. K7H 3K5.

**DANSEREAU, Jean-Claude;** retired petroleum executive; political party executive; b. Montreal, Que. 11 July 1930; s. late Gaston and late Flore (Guimond) D.; e. Externat Ste-Croix, Classical Studies; Univ. of Chicago, Adm. Course; m. Jeannine d. late Ls.-Theophile Ayotte 24 Apr. 1954; one d. Danielle; Services Coordinator, Imperial Oil Ltd., joined Co. 1949, retired 1985; former Pres., Les Entreprises J.P.C. Inc.; former Vice Pres. Erenaure Inc.; Regional Dir. (Que.), Lib. Party of Can. 1966, Co-Chrmn. Prov. Convention 1968, Secy. 1968–70 and 1972–79, Acting Pres. 1979, Pres. 1979 and 1982–83, Chrmn. L.P.C. Organ. Comte. 1984–85; mem. Organ. Comte. Jean Lesage Team 1960; Organ. Secy. and Jt. Dir. Trudeau Leadership Team 1968; Qué. Dir. Turner leadership team 1984; Pres., Lib. Assn. Mercier Riding 1971–85; former Vice Pres. Bd. Dirs. Louis-Hyppolite Lafontaine Hosp.; K. of C.; Liberal; R. Catholic; recreations: golf, tennis, swimming; Club: Kiwanis Metropolitan (Past Pres.); Home: 2735 Mercier St., Montreal, Que. H1L 5H8.

**DANSEREAU, Hon. Jean-Paul,** B.A., LL.B.; judge; b. Montréal, Qué. 7 Apr. 1921; s. Clovis and Laurette (Piché) D.; e. Externat classique Ste-Croix B.A. 1942; Univ. de Montréal LL.B. 1945; m. Gabrielle d. Georges and Anna Manseau 12 Oct. 1946; m. 2ndly Marie-Paule d. J. Anthony and Brigitte Kennedy 30 July 1990; children (from previous marriage): Jean-Paul jr., Hélène, Michel; JUDGE, QUEBEC SESSIONS COURT 1975–..; called to Bar of Qué. 1946; cr. Q.C. 1962; gen. law practice until present appt.; Asst. Enforcement Counsel Wartime Prices & Trade-Bd. 1946–47; Partner, Bertrand, Grégoire & Dansereau 1947–53; Grégoire, Dansereau, Daoust & Associates 1953–73; Dansereau, Daoust, Duceppe, Beaudry, Rouleau, Filion & Jolicoeur 1973–75; Mun. Court Judge: cities of St-Léonard and Rivière-des-Prairies 1960–65, cities of Montréal-Est and Pointe-aux-Trembles 1965–75; Prosecutor for Dept. of Revenue (Qué.) Sales Tax Div. 1961–67; mem. Disciplinary Ctte. Bar of Montréal 1967–75; mem. Bd. Fondation Charles-Lemoyne; Pres. Young Libs. Assn. Montréal-Maisonneuve 1947–50; Founding mem. Fédération Libérale du Qué. 1955; mem. Adv. Council Nat. Lib. Fedn. Can. 1958; Founding Ctte. Fédération Libérale du Can. (Qué.) 1966; Pres. Constitution Ctte. 1958–62; Hon. mem. Regt. Les Fusiliers Mont-Royal; K. of C.; Kinsman; R. Catholic; Liberal; recreation: reading.

**DANSEREAU, Pierre,** C.C. (1969), G.O.Q., B.Sc., D.Sc., F.R.S.C.; university professor (emeritus); b. Montréal, Qué. 5 Oct. 1911; s. Jean-Lucien and Marie (Archambault) D.; e. Coll. Ste-Marie, B.A. 1931; Inst. Agricole d'Oka, B.Sc. (Agric.) 1936; D.Sc. Univ. de Genève 1939; hon. degrees: Univ. of N.B. 1959, Sir George Williams 1971; Univ. of Sask., LL.D. 1959; Univ. de Strasbourg 1970; Sherbrooke 1971; Memorial 1974; Guelph 1973; Western Ont. 1973; McGill 1976; Ottawa 1978; Royal Mil. Coll. (St-Jean) 1990; Univ. Laurentienne 1993; Dr. Environmental Studies Waterloo 1972; m. Françoise, d. Henri Alexandre Masson, 29 Aug. 1935; Prof. of Ecol., Centre de Recherche en Sciences de l'Environnement, Univ. du Qué. à Montréal 1972–76; Prof. Emeritus, Univ. du Qué. à Montréal since 1976; mem. Science Council of Can. 1968–73; Vice Pres. Candn. Comte for the Internat. Biol. Program 1969; Bot., Montréal Bot. Gdn., 1939–42; Dir., Service de Biogéographie, Montréal, 1943–50; Asst. and Assoc. Prof. Dept. of Bot., Univ. of Mich., 1950–55; Dir., Inst. Botanique, Univ. de Montréal, and Dean, Faculty of Science, 1955–61; Asst. Dir., N.Y. Bot. Gdn., Prof. of Bot. and of Geog., Columbia Univ., 1961–68; Prof. Institut d'Urbanisme, Université de Montréal, 1968–71; Scientific Dir., Centre de Recherche Écologique de Montréal, 1971–72; Trustee, Cranbrook Inst. of Science, Mich., 1953–62; received Médaille Fermat, Toulouse, 1960; Consejero de Honor – Consejo Superior de Investigaciones Científicas, Madrid, 1960; Massey Medal, Royal Canadian Geog. Soc. 1973; co-winner of Molson Prize 1974; NATO Sen. Scientist Fellowship 1977; Prix Esdras-Minville 1983; Prix Marie-Victorin 1983; Izaak Walton Killam Prize (Canada Council) 1985; Ordre national du Qué. 1985 (Pres. 1987); Lawson Medal, Candn. Botanical Assn. 1986; Lifetime Achievement Award (Environment Canada) 1989; Prix Interamerica 1990; Quebec Youth Education Excellence prize 1990; Grand Prix du Mérite forestier 1990; Grand Offr., Ordre National du Québec 1992; author: 'Biogeography: An Ecological Perspective' 1957; 'Contradictions & Biculture' 1964; 'Inscape and Landscape' 1973; 'La terre des hommes et le paysage intérieur' 1973; 'Harmony and Disorder in the Canadian Environment' 1975; 'Harmonie et désordre dans l'environnement canadien' 1980; 'Essai de classification et de cartographie écologique des espaces' 1985; 'Les dimensions écologiques de l'espace urbain' 1987; 'Interdisciplinary perspective on production - investment - control processes in the environment' 1990; 'L'envers et l'endroit: le désir, le besoin et la capacité' 1991; ed. 'Challenge for Survival: Land, Air, and Water for Man in Megalopolis' 1970; contrib. to many Candn. and foreign journs.; also chapters in several books; author, series of films on environment for TV; Pres. Candn. Mental Health Assn. (Que. Div.) 1972–74; Vice-Chrmn. Candn. Env. Adv. Council 1972–76; member, Ecological Soc. of Amer. (Vice Pres. 1969); Royal Soc. of Canada; Royal Soc. N.Z. (hon.); Candn. and Am. Geog. Socs.; R. Catholic; recreation: swimming, skiing; Home: 76 Maplewood, Outremont, Montréal, Qué. H2V 2M1.

**DANSON, Andrew;** photographer; designer; b. Bournemouth, Eng. 12 Jan. 1945; s. Bertram Wolfe and Theodora (Markowitz) D.; e. Univ. of Guelph 1967; one child: Akira; First Exhn. 1974; 16 solo exhns. 1975– , 25 group exhns.; Curator 2 exhns. Yr. of the Child Show Toronto 1979, Documentary Styles Show Burlington 1988; Guest Lectr. Meml. Univ. Nfld. 1983; Official Photographer '76 Olympics; rep. in private and pub. colls.; Can. Council Awards, Secy. of State Award and part-time teaching positions 1976–79; Authored Candn. Best Seller 'Unofficial Portraits' 1987; Guest Lectr., Emily Carr College of Art & Design 1987; Portrait series of Great Canadian Authors for Candn. Booksellers Assoc.; author 'Unofficial Portraits' 1988; Mag. articles, 'Art Magazine' 1979, 1989; 'Macleans' 1982, 1987; 'Books in Canada' 1987; 'Vanguard' 1988; 'Camera Canada' 1988; 'American Photographer' 1988; Collections: City of Toronto Archives; Candn. Mus. of Contemp. Photog.; Nat. Archives Can.; recipient, Can. Council Awards; Secy. of State Award; Ont. Arts Council Awards; Art Directors Club of Toronto Award 1988 (editorial photo journalism); First Prize Colour Photo, International Assn. of Business Communications (IABC) 1988; mem. Toronto Photographers Workshop; Candn. Assn. Photogs. & Illustrators in Communication; Address: 289A Monarch Park, Toronto, Ont. M4J 4T2.

**DANSON, Hon. Barnett J.,** P.C. (1974); b. Toronto, Ont. 8 Feb. 1921; s. late Joseph B. and late Sadie W. D.; e. Pub. and High Schs., Toronto; m. Isobel, d. J. Robert Bull, London, Eng., 6 Feb. 1943; four s.: Kenneth B., John A.H., Timothy S.B., Peter T.J.; CONSULTANT; Dir., Algoma Central Corp.; el. to H. of C. for York N. in g.e. 1968; re-el. 1972 and 1974; Parlty. Secy. to Prime Min. 1970–72; Min. of State for Urban Affairs 1974–76; Min. of Nat. Defense 1976–79; Consul Gen. for Canada, Boston 1984–86; Danson Corporation Limited established 1953; Former Chrmn. & Dir., The Dehavilland Aircraft of Can. Ltd.; served with Q.O.R. of Canada 1939–45; rank Lt. on discharge; Hon. L.Col. Q.O.R. of C., 1974–9; Dir., Atlantic Council; Organization for Rehabilitation through Training; Dir. Emeritus, Candn. Counc. on Native Business; Chrmn., Inst. for Political Involvement; Dir. & Chrmn., Nat. Co-ordinating Ctte., CESO (Candn. Extve. Services Orgn.); Dir., Candn. Inst. for Strategic Studies; Candn. Counc. of Christians & Jews; Empire Club of Can.; Jewish; recreation: fishing; Clubs: Donalda; Craigleith Ski; Home: 1501 – 1132 Bay St., Toronto, Ont. M5S 2Z4.

**DANZIGER, Kurt,** M.Sc., D.Phil., F.R.S.C.; b. Breslau, Germany 3 June 1926; s. Ludwig and Margarethe D.; e. Univ. of Cape Town M.Sc. 1948; Oxford Univ. D.Phil. 1952; m. Flora d. Wilhelm and Rosa de Swardt 5 Dec. 1970; children: Ruth, Eve, Peter; PROF. OF PSYCH. YORK UNIV. 1965– ; prior to 1965 held acad. positions and conducted rsch. univs. Australia, S.Africa and Indonesia; Visiting Prof. Univ. of Konstanz, Germany; author 'Socialization' 1971; 'Interpersonal Communication' 1976; 'Constructing the Subject: Historical Origins of Psychological Research' 1990; numerous rsch. papers social, devel. & gen. exper. psychol.; articles theory & hist. psych.; ed. cons. various sci. jours. and acad. pubs.; Fellow, Candn. Psychol. Assn.; mem. Cheiron Soc. (Eur. and Am. Brs.); Hist. Sci. Soc.; recreations: travel, swimming; Home: 32 Greengate Rd., Don Mills, Ont. M3B 1E8; Office: 4700 Keele St., North York, Ont. M3J 1P3.

**DAOUST, Fernand,** B.S.S.; labour union executive; b. Montréal, Qué. 26 Oct. 1926; e. Univ. de Montréal B.S.S.; m. Ghyslaine Coallier 1956; two d. Marie-Josée, Isabelle; PRES. QUE. FEDN. OF LABOUR 1991– ; union rep. Hatters Internat. Union 1950 and subsequently Candn. Cong. of Labour, Oil & Chem. Workers; Qué. Dir. Candn. Union Pub. Employees; Gen. Sec. present Fedn. 1969; former Comnr. Montréal Cath. Sch. Bd.; NDP Cand. 1962, 1963; Founding Pres. Parti socialiste du Qué.; Sec. Bd. Dirs. Fonds de solidarité des travailleurs du Qué.; Dir. Institut de recherche appliquée sur le travail; Office de la langue française; Candn. Labour Market & Productivity Centre; Office franco-québécois pour la jeunesse; Institut canadien d'éducation des adultes; recipient Grande Médaille Mouvement national des Québécois; Founding mem. Mouvement Qué.; Office: 17F, 545, Crémazie Blvd. Est, Montréal, Qué. H2M 2V1.

**DAOUST, Sylvia,** R.C.A., M.C., C.Q.; sculptor; b. Montreal, P.Q. 24 May 1902; e. Beaux-Arts, Montreal; winner of 1st Prize, Ex-AEQUE Willingdon Arts Compet. 1929; P.Q. Schol. to Europe, 1929; assoc., Roy. Candn. Acad., 1943; has executed portraits busts for Candn. Bar Assn. and Que. Govt.; has exhibited in Can. and U.S., and at Rio 1946; awarded Scholar., Soc. Royale du Can. 1955–56; Royal Arch. Inst. Can. Medal and Allied Arts Award, Sculpture 1961; executed 'Edouard Montpetit' Monument, Univ. de Montréal 1967; 'Marie-Victorin E.C.' Monument, Jardin Botanique de

Montréal 1954; one-man Exhns. incl. Musée du Qué. 1974; Dorval Cultural Centre 1975; Exhn.: 'Trois Sculpteurs,' Museum of the St. Joseph Oratory of Mt. Royal, 1979–80; Gold Medal, City of Dorval 1975; Prix Philippe-Hébert de la Société Saint-Jean-Baptiste de Montréal 1975; Member, Order of Canada 1976; Mérite-Diocésain, 'Monseigneur-Ignace-Bourget,' Archdiocèse de Montréal 1983; Élue Chevalier de l'Ordre National du Québec 1987; mem., Sculptors' Soc. Can.; Address: Apt. 651, 505 Boul. Gouin ouest, Montréal, Qué. H3L 3T2.

**d'AQUINO, Thomas,** B.A., LL.B., LL.M.; lawyer; assoc. executive; b. Trail, B.C. 3rd Nov. 1940; e. Univ. of B.C., B.A. 1962; Queen's Univ. and Univ. of B.C. LL.B. 1965; Univ. of London LL.M. 1967; m. Susan Marion Peterson, 1965; PRESIDENT & C.E.O., BUSINESS COUNCIL ON NATIONAL ISSUES, Ottawa 1981– ; Pres., Intercounsel, Ottawa; Special Asst. to Prime Minister 1969–72; strategic business consulting, London, Paris, New York 1972–75; Adjunct Prof. of Law, Univ. of Ottawa 1976–83; Special Counsel, McCarthy & Tétrault, Barristers & Solicitors, Toronto 1987–89; Founder & Co-Chrmn., Candn. Labour Market & Productivity Centre 1988–90; acted as Legal Counsel and Advisor various govts. and major enterprises Canada and abroad, past fifteen yrs., incl. periods in London and Paris; frequent Guest Lectr.; author numerous publs.; mem., Candn. Bar Assn.; Internat. Bar Assn.; Law Soc. B.C.; a founder and Extve Ctte. mem., Candn. Alliance for Trade and Job Opportunities; mem. Ed. Bd., 'Policy Options' Inst. for Rsch. on Publ. Pol.; mem., Internat. Trade Adv. Ctte. to the Min. of Internat. Trade; Defence Industrial Preparedness Adv. Ctte. to the Min. of Nat. Defence; Internat. Inst. for Strategic Studies; Office: 806 Royal Bank Centre, 90 Sparks St., Ottawa, Ont. K1P 5B4.

**DARCY, Judy;** union executive; b. Grinsted, Denmark 25 Nov. 1949; d. Jules and Else Margrethe (Rich) D.; m. Gary Caroline 10 Dec. 1977; 1 son: Darcy Caroline; NATIONAL PRESIDENT, CANADIAN UNION OF PUBLIC EMPLOYEES (CUPE) 1991– ; active in CUPE since 1972; Regional Vice-Pres. 1983–89; Pres., CUPE Metro Toronto Council 1984–89; Ont. Div. Extve. Bd. Mem. 1984–89; Nat. Sec.-Treas. 1989–91; Vice-Pres., Candn. Labour Congress 1990–91; Gen. Vice-Pres. 1991– ; Home: 750 Eastbourne Ave., Ottawa, Ont. K1K 0H7; Office: 21 Florence St., Ottawa, Ont. K2P 0W6.

**DARDICK, Simon Stephen;** publisher; b. Kingston, Ont. 5 Dec. 1943; s. Herman and Lillian (Levin) D.; e. Kingston C.V.I.; Loyalist C.V.I.; Concordia Univ.; m. Nancy d. Mary and Joseph Marrelli 1976; children: Rosemary, Anne; PUBLISHER, VÉHICULE PRESS 1981– ; Founding Partner of Véhicule Press 1973; Editor, 'Dossier Québec' an ongoing series of non-fiction titles which document Que. soc.; co-ord. pub. of over 150 books focussing on Candn. lit., soc. hist., translation & urban studies; Co-founder, Que. Soc. for the Promotion of English Language Lit. (QSPELL) and Assn. des editeurs anglophones du Qué. (AEAQ); Sec., AEAQ 1987–88, 1990–94; Pres. 1989; Teacher, Editing & Publishing course, Concordia Univ.; Dir., ARTEXTE (Contemp. art information ctr.) 1983–88; Mem. Bd. of Dirs., Atwater Library, Mechanics' Institute of Montreal; Mem., Assn. of Candn. Publishers; Literary Press Group (Co-chair 1986–87); Que. Soc. for the Promotion of English Language Lit. (Vice-Pres. 1990–91); Office: P.O. B. 125, Place du Parc Station, Montreal, Que. H2W 2M9.

**DARKE, Raymond George,** M.B.A. C.M.A., F.C.M.A.; banker; b. United Kingdom 18 May 1937; s. Alfred George and Frances May (Dolman) D.; e. McMaster Univ. M.B.A. 1979; C.M.A. 1974; F.C.M.A. 1991; m. Sandra d. Harry and Grace Koehler June 1989; children: Peter, Stephen, Jason; SENIOR VICE-PRES., SCOTIA CORP. & COMMERCIAL AUTOMATED SERVICES, BANK OF NOVA SCOTIA 1983– ; Consultant, Peat Marwick & Partners 1967–69; various mngt. positions, Toronto-Dominion Bank 1970–83; Chair, Toronto Regional Council, Inst. of Candn. Bankers 1992; Pres., Soc. of Mngt. Accts. of Ont. 1991; Mem., MBA Alumni Bd., McMaster Univ. 1991; recreations: golf; clubs: Boulevard; Office: 44 King St. W., Toronto, Ont. M5H 1H1.

**DARLING, Alexander L.,** B.Sc., M.Ed., F.K.C.; university administrator; b. Bishop Auckland, England 5 July 1944; s. James H.B. and Ethel L. (Todd) D.; e. Univ. of London, B.Sc. (1st class hons. in chem.) 1965; Univ. of Alta., M.Ed. (Edn. Admin.) 1976; m. Jenifer E. d. John W. and Helene Williams 20 Mar. 1971; children: Elizabeth K., Ian W.A., Ruth C.; VICE-PRESIDENT (ADMINISTRATION), MCMASTER UNIV. 1988– ; Admin. Asst., Univ. of London King's Coll. 1965–67; Asst. to the Registrar, Univ. of Alta. 1967–70; Asst. Registrar 1970–74; Univ. Registrar, present univ. 1974–79; Univ. Registrar & Dir. of Institutional Analysis 1979–88; Mem., Counc. of Ont. Univ. Ctte. on Enrollment Statistics & Projections 1976–89 (Chair 1987–89); Counc. of Sr. Administrative Officers, Univs. of Ont. (Vice-Chair 1991–92, Chair 1992– ;); Goldsmith's Co. Travel Scholarship 1964; Jelf Medal 1965; Fellow of King's Coll. 1988; Chrmn. of Bd., Bach-Elgar Choral Soc., Hamilton 1980–81; Mem., Edmonton Opera Chorus 1968–73; Opera Hamilton Chorus 1981–86; Depy. Co-Chair, United Way of Burlington-Hamilton Wentworth; Campaign Co-Chair 1990; Mem., Candn. Soc. for Studies in Higher Edn. (Prog. Chair 1987, 1989; Extve. Ctte. 1986–88); Past Mem., Extves. of Candn. & Ont. Registrars Assn.; Christ's Ch. Cathedral Hamilton (Warden 1978–80 and 4 other extve. positions involving fundraising) Sec.-Treas., Friends of King's Coll. London 1983–92; author of several papers; recreations: nordic skiing, walking, gardening; Home: R.R. #2, Dundas, Ont. L9H 5E2; Office: Hamilton, Ont. L8S 4L8.

**DARNLEY, Arthur George,** M.A., Ph.D., C. Eng., C. Geol.; geoscientist; b. West Hartlepool, Co. Durham, Eng., 28 Feb. 1930; s. Arthur and Dora Lilian (Archer) D.; e. Christ's Coll., Cambridge Univ., B.A. 1952, M.A. 1956, Ph.D. 1958; m. Joan, d. Frederick Allen, Cheltenham, Eng., 28 Aug. 1954; children: Robert Arthur, Elizabeth Ann, Ian Gordon; SR. ADVISOR, RESOURCE EXPLORATION, GEOL. SURVEY OF CAN. 1988– ; Geol., Rhodesian Selection Trust (Services) Ltd., N. Rhodesia, 1952–54; Geol., Geol. Survey of Gt. Brit., London, Eng., 1957–66; Head, Remote Sensing Methods, Geol. Survey of Can. 1966–71; Chief of Exploration Geophysics 1971; Dir., Resource Geophysics & Geochem., 1972–86; Dir. New Technology & International Programs 1986–88; served as consultant to Internat. Atomic Energy Agency since 1965, also to OECD Nuclear Energy Agency and Asian Development Bank; Chief Technical Adviser, Canada-Brazil Projeto Geofisico, 1972–79, Thailand Airborne Geophysical Survey 1983–89; Chrmn., UNESCO/IUGS Internat. Geochemical Mapping Project 1988– ; gen. chrmn. conferences on mineral exploration Vienna 1976, Ottawa 1977, Paris 1982; served with R.A.F. and R.A.F.V.R. 1948–57; author of more than 100 publications; mem., Canadian Institute of Mining & Metall.; Geol. Assn. of Can.; Assn. of Exploration Geochemists; Instn. of Mining and Metall. London; Geol. Soc. London; recreations: flying, travel, carpentry; Home: 39 Trimble Cres., Ottawa, Ont. K2H 7M9; Office: 601 Booth St., Ottawa, Ont. K1A 0E8.

**da ROZA, Gustavo Uriel,** O.C., C.O.H., B.Arch.(Hons.), F.R.A.I.C., R.C.A.; architect; b. Hong Kong 24 Feb. 1933; s. late Gustavo Uriel and Cecilia Maria (Alves) da R.; e. Liceu Nacional, Macau, 1945–47; La Salle Coll., Kowloon, Hong Kong, 1947–50; Univ. of Hong Kong, B.Arch. (1st class hons.) 1955; m. Gloria, d. late Stephen Go, 17 June 1961; children: Guia Maria, Gabriella Maria, Gina Maria, Gustavo Uriel III, Gil Vasco; in private practice since 1961, principal of DA ROZA WARNER ARCHITECTS; former Prof. and Head, Dept. of Arch., Univ. of Manitoba; Visiting Lectr. and Design Critic numerous Univ. in N.Am. and Far East; Asst. Arch to R. Gordon Brown, Hong Kong, 1955–56; joined teaching staff, Univ. of Hong Kong and began practice, 1956; taught at Coll. of Environmental Design, Univ. of California, Berkeley, 1958–60; joined teaching staff, Univ. of Man., 1960, apptd. Head, Dept. of Arch. 1984; apptd. Officer of the Order of Canada 1988; apptd. Cmdr. of the Order of Prince Henry by Pres. of Portugal, 1985; winner: 3 Design Awards for Infill House Design Comp., 1982; C.H.D.C. Hon. Mention Award for 'Nassau Square' Residential Project, Winnipeg, 1981; two Hon. Mention Awards Arch./Eng. National Comp. for Low Energy Bldg. Designs, 1980; Mention Award for Affordable Housing Project in Vancouver C.H.D.C. Comp., 1979; Finalist in Limited Arch. Comp. for Nat. Gallery of Canada, 1977; Sr. Arts Award, Can. Counc., 1975; First Prize and comm. Winnipeg Art Gallery Nat. Arch. Comp., 1967; Arts Award, Can. Counc. to study arch. in Scandinavia, 1966; 1st Prize and 2 Hon. Mentions in Nat. House Design Comp. 1965, winning design built as 'Man and His Home' Pavilion, Expo 67; winner (with assoc.), nat. Comp. for design of 1968 Winter Olympic Games Project in Banff; drawings exhbtd. at Royal Acad., London, 1956 and 1958; major comm.: Winnipeg Art Gallery; Gull Harbour Resort Hotel, Hecla, Man.; Church of Immaculate Conception, Winnipeg; Design of Owens Art Gall., Sackville, N.B. (with Brown Brisley Brown Archs.); numerous residential and commercial projects; resorts in South Padre Island, Texas (with assoc.); over 60 residences acress Can.; work exhbd. at individual and group exhbns. and published across Can., the U.S., Europe and Far East; Chrmn., Can. Housing Design Counc. 1975–77; mem. Arch. Adv. Bd., Wascana Centre Auth. Regina; Apptd. Hon. Consul of Portugal in Winnipeg, 1970; el. Vice Dean Consular Corps of Winnipeg 1982–88; mem. Bd. of Govs., Winnipeg Art Gall. 1980–82 and el. mem. of Founders Soc.; past Pres. Winnipeg Horsemens Club; past Chrmn., Manitoba Horse Counc. Inc.; past mem. Bd. of Dir., Candn. Equestrian Fed.; mem., Manitoba Assn. Archs.; mem., Arch. Inst. of B.C.; Consular Corps of Winnipeg; Port. Assoc. of Man.; Vancouver Bd. of Trade; Club: St. Charles Golf and Country: R. Catholic; recreations: travel, ski, equestrianship, music; Home: 5650 Eagle Court, North Vancouver, B.C. V7R 4T9.

**DARRAGH, Ian,** B.A., B.J.; magazine editor and writer; b. Montreal, Que. 28 Sept. 1953; s. Dr. James H. and Marna A. (Gammell) D.; e. Special Student, Univ. of Nairobi 1970–71; Carleton Univ. B.A. (Hons.) 1976, B.J. (Hons.) 1980; m. Maria J. d. Luis and Clementina Afonso 26 Nov. 1974; children: Michael, Patrick, Margaret, Alan; EDITOR, CANADIAN GEOGRAPHIC MAGAZINE 1989– ; Assistant Editor, Canadian Geographic 1978–81; Book Review Ed. 1981–88 (expanded coverage of Candn. non-fiction); Assoc. Ed. 1981–84; Managing Ed. 1984–89; editor: 'Environment in Peril' 1990, 'The Great Lakes: Can These Ailing Giants Be Saved?' 1991, etc. (series of maps); Seminar Leader & Guest Lectr. to journalism students & writers' assns. 1984– ; Instr., Algonquin Coll. 1986; Mem., Lectures Ctte., Royal Candn. Geographical Soc. 1986– ; Mem., Candn. Science Writers' Assn.; Candn. Assn. of Geographers; Can. Soc. of Magazine Editors; author of numerous feature articles in Canadian Geographic and other periodicals; co-editor: 'Northwest Passage: The Quest for an Arctic Route to the East' by Edward Struzik 1991; Script Editor & Consultant, 'Search for a Tropical Arctic' 1989 (TV documentary); recreations: canoeing, nordic skiing; Office 39 McArthur Ave., Ottawa, Ont. K1L 8L7.

**DARVILLE, Jack Steven,** B.Comm., M.B.A.; accountant; b. Brantford, Ont. 10 Dec. 1946; s. Jack Stanley and Doris Laurine (Stuart) D.; e. McMaster Univ. B.Comm. 1968; Univ. of Michigan M.B.A. 1970; m. Pamela Bryant d. Thomas and Susan Bryant; PARTNER, PRICE WATERHOUSE 1983– ; joined Price Waterhouse Toronto 1970; London, England 1973–75; Teacher, Univ. of Toronto 1972–73, 1976–79; Ont. Inst. of C.A.s 1976–79; Candn. Inst. of C.A.s 1978–80; Paton Scholar, Univ. of Michigan; C.A. Ont. 1972; Pres., Bd. of Dir., Children's Aid Soc. of Metro Toronto 1992–94; Surrey Place Centre 1991–93; Chair, Bd. of Gov., Candn. Inst. for Radiation Safety 1990–93; recreations: fitness, hockey, travel, music; clubs: National, Fitness Inst.; Home: 32 Palmerston Gardens, Toronto, Ont. M6G 1V9; Office: 1 First Canadian Pl., Ste. 3300, Toronto, Ont. M5X 1H7.

**DAS, Jagannath Prasad,** M.A., Ph.D.; educator; b. Puri, India, 20 Jan. 1931; s. Sri Biswanath and Nilomoni (Mohanty) D.; came to Canada 1967; e. Utkal Univ. B.A. 1951; Patna Univ. M.A. (Gold Medallist) 1953; Univ. of London, Inst. of Psychiatry, Ph.D. 1957; m. Gita, d. R.C. Dasmohapatra, Jamirapalgarh, India 1955; children: Satya, Sheela; PROF. OF EDUCATIONAL PSYCHOL., UNIV. OF ALBERTA and Dir. Developmental Disabilities Centre there; began teaching in India; subsequently at George Peabody Coll. and Univ. of Calif. at Los Angeles before present position;rec'd Kennedy Foundation Fellowship 1963–64; Nuffield Fellowship 1972; Harris Award of International Reading Assoc.; University Research Prize 1987; Fellow, Am. Psychol. Assn.; Candn. Psychol. Assn.; Intl. Assoc. Rsch. on Learning Disabilities; mem., Assn. Cross-cultural Psychol.; author of 'Assessment of Cognitive Processes' 1994; 'A textbook of Psychology' 1985; 'Theory and Research in Learning Disabilities' 1982; 'Intelligence and Learning' 1981; 'Simultaneous & Successive Cognitive Processes' 1979; 'Mental Retardation for Special Educators' 1978; 'Verbal Conditioning and Behaviour' 1969; 'Manasika Byadhi' (Mental Illness) 1962; 'Samaja' (Society) 1956; also numerous scient. articles in learned and prof. journs.; Home: 11724–38a Ave., Edmonton, Alta. T6J 0L9; Office: Edmonton, Alta. T6G 2E5.

**DAS GUPTA, Sankar,** M.Sc., Ph.D., D.I.C.; scientist; executive; b. New-Delhi, India 3 Feb. 1951; s. Manindranath and Pratima (Sen) D.; e. Presidency Coll. Calcutta Univ. B.Sc. 1970; Imp. Coll. Univ. of London M.Sc. 1972, Ph.D., D.I.C. 1975; m. Suzanne Geddes 1979; children: Gitanjali, Raj Shekar, Maya, Bhaskar; PRES. THE ELECTROFUEL MANUFACTURING CO. 1983– ; Postdoctoral Rsch. Assoc. Imp. Coll. London

1975; Vice Pres. and Dir. HSA Reactors Ltd. 1976–81; Dir. Environmental Monitoring & Control 1980–85; Adjunct Prof. of Metall. and Mat. Sci. Univ. of Toronto 1987– ; mem. Candn. Adv. Ctte. on Hydrogen 1978; recipient Lash Miller Award 1986; C.Howard Smith Award & Medal 1979; Nat. Scholar India 1967; author over 100 patents, publs., conf. proceedings, book chapters; Dir. and Founding mem. Candn. Univ. Ind. Council Advanced Ceramics 1987; mem. Exec. Electrochem. Soc. Can. 1978–85; mem. various sci. assns.; Hindu; recreation: travel; Home: 29 Sullivan St., Toronto, Ont. M5T 1B8; Office: 9 Hanna Ave., Toronto, Ont. M6K 1W8.

**DASKO, Donna Anne,** M.A., Ph.D.; pollster; b. Winnipeg, Man. 19 Aug. 1951; d. William and Helen D.; e. Univ. of Man. B.A. 1973; Univ. of Toronto, M.A. 1974, Ph.D. 1982; VICE PRES. ENVIRONICS RESEARCH GROUP LTD. 1987– ; Lectr. Univ. of Man. 1974–75, Univ. of Toronto 1983–84; Sr. Assoc. present firm 1982–87; Pres. St. Stephen's Community House 1985–88; recipient Gov. Gen. Medal 1969; co-author 'The Globe-Environics Poll' series 1984–89; author various acad. & popular articles pub. opinion, politics & current issues; commentator radio and TV; Bd. of Dirs., United Way of Greater Toronto; Office: 45 Charles St. E., Toronto, Ont. M4Y 1S2.

**DATARS, W. Ross,** B.Sc., Ph.D., FRSC; university professor; b. Desboro, Ont. 14 June 1932; s. Albert John and Leona Alberta (Fries) D.; e. McMaster Univ., B.Sc. 1955, M.Sc. 1956; Univ. of Wisconsin, Ph.D. 1959; m. Eleanor d. Clarence and Violet Wismer 10 Oct. 1959; children: Timothy, Andrew, David; PROF., DEPT. OF PHYSICS, MCMASTER UNIV. 1962– ; Scientist, Defence Rsch. Bd. 1959–62; Asst. Prof., present univ. 1962–65; Assoc. Prof. 1965–69; Prof. 1969– ; E.W.R. Steacie Fellow, NRC 1968–70; Mem., Candn. Assn. of Physicists; Am. Physical Soc.; Royal Soc. of Can.; author of 185 papers & books incl. 'The Infinite Linear Chain Compounds' in Extended Linear Chain Compounds ed. by J.S. Miller 19..; Home: R.R. 2, Lynden, Ont. L0R 1T0; Office: 1280 Main St. W., Hamilton, Ont. L8S 4M1.

**DATO, Edward J.,** M.B.A., C.M.A.; financial executive; b. Malta 24 July 1945; s. Lawrence and Edwige (Mallia) D.; e. York Univ. B.A. (Hons.) 1975, M.B.A. 1978; F.I.C.B. 1970; C.M.A. 1978; m. Angela d. Robert and Eleanor Dotey 25 July 1970; children: Stephanie, Edward Jr.; SENIOR VICE-PRESIDENT & CHIEF FINANCIAL OFFICER, MARATHON REALTY COMPANY LIMITED 1991– ; executive with major Candn. chartered bank where he gained 20 years experience in corp., commercial & real estate lending opns. in Toronto, Vancouver, N.Y. & San Francisco; Chief Financial Offr. for major Candn. developer 2 years; recreations: squash; clubs: RCYC, Cambridge Club, Vancouver Club; Home: 186 Golfdale Rd., Toronto, Ont. M4N 2B9; Office: 200 Wellington St. West, Suite 400, Toronto, Ont. M5V 3C7.

**DATTELS, Stephen Roland,** B.A., LL.B.; b. Kitchener, Ont. 11 Sept. 1947; s. David Roland and Norma Elliott (Emblem) D.; e. St. Andrew's Coll. Aurora, Ont. 1965; McGill Univ. B.A. 1969; Univ. of W. Ont. LL.B. 1972; m. Jennifer Jane d. William D. Robb 4 June 1970; two s. Graham Roland, David Robb; PRES. & DIR., INTERNATIONAL DUNRAINE LIMITED 1988– ; PRES. & DIR. INTERNATIONAL PURSUIT CORPORATION 1987– ; law practice Messrs. Perry, Farley & Onyschuk, Toronto 1974–76; Venturetek International Ltd., Candn. Venture Capital Co. 1976–82; Exec. Vice Pres. & Dir., American Barrick Resources Corp., 1982–87; recreations: skiing, squash; Clubs: Caledon Ski; Badminton & Racquet; Home: 100 Glengowan Rd., Toronto, Ont. M4N 1G4; Office: 172 King St. E., Toronto, Ont. M5A 1J3.

**DAUB, Mervin Austin Conrad,** B.Comm., M.B.A., Ph.D.; university professor; b. Kitchener, Ont. 11 Sept. 1943; s. Alvin Henry and Lulu Nancy Johanna (Roeder) D.; e. Queen's Univ. B.Comm. 1966; Univ. of Chicago M.B.A., Ph.D. 1971; m. Agnes d. Aubert and Marthe Lefas 28 Oct. 1972; PROF., SCH. OF BUSINESS, QUEEN'S UNIV. 1971– ; Vis. Prof., Cambridge Univ. 1973; Monash Univ. 1979; Harvard Univ. 1986; Helsinki Univ. 1993; Extve. Interchange Prog., Govt. of Can. 1981–82; apptd. by Ont. to OEB 1986–90; Guest Lectr., var. orgns., referee, book reviewer, contbr. to acad. confs.; main rsch.: forecasting, macroecon., public policy; var. acad. awards; Beta Gamma Sigma; Mem., Candn., Am. & Euro. Econ. Assns.; Candn. Assn. of Bus. Econ.; author: 'Canadian Economic Forecasting' 1987 and var. articles in profl. jours.; recreations: photography, travel, fiction writing; Home: Village of Upper Brewers Mills, R.R. 1, Seeley's Bay, Ont. K0H 2N0; Office: Kingston, Ont. K7L 3N6.

**DAUBNEY, David Bruce,** B.A., LL.B.; lawyer; b. Windsor, Ont. 23 July 1947; s. Edwin Bruce and Mary Margaret (Strong) D.; e. Oakville-Trafalgar High Sch. 1966 (Ont. Scholar); Queen's Univ. B.A. 1969; Univ. of W. Ont. LL.B. 1972; Osgoode Hall 1974; m. Mary d. Alexander and Eleanor Devine 28 June 1974; children: Jennifer Catherine, James Alexander; GENERAL COUNSEL, CRIMINAL AND SOCIAL POLICY, DEPT. OF JUSTICE 1991– ; Chief of Staff to Rt. Hon. Joe Clark, Secy. of State for External Affairs and Pres., Privy Council and Min. Responsible for Constitutional Affairs 1991; Solr. Perley-Robertson, Panet, Hill & McDougall Ottawa 1974–80; Legal Offr. Dept. of Justice Can. 1981–84; el. to H. of C. for Ottawa W. 1984; Chrmn. Standing Ctte. on Justice and Solr. Gen.; Lawyer, Soloway, Wright, Ottawa 1988–90; Dir. Ont. Lottery Corp. 1978–81; Interprovl. Lottery Corp. 1980–81; mem. Assessment Review Court 1980–81; Dir., Internat. Centre for Human Rights and Democratic Develop. 1990–91; Dir., Forum for Young Canadians, New Beginnings for Youth, Kiwanis Club of Ottawa; Depy. Campaign Chrmn., 1990 United Way of Ottawa Carleton Campaign; author various publs.; mem. Law Soc. Upper Can.; R.Catholic; P. Conservative; Club: Kiwanis; Home: 5 Winslow Court, Ottawa, Ont. K2B 8H8.

**DAUDELIN, Charles,** R.C.A.; sculptor; b. Granby, Que. 1 Oct. 1920; s. Aimé and Berthe (Lamothe) D.; e. Ecole du Meuble Montreal 1943; studied painting with Fernand Léger N.Y. 1943–44 and 1947–48 also with Henri Laurens (sculptor) Paris; m. Louise d. Marc Bissonnette 1 Oct. 1946; children: Eric, Nanouk, Rémy, Katia, Valérie; Concepts and realizations: monumental public sculptures and fountains in various cities and for mural and religious works within churches; recipient French Govt. Scholarships Paris 1946–48; Can. Council Arts Award 1968–69, 1972–73 (Lynch-Staunton); Can. and Ont. Arts Council to make sculpture with students at Charlebois Sch., Ottawa 1981; sculpture prizes (incl. commissions): Nat. Arts Centre Ottawa 1966; Place des Arts Montreal 1967; Nouveau Palais de Justice Montréal 1972; Cégep du Vieux Montréal 1975; Ecole Joseph-Charbonneau Montréal 1978; Place du Québec, Paris, France 1981; environmental sculptures: Centre d'accueil Pierre-Joseph-Triest in Montreal 1985; C.A. Champlain-Châteauguay in Châteauguay 1989; Fernand-Seguin Sch., Candiac 1992; Mount-Royal Cemetery, Outremont 1992; commissions: 'Paulia' fountain, Provincial Parliament, Charlottetown, P.E.I. 1967; retable Sacred Heart Chapel, Notre Dame Church 1982; sculpture, Palais des Congrès, Montréal 1983; National Bank of Canada Head Office, Montreal 1983; Lt.-Gov. of Canada Residence, La Citadelle, Que. 1984; concept for Viger Square incl. sculpture, Montreal 1984; fountain, bronze, environment for library in Saint-Laurent 1990; signaling system and sculpture for Musée d'art de Joliette 1992; 'sculpture pieces' stainless and glass and stained-glass window for Résidence l'Amitié, Montréal 1992; awards: Royal Arch. Inst. Can. Allied Arts Award 1973; Philippe Hébert Award, Soc. St-Jean-Baptiste, Montréal 1981; Paul-Emile-Borduas Award, Que. Govt. 1985; médaille from l'Université Québec à Trois-Rivières 1992; Address: 17166 chemin Ste-Marie, Kirkland, Que. H9J 2K9.

**DAUDLIN, Hon. Mr. Justice Robert Mose Patrick,** LL.B.; judge; b. Port Crew, Ont. 3 March 1940; s. Antoine Joseph and Florence D.; e. Tilbury Dist. High Sch.; Ottawa Univ. High Sch.; King's Coll. London, Ont. 1961; Univ. of W. Ont. LL.B. 1964; m. Linda Darlene d. Edward and Estelle Wideman 25 June 1966; children: Matthew Anthony Edward, Jason Joel, Chantalle, Jennifer Suzanne; JUDGE, ONT. COURT OF JUSTICE, GEN. DIV. 1990– ; called to Bar of Ont. 1966; el. to H. of C. g.e. 1974, re-el. 1979, 1980; Parlty. Sec. to Sec. of State for Can. 1977, Pres. Treasury Bd. 1980; Judge, Dist. Court of Ont. 1984; Chrmn. Special Ctte. Visible Minorities in Candn. Soc.; Chrmn. Separate Sch. Bd. Tecumseh, Ont. 1967–69; Chrmn. 185 EAA Windsor, Ont. K. of C.; mem. Exper. Aircraft Assn. Can.; Home: 225 Victoria Ave., Chatham, Ont. N7L 3A7; Office: 21 Seventh St., Chatham, Ont. N7M 4K1.

**DAUPHIN, Claude,** LL.B., M.N.A.; lawyer, politician; b. Lachine, Que. 17 Dec. 1953; s. Médéric and Cécile (Bouchard) D.; e. Laval Univ. LL.B. 1977; called to Quebec Bar 1978; m. Maria d. Giacomo and Rosa Mazzuca 24 Sept. 1984; children: Eric, Lavra; MEMBER OF THE NATIONAL ASSEMBLY OF QUEBEC FOR MARQUETTE (ISLAND OF MONTREAL) 1981– ; Lawyer in Lachine 1978–81; Parliamentary Asst. to the Justice Min. 1985–89; Pres., Institution Committee 1989–93; Home: 3910 St. Joseph Blvd., Lachine, Que.; Office: 1015 Notre-Dame St., Room 200, Lachine, Que. H8S 2C3.

**DAVENPORT, Alan Garnett,** M.A.Sc., M.A., Ph.D., F.R.S.C.; engineer; b. Madras, India 19 Sept. 1932; s. late Thomas and May (Hope) D.; e. Cambridge Univ. B.A. 1954, M.A. 1958; Univ. of Toronto M.A.Sc. 1957; Univ. of Bristol Ph.D. (Civil Engn.) 1961; Dr. of App. Sc. (Hon. causa) Univ. of Louvain 1979; D.Eng. (Hon. causa) Technical Univ. of Denmark 1983; D.Sc. (Hon. causa) McGill Univ. 1984; D.Eng. (Hon. causa) Univ. of Waterloo 1986; D.Eng. (Hon. causa) Univ. of Toronto 1989; D.Sc. (Hon. causa) Univ. of La Plata, Argentina 1993; D.Sc. (Hon. causa) Univ. of Guelph 1993; m. Sheila Rand d. late Sidney Earle Smith 13 Apr. 1957; children: Thomas Sidney, Anna Margaret, Andrew Hope, Clare Rand; PROF. AND DIR., BOUNDARY LAYER WIND TUNNEL LAB., FAC. OF ENGINEERING SCIENCE & DIR., CENTRE FOR STUDIES IN CONSTRUCTION, UNIV. OF W. ONT.; recipient Noble Prize 1963; Gzowski Medal, Engn. Inst. Can. 1963, 1978, Duggan Medal 1965; Golden Plate Award, Am. Acad. of Achievement 1965; Prize in Applied Meteorol., Candn. Meteorol. Soc. 1967; Can-Am Civil Eng. Amity Award, Am. Soc. Civil Engrs. 1977; Silver Medal, Assn. Prof. Engrs. Prov. Ont. 1977; co-recipient State-of-Art Civil Engn. Award for report 'Structural Safety,' Am. Soc. Civil Engn. 1973; cited in 1981 by Engineering News Record for service to the construction industry; CANCAM medal, Candn. Congress of Applied Mechanics 1983; A. B. Sanderson Award for Structural Engineering, Can. Soc. Civ. Engn.; Gold Medal, Inst. of Structural Engr. (UK) 1987; Manning Award of Distinction for Innovation 1990; Bell Canada Forum Award 1992; Izaak Walter Killam Memorial Prize 1993; Julian C. Smith Award, Eng. Inst. Canada 1993; awarded Commemorative Medal for 125th Anniversary of Candn. Confederation 1993; Canada Gold Medal for Science & Engn. 1994; served with RCN (Air Br.) VC 920 Sqdn. 1957–58; Fellow, Royal Soc. of Can. 1972; Candn. Acad. of Engr. 1987 (Past Pres.); Foreign Assoc., Nat. Acad. of Engr., U.S.; Foreign Mem., Royal Acad. of Engr., U.K.; mem. Assn. Prof. Engrs. Prov. Ont.; Am. Meteorol. Soc.; Candn. Meteorol. & Oceanographic Soc.; Royal Meteorol. Soc.; Candn. Soc. Civil Engn.; Engn. Inst. Can.; Internat. Assn. Bridge & Structural Engn.; Internat. Assn. Shell & Spatial Structures; Am. Acad. Mechanics; Seismol.Soc. Am.; Am. Soc. Civil Engrs.; Am. Concrete Inst.; recreations: tennis, squash; sailing; Home: 412 Lawson Rd., London, Ont. N6G 1X8; Office: London, Ont. N6A 5B9.

**DAVENPORT, Barry M.;** banker; b. Oxford, England 30 April 1947; m. Anita; SENIOR VICE-PRESIDENT, TREASURY GROUP, BANK OF MONTREAL; Past Pres., Forex Assn. of Canada; Pres., St. George's Society of Toronto; recreations: skiing; Office: 17th Floor, First Canadian Place, Toronto, Ont. M5X 1A1.

**DAVENPORT, Paul Theodore,** M.A., Ph.D.; university executive; b. Summit, N.J. 24 Dec. 1946; s. Theodore and Charlotte Lomax (Paul) D.; e. Stanford Univ. B.A. 1969 (Phi Betta Kappa); Univ. of Toronto M.A. 1970, Ph.D. 1976; m. Josette d. Henri and Yvonne Brotons 12 July 1947; children: Eric, Leslie, Audrey; PRESIDENT & VICE CHANCELLOR, UNIV. OF WESTERN ONTARIO 1994– ; Asst. Prof. of Econ. McGill Univ. 1973 becoming Assoc. Prof. and Prof., Assoc. Dean of Grad. Studies & Rsch. 1982–86, Vice Prin. (Planning & Computer Services) 1986–89; Pres. & Vice-Chancellor, Univ. of Alta. 1989–94; former mem. Conseil des universites and served on Organizing Ctte. Nat. Forum on Post-Secondary Edn. Saskatoon 1987; Past Dir. Vanier Coll. Montreal; mem. Bd. Govs.: Alta. Heritage Found. for Med. Rsch.; St. Joseph's Coll.; Univ. of Alta. Hosps.; Bd. mem., Economic Development Edmonton; mem. Premier's Council on Sci. & Technol.; presented some 50 lectures and papers acad. meetings since 1973; co-ed. 'Reshaping Confederation: The 1982 Reform of the Canadian Constitution' 1984; Life mem. Grads. Soc. McGill Univ.; mem. Candn. Assn. Econs.; Am. Econ. Assn.; recreations: swimming, trail biking, photography; Office: London, Ont. N6A 3K7.

**DAVEY, Clark W.,** B.A.; newspaper publisher; b. Chatham, Ont. 3 March 1928; s. William and Marguerite (Clark) D.; e. Chatham Collegiate; Univ. of W. Ont. B.A. (Journalism) 1948; Univ. of W. Ont. LL.D. 1986; m. (Katherine) Joyce d. Rowley Archibald and Ruth Gordon 13 Sept. 1952; children: Richard Gordon, Kevin William, Clark Michael; Vice Pres., Southam and Publisher, The Ottawa Citizen 1989–92; served as reporter 3 yrs. Chatham News; Manag. Ed., Northern Daily News, Kirkland Lake; 27yrs. The Globe & Mail becoming Manag. Ed. last 15 yrs.; Publisher, The Vancouver Sun 1978; Dir., Candn. Press 1974–86, Vice Pres. 1979–

81, Pres. 1981–82, Chrmn. 1982–83; Vice Pres. & Dir., Pacific Press Ltd. 1981–83; Publisher, The Gazette (Montreal) 1983–89; Past Pres., Candn. Mang. Eds. Conf. and Editorial Div., Candn. Daily Newspaper Assoc.; Dir., Am. Press Inst.; Adv. Comtes., Univ. of W. Ont. Sch. of Journalism; Pres., Michener Awards Foundation; Gov., Nat. Newspaper Awards Board; lectr., in journalism various colls. and univs.; recreations: golf, reading, swimming; Clubs: Rideau (Ottawa); Canadian; University (Montreal); Royal Montreal Golf and Country; Rivermead Golf & Country; Home: 29 Madawaska Dr., Ottawa, Ont. K1S 3G5; Office: 1101 Baxter Rd., Ottawa, Ont. K2C 3M4.

**DAVEY, Frank W.,** M.A., Ph.D.; poet; educator; b. Vancouver, B.C. 19 Apr. 1940; s. Wilmot Elmer and Doris (Brown) D.; e. Univ. of B.C., B.A. 1961, M.A. 1963; Univ. of S. Cal., Ph.D. 1968; m. Linda Jane, d. W. E. McCartney, Vancouver, B.C., 20 Nov. 1969; children: Michael Gareth, Sara Genève; CARL F. KLINCK PROF. OF CANDN. LIT., UNIV. OF W. ONT. 1990– ; Teaching Asst., Univ. of B.C. 1961–63; Lectr., Royal Roads Mil. Coll., Victoria 1963–66, Asst. Prof. 1967–69; Writer-in-Residence, Sir George Williams Univ., Montreal 1969–70; Asst. Prof., York Univ., Downsview, Ont. 1970, Assoc. Prof. 1972, Prof. 1980–90, Chrmn., Dept. of English 1985–90; rec'd Can. Council Grants or Fellowships 1966, 1971–73, 1974–75; Dept. of Nat. Defence Arts Research Grant 1965, 1966, 1968; author 'D-Day and After' 1962; 'City of the Gulls and Sea' 1964; 'Bridge Force' 1965; 'The Scarred Hull' 1966; 'Five Readings of Olson's Maximus' 1970; 'Four Myths for Sam Perry' 1970; 'Weeds' 1970; 'Earle Birney' (Studies in Candn. Lit. No. 11) 1971; 'Griffon' 1972; 'King of Swords' 1972; 'L'an Trentiesme' 1972; 'Arcana' 1973; 'The Clallam' 1973; 'From There to Here: a Guide to English-Canadian Literature since 1960,' 'WarPoems' 1979; 'The Arches' 1980; 'Louis Dudek and Raymond Souster' 1981; 'Capitalistic Affection!' 1982; 'Surviving the Paraphrase' 1983; 'Edward and Patricia' 1984; 'Margaret Atwood: A Feminist Poetics' 1984; 'The Louis Riel Organ and Piano Company' 1985; 'The Abbotsford Guide to India' 1986; 'Reading Canadian Reading' 1988; 'Popular Narratives' 1990; 'Post-National Arguments: The Politics of the Anglophone-Canadian Novel since 1967' 1993; 'Reading "KIM" Right' 1993; Founding ed. two lit. mags.: 'Tish' 1961–63, 'Open Letter' 1965– ; Founding ed. 'Swift Current' (electronic lit. mag. and database) 1984; Humanities Research Council Subvention 1974, 1979; mem., Ed. Bd., Coach House Press, 1974– ; mem., Candn. Assn. Univ. Teachers; Assn. Candn. College and Univ. Teachers Eng. (Vice-Pres.); Assn. Can. Que. Lit.; Office: Univ. of Western Ont., London, Ont. N6A 3K7.

**DAVEY, Hon. Keith;** senator; b. Toronto, Ont. 21 Apr. 1926; s. Charles Minto and Grace Viola (Curtis) D.; e. North Toronto Coll. Inst.; Victoria Coll., Univ. of Toronto, B.A. 1949; children: Douglas, Ian, Catherine; married Dorothy Elisabeth 1 Dec. 1978; estbd. own communications consultancy 1969; after graduation became Sales Mgr., Radio Stn. CKFH, Toronto, for 11 yrs.; apptd. Nat. Campaign Dir., Liberal Party Can. 1961, 1962, 1963, 1965; concurrently Nat. Organizer of the Party and Extve. Dir., Lib. Fed. of Can. till summoned to the Senate, Feb. 1966; Co-Chrmn. Nat. Campaign 1973, 79, 80, 84 (last half); Commr. of Candn. Football League, 1967; mem. Bd. Govs., Toronto Central Hosp.; Candn. Oldtimers Hockey Assn.; Liberal; United Church; author: 'The Rainmaker – A Passion for Politics' (political memoir) 1986; Home: 33 Warren Rd., Toronto, Ont.; Office: 1881 Yonge St. Ste. 600, Toronto, Ont. M4S 1Y6 and The Senate, Ottawa, Ont. K1A 0A4.

**DAVEY, Kenneth George,** M.Sc., Ph.D., F.R.S.C., F.E.S.C.; b. Chatham, Ont. 20 Apr. 1932; s. William and Marguerite (Clark) D.; e. McKeough Pub. Sch. and Chatham (Ont.) Coll. Inst. 1950; Univ. of W. Ont. B.Sc. 1954, M.Sc. 1955; Cambridge Univ. Ph.D. (Insect Physiol.) 1958; m. Jeannette Isabel d. late Dr. Charles S. Evans 28 Nov. 1959 (separated); children: Christopher Graham, Megan Jeannette, Katherine Alison; DISTINGUISHED RSCH. PROF., YORK UNIV. 1984– , Prof. of Biol. there 1974, Dean of Fac. of Sci. 1982–85, Vice-Pres. (Academic Affairs), York Univ. 1986–91; Nat. Research Council Post-doctoral Fellow, Dept. Zoo. Univ. of Toronto 1958–59; Drosier Fellow, Gonville and Caius Coll. Cambridge Univ. 1959–63; Assoc. Prof. Inst. Parasitol. McGill Univ. 1963–66, Dir. of Inst. 1964–74, Prof. of Parasitol. and Biol. 1966–74; Chrmn. of Biol., York Univ. 1974–81; Dir., Huntsman Marine Lab., St. Andrews, N.B. (Pres. and Chrmn. 1977–80); mem.: Tropical Med. & Parasitol. Panel, US Nat. Insts. Health 1978–82; Animal Biol. Comte., Nat. Sciences and Engn. Research Council Can. 1969–72, 1980–83 (Chrmn. 1982–83); Comte. on Grants & Scholarships, NSERC 1983–86; author 'Reproduction in the Insects' 1965, Spanish ed. 1966; over 100 scholarly articles in various scient. journs. dealing with endocrinology of invertebrate animals; Ed. Bd. 'International Journal for Parasitology'; rec'd Queen's Silver Jubilee Medal; Gold Medal, Entomological Soc. of Can. 1984; Fry Medal, Candn. Soc. Zools. 1987; Gold Medal, Biol. Counc. Can. 1987; Pres., World Extve. Counc., Institut de la Vie; mem. Candn. Soc. Zools. (Extve., Nominating Comtes. V.P. 1979, 1980, Pres. 1981); European Soc. Nematol.; Soc. Exper. Biol.; Entomol. Soc. Can. (Fellow 1976); Candn. Comte, Univ. Biol. Chrmn. 1974–81 (Chrmn. 1975–77); Biol. Council Can. (Pres. 1979–81); Secy. Acad. of Science, Royal Soc. of Can. 1979–85; recreation: hand weaving, wine and food; Home: 96 Holm Cres., Thornhill, Ont. L3T 5J3; Office: 4700 Keele St., Downsview, Ont. M3J 1P3.

**DAVEY, Thomas Peter (Tom);** writer; publisher; b. Wigan, Eng. 8 June 1930; s. Peter and Nellie (Prescott) D.; e. Univ. of Toronto; Univ. of Tasmania; m. Sandra d. Stephen Woodward and Elsie Turner 19 June 1959; children: Stephen Thomas, Penelope Helen; CO-FOUNDER AND PUBLISHER ENVIRONMENTAL SCIENCE AND ENGINEERING MAG. 1988– ; freelance writer Can. 1959 followed by editorial posts in London, Eng.; newspaper reporter Australia 1964; Sub-ed. Australian Broadcasting Corp. Radio Australia, radio and TV news progs., Melbourne and Tasmania; ed. Southam Communications Can. environmental features 1967; became publs. and sci. ed. Inst. for Environmental Studies Univ. of Toronto; founded Davcom Communications Inc. 1975; guest lectr., special sci. conf. chem. spills, WHO, Rome 1982, Queen's Univ. 1989; part-time lectr. in mag. jour. Humber Coll.; Assoc., Inst. for Environmental Studies Univ. of Toronto; recipient Environment Canada Award 1992; Cert. of Hon. Environment Can. 1989; J.H. Neal Award (1st Candn.) Am. Bus. Press 1970; Schlenz Medal (1st Candn.) Water Environment Federation 1980; over 30 awards for writing; author 'All the Views Fit to Print' satirical essays 1985; 'The Invisible Profession' drama-documentary 1987; various articles hist., travel, environment; Pres. Candn. Sci. Writers Assn. 1978–79; recreations: swimming, windsurfing; Address: 10 Petch Cres., Aurora, Ont. L4G 5N7.

**DAVID, Jacques Lefaivre,** B.Arch., F.R.A.I.C., R.C.A.; architect; b. Montreal, Que. 11 Nov. 1921; s. Charles, F.R.A.I.C., F.R.I.B.A., D.Sc.(Hon.) and Pauline (Lefaivre) D.; e. Coll. Mont-St-Louis Montreal Dipl. Science & Math. 1941; McGill Univ. B.Arch. 1946; children: Danielle (Engle); Christiane (Bourbonnière); Marie; Nathalie; SR. PARTNER, DAVID, BOULVA, CLEVE-ARCHITECTS; maj. projects incl. Palais de Justice de Montréal; Dow Planetarium Montreal; Place des Arts Master Plan; Théâtres Port-Royal & Maisonneuve; Hdqrs.: Banque Canadienne Nationale; Banque Nationale du Can.; Bell Canada Que. Region; Mercantile Bank of Can.; Alliance-Mutuelle-Vie Montreal; Royal Bank Centre Ottawa; Fed. Govt. Accommodation Program Hull, Que. (Phase III); Le Régence Hyatt Hotel Montreal; mem. Ordre des Architectes du Qué.; Ont. Assn. Archs.; Royal Arch. Inst. Can.; Zeta Psi (Past Pres.); R. Catholic; recreations: golf, tennis, reading, writing; Club: Mount Bruno Country; Home: 1455 Sherbrooke St. W., Apt. 2601, Montreal, Que. H3G 1L2; Office: 1155 René-Lévesque Blvd. W., Suite 2400, Montreal, Que. H3B 3X7.

**DAVID, Paul,** C.C., G.O.Q., M.D.; senator; b. Montréal, Que. 25 Dec. 1919; s. Athanase and Antonia (Nantel) D.; e. Univ. of Montréal, M.D. 1944; certified specialist in cardiology and internal medicine, 1952; m. 1stly Nellie, d. Charles Maillard, 17 July 1943; m. 2ndly Yvette, d. Donat Lemire, 30 June 1972; children: Pierre, Françoise, Thérèse, Anne-Marie, Hélène, Charles; SENATOR OF CANADA 1985; Hôpital Notre-Dame, Montréal 1948–53; founded Montréal Heart Inst. 1954: Chief of Cardiology Dept. and Med. Dir. 1954–65, Exec. Dir. 1966–74; Med. Director, Montreal Heart Inst. 1966–84; Assoc. Prof., Fac. of Med., Univ. of Montréal 1957; Expert in cardiovascular disease, World Health Orgn. 1972–77; Pres., Cardinal Léger Inst. against leprosy; Acad. of Great Montréalers; Admin., Foyer Rousselot; Vanier Inst. for the Family; awards: Centennial Medal of Can. 1967; Service Medal; Order of Can. 1968; Hippolyte Unanue Order (Perou) 1968; Ann. Award of Assn. des Diplômés de l'Univ. de Montréal 1968; Archambault Medal (A.C.F.A.S.) 1969; Honoris Causa Doctorates, Univ. of Lyon (France) 1970; Hon. Causa Doctorate Univ. of Ottawa 1971; Great Montréaler 1981; Companion, Order of Can. 1981; Hon. Fellow, Candn. Coll. of Health Directors 1985; Commandeur, Ordre de Malte 1985; Hon. Fellow, Am. Coll. of Cardiology 1985 (Fellow 1964–84); Hon. Fellow, Am. Heart Assn. 1985 (Fellow 1966–84); Hon. Pres., Rsch. Fund, Montréal Heat Inst. 1986; Grand Officier, Ordre National du Québec 1988; CPQ Annual Career Award, Montréal Chamber of Comm. 1988; Hon. Fellow, Royal Coll. of Physicians & Surgs. of Can. 1989; Merit Prize de l'Association des médecins de langue française du Canada 1989; Annual Award, Carrefour des chrétiens du Québec pour la Santé 1991; Chevalier, Ordre de la Pléiade 1991; Annual Award, Que. Heart Found. 1991; mem.: Assn. des Médecins de Langue Française du Can.; Candn. Cardiovascular Soc.; Académie de Médecine de France; Bur. des Gouverneurs de la Corp. des Célébrations du 350e anniversaire du Montréal (Celebration Montréal 1992) 1989; author of numerous works on medical subjects; Home: 2 Terrasse Les Hautvilliers, Outremont, Qué. H2V 4P1; Offices: 5000 East, Bélanger St., Montréal, Qué. H1T 1C8 and Senate of Canada, Ottawa, Ont. K1A 0A4.

**DAVID, Robert H. (Bob),** B.Sc., M.Sc., P.Eng.; b. Rosetown, Sask. 18 Feb. 1938; e. Univ. of Sask. B.Sc. (Civil Engr.) 1962; Univ. of Alta. M.Sc. (Transport. Engr.) 1970; m. Edna; children: Dianne, Bruce; PRESIDENT, CHIEF EXECUTIVE OFFICER & DIR., EDMONTON TELEPHONES CORP. 1988– ; RCAF Pilot, Univ. of Sask. Reserve Squadron 1956–61; extensive municipal govt. experience incl. appts. as Gen. Mgr. of var. Civic Depts.: Traffic Engr., City of Saskatoon 1962 and City of Edmonton 1965; Roadway Functional Planner, Mgr. of Opns. for Edmonton Transit, City Engineer, Gen. Mgr. Transporation Dept., City of Edmonton; former Sr. Transportation Engr., Stanley Associates Engineering Ltd.; Bd. of Dirs., Edmonton YMCA; TRLabs; Campaign Chrmn., Edmonton and Area United Way Campaign 1992; mem., Assn. of Profl. Engineers, Geologists & Geophysicsts of Alta. (former mem., Practice Standards, Builders' Liens, Engrg. Technol. Liaison Cttes.; current mem., Honours and Awards Ctte.); Mem., United Ch. of Canada; recreations: running, hiking, reading, sailing; Home: 16111 Patricia Dr., Edmonton, Alta. T5R 5N3; Office: #1270, 10044 – 108 St., Edmonton, Alta. T5J 3S7.

**DAVID, Tirone E.,** M.D., F.R.C.S.(C), F.A.C.S.; physician, hospital administrator; b. Brazil 20 Nov. 1944; s. Antonio E. and Carolina (Gulinelli) D.; e. Univ. of Parana, Brazil M.D. 1968; m. Jacqueline d. Gerald and Monica Shumaker 15 Feb. 1974; children: Adriane, Carolyn, Kristen; CHIEF OF CARDIOVASCULAR SURGERY, THE TORONTO HOSPITAL 1988– ; immigrated to USA 1970 for training in surgery; internship, State Univ. of N.Y., Downstate Med. Ctr.; general surgery residency, Cleveland Clinic Found. 1971–75; cardiovascular surger res., Univ. of Toronto 1975–77; Rsch. Fellowship, Ont. Heart Found., Toronto Gen. Hosp. 1977–78; Cardiovascular Surgeon, Toronto Gen. Hosp. & Asst. Prof. of Surgery, Univ. of Toronto 1978–80; Chief of Cardiovascular Surger, Toronto Western Hosp. 1980–88; Prof. of Surgery, Univ. of Toronto 1989– ; Consultant, St. Jude Medical Inc.; Medtronics; Edit. Bd. Mem., 'J. of Cardiac Surgery,' 'J. of Heart Valve Disease,' 'Annals of Thoracic Surgery' and 'Australasian Journal of Cardiac and Thoracic Surgery'; Mem., Royal Coll. of Phys. & Surg. of Canada; Am. Coll. of Surg.; Am. Assn. of Thoracic Surg.; Soc. of Thoracic Surg.; Am. Heart Assn.; Candn. Cardiovascular Soc.; Am. Assn. of Clin. Cardiac Surg.; Candn. Med. Assn.; Ont. Med. Assn.; author of 81 peer-reviewed original med. articles & 8 med. textbooks chaps. and one book; Order of Ontario 1993; Home: 100 Dunvegan Rd., Toronto, Ont. M4V 2P7; Office: 200 Elizabeth St., EN 13-219, Toronto, Ont. M5G 2C4.

**DAVIDS, Leo,** B.A., M.A., Rabbi, Ph.D.; university professor, sociologist; b. Amsterdam, The Netherlands 22 July 1938; s. Eliazer and Bertha (Perlberg) D.; e. City Coll. of N.Y., B.A. (magna cum laude) 1959, M.A. 1961; ord. Rabbi (Orthodox) 1960; Columbia Univ., part-time; New York Univ., Ph.D. 1968; m. Faigie d. Nathan and Annie Shields 23 Dec. 1968; children: Elliot, Haviva, Rifka, Naomi; ASSOC. PROF., ATKINSON COLL., YORK UNIV. 1972– ; (Chair of Dept. 1991–94); Rabbi, Cong. Agudat Achim, Bridgeport, Conn. 1962–64; Soc. Teacher, City Univ. N.Y. 1961–66; Stern Coll. for Women, Yeshiva Univ., N.Y. 1966–68; Asst. Prof., present univ. 1968–72; Vis. Prof., Bar-Ilan Univ. 1974–75; Tel Aviv Univ. 1981–82; Vis. Researcher, Demographic Ctr. (Jerusalem, Israel) 1981–82; Rsch. Cons., B'nai Brith Can. (Divorce Project) 1986–87; Lectr., Univ. of Toronto, Brandeis Univ. (Jerusalem Ctr.), Trent Univ. & others; Phi Beta Kappa, Kappa Delta Pi, Alpha Kappa Delta; rsch. grants, Min. of State for Multiculturalism & SSHRCC; CBC Radio interviewee; Judge, Nat. Bible Contest, Candn. Zionist Fed. 1985, 1987, 1989; nom. several times for Teaching Excellence Award,

O.C.U.F.A.; mem., Candn. Prof. for Peace in the Middle East, Candn. Soc. & Anthrop. Assn., Assn. for Jewish Demography & Statistics, etc.; author: 'Defining Sociology/Anthropology' 1982; author of scholarly articles; Founding & Current Co-chair, Jewish Marriage Edn. Ctte., Toronto; recreations: Torah-scroll reading; Home: 242 Armour Blvd., Downsview, Ont.; Office: 338, Atkinson Coll., 4700 Keele St., North York, Ont. M3J 1P3.

**DAVIDSON, Alexander Thomas,** M.A.; public servant; b. Fort William, Ont. 11 Jan. 1926; s. Oliver Mowat and Charlotte Emma (Potter) D.; e. Queen's Univ., B.A. 1948; Univ. of Toronto, M.A. 1951; Univ. of Waterloo, Honorary Doctorate 1991; m. Joan Adeline, d. Frederick Alexander, 6 Aug. 1955; four s.: Chuck, Ronald, James, John; Adm. Asst. to Depy. Min. of Nat. Resources, Sask. 1950; Sr. Planning Offr. 1951; Asst. Depy. Min. 1953; Chief, Resources Div., Dept. N. Affairs & Nat. Resources 1958; Dir., Agric. Rehab. & Devel., Dept. of Agric. 1961–65; Asst. Depy. Min., Rural Devel., Dept. of Forestry 1965–66; Asst. Depy. Min. (Water), Dept. Energy, Mines and Resources 1966–71; Policy, Planning and Research, Dept. of the Environment 1971–73; Asst. Depy. Min. Parks Canada 1973–86; Pres., Royal Candn. Geographical Soc. 1986–92; Environmental Advisor, Inst. for Rsch. on Public Policy 1987– ; served in 2nd World War in R.C.N.V.R., 1944–45; Past Pres., Candn. Assn. of Geographers; Past Pres., Royal Candn. Geographical Soc.; Vice Pres., Candn. Wildlife Found.; Trustee, Nature Conservancy of Can.; mem., Candn. Inst. of Forestry; United Church; recreations: fishing, skiing, curling; Home: 5 Okanagan Dr., Nepean, Ont. K2H 7E7.

**DAVIDSON, Colin H.,** M.Arch.; architect; educator; b. Exeter, U.K. 4 March 1928; s. Douglas Nangle and Dulcie Rose (Winter) D.; e. Marlborough Coll. 1946; Brussels City Royal Acad. Dipl. Arch. 1951; Mass. Inst. of Technol. M.Arch. 1955; m. Lucienne d. Lucien and Marie Fiant 1958; children: Dominique, Philip; DEAN, FACULTE DE L'AMENAGEMENT, UNIV. DE MONTREAL 1976–85, Prof. of Arch. there 1968– ; Arch. Asst., Luccichenti Monaco, Rome 1951–54; The Architect's Collaborative Cambridge 1954–55; Arch., London Co. Council 1957–60; Arch. Asst. Sir Hugh Casson, London 1960–61; Pres., C.H. Davidson, Consultants, London 1961–68; Visiting Prof. Univ. of Wash. 1964; Washington Univ. 1967–69; Visiting Lectr. Harvard Grad. Sch. of Design 1973–75; author: 'Canadian Thesaurus of Construction Science and Technology' 2 vols. 1978; 'Canadian Urban Thesaurus' 1979; 'Conception des Espaces Industriels et amélioration des conditions de travail, Actes d'un colloque' 1982; Founder-Ed. 'Industrialisation Forum' 1969–79; Pres., IF Research Corp.; Mem., Internat. Council for Building Rsch., Studies and Documentation - CIB; Mem., Order of Architects of Que. 1987– ; Mem. Bd., Cibât, Internat. Bldg. Centre in Montréal 1990– ; Office: Univ. de Montréal, C.P. 6128, Succursale A, Montréal, Qué. H3C 3J7.

**DAVIDSON, Donald Robert,** C.A.; chartered accountant; b. Orillia, Ont. 5 Oct. 1943; s. Robert Sydney (dec'd) and Lottie May (Goodchild) D.; e. Park St. C.I. 1962; C.A. 1968; m. Bernice d. James and Isobel Buckingham 31 July 1965; one s.: Robert James; PARTNER, FULLER JENKS LANDAU 1975– ; Partner, Davidson, Mostov & Company 1971; Council Mem., HLB International 1976–88; Chrmn. 1989; club: Ontario; Home: R.R. 1, Hawkestone, Ont. L0L 1T0; Office: 280 Jarvis St., Toronto, Ont. M5B 2C5.

**DAVIDSON, Dorothy Louise;** retired executive; b. Joliette, Que. 29 July 1911; d. Harold and Louisa Alberta (Stafford) Crabtree; e. King's Hall, Compton 1929; McGill Univ. 1933; m. Edgar s. Maxwell and Emilia (Birkholz) D. 5 Aug. 1943; LL.D., Mount Allison Univ.; Former Pres., The Harold Crabtree Foundation, Retired 1993; Home: 2411 – 400 Stewart St., Ottawa, Ont.; Office: 130 Albert St., Suite 2005, Ottawa, Ont. K1P 5G4.

**DAVIDSON, Frederick W.,** B.A., M.B.A.; financial executive; b. Toronto, Ont. 10 Sept. 1947; s. Alfred William and Virginia Caldwell (McBean) D.; e. Simon Fraser Univ. B.A. 1969; Univ. of B.C. M.B.A. 1970; m. Linda Ryckman; children: Kirsten, Ryan; Pres. & C.E.O., Energold Minerals Inc. 1993–.; received C.A. Price Waterhouse 1972; Chief Financial Officer, Erickson Mining Corp. 1978; Chief Financial Offr., Total Energold Corp. 1985–92; Dir., North American Metals; British Columbia Mining Museum 1991– ; Mining Assn. on B.C. 1991– ; Mem., Prospectors & Developers Assn. of Canada; Candn. Equestrian Fed.; recreations: equestrian; clubs: Vancouver, Hollyburn Country; Home: 1444 Sandhurst Place, West Vancouver, B.C. V7S 2P4.

**DAVIDSON, George Forrester,** C.C. (1973), Grand Silver Cross of Honour (Govt. of Austria, 1985), M.A., Ph.D., LL.D., L.H.D., D.Litt.; b. Bass River, N.S. 18 Apr. 1909; s. Oliver Wendell and Emma Jane (Sullivan) D.; e. Elem. Sch., Bass River; Duke of Connaught High Sch., New Westminster, B.C.; Univ. of Brit. Columbia, B.A. 1928, LL.D. 1955; Harvard Univ., M.A. 1930, Ph.D. 1932; L.H.D. Brandeis Univ. 1961; LL.D., Univ. of Victoria, 1968; D.Litt. Acadia 1973; LL.D. McMaster 1973; D. Adm., Univ. of Ottawa, 1977; m. Elizabeth Ruth, d. Frank Henderson, Vancouver, 9 July 1935; children: Roger Reynolds, Craig Sullivan, Barbara Louise; Prov. Supt. of Welfare and Neglected Children, Prov. of B.C., 1934–35; Extve. Dir., Vancouver Welfare Fed. and Council of Social Agencies, 1935–39; Dir. of Social Welf., Prov. of B.C., 1939–42; Extve. Dir., Candn. Welf. Council, 1942–44; Depy. Min. Dept. National Health & Welfare 1944–60; Depy. Min. Dept. Citizen & Immig. 1960–62; Dir., Bureau of Govt. Organ., Privy Council Office 1963–64; Secy. of Treas. Bd., Dept. of Finance, 1964–68; Pres. CBC 1968–72; Under Sec'y. Gen. for Admin. & Management, U.N. 1972–79; Special Adviser to Extve. Dir., United Nations Fund for Population Activities 1980–86; Candn. Rep. to U.N. Social Comn., 1947–50; mem. of Candn. del. to U.N. Econ. and Social Council on numerous occasions, 1946–52; Chairman, Social, Humanitarian and Cultural Committee United Nations General Assembly, 1953; Pres., U.N. Econ. & Social Council, 1958; President, Can. Conf. on Social Work, 1952–54; Internat. Conf. of Social Work, 1956–60; Chrmn., Nat. Jt. Council of the Pub. Service of Can., 1954–60; has written numerous reports and articles on social welfare and U.N. problems; United Church; Home: 1120 Beach Dr., Apt. 603, Victoria, B.C. V8S 2N1.

**DAVIDSON, Melville Whitelaw,** B.A., M.A., A.F.C.; writer; b. Calgary, Alta. 12 June 1912; s. David and Jean (Whitelaw) D.; e. McGill Univ. B.A. 1936; Sch. of Internat. Studies, Geneva, Switzerland 1936; Columbia Univ. M.A. 1939; War Staff Coll. 1944; Harvard Univ. Advanced Mgmt. Prog. 1967; m. Audrey d. Herbert A. Locke 18 Nov. 1944; children: Mrs. Douglas Scott, Ian David C.A., Derek Locke, Leigh Anthes; Navigator, Royal Candn. Air Force 1939–45; Wing Commander Ret.; joined Canada and Dominion Sugar, Chatham, Ont. Dec. 1945; transf. to HQ in Montreal 1960; Resident Vice-Pres., Redpath Ind., Toronto, Ont. 1968–75; Pres., Candn. Sugar Inst. 1975–82; author 'The Canadian Sugar Industry: A Basic Study,' several fact sheets on sugar industry, three company histories; awarded Air Force Cross; Polish Air Force Award; Pres. Internat. Sugar Rsch. Found., Bethesda, Md. 1970–71; Anglican; Address: 72 Highbourne Rd., Toronto, Ont. M5P 2J4.

**DAVIDSON, Neil Anderson,** Q.C., LL.B.; b. Stettler, Alta. 23 Feb. 1916; s. Robert Anderson and Jane Simpson (Ogg) D.; e. Univ. of Alta., LL.B. 1940; m. Isabel Muriel, d. Russell Stanley, Edmonton Alta., 29 Apr. 1942; children: Diane Isabel Beaumont, Barbara Jean Davidson, Margaret Muriel Newell, Gordon Neil Stanley Davidson; Sr. Partner, Davidson & Co. 1966–89; called to Bar of B.C. 1941; cr. Q.C. 1969; com. practice of law in Vernon, B.C. as Partner in firm of Morrow and Davidson, 1946; firm became Morrow, Davidson & Seaton 1951; Sr. Partner, Davidson & Co. 1966–77; Chrmn. of B.C. Liquor Board 1973–77; Mayor, City of Vernon, B.C. 1979–81; served with RCAF for 4 yrs. during World War II; recipient, Canada Bar Assn. Georges C. Goyer Q.C. Award for Distinguished Service 1993; served on Silver Star Parks Board (Chrmn. 15 yrs.) and with Coll. and Prof. Groups; mem., Candn. Bar Assn.; B.C., Vernon and Yale Bar Assn. (Past Pres.); Senate, Univ. of B.C.; Liberal; Un. Ch.; recreation: outdoor sports; Home: 1801 - 27th Ave., Vernon, B.C. V1T 1R3; Office: 4th Floor, 3205 - 32nd St., Vernon, B.C. V1T 2M4.

**DAVIDSON, Paul James,** B.Eng., LL.M.; educator; barrister & solicitor; b. Owen Sound, Ont. 5 Oct. 1947; s. Melville James and Lois Elizabeth (Stevens) D.; e. Carleton Univ. B.Eng. 1969; Univ. of Ottawa LL.B. 1972; Univ. of London, London Sch. of Econ. & Pol. Sci. LL.M. 1975; m. Brenda d. Joseph and Sadie Morrison 3 June 1971; two children: Shainen, Lian; ASSOC. PROF. OF LAW CARLETON UNIV. 1983– , Asst. Prof. 1976–83; Rsch. Fellow, Candn.-Southeast Asian Relations, Inst. of Southeast Asian Studies, Singapore 1992–93; Policy Analysis Group Dept. Consumer & Corporate Affairs Ottawa 1974; private law practice Ottawa 1975–76; Lectr. in Law Univ. of Ottawa 1976–77, 1987–89; Visiting Fellow in Law Nat. Univ. of Singapore 1982–83, co-ed. Current Problems Internat. Trade Financing Proceedings Inaugural Conf. 1983, 2nd ed. 1990; Group Instr. and Lectr. Bar Admission Course Law Soc. Upper Can. 1978–84; legal cons. internat. trade & invest. issues; Co-ord. Asian Pacific Rsch. & Resource Centre; Pres. Candn. Arbitration, Conciliation & Amicable Composition Centre; Sec. Internat. Fedn. Comm. Arbitration Instns.; Vice Pres., Candn. Sect. Inter Am. Comm. Arbitration Comn.; Mem., Adv. Bd., World Arbitration & Mediation Report; author 'ASEAN Business Laws and Investment Procedures' 1987; co-author 'Commercial Arbitration Institutions: An International Directory and Guide' 1986, 2nd ed. 1992; editor: 'International Commercial Arbitration - Commercial Arbitration Law in Asia and the Pacific'; 'Law & Practice Under the GATT and Other Trading Arrangements - The Association of Southeast Asian Nations: ASEAN'; numerous articles and papers; mem. Law Soc. of Upper Can.; Candn. Asian Studies Assn.; Candn. Council Internat. Law; Home: 290 Clemow Ave., Ottawa, Ont. K1S 2B8; Office: Ottawa, Ont. K1S 5B6.

**DAVIDSON, Robert William,** C.A.; chartered accountant and management consultant; b. Croydon, England 24 May 1947; s. William Thomson and Vera (Noton) D.; e. Ashford Grammar Sch.; Isleworth Polytech. Coll.; m. Heather d. John and Joan Bisson 27 May 1972; children: Mark Robert, Matthew James; articled at Bolton Colby & Co., England qualifying as C.A. 1972; Mgr., Longcrofts 1972–73; immigrated to Canada 1973; Auditor, then Supvr., Price Waterhouse 1973–78; Controller, Consolidated Graphics Ltd. (now Cairn Capital Inc.) 1978; Treas. & Dir., Abstainers Insurance Co. and Maplex General Insur. Co. (both owned by Maplex Management & Holdings Ltd.) 1986; Vice-Pres. & Chief Operating Offr., Maplex Management & Holdings Ltd. 1983–86; started own C.A. & management consulting practice providing serv. to small & medium business 1987; Dir. & majority shareholder, Robert Davidson Consulting Inc.; F.C.A. (England & Wales) 1979; Mem., Church of England; Ont. Soccer Referees Assn.; Chief Refereee, Markham Soccer Club 1991–92, 1992–93 seasons; recreations: golf, soccer referee; Home: 47 Squire Bakers Lane, Markham, Ont. L3P 3G8; Office: 178 Main St., Unionville, Ont. L3R 2G9.

**DAVIDSON, Roger Reynolds,** B.Sc., M.A., Ph.D.; university professor; b. Vancouver, B.C. 14 June 1938; s. George Forrester and Elizabeth Ruth (Henderson) D.; e. Queen's Univ. B.Sc. 1960; Univ. of Toronto M.A. 1961; Florida State Univ. Ph.D. 1966; m. Cherie Elizabeth d. Thomas and Myrtle MacKenzie 11 Aug. 1962; children: Heather, Colleen, Michael; PROF., MATH. AND STATISTICS, UNIV. OF VICTORIA 1979– ; Instr., Florida State Univ. 1964–65; Asst. Prof., Univ. of Vict. 1966–71; Asst. Prof., Cornell Univ. 1971–73; Assoc. Prof., Univ. of Vict. 1971–79, Chrmn., Dept. of Math 1977–81, Dean of Arts & Science 1981–84, Dean of Science 1984–85; author of technical papers appearing in following journals: Biometrika, Biometrics, Communications in Statistics, J. Am. Statist. Assn., J. Combinatorial Theory and Sankhyā; Book Reviews Ed. Candn. Jour. of Statistics 1980–83; Bd. of Gov., Univ. of Victoria 1980–84, Senate 1990– ; mem., Statistical Soc. of Can. (Bd. of Dir., Rep. from B.C., Alta., Yukon 1980, 1981); Internat. Statistical Inst.; Royal Statistical Soc.; Am. Stat. Assn.; Biometrics Soc.; Bernoulli Soc. for Math. Stats. & Probability; Inst. of Math. Stats.; Soc. of Sigma Xi; United Church; recreations: skiing, sailing, camping, theatre; Office: P.O. Box 3045, Victoria, B.C. V8W 3P4.

**DAVIDSON, Roy Mitchell,** M.A.; economic consultant; b. Los Angeles, Cal. 5 July 1923; s. William and Margaret Lawson (Mitchell) D.; e. Pub. and High Schs., Calgary, Alta.; Univ. of Alta., B.A. 1944; Univ. of Toronto, M.A. 1947; Depy. Head, Bureau of Competition Policy, Dept. of Consumer & Corp. Affairs, 1974–82 (formerly Sr. Econ. Adv.); joined govt. service as Jr. Adm. Asst., Dept. of Justice, 1947; apptd. Combines Offr. 1948; Dir. of Merger & Monopoly Br., Combines Investigation Office, 1960; served with RCAF 1944–45; Vice-Chrmn., Bd. of Trustees, Dominion Chalmers United Church; recreations: handball, squash; Home: 121 Buell St., No. 66, Ottawa, Ont. K1Z 7E7.

**DAVIDSON, Thomas Noel,** B.Sc.; executive; b. Evansville, Indiana 4 Oct. 1939; s. Harry R. and Helen E. D.; e. Michigan State Univ., B.Sc. (High Hons.) 1961; m. Sally d. Paul and Ernestine Fries, 25 Sept. 1958; children: Tom Noel, John Cullen, James Robert, Jennifer Jill; Chairman of the Board: Cardinal Crest Partners; Nutech Precision Metals Inc.; Quarry Hill Partners; Sklar-Peppler of Am. Inc.; Young Presidents Organization Inc. (past Internat. Pres.); Chrmn., Ocean Reef Club; Past Chrmn.: Metro Toronto Convention Centre; Soc. of the Plastics Industry; Ontario Open Golf Tournament; Candn. PGA Golf Championship; Past Chrmn. and Dir.: Hugh MacMillan Rehabilitation Centre; Griffith Island (Past Chrmn.), Wiarton; General Trust Corp.; PCL Industries Ltd.; Hanson Inc.; Director: Canada Publishing Corp.; Derlan Industries Ltd.; MDC Corp.; Nutech Precision Metals LP; The Am. Museum of Fly Fishing; Varity Corp. (Massey Ferguson, Kelsey Hayes, Perkins Diesel); Panstwowe Wydawnictwo Naukowe (PWN Publishing); Past Director: PCL Packaging; Am. Brass Co.; Ansonia Brass; Atco Controls Inc.; Buffalo Brass Co.; Dorr-Oliver Inc.; Sandbright & Co.; Volstatic Inc.; LUSF & G Insurance of Can.; Plasti-Fab Ltd.; Westhem Corp.; Soc. of Plastics Engineers; Variety Village; Past Mem.: C.D. Howe Institute; Con Smythe Rsch. Found.; Dorset Resources; Carborondam Abrasives Inc.; Jensen Fittings Inc.; Consolidated Brinco Inc.; Blissymbonic Found.; Stephensons Rent-all; Canadian Club; Honours: Entrepreneur of the Year, Financial Post 1979; SPI Man of the Year 1985; Fraternities: Tau Beta Pi (Technical Hon.); Pi Tau Sigma (Technical Hon.); Clubs: Toronto Rosedale Golf; Bayview Country (Past Dir.); Caledon Mountain Trout; Ocean Reef Yacht, Key Largo; Key Largo Anglers; Card Sound Golf, Key Largo; Canadian, N.Y.; Canadian, Toronto; English Turn Golf & Country, New Orleans; Harbour Course, Key Largo; Residence: 29 Cardinal Lane, Ocean Reef Club, Key Largo, Fla. 33037.

**DAVIDSON, William Scott,** B.Sc., Ph.D.; educator; b. Ballater, Scot. 16 Apl. 1952; s. Scott Cairns and Lily (Ritchie) D.; e. Banchory (Scot.) Acad. 1970; Edinburgh Univ. B.Sc. 1974; Queen's Univ. Kingston Ph.D. 1978; m. Evelyn d. Alexander and Irene Purves 17 Aug. 1974; children: Lindsay Anne. Calum Scott Laurie; PROF. OF BIOCHEM., MEMORIAL UNIV. OF NFLD. 1992– ; Med. Rsch. Council Fellow Biochem. Dept. Univ. of Cal. Berkeley 1978–80; M.R.C. Centennial Fellow in Biochem. Univ. of Conn. 1980–81; Asst. Prof. of Biochem. present Univ. 1981; Assoc. Prof. of Biochem. 1987; Prof. of Biochem. 1993; NSERC/Royal Soc. Bilateral Exchange Fellow 1987; Bensinger-Lidell Fellow of Atlantic Salmon Fedn. 1988; mem. Med. Rsch. Council Grants Panel (Biochem.) 1989–92; mem. NSERC Grants Panel (Strategic/Biotech.) 1993– ; author or co-author numerous sci. publs. biochem. rsch.; assoc. ed. Biochem. Cell Biol. 1989–93; mem. Candn. Biochem. Soc.; Am. Soc. Biochem. & Molecular Biol.; Protein Soc.; Genetical Soc.; Atlantic Salmon Fedn.; Sigma Xi; recreations: sports, gardening, fishing; Home: 15 Dartmouth Place, St. John's, Nfld. A1B 2W1; Office: Biochemistry Dept., Memorial Univ., St. John's, Nfld. A1B 3X9.

**DAVIES, Alan Trewartha,** B.A., B.D., S.T.M., Ph.D.; university professor; b. Westmount, Que. 24 June 1933; s. Albert Victor and Florence Elsie (Clendenning) D.; e. Westmount H.S. 1950; McGill Univ. B.A. 1954, B.D. 1957; Union Theological Seminary N.Y. S.T.M. 1960, Ph.D. 1966; m. Marilyn d. Joshua and Mary Kiefer 22 Sept. 1962; children: Andrew Mark, Alison Anne; PROF. OF RELIGION, VICTORIA COLLEGE, UNIV. OF TORONTO 1989– ; Ordained Minister, United Ch. of Canada 1957; Minister, N.W. Interlake Pastoral Charge, Manitoba 1957–59; Wesley United Ch., Toronto 1964–67; McGill Delta Epsilon travelling Fellowship 1959; J. Clarence & Corale B. Workum Post-doctoral Fellowship, Hebrew Union College Cincinnati 1967–68; Visiting Mem., Senior Common Room, Mansfield College, Oxford (summer) 1975; Lectr., Victoria College, Univ. of Toronto 1969–71; Asst. Prof. 1971–77; Assoc. Prof. 1977–89; Mem., Un. Ch. of Canada; author: 'Anti-Semitism and the Christian Mind' 1969, 'Infected Christianity: A Study of Modern Racism' 1988; editor: 'Antisemitism and the Foundations of Christianity' 1979, 'Antisemitism in Canada: History and Interpretation' 1992; Home: 9 Torrington Dr., Etobicoke, Ont. M9C 3V3; Office: Toronto, Ont. M5S 1K7.

**DAVIES, Arthur Llewellyn;** publisher (retired); b. Brantford, Ont. 18 Aug. 1903; s. late Senator William Rupert (Past Pres., The 'Kingston Whig-Standard') and Florence (MacKay) D.; e. Renfrew (Ont.) Coll. Inst.; Central Tech. Sch., Toronto; m. Dorothy Eleanor, d. Dr. S. E. Porter, 5 May 1934; two s., Michael, Christopher; m. 2ndly Jean Rowe, 8 July 1969; Pres., Alda-Llyn Ltd.; Officer Order of St. John; Hon. Doctor of Laws (Queen's); Past Pres., The Kingston Whig-Standard Co. Ltd.; The Peterborough Examiner Co. Ltd.; Frontenac Broadcasting Co. Ltd.; Past Chrmn. of Extve. Comte., Queen's Univ.; Past Chrmn., Kingston Gen. Hosp.; Past Pres., Kingston and District United Fund; Kingston Chamber of Comm.; Ont. Prov. Dailies Assn.; Candn. Daily Newspaper Publishers Assn.; Kingston Community Chest; Freemason; Clubs: Kingston Yacht; Home: 245 Alwington Place, Kingston, Ont. K7L 4P9; Office: c/o The Davies Found., 165 Ontario St., Kingston, Ont. K7L 2Y6.

**DAVIES, Bryan Phillip,** B.Comm., M.P.A.; university administrator; b. Toronto, Ont. 24 Sept. 1948; s. Benjamin and Beulah (Davis) D.; e. Oakwood Collegiate; Univ. of Toronto B.Comm. 1971; Queen's Univ. M.P.A. 1973; VICE-PRES., BUSINESS AFFAIRS AND CHIEF ADMINISTRATIVE OFFICER, UNIV. OF TORONTO 1992– ; Dir., Govt. Prog., Ernst & Ernst 1973–75; Policy Advisor, Min. of Treas., Econ. & Intergovt. Affairs, Ont. 1975–79; Dir., Econ. Devel., Treas. & Econ. 1979–81; Asst. Dep. Min., Econ. Policy 1981–83; Taxation & Intergovt. Finance 1983–85; Dep. Min., Citizenship & Culture 1985–86; Financial Institutions 1986–88; Housing 1988–89; Dep. Treas. & Dep. Min. of Econ. 1989–92; Dir., Suncor Inc.; University of Toronto Press Incorporated; Nat. Treas., Inst. of Public Admin. of Canada 1991– ; recreations: cottaging, cooking; clubs: University; Home: 87 Old Mill Rd., Etobicoke, Ont. M8X 1G9; Office: 27 King's College Circle, Room 220, Toronto, Ont. M5S 1A1.

**DAVIES, Christine E.,** B.A., M.B., B.Ch., BAO, CCFP; family physician; association executive; b. N. Ireland 25 Jan. 1948; d. John and Doreen Ursula (Spragg) Rountree; e. Glenlola Coll. Sch., Bangor, N. Ireland; Trinity Coll., Dublin, B.A. 1970, M.B. B.Ch. BAO 1972; Certificant, College of Family Physicians of Canada 1980; m. Dr. E. Colin s. Clifford and Nancy D. 19 Sept. 1969; children: Gareth, Rachel, Elaine; PRES., FED. OF MEDICAL WOMEN OF CANADA 1988–89; Family Physician, Montreal 1973–82; Clinical Teacher; Staff and Asst. Chief, Family Med. Dept., Queen Elizabeth Hosp. and family physician, Saint John, NB 1983– ; Staff, Saint John Reg. Hosp., St. Joseph's Hosp.; Faculty Mem., Family Med., Dalhousie Univ.; Co-Chair, Saint John Health Action Counc.; special interest in adolescents; has developed & teaches course on Sexuality for Teens; Elder, Saint Andrew & St. David's Un. Ch.; Mem. of Council, College of Physicians & Surgeons of N.B. 1993– ; Mem., Soc. for Adolescent Med.; Candn. Physicians for Prevention of Nuclear War; recreations: gardening, cross country skiing, boating, reading; Office: 28 King St., Suite 3B, Saint John, N.B. E2L 1G3.

**DAVIES, David Ioan,** B.Sc., Ph.D.; university professor; b. Ibambi-Wamba, Zaire 28 Aug. 1936; s. Ivor and Rosalie Deborah (Sore) D.; e. Arbroath H.S.; Central Polytechnic (UK); London Sch. of Econ. and Pol. Science B.Sc. 1962; Univ. of Essex Ph.D. 1970; m. Diane d. Alex and Sally Bellan 19 May 1975; children: Miranda, Eric Mervyn, Thomas Oliver, Justin, Benjamin; PROFESSOR, SOCIOLOGY, YORK UNIV. 1977– ; Senior Tutor, Univ. of Cambridge 1962–65; Sr. Lectr., Univ. of Essex 1965–70; Assoc. Prof., Queen's Univ. 1970–72; Assoc. Prof., York Univ. 1972–77; Visiting Prof., Univ. of Guyana 1970; London Sch. of Econ. 1977–78; Editor, 'Borderlines' mag. 1984– ; Edit. Ctte. Mem., 'Stand' 1960–65, 'Canadian Forum' 1972–84, 'Can. J. of Pol. & Soc. Theory' 1982–85; author: 'African Trade Unions' 1966, 'Social Mobility and Political Change' 1970; 'Writers in Prison' 1990, 'Cultural Marxism' 1994; co-editor: 'Social Space: Canadian Perspectives' 1971; recreations: theatre, fine arts, gardening; Home: 162 Roselawn Ave., Toronto, Ont. M4R 1E6; Office: 309 Bethune College, 4700 Keele St., North York, Ont. M3J 1P3.

**DAVIES, Donald Harry,** B.Sc., Ph.D., F.C.I.C.; university professor, business executive; b. Ottawa, Ont. 26 Jan. 1938; s. Don and Eleanor May (Carson) D.; e. Glebe C.I. 1956; Carleton Univ. B.Sc. (Hons.) 1960; Univ. of Bristol Ph.D. 1963; m. Sherill d. Alice and Sanford Doleman 30 Dec. 1978; children: Donald Cedric, Allison Ruth; PRES., NOVA CHEM LIMITED 1978– ; & PROF. OF CHEMISTRY, SAINT MARY'S UNIV. 1979– ; Postdoct. Fellow, Nat. Rsch. Counc. 1963–65; Sess. Lectr., Carleton Univ. 1964–65; Asst. Prof. of Chem., Dalhousie Univ. 1965–69; Saint Mary's Univ. 1969–71; Assoc. Prof. 1971–79; Chrmn., Dept. of Chem. 1973–78; Chrmn., Atlantic Sect., Chem. Inst. of Can. 1977–78; Chrmn. Nat. Conf. Ctte., Chem. Inst. of Can. 1978–81; F.C.I.C. 1978; Pres., Shooting Fed. of N.S. 1973– ; Dir., Shooting Fed. of Canada 1975– ; Pres., Sport N.S. 1980–82; Chrmn., Candn. Counc. of Prov. & Territorial Sport Feds. Inc. 1982–85; Extve. Vice-Pres. and/or Treas., Sports Fed. of Can. 1984–93; Treas. N.S. Inst. of Science 1988– ; awarded Commemorative Medal for 125th Anniversary of Candn. Confederation 1992; recreations: shooting, equestrian; Home: 2651 Oxford St., Halifax, N.S. B3L 2T7; Office: Box 8746 Stn. A, Halifax, N.S. B3K 5M9.

**DAVIES, Hon. Francis William Harding;** record producer; music publisher; b. Northampton, Engl. 22 Nov. 1946; s. Rt. Hon. John Emerson Harding D. and Rt. Hon. The Lady Vera Georgina (Bates); e. Windlesham House Sch., Engl.; The Nautical Coll., Pangbourne, Engl.; Strasbourg Univ., France; m. Lynda d. Leo and Ruth Squires 1 June 1972; children: Meghan Mae Harding, Emily Gwyneth Emerson; Kate Theresa Georgina; PRESIDENT, T.M.P. - THE MUSIC PUBLISHER 1986– ; Corr. Billboard Mag., France 1964–65; Asst. Mgr. Internat. Promotion EMI Records Ltd., Engl. 1966–67; Export Mgr. Liberty Records Ltd., Engl. 1967–68; Pres. Love Prodns. Ltd., Can. 1970–78; Pres. Partisan Music Prodns. Inc. 1978–82; Pres., ATV Music Group, Can. 1982–85; Trustee, Candn. Acad. of Recording Arts and Sci. (CARAS); Chrmn., Candn. Mech. Reproduction Rights Agy. (CMRRA); The SOCAN Foundation; Dir., Soc. of Composers, Authors and Music Publishers of Can. (SOCAN); Candn. Music Publ. Assn. (CMPA); Love Prodns. Ltd.; Partisan Music Prodn. Inc.; mem. CIRPA; CCMA; CMA; SAC; SOCAN; recreations: photography, music; Home: P.O. Box 615, Don Mills, Ont. M3C 2T6; Office: 1670 Bayview Ave., Ste. 300, Toronto, Ont. M4G 3C2.

**DAVIES, Gareth John;** association executive; b. Neath, Wales 30 Jan. 1944; s. Gwyn and Molly (Blann) D.; e. Neath Grammar Sch.; Coll. of Law (U.K.); m. Maureen d. Alan and Trudy Martin 1 Sept. 1973; children: Trudy, Allison; SECY./GEN., UNIVERSAL FEDERATION OF TRAVEL AGENTS' ASSOC. 1989– ; (represents Nat. Travel Agents' Assns. of more than eighty countries); Pros. Solicitor, South Wales Police Authority 1969–70; Asst. Co. Sec., Beecham Rsch. Internat. 1970–71; Partner in U.K. law firm 1972–76; Chief Admin., Ont. Travel Indus. Conf. 1977–78; Extve. Dir., Alliance of Candn. Travel Assns. 1978–89; Solicitor and Notary; Mem., IATA/UFTAA; Passenger Agency Travel Agent (PATB); World Travel Market Council (WTM); Advisory Council, PATA Europe; Mem. & Hon. Sec., Young Solicitor's Nat. Ctte. of Law Soc. of England and Wales 1975–76; Brit. Rep. to Internat. Fed. of Law Students 1968–69; Chrmn., Assoc. Mem. Group, Law Soc. (England & Wales) 1968–69; Mem., Royal Ocean Racing Club; Yacht Club of Monaco; Rideau Club; Law Soc. of U.K.; Home: 823 Les Cyclades, Fontvieille, Monaco 98000; Office: Ave. du Prince Héréditaire Albert, Stade Louis II - Entrée H, 98000 Monaco.

**DAVIES, Glynn Gareth,** B.Sc., F.C.A.; executive; b. Wellingborough, UK 19 Apr. 1944; s. Joseph Thomas and Bettina Olive (Johnson) D.; e. Palmers Sch. Grays, Essex, UK 1962; Hull Univ. B.Sc. 1965; m. Judith d. Harry and Dorothy Taylor 16 May 1970; children: Sarah Carolyn, James Philip; PRES. AND CHIEF EXEC. OFFR. DRECO ENERGY SERVICES LTD. 1987– ; C.A., Deloitte, Haskins & Sells, London, UK 1965–71; Corporate Auditor, Mobil Oil Corp. New York 1971–74; Project Finance Coordinator, Mobil Oil Indonesia Jakarta 1974–78; Controller, Mobil Oil Canada Calgary 1978–82; Finance Mgr. Mobil Producing Cameroon, Douala 1982–83; Planning & Finance Exec. P.T. Arun NGL Co. Jakarta 1983–84; Vice Pres. Finance present Co. 1984–87; Office: 3716 – 93 St., Edmonton, Alta. T6E 5N3.

**DAVIES, Haydn Llewellyn,** R.C.A.; sculptor; b. Rhymney, Wales 11 Nov. 1921; s. Emrys and Rosina (Gallop) D.; e. Central Tech. Sch. (Art) Toronto grad 1939; Ont. Coll. of Art (Fine Art) grad. A.O.C.A. 1947; Univ. of W. Ont. Marketing Management 1964; Univ. of Toronto Fine Art 1972–74; m. Eva d. John Koller 26 June 1948; two s. Haydn Bryan, Trevor Koller; following grad. O.C.A. entered film, TV and advertising business becoming Sr. Vice Pres. and Dir. McCann-Erickson Advertising of Canada Ltd. and Pres. Trevan Properties; resigned 1976 to become full-time sculptor; Artist-in-Residence, Center for the Arts, Vero Beach, Fla. 1986; rep. in pub., corporate and private colls. incl. Lambton Coll. of Arts and Technology, Sarnia, Ont.; Ont. Govt. Offices, Windsor; Burlington Cultural Centre; Galleria Nazionale d'Arte Moderna e Contemporanea, Rome; Museo d'Arte Moderna, Venice; Musée Royaux des Beaux-Arts de Belgique, Brussels; Nat. Museum of Wales; Victoria & Albert Museum, London, England; Art Museum of SouthEast Texas, Beaumont, TX; Art Collection of the Govt. of Ont., Toronto; rep. various exhns. incl. Wood Sculpture of the Americas 1977; Monumental Sculpture-7 Sculptors Toronto 1978; Steel-the Engineer and the Sculptor Univ. of W. Ont. 1980; Contemporary Sculpture at the Guild 1982; Centenary Exhbn. of the RCA 1980; Pratt Inst. Brooklyn Bridge Centenary 'Bridges' exhbn., NY 1983; solo exhns.: 'Planar Constructions' Burlington Cultural Centre, Burlington, Ont. 1989; The Gallery/Stratford, Stratford Ont. 1989; Center for the Arts, Vero Beach, Fla. 1990; Anita Shapolsky Gall., New York City, NY 1991; Art Museum of SouthEast Texas, Beaumont, TX 1992; Asheville Art Museum, Asheville NC 1993; served with RCAF 1941–45; recreation: collecting antiques, art; Club: R.C.Y.C.; Homes: 10 Rose Park Cres., Toronto, Ont. M4T 1P9.

**DAVIES, Ioan,** B.Sc., Ph.D.; university professor; b. Ibambi-Wamba, Zaire 28 Aug. 1936; s. Ivor and Rosalie Deborah (Sore) D.; e. Arbroath H.S. (Scotland) 1954; Univ. of London L.S.E., B.Sc. 1961; Essex Univ. Ph.D. 1970; m. Diane d. Alec and Sally Bellan 26 May 1975; children: Justin, Benjamin, Eric, Thomas, Miranda; PROF., YORK UNIV. 1972– ; Journalist, Dundee 1954–55; London 1961–62; Brit. Army Offr. 1955–57; Lectr., Cambridge Univ. 1962–65; Sr. Lectr., Essex Univ. 1965–70; Vis. Lectr., Univ. of Guyana 1970; Assoc. Prof., Queen's Univ. 1970–72; Vis. Prof., L.S.E. 1977–78; Visitor, Soviet Acad. of Sci., 1990 and 1991; Cons., J. Walter Thompson 1967; U.K. Cabinet Office 1968–69; Canatom 1984; Control Data 1985; Mem., Candn. Assn. of Sociol. & Anthropol.; Internat. Sociol. Assn.; Candn. Commun. Assn.; Modern Languages Assn.; Inst. of Contemporary Arts (London); author: 'African Trade Unions' 1966, 'Social Mobility and Political Change' 1970, 'Politics and Labour in Africa' 1975; 'Writers in Prison' 1990; co-author: 'Social Space – Canadian Perspectives' 1972; freelance journalist, 'Toronto Star,' 'Globe & Mail,' 'Canadian Forum,' CBC, BBC, and others; Founder-Dir.-Ed., 'Borderlines' 1984– ; Ed. Bd., 'Canadian Forum' 1972–86; 'Canadian Journal of Political and Social Theory' 1981–83; recreations: travel, swimming, reading; Home: 162 Roselawn Ave., Toronto, Ont. M4R 1E6; Office: Norman Bethune Coll., York Univ., 4700 Keele St., Downsview, Ont. M3J 1P3.

**DAVIES, John Arthur,** M.A., Ph.D., F.C.I.C., F.R.S.C.; research scientist; b. Prestatyn, N. Wales, U.K. 28 March 1927; s. late Francis James and Doris (Edkins) D.; e. Univ. of Toronto B.A. (St. Michael's Coll.) 1947, M.A. 1948, Ph.D. 1950; Univ. of Leeds Post-doctoral Fellow 1954–56; D.Sc. (Hon.) Royal Roads Mil. Coll. 1984; D.Sc. (Hon.) Univ. of Salford (UK) 1993; m. Florence Mary d. late Alfred Smithson 29 July 1950; children: Susan Mary, J. Christopher, Catherine M., Paul M., James N., Anne E.; PROF. EMERITUS, ENGINEERING PHYSICS, MCMASTER UNIV.; and Salford Univ. (U.K); joined Chalk River Nuclear Labs., Atomic Energy of Canada Ltd. 1950, becoming Princ. Rsch. Offr. until retired 1985; Visiting Prof. Inst. of Physics, Aarhus Univ. Denmark 1964–65, 1969–70; Cal. Tech. Pasadena 1969; Univ. of Osaka, Japan 1972; Noranda Award Chem. Inst. Can. 1965; T.D. Callinan Award Am. Electrochem. Soc. 1968; mem. Deep River & Dist. High Sch. Bd. 1959–68, Chrmn. 1 term; Renfrew Co. Bd. Educ. 1969; Deep River & Dist. Hosp. Bd. 1977–83; author 'New Uses for Low-Energy Accelerators' 1968; 'Ion Implantation of Semiconductors' 1970; 'Channeling – Theory, Observation and Applications' 1972; over 200 research papers; Fellow, Danish Royal Akademy of Arts & Sciences; Royal Soc. of Can.; Chem. Inst. of Can.; Bohmische Physikaliches Gesellschaften; R. Catholic; recreations: canoeing, cross-country skiing; Home: 7 Wolfe Ave., Deep River, Ont. K0J 1P0; Office: McMaster Univ., Hamilton, Ont. L8S 4L8.

**DAVIES, His Hon. John Llewellyn,** B.A., LL.B.; judge, retired; b. Sayward, B.C. 19 Feb. 1923; s. Daniel and Janet (Brain) D.; e. Univ. of B.C., B.A. 1953, LL.B. 1954; m. Vera d. Lewis and Rosalie McLean 16 May 1953; children: Barbara Lea, Brian Daniel; Judge, Provincial Court of B.C. 1969–91; read law with Cyril White; called to Bar of B.C. 1955; Clk. Silbak Premier 1940; Able Seaman, Union Steamships Ltd.; served with RCAF 1942–46; Bomb Aimer, 427 (Lion) Squadron; Deputy Game Warden and Bonus Cougar Hunter 1950– ; Barrister and Solr. White & Shore 1955; White, Shore, Davies & Co. 1956; Sr. mem. Davies & Associates 1962; Magistrate 1969; past Treas. B.C. Provincial Judges Assn.; Past Treas. Hastings E. Br. Royal Cand. Legion; Past Hon. Counsel Burnaby Boy Scouts; Shriner; Freemason; Protestant; recreations: hunting, fishing, photography, dog training, shooting; Clubs: Lions (Past Zone Chrmn.; Hon. mem. Burnaby N.); Totem Fly Fishers (Past Treas. and Hon. mem.); Coast Marksmen; Sayward and District Fish and Game Assn.; Home: 120 N. Warwick, Burnaby, B.C. V5B 1K7.

**DAVIES, Michael Rupert Llewellyn,** O.C. (1982), C.M., B.A., F.R.S.A.; b. Kingston, Ont. 22 July 1936; s. Arthur Llewellyn and Dorothy Eleanor (Porter) D.; e. Kingston (Ont.) Pub. Sch.; Trinity Coll. Sch., Port Hope (Ont.); Queen's Univ., B.A. 1959; m. Elaine, d. Earl Stephens, 8 Oct. 1960; children: Gregory, Eric, Andrew, Timothy, Jennifer; FOUNDER AND PRES., THE DAVIES CHARITABLE FOUND., Kingston, Ont.; Chrmn., Kasten Chase Applied Research, Toronto; Chrmn., Bd. of Govs., Trinty Coll. Sch.; Former Owner & Publisher, The Kingston Whig-Standard Co. Ltd. (1969–90), pub. of 'The Kingston Whig-Standard' daily newspaper; Gen. Mgr. 1962; Publisher 1969; Sole Prop. 1976; Past Chrmn., Commonwealth Press Union, Candn. Sec.; Past Pres., Candn. Daily Newspaper Publishers' Assn.; Ont. Prov. Dailies Assn.; Past Dir., Canadian Press; Past Pres., Ont. Fed. of Symphony Orchestras; Past Pres., Kingston Symphony Orchestra; Mem., Ontario Arts Counc. 1967–76; Mem., Stratford Shakespearean Festival 1970–76; Past Chrmn., Grand Theatre Bd.; Mayor's representative to obtain and install large outdoor sculptures to commemorate Kingston's Tercentenary, 1973; mem. Olympic Organizing Comte. 1976; mem. Mang. Comte. (1965–76) and Pres. (1975), Kingston General Hosp.; Past Dir., Young Naturalist Foundation; Past Pres. Marine Museum of the Great Lakes, Kingston; Past-Pres. (Founding), Kingston Rowing Club; mem. & Past Vice Chrmn., Bd. of Trustees, Queen's Univ.; Life Gov. and Vice Chrmn. of Extve. Ctte., Trinity Coll. School; Campaign Chrmn., Combined 3 Hospital Appeal for Kingston Health Sciences Centre; mem., Fund-Raising, St. Mary's of the Lake Hosp.; Founding Pres., Martello Tower Soc. of Kingston; mem., Disciplinary Tribunal, Inst. of Chartered Accountants of Ont. 1988–91; Past Dir., The Trillium Found. of Ont.; rec'd. Queen's Jubilee Medal 1977; Member, Order of Canada 1982; Kingston Award, Queen's Alumni Assoc. 1987; Commemorative Medal (for leadership and promotion of the concept of a smoke-free society), The World Health Organization 1988; Commemorative Medal, 125th Anniversary of Candn. Confedn. 1992; recreations: sailing, music, tennis; Clubs: Kingston Yacht; Toronto; Royal Dart Yacht & Ocean Cruising; Home: 226 Alwington Place, Kingston, Ont. K7L 4P8; Office: 165 Ontario St., Kingston, Ont. K7L 2Y6.

**DAVIES, Patricia Anne,** B.A.; writer; editor; b. Toronto, Ont. 23 Nov. 1945; d. Norman Robert and Wilma Dorothy (Rogers) Nash; e. Univ. of Toronto Victoria Col. B.A. 1968; children: Evan, Elizabeth; ed. specializing in news features The Globe and Mail 1976–85; freelance mag. writer since 1986; recipient Nat. Mag. Award (Gold) 1989; mem. Bd. Simpson Ave. Un. Ch. and Head Min. & Personnel Ctte. 1989–90; mem. Bd., Bain Ave. Daycare 1990–91, 1991–92; mem., Bellefair United Church; recreations: tennis, cross-country skiing, aerobics, quilting, cooking; Club: St. Clair; Address: 11 Sparkhall Ave., Toronto, Ont. M4K 1G4.

**DAVIES, Peter D.R.;** diplomat; b. 29 Nov. 1936; m. Elizabeth Mary Lovett Williams 1967; children: one son & two daughters; BRITISH CONSUL-GENERAL, TORONTO & DIRECTOR OF TRADE & INVESTMENT, CANADA 1991– ; joined British Foreign Service 1964; served in Nicosia 1966–67; 1st Sec. in Budapest 1968–71; Commercial Consul, Rio de Janeiro 1974–78; Commercial Counsellor, The Hague 1978–82; Deputy High Comnr., Kuala Lumpur 1982–85; attended Royal College of Defence Studies (London) 1986; Head of Arms Control & Disarmament Dept., FCO 1987–91; clubs: National, Ontario, Waterfront; Office: #1910, 777 Bay St., Toronto, Ont. M5G 2G2.

**DAVIES, Robert Henry;** C.A.E.; executive; b. Liverpool, Eng. 13 Jan. 1929; s. Joseph and Delia (Dignum) D.; e. De La Salle Grammar Sch. 1946 and Liverpool Tech. Coll. 1949; Univ. of B.C. Extve. Mang. Dipl. 1958; m. Helen, 27 July 1957; four d. Carolyn, Diana, Rita, Linda; R.H.DAVIES, CONSULTANT; Consultant, Heart & Stroke Found., B.C. & Yukon; Dir., Regional Services, The Nature Trust of B.C.; Lectr., Vancouver Jr. Chamber and Fac. of Comm. and Bus. Adm., Univ. B.C.; Candn. Cancer Soc. 1961–68; Sr. Adv. Counc., Heart & Stroke Found., B.C. & Yukon (Extve. Dir. 1968–90); served several engn. consulting firms for 13 yrs.; served with Royal Naval Air Service 1947–1949; Hon. Life Mem., Certified Assn. Extve. and Examiner, Candn. Soc. of Assoc. Extves. (Past Chrmn. of the Bd.; Past Chrmn., Hon. Life Mem., B.C. Chapter); Consultant, Amer. Heart Assn.; Int. Soc. & Fed. of Cardiology; mem., Amer. Soc. Assoc. Executives; mem. Welsh Soc.; Vice-Pres., Independent Immigration Aid Assn.; R. Catholic Lay Lector; Club: Marine Drive Golf (Past Pres.; Bd. Trustees); Office: 3295 West 23rd Ave., Vancouver, B.C. V6L 1P9.

**DAVIES, Robertson,** C.C. (1972), B. Litt., D.Litt., D.C.L., LL.D., D.Hum. Litt., F.R.S.C. (1967), F.R.S.L. (1984); author; educator; b. Thamesville, Ont., 28 Aug. 1913; s. Senator William Rupert and Florence (MacKay) D.; e. Upper Can. Coll.; Queen's Univ.; Balliol Coll., Oxford, B.Litt.; LL.D.: Univ. of Alta. 1957; Queen's Univ. 1962; Univ. of Man. 1972; Univ. of Calgary 1975; Univ. of Toronto 1981; Univ. P.E.I. 1989; D.Litt.: McMaster Univ. 1959; Univ. of Windsor 1971; York Univ. 1973; Mt. Allison Univ. 1973; Memorial Univ., Univ. of W. Ont., McGill Univ., Trent Univ. 1974; Univs. of Lethbridge and Waterloo 1981; Univ. of B.C. 1983; Univ. of Santa Clara 1985; Trinity Coll., Dublin 1990; Oxford Univ. 1991; D.C.L., Bishop's Univ. 1967; D.Hum. Litt., Univ. of Rochester 1983; Dowling College, N.Y. 1992; D.S.L., Thornloe Univ., Sudbury, 1988; m. Brenda Mathews, 2 Feb. 1940; children: Miranda, Jennifer, Rosamond; Master, Massey College, Toronto 1963–81; Professor of Eng., Univ. of Toronto until retirement 1981; PROFESSOR EMERITUS AND FOUNDING MASTER, MASSEY COLL., UNIV. OF TORONTO; Senator, Stratford Shakespearean Festival 1953; sometime actor and mem. Old Vic Repertory Co. and teacher in Old Vic Theatre Sch., Eng.; returned to Can. as Lit. Ed., 'Saturday Night' 1940; became Ed., 'Examiner' 1942; author of 'Shakespeare's Boy Actors' 1939; 'Shakespeare for Young Players' 1942; 'Diary of Samuel Marchbanks' 1947; 'Eros at Breakfast and Other Plays' 1949; 'Fortune My Foe' 1949; 'The Table Talk of Samuel Marchbanks' 1949; 'At My Heart's Core' 1950; 'Tempest Tost' 1951; 'A Masque of Aesop' 1952; 'Leaven of Malice' 1954; 'A Jig for the Gypsy' 1954; 'A Mixture of Frailties' 1958; 'A Voice from the Attic' 1960; 'A Masque of Mr. Punch' 1963; 'Marchbanks' Almanack' 1967; 'Stephen Leacock' 1970; 'Feast of Stephen' 1970; 'Fifth Business' 1970; 'The Manticore' 1972; 'Hunting Stuart and Other Plays' 1972; 'World of Wonders' 1975; (with others) 'The Revels History of Drama in English' (Vol. 6, 1750–1880) 1975; 'One Half of Robertson Davies' 1977; 'Question Time' 1975; 'The Enthusiasms of Robertson Davies' (ed. by Judith Skelton Grant) 1979; 'Robertson Davies: The Well-Tempered Critic' (ed. by Judith Skelton Grant) 1981; 'The Rebel Angels' 1981; 'High Spirits' 1982; 'The Mirror of Nature' 1983; 'What's Bred in the Bone' 1985; 'The Papers of Samuel Marchbanks' 1985; 'The Lyre of Orpheus' 1988; 'Murther & Walking Spirits' 1991; 'Reading and Writing' 1993; author (with Sir Tyrone Guthrie) 'Renown at Stratford' 1953; 'Twice Have the Trumpets Sounded' 1954; 'Thrice the Brinded Cat Hath Mew'd' 1955; 3–act plays produced: 'Fortune My Foe' 1948; 'King Phoenix' 1950; 'At My Heart's Core' 1950; 'A Jig for the Gypsy' 1954; 'Hunting Stuart' 1955; 'Love and Libel' 1960; 'Brothers in the Black Art' (TV) 1974; 'Question Time' 1975; 'Pontiac and the Green Man' 1977; 'World of Wonders' (stage version) 1992; awarded Louis Jouvet Prize for direction 'Taming of the Shrew,' Dom. Drama Festival 1949; Stephen Leacock Medal 1955; Lorne Pierce Medal for Lit., R.S.C. 1961; Gov.-Gen.'s Award for Fiction 1973; Hon. mem., Am. Acad. & Inst. of Arts & Letters 1980; Hon. Fellow, Balliol Coll., Oxford 1986; Hon. Fellow, Trinity Coll., Univ. of Toronto 1987; City of Toronto Book Award 1986; Candn. Authors' Assoc. award for fiction 1986; Banff Sch. of Fine Arts Nat. Award 1986; Toronto Arts Awards: Lifetime Achievement Award 1986; Nat. Arts Club, N.Y., Medal of Honour for Lit. (1st Candn.) 1987; Scottish Arts Counc., Neil Gunn Internat. Fellowship 1988; Order of Ontario 1988; Diplôme d'honneur, Candn. Conf. of the Arts 1988; Canada Counc. Molson Prize in the Arts 1988; Author of the Year award, Foundation for the Advancement of Candn. Letters & the Periodical Marketers of Canada 1990; Anglican; recreation: music; Clubs: Long Christmas Dinner; York (Toronto); Athenaeum (London); Address: Massey College, 4 Devonshire Pl., Toronto, Ont. M5S 2E1.

**DAVIES, Ronald Wallace,** Ph.D., D.Sc.; educator; b. London, UK 23 Dec. 1940; s. Wallace George and Hazel May (Crocker) D.; e. Univ. of Wales, Bangor B.Sc. (Botany) 1962, B.Sc. (Zoology) 1963, Ph.D. 1967, D.Sc. 1986; Univ. of Wales, Cardiff Dip. Edn. 1964; m. Mary M.E. d. Gwilym and Elyned Harries 20 July 1963; children: Calvin M.W., Neal M., E. Lynne; PROF. OF BIOL. UNIV. OF CALGARY 1980– , Head of Biol. Sci's 1989– ; Asst. Lectr. in Zool. Univ. of Wales, Bangor 1967–68; Rsch. Sci. Candn. Internat. Biol. Prog. Marion Lake Project Univ. of B.C. 1968–69; Asst. Prof. of Biol. present Univ. 1969, Assoc. Prof. 1971–80; author over 150 sci. papers internat. jours.; mem. Brit. Ecol. Soc.; Ecol. Soc. Am.; Candn. Soc. Zools.; Freshwater Biol. Assn. (G.B.); Am. Soc. Limnol. & Oceanog.; N.Am. Benthol. Soc.; Alta. Assn. Profl. Biols.; Societas Internat. Limnologiae; Royal Commonwealth Soc.; Sigma Xi; recreation: sports; Home: 2912 University Place N.W., Calgary, Alta. T2N 4H5; Office: 2500 University Dr. N.W., Calgary, Alta. T2N 1N4.

**DAVIES, Walter,** F.R.I.C.S., C.R.E.; Chartered Surveyor / real estate consultant; b. Middlesbrough, England 13 Aug. 1946; s. Walter and Audrey E. (Morgan) D.; e. Univ. of London (U.K.), Estate Mngt. 1970; F.R.I.C.S. 1984; C.R.E. 1991; m. Jane d. Ralph and Joan Hodgson 4 Sept. 1976; children: Ralph Walter, Alexandra Jane, Amy Elizabeth; PRES., DRIVERS JONAS (CAN.) LTD. 1983– ; Sr. Devel. Mgr., Capital & Counties Ltd., England 1972–76; Gen. Mgr., Straits Prop., Singapore 1976–79; Vice-Pres., A.E. LePage Comm. Real Estate, Toronto 1979–83; Dir. & Pres., Drivers Jonas (Can.) Ltd.; Partner, Drivers Jonas – A U.K. Partnership; Dir., Economics Research Associates, (U.S. Corp.); recreations: sailing, skiing; clubs: Ontario, Boulevard, Tanglin (Singapore); Home: 33 Halford Ave., Toronto, Ont. M6S 4G1; Office: Scotia Plaza, Box 218, Ste. 4812, 40 King St. W., Toronto, Ont. M5H 3Y2.

**DAVIES, Hon. William Hugh,** LL.B.; Justice; b. Chilliwack, B.C. 2 June 1931; s. John Lorimer D. and Mabel Helen (Currie) D.; e. Chilliwack High Sch.; Univ. of B.C. LL.B. 1955; m. Judith Ann d. Harry Jack Stevens, Chilliwack, B.C. 16 June 1962; children: Steven John, Jacklyn Ann; JUSTICE, SUPREME COURT OF B.C.; Past Chrmn.: Candn. Judges Conf.; Cultus Lake Park Bd.; Past Pres., Fraser Valley Bar Assn.; rec'd Silver Jubilee Medal; served with RCAF, rank Flying Offr.; Delta Upsilon (Past Pres.); Baptist; recreations: golf, tennis; Home: 48489 Camp Road, R.R. 2, Chilliwack, B.C. V2P 6H4; Office: The Law Courts, 9391 College St., Chilliwack, B.C. V2P 4L7.

**DAVIS, Andrew,** Mus.B.; conductor; b. Herts., Eng. 2 Feb. 1944; s. Robert James and Florence Joyce D.; e. King's Coll. Cambridge, Organ Scholar, (Mus.B.) 1967; studied conducting with Franco Ferrara, Rome 1967–68; MUSIC DIR., BBC SYMPHONY ORCHESTRA (in succession to Sir John Pritchard) Oct. 1989– ; Music Dir., Glyndebourne Festival Opera 1988– ; Conductor Laureate, The Toronto Symphony 1988– , Music Dir. 1975–88; first maj. conducting Janacek's 'Glagolitic Mass' with BBC Symphony Orchestra 1970 followed by 2 yrs. with BBC Scottish Symphony Orchestra, Glasgow; apptd. Assoc. Conductor New Philharmonia Orchestra 1973; served 3 seasons as Princ. Guest Conductor Royal Liverpool Philharmonic Orchestra; has appeared at many maj. internat. festivals incl. Edinburgh, Flanders, Berlin, Glyndebourne where he conducted his first Opera debut in 1973 and has since led numerous productions; apptd. Mus. Dir. of Glyndebourne in succession to Bernard Haitink 1988; has guest conducted all of the world's major orchestras; has led Toronto Symphony many national and internat. tours, including historic 1978 tour of The People's Republic of China and 16–city tour of Europe in 1986; Metropolitan Opera debut conducting Richard Strauss' 'Salome' 1981; Paris Opera 1981 and Covent Garden 1983 conducting Richard Strauss' 'Der Rosenkavalier'; returned to Metropolitan Opera to conduct Rossini's 'Barber of Seville' 1982 and Strauss' 'Ariadne auf Naxos' 1985; led BBC Symphony Orch. to the Far East 1990; recent operatic engagements incl. productions at Glyndebourne and at the Lyric Opera of Chicago; recent guest conducting engagements incl. the Los Angeles Philharmonic, the Cleveland Orch., the Cincinnati Symphony; furture guest conducting engagements incl. the New York Philharmonic and the Dallas Symphony; rec'd 2 Grand Prix du Disque awards (Orchestral & Lyric) for recording of Maurice Duruflés 'Requiem' with Philharmonia Orchestra; Gramophone Record of the Year Award 1987 and Grand Prix du Disque 1988 for Sir Michael Tippett's 'The Mask of Time'; Hon. D.Litt., York Univ., Toronto 1984; Office: c/o Roy Thomson Hall, 60 Simcoe St., Toronto, Ont. M5J 2H5.

**DAVIS, Angela Elizabeth,** B.A., M.A., Ph.D.; historian; author; b. London, England 22 Sept. 1926; d. George Frederick and Winifred (Remnant) Pizzey; e. Lady Eleanor Holles School (U.K.) 1945; King's Coll. Hospital S.R.N. 1948; Univ. of Winnipeg B.A. (Hons.) 1977, M.A. 1979; Univ. of Manitoba Ph.D. 1987; m. Royden A. Davis F.R.C.P.(C) 27 April 1950; children: Sara, Christopher, Jonathan, Rowan, Michael; Co-founder with the late David Williams of the Osborne Gallery (Winnipeg) 1976; Art Consultant for the Gall. 1977–86; Lectr. in History, Univ. of Winnipeg 1980–84; Asst. Prof. in History, Univ. of Manitoba 1986–93; Rsch. Cons., 'No Man's Land,' a film on the life of Candn. artist Mary Riter Hamilton; Guest Curator, 'No Man's Land: the Battlefield Paintings of Mary Riter Hamilton,' Univ. of Winnipeg Gall. 1989; Guest Curator, Univ. of Winnipeg Gallery 1989; National Archives of Canada 1992; Candn. Hist. Assn. (Reg. Awards Ctte. 1990–92); Manitoba Hist. Soc. (Chair, Prog. Ctte. 1989–92); Candn. Ctte. on Women's History; author: 'No Man's Land: The Battlefield Paintings of Mary Riter Hamilton 1919-1922' 1989, 1992; 'The Grand Western Canadian Screen Shop: Printing, People and History' 1992; recreations: reading, travelling; clubs: University Women's Club of Winnipeg; Home: 187 Cambridge St., Winnipeg, Man. R3M 3E7.

**DAVIS, (Horace) Chandler,** B.Sc., M.A., Ph.D.; mathematician; writer; b. Ithaca, NY 12 Aug. 1926; s. Horace Bancroft and Marian (Rubins) D.; e. Harvard Univ., B.Sc. 1945, M.A. 1947, Ph.D. 1950; m. Natalie d. Julian & Helen Zemon 16 Aug. 1948; children: Aaron B., Hannah P., Simone W.; PROF., DEPT. OF MATH., UNIV. OF TORONTO 1965– ; Teacher, Univ. of Michigan (& other U.S. univs.) 1950–57; Assoc. Ed., 'Mathematical Reviews' 1958–62; Assoc. Prof., Univ. of Toronto 1962–65; fellowships & vis. appts. at Inst. for Adv. Study, New York Univ., Univ. of Calif. at Berkeley, Univ. de Paris, Steklov Inst. (Moscow) & elsewhere; rsch. in operator theory, matrix theory, analysis, applications; num. pub. sci.-fiction stories, poems, essays; challenged constitutionality of US House Ctte. on Un-Am. Activities 1954; served sentence for contempt of Cong. in US fed. prison 1960; Co-chair, 'Stop War Goods to the US' campaign 1967–68; many other civil liberties & anti-war activities; co-ed.: 'The Geometric Vein: The Coxeter Festschrift' 1981; Ed.-in-Chief 'Mathematical Intelligencer' 1991– ; Vice-Pres., Am. Math. Soc. 1991– ; Home: 52 Follis Ave., Toronto, Ont. M6G 1S3; Office: Toronto, Ont. M5S 1A1.

**DAVIS, Charles Carroll,** M.A., Ph.D.; biologist; educator; b. Calif. 24 Nov. 1911; s. William Allen and Maude (Snyder) D.; e. Pasadena Jr. Coll. 1929; Oberlin Coll. B.A. 1933; Univ. of Wash. M.A. 1935, Ph.D. 1940; m. Sally May d. John P. Jacobsen June 1936; children: Peter T., Betsy A. Gimbel; PROF. EMERITUS OF BIOL., MEM. UNIV. OF NFLD. 1984– ; Instr. Jacksonville Jr. Coll. 1945–46; Asst. Prof. Univ. of Miami 1946–48; Case Western Reserve Univ. Asst. Prof., Assoc. Prof., Prof. of Biol. 1948–68; Prof. of Biol. Mem. Univ. of Nfld. 1968–77 (when retired); Gjeste-professor, Universitetet i Tromsø 1975–76; Adjunct Prof. of Biol. Univ. Waterloo (at Addis Ababa Univ.) 1986–87; author 'The Pelagic Copepoda of the Northeastern Pacific Ocean' 1949; 'The Marine and Freshwater Plankton' 1955; over 120 papers prof. journs.; Fellow, Am. Assn. Advanc. Science; Ohio Acad. Science; mem. Am. Soc. Limnology & Oceanography; Ecol. Soc. Am.; Candn. Soc. Zool.; Plankton Soc. Japan; Marine Biol. Assn. UK; Freshwater Biol. Assn. UK; Internat. Soc. Limnology; Soc. Candn. Limnols.; Crustacean Soc.; recreations: gardening, cooking, hiking, reading; Home: 270 Portugal Cove Rd., Apt. 201, St. John's Nfld. A1B 4N6; Office: Dept. of Biology, Memorial Univ., St. John's, Nfld. A1B 3X9.

**DAVIS, David Homer,** B.A., L.Mus.; musician; b. Halifax, N.S. 11 April 1951; s. Samuel Warren and Margaret Joan (Covey) D.; e. Dartmouth H.S. 1969; Dalhousie Univ. B.A. (Mus.) 1973; McGill Univ. L.Mus. 1975; m. Mary Jane d. William and Mary Lemon 7 July 1973; children: Samuel William, (Daniel) Ehren, Sarah Eleanor, Nicholas Rhodes; ORGANIST/CHOIR DIR., PARISH CHURCH OF ST. LUKE, BURLINGTON 1991– ; Music Dir., Westboro Un. Ch. Ottawa 1975–78; Organist & Choir Master, Christ Church Cathedral Fredericton 1978–84; Founder/Dir., Fredericton Choral Soc. 1978–81; Bel Canto Singers 1979–84; Organist/Choir Master, Christ's Ch. Cathedral Hamilton 1984–91; Artistic Dir., Hamilton Children's Choir 1985– ; Founder/Dir., Ars Antigua (formerly St. Luke's Chamber Singers); private teacher: organ, piano, theory 18 years; Music Teacher, Hillfield-Strathallan Coll. 1985–86; Teacher (set up prog. as Specialist in Vocal Performance), St. Thomas Aquinas Ctr. for the Arts Hamilton 1987–90; Classroom Music Teacher, Robert Land Acad. 1990–91; Vocal Instr., St. Mildred's Lightbourne School 1992– ; Instructor for conducting courses, Mohawk College, Fennell Campus 1993/94; has made 4 recordings of his choirs; has performed concerts solo & with choirs on National CBC and live in Maritimes, Que., Ont., N.Y. State; Mem., Royal Candn. Coll. of Organists (Chair 1990–91, 1991–92); N.B. Choral Fed. (Chair 1983–84); Assn. of Candn. Choral Conductors; Ont. Choral Fed.; has composed numerous choral works for children's choir, adult S.A.T.B. choirs, mainly of a religious nature; comnd. to write choral works for other children's and adult's choirs and soloists; compositions have rec. favourable reviews; Home: 194 Sanford Ave. S., Hamilton, Ont. L8M 2H2; Office: 1382 Ontario St., Burlington, Ont. L7S 1G1.

**DAVIS, George R.;** executive; s. George B. and Jessie Florence (Rose) D.; e. Ryerson Polytech. Inst. Toronto Cert. Arch. Technol.; m. Norma d. Robert McBride; children: Douglas, Stephen, Susan, Sharon; PRES. & OWNER, DAICON CONTRACTORS LTD. 1989– ; Project Mgr. maj. contracts present co. 1964–71, Dir. Labour Relations 1965–68, Asst. Chief Estimator H.O. London 1971–72, Vice Pres. Aztec Contractors Ltd. (subsidiary) 1972–73, Project Mgr. 1974–75, Mgr. N. Ont. Operations 1975–78, Mgr. Central, N. and E. Ont. 1978–80, Vice Pres. Ont. 1980, Sr. Vice Pres. E. Ont. 1983–85; Exec. Vice Pres., Gen. Mgr. and Dir., Ellis-Don Ltd. 1985–89; Dir. Ont. Gen. Contractors' Assn.; mem. Bd. Trade Metrop. Toronto; Club: Ontario; Home: R.R. #1, Gormley, Ont. L0H 1G0; Office: 21 Cardico Dr., P.O. Box 207, Gormley, Ont. L0H 1G0.

**DAVIS, Hank,** B.A., M.A., Ph.D.; university professor; music journalist; b. New York City, N.Y. 6 July 1941; s. Alfred H. and Sarah (Lowen) D.; e. Columbia Univ. B.A. 1963; Boston Univ. M.A. 1965; Univ. of Maryland Ph.D. 1968; PROF., DEPT. OF PSYCHOLOGY, UNIV. OF GUELPH; involved in formation of Centre for Study of Animal Welfare, Univ. of Guelph; Mem., Psychonomic Soc.; Animal Behaviour Soc.; author of 2 books & approx. 100 sci. papers on experimental psych., animal learning & cognition; music journalist; former recording artist; specialist in '50s music; annotator-producer-compiler of record albums for cos. in Canada, U.S., Germany, France, U.K., Sweden; co-editor: 'Operant – Pavlovian Interactions' 1977, 'The Inevitable Bond' 1991; recreations: baseball, music; Home: R.R. 1, Puslinch, Ont. N0B 2J0; Office: Guelph, Ont. N1G 2W1.

**DAVIS, Harry Floyd,** S.M., Ph.D.; mathematician; educator; b. Colby, Kans. 2 Oct. 1925; s. Leo Lloyd and Edna Miars D.; e. Mass. Inst. Tech. S.B. (Physics) 1948, S.M. (Math.) 1953, Ph.D. (Math.) 1954; m. Myrna Joan d. late Harold Hugh MacPhie 9 Sept. 1961; two s. Harry Floyd, Kenneth Hugh; ADJUNCT PROF., UNIV. OF WATERLOO 1991– ; Prof. of Math., Univ. of Waterloo 1961–91; Instr., Armed Forces Inst. 1945–46; Lowell Inst. Sch. Cambridge 1948–54; Mass. Inst. of Technol. 1948–54; Asst. Prof., Miami Univ. of Ohio 1954–55; Univ. of B.C. 1955–58; Assoc. Prof. Royal Mil. Coll. Can. 1958–61; served with U.S. Navy 1944–46; author 'Fourier Series and Orthogonal Functions' 1963 and 1989; co-author 'Introduction to Vector Analysis' 6th rev. ed. 1991; mem. Cdn. Math. Soc.; Soc. Indust. & Applied Math.; Am. Math. Assn.; Sigma Xi; Beta Theta Pi; Home: 355 Pommel Gate Cres., Waterloo, Ont. N2L 5X7; Office: Applied Math Dept., Univ. of Waterloo, Waterloo, Ont. N2L 3G1.

**DAVIS, Henry Francis,** C.V.O., C.M., B.A., M.A., B.C.L.; retired Canadian public service; b. Ottawa, Ont. 30 Jan. 1914; s. Michael Patrick and Gertrude Ann (McGrady) D.; e. Lisgar Collegiate, Ottawa; Bishop's Univ., B.A. 1932; McGill Univ., B.C.L. 1935; Nat. Defence Coll. 1951; Carleton Univ., B.A. (Hons.) 1983; M.A. (Classics) 1986 and 1991; m. Isobel Margaret, d. James O'Reilly, 9 Jan. 1946; children: Ann, Martha, Thomas H.P., Jane; read law with Col. J. L. Ralston, Q.C.; called to the Bar of Que. 1936; Extve. Asst. Gen. Mgr., Royal Trust Co., Montreal, Que. 1936–40; served in 2nd World War with R.C.A.F. 1940–46 (Overseas, Bomber Pilot); with Dept. of External Affairs, Ottawa 1946–47; Secy., Candn. Embassy, Buenos Aires 1947–50; Ottawa 1951–54; Min. Counsellor, Candn. Embassy, Paris 1954–58; Head of European Div., Ottawa 1958–61; (periods as Acting Asst. Under Secy. of State for External Affairs); Chief of Protocol and Chrmn. of Govt. Hospitality Comte. 1961–64; Special Adv. Privy Council 1964–69; Secy. Constitutional Conf. 1969–72; Secy., Candn. Intergovernmental Conferences 1973–82; former Candn. Secy. to Her Majesty the Queen; Co-ord. for 1978 and 1982 Royal Visits; Past Pres.: Nat. Council of YMCA of Can.; Ottawa YM/YWCA; Ottawa Red Cross; Nat. Gallery Assn.; Past Dir., Ottawa Social Planning Council; past mem., Extve. Comte. World Alliance of YMCA; Trustee, Candn. Mediterranean Inst.; apptd. Commdr. Royal Victorian Order 1978; apptd. by Queen to be Extra Gentleman Usher to Her Majesty 1984; Member, Order of Canada 1985; Companion, YMCA Fellowship of Honour; Roman Catholic; Clubs: Rideau; Canadian (Past Pres.); Home: 80 MacKinnon Rd., Rockcliffe Park, Ont. K1M 0G3.

**DAVIS, J(ames) R(obert) Leighton,** B.F.A.; curator; artist; b. Winnipeg, Man. 14 May 1941; s. Robert Leighton Davis; City Mgrs.' Assn. Planning Adm. Dipl. Washington, D.C. 1969; Capilano Coll. Vancouver 1969–76; Dalhousie Univ. grad. studies Personnel & Financial Adm. 1978–79; N.S. Coll. of Art & Design B.F.A. 1979; m. Arlene I. d. J.E. Graham, Winnipeg, Man. 14 Sept. 1963; DIR./CURATOR, ST. MARY'S UNIV. ART GALLERY; Artist in Residence, St. Mary's Univ. 1980– ; printmaker, watercolourist; 16 solo exhns. 1977–86; rec'd Vancouver Foundation Scholarship, Helen Pitt Fund for Fine Arts 1977; Pres., Atlantic Provs. Art Gallery Assn. 1983; Address: St. Mary's University Art Gallery, Halifax, N.S. B3H 3C3.

**DAVIS, John Christopher,** B.Sc., M.B.A., P.Eng.; real estate executive; b. Talara, Peru 27 Aug. 1941; s. Basil

Vernon and Annabel Begg (Rymer) D.; e. South Porcupine (Ont.) High Sch. 1959; Queen's Univ. B.Sc. (Civil Eng.) 1963; Univ. of W. Ont. M.B.A. 1969; m. Sherrill Anne d. Air Vice Marshall Lawrence E. and Audrey Garland Wray 28 Feb. 1975; children: Brenton Basil, Mark Christopher; Vice-Pres., Royal LePage Limited 1988–..; Project Eng. EG.M. Cape & Co. 1963–65; Project Eng., Bechtel Corp. Libya, N. Africa 1965–67; Asst. to Pres., A.E. LePage Ltd. 1969 becoming Comml. Sales Rep., Vice Pres. & Sales Mgr. Comml. Devel. Div.; Pres., Royal LePage Commercial Real Estate Services 1980–88; mem., Assn. Prof. Engs. prov. Ont.; recreations: skiing, sailing, fitness; Clubs: National; Fitness Inst.; RCYC; Home: 153 Douglas Dr., Toronto, Ont. M4W 2B6.

**DAVIS, Sir John G.,** Bart.; executive; b. London, Eng. 17 Aug. 1936; s. Sir Gilbert D. Bart. and Kathleen (Ford) D.; e. Oundle Sch.; Royal Naval Coll. (Dartmouth, Eng.); m. Elizabeth, d. Robert and Greta Turnbull, 16 Jan. 1960; children: Wendy; Linda; Richard; Extve. Vice-Pres., Abitibi-Price Inc. 1987–90, retired after 33 yr. career with Abitibi-Price to pursue new entrepreneural opportunities; Past Pres., Candn. Arthritis Soc.; served 2 years Royal Navy; Clubs: Donalda; Toronto; Rosedale Golf; recreations: golf; squash; reading; music; Home: 5 York Ridge Rd., Willowdale, Ont. M2P 1R8.

**DAVIS, Murdoch Anthony,** B.A.; newspaper editor, manager; b. New Waterford, Cape Breton, N.S. 19 Feb. 1954; s. Robert Anthony and Rita Mary (MacDonald) D.; e. Ryerson Polytech. Inst., B.A. in Journalism 1975 (Joe Perlove Award, best journalist, grad. class & Maclean-Hunter Award, highest standing); EDITOR, EDMONTON JOURNAL 1992– ; Reporter, Toronto Star 1976–78; Ottawa Citizen 1978–79; Asst. City Editor 1979–80; Night News Editor 1980–81; City Editor 1981–83; Asst. Mng. Ed. 1983–89; Mng. Ed., Edmonton Journal 1989–92; recreations: sailing, bridge, baseball; Office: Box 2421, Edmonton, Alta. T5J 2S6.

**DAVIS, R. Frank,** B.Eng., P.Eng.; utilities executive; b. Carbonear, Nfld. 10 June 1946; s. G. Benjamin and Clarinda D.; e. Memorial Univ. 1967; N.S. Technical College B.Eng. 1969; m. Deli d. Rita and Jack Jacobs 10 Aug. 1974; children: Stephanie, Erin, Frank Benjamin; VICE PRES., TECHNOLOGY, NEWFOUNDLAND TELEPHONE CO. 1991– ; joined Newfoundland Tel 1969 and has held various positions in Engineering, Marketing & Operations; Vice-Pres. Marketing & Planning 1990; Dir., Paragon Information Systems Ltd.; Mem., BOD Atlantic Div., Multiple Sclerosis Soc. (Bd. Treas. 1991–92); Soc. of Nfld. Radio Amateurs (Past Pres.); radio callsign: VO1HP; recreations: music, computers; clubs: Soc. of Nfld. Radio Amateurs; Home: 159 Highland Dr., St. John's, Nfld. A1A 3C6; Office: P.O. Box 2110, St. John's, Nfld. A1C 5H6.

**DAVIS, Rick,** B.A.; advertising executive; b. Peterborough, Ont. 5 Jan. 1950; s. Lester Ralph and Josephine Laura (Rowat) D.; e. Adam Scott H.S. 1969; Univ. of Western Ont. B.A. (Hons.) 1973; m. Wendie Scott Davis d. Charles and Patricia Scott 1 Aug. 1981; children: Laura Patricia; Matthew Richard; SENIOR VICE-PRES. & CREATIVE DIRECTOR, YOUNG & RUBICAM LTD. 1987– ; Sr. Mktg. Writer, London Life Insur. Co. 1973–77; Advtg. & Promotions Mgr., United Way of Metro Toronto 1977–78; Copywriter, Saatchi & Saatchi Advtg. 1978–79; Assoc. Creative Dir., Ambrose, Carr, Linton, Kelly 1979–83; Vice-Pres. & Sr. Writer, DDB Needham Worldwide 1983–87; Vice-Pres. & Group Creative Dir., MacLaren: Lintas 1987; Lectr., Univ. of Syracuse; Adv. Bd. Mem., Studio mag.; Chair & Past Chair, Candn. Mktg. Awards; Past Chair, Candn. Radio Awards ('The Crystals'); over 200 awards nationally & internationally for creative advtg.; Home: 113 Brooke Ave., Toronto, Ont. M5M 2K3; Office: 60 Bloor St. W., Toronto, Ont. M4W 3B8.

**DAVIS, S. James,** B.A.; executive compensation consultant; b. Montreal, Que. 12 April 1938; s. Roberts Samuel and Margaret Russell (Pitts) D.; e. Sir George Williams Univ. B.A. 1963; m. Elisabeth d. Birger and Kirsten Lund 15 May 1981; children: Barry, Christopher, Leina, Heather, Julie; VICE-PRESIDENT, TOWERS PERRIN 1982– ; Sun Life Assur. Co. of Canada 1959; Asst. Sec., The Bristol Aeroplane Co. of Canada 1964; Dir., Compensation & Benefits, Celanese Canada Limited 1966; Compensation Consultant, Towers Perrin, Montreal 1970; Vancouver 1973; Principal 1976; Vice-Pres. 1982; Manager, Vancouver 1984; Candn. Practice Leader for Extve. Compensation, Toronto 1987; Coordinator of cert. course on Extve. Compensation, Candn. Compensation Assn. 1987– ; Mem., Candn. Compensation Assn. (Edn. Ctte. 1989– ;); Industrial

Relations Management Assn. of B.C. (Vice-Pres. 1976–78); Editor, 'Davis on Executive Compensation' Federated Press newsletter 1991– ; recreations: golf, nordic skiing, hiking; clubs: Ontario, Spring Lakes Golf & Country; Home: 60 Bannatyne Dr., North York, Ont. M2L 2P1; Office: 175 Bloor St. E., Suite 1501, Toronto, Ont. M4W 3T6.

**DAVIS, Stephen Alexander,** B.A., M.A., D.Phil.; university professor; b. Edmonton, Alta. 15 July 1949; s. Alexander Miller and Marie Stella (McNeil) D.; e. Univ. of N.B., B.A. 1971; Mem. Univ. of Nfld. M.A. 1975; Univ. of Oxford, Doctoral student 1978–80, D.Phil. 1987; m. Elizabeth Myra d. Jake and Olive Button 30 April 1983; children: Bronwen Elizabeth, Myra Alexandra; ASSOC. PROF., DEPT. OF ANTHROPOL., SAINT MARY'S UNIV. 1987– ; Pres., Davis Archaeological Consultants Ltd. 1989– ; Lectr., Dept. of Anthrop., Saint Mary's Univ. 1973–78; Asst. Prof. 1981–86; Chairperson 1981–89; Rsch. Asst., Deya Archaeological Mus. & Rsch. Mus., Deya, Majorca, Spain; Rsch. Assoc., N.S. Mus.; Arts Extve. Ctte., Saint Mary's Univ. 1981–87; Univ. Senate 1982, 1984–86; co-author: 'An Archaeological Bibliography of the Maritime Provinces' 1986, 'Artifacts from Eighteenth Century Halifax' 1987; 'Micmac' 1991; recreations: camping; Home: 6519 Oak St., Halifax, N.S.; Office: Halifax, N.S. B3H 3C3.

**DAVIS, Hon. William Grenville,** P.C., C.C., Q.C.; barrister and solicitor; b. Brampton, Ont. 30 July 1929; s. late Albert Grenville and Vera (Hewetson) D.; e. Brampton (Ont.) High Sch.; Univ. of Toronto, B.A. 1951; Osgoode Hall Law Sch.; LL.D. (Hon.): Waterloo Lutheran Univ. 1963, Univ. of W. Ont. 1965, Univ. of Toronto 1967, McMaster Univ., Queen's Univ. 1968, Univ. of Windsor 1969, Univ. of Waterloo 1982; Law Soc. of Upper Canada 1983; D.U.C. (Hon.) Ottawa 1980; m. 1stly Helen (died 1962) d. Neil MacPhee, Windsor, Ont.; m. 2ndly Kathleen Louise, d. Dr. R.P. Mackay, Illinois; children: Neil, Nancy, Catherine, Ian, Meg; COUNSEL, TORY TORY DESLAURIERS & BINNINGTON; Dir.: Algoma Steel Inc.; Corel Corporation; First American Title Insurance Co.; Fleet Aerospace Corp.; Ford Motor Co. of Canada, Limited; Inter-City Products Corp.; Magna International Inc.; NIKE Canada Ltd.; Olympia & York Companies U.S.A.; Power Corp. of Canada; The Seagram Company Ltd.; Canadian Imperial Bank of Commerce; Lawson Mardon Group Ltd.; Honeywell Limited; St. Lawrence Cement; Hemlo Gold Mines; Bd. Chrmn., Bramalea Limited; Vice Chrmn., Stadium Corp. of Ont. Ltd.; called to Bar of Ont. 1955; practiced general law with Brampton firm until first el. to Ont. Leg. 1959; M.P.P. 1959–85 (rep. Peel, Peel North and Brampton); mem., Select Comte of Ont. Leg. to study Adm. and Extve. Problems of Govt. of Ont. 1960–63; 2nd Vice-Chrmn., Ont. Hydro-Electric Power Comn. 1961–62; Min. of Educ. 1962–71 and Min. of Univ. Affairs 1964–71; attached to Candn. Del. to UNESCO Conf., Paris, Nov. 1966; el. first Chrmn., Council of Mins. of Educ., Can. 1967; el. Leader, P.C. Party, Ont. 1971; Premier of Ontario and Pres. of the Council of Ontario 1971–85; retired as Premier and as M.P. 1985; Special Envoy on Acid Rain 1985–86; rec'd Greer Mem. Award, Ont. Educ. Assn. 1966; Award of Merit, Phi Delta Kappa, Univ. of Toronto Chapter 1967; publications: 'The Government of Ontario and the Universities of the Province' (Frank Gerstein Lectures, York Univ.) 1966; 'Education in Ontario' 1965; 'Building an Educated Society 1816–1966' 1966; 'Education for New Times' 1967; Cert. of Merit, Edinboro Univ., Pa.; Am. Transit Assn. Man of the Year 1973; mem. Privy Council 1982; Companion of the Order of Canada 1986; Candn. Bar Assn.; Ont. Bar Assn.; Freemason; United Church; P. Conservative; Clubs: Kiwanis; Albany; Home: Brampton, Ont.; Office: Suite 3000, Aetna Tower, P.O. Box 270, Toronto-Dominion Centre, Toronto, Ont. M5K 1N2; European Office: Tory Ducharme Lawson Lundell, 44/45 Chancery Lane, London WC2A 1JB England.

**DAVIS, William M.;** business executive; b. Columbia, South Carolina 27 Oct. 1940; e. Univ. of S.C., B.Admin. 1962; m. Patricia; children: Dana, Kristin; Pres. & Chief Extve. Offr., Uniroyal Goodrich Canada Inc. 1989–92; Vice-Pres. Bus. Mgmt., BFG Brands, Uniroyal Goodrich Tire Co. (U.S.) 1986–88; Vice-Pres. and Gen. Mgr., Textiles 1983–86; Gen. Mgr., Textiles 1977–83.

**DAVISON, Edward Joseph,** B.A.Sc., M.A., Ph.D., Sc.D., F.I.E.E.E., F.R.S.C.; educator; b. Toronto, Ont. 12 Sept. 1938; s. Maurice John and Agnes (Quinlan) D.; e. Royal Conserv. of Music Toronto A.R.C.T. Piano 1957; Univ. of Toronto B.A.Sc. 1960, M.A. (Applied Math.) 1961; Cambridge Univ. Ph.D. (Control. Engn.) 1964, Sc.D. 1977; m. Zofia d. M.C. Perz; 4 children; PROF. OF ELECT. ENGN. UNIV. OF TORONTO since 1974; el.

Hon. Prof., Beijing Inst. of Aeronautics and Astronautics 1986; Vice-Pres., (Technical Affairs), IEEE Control Systems Soc., 1979–81 (Pres.-el. 1982; Pres. 1983); mem of Edit. Adv. Bd. 'Proceedings of the IEEE' 1980–81; Dir. of IEEE Control Systems Soc. Magazine, 1980–82; Dir., Elect. Engineering Consociates Ltd., Tor., 1977–82, 1984– ; Vice-Chrmn., Theory Comte., Internat. Fed. of Automatic Control (IFAC) 1978–86, Chrmn., Theory Comte. (IFAC) 1987–90, Vice-Chrmn., Technical Bd. (IFAC) 1990–93, Counc. mem. (IFAC) 1990–93, 1994–96; Asst. Prof. Univ. of Toronto 1964–66, 1967–68, Assoc. Prof. 1968–74; Asst. Prof. Univ. Calif. Berkeley 1966–67; Athlone Fellow 1961–63; E.W.R. Steacie Mem. Fellow 1974–77; Fellow, Inst. Elect. & Electronic Engrs. (1978); Fellow, Royal Society of Canada (1977); Killam Research Fellowship 1979–80, 1981–83; IEEE Centennial Medal 1984; Distinguished Mem., IEEE Control Systems Soc. 1984; Awarded Internat. Federation of Automatic Control (IFAC) Quazza Medal 1993; author over 350 scient. articles math. system theory, multivariable control systems, large scale system theory, computational methods, application system theory to biol.; consulting ed., IEEE Transactions on Automatic Control 1985; assoc. ed., Automatica 1974–87; Large Scale Systems: Theory and Applications 1979–90; Optimal Control Appl. and Methods 1983– ; IEEE Trans. on Automatic Control 1974–76; Designated Consulting Engr. Prof. Engrs. Prov. Ont.; Office: Toronto, Ont. M5S 1A4.

**DAVY, Diane Elizabeth;** communications executive; b. Winnipeg, Man. 3 Aug. 1947; d. Roy Arthur and Nora Camilla (Morrison) Dingle; e. Don Mills Collegiate; Univ. of Toronto Fine Arts; m. Henry Mowat s. Henry and Dorothy Davy 6 Sept. 1969; EXECUTIVE VICE-PRES., YOUNG NATURALIST FOUNDATION / GREEY DE PENCIER BOOKS; Promotion Manager, Nelson Canada 1971–75; Promotion Mgr., Sch. of Contg. Studies, Univ. of Toronto 1975–77; Extve. Dir., Canadabooks 1977–79; Managing Editor, Key to Toronto 1979; joined present firm 1979 as Business Affairs Manager; Pres., Candn. Magazine Publishers Assn. 1993– , Treas./Chair, Environment Ctte. 1988–93; Treas., Candn. Children's Book Centre 1986–88; current mem., Magazine Advisory Ctte., Ont. Publishing Centre; recreations: photography, hiking, sailing, reading; Office: 56 The Esplanade, Suite 302, Toronto, Ont. M5E 1A7.

**DAWE, Chester;** company director; b. Bay Roberts, Conception Bay, Nfld. 17 May 1904; s. William and Mary E. (Russell) D.; both of Bay Roberts, Nfld.; m. Phyllis May, d. late William J. Carson, Montreal, Que., 30 Sept. 1930; two d. Janet (Gardiner), Sonia (Dawe Ryan); PRESIDENT, CHESTER DAWE LIMITED and associated companies; Freemason; Anglican; Home: 50 Circular Rd., St. John's A1C 2Z1 & North Arm, Holyrood, Nfld.; Office: P.O. Box 8280, St. John's, Nfld. A1B 3N4.

**DAWSON, Eleanor Ruth,** B.Sc., LL.B., Q.C.; lawyer; b. Burnaby, B.C. 21 Feb. 1953; d. Arnold John and Julia Eleanor (Gill) D.; e. Univ. of Manitoba B.Sc. 1973, LL.B. 1976; PARTNER, AIKINS, MacAULAY & THORVALDSON 1986– ; called to Manitoba Bar 1977; practised civil litigation, A. Kerr Twaddle, Q.C. 1977–84; Counsel, Law Soc. of Man. 1984–86; Lectr., Fac. of Law, Univ. of Man. 1986–92; Comnr., Uniform Law Comn. of Canada 1987–89; Comnr., Law Reform Comn. of Man. 1987– ; Q.C. 1988; Pres., Winnipeg Humane Soc. 1985– ; (Pres. 1989–92); Pres., Candn. Federation of Humane Societies (Pres. 1992– ;); Mem., The Advocates Soc. of Man.; The Selden Soc.; Office: 30th floor, 360 Main St., Winnipeg, Man. R3C 4G1.

**DAWSON, Graham Russell,** B.A.Sc., P.Eng.; contractor; b. Vancouver, B.C. 18 Nov. 1925; s. Frederick James and Marion Patterson (Russell) D.; e. Prince of Wales High Sch., Vancouver, 1943; Royal Canadian Naval Coll., grad. 1945; Univ. of B.C., B.A.Sc. 1949; Lieut. (Ret'd.), R.C.N.; m. Dorothy Eva Drape, d. late Col. R.D. Williams, 19 May 1949; children: Rebecca, Bruce, Ian, Murray, Marion; Chrmn., Pres. & Dir., Pe Ben Oilfield Services Ltd.; Chrmn. and Dir.: Dawson Construction Ltd.; Interior Roads Ltd.; mem. Adv. Bd., Nat. Victoria and Grey Trust Co.; Dir.: Bank of Montreal; Canada Life Assurance Co.; Andres Wines Ltd.; Candn. Environmental Energy Corp.; A.D.I. Technologies Inc.; mem., Vancouver Board Trade (Past President); Bd. of Govs., Vancouver Public Aquarium; mem. Convocation, Univ. of B.C. and Simon Fraser Univ.; Past Pres., B.C. Div., Candn. Arthritis Soc.; Phi Delta Theta; United Church; recreations: golf, fishing, skiing; Clubs: Vancouver; Shaughnessy Golf & Country; Home: 1459 McRae Avenue, Vancouver, B.C. V6H 1V1; Office: 1066 - 999 W. Hastings St., Vancouver, B.C. V6C 2W2.

**DAWSON, John A.,** B.Sc., M.S., Ph.D.; economist; b. Montreal, Que. 14 Sept. 1923; s. Carl Addington and Mary Alice (Dixon) D.; e. McGill Univ., B.Sc. (Agric.) 1947; Univ. of Ill., M.S. (Agric. Econ.) 1949; Univ. of Chicago, Ph.D. (Econ.) 1957; m. Eunice Irene, d. Joseph William Hutchison, 20 Sept. 1947; children: Robert John, Kathleen Eunice; CONSULTANT, 1980– ; Econ., Can. Dept. of Agric. 1947; Sr. Econ. Advisor, Bd. of Broadcast Govs. 1960; joined Economic Counc. of Can. as Staff Econ. 1964, Dir. 1973–76; Extve. Dir., Candn. Energy Research Inst., 1976–80; served with RCNVR 1942–45; United Church; recreations: golf, skiing; Address: 1837 Beattie Ave., Ottawa, Ont. K1H 5R7.

**DAWSON, John H.,** B.A., B.C.L.; lawyer; insurance executive; b. Montreal, Que. 11 July 1934; s. Dr. Howard Le Rossignol and Virginia Vorys (Douglas) D.; e. Sedbergh Sch. Montebello, Que. 1951; Lower Can. Coll. Montreal; McGill Univ. B.A. 1956, B.C.L. 1959; m. Julia F. d. Dr. Leyland and Barbara Adams 21 Oct. 1961; children: Andrew L., Lynne F., Barbara D., Michael J.; VICE PRES., GEN. COUNSEL AND SEC. THE STANDARD LIFE ASSURANCE CO. 1988– ; Dir. and Sec. Standard Life Portfolio Management Ltd.; Sec. The Standard Life Assurance Co. of Canada; called to Bar of Que. 1960; Associate, Laidley, Campbell, Walsh & Kisilenko 1960–62; McDonald & Dessaulles 1962–64; Partner, Dessaulles & Dawson 1964–67; Byers, McDougall, Casgrain & Stewart 1967–71; Legal Offr. present Co. 1971, Gen. Counsel 1974, Vice Pres. 1976, Sec. 1988; Dir. Montreal Protestant Homes Found.; Gov. Montreal Gen. Hosp. Found.; Que. Bar Found.; mem. T.J. Wood Found.; Trustee Sedbergh Sch. Assn. 1975–90; mem. Council Montreal Bd. Trade 1978–81; Sec. Lake Manitou Improvement Co.; mem. Candn. Bar Assn.; Que. Bar Assn.; United Church; recreations: curling, jogging, tennis, skiing, music; Clubs: Royal Montreal Curling; Montreal Badminton & Squash; Off the Record; Home: 4379 Westmount Ave., Que. H3Y 1W8; Office: 206, 1245 Sherbrooke St. W., Montreal, Que. H3G 1G3.

**DAWSON, Joseph P.,** B.Comm., LL.B.; lawyer; b. Peterborough, Ont. 19 Feb. 1940; s. Joseph C.C. and Muriel T. D.; e. Peterborough C.V.S. 1958; Univ. of Toronto B.Comm. 1962, LL.B. 1965; m. Margot d. Ilse and Gerhardt Belling 20 Dec. 1970; children: Amanda Lee, Elinore Jane, Ian Joseph; LAWYER, AIRD & BERLIS 1968– ; commenced practice at Fraser, Beatty, Tucker, McIntosh & Stewart 1967; Dir., Interprov. Diversified Holdings Ltd.; Candn. BBR (1980) Inc.; Allgrant Industries Ltd.; recreations: skiing, tennis, sailing; Home: 240 Cortleigh Blvd., Toronto, Ont. M5N 1P7.

**DAWSON, Mary E.,** B.A., B.C.L., D.E.S.D., LL.B.; public servant; b. Halifax, N.S. 23 June 1942; d. Thomas Paul and Florence Margaret (Thurston) McMillan; e. McGill Univ., B.A. (Hons. in Philos.) 1963, B.C.L. 1966; Univ. of Ottawa, D.E.S.D. 1968; Dalhousie Univ., LL.B. 1970; Que. Bar 1967; N.S. Bar 1970; m. Peter s. Sydney and Joan D. 30 Aug. 1969; children: David, Emily; ASSOC. DEPY. MINISTER, PUBLIC LAW, DEPT. OF JUSTICE 1988– ; Tax Researcher, Revenue Can. 1967–68; Legal Couns. 1968–69; Teaching Fellow, Dalhousie Univ. 1969–70; Legislative Drafter, Dept. of Justice 1970–79; Assoc. Chief Legis. Couns. 1980–86; Asst. Depy. Min., Public Law 1986–88; Assoc. Depy. Min. 1988– ; University Scholar, McGill 1960; Lyon William Jacobs, Q.C. Award (McGill Law) 1965; Q.C. 1978; active mem., Parkdale United Ch.; recreations: nordic skiing, swimming, theatre, reading; Home: 97 Reid Ave., Ottawa, Ont. K1Y 1T1; Office: Ottawa, Ont. K1A 0H8.

**DAWSON, Robert Frederick,** B.Sc., LL.B.; orchard grower; lawyer; b. Kelowna, B.C. 18 Nov. 1946; s. James Frederick and Margaret Dawn (Couglin) D.; e. Similkameen Secondary Sch. 1963; Univ. of B.C. B.Sc. 1967, LL.B. 1970; m. Bonna 3 June 1978; children: Rhiannon, Meaghan, Cara; OWNER/MANAGER, DAWSON ORCHARDS LTD. 1978– ; Chrmn. Okanagan Valley Tree Fruit Authority 1990– ; Chrmn., Sun-Rype Products Ltd. 1990–92, Dir. 1981– ; mem. Internat. Dwarf Fruit Tree Assn. (Distinguished Grower Award 1989); B.C. Fruit Growers' Assn. (Compact & Golden Orchard Award 1988, 1991); Okanagan Similkameen Co-op. Growers Assn. (Dir. 1981– , Pres. 1984–87); Pacific Northwest Fruit Testers Assn. (Dir.); Hakai Land & Sea Soc.; recreations: skiing, boating, fishing; Office: 1473 Water St., Kelowna, B.C. V1Y 1J6.

**DAWSON, Ronald Curtis;** executive; b. London, Ont. 27 Feb. 1930; s. Francis Alexander Mirehouse and Viola Louise (Jacobs) D.; e. Ryerson P.S. 1942; London Cent. C.I. 1947; Univ. of W. Ont. 1949; m. June d. James and Elizabeth Craig 2 Aug. 1952; children: Craig Alexander, David Ronald, Laurie Helen; PRESIDENT, R.C. DAWSON CO. LTD. 1970– ; Office Mgr. London Motor Products Ltd. 1950–54; Sec.-Treas. & Off. Mgr. Dawson, McLean & Co. Ltd. 1954–55; Vice-Pres. & Gen. Mgr. Towne & Country Furn. Mfg. Ltd. 1955–60, Pres. 1960–67; Vice-Pres. Sales, Honderich Industries Ltd. 1967–69; Pres. Piccadilly Holdings Ltd. 1955– ; Pres., F.A.M. Dawson Co. Ltd. 1987– ; 1st Lieut. Candn. Fusiliers, City of London Regt. 1950; Capt. 2 R.C.R. (ret.); Dir. London Health Assn. 1982–86; Univ. Hosp. 1982–86; London West P.C. Assn. 1982–85; Ont. Motor Vehicle Licence Issuers Assn. 1983–86; Rotary Club of London 1979–81; Pres., London South P.C. Assn. 1980–86; Founding Pres., London & Area P.C. Business Assn. 1982–83; Pres. London Chamber of Comm. 1986–87; Dir., Candn. Chamber of Comm. 1987–93 (Chrmn., Small Business Ctte. 1985–87 and 1990–91; Chrmn., Extve. Ctte. 1988–89); mem. National Panel, Better Business Bureau of Can. 1983–92; Mocha Temple, Shrine Club 1975– ; Toronto Bd. of Trade 1983– ; London Press Club 1956–90; Dir., A.I.E.S.E.C., Western 1987–90; Chrmn., Adv. Panel, Fanshawe Coll., Sch. of Design 1987–88, Chrmn., Applied Arts Adv. Ctte. 1989–90; Founding Chrmn., London Medical Development Counc. 1987– ; Chrmn., Adjudication Ctte., Can. Awards for Bus. Excellence (Small Bus. Category) for D.R.I.E. 1987; Secy., London Regional Art and Historical Museums 1989–90 (1st Vice-Chrmn. 1990–91); Hon. Chrmn., Small Business Week, City of London & Area, F.B.D.B. 1989; Mem., Small Business Adv. Ctte., Revenue Canada Taxation Dept. 1991– ; Mem., Community Relations Task Force, U.W.O. 1992– ; Mem., Community Groups Adv. Ctte., Victoria Hospital 1993– ; Mem., Project Adv. Group, Candn. Found. for Economic Education 1993– ; Winner, David J. Gibson Award (Chairman's Award), Candn. Chamb. of Comm. 1992; awarded Commemorative Medal for 125th Anniversary of Candn. Confederation 1993; Home: 308 Ramsay Rd., London, Ont. N6G 1N8; Office: 544 Egerton St., London, Ont. N5W 3Z8.

**DAY, Bruce Donald,** C.A.; financial executive; b. Haileybury, Ont. 1956; e. Univ. of Waterloo B.Math (Hons.) 1979; m. Sheila Casey; three children; VICE-PRESIDENT, CORPORATE, ROGERS COMMUNICATIONS INC. 1991– ; Manager, Peat Marwick Thorne (formerly Thorne Riddell) 1979–83; Vice-Pres. & Treas., Rogers Communications Inc. 1983–89; Vice-Pres., Finance, Rogers Cantel Mobile Communications Inc. 1989–91; Office: Suite 2600, Commercial Union Tower, Toronto, Ont. M5K 1J5.

**DAY, Geoffrey Walter Gordon;** banker; b. London, Eng. 21 Dec. 1929; s. Francis William and Ada Beatrice (Norris) D.; e. Ilford Co. High Sch. 1945; Banff (Alta.) Sch. Advanced Mang. 1968; m. Karen Audrey d. late Arthur Kemp 4 Nov. 1960; children: Anne Louise, Hilary Lee, Kevin Geoffrey Kemp; Sr. Vice Pres., Corporate & Government Banking, Bank of Montreal 1981–90; Law Student, Thomas Cooper & Co., London, Eng. 1950–53; joined Bank of Montreal 1953 holding various positions Kelowna and Vancouver, B.C., Sr. Asst. Mgr. Main Office, Victoria, B.C. 1965 and Calgary 1967, Dist. Mgr. E. Ont. 1969, Mgr. Main Office Hamilton, Ont. 1971, Comm. Marketing Mgr. H.O. Montreal 1974, Vice Pres., Corporate Banking, Toronto 1976–79; Vice Pres., Internat. Banking 1979–81; served with R.A.F. 1948–50, Radar Operator, rank Cpl.; P. Conservative; United Church; recreations: tennis, curling, golf; Clubs: Vancouver; University of Vancouver; Shaughnessy Golf and Country; Address: 557 Tralee Pl., Delta, B.C. V4M 3V7.

**DAY, Howard M.,** B.A.Sc., P.Eng.; computer and telecommunications executive; b. Toronto, Ont. 24 June 1948; s. Milton C. and Eileen M. D.; e. Humewood P.S.; Vaughan Rd. Collegiate; Univ. of Toronto B.A.Sc. (Hons.) 1972; P.Eng.; m. Connie J. d. Donald and Anne Gloin 21 July 1973; children: Cindy C., Laura M.; e. Vice-President. Fujitsu Canada Inc. 1985–..; Sr. Account Mgr., Burroughs Business Machines 1972–76; Nat. Sales Mgr., Control Data Canada 1976–85; recreations: tennis, skiing, photography; Home: 3342 Sawmill Valley Dr., Mississauga, Ont. L5L 2Y1.

**DAY, James Halliday,** B.A., M.D., C.M.; physician; professor; b. Kingston, Ont. 8 June 1931; s. David John and Belva Inez (Halliday) D.; e. Queen's Univ., B.A. (Hon.) 1953; McGill Univ., M.D. 1959; F.R.C.P.(C) 1967; Am. Bd. of Allergy & Immunology, dipl. 1977; m. Maureen d. John and Evelyn Briscoe 1968; one d.: Jennifer Anne; PHYSICIAN, PROFESSOR AND HEAD, DIV. OF ALLERGY & IMMUNOLOGY, DEPT. OF MED., QUEEN'S UNIV.; Intern & Res., Royal Victoria Hosp. 1959–61; specialist training, Scipps Clinic & Rsch. Found. (U.S.) 1962–65; St. Mary's Hosp. (U.K.) 1966– ; attending privileges Kingston Gen., Hotel Dieu, St. Mary's of the Lake, Lennox & Addington hosps.; Cons. on Immunotoxicol. & Environmental Toxicology, World Health Orgn. 1982–90; Cons. on Indoor Air Quality, NATO 1991– ; several positions with nat. & internat. cttes. & socs. incl. Pub. Health Ctte. O.M.A. (Chrmn. 1978–83); Min. of Health Ctte.; Test Ctte. for Royal Coll. of Phys. & Surgs.; Internat. Joint Comn.; Schering Travelling Award 1963; R. Samuel McLaughlin Travel. Fellowship 1966; Fellow, Royal Coll. of Phys. (Can.); Am. Coll. of Phys.; Candn. Soc. for Allergy & Immunol. (Pres. 1972); Am. Acad. of Allergy & Immunol.; Am. Coll. of Allergy and Immunology; author of num. articles; recreations: outdoors; Home: 827 Wartman Ave., Kingston, Ont. K7M 4M3; Office: Kingston Gen. Hosp., 76 Stuart St., Kingston, Ont. K7L 2V7.

**DAY, Peggy Lynne,** Ph.D.; educator; b. Winnipeg, Man. 26 Feb. 1954; d. Robert David and Renee Caroline (Cole) D.; e. Univ. B.C., B.A. 1975, M.A. 1977; Harvard Univ. M.T.S. 1979, Ph.D. 1986; ASSOC. PROF., RELIGIOUS STUDIES, UNIV. OF WINNIPEG 1989– ; Instr. in Biblical Hebrew, Summer Lang. Prog., Harvard Divinity Sch. 1983–86; Asst. Prof. of Old Testament, Trinity Coll., Univ. of Toronto 1986–89; mem. Candn. Nat. Women's Volleyball Team 1972–73; co-editor and contributor, 'The Bible and the Politics of Exegesis' 1991; editor & contributor 'Gender and Difference in Ancient Israel' 1989; author 'An Adversary in Heaven: sāṭān in the Hebrew Bible' 1988; mem., DL Invest. Club (Pres. 1987–89); mem. Soc. Biblical Lit.; Candn. Soc. Biblical Studies; recreations: folk dancing, volleyball, basketball; Home: 188 Montrose St., Winnipeg, Man. R3M 3M7; Office: 515 Portage Ave., Winnipeg, Man. R3B 2E9.

**DAY, Peter John,** L.S.I.A.; creative director; b. Middlesex, England 29 Aug. 1947; s. John Francis Robert and Marie Louise (Prosper) D.; e. St. Columbas College, St. Albans U.K. 1963; Central School of Art London 1963–65; Watford School of Art L.S.I.A. 1965–68; m. Shirley d. Harry and Eileen Drake 27 Dec. 1977; children: Joshua John, Katherine Scarlet Louise; FOUNDING PARTNER, VICE-PRESIDENT & CREATIVE DIR., DEACON DAY ADVERTISING TORONTO 1987– ; Art Director, J. Walter Thompson London (U.K.) 1968–76 (worked in offices in Paris, Amsterdam, Istanbul); Senior Art Dir., Young & Rubicam Toronto 1976–78; Founding Partner & Creative Dir., Angus Baldwin & Partners 1979–84; Senior Art Dir., Doyle Dane Bernbach Ltd. 1984–87; Dir., Deacon Day Advertising; recipient of various nat. & internat. advertising awards; recreations: painting, horticulture; clubs: West Hartlypools Ferret; Home: Chestnut Farm, R.R. 3, Mount Albert, Ont. L0G 1M0; Office 20 Richmond St. E., Toronto, Ont. M5C 2R9.

**DAY, Richard Bruce,** M.A., Ph.D.; educator; b. Toronto, Ont. 22 July 1942; s. Raymond Victor and Dorothy Mabel (Witney) D.; e. Univ. of Toronto B.A. 1965, M.A. 1967, Dip. REES 1967; Univ. of London Ph.D. 1970; m. Judith d. Owen and Norma Sheffield 5 Aug. 1969; children: Tara Nicole, Geoffrey Bruce, Christine Michelle; PROF. OF POL. SCI. ERINDALE COLL. UNIV. OF TORONTO 1979– ; Asst. Prof. present Univ. 1970, Assoc. Prof. 1974, Discipline Rep., Asst. Chrmn. of Pol. Sci., Erindale Campus 1973–76, 1981–84, 1991–93; Mem., Internat. Soc. for the Study of European Ideas; mem. Appraisals Ctte. Ont. Council Grad. Studies 1983–86; mem. S.S.H.R.C. Appraisals Ctte. 1987–88; Killam Sr. Rsch. Fellow 1978, 1979; mem. Mun. Council Town of Kearney, Ont. 1978–81; author 'Leon Trotsky and the Politics of Economic Isolation' 1973, Italian transl. 1979; 'The "Crisis" and the "Crash" – Soviet Studies of the West (1917–1939)' 1981; ed. and transl. 'Selected Writings on the State and the Transition to Socialism' by N.I. Bukharin, 1982; 'The Decline of Capitalism' by E.A. Preobrazhensky, 1985; co-editor (with Ronald Beiner and Joseph Masciulli) 'Democratic Theory and Technological Society' 1988; Assoc. Ed. Candn. Slavonic Papers 1982–89; Contributing Ed., Internat. Journal of Political Economy 1989– ; mem. Candn. Assn. Slavists; Candn. Political Science Assoc.; recreations: municipal politics, ratepayer activities, skiing; Home: 2601 Truscott Dr., Mississauga, Ont. L5J 2B6; Office: Crossroads Bldg., Erindale Campus, Mississauga, Ont. L5L 1C6.

**DAY, Hon. Stockwell B.,** M.L.A.; politician; auctioneer; b. Barrie, Ont. 16 Aug. 1950; s. Stockwell and Gwendolyn (Gilbert) D.; e. Westmount H.S. 1967; Univ. of Victoria 1970–71; m. Valorie d. Richard and Violet Martin 2 Oct. 1971; children: Logan, Luke, Benjamin; MIN. OF LABOUR, ALTA. 1992– ; professional auctioneer; Auction Bus. Co-owner & Auctioneer 1972–74; Dir., Teen Challenge Ministries 1974–75; Commercial Interiors Contractor 1976–78; former Asst. Pastor &

Christian Sch. Admin., Bentley Christian Ctr. 1978–85; el. M.L.A., Red Deer, Alta. 1986– ; Govt. Caucus Whip 1989; Chrmn., Alta. Tourism Edn. Council; Chrmn., Premier's Council on the Family; Office: Legislative Buildings, Edmonton, Alta. T5K 2B6.

**DAYA, Azmin F.,** F.C.C.A., M.S.M., C.M.A.; financial executive; b. Astrida, Rwanda 6 Dec. 1956; s. Firoz Merali and Begum Baradali (Talib) D.; e. F.C.C.A. (U.K.) 1976; Boston Univ. M.S.M. 1982; C.M.A. 1985; divorced; children: Hussein, Farah; VICE-PRESIDENT, ACCOUNTING & FINANCE, THE GREAT LAKES REINSURANCE CO. 1987– ; Accountant, Travelers Indemnity Co. (Brussels, Belgium) 1977–78; Admin. Supvr. 1978–80; Asst. Mgr., Financial 1980–82; Supervisor, Great Lakes Reinsurance Co. 1982–84; Manager 1984–87; Mem., Admission & Awards Ctte., Soc. of Mngt. Accountants of Ont. (Mem. 1986–88, Vice-Chair 1988–89; Chair 1989–92); Insur. Acctg. & Systems Assn., Candn. Chap. (Sec. & Treas. 1988–89; Vice-Pres. 1989–90; Pres. 1990–91; Past Pres. 1991–92); recreations: squash, tennis, travel; Home: 804 Strouds Lane, Pickering, Ont.; Office: 390 Bay St., Suite 2100, Toronto, Ont. M5H 2Y2.

**DAYA, Salim,** M.B.,Ch.B., M.Sc., F.R.C.S.(C), F.A.C.O.G.; educator; gynaecologist; b. Nairobi, Kenya 16 July 1953; s. Haiderali M. and Gulshan K. (Sayani) D.; e. Prince of Wales Sch. Nairobi 1972; Manchester Univ. M.B.,Ch.B. 1977; Univ. of Toronto 4 yrs. postgrad. training Obstetrics & Gynaecol., one yr. Reproductive Endocrinol.; McMaster Univ. M.Sc. 1987; m. Yasmin d. Badrudin and Kulsum Bapoo 17 Nov. 1978; children: Rahim, Jamil; DIR. DIV. REPRODUCTIVE ENDOCRINOL. AND INFERTILITY McMASTER UNIV. 1988– , Assoc. Prof. of Health Sci's 1989– ; Chief of Service Endocrinol.-Infertility Div. Chedoke-McMaster Hosps. 1988– ; Chrmn., Reproductive Biology Section, Ont. Med. Assoc.; Assoc. Ed., J. of the Soc. of Obstetricians and Gynaecologists of Can.; came to Can. 1977; Asst. Prof. present Univ. 1985; Career Sci. Ont. Min. of Health 1986– , Award since 1986; recipient 7 awards best sci. paper sci. meetings since 1984; Mackid Lectr. Calgary 1989; Ismaili Award of Excellence 1989; author over 50 papers sci. jours., book chapters; Fellow, Am. Coll. Obstetricians Gynaecols.; mem. Am. Fertility Soc.; Candn. Fertility & Andrology Soc.; Am. Soc. Reproductive Immunol.; Home: 1400 Livingston Rd., Oakville, Ont. L6H 3G4; Office: 1200 Main St.W., Hamilton, Ont. L8N 3Z5.

**D'CRUZ, Joseph R.,** D.B.A.; educator; b. Karachi, Pakistan 19 June 1941; s. Robert and Dorothy (Gomes) D'C.; e. Karachi Univ. M.B.A. 1965; Harvard Bus. Sch. D.B.A. 1979; m. Filomena d. Orfino and Ida D'Sa 24 Aug. 1974; three s. Jason, Andrew, Geoffrey; ASSOC. PROF. OF STRATEGIC MGMT. UNIV. OF TORONTO 1979– ; Adjunct Prof. IMD Internat. Lausanne, Switzerland 1988– ; Dir. Strategic Analysis Dept. of Regional Ind. Expansion Can. 1984–85; adv. to multinat. corps. on exec. edn. and strategic mgmt.; frequent speaker nat. competitiveness & ind. strategy; recipient Touche Ross Award best article Business Quarterly 1988; co-author 'Canada Can Compete: Strategic Management of Canada's Industrial Portfolio' 1984; 'Yankee Canadians: Strategic Management of U.S. Subsidiaries After Free Trade' 1987; mem. World Econ. Forum; R. Catholic; recreation: travel; Home: 94 Highland Cr., Willowdale, Ont. M2H 1L1; Office: 246 Bloor St. W., Toronto, Ont. M5S 1V4.

**DEACON, D. Campbell,** B.A.; investment dealer, stock broker; b. Unionville, Ont. 30 Mar. 1948; s. Donald M. and Florence (Campbell) D.; e. Univ. of Guelph; York Univ., B.A. 1972; m. Jennifer Jeffrey; 3 children; CHRMN. & CHIEF EXTVE. OFFR., DEACON BARCLAYS de ZOETE WEDD LTD. 1986– ; Research Analyst, Read, Hurst-Brown & Co. (U.K.) 1973; Mgr., Eur. Dept., F.H. Deacon, Hodgson Inc. 1974; Vice-Pres. & Dir. 1976–86; mem., United Church; recreations: golf, skiing, tennis; clubs: Toronto Club, York Downs Golf & Country; Cambridge Club; Office: 304 Bay St., Toronto, Ont. M5H 4A5.

**DEACON, David Emmerson;** advertising executive; b. Toronto, Ont. 22 July 1949; s. Donald Mackay and Florence Isabelle (Campbell) D.; e. Rothesay Coll. Sch. 1968; Brock Univ. 1970; Casa Sch. of Fine Art (France) 1971; m. Mary d. Edward and Dorothy Eberle 23 July 1982; PRES., DEACON DAY ADVERTISING 1988– ; Gen. Mgr., Porsche, Volkswagen Canada Inc. 1984–87; Chrmn. Political Alerts, F.H. Deacon, Hodgson Inc. 1976–84, Vice-Pres. Retail Sales 1981–84; Ont. Chrmn. J. Turner Leadership Campaign 1984; Pres. Ont. Liberal Party 1984–85; Candn. Endurance Racing Champ., Sports Cars 1980; first Candn. to drive for factory team, 24 hrs. of LeMans 1981; one-man art exhbn. Brock Univ. 1970; Vice-Pres., Inst. for Political Involvement 1977–81; Hon. Dir., Candn. Environmental Law Resch. Found. 1979–83; ed. 'Political Alerts' 1976–80; illustrator 'Pen & Inks' 1969; recreations: skiing, tennis, windsurfing, sailing, riding; Club: Toronto; Craigleith Ski; Home: 30 Wellington St. E., Toronto, Ont. M5E 1S3; Office: 7th Flr., 20 Richmond St. E., Toronto, Ont. M5C 2R9.

**DEACON, Donald MacKay,** M.C., C.M., B.A.; b. Toronto, Ont. 24 Apr. 1920; s. late Frederick Herbert and Ethel Record (Emmerson) D.; e. Univ. of Toronto Schs. (1937); Univ. of Toronto, B.A. 1940; m. Florence, d. late Gordon D. Campbell, F.C.A., Toronto, Ont. 17 May 1947; children: Campbell, David, Martha, Douglas, Richard, Colin; Dir., Czar Resources Ltd.; Orbit Oil & Gas Limited; Chrmn., Atlantic Provinces Economic Counc. 1987–89; Nat. Comm. Scouts Can. 1982–87; Pres., Canadian Club of Toronto, 1968–69; M.L.A.-York centre 1967–75 Deputy-Reeve, Twp. of Markham, Ont., 1957; served in 2nd World War, 1941–46 with Royal Candn. Arty., awarded M.C.; Member, Order of Canada 1987; Liberal; United Church; recreations: skiing, hiking, cycling; Clubs: Toronto; United Services Officers Club, Charlottetown; Home: 271/2 Water St., Charlottetown, P.E.I. C1A 1A2.

**DEACON, Paul Septimus,** B.A., M.Com.; b. Toronto, Ont. 9 June 1922; s. Frederick Herbert and Ethel Record (Emmerson) D.; e. Univ. of Toronto Schs.; Univ. of Toronto, B.A. 1943, M.Com. 1947; m. Charlotte Adelle, d. Kenneth M. Smith, 25 Feb. 1950; children: (Charlotte) Anne, Wendy (Elizabeth), James (Kenneth), Andrew (Paul Donald), Jennifer (Emmerson); Vice-Pres., Maclean Hunter Ltd. 1979–92; Dir., Key Radio Ltd.; joined The Financial Post, July 1947; Montreal Office, 1948–52; Investment Editor, 1952–64; Editor 1964–77; Publisher 1968–79; Dir., Maclean Hunter Ltd. 1972–88; served in 2nd World War, with R.C.A.F., July 1942–Nov. 1945 as Pilot; served Overseas with No. 620 R.A.F. Sqdn.; Commissioned Apr. 1943; discharged with rank of Flight Lieut.; Mentioned in Dispatches; Pres., Michener Awards Foundation 1983–90; Toronto Soc. of Financial Analysts 1961–62; Nat. Ballet of Canada 1975–78; Kappa Sigma; United Church; recreations: golf, tennis; Clubs: Rideau (Ottawa); Royal Ottawa Golf; University (Toronto); Rosedale Golf (Toronto); Canadian (Ottawa) (Pres. 1982–83); Home: 112 Acacia Ave., Rockcliffe Park, Ont. K1M 0P9.

**DEACON, Peter,** Dip.A.D., A.T.D., H.D.F.A.(Lond); university professor, artist; b. Newport, Isle of Wight, England 3 Oct. 1945; s. Ronald Frank and Maisie Kathleen (Sanders) D.; e. Portsmouth Coll. of Art, dipl. in art & design (1st class hons.) 1963–67; Univ. of Wales, Art Teachers dipl. 1968; Slade Sch. of Art, Univ. of London (U.K.) H.D.F.A. 1970; PROF., UNIV. OF CALGARY 1990– ; awarded Abbey Major Scholarship in Painting tenable at Brit. Sch. at Rome 1970–72; appt. Fellow in Fine Art, Nottingham Univ. 1973–75; joined present univ. as Instructor 1975; Co-ord., Grad. Prog., Dept. of Art & Co-ord., painting & drawing areas; has exhibited artistic work widely incl. exhibs. in Can., Great Britain, U.S.A., Italy, Germany, Korea & Japan; received num. internat. prizes & awards; twenty one-person exhibs. since 1972; rep. in many public & corp. collections in several countries incl. The Victoria & Albert Mus., Can. Counc. Art Bank. & Alta. Art Found.; Artist-in-Res., Leighton Artists Colony, Banff, The Gushul Studio (Univ. of Lethbridge); Mem., Leighton Found.; Alta. Soc. of Artists; Hon. Mem., Mackenzie Art Gall. Regina; Midland Group Gall. England; has served on num. cttes. & juries for prov. arts orgns.; Office: Calgary, Alta. T2N 1N4.

**DEAHL, James;** writer; editor; b. Pittsburgh, Pa. 5 Dec. 1945; s. Henry Vance and Dorothy Ella (Dauber) D.; m. 2ndly Gilda L. d. Bernard and Lucy Mekler 23 May 1982; three d.: Sarah Llewellyn, Simone Dorothy, Shona Rachel; taught Centennial Coll. 1980; Seneca Coll. 1986; Ryerson Poly. Inst. 1986 and 1988; author: 'Real Poetry' (monograph) 1981; books of poetry: 'In the Lost Horn's Call' 1982; 'No Cold Ash' 1984; 'Blue Ridge' 1985; 'Geschriebene Bilder' 1990; 'Opening The Stone Heart' 1992; co-author: (with R. Souster) 'Into This Dark Earth' 1985; (with M. Acorn) 'A Stand of Jackpine' 1987; ed.: 'The Uncollected Acorn' 1987; 'The Northern Red Oak' 1987; 'I Shout Love and Other Poems' 1987; 'Hundred Proof Earth' 1988; Ed., Milton Acorn Series, The Mercury Press; Candn. Ed., 'The Pittsburgh Quarterly'; recipient Mainichi Award 1985; Vice-Chrmn., Candn. Poetry Assn.; mem., Workers' Ednl. Assn. of Can.; League of Candn. Poets; Internat. PEN; Haiku Can.; Acad. of Am. Poets; Poetry Soc. (U.K.); Address: Box 20, 99 Kimberley Ave., London, Ont. N5Z 5A1.

**DEALY, John Michael,** Ph.D.; educator; consulting engineer; b. Waterloo, Iowa 23 March 1937; s. Milton David and Ruth Marion (Dorton) D.; e. Univ. of Kansas B.S.Ch.E. 1958; Univ. of Mich. M.S.E. 1959, Ph.D. 1963, postdoctoral Fellow 1963–64; m. Jacqueline Mary Barbara d. Leo Déry, Town of Mount Royal, Que. Aug. 1964; one d. Pamela Ruth; PROF. OF CHEM. ENGN., McGILL UNIV. 1973– ; Dept. Chair 1993– ; Asst. Prof. Chem. Engn. McGill Univ. 1964, Assoc. Prof. 1967; Visiting Prof. Univ. of Cambridge 1970; Univ. of Del. 1978–79; Visiting Prof. Univ. of Wisconsin 1986–87; author 'Rheometers for Molten Plastics' 1982; 'Melt Rheology and its Role in Plastics Processing' 1990; 60 research publs. and patents: chem. engn., polymer rheol., plastics processing; mem. Candn. Soc. Chem. Engn.; Order Engrs. Que.; Am. Inst. Chem. Engrs.; Soc. Plastics Engrs.; Soc. Rheol. (Pres. 1987–89); Candn. Rheol. Group (Founding Pres.); McGill Assn. Univ. Teachers (Pres. 1968–69); Sigma Xi Scient. Rsch. Soc. (Pres. McGill Chapter 1972–73); Pres. McGill Faculty Club 1972–73; recreations: music, reading; Home: 315 Roslyn Ave., Westmount, Qué. H3Z 2L7; Office: 3480 University, Montréal, Qué. H3A 2A7.

**DEAN, Diana;** artist; b. 1942; e. Bath Acad. of Art (U.K.), dipl. in art & edn. with distinction in sculpture; exhibitions: solo, Nancy Poole's Studio 1987–93; 'Personal Vision in Landscape' Cambridge Pub. Gall. 1987; 'Canadian Genre,' Mem. Univ. Gall. 1987; one-woman exhibs., Nancy Poole's Studio 1978, 79, 81, 82, 84, 85; 2-person show, Surrey Art Gall. 1983; 'Works on Paper,' London Reg. Gall. 1981; York Gall. 1978; Studio Exhib. 1976, 77; Lancaster Univ. 1973; Arts Spectrum North, Arts Counc. of Britain 1973; Mid-Penine Nat. Sculp. Exhib. (purchase prize) 1971; sculpture comn., Castleford Civic Ctr. 1970; A.I.A., One Woman Sculpture Exhib. London 1966; A.I.A. Group Sculpture Show London (1st prize) 1965; 'Midlands 21' Nottingham Group Show 1963; collections: Confederaton Ctr. Mus. & Art Gall. P.E.I.; Dupont Can. Inc. Coll.; Candn. Paraplegic Assn.; Norcen Corp. Coll., Canada Council Art Bank; Owens Art Gall. Mt. Allison Univ.; Texaco Can. Inc.; Lancaster Univ.; Northern Arts Assn. (Brit. Counc.); Royal Bank of Can. Corp. Coll.; Teleglobe Can. Montreal; General Electric Can. Inc.; Borden & Elliot; Glaxo Canada Inc.; The Blackburn Group; subject of several reviews; Office: c/o Nancy Poole's Studio, 16 Hazelton Ave., Toronto, Ont. M5R 2E2.

**DEAN, Geoffrey,** B.A.; publisher; b. Newcastle-on-Tyne, Eng. 18 Sept. 1940; s. Thomas Craig D.; e. Heaton Grammar Sch. Newcastle-on-Tyne; N. Toronto Coll. Inst. 1957; Victoria Coll. Univ. of Toronto B.A. 1961; m. Philma Marina Patterson 10 Aug. 1963; children: Andrea Samantha, Christopher Michael; Coll. Rep. and subsequently Coll. Ed. McGraw-Hill Co. of Canada Ltd. 1961–65; Sales Mgr. Methuen Publications (Div. of Carswell Co.) 1966–69; Van Nostrand Reinhold Ltd. 1970–76 (Marketing Mgr., Vice Pres. Marketing 1972); Vice Pres. and Gen. Mgr., John Wiley & Sons Canada Ltd. 1976; Pres. and Dir. 1977–86; Pres. and Dir., Wiley Publishers of Canada Ltd. 1977–81; Consultant, Geoffrey Dean Enterprises 1986– ; Pres., Technical Instructional Products Inc. 1987–89; Pres., Scriptographic Communications Ltd. 1989–91; Offr., Candn. Book Publisher's Counc. 1981–83, Pres. 1983; Hon. Pres., Ont. Bus. Education Assn. 1982–84; mem. Adv. Bd. on Sci. Pub., Nat. Research Council of Can. 1982–85; Mem., Project Assessment Ctte., Book Publishing Industry Development Program, Govt. of Can. 1987–91; Chrmn., Book & Periodical Devel. Counc. 1988–89; Dir., Candn. Diabetes Assn. 1987–89; Vice Pres., Alumni of Victoria Coll. 1989; Protestant; recreation: music, curling, badminton; mem., Bd. of Trade of Metropolitan Toronto; Clubs: Granite; Arts & Letters.

**DEAN, Simon Paul,** B.A., M.B.A.; b. England 23 Apr. 1949; s. Denis A. and Kathleen D.; e. York Univ., B.A. (Econ.) 1972; Univ. of Western Ont., M.B.A. 1974; m. Wendy d. Dr. Robert and Joan Vince 3 Sept. 1971; children: Rachael, Nicholas; Pres., C.E.O. ROGERS RETAIL 1992– ; Vice-Chrmn., C.E.O. & DIR., CANADIAN HOME SHOPPING NETWORK (CHSN) LTD. 1988– ; C.E.O., ROGERS CANTEL MOBILE INC. - RETAIL DIV. 1991– ; C.E.O., ROGERS VIDEO 1992– ; Dir., Corp. Devel., John Labatt Limited 1981–82; Vice Pres., Mktg. & Sales, Mattel Canada Inc. 1982–83, Pres. 1984–87 and Vice Pres., Mattel Toys, U.S.A. 1984–87; mem., YPO; past Pres., Am. Marketing Assn. Toronto; recreations: music, squash; Clubs: Toronto Cricket Skating & Curling; Fitness Institute (Toronto); Home: 27 Woodland Court, Belfountain, Ont. L0N 1B0;

Office: 1 Valleybrook Dr., 5th Floor, Don Mills, Ont. M3B 2S7.

**DEAN, William George,** M.A., Ph.D.; retired university professor emeritus; b. Toronto, Ont. 29 Nov. 1921; s. William Ashton and Alice Mary (Firstbrook) D.; e. Brown Pub. Sch. and Upper Can. Coll., Toronto; St. Andrew's Coll., Aurora, 1940; Univ. of Toronto, B.A. (Trinity Coll.) 1949, M.A. (Geophysics and Geog.) 1950; McGill Univ., Ph.D. 1959; m. Elfreda Elizabeth, d. R. B. Johnston, Q.C., St. Catharines, Ont., 18 Sept. 1948; children: Peter Hugh, Robin Elizabeth; PROF. OF GEOG., UNIV. OF TORONTO, since 1969; Lab. Asst., Dept. of Geog. at present Univ. 1947; Lab. Demonst. 1948–49; Teaching Fellow 1949–50; Lectr. 1956–58; Asst. Prof. 1958–63; Assoc. Prof. 1963–69; Dir. of Field Camps 1958–67; Research Asst., Meteorol. Br., Dept. of Transport, 1947; Geog., B.C. Dept. of Lands, Victoria, 1951–53; Asst. Prof. and Chrmn. of Geog., Un. Coll., Winnipeg, 1953–56; Research Consultant on Arctic for Rand Corp., Santa Monica, Cal., 1954–56; Research Geog., Dept. of Mines and Tech. Survey, Ottawa, 1956–57; Visiting Fellow, Univ. Coll.,Cambridge Univ., 1969–70; Project Supvr., Ont. Jt. Hwys. Research Programme on N. Ont. Roads Survey, 1961–64; Research Consultant, Bd. of Govs., Georgian Coll. of Applied Arts and Technol., 1967–68; has also served as consultant for various firms and govt. depts.; summer research and field work incl. N.W.T., N. Ont. and Ottawa; served with RCA (Militia), Toronto, 1940–42 and with RCA in Can., UK and N.W. Europe 1942–46; rank Lt.; Capt., C.O.T.C., Univ. of Man., 1954–56; awarded D.V.A. Schols. 1947–52; Archibald Lampman Schol. 1947; Trinity Coll. Prize for Proficiency 1949; Carnegie Arctic Research Fellow 1950–52; U.S. Nat. Science Foundation Fellowship 1963; Can. Council Fellowship 1969 and 1977; Ed. 'The Canadian Geographer' 1960–67; Research Dir. and Ed., 'Economic Atlas of Ontario' (Gold Medal, Leipzig 1970); W.W. Atwood Gold Medal, Pan. Am. Inst. of Geography and History 1973; Dir., 3 volume 'Historical Atlas of Canada' (RCGS Gold Medal 1988); Special Citation, Assoc. of Am. Geographers 1990; recreations: curling, sailing, reading, music; Clubs: Faculty Club; Royal Canadian Curling; National Yacht; Sigma Xi; Home: 34 Dinnick Cres., Toronto, Ont. M4N 1L6.

**DEANE, Colin Michael,** B.Sc., Dp.B.A., CMC; management consultant; b. Whitehaven, England 29 August 1951; s. Arthur Michael and Georgina Eudith (Andrews) D.; e. John Mason H.S.; Univ. of Manchester Inst. of Sci. & Technol. B.Sc. (Hons.) 1973; Manchester Business School Dp.B.A. 1974; m. Leslie d. Ian and Dorothy Dutton 18 June 1988; PRINCIPAL, FINANCIAL SERVICES GROUP, ERNST & YOUNG MANAGEMENT CONSULTANTS (formerly Woods Gordon) 1978– ; Business Devel. Mgr., BTR Industries Group U.K. 1974–76; Indus. Marketing Consultant, METRA Consulting Group (London, U.K. & Saudi Arabia) 1976–78; author of Ernst & Young in-depth studies on mutual funds, RRSPs, the distbn. of wealth in Canada, and several edns. of 'Tomorrow's Customers' (annual pubn.); recreations: skiing, auto racing, reading, philately; clubs: CASC; Home: 7 Southlea Ave., Toronto, Ont. M4G 3L8; Office: P.O. Box 251, Ernst & Young, Toronto-Dominion Ctr., Toronto, Ont. M5K 1J7.

**DE BANE, Hon. Pierre,** P.C., M.P., Q.C., B.A., LL.L., Doc. Sc. Adm. (hon.); senator; b, Haifa, Palestine 1938; came to Can. 1951, naturalized 1956; S. Gabriel and Marie (Gahel) De B.; Coll. St-Alexandre B.A. (magna cum laude); post-grad. Séminaire Trois-Rivières, Laval Univ., Univ. of Ottawa; m. Elisabeth Nadeau 22 Dec. 1980; one s. Jean-Manuel; MEMBER OF THE SENATE 1984– ; called to Bar of Que. 1964; Prof. of Law, Fac. of Law, Laval Univ.; journalist, 'Le Soleil' and 'L'Action' Que.; Special Asst. to Min. of Justice, Gov't. of Can. 1967–68; mem. H. of C. from Matapedia-Matane, Can. 1968–84; Parlty. Secy. to Min. of Ext. Affairs 1972–74; Parlty. Secy. to Min. Urban Affairs 1974; Min. of Supply and Serv. 1978–90; Min. of Regional Econ. Expansion 1980–82; Min. of State for External Relations 1982; Min. of Fisheries and Oceans 1982–84; apptd. to Privy Council 1978; apptd. to Senate 1984; cr. Q.C. 1985; Liberal; Address: The Senate, Ottawa, Ont. K1A 0A4.

**DeBARDELEBEN, Joan,** M.A., Ph.D.; educator; b. Park Falls, Wis. 12 Oct. 1950; d. Lionel Arthur and Helen (Thompson) DeB.; e. Univ. of Wis. Madison B.A. 1972, M.A. 1974, Ph.D. 1979; m. Randall B. s. Charles and Ritta Droll 18 Dec. 1979; children: Andrew, Larisa; PROFESSOR 1993– ; and DIRECTOR 1992– , INST. OF CENTRAL/EAST EUROPEAN AND RUSSIAN-AREA STUDIES, CARLETON UNIV., Ottawa; Assoc. Prof. 1991–93; Asst. Prof. Colo. State Univ., Fort Collins 1978–80; Asst. Prof. 1980, Assoc. Prof. of Pol. Sci. 1985–91, Dir. of Grad. Studies, McGill Univ. 1983–85, 1989–90; guest lectr., rsch. politics in the Soviet successor states; media commentator; author 'Soviet Politics in Transition' 1992; 'The Environment and Marxism-Leninism: The Soviet and East German Experience' 1985; co-author ' European Politics in Transition' 1987, 1992; ed. and co-author 'To Breathe Free: Eastern Europe's Environmental Crisis' 1991; author numerous articles; Vice Pres., Candn. Assn. Slavists; Extve. Bd., Am. Assn. Advanc. Slavic Studies; Mem., Candn. Assn. Univ. Teachers; recreations: hiking, gardening, swimming; Office: CERAS, Paterson Hall, 1125 Colonel By Drive, Carleton Univ., Ottawa, Ont. K1S 5B6.

**de BELLEFEUILLE, Pierre,** O.C. (1967), B. Phil.; b. Ottawa, Ont. 12 May 1923; s. Lionel Lefébure and Annette (Senécal) de B.; e. Univ. of Ottawa, B.Phil. 1944; children: Louis, Anne; with Le Droit, Ottawa, as Reporter, Music Critic, Foreign Ed. and Parlty. writer, 1945–51; joined Nat. Film Bd. of Can. as Chief of Ed. and Cataloguing Services and Co-ordinator of French Distribution, 1951–60; Founding Ed., 'Le Magazine Maclean' 1960–64; apptd. Dir. of Exhibits, Candn. Corp. for the 1967 World Exhn., 1964–68; Free-lance journalist, writer, broadcaster and information consultant 1968–76; el. M.N.A. (Parti Québécois) for Deux-Montagnes, 15 Nov. 1976; apptd. Parlty. Asst. to Min. Cultural Affairs 1976, to Min. Inter-govt. Affairs 1978; re-el. 1981; Pres., Le Conseil de la Culture des Laurentides; Past Pres., Le Parti indépendantiste; la Société d'histoire de Deux-Montagnes; Les Semences Laval inc.; l'Institut Canadien des Affaires publiques; Ottawa Press Club; Le Syndicat des Journalistes d'Ottawa; Past Vice-Pres., Candn. Citizenship Council; l'Union Canadienne des Journalistes de langue française; mem. Québec Press Council (1974–76); awarded Gold Medal, Czechoslovak Soc. of Internat. Relations; author: 'La bataille du livre au Québec' (in collaboration 1972); 'Sauf vot' respect - lettre à René Lévesque 1984; 'L'ennemi intime' 1992; Address: 83, rue Chénier, Saint-Eustache, Qué. J7R 1W9.

**DEBER, Raisa Rebecca Sarah Berlin,** S.M., Ph.D.; educator; b. Toronto, Ont. 8 Oct. 1949; d. Abraham David and Norda Adelaide (Bennett) Berlin; e. Mass. Inst. of Technol. S.B. 1971, S.M. 1971, Ph.D. 1977; m. Charles Michael s. Solomon and Judith Deber 2 Jan. 1971; one s. Jonathan Arthur; PROF. OF HEALTH ADM., UNIV. OF TORONTO 1990– , cross appts. Dept. of Pol. Sci., Inst. of Med. Sci.; Asst. Prof. of Pol. Sci. Univ. of Wis. 1975–77; Asst. Prof. of Health Adm. present Univ. 1977–82, Assoc. Prof. 1982–90; co-editor: 'Case Studies in Canadian Health Policy and Management' 2 vols. 1992; 'Restructuring Canada's Health Services System' 1992; numerous publs. health policy and med. decision making; mem. various ed. bds.; mem. Soc. Med. Decision Making (Sec.-Treas. 1983–84); Internat. Soc. Technol. Assessment; Judgement/Decision Making Group; Candn. Health Econ. Rsch. Assn. (Bd. mem. 1987– ;); Candn. Pol. Sci. Assn.; Policy Studies Orgn.; Phi Beta Kappa; recreations: computers, reading; Home: 513 St. Clements Ave., Toronto, Ont. M5N 1M3; Office: 12 Queen's Park Cres. W., Toronto, Ont. M5S 1A8.

**de BEVER, Leo J.,** M.A., Ph.D.; economist; b. Zevenbergen, Netherlands 4 June 1948; s. Matthijs Johannus and Adriana Johanna (Verhagen) de B.; e. Univ. of Ore. B.A. 1970; Univ. of Wisc. M.A. 1972, Ph.D. 1976; m. Anne d. William and Eleanor O'Keefe 12 Apr. 1975; two s. Ian, Joshua; VICE PRES. & CHIEF ECONOMIST, NOMURA CANADA INC. 1991– ; Rsch. Assoc., Univ. of Wisc. 1975; Econ. Bank of Canada 1975–78, Chief Forecaster 1978–80; Chief Econ. & Mng. Dir. Chase Econometrics Canada, Toronto 1980–86; Vice Pres., Investment Admin. & Chief Econ., Crown Life Insurance Co. 1986–91; Econ. Cons., Ont. Energy Bd. hearings; co-author various articles, rsch. reports incl. 'The Impact of Microelectrons on Canadian Growth and Employment' 1981; Phi Beta Kappa; Home: 94 Cambridge Cres., Richmond Hill, Ont. L4C 6G2; Office: 1 First Candn. Place, Ste. 5830, Toronto, Ont. M5X 1E3.

**de BILLY, Jacques,** Q.C.; solicitor; b. Levis, P.Q. 25 June 1916; s. Valmore A. and Imelda (Gosselin) de B.; e. Laval Univ. B.A.; Osgoode Hall Law Sch.; m. Juliette, d. Laurence and Romeo Parent 15 Dec. 1947; children: Michel; Jose; Christiane; Claire; COUNSEL, LAVERY, de BILLY; Dir., United Accumulative Fund and Assoc. Companies; called to the Bar of Que. 1938; created Queen's Counsel 1950; past Pres. Que. Jr. Bar; Candn. Bar Assn., Que. Div.; served in Can. and overseas with Royal Candn. Artillery, Candn. Army during WW II; Hon. Col., 6th Field, Artillery Regt., Levis 1980–85; Gov., Laval Univ. Found.; recreations: fishing; reading; Clubs: Quebec Garrison; Candn. Inst. of Internat. Affairs; Home: 1155 Turnbull, #812, Quebec, P.Q. G1R 5G3; Office: 925, Chemin St-Louis, #500, Québec, Qué. G1S 1C1 (P.O. Box 970, Upper Town, Quebec, Qué. G1R 4W8).

**DE BLOIS, The Hon. Louis,** B.A., LL.L.; judge; b. Que. 26 Mai 1935; s. Rodolphe and Cecile (Michaud) D.; e. Laval Univ. B.A. 1957; Laval Univ. Fac. of Law LL.L. 1960; Amis au Bareau du Que. 1961; m. Denise d. Roland and Laure (Bellau) Champoux 27 Aug. 1960; children: Guy, Michel, Lucie; JUGE PUÎNÉ DE LA COUR SUPÉRIEURE À QUÉBEC, DIVISION D'APPEL DE QUÉBEC 1991; Stagiaire attaché à la Cour Municipale de Que. 1957–60; Stagiaire au Bur. Noel, Alleyn & Rioux 1959–61; Avocat au Bur. de Noel, Alleyn & Rioux 1961–62; Assoc. de l'etude de Blois & Sirois 1962–65; Assoc. de l'étude Letarte, St-Hilaire, de Blois & Assoc. 1965–70; Associe Sr. de St-Hilaire, de Blois, Leclerc, Gingras, Delage and Assoc. 1970–84; Admin. Régie des Loyers du Qué. 1966–70; Chargé de la formation et entrainement du Dept. des Fraudes Econ., Min. de la Justice de la Prov. 1966–70; Prof. Ecole Profl. du Barreau du Qué. 1977–81; Juge Puîné de la cour supérieure à Québec 1984–91; mem. du Conseil du Jeune Barreau du Qué.; Conferencier-Prof. à l'Assn. des Banquiers Candn. du Qué.; Procureur de corp. et soc. à carractere nat. et mulitnational; mem. Club de service Kiwanis 1966– ; mem. et Dir. de differents clubs sportifs; Dir. et Sec. de diverses corps. commerciales; recreations: tennis, peche, chasse, ski, musique; Adresse résidence: 9, Jardins Mérici, app. 1303, Québec, Qué. G1S 4S8.

**de BOLD, Adolfo J.,** O.C., M.Sc., Ph.D., F.R.S.C.; educator; research scientist; b. Parana, Argentina 14 Feb. 1942; s. Adolfo E.G. and Ana (Patriarca) de B.; e. Nat. Univ. of Cordoba B.Sc. (Hon.) 1968; Queen's Univ. M.Sc. 1972, Ph.D. 1973; m. Mercedes L. d. Agustin and Ercilia Kuroski 26 Apr. 1968; children: Adolfo A., Alejandro J., Cecilia I., Gustavo A., Pablo G.; PROF. OF PATHOL. AND PHYSIOLOGY, UNIV. OF OTTAWA 1986– ; Demonst. in Physics 1961–62 and in Normal & Pathol. Histol. 1964–67, Nat. Univ. of Cordoba, Argentina; Resident 1966–68 and Chief Resident 1967–68 Central Lab. Hosp. Nacional de Clinicas Cordoba; Lab. Sci. Hotel-Dieu Hosp. Kingston 1974–86; Asst. Prof. of Pathol. Queen's Univ. 1974–82, Assoc. Prof. 1982–85; Prof. 1985–86; Dir. of Rsch., Univ. of Ottawa and Ottawa Civic Hosp. Heart Inst. 1986–93; chief sci. contribution discovery heart hormones (atrial natriuretic factor/cardionatrins); Cons., USA Nat. Inst. of Health; Queen's Univ. Prize for Excellence in Rsch. 1985; E.C. Manning Principal Award 1986; Candn. Cardiovascular Soc. Rsch. Achievement Award; Am. Soc. for Hypertension Rsch. Award; Internat. Soc. for Hypertension Scientific Achievement Award 1990; Gairdner Found. Internat. Award 1986; McLaughlin Medal In Med. Rsch.; Officer, Order of Canada 1993; Fellow, Royal Soc. of Can.; Hon. Fellow, Royal Coll. of Physicians and Surgeons (Can.); mem. Candn. Soc. for Cell Biol.; Am. Soc. for Cell Biol.; Internat. Acad. Pathol.; Am. Assn. of Pathol.; Fedn. Am. Soc. for Experimental Biol.; Microscopical Soc. Can.; Soc. Exper. Biol. & Med.; Candn. Soc. Anat.; New York Acad. Sci.; New York Acad. of Sciences.; Am. Assn. for the Advancement of Sci.; author or co-author over 100 sci. publs. prof. jours. and books; R. Catholic; recreations: classical guitar, fine woodwork; Home: 5503 Island Park Drive, Manotick, Ont. K4M 1J2; Office: Heart Institute, Ottawa Civic Hospital, 1053 Carling Ave. Ottawa, Ont. K1Y 4E9.

**de BONDT, John Jaap;** writer; automotive historian; b. Baarn, Netherlands 7 Feb. 1924; s. Leendert and Krijntje (Groeneveld) de B.; e. Eerste Christelijke Hoogere Burger Sch. The Hague 1942; m. Corry d. Willem Frederik and Amélie Alice Heshusius 13 Sept. 1952; Acting Chief Pub. Info. KLM The Hague 1946, Chief Pub. Info. KLM Curaçao 1946–48; Founder, Publisher and Ed. 'Today' (Curaçao's first daily morning newspaper) 1949; Advt. Mgr. Julius L. Penha & Sons Inc. Curaçao 1950–52; Advt. Dept. 'Edmonton Journal' 1952–54; Promotion Mgr. 'Ottawa Journal' 1955–58; Public info. positions various Candn. Govt. depts. 1958–81 incl. Chief Media Relations CIDA 1975–81; Ed. 'Development Business' newspaper UN Geneva and New York 1981–84; Exec. Ed. 'Development' CIDA Ottawa 1984–85; author: 'Canada on Wheels' 1970; 'They Don't Make 'Em Like That Any More' 1987; numerous articles early cars Candn. and US publs.; mem. various ed. bds. car mags.; mem. Antique Automobile Club of Am.; recreations: cars, old car ads (coll. 10,000 car ads 1898–present), car models, music (classical & big band), old movies, art, animal welfare, environment, mystery stories; Address: 1750 Barrett Dr., Sidney, B.C. V8L 4V1.

**DECARIE, (Malcolm) Graeme,** B.A., M.A., Ph.D.; university professor; b. Montreal, Que. 27 Aug. 1933; s. Malcolm Stanley and Jessie (Miller) D.; e. Sir George Williams Univ. B.A. 1960; Acadia Univ. M.A. 1965; Queen's Univ. Ph.D. 1972; divorced; children: Ann Catherine, Christina Louise; m. 2ndly Catherine Gray 1992; Chrmn., History Dept., Concordia Univ. 1986–93; Teacher, Protestant School Bd. of Greater Montreal 1957–63; Prince of Wales College, Univ. of P.E.I. 1968–71; Loyola College/Concordia Univ. 1971– ; freelance broadcaster & writer (CBC, CJAD Radio Montreal Gazette) 1972–91; Boy Scout (second class); Captain-Lieutenant, 78th Fraser Highlanders; Mem., Alliance Quebec (Prov. Extve. 1987–90; Chair 1989–90, Adv. Bd. 1991– ;); recreations: public speaking, sailing; Home: 25 Oxford Rd., Baie d'Urfé, Que.; Office: 7141 Sherbrooke St. W., Montreal, Que. H4B 1R6.

**DECARIE, Guy,** P.Eng.; b. Montreal, Que. 10 Nov. 1925; s. Wilbrod and Mercedes (Ouimet) D.; e. Ecole Notre-Dame de Grâce; D'Arcy McGee High Sch. 1944; McGill Univ., B.Eng. 1948; m. Solange, d. Ernest Lapointe, 24 June 1952; children: Guy Philippe, Jacques, François; President and Gen. Mgr., Quebec Engineering Inc.; with Harney Construction Co. Ltd., Quebec, Que. as Dir. and Secy. 1948–50; Project Mgr., North Shore Construction Co. Ltd., Montreal 1950; Marine Div. Engr., E. Area Engr., Mannix Ltd., Calgary and Chief Engr. and Dir., Mannibec Ltd. (Mannix subsidiary Calgary and Montreal) 1952; Vice-Pres and Operations Mgr., J. D. Stirling Ltd. 1957–59; mem. Corp. Engrs. Que.; Engn. Inst. Can.; R. Catholic; recreations: golf, tennis, skiing, swimming; Clubs: M.A.A.A.; Rosemere Golf; Home: 140 Jardin des Tourelles, Rosemere, Qué. J7A 4M7.

**DECARIE, Thérèse Gouin,** O.C. (1977), B.A., Ph.D.; professeur; née Montréal, Qué., 30 sept. 1923; f. Léon et Yvette (Ollivier) Gouin; é. Univ. de Montréal, B.A. 1945, L.Ph. 1947, Ph.D. 1960; ép. Vianney D. 1948; doctorat honorifique, Univ. d'Ottawa 1981; enfants: Pascale, Dominique, Jean-Claude, Emmanuel; PROF., DEPT. DE PSYCHOLOGIE, UNIV DE MONTREAL; auteur de 'Le développement psychologique de l'enfant' 1953 (5e éd. 1971); 'De l'adolescence à la Maturité' 1955 (3e éd. 1971); 'La Fasi della Crescita' (éd. italienne abrégée des deux livres précédents) 1960; 'L'intelligence et l'affectivité chez le jeune enfant' 1961 (traduction anglaise 1965, espagnole 1970 et italienne 1980); éditeur, 'La réaction du jeune enfant à la personne étrangère' (1972) (traduction anglaise 1974); aussi divers articles en français et en anglais sur les mêmes sujets; mem. Soc. Candnne. de Psychol. (Prés. hon. 1984–85); Corp. des Psychol. de la P.Q.; Soc. for Research in Child Devel.; Soc. de Psychanalyse; Soc. Royale; Conseil Nat. de Recherches du Canada 1970–76; Ordre du Canada; Prix Marcel-Vincent de l'ACFAS 1986; Prix du Québec Léon-Gérin 1988; Distinguished Fellow, Internat. Conference on Infant Studies 1990; Médaille Inis-Gérin de la Société Royale du Canada 1991; catholique r.; résidence: 77 McNider, Outremont, Qué. H2V 3X5; bureau: B.P. 6128, Montréal, Qué. H3C 3J7.

**DECARY, Hon. Raymond Gervais,** Q.C., B.A., LL.B.; retired judge; b. Montreal, Que. 16 Oct. 1921; s. Louis-Amédée and Germaine (Marchand) D.; e. Brebeuf Coll. (Jesuits) B.A. 1942; Univ. of Montreal LL.B. 1945; N.Y. Univ. 1946; divorced; children: Raymond Jean, Claude Champagne, Matthieu; read law with C.G. Heward, Q.C.; called to Bar of Que. 1945; cr. Q.C. 1961; practised law Satterlee, Warfield & Stephens, New York 1945–46; Counsel Taxation Div. Dept. Nat. Revenue 1947–55; Geoffrion & Prud'homme 1955–69; Decary, Guy, Vaillancourt, Bertrand & Bourgeois 1970–73; Justice, Federal Court of Canada 1973–84 (ret.); Gov. Business Adm. Faculty Sherbrooke Univ.; mem. Candn. Bar Assn. (Pres. Tax Sub-Sec.); Candn. Tax Foundation (Extve.); R. Catholic; recreations: skiing, tennis, hiking; Address: 3470 Stanley, #1602, Montreal, Qué. H3A 1R9.

**DÉCARY, The Hon. Mr. Justice Robert,** LL.L., LL.M., Q.C.; federal court judge; b. Montreal, Que. 26 May 1944; s. Jacques and Madeleine (Toupin) D.; e. Coll. Jean de Brébeuf, B.A. 1963; Univ. of Montreal, LL.L. 1966; University Coll., London LL.M. 1968; JUDGE, FEDERAL COURT OF CANADA, APPEAL DIV.; JUDGE, COURT MARTIAL APPEAL COURT; Spl. Asst. to Sec. of State for Ext. Aff. 1970–73; practiced law with Deschênes, de Grandpré, Montreal 1973–79; Co-Dir. of Rsch., Task Force on Candn. Unity 1978–79; Partner, Noël, Décary, Aubry & Assoc. 1979–90; Columnist, Le Devoir and La Presse 1977–90; monthly columns in The National and Journal Barreau; Ed., Supreme Court News 1985–90; Agt. of the Atty. Gen. of Que. in the Supreme Ct. of Can. 1980–90; Law Review Ed., Univ. of Montreal 1964–66; Commonwealth Scholar 1967; Dir., Les Grands Ballets Canadiens 1970–73; Mem., Arts Counc. of the City of Montreal 1977–79; author: 'Chère Elize (ou la petite histoire du rapatriement)' 1983; 'L'appel à la Cour Suprême' 1988; co-author: 'The Court and the Constitution' 1982; 'La réponse du Québec' 1980; Home: 330 Lévis, Hull, Que. J8Z 1A4; Office: Supreme Court Bldg., Ottawa, Ont. K1A 0H9.

**de CHANTAL, René,** B.A., L. ès L., Dr. de l'U. (Paris), Dr. de l'Université d'Ottawa (hon. causa), F.R.S.C.; retired university professor; b. Moose Creek, Ont. 27 June 1923; s. William Joseph and Antoinette (Ladouceur) de C.; e. McGill Univ., B.A. 1948; Univ. de Paris, L. ès L. 1951, Dr. de l'U. 1960; Univ. de Paris, Diplôme de professeur de français à l'étranger 1951; m. Geneviève Marguerite Andrée. d. late Raoul Penot, 1951; children: Marie-Laure, François; CONSULTANT (writer, rewriter and reviser); Lectr., Faculty of Arts, Univ. of Ottawa, 1951; Asst. Prof. 1955; Assoc. Prof. 1961; joined Univ. of Montreal as Assoc. Prof., Faculty of Letters and Head, Dept. of French Lit., 1962; Prof. of Modern French Lit. and French-Candn. Linguistics 1964; Dean, Faculty of Letters 1967–71; Dean, Faculty of Arts and Sciences 1971–75; Vice Rector Academic Affairs 1975–79; Minister, Cultural Affairs and Information, Candn. Embassy in Paris 1979–83; Dir., Academic Relations Div., Dept. of External Affairs 1983–87; participant in Weekly CBC program 'La langue bien pendue' from 1964 and in 'La Parole est d'or' until 1968; Head of Cultural Affairs, Dept. of External Affairs 1966–67; Mem. and Pres., National Library Adv. Bd. 1975–79; served with RCAF 1942–45; author: 'Chroniques de français' 1956, rev. ed. 1961; 'Marcel Proust, critique littéraire' 2 vols. 1967; other writings incl. articles for various newspapers and journs. and a weekly column on linguistics problems for 'Le Droit' from 1953–63; Dir. and Founder, 'Etudes françaises' 1965; mem., Académie canadienne-française 1967– , Sec. perpétuel 1974–79; Royal Soc. of Canada 1966– ; Pres., Académie des lettres et des sciences humaines 1977–78; Conseil internat. de la langue française 1967– , Vice-Pres. 1976– ; Assoc. Mem., Acad des Sci., Belles-Lettres et arts de Rouen 1981– ; Acad. de Marseille 1981– ; R. Catholic; recreations: skiing, swimming; Address: 7 Birch Ave., Ottawa, Ont. K1K 3G4.

**de CHASTELAIN, Gen. Alfred John Gardyne Drummond,** CMM, OC, CD, B.A.; diplomat; b. Bucharest, Rumania 30 July 1937; s. Alfred George Gardyne and Marion Elizabeth (Walsh) de C.; e. Fettes Coll. Edinburgh 1955; Mount Royal Coll. Calgary 1956; Royal Mil. Coll. Can. Kingston B.A. 1960; Brit. Army Staff Coll. Camberley grad. 1966; m. MaryAnn d. Rev. Dr. A. M. Laverty, Kingston, Ont. 9 Sept. 1961; children: Duncan John Drummond, Amanda Jane; CHIEF, NATIONAL DEFENCE H.Q. 1993– ; comnd. 2nd Lt. 2 Bn. PPCLI Edmonton 1960; promoted Capt. and named aide-de-camp to Chief of Gen. Staff Army HQ Ottawa 1962–64; Co. Commdr. 1 PPCLI Hemer, Fed. Republic Germany 1964–65; promoted Maj. and Co. Commdr. 1 PPCLI Edmonton and later served with 1 Bn. UN Force Cyprus 1967–68; appointed Bgde. Maj. 1 Combat Group Calgary 1968–70; Commanding Officer 2 PPCLI Winnipeg 1970–72 and promoted Lt. Col.; attended Laval Univ. under Federal Bicultural Program 1972–73; Sr. Staff Offr. Quartier Général Dist. 3 Qué. (Milice) Québec City 1973; promoted Col. and Commdr. Candn. Forces Base Montreal 1974; Depy. Chief of Staff HQ UN Forces Cyprus and Commdr. Candn. Contingent 1976; promoted to Brig. Gen. 1977 and apptd. Commandant Royal Mil. Coll. Can. Kingston; assumed command 4 Candn. Mechanized Bgde. Group Lahr, Fed. Republic Germany 1980–82; appointed Director General Land Doctrine and Operations NDHQ, Ottawa 1982–83; promoted Maj. Gen. 1983 and apptd. Depy. Commdr. Mobile Command, St Hubert, Que.; promoted Lt. Gen. 1986 and appointed Asst. Depy. Min. (Personnel) at NDHQ Ottawa; Vice Chief, Defence Staff 1988; promoted Gen. 1989 and apptd. Chief of the Defence Staff; Candn. Ambassador to the United States Jan. 1993–Dec. 1993; Past Vice-Pres., Nat. Counc., Boy Scouts of Can.; Past Pres., Dominion of Canada Rifle Assoc.; Vice-Pres., Nat. Rifle Assn. (UK); apptd. Commander of the Order of Military Merit 1984; Officer of the Order of Canada 1993; Officer of the Order of St. John 1987, Commander 1991; Conference of Defence Assns. VIMY Award 1992; Presbyterian; recreations: fishing, painting, jogging, Scottish country dancing; Clubs: Royal Military College of Canada Club; Royal Kingston Un. Services Inst.; St. Andrew's Soc. of Montreal; Royal Scottish Country Dance Soc.; Office: 101 Colonel By Dr., Ottawa, Ont. K1A 0K2.

**DECKER, Franz-Paul;** music director; b. Cologne, Germany; s. Kaspar and Elisabeth (Scholz) D.; e. Cologne Univ. and State Conserv.; CHIEF CONDUCTOR, NEW ZEALAND SYMPHONY 1990– ; Music Dir., Barcelona Symphony 1986– ; Principal Guest Conductor, National Arts Center, Ottawa 1991– ; Choir Dir. and Music Dir., Municipal Theatre, Giessen and Music Dir., Cologne Opera 1945; Perm. Conductor, Krefeld Opera and Orchestra 1946–50; Conductor, Wiesbaden State Opera 1950–53; Wiesbaden Mun. Orchestra 1953–56; Gen. Dir., Bochum Orchestra 1956–64; and Rotterdam Orchestra 1962–68; Conductor and Music Dir., Montreal Symphony Orchestra 1966–76; Principal Guest, New Zealand Symphony 1980–89; has conducted all maj. orchestras in Athens, Berlin, Brussels, Vienna, Salzburg, Paris, Zurich, Geneva, London, Edinburgh, Munich, Lisbon, Madrid, Buenos Aires, Rio de Janeiro, Moscow, Leningrad, Rome, Australia and New Zealand; regular Guest Conductor for Opera in Germany, USA (Chicago, Dallas, Houston, Tulsa), Buenos Aires (Teatro Colon), and Barcelona (Teatro Liceo); rec'd German 'Bundesverdienst Kreuz' 1st Class; Edgard Roquette Pinto-Medaille, Brazil and 'Herscheppend schepik' Medal, Holland; Professor Dr. (hon. causa); mem., Soc. Contemporary Music; Address: Kronenburger Str. 2, Cologne (Koeln) or 486 B Mount Pleasant Ave., Westmount, Que. H3Y 3H3.

**DECORE, Laurence G.,** C.M., B.A., LL.B., Q.C.; politician; b. Vegreville, Alta. 28 June 1940; e. Univ. of Alberta, B.A. 1961, LL.B. 1964; Clinton J. Ford 3rd yr. law Moot Court Award 1964; LEADER, ALTA. LIBERAL PARTY 1988– ; M.L.A. (Edmonton Glengarry); Lieut., Royal Candn. Navy; Jr. Offr. Judge Advocate Gen. Dept. 1963; Most Proficient Jr. Offr. HMCS Nonsuch 1965; Alderman, City of Edmonton 1974–77; former Chrmn., City of Edmonton, Econ. Aff. Ctte.; Budget Ctte. 1976; Pub. Aff. Ctte.; former Chrmn., Nat. Candn. Cons. Council on Multiculturalism (CCCM) 1980–83; Mayor, City of Edmonton 1983–88; Edmonton Multiculturalism Ctte.; Former Vice-Chrmn., Development Appeal Bd.; Former Dir., Local Bd. of Health 1974–77; Royal Alexandra Hosp. Bd. 1975–77; Greater Edmonton Found.; Mem., Ukrainian Community Ctte. on Multiculturalism; Former & 1st elected Chrmn., Alta. Heritage Council; Past Pres., Ukrainian Prof. & Businessmen's Club; Ukr. Prof. & Bus. Fed. of Canada; Former Sec., Ukr. Candn. Ctte., Edmonton; Past Dir., Candn. Found. of Ukr. Studies; mem., several cttes. & spokesman on many occasions for CCCM; Dir. of several private companies in Alta.; Co-founder, QCTV Ltd.; Prov. of Alta. Achievement Award for Outstanding Community Serv. 1982; Order of Canada 1983; SKIP, Edmonton H.S. Curling Champs.; Former Admin. Sec., Edmonton & Dist. Soccer Assoc. and Alta. Soccer Assn.; Dir. & Fin. Chrmn., Elizabeth Fry Soc.; mem., Alta. Law Soc.; Candn. Bar Assn. (Alta.); St. John's Ukrainian Greek Orthodox Parish; Office: 601 Legislature Annex, Edmonton, Alta. T5K 1E4.

**de CORNEILLE, Rev. Roland,** B.A., S.T.B., M.Th.; b. Switzerland 19 May 1927; s. Jacques Andre and Muriel Hilda (Schlager) de C.; e. Amherst (Mass.) Col. B.A. 1946; Trinity Coll. Univ. of Toronto L.Th. 1953, S.T.B. 1954; M.Th. 1961; m. Elizabeth d. Charles and Marion Cleland 6 June 1954; children: Christopher, Michelle; INCUMBENT, CHURCH OF ST. JUDE, TORONTO 1993– ; el. to H. of C. as Lib. for Eglinton Lawrence 1979–88; Official Opposition Critic for Secy. State 1984–86; Official Opposition Critic for External Relations and for Human Rights 1986–88; o. Anglican Priest 1953; Statistician, Time Inc., N.Y. 1946–48; Advertising and Brand Promotion, Proctor & Gamble, Ohio 1948–51; Curate and Rector Parish Chs. Montreal and Toronto 1952–62; founder and Dir. 1st Christian-Jewish Dialogue Prog. 1962–70; Nat. Dir. League for Human Rights B'nai B'rith 1971–79; Parlty. Sec. to Min. of Veterans' Affairs 1981–83; Chrmn. Toronto & Region Lib. Caucus 1984–85; Can.-Italy Parlty. Friendship Grp.; Founding Chrmn. Can.-Israel Parlty. Friendship Grp. and other parlty. assns. incl. Commonwealth, Can.-Europe, Can.-U.S. and NATO; mem. many Ch. and Inter-Religious Cttes. incl. World Council Chs., Nat. Counc. Chs., Candn. Counc. Chs., Ang. Diocese Toronto; shared Brotherhood Book Award Nat. Conf. Christians & Jews with Martin Luther King Jr. 1966; recipient first Claude Uzielli Award for pioneering Christian-Jewish Dialogue 1982; Cert. Appreciation Jamaican-Candn. Assn. 1983; Spiritual Father of Year Award, Pioneer Women 1984; author 'Christians and Jews' 1966; Phi Beta Kappa; Freemason (Past Grand Chaplain; Hon. Grand Chaplain Israel); Home: 9 Bernick Rd., Willowdale, Ont. M2H 1E3.

**DE COTRET, Hon. Robert Rene,** P.C., B.A., M.B.A.; b. Ottawa, Ont. 20 Feb. 1944; s. Robert and Carmen (Laperrière) René de Cotret; e. Univ. of Ottawa B.A. 1964; McGill Univ. M.B.A. 1966; Univ. of Mich. C.Ph.

(Business Econ.) 1969; m. Diane d. Gérard Chénier 14 May 1966; children: Lynne A., Marc R., Michel J.; Secretary of State of Canada and Min. Responsible for the Status of Disabled Persons 1991–93; Lectr. in Banking and Finance, Univ. of Mich. 1969–70; Sr. Econ. Council Econ. Advisors to Pres. of U.S.A., Washington 1970–71; Advisor on Monetary Affairs Dept. Finance, Ottawa 1971–72; Dir. to Pres. Conf. Bd. Can. 1972–78; P. Cons. Cand. for Ottawa Centre g.e. 1978; apptd. to Senate of Can. 1979; Min. of Industry, Trade & Comm. and Min. of State for Econ. Devel. 1979; First Extve. Vice Pres. and Gen. Dir., National Bank of Canada 1980; Extve. Vice Pres. Internat., Nat. Bank of Can. 1982–84; el. M.P. for Berthier-Maskinongé-Lanaudière Sept. 1984, re-el. 1988 for Berthier-Montcalm; apptd. Pres., Treasury Bd. 1984–87, 1989–90; Min. of Regional Industrial Expansion & Min. of State for Science & Technology 1987–89; Acting Min. of the Environment May 1990; Min. of the Environment Sept. 1990; apptd. Secy. of State and Min. Responsible for the Status of Disabled Persons 1991–93; mem. Ont. Econ. Council 1976–78; Adv. Comte. on Confed. to Premier of Ont. 1977–78; Candn. Econ. Policy Comte. C.D. Howe Research Inst. 1977; Candn. Foundation for Econ. Educ. 1977; Dir. Alphatext Ltd. 1974–79, 1980–81 (Chrmn., Extve. Comte. of Bd. 1976–79); Campaign Chrmn. Que. Heart Foundation; Chrmn. Fondation de l'Hôpital Saint-Luc.

**de COURVILLE NICOL, Jacques,** B.Adm., B.A.; communications executive; b. Outremont, Qué. 18 Sept. 1941; s. Jean and Thérèse (Leclerc) de Courville Nicol, L.L.L., Q.C.; e. Hamilton Inst. of Technol. New York B.Adm. 1960; Laurentian Univ. B.A. 1966; Univ. of Ottawa Adm. Law Prog. 1970; Sr. Exec. Mgmt. Training Prog. Fed. Govt. 1974; m. Michelle d. J. Conrad and Jeanne (Cannie) Lavigne 12 Sept. 1965; children: Alexandre, Valérie, Isabelle, Pascale; FOUNDER. PRES. & C.E.O.: CHROMAVISION INTERNATIONAL INC. 1984– ; TURNELLE CORP. 1980– ; NORACOM Consultants Inc. 1982– ; 137462 Canada Inc. 1983– ; Decogescom Inc. 1985– ; Video Newsletter (VNL) Inc. 1988– ; Educasat Communications Inc. 1991; Dir., Capital CanWest TV Inc. 1989– ; mem. Exec. Ctte. and Dir., Teleglobe Canada 1981– ; Co-Founder, Treas. and Dir., TEVEMEDIA Internat. Investments Inc. 1985– ; Co-Founder and Dir., Ontario Film Devel. Corp. 1986–88; Dir., Candn. Film Inst. 1986; Founder of Le Regroupement des Gens d'Affaires de l'Outaouais Inc. (Hon. Life Pres.) 1983– ; Founder and Chrmn., Videoglobe Inc. 1983–85; Co-Founder and Vice-Chrmn., The Canadian Entertainment Network Inc. (Pay TV) 1981–83; part-time Cons., Nordicity Group since 1976; Vice Pres., Mid-Canada Communications Canada Inc. (Radio and Television Network) 1976–80; Founder, Sec.-Treas. and Dir., Télévision de l'Est du Canada (TVEC) Inc. 1982–85; Dir. Gen., Training & Info., Fed. Treasury Bd. 1972–76; Head, Information & Training, Secretary of State for Canada 1968–71; Exec. Dir., Candn. Assn. of Medical Students, Interns and Residents (CAMSIR) 1966–67; Publisher, 'L'Information,' French weekly, N. Ont. 1964–68; 'Franc-Jeu,' 'Ici L'Outaouais,' 'Le Lien' and other mags. and publs. 1960–68; Agency Mgr., R.L. Crain Ltd. 1960–64; apptd. Chrmn., Nat. Capital Aquarium Corp. (NCAC) 1990– ; Chrmn., Nat. Capital Aquarium Task Force (NCATF) 1989–90; apptd. Vice Pres. of Bd., Gloucester C. of C. 1989; awarded Commemorative Medal for 125th Anniversary of Candn. Confederation 1993; named Businessman of Yr., Nat. Capital Region 1986; apptd. by Fed. Govt. to rep. communications ind. at Anik C-3 launching 1985; apptd. mem., La Société des Cent Associés d'Amérique 1991– ; Past Trustee: Children's Hosp. E. Ont.; Ottawa-Carleton Cath. Sch. Bd.; Bd. Regents Univ. of Sudbury; Ottawa-Carleton Learning Enhancement Found.; Council Candn. Unity; Nat. Council Econ. Devel.; mem. Gloucester C. of C.; Canada's Capital Visitors and Convention Bureau; Ottawa-Carleton Econ. Devel. Corp.; Candn. Cable TV Assn.; Internat. TV Can.; Nat. Audio-Visual Assn. Can.; Univ. of Ottawa Innovacom Centre; Internat. Import/Export Assn.; Nat. Mktg. Conf. & Expn.; R.G.A.; Clubs: Pineview Golf; Cercle Universitaire d'Ottawa; Club des Ambassadeurs (Montréal); Home: 621 Gaines Dr., Gloucester, Ont. K1J 7W7; Office: 1172 Rainbow St., Gloucester, Ont. K1J 6X7.

**DECTER, Michael Barry Rice,** A.B.; b. Winnipeg, Man. 25 Sept. 1952; s. Percy Harry and Una Barry (McGilligan) D.; e. Kelvin H.S. Winnipeg 1969; Harvard College, A.B. (Hons. magna cum laude) 1974; m. Lucille d. Louis and Delia Roch 16 April 1981; children: Riel Percy and Genevieve Sarah Roch-Decter; RSCH. SCHOLAR, CENTRE FOR BIOETHICS, UNIV. OF TORONTO 1993– ; various positions Manitoba govt. & private sector 1974–81; Clerk of Extve. Council & Cabinet Sec., Manitoba Govt. 1981–86; Partner, The October Partnership (Winnipeg) 1986–88; Peat Marwick Consulting Group (Winnipeg, Montreal) 1988–90; Managing Partner, Roch-Decter Associe's & Pres., VISTA (Montreal) 1990–91; Chair & Dir., Shawinigan Energy 1990–91; Deputy Min. of Health, Govt. of Ontario 1991–93; Chief Negotiator, Ont. Social Contract 1993; Hon. Research Fellow, IPAC 1986–87; Nat. Chair, Stanley Knowles Distinguished Professorship Endowment Campaign, Brandon Univ.; Mem., Brandon Univ. Found. Bd.; Dir., Border Crossings Magazine; recreations: skiing; clubs: Toronto Bd. of Trade; Home: 89 Kingswood Road, Toronto, Ont. M4E 3N4; Office: 88 College St., Toronto, Ont. M5G 1L4.

**DEEKS, Harley Ross,** B.S.A.; retired brewing executive; b. Morrisburg, Ont 14 June 1927; s. Merle J. and Eva Belle (Beckstead) D.; e. Univ. of Guelph B.S.A. 1950; Brit. Inst. of Brewing Dip. 1956; Am. Mgmt. Dip. 1964; m. Barbara d. George and Agnus Herring 6 March 1948; children: Donald, Gordon, Gregory, James, Peter, Sandra, Paula; Vice Pres., Ops., Western Div., Molson Breweries 1989–90; retired; Asst. and Head Brewer O'Keefe Brewing Co. Ltd. 1950–60; Gen. Mgr. O'Keefe Old Vienna Brewing Co. (B.C.) Ltd. 1960–63, Vice Pres. and Gen. Mgr. 1963–65; Dir. of Operations W. Div. National Breweries of Canada Ltd. 1965–66; Asst. to Vice Pres. Prodn. Molson Western Breweries Ltd. 1966–70; Gen. Mgr. Molson Saskatchewan Brewery Ltd. 1970–73, Pres. 1975–83; Gen. Mgr. present Brewery 1973–75; Pres. present Brewery 1983–88; Convocation Founder Simon Fraser Univ.; Chrmn. Council for Candn. Unity Sask. 1976–79; Pres. Regina Rotary 1978–79; Pres. Regina Chamber of Commerce 1979–80; recreations: golf, hunting; Club: Mayfair Golf & County; Home: 214 Wolf Willow Cres., Edmonton, Alta. T5T 1T2.

**DEEP, Albert Ross,** M.D.,C.M., F.R.C.P.(C); physician; b. Windsor, Ont. 1 Oct. 1935; s. Ab and Anne (Teraz) D.; e. The Hon. J.C. Patterson Coll. Inst. Windsor 1953 (Alice Wilson Graybiel Mem. Scholar Essex Co. 1953); Queen's Univ. M.D.,C.M. 1959 (Univ. Scholarship Med. (for first place standing in class) 1956, Univ. Prize Biochem., Pharmacol. & Physiol., Edgar Forrester Faculty Prize 1959); m.Janet d. N. Wainwright Cleary, 31 May 1958; children: Albert Ross II, Bruce Wainwright, James Edward, Mark Elliott; private practice Cardiol. and Internal Med. 1969– ; internship and residency training, Montreal Gen. Hosp. 1959–65; positions incl. Clin. Fellow in Cardiol., Chief Resident Internal Med., also Resident and Teaching Fellow McGill Univ.; Clin. Fellow Nat. Inst of Health, Mass. Gen. Hosp. Boston and Teaching Fellow Harvard Univ. (Cardiology & Int. Med.) 1965–67; Assoc. Physician Toronto Western Hosp. 1967–68; Toronto Gen. Hosp. 1970–71; Intensive Care Unit and Dept. of Medicine, Reddy Memorial Hosp., Westmount, Que. 1990–91; Fellow of the Royal College of Physicians (Canada); First Dir. Heart Sunday, Queen's Univ., mem. Extve. Alma Mater Soc., Pres. Aesculapian (Med.) Soc. 1957–58; Pres. Interns & Residents Assn. Montreal Gen. Hosp. 1964–65; mem. Ont. Coll. Phys. & Surgs.; Que. Coll. Phys. & Surgs.; Ont. Med. Assn.; Que. Med. Assn.; Am. Heart Assn.; Paul Dudley White Soc.; Fed. Internists Prov. Que.; Past mem., Acad. of Medicine, Toronto; New York Acad. of Sciences; publ.: Pharmacy Practice: Treatment of Hypertension; FOCUS: Calcium Channel Blockers; An Overview; recreations: tennis, golf, skiing, music, economics, law, politics; Home: 279 Glengrove Ave. W., Toronto M5N 1W3; Office: Suite 206, 200 St. Clair Ave. W., Toronto, Ont. M4V 1R1.

**de FAYER, Thomas L.,** M.A.; economist; b. Budapest, Hungary 5 March 1919; s. Alexander L. and Dorothea (Meszaros) de F.; e. Franz Joseph Royal Cath. Acad., Budapest 1937; Bishop Peter Pazmany Univ. of Budapest (Absolutorium, Doctorandus) 1941; Pembroke Coll. Cambridge B.A. (Hons.) 1941, M.A. 1944; m. H. Joyce d. Benjamin Wild and Ann Schofield 29 July 1944; children: Andrea Struthers, Geraldine Thomas, Paul, Nicholas; Market Rsch. Mgr., Imperial Chemical Industries Ltd. Eng. 1941–64; I.C.I. China Ltd. Shanghai 1946–47; Advr. on Chem. Ind. to Brit. Govt. in trade negotiations and to OECD Paris; British del. to internat. chemical business negotiations; Lectr. in Market Rsch. and Forecasting, Univs. of Manchester and Birmingham (England); Br. Dir. and Chief Econ. Nat. Energy Bd. Can. 1964–70; Sr. Policy Advr., Environment Can. 1970–84; Co-Chrmn. Econ. Adv. Grp. Can./U.S. Internat. Jt. Comn.; Chrmn. and Advr. OECD Group Experts on State of Environment; Candn. del. to E.C.E. (U.N.) on Environmental Statistics (Geneva, Switzerland and Warsaw, Poland); Advr. to 'Goals for Mankind' Report to Club of Rome 1977 and to 'The Global 2000 Report to the President of the U.S.A.' 1977–80; Kt. St. Gregory the Great 1982; Hon. mem., Candn. Assn. for the Club of Rome (and of its Bd. of Dirs.) 1977–86; founding mem. and 1st Chrmn. Eur. Chem. Market Rsch. Group. 1955–64; R. Catholic; recreations: travel, philosophy, futures research; Home: 1405, 415 Greenview Ave., Ottawa, Ont. K2B 8G5.

**DE FOREST, Jon Michael,** C.A.A.P.; broadcasting executive; b. Hamilton, Ont. 28 Mar. 1942; s. Norman Edger and Ruth Rachel (Williamson) D.; e. Nelson H.S. 1961; Inst. of Candn. Advtg. C.A.A.P. 1966; Univ. of West. Ont.; The Wharton Sch., Univ. of Pennsylvania 1989; m. Mary d. John and Margaret Fothergill 10 Sept. 1965; children: Jon David, Pamela Anne; Pres., Radio Bureau of Can. 1988–.; Vice-Pres., Acct. Group Supvr., Goodis Goldberg & Soren 1963–73; Vice-Pres., Dir. of Client Serv. & Founding Partner, Ambrose Carr, De Forest & Linton 1973–87; Mem., Bd. of Dir., Radio Bur. of Can.; Bureau of Broadcast Measurement; Candn. Assn. of Broadcasters & Broadcast Extves. Soc.; Pres., Financo Investments Ltd.; crew member, 1963 N. Am. champions for six metre sailing yachts; trumpet, coronet & flugelhorn musician; recreations: sailing, music; Home: 1279 Cambridge Dr., Oakville, Ont. L6J 1R9.

**DeFRANCESCO, Lorenzo;** sculptor, marble contractor; b. Rome Italy 20 Oct. 1947; s. Carmelino and Iolanda (Risa) D.; e. ITI, G.L. Bernini Rome, Chem. Img. 1969; Vanc. Sch. of Art, dipl. in sculpture (Hons.) 1979; m. Nancy d. Muriel and Fred Myers 13 Sept. 1985; children: Michael-David, Joy-Noel; Faberwerk Hoechst, Frankfurt, Germany 3 years; started business, 3D Marble Ltd. (designing floor, furniture & hand rolling in marble) 1980; first one-man show 1987; next show scheduled for 1991; Mem., Born Christian 1984– ; Bd. Mem., First Ch. of the Nazarene, Vanc.; recreations: sculpting; Office: 655 Renfrew North, Vancouver, B.C. V5K 4V9.

**DEGAGNE, Alcide J.,** MBA, FCGA; city manager / strategic management consultant; b. Fort Frances, Ont. 11 Apr. 1943; s. Alcide Donat and Roseanna (Chartier) D.; e. Univ. of Ottawa, MBA; Univ. of B.C., C.G.A.; m. Angele L. d. Ernest and Therese Meilleur 15 Aug. 1964; children: Thomas, Debra; PRES., THE DELTA PARTNERS 1989– ; Dir. of Acctg., The City of Oshawa 1967–72; Depy. Treas. 1972–73; Comnr. of Finan. & City Treas. 1974–75; Dir. Gen., Fin. Planning & Policy, Transp. Can. 1976–79; Dir. Gen., Finan., Statistics Can. 1980; Asst. Depy. Min., Veterans Affairs 1981, 1982; Comnr., Mngt. Serv., Metro Toronto 1982–85; Chief Admin. Offr., The City of Ottawa 1985–89; Past Pres., Candn. Assn. of Municipal Admin.; Lectr., Univ. of Ottawa; Seminar Leader to Trans. Can. Train Inst.; CANMA Profl. Award 1989; 1989 Fellow Award, The Cert. Gen. Accts. Assn. of Can.; mem., Internat. City Mngt. Assn.; recreations: alpine & nordic skiing; club: Le Cerlce Universitaire; Home: 32 Burrows Rd., Ottawa, Ont. K1J 6E6.

**DEGEER, William Ross;** executive; b. Toronto, Ont. 31 July 1936; s. William Nelson and Elizabeth D.; e. Weston Collegiate; m. 2ndly Frances d. George and Veronica Dunn 3 Aug. 1973; children: Lynn, Gale, Drew; SR. VICE PRES. & MNG. DIR., BURSON-MARSTELLER 1987– ; Vice-Pres. and Dir. St. Lawrence Securities 1956–71; Exec. Dir. Prog. Cons. Party of Ont. 1971–76; Princ. Sec. to Premier William Davis of Ont. 1977–78; Agent Gen. for Govt. of Ont. in U.K. 1978–85; Vice Pres., Mktg. Geac Computer Corp. 1985–86; mem. Ch. of England; Commonwealth Soc.; European Atlantic Group; Roy. Overseas League; Can.-Un. Kingdom C. of C.; Bd. of Trade Metrop. Toronto; recreation: hiking; Clubs: Empire; Albany; East India; Royal Automobile; Rambler; Home: Sonning House, 181 Ontario St., Cobourg, Ont. K9A 3B6; Office: 80 Bloor St. W., Toronto, Ont. M5S 2V1.

**de GRANDPRE, A. Jean,** CC (1987), Q.C.; b. Montreal, Que. 14 Sept. 1921; s. Roland and Aline (Magnan) de G.; e. Coll. Jean-de-Brebeuf, Montreal, Que., B.A. 1940; McGill Univ., B.C.L. 1943; Ph.D. (Hon.) Univ. of Que. 1979; D.C.L. (Hon.) McGill Univ. 1981; D.Univ. (Hon.) Univ. of Ottawa 1982; D.C.L. (Hon.) Bishop's Univ. 1983; Univ. de Montréal 1989; m. Hélène, d. Azarie Choquet, Montreal, Que., 27 Sept. 1947; children: Jean-François, Lilianne, Suzanne, Louise; Founding Dir. & Chrmn. (Emeritus), BCE Inc. 1989– , Chrmn. 1983–89; Dir., Bell Canada; BCE Inc.; Chemical Bank (mem. Internat. Adv. Bd.); Chrysler Can. Ltd.; Chrysler Corp.; Northern Telecom Ltd.; Textron Canada Ltd.; former partner, Tansey, de Grandpré, de Grandpré, Bergeron & Monet; read law with Hon. F. Philippe Brais, Q.C.; called to the Bar of Que., 1943; Legal Counsel, Roy. Comn. on Broadcasting 1956–57; cr. Q.C. 1961; Hon. Pres. la chambre de commerce france-canada; Hon. Assoc., Conf. Bd. of Can.; Dir., The Jeanne Sauvé Youth

Found.; created Companion, Order of Canada 1987; Life mem., Candn. Bar Assn.; mem. Montreal Chamber Comm. (Dir. 1969–70); Assn. Candn. Gen. Counsel (emeritus); Bar of Que.; R. Catholic; Clubs: St. Denis; Mt. Bruno Golf; University Club of Montreal; Home: 2333 Sherbrooke St. W., Apt. 903, Montréal, Qué. H3H 1G6; Office: 1000 de la Gauchetière St. W., Suite 3700, Montréal, Qué. H4Y 2W8.

**de GRANDPRÉ, Jean-François,** B.A., B.C.L.; lawyer; b. Montreal, Que. 12 Nov. 1948; s. A. Jean and Hélène (Choquet) de G.; e. Coll. Jean-de-Brébeuf, B.A. 1967; McGill Univ., B.C.L. 1970; m. Michelle d. Jacques and Madeleine Décary 20 June 1970; children: Louis, Jean-Marc, Françoise; PARTNER, LAVERY, de BILLY 1979– ; admitted to Bar, Prov. of Que. 1971; joined predecessor firm Tansey, de Grandpré, Bergeron, Lavery et al. 1971, Partner, Lavery, Johnston 1978; mem., Barreau du Québec; Candn. Bar Assn.; Dir., Gold Circle Insur. Co. 1980–83; Dir., Vice-Pres., Pres., Quebec Special Olympics 1980–88; Dir., Candn. Special Olympics 1989–92; Dir. & Vice-Pres., Candn. Club Montreal 1987– ; Pres., University Club of Montreal 1993– ; recreations: tennis, golf, skiing; club: University Club of Montreal; Home: 530 Powell, Town of Mount Royal, Quebec H3R 1L6; Office: 1, Place Ville Marie, 40th Floor, Montreal, Que. H3B 4M4.

**de GRANDPRE, Louis-Philippe,** C.C., Q.C., B.A., B.C.L., LL.D.; b. Montreal, Que. 6 Feb. 1917; s. Roland and Aline (Magnan) de G.; e. Coll. Sainte-Marie, Montreal; Univ. of Montreal, B.A. 1935; B.C.L., McGill Univ. 1938; LL.D. (hon.) McGill Univ. 1972; LL.D. (hon.) Ottawa Univ. 1973; m. Marthe Gendron d. late Hon. Lucien H. Gendron, P.C. Q.C., Montreal, 25 October 1941; children: Michel, Ivan, Sylvie, Francine; SR. COUNSEL, LAFLEUR BROWN; called to Bar of Que. 1938; K.C. 1949; Bâtonnier, Montreal Bar 1968–69; Prov. Que. 1968–69; Pres. Canadian Bar Assn. 1972–73; apptd. Companion, Order of Canada 1971; practised law in Montreal 1938–73; Justice, Supreme Court of Can. 1974–77; admitted to the Law Soc. of Upper Can. 1978, and the Law Soc. of Sask. 1981; R. Catholic; Club: The Mount Royal; Home: 310 Trenton Ave., Town of Mount Royal, Que. H3P 1Z9; Office: 1 Place Ville Marie, 37th Floor, Montreal, Que. H3B 3P4.

**DEGROAT, Meredith A.,** H.B.A., M.A.; business executive; b. Newmarket, Ont. 14 Feb. 1955; d. David Hugh Meredith and Diana Lois (Windeyer) McLean; e. Univ. of Windsor B.A. (Hons.) 1978, M.A. 1980; m. Richard Degroat 9 June 1979; VICE PRES., LEVESQUE BEAUBIEN GEOFFRION 1987– ; Investment Advisor, Bell Gouinlock 1980–82; Pitfield Mackay Ross & Dominion Securities 1982–84; estab. Calgary office of Levesque Beaubien Geoffrion Inc. 1984; Gov., Alta. Stock Exchange 1986– ; (Chrmn., Audit & Capita Ctte. 1990– ;); Chrmn., Min. Adv. Ctte. on Finan. Planning, Prov. of Alta. 1989–90; Cont. Edn. Lectr., Mount Royal Coll.; Dist. Counc. Mem., The Investment Dealers Assn.; recreations: skiing, golf; clubs: Calgary C. of C.; Glencoe Golf & Country; Home: 1223 Baldwin Cres., Calgary, Alta. T2V 2B6.

**DeGROOT, Lois C.,** B.A.Sc., Dip.Bus.Admin., P.Eng.; consultant; b. Detroit Mich. 28 Feb. 1930; d. Gordon Graham (Hutchings) and Callista (Pittman); e. North Toronto C.I. 1947; Univ. of Toronto B.A.Sc. 1952, Dip.Bus.Admin. 1977; m. John M. D. 28 April 1951; children: Philip, Nancy, Eric; PRESIDENT, BRIDGINGS INTERNATIONAL INC. 1986– ; Mem., Environ. Appeal Bd., Prov. of Ont. 1971–87; Chrmn. 1978–87; Chrmn., Scarborough Public Library Bd. 1974, '75; Dir., AECL Limited 1987–92; Chrmn., Awards Comm., Assn. of Profl. Engineers of Ont. 1990–91, 1991–92; Officer, Order of the Sons of Martha; Home: 18 Perivale Cres., Scarborough, Ont. M1J 2C1.

**DEHEM, Roger,** Dr.sc.écon.; educator; b. Wemmel, Belgium 24 July 1921; s. Charles Louis and Elise Marguerite (Masschelein) D.; Univ. of Louvain Lic.sc.comm. 1942, Lic.sc.écon. 1943, Lic.sc.pol. et soc. 1944, Dr.sc.écon. 1952; children: Charles, Astrid, Francis, Denise, Irène, Elise; PROF. OF ECON. UNIV. LAVAL 1961– ; Lectr., McGill Univ. 1947–49; Asst. Prof., Univ. de Montréal 1948–54, Prof. 1954–58; Prin. Adm. OEEC Paris 1958–59; Rockefeller Foundation Fellow 1946–48; author, 'L'efficacité sociale du système économique' 1952; 'Traité d'analyse économique' 1958; 'Planification économique et fédéralisme' 1968; 'L'utopie de l'économiste' 1969; 'L'équilibre économique international' 1970; 'De l'étalon-sterling à l'étalon-dollar' 1972; 'Précis d'histoire de la théorie économique' 1978; 'Précis d'économie politique' 1980; 'Précis d'économie internationale' 1982; 'Histoire de la pensée économique' 1984; 'Les économies capitalistes et socialistes: leçons d'histoire'; el. to Royal Soc. Can. 1981; mem., Candn. Econ. Assn. (Pres. 1973–74); Hist. of Econ. Soc.; Am. Econ. Assn.; Home: 2000 rue Chapdelaine, Ste-Foy, Qué. G1V 1M3; Office: Ste-Foy, Qué. G1K 7P4.

**deKERGOMMEAUX, Duncan Chassin,** R.C.A.; artist; educator; b. Premier, B.C. 15 July 1927; s. Robert Chassin and Cecilia Roberts (Halliwell) deK.; e. Banff Sch. of Fine Arts 1951; Hans Hoffman Sch. of Fine Arts, Provincetown, Mass. 1955–57; Instituto Allende, Mexico 1958; full-time student of Jan Zach, Victoria, B.C. 1951–54; m. Mary-Anne Carrieres 1974; children (from previous marriage): Davin Jay, Byron Drew, Laurie Gillian; PROF. EMERITUS, UNIV. OF WESTERN ONTARIO 1993– ; Project Designer Expo 67, Dir. Candn. Pavilion Art Gallery Expo 67; Project Designer Dept. of Secy. of State and Man. Govt., Man. Centennial Caravan 1970; Instr. Univ. of W. Ont. 1970, Asst. Prof. 1972, Assoc. Prof. 1974–80, Prof. of Visual Arts 1980–93 (and Chrmn. of Dept. 1981–86);taught summer sch.: Banff Sch. of Fine Arts 1974, 1975; N.S. Coll. of Art 1980; Univ. of Victoria 1984; over 30 solo exhns. since 1956; rep. many maj. group exhns. Can. and abroad; paintings toured Can. by Nat. Gallery 1967–68; several comns. Fed. Govt. and private architects; major works: 'Cube Route'; 'My Rainbow'; 'Square Root'; 'New York Maple Leafs'; 'Take Two'; 'An Art of Ordered Sensations' London Regional Art Gallery 1987; Lake Huron 1988; Artists' Tombs & Monuments 1985–92; rep. maj. pub. colls. Can. and several abroad incl. Nat. Gallery Can., Art Gallery of Ont.; London Regional Art Gall.; awarded Can. Counc. Studio in Paris 1990; mem. The Loons; recreations: skiing, garden, travel; Home: 35 Woodgate Court, London, Ont. N6K 4A4; Dealer: Mira Godard Gall., 22 Hazleton Ave., Toronto, Ont.

**DeKESEREDY, Walter S.,** B.A., M.A., Ph.D.; university professor; b. Vancouver, B.C. 6 March 1959; s. Stephen and Eva (Jantz) D.; e. York Univ. B.A. 1982, M.A. 1984, Ph.D. 1988; m. Patricia d. Allan and Marie Barger 22 July 1989; one d.: Andrea; ASSOCIATE PROFESSOR, SOCIOLOGY & ANTHROPOLOGY, CARLETON UNIV.; conducted first Nat. Candn. Survey on Woman Abuse in University and College Dating Relationships with Katharine Kelly 1992–93; Mem., Bd. of Dir., House of Hope; Pres., DeKeseredy Rsch. Associates; Carleton Univ. Research Achievement Award 1993; Mem., Am. Soc. of Criminology (Extve. Counsellor, Div. on Critical Criminology 1992–93); Soc. for the Study of Social Problems; Acad. of Criminal Justice Sciences; author: 'Woman Abuse in Dating Relationships' 1988 and 30 sci. journal articles; co-author: 'Woman Abuse: Sociological Perspectives' 1991; co-editor: 'The Critical Criminologist'; Assoc. Ed., 'Justice Q.'; Home: 335 Riverdale Ave., Ottawa, Ont. K1S 1R6; Office: Carleton Univ. K1S 5B6.

**DE KONINCK, Joseph-M.,** Ph.D.; university professor and administrator; b. Québec, Qué. 12 Apr. 1947; s. Charles and Zoé (Decruydt) D.; e. Laval Univ., B.A. 1966, B.A. 1969, M.A. 1970; Univ. of Manitoba, Ph.D. 1973; PROF. OF PSYCHOL., UNIV. OF OTTAWA 1987– ; Asst. then Assoc. Prof. present univ. 1972–87; Dir., Sch. of Psych. 1978–87; Assoc. Dean, Fac. of Soc. Sci. 1978–87; Vice-Dean, Sch. of Grad. Studies & Rsch. 1987–90; Visiting Scholar, Univ. of Calif., San Diego 1990–91; Mem., Soc. canadienne de Psych.; Am. Psychol. Assns.; Assn. de psych. sci. de la langue française; Sleep Rsch. Soc. & Assn. of Profl. Sleep Soc.; Assn. for the Study of Dreams; Soc. Qué. pour la rech. en Psych.; Soc. Royale d'Astron. du Can./Royal Astron. Soc. of Can.; Fellow, Candn. Psych. Assn.; author of 90 sci. publications; recreations: astronomy, swimming, squash; Home: 360 Templeton St., Ottawa, Ont. K1N 6X9; Office: 125 University, Univ. of Ottawa, Ottawa, Ont. K1N 6N5.

**DELAGE, Maurice Allan,** B.S.A., M.Sc., P.Ag.; executive; b. Tisdale, Sask. 16 Aug. 1946; s. Aimé L. and Mary A. D.; e. Univ. of Sask. B.S.A. 1969, M.Sc. 1972; m. Janet d. Laurent and Antoinette Duhaime 1982; children: Tracy, Cara, Marc, Aimée; CORP. VICE PRES. HOECHST CANADA INC.; joined F.M.C. Canada 1972–74, product mgmt. and mktg.; present co. 1974, rsch. and devel., sales, mktg., gen. mgmt.; Guest Lectr. in Bus. Adm. Univ. of Regina; Dir. and mem. Exec., Crop Protection Inst. of Can.; Dir., Nat. Agricultural Chemicals Assn., U.S.A.; recreations: reading, hockey, golf; Clubs: Assiniboa; Wascana Country; Home: 69 Academy Park Rd., Regina, Sask. S4S 4T8.

**DELAMERE, D.R. (D'Arcy),** B.A., M.B.A., F.I.C.B.; banker; b. Ottawa, Ont. 27 Jan. 1948; e. Dalhousie Univ. B.A. 1968; Univ. of W. Ont. M.B.A. 1976; m. Marcia 1966; two s.; VICE PRES. RETIREMENT INCOME SERVICES, THE ROYAL BANK OF CANADA 1992– ; trainee present Bank Halifax 1968, Asst. Mgr. Toronto Main Br. 1976; joined Global Travel Computer Services 1978 returning to present Bank's Financing Services group 1981; held various managerial positions becoming Area Mgr. Ottawa Downtown 1987; Vice-Pres., Public Affairs 1988–92; Vice Chrmn. & Treas., Candn. Council for Internat. Business (CCIB); mem., Task Force on Consensus Decision-Making of The National round Table on the Environment and the Economy; mem., The United Nations Environment Programme Executive Director's Advisory Group on Banks and the Environment; mem., Ontario Council of The Boy Scouts of Canada; Office: 26th Floor, South Tower, Royal Bank Plaza, Toronto, Ont. M5J 2J5

**de LAMIRANDE, Claire,** M.A.; écrivain; née Sherbrooke, Qué. 6 août 1929; f. J.O. et Rose Alma (Cousineau) Bourget; e. Coll. du Sacré-Coeur; Univ. de Montréal M.A. 1951; ép. Dr. Gaston f. J.B. René de Lamirande 26 août 1950; enfants: Mireille, Eve, Hughes; Auteur (romancière)) 'Aldébaran ou la fleur' 1968; 'Le grand élixir' 1969, Réédition 1980; 'La baguette magique' 1971; 'Jeu de clef' 1974; 'La pièce montée' 1975; 'Signé de biais' 1976; 'L'opération fabuleuse' 1978; 'Papineau ou l'épée à double tranchant' 1980; 'L'occulteur' 1982; 'La rose des temps' 1984; 'Voir le jour' 1986; 'Neige de Mai' 1988; Critique littéraire 'Le Droit' Ottawa 1983–1986; mem. PEN; Nombreux jurys: Prix littéraire de la CUM; Prix du gouverneur général; Adresse: 9925 Verville, Montréal, Qué. H3L 3E4.

**DELANY, Paul,** B.Comm., A.M., M.A., Ph.D., F.R.S.C.; university professor; b. Purley, England 18 July 1937; s. George Foster and Clare Josephine (Parfait) D.; e. McGill Univ. B.Comm. 1957; Stanford Univ. A.M. 1958; Univ. of Calif. at Berkeley M.A. 1961, Ph.D. 1965; m. Elspeth d. Patrick and Ina McVeigh 11 June 1981; children: Nicholas, Lev (by 1st marriage), Katherine; PROF. OF ENGLISH, SIMON FRASER UNIV. 1977– ; Economist, Internat. Labour Office Geneva 1958–59; Instructor, Dept. of English, Columbia Univ. 1964–66; Asst. Prof. 1966–70; Assoc. Prof. of English, Simon Fraser Univ. 1970–77; Exchange Prof., Univ. of Waterloo 1985–86; Guggenheim Fellowship 1973; Killam Research Fellowship 1992, 1993; Fellow, Royal Soc. of Literature; Fellow, Royal Society of Canada; N.D.P.; Mem., MLA; ACUTE; Pres., D.H. Lawrence Soc. of N. Am. 1990–92; author: 'British Autobiography in the Seventeenth Century' 1969, 'D.H. Lawrence's Nightmare' 1978, 'The Neo-Pagans' 1987; co-editor: 'Hypermedia and Literary Studies' 1991; 'The Digital Word' 1993; recreations: walking; Office: Burnaby, B.C. V5A 1S6.

**DE LA TORRE, Jack C.,** M.D., Ph.D.; university professor; physician; b. Paris, France 2 Dec. 1937; s. Rafael and Maria (Parodi) D.; e. American Univ., B.S. 1961; Univ. of Geneva, Ph.D. 1968 (Summa cum laude); Univ. of Juarez, M.D. 1979; Univ. of Miami Hosp., post-grad. 1979–80; PROF. OF NEUROSURG. & PHARMACOLOGY, UNIV. OF OTTAWA 1983– ; Dir., Neurosurg. Labs. 1983– ; Asst. Prof., Univ. of Chicago 1969–75; Assoc. Prof. 1975–77; Assoc. Prof. & Dir. of Rsch., Univ. of Miami 1980–82; Assoc. Prof. Northwestern Univ. 1982–83; Dir., Experimental Surgery, Univ. of Ottawa 1983–85; Chrmn., Internat. Symposium on Med. Uses of DMSO 1983; mem. Soc. for Neurosci.; Internat. Brain Rsch. Orgn.; Royal Soc. of Med.; Am. Acad. of Neurology; Interam. Coll. of Phys. & Surg.; Coll. of Phys. & Surg. of Ont.; Cajal Club; Fellow, Stroke Counc., Am. Heart Assoc.; author 'Dynamics of Brain Monoamines' 1972; ed. 'Biological Actions and Medical Applications of Dimethyl Sulfoxide' 1983; co-ed. & transl. 'The Neuron and the Glial Cell' 1984; author of more than 200 articles & publs.; recreations: music, tennis, oil painting, chess; Home: 221 Lyon St., #1808, Ottawa, Ont. K1R 7X5; Office: 451 Smyth Rd., Ottawa, Ont. K1H 8M5.

**DE LAUNAY, Leon 'David' Ward;** director; b. Ottawa, Ont. 30 Mar. 1950; s. Leon Henry Ward and Daisy Selma (Pallo) d.; e. Lindsay Place H.S. (Que.) 1968; Carleton Univ.; Royal Cons. of Music; DIR., ABORIGINAL POLICY AND OPERATIONS BR., MIN. OF NATURAL RESOURCES (ONT.) 1993– ; composer, lyricist, performer (piano) & music teacher 1969–82; Legal Worker, Sudbury Community Legal Clinic 1983–85; Asst. to Floyd Laughren, MPP Nickel Belt 1985–86; Rsch. Assoc., Ont. NDP Caucus 1986–90; Co-ordinator, Health and Safety Clinics, Ont. Fed. of Labour 1990; Extve. Asst., Ont. Govt. House Leader 1990–91; Extve. Asst., Min. for Northern Development and Mines 1990–91; Prov. Rep., Moose River Basin 1991–92; Extve. Asst. to Ont. Min. of Natural Resources (also Min. Resp. for Native Affairs) 1992–93;

Mem., Project Ploughshares 1982– ; (past mem., Nat. Bd., Nat. Extve. & past Chair, Personnel Ctte.); Founding Mem., Candn. Peace Alliance Steering Ctte. 1985–88; Dir., Toronto Workers' Health & Safety Legal Clinic 1989–90; Dir., 'Peace' magazine 1986–87; Mem., Soc. of Composers, Authors & Music Publishers of Can. 1972– ; Ont. Public Serv. Employees' Union (local extve. positions) 1986–90; Ont. Fed. of Labour (var. subcttes.) 1984–90; Un. Steelworkers of Am. (local extve. positions) 1983–85; author of numerous articles; composer and lyricist; recreation: music; Home: 119 Gore Vale Ave., Toronto, Ont. M6J 2R5; Office: Whitney Block, 6th Fl., 99 Wellesley St. W. Toronto, Ont. M7A 1W3.

**DeLAURIER, James Duncan,** M.S., Ph.D.; educator; b. Pontiac, Mich. 1 March 1941; s. John James and Bonita Amelia (Gasparin) DeL.; e. Univ. of Ill. B.S. 1964; Stanford Univ. M.S. 1965, Ph.D. 1970; m. Susan d. Victor and Lili Lawrence 18 June 1966; children: April Felicia, Bradley James; PROF. OF AEROSPACE STUDIES, UNIV. OF TORONTO 1974– ; Pres. Aeronautical Design Inc. Toronto; Cons. American Blimp Corp. and TCOM L.P.; joined McDonnell Aircraft St. Louis, Mo. 1964; NASA Ames Rsch. Labs. Moffett Field, Cal. summers 1965, 1966; Von Karman Inst. for Fluid Dynamics, Rhode-St-Genese, Belgium 1970; G.T. Schjeldahl Co. Northfield, Minn. 1970–72; Battelle Meml. Inst. Columbus, Ohio 1972–74; recipient Bronze Tablet Honors Grad. & Distinguished Alumni Univ. of Ill.; F.W. (Casey) Baldwin Medal Candn. Aeronautics & Space Inst.; FAI Award (for first flight microwave-powered aircraft); Popular Science 'Best of What's New' Award and Popular Mechanics 'Design and Engineering' Award for successful engine-powered flapping-wing airplane (ornithopter); designer several vehicles incl. large tethered aerostats, towed underwater bodies, meteorol. kites, ornithopters & SHARP microwave-powered airplane; author tech. papers & reports various jours.; Assoc. Fellow, Am. Inst. Aeronautics & Astronautics; mem. Royal Aeronautical Soc.; Candn. Aeronautics & Space Inst.; Assn. Unmanned Vehicle Systems; Airship Assn.; recreations: photography, model airplanes & kites; Home: 60 Cherry Hills Rd., Concord, Ont. L4K 1M4; Office: 4925 Dufferin St., Downsview, Ont. M3H 5T6.

**DELICAET, Leonard George,** B.Sc., B.Eng., M.Sc., D.D. (hon.), F.C.M.C., P.Eng.; b. Cowansville, Que. 24 Sept. 1931; s. Franz Joseph and Kathleen Angela (Cusack) D.; e. Loyola H.S.; Univ. of Montréal (Loyola Coll.) B.Sc. (Hon.) 1952; McGill Univ., B.Eng (Mechanical) 1954; Carnegie-Mellon Univ., M.Sc. (Hon.) 1956; D.D. (hon.) Regis Coll., Univ. of Toronto 1992; m. Anne Margaret d. Joseph F. and Mary Kuna 27 Dec. 1965; children: Leonard Jacques, Mary-Kathleen, Kendra Anne Francesca; PARTNER, ERNST & YOUNG (resp. for Nat. Forest Industry Practice); Former Chrmn., Woods Gordon and Extve. Partner of Ernst & Young; Fin. Analyst, Candn. Chem. Co. Ltd. 1956–58; Mktg. Analyst, Chemcell/Columbia Cellulose 1958–60; Cons., Woods Gordon 1960; Sr. Cons. (Vanc.) 1964; Mng. Partner (Vanc.) 1968; (Toronto) 1975; Executive Partner 1973–78, 1981–90; Mem., Assn. of Profl. Engrs. (Que. 1954; Ont. 1960; B.C. 1964); Insts. of Mngt. Cons. of Ont. 1977; B.C. 1975; Vice-Pres. and Mem. Extve. Ctte., Candn. Assn. of Mngt. Cons. 1986–89, Pres. 1989–90; Adv. Bd., Sch. of Bus., Dalhousie Univ. 1985– ; Fellow, Inst. of Mgmt. Consultants of Ont. 1987; Past Chrmn., Exam. Ctte., Inst. of Mngt. Cons. of Ont.; Founding Vice-Pres., Inst. of Mngt. Cons. of B.C.; William Larimer Mellon Scholar 1955–56; Ford Found. Scholar 1955; Dir., Ont. Forestry Assoc. 1991– ; Candn. Pulp & Paper Assoc. 1990– ; Bd. of Govs. (Extve. Ctte.) & Chrmn., Fin. Ctte., Regis Coll., Univ. of Toronto 1984– ; Bd. mem. & Chrmn., Pension Ctte., Catholic Charities of the Archdiocese of Toronto 1984–88; Toronto Vice-Chrmn., McGill Univ. Campaign 1985; Toronto Co-Chrmn., Loyola Montreal Campaign 1989; Bd. of Dirs. & Corp. Campaign, Candn. Opera Co. 1976–79; Dir., Vancouver Playhouse Theatre Co. 1973–75; Internat. Adv. Bd., Frederic Remington Art Museum, N.Y. 1987– ; Assoc. Sr. de la Conf. Entonneurs Rabelasiens (Chinon); Dir., Community Arts Serv. of Toronto; Nat. UNICEF Ctte.; Lt. (Res.) Royal Candn. Electr. & Mech. Engrs.; recreations: opera, coaching youth hockey, teaching Sunday sch., curling, standard bred racing; Clubs: Arbutus (Vanc.); Granite; Toronto Bd. of Trade; Home: 21 Doncliffe Dr., Toronto, Ont. M4N 2E5; Office: P.O. Box 251, Toronto-Dominion Ctr., Ernst & Young Tower, Toronto, Ont. M5K 1J7.

**DELISLE, Jacques;** judge; b. Montréal, Que. 4 May 1935; S. Roch and Cecile (Miller) D.; e. Collège de Jésuites, Québec B.A. 1954; Univ. Laval, Québec, LL.L. 1957; Univ. de Paris 1958–59; Univ. of Toronto 1959–60; m. Nicole Rainville 17 Sept. 1960; children: Elène, Jean; JUDGE, QUEBEC COURT OF APPEAL 1992– ; called to Bar of Qué. 1958; Q.C. 17 Sept. 1973; Judge, Quebec Superior Court 1983–92; Home: 2201, Chemin Saint-Louis, app. 605, Sillery, Qué. G1T 1P9; Office: 300 Boul. Jean-Lesage, #R-451, Québec, Qué. G1K 8K6.

**DELISLE, Jean,** D.Trad.; university professor; translator; b. Hull, Que. 13 Apr. 1947; s. Marcel and Rolande (Chartrand) D.; e. Laval Univ., B.A. 1968; Univ. of Montreal, L.Trad. 1971, M.Trad. 1975; Sorbonne Nouvelle, Paris, D.Trad. 1978; m. Michèle d. Lionel and Yolande Plante 22 Aug. 1970; children: Christian, Isabelle, Jean-Philippe; PROF., SCH. OF TRANSL. & INTERPRETERS, UNIV. OF OTTAWA 1974– ; Reviser and Transl., Sec. of State 1971–74; Cert. Transl. 1973; Terminologist 1979; Can. Counc. Scholarship 1976; Mem., Soc. des traducteurs du Qué. 1972–92; Union des écrivains québécois 1987–94; Candn. Assn. for Transl. Studies 1987– ; Pres., Ctte. for the History of Translation (Fédération internationale des traducteurs, FIT) 1990– ; Pres., Candn. Assn. for Transl. Studies 1991–93; Co-founder & Pres., SOPAR-LIMBOUR, non-profit orgn. helping poor people in India; author 'L'Analyse du discours comme méthode de traduction' 1980 (transl. into Chinese, Eng., and Spanish); 'Les Obsédés textuels' (novel) 1983; 'Au coeur du trialogue canadien/Bridging the Language Solitudes' 1984; 'La Traduction au Canada/Translation in Canada, 1534–1984' 1987; 'Les Alchimistes des langues' (La Société des traducteurs du Québec 1940–90), 'The Language Alchemists' Eng. transl. 1990; 'La Traduction raisonnée' 1993; 'International Directory of Historians of Translation' 1993; co-author 'Bibliographic Guide for Translators, Writers & Terminologists' 1979; ed. 'L'enseignement de l'interprétation et de la traduction: de la théorie à la pédagogie' 1981; founder of two collections: 'Translatione Studies' 1979 and 'Pédagogie de la traduction' 1993 at the Univ. of Ottawa Press; R. Catholic; recreations: reading, music; Home: 23, rue Ville Franche, Gatineau, Que. J8T 6E1; Office: Ottawa, Ont. K1N 6N5.

**DELISLE, Jean-Louis,** B.A., M.A., LL.L.; diplomat (retired); b. Quebec City, Que. 14 Jan. 1912; s. François and Antoinette (Côté) D.; e. Petit Seminaire de Québec, B.A. 1933; Laval Univ., LL.L. 1936; Rhodes Scholar, Oxford Univ., B.A. (Hons.) 1939; M.A. 1968; m. Constance, d. Ovila and Léda (Lajoie) Charette, Ottawa, Ont., 28 Oct. 1946; children: Martin, Sylvie; called to the Bar of Quebec, 1936; Lectr., Laval Univ. 1940–42; Secy., Prime Minister's Office, Ottawa, Ont., 1942–46; 2nd Secy., Canadian Embassy, Rio de Janeiro, 1946–49; Lectr., Ottawa Univ. 1950–51; Consul of Canada, Boston, Mass., 1951–54; studied Internat. Law, Harvard Univ. 1953–54; Chargé d'Affaires and Head of Post Canadian Legation, Warsaw, 1954–56; mem., United Nations Comn. on French Togoland, 1957; Head of Legal Div., Dept. of External Affairs, Ottawa, Ont., 1958–59; Counsellor, Press and Cultural Affairs, Candn. Embassy, Paris, 1959–61; Ambassador to Costa Rica, ElSalvador, Honduras, Nicaragua and Panama, 1961–64; Ambassador to Turkey 1964–67; Ambassador and Permanent Rep. to the U.N. and other internat. organs. in Geneva 1967–70; Dir., Academic Relations, Dept. External Affairs 1970–73; Consul Gen. of Can., Boston, Mass. 1973–76; Lectr., Laval Univ. 1977; Founding Pres., Internat. Assn. of Francophone Elders; Hon. Secy., Oxford Univ. Soc. for the Province of Qué. 1987–91; Hon. Life Mem., Candn. Assn. of Rhodes Scholars; Catholic; recreations: swimming, skiing; Address: Le St-Amable, 1155, ave Turnbull (app 811), Quebec, Que. G1R 5G3.

**DELISLE, Jules,** L.Ph., B.Sc.A., M.Sc.A.; engineer; university professor; b. Quebec City, Que. 9 Apr. 1929; s. Gérard and Anna (Girard) D.; e. Univ. of Ottawa L.Ph. 1954; Univ. Laval, Que., B.Sc.A. 1959; Ecole Nat. Sup. de l'Aréronatique, Paris, M.Sc.A. 1960; Faculté des Sciences, Paris, D.Sc. 1966; m. Mariette d. Emile Cantin 1 Aug. 1959; children: Sylvie, Pierre, Alain; ENGINEER and PROFESSOR, UNIVERSITE DE SHERBROOKE; Head of Elec. Engn. Dept. 1967–71; Dean of Engn. Faculty, 1973–81; Registrar 1983–87; Chrmn. Candn. Accreditation Bd., 1982–83; co-author of 'Introduction aux circuits logiques,' 'Travaux pratiques en CCTS logiques'; publ. articles on switching circuit designs and automatic audiometric measurement; 6 patents in the fields of electrical load controllers and automatic audiometry; mem., Ordre des Ingénieurs du Québec; Inst. of Electronics and Electrical Engn.; R. Catholic; recreations: jogging, swimming, skiing, reading, movies; Home: 275 Rioux, Sherbrooke, Que. J1J 2W9; Office: 2500 Blvd. Université, Sherbrooke, Que. J1K 2R1.

**DELLANDREA, David Aubrey,** C.D., B.Sc., M.D., F.C.A.S.I.; physician; educator; b. Port Loring, Ont. 25 May 1941; s. Aubrey C. and Ena Rebecca (de Bernard) D.; e. Univ. of Toronto B.Sc. (Victoria Coll.) 1962, M.D. 1966; Dalhousie Univ. Residency Gen. Surg. 1967–69; Flight surgeon Dipl. in Aviation Med. 1969; m. Carol d. Joseph and Elsie McJury 2 Dec. 1967; children: Meredith, Allison; mem., Active Staff and Consultant in Aviation Med. North Bay Civic and St. Joseph's Hosps. 1970– , Chief of Emergency Services 1980–86; Lectr. and Consultant, Canadore Coll. 1971– ; Coroner Ont. 1982– ; Base Surgeon and Sr. Flight Surgeon Air Defence Command, Candn. Forces 1969–70; Grad., Commercial Helicopter Pilot Training, Canadore Coll. 1971; mem., Candn. Aeronautics & Space Inst.; Internat. Acad. Aviation & Space Medicine; author 'Drug Ingestion and Flying' 1981; various articles prof. journs.; Asst. Ed., 'University of Toronto Medical Journal' 1965–66; Pres., Candn. Soc. Aviation Med. 1976–77; mem., Aerospace Med. Assn.; Am. Scient. Affiliation; Internat. Soc. Air Safety Investigators; Pres. Candn. Soc. of Aerospace Med. 1987–88; Assoc. Fellow, Aerospace Med. Assoc. 1988; Mem., Internat. Acad. of Aviation and Space Med. 1988; Fellow, Candn. Aeronautics and Space Inst. 1989; Fellow, Aerospace Med. Assoc. 1990; recreations: skiing, photography, golf; Home: 135 Wallace Heights Dr., North Bay, Ont. P1B 8G2; Office: Medical Arts Bldg., 1950 Algonquin Ave., North Bay, Ont. P1B 4Z2.

**DELMOTTE, Daryl James Arthur,** M.A., A.R.I.C.S.; real estate executive; b. Kent, England 7 Sept. 1937; s. Edmond Joseph and Dorothy (Staples) D.; e. Westminster Sch.; Cambridge Univ. M.A.; Royal Inst. of Chartered Surveyors; m. Felicity d. Keith and Angela Jenkins 25 Apr. 1964; children: Penelope, James, Stuart; GROUP CHIEF EXTVE. & PRES., GROSVENOR INTERNAT. 1989– ; joined present co. 1967; Richard Costain 1962–65; Dir., Grosvenor Internat. Holdings Limited; Internat. Freehold Properties; Internat. Sailors' Soc. (Can.); Mem., Hakluyt Soc.; recreations: sailing, skiing, golf; clubs: Capilano Golf & Country, Royal Vancouver Yacht; Home: 240 Sandringham Cres., N. Vancouver, B.C. V7N 2R6; Office: 2100 – 1040 W. Georgia St., Vancouver, B.C. V6E 4H1.

**DELORME, Jean-Claude,** O.C., C.R., O.N.Q., B.A., LL.L.; exécutif; né 22 mai 1934; f. Adrien et Marie-Anne (Rodrigue) D.; é. Coll. Sainte-Marie Montréal B.A.; Univ. de Montréal LL.L. 1959; ép. Paule f. Gérard et Lucille Tardif 2 septembre 1961; enfants: Catherine, Marie-Eve; PRÉS. DU CONSEIL ET CHEF DE LA DIRECTION, CAISSE DE DÉPÔT ET PLACEMENT DU QUÉBEC 1990– ; admis au Barreau 1960; cabinet juridique de Martineau, Walker Montréal 1960; secrétaire juridique de la Compagnie canadienne Expo '67 1963; Conseiller juridique et adjoint au président du conseil et chef de la direction Standard Brands Ltée 1968; vice-président de l'adm. et conseiller juridique Télésat Canada 1969; Président-directeur général Téléglobe Canada 1971–90; Pres. du Conseil, Musée des Beaux-Arts du Canada et membre Conseil d'adm.: COBEPA; Conf. Bd. of Can.; Univ. de Montréal; COMIPAR; PARGESA; A été membre jusqu'en 1990 du Conseil de diverses entreprises et associations notamment; Mem. du conseil d'admin. de l'Assoc. canadienne des courtiers en valeurs mobilières, Toronto; Bureau de commerce de Montréal; prés. du comité exécutif et mem. du Bd. of Trustees de l'Internat. Institute of Communications, Londres, Royaume-Uni; rep. permanent du Canada au Conseil du Commonwealth Telecommunications Organization pendant 17 ans (ancien prés.); mem. du conseil d'admin.: Memotec Data Inc.; Téléglobe Canada Inc.; Teleglobe International Inc.; Teleglobe Marine Inc.; Banque Royale du Canada; Pirelli Canada; Les Provinces Unies compagnie d'assurances; AXA International; Interprovincial Pipeline Ltd.; Lakehead Pipeline Ltd.; Expo '86 Vancouver; Société Radio-Canada; Chambre de commerce de Montréal; Chambre canadienne allemande de l'industrie et du comm. (ancien prés.); Assn. canadienne des entreprises de télécommunications (ancien prés.); mem. du conseil d'admin. et du comité exécutif, Musée des Beaux-Arts de Montréal; Centraide Montréal; prés. du conseil, Fondation des Jeûnesses musicales du Canada; prés., Société Place des arts de Montréal; premier prés., l'Opéra de Montréal; prés., Grands Ballets Canadiens; mem. Bureau des Govs., l'École nationale de théâtre du Canada; Distinctions: O.C. 1967; Médaille du Centenaire du Can. 1967; Médaille d'or Soc. tchécoslovaque pour les relations internationales; Médaille du Mérite des Diplômés de l'Univ. de Montréal 1983; doctorat Honoris Causa de l'Univ. de Montréal 1985; récip., 'Distinguished Friend of Education Award' de l'organisme américain Council for Advanc. & Support of Education 1986; O.N.Q. 1987; commandeur Ordre du mérite Répub. italienne 1987; Management Achievement Award, l'Univ. McGill 1987; prix des Communications du Qué. 1989; Clubs: Saint-

Denis; Mont-Royal; Forest and Stream; Adresse: 3 ave. Glendale, Beaconsfield, Qué. H9W 5P6; Bureau: 1981 ave. McGill College, Montréal, Qué. H3A 3C7.

**DELROY, Stephen Henry,** B.A., M.Phil.; curator; b. Montreal, Que. 15 Jan. 1949; s. Mortimer Samuel and Inez Mulray (Tourangeau) D.; e. Carleton Univ. B.A. (Hons.) 1972; Univ. of Edinburgh M.Phil. 1980; m. Alexa d. Dennis and Anne Olliver 9 May 1970; children: Nicholas, Rosalind, Diana, Sarah, Peter; CURATOR (FIRST), HOUSE OF COMMONS 1989– ; various curatorial positions at National Museum of Man 1974–82; Chief Research and Consulting and other positions at Canadian Heritage Information Network 1982–89; Tutor, Univ. of Edinburgh 1972; Chair, Museum Technology Adv. Ctte., Algonquin College; Mem., Candn. Museums Assn.; The Conservation of Bronze Sculptures & Architectural Bronze Ctte.; co-author: 'Humanities Data Dictionary of the Canadian Heritage Information Network' 1988, 'Natural Sciences Data Dictionary of the Canadian Heritage Information Network' 1988; Home: 42 Priam Way, Nepean, Ont. K2H 8S8; Office: P.O. Box 659, West Block, House of Commons, Wellington St., Ottawa, Ont. K1A 0A6.

**DELUCE, William Stanley,** B.A.Sc.; airline executive; b. Chapleau, Ont. 29 Jan. 1949; s. Stanley Matthew and Angela Marie (Spadoni) D.; e. St. Michaels Coll. H.S.; Univ. of Toronto, B.A.Sc. 1971; m. Ann d. Ken and Mary Larkin 16 Dec. 1972; children: Aynsley, Dana, Lindsey, Andrew; PRES. & C.E.O., LARDEL HOLDINGS INC. 1992– ; Gen. Mgr., NorOntair 1971–74; Vice-Pres. & Gen. Mgr., Austin Airways Ltd. 1974–81; Extve. Vice-Pres., Austin Airways Ltd. 1981–86; Vice-Pres., Air Ontario Inc. 1981–86, Pres. & C.E.O. 1987–91; Pres. & C.E.O., C & C Yachts 1985; Dir., Air Ontario Inc.; Air Alliance; Candn. Tire Corp.; South China Industries; Northern Greenhouse Farms Ltd.; Mission Air Transporation Network; St. Michael's Hosp.; recreations: flying, skiing, sailing, hockey, tennis; Clubs: St. George Golf & Country; Granite; Young Presidents' Orgn.; Home: 15 Highland Ave., Toronto, Ont. M4W 2A2; Office: 70 University Ave., Ste. 250, Toronto, Ont. M5J 2M4.

**DELVOIE, Louis Andre,** B.A. M.A., NDC; diplomat; b. Paris, France 5 May 1939; s. Maurice Robert and Mary Millicent (Lee-Graham) D.; e. Loyola Coll., B.A. 1960; Univ. of Toronto, M.A. 1962; McGill Univ., postgrad. study 1963–64; Nat. Defence, Coll., NDC 1976; m. Frances R. d. Wesley and Roberta Morey 7 Dec. 1968; one. d.: Sandra M.; HIGH COMMISSIONER TO PAKISTAN 1991– ; joined Candn Fgn. Serv. 1965; var. positions, Dept. of External Affairs and posts in Lebanon, Egypt, Algeria, Belgium 1966–78; Dir. Intelligence Div. 1978–80; Ambassador to Algeria 1980–82; Dir. Gen., Bur. of Internat. Security and Arms Control 1982–85; Depy. High Comnr. to United Kingdom 1985–89; Asst. Depy. Min. (Policy), Dept. of National Defence, Ottawa 1989–91; Mem., Internat. Inst. of Strategic Studies; author of articles on Candn. Fgn. Policy; recreations: reading, music; Office: Canadian High Commission, Diplomatic Enclave, Islamabad, Pakistan.

**DeMAIO, Dominic Michael,** H.B.A.; business executive; b. Toronto, Ont. 8 May 1938; s. Frank and Phyllis (Sacco) D.; e. Royal York Collegiate 1957; Univ. of West. Ont., H.B.A. (Hons.) 1961; m. Jean d. Joseph and Viola Omanique 2 Sept. 1961; children: Michael, Natalie, Valerie, David, Peter; PRES. & CHIEF OPERATING OFFR., THE JOHN FORSYTH CO. LTD. 1992– ; Mngt. Trainee then Salesman, Westinghouse Canada 1961; Sales Mgr. 1963; Nat. Serv. Mgr. 1967; Div Mgr., Portable Prod. 1969; Div. Mgr., Major Appliances 1972–77 (this div. was purchased by CAMCO Inc. in 1977); Gen. Mgr., CAMCO Inc. 1977–78; Vice-Pres. 1979–88; Pres. & Dir., Work Wear Corp. of Can.; Vice-Pres., Work Wear Internat. 1988–90; Pres. & C.E.O. Work Wear Corp. of Can.; Dir., Work Wear Inc. 1989–90; Pres., Shirt Div., The John Forsyth Co. Ltd. 1991–92; Dean's Hon. List, U.W.O., Bus. Admin.; recreations: tennis, cycling, reading; club: Fitness Inst.; Home: 1231 Woodland Ave., Mississauga, Ont. L5G 2X8.

**DE MARA, Ronald;** realtor; b. Hamilton, Ont. 12 June 1932; s. Cyril R. and Kathleen (Hall) D.; e. Upper Can. Coll.; m. Patricia Blagden Robinson 1980; children: Leize Perlmutter, Kathleen Cornish, Persis Craik; stepchildren: Stephen, David & Carolyn Robinson; PRES. DE MARA INC. 1960– ; Past Pres.; I.C.I. Div. Toronto Real Estate Bd.; Soc. Ind. Realtors Cent. Candn. Chapter; recreations: tennis, golf, sailing; Clubs: Granite; Lyford Cay (Bahamas); Pelican Bay (Fla.); Muskoka Lakes Golf & Country; Address: 390 Russell Hill Rd., Toronto, Ont. M4V 2V2.

**DeMARCO, Frank Anthony,** M.A.Sc., Ph.D., F.C.I.C.; university administrator; b. Podargoni, Reggio Calabria, Italy 14 Feb. 1921; s. Frank and Carmela (Scappatura) DeM.; e. North Bay (Ont.) Coll. Inst. 1938 (Robert Simpson Scholar.); Univ. of Toronto, B.A.Sc. 1942, M.A.Sc. 1943 (International Nickel Co. Scholar.), Ph.D. (Chem. Engn.) 1951 (Sch. of Engn. Fellowship); Inst. of Coll. Adm. & Coll. Prof.'s Workshop, Univ. of Mich., 1956; Computer Systems for Univ. Pres. course, 1969; Systems Analysis & Research course, 1970; m. Mary, d. late Tony Valenti, Toronto, Ont., 1 May 1948; children: Maria, Anna (Mrs. John Moore), Jean, Paula, Christine, John, Dante, Thomas, James, Teresa, Robert, Jerry; Sr. Vice-Pres., Univ. of Windosr 1973–86; Instr., Univ. of Toronto 1943–46; Asst. Prof. and subsequently Prof. and Head, Chem. Dept., Assumption Coll. (became Assumption Univ. 1953), 1946–57, Dir. of Athletics 1949–55, Chrmn. Staff Comte., Essex Coll. of Univ. 1956–59, Acting Head, Engn. Dept. 1957–59, Princ., Essex Coll.1959–63, Assoc. Dean of Arts & Science 1958, Dean, Faculty of Applied Science 1959–64; Vice Pres., Univ. of Windsor 1963–73, Acting Dean of Engn. 1972–73, Acting Dean of Extension and Continuing Educ. 1975–76; Chrmn., Univ. Div. Devel. Fund 1963–68; has served industry in various fields incl. research and as consultant in polyester resins, fiberglass laminates, fire-resistant cardboard; has held various offices Council Ont. Univs.; mem. 1st Council, Ont. Educ. Communications Authority Regional Council; mem. Organ. Comte. and Adv. Council, W. Ont. Inst. Technol.; Founding Chrmn. St. Clair Coll. of Applied Arts & Technol.; mem. Windsor (Ont.) Suburban Dist. High Sch. Bd.; Essex Co. Bd. of Educ. (mem. various comtes.); former Dir., Willistead Art Gallery; mem. Mang. Comte. and Chrmn. Inst. Div., Un. Fund Windsor; rec'd Coronation Medal 1953; Centennial Medal 1967; CKWW Citizen of Week Award for educ. and community work; Univ. of Windsor Alumni Award 1971; St. Clair Coll. Alumni Award; has conducted research in coordination compounds, brittle copper (electro-deposition), synthesis of cyanine dyes, solubilization properties of non-ionics; author of various articles in prof. journs.; Councillor and Chrmn. Chem. Educ. Div., Chem. Inst. Can.; mem. Am. Soc. Engn. Educ.; Assn. Prof. Engrs. Ont.; Candn. Soc. Study Higher Educ.; Windsor Art Gallery; mem. Ont. Min. of Health Comte. on the effects on Human Health of lead from the Environment; R. Catholic; recreations: curling, golf, squash, canoeing, art, travel; Clubs: Essex Golf; Windsor Curling; Home: 7750 Matchette Rd., Windsor, Ont. N9J 2J4.

**de MAYO, Paul,** Ph.D., D.és Sc., F.R.S.C., F.R.S.; educator; b. London, Eng. 8 Aug. 1924; e. Univ. of London, B.Sc. 1944, M.Sc. 1952, Ph.D. 1954; Univ. of Paris, D.és Sc.1969; m. Mary Turnbull, 28 May 1949; children: Ann Gabrielle, Philip Nicholas; PROF. EMERITUS, UNIV. OF WESTERN ONT. 1990, Prof. of Chem. 1959–90; Dir., Photochem. Unit there 1969–73; rec'd Merck, Sharp and Dohme Lecture Award 1966; Centennial Medal 1967; Chemical Inst. of Can. Palladium Medal 1982; E.W.R. Steacie Award in Photochemistry 1985; Steacie Award, Can. Soc. Chem. 1992; author 'The Higher Terpenoids' 1959; 'Mono- and Sesquiterpenoids' 1959; Ed. 'Molecular Rearrangements' 1963; Ed. 'Rearrangements in Ground and Excited States' 1980; also numerous publs. in scient. lit.; Home: 436 St. George St., London, Ont. N6A 3B4; Office: London, Ont. N6A 5B7.

**DEMERS, François,** B.A.; university professor and administrator; b. Sudbury, Ont. 14 July 1943; s. Roland and Thérèse (Blais) D.; e. Univ. of Montreal B.A. (Theol.) 1965; Laval Univ. B.A. (Phil.) 1977; m. Nicole d. Charles-Emile and Jeannette Ménard 26 March 1968; one d.: François-Nicola; PROFESSOR, LAVAL UNIVERSITY 1980– ; Journalist 1965–80; Dean of the Faculty of Arts, Laval Univ. 1987– ; author: 'Communication et syndicalisme-des imprimeurs aux journalistes' 1988, 'Chroniques impertinentes du troisième Front commun syndical' 1982; co-editor: 'Challenges for International Broadcasting' 1993, 'America and the Americas' 1992; Home: 182 Aberdeen, Quebec, Que. G1R 2C8; Office: Pavillon Casault, Laval Univ., Sainte-Foy, Que. G1K 7P4.

**DEMERS, Jean,** B.A., B.Eng., M.Eng.; consulting engineer; b. Quebec, Que. 16 March 1942; s. Georges and Lucile (Besner) D.; e. Coll. Brébeuf, B.A. 1961; Laval Univ. B.Eng. 1966; Univ. of California M.Eng. 1967; Ecole des Hautes Etudes Comm. dipl. 1972; m. Louise d. Jean and Madelein (Duhamel) Monty 15 March 1969; children: Marie-Hélène, Julie; PRINCIPAL & OWNER, JEAN DEMERS & ASSOC. 1991– ; Project Engr. & Bus. Devel. Dir., Geo. Demers Cons. Engrs. 1967–72; Project Dir. & Envir. Dept. Mgr., Telsut Inc. 1973–78; Project Control. Dept. Dir., Lavalin Inc. 1978–82; Principal & Consulting Assoc., Touche Ross & Partners 1982–91; Dir. & Co-ord., Railway Technol. Rsch. Consortium Project, Ecole Polytech. of Montreal 1992– ; Dir., Atomic Energy of Canada Ltd. 1991– ; Mem., Order of Engrs. of Que.; Cert. Mngt. Cons. Inst. of Que.; Bd. Mem., Théâtre de 4 sous de Montréal; Pres., Project Mngt. Inst. Mtl. Chapter 1982–86; Mem., Montreal Bd. of Trade (Transp. Ctte.); recreations: skiing, tennis, golf; clubs: Chantecler, Tennis Joyce; Home: 732 ave Davaar, Outremont, Que. H2V 3B2; Office: 75, rue de Port Royal est, Bureau 60, Montreal, Que. H3L 3T1.

**DEMERS, Robert,** B.A., B.C.L.; investment dealer; b. Montreal, Que. 10 Oct. 1937; s. André and Berthe (Bélander) D.; e. Coll. Stanislas B.A. 1957; Univ. McGill B.C.L. 1960; m. Liliane d. Paul Densky 14 May 1960; children: François, Catherine; Vice-Chrmn., McNeil Mantha Inc. 1981–..; called to the Bar of Que. 1961; Legal Couns. & Dir. of Listings, Montreal & Candn. stock exchanges 1962; Finan. Advr., Que. Dept. of Edn. 1964; Legal Advr., Desjardins, Ducharme 1966; Legal Couns., Prime Minister of Que. 1970; Chrmn., Que. Securities Comn. 1972; Pres. & Gov., Montreal Stock Exchange 1976; Bd. Mem., Hydro-Québec; PEMP Investment Advisors, Inc.; Klockner Stadler Hurter Ltd.; La Société d'energie de la Baie James; Nouveler Inc.; Constitution Insur. Co. of Can.; Officer, l'Ordre de la couronne de chêne du Luxembourg; Mem., Que. Bar Assn.; Que. Liberal Party; recreations: fishing, hunting, swimming; Home: 3537, Aylmer, Montreal, Qué. H2X 2B9.

**DEMERS, Rock,** C.M., B.A.; film producer; b. Ste-Cécile de Lévrard, Qué. 11 Dec. 1933; s. Adrien and Marie (Carignan) D.; e. Ecole Normale Jacques Cartier B.A. 1957; Ecole Normale Supérieure de St-Cloud (Paris, France) Dip. Audio-Visual Techniques Applied to Edn. 1958; m. Viviane d. Alphonse and Alice Julien 29 Nov. 1974; two s. Jean, Eric; PDG OF LES PRODUCTIONS LA FÊTE 1982– ; Dir. Gen. Montréal Internat. Film Festival 1962–67; PDG of Faroun Film (Can.) Inc. 1965–78; Dir. Gen. Qué. Film Inst. 1978–79; Co-founder 'Images' movie mag. 1956; La Cinémathèque Québécoise 1963, also served as mem. Bd. Dirs. many yrs.; mem. consultative ctte. for est. Candn. film policy 1973; film course given UQUAM Univ. 1983–84; recipient Gov. Gen.'s Medal for service to Candn. film ind. 1978; Order of Canada 1992; nominated 'Chevalier des Arts et des lettres' by French Govt. 1992; Pres. Qué. Film Distributors Assn. 1974–78; Qué. Film Prod. Assn. 1986–88; recreations: reading, gardening; Home: 320 Carré St-Louis, Montréal, Qué. H2X 1A5; Office: 225 est rue Roy, Montréal, Qué. H2W 1M5.

**de MESTRAL, Armand L.C.,** A.B., B.C.L., LL.M.; educator; b. Montréal, Qué. 17 Nov. 1941; s. Claude B.R. and Lulu-Dell (Bates) de M.; e. Whitgift Sch. South Croydon, UK 1959; Harvard Univ., A.B. 1963, LL.M. 1968; McGill Univ., B.C.L. 1966; m. Rosalind d. Edward and Esmée Pepall 26 Sept. 1979; children: Philippe, Charles; PROF. OF LAW, McGILL UNIV. 1976– ; served UN Secretariat 1969–70; Dept. of Justice, Ottawa 1970–76; Special Adv. Dept. External Affairs 1979–80; Barreau du Quebec 1967– ; Mem., Canada-U.S. Bi-national Disputes Panel; Nat. Marine Counc.; Legal Counsel, Gottlieb & Associates, Montréal; Dir., Inst. Comparative Law McGill 1984–89; Pres., Candn. Council on Internat. Law 1987–90; co-author 'Introduction to Public International Law' 1979, 2nd ed. 1987; 'International Business Transactions' 1986; 'Extraterritorial Application of Export Control Legislation' 1990; 'The Canadian Law & Practice of International Trade' 1991; ed. 'The Limitation of Human Rights in Comparative Constitutional Law' 1986; co-ed. 'Canadian Year Book of International Law'; recreations: farming, skiing, hiking; Home: Montréal, Qué.; Office: 3644 Peel St., Montréal, Qué. H3A 1W9.

**DEMIRJIAN, Arto,** D.D.S., M.Sc.D.; educator; b. Istanbul, Turkey 11 Feb. 1931; s. Karekin and Teshkoyan A.; e. Coll. St-Michel, Istanbul, B.A. 1949; Univ. of Istanbul Dipl. Dental Surg. 1953; Univ. de Montréal D.D.S. 1959; Univ. of Toronto M.Sc.D. Anat. 1961; m. Sona, Montreal, Que; 2 children; PROF. OF ANAT., FACULTY OF DENTAL MED., UNIV. DE MONTREAL 1971– ; Dir. Growth Research Center 1970– ; Asst. Prof. of Anat. Dept. Oral Biol. Faculty of Dentistry present Univ. 1961–65, Assoc. Prof. 1965–71; recipient Candn. Dental Assn.'s War Mem. Award; served with Turkish Army 1955, rank Capt.; author or co-author numerous publs.; mem. Armenian Gen. Benevolent Union; Soc. Armenians from Istanbul; Med. Research Council Dental Sciences Comte. 1971–74 (Chrmn. 1973–74); Candn. Dental Assn.; Coll. Dental Surgs. Prov. Que.; Internat. Assn. Dental Research; Am. Assn. Phys. Anthrop.; Internat. Assn. Anthropobiols.;

Candn. Assn. Anats.; Am. Assn. Anats.; Internat. Soc. Cranio-Facial Biol.; Candn. Assn. of Dental Rsch. (Pres. 1984– ; mem. Task Force on Dental Rsch. in Can.) and other prof. assns.; Armenian Apostolic; recreations: camping, photography; Home: 1545 Lucerne Rd., Town of Mount Royal, Qué. H3R 2J1; Office: 2900 Edouard-Montpetit, Montréal, Qué. H3T 1J4.

**DEMONE, Henry,** B.Sc.; fishery executive; b. Lunenburg, N.S. 29 May 1954; s. Earl Harold and Rena Martha (Ritcey) D.; e. Acadia Univ. B.Sc. 1976; m. Rena d. Percy and Barbara Morash 22 July 1978; children: Tiffanie, Elliott, Andreas; PRES. NATIONAL SEA PRODUCTS 1989– ; joined present Co. 1977–80; AB Franz Witte, Gothenburg, Sweden 1980–84; recreations: sailing, skiing, running; Home: 845 Tower Rd., Halifax, N.S. B3H 2Y1; Office: 1959 Upper Water St., P.O. Box 2130, Halifax, N.S. B3J 3B7.

**DeMONE, Robert Stephen,** B.Com., C.A.; hotel company executive; b. Dartmouth, N.S. 13 June 1932; s. Urban Roy and Effie Elfreda (Meisner) D.; e. Dartmouth pub. and high schs. 1949; Dalhousie Univ. B.Com. 1952; C.A. 1954; Univ. of W. Ont. Dipl. Business Mgmt. 1970; m. 1stly late Jean Valerie Ann d. Charles William Snedden 26 June 1954; two d. Susan Liane, Jill Carol; m. 2ndly Joanna Stefania d. Zygmunt M. Tchorek 22 Mar. 1985; CHRMN., PRES., C.E.O. & DIR., CANADIAN PACIFIC HOTELS CORP. 1987– ; Corporate Tax Assessor, Revenue Can. Halifax 1955–56; Works Acct. Canadian Rock Salt Co. Ltd. Pugwash, N.S. 1956–62; Comptroller, Ben's Ltd. Halifax 1962–67; various sr. finance and acctg. positions Canadian Pacific Ltd. Montreal and Toronto 1967–79; Chrmn. and C.E.O. Canadian Pacific Securities Ltd. Toronto 1977–81; Vice Pres. Finance & Accounting Canadian Pacific Enterprises Ltd. Toronto 1979–81; Pres., Chief Oper. Offr. & Dir., Maple Leaf Mills Ltd. 1981–83; Pres., C.E.O. & Dir. 1984–85; Chrmn., Pres., C.E.O. & Dir. 1985–87; Dir., The Sumitomo Bank of Canada 1992; author various articles; Anglican; Clubs: Canadian; Freemason; Home: 68 Rathnelly Ave., Toronto, Ont. M4V 2M6; Office: 1 University Ave., Suite 1400, Toronto, Ont. M5J 2P1.

**DE MONTIGNY, Jean-Pierre,** B.A.A., B.Sc., M.B.A.; financial executive; b. Montreal, Que. 29 May 1956; s. Jean-Paul and Pierrette (Lapointe) D.; e. Univ. du Qué. à Montréal, B.A.A. 1977, B.Sc. 1980; McGill Univ., M.B.A. 1980; m. Lynda d. Lucien and Cecile Deschambault 14 Feb. 1981; children: Jean-Philippe, Caroline, Marie-Claude; MANAGING DIRECTOR, QUEBEC, RICHARDSON GREENSHIELDS OF CANADA LTD. 1993– ; Investment Offr., Royal Trust 1977–78; Corp. Fin. Assoc., McLeod Young Weir Ltd. 1980–83; Vice-Pres., Lévesque, Beaubien Inc. 1983–85; Vice-Pres. & Dir. 1985–86; Sr. Vice Pres. & Dir. 1986–88; Sr. Vice Pres. & Dir., Merrill Lynch Canada Inc. 1988–91; Managing Partner, Bennett, De Montigny, Echenberg & Partners 1991–93; Grilli Property Group Inc.; Laperrière & Verreault Inc.; Trustco General Inc.; Chartered Fin. Analyst (CFA); Fellow, Candn. Securities Inst.; Dir., Jr. Achievement of Qué. Inc.; recreations: golf, squash, skiing; Club: Laval-sur-le-Lac; Home: 9234 Rossini, Brossard, Qué.

**DEMPSTER, Barry;** writer; b. Toronto, Ont. 17 Jan. 1952; s. Albert Edward and Helen Florence (Robinette) D.; e. Centennial Coll.; m. Karen d. Arthur and Isabelle Ruttan 26 Sept. 1981; author 'Fables for Isolated Men' (poetry) 1982; 'Globe Doubts' (poetry) 1983; 'Real Places and Imaginary Men' (short stories) 1984; 'David and the Daydreams' (children's novel) 1985; 'Writing Home' (short stories) 1989; 'Positions To Pray In' (poetry) 1989; 'The Unavoidable Man' (poetry) 1990; 'Letters From a Long Illness with the World, the D.H. Lawrence Poems' (poetry) 1993; 'The Ascension of Jesse Rapture' (novel) 1993; ed. 'Tributaries, An Anthology: Writer to Writer' (poetry) 1978; co-author 'Best Canadian Stories' 1980; 'Third Impressions' 1982; contbr. anthols. 'Canadian Poetry Now: 20 Poets of the 80's' 1984; 'Christian Poetry in Canada' 1989; 'More Garden Varieties Two' 1990; 'The Oberon Reader' 1991; Book Review Ed. and Poetry Ed., Poetry Can. Review 1984– ; lectr. poetry workshops League Candn. Poets and Ont. Arts Council Artists in Sch. Prog.; nominated Gov. Gen.'s Award Poetry 1982; mem. League Candn. Poets; recreation: writing, film criticism, travel, music, gardening, bicycling; Address: 45 French Cres., Holland Landing, Ont. L9N 1J8.

**DENAULT, Hon. Pierre,** J.F.C.C.; judge; b. Verdun, Que. 8 Nov. 1938; s. Gérard and Cécile (Levasseur) D.; e. Séminaire St-Charles Borromée, B.A. 1959; Univ. d'Ottawa, B.Sc. Pol. 1960, LL.L. 1963; m. Thérèse d. Paul-Bruno and Rachel (Vézina) Bécotte 28 May 1966; children: Michel, Anne-Andrée, Bernard; JUDGE, TRIAL DIV., FEDERAL COURT OF CANADA 1984– ; practiced law, Denault, Allard, Dubois, Caron, Arpin 1964–84; Administrator, Caisse Populaire de Victoriaville 1968–84; Pres., Athabaska Bar; Mem., Admin. Ctte., Que. Bar; recreations: golf, skiing, jogging; Office: Supreme Court of Canada Bldg., Kent & Wellington Sts., Ottawa, Ont. K1A 0H9.

**DENGLER, William Robert,** B.Sc., D.Sc.; mining engineer / executive; b. Kirkland Lake, Ont. 4 June 1940; s. William J. and Marian I. (Taylor) D.; e. Queen's Univ. B.Sc. 1965, Hon. D.Sc. 1988; m. Patricia d. Frank Ducheck July 1987; children: Steven, Sandra, Andrea, Heather; CHAIRMAN AND CHIEF EXECUTIVE OFFICER, DYNATEC INTERNATIONAL LIMITED 1988– ; Project Engineer, J.S. Redpath Ltd. (North Bay, Ont.) 1965; Area Manager 1969; Vice-Pres. & General Manager 1971; Founding Partner & Pres., Dynatec Mining Limited 1980; Dir., Dynatec International Limited; Mining Assn. of Canada; Great Lakes Minerals; Donald J. McParland Award, Candn. Inst. of Mining & Metallurgy 1990; Mem., Assn. of Profl. Engrs. of Ont. (Designated Consultant); Corp. of Engrs. of Que.; Candn. Inst. of Mining & Metallurgy; Am. Inst. of Mining Engineers; Tunnelling Assn. of Can.; Inst. of Shaft Drillers; author of num. technical pubns. for industry meetings & confs.; co-lecturer 'Mining Access' (Donald Gordon Ctr., Queen's Univ. 1982; recreations: tennis, running; club: Richmond Hill Country; Home: 28 Hill Farm Rd., Nobleton, Ont. L0G 1N0; Office: 2 East Beaver Creek Rd., Richmond Hill, Ont. L4B 2N3.

**DENHAM, David Alexander;** food service executive; b. Birmingham, England 26 Nov. 1937; s. Frederick Albert and Nora Susan (Langford) D.; e. King Edward VI Grammar Sch.; m. Janet d. William and Beattie Harris; children: David Antony, Claire, Matthew; Vice-Pres., Group Vice-Pres., Extve. Vice-Pres. & Gen. Mgr., VS Services Ltd. 1981–..; Treas. Dept., City of Birmingham 1954–56; Nat. Serv., Royal Army Ordnance Corps 1956–58; Ault & Co. Chartered Accts. 1958–69; Controller, Devel. Dir. & Airport Opns. Dir., Grand Metro. Hotels 1969–81; emigrated to Can. 1981; Dir., Candn. Restaurant and Foodservice Assn.; Mem., Anglican Ch. of Can.; recreations: golf, bridge, travel, antique refurbishment & collection, piano; Home: 4 Burnhamill Pl., Etobicoke, Ont. M9C 3S4; Office: 811 Islington Ave., Etobicoke, Ont.

**DENHAM, Frederick Ronald,** B.Sc., Ph.D., M.B.A., F.E.I.C., F.M.C.; management consultant; b. Middlesbrough, Eng. 21 Oct. 1929; s. Frederick and Gladys (Tattersall) D.; e. Univ. of Durham B.Sc. 1950, Ph.D. (Mech. Engn.) 1953; Univ. of Buffalo M.B.A. 1960; m. Enid Lynn Hughes 19 Sept. 1953; children: John Frederick Hughes, Gillian Helen, Michael Edmund Graham; VICE CHRMN., PEAT MARWICK STEVENSON & KELLOGG 1989; Scient. Offr. Defence Research Bd. 1953–54; Ford Motor Co. of Canada 1954–56; Union Carbide Canada 1956–61; joined Stevenson & Kellogg 1961, Partner 1967, Dir. 1966; Prof. of Adm. Studies York Univ. 1967–71; Vice Pres. and Dir., Stevenson & Kellogg 1973–89; Trustee, N. York Bd. Educ. 1974–78; author 'Distribution Management Handbook' 1981; 'Profitable Logistics Management' 1989; various articles; Fellow, Inst. Mgmt. Consultants Ont. (Pres. 1982–83); Assn. Prof. Engrs. Prov. Ont.; Beta Gamma Sigma; Freemason; Liberal; Anglican; recreations: skiing, squash; Clubs: Rotary (Pres.-Eglinton 1972–73, District Governor 1993–94); Donalda; Home: 15 Danville Dr., Willowdale, Ont. M2P 1H7; Office: 2300 Yonge St., Toronto, Ont. M4P 1G2.

**DEN HERTOG, Johanna Agatha;** political/labour relations executive; b. Rijswijk, Netherlands 19 Aug. 1952; d. Willem and Johanna (Ann) Maria (Smits) D.; e. Strathcona Comp. H.S., 1st class hon. 1970; McGill Univ. 1970–72; m. Ron s. Joan and Loyle Johnson 4 May 1985; one s. Alexander Pieter den Hertog Johnson; one d. Kirstin Anna den Hertog Johnson; DIRECTOR OF TRADE AND ECONOMIC LIAISON FOR THE PREMIER (B.C.) 1992– ; Co-Founder, Vanc. Rape Relief 1973–75; Ombudsperson, Vanc. Status of Women 1975–76; Dir. of Legis. & Rsch., B.C. Fed. of Labour 1977–79; Bd. Mem., Candn. Ctr. for Arms Control 1985– ; Extve. Asst. to the Pres. and Vice Pres., Telecommunications Workers Union 1987–92 (Dir., communications 1979–87); National Comnr. on Citizen's Inquiry into Peace and Security 1991–92; cand., Vancouver Ctr. 1984 and 1988 fed. election; Pres., Fed. New Democrats 1987–89; Co-chair, Mike Harcourt Leadership Campaign; First Vice-Pres., B.C. NDP 1984–85; Fourth Vice-Pres. 1982–83; immigrated to Canada 1956; Candn. citizen 1961; author of book chapter and articles in 'SI Affairs'; recreations: viola player, world travel, hiking, reading, camping; speaks Dutch, French, German, English; Home: 2866 West 15th Ave., Vancouver, B.C. V6K 2Z9; Office: 740–999 Canada Place, Vancouver, B.C. V6C 3E1.

**DENHEZ, Marc Charles McCarthy,** B.A., B.C.L.; lawyer; b. Montreal, Que. 15 Sept. 1949; s. Charles Henri and Marie Berry (McCarthy) D.; Univ. de Montréal (Loyola), B.A. (Hons.) 1970; McGill Univ., B.C.L. 1973; m. Robin d. C. Ernest and Patricia Anderson 14 Sept. 1985; two s. Charles Ian, Christophe; Bar of Qué. 1975, Ont. 1978, N.W.T. 1979; priv. practice 1982– ; Sr. Couns., Inuit Tapirisat of Can. 1979–82; Couns., Heritage Can. Found. 1975–77; Rsch. Dir. 1977–79; Life Mem.; Pres., Hist. Ottawa Devel. Inc.; Hon. Dir., Candn. Inst. for Envir. Law & Policy; Hon. Couns., Candn. Artists Rep.; Candn. del., UNESCO Heritage Conf., W. Germany 1976, Italy 1977; RAI conf., Siena 1981; Edit. Writing Award, Internat. Assn. of Bus. Communicators 1987; Nat. Heritage Award (Environment Can.) 1989; solo art shows: Mt. Royal Pub. Lib. 1973 (paintings); Braam Gallery 1986 (photos); Dir., Heritage Ottawa (Pres. 1986–88); McGill Soc. of Ottawa (Pres. 1982–84); Assn. for Preservation Technol. 1987–91 (Vice-Pres. 1993– ;); SAW Gallery 1984–85; Algonquin Coll. (visual arts program) 1980–82; United Way Ottawa-Carleton 1978–84; Inuit Art Found. 1988–89; mem. Internat. Counc. on Monuments & Sites; Dir., Candn. Renovators Counc.; Candn. Hunger Found.; author: 'Heritage Fights Back' 1978; 'The Canadian Home' 1994; co-author: 12 books and several articles (worldwide); recreations: photo, skiing, tennis; Home: 62 Ipswich Terrace, Kanata, Ont. K2K 2R3; Office: 200 – 150 Laurier Ave. W., Ottawa, Ont. K1P 5J4.

**DENHOFF, Eric Anthony Stockton;** provincial civil servant; b. Unity, Sask. 27 June 1953; s. Jacob William and Patricia Witham (Stockton) D.; e. Prince Albert Coll. Inst. Sask.; CHAIRPERSON, B.C. TRANSIT 1992– ; journalist and pub. 1969–80; joined Min. of Health B.C. 1980; Asst. Dep. Min. of Native Affairs 1987, Assoc. Dep. Min. 1988; Chief Negotiator Leads Prov. Land Claims Negotions; Sec. Premier's Council Native Affairs; taught journalism Grant McEwan Community Coll. Edmonton; served as adv. to Indian orgns. Alta. and B.C.; Past Dir. Greater Victoria Hosp. Soc.; mem. Victoria Hosp. Bd. and Found.; Dir., Grace Hosp. Found.; mem. Child Development Found. Community Adv. Ctte.; R.Catholic; recreations: fishing, canoeing; Home: 2888 Dooley Rd., Victoria, B.C. V8Y 1R7; Office: 1500–1200 W. 73rd Ave., Vancouver, B.C. V6P 6M2.

**DENISON, David F.,** B.A., B.Ed., C.A.; financial executive; b. Gander, Nfld. 28 June 1952; s. Paul J. and Margaret M. (Strath) D.; e. Univ. of Toronto B.A. 1973, B.Ed. 1974; m. Maureen d. Wally and Nora Flanagan 18 May 1991; CHIEF FINANCIAL OFFICER, WILLIAM M. MERCER LIMITED 1991– ; Teacher, Metropolitan Separate Sch. Bd. 1974–80; various positions, Price Waterhouse 1981–84; Treas., Merrill Lynch Canada Ltd. 1984–87; Extve. Dir., Finance, Merrill Lynch Europe 1987–88; Chief Financial Officer, S.G. Warburg Canada Ltd. & Bunting Warburg Inc. 1988; Chief Financial Officer, Midland Doherty & Midland Walwyn Capital Corp. 1989–90; Mem., Financial Executives Inst.; Bd. of Trade; recreations: golf, tennis, running, skiing, squash; clubs: Granite; King Valley Golf; Winston Churchill Tennis; Home: 63 Lynwood Ave., Toronto, Ont. M4V 1K5; Office: 161 Bay St., P.O. Box 501, Toronto, Ont. M5J 2S5.

**DENLEY, Randall Warren,** B.A.; journalist; b. London, Ont. 25 March 1951; s. Richard Alfred and Eileen Grace (Biggs) D.; e. Univ. of W. Ont., B.A. 1973; m. Linda d. Cecil and Marion Jenkins 24 June 1972; children: Jake, Luke; CITY COLUMNIST, OTTAWA CITIZEN 1992– ; worked for Dept. of Univ. Relations & Info., Univ. of W. Ont. 1973–75; Wire Ed., Owen Sound Sun-Times 1975–82; Asst. News Ed., Ottawa Citizen 1983–86; Day News Ed. 1986–87; City Ed., Ottawa Citizen 1987–92; Assoc. Prof. Journalism, Carleton Univ. 1992–93; Home: R.R. 7, Nepean, Ont.; Office: 1101 Baxter Rd., Ottawa, Ont. K2C 3M4.

**DENNETT, Lauraine (Laurie) Diane,** B.A., M.A.; writer; b. Toronto, Ont. 29 Sept. 1946; d. Jack and Norma Alice (Moritz) D.; e. Agincourt C.I. 1964; Univ. of Toronto B.A. (Hons.) 1969; McMaster Univ. M.A. 1971; writer, business historian & hist. cons., London, England 1975– ; walked from Chartres, France to Santiago de Compostela, Spain along ancient pilgrim roads to raise nearly $100,000 for med. rsch. for multiple sclerosis 1986; walked from London, Engl. to Rome, Italy along pilgrim routes to raise over $220,000 in nine countries ($207,000 in Canada) for med. rsch. for multiple sclerosis 1989; pilgrimage from Canterbury to Jerusalem (arrived Christmas Eve, 1992) for multiple sclerosis rsch. 1992; Vice-Chrmn., Confraternity of St. James; Hon. Dir., Multiple Sclerosis Soc. of Can. 1989– ; author: 'A Hug for the Apostle' 1987 (account of journey for M.S.); 'The Charterhouse Group' 1979; 'Slaughter and May: The City Law Firm 1889–1989,' 'Slaughter and May 1889–1989: A Short History'; contbr.: 'Macadam, Colossus of Roads' 1982; trans. (from Spanish); 'La Guiá del Peregrino' (author, Elias Valiña Sampedro) 1991; 'The Way of St. James: The Pilgrimage Route to Santiago de Compostela' (cartography created by Elias Valiña Sampedro) 1993; currently commissioned to write history of the Prudential (Ins.) Corp. for its 150th anniversary in 1998; recreations: reading, travel, looking at paintings, walking, gardening, music; Home: 24 Andrewes House, Barbican, London EC2Y 8AX, England.

**DENNIS, David Lewis,** Q.C., LL.B.; lawyer; developer; hotelier; restaurateur; b. Toronto, Ont. 19 May 1935; s. Reuben R. and Helene D.; e. Univ. of West. Ont. 1956; Osgoode Hall Law Sch. 1957–60; called to Bar 1960; Q.C. 1972; children: Jeffrey, Anthony, Leslie, Mitchell; PRES., THIRD GENERATION REALTY LTD; associated with Samuel Gotfrid, Q.C. 1960–67; estab. Dennis Commercial Properties 1968; Pres., Sutton Place Hotel 1968; opened Bristol Place Hotel 1973; acquired Park Plaza Hotel 1987; Chrmn. & Chief Exec. Offr., Dennis Commercial Properties; Pres., Ardwold Realty Investments Ltd.; Bristol Place Hotel; Park Plaza Hotel; Gov., Mount Sinai Hosp.; Mem., Jewish Nat. Fund of Can.; Cdn. Soc. for the Weizmann Inst. of Sci. (Chrmn. of Toronto Chap.); XPO – Grad. Mem., Young Pres. Orgn.; Mem., Nat. Ballet of Can.; Ont. Art Gallery; Royal Ont. Museum; Hadassah-Wizo of Can.; Conf. de la Chaine des Rotisseurs; Campaign Ctte., Counc. of Christians & Jews, Holy Blossom Temple; recreation: tennis; Clubs: York Racquets, Oakdale Golf & Country; Office: Ste. 300, Plaza Tower, Park Plaza Hotel, 4 Avenue Rd., Toronto, Ont. M5R 2E8.

**DENNIS, David Thomas,** B.Sc., Ph.D., FRSC; university professor; b. Preston, England 2 Nov. 1936; s. Thomas Richard and Lilian (Riding) D.; e. Preston Grammar Sch., England; Leeds Univ. B.Sc. 1959, Ph.D. 1962; m. Marjory d. Jack and Charlotte Bowmer 19 April 1960; children: Roger, Bruce; PROFESSOR, BIOLOGY DEPT., QUEEN'S UNIV. 1974– ; postdoctoral fellow, NRC Ottawa 1962–63; UCLA Calif. 1963–65; Scientist, Unilever Ltd. UK 1965–68; Assoc. Prof., Queen's Univ. 1968–74; Head, Biol. Dept. 1984–92; Visiting Scholar, UCLA, Calif. 1974–75; John Innes Inst. UK 1982–83; Fellow, Royal Soc. of Canada; Mem., Am. Soc. for Plant Physiol.; Am. Soc. for Biological Chem.; Internat. Soc. Plant Molecular Biol.; Candn. Soc. Plant Physiol.; author: 'The Biochemistry of Energy Utilization in Plants' 1987; co-editor: 'Plant Physiology, Biochemistry and Molecular Biology' 1990; recreations: horse riding, squash, badminton; Home: RR 1, Elginburg, Ont. K0H 1M0; Office: Kingston, Ont. K7L 3N6.

**DENNIS, Ian Frederick,** B.A., M.A., Ph.D.; writer; b. Kingston, Ont. 10 Aug. 1952; s. Frederick John and Patricia Irene (Murphy) D.; e. Ajax H.S.; Univ. of Toronto, B.A. 1975, M.A. 1976, Ph.D. 1994; var. positions, Queen's Park Computing Ctr. 1977–86 ending as Shift Supvr., Opns.; Computer Consultant 1986–92; author: 'Bagdad' 1986; 'The Prince of Stars' 1987 (fiction-romance); 'Theodora and Her Sisters' forthcoming; recreations: hockey, music; Home: 33 Erskine Ave., Toronto, Ont. M4P 1Y6.

**DENNIS, Lloyd A.,** O.C. (1971), B.A., B.Ed., D.F.A., D.Litt.; educator; b. Aspdin, Ont. 9 Nov. 1923; s. Alfred James and Elizabeth (Grimes) D.; e. Pub. and High Schs., Muskoka Dist. and Huntsville, Ont.; Univ. of Toronto, B.A., B.Ed.; N.S. Coll. Art and Design, Hon. D.F.A.; York Univ., D.Litt.; m. 3 Dec. 1942; two d., Gale Sandra, Susan Elizabeth; former Dir. of Educ. and Secy., Leeds and Grenville Co. Bd. of Educ.; served as teacher, princ. and consultant in Toronto following World War II; served with Ont. Dept. of Educ. as Secy. and Research Dir., Prov. Comte. on Aims and Objectives of Educ. in Schs. of Ont. (Living and Learning); subsequently became Co-chrmn.; author, writer and commentator in field of educ.; author 'Marching Orders' (memoir); lectures widely to sch. and service groups in N.Am.; served with Candn. Army, Active Service, 1942–46; Officer of Order of Canada, 1971; rec'd. Greer Award for 'outstanding service in educ.'; Ont. Pub. Sch. Men Teachers' Fed. Meritorious Award; Col. Watson Award for 'outstanding contrib. to curriculum devel.'; mem. Ont.Assn. Educ. Adm. Officials; Fellow, Ont. Inst. Studies in Educ.; Home: 749 Broadview Ave., Orillia, Ont. L3V 6P1.

**DENNIS, Michael,** A.B., B.C.L.; lawyer; b. Montreal, Que. 10 Dec. 1936; s. William Gerald and Margaret MacLaren (Smith) D.; e. Selwyn House Sch. 1952; Lower Can. Coll. 1954; Princeton Univ., A.B. 1958; McGill Univ., B.C.L. 1961; m. Kathleen d. Glyde and Dorothy Gregory 14 Sept. 1962; children: Sara, Gregory; PARTNER, McCARTHY TÉTRAULT; called to Bar of Quebec 1962; Mem., Candn. Bar Assn.; Am. Bar Assn. (Assoc. Mem.); Dir., Petromont Inc.; Presbyterian; recreations: tennis, sailing; clubs: Mount Royal, Montreal Racket, Montreal Indoor Tennis, Northeast Harbor Tennis, Pot and Kettle; Home: E110, 1321 Sherbrooke St. W., Montreal, Que. H3G 1J4; Office: 1170 Peel St., Montreal, Que. H3B 4S8.

**DENNIS, Michael Mark,** LL.M.; business executive; b. Toronto, Ont. 4 March 1942; s. Samuel and Sade (Iscovitz) D.; e. Univ. of Toronto 1959–61; Osgoode Hall Law Sch. LL.B. 1963; Univ. of Cal. Berkley LL.M. 1964; EXEC. VICE PRES., OLYMPIA & YORK DEVELOPMENTS LTD. 1985– ; Extve. Dir., Olympia & York Canary Wharf Ltd.; Asst. Prof. Osgoode Hall Law Sch. 1965–67; Fellow, Internat. Legal Centre 1967; Assoc., Blake Cassels & Graydon 1969–70; Chrmn. Fed. Govt. Task Force on Low Income Housing 1971–72; Special Asst. to Mayor of Toronto 1973; Comnr. of Housing City of Toronto 1974–79; Exec. Vice Pres. O & Y Equity Corp. 1980; Exec. Dir., Olympia & York Canary Wharf Ltd. 1987–90; co-author 'Programs in Search of A Policy' 1973; Home: 101 Woodlawn Ave. W., Toronto, Ont. M4V 1G6; Office: 29th Floor, 2 First Canadian Place, Toronto, Ont. M5X 1B5.

**DENNYS, Louise,** B.A.; publisher; b. Ismailia, Egypt 7 Dec. 1948; d. Rodney Onslow and Elisabeth Katherine (Greene) D.; e. Notre Dame des Oiseaux (France) 1958; Rosemead Sch. U.K. 1964; St. Hilda's Coll., Oxford B.A. Hon. 1969; m. Eric Peter s. Beatrice and Jack V. Young Aug. 1984; PUBLISHER, ALFRED A. KNOPF CANADA and VICE-PRES., RANDOM HOUSE OF CANADA 1991– ; Bookseller, Blackwell's & Sons Ltd. 1969; Mgr., Oxford Univ. Press Bookshop 1970–72; Ed. Asst., Clarke Irwin Publishing Co. Toronto 1972–74, Ed. 1974–75; Dir. and Ed.-in-Chief, Anson-Cartwright Editions Ltd. 1975–78; Publisher, Vice-Pres. and Corp. Secy., Lester & Orpen Dennys 1979–91; Lectr. in Publishing, Banff Sch. of Fine Arts; author: 'The Changing Resource' 1975; Past-Chairwoman, Internat. Trade Comte., Assn. of Candn. Publishers; Past Pres., P.E.N. Canadian Centre; Office: Alfred A. Knopf Canada, 33 Yonge St., Suite 210, Toronto, Ont. M5E 1G4.

**DENTON, Frank T.,** B.A., M.A.; professor; b. Toronto, Ont. 27 Oct. 1930; s. Frank William and Kathleen Margaret (Davies) D.; e. Univ. of Toronto, B.A. 1952, M.A. 1954; m. Marilyn d. Edwin and Marguerite Shipp 8 Oct. 1953; children: Diana, Frank, Alan, Brian; PROF. OF ECON., MCMASTER UNIV. 1968– ; & DIR., QUANT. STUDIES IN ECON. & POPUL. 1981– ; Econ., Govt. of Ontario 1953–54; Govt. of Can. 1954–59; Philips Electronics Indus. Ltd. 1959–60; Senate of Can. ctte. staff 1960–61; Govt. of Can. 1961–64; Dir. of Econometrics, Dominion Bureau of Statistics 1964–68; Cons., Econ. Counc. of Can. 1964–68; Cons., var. appts.; F.R.S.C.; Fellow, Am. Stat. Assn.; Fellow, Royal Statistical Soc.; Elected Mem., Internat. Stat. Inst.; Internat. Union for the Sci. Study of Population; var. assn. memberships; author: 'Growth of Manpower in Canada' 1970; co-author: 'Historical Estimates of the Canadian Labour Force' 1967, 'Working-Life Tables for Canadian Males' 1969; 'Population and the Economy' 1975, 'The Short-Run Dynamics of the Canadian Labour Market' 1976, 'Unemployment and Labour Force Behaviour of Young People' 1980, 'Pensions and the Economic Security of the Elderly' 1981; num. monographs, articles & tech. papers; Home: 382 Blythewood Rd., Burlington, Ont. L7L 2G8; Office: Dept. of Econ., McMaster Univ., Hamilton, Ont. L8S 4M4.

**DENTON, Kady MacDonald,** B.A., D.T.R.P.; author, illustrator; b. Winnipeg, Man. 22 July 1942; d. George L. and Florence (Gibson) MacDonald; e. Branksome Hall School; Trinity College, Univ. of Toronto B.A. (Hons.) 1963; School of Architecture, Univ. of Toronto graduate studies; m. Trevor Davies Denton; children: William, Dorothy; Art Instructor, Art Gallery of S.W. Manitoba 1980–94; Amelia Frances Howard-Gibbon Illustration Award 1990; Mr. Christie Book Award 1991; awarded Commemorative Medal for 125th Anniversary of Candn. Confederation; Mem., Save the Children-Canada (Brandon Br.); Candn. Soc. of Children's Authors, Illustrators and Performers; author: 'The Picnic' 1988, 'Granny Is a Darling' 1988, 'Dorothy's Dream' 1989 (also a ballet, 1991), 'The Christmas Boot' 1990, 'Janet's Horses' 1990; illustrator: 'Til All the Stars Have Fallen: Canadian Poems for Children' selected by David Booth 1989, 'The Story of Little Quack' by Betty Gibson 1990, 'Before I Go to Sleep' by Ann Pilling 1990, 'The Travelling Musicians' by P.K. Page 1991, 'Realms of Gold: Myths and Legends from around the World' by Ann Pilling 1992, 'The Kingfisher Children's Bible' 1993; exhibits: Picture Books: A Process (solo show), Art Gall. of S.W. Manitoba 1990 and Visual Arts Manitoba Tour 1990; participant in numerous group shows incl. 'Canada at Bologna' 1990, an exhibit of Candn. children's book illustrators; 'Books From Far' 1992, Rome; CANSCAIP 1992 exhibit; Home: Brandon, Man.

**D'ENTREMONT, R. Irene;** business executive; b. West Pubnico, N.S. 19 Apr. 1943; d. Ulysse and Goldie (d'Eon) D'E; e. Cert. in Acctg., Dip. in Bus. Mgmt.; m. Theodore s. Modeste and Mandee d'Entremont 23 Apr. 1962; children: Wayne, Gary; PRES., M.I.T. ELECTRONICS INC. 1980– ; also Sec./Treas., Wesmar Electronics Canada Ltd. 1973– ; and Pres., Women's Up-To-Date Shop Inc. 1988– ; Counc., Yarmouth Town 1985–88; Pres., Yarmouth Y.M.C.A. 1983–84; Pres., Yarmouth Ch. of Comm. 1985– ; apptd. mem., Yarmouth Community Futures Bd. of Dirs. 1987– ; elected, Council for Candn. Unity, Nova Scotia 1990; Chrmn., N.S. Ch. of Comm. 1987 and 1990; Vice-Chrmn., Atlantic Prov. Ch. of Comm. 1987 and 1990; Bd. of Govs., L'Universite Ste. Anne 1990; Chrmn., Atlantic Provinces/New England Bus. Counc. 1991; Chrmn., Atlantic Provinces Chamber of Commerce 1992; recreation: singing; Home: 99 Brunswick St., Yarmouth, N.S. B5A 2G7; Office: P.O. Box 514, Yarmouth, N.S. B5A 4B4.

**de PAIVA, Henry Albert Rawdon,** M.Sc., Ph.D., P.Eng.; educator; b. Edmonton, Alta. 29 Feb. 1932; s. Henry Albert and Louise Anna (Rowell) deP.; e. Univ. of Alta. B.Sc. (Civil Engn.) 1955; Univ. of Ill. M.Sc. 1960, Ph.D. (Engn.) 1961; m. Dorothy Anne Magee 19 Dec. 1964; three s. Allan, Stewart, Jeffrey; EMERITUS PROF. OF CIVIL ENGINEERING, UNIV. OF CALGARY 1992– ; Asst. Dean of Engn. Univ. Calgary 1964–67, Acting Dean 1967–68, Prof. of Civil Engineering 1968–92; Head of Civil Engn. 1969–72; Acting Vice Pres. (Capital Resources) 1971–72; Vice Pres. (Services) 1972–85; Dir., Project Management Specialization 1986–91; Nat. Research Council Sr. Research Fellow 1968–69; Engn. Inst. Can. Gzowski Medal 1971; Am. Soc. Civil Engn. State of Art Award 1974; L.C. Charlesworth Award, APEGGA 1985; author various papers reinforced and prestressed concrete structures; mem. City of Calgary Bldg. Appeal Bd. 1969–72: Cub Leader Scouts Can. 1975–77; Rotary Club of Calgary; APEGGA (Council mem. 1978–82, 2nd V.P. 1986–87); Candn. Engineering Accreditation Bd. (Chair 1991–92) 1984–93; Calgary Zool. Soc. (Pres. 1982); Social Orientation Services; Fellow, Engn. Inst. Can.; Candn. Soc. Civil Engn.; Project Mgmt. Inst.; Liberal; R. Catholic; recreations: skiing, hiking, camping, sailing; Home: 20 Lakeview Dr., Blissfull Beach, Sylvan Lake, AB T0M 1Z0; Office: 2500 University Drive N.W., Calgary, Alta. T2N 1N4.

**de PEDERY-HUNT, (Mrs.) Dora,** O.C. (1974), R.C.A.; sculptor; designer; b. Budapest, Hungary 16 Nov. 1913; d. Attila and Emilia (Festl) de Pédery; e. State Lyceum, Budapest 1932; Royal Sch. of Applied Art, Dipl. in Sculpture and M.A. 1943; came to Canada 1948; apptd.to Can. Council 1970–73; one-man shows and exhns.: Laing Galleries, Toronto; Internat. Exhn. of Contemp. Medals, The Hague 1963, Athens, Paris, Prague; Biennial of Christian Art, Salzburg; Dorothy Cameron Gallery; Douglas Gallery, Vancouver; Wells Gallery, Ottawa, 1967; Candn. Govt. Pavillion, Expo 67; Cologne 1971; Helsinki 1973; Cracow 1975; Budapest 1977; Lisbon 1979; Intern. Sculpture Symposium, Toronto 1978; Prince Arthur Gallerie, 1978; Hamilton Art Gallery, 1979; Gallery Stratford, 1979; rep. in pub. colls. of The Nat. Gallery of Canada, Ottawa; Art Gallery of Ontario, Toronto; Dept. of External Affairs, Ottawa; Museum of Contemp. Crafts, Charlottetown; Royal Cabinet of Medals, The Hague and Brussels; Pub. Archives, Ottawa; Smithsonian Inst., Wash., D.C.; The Massey College of Crafts; maj. comns. incl.: Can. Council Medal; Candn. Centennial Medal (rec'd. 1st Prize for design); Candn. Govt. Expo 70; rec'd Centennial Medal 1967; The Olympic Gold 100 Dollar Coin, 1976; The Ont. Arts Council Medal; Can. Natl. Arts Centre Medal; The Queen's Jubilee Medal 1977; The Can. Medal of Service; mem., Sculptors Soc. Can. (Past Pres.); Ont. Soc. Artists; Fed. Internat. de la Médaille, Paris (Candn. Rep.); R. Catholic; Address: Apt. 902, 360 Bloor St. E., Toronto, Ont. M4W 3M3.

**DE PELLEGRIN, Mirto Luigi,** P.Eng., M.B.A., M.A.; business executive; b. 9 June 1938; e. McGill Univ. B.Eng. 1965, M.B.A. 1967; Sir Georges Williams Univ.

M.A. 1969; m. Lucille Paquet July 1965; children: Carina, Robert; VICE PRES. MARKETING, CANAC INTERNAT. DIVISION 1991– ; pre-grad., worked for Bell Can., Hydro-Que., Canadair; Rsch. Offr., Planning Econ., CNR 1967–70; Mktg. & Sales 1970–73; Gen. Mgr., Francophone Cos., CANAC Consultants Ltd. 1973–79; Vice-Pres. & Gen. Mgr. 1979–83; Pres., C.E.O.and Dir. 1983–85; Pres., C.E.O. and Dir., Canac Internat. Inc. 1986–90; Dep. Chrmn. of Bd., CANAC Internat. Ltd. (USA) 1986–90; Prof. of Rsch., Univ. du Qué. à Mont. 1978; recreations: skiing, reading, swimming; Home: 23 Finchley Rd., Hampstead, Que. H3X 2Z6; Office: 1100 University, Montreal, Que. H3B 3W7.

**de PENCIER, John D.,** F.I.I.C.; insurance executive; b. Toronto, Ont. 5 May 1930; s. late Joseph Christian and Evelyn Margaret (Richardson) de P.; e. Toronto and Ottawa pub. schs. Trinity Coll. Sch. Port Hope, Ont. 1949; grad. Ins. Insts. Ont. and Can.; Univ. of W. Ont. Mang. Training Course; m. Marianne Frazer d. late James Hector Lithgow 29 June 1954; children: Joseph C., Jan S., Adam R., Michèle L.; NORTH AM. DIR., BANKSIDE UNDERWRITING AGENCIES LTD.; Consultant, Reed Stenhouse Ltd.; Chrmn., Dartwell Corp.; Dir. Bankside Harmon Ltd., Bankside Members Agency Ltd. (London, Eng.); Perfect Mix Ltd.; Lionglen Limited; joined Richardson Brothers 1949, General Accident Assurance Co. 1949–50, el. Partner 1955; Vice Pres. and later Pres. Richardson, de Pencier Ltd.; formed Richardson, Garratt, de Pencier 1966; merger with Reed Shaw Osler 1970; Head Sales and Service Toronto Br.; 1973 trans. to Head New Business Development Group; Sr. Vice Pres., Reed Stenhouse Ltd. 1973–89; el. Underwriting mem. Lloyd's of London 1973; Life Gov. and Former Chrmn.: Trinity Coll. Sch., Port Hope; Former Chrmn. & Hon. Mem. of the Bd., Trent Univ.; el. Hon. Fellow, Champlain Coll.; Chrmn., Counc. of Chrmn., Ont. Universities; Inst. of Corporate Dirs.; Dir. Toronto Symphony; Belmont House; Adv. Bd. Family Day Care Centre; Candn. Parks & Wilderness Soc.; English Speaking Union; former Dir.: Assoc. of Independent Schools; Canadian Music Centre; Nat. Ballet of Can.; Candn. Paraplegic Assn.; Counc. for Candn. Unity; Young Naturalist Foundation; Past Pres. Soc. Fellows Ins. Inst. Can.; served with 48th Highlanders of Can. 1951–55, rank Lt. (Reserve); Anglican; recreations: skiing, golf, tennis, flying; Clubs: Toronto; York; Toronto Golf; Badminton & Racquet; Royal and Ancient Golf (Scotland); Lloyd's Club, London; Home: 190 Glenrose Ave., Toronto, Ont. M4T 1K5; Office: Reed Stenhouse Tower, 20 Bay St., Ste. 2400, Toronto, Ont. M5J 2N9.

**de PENCIER, Michael Christian,** B.A., M.A.; publisher; b. Toronto, Ont. 19 Jan. 1935; s. Joseph Christian and Evelyn Margaret (Richardson) de P.; e. Trinity Coll. Sch., Port Hope, Ont. 1953; Trinity Coll., Univ. of Toronto, B.A. 1958; Univ. of Mich., M.A. 1960; m. Honor Barbara, d. Richard H.G. Bonnycastle, 14 Apr. 1962; children: Nicholas John, Miranda Augusta, Mark Dumaresq; PRES., KEY PUBLISHERS CO. LTD.; Toronto Life Publishing Co.; Past Chrmn., Magazine Assn. of Can.; Can. Periodical Publishers Assn.; National Magazine Awards Foundation; Dir. Candn. Art Foundation; Perfect Mix Ltd.; Trinity College Sch.; CB Media Co. Ltd.; Lionglen Inc. (U.K.); Candn. Civil Liberties Assoc.; Key Porter Books; Chair of Found., Ont. Coll. of Art; past Dir.: Toronto Arts Counc.; Candn. Opera Co.; Shaw Festival; Toronto Arts Productions; Can. Nat. Sportsmen's Shows; Young Naturalist Foundation; Womens College Hospital; Clubs: Toronto Golf; Badminton & Racquet; Mid-Ocean Club (Bermuda); Beaver Winter Club; York Club; Home: 87 Woodlawn Ave. W., Toronto, Ont. M4V 1G6; Office: 70 The Esplanade, 4th Flr., Toronto, Ont. M5E 1R2.

**De PETRILLO, Amodio Denny,** M.D., F.R.C.S.(C).; surgeon; educator; b. Toronto, Ont. 1 May 1939; s. Guido and Josephine (Ciufo) de P.; e. Univ. of Ottawa, M.D. 1966; Univ. of Toronto & McMaster Univ. F.R.C.S.(C). 1971; Univ. of S. Cal. Gynecol. Oncology 1973; m. Dr. Jennifer Blake 2 July 1988; children: Alessandra, Dani, Santino; CHIEF, SURGICAL ONCOLOGY, PRINCESS MARGARET HOSP. 1990– ; Prof. of Obstetrics & Gynecol. Univ. of Toronto 1984, Dir. Div. Gynecol. Oncol. 1984; Chief of Obstetrics & Gynecol., Wellesley Hosp. 1984–90; Pres., PCM Convention Mgmt.; Sec.-Treas., Internat. Gynecol. Cancer Soc.; recreation: horse breeding & racing; Club: Turf Woodbine; Home: 79 South St., Dundas, Ont. L9H 4C7; Office: 500 Sherbourne St., Toronto, Ont. M4X 1K9.

**de RAPPARD, George F.,** B.A.; business management consultant; b. Westlock, Alta. 1 May 1935; s. Rene E. and Sophie (Biggeman) de R.; e. Colorado Coll. B.A. (Bus. Adm.) 1958; m. Jackie d. Walt and Madelaine Muller 15 Feb. 1958; children: Dee Ann, Sherry, Michele; Chief Dep. Min. of Econ. Devel. and Trade, Alta. 1986–89; joined National Lead Co. 1958; Sinclair Refining Co. 1961; estbd. ind. and automotive equipment mfg. agency 1963; Exec. Dir. P. Cons. Assn. Alta. 1971, Exec. Dir. Premier's staff 1975–79; Exec. Dir. Sparrow Industries Ltd. 1979–83; Devel. Mgr. Govt. Alta. XV Olympic Games 1983; Dep. Min. of Exec. Council 1983–86; Past Nat. Pres. Can. Jaycees and Past Vice Pres. Jaycees Internat.; Dir. & mem. Extve. Ctte., Organizing Ctte. for the XV Olympic Winter Games 1983–89; Chrmn. Venue Protocol Edmonton Commonwealth Games Ctte. 1977; V.I.P. Coordinator Pope John Paul's visit to Edmonton 1984; Chrmn. Project Concern Internat. 1993 (Dir. seventeen yrs.); named Outstanding Prov. Pres. Can. Jaycees 1969, 1970 and rec'd Jaycees Internat. Senator Award 1969; Alta. Achievement Award 1974; Vanier Award 1974; Home: 4207 – 106B Ave., Edmonton, Alta. T6A 1K7.

**de REPENTIGNY, Guy,** M.Com.; retired executive; b. Ste. Anne de Bellevue, Que. 12 May 1918; s. Aldéric and Louise (Deslauriers) de R.; e. Mont Saint Louis, Montréal; Ecole des Hautes Etudes Commerciales, Univ. de Montréal, M.Com. 1941; m. Jeanne Lemay, 22 May 1948; children: Muriel, Marc, Nicole, André, Louise (d.); formerly Vice Pres. Lukis, Stewart, Price, Forbes; Mang. Dir. for Canada, Marsh & McLennan Ltd.; Dir. Marsh & McLennan International; Exec. Vice Pres. William M. Mercer Ltd.; Pres. Pratte-Morrissette, Inc.; formerly Trustee, Montreal Museum of Fine Arts; recipient of 'Mérite H.E.C.' award; R. Catholic; recreations: art, literature, travel, swimming; Home: 23 chemin Senneville, Senneville, Que. H9X 1B7.

**DERKSEN, Jeffery Allen,** B.A.; writer, editor; b. Murrayville, B.C. 5 July 1958; s. Henry Lawrence and Peggy Veronica (Sopel) D.; e. David Thompson University Centre B.A. 1984; Founding Mem., Kootenay School of Writing 1984; Founding Bd. Mem., Artspeak Gallery 1985; Editor, 'Writing' magazine 1988; Bd. Mem., Canadian Magazine Publishers Assn. 1990–92; B.C. Book Prizes, Dorothy Livesay Poetry Award 1991; author: 'Memory Is the Only Thing Holding Me Back' 1984, 'Until' 1987, '89, 'Down Time' 1990, 'Dwell' 1993 (poetry); recreations: baseball, pre-1966 Plymouth Valiants; Home: 303 - 804 18th Ave. S.W., Calgary, Alta. T2T 0G8.

**DeROO, Mt. Rev. Remi Joseph,** S.T.D. (R.C.); bishop; b. Swan Lake, Man. 24 Feb. 1924; s. Raymond and Josephine (DePape) DeR.; e. St. Boniface (Man.) Coll. and Semy.; Dominican Pontifical Univ., Rome S.T.D. 1952; BISHOP, DIOCESE OF VICTORIA, B.C. since Dec. 1962; o. priest, 8 June 1950; formerly Pastor, Holy Cross Parish, St. Boniface, Man.; Chrmn., Human Rights Comm. of Prov. of B.C. (1974–77); LL.D (hon. causa): Univ. of Antigonish, N.S. 1983; Univ. of Brandon, Man. 1987; Univ. of Victoria, B.C. 1991; D.D. (hon. causa): Univ. of Winnipeg, Man. 1990; Hon. Fellow, Ryerson Polytechnical Inst. 1987; Mem., C.C.C.B. Theology Comn. 1987–91; mem., Am. Cath. Theol. Assn.; mem. C.C.C.B. Social Action Comm. 1973–87, 1991– ; mem. Candn. Cath. Mariol. Assn.; Pres., Western Conf. of Bishops (W-CC-O) 1984–88; Address: #1, 4044 Nelthorpe St., Victoria, B.C. V8X 2A1.

**DERRICKSON, Ronald Michael;** businessman; b. Kelowna, B.C. 6 Oct. 1941; s. Theodore Mathew and Margaret Mary D.; e. George Pringle H.S.; Chief Westbank Indian Band 1974–86; Owner/Operator of Shelter Bay Marine Resort (Marina, Houseboat Rentals, Marine Pub, Campground), trailer parks, theme parks, rental units, campground, vineyard/orchard; Developer, Contractor; Owner, Inland Realty; Owner/Pres., Westbank Property Mgmt. Ltd. Group of Cos.; Negotiator for Natives in Canada re property acquisition; Business Consultant specializing in business turn-a-rounds and property development; World Champion Hydroplane record holder; R. Catholic; Liberal; Home: Box 768, Westbank, B.C. V0H 2A0; Office: Kelowna, B.C.

**DERRY, Douglas L.,** F.C.A.; chartered accountant; b. Toronto, Ont. 3 Feb. 1946; s. Duncan Ramsay and Esther Alice (Langstaff) D.; e. Trinity Coll. Sch. 1964; Univ. of W. Ont. B.A. (Bus. Admin.) 1968; C.A. 1971; F.C.A. 1982; m. Margaret E. d. William and Elsinor DeRoche 21 Sept. 1968; children: Alison M., David D.; PARTNER, PRICE WATERHOUSE 1979– ; joined firm 1968; Dir., Vice-Pres. & Finance Ctte. Chair, Toronto Symphony; Immed. Past Chair of Bd. of Gov., The Bishop Strachan Sch.; Life Gov., Trinity Coll. Sch.; Past Pres. (1983–84), The Empire Club of Canada; mem. of Counc. and Vice Pres., Inst. of C.A.'s of Ont.; Anglican; author of articles in various magazines; recreations: skiing, tennis, golf; Clubs: Caledon Ski (past Dir.); Toronto; Toronto Golf; Home: 49 Hillholm Rd., Toronto, Ont. M5P 1M4; Office: 1 First Canadian Place, Toronto, Ont. M5X 1H7.

**de SACVILLE, Michael Anderson (nom de plume Michael Bradley);** researcher, author, amateur historian and anthropologist; b. Talladega, Alabama 12 May 1944; s. Herman Maurice and Scottibelle Hunt (Robertson) D.; e. Agincourt Collegiate 1963; Dalhousie Univ. 1964–67; m. Freda Winnifred d. Rev. Hubert and Anne Doody 11 June 1966; divorced 1980; one s.: Jason Balthazar Bradley; Candn. citizen 1 Dec. 1965; nom. for Nobel Prize (Biology) by Nobel Laureate, Konrad Lorenz 1979; refused special Doctoral degree prog. offered by Dalhousie Univ. 1980; Lectr., Princeton Inst. for Advanced Study, Vanderbilt Univ., York Univ., Yale Sch. of Divinity, Kennedy-King Coll. (Chicago), etc.; DeMille Writing Award (poetry) and Dennis Writing Award (prose) (both Dalhousie Univ.); elevated to rank of Knight of Malta 1989 for activities in carrying med. supplies to remote villages in Central Am. 1983 while cons. to Candn. Internat. Devel. Agency in design & mfr. of 5 & 10 m. boats for impoverished village fishermen in Caribbean; author of 15 pub. books incl. 'Imprint' 1978, 'The Mantouche Factor' 1979 (novels); 'The Cronos Complex' 1973, 'The Iceman Inheritance' 1978, 'Chosen People from the Caucasus' 1992 (non-fiction); 'The Black African Discovery of America' 1981, 'Holy Grail Across the Atlantic' 1988 (new hist. interpretations).

**DESAI, Rashmi C.,** B.Sc., Ph.D.; professor of physics; b. Amod, India 21 Nov. 1938; s. Chimanlal P. and Savita C. (Vakil) D.; e. Bombay, India B.Sc. (Hons.) 1957; Cornell Univ. Ph.D. 1966; m. Kalpakam d. M.V. and Janaki Shankar 2 May 1963; children: Anuj, Aparna; PROFESSOR OF PHYSICS AND ASSOCIATE CHAIR, GRADUATE STUDIES, UNIV. OF TORONTO 1992– ; Scientific Officer, Bhabba Atomic Research Center Bombay 1957–62; Research Assoc., MIT 1966–68; Asst. Prof., Univ. of Toronto 1968–71; Assoc. Prof. 1971–78; Prof. 1978– ; Prof. of Physics and Coord. of Grad. Studies 1983–87; Visting Assoc., CALTECH 1975; Visiting Scientist, IBM San Jose, Calif. 1981–82 Visiting Prof., Univ. of Mainz, Germany 1987; UCSD, Inst. for Nonlinear Science, Calif. 1988; Trustee and Chair, Nirvan Bhavan, Toronto 1979– ; NSERC Grantee 1968– ; Mem., NSERC grant selection ctte. on condensed matter physics 1990–93; Candn. Assn. of Physicists; Am. Physical Soc.; Am. Assn. of Physics Teachers; Materials Rsch. Soc.; contributor to many profl. journal articles; author of review articles in 'Advances in Chem. Physics,' 'Annual Reviews of Physical Chem.,' 'Fluid Interfacial Phenomena' (book) 1986; co-editor: Jan. 1985 issue of 'Can. J. of Physics'; recreations: gardening, chess, travel; Home: 173 Cassandra Blvd., Don Mills, Ont. M3A 1T4; Office: Dept. of Physics, Univ. of Toronto, Toronto, Ont. M5S 1A7.

**DESAULNIERS, André;** executive; b. Quebec City 30 Apr. 1941; CHAIRMAN McNEIL, MANTHA INC.; Dir., Macyro Group Inc.; Quebec Growth Fund; Cascades Inc.; Datamark Business Forms; Investment Dealers Assoc. of Can.; Home: 99, 388th Ave., St.-Hippolyte, Qué. J0R 1P0; Office: 1080 Beaver Hall Hill, Montreal, Qué. H2Z 1S8.

**DESBARATS, Guy Edouard André Joseph,** LL.D., F.R.A.I.C.; R.C.A.; architect; b. Montreal, Que. 30 July 1925; s. Edward William and Marie Marguerite (Jobin) D.; e. McGill Univ. B. Arch. 1948; LL.D. (Hon.causa) Concordia Univ. 1977; m. Aileen Anne, d. Alexander Allan Cobban 14 Aug. 1954; children: Alexandre Jean; Guy Edouard André; Catherine; ARCHITECT IN PRIVATE PRACTICE 1985– ; and PRES., JACQUES-VIGER COMMN. OF THE CITY OF MONTREAL; former Pres. C.C.I.S. (Candn. Construction Information Services); former mem., Candn. Construction Rsch. Bd., National Rsch. Counc.; architect with Abra Balharrie & Shore, Ottawa 1948–52; C.M.H.C. Research Scholar, McGill Univ., Montreal 1953; Spec. Asst., Sch. of Arch., McGill Univ. 1953–58; formed private partnership with Raymond T. Affleck, Montreal 1953; firm became Affleck, Desbarats, Dimkopoulos, Lebensold, Sise in 1954 (dissolved 1970); Dean, Ecole d'Arch., Univ. of Montreal 1964; founder and Dean, Faculté de l'Aménagement there 1968; Acting Dir. and Chrmn., Centre de Recherches et d'innovation urbaine, Montreal Univ. 1971; Consultant, Council of Ont. Univs. 1974; Asst. Depy. Min., Design, Public Works Can. 1975; Asst. Depy. Min., Design & Construction, Public Works Can. 1976–85; awarded numerous prizes and commissions in field; serves or has served on many comtes. and commns.; frequent speaker at conferences in field; author of articles in profl. and popular publications; Fellow, Royal Arch. Inst. of Can.; mem., L'ordre des Arch. du Que.;

Assoc. Mem., Ont. Assn. of Archs.; hon. mem. L'Assn. des Architectes-Paysagistes de la Prov. de Que.; L'Assn. des Designers Industriels de la Prov. de Que.; R. Catholic; recreations: country living; sailing; reading; skiing; gardening; sculpture; Address: 35 Ch. McGowan, C.P. 76, Georgeville, Que. J0B 1T0.

**DESBARATS, Peter;** journalist; b. Montreal, Que. 2 July 1933; s. Hullett John and Margaret Ogston (Rettie) D.; e. Loyola High Sch., Montreal; Loyola Coll.; DEAN, GRADUATE SCH. OF JOURNALISM, UNIV. OF WEST. ONT. 1981– ; Feature Writer, The Gazette, Montreal 1953–55; Local Reporter, Reuters, London, Eng. 1956; Pol. Reporter, The Winnipeg Tribune 1956–60; Pol. Reporter and Feature Writer, The Montreal Star, 1960–65; Ed., Parallel Magazine, Montreal 1966; Assoc. Ed., Saturday Night, Toronto 1966–71; host 'Hourglass' nightly public affairs show, CBC-TV 1966–71; Ottawa Ed., Toronto Star 1971–73; Ottawa Bureau Chief, Global Television 1974–80; Sr. Consultant, Royal Commission on Newspapers 1980–81; Consultant, 'London Magazine' (London, Ont.) 1986–90; Media Critic ('Eye on the Media'), 'The Financial Post' 1985–87; Columnist (weekly), London Free Press 1991– ; Founding Pres., Assn. Dirs. of Journalism Programs in Candn. Univs. 1983– ; mem. Adv. Comte. on Communications, Candn. Comn. for UNESCO 1985– ; Consultant, Radio and Television News, Task Force on Broadcasting Policy, Ottawa 1986; Consultant, Royal Comn. on Electoral Reform 1990; Consultant, External Affairs, Ottawa, monitoring media and elections in Romania 1992; Consultant 'Vision 96' (urban planning group) 1993; mem., Editorial Adv. Bd., Pelmorex Communications, Montreal and Toronto 1993– ; author: 'The State of Quebec' 1965; 'Halibut York and More' and 'Gabrielle and Selena' 1966 (both children's books and latter subject of an animated film); 'Canada' (official publication Candn. Pavilion Expo 70, Osaka); 'The Canadian Illustrated News' 1970; freelance contrib. to various mags.; author: play on Sir George Williams Univ. student sit-in, produced by Centaur Theatre, Montreal 1970; 'René: A Canadian in Search of a Country' 1976; 'The Hecklers' 1979 (a history of political cartooning in Canada); 'Canada Lost/Canada Found: The Search for a New Nation' 1981; 'Colin and the Computer' (children's book) 1985; 'Lucretia' (NFB animated film for children) 1987; 'Guide to Canadian News Media' 1990; 'Actra Award ('Best News Broadcaster') 1977; recreations: literature, cross-country skiing; cycling; Office: Grad. Sch. of Journalism, Univ. of W. Ont., London, Ont. N6A 5B7.

**DesBOIS, L. Cameron,** Q.C., B.A. B.C.L.; lawyer; transportation executive; b. Outremont, Que. 20 July 1931; s. Louis Philippe and Helen Elizabeth (Cameron) DesB.; e. Coll. Jean-de-Brébeuf 1952; Univ. de Montréal, Lt.-Gov.'s Medal & B.A. (summa cum laude) 1952; McGill Univ. B.C.L. 1955; Queen's Coll. Oxford Air Transport course 1965; m. Louise d. Paul Gareau Apl. 1959; children: Valerie, Nicolas, Jean-François; VICE PRES. AND GENERAL COUNSEL AIR CANADA 1986– ; Dir. Domaine d'Iberville (est) Ltée; Domaine d'Iberville Ltée; Matac Cargo Limited; Penair Investments (1982) Limited (and Secretary); called to Bar of Que. 1956; cr. Q.C. 1974; practised law, Howard & Stalker, Montreal 1956–61; Solicitor, Air Canada 1961–69; Gen. Attorney 1969–77; Corp. Sec. 1977–79; Gen. Counsel & Chief Legal Offr. 1979–86; Vice Pres. & Gen. Counsel 1986– ; Affiliations: The Antiquarian and Numismatic Soc. of Montreal; Château Ramezay (owner, Hon. Pres. & Life Gov.); Montreal Museum of Fine Arts; Candn. Bar Assn. (former Nat. Chrmn., Air Law Section); Internat. Law Assn. (Pres., Candn. branch 1990– , former Sec., Montreal section); Air Transport Assn. of America Law Counsel; Internat. Air Transport Assn. (Legal Ctte.) current chairman; recreations: swimming, skiing, gardening, art collecting, travel; Home: 102 de Touraine, Préville, St-Lambert, Que. J4S 1H2; Office: 500 west boul. René Levesque, Montreal, Que. H2Z 1X5.

**DesBRISAY, Richard Blakeny,** B.Sc.; business executive; b. Moncton, N.B. 31 Aug. 1944; s. Lestock Graham and Margaret Alice (Blakeny) D.; e. Bishops Coll. Sch. Lennoxville, Qué.; Mount Allison Univ., B.Sc. 1965; m. Patricia d. Clifford and Lorraine Chappell 24 Aug. 1968; children: Craig, Julie, Laura; PRES. PROCESS TECHNOLOGY (1988) LIMITED 1988– ; DesBrisay Holdings Corp. 1979– ; Pres., Business Roundtable 1991– ; Chamber Publications Inc. 1986–87; Vice Pres. Blakeny and Son Ltd. 1968–79; Pres. Blakeny and Son (1979) Ltd. 1979–83; Pres. Sumner Co. (1984) Ltd. 1984–87; Pres., Eastern Enterprises Ltd. 1987–92; Dir. Greater Moncton Found.; Past Nat. Vice Pres. Boy Scouts Can. (Past Pres. N.B. Council); Past Vice Pres. Better Bus. Bureau Can. (Past Chrmn. N.B.); Dir. and Sec. Greater Moncton YMCA; Past Dir. Moncton Industrial Development Ltd.; Past Dir. Atlantic Provs. Transp. Comn.; Past Dir. Atlantic Provs. Econ. Council; Past Chrmn. Atlantic Provs. C. of C.; mem. and Past Pres. Greater Moncton C. of C.; mem. Young Pres. Orgn.; United Church; Liberal; recreations: squash, tennis, sailing; Home: 37 Chandler Cres., Moncton, N.B. E1E 3W6; Office: 286 Restigouche Rd., Oromocto, N.B. E2V 2H5.

**DESCHAMPS, Jean,** B.A.; business executive; b. Montreal, Que. 22 Aug. 1923; s. Robert and Adrienne (Maisonneuve) D.; e. Univ. of Montreal, B.A. 1944, Lic. 'Sci. comml.' 1947; m. Gisèle d. Alcide and Berthe Gagnon 16 Oct. 1947; children: Michel, Danielle, Benoît, Marie, Claire, André, Anne, Elizabeth; Pres. & C.E.O., Regie des Installations Olympiques 1982–90; Lectr., Assoc. Prof., Prof., Dir., Bus. Admin. Dept., Bd. Mem. & Dir., Extve. Mngt. Program for Bus. Extves. 1947–63; Depy. Min., Industry and Comm., Que. Govt. 1963–66; Pres. & Chief Extve. Offr., Soc. Gén. de Fin. de Qué. 1966–73; Que. delegate-gen. in Belgium 1973–77; in France 1977–79; Assoc. Sec.-Gen. in charge of Crown Corps. to Extve. Ctte. of Govt. of Que. 1979–82; Comdr., Ordre Nat. du Mérite; Gov., Hospital Le Gardeur; Unit Pres., Wally Byam Caravan Club Internat.; recreations: outdoors; Home: 75 Notre Dame, Repentigny, Qué.

**DESCHÊNES, Bernard M.,** B.A., B.C.L.,Q.C.; retired aviation safety executive; b. Sayabec, Qué. 8 Apr. 1926; s. Louis and Rose-Alma (Dufault) D.; e. Univ. of Montreal, B.A. 1946; McGill Univ., B.C.L. 1949; m. Lise d. Gaston and Paule Caron 10 May 1952; children: Hélène, Louis, Geneviève, Philippe, Charles; Occasional Lectr., Internat. Aviation Mgmt. Training Inst., Montreal, Kuala Lumpur and Bali; Internat. Maritime Orgn., Acad. of Trieste, Italy; Sr. Partner, de Grandpré, Deschênes, Godin, Paquette, Lasnier, Alary 1949–84; apptd. Q.C. 1965; Couns., Transp. Can., Royal Comn. of Inquiry into Bilingual Air Traffic Serv. in Qué. 1977–79; mem., Aircraft Accident Rev. Bd. 1979–84; Min. of Transp. Adv. Ctte., Implementation of Report, Comn. of Inquiry on Aviation Safety 1981–83; Chrmn., Candn. Aviation Safety Bd. 1984–88; Dir., Canadair Ltd. 1978–84; Pres., Ctte. on Legal Ethics, Qué. Bar Assn. 1976–84; mem., Candn. Maritime Law Assn.; Fellow, Chartered Inst. of Transport; Distinguished Service Award, U.S. Nat. Transportation Safety Bd. 1988; author: 'Study on Marine Casualty Investigations in Canada' 1984; recreations: golf, fishing; Club: Club de Golf de la Vallée du Richelieu; Home: 6887 – 20th Ave., Montréal, Qué. H1X 2J6.

**DESCHÊNES, Hon. Jules,** O.C., Q.C., B.A., LL.M., LL.D., F.R.S.C.; retired Chief Justice; b. Montréal, Qué. 7 June 1923; s. Wilfrid and Berthe (Bérard) D.; e. Ecole St-Jean Baptiste Montréal; Coll. André-Grasset, Coll. de Montréal and Séminaire de Philosophie B.A. 1943; Univ. of Montreal LL.M. 1946 (Gov. Gen. & Lt. Gov. Medals); Concordia Univ. LL.D. 1981; McGill Univ. LL.D. 1989; m. Jacqueline d. Joseph-Edouard Lachapelle, Montréal, Qué. 26 June 1948; children: Louise, Mireille, Pierre, Yves, Jean-François; Chair, ILO Comm. Inq. on Rumania 1989–91; Chair, Comm. Inq. on War Criminals 1985–87; Consultant, U.N. Centre for Social Devel. and Humanitarian Affairs, Vienna 1983–85; el. mem., U.N. Sub-Commn. on Prevention of Discrimination and Protection of Minorities, Geneva 1984–87; Vice Pres., World Assn. of Judges 1985–87; called to Bar of Qué. 1946; cr. Q.C. 1961; Barrister and Solr. 1946–72; Sr. Partner Deschênes, de Grandpré, Colas, Godin & Lapointe 1966–72; Justice, Court of Appeal Qué. 1972–73; Chief Justice, Superior Court of Que. 1973–83; Lectr. in Private Internat. Law Univ. of Montréal 1962–69; Fellow, Royal Soc. Can. 1977; rec'd Order of Malta 1978; Officer, Order of Canada 1989; Mem., Extraordinary Challenge Ctte. under Canada-USA Free Trade Agreement 1989–94; Pres., Royal Soc. of Can. 1990–92; Pres., Montréal Port Council 1969–70; Qué. Adv. Council on Justice 1972; Qué. Br. Defence Research Inst. 1965–67; Warden, Paroisse St-Germain d'Outremont 1970–73; Trustee, Foundation for Law Research in Can. 1967–78; mem. Bd. Govs. 1967–73, Extve. Comte. 1970–73 and Hon. Gov. 1977, Univ. of Montréal; mem. Council Bar of Montréal 1962–64; Gen. Council Bar of Prov. Qué. 1963–64; First Pres. Qué. Interprof. Council 1965–67; mem. Extve. Comte. Candn. Judicial Council 1977–83; Pres., World Assn. Judges' Comte. on Expanding Jurisdiction of Internat. Court of Justice 1977–82; mem. Council World Peace Through Law Center 1980–82; Bd. Govs. and Extve. Comte. Candn. Inst. Advanced Legal Studies 1978–82; First Vice Pres. Candn. Inst. Adm. Justice 1980–82; Chrmn., First World Conference on the Independence of Justice, Montréal June 1983; author 'The Sword and the Scales' 1979; 'Les plateaux de la balance' 1979; 'L'école publique confessionnelle au Québec' 1980; 'Ainsi parlèrent les Tribunaux ... Conflits linguistiques au Canada 1968–1980' 1981; 'Justice et Pouvoir/A Passion for Justice' 1984; 'Ainsi parlèrent les Tribunaux II' 1985; co-author 'L'Université: Son rôle, le rôle de ses composantes, les relations entre ses composantes' 1969; 'Maîtres chez eux/Masters in their own House' 1981; 'Judicial Independence: The Contemporary Debate' 1985; numerous articles; Life mem. Montréal Lawyers' Benevolent Assn.; mem. Internat. Law Assn.; Internat. Comn. Jurists; Candn. Council on Internat. Law; Assn. québecoise pour l'étude comparative du droit; Hon. mem. Phi Delta Phi; R. Catholic; recreation: music; Home: 4854 Côte des Neiges, Montréal, Qué. H3V 1G7.

**DESCOTEAUX, Claude,** B.A., L.Ph., LL.L.; utilities executive; b. Baie de la Trinité, Qué. 27 Feb. 1938; s. Jacques and Claire (Rouleau) D.; e. Univ. of Ottawa B.A. 1958, L.Ph. 1959; Univ. of Montreal LL.L. 1962; McGill Univ. 1963; Univ. de Paris, Inst. d'Etudes Politiques Dipl. Internat. Relations 1965, Faculté de Droit et de Sciences Economiques 3rd Cycle dipl. in Econ. 1966, Ecole Nationale d'Adm. de France Dipl. 1967; m. Micheline d. Jean Paul Crête, Montreal, Que. 15 July 1961; children: Paule, Jacques, Annie; EXTVE. VICE PRES., PROV. OF QUE. CHAMBER OF COMMERCE; called to Bar of Que. 1963; joined Dept. Industry & Comm. Que. 1967, Asst. Depy. Min. 1969 (and Asst. Gen. Secy. Que. Extve. Counc. and Secy. of Perm. Ministerial Comte. on Econ. Matters 1973; and Pres. and C.E.O. Que. Indust. Rsch. Centre 1974), Depy. Min. 1977; Depy. Min. of Industry, Trade & Tourism, Que. 1977–82; Depy. Min. Energy and Resources 1982–84; Vice Pres. for United States Affairs, Hydro Quebec 1984–87; Pres. & C.E.O., Hydro Québec International 1987–89; served with Candn. Army 1961–63 Ottawa and Montreal, rank Capt.; mem. Que. Bar Assn.; R. Catholic; Clubs: Garrison, Quebec City; St. Denis, Montreal; Home: 909 Antonine Maillet, Outremont, Que. H2V 2Y8; Office: 500 Place d'Armes, Montreal, Que. H2Y 2W2.

**DeSERRES, Roger,** B.en Com.; exécutif; né Montréal, Qué. le 5 sept. 1914; fils Omer et Eugénie (Saucier) D.; é. Coll. Mont St-Louis, gradué Cours scient. 1934; Univ. McGill, B.en Com. 1937; ép. Monique, fille Rolland Préfontaine 1943; cinq enfants; PRESIDENT DU CONSEIL, OMER DeSERRES CANADA INC.; Pres. Conseil, S.P.B. Canada Inc.; Formula Growth Ltd.; Prés. Nat., Chambre de Comm. du Can. 1966–67; Prés. Chambre de Comm. du Dist. de Montréal 1959–60; Prés. Inst. Candn. de Plomberie & Chauffage 1954–55; Prés., Fondation Hôpital Nôtre-Dame 1976–79; Grand Offr. de l'Ordre Equestre du St-Sépulcre de Jérusalem; Clubs: Mont Bruno Golf; Saint-Denis; Laval-sur-la-Lac; loisirs; golf, voyages; résidence: 6000 chemin Deacon, app P4, Montréal, Qué. H3S 2T9; bureau: 334 Ste. Catherine Est, Montréal, Qué. H2X 1L7.

**des GAGNIERS, Jean,** B.A., L.Ph.; educator; author; b. St-Joseph-de-la-Rive, Qué. 7 Feb. 1929; e. Coll. Jean de Brébeuf Montréal B.A. 1949; Diplôme de l'Ecole de Marine Rimouski 1951; Univ. Laval L.Ph. 1953; Diplôme de l'Ecole du Louvre, Paris 1956; ASST. TO VICE RECTOR, LAVAL UNIV. 1976– ; in charge new museum project (CENTRE MUSEOGRAPHIQUE) 1979– ; Laodikaia Excavations Turkey 1961–64; Soli Excavations Cyprus 1964–74; Trustee, Nat. Museums of Canada 1972–79; Pres., Adv. Ctte. Nat. Gallery of Canada 1977–79; author 'Fouilles de Laodicée du Lycos'; 'L'Acropole d'Athènes'; 'La céramique chypriote à décor figuré'; 'Vases et figurines de l'Age du Bronze'; 'Objets d'art grec du Louvre'; 'L'Acropole d'Athènes'; 'La céramique chypriote à décor figuré'; 'Vases et figurines de l'Age de Bronze'; 'Soloi: dix campagnes de fouilles'; 'La conservation du patrimoine muséologique du Québec'; 'L'Ile-aux-Coudres'; 'Charlevoix, pays enchanté' (en préparation); mem., Royal Soc. Canada; recreations: gardening, reading; Home: St-Joseph-de-la-Rive, Charlevoix, Qué. G0A 3Y0; Office: 3640, Pavillon Louis-Jacques-Casault, Univ. Laval, Québec, Qué. G1K 7P4.

**De SHANE, William Wesley,** C.A.; financial executive; b. London, Ont. 23 Sept. 1938; s. Joel and Gertrude Alberta (Kelley) D.; e. C.A. 1962; m. Louise d. Mabel and Gordon Sperry 26 June 1965; one s.: Peter Joel; VICE-PRES., CHIEF FINAN. OFFR. & SEC., CANADA MALTING CO. LIMITED 1990– ; var. finan. posts with Emco Ltd. & Candn. Gen. Electric 1962–73; Comptroller & Asst. Sec., Emco Ltd. 1973–78; Sec.-Treas. & C.F.O. 1978–89; Past Pres., United Way of Greater London; Finan. Extves. Inst., S.W. Ont. Chap.; Dir. & Treas., Grand Theatre 1968–90; Mem., FEI, Toronto Chap.; Inst. of C.A.s of Ont.; recreations: theatre, music; club: London; Home: 33 Harbour Sq., Apt. 1404,

Toronto, Ont. M5J 2G2; Office: 10 Four Seasons Pl., Ste. 600, Toronto, Ont. M9B 6H7.

**DÉSILETS, Andrée,** M.A., D.ès L., M.S.R.C., F.S.R.C.; professeure; née Sherbrooke, Qué. 27 mars 1928; f. Albert et Lucienne (Verret) D.; é. Univ. de Montréal B.A. 1949; Bishop's Univ. M.A. 1954; Univ. Laval D.ès L. (Histoire) 1968; Bishop's Univ. D. en Droit civil (honoris causa); PROFESSEURE ÉMÉRITE, UNIVERSITÉ DE SHERBROOKE 1991; Professeure d'Histoire, Université de Sherbrooke 1970–90; enseignement au Coll. Marguerite-Bourgeois (Montréal), Coll. de la Gaspésie et Université de Sherbrooke; mem., Comn. des lieux et monuments historiques du Can., 1974–88; Com. de toponymie du Qué., 1981–87; Institut d'histoire de l'amérique française (prés. 1985–89 et directrice de la 'Revue' 1982–85); auteure 'Hector-Louis Langevin: Un Père de la Confédération Canadienne 1826–1906,' (1969); 'Les Vingt-Cinq Ans de l'Université de Sherbrooke 1954–79,' (1982); 'Un Seigneur sans Titres: Louis-Rodrique Masson 1833–1903,' (1985); Adresse: 2495 Laurentie, Sherbrooke, Qué. J1J 1L3; Bureau: Université de Sherbrooke, Sherbrooke, Qué. J1K 2R1.

**DESILETS, Lisa Marie,** B.F.A., B.Ed.; art educator, independent art curator, critic; b. Winnipeg, Man. 28 Aug. 1962; d. Ronald Richard Joseph and Anna Marie (Molgat) D.; e. Coll. secondaire de Saint-Boniface 1980; Univ. of Manitoba B.F.A. 1984; Coll. universitaire de St-Boniface B.Ed. 1992; m. David s. Leonard and Dorene Manahan 14 Oct. 1989; one son: Louis Leonard Desilets Manahan; INDEPENDENT CONSULTANT/ART EDUCATOR 1990– ; Curator/Visual Arts Coord., Le Centre Culturel Franco-Manitobain 1986–90; Resource Asst. to Devel. of Visual Arts Curriculum for French & Immersion Schools, Dept. of Edn. & Profl. Training, Govt. of Manitoba 1989–92; Assoc. Prof., Coll. universitaire de St-Boniface 1993 (chargée de cours 1992); Trustee, Nat. Gallery of Canada 1990–94; interests: travel, music, all forms of art; Home: 58 Cathedral Ave., Winnipeg, Man. R2W 0W5; Office: National Gallery of Canada, 380 Sussex Dr., Ottawa, Ont. K1N 9N4.

**DESJARDINS, The Hon. Justice Alice,** B.A., LL.L., LL.M.; b. Montréal, Qué. 11 Aug. 1934; d. Louis and Alexandrina (Venne) D.; e. Univ. de Montréal; Harvard Law Sch.; JUDGE, FEDERAL COURT OF CANADA, APPEAL DIVISION, and ex officio mem. of the Federal Court of Can., Trial Div., July 1987; Judge of the Court Martial Appeal Court of Can., Sept. 1988; Ottawa, Ont.; called to Qué. Bar 1958; apptd. Q.C. 1974; Asst. Prof., Fac. of Law, Univ. de Montréal 1961–68; Assoc. Prof. 1968–69; Legal Couns., Privy Counc. Office, Ottawa 1969–74; Dir., Adv. & Admin. Law, Dept. of Justice, Ottawa 1974–81; apptd. Judge, Superior Court of Québec 1981; MacKenzie King Travelling Scholarship 1958–59; Ford Found. Scholarship 1966; Mem., Bd. of Govs., Donner Candn. Found. 1974–81; Bd., Found. Internationale Roncalli 1982– ; Chairperson, Québec Selection Ctte. for Rhodes Scholarships 1989–93; Mem. Bd. of Advisors, Internat. Section of the Harvard Law School Assn. 1992– ; Assn. of Qué. Law Teachers 1968–69; Pres., Local Chap. Ottawa, Candn. Br., Internat Law Assn. 1977–79; Vice-Pres. Candn. Branch Internat. Law Assoc. 1984; Inst. of Pub. Admin. 1975 (Nat. Bd. 1975–78, Pres., Local Chapt. Ottawa 1975); Ctte. Mem., Am. Soc. of Internat. Law 1971–72; Nat. Bd., Candn. Assns. of Univ. Profs. (Ottawa) 1968–69; Club: Mount Royal Tennis (Extve. Ctte.); Catholic; Office: The Federal Court of Canada, Ottawa, Ont. K1A 0H9.

**DESJARDINS, Hon. Gaston,** L.ès D.; juge; né Baker Brook, N.B. 2 oct. 1932; f. J. Antoine et Marie (Bouchard) D.; é. Baker Brook, N.B. ecole primaire; Univ. Saint-Louis d'Edmundston gradué 1955; Univ. Laval L.ès D. 1958; ép. Louise f. Alphonse et Annette (Picard) Cyr, Edmundston, N.B. 27 août 1957; enfants: Mireille, Yves; JUGE DE LA COUR SUPERIEURE DE LA PROV. DE QUE.; admis au Barreau de Qué. 1959; cr. Q.C. 1974; élu député libéral de Louis Hébert à l'Assemblée nationale du Qué. à l'élection de 1973; renouvellement de mandat non sollicité; catholique; récreations: tennis, skiing, pêche; Adresse: 3631, chemin St-Louis, Sainte-Foy, Qué. G1W 1T2; Bureau: 300, boul. Jean Lesage, Québec, Qué. G1K 8K6.

**DESJARDINS, Jean A.,** Q.C., B.A., LL.L.; lawyer; b. Montréal, Qué. 5 Sept. 1931; s. Henri and Marguerite (Denault) D.; e. Loyola Coll. B.A. 1952; Univ. de Montréal LL.L. 1955; McGill Univ. 4th yr. Law; children: Jean-François, Valérie, Frédéric; PRES. AND DIR., DESJARDINS DUPONT REALTY INC. and DESJARDINS DUPONT INTERNATIONAL INC. 1989– ; Dir., Marché Central Métropolitain Inc. (and since 1987, mem. Extve. Ctte.) 1983–92; Law Clk. Lavery, O'Brien 1952–55; articled 1955–56, and practiced law, Ogilvy, Renault 1956–59; Partner, Desjardins Ducharme 1959–88; Sr. Partner, Desjardins Dupont, Barristers, Solicitors and Trademark Agents 1989–93; Dir., Normick Perron Inc. 1975–89; Corp. de Gestion La Vérendrye 1982–90; called to Bar of Qué. 1956; apptd. Q.C. 1972; cr. mem., legal ctte. revision Can. Corps. Act.; sometime lectr. in corporate law Qué. Bar Prof. Training Prog.; participated Legal Aid Program Bar of Montréal; served with RCN (R) 1950–56, rank Lt. (S); mem., Candn. Power Squadrons (advanced pilotage); mem., Bd. Govs. and Bd. Mgmt. Qué. Div. Candn. Red Cross Soc. 1964–77: Hon. Counsel 1966–71, Hon. Treas. 1970–72, Exec. Vice Pres. 1972–73, Pres. 1973–76, Pres. Div. Council 1976–77; Regional Pres., Shefford-Brome-Missisquoi 1989–91; mem., Central Council of Soc. 1969–79: Nat. Hon. Comptroller 1975–77, Nat. Pres. 1977–78, Nat. Imm. Past Pres. 1978–79; mem., 1977–80 and Vice Chrmn. 1980–81 Fin. Comm. of League of Red Cross and Red Crescent Socs.; mem., Perm. Scale Contributions Comn. of League 1981–85; apptd. Hon. Vice Pres., Qué. Div., Candn. Red Cross 1977; apptd. Hon. Vice Pres., Candn. Red Cross 1979; apptd. Hon. Counsellor, Candn. Red Cross Soc. 1980; apptd. Hon. Gov., Qué. Div., Candn. Red Cross 1991; mem., Bedford, Qué. Bar Assn.; Trademark Agent 1960–93; Real Estate Broker since 1989; recreations: swimming, yachting, flying (private pilot licence, valid day and night, land and sea, single and multi-engine), fishing, alpine and cross-country skiing, golf, tennis; Address: 44, rue des Cygnes, Granby, Qué. J2H 1X6.

**DESJARDINS, Jean-Paul,** Phm.B.; pharmacist; b. Ottawa, Ont. 4 Jan. 1926; s. Horace Alphonse and Marie Louise (Boyle) D.; e. Univ. of Ottawa 1945; Univ. of Toronto Phm.B. 1950; m. Liliane d. Emile and Marie-Antoinette Charette 24 June 1952; children: Andrée, Jean, Louis, Pierre; PRES. DESJARDINS PHARMACIES LTD. 1960– ; Founder, Ontario Medical Supply Ltd.; Dir. Candn. Found. for Pharm.; mem. Internat. Fedn. Pharm. The Hague; mem. Exec. Ctte. Bd. Govs. Univ. of Ottawa; Patron, Med. Friends of Peru; Life mem. & Patron French Candn. Inst.; guest speaker prov. and nat. pharm. seminars; Fellow, Am. Coll. Apothecaries; Founder and Pres. Dalhousie Profl. Assn. 1955; mem. Ottawa Exec. Assn.; Pres.: Ottawa Pharms. Assn. 1960; Ont. Pharm. Assn. 1977 (Squibb Can. Award 1977); Cercle Universitaire d'Ottawa 1978; Found. St. Louis Residence for Aged; Dir. Candn. Pharm. Assn. 1984 (Award of Appreciation 1982); Vice Pres. Qué. Assn. Advanc. Pharm.; recipient A.H. Robins Bowl of Hygeia Award 'outstanding community service in Pharmacy' 1979; Cross Order Malta, Kt. Magistral 1985; recreation: golf, skiing, tennis, fishing; Clubs: Gatineau Fish & Game; Nautilus; Home: 1917 Fairmeadow Cres., Ottawa, Ont. K1H 7B8; Office: 298 Dalhousie St., Ottawa, Ont. K1N 7E7.

**DESJARDINS, Léandre,** Ph.D.; university professor; n. New Brunswick, 23 Mar. 1942; s. Wilfrid N. and Cecile (Richard) D.; e. Univ. St-Joseph (Moncton), B.A., 1963; Univ. Moncton, M.A.Ps 1968; Univ. Colorado, Ph.D. 1971; m. Doris, d. Carlos Alfonso, 27 Nov. 1965; children: Clarissa; Mireille; Renelle; VICE-PRES., ACADEMIC, UNIV. OF MONCTON 1990– ; joined present univ. as Prof. Psychology 1966; Dept. Head 1975–77; Dean, Social Sciences 1979–90; Reviewer, grant applications Dept. Nat. Health & Welfare, Can. Counc., Candn. Environmental Rsch. Counc.; mem. Premier's Counc. Status of the Disabled 1982–85; mem. Assn. des Professeurs de l'Univ. de Moncton (Pres. 1967–68); Assn. des Psychologues du N.B. (Past Pres.); Mental Health N.B. (Past Pres.); Lepreau II Environmental Assessment Panel (Co-Chrmn. 1984); Home: 76, ave. Massey, Moncton, N.B. E1A 3E2; Office: Université de Moncton, Moncton, N.B. E1A 3E9.

**DESJARDINS, Marcel,** B.A., B.Sc.A., M.B.A.; consultant; b. Ste-Thérèse, Qué. 28 May 1939; s. Laurent and Fernande (Leroux) D.; e. Séminaire de Ste-Thérèse (Qué.) B.A. 1960; Ecole Polytechnique de Montréal B.Sc.A. 1964; Harvard Grad. Sch. of Business Adm. M.B.A. 1967; m. Madeleine d. Dr. Larose, Ste-Thérèse, Qué. 1963; children: Annie, Natalie, Eric; SPECIAL ADVISOR TO PRESIDENT & C.E.O. TELEGLOBE INC.; Ordre des ingénieurs Qué.; R. Catholic; recreations: skiing, golf, reading, music; Clubs: St-Denis; Rosemère Golf; Home: 706 Presseault, Ste-Thérèse-en-Haut, Qué.

**DESJARDINS, Pierre,** B.A., B.Sc.; brewery executive; b. Montreal, Que. 28 Oct. 1941; s. Henri and Azilda (Tremblay) D.; e. Univ. of Montreal, B.A. 1962; Univ. of Wyoming, B.Sc. 1966; children: Andre, Danielle, Patrick, Christian; Pres., Labatt Breweries of Can. 1986–..; Vice Pres., John Labatt Ltd.; Dir., Domtar Inc.; Mem., Montreal Alouettes Football Club 1966–72; Vice-Pres., Admin. & Sales, Imperial Tobacco 1967–79; Pres., La Brasserie Labatt Ltee. 1979–86.

**DESLONGCHAMPS, Pierre,** O.C., B.Sc., Ph.D., F.R.S.C., F.R.S., F.C.I.C.; educator; b. Laurentides, Que. 8 May 1938; s. Rodolphe and Madeleine (Magnan) D.; e. Univ. de Montréal B.Sc. 1959; Univ. of N.B. Ph.D. 1964; Doctorat (hon. causa): Univ. Pierre et Marie Curie, Paris 1983; Bishop's Univ., Univ. de Montréal, Univ. Laval 1984; Univ. of N.B. 1985; children: Ghislain, Patrice; PROF. DE CHIMIE, UNIV. DE SHERBROOKE; Research Fellowship Harvard Univ. 1964; A. P. Sloan Fellowship 1970–72; Scient. Prize Que. 1971; E.W.R. Steacie Fellowship 1971–74 and Prize 1974; Médaille Vincent de l'ACFAS 1975; Izaak Walton Killam Mem. Scholarships in Science 1976–77; Merck, Sharp and Dohme Lectures Award Chem. Inst. Can. 1976; Fellowship 'John Simon Guggenheim Memorial Foundation' (New York), 1979; Prize winner 'Médaille Pariseau de l'ACFAS,' 1979; Fellow of the Chem. Inst. of Can. 1980; Fellow, Royal Soc. of London 1983; recipient Marie-Victorin Prize, Prov. of Que. 1987; Officer of the Order of Canada 1989; Alfred Bader Award in Organic Chem. (Candn. Soc. for Chem.) 1991; Canada Gold Medal for Science and Engn. (NSERCC) 1993; author 'Stereoelectronic Effects in Organic Chemistry' 1983; over 140 scient. publs. organic chem.; Fellow, Am. Assn. Advanc. Science 1988; mem. Swiss Chem. Soc.; Royal Soc. Can.; Am. Chem. Soc.; Chem. Inst. Can.; Assn. Harvard Chems.; Ordre des Chimistes du Qué.; Assn. Canadienne-Française pour l'Avancement des Sciences; Assn. for the Advancement of Sci. (AASC); Candn. Ctte. of Scientists and Scholars (CCSS) 1993– ; Home: R.R. 1, North Hatley, Qué. J0B 2C0; Office: Sherbrooke, Qué. J1K 2R1.

**DESMARAIS, André,** B.Comm.; executive; b. Ottawa, Ont. 26 Oct. 1956; s. Paul and Jacqueline (Maranger) D.; e. Loyola Univ. B.Com. 1978; m. France d. Hon. Jean Chrétien and Aline (Chaîné) 23 May 1981; four children; PRES. AND CHIEF OPERATING OFFICER, POWER CORP. OF CANADA 1991– ; Chrmn. & C.E.O., Power Broadcasting Inc.; Pres. & C.O.O., Gesca Ltée; Dir. & Mem. Extve. Ctte. and Audit Ctte.: Gesca Ltée; La Presse Ltée; Les Publications J.T.C. Ltée; Dir. & Mem. Extve. Ctte., Power Financial Corp.; Dir., Bombardier Inc.; C.G.C. Inc.; Groupe Bruxelles Lambert S.A.; Great-West-Lifeco Inc.; The Great-West Life Assurance Company; Northstar; Dir. & Mem. Audit Ctte., Investors Group Inc.; Dir. & Mem. Extve. Ctte. and Compensation Ctte., Southam Inc.; Mem., Extve. Ctte., La Compagnie Luxembourgeoise de Télédiffusion; Exec. Asst. to Chrmn. and Chief Exec. Offr. present Co. 1978–79; Devel. Offr. Campeau Corp. Ltd. 1979–80; Press Sec. and Special Asst. to Min. of Justice and Atty. Gen. of Can. 1980–81; Extve. Asst. to the Chrmn. & C.E.O. 1981–82, Extve. & Development Offr., Power Communications, present co. 1983–84; Vice Pres. (1984), Dir. & Mem. Extve. Ctte. 1988; Instl. Salesman Options, Richardson Greenshields of Canada Ltd. 1982–83; Vice-Chrmn. & Mem. Extve. Ctte., Canada-China Trade Counc. 1984; Mem. Chrmn.'s Internat. Adv. Counc., Americas Society Inc. 1988; Dir., Lester B. Pearson Coll.; Les Partenaires du Cardinal (Dir. & Treas.); Montréal Children's Hosp. Found.; Montréal Gen. Hosp.; Hon. Lt.-Col., 'Les Voltigeurs de Québec'; Clubs: Mount Royal; Murray Bay Golf; University; Toronto; Royal St-Lawrence Yacht; Office: 751 Square Victoria, Montréal, Qué. H2Y 2J3.

**DESMARAIS, Chantal;** chartered accountant; b. Montreal, Que. 23 Aug. 1958; e. McGill Univ.; m. Derek Patterson 12 Nov. 1988; two s.: Michael Derek, Brandon Alexander; PARTNER, ZITTRER, SIBLIN, CARON, BÉLANGER, ERNST & YOUNG; Home: 11 O'Reilly, Nun's Island, Que.; Office: 1 Pl. Alexhis Nihon, Montreal, Que. H3Z 3E8.

**DESMARAIS, Paul,** P.C., C.C., B.Com.; businessman; b. Sudbury, Ont. 4 Jan. 1927; s. late Jean Noel (Q.C.) and Lebea (Laforest) D.; e. Univ. of Ottawa, B.Com.; m. Jacqueline, d. Ernest Maranger, Ottawa, Ont., 8 Sept. 1953; two s., two d.; CHRMN. & CHIEF EXTVE. OFFR. (AND CHRMN. EXTVE. COMTE.) POWER CORPORATION OF CANADA; Chrmn., Pargesa Holding S.A. (Switzerland); Parfinance (France); Chrmn., La Presse, Ltée; Dir., Compagnie Luxembourgeoise de Télédiffusion; Electrafina S.A.; Great-West Life Assurance Co.; Great-West Lifeco Inc.; Groupe Bruxelles Lambert, S.A.; Investors Group Inc.; Parfinance; Pargesa Holding, S.A.; Petrofina S.A.; La Presse Ltée; Power Financial Corp.; The Seagram Co. Ltd.; Southam Inc.; Office: 751 Victoria Square, Montréal, Qué. H2Y 2J3.

**DESMARAIS, Paul Jr.,** B.A., B.Comm.; financial executive; b. Sudbury, Ont. 3 July 1954; s. Paul Guy and Jacqueline (Maranger) D.; e. European Inst. of Bus. Admin. France B.A. 1979; McGill Univ. B.Comm. 1977; m. Hélène d. Yolande and Edouard Blouin 8 Sept. 1979; CHRMN., POWER FINANCIAL CORPORATION 1990– ; and VICE-CHRMN., POWER CORP. OF CAN. 1991– ; S.G. Warburg & Co. Ltd. (U.K.) 1979–80; Planning Mgr., Standard Brands. Inc. (U.S.) 1980–81; Dir. of Planning, Power Corp. of Can. 1981–82; Vice-Pres. 1982–91; Vice-Pres., Power Finan. Corp. 1984–86; Pres. & Chief Op. Offr. 1986–89; Vice-Chrmn. 1989–90; Dir. & Extve. Ctte. Mem., Power Corp. of Can., Power Finan. Corp., Investors Group Inc., The Great West Life Assur. Co., Groupe Bruxelles Lambert S.A. (Belgium), Pargesa Holding S.A. (Switz.); Dir., H.D. Internat. Limited (England), Parfinance (France), Imetal (France), Petrofina (Belgium), Fibelpar S.A. (Belgium), Royale Belge S.A. (Belgium), Royale Vendôme S.A. (Belgium), Great-West Life & Annuity Insurance Company (USA), G.W.L. Properties Inc. (USA), G.W.L. Properties Ltd., Great-West Lifeco Inc., Gesca Ltd., La Presse Ltd., Les Pubs. J.T.C. Ltd. (Can.); Vice-Chrmn. of the Bd., Olympic Trust of Can.; Co-Pres. of the Candn. Chapter, Canada-Belgium Ctte.; Chrmn., Adv. Bd., McGill Univ.; Mem., INSEAD Internat. Counc.; recreations: tennis, skiing, hunting, fishing; clubs: Mount-Royal, Toronto, Hillside Tennis, Montreal Indoor Tennis, Royal St. Lawrence Yacht, Mount-Bruno Country, Club Polo de Bagatelle (Paris), The Travellers (Paris); Office: 751 Victoria Square, Montreal, Que H2Y 2J3.

**DES MARAIS, Pierre II;** company president; b. Montreal, Que. 2 June 1934; s. Pierre and Rolande (Varin) Des Marais ; e. Coll. Jean-de-Brébeuf, 1946–50; Coll. Sainte Marie, B.A. 1954; Graphic Arts Course, Toronto, 1954; Univ. of Montreal, Business Adm., H.E.C. 1958; m. Lise Blanchard, Jan. 21, 1956; children: Suzanne, Lison, Pierre III, Jean, Danielle, Stéphane, Sophie, Philippe, Anik; PRESIDENT & C.E.O., UNIMEDIA 1987– ; Dir., Rothman's Inc.; Royal Bank of Canada; Imperial Oil Ltd.; Hollinger Inc.; Ouimet-Cordon Bleu Inc.; Alumax Inc.; The Royal Candn. Geographical Soc.; Chrmn., Corp. de l'Hôpital Maisonneuve-Rosemont; Hon. mem. Order of St-John, Que.; Fellow, Royal Geographical Soc.; recreations: skiing, yachting; Clubs: Saint-Denis; Mt. Royal; Forest & Stream; Office: 600 de Maisonneuve W., Ste. 3200, Montreal, Que. H3A 3J2.

**DESMARAIS, The Hon. Mr. Justice Robert C.,** Q.C., B.Sc., LL.B., LL.D.; b. Sudbury, Ont. 16 Aug. 1936; s. Jean-Noel and Lebea (Laforest) D.; e. Univ. Ottawa, B.Sc. Pol. Sc. 1962; LL.B. 1963; Laurentian Univ., LL.D. (Hon.) 1990; m. Jeanne, d. Dr. Mrs. G. Rheault, 20 Aug. 1962; children: Robert Jr., Daniel, Alain, and Chantal (dec.); REGIONAL SENIOR JUSTICE, ONT. COURT OF JUSTICE (GEN. DIV.) EAST REGION 1990– ; called to the Bar Ont. 1965; apptd. Q.C. 1976; Sr. Partner, Desmarais, Keenan 1967–82; apptd. County and District Court Judge, Ont. 1982; apptd. Sr. Judge, Judicial District of Ottawa-Carleton, 1990; apptd. to Ont. Court of Justice (Gen. Div.) 1990; apptd. Sr. Regional Justice, Ont. Court of Justice (Gen. Div.) East Region 1990; elected Alderman, City of Sudbury 1965; el. Deputy Mayor 1967; Founding Dir., Pres., Sudbury Regional Devel. Corp.; Founding Dir., Sudbury Regional Sch. Nursing; Founding mem. and Chrmn., Sudbury Regional Police Commission; Founding Dir., Vice-Pres. and Hon. Life Mem., Science North; Dir. Sudbury Youth Centre; Centre des Jeunes; Hon. Dir., The Thomas More Lawyers Guild of Ottawa; mem., Candn. Bar Assoc.; Candn. Inst. for the Admin. of Justice (Life Mem.); Ont. Superior Court Judges Assoc.; Office: Court House, 161 Elgin St., 6th Flr., Ottawa, Ont. K2P 2K1.

**DESMEULES, André,** B.A., LL.L.; superior court judge; b. Quebec, Que. 2 Aug. 1931; s. Roland and Beatrice (Miller) D.; e. Jesuit Coll.; Laval Univ., B.A. 1952, LL.L. 1955; dipl. d'études sup. en droit 1960; m. Hèléne d. Jules Caouette 7 Oct. 1961; children: Julie, Georges, Claude, Michel; JUDGE, SUPERIOR COURT FOR THE PROV. OF QUE. 1973– ; law practice, St.-Laurent, Monast, Desmeules & Walters 1956–73; Q.C. 1971; Former Bd. Mem., St.-Sacrement Hosp.; recreations: tennis, golf, skiing; Clubs: Quebec Garrison; Cap Rouge Golf Club; Club de Tennis Avantage; Home: 915 Cardinal-Rouleau, Québec, Qué. G1S 3L1; Office: 300 boul. Jean-Lesage, Québec, Qué. G1K 8K6.

**DE SOUSA, Ronald Bon,** B.A., Ph.D.; university professor / philosopher; b. Lausanne, Switz. 25 Feb. 1940; s. Manuel Julio Bon de Sousa Pernes and Lucile Odier; e. Bryanston Sch. (U.K.) 1955; Lycée français, London 1956; Internat. Sch. of Geneva (Baccalauréat) 1958; New Coll., Oxford Univ., B.A. 1962; Princeton Univ., Ph.D. 1966; children: Hannah Carolan, Nathan Carter; PROF., DEPT. OF PHILOSOPHY, UNIV. OF TORONTO 1981– ; Asst. Prof. of Philos., present univ. 1966–70; Assoc. Prof. 1970–81; Vis. Assoc. Prof., Univ. of Calif. at Santa Barbara 1971–72; Vis. Prof., Univ. of B.C. 1984; Dartmouth Coll. 1989; Lanzhou (P.R. of China) 1989, 1993; Assoc., Inst. of the Hist. & Philos. of Sci. & Technol., Univ. of Toronto; Cons., Ont. Counc. of Grad. Studies; Lectr., numerous universities in Can., U.S., U.K. Argentina, France, Poland, Yugoslavia, China, etc.; religion: Atheist; politics: vaguely left-libertarian-anarchist; Mem., Candn. Philos. Assn. (Past Dir.); Am. Philos. Assn.; Internat. Soc. Rsch. on Emotions; Assoc., Behavioral & Brain Sci.; author: 'The Rationality of Emotion' 1987; recreations: acting, Chinese language and literature; Home: 82 Salisbury Ave., Toronto, Ont. M4X 1C4; Office: 215 Huron St., #907, Toronto, Ont. M5S 1A1.

**de SOUZA, Ivan Xavier,** B.Com., M.B.A., O.C.M.; stockbroker; financial consultant; b. London, Eng. 12 Dec. 1935; s. Arthur Francis (dec.) and Lilian Antonette (Pereira) de S. (dec.); e. Cambridge Univ.; Univ. Laval B.Com. 1957, M.B.A. 1959; m. Anna Maria Marcolini d. Amadeu and Honorina Guidi 22 Dec. 1982; one s. (by previous marriage) John Arthur; PRESIDENT, IXD HOLDINGS INC.; Pres. Investcan Securities Ltd.; Pres., Investcan Financial Corp.; Chrmn. & Dir. Wilshire Energy Resources Inc.; Dir., Environmental Technologies Inc.; Asst. Corporate Econ. DuPont of Canada 1959–64; Candn. OECD Rep. and Econ. Adv. Dept. Industry Trade & Comm. Can. 1964–69; Mgr. Marketing Research & Devel. Imperial Oil Ltd. 1969–70; Vice Pres. and Dir. Canavest House Ltd. 1970–75; Extve. Vice Pres. Canergy Resources Ltd. 1973–75; Sr. Vice Pres. and Dir. McLeod Young Weir Ltd. 1975–81; mem. Ont. Petrol. Inst.; Knight, Internat. Constantian Order (Ordo Constantini Magni); Knight, Order of St. Gregory; Knight, Order of St. George; Knight, Order of St. Basil; mem., L'Accademia Italiana della Cucina; recreations: tennis, fishing; Clubs: Granite; Toronto Lawn Tennis; Office: Royal Bank Plaza, North Tower, P.O. Box 75, 200 Bay St., Toronto, Ont. M5J 2J1.

**DESPLAND, Michel;** educator; author; b. Lausanne, Switzerland 25 July 1936; s. Amy and Lisette (Vuagniaux) D.; e. Univ. de Lausanne Lic. Theol. 1958; Edinburgh Univ. n.d.; Harvard Univ. Th.D. 1966; m. Francine Lichtert; children: Emma Geneviève, Alexis Martin, Joachim Adrien, Noémie Fabienne; PROF. OF RELIGION, CONCORDIA UNIV. 1974– ; mem., Conseil des Universites Gouvernement du Qué.; author: 'Kant on History and Religion' 1973; 'Le Choc des Morales' 1973; 'La Religion en Occident' 1979; 'The Education of Desire: Plato and the Philosophy of Religion' 1985; 'Christianisme: dossier corps' 1987; 'Les sciences religieuses au Québec depuis 1972' 1988; 'La tradition française en sciences religieuses' 1991; 'Religion in History' 1992; Home: 4070 Grand Blvd., Montréal, Qué. H4B 2X5; Office: 1455 Boul de Maisonneuve Ouest, Montréal, Qué. H3G 1M8.

**DESPRÉS, Monique,** LL.B.; lawyer; b. Montmagny, Prov. of Que. 17 Nov. 1950; d. Jean Baptiste and Laurette (Boulet) D.; e. Univ. of Montreal LL.B. 1980; Mem. of the Quebec Bar 1981; single; VICE PRESIDENT, GENERAL COUNSEL & SECRETARY, TELEMEDIA INC. 1992– ; General Counsel & Secy., Telemedia Inc. 1990– ; Legal Counsel, Telemedia Inc. 1981–90; Teaching Asst., Univ. of Montreal 1981–84; Dir., L'Assn. canadienne de la radio et de la TV de langue française 1984–88; Vice-Pres. Radio de l'Ass. Can. de la radio et de la TV de langue français 1987–88; Office: 500, 1411 Peel St., Montreal, Que. H3A 1S5.

**DESPRÉS, Robert,** O.C., M.Comm., FCGA, FSMAC; executive; b. Quebec, Que. 27 September 1924; e. Laval Univ.; m. Marguerite Cantin, 1949; 4 children; DRM Holdings Inc.; Dir., Camdev Corp.; Camdev Properties Inc.; Canada Malting Co. Ltd.; CFCF Inc.; Domtar Inc.; Greyvest Inc.; Greyvest Financial Services Inc.; Manulife Financial; UniMédia Inc.; Univa Inc.; National Optics Inst.; National Trust Co.; Norcen Energy Resources Ltd.; PMG Financial Inc.; Provigo Distribution Inc.; Réseau de télévision Quatre Saisons Inc.; Sidbec and Sidbec-Dosco Inc.; Solivar Inc.; South Shore Industries Ltd.; Wajax Ltd.; former mem. Roy. Comm. on Finan. Mang. & Accountability in Govt. of Can.; Que. Comm. of Inquiry on Finan. Institutions; Comptroller, Quebec Power Company, 1959–1963 and mem. Extve. Comte.; Mgr., Que. Regional Br., Administration and Trust Co., 1963–65; Depy. Min. of Revenue, Que., 1965–69; Pres. and General Manager, Quebec Health Insurance Board, 1969–73; Pres., Univ. of Quebec, 1973–78; Pres. & CEO, Netcom Inc., 1978; Nat. Cablevision 1978–80; Bd. Chrmn., Atomic Energy of Can. Ltd. 1980–86; Counsel, Raymond, Chabot, Martin, Paré, Chartered Accountants and Mgmt. Consultants 1987; Dir. Soc. du Musée du Séminaire de Qué.; Counc. for Candn. Unity; (and Pres.) Que. Heart Inst.; mem., Soc. of Mgmt. Accountants; Certified Gen. Accountants; Officer Order of Canada 1978; Fellow Soc. of Mgmt. Accountants of Can. 1979; Fellow Candn. Certified Gen. Accts. Assn. 1981; Hon. Doctorate, Univ. du Québec 1986; R. Catholic; recreations: golf, reading; Clubs: Cercle de la Garnison de Qué. Inc.; Lorette Golf; La Gorce Country; Home: 888, rue St-Jean, Ste. 200, Quebec, Que. G1R 5H6.

**DESROCHERS, Jean-Claude,** B.Sc., M.Sc.; food industry executive; b. St. Jacques, Co. Montcalm 3 April 1943; s. Firmin and Bibianne D.; e. Univ. Laval B.Sc. 1967; Maine Univ. M.Sc. (horticulture) 1969; m. Diane d. Roland Couture 9 July 1967; children: Nathalie, Stephane, Sebastien; SENIOR VICE-PRES., MERCHANDISING AND MARKETING, PROVIGO DISTRIBUTION INC. 1991– ; Quebec Govt. 1969–74; Gen. Mgr., Produce Div., Que., Provigo 1974–81; Montreal & Que. 1981–87; Vice-Pres., Perishables 1987–89; Sr. Vice-Pres., Perishables & Food Serv. 1989–91; Mem., Que. Produce Marketing Assn.; Candn. Produce Marketing Assn.; Bronze Prisme 1990; recreations: golf, gardening; club: St. Hyacinthe Golf; Home: 721, Pacifique Duplessis, Boucherville, Que. J4B 7V7; Office: 1611 Cremazie E., Montreal, Que. H2M 2R9.

**DesROCHES, Antoine;** publishing executive; b. Quebec City, Que. 9 Jan. 1924; s. Francis and Antoinette (Dubois) D.; e. St. Sacrement Superior Sch. 1939; Columbia Univ. Sch. of Journalism; Les Hautes Etudes Commerciales, Business Adm. 1967; Micrographics & Computer Output Microfilm Advanced Mgmt. Studies, Toronto 1974; m. Monique d. Fernand Nuytemans 24 Jan. 1969; children: Claude, Alain, José-Anne, France, Gisèle; SPECIAL ADV. PRES., LA PRESSE LTEE 1988– ; Pres., Les Editions La Presse Ltée 1981–86; Information Expert UNESCO 1962–63; Treas. Que. Press Council 1974–79; mem. Candn. Consultative Videotex Comte. 1980–81; Pres. Assn. des Editeurs Canadiens 1983–84; Asst. to the Pres. and Dir. of Publ. Relations 1980–88; mem. Internat. Press Inst.; Candn. Daily Newspaper Publishers Assn.; R. Catholic; recreations: skiing, tennis, travel; Home: 24 Buttonwood, Dollard-des-Ormeaux, Que. H9A 2N2; Office: 7 St-Jacques, Montreal, Que. H2Y 1K9.

**DES ROCHES, Kenneth Francis,** B.A., B.Ed.; civil servant; b. Charlottetown, P.E.I. 21 Aug. 1948;s. Francis Augustus and Elizabeth Anne (Deagle) Des R.; e. Saint Dunstan's Univ. B.A. 1969; Univ. of P.E.I. B.Ed. 1972; m. Anne Marie d. Nazaire and Gertrude Gallant 26 June 1971; children: Jennifer Anne, Monica Jane, Rebecca Marie; PRINCIPAL, KENNETH F. DESROCHES AND ASSOCIATES 1993– ; Teacher, Charlottetown Sch. Bd. 1969–70; Core Counsellor Rural Devel. Council P.E.I. 1970–73; Exec. Dir. Occupational Training Centre 1973–77; Asst. Mgr. Charlottetown Area Development Corp. 1977–81, Chief Exec. Offr. 1981–86; Depy. Min., Community & Cultural Affairs P.E.I. 1986–89; Depy. Min. of the Environment 1989–91; Chief Operating Offr., P.E.I. Business Development Agency 1991–93; C.E.O., Enterprise P.E.I. 1993; former Dir., Charlottetown Area Development Corp.; former Vice Chrmn.: Harbourside Development Ltd.; Confederation Court Mall Ltd.; Hon. mem. P.E.I. Div. Candn. Mental Health Assn.; R. Catholic; recreation: reading; Home: 15 Shell Court, Charlottetown, P.E.I. C1A 2Z8; Office: West Royalty Industrial Park, Charlottetown, P.E.I. C1E 1B0.

**DESROCHES, Pierre;** b. Montreal, Que. 24 Aug. 1931; s. Léo and Marguerite (Létourneau) D.; e. Collège Ste-Marie; m. Denise d. Adrien and Bernadette MacBeth 11 Apr. 1955; children: Daniel, Anne-Marie; EXTVE. DIR., TELEFILM CANADA 1988– ; CBC 1952–86: TV Prod. 1955–61; Mng. Dir., French Radio 1970–71; Vice-Pres., Planning 1973–75; Extve. Vice-Pres. 1975–82; Vice-Pres. & Gen. Mgr., French Broadcasting Serv. 1982–86; loaned by Candn. govt. to Ctte. Resp. for the Follow-up to the Paris Summit Mtg. of Francophone Heads of State & Govts.; 1986–88; Mem., Bd. of Gov., Univ. of Ottawa 1975– ; Home: St. Lambert, Que.; Office: 600 de la Gauchetière St. W., 14th fl., Montreal, Que. H3B 4L8.

**DESROSIERS, Roger,** B.Comm., M.Comm., F.C.A.; financial executive; b. St-Cléophas, Matapédia County 24 Oct. 1938; s. Robert and Antoinette (Chouinard) D.; e. Laval Univ. B.Comm. 1961, M.Comm. 1962, C.A. 1963; m. Agathe Beaupré-Landry; children: Marie-Claude, Michel; PRESIDENT & CHIEF EXECUTIVE

OFFICER, LE GROUPE MALLETTE MAHEU 1989– ; C.A., Coopers and Lybrand 1963–68; Asst. to Gen. Mgr., Acctg. & Finance, then Gen. Mgr., Quebec Telephone 1968–73; Co-founder, Desrosiers, Lepage and Associates 1973; merged with Mallette, Benoît, Boulanger, Rondeau & Assoc. 1980; and with Maheu Noiseux 1991; Mem., Adv. Ctte., Chaire des Sci. Comptables, Hautes Etudes Commerciales; Audit & cons. work for a number of credit unions, coops & telecomm. businesses; Consultant for several large & mid-sized independent business; Fellow de l'Ordre des comptables agréés du Québec; Mem. Bd. of Dirs., Société Innovatech du Grand Montréal; Dir., Horace Boivin Found.; Chrmn. of the Bd., I Musici, Chamber Orch.; Hon. Pres. (Prov. of Que.), The Candn. Red Cross Soc. Fundraising Campaign 1992; Mem., Bd. of Dir. & Chair, Groupe Desjardins, Assur. gén. 1989–90; Mem., Bd. of Dir., Féd. des caisses popularies Desjardins du Bas-Saint-Laurent 1977–90 (Pres. 1984–90); recreations: skiing, golf, tennis; clubs: Saint Denis, Saint James's; Home: 11 O'Reilly, Suite 809, Ile des Soeurs, Que.; Office: 5 Place Ville-Marie, Suite 1000, Montreal, Que. H3B 4X3.

**DEUGAU, Kenneth Victor,** B.Sc., Ph.D.; biochemist; b. Edmonton, Alta. 25 Sept. 1947; s. Albert Victor and Doris Eleanor (Little) D.; e. William Aberhart High Sch. Calgary 1965; Univ. of Calgary B.Sc. 1970; McMaster Univ. Ph.D. 1975; m. Kathleen d. Michael and Kathleen Malfesi 18 Oct. 1969; one s. Kristen Graham; SCIENTIST, RAD. BIOL., AECL CHALK RIVER 1993– ; and DIR. DNA LAB, QUEEN'S UNIV.; Adjunct Asst. Prof. Queen's Univ. 1986– ; postdoctoral rsch. in med. biochem. and pediatrics Univ. of Calgary 1975, Profl. Assoc. 1979; Visiting Sci. Fellowship NSERC Biol. Div. AECL Chalk River 1980, Staff Biochem. with Bio Logicals 1981–83; Dir. Oligonucleotide Synthesis Lab., Dept. of Biochem., Queen's Univ. 1983–93; author various papers, abstracts, presentations; mem. Candn. Biochem. Soc.; Home: 1069 Bauder Cres., Kingston, Ont. K7P 1M6; Office: Kingston, Ont. K7L 3N6.

**DEUTSCH, Antal,** B.Com., Ph.D.; educator; b. Budapest, Hungary 11 May 1936; s. Ervin and Isabella M. (Fabri) D.; e. Sir George Williams Coll. Montreal B.Com. 1959; McGill Univ. Ph.D. 1967; m. Hanna d. Apolonia and Macies Zowall 26 July 1986; one d. Julia Alexandra Karen; CHAIR, DEPT. OF ECONOMICS 1992– ; and PROF. OF ECON. McGILL UNIV. 1979– ; Lectr. present Univ. 1962–64, Asst. Prof. 1966–67, Assoc. Prof. 1967–79; Asst. Prof. Queen's Univ. 1964–66; Visiting Scholar Harvard Univ. 1979–80; Cons. Pension Reform Tax Policy Div. Dept. Finance Ottawa 1983; Visiting Fellow Inst. S.E. Asian Studies Singapore 1986–87; Mem., Taskforce on Hungary, Harvard Inst. for Internat. Development 1990; Advisor on pension reform, Min. of Finance and Min. of Welfare, Republic of Hungary 1991– ; Gov. McGill Univ. 1975–77; author or co-author various publs.; mem. Candn. Econ. Assn.; Am. Econ. Assn.; McGill Assn. Univ. Teachers (Pres. 1971–72); recreations: fishing, reading; Home: 462 Lansdowne, Westmount, Que. H3Y 2V2; Office: 855 Sherbrooke St. W., Montreal, Que. H3A 2T7.

**DEVENYI, Robert G.,** M.D., FRCS(C), FACS.; vitreoretinal surgeon, university professor; b. Hamilton, Ont. 28 Dec. 1958; s. Paul and Mary Eve D.; e. Don Mills C.I. (Hons.); Univ. of Toronto M.D. (Hons.) 1983; Ophth. Residency FRCS(C) 1987; Med. Coll. of Wisconsin, Retinal Surgery Fellow 1988; m. Diane M. d. Bohdan and Micheline Slonetsky 10 June 1984; children: Tyler, Simon, Aliza; DIRECTOR, RETINAL SERVICE, THE TORONTO HOSPITAL, UNIV. OF TORONTO 1992– ; Vitreoretinal Surgeon, Hosp. for Sick Children, Mt. Sinai Hosp. and Women's Coll. Hosp. 1988– ; performs between 500–600 complicated vitreoretinal surgeries per year & 1500–2000 vitreoretinal laser surgeries per year; Asst. Prof. of Ophthal., Univ. of Toronto; Dir., Technical Services, Dept. of Ophthal., Univ. of Toronto; Chair, Operating Room Ctte., Ophth., The Toronto Hosp.; Alpha Omega Alpha Honor Med. Soc.; Summa Cum Laude Grad. (Med.), Univ. of Toronto 1993; Fellow, Royal Coll. of Surgeons of Canada; Am. Coll. of Surgeons; author of over 40 sci. articles, abstracts & presentations; recreations: golf, running, squash; Home: 65 Gordon Rd., Willowdale, Ont. M2P 1E3; Office: 399 Bathurst St., 6EC-036, Toronto, Ont. M5T 2S8.

**DEVER, Donald A.,** B.S.A., M.Sc., Ph.D.; agricultural scientist; b. Sudbury, Ont. 18 Sept. 1926; s. late John Andrew and Vona Mae (Chisholm) D.; e. Ont. Agric. Coll. (now Univ. of Guelph), B.S.A. 1949; Univ. of Wis., M.Sc. 1950, Ph.D. 1953; m. Elva May, d. late Charles Evan Carter, Guelph, Ont.; EXTVE. DIR., CANADIAN SPECIAL CROPS ASSOC. 1992– ; former Pres., Canada Grains Council; Past Dir., Western Transportation Adv. Council; past Chrmn., Biomass Energy Inst., Winnipeg; Villa Rosa, Wpg.; past Pres., Manitoba Club (Winnipeg); Project Leader, Fruit Insect Project, Biol. Control Laboratory, Canada Dept. of Agric., Belleville, Ont., 1946–49; Asst. Prof., Dept. of Entom., Univ. of Wis., 1953–56; Co-ordinator Fungicide Devel., Ortho Div., Chevron Chemical Co. (Div. of Standard Oil of Cal.), 1956–62; Tech. Dir., Niagara Chemicals (Div. of FMC Machinery & Chemicals Ltd.) 1962; Mgr. Internat. Devel., New York 1968–69; served with RCAF as Wireless Air Gunner, 1943–45; author or co-author of over 50 scient. and popular articles; el. Pres., Candn. Agric. Chemicals Assn., 1967; mem., Agric. Inst. Can. (Vice-Pres., Agric. Pesticide Tech. Soc., 1966–67); Entom. Soc. Am.; Entom. Soc. Can.; Past Dir., GIFAP, Brussels, Belgium; Anglican; recreations: golf, painting, woodworking; Home: 18 Holdsworth Ave., Winnipeg, Man. R3P 0P2; Address: 900 – 360 Main St., Winnipeg, Man. R3C 3Z3.

**DEVERELL, Rex Johnson,** B.A., B.D., S.T.M.; playwright; b. Toronto, Ont. 17 July 1941; s. Joseph and Ruby Gwendolyn (Johnson) D.; e. McMaster Univ., B.A. 1963, B.D. 1966 (Pres., Dramatic Soc. & Mem., Hon. Soc. 1963); Union Theol. Sem., S.T.M. 1967; m. Rita d. Versie and Hugh Shelton 24 May 1967; one s.: Shelton Ramsay; playwright; Res. Playwright, Globe Theatre 1975–90; Pastor, Baptist Church, St. Thomas, Ont. 1967–70; Performer & Writer, Studio Lab Theatre 1970–71; author: 'The Riel Commission' 1986 (Major Armstrong Award) and other radio & tv scripts; 'Shortshrift' 1972, 'The Copetown City Kite Crisis' 1973, 'Sarah's Play' 1974, 'Underground Lake' 1975, 'The Shinbone General Store Caper' 1975, 'The Uphill Revival' 1976, 'Superwheel' 1978, 'You Want Me To Be Grown Up, Don't I?' 1978, 'The Gadget' 1979, 'Melody Meets the Baglady' 1985, 'Fallout' 1985, 'Switching Places' 1986, 'Weird Kid' 1987, 'Inventor' 1988, 'Video Wars' 1991, 'The Short Circuit' 1993 (children's plays); 'Boiler Room Suite' 1976, 'Medicare!' 1980, 'Drift' 1980, 'Black Powder' 1981, 'Righteousness' 1983, 'Mandarin Oranges' 1984, 'Beyond Batoche' 1985, 'Resuscitation of a Dying Mouse' 1986, 'Quartet for Three Actors' 1987, 'Afternoon of the Big Game' 1988, 'Mandarin Oranges II' 1989, 'The Realm of Possibilities' 1993 (adult plays) (dates refer to 1st prodns.); librettist: 'Boiler Room Suite' (composer Q. Doolittle) 1989; 'Land' (composer Stephen McNeff) 1990; translator: 'The Oresteia' (Aeschylus) 1981; 'Servant of Two Masters' 1990; recipient, Candn. Authors Assn. Award 1978; mem., Amnesty Internat.; A.C.T.R.A.; Equity; Sask. Writers' Guild; Past Chair, Playwrights Union of Can.; Past Extve., Guild of Candn. Playwrights; recreations: reading, walking, violin scraping, choir, cycling; Address: 36 Dentonia Park Ave., Toronto, Ont. M4C 1W7.

**DEVERELL, William Herbert,** B.A., LL.B.; lawyer; author; b. Regina, Sask. 4 March 1937; s. Robert J. and Grace Amy (Barber) D.; e. Univ. of Sask. B.A., LL.B.; m. Tekla; children: Daniel Mark, Tamara Lise; called to Bar of B.C. 1964; Hon. Dir., B.C. Civil Liberties Assn.; Writers Guild of Canada; Writers Union Can.; author 'Needles' 1979; 'High Crimes' 1981; 'Mecca' 1983; 'The Dance of Shiva' 1984; 'Platinum Blues' 1988; 'Mindfield' 1989; 'Fatal Cruise' (non-fiction novel) 1991; created TV series 'Street Legal'; Home: North Pender Island, B.C. V0N 2M0.

**de VILALLONGA, Jesus Carlos;** artist; b. Sta. Coloma de Farners, Spain 10 Mar. 1927; e. Univ. of Madrid and Barcelona, Arch., 1944–49; Escola de Belles Arts de St. Jordi, Barcelona, 1948–51; Ecole des Beaux Arts, Paris 1952–54; one man exhbns. incl.: Dominion Gallery, Montreal 1959, '73, '77, '80, '83, '86, 88; Galerie Art Contemporaine, Paris, 1982, '87; Galerie Esperanza, Montreal 1988, '89; EP Galerie, Düsseldorf 1984, '85; Galeria Juana Mordó, Madrid 1976, '82; Dau al Set, Barcelona 1976, '79, '81; Sagittarius Gall., New York 1970; Portal Gall., London 1965; rep. in permanent colls.: Musée des Beaux-Arts de Montreal, Musée d'Art Contemporain, Montreal; Bibliothèque Nationale, Paris; Museo Español de Arte Contemporaneo, Madrid; Univ. of Toronto; Museum of Fine Arts, Boston; Museu d'Art Contemporani, Barcelona; Musée de la Province de Québec, etc.; Address: 4050 Marlowe, Montreal, Que. H4A 3M3 and Calvet 31, ático 4a, 08021 Barcelona Spain.

**de VILLIERS, Marq,** B.A.; journalist; b. Bloemfontein, S. Africa 22 Oct. 1940; s. Rene Marquard and Moira Grace (Franklin) de V.; e. Univ. of Cape Town B.A. 1959; London Sch. of Econ. Dip. Internat. Relations 1961; m. Sheila d. John and Edythe Hirtle 20 March 1965; EDITORIAL DIRECTOR, WHERE MAGAZINES INTERNATIONAL 1993– ; Reporter and writer S. African newspapers 1959–60; Reporter and ed. writer Toronto Telegram 1962–65, Feature Writer 1967–69, Moscow Bureau 1969–71; Reporter Reuters London and Spain 1965; Cape Times, S. Africa 1966; Prof. Ryerson Polytech. Inst. 1971–77; Rsch. Fellow Biblioteque Nationale Paris 1977; Exec. Ed. 'Toronto Life' 1978–82, Editor 1982–92, Publisher 1992–93; author: 'White Tribe Dreaming: Apartheid's Bitter Roots. Notes of an 8th generation Afrikaner' 1987; 'Down the Volga in a Time of Troubles: a Journey through post-perestroika Russia' 1991; 'The Heartbreak Grape: the Search for the Perfect Pinot Noir' 1993; Office: 70 The Esplanade, Toronto, Ont. M5E 1R2.

**DEVINE, Hon. Grant,** M.L.A., B.S.A., M.Sc., M.B.A., Ph.D., P.Ag.; politician; b. Regina, Sask. 1944; e. Univ. of Sask. B.S.A. (Agric. Econ.) 1967; Univ. of Alta. M.Sc. (Agric. Econ.) 1969, M.B.A. 1970; Ohio State Univ. Ph.D. (Agric. Econ.) 1976; m. Chantal Guillaume July 1966; children: Michelle, Monique, David, John William, Camille; PRESIDENT, GRANT DEVINE MANAGEMENT INC.; Bd. of Dirs., Cominco Fertilizers; Upton Oil; Earthwhile Developments; NuGrain Inc.; Specializing in agriculture, marketing, energy and Chinese business development consulting; Marketing Specialist Fed. Govt. Ottawa, Agric. commodity Leg. 1970–72; Adv. to Food Prices Review Bd. and Prov. Govts.; el. Assoc. Prof. of Agric. Econ. Univ. of Sask. 1975–79; author numerous papers Candn. and U.S. prof. journs.; mem. Am. Econ. Assn.; Am. Marketing Assn.; Am. Assn. Consumer Research; Candn. Agric. Econ. Soc. (recipient Cert. of Merit); Consumer's Assn. Can.; Leader of P.C. Party of Saskatchewan and Leader of the Opposition 1991–92; Leader of P. Cons. Party of Sask. 1979–92; el. M.L.A. for Estevan and Premier of Sask. 1982–91; Min. of Agriculture 1985–91; re-el. 1986; Hon. Trustee, Institute for Society and Humanity, Univ. of Saskatchewan; Hon. Patron, The Diefenbaker Society; actively involved in family farm Lake Valley, Sask.; previously engaged in studying grain and livestock marketing opportunities, inland terminals and freight rate structures; recipient 1983 Vanier Award; named 'Free Trader of the Year', Sask. Chamber of Commerce 1988; recreations: golf, skiing, baseball; Office: 265 Legislative Bldg., 2405 Legislative Dr., Regina, Sask. S4S 0B3; Business: Suite 1000, 1777 Victoria Ave., Regina, Sask. S4P 4K5.

**DEVINE, Robin Lynn;** automobile executive; broadcaster; journalist; lecturer; b. Toronto, Ont. 12 Oct. 1954; d. Roy Bruce and Margaret (Mitchell) D.; m. Kazimierz s. Anne and Edward Konkel 17 Feb. 1979; one d: Laura Grace Konkel; OWNER/OPERATOR, CLASSICALLY YOURS...AUTOMOBILES LTD. 1983– ; Dir., Ontario Development Corp. 1988; 1st & only woman in Can. to own & operate major auto. distributorship, Checker Automobiles 1978–82; President/Principal, Classically Yours...Automobiles Ltd. 1983–87; Creator, 'Wannabee' ® concept & characters 1985; Bd. Chrmn., Auto Group Internat., 1st mfr. of reproduction automobiles in N.A. to become a publicly owned co. (predecessor-Classically Yours...) 1987; 1st person in Can. to mass market repro. autos. entrenching Replicar Industry; Bus. Expert, CKO Radio nat. prog., 'Cover to Cover...About Business' 1986; Contbr. Ed. & Writer for AfterMarket Canada (internat. bus. pub.) 1985– ; Lectr., Ont. Women's Directorate; Founding mem., Bus. Adv. Bd., Mount Saint Vincent Univ., Halifax 1987; Mem., Empire Club of Can.; Metro. Toronto Bd. of Trade (Community Issues Ctte.).

**DEVINS, Jeffrey P.,** B.Comm., M.B.A.; executive; b. Winnipeg, Man. 18 Apr. 1949; s. Martin R. and Sandra (Love) D.; e. Univ. of Alta. B.Comm. 1972, M.B.A. 1973; PRES. J.P. DEVINS & ASSOCIATES LTD. 1976– ; and URBANEX DEVELOPMENT CORP. 1986– ; Dir., Primary Investments Ltd.; Duchess Holdings Ltd.; joined IBM Canada 1973; Vice Pres. Edmonton Properties Ltd. 1973–83; Pres. Norcan Properties Ltd. 1978–83 and Norcan Properties Inc. 1980–84; Exec. Vice Pres. and Chief Operating Offr., N.A. Properties Ltd. 1984–86; Exec. Vice Pres., Real Estate, North West Trust Co. 1984–86; former Bd. mem. Un. Way of Edmonton; former Dir., North West Trust Co.; Edmonton City Centre Assn; former mem. Adv. Bd. AISEC Edmonton; recreations: squash, tennis, golf, skiing; Home: Vancouver, B.C.

**de VISSER, John,** R.C.A.; photographer; b. Veghel, North-Brabant, The Netherlands 8 Feb. 1930; s. Sebastian and Christine (van Hout) de V.; e. High Sch. Holland; children: Carole, Joanne, John; freelance photographer John de Visser Photographer Ltd.; 4 one-man exhns., several group exhns.; author 'Portrait of Canada' New York Times 1970; 'The North East Coast' 1973; 'Toronto' 1977; 'Pioneer Churches' 1976; 'Newfoundland and Labrador' 1979; 'Quebec and the St. Lawrence' 1980; 'Treasures of Canada' 1980; 'Upper Canada Village' 1981; 'Southwestern Ontario' 1982; co-author 'This Rock Within the Sea: A Heritage Lost' (with Farley Mowat) 1968; 'Heritage, A Romantic Look at Early Canadian Furniture' (with Scott Symons) 1971; 'Rivers of Canada' (with Hugh McLennan) 1974; 'Winter' (with Morley Callaghan) 1974; photographic author: 'Canada. A Celebration' (with Robert Fulford) 1983; 'City Light. A Portrait of Toronto' (with Robert Fulford) 1983; 'The Farm' (with Jock Carroll) 1984; 'Visions of Canada' 1982; 'The Inland Seas' 1987; 'Port Hope. A Treasury of Early Houses' 1987; 'The University of Western Ontario' 1988; 'Montreal. A Portrait' 1988; 'Historic Newfoundland' (with Harold Horwood) 1986; 'Muskoka' (with Judy Ross) 1989; maj. contrib. to 'Canada: A Year of the Land,' 'Call Them Canadians,' 'Between Friends/Entre Amis,' 'This was Expo,' 'Windows,' 'Doors,' 'The Yellowhead Route'; maj. mag. credits incl. 'Life,' 'Time,' 'Macleans,' 'National Geographic,' 'Paris Match'; clients incl. Govts. of Can., Ont., India and maj. business firms; Past Council mem. R.C.A.; rec'd Nat. Film Bd. Gold Medal; Awards of Merit Art Dirs. Clubs Toronto, Montreal and N.Y.; Address: 317 King St. W., Cobourg, Ont. K9A 2N4.

**DEVLIN, Gerald M.,** Q.C., B.A., LL.B.; lawyer; b. Detroit, Mich. 23 Nov. 1930; s. James Joseph and Kathrine Agnes (Loewen) D.; e. Univ. of Toronto B.A. 1954; Osgoode Hall Law School LL.B. 1959; m. Irene M. d. Helen and Frank Trace 5 Oct. 1957; children: Joseph, Mary Teresa, John, Anne, Michael; VICE-PRES., GENERAL COUNSEL & SECRETARY, ONTARIO BLUE CROSS 1992– ; private law practice 1959–60; Vice-Pres., Gen. Counsel & Secy., North Am. Life Assur. Co. 1960–77; Pres., Candn. Life and Health Insur. Assoc. Inc. 1977–89; Counsel, Lang Michener Lawrence Shaw 1989–92; Vice-Pres., Gen. Counsel & Secy., Ontario Blue Cross 1992– ; Mem., Candn. Bar Assn. (Past Pres. Insurance Section); Law Soc. of U.C.; Thomas More Lawyers Guild (Past Pres.); Q.C. 1975; recreations: golf, tennis, walking; clubs: National, University; Home: 36 Butterfield Dr., Don Mills, Ont. M3A 2L8; Office: 150 Ferrand Dr., Don Mills, Ont. M3C 1H6.

**DEVLIN, M. Corinne,** M.D., FRCS(C), FACOG, FSOGC, FIBA, Dpl ABS; professor; b. St. Catharines, Ont. 12 Nov. 1937; d. Charles William and Margaret Jamesina D.; e. Mack Sch. of Nursing, grad. nurse 1958; Univ. of West. Ont., M.D. 1967; FRCS(C) 1972; FACOG 1978; FSOGC 1984; FIBA 1989; Diplomate, Am. Bd. of Sexology 1990; PROF. OF OBSTETRICS & GYNECOLOGY, MCMASTER UNIV. 1984– ; complementing clin. role as cons. obstetrician & gynecol. is interested in sex-related health care from consumer & provider perspective as well as fertility control (funded rsch. in progress); Mem., N.S.O.G.C.; S.S.S.S.; F.M.W.C.; CSRF; Ont. Coll. Phys. & Surg.; N.Y. Acad. of Sci.; author of sev. presentations & papers; recreation: naturalist activities; Office: 1200 Main St. W., Hamilton, Ont. L8N 3Z5.

**DeVOE, Irving Woodrow,** Ph.D.; scientist; educator; corporate executive; b. Brewer, Me. 4 Oct. 1936; s. Woodrow Donnison DeVoe; e. Aurora Coll. Ill. B.Sc. 1964; Univ. of Ore. Med. Sch. Ph.D. (Microbiol.) 1968; McGill Univ. post-doctoral fellow 1968–69; m. Lynne Rae d. Arthur Brookfield Parker 21 June 1960; children: Scott Irving, David Brookfield, Steven Patrick (dec.), Christopher James, Samantha Rae; PRES., METANETIX CORPORATION 1993– ; Rsch. Assoc. Argonne Nat. Lab. U.S. Atomic Energy Comn. 1969–70; Asst. Prof. Aurora Coll. Ill. 1969–70; Asst. Prof., McGill Univ. 1970, Assoc. Prof. 1975, Prof. and Chrmn. of Microbiol. & Immunol. 1978–84; Managing Dir., DeVoe-Holbein Internat. 1983–86; Dir., DeVoe-Holbein Australia Pty. Ltd. 1985–86; Chrmn., Dir. of Rsch., Metanetix Inc. 1988–91; Pres., Devoe Environ. Lab. 1991–93; Nat. Inst. of Health (U.S.) Predoctoral Fellow; served with U.S. Army (Arty.) 1954–58, U.S. Navy (Aviation) 1958–61, Vietnam; author 'Microbiology' 1977; numerous scient. papers and reviews; co-inventor and holder of numerous patents world-wide; Candn. citizen; Sigma Xi; Protestant; Address: 454 Elm St., Westmount, Qué. H3Y 3J1.

**DE VRIES, John,** B.A., M.Sc., Ph.D.; university professor; b. Eindhoven, the Netherlands 15 Dec. 1938; s. Willem and Jacoba (Koudijs) d.; e. Univ. of Utrecht, B.Sc. 1960; Sir George Williams Univ. B.A. 1965; Univ. of Wisconsin, M.Sc. 1968, Ph.D. 1973; m. Gerda d. Hendrik and Maria Sanderse 27 July 1961; children: Ingrid, Jacqueline, Erik, Lex; PROF., DEPT. OF SOCIOL. & ANTHROPOL., CARLETON UNIV. 1969– ; Actuarial clerk to chief clerk, Sun Life Assur. Co. of Can. 1961–66; Rsch. asst./systems analyst, Soc. Sci. Rsch. Inst., Univ. of Wisc. 1966–68; Rsch. Assoc., Poverty Rsch. Ctr. 1968–69; Vis. Prof. of Sociol., Univ. of Helsinki 1975–76; of Linguistics, Tilburg Univ. 1983–84; of Sociology, European Univ. Institute, Florence; Mem., Senate & Senate Extve. Ctte., Presbyterian Coll., Montreal 1986–89; Presbyterian; Mem., Internat. Sociol. Assn.; Candn. Sociol. & Anthropol. Assn.; author: 'Towards a Sociology of Language in Canada' 1986, 'Language Use in Canada' 1980; recreations: duplicate bridge, music (jazz); Home: 50 Bowhill Ave., Nepean, Ont. K2E 6S7; Office: Ottawa, Ont. K1S 5B6.

**DEVROYE, Luc,** B.Eng., Ph.D.; university professor; b. Tienen, Belgium 6 Aug. 1948; s. Frans and Lucia (Thiry) D.; e. Univ. Louvain, B.Eng. 1971; Univ. of Texas at Austin, Ph.D. 1976; m. Beatrice d. Eugene and Huguette Van Nuffel 19 May 1971; children: Natasha, Birgit; PROF., SCHOOL OF COMPUTER SCIENCE, MCGILL UNIV. 1977– ; current rsch. in probability theory & its applications in computer sci.; Steacie Fellowship 1987; author: 'Nonparametric Density Estimation: The L1 View' 1985, 'Lecture Notes on Bucket Algorithms' 1986, 'Non-Uniform Random Variate Generation' 1986, 'A Course in Density Estimation' 1987; recreations: running (best marathon to date $2^{h}$–58'06'); Home: 1250 Pine W., #950, Montreal, Que. H3G 2P5; Office: Sch. of Computer Sci., McGill Univ., Montreal, Que. H3A 2A7.

**DEWAR, Daniel Bevis,** B.A.; retired Canadian public servant; b. Kenmore, Ont. 21 Aug. 1932; s. Daniel Peter and Greta Mae (Loney) D.; e. Kenmore, Ont.; Queen's Univ. B.A. 1953; m. Barbara Ann d. late William J. Sweeney 24 Apr. 1965; children: Peter, Sarah; Cabinet Secretariat, Privy Council Office 1954–63; Treasury Bd. Secretariat 1963–73; Asst. Depy. Min. Med. Services, Dept. Nat. Health & Welfare 1973–75; Asst. Secy. Govt. Br., Ministry of State for Science and Technol. 1975–79; Depy. Secy. (Operations), Privy Council Office, 1979–82; Depy. Min., Dept. of National Defence 1982–89; Assoc. Secy. to the Cabinet and Depy. Clerk, Privy Council 1989–90; Principal, Candn. Centre for Management Development 1990–92; Protestant; Home: 9 Pellan Cres., Kanata, Ont. K2K 1J6.

**DEWAR, Garry J.;** wheat pool executive; b. Vancouver 1937; e. Vancouver; m. Shirley; 2 children; 4 grandchildren; CHIEF EXECUTIVE OFFICER, ALBERTA WHEAT POOL 1992–present; joined Pacific Elevators Limited 1957; Foreman 1974; Asst. Supt. 1975; Asst. Dir., Terminal Opns., Alberta Pool 1976; Dir., Terminal Opns. 1977; Acting Gen. Mgr. 1989; Gen. Mgr., Terminal Opns. & Deputy C.E.O. 1990; Drummond Brewing Company Ltd.; Maalsa Investments Ltd.; Pacific Elevators Limited; Western Pool Terminals Ltd.; Prairie Sun Grains Ltd.; Prince Rupert Grain Ltd.; Western Co-op. Fertilizers Limited; XCAN Grain Ltd.; Past Pres., B.C. Terminal Elevator Operators Assn.; clubs: Calgary Petroleum, Calgary C. of C., Vancouver Bd. of Trade, Bellingham Golf & Country, Richmond Winter Club; Office: P.O. Box 2700, Calgary, Alta. T2P 2P5.

**DEWAR, John Stuart,** B.Sc.; retired industrialist; b. Guelph, Ont. 24 June 1918; s. John George and Effie (Marshall) D.; e. Brown Pub. Sch. and Upper Can. Coll., Toronto, Ont.; Queen's Univ., B.Sc. (Chem. Engn.) 1941; children: Helen, John, Peter, Kenneth; m. 2ndly (Mrs.) Marian E. Prowse (who has 3 children) 1968; joined Nat. Carbon Co., Div. of Union Carbide Can. Ltd. in 1943 as Chem. Engr.; apptd. Pres. in 1955; apptd. Vice-Pres. of Union Carbide Can. Ltd. in 1956; Dir. 1959; Pres. 1965; Chrmn. and C.E.O. 1981; Dir., Can. Chemical Producers' Assn. (Chrmn. 1970); Candn. Council, Conf. Bd. of U.S. (Chrmn. 1972); Anglican; Clubs: Rosedale Golf; Lost Tree (N. Palm Beach Fla.); Home: 1007, 63 St. Clair Ave. W., Toronto, Ont. M4V 2Y9.

**DEWAR, Marion,** R.N., B.ScN., Dip. P.H.N.; former politician; b. Montreal, P.Q. 17 Feb. 1928; d. Wilson Edward and Agnes (Cunningham) Bell; e. St. Joseph's Sch. Nursing (Kingston, Ont.) 1949; Univ. Ottawa, Nursing Sci./Public Health 1969; m. Kenneth J., s. Cecil and Kathleen (Lynch) Dewar, 15 Sept. 1951; children: Robert, Elizabeth, Cathy, Paul, Elaine; EXTVE. DIR., CANDN. COUNC. ON CHILDREN & YOUTH 1989– ; Nurse, Ottawa region 1949–52; P.H.N., Ottawa 1969–71; elected Alderman 1972; Sr. Controller and Deputy Mayor 1974; Mayor of Ottawa 1978–85; Pres., New Democratic Party of Canada 1985–87; Mem. of Parliament (Hamilton Mountain) 1987–88; Bd. Dirs., Candn. Centre for Arms Control & Disarmament; Candn. Centre for Policy Alternatives; Internat. Inst. of Concern for Public Health; Counc. of Canadians; mem., Group of 78; World Federalists of Canada and others; NDP; Club: Sussex; recreations: curling; bridge; swimming; reading; Home: 869 Rex Ave., Ottawa, Ont. K2A 2P6.

**DeWARE, Hon. Mabel M.;** senator; b. Moncton, N.B. 9 Aug. 1926; d. Hugh Fraser and Mary Elizabeth Ann (Adams) Keiver; e. Moncton schools; m. Dr. Ralph B. D. 1 Aug. 1945; children: Kimberley, Peter, Michael, Joanne; SENATOR, THE SENATE OF CANADA 1990– ; first elected to N.B. Legislature general election 1978; re-elected g.e. 1982; defeated g.e. 1987; Min. of Labour and Manpower, N.B. Leg. 1978–82; Min. of Community Colleges 1983–85; Min. of Advanced Education 1985–87; Chair, Canadian Delegation to World Health Conf. on Occupational Health & Safety, Norway; Candn. Delegation to Geneva on Edn.; Delegate, Internat. Conf. on Decade for Women, Copenhagen; World Conf. on Labour Issues, Paris; N.B. Sports Hall of Fame 1976; Candn. Curling Hall of Fame as Curler/Builder Feb. 1987; received Queen's Medal for contbn. to sports 1983; Elmer Freytag Memorial Award 1983 (1st female recipient); Past Pres., Y.W.C.A. & Y.M.C.A.; Beaver Curling Club; Ladies Curling Assn.; Cyrette Club of Moncton; Second Vice-Pres., Moncton Hosp. Found.; P.C.; Baptist; recreations: bridge, golf; Home: P.O. Box 1898, Shediac, N.B. E0A 3G0; Office: Room 802, 140 Welllington St., Ottawa, Ont. K1A 0A6.

**DEWART, Leslie,** M.A., LL.B., Ph.D.; philosopher; b. Madrid, Spain 12 Dec. 1922; s. Gerardo Gonzalez and Adamina (Duarte) D.; e. Univ. of Toronto B.A. 1951, M.A. 1952, Ph.D. 1954, LL.B. 1979; m. Doreen Brennan 20 Aug. 1976; children (by first marriage): Leslie (Mrs. Philip Giroday), Elizabeth (Mrs. David McEwen), Sean, Colin; PROFESSOR EMERITUS, CENTRE FOR THE STUDY OF RELIGION, UNIV. OF TORONTO 1991– ; Prof. of Philosophy of Religion, St. Michael's Coll., Univ. of Toronto 1956–88; called to Bar of Ont. 1981; served with RCAF 1942–47; author: 'Evolution and Consciousness: The Role of Speech in the Origin and Development of Human Nature' 1989; Home: 14 Prospect St., Toronto, Ont. M4X 1C6; Office: Toronto, Ont.

**DEWDNEY, Alexander Keewatin,** M.A., Ph.D.; educator; b. London, Ont. 5 Aug. 1941; s. Selwyn Hanington and Irene Maude (Donner) D.; e. London South S.S. 1959; Univ. of W. Ont. B.A. 1964; Univ. of Waterloo M.A. 1965, Ph.D. 1974; Univ. of Mich.; m. Patricia d. Dudley and Aileen Pegg 23 May 1964; one s. Jonathan Woodsworth; ASSOC. PROF. OF COMPUTER SCI. UNIV. OF W. ONT. 1978– ; Pres. Turing Omnibus Inc. London, Ont. 1985– ; mem. Adv. Panel Prince Investments New York 1988; Cons. Bell Communications Research, Morristown, N.J. 1986–88; Cons., Info-Quest, Toronto 1988–89; Lectr. present Univ. 1968, Asst. Prof. 1974, Assoc. Prof. 1981; author: (poetry & collage) 'The Maltese Cross Movement' 1966; (novel) 'The Planiverse' 1984; (non-fiction) 'The Armchair Universe' 1988; 'The Turing Omnibus' 1989; 'The Magic Machine' 1990; 'The Tinkertoy Computer and Other Machinations' 1993; 'The New Turing Omnibus' 1993; 'Two Hundred Percent of Nothing' 1993; Editor, 'Algorithm', a programming periodical 1989–93; Columnist 'Scientific American' mag. 1984–91; recipient Hopwood Prize, Univ. of Mich. (novel) 1967; Candn. Artists '68 Award (non-narrative film) 1968; frequent speaker ednl. seminars; Bd. mem., Near E. Cultural & Ednl. Found.; recreations: bicycling, tree culture; Home: 42 Askin St., London, Ont. N6C 1E4; Office: London, Ont. N6A 5B7.

**DEWDNEY, Christopher;** poet; writer; b. London, Ont. 9 May 1951; s. Selwyn Hannington and Irene Maude (Donner) D.; e. Victoria Pub., South and Westminster Secondary Schs.; H.B. Beal Art Annex Sch. of Art; m. Suzanne Dennison; one child Calla Xanthoria Kirk; m. Lise d. William and Susan Downe; one child Tristan Alexander Downe; author 'Golders Green' 1972; 'A Palaeozoic Geology of London, Ontario' 1973, (Design Can. Award of Excellence) 1974; 'Fovea Centralis' 1975; 'Spring Trances in the Control Emerald Night' 1978; 'Alter Sublime' 1980; 'The Cenozoic Asylum' 1983; 'Predators of the Adoration, Selected Poems' 1972–82) 1983; 'The Immaculate Perception' 1986 (essays on biol. nature of consciousness); 'Permugenesis' 1987; 'The Radiant Inventory' 1988; 'Concordat Proviso Ascendant' 1991; appeared in Candn. film 'Poetry in Motion' 1982; prodn. prose poem Theatre Centre Toronto 1982; Assoc. Fellow, Winters Coll. York Univ. 1984; recipient CBC Lit. Competition 1st Prize Poetry 1986; Editor, Coach House Press 1988, Dir. 1989; Address: c/o McClelland and Stewart, 481 University Ave., Ste. 900, Toronto, Ont. M6G 2E9.

**de WEERDT, Hon. Mark Murray,** M.A., LL.B.; b. Cologne, Germany 6 May 1928; s. Hendrik Eugen and

Ina Dunbar (Murray) de W.; e. various schs., Belg. and Scot., 1935–46; Univ. of Glasgow, M.A. (Math. & Econ.) 1949; Univ. of B.C., LL.B. (Norgan Law Scholar 1953) 1955; m. Linda Anne, d. I.S.A. Hadwen, D.V.Sc., F.R.S.M., Toronto, 31 March 1956; children: Simon André, Murray Hadwen, David Lockhart, Charles Dunbar; JUDGE OF THE SUPREME COURT OF THE NORTHWEST TERRITORIES AND JUSTICE OF APPEAL OF THE COURTS OF APPEAL OF THE NORTHWEST TERRITORIES AND OF THE YUKON; read law with T.P. O'Grady, Q.C., City Solr., Victoria, B.C.; called to Bar of B.C. 1956 and to Bar of N.W.T. 1958; cr. Q.C. (Fed.) 1968; Cross & O'Grady, Victoria, Assoc. Solr. 1956–57; Adv. Counsel, Dept. of Justice, Ottawa 1957–58; Crown Atty., Yellowknife, N.W.T. 1958–63; Agt. of Atty. Gen. of Can., Yellowknife 1958–66; Pub. Adm. for N.W.T. 1965–67; formed de Weerdt & Searle 1963–64 and successor firms to 1971; Magistrate, Northwest Territories 1971–73; General Solicitor, Insurance Corp. of B.C. 1974–76; Senior Counsel, Dept. of Justice at Vancouver 1976–79; Gen. Counsel and Dir., Dept. of Justice Vancouver 1979–81; Extve. mem., Yellowknife Bd. Trade 1960–62; mem., Nat. Comte., N. & Arctic Scouting, Boy Scouts of Can. 1966–70; Trustee and Bd. Vice-Chrmn., Yellowknife Pub. Sch. 1964–68; Pres., N.W.T. Bar Assn. 1964–66, 1969–70; Life Mem., Candn. Inst. for Admin. of Justice; Dir., Candn. Judges' Conf. 1982–89; mem., Candn. Judicial Council 1985–87, 1989–91, 1993–95; Internat. Comm. of Jurists; Candn. Bar Assn.; Candn. Human Rights Foundation; United Nations Assn. (Canada); Osgoode Soc.; Selden Soc.; Address: PO Box 1439, Yellowknife, N.W.T. X1A 2P1; Chambers: The Court House, Yellowknife, N.W.T.

**DEWEY, John M.,** B.Sc., Ph.D., F.Inst.P.; educator; b. Portsmouth, Eng. 23 Mar. 1930; s. Stanley George and Ilva (Hollingsworth) D.; came to Canada 1956; e. St. John's Coll., Portsmouth, Eng. 1947; Portsmouth Coll. of Technol. 1947–50; B.Sc. (London) 1950, Ph.D. (London) 1964; m. Jean Evelyn, d. Arthur Frederick Moon, 16 Aug. 1951; children: Elizabeth Sarah, Richard Kelvin; PROF. OF PHYSICS, UNIV. OF VICTORIA since 1965; Sr. Science and Math. Master, De La Salle Coll., Jersey, Channel Islands 1950; Head Aerophysics & Shock Tubes Sect., Suffield Exper. Station, Ralston, Alta. 1956; Dean of Grad. Studies, Assoc. Vice Pres. Academic (Rsch.), Univ. of Victoria 1977–1985; Depy. Min. for Universities, Science and Communications, B.C. 1985; Depy. Min. for Post Secondary Education, Prov. of B.C. 1986–87; Pres. & C.E.O., Dewey McMillin & Assoc. Ltd. 1988– ; Fellow, Inst. Physics (U.K.); mem., Candn. Assn. Physicists; Am. Inst. Physics; Candn. Assn. Univ. Research Administrators (Pres. 1985); Candn. Assoc. Graduate Schools (Pres. 1980–81); recipient, Fraunhofer Gesellschaft Ernst Mach Medal 1990; has published numerous research reports and papers in learned and prof. mags. and journs. on shock and blast waves, and high speed photography; recreations: sailing, badminton, tennis; Club: Royal Victoria Yacht; Home: 1741 Feltham Rd., Victoria, B.C. V8N 2A4.

**DEWHURST, Margaret,** B.Comm., R.S.W. (Alta.); social worker; b. Widnes, Lancs. England 24 Aug. 1933; d. Frank and Grace (Brown) Dransfield; e. Wyggeston Girls Sch.; Purley Co. Sch. for Girls (County Scholarship) 1952; Univ. of Birmingham B.Comm. (Hons.) 1955; Univ. of London, London Sch. of Econ. Cert. in Mental Health 1959; m. William George s. William and Elspeth Dewhurst 17 Sept. 1960; children: Timothy A., Susan J.; DIRECTOR, PERSONNEL & SUPPORT SERV., CITY OF EDMONTON COMMUNITY & FAMILY SERVICES 1986– ; var. social work positions U.K. 1955–69; Sr. Social Worker, Edmonton Gen. Hosp. 1971–77; Sr. Social Worker, City of Edmonton Community & Family Serv. 1977–78; Soc. Serv. Ctr. Supvr. 1978–84; Dir., Personnel and Support Services 1985; extensive presentations on social work, etc.; Keynote Speaker, Alta. Assn. of Social Workers 1991; Consultant, Russian Assn. of Social Pedagogues & Social Workers 1991; Past Pres. & Bd. Mem., Candn. Social Work Foundation 1985– ; Pres., Community Orgn. Employee Benefit Soc. of Alta. 1988– ; Mem., Alta. Assn. of Social Workers (Past-President 1985–89); Candn. Assn. of Social Workers (Pres. 1991–93); Internat. Fed. of Social Workers (Treas. 1992– ;); extensive executive ctte. work; Nom., Edmonton YWCA Woman of the Year Award 1989, '90; volunteer awards, United Way & Christmas Bur. of Edmonton; Mem., United Way of Edmonton & Area; co-author: 'Effects of Late Onset Epilepsy' 1961, 'The Canadian Health Care System with Speical Reference to Mental Health Services' 1992; editor: 'On Track' (newsletter) 1985–88; author of various articles & commentaries; reviewer; Home: 92 Fairway Dr., Edmonton, Alta. T6J 2C5; Office: 5th Floor, Centennial Library, 7 Sir Winston Churchill Sq., Edmonton, Alta. T5J 2V4.

**DEWHURST, William George,** B.M., B.Ch., F.R.S.M., F.R.C.P.(C), F.R.C. Psych., F.A.C.P., F.A.P.A.; F.A.P.P.A.; physician; educator; b. Frosterley, Eng. 21 Nov. 1926; s. William and Elspeth Leslie (Begg) D.; e. Open Exhibitioner (Natural Sciences) Oxford Univ. B.A. 1947, B.M., B.Ch. 1950, M.A. 1962; M.R.C.P. 1955; London Univ. Acad. Postgrad. Dipl. in Psychol. Med. with Distinction 1961; Cert. Specialist Alta. 1970; Foundation mem. Royal Coll. Psychiatry 1971; m. Margaret d. Frank Dransfield, Southwater, Sussex, Eng. 17 Sept. 1960; children: Timothy Andrew, Susan Jane; PROF. & DIR. EMERITUS OF PSYCHIATRY AND NEUROCHEM. RESEARCH UNIT, UNIV. OF ALTA. 1990– , Assoc. Prof. 1969, Prof. 1972– ; and Chrmn. of Psychiatry 1975–90; Co. Dir., Neurochem. Research Unit 1979–90; Hon. Prof., Pharmacy and Pharmaceutical Sci. 1979– ; Hon. Prof., Oncology 1983– ; Mem., Alta. Attorney Gen. Bd. of Review 1991– ; Mem., N.W.T. Bd. of Review; Vice-Pres. Bd., Children's Assoc. (CASA) 1991– ; Consultant Psychiatrist, Royal Alexandra Hosp., Edmonton Gen. Hosp. and Univ. of Alberta Hosps.; Ponoka General Hospital and Alta. Hospital Ponoka; Past Chrmn., Ethics Consultative Ctte, Univ. of Alta. Hosps., Vision 2000 (Planning) Ctte., Univ. of Alta Hosps.; Past Chrmn., Med. Staff Adv. Bd., Past Chrmn., Edmonton Psychiatric Services Planning Ctte.; Past Mem., Bd. of Dir., Centre for Gerontology, Univ. of Alta.; Lectr. Inst. Psychiatry, London Univ. 1962–64; Sr. Lectr. and Consultant Physician, Inst. Psychiatry, Maudsley Hosp. London 1965–69; served as Offr. in charge of med. wards 33rd Gen. Hosp. Hong Kong 1952–54, rank Capt.; mem. Edmonton Local Bd. Health 1974–76; Past Univ. of Alta. Rep. on Prov. Mental Health Adv. Council and mem. Rsch. Comte.; mem. Prof. Scient. Adv. Comte. Candn. Psychiatric Rsch. Foundn; mem. various ed. bds.; author or co-author numerous med. publs.; co-editor 3 books; past Pres. Candn. Psychiatric Assn. (past Rep., Scient. Counc.); past Pres. Alta. Psychiatric Assn.; past Pres. Candn. Coll. Neuropsychopharmacol.; Awarded College Medal 1993; past Chrmn. Candn. Assn. Profl. Psychiatry; Councillor, W. Candn. Dist. Br. Am. Psychiatric Assn.; mem. various other internat. and nat. socs.; Anglican; recreations: books, football, athletics, hockey, music, chess; Home: 92 Fairway Dr., Edmonton, Alta. T6J 2C5; Office: Mackenzie Centre, Univ. of Alta., Edmonton, Alta. T6G 2B7.

**DEWITT, David B.,** M.A., Ph.D.; educator; b. London, Eng. 11 Sept. 1948; s. Vernon L. and Marion (Berghold) D.; e. The Hebrew Univ. of Jerusalem 1967–68; Univ. of B.C. B.A. 1971; Univ. of Chicago 1971–72; Stanford Univ. M.A. 1973, Ph.D. 1977; m. Susan d. Abraham and Goldie Davis 25 Aug. 1983; three children; DIR. CENTRE FOR INTERNAT. AND STRATEGIC STUDIES, YORK UNIV. 1988– , Prof. of Pol. Sci. 1993– ; Postdoctoral Fellow, Inst. Internat. Relations Univ. of B.C. 1976–79; Asst. and Assoc. Prof. of Pol. Sci. Univ. of Alta. 1979–83; Assoc. Prof. of Pol. Sci. present univ. 1983–92 and Dir. Undergrad. Studies 1985–87; co-author 'Canada as a Principal Power' 1983; ed. and contbg. author 'Nuclear Non-Profileration and Global Security' 1987; co-ed. and contbg. author 'The Middle East at the Crossroads' 1983; 'Conflict Management in the Middle East' 1987; 'East-West Arms Control: Challenges for the Western Alliance' 1992; 'Building a New Global Order: Emerging Trends in International Security' 1993; 'Confidence-Building in the Arab-Israeli Conflict' 1993; 'Common, Comprehensive and Cooperative Security in Asia Pacific' 1994; 'Canada's International Security Policy' 1994; mem. Internat. Inst. Strategic Studies; Internat. Studies Assn.; Candn. Pol. Sci. Assn.; Candn. Inst. Internat. Affairs; Candn. Inst. Strategic Studies; Office: 4700 Keele St., North York, Ont. M3J 1P3.

**DEWITT, Frank J.,** B.Sc., M.B.A.; cement executive; b. Perth, Ont. 16 Nov. 1929; s. Thomas Zephenia and Loretta Ellen (Nagle) D.; e. St. Patrick's Coll. B.Sc. 1950; Queen's Univ. B.Sc. (Hons. Civil Eng.) 1954; York Univ. M.B.A. 1974; m. Melba V. Hughes 30 July 1955; children: Constance, Matthew, Virginia; PRESIDENT & CHIEF EXECUTIVE OFFICER, ST. LAWRENCE CEMENT 1989– ; General Mgr., Dufferin Aggregates / Dufferin Concrete 1969–72; Pres., Dufferin Aggregates 1972–81; Sr. Vice-Pres., Ont. Div. 1981–88; Extve. VIce-Pres. & Chief Operating Offr. 1988–89; Dir., Holnam Inc. (US); Portland Cement Assn. (US); Philip Environment Corp. (Can.); recreations: golf, gardening, reading, travel; clubs: Mount Stephen, Rideau, Kanawaki; Home: 3577 Atwater St., Central Bldg., Apt. 1010, Montreal, Que. H3H 2R2; Office: 1945 Graham Blvd., Mount Royal, Que. H3R 1H1.

**DeWOLF, Vice-Admiral Harry George,** C.B.E. (1946), D.S.O. (1944), D.S.C.; R.C.N. retired; b. Bedford, N.S. 26 June 1903; s. Henry George and Kate A. (Fitzmaurice) D.; e. Roy. Naval Coll. of Can., Grad. 1921; Roy. Naval Staff Coll., Greenwich, Eng., Grad. 1937; m. Gwendolen Fowle, d. Thomas St. George Gilbert, Bermuda, 5 May 1931; children: Suzette (dec.), James; joined R.C.N., 1918; Commdr. H.M.C.S. 'St. Laurent' 1939–40, 'Haida' 1943–44, 'Warrior' 1947, 'Magnificent' 1948; Rear Adm., Flag Offr. Pacific Coast 1948–50; Vice Chief of Naval Staff 1950–52; Chrmn., Candn. Jt. Staff, Wash., D.C. 1952–55; promoted Vice-Adm. 1956; Chief of Naval Staff 1956–60; retired 1961; Offr., Legion of Merit (U.S.A.) 1946; Legion of Hon. (France) 1947; King Haakon Cross of Liberation, 1948; D. M.Sc. h. RMC 1966, RRMC 1980; Presbyterian; recreation: golf; Homes: 200 Rideau Terrace, Apt. 1006, Ottawa, Ont. K1M 0Z3.

**DEWSON, Michael Richard James,** B.Sc., M.A., Ph.D.; university professor/administrator; b. Edmonton, Alta. 25 Dec. 1948; s. Raymond Brian and Joan Evelyn (White) D.; e. McGill Univ. B.Sc. 1969; Univ. of Man. M.A. 1971, Ph.D. 1981; m. Monique d. Georges and Aline Lamarche 13 June 1970; children: François Sébastien, Vanessa Stéphanie; DIRECTOR, OFFICE OF INSTITUTIONAL RESEARCH, LAURENTIAN UNIV. 1993– ; joined Dept. of Psychology, Laurentian Univ. 1975; Chrmn., Dept. of Psychology 1980; Dean of Social Sciences 1984–89; Vice Pres., Academic (Faculty & Services) 1989–91; Ctr. for Rsch. in Human Devel.; Registered Psychologist, Prov. of Ont.; Mem., Candn. Psychol. Assn.; Soc. for Rsch. in Child Devel.; author of several sci. articles in psychology jours.; recreations: sailing; Home: Box 19, Site ll, SS #1, 709 Bedford Court, Sudbury, Ont. P3E 2V3; Office: Sudbury, Ont. P3E 2C6.

**DEXTER, Robert Paul,** B.Comm., LL.B.; barrister; b. Halifax, N.S. 11 Dec. 1951; s. Carl Edmund and Jean Rankin (Collins) D.; e. Queen Elizabeth H.S. 1970; Dalhousie Univ. B.Comm. 1973 (I.W. Killam Scholar), LL.B. 1976 (Sir James Dunn Scholar); one d.: Angela Elizabeth; PARTNER, STEWART McKELVEY STIRLING SCALES 1982– ; joined firm in 1977; Chrmn., Chief Extve. Offr. & majority shareholder, Maritime Travel Limited 1978– ; Vice Chrmn., N.S. Bus. Devel. Corp. 1992– ; Dir., Empire Co. Limited 1987– ; Wajax Limited 1988– ; Sobeys Inc. 1989– ; Merchant Private Ltd. 1989– ; Lawton's Drug Stores Limited 1990– ; National Sea Products Ltd. 1992– ; Pres., Halifax Bd. of Trade 1993; Mem., N.S. Barristers' Soc.; Candn. Bar Assn.; Young Pres. Orgn., Atlantic chap.; recreations: sailing, skiing, tennis; Home: 6931 Tupper Grove, Halifax, N.S. B3H 2M7; Office: Purdy's Wharf, Tower One, 1959 Upper Water St., P.O. Box 997, Halifax, N.S. B3J 2X2.

**DEY, Janet Cummins,** B.A.; real estate executive; b. London, Ont.; d. Charles Richard and Alma Esther Patricia (Mark) Cummins; e. Lachine and Montréal High Schs. 1959; Queen's Univ. B.A. 1962; two d. Sarah, Claudia; VICE PRES., DEVELOPMENT, WESTNOR (one of the Weston group of companies) 1990– ; Prog. Dir. and Cons. YWCA Halifax, Boston and Nat. Office Toronto 1963–70; Cons. Nat. Health & Welfare and Nat. Film Bd. Toronto 1971–73; City Planner, City of Toronto 1974–80; CBC 1980–90: in various senior positions responsible for the CBC's Broadcast Centre Devel. Project, last position as Corporate Dir., Real Estate and Development; mem. Council Ont. Assn. Archs. 1985–89; mem., ACPRAM, NCC (Adv. Ctte. on Planning and Real Asset Mgmt., National Capital Commission) 1991–93; Mem. of Bd., Chair of Long Range Planning Ctte. 1992–94; Lectr., York Univ. MBA Program, Real Property Development 1993–94; Club: Toronto Lawn Tennis; Home: 193 Cottingham St., Toronto, Ont. M4V 1C4; Office: 22 St. Clair Ave. E., Ste. 200, Toronto, Ont. M4T 2S5.

**DEY, Peter,** Q.C., B.Sc., LL.B., LL.M.; lawyer; b. Ottawa, Ont. 3 Mar. 1941; s. James Jardine and Jesse Elizabeth (Comba) D.; e. Queen's Univ. B.Sc. Mech. Engr. 1963; Dalhousie Univ. LL.B. 1966; Harvard Univ. LL.M. 1967; m. Phyllis Ortved; children: Sarah, Claudia, Anouk; stepchildren: Allie, Chat, John; PARTNER, OSLER, HOSKIN & HARCOURT 1973 and 1985– ; articled with Osler, Hoskin & Harcourt 1967–68; admitted to Bar of Ont. 1969; Chairman,Ontario Securities Commission 1983–85; author several articles on Candn. securities industry and law; cr. Q.C. 1983; recreations: skiing, tennis, fishing; Clubs: Toronto Lawn Tennis; le Club de Pèche Lac Claw; Office: Box 50, First Canadian Place, Toronto, Ont. M5X 1B8.

**DEYELL, The Honourable Mr. Justice Roy Victor;** Court of Queen's Bench; b. Frobisher, Sask. 23 Apr. 1925; s. Albert and Amy Mary (Mulligan) D.; e.

Estevan C.I.; Univ. of Toronto; Univ. of Sask., B.A. 1948, LL.B. 1950; m. Barbara d. Stuart and Mattie Kendry 24 June 1950; children: Bert, Brian, Colleen; Lawyer, McLaws & Co. 1951–86; Parlee McLaws 1986–87; admitted to Alta. Bar 1951; Q.C. 1967; Chrmn., Real Property Section, Candn. Bar 1973–75; Dir., Petro-Can. 1984–87; Columbia Seed Co. Ltd. 1982–87; Chrmn., Alta. Blue Cross 1980–90; Blue Cross Life Insur. Co. of Can. 1986–87; Life Mem., Calgary S. Progressive Conservative Assn. 1968 (has held num. extve. party positions locally & nationally, most recent Vice-Chrmn., P.C. Can. Fund 1977–83); Pres. P.C. Assn. Alta. 1958–59 & 1985–87; Heritage Park Soc. 1970 (Dir. 1963–64); (Hon.), Calgary Real Estate Bd. 1978; Alta. Hosp. Assn. 1984; recipient Queen's Silver Jubilee Medal 1977; Alta. Achievement Award 1986; City of Calgary Centennial Award of Merit 1987; Chrmn., Bd. of Govs., Mount Royal Coll. 1981–87; Citizen of the Year 1989; Mem., Calgary Gen. Hosp. Bd. 1963–65; Metro. Calgary & Rural Gen. Hosp. Bd. Dt. #93 1968–80 (Chrmn. 1969–72, 1975–78); Trustee, Alta. Hosp. Assn. 1972–78 (Pres. 1976–77); Robert & Mary Stanfield Found.; United Ch. (Pres., Knox Un. Ch. A.O.T.S. 1959; Past Chrmn., Bd. of Stewards); Alderman, City of Calgary 1963–65; clubs: Calgary Petroleum, Glencoe, Kiwanis of Calgary, Downtown (Dir. 1963–65, Pres. 1966, mem. 1959–88); Home: 104, 5555 Elbow Dr. S.W., Calgary, Alta. T2V 1H7.

**DIAMOND, Abel J.,** M.A.(Oxon.), M.Arch.(Penn.), F.R.A.I.C., A.R.I.B.A., N.C.A.R.B.(Cert.), M.C.I.P., M.A.I.P., R.C.A.; architect; b. S. Africa 8 Nov. 1932; s. Jacob and Rachel (Werner) D.; e. Durban High Sch. 1950; Univ. of Capetown B.Arch (with Distinction) 1956; Oxford Univ. M.A. 1958; (Rugby Blue 1957); Univ. of Pa. M.Arch. 1962; m. Gillian Mary d. Kenneth Huggins 11 Aug. 1959; children: Andrew Michael, Alison Suzanne Katherine; SR. PARTNER, A.J. DIAMOND, DONALD SCHMITT AND CO. 1975– ; Pres. A.J. Diamond Planners Limited; Arch., Durban, S. Africa 1956; Partner, Cameron, Phillips & Diamond, Durban 1959–61; Asst. Arch., Louis I. Kahn, Philadelphia 1963–64; Arch., Toronto 1965–68; Princ., Diamond & Myers, Toronto 1969–75; Instr. in Arch. Univ. of Pa. and Drexel Inst. of Technol. Philadelphia 1962–63; Asst. Prof. Univ. Pa. 1963–64; Asst. Prof. Univ. of Toronto 1964, Assoc. Prof. (inaugurated postgrad. Urban Design) 1967–70; Assoc. Prof. (part-time) of Environmental Studies York Univ. 1970–72, Prof. (part-time) 1970–72; Tutor in Arch. Univ. of Toronto 1980–81; Adjunct Prof. Univ. of Texas, Arlington 1982–84; keynote speaker various meetings incl. 150th Anniversary Royal Inst. Australian Archs. Perth 1979; recipient Thornton White Prize in Arch. Univ. Capetown 1951; Graham Foundation Scholarship (USA) 1962; Marley Scholarship (S.Africa) 1962; recipient 30 nat. and internat. awards for architectural design including Toronto Arts Award, Design and Architecture 1989; Governor General's Gold Medal, for the Metropolitan Central YMCA, Toronto and the 1986 Credit Foncier Prix for the Burns Bldg. restoration, Calgary; Gold Medal, Olympic Arts Festival 1988; visiting critic and guest lectr. various Candn. and U.S. univs.; author various publs. arch. and planning; Assoc. Ed. 'Architecture Canada' 1965–69; mem. ed. bd. 'Canadian Forum'; Dir., Bach 300 Bd. 1984–85; Music Toronto 1984–88; Comnr., Ont. Human Rights Comn. 1986–89; Adv. Bd., Sch. of Architecture, Univ. of Toronto 1987– ; Bd. of Govs., Mount Sinai Hosp., Toronto 1988– ; Fellow, Royal Arch. Inst. Can.; mem. Ontario Assn. Archs. mem., Royal Canadian Academy of Arts; Registration Board 1976–79; Chrmn., National Capital Commission Design Adv. Comte. 1984–86; Royal Inst. Brit. Archs.; mem. Candn. Inst. Planners; Am. Inst. Planners; Nat. Cert., Arch. Registration Bds. (U.S.A.); recreations: drawing, music; Clubs: Vincents (Oxford); Office: 2 Berkeley St., Toronto, Ont. M5A 2W3.

**DIAMOND, Allen Ephraim,** B.Sc., P.Eng.; real estate developer; b. Montreal, Que. 1 Mar. 1921; s. Meyer and Alice (Chowsky) D.; e. Queen's Univ. B.Sc. P.Eng. (cum laude) 1943; Radar Offr., Royal Candn. Navy 1943–46 (Lt. at discharge); m. Shirley d. Charles and Ida Greenberg 15 Sept. 1946; children: Michael, Stephen, Carey, Mark; PRES., WHITECASTLE INVESTMENTS LIMITED 1987– ; Project Mgr. Constr., Real Estate Devel. Co. 1946–53; Founding Partner & Pres., Cadillac Devel. Corp. 1953; Chrmn. & C.E.O., The Cadillac Fairview Corp. 1974–79; Extve. Ctte., Bd. of Dir. 1979–87; Past Pres. & Hon. Dir., Candn. Inst. of Pub. Real Estate Co.; Dir., Clairvest Group Inc.; Israel Discount Bank; Candn. Counc. of Christians & Jews Human Relns. Award 1980; inducted Candn. Bus. Hall of Fame 1988; Founding Chrmn., The Ballet Opera House Corp.; Dir., Mount Sinai Hosp.; Raymond F. Kravis Ctr. for the Performing Arts (USA); Baycrest Ctr. for Geriatric Care; Adv. Bd., U. of T. Ctr. for Rsch. for Neuro-Degen. Diseases; Mem., Assn. of Profl. Engrs.; Lambda Alpha Internat.; recreations: golf, bridge; clubs: Primrose, Oakdale Golf & Country, Palm Beach Country; Home: 1166 Bay St., Suite 2204, Toronto, Ont. M5S 2X8 and 110 Sunset #3A, Palm Beach, Fla. 33480; Office: 22 St. Clair Ave. E., Ste. 1010, Toronto, Ont. M4T 2S3.

**DIAMOND, Ann (Anne McLean),** B.A.; writer; b. Montreal, Que. 11 Apr. 1951; d. Donald Alexander and Thérèse Anne Marie (Bouthillier) M.; e. Baron Byng H.S.; St. Laurent H.S. 1968; Concordia Univ., B.A. 1974; writer of fiction and poetry; literary journalist; frequent book reviewer of The Montreal Gazette, Books in Canada, etc.; winner, Creative Non-Fiction Contest, Event Magazine 1991; publ. in 'Best Canadian Short Stories' 1991; 'The Thinking Heart: Best Canadian Essays' 1991; 'The Third MacMillan Anthology' 1990; poetry adapted for theatre by Robert Lepage and dance by Janet Oxley; author: 'Lil' 1977, 'A Nun's Diary' 1984 (poetry); 'Mona's Dance' 1988 (novel); 'Snakebite' 1989 (short stories); 'Terrorist Letters' 1992 (poetry); Home: 4312 St. Dominique, Montreal, Que. H2W 2B1.

**DIAMOND, Michael Peter,** M.Ed., LL.B.; business executive; b. Toronto, Ont. 13 June 1949; s. Ephraim Allan and Shirley (Greenberg) D.; e. Univ. of W. Ont. B.A. 1971; Althouse Coll. B.Ed. 1972; O.I.S.E. Univ. of Toronto M.Ed. 1975; Osgoode Hall York Univ. LL.B. 1980; m. Janette d. Jack and Mila Penn 5 March 1976; children: Jesse, Cole, Ari; PRES. AND CHIEF EXEC. OFFR. MINICOM DATA CORPORATION & HONICKMAN & ASSOCS. 1989– ; Vice Pres. and Dir. Whitecastle Investments Ltd.; Teacher, Sir Robert L. Borden Secondary Sch. Scarborough 1972–74, Emery Coll. Inst. N. York 1975–77; articled with Goodman & Goodman 1981; called to Bar of Ont. 1982; Exec. Vice Pres. present Co. 1982–88, Pres. of Co. and of Honickman & Associates Ltd. 1988; recreations: bicycling, squash; Home: 75 Strathearn Rd., Toronto, Ont. M6C 1R5; Office: 185 Renfrew Dr., Markham, Ont. L3R 6G3.

**d'IBERVILLE-MOREAU, Luc,** B.A., M.A., Ph.D.; museum director; b. Iberville; s. Hector and Hectorine (de la prairie) D.; e. Univ. of Montreal B.A. 1959; Parson's School of Design; Univ. of New York, Inst. of Fine Arts M.A. 1964; Univ. of London, Courtauld Inst. Ph.D. 1966; DIRECTOR, MUSEUM OF DECORATIVE ARTS MONTREAL 1976– ; General Curator, Musée des beaux arts de Montréal 1966–69; Gov., Heritage Canada; Pres., Decorative Arts Soc.; author: 'Lost Montreal' and numerous catalogues and articles; Office: Box 12,000, Station A, Montreal, Que. H3A 2P3.

**DICERNI, Richard,** B.A., M.P.A.; public servant; b. Montreal, Que. 2 Feb. 1949; s. Dominic and Jeannette (Richard) D.; e. Univ. de Montréal B.A. 1969; Harvard Univ. M.P.A. 1981; m. Ruth d. Frank and Hazel Bateman; children: Suzanne, Patrick; DEPUTY MINISTER, ONTARIO MIN. OF THE ENVIRONMENT & ENERGY 1992– ; Ministerial Asst. to Hon. Robert Andras 1969–73; Corp. Sec., Unemployment Insur. Comn. 1973–74; Dir., Planning & Evaluation, Que. Region 1973–76; Dir. Gen., Candn. Unity Information Office 1977–80; Asst. Under Sec. of State (Corp. Policy & Public Affairs) 1981–84; Acting/Asst. Under Sec. of State (Regional Opns.) 1986–87; Asst. Under Sec. of State (Citizenship) 1985–89; Senior ADM, Health & Welfare 1990; Deputy Sec. to the Cabinet FPRO 1991–92; Bd. of Dir., ABC Canada; Hydro Ontario; Ont. Clean Water Agency (O.C.W.A.); Home: 3510 Kingbird Court, Mississauga, Ont. L5L 2R1; Office: 135 St. Clair Ave. W., 15th floor, Toronto, Ont. M4V 1P5.

**DI CICCO, Pier Giorgio,** B.A., B.Ed.; poet, editor, literary consultant, b. Arezzo, Toscana, Italy 5 July 1949; s. Giuseppe and Primetta D.; e. Univ. of Toronto B.A., B.Ed. 1973, M.Div. 1990; a Brother in the Order of St. Augustine; ASSOC. PASTOR, ST. MARGARET MARY CHURCH; author: 'We are the Light Turning' 1975 (rev. ed. 1976); 'The Sad Facts' 1977; 'The Circular Dark' 1977; 'Dancing in the House of Cards' 1978; 'A Burning Patience' 1978; 'The Tough Romance' 1979; 'Flying Deeper into the Century' 1982; ed.: 'Roman Candles: An Anthology of 17 Italo-Canadian Poets' 1978; recent books include 'Dark to Light: Reasons for Humannness' 1983, 'Women We Never See Again' 1984, 'Post-Sixties Nocturne' 1985; 'Virgin Science' 1986; anthology contribs: 'The Oxford Book of Canadian Verse,' 'The New Canadian Poets' (M&S), 'Storm Warning 2' (M&S), 'Twenty Poets of the Eighties' (Anansi), 'Italo-Canadian Voices' (Mosaic), 'The Oxford Companion to Canadian Literature'; contrib. ed.: 'Argomenti Canadesi' (Rome); 'Italia/America' (San Francisco); former ed. 'Books in Canada'; 'Descant'; 'Waves'; 'Poetry Toronto'; poems publ. in over 200 magazines in Can., the U.S., Britain, Australia, Italy; over 300 readings and lectures given in Can. and abroad; Office: St. Margaret Mary Church, 8500 Islington Ave., Woodbridge, Ont. L4L 1X4.

**DICK, Eric Lyle,** M.A.; historian; b. Brandon, Man. 19 Nov. 1951; s. John David and Phyllis Marion (Lee) D.; e. Brandon Univ. B.A. 1972; Univ. of Manitoba M.A. 1978; HISTORIAN, DEPT. OF CANADIAN HERITAGE, PARKS CANADA, NATIONAL HISTORIC SITES DIRECTORATE 1992– , Prairie & N. Region 1977–92; mem. City of Winnipeg Hist. Bldgs. Ctte. 1980–90; Hist. Rsch. Group Exec., Profl. Inst. Pub. Service Can. (Local Rep. Can. Parks Service 1986–90); Dir. Project Lambda Inc. 1982–85, 1987 (Pres. 1983–84); Mem., Program Planning & Evaluation Ctte., Manitoba Museum of Man and Nature 1986–88; mem., Oral Hist. Grants Ctte., Province of Man. 1986–87; mem., Program Ctte., Man. Hist. Soc. 1990–92; mem., Newspapers Ctte., Man. Lib. Assoc. 1988–89; Adjunct Prof., Dept. of Landscape Arch., Univ. of Man. 1991–92; mem. Nat. Archives Appraisal Bd. 1985– ; author 'Farmers "Making Good": The Development of Abernethy District, Saskatchewan 1880–1920' in 'Studies in Archaeology, Architecture and History' 1989; 'A History of Prairie Settlement Patterns, 1870–1930' Can. Parks Service 1987; various scholarly articles Candn. agric. hist., hist. criticism, arch. hist., arctic hist.; contr. 'The Canadian Encyclopedia' entry on 'History of Agriculture' 1985, 1988 rev. ed.; co-recipient, Candn. Hist. Assn. Regional History Certificate of Merit 1990; Merit Award, City of Winnipeg 1990; mem. Candn. Hist. Assn.; Soc. Study Arch. Can.; Man. Hist. Soc.; recreations: golf, swimming, movies, music; Address: #307, 475 Laurier Ave. W., Ottawa, Ont. K1R 7X1.

**DICK, Ernest J.,** B.A., M.A.; corporate archivist; b. Leamington, Ont. 6 March 1946; s. John H. and Helen Marie (Bergen) D.; e. Univ. of Waterloo B.A. (Hons.) 1969; Trent Univ. M.A. 1972; m. Nancy d. George and Velzyn Parker 27 June 1970; children: Janette, Sheila; CORPORATE ARCHIVIST, CANADIAN BROADCASTING CORP. 1991– ; historical researcher in Ottawa 1968–74; Archivist, Nat. Archives of Canada 1974–89; Supervisor, Nat. Film, TV & Sound Archives Acquisitions 1982–88; Dir., Moving Image & Sound Archives, Nat. Archives of Can. 1989; consultant on archives at Candn. Broadcasting Corp. 1989–91; consultant, Nat. Film & Sound Archives of Australia 1986; Judge, Candn. Assn. of Broadcaster Awards 1988; Grant Assessor, Candn. & US academic & archival granting agencies 1980– ; consultant, Globalmic 1991– ; Founding Mem., Assn. of Candn. Archivists; Assn. for the Study of Candn. Radio & TV; Assn. of Moving Image Archivists; Mem., Internat. Fed. of TV Archives & Internat. Assn. of Sound Archives; editor: 'Guide to CBC Sources at the Public Archives' 1987; 'Beyond the printed word ... newsreel and broadcast reporting in Canada' 1988; author: 'Courage, Courage, the Lord Will Help: the Family History of Johann P. Dück of Schönfeld, Southern Russia'; and num. chapters, articles, reviews etc.; has made dozens of presentations (audio-visual) on history of Candn. broadcasting; curator of audio-visual exhibitions; recreations: basketball, tennis, nordic skiing; Home: 474 Highland Ave., Ottawa, Ont. K2A 2J6; Office: 1500 Bronson Ave., Ottawa, Ont. K1G 3J5.

**DICK, Paul Wyatt,** P.C., Q.C., B.A., LL.B.; lawyer; b. Kapuskasing, Ont. 27 Oct. 1940; s. Wyatt and Constance Grace (Harrison) D.; e. elem. sch. Arnprior, Ont.; high sch. Trinity Coll. Sch., Port Hope, Ont.; Univ. of W. Ont. B.A. 1962; Univ. of N.B. LL.B. 1967; twin s. Wyatt, Andrew; Min. of Supply and Services 1989–93; Min. of Public Works and Minister-Designate of Govt. Services 1993; called to Bar of Ont. 1969; cr. Q.C. 1981; Asst. Crown Atty. Co. of Carleton 1969–72; private law practice Dick & Nichols, Ottawa 1972–86; el. to H. of C. for Lanark-Renfrew-Carleton g.e. 1972, re-el. 1974, 1979, 1980, 1984, 1988; Chrmn. Ont. Federal P.C. Caucus 1974–78; P.C. Youth Critic 1976–79; P.C. Depy. House Leader 1983–84; Parliamentary Secretary to the President of the Queen's Privy Council of Canada 1984–85; Parlty. Secy. to Pres. of Treasury Bd. 1985–86; Assoc. Min. of Nat. Defence 1986–89; Min. of Supply & Services 1989–93; Home: 104 Stratas Ct., Kanata, Ont. K2L 3K4.

**DICK, Ronald Albert,** M.Arch., R.I.B.A., F.R.A.I.C.; b. Paris, France 3 June 1920; s. Leonard Albert and Elfrieda Annie (Gindle) D.; e. Sutton Valence Sch., Kent Eng.; Ecole Nationale Superieure des Beaux Arts, Paris, France; Bartlett Sch. of Arch., London Univ.; Cornell Univ.; Ithaca, N.Y.; m. Louise Spencer, d. Spencer Ervin, 24 June 1950; children: David Leonard, Andrew

Ronald, Edwina Louise; Sr. Partner, Rounthwaite, Dick & Hadley 1981–.; joined Marani & Morris, Archs. 1949; Partner, Marani, Morris & Allan 1953; Sr. Partner Marani, Rounthwaite & Dick 1964; served in 2nd World War with Royal Engrs., 1939–46, in U.K., S.E. Asia Command and N.W. Europe; attained rank of Major; with Candn. Militia, 1951–56; Fellow, Royal Arch. Inst. Can.; Trustee, Rotary Laughlen Centre Toronto; Anglican; Clubs: Badminton & Racquet; University; Home: 319 Inglewood Drive, Toronto, Ont. M4T 1J4.

**DICK, Susan Marie,** M.A., Ph.D., F.R.S.C.; university professor; b. Battle Creek, Mich. 6 Nov. 1940; d. James Allen and Mildred Marie (Thomas) D.; e. Western Mich. Univ., B.A. (Hons.) 1963; Northwestern Univ., M.A. 1964, Ph.D. 1967; PROF., DEPT. OF ENGLISH, QUEEN'S UNIV. 1967– ; F.R.S.C. 1989; author: 'Virginia Woolf' 1989; editor: (George Moore) 'Confessions of a Young Man' 1972, (Virginia Woolf) 'To the Lighthouse: The Original Holograph Draft' 1982, 'The Complete Shorter Fiction of Virginia Woolf' 1985, 2nd enlarged ed. 1989; co-editor: 'Omnium Gatherum: Essays for Richard Ellmann' 1989, (Virginia Woolf) 'To the Lighthouse' 1992; recreations: gardening, reading; Home: 177 Churchill Cres., Kingston, Ont. K7L 4N3.

**DICKASON, Olive Patricia,** B.A., M.A., Ph.D., D.Litt.; university professor; b. Winnipeg, Man. 6 Mar. 1920; d. Francis Leonard and Phoebe Philomène (Coté) Williamson; e. Notre Dame Coll., B.A. 1943; Univ. of Ottawa, M.A. 1972, Ph.D. 1977; Univ. of N.B. D.Litt. 1993; m. Anthony Willis s. George and May D. Feb. 1946; children: Anne-May, Clare Francesca, Roberta Marie; Prof. of History, Univ. of Alta. 1985–92; Gen. & City Hall Reporter, The Leader-Post 1944–56; Reporter, Sub-ed., The Winnipeg Free Press 1946–47; freelance writer 1947–50; Reporter, Sub-ed., Women's Ed., The Gazette 1950–55; various posts, The Globe and Mail 1955–67; Chief of Inform. Serv., Nat. Gall. of Can. 1967–70; Asst. Prof., present univ. 1976, Assoc. Prof. 1979, Prof. 1985; Sr. Rockefeller Fellowship 1989; SSHRCC Rsch. Grant 1985; other grants; Bd. Mem., Louis Riel Hist. Soc.; Women of the Metis Nation; Candn. Indian/Native Studies Assn.; Mem., Champlain Soc.; Candn. Hist. Assn.; Am. Soc. for Ethnohist.; French Colonial Hist. Soc.; Soc. française d'hist. d'outremer; Soc. d'hist. de l'Amér. française; author: 'Indian Arts in Canada' 1972, 'The Myth of the Savage and the Beginnings of French Colonisation in the Americas' 1984, 'Canada's First Nations: A History of Founding Peoples From Earliest Times' 1992 and numerous scholarly articles; co-author: 'The Law of Nations and the New World' 1989; recreations: visiting early Indian archaeological sites; Home: 6843 – 112 St., Edmonton, AB T6H 3K2; Office: Edmonton, Alta. T6G 2H4.

**DICKENS, Bernard Morris,** Ph.D., LL.D.; educator; b. London, Eng. 4 Nov. 1937; s. David and Rose (Jacobs) D.; e. King's Coll. Univ. of London LL.B. 1961, LL.M. 1965, Ph.D. 1971, LL.D. 1978; m. Rebecca d. John R. Cook 26 Apr. 1987; PROF. OF LAW, UNIV. OF TORONTO 1981– , cross appts. Faculty of Med., Centre of Criminol. and Centre for Bioethics; Tutorial Student in Laws, King's Coll. Univ. of London 1962–63; called to English Bar (Inner Temple) 1963, Bar of Ont. 1977; Lectr. Coll. of Law London, Eng. 1964, Sr. Lectr. 1968, Prin. Lectr. 1972–74; Rsch. Prof. of Law present Univ. 1974, Assoc. Prof. 1980; Visiting Heritage Prof. Univ. of Alta. 1986; Visiting Scholar The Hastings Center New York 1987; Julius Silver Fellow Sch. of Law and Visiting Prof. Sch. of Pub. Health Columbia Univ. 1987; Cons. World Health Orgn. Project Guidelines Human Rsch. 1978–83, 1991–93; Project Guiding Principles for Organ Transplantation 1990–91, Guidelines for Epidemiological Rsch. 1990–91; Ont. Law Reform Comn. Project Human Artificial Reproduction & Related Matters 1982–85; Med. Rsch. Council Can. Ctte. Ethics in Experimentation 1984–92; Legal Cons. Center Population & Family Health Columbia Univ. 1984– ; Nat. Rsch. Council Can. Ethics Ctte. 1992– ; author: 'Abortion and the Law' 1966; 'Medico-Legal Aspects of Family Law' 1979; co-author: 'Abortion Laws in Commonwealth Countries' 1979; 'Deciding Dangerousness: Policy Alternatives for Dangerous Offenders' 1983; 'Issues in Reproductive Health Law in the Commonwealth' 1986; 'Bioethics in Canada' 1993; editor: 'Medicine and the Law' 1993; Legal Ed. 'Law, Medicine and Ethics' 1987– ; Cons. Ctte. Ethics, Candn. Med. Assn. 1982–89; Am. Soc. Law, Med. & Ethics (Dir. 1986–92, Sec. 1987–89, Pres. 1990–91); recreation: walking; Club: National Liberal (London, Eng.); Home: 10, 31 Walmer Rd., Toronto, Ont. M5R 2W7; Office: 84 Queen's Park, Toronto, Ont. M5S 2C5.

**DICKEY, James Ross,** B.A., B.D.; editor/clergyman; b. Prescott, Ont. 11 Jan. 1943; s. Mervyn Elden and Nell (Ross) D.; e. Sir. George Williams Univ. B.A. 1964; The Presbyterian Coll. B.D. 1967; m. Carol d. Dorothy and Alexander Edgley 13 May 1967; children: Alice, Stephen, Rachel; Minister, St. Andrew's Presbyterian Church, Stratford, Ont. 1988– ; Minister, St. Stephens (Creston, B.C.) 1967–69; Christ Church (Wabush, Lab.) 1969–72; St. Andrew's (Thompson, Man.) 1972–77; Editor, The Presbyterian Record 1977–88; Information Offr., Presbyterian Ch. 1977–88; Pres. Candn. Church Press 1980–81; Hon. Life Mem. 1989– ; Dir., Assn. Church Press 1983; Commentator: 'Godshow' (CFRB) 1982– ; author and host: 'Signposts' CHTM 1972–77; Chrmn. Lab. West Integrated Sch. Bd. 1970–72; Speech writer, New Labrador Party 1970–72; occasional columnist for The London Free Press, Toronto Star; magazine contributor 'These Days' and 'The Presbyterian Record'; Home: 46 Church St., Stratford, Ont. N5A 2R1; Office: 25 St. Andrew St., Stratford, Ont. N5A 1A2.

**DICKEY, John Horace,** Q.C.; lawyer; b. Edmonton, Alta. 4 Sept. 1914; s. Horace Arthur and Mary Catharine (Macdonald) D.; e. Morrison Sch., Antigonish, N.S.; Coll. St. Sch. and St. Mary's Coll., Halifax, N.S., B.A. 1936; Dalhousie Univ., LL.B. 1940; St. Marys Univ., LL.D. 1980; Mount St. Vincent Univ., D.Hum.L. 1981; m. Eleanor Joyce, d. Mrs. E.E. Carney and the late Dr. M.J. Carney, Halifax, N.S., 18 Apr. 1959; Counsel, McInnes, Cooper & Robertson 1985–90; Hon. Chrmn., Stora Forest Industries; Dir., Dover Mills Ltd.; Dir., Atlantic Industrial Minerals Inc.; read law with W.C. MacDonald, K.C., M.P.; called to Bar of N.S. 1940; cr. Q.C. 1957; 1st el. to H. of C. for Halifax in by-el. 1947; re-el. g.e. 1949 and 1953; apptd. Parlty. Asst. to Min. of Def. Production 1952; def. in g.e. 1957, 1958; mem., Candn. del. to U.N. 1950; Candn. Rep. on Econ. and Social Council of U.N., 1950; Assoc. Prosecutor with Candn. War Crimes Liaison Detachment Far East; served in World War 1942–47 as Maj. with Candn. Army; Pres., N.S. Barristers Soc. 1966–67; Vice Pres., Candn. Bar Assn. 1967–69; Liberal Fed. of Can.; Phi Delta Theta; Knight, Order of St. Gregory; Knight Comm., Order of St. Lazarus; Liberal; R. Catholic; recreations: swimming, tennis, boating, skiing, golf; Home: 1991B Prince Arthur St., Halifax, N.S. B3H 4H2; Office: 6021 Young St., Halifax, N.S. B3K 2A1.

**DICKIE, Lloyd Merlin,** M.Sc., Ph.D., F.R.S.C.; oceanographer; b. Kingsport, N.S. 6 March 1926; s. Ebenezer Cox and Pearl Amanda (Sellars) D.; e. Kings Co. Acad.; Acadia Univ. B.Sc. 1946; Yale Univ. M.Sc. 1948; Univ. of Toronto Ph.D. 1953; m. Marjorie d. Ervin and Phoebe Bowman 6 Sept. 1952; children: Catharine Elizabeth, Sarah Jane, Allan Lloyd; SCIENTIST, BEDFORD INST. OF OCEANOGRAPHY 1978– ; Participant in Ocean Production Enhancement Network (OPEN) 1990– ; Adjunct Prof. of Biology, Dalhousie Univ. 1990– ; Sci. Investigator Fisheries Rsch. Bd. Can. Biol. Stn. St. Andrews, N.B. 1951–61, seconded to Great Lakes Inst. Univ. of Toronto 1961–65; Dir., Marine Ecology Lab. present Inst. 1965–74; Prof. of Oceanography Dalhousie Univ. 1974–78, Chrmn. 1974–77; Dir., Inst. Environmental Studies 1974–75, Acting Dir. Govt. Studies Prog. 1974–75; mem., Special Study Marine Sci. in Can., Sci. Council Can. 1969–70; mem., Council Nat. Rsch. Council Can. 1972–75; Adv. Ctte. Marine Resources Rsch. Food & Agric. Orgn. U.N. 1973–76; author or co-author over 80 papers sci. jours. and books; Home: 7 Lakewood Ct., Dartmouth, N.S. B2X 2R6; Office: P.O. Box 1006, Dartmouth, N.S. B2Y 4A2.

**DICKINSON, Donald Percy,** B.A., M.F.A.; writer; b. Prince Albert, Sask. 28 Dec. 1947; s. John Crabtree and Grace Lily (Green) D.; e. Univ. of Sask. B.A. (P.E.) 1970, B.A. (Hons. English) 1973; Univ. of B.C., M.F.A. (creative writing) 1979; m. Chellie d. Newton and Margaret Eaton 1 May 1970; children: Luke, Paul, Alice; began writing fiction 1973; short stories pub. in lit. mags. & anthologies; stories anthologized in 'Third Impressions' 1982, 'Metavisions' 1983, 'Best Canadian Short Fiction' 1984, 'Volk und Veldt' 1984, 'Words We Call Home' 1990, anthologized in 'The New Story Writers' 1992; spent 7 yrs. travelling in Eur. Australia, Asia working as landscape gardener, shepherd, fitness instr., farm labourer, surveyor's asst., etc.; Teacher, Lillooet, B.C.; author: 'The Crew' 1993; 'Blue Husbands' 1991 (nominated for Gov. Gen.'s Award), winner Ethel Wilson Fiction Prize 1991; 'Fighting the Upstream' 1987 and co-author: 'Third Impressions' 1982 (short stories); recreations: weight-training, canoeing, hockey; Lillooet Old Timers' Hockey Team; Home: Box 341, Lillooet, B.C. V0K 1V0.

**DICKINSON, Garth Edwin,** B.A., M.D., F.R.C.P.(C); physician; b. Hamilton, Ont. 12 Jan. 1953; s. Lawrence Edwin and Virena Josephine (Carslake) D.; e. Queen's Univ. B.A. 1973, M.D. 1977, Univ. of B.C. 1977–78; Univ. of W. Ont. 1978–80; Univ. of Ottawa 1981–82; m. Kathryn d. Eileen and Hubert Dunlop 21 Sept. 1978; children: Bart, Emma; EMERGENCY PHYSICIAN, OTTAWA GENERAL HOSPITAL 1993– ; Clinical Asst. Prof., Depts. of Med. & Family Med., Univ. of Ottawa 1983– ; Emergency Physician, King Edward VII Meml. Hosp., Bermuda 1980–81; Ottawa Gen. Hosp. 1982– ; Dir., Dept. of Emerg. Med., Ottawa Gen. Hosp. 1983–91; Health Consultant, Cairo, Egypt 1991–93; F.R.C.P.C. (Internal Med.) 1982, (Emergency Med. 1983); mem. Prov. Emergency Health Services Adv. Ctte., Ont. Min. of Health 1987–92; mem. Ont. Med. Assn., Candn. Med. Assn.; founding mem. Candn. Assn. of Emergency Physicians 1978; author of various papers pub. in med. jours.; recreations: photography, boating; Home: 3691 Revelstoke Dr., Ottawa, Ont. K1V 7C2.

**DICKINSON, Terence;** science writer; b. Toronto, Ont. 10 Nov. 1943; s. Reginald Chapman and Anna Teresa (Duz) D.; m. Susan d. Sidney and Julia Beard 24 June 1967; freelance writer since 1976; Part-time Teaching Master St. Lawrence Coll. Kingston, Ont. 1977– ; Astron. Columnist 'Toronto Star' 1981– ; Astron. Commentator CBC Radio 'Quirks & Quarks' 1978– ; contbg. ed. 'Equinox' mag. 1983– ; 'Harrowsmith' mag. 1987– ; Tech. Transp. & Communications Ont. Govt. 1964–67; Sci. Asst. McLaughlin Planetarium Royal Ont. Museum 1967–70; Asst. Dir. Stasenburgh Planetarium Rochester, N.Y. 1970–73; Ed. 'Astronomy' mag. Milwaukee, Wis. 1973–75; Ed./Publs. Ont. Sci. Centre Toronto 1975–76; author 'Exploring the Moon and the Solar System' 1971; 'Nightwatch' 1983; 'Halley's Comet: Mysterious Visitor From Outer Space' 1984; 'The Universe and Beyond' 1986; 'Exploring the Night Sky' 1987; 'Exploring the Sky by Day' 1988; 'From the Big Bang to Planet X' 1993; 'Extraterrestrials' 1994; co-author 'Sky Guide' 1977; 'Mag-Six Star Atlas' 1982; 'Backyard Astronomer's Guide' 1991; over 300 articles various mags.; over 1000 newspaper articles; cons. to various museums, sci. centres and ednl. instns.; recipient 1st Place Award Candn. Sci. Writers Awards 1984, 1992; Author's Award Found. Advan. Candn. Letters 1982, 1984, 1986; 1st Place Hughes Aerospace Astron. Writing Awards 1985; Hon. Mention Nat. Mag. Awards 1983, 1985; New York Acad. of Sciences Outstanding Children's Science Book Award 1988; Children's Lit. Roundtables of Canada Information Book Award 1989; Sandford Fleming Medal, Royal Candn. Institute 1992; Life mem. Royal Astron. Soc. Can.; mem. Candn. Astronomical Soc.; Candn. Sci. Writers Assn.; Am. Inst. Aeronautics & Astronautics; Am. Assn. Advanc. Sci.; recreations: snooker, photography, horseback riding; Address: P.O. Box 10, Yarker, Ont. K0K 3N0.

**DICKMAN, Michael David,** B.A., M.Sc., Ph.D.; educator; b. Pittsburgh, Pa. 30 June 1940; s. Avrom Isaac and Harriet (Trasin) D.; e. Univ. of Cal. Santa Barbara B.A. 1962; Univ. of Ore. M.Sc. 1965; Univ. of B.C. Ph.D. 1968; Univ. of Uppsala, Sweden, Thord-Gray Post-doctoral Fellow 1969; m. Daryl Ann d. Dr. and Mrs. George Dubpernell 11 Aug. 1962; children: Sven Dubpernell, Timothy Avrom; PROF. OF BOTANY, UNIV. OF HONG KONG 1993– ; Adjunct Prof. McMaster Univ. 1980– ; Asst. Prof. Univ. of Ottawa 1969 and Dir. Ottawa-Carleton Municipalities Pollution Abatement Prog. 1972; Assoc. Prof. Brock Univ. 1974, Prof. 1985–93; Prof., Ecology Dept., Univ. of Hong Kong 1993– ; Chrmn. Senate Cttes. Acad. Planning 1981–82, Budget Adv. Standing Ctte. 1982–83, Rules Ctte. 1983–84; Vice Chrmn. Regional Niagara Environmental Ecol. Adv. Ctte. 1985–88; apptd. to Ont. Environmental Appeal Bd. 1990– ; Univ. Court 1993– ; Senate 1993– ; Faculty Bd. 1993– ; recipient numerous awards & grants aquatic ecol. incl. Fisheries Rsch. Bd. Can. Scholarship 1967–68; Thord-Gray Post-Doctoral Fellow 1968–69; Natural Sci's Eng. Council Can. 1974–92; NSERC Sabbatical Travel Awards Black Sea Rsch. 1978; Geol. Survey Ont. 1979–86; Polar Continental Shelf 1980–86; Candn. Scouting Assn. Silver Pin Environmentalist Award 1982; Acid Rain Rsch. Netherlands 1985; Rawson Acad. Aquatic Sci's Candn. Touring Lectureship Award 1986; NSERC Sabbatical Year, Internat. Collaborative Rsch. Grant for Rsch. in Iceland and France 1991; Niagara Peninsula Conservation Authority Professional Conservation Award 1992; World Wildlife Found. & Environment Can. Grants 1986–89; Ont.-Jiangsu (China) Ednl. Exchange Award Acid Rain Rsch. China 1987, Palaeolimnology Rsch. 1989; mem., Ont. Grad. Student Awards Ctte. 1979–81, 1987–88; author or co-author 66 sci. publs.; mem., Soc. Candn. Limnols. (Pres. 1983–85); Candn. Environmental Law Assn. (Bd. of Dir. 1982–85); Bd. of Dirs., Great Lakes United 1992; Soc. Internat. Limnol.; Green Peace; Niagara Ecosystems Taskforce (Pres. 1986–93); Mem. Bd. of Dirs., Candns. For A Clean Environment 1991–93; N. Am.

Diatomists; Soc. Wetlands Sci's; Environmental Ecological Adv. Ctte. for Regional Niagara 1984–89; recreations: hiking, sailing, chess, scuba; Home: 16 Leawood Court, St. Catharines, Ont. L2T 3R6; Office: Univ. of Hong Kong, Pohfulam Road, Hong Kong.

**DICKSON, The Rt. Hon. Brian,** P.C., C.C., K. St. J., LL.B., LL.D. (Hon.), D.Cn.L. (Hon.), D.C.L. (Hon.), C.D.; judge; b. Yorkton, Sask. 25 May 1916; s. Thomas and Sarah Elizabeth (Gibson) D.; e. Regina (Sask.) Coll. Inst.; Univ. of Man.; Man. Law Sch., LL.B. 1938 (Gold Medallist); Hon. Degrees: D.Cn.L., St. Johns Coll. 1965; LL.D. Univ. of Man. 1973; Univ. of Sask. 1978; Univ. of Ottawa 1979; Queen's Univ. 1980; Dalhousie Univ. 1983; York Univ. 1985; Univ. of B.C. 1986; Univ. of Toronto 1986; Laurentian Univ. 1986; Yeshiva Univ. 1987; McGill Univ. 1987; Carleton Univ. 1988; Law Society of Upper Canada 1993; Univ. of Victoria 1993; D.C.L., Univ. of Windsor 1988; Mount Allison Univ. 1989; Brock Univ. 1990; Univ. of Winnipeg 1991; Univ. of Western Ont. 1992; Hon. Prof. Univ. of Manitoba 1985; m. Barbara Melville d. Henry E. Sellers 18 June 1943; children: Brian H., Deborah I. (Shields), Peter G., Barry R.; Chief Justice of Canada, Supreme Court of Canada 1984–90; called to Bar of Man. 1940; practised law with Aikins, MacAulay 1945–63; Lectr., Manitoba Law Sch. 1948–54; cr. Q.C. 1953; apptd. to Court of Queen's Bench, Manitoba 1963, Court of Appeal 1967, Supreme Court of Can. 1973; served with Royal Candn. Arty., 1940–45 (wounded, despatches); Hon. Col., 30th Field Regiment, RCA, retired; Life Bencher, Law Soc. Man.; The Order of the Buffalo Hunt (Man.); Hon. Bencher, Lincoln's Inn, London 1984; Knight, Order of St. John, 1985; Hon. Fellow, American Coll. of Trial Lawyers 1986; recipient, Prix Archambault-Fauteux 1990; Churchill Society Award 1990; Order of Ste Agathe (San Marino) 1991; Roayl Bank Award 1992; Chrmn. Bd. of Govs., Univ. of Man. 1971–73; Anglican Church of Can. (Chancellor, Dioc. of Rupert's Land 1960–71); recreation: riding; Club: Rideau.

**DICKSON, Hon. Frank Gordon William,** B.A., LL.B.; judge; b. Regina, Sask. 22 Aug. 1931; s. Frank James and Edna Marion (Lewis) D.; e. Albert and Victoria Schs. Regina; Swift Current (Sask.) Coll. Inst. 1949; Univ. of Sask. B.A. 1962, LL.B. 1963; m. Jennie Ruth d. Andrew Anderson, Chaplin, Sask. 10 Aug. 1957; children: Gail Marion, Donna Helen, Joseph Andrew, David Frank; PUISNE JUDGE, COURT OF QUEEN'S BENCH, SASK.; called to Bar of Sask. 1964; practiced law with MacDermid & Co. Saskatoon 1963–78; mem. Saskatoon Bar Assn. (Past Pres.); Law Soc. Sask.; Candn. Bar Assn.; Protestant; recreations: golf, badminton, swimming, camping, fishing; Clubs: Riverside Golf; Saskatoon Badminton; Home: 504 – 415 Heritage Cresc., Saskatoon, Sask. S7H 5M5; Office: Court of Queen's Bench, Court House, Regina, Sask. S4P 3V7.

**DICKSON, George H.,** B.S.A.; retired company executive; b. Westbourne, Manitoba, 4 July 1915; s. Rev. G. A., B.D., D.D., and Lillian (McLachlan) D.; e. Western Canada High Sch., Calgary, Alta. (1934); Ont. Agric. Coll., Guelph, Ont., B.S.A. 1938; m. Margaret Eleanor, d. late Matt Leggat, 18 May 1938; children: Beverley Ann, George Kent; Extve. Vice Pres. and Dir., Canada Packers Ltd., 1962–78; Dir., Canada Packers Inc. 1956–86; joined Canada Packers Ltd. in 1937 as Mail Clerk; Office and Plant Training, 1937–39; Hog Buying Operations, 1940; Pork Trading Operations, 1941; Mgr., Pork Operations at Toronto Plant, 1951, and Gen. Mgr. of Co's. Pork Operations, 1954; Dir. and Dir. of Marketing, 1956; Dir. and Gen. Mgr., 1960; Extve. Vice Pres., Chief Operating Offr. and Dir., 1962–77; Past Pres., Ontario Agricultural Coll. Alumni Assn.; mem. of Senate, Univ. of Toronto, 1953–56; mem. Bd. Govs., Univ. of Guelph; (1976–82); Agric. Inst. of Can. (Past Pres., Central Ont. Local); mem., Toronto Bd. of Trade; United Church; recreations: golf, curling, gardening; Clubs: St. George's Golf & Country; Home: 5 Edenbridge Drive, Islington, Ont. M9A 3E8.

**DICKSON, Jennifer,** R.A., LL.D.; artist; b. Piet Retief, S. Africa 17 Sept. 1936; d. late John Liston and late Margaret Joan (Turner) D.; e. Goldsmiths Coll., Sch. of Art, Univ. of London 1954–59; Atelier 17, Paris 1960–65; m. Ronald Andrew Sweetman 13 Apl. 1961; one s. William David; ARTIST, PHOTOGRAPHER AND GARDEN HISTORIAN; Teacher, Eastbourne Sch. of Art 1959–62; directed and developed Printmaking Dept. Brighton Coll. of Art 1962–68; Graphics Atelier, Saidye Bronfman Centre Montreal 1970–72; Visiting Artist, Ball State Univ. 1967, Univ. of W. Indies 1968, Univ. of Wis. 1972, Ohio State Univ. 1973, W. Ill. Univ. 1973, Haystack Mountain Sch. of Crafts Me. 1973; Sessional Instr., Concordia Univ., Montreal 1972–79; Université d'Ottawa 1980–85; Head, Dept. of Art Hist., Saidye Bronfman Centre, Montreal 1985–88; Visiting Artist Queen's Univ. 1977–78; rec'd Prix des Jeunes Artistes (Gravure) Biennale de Paris 1963; Maj. Prize World Print Competition San Francisco 1974; Biennale Prize 5th Norwegian Internat. Print Biennale 1980; LL.D. (Hon.), Univ. of Alta., Edmonton 1988; author suites of original etchings: 'Genesis' 1965; 'Alchemic Images' 1966; 'Aids to Meditation' 1967; 'Eclipse' 1968; 'Song of Songs' 1969; 'Out of Time' 1970; 'Fragments' 1971; 'Sweet Death and Other Pleasures' 1972; 'Homage to Don Juan' 1975; 'Body Perceptions' 1975; 'The Secret Garden' 1976; 'Openings' 1977; 'Three Mirrors to Narcissus' 1978; 'Il Paradiso Terrestre' 1980; 'Il Tempo Classico,' 1981; 'Grecian Odes' 1982/83; 'Aphrodite Anadyomene' 1984/85; 'The Gardens of Paradise' 1984; 'The Gilded Cage' 1986; 'The Hospital for Wounded Angels' (publ. in book form) 1987; 'The Water Gardens' 1987; 'The Gardens of Desire' 1988; 'Pavane for Spring' 1989; 'Sonnet to Persephone' 1990; 'Cadence and Echo: The Song of the Garden' 1991; 'The Spirit of the Garden' 1992; 'The Haunted Heart' 1993; author: 'The Royal Academy Gardener's Journal' 1991; subject of CBC Special TV programs 1980, 1982 and 1990; awarded LL.D. (h.c.), Univ. of Alberta, Edmonton for her contribution to Candn. culture 1988; major exhibition 'The Last Silence' toured Italy (Feb.-May 1993) under auspices of Dept. of External Affairs, to be exhibited in Ottawa (Nov. 1993-Jan. 1994) at the Candn. Museum of Contemporary Photography, an associate Museum of the National Gallery of Canada; rep. in maj. internat. museums incl. Metropolitan Museum New York, Victoria and Albert Museum, Hermitage Museum Leningrad; Can. Council Art Bank; National Gallery of Canada; Founding mem. Brit. Printmakers' Council; Print & Drawing Council Can.; Fellow, Royal Soc. Painter-Etchers & Engravers; Anglican; Address: 20 Osborne St., Ottawa, Ont. K1S 4Z9.

**DICKSTEIN, Joseph,** B.Com., M.B.A., C.L.U.; insurance executive; b. Montreal, Que. 26 Jan. 1930; s. Moses and Lena (Feinberg) D.; e. McGill Univ., B.Com. 1951; Wharton Sch. of Finance and Economics; Univ. of Penna., M.B.A. 1952; C.L.U. 1953; m. Sibylle, d. Kurt Otto, 1 Oct.1974; children: Michael, Melanie, Oliver, Stephanie, Jeremy; PRES., P.P.I. FINANCIAL GROUP (EASTERN) LTD. 1982– ; Dir., Prudential of America Life Insurance Co. (Canada) 1991– ; with Crown Life Ins. Co., 1952–62; Pres., Westmount Life Ins. Co. 1962–76; Pres., Dickstein Insurance Agencies Ltd. 1977–82; Home: 31 Medalist Rd., Willowdale, Ont. M2P 1Y3.

**DiCOSIMO, Joanne V.,** B.A.; museum director; b. Winnipegosis, Man. 2 Feb. 1953; d. Bui Oscar and Lois Dawn (Tomes) Fredrickson; e. Univ. of Winnipeg B.A. (Hons.) 1974; EXECUTIVE DIRECTOR, MANITOBA MUSEUM OF MAN AND NATURE 1988– ; Candn. Studies Coord., Manitoba Dept. of Education 1974–78; Chief of School & Public Programs, Man. Mus. of Man and Nature 1978–86; Dir. of Programs 1986–88; Councillor, Candn. Mus. Assn. 1988–89; Treas. 1989–90; Founding Vice-Pres., Winnipeg Internat. Children's Fest.; Founding Pres., West End Cult. Ctr.; Bd. Mem., Candn. Learning Materials Centre 1985–91; author of some journal articles; recreations: reading, swimming, skiing; Home: Winnipeg, Man.

**DIEBEL, Kenneth R.,** C.I.A., C.M.A., F.C.M.A.; financial executive; b. Kitchener, Ont. 26 Oct. 1935; s. Robert William and Florence Ann (Kilian) D.; e. Certified Management Accountant 1964; The Soc. of Mngt. Accountants' Mngt. Devel. for Extve. Accountants Course 1971; Certified Internal Auditor 1973; m. Ann d. Jon and Eileen Cubberley 17 Oct. 1964; children: Adam, Sarah; CHIEF FINANCIAL OFFICER, WM. ROBERTS ELECTRICAL & MECHANICAL; Treasurer, Morval Durofoam; Budd Automotive; Pres., The Soc. of Mngt. Accountants of Canada 1991–92; The Soc. of Mngt. Accountants of Ont. 1984–85; Fellow, The Soc. of Mngt. Accountants of Canada F.C.M.A. 1985; Pres., St. John's Memorial Found.; Pres., St. John's Lutheran Ch. 1982–85; Extve. Mem., Waterloo North Scouting Assn. 1992; Treas. & Vice-Pres., Kitchener Waterloo Symphony Orch. 1982–87; Dir. & Extve. Mem., Waterloo Lutheran Seminary 1992–95; Dir., Wilfred Laurier Univ. 1992–96; clubs: University Club, Univ. of Waterloo; Home: 284 Shakespeare Dr., Waterloo, Ont. N2L 2T6; Office: 85 Edwin St., Kitchener, Ont. N2G 4H3.

**DIEHL, Alden Edgar;** radio broadcasting executive; b. Cypress River, Man. 10 June 1931; s. James Edgar and Iva Irene (Campbell) D.; e. Souris Coll. 1950; m. Margaret Alice d. Louis and Mabel Kilmury 10 June 1953; children: Debra Ann, Janis Lori, Darin James, Kathy Margaret; HEAD, INDUSTRY RELATIONS AND STAFF DEVELOPMENT, SHAW RADIO LTD. 1993– ; Clerk-Embalmer, Diehl's Funeral & Furniture Store 1949–51; Mgr. 1957; Music Lib. Asst., Writer, Performer, CJCA 1951–56; freelance actor/singer/-writer, Toronto stage, TV (CBC) 1956; Copy Chief/-Prog. Dir., CKBI TV & Radio Prince Albert 1958; Promo. Dir., CKLW Windsor 1964; Prog. Dir. 1965; CFRA Ottawa 1967; Vice-Pres. Prog., CKLW Windsor 1970–73; applied for license in Thunder Bay 1973; Cons.; Vice-Pres., CKY AM & FM Winnipeg, Moffat Commun. 1973–82; Vice-Pres. & Gen. Mgr., L973, CFOX FM, Moffat Commun. 1982–93; Treasurer, Candn. Assn. of Broadcasters (C.A.B.); Chrmn., B.C. Broadcast Standards Counc.; Vice-Chrmn., B.C. & Yukon Advtg. Stan. Counc.; Dir., B.C. Assn. of Broacasters (Convention Chrmn. 1987, 1991); Dir. & Bd. of Adv., A.I.E.S.E.C. (Simon Fraser Univ. br. of internat. bus. students exchange prog.); tenor soloist in many Un. Ch. choirs, currently Tsawwassen U.C.; wrote & performed 'Fight on Manitoba – Winter and Summer' successful mid-70s recording; recreations: golf, walking, long-time curler; club: Beach Grove Golf & Country; Home: 5700 Golden Rod Cres., Delta, B.C.; Office: 1006 Richards St., Vancouver, B.C. V6B 1S8.

**DIELSCHNEIDER, Peter J.;** queen's bench judge; b. Macklin, Sask. 7 Jan. 1928; s. Christopher Jacob and Josephine (Bichel) D.; e. St. Thomas Coll.; Coll. of Law & Arts., St. Thomas More Coll., Univ. of Sask.; m. Joyce d. Albert and Beatrice Killick 15 Sept. 1956; children: Joanne, Thomas, Beverley; JUDGE, COURT OF QUEEN'S BENCH, SASK. 1981– ; priv. prac., Melville, Sask. 1955–73; Dist. Court Judge 1973–81; Home: Box 1267, Humboldt, Sask. S0K 2A0; Office: Box 490, Court House, Humboldt, Sask. S0K 2A0.

**DIEM, Tadeusz;** diplomat; b. Warsaw, Poland 1 June 1940; s. Otto and Maria Klara (Wypych) D.; e. A. Mickiewicza Licee 1958; Warsaw Tech. Univ. 1963, Ph.D. 1971; m. Ada d. Józef and Wanda Bogdaska 17 Dec. 1968; children: Magdalena, Joanna; AMBASSADOR TO CANADA FROM POLAND; Assoc. Prof., Warsaw Tech. Univ. 1963– ; Researcher and Visiting Prof., Univ. of Akron, Marquette Univ. & Lehigh Univ. 1975–76, 1985–86; Dep. Min. of Edn., Govt. Plenipotentiary, Orgn. of Utilization, 24 Western Countries Aid in Area of Devel. of Human Resources 1989; Pres., Polish Ctte., F. Miterrand Found.; Mem., Mngt., 'East-West Inst.' United Nations; Mem., Extve. Ctte., Euro. Dist. Edn. Network; awarded Legion of Hon., Rep. of France; club: Le Cercle Universitaire; Home: 323 Stewart St., Ottawa, Ont. K1N 6K5; Office: 443 Daly St., Ottawa, Ont. K1N 6H3.

**DIENER, Erwin,** Ph.D., F.R.S.C.; scientist; b. Luzern, Switzerland 6 Jan. 1932; s. Reinhold and Alice Sophia (Treichler) D.; e. high sch. Switzerland; Univ. of Zurich, Ph.D. 1963; m. Eva Schaufelberger 15 Oct. 1957; PROF. EMERITUS 1989– ; Prof. of Immunol., Univ. of Alta. 1970–89, Chrmn. of Immunol. 1973–89; Roche Fellow, Walter and Eliza Hall Inst. of Med. Rsch. Australia 1964–70; recipient Univ. of Alta. Prize Excellence in Rsch. 1987; Fellow, Royal Soc. of Can.; Home: R.R. #1, Browning Site, Sechelt, B.C. V0N 3A0; Office: 8–60 Medical Sciences Bldg., Edmonton, Alta. T6G 2H7.

**DIENES, Zoltan,** Ph.D.; mathematician; educator; b. Budapest, Hungary, 11 Sept. 1916; s. Paul Alexander and Valérie (Geiger) D.; e. Hungary, Paris and Eng.; Dartington Hall Sch., Devon, Eng., Matric. 1934; Univ. of London, B.A. (Maths & Psychol.) 1937, Ph.D. 1939; Dipl. in Educ., Leicester Univ.; hon. doctorates: Mount Allison, Caen & Siena; Invited Prof. of Math. Educ., Univ. of Siena, Italy 1984–86 and 1990; Dir., Ravenna Computer Project 1985–87; Consultant, IRRSAE Bologna 1984–86; Pres. International Study Group for Math. Learning; Teacher, Highgate and Dartington Hall Schs., Eng. 1940–41; taught math. at Southampton Univ. 1941–43, Sheffield Univ. 1943–45, Manchester Univ. 1945–47, Leicester Univ. 1947–59; Dir. of Research Unit for investigation of generation insights, Brit. Assn. for Advanc. of Science 1959–61; Research Fellow, Center for Cognitive Studies, Harvard Univ. 1960–61; Assoc. Prof. in Psychol., Adelaide Univ., Australia; Prof. of Educ. 1961–65; Math. Consultant: Leicestershire Educ. Authority 1957–60; Organ. for European Econ. Co-op. 1960; Peace Corps, Hilo Campus, Univ. of Hawaii 1960–61; Educ. Dept., State of S. Australia 1962–65; Territory of Papua New Guinea 1964–65; Minnemath Program, Univ. of Minn. 1965; Teachers Coll., Columbia Univ. 1966; Ministry of Educ., Paris 1965; UNESCO, Paris, Budapest and Hamburg 1962–68; Dir. Rsch. in Math Learning, Univ. of Sherbrooke 1966–75; Prof. of Educ., Brandon Univ., Man. 1975–78; Consultant for Tahiti 1976, State of Victoria, Aust. 1976, Univ. of Qué. 1978; Fellow of Howe Green Trust for developing interdisciplinary education in South Devon 1978–81; chief maths consultant Giunti-Marzocco 1978–87; Guest Prof., Goëthe Univ., Frankfurt 1979–80; consultant Ospedale Policlinico Milano for maths learning of deaf children 1982; Centro di Riabilitazione BARI for retarded children 1982–84; Consultant, Kent County 1987–89; Rsch. Assoc., Acadia Univ., Wolfville, N.S. 1986–94; consultant for Petö Inst. for cerebral palsy children, Budapest 1990; Consultant to Associazione Italiana per l'Assistenza agli Spastici 1991–93; Consultant to Szekszárd Schools, Hungary 1993; author: 'Concept Formation and Personality' 1959; 'Building Up Mathematics' 1960, 2nd ed. 1964; 'An Experimental Study of Mathematics Learning' 1964; 'The Power of Mathematics' 1964; 'Mathematics in the Primary School' 1964; 'Modern Mathematics for Young Children' 1965; 'Geometry Through Transformations' (Parts I, II and III) 1967; 'Fractions' 1968; 'Power Roots and Logarithms' 1968; 'L'albero delle storie' (3 vols.) 1984; (with M. Jeeves) 'Thinking in Structures' 1965; (with N. Golding) 'First Years in Mathematics' (Parts I, II and III) 1966; 'The Arithmetic and Algebra of Natural Number' 1966; 'The Effects of Structural Relations on Transfer' 1968; (with M. Jeeves) 'Les six étapes de l'apprentissage de la mathématique' 1970; 'Elements of Mathematics' 1971; 'Mathematique Vivante' 1979; 'Giochi e Idee' (I & II) 1979; 'Parole e Idee' 1980; 'Ambiente, Uomini, Idee' (3 vols.) 1980; 'Rinnovamento dell' insegnamento della matematica al livello elementare' 1985; 'Psicodinamica del processo di astrazione' 1988; 'Il piacere della matematica' 1991; Dienes professzor játékai 1988; Apprendimento Dei Concetti Matematici E Processi Mentali, A.I.A.S. 1991; series of films on mathematical games for Hungarian TV 1985; Mathematical games: Factor game, Sixteen game, Keep-Add-and-Exchange game 1989; Educational Videotapes for Acadia Univ. and for Nova Scotia Education Dpt (1993); other writings incl. articles and papers in field of math. for journs. and confs.; Quaker; Home: 14 Grandview Dr., P.O. Box 482, Wolfville, N.S. B0P 1X0.

**DIETRICH, Sister Dominica,** M,A., LL.D.; b. Dashwood, Ont. 3 March 1916; d. Noah and Christine (Foster) D.; e. The Pines, Chatham, Ont.; Univ. of Toronto, B.A. 1943, M.A. 1945; St. Michael's Hosp., Toronto, Dipl. Dietitian 1944; Cornell Univ., pre-doctoral courses; Univ. of W. Ont., LL.D.; Superior Gen., Ursuline Religious of Chatham, 1969–77; Prof. and Head of Home Econ. Dept., Brescia Coll., London, Ont., 1945–69; Superior of Coll. 1954–60; Dean 1963–69; mem. Senate of Univ. of W. Ont. during same period; mem., Candn. Dietetic Assn. (Pres. 1968–69); Candn. Catholic Orgn. for Development and Peace; Women's Ordination Conf.; R. Catholic; recreation: bridge; Address: The Pines, Chatham, Ont. N7L 3L8.

**DIETRICH, Harold A.,** LL.B., LL.D., F.L.M.I.; insurance executive; b. Regina, Sask. 13 July 1930; s. Jacob and Rosina (Manz) D.; e. Univ. of Sask. LL.B. 1952; m. Joyce d. Jon and Rosa Johnson 16 June 1956; children: John, Rosanne, Norma, Robert; Pres., Lutheran Life Insurance Soc. of Can. 1974–90 (Extve. Vice Pres. 1973); law practice Regina, Sask. to 1973; Pres. Candn. Fraternal Assn. 1977–78; Pres., Insurance Inst. of Can.; Chrmn. Lutherwood Child and Family Foundation, Waterloo; Pres., YMCA Kitchener-Waterloo; Past Chrmn., Canada World Youth; Fellow, Life Office Mang. Assn.; mem. Candn. Bar Assn.; Law Soc. Sask.; recreations: amateur radio, automobile restoration; Home: 12 Post Horn Pl., Waterloo, Ont. N2L 5E9.

**DI GIACOMO, Thomas A.,** B.Comm., M.B.A.; insurance executive; b. Toronto, Ont. 22 Dec. 1941; s. John R. and Alice M. (Caruso) C.; e. Univ. of Toronto, B.Comm. 1964; Univ. of Chicago, M.B.A. 1966; CHRMN. OF THE BD., PRES. & CHIEF EXTVE. OFFR., THE MANUFACTURERS LIFE INSUR. CO. 1990– ; Portfolio Mgr., U.S. Equities, The Manufacturers Life Insur. Co. 1966; joined Andresen & Company 1968; returned to prev. position at The Manufacturers 1971; Financial Vice-Pres.: U.S. Securities 1972; U.S. Investments 1974; N. Am. Securities 1975; N. Am. Securities & Internat. Investments 1976; Vice-Pres., Investments 1977; Sr. Vice-Pres., Investments 1979; Extve. Vice-Pres. 1984; apptd. to Bd. of Dir. 1984; Pres. & Chief Op. Offr. 1985; Pres. & C.E.O. 1987; Chrmn., Pres. & C.E.O. 1990; Dir.: ManuLife Investment Mgmt. Corp.; Cabot Devel. Corp.; The Manufacturers Life Ins. Co. (U.K.) Limited; ManuLife Mgmt. Limited; Simcoe Erie Investors Limited; Pres. & Chief Extve. Offr., Manufacturers Life Capital Corp. Inc.; Chrmn., Manufacturers Life Property Corp.; recreations: golf, fishing; Home: Toronto, Ont.; Office: 200 Bloor St. E., NT-11, Toronto, Ont. M4W 1E5.

**DIGNAM, Michael John,** B.A., Ph.D.; university professor; b. Toronto, Ont. 25 May 1931; s. Hugh Molenue and Elizabeth Katheline (Skey) D.; e. Trinity Coll. Sch. Port Hope 1949; Trinity Coll., Univ. of Toronto B.A. (Hons.) 1953; Dept. of Chem., Univ. of Toronto Ph.D. 1956; m. Nancy d. John and Dorothy Dumbrille 23 May 1953; children: Donald R., Carol S., H. Timothy, Darcy J., Marc M.; PROFESSOR OF CHEMISTRY, UNIV. OF TORONTO 1966– ; Rsch. Chem., Aluminium Labs. Ltd. 1956–58; Asst. Prof. of Chem., Univ. of Toronto 1958–62; Assoc. Prof. 1962–66; Assoc. Chair, Dept. of Chem. 1970–72, Chair 1988–93; Chair, Connaught Adv. Ctte., Physical Sciences, Univ. of Toronto 1974–76; Univ. of Toronto Computer Ctr. 1974–76; Divisional Ed., Div. of Phys. Electrochem., 'J. of the Electrochem. Soc.' (Am.) 1976–81; Dir., Surface Science & Catalysis Group, Univ. of Toronto 1980–85; Dir., H.M. Dignam Corp. (Barrie, Ont.); Chair, Chem. Grant Slection Ctte., NSERC 1987–88; author/co-author of over 110 articles in sci. journals & books; recreations: skiing, squash, bridge; clubs: Caledon Ski, Univ. of Toronto Faculty; Home: R.R. 2, Erin, Ont. N0B 1T0; Office: Toronto, Ont. M5S 1A1.

**DiIORIO, Alido,** B.A.Sc., P.Eng.; real estate developer; b. Italy 16 Jan. 1949; s. Antonio G. (dec.) and Anna Teresa (Zarlenga) D.; e. Univ. of Toronto B.A.Sc. 1972; m. Angela d. Euginio and Guilia Ferrari 31 May 1975; PRES., ALTERRA GROUP OF COMPANIES 1973– ; Past Dir., Ont. New Home Warranty Prog.; Past Pres., Ont. Home Builders Assn. (OHBA) 1989; Hamilton and Dist. Home Builders Assn. (HHBA) 1985; HHBA, Member of the Year Award 1986; OHBA Member of the Year Award 1989; Candn. Home Builders Assn., Beaver Award 1989; Mem., Assn. of Profl. Engrs.; Office: 920 Yonge St., Suite 1000, Toronto, Ont. M4W 3C7.

**DILLON, Richard Maurice,** M.C., C.M., E.D., B.A., S.M., LL.D., F.E.I.C., F.C.A.E., P.Eng.; consultant; b. Simcoe, Ont. 4 Aug. 1920; s. late Brig. Murray M., M.C., E.D. and Muriel Talbot (Hicks) D.; e. Pub. and High Schs., London, Ont.; Univ. of W. Ont., B.A. 1948, LL.D. Hon. 1979; Mass. Inst. of Technol., S.M. 1950; m. Elizabeth, d. late Henry Herbert Dempsey 1945; children: Kelly, Ann, Katherine; former Prof. of Engn., Univ. of W. Ont. and sometime Dean Faculty of Engn. Science there; Design Engr., M. M. Dillon & Co., later Partner and Dir., 1951–60; Design Engr., Dominion Bridge Co. Ltd., Toronto, 1950–51; founding Dean of Engn. Science at Univ. of W. Ont., 1960–71; Project Offr., Scient. Research & Devel. Comn. on Govt. Organ. (Glassco Comn.) 1961–62; Colombo Plan Consultant on Eng. Educ. to Govt. of Thailand, 1963; mem. Prov.of Ont. Adv. Comte. on Confed., 1965–67; seconded to Extve. Dir., Task Force Hydro Comte. on Govt. Productivity, Toronto, 1971; Depy. Min. of Energy, Ont. 1973–76; Depy. Prov. Sec. for Resources Development, Ont. 1976–79; Depy. Min. of Municipal Affairs and Housing 1979–82; founding partner, Alafin Consultants Ltd. 1982–90, sole proprietor Alafin Consultants 1990– ; lead People-to-People, Energy and Transportation delegation, Candn. Engrs. to China 1984; served with Candn. Army 1933–56; served in Can., U.K., Italy 1939–45; retired as O.C. 3rd Bn. RCR 1956; apptd. Hon. Lt. Col. 4th Bn. RCR 1986–96, apptd. Col. of the Regt. The RCR 1993; rec'd. M.C. 1942, E.D. 1953, Elizabeth II Coronation Medal 1953; Jubilee Medal, 1977; Commemorative Medal, 125th Anniversary of Candn. Confedn. 1992; recipient, Gold Medal for Mathematics, Univ. of W. Ont. 1948; Sigma Xi, MIT 1950; Assn. Prof. Engrs.-Sons of Martha Medal 1972, Companion Order of Sons of Martha 1981, CCPE Meritorious Service Medal 1984; Member, Order of Canada 1986; Fellow, Candn. Acad. of Engr. 1988; Past Pres., London and Ont. Brs. V.O.N.; Dir. London Div. Candn. Corps of Commissionaires 1950–76; mem. Toronto Div. 1977– ; (Chrmn. 1988–91); Dir., Arbitration and Mediation Inst. of Ont.; Vice Chrmn. and mem. Bd. of Govs., Fanshawe Coll. of Applied Arts & Technol., 1967–71; Gov., Ont. Research Foundation 1964–89; Dir., Inst. for Hydrogen Systems 1983–87; Mem., Sci. Counc. of Can. 1987–92; sometime Fellow Am. Soc. Civil Engn.; Fellow Engr. Inst. of Can.; mem. Assn. Prof. Engrs. Ont. (Vice-Pres. 1978; Pres. 1979–80); recreations: reading, skiing, travel, oenology; Clubs: Toronto Hunt; Albany; Commanderie de Bordeaux de Toronto; London; Home: 11 Meredith Cres., Toronto, Ont. M4W 3B7.

**DILWORTH, Thomas,** B.A., M.A., Ph.D.; university professor; b. Detroit, Mich. 31 March 1945; s. Thomas Murphy and Mary Louise (Kaiser) D.; e. Catholic Central H.S. 1963; St. Michael's College B.A. 1969; Univ. of Toronto M.A. 1971, Ph.D. 1977; m. Kathleen d. William and Ailein Connors 15 March 1976; children: Alison, Molly, Christine; PROFESSOR, ENGLISH, UNIV. OF WINDSOR 1986– ; Lecturer, St. John Fisher College (N.Y.) 1970–72; Asst. Prof., Univ. of Windsor 1977; Assoc. Prof. 1982; Chair, Comp. Literature Prog. 1979– ; referee for SSHRC rsch. grants; Candn. Fed. for the Humanities; Killam Fellow 1992–94; British Council Prize in the Humanities 1989; SSHRC research grants 1986–89, 1989–90, 1989–94; Woodrow Wilson Fellowship 1969; Christian; author: 'The Shape of Meaning in the Poetry of David Jones' 1988, 'The Liturgical Parenthesis of David Jones' 1979; co-author: 'The Talented Intruder: Wyndham Lewis in Canada 1939–45' 1992; editor: 'Inner Necessities: The Letters of David Jones to Desmond Chute' 1984; recreation: meditation, bicycling; Office: Windsor, Ont. N9B 3P4.

**DIMAKOPOULOS, Dimitri,** B.Arch., F.R.A.I.C., R.C.A.; architect; Chevalier, National Order of Que.; b. Athens, Greece 14 Sept. 1929; came to study in Can. 1948; e. Experimental Sch., Univ. of Athens 1947; McGill Univ. B.Arch. 1955; m. Lydia d. Dimitri Chabaline 15 June 1954; children: Irene, Marina; PRINCIPAL, DIMITRI DIMAKOPOULOS & PARTNERS; Prof., Univ. of Montreal 1965; Visiting Prof. and Critic, McGill Univ.; Trustee, Hellenic College U.S.A. 1975; past Dir., St. George's Sch. of Montreal; Fellow, Royal Arch. Inst. of Can.; mem., Order of Archts. of Que.; Ont. Assn. of Archts.; Royal Candn. Academy of the Arts; Bd. of Dirs., Candn. Archaeol. Inst. Athens 1980; Pres., Design Comte., Nat. Capital Comn., Ottawa 1983; recipient of numerous prizes & awards in nat. and internat. arch. competitions; participated in design of Salle Wilfrid Pelletier, Place des Arts, Place Ville Marie (in assn. with I.M. Pei of N.Y.), Greek Orthodox Cathedral, Place Bonaventure, Univ. du Qué. Campus, Inst. de Recherches en Biotechnologie, N.R.C., 'La Laurentienne' tower, 1000 de La Gauchetière Complex (all in Montreal); Concert Hall and Theatre (Vancouver); Cultural Centre, The Freiman Mall (both Ottawa); Portage III, Place d'Accueil (both Hull, Que.); Fathers of Confederation, Govt. Bldgs. (both PEI); Centre Scientifique INRS, Palais de Justice (Quebec City); and planning in cities of Calgary, Quebec, Ottawa and Winnipeg; designed projects in Greece, Italy, Saudi Arabia, U.S.A., Algeria, Hong Kong and China; Greek Orthodox; Home: 461 Clarke Ave., Westmount, Que. H3Y 3C5; Office: 1253 McGill College Ave., Suite 885, Montreal, Que. H3B 2Y5.

**DIMANT, Frank;** association executive; b. Munich, W. Germany 5 Apr. 1946; s. Morris and Nechama (Schwartsbrem) D.; e. Yeshiva Univ. New York Undergraduate Sch.; McGill Univ. Grad. Sch. Sociol.; m. Florence Kupfert d. Morris and Eva K. 8 Oct. 1972; children: Aviva Shoshana, Miriam Yael, Arie Zvi; EXEC. VICE PRES. B'NAI BRITH CANADA 1978– , Chief Exec. Offr. League for Human Rights 1978– ; former Exec. Dir., Candn. Zionist Fedn., Central Region, Toronto 1974; Nat. Exec. Sec., Candn. Friends of Hebrew Univ., Montréal 1970; Asst. Dir. B'nai Brith Youth Orgn. Montréal 1969; joined present orgn. 1978; Exec. Can.-Israel Ctte. 1978– ; Dir. Levi Arthritic Hosp., Hot Springs, Ark.; Chrmn. New York Zionist Youth Council 1966, Am. Zionist Youth Council 1967; Spokesman N.Y. Youth Conf. on Soviet Jewry 1966; Exec. Bd. Un. Zionist Revisionist Orgn. 1964–68; Pres. Betar Zionist Youth U.S. & Can. 1967; Del. First Brussells Conf. on Soviet Jewry, Third Conf. Jerusalem; Chrmn., Ed. Bd., Candn. Zionist 1969–72; Vice Pres., Zionist Revisionist of Can. 1974; Exec. Bd. Mem., Mazon – A Jewish Response to Hunger; Bd. of Gov., Tel Aviv Found. 1988; Bd. of Dirs., Community Hebrew Academy High Sch.; Education Ctte., Assoc. Hebrew Day Schools; Adv. Bd., Candn. Jewish News; Yellow Brick House home for battered women 1988–89; co-ordinated leadership missions to Israel, Lebanon, Ethiopia, Spain, South Africa, Hungary, Poland, Romania, The Soviet Union; recreation: reading, travelling; Home: Thornhill, Ont. L4J 2T4; Office: 15 Hove St., Downsview, Ont. M3H 4Y8.

**di MICHELE, Mary,** B.A., M.A.; writer; b. Lanciano, Italy 6 Aug. 1949; d. Vincent and Concetta Andreacola D.; e. Univ. of Toronto, B.A. 1972; Univ. of Windsor, M.A. 1974; divorced; one d.: Emily; TEACHER, CREATIVE WRITING PROGRAM, CONCORDIA UNIV.; Poetry Ed., 'Toronto Life' 1980–81, 'Poetry Toronto' 1982–84; Writer-in-Res., Univ. of Toronto 1985–86; Writer-in-Res., Metro Reference Lib. (Toronto) May-Sept. 1986; Writer-in-Res., Regina Public Lib. Sept. 1987–July 1988; Writer-in-Lib., Etobicoke Libs. Sept.-Dec. 1989; Writer-in-Residence, Concordia Univ. Jan.-May 1990; 1st Prize for Poetry, C.B.C. Lit. comp. 1980; Silver Medal DuMaurier Poetry Award, Nat. Mag. 1982; Air Can. Writing Award 1983; Italian-Candn. Writers' Assn.; Writers' Union; author: 'Tree of August' 1978, 'Bread and Chocolate' 1980, 'Mimosa and Other Poems' 1981, 'Necessary Sugar' 1983, 'Immune to Gravity' 1986; 'Luminous Emergencies' 1990; 'Under

My Skin' 1994; editor: 'Anything is Possible' 1984; Address: c/o English Dept., Concordia Univ., 1455 de Maisonneuve Blvd. W., Montréal, Qué. H3G 1M8.

**DIMITROV, Olga,** R.C.A. (1975); costume designer; b. Czechoslovakia 5 Jan. 1933; d. Svetoslav and Miskovska (Antonie) Dimitrov; e. Sch. of Ceramics Karls-Bad Czechoslovakia 1947–49; Acad. of Applied Arts Prague 1949–52; m. 7 Feb. 1957; one child; Prop., Dimitrov Design Services Ltd.; served as Resident Designer Civic Theatre Kladno and later at the Civic Theatre Presov; guest designer throughout Czechoslovakia creating designs for over 360 stage productions encompassing drama, opera, ballet and musical comedy; designed costumes for 18 feature films between 1964–68 incl. Acad. Award winning 'Closely Watched Trains' and 'The End of August in Hotel Ozone' (Vatican Peace Prize); came to Can. 1968; became Resident Costume Designer Neptune Theatre Halifax; Costume Designer Ind. Univ. Sch. of Music's Opera Dept. 1971–73; Resident Costume Designer Theatre London Co. and during this period also designed costumes for Toronto Arts Productions and Nat. Arts Centre Ottawa; Costume Designer 'Fantastica' 42 short films for children; since 1977 freelance costume designer (film, theatre, TV); costume design for 'In Praise of Older Women'; 'Agency'; 'Silence of the North'; 'Death Hunt'; 'Harry Tracy'; 'Dead Zone'; designed films 'The Undergrads,' 'Beer,' 'Samuel Lount,' 'One Magic Christmas,' 'John and the Missus,' 'Bethune - Making of a Hero' 1987–88, 'Millennium' 1988, 'Agaguk' (French-Candn. co-production) 1990–91; 'Agaguk' 1992; 'Woman on Trial' 1993; 'Squanto - Indian Warrior' 1993; nominated for Dora Mavor Moore Award (Best Costumes in Musical – 'The Boyfriend') 1981; nominated for Genie Award for costumes ('Silence of the North'); won Dora Mavor Moore Award (Best Costumes – 'Man of La Mancha') 1982; nominated for Prix Genie Award ('One Magic Christmas' and 'Samuel Lount') 1985, ('Millennium') 1990; received Genie Award for best costume design for 'Bethune - Making of the Hero' 1991; Address: 132 Indian Rd., Toronto, Ont. M6R 2V5.

**DIMMA, William Andrew,** B.A.Sc., P.Eng., M.B.A., D.B.A., D.Comm. (Hon.); b. Montreal, Que. 13 Aug. 1928; s. William Roy and Lillian Norine (Miller) D.; e. Univ. of Toronto B.A.Sc. 1948; P.Eng. 1950; Harvard Univ. Middle Mgmt. Prog. 1956; York Univ. M.B.A. 1969; Harvard Univ. D.B.A. 1973; m. Katherine Louise, d. William Matthews Vacy Ash, 13 May 1961; children: Katherine, Suzanne; Bd. Chrmn., CB Media Ltd.; Fleet Aerospace Corp.; Toronto Commercial Advisory Council; Royal LePage Ltd.; Monsanto Canada Inc.; York University; Director: Canadian Reassurance Co.; Canadian Reinsurance Co.; CB Media Ltd.; Continental Bank of Canada; Fleet Aerospace Corp.; Home Oil Inc.; Interprovincial Pipe Line Inc.; London Life Insur. Co.; Monsanto Canada Inc.; Sears Canada Inc.; Sears Canada Acceptance Inc.; Silcorp Ltd.; SwissRe Management Ltd.; Trilon Financial Corp.; Trizec Corp. Ltd.; Former Directorships: Canron Inc. 1982–90; Capstone Investment Trust 1979–86; Costain Ltd. 1977–79; Delta Hotels Ltd. 1981–85; General Accident Insur. Co. of Canada 1981–85; Harlequin Enterprises Ltd. 1976–78; Interhome Energy Inc. 1986–91; A.E. LePage Ltd. 1979–84; Royal LePage Ltd. 1984–93; Polysar Chem. Co. 1974–87 (Chrmn. 1977–87); Polysar Energy & Chem. Corp. (Canada Develop. Corp.) 1987–88; Torstar Corp. 1976–78; Toronto Star Newspapers Ltd. 1974–78; Union Carbide Canada Ltd. 1967–70; Former Directorships (non-profit): Ballet-Opera House Corp.; Governor 1987–89; Bishop Strachan School 1978–81; Mem., Business Council on National Issues 1984–87; Canada-Japan Business Ctte. (Secretary) 1989–92; Canadian Club of Toronto 1977–83 (Pres. 1981–82); Mem., Candn. Council for Native Business 1984–87; Candn. Opera Co. 1986–89; Economic Council of Canada 1977–80; Chrmn., Federal Advisory Ctte. on Financial Institutions 1984; Mem., Govt. of Ont. Labour Management Study Group 1977–86; Trustee, Hospital for Sick Children 1977–92; C.D. Howe Institute 1985–92; Industrial Accident Prevention Assn. 1976–78; Niagara Institute 1976–88 (Chrmn. 1983–86); Ontario Press Council 1986–92; Mem. of Premier's Advisory Ctte. on the Economic Future (Ont.) 1976–83; Dir., Toronto Symphony Orchestra 1979–82; Trillium Foundation 1986–89; Career: Union Carbide Canada Ltd. 1948–70; Extve. Vice Pres. & Dir. 1967–70; Prof. and Dean, Fac. of Administrative Studies, York Univ. 1974–76; Pres. & Dir., Torstar Corp. and Toronto Star Newspapers Ltd. 1976–78; Pres. & Dir., A.E. LePage Ltd. 1979–84; Pres. & C.E.O., Royal LePage Ltd. 1984–86; Depy. Chrmn., Royal LePage Ltd. 1986–93; Gov., Candn. Journalism Found.; Hon. Trustee, Hospital for Sick Children; Chrmn. of the Bd. of Govs., Jr. Achievement of Metro. Toronto; Honorary Dir., Niagara Institute; Chrmn. & Gov., York Univ.; Chrmn., York Univ. Devel. Corp.; Awards: Elmslie Memorial Scholarship 1944; Canada Council Fellowship 1970–73; Gold Medal, Doctoral Programme, Grad. Sch. of Bus. Admin., Harvard Univ. 1971; York Univ. Business Sch. Alumni Award for Outstanding Corporate Leadership 1992; author: 'Canada Development Corporation: Diffident Experiment on a Large Scale'; Beta Theta Pi; Kt. Comdr., Order of St. Lazarus of Jerusalem; Anglican; recreations: cross-country skiing, swimming, cycling; Clubs: Toronto; Toronto Golf; York; Home: 17 Dunloe Road, Toronto, Ont. M4V 2W4.

**DIMOCK, John Leslie,** M.B.,Ch.B., F.R.C.P.(C); psychiatrist; b. Birmingham, Eng. 1 Sept. 1951; s. Ernest Leslie and Lillian Grace (Harvey) D.; e. King Edward Grammar Sch. Birmingham; Birmingham Univ. M.B.,Ch.B. 1975; LMCC 1977, Dip.Psych 1978 FRCPC 1980; divorced; children: Emma, Amy, Stephen; PRIVATE PRACTICE OF PSYCHIATRY (speciality Forensic); Dir., Family Court Clinic, Royal Ottawa Hosp. 1981–89; Founding mem. Candn. Acad. Psychiatry & Law; recreations: rugby football, basketball; Club: Ottawa Scottish Rugby (Past Pres.); Home: 5 Lakewood Dr., R.R. 1, Richmond, Ont. K0A 2Z0; Office: Suite 900, 155 Queen St., Ottawa, Ont. K1P 6L1.

**DIMOND, Michael Frank,** B.A., C.G.A.; financial executive; b. Niagara Falls, Ont. 15 Feb. 1946; s. Frank Thomas and Margaret Melitta (Scott) D.; e. Wilfrid Laurier Univ., B.A. 1969; C.G.A. 1979; m. Carol d. James and Susan Bright 13 July 1983; children: Scott, Julie; PRES., CHEP CANADA INC. 1988– ; Mgr., Finan. Analysis, Becton Dickinson & Co. 1981; Corp. Controller, Canvin Prod. Ltd. 1982; Controller/Sec., CHEP Can. Inc. 1983; Vice-Pres., Finan. & Admin. 1988; recreations: sailing; Club: Port Credit Yacht; Home: 2021 Granby Dr., Oakville, Ont.; Office: 76 Wentworth Court, Brampton, Ont. L6T 5M7.

**DIMSON, Theo,** R.C.A., F.G.D.C., A.O.C.A., A.G.I.; creative designer; b. London, Ont. 8 Apr. 1930; s. Nicholas and Helen (Papadopoulos) D.; e. Pub. Sch. London, Ont.; Tech. Sch., Toronto; Ont. Coll. Art (scholar.), grad. 1950; m. Judith Donoahue d. the late Olav Gjevre and the late Tyra Eriksson 30 May 1993; Children: Lisa, Benjamin, Nicole, Emily Victoria; PRESIDENT AND CREATIVE DIR., THEO DIMSON DESIGN INC. 1983– ; began with Art Associates Ltd. as Graphic Designer 1950; Freelance 1953–60; rejoined Art Associates Ltd. as Vice-Pres., Creative Dir. 1960–65; Pres. & Creative Dir., Dimson & Smith Ltd. 1965–83; gold & silver awards of Excellence: Art Directors and Graphica Clubs of Toronto 1951–91 and of Montreal; Communication Arts Exhn., Los Angeles; Sr. Arts Fellowship by Can. Council 1961, 1971; Award of Excellence, 10th Candn. TV Commercials Festival; Best Show Award Gold and (triple) Silver Medallist, Art Dirs. Club of Toronto; 1st Prize Nat. Retail Merchants Assn. TV Conf. N.Y. and 21st Annual Retail Advertising Conf., Chicago 1973; exhibited in '100 Years of the Poster in Canada' A.G.O. 1979; 2 gold, 5 silver awards, Art Dirs. Club, Toronto, 1980; The Usherwood Award 1984; exhibited 8th Internat. Poster Biennale, Warsaw, Poland; The Colorado Internat. Invitational Poster Exhibition U.S.A. 1984, 1985, 1987, 1989–93; Lahti Poster Biennial, Finland 1983; The 1st Internat. Triennial of Posters, Japan 1985; First Internat. Theatre Poster Exhibition, Chaumont, France 1990; Gitane Poster Exhib. Paris, France 1991; Litfass-Kunst Biennale (International) Munich, Germany 1992; The Advertising and Design Club of Canada 1993; work exhibited internationally and rep. in internat. journals; one man articles in Idea Magazine (Japan), C.A. Magazine (U.S.A.), Studio Magazine, Creativity Magazine, Applied Arts Quarterly & Toronto Star (Canada); Who's Who in Graphic Art (Intnl.) De Clivo Press, Switzerland (Vol. 1 1962, Vol. 2 1984); one man show, Toronto, 1978; Retrospective of work, Royal Ontario Museum, Toronto Oct. 1993–Jan. 1994; Author, 'Great Canadian Posters' 1979; Pres., Art Directors Club, Toronto 1986–88; mem. A.G.I.; Art Directors Club, Toronto; Am. Inst. Graphic Arts, New York; Fellow, Graphic Designers of Canada; Assoc., Ont. Coll. of Art; Greek Orthodox; Home: Box 358, Mount Albert, Ont. L0G 1M0.

**DINGLEDINE, Paul Stewart,** B.A., M.B.A.; diplomat; b. Hamilton, Ont. 6 May 1946; s. Elden Wyatt and Helen Elizabeth (Bennett) D.; e. McMaster Univ. B.A. 1967, M.B.A. 1969; CANADIAN AMABASSADOR TO TEHRAN, IRAN 1990– ; Candn. Govt. Trade Comnr., Trinidad, Israel & India 1971–77; Advisor to Sr. Vice-Pres., McMillan Bloedel Ltd. Vancouver 1978; Policy Advisor to Asst. Dep. Min., Dept. of Indus., Trade & Commerce Ottawa 1979–81; Candn. Consul, Hamburg Germany 1981–82; Sr. Asst. to Min. for Internat. Trade Ottawa 1983–84; Dir. of Investment Promotion, Investment Canada 1985; Dir., Middle East Trade, External Affairs 1986–90; Hom: P.O. Box 500 (Teran), Station A, Ottawa, Ont. K1N 8T7; Office: Canadian Embassy, P.O. Box 11365 – 4647, Tehran, Iran.

**DINGWALL, David Charles,** B.Comm., LL.B., M.P.; politician; b. South Bar (Cape Breton), Nova Scotia 29 June 1952; s. George R. and Isabell L. D.; e. College of Cape Breton; St. Francis Xavier Univ.; Dalhousie Univ. B.Comm. 1974, LL.B. 1979; children: Jay David, Leigh-Ann, Jennifer Rae; MINISTER OF PUBLIC WORKS and GOVERNMENT SERVICES and Min. resp. for the Atlantic Canada Opportunities Agency 1993– ; also Min. responsible for Canada Post Corporation, the Royal Candn. Mint and Canada Mortgage and Housing Corporation; Spec. Asst., Office of the Min. of Public Health & Attorney-General, Govt. of N.S. 1974–76; private law practice 1979–80; Parly. Secy. to Min. of Energy, Mines & Resources, House of Commons 1982–84; Member of Parliament for Cape Breton-East Richmond, House of Commons 1980– ; 1st elected general election 1980; re-elected 1984, 1988; various Assoc. & Official Opposition Critic posts 1984–90; Chair (Atlantic), Liberal Caucus, Parl. of Can. 1985–86; Nat. Extve. 1986–87; Chief Opposition Whip, House of Commons 1990–91; Opposition Leader in the House 1991–93; Roman Catholic; recreations: athletics, reading, travelling; Office: Room 607, Confederation Block, House of Commons, Parl. Bldgs., Ottawa, Ont. K1A 0A6.

**DINGWALL, William Gray,** B.A., Q.C.; lawyer; b. Rosetown, Sask. 11 Aug. 1929; s. Roderick and Janet Elizabeth (Gray) D.; e. Univ. Toronto; Osgoode Hall Law Sch. 1955; m. Karen, d. Frederick Taylor, 8 Aug. 1959; children: William, Suzanne, Brian, John; LAWYER, WOOLLEY, DALE & DINGWALL since 1976; Dir., Vital Pacific; Davidson Tisdale Mines Ltd.; Partner, Willis, Dingwall 1960; Clarke, Dingwall, Newall 1971; Hames, Dingwall 1975; Clubs: Albany; Granite; Home: 59 Chestnut Park Rd., Toronto, Ont. M4W 1W7; Office: Box 65, Toronto-Dominion Centre, Toronto, Ont. M5K 1E7.

**DI NINO, Honourable Consiglio;** senator; b. Italy 24 Jan. 1938; e. St. Michael's College, Univ. of Toronto; York Univ.; m. Sheila Marlyn McWhirter 1960; children: Frank, Karen; SENATOR, THE SENATE OF CANADA 1990– ; 36 years in the financial services industry incl. nine years with a major Candn. chartered bank; Co-Founder, Pres. & Chief Extve. Offr., Cabot Trust Company 1979–91; summoned to the Senate of Canada 30 Aug. 1990 by The Right Honourable B. Mulroney; Chair, Italian Candn. Benevolent Corp.; Vice-Pres., Boy Scouts of Canada; Past Chair, Harbourfront Corp.; Past Pres., Candn. Italian Bus. & Profl. Assn.; Villa Colombo Home for the Aged; Columbus Ctr. of Toronto; Scouts Canada (Greater Toronto Region); recreations: travel; clubs: Scouts Canada; Office: 212 East Block, Ottawa, Ont. K1A 0A4.

**di NORCIA, Vincent,** M.A., Ph.D.; educator; b. Toronto, Ont. 18 March 1937; s. Jimmy and Mary Teresa (Gorassi) di N.; e. De La Salle Oaklands Toronto; Gonzaga Univ. Spokane, Wash. M.A. 1964; Univ. of Toronto Ph.D. 1969; m. Linda Blakeley Ross 25 Nov. 1966; children: Andrea, Alexander; PROF. OF PHILOS. UNIV. OF SUDBURY 1966– ; Jesuit 1956–63; Lib. Brebeuf High Sch. Willowdale 1963–64; part-time faculty Laurentian Univ. Sch. of Comm. since 1984, Chrmn. Philos. Dept. 1971–72, 1978–82, mem. Senate 1969–72, 1977–80, 1983–87, 1992– ; Acad. Visitor Mgmt. Sci's Dept. Univ. of Waterloo 1989–90; Dept. of Govt. London Sch. of Econ. 1982; Ethics Rsch. Centre Univ. of Del. 1983; Scarborough Coll. 1972–73; Prog. Ctte. Niagara Inst. 1986–89; Govt. of Italy Grant for Rsch. Early Renaissance Democratic Theory 1982; Mem., Ethics Ctte., Sudbury Cardio-Thoracic Found. 1989–91; Part-time Fac., Sch. of Commerce, Laurentian Univ. 1986–91; Leader and Cons., Values Mgmt. Workshop 1987–91; Dir., SSHRC Rsch. project on 'Environmental Values and Technological Innovation' 1991; Dir. Sudbury Symphony 1988–89; St. Andrew's Concert Series 1986–88; Pres. and Vice Pres. John Howard Soc. 1976–79; Dir. Children's Aid Soc. 1973–76; mem. Sudbury 2001 Rsch. Ctte. 1978–80; mem., Environment Ctte., Sudbury Chamb. of Comm.; Chair, Environmental Technology Ctte., Sudbury Next 10 Years Conference 1992; Forum Ed. 'Corporate Ethics Monitor' 1989– ; Mem. Bd., Sudbury Children's Mental Health Assn. 1992– ; recreations: tennis, squash; Home: 18 Aspenwood, Sudbury, Ont. P3E 5W1; Office: Sudbury, Ont. P3E 2C6.

**DI NOVI, Gene;** musician; b. Brooklyn, N.Y. 26 May 1928; s. Antonio and Philomena (Pecchio) D.; e. Fort

Hamilton High Sch. Brooklyn; m. late Patricia d. Alexander and Mary Gertrude McNeil 1 May 1949; children: Denise, Michelle; remarried May 7th 1983 to Deirdre Bowen d. Rev. Dr. Desmond and Jean Bowen; one son: William Desmond; started as Jazz Pianist, 52nd St. N.Y.C.; records with Benny Goodman, Artie Shaw, Lester Young; Musical Dir. for Lena Horne, Peggy Lee, Tony Bennett, Dinah Shore; concert tours: 'I can Hear the Music' (with vocalist Kirstin Campbell); 'Jazz in a Classical Key' (clarinet and piano duo with James Campbell); popular concerts with conductor Howard Cable; engagements with own jazz trio (David Young, bass; Memo Acevedo, drums); film composer – Candn. credits: 'I Married the Klondike' C.B.C.; 'The Woodland Indians' C.B.C.; 'Toronto the Good' for Cinesphere, Ont. Place; actor: 'Scales of Justice' C.B.C. drama; 'Top Cops'; 'Cement Soul' C.B.C.; 'Perfectly Normal' etc.; teaches private class, 'The Playing, Arranging and History of the American Popular Song'; A.C.T.R.A. Award Nominations 1978, 1981; Home: RR 1, Orangeville, Ont. L9W 2Y3; Office: 680 Queen's Quay W., Apt. 602, Toronto, Ont. M5V 2Y9.

**DINSDALE, Henry Begg,** M.D., C.M., F.R.C.P.(C), F.A.C.P.; physician; educator; b. Kingston, Ont. 22 Sept. 1931; s. Harry Hamlin and Doris Eileen (Donnelly) D.; e. Queen's Univ. M.D., C.M. 1955; m. Lyla June d. Bert T. Yates 11 June 1955; children: Janyce Hall, John Scott, Henry Yates, Martha Jane; ASSOC. DEAN FOR RESEARCH 1993– ; and PROFESSOR, DEPT. OF MEDICINE (NEUROLOGY), QUEEN'S UNIV. 1983– ; Regional Dir., Medical Rsch. Council 1993– ; Head, Dept. of Medicine 1983–93; Physician-in-Chief, Kingston Gen. Hosp. and Hotel Dieu Hosp. (Kingston) 1983–93; Prof. and Chrmn. Div. of Neurol. Queen's Univ. 1971–1983; Resident in Med., Kingston Gen. Hosp. 1955–57; Registrar, Maudsley Hosp. London, Eng. 1957–59; Nuffield Fellow, Nat. Hosp. Queen's Sq. London, Eng. 1959–60; Resident and Research Fellow, Harvard Neurol. Unit Boston City Hosp. 1960–63; Past Chrmn. Ont. Heart Foundation, Ont. Mental Health Foundation and Ministry of Health Ont. Med. Research Comtes.; mem. various fed. and prov. task forces on Cerebrovascular Disease, Med. Manpower, High Technol. and Hypertension; mem. Med. Research Council Can. (Council 1977–84, Extve. 1979–84, Vice-Pres. 1983–84); mem. Counc., Royal Coll. of Physicians and Surgeons of Can. 1984– ; (Vice-Pres., Med. 1991); recipient Brown Prize 1950; Morris Prize 1958; MacLachlan Fellow 1961–62; Bullard Fellow 1962–63; Weil Award Am. Assn. Neuropathol. 1976; author 'The Nervous System, Structure and Function in Disease' 1972; numerous research articles and book chapters dealing with neurology, cerebrovascular disease and hypertension; mem. Candn. Neurol. Soc. (Past Councillor, Pres. 1981–82); Am. Acad. Neurol. (mem. Extve. 1979–83); Colls. Phys. & Surgs. Ont. and Que.; Am. Neurol. Assn.; Candn. Soc. Clin. Investig.; Soc. Neurosciences; Candn. Assn. Neuroscientists; Internat. Soc. Cerebral Circulation & Metabolism; Candn. Stroke Soc.; Am. Heart Assn. (Council Cerebrovascular Div.); PanAm. Soc. Neurol.; Ont. Heart and Stroke Foundn. (Dir. 1985–91); Alzheimer Soc. Canada (Bd. Mem., Chair Rsch. Policy); Protestant; recreation: tennis; Home: 95 Hill St., Kingston, Ont. K7L 2M8; Office: Kingston General Hospital, Connell 725, 76 Stuart St., Kingston, Ont. K7L 2V7.

**DINSHAW, Nadine,** B.Sc., M.Sc.; astronomer; b. New Delhi, India 30 Sept. 1964; d. Jal and Mithoo (Contractor) D.; e. Univ. of B.C. B.Sc. 1989, M.Sc. 1992; ASTRONOMER, STEWARD OBSERVATORY, UNIV. OF ARIZONA 1992– ; research and pubns. on the radial velocity variations of cepheid variable stars, Univ. of B.C. 1987–88; on the polarisation properties of stars with circumstellar disks and of spectral features arising in the interstellar medium 1989–91; present research into the large-scale structure of the universe using absorption lines of heavy elements observed in the spectra of quasars; work on the cepheid Polaris, suggesting the imminent cessation of its pulsations, was pub. in a number of popular magazines incl. 'Sky & Telescope,' 'New Scientist,' and 'Equinox'; Mem., Am. Astronomical Soc.; Candn. Astronomical Soc.; recreations: skiing, tennis, travel; Office: Tucson, Arizona.

**DION, Claude G.,** B.A., B.Com., M.Com., C.A.; executive; b. Québec, Qué. 12 Oct. 1942; s. Gérard O. and Juliette (Bilodeau) D.; e. Coll. de Lévis, B.A. 1963; Laval Univ. B.Com. 1965, M.Com. 1966, Licence in Acctg. 1967; C.A. 1967; m. Andrée d. Charles Côté 7 Aug. 1965; children: Marc, Isabelle; PRES. WILLIAMS & WILSON LTD. 1988– ; Dir. La Société Therapprouve Inc.; Dir., Groupe Soprin; Auditor, Coopers & Lybrand 1966–69; Controller and Sec.-Treas. DCB Industries Ltd. 1970–73; Controller, Piedmont Equipment Ltd. 1974, Vice Pres. Finance 1977, Exec. Vice Pres. 1981–83; Vice Pres. Finance present Co. 1983, Exec. Vice Pres. 1987–88; mem. AMTDA; IDA; Montréal C. of C.; Montréal Bd. of Trade; recreations: skiing, golf, tennis; Clubs: Richelieu (Pres. 1981); Carrefour Le Moutier (Pres. 1983–86); Montréal Golf & Country; Home: 30 Place Calédonie, Candiac, Qué. J5R 4G8; Office: 1300 Rue St-Patrick, Montréal, Qué. H3K 1A4.

**DIONNE, Major George Burton, CD (Ret'd),** F.R.G.S.; company executive; b. Montreal, Que. 17 Jan. 1922; s. Telesphore Octave and Louise Helen (Drolet) D.; m. Beryl Emily, d. Cyril DesCôtes and Lillian (Haney), 26 Sept. 1942; children: Carolyn Lois, Bruce Charles, Arlene Beryl; PAST DIRECTOR, J.A. PRESTON OF CANADA LTD.; Frank W. Horner Ltd., 1939–54; served as Asst. to Vice Pres.-Marketing and Export Mgr.; Arbuthnot Ewart (Canada) Ltd. (subsidiary of The Anglo-Thai Corp. of Great Britain), 1954–57; served as Resident Mgr. for Can.; Mead Johnson of Canada Ltd., 1957–61; Dir. of Merchandising and subsequently Pres. of Mead Johnson of Quebec Ltd.; Schering Corp. Ltd., 1961–69; Dir. of Marketing and subsequently Vice Pres. of Corp. also Dir. and Vice Pres. of Pharmaco Canada Ltd. and White Laboratories; USV of Can. Ltd., 1969–73; Managing Dir. & Chief Exec. Officer of this Revlon Inc. Subsidiary; subsequently worked with Organizing Comm. 1976 Olympic games (Revenue Division) and as Exec. Vice-Pres. of Better Bus. Bureau of Canada; served with Candn. Active Army in Can. and Overseas during World War II; served with Victoria Rifles of Can. before and after War, currently Mem., Regimental Officers' Mess, The British Columbia Dragoons, rank Major; Past Pres. YCC 212; Past Dir. & Chrm., Membership Comm., Pharmaceutical Manufacturers Assoc. of Can.; Past Dir. & Hon. Treas., Candn. Foundation for the Advancement of Pharmacy; Past Dir., St. Lawrence Yacht Co.; Past Consul, ad honorem, Republic of Paraguay; Past Pres. and Treas., Archdiocesan Union of Montreal; Parents' Assoc. of Mt. Royal and St. Laurent, Que.; Past Dir. and Past Treas., Fed. of Home & Sch. Assns. Prov. of Que.; Past Dist. Treas., St. Lawrence Dist. of Candn. Power Squadrons and Past Commander, Montreal Squadron; Nat. Treas., Candn. Power Squadron 1970 conf.; Chrmn., Okanagan Br., The Monarchist League of Can.; Fellow, Royal Geographical Soc., 1979; Past mem., Royal Candn. Military Inst.; recreations: yachting, curling, duplicate bridge (Life Master); Club: Kelowna Yacht; Home: 'The Fountains,' 81 – 2200 Gordon Dr., Kelowna B.C. V1Y 8T7.

**DIONNE, René,** M.A., L.Ph., L. ès L., D. ès L.; professeur titulaire; né Saint-Philippe-de-Néri, Qué. 29 janvier 1929; f. Ferréol (déc.) et Marie-Anne (Massé) D.; é. Coll. de Sainte-Anne-de-la-Pocatière; Univ. Laval B.A. 1950; Univ. de Montréal M.A. 1955, L. ès L. 1960; L'Immaculée-Conception Montréal L.Ph. 1958; Univ. de Sherbrooke D. ès L. 1974; Univ. de Strasbourg (études de théologie); Georgetown Univ. Washington, D.C. (études de linguistique); Cambridge Univ., Univ. of Edinburgh, Oxford Univ. (études de littérature anglaise); ép. Gabrielle f. Charles-Édouard et Estelle Poulin 1970; PROFESSEUR DE LETTRES FRANÇAISES, UNIV. D'OTTAWA 1970– ; Professeur au Coll. Saint-Ignace Montréal 1954–56, 1958–59, au Coll. Sainte-Marie Montréal 1965–69, à l'Univ. de Montréal (littérature québécoise) 1967–69, à l'Univ. de Sherbrooke 1969–70; Directeur du Département des lettres françaises, Univ. d'Ottawa 1975–78; Professeur invité à l'Univ. de Kiel, R.F.A. 1988; Professeur associé à l'Univ. de Moncton 1989–95; Prix de l'Ambassade suisse 1960; Prix littéraire de 'La Presse' 1979; Prix littéraire Champlain 1980; collaborateur aux revues suivantes: 'Relations' 1966–80; 'Collège et famille' 1968–69; Univ. of Toronto Quarterly 1974–77; 'Lettres québécoises' 1976–81; directeur adjoint des 'Lettres du Bas-Canada' 1957–58; membre du comité de rédaction de 'Voix et images du pays' 1972–75; directeur-fondateur de la 'Revue d'histoire littéraire du Québec et du Canada français' 1979–87; Comité de recherche francophone de l'ALCQ 1976–79; coordonnateur du Groupe interuniversitaire d'études franco-ontariennes 1975–79, du Regroupement des Centres de recherches et d'études en civilisation canadienne-française 1980–82; membre du Comité de parrainage et des Comités scientifique et multiculturel du projet 'Histoire de l'institution littéraire au Canada' 1987– , du Comité de rédaction du 'Dictionnaire des écrits de l'Ontario français' 1987– , de l'Institut franco-ontarien 1988– ; auteur 'Antoine Gérin-Lajoie, homme de lettres' 1978; 'La Patrie littéraire 1760–1895' 1978; 'Bibliographie de la littérature outaouaise et franco-ontarienne' 1978, 1981; 'Répertoire des professeurs et chercheurs (littérature québécoise ou canadienne-française) 1978, 1980; 'La Littérature canadienne de langue française' 1988; 'Anthologie de la poésie franco-ontarienne, des origines à nos jours' 1991; 'La Littérature régionale aux confins de l'histoire et de la géographie' 1993; co-auteur 'L'Age de l'interrogation 1937–1952' 1980; 'Bibliographie de la critique de la littérature québécoise et canadienne-française dans les revues canadiennes (1974–1978)' 1988, '(1979–1982)' 1991, '(1760–1899)' 1992; éd. 'Propos littéraires' 1973; 'Propos sur la littérature outaouaise et franco-ontarienne' (4 tomes 1978–83); 'Situation de l'édition et de la recherche' 1978; 'Quatre Siècles d'identité canadienne' 1983; 'Le Québécois et sa littérature' 1984; coll. 'Histoire littéraire du Québec et du Canada français' (14 tomes 1979–87); membre Union des écrivains québécois, ALCQ (président 1976–78), Association des études canadiennes, Société des écrivains canadiens, Société bibliographique du Canada, Association des auteurs de l'Ontario; récréations: lecture, cinéma, marche, voyages; Adresse: 1997 avenue Quincy, Ottawa, Ont. K1J 6B4; Bureau: Université d'Ottawa, Ottawa, Ont. K1N 6N5.

**DIONNE-MARSOLAIS, Rita,** B.A., B.Sc., M.A.; economist; b. Sherbrooke, Que. 20 April 1947; d. Charles-H. and Alice (Létourneau) D.; e. Univ. de Montréal B.A. 1967, B.Sc. 1970, M.A. 1971; m. Jean s. A. Marsolais 8 Aug. 1970; SENIOR MANAGER, PRICE WATERHOUSE (MONTREAL) 1991– ; Extve., Hydro-Québec 1971–79; Vice-Pres., Corp. Devel., Soc. Gén. de Financement du Qué. 1979–82; Pres., Bio-Endo 1982–84; Delegate Gen. for Que. in N.Y. 1984–87; Pres., Les Consultants Nunc Inc. 1987–91; Bd. Mem., Fond. Hôpital Saint Luc; Mem., Economic Club of N.Y.; Nat. Treas., Parti Québécois; Ed. Bd. Mem., 'Ecodecision'; Address: 1250 boul. René-Lévesque ouest, Bureau 3500, Montreal, Que. H3B 2G4.

**D'IORIO, Antoine,** B.Sc., M.Sc., Ph.D.; educator; b. Montreal, Que. 22 Apr. 1925; s. Giuseppe and Assunta (Torino) D'I.; e. Univ. of Montreal, B.Sc. 1946, M.Sc. 1947, Ph.D. (Biochem.) 1949; Scholar Am. Heart, Univ. of Wisconsin 1952; Post-doctoral Fellowship, Oxford Univ. 1955; m. late Ghislaine Chatel Sept. 1950; seven children; PRES., CANADIAN MEDITERRANEAN INST. 1990– ; Asst. Prof. of Physiol. Univ. of Montreal 1949–55, Assoc. Prof. 1956–61; Prof. of Biochem. & Chrmn. of Dept. present Univ. 1961–69; Dean, Fac. of Sci. & Engn. there 1969–76, Vice-Rector (Acad.) 1976–84; Rector & Vice-Chancellor, Univ. of Ottawa 1984–90; Publications: about 90 research papers in field of biol. sciences; Ed. Candn. Journl. of Biochemistry; acted as Editor of 'Revue Canadienne de Biologie,' 1956–60; mem. Am. Chem. Soc.; Am. Assn. Biological Chemists; Am. Soc. of Neurochemistry; The Biochem. Soc. (Eng.); Candn. Soc. of Biochem. (Vice-Pres. 1969–70; Pres. 1969–70); Soc. of Experimental Biology & Med.; Orgn. Internat. de rsch. sur le cerveau; Internat. Soc. of Neurochemistry; Roy. Soc. of Can. (Sec. 1974–77); Candn. Soc. of Physiology (Treas. 1958–61); Candn. Fed. of Biological Socs. (Treas. 1962–66, Pres. 1971); Assn. Candn.-Francais pour l'avancement des sci. – ACFAS (Vice-Pres. 1969–71, Pres. 1971); Dir., Nation's Capital Television Inc. 1989; R. Catholic; Chevalier, Ordre du Mérite National (France) 1988; Hon. D.Sc., Carleton 1990; Home: 405 - 15 Murray St., Ottawa, Ont. K1N 9M5; Office: Ottawa, Ont. K1N 6N5.

**DIOSADY, Levente Laszlo,** Ph.D., P.Eng., C.Eng., F.C.I.C.; university professor; b. Hungary 2 Oct. 1943; s. Paul L. and Irene A. (Szabo) D.; e. Univ. of Toronto B.Sc. 1966, M.Sc. 1968, Ph.D. 1971; m. Klara M. d. Lajos and Clara Lendvay 10 July 1971; children: Andrew, Laslo; PROF. OF FOOD ENGR., DEPT. OF CHEM. ENGR., UNIV. OF TORONTO 1979– ; Proc. Engr., The Cambrian Engr. Group 1972; Dir., 1974; Pres., Food Biotek Corp.; Dir., Chem. Engr. Rsch. Cons. Limited; Mem., Expert Ctte. on Food Engr.; Can. Awards of Bus. Excellence, Inventions Category 1987; Sec. Treas., Hungarian Rsch. Inst. of Can.; Rsch. Ancillary of Univ. of Toronto; Vice-Pres., Rakoczi Found.; Past Pres., Hungarian Candn. Engrs. Assn.; P.Eng. and C.Eng., Prov. of Ont.; Mem., Candn. Inst. of Food Sci. & Technol.; Inst. of Food Technol.; Am. Oil Chem. Soc.; Candn. Soc. for Chem. Engr.; Assn. of Official Analytical Chem.; author of some 60 referred pubns. & 9 patents/patent applications; Home: 20 York Rd., Willowdale, Ont. M2L 1H5; Office: Toronto, Ont. M5S 1A4.

**DIOUF, Pierre;** diplomate; né Fadiouth, Sénégal 26 mars 1943; é. Univ. de Dakar Licence en Droit Public internat. 1970; Brevet de l'Ecole nationale d'Adm. du Senegal 1972; marié; enfants: quatre; AMBASSADEUR DU SENEGAL AU CAN. 1989– ; Chef de la Div. 'Conventions et Accords internationaux' de la Direction des Relations extérieures du Ministère des Affaires étrangères 1972–74; Conseiller puis Premier Conseiller

Rome 1974–76; Conseiller diplomatique du Président de la République 1976–78; Ministre-Conseiller Paris 1978–81; Secrétaire exécutif du Comité inter-Etats Sénégalo-gambien à Banjul 1981– ; Secrétaire général de la Présidence de la Confédération de la Sénégambie 1982–89; Bureau: 57 Marlborough Ave., Ottawa, Ont. K1N 8E8.

**DIRKS, John Herbert,** B.Sc. (Med.), M.D., F.R.C.P.(C), F.A.C.P., F.R.S.C.; educator; b. Winnipeg, Man. 20 Aug. 1933; s. Alexander P. and Agnes (Warkentin) D.; e. Mennonite Brethren Coll. Inst. Winnipeg 1950; Univ. of Man. B.Sc. and M.D. 1957; m. Fay Ruth d. Mark K. Inman, Ph.D., London, Ont. 3 July 1961; children: John Mark, Dr. Peter Benjamin, Dr. Martha, Carol; PROF. OF MEDICINE & HEALTH ADMIN., UNIV. OF TORONTO; Rotating Intern and Jr. Asst. Resident Winnipeg Gen. Hosp. 1957–59; Renal Fellow, Deer Lodge Veterans Hosp. Winnipeg 1959–60; Med. Resident Montreal Gen. Hosp. and M.R.C. Fellow McGill Univ. 1960–62; M.R.C. Fellow and Visiting Scient. Lab. of Kidney & Electrolyte Metabolism, Nat. Heart Inst. Bethesda, Md. 1963–65; Dir. Renal Lab. Royal Victoria Hosp. 1965–76, Sr. Phys. 1971–76, Dir. Renal & Electrolyte Div. 1965–76; Med. Rsch. Council Scholar, McGill Univ. 1965–70, Prof. of Med. 1971, Prof. of Physiol. 1974, John Fraser Rsch. Assoc. 1971–76; Eric W. Hamber Prof. and Head of Med., Univ. of B.C. 1976–87; Dir. G.F. Strong Labs UBC, Prof. of Physiol. 1978–87; Phys.-in-Chief, Vancouver Gen. Hosp. 1976–86; Head, Dept. of Med., Health Sciences Centre Hosp., UBC 1984–87; Dean of Faculty of Med., Univ. of Toronto 1987–91; Special Advisor, Min. of Health, Prov. of Ont. 1992–93; Chair, United Nations University Feasibility Study on Environment Water and Health 1992–93; mem. Endocrinol. & Nephrol. Grants Comte. Med. Research Council Can. 1972–77, Program Grants & Core Comte. 1977; Visiting Prof. Univ. Coll. Hosp. London 1973; mem. Scient. Adv. Bd. Nat. Kidney Foundation 1972, mem. Counc. 1984–88; Vice Pres. C.O.S.C.I.N. Internat. Cong. Nephrol. 1974–78; Chrmn. VIth Internat. Urolithiasis Workshop 1988; Program Chrmn. ASN 1987; Assoc. Ed. 'Canadian Journal of Physiology & Pharmacology' 1968–73; mem. Ed. Bd. several prof. journs.; author or co-author numerous publs. Candn. and foreign prof. journs.; Fellow, Royal Soc. of Can. 1982; mem. Candn. Soc. Clin. Investigation (Secy.-Treas. 1972–75, Pres. 1976–77); Candn. Soc. Nephrol. (Councillor); Coll. Phys. & Surgs. Prov. Que.; Fed. Med. Specialists Que.; Internat. Soc. Nephrol. (mem. Counc. 1984–93) Chrmn. Nomin. Ctte. 1984–87; MRC Council 1978–84, Mem. of Extve. 1981–84; Chrmn., Scientific Advisory, Kidney Foundation of Canada 1982–86; mem. Med. Advisory Bd., Gairdner Found. 1983– , mem. Bd. of Trustees 1987– , Pres. 1993– ; Candn. Assn. Professors of Med. (Pres. 1984–85); B.C. Science Counc. (Dir. 1986–87); Royal College Research Ctte. 1986–88; Assn. Am. Phys. and other Candn. and Am. prof. assns.; recipient Queen Elizabeth Jubilee Award; Medical Award, Kidney Foundn. of Can. 1985; Protestant; Home: 60 Admiral Rd., Toronto, Ont. M5R 2L5; Office: EN1 - 222 Toronto Hospital, 200 Elizabeth St., Univ. of Toronto, Toronto, Ont. M5G 2C4.

**Di SALLE, Hon. Mario Crescenzo,** B.A., LL.B.; judge; b. Copper Cliff, Ont. 30 Aug. 1935; s. Donato and Amalia (Cercone) DiS.; e. elem. and high schs. Copper Cliff; Assumption Univ. of Windsor B.A. 1958; Univ. of Ottawa LL.B. 1961; m. Joan Ann d. Kenneth and Rita Beresford, Windsor, Ont. 19 aug. 1961; children: Michael, Lisa; JUDGE, ONT. COURT OF JUSTICE (GEN. DIV.), formerly District Courts of Ont. (Algoma Dist.) 1982– ; articled Hawkins & Gratton, Sudbury; called to Bar of Ont. 1963; Partner, Wilkins DiSalle Poupore & Wilkins, Sudbury 1963–82; Past Chrmn., Sudbury Planning Bd.; Past Pres., Club Montessori Sudbury; mem., Candn. Bar Assn.; R. Catholic; recreations: golf, squash, tennis; Club: Idylwylde Golf; Home: 1102 - 2000 Regent St. S., Sudbury, Ont. P3E 5T5; Office: Court House, Sudbury, Ont. P3C 1T9.

**DISNEY, David M.,** B.A., M.Ed., Ed.D.; education executive; b. Oshawa, Ont. 30 June 1938; s. Everett George and Helen Doreen (Michael) D.; e. Queen's Univ. B.A. 1966; Univ. of Ottawa M.Ed. 1971; Univ. of Toronto Ed.D. 1975; m. Marie d. Edward and Elenor Fulton 26 March 1960; children: Shari, Dana; DIR. OF EDN. AND SEC. TO THE BD. VICTORIA CO. BD. OF EDN. 1981– ; elem. sch. teacher 6 yrs.; sec. sch. teacher 2 yrs.; elem. sch. prin. 12 yrs.; Eng. as a second lang. teacher 2 yrs.; Instr.: Ministry Prin. Course 1974; OISE 1975–77; Queen's Univ. 1977; Supt. of Human Resources, York Co. Bd. of Edn. 1978–81; author various papers, articles; Chair, Local Adv. Counc., Chair Victoria County, United Way; United Church; Clubs: Kiwanis (Past Distinguished Pres.); Rotary (Past Pres.); Office: P.O. Box 420, Lindsay, Ont. K9V 4S3.

**DISSETTE, G. Keith,** B.A., RPA; commercial real estate executive; b. Cleveland, Ohio 6 July 1944; s. Vaughn Kester and Gertrude Alice (Singleton) D.; e. Miama Univ. B.A. 1967; m. Judith d. James and Lea Madden 26 June 1969; children: Danielle Leonora, Alexandra Kristine; VICE-PRESIDENT & GENERAL MANAGER, DOWNTOWN REGION COMMERCIAL PROPERTIES GROUP, BRAMALEA LIMITED 1978– ; Captain, U.S. Air Force 1967–71 (architectural-engr. services); Asst. Sec. Treas., Empire Realty (Bank of N.S. subsidiary) 1971–75; Property Mgr., S.B. McLaughlin & Assoc. 1975–78; Dir. & Mem., Building Owners & Mgrs. Inst. of Can. (Chapter. Dir. 1975–77, 1987–89); Mem., Crossroads Un. Ch. (Dir. 1983–85); Home: 3579 Ash Row Cres., Mississauga, Ont. L5L 1K3; Office: Suite 2300, One Queen St. E., Toronto, Ont. M5C 2Y9.

**DISTON, David George,** F.C.A., C.M.A.; wine industry executive; b. Wembley, England 10 Aug. 1932; s. Roland and Nina Frances (Sherlock) D.; e. Gunnersbury Gr. Sch. 1948; Assoc., Inst. of C.A.'s England & Wales 1954; Fellow 1964; cert. Mngt. Acct., Ont. 1968; m. Gudrun d. Alfred and Kaethe Anderschd 29 June 1957; children: Carmen, Michael, Dolores, Marion, Maria Teresa, Yolanda; VICE PRES., CORPORATE DEVELOPMENT, BRIGHTS WINES LTD. 1988– ; Chief Acct., Chase Protected Cultivation Ltd. 1954–57; Office Mgr., Chateau-Gai Wines Ltd. 1957–62; Winery Mgr. 1962–73; Vice-Pres., Prodn. 1973–75; Vice-Pres., Admin., Jordan Valley Wines Ltd. 1975–78; Vice-Pres., Opns., T.G. Bright & Co. Ltd. 1978–80; Vice-Pres. & Gen. Mgr., Ont. 1980–88; Dir. & Vice Chrmn., Candn. Wine Inst.; Chrmn., Wine Counc. of Ont. 1984–85; Mem., Ont. Govt. Long Range Task Force on Grape & Wine Indus. 1984–86; Gov., Greater Niagara Gen. Hosp. 1983–93, Chrmn. 1990–92, Sec. Treas. 1986–88, Vice-Chrmn. 1988–90; var. Bds. of Edn. (9 yrs.); Past Chrmn., Loretto Acad. Lay Adv. Bd.; Saint Paul H.S. Bd. of Govs.; Roman Catholic; recreation: travel; Home: 3813 Potter Heights, Niagara Falls, Ont. L2J 3E1; Office: P.O. Box 510, Niagara Falls, Ont. L2E 6V4.

**DIXON, Brian,** M.Com., Ph.D.; sculptor; professor; b. Winnipeg, Man., 13 Jan. 1930; s. William Armstrong and May Alice (O'Brien) D.; e. Univ. of Man., B.A. 1950; Univ. of Toronto, M.Com. 1953; Univ. of Michigan, Ph.D. 1959; PROF. EMERITUS AND SR. SCHOLAR, YORK UNIV., Prof., Bus. Adm. 1967–90; Founding Dir., Program in Arts Adm., York Univ., 1969–70; Assoc. Dean 1972 & Acting Dean 1973–74, Fac. of Admin. Studies, York Univ.; 23 solo and group exhns. of sculpture: Montreal, N.Y., Toronto, Kingston, Motril, Marbella and Almuñecar, Spain; Co-ordinator, Project for Restoration of Egyptian Antiquities Museum, Cairo 1980–81; author of 3 books and numerous articles in learned and popular journs.; recreations: bicycling, poetry, travel; Home: P.O. Box 423, Gananoque, Ont. K7G 2T9; Office: 4700 Keele, North York, Ont. M3J 1P3.

**DIXON, Gordon H.,** O.C., M.A., Ph.D., F.R.S.C. (1970), F.R.S. (1978); university professor; b. Durban, S. Africa, 25 Mar. 1930; s. Walter James and Ruth (Nightingale) D.; e. High Sch., Cambridge, Eng.; Trinity Coll., Cambridge Univ., M.A.; Univ. of Toronto, Ph.D. 1956; came to Canada Nov. 1951; m. Sylvia Weir (Gillen) 20 Nov. 1954; children: Frances Anne, Walter Timothy, Christopher James, Robin Jonathan; PROF. OF MED. BIOCHEM., UNIV. OF CALGARY 1974– ; (and Head of Dept. 1983–88); Research Adv. Comte., Research Inst., Hospital for Sick Children, Toronto 1981–84; Research Adv. Ctte., Clinical Rsch. Inst. of Montreal 1983–90; Trustee of the E.W.R. Steacie Memorial Found. 1978– ; served RCAF Reserve, Air Intelligence 1952–54; Rsch. Assoc., Univ. of Washington 1954–55 (Asst. Prof. 1956–58); Staff mem., Med. Research Council Unit for research in cell metabolism, Univ. of Oxford 1958–59; Asst. Prof., Biochem., Univ. of Toronto 1960–62, Assoc. Prof. 1962–63; Assoc. Prof., Univ. of B.C. 1963–66, Prof. 1966–72; Prof. and Head, Biochem. Group, Sch. of Biol. Sci., Univ. of Sussex 1972–74; author more than 200 articles in scient. journs.; winner of Ayerst Award, Candn. Biochem. Soc. 1966 and Steacie Prize for 1966; Josiah Macy Jr. Faculty Scholar Award 1979; Visiting Fellow, Trinity Coll., Cambridge 1979–80; Flavelle Medal, Royal Soc. of Can. 1980; Izaak Walton Killam Memorial Prize 1991; apptd. Officer, Order of Canada 1993; mem., Candn. Biochem. Soc. (Pres. 1982–83); Pres., Pan-American Assoc. of Biochem. Soc. 1987–1990 (Vice-Pres. 1984–87); Extve., Internat. Union of Biochem. 1988–97; Chrmn., Candn. National Comte. for the Internat. Union of Biochemistry 1984–88; Am. Soc. Biochem. Mol. Biol.; Candn. Soc. Cell. Biol.; Am. Soc. Cell Biology; Assoc. Ed., 'Journal of Molecular Evolution'; 'Biochemistry International'; recreations: hiking, gardening, reading; Home: 4402 Shore Way, Victoria, BC V8N 3T9; Office: Fac. of Med., Dept. Med. Biochem., Health Sciences Centre, 3330 Hospital Dr. N.W., Calgary, Alta. T2N 4N1.

**DIXON, Harold Collier,** B.Comm., LL.D. F.C.A.; b. Toronto, Ont. 22 July 1910; s. George Ernest and Elinor Gertrude (Dadson) D.; e. Univ. of Toronto, B. Comm. 1932; LL.D., Honoris Causa, McMaster Univ., 1979; m. Norma Irene, d. Howard Fife, Sharon, Ont. 11 June 1938; children: Joan Elaine, Barbara Jean, Robert Harold; Partner, Clarkson, Gordon & Co., 1947–75; Hon. mem. Bd. Govs., McMaster Univ.; joined firm 1932; C.A. 1936; F.C.A. 1956; Pres., Hamilton Assn. for Advanc. of Lit., Science and Art (1978–80); Baptist; recreation: gardening; Home: 119 Dalewood Cres., Hamilton, Ont. L8S 4B8.

**DIXON, Jack Edmund Garrard,** C.D., M.A., Ph.D.; scholar; translator; writer; b. Broadstairs, Eng. 20 Jan. 1924; s. Howard George and Joan Irene (Bramley) D.; e. St. Lawrence Coll. Ramsgate, Eng. Sch. Cert. 1939; Inst. de Touraine, Univ. de Poitiers Diplôme d'Études Supérieures 1949; Merton Coll. Oxford B.A. (Hons.) 1952, M.A. 1956; Stanford Univ. Ph.D. 1970; m. Rika d. Wilhelmus and Henrika Moerkes 1 Aug. 1959; one d. Jacqueline Joan; served with RAF 1940–48 UK and S. Africa, Pilot 1943–48; RAF Volunteer Reserve Oxford 1950–52; RCAF 1953–57, Security Offr., NATO 1955–57, Reserve 1957–63 Winnipeg; Awarded, Candn. Forces Decoration by Gen. GCE Thériault, Chief of Defence Staff, for 'many years of distinguished service' 1985; Lectr. to Prof. of French Lit. Univ. of Winnipeg 1959–89, Head of French 1966–78; writer (with special interest in military aviation) 1989– ; 'Concordance des "Œuvres" de Rabelais' 1992; editor: Laddie Lucas 1985, 1989; contbr. 'Out of the Blue. The Role of Luck in Air Warfare 1917–1966'; 'Thanks for the Memory. Unforgettable Characters in Air Warfare 1939–45'; mem. RCAF Assn.; Aircrew Assn.; N.W. Pacific Renaissance Assn.; RAF Historical Soc.; RAF Club London; recreations: theatre, bridge, walking; Address: 1470 Derby Rd., Victoria, B.C. V8P 1T3.

**DIXON, John Edward,** B.A., Ph.D.; federal official; educator; b. New Westminster, B.C. 14 Nov. 1943; s. Frank George and Annis Victoria (Dickinson) D.; e. Vancouver Coll.; Univ. of B.C. B.A. 1965, Ph.D. 1974; m. Sandra d. Douglas and Edith Ross 27 Aug. 1977; two s. Matthew, Alister; Special Policy Advisor on Defence to the Min. of Defence 1993; Instr. in Philos. Capilano Coll. 1973– , Coordinator Depts. Fine Arts, Religious Studies, Theatre and Philos. 1976–79, 1985–86; Pres. and Dir., B.C. Civil Liberties Assn. 1984–91 (Dir. 1981); recipient, Can. Counc. Fellowship 1968–72; Begbie Public Service Award for 'outstanding contribution ... in advancing justice, law reform, and the standards of the legal profession' Univ. of Victoria, Fac. of Law, Alumni Assoc. 1990; author 'Catastrophic Rights' 1990 (Fr. transl. 'Sida et Médicaments Expérimentaux: Des Droits Catastrophiques'); mem. YMCA; recreations: handball, hunting, fishing; Home: 20 Rideau Terrace, Ottawa, Ont. K1M 1Z9.

**DIXON, Langford;** poet and recitalist; b. Toronto, Ont. 2 June 1915; s. Henry and Margaret Diana (Rennie) D.; e. Balmy Beach public Sch.; Malvern Coll., Toronto; Private Tuition before attending London Sch. Engn. Tech. (U.K.); Oxford Univ. 1945; Hons. Grad., Lorne Greene's Acad of Radio Arts; m. Grace Marion, d. late George Morris Watson, 23 Aug. 1947; for some time Music Critic, CKEY, Toronto and later with Globe and Mail; Social Worker on Pilot Project sponsored by Bickell Foundation at core of Toronto's Gang Problems; Co-ordinator, Poetry Exchange Programme between B.W.I. and Ont. Schs., Ont. Dept. Educ.; Pres., Wilson MacDonald Poetry Soc.; Candn Chrmn.; World Poetry Day Comte.; author of 'The Ballad of Willy' 1964; 'Comment' 1965; 'The Devil You Say' 1965; 'The Birds and Bees' 1965; 'Seven' 1967; 'When Laughter Put to Sea' 1968; 'Once Upon a Time' 1970; 'Though the World Cry' 1979; 'On Reading Poetry in the Schools' 1981; 'To Wake in a Dream' 1989; 'Let Eloquence But Speak' (a study of Candn. poetry) 1990; has read his work widely throughout Ont. and U.S. in schs., colls., univs., theatres and on radio and TV; World Poetry Day Citation 'for his contribution to International Understanding through Poetry' by World Poetry Day Comte., N.Y. 1971; Diploma di Benemerenza (for literary activities), Centro Studi e Scambi Internazionali 1972; officially apptd. Ontario's Bicentennial Poet; Protestant; recreations: photography, furniture making and refinishing: Home: 33 Fairway Ave., Belleville, Ont. K8N 4B4.

**DIXON, Michael A.,** M.Sc., Ph.D.; educator; b. Maniwaki, Qué. 21 June 1952; s. Arthur Curtis and Isabel Jean (Swetnam) D.; e. Mount Allison Univ. B.Sc. 1975, M.Sc. 1976; Edinburgh Univ. Ph.D. 1982; U.R.F., ASSOC. PROF. OF HORTIC. UNIV. OF GUELPH 1985– ; Pres., Plant Water Status Instruments, Inc.; Rsch. Asst. Mount Allison Univ. 1975–76; Asst. Check Scaler, N.B. International Paper Co. 1976–78; Rsch. Assoc. Edinburgh Univ. 1978–82; Post-Doctoral Fellow, Univ. of Toronto 1982, Rsch. Assoc. 1984–85; Home: 7 Elmhurst Cr., Guelph, Ont. N1H 6C8; Office: Dept. of Hort. Science, Univ. of Guelph, Guelph, Ont. N1G 2W1.

**DIXON, Michael E.,** M.D., C.M., M.Sc., F.R.C.P.(C); medical executive; b. Toronto, Ont. 16 June 1936; s. John Harkness and Edith Millicent (Bailey) D.; e. Lower Can. Coll. Montreal 1953; McGill Univ. B.Sc. 1958, M.D., C.M. 1960, M.Sc. 1963; m. Gail Susan d. F. Thurston Gunning 21 June 1958; children: Susan, Julia, Leanne, Andrew; REGISTRAR, THE COLL. OF PHYSICIANS & SURGEONS OF ONT. 1980– ; postgrad. training Royal Victoria Hosp., Montreal Gen. Hosp. and Queen Mary Veterans Hosp., Montreal 1960–65; hosp. appts. Montreal Gen. Hosp. 1967–69, Queen Mary Veterans Hosp. 1966–69, Oshawa (Ont.) Gen. Hosp. 1970–72, Toronto Gen. Hosp. 1972–79; Lectr. in Med. McGill Univ. 1968–70, Univ. of Toronto 1972–75, Asst. Prof. 1975–79; Dir. of Med. Services, Ont. Med. Assn. 1972–74; Vice Pres. Med. Affairs, Toronto Gen. Hosp. 1974–79; recreation: sailing; Clubs: R.C.Y.C.; Home: 106 Cortleigh Blvd., Toronto, Ont. M4R 1K6; Office: 80 College St., Toronto, Ont. M5G 2E2.

**DJWA, Sandra Ann,** B.Ed., Ph.D.; writer and educator; b. St. John's, Nfld. 16 Apr. 1939; d. Walter William and Dora Beatrice (Hancock) Drodge; e. Mem. Univ. of Nfld. Teacher Training 1955–56; Univ. of B.C., B.Ed. 1964, Ph.D. 1968; m. Peter Djing Kioe Djwa 6 Sept. 1958; divorced 1987; one s. Phillip John; m. secondly, Lalit Srivastava 14 July 1991; CHAIRWOMAN, DEPT. OF ENGLISH, SIMON FRASER UNIV. 1986– ; Asst. Prof. of Engl. there 1968–75, Assoc. Prof. 1976–80, Prof. 1980– ; rec'd Killam Post-Doctoral 1970–72, Sr. Killam Family Fellowship 1981–82, 1982–83; author 'E.J. Pratt: The Evolutionary Vision' 1974; 'Saul and Selected Poetry of Charles Heavysege' 1976; 'The Politics of the Imagination: A Life of F.R. Scott' 1987; various articles, book chapters; co-ed. 'On F.R. Scott: Essays on his Contributions to Law, Literature and Politics' 1983; 'E.J. Pratt: Complete Poems' (2 vols.); sometime ed. Annual Review of 'Poetry,' Letters in Canada, 'Univ. of Toronto Quarterly' 1979–84; mem. Assn. Candn. Univ. Teachers Eng.; Assn. Candn. & Que. Lits.; United Church; recreations: gardening, writing; Home: 2947 Marine Dr. W., Vancouver, B.C. V7V 1M3; Office: Burnaby, B.C. V5A 1S6.

**DLAB, Vlastimil,** RNDr., C.Sc., Ph.D., D.Sc., F.R.S.C.; educator; b. Bzí, Czechoslovakia 5 Aug. 1932; s. Vlastimil and Anna (Stuchlíkova) D.; e. elem. Sch. Bzí 1943; Real Gymnasium, Turnov 1951; Charles Univ. R.N.Dr. 1956, C.Sc. 1959; Habilitation 1962, D.Sc. 1966; Khartoum Univ. Ph.D. 1962; (div.); m. Helena d. František Briestenský 18 Dec. 1985; children: Dagmar, Daniel Jan, Philip Adam, David Michael; PROF. OF MATH. CARLETON UNIV. 1968– ; and DIRECTOR, OTTAWA-CARLETON INSTITUTE OF MATHEMATICS AND STATISTICS 1992– ; Fellow, Czech. Acad. Science 1956; Lectr. and Sr. Lectr. Charles Univ. 1957–59, Reader 1964–65; Lectr. and Sr. Lectr. Univ. of Khartoum 1959–64; Research Fellow and Sr. Research Fellow, Inst. Advanced Studies, Australian Nat. Univ. 1965–68; Chrmn. of Math. Carleton Univ. 1971–74; Visiting Prof. Univ. de Paris VI, Brandeis Univ. and Universität Bonn 1974–75, Univ. Leeds 1975, Univ. of Tsukuba 1976, Univ. de Sao Paulo 1976, Univ. Stuttgart 1977, Univ. de Poitiers 1978, Univ. Nat. Auton. Mexico 1979, Universität Essen 1979; Univ. Trondheim 1979, 1991; Univ. of Tsukuba 1981; Univ. Bielefeld 1980, 1983, 1985, 1990, 1991; Hungarian Academy of Sciences 1985, 1990, 1993; Czechoslovak Academy of Sciences 1985; Univ. Beijing, Univ. Warsaw and Univ. Vienna 1988; U.C.L.A. 1989; Univ. Virginia 1990; Univ. Paderborn 1993; rec'd Can. Council Leave Fellowship 1974; Nat. Research Council Can. Scient. Exchange 1978; Japan Soc. for the Promotion of Sci., Sr. Research Fellowship 1981; NSERC Science Exchange 1983, 1985, 1988, 1991; Dipl. of Hons. Union of Czechoslovakia Mathematicians 1962; author over 90 research papers group theory, theory of rings and modules, gen. algebra, representation theory; mem. Royal Soc. Can. (Convenor & mem. of Counc. 1980–81); Candn. Math. Soc. (Council 1973–77, Chrmn. Rsch. Comte. 1973–77, Ed., Can. Jour. of Math.); Am. Math. Soc.; London Math. Soc.; Math. Assn. Am.; European Mathematical Soc.; recreations: sports, music; Home: 277 Sherwood Dr., Ottawa, Ont. K1Y 3W3; Office: Ottawa, Ont. K1S 5B6.

**DOAK, James Crosland,** Q.C. (Man.), LL.B.; barrister and solicitor; b. Portage La Prairie, Man. 18 May 1919; s. Haughton Augustus and Rosalind (Crosland) D.; e. Univ. of Man., LL.B. 1942; m. Shirley Mae d. E.C. and E.M. Smith 11 Aug. 1945; children: Russell, Graeme, Crosland; Couns., Winnipeg 1945–53; Sr. Partner, Doak, Buckingham & Co. (Man.) 1953–69; Partner, Salloum Doak 1970–77; General Counsel, Salloum Doak 1977–91; Couns. on Transp. before Hall Comn., Snavelly Comn., Candn. Transp. Comn.; Former Dir., VIA Rail Canada Inc.; Past Adv. Bd., Montreal Trust Co. of Can.; Hon. Mem., Real Estate Bd. (Okanagan Mainline); Q.C. 1960; six military medals; Pres. & Past Chrmn., Nat. Extve., Assn. of Candn. Clubs; Past Vice-Chrmn., Univ. Grants Comn. (Man.); Mem., Candn. Bar Assn. (Past Vice-Pres.; Past Nat. Chrmn., Energy & Natural Resources and Petroleum & Gas); Law Soc. of B.C. 1969–93, of Man. 1945–93, of Sask. 1955–93; P.C. Party of Can. (Past Nat. Treas.; Past Nat. Vice-Pres.); P.C. Party of Man. (Past Pres.); recreations: golf; Address: 16 – 880 Christina Place, Kelowna, B.C. V1V 1S2.

**DOANE, Harvey Lawrence,** B.Comm., C.B.V., F.C.A.; chartered accountant; b. Halifax, N.S. 18 March 1934; s. Harvey Roy and Anne Margaret (Hayden) D.; e. Dalhousie Univ., B. Comm. 1955; Inst. of C.A.s of N.S., C.A. 1957, F.C.A 1978; m. Elise d. Temple and Frances Lane 21 May 1958; children: Stephen, Thomas, Edward, Jennifer; Lectr., part-time, Dalhousie Univ. 1957–58; Partner, Doane Raymond 1958–92; Head, New Glasgow office, Doane Raymond 1962–67; Sr. Tax Partner 1970; Chrmn., Mngt. Ctte. 1974–88; Pres., Inst. of C.A.s of N.S. 1968; Chrmn., Candn. Inst. of C.A.s 1982–83; Chrmn., Candn. Tax Found. 1985–86; Chrmn., Halifax Dartmouth Bridge Comn. 1992– ; Mem., Candn. Inst. of Bus. Valuators; Former mem., Adv. Bd., Revenue Can.; Joint Ctte. on Taxation, Candn. Bar Assn. & C.I.C.A.; Former Dir., Issac Walton Killam Hosp. for Children; Tech. Univ. of N.S.; Dalhousie Univ.; author of various articles & papers; recreations: sailing, skiing; Clubs: Royal N.S. Yacht Squadron; Home: 931 Beaufort Ave., Halifax, N.S. B3H 3X8.

**DOBBIE, George Herbert;** textile manufacturer; b. Galt, Ont. 15 Nov. 1918; s. late George Alexander and Jean Edith (Scott) D.; e. Lakefield Coll.; Bishop Ridley Coll.; McGill Univ. (Comm. & Finance); m. Marie Louise, d. C. A. Reiser, Montreal, Que., 15 Mar. 1941; four s. George, Murray, Brian, Alexander; Chrmn., GLENELG TEXTILES LTD.; Chrmn., Agatex Devels. Ltd.; Past Pres., Candn. Woolen & Knit Goods Mfrs. Assn.; Past Chrmn., Can. Textiles Inst., Galt Bd. of Trade; Galt Bd. of Ed.; Past Pres., Dobbie Industries Ltd.; Newlands & Co. Ltd.; Past Vice-Pres., Can. Manufacturing Assn.; Can. B.I.A.C.; Can. Comte. of the Pacific Basin Economic Council; Past Governor, Univ. of Waterloo; Lakefield College School; served in 2nd World War with Candn. Army, 1941–45; discharged with rank of Capt.; Anglican; recreations: hunting, fishing; Home: 45 Blair Road, Galt, Ont. N1S 2H8; Office: 1201 Franklin Blvd., Galt, Ont. N1R 6R7.

**DOBBIN, D. Michael,** B.Ed.; producing director; freelance actor/director; b. Calgary, Alta. 23 March 1948; s. Robert Campbell and Maureen Martha (James) D.; e. Univ. of Calgary B.Ed. 1971; PRODUCING DIR. ALBERTA THEATRE PROJECTS 1983– ; Founding Artistic Dir. Palisade Arts Alta.; Former Instr. in Theatre Mngmt., Univ. of Calgary Dept. of Drama; served as Theatre Mgr. Round House, London, Eng.; joined Vancouver Playhouse as Mng. Dir. and co-founder of Acting Sch.; Artistic Dir. Western Can. Theatre Co., Kamloops 1979–83; conceived and produced for 7 years playRites Festival; co-founder and Past Chrmn. Profl. Assn. Candn. Theatre; Founding Chrmn. B.C. Touring Council for Performing Arts; served numerous panels, juries and as adjudicator; Participant, Gov. General's Candn. Study Conference 1991; served one term Bd. Candn. Conf. Arts; mem. Calgary Econ. Adv. Council; Founding Bd. Mem., Calgary Winter Festival; Bd. Nat. Theatre Sch.; Adv. Ctte. Theatre Depts. Mount Royal Coll. and Banff Centre for the Arts; recipient Queen's Silver Jubilee Medal 1977; Outstanding Citizen Cert. from H. of C. 1983; Govt. Can. Cert. of Merit 1988; Alta. Achievement Award 1988; Harry and Martha Cohen Award for Sustained and Significant Contribution to Theatre 1992; Home: Calgary, Alta.

**DOBBS, Kildare Robert Eric,** M.A.; writer, travel correspondent and broadcaster; b. Meerut, Uttar Pradesh, India, 10 Oct. 1923; s. late William Evelyn Joseph, I.C.S., and Maud Clifford (Bernard) D.; e. St. Columba's Coll., Rathfarnham, Ireland 1937–41; Jesus Coll., Cambridge, (Exhibitioner), B.A. 1947, M.A. 1952; Inst. of Educ. London Univ., Teacher's Dipl. 1948; m. 1st Patricia Marjorie Agnes Parsons, 1944 (div.); children: Kildare John Evelyn, Christian Tracey Allan; 2nd Mary L. McAlpine 1958 (div.); children: Lucinda Favell, Sarah Williams; 3rd Linda Kia Kooluris, 7 May 1981; formerly Staff Writer, Toronto 'Star Weekly' 1962–65; Book Editor and Columnist, 'Toronto Star' 1970–73; Educ. Offr., Moshi, Tanganyika 1948–50; Dist. Offr., Iringa, Tanganyika 1950–52; came to Canada 1952; worked in Heinz' warehouse, Toronto; Teacher, High Sch., Lambton-Kent Co. 1953; Ed., Trade Books, Macmillan Co. of Canada Ltd., Toronto 1953–61; Assoc. Ed., 'Saturday Night' Dec. 1961–June 1962, Managing Ed. 1965–68; mem. Ed. Bd., 'The Canadian Forum'; Co-Founder, 'The Tamarack Review'; rep. in 'The Norton Reader' and other anthologies; served in 2nd World War with Royal Navy, 1942–46; author of 'Running to Paradise' (winner of 1963 Gov.-Gen's. Award) 1962; 'Canada' (with Peter Varley) 1964; 'Reading The Time' 1968; 'The Great Fur Opera' (with Ronald Searle) 1970; 'Pride and Fall' (short stories) 1981; 'Historic Canada' (with Marjorie Harris) 1984; 'Coastal Canada' 1985; 'Away from Home: An Anthology of Canadian Travel-Writing' 1986; 'Anatolian Suite: Travels and Discursions in Turkey' 1989; 'Ribbon of Highway' 1992; Nat. Magazine Award for travel essay 1986; recreations: music, walking, photography; Address: Ste. 1005, 330 Spadina Rd., Toronto, Ont. M5R 2V9.

**DOBELL, (Alan) Rodney,** Ph.D.; professor; b. Vancouver, B.C. 27 Apr. 1937; s. Colin and Sophie Elizabeth (Freeman) D.; e. Univ. of B.C., B.A. 1959, M.A. 1961; Massachusetts Inst. of Technology Ph.D. 1965; m. Marnie d. Victor and Ruth Rogers 16 June 1962; children: Lauren Lisa, Darcy Jean, Kenneth Rogers; FRANCIS G. WINSPEAR PROF. OF PUBLIC POLICY, UNIV. OF VICTORIA 1991– ; Asst. Prof. of Econ. Harvard Univ. 1964–68; Prof. of Pol. Econ. Univ. of Toronto 1968–73; Dep. Sec. Planning Br. Treasury Bd. Secretariat Ottawa 1973–76; Dir., Gen. Econ. Br. OECD Paris 1976–78; Rsch. Dir. Parlty. Task Force on Fed.-Prov. Fiscal Arrangements 1981 and on Pension Reform 1983, co-author Reports 'Fiscal Federalism in Canada ' 1981, 'Pension Reform' 1983; Chrmn. Jt. Productivity Ctte. B.C. Govt/B.C Govt. Employees' Union 1982–83; Prof. and Dir. Sch. Publ. Adm. Univ. of Victoria, B.C. 1977–84; Pres. The Inst. for Research on Public Policy 1984–91; co-author 'Mathematical Theories of Economic Growth' 1970; co-ed. 'Economic Analysis of Telecommunications: Theory and Applications' 1983; 'Public Purse, Public Purpose' 1991; 'Learning for Life' 1992; Home: 3456 Plymouth St., Victoria, B.C. V8P 4X4; Office: Univ. of Victoria, P.O. Box 1700, Victoria, B.C. V8W 2Y2.

**DOBIE, Edgar Hampton Jr.,** B.A., M.A.; arts administrator and manager; b. Vernon, B.C. 12 Apr. 1953; s. Edgar Hampton and Constance Irene (Smith) D.; e. Univ. of B.C. B.A. (1st class) 1977; Univ. of Leeds M.A. 1978; m. Elizabeth d. Gordin and Sylvia Kaplan 12 May 1981; children: Anna Elizabeth, Samuel Jacob Edgar; Extve. Vice Pres. and Mng. Dir. (North, South, Central America) for Sir Andrew Lloyd Webber's Really Useful Company Inc. 1992– ; Teacher, H.S. drama 1972–73; Mgr., Frederick Wood Theatre 1976; Electrician/Scenic Carpenter 1976–77; post-grad. student seconded to The Leeds Playhouse, The Sheffield Crucible & The Royal Exchange Theatre 1977–78; Gen. Mgr., The New Play Centre, The Waterfront Theatre and Project Mgr., Waterfront Theatre Capital Prog. 1978–83; Admin., Theatre Dept., Nat. Arts Ctr. 1983–85; Gen. Mgr., CentreStage Co. 1985–88, and Toronto Free Theatre 1986–88; Vice Pres., Live Entertainment, Cineplex Odeon Corp. 1988–89; Sr. Vice-Pres., Live Entertainment Corp. of Can. 1989–91; Corp. of Dir., Toronto Reg., Profl. Assn. of Candn. Theatres; Toronto Theatre Alliance; Club: Arts & Letters; Home: 171 Robert St., Toronto, Ont. M5S 2K6.

**DOBROWOLSKI, Jerzy Adam,** M.Sc., Ph.D.; research scientist; b. Katowice, Poland 9 May 1931; s. Józef and Irena (Iberal) D.; e. Univ. of London B.Sc. 1953, Imp. Coll. Sci. & Technol. M.Sc. 1954, Ph.D. (Optics) 1955; m. Jadwiga d. Wiktor and Nadzieja Duduk 6 June 1959; children: John, Andrew, Barbara; GUEST WORKER, INST. FOR MICROSTRUCTURAL SCIENCES, NAT. RSCH. COUNCIL 1991– ; Post-doctoral Fellow present Council 1955–56; Asst. Rsch. Offr. 1956–69, Assoc. Rsch. Offr. 1969–71, Sr. Rsch. Offr., Div. Physics 1971–90; Principal Rsch. Offr., Inst. for Microstructural Sciences 1990–91; co-author 'Handbook of Optics' 1978; recipient Joseph Fraunhofer Award Optical Soc. Am. 1987; Moët Hennessy-Louis Vuitton 'Science pour l'Art' Prize 1989; Fellow, Optical Soc. Am.; mem. Internat. Soc. Optical Eng.; Office: Ottawa, Ont. K1A 0R6.

**DOBSON, Thomas Smith;** banker; b. Glasgow, Scot. 5 Aug. 1917; s. James Frederick Gordon and Ellen (McTole) D.; came to Canada 1919; e. Dundas (Ont.) High Sch., Sr. Matric.; m. Wilma Flora, d. William John McKee 7 July 1943; children: Richard, Virginia, Nancy; CHRMN., EASTON UNITED HOLDINGS LTD.; Pres. & Dir., T.S. Dobson Consultant Ltd.; Camarco Investments Ltd.; Commercial Trust Co. Ltd.; Threadneedle Holdings Ltd.; Lothian Holdings Ltd.; Dir., Internat. Trust Co.; Robt. Mitchell Inc.; Candn. Marconi Co.; Murphy Oil Co. Ltd.; Canadian Roxy Petroleum Ltd.; Bovar Inc.; former Exec. Vice-Pres., Royal Bank of Canada; Fellow, Inst. Candn. Bankers; Presb.; recreations: golf, curling, fishing, hunting; Clubs: Calgary Petroleum; Ranchmen's (Calgary); Calgary Golf and Country; Home: 2110, 720 – 13th Avenue S.W., Calgary, Alta. T2R 1M5; Office: 400 – 407 8th Ave. S.W., Calgary, Alta. T2P 1E5.

**DOBSON, Wendy K.,** B.ScN., S.M., M.P.A., Ph.D.; economist; executive; b. Vernon, B.C. 23 Nov. 1941; d. W. Kenneth and Una Grace (Osborn) D.; e. Univ. of B.C., B.ScN. 1963; Harvard Univ. M.P.A. 1971, S.M. 1972; Princeton Univ. Ph.D. 1979; PROFESSOR & DIRECTOR, CENTRE FOR INTERNATIONAL BUSINESS, UNIV. OF TORONTO 1990– ; Visiting Fellow, Inst. for Internat. Economics, Washington DC 1989– ; Dir., DuPont Canada Inc. 1989– ; IBM Canada Ltd. 1989– ; Pratt & Whitney Canada Inc. 1990– ; Toronto Dominion Bank 1990– ; Working Ventures 1990– ; Trans Canada Pipelines Ltd. 1992– ; Bd. Mem., Univ. of Toronto Press 1991– ; Dir., Japan Soc. 1993– ; Dir. Indian Family Planning Prog. CUSO 1966–68; Prog. Offr. CIDA 1968–70; Cons. UN Devel. Prog. 1972–74; Special Asst. to Pres. Internat. Devel. Rsch. Centre 1972–75; Lectr. in Econ. Princeton Univ. 1978, Concordia Univ. 1979–80; Econ., C.D. Howe Inst. 1979–81, Pres., 1981–87, Dir. 1982–87; Publ. Gov. Toronto Stock Exchange 1984–87; mem. Internat. Trade Adv. Ctte. 1986–87; Comnr., Study of Public Expectation of Audits, CICA 1986–87; mem. Ministerial Adv. Ctte. Inflation & Taxation 1982; Rsch. Adv. Ctte. Macdonald Royal Comn. 1983–85; Gov. Waterloo Univ. 1985–87; Dir. North-South Inst. 1984–87; mem., National Statistics Counc. 1986–87; Alternate Gov., Internat. Monetary Fund 1987–89; Assoc. Depy. Min. of Finance, Govt. of Can. 1987–89; mem. Selection Ctte., Manning Found. Innovation and Entrepreneurship Awards 1988–93; Mem., Adv. Ctte., Internat. Centre, Univ. of Calgary 1989– ; Adv. Ctte., Banff Centre for Mgmt. 1989– ; mem., Toronto Stock Exchange Ctte. on Corporate Governance 1993– ; mem., Japan-Canada Forum 2000 Advisory Ctte. 1993– ; author 35 publs.; mem. Candn. Econ. Assn.; Am. Econ. Assn.; recreations: tennis, hiking, skiing, photography, music; Club: Queen's; Office: Fac. of Mgmt., Univ. of Toronto, 246 Bloor St. W., Toronto, Ont. M5S 1V4.

**DODD, Lionel G.,** B.Comm., M.B.A.; business executive; b. Regina, Sask. 1 Feb. 1940; e. Univ. of Saskatchewan B.Comm. 1962; Univ. of Calif. at Berkeley M.B.A. 1963; married; 4 children; Chief Operating Offr., O&Y Enterprises Inc. and Pres. & C.E.O, GW Utilities Ltd. 1988–..; various positions ending as Controller, Ford Motor Company 1963–79; Gulf Canada 1979–88 (left as Senior Vice-Pres. & Chief Financial Officer); Dir., Abitibi-Price Inc.; Camdev Corp.; Gulf Canada Resources Limited; GW Utilities Limited; Home Oil; Santa Fe Energy Resources Inc.; Scurry-Rainbow; Mem., Financial Executives Inst.; recreations: biking, skiing, hiking; clubs: National.

**DODDS, Colin James,** B.Sc., B.A., M.A., Ph.D.; university professor and administrator; b. Morpeth, U.K. 26 Nov. 1944; s. James and Evelyn D.; e. Univ. of Hull B.Sc.(Econ.) 1966; Sheffield Univ. M.A. 1969, Ph.D. 1978; Open Univ. B.A. 1982; m. Carol d. John and Margaret Jennings 14 Aug. 1969; children: James Alexander, Elizabeth Caroline; VICE-PRESIDENT, ACADEMIC & RESEARCH, SAINT MARY'S UNIV. 1991– ; Rsch. Asst./Fellow, Univ. of Sheffield 1969–78; Lectr. in Acctg. & Finance 1979–82; Visiting Lectr., Birmingham Univ. 1976; Assoc. Prof., Saint Mary's Univ. 1982–84; Prof. 1984– ; Chair, Dept. of Finance & Mngt. Sci. & M.B.A. Dir. 1984–87; Dean of Commerce 1987–91; Visiting Assoc. Prof., McMaster Univ. 1978–79; Brock Univ. summer 1979; Visiting Prof., Xiamen Univ. (PRC) 1985; Nat. Inst. of Devel. Admin., Bangkok 1986; Mount St. Vincent Univ. 1984–88; Dalhousie Univ. 1984–91; Dir., Halifax Bd. of Trade 1990– ; FBIM; Edit. Bd. Mem., 'Journal of Business Finance and Account-

ing'; 'British Accounting Review'; 'American Business Review'; Mem. & Chair, SSHRC adjudication panels; Dir., Candn. Fed. of Deans of Mngt. & Admin. Studies 1988–91; Vice-Chair 1989–91; Candn. Consortium of Mngt. Schools 1990–93; Mem., Rotary 1990– ; Dartmouth East Black Learning 1989– ; Dartmouth C. of C.; Nova Scotia Trades Council; World Trade Inst. 1988– ; Dir., Halifax Dance; co-author: 'Expectations, Uncertainty and the Term Structure of Interest Rates' 1974, 'Managerial Decision Making' 1975, 'Planning and Growth of the Firm' 1978, 'The Investment Behaviour of British Life Companies 1963–76' 1979, 'Financial Management' 1988; clubs: Halifax, Waegwoltic; Home: 44 Birchview Dr., Halifax, N.S. B3P 1G4; Office: Halifax, N.S. B3H 3C3.

**DODDS, Richard (Dick) Albert,** B.A., M.Ed.; educational executive; b. Ailsa Craig, Ont.; s. Donald Roy and Frances Anne (Hatter) D.; e. Queen's Univ. B.A. 1962; Univ. of Toronto B.Ed, M.Ed 1967; m. Wilma d. Ila and William Wagar; children: Nancy, Richard; DIRECTOR OF EDUCATION & SECRETARY-TREASURER, THE BOARD OF EDUCATION FOR THE BOROUGH OF EAST YORK 1980– ; Classroom Teacher, K–8, Kingston; Counsellor, 9–13; Consultant, Spec. Edn. & Guidance; Vice-Principal & Principal; Principal, Germany (DND); Teacher Trainer, E. Africa (Uganda) & W. Africa (Sierra Leone); Supt. of Schools, Lennox & Addington Co. 1969–77; Peel Bd. of Edn. 1977–79; Supt. of Programme 1979–80; Prov. Pres., Ont. Assn. of Edn. Admin. Officials 1978–79; Nat. Pres., Candn. Assn. of School Admin. 1981; Pres., The Candn. Edn. Assn. 1992– ; Chrmn., Business Edn. Relns. Ctte., Bd. of Trade; Bd. of Dir., Candn. Nat. Exhibition Assn.; Chrmn., Edn. Div., United Way for Metro. Toronto; Mem., Queen's Univ. Council 1989–95; Vice-Chrmn., Metro Econ. Devel. Council, Metro. Toronto Corp.; Chrmn., Econ. Devel. Council Image Ctte.; Fellowship, Ont. Teachers' Fed. 1984; Life Mem., Ont. Fed. of Home & School Assns. 1985; Andre Lecuyer Award, Ont. S.S. Teachers' Fed. 1985; Distinguished Serv. Award, Candn. Assn. of School Admin. 1986; Award of Honor, Nat. School Public Relns. Assn. (U.S.) 1988; Fred L. Bartlett Award, Ont. Public School Bds. Assn. 1990; Educator Award, Fed. of Ont. Home & School Assns. 1990; Distinguished Educator Award (OISE); Distinguished Service Award, Am. Assoc. of Sch. Administrators; author of many magazine articles; recreations: golf, hockey; Home: 29 Sari Cres., Scarborough, Ont. M1E 4W3; Office: 840 Coxwell Ave., Toronto, Ont. M4C 2V3.

**DODDS, Richard Webster,** B.A.; investment and development executive; b. Toronto, On. 22 Nov. 1928; s. Clarence William Richard and Anna Munro (Davidson) D.; e. Univ. of Toronto, B.A.; Queen's Univ.; m. Lois M. d. Wilfrid and Frances Buckley 27 June 1953; children: David Richard, Douglas Buckley, Jill Margaret; OWNER/OP., RICHARD W. DODDS & ASSOC. INC. 1988– ; Naval Offr., Dept. of Nat. Defence; var. posts; Extve. Asst. to Donald Gordon (Chm. & Pres., CNR) 1957–61; Asst. Mgr., Freight Mktg. 1962–66; seconded to Centennial Project of Internat. Scope 1966–67; var. posts ending as Vice-Pres., Kerrybrooke Dev. of Sears Can. 1967–88 (voluntary 'retirement'); Past Pres., Quintum Investment Group; Fellow, Royal Candn. Geog. Soc.; Perm. Hon. Mem., Trinity Coll. Corp. (Past Vice-Chrmn., Extve. Ctte.); Past Chrmn., Quetico Found.; Past Dir., Nat. Ballet of Can. (Past Extve. Ctte. Mem.); Chrmn., Ballet Jörgen; Dir., Internat. Chorals Fest. 1989; Mozart Fest. 1990; Founding Dir. & First Vice-Pres., Ballet Opera House Corp.; Vice Pres. & Dir., Royal Candn. Geog. Soc.; recreations: wilderness canoeing, sailing, skiing; Home: 35 Wimbleton Rd., Islington, Ont. M9A 3R9.

**DODGE, David A.,** B.A., Ph.D.; b. Toronto, Ont. 8 June 1943; s. Andrew A. and C. Louise (Beatty) D.; e. Queen's Univ. B.A. 1965 (Medal in Econ.); Princeton Univ. Ph.D. 1972 (Woodrow Wilson Fellowship 1965–66, Princeton Nat. Fellowship 1966–67, Can. Council Fellowship 1968); m. two children; DEPY. MIN., DEPT. OF FINANCE, Ottawa 1991– ; Asst. Prof. of Econ. Queen's Univ. 1968–72; Sr. Research Offr. Dept. Finance Ottawa 1972–73, Chief Quantitative Tax Analysis 1973–75; Extve. Dir. Indust. and Market Analysis Central Mortgage and Housing Corp. 1975–76; Dir. Gen., Econ. Research Br., Anti-Inflation Bd. 1976–77; Prof. of Candn. Studies, Johns Hopkins Univ., Wash. D.C. 1978–80; Dir., Inter. Economics Program, Inst. for Research on Public Policy, Ottawa, 1979–80; Extve. Coord., Labour Market Develop. Task Force, Employment and Immigration Canada 1980–82; Asst. Depy. Min., Strategic Policy & Planning, Employment & Immigration Canada 1982–84; Asst. Depy. Min., Fiscal Policy & Economic Analysis, Dept. of Finance, Ottawa 1984–86;

Asst. Depy. Min., Tax Policy and Legislation, Dept. of Finance, Ottawa 1986–87; Sr. Asst. Depy. Min., Tax Policy and Legislation, Dept. of Finance, Ottawa 1987–89; Assoc. Depy. Min., Dept. of Finance 1989–91; author 'Returns to Investment in University Training: The Case of Canadian Accountants Engineers and Scientists' 1973; 'Structure of Earnings of Professional Engineers in Ontario' 1972; author or co-author various articles, papers and book chapters; Home: 3 Monkland Ave., Ottawa, Ont. K1S 1Y7; Office: 140 O'Connor St., Ottawa, Ont. K1A 0G5.

**DODINGTON, John Edward,** Mus.B.; bass; b. Toronto, Ont. 3 July 1945; s. James Lucius and Margaret Evelyn (Thompson) D.; e. Univ. of Toronto Mus.B. 1972; Royal Conserv. of Music ARCT 1973; m. Catherine d. Cormac and Una Robbin 2 Aug. 1975; 2 d. Leigh Anne Louise, Erin Patricia; began career with Festival Singers of Can.; became mem. chorus Royal Opera House, Covent Garden; has performed with maj. Candn. opera co.'s, orchs., festivals and choral soc.'s; opera incl. 'The Marriage of Figaro,' 'Carmen,' 'Cinderella,' 'Simon Boccanegra,' 'Werther,' 'Peter Grimes,' 'Falstaff,' 'The Magic Flute,' 'The Barber of Seville,' 'Trovatore,' 'Aida'; appeared as Sparafucile in 'Rigoletto' Vancouver Opera Assn.; title role 'The Mikado' Calgary Opera; performed in premiere of Handel's 'Rinaldo' Nat. Arts Centre 1982; oratorio appearances incl. Handel's 'Messiah,' Bach 'Passions,' Mozart and Verdi 'Requiem'; musical theatre appearances include Andrew Lloyd Weber's Phantom of the Opera as 'Buquet'; Address: R.R. 4, Alliston, Ont. L9R 1V4.

**DODSON, T. Stephen,** M.Sc.; astronomer; b. San Francisco, Cal. 26 Dec. 1943; s. Edward O. and Mary Kay (Street) D.; e. Univ. of Ottawa High Sch. 1961; Univ. of Ottawa B.Sc. 1967, M.Sc. 1971; m. Hélène d. Guy and Flo Stein 12 Oct. 1968; children: Natalie, Patrick, Marc-André; ASTRONOMER, SCIENCE NORTH 1982– ; Sci. and Physics Teacher Ecole Secondaire Thériault, Timmins, Ont. 1969–73, Ecole Secondaire Algonquin, North Bay, Ont. 1973–82; designed and built largest mobile telescope in Can. during this time; proposed and designed complete pub. solar observatory and designed 'Starwall' (interactive computer-controlled fibre-optic 3-D sky display) Science North; recipient 2 awards Stellafane Convention Springfield, Vt. for innovative telescope design 1981, 1983; designed and offers numerous telescope-making projects for students and adults; author numerous astron. publs.; mem. Royal Astron. Soc. Can. (Chrmn. National Astronomy Day Ctte.); Mem. Am. Assoc. of Variable Star Observers; R.Catholic; recreations: cycling, cross-country skiing, photography, telescope-making, astronomical observing; Club: Sudbury Astronomy; Home: 1752 Rutherglen Cres., Sudbury, Ont. P3A 2K3; Office: 100 Ramsey Lake Rd., Sudbury, Ont. P3E 5S9.

**DODWELL, Peter C.,** B.A., M.A., D.Phil., F.R.S.C.; university professor, writer; b. Ootacamund, India 13 Mar. 1930; s. David William and Marcia A. Bausor (Bradley) D.; e. Michael Hall Sch., Oxford Univ., B.A. 1953, M.A. 1957, D.Phil. 1958; m. Elizabeth d. Peter and Vera Dobrowolsky 1989; children (by prev. marriages): Nicholas M., Karen A., Tobias M., Andrea H., Emily R.; PROF. EMERITUS OF PSYCHOLOGY, QUEEN'S UNIV. 1993– ; Asst., Assoc. & Head of Dept. 1964–66, 1972–81, Full Prof. 1965–93; Vis. Prof., Harvard Univ. 1970; var. hon. visiting appts. in U.K., Can., U.S.A., Australia & New Zealand; Editor, 'Can. J. of Psych.' 1974–81, 'Spatial Vision' 1984–91; Fellow, Candn. Psych. Assn. 1972 (Dir. 1971–82, Pres. 1985); F.R.S.C. 1989; Cons., Nat. Rsch. Counc.; Med. Rsch. Counc.; NSERC; Med. Rsch. Counc. (U.K.); Australian Grants Counc.; Editor, Cognitive Science Series, Penguin Books (U.K.); Ed. Advr. to several companies & rsch. jours.; War Memorial Scholar, Balliol Coll., Oxford 1954; C.D. Howe Fellow 1966; Guggenheim Fellow & Resident Fellow, Ctr. for Adv. Study, Stanford 1968; Can. Counc. Fellow & Vis. Fellow, Wolfson Coll., Oxford 1975; Killam Rsch. Fellow 1982–84; recipient, Catell Award 1988; D.O. Hebb Award 1992; Mem., Candn. Psych. Assn. 1958– ; Experimental Psych. Soc. 1959– ; Sigma Xi 1970– ; author: 'Visual Pattern Recognition' 1970; co-author: 'Figural Synthesis' 1984; editor: 'New Horizons in Psychology' 1972, 1980, 'Perceptual Learning & Adaptation' 1970, 'Perceptual Processing' 1971; approx. 100 sci. & tech. articles in profl. jours.; recreations: classical music, tennis, sailing; Home: 3759 Waring Place, Victoria, B.C. V8P 5E9.

**DODWELL, Roland Bodington,** M.A.; financial consultant; b. Williams Lake, B.C. 23 Feb. 1921; s. Claude Henry Dodwell; e. Oak Bay High Sch. Victoria, B.C. 1939; Univ. of B.C. B.A. 1944; Univ. of Toronto M.A. 1947; m. Audrey Joyce d. Harry Roy Day 5 June 1946;

children: Lesley Joyce, Philip Henry; Dir. Emeritus, Spar Aerospace Ltd.; Dir., Internat. Scholarship Found.; Lectr. Univ. of B.C. 1947–49; Invest. Dealer (Dir.) Mills Spence & Co. 1949–68; Walwyn Stodgell & Co. 1968–74; Pres. and Dir., R.B. Dodwell Ltd. 1977–93; served with RCNVR during World War II, rank Lt.; mem. Financial Analysts' Assn.; United Church; recreations: golf, fishing, hunting; Clubs: Oakville Golf; Canard Gun; Home: 1112 Linbrook Rd., Oakville, Ont. L6J 2L1; Office: 145 King St. W., Ste. 2700, Toronto, Ont. M5H 1J8.

**DOE, Roger Graham,** Q.C., B.A.; b. Bermuda 25 June 1933; s. William Lestock and Helen M. O. (Franklin) D.; e. Saltus Grammar Sch. Bermuda 1945; Glebe Coll. Inst. Ottawa 1949; Univ. of W. Ont. B.A. (Hon. Bus. Adm.) 1953; Osgoode Hall Law Sch. 1958 (Silver Medal); Queen's Counsel 1979; m. Margaret Parker 1981; children: Linda, Peggy, Gail, Douglas, Darrin; law practice Campbell, Godfrey & Lewtas since 1958, merged into Fasken Campbell Godfrey 1989; Dir. Dofasco Inc.; mem. Candn. Bar Assn.; Co. York Law Assn.; recreations: golf, skiing; Clubs: Toronto; Toronto Golf; Home: 159 Glen Rd., Toronto Ont. M4W 2W7; Office: P.O. Box 20, Toronto-Dominion Centre, Toronto, Ont. M5K 1N6.

**DOEHRING, Donald Gene,** M.A., Ph.D.; psychologist; educator; b. Pittsburgh, Pa. 7 Apr. 1927; s. Walter Alan and Frances Elizabeth (Mehnert) D.; e. Montgomery Blair High Sch. Silver Spring, Md. 1944; Univ. of Buffalo B.A. 1949; Univ. of New Mexico M.A. 1951; Ind. Univ. Ph.D. 1954; children: Nancy, Carrie, Carl, Laura, Peter; PROF. EMERITUS OF HUMAN COMMUNICATION DISORDERS & PSYCHOL. McGILL UNIV.; Research Assoc. Central Inst. for Deaf, St. Louis, Mo. 1954–59; Asst. to Assoc. Prof. Ind. Univ. Med. Center 1959–63; joined McGill Univ. as Assoc. Prof. 1963; First Dir. Sch. Human Communication Disorders 1963–68; Visiting Scient. of Med. Research Council, Cambridge Univ. 1971–72; founded first Ph.D. program in speech & hearing in Can.; served with US Army 1944–47; author 'Patterns of Impairment in Specific Reading Disability' 1968; 'Reading Disabilities' 1981; 'Research Strategies in Human Communication Disorders' 1988; various book chapters, papers in scient. journs.; mem. Am. Sp. & Hear. Assn.; Liberal; recreations: music, reading, writing; Home: 4437 King Edward Ave., Montreal, Que. H4B 2H4; Office: 1266 Pine Ave. W., Montreal, Que. H3G 1A8.

**DOERING, John Harris;** manufacturing executive; b. Bermuda 18 Sept. 1939; s. Rev. Roderick Edmund and Bessie Margaret (Harris) D.; e. Kings Coll. Sch.; Univ. of Kings Coll.; Univ. of West. Ont.; m. Suzanne Gamble 25 Aug. 1962; children: Stephen, Carolyn; VICE-PRES., C.E.O. & DIR., DOVER MILLS LIMTED 1983– ; Accountant, Swift & Co. Ltd. (U.K.) 1960–63; Office Mgr., Controller, Swift Candn. Co. Ltd., Ont. & N.S. 1963–76; Controller, Asst. Sec.-Treas., present firm 1976–83; Vice-Pres. & Dir., Dover Indus. Limited; Candn. Nat. Millers Assn.; Candn. Mfrs. Assn. (N.S. Div.); Maritime Reg. Adv. Bd., Ports Can.; Mem., Eastern Expert Ctte. of Cereals & Oilseeds; Dir., Halifax-Dartmouth Port Development Comn.; Chrmn., Bd. of Gov., Northwood Care Inc.; Dir. & Chrmn., Missions to Seamen; Northwood Found. (Chrmn. 1990–92); Halifax Citadel Found.; Anglican; Diocesan Layreader, Diocese of N.S.; Chrmn., Evangelism & Renewal 1983–85; Dir., City Centre Ministry 1986–89; recreations: fine arts, musical theatre; clubs: The Halifax, The Rotary of Halifax; Home: 155 Eaglewood Dr., Bedford, N.S. B4A 3B6; Office: P.O. Box 2183, Halifax, N.S. B3T 3C4.

**DOHANEY, M.T. (Jean),** Ed.D.; educator; writer; b. Point Verde, Nfld. 15 Sept. 1930; d. Roger John and Anastasia Mary (King) Judge; e. Univ. of N.B. B.A. 1967; Univ. of Maine M.Ed. 1970; Boston Univ. Ed.D. 1978; m. Walter Joseph Dohaney (dec.) 4 Oct. 1952; children: Steven, Susan; PROF. OF TECH. COMMUNICATIONS FACULTY OF FORESTRY UNIV. OF N.B. 1980– ; Teacher of Eng. students with reading disabilities N.B. Pub. Sch. 1968–69, 1971–73; operated writing lab. for students with writing deficiencies present Univ. 1973–78, Lectr. in Writing & Reading Faculty of Edn. 1978–80; author (novel) 'The Corrigan Women' 1988; 'When Things Get Back to Normal' (Journal) 1989; 'To Scatter Stones' (novel) 1992; numerous short stories, articles; mem. Writer's Union of Canada; Candn. Assn. Teachers Tech. Writing; Writers Fedn. N.B.; R.Catholic; Office: Fredericton, N.B. E3B 2W1.

**DOHENY, Daniel O'C.,** Q.C., B.A., B.C.L.; advocate; b. Montreal, Que. 27 July 1915; s. Hugh and Mary Roycroft (O'Connell) D.; e. Selwyn House Sch., Montreal; Bishop's Coll. Sch., Lennoxville, Que.; McGill Univ., B.A. 1939, B.C.L. 1947; m. late Norah Deane, d. A.F. Baillie, 20 June 1946; m. 2ndly Marion, d. late R.M. Trow, Stratford; children: (from 1st m.) Patrick, Norah Deane, Mary Lucille, Lisa Margot; (from 2nd m.) David, Kathleen; COUNSEL, MACKENZIE GERVAIS (a member of Borden DuMoulin Howard Gervais); former Dir., R.C.A. Inc.; Ritz-Carlton Inc.; Trust General du Canada; The Guarantee Co. of N.A.; called to the Bar of Que. 1947; cr. Q.C. 1958; Chrmn. of Bd., Butters Foundation; served with Fifth Field Regt., R.C.A. overseas 1940–42 as Lieutenant; prisoner of War 1942–45; Alpha Delta Phi; Roman Catholic; recreations: golf, tennis, skiing, fishing; Clubs: Montreal Racquet; Mount Bruno Golf; Hillside Tennis; Montreal Indoor Tennis; Coral Beach (Bermuda); Home: 41 Barat Rd., Westmount, Que.; Office: 770 Sherbrooke St. W. Montreal, Que. H3A 1G1.

**DOHERTY, Edward Joseph,** M.D.; physician; b. Moncton, N.B. 22 May 1949; s. Joseph Martin and Marion Elizabeth (McMackin) D.; e. St. Francis Xavier Univ. pre-med. 1970; Dalhousie Univ. M.D. 1974, postgrad. studies 1983; m. Mary C. d. Robert Reid 27 June 1987; children: Teresa (Hynes), Robert (Hynes), Catherine (Doherty); general ophthalmology practise with specialty in contact lens Saint John N.B. 1983– ; Internship, Jewish Gen. Hosp. Montreal 1975; family practise Antigonish N.S. 1975–80; Lecturer, Continuing Med. Edn., Dalhousie Univ.; Vice-Chair, St. Joseph's Hosp. Bd. of Dir. 1990–92; Bd. of Gov., Univ. of N.B. 1993– ; Co-Chair, 'Yes' Ctte. for Canada 1992; Chair, L'Arche Home for the Mentally Handicapped 1986; Dir., Saint Joseph's Hosp. Found. 1985–88; Mem., St. Francis Xavier Univ. Alumni Assn.; Saint John Med. Soc.; N.B. Med. Soc.; The Royal Soc. of the Arts & Commerce; N.B. Liberal Assn.; Liberal Assn. of Can.; St. Patrick's Soc.; Laurier Club of Canada; N.B. Museum; N.B. Conservation Council; Irish Cultural Assn. of N.B.; Nature Conservancy of Can.; Atlantic Salmon Assn.; recreations: swimming, skiing, sailing, photography, nature, genealogy, salmon fishing; clubs: Saint John Masters Swim, Can. Assn. of Disabled Skiers, Can. Nature Federation; Royal Kennebecasis Yacht; Home: 30 Westview Dr., Saint John, N.B. E2K 2G7; Office: 28 King St., Saint John, N.B. E2C 1G3.

**DOHERTY, James Patrick,** B.Sc.; business manager; b. Winnipeg, Man. 29 Sept. 1927; s. James Joseph and Catherine Loretto (Blute) D.; e. Univ. of Manitoba B.Sc. 1948; m. Doreen d. Frank H. Hoefer 1 July 1950; children: Kathy, Shannon, James, Patrick, Mary, Kerry; VICE-CHRMN. & DIR., DEPRENYL RESEARCH LIMITED 1990– ; and DIR., DUSA PHARMACEUTICALS INC. 1991– ; Pres. & Gen. Mgr., Mead Johnson Canada 1968–72; Schering Canada 1972–81; Vice-Pres., Connaught BioSciences 1981–90; Dir., Emmanuel Convalescent Found.; Toronto Med. Corp.; recreations: golf, curling, reading; clubs: Granite, Toronto Bd. of Trade; Home: #1 Bachelor Place,Willowdale, Ont. M2L 1W9; Office: 337 Roncesvalles Ave., Toronto, Ont. M6R 2M7.

**DOHM, Bernard A. (Barney),** B.Comm.; general management executive; b. Vancouver, B.C. 30 Nov. 1948; s. The Hon. Thomas Anthony and Faith Alexandria (Cameron) D.; e. Univ. of Alta., B.Comm. 1974; m. Roxanna d. George and Marilyn Moroz 11 Aug. 1984; two s.: Justin Anthony, Quintin Andrew; GEN. MGR. & CHIEF OPERATING OFFR., WORKERS' COMPENSATION BD., N.W.T. 1988– ; Div. Mgr., Fin. & Admin., Dillingham Corp. (Edmonton) 1978–82; Mgr., Internal Audit (N. Vanc.) 1982–84; Mgr., MIS Implementation (Calif.) 1984–85; Regional Operations Mgr., Philips Electronics (Vanc.) 1985–88; Past Chrmn., Carpenters' Trust Funds Local 1325; recreations: fishing, travel, reading; club: YK Racquet; Home: 2 Rycon Dr., Yellowknife, N.W.T. X1A 2V8; Office: P.O. Box 8888, Yellowknife, N.W.T. X1A 2R3.

**DOLAN, Terence Manley,** B.A., LL.B.; barrister & solicitor; b. Toronto, Ont. 27 Jan. 1942; s. John Campbell and Margaret Anne (Manley) D.; e. St. Michael's Coll., Univ. of Toronto, B.A. 1964; Osgoode Hall Law Sch., LL.B. 1967; divorced; children: Siobhan, Brendan; PARTNER, McCARTHY TÉTRAULT, BARRISTERS & SOLICITORS 1982– ; joined present firm 1980; called to Ont. Bar 1969; practised law with firms of Lash Johnston and Harries Houser until 1980; frequent lectr.; Extve. Mem., Insolvency Subsection, Candn. Bar Assn.; author of a book chapter on 'Statutory Owners' in 'The Construction Lien Act Issues and Perspectives'; recreations: skiing, sailing; clubs: Royal Candn. Yacht, The Fitness Inst.; Home: 68 Crescent Rd., Toronto, Ont. M4W 1T5; Office: Suite 4700, Toronto Dominion Bank Tower, Toronto-Dominion Centre, Toronto, Ont. M5K 1E6.

**DOLBEC, André,** B.A., B.Ps., M.Ps., Ph.D.; university professor; b. Shawinigan, Que. 9 April 1949; s. Jacques and Rolande (Lamothe) D.; e. Université Laval B.A. 1969, B.Ps. 1972, M.Ps. 1976; Gestalt Inst. Cleveland postgrad. program in edn. 1980; Univ. of Lancaster Ph.D. in Systems 1989; one s.: François; PROFESSOR, DEPARTMENT OF EDUCATION, UNIVERSITÉ DU QUÉBEC À HULL 1976– ; Course Dir., Bur. of Staff Devel. & Training, Public Service Comn. 1973–76; Head, Master's Degree Program in Edn., Univ. du Qué. à Hull 1986–90; Dir., Dept. of Edn. Sciences 1988–90; Mem., Bd. of Trustees 1988– ; Dir., Lab. for Research and Intervention in Edn. 1990– ; Fellow, Internat. Systems Inst. 1992– ; Sec.-Treas., Candn. Soc. for the Study of Edn. 1992– ; consultant on study trips in Sweden, France, Italy to evaluate these country's policies for special ed. children 1990– ; Guest Lecturer, Candn. Center for Mngt. Development 1991– ; consultant for many depts., federal govt. in field of orgn. behaviour 1978– ; Candn. Rep., Bd. of the Internat. Soc. for Systems Sci. 1989– ; Pres., Bd. of Trustees, Centre de réadaptation 'Les Jeunes de l'Outaouais' 1990–92; Mem., Candn. Soc. for Rsch. in Edn.; Am. Assn. for Rsch. in Edn.; British Assn. for Rsch. in Edn.; Conf. on Action Rsch. Network; Internat. Soc. for Systems Sciences; Internat. Systems Inst.; Assn. of Humanistic Psychology; Assn. can.-française pour l'avancement de la science; author of several articles; Home: 37 Higgins Rd., Nepean, Ont. K2G 0R3; Office: C.P. 1250, Succ. B., Hull, Que. J8X 3X7.

**DOLEZEL, Lubomir,** Ph.D.; educator; b. Lesnice, Czechoslovakia 3 Oct. 1922; s. Oskar Dolezel; e. Gymnasium Zabreh and Litovel, Czechoslovakia 1941; Charles Univ. Prague grad. 1949; Czechoslovak Acad. of Sciences Ph.D. 1958; div.; children: Marketa Evans, Milena, Pavla Kollert, Lubomir; PROF. EMERITUS OF SLAVIC AND COMPARATIVE LIT., UNIV. OF TORONTO 1988– ; High Sch. Teacher Czechoslovakia 1949–54; Research Fellow, Inst. for Czech Lang., Czechoslovak Acad. of Sciences 1958–68; Assoc. Prof. (Docent) of Czech Lang. Charles Univ. Prague 1961–68; Visiting Prof. of Slavic Langs. & Lits., Univ. of Mich. 1965–68; Univ. of Toronto 1968–71, Prof. 1971–88; Visiting Prof. Univ. of Amsterdam 1976; Can. Council Research Leave Fellow 1977–78; Chrmn., Dept. of Slavic Languages & Literatures, Univ. of Toronto 1980–83; Acting Dir., Ctr. for Comparative Lit., Univ. of Toronto 1988–89; Connaught Sr. Fellow 1983–84; author 'O Stylu Moderni Ceské Prozy' (On the Style of Modern Czech Prose Fiction) 1960; 'Slovnik Spisovneho Jazyka Ceskeho' (Dictionary of Standard Czech) Vol. 1 1960 (co-author); 'Narrative Modes in Czech Literature' 1973 (Czech. ed. Prague 1992); 'Occidental Poetics: Tradition and Progress' 1990; Ed. 'Teorie Informace a Jazykoveda' (Information Theory and Linguistics) 1964; co-ed. 'Statistics and Style' 1969; various studies in stat. linguistics, stylistics, hist. of poetics, theory of fiction, Czech and Russian lit.; served with Anti-Nazi Resistance 1943–45; rec'd Mem. Medal of Resistance; mem., Toronto Semiotic Circle; Candn. Comparative Lit. Assn.; Assoc. of Czech Writers; F.R.S.C.; recreations: swimming, gardening; Home: 79 Midland Ave., Scarborough, Ont. M1N 3Z8; Office: Robarts Lib., 14th Flr., Toronto, Ont. M5S 1A1.

**DOLEŽELOVÁ-VELINGEROVÁ, Milena,** M.A., Ph.D.; university professor; b. Prague, Czechoslovakia 8 Feb. 1932; d. Josef and Marie (Vichrová) Velinger; e. Charles Univ. (Prague) M.A. 1955; Oriental Inst., Czechoslovak Academy of Sciences, Prague Ph.D. 1965; children: Markéta, Milena; PROFESSOR, DEPT. OF EAST ASIAN STUDIES, UNIV. OF TORONTO 1975– ; Research Assoc., Oriental Inst., Czech. Acad. of Sciences 1954–68; Inst. of Literature, Chinese Academy of Sciences 1958–59; Center for Chinese Studies, Univ. of Michigan 1967–68; Associate Prof., Univ. of Toronto 1969–75; Senior Visiting Fellow, Corpus Christi College, Univ. of Cambridge 1984–85; Resident Scholar, Rockefeller Found. Study & Conf. Center (Bellagio, Italy) June 1985; Visiting Scholar, John King Fairbank Center for East Asian Research, Harvard Univ. 1990–91; Visiting Prof., East Asian Studies, Charles Univ. (Prague) Sept. 1991 and May 1992; recipient of num. research grants from SSHRCC; Organizer of 6 internat. confs. in Canada, U.S. and Czech Republic; Mem., Assn. for Asian Studies 1968– ; Candn. Comp. Lit. Assn.; Toronto Semiotic Circle (Pres. 1986–87); 9th Internat. Inst. for Semiotic & Structural Studies (Pres. 1–26 June 1987); co-author & translator: 'Ballad of the Hidden Dragon' 1971; co-author & editor: 'The Chinese Novel at the Turn of the Century' 1980, 'A Selective Guide to Chinese Literature 1900–1949' 4 vols. 1988–90, 'Poetics

East and West' 1989; Home: 131 Bloor St. W., #917, Toronto, Ont. M5S 1S3; Office: Robarts Library, 14th floor, Toronto, Ont. M5S 1A5.

**DOLIN, Samuel Joseph,** Mus.D.; composer; educator; b. Montreal, Que. 22 Aug. 1917; s. Joseph and Freda (Levin) D.; e. Baron Byng High Sch. Montreal 1933; Univ. of Toronto Mus.B. 1942, Mus.D. 1958; Toronto Conserv. of Music ATCM 1945; m. Inthia Leslie d. A. L. Pidgeon, Burlington, Ont. 7 March 1953; children: Elizabeth L., John J.; CHAIRMAN EMERITUS, COMPOSITION DEPT., AND TEACHER COMPOSITION THEORY & PIANO, ROYAL CONSERVATORY OF MUSIC TORONTO; Founder Electronic Music Studio 1966; joined present Conserv. 1945; served 3 yrs. as Music Supvr. of Schs. Durham and Northumberland, Ont. prior to 1945; compositions incl.: (opera) 'Casino' 1966–67; (orchestra) 'Scherzo' 1950; 'Serenade for Strings' 1951 (premiered by Finnish Nat. Radio during 1952 Olympiad); 'Sinfonietta' 1950; 'Sonata for String Orchestra' 1962; 'Symphony No. 1 (Elk Falls)' 1956; 'Symphony No. 2' 1957; 'Symphony No. 3' 1976; (soloist(s) with orchestra) 'Concerto for Piano and Orchestra' 1974; 'Drakkar' 1972; 'Fantasy for Piano and Chamber Orchestra' 1967; 'Isometric Variables' 1957; (instrumental ensemble) 'Adikia' 1975; 'Barcarolle' 1962; 'Concerto Grosso (Georgian Bay) 1970 (premiered CBC Summer Festival Toronto 1971); 'Duo Concertante' 1977; 'Little Sombrero' 1964; 'Portrait' 1961; 'Sonata' 1960; 'Sonata' 1978; 'Blago's Trio' 1979; 'Sonata fantasia' 1980; 'Sonatina' 1954; (instrumental solo) 'Little Toccata' 1959; 'Prelude, Interlude and Fantasy' 1976; 'Ricercar and Fantasy' 1975; 'Sonata' 1970; 'Stelcel' 1978; 'Psalmody for Solo Oboe' 1982; 'Three Sonatas' 1973; (voice) 'Chloris' 1951; 'Deuteronomy XXXII' 1977; 'Julia' 1951; 'Ozymandias' 1951; (chorus) 'The Hills of Hebron' 1954; 'Marchbankantata' 1971; 'Mass' 1972; (piano) 'If' 1972; 'Little Suite' 1954; 'Little Toccata' 1959; 'Prelude for John Weinzweig' 1973; 'Queekhoven and A.J.' 1975; 'Slightly Square Round Dance' 1966; 'Sonata' 1950; 'Sonatina' 1959; 'Three Piano Preludes' 1949; (2 pianos) 'Concerto for Four' 1977; 'Variation for Two Pianos' 1967; (incidental music) 'Machina' 1970; 'Missionaries' 1971; 'Music from "The Meeting Point"' 1971; 'Concerto for Accordion and orchestra' 1984; 'The Hero of our World' (lyrics: Leonard Peterson) 1985; Double Concerto for Oboe, Violoncello and Orchestra 1988; Sonata for Organ and Trumpet (dedicated to Karen Rymal); 2 x 3 for Eugene Kash (violin & piano) 1992; 'Variables for Cello and Piano' 1993; Queekhoven and A.J. (Centre disc); (discography) 'Ricercar'; 'Sonata for Accordion'; 'Sonata for Violin and Piano'; 'Concerto for 4,' (Melbourne); 'Fantasy for Guitar' (Hohner); 'Slightly Square Round Dance'; 'April March'; comns. many organs. and individuals incl. Stratford Festival, Toronto Repertory Ensemble, Royal Conserv. Music Toronto, Etobicoke Philharmonic Orchestra, CBC; mem. Adjudication Comte. Guitar Soc. Toronto's Internat. Guitar Festival 1978; mem. Candn. League Composers (Founding mem., Vice Pres. 1967–68, Pres. 1969–73); Internat. Soc. Contemporary Music (Vice Pres. 1972–76, Chrmn. Candn. Sec. 1972–74); Assoc. Composer, Candn. Music Centre (past Bd. mem.); mem. SOCAN; mem., Bd. of Gov., North Simcoe Arts Counc. 1986; former Artistic Dir., Candn. Contemp. Music Workshop; recipient Can. Council, Ont. Arts Council, Laidlaw Foundation and CBC grants or commissions; Office: SS # 2, Site 9, Comp 124, Penetang, Ont. L0K 1P0.

**DOLOVICH, Jerry,** M.D., FRCPC; physician, allergist; b. Winnipeg, Man. 2 April 1936; s. Joseph and Raechel (Pelonsky) D.; e. Univ. of Manitoba, Faculty of Science 1952–55, M.D. 1959; m. Myrna d. Frank and Sarah Gersovitz 7 July 1963; children: Lisa, Sharon, Pauline; ALLERGIST, CHEDOKE MCMASTER HOSPITALS & ST. JOSEPH'S HOSPITAL HAMILTON; postgrad. training Winnipeg, Montreal, Buffalo; recruited Dept. of Pediatrics, Fac. of Health Sciences, McMaster University 1968; Prof., Dept. of Pediatrics, McMaster Univ.; clinical allergist & researcher in the field of allergy / immunology; Office: Hamilton, Ont. L8S 4L8.

**DOLPHIN, David,** Ph.D., D.Sc., F.C.I.C., F.R.S.C.(London); educator; b. London, Eng. 15 Jan. 1940; e. Grocer's Company Sch. London; Univ. of Nottingham B.Sc. 1962, Ph.D. 1965, D.Sc. 1982; PROF. OF CHEM., UNIV. OF B.C. 1974– , Acting Dean of Sci. 1988–90 (Assoc. Dean of Sci. 1985–88); Postdoctoral Fellow, Harvard Univ. 1965–66, Instr. to Assoc. Prof. 1966–73; Assoc. Prof. present Univ. 1974; Cons. numerous chem., biochem. and high technol. cos. incl. Ballard Technologies Ltd. (N. Vancouver), Repligen – Sandoz Research Corp. (Lexington, Mass.), Scott Paper International (Philadelphia); Vice Pres., Technology Develop., Quadra Logic Technologies (Vancouver); Guggenheim Fellow 1980; Fellow, Japanese Soc. Promotion Sci. 1987; recipient, Gold Medal in Health Sci., Sci. Counc. of B.C. 1990; The 1993 Syntex Award, Candn. Soc. for Chemistry; Bell Canada - Forum 1993 Award; co-author 'Tabulation of Infrared Spectral Data' 1977; ed. 'The Porphyrins' Vols. 1–7 1977–78; 'B12' Vols. 1, 2 1982; co-ed.: 'Coenzymes and Cofactors' numerous vols. 1986–89; mem., Candn. Inst. of Chem.; Chem. Soc., London; Am. Chem. Soc.; Electrochem. Soc.; recreations: squash, scuba diving; Office: 2036 Main Mall, Vancouver, B.C. V6T 1Y6.

**DOMARADZKI, Theodore F.,** M.A., Litt.D.; educator; writer; b. Warsaw, Poland 27 Oct. 1910; s. Joseph Felix and Maria Helena (Tomaszewska) D.; e. Acad. of Pol. Sci., Warsaw, Pol. Sci. Dipl. 1936; Univ. of Warsaw, M.A. (Hist.) 1939; Univ. of Rome Litt.D. (Slavic Philol.) 1941; m. Maria Teresa d. Kazimierz and Julia Dobija 20 Apr. 1954; PROF. AND DIR. INST. OF COMPARATIVE CIVILIZATIONS OF MONTREAL 1976– ; Asst., Acad. Pol. Sciences Warsaw 1936–39; Lectr. Univ. of Rome 1941–47; Assoc. Prof. Pontificio Istituto Orientale Rome 1943–47; Rep. in Italy Polish Ministry of Educ. 1942–45, Head, Educ. Div. Poles, Brit. Embassy Rome 1945–46; Dir., Prof. and Founder Dept. Slavic Studies and Centre Polish & Slavic Research Univ. of Montreal 1948–76; Head, Polish Studies Program and Visiting Prof. Fordham Univ. 1948–50; Prof. and Dir. of Slavic Studies Univ. of Ottawa 1949–53; Scient. Advisor (Slavistics) Univ. of Windsor 1950–52; Hon. Pres., Candn. World Univ. Comte.; Paderewski Foundation (Can.); decorations: Member, Order of Canada; Kt., Order Polonia Restituta; Kt. Commdr. Papal Order St. Gregory the Great; Commdr. R.Y. Order of St. Sava; Kt. Ordo Constantini Magni; Kt. Commdr. Sovereign Order St. John of Jerusalem; Kt. French Underground Forces Order; Polish Golden Cross of Merit; Cross Allied Vol. Combattants; Medal Polish Educ. Merit and many others; author 'Idea pokoju na przestrzeni wiekow' 1939; 'Le concezioni antiche della guerra e della pace' 1939; 'Il problema sociale nell' opera di B. Prus' 1941; 'Les considérations de C. Norwid sur la liberté de la parole' 1971; 'Le symbolisme et l'universalisme de C.K. Norwid' 1974; 'La réalité du mal chez C. Baudelaire et C. Norwid' 1966; Master of Archetypal Lang. (Mistrz archetypicznego jezyka) in 'Norwid z dziejow recepcji tworczosci,' ed. M. Inglot, Warszawa 1983; 'Norwid poet of Christianity' (Norwid piewca kultury chrzescijanskiej) 1984; ed. 'Slavic and East-European Studies' 1956–76; Ed., 'Slavic Publications'/'Publications Slaves' 1973– ; 'Entre le romantisme et le symbolisme: C. Baudelaire et C. Norwid' in Les Cahiers de Varsovie 1986; 'C.K. Norwid in Canada' 1989; 'Personnalités ethniques au Québec' 1991; Hon. Life mem., Candn. Assn. Slavists and Candn. Soc. Comparative Study Civilizations; mem. Candn. Internat. Acad. Humanities & Social Sciences (Vice Pres. 1975– ;); Que. Ethnic Press Assn. (Adv. 1980– ;); P.E.N. Club Internat. (Candn. Francophone Centre) 1988– ; Soc. des Ecrivains Canadiens; Istituto Italiano di Cultura; Royal Candn. Legion; recreations: chess, classic music; Clubs: United Services; Cercle Universitaire; Home: 6100 Deacon Rd., Apt. 4E, Montréal, Qué. H3S 2V6; Office: P.O. Box 759, Succ. Outremont, Montreal-Outremont, Qué. H2V 4N9.

**DOMARATZKI, Zygmund,** B.Sc.; nuclear regulator; b. Ethelbert, Man. 3 Jan. 1938; s. Nicholas and Mathilda (Belinski) D.; e. Univ. of Manitoba B.Sc. 1959; m. Patsy Ruth d. James and Ethel Patterson 1961; children: Nicholas James, Jeanette, Reginald; DIRECTOR GENERAL, REACTOR REGULATION, ATOMIC ENERGY CONTROL BOARD 1981– ; Research, Chalk River Nuclear Labs., Atomic Energy of Canada Limited 1959–69; Sci. Advisor, Pickering Nuclear Generating Station 1969–75; Manager, Reactor Licensing 1975–81; Mem., IAEA Internat. Nuclear Safety Adv. Group 1988–91; Chair 1992– ; Home: 75 Southpark Dr., Ottawa, Ont. K1B 3B5; Office: P.O. Box 1046, Ottawa, Ont. K1P 5S9.

**DOMB, Uriel,** B.Sc., M.Sc., P.Eng.; aerospace scientist, executive; b. Haifa, Israel 18 Aug. 1942; s. Solomon and Aviva (Hanina) D.; e. Polytechnic Inst. of N.Y. B.Sc. 1962, M.Sc. (Astro.) 1964; Columbia Univ. M.Sc. (Ops. Res.) 1968; Cornell Univ. postgrad. studies 1964–65; m. Elizabeth (Watts) 17 Jan. 1987; children: Sharon B., Ilana, Gabrielle M., Arielle H.; FOUNDER & PRESIDENT, TELESPACE LTD. 1979– ; System Analyst, IBM Corp. 1962–63; Manager of System Analysis, NASA 1967–70 (participant in first lunar landing mission 1969; citation for support role); Mgr., Satellite Control, Telesat Canada 1970–78 (participant in launch of world's first domestic satellite ANIK I 1972 and all other ANIK launches until 1978); Canada's Rep. to Internat. Astronautical Fed. 1978–80; Founder & Chair, Candn. Astro. Soc. 1977–79; Adjunct Assoc. Prof. (Telecomm.), York Univ. 1981–85; Dir., Canada-Israel C. of C.; Assoc. Fellow, Am. Inst. of Aero. & Astro.; NASA medal; Organizer & Chair, AIAA Internat. Comm. Satellite Conf. 1977; Mem., Internat. Affairs Ctte. on B'nai B'rith; Miltiary service, Israeli Air Force and Reserves; co-author: 'Oceans from Space' 1985; recreations: music, jogging; Office: 174 Ava Rd., Toronto, Ont. M6C 1W5.

**d'OMBRAIN, J. Nicholas,** B.A., M.A., D.Phil.; government official; b. London, Eng. 11 Nov. 1944; s. George Lee and Kathleen (Cullen) d'O.; e. Loyola H.S.; McGill Univ. B.A. (1st Class Hons.) 1965, M.A. 1966; Oxford Univ. D.Phil. 1969; Research Fellow (postdoctoral), Ctr. for Internat. Affairs, Harvard Univ. 1969–70; m. Elodie d. Emile and Emilienne Cormier 5 May 1973; DEP. SEC. TO THE CABINET with the rank of Deputy Minister 1991– ; entered Public Service 1970; variety of positions principally in Privy Council Office & Dept. of the Solicitor Gen.; apptd. Asst. Sec. to the Cabinet for Security & Intelligence 1982; for Machinery of Govt. 1986; Mem., Internat. Inst. for Strategic Studies; author: 'War Machinery and High Policy' 1973; Home: 704 Island Park Dr., Ottawa, Ont. K1Y 0B7; Office: 80 Wellington St., Ottawa, Ont. K1A 0A3.

**DOMVILLE, Eric William,** Ph.D.; university professor/writer; b. Liverpool, England 27 April 1929; s. Wilfred Lawton and May (Priestman) D.; e. St. Edward's Coll. 1945; Strawberry Hill Training Coll. 1958; Univ. Coll., Univ. of London B.A. (Hons.) 1961, Ph.D. 1965; m. Jean d. Christopher and Bertha MacPhail 13 July 1987; one d. (prev. m.): Elspeth Jane; PROF., DEPT. OF ENGLISH, TRINITY COLL., UNIV. OF TORONTO 1987– ; Lectr., Dept. of English, Univ. of Toronto 1964–66; Asst. Prof. 1966–69; Assoc. Prof. 1969–87; major undergrad. teaching: 19th & 20th century fiction; grad. teaching: 20 cent. Am. poetry & the city in Brit. & Am. Lit.; major rsch.: W.B. Yeats, Ezra Pound, Richard Wagner, the city in lit.; Chrmn., Toronto Wagner Soc. 1981–85; editor: 'A Concordance to the Plays of W.B. Yeats' 2 vols. 1972, 'Editing British and American Literature, 1880–1920' 1976; co-editor: 'The Collected Letters of W.B. Yeats' Vol. I 1986; author of 3 unpub. novels; Candn. Corr., 'Opera' (U.K.) 1983–88; contbr., 'Opera Can.'; broadcaster on opera; guest lectr.; recreations: music, badminton, tennis; club: Savile (U.K.); Home: 342 Brunswick Ave., Toronto, Ont. M5R 2Y9; Office: Toronto, Ont. M5S 1H8.

**DOMVILLE, James de Beaujeu,** B.A., B.C.L.; b. Cannes, France 1933; s. Henri de Gaspé and Elsie Welsh (Saltus) D.; e. Selwyn House Sch. Montreal; Trinity Coll. Sch. Port Hope, Ont.; Univ. de Fribourg Diplôme d'aptitude à l'enseignement du français à l'étranger 1951; McGill Univ. B.A. 1954, B.C.L. 1957; GOVT. FILM COMMR. AND CHRMN. NAT. FILM BD. OF CAN. 1979–84; Dir. CBC 1979–84; Ex-officio mem. Bd. Dirs. Candn. Film Devel. Corp. and Bd. Trustees Nat. Arts Centre 1979–84; Dir. Institut de la musique du Can. 1973–82; Gov. Le Théâtre du Nouveau Monde since 1972; mem. Bd. Govs., Extve. Comte. and Consultant Nat. Theatre Sch. 1968, Life Gov. 1968– ; (Co-founder and 1st Adm. Dir. 1960–64, Dir. Gen. 1964–68, Teacher 1960–70); Asst. Dir. of Eng. Production Nat. Film Bd. 1972, Extve. Producer Studio B. 1974–75, Depy. Govt. Film Commr. 1975–79; Producer, co-author, composer Candn. musical 'My Fur Lady' 1956–58; Founder, Pres. Quince Productions Montreal 1958– ; co-producer theatrical productions incl. 'Jubilee!' 1959, 'Spring Thaw' 1960; Extve. Dir. Le Théâtre du Nouveau Monde 1968–72; Adviser and Consultant Entertainment Br. Candn. Fed. Pavilion Expo '67 1963–66; Rep. Internat. Theatre Symposia Rumania, Germany, Italy (Chrmn.), Sweden (Chrmn.) and Czechoslovakia 1964–68; guest lectr. various univ. theatre depts. 1964–68; Theatre Consultant to archs. Nat. Arts Centre Ottawa 1964–68; Theatre Rep. Internat. Colloquium on Can. Centre Culturel Internat. Cérisy la Salle, France 1968; mem. Selection Comte. First World Jewish Film Festival Jerusalem 1977; Gov. and mem. Extve. Dom. Drama Festival 1961; Chrmn. Festivals & Cultural Activities sub-comte. Candn. Centenary Council 1963; Treas. and Dir. Candn. Theatre Centre 1962, Secy. 1964–68; mem. Am. Educ. Theatre Assn.; Dir. U.S. Inst. Theatre Technol. 1966; mem. Comte. Prof. Training Internat. Theatre Inst. 1966–69; Co-chrmn. Theatre of Tomorrow Panel N.Y. 1967; mem. Adv. Arts Panel Can. Council 1968–69, Chrmn. 1969–72; Gov., Senator McGill Univ. 1969–74; Gov. Candn. Conf. of Arts 1975–77; recipient Candn. Centennial Medal 1967; Queen's Silver Jubilee Medal 1977; Home: 227 Clarke St., #2, Westmount, Que. H3Z 2E3.

**DON, Conway Joseph,** M.B., B.S., F.R.C.R., F.R.C.P.(C), F.R.C.P.; radiologist; educator; b. Newcastle-on-Tyne, Eng. 1 Dec. 1922; s. Frank Austin and Rosanna (McHatton) D.; e. Univ. Coll. London 1941–43; Univ. Coll. Hosp. London 1943–46 (Liston Gold Medal in Clin. Surg. 1945), M.B., B.S. 1946; children: Felicity, Rosemary, Caroline, Paul, Penelope; PROFESSOR OF RADIOLOGY, UNIV. OF OTTAWA; Chrmn. 1960–86; Emeritus Radiologist, Ottawa Gen. Hosp., Chrmn. Med. Adv. Comte. and Chief of Med. Staff 1966–71, 1977–80; Consultant in Radiol., Ont. Cancer Foundation (Ottawa Clinic); Consultant in Chest Radiol., Immigration Medical Service, Dept. of Health & Welfare; Resident Med. Officer, Univ. Coll. Hosp. London 1948–50; Med. Registrar, Univ. Coll. Hosp. London 1950–51, Registrar and Sr. Radiological Registrar 1951–56; Clin. Fellow, Mass. Gen. Hosp. and Teaching Fellow, Harvard Univ. 1956–57 (Richman Godlee Fellowship); Visiting Fellow, Mass. Gen. Hosp. 1968; Visiting Prof. Vanderbilt Univ. 1976–77; King Abdulaziz Univ., Saudi Arabia 1980; Univ. of Calif., San Francisco 1984; Vanderbilt Univ. 1988; RSNA Internat. Visiting Prof., Univ. of Malaya 1992–93; Chrmn., Candn. Heads of Academic Radiology Depts. 1986–87; Research Grant Referee, Research Programs Br. Nat. Health & Welfare; Cons. in Radiology, Dept. of Health & Welfare; author or co-author numerous scient. publs.; mem. Ont. Med. Assn.; Faculty of Radiols.; Candn. Assn. Radiols. (Councillor for E. Ont. 1965–67, Past Chrmn./mem. various comtes.); Gordon Richards Lecturer, Can. Assn. Radiol. 1987; Candn. Med. Assn.; E. Ont. Assn. Radiols.; Radiol. Soc. N. Am.; P. Conservative; recreations: tennis, skiing, swimming, reading; Clubs: Rideau Tennis & Squash; Home: #1801, 1785 Riverside Dr., Ottawa, Ont. K1G 3T7; Office: Ottawa General Hospital, Ottawa, Ont. K1H 8L6.

**DONAHOE, Arthur Richard,** Q.C., B.Com., LL.B.; lawyer; politician; b. Halifax, N.S. 7 Apl. 1940; s. Richard Alphonsus and Mary Eileen (Boyd) D.; e. Halifax pub. schs.; St. Mary's Univ. B.Com. 1959; Dalhousie Univ. Law Sch. LL.B. 1965; m. Carolyn d. Douglas and Alice MacCormack 16 Dec. 1972; SECRETARY-GENERAL, COMMONWEALTH PARLIAMENTARY ASSN. 1992– ; Exec. Asst. to Leader of Opposition Senate of Can. 1967; Barrister & Solr. since 1968; el. M.L.A. for Halifax-Citadel 1978, 1981, 1984 and 1988 (resigned Nov. 1992); Speaker, N.S. House of Assembly 1981–91; former Lectr. in Comm. Law St. Mary's Univ.; Past Chrmn. Bd. Mgmt. St. Vincent's Guest House; Past Pres. Charitable Irish Soc. Halifax; N.S. Br. Candn. Bar Assn.; N.S. Med.-Legal Soc.; recreation: golf; Clubs: Halifax; Ashburn Golf (Past Pres.); Home: 128 Kenilworth Court, Lower Richmond Rd., Putney, London, UK SW15 1HB; Office: Suite 700, Westminster House, 7 Millbank, London, UK SW1P 3JA.

**DONAHOE, Richard Alphonsus,** Q.C., B.A., LL.B., K.S.G.; Senator; b. Halifax, N.S., 27 Sept. 1909; s. late James Edward and Rebecca Margaret (Duggan) D.; e. St. Mary's Coll., Halifax, N.S.; Dalhousie Univ., B.A. 1930, LL.B. 1932; Hon. LL.D., St. Mary's Univ. 1981; m. Mary Eileen, d. late Donald D. Boyd, 22 Sept. 1936; children: Arthur, Cathleen, Terence, Sheila, Nora, Ellen; read law with Burchell, Smith, Parker & Fogo, Halifax, N.S.; called to the Bar of N.S. 1932; cr. Q.C. 1950; contested N.S. Prov. el., 1937, in Halifax S.; Fed. el. 1940; contested Halifax N. (Prov.) 1949; el. Alderman for Ward 4, Halifax City, 1951, Mayor, 1952, re-el. by acclamation, 1953 and 1954; el. to Prov. Leg. for Halifax S., by-el. 1954; apptd. Atty. Gen., Min. Public Health, 1956; (both portfolios held until 1970); appointed Knight of St. Gregory the Great, 1969; appointed to Senate of Canada, 1979; mem., (Past Pres.) Charitable Irish Soc.; Past Pres., Dominion (Candn.) Curling Assoc.; (Past Vice-Pres.) Royal Caledonian Curling Assn. of Scotland; (Past Pres.) Halifax City & County P.C. Assn.; K. of C.; P. Conservative; Roman Catholic; recreations: curling, fishing; Clubs: Halifax Curling; Canadian; Home: #601, 5524 Heatherwood Court, Halifax, N.S. B3K 5N7.

**DONAHOE, Hon. Terence Richard Boyd,** M.L.A., B.Com., LL.B., D.Ed. (Hon.); politician; b. Halifax, N.S. 30 Oct. 1944; s. Senator Richard Alphonsus and Mary Eileen (Boyd) D.; e. St. Mary's Univ. High Sch. 1960; St. Mary's Univ. B.Com. 1964; Dalhousie Univ. Law Sch. LL.B. 1967; Hon. D.Ed.: Univ. Ste. Anne 1985; m. Lynne Marie d. Bernard Harrison Sheehan 30 Dec. 1967; one d. Moira Eileen; LEADER OF HER MAJESTY'S LOYAL OPPOSITION AND INTERIM LEADER, NOVA SCOTIA PROGRESSIVE CONSERVATIVE PARTY 1993– ; Min. of Educ. N.S. and Min. Responsible for Status of Women 1978–85; Chrmn. Policy Bd. N.S. and Min. of Vocational and Technical Training 1985; Attorney Gen. and Provincial Sec. 1987–89; apptd. Min. of Labour 1987 and Attorney General 1988; Min. of Govt. Services, Min. of Intergovernmental Affairs, Min. responsible for the Civil Service Act, Chrmn. Mgmt. Bd. 1989–91; Min. of Tourism and Culture, Min. responsible for the Heritage Property Act, Min. responsible for the Multiculturalism Act 1991–92; Min. of the Environment, Min. responsible for the Emergency Measures Organization Act, co-chair on the Nova Scotia Roundtable on Environment and Economy 1992–93; called to Bar of N.S. 1967; former Partner, Blois, Nickerson, Palmeter & Bryson; el. M.L.A. for Halifax Cornwallis prov. g.e. 1978; re-el. 1981, 1984, 1988, 1993 (Halifax Citadel); mem. Bd. of Gov. (& mem. Exec. Ctte.) St. Mary's Univ. 1975–78; Head Candn. Del., Third Conf. Mins. of Educ. Europe Region, UNESCO, Sofia, Bulgaria 1980; Head Educ. Sector, Candn. Del., 21st Gen. Conf. UNESCO, Belgrade, Yugoslavia 1980; Head Candn. Del., meeting of Min. of Educ. of Europe, Dublin, Ireland 1983; Head Candn. Del., meeting of Min. of Educ. of Commonwealth, Nicosia, Cyprus 1984; served Min. of Social Services' Comte. to review Family Court rules N.S.; former mem. Children & Youth Action Comte. on Child Welfare; former State Advocate K. of C.; former mem. Prov. Extve. and former Hon. Treas., N.S. Div. Candn. Red Cross Soc.; former mem. Prov. Extve. John Howard Soc.; Past Pres. Halifax-Cornwallis P. Cons. Assn.; Hon. Prov. Vice Pres., Hon. Counc., St. John Ambulance N.S.; mem. and past Chrmn., Council of Mins. Educ. Can.; Candn. Comn. for Unesco; P. Conservative; R. Catholic; recreations: golf, skating; Club: Ashburn Golf & Country; Home: 456 Francklyn St., Halifax, N.S. B3H 1A9; Office: P.O. Box 1617, Halifax, N.S. B3J 2Y3.

**DONALD, Graham Edward Bruce,** B.A., F.C.A.; chartered accountant; b. Warren, Ohio 23 Nov. 1926; s. Bruce and Joan (Clowes) D.; e. Brantford (Ont.) Coll. Inst.; Univ. of Toronto B.A. 1948; C.A. 1954; F.C.A. 1976; m. Joyce d. Roy P. Findlay 4 June 1955; children: Elizabeth, Stephen, Sarah, Anne, Graham; formerly Depy. Chrmn., Thorne Ernst & Whinney; joined Ernst & Whinney 1953, Montreal 1958; Partner-in-Charge Hamilton Office 1962, Toronto 1970, Vice Chrmn. 1981; on merger of Ernst & Whinney and Thorne Riddell, became Depy. Chrmn., Thorne Ernst & Whinney 1986; retired 1988; Hon. Treas. Red Cross Hamilton Br. 1965–70; Ont. Div. Candn. Red Cross Soc. 1972–77; Campaign Extve. Un. Way Metrop. Toronto 1974–76; Gov. Hillfield-Strathallan Colls. 1966–71; Comte. Chrmn. Hamilton Chamber Comm. 1964–69; Warden, Christ Church Deer Park 1982–83; Bd. mem., Candn. Life and Health Ins. Assoc. Compensation Corp. 1990– ; served with RCA, rank Capt.; mem. Inst. C.A.'s Ont.; Candn. Inst. C.A.'s (Accounting Research Comte. 1973–77; Chrmn. Jt. Task Force on Ins. 1975–82); Delta Tau Delta (Treas. 1946); Anglican; recreations: golf, gardening; Clubs: Toronto Badminton & Racquet; Rosedale Golf (Bd. mem. 1989–92); Albany; Quail Creek (Naples, Fl.); Home: 120 Roxborough St. E., Toronto, Ont. M4W 1W1 and Vanderbily Club, Naples, Fla.

**DONALD, Jack C.;** executive; b. Edmonton, Alta. 29 Nov. 1934; s. Archibald Scott and Margaret Catherine (Cameron) D.; e. Univ. High Sch., Edmonton; Tech. Sch., Southern Inst. Art & Tech.; m. Joan M., d. Carl & Annie Schultz, 29 Oct. 1955; children: Katherine Ann Lacey; John Scott; PRES. & C.E.O., PARKLAND INDUSTRIES LTD. since 1977; Pres. & Dir., Parkland Properties Ltd.; Vice Pres. & Dir., Brandt Industries Ltd.; Chrmn. & Dir., Alberta Opportunity Co.; Drummond Brewing Co. Ltd.; Candn. Western Bank; Dir., Ensign Resource Service Group; Petrostar Petroleums Inc.; TransAlta Utilities Corp.; Red Deer South Progressive Conservative Assoc.; service station 1951–56; Lab Technician, oil refinery 1955; service station owner 1957; sales & mgmt., oil co. 1960; Owner & Mgr., oil co. 1964; Vice-Pres., Marketing, oil co. 1971–77; Past Pres. Westerner Exposition Assn.; Former Alderman, City of Red Deer; Former Mem. Bd. Govs., Red Deer College; Former Pres., Optimist Club Red Deer; recreations: fishing; camping; hunting; Club: Rotary of Red Deer; Home: c/o River Ridge Ranch, RR 4, Red Deer, Alta. T4N 5E4; Office: 4919 - 59 St., Ste. 236, Red Deer, Alta. T4N 6C9.

**DONALD, Joan M.;** business executive; b. Wetaskiwin, Alta. 29 May 1935; d. Charles and Anne (Metke) Schultz; e. Garneau H.S.; Reeves Bus. Coll.; m. Jack C. s. Archie and Margaret D. 29 Oct. 1955; children: Katherine A. Lacey, John S. Donald; ASST. CORP. SEC., PARKLAND INDUS. LTD. RED DEER 1976– ; Sec., Parkland Oil Products Ltd. 1964–71; Dir. & Sec. Treas., Parkland Properties Ltd.; Dir., Alberta Energy Co. Ltd.; Dir. & Ex. Com., Westerner Exposition Assn.; Dir., Red Deer Federal P.C. Assoc.; recreations: gardening, camping; clubs: Rotaryanns, Quarter Horse Assn. of Alta.; Home: River Ridge Ranch, R.R. #4, Red Deer, Alta. T4N 5E4; Office: #236, 4919 – 59 Street, Red Deer, Alta. T4N 6C9.

**DONALD, Rodney Stewart Craik,** M.A., M.B.A.; investment manager; b. London, Eng. 25 June 1928; s. Charles and Amy Stewart (Walker) D.; e. Charterhouse Sch. 1946; Oxford Univ., M.A. 1949; Harvard Bus. Sch., M.B.A. 1954; m. Susan d. James and Audrey Passant 26 Apr. 1957; children: Caroline Margaret, James Maitland, Fiona Stewart; Chrmn., McLean, Budden Limited 1977–90; Invest. Mgr., Mutual Funds, Management Corp. 1954–59; Pres., United Funds Mngt. 1959–70; Extve. Dir., S.G. Warburg & Co. (UK) 1970–77; Dir., The Mercantile & Gen. Reinsur. Co. of Can.; The Mercantile & Gen. Life Assur. Co. of Am.; Warburg Asset Mgmt. Canada Ltd.; Pres., The Oxford Union Soc. 1949; The Ticker Club 1985; Home: 106 Elm Ave., Toronto, Ont. M4W 1P2.

**DONALDSON, Edward Mossop,** Ph.D., D.Sc., F.R.S.C.; research scientist; b. Whitehaven, England 25 June 1939; s. Edward and Margaret Elizabeth (Mossop) D.; e. Whitehaven Grammar Sch. 1958; Univ. of Sheffield, 1958–61, B.Sc. (Hons.), D.Sc. 1975; U.B.C., Ph.D. 1964; Univ. of Minnesota post-doct fellow, 1965; m. Judith D. d. William and Eleanor Selwood 8 Aug. 1964; one d.: Heather Jean; RESEARCH SCIENTIST, DEPT. OF FISHERIES & OCEANS 1965– ; Rsch. Sci. 4 1984; Rsch.Sci. 5 1991– ; Section Head, Fish Cult. Rsch. 1981–89; Biotech., Genetics & Nutrition 1989– ; Head, DFO Ctr. for Disciplinary Excellence (CODE) for Biotech. & Genetics in Aquaculture 1986– ; Adjunct Prof. of Zool., U.B.C. 1988– ; doct. & masters suprvr., U.B.C. & S.F.U.; Cons., IDRC, CIDA, NSERC, NRC, CESO, EIFAC, FAO, UNDP, SGOMSEC, SCOPE/WHO, NSF, ICLARM, USAID, Office of Tech. Assessment US Congress, U.S. Sea Grant, U. of Calif., State of Alaska, Inst. of Fisheries (Portugal), Ruder Boskovic Ins. (Yugoslavia), and indus.; Am. Fish. Soc. citation for most significant paper in Soc. Transactions 1977; F.R.S.C. 1988 (Acad. III Life Mem.); Dept. of Fish. & Oceans, Merit Award for rsch. on monosex female salmon 1989; Ed. Bd., 'Gen. Comp. Endocrinol.' 1971–78, 'Aquaculture' 1983– , 'Can. J. Zool.' 1986–91, 'Can. J. Fish. Aquat. Sci.' 1986–88; Mem., Can. Soc. Zool. 1971–91 (Counc. 1980–83); Am. Soc. Zool. 1972–92; World Aqua. Soc. 1986– ; Aquac. Assn. Can. 1987– ; Asia & Oceania Soc. Comp. Endocrinol. 1987– ; Chrmn., Royal Soc. of Canada Symposium on 'The Marine Resources of the North Pacific Ocean' June 1990; Candn. Co-Chrmn., Canada/Japan Workshop on Aquaculture Biotechnology 1991; author of over 300 pubs. in sci. jours., conf. proceedings & books; co-editor: 'Fish Physiology' vol. 9A & vol. 9B 1983; Editorial Bd., 'Revista Italiana di Aquacoltura' 1991– ; recipient, Gold Medal in Natural Sciences, B.C. Science Council 1992; recreations: photography, swimming, kayaking, hiking; Home: 5492 Greenleaf Rd., West Vancouver, B.C. V7W 1N6; Office: W. Vanc. Lab., DFO, 4160 Marine Dr., W. Vancouver, B.C. V7V 1N6.

**DONALDSON, Jeffery William,** B.A., M.A., Ph.D.; university professor, writer; b. Toronto, Ont. 5 Oct. 1960; s. Harold James and Barbara Joyce (Westfall) D.; e. Huron Heights S.S.; Univ. of Toronto B.A. (Victoria College) 1983, M.A. 1985, Ph.D. 1989; PROF., McMASTER UNIV. 1989– ; began publishing poems in U.S. journals 1985; author: 'Once Out of Nature' 1991 (book of poems); Home: #11 – 4 Paislay Ave. S., Hamilton, Ont. L8S 1T7; Office: Dept. of English, McMaster Univ., Hamilton, Ont. L8S 4L9.

**DONALDSON, Marianne B.,** B.A.; human resources consultant; b. Toronto, Ont. 24 March 1944; d. Herbert J. and Margaret J. (Kennedy) Bellmore; e. Univ. of Toronto St. Michael's Coll. B.A. 1964; Ont. Coll. Edn. Cert. in Edn. 1966; m. James M. Donaldson 3 May 1975; PARTNER, ROURKE, LIZOTTE & ASSOCIATES 1986– ; Teacher Vincent Massey Coll. Inst. Windsor, Ont. 1964–66; News Broadcaster Expo '67 Montreal 1967; Touche Ross & Co., Montreal 1967–71; joined present firm 1971; Gov. Concordia Univ. Montreal; Adv. Bd., St. Mary's Hosp.; Former Adv. Bd., Financial Post; Former Dir. Tambrands Canada Inc.; recreations: tennis, skiing, fitness; Clubs: Canadian; Mount Royal Tennis; MAAA; Office: P.H., 1130 Sherbrooke St. W., Montreal, Que. H3A 2M8.

**DONEGAN, Edward L.,** Q.C., B.A.Sc., LL.B.; lawyer; b. Sudbury, Ont. 17 May 1935; s. Edward J. and Kathleen Spencer (Purvis) D.; e. Univ. of Toronto B.A.Sc. (Elec. Eng.) 1957, LL.B. 1960; PARTNER, BLAKE CASSELS & GRAYDON 1968– ; called to Bar of Ont. 1962; cr. Q.C. 1981; joined present firm 1962; Dir., Candn. Imperial Bank of Comm.; Dir., Torstar Corp.; Candn. High-Sch. Pub. Speaking Champion 1952;

mem., Business Law Sect. Internat. Bar Assn.; Licensing Exec. Soc.; R. Catholic; recreation: golf; Clubs: York; Toronto; National; Rosedale Golf; Home: 4409, 44 Charles St. W., Toronto, Ont. M4Y 1R8; Office: (P.O. Box 25) Commerce Court W., Toronto, Ont. M5L 1A9.

**DONEGAN, Rosemary Anne,** B.F.A., M.A.; curator; writer; b. Pretoria, S. Africa 15 Feb. 1949; d. Edmund and Eileen (Leyden) D.; e. Univ. of Sask. B.F.A.; Univ. of Toronto M.A.; Edn. & Extension Offr., Mendel Art Gallery, Saskatoon 1973–74; Co.-Manager, DEC Films 1976–78; curatorial projects include 'Reflections of our labour/Reflet de notre travail,' CLC Labour Studies & Edn. Centre, Ottawa 1980; 'Spadina Avenue: A Photo-history,' A Space Gallery, Toronto 1984; 'Industrial Images/Images Industrielles,' Art Gallery of Hamilton 1987–88; research assignments for Nat. Gallery of Can., Dalhousie Art Gallery, Art Gallery of Hamilton, Candn. Conf. of the Arts; Spl. Collections Proj., Urban Design Grp., City of Toronto; Candn. Auto Workers, Dunlop Art Gall.; author: 'Spadina Avenue' 1985; 'Industrial Images/Images Industrielles' 1988; Vice-Pres., Devel. Edn. Centre 1979–88, Pres., 1988– ; Mem., Ed. Collective & Dir., BorderLines Magazine 1984– ; Founding Mem. & Past. Pres., Women's Cultural Bldg., Toronto; Founding Mem., Candn. Women's Ednl. Press 1972; Regional Hist. Award, Candn. Hist. Assn. 1987; Home: 54 Delaware Ave., Toronto, Ont. M6H 2S7.

**DONEGANI, Jack,** B.Sc., M.Sc., M.B.A.; b. Montreal, Que. 6 Dec. 1946; s. Eric Edward and Daisy Harriet (Welch) D.; e. Sir George Williams Univ. B.Sc. Physics 1969; Univ. of Toronto M.Sc. Physics 1975; York Univ. M.B.A. Pub. Admin. 1980; m. Denise d. Sydney and Sheila Ballagh; 1 s.: Neal; Pres., Professional Institute of the Public Service of Canada 1980–..; Actuarial student Sun Life Corp. 1969–71; Meteorological Offr. CFB Greenwood 1971–73; Edn. leave 1973–75; Arctic Project Meteorologist 1975–76; Head Mktg. Services, Computing Centre 1976–77; Meteorological Support Offr., Computing Centre 1977–78; Head Surface Standards, Network Standards Div. 1978; Head, Climate Archives Section, Data Mgmt. Div. 1979; Atmospheric Environment Service, Environment Can. 1970–80; author: 'L'excellence scientifique canadienne en danger' in Interface 1985; Feature Ed. Greenwood Argus 1972–73; Ed. staff 'Pro-Forum' and 'Communications'; Guest Lectr. in Labour Relations at Universities, confs. and socs. such as C.P.P.M.A., F.M.I.; Order-in-Council appointee, Adv. Ctte. to Pres. of Treas Bd. on Pub. Service Superannuation Act; co-Vice-Chrmn. Nat. Joint Counc.; mem. Adv. Bd. on Health and Safety, Candn. Standards Bd.; mem. Un. Way; Inst. of Pub. Admin. of Can.; Candn. Pub. Personnel Policy Assn.; frequently on Bds. and panels, Conf. Bd. of Can.; awarded Gold Medal for Highest Marks in Fac. of Sci., Sir George Williams Univ. 1969; Grad. 2nd highest in Prov. of Que. Sr. Matric. 1963; recreations: golf, racquetball, nautilus; Clubs: Ottawa Athletic; The Canadian, Ottawa.

**DONGIER, Maurice Henri Jacques,** M.D., F.R.C.P.C.; educator; b. Sorgues (Vaucluse), France 27 Nov. 1925; s. Raphael and Yvonne (Jouanen) D.; e. Univ. de Marseille, Cert. d'études physiques, chimiques et biologiques 1943, Thèse de doctorat en médecine 1951; McGill Univ. Dipl. in Psychiatry 1953; m. Suzanne d. Louis Montagnac, Cannes; France 1952; children: Pierre, François, Isabelle, Philippe; Prof. and Chrmn. of Psychiatry, McGill Univ. 1974–85; Boursier du Ministère des Affaires culturelles de France 1951–52; Chef de Clinique adjoint, Clinique des maladies nerveuses Univ. de Marseille 1954–57; Chef de Clinique titulaire 1957–60; Psychiatre chargé de recherches, Laboratoire de neurophysiologie clinique, Hôpital de la Timone, Marseille 1960–63; Professeur et Directeur, Département de Psychologie médicale et médecine psychosomatique, Univ. de Liège, Belgique 1963–71; Prof. of Psychiatry and Dir. Allan Mem. Inst., McGill Univ. 1971–80; Co-dir., Alcohol Rsch. Center, Douglas Hosp. 1982– ; named Officier de l'ordre de Léopold (Belg.); Chevalier de la Légion d'Honneur (Fr.); author 'Névroses et troubles psychosomatiques' 1966–1967–1969–1972–1980–1984, édit néerlandaise 1967; German transl. 1984; co-author 'Contingent Negative Variations' 1969; 'Divergent Views in Psychiatry' 1981; numerous book chapters, 250 articles, mem. Soc. Médico-Psychologique de Paris;Groupe de l'Evolution psychiatrique Paris; Soc. d'Electroencéphalographie de Langue Française; Soc. de Psychiatrie de Marseille; Internat. Coll. Psychosomatic Med. (Founding mem.); Candn. Psychoanalytic Soc. (Secy. Que. Eng. Sec. 1975–77); Candn. Psychiatric Assn.; Que. Psychiatric Assn.; Candn. Psychoanalytic Inst. (Dir. 1990– ;); Fellow, Am. Psychiatric Assn.; Am. Psychopathol. Assn.; Fellow, Am. Psychosomatic Soc.; R. Catholic; recreations: sailing, flying; Home: 501 Roslyn Ave., Westmount, Que. H3Y 2T6; Office: 1033 Pine Ave. W., Montreal, Que. H3A 1A1.

**DONISON, Christopher John,** B.Mus.; musician: composer, conductor, arranger, pianist; b. Halifax, N.S. 26 Dec. 1952; s. Wesley S. and Rosemary Florence (Gray) D.; e. Esquimalt H.S. 1971; Univ. of Victoria, B.Mus. 1976; m. Brenda d. Viviani and Joyce Maree 1 Jan. 1983; DIR. OF MUSIC, SHAW FESTIVAL 1988– ; began performing as pianist in jazz & rock ensembles in Victoria area late 1960s while pursuing rigorous classical training; Teacher, Victoria Conserv. of Music 1976–79; theatre productions, Belfry Theatre 1979–81; has worked exclusively in theatre as composer, conductor, arranger & pianist primarily with Shaw Festival 1981– ; original scores incl. 'You Never Can Tell' by George Bernard Shaw for Olympic Arts Fest. & 'Peter Pan' 1987, 1988; 'Man and Superman' 1989; 'Waltz of the Toreadors' 1990; 'Lulu' 1991; '7 Encounters for Soprano & Flute' 1992; 'The Silver King' 1993; 'Theme & Conversations for Orchestra' 1993; Dora Mavor Moore award for Musical Direction, City of Toronto 1986; Mem., C.A.P.A.C., A.F. of M. (Toronto local); Home: 408 Simcoe St., Niagara-on-the-Lake, Ont.; Office: Box 774, Niagara-on-the-Lake, Ont. L0S 1J0.

**DONNAN, David Charles,** B.A.Sc., M.B.A., P.Eng., C.M.C.; management consultant; b. Toronto, Ont. 18 Apr. 1955; s. Hugh and Amie (Dickson) D.; e. Univ. of Toronto B.A.Sc. 1978, M.B.A. 1982; m. Karen d. Doug and Margorie Goss 1979; children: Michael, Peter; PARTNER, PEAT MARWICK STEVENSON & KELLOGG 1990– ; Cons., Stevenson & Kellogg 1978–81; Sr. Cons., Opns. Rsch., Canada Packers Inc. 1981–82; Mgr., Corp. Indus. Engr. 1982–87; Opns. Mgr. 1987–88; Principal, present firm 1988–90; Mem., Experience Requirements Ctte., Assn. fo Profl. Engrs. of Ont.; Business Adv. Bd., Dept. of Indus. Engr., Univ. of Toronto; Lectr., Fac. of Business; recreations: cycling, camping; Home: 257 Riverside Dr., Oakville, Ont.; Office: 18th fl., 2300 Yonge St., Toronto, Ont. M4P 1G2.

**DONNAY, J(oseph) D(ésiré) H(ubert),** Ph.D., F.M.S.A., F.G.S.A.; educator; b. Grandville-Oreye, Belgium 6 June 1902; s. Désiré Mathieu Joseph and Madeleine (Doyen) D.; e. Athenaeum Liège, Belgium 1920; Univ. Liège Candidat Ingénieur 1922, Ing. civil des Mines 1925; Stanford Univ. Ph.D. (Geol.) 1929; m. 1stly Marie-Madeleine Hennin 23 Dec. 1931; children: Robert V.J., Nicole; m. 2ndly Gabrielle Hamburger 25 July 1949; children: Albert H., Victor J.; Research Assoc. in Crystallography, McGill Univ. 1975–86; Research Assoc. in Geol. and Teaching Fellow in Mineral. Stanford Univ. 1930–31; Assoc. in Mineral. & Petrography The Johns Hopkins Univ. 1931–39, Visiting Prof. of Chem. Crystallography & Mineral. 1945 and Prof. 1946–71, Prof. Emeritus 1971, Chrmn. Phys. Sciences Group 1951–53, Visiting Prof. 1972; Prof. agrégé Univ. Laval 1939–40, prof. titulaire 1940–45; Research Chem. Hercules Powder Co. Exper. Stn. Wilmington, Del. 1942–45; Prof. ordinaire à la Faculté des Sciences Univ. de Liège 1946–47, Prof. honoraire 1948, rec'd médaille de l'Université 1959; Fulbright Lectr. Univ. de Paris (Sorbonne) 1958–59; Guest Investigator, Carnegie Inst. of Washington, Geophys. Lab. 1959–70; Chargé de cours Univ. de Montréal 1970–72, Prof. invité 1972–76; Visiting Lectr. Univ. of Utah 1950, Ballistic Research Lab. Aberdeen Proving Ground, Md. 1961, Emory Univ., Ga. Inst. Technol., Univ. of Ga. 1963; Tokyo and other Japanese universities 1951, 1962, 1974; Visiting Scient. U.S. Naval Postgrad. Sch. Monterey, Calif. 1955; Brookhaven Nat. Lab. 1957; Gastprof. Universität Marburg, Mineralogisches Inst. 1966, 1968; Guest Worker, U.S. Nat. Bureau of Standards 1967–73; rec'd Queen's Silver Jubilee Medal 1977; ed. 'Crystal Data' 1st ed. 1954, 2nd ed. 1963, 3rd. ed. vol. 1 1972, vol. 2 1973, vols. 3 and 4 1978 (hon. ed.); author 'Spherical Trigonometry' 1945; co-ed. 'Internat. Tables of Crystallography' 1952, 1974; co-author, 'Space Groups and Lattice Complexes' 1973; over 163 papers scient. journs.; U.S. patent, Highway intersection system (3,399,379 Aug. 27 1968); Fellow, Mineral. Soc. Am. (Pres. 1953; Roebling Medal 1971); Geol. Soc. Am. (Vice Pres. 1954); membre correspondant, Société royale des Sciences de Liège; membre honoraire, Soc. géologique de Belgique (Vice Pres. 1946–47); Soc. française de Minéralogie et de Cristallographie (Vice Pres. 1949, mem. d'honneur 1978); Charter mem., Am. Soc. X-Ray & Electron Diffraction (Secy.-Treas. 1944, Secy. 1945–46); Crystallographic Soc. Am. (Pres. 1949); Am. Crystallographic Assn. (Pres. 1956); Geochem. Soc.; Vice Pres. Assn. française de Cristallographie 1959–60; mem. Assn. Ingénieurs Liège A.I.Lg. (médaille Trasenster 1977; adm. Sect. canadienne 1983–86); Sigma Xi; Mineral. Soc. (UK); The Philadelphia Mineral. Soc. (emeritus); Phi Beta Kappa; del. various gen. assemblies and congs. Internat. Union Crystallography; Società Italiana di Mineralogia e Petrologia; Mineral. Assn. Can.; (mem. associé) Académie royale des Sciences, des Lettres et des Beaux-Arts de Belgique; hon. mem. Mineral Soc. Japan; recreation: philology; Home: 516 rue d'Iberville, Mont-St-Hilaire, Que. J3H 2V7; Office: 3450 University St., Montreal, Que. H3A 2A7.

**DONNELLY, James;** executive; b. Wishaw, Scot. 22 March 1931; s. Peter and Mary (Morris) D.; e. Royal Tech. Coll. Glasgow 1949–53; m. Brenda d. Ernest John Marks 29 March 1954; one d., three s.; PRESIDENT, JAMES DONNELLY & ASSOC., EXECUTIVE CONSULTANTS; held extve. positions General Electric of Eng. and English Electric Co. 1954–74; Vice Pres. Forestry Products, International Systems & Controls Corp. Inc. Montreal 1974; Pres. and C.E.O., Atomic Energy of Canada Ltd. 1978–89; Extve. Vice Pres. & C.E.O., Stadler Hurter, Montreal; Commercial Dir., GECK T.G., U.K.; Program Chrmn., WEC '89, Montreal; Assoc., Royal Tech. Coll. Glasgow; mem. U.K. Inst. Elect. Engrs.; recreations: tennis, fishing, golf.; Clubs: Cercle Universitaire; Royal Ottawa Golf; Ottawa Athletic; Ottawa Hunt; Home: Benson Lake, Elgin, Ont.; Office: 23 – 255 Botanic Pr., Ottawa, Ont. K1Y 4P8.

**DONNELLY, Michael Wade,** B.S., M.A., Ph.D.; educator; b. Buffalo, N.Y. 28 Feb. 1939; s. Edward Glen and Frances (Knight) D.; e. Columbia Univ. B.S. 1966, M.A. 1975, Cert. E. Asian Inst. 1975, Ph.D. 1978; m. Lynne Kutsukake 31 Aug. 1987; one d. Michaela Elisabeth; ASSOC. DEAN, FACULTY OF ARTS AND SCIENCE, UNIV. OF TORONTO 1992– , Lectr. 1975–78, Asst. Prof. 1978–81, Assoc. Prof. 1981– ; Visiting Rsch. Fellow Inst. Developing Economies Tokyo 1970–73, 1981–82; Staff, Social Sci. Rsch. Council N.Y. 1973–74; Visiting Prof. Keio Univ. Tokyo 1981–82; Visiting Rsch. Scholar Japanese Soc. Promotion Sci., Japan 1986; Visiting Prof., Meiji Univ. 1989–90; Assoc. Dir. Jt. Centre for Asia Pacific Studies 1979–81, Dir. 1985–88; Dir. Japan Rsch. Prog. 1986–89; Assoc. mem. Inst. Fiscal & Monetary Policy and Found. for Advanced Info. & Rsch. Japan; mem. Candn. Nat. Ctte. Econ. Co-op. 1988–89; recipient Woodrow Wilson Fellowship 1966; Fellow of Faculty Columbia Univ. 1966–1970; Foreign Area Fellowship SSRC (US) 1970–72; John Lindbeck Award (Columbia) 1975; Yoshida Internat. Edn. Found. Fellowship 1972; author of 36 book chapters and articles on contemporary Japan; mem. Am. Pol. Sci. Assn.; Candn. Pol. Sci. Assn.; Candn. Asian Studies Assn.; Dir., Can.-Japan Soc. Toronto; Can.-Japan Trade Council; Japan Social Sci. Assn. Can.; Home: 796 Palmerston Ave., Toronto, Ont. M6G 2R7; Office: Toronto, Ont. M5S 1A1.

**DONNER, Gail J.,** R.N., B.Sc.N., M.A., Ph.D.; nursing educator; b. Winnipeg, Man. 2 June 1942; d. Sydney R. and Anne R. Gitterman; e. Winnipeg Gen. Hosp. Sch. Nursing R.N. 1962; Univ. of Pa. B.Sc.N. 1967; New York Univ. M.A. 1969; Univ. of Toronto Ph.D. 1986; m. Arthur s. Fred and Edith Donner 18 Nov. 1962; children: Simon, Elizabeth; ASSOC. PROF., FAC. OF NURSING, UNIV. OF TORONTO; med., surgical, psychiatric nursing hosps., community centres, student health services 1962–67; Instr. in Nursing 1969–74; Prof. of Nursing Ryerson Polytech. Inst. 1974–84, Chair 1976–82; Exec. Dir., Registered Nurses' Assoc. of Ont. 1986–89; Dir., Nursing Education, Hospital for Sick Children, Toronto 1989–92; Extve. Mem., Bd. of Trustees, United Way of Metro. Toronto; Vice-Chair, Director's Ctte. on the Future of the Ontario Institute for Studies in Education 1992– ; Mem., Presidential Comn. on Future of Health Care in Ont., Univ. of Toronto 1990–91; Bd. of Dirs., Home Care Prog. Metro Toronto 1987–90; Mem. Ctte. on Hosps., Ont. Med. Assoc.; Mem. Adv. Ctte., Hosp. Mgmt. Rsch. Unit, Univ. of Toronto; author various nursing articles; Office: 50 St. George St., Toronto, Ont. M5S 1A1.

**DONOAHUE, James Thomas,** R.C.A.; graphic designer; b. Walkerton, Ont. 15 Oct. 1934; s. Frank and Helene (Montpetit) D.; e. Central Tech. High Sch. Hamilton 1952; Ont. Coll. of Art 1956; children: Zoe, Noah, Colin; PROP., JIM DONOAHUE & ASSOCIATES LTD.; recipient numerous nat. and internat. awards from design organs. Toronto, Montreal, New York, Chicago; work featured in design publs. USA, Europe and Japan; mem. Art Dirs. Club Toronto (Past Pres.); Alliance Graphique Internationale; Offices: 544 Richmond St. W., Toronto, Ont. M5V 1Y4 and 353 Newdale Court, N. Vancouver, B.C. V7N 3H3.

**DONOVAN, D. Peter,** B.A., C.A., M.B.A.; financial executive; b. Toronto, Ont.; s. Daniel and Dorothy D.; e. Univ. of Toronto B.A. (Hons.) 1963; Univ. of Western Ont. M.B.A. 1968; m. Elizabeth d. James and Clara

Martin 23 Dec. 1967; children: Daniel, Mathew; COMPTROLLER, GENERAL ELECTRIC CANADA INC. 1987– ; and TREASURER 1992– ; Dir. & Vice-Pres., General Electric Capital Canada Inc.; Dir. & Treas., General Electric Capital Candn. Holdings Ltd.; Dir., Comptroller & Treas., General Electric Candn. Holdings Ltd.; General Electric Canada Internat. Inc.; Financial Specialist, Alcan Internat. Ltd. 1968–70; Mgr. Financial Planning, Alcan Aluminio do Brasil 1970–72; Controller 1972–74; Asst. Treas. Finance, Alcan Canada Products Ltd. 1974–78; Chief Finan. Offr. & Sec., Aughinish Alumina Ltd. 1978–83; Vice-Pres., Finance, Alcan Can. Prod. Ltd. 1983–85; Vice-Pres., Finance & Chief Finan. Offr., Jannock Limited 1985–86; C.A. 1966; Mem., Ont. Inst. of C.A.s; Dir., Financial Extve. Inst. 1989– ; Tax Extve. Inst.; recreations: music, reading, gardening; club: Granite; Home: 101 Chudleigh Ave., Toronto, Ont. M4R 1T5; Office: 2300 Meadowvale Blvd., Mississauga, Ont. L5N 5P9.

**DOOB, Anthony N.,** A.B., Ph.D.; educator; b. Washington, D.C. 28 Apr. 1943; s. Leonard W. and Eveline (Bates); e. Harvard Univ. A.B. 1964; Stanford (Calif.) Univ. Ph.D. 1967; m. Patricia d. Frank and Gemma Baranek 17 Aug. 1980; children: Joshua; PROFESSOR OF CRIMINOLOGY, UNIVERSITY OF TORONTO 1976– ; Instr. Stanford Univ. 1967; Asst. Prof. present Univ. 1968; Assoc. Prof. 1971; Prof. 1976; Dir., Ctr. of Criminology, Univ. of Toronto 1979–89; Office: Centre of Criminology, Univ. of Toronto, Toronto, Ont. M5S 1A1.

**DOODY, Hon. C. William;** politician; b. St. John's, Nfld. 26 Feb. 1931; s. Matthew and Florence (O'Neil) D.; m. Doreen Jessop, 30 July 1961; children: Christine, Liam, Steven; SENATOR since 1979; Depy. Leader Government Senate 1984–91; el. Harbour Main Dist. 1971; Min. of Mines and Resources 1972, of Indust. Devel. 1973, of Finance 1975–78; of Trans. and Comm., for Intergov. Affairs, of Pub. Works and Serv., 1978–79; P. Conservative; R. Catholic; Home: 94 Merrymeeting Rd., St. John's Nfld. A1C 2W1; Office: The Senate, Ottawa, Ont. K1A 0A4.

**DOOLITTLE, Quenten,** B.Sc., M.M., A.M.D.; b. Elmira, N.Y. 21 May 1925; s. Guy Cornell and Ruby Edith (Sisson) D.; e. Ithaca College B.Sc. 1950; Indiana Univ. M.M. 1952; Eastman School of Music, Univ. of Rochester A.M.D.; m. Joyce d. Terence and Irene Donahue 29 June 1949; children: Megan, Eric, Lisa, Amy; PROFESSOR EMERITUS OF MUSIC, UNIV. OF CALGARY; Candn. citizen 1969; in 1965 he began music composition during an active career as a soloist, conductor, prof. of music & principal violist for Calgary Philharmonic; his compositions have been heard in Canada, U.S., U.K., France, & Eastern Europe; composer of over 40 works including three operas: 'Charlie the Chicken,' 'Silver City,' and 'Boiler Room Suite' (heard in London, Cardiff, Birmingham, Toronto, Banff); Pres., New Works Calgary Society; Chrmn., Candn. Music Centre, Prairie Region; recipient Killam Fellowship; Canada Council Senior Arts Grant; Mem., Candn. League of Composers; Candn. Music Centre; Home: 2108 7th St. S.W., Calgary, Alta. T2T 2X2.

**DORAIS, Léo A.,** B.A., B.Ph., L.Ps., M.B.A., Ph.D.; educateur; né Montréal 21 sept. 1929; f. J. Armand et Lucienne (Cormier) D.; é. Univ. Montréal, B.A. 1952, B.Ph. 1953, L.Ph. 1955; Univ. Chicago, M.B.A. 1962; Univ. Chicago, Ph.D. 1964; ép. Suzanne, f. J. Roland Dansereau, 3 sept. 1955; enfants: André-R., Anne-Marie, Catherine, Jean-A.; CONSEILLER SPECIAL AUPRES DU SOUS-MINISTRE DES COMMUNICATIONS ET PROFESSEUR INVITE À LA FACULTÉ D'ADMINISTRATION DE L'UNIV. D'OTTAWA 1987– ; Secrétaire Général des Musées Nationaux de Canada; Sous-Ministère Adjoint aux Arts et à la Culture 1980–87; mem. du Comité d'étude de la politique culturelle Fédérale (Comité Applebaum-Hébert); sous-secrétaire d'Etat adjoint aux Arts et à la culture 1979–80; vice président principal, Agence Canadienne de Développement International 1976–79; Recteur, Univ. du Quebec (Montreal) 1969–74; Vice-prés., Faroun Films (Canada) Ltée; Dir., Service d'education perm. Univ. Montréal, 1967–69; Dir. associé Service audiences Comn. Royale d'enquête sur le bilinguisme et le biculturalisme, 1964–65; membre; Comité planification de la recherche pédagogique 1967–68; Coordonnateur Comité élab. système informatique gestion universités 1968; membre: Canadian Indust. Trainers' Assn.; Candn. Assn. Adult Educ.; Musée Beaux-Arts, Montréal; Corporation des psychologues de la P.Q.; Soc. can. de psychologie; Soc. can. anthropologie et sociologie; Vice-Prés., Soc. de Math, appliquées; auteur du: 'Manuel de méthodologie de la recherche,' 1956; 'l'Autogestion Universitaire: autopsie d'un mythe' 1977; de nombreux articles, Revue de Livres dans des périodiques; Catholique; Récréations: photographie, musique; sports aquatiques; Résidence: 333 Chapel, Ottawa, Ont. K1N 8Y8.

**DORAIS, Marcel,** B.A.Sc.; retired mining executive; b. Montreal, Que. 25 June 1924; s. Honoré and Albertine (Ladouceur) D.; e. Ecole Supérieure St-Stanislas and Mont St-Louis, Montreal 1944; Ecole Polytech., Univ. de Montréal, B.A.Sc. (Civil Engn.); m. Marcelle, d. Marcel Rigaud, 4 Jan. 1947; children: Michel, Daniel, Anne; Mgr. (Constr.) C. Jobin Ltée, Québec City, 1950; Chief Engr. (Constr.) Michaud & Simard, 1959; Vice Pres. (Constr. Div.) Compagnie Miron Ltée, Montreal 1961–71; Pres., C.E.O. and Dir., Bell Asbestos Mines Ltd., 1971; Pres., C.E.O. & Dir., Société Asbestos Ltee 1982–85, Chrmn. & Dir., 1985–86; Retired 1986; Mem., Corp. des Ingénieurs du Qué.; Engn. Inst. Can.; R. Catholic; recreations: photography, swimming, travel, art; Home: 11 Oreilly, Apt. 709, Ile des Soeurs, Verdun, Qué. H3E 1T6.

**DORAIS, Michel,** D.E.C., B.Sc., D.E.A.; public servant; b. Valleyfield, Que. 6 March 1952; d. Henri and Muguette (Lavigne) D.; e. Classical Studies, Valleyfield 1969; D.E.C. Health Sci., Valleyfield 1971; Univ. of Ottawa B.Sc. 1974; Univ. Paul Sabatier, D.E.A. (UNESCO) 1975; m. Odette d. Gérard Mercier 22 Dec. 1984; one s.: François-Olivier; EXECUTIVE CHAIRMAN, FEDERAL ENVIRONMENTAL ASSESSMENT REVIEW OFFICE 1991– ; and FEDERAL ADMINISTRATOR, James Bay & Northern Quebec Agreement; Senior Policy Analyst, Parks Canada 1975–80; Analyst & Sr. Offr., Machinery of Govt., Privy Council 1980–84; Dir. Gen., Labour Canada 1984–86; Dir., Investment Promotion, Investment Canada 1986–87; Chief of Staff for Que. Min. of Communication, Sci. & Tech. and Supply & Services 1987–89; Vice-Pres., Que. Environ. Assessment Office 1989–90; Pres. 1990–91; Office: Fontaine Bldg., Hull, Qué. K1A 0H3.

**DORAN, Anthony Burke,** Q.C., LL.B.; barrister; b. Ottawa, Ont. 17 May 1937; s. Anthony Burke and Margaret Felicite (Heney) D.; e. Univ. of Ottawa High Sch. 1954; Univ. of Ottawa 1955–56; McGill Univ. B.A. 1958; Osgoode Hall Law Sch. LL.B. 1961; m. Janet; one s. Patrick John Wentworth; PARTNER, LANG MICHENER; called to Bar of Ont. 1963; cr. Q.C. 1979; author various articles legal topics; mem., Candn. Bar Assn. (Past Chrmn. Family Law Sec. Ont. Br.; past Chrmn., Nat. Judicial Appts. Comte); Advocates' Soc.; Thomas More Guild; Kappa Alpha; Phi Delta Phi; Liberal; R. Catholic; Club: Univ. Club of Toronto; Office: P.O. Box 747, BCE Place, 181 Bay St., Toronto, Ont. M5J 2T7.

**DORAN, John Lloyd,** C.A.; auditor; b. Meaford, Ont. 17 July 1936; s. Frank Norton and Olive Agnes (Gifford) D.; e. Ryerson Polytech. Inst. 1958 (Ist in Class); Ont. Inst. C.A.'s 1963; Trust Co's Assn. Course (highest standing in Can.) m. Joan d. Norman and Marion Crawley 1958; children: Brian John, Nancy Lyn; VICE PRES. AUDIT SERVICES CT FINANCIAL SERVICES 1991– ; systems analyst 1968–72; AVP Audit Services 1972–78; Product Mgr. AVP Demand Savings Services 1978–81; Vice Pres. Comptroller present Co. 1981–91; Dir. S.W. Ont. Chapter Financial Execs. Inst.; Founding Pres. London Chapter Inst. Internal Auditors; recreations: golf, personal computing, reading; Club: Highland Golf & Country; Home: 46, 2 Cadeau Terrace, London, Ont. N6K 4G4; Office: 4F, 114 Dundas at Talbot, London, Ont. N6A 4S4.

**DORÉ, Jean,** (Col. Ret.), SB St.J, CD, KCLJ; dignatary; b. Montreal, Que. 5 April 1928; s. Dr. Réal and Henriette (Leclerc) D.; e. Acad. Querbes, Outremont; Univ. of Montreal; McGill Univ.; m. Marilyn d. Myrtle and Archibald Rogers 23 April 1960; GENTLEMAN USHER OF THE BLACK ROD, THE SENATE OF CANADA 1990– ; joined Les Fusiliers Mont-Royal Regiment 1950; served in Germany 1952–53; Candn. Guards 1953–59; Lt. Col., Commanding 6 bn R22R Mil., 1967–70; promoted to Col. & Comdr. No. 1 Mil., Dist., Montreal 1970–71; Comnr., St. John Ambulance, Montreal Reg. 1970–73; ex Deputy Refinery Mgr., Redpath Sugar; Mgr., Eastern Can., Pop Shoppe Group; Grad. Militia Staff Coll. with Hon. 1967; Life Mem., La Fond. Vanier; Footguards Assn.; Gov., Le Club des Officiers, FMR; Mem., Army Officers Mess Ottawa; Officers Mess at la Citadelle, Que., Ste Hyacinthe & Montreal; Dir., Candn. Legion Br., Jean Brillant, VC; Mem. Candn. Power & Sail Squadron; recreations: sailing, golf, chess; club: National Press; Home: 1449 Waltham, Gloucester, Ont. K1T 2T4; Office: Ottawa, Ont. K1A 0A4.

**DORE, Karl J.,** Q.C., B.B.A., B.C.L., LL.M.; professor; b. Fredericton, N.B. 17 May 1943; s. Karl H. and Geraldine E. (Morehouse) D.; e. Univ. of N.B., B.B.A. 1965, B.C.L. 1967; Yale Univ., LL.M. 1968; m. Shirley d. Irvine and Mabel Hagerman 15 July 1967; children: Natalie, Mitchell, Katherine; PROF. OF LAW, UNIV. OF NEW BRUNSWICK 1991– ; Asst. Prof., present univ. 1968–73; Assoc. Prof. 1973–76; Prof. 1976–77; Dean of Law 1984–91; Vis. Prof., Osgoode Hall 1976; Dir., Consumer & Corp. Affairs, N.B. Govt. 1977–84; Q.C. 1987; Home: 837 Mitchell St., Fredericton, N.B. E3B 6E8; Office: P.O. Box 4400, Fredericton, N.B. E3B 5A3.

**DORE, Raymond,** C.A.; banker; b. Sudbury, Ont. 25 March 1939; s. the late Albert and Anna (Leschishin) D.; e. Public and High Schs. Sudbury, Ont.; children: Steven, Glenn; PRES., C.E.O. & DIR., THE MUTUAL TRUST CO. 1981– ; Dir., Mutual Trustco Inc.; Interior Capital Corp.; The Northwest Co. Inc.; C.A. with Arthur A. Crawley and Co., Montreal 1965; Treas., Commercial Trust Co., Montreal 1966–74; Vice Pres., Mercantile Bank of Can., Toronto 1975–77; C.E.O., Rolfe Reeve Group Ltd. 1977–78; Chrmn., Merchant Trust Co. 1978–79; Chrmn., Doré, Sutherland & Stuebing Inc. 1980; recreations: golf, squash; Clubs: Montreal Badminton & Squash; Royal Montreal Golf; Home: 22 Lowther Ave., Toronto, Ont.; Office: 70 University Ave., Suite 400, Toronto, Ont. M5J 2M4.

**DORÉ, Roland,** O.C., Ph.D., M.S., B.A.Sc., P.Eng.; educator and administrator; b. Montreal, Que. 16 Feb. 1938; s. Gaston D. and Alice (Laverdure) D.; e. École Polytechnique, Montreal; B.A.Sc. 1960; Stanford Univ. M.S. 1965, Ph.D. 1969; m. Céline d. Achille and Blanche Bergeron 16 Sept. 1958; children: Sylvie, François, Eric; PRES., CANADIAN SPACE AGENCY 1992– ; Asst., Dept. of Mechanical Engineering, École Polytechnique 1960–63; Asst. Prof., Dept. Mech. Eng. 1963–69 (grad. studies 1964–65 and 1967–69); Assoc. Prof., Dept. of Mech. Eng. 1969–76; mem. Bd. of Dir. 1971–76; Head, Mech. Eng., Machine Design Section 1972–75; Head, Mech. Eng. 1975–78; Prof. 1976– ; Asst. Dir. Rsch. 1979–80; Dir. Rsch. 1980–82; Dir. 1982–89; Pres. 1989–92; Vice-Pres., Natural Sciences and Engineering Rsch. Counc. of Can. 1988–92; Fellow, Engrg. Inst. of Canada; Ordre des Ingénieurs du Qué.; Fellow, Candn. Soc. for Mech. Engineers; Candn. Acad. of Engrg.; Am. Soc. for Mech. Engineers; Assn. des Diplômés de Polytechnique; Montreal Cham. of Comm.; author of more than 60 technical publications in applied mechanics and biomechanics; Scholarships and awards: Kennecott Copper Corp Schol. 1959; Silver Medal, Assn. des Diplômés de Polytechnique; Award from Am. Soc., Heating, Refrigerating & Air Conditioning Engineers 1960; Symbolic Schol., Prov. of Que.; Schol. from Hydro-Québec 1967–69; Officer, Order of Canada 1992; Julian C. Smith Award, Candn. Council of Professional Engineers 1992; Grand Prix D'Excellence 1993; Order of Engineers of Quebec 1993; Honorary doctorate: College militaire royal de St-Jean 1992; McGill Univ. 1992; mem., Club St-Denis; recreations: jogging, skiing, golf, reading, music listening; Home: 2941, rue Fendall, Montreal, Qué. H3T 1N2; Office: Canadian Space Agency, 6767 Route de L'Aéroport, St-Hubert, Qué. J3Y 8Y9.

**DOREEN, Dale,** B.S., M.A., Ph.D.; university professor; b. Rochester, NY 8 March 1943; d. John Dan and Helen Vanetta D.; e. Univ. of Alabama B.S. 1965, M.A. 1967, Ph.D. 1972; ASSOC. PROF. OF DECISION SCIENCES & MNGT. INFORMATION SCIENCES, CONCORDIA UNIV. 1971– ; joined Concordia as Asst. Prof. 1971; Acad. Dir., Concordia Extve. MBA Prog. 1986–92; Chair, Dept. of Decision Sci. & Mngt. Information Systems 1978–80; Visiting Prof., Valbonne France 1988; Peoples Univ. Beijing China 1986; Nat. Univ. of Singapore 1982 Beta Gamma Sigma (Nat. Bus. Hon.); Phi Mu Epsilon (Nat. Math. Hon.) Omnicron Delta Epsilon (Nat. Econ. Hon.); Reg. Dir., A.I.E.S.E.C. U.S. (1967–70; Mem., Internat. Council for Small Business; contbg. author: 'The World Book Encyclopedia' 1988, 'Mediterranean Europe and the Common Market' 1976; author/co-author 27 acad. articles; club: Montreal Amateur Athletic Assn.; Home: 1469 Argyle Ave., Montreal, Que. H3G 1V5; Office: 1455 de Maisonneuve Blvd. W., Montreal, Que. H3G 1M8.

**DORIN, Hon. Murray William,** C.A., M.P.; politician, accountant; b. Viking, Alta. 21 May 1954; s. William and Lillian (Teske) D.; e. Univ. of Alta. B.Comm. 1976; articled with Price Waterhouse qualifying as CA 1978; married with two children; Member of Parliament, Govt. of Canada 1984–93; Comptroller, Terra Mines Limited; 1st elected 4 Sept. 1984; re-elected 21 Nov. 1988; Chair, Standing Ctte. on Finance (former Vice-Chair); Former Campaign Mgr., P.C. Party of Alberta; Fundraiser, PC Canada Fund; Former Mem., Nat. Extve., PC Party of Canada (Vice-Pres., Alta.); Mem., Phi Gamma Delta; recreations: skiing, golfing.

**DORION, Robert Bernard Joseph,** B.Sc., D.D.S., Diplomate A.B.F.O.; b. Montreal, Que. 16 Oct. 1944; s. Eugene Squires and Marcelle Fernande Sarah (Rochon) D.; e. St. Francis Xavier Univ. B.Sc. 1968; McGill Univ. D.D.S. 1972; Am. Armed Forces Inst. of Pathology Cert. in Forensic Dent. 1972; Dipl. Am. Bd. Forensic Odontology 1976; Licensure Coll. Dent. Surgeons Prov. Quebec 1972; m. Patricia Ann d. Alexander James Boyd, Morristown, Antigonish, N.S. 19 Aug. 1972; s. Robert Peter James; d. Melissa Sarah Jane; Clinician, Operative Dent., Univ. of Montreal since 1972, Lectr. in Forensic Dent. 1974–80; Guest Lectr. Forensic Dent. McGill Univ. 1972–1974, Sessional Lectr. since 1974; Dir. of Forensic Dent., Laboratoire de Medecine Legale, Ministry of Public Security, Que. since 1973; Lectr. in Forensic Dent. Univ. Laval 1977–85; Lectr. Can. Police College, 1978–80; Vice-Pres., Assn. Prof. des Charges Clinique, Univ. of Montreal Fac. of Dent. 1980–86; Co-Chrmn., Med. Ctte. Vietnamese Refugees, St. Veronica's Parish, Dorval 1979–80; mem., Am. Acad. Forensic Sciences 1975– ; (Chrmn. Ctte. Recommended Methods, Odont. Sect. 1976–77, Fellow 1977, Mem. Methods Examination Ctte. Odont. Sect. 1977–78, Mem. Rsch. Ctte. Bite Mark Evidence Odont. Sect. 1977–78, Mem. Internat. Relns. Ctte. 1980–82); Mem. Ed. Bd., J. Candn. Soc. Forens. Sci. 1975–77, 1978– ; Specialty Contrib. Forens. Dent., J. Can. Dent. Assn. 1980– ; Chrmn. Can. Soc. Forensic Science 1972– ; (Pres. Que. Nucleus Odont. Sect. 1972–74, Vice Pres. Odont. Sect. 1974–75, Pres. Odont. Sect. 1975–77, Dir. 1975–79, Chrmn., Sci. Prog. Odont. Sect. National Convention 1976, 2nd Vice Pres. 1976–77, Mem. Finance Ctte. 1977–78, Pres. 1978–79, Chrm. of Bd. 1978–79, Ed. Bd. 1975– , Chrmn. Nominating Ctte. 1980–81, Chrmn. Publicity and Public Relns. Ctte. 1981–82, Mem. Nominating Ctte. 1981–83); Cons., Forens. Odont. Investigative Tests, Law Reform Comn. of Can. 1982–83; mem., Am. Bd. Forensic Odontology (Dir. 1976–82, 1985–88; Co-Chrmn., Ctte. Bylaws 1977–78; Acting Chrmn., Bylaws Ctte. 1984–85; Pres. & Bd. Chrmn. 1985–86; Mem. Ethics Ctte. 1986–90 (Chrmn. 1989); Mem. Cert. and Examination Ctte. 1987–91 (Chrmn. 1989)); mem., Candn. Dent. Assn. 1972– ; Order Dents. Que. 1972– ; Candn. Soc. Forens. Odont. 1971–73; Montreal Dent. Club 1972–87 (Mem., Continuing Educ. Ctte. 1973–76); Montreal Endodontia Soc. 1973–74; Mem. Internat. Soc. Forens. Odonto-Stomatology 1974–76; Dir., Profl. Relns., Prov. of Que., Future Focus Health Systems, Ltd. 1987–88; Clinical surveyor, univ. accreditation prog. ed. and Accredit. Commn. Candn. Dent. Assn. 1987; author various articles prof. journs. and contr. author to books on forensic evidence; numerous lecture presentations in Can., U.S. and abroad; recreations: photography, video recording, painting, skiing, swimming, chess, sculpturing, writing, research and computerisation; Office: 1 Place Ville-Marie, Ste. 1521, Montreal, Que. H3B 2B5.

**DORN, A. Walter,** B.Sc., M.Sc., Ph.D.; scientist; educator; b. Toronto, Ont. 11 July 1961; s. Paul Carl and Trudy (Veen) D.; e. Toronto French Sch. 1979; Univ. of Toronto B.Sc. 1983, M.Sc. 1986, Ph.D. 1994; RSCH. ASSOCIATE, INTERNATIONAL RELATIONS, UNIV. OF TORONTO 1994– ; rsch. asst. in chem. Univ. of Toronto summer 1981, 1982, teaching asst. Scarborough Coll. 1982–87, teaching asst. in chem. 1987, 1990, grad. student researcher 1987–92, 1993– ; program coordinator for arms control verification, Parliamentarians for Global Action 1992–93; rsch. asst. Ont. Cancer Inst. summer 1983; cons., researcher Candn. Inst. Internat. Peace & Security 1986–87; sci. cons., York Energy Conserv. 1989; Keymolecular Corp. 1990; International Surgical Products 1991; cons. to Chrmn. of First Ctte. (UN) 1990; mem. Fed. Am. Scientists Expert Working Group on Biological Weapons Verification 1989–90; physical sciences don, Trinity Coll. 1990–92; Jr. Fellow, Massey Coll. 1990–91; recipient Candn. Inst. Internat. Peace & Security Award 1987/88, 1989/90; mem. Scarborough Coll. Council 1982/83; Bd. mem. Sci. for Peace 1982– , UN Rep. 1983– ; Chrmn. Working Group Internat. Surveillance & Verification 1986– ; Chrmn. Organizing Ctte. Workshops on Peace-keeping Satellites 1986, Satellite & Airborne Surveillance 1987, Control of Chem. & Biol. Weapons 1989; over 50 publications; Numerous lectures and presentations, incl. address to UN Special Session on Disarmament 1988; Bd. NGO Ctte. on Disarmament (New York) 1991–93; mem. Candn. Pugwash 1991– ; mem. Sri Chinmoy Centre 1981– ; author 'Peace-keeping Satellites: The Case for International Surveillance and Verification' 1987; co-author 'Disarmament's Missing Dimension: A UN Agency to Administer Multilateral Treaties' 1990; ed. 'Controlling the Global Arms Threat: Technology for Arms Control Verification in the 1990s' 1992; mem. Acad. Council UN System; Biophys. Soc.; Candn. Inst. Internat. Affairs; Chem. Inst. Can.; Group of 78; UN Assn. Can.; Sri Chinmoy Marathon Team (1st place Sri Chinmoy 12 Hr. Walk (61 miles) 1990); Ont. Track & Field Assn.; recreations: marathon running, race walking, tennis, skiing; Address: Trinity College, 6 Hoskin Ave., Toronto, Ont. M5S 1H8.

**DORN, Peter Klaus,** R.C.A.; F.G.D.C. graphic designer; educator; b. Berlin, Germany 30 June 1932; s. Robert and Charlotte (Lemme) D.; e. Berufsschule für Grafisches Gewerbe Berlin 1949–51; Ont. Coll. of Art (evenings) 1962–63; Akademie für Grafik und Buchkunst Leipzig 1968; m. Charlotte d. Hans Graffunder, Berlin, Germany 25 Dec. 1954; children: Gregory, Jennifer, Jeffrey; DIR., GRAPHIC DESIGN UNIT, QUEEN'S UNIV. 1971– ; Dir., Graphic Services, North Hatley Group; King Abdulaziz Univ. Review Office, North Hatley, Que. and Camberley, England, 1982–83; part-time Teaching Master, St. Lawrence Coll. Kingston 1979–86; Prop., Heinrich Heine Press; came to Can. 1953; Howarth & Smith, Typographers, Toronto 1954–59; Cornish & Wimpenny, Toronto 1960–63; Univ. of Toronto Press 1964–70; Guest Lectr. Sheridan College, Oakville; Univ. of Manitoba, Winnipeg; N.S. Coll. Art & Design 1980; Dir. Candn. Book Design Comte. 1975–78; Guild of Hand Printers 1963–70; designed New Brunswick Bicentennial stamp 1984; Principal's Adv. Ctte. on Colours and Emblems 1984–85; awarded Best Journal Design, CELJ Internat. Awards Competition 1991; rec'd Can. Council Grant 1968; over 70 nat. and internat. design awards; Distinguished Service Award, Queen's Univ. 1991; el. mem. Royal Canadian Academy, 1974; Fellow, Graphic Designers Can. (Nat. Pres. 1978–79); mem. Soc. Graphic Designers Can. (Pres. Kingston Br. 1977–79); Amer. Inst. of Graphic Arts; Extve. mem., Pittsburgh Historical Soc.; Lutheran; recreations: private printing, sports; Home: R.R. #2, Kingston, Ont. K7L 5H6; Office: 207 Stuart St., Kingston, Ont. K7L 3N6.

**DOROSZ, Wanda M.,** B.Ed., LL.B.; lawyer, business executive; b. Regina, Sask. 30 Nov. 1950; d. Edmund Casmir and Stephania Helen (Belza) D.; e. Univ. of Regina B.Ed. (secondary) with distinction 1971; Univ. of B.C. LL.B. (first quartile) 1975; Mem., Law Soc. of B.C. 1976; Law Soc. of U.C. 1978; m. Richard Dole 4 April 1981; PRESIDENT & CHIEF EXECUTIVE OFFICER, QUORUM GROWTH INC. 1987– ; Lawyer (spec. in tax), Goodman & Goodman 1976–81; Partner, Dorosz, Barristers & Solicitors 1981–85; Vice-Pres., Corp. Devel. of a multi-information technol. corp. 1985–87; Dir. of num. private, public & 'not-for-profit' entities such as China Trust Quorum Corp., ISG Technologies Inc., Promis Systems, Home Products Inc., Minicom Data Corp., Rand Technologies, Quartex Corp., Internat. Systems Group Ltd., Computer Talk Technology Inc., Atlantis Aerospace Corp., Univ. of Toronto Innovation Found., Nat. Adv. Bd. on Sci. & Technol. and Advisory Bd., Andersen Consulting Inc.; Office: 150 King St. W., P.O. Box 5, Suite 1505, Toronto, Ont. M5H 1J9.

**DORRICOTT, Keith O'Neill,** B.Comm., M.B.A., F.C.A.; chartered accountant; b. Scotland, U.K. 6 Feb. 1943; s. Albert Joseph and Audrey May (Beadsworth) D.; e. Weston C.I. 1959; Univ. of Toronto, B.Comm. 1964; York Univ., M.B.A. 1975; m. Sandra d. James and Susan Philp 9 Sept. 1967; children: Adele, Jennifer, Andrew; VICE-CHRMN., CORPORATE SERVICES, BANK OF MONTREAL 1992– ; Partner, Deloitte Haskins & Sells 1972–83; Sr. Vice-Pres. & Chief Auditor, Bank of Montreal 1983–85; Extve. Vice-Pres. & Chief Finan. Offr. 1986–92; Pres., Pension Fund Soc., Bank of Montreal 1989– ; Dir.: The Nesbitt Thomson Corp.; Bank of Montreal Securities Canada Ltd.; Concordia Life Insurance Corp.; Concordia Assurance Corp.; Concordia Financial Corp.; Kids Help Phone Found.; Chrmn. C.I.C.A. Computer Ctte. 1978–83; Dir., Daystar Found.; EDP Ed., CA Magazine 1980–83; author: '1983 Canadian Business Guide to Micro-Computers'; Elder, Churches of God (Brethren); recreations: golf, tennis; Clubs: St. George's Golf & Country; Bd. of Trade; Home: 44 Poplar Heights Dr., Islington, Ont. M9A 5A6; Office: First Bank Tower, 1st Candn. Pl., Toronto, Ont. M5X 1A1.

**DORSEY, Candas Jane,** B.A., B.S.W.; writer; editor; b. Edmonton, Alta. 16 Nov. 1952; d. Frederick Jack and Frances Marie (Dezall) D.; e. Univ. of Alta. B.A. 1975; Univ. of Calgary B.S.W. 1979; author (poetry) 'this is for you' 1973; 'Orion Rising' 1974; 'Results of the Ring Toss' 1976; (short fiction) 'Machine Sex and Other Stories' 1988 (British ed. 1990); co-author (fiction) 'Hardwired Angel' 1987; various acad. publs.; co-ed. 'Tesseracts $^3$' 1990 (anthol. Candn. short speculative fiction); (poetry) 'Leaving Marks' 1992; freelance writer and ed. since 1980 incl. ednl. TV scripts, arts journalism, communications planning, book reviews, non-fiction articles and profiles regional and nat. mags.; Co-founder arts periodical 'The Edmonton Bullet' 1983, Assoc. Ed. 1983–86, Ed. 1986–88; Founding mem. SF Workshop Ink and Inst. for Future Studies; teacher writing theory and practice workshops and classes; Writer-in-Residence Edmonton Pub. Lib. 1990; recipient Edmonton Arts Award 1987; Candn. Sci. Fiction & Fantasy Award 1989, Best Short Form Work Eng. 1988; mem. Bd. The Books Collective/River Books; mem. Writers Guild Alta. (Vice Pres. 1992–93, Pres. 1993–94); Writers Union Can.; Periodical Writers Assn. Can.; ACTRA; Founding Mem., SFCanada (Speculative Writers Assn. Can./Assn canadienne des écrivains speculatifs); Home: 10438 – 86 Ave., Edmonton, Alta. T6E 2M5; Office: c/o Wooden Door, 3rd Floor M & M Building, 10022 - 103 St., Edmonton, Alta. T5J 0X2.

**DORTELUS, Daniel,** LL.B.; lawyer; b. Haiti 20 July 1953; s. Dorcius and Louise Evna (Jean-Gilles) D.; e. Univ. of Que. at Montreal LL.B. 1985; m. Christiane d. Luc and Clericie Constant 18 Aug. 1973; children: Lynda, Danny; SENIOR LAWYER, DORTELUS LEGAL FIRM 1988– ; Registered Nurse (Emergency & Psych. Nursing) 1985–88; Lawyer, Pointe-St-Charles & Little Burgundy Community Legal Serv. 1986–88; field of practice: family, admin. & labour law, human rights, civil litigation, criminal & immigration law; Mem., Can. Employment & Immigration Adv. Counc. 1990–92; Que. Human Rights Tribunal 1991– ; Jacky Robinson Award for Professional of the Year (Law), Montreal Assn. of Black Business Persons & Profls. 1990; Dir., Que. Civil Liberty Union 1988–90; Dir., Ctr. for Rsch. on Race Relns. 1987–90; consultant for several orgns. 1982–91; Home: 3955 Lausanne, St-Hubert, Que. J3Y 4C6; Office: 2565, #105, Centre, Montreal, Que. H3K 1J9.

**DORTON, Roger Anthony,** Ph.D., D.Eng., D.Sc., P.Eng.; civil engineer; b. London, Eng. 23 March 1929; s. Harold William D.; e. Lexington (Mass.) High Sch. 1944; Hitchin Grammar Sch. Herts. Eng. 1947; Univ. of Nottingham B.Sc. (Engn.) 1951, Ph.D. 1954; Univ. of Waterloo D.Eng. (hon. causa) 1989; Queen's Univ. D.Sc. (hon. causa) 1990; m. Patricia Mary d. Horace George Upshall 4 Oct. 1958; children: Peter, Mary, Anne, Catherine; MANAGER, ONTARIO OFFICE, BUCKLAND & TAYLOR LTD., Structural Engineers; came to Can. 1954; joined Dept. of Highways Ont. 1954–56; P.L. Pratley, Consulting Engrs. Montreal 1956–58; Chief Engr. H.H.L. Pratley Montreal 1958–65 (Champlain Bridge Montreal, Cornwall Bridge, Ogdensburg-Prescott Bridge); Partner, Pratley & Dorton Montreal (19 canal bridges Expo '67; A. Murray Mackay Suspension Bridge Halifax) 1965–72; joined Ministry of Transportation, Ont. 1972 serving as Sr. Research Offr., Princ. Research Offr. R & D Div., Manager Structural Office 1976–92; recipient 1st Prize Nat. Bridge Design Competition Expo '67 1965; Award of Merit A. Murray Mackay Bridge Assn. Consulting Engrs. 1970; Gzowski Medal Engn. Inst. Can. for Best Paper of Yr. 1976; Candn. Soc. Civil Engn. 1977 Nat. Tour Lectr.; James A. Vance Award 1984; A.B. Sanderson Award 1988; Assn. Prof. Engrs. Prov. Ont. Engn. Medal for Distinguished Engn. Achievement 1980; Queen's Silver Jubilee Medal 1977; Am. Assoc. of State Highway and Transportation Officials, Alfred E. Johnson Achievement Award 1988; Chrmn. Ont. Highway Bridge Design Code Comte.; author 'The Champlain Bridge' 1962; 'The Ontario Highway Bridge Design Code' 1983, 1991; various articles bridge design, research and testing, transit guideways; mem. Assn. Prof. Engrs. Prov. Ont.; Chrmn., CSA Loads Ctte., Candn. Highway Bridge Design Code; Hon. Mem. and Vice-Pres., Internat. Assn. Bridge & Structural Engn.; Fellow, Candn. Soc. Civil Engn.; Fellow, Am. Concrete Inst.; Fellow, The Candn. Academy of Engineering; Fellow, Engn. Inst. Can.; R. Catholic; recreations: golf, music, reading, photography, history of bridges, antique prints; Home and Office: 34 Kingland Cres., Willowdale, Ont. M2J 2B7.

**DORVAL, Bernard,** B.Sc.Ac., F.C.A.S., F.I.C.A.; exécutif; né Ville de Québec, Qué. 4 décembre 1952; f. Dr. Charles-Henri et Marthe (Guérin) D.; é. Univ. Laval, B.Sc.Ac. 1973; ép. Francine Côté 17 août 1974; VICE-PRESIDENT EXECUTIF ET CHEF DE L'EXPLOITATION, LAURENTIENNE FINANCIERE INC. 1993– ; Recherche pour le Comité d'Étude sur l'assurance automobile (Comn. Gauvin) 1973; Actuaire pour La Prévoyance Compagnie d'Assurance 1974, puis les compagnies membres du Groupe La Laurentienne 1975; Dir. et actuaire-chef de La Prévoyance 1979; Vice-Prés.

de La Prévoyance et actuaire-chef des co. IARD mem. du Groupe La Laurentienne 1982; Vice-prés. actuariat et assurance des particuliers 1984; Premier vice-prés. opérations d'assur. 1986; Vice-prés. exec. et chef des opérations corporatives de La Laurentienne Gén., Co. d'Assur. inc. 1988; Prés. et chef de la direction, La Compagnie Laurentienne/Impériale 1990; membres des conseils de Inter-Ocean Re. of Bermuda; Medisys Group; Jeune homme d'affaires de l'année 1983 par la Jeune C. de C. de Montréal; Prof. invité au prog. d'actuariat de l'Univ. Laval à Québec 1979–85; Adresse Bureau: 1100 boul. René-Lévesque O., Montréal, Qué. H3B 4N4.

**DOSCH, Hans-Michael,** M.D.; professor of paediatrics and immunology; b. Frankenberg / Eder, W. Germany 20 May 1946; s. Hans and Ina (Hackbusch) D.; e. Univ. of Marburg M.D. 1971, doctor medicinae 1972; PROFESSOR OF PAEDIATRICS, UNIV. OF TORONTO 1989– ; AND PROFESSOR OF IMMUNOLOGY 1990– ; Lectr., Univ. of Toronto & Scientist, Rsch. Inst., Hosp. for Sick Children 1977; Asst. Prof. of Paed. 1978; Assoc. Prof. of Paed. 1983; of Immunology 1985; Head (Acting), Div. of Immunology & Rheum., Rsch. Inst., Hosp. for Sick Children 1987–90; Sci. Fac., Ctr. for Drug Safety Rsch., Univ. of Toronto 1988; Mem., Extve. Council, C.E.D.I.; Scientific Officer, MRC; Gold Medal in Medicine, Royal College of Physicians & Surgeons for Studies in Antibody Deficiency Syndromes 1981; Scientific Chair, 10-year Multinat. Childhood Diabetes Prevention Trial & Nat. Chair of Candn. Trial Branch; senior author of over 200 orig. rsch. articles & book chapters in human immunology, oncology & childhood diabetes; recreations: yacht racing; club: National Yacht; Home: 77 Harbour Square, Suite 2908, Toronto, Ont.; Office: 555 University Ave., Toronto, Ont. M5G 1X8.

**DOSHEN, Lawrence Thomas,** CD, B.E.; military officer; b. Kenaston, Sask. 11 July 1940; s. Leopold and Mary Rose (Sulik) D.; e. Kenaston H.S. 1958; Univ. of Sask. B.E. 1962; Candn. Forces Staff College 1971; Nat. Defence College 1984; m. Linda d. Sinclair and Joy Elliott 11 Dec. 1965; children: Samantha Coreen, Nanette Christine; DIRECTOR GENERAL, PERSONNEL POLICY, CANADIAN ARMED FORCES 1993– ; joined Royal Candn. Air Force 19 Sept. 1958; flying tours as an air navigator in Maritime Patrol & training opns.; Directing Staff, Candn. Forces Command & Staff Coll. 1975–78; Comndg. Offr., Candn. Forces Station Dana, Sask. 1978–80 Dep., Opns., Candn. NORAD Region, North Bay, Ont. 1985–88; Dep. Comndr. Alaskan NORAD Region, Elmendorf, Alaska 1988–91; Director General, Intelligence, National Defence H.Q. 1991–93; Roman Catholic; Mem., Candn. Inst. of Strategic Studies; Candn. Geog. Soc.; Candn. Assn. for Security & Intelligence Studies; recreations: hockey, running; Home: 1799 Dorset Dr., Ottawa, Ont. K1H 5T7; Office: 101 Colonel By Dr., Ottawa, Ont. K1A 0K2.

**DOSMAN, James A.,** M.D., F.R.C.P.(C); university professor; b. Humboldt, Sask. 24 Apr. 1938; s. Harold Charles and Gesina Marie (Vanderlinde) D.; e. Univ. of Sask. B.A. 1959, M.D. 1963; m. Susan McKay d. Marian and Peter Fairclough 26 May 1962; children: Audrey Susan, Jill Marie, Andrea Jane, Cara Fairclough, John Harold; DIR., CENTRE FOR AGRICULTURAL MEDICINE, UNIV. OF SASKATCHEWAN 1986– ; interned at St. Paul's Hosp., Saskatoon; family med. practice, Saskatoon 1965–69; specialty training, Respiratory Diseases & Rsch., McGill Univ. 1969–75; Past Scholar, Med. Rsch. Counc. of Can.; Scholar, Health & Welfare Can.; Life Mem., Sask. Anti-Tuberculosis League; Past Pres., Candn. Thoracic Soc.; co-author: 'Occupational Pulmonary Disease' 1980, 'Principles of Heatlh and Safety in Agriculture' 1989, Obstructive Lung Disease' 1990; recreations: skiing, skating, water sports; clubs: Faculty; Home: 614 Leslie Ave., Saskatoon, Sask. S7H 2Z2; Office: Ctr. for Agric. Med., Royal Univ. Hosp., Saskatoon, Sask. S7N 0X0.

**DOTTO, Lydia Carol,** B.J.; freelance science writer; b. Cadomin, Alta. 29 May 1949; d. late August and Assunta (Paron) D.; e. Austin O'Brien High Sct. Edmonton 1968; Carleton Unv. B.J. 1971 (Class Medal); FREELANCE WRITER 1978– ; joined Edmonton Journal 1969; Toronto Star summers 1970–71; sci. writer Toronto Globe and Mail 1972–78; Extve. Editor, Candn. Science News Service 1982–92; freelance writer participant zero-gravity training flight Johnson Space Center, Houston 1983; 2 dives under Arctic ice Resolute Bay, NWT 1974; coverage space missions since 1972 incl. recovery Skylab astronauts U.S.S. Ticonderoga 1973 (first woman aboard aircraft carrier at sea); holder private pilot's licence; frequent pub. speaker space prog., sleep, the environment, science literacy, science journalism/public awareness of science & women in sci.; past Mem. Adv. Ctte. on Public Awareness of Science, Royal Soc. of Can.; Past Pres., Candn. Science Writers' Assn. 1979–80; recipient Royal Candn. Inst. Sandford Fleming Medal 1982–83; Candn. Sci. Writers Awards for newspaper & mag. articles 1974 (nuclear terrorism), 1981 (high energy physics), 1984 (women in sci.); Candn. Meteorol. Soc. Award 1975; author: 'Thinking the Unthinkable: Civilization and Rapid Climate Change' 1988; 'Canada in Space' 1987; 'Planet Earth in Jeopardy: The Environmental Consequences of Nuclear War' 1986; 'Asleep in the Fast Lane: The Impact of Sleep on Work' 1990; 'Losing Sleep: How Your Sleeping Habits Affect Your Life' 1990 (U.S. version of 'Asleep in the Fast Lane'); 'Blue Planet' 1991; 'Ethics and Climate Change' 1993; 'The Astronauts: Canada's Voyageurs in Space' 1993; co-author 'The Ozone War' 1978; recreations: computers, swimming, theatre; Office: 2650 Marsdale Dr., Unit 303, Peterborough, Ont. K9L 1Y1.

**DOUCET, Clive Robert Oliver,** B.A., M.Sc.; writer; b. London, England 20 March 1946; s. Fernand Joseph and Katherine Emma (Oliver) D.; e. Univ. of Toronto B.A. (Hons.) 1970; Univ. of Montreal M.Sc. 1971; m. Patricia d. Niel and Barbara Steenberg; children: Julian, Emma; INFORMATION OFFICER, CANADA DEPT. OF JUSTICE, GUN CONTROL PROJECT; Co-ord., Fed. of Citizens Assns. of Ottawa-Carleton 1975–76; Communications Manager, False Creek B.C., Vieux Port, Montreal, Le Breton Flats, Ottawa, Maryfield, P.E.I. 1976–80; Communications Mgr. for David MacDonald during 1985 Ethiopian famine; Mem., Playwrights Union of Canada; Ottawa Independent Writers; author: 'Hatching Eggs' (play) 1976; 'A Very Desirable Resident' (play) 1978; 'Disneyland Please' (novel) 1978, pbk 1979 (nom. for Books in Canada first novel award); 'Chicken Delight' (radio broadcast) 1979; 'May the Best Man Win' (play) 1980; 'My Grandfather's Cape Breton' (memoir) 1980, sch. edn. 1981; 'Before Star Wars' (poetry) 1981; 'John Coe's War' (novel) 1983; 'Echoes I' (anthology for schools) 1983; 'Tout pres d'ici, prise de parole' (anthology for schools) 1984; 'The Cape Breton Collection' (anthology for schools) 1984; 'The Chez Lucien is Closed' (play) 1984; 'The Unknown Town' (radio broadcast) 1985; 'The Apprentice Shoemaker' (radio broadcast) 1985; 'Icetime' (TV drama) 1985; 'Your Voice and Mine' (anthologies for schools) 1987; 'The Gospel According to Mary Magdalene' (novella) 1990; 'Seduced by Moonlight' (play) 1990; 'The Priest's Boy' (short stories) 1992; 'The Debris of Planets' (poetry) 1993; Globe and Mail, literary reviews, Mermaid Inn (newspaper); two Canada Council grants; clubs: Bytown Boat; Home: 38 Muriel St., Ottawa, Ont. K1S 4E1.

**DOUCET, (Jean Alfred) Fred,** B.Sc., B.Ed., M.Ed., Ph.D.; government relations consultant; b. Grand Etang, N.S. 30 Jan. 1939; s. Joseph Simon and Marie Antoinette (Aucoin) D.; e. St. Francis Xavier Univ. B.Sc. 1960; Mt. Allison Univ. B.Ed. 1964, M.Ed. 1966; Univ. of Ottawa Ph.D. 1976; m. Alina d. Greg and Ida Kawecki 21 March 1986; children: Marie, Mark, Glen, Terrence; CHIEF EXECUTIVE OFFICER, THE GOVERNMENT BUSINESS CONSULTING GROUP INC. 1988– ; H.S. Teacher, Manitoba 1960–62; H.S. Principal, Quebec 1962–65; Dean of Studies, St. Lawrence College, Laval Univ. 1965–68; Admin. Asst. to Pres., St. Francis Xavier Univ. 1968–74; Doctoral Study Leave 1974–76; Dir. of Student Serv. & Prof., Orgn. Behaviour & Admin. Theory, St. Francis Xavier Univ. 1976–79; Dir. of Devel. 1979–82; Chief Extve. Offr., East Coast Energy Limited 1982–83; Chief of Staff, Office of the Leader of the Opposition, Ottawa 1983–84; Senior Advr. to Prime Minister of Canada 1984–87; Ambassador & Chrmn., Orgn. Ctte. for Internat. Summits, Dept. of External Affairs Canada 1987–88; participant in num. nat. & internat. events 1984–88; Bd. Mem., Ottawa Civic Hospital, Heart Inst.; Bd. of Gov., Mt. Allison Univ.; author of two articles; recreations: fishing, gardening, raising standardbred race horses; clubs: Founder's Club, Skydome, Toronto; Home: 68 – 3691 Albion Rd., Ottawa, Ont.; Office: Suite 320, 440 Laurier Ave. W., Ottawa, Ont. K1R 7X6.

**DOUCET, G. Raymond,** P.Eng.; business executive; b. Cheticamp, N.S. 16 Sept. 1942; s. Joseph Simon and Marie Antoinette (Aucoin) D.; e. N.S. Tech. Coll., B.E.E. 1965; St-Francis Xavier Univ., cert. of Engr. 1963; grad. with Hons. & Distinction; Union Carbide & Inco scholarships; m. Carol d. Allistair and Evelyn McInnis 1 May 1965; children: Lise Marie, Kevin Raymond, Joanne Lynn; PRES. & CHIEF EXTVE. OFFR., DOUSERV MANAGEMENT INC. 1980– ; Engr., Bell Can. 1965–74; Pres., Doucet & Assoc. Cons. Ltd. 1974–80; Chrmn. & C.E.O., Radcel Communications Inc. 1984–91; Dir., Doucet & Assoc. Cons. Ltd.; Servco Quebec Inc.; Telezone Corp.; mem., Assn. of Cons. of Engrs. of Can.; Texas St. Bd. of Profl. Engrs.; recreations: golf, ski; Clubs: Summerlea Golf; University Club (Montreal); IBIS Golf & Country (West Palm Beach); City Club of the Palm Beaches; Home: 489 Olympic Dr., Beaconsfield, Que. H9W 1A3; Office: 1550 – 2000 McGill College Ave., Montreal, Que. H3A 3H3.

**DOUCET, Gerald,** B.A., M.A.; public servant / consultant; b. Vancouver, B.C. 21 Aug. 1943; s. Gerald Thomas and Margaret Caterall (Dempster) D.; e. St. Paul's H.S. (Winnipeg) 1960; Univ. of Ottawa, B.A. 1967; Carleton Univ., M.A. 1969; children: Alison, Suzanne, John, Alexander, Nicolas; PRESIDENT, EUROPE-CANADA DEVELOPMENT ASSN. 1992– ; Econ. & Trade Comnr., Govt. of Can. 1967–76; Advr. to Privy Counc. Office & Min. of State for Econ. Devel. 1976–81; estab. G.W. Doucet & Assoc. Ltd. 1981; Sr. Vice-Pres., Retail Counc. of Can. 1982–87; Agent Gen. for Ont. in Europe 1988–92; part-time lectr., York Univ. 1982–86; Dir., Candn. Coalition of Serv. Indus.; Europe-Canada Devel. Assn.; Past Chrmn., Employers' Counc. on Workers Comp. (Ont.); Past Gov., Frontier Coll. & Business Task Force on Illiteracy; Adv. Bd., Cabbagetown Community Arts Ctr.; author of several books and articles; recreations: bicycling, windsurfing; club: Cercle de l'Union Interalliée, Paris; Home: 3, rue des Capucins, Meudon 92190, France.

**DOUCET, Gerald Joseph,** Q.C., B.A., LL.B.; government relations consultant; b. Grand Etang, N.S. 4 May 1937; s. Joseph Simon and Marie Antoinette (Aucoin) D.; e. St. FrancisXavier Univ. B.A.; Dalhousie Univ. LL.B.; m. Vida Mae d. Clayton and Hulda Eisenhauer 30 June 1978; children: Michelle, Dana, Gerry Jr., Paul, Denise; step-children: Brian, Brad; CONSULTANT, THE GOVERNMENT BUSINESS CONSULTING GROUP INC.; Dir. of several companies; mem. N.S. Leg. 1963–74, mem. N.S. Cabinet 1964–70 (Prov. Secy., Min. of Educ., Min. in Charge of Youth Agency, Min. of Emergency Measures); Past Chrmn. Atlantic Provs. Econ. Council; past mem. Council Chief Extve. Offrs. Conf. Bd. of Can.; Chrmn. 1984 CORE Conference; mem., many community assocs.; frequent speaker confs. and seminars; recreations: golf, reading; Home: 6970 Armview Ave., Halifax, N.S.; Office: Suite 320, 440 Laurier Ave. W., Ottawa, Ont. K1R 7X6 and 6970 Armview Ave., Halifax, N.S.

**DOUCET, Jean-Louis,** Q.C.; Quebec, public service; b. St-Jacques-des-Piles, Co. Laviolette, Que. 23 Nov. 1909; s. Arthur and Aurore (Massé) D.; e. Séminaire Saint-Joseph, Trois-Rivières, Que., B.A. 1935; Laval Univ., LL.L. 1938; m. Claire, d. E. Alexandre Frenette, Quebec, 23 Sept. 1941; children: Danièle, Luc; Pres., Greater Québec Water Purification Bd., Jan. 1969–79 (Depy. Min. of Mun. Affairs 1950–69); Prof., Faculty of Law, Laval Univ.; called to the Bar of Quebec 1938; created K.C. 1951; was associated with his father's industry (J. Arthur Doucet, St-Jacques-des-Piles, Que.), 1932–35; apptd. Law Offr., Atty. Gen. Dept., Que., 1938; Assoc. Depy. Min. of Mun. Affairs, Dec. 1947; mem. of Prov., Nat. and Internat. Municipal Assns.; K. of C.; R. Catholic; recreation: reading, golf; Home: 2144 rue Boisjoli, Sillery, Que. G1T 1E5.

**DOUCETT, Hon. Rayburn Donald,** M.L.A.; politician; b. Campbellton, N.B. 2 Jan. 1943; s. Raymond Daniel and Catherine Ila (Lutes) D.; e. Jacquet River High Sch.; Albert Coll. Belleville, Ont. m. Della d. Arthur and Yvonne Hickey; children: Ryan, Richard, Kimberly, Rhonda; MIN. OF PROVINCE OF N.B. responsible for Regional Development Corporation 1993– ; M.L.A., Restigouche East, N.B. 1970– ; Min. of Energy, N.B. and Chrmn. The New Brunswick Electric Power Comn. 1987–90; Min. of Economic Development 1990–91; Pres. Q & A Marketing; SUNOW Holdings Ltd.; Office: 377 York St., 2nd Floor, P.O. Box 428, Fredericton, N.B. E3B 5R4.

**DOUGAN, John Alpine,** M.C., B.A., M.A.(Oxon); retired Candn. diplomat; b. Lethbridge, Alta. 7 Apr. 1921; s. John Andrew and Carine (Vadnais) D.; e. Claresholm (Alta.) H.S. 1939; Univ. of Alta. B.A. 1942; Rhodes Scholar, Balliol Coll., Oxford B.A. (Hons.) 1948, M.A. 1954; m. Hendrika d. Hendrik Koopman 27 Aug. 1945; children: Elisabeth, Maureen, Barbara, Jacqueline; served WW II as Major with The Loyal Edmonton Regt. overseas 1942–45; Military Cross and Bar; joined Dept. of Secy. of State 1948; Foreign Serv. Offr., Dept. of External Affairs 1949; various posts, Can. and abroad 1949–64; Perm. Chargé d'Affaires A.I. Uruguay 1964–67; High Comnr., Guyana 1967–70; New Zealand 1970–74; accredited to Tonga & W. Samoa; Dir. Gen., Candn. Habitat Secretariat, UN Conf. on Human Settlements 1975; High Comnr., Malaysia 1976–78; ret. 1978; R. Cath.; Pres., Vancouver Is. Br., Royal Commonwealth Soc. 1981–85; Mem., Candn. Inst. of Internat. Affairs;

Candn. Diabetic Assoc.; Pres., B.C. Branch, The Loyal Edmonton Regiment Assoc.; RHOMA; recreations: fishing, golf, reading, photography; Clubs: Faculty; Ardmore Golf; Home: 6701 Welch Rd., R.R. 3, Victoria, B.C. V8X 3X1.

**DOUGHERTY, Geoffrey E.,** B.A., M.A., M.S.C., M.D.C.M., F.R.C.P.C., C.S.P.Q., F.A.A.P.; physician; b. Montreal, Que. 19 June 1953; s. Donald Bruce and Joan (Mason) D.; e. Middlebury Coll. 1970–72; Oxford Univ. B.A. 1976; M.A. 1983; McGill Univ. M.D.C.M. 1979, M.S.C. 1986; Rhodes Scholar (Que.) 1973–76; ASST. PROFESSOR OF PEDIATRICS & EPIDEMIOLOGY AND BIOSTATISTICS, MCGILL UNIV. 1986– ; DIR., INTENSIVE AMBULATORY CARE SERVICE & ATTENDING PHYSICIAN, PEDIATRIC MEDICINE, MONTREAL CHILDREN'S HOSP. 1986– ; Resident, Pediatrics and Community Medicine 1980–85; F.R.S.Q. Post-doc. Fellow in Epidemiology, McGill Univ. 1983–84, 1985–86; F.R.S.Q. Chercheur Boursier Clinicien 1990– , Rowland Frazee Post Grad. Scholarship in Neuromuscular Disease 1988–93; mem. Candn. Med. Assn.; Candn. Pediatric Soc.; Ambulatory Pediatric Assn.; recreations: cross-country skiing, mountaineering, tennis; Clubs: Viking Ski; Home: 160 Metcalfe Ave., Westmount, Que. H3Z 2H4; Office: Montreal Children's Hosp., 2300 Tupper St., Montreal, Que. H3H 1P3.

**DOUGLAS, Bryce Wolfram;** investment dealer; b. Winnipeg, Man. 8 Sept. 1941; s. Bryce Grierson and Johanna D.; e. Kelvin High Sch.; United College (Winnipeg); m. Helen Nixon, d. Kenneth and Eleanor McGibbon, Oct. 1966; children: Bryce Charles; Victoria Jean; Kenneth David; VICE-CHRMN., RBC DOMINION SECURITIES INC.; Dir., Nowsco Well Service Ltd.; Dir., Regal Greetings & Gifts Corp.; Anglican; recreations: golf, shooting; fishing; tennis; Clubs: Toronto Club (Toronto); Badminton and Racquet (Toronto); Toronto Hunt (Toronto); Mount Royal (Montreal); Ranchmens (Calgary); Home: 140 Glen Rd., Toronto, Ont. M4W 2W3; Office: Commerce Court South, Toronto, Ont.

**DOUGLAS, G. Ross,** C.L.S., B.Sc.; hydrographer; b. Gull Lake, Sask. 25 Nov. 1939; s. Gordon William and Jeanne Margaret (Douglas); e. Southern Alta. Inst. of Tech. 1960; Dalhousie Univ., B.Sc. 1978; m. Loretta d. Egbert and Keitha Young 24 Nov. 1962; children: Michelle, Lynda; DOMINION HYDROGRAPHER, CANDN. HYDROGRAPHIC SERV., DEPT. OF FISHERIES & OCEANS 1987– ; joined Candn. Hydrographic Serv. 1960; developed first Hydrographic Data Logger 1968; completed 5 years of survey in High Arctic; Dir. of Hydrography, Can. Ctr. for Inland Water 1978; Adjunct Prof., Univ. of Toronto 1978; club: Marine; Home: 9 Grouse Ave., Nepean, Ont. K2J 1R2; Office: 615 Booth St., Ottawa, Ont. K1A 0E6.

**DOUGLAS, James Jardine,** LL.D.; book publisher; b. Edinburgh, Scot. 26 March 1924; s. Peter Jardine and Isabella Black (Brand) D.; e. Darroch Tech. High Sch. Edinburgh 1939; RAF Apprentice Sch. Cranwell 1942; RAF Tech. Staff Coll. Debden, grad. Inst. Radio Engn. 1950; children: Diana Ritch, Christopher Jardine, Alan James; FOUNDER, DOUGLAS AND McINTYRE LTD. 1972; Publisher, J.J. Douglas Ltd.; Dir. Self-Counsel Holdings Ltd.; served with RAF 1940–46, Radio/Gunner, rank Flying Offr.; Tech. Staff Offr. 1949–54, rank Flight Lt.; Bookseller, Edinburgh 1946–49; came to Can. 1954; Publisher's Agt. Douglas Agencies Ltd. 1957–72; J.J. Douglas Ltd. 1963–66; Publisher, Douglas, David & Charles Ltd. 1974–78; Dir., Canongate Publishing, Edinburgh 1977–80; mem. Assn. Publishers B.C. (Founding Pres. 1974–75); Assn. Candn. Publishers (Pres. 1975–76, 1983); LL.D. (hon. causa), Simon Fraser Univ. 1991; recreations: travel, music, hill walking; Club: Scottish Arts (Edinburgh); Home: 303–1930 Marine Dr., W. Vancouver, B.C. V7V 1J8; Office: 1615 Venables St., Vancouver, B.C. V5L 2H1.

**DOUGLAS, John Macdonald,** B.E., M.Sc., P.Eng.; retired industrial executive; b. Zealandia, Sask. 10 Aug. 1917; s. John Macdonald and Marjorie May (Sweney) D.; e. Univ. of Sask., B.E. (Geol. Engn.) 1940; McGill Univ. M.Sc. (Geol.) 1941; m. Jessie Lucille, d. Col. J.G. Robertson, New Glasgow, N.S., 28 Nov. 1942; one d. Jill Robertson D.; with Consolidated Mining & Smelting Co. of Canada 1946–55 (Property Supt., Pine Point Mines, N.W.T., for last 2 yrs.); with Eldorado Mining and Refining Ltd. 1955–63 (Mine Mgr., Beaverlodge Mine, Uranium City, Sask., for last 4 yrs.); joined Babcock & Wilcox Canada Ltd. as Extve. Asst. to the Pres. 1963–65; apptd. Gen. Mgr. 1965; Vice Pres. and Gen. Mgr. 1966; Pres. and Chief Extve. Offr. 1968–76; Chrmn. 1976–78; Dir., Reuter-Stokes Inc. and Reuter-Stokes Canada Ltd. 1977–84; Consultant, Gen. Mgr. and Secy., for Organ. of CANDU Industries 1979–86; Dir., Numet Engineering Co. 1983–84; served with R.C.A.F. 1942–46, in Aero Engn. Br. (rose from Pilot Offr. to Squadron Leader); mem., Educ. Services Comte. 4 yrs., Hosp. Bd. 2 yrs., Councillor 4 yrs., Uranium City, Sask.; mem., Adv. Vocational Comte., Galt Bd. Educ. 1966; mem., Assn. Prof. Engrs. Ont.; Candn. Inst. Mining & Metall.; Pres. (1974–75), Dir. (1980–81) Candn. Nuclear Assn.; Chrmn. Ont. Div., Candn. Mfrs. Assn. 1973–74; Gov., Univ. of Waterloo 1977–81; Trustee, Royal Ont. Museum 1983–86; Protestant; recreations: golf, curling, reading; Home: 24 Ridgewood Pl., Cambridge, Ont. N1S 4B4.

**DOUGLAS, Keith A.,** C.A.E.; association executive; b. North Bay, Ont. 19 Aug. 1937; s. James Alton and Susan Harriet (Sauer) D.; e. North Bay Coll. Inst.; Univ. of B.C.; m. 2ndly Janet d. Erik and Mildred Feldthusen 22 Dec. 1983; children: Heather, Mark, Jeffrey, Laura; PRINCIPAL, KEITH DOUGLAS ASSOCIATES 1991– ; various posns., Montreal Trust Co. 1957–75; Pres., Investment Funds Inst. of Canada 1976–91; mem., Certification Counc., Candn. Soc. of Assn. Extves.; Certified Assn. Extve. (C.A.E.) Designation 1981; Protestant (United); author of magazine articles and columns; recreations: tennis, badminton, sailing; Club: National; Address: 61 Shaw St., Toronto, Ont. M6J 2W3.

**DOUGLAS, Leith Garrett,** C.D., M.D., F.R.C.S.(C), F.A.C.S.; plastic surgeon; b. Charlottetown, P.E.I. 20 Jan. 1931; s. Ira Winfred and Ella Priscilla (Garrett) D.; e. W. Kent Sch., Prince of Wales Coll. Charlottetown; Dalhousie Univ. M.D. 1962 (Gold Medal); m. Lorna d. Harris and Muriel Jordan 9 May 1953; one d. Ellen Rosemary (Mrs. Peter Woodward); PLASTIC SURG. THE WELLESLEY HOSP. 1969– ; Cons. Plastic Surg. Princess Margaret Hosp. 1980– ; Asst. Prof. of Surg. Univ. of Toronto 1975– , Lectr. 1969–75; Plastic Surg. Toronto Maple Leafs Hockey Team 1969– ; served with R.C.N.R. 1948–67, rank Surg. Lt.; Candn. Forces Decoration, 125th Anniversary Confederation Medal; author 'History of the Canadian Society of Plastic Surgeons' 1983; contbg. author 'Current Therapy in Sports Medicine' 1989; numerous sci. papers; mem. Candn. Soc. Plastic Surgs. (Pres. 1989–90); Candn. Med. Assn.; Ont. Med. Assn.; Am. Soc. Plastic & Recons. Surgs.; Tord Skoog Soc. Plastic Surgs.; Naval Offrs. Assn. Can.; Presbyterian; recreations: fishing, med. & mil. hist., militaria collecting; Home: 94 Whitehorn Cres., Willowdale, Ont. M2J 3B2; Office: 324 E.K. Jones Buillding, 160 Wellesley St. E., Toronto, Ont. M4Y 1J3.

**DOUGLAS, Lloyd Robert,** C.D., B.Sc.; retired executive; b. Silverton, Man., 4 Aug. 1916; s. John Faircleugh and C. Mabel (Todd) D.; e. Strathclair (Man.) High Sch.; Univ. of Man., B.Sc. (Elect. Engn.) 1938; m. Frances Mary, d. T. L. Edwards, 12 Oct. 1940; children: Caroline, Elizabeth, William; Test Engr., Canadian General Electric Co. Ltd., Peterborough, Ont., 1938, Sales Engr., Toronto, 1946, Mgr. Apparatus Marketing, Peterborough, 1955, Gen. Mgr., Apparatus Dept., 1964; Mgr. Bus. Dev. Apparatus & Heavy Machinery Division 1979; Vice-Pres. & Mgr. Bus. Develop. until retirement 1981; served in 2nd World War, 1940–45, Lt.-Col., Royal Candn. Signals; served overseas in Eng., N. Africa, Sicily, Italy, France, Germany and Holland; Mentioned in Despatches, 1944; Candn. Army Reserve, 1945–52; mem. Assn. Prof. Engrs. Ont.; Corp. Prof. Engrs. Que.; Engn. Inst. Can.; recreations: curling, golf; Clubs: Thornhill Golf & Country; Home: 9 Cachet Parkway, Markham, Ont. L6C 1C4.

**DOUGLAS, Susan (Mrs. Jan Rubes),** O.C.; actress; producer; b. Vienna, Austria, 13 March 1928; m. Jan Rubes, 22 Sept. 1950; children: Christopher, Jonathan, Anthony; came to Can. 1959; HEAD OF RADIO DRAMA FOR CBC DRAMA CANADA since 1979; as an actress has played on Broadway in 'He Who Gets Slapped' (won Donaldson Award for best supporting performance 1946); 'Druid Circle'; 'Heart Song'; 'Taming of The Shrew'; in Hollywood 'Private Affairs of Bel'Ami' with George Sanders; 'Lost Boundaries' with Mel Ferrer; 'Five'; 'Forbidden Journey' with husband; has acted in various TV shows incl.; 'Studio One,' 'Kraft Playhouse,' 'Montgomery Presents'; played Kathy for 10 yrs. in 'Guiding Light'; radio performances incl.: 'Theatre Guild on the Air,' 'March of Time,' 'Inner Sanctum Mystery,' 'Helen Trent,' 'Backstage Wife,' 'Big Sister'; producer and founder of Young People's Theatre (estbd. 1965) and responsible for production of such plays as 'Dandy Lion,' 'Popcorn Man,' 'The Diary of Anne Frank' with the Wallach family, and Laterna Magika's 'The Lost Fairy Tale' (from Czechoslovakia); Pres., The Family Channel, TV Canada 1987– ; Bd. mem. of St. Lawrence Centre; Ont. Arts Counc.; awarded Order of Canada in 1977; voted 'Woman of the Year' by B'nai Brith, Toronto, 1979; Home: Suite 2813, 44 Charles St. W., Toronto, Ont. M4Y 1R7 and 1510 Pelican Point, Apt. B166, Sarasota, Fla. 43231.

**DOUGLAS, William D.,** B.Comm.; insurance executive; b. Toronto, Ont. 12 Jan. 1940; s. William D.A. and Dorothy G. (Mason) D.; e. Univ. of Toronto B.Comm. 1965; m. Sharon Margaret d. John and Jane Healey 29 June 1965; children: Andrew, Barbara, Cathy; SR. VICE-PRES., CORP. DEVEL., CONFEDERATION LIFE 1990– ; Supvr. of Rsch., Candn. Bus. Serv. 1957–66; Sr. Investment Analyst, Investment present firm 1966; Asst. Treas. for Candn. Common Stocks 1968; Mgr., Common Stocks, 1968; Corp. & Tax Planning 1969; Asst. Vice-Pres., Corp. & Tax Planning 1971; Corp. Planning & Rsch. 1974; Corp. Vice-Pres., Planning & Acctg. 1979; Vice-Pres., Corp. Devel. 1983; Chrmn., Confederation Leasing Limited; Confederation Tres. Serv. Limited; recreations: golf, tennis, cycling; clubs: York Downs Golf; Home: 55 Normandale Rd., Unionville, Ont. L3R 4J8; Office: 321 Bloor St. E., Toronto, Ont. M4W 1H1.

**DOUTRIAUX, Jérôme,** Ing. ICAM, Ing. ESE, M.Sc., Ph.D.; university professor; b. Marcq-en-Baroeul, France 6 April 1945; s. Pierre Germain and Bernadette (Rigot) D.; e. Inst. Cath. des Arts et Métiers, Lille, France, Engr. 1966; Ecole Sup. d'Electricité, Paris, France, Engr. 1968; Carnegie-Mellon Univ. M.Sc., Ph.D. 1970–72; m. Carol May d. Walter and Catherine (Cooley) Woodward 21 Aug. 1971; children: Miriam, Stéphane, Sylvie, Timothée; PROFESSOR, FACULTY OF ADMIN., UNIV. OF OTTAWA 1992– ; joined Faculty, Univ. of Ottawa 1971; Assoc. Dean, Fac. of Admin. 1994– ; Chair, Comm. for Grad. Studies in the Humanities 1990–93; Asst. Dean & Dir. of Grad. Prog. in Admin. 1982–90; Mem., Chair, Grants Comm., Ont. Grad. Scholarships 1983–85, 1990, Soc. Sci. Humanities Rsch. Council 1987–88; Chair, Systems Sci. Prog. 1982–85; Visitng Prof., Grad. Sch. of Business, Reims, France 1985–86; Harvard Inst. for Internat. Devel., Indus. Advisor on assistance project in Venezuela 1977–79; previous profl. experience in engr. in U.S. & France (limited duration); Principal, Management Services Internat., Mansi Corp.; consultant to private sector & Govt. of Can.; Prof. Honorario, Universidad Catolica, Santa Maria, Arequipa, Peru, Best paper awards for communications on high-technol. entrepreneurship; Bd. Mem., AFS-Interculture Can. 1989– ; recognized expert in field of high-technol. entrepreneurship, spin-offs & univ.-indus. technol. transfer; Mem., Internat. Council for Small Business; Candn. Operational Rsch. Soc.; I.E.E.E.; co-author of several textbooks, most recent: 'Economie et gestion' 1989, 'Ceres, simulation de politique gén. d'entreprises' 1985; author of many refereed pubs., conf. communications & technical reports; recreations: sheep farming; Home: 173 Huntmar Dr., S.S. 1, Stittsville, Ont. K2S 1B9; Office: 136 Jean-Jacques Lussier, Ottawa, Ont. K1N 6N5.

**DOUVILLE, Jean R.,** LL.D.; automotive parts industry executive; b. Montreal, PQ 26 June 1943; s. Jean-Paul and Louise (Lavoie) D.; e. Coll. Jean de Brébeuf 1958; Univ. of Ottawa B.A.Sc. 1964, law grad. 1967; children: Sophie, Valérie; PRES. & CHIEF EXTVE. OFFR., UAP INC. 1982– ; Corp. Sec., present firm 1971; var. posts incl. Div. Mgr. 1972–77; Extve. Vice-Pres., Western Tire (UAP subs.) 1978; Vice-Pres., Admin., UAP 1980; Pres. 1981; Dir., Maclean Hunter Limited 1987; Nat. Auto. Parts Assn. 1990; Banque Nationale du Canada 1991; Genuine Parts Co., Atlanta, USA 1992; Unigesco Inc. 1992; Sodisco-Howden Group Inc.; Gov., Fond. du Théâtre du Nouveau Monde 1987; Found. for Que. Univ. Athletics 1986; Dir., Montreal Symph. Orch. 1987; Homme du Mois, Revue Commerce 1988; Meritas, Univ. of Ottawa 1990; recreations: owns a 100-acre farm in Bedford, PQ, fishing, hunting, golf, reading; club: Saint-Denis; Home: 120 Ferland, Apt. 10A, Ile des Soeurs, Verdun, Qué. H3E 1L1; Office: 7025 Ontario St. E., Montreal, Qué. H1N 2B3.

**DOUVILLE, Jean-Francois,** B.B.A.; food industry executive; b. New York, N.Y. 14 Nov. 1950; s. Rolland and Madeleine (Delisle) D.; e. Ecole des Hautes Etudes Commerciales, B.B.A. 1973; Harvard Business School, P.M.D. 1990; m. Lucie Martineau 8 June 1985; VICE-PRES. & GEN. MGR., CULINAR FOODS 1992– ; Vice-Pres. & Gen Mgr., Client Serv., A.C. Nielsen (Montreal) 1979–83; Vice-Pres. & Gen. Mgr., New Business Development, A.C. Nielsen (Toronto) 1983–86; Vice-Pres. & Gen. Mgr., Unico Foods 1986–89; Pres., Unico Foods 1989–92; Home: 94, Côté-Ste-Catherine, Outremont, Que. H2V 2A3; Office: 4945 E. Ontario St., Montréal, Qué. H1V 1M2.

**DOUVILLE, Raymond,** B.Sc.; newspaper man; historian; b. La Pérade, Qué. 17 Sept. 1905; s. Alphonse and Alice Chavigny de La Chevrotière D.; e. Nicolet, Qué. Semy.; Univ. of Montréal B.Sc. (Journalism); m. Bella d. late Dr. Henri Beaulac 25 Sept. 1937; children: Renée (Mrs. Rejean Bouchard), Louise (Mrs. Cyrille Bernard), Charlotte (Mrs. Hubert Gaudry); Former Depy. Min. and Registrar Qué. Prov. Secy.; author 'La vie quotidienne en Nouvelle-France' 1964; 'La vie quotidienne des Indiens du Canada' 1967; 'Daily Life in Early Canada' transl. 1967; 'Na Nova França O Canada' transl. 1970; Ed. Françaises 'La Vie d'Arthur Buies' 1933; Ed. du Bien Public 'Aaron Hart' 1938; 'Premiers Seigneurs et Colons de La Pérade' 1948; 'Visages du Vieux Trois-Rivières' 1956; various hist. studies, booklets Candn. hist.; collab. 'Biographical Dictionary of Canada'; mem. Royal Soc. Can.; Société des Dix; recreation: historial research, travel; Address: 650, Murray Ave., Apt. 803, Québec, Qué. G1S 4V8.

**DOVER, William P.,** B.A., M.B.A.; consultant to the service industry; b. Pembroke, Ont. 28 Aug. 1942; s. Cornelius Conn and Irene (Boucher) D.; e. Ryerson Polytech. Inst., dipl. Hotel, Resort & Rest. Admin. 1962; York Univ., B.A. 1973; Simon Fraser Univ., M.B.A. 1979; m. Ruth d. Stanley and Marjorie Lounds 10 July 1964; children: Jeffrey, Michael; PRES., W.P. DOVER & ASSOCIATES 1992– ; Restaurant Mgr., Grenadier Rests. Ltd. 1962–65; Dist. Mgr., Alta., V.S. Serv. 1965–70; Gen. Mgr., B.C. then 'The Great Candn. Soup Co.,' Parnell Foods Ltd. 1970–80; Vice-Pres., Urban Rest. Div. then Gen. Mgr., Harvey's Restaurants, Cara Operations Ltd. 1980–85; Pres., Randa Food Systems Ltd. 1985–86; Pres., Red Lobster Canada 1986; Pres., General Mills Restaurants Canada 1988; Vice-Chrmn. 1992; Past Pres., Toronto and Ont. Rest. & Food Serv. Assns.; Past Chrmn., Candn. Rest. & Food Serv. Assn.; Chrmn., Candn. Hospitality Found.; Adv. Bd. Mem., Adv. Mngt. Prog. for Hospitality Indus., Univ. of Guelph; Recipient, 'The Fran Deck Award' for leadership in the hospitality industry 1986; Gold Award, Ont. Hostelry Assoc. 1989; inducted into the 'We Care' Hall of Fame 1991; 1992 Extve.-in-Residence, Univ. of Guelph, School of Hotel & Food Administration; Office: 6 Tallforest Court, Etobicoke, Ont. M9C 2X2.

**DOWIE, Ian R.,** M.A.; industrialist (retired); b. London, Eng., 4 Oct. 1907; s. George and Annie (Gollan) D.; e. George Heriot's Sch., Edinburgh, Scot.; Edinburgh Univ. M.A. 1929; m. the late Frances Margaret, d. J.A. Campbell, Toronto 12 May 1937; children: Mark Ian George Campbell, Frances Elizabeth Anne Campbell, John Rodney Campbell; m. Barbara Fleury, d. Dr. N.S. Shenstone, Toronto 28 Jan. 1986; formerly with Canadian Breweries Ltd. (Pres. 1958–65); Chrmn., Ont. Comte. on the Healing Arts 1967–70; Campaign Chrmn., Ont. Red Cross 1942–46; Red Cross, Cleveland, Ohio 1950–51; Trustee, Cleveland Orchestra, Cleveland Community Fund; Presbyterian; recreation: golf; Clubs: Toronto Golf; Oakville Golf; Home: 5 Chartwell Rd., Oakville, Ont. L6J 3Z3.

**DOWLING, Robert Wagner,** B.A., Sc.; pharmacist; b. Camrose, Alta. 28 Sept. 1924; s. Harold James and Emma Maude D.; e. Univ. of B.C. B.A. 1952; Univ. of Alta. B.Sc. 1955; m. Olga L. d. Samuel and Theodora Yewchin 6 Sept. 1952; children: Lori S., Robert J.; OWNER, CAVELL DRUGSS & WHISTLERS DRUGSTORES (JASPER NAT. PARK) 1958– ; Pilot, R.C.A.F. 1942–45; active in pharmacy since 1955; Mem., Alta. Pharm. Assn.; Past Mem., B.C. Pharm. Assn.; Former Chair, Jasper Sch. Bd.; Vice-Pres., Candn. Legion; Pres., Alta. C. of C.; Rocky Mtn. P.C. Assn. 1969; active in many community & prov. groups incl. Boy Scouts, Cancer Soc., Air Cadets, Anglican Ch., etc.; elected to Legislation Assembly of Alberta in Edson riding by-election 1969 as P.C. mem.; re-elected & apptd. Min. resp. for Tourism 1971; Min. of Consumer Affairs & Tourism 1973; re-elected in g.e. & apptd. Min. of Business Devel. & Tourism 1975; Bd. Mem., Canada Ports Corp.; Edmonton Flying Club; Alta. Aviation Heritage Soc.; Past Bd. Mem., Union Oil of Calif.; Bank Nat. de Paris; Heritage Trust Co. and others; Comn. 75th Anniv. of Alberta 1980; Comnr. Gen., Alberta Pavilion, Expo '86 1986; Mem., Anglican Ch.; Royal Candn. Legion; Masonic Lodge & Shrine; active in Candn. Extve. Serv. Assn.; recreations: skiing, hiking, golf; clubs: Kiwanis, Lions, SKAL; Home: 825 Giekie St., Box 370, Jasper, Alta. T0E 1E0 and 319 Lessard Dr., Edmonton, Alta. T6M 1A6; Office: P.O. Box 370, Jasper, Alta. T0E 1E0.

**DOWN, Jane Lillian,** B.Sc.; conservation scientist; b. Leamington, Ont. 12 May 1950; d. Russell Saward and Gladys Bertha (Bignell) D.; e. Leamington Dist. S.S. 1969; Queen's Univ. B.Sc. (Hons.) 1973; m. Robin Walter s. Margaret and Walter Souchen 17 Dec. 1983; one s.: Russell Alexander; CONSERVATION SCIENTIST, CANADIAN CONSERVATION INST., DEPT. OF COMMUNICATIONS 1978– ; radiation analysis of gun residues, Centre of Forensic Science, Toronto summer 1971, '72; rsch. on D-Glucuronate Reductase, Queen's Univ. 1973–74; neur. rsch. of histamine, Univ. of Ottawa 1974–77; rsch. on lindane & oxytetracycline pesticides, Chem. & Biol. Rsch. Inst., Agric. Canada 1977–78; current rsch. on epoxy resin, poly(vinyl acetate) & acrylic adhesives for the conservation of historic & artistic works; created & developed a materials & suppliers database for Conservation Information Network; Mem., Un. Ch. of Canada; Internat. Inst. for Conserv. Candn. Group (Treas. 1984–86); Internat. Inst. for Conserv. of Historic & Artistic Works; author/co-author of several scientific articles and symposium reports; Ontario Scholar 1969; recreations: tennis, bridge, piano, geneology, travel; Home: 1843 Burfield Ave., Gloucester, Ont. K1J 6S9; Office: 1030 Innes Rd., Ottawa, Ont. K1A 0C8.

**DOWNER, Roger G.H.,** Ph.D., D.Sc., F.R.S.C.; educator; university executive; b. Belfast, N.Ireland 21 Dec. 1942; s. Leslie G. and Edith P. (Hamill) D.; e. Queens Univ. Belfast B.Sc. 1964, M.Sc. 1967, D.Sc. 1984; Univ. of W. Ont. Ph.D. 1970; m. Jean E.N. Taylor 2 Apl. 1966; children: Kevin G., Kathleen P., Tara S.; VICE PRES. UNIV. RELATIONS, UNIV. OF WATERLOO, Prof. of Biol. and Chem. 1981– ; joined present Univ. 1970 serving as Asst. Prof., Assoc. Prof., Prof. and Chrmn. of Biol., Acting Dean of Sci., mem. Senate & Bd. Govs. 1988–90, recipient Distinguished Teacher Award 1982; Visiting Prof. of Biochem. Hokkaido Univ. Japan 1976, Oxford Univ. 1977; cons. several multinat. agrichem. co's; cons. InterAm. Inst. for Coop. in Agric. (report on Implementation Biotechnol. into Agric. Practice Latin Am. and Caribbean); mem. Nat. Sci. Eng. Rsch. Council Grant Selection Ctte. Food & Agric. 1986–89 (Chrmn. 1988–89); Vice Pres. (Rsch.) Huntsman Marine Lab. 1985–86; mem. Internat. Adv. Ctte. Neurotox 1988, 1991; Vice Pres. Biol. Council Can. 1986–90; Dir. Insect Biotech. Can. 1989–90; mem. Grant Selection Ctte. Nat. Sci. Found. 1988–90; Vice Pres. Candn. Council Univ. Biol. Chrmn. 1987–88, Pres. 1988–89; author or coauthor over 140 scholarly articles; ed. 4 scholarly books; ed. bd. Candn. Jour. Zool., Archives Insect Physiol. & Biochem.; Fellow, Royal Society of Canada; Fellow, Royal Society of Arts; Fry Medal, Candn. Soc. Zools. 1990; Gold Medal, Entomological Soc. of Can. 1991; mem. City of Waterloo Cultural Develop. Ctte.; mem. Candn. Soc. Zools. (Vice Pres. 1984–86, Pres. 1986–87); Entomol. Soc. Can. (Dir. 1984–87); Anglican; recreations: squash, golf, skiing, walking, theatre, reading; Club: University; Home: 15 Wildwood Pl., Waterloo, Ont. N2L 4B2; Office: Waterloo, Ont. N2L 3G1.

**DOWNEY, James,** B.A., B.Ed., M.A., Ph.D., D.H.L., D.Litt., LL.D.; educator; b. Winterton, Nfld. 20 Apl. 1939; s. Ernest Fletcher and Mimy Ann (Andrews) D.; e. Winterton (Nfld.) Un. Ch. Sch. 1955; Mem. Univ. of Nfld. B.A. 1962, B.Ed. 1963, M.A. 1964; Univ. of London Ph.D. 1966; m. Laura Ann d. late William Parsons 25 July 1964; children: Sarah Elizabeth, Geoffrey James; PRES., UNIV. OF WATERLOO 1992– ; Dir., Tennis Canada 1991– ; Hewlett-Packard Ltd. (Canada) 1993– ; Co-chair, Commission on Excellence in Educ., N.B. 1991–92; Pres., Univ. of New Brunswick 1980–90; Vice-Pres., (Academic), Carleton Univ. 1978–80; Dean, Faculty of Arts, Carleton Univ. 1975–78; Pres., pro-tempore, Jan. to May 1979; Chrmn. Dept. Eng., Carleton Univ. 1972–75, author 'The Eighteenth Century Pulpit' 1969; co-editor 'Fearful Joy' 1974; articles and reviews various learned journs.; Fellow, Univ. of Georgia, 1985; Doctor of Humane Letters, Univ. of Maine 1987; Doctor of Letters, Memorial Univ. of Nfld. 1991; Doctor of Laws, Univ. of N.B. 1991; United Church; recreations: tennis, book collecting; Home: 272 Mary St., Waterloo, Ont. N2J 1S6; Office: Univ. of Waterloo, Waterloo, Ont. N2L 3G1.

**DOWNEY, (Richard) Keith,** O.C., B.S.A., M.Sc., Ph.D., F.A.I.C., F.R.S.C.; agrologist; research scientist; b. Saskatoon, Sask. 26 Jan. 1927; s. Richard Albert and Alberta Georgina (Amy) D.; e. Univ. of Sask. B.S.A. 1950, M.Sc. 1952; Cornell Univ. Ph.D. 1961; m. Edna d. Charles and Edith Brewer 23 Aug. 1952; children: Debra Anne, Patricia Grace, Karen Elaine, Richard Douglas, Kevin Donald; PRIN. RSCH. SCIENT. (OILSEED BREEDING), AGRIC. CAN. RSCH. STN. SASKATOON 1958– ; Adjunct Prof., Crop Sci. Univ. of Sask. 1970– ; Student Asst., Dominion Forage Crops Lab. Saskatoon 1946–52; Rsch. Offr., Agric. Can. Rsch. Stn. Lethbridge 1951–57; Internat. Cons. Insternat. Devel. Rsch. Centre, Candn. Internat. Devel. Agency, Orgn. Am. States, FAO; Chrmn., Internat. Rapeseed Plant Breeders' Ctte. Groupe Consultatif Internat de Recherche sur le Colza 1974– ; recipient Bond Gold Medal Am. Oil Chems.' Soc. 1963; Pub. Service of Can. Merit Award 1969; Grindley Medal Agric. Inst. Can. 1973; Royal Bank Award 1975 (jt. holder); O.C. 1976; Queen's Silver Jubilee Medal 1977; Century Saskatoon Agric. Award 1982; Gold Medal Award (Pure or Applied Science) Joint Award, Professional Inst. of the Public Service of Can. 1989; Commemorative Medal, 125th Anniversary of Candn. Confedn. 1992; author or co-author over 215 sci. publs., rsch. papers, book chapters, maj. reports; Nat. Dir., Agric. Inst. Can. 1970–72; Hon. Life mem., Candn. Seed Growers' Assn. (Chrmn. Plant Breeders' Ctte. 1975– ;); Sask. Rapeseed Growers' Assn.; mem., Sask. Inst. Agrols. (Pres. 1967–68); Candn. Soc. Agronomy (Pres. 1960–61); Am. Soc. Agronomy; Am. Oil Chems.' Soc.; Sigma Xi; United Church; recreations: curling, cycling; Club: Nutana Rotary; Home: 23 Simpson Cres., Saskatoon, Sask. S7H 3C5; Office: 107 Science Pl., Saskatoon, Sask. S7N 0X2.

**DOWNEY, Patrick D.,** B.Comm., C.A.; mining executive; b. Chapleau, Ont. 9 Dec. 1943; s. Lawrence Thomas and Sybil Isobel (McCoshen) D.; e. Laurentian Univ. B.Comm. (Hons.) 1974; C.A. Ont. 1976; m. Lynne d. Raymond and Ida Allaire 1967; children: Chantal, Dennis, Trisha; PRESIDENT & CHIEF EXECUTIVE OFFR., NORTHGATE EXPLORATION LIMITED 1980– ; Auditor, Price Waterhouse 1974–76; Manager, Finance & Tax, Northern & Central Gas 1976–79; Dir., Northgate Exploration; Sonora Gold Corp.; Northwest Gold Corp.; Office: Suite 2701 – 1 First Canadian Place, Toronto, Ont. M5X 1C7.

**DOWNEY, Terrence James,** B.A., M.A., Ph.D.; educator; b. Peel Twp. Ont. 20 Dec. 1944; s. the late William Joseph and Margaret Agnes (Jordan) D.; e. Arthur Dist. High Sch. 1963; Univ. of Waterloo B.A. 1966; Univ. of W. Ont. M.A. 1972, Ph.D. 1977; m. Margaret Elizabeth d. Patrick and Ann Brown 22 June 1968; children: Patrick, William, Mary, Kathleen, Elizabeth, Margaret, James, Michael, Sarah, Christine, Erin; PROF. OF POL. SCI. UNIV. OF WATERLOO 1977– ; High Sch. Teacher, Cannington, Ont. 1966–69, Lindsay, Ont. 1969–71, 1972–74; Lectr. in Pol. Sci. (Part-time) Univ. of W. Ont. 1974–77; Lectr. in Pol. Sci. present Univ. 1977, Asst. Prof. 1978, Assoc. Prof. 1991, Chrmn. of Dept. 1985–88; Dir., Personnel and Management Studies Programs 1991– ; Distinguished Teacher Award 1988; Co-recipient (with spouse), Father Norm Choate Distinguished Graduate Award, St. Jerome's Coll., Univ. of Waterloo 1990; Special Visiting Appt. Grad. Faculty (Part-time) 1983–88, Wilfrid Laurier Univ.; Cons. Waterloo Region Review Comn. 1978; Expert Witness Legis. Ctte. H. of C. 1988; author various articles: Candn. resource development; economic, trade, and environmental policy; constitutional reform; Catholic Church-state relations in Canada; Ont. regional govt. reform; mem. Inst. Pub. Adm. Can. (Exec. Hamilton Regional Group 1983–84); Candn. Pol. Sci. Assn.; Counc. of Canadians; R. Catholic; recreations: baseball, hockey, music; Home: 303 Dale Cres., Waterloo, Ont. N2J 3Y4; Office: Waterloo, Ont. N2L 3G1.

**DOWNIE, Bryan McKay,** B.A., M.B.A., Ph.D.; university professor; b. Winnipeg, Man. 27 June 1938; s. Irwin McKay and Agnes Viola (Atkins) D.; e. Concordia College B.A. 1959; Univ. of Chicago M.B.A. 1970, Ph.D. 1970; m. Mary d. Douglas and Norma McClellan 29 March 1984; children: Diana, Mark; DIRECTOR, SCHOOL OF INDUSTRIAL RELATIONS & DIRECTOR, INDUSTRIAL RELATIONS CENTRE, QUEEN'S UNIV. 1991– ; Third Party Neutral in Labour Disputes 1975– ; Chrmn., College Relations Comn., Ont. Govt. 1979–87; Education Relations. Comn. 1979–87; Prof., Sch. of Business, Queen's Univ. 1965–90; Pres., Candn. Industrial Relations Assn. 1984–85; Candn. Dir., Soc. of Professionals in Dispute Resolution 1982–87; 1st recipient, Annual Teaching Award, Sch. of Bus., Queen's Univ.; author: 'Strikes, Disputes and Policymaking' 1992; 'The Changing Face of Industrial Relations and Human Resource Management' 1993; Home: 44 - 100 Medley Court, Kingston, Ont. K7K 6X2; Office: Kingston, Ont. K7L 3N6.

**DOWNIE, Mary Alice Dawe (Hunter),** B.A.; writer; b. (of Candn. parents) Alton, Ill. 12 Feb. 1934; d. Robert Grant and Doris Mary (Rogers) Hunter; came to Canada 1940; e. Univ. of Toronto B.A. 1955; m. John Downie 27 June 1959; children: Christine Avery, Jocelyn Grant, Alexandra Duncan; Stenographer, Maclean-Hunter 1955; Reporter, Marketing Magazine 1956; Editorial Assistant, Candn Medical Assn. Journal 1956–57; Librarian and Publicity Manager, Oxford Univ. Press. 1958–59; Freelance Reviewer 1959–78; Book Review Editor, Kingston Whig Standard 1973–78; co-compiler (with Barbara Robertson) 'The Wind Has Wings' 1968; 'Scared Sarah' 1974; 'The Magical Adventures of Pierre' 1974; 'Dragon on Parade' 1974; 'The Witch of the North' 1975; 'The King's Loon' 1979; 'The Last Ship' 1980; co-compiler 'And Some Brought Flowers' (with Mary Hamilton) 1980; 'Jenny Greenteeth' 1981; 'The Wicked Fairy Wife' 1983; co-author (with John Downie) 'Honor Bound' 1971; 'Alison's Ghosts' 1984; (with George Rawlyk) 'A Proper Acadian' 1981; 'Acadien pour de bon' 1982; (with Jillian H. Gilliland) 'Seeds and Weeds' 1981; 'Stones and Cones' 1984; (with Barbara Robertson) 'The New Wind Has Wings' 1984; (edited with Elizabeth Greene & M.-A. Thompson) 'The Window of Dreams' 1986; co-author (with Barbara Robertson) 'The Well-Filled Cupboard' 1987; 'How the Devil Got His Cat' 1988; co-author (with Mann Hwa Huang-Hsu) 'The Buffalo Boy and the Weaver Girl' 1989; co-compiler (with Barbara Robertson) 'Dr. Dwarf & Other Poems for Children, by A.M. Klein' 1990; 'Cathal the Giant Killer & the Dun Shaggy Filly' 1991; 'The Cat Park' 1993; co-compiler (with M.A. Thompson) 'Written in Stone' 1993; author various articles, stories and profiles in anthologies, The Hornbook Magazine, Candn. Children's Annual; creator and initial editor 'The Northern Lights Series' and 'Kids Canada Series'; rec'd Canada Council Arts Awards 1971–72, 1981–82; various Ontario Arts Council Awards; recreations: reading, travel, plants, music; Address: 190 Union St., Kingston, Ont. K7L 2P6.

**DOWNIE, Peter Wilson,** B.A.; journalist; b. Montreal, Que. 30 Jan. 1951; s. Thomas Gordon and Doreen (Beck) D.; e. Univ. of N.B. B.A. 1973; HOST, 'MAN ALIVE,' CBC TV & 'FRESH AIR,' CBC RADIO; joined CBC Radio & TV 1973; has worked in various positions across country: Announcer, Host, Producer & Manager; regional radio programs hosted in Fredericton, Calgary, Montreal & produced in Sudbury; network programs: 'Cross Country Check Up' in Montreal and 'Entertainment Section' (arts program) on FM Network Toronto; also fill in work on 'As It Happens' and 'Morning Side'; TV since 1984 incl. 'Midday' and 'Man Alive'; 2 ACTRA nom. for Best Host/Interviewer 1983, '84; 2 Gemini nom. for Best Host 1987, '92; Co-Host, Best Remote Broadcast 1984, Candn. Music Council; Patron, Child Haven International; Foster Parent; Mem., World Wildlife Fund; Amnesty Internat.; Candn. Wildlife Fed.; Toronto Humane Soc.; recreations: painting, gardening, cooking, fishing; Home: P.O. Box 423, Mt. Albert, Ont. L0G 1M0; Office: 790 Bay St., 3rd Floor, Toronto, Ont.

**DOWNIE, Ronald J.,** Q.C., B.A., LL.B., LL.M., LL.D. (Hon.); barrister; b. Halifax, N.S. 24 Oct. 1927; s. William A. and Mabel A. (Clancey) D.; e. St. Mary's Coll. H.S. 1944; St. Mary's Univ. B.A. 1948; Dalhousie Law Sch. LL.B. 1951; Harvard Law Sch. LL.M. 1952; St. Mary's Univ. LL.D. (Hon.) 1990; m. V. Marie d. Leo and Veilchen Merritt 21 May 1955; children: Brian W., Kevin P., Jennifer A., Laura E., Liane M.; PARTNER, COX, DOWNIE 1952– ; admitted to Bar of N.S. 1952; apptd. Q.C. 1967; Fellow, Am. Coll. of Trial Lawyers 1979; clients incl. Maritime Telegraph & Telephone Co. Ltd., Candn. Med. Protective Assn., N.S. Teachers' Union, N.S. Inst. of C.A.s; Assoc. Profl. Engrs., N.S.; Past Pres., N.S. Barristers Soc.; Charitable Irish Co.; Founding Chrmn., Law Found. of N.S.; Past Counc. Mem., Candn. Bar Assn.; Past Dir., Public Legal Edn. Soc.; Past Chrmn., St. Mary's Univ.; Past Pres., Dalhousie Law Alumni; Founding Chrmn., Archdiocese of Halifax, Diocesan Pastoral Counc.; Past Comnr., Archdiocese of Halifax, Fin. Comn.; Trustee, Saint Vincent Guest House Found.; recreations: reading, skating, cross-country skiing, gardening, travel; Club: Halifax; Home: 5925 Emscote Dr., Halifax, N.S. B3H 1B3; Office: Purdy's Wharf, Upper Water St., Halifax, N.S. B3J 3E5.

**DOWNING, John Henry,** B.A.; journalist; b. Toronto, Ont. 10 June 1936; s. Dr. John Henry and Lena (Hoogstad) D.; e. Weston Coll. Inst.; Univ. of Toronto; Ryerson Polytech. Inst.; m. Mary d. Ignac and Barbara Horvat 8 July 1961; three s. John Henry Jr., Brett, Mark; EDITOR, THE TORONTO SUN 1985– ; Ed. Whitehorse Star 1957; joined Toronto Telegram 1958–71 serving as Reporter, Ed. incl. City Ed. and Asst. Mng. Ed.; Toronto Sun 1971– , Pol. Columnist, Assoc. Ed.; Trustee Metro Safety Counc.; Past Pres. Fedn. Press Clubs Can.; mem. Candn. Nat. Exhn. Ctte.; Life Mem., Metro & Region Conservation Authority; Dir., Runnymede Chronic Care Hosp.; Candn. Chrmn., Internat. Press Inst.; Hon. Dir., Toronto Outdoor Art Exhbn.; recipient various awards Metro Toronto Police Assn.; Ont. Safety League; service medal, Toronto City Counc.; awarded Commemorative Medal for 125th Anniversary of Candn. Confederation 1992; Award of Merit, Metro Caravan; St. John Priory Honor; co-author 'Mayor of All the People' 1967; 'Once Upon a Country' 1978; author various book chapters local hist.; pol. commentator, radio and TV; recreations: urban history, reading, swimming; Club: Toronto Press (Past Pres.); Home: 92 Elsfield Rd., Etobicoke, Ont. M8Y 3R8; Office: 333 King St. E., Toronto, Ont. M5A 3X5.

**DOWNING, Robert James,** R.C.A.; artist; b. Hamilton, Ont. 1 Aug. 1935; s. Albert James and Dora Florence (Figgins) D.; e. grade sch. (self taught); m. Miriana d. Ratko and Milica Kaludjerovic, Toronto, Ont. 27 Sept. 1980; children: Sara Lynn, Michael John (by previous marriage); sculptor, conceptual artist and designer; served with RCN as Photographer 1952–57 (awarded hon. mention for photog.); Police Constable City of Hamilton, co-founder Can.'s first police choir 1957–60; began sculpting 1960; apprenticeship with Ted Bieler, Prof. of Sculpture, Univ. of Toronto 1963 and in 1966 went into partnership with Bieler to complete largest precast concrete sculpture project ever attempted: Med. Sciences Bldg., Univ. of Toronto; Lectr. in Sculpture Univ. of Toronto 1967–69, completed series of 108 sculptures derived from the Cube and became first artist to represent Canada with a solo exhibition at a major European public gallery: Whitechapel Art Gallery, London, Eng. 1969; Part-time Lectr. in Art & Arch. Fanshawe Coll. of Art & Technol. London, Ont. 1969–71 and in Formative Processes & Structural Systems Ont. Coll. of Art 1971–72; Dir. of Art, Appleby Coll. Oakville, Ont. 1972; Visiting Lectr. in Sculpture, Banff Sch. of Fine Art 1973; Part-time Lectr. on 3–D form, Cal. State Univ. Long Beach and completed series of sculptures exploring relationships between Platonic Solids and Fibonacci Ratio 1974–77; taught Industrial Design, O.C.A. 1981–82; prepared and implemented a visual & tactile awareness program for secondary sch. art & design teachers, Molepolole Coll. of Educ., Botswana 1985–86; part-time lectr., sculpture & three-dimensional design, La Salle, Singapore 1987–88; prod. several learning aids incl. 'Cosmokit' an intermodulated printing set based on hexagonal plane tessellations 1973; 'Transentials of Space' based on multicultural expressions of elementary geometries, in Math., Art & Nature 1984; solo exhns. in Canada incl. Dunkelman Gallery Toronto 1968; Galerie Agnes Lefort Montreal 1968; York Univ. Art Gallery Toronto 1970; Robert McLaughlin Gallery Oshawa (travelling Ont.) 1972; Univ. of Alberta 1973; College Park, Toronto 1981; Art Gallery of Hamilton (The Robert Downing Archive) 1992; rep. in over 60 exhns. in 8 countries, incl. National Gallery of Canada, Sculpture '67 Exhibit; Brooklyn Museum E.A.T. Competition, New York 1968; 11th Biennale of Middleheim, Antwerp, Belgium 1971; Long Beach Museum of Art, California 1975; Smithsonian Inst. 1978; National Gallery of Botswana 1985; Science Centre, Republic of Singapore 1988; rep. in various pub. and corporate colls. on four continents; founded Art Collection Program Texaco Canada Inc. 1980; wrote and published limited edition of early memoirs: 'Confessions of a Canadian Sculptor' 1991; rec'd Ont. Arts Council Awards 1967, 1978–79 and seven Can. Council Awards between 1967 and 1985; Founding mem. (1967) Candn. Artists Reps.; mem. (1979–80) Ont. Soc. Artists (Extve. Council); Address: 270 Scarlett Rd., Suite 1506, Toronto, Ont. M6N 4X7.

**DOWNS, Allan Rae,** M.D., F.R.C.S.(C), F.A.C.S.; surgeon; educator; b. Preeceville, Sask. 14 Oct. 1930; s. Walter Harold and Violet Ellen (White) D.; e. Preeceville (Sask.) High Sch.; Univ. of Man. 1947–49; Man. Med. Coll. M.D. 1954; m. Janet P. Curran; children: Allan Craig, Allyson Merren, Christopher Ian; Kathleen Mary-Ellen; PROF. FACULTY OF MED. UNIV. OF MAN.; Head, Section of Vascular Surg., Dept. of Surg., Faculty of Med., Univ. of Man.; Health Sciences Centre; mem., Society of Vascular Surg.; author or co-author various publs. and presentations; Past Pres. Candn. Soc. Vascular Surg.; mem. Candn. and Man. Med. Assns.; Candn. Cardiovascular Soc.; Candn. Assn. Clin. Surgs.; Internat. Cardiovascular Soc.; Soc. of Vascular Surgery; Central Surg. Assoc.; Candn. Univ. Surg. Chrmn., Amer. Surgical Assoc.; Ed. Bd., Jour. of Vasc. Surg.; and other med. assns.; P. Conservative; Protestant; recreations: golf, tennis, hockey; Club: Wildewood; Home: 312 Hosmer Blvd., Winnipeg, Man. R3P 0H6; Office: 820 Sherbrook St., Winnipeg, Man. R3A 1R9.

**DOWNS, Barry Vance,** B.Arch., R.C.A., F.R.A.I.C.; architect; b. Vancouver, B.C. 19 June 1930; s. William Arthur and Milada Marie (Ruziska) D.; e. Queen Mary Primary Sch.; Lord Byng High Sch. 1947; Univ. of B.C. 1948–49; Univ. of Wash. B.Arch. 1954; m. Mary Hunter d. late Allan Stewart 24 Feb. 1955; children: William Stewart, Elizabeth Mary; PARTNER, DOWNS/ARCHAMBAULT ARCHITECTS 1969– ; Design Arch. Thompson, Berwick, Pratt Archs. 1956–63; private arch. practice 1963; Visiting Lectr. Univ. of B.C. 1960–63; recipient Massey Medal and numerous awards incl. Nat. Housing Design Awards, Candn. Arch. Yearbook Awards, RAIC Awards of Merit, Heritage Can. Regional Award; author 'Sacred Places, British Columbia's Early Churches' 1980; various journ. articles; work cited numerous publs.; mem. Vancouver Civic Design Panel 1967–68; Hist. Adv. Bd. 1971–73; Heritage Adv. Comte. 1974–76; Candn. Housing Design Council Can. W. Region 1969–73; mem., West Vancouver Planning Comn. 1986–90; mem. Arch. Inst. B.C.; Phi Delta Theta; United Church; recreations: tennis, hiking; Clubs: Vancouver Central Lions; Vancouver Lawn Tennis; Home: 6664 Marine Dr., West Vancouver, B.C. V7W 2S9.

**DOWNS, Philip George,** B.A., Mus.M., Ph.D.; professor; b. Leeds, England 5 Mar. 1928; s. Harold Bailey and Dorothy (Axon) D.; e. Roundhay Sch.; Leeds Univ., B.A. 1949; Royal Coll. of Mus.; Univ. of Toronto, Mus.M. 1960, Ph.D. 1964; 1st m. the late Marianne Katharine d. John and Anna Bell 1960; 2nd m. Mary Annabella d. William and Eileen Leggatt 1973; children: Philip Robin, Dorothy Katharine, Mary Margaret Louise; CHRMN., DEPT. OF MUS. HIST., UNIV. OF WEST. ONT. 1985– ; Nat. Serv., Comn. Offr., Brit. Army 1950; emigrated to Can. 1955; Teacher, Mount Allison Univ. 1955–56; worked in advtg. 1956–58; Teacher, Western Tech. Sch. 1960–61; post-doct. study England 1964–65; Sr. Lectr., Fac. of Music, Univ. of Melbourne 1966–69; Assoc. Prof., Dept. of Mus. Hist., Univ. of West. Ont. 1969; Prof. 1973– ; U. of T. Open fellowships; Ont. Grad. scholarships; Can. Counc. post-doct. fellow; Jr. Fellow, Massey Coll. 1963; Founder mem., London Mus. Scholar. Found. (Pres. 1981–86); Former Bd. Mem. & Chrmn., Prog. Ctte., London Orch.; Mem., Am. Musicol. Soc.; author: 'Thérèse Raquin' 1953, 'The Development of the "Great Repertoire" in the Nineteenth Century' 1964, 'Classical Music: the Era of Haydn, Mozart, and Beethoven' 1992, 'Anthology of Classical Music' 1992; recreations: chamber music, horses; Home: 2–1025 Brough St., London, Ont. N6A 3N5; Office: Room 221, Talbot College, Univ. of West. Ont., London, Ont. N6A 3K7.

**DOWSETT, Robert Chipman,** O.St.J, B.A., F.S.A., F.C.I.A., M.A.A.A.; employee benefits and actuarial consultant; b. Toronto, Ont. 27 June 1929; s. Reginald Ernest and Jean Shillington (Rose) D.; e. Univ. of Toronto Schs.; Univ. of Toronto, B.A. (Hon. Math. & Physics) 1950; VICE CHRMN., WILLIAM M. MERCER LTD. 1984– ; Managing Dir., William M. Mercer Cos. Inc. (New York); Dir., CT Financial Services Inc.; Canada Trustco Mortgage Co.; Dofasco Inc.; The Donwood Inst.; joined Crown Life 1950; promoted successively to Asst. Actuary 1955, Assoc. Actuary 1959, Actuary 1964, Vice-Pres. and Actuary 1969, Extve. Vice-Pres. 1970, Pres. and Dir. 1971, Hon. Dir. 1982– ; joined William M. Mercer Ltd. as Director 1982; Fellow, Soc. of Actuaries 1954 (Secy. 1969–71; mem. Bd. of Govs. 1971–74, 1975–78, Vice Pres. 1986–88); mem. Candn. Assn. of Actuaries since 1953 (Secy. 1960) and its successor (1964) Candn. Inst. of Actuaries (Fellow, Pres. 1973–74); mem., Am. Acad. of Actuaries 1965; el. Pres., The Candn. Life and Health Ins. Assn. 1974–75; Chrmn., Council for Cdn. Unity, 1979–81 (Gov. 1981– ;); mem., Div. of Finance, United Church; recreations: skiing, water sports; Home: 5 Sylvan Valleyway, Toronto, Ont. M5M 4M4; Office: BCE Place, 161 Bay St., P.O. Box 501, Toronto, Ont. M5J 2S5.

**DOXEY, George Victor,** B.Sc., M.A.; educator; b. Capetown, S. Africa 26 May 1926; s. Charles and Mary Lea (De Wet) D.; e. Univ. of London B.Sc. (Econ) 1948; Lincoln's Inn, Barrister-at-Law 1954; Univ. of Capetown M.A. 1956; m. Isabel d. Stanley and Bessie Bullis 11 Dec. 1968; children: Lea, Michael; PROF. EMERITUS & SENIOR SCHOLAR, YORK UNIV. 1992– ; S. African Foreign Service Offr. 1948–53; Lectr. Univ. of Capetown 1953–58; Sr. Lectr. in Econ. Univ. of Witswatersrand 1959–60; Lectr. Univ. of London and Adv. to Brit. Foreign Office 1961; Prof. of Econ., York Univ. 1962–92 (and Master McLaughlin Coll. 1978–88), Founding Chrmn. of Econ. 1964–67; Candn. mem. Tripartite economic survey of Eastern Caribbean 1966; Visiting Prof. Univ. of the West Indies, Barbados 1968–70; Cons. to Fed. Govt. Can., Candn. Bankers Assn., Candn. Manpower Service, Tourism Devel. & Edn.; undertook study which led to creation Candn. Inst. Bankers 1964; Ayres Fellow, Grad. Sch. Am. Banking Assn. 1966; Visiting Fellow, Univ. of Otago, New Zealand 1986; Councillor, Town of Kearney, Ont. 1982–88 and 1993– , Depy. Mayor 1987, mem. and Chrmn. Kearney Planning Bd. and Adv. Ctte., Chrmn., Finance Ctte.; mem. Parry Sound & Area Development Counc. 1987–93, Chrmn. 1989; author 'The Industrial Color Bar in South Africa' 1962; 'South Africa and the High Commission Territories' 1962; 'Free Trade – Canada and the Caribbean' 1967; 'The Tourist Industry in Barbados' 1970; co-author 'Tourism in Canada in the 1980's' 1985; recreations: gardening, cooking; Address: Kearney, Ont. P0A 1M0.

**DOYLE, Anne Marie,** B.A.; public servant; b. Toronto, Ont. 6 July 1946; d. Philip Ernest and Mary Catherine (MacDonnell) D.; e. St. George's Grade Sch.; St. Joseph's H.S.; Univ. of Toronto B.A. 1967; CANADIAN AMBASSADOR AND PERMANENT REP. TO THE ORGN. FOR ECONOMIC COOPERATION & DEVELOPMENT 1991– ; Fgn. assignments incl. Candn. High Comn. in Nairobi and Candn. Del. to NATO in Brussels, Dept. of External Affairs 1967–72; worked on Internat. Trade Policy incl. Tokyo round of negotiations, Dept. of Finance 1974–79; Economic Counsellor, OECD Paris 1979–82; Dept. of Finance incl. period as Dir, Internat. Finance & Devel. Div. 1982–86; Candn. Comnr. to Hong Kong and Consul Gen. to Macau 1986–89; Asst. Sec. to Cabinet for Foreign & Defence Policy 1989–91; recreations: tennis, travel, walking, music, theatre, film; Home: 26 Av. Foch, Paris 75116, France; Office: 15 bis Rue de Franqueville, Paris 75116, France.

**DOYLE, Arthur T.,** B.B.A.; publisher; b. Saint John, N.B. 15 June 1938; s. Gregory Arthur and Barbara St. Clair (Morris) D.; e. St. Malachy's High Sch. 1958; Univ. of N.B. B.B.A. 1962; m. Bonita d. Edmund and Jennie Chandler 13 Sept. 1963; children: Heather, Natalie, Arthur, Bonnie, Nancy; Publisher, The Telegraph-Journal and The Evening Times-Globe 1990–..; Project Exec. and Cons. N.B. Govt. 1962–71; Dir. Alumni Affairs Univ. of N.B. 1971–90, mem. Senate and Bd. Govs. 1975–90; author 'Front Benches And Back Rooms' 1976; 'Premiers Of New Brunswick' 1981; 'Heroes of New Brunswick' 1982; 'How To Get Elected' 1983; R. Catholic; Club: White Rapids Fishing; Home: 289 Oxford St., Fredericton, N.B. E3B 2R4.

**DOYLE, Brian,** B.A., B.J.; writer; b. Ottawa, Ont. 12 Aug. 1935; s. Hulbert and Lottie (Duff) D.; m. Jackie d. Jack and Deedee Aronson 1960; children: Megan, Ryan; author of children's books: 'Hey, Dad' 1978, 'You Can Pick Me Up at Peggy's Cove' 1980 (made into film by Atlantis Films), 'Up to Low' 1983 (Candn. Library Assn. Award for Book of the Year 1983), 'Angel Square' 1986 (adapted for the stage & perf. at Nat. Arts Centre 1987; short list for Gov. Gen. Award), 'Easy Avenue' 1988 (Candn. Library Assn. Award for Book of the Year 1988; short list for Gov. Gen. Award); 'Covered Bridge' 1990 (short list for Gov. Gen. award; winner of Mr. Christie Book Award 1990); author's body of work winner of Vicky Metcalf Award 1991; 'Spud Sweetgrass' 1992; Home: 539 Rowanwood Ave., Ottawa, Ont. K2A 3C9.

**DOYLE, Denzil J.,** B.Sc., D.Eng.; innovation consultant; b. Vinton, Que. 16 Apr. 1932; s. Michael Ambrose and Florence Catherine (Kelly) D.; e. Queen's Univ. B.Sc. 1956; D.Eng. (Hon.) Carleton Univ. 1981; m. Marion Patricia d. Allen Merritt 21 July 1956; children: Karen, Michael, Christopher, Jeffrey; PRESIDENT, DOYLETECH CORPORATION 1981– ; Design Engr., Computing Devices Co. 1956–57; Scientific Offr., Defense Rsch. Bd. 1957–63; 1st employee, Digital Equipment of Canada Ltd. 1963–81, resigned as Pres. leaving a staff of 1600; Founding shareholder various technology-intensive firms 1981– ; Chrmn. Instantel Inc.; Chrmn., Rockcliffe Research & Technology Inc.; Newbridge Networks Corp.; Canadian Astronautics Ltd.; Gennum Corp., LNS Systems, Advanced Systems Integration; Consultant, Govt. of Sask. (Dept. Sci. & Tech.); Govt. of Can. (Min. of State for Sci. & Tech.); Govt. of N.B. (Commerce & Technology); Marketer of the Yr. Award, Am. Mktg. Assn. 1982; Commercial & Indus. Devel. Corp. of Ottawa-Carleton; served on adv. cttes. for NRC & Min. of Industry & Commerce; Guest lectr., USSR State Ctte. on Higher Educ. 1991; author: 'New Ventures Planning Handbook'; 'Technology Management Handbook' 1984; 'Technology Exploitation Handbook' 1986; 'Making Technology Happen' 1988; several articles; Home: 3 Sherk Cres., Kanata, Ont. K2K 2L5; Office: 362 Terry Fox Dr., Kanata, Ont. K2K 2P5.

**DOYLE, Francis Patrick,** M.D., B.Sc., L.M.C.C.; physician; b. St. Boniface, Man. 28 Feb. 1922; s. Joseph Pierce and Margaret Jane (King) D.; e. Provencher Sch.; Univ. of Man. B.Sc. 1943; Laval Univ. M.D. 1948; m. Marie-Thérèse d. Joseph and Germaine Arbez 27 Dec. 1949; children: Rosemary, Patricia, Elaine, Paul; private practice, Ste. Anne, Man. 1948– ; Co-founder, Ste-Anne Hosp. 1954; Coroner, Prov. of Man. 1954, subsequently Medical Examiner; Staff mem., Ste-Anne and St. Boniface hosps.; Mem., Coll. of Family Practice of Can.; Senior Mem., Manitoba Med. Assn.; Counc., Coll. of Physicians & Surgeons 1976–88 (Pres. 1984–85); Man. Hosp. Comn. and Man. Health Serv. Comn. 1962–73; Dir., St. Boniface Gen. Hosp. 1974–88 (Chrmn. 1978–88); mem. & Chrmn. Seine River Sch. Div. 1967–73; Past Pres., Catholic Health Conf. of Man.; Catholic Health Assn. of Can.; Catholic Physicians Guild of Man.; Assn. des Commisaires de langue française du Man.; Past Bd. Mem. CBC; St. John's Ambulance Ste. Anne Div. bears name in its title; recipient, Judge J.M. George Memorial Award, Manitoba Health Orgn. 1988; Prix Evangelium Award, Archdiocese of St. Boniface 1991; Physician of the Year, Manitoba Med. Assn. 1992; Home: PO Box 9, 259 Central Ave., Ste. Anne, Man. R0A 1R0; Office: 142 Central Ave., Ste. Anne, Man. R0A 1R0.

**DOYLE, Frank Patrick,** B.A.; retired securities industry executive; b. Hamilton, Ont. 29 Jan. 1930; s. Albert and Sara Ellen (McGrath) D.; e. Cathedral High Boys School; McMaster Univ. B.A. 1972; m. Marietta Johanna d. Emmanuel and Anna Weiser 16 Aug. 1952; children: Timothy John, Peter Jeffrey, Ellen Jane; Pres. & C.E.O., Canadian Securities Institute 1990–94, Retired; Supvr., Service Parts Purchasing, International Harvester Co. of Canada; Dir., Admin. Serv., McMaster Univ.; Sec., Investment Dealers Assn. 1979; Extve. Vice-Pres. 1980–90; recreations: golf, hiking, antique watch collecting; clubs: Ontario, Metro Toronto Bd. of Trade; Home: 77 Rockcliffe Rd., Hamilton, Ont. L9J 1B8.

**DOYLE, Kevin,** M.Sc.; editor; b. Fitzroy Harbour, Ont. 6 Feb. 1943; s. John and Teresa D.; e. Univ. of Ottawa, B.A. (Politics and Econ.) 1965; London Sch. of Econ. M.Sc. 1971; m. Marion d. James and Helen Edmonds 25 June 1970; one d. Hilary; EDITOR, MACLEAN'S MAGAZINE 1982; Gen. Reporter The Windsor Star 1965–67; Parliamentary Reporter, Ottawa Bureau, The Canadian Press 1967–70, Reporter London, Eng. (covering Asia, Europe, Africa & Middle E.) 1970–75, Washington Bureau 1975–76; Foreign and Nat. Ed. Maclean's Mag. 1976–77, Managing Editor 1977–79; Depy. Ed. 1981–82; Ed. The FP News Service 1979–80; Gen. Ed. Newsweek 1980–81; recreations: tennis, reading, classical music; Home: 10 Heather Rd., Toronto, Ont. M4G 3G3; Office: Maclean Hunter Building, 777 Bay St., Toronto, Ont. M5W 1A7.

**DOYLE, Kevin Barry,** B.Comm., M.C.I.T.; transportation executive; b. Sudbury, Ont. 14 May 1938; s. Edward Michael and Mary Irene (Bolton) D.; e. Sir George Williams Univ. B.Comm. 1967; Univ. of Syracuse, Industrial Engineering Cert.; m. Carole d. Margaret and Gordon Westerby 15 Sept. 1961; children: Karen Lynn, Kevin Brian; PRES. & CHIEF EXTVE. OFFR., SULTRAN LTD. & PACIFIC COAST TERMINALS CO. LTD. 1978– ; various transp. positions, Allied Chem. Canada Ltd. 1958–65; Mgr., Transp. & Distrib., Falconbridge Nickel Mines Ltd. 1966–70; Dir. of Transp., Canada Post Office 1970–72; Dir. of Distrib., Canpotex Ltd. 1972–76; Vice-Pres., Opns., Sultran Ltd. 1976–78; Dir., Sultran Ltd.; Pacific Coast Terminals Co. Ltd.; PDS Rail Car Services Corp.; PLM Railcar Mngt. Serv. Can. Limited; Alberta Sulphur Rsch. Limited; Sr. Assoc., Calgary Exhibition & Stampede; Home: Box 36, Site 36, R.R. #4, Calgary, Alta. T2M 4L4; Office: 2840, 205 – 5th Avenue S.W., Calgary, Alta. T2P 2V7.

**DOYLE, Michael J.;** business executive; b. Orillia, Ont. 13 Oct. 1940; s. Hugh J. and Ellen J. (O'Connel) D.; m. Sandra J. d. Anne Murray 11 Feb. 1961; children: Kimberley Anne, Donald, Kirk; PRESIDENT, AVESTA SHEFFIELD INC. CANADA 1992– ; and PRESIDENT, AVESTA WELDING PRODUCTS INC. U.S. 1987– ; active in steel industry for 30 years; Founder, Concept Metals 1971; sold company 1974; Mgr., Wilkinson Co. Steel Service Centre 1974–82; Vice-Pres. & Gen. Mgr., Axel Johnson Metals Div. 1982–84; Pres., Avesta Stainless Inc., Canada 1984–92; Owner & Pres., Dundee Golf & Country Club, Kitchener; Past Chrmn., Candn. Steel Service Centre Inst. 1990–92; Bd, Mem., Avesta Sheffield Holding Co. and Steel Service Centre Institute, U.S.; recreation: golf, tennis, travel; club: Cutten Golf; Home: 25 Manor Park Residence 4, Guelph, Ont. N1G 1A2; Office: 2140 Meadowpine Blvd., Mississauga, Ont. L5N 6H6.

**DOYLE, Peter Ronald,** B.Eng., M.Ed., P.Eng.; education consultant; b. Quebec City, Que. 5 Apl. 1930; s. Peter Emmett and Jean Orr (Robb) D.; e. McGill Univ. B.Eng. 1954; Queen's Univ. M.Ed. 1974; Mich. State Univ. doctoral studies in edn.; m. Loretta d. Joseph and Mary Foley 25 Sept. 1954; children: Maureen, Brian, Michael, John, Allan; Pres. Sault Coll. of Applied Arts & Technol. 1979–93, retired; currently pursuing a Ph.D. in Educ. Admin., Michigan State Univ., East Lansing, Mich.; profl. eng. various assignments Canadian General Electric and General Electric USA 1954–63; Mgr. Mktg. Meters & Instruments Canadian General Electric Quebec 1963–68 and Lamp Div. 1969–71; lectr. in Bus. St. Lawrence Coll. Kingston 1968–69, Acad. Chrmn. 1969, Prin. Brockville Campus 1971–77, Vice Pres. Adm. 1977–79; Dir. Ont. Idea Corp. 1986–87; Econ. Devel. Corp. of Sault Ste. Marie 1986–88; Chrmn. Ont. Ctte. Pres. Colls. Applied Arts & Technol. 1984–85; recreations: skiing, hunting; Address: P.O. Box 73, Plevna, Ont. K0H 2M0.

**DOYLE, Richard J.,** O.C. (1983); former newspaper editor; senator; b. Toronto, Ont. 10 Mar. 1923; s. James A. and Lillian (Hilts) D.; hon. LL.D., St. Francis Xavier Univ. 1981, King's Coll. Univ. 1983; m. Florence, d. late Francis Chanda, Jan. 1953; children: Kathleen Judith, Sean Gibson; summoned to The Senate March 1985; former Editor-in-Chief and Editor Emeritus, 'The Globe & Mail'; served in 2nd World War with R.C.A.F.; retired 1945 with rank of Flying Offr.; author 'Hurly-Burly: A Time at the Globe' 1989; 'The Royal Story' 1952; inducted into the Candn. News Hall of Fame 1990; United Church; Home: 36 Long Crescent, Toronto, Ont. M4E 1N6; Office: The Senate, Ottawa, Ont. K1A 0A4.

**DOYLE, Thomas Durham,** B.Sc., P.Eng.; pipeline executive; b. Kirkland Lake, Ont. 7 April 1937; s. John and Evelyn D.; e. Univ. of N.B., B.Sc. 1960; Banff Sch. of Adv. Mngt. 1966; m. Patricia d. Douglas S. Paris 1 March 1968; children: Douglas, Kindrey; EXTVE. VICE PRES., CHIEF OP. OFFR. & DIR., TRANS MOUNTAIN PIPE LINE CO. LTD. 1988– ; Pipe Line Engr., Hudson's Bay Oil & Gas Co. Limited 1960–61; Chief Construction Inspector 1961–62; District Foreman 1962–65; Supt. of Opns. 1965–68; Mgr., Pipe Line Div. 1968–74; Dir., Coal Projects 1974–78; Gen. Mgr., Minerals & Coal 1978–82; Pres., Doyle Cons. Serv. Ltd. 1982–85; Extve. Vice-Pres., Trans Mountain Pipe Line Co. Ltd. 1985–88; Extve. Vice Pres. & C.O.O. 1988– ; Dir., Trans Mountain Petroleums Ltd.; Trans Mountain Pipe Line Co. Ltd.; Candn. Energy Pipelines Assn.; Chrmn., Burrard Clean; mem., CSA, Standards Steering Ctte.; Assoc. of Profl. Engrs. of B.C. & Alta.; Candn. Heavy Oil Assn.; Am. Petroleum Inst.; recreations: sailing, golf, skiing; clubs: Royal Vancouver Yacht, Hollyburn Country; Home: 4705 Woodburn Court, W. Vancouver, B.C. V7S 3B3; Office: 900 – 1333 W. Broadway, Vancouver, B.C. V6H 4C2.

**DOYLE, Mt. Rev. Wilfred Emmett,** B.A., J.C.D. (R.C.); bishop; b. Calgary, Alberta, 18 Feb. 1913; s. John J. and Mary Anne (O'Neill) D.; e. Sacred Heart Sch., St. Joseph's High Sch., and St. Joseph's Semy., Edmonton, Alta.; Univ. of Alberta, B.A. 1935; Univ. of Ottawa, J.C.D. 1949; Asst. at St. Joseph's Cath., Edmonton, Alta., 1938–43, Asst. Chancellor, Archdiocese of Edmonton, 1938–43, and Chancellor, 1943–46 and 1949–58; Bishop of Nelson, 9 Oct. 1958 – 6 Feb. 1990; Chancellor, Notre Dame Univ., Nelson, B.C. 1963–68 and Chrmn. of Bd. of Govs. 1963–74; Bishop Emeritus of Nelson; Address: 10661 - 82 Ave., Edmonton Alta. T6E 2A6.

**DOYLE-RODRIGUE, Jocelyne,** B.A.; translator; b. Montréal, Qué. 17 Sept. 1951; d. Gabriel and Jacqueline (Lagarde) Doyle; e. Univ. de Montréal B.A. (Transl.) 1973; m. Nelson s. Roland and Liliane Rodrigue 31 May 1975; children: Philippe, Andréane; PRES. AND OWNER EXCELCOM/TRANSLEX TRANSLATION INC. 1980– ; Translator Fed. Govt. Ottawa 1973; Pres. Candn. Union Profl. & Tech. Employees 1975; Head of Transl. Service CRTC 1977; estbd. Translex Inc. 1980; Translex Toronto Inc. 1986; acquired The House of Translation Ottawa 1986 and Therrien & Rheault Montreal 1987; recipient Women's Achievement Award, Women's Business Network of Ottawa 1991; Pres., Assn. of Transl. and Interpreters of Ont.; Mem., Women's Invest. Club; Women's Bus. Network; Am. Transl. Assn.; Home: 33 St-Malo, Aylmer, Que. J9J 1J6; Office: 116 Albert St. 9th Floor, Ottawa, Ont. K1P 5G3.

**DOYON, J. Michel,** Q.C., B.A., M.A., D.E.N.S., LL.L., Ph.D.; lawyer; b. Québec 20 April 1943; s. Josaphat and Cecile (Gingras) D.; e. Laurentian Univ. B.A. 1964; Laval Univ. M.A. 1966, D.E.N.S. 1967, LL.L. 1971, Ph.D. (Hist.) 1978, Ph.D. (Phil.) sch. completed 1986; m. Pauline d. Marthe (Lagueux) and Sévère Théberge 27 Aug. 1966; children: Jean-François, Marie-Hélène; PARTNER, MESSRS. GAGNE, LETARTE, SIROIS, BEAUDET 1984– ; Lectr., Laurentian Univ. 1966; Prof., CEGEP de Ste- Foy 1967–70; called to Bar 1972; Lectr., Bar Admission Course & Bar Cont. Edn., Bar of the Prov. of Que.; Lectr., Laval Univ. 1988–93; Dir.,

Candn. Broadcasting Corp.; Les Mutuelles du Mans Canada (Assurances) inc.; L'Équitable, Compagnie d'assurances générales; Quebec Symphonic Orchestra; Pres. CBC Pension Board of Trustees; Officer of the Military and Hospitaller Order of Saint Lazarus of Jerusalem 1989, Commander of the Quebec Commandery; Past Pres., François Charon Found.; Past Dir., Le Centre d'Enseignement et de recherches en informatique Clément Lockwell; 'Fiducie Roger Demers'; Roman Catholic; Mem., Bar of the Prov. of Que.; Candn. Bar; Internat. Union of Lawyers; L'Assn. des Gens l'Air (Dir. 1979–81; Pres. 1981); ALAI Canada; Quebec Nat. and Internat. Commercial Arbitration Ctr.; author: 'Quebec, Capitale de la Neige' 1976; recreations: golf, skiing; club: Royal-Quebec Golf; Home: 1146, rue Charleroi, Ste-Foy, Que. G1W 4H7; Office: 79, Boul. St-Cyrille Est, Bureau 400, Québec, Qué. G1R 5N5.

**DRABBLE, Bernard J.,** B.A.; economic consultant; b. Eng. 1925; e. schs. Eng.; McGill Univ. B.A. (Hon. Econ.); entered Bank of Canada 1947, holding various positions up to Depy. Gov. 1974–81; Extve. Dir. for Can., Ireland and others International Monetary Fund, Washington, D.C. 1974–81; Assoc. Depy. Min. of Finance, Can. 1981–87; Home: 2406 – 400 Stewart St., Ottawa, Ont. K1N 6L2.

**DRABBLE, Margaret (Holroyd),** B.A., C.B.E.; writer; b. Sheffield, U.K. 5 June 1939; d. John Frederick Drabble and Kathleen Marie (Bloor) D.; e. Mount Sch. York; Newnham Coll., Cambridge Univ. B.A. (Hons.) 1960; m. Michael s. Basil and Vlla H. 14 Sept. 1982; children (from 1st marriage): Adam, Rebecca, Joseph Swift; novelist, critic, editor; Hon. D.Litt. Sheffield; Hon. Fellow, Manchester Bradford Bard Coll.; F.R.S.L., Sheffield Polytech.; Patron, Child Psychotherapy Trust 1988– ; Founder & Memn., Charter 88 1988; author: 'A Summer Birdcage' 1963 and 11 other works of fiction incl. 'The Radiant Way' 1985, 'A Natural Curiosity' 1987, 'The Gates of Ivory' 1991; editor: 5th ed., 'Oxford Companion to English Literature' recreations: walking, talking; Office: c/o Peters, Fraser & Dunlop, Fifth Floor, The Chambers, Chelsea Harbour, London SW10 OXF, England.

**DRABEK, Jan,** B.A.; writer; b. Prague, Czechoslovakia 5 May 1935; s. Jaroslav and Jarmila (Kucera) D.; e. American Univ. Washington, D.C., B.A. 1960; m. Joan M. d. Norman M. and Jean S. Sanders 24 Oct. 1964; two d. Katherine M., Alexandra J.; AMBASSADOR OF THE CZECH REPUBLIC TO THE REPUBLIC OF KENYA 1992– ; Chrmn., Ctte. of Permanent Representatives to the United Nations Environment Programme in Nairobi 1994– ; (Vice-Chrmn. 1992–94); Chrmn., author (fiction) 'Whatever Happened to Wenceslas' 1975; 'Report on the Death of Rosenkavalier' 1977; 'The Lister Legacy' 1980; 'The Statement' 1982; 'The Exotic Canadians' 1990; (non-fiction) 'Blackboard Odyssey' 1973; 'The Golden Revolution' 1989; 'Thirteen' 1991; (children's) 'Melvin the Weather Moose' 1976; former refugee resettlement offr., broadcaster, travel clk., high sch. teacher; freelance writer since 1976; Past Chrmn. Fedn. B.C. Writers; Past Chrmn. B.C. Caucus Writers Union Can.; Address: The Embassy of the Czech Republic, P.O. Box 48785, Nairobi, Kenya.

**DRABINSKY, Garth Howard,** LL.B.; lawyer; entrepreneur; b. Toronto, Ont. 27 Oct. 1948; s. Philip D.; e. N. Toronto Coll. Inst.; Univ. of Toronto LL.B. 1973; m. Pearl, d. Harry Kaplan 22 June 1971; children: Alicia Monica, Marc Lorne; CHRMN., LIVE ENTERTAINMENT OF CANADA INC. (LIVENT); called to Ont. Bar 1975; law practice Thomson, Rogers 1975–78; Producer motion pictures: 'The Silent Partner' (Cdn. Film Award Best Picture 1978) 1977, 'The Changeling' (Cdn. Film Award Best Picture 1980) 1979, 'Tribute' (Jack Lemmon Acad. Award nomination Best Actor 1981); Chrmn., LIVENT, which operates the Pantages Theatre (Toronto) and which has produced 'Phantom of the Opera,' 'Aspects of Love,' 'Joseph and the Amazing Technicolor Dreamcoat,' 'The Music of Andrew Lloyd Webber,' 'Love and Anger,' 'Out There Tonight,' 'Me and My Girl,' 'Cabaret'; LIVENT produced the acclaimed musical version of 'Kiss of the Spider Woman' (the Broadway production rec'd. seven 1993 Tony Awards incl. 'Best Musical' and was the recipient of both the Drama Desk and the New York Drama Critics' Circle Awards for 'Best Musical'); LIVENT manages and operates the new North York Performing Arts Centre, opening Oct. 1993 with a new production of 'Show Boat'; Mem. Bd. of Dirs.: The Actors Studio Inc. (New York); American Cinematheque (Los Angeles); Trustee (and Mem. Second Decade Counc.), American Film Inst. (Los Angeles); Mem., Acad. of Motion Picture Arts and Sciences (Los Angeles); Mem. Bd. of Dirs., Mt. Sinai Hosp. (Toronto); Mem. Bd. of Govs., Baycrest Ctr. for Geriatric Care (Toronto); Mem. Adv. Bd., Ctr. for Rsch. in Neurodegenerative Diseases, Univ. of Toronto; recipient, Heart of Variety Award, Variety Club of Gter. Washington 1989; B'nai B'rith Internat. Distinguished Achievement Award 1989; Nat. Assn. of Theatre Owner's (NATO) ShoWest award as The Industry's Consummate Showman 1988; named 'The Renaissance Man of Film,' Montreal World Film Festival 1987; recipient, Vanier Award, Can. 1987; Air Canada Award for Outstanding Contribution to the Business of Filmmaking in Canada 1987; Lifetime Achievement Award, The Canada California Chamber of Comm. 1987; Hon. Fellowship, Ryerson Polytechnical Inst., Toronto 1987; Award for Marketing Excellence, Am. Mktg. Assn. 1986; Chetwynd Award for Entrepreneurial Achievement, Cdn. Film & Television Assn. 1986; author 'Motion Pictures and the Arts in Canada: The Business and the Law' 1976; mem. Cdn. Bar Assn.; Co. York Law Assn.; mem., Founder's Council of the Candn. Film Centre; recreations: sailing, squash, motion pictures, theatre, music, collecting Cdn. art; Office: 165 Avenue Rd., Toronto, Ont. M5R 2H7.

**DRACHE, Arthur Barry C.,** Q.C., LL.M.; lawyer; writer; b. Winnipeg, Man. 1 Nov. 1939; s. Samuel Joshua and Marjory (Tadman) D.; e. Brandeis Univ. B.A. 1961; Univ. of Toronto LL.B. 1966; Harvard Univ. LL.M. 1968; m. Sharon d. Murray and Edythe Abron 20 Dec. 1965 (divorced); m. 2ndly, Judy Young 1 Nov. 1992; children: Deborah, Ruth, Joshua, Mordecai; LAWYER, FRASER & BEATTY (Ottawa, Ont.) 1990– ; Partner, Drache, Rotenberg 1976–90; Prof. of Law Queen's Univ. 1969–73; Chief, Personal Tax Sect. Dept. Finance Ottawa 1972–76; Pres. Audrac Information Services Inc.; Lectr. in Law, Queen's Univ.; Past Lectr. in Law, Univ. of Ottawa; cr. Q.C. 1983; Nat. Bus. Writing Award 1977; Dir. Jack Chambers Meml. Found.; Ethos Cultural Found.; St. Boniface Hosp. Rsch. Found.; author: 'Deferred Income Plans' 1977; 'Tax Tactics' 1979; 'The Great Tax Rip-Off' 1982; 'It's Your Future' 1983; 'Taxation and the Arts' 1987; 'Canadian Taxation of Charities' 1987; 'Dollars and Sense' 1987; co-author: 'Head and Heart' 1987; ed.: 'The Canadian Taxpayer'; 'The Canadian Tax Planning Service'; 'Non-Share Capital Corporations'; 'Canadian Not-For-Profit News'; over 900 articles; contbg. ed. 'Financial Post' 1978– ; mem. Candn. Bar Assn.; Candn. Tax Found.; Internat. Fiscal Assn.; recreation: reading; Club: Le Cercle Universitaire d'Ottawa; Home: 21 McLeod St., Ottawa, Ont. K2P 0Z4; Office: Ste. 1200, 180 Elgin St., Ottawa, Ont. K2P 2K7.

**DRACHE, Sharon Abron,** B.A.; writer; b. Toronto, Ont. 22 March 1943; d. Murray and Edythe Claire (Levinter) Abron; e. Univ. of Toronto, B.A. 1965, Dip. C.S. 1966; m. Arthur B.C. s. Samuel J. and Marjory Drache 20 Dec. 1965 (divorced, June 1990); children: Deborah, Ruth, Joshua, Mordecai; psychometrician, Ont. Crippled Children's Centre Toronto 1966–68; freelance book reviewer since 1980 various newspapers incl. The Globe and Mail, The Ottawa Citizen, Whig-Standard and The Jerusalem Post (Israel); Book Review Ed., Ottawa Jewish Bulletin 1980–90; regular book columnist The Glebe Report (Ottawa) 1980– ; Instr. in Anglo-Jewish Writing in Can. Carleton Univ. 1984–85; Writer-in-Residence Port Hope (Ont.) Pub. Lib. 1987; Trustee, Ottawa Pub. Lib. 1986–89; author: 'The Mikveh Man' (short stories) 1984; 'Ritual Slaughter' (novel) 1989; 'The Golden Ghetto' (short stories) 1993; ed. bd. Viewpoints Mag. 1981–82, Candn. Jewish Cong. Montréal; Nat. Extve., The Writers' Union of Can. 1988–90; Address: 29 Clemow Ave., Ottawa, Ont. K1S 2B1.

**DRAINIE, Bronwyn Deborah Ann,** M.A.; writer; journalist; radio and television broadcaster; b. Toronto, Ont. 8 June 1945; d. John Robert Roy and Claire Paula (Wodlinger) D.; e. Whitney and Rosedale Pub. Schs., Jarvis Coll. Inst., Toronto; Univ. of Toronto B.A. 1967, M.A. 1969; m. Patrick Allen Martin 1980; two sons: Gabriel Dunbar Martin, Samuel John Martin; FREELANCE WRITER 1985– ; Researcher, CJOH TV Ottawa 1969–70; Story Producer 'Weekday' CBLT Toronto 1970–71; Student Counsellor, Scarborough Coll. Univ. of Toronto 1971–73; writing and language study, Crete, Greece 1973–74; B.B.C. and C.B.C. Radio London Eng. 1974–75; C.B.C. announcer, Toronto 1975–85, incl. 'World at 6,' 'World at 8,' 'Identities,' 'Offstage Voices,' 'Celebration,' 'New Releases,' 'Anthology'; Host of C.B.C. Radio 'Sunday Morning' 1976–81 (ACTRA Award, Best Host-Interviewer on Radio 1980); freelance writer 1985– , incl. articles for 'Saturday Night,' 'Toronto Life,' 'Report on Business Magazine,' 'Chatelaine,' 'London Magazine', Globe & Mail book reviews, 'Books in Canada', 'Canadian Forum'; National Arts Columnist, Globe and Mail, 1989–91, 1993– ; T.V. book panelist, 'The Journal,' C.B.C. 1988–91; T.V. book critic, 'TVO Imprints,' T.V.O. 1989–91; recipient, Nat. Magazine Award (gold) in Service Journalism for 'Happier Endings' Toronto Life 1987; author 'Living the Part: John Drainie and the Dilemma of Canadian Stardom' 1988 (Ann Saddlemyer Book Prize 1988); Home: Toronto, Canada.

**DRAKE, John J.,** M.A., M.Sc., Ph.D.; educator; b. Maidstone, Kent, Eng. 3 Feb. 1947; s. Frederick John and Joan Beatrice (Vaizey) D.; e. Chatham House Grammar Sch. 1964; Oxford Univ. B.A. 1968, M.A. 1972; McMaster Univ. M.Sc. 1970, Ph.D. 1974; m. Pamela d. Walter (Ike) and Ethel Iredale 6 Feb. 1970, separated 1990; two s. Paul, Tom; PROF. OF GEOG. MCMASTER UNIV. 1986– , Asst. Vice Pres. Info. Serv. & Tech. 1987– ; Asst. Prof. of Geog. McGill Univ. 1973, Assoc. Prof. 1978–79, Sci. Dir. Subarctic Rsch. Lab. 1978–79; Assoc. Prof. present Univ. 1979; Chair, ONet Management Bd.; mem. Water Mgmt. Bd.; Hamilton Region Conserv. Authority; Past mem. and Chrmn. Dundas Community Services; co-ed. 'Steel City' 1987; author or co-author over 50 sci. articles; Home: 57 East St. N., Dundas, Ont. L9H 1P2.

**DRAKULIC, Slobodan,** B.A., M.A.; research associate; b. Zagreb, Croatia 29 Nov. 1947; s. Nikola and Zagorka (Avdalovic) D.; e. Univ. of Zagreb B.A. 1975, M.A. 1979; children: Rujana, Justin; RESEARCH ASSOC., CENTRE FOR RUSSIAN AND EAST EUROPEAN STUDIES, UNIV. OF TORONTO 1991– ; Sociology & Anthropology Teacher, Univ. of Rijeka 1975–80; Univ. of Zagreb 1980–86; Mem., Presidency, Sociological Soc. of Croatia 1978–86; freelance lecturer on ethnic relations, specifically on the breakup of Yugoslavia; author: 'Education and Order' 1981 and numerous academic and popular articles; co-author: 'Urban Guerrilla in Italy 1979–1980' 1983, 'Formation and Development of Ideological Orientation of Youth in Rijeka' 1978, 'Ideological Orientations and Practical Preoccupations of Students of Rijeka'1978; Home: 48 Garnock Ave., Toronto, Ont. M4K 1M2; Office: 140 St. George St., Toronto, Ont. M5S 1A1.

**DRANCE, Stephen Michael,** O.C., M.D., F.R.C.S.; ophthalmic surgeon; b. Bielsko, Poland 22 May 1925; s. George Henry and Ida (Berger) C.; e. Univ. of Edinburgh, M.B. Ch.B. 1948, M.D. (Clin. Med.) 1949; Coll. of Surgs. of Eng., Dipl. of Ophthal. 1953; m. Betty Joan, d. Fred Palmer, Stamford, Eng., Jan. 1952; children: Jonathan Stephen, Michael George, Elisabeth Joan; PROF. & PAST HEAD OF OPHTHAL., UNIV. OF BRIT. COLUMBIA; past mem., Med. Research Council; Past Chrmn., Sci. Adv. Comte., B.C. Health Sciences Research Found.; Research Asst. Ophthal., Oxford Univ. 1955–57; Asst. Prof. and Assoc. Prof., Univ. of Sask. 1957–63; joined present Univ. as Assoc. Prof. 1963; served with RAF Med. Service, rank Sqdn. Leader; former Ed., 'Canadian Journal of Ophthalmology'; past Council mem., Candn. Ophthal. Soc. (past Pres.); rec'd McKenzie Medal, Glasgow Univ. 1971; Stewart Lectr., Dalhousie Univ. 1974; Doyne Medal, Oxford Ophthal. Cong. 1975; Spaeth Medal, Philadelphia 1977; Richardson Cross Medal, S.W. England Soc. Ophthalmology 1980; Bedell Lectr. Philadelphia 1981; Wright Lectr. Toronto 1983; Irvine Lectr., Los Angeles 1984; Shafer Lectr., Am. Acad. Ophth., Atlanta 1984; Proctor Lectr., San Francisco 1984; Frosst Lectr., Australia/New Zealand 1985; Duke Elder Medal, Soc. Contemporary Ophthalmol. 1986; Ida Mann Lectr., Oxford 1986; Gifford Lectr., Chicago 1987; Phelps Lectr., Iowa City 1987; Adler Lectr., Philadelphia 1988; Officer, Order of Canada 1987; A.E. McDonald Award for Prevention in Blindness 1987; Semi Centennial Honor Award, Candn. Ophthalmological Soc. 1987; Hon. Fellow, The Royal Australian Coll. of Ophthalmol. 1988; Hon. Pres., XXVII Internat. Congress of Ophthalmology, Can. 1994; Jean Lacerte Lecture, Que. 1990; A.J. Elliot Lectr., Vancouver 1990; Demorest Lect., Sacremento 1990; Krieger Lecture, Baltimore 1990; Schoenberg Lectr., Univ. of Chicago 1991; Bowman Lectr., Coll. of Ophthalmologists, U.K. 1992; Sir Norman Gregg Lect., Royal Australian Coll. of Ophthalmologists 1992; Past Vice-Pres. Amer. Academy Ophthalm.; Past Pres. Internat. Perimetric Soc.; Past Pres. Internat. Glaucoma Soc.; Liberal; recreations: swimming, music, cartography; Home: 1561 Wesbrook Cr., Vancouver, B.C. V6T 1V9.

**DRANOFF, Linda Silver,** B.A., LL.B.; lawyer; b. Toronto, Ont. 14 Oct. 1939; d. Joseph J. and Ethel (Rubenstein) Silver; e. Univ. of Toronto Hons. B.A. (History) 1961; Osgoode Hall Law Sch. York Univ. LL.B. 1972; called to Ont. Bar 1974; m. Jack Marmer 27 May 1990; one d. Beth; PRIN., LINDA SILVER DRANOFF AND ASSOCIATES specializing in family law 1974– ; counsel on a number of precedent-setting family law decisions; spearheaded drive for revised family laws in particular those laws providing for equal sharing of all matrimonial property between husband and wife (Family Law Act passed by Govt. of Ont. 1986); mem. Ont. Status of Women Council, Exec. 1979–82, Vice Chairperson 1980–82; guest speaker numerous profl. and pub. panels and confs.; frequent radio and TV appearances on legal and community issues; Instr. in Family Law Bar Admission Course Law Soc. Upper Can. 1978–83; legal adv. CITY TV's City Line phone-in advice show 1985– ; recipient, Ont. Award for Distinguished Service, Candn. Bar Assn. 1993; author 'Women in Canadian Law' (a history) 1977; 'Every Woman's Guide to the Law' 1985; columnist, legal questions, Chatelaine mag. 1979– ; guest columnist Toronto Star and other newspapers and mags. on contemporary legal, political, and women's issues; Chair, Feminist Legal Analysis Section, Can. Bar (Ont.); mem., Candn. Bar Assn.; County of York Law Assoc.; Candn. Coalition on the Constitution; Counc. of Canadians; Candn. Civil Liberties Assoc.; Women's Law Assn. Ont.; Nat. Assn. Women & Law; Osgoode Soc.; Lawyers for Social Responsibility; ACTRA; Women in Educational Administration (Adv. Bd.); Planned Parenthood (Hon. Dir.); Club: McGill; Office: 314, 1033 Bay St., Toronto, Ont. M5S 3A5.

**DRAPEAU, Arnold J.,** B.Sc.A.; Dipl. Bact.; professor; b. East-Angus, Qué. 5 Aug. 1928; s. Arthur and Albertine (Tardif) D.; e. École Sup. de Sherbrooke 1949; Univ. Laval, B.Sc.A. 1954; Univ. of Toronto, Dipl. Bact. 1960; m. Denyse d. Aimé Paquet 9 Oct. 1954; one s.: Serge; PROF., ÉCOLE POLYTECHNIQUE DE MONTRÉAL 1967–92, retired; Merck Sharp & Dohme 1954–57; Aluminum Co. of Can. 1957–58; Min. de la Santé du Qué. 1958–67; Am. Water Works Assn. 'Fuller Award' 1978; Fed. of Assns. of Candn. Environ. 'Face Award' 1978; Assn. Can.-Fran. pour l'avancement des sci. 'Sciences de l'Eau Award' 1985; Sovereign Military Order of Saint John of Jerusalem, Knights of Malta 'Knight of Merit' 1986; 'Ordre des Francophones d'Amérique Award' du Conseil de la langue française 1988; Bd. Mem., Assn. Lavalloise de parents pour le bien-être mental; author: 'Manuel de microbiologie de l'environnement' WHO 1977, 'La langue d'usage dans les communications et les publications des chercheurs d'institutions francophones du Québec' 1985 and 90 articles and num. interviews, confs., TV & radio broadcasts; Mem., Ed. Bd.: 'Sciences de l'eau' 1984–90; initiateur de ce que l'on appelle 'l'Affaire de l'Institut Pasteur'; recreations: dancing, reading; Home: 2495 boul. de Blois, Laval, Qué. H7E 1P8.

**DRAPEAU, Jean,** C.C., (1967), C.R., B.A., L.Sc.Soc. Econ. Pol., LL.D.; né Montréal, Qué. 18 fév. 1916; é. Ecole Jean-de-Brébeuf; Le Plateau; Univ. de Montréal, L. Sc. Soc. Econ. Po., 1937; B.A., 1938; LL.B. 1941; D.Hon., Univ. de Moncton, 1956; Univ. de Montréal, 1964; Univ McGill, 1965; Univ Loyola, Nouvelle-Orléans, 1966; Univ. Sir G. Williams et Laval, 1967; marié, 3 enfants; admis au Barreau de Montréal, 1943; nommé C.R., 1961; maire de Montréal 1954–57; réélu maire de Montréal, 1960, 1962, 1966, 1970, 1974, 1978 et 1982; nommé Ambassadeur, Délégué permanent du Canada auprès de l'UNESCO à Paris de 1987 à 1991; oeuvres: Place des Arts, le Métro, Expo '67; C'est également grâce à son esprit de persévérance et de travail que la Ville de Montréal a été choisie comme lieu des Jeux Olympiques d'été de 1976; mem.: Am. Bar Assn. (hon.); autres assoc. nat. et internat.; trophée des Min. du Comm. et Indust. des dix prov. du Can. au can. ayant le plus contribué au dévelop. indust. du Can., 1965; Médaille d'Or, Inst. Royal d'Architect. du Can., 1967; Compagnon de l'Ordre du Can., 1967; représ. du Can. au Bur. Internat. des Expos. à Paris, 1967–71; commandeur dans l'Ordre de la Légion d'Honneur (France) 1984; Grand officier de l'Ordre national du Québec 1987; Adresse: 5700, av. des Plaines, Montréal, Que. H1T 2X1.

**DRAY, William Herbert,** M.A., D. Phil., F.R.S.C.; university professor (retired); b. Montréal, Qué. 23 June 1921; s. William John and Florence Edith (Jones) D.; e. Rosedale Pub. Sch. and West Hill High Sch. Montréal 1938; Univ. of Toronto B.A. 1949; Oxford Univ. B.A. 1951, M.A. 1955, D. Phil. 1956; m. Doris Kathleen d. Gilbert Best, Toronto, Ont. 18 Sept. 1943; children: Christopher Reid, Jane Elizabeth; Lect. in philosophy, Univ. of Toronto 1953–55; Asst. Prof. 1956–61; Assoc. Prof. 1961–63; Prof. 1963–68; Prof., Trent Univ. 1968–76 and Chrmn. of Dept., 1968–73; Prof., Univ. of Ottawa 1976–85; Prof. Emeritus 1986– ; Visiting Prof., Case Inst. of Tech. 1966–67, Duke Univ. 1973–74; served with RCAF 1941–46, Air Navig. Can. W. Indies UK S.E. Asia, RCAF (R) 1956–66, Wing Commdr.; author 'Laws and Explanation in History' 1957; 'Philosophy of History' 1964, 2nd ed. 1993; 'Perspectives on History' 1980; 'On History and Philosophers of History' 1989; ed. 'Philosophical Analysis and History' 1966; co-ed., 'Substance and Form in History' 1981; 'Philosophie de l'histoire et la pratique historienne d'aujourd'hui' 1982; numerous articles in learned journals on philos. of hist., mind, action and social sciences; mem. Royal Society of Canada; Candn. Hist. Assn.; mem. Ed. Bd., 'History and Theory,' 'Philosophy of the Social Sciences'; Ed. Advis., 'Clio' and 'Metaphilosophy'; ACLS Fellow 1960–61; Killam Fellow 1980–81; National Humanities Center Fellow 1983–84; Molson Prize, Canada Counc. 1986; Hon. LL.D., Trent Univ. 1987; Home: 32 Clarissa Dr., Apt. 818, Richmond Hill, Ont. L4C 9R7.

**DRAYCOTT, Anita Lynn,** B.A.; magazine editor; b. Toronto, Ont. 16 May 1949; d. Clifford and Eileen May (Sloan) D.; e. East York C.I. 1968; Victoria Coll., Univ. of Toronto 1972; m. William Orr 11 Dec. 1981; EDITOR, CITY & COUNTRY HOME 1984– ; Editor, Teen Generation 1978–82; Program Guide 1982–84; club: Victoria Tennis; Home: 222 Cortleigh Blvd., Toronto, Ont.; Office: 777 Bay St., 8th Floor, Toronto, Ont. M5W 1A7.

**DREA, Hon. James Francis,** B.A., L.H.D.; former politician; b. St. Catharines, Ont. 7 July 1933; s. John Thompson and Joan Lavene (McCarthy) D.; e. Canisius Coll. Buffalo; m. Jeanne Elizabeth d. William Campbell, New Toronto, Ont. 22 Oct. 1955; children: Catherine Elizabeth, Denise Margaret, Kevin John; CHRMN., ONT. RACING COMMISSION 1986– ; Min. of Community & Social Services, Ont. 1981–85; journalist; rec'd Heywood Broun Award for Crusading Journalism 1961; mem. Nat. Comte. Cath. Social Life Conf. 1963–65; Internat. Rep. Un. Steelworkers Am. 1963–65; Vice Pres. and Dir. Candn. Register 1967–69; Vice Chrmn. Bd. of Review Ont. Dept. Social & Family Services 1969–72; Pres. Candn. Soc. Prof. Journalists 1970–72; Founding Dir. Credit Counselling Service Toronto; Dir. Candn. Scene; el. M.P.P. for Scarborough Centre prov. g.e. 1971, re-el. until 1981 (did not contest 1985 el.); Parlty. Asst. to Min. of Consumer & Comm. Relations 1974; Min. of Correctional Services 1977; Min. of Consumer & Comm. Relations 1978; P. Conservative; R. Catholic; Office: 14th Floor, 180 Dundas St. W., Toronto, Ont. M5G 1Z8.

**DREIMANIS, Aleksis,** D.Sc., D.geogr., F.R.S.C.; university professor; geologist; consultant; b. Valmiera, Latvia 13 Aug. 1914; s. Peteris and Marta Eleonora (Leitis) D.; e. Latvian Univ., Mag. rer nat. 1938, habilitation 1942; Univ. of Waterloo, D.Sc. 1969; Univ. of W. Ont., D.Sc. 1980; D.Geogr., Univ. of Latvia 1991; m. Anita, d. late Rudolfs Kana, 18 Apl. 1942; children: Mara Love, M.D., Aija Downing, M.A.; Assist.-Lectr.-Privatdocent, Inst. of Geol., Univ. of Latvia, Riga, 1937–44; Consultant, Inst. of Mineral Resources (Z.B.P.I.) of Latvia, 1942–44; Mil. Geol., Latvian Legion, 1944–45; Assoc. Prof. Baltic Univ., Hamburg and Pinneberg, 1946–48; Lectr. to Prof., Dept. of Geol., Univ. of W. Ont., 1948–80; Prof. Emeritus 1980–; Consultant on Pleistocene Geol. and Ground Water for various Candn. and U.S. Govt. agencies and private co.'s; mem. Candn. Nat. Adv. Comte. on Research in Geol. Sciences and Chrmn. of its sub-comte. on Quaternary Geol., 1967–72; Candn. Del.to Internat. Geol. Cong. 1960 and to Congress Internat. Assn. Quaternary Research 1965, 69, 73, 77, 82; Assoc. Ed., Geosciences Canada 1976–78, Quaternary Sci. Reviews 1981–87, Technical Reviews (in Latvian) 1978– ; served with Latvian Army 1939–40 and Latvian Legion 1944–45; rank 2nd Lt.; rec'd Kr. Barons' Prize 1935; Latvian Univ. Gold Medal 1936; Centennial Medal 1967; Silver Jubilee Medal, 1977; Hon. Award, Latvian Cultural Foundation 1977; Logan Medal 1978; Teaching Award of Ont. Confed. of Univ. Fac. Assoc. 1978; Centennial Medal of Geological Survey of Finland 1986; Distinguished Career Award, Quaternary Geology and Geomophology Div., Geol. Soc. of Am. 1987; Albrecht Penck Medal, German Quaternary Assoc. (DEUQUA) 1988; W.A. Johnston Medal, Candn. Quaternary Assoc. (CANQUA) 1989; author, 'Latvijas minerali un iezi' 1942; other writings incl. about 200 scient. publs. mainly in Pleistocene and glacial geol.; mem. London Latvian Soc. (Pres. since 1948); fraternity 'Lidums' (Pres. 1935–36, editor of its newsletter 'Teicejs' 1969– ;); Royal Soc. of Can.; Latvian Acad. of Sciences (foreign mem.); Geographical Soc. of Latvia (Hon. Mem. since 1990); Assoc. of Latvian Geologists (Hon. Mem. since 1991); Internat. Union for Quaternary Rsch. (INQUA: Hon. Mem. since 1987); Geol. Assn. Can.; Geol. Soc. Am.; Soc. Econ. Paleontol. & Mineralog.; Geol. Soc. Finland (Correspond. Member); Geol. Soc. in Stockholm (Correspond. Member); Estonian Geological Soc.; Baltic Research Inst. (Correspond. Member); Assn. for Advanc. of Baltic Studies; Latvian Nat. Fedn. in Can. (Chrm., Counc. 1953–71, Hon. Mem. since 1972); Latvian Cultural Found. (Extve. Ctte. 1973–77); Latvian Am. Assn. of Univ. Profs. and Scientists (Vice-Pres. 1982–83; Pres. 1983–85); Quaternary Res. Assn.; AMQUA (Am. Quatenary Assn.) Councilor 1974–78, Pres.-elect 1978–80, Pres. 1980–82; Candn. Quaternary Assn.; Pres. of INQUA (Internat. Union for Quaternary Research) Comm. on Genesis and Lithology of Quaternary Deposits 1973–87; leader, Can. Work Group, IGCP Project 24, 1975–82; recreation: photography, gardening, travel; Home: 287 Neville Dr., London, Ont. N6G 1C2.

**DREMAN, I.J.,** investment broker; b. Winnipeg, Man. 3 June 1910; s. Israel Jacob and Lea Yetta (Stark) D.; e. St. John's Tech. Sch.: m. Rae, d. Michael Trojan, 17 Feb. 1935; children: David Nasaniel, Prof. Solomon Bernard, Sherrill Elaine Hershberg; PRESIDENT, DREMAN & CO. LTD. (Estbd. 1919); Pres., Hartford Investments Ltd. since 1963; Gov., Winnipeg Grain Exchange; joined Campbell Grain Co. Ltd., Winnipeg, Man. in July 1928 becoming Mgr. in 1929; joined North West Commission Co. Ltd. in 1932; became a member of Winnipeg Grain Exchange in 1937 and apptd. Pres. of North West Commission Co. Ltd. in 1951 (engaged entirely in grain business); el. an Assoc. mem. of Winnipeg Stock Exchange in 1957 and a full mem. in 1960; mem. of Winnipeg Clearing House Assn. (1951); former Pres. of Winnipeg Commodity Futures Brokers Assn. (for 18 yrs.); Pres., Hartford Investments Ltd.; Chairman of B'Nai B'rith Fresh Air Camp ($150,000) Campaign, Winnipeg; assisted in campaigns of Winnipeg Crippled Children's Soc. and Univ. of Manitoba Bldg. Fund; Dir., Winnipeg Talmud Torah; Chess Fed. of Can.; Mammonides Coll.; Shaarey Zedek Sch.; Candn. Foundation; mem., Winnipeg Grain & Produce Clearing Assn. Ltd.; Hebrew; recreations: chess, golf, travelling; Club: Glendale Country; Home:600 Queenston St., Winnipeg, Man. R3N 0X5; Office: 6th Floor, 238 Portage Ave., Winnipeg, Man. R3C 0B1.

**DRENNAN, Joseph Albert,** B.A.Sc., P.Eng.; retired utilities executive; b. Duncan, B.C. 24 Oct. 1931; s. Joseph Francis and Edith (Ramsey) D.; e. Duncan H.S. 1950; Univ. of B.C., B.A.Sc. 1956; Banff Sch. Advanced Mgmt. 1971; m. Roberta d. Jim and Florence Ferguson Feb. 1960; three d. Theresa, Katherine, Joanne; Pres., C.E.O. & Dir., West Kootenay Power Ltd. 1980–93, Retired; joined B.C. Power Comn. and B.C. Hydro 1956–66; joined present co. 1966 serving as Supt. Resources, Mgr. Resources, Vice Pres. and Gen. Mgr., Pres. & C.E.O. 1980; Dir. Northwest Electric Light & Power Assn.; Dir., Candn. Electrical Assn.; Office: 1290 Esplanade, Trail, B.C. V1R 4T2.

**DREW, Stephen A.W.,** B.A., B.Sc., Ph.D.; university professor; b. Norwich, U.K. 13 Mar. 1948; s. David Ralph and Simone Josephine (Bosmans) D.; e. Trinity Coll., Cambridge Univ. B.A. 1970, Ph.D. 1976; London Univ. B.Sc. 1978; children: Daniel, Maya; PROF., FAC. OF BUSINESS, MCMASTER UNIV. 1990– ; Shell Internat. (London & Amsterdam) 1975–82; Bell Northern Rsch. 1982–83; Ernst & Whinney 1983–84; Internat. Treas., Bank of Montreal 1984–88; Ryerson Polytech. Inst. 1988–90; Pres., Daimyo Inc.; Pres., Toronto Chapter, Planning Forum 1990–91; Mem., Acad. of Management; Acad. of Internat. Business; recreations: tennis, sailing; Home: 25 Maitland St., Ste. 1505, Toronto, Ont. M4Y 2W1; Office: 1280 Main St. W., Hamilton, Ont. L8S 4L8.

**DRIEDGER, Jake,** B.Comm.; banker; b. Saskaton, Sask. 7 Nov. 1940; s. Helen Green; e. Univ. of Sask. B.Comm. (Hons. & Distinction) 1973; m. Lily Agar 21 July 1984; children: Darren, Deanna, Colleen, Cindy; VICE-PRESIDENT, LENDING – ONT., ROYAL BANK OF CANADA 1992– ; RCAF Reserve, 5 years; joined Royal Bank in Saskatchewan 1960; various branch positions 1960–69; awarded Univ. Scholarship 1969; seconded to a multinat. consortium bank, Nassau, Bahamas 1975; transferred to Head Office Montreal 1978; Vice-Pres. 1981; var. comm. & corp. extve. lending positions 1981–89; Vice-Pres. & Mgr., Toronto, Bloor & Yonge Corp. Banking Ctr. 1989–92; Muir Scholarship; Fellow, Inst. of Candn. Bankers; recreations: golf, swimming; clubs: Credit Valley Golf, Fitness Inst.; Home: 1042 Veroli Court, Mississauga, Ont. L5H 4B9; Office: 1100 Burloak Dr., 2nd Floor, Burlington, Ont. L7L 6B2.

**DRIEDGER, Otto H.,** B.A., M.S.W.; educator; b. Osler, Sask. 11 Jan. 1932; s. Cornelius M. and Maria (Pauls) D.; e. Candn. Mennonite Bible Coll. Winnipeg B.Ch.Ed. 1952; Bethel Coll. Kans. B.A. 1953; Paedogogische Akademie Wuppertal, W. Germany Educ.

Dipl. 1954; McGill Univ. M.S.W. 1958; m. Florence d. Jake Hooge 10 Oct. 1954; children: Joan Louise Grace, Karen Ruth; PROF. OF SOCIAL WORK, UNIV. OF REGINA 1986– ; Consultation to Odessa, Ukraine on development of social services and social work education 1991– ; Social Worker 1954–56, 1958–61; Dir. Swift Current Regional Office Prov. Social Services 1961–65; Dir. of Child Welfare Prov. of Sask. 1965–68; Extve. Dir. Institutional Services Sask. 1968–71; Assoc. Prof. of Social Work present Univ. 1971–75, Dir. Sch. of Human Justice 1975–80; Dean of Social Work 1980–86; Prof. of Social Work, Univ. of Regina 1986– ; Consultant, NWT Dept. Social Services 1974, 1981; Candn. Assn. in Support of Native Peoples 1976–79; Sask. Dept. Social Services 1971–83; recipient Queen's Silver Jubilee Medal 1977; Moderator, Conf. Mennonites Sask. 1970–73; Bd. mem. Candn. Council on Social Devel. 1975–81; Bd. mem. John Howard Soc. 1970–78, Chrmn. 1974; Bd. Mem., MCC Can. 1980–89; Extve. Ctte. mem., MCC Can. 1986–89; Pres., Inter-Faith Ctte. on Chaplaincy of the Correctional Service of Canada 1990– ; (Extve. Ctte. mem. 1986–90); author of book chapter 'Development of Social Work Education in the Commonwealth of Independent States' in the International Handbook on Social Work Education (edited by T.D. Watts) 1992; co-author (with Florence Driedger) 'Social Policy and Service in the Chaco (Paraguay) Mennonite Communities' 1986; co-author 'Corrections: An Historical Perspective of the Saskatchewan Experience' 1981; recreations: reading, skiing, fishing; Home: 3833 Montague St., Regina, Sask. S4S 3J6; Office: College West Bldg., Regina, Sask. S4S 0A2.

**DRINKWATER, William Stanley,** B.J.; retired Canadian civil servant; b. Toronto, Ont. 23 May 1921; s. (late) William and Ellen (Duckworth) D.; e. Scarborough Coll. Inst., Ont.; Carleton Univ., B.J. 1949; m. June Mary, d. late Kenneth and Irene (Dell) Goudie, 22 May 1948; children: David, Dulce; Editor, 'Labour Gazette,' Dept. of Labour 1958–64; Chief, Publications Div., Dept. of Labour 1964–78; with Ottawa 'Citizen' 1940–41, 1946–49; Editor, 'Teamwork in Industry' (Dept. of Labour) 1950–51; Asst. Editor, 'Labour Gazette' 1951–58; served in R.C.A.S.C. 1941–46, 1949–50; mem., Prof. Inst. of Public Service of Can. (Editor of 'Professional Public Service' 1958–61); Chrmn., Publicity Comte. Ottawa and Ottawa Valley Br., Candn. Red Cross Soc. 1955–59; mem., Corporate Communicators Can. 1951–78; Information Services Inst. 1964–78; Riverside Kiwanis Club; Lectr., Carleton Univ. 1968–73; Anglican; Home: 1517 Caverley St., Ottawa, Ont. K1G 0X9.

**DRISCOLL, Frederick Leo,** M.A.; b. Mt. Herbert, P.E.I. 18 Aug. 1932; s. Joseph J. and Isabelle Suzanna (Coady) D.; e. St. Dunstan's Univ.; Univ. of N.B.; Univ. of Ottawa; m. Bernadette Mary d. William McManus, Charlottetown, P.E.I. 26 Oct. 1957; children: James William, Jennifer Elizabeth; PROF. OF CANDN. HIST., UNIV. OF P.E.I. 1969– , (and of St. Dunstan's Univ. 1965–69); Chrmn., Dept of History 1967–68, 1975–79, 1992– ; Faculty Rep., Univ. Senates 1966–78; Faculty Rep., Bd. of Gov., Candn. Assoc. of Univ. Teachers 1971–78; Pres., Faculty Assoc. 1967–69; Mem., various Senate, Faculty and Faculty Assoc. Cttes.; served with Candn. Army Militia 1955–65, rank Lt.; el. M.L.A. for 3rd Queens prov. g.e. 1978, re-el. 1979, 1982; Min. of Health 1979–81; Minister of Education 1979–82; Min. of Energy and Forestry 1982–86; Govt. House Leader 1982–86; Min. Responsible for Native Affairs 1979–86; for Trade 1982–86; Chrmn., Policy and Priorities Comm. of Cabinet 1979–82; Chrmn., Economic Develop. Comm. of Cabinet 1982–86; Mem., Inter-governmental Affairs Comm. of Cabinet 1979–86; apptd. as a one-man Royal Comn. to report on the P.E.I. potato industry Oct. 1986; Report submitted, Nov. 1987; apptd. Mem., Elections Act and Electoral Boundaries Commission of P.E.I. 1993; apptd. Mem., P.E.I. Museum and Heritage Foundation 1993; P. Conservative; R. Catholic; Clubs: United Services Officers'; Stanhope Golf & Winter; Residence: 33 Hillside Dr., Charlottetown, P.E.I. C1A 6H9; Office: History Dept., Univ. of P.E.I., 550 University Ave., Charlottetown, P.E.I. C1A 4P3.

**DRISCOLL, John F.,** B.Sc., P.Mgr.; executive; b. Boston, Mass. 1 Apr. 1942; e. Boston Coll. B.Sc. (Bus. Adm.) 1964; N.Y. Inst. of Finance 1967; Candn. Inst. of Mgmt. P.Mgr. 1976; m. Merrilyn Macdonald 6 Apr. 1968; children: Sean and Blair; PRES. & CHRMN., J.F. DRISCOLL INVESTMENT CORP. & NCE RESOURCES GROUP 1981– ; Chrmn. & Pres., Northfield Petroleum Corp.; Interfirst Oil Corp.; NCE Income Resources Corp.; NCE Petrofund Management Corp.; Intercoastal Petroleum Inc.; Petro Management Services Inc.; Capital Access Securities Corp.; Mgr. Western Candn. Operations, Technical Tape Corp. 1964–67; Account Extve., Retail Financial Services, Paine Webber Jackson & Curtis 1967–69; Mgr. Candn. Institutional Services, Thomson McKinnon & Auchincloss 1969–71; Acct. Extve., Business Development, Dominick Corp. 1971–73; Vice-Pres. Corp. Affairs and Extve. Asst. to Pres., Acklands Ltd. 1973–81; served with U.S. Marine Corps Reserve 1960–66; mem. Candn. Mgmt. Assn.; Toronto Soc. of Financial Analysts; National Investor Relations Inst.; Candn. Inst. of Mgmt.; Prospector and Developers Assn.; Independent Petroleum Assn. of Canada (IPAC); Ontario Petroleum Assn.; Office: 150 York St., Ste. 802, Toronto, Ont. M5H 3S5.

**DRIVER, Alan G.,** B.Sc., M.Sc., D.I.C., M.B.A., C.A.; chartered accountant; b. London, Eng. 11 Aug. 1947; s. John and Winnifred (Bellingham) D.; e. Birkbeck Coll., London, B.Sc. 1968; Imp. Coll. of Sci. and Technol., London, M.Sc., D.I.C. 1969; C.A. 1972; York Univ., M.B.A. 1974; m. Zillah d. Cecil and Muriel Phillips 2 Sept. 1967; children: Tanya, Keith; PRESIDENT, COOPERS & LYBRAND LIMITED 1993– ; Accountant 1977– ; with Clarkson, Gordon 1969–77; Pres., Candn. Insolvency Practitioners Assn. 1987–88; Home: 24 Annesley Ave., Toronto, Ont. M4G 2T7; Office: 145 King St. W., Toronto, Ont. M5H 1V8.

**DROBOT, Eve,** B.A.; journalist; b. Krakow, Poland 7 Feb. 1951; d. Jan and Wanda (Wander) D.; e. schs.India, Eng., USA, Switzerland; Am. Internat. Sch. New Delhi Dip. 1969; Univ. d'Aix-Marseille, France Baccalaureat 1971; Tufts Univ. B.A. (magna cum laude) 1973; m. Jack s. Chester and Lucia Kapica 9 Apr. 1983; one d. Thalia Louise; Contbg. Ed. Saturday Night mag. 1988– ; Toronto Corr. L'Actualité mag. 1990–92; Book Review Columnist The Globe and Mail 1990–93, columnist 1980–82; freelance writer since 1974; Sr. Story Ed. Canada A.M., CTV 1983–85; ed. writer Toronto Star 1982; freelance broadcaster CBC Radio 1973–76; recipient Gold Medal 1989 Nat. Mag. Awards; Candn. Author's Award 1989; Advisory Bd., Somerville House Publishers; author: 'Amazing Investigations: Money' 1987; 'Chicken Soup and Other Nostrums' 1987; 'Class Acts: Etiquette for Today' 1982; co-author 'Zen and Now: The Baby-Boomer's Guide to Middle Life' 1985; co-ed. 'Words for Sale' 1979; mem. Internat. P.E.N.; recreation: swimming; Club: Mayfair Lakeshore; Home: 17 Simpson Ave., Toronto, Ont. M4K 1A1.

**DROHAN, Walter,** R.C.A.; artist (painter); b. Calgary, Alta. 27 July 1932; s. Nikita and Nancy (Billey) Drahanchuk; e. Alta. Coll. of Art, dipl. (Ceramics major) 1956; Cranbrook Acad. of Art 1957–58; Sr. Can. Counc. Grant, studied in Germany for 1 year 1968; m. Patricia d. Annabel and Harry Banks 10 Aug. 1957; children: Nicholas, Nelson, Wendy; career at Alberta College of Art 1958–88: Instructor, ceramics, sculpture, watercolour, drawing; Instr. Supvr. 1965–88; Program Coord., Ceramics Dept. 1972–88; Interim Head of Coll. 1982; Academic Dean 1987–88; elected Royal Candn. Acad. 1975; recreations: golf; Home: Box 112, Cochrane, Alta. T0L 0W0.

**DROLET, Jean-Paul,** B.A., B.Sc.A., M.S., D.Sc.; mining engineer; b. Québec City, Qué. 15 July 1918; s. Samuel and Florida (Bouré) D.; e. Laval Univ., B.A., B.Sc.A. (Engn.); Columbia Univ., M.S. (Mineral Econ.); D.Sc. (hon. causa): McGill Univ. 1978, Laurentian Univ. 1979; m. Françoise, d. Edouard Desrochers, 1949; Fellow, Royal Candn. Geograph. Soc.; Fellow, Candn. Acad. of Engineering; with Qué. Dept. of Mines as Engr.-Geologist 1943–56; joined Qué. Cartier Mining Co. as Prospector-Engr. 1956–63; became Dir. and mem. of Bd. of Co., Hart Jaune Power Co., Cartier Railway Co.; Sr. Asst. Depy. Min., (Inter. Min.) Dept. of Energy, Mines and Resources 1963–83; Lectr. in Mineral Econs., McGill Univ. 1963–83; Past Pres., Can. Inst. of Mining & Metallurgy; retired mem., Am. Inst. Mining Engrs.; Life mem., Can. Int. of Mining & Metallurgy; Prospectors & Developers Assn. Can.; Corp. Prof. Engrs. Qué.; R. Catholic; recreations: golf, Clubs: University; Home: 1294 Park Hill Circle, Ottawa, Ont. K1H 6K3.

**DROLET, Michel,** B.A.; actuary; b. Quebec City, PQ 1 June 1947; s. Rolland and Geneviève (Pigeon) D.; e. Coll. des Jésuites Qué. B.A. 1966; Univ. Laval Bus. Admin. lic. 1970; F.C.I.A. 1976; F.S.A. 1976; children: Martin, Louis; PRINCIPAL, SOC. CONSEIL MERCER LTEE. 1989– ; Actuarial Student, Crown Life Insur. Co. 1970–73; Metro. Life Insur. Co. 1973–77; Actuary 1977–83; Mgr. (Que. City), Blondeau & Comp. 1983; Vice-Pres., MLH & A Inc. 1983–89; Mem., Am. Acad. of Actuaires 1976; Pres., La Caisse Popl Desjardins de Sillery 1989– ; Mem. of the Bd., La Fondation de la Maison Michel Sarrazin 1992– ; Mem., Candn. Pension Conf.; Assn. of Fiscal & Finan. Planners; Metro. Que. Bd. of Trade; recreations: golf, skiing; club: Club de Golf Royal Quebec; Home: 2352 Maire Blais, Sillery, Qué. G1T 2W6; Office: 1175, rue Lavigerie, Ste. 480, Sainte-Foy, Qué. G1V 4P1.

**DROUIN, Jacques A.,** B.Eng., M.B.A.; businessman; b. Montreal, Que. 4 Jan. 1942; s. Laurent and Fernande D.; e. Ecole Polytechnique, Univ. of Montreal B.Eng. 1964; McGill Univ. M.B.A. 1966; m. Denise Perrault; children: Dominique, Isabelle, Jacques Jr., Geneviève, Vincent; CHAIRMAN & CHIEF EXECUTIVE, THE LAURENTIAN GROUP CORP.; Pres., Drouin, Paquin & Assoc. (part of Currie, Coopers & Lybrand – Partner & Dir.); joined The Laurentian Group Corp. 1983; Bd. Mem., Laurentian Group Corp.; Laurentian Financial; Laurentian Bank of Canada; Laurentian Capital Corp. (U.S.); Laurentian Financial Group plc (U.K.) and others Laurentian Groups cos.; Boreal Insurance Inc.; Dir., Compagnie Industrielle Pallas (Paris); Domtar Inc.; DMR Group Inc.; The SNC Group Inc.; C.D. Howe Institute; and other Candn. cos.; Bd. of Dir. & Extve. Ctte., Montreal Symphony Orch.; club: St-Denis, Mount-Royal; Home: 1321 Sherbrooke St. W., #E-40, Montreal, Qué. H3G 1J4; Office: 1100 René-Lévesque Blvd. W., 25th Fl., Montreal, Qué. H3B 4N4.

**DRUCKER, Daniel J.,** M.D.; university professor and administrator; b. Montreal, Que. 23 June 1956; s. Ernest Robert and Cila (Bernstein) D.; e. Univ. of Toronto M.D. 1980; m. Cheryl F. d. Hank and Ruth Rosen 21 June 1981; children: Aaron, Jeremy, Mitchell; ASSOCIATE PROF. OF MEDICINE, UNIV. OF TORONTO 1991– ; Fellow, Johns Hopkins Univ. 1980–81; Chief Med. Resident, Toronto Gen. Hosp. 1984–84; Research Fellow, Harvard Med. School 1984–87; Asst. Prof. of Med., Univ. of Toronto 1987–89; Dir., Div. of Endocrinology; Office: Toronto Gen. Hosp., Div. of Endocrinoloy, 200 Elizabeth St., CCRW 3-838, Toronto, Ont. M5G 2C4.

**DRUM, Sydney Maria,** B.F.A., M.F.A.; artist; b. Calgary, Alta. 20 Nov. 1952; d. Ian Mondelet and Dorothy Mary (Weaver) D.; e. Univ. of Calgary B.F.A. (with distinction in Art) 1974; York Univ. M.F.A. 1976; m. Frank s. Frank and Helen DeSalvo 7 Nov. 1987; son: Christopher; selected solo & 2-person exhibitions: Museum am Ostwall, Dortmund, Germany 1994; Bau-Xi Gall. Toronto 1992, '90, '87; Univ. of Pittsburgh 1984; 'Five Years of Prints,' travelling solo in Yugoslavia 1983; Gallery Pascal 'Works on Paper' 1983; Getler/Pall Gall. N.Y. 1981; Condeso/Lawler Gall. N.Y. 1981; Art Gall. of Ont. 1978; selected public collections: Canada Counc. Art Bank; Univ. of Toronto; Toronto-Dominion Bank; Petro Canada; Teacher, Univ. of Illinois 1978–83; Governors State Univ. 1983–84; Rutgers Univ. 1984–87; works in public colls.: Can. Counc. Art Bank; Mus. of Modern Art, N.Y.; Philadelphia Mus. of Arts; Robert McLaughlin Gall. Oshawa; Can. Counc. 'B' Grant 1978; commissions: Pope, Ballard, Shepard & Fowle (Chicago) 1983; Zimmerli Museum, Rutgers Univ. 1990; regular reviewer of art exhibs., 'New Art Examiner' (Chicago) 1983–84; Home: 138 West 120th St., New York, N.Y. 10027-6401.

**DRUMMIE, Frederic Reid,** B.A., M.A.; public servant; b. St. John, N.B. 9 Mar. 1934; s. J. Harold and Winifred C. (Blair) D.; e. Univ. of N.B., B.A. (Hons) 1956,; Oxford Univ., B.A., M.A. 1956–58; Rhodes Scholar 1956; m. Mary Aletha d. Edward and Marie Erck 1961, separated 1991; children: Eric Reid, Ann Marie; EXECUTIVE ASSISTANT, MINISTER OF TRANSPORT CANADA 1993– ; Asst. to Pres., Ganong Bros. Ltd. 1958–61; var. positions, including Econ. Adv. & Sec. to the Treasury Board and ending as Extve. Dir., Maritime Union Study, Prov. of N.B. 1961–70; Depy. Min., Dept. of Extve. Counc. Office & Sec. to Cabinet, Prov. of N.S. 1970–72; Liaison Dir., Dept. of Regl. Econ. Expansion 1972–74; Vice-Chrmn., Min. Inflation Cons. Secretariat 1974–75; Asst. Sec. to Cabinet, Privy Counc. Off. & Dir. Gen. Inflation Opns. Secretariat 1975–76; Chrmn., Task Force on Decentralization 1976–78; Sr. Asst. Sec. to Cabinet, Machinery of Govt. & Depy. Sec. to Cabinet (Orgn.) 1979–80; Depy. Sec. to Treasury Bd. 1980–84; Assoc. Depy. Min., Indian & Northern Affairs Can. 1984–93; retired from the public service of Canada March 1993; Skelton/Clark Visiting Fellow, Queen's Univ. 1991–92; Sec., N.B. Rhodes Scholarship Selection Ctte. 1965–70; Prov. Vice-Pres., Inst. of Pub. Admin. in Can. 1966–68 (Chrmn., N.B. Regl. Group); Hon. Lectr., Univ. of N.B.; Mem., Ed. Bd. 'Canadian Public Policy'; Centennial Medal 1967; recreations: golf, alpine skiing; Club: Kanata Lakes Golf & Country; Home: P.O. Box 7077, Vanier, Ont. K1L 8E2; Office: Place de Ville, Tower C, Ottawa, Ont. K1A 0N5.

**DRUMMOND, Brian Paul,** M.B.A.; investment dealer; b. Montreal, Que. 17 Feb. 1931; s. Paul Catherin and Elizabeth Pettingill (Sise) D.; e. Westmount (Que.) High Sch.; Dalhousie Univ.; Univ. of W. Ont., M.B.A.; m. Althea Margaret, d. Archibald D. McQueen, Town of Mount Royal, Que., 28 Oct. 1960; children: Kim Ann, Jeffrey Sise, Willa McQueen; VICE-CHRMN., RICHARDSON GREENSHIELDS OF CANADA LTD. 1982– ; Dir., Atco Ltd.; Atco Enterprises Ltd.; Atcor Resources Ltd.; Brican Investments Limited; Drumcan Ltd.; Global Government Plus Fund Ltd.; Dir., Montreal Gen. Hosp. Found.; Chrmn., Investment Ctte., Montreal Gen. Hosp. Found.; mem., Adv. Council, Sch. of Bus. Admin., Univ. of Western Ont.; Past Chrmn.: Investment Dealers Assn.; The Montreal Exchange; XPO, Montreal; joined Greenshields Inc., Corporate Finance 1958; Mgr., Calgary Office 1964–67; Mgr. Corporate Finance, Montreal 1967; Dir. 1968; Extve. Vice-Pres. 1969; Pres. and Chrmn. of the Extve. Ctte. 1970–82; Zeta Psi; Anglican; recreations: skiing, squash, tennis; Clubs: Mount Royal; Mount Bruno Golf & Country; Montreal Badminton & Squash; Hillside Tennis; St. James's; Home: 371 Metcalfe Avenue, Westmount, Que. H3Z 2J2; Office: 4 Place Ville Marie, Montreal Que. H3B 2E8.

**DRUMMOND, Ian M.,** M.A., Ph.D., F.R.S.C.; educator; b. Vancouver, B.C. 4 June 1933; s. George Finlayson and Laura (Milne) D.; e. Univ. Hill Sch. Vancouver; Univ. of B.C., B.A. 1954; Univ. of Toronto M.A. 1955; Yale Univ. Ph.D. 1959; PROF. OF ECON. UNIV. OF TORONTO 1972– , Vice Dean of Arts and Sciences 1982–87; Lectr. in Econ. Yale Univ. 1958–60; Lectr. in Econ. present Univ. 1960, Asst. Prof. 1962, Assoc. Prof. 1966, Chrmn. of Pol. Econ. 1977–79; Visiting Prof. of Econ. Princeton Univ. 1966; Visiting Prof. of Candn. Studies Edinburgh Univ. 1975–76; Cons., Labour Can. 1961; Royal Comn. Taxation 1963; Orgn. for Econ. Co-op. & Devel. 1962; Devel. Adv. Service 1965; Ang. Ch. Can. 1965–66; author 'The Canadian Economy' 1966, 2nd ed. 1972, Japanese ed. 1976; 'Economics' 1976; 'British Economic Policy and the Empire' 1972; 'Imperial Economic Policy' 1974; 'The Floating Pound and the Sterling Area' 1981; 'Political Economy At Toronto' 1983; 'The Gold Standard and the International Financial System 1900–1939' 1987; 'Progress without Planning' 1987; co-author 'Canada Since 1945' 1981 (2nd ed. 1989); 'Canada 1900–1945' 1987; 'Negotiating Freer Trade' 1989; mem., Candn. Econ. Assn. (Council 1980–83); Candn. Hist. Assn.; recreations: squash, swimming, theatre, music; Home: 190 St. George St., Toronto, Ont. M5R 2N4; Office: Trinity Coll., Hoskin Ave., Toronto, Ont. M5S 1H8.

**DRYER, Douglas Poole,** Ph.D., F.R.S.C.; educator; b. Toronto, Ont. 27 Nov. 1915; s. William Poole and Mabel (McLeod) D.; e. Harvard Coll. A.B. 1936, A.M. 1939; Ph.D. 1980 m. 1stly Pegeen (d. 1963) d. J. L. Synge, Dublin, Ireland 22 March 1946; children: Dagny, Matthew, Moira; m. 2ndly Ellice d. late James Baird 29 May 1965; one step-d. Eleanor; PROF. EMERITUS OF PHILOS. UNIV. OF TORONTO 1981– ; Instr. in Philos. Union Coll. Schenectady, N.Y. 1939–41, Harvard Coll. 1943–45; Lectr. in Philos. Tufts Coll. 1944–45; joined Univ. of Toronto 1945; author 'Kant's Solution for Verification in Metaphysics' 1966; 'Introduction to J.S. Mill' in 'Collected Works' Vol. X 1969; articles on Kant and on pol. and social philos.; mem. ed. staff 'Kant-Studien'; mem. Royal Scot. Country Dancing Soc.; Bruce Trail Assn.; Am. Philos. Assn.; Candn. Philos. Assn.; Liberal; United Church; Club: Alpine; Home: 61 Lonsdale Rd., Toronto, Ont. M4V 1W4; Office: 215 Huron St., Toronto, Ont. M5S 1A6.

**DUBÉ, Hon. André,** L.Ph., L.Sc.S., M.A., LL.L.; juge retraité; né Matapédia, Qué. 12 mars 1918; f. J. Albert et Flore (Poirier) D.; é. Seminaire de Rimouski B.A. 1934; Univ. d'Ottawa L.Ph., L.Sc.S., M.A. 1937; Univ. Laval LL.L. 1947; ép. Lucile f. Jos. A. DesRosiers, Mont Joli, Qué. 5 mai 1941; enfants: Myreille, Michelle, Marc, Jean, Nicole, Suzanne; Juge en Chef Adjoint Cour d'Appel 1986–93; Administrateur de la Prov. de Qué. 1986–93; Bar de Qué. 1947; Q.C. 1963; ouverture bureau legal New Carlisle 1947; fonde bureau legal Dube & Arsenault, New Carlisle 1957; substitut Min. de la Justice 1963; Juge, Cour Superieure 1966; Juge, Court d'Appel du Qué. 1973; Cand. Lib. prov. 1948, 1952, fed. 1958; Vice Pres. Fed. Liberale Provinciale 1965; Pres.-Fondateur Fed. Liberale Federale (Prov. Qué.) 1966; enrolement volontaire 1940, licencié en 1945 au rang de Maj.; servit successivement dans Fusiliers du St-Laurent, le Regt. de Hull et le Royal 22ième Regt.; prit part à la campagne d'Italie, de France, de Hollande et d'Allemagne; Etoile d'Italie; Etoile de France-Allemagne; Etoile de Hollande; Croix d'or du mérite de la Pologne; Chevalier de l'ordre militaire et hospitalier de St. Lazare de Jerusalem; Croix du combattant de l'Europe; Queen's Silver Jubilee Medal; Pres., Fond. du Rein (section de Qué.) 1988 et 1989; Patron d'Honneur, Fond. du Rein (prov. Qué.); mem. Legion Canadienne (ancien Pres. New Carlisle); Chev. de Colomb (ancien depute de dist.); Assn. R22ième Regt. (ancien Pres.); récreations: golf, ski, natation, chasse, pèche; catholique; Club: Garnison; Adresse: 7 Jardins Merici, Apt. 1205, Québec City, Qué. G1S 4N8.

**DUBÉ, Ian David,** M.Sc., Ph.D.; geneticist; educator; b. Trinidad and Tobago; s. Joseph M. and Vilma V. (Meghu) D.; e. Univ. of B.C. B.Sc. 1977, M.Sc. 1980, Ph.D. 1984; Clin. Fellow in Cytogenetics, Hosp. for Sick Children, Toronto 1984–86; m. Margrete d. Magnar and Astrid Innerdal 7 Jan. 1981; children: Karina, Kristin, Christopher, Melissa; HEAD OF CANCER CYTOGENETICS, DEPT. OF PATHOL. TORONTO GENERAL HOSP. 1986– , Sci. in Pathol. and in Oncology Rsch. Prog.; Assoc. Prof. of Pathol. and of Paediatrics Univ. of Toronto 1986– ; Mem., School of Graduate Studies, Univ. of Toronto and of Univ. of Guelph; Cons. in Paediatrics Div. Haematol./Oncol. Hosp. for Sick Children 1986– ; Cons. Med.-Dental staff Lab. Haematol. Sunnybrook Med. Centre; Cons. Med. staff Pathol. The Wellesley Hosp., The Princess Margaret Hosp.; recipient Nat. Cancer Inst. Studentship, Terry Fox Special Award 1982–83; Terry Fox Training Centre Fellowship Nat. Cancer Inst. and Hosp. for Sick Children 1984–86; Leica Canada Scientific Award 1993; author or co-author numerous publs., 7 book chapters; nat. and internat. sci. presentations; mem. Am. Soc. Human Genetics & Am. Soc. Hematology; Home: 104 Glendonwynne Rd., Toronto, Ont. M6P 3E4; Office: 77, Banting Institute, 100 College St., Toronto, Ont. M5G 1L5.

**DUBÉ, Jean-Claude,** Ph.D., F.R.S.C.; university professor; b. Rivière-du-Loup, Qué. 12 Jan. 1925; s. Antoine and Augustine (Plourde) D.; e. Univ. of Ottawa, Lic. in Phil. 1946, in Theol. 1950, M.A. 1961; Univ. of Paris, Ph.D. 1966; m. Denise d. Gaston and Marie-Anne (Goyette) Daigle 5 Oct. 1973; PROFESSOR EMERITUS, DEPT. OF HIST., UNIV. OF OTTAWA 1990; Chargé de cours, present univ. 1961, Asst. Prof. 1966, Assoc. Prof. 1968, Prof. 1976; Founder & 1st Dir., Ctr. de rech. en hist. relig. du Canada (St. Paul Univ.); Book review ed., 'Histoire sociale/Social History' 1984– ; Mem. correspondant, 'Histoire, économie et société' (Paris); Prix litt. du Qué. (Hist.) 1970; F.R.S.C. 1989; Mem., Soc. d'Hist. de France (Paris); Soc. archéol. de Tours; author: 'Claude-Thomas Dupuy, intendant de la Nouvelle-France' 1969, 'Les intendants de la Nouvelle-France' 1984, 'Les Bigot du XVIe siècle à la Révolution' 1987; co-editor: 'Rencontres de l'historiographie française avec l'histoire sociale' 1978; Home: 103, rue Cholette, Hull, Que. J8Y 6L7; Office: Ottawa, Ont. K1N 6N5.

**DUBÉ, Hon. Jean-Eudes,** P.C. (1968), Q.C., B.A., B.Ph., L.Ph., B.S.F.S., B.C.L., LL.D. (N.B.) 1971, D.C.L. (Moncton) 1973; barrister; b. Matapédia, Que. 6 Nov. 1926; s. J. Albert and Flore (Poirier) D.; e. College of Gaspé, Que.; St. Joseph University, N.B.; Ottawa University, B.A., B.Ph., L.Ph.; Georgetown Univ., Sch. of Foreign Service, B.S.F.S.; Univ. of New Brunswick, Law Sch., B.C.L.; m. Noella, d. J. Edgar Babin, 25 June 1956; children: Marie Flore Rachelle, Jean-François; FEDERAL COURT OF CAN. 1975– ; Ald., Campbellton (N.B.) City Council, 1959–63; Crown Prosecutor 1960–61; 1st el. to House of Commons for Restigouche-Madawaska, 1962, re-el. 1963, 65, 68, 72, 74; Pres., Candn. NATO Parlty. Assn., 1963 and re-el. 1964, 1965; Pres. (1st Candn.), N. Atlantic Assembly 1967; Chrmn., H. of C. External Affairs Comte., 1966 and 1967; sworn of Privy Council 1968; Min. Veterans' Affairs 1968–72; Min. of Public Works 1972–74; apptd. to Fed. Court of Can. 9 Apr. 1975 and to Court Martial Appeal Court of Can. 17 July 1975; Q.C. (N.B.) 1969, and Q.C. (Fed.) 1974; Roman Catholic; Club: Hylands Golf; Home: 1694 Playfair Dr., Ottawa, Ont. K1H 5S6.

**DUBÉ, Laurent,** B.A., LL.B.; judge; b. St-Paul-de-la-Croix, Que. 21 Aug. 1935; s. Isidore and Medora (Gagnon) D.; e. Sem. de Rimouski B.A. 1957; Sherbrooke Univ. LL.B. 1961; 1st m. Louise d. Louis Edmond and Regina (Marquis) Lefebvre; 2nd m. Nancy d. Guy and Thérèse (Roy) Jenniss 14 May 1988; children: Julie, Marina (from 1st m.), Eugénie, Thomas (from 2nd m.); JUDGE, QUEBEC COURT, CRIMINAL DIVISION 1988– ; called to Quebec Bar 1961; general practice in civil law 1961–78; apptd. Judge 1978; was very active in Quebec Bar Assn. 1961–78; now active in Quebec Judges Conf.; author: 'La Mariakèche' 1981, 'Damnée Aimée' 1983, '29, rue Couillard' 1992 (novels); Office: 300 boul. Jean Lesage, Quebec, Que. G1K 8K6.

**DUBÉ, Yvon,** M.Sc.F.; forest engineer; commissioner; b. Cabano, Qué. 21 March 1929; s. Rosaire and Eva (Pelletier) D.; e. Colls. of Cabano and Victoriaville B.Sc. 1947; Laval Univ. Bac. Land Surveying 1950, B.Sc.F. 1951, M.Sc.F. 1960; m. Monique d. Albert Sévigny and Rose-Anna Pelletier 23 June 1956; children: Louis-Pierre, François, Geneviève; COMNR. BUREAU OF PUB. HEARINGS ON ENVIRONMENT QUÉ. 1988– ; Field Eng. Beaupré, Sanmaur, La Tuque 1951–60; Asst. Chief Forest Eng. CIP Montréal 1960–67; Dir. Gen. Woods & Forests Qué. Govt. 1967–71; Chief Forestry Mission CIDA Zaire, Kinshasa 1971–73; Dir. Gen. Parks Québec 1973–78; Councillor Sup. Devel. Amazonia, Belém, Brazil 1978–80; Councillor Parks Service Policy Qué. Govt. 1980–82; Dir. Gen. Environment NWT-Yukon (DIAND) Ottawa 1982–84; Coordinator Indian Affairs (Fish & Game) Qué. 1984–88; author various publs. forestry, land use planning; Pres., Corp. Forest Engs. Qué. 1975–76; Pres., Qué. Forestry Assn. 1986–88; Pub. Relations Qué. Land Surveyors 1964–70; Pres., Charlevoix UNESCO Biosphere Reserve 1984–89; Environment Ctte. Arbitrage Centre 1988–89; Sec. Friends Earth Can. 1988–92; mem. UNESCO Man and Biosphere Can. 1984–92; Environment Ctte. Candn. Assn. UN 1989–92; N.Am. Assn. Environmental Edn. 1985–92; recipient, Medal of Honor 1992, Order of Quebec Forest Engineers; Dir., Arctic Institute of N. Am. 1992– ; Mem. Quebec Forestry Assn. 1950– ; Mem., Order of Quebec Forest Engineers 1951– ; recreations: bicycling, walking, skiing; Home: 1430, av. Belcourt, Sillery, Qué. G1T 2S8; Office: 2e étage, 625 rue Saint-Amable, Québec, Qué. G1R 2G5.

**DUBEAU, Angèle;** violinist; b. St-Norbert, Que. 24 March 1962; d. Jules and Lucette (Dauphin) D.; e. student of Dorothy DeLay, Julliard School of Music and of Stefan Georghiu in Romania; awarded First Prize from Conservatoire de musique de Montréal where she studied with Raymond Dessaints; m. Mario s. Eddy and Annie Labbé 1 Aug. 1987; one d.: Marie; while studying she began an impressive career thanks to her remarkable success in numerous competitions in Canada & abroad; First Prizes: Candn. Music Competitions 1976; CBC Talent Festival 1979; Montreal Symphony Orch. Competition 1976; Sylva-Gelber Award from Canada Council 1982; 'Soloist of the Year 1987,' of the Internat. Community of French Speaking Radios, etc.; has toured in over 20 countries (Asia, Canada, Europe & S. Am., among others), appearing in major concert halls and festivals; her exceptional talent, warm tone and strong musical personality have been praised by critics throughout the world; her violin, the Des Rosiers,was built in 1733 by the famous Antonio Stradivarius; Teacher, Conservatory of Montreal; Mem., Guilde des musiciens de Montréal; recordings: RCI 612, Fauré, Contant, Champagne; AN 8701, Analekta, Fauré, Leclair, Debussy; AN 8702, Analekta, Prokofiev, Kabalevsky, Tchaïkovsky; AN 8703, Analekta, Schubert's Sonatas with Anton Kuerti; AN 8704, Analekta, Adoration, Sacred Music with Les Petits Chanteurs du Mont-Royal; AN 8705, Analekta, Sibelius Concerto; AN 2 8706 Piazzolla, De Falla, Paganini with guitarist Alvaro Pierri; AN 2 8707 Glazunov, The Seasons; AN 2 8708 Telemann, 12 Fantasies for violin without bass; AN 2 8709 Bohuslav Martinu, Trio Sonatas with pianist Marc-André Hamelin & flutist Alain Marion; Office: 841, rue Querbes, Outremont, Que. H2V 3X1.

**DUBIENSKI, Hon. Ian Ventress,** LL.B.; judge; b. Winnipeg, Man. 4 Mar. 1921; s. late Bernard Bronislaw, O.C. and late Amy Elizabeth (Ventress) D.; e. elem. and high schs. St. James, Man.; Univ. of Man. LL.B. 1945; m. Naomi d. Louis and Sophie Levine 7 May 1983; children (by previous marr.): Ian, Jennifer, Peter, Phillip, Michael, Marie-Louise; SUPERNUMARY JUDGE 1989; Deputy Judge, Tax Court of Can. 1989; called to Bar of Man. 1947; cr. Q.C. 1961; Judge of Prov. Court 1962; Chief Judge, Prov. Court of Man. Criminal Div. 1982–88; recipient St. John's Ambulance Commendation 1963; Candn. Mental Health Cert. of Honour 1966; Centennial Medal 1967; Queen's Silver Jubilee Medal 1977; awarded Commemorative Medal for 125th Anniversary of Candn. Confederation 1992; First Cert. of Honour Man. Soc. Criminol. 1982; Nat. Pres. Candn. Assn. Prov. Court Judges 1985–86; author various rsch. papers, reports; co-author 'Law and Mental Disorder: Civil Rights and Privileges' 1964; 'The Law and Mental Disorder: Criminal Law' 1965; 'Police Function in Canada' 1981; Home: 8500 Roblin Blvd., S. Headingley, Man. R4J 1B3; Office: 408 York Ave., 5th Flr., Winnipeg, Man. R3C 0T9.

**DUBIN, Anne R.,** Q.C.; b. Toronto, Ont. 19 Nov. 1926; e. Univ. of Toronto, B.A., LL.B., 1948; Osgoode Hall Law Sch., Toronto, Ont. (with Hons., Matthew Wilson Mem. Scholarship; Bronze Medal); m. The Hon.

Charles L. Dubin, Chief Justice of Ont.; PARTNER, TORY, TORY, DESLAURIERS & BINNINGTON; Trustee, Tor. Gen. and Western Hosp. Foundn.; Dir., Petro Canada Ltd.; Public Gov., Tor. Stock Exch. 1976–84; called to Bar of Ont. 1951; cr. Q.C. 1961; Clubs: Queen's; Toronto Lawn Tennis; The Toronto Hunt; Home: 619 Avenue Rd., Toronto, Ont. M4V 2K6; Office: Box 270, Aetna Tower, Toronto Dominion Centre, Toronto, Ont. M5K 1N2.

**DUBIN, Hon. Charles L.;** b. Hamilton, Ont. 4 Apr. 1921; s. Harry and Ethel Dubin; e. Central Coll. Inst., Hamilton, Ont.; Univ. of Toronto, B.A. 1941; Osgoode Hall (with Hons.; Gold Medal; Chancellor Van Koughnet Schol.; Clara Brett Martin Mem. Schol. and Gurston Allen Prize); m. Anne Ruth Levine, 1951; CHIEF JUSTICE OF THE ONTARIO COURT OF APPEAL 1990– ; read law with Mason, Foulds, Davidson & Kellock; called to the Bar of Ont., June 1944; cr. K.C., Dec. 1950; formerly Sr. Partner, Kimber, Dubin, Brunner & Armstrong; Bencher, Law Society of Upper Canada 1966–73; Assoc. Chief Justice, Court of Appeal, Supreme Court of Ont. 1973–90; apptd. Royal Comm. to enquire into air safety in Canada 1979; Head, Inquiry into the Use of Drugs in Amateur Sport (The Dubin Inquiry) 1989–90; Clubs: Toronto Lawn Tennis; Queens; Home: 619 Avenue Road, Toronto, Ont. M4V 2K6; Office: Osgoode Hall, 30 Queen St. W., Toronto, Ont. M5H 2N5.

**DUBOWEC, Walter,** F.C.A.; chartered accountant; b. Winnipeg, Man. 23 March 1932; s. Wasyl and Petrunelia (Hrushka) D.; e. Kelvin H.S. 1949; Inst. of C.A.s of Man. 1956; F.C.A. 1973; Licence Trustee in Bankruptcy 1972; m. Alice d. Frank and Anne Kilimnik 4 June 1955; children: Walter, Teresa, Nadine, Michael; SENIOR PARTNER, DELOITTE & TOUCHE; joined Deloitte & Touche 1956; Office Managing Partner 1975–93; has acted as advisor to govts., crown agencies, credit unions, non-profit orgns.; Chair & Pres., J.M.B. Candn. Explorations Ltd.; past part-time lectr., Univ. of Man., The Man. Inst. of C.A.s; Bd. of Examiners, Candn. Inst. of C.A.s; Past Mem., Man. C.A. Inst. (served on 10 cttes.; chair of 5); Candn. Indus. Renewal Bd.; ranked amongst 25 most influential Manitobans by Winnipeg Business People Mag.; Chair & Pres., The Joe Brain Found.; Hon. Life Mem., The Holy Family Nursing Home; Treas., Joint Capital Campaign, Foundations for Health Inc.; Mem., Holy Family Ukrainian Cath. Parish; lecturer on profl. topics and author of articles on business interruption insur. claims; recreations: reading, gardening, woodwork; clubs: Manitoba, Carleton; Home: 609 Holland Blvd., Winnipeg, Man. R3P 1X1; Office: Suite 2200, 360 Main St., Winnipeg, Man. R3C 3Z3.

**DUCHARME, Claude,** Q.C.; LL.; lawyer; b. Richelieu, Que. 2 Oct. 1923; s. Alexandre and Bernadette (Préfontaine) D.; e. Coll. Saint-Laurent, Montreal, B.A. 1944; Univ. of Montreal, LL.L., 1947; m. Marie, d. Elie Beauregard, 1950; children: Bertrand, Paule, Bruno; called to Bar of Quebec 1947; Partner, Desjardins Ducharme; Chrmn. of Bd.: UAP Inc. (Bd. mem. since 1966); Bd. Mem.: Rogers Communications Inc. (1969); Sodarcan Inc. (1972); National Reinsurance Co. of Canada; Dale-Parizeau Ltd.; Hachette Canada Inc.; Les Messageries de Presse Internationale Inc.; Pres. (1970–71) Chambre de Comm. de Montréal; Dir.: Clinical Research Inst. of Montreal; Past Pres.: Fondation de Théâtre du Nouveau-Monde; Past Vice Pres. Conseil consultatif de la justice; R. Cath.; Liberal; Club: Mount Bruno Country; Home: 1250 Pine Ave. W., Apt. 860, Montreal, Que. H3G 2P5.

**DUCHARME, Hon. Gerald,** M.L.A.; insurance agent; b. Winnipeg, Man. 21 March 1939; s. Jean Louis and Michaelena (Andreychuck) D.; e. Glenlawn Collegiate; Univ. of Man.; m. Yvonne Marie d. Ralph and Madeline Normandeau 14 Sept. 1963; children: Michael, Marc, Monique; MIN. OF URBAN AFFAIRS AND MIN. OF HOUSING, MAN. LEGIS. ASSEMBLY 1988– ; formed Ducharme Agencies 1959; Trustee, St. Vital Sch. Div. 1974–80; Winnipeg City Councillor 1980–86; el. to Man. legis. 1986; Past Pres., St. Vital Jaycees; Former Dir., Winnipeg Enterprises; Winnipeg Convention Centre; Former Chrmn., Winnipeg City Counc.; St. Vital Sch. Div.; Hon. Life Mem., St. Vital Curling Club 1987; R. Catholic; P. Conservative; recreation: golf; club: Niakwa Country; Home: 66 Kilmarnock Bay, Winnipeg, Man. R2M 4Z8; Office: Rm. 317, Legislative Bldg., 450 Broadway Ave., Winnipeg, Man. R3C 0V8.

**DUCHARME, Jacques R.,** B.A., M.Sc., M.D.; b. Montreal, Que., 1 Jan. 1928; s. J. Oscar and Antonia (Gagnon) D.; e. Brébeuf Coll., Univ. of Montreal, B.A. 1948, M.D. 1954; Univ. of Pennsylvania, M.Sc. (Med.) 1961; Dipl. Am. Bd. of Pediatrics; Cert. Pediatrician and Endocrinologist, Que.; m. Monique, d. late Charles G. Smith, M.D., 4 June 1955; children: Andrée, Marie, Jean, Raymond, Anique; PROFESSOR EMERITUS, UNIV. OF MONTRÉAL 1991– ; Chrmn., Dept. of Pediatrics, Univ. of Montreal and l'Hôpital Ste Justine, Montreal 1968–75; Dir., Pediatric Research Center, l'Hôpital Ste-Justine, Montreal 1975–78; Dir., Pediatric Endocrine Lab. 1960–92; Endocrine Sect., Dept. of Biochem., Hôpital Ste Justine 1980–92; Chief, Endocrine Div., Hôpital Ste Justine 1988–91; Scientific Dir., Quebec Health Rsch. Fund (FRSQ) 1990–92; Chrmn. Bd. Trustees, Queen Elizabeth II Research Fund to aid research in diseases of children; has engaged in full-time acad. career since 1959 and research particularly in field of hormonal steroids, regulation of sexual maturation, testicular steroidogenesis; Doctor (hon. causa) Medicine-Sciences, Univ. Claude Bernard, Lyon 1, 1987; Michel Sarrazin Prize, Club de Recherches, Cliniques du Qué., for excellence in teaching and rsch. 1984; Pres., Candn. Soc. for Clin. Inves., 1966; Secy. Que. Med. Research Council 1964–69; mem., Candn. Med. Assn.; Endocrine Soc.; Candn. Soc. Endocrinology & Metabolism; Am. Pediatric Soc.; Club de Recherche Clinique du Que.; Candn. Pediatric Soc.; Corresponding mem., Soc. Française de Pediatrie and European Soc. for Pediatric Endocrinology; Lawson Wilkins Pediatric Endocrine Soc.; Assn. des Médecins des Langue Française du Can.; R. Catholic; recreations: skiing, windsurfing, swimming, foreign languages; Home: 505 Stuart Ave., Outremont, Que. H2V 3H1.

**DUCHESNEAU, François Bruchési,** B.A., L.Ph., Ph.D.; educator; b. Montréal, Qué. 13 Apl. 1943; s. Francis Allen and Madeleine (Bruchési) D.; e. Coll. Stanislas Montréal bacc. français 1961; Univ. de Montréal B.A. 1962; Univ. de Paris L.Ph. 1964, D.E.S. philosophie 1966; Univ. de France Agrégation de philosophie 1968; Univ. de Paris-I Doctorat de 3e cycle philosophie 1971, Doctorat d'Etat philosophie 1980; m. Odette d. Jules and Adrienne Vaisset 2 March 1965; children: Michel, Dominique; PROF. OF PHILOS., UNIV. DE MONTRÉAL 1979– ; Asst. Prof. Univ. of Ottawa 1971–73, Assoc. Prof. 1973–78, Prof. 1978–79, Vice Dean of Grad. Studies 1974–77; Prof. of Philos., Univ. de Montréal 1979– , Chrmn. of Philos. 1981–91, Vice Dean of Arts and Sciences 1991–93; Pres. Candn. Fedn. for Humanities 1986–88; mem. Nat. Adv. Bd. Sci. & Technol. 1988–91; mem. Social Sci's & Humanities Rsch. Council Can. 1988– ; author 'L'empirisme de Locke' 1973; 'La Physiologie des Lumières' 1982; 'Genèse de la théorie cellulaire' 1987; 'Leibniz et la méthode de la science' 1993; 'La dynamique de Leibniz' 1994; ed. 'Locke' 1988; 'Analytiques' 1987; co-ed. 'Dialogue' 1974–91; 'Proceedings of the Ottawa Conference on Kant' 1976; mem. ed. bd. Internat. Archives Hist. of Ideas; Conseil scientifique 'Encyclopédie philosophique universelle'; Adv. Ctte. 'Encyclopedia Britannica'; recipient, André Laurendeau prize, ACFAS 1992; mem. Royal Soc. Can.; Candn. Philos. Assn.; Candn. Soc. Hist. & Philos. Sci. (Pres. 1981–84); Candn. Soc. 18th Century Studies; Hist. Sci. Soc.; Philos. Sci. Assn.; Leibniz Gesellschaft; Soc. française d'étude du 18e siècle; Soc. de philos. du Qué.; Home: 157 Trenton Ave., Mont-Royal, Qué. H3P 1Z3; Office: Faculté des arts et des sciences, Direction, Univ. de Montréal, CP 6128 Succ. A, Montréal, Qué. H3C 3J7.

**DUCKWORTH, Henry Edmison,** O.C. (1976), B.A., B.Sc., Ph.D., D.Sc., LL.D., F.R.S.C.; educator; b. Brandon, Manitoba, 1 Nov. 1915; s. Rev. Dr. Henry Bruce and Ann Hutton (Edmison) D.; e. Univ. of Manitoba B.A. 1935, B.Sc. 1936; Univ. of Chicago, Ph.D. 1942; D.Sc. Ottawa 1966, McMaster 1969; Laval 1971; Mount Allison 1971; New Brunswick 1972; Queen's 1978; Western Ont. 1979; Brandon 1982; LL.D., Manitoba 1978; Winnipeg 1984; m. Katherine Jane (dec.), d. W.J. McPherson, Winnipeg, Man., 21 Nov. 1942; children: Henry William, Jane Edmison Maksymiuk; PRESIDENT EMERITUS, UNIV. OF WINNIPEG 1981– ; Instr. in Math., Stonewall, Man. 1937–38; Lectr. in Physics, United Coll., Winnipeg, Man. 1938–40; Royal Candn. Corps of Signals 1942, but assigned to Jr. Scientist N.R.C., Ottawa, 1942–44 and Asst. Research Physicist, Hamilton, Ont. 1944–45; Asst. Prof. of Physics, Univ. of Manitoba 1945–46; Assoc. Prof. of Physics, Wesleyan Univ., Middletown, Conn. 1946–51; Prof. of Physics. Hamilton Coll., McMaster Univ. 1951–65, Dean of Graduate Studies 1961–65; Vice Pres. (Devel.) Univ. of Manitoba 1965–66, Vice Pres. (Acad.) 1966–71; Pres. & Vice Chancellor, Univ. of Winnipeg 1971–81, Pres. Emeritus 1981– ; Prof. Emeritus, Univ. of Manitoba 1983– , Chancellor 1986–92; Prof. Visiteur, Univ. Laval 1970–71; Nuffield Foundation Travelling Fellowship, 1955; Dir., Wawanesa Mutual Ins. Co.; Past Chrmn.: Advisory Ctte. on Nuclear Safety of Atomic Energy Control Bd.; Council of Assn. of Commonwealth Univs.; Past Pres., Royal Soc. of Can.; Assoc. of Univ. and Coll. of Can.; Candn. Assn. of Physicists; former mem., Nat. Rsch. Counc. of Can.; Defence Rsch. Bd. of Can.; Sci. Counc. of Can.; Natural Sciences and Engr. Rsch. Counc.; Candn. Adv. Environmental Counc.; Nat. Lib. Bd.; Fellow, Am. Physical Soc. 1954; recipient Candn. Assoc. of Physicists Medal 1964; Tory Medal of Royal Soc. of Can. 1965; Officer of the Order of the Buffalo Hunt, Prov. of Manitoba 1992; Distinguished Service Medal, Univ. of Manitoba 1992; United Church; recreation: philately; Club: Manitoba; Home: 76 Wilton St., Winnipeg, Man. R3M 3C1.

**DUCKWORTH, John Walter Adam,** M.B., Ch.B., M.D.; university professor; e. Harrow; Edin. Univ.; PROF. OF ANATOMY, Candn. Memorial Chiropractic College; EMERITUS PROF. OF ANATOMY, FACULTY OF MED., UNIV. OF TORONTO 1979– ; before coming to Canada was House Surg. in Royal Simpson Maternity Hosp., and in Royal Infirmary, Edinburgh, and later Lect. at Edin. Univ.; served in 2nd World War (Comn. Surg.-Lieut. in R.N.V.R. 1938) with Royal Navy and promoted to Surg. Capt. R.C.N.R. in 1958; Assoc. Prof. of Anatomy, Univ. of Toronto, 1952–56; Prof. and Chrmn., Dept. of Anatomy, 1956–64; research interests are the human heart and congenital heart disease; mem., Candn. Assn. of Anatomists; awarded V.R.D. 1962, C.D. 1965; Hon. Physician to Queen 1975; Address: 1477 Bayview Ave., B4, Toronto, Ont. M4G 3B2.

**DUCORNET, Rikki,** B.A.; writer, university professor; b. Canton, N.Y. 19 April 1943; d. Gerard and Muriel (Harris) DeGré; e. Bard College B.A. 1964; separated; one s.: Jean-Yves; PROF. OF ENGLISH, DENVER UNIV.; grants: The Eben Demarest Trust 1990; The Mary Ingram Bunting Inst. 1987–88; The Ingram Merrill Foundation 1988; Ontar Arts Council grants 1977, '76, '83, '87; Copeland Colloquium 1992; Lannan Foundation Fellow 1993; subject of scholarly article: 'Rikki Ducornet's No-Nonsense Almost Fairy Tales' by J.H. Matthews; author: 'The Complete Butchers Tales' 1994; 'The Jade Cabinet' 1993, 'The Fountains of Neptune' 1989, 'Entering Fire' 1986, 'The Stain' 1984 (2 pubs.), 1986 (novels); 'Butcher's Tales 1991 (fiction); 'The Volatilized Ceiling of Baron Munodi' 1991, 'Haddock's Eyes' 1987 (short fiction); 'The Butcher's Tales' 1980; 'The Cult of Seizure' 1989, 'The Illustrated Universe' 1979, 'KnifeNotebook' 1977, 'Weird Sisters' 1976 (poetry), etc.; Address: Denver, Co. 80208.

**DUCROS, Pierre Y.,** B.A., B.Eng.; business executive; b. Montreal, Que. 1939; s. François-Joseph D.; e. Coll. Stanislas B.A.; Royal Military College of Canada 1960; McGill Univ. B.Eng. 1961; m. Francine Perron; children: Eliane, Alain, Philippe; CHAIRMAN, PRESIDENT & CHIEF EXTVE. OFFICER, DMR GROUP INC. 1973– ; Officer, Royal Candn. Navy 1961–64; various mngt. positions, IBM Canada Ltd. 1964–73; Dir., Laurentian Group Corp.; Unigesco Inc.; Cognos Inc.; Les Grands Ballets Canadien; Univ. du Qué. à Montréal; Conference Bd. of Canada; Member and Past Chair, Information Technol. Assn. of Canada 1991–93; Ordre le la Courone of Belgium; CIPS Profl. Achievement Award 1992; HEC, Revue Comm. Vision sans frontière Award 1993; Conseil du Patronat's Entrepreneurs Club 1993; Bd. Mem., Council on National Unity; C. of C. of Metro. Montreal 1985–86; Mem., Public Policy Forum Steering Ctte. on the Future Governance Initiative; Policy Ctte. of Bus. Council on Nat. Issues; Candn. Coun. of Profl. Engrs.; L'Ordre des ingén. du Qué.; Le Cons. du patronat du Qué.; Pres., Candn. Assn. of Mngt. Cons. 1982–83; Candn. Inst. of Mngt. Cons. 1981; Inst. of Cert. Mngt. Cons. of Qué. 1979–81; recreations: tennis, skiing; clubs: Saint-Denis; Office: 1200 McGill College Avenue, Suite 2400, Montreal, Que. H3B 4G7.

**DUDEK, Louis,** O.C., M.A., Ph.D.; poet; teacher and editor; b. Montreal, Que., 6 Feb. 1918; s. Vincent and Rozynski (Stasia) D.; e. Montreal High Sch. (Sr. Matric 1936); McGill Univ., B.A. 1939; Columbia Univ., M.A. (History) 1947; Ph.D. (English and Comparative Lit.) 1955; m. Stephanie Zuperko 1943 (div. 1965); one s., Gregory; m. 2ndly Aileen Collins 1970; joined McGill 1951 as Lectr. in Eng.; Asst. Prof. 1953; Greenshield Prof. of English 1969–84; Prof. Emeritus 1984– ; Founder with Raymond Souster and Irving Layton of Contact Press, poetry publishing; Editor and Publisher of 'Delta,' literary mag. 1957–66 (ceased publ.); helped to edit and produce 'First Statement' with John Sutherland and Irving Layton 1941–43; assoc. with CIV/n magazine in Montreal 1953–55; Ed. of Delta Canada, (later DC Books) book publishers; Instr. in English, City Coll. of New York 1946–51; Publications; (poetry) 'East of the City' 1946; 'The Searching Image' 1952; 'Twenty-Four

Poems' 1952; 'Europe' 1954, reprint 1991; 'The Transparent Sea' 1956; 'Laughing Stalks' 1958; 'En Mexico' 1958; a prose work, 'Literature and the Press' 1956; poems published in books: 'Unit of Five' 1944; 'Other Canadians' 1947; 'Cerberus' 1952; co-ed. with M. Gnarowski 'The Making of Modern Poetry in Canada' 1967; ed. 'Poetry of Our Time' (anthology of modern poetry) 1965; publ. long poem 'Atlantis' 1967; 'The First Person in Literature' 1967; 'Collected Poetry' 1971; 'Selected Essays and Criticism' 1978; 'Technology and Culture' 1979; 'Cross-section: Poems 1940–1980' 1980; 'Poems from Atlantis' 1980; 'Continuation I' 1981; 'Continuation II' 1990; 'Louis Dudek: Open Letter' Nos. 8–9, 1981; 'In Defence of Art' (essays) 1988; 'Small Perfect Things' 1991; 'Infinite Worlds' selected poetry, preface by Robin Blaser, 1988; 'Paradise: Essays on Art, Myth and Reality' 1992; 'The Birth of Reason: Miletus and the Ionians in Greek Philosophy' 1994; articles in 'Dalhousie Review'; 'Queen's Quarterly'; 'Culture'; 'Canadian Forum'; 'Tamarack Review'; 'Delta,' etc.; biographical-critical study by Frank Davey: 'Louis Dudek & Raymond Souster' 1980; 'Ideas for Poetry' 1983; bibliography by Karol W.J. Wenek: 'Louis Dudek: A Check-list' 1975; biog. study by Susan Stromberg-Stein: 'Louis Dudek: A Biographical Introduction to His Poetry' 1983; autobiographical essay in 'Contemporary Authors: Autobiography Series' Gale Rsch., Detroit 1991; Order of Canada 1984; Doctor of Letters, York Univ. 1983; Hon. Diploma, Dawson College, Mtl. 1984; Address: 5 Ingleside Ave., Montreal, Que. H3Z 1N4.

**DUERR, Al,** B.A.; mayor; b. Humboldt, Sask. 29 Jan. 1951; s. Alfred John and Viola Catherine (Weber) D.; e. Humboldt Coll. Inst. 1969; Univ. of Sask. B.A. 1973, M.Sc. courses 1974–75; Univ. of B.C. 1973; m. Kit Chan d. Tak Ming 1979; children: Carly, Ryan; MAYOR, CITY OF CALGARY 1989– ; Planning Cons. Saskatoon and Calgary 1973–76; Policy & Devel. Planner City of Calgary 1976–79; Project & Dist. Mgr. Melcor Development Ltd. Calgary 1979–85; Pres. & Mng. Dir. ALPAC Technologies Ltd. Calgary and Mng. Dir. ALPAC (Malaysia) Sdn., Bhd., Kuala Lumpur 1985–89; Ald. City of Calgary 1983–89; Chrmn. Calgary Econ. Devel. Authority 1989– ; mem. Rotary Internat.; Calgary C. of C.; recreations: skiing, camping; Clubs: Calgary Golf & Country; Glencoe; Calgary Professional; Ranchman's; Home: 719 Madison Ave. S.W., Calgary, Alta. T2S 1K2; Office: City Hall, P.O. Box 2100 Stn. M, Calgary, Alta. T2P 2M5.

**DUFF, Ann MacIntosh,** R.C.A.; artist; b. Toronto, Ont. 14 July 1925; d. John MacIntosh Duff, Q.C., and Constance Hamilton (Townsend) D.; e. Branksome Hall Sch., Toronto, Ont.; Central Tech. Sch., Toronto, Ont.; Queen's Univ. Sch. of Fine Arts (summer); has exhibited with major group shows in Toronto, Montreal, Winnipeg, etc., since 1946; solo shows at Picture Loan Soc., 1959, 1961, 1963, 1964, Gallery Ustel 1968, Merton Gall. 1970, '74, Sisler Gall. 1975, Prince Arthur Galleries 1980–82, Gadatsy Gallery 1984, 1985, 1988, Lake Galleries 1990, 1991, 1993; also with four Toronto painters at Montreal Museum of Fine Arts and group show at Art Gallery of London, Ont.; exhibited at Candn. Nat. Exhn. (1951, 1954, 1956); incl. in 8th Burnaby Biennial 1975; Graphex 1, 2 and 3, 1973, 74, 75; 'Fifty Years of Watercolour Painting' Art Gall. Ont. 1975; 'Watercolours Japan-Canada' Tokyo, Montreal 1976–78; work in coll. of Nat. Gallery of Can., Dofasco Inc., City of Toronto Archives, Extendicare, Art Gallery of Ont., Huron Coll., Agnes Etherington Gall., Sarnia Art Gall., London Art Gall., Toronto Dominion Bank, Princess Margaret Hosp., Nat. Paper Goods, Esso Resources; Citibank, Toronto; Kitchener-Waterloo Art Gallery, Ont. Inst. for Studies in Education, John Labatt Ltd., Oregon State Univ., Corvallis, U.S.A., The Royal Coll. of Drawings and Watercolours, Windsor Castle; and many private colls. in Toronto, Montreal, Edmonton, Winnipeg and Vancouver and abroad; mem., Roy. Can. Acad. of Arts; Print and Drawing Council Can.; Candn. Soc. of Painters in Water Colour; Queen's Jubilee Medal 1977; Candn. Soc. of Painters in Watrcolour Hon. Award 1984; Anglican; Address: 133 Imperial St., Toronto, Ont. M5P 1C7.

**DUFF, Donald James,** B.Ed., M.Sc., K.L.J., F.R.S.A.; fund raising and community relations counsel; b. Calgary, Alta., 18 Sept. 1926; s. James and Julia Isobel (Middleton) D.; e. Central Coll. Inst., Calgary, Alta.; Calgary (Alta.) Business Coll., 1946; Univ. of Alta., B.Ed. 1949; Columbia Univ., M.Sc. (Grad. Sch. of Journalism), 1950; m. Beth Elinor, d. Connor W. Edwards, 19 Feb. 1948; children: James Connor, Julie Anita, Donald Jonathan; Chrmn., The Duff Consulting Group, fund raising and communications consultants; journalist with Southam newspapers, 1945–50; Dir., Pub. Relations, Vancouver Gen. Hosp. and B.C. Med. Centre, 1951–54; Vice-Pres., G.A. Brakeley & Co. Ltd. 1954–61; Pres., Donald J. Duff & Associates Ltd. 1961–82; Dir. of Devt., Queen's Univ. 1982–88; Vice-Pres., External Affairs, Ottawa Civic Hosp. 1988–90; served with Candn. Army (Calgary Tank Regt.) 1943–45; author of articles on philanthropy and Candn. art and sculpture; Pres., Gallery Assn., Agnes Etherington Art Centre; Dir., Kingston Symphony Assn.; St. Andrew's Society (Kingston); Gov., Kingston Gen. Hosp.; Anglican; recreations: golf, gardening, writing, photography; Clubs: Rideau; M.A.A.A.; Arts & Letters (Toronto); Kingston Yacht; Glen Lawrence Golf; Home: 14 Kinogama Rd., Kingston, Ont. K7L 4V1; Office: Box 1745, Kingston, Ont. K7L 5J6.

**DUFF, George Francis Denton,** M.A., Ph.D., F.R.S.C.; university professor; b. Toronto, Ont., 28 July 1926; s. George Henry and Laura (Denton) D.; e. Univ. of Toronto Schs.; Univ. of Toronto, B.A. 1948, M.A. 1949; Princeton Univ., Ph.D. 1951; m. Mary Elaine Wood 1951 (div. 1985); m. Patricia Margaret Sauerbrei 1991; Prof. of Math., Univ. of Toronto 1961–..; Chrmn., Dept. of Math. 1968–75; Editor, 'Canadian Journal of Mathematics' 1958–61, 1978–81; Moore Instr., Mass. Inst. Tech. 1951; Asst. Prof. Math., Univ. of Toronto 1952–57; Assoc. Prof. 1957–61; Visiting Prof. of Math., Univ. of Sask. 1957; Publications: 'Partial Differential Equations' 1956; 'Differential Equations of Applied Mathematics' 1966; various math. papers in tech. journs.; mem., Am. Math. Soc.; Candn. Math. Soc. (Pres. 1971); Home: 92 Chatsworth Dr., Toronto, Ont. M4R 1R7.

**DUFFETT, Harold William;** business executive; b. St. John's, Nfld. 11 June 1938; s. late Eric and Mildred D.; e. Bishop Field Coll. 1954; CHRMN. & CHIEF EXTVE. OFFR., EASTERN CAPITAL CORP.; founded Nat. Office Equipment Ltd. 1957 (Chrmn.); Chrmn. & Chief Extve. Offr., T. & M. Winter Ltd.; Matchless Inc.; Gerald S. Doyle Ltd.; Sanitary Products Ltd.; Jespersons Press Ltd.; Jesperson Printing Ltd.; Bradlea Ltd.; Matchless Paints Ltd.; Future Ltd.; Happy Adventures Ltd.; Fannings National Office Inc.; Dir., Atlantic Shopping Centres Ltd.; Keltic Inc.; Maritime Chemicals Equipment Ltd.; Past Chrmn., Found. for the Lt.-Gov.'s Inst. on Family Life Inc.; Dir., World Wildlife Fund; Past. Pres., Young Pres. Orgn. (Atlantic Chap.); Mem. Bd. of Govs., Nfld. & Labrador Business Hall of Fame; Advisory Bd., Memorial Univ. School of Business; recreations: boating, fishing, tennis, skiing; Clubs: Royal Nfld. Yacht (Past Commodore); St. John's Bd. of Trade; Saraguay Club, Halifax; Bally Haly Golf & Country; St. John's Shrine; St. John's Rotary; Halifax; Home: 1 Frasers Lane, St. John's, Nfld. A1B 1A1; Office: P.O. Box 1654, St. John's Nfld. A1C 5P3.

**DUFFIE, Paul Edward,** B.B.A., LL.B., M.L.A.; lawyer, politician; b. Neguac, N.B. 14 June 1951; s. Theodore Edward and Dorina Marie (Breault) D.; e. Ricker Coll. B.B.A. 1975; Univ. of New Brunswick LL.B. 1978; m. Constance d. Wilfrid and Olive Bowlin 9 June 1973; children: Michèle, Renée, Danielle, Kevin; MINISTER OF EDEUCATION, GOVT. OF N.B. 1991– ; Lawyer, Duffie & Friel 1978–91; elected Mayor, Town of Grand Falls 1986; 1st elected M.L.A. for Grand Falls, N.B. Legislative Assembly 1987; re-elected 1991; Elected Mem., Alpha-Chi Maine Gamma Chapter 1975; Wall Street Journal Student Achievement Award 1975; Mem., Univ. of N.B. Bd. of Gov. 1991– ; recreations: curling, golf, tennis; club: Grand Falls Golf; Home: P.O. Box 747, Grand Falls, N.B. E3Z 1C2; Office: Legislative Bldg., Fredericton, N.B. E3B 5H1.

**DUFFUS, Henry John,** B.A.Sc., B.A., D.Phil., P.Eng.; physicist; educator; b. Vancouver, B.C. 27 Aug. 1925; S. Henry Cleveland and Elizabeth Helen (Dorsey) D.; e. Univ. of B.C., B.A.Sc. 1948, B.A. 1949; Oxford Univ. D.Phil. 1953; Nat. Defence Coll. 1976; m. Maureen d. Robert and Alice Yates 16 Aug. 1948; two s. Robert, James; retired 1989; Dean of Science and Engn., Royal Roads Mil. Coll. 1978–88; Lectr. in Physics, Carleton Univ. 1948–51; Rsch. Physicist, Defence Research Estab. Pacific 1953–59; Prof. and Head of Physics present Coll. 1959–78, Acting Princ. of Coll. 1982; Sch. Trustee 1973–76; Dir., Vancouver Island Ballet Soc. 1978–82; mem., Assn. prof. Engrs. B.C.; Candn. Assn. Physicists (chrmn. Educ. Div. 1975); Home: 139 Atkins Ave., Victoria, B.C. V9B 2Z9; Office: FMO Victoria, B.C. V0S 1B0.

**DUFFY, (John) Dennis,** M.A., Ph.D.; educator; b. Louisville, Ky. 8 Oct. 1938; s. John Raymond and Agnes (Shouse) D.; e. St. Xavier High Sch. Louisville 1956; Georgetown Univ. Washington 1956–60; Univ. of Toronto M.A. 1962, Ph.D. 1964; m. Mary Ann d. Emory J. Gary, Louisville, Ky. 11 June 1960; children: Aubrey, Elaine, John Raymond; PROF. OF ENG., UNIV. OF TORONTO; Principal, Innis College 1979–84; Shastri Indo-Candn. Inst. Lectr. on Candn. Lit. in India 1982; Indian Assn. for Candn. Studies Lectr. on Candn. Lit. in India 1992–93; Fulbright Fellowship 1993; author 'Marshall McLuhan' 1968; 'Gardens, Covenants, Exiles: Loyalism in the Literature of Upper Canada' 1982; 'John Richardson and His Works' 1983; 'Sounding the Iceberg, an essay on Canadian historical novels' 1986; 'Introducing John Richardson's 'Wacousta'' 1993; broadcasting, numerous reviews, articles on Candn. lit.; R. Catholic; Home: 110 Cottingham St., Toronto, Ont. M4V 1C1; Office: Innis College, Toronto, Ont. M5S 1J5.

**DUFFY, John Michael,** B.A., C.A.; financial executive; b. Toronto, Ont. 14 March 1943; s. John Edwin and Mary Wilma (Hodgson) D.; e. Malvern Coll. Inst. 1961; Univ. of Toronto B.A. 1965; C.A. 1969; m. Denyse d. Joseph and Blanche Tremblay 17 March 1971; children: Brian, Stephanie; JOHN M. DUFFY, FINANCIAL MANAGEMENT SERVICES 1991– ; Vice Pres. The Bitove Corp. 1987–91; articled with Clarkson, Gordon & Co.; Controller Dexleigh Corp. 1972, Vice Pres. Adm. 1976, Vice Pres. Finance & Adm. 1980–87; Dir. Groveside Cemetery Bd. 1985– ; Vice Chrmn. Whitby Dist. Boy Scouts 1976–78; Anglican (Treas. All Saints, Whitby 1982–87); recreations: skiing, hiking; Address: 156 Pringle Dr., Whitby, Ont. L1N 6K5.

**DUFFY, Michael Dennis (Mike);** broadcast journalist; b. Charlottetown, P.E.I. 27 May 1946; s. Wilfred Francis and Lillian (McCarron) D.; e. Charlottetown Pub. Schs.; m. Heather J. d. K. McLeod and Margaret Collins of Pembroke, Ont. 13 June 1992; children: Miranda S., R. Gavin; Host, Baton Broadcasting's SUNDAY EDITION 1988– ; Commentator, CTV's W 5; Columnist, Sun Newspapers; former newspaper reporter Charlottetown and private radio stations in Amherst and Halifax, N.S.; CFCF TV, Montreal 1969; CHUM Group, Ottawa 1971; Parliamentary Correspondent CBC Radio 1974; CBC TV 1977–88; frequent speaker on Candn. politics and workings of Parlt.; Visiting Fellow, Duke Univ., Durham N.C., U.S.A. 1986; cited in H. of C. for efforts to assist Vietnamese refugees 1975; winner ACTRA Award 1986 for live TV reporting, (Armenian terrorist attack on Turkish Embassy); twice nominated 'Best in the Business' by Washington Journalism Review; Hon. Doctorate, Univ. of P.E.I. 1990; R. Catholic; Clubs: Rideau; National Press; Office: Nation's Capitol Television Inc., 1500 Merivale Rd., Ottawa, Ont. K2E 6Z5.

**DUFOUR, Gary,** B.F.A., M.F.A.; curator; b. Tisdale, Sask. 25 Sept. 1954; s. Edward Victor and Searle Sadie (Pawson) D.; e. Univ. of Regina B.F.A. (distinction) N.S. Coll. of Art and Design M.F.A. 1979; m. Sine Mary d. Donald K. and Elizabeth MacPherson 14 Aug. 1976; children: Hollis Elizabeth, Meredith Searle, Hilaire Ruth; SENIOR CURATOR, VANCOUVER ART GALLERY 1988– ; Sessional lectr. in art, N.S. Coll. of Art & Design 1980; Asst. Prof. of Art, Univ. of Regina 1980–83; Curator of Prints & Drawings, The Art Gall. of West Australia 1983–87; Curator, Mackenzie Art Gall., Univ. of Regina 1987–88; Candn. Commissioner, The Biennale of Sydney 1992; author: 'Dan Graham' 1985, 'Howard Taylor Sculptures, Painting, Drawings 1942–1984' 1985, 'Max Pam: From Eastern Fluency to Southern Recall Photographs 1980–1985' 1986, 'Guido Molinari 1951–61 The Black and White Paintings' 1989, 'Jeff Wall 1990' 1990; 'Pastfuturetense' 1990; 'Sara Diamond: Patternity' 1991; 'Out of Place' 1993; editor: 'Ffarington's Folio South West Australia 1843–1847' 1986; recreation: sailing; Office: 750 Hornby St., Vancouver, B.C. V6Z 2H7.

**DUFOUR, Ghislain,** O.C., M.A.; executive; b. Sainte-Jeanne-d'Arc, Qué. 28 Sept. 1934; s. Thomas and Marie-Rose (Beaulieu) D.; e. Univ. de Montréal M.A. 1958; m. Denise d. Aimé and Simone Léonard Pilon 27 June 1959; children: Hélène, Johane, Lucie, Marie-Josée; PRES. CONSEIL DU PATRONAT DU QUÉBEC 1985– ; Dir. Personnel & Adm. Hôpital Maisonneuve, Montréal 1958–66; Cons. and Asst. Gen. Mgr. Centre des dirigeants d'entreprise Montréal 1966–69; Asst. Gen. Mgr., Gen. Mgr. and Exec. Vice Pres. present Conseil 1969–85; mem. Occupational Health & Safety Comn.; Adv. Council on Labour & Manpower Qué.; Comn. on the Political and Constitutional Future of Qué., Oct. 1990 to Apr. 1991; co-author 'La Gestion des relations du travail au Québec' 1980; 'Vingt-cinq ans de pratique en relations industrielles' 1990; mem., Candn. Soc. of Assn. Extves.; Am. Soc. Assn. Execs.; Profl. Corp. Ind. Relations Counsellors; Recipient, Fond. Edouard Montpetit 1988; Pinacle Award 1990; Officer of the Order of Canada 1989; Commemorative Medal,

125th Anniversary, Candn. Confedn. 1992; recreations: tennis, dramatic art, music; club: University; Home: 871 rue Pierre Viger, Boucherville, Qué. J4B 3W1; Office: 606, 2075 rue University, Montréal, Qué. H3A 2L1.

**DUFRESNE, Cyrille,** B.A., B.Ap.Sc., M.Sc., Ph.D., P.Eng.; retired industrial executive; geologist; consultant; b. Quebec, Que. 28 Aug. 1919; s. Alphonse-Olivier and Louise (L'Espérance) D.; e. Primary Sch., Que.; St. Charles Garnier Classical Coll., Que., 1930–39; Laval Univ., B.A. 1939, B.Ap.Sc. (Mining) 1943; McGill Univ., M.Sc. (Geol.) 1948, Ph.D. (Geol.) 1952; m. Mabel, d. Solyme Tremblay, Pointe Claire, Que. 30 April 1949; children: Marc, Anne, Monique, Thérese, Paul, Jean Louis, Marie Edith, François; Pres., Sidbec Normines Inc. 1977–82; with various mining cos. during summers 1937–48; joined Labrador Mining & Exploration Co. Ltd. Geol. 1949–50; with Iron Ore Co. of Can. as Geol. 1950–51; Supvr. (Geol.) 1952–55; Exploration Supervising Engr. 1956–58; Chief Engr., Carol Project 1958–63; Govt. Prov. of Que. Comité de Sidérugie 1963; joined Sidbec as Tech. Adv. to Bd. of Dirs. 1964; apptd. Asst. to the Pres. 1965; Vice-Pres., Supply, Sidbec Dosco Ltee. 1970–76; served with R.C.E. as Lt. 1943–45; Founder and 1st Chrmn., Schefferville R.C. Sch. Bd. 1956–58; Labrador R.C. Sch. Bd. 1961–63; mem., Corp. Prof. Engrs. Que.; Geol. Assn. Can.; Candn. Inst. Mining Metall.; Assn. des Anciens de Laval; McGill Grad. Soc.; Candn. Extve. Service Orgn. (CESO); R. Catholic; recreations: fishing, swimming, golf; Address: 418 Greenwood Dr., Beaconsfield, Qué. H9W 4Z8.

**DUFRESNE, Col. F. Gérard,** C.M. (1976), O.St.J., E.D., C.D.; insurance executive; b. East Angus, Que. 22 July 1918; s. Dr. Albert and Laetitia (Milette) D.; e. Shawinigan (Que.) Tech. Inst., 1939; m. Madeleine, d. Louis A. Cyr. Shawinigan, Que., June 1949; children: Monique, Luc, Suzanne; served with Candn. Militia, 1937–40, 1947–63; Candn. Army Overseas with Fusiliers Mont-Royal and 3rd Div. H.Q., 1940–46; C.O. 62 Regt. R.C.A. and G.S.O. 11 Mil. Gp.; Hon. Col., 62 Rgt. RCA; former Mayor of Shawinigan; Gov., Candn. Commissioners Corps; Past Pres., local Junior Chamber of Comm.; Chamber Comm.; Corp. Prof. Techs.; Past Vice-Pres., Insurance Brokers Assoc., Province Quebec; R.C.A. Assn.; Dir., Que. Council, St-John Ambulance; Gov. Foundation of Laval Univ.; Member, Order of Canada; Officer of Order of St. John of Jerusalem; Liberal; Roman Catholic; recreations: hunting, fishing; Club: Shawinigan Golf; Home: 1363 Maple Ave., Shawinigan, Que.; Office: 500 Broadway, Shawinigan, Que. G9N 1M3.

**DUFRESNE, Guy G.,** B.A., B.Eng., M.Eng., M.B.A.; executive; b. Montreal, Que. 28 Oct. 1941; s. André M. and Anita (Lacoste) D.; e. Univ. of Montreal, B.A. 1960, B.Eng. 1964; M.I.T., M.Eng. 1965; Harvard Univ., M.B.A. 1967; m. Lucie d. Dr. and Mrs. R. Pellerin 4 Sept. 1965; children: Johanne, Sylvie, Robert, Louise; PRES. & CHIEF EXTVE. OFFR., QUÉBEC CARTIER MINING CO. 1992– ; various functions, Consolidated-Bathurst Inc. 1967–74; Gen. Mgr., Woodlands, Que. Region, Domtar Inc. 1974–76; Vice-Pres., Mktg., Consolidated-Bathurst Inc. 1976–79; Vice-Pres., Mktg. & Prod. Mgr., Newsprint & Pulp 1979–82; Sr. Vice-Pres., Opns., Pulp & Paper 1982–85; Sr. Group Vice-Pres., N. Am. Pulp & Paper 1985–89; Pres. & C.O.O., Kruger Inc. 1989–92; Dir., Groupe La Laurentienne; Carbonic Liquid Inc.; Ecole Polytechnique; Repap Inc.; club: Saint-Denis; Mount Royal; Home: 641, rue St-Germain, Outremont, Que. H2V 2V7; Office: 1801 McGill College Ave., Suite 1400, Montreal, Que. H3A 2N4.

**DUGAN, James Shackelford,** B.A., M.A., Ph.D.; university professor, professional actor; b. Huntington, W.V. 26 May 1943; s. George McCans and Charlotte Plunkett (Burns) D.; e. St. Andrew's H.S. 1961; Lehigh Univ. B.A. (cum laude) 1965, M.A. 1971; Univ. of Toronto Ph.D. 1979; m. Guidonna Lee d. Guido and Mathilde Terzi 19 Dec. 1987; children: Gabriel, Zachary, Aidan; HEAD OF DRAMA, UNIV. OF CALGARY 1983–94; immigrated to Canada 1969, now a Candn. citizen; doct. degree compl. under supervision of Robertson Davies; Faculty, Theatre Dept., Univ. of Ottawa 1976–80; Theatre Reviewer, CBC Radio, Ottawa 1978–79; Co-devel. & actor 'The Ziggy Effect' 1980; freelance performer 1980–83; received critical acclaim for performance in Mark Medoff's 'When You Comin' Back, Red Ryder?' (Ottawa) 1978, (Toronto) 1979; cast in running principal role of 'Sergeant Striker,' CBC-TV series 'The Great Detective' (with Douglas Campbell) 1980, '81; Dir., Theatre Calgary 1983–92; Co-Founder, Theatre Alberta (Pres. 1990– ;); Mem., Alliance of Canadian Film, Radio & TV Artists; Candn. Actors' Equity Assn.; co-author of one article, one monograph; recreations: tennis, swimming; Home: 1924 Cayuga Dr. N.W., Calgary, Alta. T2L 0N3; Office: Univ. of Calgary, Dept. of Drama, Calgary, Alta. T2N 1N4.

**DUGDALE, John Sydney,** M.A.(Oxon), D.Phil.(Oxon); professor emeritus; b. Settle, Yorkshire, England, 10 Feb. 1922; s. William Eddy and Harriet Gertrude (Harger) D.; e. Giggleswick Sch., Settle 1932–40; Univ. of Oxford, M.A. 1949, D.Phil. 1951; m. Barbara Baird Henderson, 30 Oct. 1954; children: Elizabeth, John; Prof. of Solid State Physics, Univ. of Leeds, U.K., 1965–87; Nat. Rsch. Counc. of Can.: postdoctoral fellow 1951–53, mem. of staff 1953–63, head of Low Temperature and Solid State Physics Group 1963–65; J. Phys. F. (Inst. of Physics): Ed. Bd. 1970–73, Dep. Ed. 1978–80; Vice-pres. for Meetings, Inst. of Physics 1980–83; F.R.S.C. 1964; author: 'Entropy and Low Temperature Physics' 1966, 'Electrical Properties of Metals and Alloys' 1977; ed. Contemporary Physics 1981–92; Home: 14 Weetwood Cres., Leeds LS16 5NS, U.K.; Office: Univ. of Leeds, Leeds LS2 9JT, U.K.

**DUGGAN, Michael Bruce,** B.Sc., B.A.; filmmaker; b. Belleville, Ont. 24 Jan. 1957; s. John Edgar and Betty Jean (Sinclair) D.; e. Univ. of Winnipeg B.Sc. 1979, B.A. 1983; Univ. of Man. postgrad. social work 1983; m. Darcy d. John and Selma Redekop 9 July 1983; one s. Michael John; DIR. OF DEVELOPMENT, PRAIRIE THEATRE EXCHANGE 1992– ; Extve. Dir., Winnipeg Film Group 1987–91; former social worker and performance poet; author, dir. and ed. 7 films incl. 'Bite' 1986, 'Mike' 1989, 'Smoked Lizard Lips' 1991; Pres. Artspace 1988–90, Man. Arts Alliance 1989–90; mem. Can. Council Media Arts Adv. Ctte. 1990–91; Organiser Nat. Coalition Non-Theatrical Fund 1991; mem. Man. Coalition on Mental Health 1985–88; Planning & Review Ctte. Child & Family Services Central Winnipeg 1985–87; Ctte. to est. Child Ombudsman 1983–84; films received 2 Golden Sheafs, Gold Apple; nominated for Blue Ribbon, Genie; author 'Incisions' (haiku) 1985; poetry pub. over 25 lit. jours.; Anglican; Home: 402 Lipton St., Winnipeg, Man. R3G 2H1; Office: Y300 – 393 Portage Ave., Winnipeg, Man. R3B 3H6.

**DUGUAY, Gilles,** B.A., LL.L.; diplomat; b. Montreal, Que. 16 Jan. 1936; s. Gerard and Blanche (Rioux) D.; e. Coll. Stanislas Montreal B.A. 1955; Univ. de Montréal LL.L. 1959; Northwestern Univ. Chicago 1959–60 (Ford Foundation Scholar); Univ. Coll. Oxford England 1960–62 (Rhodes Scholar); m. Anne d. Arkady Demine 6 June 1964; children: Romain, Alexandra, Natalie, Barbara, Delphine, Laurence, Raphaël; PERMANENT REP. OF CANADA ON THE COUNCIL OF THE INTERNAT. CIVIL AVIATION ORGANIZATION in Montreal 1989– ; called to Bar of Que. 1959; Prof. of Law, Nat. Sch. of Law and Pub. Adm. Kinshasa, Zaïre 1962–64; Vice Dean of Social and Econ. Sciences, Nat. Univ. of Rwanda 1964–67; Foreign Service Offr. Ottawa 1967; Second Secy. Dakar, Senegal 1968–70; First Secy. Ankara, Turkey 1970–71; Counsellor for Francophone Africa, Dakar, Senegal 1971–73; Cultural Counsellor Paris 1973–76; Ambassador to Cameroun 1978–80; Canadian Ambassador to Morocco 1980–83; Public Affairs Minister (Information & Culture) Paris 1983–87; Chief of Staff for Mr. Paul Desmarais, Chrmn. of the Board & C.E.O., Power Corp. of Canada, Montreal 1987–89; served with RCN Reserve, rank Lt. (retired); mem. Que. Bar Assn.; Office: #876, 1000 Sherbrooke St. W., Montreal, Que. H3A 3G4.

**DUHAIME, André;** enseignant; auteur; né Montréal, Qué. 19 mars 1948; é. Univ. de Montréal Baccalauréat en pédagogie 1970; professeur au C.O.F.I. (Ministère des Communautés culturelles et de l'Immigration du Qué.) Hull 1978–93; Auteur (poésie) 'Peau de fleur' 1979; 'Haikus d'ici' 1981; 'Visions outaouaises/Ottawax' 1984; 'Pelures d'oranges/Orange Peels' (traduction D. Howard) 1987; 'Au jour le jour' 1988; 'Clairs de Nuit' 1988; 'Voyage parallèle/Parallel Journey' (coll. L. Gorman) 1989; 'Traces d'hier' 1990; 'D'une saison à l'autre' (coll. L. Carducci) 1993; (Jeunesse) 'Le soleil curieux du printemps' 1990; 'Châteaux d'été' 1990; 'Haiku; anthologie canadienne/Canadian Anthology' (coll. D. Howard) 1985; Mem. Union des écrivains québécois; Adresse: 90 Eardley, #203, Aylmer, Qué. J9H 4K2.

**DUINKER, Peter Norman,** B.Sc.Agr., M.E.S., Ph.D.; b. Newmarket, Ont. 16 July 1953; s. Johan Nanning and Guurtje (Bakker) D.; e. Univ. of Guelph B.Sc.Agr. 1978; Dalhousie Univ. M.E.S. 1981; Univ. of N.B. Ph.D. 1986; m. Margaret d. Donald and Doreen Linklater 9 May 1976; children: Kate Emily, Benjamin Johan, Oriana Elizabeth, Nelle Regina; ASSOC. PROF. AND CHAIR OF FOREST MGMT. & POLICY LAKEHEAD UNIV. 1988– ; Rsch. Assoc. Dalhousie Univ. 1981–83; Rsch. Scholar Internat. Inst. Applied Systems Analysis, Austria 1986–88; Adjunct Prof. of Forestry Univ. of Toronto 1989– ; Killam Scholar Dalhousie Univ. 1979–80; NSERC Scholar Univ. of N.B. 1983–86; author or co-author some 100 jour. papers, tech. reports and conf. papers environment & natural resources; mem. Candn. Inst. Forestry; Internat. Assn. Impact Assessment; World Future Soc.; Anglican; recreation: choral singing; Home: 480 Van Norman St., Thunder Bay, Ont. P7A 4E2; Office: Thunder Bay, Ont. P7B 5E1.

**DUKE, Richard Harold,** P.Eng.; oil and gas executive; b. Montreal, Que. 4 Oct. 1939; s. Harold N. and Eileen (Crane) D.; e. McGill Univ. civil engineering 1961; m. Orlaith d. Walter and Dorothy Graham 12 May 1962; children: Stephen, Elizabeth; VICE-PRES., COMMERCIAL MARKETS, SHELL CANADA LTD. 1990– ; Engr., Building Products of Can. Ltd. 1961–66; Engr., present firm 1966–70; various mktg. & mngt. positions 1970–84; Gen. Mgr. Sales, Western Can. 1984–90; Dir., Candn. Business Aviation Assn.; Mem., Candn. Commission for Building and Fire Codes; recreations: golf, tennis; club: Glencoe; Home: 920 Sydenham Rd. S.W., Calgary, Alta. T2T 0T2.

**DUKSZTA, Annette Marie,** B.A., M.B.A.; agency executive; b. Preston, Eng. 19 Nov. 1950; d. Henry Kenneth and Margaret Neil Kane (McNair) Millray; e. Univ. of Toronto B.A. 1972, M.B.A. 1977; m. Dr. Andrzej s. Stanislaw and Stanislawa Dukszta 4 Apl. 1985; one s. Adam Stas Millray; EXEC. DIR., CANDN. BRAIN TISSUE BANK 1985– ; Extve. Dir., Tourette Syndrome Foundation of Canada 1987– ; Pres., Office Solutions 1984– ; Partner, Children's Custom Characters 1988– ; Mgr. Adm. & Edn. Toronto Humane Soc. 1972–80; Mgmt. Cons. Ont. and Toronto Hydros 1980–83; Exec. Dir. ALS Soc. Can. 1983–85; Cons. to various voluntary health agencies; Dir. Stepfamily Survival Project 1988– ; Dir. Candns. for Health Rsch. 1986; Dir. Candn. Neurological Coalition 1983–85; mem. variou govt. cttes. on advocacy for the handicapped 1986– ; mem. Univ. of Toronto Animal Care Ctte. 1986; City of Toronto Animal Control Ctte. 1978; contbg. ed.: 'Digest' 1986– ; 'Green Leaflet' 1990– ; Founding ed. 'ALS News' 1983–85; author various publs.; frequent guest speaker voluntary health groups; recreations: reading, music, travel; Club: RCYC; Home: 104 Madison Ave., Toronto, Ont. M5R 2S4; Office: 126, 100 College St., Toronto, Ont. M5G 1L5.

**DULUDE, Claude,** R.C.A.; peintre et graveur; né à Montréal, Qué. 30 mars 1931; f. Julien et Hélène (Lafleur) D.; é. école Victor-Doré 1949; école Chomedey-de-Maisonneuve 1951; Ecole des Beaux Arts de Montréal diplôme 1957; atelier de gravure J. Friedleander à Paris 1961; Ecole du Musée du Louvre 1961; ép. Suzanne f. Guy Bélanger Montréal, Qué. 8 août 1967; enfant: Mathieu; Bourses: Conseil des Arts du Canada 1961; Ministère des Affaires culturelles du Québec 1975; Expositions personnelles: Galerie Libre Montréal 1960; Galerie Claude Haeffely Montréal 1964; Musée d'Art Contemporain Montréal, 1965; Centre d'art du Mont-Royal 1968; Galerie Gilles Corbeil Montréal, 1971–72–75 Galerie Dresden Halifax 1981; Forest Art Gallery Yarmouth, 1981; Galerie Frédéric Palardy Montréal 1981–82–85–87 and 1989; Galérie La Belle Epoque 1984; Délégation du Qué., Milan 1986; Alex Gallery, Washington, D.C. 1988; Art Dialogue Gall., Toronto 1990; Livres d'Art: Emile Nelligan, poésies, accompagné de 5 eaux-fortes couleur, 1967; Cinquante contines québécoises illusrées de 19 sérigraphies couleurs, 1970; Dir. du secteur des Arts au cegep du Vieux Montréal, 1969–75; Professeur à ce même cegep de 1975–92; Mem. de l'académie Royale des Arts du Can.; adresse: 58 du Crochet, Laval, Qué. H7N 3Z4.

**DUMAS, Antoine,** B.A., R.C.A.; artist; educator; b. Québec City, Qué. 8 Dec. 1932; s. Calixte and Thérèse (Laflamme) D.; e. Séminaire de Qué. 1950; Coll. des Jésuites B.A. 1953; Ecole des Beaux-Arts de Qué. 1954–58 (Lt. Gov.'s Silver Medal); Acad. of Arts San Francisco 1969–70; m. Marie (dec. Jan. 1986) d. Rodolphe Deschênes, M.D. 7 June 1958; children: Hélène, Caroline, Emilie; PROF. ECOLE DES ARTS VISUELS, UNIV. LAVAL; Prof. Ecole des Beaux-Arts de Qué. 1962–69; Dir. Graphic Communication present Univ. 1970–73; Exhns. incl. Galerie Zanettin Québec City 1968, 1971; Galerie Gilles Corbeil Montreal 1973; Art retrospective Québec, Montréal, Rimouski 1973; Consulate Gen. Can. New York 1975; Nancy Poole's Studio Toronto 1977, '78, '80, '85, '91, '92; Itinerant Exhn. St. Catharines, Sudbury, London, Sarnia 1980–81; Galerie Bernard Desroches, Montreal 1981, '83, '87; Galerie Lacerte Guimont, Québec City, 1982; Galerie Madeleine Lacerte, Quebec City 1989, '91, '92 and La Villa Bagatelle, Sillery 1989, '92; Silk Screen Production Montréal Graphic Guild 1973–79; rep. various group exhns. incl.

Graphic Designers Soc. Qué. 1966; Montreal Museum of Fine Arts 1974, 1975; Forum '76; illustrations for luxury ed. 'Kamouraska' 1977; 'Chansons dans la mémoire longtemps' 1981; Stamps Design Can. Post 1976, '78, '79 and '92; Tapestries designs, The Edinburgh Tapestry Co., Scotland 1983 and Ivory Tapestry, Scotland 1992; author 'A l'Enseigne d'Antan' 1970; 'Antoine Dumas' Edit. Chéma 1980; 'Antoine Dumas' Edit. Alain Stanké 1983; Honorary member, Société des Graphistes du Québec; Hon. mem., Quebec Garrison Club; Hon. mem., A.I.I.Q. (Assn. des Illustrateurs et Illustratrices du Qué.); R. Catholic; Home: 1100 Marguerite-Bourgeoys, Sillery, Qué. G1S 3X9; Office: Pavillon Casault, Univ. Laval. Ste-Foy, Qué. G1K 7P4.

**DUMAS, Michael Godfrey Joseph;** artist (painter); b. Whitney, Ont. 20 Sept. 1950; s. Alphyr Adrian and Caroline Anna (Cenzura) D.; e. North Hastings H.S. 1968; Art Instruction School Minneapolis 1968; Humber College 1970, post-grad. studies 1971; Lab. of Ornithology, Cornell Univ. 1984; m. Ellen d. Frank and Harriett Kocsis 19 July 1975; one d.: Shannon-Mae; Apprentice to hist. painter Lewis Parker, Lazare & Parker Studios 1971–72; In-house Staff Artist, Ginn & Co. 1973–74; full-time painting of nature oriented themes was realized in 1974; rep. by Edwin Matthews and The Buckhorn Fine Art Group Inc.; Adv. Bd. Mem., Art Impressions mag.; Advisor & Volunteer Ctte., Buckhorn Wildlife & Art Fest. 1978– ; conducted quarterly weekend seminars & workshops, Buckhorn Sch. of Fine Art 1984–90;; Artist of the Year, Ont. Fed. of Anglers & Hunters 1993; Internat. 'Flyway' Artist, Ducks Unlimited Inc. 1992; Bronze Teal Conservation Award, Ducks Unlimited 1989; 'Artist of the Year' Candn. Collector's Clubs 1987; Wildlife Conserv. Award, Ont. Min. of Nat. Resources 1987; Carling-O'Keefe Profl. Conserv. Award 1986; Waterfowl Art Award, Ducks Unlimited 1983–84; First Winner by Comp., Wildlife Habitat Can. 1990; perm. public collections: Internat. Ctr. for Wildlife Art Gloucester England, Yamanakako-Takamura Mus. of Art Japan; major exhibits: Japan Touring Exhbit 1995; Mitsukoshi Galleries (Tokyo) 1994; Nat. touring exhibit 1993–95,Yamanakako-Takamura Mus. of Art 1991, R.O.M. (group) 1987–88, Royal Botanical Gardens Hamilton 1985, McMichael Candn. Coll. Kleinburg Ont. 1981, Theodore Roosevelt Inaugural Nat. Hist. Site Buffalo N.Y. 1977, Nat. Mus. of Nat. Sci. Ottawa Ont. 1977; major conservation events: Kenya Wild Elephant fundraiser Toronto 1987, '91, Bird Preservation fundraiser Osaka Japan 1990; Conservation fundraiser Regina 1987, 'The Spirit of the Wild' fundraiser & exhibit 1982; special projects: 'The Antarctic Experience' 1990, 'Rare Birds of the World' 1990– ; Candn. commemorative postage stamps: Vanc. Is. Marmot and Acadian Whitefish 1981, 'Candn. Endangered Species' collection 1978–84; film: 'Nature's Gallery' 1981, 'Waterfowl of N. Am.' 1987, 'The Mammals of Peterborough Co.' 1987, 'The Art of Survival' 1987, 'Vegetation Management for Wildlife in Ont.' 1979; Mem., Soc. of Animal Artists 1987– ; Soc. of Wildlife Art of the Nations (U.K.) Charter Mem. 1988; author of numerous magazine articles incl. column in Angler & Hunter 1976–83 and 'Nature in Art' (book) 1991; recreations: travel, photography, camping; Address: P.O. Box 8314, R.R. 1, Peterborough, Ont. K9J 6X2.

**DUMETT, Clement Wallace Jr.,** B.Sc.; petroleum executive; b. Tacoma, Wash. 30 Dec. 1927; s. Clement Wallace and Dilma (Arnold) D.; e. Primary Sch. Seattle, Wash.; High Sch. Whittier, Cal.; Stanford Univ. B. Sc.(Petroleum Engn.) 1951; m. Carolyn Jane d Harold Coulthurst 9 March 1957; children: Daniel Wallace, Joanne Margaret, Patricia Jane; DIR., TALISMAN ENERGY INC.; Engr. Unocal Corp., Whittier 1951; Engr. present co. Calgary, Alta. 1955, Chief Engr. 1966, Vice Pres. Exploration 1967, Vice Pres. Production 1971; President, Unocal Canada Ltd. 1975–93, Retired; served with US Army Mil. Police Bn. 1945–46; Dir., Kahanoff Foundation; Glenbow-Alberta Institute; Candn. Petrol. Assn.; Mem., Soc. Petrol. Engrs.; Am. Inst. Mining Engrs.; Assn. Prof. Engrs. Prov. Alta.; Anglican; recreations: golf, fishing, hunting; Clubs: Calgary Petroleum; Ranchmen's; Calgary Golf & Country; Home: 6 - 712 Memorial Dr. N.W., Calgary, Alta. T2N 3L7.

**DUMONT, Fernand,** B.ès A., M.en Sc., D.en Soc., D.en Théol.; éducateur; né Montmorency, Qué. 24 juin 1927; f. Philippe et Léda (Pilote) D.; é. Univ. Laval B.ès A. 1949, M.en Sc. 1953, D.en Théol. 1987; Univ. de Paris, Sorbonne D.en Soc. 1964; Docteur honoris causa: Sorbonne, Univ. du Qué., Univ. de Sherbrooke; ép. Cécile f. Albert Lafontaine 15 septembre 1953; enfants: Marie, François, Geneviève, Hélène, Véronique; PROF. TITULAIRE DE SOCIOLOGIE UNIV. LAVAL, Chargé d'enseignement à la faculté de théologie, Dir. du dépt. de sociologie, Dir. Institut supérieur des sciences humaines; Prés.-Dir. scientifique de l'Institut québécois de recherche sur la culture 1979–1990; Distinctions: Boursier Soc. royale du Can. 1953–55 et Fondation Killam 1973–75; Prix littéraire de la ville de Montréal 1969; Prix du gouverneur général 1969; Médaille Parizeau; Prix David 1975; Prix Esdras-Minville; Prix Rousseau (ACFAS); Médaille La Gloire de l'Escolle Univ. Laval 1990; Prix Léon-Gerin 1990; auteur 'L'Ange du Matin' poèmes 1952; 'Pour la conversion de la pensée chrétienne' 1964, Editions françaises 1965; 'Le lieu de l'homme' 1968; 'La dialectique de l'objec économique' 1970, Traduction espagnole; 'Parler de septembre' poèmes 1970; 'La vigile du Québec' 1971, Traduction anglaise; 'Chantiers. Essais sur la pratique des sciences de l'homme' 1973; 'Les idéologies' 1974, Traduction espagnole; 'L'anthropologie en l'absence de l'homme' 1981; 'L'institution de la théologie' 1987; 'Le sort de la culture' 1987; co-auteur 'L'Analyse des structures sociales régionales' 1963; Prés. d'honneur Assn. internationale des sociologues de langue française; mem. Académie canadienne-française; Ordre national du Québéc; Officier, Ordre des Arts et des Lettres (France); Catholique; Adresse: 1025 rue Gauthier, Sillery, Qué. G1S 3R8; Bureau: Sainte-Foy, Qué. G1K 7P4.

**DUMONT, Jean,** M.B.A.; investment executive; b. Val D'Or, Qué. 15 June 1948; s. Wilfrid and Juliette Caza D.; e. Univ. of Montréal, B.A. 1968; McGill Univ. B.B.A. 1970; Univ. of W. Ont. M.B.A. 1972; 4 children; PRES. GESTION FINANCIERE TALVEST INC./TALVEST FUND MANAGEMENT INC. 1985– ; Vice Pres. T.A.L. Investment Counsel 1984– ; Financial Analyst, Pitfield, MacKay, Ross & Co. 1972–76; Sr. Cons. Currie Coopers Lybrand 1976–79; Vice Pres. and Dir. Groupe Cayouette Superseal 1979–83; Office: 1800 Place du Canada, Montréal, Qué. H3B 2N2.

**DUMONT, Micheline,** B.A., L.ès L., D.E.S.; éducatrice; née Verdun, Qué. 2 juillet 1935; f. Robert et Lucile (Cousineau) D.; é. Univ. de Montréal B.A. 1957, L.ès L. 1959; Univ. Laval D.E.S. 1964; ép. Rodrigue f. Raoul Johnson 24 juin 1964; enfants: Marie, Laurence, Hélène; PROF. DE SCIENCES HUMAINES, UNIV. DE SHERBROOKE 1970– ; éducatrice histoire Institut Cardinal-Léger, Montréal 1959–68; auteure 'L'Histoire apprivoisée' 1979; co-auteure 'Histoire des femmes au Québec depuis quatre siècles' 1982, 2e édition 1992, Traduction anglaise 'Quebec Women. A History' 1987; 'Les couventines' 1986; mem. Institut d'histoire d'Amerique Française; Candn. Hist. Assn. (Council 1989–92); Soc. des professeurs d'histoire du Qué. (vice-prés. 1975–77); élue à l'Acamédie I de la Société Royale du Canada 1993; Adresse: 474 Québec, Sherbrooke, Qué. J1H 3L8; Bureau: Univ. de Sherbrooke, Sherbrooke, Qué. J1K 2R1.

**DUMONT, Paul;** industriel; né Montreal, Que., 21 mars 1918 f. Wilfrid et Radégonde (Arseneault) D.; B.A. à Montréal; Univ. d'Ottawa (Traduction); Univ. Laval (Espagnol); ép. Françoise, f. Henri St. Jacques, 9 mai 1942; enfants: André, Francois, Louis, Michel, Marie; 34 mois en Europe en 2e Guerre; Prés., Paul Dumont, Inc. 1956–84; administrateur fondateur CEGEP de Lévis-Lauzon; Cndn. Mfrs. Assn.; Dir., 6 ans, Prés., 19 mois, (Chapitre de la ville de Québec); Administrateur, Groupe OPTIMUM International; bénévole, SACO: 26 projets d'expertise auprès des autochtones du Canada et d'entreprises en Afrique et en Amérique centrale et du sud; récréations: bicyclette, natation, ski, voyages; Résidence: 1886 du Sault, St-Romuald, Que. G6W 2L4.

**DUNBAR, A. Carlyle;** journalist; b. Timmins, Ont. 2 Oct. 1930; s. W. Roy and Molly (Gordon) D.; e. Timmins High & Voc. School; McGill Univ.; m. Phyllis d. Herbert and Marion Gunning 8 June 1957; children: Iain, Gavin, Carolyn; Asst. Ed., Liberty Magazine 1953–55; Asst. Financial Ed., Toronto Star 1955–62; joined Financial Post 1962; News Ed. 1969–78; Admin. Ed. 1978–80; Investment Ed. 1980–85; Assoc. Ed. 1985; Publisher and Editor, Investor's Digest 1985–91; Columnist, Investor's Digest of Canada 1992– ; freelance journalist 1992– ; Mem., Empire Club of Canada (Dir. 1972– ;); Home: 135 Douglas Ave., Oakville, Ont. L6J 3R6.

**DUNBAR, Laurence James Edward,** LL.B., B.C.L.; lawyer; b. Montréal, Qué. 17 Oct. 1952; s. Alexander Gilmour and Marjorie Lomax (Ball) D.; e. Queen Elizabeth H.S. Halifax 1971 (Birks Medal 1971); Dalhousie Univ. Law Sch. LL.B. 1976 (Criminal Law Prize 1974, Constitutional Law Prize 1975); Oxford Univ. (Rhodes Scholar) B.C.L. 1978; m. Judith d. Dr. and Mrs. Alvin Macrae 17 Dec. 1977; two d.: Jennifer Nicole, Kristen Alexandra; Partner, Johnston & Buchan 1981–..; part-time Prof. of Communications Law, Univ. of Ottawa Law Sch. 1989– ; Cons. Dalfen Associates Consulting Inc.; Dir., Ottawa Distress Centre 1988– ; articled with Stewart, MacKeen and Covert, Halifax 1975–76 and with Gowling and Henderson, Ottawa 1978–79, Assoc. with latter firm 1980–81; called to Bar of Ont. 1980; co-author of report for Macdonald Royal Comn. on Econ. Union & Devel. Prospects for Can. 1985; study for Dept. Communications 'New Entry into Telecommunications Service Markets in Canada' 1982; mem. Law Soc. Upper Can.; Candn. Bar Assn. (Vice Chrmn., Media and Communications Ctte.); Candn. Assn. Rhodes Scholars 1978–85; recreations: squash, hockey, skiing; Club: Canadian; Home: 161 Manor Ave., Village of Rockcliffe Park, Ont. K1M 0H1.

**DUNBAR, Maxwell John,** O.C., M.A., Ph.D., F.L.S. (Lond.), F.R.S.C. (1954); university professor emeritus; b. Edinburgh, Scot. 19 Sept. 1914; s. William and Elizabeth Mary (Robertson) D.; e. Dalhousie Castle and Fettes Coll., Edinburgh; Oxford Univ., 1933–37, B.A., M.A.; Henry Fellow to Yale Univ. from Oxford, 1937–38; McGill Univ., Ph.D. 1941; D.Sc. (Hon.) Memorial Univ. of Nfld. 1979; D.Sc. (Hon.) Univ. of Copenhagen 1991; m. Joan Suzanne, d. Lloyd D. Jackson, Hamilton, Ont., 1 Aug. 1945; m(2) Nancy Jane Wosstroff, Montreal, Que., 14 Dec. 1960; PROF. EMERITUS OF OCEANOGRAPHY, McGILL UNIV., since 1982; Climate Rsch. Group, Dept. Atmospheric and Oceanic Sciences, McGill Univ. since 1988; Chrmn., Marine Sciences Centre, 1963–77; Gov., Arctic Inst. of N.Am. (Fellow 1947); mem. Que. Wildlife Conservation Assn.; mem. of Oxford Univ. Expdns. to Greenland, 1935 and 1936; to Glacier Bay, Alaska, 1948; mem. of Govt. Party, E. Arctic Patrol, 1939 and 1940; Expdns. to Ungava Bay (marine investigations), 1947, 1949, 1950, 1951, and to Hudson Bay, 1954, 1958; apptd. Asst. Prof. Zool., McGill Univ., 1946, Assoc. Prof. 1948, Prof. 1959; Guggenheim Fellowship to Denmark, 1952–53; Candn. Acting Consul to Greenland, Dept. of External Affairs, Ottawa, 1941–46; awarded Bruce Medal for Polar Exploration, 1950 (Royal Soc. of Edin.); Fry Medal, Can. Soc. of Zoologists, 1979; mem., Soc. for Study of Evolution; Fellow, Am. Assn. Advanc. Science; Hon. Fellow (1966), Am. Geog. Soc.; Publications: 'Ecological Development in Polar Regions'; 'Environment and Good Sense' and about 100 scient. papers; Internat. Convenor-Marine Sec. IBP 1971–75; Scient. Leader, Gulf of St. Lawrence Project, Bedford Inst., Dartmouth, N.S. 1972–73; First Fellows Award, Arctic Inst. of N. Am. 1973; awarded the North Slope Borough (Alaska) Arctic Science Prize 1986; Northern Science Award (Dept. Indian and Northern Affairs) 1987; J.P. Tully medal in Oceanography, Candn. Meteorology and Oceanography Soc. 1988; apptd. Officer of the Order of Canada 1990; Sigma Xi; Protestant; recreations: music, fishing; Clubs: McGill Faculty; Home: 488 Strathcona Ave., Westmount, Que. H3Y 2X1.

**DUNBAR, (Isobel) Moira,** O.C., M.A., F.R.S.C.; glaciologist (retired 1978); b. Edinburgh, Scot. 3 Feb. 1918; d. William and Elizabeth Mary (Robertson) D.; e. Cranley Sch. for Girls, Edinburgh 1935; Oxford Univ. B.A. 1939, M.A. 1948; U.S. Army Lang. Sch. Russian 1958; joined Defence Research Bd. Arctic Research Sec. (later Div. Earth Sciences) 1947, Acting Dir. Earth Sciences 1975–77; mem. Del. to study icebreaker operations in USSR 1964; mem. Comte. on Glaciology, Polar Research Bd., US Nat. Research Council 1976–80; prior to 1947 served in prof. theatre UK; rec'd Centennial Award 1971, Candn. Meteorol. Service; Massey Medal 1972; mem. Candn. Environmental Adv. Council 1972–78; author 'Arctic Canada From the Air' (with K. R. Greenaway) 1956; numerous scient. papers in field sea ice research; Fellow Arctic Inst. N. Am. (Gov. 1966–69); Fellow Royal Candn. Geog. Soc. (Dir. 1974–88); Internat. Glaciol. Soc.; Anglican; recreations: horseback riding, theatre, music, arctic history: Address: RR 1 Dunrobin, Ont. K0A 1T0.

**DUNBERRY, Jean;** financial executive; b. Montreal, Que. 7 July 1930; s. Ernest and Lucie (Leonard) D.; e. McGill Univ., commercial law; m. Yolande d. Emile Paquin 1 Aug. 1953; children: Lucie, Patricia, Max, Eric; former Vice-Pres., Avco Financial Serv.; started as a field rep.; 36 years experience in the finance business; recreations: golf, tennis; club: Mount Stephen.

**DUNCAN, Alastair Robert Campbell,** M.A.; D.Litt. (Lakehead Univ. 1979); university professor emeritus of philosophy; b. Blackhall, Midlothian, Scot., 12 July 1915; s. Leslie and Jean (Anderson) D.; e. George Watson's Boys' Coll., Edinburgh, 1933; Univ. of Edinburgh, M.A. with 1st Class Hons. in Philos., 1936; Univ. of Marburg, Germany, 1936–37; m. Francoise Anne Marie, d. Emile Pellissier, Vernoux, Ardeche, France, 11 June 1938; three s., Alain Campbell Bruce, Gregor Alastair Francois, Colin Adrien McKinley; PROF. & HEAD,

DEPT. OF PHILOSOPHY, QUEEN'S UNIV., 1949–80; Asst. Lect., Univ. of Edinburgh, 1937–38; Lect., Univ. Coll., Univ. of London, 1938–39; Lectr. and Dir. of Studies, Faculty of Arts, Univ. of Edin., 1945–49; Dean, Faculty of Arts & Science, Queen's Univ., 1959–64; served in 2nd World War 1939–45; commd. 2nd Lieut. March 1940, Royal Arty.; promoted Capt., Mar. 1941; seconded to Mil. Intelligence, Sept. 1942; in North Africa and Italy, 1942–44; War Office, 1944–45; mem., Mind Assn.; Aristotelian Soc.; Royal Inst. of Philos.; Candn. Philos. Assn. (Pres. 1961 and 1967); Dante Soc. of N. Am.; Truax Visiting Prof., Hamilton Coll., N.Y. 1974; visiting Prof., Sir Wilfred Grenfell Coll., Nfld. 1982; author of 'Practical Reason & Morality,' 1957 transl. of 'Development of Kantian Thought' by Vleeschauwer, 1962; Moral Philosophy (6 C.B.C. Talks, 1965); 'On the Nature of Persons' 1990; and various articles on philos., educ. and Dante; Presbyterian; recreation: golf; Home: 47 Sydenham St., #2, Kingston, Ont. K7L 3H2.

**DUNCAN, Carson M.,** B.Comm., M.B.A., Ph.D.; university professor; b. Goshen, N.B. 9 July 1944; s. late George Frederick and late Mary Alice (Layden) D.; e. St. Francis Xavier Univ. B.Comm. 1965; Harvard Univ. M.B.A. 1967; Univ. of Western Ont. Ph.D. 1978; m. Margaret d. Hubert and Mary Rideout 27 Dec. 1966; children: Jennifer, Stephen; FACULTY MEMBER, DEPT. OF BUSINESS ADMIN., ST. FRANCIS XAVIER UNIV. 1967– ; Chair of Dept. 1974–77, 1988–91 Consultant to several business, govt. & acctg. orgns.; course devel. & delivery for several acctg. & mngt. devel. programs; active in several community groups; Pres., Bd. of Dir., St. Martha's Regional Hosp.; recreations: skiing, golf, hockey, tennis; clubs: Antigonish Golf & Country; Home: 57 Brookland St., Antigonish, N.S. B2G 1V8; Office: St. Francis Xavier Univ., Antigonish, N.S. B2G 1C0.

**DUNCAN, G.R.,** M.Sc.Phm., D.Phil.; educator; b. Windsor, Ont., 22 Feb. 1934; s. Albert and late Edith (Vollans) Brackett; adopted by Mabel Gladys (Vollans) Wright and late Robert Duncan; e. Univ. of Toronto, B.Sc.Phm. 1957, M.Sc.Phm. 1959; Univ. of Basel, D.Phil. 1962; m. Elinor Joan, d. Leo Svirplys, 13 Aug. 1955; two d., Wendy Carolyn, Colleen Suzanne; DIRECTOR, SCH. OF PHARMACY, MEMORIAL UNIV. OF NFLD.; Prof. of Pharmaceutical Chem., Univ. of Toronto and past Chrmn., Grad. Programme in Pharm. there; sometime Visiting Prof., Univ. of B.C.; Univ. of Alta.; author of over 30 scient. papers and abstracts; mem., Chem. Inst. Can.; A.A.C.P. & A.F.P.C; recreations: gardening, hunting, fishing, carpentry; Home: R.R. 1, Box 99, Paradise, Nfld. A1L 1C1; Office: Rm. 83436, Health Science Centre, Memorial Univ. of Nfld., P.O. Box 4200, St. John's, Nfld. A1B 3V6.

**DUNCAN, H. James,** B.F.A.; association executive; human resources consultant; b. Ottawa, Ont. 18 June 1948; s. late Hugh and Mary Clare (McIntosh) D.; e. Concordia Univ. B.F.A. 1977; Candn. Soc. of Assoc. Extves. CAE 1987; EXTVE. DIR., CONSTRUCTION SPECIFICATIONS CANADA 1990– ; various human resource positions Price Waterhouse Canada, Toronto and Montréal 1966–77, Nat. Personnel 1977–81; Nat. Personnel Dir. Dunwoody and Co. Toronto 1981–85; Employer Dir., Univ. & Coll. Placement Assn. 1981–84; Exec. Dir., ACCIS – The Graduate Workforce professionals 1985–88; Dir., Human Resources, Mintz & Partners 1988–90; mem. Council Sch. Continuing Studies Univ. of Toronto 1979–81; Human Resources Professionals Assn. of Ont. (C.H.R.P.) 1989; Dir. Candn. Career Planning & Employment Inst. 1981–83; Friends of Seneca 1986–88; author or ed. various human resources and career counselling material mags. and newspapers; first recipient, Alta. Executive Development Scholarship Award, Found. for Assn. Rsch. and Education 1993; mem. Candn. Soc. of Assn. Execs., Toronto; Am. Soc. Assoc. Adm.; Human Resources Profls. Assoc. of Ont.; Toronto Central YMCA; recreations: aerobics, piano, ancient history; Home: 256 Jarvis St., Penthouse B, Toronto, Ont. M5B 2J4; Office: 100 Lombard St., Ste. 200, Toronto, Ont. M5C 1M3.

**DUNCAN, Ian Bonthrone Rae,** MB, Ch.B, MD, FRCP(C), FRCPath, FACP; physician, medical microbiology specialist; b. Kilmarnock, Scotland 10 Oct. 1926; s. David Bonthrone and Agnes Richardson (Rae) D.; e. Univ. of Glasgow; m. Norma Helen d. Roy and Bessie Davis 27 July 1957; children: David, Sheila; PROFESSOR EMERITUS OF MICROBIOLOGY, UNIV. OF TORONTO 1992– ; Asst. Prof., Univ. of Glasgow 1951–60; Asst. & Assoc. Prof., Univ. of Western Ont. & Dir. of Microbiology, St. Joseph's Hosp. 1960–67; Dir. of Microbiology & Infection Control, Sunnybrook Health Science Centre & Prof. of Microbiology, Univ. of Toronto 1967–92; Consultant, Infection Control & Lab. Management; Home: 23 Colin Ave., Toronto, Ont. M5P 2B6.

**DUNCAN, Martin James,** B.Sc., M.Sc., Ph.D.; university professor; b. London, England 27 Jan. 1950; s. Peter Rhys and Elizabeth (Pollock) D.; e. McGill Univ. B.Sc. (Hons.) 1971; Univ. of Toronto M.Sc. 1973; Univ. of Texas at Austin Ph.D. 1980; m. Martha d. Blanche Hill 22 March 1980; children: Alexander, Claire; ASSOCIATE PROFESSOR OF PHYSICS, QUEEN'S UNIV. 1988– ; postdoctoral fellow, Cornell Univ. 1979–81; Asst. Prof., Astronomy, Univ. of Toronto 1982–87; Univ. of Calif. at Santa Cruz 1987–88; Visiting Prof., Inst. for Theoretical Physics (Santa Barbara, Ca.) 1992; Consultant, S.W. Research Inst., San Antonio, Tx.; NSERC postgrad. fellowship 1971–73; NSERC postdoct. fellow 1981; NSERC Univ. Rsch. Fellow 1982–87; Mem., Candn. Astron. Soc.; Am. Astron. Soc.; author of numerous sci. papers & review articles; recreations: tennis, hockey; Office: Physics Dept., Queen's Univ., Kingston, Ont. K7L 3N6.

**DUNCAN, Robert Murray,** B.Sc., M.Sc., P.Eng.; engineer, government executive; b. St. Boniface, Man. 5 July 1938; s. David Murray and Marie Antoinette (Smith) D.; e. Univ. of Man. B.Sc. 1960; Univ. of Birmingham M.Sc. 1962; m. Katherine d. Gerald and Anna Mae Carlin 8 Oct. 1966; children: Anne Marie, David, Emily, Alison; MANAGER, DIRECTOR, DIR. GEN. & MEM., EXTVE. CTTE., ATOMIC ENERGY CONTROL BOARD 1984– ; Mech. Engineer, Greater Winnipeg Water Dist. 1960; Mech. Engineer, Assoc. Electrical Indus. Limited U.K. 1960; Researcher, The Nuclear Power Group U.K. 1961; Nuclear Safety Engr., Candn. General Electric Co. Ltd. 1962–67; Sci. Advr. & Asst. Dir., Atomic Energy Control Bd. 1967–82; Sci. Counsellor to Candn. Ambassador, Vienna, Austria 1982–84; Candn. Rep. & Mem., Extve. Ctte. of several sci. cttes., Nuclear Energy Agency, OECD (Paris), Internat. Commission on Radiological Protection (U.K.) and Internat. Atomic Energy Agency (Vienna); Isbister Scholarship; Governor General's Medal; Athlone Fellowship; Mem., Assn. of Profl. Engrs. of Ont.; Delta Kappa Epsilon Frat.; recreations: skiing, swimming, vintage motor racing; Home: R.R. 2, Almonte, Ont. K0A 1A0; Office: P.O. Box 1046, Ottawa, Ont. K1P 5S9.

**DUNELL, Basil Anderson,** M.A.Sc., M.A., Ph.D., F.C.I.C.; educator; b. Vancouver, B.C. 5 Apl. 1923; s. Basil and Elizabeth Dodd (Allan) D.; e. Univ. of B.C., B.A.Sc. (Chem. Engn.) 1945, M.A.Sc. 1946; Princeton Univ. M.A. 1948, Ph.D. (Phys. Chem.) 1949; Prof. Emeritus, Univ. of B.C. 1985– ; Textile Research Inst. Fellow, Princeton Univ. 1946–49; Asst. Prof. Univ. of B.C. 1949, Assoc. Prof. 1961; Univ. Fellow Physics Dept. Univ. of Nottingham 1978–79; Prof. of Chemistry, Univ. of B.C. 1965–85; co-author 'Problems for Introductory University Chemistry with Complete Solutions' 1967; scientific articles on polymer rheology and studies in molecular motion in solids by nuclear magnetic resonance; mem. Council, Chem. Inst. Can. 1965–70, Dir. Scient. Affairs 1967–70; Assoc. mem. Royal Soc. Chem. (London); Anglican; Club: Alpine of Canada; Home: 3893 W. 9th Ave., Vancouver, B.C. V6R 2C2; Office: Dept. of Chemistry, Univ. of B.C., Vancouver, B.C. V6T 1Z1.

**DUNFORD, Robert A.,** B.A., LL.B.; lawyer; business executive; b. Toronto, Ont. 7 June 1931; s. Horatio Alfred D. and Ellen (Brown); e. East York Coll. Inst. 1949; Univ. of Toronto B.A. 1953; Osgoode Hall Law Sch., Barr. & Sol. 1960; m. Sofie d. Vincent and Helen Pyzyna 26 May 1956; children: Lisa Gay, Paul Robb; VICE CHRMN. BRASCAN LIMITED 1993– ; private practice, Dunford & Martin 1960–63; Corp. Solicitor, The T. Eaton Co. Ltd. 1963–67; Atty. & Corp. Secy., Cyanamid of Canada Ltd. 1967–70; Chief Legal Counsel, Corp. Secy. & Vice-Pres., Eaton Financial Serv. Ltd. 1970–77; Exec. Vice-Pres. & Chief Admin. Offr., Brascan Ltd. 1977–93; Group Chrmn., Utilities, Edper-Brascan Group; Chrmn. & Dir., Unicorp Energy Ltd.; Great Lakes Power Inc.; Dir., Brascan Ltd.; Brascade Resources Inc.; Hemlo Gold Mines Inc.; recreations: tennis, skiing, sailing; Office: 4400, BCE Place, Toronto, Ont. M5J 2T3.

**DUNGAN, D. Peter,** Ph.D.; educator; b. Bobcaygeon, Ont. 19 Dec. 1949; s. George B. and Dorothy B. (Dash) D.; e. Glendon Coll. York Univ. B.A. 1972; Princeton Univ. Ph.D. 1980; m. Eshrat Sayani, M.D. d. Gulamhusein and Malek S. 8 Dec. 1984; two d. Sarah, Sophia; ASSOC. DIR. POLICY & ECON. ANALYSIS PROG., INST. FOR POLICY ANALYSIS, UNIV. OF TORONTO 1981– , Adjunct Assoc. Prof. of Econ. 1991– ; joined present Univ. 1977, Asst. Prof. of Econ. 1977–91; co-author 'The Focus Model of the Canadian Economy' 1991; 'The Ontario Economy 1982–1995' 1983; Home: 6 Ellenhall Squ., Scarborough, Ont. M1W 3B2; Office: 140 St. George St., Rm. 325, Toronto, Ont. M5S 1A1.

**DUNLAP, Air Marshal Clarence R.,** C.B.E., C.D., D.C.L., D.Eng., B.Sc.; Royal Canadian Air Force (retired); b. Sydney Mines, N.S., 1 Jan. 1908; s. late Frank Burns and Flora L. (Whitman) D.; e. Acadia Univ. and Tech. Univ. of N.S., B.Sc. in E.E., 1928; D.C.L. Granted Hon. (Acadia 1957); Hon. D. Eng. (N.S.T.C. 1967); m. Hester, d. late Dr. E.A. Cleveland, Vancouver, B.C., 3 Aug. 1935; one s., Dr. David; joined R.C.A.F. in 1928 and commissioned in the rank of Pilot Offr.; for a number of years prior to 2nd World War was engaged in R.C.A.F.'s aerial photographic survey program; later specialized in air armament and attended special training courses in U.K.; at outbreak of war in 1939 was serving as Dir. of Armament at Air Force Hdqrs., Ottawa; early 1942 assumed command of the RCAF Station, Mountain View, Ont., the home of Air Armament School & No. 6 Bombing & Gunner School; late in 1942 posted overseas to become C.O. at R.C.A.F. Stn. at Leeming, Yorks, a station in No. 6 Candn. Bomber Group; in 1943 went to N. Africa as C.O.of No. 331 wing located in Tunisia; R.C.A.F. Sqdns. under his command carried out strategic and tactical bombing in support of campaigns in Sicily, and mainland Italy; returning to U.K. took command of a medium bomber wing (No. 139 Wing) engaged in daylight operations (2nd Tactical Air Force); awarded American Silver Star and Fr. Croix de Guerre; in Jan. 1945 after promotion to Air Commodore, posted back to U.K. taking command of Candn. bomber bases at Middleton-St. George, and Croft; returned to Can., May 1945 and apptd. Depy. Air Member for Air Staff at A.F.H.Q.; in 1946 attended Bikini atomic bomb tests as a Rep. of R.C.A.F., and before his appt. as Air Member for Air Plans in Oct. 1948 was priveledged to attend The Nat. War Coll., Wash., D.C., for one year; in Nov. 1949 assumed duties of A.O.C., N.W. Air Command with hdqrs. at Edmonton, Alta., and was trans. to Air Defence Command, St. Hubert, P.Q., in May 1951 to fill a similar position; apptd. Commandant of Nat. Defence Coll., Kingston, Ont., 1 Aug. 1951; Vice Chief of Air Staff, June 1954; in June 1958 assumed position of Depy. Chief of Staff Operations and was later designated Asst. to the Chief of Staff at Supreme Hdqrs., Allied Powers Europe, Paris, France; Chief of the Air Staff, Canada, 15 Sept. 1962–14 Aug. 1964; Depy. Commdr.-in-Chief, North American Air Defence Command (NORAD), 1964–67; placed on retired list (R.C.A.F.) July 1968; Hon. Pres., RCAF Mem. Fund; recreations: golf, fishing, painting, bridge; Clubs: Victoria Golf; Royal Ottawa Golf; Union of B.C.; Home: Apt. 203, 1375 Newport Ave., Victoria, B.C. V8S 5E8.

**DUNLOP, James Dennis,** B.Comm., M.B.A.; financial services executive; b. Vancouver, B.C. 10 Sept. 1944; s. Robert Crawford and Violet May (McLeod) D.; e. King Edward H.S. 1962; Univ. of B.C. B.Comm. 1967; Univ. of Washington M.B.A. 1969; Univ. of Western Ont., 'Western Executive Prog.' 1986; m. Shirley d. Norman and Mary Skleryk 12 Dec. 1980; VICE-PRES., MIDDLEFIELD GROUP & PRES., MIDDLEFIELD REALTY LTD. 1992– ; Asst. Mgr., Transp. Serv., Johnston Terminals Ltd. 1967–69; Terminal Mgr. 1970–71; extensive internat. training positions in prodn. & mktg. with renowned wineries & distilleries in France, Italy, Germany, Spain, Portugal, UK, Ireland, Greece, Australia, Calif. USA, Brazil, Argentina and Chile 1972–77; Mktg. Mgr., Meagher's Distillery Ltd. 1977; Vice-Pres., Mktg., William Mara Co. 1979; J.M. Douglas Internat. (Corby Distilleries Ltd.) 1984; William Mara Co. 1987; merged with McGuinness Distillers Ltd. 1988; Vice-Pres. Mktg., Corby Distilleries Ltd. 1991; Past Grand Master, Kappa Sigma Fraternity 1967; Past Dir., Independent Wine Education Guild 1981–84; Past Mem., Adv. Bd., Food Service and Hospitality magazine 1982–84, 1990–91; recreations: wine appreciation, swimming, travel; clubs: North York Health, Univ. of B.C. Faculty of Comm. Alumni, Univ. of Western Ont. Business; Home: 131 Beecroft Rd., Ste. 2410, North York, Ont. M2N 6G9; Office: One, First Canadian Pl., 58th floor, P.O. Box 192, Toronto, Ont. M2N 6G9.

**DUNLOP, Marilyn Elizabeth,** B.A.; retired journalist; b. Detroit, Mich. 5 May 1928; d. James Thyne and Florence Ethel (Morgan) Bell; e. London S. S.S.; Univ. of West. Ont. B.A. 1949; divorced; children: Stephanie, Douglas; Medical Reporter, Toronto Star 1968–92, Retired; General Reporter, Toronto Telegram 1949–54; Toronto Star 1964–68; London Correspondent (England) 1977–79; Nat. Newspaper Award 1987; Candn.

Sci. Writers Awards 1976, 1980, 1985; author: 'Understanding Cancer' 1985, 'Body Defences – Immunology' 1987, 'Biography of Dr. William Mustard' 1989; Home: 81 Bywood Dr., Islington, Ont. M9A 1M2.

**DUNLOP, Robert Gray,** B.A.Sc., P.Eng.; consulting engineer; b. Windsor, Ont. 19 Feb. 1953; s. Francis Mason and Georgina Rae (Sharp) D.; e. Univ. of Waterloo B.A.Sc. 1976; m. Janice d. Arthur and Anne Trudelle 22 Dec. 1984; FOUNDER, CARSON, DUNLOP & ASSOC. LTD. 1978– ; lectr. tech. aspects houses and other bldgs to pub., appraisers and real estate community; co-author 'Inspecting a House: A Guide for Buyers, Owners and Renovators' 1982; 'The Home Reference Book' 1988; Sr. mem. Am. Soc. Home Inspectors; mem. Assn. Prof. Engs. Ont.; recreations: squash, sailing, windsurfing; Office: Suite 407, 120 Carlton St., Toronto, Ont. M5A 4K2.

**DUNN, Gerald Fitzpatrick,** F.C.A. (1957); b. Victoria, B.C. 21 Aug. 1911; s. late Henry Josias and Caroline H.G. (Patten) D.; e. Public and High Schs., Victoria, B.C.; admitted to B.C. Inst. of Chart. Accountants, 1942; m. Jean MacDonald 1943 (dec. 1979); m. Joan Procter (née Fraser) 1985; two d., Patricia Ann, Sheelah Jean; retired Partner, Peat, Marwick, Thorne; Hon. Dir., Ducks Unlimited (Canada); Past Pres., Victoria Chamber of Comm.; Pres., B.C. Inst. of Chart. Accts., 1953–54, (mem. of Council, 1949–56); B.C. Dir. Candn. Inst. of Chart. Accts., 1952–53–54; Gov., Candn. Tax Foundation; Pres., B.C. Chamber of Comm., 1958–59; Past Pres., Ducks Unlimited (Canada); Freemason; Anglican; recreations: shooting, fishing, golf; Clubs: Union; Victoria Golf; Canadian (Past Pres.); Address: 2750 Thorpe Place, Victoria, B.C. V8R 2W4.

**DUNN, Maj. Gen. John J.,** C.M.M., C.D.(Ret.), B.A., D.B.A., C.I.B.; insurance executive; b. Sherbrooke, Que. 20 Apr. 1930; s. Cecil William and Jeanne (Couture) D.; e. St-Patrick's Acad. Sherbrooke 1946; Loyola Coll. 1946; Bishop's Univ. B.A. 1950; Univ. of W. Ont. Dipl. in Business Adm. 1952; m. Françoise d. Wilfrid and Adele Rousseau 12 May 1951; children: Robert, Nina, Peter, John; PRESIDENT AND DIR., GESTION J.R.D. 1960– ; Pres., Dunn, Parizeau Inc. 1983– ; Vice Pres., Dale Parizeau Que.; Chief of Reserves Candn. Forces 1981–1983; Hon. Col., Les Fusiliers de Sherbrooke, 1983; Mgr. Printing Plant La Tribune Ltée 1952–55; joined family ins. business 1955, Dir. 1957; joined Les Fusiliers de Sherbrooke 1948, rank Lt.; promoted Col. and apptd. W. Que. Adv., Asst. to Commdr. Secteur de l'Est 1970, Commdr. Dist. No. 1 Secteur de l'Est 1973, Brig. Gen. and Commdr. Secteur de l'Est 1974, Sr. Militia Adv. to FMC 1977, Maj. Gen. 1981; Trustee, Bishop's Univ. 1967; CMM 1982; CD with 3 Bars; Commdr. Order St. John and St-Lazare; Order of Malta, St-Hubert; recreations: sailing, tennis, skiing, hunting; Clubs: Social Sherbrooke; United Services (Montreal); Office: 300 nord, rue Belvedere, Sherbrooke, Que. J1H 4B1.

**DUNN, Michael Stephen,** M.D., FRCP; medical doctor / neonatologist; b. Toronto, Ont. 8 Sept. 1953; s. Kenneth Currie and Alice (Humphries) D.; e. Saltfleet H.S. (Hons.) 1972; Trinity Coll., Univ. of Toronto, undergrad. sci. 1972–74; Univ. of Toronto, Fac. of Med. M.D. 1978; m. Marie Elaine d. Russell and Cecile Brown 9 Aug. 1986; two s.: Maxwell Michael David, Alexander Christopher Kenneth; STAFF NEONATOLOGIST, WOMEN'S COLLEGE HOSP. 1986– ; Active Staff (cross appt.) with Hosp. for Sick Children; Asst. Prof., Depts. of Paed. & Obst. & Gyn., Univ. of Toronto, Fac. of Med. 1989; extensive involvement in clin. rsch. involving premature newborn infants, esp. involving the respiratory system & nutrition; assisted in devel. of surfactant replacement therapy for neonatal resp. distress syndrome (immature lungs in the premature infant); Consultant, Candn. Medical Protective Assn.; Candn. Paed. Soc., Nutrition Ctte.; research grants: Hosp. for Sick Children Found.; Genesis Rsch. Found.; Physician's Serv. Incorp. Found.; The Easter Seal Soc.; FRCP; Mem., Candn. Paed. Soc.; recreations: music, baseball, travel, photography; Home: 170 Hammersmith Ave., Toronto, Ont. M4E 2W8; Office: 76 Grenville St., Toronto, Ont. M5S 1B2.

**DUNN, Patrick J.,** B.Sc., M.Sc., Ph.D.; tobacco industry executive; b. Windsor, Ont. 5 June 1947; s. Lawrence P. and Ellen (Kavanagh) D.; e. St. Clair Coll., Tech.Dipl. 1968; Inst. Tech., Detroit, Mich. B.Sc. 1969; Univ. of Detroit 1970; Univ. of Windsor M.Sc. 1971, Ph.D. 1974; m. Kathleen d. Laura and Tom Coughlin 7 Oct. 1978; one d.: Julia; VICE-PRES., RSCH. & DEVEL., IMPERIAL TOBACCO LTD. 1982– ; Chem. Technol., Imperial Oil; Teaching Asst., Univ. of Detroit 1969–70; Univ. of Windsor 1970–71, 1971–74; Analyst, Windsor Utilities 1971–73; Mgr., Labs., Imperial Tobacco 1975; Dir. and Vice-Pres., Hosp. In-Common Lab. Inc.; Mem. Tech. Ctte., Candn. Tobacco Mfrs. Counc.; Mem., Chem. Inst. of Can.; Am. Chem. Soc.; Candn. Rsch. Mngt. Assn.; Ordre des Chim. du Qué.; Univ. of Windsor Alumni Assn.; author: 'The Kinetic Anation Reactions of Some Rhodium Cyclam Complexes' 1971, 'The Chloroform Extraction of the Alkyl and Cycloalkyl Ketoxime Complexes of Palladium (II) from Aqueous Acid Solutions' 1974; recreations: swimming, skiing; Home: 241 Ballantyne North, Montreal W., Que. H4X 2C3; Office: Box 6500, Montreal, Que. H3C 3L6.

**DUNN, Peter Arthur,** B.A., M.S.W., Adv. Dip.S.W., Ph.D.; university professor; b. Hamilton, Ont. 26 Dec. 1946; s. Charles William and the late Patricia (Campbell) D.; e. Browne & Nichols Sch., Cambridge Mass. 1965; Univ. of Mass. B.A. 1969; Univ. of Toronto M.S.W. 1973, Adv.Dip.S.W. 1981; Brandeis Univ. Ph.D. 1988; ASSOC. PROF., FAC. OF SOCIAL WORK, WILFRID LAURIER UNIV. 1986– ; Extve Dir., Human Serv. of Scarborough 1981–83; numerous rsch., cons. & human serv. positions in Can., U.S. & U.K.; Mem., Profl. Adv. Bd., Ontario Easter Seals Soc.; Men Opposed to Violence Against Women; Founding Bd. Mem., Integrated Employment Serv.; scholarships: Ont. Min. of Community & Social Serv., Can. Mortgage & Housing Corp.; Rsch. Student, London Sch. of Econ. & Pol. Sci.; SSHRC rsch. grant; author: 'Barriers Confronting Seniors with Disabilities in Canada' 1990 and var. articles & govt. reports on disability concerns, social housing issues & internat. comp. social policies; recreations: nordic skiing, sailing, antique collecting; Home: 481 Beechwood Dr., Waterloo, Ont. N2T 1H8; Office: 75 University Ave. W., Waterloo, Ont. N2L 3C5.

**DUNN, Wesley John,** D.D.S., F.A.C.D., F.R.C.D.(C) (Hon.), F.A.D.I. (Hon.), F.I.C.D. (Hon.); b. Toronto, Ont. 21 May 1924; s. late John James and late Grace Eleanor (Bryan) D.; e. Bloor Coll. Inst., Toronto, 1938–42; Univ. of Toronto, Victoria Coll. 1942–43. Faculty of Dent., D.D.S. 1947 (Student Parlt. Prize, Univ. Honour Award 1947); m. Jean Mildred, d. late George Leclair Nicholls and late Ida (Harris) Nicholls, 6 Nov. 1948; three s., Steven Craig, Brian Wesley, Bruce Edward James; private dental practice, Toronto, 1947–56; Registrar-Secy. and Treas., Royal Coll. of Dental Surgs. of Ont., 1956–65; Special Lectr., Univ. of Toronto, Faculty of Dent. 1956–64, Sch. of Hygiene 1957–64; joined Univ. of W. Ont., Faculty of Dent. 1965, Founding Dean of Faculty 1965–82, Asst. Prof. 1965, Assoc. Prof. 1966, Prof. 1974, Prof. Emeritus 1989; mem., Pres.'s Adv. Comte. there and Ex Officio mem., Senate and offr. or mem. of various other univ. Comtes.; Royal Coll. Dent. Surgs. Ont. (Dir. of Coll. 1966–70, Councillor 1985–90, and Pres. 1989–90); Gov., Women's College Hospital, Toronto, 1959–64; Dir., London YMCA-YWCA, 1965–70 (Chrmn. Boys' Dept. Comte 1968–70); mem., Health & Welfare Related Programs Adv. Comte., Fanshawe Coll, 1967–69 and Chrmn., Dent. Assisting Course Adv. Comte.; Dir., Un. Community Services, 1968–70; Chrmn., Ont. Council of Univ. Health Sciences, 1974–76; mem., Ont. Council of Health, 1966–71 (Extve. Comte. 1966–69; Chrmn. Comte on Educ. of Health Disciplines 1966); Asst. Ed., Ont. Dent. Assn. Journ., 1948–50; Ed., 'Oral Health' 1950–53 and Candn. Dent. Assn. Journ. 1953–59; author of numerous articles for various prof. journs.; recipient, Barnabus W. Day Award, Ont. Dent. Assn. 1988; Pres., Assoc. of Candn. Fac. of Dentry, 1976–78; Hon. Mem., Hamilton Acad. Dent.; London & Dist. Dent. Soc.; mem., Omicron Kappa Upsilon; Candn. Soc. Dent. Children (Organ. Secy. 1951–53); Am. Assn. Dent. Ed's (Pres. 1958); Can. Dent. Assn.; (Chrmn. various comtes.); Fellow Am. Coll. Dents.; Hon. Fellow, Royal Coll. of Dent. of Can.; Hon. Fellow, Acad. of Dent. Internat.; Hon. Fellow, Internat. Coll. of Dentists; Candn. Dent. Service Plans Inc. (Dir. and mem. Extve. Comte. 1959–65); Ont. Dent. Nurses' & Asst.'s Assn. (Adv. Bd. 1961–64); Dentists Legal Protective Assn. Ont. (Secy.-Treas. 1956–65); Award of Merit, Alumni Assn., Univ. of Western Ont. 1984; Hon. Mem., Ont. Dental Assoc. 1991; Candn. Dental Assoc. 1991; Award of Merit, Dental Alumni Assoc., Univ. of Toronto 1991; Inaugural Award for Distinguished Service, Am. Coll. of Dentists - Ont. Section 1993; Chrmn., Fluoridation Comte., Health League of Can., 1957–62; Christmas Seals & Fund Raising Comte. Chrmn., London; Middlesex Lung Assn. 1984–86; Exec. Secy., Ont. Commission on Interuniversity Athletics 1990– ; mem., Thames Valley District Health Counc. 1992– ; United Church; Home: 134 Wychwood Park, London, Ont. N6G 1R7.

**DUNNET, Hon. Tamarin,** B.A., LL.B.; judge; b. Halifax, N.S. 4 Feb. 1949; d. Gordon and Melda (Nightingale) D.; e. Univ. de Neuchatel, Switzerland 1970; Dalhousie Univ. B.A. 1971, LL.B. 1974; children: Frederick and Tiffany Sagel; JUDGE, ONTARIO COURT OF JUSTICE, apptd., High Court of Justice Ont. and ex officio mem. Court of Appeal Ont. 1990– ; law practice (civil litigation) Thomson, Rogers, Toronto 1976–90; frequent guest speaker, lectr. legal seminars; Lectr. Law Soc. Upper Can. Bar Admission Course 1990; author various legal publs.; mem. Candn. Bar Assn. (Nat. Exec. Ctte. 1987–89, Nat. Council 1982–90), Ont. Br. (Chair Prov. Judiciary Ctte. 1986, Exec. mem. Jt. Ctte. Court Reform, mem. Council 1982–90); Co. of York Law Assn. (Pres. 1990, Trustee 1982–90); Women's Law Assn. Ont. (Pres. 1980–83); Medico-Legal Soc. Toronto (Dir. 1983–86); Pi Beta Phi (Pres. 1970–71); recreations: Golf, skiing, tennis; Club: Mississauga Golf & Country; Home: 39 Pinewood Trail, Mississauga, Ont. L5G 2L2; Office: Osgoode Hall, Toronto, Ont. M5H 2N5.

**DUNNIGAN, Gerald George,** B.A., M.B.A.; executive; b. Montreal, Que. 12 Dec. 1931; s. late John George and late Olive Catherine (Brophy) D.; e. Univ. of Montreal B.A. 1954; Labour Coll. Can. Dipl. 1965; McGill Univ. Dipl. Business Mang. 1968; Nat. Defence Coll. 1968–69; Sir George Williams Univ. M.B.A. 1972; m. Constance Barbara d. late Clarence Fleming 22 May 1954; three s. Sean, Paul, Frank; CHRMN., TECHSPAN INDUSTRIES INC.; joined Northern Electric Co. (Northern Telecom Ltd.) Montreal 1951, Product Mgr. Quebec City 1959, Trois Rivieres Mgr. 1961, N.S. Mgr. Halifax 1963, Labour Relations Mgr. 1965, Gen. Mgr. Distribution Sales Div. Montreal 1969, Vice Pres. Product Mang. 1971 and Vice Pres. Marketing Nedco Ltd. 1972; Vice Pres. 1974 and Pres., Distribution Group Steetley Ind. Ltd. 1977; Pres. and C.E.O., Eutectic Can. Ltd. and Pres., N. Amer. Div. Eutectic Corp. N.Y. 1979; Pres. & C.E.O., Westcan Electric Heating Inc. 1982–90; Pres. Electromode Inc. Auburn N.Y. 1985–90; served with RCN (R) 1951–56, rank Lt.; Past Pres., Candn. Elec. Distributors Assn. (1977–78); Dir. Electrical & Electronics Mfrs.' Assn. of Can.; R. Catholic; recreations: golf, skiing, reading; Clubs: Weston Golf & Country (Dir.); Mount Stephen (Montreal); Home: 2010 Islington Ave., Suite 2406, Toronto, Ont. M9P 3S8; Office: 2 - 3131 Pepper Mill Court, Mississauga, Ont. L5L 4X6.

**DUNSMORE, Rosemary,** B.F.A.; actress; b. Edmonton, Alta. 13 July 1952; d. Robert James and Florence Ruth (MacQuarrie) D.; e. Sarnia Central C.I. 1968; Neuchatel Jr. Coll. 1969; York Univ. B.F.A. 1973; profl. actress since 1974 performing in theatres across the country; highlights: Nat. & Eur. tour of 'Ten Lost Years,' Candn. premieres of 'Buried Child,' 'Getting Out,' 'Single' (a one-woman show), 'Straight Ahead/Blind Dancers' (also at Edinburgh Fest.), leading roles at Stratford Fest. 1983, 1984; recent film & TV: 'Liar, Liar' (CBC Movie), 'Anne of Green Gables: The Sequel,' 'Road to Avonlea,' 'Blind Faith' (CBC, For the Record), 'Skate' (CBC Movie), 'Dancing in the Dark,' 'The Campbells' (Series), 'Mom P.I.' (Series) and featured roles in US film and television; Acting teacher, Ctr. for Actors Study in Toronto; Equity Showcase; Guest Teacher, Langara Coll., Vancouver; Workshop for Profl. Actors, Vancouver; Actra Nellie for Best Actor 'Blind Faith' 1982; Toronto Theatre Alliance Dora 'Straight Ahead/Blind Dancers' 1982; Dora nom. 'Buried Child' 1980, 'Single' 1984 and 'Fallen Angels' 1992; Kari Award Best Actress in Commercial 'Griswald,' Candn. Telecom 1982; Gemini nomination 'Skate' 1988; McLeans Magazine Honour Roll 1990; recreations: tennis, cooking; Address: c/o Ms. Pam Friendly, Premiere Artists, 671 Danforth Ave., Suite 305, Toronto, Ont. M4J 1L3.

**DUNSTAN, Harold A.,** B.Comm.; human resources executive; b. Winnipeg, Man. 23 Oct. 1944; e. McGill Univ. B.Comm.; m. Dianne; VICE-PRESIDENT, HUMAN RESOURCES AND ADMIN., CANADA POST CORP. 1990– ; joined CP Telecommunications 1960; Manager Labour Relations CNCP Telecommunications 1979–82; Nat. Dir, Labour Relations, Canada Post Corp. 1982–84; Nat. Dir., Industrial Relations Res. 1984–85; Gen. Mgr., Labour Relations 1985–89; Vice-Pres., Personnel and Labour Relations 1989–90; Office: Sir Alexander Campbell Bldg., Station 44, Ottawa, Ont. K1A 0B1.

**DUPERVAL, Raymond,** M.D., FRCP(C); professor of medicine; b. Jérémie, Haiti 1 July 1944; s. Favard and Yolande (Staco) D.; e. Ecole St. Louis de Gonzague Haiti B.Sc. 1962; Univ. Louis Pasteur France M.D. 1970; Univ. de Sherbrooke, CSPQ, Med. Interne 1975; Univ. of Minnesota, Mayo Grad. Sch. 1976 (infectious diseases); m. Mimose d. Charles and Gisèle (Cham) Dambreville 13 Aug. 1965; children: Richard, Laurent,

Jean-Sebastien, Valérie; PROF. OF MEDICINE, UNIV. HOSPITAL CENTRE, UNIV. DE SHERBROOKE 1993– ; Asst. Prof. of Med., Univ. de Sherbrooke 1976; LMCC 1971; FRCP(C) 1976; Infectious Diseases Consultant, Sherbrooke Univ. Hosp. Ctr. & affiliated hospitals 1976; Assoc. Prof. of Med. 1981; Head, Div. of Infectious Diseases 1990; Home: 1900 Rochefoucauld, Sherbrooke, Que. J1J 1E2; Office: 3001 12th Ave. N., Fleurimont, Que. J1H 5N4.

**DU PLESSIS, M.P. (Duke),** B.Sc., M.Sc., Ph.D.; research executive; b. Potchefstroom, S. Africa 3 Feb. 1933; s. David J. and Dorothy D.; e. Potchefstroom Univ. B.Sc. 1953; Univ. of Natal B.Sc. 1956, M.Sc. 1957; Univ. of Alberta Ph.D. 1965; m. Elizabeth Mary d. William and Sophia Gamble 10 Nov. 1962; children: Robyn, Melanie, Andre; VICE-PRES., RESOURCE TECHNOLOGIES DIV., ALBERTA RESEARCH COUNCIL 1992– ; Process Engr., SASOL, S. Africa 1953–56; Sr. Process Engr., Cities Service Athabasca Inc. 1959–64; Prof. & Chair, Mech. Eng., Concordia Univ. 1965–76; Mgr., Coal Conversion & Hydrocarbon Tech., Shawinigan/STEAG Eng. Calgary 1977–79; Head, Coal & Hydrocarbon Proc. Dept., Alta. Rsch. Council 1979–85; Oil Sands & Hydrocarbon Recovery Dept. 1985–91; Mem., Bd. of Dir., Alta. Office of Energy, Rsch. & Tech.; Petroleum Recovery Inst.; Sci. Rsch. Ctte., Hydrogen Indus. Council; Forest Rsch. Adv. Council; Nat. Adv. Council on Coal Rsch.; holder of 3 patents; Registered Profl. Engr. in Alta., Sask. & Que.; Mem., Am. Inst. of Chem. Eng.; Candn. & Am. societies of Mech. Engrs.; Petroleum Society of CIM; author/co-author/editor of 40 sci. articles and papers; recreations: skiing, swimming, running; Office: P.O. Box 8330, Stn. F., Edmonton, Alta. T6H 5X2.

**du PLESSIS, Raymond L.,** Q.C., B.A., LL.L.; lawyer; b. Montreal, Que. 8 Dec. 1928; s. Edgar and Gladys (McGivern) du P.; e. Univ. of Ottawa B.A. 1950, LL.L. 1956; m. Helen d. James Burleigh and Marjorie Sutherland 18 Apr. 1959; children: Catherine, Valerie, Philip; LAW CLERK & PARLIAMENTARY COUNS. TO THE SENATE OF CAN. 1976– ; admitted to Que. Bar 1957; Solicitor, Can. Mortgage & Housing Corp. 1957–62; Fed. Bus. Devel. Bk. 1962–67; served with Fed. Dept. of Justice as Legal Adviser to Statute Revision Comn. 1967–72 and Sr. Adv. Counsel, Legis. Sect. 1972–75; cr. Q.C. 1972; President, Candn. Psoriasis Found.; mem. Assn. of Parlty. Couns. in Can.; Commonwealth Assn. of Legislative Couns.; Candn. Bar Assn.; Que. Bar Assn.; Pres., Federal Lawyers Club 1977–78; Exec. Mem., Candn. Study of Parliament Group 1983–86; Dir., Human Rights Inst. of Can. 1983–87; recreations: tennis, badminton, theatre; Clubs: Blackburn Hamlet Tennis & Badminton; Home: 33 Parkwood Cres., Gloucester, Ont. K1B 3J5; Office: Senate of Canada, Parliament Bldgs., Ottawa, Ont. K1A 0A4.

**DUPLESSIS, Suzanne,** B.A.; politician; b. Chicoutimi, Que. 30 June 1940; d. Jean-Julien and Pearl (Tremblay) Fortin; e. Ecole des Beaux Arts de Qué.; Ste-Foy Cegep; Laval Univ. B.A., dipl.Psycho-ped.; m. Maurice s. Ernest and Jeanne (Laroche) D. 26 Dec. 1959; children: Jean-Maurice, Claude; Mem. of Parliament, Louis-Herbert & Parl. Sec. to Min. for External Relations and Internat. Development 1991–93; Dir., Louis-Hébert P.C. Assn. 1979–80; 1st Active Mem., Cons. Party Prov. Assn., Prov. of Que. 1976– ; elected 1st Vice-Chrmn. 1979, 1982; Pres., O.U.I., Louis-Hébert riding 1980; elected Munic. Coun., Ste-Foy City (1st woman) 1981; elected official cand., Louis-Hébert Cons. Party 1982; Parl. Sec. to Min. of State for Sci. & Tech., Govt. of Can. 1987–91; chrmn./vice-chrmn., sev. govt. cttes.; Mem., Ste-Foy C. of C. & other local cttes.; Dir., OTJ 1966; Churchwarden St-Mathieu Parish 1970–74; Mem., Féminin des Anciens de Laval 1970– ; (Ctte. Pres. 1980; Admin. Counc. 1980); sec. past extve. assn. posts; Plastic Arts Prof., Rég. Louis-Frechette; recreations: golf, swimming; club: Richelieu, Mont Tourbillon Golf (Pres.); Home: 1070, ave du Long Sault, Ste-Foy, Que. G1W 3Z9.

**DUPONT, Claude J.E.,** B.A., LL.L., M.B.A.; lawyer; b. Montréal, Qué. 29 July 1942; s. Joseph Arthur and Kathryn K. (Kavanagh) D.; e. Coll. Jean-de-Brébeuf B.A. 1962; Univ. de Montréal LL.L. 1965; York Univ. M.B.A. 1970; m. Paule d. Brig. général Guy and Louise (Laurendeau) Gauvreau 24 Sept. 1971; children: Marc, Michel, Francis Sean; PARTNER, BÉLANGER, SAUVÉ 1979– ; Vice-Pres. & Co-Owner, Manex Inc. 1970; Vice Pres., Gen. Counsel & Secy. Construction and Cement Products, Miron Co. Ltd. 1971–79; Adminstrator, SOQUIP; Sceptre Resources Ltd. (mem. Audit Ctte.); Flintkote Mines Ltd.; Pres., T.M.R. Old Timers Hockey League; mem., Candn. Bar Assoc.; Coll. Jean-de-Brébeuf Alumni Assoc.; York Univ. Alumni Assoc.; Montreal Univ. Alumni Assoc.; recreations: hockey, jogging, skiing; Clubs: Club du Lac Epinette (fishing); Club de la Baie du Lac deux Montagnes Inc. (duck hunting); Home: 2235 Sheridan, Town of Mount Royal, Qué. H3P 2N7; Office: 1, Place Ville Marie, Suite 1700, Montréal, Qué. H3B 2C1.

**DUPONT, Jean-Claude,** D.ès L.; professeur; né Saint-Antonin, Rivière-du-Loup, Qué. 27 avril 1934; f. Vilmaire et Marie-Anne (Castonguay) D.; é. Univ. Laval L.ès L. 1964, Diplôme d'études supérieures (maîtrise) 1967, D.ès L. 1975; Centre d'Ethnologie française, Paris, Études post-doctorales 1973–74; PROF. TITULAIRE D'ETHNOLOGIE DE L'AMÉRIQUE FRANÇAISE, UNIV. LAVAL 1968– ; Auparavant, Meml. Univ. of Nfld. 1964–65; Univ. de Moncton, N.B. 1966–68; Dir., Centre d'études sur la langue, les arts et les traditions populaires des francophones en Amérique du Nord (Célat) 1976–82; Prof. invité, Univ. of N.Y. at Albany 1988; Prés., Editions J.-C. Dupont; auteur 'Le Légendaire de la Beauce' 1974, 1978; 'Le Pain d'habitant' 1974; 'Le Sucre du pays' 1975; 'Contes de bûcherons' 1976; 'Héritage d'Acadie' 1977; 'Histoire populaire de l'Acadie' 1979; 'L'Artisan forgeron' 1979; 'Héritage de la francophonie' I 1986; 'Légendes des villages' 1987; Mem. de la Société royale du Can.; Mem. de l'Ordre des Francophones d'Amérique; Récipiendaire de la Médaille Marius-Barbeau; Mem. honoraire de la tribu des Abénakis, Odanak, Qué.; Am. Folklore Soc.; Assn. canadienne pour l'étude du folklore; Soc. québécoise des ethnologues; Union écrivains québécois; recreation: peintre; Adresse: 2700 rue Mont-Joli, Sainte-Foy, Qué. G1V 1C8.

**DUPONT, Luc,** M.A.; advertising man; journalist; b. St. John's, Nfld. 19 Oct. 1964; s. Jean-Claude and Jeanne (Pomerleau) D.; e. Coll. Arts & Math., Coll. F-X-G, Québec 1985; Laval Univ. B.A. 1988; Univ. Qué. à Montréal M.A. 1991; campaign mgr. fed. el. cand. 1984; Host weekly radio prog. advt. & mktg. Stn. CKRL-FM Québec 1985–86; Jour. 'L'Exclusif' 1986–87; Host weekly television prog. advt. & mktg. Stn. Tele-Plus 24 1991–92; Asst. Ed., 'Journal Économique de Québec' 1992– ; Chronicler Les Nordiques magazine 1992– ; Asst. Prof., Communication Dept., Laval Univ. 1992– ; guest lectr. Laval Univ.; UQTR; Montréal Bus. Exhn.; ACFAS 1993; Learned Society 1993; Qué. Bus. Exhn.; advt. cons.; author '1001 Trucs Publicitaires' 1990, 1993; mem. Advt. Club Montréal; Laval Univ. Alumni Assn.; Union des écrivains du Qué.; recreation: reading; Home: 2700 rue Mont-Joli, Sainte-Foy, Qué. G1V 1C8.

**DUPONT, Rosaire François;** food executive; b. Hull, Qué. 10 Oct. 1927; s. Victor and Marie-Rose (Berube) D.; e. Hull H.S.; m. Laurianne d. Edouard and Violette Trudel 17 June 1950; children: Serge, Diane, Marc; DIRECTOR, MORRISON LAMOTHE INC.; Exec. Vice Pres. and Gen. Mgr. 1978–91; Past Vice Pres., Outaouais Development Corp.; former Asst. Gen. Credit Mgr. Canada Packers Ltd.; Gen. Mgr. Morrison Lamothe Inc. 1970–78, Vice-Chrmn. 1991–93, Retired; Past Vice Pres.: Outaouais CEGEP Coll.; Bakery Counc. Can.; Past Pres. Hull C. of C.; Former Treas. Candn. Food Processors Assn.; mem. Candn. Restaurant Assn.; Club: Rivermead Golf (Aylmer, Qué.); Office: 1603, 275 Slater St., Ottawa, Ont. K1P 5H9.

**DuPONT, His Hon. Wilfred Roland;** judge; b. Foleyet, Ont., 16 Feb. 1926; s. Alexander and Aldea (St. Aubin) D.; e. Osgoode Hall Law Sch., 1950; m. Jeannine, d. Joseph David Levesque, 11 Feb. 1956; children: Linda, Louise, Julie, David, Denise, Richard; Justice, Supreme Court of Ont., Ex Offico, Mem., Ont. Court of Appeal 1977–..; called to Bar of Ont. 1950; cr. Q.C. 1963; private law practice, Timmins, Ont., 1950–53; Asst. Crown Atty. for Dist. of Cochrane, 1953–66; Crown Atty. for Prov. of Ont., 1966–68; Sr. Judge of Cochrane District Court, 1969–77; served with RCAF 1943–45; rank Flying Offr.; Chrmn. and Trustee, Cochrane High Sch. for 9 yrs. and Lady Minto Hosp. for 10 yrs.; R. Catholic; recreations: flying, hunting; Home: R.R. #3, Caledon East, Ont. L0N 1E0.

**DUPRAS, Yves,** LL.L.; lawyer, CRTC commissioner; b. Montreal, Que. 7 Sept. 1958; s. Claude and Manon (Dufresne) D.; e. Univ. of Montreal, Econ. 1978; Univ. of Ottawa, Pol. Sci. 1979, LL.L. 1982; called to Quebec Bar 1983; QUEBEC REGIONAL COMMISSIONER, CANADIAN RADIO-TELEVISION & TELECOMMUNICATIONS COMMISSION 1993– ; Lawyer, Heenan Blaikie; Legault Longtin; primary practice was entertainment, business and corporate law; Mem., Nat. Assn. of Regulatory Utility Comissioners; Candn. Bar Assn.; Barreau du Québec; Office: Place Montreal Trust, 1800 McGill College Ave., Suite 1920, Montreal, Que. H3A 3J6.

**DUPRE, John,** M.A., B.Sc., B.M., B.Ch., F.R.C.P., F.A.C.P.; university professor/physician; b. Bristol, England 20 Feb. 1931; s. William Edward and Dorothy Emily (Clark) D.; e. The Merchant Taylors' Sch. 1944–50; St. John's Coll., Oxford 1950–55 (Sir Thomas White Scholar in Nat. Sci. 1950–54; Theodore Williams Scholar, Dept. of Physiol. 1954; Life Mem., Sr. Common Rm.); St. Thomas' Hosp. Med. Sch. 1955–58; m. Gillian d. Col. & Mrs. R.C. Molesworth 25 June 1959; children: Matthew Guy, Louisa Jane, Richard Edward Luke; PROF. OF MED., UNIV. OF WEST. ONT. 1976– ; & CHIEF OF ENDOCRINOL. & METABOLISM, UNIV. HOSP., LONDON 1987– ; Lectr. in Med., London Univ. at St. Thomas Hosp. 1963–66; Radcliffe Travelling Fellow in Med. Sci., Univ. Coll., Oxford 1964–65; C.D. Howe Travelling Fellow, Assn. of Candn. Univ. & Coll. 1967–68; Scherring Fellow, Can. Soc. for Clin. Investig. 1967–68; Dir., Fraser Lab. for Rsch. in Diabetes, McGill Univ./Royal Victoria Hosp. 1969–74; Charles Best Medal & Prize for rsch. in diabetes in Can. 1974; Frederick Banting Award 1984; Mem., Am. Soc. for Clin. Investig.; The Endocrine Soc.; The Royal Soc. of Med. (UK); N.Y. Acad. of Sci.; author of articles & book chapters; Assoc. Ed., 'Pancreas'; former Assoc. Ed. 'Can. J. Phys. & Pharm.'; recreations: print collector & Oenophilist; club: Royal Can. Military Inst.; Home: 72 Sherwood Ave., London, Ont. N6A 2E2; Office: 339 Windermere Rd., London, Ont. N6A 5A5.

**DUPRE, Joseph Stefan,** O.C., O.Ont., A.M., Ph.D.; university professor; b. Quebec, Que. 3 Nov. 1936; s. late Hon. Maurice, P.C., K.C. and Anita Arden (Dowd) D.; e. St. Patrick's Sch., Quebec, Que.; Univ. of Ottawa, B.A. 1955; Harvard Univ., A.M. 1957, Ph.D. 1958; Hon. degrees: D.Sc.Soc., Laval, 1976; LL.D., McMaster, 1977; D.U., Univ. of Ottawa, 1977; m. Anne Louise, d. Dr. J. Robert Willson, Philadelphia, Pa., 6 July 1963; children: Daphne, Maurice; PROF. OF POL. SCIENCE UNIV. OF TORONTO since 1966, Chrmn. of the Dept. of Pol. Econ. 1970–74; Dir., Centre for Urban and Community Studies 1966–70; Teaching Fellow in Govt., Harvard Univ., 1956–57; Instr. 1958–61; Asst. Prof. 1961–63; Secy., Grad. Sch. of Pub. Adm., 1960–63; Mackenzie King Professor 1978–79; Research Fellow, The Brookings Inst., Washington, D.C., 1957–58; joined present Univ. as Assoc. Prof. of Pol. Science, 1963; Ed. Dir., Ont. Comte. on Taxation, 1964–67; mem., Ont. Civil Service Arbitration Bd., 1965–68; Science Council-Can. Council Study Group on Fed. Support of Univ. Research, 1967–68; Nat. Research Council of Can., 1969–77; Chrmn., Ont. Council on Univ. Affairs, 1974–77 and mem. 1977–83; Chrmn., Royal Com. on Asbestos 1980–84; Ont. Task Force on Financial Institutions 1985–86; Chrmn., Industrial Disease Standards Panel (Ont.) 1988–90; Chrmn., Natl. Innovation Advisory Ctte., Employment and Immigration Canada 1992– ; author: 'Intergovernmental Finance in Ontario: A Provincial-Local Perspective' 1968; 'Post-Secondary Operating Grants in Alberta' 1987; co-author 'Federalism and Policy Development' 1973; 'The Role of the Federal Government in the Support of Research in Canadian Universities' 1969; 'Science and the Nation' 1962, Japanese ed. 1965; also numerous contributions to books and scholarly journs.; mem., Inst. Pub. Adm. Can. (Nat. Vice Pres. 1967–69; Pres. 1969–70); Soc. Sciences and Hum. Research Council of Canada; Council of Trustees, Inst. for Research on Public Policy; Prof. Organizations Comte of the Atty. Gen. of Ont.; Candn. Pol. Science Assn. (Secy.-Treas. 1965–66); Candn. Tax Foundation; Officer of the Order of Canada 1986; Order of Ontario 1992; R. Catholic; Home: 422 Glencairn, Toronto, Ont. M5N 1V5.

**DUPREY, Donald Philip,** B.A.; broadcasting executive; b. Morris, Man. 24 Oct. 1940; s. Philip E. (dec.) and Jeanne (Alarie) D.; e. Portage La Prairie Coll. Inst. 1958; Univ. of Man. B.A. 1961, Cert. in Edn. 1962, M.A. studies 1965; m. Alexandria d. David and Diane Spindel 5 Sept. 1982; children, from previous marriage: David, Natasha; from present marriage: Jacob, Ethan; MNG. DIR. ENGLISH PROG. SERVICES, TV ONT. 1988– ; served with Royal Cdn. Arty. (Capt. (M)) 1958–62; High Sch. Teacher Winnipeg 1962–64; National Film Bd. Can. 1965–72, various positions incl. Exec. Producer; Vice Pres. and Gen. Mgr. International Cinemedia Centre Ltd. 1972–78; Pres. M.L.V. Media 1978–82; Mng. Dir., French Prog. Services 1982–88; Mem., Banff Television Festival Bd., Program Ctte., Assoc. Educational Television of Can.; major prodn. credits: Assoc. Prod. 'Apprenticeship of Duddy Kravitz'; Producer, CBC drama 'His Mother'; 'The Chinese' (6 part series); Home: 28 Strathearn Blvd., Toronto, Ont. M5P 1S7; Office: P.O. Box 200 Station Q, Toronto, Ont. M4T 2T1.

**DUPUIS, Pierre,** B.A.; corporate executive; b. Montreal, Que. 31 July 1944; s. Ladislas and Claire (Hartenstein) D.; e. Univ. de Montreal B.A. 1965; post grad. studies McGill Univ. 1965–67; m. Maureen d. Maurice and Doris Cloutier 28 May 1966; children: Francois, Simon; PRES., CONSTRUCTION MATERIALS & PACKAGING, DOMTAR INC. & VICE-PRES. OF CORP. 1985– ; Mktg. Extve., Imperial Oil Ltd. 1968–79; Vice-Pres., Petrochem., Groupe SGF 1979–81; Pres. & Chief Extve. Offr., Cegelec Industries 1981–83; Sr. Vice-Pres., Petrocanada Products 1983–85; Dir., Groupe Transcontinental GTC; Groupe GCI; Past Dir., Montreal C. of C.; Vice-Chrmn., Candn. Manufacturers' Assn.; Past Chrmn., Orch. Metropolitain; Gov., Orford Arts Center; Dir., Fond. Hop. Charles Lemoyne; Office: 395 de Maisonneuve W., Montreal, Que. H3A 1L6.

**DUPUIS, Yvon C.,** P.Eng., F.E.I.C.; consultant; b. Montreal, Que. 31 March 1932; s. Charles Joseph and Hélène (Tarte) D.; e. McGill Univ. B.Eng. Civil Engr. 1959; Loyola Coll. B.Sc.; m. Louise Demeules 30 May 1980; children: Danielle, Jean-Charles, Louis-Philippe, Marie-Claude; PRES., CONSULTANTS DELMONT INC. 1990– ; served in senior capacities with several leading engr. and construction firms prior to founding his own consulting company; has construction and consulting experience in 29 countries on 4 continents; Pres., Ordre des ingénieurs du Québec 1973–75; Pres. Conseil Interprofessionnel du Qué. 1974–76; Regional Vice Pres., Engineering Inst. of Can. 1975–76; Chrmn., A.C.E.C./C.I.D.A. Liaison Ctte., Assn. of Consulting Engrs. of Can. 1978–80; Pres., Consultants Dutech Inc. 1983–90; Pres., Can. Counc. of Professional Engineers 1986–87; Past bd. mem., Can. Coll. of Advanced Engineering Practice; Dir. & Extve. Ctte. Mem., Corporation Professionnelle des Médecins du Qué. 1986–1990; Mem., Nat. Adv. Bd. for Science and Technology 1987–91; Fellow, Engr. Inst. of Can.; Mem., Ordre des ingénieurs du Qué.; Assoc. of Profl. Engrs. of Ont.; recreations: skiing, riding, breeding and showing of thoroughbred beef cattle; Address: 40 chemin Thomson, Arundel, Que. J0T 1A0.

**DUPUY, Diane Lynn,** C.M., L.L.T.; arts executive; b. Hamilton, Ont. 8 Sept. 1948; d. the late Robert Stanley and Mary Christine (Gioberti) Thornton; e. Loretto Academy Hamilton, grade 8; m. Bernard Pierre Henri s. Adine and Jean-Paul (both dec.) D. 22 June 1974; children: Jeanine, Joanne; FOUNDER, PRESIDENT & ARTISTIC DIRECTOR, FAMOUS PEOPLE PLAYERS 1974– ; founded co. with small govt. grant & a dream of integrating developmentally challenged young people into the community & grooming them to be profl. performers; troupe is now a profl. theatre co. with 30 full-time staff, a prop construction unit & an understudy program which teaches performers life skills; tours to 60 N. Am. cities each year; Famous People Players (FPP) has appeared on Broadway, with Liberace in Las Vegas, Radio City Music Hall & the People's Rep. of China; FPP Theatre Centre Toronto scheduled to open 1993 (fully accessible to all people with disabilities); profl. motivational speaker; Order of Canada 1981; Woman of the Year Award, B'Nai Brith Women 1981; Vanier Award, Order of Canada, Jaycees of Canada 'Outstanding Young Canadian' Award 1982; Ernest C. Manning Award of Merit 1984; Candn. for Progress Award, Candn. Progress Club 1988; Service to Mankind Award, Hamilton Sertoma Club 1991; Hon. Doctorate of Law, Univ. of Calgary 1991; Hon. Doctorates, Univ. of Windsor & Trent Univ.; co-author: 'Dare to Dream' (with Liane Heller) 1988 (biography); Office: 45 Lisgar Ave., Toronto, Ont. M6J 3T3.

**DUPUY, Michel,** B.A., LL.D., Ph.D., M.P., P.C.; politician; b. Paris, France 11 Jan. 1930; Canadian citizen; e. Collège Stanislas B.A. 1946; Oxford Univ. 1950; Inst. of Pol. Studies Paris 1952; Univ. of Paris LL.D. 1954; m. Micheline D'Allaire; HERITAGE MINISTER (CANADA) 1993– ; Chief Govt. Negotiator, Canada-U.S. Air Agreement; Econ. Coop. Agreement with the Eur. Community; Negotiator, various nuclear co-op. and non-proliferation agreements; Asst. Under-Sec. of State for External Affairs (Econ. Relations); Canadian ambassador at the U.N. in Yew York; Canadian ambassador to France; Pres., Canadian International Development Agency; Chief Foreign-Policy Adviser to Jean Chrétien 1991–93; Gov., Internat. Devel. Rsch. Centre; Alternate Gov., World Bank, Inter-Am. Devel. Bank, Asian Devel. Bank, African Devel. Fund, Caribbean Devel. Bank; Bd. Mem., Export Devel. Corp.; author: 'La Source et le Feu' (novel) 1954; weekly articles for 'Le Droit' 1974–76; recreations: skiing, tennis, swimming; Home: 200 Rideau Terrace, Ottawa, Ont. K1M 0Z3; Office: Ottawa, Ont. K1A 0A6.

**DUQUETTE, Jean-Pierre,** L.èsL., de l'Acad. des Lettres du Qué.; university professor; b. Valleyfield, Que. 27 June 1939; s. Armand and Marguerite (Besner) D.; e. Univ. de Montréal L.èsL. 1963; Doctorat de 3e cycle Lettres modernes, Parix X 1969; PROF., DEPT. OF FRENCH, MCGILL UNIV. 1985– ; Asst. Prof., Dept. of French, McGill Univ. 1969; Assoc. Prof. 1973; Chair 1985–93; Vice-Pres., Centre québécois de P.E.N. Internat.; Sec. général, Acad. des Lettres du Qué.; author: 'Flaubert ou l'architecture du vide' 1972, 'Germaine Guèvremont: une route, une maison' 1973, 'Fernand Leduc' 1980, 'Colette, l'amour de l'amour' 1984; editor: 'Centenaire de Jean Cocteau' 1990; club: Faculty; Home: 3421 Drummond St., Apt. 74, Montreal, Que. H3G 1X7; Office: 3460 McTavish St., Montreal, Que. H3A 1X9.

**DURAND, Hon. Roland Louis Henri Gaston,** B.C.L.; judge; b. Montréal, Qué. 21 March 1932; s. Gaston Julien and Solange Estelle (Guillaudin) D.; e. Lycée Champollion and Univ. of Grenoble, France 1950; McGill Univ. B.C.L. 1957; m. Anne d. Lt. Col. Henri and Renée (Geoffrion) Vautelet, C.B.E., 28 apl. 1962; PUISNE JUDGE, SUPERIOR COURT OF QUE. 1982– ; called to Bar of Que. 1958; cr. Q.C. 1973; law practice 12 yrs. Brais, Campbell, Pepper & Durand, later Campbell, Pepper durand & Laffoley and with firms Yanofsky, Kahn, Durand, Marcovitch & Brull and Durand & Marcovitch; Mayor, Town of Rosemère 1970–82; Dir., CBC 1981–82; mem., Appeal Tribunal Rental Comn. 1971–82; Councillor, Treas., Vice Pres. Jr. Bar Montreal 1960–63; Pres., Jt. Town Planning Comn. Greater Ste-Thérèse 1971–78; Vice Pres. 1971–75, Pres. 1975–78 Planning Comn. Mirabel Airport Region; recipient Queen's Silver Jubilee Medal 1977; Home: 264 Willowtree, Rosemère, Qué. J7A 2E3; Office: 1 est, Notre Dame, Montréal, Qué. H2Y 1B6.

**DURHAM, Thompson Seelye,** C.D., B.A., M.B.A.; b. Sault Ste. Marie, Ont. 23 Mar. 1930; s. T. Edwin and Jessie (Seelye) D.; e. Queen's Univ., B.A., (Gen.) 1954; M.B.A. Univ. of West. Ont. 1959; m. Leone A., d. Engner Lindstrom, Kenora, Ont., 30 June 1956; MGR., BETTER BUSINESS BUREAU OF WINNIPEG AND MANITOBA INC.; TEXPEX principal; Service Affiliation, Naval Rank CDR (R) Ret'd HMCS Chippawa; recreations: outdoors, telecommunications; Club: Rotary; Home: 118 Talon Bay, Winnipeg, Man. R2M 2B7; Office: 204 - 365 Hargrave St., Winnipeg, Man. R3B 2K3.

**DURIEUX-SMITH, Andrée,** B.èsA., B.Sc., M.Sc., Ph.D.; audiologist; b. Montreal, Que. 3 Jan. 1943; d. Maurice and Emilienne (Cristel) D.; e. Collège Marie de France B.èsA. 1960; McGill Univ. B.Sc. 1964, M.Sc. 1968, Ph.D. 1974; m. Roger B. s. Arthur and Elsie Smith 8 Oct. 1970; children: Dominique, Michel; DIR. AND PROF., PROGRAM IN AUDIOLOGY AND SPEECH-LANGUAGE PATHOLOGY, FACULTY OF HEALTH SCIENCES, UNIV. OF OTTAWA 1993– ; Dir., Audiology Dept., Children's Hosp. of Eastern Ont. (CHEO) 1974–91; Dir., Dept. of Communication Disorders, Children's Hosp. of Eastern Ont. 1991–93; Assoc. Ed., 'J. of Speech-Language Path. & Audiology'; Chair, Candn. Joint Ctte. on Hearing-Impairment, Health Serv. Directorate, Health & Welfare 1989– ; Mem., Review Ctte. on Rehab. & of several task forces addressing hearing loss, Health & Welfare Can. 1978–90; Founding & Active Mem., CHEO Rsch. Inst. 1985– ; recipient of var. peer-reviewed rsch. grants; Prof., Otolaryngology, Fac. of Med., Univ. of Ottawa; Mem., Candn. Assn. of Speech-Language Pathol. & Audiol. (Past Pres.); Ont. Assn. of Speech-Language Pathol. & Audiol.; Am. Auditory Soc.; Am. Speech & Hearing Assn.; Honours, Candn. Assn. of Speech-Language Pathol. & Audiol. for Outstanding Scholarly Contbns. 1987; Award for Most Outstanding Paper, Am. Auditory Soc. 1986; author/co-author of over sixty peer-reviewed articles, abstracts & chapters in books; recreations: alpine skiing, running, tennis: Home: 4804 Massey Lane, Gloucester, Ont. K1J 8W9; Office: 545 King Edward, Ottawa, Ont. K1N 6N5.

**DURNAN, William (Bill) David,** CAAP; b. Ottawa, Ont. 17 July 1951; s. William Ronald and Amanda (Kent) D.; e. George Vanier; Cert. Advtg. Agency Practioners Course (CAAP), 3 yrs.; m. Indra d. Uldis and Tatjana Kiesners 30 Sept. 1983; children: Sandra, Matthew; SR. VICE-PRES. NAT. CREATIVE DIR., MACLAREN: LINTAS INC.; Acct. Coord., Vickers & Benson Advtg. 1972; Acct. Extve., (Gulf Oil) 1973; (Loblaws, IAC Fin., Bell Can.) 1977; Acct. Extve., (Molson Breweries, Molson Lite Intro., Molson Brador Promotions), MacLaren Advtg. 1977; Sr. Acct. Extve. 1978; Acct. Supvr. (Molson – All Brands) 1979; Copywriter (John Deere, Boots No. 7, Imperial Oil, Molson Cdn., Lever Bros.) 1980; Vice-Pres. Toronto Creative Dir. 1984; awards: 'Gold Clio,' 'Bessie' Campaign of the Year, Molson Cdn. 1985, 1988; 'IBA Gold' for Molson Cdn. Radio; 'Art Dir. Club of Toronto' Campaign gold medal & over 50 internat. cert. of excellence incl. Cannes, Clios, New York A.D., Art Direction Mag., Internat. Film & TV Fest. of N.Y., London Internat., Mktg.; Home: 1436 Crescent Rd., Mississauga, Ont.; Office: 20 Dundas St. W., Toronto, Ont. M5G 2H1.

**DUROCHER, The Hon. Denis,** B.A., LL.L., D.E.S.D.; judge; b. Montreal, Que. 12 Dec. 1933; s. Roland Joseph and Gabrielle (Desjardins) D.; e. Univ. of Ottaw, B.A. 1955, LL.L. 1958; McGill Univ., admitted to Que. Bar 1959; Univ. of Ottawa Law Sch., D.E.S.D. 1968; m. Claire d. Edouard and Stella Robert 19 Sept. 1960; children: Benoit, Geneviève, Antoine, Nicolas, Mathieu; JUDGE, SUPERIOR COURT OF QUE. 1980– ; Dept. of Trade & Comm. 1959; gen. legal prac., Laprairie, Que. 1959–63; civil, comml. & bankruptcy prac., Birtz, Leduc & Durand; and Pouliot, Mercure 1968–71; labour, Marcoux, Durand, Brunet & Durocher 1971–75; labour arbitrator, Que. 1975–80; Rental Appeal Bd. Comnr. 1971–80; Pres., discipl. cttes. of some profl. corps. under the Profl. Code of Que.; Private Bills in Parls. in Ottawa & Que.; Former Dir., Que. Conf. of Arbitrators; Beloeil Golf Club; Lectr., Univ. du Qué. à Montréal; Past Pres., Club Richelieu, Laprairie & St-Bruno; recreations: skiing, golf; Office: 1, rue Notre-Dame est, Bureau 16.45, Montréal, Qué. H2Y 1B6.

**DUROCHER, Brig. Gen. Jean Yvon,** C.D., M.Eng.; Candn. Forces; b. Fort Coulonge, Que. 28 May 1940; s. Romeo Joseph and Marie Jeanne (Rivet) D.; e. Coll. Militaire Royal de Saint Jean; Royal Mil. Coll. Kingston B.E. (Elect. Engn.) 1962, M.Eng. 1971; m. Patricia G. d. George and Margaret Mabee 4 May 1963; children: Grant, Suzanne, Kyle, Patricia; COMPTROLLER, COMM. SECURITY ESTABLISHMENT 1987– ; Organization & Establishments Defence HQ 1985–87; joined RCAF 1957; held various staff and operational appts. Maritimes, Ontario, Quebec; Commandant Coll. Militaire Royal de Saint Jean 1981; Candn. Amateur Radio Fed.; recreation: amateur radio; Home: 33 Hawk Cres., Ottawa, Ont. K1V 9G8; Office: 719 Heron Rd., Ottawa, Ont.

**DUROCHER, René,** B.A., B.Péd., L.ès L., D.E.S., F.R.S.C.; historian; b. Montréal, Qué. 28 June 1938; s. Roger and Germaine (Doucet) D.; e. Univ. de Montréal B.A. 1960, B.Péd. 1960, L.ès L. 1965, D.E.S. Histoire 1968; m. Raymonde d. Joseph and Solika Sabbah 18 Dec. 1981; one s. Eric; VICE-DEAN, FACULTY OF ARTS ET SCIENCES 1987– ; & PROF. OF HISTORY, UNIV. DE MONTREAL 1974– ; Asst. and Assoc. Prof., York Univ. Toronto 1971–74; Maître de Conférences Institut d'Etudes Politiques Univ. de Bordeaux, France 1975–76; Professeur invité Univ. of Calgary summer 1972, Israel summer 1980; Prés. Institut d'Histoire de l'Amérique française 1977–81; Chrmn., Prog. d'études québécoises 1982–85; Chrmn. of the Dept., present univ. 1984–87; mem., Conseil de la Sci. et de la Technologie du Qué. 1981–86; Pres. Candn. Historical Assn. 1986–87; co-author 'Le retard du Québec et l'infériorité économique des Canadiens français' 1971; 'Histoire du Québec contemporain 1867–1929' 1979; 'Nouvelle histoire du Canada et du Québec'; 'Histoire du Québec contemporain'; 'Le Quebec depuis 1930'; Office: C.P. 6128, Succ. A, Montréal, Qué. H3C 3J7.

**DURR, Pat,** B.A.Ed.H., R.C.A.; visual artist; b. Kansas City, Missouri 18 Sept. 1939; d. Martin Max and Lorraine (Lueking) Goldberg; e. Univ. of Kansas B.A.Ed. (Hons.) 1961; Univ. of Southampton England 1961–62; Kansas City Art Inst. 1963; Ottawa Sch. of Art 1965; m. Laurence s. James and Edith D. 16 March 1963; children: Tanya M. and T. Sean; 18 solo exbns. incl. most recent: Ottawa Public Art Gall. 1993; Le Centre d'Exposition L'Imagier, Aylmer, Que. 1993; MacLaren Art Gall., Barrie, Ont. 1992; Art Gall. of Algoma Sault Ste-Marie, Ont. 1990, Confederation Ctr. Art Gall. Charlottetown, P.E.I. 1989; over 30 group exbns. incl. most recent: 'Just A Taste of the Claridge Collection, 25th Anniversary Exhibition' Saidye Bronfman Centre, Montreal 1992; 'Canadian Printmakers' Gallery 206, Missouri Western State College, St. Joseph, Missouri 1992; 'Okanata' A-Space and Workscene Galleries, Toronto 1991; 4-person show 1990; 'Print Types' Owatonna Art Ctr. Minnesota 1991; 'Twelve Ottawa Painters' Arts Court Gall. Ottawa 1990; 'Papier' Arts Court Municipal Art Gall. 1990; works in num. public and private collections incl. Esso Resources Calgary, Petro Canada, Canada Capital Congress Ctr., Canada Council Art Bank, Ont. Min. of Govt. Serv., Corp. of the City of Ottawa, Toronto Dominion Bank, Univ. of Kansas, etc.; public comns.: Ottawa Bd. of Edn., City of Ottawa, Ottawa-Carleton Regional/O.C. Transpo; awards: 5

Ont. Arts Council grants 1979–92; Regional Municipality of Ottawa-Carleton Artist 'A' Grant 1992, Victor Tolgesy Arts Award City of Ottawa 1989, Leighton Colony Artist in Residence Banff Alta. 1988, Loomis & Toles Reg. Juried Exbn. First Prize Painting 1983, Canada Council Travel Grant 1981–82, Univ. of Kansas/Univ. of Southampton Exchange Grant/Fellowship 1961–62, Fulbright Found. Travel Grant 1961; extensive involvement in design, development & implementation of municipal & educational architectural projects; has participated at project team level, executed public art comns. & initiated public consultation; Nat. Spokesperson, CARFAC 1982–84; Chair, Jack Chambers Found. 1984–86; Chair, CAR-Ottawa 1978–80; Chair, Tax Ctte., Candn. Conf. of The Arts 1984–86; subject of num. articles in magazines and newspapers; author of 12 articles and numerous reviews of art exbns.; recreations: gardening; Address: 167 First Ave., Ottawa, Ont. K1S 2G3.

**DURRANT, Geoffrey Hugh,** D. Litt. et Phil., F.R.C.S.; educator; b. Pilsley, Eng. 27 July 1913; s. John and Charlotte (Atkinson) D.; e. Chesterfield Sch. Eng.; Jesus Coll. Cambridge Univ. (Open Scholarship 1932–35, Kitchener Scholarship 1932–36) B.A. 1935; King's Coll. Univ. London Ed. Dipl. 1936; Univ. of Tuebingen 1937–39; Univ. of S. Africa D. Litt. et Phil. 1970; m. Barbara Joan d. late John Altson, Natal, S. Africa June 1942; children: John Guy, Catherine Jane; Prof. of Eng. Univ of B.C. 1966–81; Prof. Emeritus 1981; Head Dept. Eng. 1966–69; Head Dept. Eng. Univ. of Natal 1944–60, Univ. of Man. 1965–66; Visiting Prof. Univ. York (Eng.), Univ. of N.Y. Buffalo, Australian Nat. Univ., Univ. of Tuebingen, Univ. of Waterloo, Univ. of York, Eng., La Trobe Univ. Australia; rec'd Carnegie Fellowship 1960; Master Teacher Award U.B.C. 1973; Killam Sr. Fellowship 1976; active in adult educ. and S. African pol. movements 1945–60; Moderator in Eng. Jt. Matric. Bd. S. African Univs. 1948–60; awarded Coronation Medal 1953; served with 1st S. African Div. E. Africa, Egypt 1941–42, S. African Intelligence 1942–44; author 'William Wordsworth' 1969; 'Wordsworth and the Great System' 1970; monographs and articles on Shakespeare, Wordsworth, Malcolm Lowry and on educ. topics; el. Fellow of Royal Soc. of Can. 1977; mem. Assn. Candn. Univ. Teachers Eng.; recreations: fishing, chess; Home: 3994 W. 34th Ave., Vancouver, B.C. V6N 2L5.

**DUSCHENES, Mario,** C.M., LL.D.; conductor; b. Altona 27 Oct. 1923; s. Frank and Greta (Winman) D.; e. Cons. de Genève, Switzerland, Prix de Virtuosité 1946; m. Ellyn d. Hugo and Madeleine Simons 21 Sept. 1951; children: Jeremy, Monica, Michael, Peter, Christopher; GUEST CONDUCTOR, NFLD. SYMPHONY ORCHESTRA; Music Dir., Nfld. Symphony Orch. 1985–..; Soloist, Ars Antiqua Ensemble 1946–48; Principal flute, CBC Montreal Symphony Orch. 1950–55; Prof., McGill Univ. 1952–72; Mem., Baroque Trio 1957–71; Host. & Cond., 'Initiation a la mus. avec M. Duschenes' (Radio-Canada) 1970–85; Dir., CAMMAC; Noon Concerts, Place des Arts Montreal; conducts 100 concerts annually nationwide; over thirty recordings; Order of Canada 1985; 1st prize Geneva Internat. Music. Comp. 1947; Candn. Music Counc., best edn. TV prog. 19..; Hon. doct., Concordia Univ. 1982; Nat. Pres., 'Jeunesses Mus. du Can.' 1983–85; author: 'Method for the Recorder Mario Duschenes' 19..; recreations: tennis, cross country skiing; Address: 4214 Ostell Place, Montreal, Qué. H4P 1N4.

**DUSCHENES, Rolf,** C.M., B.Arch., F.R.A.I.C., F.R.S.A.; architect; b. Hamburg, Germany 6 Jan. 1918; s. Franz and Grete Marie Sophie (Winsemann) D.; e. Sr. Matric. Marienau, Germany 1937; Prague Univ. 1938; Ecole des Beaux Arts, Geneva 1939; S.E. Essex Sch. of Design 1940; McGill Univ., Montreal B.Arch. 1945; m. Ermon Fay d. Guy and Ora Johnson 13 Dec. 1946; children: Ellis Lynn, Jennifer, Julie, Claudia, Wendy; ARCHITECT AND PARTNER, DUSCHENES, FISH & START, SAINT JOHN 1988– ; AND DUSCHENES & FISH MONTREAL 1978– ; Pres. Endec Ltd.; Archit. Ross, Patterson, Townsend & Heughan, Montreal 1946; Mgr. Saint John office of that co. 1948; Partner, Ross, Fish, Duschenes & Barrett, Montreal and Saint John 1958; Fellow, Royal Archit. Inst. of Can.; Order of Archit. of Que.; Archit.'s Assn. of N.B. (Pres. 1957–58); Sec. N.B. Youth Orchestra Found. Inc.; Past Pres. N.B. Youth Orch. 1972–87; Founding Dir. 1973 and Pres. 1981–83 Candn. Assn. of Youth Orchs.; Vice-Pres. Nat. Youth Orch. 1980; Dir. Saint John Symphony Orch.; Dir. Candn. Assn. of Orchs. 1978–80; Gov. Candn. Conf. of the Arts 1981–85; mem. Order of Can.; Fellow, Royal Soc. of Arts; mem. McGill C.O.T.C. Contingent 1942–45; McGill Scarlet Key Soc. 1944–45; Pres. McGill Archit. Undergrad. Soc. 1944–45; Pres. N.B. Br., McGill Grad. Soc. 1966–67; Pres. Saint John Exec. Assn. 1966–67; recreations: tennis, skiing, music; Home: R.R. 2-13-1, Westfield, N.B. E0G 3J0; Office: P.O. Box 2204, Saint John, N.B. E2L 3V1.

**DUSCHESNE, Robert,** B.A., B.A.A. (Elec. Engr.); business executive; b. Rimouski, Que. 26 April 1939; e. Séminaire de Rimouski, B.A. 1960; Laval Univ., B.A.A. (Elec. Engr.) 1964; m. Michèle Desmeules 15 April 1967; children: Marie-Claude, Marjorie; VICE PRES., MKTG. & BUS. DEVEL. AND DIR., QUE. TELEPHONE 1987– ; Vice Pres., Consortel 1987– ; Dir., Conseil économique de Rimouski 1986– ; joined Que. Telephone as Engr., Toll Equipment 1964; held various engr. positions 1964–77; Gen. Mgr., N. Shore Region 1977; Dir., Switching Services 1981; Vice Pres., Network Engr. & Constrn. 1981; Vice Pres., Mktg. & Customer Service 1986; Mem. Extve. Ctte., Que. Region, Candn. Cancer Soc.; Club de nage synchronisée Vivelo de Rimouski; mem. Order of Engrs. of Que.; recreations: music, photography, skiing, horticulture, handiwork; Home: 33, de Touraine, Rimouski, Que. G5L 5N5; Office: 6, Jules-A.-Brillant, Rimouski, Que. G5L 7E4.

**DUSSAULT, Hon. René,** B.A., LL.L., Ph.D.; judge; b. Quebec, Que. 23 Nov. 1939; s. Daniel and Madeleine (Pelletier) D.; e. Laval Univ. B.A. 1959, LL.L. 1962; London Sch. of Econ. & Pol. Sci. Ph.D. 1965; m. Marielle d. Roger and Yvette Godbout 8 July 1967; children: François-René, Louis-Martin; JUDGE. QUE. COURT OF APPEAL 1989– ; Co-Chrmn., Royal Comn. on Aboriginal Peoples 1991– ; lectr. in law Laval Univ. 1966–70; legal counsel Que. Health & Welfare Inquiry Comn.; special adv. to Min. of Social Affairs Que. 1970–73; Chrmn. Que. Professions Bd. 1973–77; Dep. Min. of Justice Que. 1977–80; Prof. Nat. Sch. Pub. Adm. 1981–89; held Laskin Chair in Pub. Law Osgoode Hall Law Sch. 1983–84; legal cons. law firm Kronströon, McNicoll & Associates, Quebec City; el. mem. Royal Soc. Can. 1987; recipient Que. Bar Assn. Medal 1987; Que. Interprofessional Counc. Prize 1991; York Univ. LL.D. (Hon.) 1992; author 'Le contrôle judiciaire de l'administration au Québec' 1969; 'Traité de droit administratif' tomes 1 et 2 1974, 1st ed.; co-author tomes 1,2,3 1984, 1986, 1989, 2nd ed.; co-author 'Administrative Law: A Treatise' vols. 1,2,3,4,5 1985, 1988, 1989, 1990; asst. ed. Candn. Pub. Adm. review 1982–89; Home: 1332 James-Lemoine, Sillery, Que. G1S 1A3; Office: 300 boul. Jean Lesage, Quebec City, Que. G1K 8K6.

**DUTIL, Marcel,** C.M.; industrial executive; b. Ville St. Georges, Beauce, Qué. 17 Aug. 1942; s. Roger and Gilberte (Lacroix) D.; e. St. Georges Primary Sch.; Académie de Qué.; m. Hélène d. Odule Giguère 1 Feb. 1964; children: Marc, Charles, Anne-Marie, Sophie; CHRMN., THE CANAM MANAC GROUP INC., Founder 1973; Chrmn., Canam Steel Works; Pitt Steel; Manac Inc.; Biltrite Nightingale Inc.; Canam Steel Corp.; Murox Inc.; Dir. Roins Holdings Ltd.; National Bank of Canada; Noverco Inc.; Textiles Dionne Inc.; Groupe Transcontinental; G.T.C. Ltée; Compagnie d'Assurance du Québec; Inter-Canadien; Québec Téléphone; joined Canam Steel Works Inc. 1963, Gen. Mgr. 1966; Founded Manac Inc. 1966; named Business Man of Month, Revue Commerce Oct. 1978; mem., Order of Canada 1985; D.U., Univ. de Sherbrooke 1989; R. Catholic; recreations: bridge, hunting, jogging; Home: 1296 Redpath Cres., Montréal, Qué. H3G 2K1; Office: 11535 1re Ave., Suite 700, Ville St. Georges, Beauce, Qué. G5Y 7H5 and 1800 McGill Coll., 27th Flr., Montréal, Qué. H3A 3J6.

**DUTIL, Hon. Robert,** B.P.E., M.B.A.; politicien; né St. Georges de Beauce, Qué. 16 avril 1950; f. Roger et Gilberte (Lacroix) D.; é. Seminaire St-Georges, St-Georges de Beauce, Que., Diploma in Collegial studies in Sciences 1969; Univ. Laval B.P.E. 1973, M.B.A. 1982; MINISTRE DES APPROVISIONNEMENTS ET SERVICES 1989– ; Directeur général centre sportif St. Georges de Beauce 1973–75; Directeur général adjoint et co-propriétaire Vélo-Sport Inc. 1975–77; Administrateur et co-propriétaire Sports Experts St. Georges 1976–84; Vice-prés. et co-propriétaire de Procycle inc. 1977–86; Prés. et co-propriétaire du Beauce-Bois Inc. 1985; Conseiller municipal St. Georges de Beauce 1975–79, Maire 1979–85; Préfet MRC Beauce-Sartigan 1982–85; Député provincial de Beauce-Sud 1985– , Ministre délégué aux pêcheries 1985; Min. délégué à la Famille à la Santé et aux Services Sociaux 1987; Min. des Communications 1988; Min. des Approvisionnements et Services 1989; récréations: tennis, skiing, lecture, echecs, cinéma, bicyclette; Adresse: 10555 Blvd. Lacroix, Ville St-Georges de Beauce, Qué. G5Y 1K2; Bureaux: 575, rue St-Amable, 5e étage, Québec, Qué. G1R 5N9 et 12435, 1ère Avenue, St-Georges, Qué. G5Y 2E3.

**DUTKA, Randall Joseph,** F.S.A., F.C.I.A.; consulting actuary; b. Winnipeg, Man. 11 Nov. 1946; s. Joseph and Mary (Zubricki) D.; e. Univ. of Man., B.Comm. (Hons.) 1968; Univ. of Toronto, Fac. of Mgmt. Studies 1973–74; m. Catherine d. Joseph and Phyllis Eansor 26 Feb. 1972; children: Christine Marie, Jillian Louise, Joseph Randall; PARTNER-IN-CHARGE, PEAT MARWICK THORNE ACTUARIAL & BENEFITS INC.; var. positions ending as Actuarial Asst., Canada Life 1968–72; Group Extve. Actuar. Offr., Commercial Union 1972–73; Mgr., Employee Benefit Practice Vanc., Peat Marwick Consulting Group 1974–78; Mgr., Actuar. Serv. Toronto 1978–81; Partner, Compensation & Benefits 1981–89; Partner & Dir., Peat Marwick Stevenson & Kellogg 1989–91; F.S.A., F.C.I.A.; Counc., Candn. Inst. of Actuaries; Dir., Actuar. Edn. & Rsch. Fund; Adv., CEBS Program; Mem., Assn. of Candn. Pension Mgmt.; Candn. Pension & Benefits Conf.; World Future Soc.; Human Resource Professionals Assn. of Ont. (C.H.R.P.); Candn. Compensation Assn.; co-author: 'Pensions and Retirement Planning' 1985; 2nd ed. 'Pensions and Retirement Income Planning: New Rules and Strategies' 1987; 'Pensions and Retirement Income Planning: New Tax Rules and Strategies' 1990–91; 'Pensions and Retirement Income Planning' 1993; co-editor 'Canadian Employment Benefits & Pension Guide'; frequent lectr., speaker, writer; recreations: photography, computers, travel; Club: Ont.; Home: 2163 Adair Cres., Oakville, Ont. L6J 5J6; Office: P.O. Box 31, Commerce Court P.S., Toronto, Ont. M5L 1B2.

**DUTOIT, Charles Edouard;** conductor; artistic director; b. Lausanne, Switzerland 7 Oct. 1936; s. Edmond and Berthe (Laedermann) D.; e. Conservatory of Lausanne, Acad. Music, Geneva; Academia Musicale Chigiana, Siena; Conserv. Benedetto Marcello, Venice, Italy; m. Marie-Josée Drouin; children: Ivan, Anne-Catherine; ARTISTIC DIR., ORCHESTRE SYMPHONIQUE DE MONTREAL 1977– ; debut with Bern Symphony Orch. 1963, Assoc. Conductor 1964, Music Dir. 1966–68; invited to conduct Vienna Opera and apptd. Music Dir. Radio-Zurich Orch. 1964; Music Dir. Mexico's Nat. Orch. 2 yrs.; regular Conductor Göteborg Orch., Sweden 1975–78; regularly conducts London Symphony, London Philharmonic, Royal Philharmonic and New Philharmonia orchs.; regular guest conductor, Berlin Philharmonic Orch., La Scala de Milan, Concertgebouw-Amsterdam, Boston Symphony Orch., Philadelphia Orch., New York Philharmonic, Cincinatti, Los Angeles, Minnesota, and Cleveland Orchs.; debut with present Orch. 1977; will make his debut at the Metropolitan Opera as guest conductor Dec. 1987; has conducted over 2,000 concerts with world's greatest orchestras; tours regularly Europe, S. Am., & Japan; over 60 recordings on DECCA-LONDON, DGG, PHILLIPS & ERATO; more than 25 international record awards including Platinum status for sales in excess of 100,000 records of Ravel's Bolero in Canada alone; with present world acclaimed orch. toured Can. and Am. W. Coast 1981; high success European tour 1984; Japan and Hong Kong Festivals 1985; toured United States and Western Canada (EXPO 86) 1986; plays Carnegie Hall annually; Protestant; recreations: swimming, reading, travel; Address: 85 St. Catherine St. W., Suite 900, Montreal, Que. H2X 3P4.

**du TOIT, Roger,** M.Arch.; architect; b. Cape Town, S. Africa 20 Dec. 1939; s. Reginald FitzRoy and Violet Mary (Marx) du T.; e. Univ. of Cape Town, B.Arch. 1963; Univ. of Toronto, M.Arch. 1966; m. Sheila d. Fuller and Gwendolyn Kingston; children: Robert Nicholas, Andre Christopher Karel; PRIN., ROGER du TOIT ARCHITECTS LIMITED 1975– ; and PRIN. du TOIT, ALLSOPP, HILLIER, PLANNERS & LANDSCAPE ARCHS. 1985– ; joined H.G. Huckle and Partners London, Eng. 1963 and taught at Coll. of Technol. Arch. Sch., Oxford; joined John Andrews Archs. Toronto 1966, Assoc. 1969, Partner 1970; estbd. John Andrews International/Roger du Toit, Toronto 1973; Co-founded Planning Services International 1978–83 and Cunningham du Toit Edmonton 1981–87; present firms have completed numerous private and pub. sector projects and studies Can., USA and Hong Kong; completed urban design work incls. long range devel. plans Univ. of Minn.'s St. Paul and Minneapolis Campuses, Univ. of B.C., S. Downtown Vancouver, Ceremonial Routes Ottawa, site selection Candn. Museum of Civilization and Nat. Gallery of Can., long range development plan for Houses of Parlt. and Supreme Court area Ottawa; completed arch. projects incl. (in jt. venture) CN Tower Toronto, Garneau Student Housing Univ. of Alta., Designers Walk Toronto, Windward Co-operative Housing Harbourfront Toronto; Univ. of Windsor Fac. of Bus.; Sun Parlour Home for Aged, Leamington; completed landscape arch. projects incl. numerous downtown revitalization streetscapes; comnd. Arch./Planner and Chrmn. of Arch. Adv. Ctte. Wascana Centre Regina since 1979; winner landscape competition Winston Churchill Square Edmonton; numerous arch. and landscape design awards; City of Toronto Medal of Service to Community 1982; served several civic adv. cttes. and juries; lectr., design critic and adv. various arch. schs.; author numerous articles; mem. Royal Arch. Inst. Can.; Ont. Assn. Archs.; Candn. Inst. Planners; Am. Inst. Cert. Planners; Ont. Assn. Landscape Archs.; Home: 108 Park Rd., Toronto, Ont. M4W 2N7; Office: 50 Park Rd., Toronto, Ont. M4W 2N5.

**DUTTON, John Edgar,** B.A., B.L.S.; retired librarian; b. Lethbridge, Alta. 30 Aug. 1924; s. Edgar Evans and Hannah Eleanor (Turner) D.; e. Lethbridge Coll. Inst. 1942; Univ. of Alta. B.A. 1950; Univ. of Toronto B.L.S. 1951; m. Helen Irene d. Frank Dudley Stapley 28 Nov. 1945; children: Corinne Eleanor, Carolyn Ann, Dianne Lillian; Dir., Calgary Public Library 1979–91; joined Univ. of Alta. Lib. 1951–53; Chief Lib. Lethbridge Pub. Lib. 1953–63 and North York Pub. Lib. 1963–77; City Lib. Winnipeg Pub. Lib. 1977–79; served with RCAF 1943–46; author encyclopedia articles, papers on librarianship; rec'd Outstanding Service to Librarianship Award, Candn. Lib. Assn. 1987; Distinguished Graduate Award, Univ. of Toronto 1989; mem. Lib. Assn. Alta. (Pres. 1962); Candn. Lib. Assn. (2nd Vice Pres.); Ont. Lib. Assn. (Pres. 1969–70); United Church; recreations: canoeing, tennis, skiing, hiking, photography, theatre, reading; Home: 4240 – 40 St. N.W., Calgary, Alta. T2A 0H6.

**DUTTON, William Ross;** oil & gas industry executive; b. Virden, Man. 6 May 1933; s. William L. and Dorothy J. (McMillian) D.; e. Virden C.I. 1952; numerous spacial engr. & special business course; m. Donna d. Ed and Tena Hagan 23 July 1954; children: W. Craig, G. Scott, A. Brad, E. Drew; PRES. & CHRMN., UPTON RESOURCES INC.; has spent his lifetime in oil & gas exploration & drilling in Western Canada, N.W.T. & N.W. U.S.A.; Pres., Clan Resources Ltd.; Dag Resources Ltd.; Dir., Small Explorers & Producers Assn. of Can.; Alliance to Promote & Preserve Rural Sask.; Past Pres. & Dir., Estevan Flying Club & Sask. Aviation Counsel; Past Pres., Estevan Bruin Hockey Club Jr.; Estevan Oil Tech. Soc.; recreations: golf, hunting; clubs: Assiniboia Club Regina, Canadian Oldtimers Hockey Assn.; Home: 1429 – 2nd St., Estevan, Sask.; Office: 322 – 4th St., Estevan, Sask. S4A 2G1.

**DUVAR, Ivan E.H.,** B.E., P.Eng., D.C.L.; public utility executive; b. Charlottetown, P.E.I. 30 March 1939; e. Prince of WalesColl. Charlottetown 1956; Mt. Allison Univ. Engn. 1960; Tech. Univ. of N.S. Elect.Engn. 1962; St. Mary's Univ. Candn. Inst. Mgmt. 1973; D.C.L. (Hon.), Acadia Univ.; CHRMN., PRESIDENT & CEO, MARITIME TELEGRAPH & TELEPHONE CO., LTD. 1985– ; Chrmn., The Island Telephone Co. 1975– ; Dir., Stentor Resource Centre Inc.; Air Nova; Candn. Imperial Bank of Commerce; Halifax Insurance; NN Financial Co. of Can.; Eastern Telephone & Telegraph Co.; Oxford Frozen Foods; Conference Bd. of Can.; Chrmn., Bd. of Govs., Tech. Univ. of N.S.; Adv. Bd., Dalhousie Sch. of Business; IWK Hosp. Found.; joined Bell Canada, Engn. 1962–66; Maritime Telegraph and Telephone Co. Ltd., Engn. 1966–68, Business Information Mgr. 1968–72, Chief Engr. 1973, Vice Pres. Planning 1975; Pres. The Island Tel. 1975; Vice Pres. Operations 1982 and V.P. Marketing 1984; served with COTC, rank Lt.; Past Pres., Halifax Bd. of Trade; Fellow, Candn. Acad. of Engr.; mem., Halifax Club; Assn. Prof. Engrs. N.S.; Inst. Elect. & Electronic Engrs.; Candn. Inst. Mgmt.; Home: 52 Edward Laurie Dr., Halifax, N.S. B3M 2C7; Office: 1505 Barrington St., Halifax, N.S. B3J 2W3.

**DYBA, Kenneth,** B.A.; writer; stage director; researcher; archivist; b. Nordegg, Alta. 9 May 1945; s. Walter and Stefania (Filipowicz); e. West. Can. H.S.; Univ. of B.C., B.A. 1966; 1960s: Reporter & other positions, The Calgary Herald; News Announcer & other positions, CHQR Radio, Calgary; Artistic & Public Relations Dir., MAC 14 Theatre; Freelance Dir., Calgary Arts Ctr. Theatre Co. & Theatre Can.; freelance stage direction for many profl. prodns.; 1970s: Dir., Dramaturge, Theatre Calgary; Dir., Script Devel., Que. Drama Fest.; Art. Dir., Admin., Dramaturge, Pleiades Theatre; Archivist, Radio Archives, CBC Toronto 1980–91; Lectr., Banff Playwrights Colony; Notre Dame Summer Sch.; Okanagan Summer Sch. of the Arts; Alta. Gov. Achievement Award; Ford of Can. Achievement Award; City of Calgary Achievement Award; Can. Counc.; Ont. Arts Counc.; Mem., Candn. Actors Equity; Playwrights Union of Can.; author: 'Sister Roxy' 1973, 'Lucifer and Lucinda' 1977, 'The Long (and Glorious) Weekend of Raymond (and Bingo) Oblongh' 1983 (novels); 'Betty Mitchell' 1986 (biog.); 'Teaser!' 1975, 'The Sun Runner' 1983, 'Lilly, Alta.' 1986 (formerly radio play prod. on CBC 1980) (stage plays); 'Peggy's Miranda' 1988 (children's play); 'Yerma' 1978 (transl./adapt. of Garcia Lorca play); over 80 short stories and one-act plays; cond., num. workshops in writing & theatre; script adjudication; recreations: bicycling, reading, flying, working with writers on devel. of their work, movies; Home: Victoria, B.C.

**DYCK, Edward Frank,** M.Ed., M.A., Ph.D.; writer, teacher; b. Turnhill, Sask. 3 Sept. 1939; s. Peter P. and Anna Nora (Klassen) D.; e. Univ. of Sask., M.Ed. 1964; Univ. of Minn., M.A. (Math'l. logic) 1973; Univ. of Man., M.A. (Engl.) 1980, Ph.D. 1988; has lived with Gloria Jane Forbes and her daughter, Lara Jane since 1979; English Teacher, Univ. of Man. 1989–90; Guest Prof., Univ. Augsburg 1989; sess. lectr., Univ. of Man. & Sask. 1980–87; Math. Teacher, Gustavus Adolphus Coll. 1968–69; Univ. of Missouri 1971–72; Sask. Tech. Inst. 1975–78; Creative Writing Teacher, Univ. of Sask. 1981–82, 1985; Cypress Hills Comm. Coll. 1981, 1983; Sask. Summer Sch. of the Arts 1985; plus many workshops; Readings: Canada 1978– ; Germany 1989; Chrmn. of Bd., AKA Art Gall. 1982–83; Bd. Mem., CPPA 1981–83; Sask. Arts Bd. Sr. Grant 1988; SSHRCC doct. fellowship 1984–87; Alfred R. Tucker Scholarship 1983; Sask. Writers Guild Poetry Ms. Prize 1983; WUSC Exchange Scholarship (Munich) 1964; Mem., SWG (Regina); Can. Soc. Hist. Rhetoric; author: 'Odpeoms &' 1978, 'The Mossbank Canon' 1982, 'Pisscat Songs' 1983, 'Apostrophes to Myself' 1987 (poetry); editor: 'Chapbook' 1983 (prose & poetry), 'Essays on Saskatchewan Writing' 1987 (criticism); 'Grain' 1980–83; recreations: cycling, jogging, skiing, trout-fishing; Address: c/o Oolichan Books, P.O. Box 10, Lantzville, B.C. V0R 2H0.

**DYCK, Howard,** A.M.M., A.R.C.T., B.A.; conductor, music broadcaster; b. Winkler, Man. 17 Nov. 1942; s. John Peter and Mary Ann (Wiebe) D.; e. Winkler C.I. 1961; Mennonite Brethren Coll. of Arts 1961–63; Univ. of Man. A.M.M. 1963; Royal Conservatory of Music A.R.C.T. 1963; Goshen College B.A. 1964; Nordwestdeutsche Musikakademie 1967–69; Internat. Bachakademie 1981; m. Magdalene d. Aron and Gertrude Baerg 1 Aug. 1964; children: Anthony Christian, Kristine Marie, Jeremy Nathan; CONDUCTOR, KITCHENER WATERLOO PHILHARMONIC CHOIR 1972– ; Visiting Prof., Mennonite Brethren Coll. of Arts 1969–71; Prof., Wilfrid Laurier Univ. 1971–76; Programme Host, CBC ('Mostly Music,' 'Choral Concert,' 'Saturday Afternoon at the Opera') 1976– ; Conductor, London Pro Musica 1975–78, 1982–87; Kitchener Bach Choir 1972–81; Stratford Concert Choir 1981–84; Guest Conductor, Kitchener Waterloo Symph.; Sask. Symph. Orch.; Orch. London Canada; Metro. Festival Choir and Orch.; Polish Radio Chamber Orch.; Stratford Fest. (La Vie Parisienne 1974); Cochair, Steering Ctte., Podium '92 (nat. biennial conf., Assn. of Candn. Choral Conductors); Manitoba H.S. Public Speaking Championship 1960; Mary L. Robertson Meml. Scholarship, Western Bd. of Music 1963; Canada Council grants 1972, '81; Deutscher Akademischer Austauschdiesnst 1967, '68; Music Mag. Choral Recording of the Year 1985; Kitchener Waterloo Arts Award 1990; Home: 273 Old Post Rd., Waterloo, Ont. N2L 5B8; Office: CBC Radio Music, P.O. Box 500, Station A, Toronto, Ont. M5W 1E6.

**DYE, Kenneth M.,** M.B.A., C.A., F.C.A.; retired Offr. of Parliament; b. Vancouver, B.C. 16 Jan. 1936; s. Allan Edward D.; e. Magee and Lord Byng High Schs.; Univ. of B.C.; Simon Fraser Univ. M.B.A. 1971; Lakehead Univ. Hon. D.Com.; Simon Fraser Univ., LL.D. (Hon.); Univ. of Waterloo D.L. (Hon.); Univ. of Ottawa D.U. (Hon.); Inst. of C.A.'s B.C., C.A. 1962; m. Frances Marion d. Ralph Kenneth Johnson, West Vancouver, B.C. 13 Dec. 1958; children: Elizabeth Georgia, Lesleigh Marion, James Kenneth; PRINCIPAL, COWATER INTERNATIONAL INC. 1993– ; trained as C.A. with Frederick Field & Co. (later known as Doane, Raymond, Pannell Chartered Accountants), apptd. Partner 1966–81; Auditor Gen. of Canada 1981–91; Pres. & C.E.O., Workers' Compensation Bd. of B.C. 1991–93; Retired Partner, Pannell Kerr Forster, Mang. Consultants; served as Flight Cadet 1955–57; Pres. Inst. C.A.'s of B.C. 1979–80; Gov. Candn. Inst. C.A.'s 1977–80; F.C.A. (B.C.) 1975; F.C.A. (Ont.) 1982; F.C.A. (Que.) 1984; Delta Kappa Epsilon; Anglican; recreations: skiing, hiking, canoeing, reading; Clubs: Hollyburn Country; Vancouver; Home: 1907 Highland Terrace, Ottawa, Ont. K1H 5A5; Office: 411 Roosevelt Ave., Ottawa, Ont. K2A 3X9.

**DYER, Gerald B.,** B.Sc.; retired chemical industry executive; b. Port Arthur, Ont. 9 Nov. 1929; s. Charles Benjamin and Gwynneth Elizabeth (Sheldon); e. Port Arthur C.I. 1948; Queen's Univ. B.Sc. (Hons.) 1952; m. Margaret d. Robert and Daisy Goodrich 27 Dec. 1952; children: Gregory, Timothy, Lisa, Stephen; Director of Rsch., Du Pont Canada Inc. 1982–93, Retired; Technical Asst., Du Pont (CIL) 1952; Research Engineer 1956; Research Supvr. 1967; Lab. Manager 1972; Research Div. Manager 1978; Bd. Mem., Ont. Laser & Lightwave Rsch. Ctr.; Past Mem., Science Counc. of Canada; Mem. & Past Chair, Mngt. Ctte., Inst. for Chem. Sci. & Technol.; Mem., Bd. of Trustees, Queen's Univ; Research & Devel. Ctte., Kingston Gen. Hosp.; Mem. & Past Chair, Candn. Rsch. Mngt. Assn.; APEO; recreations: nordic skiing; Home: 195 Country Club Dr., Kingston, Ont. K7M 7G8.

**DYKE, Doris Jean,** M.A., M.Ed., Ed.D.; educator; b. Ont. 4 June 1930; d. Oliver E. and Cassie J. (McFadden) Scott; e. Queen's Univ. B.A. 1959; Univ. of Toronto B.Ed. 1960, M.Ed. 1963; Columbia Univ. M.A. 1962, Union Theol. Semy. Ed.D. 1967; m. Donald Milne s. Jack and Olive Milne 9 Sept. 1989; three d. Catherine, Brenda, Tanya; PROF. EMMANUEL COLL., UNIV. OF TORONTO 1977– ; former teacher Scarborough; Head of Ednl. Founds. and Prof. of Philos. of Edn., Univ. of Sask. 1964–72; Dean of Edn. Dalhousie Univ. 1973–77; recipient Sr. Rsch. Award Assn. Theol. Schs. Can. & U.S. 1989; mem. Bd. Three Guineas Found. 1984– ; Bd. mem. NFB Women's Film Program Advisory Ctte.; author: 'The Crucified Woman' 1991; co-ed. 'Education and Social Policy: Local Control of Education' 1969; Home: 82 Admiral Rd., Toronto, Ont. M5R 2L6; Office: 75 Queen's Park Cres., Toronto, Ont. M5S 1K7.

**DYKEMAN, Floyd Wallace,** B.A., M.PL., M.C.I.P.; university administrator; b. Bathurst, N.B. 21 May 1950; s. Charles Wallace and Marie Ida (Black) D.; e. Saint Thomas Univ., B.A. 1973; Queen's Univ., M.PL. 1975; m. Patricia Margaret d. Wilfred and Geraldine Coyne 28 June 1975; children: Alison Monica, Sarah Emily Marie, Gillian Elizabeth; SENIOR ADVISER, PLANNING, PARTNERSHIPS AND PROFESSIONAL SERVICES 1993– ; and DIR., RURAL & SMALL TOWN RSCH. & STUDIES PROG., MOUNT ALLISON UNIV. 1985– ; Planner, N.B. Dept. of Municipal Affairs 1975–77; Dir. of Planning, Reg. Dist. of Central Kootenay, Nelson, B.C. 1978–85; numerous special assignments & cons. serv. provided; numerous guest lectures, confs.; cons. by reg. & nat. media; Mem., Candn. Inst. of Planners 1975– ; Mem., Planning Inst. of B.C. 1978–85 (Extve. Mem. 1985); Atlantic Planners Inst. 1975–77, 1985– ; Inst. of Public Admin. of Can. 1975– ; Am. Planning Assn.; Ed. Bd., 'Plan Canada' 1986, 1987; Ed. Adv. Bd., 'Progress in Rural Policy and Planning' annual pub.; author of numerous papers & book reviews; editor: 'Integrated Rural Planning and Development' 1988, 'Entrepreneurial and Sustainable Rural Communities' 1990; 'Rural Land Management: Canadian and United States Perspectives' 1991; recreations: sailing, skiing, tennis; Home: 30 Raworth Heights, Box 1930, Sackville, N.B. E0A 3C0; Office: Sackville, N.B. E0A 3C0.

**DYKES, James Grant,** B.Com.; association manager (retired); b. Norwood Grove, Man. 11 May 1920; s. John and Marion (McDonald) D.; e. Univ. of Manitoba, B.Com., 1941; m. Jeanne Elizabeth Wyndels, 27 March 1944; one d. Jennifer Mary; Foreign Service Offr. (Trade Commr.), Dept. of Trade & Commerce, Ottawa and London, Eng., Jan. 1945–Oct. 1946; with Great-West Life Assnce. Co., Winnipeg, Man., 1946–48; Asst. Dir., Dept. of Industry & Comm., Prov. of Man., 1948–49; Industrial Commr., Windsor, Ont., 1949–54; Pres., Motor Vehicle Mfrs. Assn. 1954–85; Member, Sectoral Advisory Group on International Trade 1986–88; served in 2nd World War, 1941–45, with R.C.N.; Lieut.-Commdr. (S) R.C.N.(R) retired; author: 'Canada's Automotive Industry' 1970; United Church; Home: 16 Moorehill Drive, Toronto, Ont. M4G 1A1.

**DYMENT, Frederick John,** C.A.; petroleum executive; b. Toronto, Ont. 8 Dec. 1948; s. William and Evelyn Anne (Brunne) D.; e. Bloor Coll. Inst. 1967; C.A. 1972; m. Shirley Felske 31 May 1980; two s. Matthew, Christopher; PRES., DIR. & CHIEF EXECUTIVE OFFICER, RANGER OIL LIMITED 1991– , Corporate Comptroller 1978, Vice Pres. Finance 1984; Office: 2700, 425 1st St. S.W., Calgary, Alta. T2P 3L8.

**DYMENT, John J.,** C.A., B.Comm., M.B.A.; financial executive; b. Ottawa, Ont. 16 April 1933; s. John Talbot and Josephine Beatrice (Bull) D.; e. McGill Univ. B.Comm 1953, lic. in accountancy 1955; Harvard Business Sch. M.B.A. (with distinction) 1962; m. Judith

Gayle d. Lorne and Dorothy Jowsey 25 Feb. 1961; children: John, Jeffrey, Jennifer; Vice Pres. Finan. & Treas., Bruncor Inc. 1990–92; articled with Price Waterhouse Montreal 1953–55; Mngt. Cons., Urwick Currie Limited 1955–62; Arthur Young & Company 1962–63; Hemphill Noyes & Co. 1964; Partner, Arthur Young & Co. 1968–87; Exec. Vice-Pres., MML Internat. Inc. 1987–90; Adjunct Prof., Internat. Business, Univ. of Connecticut 1989; Baker Scholar, Harvard Bus. Sch.; Trustee & Chrmn., Finan. Ctte., Am. Sch. of Paris, St. Cloud, France 1973–79; author: 'Meet the Men Who Sails the Seas' 1967 (Random House, 1967; Grolier's Book Club Selection); recreations: skiing, sailing; Home: 61 Haskell Cres., Aurora, Ont. L4G 5T6.

**DYMOND, The Hon. Sidney,** B.A., LL.B.; b. Toronto, Ont. 9 Nov. 1923; d. Arthur Allan and Dorothy Kathleen (Denton) D.; e. St. Clements Sch.; Trinity Coll., Univ. of Toronto B.A. (Hon.) 1946; Osgoode Hall Law Sch. 1949; private law practice 1949–65; Vice-Provost, Rsch. Admin., Univ. of Toronto 1965–73; Judge of the County and then District Court 1973–90; Justice, Ont. Court of Justice (Gen. Div.) 1990–92; Past Bd. Mem., Toronto Gen. Hosp.; Ont. Coll. of Art; Rosalie Hall; Past Counc. Mem., SSHRCC; Mem., Medico-Legal Soc. of Toronto; Judicial Conf. of Can.; Candn. Bar Assn., etc.; recreations: swimming, gardening; Club: Granite.

**DYMOND, William R.,** M.A., Ph.D.; economist; educator; b. Toronto, Ont. 10 June 1921; s. late John Richardson, F.R.S.C., and late Hilda (Freeman) D.; e. Upper Canada Coll., Toronto, Ont.; Univ. of Toronto, B.A. 1943; M.A. 1946; Cornell Univ., Ph.D. 1950; m.; Asst. Prof. of Econ., Univ. of Mass. 1949–51; Chief of Manpower Div., Econ. & Research Br., Dept. of Labour, Ottawa 1951–56; Dir., Econ. & Research Br. 1957–61; Asst. Depy. Min. of Labour 1961–65; Chrmn., Manpower & Social Affairs Comte. of Organ. for Econ. Cooperation and Devel., Paris 1965–70; Asst. Depy. Min., Manpower and Immigration 1966–70; Chrmn., Dept. Public Adm., Univ. of Ottawa 1970–74; Depy. Dir., Social Affairs, Manpower and Educ., Organ. for Econ. Cooperation and Devel. 1974–86; Consultant, Organ. for Econ. Co-operation and Devel. 1986– ; Moderator, Amer. Church in Paris 1980–84; recreation: photography; Address: 20 - 23100 129th Ave., Maple Ridge, B.C. V2X 0M5.

**DYNES, Henry Edwin;** retired; b. Quebec, P.Q. 2 July 1916; s. Edwin John and Ruth Olive (Conner) D.; m. Gertrude, d. late Joseph Pleau, 10 Sept. 1945; children: Elizabeth Ann, Charles Henry, Helen Gertrude, Lynne; TRUSTEE, FIRST CANADIAN MUTUAL FUNDS and Chrmn. of the Audit Cttes.; formerly: CEO, Traders Group Ltd.; Chrmn., Guaranty Trust Co. Ltd.; served in 2nd World War with R.C.A.P.C. as Captain; Protestant; recreations: golf, swimming; Clubs: Bayview Country; Canadian; Home: 2330 Bridletowne Circle #1103, Scarborough, Ont. M1W 3P6.

**DYSART, Hon. Shirley,** M.L.A.; politician; e. N.B. Teachers Coll.; Univ. of N.B.; Univ. of London (Beaverbrook Overseas Scholarship); m. Dr. H. Eric Dysart; one son; SPEAKER OF THE LEGISLATIVE ASSEMBLY OF N.B. 1992– ; taught Hist. and Eng. St. Vincent's High Sch. Saint John; el. M.L.A. for Saint John Park 1974, re-el. since; Interim Leader of Lib. Party 1985; Min. of Edn. N.B. 1987–91; Pres. N.B. Competitive Festival of Music; mem. Exec. Ctte. N.B. Saint John Bicentennial Inc.; Gov. Beaverbrook Art Gallery; Dir. Saint John Family Services; Past Pres. Cath. Women's League Council; Past Pres., Univ. of N.B. Alumni Council; former Chairperson Dist. 20 Saint John Area Sch. Bd.; Office: P.O. Box 6000, Fredericton, N.B. E3B 5H1.

# E

**EADIE, Thomas Michael** to **EASTON, David**
Please see Addenda page 1247.

**EASTON, Melvin Donald,** LL.B.; b. Vancouver, B.C. 9 Feb. 1923; s. Albert Edward and Mattie (Harrison) E.; e. Cecil Rhodes Jr. Secondary Sch. and Kitsilano High Sch., Vancouver, 1942; Univ. of B.C., LL.B. 1950; m. Elaine Louise; one s. Michael Donald Leary; PARTNER, HARPER, GREY, EASTON & CO.; read law with Hon. Mr. Justice John Groves Gould; called to the bar of British Columbia 1950; Partner, Gould, Thorpe & Easton, 1950–65; joined present firm (then Harper, Gilmour, Grey & Co) 1965, Partner 1966; served with RCAF 1942–45; served overseas with 432 Hvy. Bomber Sqdn.; rank Fly. Offr.; mem. Law Soc. B.C.; Candn. Bar Assn.; Candn. Tax Foundation; Air Force Offrs. Assn.; Phi Gamma Delta; Freemason; Anglican; recreations: boating, fishing, shooting; golfing; Clubs: Royal Vancouver Yacht; Vancouver; Men's Canadian; Shaughnessy Golf & Country; Home: #810 – 1450 Pennyfarthing Dr., Vancouver, B.C. V6J 4X8; Office: 3100 – 650 West Georgia St., Vancouver, B.C. V6B 4P7.

**EASTWOOD, Gordon Stuart;** news executive; b. Halifax, Eng. 12 Aug. 1936; s. Arthur Shaw and Nellie (Lees) E.; e. Central Kaye's Coll. 1952; Percival Whitley Coll., B.J. 1956; m. Esther d. Arthur and Jessie LeBlanc 30 Dec. 1961; children: Marie, Patricia; PRES. & CHIEF EXTVE. OFFR., CANADA NEWS WIRE LTD. 1980– ; Flying Training Comnd., Royal Air Force 1956–58; Reporter, 'Northern Echo' (UK) 1958–59; News Ed./Asst. Mng. Ed., Monitor Pub. (Can.) 1961–62; Admin. Offr., Candn. Marconi 1959–61, 1962–63; Info. Offr., Manpower & Immigr., Candn. Govt. 1966–68; Reporter/Night Ed./City Ed./Saturday Ed., 'Ottawa Journal' 1963–80; Home: 248 Langstaff Rd. W., Richmond Hill, Ont. L4C 6N7; Office: 10 Bay St., Ste. 914, Toronto, Ont. M5J 2R8.

**EATON, Fredrik Stefan,** B.A.; diplomat; b. Toronto, Ont. 26 June 1938; s. late John David and late Signy Hildur (Stephenson) E.; e. Upper Canada College; Univ. of New Brunswick B.A., LL.D. (honoris causa); m. Catherine d. of late D.A.C. Martin 16 June 1962; one s. and one d.; HIGH COMMISSIONER FOR CANADA TO THE UNITED KINGDOM OF GREAT BRITAIN AND NORTHERN IRELAND; joined The T. Eaton Co. Ltd. serving in various positions in Victoria, B.C., London, England, and Toronto 1962; apptd. Dir., The T. Eaton Co. Limited 1967; Pres. & Dir., Eaton's of Canada 1969; apptd. Chrmn., Pres. and C.E.O., The T. Eaton Co. Limited 1977; Chrmn. 1988–91; apptd. Chancellor, Univ. of New Brunswick 1993; served as Director of Baton Broadcasting Inc.; Toronto-Dominion Bank; Hollinger Inc.; Maple Leaf Foods; Norcen Energy; Ritz Hotel; served as Patron Founder, Trustee and Pres., The Art Gallery of Ont.; Gov., The Eaton Foundation; Trustee amd Vice-Chrmn., The Toronto Hospital; Patron, Outward Bound; Dir., World Wildlife Fund (Canada); Bata Shoe Museum; Member, ICBP Rare Bird Club; The Conference Board of Canada; Candn. Institute of Internat. Affairs; Ontario XPO; Fellow, The Royal Society for the encouragement of Arts, Manufacturers & Commerce; named Internat. Retailer of the Year, National Retail Merchants Assn. of New York 1978; recipient, McGill Univ. Management Award 1987; appointed, Officer of the Order of Canada 1990; Freeman of the City of London 1993; Office: Canadian High Commission, 1 Grosvenor Square, London, England, W1X 0AB.

**EATON, John Craig,** O.O., C.St.J., KCLJ; executive; b. Toronto, Ont. 30 May 1937; s. of late John David Eaton and late Signy Hildur (Stephenson) E.; e. Upper Canada College; Harvard Univ.; m. 2ndly Sherrill Joan d. Mr. & Mrs. John Howard Taylor Nov. 1975; children: two s. one d. (by 1959 m.) two d. (by 1975 m.); BD. CHRMN., EATON'S OF CANADA LTD. (parent co.) 1969– ; Pres., Cresta Canada Ltd.; Dir., The Toronto Blue Jays Baseball Club; Yes Canada (Youth Employment Skills Canada Inc.); joined The T. Eaton Co. Limited 1954, apptd. Dir. 1967; Past Chrmn. and Mem. Bd. of Govs., Upper Canada Coll.; Past Pres. and Dir., Royal Agricultural Winter Fair; Trustee, E. P. Taylor Equine Rsch. Fund; Gov., The Easter Seal Soc.; Candn. Atherosclerosis Soc.; The Eaton Foundation; The Olympic Trust of Canada; Dir. The John Augustus Soc.; Chrmn., Ducks Unlimited (Canada); National Employers' Support Ctte.; Hon. Chrmn., The Canadian Hearing Soc. Foundation; The Hugh MacMillan Medical Centre; mem., Metro Toronto Adv. Bd., The Salvation Army; Canadian Council of Christians & Jews; Adv. Counc., Y.M.C.A. of Metro Toronto; Bd. of Trade of Metro Toronto; Senate mem. Stratford Festival Foundation of Canada; former Chrmn., The Trillium Found.; former National Chrmn. and Mem., The Charlie Conacher Rsch. Fund; former Pres. and Dir., National Youth Orch.; former Gov., York Univ.; Order of Ontario; Commander (Brother) of the Most Venerable Order of the Hospital of St. John of Jerusalem; Mem. of Senate, and Knight of the Military and Hospitaller Order of Saint Lazarus of Jerusalem; recreations: music, fishing, hockey, golf, deep sea diving; Clubs: Rosedale Golf; Toronto Badminton & Racquet; Toronto; London Hunt; London; York; Goodwood; Caledon Ski; Craigleith Ski; Office: 250 Yonge St., Toronto, Ont. M5B 1C8.

**EAYRS, Catherine Elizabeth (Lofft),** B.A., M.A.; politician; volunteer; b. Toronto, 30 June 1927; e. Univ. of Toronto B.A. 1949; Univ. of Western Ont. M.A. 1950; m. James G. Eayrs 16 Sept. 1950; children: Jonathan Michael, 'Betsy' Elizabeth Catherine, James Wild, Emily Ann (Babiak), Susanna Ella (Paynter); City of Toronto alderman 1972–78; Metropolitan Toronto Councillor 1972–74, 1976–78; founder and co-ord. Tinnitus Assoc. of Canada 1989– ; Ont. Medal for Good Citizenship 1990; Address: 23 Ellis Park Rd., Toronto, Ont. M6S 2V4.

**EAYRS, James George,** O.C., B.A., A.M., Ph.D., F.R.S.C.; educator; b. London, Eng. 13 Oct. 1926; e. Univ. of Toronto B.A. 1948; Columbia Univ. A.M. 1950, Ph.D. 1954; m. C. Elizabeth Lofft 16 Sept. 1950; children: Jonathan Michael, 'Betsy' Elizabeth Catherine, James Wild, Emily Ann (Babiak), Susanna Ella (Paynter); mem. acad. staff Univ. of Toronto 1952–80; Dalhousie Univ. 1980–92; recipient Gov. Gen.'s Award 1965; Guggenheim Fellow 1967; Molson Prize 1984; Address: 23 Ellis Park Rd., Toronto, Ont. M6S 2V4.

**EBACHER, Mgr. Roger,** B.A., L.Th., D.en Ph.; évêque; né Amos, Qué. 6 octobre 1936; f. Louis et Lucienne (Cossette) E.; é. Univ. Laval B.A. 1957; Univ. d'Ottawa L.Th. 1961; Institut Catholique de Paris D.en Ph. 1966; nommé ARCHEVÊQUE MÉTROPOLITAIN DE GATINEAU-HULL le 30 octobre 1990; Ordonné prêtre catholique 1961; Professeur de philosophie 1961–67; Travaux divers en pastorale diocésaine (diocèse d'Amos) et curé de paroisse; Vicaire général du diocèse d'Amos; Ordonné évêque à Hauterive (Qué.) 1979; Transféré au siège épiscopal de Gatineau-Hull 1988; Évêque de Gatineau-Hull 1988– ; Membre de divers comités épiscopaux; Auteur de très nombreux articles philosophiques et religieux dans des revues et des journaux; 'L'Eglise d'Amos à la recherche de son avenir' 1975; 'La religieuse animatrice de paroisse' 1978; 'Ma vie au fil des jours' 1981; 'Mes jours et mes saisons devant toi' 1978; 'Education de la foi (un diocèse engage ses laics)' 1979; 'Marie et notre pèlerinage de foi' 1988; Bureau: 180, boul. Mont-Bleu, Hull, Que. J8Z 3J5.

**EBANKS, G. Edward,** B.A., M.A., Ph.D.; university professor; b. Jamaica 1 March 1938; s. William Joshua and Emmie Rita (Falconer) E.; e. Univ. College of the West Indies & London Univ. B.A. 1962; Cornell Univ. M.A. 1965, Ph.D. 1968; divorced; one d.: Natasha Ann; PROFESSOR, SOCIOLOGY, UNIV. OF WESTERN ONTARIO 1968– ; High School Teacher, Jamaica 1962–63; Rsch. Asst., Population Council 1966–67; Consultant, Ford Found. 1968–69; U.N. Expert, Family Planning Working Group 1976, '78; U.N. ECLAC Visiting Scholar 1984; UNECLAC Visiting Sci. 1990–91; WFS/ISI Visiting Fellow 1983; Consultant, U.N. ECLAC 1992; Population Council Fellow 1964–66, 1968; Vice-Pres., Candn. Population Soc. 1980–82; Pres.-Elect, Planned Parenthood Fed. of Can. 1981–83; Senate Mem., Univ. of W. Ont. 13 years; Bd. of Gov. 1992–96; Chair, Fac. Assn. 1980–81; Pres. 1987–88; area of expertise: demography, Latin Am. & the Caribbean; Mem., PAA, ASA, CPS, CSAA, CALACS, IUSSP; author: 'Socio-economic Determinants of Internal Migration in Latin America and the Caribbean' 1993, 'Infant and Child Morality and Fertility' 1985; recreations: jogging, tennis, golf; Home: 7, 1050 Brough St., London, Ont. N6A 3N4; Office: London, Ont. N6A 5C2.

**EBERDT, Frank Lothar,** B.A.Sc., M.B.A.; cable TV executive; b. Isernhagen, W. Germany 8 Feb. 1947; s. Edmund Otto Julius and Eleonore Mathilde Margarete (Bar) E.; e. Univ. of Waterloo, B.A.Sc. 1970; Univ. of W. Ont., M.B.A. 1974; m. Karen d. Margaret and Steve Armstrong 28 Apr. 1973; children: Brian, Caroline; EXEC. VICE-PRES. & C.O.O., ROGERS CABLE TV LTD., Western Region 1989– ; Dir. of Mktg., Candn. Cablesystems 1974–76; Vice-Pres. & Gen. Mgr., Cornwall Cablevision 1977–78; Extve. Vice-Pres. & Gen. Mgr., Rogers Cable TV-Kitchener 1978–81; Vice-Pres., Tech. Opns., Rogers Cablesystems Inc. (Toronto) 1981–82; Extve. Vice-Pres. & Gen. Mgr., Valley Cable TV (US) 1982–83; Rogers Cable TV (Vanc.) 1983–88; recreations: swimming, sailing, racquetball; Home: 3222 West 26th Avenue, Vancouver, B.C. V6L 1W1; Office: Rogers Cantel Tower, 1600 - 4710 Kingsway, Burnaby, B.C. V5H 4M5.

**EBERLE, Hon. John Edward,** B.A.; judge; b. Owen Sound, Ont. 10 June 1928; s. Charles Addison and Grace Cecilia (Keenan) E.; e. Owen Sound Coll. & Vocational Inst. 1946; Univ. of Toronto B.A. 1950; Osgoode Hall Law Sch. 1955; m. Dorothy d. James and Mary Doran 24 Aug. 1957; children: Margaret, Mary, Ted, David; JUDGE, ONTARIO COURT OF JUSTICE (GEN. DIV.) 1990– ; Judge, Supreme Court of Ont. 1977–90; former

Partner, Kimber Dubin & Eberle; Goodman & Goodman; former Chrmn. Bd. Dirs. Providence Hosp.; mem. Candn. Bar Assn.; Advocates Soc. Ont.; recreations: tennis, skiing; Clubs: Toronto Lawn Tennis; Queens; Home: 146 Underhill Dr., Don Mills, Ont. M3A 2K5; Office: 130 Queen St. W., Toronto, Ont. M5H 2N5.

**EBERLEE, Peter C.,** B.A.Sc., P.Eng.; consulting engineer; b. Ottawa, Ont. 1 Aug. 1934; s. Col. Thomas Harley and the late Gwen (McKay) E.; e. Lindsay (Ont.) Coll. Inst. 1952; Univ. of Toronto B.A.Sc. 1956; m. Altamae d. Jean and late Dr. W.D. Thomas 18 May 1957; children: Jennifer, Douglas; SENIOR VICE-PRES. AND GEN. MGR., ONTARIO, SNC-LAVALIN INC. 1992– ; Pres., Fenco MacLaren Inc. 1992– ; Chrmn., Simon-Carves Fenco Inc. 1992– ; James F. MacLaren Assoc. 1954–57; Gore & Storrie Ltd. 1957–66; Totten Sims Hubicki Associates 1966–91, Dir. 1968–90, Vice Pres. 1968–81, 1984–87; Pres. 1981–84, 1987–90; Chrmn., C.E.O. and Pres., Spectrum Engineering Corp. Ltd. 1991–92; Bd. Mem.: Trafalgar Castle Sch. Whitby 1979–91 (Pres. and Chrmn. 1981–86); Whitby Gen. Hosp. (Chrmn. 1985–87); mem. Assn. Prof. Engs. Prov. Ont.; Eng. Inst. Can.; Candn. Soc. Civil Eng.; Ontario Waste Mgmt. Adv. Bd. 1975–80 (Vice Chrmn. 1978–80); recreations: sailing, cross country skiing, classical music, gardening; Address: 244 Wellington St., Whitby, Ont. L1N 5L8.

**EBERLEE, Thomas McKay,** B.A.; labour relations consultant; b. Toronto, Ont. 2 Aug. 1930; s. Thomas Harley and the late Gwen (McKay) E.; e. Univ. of Toronto, B.A. 1951; m. Elinor d. the late Lindley and Elinor Calnan 6 June 1953; children: Susan Elizabeth, John C.; LABOUR RELATIONS CONSULTANT, specializing in arbitration and mediation 1992– ; Reporter, Toronto Star 1951–58; Asst. Sec of Cabinet, Ont. Govt. 1959–62; Sec., Royal Comn. on Labour Mgmt. Relns. in Ont. Construction Indus. 1961–62; Sec. & Mem. of Ont. Human Rights Comn. 1959–71 (drafted Ont. Human Rights Code 1961); Asst. Depy. Min., Labour Dept. 1962–66; Depy. Min. 1966–71; Mgmt. Policy 1971–72; Community & Social Serv. 1972–74; Candn. Dept. of Labour 1974–82; Vice Chrmn., Candn. Labour Relations Bd. 1982–92; Ont. Civil Serv. Comnr. 1969–74; Chrmn., Construction Indus. Review Panel 1972–74; Labour Safety Counc. of Ont. 1967–70; Mem., Counc. of Candn. Ctr. for Occup. Health & Safety 1979–82; recreations: reading, gardening; Home: 1867 Featherston Dr., Ottawa, Ont. K1H 6P6.

**EBERTS, Edmond Gordon,** B.Sc.; executive; b. Montréal, Qué. 27 Apr. 1938; s. Edmond Howard and Elizabeth Evelyn (MacDougall) E.; e. Bishop's Coll. Sch. 1956; McGill Univ. B.Sc. 1960; m. Maureen d. Frederick and Margaret Mannix 30 Aug. 1979; three d. Jennifer, Rachael, Katherine; PRES., RAPPORT CAPITAL FORMATION STRATEGISTS INC. 1975– ; joined Union Carbide Canada Ltd. 1959–65; C.J. Hodgson Securities Inc. 1965–73; Gordon Securities Ltd. 1973–74; present Co. 1975; Hon. Dir. The Country Day Sch. mem. Toronto, Montréal, Calgary Soc.'s Financial Analysts; recreations; golf, skiing; Clubs: Mount Bruno Country; Glencoe Golf & Country; Beacon Hall Golf; PGA West; Royal and Ancient; Ranchmen's; Cambridge Club; Calgary Petroleum; Home: 494 Beacon Hall Dr., Aurora, Ont. L4G 3G8; Office: 703, 141 Adelaide St. W., Toronto, Ont. M5H 3L5.

**EBERTS, Mary (Anne),** L.S.M., B.A., LL.B., LL.M., LL.D., D.Hum.L.; lawyer; b. St. Thomas, Ont. 18 Jan. 1947; d. James Ellsworth and Martha Patricia (Perrott) E.; e. Univ. of West. Ont. B.A. 1968, LL.B. 1971; Harvard Law Sch. LL.M. 1972; called to Bar of Ont. 1974; m. The Hon. Robert A.F. s. John W. and Marjorie (Fraser) Sutherland 6 May 1977; children: Alexandra Marjorie McLean, Brian James McLean, Simon Dugald Andrew; PARTNER, TORY TORY DesLAURIERS & BINNINGTON 1984– ; Fac. Mem. (ending as Assoc. Prof.), Fac. of Law, Univ. of Toronto 1974–80; joined present firm 1980; practises (and teaches at Univ. of Toronto) civil & constitutional litigation; writes & lectures extensively on equality rights & const. litigation; Mem. & Chair, Transitional Counc., Coll. of Midwives 1993; Chair, Interim Regulatory Counc. on Midwifery in Ont. 1989–93; Judges' Nominee, Prov. Judges Remuneration Comn. (Ont.) 1989–93; Chair, Task Force on the Implementation of Midwifery in Ont. 1986–87; Mem., Spec. Ctte. on Pornography & Prostitution 1983–85; Vice-Chair, Crown Employee's Grievance Settlement Bd. (Ont.) 1978–79; recipient, Merit Award, Federation of Women Teachers' Assns. of Ont. 1993; President's Award, Women's Law Assoc. (Ont.) 1993; LL.D., Queen's Univ. 1992; LL.D., Concordia Univ. 1993; Law Soc. Medal, Law Soc. of U.C. 1989; D.Hum.L. (Hon.), Mt. St. Vincent Univ. 1988; Woman of Distinction Award, YWCA of Metro. Toronto 1982; Co-Founder, Women's Legal Edn. & Action Fund; Catharina Shrader Found. for Midwifery Rsch.; Bd. of Dir., Naruth Found. 1989– ; Candn. Women's Found. 1987–89; Metro Action Ctte. on Public Violence against Women & Children 1986–92; Bd. of Dir., Calmeadow Found. 1986–87; Harshman Scholarships Found. 1977–85; Vice-Pres., Candn. Civil Liberties Assn. 1979–83; Mem., Bd. of Dir. 1978–85; author of numerous articles & book chapters; co-author: 'Women and Legal Action' 1984, 'Athlete's Rights in Canada' 1982; co-editor: 'Equality Rights under the Canadian Charter of Rights and Freedoms' 1985, 'The Child and the Courts' 1978; recreations incl. Ont. history, women's diaries, quilting; Home: 46 Nanton Ave., Toronto, Ont. M4W 2Y9; Office: Ste. 3000, Aetna Tower, Box 270, Toronto-Dominion Ctr., Toronto, Ont. M5K 1N2.

**EBSEN, Alf K.,** R.C.A.A.; calligrapher. b. Berlin, Germany 29 July 1908; s. Carl and Minna (Stüber) E.; e. Realschule vor dem Lübeckertor, Hamburg 1926; lithographer apprentice 1927–31; Kunstgewerbeschule, Hamburg 1931–33; m. 25 Aug. 1960 Florence Irene d. Walter John Bowyer; one d. Andrea; Prop., calli*GRAFIK*design 1962– ; advertising designer for cigarette mfr. prior to war; own design firm from 1947; client Volkswagenwerk AG 1950–54; came to Can. 1954; Dir. of Graphic Arts, Eddy Match Co. Pembroke, Ont. 1955–63; originator Candn. System of Calligraphy and Handwriting; author & publisher 'CALLIGRAPHY: practice book one'; 'Making Thoughts Visible: teaching book two'; Founder Handwriters Guild Toronto; Calligraphic Arts Guild Toronto; mem. Royal Candn. Acad. of Arts; recreations: incunabula, sports; Address: Calligraphy & Handwriting Oasis, Roseneath Landing, 21 Edgewater Drive, Roseneath, Ont. K0K 2X0.

**EBY, John C.,** B.Sc., M.B.A.; banker; b. Haileybury, Ont. 14 May 1951; s. J. Graham and Lois V. (Locke) E.; e. Queen's Univ. B.Sc. 1973, M.B.A. 1973; m. Shelley d. Jack and Kaye Smith 25 Aug. 1973; children: Gordon, Duncan, Cameron; SENIOR VICE PRES. (RESP. FOR EUR. CORP. BANKING), BANK OF NOVA SCOTIA (LONDON, ENGLAND) 1991– ; Jr. Profl., Inter-Am. Devel Bank Washington 1973–75; Treasury Group, The Bank of N.S. Toronto 1975–78; Agent Treas., N.Y. 1978–82; various positions in Credit & Corp. Banking functions Toronto 1982–91; Dir., Scotiabank (U.K.) Limited; Home: 6a Cranley Rd., Burwood Park, Walton-on-Thames, Surrey, England KT12 5BP; Office: Scotia House, 33 Finsbury Square, London EC2A 1BB, England.

**EBY, Peter Blair Mara,** B.Com., M.B.A.; investment dealer; b. Toronto, Ont. 17 May 1938; s. late Blair Smart and late Lorna Lee (Mara) E.; e. Upper Can. Coll. Toronto; Univ. of Toronto B.Com. 1960; Univ. of Cal. M.B.A. 1961; m. Jane Margaret d. Dr. William Apted 22 Dec. 1972; children: Brian, Stephen, Christopher, Blaire; VICE CHRMN. AND MEM. EXTVE. COMTE., BURNS FRY LTD.; joined Burns Bros. and Denton Ltd. (now present firm) 1961; Gov., Upper Canada College; Gov., Olympic Trust of Canada; recreations: golf, tennis, squash; Clubs: Badminton & Racquet; Toronto; Cambridge; Rosedale Golf; Toronto Golf; Beacon Hall; Mid-Ocean (Bermuda); Loxahatchee (Fla.); Home: 143 Dunvegan Road, Toronto, Ont. M5P 2N8; Office: (P.O. Box 150) First Canadian Place, Toronto, Ont. M5X 1H3.

**EBY, Thomas G.,** C.A., M.B.A.; financial executive; b. Toronto, Ont. 26 May 1940; s. Glynn Fisher and Susan Isabel (Watt) e.; e. Univ. of Western Ont. M.B.A. 1968; m. Karen d. Ethel and Lenard Chambers 13 Sept. 1968; PRES., ADMIN., GENERAL ACCIDENT ASSURANCE CO. OF CANADA 1987– ; articled with Deloite and Touche C.A. 1964; Comptroller, Merry Packaging Limited 1968–69; The General Accident Assur. Co. of Canada 1969–73; Asst. Treas., DRG Packaging 1973; Chief Financial Offr. 1976; Vice-Pres., Finance 1980–86; Dir., Candn. Insur. Acctg. Assn.; Insurance Bur. of Can. (Fin. Analysis Ctte.); Dir., Amici Camping Charity; frequent contbr. to insur. mngt. journals; recreation: hiking, photography, wilderness canoeing; clubs: Western Business Sch. Club of Toronto, Fitness Inst., Toronto Camera, Metro Toronto Bd. of Trade; Home: 86 Glenvale Blvd., Toronto, Ont. M4G 2V6; Office: 2 First Candn. Place, Suite 2600, P.O. Box 410, Toronto, Ont. M5X 1J1.

**EBY, Todd D.G.,** CMA; financial executive; b. Kitchener, Ont. 10 Sept. 1950; s. Foster and Mary E.; e. York Univ.; Conestoga College, Business Admin. 1973; Soc. of Mngt. Accountants CMA 1976; m. Ursula Madison; VICE-PRESIDENT, FINANCE, BONAR INC. 1991– ; Corp. Acctg. Mgr., Electrohome Limited 1973–78; Controller, Loblaw Companies Limited 1978–85; Husky Injection Molding Systems Ltd. 1985–86; Vice-Pres. Finance, Admin., Lumsden Bros. Ltd. 1986–88; Jack Austin Ltd. 1988–91; Mem., Financial Extves. Inst. 1980; Mem., Toronto Board of Trade 1993; recreations: hockey, squash, fitness; clubs: Curzon; Office: 2380 McDowell Rd., Burlington, Ont. L7R 4A1.

**ECCLES, William John,** M.A., Ph.D., LL.D.; university professor; author; b. Thirsk, Yorks, Engl. 17 July 1917; s. John and Jane Ellen (Thorpe) E.; came to Can., 1928; e. McGill Univ., B.A. (Hons.) 1949, M.A. 1951, Ph.D. 1955; Sorbonne, Paris, 1951–52; French Govt. Scholar, 1951–52; McGill Univ. Grad. Fellowship, 1952–53; Humanities Research Council Fellowship, 1956; Ewart Foundation Fellowships, 1955, '56, '57, '58; Can. Council Fellowship, 1959, 1964, 1968, 1977–78; Dottore in Lettere honoris causa, Università di Genova 1992; m. Margaret Jean Jaffray, d. Arthur Alexander Low, Stratford, Ont., 18 Sept. 1948; children: late Michael John, Robin Christina, Peter Alexander; PROF. EMERITUS, UNIV. OF TORONTO 1983– ; Lectr., Dept. of Hist., Univ. of Manitoba, 1953–57, Asst. Prof., 1957; Asst. Prof., Dept. of Hist., Univ. of Alberta, 1957–59; Assoc. Prof. 1959–63; Prof. of History, Univ. of Toronto 1963–83; rec'd Sr. Killam (Fellowship) Award 1969–72; Tyrrell Medal 1979; Senior Connaught Fellow 1980–81; Publications: 'Frontenac: The Courtier Governor,' 1959 (awarded 1959 prize by Pacific Coast Br., Am. Hist. Assn.); 'Canada Under Louis XIV' 1964; 'Canadian Society During the French Régime,' 1968; 'The Canadian Frontier 1534–1760,' 1969, rev. ed. 1983; 'France in America' 1972, rev. ed. 1990 (rec'd Inst. français de Washington Gilbert Chinard Award, 1974); 'Essays on New France' 1987; various articles and reviews; Assoc. Ed., 'Encyclopedia of the North American Colonies' 3 vols. 1993; Visiting Prof., Univ. of Chile, Santiago, 1966; McGill Univ., 1966–67; Guest Lectr., Am. Univ. of Beirut, Lebanon, 1967; James Pinckney Harrison Professor, Coll. of William and Mary 1983–84; Messecar Prof., McMaster Univ. 1987–88; mem., Council Inst. Early Am. History and Culture 1976–79; club: University (Montreal); Home: 108 Cluny Drive, Toronto, Ont. M4W 2R4.

**ECHALOOK, Noah;** artist; b. Elsie Island, Québec 13 May 1946; nephew of Lucassie Echalook who encouraged him to carve as a youth; medium: sculptures, prints; 30 group exbns. incl. most recent: Musée des Beaux-arts de Montréal 1992, National Gallery of Canada Ottawa 1992, Houston North Gall. Lunenburg, N.S. 1988; Le Fed. des Coop. du Nouveau Que. Montreal, Que. (tour) 1988–90; solo exbns.: Inuit Galerie Mannheim, Germany 1991, The Innuit Gallery of Eskimo Art Toronto 1983, Raven Gallery Minneapolis, Minn. 1979; works in 7 collections: Candn. Mus. of Civilization Hull, Que., La Fed. de Coop. du Nouveau-Que., Min. des affaires culturelles du Que., Musée de la civilisation Que., Que., Nat. Gallery of Can., Royal Ont. Mus., Winnipeg Art Gallery (Swinton & Twomey colls.); spent two months demonstrating carving at Montreal Olympics 1967; attended Internat. Art Fair Toronto 1982; subject of articles and catalogues; Home: Inukjuak, Québec; Office: c/o La Fédération des Coopératives du Nouveau-Québec, 19950 Clark Graham, Baie D'Urfe, Qué. H9X 3R8.

**ECHLIN, Randall Scott,** B.A., LL.B.; barrister & solicitor; b. Toronto, Ont. 29 Nov. 1950; s. Dr. Robert Edward and Madeleine Lillian (Foreacre) E.; e. Victoria College, Univ. of Toronto B.A. 1972 (Gold Medalist, Prince of Wales Gold Medal), Fac. of Law LL.B. 1975; m. Ann d. Jack and Ethel Mackenzie 24 Aug. 1973; children: Elizabeth Ann, Robert Edward; PARTNER, BORDEN & ELLIOT 1984– ; called to Ont. Bar 1977; Chair, Civil Litigation Section, Candn. Bar Assn. (Ont.) 1986–87; cert. by Law Soc. of U.C. as Specialist in Civil Litigation 1990; Teacher, Law Soc. of U.C. Bar Admission Court on Employment Law 1986; Civil Litigation Advocacy 1989, 1990; Lectr., Univ. of Toronto 1990– ; Special Citation, City of Burlington 1972; Candn. Baseball Hall of Fame and Museum, 'Man of the Year' 1988; Nat. Sec. & Mem., Bd. of Dir., Crohn's Colitis Found. of Canada 1989–92; Mem., Advocate's Soc.; Co. of York Law Assn.; Lawyers' Club of Toronto; Osgoode Soc.; Defence Rsch. Inst.; Candn. Bar Assn.; Assn. of Trial Lawyers of Am.; Candn. Inst. for the Admin. of Justice; Human Resources Profls. Assn. of Ont.; President's Ctte., Univ. of Toronto; Chancellor's Council, Victoria Univ.; Leaside Un. Ch.; Editor-in-Chief, 'The University of Toronto Faculty of Law Review' 1975; Assoc. Ed., 'Canadian Cases on Employment Law' 1983– ; recreation: squash, snorkelling, baseball, photography; clubs: National, Adelaide, Bd. of Trade of Metro. Toronto; Home: 76 Bessborough Dr., Toronto, Ont. M4G 3J1; Office: 40 King St. W., Toronto, Ont. M5H 3Y4.

**ECK, Paul Barr;** arts administrator; b. Rochester, N.Y. 16 June 1938; s. Walter Edmund and Christie Ann (Barr) E.; e. York Univ. 1973; Harvard Univ. 1974; m. Mary Gwen d. Elizabeth and Harold Brownlee 27 Sept. 1958; children: Kevin, Karen, Jamie; PRES., ECK TALENT ASSOCIATES LTD. 1979– ; Founder and Artistic Dir. Everyman Players 1967–78; Admin. Dir. Theatre London 1973–81; Gen. Mgr. Orchestra London 1981–83; Exec. Dir. Stratford Summer Music 1983, 1984; Gen. Mgr. Hamilton Philharmonic Orchestra 1983–87; Exec. Dir. Quinte Summer Music 1984–88; Gen. Mgr. Toronto Pops Orchestra 1987–90; Theatre Mgr. Meadowvale Theatre, Mississauga 1988– ; Performing Arts Associate, Lord Cultural Resources, Toronto; Pres., Campus & Community Impresarios; Past Chrmn. of the Bd., Theatre Ontario; Bd. Mem., Mississauga Living Arts Centre; Past Pres., Nat. Assn. of Cultural Execs.; Dir. Ont. Fed. of Symphony Orchs.; Adv. Bd. Confederation Coll. Performing Arts Mgmt.; Dean, Arts Admin. Extve. Development Program, Northwest Enterprise Center 1988; Instr.: Ryerson Inst. Prog. in Theatre; Inst. Theatre Ontario Summer Courses; Lectr., Univ. of Toronto Arts Admin.; York Univ., Arts Marketing; Confederation Coll., Arts Mgmt.; Univ. of Waterloo, Bd. Development; Lectr., Arts Management, Brock Univ., St. Catharines; Prof., Fund Raising, Humber Coll., Toronto; Advr., Can. Counc. and Ont. Arts Counc.; Nat. Study Team – Arts Administration Training; mem., Candn. Theatre Rsch. Assn.; Candn. Assoc. of Arts Admin. Educators; Bronfman Found. 1974; Harvard Study Can. Counc. 1974; Candn. Silver Jubilee Medal 1978; Can. Counc. Special Projects, Hist., Grand Theatre, London, Ont. 1978; Mayor's New Year's Honours List, City of London (Ont.) 1979; Prov. of Ontario Volunteer Service Award 1985 and 1988; mem., Trinity Anglican Church; Home: 2377 Cobbinshaw Circle, Mississauga, Ont. L5N 2G2.

**ECKERSLEY, John Alan,** B.Sc., LL.B.; mining executive; b. Vancouver, B.C. 14 Feb. 1945; s. Gilbert and Rosa (Württemburger) E.; e. Univ. of B.C. B.Sc. 1965, LL.B. 1970; m. Debbie d. Tjin and Kwan Tjoei 12 May 1971; two d.: Rica, Olivia; VICE-PRES., SECRETARY & GENERAL COUNSEL, PLACER DOME INC. 1991– ; Asst. Sec., subsidiary cos., Placer Development 1973–75; Solicitor, Legal Dept. 1975–80; Sec., Placer U.S.Inc. 1980–84; Sec., Placer Development Limited 1984–87; Gen. Mgr., Corp. Admin., Placer Pacific Limited Sydney Australia 1987–88; Sec., Placer Dome Inc. 1988–91; Mem., Law Soc. of B.C.; Office: P.O. Box 49330, Bentall Postal Stn., Vancouver, B.C. V7X 1P1.

**ECKLER, H. James,** B.Math, M.S., CMC; management consultant; b. Toronto, Ont. 20 May 1950; s. Samuel and Beula (James) E.; e. Univ. of Waterloo B.Math 1973; Wharton Sch., Univ. of Pennsylvania M.S. 1977; children: Allison, Joshua; SENIOR VICE-PRESIDENT, LOGISTICS PLANNING, LIVINGSTON GROUP INC. 1993– ; Analyst, Busch Ctr., Philadelphia 1975–77; Sr. Cons., Transp. Cons. Div., Booz Allen & Hamilton, Bethesda, MD 1977–82; Partner, Peat Marwick Stevenson & Kellogg 1982–93; Past Pres. & Dir., Candn. Assn. of Logistics Mngt.; Lectr., York Univ., McGill Univ. & Univ. of B.C.; certified management consultant; editor: 'Principles of Transportation'; recreations: skiing, jogging, cycling; Home: 20 Carnwath Cr., Willowdale, Ont. M2P 1J5; Office: 405 The West Mall, Etobicoke, Ont. M9C 5K7.

**ECKLER, Norman S.,** C.A.; executive; b. Toronto, Ont. 22 Sept. 1941; e. C.A. 1964; children: Alana Cher, Gregory, Amy Leigh; CHIEF FINANCIAL OFFR., NOMA INDUSTRIES LIMITED 1978– ; Vice Pres. Finance, Seaway MultiCorp Ltd. 1973–78; Home: 62 Wellesley St. W., #1505, Toronto, Ont. M5S 2X3; Office: 4211 Yonge St., Suite 315, Willowdale Ont. M2P 2A9.

**ECKLER, Samuel;** B.Comm., F.S.A., F.C.I.A.; actuary; b. Toronto, Ont. 4 Sept. 1914; s. Hyman and Lillian (Godfrey) E.; e. Parkdale Collegiate Inst. 1931; Univ. Toronto, B.Comm. 1935; m. Beula, d. Hyman and Augusta James, 3 Sept. 1945; children: Henry James; John David; FOUNDING CHRMN., ECKLER PARTNERS LTD. (Chrmn. 1947–88); Dir., Independent Order of Foresters 1973–93; Actuary, Independent Order of Foresters 1947–79; Commissioner reporting on finances, Workers' Compensation Bd. B.C. 1976; collaborator, study of Candn. Univ. Pensions Systems 1966; advisor to Govt. Bermuda on hospital insurance 1970; mem. Candn. Assn., Actuaries (Pres. 1961–62); mem. Soc. Actuaries (Bd. Govs. 1979–82); Internat. Actuarial Assn. (Vice-Pres. 1969–73); Candn. Fraternal Assn. (Pres. 1970); Hon. Vice-Pres. Jewish Community Centre Toronto; recreations: golf; skiing; travel; reading; Club: Oakdale Golf & Country; Home: 55 Prince Arthur Ave., #1006, Toronto, Ont. M5R 1B3; Office: 789 Don Mills Rd., Don Mills, Ont. M3C 1T8.

**ECROYD, Lawrence Gerald,** M.B.A.; C.A.E.; association executive; b. Montreal, Que., 14 Sept. 1918; s. the late George Smith and the late Marie E. (Guibord) E.; e. High Sch. of Montreal (Que.), 1936; Colscott Sch. of Comm., Montreal, 1940; London Sch. of Econ., 1957–60; Univ. of B.C., 1957–59; Fla. Atlantic Univ., 1970–72; m. Dorothy Gertrude, d. late Thomas Albert Howson, 26 Dec. 1949; children: Lynn Doreen, Claire Gail, Beverly Ann, Bruce Lawrence; CONSULTANT, 1984– ; General Steel Wares Ltd., Montreal, 1936–40; Hinde & Dauch Paper Co., Montreal, 1940–41; Candn. Chamber of Comm., Montreal, Maritimes and B.C., 1946–53; Extve. Dir. and Asst. Publisher, Mitchell Press Ltd., Vancouver, 1953–61; Travel Industry Assn. of Can. (then Candn. Tourist Assn.) 1961; served as Gen. Mgr., Extve. Vice Pres.; Pres. & C.E.O., Candn. Inst. of Plumbing and Heating 1973–84; served with RCN 1941–45; Asst. Naval Secy. 1945; rank Lt. Commdr. (S); mem. Adv. Comte. Ont. Govt. Project on Productivity Improve., 1971; Pres. & Dir., B.C. Borstal Assn., 1952–61; Dir., B.C. Narcotics Addiction Foundation, 1960–61; rec'd Dr. Milton Hersey Gold Medal for Pub. Speaking, 1947; Kenneth R. Wilson Award for Business Journalism, 1954; Award of Merit for Mang. Achievement (Am. Soc. Assn. Extves.), 1971; Life mem., Am. Soc. Assn. Extves.; Cert. Assn. Extve 1973; Past Chrmn. of Bd., Dir. and Hon. Life Mem., Inst. Assn. Extves.; Hon. Life Mem., Candn. Inst. of Plumbing and Heating; Hon. Life Mem., Candn. Assn. of Exposition Mgrs.; R. Catholic; recreations: reading, philately, fishing; Home: 95 La Rose Ave., Apt. 307, Etobicoke, Ont. M9P 3T2.

**EDDY, Hon. Alec Louis,** B.A., LL.B.; judge; b. Shedden, Ont. 12 March 1930; s. Rev. William Thomas and Mary Freeman (Hudson) E.; e. McGill Univ. B.A. 1952; Osgoode Hall Law Sch. 1956; m. Selma d. Alex and Alma Tarkpea 7 Sept. 1952; children: Mary Ann, Robert Alexander; JUDGE, PROVINCIAL COURT OF ONT. 1982– ; called to Bar of Ont. 1956; cr. Q.C. 1966; Past Solr. Co. of Lambton; Paul Harris Fellow Rotary Internat.; Pres. Lambton Law Assn. 1970; past mem., Candn. Bar Assn.; Med.-Legal Assn. Ont.; Past Pres.: Sarnia C. of C.; Rotary Club Sarnia (Hon.); Past Dir. Ont. C. of C.; recreations: skiing, sailing, diving; Home: 151 Norman St., Sarnia, Ont. N7T 6V6; Office: 700 N. Christina St., Sarnia, Ont. N7T 7L1.

**EDDY, Larry Alan,** F.C.A.; packaging industry executive; b. Toronto, Ont. 28 Sept. 1942; s. Arthur W. and Irene G. (Smith) E.; e. Oakwood C.I. 1960; C.A. (Candn. hon. list & Ont. 3rd prize) 1965; F.C.A. 1976; m. Dorothy Ann d. Albert and L. May Adams 19 Feb. 1966; children: Kimberley Ann, Kevin Adrian; SR. VICE-PRES., CORP. DEVEL., CCL INDUSTRIES INC. 1988– ; Student, Thorne, Mulholland, Howson & McPherson 1960–65; Partner, Thorne Gunn 1971; Ont. Reg. Tax Dir., Thorne Riddell 1974–81; Nat. Dir. of Tax Training 1981–83; Nat. Tax Dir. 1983–84; Vice-Pres., Admin., CCL Indus. Inc. 1984–88; Mem., Ont. Inst. of C.A.'s 1965 (Fellow 1976); Can. Inst. of Chartered Bus. Valuators 1975; Internat. Fiscal Assn.; Candn. Tax Found.; past chmn./mem. several orgns.; Past Lectr., York Univ.; Home: 1 Edmund Cres., Richmond Hill, Ont. L4B 2X9; Office: 105 Gordon Baker Rd., Willowdale, Ont. M2H 3P8.

**EDEL, (Joseph) Leon,** M.A., D.ès L.; writer and educator; b. Pittsburgh, Pa. 9 Sept. 1907; s. Simon and Fannie (Malamud) E.; came to Canada in 1910; e. Pub. and High Sch., Yorkton, Sask.; Yorkton Coll. Inst., 1920–23; McGill Univ., B.A. 1927, M.A. 1928; Que. Provincial Scholarship for study abroad 1928–32; Univ. of Paris, D.ès L. 1932; Hon. D.Litt. Union Coll. 1963; McGill Univ., 1963; Univ. of Sask. 1982; Hawaii Loa Coll. 1988; Guggenheim Fellow 1936–38 and 1965–66; Bollingen Fellowship 1958–60; m. 1stly Bertha Cohen 1935, divorced 1950; 2ndly Roberta Roberts 1950, divorced 1979; 3rdly Marjorie Putnam Sinclair 1980; Ed. (with F.R. Scott and A.J.M. Smith) of McGill Fortnightly Review 1925–27; Teaching Assoc., McGill Univ. 1927–28; Asst. Prof., English, Sir George Williams Coll., Montreal, Que. 1932–34; Cable editor, Agence Havas, N.Y. and Paris 1934–38; cable editor Canadian Press, N.Y. 1939–41; Foreign Desk, newspaper 'PM' 1941–43; UN correspondent 'PM' 1947–50; occasional commentator CBC (on UN) 1947–50; contrib. articles, reviews to 'Canadian Forum' 1930–35; N.Y. Univ., Assoc. Prof. of English 1953, Prof. 1955–66; Henry James Prof., Eng. & American Letters, New York Univ. 1966–73; Emeritus 1973; Citizens Professor of English, Univ. of Hawaii 1971–78; Emeritus 1978– ; Visiting Prof., Harvard Univ. 1959–60; Visiting Critic, Indiana Univ. 1954–55; Christian Gauss Seminar in Criticism, Princeton Univ. 1953; Univ. of Toronto, The Alexander Lect. 1956; Centenar Prof. 1967; served in 2nd World War 1943–46, Field Comm., Bronze Star Medal, 1945; German Occupation 1945–46 (organized News Agency in U.S. Zone); author: 'Life of Henry James' Vol. I 'The Untried Years' 1953; Vol: II 'The Conquest of London' 1962, Vol. III 'The Middle Years' 1962, Vol. IV 'The Treacherous Years' 1969, Vol. V 'The Master' 1972; co-author: 'Willa Cather' 1953; 'The Psychological Novel' 1955; 'Literary Biography' 1957; 'Henry David Thoreau' 1969; 'Bloomsbury, A House of Lions' 1979; 'Stuff of Sleep and Dreams' 1982; 'Writing Lives' 1984; 'Henry James: A Life' 1985; 'Some Memories of Edith Wharton' 1993; editor: The Complete Plays, Complete Tales (12 vols), Selected Letters (4 vols) and co-editor 'The Complete Notebooks' of Henry James; ed. The Diary of Alice James 1964; the Edmund Wilson Papers 'The Twenties' 1975, 'The Thirties' 1980, 'The Forties' 1983; 'The Fifties' 1986; awarded Pulitzer Prize for Biography 1963; Nat. Book Award for non-fiction 1963; Gold Medal for Biography of Academy – Inst. of Arts and Letters 1976; Nat. Book Critics' Circle Award for biography 1985; address Westminster Abbey 1976 unveiling tablet to Henry James in Poets' Corner; E.J. Pratt Lecture, Memorial Univ., Nfld. 1984; first annual Frank Scott Memorial Lectr., McGill Univ. 1989; Hawaii Literary Award (1977); el. mem., Nat. Inst. Arts, Letters 1964 (Secy., 1965–67); American Academy of Arts and Letters (1972); Fellow, Royal Society of Literature (Gt. Br.) 1970; Am. Acad. Arts & Sciences, 1959; Ed. Bd., P.M.L.A. 1963–68; Hon. mem., W.A. White Psychoanalytic Soc. and American Acad. of Psychoanalysis; mem. P.E.N. (Pres. U.S. Center, 1957–59); Authors' Guild (Pres. 1968–70); Soc. of Authors (Britain); recreations: music, swimming; Clubs: Century (N.Y.); Address: 3817 Lurline Drive, Honolulu, Hawaii 96816.

**EDEN, Ronald William,** B.A.; business executive; b. Winnipeg, Man. 12 May 1931; s. Harry and Dorothy Arnott (Yelland) E.; e. Univ. of West. Ont., B.A. (Hons.) 1953; m. Janet d. Dr. and Mrs. T. Barnby 18 Sept. 1954; children: Mark, Brian, Kevin; PRES. & CHIEF EXTVE. OFFR., CANADA MALTING CO. LIMITED 1988– ; Ford Motor Co. of Can. 1953–57; Asst. to Pres., Guthrie Candn. Investments Limited 1958–62; Vice-Pres., Guthrie & Gen. Mgr., Trench Electric 1962–72; Pres. & Chief Extve. Offr., Guthrie Candn. Investments Limited 1969–88; Dir., Dominion Textile, Inc.; Protection Mutual Insur. Co.; Can. Malting Co. Limited; recreations: golf, bridge, reading; clubs: St. Georges Golf & Country; Ontario; Beaumaris Yacht; Home: 21 King Georges Rd., Toronto, Ont. M8X 1K9; Office: 10 Four Seasons Place, Suite 325, Etobicoke, Ont. M9B 6H7.

**EDGE, Charles Geoffrey,** B.Sc., F.I.S., F.C.M.A., C.M.A.; consultant; b. Wilmslow, Chesire, Eng. 8 Aug. 1920; s. Charles Edmund E.; e. Varndean Secondary Sch. Brighton, Eng.; Univ. of London B.Sc. (Econ.) 1950; m. Madeline Rita d. Henry Lester Butler Tarrant, M.B.E. 25 May 1940; two d. Christine Dorothy (Jeffery), Jennifer Wendy (Doyle); PRESIDENT, C.G. EDGE & ASSOCIATES INC.; Tax Offr. Brit. Civil Service 1937–39, Higher Extve. Offr. 1946–51; came to Can. 1951; Canadian Industries Ltd. 1951–56; Mgr. Financial Analysis Canadian Chemical & Cellulose Co. Ltd. 1956–59; Asst. Treas. Chemcell Ltd. 1959–62, various sr. positions incl. Vice Pres. Corporate Devel. 1962–70; Dir. Bralorne Oil and Gas Co. Ltd. 1969–70; joined National Energy Bd. 1971 serving as mem., Assoc. Vice Chrmn., Vice Chrmn., Chrmn. until 1986; rec'd Queen's Silver Jubilee Medal; author 'A Practical Manual in the Appraisal of Capital Expenditure' 1960, revised 1964, 1981; co-author 'The Impact of Systems and Computers on Management and on the Accountant' 1966; served with RA 1939–46, rank Lt.; Fellow, Soc. Mgmt. Accts.; Certified Mgmt. Acct.; Unitarian; Address: 2056 Brant St., Unit 6, Burlington, Ont. L7P 3A6.

**EDIGER, Nicholas Martin;** business consultant; b. Winnipeg, Man. 25 June 1928; s. Nicholas and Anna (Hamm) E.; e. Univ. of Man. B.Sc. 1950; m. Elizabeth Durden d. Prof. R.E.D. Cattley 18 Sept. 1973; one d. Julia Anne; MANAGING DIR., SENTINEL ASSOCIATES LTD. 1988– ; Chrmn. and Chief Extve. Offr. Eldorado Aviation Ltd.; Eldorado Resources Ltd.; Eldor Resources Ltd. 1974–88; Gulf Oil Corp. and affiliates 1950–74; Vice Pres. Gulf Minerals Canada Ltd. to 1974; Pres. and C.O.O., Eldorado Nuclear Ltd. 1974–88; Office: 165 University Ave., Ste. 200, Toronto, Ont. M5H 3B9.

**EDINBOROUGH, Arnold,** O.C., M.C., M.A., LL.D., Litt. S.D.; b. Donington, Eng. 2 Aug. 1922; s. Frank and Sarah Ann (Clark) E.; e. Spalding (Eng.) Grammar Sch., 1932–40; St. Catharine's Coll., Cambridge, B.A. 1947, M.A. (Hons. English) 1949; Univ. of Guelph, LL.D.

1968; Litt. S.D., Wycliffe Coll. 1980; Hon. Fellow, St. John's College, Winnipeg 1976; m. Letitia Mary, d. late Ralph Henry Woolley, 14 Jan. 1947; children: Christine Ann, Alastair Michael, Sarah Jane; PRES. EDINA PRODUCTIONS LTD.; Chrmn., Intern. Scholarship Found.; own imprint., Stoddart Publishing; formerly Pres. & C.E.O., Council for Business and The Arts in Canada 1974–89; Asst. Prof. of English, Queen's Univ., 1947–54; Visiting Lect., Univ. of Lausanne, 1947; Dir. of Studies in Eng., St. Catharine's Coll., Cambridge, 1952–53; Editor, 'Kingston Whig-Standard,' 1954–58; Editor, 'Saturday Night,' 1958–62; Pres. and Publ., Sat. Night Publs. Ltd., 1963–70; Contr. Ed., 'The Financial Post' 1970–90; Columnist, 'Anglican Journal Episcopal' 1963–90; Dir. of Sch. of Eng., Queen's Univ., Summer Sch., 1950–53; Special Lectr. Royal Mil. Coll., 1957–58; Special Lectr., in Eng., Royal Mil. College Canada, 1948–52; Candn. Corr. for 'Shakespeare Quarterly' and 'Shakespeare Survey' 1950–70; served in 2nd World War; Capt., Royal Arty., with 23rd Field Regt., R.A.; 1st Army, N. Africa, 1942; 5th and 8th Army in Italy, 1942–45; awarded M.C. 1945; Mem. of Extve., John Howard Soc. of Kingston, 1955–58; Chrmn., New Symphony Assn. of Kingston 1954–58; Chrmn., Eastern Ont. Drama League, 1955–56; former Gov., Dom. Drama Festival; Hon. Dir., John Howard Soc. of Ont.; Senator Stratford Fest. Foundn.; former Vice Pres., The Corp. of Massey Hall and Roy Thomson Hall, Toronto; Past Chrmn., Elliot Lake Centre; Officer, Order of Canada 1983; awarded Centennial Medal 1967; Silver Jubilee Medal 1977; awarded Commemorative Medal for 125th Anniversary of Candn. Confederation 1992; Publications: 'One Church, Two Nations' 1967; 'Some Camel, Some Needle' 1974; 'The Enduring Word' 1978; 'The Festivals of Canada' 1981; 'Winston's: The Life and Times of a Great Restaurant' 1988; 'Arnold Edinborough: An Autobiography' 1991; Former mem., several national and diocesan comtes., Anglican Church of Canada; Dir. (1963), Nat. Ballet Sch.; mem. (1965) Toronto Planning Bd.; Anglican; Clubs: Albany; Arts & Letters; recreation: reading; fishing; Home: #2405, 355 St. Clair Ave. W., Toronto, Ont. M5P 1N5.

**EDISON, Noel;** artistic director and conductor; b. Toronto, Ont. 16 Nov. 1958; s. George and Marian Clarissa (Frost) E.; e. Jarvis Collegiate 1978; Laurier Univ. 1985; ARTISTIC DIRECTOR, ELORA FESTIVAL (FORMERLY THREE CENTURIES FESTIVAL) 1983– AND CONDUCTOR, ELORA FESTIVAL SINGERS 1981– ; Organist and Choirmaster, Church of St. John the Evangelist, Anglican, Elora 1984– ; Past Teacher, St. John's Kilmarnock School and Guelph Univ.; Lectr., Laurier Univ. 1991– ; Young Achievers Award from the Office of the Prime Minister 1982; Conductor, 'Nine Lessons and Carols for Summer' 1987 (tape cassette), 'Christmas in Elora' 1992 (compact disc and cassette); Home: 48 Mill St., Elora, Ont. N0B 1S0; Office: 33 Henderson St., Elora, Ont. N0B 1S0.

**EDMONDS, Edward Leslie,** M.A., Ph.D., D.Litt.; university professor; b. Royston, England 15 Mar. 1916; s. Edward Oliver and Olive (Foster) E.; e. Normanton and Oxford Univ., B.A. 1937, B.A. 1939, M.A. 1940; Sheffield Univ., M.A.(Edn.) 1955; Leeds Univ., Ph.D. 1960; Somerset Univ., D.Litt. 1990; university diplomas in teaching, public admin., educational administration; m. Ruth Isabel (dec.), d. David and Mary Auty, 1950; m. 2ndly, Jane Mary d. Sybil Wardle 1985; children: (from previous m.) Iain David Foster, Kirsteen Fiona; DEAN AND PROF., UNIV. OF PRINCE EDWARD ISLAND, (ret. 1982); Sr. Eng. master; major in H.M. Forces; tutor at coll. of edn.; Chief Insp. of Schools and Colls.; Dept. Head, Univ. of Sask.; Fellow: Royal Hist. Soc., Royal Soc. of Arts, Eng. Speaking Bd.; Pres., Nat. Assn. of Insps. 1962; Hon. Chief, Micmac 1972; Pres., W.C.C.I. 1975–78; Pres., Royal Commonwealth Chapter P.E.I. 1974–76, 1981–88; St. John Ambulance: Prov. Comnr. 1972–81, First Vice-pres. 1983–90, President Emeritus 1990– ; Prov. Historian 1981– ; mem. Priory Chapter of the Priory of Canada 1984–90, Almoner 1990– ; Bd. of Dirs., Laubach Literacy Can. 1981–85; Pres., P.E.I. Counc. on Drug Education 1972– ; rec'd. Qantas Travel Scholarship 1973, World Federalist Essay Prize 1976, White House Award 1976; became Hon. Citizen of Texas 1977, Knight of Justice, Order of St. John 1983; Officer, Order of St. Lazarus 1987; author of numerous scholarly works; religion: Anglican; recreations: lay-reader, masonry, bridge, music, heraldry, theatre; clubs: Un. Services Officers Club; Address: R.R. #2, Cornwall, P.E.I. C0A 1H0.

**EDMUNDS, Charles C.,** A.B., M.A., Ph.D.; university professor; b. St. Louis, Missouri 24 Nov. 1946; s. Bernard Claiborne and Margaret Elizabeth (Hon) E.; e. Webster College A.B. 1968; Univ. of Manitoba M.A. 1971, Ph.D. 1973; m. Jean d. Charles and Virginia Ligertwood 8 June 1968; children: Charles, Susanne; PROFESSOR OF MATHEMATICS, MOUNT SAINT VINCENT UNIV. 1975– ; consulting and authoring, Houghton-Mifflin, Oxford Univ. Press; Dir., Candn. Math. Soc.; Mt. St. Vincent Univ. Teaching Excellence Award; Roman Catholic; Mem., AMS; MAA; CMS; author: 'Houghton Mifflin Mathematics Achievement Tests' (9, 10, 11, 12), 1987, '88, '91, '91 (textbooks); recreations: barbershop singing, slowpitch, baseball, weight lifting; clubs: SPEBSQSA, Inc.; Home: 25 Deerbrooke Dr., Dartmouth, N.S. B2V 1W4; Office: Bedford Highway, Halifax, N.S. B3M 2J6.

**EDWARD, John Thomas,** Ph.D., D.Phil., Sc.D., F.R.S.C., F.C.I.C.; F.A.A.A.S.; educator; b. London, Eng. 23 Mar. 1919; s. John William and Jessie C. (Simpson) E.; e. Town of Mount Royal (Que.) High Sch. 1935; McGill Univ. B.Sc. 1939, Ph.D. 1942; Iowa State Coll. 1942–43; Oxford Univ. D.Phil. 1949; Trinity Coll. Dublin M.A. 1955, Sc.D. 1972; m. Deirdre Mary d. Cyril Waldron, Birmingham, Eng. 21 March 1953; children: John Valentine, Jeremy Bryan, Julian Kevin; EMERITUS PROF. OF CHEM. McGILL UNIV. since 1986; Research Offr. Explosives, Nat. Research Council, Ottawa and C.A.R.D.E. Valcartier 1943–45; Imp. Chem. Ind. Research Fellow in Chem. Univ. of Birmingham 1949–52; Lectr. in Organic Chem. Trinity Coll. Dublin 1952–56; joined McGill Univ. 1956; Visiting Scient. Copenhagen 1953, Stanford 1965, Paris 1972–73 and 1979–80, Prague 1977, São Paulo 1978, Umeå, Sweden 1980 and 1982, Sofia 1986; Science Scholar Royal Comn. Exhn. 1851, Oxford 1946–49; author various articles on structures organic molecules, mechanisms organic reactions, conformational effects; Fellow, Am. Assn. Advanc. Science; mem. Am. Chem. Soc.; Sigma Xi; recreations: hiking, gardening; Home: 51 Chesterfield Ave., Westmount, Que. H3Y 2M4; Office: 801 Sherbrooke St. W., Montreal, Que. H3A 2K6.

**EDWARDS, Hon. Anne,** B.A., M.A., M.L.A.; journalist, college instructor, politician; b. Tisdale, Sask. 6 June 1935; s. Isaac F. and J. Leone (Thorpe) Stothers; e. Tisdale Sch. System; Univ. of Sask. B.A. 1955, M.A. 1958; m. Russell E. 22 March 1958; children: Robert, Elizabeth, Gregory, Allan; MINISTER, ENERGY, MINES & PETROLEUM RESOURCES, GOVT. OF B.C. 1991– ; 1st elected to B.C. legislature g.e. 1986; re-elected 1991; Critic for Tourism, Recreation & Culture 2 yrs.; Former Critic, Energy, Mines & Petroleum Resources; has also worked with Bd. of Referees for U.I.C. & Reg. Bd. of Variance; N.D.P.; co-author: 'Exploring the Purcell Wilderness'; Home: Box 576, Cranbrook, B.C. V1C 4J1; Office: Room 133, Legislative Bldgs., Victoria, B.C. V8V 1X4.

**EDWARDS, Anthony William,** M.A.; b. Wells, Somerset, Eng. 3 June 1939; s. William Bell and Lavinia Margaret (Tyson) E.; e. Taunton Sch. Somerset, Eng. 1957; St. Andrews Univ. Scot. M.A. (Hons.) 1961 (James Cunningham Prize in Geog. 1961); C.E.O., ROYAL SOCIETY FOR THE PREVENTION OF ACCIDENTS; C.E.O., Assn. for Internat. Cancer Rsch. 1992; Chrmn. & C.E.O., Hartz Holdings Ltd. & Thomas Cork SM 1986–90, Harmon Savory Ltd. 1988–90; Chrmn. Hartz International Ltd. 1978–90, Mng. Dir. 1974–78; Div. Dir. Spillers International Ltd. 1971; Fellow, British Inst. Mgmt.; recreations: French wine and food, Scottish islands; Clubs: Caledonian (London, Eng.); London (Ont.); Home: The Orchards, Old Somerby, Grantham, Lincs. NG33 4AG England.

**EDWARDS, Clifford Henry Coad,** Q.C., LL.B.; educator; b. Jamalpore, India 8 Nov. 1924; s. George Henry Probyn and Constance Ivy (Coad) E.; came to Canada 1958; e. King's Coll. Sch., Wimbledon, Eng.; King's Coll., Univ. of London, LL.B. (1st Class Hons.) 1945; post-grad work 1946–47; m. Kathleen Mary, d. late Jacob Ernest Faber, 6 Jan. 1951; two s., John Philip and Michael Hugh; two d., Jeanette Marie and Margaret Susan; PRESIDENT, MANITOBA LAW REFORM COMMISSION 1979–86 and 1988– ; former Dean, Fac. of Law, Univ. of Manitoba, 1966–79; apptd. Dean Emeritus 1986; served articles of Clerkship, London, Eng.; admitted as a Solr., Supreme Court of Eng. 1949; called to Bar of Man. 1964; in practice with firm of Solrs., London, Eng., 1948; Legal Advisor, Sudan Interior Mission, W. Africa 1952; apptd. Lectr. at Law, Kumasi Coll., Ghana 1956, Sr. Lectr. 1957; apptd. to acad. staff, Manitoba Law Sch. 1958, Sch. Recorder 1960, Assoc. Prof. 1962, Prof. and Dean, Sch. of Law 1964; past mem. Extve. Comte. Commonwealth Legal Educ. Assn.; Past Pres., Assn. Candn. Law Teachers; apptd. mem. of the Uniform Law Conf. of Can., 1979; Various reviews, case comments and articles in leading law journs.; contributor, Casebook on Candn. Law of Contract, 1978; Baptist; recreations: tennis, reading, public speaking; Home: 301–180 Tuxedo Ave. Winnipeg, Man. R3P 2A6; Office: c/o Univ. of Manitoba, Faculty of Law, Winnipeg, Man. R3T 2N2.

**EDWARDS, David Francis,** B.Sc.; heavy equipment executive; b. Broadview, Sask. 19 Sept. 1938; s. Donald Albert and Hilda E.; e. Univ. of Alberta B.Sc. 1960; m. Patricia d. Henry Archibald and Lydia Logan 22 July 1961; children: Hugh, Paul, Jill; VICE-PRESIDENT OF OPERATIONS, FINNING LTD. 1992– ; Technical Support Engr., Street & Robbins Morrow 1960; later moved into sales; Major Accounts Sales Rep., R. Angus (purchased Street & Robbins Morrow) 1968; Calgary Mgr. 1971; Edmonton Mgr. 1974; Gen. Mgr., Northern Opns. 1977; Gen. Sales Mgr. 1980, then Regional Mgr. Edmonton 1989; Finning Ltd. (acquired R. Angus) 1989; General Parts Mgr. (Vancouver) 1990; Home: 1785 137A St., Surrey, B.C. V4A 9E6; Office: 555 Great Northern Way, Vancouver, B.C. V5T 1E2.

**EDWARDS, Iwan,** B.Mus.; choral director; b. Swansea, Wales, U.K. 5 Oct. 1937; s. Kenneth Thomas and Sarah Jane (Morgan) E.; e. Gowerton Boys' Grammar Schoo; Univ. College of Wales B.Mus. (Hons.) 1960; Teachers' Diploma 1961; m. Undeg d. Rhys and Gwyneth Gruffydd 28 Dec. 1961; children: Aled Morgan, Owain Rhys; PROFESSOR, MUSIC FACULTY, MCGILL UNIV. 1991– ; Head, Music Dept., Holyhead S.S. (N. Wales) 1961–65; Music Dir., Lachine H.S. 1965–79; F.A.C.E. School Montreal 1979–90; Founder-Dir., St. Lawrence Choir 1972; F.A.C.E. Treble Choir 1981; Dir., Montreal Symphony Orch. Chorus 1986; Asst. Prof., Music Fac., McGill Univ. 1989; Chrmn., Performance Dept. Music Fac., McGill Univ.; Artistic Dir., Ottawa Choral Soc. 1992; Guest conductor for num. choral groups in Canada & the U.S.; clinician and adjudicator; choirs have won awards in Canada (C.B.C. Choral Competitions) and Europe (Llangollen Internat. Eisteddfod, Wales), Vienna and Arnhem; 1978 Queen's Silver Jubilee Medal 1978; 1st recipient, 'Merité Culturel,' City of Lachine 1987; 'Certificate of Recognition,' Protestant Sch. Bd. of Montreal 1989; Mem., St. David's Soc. of Montreal (Sec. 1971–73; Pres. 1974); Trustee, Welsh Nat. Gymanfa Ganu Assn. 1987– ; recreations: reading, cycling; Home: 840 – 38th Ave., Lachine, Qué. H8T 2C3; Office: 555 Sherbrooke St. W., Montreal, Qué. H3A 1E3.

**EDWARDS, James Stewart,** M.P., B.A.; politician; b. Edmonton, Alta. 31 Aug. 1936; s. Donald Stewart and Verna May (Armstrong) E.; e. Victoria Composite High Sch. Edmonton; Univ. of Alta. B.A. 1962; m. Sheila Mary d. Francis Patrick and Mary Helena Mooney 10 Sept. 1960; children: Mary-Caroline (Mrs. Henry T. Tillman III), John, Sarah (Mrs. Seth W. Frater), Gweyn; Treasury Board President 1993; el. to H. of C for Edmonton South 1984, re-el. Edmonton Southwest 1988, def. 1993; Chrmn. Standing Ctte. Communications & Culture 1986–87, Standing Ctte. Official Langs. 1991; Parlty. Sec. to Min. of Communications 1985–86, 1989–91, Min. of Indian Affairs & N. Devel and Min. W. Econ. Diversification 1988; Co-Chrmn. Special Jt. Ctte. Process for Amending Constitution Can. 1991; Parlty. Sec. to Min. of Consumer and Corporate Affairs 1991–92; Parliamentary Secretary, Government House Leader 1992–93; Sec.-Treas. Alta. Caucus 1986; mem. Legis. Ctte. Can.-U.S. Free Trade Agreement; Rapporteur Strasbourg II Conf. Parlty. Democracy, France 1987; served as Can.'s Gov. ad interim Asian Devel. Bank Conf. Manila 1986; Chrmn. Can.-Germany Friendship Group Chrmn. 1986; served various positions broadcasting Edmonton & Vancouver 1955–84; served Bds. Edmonton Symphony, Misericordia Hosp., Grant MacEwan Community Coll.; mem. Quarter-Century Club Candn. Assn. Broadcasters; Home: 13616 – 82 Ave., Edmonton, Alta. T5R 3R4.

**EDWARDS, John,** M.A.; public servant; b. Cairo, Egypt 18 Oct. 1940; e. Charterhouse Sch. (UK) 1957; Univ. of B.C., B.A. 1961; Cambridge Univ. 1962; Manchester Univ. 1966, M.A. 1967; COMMISSIONER OF CORRECTIONAL SERVICES CANADA; UK Overseas Civil Service 1962–64; Statistics Can. 1967–70; Efficiency Evaluation, Treasury Bd. 1970–71; Orgn. Div. 1971–76; Comnr., Pub. Serv. Comn. 1976–82; Assoc. Dep. Min./Vice-Chrmn., Employment & Immigr. Can. 1982–87; Sec.-Gen., Nat. Museums of Can. 1987–90; Manager, Public Service 2000, Privy Council Office 1989–..; Office: 340 Laurier Ave. N., Ottawa, Ont. K1A 0P9.

**EDWARDS, John Llewelyn Jones,** LL.B., M.A., Ph.D., LL.D., LL.D. (Hon.); university professor emeritus; b. Aberystwyth, Cardiganshire, Wales, 16 May 1918; s. David and Sarah (Jones) E., e. Univ. Coll. of Wales, LL.B. 1939; St. John's Coll., Univ. of Cambridge,

B.A. 1947, M.A. 1952, LL.D. 1964; Univ. of London, Ph.D. 1953, and Hon. LL.D. Univ. of Wales, 1976, York University, Canada, 1982 and Dalhousie Univ. 1984; m. Monica Mary d. Cuthbert and Jessie Haysey, Leigh-on-Sea, Essex, Eng., 24 March 1945; children: Alexandra Mary, Mark Llewelyn John, Stephen Gordon Patrick; PROF. OF LAW, FACULTY OF LAW since 1963, AND FIRST DIR. OF THE CENTRE OF CRIMINOLOGY, UNIV. OF TORONTO, 1963–76; called to Bar at Middle Temple, London, Eng. 1948; McMahon Studentship, St. John's College, Cambridge 1947–48; Harmsworth Scholar, Middle Temple, 1948–51; called to Bar of Ont. 1971; called to Bar of The Bahamas 1989; Lect., Faculty of Law, Univ. Coll., London., 1947–51; Queen's Univ. of Belfast (N. Ireland) 1951–53, Reader in Law 1953–58; came to Canada 1958; Sir James Dunn Prof. of Law, Faculty of Law, Dalhousie Univ., 1958–63; served in 2nd World War, Terr. Army, 1939; served with R.A. in W. Africa; staff appts. with H.Q., Br. Airborne Corps and Directorate of Staff Duties, War Office; Legal Corr., 'Manchester Guardian' 1948–52; author: 'Mens Rea in Statutory Offences' 1955, reprinted 1968; 'Law Officers of the Crown' 1964, reprinted 1977, 1979; 'Ministerial Responsibility for National Security' 1980; 'The Attorney General, Politics and the Public Interest' 1984; 'Walking the Tightrope of Justice' 1990; honoured in *festschrift* 'Perspectives in Criminal Law' (A.N. Doob and E.L. Greenspan, eds.) 1985; Founding mem., Conf. of Chief Justices of Canada (precursor to the Candn. Judicial Council) 1964–65; Dir., 1st Judicial Conf. on Sentencing in Brit. Commonwealth, Dalhousie Univ., N.S. 1962; Dir., National Conf. of Judges on Sentencing, Univ. of Toronto 1964; Dir., National Conf. on Prevention of Crime, Univ. of Toronto 1965; Chrmn., 1st Conf. of Dirs. of N. American Criminological Rsch. Insts. 1966; Dir., National Conf. on Disposition of Offenders in Canada, Univ. of Toronto 1972; Dir., National Symposium on Medical Sciences and the Criminal Law, Univ. of Toronto 1973; mem., Secy.-Gen.'s Review Comte. on Commonwealth Legal Co-operation 1974; Overseas Fellow, Churchill Coll., Cambridge 1967–68 and 1976–77; Ford Foundation Travelling Fellow 1967–69; Visiting Prof. & Fellow, Univ. of Wales 1974; Commonwealth Prestige Fellow, N.Z. Univs. 1977; Viscount Bennett Memorial Lectr., Univ. of New Brunswick 1986; Visiting Prof., Salmon P. Chase Coll. of Law, N. Kentucky Univ. 1987; Pres. Medico-Legal Soc. of Toronto 1970–71; Spec. Advr. to McDonald Comn. on National Security 1977–81; Spec. Advr. to Nova Scotia Royal Comn. on the Donald Marshall Jr. Prosecution 1987–90; Special Adv., Law Reform Comn. of Can. 1988–90; recipient, G. Arthur Martin Award, Ont. Criminal Lawyers' Assn. 1993; Anglican; Recreations: lawn bowling, music, reading and walking; Home: 66 Baby Pt. Cres., Toronto, Ont. M6S 2C1.

**EDWARDS, K. Michael,** B.Comm., F.C.S.I.; financial executive; b. Hamilton, Ont. 9 Feb. 1947; s. Kenneth and Jane (Callaghan) E.; e. Univ. of Alberta B.Comm. 1971; m. Rosemary J. McCarten 10 May 1969; children: Jane, Cynthia, Amy, Michael; PRESIDENT & CHIEF OPERATING OFFICER, RICHARDSON GREENSHIELDS OF CANADA LIMITED 1991– ; Nat. Sales Mgr. & Dir., McLeod Young Weir 1971–84; Pres. & C.O.O. , Dean Witter/Gardiner Watson 1984–87; Extve. Vice-Pres., Richardson Greenshields of Can. Limited 1987; Extve. Vice-Pres. & C.O.O. 1989; Dir., Richardson Greenshields Limited; Richardson Greenshields Securities Inc.; Chair, Candn. Investors Protection Fund 1992; Bd. of Gov., Toronto Stock Exchange 1985–89; Vice-Chair 1989–91; Chair 1991–93; Dir., Candn. Securities Inst.; Chair, Children's Aid Soc. Found. 1993; Fac. of Bus. Advisory Council, Univ. of Alta. 1991; recreations: golf, skiing, sailing; clubs: National, Lambton Golf & Country, Muskoka Lakes Golf & Country; Home: 33 Queen Mary's Dr., Etobicoke, Ont. M8X 1S3; Office: 130 Adelaide St. W., 12th fl., Toronto, Ont. M5H 1T8.

**EDWARDS, Mark Edward,** B.A., LL.B.; lawyer, insurance executive; b. Montreal, Que. 24 Nov. 1947; s. Edward and Gwendolyn Jessie E.; e. Lower Canada Coll. 1960–65; Queen's Univ. B.A., LL.B. 1965–71; m. Diane Alaine Sweanor 29 Aug. 1970; children: Bryce, Jessica, Derek; VICE-PRES., GEN. COUNSEL & SECRETARY, CONFEDERATION LIFE INSUR. CO. 1973– ; Articling Student, Good Year Tire & Rubber Co. 1971–72; Asst. Counsel, present firm 1973–76; Assoc. Couns. 1976–78; Asst. Vice-Pres. & Couns. 1978–80; Legal Vice-Pres. & Assoc. Gen. Couns. 1980–82; Legal Vice-Pres., Gen. Couns. & Sec. 1982–83; Dir., Confed Realty Serv. Limited; Dolphin Investments, Properties, Financial Serv. and Funds Limited; CL Finan. Limited; Confed. Finan. Serv. (Can.) Limited; Confed. Leasing Limited; Confederation Trust Company; Home: 26 Baby Point Cr., Toronto, Ont. M6S 2B8; Office: 321 Bloor St. E., Toronto, Ont. M4W 1H1.

**EDWARDS, Mary Jane,** M.A., Ph.D.; educator; b. St. Thomas, Ont. 21 March 1939; d. Frederick John and Winnifred Idette (Billingsley) E.; e. West Hill High Montréal 1953; Galt Coll. Inst. & Vocation Sch. 1956; Trinity Coll. Univ. of Toronto B.A. 1960, Ph.D. 1969; Queen's Univ. M.A. 1963; DIR. CENTRE FOR EDITING EARLY CANDN. TEXTS, CARLETON UNIV. 1981– , Gen. Ed. CEECT Series, Prof. of English 1982– ; Lectr. in Eng. Acadia Univ. 1961–63; Instr. in Eng. Univ. of B.C. 1966–69, Asst. Prof. 1969–70; Asst. Prof. of Eng. present Univ. 1970, Assoc. Prof. 1973; ed. 'The Evolution of Canadian Literature in English: Beginnings to 1867' 1973; co-ed. 'The Evolution of Canadian Literature in English: 1867–1914' 1973; 'Canadian Literature in the 70's' 1980; ed. 'The History of Emily Montague' by Frances Brooke 1985; gen. ed. 'Canadian Crusoes' by Catharine Parr Traill 1986; 'A Strange Manuscript Found in a Copper Cylinder' by James De Mille 1986; 'Wacousta' by John Richardson 1987; 'Roughing It in the Bush' by Susanna Moodie 1988; 'Antoinette De Mirecourt' by Rosanna Leprohon 1989; 'The Mephibosheth Stepsure Letters' by Thomas McCulloch 1990; 'St. Ursula's Convent' by Julia Catherine Beckwith Hart 1991; 'The Canadian Brothers' by John Richardson 1992; mem. Ed. Ctte., 'Collected Works of Northrop Frye'; Chair, Queen Elizabeth II Scholarship Selection Ctte.; mem. Bd. of Dirs., and mem. Candn. Studies Ctte., Shastri Indo-Canadian Inst.; Anglican; Home: 1, 35 Glen Ave., Ottawa, Ont. K1S 2Z6; Office: 1901 Dunton Tower, Carleton University, Ottawa, Ont. K1S 5B6.

**EDWARDS, Oliver Edward,** B.Sc., M.S., Ph.D., F.R.S.C., F.C.I.C.; organic chemist; b. Wattsville, Wales 8 Jan. 1920; s. Oliver Edward and Anna E.; came to Canada 1926; e. Univ. of Alberta, Bsc. (Hons. Chem.) 1941; Northwestern Univ., M.S. 1943, Ph.D. 1948; m. Isobel Mary, d. Samuel George Gregg, 4 Aug. 1945; children: Sheryl Anne, Laurel Ruth; ADJUNCT PROF., DEPT. OF CHEMISTRY, CARLETON UNIV. 1985– ; former Prin. Research Offr., Div. of Biol. Sciences, Nat. Research Council, which he joined in 1948; served in Candn. Army, 1943–46, retiring with rank of Capt.; mem., Eastview, Ont., Sch. Bd. 1956–58; mem., Am. Chem. Soc.; Chem. Inst. Can.; (1960 Merck, Sharpe & Dohme Award); author: over 106 scientific papers; United Church; Home: 678 Portage Ave., Ottawa, Ont. K1G 1T4; Office: Carleton Univ., Ottawa, Ont. K1S 5B6.

**EDWARDS, Robert John Conway,** B.Ed., M.A.; writer; teacher; b. London, Eng. 12 Jan. 1946; s. Newton Alun and May (Alcock) E.; e. Victoria Coll., Jersey; Oak Bay H.S., Victoria; Univ. of Victoria B.A. 1967; Oxford Univ. (Rhodes Scholar, B.C. & Hertford) 1967–69; Univ. of Washington M.A. 1972; Univ. of Victoria M.A. 1973; McMaster Univ. M.A. 1974; Ont. Teacher's Coll. B.Ed. 1975; m. Gillian d. Norman and Diana Lockyer 12 March 1978; one s. John Tecwyn; Classics instr., Camosun Coll., Victoria 1971–73; Primary sch. teacher, Cortez, Hornby and Saltspring Islands 1976–84; Galiano Elementary Sch. 1984– ; English Instr., Camosun Coll. 1991– ; Student, Victoria College of Art 1991–92; mem. Anglican Ch.; Candn. Assn. of Rhodes Scholars; author: 'Jordan River Poems' 1974; 'The Roman Cookery of Apicius' 1984; 'Roman Cookery, Elegant and Easy Recipes From History's First Gourmet' 1986; Newspaper . columnist 'Country Gourmet' 1988– ; recreations: running, woodwork; Home: R.R. #1, Fulford Harbour, Salt Spring Island, B.C. V0S 1C0.

**EDWARDS, Brig.-Gen. Robert Martin,** A.F.C., C.D.; transportation executive; b. Lucky Lake, Sask. 20 Aug. 1928; s. Frederick and Doris Martha (Chell) E.; e. rural schs. Sask.; St. James Coll. Inst. Winnipeg 1946; Univ. of Man. 1946–47; RCAF Aircrew Training 1948; RCAF Staff Coll. 1960; RAF Coll. of Air Warfare UK 1968; Nat. Defence Coll. Kingston 1972; m. Lucile d. Warren and Patti Hunt 2 July 1981; children: Martha Louise, Charles Frederick; DIR. OF OPERATIONS, BUSINESS FLIGHTS 1990– ; joined RCAF 1947; flew North Star aircraft 1949–56; awarded the Air Force Cross during the Korean War; assigned world's first jet airliner (DH Comet) 1952–54; pilot 412 VIP Sqn. Ottawa 1952–56; Staff Offr. Air Transport Command HQ 1956–59; Sqdn. Commdr./Ops Offr. RCAF Air Div. Eur. 1961–68; C.O. RCAF Stn. Uplands Ottawa 1968–71; Dep. Chief of Staff Transport Command 1972–76; Gen. Mgr./Vice Pres. Operations, Business Flights 1976–86; Vice Pres., Westair Resources Ltd. 1987–90; Dir. of Operations, Business Flights 1990– ; recreations: golf, skiing; Clubs: Glencoe Golf & Country; Glencoe; Calgary Polo; Office: 1441 Aviation Park NE, Calgary, Alta. T2E 8M7.

**EDWARDS, Roy Lawrence,** M.A., D.Phil.; educator; b. Southampton, Eng. 2 Dec. 1922; s. Bertram Frank and Ellen Mary Jane (Hicks) E.; e. Price's Sch. Fareham, Hants 1933–41; Borough Rd. Coll. Isleworth, Teacher's Cert. 1943; Keble Coll. Oxford B.A. 1950, M.A., D.Phil. 1952; m. Joy d. Bertie and Amy Sanders 27 Aug. 1949; children: Rachael (d.), Diana, Sylvia; ACTING VICE-PRES. (ACAD.), TRENT UNIV. 1983–84; Lectr. in Entomol. Hull Univ. Yorks., Eng. 1952–57; Nat. Research Council Post-doctoral Fellow, Agric. Research Stn. Belleville, Ont. 1957–58; Research Offr. Can. Agric. Research Stn. Saskatoon 1958–61; Asst. Prof. of Biol. Univ. of Sask. 1961–64; Assoc. Prof. of Biol. Trent Univ. 1964–66; Chrmn. of Biol. 1964–69 and 1979–83; Prof. of Biol. there 1966–88; now retired; served on CSS Hudson during 'Hudson 70' Expedition to Antarctic 1970; mem. Fed. Mil. & Un. Services Insts.; author or co-author several articles ecol. and entomol. in scient. journs.; Pres., Entomol. Soc. Ont. (1982–83); recreation: sailing; Home: 619 Walkerfield, Peterborough, Ont. K9J 4V9.

**EDWARDS, Stanley Ewart,** Q.C., B.A., LL.B., LL.M.; b. Airdrie, Alta. 20 Nov. 1921; s. William Frederick and Anna Lamont (McCracken) E.; e. Public and High Schs., Airdrie, Alta.; Univ. of Alberta (B.A. 1942, LL.B. 1943); Harvard Law School (LL.M. 1947); m. Margaret Jean, d. Frank Duncan Patterson, 11 Nov. 1949; children: Paul Donald, Stanley David, Douglas William, James Richard, John Glen; CONSULTANT, FRASER & BEATTY; Dir., Texas Refinery Corp. of Can. Ltd.; Schlumberger Canada Ltd.; mem., Edit. Bd. CCH Canadian Tax Reporter, since 1949; Adv. to Royal Commission on Taxation, 1966–67; served with R.C.N.V.R.; read law with Hannah, Nolan, Chambers, Might and Saucier, Calgary, Alberta; called to the Bar, Alta., 1946; Ont. 1949; cr. Q.C. 1962; Lectr., Osgoode Hall, Toronto, 1947–49; joined Fraser, Beatty & Co. 1949; Partner 1955; Consultant 1991; mem., Candn. Bar Assn.; Candn. Tax Foundation (Past Chrmn.); Alta. and Ont. Bar Assns.; Bd. Trade Metrop. Toronto (Past Pres.); Past Pres., Estate Planning Council; United Church; recreations: golf, skiing, Clubs: National; Alpine Ski (Past Pres.); Home: 242 Cottingham St., Apt. 3, Toronto, Ont. M4V 1C6; Office: P.O. Box 100, First Canadian Place, Toronto, Ont.

**EFFRAT, Andrew,** Ph.D.; educator; b. New York City, N.Y. 31 Oct. 1939; s. John and Anne (Zwilling) E.; e. Princeton Univ. B.A. 1961; Harvard Univ. Ph.D. 1970; m. Nola d. James and Beth Stephen 2 Aug. 1980; one s.: Jonathan; PROF. OF SOCIOL. IN EDUC., YORK UNIV. 1980– ; Dean of Education 1980–90; Chair, Ont. Assoc. of Deans of Educ. 1988–90; Chair, Teacher Educ. Counc., Ont. 1989–90; Assoc. Prof. and Asst. Coordinator of Grad. Studies 1976–80 at O.I.S.E.; ed. 'Interchange: A Journal of Educational Studies' 1969–76; 'Sociological Inquiry' 1968–76; 'Perspectives in Political Sociology' 1973; co-ed. 'Explorations in Social Science Theory' 1976; Office: 4700 Keele St., North York, Ont. M3J 1P3.

**EGAN, Timothy,** B.A., R.F.P.; financial executive; b. England 11 March 1945; s. Samuel Frank and Betty (Grindley) E.; e. Concordia Univ., B.A. 1972; Humber Coll., C.E.B. 1969; Registered Financial Planner (R.F.P.) 1987; children: Amanda, Bridget, Robyn; CHRMN. & C.E.O., T.E. FINANCIAL CONSULTANTS LTD. 1972– ; Pres., The Egan Macdonald Shymko Group Inc.; various pos. at National Trust Co. Ltd. 1966–72; former Chrmn., Candn. Assn. of Fin. Planners; former Regent Candn. Inst. of Fin. Planning; recreations: tennis, badminton, squash, scuba, running, music, reading, sailing; Clubs: Montreal Badminton & Squash; National; Boulevard; Home: Ste. 506W, 480 Queen's Quay W., Toronto, Ont. M5V 2Y5; Office: Ste. 1810, 141 Adelaide St. W., Toronto, Ont. M5H 3L5.

**EGBERT, Hon. William Gordon Neil,** B.A., LL.B.; judge; b. Calgary, Alta. 21 Dec. 1928; s. His Hon. William Gordon and Gladys (McKelvie) LL.D., F.R.A.M., Egbert; e. Strathcona Sch. for Boys Calgary 1941; Rideau Park Jr. High Sch. and Central Coll. Inst. Calgary 1947; Univ. of Alta. B.A., LL.B. 1952; m. Margot d. Eugene Burton, Medicine Hat, Alta. 24 May 1952; children: Sherri, Cynthia, Michael, William; JUDGE, COURT OF QUEEN'S BENCH ALTA. 1979– ; called to Bar of Alta. 1953; cr. Q.C. 1969; Assoc. Macleod Dixon 1953–58; Corporate Secy. and Gen. Counsel, Alberta Coal Ltd. 1958–60; Partner, Stack, Egbert & Stack 1960–63; Walsh, Egbert & Harkness 1963–69; Gill Cook 1969–79; Hon. Life Dir., Calgary Ex. & Stampede; Bencher, Law Soc. Alta. 1970–71, 1974–79; Past Pres. Calgary Bar Assn.; mem. Candn. Bar Assn.; Anglican; recreation: golf; Club: Calgary Golf & Country (Past Pres.); Home: 340, 540 14th Ave. S.W., Calgary, Alta.

T2R 0M7; Office: Court House, 611 – 4th St. S.W., Calgary, Alta. T2P 1T5.

**EGELSTAFF, Peter A.,** B.Sc., Ph.D., D.Sc., F.Inst.P., F.R.S.C.; educator; b. London, Eng. 10 Dec. 1925; s. Walter and Ethel (Seabrook) E.; e. Univ. of London B.Sc. 1946, Ph.D. 1954; m. Joyce Marie Salter 13 Dec. 1947; children: Robert, Richard, Paul, Janet, Katherine; Prof. of Physics Univ. of Guelph 1975–90, Chrmn. of Physics 1970–75, mem. Bd. Govs. 1983–86, retired 1990; Prin. Sci. Offr. Atomic Energy Rsch. Est. Harwell, Eng. 1947–57, Special Merit Sr. Appt. 1959–70; Group Leader Atomic Energy of Canada Ltd. Chalk River, Ont. 1957–59; recipient Spiers Meml. Medal Chem. Soc. London 1978; elected Fellow Royal Society of Canada 1980; recipient, Distinguished Rsch. Award Univ. Guelph 1989; D.Sc. (hon. causa) Univ. of Waterloo 1992; author 4 books and 195 articles; mem. Candn. Assn. Physicists (Physics Achievement Medal 1983; Pres. 1987–88); Eur. Phys. Soc.; Am. Phys. Soc.; recreation: gardening; Office: Guelph, Ont. N1G 2W1.

**EGERVARI, Tibor Janos;** university professor; stage director; b. Budapest, Hungary 21 May 1938; s. Laszlo and Klara (Peto) E.; e. Madach Imre Gimnazium, Budapest, Baccalaureat 1956; Ecole Supérieure d'Art Dramatique de l'Est, Strasbourg, Diplôme 1960; PROF. OF THEATRE, UNIV. OF OTTAWA 1980– ; Stage Dir., Centre Dramatique de l'Est and Prof., Ecole Supérieure d'Art Dramatique de l'Est, Strasbourg 1960–65; founding mem. Théâtre des Drapiers, Strasbourg 1962; Asst. Artistic Dir., French Sect., Nat. Theatre Sch. of Can. 1965–71; joined Univ. of Ottawa 1971; Chrmn., Dept. of Theatre 1979–85, 1987–92; Mem., University Sénat 1980; Mem., Bd. of Govs. 1986–92; Artistic Dir., Théâtre du Peuple, Bussang, France 1972–85; Founder, Théâtre Distinct Theatre 1989; has directed over 70 plays in France and Can.; Mem., Bd. of Gov., Nat. Theatre Sch. of Can. 1975–92; Mem., Conseil d'administration Lycée Claudel 1988–92; Prés. Lycée Claudel 1990–92; Jewish; author of several articles on theatre; Ordre des Arts et des Lettres (France) 1990; Ordre des Palmes Académiques (France) 1993; recreations: skating, bicycling, swimming; Home: 33 Hadley, Hull, Que. J8Y 3K6; Office: Ottawa, Ont. K1N 6N5.

**EGGENS, Jack Lambert,** M.Sc., Ph.D.; educator; b. Ottawa, Ont. 2 March 1936; s. John Herman and Gladys Emma (Turpin) E.; e. Royal Mil. Coll. Kingston B.Sc. 1960; Univ. of Guelph B.Sc. 1965, M.Sc. 1966, Ph.D. 1970; m. Patricia d. Maurice and Sis Conway 7 July 1962; PROF. OF HORTIC. SCI. UNIV. OF GUELPH 1986– ; served with Candn. Army 1956–63; Lectr. present Univ. 1966, Asst. Prof. 1970, Assoc. Prof. 1973, Prof. 1985; recipient OAC Alumni 'Outstanding Teacher Award' 1984; Home: 2 Berkley Pl., Guelph, Ont. N1E 1E6; Office: Guelph, Ont. N1G 2W1.

**EGGLESTON, Anne Elisabeth,** Mus. M.; composer; b. Ottawa, Ont. 6 Sept. 1934; d. John Wilfrid (dec.) and Magdelana (Raskevich) E.; e. Glebe Coll. Inst., Ottawa, 1952; Assoc. of Royal Conserv. of Music of Toronto (piano) 1952; Univ. of Toronto, Artist Dipl. (musical comp.), 1956; Eastman Sch. of Music, Mus.M. 1958; master's thesis, 'Autumnal Clouds' (poem for baritone voice and orchestra) performed by Eastman Rochester Symphony Orchestra, 1958; rec'd commission from Ottawa Bd. of Ed. to write, 'Lets Celebrate,' for S.A.T.B. Recorders and percussion, first performed 1979; arranged 'Fifteen Canadian Folk Songs' for piano solo (easy) 1979; arranged 'Six variations on the Squid-Jiggin' Ground,' dedicated to Ken Prior, 1979; rec'd comns. from Candn. Music Centre to write educ. music 1963, a work for string orchestra 'On Citadel Hill,' and from the Charlottetown Festival (1966) an orchestral overture; has orch. and chamber music scores in lib. of Candn. Music Centre; 'String Quartet' and 'Sonatine (piano)' won prizes in the First Competition for Ottawa composers 1964–65; orch. works, chamber music, vocal and instrumental music have been performed over CBC, quartet for piano and strings was performed at Stratford Festival, 1966; concert of compositions given by Musical Arts Club of Ottawa in Nat. Gallery. 1967; 'Fanfaron' (for orchestra) performed by Atlantic Symphony over C.B.C. Oct. 1971; 'Quartet for Piano and Strings' 1972; 'Five Lullabies of Eugene Field' (CBC record) 1972; 'Ascent' (for carillon) commnd. by Percival Price and performed by him on Parlty. Bldgs. Peace Tower carillon July 1973; 'Quintessence' (for solo cello) performed by Janet Covington, 1975; 'Serenade' (for flute, cello, and harpsichord) commissioned by CAMMAC 1975; 'Toccata' (for piano) commissioned by and performed by Suzanne Chapin, 1976; 'Seven Variations' (for piano) published in 'Piano Solos by Ottawa Composers,' 1977; 'Musical Christmas Cards' for piano 1980; in Night on the Ottawa River S.S.A.' (lyrics by Arthur Bourinot), commissioned by Ottawa Bd. of Ed., 1982; 'Sonatine' performed by Beverley Gertsman in Brazil, S.A., in recital at McGill Univ., Montreal (taped and aired by CBC), and performed at the residence of the Candn. Ambassador to the Holy See in Rome 1991; 'Piano Quartet' performed at Indiana State Univ., Bloomington, Ind. and by members of MusiCamerata in Que.; several songs sung in Switzerland; SOCAN; Canadian League of Composers; bilingual; recreations: reading, handicrafts; Address: 234 Clemow Ave., Ottawa, Ont. K1S 2B6.

**EGGLETON, Arthur C.;** b. Toronto, Ont. 29 Sept. 1943; m. Brenda Louise (Clune) Dec. 1981; children: Stephanie; TREASURY BOARD PRESIDENT and INFRASTRUCTURE MINISTER, GOVERNMENT OF CANADA 1993– ; Mayor, City of Toronto 1980–91; first el. to City Council for Ward 4 1969, re-el. since; el. by Council to City of Toronto Extve. Comte. after each re-el. and apptd. each time by the Mayor and Extve. as Budget Chief; served 2 terms as Pres. City Council and Vice Chrmn., Extve. Comte.; Chrmn. Mun. Liaison Comte. 1975; served various comtes. City, Metro and FCM; Metro Extve. Comte., Metro Council; Past Mem., Metro Police Comn.; Bd. of Gov. Can. Nat. Exhn.; Past Pres., City of Toronto Non-Profit Housing Corp.; mem. Soc. Mgmt. Accts.; recreations: skiing, tennis, horseback riding; Office: Ottawa, Ont. K1A 0A6.

**EGOYAN, Atom,** B.A.; film director; writer; b. Cairo, Egypt 19 July 1960; s. Joseph and Shushan (Devletian) E.; e. Univ. of Toronto Trinity Coll. B.A. 1982; writer, dir. and producer feature films incl. 'Exotica' 1993 feature film; 'Gross Misconduct' 1992 (winner of the Golden Gate Award, San Francisco Film Festival) dramatic telefilm produced for CBC; 'Calendar' 1992 dramatic telefilm produced for German television and shot in Armenia in the summer of 1992; 'The Adjuster' 1991 (winner Toronto City Award for Excellence in Candn. Prodn., Toronto Film Festival, Special Jury Prize, Moscow Film Festival); invited to Cannes Film Festival and New York Film Festival; 'Montreal Vu Par' co-director of six part anthology film 1991; 'Speaking Parts' 1989 (Cannes Film Festival, New York Film Festival); 'Family Viewing' 1987 (winner Toronto City Award for Excellence in Candn. Prodn. Toronto Film Festival; acclaimed at festivals in Berlin, Montréal, Miami, Hong Kong, Locarno and Los Angeles; invited to New Dir./New Films series Museum of Modern Art New York); 'Next of Kin' 1984 (winner Gold Ducat Award Mannheim Internat. Filmweek, W. Germany); Dir. numerous short films and TV prodns.; award-winning playwright; classical guitarist; mem. ACTRA; Dirs. Guild Can.; recreation: music; Office: 80 Niagara St., Toronto, Ont. M5V 1C5.

**EHRICHT, Horst Hermann,** R.C.A.; photojournalist; photographer; b. Berlin-Charlottenburg, Germany 13 Nov. 1928; s. Herman Gottfried Ehricht; e. Staatl. Martin Luther Oberschule, Eisleben, Germany 1948; Ryerson Polytech. Inst. Toronto 1952–55; came to Can. 1951; m. Wilhelmina d. late Jacobus Cornelius van Klaveren, Creemore Ont. 3 Sept. 1955; children: Mark, Lucas, Peter; freelance photojournalist 1955–65; Dir. of Photography 'Maclean's' mag. 1965–71; work incls. edit. photography, photographic illustrations, corporate and advertising photography, documentary films; served with German Army 1944–45; mem. Dom. of Can. Rifle Assn.; Ont. Rifle Assn.; Service Rifle Shooting Assn.; CAPIC Lifetime Achievement Award 1991 for Photography; National Archives of Canada acquired Life's Work of Photography 1991; Protestant; recreations: photography, reading, military history, skiing, shooting; Address: Box 253, Kleinburg, Ont. L0J 1C0.

**EHRLICH, David S.,** LL.B.; lawyer; b. New York, N.Y. 18 Mar. 1951; s. Milton M. and Carole M. (Wiener) E.; e. Tenafly H.S. 1969; Rutgers Univ. 1970–73; Dalhousie Law Sch. LL.B. 1977; m. Dr. Lisa d. Sheldon and Irene Cohen 24 June 1973; children: Jeremy Simon, Molly Jessica; PARTNER, TORY TORY DesLAURIERS & BINNINGTON 1986– ; called to bars of N.S. 1979 and Ont. 1986; Sr. Partner, Goldberg, Ehrlich & Macdonald until 1986; practice in real estate finan., incl. real estate securities, joint ventures, pension fund investments & hotel finance; Lectr., real estate finance confs.; part-time faculty, Dalhousie Law Sch. 1983–85; Mem., Law Soc. of U.C.; N.S. Barristers Soc.; Candn. Bar Assn.; Temple Emanu-El; 1818 Soc. (Dalhousie Law Sch.); Founding Ed., 'Nova Scotia Annotated Rules of Practice' 1980 (updated annually); Past Assoc. Ed., 'Carswell's Practice Cases'; recreations: skiing, watching sports; club: Fitness Inst.; Home: 105 Dinnick Cr., Toronto, Ont. M4N 1L9; Office: Box 270, #3000, T-D Centre, Toronto, Ont. M5K 1N2.

**EHRMAN, Joachim Benedict,** A.M., Ph.D.; educator; b. Nuremberg, Germany 12 Nov. 1929; s. late Dr. Fritz S. and late Ilse (Benedict) E.; e. Univ. of Pa. A.B. 1948; Princeton Univ. A.M. 1949, Ph.D. 1954; m. Gloria Jeanette d. late Stephen Gould 24 Jan. 1961; one s. Carl David; PROF. OF APPLIED MATH., UNIV. OF W. ONT. 1968– ; Research Engr. Atomic Energy Dept. North American Aviation Inc., Downey, Calif. 1951–53; Instr. in Physics Yale Univ. 1954–55; Research Physicist U.S. Naval Research Lab. Washington, D.C. Nucleonics Div. 1955–66, Plasma Physics Div. 1966–68 (part-time Consultant 1969–70); Visiting Staff Theoretical Div. Princeton Univ. Plasma Physics Lab. 1975–76; Assoc. Prof. (part-time) of Physics George Washington Univ. 1956–57; part-time lectr. in Physics Univ. of Md. (at U.S. Naval Research Lab. Washington) 1963–64; author or co-author various articles prof. journs.; Phi Beta Kappa; Jewish; Office: London, Ont. N6A 5B7.

**EICHLER, Margrit,** M.A., Ph.D., LL.D.; university professor; b. Berlin, Germany 28 Sept. 1942; d. Wolfgang and Grete (Brischke) E.; e. Univ. of Goettingen 1962–65; Free Univ. of Berlin 1965–66; Duke Univ. M.A. 1968 (grad. student 1966–70; exchange fellowship; Fulbright Travel grant; two fellowships; Woodrow Wilson Diss. fellowship), Ph.D. 1972; child: Jens Kohler; PROF., DEPT. OF SOCIOLOGY, ONT. INST. FOR STUDIES IN EDUCATION 1980– ; Lectr., Dept. of Sociology, Univ. of Waterloo 1971; Asst. Prof. 1972–75; Adjunct Prof. 1975–77; Assoc. Prof., Dept. of Sociology, Ont. Inst. for Studies in Edn. 1975–80; cross-appt., Dept. of Sociol., Univ. of Toronto 1981– ; Prof., Dept. of Sociology, OISE 1980– ; Mem., Profl. Adv. Bd., Addiction Rsch. Found. 1983–86; Mem., Adv. Bd., Ont. Law Reform Comn. 1989– ; Mem., Adv. Bd., 'Atlantis. A Women's Studies Journal' 1975– , Candn. Corr., 'Signs, Journal of Women in Culture and Society' 1977– ; Cons. Ed., 'Interchange' 1978– ; Past Mem. 5 other ed. bds.; acted as Cons. for 21 agencies; recipient of 39 rsch. & devel. grants; author: 'Martin's Father' 1971 (children's); 'The Double Standard' 1980, 'Women in Future Research' 1982, 'Canadian Families Today' 1983, 2nd ed. 1988, 'Nonsexist Research Methods' 1988, 'Misconceptions' 1993/4 and numerous articles, bibliographies, book chapters, reports, book reviews, etc.; has also presented numerous papers at sci. assn. meetings; extensive public speaker, symposia participant & ctte. mem.; Mem., Am. Sociol. Assn.; Candn. Sociol. & Anthropol. Assn. (Pres. 1990–91); Candn. Rsch. Inst. for Adv. of Women (Pres. 1981–82); Candn. Women's Studies Assoc.; Founder & Co-ord. Candn. Coalition for a Royal Commission on New Reproductive Technologies 1987–89; Nancy Rowell Jackman Chair in Women's Studies, Mt. St. Vincent Univ. 1992–93; Woman of Distinction, YWCA 1990; LL.D. (hon. causa), Brock Univ. 1991; Office: 252 Bloor St. W., Toronto, Ont. M5S 1V6.

**EICHNER, Hans,** Ph.D., LL.D.; educator; professor, retired; b. Vienna, Austria 30 Oct. 1921; s. Alexander and Valerie (Ungar) E.; e. Univ. of London B.A. 1944, B.A. (Hons.) 1946, Ph.D. 1949; Queen's Univ. LL.D. 1974; children: Elizabeth Jane, James Alexander; EMERITUS PROFESSOR, UNIV. OF TORONTO 1988; Asst. Lectr. Bedford Coll. London 1948–50; Asst. Prof. Queen's Univ. 1950, Assoc. Prof. 1956, Prof. 1962–67; Prof. of German, present Univ. 1967–88, Chrmn. Grad. Dept. German 1967–72, Chrmn. of German 1975–84; Hon. Prof. of Humanities, Univ. Calgary 1978; Adjunct Prof., Queen's Univ. 1990– ; author 'Thomas Mann' 1953, 2nd rev. ed. 1961; 'Reading German for Scientists' 1959; 'Four German Authors: Mann-Rilke-Kafka-Brecht' 1964; 'Friedrich Schlegel' 1970; 'Deutsche Literatur im klassisch-romantischen Zeitalter, 1795–1805' 1. Teil, 1990; Ed. 'Friedrich Schlegel: Literary Notebooks 1797–1801' 1957, 2nd (German) ed. 1980; 'Kritische Friedrich Schlegel-Ausgabe' Vols. 2–6 and 16, 1959–81; ''Romantic' and its Cognates: The European History of a Word' 1972; Gen. Ed. 'Canadian Studies in German Language and Literature' 1970 ff.; various articles Thomas Mann, Friedrich Schlegel, Goethe and others; mem. Candn. Assn. Univ. Teachers German (Pres. 1976–78); Fellow of the Royal Society of Canada, since 1967; Jewish; recreation: sailing; Home: Box 41, Rockwood, Ont. N0B 2K0.

**EINSIEDEL, Edna F.,** Ph.D.; university professor; b. Philippines 23 July 1946; d. Dr. Florencio M. and Vicenta T. Flores; e. Indiana Univ. Ph.D. 1975; m. Dr. Albert A. s. Albert and Luz E. 25 June 1968; one s.: Erik Miguel; PROF., COMMUNICATIONS STUDIES, UNIV. OF CALGARY 1986– ; Prof., Kent State Univ. 1975–78; Newhouse Sch. of Public Communications, Syracuse Univ. 1978–85; Staff Soc. Scientist, U.S. Comn. on Pornography 1985–86; recipient of SSHRC & Industry, Sci. & Technol. grants to study sci. literacy among Candn. adults 1989–90; nominated YWCA's 'Women of Distinction' Calgary 1991; Dir., Grad. Prog. of Communication Studies, Fac. of Gen. Studies; author of several book chapters; has published in areas of sci. & health communications, public opinion & the mass media, and the production of sci. news; co-author: 'Public Opinion: Issues and the News' 1991; Home: 2020 Urbana Rd. N.W., Calgary, Alta. T2N 4B8; Office: Calgary, Alta. T2N 1N4.

**EISEN, Andrew A.,** M.D., F.R.C.P.(C); doctor and professor of medicine; b. Berlin, Germany 7 Feb. 1936; s. Arnold and Ursula (Ansbach) E.; e. Univ. of Leeds MRCS, LRCP 1960; FRCP(C) Neurology 1968; FMSPQ Neurology 1970; m. Kathleen Baucaud 15 May 1965; PROF. OF MEDICINE (NEUROLOGY), UNIV. OF B.C. 1980– ; Asst. Prof., McGill Univ. 1968–76; Assoc. Prof. 1976–80; Asst. Neurologist, Montreal Neurol. Inst./Hosp., Royal Victoria Hosp. 1967–76; Assoc. Neurol. 1976–80; Dir., Electromyography 1968–80; Assoc. Dean for Rsch. & Grad Studies, Univ. of B.C. 1984–87; Acting Dir., TRIUMF PET Prog. 1987–89; Acting Head, Dept. of Med. 1987–92; Mem., Candn. Soc. of Clin. Neurophysiol. (Pres. 1980–82); Am. Assn. of Electrodiagnostic Med. (Pres. 1989–90); Am. Soc. for Clin. Evoked Potentials (Dir. 1986– ;); Am. Acad. of Clin. Neurophysiol. (Dir. 1986– ;); Med. Adv. Bd., MS Soc. of Can. 1983–83; Profl. Adv. Bd., Vanc. Neurol. Inst. 1981–84; ALS Soc. of B.C. (Vice-Pres. 1984– ;); B.C. Cancer Found. Adv. Bd. 1984–90; Ad Hoc Reviewer: 'Neurology,' 'Annals of Neurology,' 'Brain,' 'Electroencephalography & Clin. Neuro.,' 'Cdn. J. of Neuro. Sci.'; author of 107 papers, 23 book chaps. & 106 abstracts; co-author: 'Diseases of the Spinal Column'; recreations: alpine & nordic skiing, golf; Office: Neuromuscular Diseases Unit, 1st Floor, Willow Pavilion, Vanc. Gen. Hosp., 855 West 12th Ave., Vancouver, B.C. V5Z 1M9.

**EISEN, Leonard,** B.A., F.C.A.; food distributor executive; b. Toronto, Ont. 14 Oct. 1934; s. Harry Mendle and Anne Miriam (Grossman) E.; e. C.A. 1957; York Univ. B.A. 1977; el. F.C.A. (Inst. of C.A.s Ont.) 1985; m. Merle Faye d. late Harry Dover 18 June 1958; two d. Rhonda Lynn, Beth Francis; TREAS., THE OSHAWA GROUP LTD. 1974– ; Mgr. Corporate Finance, Vise, Rumack, Seigel, Kurtz & Co. (Chartered Accountants) 1960–63; Partner, Bernard C. Kurtz & Co. (Chartered Accountants) 1963–64; Vice Pres. Finance and Adm., Dir., WIMCO Steel Sales Ltd. 1964–68 and Toronto Iron Works Ltd. 1965–68; Dir. Corporate Accounting present co. 1968, Asst. Treas. 1970; mem. Inst. C.A.'s Ont.; Order C.A.'s Que.; Tax Extve. Inst.; Nat. Assn. Accts.; Chrmn. Investment Comte., past Gov. and past Chrmn. Audit & Finance Comte., Candn. Tax Foundation; Toronto Cash Mgmt. Soc. (Past Pres.); Inst. of C.A.'s Ont. (Chrmn., Taxation Comte. 1981–84); Retail Council Can. (Tax Comte.); Gov., Beth Tzedec Synagogue; Jewish; recreations: squash, swimming, golf; Home: 15 Cobden St., North York, Ont. M2R 1R8; Office: 302 The East Mall, Etobicoke, Ont. M9B 6B8.

**EISEN, Sydney,** B.A., Ph.D.; university professor and administrator; b. Poland 5 Feb. 1929; s. David and Eva (Singer) E.; e. Orde and Lansdowne Pub. Schs., Harbord Coll. Inst. Toronto 1946; Univ. Education Toronto B.A. 1950; Johns Hopkins Univ. Ph.D. 1957; Cornell Univ. 1950–51; London Sch. of Econ. 1953–54; m. Doris Ruth d. Ben Kirschbaum 22 Jan. 1957; children: Daniel, Robert Joseph, Sarah Anne, Miriam Malka; UNIVERSITY PROFESSOR, YORK UNIVERSITY 1993– ; Dir., Centre for Jewish Studies York Univ. 1989– ; Instr. Williams Coll. Williamstown, Mass. 1955, Asst. Prof. 1958–61; Asst. Prof. The City Coll. of New York 1961–65, Acting Asst. Dean 1964–65; Visiting Assoc. Prof. Univ. of Toronto 1965–66; Assoc. Prof. of Hist. and Humanities York Univ. 1965–68, Acting Chrmn. Div. of Humanities 1967–68, Prof. of History and Humanities 1968–93, Chrmn. Dept. of Hist. 1970–72; Dean, Faculty of Arts 1973–78; Consultant, Reader and Examiner for Coll. Entrance Exam. Bd. and Educ. Testing Service 1959–66; Nat. Humanities Faculty, (U.S.A.), since 1972 (Trustee & mem. Extve. Comte. 1974–82, Pres. & Chrmn. 1976–80); mem. Bd. Jewish Educ. Toronto 1970–74; Life Mem. & Dir. Community Hebrew Acad. Toronto (Chrmn. 1982–86); Dir. Assn. Hebrew Schs., Life Mem., (Mgmt. Comte. 1978–88; Secy. 1979–85; Chrmn., Bd. of Ed. 1985–88); Gov., Ont. Inst. for Studies in Educ. 1970–72; Toronto Jewish Congress, Shem Tov Award 1988; rec'd Louis Rosenfeld (1946), Univ. Coll. Alumni (1948) and John Fraser Gray (1949) Scholarships; Cody Prize 1950; Vincent Fellow 1951–53, and Bissing Fellow 1954–55, Johns Hopkins Univ.; Social Science Research Council of Can. Fellowship 1953–54; Morris Ernst Prize Williams Coll. 1961, 1900 Fund Grant 1961; Can. Council Summer Grant 1967 and Leave Fellowship 1968–69; co-author 'The Human Adventure: Readings in World History' 2 vols. 1964; 'Victorian Science and Religion: A Bibliography' 1984; Gen. Ed. 'The West and the World' (various books & pamphlets); Introd., 'Victorian Faith in Crisis' 1990; author various articles and reviews; mem. Victorian Studies Assn. Ont.; Conf. on Brit. Studies; Hist. Science Soc.; Am. Hist. Assn.; Home: 5 Renoak Dr., Willowdale, Ont. M2R 3E1; Office: 4700 Keele St., Downsview, Ont. M3J 1P3.

**EISENBERG, Adi,** Ph.D.; educator; b. Breslau, Germany 18 Feb. 1935; s. Oscar and Helene (Weiss) E.; came to Can. Aug. 1967; e. Worcester Polytechnic Inst., Mass. B.Sc. 1957; Princeton Univ., M.A. 1959; Ph.D. 1960; div.; one s., Elliot; OTTO MAASS PROFESSOR OF CHEMISTRY, MCGILL UNIVERSITY 1975– ; Dir., Polymer McGill 1991– ; Postdoctoral fellow, Princeton Univ. 1960; Postdoctoral fellow, Univ. of Basel 1961; Asst. Prof. U.C.L.A. 1962; Assoc. Prof., McGill Univ. 1967; co-author (with M. King) 'Ion Containing Polymers: Physical Properties and Structure' 1977; co-author (with J.E. Mark, W.W. Graessley, L. Mandelkern, E.T. Samulski, J.L. Koenig & G.D. Wignall) 'Physical Properties of Polymers' 2nd ed. 1993; ed. 'Ion Containing Polymers' 1974; 'Ions in Polymers' 1980; co-ed. 'Perfluorinated Ionomer Membranes' (with H.L. Yeager) 1982; 'Coulombic Interactions in Macromolecular Systems' (with F.E. Bailey) 1986; 'Structure and Properties of Ionomers' (with M. Pineri) 1987; over 200 articles in profl. journals; holds internat. patents on 'Dispersion Imaging Material and Method'; Killam Research Fellow 1987–89; rec'd C.I.C. Dunlop Award 1988; NATO Fellow 1961–62; Fellow, Amer. Phys. Soc. (Chrmn. Div. High Polymer Physics 1975–76); Fellow, Chem. Inst. Can.; mem. Amer. Chem. Soc.; Soc. Rheol. (U.S.A.); Sigma Xi; Office: 801 Sherbrooke St. W., Montreal, Qué. H3A 2K6.

**EISENBICHLER, Konrad,** M.A., Ph.D.; university professor; b. Mali Losinj, Croatia 18 Mar. 1949; s. Erich and Johanna (Ivetta) (Martinolich) E.; e. McMaster Univ. B.A. 1973, M.A. 1974; Univ. of Toronto Ph.D. 1981; DIR., CENTRE FOR REFORMATION & RENAISSANCE STUDIES, VICTORIA UNIV., UNIV. OF TORONTO 1990– ; Curator, Ctr. for Reformation & Renaissance Studies 1979–85; Asst. Prof., Dept. of Italian Studies, Univ. of Toronto 1985–89; Assoc. Prof. 1989– ; Co-editor 'Confraternitas' 1989– ; Extve. Mem., Féd. Internat. des Soc. et Inst. d'Etudes sur la Renaissance (Paris) 1990– ; Candn. Rep., Soc. Internat. du Théâtre Médiéval 1989– ; Business Mgr., 'Renaissance and Reformation' 1985–93; Vice-Pres., Comitato Reg. per l'Emigrazione, Friuli-Venezia Giulia 1993– ; Mem., Renaissance Soc. of Am.; Candn. Soc. for Renaissance Studies; Candn. Soc. for Italian Studies; FISIER; Soc. Internat. du Théâtre Médiéval; Club Giuliano-Dalmato; Dante Alighieri; editor: 'Love and Death in the Renaissance' 1991, 'Crossing the Boundaries' 1991, 'Ragionamenti spirituali' 1986; co-editor: 'Internat. Directory of Renaissance and Reformation Associations and Institutes' 1993, 'Petrarch's Triumphs' 1990, 'Ficino and Renaissance Neoplatonism' 1986; Office: Victoria College, Univ. of Toronto, Toronto, Ont. M5S 1K7.

**EISENSTADT, David M.,** B.A., B.J.; accredited public relations consultant; b. Calgary, Alta. 8 July 1944; s. Marcus and Bessie (Shapiro) E.; e. Univ. of Alberta B.A. 1966; Carleton Univ. B.J. 1967; m. Rhoda d. Saul and Selma Coopersmith 16 June 1968; children: Harris Brett, Evan Noah; PRESIDENT & FOUNDING PARTNER, THE COMMUNICATIONS GROUP INC. (TORONTO) 1973– ; and PRESIDENT, PINNACLE WORLDWIDE (MINNEAPOLIS) 1993– ; Public Relations Officer, Candn. Film Inst. 1967–69; Information Rep., IBM Canada Ltd. 1969–71; General Manager, Courier Public Relations 1971–73; Dir., The Communications Group Inc.; Rhohar Investments Inc.; Rhoda Investments Inc.; Editorial Adv. Bd., Univ. of Calgary Alumni Magazine; Political Liaison Ctte., Candn. Jewish Congress, Ontario; Past Internat. Chrmn., Public Relations Soc. of Am. (PRSA) Counsellor Academy's Extve. Ctte.; Past Pres., Candn. Public Relations Society's Consultants' Institute (Toronto) and served on CPRS National Accreditation Bd. (Ottawa); Mem., Internat. Public Relations Assn.; IABC; Public Affairs Assn. of Canada; Candn. Writers' Assn.; serves a number of Candn. association boards and committees in a PR advisory capacity; Judaism; P.C.; author of two book chapters; recreation: reading, baseball, tennis, skiing, hockey; clubs: The Albany, Canadian Club of Toronto, Fitness Inst.; Home: 8 Gardiner Rd., Toronto, Ont. M5P 3B3; Office: 65 Overlea Blvd., 4th Floor, Toronto, Ont. M4H 1P1.

**EISNER, David Sheldon;** actor; b. Toronto, Ont. 3 March 1958; s. Stan and Janet (Bornstein) E.; e. York Univ.; Stella Adler Theatre Sch.; semi-regular (Guido Lefkowitz) 'King of Kensington' 1977–80; lead regular (Mike Difalco) 'Hangin' In' 1980–87; lead (Benji) 'Family Renunion' 1988; Phobia 1980; guest appearance 'Highway to Heaven' 1986; 'Samson & Delilah' ABC Movie of the Week 1984; guest lead 'Alfred Hitchcock Presents' 1988; nominated Best Lead Actor in a Comedy Series Gemini Award 1986, 1987; Bd. of Dir., Toronto Branch of Performers, ACTRA 1988; Second Harvest volunteer; recreations: baseball, golf, tennis; Office: 30 Westgate Blvd., North York, Ont. M3H 1M7.

**EISNER, Robert Gordon,** B.Eng., M.B.A., P.Eng., C.M.A.; financial executive; b. Wolfville, N.S. 2 Jan. 1949; s. Kenneth and Edna (Ward) E.; e. Acadia Univ. 1969; Tech. Univ. of N.S. B.Eng. 1971; registered profl. engr. 1974; McMaster Univ. M.B.A. 1975; regis. industrial accountant 1981; m. Rosemarie d. J. Anselm and M. Geraldine Blinn 1 May 1971; children: Deneige, Michael, Timothy; VICE-PRES. FINANCE & CONTROLLER, ITT CANADA LIMITED & ITT INDUSTRIES OF CANADA LTD. 1986– ; various finan. positions Procter & Gamble Inc. 1971–76; Mgr., Treas. Opns., ITT Canada Limited 1976–78; Asst. Treas. 1978–81; Treas. 1981–86; Dir., Abbey Life Insur. Co. of Can.; ITT Canada Finance Inc.; Financ. Extves. Inst. (Toronto Chap.); Greater Toronto Scout Found.; Extve. & Mngt. Cttes., Greater Toronto Region, Scouts Canada; Mem., Finan. Extves. Inst.; Assn. of Profl. Engrs. (Ont.); Soc. of Mngt. Accts. of Ont.; Assn. of Candn. Pension Mngt., Bd. of Trade of Metro. Toronto; recreations: swimming, tennis, nordic skiing, golf, skating; Home: 29 Geraldton Cres., Willowdale, Ont. M2J 2R5; Office: P.O. Box 138, 18th floor, Royal Trust Tower, Toronto-Dominion Centre, Toronto, Ont. M5K 1H1.

**EKSTEINS, Modris,** D.Phil.; educator; b. Riga, Latvia 13 Dec. 1943; s. Rudolfs Erhards and Biruta (Vajeiks) E.; e. Upper Can. Coll. Toronto 1961; Heidelberg Univ. 1963; Univ. of Toronto Trinity Coll. B.A. 1965; St. Antony's Coll. Oxford (Rhodes Scholar) B.Phil. 1967, D.Phil. 1970; m. Jayne Delbeek d. Carel and Ruby D. 20 Oct. 1984; children: Theodore, Roland, Oliver, Andra; PROF. OF HISTORY, SCARBOROUGH COLL. UNIV. OF TORONTO 1980– ; Asst. Prof. of Hist. present Coll. 1970, Assoc. Prof. 1975; Centre for Internat. Studies Univ. of Toronto, Acting Dir. 1983; recipient Woodrow Wilson Fellowship 1965; Can. Counc. Rsch. Grants 1971–72, 1974–75, Leave Fellowship 1976–77, 1981–82; SSHRCC Rsch. Grants 1981–83, 1988–89, 1991–92; Connaught Senior Fellow 1992–93; Scarborough Coll. Teaching Award 1981; Wallace Ferguson Prize, Candn. Historical Assoc. 1989; Trillium Book Award 1990; Vice Pres. St. Antony's Soc., Oxford 1985–92; Ont. Rhodes Scholar Selection Ctte. 1991– ; DAAD Scholarship Selection Ctte. 1991– ; Adv. Bd., Historial de la Grande Guerre, France 1991– ; author 'Theodor Heuss und die Weimarer Republik' 1969; 'The Limits of Reason' 1975; 'Rites of Spring' 1989; Ed. 'Stipri piesiets' 1979; 'Nineteenth-Century Germany' 1983; Office: Scarborough, Ont. M1C 1A4.

**ELDER, Richard Bruce,** M.A., B.A.A.; artist; writer; b. Hawkesbury, Ont. 12 June 1947; s. David Murdoch and Edrie Maud (Campbell) E.; e. McMaster Univ. 1969; Univ. of Toronto M.A. 1970; Ryerson Polytech. Inst. B.A.A. media studies 1976; m. Kathryn d. Luke H. and Veronica LeRoy 4 Sept. 1970; since 1975 has been creating epic film cycle 'The Book of All the Dead' of which 35 hrs. have been completed; parts of cycle exhibited Museum of Modern Art and Millennium (N.Y.C.), San Francisco Cinematheque, Hood Museum (Atlanta), Kino Arsenal (Berlin); retrospectives of film work mounted by Art Gallery of Ont. 1985, Cinémathèque Québecoise 1986, Anthology Film Archives 1988; curator film progs. for Festival of Festivals 1984, Art Gallery of Ont. 1986, 1989, Candn. Images 1982, 1983, Can. Council 1982; Internat. Exper. Film Cong. 1989; recipient Candn. Film Award Best Exper. Film 1976; Los Angeles Film Critics Circle Award Best Ind. Exper. Film 1980; Auswortiges Amt. F.G.R. Study Tour 1986; numerous film, writing and curating grants Can. Council, Ont. Arts Council; author 'The Body in Film' 1989; 'Image and Identity: Reflections on Canadian Film and Culture' 1989; critical writings film and music various mags. and jours.; manifesto 'The Cinema We Need' 1985; anthologized Candn. Film Reader, Take Two, Documents in Candn. Film; epic film cycle subject numerous articles, catalogues; Address: Unit 5, 692 St. Clarens Ave., Toronto, Ont. M6H 3X1.

**ELDON, Walter Donald Ridley,** A.M., Ph.D.; economist; b. London, Ont. 9 Aug. 1926; s. Frank Irving, M.A., and Daveda Elinor Louise (Ridley) E.; e. Univ. of

Western Ont., B.A. (Gold Medal for highest standing in honours Hist.) 1948; Harvard Univ., A.M. 1951, Ph.D. (Econ.) 1952; m. Jean Elizabeth, d. Donald McLennan, Brantford, Ont., 12 April 1958; one s. Donald McLennan; one d. Elizabeth Lucinda Louise; PRES., ELDON ASSOCIATES 1985–86, 1991– ; Asst. Econ., Candn. Nat. Rlys., Montreal 1951–55; Dir. of Research, P. Conservative Party of Can., Ottawa, Ont. 1955–58; Asst. Prof. of Econ., Univ. of W. Ont., London, Ont. 1958–61; consultant to various Roy. Comns. 1958–60; mem., Tariff Bd. of Can. 1961–63; Restrictive Trade Practices Comn. 1963–66; Prof. of Econ., Assoc. Dean of Arts & Science and other posts, Trent Univ. 1966–71; Vice Pres., Lakehead Univ. 1971–73; mem., Ont. Energy Bd. 1973–75; Sr. Adv., Gov. Relations, Imperial Oil Ltd. 1975–83; Sr. Adv., Candn. Chamber of Comm. 1983–85; Vice Pres., Economic Affairs, The Mining Assoc. of Canada 1986–91; Publications: 'American Influence in the Canadian Iron & Steel Industry' 1954 & various articles and reports; Anglican; Home: 9 – 174 Dufferin Rd., Ottawa, Ont. K1M 2A6.

**ELDRED, Gerald Marcus;** arts executive; b. Cambridge, Ont. 5 Oct. 1934; s. Albert Harold and E.E. Hope (Bardwell) E.; e. Nat. Theatre Sch. Can. Dipl. 1965; m. Marjorie Christine d. Andrew and Bessie Kidd 4 Aug. 1956; one s. Peter Marcus (dec.); DIR., OPERATIONS, HARBOURFRONT CORP. 1987– ; stage producer, dir., adm., Candn. Players Toronto 1965–66; Man. Theatre Centre Winnipeg 1966–72; Kawartha Summer Festival Lindsay, Ont. 1966; Shaw Festival Niagara-on-the-Lake 1967; Expo '67 Montreal; Rainbow Stage Winnipeg 1968; Producer Commd. Opera, Nat. Arts Centre Ottawa 1969; Adm., Nat. Ballet of Can. Toronto 1972–79; Adm. Dir., Acad. Princ., Nat. Ballet Sch. Toronto 1979–81; Extve. Dir., Stratford Shakespearean Festival Found. of Can. 1982–86; Consultant, Harbourfront Corp. 1986–87; mem. Adv. Comte. Program in Arts Adm. York Univ. 1982– ; Adv. Arts Panel Can. Council 1970–72; mem. Adv. Bd., Touring Office, Can. Council 1983–85; Arts Adv. Ctte., The Laidlaw Found. 1980–90; mem. Candn. Actors Equity Assn.; Assn. Cultural Extves.; Address: 77 Harbour Square, Apt. 803, Toronto, Ont. M5J 2H2; Office: Harbourfront Corp., 410 Queen's Quay W., Toronto, Ont. M5J 2G8.

**ELDRIDGE, Robert Huyck,** B.A., M.S.; financial consultant; b. New York, N.Y. 13 Mar. 1938; s. William A. and Barbara Franklin (Jones) E.; e. Deerfield (Mass) Acad. 1956; Harvard Univ. B.A. magna cum laude 1961; Mass. Inst. of Technol. M.S. 1966; m. Elisabeth B. d. Dr. Walter L. Palmer, Chicago, Ill. 11 Sept. 1965; children: Daniel H., Cynthia B.; PRES., CRISPIN RESOURCES LTD. (Calgary) and VICE-PRES., IDENTICARD LTD. (Toronto); Financial Consultant 1980– ; joined Banco de la Republica, Bogota, Colombia 1966–69; Rsch. Associate, Mass. Inst. of Technol. 1966–69; Kuhn Loeb & Co. New York 1969–72; Treas. Brascan Ltd. Toronto 1973–79; Vice Pres. Chamber Players of Toronto; service U.S. Marine Corps; Protestant; recreations: distance running, skiing, fishing; Home: 24 Castle Frank Cres., Toronto, Ont. M4W 3A3; Office: 59 Wynford Dr., Don Mills, Ont. M3C 1K3.

**ELGAARD, Elin (Thorpe),** B.A., M.A.; educator, writer, translator; b. Aarhus, Denmark 20 July 1950; d. Ernst Wilhelm and Dagny Caroline (Elgaard) Berg; e. Aarhus Katedralskole 1969 (1stprize, creative writing contest between all high schools within Denmark; 1st prize from Acad. Française for French proficiency); travel scholarship to England 1969; Aarhus Univ. B.A. (Top Honours in William Blake), M.A. (Hons. in translation) 1976; m. Michael s. Gordon and Muriel Thrpe 22 July 1972; one s.: Jacob Johan Thorpe; worked at Church House Westminster 1 year; began writing short stories in English on arrival in Canada; first pub. Antigonish Review, age 21; won WFNB short stories 2nd prize twice; 1st Prize, Children's Category and 1 hon. mention in Prism Internat. Contest; teaches English & Children's Lit., Continuing Edn. Prog., Mt. Allison Univ. 1987– ; Guest Lecturer & Prof., Univ. of N.B. 1993; author: 'Wafer Thin' (novel) 1992, and of many short stories in lit. mags. in Can., Brit. & U.S.; trans.: 'Bear' Marian Engel, 'The Wars' Timothy Findley, 'Nights Below Station Street' D.A. Richards (into Danish), 'Howlin' Marie' (into English) and others; reviewer: 'World Literature Today'; recreations: biking, reading, being with animals & friends; Address: P.O. Box 1456, Sackville, N.B. E0A 3C0.

**ELGIE, Robert Goldwin,** Q.C., B.A., LL.B., M.D., F.R.C.S.(C) (Neurosurgery); b. Toronto, Ont. 22 Jan. 1929; s. Goldwin Corlett and Vivian Granger (McHenry) E.; e. Univ. of Toronto Schools; Univ. of W. Ont.; Osgoode Hall Law Sch.; Univ. of Ottawa Fac. of Med.; m. Nancy Anne d. Harvey and Verna Stewart 23 June 1956; children: Allyson G., Stewart A.G., William C., Peter G., Catherine A.G.; DIR. & PROF., HEALTH LAW INST., DALHOUSIE UNIV. 1991– ; Chrmn., Nova Scotia Workers' Compensation Bd. 1992– ; neurosurgeon; el. M.P.P. for York East prov. g.e. 1977; Parlty. Asst. to Min. of Community & Soc. Services 1978; Min. of Labour, Ont. 1978–82; Min. of Consumer & Comm. Relations 1982–85; Min. of Comm. & Soc. Services 1985; Min. of Labour 1985; Chrmn., Ont. Workers' Compensation Bd. 1985–91; P. Conservative; United Church; Clubs: Albany; Office: Fac. of Law, Dalhousie Univ., Halifax, N.S. B3H 4H9.

**ELIE, Marc-Andre,** B.Sc.Com., L.Sc.Com.; investment executive; b. Montréal, Qué. 23 March 1945; s. Gaston and Aline (Labrosse) E.; e. Ecole des Hautes Etudes Commerciales, Univ. de Montréal B.Sc.Com. 1966, L.Sc.Com. 1968; m. Elisabeth d. John A. and Marguerite Burke 30 Dec. 1967; children: Madeleine, Martine, Marianne; VICE PRES. AND DIR. RBC DOMINION SECURITIES 1986– ; Pres. Les Entreprises Marcelie Inc.; Dir. Placements Cheneaux (1980) Inc.; joined Molson Rousseau (predecessor firm) 1970, Pres. and Chief Operating Offr. 1984; Chrmn., Qué. Paraplegic Foundation; Clubs: St-Denis (Dir.); Hermitage; Mount Royal; Home: 42 Sunnyside Ave., Westmount, Qué. H3Y 1C2; Offfice: 300, 2000 McGill College Ave., Montréal, Qué. H3A 3H5.

**ELIESEN, Marc,** B.Comm.; hydro executive; b. Montreal, Que.; e. Sir George Williams Univ. B.Comm. 1962; Carleton Univ, post-grad. work in economics; PRESIDENT & CHIEF EXECUTIVE OFFR., B.C. HYDRO 1992– ; Chair & C.E.O. Ontario Hydro 1991; Dep. Min. of Energy, Ontario 1990; Partner & Nat. Dir. of Govt. Serv., Peat Marwick Stevenson & Kellogg 1989–90; Dep. Min. of Energy & Mines and Chair & Extve. Offr., Manitoba Energy Authority and Chair, Board of Directors, Manitoba Hydro 1982–88; Office: 333 Dunsmuir St., Vancouver, B.C. V6B 5R3.

**ELIO, Renée Elaine,** B.S., M.A., Ph.D.; educator; scientist; b. New Haven, Conn. 19 June 1955; d. Joseph F. and Jo-anne M. (Petroski) E.; e. Smith Coll. Mass. B.S. 1977; Yale Univ. 1977–78; Carnegie-Mellon Univ. M.S., Ph.D. 1981; ASSOC. PROF. OF COMPUTING SCI., UNIV. OF ALTA. 1985– ; Mem. Bd. of Dirs., Alta. Rsch. Counc. 1989–94; Mem. Bd. of Dirs., Edmonton Council for Advanced Technology; joined Bell Laboratories Whippany, N.J. 1981; Alta. Rsch. Council Edmonton 1983, Project Mgr. and Prin. Designer METEOR (artificial intelligence system for predicting occurence & nature of severe convective storms); cons. various artificial intelligence application projects Alta. and B.C. firms; recipient Natural Sci's & Eng. Rsch. Council Can. Ind. Rsch. Fellow 1983–85, several rsch. grants; Nat. Sci. Found. Grad. Fellow 1977–80; author or co-author numerous publs. sci. jours. & conf. proceedings cognitive psychol., cognitive science and artificial intelligence; mem. Candn. Soc. Computational Studies Intelligence; Am. Assn. Artificial Intelligence; Phi Beta Kappa; recreations: downhill skiing, backpacking, theatre; Office: Edmonton, Alta. T6G 2H1.

**ELIOT, Charles William John,** C.M., B.A., M.A., Ph.D., D.C.L.; university president; b. Rawalpindi, Pakistan 8 Dec. 1928; s. William Edmund Cyril and Anne Catherine Gertrude (McDougall) E.; e. Ashbury Coll. 1945; Trinity Coll., Univ. Toronto, B.A. 1949; M.A. 1951; Ph.D. 1961; D.C.L., King's Coll. 1988; Am. Sch. Classical Studies in Athens, 1952–57; m. Mary, d. Albert and Emily Williamson, 2 Sept. 1954; children: Charles; Sophia (d. 1963); Nicholas; Johanna; Luke; PRES. & VICE-CHANCELLOR, UNIV. OF P.E.I. 1985– ; Instructor to Prof. Classics, Univ. of B.C. 1957–71; Visiting Prof., Am. Sch. Classical Studies in Athens 1966–67; Prof. Archaeology 1971–76; Prof. of Classics, Mt. Allison Univ. 1976–85; Head, Dept. Classics there 1976–81, 1983–85; Acting Dean of Faculty 1981; Vice-Pres. (Academic) 1981–83; author: 'Coastal Demes of Attika' 1962; 'Campaign of the Falieri and Piraeus in the Year 1827: The Journal of T.D. Whitcombe' 1992; also over 30 articles and 30 reviews; co-author (with K.D. Naegele, M. Prang, M.W. Steinberg, and L. Tiger) 'Discipline and Discovery: A Proposal to the Faculty of Arts at the University of British Columbia' 1965; rec'd. Can. Counc. Leave Fellowship 1965–66; Summer Fellowship, Dumbarton Oaks 1980; SSHRC Leave Fellowship 1984–85; Member of the Order of Canada 1994; Mem. Advisory Academic Panel of Social Sciences and Humanities Counc. Can. 1979–83; Vice-Chrmn. 1980–81; Chrmn. 1981–82; Am. Sch. Classical Studies at Athens, Managing Comte. 1960–71, 1973– ; Extve. Comte. 1981–85; mem. Classical Assn. Can. (mem Counc. 1963–64, 1976–80, 1987–90, Vice Pres. 1990–92, Pres. 1992–94); Arch. Inst. of Am.; The Byron Soc.; Candn. Assn. Univ. Teachers (Bd. Dirs. 1979–81); Fed. of N.B. Faculty Assns. (Pres. 1983–85); Assn. of Atlantic Univ. (Chrmn. 1989–92); Assn. of Univ. & Coll. of Can. (Bd. of Dir. 1989–92); Trustee, Candn. Mediterranean Inst. 1983–88; Gov., Holland Coll.; P.E.I. Museum and Heritage Found. (Bd. of Govs. 1986–92, Chrmn. 1989–92); Community Museums Assoc. of P.E.I. (Pres. 1986–89, 1992–94); Candn. Federation of the Humanities (Bd. of Dir. 1990– ;); Anglican; recreations: collecting first eds. of John Galt; Homes: 181 Fitzroy St., Charlottetown, P.E.I. C1A 1S3 and Box 33, Dorchester, N.B. E0A 1M0; Office: 550 University Ave., Charlottetown, P.E.I. C1A 4P3.

**ELKHADEM, Saad Eldin Amin,** Ph.D.; author; educator; b. Cairo, Egypt 12 May 1932; s. Amin Saad and Zahra Amin (Tharwat) E.; came to Can. 1968; e. Universities of Graz and Vienna, Ph.D. 1961; m. Madiha Mahmoud, d. Mahmoud Elkhadem, Cairo 16 July 1962; 1 d., Sherifa; PROFESSOR, DEPT. OF GERMAN AND RUSSIAN, UNIVERSITY OF NEW BRUNSWICK 1974– ; Ed. and Pres., York Press Ltd.; Ed.: 'International Fiction Review'; 'Authoritative Studies in World Literature'; Press Attache, Egyptian Government 1962; Dir., Office for Cultural Relations, Cairo 1965; Asst. Prof., Univ. of N. Dakota 1967; Assoc. Prof. of German, Univ. of N.B. 1968; awarded Can. Council Grant 1974–75; recipient of Min. of State (Multiculturalism and Citizenship) Awards, 1989, 1990; author of 4 scholarly books in German, 5 scholarly books in English, 7 plays in Arabic, 10 novels in Arabic, collection of short stories in Arabic; trans. 4 German books into Arabic, 4 Arabic books into English; author of several scholarly articles and book reviews; ed. of 32 scholarly books; mem. Mod. Lang. Assn. of Amer.; Candn. Assn. of Univ. Teachers of German; Internat. Fiction Assn. (Pres.); Home: 96 Meadow Green Ct., Fredericton, N.B. E3B 5L8; Office: Univ. of N.B., Fredericton, N.B. E3B 5A3.

**ELKINS, David J.,** Ph.D.; professor; b. U.S.A. 29 July 1941; e. Yale Univ., B.A. 1963; Univ. of Calif., Berkeley, M.A. 1964, Ph.D. 1971; PROF., DEPT. OF POL. SCIENCE, UNIV. OF B.C.; Inst., Univ. of Calif., Berkeley 1968–69; Asst. Prof., Assoc. Prof., Prof., Univ. of B.C. 1969– , Chrmn., Dept. of Pol. Science 1985–89; Acting Dean of Arts 1989–90; Visiting Fellow, Australian Nat. Univ. 1984; Vis. Prof., Queen's Univ., 1984–85; mem., Candn. Civil Liberties Assn.; B.C. Civil Liberties Assn.; Candn. Wildlife Fed.; Cand. Poli. Sci. Assn. (Pres. 1988–89); Am. Pol. Sci. Assn.; author: 'Electoral Participation in a South Indian Context' 1975; 'Manipulation and Consent' 1992 and numerous articles in learned journals; co-author: 'Survey Research ' 1976; 'Small Worlds' 1980; 'Two Political Worlds' 1985; recreations: skiing, hiking; Home: P1 – 1855 Nelson St., Vancouver, B.C. V6G 1M9; Office: Dept. of Political Science, Univ. of B.C., Vancouver, B.C. V6T 1W5.

**ELL, Leo Christian;** insurance executive; b. Holdfast, Sask. 18 Sept. 1933; s. Charles Joseph and Barbara Josephine (Reinbold) E.; e. elem. & high schs. Holdfast, Sask.; m. Helen d. John and Rose Frohlick 17 Oct. 1955; children: Darcy R., Janice A., Darren J., Kevin D., Garth D., Jodi A.; PRESIDENT, C.E.O. & DIR. WESTERN SURETY CO. 1978– ; Dir. McCallum Hill Ltd.; Harvard Developments Ltd.; Marathon Investments Ltd.; joined J.A. Peters & Co., C.A.'s, Regina 1955–59; McCallum Hill Ltd. Regina 1959, Office Mgr. and Treas. 1971–76; Dir., Asst. Mgr. present co. 1967–74, Sec.-Treas. 1973–78, Vice Pres. and Gen. Mgr. 1974–78; Trustee and Sec. Franciscans of W. Can.; mem. (and Pres.) Regina Eastview Rotary (Paul Harris Fellow); YMCA; Regina C. of C.; R. Catholic; recreations: jogging, skiing, golf, reading; Clubs: Assiniboia (past Dir.); Wascana Country; Home: 157 Habkirk Dr., Regina, Sask. S4S 2X5; Office: (P.O. Box 527) 20th Fl., 1874 Scarth St., Regina, Sask. S4P 2G8.

**ELLEN, Leonard,** LL.D.; executive; b. Montreal, Que. 23 Sept. 1925; CHRMN., LEONARD ELLEN CANADA INC. 1991– ; Pres., G.A. Grier Inc. 1991– ; Standard Investments Ltd.; Dir., Inter-City Products Inc.; mem. Bd. of Gov. Concordia Univ.; Bd. mem. Sir Mortimer B. Davis – Jewish General Hospital; Office: 5 Place Ville Marie, Montreal, Que. H3B 2G2.

**ELLERBECK, Karen Marie;** art consultant; b. Calgary, Alta. 19 July 1946; d. Christian P. and Annie Decore (Clustavik) Nielsen; e. Mount Royal College 1964–65; Simon Fraser Unvi. 1988; Univ. of B.C. 1988–93; m. Douglas Earl s. Albert and Alma E. 2 April 1966; children: Douglas Michael, Kirsten Anne; PRIVATE CONSULTANT ON NORTHWEST COAST INDIAN ART; Co-Owner 'The Studio' Antique store 1978; Teacher, Vanc. & Burnaby sch. boards 1976–88; Appraiser, N.W. Coast Indian art, antiques (for estate &

insur. purposes), museums 1978–88; agent for estate liquidation of N.W. Coast Indian Art Collection 1986– ; involved in heritage preservation and conservation of local sites in B.C.; Bd. Mem., Candn. Mus. of Civilization 1991; Dir., Elizabeth Found.; White Rock Festival of Strings; White Rock Hist. Soc.; Candn. Mus. of Civilization; Mem., Federal P.C. Party 1985– ; Home: 15140 Royal Ave., White Rock, B.C. V4B 1M3.

**ELLIOT, Alfred Johnston,** B.A., M.D., D.O.M.S., Med. Sc.D., F.R.C.S.(C); physician; university professor; b. Calgary, Alta., 16 Aug. 1911; s. Laurie Benjamin and late Mary Elizabeth (Howson) E.; e. Univ. of Brit. Columbia, B.A. (Hons.) 1932; Univ. of Toronto, M.D. 1937; Columbia Univ., Med. Sc.D. (Ophthalmol.) 1941; Royal Coll. Phys. and Surgs., London, Eng., Dipl. Ophthalmic Med. and Surg., 1945; m. Jean Kerr, d. Geo. Kerr MacNaughton, Cumberland, B.C., 27 June 1942; children: Mary, Heather, George, Barbara; EMERITUS PROF., OPHTHALMOL., UNIVERSITY OF B.C.; (Prof. and Dept. Head there 1961–73); Prof. and Head, Dept. of Ophthalmology, Univ. of Toronto, 1946–61; Head Dept. Ophthalmology, Tor. Gen. Hosp., 1946–61; Senior Consultant D.V.A. Toronto, 1945–61; practised with Dr. Conrad Berens, New York City, 1941; privately in Toronto, 1945–61; Visiting Prof. in Ophthalmology, Kabul Afghanistan, Oct. 1976; People's Rep. of China, Oct. 1983; served in World War, 1941–45 with R.C.A.F. as Ophthalmic Specialist, Montreal, 1943; London, Eng., 1944; promoted Flying Offr. and later Flight-Lieut. 1941; Squadron Leader 1943; Wing Commdr. 1944; mem. Am. Ophthal. Soc.; Candn. Med. Assn.; B.C. Med. Assn.; Candn. Ophthalmol. Soc.; Am. Acad. of Ophthalmol.; Hon. mem., Montreal Ophthalmol. Soc., 1961; Golden Jubilee Award, Candn. Nat. Inst. for the Blind, 1968; Prince of Good Fellows, Vancouver Med. Assn. 1974, 1975; Sen. Mem., Candn. Med. Assn. 1977; Hon. Vice Pres., Candn. Nat. Inst. for the Blind 1978; Award of Merit, Can. Ophth. Soc. 1980 and 1987; A.N. Magill Distinguished Service Award, Candn. Nat. Inst. for the Blind, 70th Annual Meeting, Toronto, 1988; Chrmn., Planned Giving & Endowment Ctte., Candn. Nat. Inst. for the Blind 1990; Publications: author and co-author of numerous books on ophthalmic diseases; Nu Sigma Nu.; Protestant; recreations: curling, fishing; Home: #47–6600 Lucas Rd., Richmond, B.C. V7C 4T1.

**ELLIOT, Beverley Vallack,** Q.C., b. Norwich, Ont. 11 Feb. 1900; s. Reginald and Jessie (Carling) E.; e. Univ. of Toronto, B.A. 1922; Osgoode Hall, Toronto; m. Iris Elaine, d. Charles E. Lanskail, Toronto, 27 Sept. 1930; PARTNER, BORDEN & ELLIOT; called to Bar of Ont. 1925; cr. Q.C. 1944; practised alone 1926–36; formed partnership with Henry Borden, C.M.G., Q.C., 1936; mem., Law Soc. of Upper Can.; Freemason; Conservative; Anglican; recreations: golf, bridge, fishing; Clubs: National; Rosedale Golf; York; Home: 2900 Yonge St., Toronto, Ont. M4N 3N8; Office: Ste. 4100, 40 King St. W., Toronto, Ont. M5H 3Y4.

**ELLIOT, Geoffrey,** B.A., M.Sc.; diplomat; b. Northampton, U.K. 4 Oct. 1939; e. Oakville Trafalgar H.S.; McMaster Univ. B.A. 1961; London Sch. of Econ. M.Sc. 1980; m. Cheryl Alicia d. Carol Fields and Cyralene Gale 29 May 1976; children: Catherine Anne, Stephen John, Adrian Edward John, Graham Spencer; CONSUL GENERAL OF CAN. IN ATLANTA, GA., TO & S.E. U.S. STATES, PUERTO RICO & U.S. VIRGIN ISLANDS 1986– ; joined govt. serv. with DNR (Customs) 1961; var. mngt. posts, Dept. of Trade & Comm. 1966; Dir., Gen. Trade Policy Branch 1974; Dir. Gen., Office of Gen. Trade Relations 1980; Asst. Undersecretary, Commodity & Indus. Trade Policy 1981; Chief Aid Negotiator 1983; clubs: World Trade Club of Atlanta, Atlanta Rotary, Atlanta Consular Corps; recreations: tennis, golf, travel; Office: 400 S. Tower, One CNN Center, Atlanta, GA 30303-2705.

**ELLIOTT, Bruce Stewart,** B.A., M.A., Ph.D.; historian, author; b. Ottawa, Ont. 26 Oct. 1954; s. Alexander 'Graeme' and Mavis 'Elizabeth' (Bonell) E.; e. Carleton Univ., B.A. (Hons.) 1977; Univ. of Leicester, M.A. 1979; Carleton Univ., Ph.D. 1984; single; ASST. PROF. OF HISTORY, CARLETON UNIV. 1990– ; Asst. Prof. & postdoct. fellow, Queen's Univ. 1984–86; Historian, City of Nepean 1986–90; Lectr., Ont. Hist. Soc. local history workshops 1984– ; numerous public lectures & addresses in Can., U.S., U.K. & Ireland; Univ. Medal 1977, 1984; Philemon Wright Award 1986; Cert. of Recognition, Ont. Geneal. Soc. 1987, Hon. Life. Mem. 1992; Cert. of Commendation, Am. Assoc. for State & Local History 1992; Mem., Pinhey's Point Found. (Dir. 1981– ; Chrmn., Hist. & Archives Ctte. 1983– ; Newsletter ed. 1986– ;); City of Nepean Archives Ctte. (Chrmn. 1980–81); Ont. Geneal. Soc. (served several extve. posts); apptd. to National Archives of Canada Researchers' Forum 1991; author: 'Irish Migrants in the Canadas' 1988 (Floyd S. Chalmers Award in Ontario History, 1988; hon. mention, Sir John A. Macdonald Prize, CHA 1989; Joseph Brant Award in ethnic and cultural history, Ont. Hist. Soc. 1990); 'The City Beyond: A History of Nepean, Birthplace of Canada's Capital 1792–1990' 1991 (Fred Landon Award, Ont. Hist. Soc. 1993) as well as numerous articles & a newspaper column, 'Nepean Advance' 1987–88; general editor: 'Index to the 1871 Census of Ontario' 30 vols 1986–92; Home: 881 Smyth Road, Ottawa, Ont. K1G 1P4.

**ELLIOTT, Rev. Clifford,** B.A., B.D., S.T.M., Ph.D., D.D. (Un. Ch.); b. Langham, Sask., 30 March 1919; s. George Wilfred and Annie (Jennings) E.; e. Univ. of Sask., B.A. 1939; St. Andrew's Coll., Saskatoon, B.D. 1944, D.D. 1967; Union Theol. Semy., N.Y., S.T.M. 1945; Columbia Univ., Ph.D. 1950; m. late Margaret Patricia, d. late Walter Kirkpatrick, 15 July 1942; children: Cherry, Kirk, Stuart, Grace (deceased); m. 2ndly Mary d. late C. F. Sanderson, June 20, 1984; Sr. Rsch. Scholar, Victoria Univ. 1987–89; o. by Saskatchewan Conf. 1942; Min., Dundurn (Sask.) 1942–44; Third Ave., N. Battleford, Sask., 1947–52; St. Giles, Hamilton, Ont., 1952–59; Robertson, Edmonton, 1959–66; Metropolitan Un. Ch. Toronto 1966–75; has travelled in Far East, Europe, Latin America, Africa, USA, China, E. Germany, Nicarauga and Middle East to see missionary and refugee work, social and political conditions 1960, 1963, 1965, 1979, 1984, 1985, 1987; served for several years as Alberta Consultant on new Hymn Book; served on various national boards of church; Chrmn. of Comte. on Overseas Relief; Chrmn., Div. of Ministry Personnel and Educ.; Pres., Alta. Conf. 1963–64; Lectr. in Homiletics, St. Stephen's Coll., Edmonton for several yrs. and also conducted several workshops there and at Vancouver Sch. of Theology, Queen's (Kingston), St. Andrew's Coll., Saskatoon, Centre for Christian Studies, Toronto and at Toronto Sch. of Theology; Chaplain (part time) of Victoria Univ., 1976–78; Adjunct Prof., Emmanuel Coll., Toronto 1979–84; travelled to Moscow as rep. of Christian Initiative for Peace 1983; Minister, Bloor United Church, Toronto, 1975–86; Pastor-in-Residence, St. Andrew's Coll., Saskatoon 1989; rec'd. two yr. Sr. Scholarship from McGeachy Scholarship Ctte. to do research and writing in the field of popular theology 1986; Visiting Prof. of Homiletics, Vancouver Sch. of Theology, Vancouver, B.C. 1986–87; Prof. of Practice of Ministry, Queen's Theological Coll., Kingston 1990–91; Lectr., Atlantic Seminar in Theological Education 1991; Lectr., Seminar on Pastoral Care of People with AIDS, Merrimack College (U.S.) 1992; involved in radio and TV broadcasting ch. services, devotional programs and educational T.V. courses; children's programs; author: 'This is Brazil'; 'A New Look at Mission'; 'Speaking for Themselves, Hearing the Gospel from the dispossessed, the undervalued and the marginalized' 1990; 'Snapshots, Glimpses of God in Ordinary Life' 1991; 'With Integrity of Heart, Living Values in Changing Times' 1991; co-author: 'Journey Into Understanding'; 'Stewardship Explorations'; 'Saying Goodbye' 1990; contrib. to 'United Church Observer' and other papers; columnist for Toronto Star; Volunteer, Casey House Hospice for People with AIDS; AIDS Ctte. of Toronto; recreation: music; Home: 6 Glen Gannon Dr., Toronto, Ont. M4B 2W4.

**ELLIOTT, David B.,** B.Sc., Ph.D., M.B.C.O.; researcher, optometrist; b. Cottingham, U.K. 10 Nov. 1961; s. David Oliver and Valerie (Cook) E.; w. Wolfreton School 1979; Bradford Univ. B.Sc. 1983, Ph.D. 1988; m. Mary d. James Patrick and Rosa McLaughlin 23 Sept. 1990; children: Danny, Róisín Amelia; ASSISTANT PROF., CENTRE FOR SIGHT ENHANCEMENT, SCH. OF OPTOMETRY, UNIV. OF WATERLOO 1991– ; Optometrist 1984– ; Research Fellow, Bradford Univ. 1988–90; Mem., Great Britain Students Rugby League 1982–86; Professional Rugby League (Hull RLFC) 1979–85; Bradford University Colours 1982; Fellow, American Academy of Optometry; Mem., The British Coll. of Optometrists; The Assn. for Research in Vision and Ophthalmology; The Applied Vision Assn.; Vision Aid Overseas; recreation: soccer, music; Home: 480 Boettger Place, Waterloo, Ont.; Office: Waterloo, Ont. N2L 3G1.

**ELLIOTT, Donald Campbell,** B.A., C.L.U.; executive, retired; b. Napanee, Ont. 23 June 1926; s. Francis Burton and Marion Jane E.; e. Univ. of W. Ont., B.A. (Hons.) 1950; C.L.U. 1957; m. Cornelia, d. Arend Berendse; children: Michael, Margaret, Catherine, Adriana, Robin; Dir., GRENEL Financial Corp.; Connecticut National Life; former Pres. and C.E.O., The Empire Life Insurance Co., retired 1991; former Pres., E-L Financial Services Ltd.; former Extve. Vice-Pres. & Dir., E-L Financial Corp. Ltd.; former Chrmn. & C.E.O., GRENEL Financial Corp.; Connecticut National Life; former Dir., Empire Life, Dominion of Canada General; joined Great-West Life Assurance Co. 1950–81; Zeta Psi; Anglican; Home: 223 Fairway Hills Cres., Kingston, Ont. K7M 2B5.

**ELLIOTT, George Arthur,** B.Sc., M.Sc., Ph.D., FRSC; research mathematician; b. Montreal, Que. 30 Jan. 1945; s. Lloyd George and Margaret Isobel (Wilson) E.; e. Dr. C.J. Mackenzie H.S.; Queen's Univ., B.Sc. (Hons.) 1965, M.Sc. 1966; Univ. of Toronto, Ph.D. 1969; m. Noriko d. Haruo and Sumiko Yui 20 July 1974; LEKTOR, UNIV. OF COPENHAGEN 1972– ; ADJUNCT PROF., UNIV. OF TORONTO 1984– ; postdoctoral fellow, U.B.C. 1969–70; Queen's Univ. 1970–71; Mem., Inst. for Advanced Study, Princeton 1971–72; Assoc. Prof., Univ. of Ottawa 1978–79; Adjunct Prof. 1979–81, 1982–85; visiting positions: Queen's Univ., Ctr. Nat. de la Rech. Sci. (Marseille), Univ. of Newcastle upon Tyne, Rsch. Inst. for Math. Sci. (Kyoto Univ.), Univ. of N.S.W., Univ. of Warwick, Australian Nat. Univ., Univ. d'Aix Marseille II (Luminy), Math. Sci. Rsch. Inst. (Berkeley), Univ. Coll. of Swansea, Tech. Univ. of Norway (Trondheim), Hokkaido Univ; FRSC 1982– ; Mem., Am., Candn., Danish, European & London Math. Societies; Internat. Assn. of Math. Physics; author/co-author of journal articles on algebras of operators in Hilbert space (esp. concerning K-theory, dynamical systems, & applications to math. physics); Assoc. Ed., 'Can. J. of Math.' & 'Can. Math. Bulletin' 1985–89; Ed., 'Math Reports Acad. Sci.' 1990– ; Home: 2350 Dundas St. W., Apt. 2814, Toronto, Ont. M6P 4B1; Office: Dept. of Mathematics, Univ. of Toronto, Toronto, Ont. M5S 1A1.

**ELLIOTT, Harry,** B.E., M.B.A.; food processing executive; b. Dublin, Ireland 28 July 1945; s. William George and Anne (McGann) E.; e. Univ. Coll., Dublin, B.E. 1967, M.B.A. 1976; m. Eadaoin d. Tomas and Vivienne de Bhaldraithe 8 Aug. 1969; children: William, Colm; PRES. & C.E.O., BEST FOODS CAN. INC. 1988– ; Chrmn., Grocery Products Manufacturers of Canada 1992; Pres., Delico Corp. 1983–88; Home: 2315 Bennington Gate, Oakville, Ont. L6J 5Z4; Office: 401 The West Mall, Etobicoke, Ont. M9C 5H9.

**ELLIOTT, James Arthur,** M.Sc., Ph.D.; scientist; b. Pierceland, Sask. 24 Feb. 1941; s. James John and Dorothy Irene (Speer) E.; e. Univ. of Sask. B.Sc. 1962; Univ. of B.C., M.Sc. 1965, Ph.D. 1970; m. Gillian d. Patrick Duncan and Margaret McTaggart-Cowan May 1967; children: Rebecca Jean, Jonathan James Patrick; DIR. ATLANTIC OCEANOGRAPHIC LAB. BEDFORD INST. OF OCEANOGRAPHY 1985– ; Hon. Rsch. Assoc. in Oceanography, Dalhousie Univ.; Sci. Offr. Bedford Inst. of Oceanography (BIO), Fed. Govt., coastal oceanography 1962; Sci. Offr. BIO, Frozen Sea Rsch. Group, arctic oceanography 1962–70; Rsch. Sci. Atlantic Oceanographic Lab. (AOL), BIO, air/sea interaction, oceanic mixing & marine technol. 1971–78; Head, Ocean Circulation Div. AOL, BIO, e. coast phys. oceanography progs. deep sea & continental shelves; Dir. A.G. Huntsman Award (excellence in marine sci's); recipient Nat. Rsch. Council and Univ. of B.C. Fellowships; author or co-author numerous publs. sci. jours., review books and tech. series air/sea interaction, oceanic mixing, ocean technol; holds patent; mem. Candn. Meteorol. & Oceanographic Soc.; Am. Meteorol. Soc., Arctic Inst. N. Am.; Am. Geophys. Union; Am. Assn. Advanc. Sci.; recreation: individual sports; Home: Site 14, Box 15, R.R. 3, Salmon River Dr., Dartmouth, N.S. B2W 5N7; Office: P.O. Box 1006, Dartmouth, N.S. B2Y 4A2.

**ELLIOTT, Maurice S.,** B.A., M.A., Ph.D.; university administrator; educator; b. Fulham, Engl. 29 June 1937; s. Thomas Ridley and Nora Ethel (Franklin) E.; e. Tiffin Boys' Sch. 1956; Christ's Coll., Cambridge B.A. 1961, M.A. 1965; Univ. of Toronto Ph.D. 1973; m. Carole d. Laurence and Freda 23 June 1962; children: Adam, Giles, Lucy; ASSOC. PROF. OF ENGLISH, YORK UNIV. 1974– , UNIVERSITY ORATOR 1987– , CHAIR, ENGLISH DEPT. 1994– ; Master of Winters Coll. 1979–88; Linguist Royal Air Force 1956–58; Lectr. Univ. of Manitoba 1961–63; Instr. Univ. of Toronto 1965–66; Asst. Prof. present Univ. 1966–74; Pres. Candn. Assn. of Irish Studies 1984–87; mem. ACUTE; Victorian Studies Assn. of Ont. (Sec. Treas. 1976–78); CAIS; IASAIL; Cambridge Union; recreations: conversation, fly fishing; Clubs: Christ's Coll., Cambridge; X-Club Stong Coll.; Home: 96 Church St., Stouffville, Ont. L4A 4T8; Office: Winters Coll., 4700 Keele St., North York, Ont. M3J 1P3.

**ELLIOTT, Robbins L.,** M.A.; b. Wolfville, N.S. 12 Aug. 1920; s. Malcolm Robertson and Jean Steadman (Haley) E.; e. Wolfville (N.S.) High Sch.; Acadia Univ., B.A. 1941; Univ. of Toronto, M.A. 1947; m. Myfanwy Esther, d. George Frederick Millward, Ottawa, Ont. 9 Sept. 1950; children: Michael Allan, Shirley Ann, Ruth Barbara, Malcolm Robbins; newspaper Reporter with Halifax and Windsor, Ont., dailies, 1941 and 1946; Editor, Candn. Citizenship Br., Dept. Secy. of State, 1947–48; Extve. Asst. to Min. of Resources & Devel., Ottawa, 1949–53; to Min. of Public Works, 1953–55; Asst. Dir. of Property & Building Management, Dept. of Public Works, 1955–56; Dir. of Personnel, Dept. of Pub. Works, 1956–58; Extve. Dir., Roy. Arch. Inst. Can. 1958–63; Dir. of Planning Br., Centennial Comn. 1963–68; apptd. Dir., Candn. Govt. Exhn. Comn. 1969–71; Gen. Dir. Office of Design, Dept. of Trade & Comm., 1971–76; Extve. Vice-Pres., Royal Architectural Inst. of Canada 1976–81; Trustee, Ottawa Bd. of Educ. 1974–76; Extve. Dir., Can. Housing Design Council 1981–87; Extve. Dir., Investment Property Owners Assoc. of N.S. 1988–89; Pres., Robbins Elliott Associates; served in 2nd World War; Platoon Commdr., North N.S. Highlanders and Field Press Censor, 1st Canadian Army H.Q.; served in U.K. and N.W. Europe; retired with rank of Capt.; mem. Adv. Comm. on Communications, National Capital Comn.; Vice Chrmn., Bd. of Dirs., Ont. Heritage Foundation; mem. Bd. of Dirs., Ont. Bicentennial Com.; Hon. Pres., Elliot Clan Soc.; Past Pres., Ottawa-Hull Chapter, Archaeological Inst. of America; Past Pres., Ottawa Chapter, John Howard Soc.; Past Pres., Kings Hist. Soc.; Chrmn., Wolfville Centennial of Incorporation 1993– ; Baptist; recreations: golf, swimming; Clubs: Rotary (Pres.; Paul Harris Fellow); Home: 10 Minas View Dr., Box 401, Wolfville, N.S. B0P 1X0.

**ELLIOTT, Robert John,** B.Comm., C.A.; forest industry executive; b. Moose Jaw, Sask. 15 July 1942; e. Univ. of Sask. B.Comm. 1964; C.A. (Alberta Gold Medal) 1967; m. Cheryl; children: Jacqueline, James; PRESIDENT, ZEIDLER FOREST INDUSTRIES LTD. 1991– ; Partner (Taxation), Price Waterhouse 1964–82; Extve. Vice-Pres. & Chief Financial Offr., Head Office, Princeton Developments Ltd. 1982–91; Dir., Vencap Equities Ltd.; Delta North Transportation Ltd.; Office: 4828 – 89 St., P.O. Box 4370, Edmonton, Alta. T6E 5K1.

**ELLIOTT, Roy Fraser,** C.M., Q.C., B.Com., M.B.A.; lawyer; b. Ottawa, Ont. 25 Nov. 1921; s. Colin Fraser and Mary Marjorie (Sypher) E.; e. Queen's Univ. B.Com.; Osgoode Hall Law Sch., Toronto, Ont.; Harvard Grad. Sch. of Business Adm., M.B.A.; m. the late Betty Ann, Westmount, Que., 24 May 1955; PARTNER, STIKEMAN, ELLIOTT (Toronto); Stikeman, Elliott (Montreal); Dir., CAE Inc.; New Providence Development Co. Ltd.; The Toronto Symphony; The Toronto Hospital; read law with Borden and Elliot, Toronto, Ont.; called to the Bar of Ont. 1946; Quebec 1948; formerly practised under firm name of Foster, Hannen, Watt, Stikeman & Elliott; author of 'Quebec Corporation Manual,' 1949; Co-ed, 'Doing Business in Canada'; Anglican; recreations: golf, tennis; Clubs: Royal Montreal Golf; Mount Royal; Lyford Cay (Nassau); Toronto Golf; Montreal Indoor Tennis; The Hon. Co. of Edinburgh Golfers; Queen's; Toronto; Lost Tree Club; Seminole Golf; Beacon Hall Golf; Homes: 54 Ardwold Gate, Toronto, Ont. and 3450 Drummond St., Apt. 1006A, Montreal, Que.; Offices: Suite 5300, Commerce Court West, Toronto, Ont. M5L 1B9, and Suite 3900, 1155 Rene-Levesque Blvd., West, Montreal, Que. H3B 3V2.

**ELLIOTT, Shirley Burnham,** M.A., S.B., D.C.L., LL.D.; librarian (retired); b. Wolfville, N.S. 4 June 1916; d. Malcolm Robertson and Jean Steadman (Haley) E.; e. Acadia Univ. B.A. 1937, M.A. 1939; Simmons Coll. Boston, S.B. (Lib. Science) 1940; Hon. D.C.L., Acadia Univ. 1984; Hon. LL.D., Dalhousie Univ. 1985; Hon. Librarian, Cambridge Military Library; Reference Asst. Brookline (Mass.) Pub. Lib. 1940–46; Asst. Librarian, Univ. of Rhode Island Library 1946–49; Asst. Ed. 'Canadian Index' Candn. Lib. Assn. Ottawa 1949–50; Chief Librarian, Colchester-E. Hants Regional Lib. Truro, N.S. 1950–54; Legislative Librarian, Legislative Library of N.S. 1954–82; mem. Staff, Duke of Edinburgh's Commonwealth Conf. Can. 1962; author 'Nova Scotia in Books, 1752–1967' 1967; 'Province House' 1966; 'Nova Scotia Book of Days' 1980; 'The Legislative Assembly of Nova Scotia 1758–1983: a biographical directory' 1984; 'Nova Scotia in Books: A Quarter Century's Gleanings' 1987; 'Nova Scotia in London: a History of its Agents General 1762–1988' 1988; Ed. and Compiler, 'Atlantic Provinces Checklist, 1957–65' (Atlantic Provs. Econ. Council); contrib. to 'Dictionary of Canadian Biography'; awarded Commemorative Medal for 125th Anniversary of Candn. Confederation; Winner, Atlantic Provinces Library Assn. Merit Award, 1981; CASLIS Merit Award 1988; Royal Commonwealth Soc., N.S. Br.; Candn. Fed. Univ. Women; IODE; Heritage Trust of N.S.; Royal N.S. Hist. Soc.; Candn. Lib. Assn.; Bibliog. Soc. Can. (Vice Pres. 1970–71); Atlantic Provs. Lib. Assn.; Baptist; recreations: music, reading, travel; Home: Box 342, 15 Queen St., Wolfville, N.S. B0P 1X0.

**ELLIOTT, Wade,** B.Comm.; marketing executive; b. Botwood, Nfld. 21 July 1961; s. Bemister George and Mary Rhoda E.; e. Dalhousie Univ. B.Comm. 1986; Memorial Univ. of Nfld.; DIR. OF MARKETING, HALIFAX-DARTMOUTH PORT DEVEL. COMN. 1990– ; seasonal work on a variety of ships to finance univ. edn. 1979–84; Rsch. Asst., Candn. Marine Transp. Ctr. 1985–86; Rsch. Assoc., Internat. Inst. for Transp. & Ocean Policy Studies 1986–87; Rsch. Analyst, Halifax-Dartmouth Port Devel. Comn. 1987–90; Assoc., Oceans Inst. of Can.; Dir., EDIPORT Atlantic Inc.; Dir., Candn. Transp. Rsch. Forum; Secy. & Treas., Halifax Shipping Assn.; Mem., Transp. Ctte., Halifax Bd. of Trade; Internat. Cargo Handling Co-ord. Assn.; Royal Inst. of Navigation; author/co-author of 2 book chapters; Home: 5278 Tobin St., Apt. 4, Halifax, N.S. B3H 1S2; Office: Suite 900, Cogswell Tower, Halifax, N.S. B3J 3K1.

**ELLIS, Alfred John,** O.C. (1983), LL.D.; board chairman; company director; b. Montreal, Que. 27 May 1915; s. Robert Louis and Frances Elizabeth (Robinson) E.; e. Argyle School, Westmount, Que.; Lower Can. Coll., Montreal, Que.; Grad. C.O.T.C., McGill Univ., Montreal; m. Christina Joan Wilson, Marlborough, Wilts, Eng.; children: Elizabeth, Susan, Robert; Chrmn., Candn. Adv. Bd., MARSH & McLENNAN LTD.; Past Mem., Mgmt. Group, Atsugi Nylon Industrial Co. Ltd. of Japan; Past Chrmn./Dir., National Investors Management; NIM Management Ltd./Gestion NIM Ltée (Vancouver); NIM Capital Corp.; Camlin Consulting Corp.; Past Hon. Chrmn. and Dir. Emeritus, Canada Development Corp.; Mem. and Internat. Counsellor, Pacific Basin Econ. Counc. (past Chrmn.: Candn. Comte.; Internat. & Candn. Trade & Finance Comte.); Past Dir., Ventures West Resources Ltd.; Dir. Penreal Advisors Ltd.; Fractal Capital Corp.; Mem. Internat. Counc., DOH Ltd., Tokyo, Japan; former mem. Special Comte. on Standard-Setting, Candn. Inst. of Chartered Accts. (former mem., Acct. Rsch. Bd.); Adv. Bd., The Royal Trust Co., Vancouver; Hon. Dir., Past Dir., Chrmn. Finance Comte. and founding Mem., Asia Pacific Foundn. of Can.; joined Bank of Montreal in 1933 in Montreal subsequently serving from coast to coast and internationally in various executive capacities, apptd. Hon. Dir. 1994; apptd. Vice-Chrmn. & Dir. 1973; resident in Vancouver from which position he retired in 1976; Past Dir., Consolidated Pipe Lines Co., Calgary 1973–86; Bank of Montreal 1973–86; Consolidated Natural Gas Ltd. 1973–86; Consolidex Gas and Oil Ltd. 1979–86; Canada China Trade Counc. 1982–86; served in 2nd World War, Inf. and Staff Offr., 1940–45; grad. War Staff course at R.M.C.; service in Can., Eng. and Europe; Mentioned in Despatches; Past Pres., Douglas Hosp.; Dir., B.C. Internat. Trade Fair 1971; mem. Prov. Counc., Boy Scouts of Can.; past mem. Adv. Bd. to Div. of Finance, Univ. of B.C.; past mem. Extve. Comte., The Asian Centre Fund; Mem., Canada Japan Business Ctte.; Canada Jorea Business Assn.; Canada Taiwan Business Assn.; The Hong Kong-Canada Business Assn.; Past Pres. and Hon. Vice Pres., Canada-Japan Soc. of Vancouver; Past Mem. Pacific Devel. Group; Past Pres., B.C. Heart Foundn.; Candn. Chamber of Commerce; retired Senate mem. Simon Fraser Univ.; Past Gen. Campaign Chrmn., United Appeals Halifax & Vancouver; Officer of the Order of Canada; awarded The Order of the Rising Sun Gold Rays with Neck Ribbon by The Emperor of Japan 1989; LL.D. Doctor of Laws (honoris causa) Simon Fraser Univ. 1992; Anglican; recreations: fishing, hunting, boating, gardening, shooting; Clubs: The Vancouver; Vancouver Lawn Tennis & Badminton; Pennask Fish & Game; President's, Simon Fraser Univ.; Office: 1300 – 510 Burrard St., Vancouver, B.C. V6C 3J2.

**ELLIS, James R. Pat;** retired banker; b. Sydney, N.S. 1920; m. Doreen Rourke; Sr. Vice Pres., Bank of Montreal, Atlantic Prov. 1973–84; mem. Candn. Adv. Bd., Marsh & McLellan Ltd. 1984–90; Mem., Atlantic Canada Opportunities Agency (Fed. Govt.) and Chrmn., Projects Review Ctte.; mem., Bd. of Dirs., Enterprise Cape Breton Corp.; Chrmn., Bd. of Govs., Acadia Univ.; Comnr., Environmental and Socioeconomic Review of Cohasset and Panuke Oil Development off Sable Island 1990; Chrmn., Victoria General Hosp. Found. 1984–89; Vice Chrmn., Voluntary Economic Planning Bd., Prov. of N.S. 1982–89; Clubs: Halifax; Waegwoltic; Ashburn Golf; Halifax Curling; Home: 1158 Dalhousie St., Halifax, N.S. B3H 3W6.

**ELLIS, Keith Audley Alexander,** B.A., M.A., Ph.D., F.R.S.C.; university professor; b. Jamaica 5 Apr. 1935; s. Charles Henry Alexander and Cora Joyce (Lazarus) E.; e. Calabar H.S. Jamaica 1953; Univ. of Toronto, B.A. 1958; Univ. of Washington, M.A. 1961, Ph.D. 1962; m. Zilpha d. Jerome and Janet Bentley 31 Aug. 1966; one d.: Carmen; PROF., DEPT. OF SPANISH & PORTUGUESE, UNIV. OF TORONTO 1962– ; Teacher, Calabar H.S.; has taught courses in most genres in modern Hispanic field, spec. in Latin Am. poetry & the short story; his scholarly writing has won him internat. recognition for his literary scholarship; writing is noted for its elucidation of lit. theory on the basis of well analysed texts & its mature social perspective; co-winner: Candn. Hispanists' Prize for Best Book; F.R.S.C.; Juror: Casa de las Américas Literary Prize, 1988; Mem., Candn. Assn. of Hispanists; Mod. Lang. Assn.; Candn. Assn. of Latin Am. Studies; Jamaican Candn. Assn.; Candn.-Cuban Friendship Assn.; author: 'El arte narrativo de Francisco Ayala' 1964, 'Critical Approaches to Rubén Darío' 1974, 'Tres ensayos sobre Nicolás Guillén' 1980, 'Cuba's Nicolás Guillén: Poetry and Ideology' 1984, 'Nicolás Guillén: poesiá e ideología' 1987, 'Nicolás Guillén (1902–1989): A Life of Poetic Service' 1991; co-author: 'Mirrors of War' 1985, 'La poesía de Emilio Ballagas' 1990; editor & translator of 4 Latin Am. Scholar in Res. Collected Lectrs. 1969–72; editor: 'La cabeza del cordero de Francisco Ayala' 1970; co-editor: 'El ensayo y la crítica literaria en Iberoamérica' 1970, 'Encyclopedia of Spanish American Literature' 1990; Office: Toronto, Ont. M5S 1A1.

**ELLIS, Peter Hudson;** health care executive; b. England 28 July 1944; s. Fredrick Hudson and Kathleen Cecily (Dodds) E.; e. Prince Henry's Sch.; Nuffield Ctr. for Health Serc. Studies cert.; m. Annette d. Hubert and Elsie Beaumont 10 Aug. 1974; PRES. & CHIEF EXEC. OFFR., SUNNYBROOK HEALTH SCIENCE CTR. 1987– ; Cons., Woods Gordon 1974–77; Dir. of Spec. & Hosp. Serv., Sunnybrook Med. Ctr. 1977–81; Asst. Admin, Prof. & Nurs. Serv. 1981–83; Vice-Pres., Nurs. & Support Serv. 1983–84; Corp. Affairs 1984–87; Dir., IST-Healthcomp Inc.; C.H.E., A.H.A.; Asst. Prof., Univ. of Toronto; mem., Candn. Coll. of Health Serv. Extve.; Bd. of Trade, Metro Toronto; Inst. of Health Serv. Mgmt. (U.K.); Inst. for Health Care Facilities of the Future; Internat. Soc. of Sys. Science in Health Care; Candn. Health Econom. Rsch. Assoc.; Internat. Adv. Bd., Gina Bachauer Internat. Piano Competition; author: 'Doing the Right Thing' 1986; 'Health Care Systems & Actors'; co-author: 'Patient Care Appraisal Handbook' 1982, 'Quality Assurance and the 1983 Standard' 1984; 'The Role of the Physician Manager' 1989 'Decentralized Hospital Management: Rationale, Potential & Two Case Examples' 1989; 'Computers in Healthcare: Information and Corporate Strategy' 1990; and book review; recreations: music, squash, running; Clubs: Royal Candn. Yacht; Headingley Rugby Football (UK); University Club; Home: 92 Admiral Rd., Toronto, Ont. M5R 2L6; Office: 2075 Bayview Ave., Rm. C-104, North York, Ont. M4N 3M5.

**ELLIS, Robert Forsyth,** M.A.; executive; b. Kitchener, Ont. 5 Dec. 1944; s. Robert Kingsbury and Joy Claudia (Forsyth) E.; e. Trinity Coll. Sch. Port Hope, Ont.; Colgate Univ. B.A. 1967; Sophia Univ.; Univ. of N.C. M.A. 1970; m. Pamela d. Albert and Harriet Schmidt 10 Sept. 1971; children: Alexis, Ainslie, Robert Benjamin; Fund Raising Consultant to Independent Schools; Pres. and Dir., Ellis Holdings Ltd. 1984– ; Asst. to Gen. Mgr. Maj. Appliance Div., Ellis & Howard 1972, Asst. to Pres. 1973, Pres. and Dir. 1974–92; Pres. Kitchener Br. and Gov. and mem. Exte. Ctte., Trinity Coll. Sch.; Past Treas. Kitchener-Waterloo Bilingual Sch.; mem. Candn. Elect. Distributors Assn. (Dir. 1979–89, Treas. 1980–81, 1983–89, Chrmn. 1981–82); Candn. Assn. Family Enterprises; recreation: reading; Clubs; Westmount Golf & Country; University (Toronto); Badminton & Racquet (Toronto); York (Toronto); Tamahaac (Ancaster, Ont.); Devils Glen Country; Willow Bank Yacht (Cazenovia, N.Y.); Gyro Kitchener (Pres. 1981–82); Confederation Kitchener (Pres. 1982–83); Address: 369 Redwood Pl., Waterloo, Ont. N2L 2P3.

**ELMAHDY, Abdelhakim H.,** B.Sc., M.Sc., Ph.D., M.B.A., P.Eng.; researcher; b. Cairo, Egypt 13 Dec. 1943; s. Hamid M. and Fathia M. (Ghanim) E.; e. Ain Shams Univ. B.Sc. 1965, M.Sc. 1970; Carleton Univ. Ph.D. 1975; Ottawa Univ. M.B.A. 1985; m. Susan d. Talat and Aisha Hassib 26 Aug. 1973; children: Nancy, Dalal, Kareem; SENIOR RESEARCH OFFICER, INSTITUTE FOR RESEARCH IN CONSTRUCTION, NATIONAL RESEARCH COUNCIL OF CANADA 1975– ; Teaching Asst., Ain Shams Univ. 1965–70; Carleton Univ. 1973–75; Guest Worker, National Research Council 1973–75; ASHRAE Best Symposium Paper Award 1993; Past Pres., Egyptian Candn. Cultural Assn. of Ottawa; member of several national standards cttes.; represents Canada on a number of internat. standards cttes. incl. ASHRAE, NFRC, ISO, IEA; author of more than 45 technical papers & reports in areas of energy analysis system simulation, testing & rating of windows; recreations: soccer, ping-pong; Office: Montreal Rd., Ottawa, Ont. K1A 0R6.

**ELMORE, Bruce James,** B.Comm., C.A.; transportation executive; b. Vancouver, B.C. 22 July 1950; e. Univ. of B.C. B.Comm. 1975; C.A. B.C. 1978; m. Dianne; two children; CHIEF FINANCIAL OFFICER, GREYHOUND LINES CANADA, LTD. 1987– ; Articling Student and C.A., Touche Ross & Co. 1975–79; Controller, Chemetics Internat. 1979–82; Dir. of Finance & Treas., The Johnston Group 1982–87; Dir., Brewster Transp. Co. Ltd.; Better Business Bur. of Calgary & S. Alta.; Jr. Achievement of Calgary & S. Alta.; Mem., Financial Extve. Inst.; Inst. of C.A.s of B.C. & Alta.; Western Financial Extves., Conference Bd. of Canada; recreation: skiing, tennis, squash, racquetball, golf, bridge; clubs: Glenmore, Glencoe; Office: 877 Greyhound Way, Calgary, Alta. T3C 3V8.

**ELOUL, Kosso,** R.C.A.; scluptor; b. Moorom, Russia 22 Jan. 1920; s. Leib and Anna (Shapiro) E.; e. Tel-Aviv Hebrew Gimnasia; Chicago Art Inst. 1939–43; m. Rita d. Héliodore Letendre; came to Canada to do sculpture 'Optimax' on Mount Royal, Montreal 1964; solo exhns. incl. Tel-Aviv Museum 1951, 1957; Jerusalem Art Pavilion 1957; Galleria Topazia Alliata Rome 1962; Galerie Camille Hébert Montréal 1964; David Stuart Galleries Los Angeles 1965, 1968; Jewish Museum N.Y., 1966; Jerrold Morris Gallery Toronto 1968; Gordon Gallery Tel-Aviv 1969; Galerie Sherbrooke Montréal 1969; O.K. Harris Gallery N.Y. 1971; Dunkelman Gallery Toronto 1971; Galerie de Montréal 1973; Arras Gallery N.Y. 1974, 1976; Marlborough-Godard Toronto 1974, Montréal 1975; West End Gallery Edmonton 1977; Koffler Centre of Arts Toronto 1979; Art Gallery of Hamilton 1980; The Municipal Art Gall. of Los Angeles 1984; rep. in many pub., corporate and private colls. Israel, Europe, USA and Can. incl. Montréal Museum of Fine Art; Musée d'Art Contemporain Montréal; Art Gallery Ont.; Smithsonian Inst.; Canada-Mexico friendship sculpture 'Signalos' (Invitational 1978); invited to represent Canada at Hakone open-air museum, Japan, with sculpture 'Zen-West' purchase prize 1980; 'Candchin' sculpture for Candn. Embassy Beijing, China 1990; 'Istorzu '90' for Toronto Symphony; solo exhibit at Royal Candn. Acad., Toronto 1991; mem. jury Olympic Coin Program '76 Ottawa; jury of 'North American Sculpture' Denver, Colorado 1989; rec'd Can. Council Sr. Art Grant 1976; Medal of Accomplishment, Mexico City 1978; served with U.S. Navy 1944–45; work cited various publs.; Hon. Fellow, Royal Acad. Fine Art The Hague; Hon. mem. Academia Tiberina Rome; Address: 288 Sherbourne St., Toronto, Ont. M5A 2S1.

**ELSAFTY, Mohamed Adel H.,** B.Comm.; diplomat; b. Tanta-Gharbia, Egypt 11 June 1938; s. Hussein Mohamed and Amina Abdel Aziz (Elkholy) E.; e. Ein Shams Univ., B.Comm. 1959; Inst. of Banking & Stat. Studies 1961; m. Ragaa Mahmoud d. Hend and Mahmoud 30 Aug. 1968; children: Hecham, Omar; AMBASSADOR OF EGYPT TO CANADA 1989– ; Acct., Auditor & Sr. Auditor, Bank El-Gomhouria 1959–62; joined Egyptian Fgn. Serv. as Attaché 1962 & served in many positions, most recent: Counsellor & Min. Plenipotentiary, Mission of Egypt to the U.N., N.Y. 1980–85; Dep. Dir. (Acting Dir.), Internat. Orgn. Dept., Min. of Fgn. Affairs 1985–89; Bd. of Dir., Egyptian Diplomatic Corps Fund 1986–89; Egyptian Shooting Club 1986–89; Teacher, Police Acad., Cairo 1989; Mem., Egyptian Assn. to the U.N. 1968– ; Egyptian Pol. Sci. Assn. 1970– ; co-author: 'International Pressures for Accounting Change' 1989 and several reports, articles & rsch. papers; recreations: tennis, squash, shooting, reading; clubs: Guizhah Sporting, Cairo Shooting, Cairo Diplomatic; Home: 741 Acacia Ave., Rockcliffe Park, Ont. K1M 0M8; Office: 454 Laurier Ave. E., Ottawa, Ont. K1N 6R3.

**ELSTON, The Hon. Murray J.,** M.P.P., B.A., LL.B.; politician; b. Wingham, Ont. 8 Oct. 1949; s. William John and Isabel Jeannette (Bowman) E.; e. F.E. Madill S.S. 1968; Univ. of W. Ont., B.A. (Hons.) 1972, LL.B. 1975; m. Trudy Isabel d. Edward and Laura McLeish 11 May 1974; children: Jeannine Louise, Erin Lynn, James Murray, Gillian Anne, Sean Edward William; called to Bar 1977; practiced law, Crawford, Mill, Davies & Elston 1977–81; M.P.P. Huron-Bruce 1981–87; M.P.P. Bruce 1987– ; (Chrmn., Standing Ctte. on Public Accts. 1984–85; Chrmn., Mgmt. Bd. of Cabinet and Chrmn. of Cabinet 1987–90); Min. of Health, Prov. of Ont. 1985–87; Min. of Financial Institutions, Prov. of Ont. 1988–90; Chrmn., Ont. Round Table on Environment and Economy 1988–90; Opposition House Leader 1990–91; Interim Leader of the Liberal Party 1991; Liberal Leadership Candidate 1992; Opposition House Leader 1992– ; Critic for Min. of Financial Institutions 1993– ; Presbyterian; Liberal: Home: Walkerton, Ont.; Office: Rm. 211, Main Legislative Bldg., Queen's Park Cres., Toronto, Ont. M7A 1A4.

**ELTING, Everett E.;** advertising agency executive; b. New York, N.Y. 14 Feb. 1936; came to Can. 1976, naturalized 1979; s. Everett Ely and Louise F.; e. Trinity Coll, Hartford, B.A. 1958; m. Judith Lass, 19 June 1960; children: Lynn, Elizabeth; PRESIDENT, C.E.O. AND DIR., GREY ADVERTISING LTD. 1980– ; Chrmn.: Grey Advertising (Vancouver) Ltd.; Kelley Advertising Inc.; Lawrence Marshall Productions Ltd.; DMG & Associates Ltd.; Pres. & Dir.: GCI Communications; Gabor Communications; former Chrmn., Grey Ronalds Smith Ltd.; served with U.S. Air Force 1958–62, rank Cpt.; Pres., Bd. of Dirs., Aisling Centre for Children & Families; former Pres. & Dir., Children's Aid Soc. of Metro Toronto; former Chrmn., Children's Aid Soc. Foundation; Home: 1132 Bay SLt., Apt. #1102, Toronto, Ont. M5S 2B4; Office: 1881 Yonge St., Toronto, Ont. M4S 3C4.

**ELTIS, David,** B.Ed., M.A., Ph.D.; economic historian; b. South Shields, England 26 June 1940; s. Charles and Stella (Davison) E.; e. Univ. of Durham B.A. (Hons.) 1962; Dalhousie Univ. B.Ed. 1965; Univ. of Alta. M.A. 1969; Univ. of Rochester Ph.D. 1979; m. Suzan d. Jack and Alice Turland 16 Dec. 1962; children: Lindsay David, Christopher John, Jonathan Kevin; QUEEN'S NATIONAL SCHOLAR, QUEEN'S UNIV. 1989– ; Economic Historian, Algonquin Coll. 1967–89; author: 'Economic Growth and the Ending of the Transatlantic Slave Trade' 1987 and num. articles in scholarly jours.; co-editor: 'Abolition of the Atlantic Slave Trade' 1981; Home: 384 Chapel St., Ottawa, Ont. K1N 7Z6; Office: Dept. of History, 99 University Ave., Kingston, Ont. K7L 3N6.

**ELWOOD, R.C.,** B.A., M.A., Ph.D.; university professor; b. Chicago, Illinois 23 July 1936; s. Calvin A. and Virginia (Carter) E.; e. Dartmouth College B.A. 1958; Columbia Univ. M.A. 1962, Ph.D. 1969; Univ. of Edinburgh; m. Jill St. Germain d. Frank St. Germain 5 May 1990; children: Bruce, Marjorie, Kenneth; PROFESSOR OF HISTORY, CARLETON UNIV. 1976– ; Visiting Asst. Prof., Univ. of Virginia 1964; Asst. Prof., Univ. of Alta. 1964–68; Carleton Univ. 1968–70; Assoc. 1970–76; Chair, History Dept. 1982– ; Visiting Scholar, St. Antony's College, Oxford 1970–71, 1974; Univ. of Fribourg 1977–78, 1985; London Sch. of Econ. 1984–85; Russian Rsch. Ctr., Harvard Univ. 1991–92; Co-ord. 1993 Learned Societies Conf.; Pres., Candn. Assn. of Slavists 1981–82; Excellence in Teaching Award 1985; Marston LaFrance Fellow 1987–88; Heldt Prize for Best Book in Field of Slavic Women's Studies 1992; author: 'Russian Social Democracy in the Underground' 1974, 'Roman Malinovsky' 1977, 'Inessa Armand' 1992; editor: 'The Russian Social Democratic Labour Party' vol. I 1974, 'Canadian Slavonic Papers' 1975–80; Gen. Ed., 'Proceedings of Third World Congress of Soviet and East European Studies' 15 vols. 1986–89; recreations: hiking, skiing; Home: 600 Queen Elizabeth Driveway, Ottawa, Ont. K1S 3N5; Office: Ottawa, Ont. K1S 5B6.

**ELWORTHY, Arthur B.,** B.Com.; company executive, retired; b. Victoria, B.C. 18 May 1922; s. Harold B. and Myrta Gladys (McDonald) E.; e. Sir James Douglas Sch. and Victoria (B.C.) High Sch.; Victoria Coll., 1940–41; Univ. of Brit. Columbia, B.Com. 1948; m. Elizabeth Anne, d. R. S. Laird, Vancouver, B.C., 20 Nov. 1948; children: Mark Barrington, Merrill Anne, Blake Barrington Elworthy (dec.); Secy., Straits Towing and Salvage Company Limited, 1942–46; Pres. of Island Tug and Barge Ltd. 1961–70; Chrmn. of Bd., Seaspan Internat. Ltd., 1970–72; Pres. and Gen. Mgr., B.C. Steamship Co. (1975) Ltd., 1976–80; Acct. Exec., Union Securities Ltd. 1990–92; served in 2nd World War with R.C.A.F. as Pilot; discharged Mar. 1946 with rank of Flying Offr.; Phi Delta Theta; Freemason; recreations: golf, fishing; Clubs: Vancouver; Terminal City; Shaughnessy Golf; Union (Victoria); Victoria Yacht; Home: 507/522 Moberly Rd., Vancouver, B.C. V5Z 4G4.

**ELZINGA, Hon. Peter,** M.L.A.; politician; b. Edmonton, Alta. 6 Apr. 1944; s. Peter and Susan E.; e. Bonnie Doon Composite High Sch. Edmonton; m. Patricia d. Ike and Jenny Nanninga 28 May 1965; 3 sons: Gregory, Roger, Peter Burl; DEPUTY PREMIER, MIN. OF FEDERAL AND INTERGOVERNMENTAL AFFAIRS, Responsible for Government Reorganization Secretariat; el. to H. of C. for Pembina 1974–86 serving on various Parlty. Standing Cttes. incl. Agric., Nat. Health & Welfare, Nat. Resources, Indian & N. Affairs, Pub. Accts.; el. M.L.A. for Sherwood Park, Alta. 1986; Min. of Agric. 1986–89; Min. of Economic Development & Trade 1989–92; acts on various Cabinet cttes. incl. Priorities, Treasury Bd., Communications, Econ. Planning, Agric. and Rural Econ. and Energy; Past Pres. P. Cons. Assn. Can. 1983–86; Chrmn. 1983 Fed. P. Cons. Leadership Convention; Past Sec. Alta. P. Cons. Caucus and P. Cons Caucus Govt. Operations; Past Pres. Clover Bar Prov. P. Cons. Assn.; mem. Candn. Wildlife Fedn.; Heritage Can.; Associated Candn. Travellers; C. of C.; named Kinsman of Yr. 1972–73; Hon. mem. Royal Candn. Legion, Rotary Club; mem. Sherwood Park Chapter Full Gospel Businessmen's Fellowship; Office: 404 Legislature Building, Edmonton, Alta. T5K 2B6.

**EMBLETON, Tony Frederick Wallace,** Ph.D., D.Sc., F.R.S.C.; scientist; b. Hornchurch, Essex, Eng. 1 Oct. 1929; s. Frederick William Howard and Lucy Violet Muriel (Wallace) E.; e. Brentwood Sch. Essex, Eng.; Imp. Coll. Univ. of London B.Sc. 1950, Ph.D. 1952, D.Sc. 1964; m. Eileen Loraine Blackall 14 Nov. 1953; one d. Sheila Margaret; Princ. Rsch. Offr., Nat. Research Council 1974–90; retired 1990; Adjunct Prof. Carleton Univ. since 1978; Fellow, Nat. Research Council 1952–53, Asst. or Assoc. Research Offr. 1954–62, Sr. Research Offr. 1962–74; Visiting Lectr. Univ. of Ottawa 1959–69; Mass. Inst. Technol. 1964, 1967, 1972; mem. Rockcliffe Park Pub. Sch. Bd. 1967–69; Village of Rockcliffe Park, Court of Revision 1975–85; Dir. Youth Science Foundation 1969–72, Ed.-in-Chief 1970–72; rec'd Acoustical Soc. Am. Biennial Award 1964 and Silver Medal in Noise 1986; Soc. Automotive Engrs. Arch T. Coldwell Award 1974; Rochester Inst. Technol. John Wiley Jones Award 1976; Founding Ed.-in-Chief 'Acoustics and Noise Control in Canada' 1972–75; author chapters 'Noise and Vibration Control' 1971; various articles scient. and tech. journs. sound propagation, machinery noise control, acoustical standards; Charter mem. Candn. Acoustical Assn. (Founding Secy. 1961–64); Fellow, Acoustical Soc. Am. (Pres. 1980–81, Vice Pres. 1977–78, Standards Dir. 1993– ; Tech. Council 1964–67, Assoc. Ed. 1970–75); Chrmn., Candn. Standards Assn. Comte., Acoustics and Noise Control (1978–82); Chrmn., Amer. National Standards Comte. S1, Acoustics (1982–85); mem., Inst. of Noise Control Engrg. (Dir., Technical Gps. and Coordination Grps. 1984–87); Dir., International INCE 1993– ; Fellow, Royal Soc. of Can. (Treasurer 1982–85); Foreign Assoc., Nat. Acad. of Engr., U.S. 1987– ; Anglican; recreations: gardening, reading and skating; Home: 80 Sheardown Dr., Nobleton, Ont. L0G 1N0.

**EMBLIN, Ian Peter,** F.C.I.I.; reinsurance executive; b. London, U.K. 23 March 1934; s. Herbert Henry and Edna Maud (Hill) E.; e. Beckenham Tech. Sch. Oxford Univ. Sch. Cert. 1951; m. Maria Ines Molano 11 July 1959; PRESIDENT AND DIR., THE GREAT LAKES REINSURANCE CO. 1982– ; AND GREAT LAKES REINSURANCE HOLDINGS LTD. 1987– ; Dir. and Vice Chrmn., Great Lakes Re Management Corp. New York; Great Lakes Reinsurance (UK) PLC; Great Lakes Re Management Co., Belgium S.A.; Dir., Munich Reinsurance Co. of Canada; Munich-Canada Management Corp. Ltd.; Munich American Consulting Corp. New York; Munich American Services Corp. New York; joined Royal Insurance Co. U.K. 1951; Seguros La Andina, Bogota, Colombia 1957; Royal Insurance Co. Caracas 1961; Royal Caribe de Venezuela, Caracas 1966 (Dir.); Segurosca Insurance Brokers, Caracas 1966 (Dir.); Pan American de Venezuela, Caracas 1969, Mgr. Gen. Ins. Operations; joined Munich Reinsurance Co., Munich 1975; The Great Lakes Reinsurance Co. Toronto 1980; Assoc., Chart. Ins. Inst.; recreations: philately, fire marks, skiing; Clubs: Albany; Canning (U.K.); Home: 197 Markland Dr., Etobicoke, Ont. M9C 1P5; Office: 2100, 390 Bay St., Toronto, Ont. M5H 2Y2.

**EMBURY, Sheila Barbara,** R.N., B.Sc.; politician; b. Calgary, Alta. 6 June 1931; d. Herbert Leonard and Beatrice Mary (Taffler) Pease; e. Calgary Gen. Hosp. Sch. of Nursing R.N. 1953; Univ. of Alta. B.Sc. (Nursing) 1971; m. David E. Embury 4 June 1955; children: B. Lynn, James Edwin; nursing and educ. service Alta. and B.C. 1953–73; Asst. Prof. Sch. of Nursing Univ. of Calgary 1973–79 (became Faculty of Nursing 1974); Research Assoc. Faculty of Nursing Univ. of Alta. 1980–81; Adjunct Assoc. Prof., Faculty of Nursing, Univ. of Calgary, 1983– ; el. M.L.A. for Calgary N.W. Alta. g.e. 1979, re-el. 1982; apptd. Party Whip 1983; retired from politics 1986; Secy., Palliser P. Cons. Fed. Constituency Assn. Bd. Dirs. 1970–72, Pres. 1975–78; Vice Pres. Volunteer Centre Bd. Dirs. 1973–74, Pres. 1974–76; Pres. and Founding mem. Calgary W.P. Cons. Fed. Constituency Assn. 1976–78; Vice Pres. Foothills P. Cons. Prov. Constituency Assn. Bd. Dirs. 1975–76; mem., Alta. Housing Corp. Bd. Dirs. 1976–79; Calgary Heritage Adv. Bd. 1979–82; Alta. Labour Legislation Review Ctte., Govt. of Alta. 1986–88; Fac. of Med., Univ. of Calgary Admissions Ctte. 1986–89; Alternate Mem., Dependent Adult's Review Ctte., Dept. of Social Services, Govt. of Alta. 1986– ; Hon. Mem., Calgary North West Progressive Conservative Assoc. 1986– ; Mem. Selection Ctte., Pinnacle Awards (Business Recognition Awards), Calgary 1987–89; Mem., Rundel Coll. Bd. of Dir. 1987– ; Chrmn., Task Force on Health Care Alternatives, Alta. Assoc. of Registered Nurses 1987–89; Chrmn., Alta. Found. for Nursing Rsch. 1991– ; (Mem. 1987– ;); Vice-Chrmn., McDougall Ctr. Adv. Bd., Calgary 1988–92; author or co-author various nursing and pol. publs.; Home: 1204 Varsity Estates Rd. N.W., Calgary, Alta. T3B 2X2.

**EMENEAU, Murray Barnson,** M.A., L.H.D., LL.D., D.Lit., Ph.D.; professor emeritus; b. Lunenburg, N.S. 28 Feb. 1904; s. Archibald and Ada Helena (Barnson) E.; e. Lunenburg Acad.; Dalhousie Univ. B.A. 1923; Oxford Univ. B.A. 1926, M.A. 1935; Yale Univ. Ph.D. 1931; Rhodes Scholar N.S. 1923–26; Gov.-Gen.'s Gold Medallist 1923; Guggenheim Fellow 1949–50, 1956–57; Faculty Rsch. Lectr., Univ. of Calif., Berkeley 1955–56; Wilbur Lucius Cross Medallist, Yale Grad. Sch. 1969; Hon. degrees: L.H.D. Univ. of Chicago 1968; LL.D. Dalhousie Univ. 1970; D. Lit. (hon. causa) Univ. of Hyderabad, India 1987; m. Katharine Fitch 16 Apr. 1940; PROFESSOR EMERITUS OF SANSKRIT AND GENERAL LINGUISTICS, UNIV. OF CALIFORNIA, BERKELEY 1971– ; Latin Instr. Yale Univ. 1926–31; anthropological linguistic resch. in India on Dravidian languages of S. India 1935–38; Asst. Prof., Univ. of Calif. (Berk.) 1940–43, Assoc. Prof. 1943–46, Prof. 1946–71, Chrmn. Dept. of Linguistics; Dir., Cdn. Assn. of Rhodes Scholars 1981–85; Pres. VIth World Sanskrit Conf., Philadelphia 1984; mem. Linguistic Soc. of Am. (Pres. 1949); Am. Oriental Soc. (Ed. 1941–51, Pres. 1954–55); Am. Philosophical Soc.; Internat. Assn. for Tamil Studies (Vice-Pres. 1966–87); Hon. Fellow Royal Asiatic Soc. 1969; Fellow Am. Acad. of Arts and Sciences 1970; Corresponding Fellow, British Academy 1993; Hon. mem. Linguistic Soc. of India 1964 (winner Citation and silver plate, Golden Jubilee of soc. 1978); author: course in Vietnamese for U.S. Army 1944; 'Kota Texts' 1944–46; 'Kolami: A Dravidian Language' 1955; 'Dravidian Linguistics, Ethnology, and Folktales' 1967; 'Toda Songs' 1971; 'Language and Linguistic Area' 1980; 'Toda Grammar and Texts' 1984; co-author 'A Dravidian Etymological Dictionary' 1961, 1968 (2nd ed. 1984); 'Sanskrit Studies: selected papers' 1988; numerous other books and articles; recreations: ballet, opera, theatre; Home: 909 San Benito Rd., Berkeley, Calif. 94707.

**EMERSON, H. Garfield,** B.A., LL.B., Q.C.; lawyer, investment banker; b. Leamington, Ont. 20 Jan. 1941; s. Donald Garfield and Eleanor Irene (Morris) E.; e. Univ. of Toronto (Hons. Hist.) B.A. 1963; Univ. of Toronto Law Sch. LL.B. 1966; called to Bar of Ont., Law Soc. of U.C. 1968; Q.C. 1980; m. Melissa Jane d. Dr. and Mrs. Alan Fowler Taylor 30 May 1964; children: Melissa Ann, Taylor Garfield; PRES. & CHIEF EXTVE. OFFR., ROTHSCHILD CANADA LTD., investment banking and corporate finance advisory services 1990– ; joined Davies Ward & Beck, Toronto law firm 1968; Partner 1970–90; specialized in corp. finan. & securities law, mergers & acquisitions, reorganizations, finan. insts. & corp. governance; advised Candn. Prov. Securities Comns. & regulatory agencies; Chrmn., Rogers Communications Inc.; Dir., Rogers Cantel Mobile Communications Inc.; CAE Inc.; Marathon Realty Co. Limited; Live Entertainment of Canada Inc.; Unitel Communications Inc.; Genstar Capital Corp.; Candn. Psychiatric Rsch. Found.; Candn. Council of Christians and Jews; author of several articles & book chaps.; former Gen. Ed., 'Canadian Corporation Precedents' 2nd & 3rd eds., 'Canadian Securities Law Precedents'; recreations: golf, tennis, skiing; clubs: Toronto, National, Granite, Mad River Golf, Devil's Glen, Cambridge; Office: Box 77, 1 First Canadian Place, Toronto, Ont. M5X 1B1.

**EMERSON, Montrose L.,** B.Comm.; company executive; b. Stratford, Ont. 17 Sept. 1931; e. McMaster Univ., B.Comm. 1956; m. Janet McCabe 29 Sept. 1956; children: Katherine (Larkin), Christine (Hassell), Edward; Pres., C.O.O. & Dir., Roman Corporation Limited 1988–92; Dir.-Finan. & C.F.O. Procter & Gamble Inc. 1976–88; Mem., Finan. Extves. Inst.; Past Treas., St. Christopher House; Past Warden, Church of St. Clement-Eglinton; Club: Toronto Cricket, Skating & Curling; Home: 54 Lytton Blvd., Toronto, Ont. M4R 1L3.

**EMERY, Alan Roy,** B.Sc., M.Sc., Ph.D.; scientist/museum director; b. West Indies 21 Feb. 1939; s. Roy W. and Ruth I. (Jackson) e.; e. Univ. of Toronto, B.Sc. (Hons.) 1962; McGill Univ., M.Sc. 1964; Inst. of Marine Sci., Univ. of Miami, Ph.D. 1968; m. Frances d. Henry and Margot Ruttan 23 June 1962; children: Katherine, Timothy; PRESIDENT, CANADIAN MUSEUM OF NATURE 1983– ; rsch. assoc., rsch. asst. & teaching asst., Univ. of Toronto, McGill Univ., Fisheries Rsch. Bd. of Can., Ont. Min. of Nat. Resources, Univ. of Miami 1959–73; Assoc. Curator, Dept. of Ichthyology & Herpetology, Royal Ont. Mus. 1973–80; Sci. Co-ord. 1976–78; Curator, Dept. of I. & H., R.O.M. & Assoc. Prof., Univ. of Toronto 1980–83; Sigma XI 1970; Citation, Sports Fishing Inst.; Found. for Ocean Rsch. Marine Environ. Award 1986; Mem., Royal Candn. Inst. (Gov. 1979–81, 2nd Vice Pres. 1981, 1st Vice Pres. 1982, Pres. 1983); Am. Soc. of Ichthyol. & Herpetol. (Gov. 1976–81, 1983–88; Ed. Bd. 1979–86); Ichthyol. Soc. of Japan; Internat. Oceanographic Found.; Internat. Assn. of Profl. Diving Scis.; Assn. of Science Mus. Dir.; Candn. Assn. for Underwater Sci. (Prof. Chrmn., 1985–86); Assn. of Systematic Collections (Vice Pres. 1985, 1986; Pres. 1987, 1988); author: 'The Coral Reef' 1981 and approx 75 pub. articles & chapters in books; recreations: music, writing, lapidary, silversmithing, photography, etc.; Office: P.O. Box 3443, Stn. D, Ottawa, Ont. K1P 6P4.

**EMMERTON, William James,** B.A., LL.B.; business executive, lawyer; b. Kincardine, Ont. 11 Sept. 1947; s. Chester Courtney and Irene Gladys E.; e. Univ. of Guelph B.A. (Hons.) 1970; Univ. of West. Ont. LL.B. 1973; called to Bar of Ont. 1975; m. Marianne d. Kurt and Elizabeth Lade 20 Apr. 1985; children: Tasha Nicole, Heather Margaret Anne, John James, Christina Courtney; VICE PRES., GEN. COUNS., JOHN LABATT LIMITED 1990– ; Bd. of Dirs. 1991– ; lawyer with Douglas A. Farr, Walkerton, Ont. 1975–76; commercial lawyer, present firm 1976–80; Secretary 1981–86; Treas. 1987–90; Dir., Mississauga Children's Choir 1988–90; First Dir., London Better Bus. Bur. 1984–85; Mem., Candn. Bar Assn. 1976– ; Law Soc. of U.C. 1976– ; Toronto Cash Mngt. Soc. 1989–90; recreations: music, golf, bridge; clubs: Founders, Toronto; Home: 1264 Old Colony Rd., Oakville, Ont. L6M 1J8; Office: 130 Adelaide St. W., P.O. Box 105, Toronto, Ont. M5H 3P5.

**EMMONS, Douglas B.,** B.S.A., M.S., Ph.D.; research scientist; b. Huntington Twp., Hastings Co., Ont. 23 May 1930; s. Thomas Edmund and Margaret Isobel (Fitchett) E.; e. Univ of Toronto (Ont. Agric. Coll.) B.S.A., 1952; Univ. Wisconsin, M.S., 1953, Ph.D., 1957; m. Mavis Jean, d. late Dr. Phillip Wharton, 19 June 1953; div.; children: Phillip, Peter, Christina, Jennifer, Beryl; RESEARCH SCIENTIST, AGRICULTURE CANADA (Food Research Centre (Ottawa), Research Br.) since 1958; Asst. Prof., Univ. Wisconsin 1957; awarded 'Pfizer Paul-Lewis Award in Cheese Research' by Am. Dairy Science Assn. 1963; William J. Eva Award by Can. Inst. of Food Sci. and Technology 1981; Merit Award, Agriculture Can. 1986; mem., Can. Inst. Food Sci. Technology; Am. Dairy Science Assn.; Prof. Inst. Pub. Service of Can.; Protestant; recreations: curling, genealogy; Home: 712 – 1171 Ambleside Dr., Ottawa, Ont. K2B 8E1.

**EMOND, Robert M.,** B.A.; public servant; b. Ottawa, Ont. 28 March 1949; s. Ernest Rosario and Elizabeth Veronica (Flintoff) E.; e. Carleton Univ. B.A. (Hons.) 1972; ASST. DEP. MIN., ADMIN. BR., DEPT. OF FINANCE/TREASURY BOARD SECRETARY 1989– ; var. personnel mngt. positions, Dept. of Nat. Defence 1972–77; Sr. Policy Analyst, Audit Br., Public Service Comn. 1977; Dir., Audit Operation 1978; Dir., Policy & Procedures, Staffing Br. 1980; Dir. Gen., Staffing Policy & Program Devel. 1982; Extve. Dir., Staffing Programs Br. 1983; Dir. Gen., Orgn. Devel., Supply and Services Canada 1985; Asst. Dep. Min., Finance, Personnel & Admin. 1986; Extve. Dir., Office of the Supt. of Finan. Institutions 1987; Home: 132 Hunter's Glen Cr., Ottawa, Ont.; Office: 5th floor, 140 O'Connor, L'Esplanade Laurier, Ottawa, Ont. K1A 0G5.

**EMORI, Eiko,** M.F.A., F.G.D.C., R.C.A.; graphic designer; b. Dairen, Japan; d. Morihisa and Fumie (Okura) E.; e. Central Sch. of Arts & Crafts London, Eng. Nat. Dipl. in Design (Graphic) 1958; Yale Univ. Sch. of Art & Arch. M.F.A. 1963; one d. Emilia Péch; PRES., EIKO EMORI INC. 1967– ; designed Algonkian syllabic typefaces; ongoing work providing communication tools in syllabics; Office: 159 Gilmour St., Ottawa, Ont. K2P 0N8.

**EMPRY, Gino;** personal manager; public relations consultant; entertainment director; b. Toronto, Ont. 11 Oct. 1945; s. Arthur and Lucy (Flaminio) Emperatori; e. St. Mary of the Angels Separate Sch. 1953; Oakwood Coll. Inst. 1959; Western Comm. 1961; FOUNDER AND OWNER, GINO EMPRY PUBLIC RELATIONS; Acct., Asst. Office Mgr. Direct Winters Transport 1962; Acct., Systems Analyst, Smith Transport 1963; became actor, director and producer; Entertainment Dir. and Public Relations Royal York Hotel and La Cage Dinner Theatre; Personal Mgmt. for William Hutt, Karen Kain, Toller Cranston, Robin Ward, Jane Corkin Gallery, Ken James, Michael Danso and others; Candn. rep. for Patrick Macnee, Tony Bennett, Peggy Lee, Eartha Kitt, Playboy Magazine, E & B Productions (London, Eng.) and others; Public Relations for Famous People Players, Havana Cigars, Limelight Dinner Theatre, Ramada Renaissance Hotels (Toronto, Montreal), Royal Alexandra Theatre, Zeidler Roberts Partnership, Ronnie Hawkins, Cinespace Studios, Shopsy's, Andre Gagnon, Serge Lavoie, Carman's Club, Johnny Lombardi, CHIN Radio, Honest Ed's, Roch Voisine, Andre Phillippe Gagnon, Ken Danby, Canadian Actor's Equity, Variety Club of Ont.; Dir., Actors Fund Can.; Supporter, Famous People Players; The Heart and Stroke Found.; The Smile Co.; coll. of Gino Empry files, Nat. Archives, Ottawa; author theatre articles, pub. in various mags.; Hon. Chrmn., Canada U.S.S.R. Assoc.; Bd. mem., Ont. Musical Arts Centre; mem., Candn. Public Relations Soc.; Candn. Italian Business and Professional Assn. Inc.; Assn. of Theatrical Press Agents & Mgrs.; Candn. Acad. Recording Arts & Sciences; Nat. Acad. Recording Arts & Sciences, U.S.; Toronto Theatre Alliance; Amer. Federation of Musicians; Acad. of Candn. Cinema & Television; Stratford Shakespearean Found. of Can.; Performing Arts Publicists Assn. of Ont.; Liberal; R. Catholic; recreations: gardening, theatre, movies, travel, collecting rare jewelry and artifacts; Clubs: Toronto Press; Variety; Empire; Home: 130 Carlton St., Apt. 1508, Toronto, Ont. M5A 4K3; Office: 120 Carlton St., Suite 315, Toronto, Ont. M5A 4K2.

**EMSON, Harry Edmund,** M.A., B.M., B.Ch., M.D., FRCP(C); pathologist; educator; b. Swinton, Lancs., Eng. 16 Nov. 1927; s. Edmund E.; e. Manchester (Eng.) Grammar Sch.; Brasenose Coll. Oxford Univ. B.A. 1948, M.A. 1953, B.M., B.Ch. 1952; Univ. of Sask. M.D. 1958; King's Coll., London, Dip. in Med. Law & Ethics 1986; m. Mary Elizabeth Lewis 18 July 1953; children: Jane Margaret, Susan Anne; PROF., DEPT. OF PATHOL., UNIV. OF SASK. since 1975; Consultant Pathol., St. Pauls and City Hosps. Saskatoon; Registrar in Pathol., Birmingham Accident Hosp. 1955–56; Resident in Pathol., St. Pauls Hosp. Saskatoon 1956–57, Univ. Hosp. 1957–58; Asst. Prof. of Pathol., Univ. Hosp. 1958–60; Dir. of Labs., St. Pauls Hosp. 1960–75; Head of Pathol., Univ. Hosp. 1975–90; served with RAMC 1953–55, rank Capt.; Candn. Forces (Militia) 1965–75, rank Maj.; author 'The Doctor and the Law' 1989, 2nd ed.; numerous articles in prof. journs.; Fellow Royal Coll. Phys. & Surgs. Can. (former Examiner, Chrmn. Comte. on Gen. Pathol.); mem. Candn. Assn. Pathols. (Past Pres.); Candn. Soc. Forensic Science (Past Pres.); recreations: theatre, hunting; Office: Univ. Hospital, Saskatoon, Sask. S7N 0X0.

**ENDICOTT, Stephen Lyon,** M.A., Ph.D.; educator; writer; b. Shanghai 5 Jan. 1928; s. James Gareth and Mary Elsie (Austin) E.; e. Candn. Sch. Chengdu, China; Vaughan Rd. Coll. Inst. Toronto; Univ. of Toronto, Victoria Coll. B.A. 1949, M.A. 1966; Sch. of Oriental & African Studies Univ. of London, Univ. of Toronto Ph.D. 1973; m. Lena d. Kenneth and Elizabeth Wilson 26 Apl. 1951; children: Marion, Lorraine, Irene, Valerie; SR. SCHOLAR, DEPT. OF HIST. ATKINSON COLL. YORK UNIV. 1990– ; mem. Nat. Fedn. Labour Youth 1949–57; Journalist 'Jeunesse du Monde' Budapest, Hungary 1952–54; mem. Labour Progressive Party Exec., Toronto 1954–57; bus. high sch. teacher Peel Co., Ont. 1960–68; Lectr. present Univ. 1972, Assoc. Prof. of Hist. 1975–90, Assoc. Prof. and Chrmn. Hist. Dept. Atkinson Coll. 1982–86; Visiting Prof. Sichuan Univ. Chengdu 1980–81, 1988; recipient Can. Council Scholarship 1975–76; Sr. Killam Fellowship 1976–78; Social Sci's & Humanities Rsch. Council Fellowship 1983–84; Atkinson Fellowship 1986; author 'Diplomacy and Enterprise: British China Policy 1933–37' 1975; 'James G. Endicott: Rebel Out of China' 1980; 'Wen Yiuzhang Zhuan' 1983; 'Red Earth: Revolution in a Sichuan Village' 1988; 'The Red Dragon: China 1949–1990' 1991; recreation: white water canoeing; Club: Wen Jiahui; Home: 10 Cherrywood Ave., Toronto, Ont. M6C 2X2; Office: 4700 Keele St., North York, Ont. M3J 1P3.

**ENDLER, Norman S.,** M.Sc., Ph.D., F.R.S.C.; educator; b. Montreal, Que. 2 May 1931; s. Elie and Pearl

(Segal) E.; e. Baron Byng H.S. 1948; Bet Berl Coll. Kfar Saba Israel 1950–51; McGill Univ., B.Sc. 1953, M.Sc. 1954; Univ. of Ill., Ph.D. 1958; m. Beatrice d. Hyman and Edith Kerdman 26 June 1955; children: Mark, Marla; PROF., PSYCHOLOGY, YORK UNIV. 1968– ; Psychol., Penn. State Univ. 1958–60; Rsch. Assoc. & Lectr., present univ. 1960–62; Asst. Prof. 1962; Assoc. Prof. 1965; Dir. Grad Prog. 1968–71; Chrmn., Psychol. 1974–79; various summer acad. appts. 1958, 1965–67; Vis. Prof., Univ. of Stockholm 1973–74; Univ. of Florence 1985–86; Vis. Scholar, Stanford Univ. 1979–80, 1986; Disting. Univ. Scholar, var. Brit. univs. incl. Oxford, Sheffield, Sussex & L.S.E. 1978; Cons. (Psychol.), Toronto E. Gen. Hops. 1964–84; Clarke Inst. of Psych. 1972–82; Sr. Rsch. Assoc., Clarke Inst. 1988– ; Dir., Counc. Suicide Prev. Metro Toronto; Profl. Adv. Bd. Addiction Rsch. Found. 1977–83; ed. bd. mem., var. psychol. jours.; Integra Found. 1971–74; Queen's Silver Jubilee Medal 1978; F.R.S.C. 1986; Killam Rsch. Fellowship 1987–89; Award of Merit Ont. Psychol. Assn. 1988; Rsch. Leave Fellowship, Can. Counc. 1967–68, 1973–74; SSHRC 1979–80, 1985–86, 1991–94; York Univ. 1981–82; Fellow, Winters Coll., York Univ.; Am. Psychol. Assn.; Candn. Psychol. Assn.; Mem., Beth Tikvah Synagogue (Jewish); author: 'Holiday of Darkness' 1982, rev. 1990; co-author: 'Electroconvulsive Therapy' 1988, 'Maturing in a Changing World' 1971; 'Coping Inventory for Stressful Situations: Manual' 1990; 'Endler Multidimensional Anxiety Scales: Manual' 1991; 'Depression: New Directions in Research, Theory and Practice' 1990; co-editor: 'Depression' 1990, 'Personality at the Crossroads' 1977, 'Interactional Psychology and Personality' 1976, 'Contemporary Issues in Development Psychology' 1968, 1976; recreations: tennis, nordic skiing, classical music, reading mystery novels; Home: 52 Sawley Dr., North York, Ont. M2K 2J5; Office: 4700 Keele St., North York, Ont. M3J 1P3.

**ENDRENYI, Laszlo,** B.Eng., Ph.D.; university professor; b. Budapest, Hungary 6 May 1933; s. Sandor and Lilly (Szegvari) E.; e. Technical Univ. of Budapest B.Eng. 1956; Univ. of Toronto Ph.D. 1965; m. Agota d. Mihaly and Piroska Barabas 21 Dec. 1956; PROFESSOR, DEPT. OF PHARMACOLOGY & DEPT. OF PREVENTIVE MED. & BIOSTATISTICS, UNIV. OF TORONTO 1977– ; Research Assoc., present univ. 1966; Asst. Prof. 1969; Assoc. Prof. 1972; Assoc. Dean, Sch. of Graduate Studies 1988–93; Mem., Statistical Soc. of Canada; Candn. Pharmacol. Soc.; Am. Statistical Assn.; author of more than 100 sci. papers; editor: 'Kinetic Data Analysis' 1981; Home: 33 Rosehill Ave., Apt. 2007, Toronto, Ont. M4T 1G4; Office: Toronto, Ont. M5S 1A8.

**ENEMARK, Tex Cyril,** B.A., LL.B.; business executive; b. Wells, B.C. 3 Sept. 1940; s. Holger Pedersen (dec.) and Margaret Mary (Watkins) E.; e. Univ. of B.C., B.A. 1967, LL.B. 1970; m. Sandra d. George (dec.) and Jean Thompson 22 Aug. 1964; children: Kiersten Alexandra, Tasha Cathalyn, Elizabeth Ashleigh; PRESIDENT, MILLER & LEONARD PUBLIC RELATIONS/PUBLIC AFFAIRS INC. 1994– ; Consultant in business mgmt. and public policy 1986–93; Vice Pres., P.R.M. Resources Ltd.; Special Asst. to Federal Min. of Consumer & Corporate Affairs 1970–72; Exec. Asst. Min. of State for Urban Affairs 1972–73; with law firm of Davis & Co. Vancouver 1973–74; Vice Pres. Executive Consultants Ltd. Ottawa 1974–76; Dep. Min. of Consumer & Corporate Affairs, B.C. 1976–79; Dir. of Deregulation, Min. of Deregulation, B.C. 1979–80; W. Mgr. Maclean Hunter Ltd. 1980–82; Pres. & C.E.O., Mining Assn. of B.C. 1982–86; Mem. Adv. Ctte., Faculty of Bus. Adm., Simon Fraser Univ.; Founder & Past Pres., Northern Inst. for Resource Studies; Founding Bd. mem., Western Magazines Awards Found.; Past Pres. Vancouver Assn., Children with Learning Disabilities; Mem., Underwater Archeol. Soc. B.C.; Founding Bd. mem., Artifical Reef Soc. of B.C.; Liberal Candidate for Parliament 1988; recreations; scuba diving, public policy, reading; Club: Vancouver; Home: 8431 Aspin Pl., Richmond (Vancouver), B.C. V6Y 3C2.

**ENESCO, Hildegard Esper,** M.A., Ph.D.; educator; biologist; b. Seattle, Wash. 16 June 1936; d. Erwin Allen and Ethel Marie (Cooke) Esper; e. Reed Coll. B.A. 1958; Columbia Univ. M.A. 1959, Ph.D. 1962; m. Mircea A. Enesco 12 July 1964; PROF. OF BIOL. CONCORDIA UNIV. 1978– ; Rsch. Assoc. McGill Univ. 1964–68; Asst. Prof. of Biol. Sir George Williams Univ. 1968, Assoc. Prof. 1969, Chrmn. of Biol. 1974–77, 1991–92; recipient rsch. grants NSERC, Health & Welfare Can.; author over 60 rsch. papers biol. jours.; mem. Candn. Assn. Gerontol. (Chrmn. Biol. Sci's Div. 1983–87 and 1993–97); Candn. Soc. Cell Biol.; Am. Soc. Cell Biol.; Am. Aging Assn.; Gerontol. Soc. Am.; Internat. Soc. Devel. Biol.; Sigma Xi; Office: 1455 de Maisonneuve Blvd. W., Montréal, Qué. H3G 1M8.

**ENG, Susan,** LL.B.; lawyer, executive; b. Toronto, Ont. 24 Aug. 1952; d. Tong and Chuey (Ting) E.; e. Jarvis C.I. 1965–70; Univ. of Toronto Commerce & Finance Programme 1970–72; Osgoode Hall Law Sch. LL.B. 1975; called to Ont. Bar 1977; CHAIR, METROPOLITAN TORONTO POLICE SERVICES BOARD 1991– ; 1st apptd. to Bd. 1989, re-apptd. 1992 (has worked to raise public awareness about the need for police forces to be more accountable to the communities they serve); Former Partner, Blaney, McMurtry, Stapells; resided in Beijing assisting clients involved in a joint venture & workplace training project Spring 1985; frequent speaker on tax matters incl. 1988 Ont. & Nat. Tax Confs.; Seminar Instr., Bar Admission Course 1984, '85, '87; Former Mem., Ont. Premier's Counc. on Technol. & Internat. Competitiveness; Past Dir., Ont. Internat. Corp.; Mem., Candn. Tax Found.; extensive community activites incl. Chinese-Candn. Nat. Counc., Urban Alliance on Race Relns., Chinese Community Nursing Home for Greater Toronto, Ont. Press Counc., Univ. Settlement House; candidate for alderman 1984 mun. by-election; author of var. articles in tax jours.;

**ENG, William Sek Fon;** chartered accountant; b. China 18 Nov. 1936; s. Eddie and Mary (Chan) E.; e. North Saanich High Sch. (Sidney, B.C.) 1958; Candn. Inst. Chartered Accountants, C.A. 1965; m. Jane, d. Wah Sing Chow, 23 July 1966; children: Daymon; Fenton; Lannette; PARTNER, ENG, ROZON, FLOOR & CLARKE 1966– ; Dir., Concord Credits Ltd.; Vice-Chrmn. and co-founder, Concord Development Corp. Ltd. 1969– ; Dir. and co-founder, Western and Pacific Bank Can. 1982–88; Dir., Bd. Govs., St. Michael's Univ. Sch. (1979–85); Mineral Land Tax Review Bd. B.C. 1977– ; Victoria Chinatown Lions Club (Pres. 1972); B.C. Human Rights Commission (Commissioner 1979–80); Founding Chrmn. & Pres., Victoria Chinese Commerce Assoc. 1991– ; recreations: golf, ski, racquet sports, weights; Club: Union; Uplands Golf; Home: 3182 Wessex Close, Victoria, B.C. V8P 5N2; Office: #400 – 915 Fort St., Victoria, B.C. V8V 3K3.

**ENGBRECHT, Henry John,** A.R.C.T., B.A., M.Mus.; professor of music; b. Whitewater, Man. 21 June 1939; s. John and Margaret (Albrecht) E.; e. Mennonite C.I.; Candn. Mennonite Bible College Sacred Music Dipl. 1961; Brandon Coll., Man. Teacher's Cert. 1962; Royal Conservatory of Music A.R.C.T. (singing) 1962; Bethel College (Newton, KS) B.A. 1966; Southern Methodist Univ. M.Mus. 1967; grad. studies at Univ. of Oregon with Helmuth Rilling, Univ. of Cincinnati 1979–83; m. Erna d. Nicholas and Helen Braun; children: Victor Charles, Geraldine Diane; PROFESSOR, SCHOOL OF MUSIC, UNIV. OF MANITOBA & DIR. OF CHORAL STUDIES & ACTIVITIES 1978– ; Elem. Sch. Teacher (Man.) 1962–63; Dir. of Music, Elim Bible Inst. 1963–65; Mennonite C.I. 1967–71; Interim Head of Music Dept. & Dir. of Choral Activities, Candn. Mennonite Bible Coll. 1971–73; H.S. Teacher & Dir. of Choral Program, Sturgeon Creek Reg. S.S. 1973–78; Chorus Master, Man. Opera Assn. 1974–79; Musical Dir. & Conductor, Winnipeg Philharmonic Choir 1975–90; Vice-Pres., Man. Music Educators Assn. (one term); Founding Pres., Manitoba Choral Assn. 1976–79; Past Pres. 1980–83; Bd. Mem., Winnipeg Bach Festivel (two terms); Adv. Bd. Mem. for renovation of Pantages Playhouse Theatre and for Prairie Performances (a concert orgn.); Dr. & Mrs. D.R. Campbell Outreach Award, Univ. of Man. 1990; Winner of CBC Amateur Choral Competitions as conductor of University Singers 1990; Church choir director for 23 years; choral adjudicator and workshop conductor throughout western Canada; frequent guest conductor, prov. youth choirs; Chair, Repertoire & Standards Ctte., Assn. of Candn. Choral Conductors; Mem., Internat. Fed. for Choral Music; Am. Choral Conductors Assn.; Home: 2313 – 80 Plaza Dr., Winnipeg, Man. R3T 5S2; Office: Sch. of Music, Univ. of Man., Winnipeg, Man. R3T 2N2.

**ENGEL, Howard,** B.A.; writer; b. Toronto, Ont. 2 Apr. 1931; s. Jack and Lollie Florence (Greisman) E.; e. St. Catharines (Ont.) Coll. Inst.; McMaster B.A. 1955; Ont. Coll. Edn. 1956; m.(1) Marian Ruth d. Frederick and Mary (Fletcher) Passmore 1962; children: William Lucas Passmore, Charlotte Helen Arabella; m.(2) Janet Evelyn d. Arthur A. and Doris (Dixon) Hamilton 1978; one s.: Jacob Harry; High Sch. Teacher 1955–56; CBC broadcaster and producer radio and TV; Exec. Producer various progs. incl. 'The Arts in Review,' 'Sunday Supplement,' 'Anthology,' 'Focus Canada' and major single documentaries on Hemingway, Faulkner, William Carlos Williams, Brendan Behan, Louis MacNeice & other literary figures; author of the Benny Cooperman Mystery Series which to date include 'The Suicide Murders' 1980; 'The Ransom Game' 1981; 'Murder on Location' 1982; 'Murder Sees the Light' 1984; 'A City Called July' 1986; 'A Victim Must Be Found' 1988; 'Dead and Buried' 1990; 'There Was an Old Woman' 1993; and, without Benny Cooperman, 'Murder in Montparnesse' 1992; author (radio scripts) 'A Child's Christmas in Scarborough' 1969; 'Ambrose Small' 1985; 'Hangman's Hands'; 'The Wrong Man' (Donald Marshall Jr. case) 1986; co-ed. (with Eric Wright) 'Criminal Shorts: Mysteries by Canadian Crime Writers' 1992; nominated for Gemini Award for CBC TV film adapted from 'The Suicide Murders' 1986; adapted 'Murder Sees the Light' for CBC TV 1986; Writer-in-Residence, Hamilton Public Lib. 1989; co-founder Crime Writers Can. (Treas. 1982–85, Chrmn. 1986–87; ed. 'Fingerprints' newsletter 1985–86; Arthur Ellis Award Crime Fiction 1984); Winner, Harbourfront Festival Prize for 'contributions to Canadian literature and the Canadian literary community' 1990; mem. ACTRA; P.O.E.T.S.; Dir., Canadian Give the Gift of Literacy Found.; Mystery Writers of Am.; The Internat. Assn. of Crime Writers (mem., founding Extve. Ctte.); recreations: swimming, canoeing, drawing; Address: 281 Major St., Toronto, Ont. M5S 2L5.

**ENGELHART, Kenneth George,** B.A., LL.B.; lawyer; b. Montreal, Que. 20 Sept. 1955; s. Frederick and Ruth (Mittler) E.; e. Univ. of W. Ont., B.A. 1977; Univ. of Toronto, LL.B. 1980; m. Susan d. William and Evelyn Paul 27 Sept. 1985; children: Katharine, Luke, Sally; VICE PRESIDENT, REGULATORY LAW, ROGERS COMMUNICATIONS; Assoc., Messrs. Turkstra Partners 1982; Assoc., Dutton, Brock, Somers, MacIntyre & Collier 1983–86; Gen. Couns. & Dir., Regulatory Affairs, Candn. Bus. Telecommunications Alliance 1987–90; author various articles on law & policy; co-author (with M. Trebilcock) 'Public Participation in the Regulatory Process: The Issue of Funding' 1981; recreations: bridge, gardening; Home: 410 Glengarry Ave., North York, Toronto, Ont. M5M 1E8; Office: Ste. 2600, Commercial Union Tower, P.O. 249, T.D. Centre, Toronto, Ont. M5K 1J5.

**ENGLISH, Gordon William,** B.Sc., M.B.A., P.Eng.; research executive; b. Minnedosa, Man. 25 May 1948; s. James Byron and Frances Mary (Blackman) B.; e. Univ. of Manitoba B.Sc. 1970; Queen's Univ. M.B.A. 1975; m. Lesley Irene Boyd; children: Graeme Geoffrey, Bryan Andrew; EXTVE. DIR., CANDN. INST. OF GUIDED GROUND TRANSPORT, QUEEN'S UNIV. 1990– ; Plant Engineer, Abitibi Manitoba Paper Co. 1970–74; Research Engineer, present institution 1975–80; Sr. Rsch. Engr. 1980–85; Mgr., Systems Engr. & O.R. 1985–90; Adjunct Assoc. Prof., Civil Engineering, Queen's Univ.; Past Bd. of Dir., Crystal Springs manor; Bd. of Dir., Camp Hyanto; Mem., I.E.E.E., I.I.E., C.T.R.F., A.P.E.O., A.R.E.A.; recreations: squash, golf, tennis; Home: 682 Milford Dr., Kingston, Ont.; Office: Kingston, Ont. K7L 3N6.

**ENGLISH, Lt. Col.-Dr. John Alan,** CD, pfsc, plsc, rmc, B.A., M.A., Ph.D.; army officer, writer, university professor; b. Delburne, Alta. 12 Oct. 1940; s. John Percival and Amelia Lydia (Stuber); e. Delburne H.S. 1958; Royal Roads Military College 1960; Royal Military Coll. of Canada B.A. 1962; Duke Univ. M.A. 1964; Candn. Forces Staff College pfsc 1972; Royal Military Coll. M.A. 1980; Candn. Land Forces Command & Staff Coll. plsc 1989; Queen's Univ. Ph.D. 1989; m. Valerie d. George and Winnifred Phillips 15 Sept. 1979; children: Shannon Elizabeth, Laura Alexandra; ASST. PROF., QUEEN'S UNIV. 1992– ; comnd. into Queen's Own Rifles of Can. 1962; served 2nd Battalion; Exchange Offr., Queen's Own Buffs & Queen's Royal Surrey Regiment 1965–67; Cyprus 1967; Staff Offr., Mobile Command H.Q. 1968–70; Company Comdr., Princess Patricia's Candn. Light Infantry 1970–71, 1972–73; Tactics Instr., Combat Arms Sch. 1974–77; Staff Offr., Dep. Chief of Defence Staff 1979–81; War Plans Offr., NATO Central Army Group Heidelberg 1981–82; Chief of Tactics Combat Training Ctr. 1982–84; Visiting Defence Fellow, Queen's Univ. 1984–85; Directing Staff Mem., Candn. Land Forces Command & Staff Coll. 1985–86, 1988–90; Rsch. Assoc., Internat. Inst. for Strategic Studies 1990–91; Staff Offr., Curriculum Planning, Nat. Defence Coll. 1991–92; UN Cyrpus Medal 1967; Queen's Jubilee Medal 1977; Second Clasp to Candn. Decoration 1990; Special Service Medal (NATO) 1993; Combat Team Comdr.'s Course 1969; Parachute course 1975; Dept. of Nat. Defence Military & Strategic Studies Doctoral Fellowship 1986; SSHRCC 2-yr. postdoct. fellowship 1992–94; Mem., Royal Candn. Military Inst.; Royal United Services Inst.; Life Mem., PPCLI Assn.; Queen's Alumni Assn.; author: 'On Infantry' 1981, '84, 'The Canadian Army and the Normandy

Campaign' 1991; co-editor: 'The Mechanized Battlefield' 1984; recreation: nordic skiing, swimming, fishing; clubs: Queen's Faculty, Fort Frontenac Officer's Mess, Royal Canadian Military Inst.; Home: 15 Riverside Dr., Milton on the St. Lawrence, Kingston, Ont. K7L 4V1; Office: Kingston, Ont. K7L 3N6.

**ENGLISH, John Richard,** A.M., Ph.D., F.R.S.C.; educator; b. Woodstock, Ont. 26 Jan. 1945; s. John and Merle (Kennedy) E.; e. Waterloo-Oxford High Sch. 1963; Univ. of Waterloo B.A. 1967; Harvard Univ. A.M. 1968, Ph.D. 1973; D.Litt. (hon. causa) Wilfrid Laurier Univ. 1992; m. Hilde Maria d. Josef and Barbara Abt 5 May 1967; one s. Jonathan Josef; MEMBER OF PARLIAMENT, KITCHENER 1993– ; PROF. OF HIST. UNIV. OF WATERLOO 1984– ; Tutor, Harvard Univ. 1970–71; Lectr. in Hist. present Univ. 1972, Asst. Prof. 1974, Assoc. Prof. 1978; Co-dir. Centre on Foreign Policy & Federalism 1981– ; Woodrow Wilson Fellow 1967; Harvard Grad. Prize Fellow 1968–72; Killam Jr. Fellow 1975–77, Sr. Rsch. Fellow 1985–87; Fellow, Royal Soc. of Can.; author 'The Decline of Politics' 1977; 'Arthur Meighen' 1977; 'Robert Borden, His Life and World' 1977; 'Years of Growth' 1986; 'Shadow of Heaven: The Biography of Lester Pearson' Vol. 1, 1989 (Macdonald Prize and Candn. Author's Assoc. Non-Fiction Prize); 'The Wordly Years: The Biography of Lester Pearson' Vol. 2, 1992 (Dafoe Prize); co-author 'Canada Since 1945' 1981; 'Kitchener: An Illustrated History' 1984; 'Canada 1900–1945' 1987; co-ed. 'Mackenzie King: Widening the Debate' 1977; 'Canadian Agriculture in the Global Context' 1986; 'Canadian Historical Review' 1985–88; 'Making a Difference' 1992; mem. various ed. bds.; Bd. mem. Champlain Soc. 1983– ; mem. Candn. Hist. Assn. (Council 1976–79); Candn. Inst. Internat. Affairs (Pres. Waterloo Br. 1982–85, Nat. Exec. Ctte. 1984–93, Vice Pres. 1987–90, Pres. 1991–92); UN Assn. (Vice Pres. Kitchener-Waterloo Br. 1981–85); Home: 134 Claremont Ave., Kitchener, Ont. N2M 2P8; Office: House of Commons, Ottawa, Ont. K1A 0H6.

**ENGLISH, John Thomas,** B.A., F.S.A., F.C.I.A.; insurance executive; b. Paris, Ont., 14 Dec. 1928; s. John Thomas and Catherine Elizabeth (Payne) E.; e. McMaster Univ., B.A. 1952; m. Joy Glendene (Nicholson); one. d.: Ann Elizabeth; PRESIDENT, TORONTO MUTUAL LIFE INSURANCE CO., since 1972; Actuarial Student, Northern Life Insurance Co., London, Ont., 1952–56; Assoc. Actuary, Commonwealth Life Insurance Co., Louisville, Ky., 1956–61; Vice-Pres. Data Processing, 1961–64; Vice-Pres., and Secy., Boston Mutual Life Insurance Co., 1964–67; joined present Co. as Mang. Dir. and Actuary 1968; mem., Bd. Trade Metrop. Toronto; Anglican; recreations; gardening, wood-working, reading; Clubs: Granite; Home: 470 St. Clements Ave., Toronto, Ont. M5N 1M1; Office: 112 St. Clair Ave. W., Toronto, Ont. M4V 2Y3.

**ENGLISH, Joseph Edward,** B.A.; insurance executive; b. Toronto, Ont. 5 May 1939; s. Emmett Patrick and Mae Ellen Anne (Mackness) E.; e. Univ. of Western Ont. B.A. 1963; m. Diane d. Charles and Evelyn Clayton; 18 Sept. 1965; children: James, Andrea; SENIOR VICE-PRESIDENT, THE CITADEL GENERAL ASSURANCE CO. 1987– ; Manager, Bell Canada 1963–64; various positions to Asst. Vice-Pres., Allstate Insur. Co. of Can. 1964–85; Asst. Vice-Pres., CIGNA Insur. Co. of Can. 1986–87; Home: 54 Emmeloord Cres., Unionville, Ont. L3R 1P8; Office: 1075 Bay St., Suite 1200, Toronto, Ont. M5S 2W5.

**ENGLISH, L. Arthur,** B.Sc., M.B.A.; banking executive; b. Winnipeg, Man. 23 July 1944; s. Leslie B. and Sarah M. (Burnell) E.; e. Univ. of Toronto B.Sc. 1968; Univ. of Western Ont. M.B.A. 1972; m. Barbara A. Langan; children: Richard, Andrew, John; EXECUTIVE VICE-PRES., FINANCIAL SERVICES DIVISION, THE TORONTO-DOMINION BANK 1993– ; Nat. Accts., Mining & Metals, Toronto-Dominion Bank 1977; Gen. Mgr., Nat. Accts. Group 1980; Vice-Pres., Corp. Banking Div. 1982; Sr. Vice-Pres., U.S.A. Div. 1984; Extve. Vice-Pres., Corp. & Investment Banking Group 1992–93; Dir., TD Mortgage Corporation; Dir., TD Pacific Mortgage Corporation; Dir., Toronto Symphony Orch.; North York Hosp.; recreations: sailing; clubs: Royal Canadian Yacht, American Yacht; Home: 124 Blythwood Rd., Toronto, Ont. M4N 1A4; Office: P.O. Box 1, Toronto-Dominion Tower, Toronto-Dominion Ctr., 55 King St. W., Toronto, Ont. M5K 1A2.

**ENNIS, Robert Malcolm;** construction executive; b. United Kingdom 11 April 1953; s. Robert Leo and Mary (Whelan) E.; m. Paula H. d. Daniel and Constance O'Reilly Sept. 1976; VICE-PRESIDENT & TORONTO AREA MANAGER, ELLIS-DON CONSTRUCTION LTD. 1992– ; Sr. Estimator, Rocca Construction 1977–80; Chief Estimator, Eton Construction 1980–83; Sr. Estimator, Ellis-Don Construction 1983–85; Chief Estimator 1985–89; Vice-Pres. & Chief Estimator 1989–92; recreations: tennis, squash; clubs: Timberlane; Home: 40 Regent St., Richmond Hill, Ont. H4C 9B9; Office: 2 Sheppard Ave. E., North York, Ont. M2N 6L5.

**ENSCH, Thomas J.,** B.A., M.B.A.; executive; b. USA 27 Dec. 1938; s. Emile E. and Margaret E. (Neff) E.; e. Marian Coll. Indiana B.A. 1960; Indiana Univ. M.B.A. 1961; m. Suzanne d. Thomas and Louise Settle 29 Dec. 1962; children: Thomas, Peter, Joan, Stephen, Kathryn, Mary; Dist. Mgr., Southern USA, B.F. Goodrich 1965–68; Mktg. Mgr., Am. Hosp. Supply Corp. 1968–70; Dir., Export Sales, Internat. B.F. Goodrich 1970–81; Vice-Pres. & Gen. Mgr., Tire Div., B.F. Goodrich Can. 1981–89; Pres., Atlas Alloys 1989–92; Teacher, Indiana Univ. 1962; Asst. Prof. (part-time), Akron Univ. 1965–66; Dir., Rio Algom Inc. (USA); Candn. Steel Serv. Centres; Roman Catholic; author of some articles; recreations: golf, hunting; club: Westmount Golf & Country; Home: 1929 Four Seasons Dr., Burlington, Ont. L7P 2Y3.

**ENSLIN, Rosemarie,** A.P.R.; public relations consultant; b. Toronto, Ont. 23 Apr. 1945; d. Hans and Marie (Halbig) Enslin; e. Mt. Royal Coll.; PRESIDENT, ENSLIN ASSOC. 1979– ; Mgr., Pub. Relations, Metrop. Toronto Conv. & Visitors Assn. 1970–72; Communications Mgr., Harbourfront 1974–76; Vice Pres., Communication Design Inc. 1976–79; Bd. mem., Toronto Brigantine Inc. 1986–89; Accredited Mem., Candn. Pub. Relations Soc.; Associate Mem., Soc. of Am. Travel Writers; Ont. Counc. Mem., Duke of Edinburgh's Award; Founding Patron, Toronto Arts Awards 1986; Past Bd. Mem., Toronto Press Club; recreation: sailing; Home: Apt. 302, 150 Balmoral Ave., Toronto, Ont. M4V 1J4.

**ENSOM, Ronald Ernest,** B.A. (Hon.), M.S.W.; social worker; b. Ottawa, Ont. 15 Aug. 1945; s. Benjamin Ernest and Albertine Amy (Latimer) E.; e. Rideau High Sch. Ottawa 1964; Carleton Univ. B.A. (Hon.) 1968, M.S.W. 1972; m. Beverly d. Victor and Eleanor Adams 27 June 1970; children: Molly, Timothy, Paul; CO-ORDINATOR CHILD PROTECTION PROG. CHILDREN'S HOSP. OF E. ONT. 1983– ; Supr. Treatment Facilities, Social Worker, Child Care Worker Children's Aid Soc. Ottawa-Carleton 1968–80; Co-ordinator Hard to Serve Children Ctte. Ottawa-Carleton 1980–83; Dir. Christie Lake Boys' Camp; Pres. Assn. Protection Little Cedar Lake 1981– ; mem. Peace Exchange Network; recreations: running, squash, swimming; Home: 1858 Sharel Dr., Ottawa, Ont. K1H 6W4; Office: 401 Smyth Rd., Ottawa, Ont. K1H 8L1.

**ENSOR, Arthur John,** R.C.A.; industrial designer; b. Llanishen, Wales 2 Jan. 1905; s. Francis Lycett E.; e. Felsted Sch. Eng.; scholarship student, Royal Coll. of Art (Design) 1926–29; Univ. of London Extension Course in Art Hist. 1925–28; Mass. Inst. Technol. summer course 1951; children: Georgina Frances, John Robert; estbd. ENSOR INDUSTRIAL DESIGN ASSOCIATES 1950, Toronto; travelled Africa collecting visual data for Empire Marketing Bd. producing posters for them and for Imperial Airways 1930–31; Designer Research Dept. Imperial Chemical Industries Plastics Div. 1935–37; estbd. own design consultant office London 1937–39; Design consultant with office of Design, Industry, Trade & Comm. Ottawa 1964–73; has devel. several patents; rec'd various competition awards; mem. Counc., Roy. Candn. Acad. of Arts; rep. Can. first Indust. Design Conf. Paris 1953; painting selected from Nat. Gallery Coll. for Can. Post Stamp 1967; author various research reports indust. design; mem. Assn. Candn. Indust. Designers (Past Pres.); Indust. Artists (U.K.); served with Royal Engr. Corps UK and N.W. Europe 1940–46, part-time War Artist for Min. of Information; Liberal; Unitarian; recreations: painting, skating, swimming; Club: Arts & Letters (Toronto); Office: 502 – 100 Gloucester St., Ottawa, Ont. K2P 0A4.

**EPP, Hon. Arthur Jacob (Jake),** P.C., M.P., B.A., B.Ed.; politician; b. St. Boniface, Man. 1 Sept. 1939; s. Rev. Jacob Peter and Margaretha (Toews) E.; e. Steinbach, Man. 1957; Univ. of Man. B.A. 1961, B.Ed. 1965; LL.D. (Hon.) Trinity Western Univ., Langley B.C. 1987; m. Lydia d. Rev. Peter W. Martens, Winkler, Man. 17 Aug. 1961; one d. Lisa Dawn; el. to H. of C. for Provencher 1972, re-el. g.e. 1974, '79, '80, '84 and 1988; serves on various Cabinet Cttes. (Priorities and Planning; Econ. Policy; Cultural Affairs and Nat. Identity; Environment); High School Teacher 1962–72; Councillor, Town of Steinbach 1970–72; Min. of Indian and Northern Affairs 1979; Min. of National Health and Welfare 1984–89; Min. of Energy, Mines & Resources 1989–93; P. Conservative; Evangelical; recreations: golf, squash; Home: 391 Southwood Dr., Steinbach, Man. R0A 2A0.

**EPP, Edward,** B.F.A., M.A.; artist, teacher; b. Saskatoon, Sask. 27 Jan. 1950; s. John and Marie (Schmidt) E.; e. Univ. of Sask. B.F.A. (with distinction) 1973, M.A. 1975; m. Leanne d. Marvin and Delores Boschman 1 Sept. 1974; children: Dawn Carol, Amelia, Nathaniel; Workshop Dir., Yorkton Art Ctr. 1967–77; Instr. of Art, Red Deer Coll. 1977–78; Coll. of New Caledonia (Prince George B.C.) 1978–81; Asst. Prof. of Art, Cuttington Univ. Coll. (Liberia W. Africa) 1982–89; Volunteer Teachers, World University Serv. of Canada, Botswana 1989–90; Instr., Emily Carr Art Coll. Outreach Prog.; Sask. Indian Fed. Coll. 1986–87; Guest Instr., Island Mountain Art (Wells B.C.) 1981, 1989; artist with long show record incl. Edmonton Art Gall. (1-man exhib.) 1983; exhibs. throughout Canada at commerical art galleries: Bau-Xi (Toronto & Vanc.), Art Placement (Sask.); included in many corp. & public collections: Toronto-Dominion, Esso, Westburne, Westin, Xerox, Nat. Bank of Can., Norman Mackenzie Art Gall., Mendal Art Gall., Nat. Gall. of Botswana, etc.; Baha'i; Mem., Assn. for Baha'i Studies; Home: RR 4, Old Lakelse Lake Rd., Terrace, B.C. V8G 4V2.

**EPSTEIN, Herbert Bernard,** B.A.; executive; b. Brooklyn, N.Y. 26 Nov. 1919; s. Morris Henry and Anne (Gitter) E.; e. Upper Can. Coll. 1938; Univ. of Toronto B.A. 1942; m. Nelle; children: Norman James, Jan Linda; former Chrmn. of Bd. and CEO, Silknit Ltd.; former Chrmn. Lovable Brassiere Co. of Canada Ltd.; served with USAF 1942–45, rank Lt.; Governor Baycrest Home for the Aged; Mount Sinai Hosp. Toronto; P. Conservative; Jewish; recreations: golf, Clubs: Oakdale Golf and Country; Longboat Key Golf (Sarasota, Fla.); Home: 228 Strathallan Wood, Toronto, Ont. M5N 1T4; Office: 504 St. Clements Ave., Toronto Ont. M5N 1M4.

**EPSTEIN, Howard Michael,** B.A., LL.B.; lawyer; association executive; b. Halifax, N.S. 17 Jan. 1949; s. Ray and late Leah Zissa (Spitz) E.; e. Carleton Univ. B.A. 1968; Dalhousie Univ. LL.B. 1973; m. Ilga d. late Ernest and Lilija Leja 30 June 1984; one d. Hannah Leja; one s. Noah Ernest; EXTVE. DIR., ECOLOGY ACTION CENTRE 1991– ; Extve. Dir., The Medical Soc. of Nova Scotia 1990–91; Lawyer Dept. Justice Ottawa 1974–76; Lectr. Carleton Univ. 1976, Osgoode Hall Law Sch. 1977–78, Saint Mary's Univ. 1983; private law practice Halifax 1978–81; Exec. Dir. N.S. Confederation Univ. Faculty Assns. 1981–84; Exec. Dir., Ont. Confederation of Univ. Faculty Assns. 1984–88; Bus. Agt. N.S. Union Pub. Employees 1979–84; Chrmn. North End Community Health Assn. Halifax 1982–84 (Dir. 1980–84); Dir. St. Joseph's Children's Centre Halifax 1981–84; Pres. Halifax Citadel N.D.P. Riding Assn. 1984; Jewish; NDP; Home: 2396 Clifton St., Halifax, N.S. B3K 4V1.

**EPSTEIN, Murray;** electronics and radio communications executive; b. Montreal, Que. 17 Oct. 1937; s. Harry and Pearl (Talisman) E.; e. McGill Univ.; Strathcona Acad.; Dewline Training Sch.; Alfred Joyce; m. Anne d. Martin and Mary Jurbin 30 Nov. 1957; children: Michelle, Harry Ian; FOUNDER & FORMER CHRMN. & CHIEF EXTVE. OFFR., SCOTCOMM RADIO INC.; Founder & Former Chrmn. & Chief Extve. Offr., Scotpage Corp. Ltd.; Former Chrmn. & C.E.O., Scotgroup Enterprises Inc.; Founder & Former Chrmn. & C.E.O., National Paging Corp. NPC; Former Pres. & C.E.O., ScoTeleterminal Inc.; Former Pres., Scotfone Corp.; Pres., Personal Radio Serv. (PRS) Ltd.; Seyton, Inc., Montreal; Seyton Ltd., Vancouver, B.C.; Murjur Holdings Ltd.; Seyco Investments Ltd.; Founder, Scott TV & Radio Serv.; Scotron; Partner and Co-Founder, Epcon Leasing; Past Dir., Candn. Radio Common Carriers Assn.; Chrmn., Mobile Satellite Ctte.; Ctte. Rep., Emergency Preparedness Canada; Nat. Emergency Coordinator, Bahamian Air Sea Rescue Assoc. (BASRA); Am. Radio Relay League; Amateur Radio Licence; Mem., CRCCA (Dir. 1981–84); author of several technical articles; Mem., Temple Emanu-El-Beth Shalom; recreations: art collecting, yachting, classical music, fishing, ham radio (licence: VE2AUU and VE0EE), N. Yacht Murjur II; Address: 3976 Du Havre St., Laval, Que. H4R 1K3.

**EPSTEIN, Philip Michael,** B.A., LL.B., Q.C.; barrister; b. England 30 Aug. 1942; s. Maurice and Esther (Bernstein) E.; e. Univ. of Toronto B.A. 1964, LL.B. 1968; called to Bar, Law Soc. of Upper Canada 1970; m. Joyce d. Samuel and Tania Rapp 25 Dec. 1966; children: David, Deborah, Sara; SR. PARTNER, EPSTEIN, COLE (Toronto); Head, Family Law Section, Bar Admission Course, Law Soc. of Upper Canada 1981– ; Bencher,

Law Soc. of Upper Canada (Gov. Mem.) 1984– ; Chrmn., Legal Education Ctte., Law Soc. of Upper Canada; Lectr. & Prog. Cons., Family Law & Solicitors' Negligence Claims, Cont. Edn. Dept., Law Soc. of Upper Canada; Lectr., Family Law, Osgoode Hall Law Sch. 1981; Family Law, Univ. of Toronto Law Sch. 1989– ; Lectr., Trial Advocacy, Univ. of Sydney Law Sch. 1991; Q.C. 1982; Mem., Attorney Gen. Ctte. on Domestic Violence 1981–82; on Mediation 1987–88; Chrmn., Family Law Section, Ont. Br., Candn. Bar Assn. 1981–82; Vice-Chrmn., Family Mediation Serv. of Ont. 1983, 1984, 1985; Pres., Temple Har Zion 1972–76; Leo Baeck Day Sch. 1978–81; author: 'Family Law' & numerous articles; editor & contbr. author, Bar Admission Course materials; legal affairs columnist, CBC Radio Noon station; Mem., Advocates Soc.; Candn. Bar Assn.; Internat. Acad. of Matrimonial Lawyers; Home: 26 Beardmore Cres., North York, Ont. M2K 2P5; Office: 3200 – 401 Bay St., Toronto, Ont. M5H 2Y4.

**EPSTEIN, Seymour,** B.E., P.Eng.; consultant; executive; b. Montreal, Que. 28 Aug. 1939; s. Harry and Pearl (Talisman) E.; e. Sir George Williams Univ. Cert. in Engn. 1960; McGill Univ. B.E. 1962; m. Gloria Jean; children: Earl Howard, John Stuart, Lauren Parla Siple; step-children: G. Scott Leslie Adair, John James Siple Adair; Chrmn. & Pres., VideoAge Limited; Chrmn. & C.E.O., Seymour Epstein Enterprises Inc.; Imagineering Ltd.; Epstein Equestrian Enterprises Inc.; Chrmn., Seyco Investments Ltd.; Seyton Ltd.; Seyton Inc.; Page Age Ltd.; Incorporated Engineers (Mich.); Pres., Incorporated Broadcasters; Dir., Canwest Broadcasting Ltd.; Enscor Inc.; Barrington Petroleum Ltd.; Paragon Entertainment Corp.; Equion Inc.; Candn. Counc. of Christians & Jews; Assn. Prof. Engrs. Prov. Ont.; Consulting Engrs. Ont.; Soc. Motion Picture & TV Engrs.; Clubs: Island Yacht; Albany; Craigleith Ski; Toronto and North York Hunt; Office: 1090 Don Mills Rd., Ste. 600, Don Mills, Ont. M3C 3R6.

**EPSTEIN, Stanley Winston,** M.D., F.R.C.P.(C); physician; educator; b. Sydney, N.S. 2 Dec. 1937; s. Maxwell and Etta Rose (Green) E.; e. Dalhousie Univ. M.D. 1962; m. Paula Rivka d. Ben and Lillian Gorman 21 March 1965; children: Eric Martin, Cheryl Rae, Ian Leonard, Neil Jordan; CHEST PHYS., RESPIRATORY DIV., DEPT. MED., TORONTO HOSP. 1968– ; mem., Med. Staff Hillcrest Hosp. Toronto 1971– ; Cons. Staff West Park Hosp. Toronto 1975– ; Asst. Prof. of Med. Univ. of Toronto 1971– ; internship and residency Victoria Gen. Hosp. Halifax, Sunnybrook Hosp. Toronto, Toronto Western Hosp., Brompton Hosp. London, Eng. 1961–67; Fellow in med. Univ. of Toronto 1964–65, Assoc. in Med. 1968–71; Hon. Rsch. Asst. Respiratory Physiol. Postgrad. Med. Sch. Hammersmith Hosp. London, Eng. 1967–68; author or co-author numerous publs.; Ed., Ontario Thoracic Reviews (1984–93); various presentations sci. meetings; recipient numerous awards incl. 3 yr. Entrance Scholarship Dalhousie Univ. 1955–58, Friends of Postgrad. Med. Sch. of London, Eng. Bursary 1967, Dr. Henry A. Beatty Scholarship Univ. of Toronto 1967–68; Visiting Lectr. Regional Chest Allergy Unit McMaster Univ. 1981; 6th Owen Clarke Meml. Lectr. Univ. of W. Ont. 1983; Fellow, Am. Coll. Chest Phys.; mem., Ont. (Pres. 1982–83) Thoracic Soc.; Candn. Thoracic Soc.; Am. Thoracic Soc.; Candn. Soc. Allergy & Clin. Immunol.; Am. Acad. Allergy; Israel Med. Assn. Candn. Chapter; Defence Med. Assn. Canada; Acad. Med. Toronto; Alpha Omega Alpha; Tau Epsilon Phi; Hebrew; recreations: Candn. and Inuit Art, woodworking, gardening; Office: Rm. 4–022, 399 Bathurst St., Edith Cavell Wing, 4th Flr., Toronto Hosp., Toronto, Ont. M5T 2S8.

**EPSTEIN, William,** O.C., B.A., LL.B., LL.D.; UN official; b. Calgary, Alta. 10 July 1912; s. Harry Louis and Masha Belle (Geffen) E.; e. Calgary (Alta.) Pub. and High Schs., 1929; Univ. of Alta., B.A. 1933, LL.B. 1935 (Chief Justice's Gold Medal in Law); London Sch. of Econ. (IODE Overseas Scholarship), Cert. in Internat. Law 1938; Univ. of Calgary LL.D. 1971; Univ. of Alta. LL.D. 1984; m. Edna Frances, d. Hyman Hyman, 22 Sept. 1946; one. s. Mark Gil; Secy., UN Disarmament Comn. 1952–72 and Dir., Disarmament Affairs Div. 1954–72; read law with A. L. Smith, K.C., M.P.; called to Bar of Alta. 1936; apptd. to Secretariat of UN as Pol. Offr. 1946; Sr. Pol. Offr., UN Mediator Staff, Palestine 1948; has rep. Secy.-Gen. at various disarmament confs. and at the negotiations that led to the 1963 Partial Test Ban Treaty, the 1968 Non-Proliferation Treaty, the 1971 Seabed Treaty, the 1972 Biological Weapons Convention and as Tech. Consultant to Comn. for Denuclearization of Latin Am. (which prepared the 1967 Treaty of Tlatelolco creating a nuclear-free zone in Latin America) 1965–67; Chrmn., Internat. Group of Consultant Experts, Report on Chem. & Biol. Weapons for Gen. Assembly, 1969; Mem. Group of Consultant Experts, Report on Comprehensive Nuclear Test Ban for Gen. Assembly, 1980; Senior Fellow, U.N. Inst. for Training & Research 1973– ; awarded Rsch. & Writing Grant, John D. and Catherine T. MacArthur Found. 1987–89; Rockefeller Foundation Fellowship 'Conflict in Internat. Relations' 1973–75; Special Consultant on Disarmament to Secy.-Gen. of U.N., 1973–81; Cecil H. and Ida Greene Visiting Prof. Univ. of B.C. 1975; Visiting Prof. Univ. of Victoria 1974–78; Visiting Prof. Carleton Univ. 1977–78; Killam Visiting Scholar, Univ. of Calgary 1978–79; Sr. Research Assoc., Carleton Univ., 1979–83; Regents Lectr. Univ. of Calif. 1981; Lectr. UN Program of Disarmament Fellowships 1979–83; lectr. many organs. and univs. in various countries; served with Candn. Army during World War II; rank Capt.; author 'Disarmament: Twenty-Five Years of Effort' 1971; 'The Last Chance: Nuclear Proliferation and Arms Control' 1976; 'The Prevention of Nuclear War: A U.N. Perspective' 1983; Ed., 'United Nations and Disarmament 1945–70'; Ed. 'A New Design for Nuclear Disarmament' 1977; Ed., 'New Directions in Disarmament' 1981; Ed., 'We Can Avert a Nuclear War' 1982; mem., Alta. Law Soc.; Calgary Bar Assn.; Candn. Inst. Internat. Affairs; Internat. Inst. Strategic Studies; Candn. Delegation to the U.N. 1st and 2nd Special Sessions on Disarmament 1978 and 1982, and to General Assembly of U.N., 1978, 1979, 1980 and 1981; Consultant on Disarmament to Candn. Govt. 1978–86; apptd. by Candn. Gov't. as a Founding Dir. of Candn. Inst. for Internat. Peace and Security 1984–86; Consultant to Parliamentarians Global Action (New York) 1985– ; Chrmn. Candn. Pugwash Group 1978–90; organizer of Pugwash Conf. on Science and World Affairs, Banff, Canada, 1981 and 25th Anniversary Commemorative Meeting, Pugwash, N.S. 1982; Arms Control Assn. (Washington); 1980s Project of Counc. on Foreign Relations (New York); North Am. Counc., Internat. Peace Acad.; Intl. Inst. for Strategic Studies (London); Council of Lawyers' Cttee. on Nuclear Policy (New York); Advisory Bd. of Proliferation Reform Project of Inst. for Resource and Security Studies (Cambridge, Mass.); Group of 78 (Ottawa); Dir. of Science for Peace (Toronto); Candn. Council on Internat. Law (Ottawa); Candn. Inst. of Intl. Affairs (Toronto); decorated by Mexican Govt. with Order of Aztec Eagle (Commander) 1977; rec'd. Peace Award, World Federalists of Canada 1978; Pomerance Award for disarmament work at U.N. 1983; Officer of the Order of Canada 1989; recreations: walking, reading, sculpting, art; Home: 400 East 58th St., New York, N.Y. 10022.

**ERASMUS, Georges Henry;** Dene Leader; b. Fort Rae, N.W.T. 8 Aug. 1948; e. Yellowknife, N.W.T. 1969; m. Sandra Knight Dec. 1984; apptd. Co-Chrmn., Royal Comn. on Aboriginal Peoples 1991– ; Sec. Band Council Yellowknife 1969–71; Organizer and Chrmn. Community Housing Assn. N.W.T. 1969–72; Fieldworker Co. of Young Candns. Yellowknife 1970–71, Regional Staff Dir. 1971–73; Chrmn. Univ. Canada North 1971–75; Dir. Community Devel. Prog. Indian Brotherhood of the N.W.T. 1973–76; Pres. of Dene Nation 1976–83; Northern Vice Chief Assmebly of First Nations 1983–85; Candn. Del. to Internat. Confs. incl. World Council of Indigenous Peoples 1984–91; Co-Chrmn., Indigenous Survival Internat. 1984–91; Nat. Chief, Assembly of First Nations 1985–91; Pres. Denendeh Devel. Corp. 1983; former Bd. mem. Candn. Assn. for Indian & Eskimo Edn.; Founding mem. 'Tree of Peace' N.W.T.; actively involved in MacKenzie Valley Pipeline Inquiry: AFN Spokesperson First Mins. Confs. on Aboriginal Rights 1983, 1984, 1985, 1987; participated in a lobby to combat the anti-fur movement in London, Eng., on behalf of Indigenous Survival Internat.; successful in convincing Greenpeace U.K. to drop their planned anti-fur campaign Oct. 1985; travelled to Soviet Union with the then Min. of Indian Affairs, Hon. David Crombie, to study the economic conditions of the indigenous people living in Siberia 1986; Dir., World Wildlife Fund of Canada 1987; appt. to the Order of Canada 1987; apptd. to Bd., Candn. Tribute to Human Rights 1987; Bd. Mem., Energy Probe Rsch. Found. 1988; Operation Dismantle 1988; Hon. Ctte Mem., Internat. Youth for Peace and Justice 1988; re-el. to Second Term as National Chief, Assembly of First Nations 1988; Mem. Adv. Counc., The Earth Circle Found.; LL.D. (Hon.): Queen's Univ. 1989; Univ. of Toronto 1992; Univ. of Winnipeg 1992; York Univ. 1992; Univ. of B.C. 1993; Bd. of Dirs., Earth Day 1990, Sept. 1989; SAVE Tour 1990; Hon. Mem., Ont. Historical Soc. 1990; co-author: 'Drumbeat: Anger and Renewal in Indian Country'; Home: Yellowknife, N.W.T.; Office: P.O. Box 1993, Stn. B, Ottawa, Ont. K1P 1B2.

**ERASMUS, Paul Jacobus,** B.Com., C.A.; company extve.; b. Senekal, S. Africa, 16 Feb. 1932; s. Paul Jacobus and Susara Cornelia (Botha) E.; e. Rhodes Univ., B.Com. 1952; C.A., S. Africa, 1956; C.A., Can., 1961; became Candn. Citizen 1964; joined Rothmans International Group 1957; transferred to New York later in that yr.; joined Rothmans of Pall Mall Can. Ltd. Feb. 1959 and apptd. Treas. in Apr.; Vice Pres., Finance, Nov. 1967; Pres. Candn. Breweries Limited 1969; Chrmn., Alpa Industry Ltd. 1972, mem. of Bd., Rembrandt Group Ltd. 1977; Managing Dir., Rupert Partnership in Industry Ltd. 1979–81; mem., Ont. Inst. of C.A.'s; Protestant; recreation: tennis; Clubs: Fresmaye, Cape Town; Home: 1A Elsinore Victoria Rd., Bantry Bay, Cape Town 8001, Republic of South Africa.

**ERDMAN, Michael H.,** B.A.; business executive; e. Xavier Univ. B.A. 1962; American Inst. of Banking; Wayne State Univ.; Vice-Pres., Marketing, General Motors of Canada Limited 1990–..; joined present firm (Chevrolet Div., Detroit) 1962; Zone Mgr. Syracuse 1974; Chicago 1975; Reg. Dir. Customer Serv. 1976; Reg. Mgr. Atlantic Coast 1980; Sales Mgr. Trucks 1981; Mktg. Mgr. Trucks, C-P-C H.Q. Warren 1984; Asst. Gen. Sales Mgr. Chevrolet Div. 1985; Mktg. Mgr. Passenger Cars & Trucks 1987; Gen. Mktg. Mgr. 1988; Dir., General Motors of Canada Limited; Volvo-GM Can. Heavy Duty Truck Corp.; Office: 1908 Colonel Sam Dr., Oshawa, Ont. L1H 8P7.

**ERICKSON, Arthur Charles,** O.C. (1973), B.Arch., A.R.C.A., D.Eng., LL.D., F.R.A.I.C., F.A.I.A. (Hon.); M.R.I.B.A.; F.R.A.I.S. (Hon.); architect; b. Vancouver, B.C. 14 June 1924; s. Oscar Ludwig and Myrtle (Chatterson) E.; e. Prince of Wales Sch., 1930–43; Univ. of B.C., 1942–44; 520 Japanese Lang. Sch., (Hons.) 1945; McGill Univ., B.Arch. (Hons.) 1950 (Lt. Gov's Bronze Medal, McLennan Travelling Schol.); Nova Scotia Technical Coll., D.Eng. (Honoris Causa) 1971; Simon Fraser Univ., LL.D. (Honoris Causa) 1973; McGill Univ., LL.D. (Honoris Causa) 1975; Univ. of Man., LL.D. (Honoris Causa) 1978; Univ. of Lethbridge LL.D. 1981; Univ. of B.C. LL.L. 1985; PRINCIPAL, ARTHUR ERICKSON ARCHITECTURAL CORPORATION since 1991; Principal, Arthur Erickson Architects 1972–91; Partner, Erickson Massey 1963–72; World War II service in India and Malaya (Capt.), Candn. Army Intelligence Corps; two Hon. Mentions in B.C. Artists Annual, Vancouver Art Gallery 1941; arch. research in Mid.-East, Mediterranean, Scandinavia, and Britain 1950–53; Asst. Prof., Univ. of Oregon 1955–56; Univ. of B.C. 1956–61; Assoc. Prof. 1961–64; Massey Medals for houses (with Geoffrey Massey) 1955–58; Western Houses Special Award 1961; Can. Council Fellowship, Arch. Research, Japan & Far East 1961; Pan Pacific Citation, Am. Inst. of Arch. (Hawaiian Chapter) 1963; Winner (with G. Massey) Simon Fraser Univ. Competition 1963; Nat. Design Awards, Candn. Housing Design Council 1964; Cert. of Merit, Candn. Wood Designs Awards 1965; Award, Tokyo Internat. Trade Fair 1965; Vancouver Citation Awards 1965–66; Pre-Stressed Concrete Inst. Award 1966–67; three Massey Medals for Simon Fraser Univ., Tokyo Pavilion & Smith House 1967; competition design winner, Candn. Pavilion, Expo '70 in Japan; shared Molson Award ($15,000) 1967; winner Royal Bank Award ($50,000) 1971; Canadian Housing Design Council Award for two residences, Jan. 1975; Internat. Union of Architects' Auguste Perret Award 1975; Am. Soc. of Landscape Architects, President's Award of Excellence for Robson Square 1979; Royal Archit. Inst. of Can., Honour Awards 1980 for Robson Square/The Law Courts, Museum of Anthropology, Eppich Residence, Habitat Pavilion; Two Awards of Merit for Sikh Temple and Champlain Heights Community Sch.; Gov. Gen's Medal for Robson Square and the Law Courts Complex 1982, Yorkdale Rapid Transit Stn. 1982, Museum of Anthropology 1983; Archit. Inst. of B.C. Award for Law Courts 1983; numerous articles and examples or work published throughout the world, T.V. series, 'Looking at Art' 1956; 'The Lively Arts' and 'House at Comox' 1960; 'A Sense of Place' etc. 1966; 'The Architecture of Arthur Erickson' 1975; 'Seven Stones' by Edith Iglauer (a New Yorker Profile) 1979; 'The Architecture of Arthur Erickson' 1988; articles in 'Time' 1972 and 1979; major comms.; Simon Fraser Univ., MacMillan Bloedel Bldg., Man in the Community and Man and His Health (Expo. 1967); Museum of Anthropology, Univ. of B.C.; Robson Sq./Law Courts Complex; Roy Thompson Hall, Toronto; California Plaza, L.A.; San Diego Convention Ctr.; Canadian Chancery, Washington; a Founder, Simon Fraser Univ.; Fellow, Royal Arch. Inst. of Can.; mem. Internat. Council, Museum of Modern Art until 1992, Americas Soc., New York until 1990; Hon. Fellow, Am. Inst. of Architects 1978; Hon. Fellow, Royal Arch. Inst. of Scotland; Hon. mem., Consejo Superior de los Colegios de Arquitectos de España; Hon. mem., Colegios de Arquitectos de Mexico; Companion of the Order of Canada 1981; Gold Medal, Royal Architectural

Inst. of Can. 1984; Chicago Architectural Award (with Philip Johnson and John Burgee) 1984; Grande Médaille d'Or, Académie d'Architecture de France 1984; Gold Medal, Amer. Inst. of Arch. 1986; recreations: architecture, skiing, travel; Club: Simon Fraser Faculty Club; Office: 1672 West 1st Ave., Vancouver, B.C. V6J 1G1.

**ERICSON, Richard Victor,** M.A., Ph.D., Litt.D., F.R.S.C.; educator; b. Montreal, Que. 20 Sept. 1948; s. John William and Elizabeth Mary (Hinkley) E.; e. Alderwood Coll. Inst. 1967; Univ. of Guelph B.A. 1969; Univ. of Toronto M.A. (Sociol.) 1971; Cambridge Univ., Ph.D. (Criminol./Law) 1974, Litt.D. (Criminol./Law) 1991; m. Dianna Lea d. Charles M. McMillan, Toronto, Ont. 31 May 1969; one s. Matthew Simon; PRINCIPAL, GREEN COLLEGE & PROF. OF LAW, SOCIOLOGY AND ANTHROPOLOGY, UNIV. OF B.C. 1993– ; Tutor, Churchill Coll. Cambridge Univ. 1971–73, Laidlaw Foundation Fellow 1971–73, Canada Council Fellow 1974; Asst. Prof. Univ. of Alta. 1973–74; Asst. Prof. Univ. of Toronto 1974, Assoc. Prof. 1979, Prof. 1982–93, Co-ordinator of Graduate Studies in Criminology, 1975–1978, 1987–89, Dir., Ctr. of Criminology & Prof. of Sociol. and Criminology 1992–93; Visiting Research Assoc., Criminology Univ. of Edinburgh, 1974; Visiting Fellow, Churchill Coll., 1979, 1984–85 and Inst. of Criminology, Cambridge Univ. 1979, 1984–85; Porter Lectr., Carleton Univ. 1983; Visiting Rsch. Prof., Coll. of Public Programs, Arizona State Univ. 1991; Parsons Lectr., Univ. of Sydney 1992; Hon. Visiting Fellow, Green College, Oxford Univ. 1993– ; Fellow, Royal Soc. of Can. 1987; research grants awarded by Canada Council 1976–78; Donner Found. 1976–78; Univ. of Toronto 1976–79; Soc. Sci. and Humanities Rsch. Council 1977–82, 1983–84, 1984–85, 1987, 1989, 1991, 1991–94; Ont. Min. of Corrections 1984–86; Solicitor-General of Canada 1987–88; author 'Criminal Reactions' 1975; 'Young Offenders and their Social Work' 1975; 'Making Crime' 1981, (reprinted 1982, 2nd ed. 1993); 'Reproducing Order' 1982 (repr. 1984, 1988); co-author 'The Ordering of Justice' 1982 (repr. 1983, 1986, 1989); 'Visualizing Deviance' 1987; 'Negotiating Control' 1989; 'Representing Order' 1991; numerous articles various law and social science journs.; co-author research monographs 'The Silent System' 1979; 'Decarceration and the Economy of Penal Reform' 1981; 'Policing Reform' 1984; 'News Accounts of Attacks on Women' 1984; 'Crime Stoppers' 1989; co-ed 'Criminology: A Reader's Guide' 1991; 'The Culture and Power of Knowledge' 1992; ed., 'Crime and the Media' 1994; founding co-ed. 'The Canadian Journal of Sociology,' Editor-in-chief 1982–86; mem., Internat. Adv. Bd., 'The British Journal of Criminology'; Corresponding Editor, 'Media, Culture and Society'; mem. Am. Sociol. Assn.; Law and Soc. Assn.; Candn. Law and Soc. Assn.; recreation: travel, walking, reading; Home: Principal's Residence, Green College, Univ. of B.C., Vancouver, B.C. V6T 1Z1; Office: Green Coll., Univ. of B.C., Vancouver, B.C. V6T 1Z1.

**ERLICH, Alan;** television and film director; b. Plymouth, Eng. 12 June 1940; s. Joseph and Belle (Lubell) E.; e. Plymouth Coll.; m. Sabina d. Paul and Elizabeth von Fircks 18 Dec. 1977; children: Sacha, Andrew; commenced career in TV Eng. 1960; emigrated to Can. 1966 becoming a Dir. CBC-TV News; Dir. and later Co-producer Fed. El. Coverages 1968, 1972, 1974; trans. to Drama 1976; dir. numerous prodns. incl. Newsmagazine, Weekend, documentaries, 'King of Kensington,' 'Flappers,' 'Hangin' In,' 'Home Fires,' 'Gift to Last,' 'Littlest Hobo,' 'Check It Out,' 'Tartuffe,' 'One for the Pot,' 'Celimare,' 'Twelfth Night'; co-recipient 1st Michener Award for Journalism 1970; Pres., Dirs. Guild Can. 1984–86 and 1988; Founding Mem., Epilepsy Rsch. Fund of Can.; recreations: sailing, skiing; Address: 122 Garfield Ave., Toronto, Ont. M4T 1G1.

**ERLICHMAN, Louis,** B.A., M.Sc.; union researcher; b. Aalen, Germany 19 Oct. 1947; s. Max and Luba (Baigelman) E.; e. Univ. of Toronto, B.A. 1970; London Sch. of Econ. & Pol. Sci., M.Sc. (Econ.) 1971; m. Sherri d. Frank and Thelma Lecker 26 July 1981; one s. Paul; RSCH. DIR. FOR CAN. INTERNAT. ASSN. MACHINISTS & AEROSPACE WORKERS 1978– ; Econ. (ODI-Nuffield Fellow) Min. of Planning, Entebbe, Uganda 1971–72; Econ. Adv. Min. of Comm. & Industries, Dar Es Salaam, Tanzania 1973–74; Econ./Comm. Offr. Ind., Trade & comm. Anti-Inflation Bd. Can. 1974–77; Chrmn. Can. Pension Plan Adv. Bd.; NDP; Home: 43 Glen Ave., Ottawa, Ont. K1S 2Z6; Office: 300, 100 Metcalfe St., Ottawa, Ont. K1P 5M1.

**ERLINDSON, Melvin E.,** C.A., M.B.A.; financial executive; b. Winnipeg, Man. 1 Jan. 1938; s. Magnus and Evelyn E.; e. Inst. of C.A.s of Man. C.A. 1960; Univ. of Western Ont., dipl. in bus. admin. 1962; Harvard Univ. M.B.A. 1963; m. Gloria d. Elmer and Martha Schneider 25 July 1964; children: Paul, Michael, Christopher; VICE-PRESIDENT, TREASURER, THE MOLSON COMPANIES LIMITED 1986– ; var. finan. positions leading to Div. Controller, The Ford Motor Co. of Can. Limited 1963–68; Consultant, The Coopers & Lybrand Cons. Group 1968–72; Treas., Polysar Limited 1972–79; Asst. Treas., Varity Corp. 1979–86; extensive background in internat. finan. mngt. (has worked in U.K., Spain & Bermuda); Pres., Sarnia C. of C. 1977; Mem., The Soc. of Internat. Treasurers (Convenor 1989–91); Financial Executives Inst.; Dir., MDB (Bermuda) Ltd.; recreation: tennis, cycling; Home: 1178 Colborne Court, Oakville, Ont. L6J 6B9; Office: Scotia Plaza, 40 King St. W., Suite 3600, Toronto, Ont. M5H 3Z5.

**ERNST, Hon. James Arthur;** politician; b. Winnipeg, Man. 19 Nov. 1942; s. Frank Luther and Stella Sarah (Bryson) E.; e. St. Paul's High Sch. and Coll. Winnipeg; m. Dorothy d. Harry and Beatrice Blom 8 July 1967; children: Shannon Lee, David James; MIN. OF CONSUMER & CORPORATE AFFAIRS and GOVERNMENT HOUSE LEADER, GOVT. OF MANITOBA 1993– ; Min. resp. for Sport and Min. resp. for Lotteries 1993– ; joined Ernst, Liddle & Wolfe Ltd. real estate and ins. brokers 1962–88 serving latterly as Pres.; MLA for Charleswood; Min. of Ind., Trade and Tourism, Govt. of Manitoba 1988–91; Min. of Urban Affairs and Housing 1991–93; Exec. Offr. Administered Acceptance Corp., Erlow Holdings Ltd., Niakwa Investments Ltd. and Northwestern Construction Co.; former Dir. Fidelity Trust Co.; Winnipeg Enterprises Corp.; Office: Rm. 317, Legislative Bldg., Winnipeg, Man. R3C 0V8.

**EROLA, Hon. Judith A.,** P.C.; b. Sudbury, Ont. 16 Jan. 1934; d. Niilo M. and Laura (Rauhala) Jacobson; m. 27 Aug. 1955; two d. Laura Elizabeth, Kelly Ann; Pres., Pharmaceutical Manufacturing Assoc. of Can.; Interviewer, Commentator, Performer, CKSO Radio and CKSO TV 1950–56; Acct. Extve. Radio Stn. CHNO prior to el. to H. of C.; Co-owner and Operator, Marina & Tourist Outfitting Business 1970–76; el. to H. of C. g.e. 1980; Min. of Consumer and Corp. Affairs, Min. Responsible for Status of Women 1980–84; def. g.e. 1984; Secy.-Treas. Nickel Belt Riding Assn.; mem. Bd. of Dirs., INCO; Ottawa Ballet; former Bd. mem. Mem. Hosp. Sudbury; mem. Advertising Comte., Sudbury Dist. Chamber Comm.; mem. Sudbury Folks Art Council; Founding mem. Sudbury Little Theatre; Liberal; Lutheran; recreations: skiing, swimming, boating; Home: R.R. 1, Whitefish, Ont. P0M 3E0 (summer) and 11 Lewis St., Ottawa, Ont. K2P 0S2.

**ESAR, Joan,** M.A.; sculptor; professor; b. Montréal, Qué. 1 Jan. 1943; s. Joseph David and Esther (Frankel) E.; e. Ecole des Beaux-Arts de Montréal, dipl. 1964, brevet spec. 1969; Concordia Univ. M.A. 1975; PROFESSOR, UNIV. DU QUÉBÉC À MONTRÉAL (UQAM) 1969– ; Founding Mem. & Pres., Atelier Sculpt Inc. 1980– ; Prof., Ecole des Beaux-Arts de Montréal 1967–69; major sculptures: designed sculpture-fountain, Parc de la Fontaine, Ile des Soeurs, Verdun, Qué. 1990; monumental sculpture-fountain, city hall, town of Ste-Anne-des-Plaines, Qué. 1987; monumental stone sculptpure, 1% project for Min. des Affaires sociales, Ile Bizard, Qué. 1982; group shows incl.: 'Expression Plurielles,' 1990, Grand théâtre du Qué. 1989, 'Dieux et Diables ...' CIRCA, Montréal 1987, Banque d'Oeuvres d'Art & 'Femmes forces,' Musée du Qué. 1984, Stone Sculpture Symposium, Iwate, Japan 1983, Guest Artist, Stone Sculp. Soc. of N.Y.; annual exhibs., Galerie Daniel 'Sculpture '85, '86, '87, '88, '89, '90' Montréal; work rep. in private & public collections; Bd. Mem., The Visual Arts Ctr., Westmount, Qué. 1976–79, 1983–85; Mem., Conseil de la Sculpture du Qué.; Stone Sculpture Soc. of N.Y.; Home: 115, ch. de la Côte Ste. Catherine, Outremont, Qué. H2V 4R3; Office: 2177 Masson, Suite 401, Montréal, Qué. H2H 1B1.

**ESAW, Johnny;** broadcasting executive; b. North Battleford, Sask. 11 June 1925; s. Sam and Miriam (Joseph) E.; e. North Battleford Collegiate Inst. (IODE Scholarship 1941); m. June d. George & Julia Docken 20 Nov. 1953; children: Patrick Alan, Wendy Ann; SPORTS, CTV TELEVISION NETWORK 1974– ; Candn. Army 1944–46; radio & newspaper work, North Battleford 1947–48; sports broadcaster, CKRM Radio, Regina 1949–56; CKRC, Winnipeg 1956–60; CFTO-TV, Toronto 1961–74; Consultant, CTV 1961–74; Pres., Johnny Esaw Enterprises; Chrmn., Sport Mktg. Counc.; Air Can. Amateur Sports Awards; Football Repts. of Can. Hall of Fame Comn.; Dir., Participaction; Toronto Rehab. Centre; Athletes Trust (Figure Skating); IOC-TV Comn.; Chrmn., Host Broadcaster, Lake Placid Olympic Games 1980; mem. United Church; recreation: golf; Clubs: Islandside & Harbourside; Longboat Key (Fla.); Home: #606 – 4 Lowther Ave., Toronto, Ont. M5R 1C6; Office: Toronto, Ont.

**ESLER, John Kenneth,** B.F.A., B.Ed.; artist; b. Pilot Mound, Man. 11 Jan. 1933; s. late William John and the late Jennie Mae (Thompson) E.; e. Silver Springs Dist. Sch. La Riviere, Man. 1948; Pilot Mound (Man.) Coll. Inst. 1951; Univ. of Man. Sch. of Art B.F.A. 1960, Dept. of Educ. B.Ed. 1961; m. Annemarie d. late Hans Schmid 26 June 1964; two s. William Sean, John Dererk; Instr. Alta. Coll. of Art, Calgary 1964–68; Prof. of Art Univ. of Calgary 1968–80; prof. artist since 1962; exhibited pub. and private art galleries Can., U.S.A., Europe, Australia, S. Am.; rep. pub. colls. Candn. and foreign galleries incl. Victoria and Albert Museum, London, Eng.; Albright-Knox Museum, Buffalo; Museum of Modern Art, New York; Nat. Gallery Can.; rep. Can. with 4 prints world exhn. fine art prints Florence, Italy 1976; recipient 30 awards for printmaking and painting; mem. Candn. Soc. Painter-Etchers & Engravers; Candn. Soc. Graphic Art; Print & Drawing Council Can. (Chrmn. 1976–78); Liberal; United Church; recreations: skiing, gardening, tree farm; Home: P.O. Box 2, Site 7, S.S.1, Calgary, Alta. T2M 4N3.

**ESQUIROL, Hubert;** farmer, association executive; b. Edam, Sask. 30 Aug. 1947; s. Elie and Estelle (Gagné) E.; e. Univ. of Sask. Sch. of Agric. 1969; m. Janice d. Scotty Cole 23 Jan. 1971; children: Trevor, Stephanie; PRESIDENT, WESTERN CANADIAN WHEAT GROWERS ASSN. 1992– ; Pres., White Mud Farms Ltd. 1973; Advisor, Western Candn. Wheat Growers Assn. 1980; Dir., Canada Grains Council 1984; Western Grain Research Found. 1989; Ctte. Mem., Fed.-Prov. Task Force on Environment Sustain. 1990; Sask. Producer, Rep. Gross Rev. Ins. Plan 1991; Facilitator, Winnipeg Commodity Exchange (options seminars) 1992; private pilot; bilingual (French); Mem., Sask. Canola Growers; Western Barley Growers; Presenter, Agric. Policy Conf. Ottawa 1989; recreation: hunting, fishing, windsurfing; clubs: Battleford Flying; Home: Box 117, Meota, Sask. S0M 1X0; Office: 201 – 4401 Albert St., Regina, Sask. S4S 6B6.

**ESSON, Andrea Elizabeth,** B.A., LL.B.; lawyer; b. Toronto, Ont. 13 Aug. 1956; d. Donald Wilfrid and Elizabeth Joanne (Shaw) E.; e. Univ. of Toronto B.A. 1978; Univ. of Ottawa LL.B. 1981; m. Christopher s. Grace and Stanley Ashby 28 Nov. 1987; children: Taryn, Neil, Simon Ashby; SENIOR COUNSEL, ONT. MINISTRY OF LABOUR 1990– ; Assoc., R. Noel Bates Burlington, Ont. 1983–85; Winkler, Filion & Wakely Toronto, Ont. 1985–86; Counsel, Ont. Min. of Labour 1986–90; recreation: skiing, tennis; clubs: Osler Bluff Ski, Badminton & Racquet Club of Toronto; Home: 36 Glengrove Ave. W., Toronto, Ont.; Office: 16th floor, 400 University Ave., Toronto, Ont. M7A 1T7.

**ESSON, The Hon. William Arthur,** B.A., LL.B.; supreme court chief justice; b. Vancouver, B.C. 1 Nov. 1930; s. John and Dolina (Morrison) E.; e. Britannia H.S. 1948; Univ. of B.C., B.A. 1953, LL.B. 1957; m. Margaret d. Adolf and Catharine Buchele 2 Aug. 1958; children: John, Catharine; CHIEF JUSTICE OF THE SUPREME COURT OF B.C. 1989– ; called to the Bar in B.C. 1958; practised with Bull Housser & Tupper 1958–79; apptd. Supreme Court of B.C. 1979; apptd. to Court of Appeal of B.C. 1983; Office: The Law Courts, 800 Smithe St., Vancouver, B.C. V6Z 2E1.

**ESTABROOK, Barry,** B.A.; editor; b. Plainfield, N.J. 11 May 1952; s. Howard Albert and Audrey Olive (Reece) E.; e. Pickering (Ont.) Coll.; Queen's Univ. B.A. 1975; m. Suzanne d. Robert and Laura Legaré 9 June 1984; Ed. Equinox Magazine and Ed. Dir. Camden House Publishing 1985–..; Assoc. Ed. Harrowsmith Magazine 1976–78; Sr. Ed. Alberta Report 1978–79; Staff Writer, Financial Times of Canada 1979–81, Sr. Ed. 1984–85; Mng. Ed. present mag. 1981–84; Office: 2031 Shelburne Rd., Shelburne, Vermont 05482.

**ESTEY, Dale,** B.A., U.E.L.; writer; b. North Minto, N.B. 19 Sept. 1948; s. Byron Caleb and Winifred Alice (Stowe) E.; e. Minto Meml. High Sch. 1966; Univ. of N.B. Fredericton B.A. 1971; joined Unipress 1966–67; high sch. teacher 1971–72; Lib. Asst. Govt. Documents 1974–76; full-time writer since 1976; mem. N.B. Arts Bd.; Dir. Maritime Writers Workshop and occasional lectr.; recipient Best Fantasy Novel U.S. Locus Poll 1980; recipient, New Brunswick Bicentennial Medal 1984; Canada Council Grant 1985; finalist CBC Lit. Contest 1988, 1989; Hon. Mention, 'Les Prix Littéraires Moncton 100 Literary Awards' 1990; recipient, Sr. Creation Grant, N.B. Govt. 1992; author (novel) 'A Lost Tale' 1980; 'The Bonner Deception' 1985; (short stories)

'The Elephant Talks to God' 1989; mem. Writers Fedn. N.B. (Pres. 1988–90); Address: 252 Charlotte St., Fredericton, N.B. E3B 1L4.

**ESTEY, Jack Burton;** executive; b. Fredericton, N.B. 18 Apr. 1922; s. Frank Burton and Mary Elizabeth (McCloskey) E.; e. Commercial High Sch., Fredericton, N.B.; m. Lucy Louise, d. Wm. Betts, Millerton, N.B., 2 June 1944; children: Carol, Joyce, Judy; PRESIDENT, A. & R. LOGGIE LIMITED; Hon. Dir., National Sea Products Ltd., Halifax, N.S.; Clerk, Royal Bank of Canada 1939–40; Paymaster, Diamond Construction Co. Ltd. 1945–47, and Purchasing Agent there 1947–52; apptd. Gen. Mgr., A. & R. Loggie Co. Ltd. 1952–59, and Monarch Cold Storage Co. (later Eagle Fisheries Ltd.); Exec. V.P. National Sea Products Ltd. 1967–74; served in 2nd World War as Navigator, R.C.A.F. 1940–45; discharged with rank of Flight Lt.; Mentioned in Despatches; Past Chrmn., Loggieville Sch. Bd.; Loggieville Local Improvement Dist.; mem. Candn. Mfrs. Assn. (Extve. Comte.; Chrmn. N.S. Br.); Pres., N.S. Fish Packers' Assn., 1968–69; Pres., Atlantic By-Products Assn.; Past Pres., N.B. Fish Packers Assn.; Pres. Fisheries Council of Canada, 1963–64; mem. Economic Council of Canada, 1964–67; mem. Fisheries Price Support Board, 1969–72; mem., R.C.A.F. Assn.; Royal Candn. Legion; Freemason (Scot. Rite); United Church; recreation: golf; Clubs: Miramichi Golf & Country (Pres.); Home: Loggieville, N.B. E0C 1L0; Office: 22 Cunard St., Chatham, N.B. E1N 3A7.

**ESTEY, Ralph Howard,** B.Sc., M.S., Ph.D., B.Ed., D.I.C.; plant pathologist; educator; b. Millville, N.B. 9 Dec. 1916; s. Walter Clay and Hazel May (Howard) E.; e. Prov. Normal Sch., Fredericton, 1st Class Teacher's Dipl. 1940; McGill Univ. B.Sc. 1951; Univ. of Maine, M.S. 1954; McGill Univ. Ph.D. 1956; Univ. of N.B. B.Ed. 1960; Imperial Coll., London, England, D.I.C. 1965; m. Dorean Elizabeth d. late Frank T. Pridham, Fredericton, N.B. 22 June 1944; children: Ronald Harry, Frank Pridham; PROFESSOR, DEPT. OF PLANT SCIENCE, McGILL UNIVERSITY 1976–82; Emeritus Prof., 1982– ; Instr., Wartime Emergency Training Prog. 1941–43 (Dir. of Prog. 1943–45); Teacher, Que. High Sch., Quebec City 1945–49; Instr., Carleton Cty. Voc. Sch. 1951–53; Lectr., Univ. of Connecticut 1956–57; Asst. Prof., Dept. of Plant Pathology, McGill Univ. 1957–61; Assoc. Prof. 1961–72; Prof. and Chrmn. 1972–76 (Dept. of Plant Pathology became Dept. of Plant Science 1976); Fellow, Linnean Soc. of London, England; author: 'Essays on the Early History of Plant Pathology and Mycology in Canada' 1994; author of chapter in 'Plant Pathology in Canada' (ed. I.L. Conners) 1972, a chapter in 'Despite the Odds, Essays on Canadian Women and Science' (ed. Marianne G. Ainley) 1990 and of more than 65 papers pertaining to plant disease research and history of plant pathology; mem. Candn. Phytopathological Soc. (Pres. 1978–79, Fellow 1986); Que. Soc. for the Protection of Plants (Pres. 1963–64, Hon. Mem. 1986); Agricultural Inst. of Can.; Candn. Science and Technology Historical Assn.; Candn. Numismatic Assn.; Candn. Soc. for Horticultural Sci.; Agricultural History Soc.; recreations: hiking, numismatics; Club: McGill Univ. Faculty; Home: 91 Devon Rd., Baie d'Urfé, P.Q. H9X 2X3; Office: Dept. of Plant Sci., Macdonald Coll., McGill Univ., Ste-Anne-de-Bellevue, P.Q. H9X 3V9.

**ESTEY, Ronald Norman,** B.A., M.B.A.; business executive; b. Halifax, N.S. 22 Mar. 1948; s. Frank Robert and Marjorie Virginia (Faulkner) E.; e. Queen's Univ., B.A. 1972; York Univ., M.B.A. 1973; children: Michael Adam, Sean Jordan; Founder & Pres., Avatar Communications 1981–..; Mgr., Candn. Analyses, Bank of N.S. 1973–76; Vice-Pres. & Gen. Mgr., A.V.S.R. Inc. 1977–80; Fellow, Inst. Candn. Bankers; Pres., Internat. Assn. Bus. Communicators 1987–88; Home: 468 Beresford Ave., Toronto, Ont. M6S 3B7.

**ESTEY, Hon. Willard Zebedee,** C.C., B.A., LL.B., LL.M.; former Canadian supreme court justice; b. Saskatoon, Sask. 10 Oct. 1919; s. James Wilfred and Muriel (Baldwin) E.; e. Univ. of Sask., B.A. 1940, LL.B. 1942; Harvard Law Sch., LL.M. 1946; m. M. Ruth, d. Norman McKinnon, 1946; children: Wilfred M., John W., Eleanor R., Paul N.; CHANCELLOR, WILFRID LAURIER UNIV.; Special Adv. to Chrmn., Bank of Nova Scotia; Counsel, McCarthy Tétrault, Barristers & Solicitors; Dir., Consolidated Talcorp. Inc.; Potash Corp. of Sask.; Mortgage Insurance Co. of Can.; Bramalea Ltd.; Nova Corp. of Alta.; called to Bar of Sask. 1942 and of Ont. 1947; Prof., Coll. of Law, Univ. of Sask. 1946–47; Lectr., Osgoode Law Sch. 1947–51; law practice, Toronto 1947–72; Mem., Court of Appeal 1973; Chief Justice of High Court, Supreme Court of Ont. 1975; Chief Justice of Ont. 1976; Justice, Supreme Court of Canada 1977–88; Commissioner, various Royal Comns.: Steel Profits Inquiry 1974; Air Canada Inquiry 1975; Comn. of Inquiry on Certain Banking Operations 1985–86; Hon. LL.D., Wilfrid Laurier Univ. 1977; Univ. of Toronto 1979; Univ. of W. Ont. 1980; Law Soc. of Upper Canada 1981; Univ. of Sask. 1984; Univ. of Lethbridge 1987; Companion of the Order of Canada; served in 2nd World War, Candn. Army and R.C.A.F.; Hon. Lifetime Mem., Bd. of Govs., York-Finch Hosp.; Chrmn., Candn. Law Scholarship Found.; former Bencher, Law Soc. Upper Can.; former Pres. (for Ont.) Candn. Bar Assn.; former Hon. Chrmn., Candn. Judges Conf.; Home: Toronto, Ont.; Office: McCarthy & Tétrault, Suite 4700, Toronto Dominion Bank Tower, Toronto-Dominion Centre, Toronto, Ont. M5K 1E6.

**ESTROV, Zeev,** M.D.; physician; cancer researcher; b. Poland 1 May 1947; s. Shabtai and Masha (Portnoy) E.; e. high sch. Rehovot, Israel 1965; Tel-Aviv Univ. M.D. 1975; Cert. Internal Med. 1981; m. Miriam d. Eliezer and Emma Metzler 19 Nov. 1970; children: Yuval, Shunit, Efrat; ASSOC. PROF. OF MED., PRINCIPAL INVESTIGATOR, HEMATOPOIESES RSCH. LAB., UNIV. OF TEXAS; M.D. Anderson Cancer Ctr., Div. of Med., Dept. of Clinical Investigation; residency The Kaplan Hosp. incl. basic rsch. Weitzmann Inst. of Sci., Rehovot, Israel 1975–80; med. teacher and tutor Hebrew Univ. and Hadassah Med. Sch. Jerusalem 1978–89, Lectr. in Internal Med. 1985–88; Sr. Lectr. in Internal Med. 1988– ; Coordinator of Postgrad. Edn. in Internal Med. for Phys., Kaplan Hosp. and Univ. Inst. Postgrad. Med. Edn. Jerusalem 1981–82; Sr. Phys. in Internal Med. 'B' Kaplan Hosp. 1981–87, teacher Nursing Sch. 1978–84; Terry Fox Found. Fellow, Lab. of Hematopoiesis Rsch., Div. of Hematol., The Hosp. for Sick Children, Toronto 1984–87; Depy. Chief, Dept. 'B', Kaplan Hosp., Rehovot, Israel 1987–89; recipient Dr. J. Rogojinski Found. Prize Kaplan Hosp. 1981; Am. Soc. Clin. Oncol. Travel Award 1986; Tisdall Award Best Rsch. Project Hosp. Sick Children 1986; Capt. in Reserve Defence Armed Forces Israel; author over 100 sci. publs. various med. jours.; mem. Israel Soc. Intern. Med.; Israel Soc. Hematol. & Blood Transfusion; Amer. Soc. Hematol.; Internat. Soc. Exper. Hematol.; Internat. Soc. Hematol.; Home: 5739 Bindwood Rd., Houston, TX 77096 U.S.A.; Office: M.D. Anderson Cancer Ctr., Clin. Invest./302, 1515 Holcombe Blvd., Houston, TX 77030 U.S.A.

**ETHANS, Harry Thomas,** B.Comm., M.B.A.; diversified manufacturing executive; b. Minneapolis, Minn. 16 Nov. 1952; s. Jordan T. and Coula (Daska) E.; e. Univ. of Manitoba B.Comm. (Hons.) 1976; Univ. of Western Ont. M.B.A. 1979; m. Margot d. Graeme and Pat Haig 22 Aug. 1980; children: Alexander, Taylor, Paula; VICE-PRES., BUSINESS DEVELOPMENT, ENSIS CORP. INC. 1991– ; Dir., Corp. Devel., Canwest Capital Corp. 1979–83; Dir., Corp. Finance, Shelter Corp. of Canada Ltd. 1983–84; Vice-Pres., Corp. Devel., Federal Industries Ltd. 1985–90; Dir., Carte Internat. Inc.; Delhi Indus. Inc.; Heron Cable Indus. Limited; Neo Indus. Limited; Dir., St. Boniface Gen. Hosp. Rsch. Found.; recreation: golf, squash; clubs: Carleton; St. Charles Country; Winnipeg Winter; Home: 141 Elm St., Winnipeg, Man. R3M 3N4; Office: Suite 1120, 200 Graham Ave., Winnipeg, Man. R3C 4L5.

**ETHELL, Col. Donald Stewart,** O.M.M., M.S.C., C.D.; Canadian armed forces; b. Vancouver, B.C. 23 July 1937; s. Noel Stubbs and Margaret Una (Hutchison) E.; e. Victoria High Sch. 1953; Candn. Forces Command and Staff Course grad.; Candn. Forces Land Forces Command and Staff Coll. grad.; m. Linda May d. Fritz and Karen Endro 27 Feb. 1960; two s. Darrell Gordon, Douglas Wayne; CHIEF OF OPERATIONS, EUROPEAN COMMUNITY MONITORING MISSION, YUGOSLAVIA; joined Candn. Forces 1956, comnd. 1972; served inf. btns. Can., Germany and Cyprus; served as staff offr. Bgde. HQ and as instr. Candn. Forces Offr. Candidate Sch.; many tours of duty with UN Peacekeeping missions incl. 2 yrs. as Sr. Candn. Mil. Observer UN Truce Supervisory Orgn. Israel, Jordan, Lebanon, Egypt and Syria; served 2 yrs. as Dep. Chief of Staff UN Disengagement Observer Force incl. supervision 1974 ceasefire between Israel and Syria on Golan Hts., implemented large-scale POW exchanges 1984, 1985, C.O. Candn. Contingent final yr. of service there; previously served 2 tours in reconnaissance and operational roles UN Force Cyprus; Dir. of Peacekeeping Operations, Nat. Defence HQ 1987–90; Chief of Liaison, Chief of Staff & Cmdr., Cdn. Contingent Multinational Force and Observers, Sinai, Egypt 1990–91; author Central Am. Peace Plan accepted by UN as model; recipient O.M.M., M.S.C., C.D. (most decorated Candn. Peacekeeper); recreations: jogging, sports, bridge; Home: 5708 Layzell Rd. S.W., Calgary, Alta. T3E 5G9; Office: HQ European Community Monitoring Mission, c/o Kablarsku 29, Sengak, 11040 Belgrad, Yugoslavia.

**ETHERINGTON, James Gordon,** B.A.; insurance executive; b. Hensall, Ont. 2 Sept. 1938; s. Archie James and Alma Matilda (Abram) E.; e. South Huron Dist. H.S. 1957; Univ. of West. Ont., B.A. (Hons.) 1961; m. Elizabeth d. Dr. Howard and Grace Ferguson 6 Apr. 1962; children: David, Timothy; VICE-PRES., CORP. AFFAIRS, LONDON LIFE INSUR. CO. 1988– ; Reporter, Kingston Whig Standard 1961–62; Public Relns. Writer, Queen's Univ. 1962–64; Reporter, London Free Press 1964–73; Public Affairs Analyst, Imperial Oil 1973–74; Mgr., Public Relns. (Ont.), Royal Bank of Can. 1974–76; Mgr., Public Relns., RBC, Montreal 1976–82; Dir., Corp. Affairs, London Life 1982–88; Dir., Downtown London Business Assoc. 1989– ; Vice Pres., Orchestra London 1992– ; Dir. & Past Chrmn., London C. of C.; Past Pres., London Reg., Boy Scouts of Can.; Chrmn., Public Relns. Ctte., Univ. Hosp. 1992– ; (Mem. 1983–92); Pub. Ctte., Univ. of Western Ont. 1983– ; Chrmn., Conf. Bd. Counc. of Public Affairs Extves.; Mem., Bd. of Govs., Univ. of Western Ont. 1993– ; Mem., London City Press Club 1982– ; Mem., Candn. Public Relns. Soc. 1974– ; Mem., Internat. Assoc. of Business Communicators 1983– ; Home: 1071 Lombardo Ave., London, Ont. N6A 2X9; Office: 255 Dufferin Ave., London, Ont. N6A 4K1.

**ETHERINGTON, William A.,** B.E.Sc.; business executive; b. Exeter, Ont. 30 Sept. 1941; s. Archie James and Alma Matilda (Abram) E.; e. Univ. of West. Ont. B.E.Sc. 1963; m. Barbara d. John William and Berendina Stewart 10 Sept. 1966; children: Jill, Michael; PRES. & CHIEF EXTVE. OFFR., IBM CANADA LTD. 1991– ; various mktg. & mngt. assignments, IBM Canada 1964–76; Internat. Assignment to IBM World Trade Americas/Far East H.Q. 1976; Vice Pres. 1980; Vice Pres., Finance & Planning & Chief Finan. Offr. 1985; Internat. Assignment to IBM Latin Am. H.Q. as Vice Pres. & Asst. Gen. Mgr., Line Opns. 1988; Dir., IBM Canada Ltd.; Ex-Officio Mem., Bd. of Dir., United Way of Greater Toronto (1993 Campaign Chrmn.); Mem. Bd. of Dirs., Ontario Hydro; Conf. Bd. of Canada; National Quality Institute; Jr. Achievement of Can.; Mem., Business Council on National Issues; Mem. Policy Ctte., Business Council on National Issues; Ont. Business Adv. Counc.; Corporate-Higher Education Forum; Chair, Engineering Sci. Adv. Counc., Univ. of Western Ont.; recreations: golf, tennis, reading, travel; clubs: Bayview Country Club Limited, Granite Club Limited, Hollyburn Country Club (Vanc.); Home: 11 Fairway Heights Cres., Thornhill, Ont. L3T 1K1; Office: 3500 Steeles Ave. E., Markham, Ont. L3R 2Z1.

**ETHIER, C. Ross,** B.Sc., M.Math., S.M., Ph.D.; university professor; b. Edmonton, Alta. 21 Oct. 1959; s. Joseph Ralph E. and Valerie Mary (Girling) E.; e. Queen's Univ. B.Sc. 1980; Univ. of Waterloo M.Math. 1982; M.I.T. S.M. 1983, Ph.D. 1986; m. Karen d. June and Gerald Ernest 25 Aug. 1984; one s.: Richard Alexander; ASSOC. PROF., MECHANICAL ENGINEERING, BIOMEDICAL ENGINEERING & OPHTHALMOLOGY, UNIV. OF TORONTO 1991– ; Asst. Prof., Mech. Engr. & Biomed. Engr., Univ. of Toronto 1986–91; Dir., King's Engineering Assoc.; Mem., Am. Soc. Mech. Engrs.; Assn. for Research in Vision and Ophthalmology; Sigma Xi; Internat. Soc. for Eye Rsch.; Office: Toronto, Ont. M5S 1A4.

**ETIENNE, Errol Herbert Russell,** R.C.A.; Artist; designer; animator; film maker; typographer; creative consultant; ilustrator; photographer; b. Edinburgh, Scotland 28 Apr. 1941; s. Russell Earl and Mary (Glover) E.; e. Los Angeles Art Centre 1961–65; m. Shawn Margaret Wigmore; two children: Michelle Alexandria Noel Etienne, Nicholas Basileo Errol Etienne; m. Wendy Dayton; one child: Christopher Adrain Vance Etienne; m. Judith Ester Goldman; one child: Hunter Alexander Galt Etienne; aka The Frog, Pres., Etienne Creative Inc., Montreal; Frog and Bison Design, Vancouver; Frog and Swan Gallery, Vancouver; Frog and Chicken Advertising, Vancouver; Number One York Street Design, Sydney, Australis; Vance and Etienne Gallery, Vancouver; Frog and Gazelle Advertising Design, Denver, Colorado; Goldman Dixon Etienne, Lancaster, Pennsylvania; Partner, in Carpenter-Etienne, Toronto; Etienne-Drummond, Montreal; guest lectr., various univs.; teaches watercolors, design, painting; exhibited internat.: over 1000 paintings in private collections, over 500 awards internationally; el. Royal Candn. Acad. 1980; articles in Communications Arts Magazine; television interviews; presently travelling on painting tours in N. Am.; exhibiting in Key West, Fla.; recreation: sailing; Address: c/o 1200 So. Glencoe St., Denver, CO 80222.

**ETKIN, Bernard,** M.A.Sc., D.Eng., F.R.S.C. (1970), F.C.A.E. (1987); university professor emeritus; b. Toronto, Ont. 7 May 1918; s. Harry and Mary (Goldberg) E.; e. Oakwood Coll. Inst., Toronto, Ont.; Univ. of Toronto, B.A.Sc. 1941, M.A.Sc. 1947, D.Eng. Carleton 1971; m. Maya, d. Samuel Kesselman, Toronto, Ont., 17 May 1942; children: Carol Elizabeth, David Alexander; UNIVERSITY PROFESSOR EMERITUS, INST. FOR AEROSPACE STUDIES, FACULTY OF APPLIED SCIENCE & ENGN., UNIVERSITY OF TORONTO; joined University of Toronto as Lecturer in Aeronautical Engn., 1942; Asst. Prof. 1948, Assoc. Prof. 1953, Prof. 1957; Chairman, Division of Engineering Science 1967–72; Dean, Faculty of Applied Sci. and Eng. 1973–79; indust. work incl. periods spent as employee and Consultant with various aircraft and other companies, and Defence Research Bd.; Past Pres. of Aercol (consulting engn. co.); Past Pres. of Infrasizers Ltd.; Publications: 'Dynamics of Flight' 1959, 2nd ed. 1982; 'Dynamics of Atmospheric Flight' 1972; technical papers and reports in sundry journs.; Fellow, Royal Society of Can.; Fellow, Candn. Acad. of Engr.; Fellow, Canadian Aero. & Space Institute; Fellow, Am. Inst. of Aero. and Astro.; Assn. of Prof. Engrs. Ont.; awards: Rupert Turnbull Lecturer (C.A.S.I.) 1965; Centennial Medal 1967; McCurdy Award (C.A.S.I.) 1969; Mechanics & Control of Flight Award (A.I.A.A.) 1975; Thomas Eadie Medal (Royal Soc. Can.) 1980; Wright Bros. Lecturer (A.I.A.A.) 1980; Hebrew; recreations: chess, golf; Home: 10 Fashion Roseway, 308N, Willowdale, Ont. M2N 6B6.

**ETROG, Sorel;** sculptor; b. Jassy, Romania; 29 Aug. 1933; s. Moritz Eserick and Toni (Walter) E.; e. High Sch., Jassey, Romania; Tel Aviv Art Inst., 1953–55; Brooklyn Museum Art Sch. (scholarship), 1958; first solo show 1958; Candn. Rep., Venice Biennale 1966; commissions: Los Angeles County Museum 1966; Candn. Pavillion, Expo 67; Olympia York Centre, Toronto 1972; Bow Valley Square, Calgary 1975; Sun-Life Canada, Toronto 1984; Olympic Park, Seoul, Korea 1988; designed and illustrated books: 'The Bird That Does Not Exist' (poem) by Claude Aveline 1967; 'Chocs' by Eugene Ionesco 1969; 'Imagination Dead Imagine' by Samuel Beckett 1972; 'Canadian Film Award' 1968; designed Toronto Symphony Anniversary Coin 1973; wrote and directed film 'Spiral' shown on C.B.C. 1975; designed sets and costumes for 'Celtic Hero' by W.B. Yeats 1978; published writings: 'Dream Chamber' (Joyce and the Dada Circus) 1982; 'Hinges' (play) 1983; 'The Kite/Le Cerf Volant' 1984; 'L'Aquilone/The Kite' 1984; 'Images from the Film "Spiral"' 1987; others; performance of 'The Kite' (A Tribute to Samuel Beckett) 1984; curated: Sculputre Exhbn. (Royal Candn. Acad. of Arts) Olympic Games, Montreal 1967; Exhbn. of Contemp. Outdoor Sculpture, Guildwood Hall, Toronto 1982; Selected Public Collections: selected public collections: Nat. Gall. of Can.; Art Gall. of Ont.; Montreal Fine Arts Museum; Tate Gall., London; St. Peter College, Oxford; Kunst Museum, Basel; Musée d'Art Moderne, Paris; Museum of Modern Art, New York; Guggenheim Museum, New York; Kroeller-Meuller Museum, Holland; Hirshhorn Museum, Washington; Jerusalem Museum; Birla Acad., Calcutta; U.C.L.A.; Hart House, Univ. of Toronto; Bank of Canada, Ottawa; selected solo exhbns.: Montreal; Toronto; New York; Paris; London; Chicago; Los Angeles; Geneva; Amsterdam; Tel Aviv; Venice; Milan; Rome; others; Monographs: William Withrow, 'Sorel Etrog: Sculpture' 1967; Theodore Heinrich, 'The Painted Constructions 1952–1960' 1968; Listed: The Canadian Encyclopedia 1985; Who's Who in American Art; International Who's Who in Art; Hebrew; mem.: Arts and Letters Club; Royal Candn. Acad.; Toronto French Sch. (Bd. of Dirs.); Celtic Arts (Bd. of Dir.); Address: Box 67034, 2300 Yonge St., Toronto, Ont. M4P 1E0.

**ETTENBERG, Elliott,** B.Com., M.B.A.; advertising executive; b. Montréal, Qué. 2 Jan. 1947; s. Bernard and Rosa (Shaffer) E.; e. Concordia Univ. B.Com. 1969, M.B.A. 1972; m. Deborah Elizabeth Sharp; children: Jodi Jennifer, Cale; CHAIRMAN AND CHIEF EXEC. OFFR. PRISM COMMUNICATIONS LTD. 1977– ; Merchandising Cons. Fashion Fibre Div. Dupont of Canada 1969–70; Acct. Supr. Grey Advertising 1970–72; Dir. of Mktg. Consumer Packaged Goods Div. Bowater Canada-Perkins Paper Ltd. 1972–74; Dir. of Mktg. & Sales FBI Foods Ltd. 1974–76; Pres., Strategic Cons., Antrum Marketing Corp. 1976–77; Grant Lectr. Dawson Coll. 1980–81; Dir. Mount Sinai Hosp. 1981–82; mem. Reconstruction Synagogue of Montreal; recreations: alpine skiing, tennis, golf; Clubs: Cavendish; Richford Golf; Nuns' Island Tennis; Home: 191 The West Mall, Ste. 500, Toronto, Ont. M9C 5K8.

**EUSTACE, David F.;** company president; b. Dublin, Ireland 31 Oct. 1931; s. Cecil Rowland Fox and Harriette (Johnson) E.; privately educated overseas; m. Roberta, d. Horace Steeves, Peace River, Alta., 5 June 1954; children; Steven, Gary, James, Talbot; PRESIDENT, CEMASCO MANAGEMENT LTD. since 1978; PROPRIETOR, NOSTALGIC CINEMA since 1982; Salesman, Mutual Life Assurance Co. of Canada, Edmonton, Alta., 1959; H.O. Agency Asst. with Life of Alta., and subsequently rose to Dir. of Agencies and then Asst. Gen. Mgr.; Sr. Consultant to life ins. co's in U.S. with Life Insurance Agency Mang. Assn., 1965–66; returned to Can. as Dir. of Agencies, Global Life Insurance Co., 1966; (subsequently apptd. Vice Pres.); Pres. and Dir., Union Mutual Life Assurance Co., 1970; Chrmn., Pres. and Dir., Constellation Assurance 1970–78; author 'Telephone Touch' 1965; 'Roll Play' 1965; 'The Intruder'; 'Something's Rotten'; 'That's Action'; 'The Eustace Ratings'; Past Area Gov., Toastmaster's Internat.; recreations: cinematography, audio, music, writing; Address: 900 Royal York Rd., Toronto, Ont. M8Y 2V6.

**EVALUARDJUK, Henry;** artist; b. Igloolik, N.W.T. 1923; medium: sculpture, drawings, paintings; 40 group exbns. incl. most recent: Westdale Gallery Hamilton, Ont. 1992, Feheley Fine Arts Toronto 1991, Arctic Artistry Hastings-on-Hudson, N.Y. 1990, 1991, Arctic Inuit Art Richmond, Va. 1991, Inuit Gall. of Vancouver 1990, Candn. Mus. of Civilization Hull, Que. 1990, 'Masters of the Arctic' UN Gen. Assembly N.Y. 1989; solo exbns.: Eskimo Art Gallery Montreal 1987, Waddington Galleries Toronto 1978, Pucker/Safrai Gall. Boston 1977, Royal Bank of Canada Montreal 1969; works in 15 collections incl. art galleries of London Region, Ontario (Klamer Family Coll.), Winnipeg, Candn. Mus. of Civilization, Inuit Cultural Inst. Rankin Inlet, N.W.T., Musée des beaux-arts de Montréal, Nat. Gallery of Can., Glenbow Museum; sculpture presented to Pres. & Mrs. Ronald Reagan during official visit to Canada 1981; subject of articles and catalogues; Home: Iqaluit, N.W.T.; Office: c/o Ingo Hessel, Indian and Northern Affairs Canada, Les Terrasses de la Chaudière, Ottawa, Ont. K1A 0H4.

**EVANGELISTA, José,** L.Sc., M.Mus., D.Mus.; composer, university professor; b. Valencia, Spain 5 Aug. 1943; s. Bernabé and Amparo (Cabrera) E.; e. studied harmony & comp. with Vicente Asencio early 1960s; Valencia Conservatory of Music dip. in composition 1967; Univ. of Valencia L.Sc. (physics); studied composition with André Prévost & Bruce Mather (Montreal); Univ. of Montreal M.Mus. 1973; McGill Univ. D.Mus. 1984; m. Matilde d. Vicente Asencio and Matilde Salvador 16 April 1968; children: Gabriel, David; PROF., FACULTY OF MUSIC, UNIVERSITY OF MONTREAL; Composer-in-residence, Montreal Symphony Orch.; Arpa de Oro Prize 1974, Prize of the Min. of Culture 1982 (both in Spain); his work 'Clos de vie' was recommended by Unesco Internat. Rostrum for Composers 1984; his music has officialy rep. Canada at Internat. Soc. for Contemp. Music 1985, '87, '90, '92, '93; num. comns. incl. Groupe Vocal de France, Kronos Quartet (San Francisco), l'Itinéraire (Paris), Radio Canada, la 'Soc. de musique contemp. du Qué.,' etc.; his music has been performed in Canada, England, France, Germany, Holland, Hungary, Italy, Norway, Romania, Spain, Switz. & the U.S.; Founding Mem., 'Les Evénements du Neuf' (new music) and 'Traditions musicales du monde' (world music) 1978–83; Bd. Mem., Soc. de musique contemp. du Qué.; main works are: 'Clos de vie,' 'Piano concertant,' 'O Bali,' and 'Monodías Españolas' (all pub. by Editions Salabert, Paris & recorded on CD: 'Salabert Actuels' SCD9102/HM83); Home: 7878 Ostell Cres., Montréal, Qué. H4P 1Y9; Office: Box 6128, Station A, Montréal, Qué. H3C 3J7.

**EVANS, Brian Llewellyn,** B.A., Ph.D.; professor of history; b. Taber, Alberta 5 Oct. 1932; s. Evan and Dora Evelyn (Lines) E.; e. Taber H.S. 1951; Univ. of Alta. B.A. 1954; Univ. of London (England) Ph.D. 1961; m. Margaret Burwash 8 Oct. 1954; PROF. OF HISTORY, UNIV. OF ALBERTA 1973– ; Asst. Prof., Univ. of Alta. 1961; Assoc. 1967; Chair, Dept. of History 1968–73; Assoc. Dean of Arts 1972–73, 1974– ; Counsellor, Canadian Embassy, Beijing 1973–74; Assoc. Vice-Pres. (Academic), Univ. of Alta. 1985–92; Dir., Ex Terra Foundation; author: 'Ronning and Recognition' 1991; co-editor: 'Korea and Canada: New Frontiers in the Asia-Pacific Era' 1989, 'Partners in a Changing World: Korea and Canada' 1990; Home: 507, 10030 – 114 St., Edmonton, Alta. T5K 1R3; Office: Edmonton, Alta. T6G 2E5.

**EVANS, Charles James;** manufacturing executive; b. London, Eng. 18 Oct. 1929; s. Charles Frederick and Ellen (Mahoney) E.; e. Sir Walter St. John's Battersea, London, Eng.; m. Andriana Lazarou d. Lazarus and Eleni Ayiotis 2 March 1957; two s. Frank Charles, James Paul; PRES. AND CHIEF EXEC. OFFR. TRIPLE CROWN ELECTRONICS INC. 1973– ; Cost Acct. Redifon Ltd. (subsidiary Rediffusion Ltd.) London, Eng. 1952, Mgmt. Acct. 1958, Chief Acct. 1962, Financial Controller 1963–66; Exec. Vice Pres., Gen. Mgr. Redifon Ltd. Toronto 1966–73; Sr. mem. Soc. Cable TV Engs.( U.S.A.); R. Catholic; Home: 3545 Ponytrail Dr. Mississauga, Ont. L4X 1V9; Office: 4560 Fieldgate Dr., Mississauga, Ont. L4W 3W6.

**EVANS, David J.,** B.Sc., Ph.D.; geologist; b. England 28 June 1947; s. Peter W. and Marjorie E.; e. Univ. of London B.Sc. (Hons.) 1969; Univ. of Wales Ph.D. 1972; m. Ann Griffith 24 Oct. 1968; children: Rupert, Frances, Holly; PRESIDENT, BARRINGTON PETROLEUM LTD. 1987– ; Robertson Research International 1972–77; Robertson Research Canada Ltd. 1977–81; Interwest Resources Ltd. 1981–87; Home: 715 Woodpark Rd. SW, Calgary, Alta. T2W 2S3; Office: P.O. Box 1958, Stn. M, Calgary, Alta. T2P 2M2.

**EVANS, Donald Dwight,** D.Phil., D.D.; educator; b. Thunder Bay, Ont. 21 Sept. 1927; s. Ira Dwight and Jessie (Milliken) E.; e. Univ. of Toronto B.A. 1950; Oxford Univ. B.Phil. 1953, D.Phil. 1962; McGill Univ. B.D. 1955; Laurentian Univ. D.D. 1982; m. Sybil Ruth Blenkinsop 28 June 1952 (div. 1983); children: Stephen, Gregory, Luke, Nicholas; m. Frances Anne Smith 21 May 1983; one s. Gareth; PROF. OF PHILOS. UNIV. OF TORONTO 1968– ; o. Un. Ch. of Can. 1955; Pastor Grand Forks, B.C. 1955–58; Asst. Prof. of Divinity McGill Univ. 1960–64; Assoc. Prof. of Philos. present Univ. 1964–68; Can. Council Killam Sr. Rsch. Scholar 1975–77; author 'The Logic of Self-Involvement' 1963; 'Communist Faith and Christian Faith' 1964; 'Struggle and Fulfilment' 1980; 'Faith, Authenticity and Morality' 1980; 'Spirituality and Human Nature' 1992; ed. and co-author 'Peace, Power and Protest' 1967; co-author 'Analytic Philosophy in Canada' 1982; ed. 'Against the Psychologist's Act' 1978; Pres. Candn. Theol. Soc. 1982–83; recreations: tennis, piano; Home: 395 Markham St., Toronto, Ont. M6G 2K8; Office: Victoria College, Toronto, Ont. M5S 1K7.

**EVANS, Douglas E.,** B.Sc., M.B.A., C.G.A., P.Eng.; b. South Porcupine, Ont. 20 March 1942; s. Edward A. and Jane A. (Doran) E.; e. Sheridan Tech. Sch. Sudbury 1958; Queen's Univ. B.Sc. 1966; Univ. of W. Ont. M.B.A. 1972; C.G.A. 1978; two d. Ann, Jane; PRES., R & D EVANS HOLDINGS INC. 1987– ; Chrmn. & Pres.: Cablecor Data Lines Ltd.; Cablecor Limited; Draftsman, Sutton-Saville, Archs. 1959–62; Project Eng. Shell Canada 1966–68; Financial Analyst Ford Canada 1968–69; Br. Adm. Mgr. Xerox of Canada 1972, Planning, Analysis & Control Mgr. 1974, Mfg. Controller 1976–78; Bus. Mgr., The Globe and Mail 1978, Dir. of Operations 1980–82, Vice Pres. Operations 1982–84; Vice Pres. and Gen. Mgr. 1984–87; recreations: skiing, tennis, travel; Club: Toronto Cricket Skating & Curling; Home: 120 Glencairn Ave., Toronto, Ont. M4R 1M9; Office; 18 Riviera Dr., Markham, Ont. L3R 5M1.

**EVANS, (David) Glyn;** professional singer, voice teacher; b. Brampton, Ont. 17 Feb. 1941; s. Evan William and Myra (Rowlands) E.; e. Brampton H.S. 1960; Lakeshore Teacher's College P.S. Teacher Cert. 1961; Ont. Dept. of Edn. Sr. Cert. in Vocal & Instrumental Music 1964; Opera Dept., Univ. of Toronto grad. 1973; m. Geraldine d. Arthur and Olive Wood 10 July 1965; one s.: Robert David; made profl. debut as tenor soloist with Toronto Mendelssohn Choir & Toronto Symph. singing Handel's oratorio 'Messiah,' Massey Hall Toronto; Eur. debut singing tenor solo in Haydn's 'Creation,' Lyon, France 1984; Canada Council Grant to study voice with Otakar Kraus, London, Eng. 1974; toured with Canadian Opera singing leading roles in 'La Boheme,' 'La Traviata' & 'The Barber of Seville' 1975–77; appeared in award-winning TV opera 'Aberfan' CBC 1977; rep. by Hart/Murdock Artists' Mngt. 1976– ; has sung with every major choral & orch. group in Canada; premiered many original Candn. works; operas: 'Aberfan' 1977, 'The Death of Enkidu' 1977, 'Winthrop' 1987; oratorio: 'Visions Through Darkness' 1988; recordings: 'Meet Me in St. Louis' and 'To God Sing Praise'; Singing Teacher, Queen's Univ. 1987–90; Fac. Mem., Scarborough Bd. of Edn. Music Camp 1988– ; Public School Teacher, Peel Bd. of Edn. 1961–66; North York Bd. of Edn. 1966–71; Home: 303 Ironwood Rd., Guelph, Ont. N1G 3G2; Office: c/o Hart/Murdock Artists' Mngt., 204A St. George St., Toronto, Ont. M5R 2N6.

**EVANS, Hon. Gregory Thomas,** Q.C., B.A., Ph.D., LL.D., K.C.S.G.; commissioner; retired chief justice; b. McAdam, N.B. 13 June 1913; s. Mary Helen (McDade) and late Thomas Vincent E.; e. St. Joseph's Univ., B.A. 1934; Osgoode Hall Law Sch., Toronto, Ont., grad. 1939; St. Thomas Univ., LL.D. 1963, Fredericton, N.B.; Univ. of Moncton, Ph.D. 1964; m. Zita, d. late Thomas Callon, 1 Oct. 1941; children: Thomas, John, Gregory, Rory, Mary, Kerry, Brendan, Catherine, Erin; apptd. Commissioner, Royal Commission on Donald Marshall, Jr., Prosecution 1987; apptd. Commissioner, Conflict of Interest (Ont.) 1988– ; apptd. Mem., Extraordinary Challenge Ctte. Review 1989; apptd. Comnr., Royal Comn. on Compensation for Donald Marshall, Jr. 1990; apptd. Conflict of Interest Comnr., Northwest Territories 1992– ; called to the Bar of Ont. 1939; cr. Q.C. 1953; before appt. to Supreme Court of Ont. in 1963 practised as Sr. Partner, Evans, Evans, Bragagnolo, Perras & Sullivan, Timmins, Ont.; Justice, Court of Appeal, Ont., 1965; Chief Justice, High Court of Ont. 1976–85; Dir., Am. Judges Assn. 1984; V.P. Can. Inst. for Advanced Legal Studies 1978–89; Gov., Am. Judges Assoc. 1986– ; Roman Catholic; Office: Commission on Conflict of Interest, 4th Flr., 101 Bloor St. W., Toronto, Ont. M5S 2Z7.

**EVANS, James Allan Stewart,** B.A., M.A., Ph.D., F.R.S.C.; university professor; b. Galt (Cambridge), Ont. 24 Mar. 1931; s. David Arthur and Isabella Jane (Stewart) E.; e. Guelph C.V.I. 1948; Univ. of Toronto, Victoria Coll., B.A. 1952; Yale Univ., M.A. 1953, Ph.D. 1957; Thos. Day Seymour Fellow, Am. Sch. in Athens 1954–55; m. Eleanor d. James Arthur Ward 16 June 1964; children: James Arthur Laird, Cecily Eleanor, Andrew Lindsay; PROF., DEPT. OF CLASSICS, UNIV. OF B.C. 1972– ; Head, Dept. of Classics 1986–93; Classics teacher, Waterloo Coll., Univ. of W. Ont. 1955–60; Vis. Spec. Lectr., Victoria Coll. 1960–61; Vis. Asst. Prof., Univ. of Texas at Austin 1961–62; Fac. Mem., Dept. of Hist., McMaster Univ. 1962–72; Non-Resident Faculty Mem., Cecil Green College 1993– ; Gertrude Smith Prof., Am. Sch. of Classical Studies, Athens 1991; Fellow, Royal Soc. of Can. 1992; Mem., Mng. Ctte., Am. Sch. of Class. Studies, Athens, Greece; Pres., Class. Assn. of Can. 1982–84; Sec.-Treas., Assn. of Ancient Hist. 1979–82; Anglican; author: 'Social and Economic History of an Egyptian Temple in Greco-Roman Egypt' 1961; 'Procopius' 1972; 'Herodotus' 1982; 'Herodotus, Explorer of the Past: Three Essays' 1991; editor: 'Polis and Imperium: Studies in Honour of Edward Togo Salmon' 1974; 'Vergilius' 1963–73; co-editor: 'Studies in Medieval and Renaissance History'; editor: 'Waterloo Review' 1957–60; literature editor: 'Commentator' 1963–71; Home: 2967 W. 43rd, Vancouver, B.C. V6N 3J2; Office: Buch C265, U.B.C., Vancouver, B.C. V6T 1Z1.

**EVANS, James Eric Lloyd,** B.Sc. (Hon.), M.A., Ph.D.; geologist; b. Miniota, Man., 25 May 1914; s. James Lloyd and Edith Eleanor (Price) E.; e. B.Sc. (Hon.), Univ. of Man. 1936; M.A. Queen's Univ. 1942; Ph.D. Columbia Univ., N.Y. 1944; m. Diana Dorothy, d. late Mark Stanley Peacock, 10 Aug. 1940; two d., Susan Louise, Deborah Anne; Prof., Dept. of Geology, Univ. of Toronto, 1980–84; CONSULTING GEOLOGIST 1979– ; Dir. of Exploration, Denison Mines Ltd. 1970–79; Geol. Survey Parties, Geol. Survey of Can. 1935–37; Sr. Asst. and Chief for Field Parties, Ont. Dept. of Mines 1938–41; Rsch. Geol. Falconbridge Nickel Mines Ltd. 1943–45; Exploration Geol., Frobisher Ltd. and Ventures Ltd. (chiefly in Ungava and Labrador) 1945–50; Mgr., Candn. Office, American Metal Co. Ltd. 1950–54; Field Mgr., Technical Mines Consultants Ltd. 1955–56; Chief Geol., Rio Tinto Canadian Exploration Ltd. 1956–70; Mgr. Exploration Planning and Research 1970; Dir. of Exploration, Denison Mines Ltd. 1970–79; Prof., Dept. of Geology, Univ. of Toronto 1980–84; rec'd Centennial Medal 1967; Fellow, Geological Soc. of Amer.; Founding mem., Candn. Geol. Foundation; Fellow, Geol. Assn. Can. (Past Pres. 1967–68); Soc. Econ. Geols.; Assn. Profl. Engrs. Prov. of Ont.; Candn. Inst. Mining & Metall.; Sigma Xi; Anglican; Home: 5810 Balmoral Rd., Halifax, N.S. B3H 1A4.

**EVANS, The Hon. Judge John David Daniel,** B.A., LL.B.; judge; b. Timmins, Ont. 5 Feb. 1944; s. Gregory Thomas and Zita Bernadette (Callon) E.; e. O'Gorman H.S. 1961; Univ. of W. Ont., B.A. 1967; Univ. of Windsor, LL.B. 1972; called to Bar 1974; m. Valerie d. Thomas and Gilberte Roscoe 25 May 1974; children: Reagan, Quentin, Jonathan; REGIONAL SENIOR JUDGE, ONT. COURT OF JUSTICE (PROVINCIAL DIV.) Sept. 1, 1990; articled to G.A. Martin 1972–73; practiced law Orillia & Toronto, Ont. 1974–76; founded Evans, Kukurin 1976; merged to form Riopelle, Evans, Chornyj & Carr 1980; in practice specialized in crim. law; Judge, Prov. Court of Ont., Crim. Div. 1984–90; Co-founder, Student Legal Aid Prog., Univ. of Windsor (Dir. 1971–72); Teacher, Law Prog., St. Clair Comm. Coll. 1970–72; Northern Coll. 1976–79; Bd. of Dir., St. Mary's Gen. Hosp. 1980–84 (Vice-Chrmn. 1982–84); Big Brothers Assn., Cobourg 1986–87; Mem., Cochrane Law Assn. 1976–84 (Vice-Pres. 1977, Pres. 1978); Candn. Bar Assn. 1974–84; recreations: playing hockey, coaching minor league hockey & soccer; Club: Rotary (Timmins) 1980–83; Home: 592 Spillsbury Dr., Peterborough, Ont. K9K 1K6; Office: 440 Kent St. W., Box 4000, Lindsay, Ont. K9V 5P2.

**EVANS, John Leslie,** B.A., M.B.A., Ph.D.; association executive; b. Seattle, Wash. 12 July 1941; s. Leslie Nathaniel and Edith Alice (Williams) E.; e. Central Wash. Univ. B.A. 1964; Univ. of Wash. M.B.A. 1966, Ph.D. 1968; m. Suzanne d. Jean and Yvette Duval 18 Oct. 1975; two d. Julie Ann, Susan Elizabeth; PRES. AND CHIEF EXTVE. OFFR. TRUST COMPANIES ASSN. OF CANADA 1987– ; Asst. Prof. of Finance, Univ. of N.C. Chapel Hill 1968–70, Univ. of B.C. 1970–75; Dir. Rsch. & Prog. Evaluation, Consumer & Corporate Affairs Can. 1975–79; el. to H. of C. for Ottawa Centre g.e. 1979, re-el. to 1984; Parlty. Sec. to Dep. Prime Min. and Min. of Finance and to Pres. Queen's Privy Council; Dep. House Leader; Chrmn. Standing Ctte. Finance, Trade & Econ. Affairs; Pres. John L. Evans & Associates 1984– ; author numerous articles profl. jours.; mem. Lib. Party Can.; Beta Gamma Sigma; R. Catholic; recreation: golf; Clubs: Rivermead Golf (Past Pres.); PGA National; The Loxahatchee; The Rideau; Royal Vancouver Yacht; Home: 1203 – 100 Bronson Ave., Ottawa, Ont. K1R 6G8; Office: 720, 50 O'Connor St., Ottawa, Ont. K1P 6L2.

**EVANS, John Robert,** C.C., O.O., M.D., D.Phil., F.R.C.P.(C) 1958, M.A.C.P., F.R.C.P. (London), FRSC; b. 1 Oct. 1929; e. Univ. of Toronto, M.D. 1952; Rhodes Scholar, Oxford Univ. 1953; Oxford Scholar, 1954; D.Phil. Oxford, 1955; m. Gay Glassco; has four s. and two d.; CHRMN., ALLELIX BIOPHARMACEUTICALS INC. 1989– ; Chrmn., Torstar Corp. 1993– ; Dir. Alcan Ltd.; Connaught Laboratories Ltd.; Dofasco Inc.; MDS Health Group Ltd.; Pasteur-Mérieux Serums & Vaccines; Royal Bank of Canada; Torstar Inc.; Trimark Financial Corp.; Def. Lib. Cand. Oct. 1978 by-election, Rosedale riding, Toronto; Trustee, Rockefeller Foundation 1982–, Chrmn. 1987– ; Trustee, Walter and Duncan Gordon Charitable Found.; post graduate training in internal medicine and cardiology at Sunnybrook Hosp., Toronto Gen. Hosp. and Hosp. for Sick Children, Toronto, Radcliffe Infirmary, Oxford, and National Heart Hosp., London 1952–58; Chief Res. Phys., Toronto Gen. Hosp. 1959; Research Fellow, Harvard Med. Sch., 1960–61; Markle Scholar in Acad. Med., Univ. of Toronto 1960–65; Assoc., Dept. of Med., Faculty of Med., Univ. of Toronto 1961–65; Dean Faculty of Med., McMaster Univ. 1965–72; Pres., Univ. of Toronto 1972–78; Dir., Dept. of Population, Health & Nutrition, World Bank 1979–83; Chrmn. and C.E.O., Alleux Inc. 1983–89; Pres., Assn. of Candn. Med. Colleges 1972; Chrmn., Counc. of Ont. Univs. 1975–77; mem., W.H.O. Adv. Comte. on Med. Research 1976–80; Chrmn., U.N. Admin. Coord. Comte (Subcomte. on Nutrition) 1981–83; mem. of Task Force on Candn. Unity 1977; numerous hon. degrees from Candn. univs., Yale and John Hopkins Univ., U.S.A., and Limbourg, Netherlands; Hon. Fellow: University Coll., Oxford; London Sch. of Hygiene and Tropical Med.; Companion of the Order of Canada 1978; Order of Ontario 1991; apptd. Med. Research Council 1969; mem. council, Inst. of Med., U.S. Nat. Acad. of Sci. 1972–80; Roy. Coll. Phys. and Surgeons 1972–80; Chrmn., National Biotechnology Adv. Ctte. 1983– ; recreations: skiing, fishing, farming; Home: 58 Highland Ave., Toronto, Ont. M4W 2A3; Office: One Yonge St., Toronto, Ont. M5E 1E6.

**EVANS, John Theodore,** B.Comm., LL.B.; lawyer; b. Toronto, Ont. 30 Apr. 1938; s. Theodore V. and Vassa (Giamou) E.; e. Univ. of Toronto B.Comm. 1961, LL.B. 1964; m. Karen d. Clara and Keith Bissell 19 Dec. 1966; children: Adrienne, Meredith; LAWYER, OSLER, HOSKIN & HARCOURT 1993– ; Dir., Maple Leaf Foods Inc.; Candn. Mini-Warehouse Properties; Internat. Semi-Tech Microelectronics Inc.; Kubota Metal Corp.; Cascades Paperboard Internat. Inc.; clubs: Toronto, Toronto & North York Hunt, The York; Home: 13 Lynwood Ave., Toronto, Ont. M4V 1K3; Office: Box 50, 1 First Canadian Place, Toronto, Ont. M5X 1B8.

**EVANS, Leonard S.,** M.L.A., M.A.; politician; b. Winnipeg, Man. 19 Aug. 1929; s. David and Gwen (Salusbury) E.; e. Transcona (Man.) Coll. Inst.; Univ. of Winnipeg, B.A. 1951; Univ. of Man., M.A. 1953; post-grad. studies 1968–69; m. Alice Mazinke, 27 June 1953; children: Brenda, Janet, Randall; NDP CRITIC FOR FINANCE, MANITOBA; Economic Critic of Opposition 1977–81; Econ., Statistics Canada 1954–62; Canada Mortgage & Housing Corp. 1962–64; Prof. of Economics, Brandon Univ. 1964–69; Min. of Ind. & Comm. 1969–77; Min. of Mines & Nat. Resources 1969; Min. of Natural Resources 1981–82; Min. Responsible for The Man. Telephone System 1981–82; Min. of Community Services & Corrections 1981–83; Min. of Employment Services & Economic Security 1983–88; NDP; Unitarian; Home: 320 Lloyd Cres., Brandon, Man.; Office: Room 111, Legislative Bldg., Winnipeg, Man. R3C 0V8.

**EVANS, Michael Harry,** B.Sc.(CE), P.Eng., C.M.C.; trustee in bankruptcy; b. Birmingham, England 10 Jan. 1932; s. Harry Frederick and Maudé (Cartwright) E.; e. King Edward VI Sch.; Kings Coll., Univ. of Durham, B.Sc. 1953; m. Jean d. David and Sally Laing 19 Oct. 1953; children: Michael David, Lisa Anne; INDEPENDENT BUSINESS CONSULTANT 1993– ; Brian R. Perry & Assoc. 1955–62; Plant Mgr., Mackinnon Struct. Steel Co. Ltd. 1962–68; Pres. & Gen. Mgr., Western Tools & Indus. Ltd. & Alwest Marine Inc. 1968–74; Principal, Woods Gordon 1974–82; Partner, & Sr. Vice-Pres., Ernst & Young Inc. 1982–92; Chief Operating Offr., Pollard Banknote Limited 1992–93; Mem., Int. of Cert. Mngt. Cons. of Man.; Gen. Mem., Candn. Insolvency Assn.; Man. Insolvency Assn. (Pres. 1984–85); recreations: golf; Clubs: St. Charles Country Club (Pres. 1989–92), Manitoba Club; Home: 202 - 3281 Pembina Highway, Winnipeg, Man. R3V 1T7; Office: 2700 - 360 Main St., Winnipeg, Man. R3C 4G9.

**EVANS, Nancy Remage,** Ph.D.; astronomer; b. Taunton, Mass. 19 May 1944; d. Russell and Esther (Swaffield) Remage; e. Wellesley Coll. B.A. 1966; Univ. of Toronto M.Sc. 1969, Ph.D. 1974; m. Martin G. s. Griffith and Dorothy B. 3 Aug. 1968; children: Lisa Remage, Kathrine Griffith; ASSOC. DIR., SPACE ASTROPHYSICS LAB., INST. FOR SPACE & TERRESTRIAL SCI., YORK UNIV. 1991– ; post-doct. fellow/rsch. assoc., Univ. of Toronto (part-time) 1975–82; Asst. Prof., Erindale Coll., Univ. of Toronto 1982–83; Res. Astronomer, Internat. Ultraviolet Explorer Satellite 1983–86; Rsch. Assoc., Univ. of Toronto 1986–88; Institute for Space & Terrestrial Sciences 1988– ; Mem., Am. & Candn. Astronom. societies; Internat. Astron. Union (Sec., Comm. 27 1979–82); author of articles in profl. jours.; Home: 183 Briar Hill Ave., Toronto, Ont. M4R 1H8; Office: 4700 Keele St., North York, Ont. M3J 1P3.

**EVANS, Steve W.;** documentary photography; b. Richmond, Ont. 5 Nov. 1955; s. William Darwin and Patricia Margaret Mary (Dallaire) E.; e. St. Philip's Separate Sch. Richmond; South Carleton High Sch., Richmond, Ont.; St. Pius X High Sch. Ottawa 1974; self taught photographer; author: 'Heart and Soul' (portraits of Can.'s Ottawa Valley); finalist, Citizen book awards 1987; 'Up the Line' (more portraits of Can.'s Ottawa Valley) 1989; 'The Back Forty' (Farm Life in the Ottawa Valley); 'The Road Home' (Images of the Ottawa Valley) 1992; Home: 199 Briston Pr., Ottawa, Ont. K2G 5R5.

**EVELYN, George E.,** B.Mus., M.Mus., D.M.A.; university professor, musician; b. Sapulpa, Oklahoma 12 Jan. 1943; s. George E. and D. Jane (Macmillan) E.; e. Tulsa Central H.S. 1960; Oklahoma Baptist Univ. B.Mus. 1968; Univ. of N. Texas M.Mus. 1970, D.M.A. 1981; m. Lottie M. d. Henry and Katherine Austin 16 Aug. 1980; children: Jeff S. Evelyn, R. Jason Evelyn, Katherine Austin-Evelyn, Jeremy Austin-Evelyn; PROF., DEPT. OF MUSIC, UNIV. OF LETHBRIDGE 1982– ; taught at Southeastern Oklahoma State Univ. 1971–73; Mt. Allison Univ. 1973–82; performed with Edmonton, Victoria, Regina, Saskatoon, Atlantic and Newfoundland symphonies, Vanc. CBC Orch., Mt. Royal Festival Chorus & Orch., Amadeus Choir & Orch.; soloist: Classical Music Fest. Eisenstadt, Austria, Montana Chorale (European tour); conductor: Vox Musica Choral Soc., U. of L. Singers, Mt. Allison Choral Soc., Alta. Youth Choir, Sask. Youth Choir; adjudicator: Toronto, Sask., Regina, Moose Jaw, Moncton Music festivals, B.C., Nfld. & Man. Prov. Finals Music festivals; Mem., Bd. of Dir., Alta. Choral Fed. (Past Pres.); Assn. of Candn. Choral Conductors; Mem., Nat. Assn. of Teachers of Singing & Am. Choral Dir. Assn.; taught at Naramata Summer School B.C., Musicamrose Alta., Saskatchewan Sings Regina & Saskatoon; Elder, St. Andrew's Presbyn. Ch.; Music Dir., Southminster United Church, Lethbridge, Alta.; clubs: Picture Butte Golf & Winter; Office: Lethbridge, Alta. T1K 3M4.

**EVERATT, Michael Roy;** network integrator; b. Toronto, Ont. 3 Dec. 1943; s. Roy Arthur and Emily Mae (Burton) E.; m. Lesley d. Jack and Dorothy Lind 3 Dec. 1965; children: Scott, Jenelle; PRES., LanSTART COMMUNICATIONS INC. 1987– ; Dir. Hedch Holdings Inc.; Terstar Enersystems Inc.; Operations Mgr. York Cablevision 1968–79; Dir. of Eng. Graham Cable 1979–83; Gen. Mgr. Cablenet Ltd. 1983–1987; Winner of 1989 Ontario Chamber of Commerce Special Merit Award for Business Achievement, and Oakville Chamber of Commerce Entrepreneur of the Year Award; mem. Candn. Cable TV Assn.; Soc. Cable TV Engs.; recreations: swimming, baseball, jogging; Club: Oakville Skating; Home: 1405 Kathleen Cres., Oakville, Ont. L6H 2G6; Office: 504 Iroquois Shore Rd., Oakville, Ont. L6H 3K4.

**EVERETT, Hon. Douglas Donald,** LL.B.; senator; b. Vancouver, B.C. 12 Aug. 1927; s. Horace and Catherine M. (Ritchie) E.; e. Maple Grove (Vancouver), Univ. (Victoria) and Ravenscourt (Winnipeg) Schs., 1943; Royal Candn. Naval Coll., Royal Roads, 1943–45; R.C.N. 1943–47 (Sub/Lieut.); Osgoode Hall Law Sch., LL.B. 1947–50; Univ. of Man., LL.B. 1951; m. Patricia G., d. Charles Vince Gladstone, 23 Feb. 1952; 6 children; Chrmn. & C.E.O., Royal Canadian Securities Ltd.; Dir. Gendis Inc.; United Canadian Shares Ltd.; Dir., Max Bell Institute of Government-Business Relations; called to Bars of Ont. 1950, Man. 1951; apptd. to Senate of Can. Nov. 1966; past Chrmn., Standing Senate Committee on National Finance; Independent; Anglican; Clubs: Manitoba; St. Charles Country; York (Toronto); Rideau (Ottawa); Mid Ocean, Bermuda; Home: 514 Wellington Cres., Winnipeg, Man. R3M 0B9; Offices: The Senate, Ottawa, Ont. K1A 0A4 and 800 – 240 Graham Ave., Winnipeg, Man. RC3 0J7.

**EVERNDEN, Lorne Leslie Neil,** M.Sc., Ph.D.; educator; b. Vancouver, B.C. 7 May 1943; s. Leslie Hal and Mary Acheson (Nesbitt) E.; e. Univ. of Alta., B.Sc. 1965, M.Sc. 1966, Ph.D. 1976; m. Frances d. Edward and Ruth Wallace 29 Apr. 1967; two s. Derek Andrew, Christopher Blake; ASSOC. PROF. OF ENVIRONMENTAL STUDIES, YORK UNIV. 1981– , Assoc. Dean 1986–88; Instr. Univ. of W. Ont. 1970–72; Rsch. Assoc. Univ. of Alta. 1975–76; Asst. Prof. York Univ. 1976–81; author 'The Natural Alien' 1985; 'The Social Creation of Nature' 1992; ed. 'The Paradox of Environmentalism' 1984; Office: 4700 Keele St., North York, Ont. M3J 1P3.

**EVERS, Frederick T.,** B.Sc., M.Sc., Ph.D.; sociologist; b. Greenport, Long Island, N.Y. 11 Mar. 1949; s. Horace Towler and Ruth Norma (Sexauer) E.; e. Cornell Univ. B.Sc. 1971; Iowa State Univ. M.Sc. 1973, Ph.D. 1979; m. Susan d. Aubrey and Eleanor Pickels 25 July 1970; children: Jerry Joyce, Courtney Ann; ASSOC. PROF. OF SOCIOL. & ANTHROPOL., UNIV. OF GUELPH 1985– ; Rsch. Asst. and Instr. Iowa State Univ. 1971–75; Social Sci. Systems Analyst, Social Sci. Computing Lab. Univ. of W. Ont. 1975, Asst. Dir. (Instrn.) of Lab. 1976; during next 8 yrs. devel. computing & quantitative methods courses & course modules social sci. students, Asst. Prof. of Sociol. 1983; co-investig. study 'Making the Match Between University Graduates and Corporate Employers in Canada' and co-author Report to Corporate Higher-Edn. Forum's Task Force Human Resources Mgmt. & Status Higher Edn., Montréal 1986; author or co-author numerous conf. papers, rsch. monographs, jour. publs., reviews; recipient New York State Regents Scholarship 1967–71; George Freeman Award Iowa State Univ. 1975; mem. Candn. Sociol. & Anthropol. Assn.; Candn. Soc. for the Study of Higher Education; Home: 45 Bishop Court, Guelph, Ont. N1G 2R8; Office: Guelph, Ont. N1G 2W1.

**EVRAIRE, Lt.-Gen. Richard Joseph,** C.M.M., C.D., B.Eng.; Canadian armed forces; b. Ottawa, Ont. 28 March 1938; s. Ernest and Fernande (Vachon) E.; e. Brébeuf and Académie La Salle, Ottawa; Coll. Militaire Royal de Saint-Jean, Qué.; Royal Mil. Coll. Kingston, Ont.; McGill Univ. B.Eng. 1960; Queen's Univ. M.P.A. (Master in Public Admin.) 1989; Candn. Army Staff Coll. Kingston 1965–66; m. Thérèse d. Jean and Eliane Valiquette 20 May 1961; COMMANDANT, NATO DEFENCE COLLEGE (ITALY); joined Royal 22e Regt. 1960 serving various positions Can., W. Germany (NATO), India & Pakistan (UN) to 1975; Commandant, Coll. Militaire Royal de Saint-Jean, Qué. 1975, Commdr. Candn. UN Contingent Middle E., Ismailia, Egypt 1978, Dir. Gen. Mgmt. Services NDHQ Ottawa 1979, Commdr. 4th Candn. Bgde. W. Germany (NATO) 1982, Commandant Nat. Defence Coll. Kingston 1984, Chief of Land Doctrine & Operations NDHQ 1986; Candn. Military Rep. to NATO (Brussels) 1988– ; Candn. Rep. Military Ctte. in Permanent Session (Brussels) 19..–..; author: 'Chambre 204' stage play 1982; co-author & ed.: 'Une brigade Canadienne à l'Otan' 1983; mem. Eng. Inst. Can.; Assns. des auteurs Francophones du Can.; Hon. 'Ancien,' NATO Defence Coll., Rome, Italy 1990; recreations: golf, running; Address: Viale della Civilta del Lavoro 38, 00144 Rome, Italy.

**EWAN, George Thomson,** B.Sc., Ph.D.; physicist; b. Edinburgh, Scot. 6 May 1927; s. Alexander Farmer and Jeannie Young (Taylor) E.; e. Univ. of Edinburgh, B.Sc. (1st Class Hons., Physics) 1948, Ph.D. (Physics) 1952; m. Maureen Louise, d. R. S. Howard, Edinburgh, Scot., 7 Aug. 1952; children: Elizabeth Louise, Robert Alexander; PROF. OF PHYSICS, QUEEN'S UNIV., since 1970; Asst. Lectr., Edinburgh Univ., 1950–52; Research Assoc., McGill Univ., 1952–53 and Nat. Research Council Post doctoral Fellow there 1953–55; Asst. Research Offr., Atomic Energy of Canada Ltd., Chalk River, Ont. 1955–58; Assoc. Research Offr., 1958–62; Sr. Research Offr., 1962–70; Ford Foundation Fellow, Niels Bohr Inst., Copenhagen, 1961–62; Visiting Scientist, Lawrence Radiation Lab., Berkeley, Cal., 1966; Head, Dept. of Physics, Queen's Univ. 1974–77; Research Associate, CERN, Geneva 1977–78 and 1984; JSPS Fellow, Tokyo 1986; contrib. author, 'Alpha-, Beta- and Gamma-Ray Spectroscopy' 1965 and 'Progress in Nuclear Instrumentation and Techniques, Vol. III' 1968; has publ. more than 90 scient. papers on topics in nuclear physics; rec'd Am. Nuclear Soc. Radiation Industry Award 1967 (for pioneering work in devel. of lithium drifted germanium gamma-ray spectrometers); rec'd. Gold Medal for Achievement in Physics, Candn. Assoc. of Physicists 1987; mem., Candn. Assn. Physics; Fellow, Royal Soc. of Canada; Royal Soc. of Edinburgh; Am. Physical Society; Royal Soc. of Arts; mem. Assn. of Profl. Engrs.; United Church; recreations: golf, skiing, canoeing; Home: 66 Fairway Hill Cres., Kingston, Ont. K7M 2B4.

**EWART, Scott L.;** soft drink industry executive; b. London, Ont. 4 Jan. 1954; e. Univ. of Toronto; Univ. of Windsor, Yale Univ.; m. Melinda Yates; DIVISIONAL COUNSEL, COCA-COLA GREAT BRITAIN & IRELAND 1993– ; Dir., Beverage Services Ltd.; Coca-Cola Ltd.; Coca-Cola Foods Canada Inc.; Coca-Cola Holdings (United Kingdom) Ltd.; Coca-Cola Distributors (Ireland) Ltd.; Associate, Osler Hoskin & Harcourt 1983–86; Securities Council & Asst. Sec., Northern Telecom Limited 1986–89; Vice-Pres., General Counsel & Secretary, Coca-Cola Ltd. 1989–93; Dean's Medal, Univ. of Windsor Law School; Bradshaw Economics Scholarship, Univ. of Toronto; Mem., Internat. Bar Assn.; Candn. & American Bar Assns.; Office: 1 Queen Caroline St., London W69 HQ, England.

**EWASCHUK, Eugene Glen;** superior court judge; b. Windsor, Ont. 23 June 1940; s. Paul and Helen Catherine (Urbanowski) E.; e. Assumption Univ., B.A. 1961; Osgoode Hall Law Sch. LL.B. 1964; m. Jean d. Joseph and Julia Kulesza 15 July 1972; children: Glen, Michael, Celeste; JUDGE, ONTARIO COURT OF JUSTICE 1990– ; admitted to Ont. Bar 1966; Asst. Crown Attorney, Co. of York 1966–72; Assoc. Law Prof., Univ. of Windsor 1972–74; admitted to Sask. Bar 1974; Dir., Crim. Justice, Prov. of Sask. 1974–76; Dir., Crim. Law Amendments, Fed. Dept. of Justice 1976–81; Gen. Couns. (Crim. Law) 1981–83; Judge, Supreme Court of Ont. 1983–90; participated in drafting & testimony re Candn. Charter of Rights & Freedoms; pleaded numerous Supreme Court of Can. cases; author: 'Criminal Pleadings and Practice in Canada' 1987, 2nd ed.; over 29 pub. articles; Office: 130 Queen St. W., Toronto, Ont. M5H 2N5.

**EWEN, Paterson,** R.C.A.; artist; educator; b. Montreal, Que. 7 Apl. 1925; s. William Paterson and Edna Mary (Griffis) E.; e. Montreal W. High Sch. 1948; Montreal Museum Sch. of Fine Art & Design (studied under Goodridge Roberts and Arthur Lismer) Dipl. in Painting, Sculpture and Teaching of Child Art 1950; retired 1987 as Professor Emeritus, Univ. of Western Ont.; D.Litt., Univ. of Western Ont. 1989; D.Laws, Concordia Univ. 1989; continues to show in Canada and internationally; one man exhbns.: Carmen Lamanna Gall. 1971–90; Equinox Gall., Vancouver, B.C. 1992, 1993; Paolo Baldacci Gallery, New York, N.Y. 1992, 1993; and numerous public galleries; served with Candn. Army 1943–46, N.W. Europe; recreations: naturalist, walking, reading; Home: 1015 Wellington St., London, Ont. N6A 3T5.

**EWENS, Douglas S.,** Q.C., LL.B.; lawyer; b. Toronto, Ont. 26 Oct. 1945; s. Sydney Eric and M. Elizabeth (McKay) E.; e. McMaster Univ. 1964–66; Osgoode Hall Law Sch., LL.B. 1969; Q.C. 1990; m. Janet d. John and Eleanor Tinkler 26 June 1968; children: Krysta, Lindsay, Steven, Jill; PARTNER, McCARTHY TÉTRAULT, BARRISTERS & SOLICITORS 1977– ; Assoc. 1971; Mem., Candn. Tax Found. (Gov. 1986–89); Ministers Adv. Counc. on Tax Admin. 1986–89; Candn. Petroleum Tax Soc.; Candn. C. of C. (Tax Ctte.); Candn. Bar Assn.; Independent Petroleum Assn. of Can. (Tax Ctte.); Law Soc. of U.C.; Law Soc. of Alta.; co-author: 'The Income Tax Law of Canada' 5th ed.; editor: 'Corporate Reorganizations Feature of the Canadian Tax Journal'; recreations: golf, skiing, hiking, trail riding; clubs: Calgary Petroleum, Willow Park Golf, Glenmore Racquet; Home: 819 Lake Placid Dr. S.E., Calgary, Alta. T2J 4B9; Office: 3300, 421 – 7th Ave. S.W., Calgary, Alta. T2P 4K9.

**EYRE, The Hon. Dean Jack;** retired diplomat; b. Westport, N.Z. 8 May 1914; e. Hamilton High Sch., N.Z.; Auckland Univ.; m. Patricia Naomi Arnoldson; two s., one d.; High Commissioner for New Zealand, 1968–73, reappointed 1976–80; Mang. Dir. Airco (N.Z.) Ltd., Auckland (founded 1936); M.P. (Nat.) for N. Shore, N.Z., 1949–66; Min. of Customs 1954–56; Min. of Social Security, Min. of Tourist and Health Resorts, 1956–57; Min. of Housing, Min. of Defence 1957, Min. of Police, 1960–63; Min. of Defence 1960–66, Min. of Tourism and Publicity, 1961–66; joined Royal Navy, Halifax N.S.; served with RNVR during World War II; rank Lt.; Pres., Jr. Nat. League, Remuera, Auckland, 1938; Roy. Commonwealth Soc.; mem., Victoria League London U.K.; recreations: golf, boating, fishing; Clubs: Royal N.Z. Yacht Sqdn.; Northern (N.Z.); Wellington (N.Z.); Officers' (Auckland); Royal Ottawa Golf; Home: 517 Wilbrod St., Ottawa, Ont. K1N 5R4.

**EYRE, Ivan,** B.F.A., R.C.A.; painter; b. Tullymet, Sask. 15 Apr. 1935; s. Thomas and Katie (Jaworski) E.; e. elem. schs. and Nutana Coll. Inst. Saskatoon 1953; Univ. of Sask. Drawing & Painting 1952; Univ. of Man. Sch. of Art B.F.A. 1957; Univ. of N. Dak. grad. asst. 1958; m. Brenda Yvonne, Winnipeg, Man. June 1957; two s. Keven Jules, Tyrone Thomas; solo exhns. incl.: Univ. of Man. 1962, 1964, 1976; Montreal Museum of Fine Arts 1964; Winnipeg Art Gallery 1964, 1966, 1969, 1974, 1982, 1988, 1992; Fleet Gallery Winnipeg 1965, 1969, 1972; Albert White Galleries Toronto 1965; Yellow Door Gallery Winnipeg 1966; Atelier Vincitore Gallery Brighton, Eng. 1967; Mount Allison Univ. 1968; Mendel Art Gallery Saskatoon 1968; Morris Gallery Toronto 1969, 1971, 1973; Frankfurter Kunstkabinett W. Germany 1973; Burnaby Art Gallery 1973; Art Gallery of Greater Victoria 1973, 1982; McIntosh Gallery Univ. of W. Ont. 1973; Siemens Werk Erlangen, W. Germany 1974; Playhouse Theatre Fredericton and N.B. Museum Saint John 1976; Nat. Gallery Can. 1978; Mira Godard Gallery Toronto 1978, 1979, 1980, 1990, 1992; Equinox Gallery Vancouver 1978, 1981; Robert McLaughlin Gallery Oshawa 1980; Rodman's Hall St. Catharines 1980; Art Gallery of Windsor; Beaverbrooke Art Gallery; London Regional Art Gallery; Sir George Williams Art Galleries, Montreal; Canadian Cultural Centre, Paris 1982; Canada House, London 1982; Talbot Rice Gallery, Edinburgh 1982; Evelyn Aimis Fine Art, Toronto 1985, 1987; Brian Melnychenko Gall., Winnipeg 1981, 1987; The National Gall. of Canada, Ottawa 1988; 'Ivan Eyre, Personal Mythologies: Images of the Milieu, Figurative Paintings 1957 to 1988' touring Winnipeg Art Gall.; Nickle Art Museum, Calgary; Edmonton Art Gallery; London Regional Art Gall.; 49th Parallel, New York, N.Y. 1988; rep. numerous group exhns. since 1956; rep. in various pub., corporate and private colls. incl. Nat. Gallery, Montreal Museum of Fine Arts, Vancouver Art Gallery, Winnipeg Art Gallery, Victoria Art Gallery, Hamilton Art Gallery, Art Gallery of Ont.; works publ. various art journs., books, catalogues, films; subject of 'Ivan Eyre' (by George Woodcock) 1981; rec'd Can. Council Sr. Grants 1965, 1977; Queen's Silver Jubilee Medal 1977; Acad. of Italy with Gold Medal 1980; The Candn. Art Portfolio Commission for Newfoundland Historic Parks Assn. 1985; Assoc., Accademia Italia Delle Arti E Del Lavoro; University of Manitoba Alumni Jubilee Award 1982; Address: 1098 rue des Trappistes, Winnipeg, Man. R3V 1B8.

**EYRE, John Lamarche,** LL.B., B.A.; shipping consultant; b. Orange, N.J. 30 Oct. 1917; s. John A. and Ethel (Lamarche) E.; e. Millbrook (N.Y.) Sch.; Yale Univ., B.A., 1940; Harvard Business Sch., Naval Supply, 1943; Fordham Law Sch., LL.B., 1949; m. Cornelia, d. Martin LeBoutillier, 17 July 1952; children: Stephen, Martin Banning, Alison; INDEPENDENT SHIPPING CONSULTANT to World Bank, U.N. and Port of Halifax 1981– ; Ship's Offr., Grace & Robin Lines, 1940–43; Port of N.Y. Authority, 1945–55; Transp. Consultant, 1955–59; Sr. Transport Consultant, Arthur D. Little Inc., Cambridge, Mass., 1959–66; Pres. & Chrmn.,

Saguenay Shipping Ltd. (and Pres. and Dir., Alcan Shipping Services, Ltd.; Dir., Alcan Ore Ltd.; Chaguaramas Terminals Ltd. (Trinidad); Sprostons (Guyana) Ltd.; Saguenay Shipping (U.K.) Ltd.) 1966–76; Pres. Genstar Overseas Ltd. 1976–80; Dir., Oceanic Finance Ltd. 1976–80; Transmode Consultants, Toronto 1986; Visiting Prof. of Transport, U.S. Merchant Marine Acad., Kings Point, N.Y. 1987; served as Lieut. during 2nd World War, with U.S. Naval Reserve, in Solomon and Philippine Island campaigns, 1943–45; Pres. 1973–74 Candn. Shipowners Assn.; mem., Candn. Comte., Amer. Bureau of Shipping; mem. Sci. Counc. of Can.; Transp. Comte., Pacific Basin Econ. Coun.; past Pres., Candn. Transp. Research Forum; Alumni Bd., Yale Univ.; recreations: sailing, beagling, fishing, skiing; Clubs: Yale & Anglers (NYC); Address: Chemin Erables, Abercorn, Que. J0E 1B0.

**EYTON, Hon. J. Trevor,** O.C., Q.C., B.A., LL.B., LL.D. (Hon.); b. Quebec City, Que. 12 July 1934; s. late John and late Dorothy Isabel E.; e. Beaupré (Que.) Pub. Sch.; Jarvis Coll. Inst. Toronto; Univ. of Toronto B.A. 1957 (Victoria Coll.), LL.B. 1960; Univ. of Waterloo, LL.D. (Hon.) 1992; m. Barbara Jane d. Dr. R.C. Montgomery, Toronto, Ont. 13 Feb. 1955; children: Adam Tudor, Christopher Montgomery, Deborah Jane (Findlay), Susannah Margaret (Belton), Sarah Elizabeth; CHRMN. AND DIR., BRASCAN LIMITED and MEMBER OF THE SENATE OF CANADA; Partner (retired), Tory Tory DesLauriers & Binnington; Dep. Chrmn. and Dir., Edper Enterprises Limited; Past Chrmn. & continuing Dir., Norcen Energy Resources Ltd.; Dir., Carena-Bancorp Inc.; General Motors of Canada Ltd.; M.A. Hanna Co.; Hees International Bancorp Inc.; The Hume Group Ltd.; John Labatt Ltd.; London Life Insurance Co.; London Life Insurance Group Inc.; Coca-Cola Beverages Ltd.; Past Dir., Canada Development Investment Corp. 1984–87; The Rouse Co. 1984–87; Past Chrmn. & Dir., The Trillium Fund 1986–91; Patron, Grenville Christian Coll.; Past Chrmn. and continuing mem., Bd. of Govs., Univ. of Waterloo 1981– ; Gov., Olympic Trust of Can.; Past Chrmn. and mem., Internat. Trade Adv. Ctte. 1988–91; Chrmn., Dome Consortium Inc. and Stadium Acquistion Inc.; read law with Tory, Tory, DesLauriers & Binnington 1960–62, Assoc. 1962–67, Partner 1967–79; called to Bar of Ont. 1962; cr. Q.C.; mem. Phi Delta Theta; Upper Can. Law Soc.; Candn. Bar Assn.; Bus. Council on Nat. Issues; P. Conservative; United Church; recreations: golf, tennis, skiing; Clubs: Founders, RCYC Toronto and York (Toronto); Caledon Ski, Caledon Mountain Trout and Devil's Pulpit Golf Club (Caledon); Rideau (Ottawa); Royal Palm Yacht and Country (Boca Raton, Fla.); Coral Beach & Tennis (Bermuda); Home: Tudorcroft, R.R. 2, Caledon, Ont. L0N 1C0; Office: P.O. Box 762, BCE Place, 181 Bay St., Toronto, Ont. M5J 2T3.

**EYTON, Rhys T.,** B.A., F.C.A., LL.D.; airline executive; b. Vancouver, B.C. 23 Sept. 1935; s. Geoffrey Tudor; e. Univ. of W. Ont. Hons. B.A. 1958; C.A. 1966; Banff Sch. of Advanced Management, 1968; m. Lynn Josephine d. Dr. Russell A. Palmer 7 Dec. 1962; children: Russell, Kathryn, Wendy; CHRMN., PRES. & C.E.O., PWA CORP.; CHRMN., CANADIAN AIRLINES INTERNATIONAL LTD.; Dir., PWA Corp.; Brascan Ltd.; Trimac Ltd.; joined Finance Dept. of present firm 1967; served as Mgr., Northern Region; Vice Pres. 1970; Vice Pres., Trucking Div. 1974–75; Extve. Vice Pres., Finance and Planning 1975; Pres. & C.E.O. 1976–86; Chrmn. & C.E.O. 1986–89; Past Chrmn. & Dir., Conference Bd. of Can.; Fellow, Candn. Inst. of C.A. (B.C. & Alta.); Hon. Mem., & Dir. Air Transport Assn. of Can. (Chrmn. 1981); Pres., Internat. Air Transport Assn. 1991–92; Hon. Doctorate, Univ. of Victoria; also serves on various educational, advisory and alumni assns. and councils; Anglican; Clubs: Ranchmen's; Calgary Golf and Country; Glencoe; Van. Lawn Tennis and Badminton; recreations: sports & arts; Office: Ste. 2800, 700 2nd St. S.W., Calgary, Alta. T2P 2W2.

# F

**FAAS, Ekbert,** Dr.phil., Dr.habil.; university professor; b. Berlin 7 May 1938; s. Adalbert and Gerda (Schulze) F.; e. universities of Munich, Dr.phil., Würzburg, Dr.habil, Madrid, Sorbonne, Paris; one s. Paul Jason; educated in Europe, now living as a teacher, writer, and editor in Toronto; author: 'Towards a New American Poetics' 1978, 'Ted Hughes' 1980, 'Young Robert Duncan' 1983, 'Tragedy and After. Euripides, Shakespeare, Goethe' 1984, 'Shakespeare's Poetics' 1986, 'Retreat into the Mind: Victorian Poetry and the Rise of Psychiatry' 1988 (scholarly monographs); 'Woyzeck's Head' 1991 (novel); co-editor: 'Robert Creeley–Irving Layton: The Complete Correspondence'; Office: 4700 Keele St., North York, Ont. M3J 1P3.

**FABBRO, Gerald,** B.Sc.; investment executive; b. Trail, B.C. 16 June 1938; s. Fiorvante and Flora (Castigloni) F.; e. high sch. Trail, B.C.; Michigan Tech. Univ. B.Sc. 1961; m. Sharon d. George and Elizabeth Platt 11 May 1957; children: Allan, Christopher, Gerri-Lynne, Stephen; SENIOR VICE-PRESIDENT & DIR., MIDLAND WALWYN LTD. 1979– ; joined Boeing Inc. 1961–64; present firm 1965; Chrmn. Vancouver Stock Exchange 1985–87, Gov. 1981–84; mem. Candn.-Italian Bus. and Profl. Assoc. of B.C.; R. Catholic; recreations: skiing, jogging, golf, tennis; Club: Vancouver; Home: 430 Walker, Coquitlam, B.C. V3K 4E3; Office: F11, 3 Bentall Bldg., 595 Burrard St., Vancouver, B.C. V7X 1C3.

**FABIAN, Robert J.,** M.S., Ph.D.; b. Cleveland, Ohio 21 March 1939; s. John and Elizabeth (Kutler) F.; e. Case Inst. of Technol. B.S. 1961, M.S. 1963, Ph.D. 1965; m. Mira d. Otto and Cornelia Matherny 12 June 1962; DIR., PRODUCT TECHNOLOGY GROUP, TELEGLOBE INSURANCE SYSTEMS 1991– ; Robert Fabian Assoc. 1990– ; former Asst. Prof. Smith Coll.; Assoc. Prof. York Univ.; Prin. Hickling-Johnston Ltd.; Mgr. Gulf Canada; Partner Gellman, Hayward; Visiting Prof. Harvard Univ., Univ. of Waterloo; Adjunct Faculty Univ. of Toronto; Candn. Info. Processing Soc.; author frequent newspaper and mag. articles; mem. CIPS; ACM; IEEE; recreation: music; Home: 71 Evelyn Ave., Toronto, Ont. M6P 2Z2.

**FACKENHEIM, Emil Ludwig,** Ph.D., LL.D., D.D., D.Hu.L., Lit.D., F.R.S.C. (1972); professor; b. Halle, Germany 22 June 1916; s. Julius and Meta (Schlesinger) F.; e. Univ. of Halle, Germany (1937–38); Aberdeen Univ. (1939–40); Univ. of Toronto (1941–43), Ph.D. 1945; LL.D. Laurentian 1969; Sir George Williams 1971; D.D. St. Andrews Coll. 1972; D.Hu.L. Hebrew Union 1974; Lit.D. Barry Coll. 1983; m. Rose Komlodi, Calgary, Alberta, 28 December 1957; children: Michael Alexander, Susan Sheila, David Emmanuel, Joseph Jonatan; PROF. OF PHILOSOPHY, UNIV. OF TORONTO since 1961; FELLOW, INST. OF CONTEMPORARY JEWRY, HEBREW UNIV., Jerusalem since 1986; Newman Distinguished Fellow, Internat. Inst. for the University Study of Jewish Civilization 1985–86; Contrib. Editor, 'Judaism'; o. as Rabbi, 1939; Rabbi, Cong. Anshe Sholom, Hamilton, Ont., 1943–48; Lectr. in Philos., Univ. of Toronto, 1948–53, Asst. Prof., 1953–56, Assoc. Prof., 1956–61; Guggenheim Fellow, 1957–58; Killam Fellow, 1977–1978; appt. University Professor 1979; Emeritus since 1981; Visiting Prof., Inst. of Contemporary Jewry, Hebrew Univ., Jerusalem 1981–84; author: 'Metaphysics and Historicity' 1961; 'Paths to Jewish Belief' 1960; 'The Religious Dimension in Hegel's Thought' 1968; 'Quest for Past and Future: Essays in Jewish Theology' 1968; 'God's Presence in History' 1970; 'Encounters Between Judaism and Modern Philosophy' 1973; 'The Jewish Return Into History' 1978; 'To Mend The World: Foundations of Future Jewish Thought' 1982; 'What is Judaism' 1987; 'The Jewish Bible after the Holocaust: A Re-Reading' 1991; subject of 'The Jewish Thought of Emil Fackenheim' ed. Michael Morgan 1987; 'Fackenheim: German Philosophy and Jewish Thought' ed. Louis Greenspan and Graeme Nicholson 1992; and many articles and reviews in scholarly journs.; rec'd. Pres.'s Medal of Univ. of W. Ont. for best scholar. article publ. in Can. in 1954; mem., Central Conf. of Am. Rabbis; Jewish; recreation: music; Home: 3/7 Elroi St., Jerusalem 92108, Israel.

**FAGAN, Cary,** B.A., M.A.; writer; b. Toronto, Ont. 29 June 1957; s. Maurice and Belle (Menkes); e. Univ. of Toronto B.A. 1980, M.A. 1991; m. Joanne d. Irving and Diana Schwartz 19 Aug. 1984; Former Editorial Staff Mem., The Canadian Forum, Seven News, Canadian Lawyer; Former Columnist, Poetry Canada Review; contbr.: Toronto Globe & Mail, Books in Canada, CBC Radio, London Free Press, Equinox, etc.; Contbg. Ed., 'Paragraph' magazine; City of Toronto Book Award 1991; Mem., Writers Union of Canada; Canadian Book Artists & Bookbinders Guild; Amnesty Internat.; author: 'History Lessons' (stories) 1990, 'City Hall and Mrs God: A Passionate Journey Through a Changing Toronto' 1990; 'The Little Black Dress' (stories) 1993; 'The Fred Victor Mission Story' 1993; co-editor: 'Streets of Attitude: Toronto Stories' 1990; Office: c/o Writers Union of Canada, 24 Ryerson Ave., Toronto, Ont. M5T 2P3.

**FAGAN, Christine Ann,** LL.B.; lawyer; b. Moncton, N.B. 7 Mar. 1950; d. Murray M. and Mary Elizabeth (Carey) Francheville; e. St. Francix Xavier Univ. B.A. 1972; Univ. of N.B. M.A. 1974, LL.B. 1977; PARTNER, CHALKER, GREEN & ROWE 1978– ; called to Bar of N.B. 1977; Nfld. 1978; Dir. National Life Assurance Co. of Can.; Past Pres. St. John's Bd. of Trade; mem. Law Soc. of Nfld.; Candn. Bar Assn.; Chrmn. Nfld. Ocean Industries Assoc (NOIA); Home: 6 Empire Ave., St. John's, Nfld. A1C 3E5; Office: P.O. Box 5939, 5th Flr., 10 Fort William Place, St. John's, Nfld. A1C 5X4.

**FAHRNI, Walter Harrison,** M.D., M.Ch.Orth. (Liverpool 1947), F.R.C.S. (Edin. 1945), F.R.C.S. (Can. 1949), F.R.S.M.; b. Gladstone, Man., 9 May 1916; s. Judge Stanley Harrison and Edith Josephine (Minaker) F.; e. Univ. of Manitoba 1933–39; m. Lana, d. of Yim Quong Lau, Hong Kong; children: Ross Harrison, Josephine Anne, Philip Grant, Jennifer Jean; mem., Hon. Attending Staff, Vancouver Gen. Hosp.; served in 2nd World War 1941–46, Capt., R.C.A.M.C.; author: 'Backache: Assessment and Treatment'; mem.; Candn. Med. Assn.; Candn. Orthopaedic Assn.; N. Pacific Orthopaedic Assn.; Protestant; Home: Suite 205, 1131 Beach Ave., Vancouver, B.C. V6E 1V6.

**FAIMAN, Charles,** M.D., M.Sc., F.R.C.P.(C); educator; b. Winnipeg, Man. 6 Dec. 1939; s. Max and Bessie F.; e. St. John's High Sch. 1956; Univ. of Man. M.D. 1962, B.Sc. (Med.) 1962, M.Sc. 1966; m. Carol Fien 16 June 1963; children: Barton Shale, Gregg Howard, Matthew Randall; CHRMN., DEPT. ENDOCRINOL., CLEVELAND CLINIC FOUND., Cleveland, Ohio, U.S.A. 1992– ; Prof. of Physiol. 1975–92 and Prof. of Med. 1978–92 Univ. of Man., Head Sec. Endocrinol. and Metabolism Health Sciences Centre 1977–92, Dir. Endocrine & Metabolism Lab. 1977–92; internship and residency, Winnipeg Gen. Hosp., University of Illinois & Mayo Clinic (Med. Research Council Can. Fellow); Asst. Prof. of Physiol. Univ. of Man. 1968, Assoc. Prof. of Physiol. & Med. 1971–75; Dir., Clin. Investig. Unit Winnipeg Gen. Hosp. 1971–74; recipient various undergrad. scholarships 1957–62, Prowse Prize for Research 1966, Med. Research Council Can. Scholarship 1968–73; mem., Specialty Cttee. in Endocrinology & Metabolism, Royal College of Physicians & Surgeons of Canada 1984–88; Grants Cttee. Canadian Diabetes Assn. 1984–87; Grants Cttee. Manitoba Health Research Council 1984–86; mem. Bd. Winnipeg Hebrew Sch. 1972–92 (Pres. 1982–83); mem. Bd. Dirs., Winnipeg Jewish Community Counc. 1986–92; author or co-author numerous publs.; mem. Endocrine Soc.; Am. Fed. Clin. Research; Soc. Exper. Biol. & Med.; Sigma Xi; Candn. Fertility & Andrology Soc. (Nat. Dir. 1988– ;); Candn. Soc. Clin. Investig.; Candn. Soc. Endocrinol. & Metabolism (Councillor 1976–79, Pres. 1979–80); N.Y. Acad. Sciences; Am. Soc. Clin. Investig.; Am. Assn. Advanc. Sciences; Am. Soc. Primatology; Jewish; recreations: jogging, symphony, opera; Home: 14 Sherwood Court, Beachwood, Ohio 44122, U.S.A.; Office: Cleveland Clinic Found., Cleveland, Ohio, 44195 U.S.A.

**FAIRBAIRN, Hon. Joyce,** B.A., B.Journalism; senator; b. Lethbridge, Alta. 6 Nov. 1939; d. late Judge Lynden Eldon and late Mary Elizabeth (Young) F.; e. Univ. of Alta. B.A. Eng. 1960; Carleton Univ. B.Journalism 1961; m. Michael s. Mack (dec.) and Mariane Gillan 28 Oct. 1967; SENATE LEADER and Min. with special responsibility for Literacy 1993– ; Journalist; News reporter Ottawa Jour. 1961–62; Pol. reporter and columnist Parliamentary Press Gallery Bur., United Press Internat. 1962–64; Pol. Corr. Parlty. Press. Gall. Bur., F.P. Publications serving The Winnipeg Free Press, The Calgary Albertan, The Lethbridge Herald, The Vancouver Sun and The Victoria Times with special assignments for The Ottawa Journ. 1964–70; apptd. Legis. Asst. to Rt. Hon. Pierre Elliott Trudeau 1970–84, with additional assignment as Communications Coordr. in P.M.'s Office 1981–83; summoned to The Senate of Canada for the Prov. of Alta. (Lethbridge) 1984; mem. Standing Senate Ctte. on Legal and Constitutional Affairs 1988–91; Standing Senate Ctte. on Agric. & Forestry (Vice Chair); Standing Senate Ctte. on Foreign Affairs; Standing Senate Ctte. on Aboriginal Peoples; Special Senate Ctte. on Terrorism and Public Safety 1986–87; mem. Special Senate Ctte. on Youth 1984–86; Vice Chair Nat. Liberal Caucus 1984–90; Vice Chair, Northern & Western Liberal Caucus 1984–90; Advocate for Literacy in Canada; Mem. of Senate, Univ. of Lethbridge; Honorary Kainai Chief 'Morning Bird Woman' of the Blood Tribe; Mem., Bd. of Dirs., Candn. Orgn. for Develop. through Educ. (C.O.D.E.); Home: 34 Harmer Ave. N., Ottawa, Ont. K1Y 0T4 and 414 – 14th St. S., Lethbridge, Alta. T1J 2X7; Office: 556–S, The Senate, Ottawa, Ont. K1A 0A4.

**FAIRCLOUGH, Rt. Hon. Ellen Louks (Mrs. Gordon Fairclough),** P.C. (Can.) 1957, O.C., F.C.A., LL.D., FRCGS; D.H., U.E.; b. Hamilton, Ont. 28 Jan. 1905; d.

Norman Ellsworth and Nellie Bell (Louks) Cook; e. Primary and Secondary Schs., Hamilton, Ont., m. David Henry Gordon Fairclough, Hamilton, Ont., 28 Jan. 1931; one. s., Howard Gordon (dec.); started own acctg. practice in 1935; Life mem., Gen. Accts. Assn. of Can.; el. Life Mem., Chart. Accts. of Ont.; Past Pres., Zonta Club of Hamilton; Past Dist. Gov., Zonta Internat. (Treas. 1972–76); Past Dom. Secy., U.E.L. Assn.; Past Offr., Prov. and Nat. Chapter, I.O.D.E.; former Vice-Pres. of Young Conservatives of Ont.; served five years on Hamilton City Council as Alderman for four yrs.and Controller for one yr.; def. cand. in Fed. gen. el. June 1949 (def. by Hon. Colin Gibson); 1st el. to H. of C. in by-el. for Hamilton W., 15 May 1950; def. g.e. 1963; Secy. of State, 1957–58; Min. of Citizenship and Immigration 1958–62; Postmaster-Gen., Aug. 1962–Apr. 1963; Advisory mem., Candn. Del. to U.N. 1950; del. to Conf. of Parliamentarians from NATO countries, Paris 1955; Ambassador Extraordinary to Argentina for inauguration of President (1958); apptd. Secy., Hamilton Trust & Savings Corp., Sept. 1963–77 (amalgamated with Canada Permanent Trust, now Canada Trust); Mem., Hamilton Chamber of Comm.; past Dir., Candn. Council of Christian and Jews; Past Hon. Treas. and Extve. Dir., Chedoke-McMaster Hospitals Found. 1982–86; Gov., Junior Achievement of Hamilton; Coronation Medal 1953; Centennial Medal 1967; Jubilee Medal 1977; Commemorative Medal, 125th Anniversary of Candn. Confedn. 1992; among 25 women receiving honours in Ontario for outstanding contributions 1975; Ont. Govt. Bldg. (Hamilton, Ont.) named after her 1982; recipient Eleanor Roosevelt Centennial Award, Hamilton Women's Div., State of Israel Bonds 1984; Humanitarian and Merit Award, Multicultural Soc. of Hamilton; invested Dame of Grace, Order of Saint John of Jerusalem, Knights Hospitaller, 1985; recipient, Persons Award (Status of Women, Can.) 1989; Hon. Life Mem., Zonta Internat. 1990 (Past Internat. Treas. 1972–76); Title 'The Right Honourable' bewtowed by Her Majesty Queen Elizabeth II, 1992; Fellow, Royal Candn. Geographical Soc.; Patron, Huguenot Soc. of Can.; Patron, U.E.L. Assn. of Hamilton; Anglican; Home: 25 Stanley Ave., Hamilton, Ont. L8P 2K9.

**FAIRGRIEVE, His Hon. Judge David Alan,** B.A., M.Sc.(Econ.), LL.B.; judge; b. Toronto, Ont. 10 Aug. 1947; s. Douglas Matson and Juanita Aileen (Cole) F.; e. Univ. of Toronto Schools 1965; Trinity College, Univ. of Toronto B.A. (Hons.) 1970; London School of Econ. & Pol. Sci. M.Sc.(Econ.) 1971; Osgoode Hall Law School LL.B. 1974; m. Catherine d. Edward and Catherine Percival 5 Aug. 1977; children: Timothy, Christopher, Benjamin; JUDGE, ONTARIO COURT OF JUSTICE, PROVINCIAL DIV. 1990– ; Asst. Crown Attorney Brampton 1976–82; Counsel, Crown Law Office Toronto 1982–86; Senior Counsel, Crown Law Office Toronto 1986–88; Counsel, Court Reform Task Force, Min. of Attorney General Toronto 1988–89; Deputy Dir., Crown Law Office – Criminal Toronto 1989–90; Anglican; Mem., Candn. Bar Assn.; Candn. Friends of L.S.E.; London House Assn.; Ont. Judges' Assn.; U.T.S. Alumni Assn.; Home: 64 Indian Trail, Toronto, Ont. M6R 1Z9; Office: Old City Hall, 60 Queen St. W., Toronto, Ont.

**FAIRHEAD, Patricia Mary,** M.A., R.C.A., O.S.A.; artist; b. Hull, Yorks., Eng. 23 Feb. 1927; d. William Bernard and Mercia (Hill) Sloane Wily; e. Ont. Coll. of Art 1946; Ont. Inst. for Studies in Edn. Dept. Adult Edn. Cert. 1972; Goddard Coll. Vt. Adult Edn. M.A. 1974; m. Robert Fairhead 20 Sept. 1946; children: John Gordon, Judith Ann Crich; common-law Peter Garstang May 1987; solo exhns. incl. Sobot Gallery Toronto 1966–67; Jacox Gallery Edmonton 1969; Art Gallery of Edmonton 1970; Shaw-Rimmington Gallery Toronto 1978–79; Braam Gallery Ottawa 1980; Pollock Gallery 1981; Roberts Gallery 1982–84, 1986, 1988, 1990, 1992; Wells Gallery Ottawa 1985; Queen Charlotte Islands Museum 1986; Thielsen Galleries London 1987 and 1991; Gallery 1667 Halifax 1988; Fraser Galleries Halifax 1990; Lydon Fine Art, Chicago, Ill., U.S.A. 1992; Mabey Gall., Richmond, Virginia, U.S.A. 1992–93; Harbour Gallery, Mississauga 1993; teacher, cons. various univs., applied arts colls., art galleries, bds. of edn. & community groups; Co-ordinator Humber Coll. Centre for Women 1971, rsch. 1st Centre in Can.; Ont. Assn. Continuing Edn. 1974–75, designed and devel. 1st Learning Network Project; Co-ordinator Resource Centre Ont. Craft Council 1975–76, designed and devel. 1st one in Can.; Co-ordinator Community Art Projects TV Ont. 1976–79, devel. on air Arts Prog. Model; author 'Colour and Composition' 1966; 'Youth, Environments and Art' 1976; 'Teaching Art with Television' 1979; mem. Candn. Soc. Painters in Water Colour (Vice Pres. 1981); Ont. Soc. of Artists; Soc. Candn. Artists (Founding mem. and Pres. 1964); recreations: swimming, canoeing, hiking, skiing, biking; Club: Arts & Letters; Home: 33 Rathnally Ave., Toronto, Ont. M4V 2M4; Studio: 390 Dupont St., Toronto, Ont. M5R 1V9.

**FAIRLEY, Albert L., Jr.,** B.S.; retired industrialist; b. Jackson, Miss. 28 Dec. 1913; s. Albert Langley and Alethe (Vardaman) F.; e. Phillips High Sch., Birmingham, Ala. (1930); Birmingham-Southern Coll., Birmingham, Ala., B.S. 1934; Johns Hopkins Univ. (Post Grad. work in Geol.) 1935; m. Claire Elizabeth, d. James Barr Haines III, Sewickley, Pa., 20 Aug. 1949; Retired Dir.: Sun Life of Canada; Sun Life of Canada (U.S.); Sun Life (New York); Canadian Imperial Bank of Commerce; Domtar; Argus Corp.; Crown Trust; Trustee, Birmingham Ala.; Bd. of Trustees, Birmingham Southern Coll.; Geol., Tennessee Val. Auth., 1935–37; Asst. Geol., Tennessee Coal Iron & Rail. Div., U.S. Steel Corp. at Birmingham, Ala., 1937–41; Asst. to Depy. Dir. of Steel Div., U.S. War Prod. Bd., 1941–43; engaged in various Operating and Extve. positions with the Shenango Furnace Co. and subsidiary organizations, Pittsburgh, Pa.; Vice-Pres. and Dir., Shenango Furnace Co., Snyder Mining Co., Lucerne Coke Co., May 1946 D1 Aug. 1958; apptd. Dir. and Extve. Vice-Pres. of Dom. Steel and Coal Corp. Ltd., Montreal, Que. 1958,and el. Pres. and Dir. 1959–64; Pres., Hollinger Mines Ltd. 1964–78 (ret.); served in 2nd World War with U.S.A.F.; enlisted in 1943 as a Pte., and discharged with rank of Capt., 1946; awarded Letter and Ribbon of Commendation; Emeritus mem., Am. Iron & Steel Inst.; Am. Inst. Mining & Metall. Engrs.; Alpha Tau Omega; Elder, 1st Presbyterian Church, Birmingham; recreations: swimming, tennis, hunting, fishing; Clubs: Downtown; The Club, Mountain Brook and Birmingham Country Club (all in Birmingham, Ala.); Duquesne (Pittsburgh); Home: 3 Ridge Dr., Birmingham, Alabama 35213.

**FAIRMAN, Carmen Royal;** executive; b. Spalding, Sask. 28 July 1936; s. John Arthur and Edith Sabena F.; e. Banff Sch. of Fine Arts Sales Force Mgmt. 1965, Exec. Devel. 1989; m. Annemarie d. Fritz and Dorothea Perschon 21 July 1978; children: Andrew, Karin, Andrea; VICE PRES. SALES PRUDENTIAL STEEL LTD. 1989– ; joined Continental Supply Co. Edmonton 1955, various managerial positions Alta., Sask. 1957–1967; Sales Rep. present Co. 1972, Sales Mgr. Oil Country Tubular Good 1976, Gen. Sales Mgr. 1986; lectr. Petroleum Ind. Training Service 1983– ; private pilot's licence 1965; mem. Petroleum Services Assn. Can. (Past Pres.); recreations: downhill & water skiing, golf, board sailing; Clubs: Canyon Meadows Golf & Country; Calgary Petroleum; Home: 631 East Chestermere Dr., Chestermere, Alta. T1X 1A5; Office: 1800, 140 – 4th Ave. S.W., Calgary, Alta. T2P 3N3.

**FAIRWEATHER, Robert Gordon Lee,** O.C., Q.C., B.C.L.; b. Rothesay, N.B. 27 March 1923; s. Jack Hall Alliger Lee and Agnes Charlotte (Mackeen) F.; e. Rothesay (N.B.) Coll. Sch.; Osgoode Hall Law Sch., Toronto, Ont.; Univ. of New Brunswick Law Sch., B.C.L. 1949; m. Nancy Elizabeth, d. late Cyril Hurd Broughall, 1 June 1946; children: Michael Gordon, Wendy Elizabeth, Hugh Alexander; Chrmn., Immigration & Refugee Bd. 1987–92; called to Bar of N.B., June 1949; cr. Q.C. Nov. 1958; practised law with firm of McKelvey, Macaulay, Machum & Fairweather, Saint John, N.B.; served in R.C.N.V.R. 1941–45; rank Lt.-Commandr. (S); 1st el. to N.B. Leg. for Kings 1952; re-el. 1956–60; Atty-Gen. N.B. 1958–60; el. to H. of C. for Royal, g.e. June 1962; re-el. 1963, 65 and for Fundy-Royal 1968, 1972 and 1974; Chief Comm. of Can. Human Rights Comm., 1977–87; Anglican; Address: P.O. Box 309, Rothesay, N.B. E0G 2W0.

**FALARDEAU-RAMSAY, Michelle,** Q.C.; b. Montreal, Que. 29 Sept. 1939; d. Jules Hector and Claire (Gareau) Falardeau; e. Coll. Marguerite Bourgeoys B.A. 1958; Univ. de Montréal LL.B. 1961; McGill Univ. bar courses 1962; Bar univ. courses 1962–71; cr. Q.C. 1983; DEPUTY CHIEF COMNR., CANADIAN HUMAN RIGHTS COMM. 1988– ; Partner, Massicotte, Levac & Falardeau 1963–68; Levac & Falardeau 1968–75; Depy. Chrmn. Public Serv. Staff Relations Bd. 1975–82; Chrmn., Immigration Appeal Bd. 1983–88; mem. Bd. of Dirs., Candn. Human Rights Found.; mem. Assoc. of Profl. Extves. of Public Service of Can.; Internat. Bar Assn., Quebec Bar; Candn. Bar Assn.; Affil.: Candn. Inst. for the Admin. of Justice; Internat. Comn. for Jurists; Membre: Fédération des femmes du Québec; Société des droits administratifs du Qué.; Office: 320 Queen St., 15th Flr., Place de Ville, Tower 'A', Ottawa, Ont. K1A 1E1.

**FALCONE, Carmine;** oil company executive; b. Cosenza, Italy 14 Oct. 1946; s. Ernesto and Lauretta (Marra) F.; e. McGill Univ. chem. engr. 1968; m. Gabriella d. Zoltan Sagi 16 Oct. 1971; children: Alicia, Roberto; EXECUTIVE VICE-PRES., PRODUCTS, SHELL CANADA LIMITED 1990– ; Opns. & Process Engr., Shell Canada Montreal East 1968; Sr. Project Engr., Head Office 1973; Mgr., Heavy Oils Dept & Mgr., Process Engr., Montreal East Refy. 1976–80; Mgr., Technical Head Office 1980; Mgr., Strategy Devel., Corp. Strategies 1982; Gen. Mgr., Corp. Strategies 1983; Vice-Pres. 1986; Vice-Pres., Western Complex 1986; Pres., Shell Canada Products Limited; Dir., Shell Canada Limited; Shell Canada Products Limited; Chair, Candn. Petroleum Products Inst.; Mem., Assn. of Profl. Engr., Geologists & Geophysicists of Alta.; Dir., West Island College; recreations: golf, skiing; clubs: Glencoe Golf & Country, Willow Park Golf, Calgary Petroleum; Home: 114 Pumpridge Place S.W., Calgary, Alta. T2V 5B1; Office: 630 – 3rd Ave. S.W., Calgary, Alta. T2P 4L4.

**FALK, Gathie;** artist; b. Alexander, Man. 31 Jan. 1928; d. Cornelius and Agatha (Penner) Falk; e. Univ. of B.C.; m. Dwight Swanson 11 Nov. 1974; divorced; solo exhns. incl.: Canvas Shack, Vancouver 1965; Douglas Gallery Vancouver 1968; Candn. Cultural Centre Paris 1974; Bau-Xi Gallery Vancouver 1976; Nat. Gallery Tour 1976–77; Forest City Gallery London, Ont. 1977; Edmonton Art Gallery 1978; Artcore Vancouver 1978; Univ. of B.C. 1980; Univ. ofS. Alta. Lethbridge 1980; Glenbow Museum Calgary 1980; Equinox Art Gallery Vancouver 1981, 82, 83, 85, 87, 88; Isaacs Gallery Toronto 1982, 84, 87, 88; Victoria Art Gallery, Painting Retrospective (touring) 1985–86; Vancouver Art Gallery, Retrospective 1962–85, 1985; 49th Parallel, New York 1987; 2 artist exhns. Vancouver Art Gallery 1970, Harbourfront Gallery Toronto 1979; group exhns. incl. Vancouver Art Gallery, Seattle Art Museum, Montréal Museum of Fine Arts, Australian Nat. Lib., Art Gallery of Ont., Nat. Gallery Ottawa; Museum of Modern Art, Toyama, Japan; commissions incl. 2 murals for the Lester Pearson Bldg., Ottawa 1973; sculptured painting for the B.C. Co-op Bldg. 1979; mural for the Candn. Embassy, Washington 1988; Odeon Cineplex IV, Vancouver 1988; cited numerous mags., jours., books since 1968; rep. various pub. and private coll.; many performance art presentations; recipient Can. Council Short Term Grant 1967, Arts Bursray 1968, 69, 71, Sr. Grant 1980; Sun Award 1968; various comns.; principal works incl. paintings, environmental sculpture, sculptured paintings, prints, sculpture, performance art, video performance art; represented by the Equinox Gallery in Vancouver and the Wynick-Tuck Gallery in Toronto; Office: c/o Wynick-Tuck Gallery, 80 Spadina Ave., 4th Floor, Toronto, Ont. M5V 2J3.

**FALK, Haim,** B.Ac., M.B.A., Ph.D., C.P.A., C.G.A.; educator; b. Berlin, Germany 20 Aug. 1929; s. Hans Jehoshua and Charlotte Leah (Kaphan) F.; e. Hebrew Univ. of Jerusalem B.Ac. 1962, Dip. Bus.Adm. 1967, Ph.D. 1971; Tel-Aviv Univ. M.B.A. 1969; C.P.A. 1962; C.G.A. (Ont.) 1989; m. Rachel d. Michael and Rasel Olanski 24 Nov. 1955; children: Bareket, Jehoshua (d), Ophir; PROFESSOR, RUTGERS UNIV. 1993– ; Jr./Sr. Mgr. Haft and Haft CPA's 1961–72; mem. Israeli Acctg./Auditing Standards Bd. 1967–72; joined The Hebrew Univ. and Tel-Aviv Univ. 1971–72; Ind. Univ. 1972–75; McGill Univ. 1975–82; Univ. of Calgary 1982–86, Asst., Assoc. & Prof. of Acctg.; Distinguished Prof. Chair in Acctg., McMaster Univ. 1986–93, Dir. Acctg. Rsch. & Edn. Centre 1986–90; Visiting Scholar: Queen's Univ., McMaster (Hooker Distinguished Prof.), Univ. of Md., Tel-Aviv Univ., Univ. of B.C., Victoria Univ. of Wellington (New Zealand), Curtin Univ. of Technology (Western Australia) 1980–92; Cons. to Israeli Govt. Co's Authority 1968–72, 1981; mem./Cons. Israeli Govt. Inquiry Cttes. Monoply of Gas Distributors and Corporate Budgets 1970–72; Dir. Gapim Enterprises 1969–72; Dir. Candn. Certified General Accountants Rsch. Found. 1990–92; Dir. and Instr. annual Social Sci's & Humanities Council Acctg. Rsch. Workshop for Candn. Profs. 1982–86; Coordinator and sole Instr. CIDA Acctg. Rsch. Methodol. Workshop for Profs. in Thailand 1987; Visiting Prof., SASIN, Grad. Inst. of Bus. Admin., Thailand 1990; External examiner for Ont. Counc. on Grad. Studies 1991–92; author: 'The Use of Financial Statements for Investment Decision Making' 1976; co-author: 'Pricing Decisions: An Empirical Study' 1981, 'The Serviceability of Financial Information – A Survey' 1986, 'Financial Reporting – Theory and Application to the Oil and Gas Industry in Canada' 1986; over 85 articles scholarly & profl. jours. and books; Founding Ed. 'Contemporary Accounting Research' 1984–89; co-editor 1990; mem. ed. bd.: Jour. Acctg. & Pub. Policy 1981– ; Contemporary Acctg. Research 1989– , The Acctg. Review 1989–94; mem. Am. Acctg. Assn.; Eur. & Candn. Acad. Acctg. Assn.; Inst. CPA's Israel; Acad. of Acctg. Historians (Chair Rsch.

Ctte. 1992–94); annual Haim Falk Award (for distinguished contribution to accounting thought) estbl. in his honour by Candn. Acad. Acctg. Assn. 1989; recreation: swimming; Home: 224 Chanticleer, Cherry Hill, NJ 08003; Office: 3rd St. Camden, NJ 08102.

**FALLDING, Harold Joseph,** B.Sc., M.A., Ph.D., F.R.S.C.; educator; b. Cessnock, N.S.W., Australia 3 May 1923; s. Frederick and Alice Bessie (Chopping) F.; e. Fort St. Boys' High Sch. Sydney 1939; Lib. Sch. Pub. Lib. of N.S.W. Cert in Librarianship 1941; Univ. of Sydney B.Sc. 1950, B.A. 1951, Dip. Ed. 1952, M.A. 1955; Australian Nat. Univ. Ph.D. 1957; m. Margaret d. George and Martha Hardy 18 Dec. 1954; children: Marion, Ruth, Helen; PROFESSOR EMERITUS, UNIV. OF WATERLOO 1989, Prof. of Sociol., Univ. of Waterloo 1965–88; served with 102nd Australian Gen. Hosp. 1942–46; high sch. teacher in Eng. and Hist. Dept. Edn. N.S.W. 1952–53; Sr. Rsch. Fellow in Sociol. Dept. Agric. Econ. Univ. of Sydney 1956–58; Sr. Lectr. in Sociol. Univ. of N.S.W. 1959–62; Visiting Assoc. Prof. of Sociol. Grad. Sch. Rutgers, State Univ. of N.J. 1963–65; author 'The Sociological Task' 1968; 'The Sociology of Religion: An Explanation of the Unity and Diversity in Religion' 1974; 'Drinking, Community and Civilization. The Account of a New Jersey Interview Study' 1974; 'The Social Process Revisited: Achieving Human Interests through Alliance and Opposition' 1990; 'Word of the Tangling Fire' (poetry) 1969; mem.: Clare Hall, Univ. of Cambridge; Stratford Shakespearean Foundation Can.; Am. Sociol. Assn.; Candn. Soc. Sociol. & Anthrop.; Internat. Sociol. Assoc.; Internat. Conf. Sociol. Religion; Candn. Inst. of Internat. Affairs Kitchener-Waterloo Br.; United Church; Home: 125 Empire St., Waterloo, Ont. N2L 2M3.

**FALLIS, Fred B.,** B.A., M.D.; medical educator; b. Vancouver, B.C. 28 March 1921; s. Rev. (Lt. Col.) George Oliver and Mabel Lavinia (Hockin) F.; e. Univ. of Toronto, B.A. 1942, M.D. 1953; m. Lois Irene, d. late William Henry Bouck and Jennie Goodman, 27 Dec. 1946; children: Mary Louise, Geordie, William, Fred Jr., Lois Anne, Joan Elizabeth; MEDICAL DIRECTOR, TELEMEDICINE CANADA; PAST PRES., TORONTO ACAD. OF MEDICINE; PROF. AND PAST CHRMN., DEPT. OF FAMILY AND COMMUNITY MEDICINE, (and Former Asst. Dean, Continuing Ed., Faculty of Medicine) UNIV. OF TORONTO; Consulting Staff Family Physician, Toronto Gen. Hosp.; Staff Phys., Med. O.P.D., Toronto Gen. Hosp. and V.D. Clinic 1954, Head, Gen. Practice Clinic, 1966–70; Staff Phys., Addiction Research Foundation, 1954–66; joined the Univ. as Clin. Teacher and Assoc., Dept. of Med., 1966–69; Phys., Bella Coola Gen. Hosp. B.C., 1960, 1963; private practice N. Toronto 1954–70; served with RCAF as Pilot 1941–45; 3rd Secy., Dept. of External Affairs, 1945–47; mem. Dept. of Nat. Health & Welfare Task Force 1971, Comte. on Manpower; author of numerous articles in various learned and prof. journs.; Certificant and Fellow, Coll. Family Phys. Can. (Past Pres.); Mem.-at-Large Nat. Extve. 1967–68; Chrmn. Nat. Comte. Patterns of Practice & Health Care Delivery 1968–74; Sustaining Fund Comte. 1977–80; Endowment and Awards Cmt. 1980–84; Mem., Continuing Education Ctte. 1985–88; Pres., N. Toronto Med. Soc. 1967–68; Tour Physician, Toronto Symphony 1983, '85, '86, '87, '88, '90, '91; Telemedicine for Ont. 1984–87; former Council mem. Ont. Med. Assn. and Family Service Assn.; Trustee, Trinity-St. Paul's Un. Ch.; Ed. 'Family Practice Manual' 1974; recreations: tree farming, photography, travel; Club: Univ. of Toronto Faculty; Home: Box 67, Bond Head, Ont. L0G 1B0.

**FALLIS, George Bryans,** B.A., Ph.D.; university professor; b. Toronto, Ont. 16 Sept. 1947; s. George Arthur and Catherine Agnes (Bryans) F.; e. Univ. of Toronto B.A. 1969; Princeton Univ. Ph.D. 1975; m. Sheila d. Nora and Mackenzie Robinson Dec. 1970; children: Jed, Brooks, Pearce, Zoe; PROF. OF ECONOMICS, YORK UNIV. 1976– ; Ministry of State for Urban Affairs, Govt. of Canada 1973–74; Ont. Econ. Council 1974–76; Consultant, Canada Mortgage and Housing Corp.; Econ. Council of Canada; Dept. of Finance; Ont. Min. of Housing; World Bank; Chair, Dept. of Econ., York Univ. 1987–90, 1991– ; author: 'Housing Programs and Income Distribution in Ontario' 1980, 'Housing Economics' 1985; co-author: 'Housing the Homeless and Poor' 1990; 'The Costs of Constitutional Change' 1992; clubs: Toronto Racquet; Home: 27 Playter Blvd., Toronto, Ont. M4K 2W1; Office: 4700 Keele St., North York, Ont. M3J 1P3.

**FALLIS, (Albert) Murray,** Ph.D., F.R.S.C.; biologist; b. Minto Twp., Ont. 2 Jan. 1907; s. William Robert and Melissa May (Millen) F.; e. Harriston (Ont.) High Sch.; Toronto Normal Sch., 1925–26; Univ. of Toronto, B.A. 1932 and Ph.D. 1937; m. Ada Ruth, d. Hon. Hewitt Bostock (former Speaker of Senate) of Monte Creek, B.C., 21 Sept. 1938; children: Alexander Graham, Hugh Murray, Bruce William; Prof. and Head of Parasitology, Sch. of Hygiene, Univ. of Toronto, 1948–72; emeritus prof. 1975; Sch. Teacher, 1926–28; Research Fellow, Ont. Research Foundation, 1932–47; Lectr. in Parasitol., Sch. of Hygiene, Univ. of Toronto, 1938–43; Assoc. Prof., 1944–48; Dir., Dept. of Parasitology, Ont. Research Foundation, 1947–66; Conslt. for W.H.O. in Ghana, 1967 and 1971; Assoc. Dean, Div. IV, Sch. of Grad. Studies, Univ. of Toronto, 1967–70; emeritus mem., Am. Soc. of Parasitol, (Vice Pres. 1970, Pres. 1979); Am. Soc. of Tropical Med.; emeritus mem., Wildlife Disease Assoc.; hon. mem. Can. Soc. Zoologists; Can. Soc. for Trop. Med. & International Health; Can. Assoc. Advancement Vet. Parasitol.; Royal Candn. Inst. (Hon. Ed. 1949–54; Pres., 1954–55); mem. Gov. Council, Univ. of Toronto 1972–73; Erskine Fellow, Univ. of Canterbury Jan.-Apr. 1975; Vis. Prof. Memorial Univ. of Nfld., Jan.-Mar. 1978; Pres. ICOPA V 1982; Freemason (P.M.); Un. Church; Home: RR #1, Caledon East, Ont. L0N 1E0.

**FALLS, Admiral Robert Hilborn,** CMM, CD, NDC, CF (ret.); retired naval officer; b. Welland, Ont. 29 Apr. 1924; s. Harry Thomas and Doris Irene (Hilborn) F.; e. Chatham C.I.; m. Isabelle d. James and Isobel Urie 27 Apr. 1946; children: Janice, Robert, David; joined RCAF 1942, tranferred to R.N. Fleet Air Arm 1945 & returned to RCN after war; flew fighter aircraft; commands incl. VF870, HMCS Chaudiere, HMCS Bonaventure; sr. positions in personnel & policy then Depy. CDS and Vice CDS; promoted to Admiral 1977 to become Chief of Defence Staff; Chrmn., NATO Military Ctte. 1980 (1st Candn. to hold position); retired 1983; Dir., Candn. Ctr. For Arms Control & Disarmament 1983; Pres. 1985–90, Dir. 1990–92, Advisor 1992– ; Commander of the Order of Military Merit; Candn. Forces Decoration; recreations: sailing; Club: Trident Yacht; Home: 15 Place Garand, Ottawa, Ont. K1H 8M1; Office: 151 Slater St., Ottawa, Ont. K1P 5H3.

**FALUDY, George;** poet; b. Budapest, Hungary 22 Sept. 1910; e. Univ. of Budapest; Univ. of Vienna; Univ. of Berlin; Hon. doctorates: Univ. of Toronto 1978; Bishop's Univ. 1982; Order of Hungary (1st class) 1990; widower; one s. Andrew; poet in Hungary 1937; exiled to France 1938; served with US Army World War II; Sec. Gen. Free Hungary Movement; returned to Hungary and imprisoned by Communists 3 yrs.; ed. Hungarian Literary Gazette, London 1957–60; emigrated to Can. 1967; visiting lectr. various acad. institutions incl. Columbia Univ.; author some 10 vols. verse; 'My Happy Days in Hell' autobiog. 1963, reprinted 1986; 'Erasmus of Rotterdam' biog. 1972; poetry transl. into Eng.: 'East and West' 1978; 'Learn this Poem of Mine by Heart' 1982; 'Selected Poems' 1986; 'Corpses, Brats and Cricket Music' 1987; 'Notes from the Rainforest' 1988; mem. Internat. PEN in Exile; recreation: travel; Offices: c/o Jacqueline d'Amboise, 129 Lorne Ave., Lennoxville, Que. J1M 1E3; Deres utca 10/B, Budapest XII, 1124 Hungary.

**FALZON, Charles John,** B.A.A.; television producer and distributor; b. Malta 26 Aug. 1957; s. Joseph V. and Jane M. (Mifsud) F.; e. York Univ. 1976–77; Ryerson Polytech. Inst. B.A.A. 1979; m. Rosalia d. Ralph and Maria DePasquale 3 Sept. 1983; children: Sarah, Rachel; PRES./PRINCIPAL, CATALYST ENTERTAINMENT 1991– ; Sales Extve., Candn. Broadcasting Corp. 1975–80; MCA-TV/Universal Pictures (N.Y.) 1980–82; Vice Pres., Internat. C.L. Taffner Ltd. 1982–85; Pres., Producers Group Internat. 1987–91; Chrmn., Canadian Film & TV Production Assn. 1991–93; executive producer of var. series for Candn., Am., & Brit. networks; Home: R.R. 2, Acton, Ont. L7J 2L8; Office: 495 Wellington St. W., Suite 212, Toronto, Ont. M5V 1G1 (Catalyst) and Candn. Film & TV Prod. Assn., 175 Bloor St. E., North Tower, Ste. 806, Toronto, Ont. M4W 3R8.

**FANJOY, Emery Myles,** B.Sc., D.I.C., LL.D., P.Eng.; public service executive; b. Saint John, N.B. 25 March 1935; s. Isaac Newton and Muriel Gertrude (Seely) F.; e. Univ. of N.B. B.Sc. 1957; Imperial College of Sci. & Technol. D.I.C. 1960; Univ. of N.B. LL.D. (Hon.) 1991; m. Agnes d. Malcolm and Janet Burgess 30 Aug. 1958; children: Stephen Myles, Bruce Smith, Andrea Seely; SECRETARY TO COUNCIL, COUNCIL OF MARITIME PREMIERS 1977– ; and CO-SECRETARY, CONFERENCE OF NEW ENGLAND GOVERNORS & EASTERN CANDN. PREMIERS 1978– ; Secretary to Conference of Atlantic Premiers 1990– ; Engr., N.B. Telephone 1957–58; Sales Engr., Candn. General Electric 1960–64; Sales Rep., IBM Canada 1964–68; Mktg. then Br. Mgr. 1968–73; Sec. to Treas. Bd., Prov. of N.B. 1973–77; Chair of Bd., Land Registration & Information Serv.; Maritime Geomatics Bd.; guest lecturer, several univs.; Lt. Gov.'s Medal for Excellence in Public Admin., N.S. 1991; Athlone Fellowship (2 yrs. in England) 1958–60; Mem., Candn. Council for European Affairs; Adv. Bd., School of Public Admin., Dalhousie Univ. (Chair 1983–85); European Community Visitor Program 1985; Mem., Inst. of Public Admin. of Canada 1973– ; (Nat. Extve. 1984–91; Chair, N.S. Branch 1983–85); North-South Inst. 1980–90; Niagara Inst. 1981–87; Assoc. of Profl. Engrs. of N.B. 1957– ; Assn. of Candn. Studies 1981– ; U.N. Assn. in Canada 1985– ; Conseil écon. du N.-B. 1985– ; New England Historic Genealogical Soc. 1984– ; Huguenot Soc. of G.B. & Ireland (Fellow) 1985– ; United Way of Metro Halifax-Dartmouth 1987–89; recreations: skiing, genealogy; Home: 6 Botany Terrace, Halifax, N.S. B3N 2Z7; Office: Box 2044, Halifax, N.S. B3J 2Z1.

**FARANO, Ronald J.,** Q.C., B.Com., LL.B.; b. Toronto, Ont. 12 Aug. 1931; s. Vincent and Rose (Lomore) F.; e. De La Salle Oaklands, Toronto, 1949; Univ. of Toronto, B.Com., 1953; Osgoode Hall Law Sch., 1957; m. Joan, d. Raymond Engholm, 20 May 1959; children: Gregory, Lisa, Christopher; PARTNER, FARANO, GREEN since 1974; A Founding Dir., Can. Fed. of Independent Business; Rep. of the Can. Fed. of Independ. Business to the Private Sector Adv. Cttee. to the Federal Gov't. Task Force Expenditure Review 1984–85; Chrmn. of Bd., Italian Cham. of Comm. Toronto (Dir. 1963–64); Mem., Toronto Olympic Counc. Adv. Bd.; Dir., Joseph D. Carrier Art Gallery; read law with Borden, Elliot, Kelley & Palmer; called to Bar of Ont. 1957; cr. Q.C. 1970; in private practice 1957–61; with Goodman & Carr 1961–66; Davies, Ward & Beck 1966–70; mem., Research Staff, Carter Royal Comn. on Taxation and Smith Comn. on Taxation (Ont.), 1963; served with C.O.T.C. summer 1950; author of 'Farano's Tax Cases' 1964, 1966, 1968, and 1981; 'Handbook on the Business Corporations Act' 1971; 'Tax Commentary,' Vol. 1 1977, Vol. 2 1979; Ed., 'Tax and Fiscal Commentary'; 'Digest of Tax Cases'; mem., Candn. Bar Assn.; Foundation for Legal Research; Phi Delta Phi; Fraser Inst.; C.D. Howe Inst.; R. Catholic; recreations: skiing, sailing, tennis; Clubs: Albany; R.C.Y.C.; Alpine Ski; Home: 23 Forest View Rd., Etobicoke, Ont. M9C 1W8; Office: 22 St. Clair Ave. E., Suite 1100, Toronto, Ont. M4T 2Z6.

**FARBER, Emmanuel,** M.D., Ph.D., F.R.S.C., F.R.C.P.(c); university professor; b. Toronto, Ont. 19 Oct. 1918; s. Morris and Mary (Madorsky) F.; e. Univ. of Toronto, M.D. 1942; Univ. of Cal., Ph.D. (Biochem.) 1949; m. late Ruth Wilma d. late Isaac Diamond, 16 Apl. 1942; one d., Naomi Beth; PROF., DEPT. OF PATHOL. & OF BIOCHEMISTRY, UNIV. OF TORONTO since 1975; mem. Surg. Gen.'s Adv. Comte. on Smoking & Health, 1962–64; Chrmn., Pathol. 'B' Study Sec., Nat. Insts. of Health, 1964–67; Chrm. Biochem. Carcinogen Rev. Panel, Am. Cancer Soc., 1972–75; mem. Cancer Research Training Grants Comte., Nat. Cancer Inst. 1971–72; mem. Adv. Council, Nat. Cancer Inst., 1967–71; mem. Bd. of Scientific Overseers, The Jackson Laboratory, 1972–81; mem. Grants Rev. Panels, Nat. Cancer Inst. Can. 1975–79; mem. Chem. Pathol. Study Sec., Nat. Inst. of Health, 1978–82; Alachlor Review Bd., Candn. Govt. 1985–87; Metabolic Pathology Study Sect., NIH 1987–89; mem. Counc. for Rsch. and Clin. Invest. Grants, Am. Cancer Soc. 1989–91; served with R.C.A.M.C. 1943–46; rank Capt. on discharge; rec'd Am. Cancer Soc. Fellowship in Cancer Research 1947–50 and Scholarship in Cancer Research 1951–55; Am. Cancer Soc. Research Professorship in Cancer Research, 1959–61, 1970–75; Second Annual Parke-Davis Award in Exper. Pathol., 1958; Fourth Annual Bertha Goldblatt Teplitz Mem. Award, 1961; Samuel R. Noble Foundation Award, 1976; elected Fellow, Royal Soc. of Can., 1980; Rous Whipple Award, Am. Soc. Exp. Pathol. 1982; G.H.A. Clowes Award, Am. Assn. Cancer Research 1984; Hon. M.D., Univ. of Torino, Italy; Eastman Kodak Award, Nat. Academy of Clinical Biochemistry 1986; Founder's Award, Chem. Industry Inst. of Toxicology (CIIT) 1987; Maude E. Abbott Lectr., Intern. Acad. Pathol. 1987; Robert E. Greenfield Lectureship in Carcinogenesis, Univ. of Nebraska Med. Ctr. 1987; Distinguished Lectr., Roswell Park Memorial Inst. 1988; Krakower Lectr., Univ. of Illinois, Sch. of Med. 1989; Distinguished Pathol. Award, US-Can. Acad. Pathol. 1992; mem. Ed. Bd., 'Int. Journal/Cancer'; 'Lab. Investig.'; 'Hepatology'; 'Liver'; 'Chemico-biological Interactions'; contrib. to nat science journs.; mem., Am. Assn. Advanc. Science; Am. Assn. Cancer Research (Bd. Dir. 1964–67, 1970–73, Pres. 1972–73); American Assn. Pathols.; Am. Chem. Soc.; Am. Soc. for Biochem. and Molecular Biol.; Am. Soc. Cell Biol.; Am. Soc. Exper. Pathol. (Pres. 1973–74); Biochem. Soc.; Histochem. Soc. (Pres. 1966–67); Internat. Acad. Pathol.; N.Y. Acad. Sciences; Soc. Exper. Biol & Med., Sigma Xi; Hebrew; Home: 17 Tranby Ave., Toronto, Ont. M5R 1N4.

**FARBER, Michael Bruce,** B.A.; journalist; b. Jersey City, N.J. 30 Sept. 1951; s. A. Jerome Lesber and Phyllis Miller (Stern) F.; e. Rutgers Univ. B.A. 1973 (Phi Beta Kappa); m. Danielle Tetrault; children: Jeremy, Gabrielle; SPORTS COLUMNIST, SPORTS ILLUSTRATED; sports writer Sun-Bulletin Binghamton, N.Y. 1973; pub. relations assoc. World Championship Tennis 1974; staff sports writer Bergen Record, Hackensack, N.J. 1975, columnist 1978–79; sports writer Montreal Gazette 1979, sports columnist 1981–84, 1988–.., city columnist 1984–88; Instr. in Jour. Concordia Univ. Montreal 1983–87; recipient Nat. Newspaper Award sports writing 1982, Cert. Merit sports writing 1980, 1986, 1988; contbr. 'Anglo Guide to Survival in Quebec' 1982; 'Unsportsmanlike Conduct' 1984; 'The Great Canadian Character Anthology' 1985; Home: 1527 Foch Ave., Verdun, Que. H4H 2R5.

**FARKAS, Peter P.,** C.A., C.B.V.; chartered accountant, trustee in bankruptcy; b. Budapest, Hungary 17 Mar. 1950; e. Univ. of West. Ont. B.B.A. 1973; C.A. 1976; Trustee 1980; Chartered bus. valuator degree 1987; m. Barbara Harris; three children; PARTNER & VICE-PRES., RICHTER & PARTNERS INC. 1983– ; C.A. student, Coopers & Lybrand; obtained C.A. & Trustee licence, Peat Marwick; joined Richter & Partners 1981; editor: 'C.A. Magazine' (insolvency section); Mem., Ont. & Candn. insts. of C.A.s; Candn. Inst. of Chartered Bus. Valuators; Pres., Ont. Insolvency Assn. 1989–90; Dir. 1987–90; Mem., Candn. Insolvency Assn.; Insolvency Inst. of Can.; Office: 90 Eglinton Ave. E., Toronto, Ont. M4P 2Y3.

**FARLEY, The Honourable Mr. Justice James M.,** LL.B., M.A.; b. Guelph, Ont. 15 Oct. 1940; s. George Albert and Charlotte M. (Thomson) F.; e. Univ. of W. Ont., B.A. 1962; Oxford Univ., B.A. (Juris.) 1964, M.A. 1968; Univ. of Toronto, LL.B. 1966; Rhodes Scholar 1962; m. Sandra Ann, d. L. Douglas Maxwell, Oakville, Ont., 16 July 1966; children: Maxwell Montague George, Michael Douglas Thomson; JUDGE, ONTARIO COURT OF JUSTICE (General Division) 1990– ; called to Bar of Ont. 1968; Assoc. Lawyer, Thomson, Rogers 1968–70, Partner 1970–74; Partner, Perry, Farley & Onyschuk 1974–87; Partner, Perry and Outerbridge 1987–89; Counsel, McCarthy & McCarthy 1989; apptd. Judge, Supreme Court of Ont. 1989; Govnr., George Brown Coll., Toronto 1980–87; Club: University; Home: 55 Colonial Cres., Oakville, Ont. L6J 4K8; Office: Osgoode Hall, 130 Queen St. W., Toronto, Ont. M5H 2N5.

**FARLEY, John Eugene,** B.A., F.C.A.; chartered accountant; b. London, Ont. 2 Sept. 1933; s. Cyril Herbert and Elizabeth Irene (Cole) F.; e. London South Collegiate 1952; Univ. of Western Ont. B.A. (Hons. Business Admin.) 1956; Chartered Accountant 1959; F.C.A. 1988; m. Donna d. Marie and Ernest Sadleir 11 Aug. 1962; children: Sarah, Michael, Andrea; AUDIT PARTNER, DELOITTE & TOUCHE 1989– ; joined Deloitte & Touche predecessor, Deloitte Haskins & Sells 1956; Mem., Policy Bd. 1979–92; Managing Partner, Toronto Office 1982–89; Mem., Junior Achievement of Canada 1984– ; (Bd. Mem.; Extve. Ctte. & Treas.; Former Program Ctte. Chair); F.C.A. 1988; Mem., Bd. of Gov., Executives Ctte. & Chair, Finance Ctte., Bishop Strachan School 1983–87; Mem., Eglinton Un. Ch.; recreations: tennis; club: The Board of Trade of Metro. Toronto; Home: 113 Strathallan Blvd., Toronto, Ont. M5N 1S8; Office: Suite 1400, BCE Place, 181 Bay St., Toronto, Ont. M5J 2V1.

**FARLINGER, David Alden,** B.Sc., FEIC, P.Eng.; consulting engineer; b. Winnipeg, Man. 22 Oct. 1938; s. David Edwin and Eveline (Partridge) F.; e. Univ. of Man. B.Sc. (C.E.) 1961; Banff Sch. Advanced Mgmt. 1969; m. Roslyn; d. Edward and Ruth Fenton 7 May 1966; children: Kristin Ruth, Scott David; Chrmn. & C.E.O., I.D. Group Inc. 1991–.., Pres. and C.E.O. 1979–91; Dir. & Chrmn. Linnet Graphics Internat. Inc.; Chrmn. and mem. Exec. Ctte. Teshmont Consultants Inc.; Constrn. Eng. Transport Can. 1961–63; Templeton Engineering Co. 1963–79, Constrn. Eng., Head Pub. Utility Economics Dept., Pres. (1976–79); Past Mem. Council & Exec. Ctte. & Past Chrmn. Assessment Ctte., Nat. Rsch. Council Can.; Past Pres. Assn. Consulting Engs. Can.; mem. Canada West Found.; Rep. Prov. Man. 3 person study directorate econ., tech., environmental & socio-econ. studies proposed W. Can. Electric Power Grid.; Chrmn., NRC Adv. Bd. for Rsch. in Constrn.; Candn. Standards Assn. (Past Chrmn. Tech. Ctte. Gas Pipeline Code Z184; mem. Standards Steering Ctte. Oil & Gas Ind. Systems & Materials); Vice-Pres., Community Support, Manitoba Theatre Centre; Protestant; recreations: summer cottage, skiing; Clubs: Manitoba; Niakwa Country; Home: 20 Victoria Cres., Winnipeg, Man. R2M 1X4.

**FARLINGER, Shirley Ruth,** B.A., B.A.A.; freelance writer and speaker; b. Toronto, Ont. 24 Jan. 1930; d. Albert Charles and Marjorie May (Reilly) Tabb; e. Lawrence Park H.S. 1945; Univ. of Toronto B.A. 1950; Ryerson Polytechnical Inst. B.A.A. (Journalism) 1980; divorced; children: Brian, Pamela, W. Craig, Leonard, David; grandchildren: Stephanie, Jessica, Mallary Davenport, Brian Farlinger; Volunteer, World Federalists of Can.; Peace Magazine; Science for Peace; Nat. Action on the Status of Women; Voice of Women; Candn. Physicians for the Prevention of Nuclear War; candidate in two federal elections; work is in the nature of teaching on global issues (usually unpaid); believes that volunteer work should be given the same recognition as paid work; Mem., Toronto-Eglinton Rotary Club; Elder, Un. Ch. of Canada, Bloor St. U.C.; editor: 'Canada in the Americas: Agenda for the 90s'; contributor to 'Peace Magazine,' 'Seeds and Sowers'; Home: 11 Thornwood Rd., Toronto, Ont. M4W 2R8.

**FARLINGER, William Alexander,** B.Com., F.C.A., LL.D.; b. Toronto, Ont. 21 Nov. 1929; s. Alexander William and Allie Margaret (Purves) F.; e. Lawrence Park Collegiate, Toronto, 1947; Univ. of Toronto (Victoria Coll.) B.Com. 1951; C.A. 1954; children: Brian Allen, William Craig, Leonard Tabb, David Lloyd, Pamela Ruth (Davenport); EXTVE. PARTNER, ERNST & YOUNG; joined Clarkson Gordon (now Ernst & Young) 1951; mem. Inst. Chart. Accts. Ont. 1954 (Fellow 1976); Phi Kappa Sigma (Pres. 1951); past Pres., Roy. Candn. Golf Assn.; Chrmn., Pres.'s Comte., Univ. of Toronto; Protestant; recreations: skiing, squash, golf, fishing; Clubs: Toronto; Founders; Caughnawana Fishing & Hunting; Beacon Hall; Lambton; Royal & Ancient Golf Club of St. Andrews; Royal Montreal Golf; Home: 3602, 65 Harbour Sq., Toronto, Ont. M5J 2L4; Office: P.O. Box 251, Toronto-Dominion Centre, Toronto, Ont. M5K 1J7.

**FARMER, Kenneth P.,** C.M., B.Com., C.A.; b. Westmount, Qué. 26 July 1912; s. John Taylor and Nora Eliza F.; e. High Sch. of Montréal 1929; McGill Univ. B.Com. 1934; Qué. Inst. C.A.s, C.A. 1937; m. Lorayne d. Howard and Mildred Strachan 2 Oct. 1945; children: Howard, Ian, Cynthia, Pamela; Gov. Montréal Corps of Commissionaires 1975– ; joined McDonald Currie & Co. (now Coopers & Lybrand) 1934, Partner 1945–77; served with Royal Montréal Regt., Man. Dragoons 1940–45, rank Maj.; Mentioned in Despatches 1945; mem. Can.'s Olympic Hockey Team 1936; Pres. Candn. Olympic Assn. 1953–61, Pres. Commonwealth Games Assn. of Canada 1977–83, Gov. Cdn. Sports Hall of Fame 1980–90; Chrmn. Nat. Adv. Council Fitness & Amateur Sports 1962–65; club: University; Home: 90 Easton Ave., Montréal West, Qué. H4X 1L2.

**FARMILOE, Dorothy;** author; b. Toronto, Ont. 1920; e. Univ. of Windsor M.A. (Eng.) 1969; author 'The Lost Island' (poetry) 1966; 'Poems for Apartment Dwellers' 1970; 'Winter Orange Mood' 1972 (poetry); 'Blue is the Colour of Death' (poetry) 1973; 'And Some in Fire' (novel) 1974; 'Creative Communication' 1974, 2nd ed. 1977 (textbook); 'Elk Lake Diary Poems' 1976; 'Adrenalin of Weather' (poetry) 1978; 'How to Write a Better Anything' (handbook for creative writers) 1979; 'Words for my Weeping Daughter' (poetry) 1981; 'Isabella Valancy Crawford: The Life and the Legends' (biography) 1983; 'Elk Lake Lore and Legend' (history) 1984; 'Dragons and Dinosaurs' (poetry) 1988; co-author '21 X 3' (poetry) 1967; Ed. 'Contraverse' (anthology of Windsor Poets) 1971; poems incl. various Candn., Am., Eng. and New Zealand mags.; rep. in 14 anthologies; featured on CBC radio 'Anthology'; co-founder and former Ed. 'Mainline' mag., 'Sesame Press'; founder and Publisher the Elk Lake Explorer; Northern Ont. Poetry Contest, Timmins Press, 1st Prize 1989; Past Pres., Temiskaming Writers' Guild; mem. League of Candn. Poets; Writers' Union of Can.; Address: P.O. Box 94, Elk Lake, Ont. P0J IG0.

**FARNON, Robert Joseph;** musician; b. Toronto, Ont. 24 July 1917; from 1934 trumpeter with Toronto orchestras of Percy Faith and Geoffrey Waddington; mem. of Happy Gang 1937–43; arranged music for Percy Faith's choral groups and for orchestras of André Kostelanetz and Paul Whiteman; completed first symphony 1940 'Symphonic Suite,' premiered by Toronto Symphony Orchestra 1941 and performed several occasions by Philadelphia Orchestra; second symphony 'Ottawa' (1942) premiered by TSO 1943 on CBC 'Concert Hour'; served overseas during World War II as Music Dir. 'The Army Show' and also conducted Candn. band of Allied Expeditionary Forces on BBC; arranged music for various Eng. dance bands incl. Ted Heath and by 1950 had own BBC radio program; in late 1940's began recording commercially under own name and as arranger for Vera Lynn; also made several LPs with Queen's Hall Light Orchestra for Chappell & Co. Mood Music; conducted orchestras BBC radio series 'Music All the Way' and 'Farnon in Concert' mid 1960's; appearances CBC TV 'Music Makers' 1961, 'The Music of Robert Farnon' 1970, 1975, 1976; arranged and conducted music for recordings by many performers incl. Tony Bennett, Lena Horne, Peggy Lee, Frank Sinatra, Sarah Vaughan; composed scores 'William Comes to Town' and 'Spring in Park Lane' 1947, 'Just William's Luck' 1948, 'Elizabeth of Ladymead' 1949, 'Captain Horatio Hornblower' and 'Circle of Danger' 1951, 'Maytime in Mayfair' 1952, 'His Majesty O'Keefe' 1953, 'Gentlemen Marry Brunettes' and 'Let's Make Up' 1955, 'The Little Hut' 1957, 'The Sheriff of Fractured Jaw' 1958, 'The Road to Hong Kong' 1962, 'The Truth About Spring' 1965, 'Shalako' 1968; other compositions incl. orchestral setting 'A la claire fontaine,' suite 'Canadian Impressions,' theme BBC TV series 'Colditz' (Novello Award 1972), 'How Beautiful is Night,' 'Jumping Bean,' 'Manhattan Playboy,' 'On the Sea Shore' (Novello Award 1960), 'Peanut Polka,' 'Portrait of a Flirt,' 'A Star is Born,' 'Westminster Waltz' (Novello Award 1956); composed 'Pleasure of Your Company' for Oscar Peterson, 'Scherzo' trumpet and orchestra, 'Rhapsody' violin and orchestra, 'Prelude and Dance' harmonica and orchestra, 'Saxophone Triparti'; film scores: 'The Disappearance' 1982; 'A Man Called Intrepid' 1985; 'Bear Island' 1986; 'Mary and Joseph: A Love Story' 1987; arranged and orchestrated music by Norman Campbell for the production by the Royal Winnipeg Ballet of 'Anne of Green Gables' 1989; arranged 12 classic popular songs for CD recording by American soprano Eileen Farrell 1989; recorded second album of songs with Eileen Farrell 1991, third album 1992; scored several concert pieces for the BBC Orchestra and Chorus tour of Canada and the USA, Oct. 1990, 1989; composed work for BBC Orchestra & Chorus 'The Last Enemy' for Battle of Britain 50th Anniversary 1990 (recorded 1991); arranged and conducted three CD albums with Pia Zadora and the Royal Philharmonic Orch. 1987, 1988, 1990; recorded CD album of original classical works with Royal Philharmonic Orch. 1991; conducted gala concert featuring pianist George Shearing and Neil Swainson, Oslo, Norway 1991; arranged and conducted CD album with George Shearing 1992; composed 'A Song of Scandia' for internat. cellist Robert Cohen 1992; composed encore piece for virtuoso percussionist Miss Evelyn Glennie 1992; CD recordings with Lena Horne, Joe Williams, J.J. Johnson, Shirley Horn, Wynton Marsalis, Nancy Wilson 1993; commissioned work 'The Grand Alliance' for Royal Marines Massed Bands Concert, Mountbatten Festival, Royal Albert Hall, London 1994; rec'd commendation from Mayor of Toronto, year of the City's Sesquicentennial 1984; rec'd Ivor Novello Award for outstanding services to Brit. music 1991; attended 75th Birthday Tribute Concert held in his honour, BBC Hippodrome, London 1992; cited various bibliogs.; mem. SOCAN; Address: La Falaise, St. Martin's, Guernsey, Channel Islands.

**FARQUHAR, Robin Hugh,** B.A. (Hons.), M.A., Ph.D.; university administrator; b. Victoria, B.C. 1 Dec. 1938; s. Hugh Ernest and Jean (MacIntosh) F.; e. elem. and high schs. Victoria, B.C.; Univ. of B.C., B.A. 1960, M.A. 1964; Univ. of Chicago Ph.D. 1967; m. Frances Harriet d. late Gordon and Frances Caswell 6 July 1963; three d. Francine Jean, Katherine Lynn, Susan Ann; PRESIDENT AND VICE CHANCELLOR, CARLETON UNIV. and Prof. of Public Admin. 1989– ; Teaching Asst. in Eng. Univ. of B.C. 1960–62; Teacher, Counselor and Coach, Edward Milne Secondary Sch., Sooke, B.C. 1962–64; Staff Assoc. Midwest Adm. Center Univ. of Chicago 1964–66; Assoc. Dir. Univ. Council for Educ. Adm. 1966–69 (apptd. as Asst. Prof. Ohio State Univ. 1967), Depy. Dir. of Council 1969–71 (Assoc. Prof. of Univ. 1970); Chrmn. of Educ. Adm. and Assoc. Prof. Ont. Inst. for Studies in Educ., Assoc. Prof. Univ. of Toronto Grad. Dept. of Educ. Theory 1971–73, Asst. Dir. Ont. Inst. Studies in Educ. 1973–76, Prof. there and Univ. of Toronto 1974; Dean, Coll. of Educ. and Prof. Univ. of Sask. 1976–81; Pres. & Vice Chancellor, Univ. of Winnipeg and Univ. Prof. 1981–89; author 'The Humanities in Preparing Educational Administrators' 1970; co-author 'Preparing Educational Leaders for the Seventies' 1969; 'Preparing Educational Leaders: A Review of Recent Literature' 1972; co-ed. 'Social Science Content for Preparing Educational Leaders' 1973; 'Educational Administration in Australia and Abroad: Issues and Challenges' 1975; 'Canadian and Comparative Educational Administration' 1980; 'The Canadian School Superintendent' 1989; 'Advancing Education: School Leadership in Action' 1991; numerous articles, book chapters; Fellow, Commonwealth Council Educ. Adm.; Hon. Dipl. in Adult Educ., Red River Community Coll.; recipient Edward L. Bernays Foundation Award 1968; Hon. Citizen, City of Winnipeg; Hon. Mem., Scouts Canada; served with RCN (Reserve) rank Lt.; mem. Candn. Soc. Study Educ. (Pres.); Commonwealth Council Educ. Adm. (Pres.); Candn. Educ. Assn. (Dir.); Inter-Am. Soc. Educ. Adm. (Dir.); Nat. Acad. Sch. Extves. (Dir.); Ottawa-Carleton Rsch. Inst. (Dir.); Ottawa-Carleton Economic Development Corp. (Dir.); Corporate-Higher Education Forum (Dir.); Chair, Candn. Bur. Internat. Educ.; Corporate Sec., Winnipeg Symphony Orchestra 1984–86; Campaign Chrmn., United Way of Winnipeg 1985; Beta Theta Pi; United Church; recreations: golf, curling, jogging, cross-country skiing; Clubs: Rideau; Le Cercle Universitaire; Rotary; Home: 1 Linden Terrace, Ottawa, Ont. K1S 1Z1; Office: Carleton Univ., Ottawa, Ont. K1S 5B6.

**FARQUHARSON, Gordon MacKay,** Q.C., B.A., LL.B.; b. Charlottetown, P.E.I. 12 July 1928; s. late Percy A. and Rachel L. (MacKay) F.; e. W. Kent Sch., Charlottetown; Lawrence Park Coll. Inst., Toronto; Victoria Coll., Univ. of Toronto, B.A.; Osgoode Hall Law Sch., LL.B.; m. June Vivienne, d. Harry V. Malabar, Toronto, Ont., 8 Sept. 1954; two s., two. d.; m. 2ndly, Judy Lynne, d. George Bridges, St. Thomas, Ont., 10th Oct. 1980, two s.; PARTNER, LANG MICHENER; Dir. and Secy., GSW Inc.; Shaw Industries Ltd.; Dir., CAMCO Inc.; Doverhold Investments Ltd.; NN Life Insurance Co. of Canada; Valleydene Corp. Ltd.; Valford Holdings Ltd.; Tambrands Canada Inc.; L'Arche International; called to Bar of Ont. 1954; cr. Q.C. 1965; Liberal; Protestant; recreations: skiing, canoeing, sailing; Clubs: The University; Craigleith Ski; Home: 419 Brunswick Ave., Toronto, Ont. M5R 2Z2; Office: P.O. Box 747, Ste. 2500, BCE Place, Toronto, Ont. M5J 2T7.

**FARQUHARSON, W. Robert,** B.Com.; executive; b. Montreal, Que. 6 Dec. 1940; s. Cyril George and Isobel M. (Macfarlane) F.; e. Upper Can. Coll. Toronto; Univ. of Toronto B.Com. 1963; Chart. Financial Analyst 1968; m. Gail d. W. Frank Morley 17 July 1964; children: Deborah, Andrew, David; VICE CHRMN. AND DIR., AGF MANAGEMENT LTD.; Invest. Counsellor Fry & Co. Toronto 1963–70; joined present co. 1963, Vice Pres. 1972, subsequently assumed presidencies of Hardit Corp., AGF Canadian Resources Fund Ltd., AGF Canadian Equity Fund Ltd., AGF Growth Equity Fund Ltd., Corporate Investors Ltd., Corporate Investors Stock Fund Ltd., apptd. Dir. 1978; Dir., Regional Cablesystems Ltd.; Gov., Investment Funds Inst. of Can.; Protestant; recreations: golf, tennis, skiing, hobby farming; Clubs: National; Badminton & Racquet; The Ticker; Queen's; Devil's Glen Country; Mad River Golf; Home: 73 Lynwood Ave., Toronto, Ont. M4V 1K5; Office: 31st Flr., Toronto-Dominion Bank Tower, Toronto, Ont. M5K 1E9.

**FARQUHARSON, Rt. Rev. Walter Henry,** B.A., B.D., D.D.; hymn writer, educator, pastor; b. Rosetown, Sask. 30 May 1936; s. James and Jessie Ann (Muirhead) F.; e. Rosetown H.S. 1954; Univ. of Sask. B.A. 1957, dipl. in edn. 1969; St. Andrew's Coll. Saskatoon B.D. 1961, D.D. 1975; m. Joan d. Henry and Phyllis Casswell 16 Sept. 1958; children: Scott, Michael, Catherine, Stephen; settled on Saltcoats-Bredenbury Pastoral Charge 1961 & has since served as clergy with only brief interruption of 2 yrs.; began teaching high & jr. high sch. in capacity of worker-priest 1967; Moderator, United Church of Canada 1990–92; Pres., Sask. Conf., Un. Ch. of Can.; Extve. Gen. Counc.; several past posts on edn. cttes. & Past Pres., Yorkton Teachers' Assn.; author of over 100 hymns & religious songs pub. worldwide; recreations: gardening; Home: Box 126, Saltcoats, Sask. S0A 3R0; Offices: Box 58, Saltcoats, Sask. S0A 3R0 and 85 St. Clair Ave. E., Toronto, Ont. M4T 1M8.

**FARR, David M.L.,** M.A., D.Phil.; b. Vancouver, B.C. 1922; s. A. Morice and Mary Norah (Marlatt) F.; e. Queen Mary Sch. and Lord Byng High Sch. Vancouver; Univ. of B.C. B.A. 1944; Univ. of Toronto M.A. 1946; Oxford Univ. (New and Nuffield Colls.) D.Phil. 1952; m. Joan Rowena d. J.R. Villiers-Fisher, Victoria, B.C. 5 Sept. 1946; children: Christopher John, Timothy Robin Wykeham, Jeremy Stuart Talbot; PROF. EMERITUS OF HISTORY, CARLETON UNIV. since 1987; Lectr. in Hist. Dalhousie Univ. 1946–47; joined present Univ. 1947; Prof. 1961; Dean of Arts 1963–69; Dir., Paterson Centre for International Programs, Carleton Univ. 1979–85; Visiting Lectr. and Assoc. Prof. Univ. of B.C. 1953, 1957–58; Visiting Assoc. Prof. Duke Univ. 1960; served with RCNVR 1944–45; author 'The Colonial Office and Canada, 1867–1887' 1955; 'A Church in the Glebe: St. Matthew's, Ottawa, 1898–1988' 1988; co-author 'Two Democracies' 1963; 'The Canadian Experience' 1969; editor 'Documents on Canadian External Relations' vol. I, 1909–1918, 1967; Subj. Ed., History, 'Carleton Library' series, 1962–69; Gen. Ed., 1970–72; articles and reviews various journs.; mem. Candn. Hist. Assn. (Eng. Lang. Secy. 1947–50, 1952–57; Pres. 1977–78); mem., Public Records Comte., 1960–67; Adv. Council on Records, 1967–83; Social Science Fed. Can. (Chrmn. Comte. on Publs. 1961–65; Council 1965–69, 1976–80); Candn. Inst. Internat. Affairs (Chrmn. National Capital Br. 1973–75); mem., Ed. Bd., Official Hist., External Affairs and International Trade Can. 1984– ; (Chrmn. 1990– ;); editor, reconstitution of House of Commons Debates, 1872–1874 (Library of Parliament) 1990– ; Jury, Gelber Prize 1991–92 (Chrmn. 1991); Council Deans Arts & Sciences Ont. Univs. (Chrmn. 1967–68); Anglican; Home: 942 Colonel By Dr., Ottawa, Ont. K1S 5C9.

**FARR, Dorothy May,** B.A., M.A.; art curator; b. Toronto, Ont. 11 Jan. 1946; d. Louis William and Lydia May (Rutherford) F.; e. Weston Coll. 1965; Univ. of Toronto B.A. 1969, M.A. 1970; CURATOR, AGNES ETHERINGTON ART CTR., QUEEN'S UNIV. 1980– ; Slide Librarian, Dept. of Art, Queen's Univ. 1970–78; Registrar, Agnes Etherington Art Ctr., Queen's Univ. 1978–80; Bd. Mem., Frontenac Hist. Found. 1981–87; Ed. Bd., 'Queen's Quarterly' 1985–93; author of many exhib. catalogues (most recent: 'Urban Images: Canadian Painting' 1990); Office: Kingston, Ont. K7L 3N6.

**FARR, Sally M. Horsfall,** R.N.; voluntary sector executive; b. Toronto, Ont.; d. Douglas and Margaret (Knox) Horsfall; e. Wellesley Hosp. Sch. of Nursing, R.N.; WEP, Univ. of W. Ont.; two s.: James Richard Henry, Richard William Orello; FOUNDING EXEC. DIR. & SEC., TRILLIUM FOUNDATION 1982– ; registered nurse, var. hosps. & disciplines, but primarily emergency; joined Candn. Hearing Soc. Hearing Aid Prog. 1977; Asst. Exec. Dir. 1977–82; Founding Managing Dir. & Vice Pres., Candn. Hearing Soc. Found. 1979–82; Dir., Niagara Inst.; Greenshield Canada; Public Rep., Appeals Ctte., Inst. of Chart. Accts. of Ont.; Past Fac. Mem., Fund Raising Mgmt. Course, Humber Coll. & Candn. Centre for Philanthropy; Founding Chrmn., Voice for Hearing Impaired Children 1973–76; Past Dir. & Exec. Ctte. Mem., Candn. Coord. Counc. on Deafness; Past Advisory Ctte. Mem., Secretariat for Disabled Persons Community Action Fund; Past Dir., Candn. Hearing Soc.; Ont. Coord. Counc. for the Hearing Impaired; Metropolitan Toronto & Region Conservation Found.; mem., Jr. Leagues of Toronto & Winnipeg 1971–79; Jr. Wimodausis Club 1966–70; author of various papers & presentations on voluntary sector mgmt.; recreations: skiing, sailing, tennis; clubs: Caledon Ski; Sturgeon Pt. Sailing, Cottingham Tennis; Office: 23 Bedford Rd., Toronto, Ont. M5R 2J9.

**FARRALL, Marjorie Jean,** B.Sc, Ph.D.; research administrator; b. Quebec City, Que. 3 Feb. 1951; d. Osman James and Jessie Mary (Allingham) Walker; e. Queen's Univ., B.Sc. (Hon.) 1973; Univ. of Ottawa, Ph.D. 1979; m. Kimberley s. Harry and Phyllis Farrall 7 Oct. 1972; children: Joanne Caitlin, Christopher James; DIR., OFFICE OF RESEARCH SERVICES, UNIV. OF OTTAWA 1987– ; NSERC postdoct. fellow 1979; Rsch. Assoc., present univ. 1980; NSERC Univ. Rsch. Fellow, Dept. of Chem. 1981–83; Grants Offr., NSERC Strategic Grants Prog. & NSERC Univ.-Indus. Prog. 1983–87; Bd. of Dir., Telecommunications Rsch. Inst. of Ont.; Bd. of Dir., Inst. for Chemical Scis. and Technology; Mngt. Bd., Ottawa-Carleton Rsch. Inst.; Mem., Chem. Inst. of Can.; Am. Chem. Soc.; Candn. Assn. of Univ. Rsch. Admin. (Extve. 1988– , Vice-Pres. 1992–93, Pres. 1993–94); Soc. of Rsch. Admin. (Can.); Technology Transfer Soc.; Home: 75 Springhurst Ave., Ottawa, Ont. K1S 0E2; Office: Room 209, Hagen Hall, 115 Seraphin Marion, Univ. of Ottawa, Ottawa, Ont. K1N 6N5.

**FARRAN, Roy Alexander,** D.S.O., M.C.; commissioner; author; farmer; b. U.K. 2 Jan. 1921; s. Stephen F. and Minnie (Tarrington) F.; e. Bishop Cotton Sch. Simla, India 1937; Royal Mil. Coll. Sandhurst 1939; m. Ruth d. William Ardern 1950; children: Sally, Peter, Teresa, David; CHRMN., ALBERTA RACING COMMISSION 1979– ; Pres., Candn. Amateur Jockeys Assoc.; comnd. The Queen's Own Hussars and served with Brit. Army 1939–48 W. Desert, Mediterranean, Brit. Special Air Service, rank Maj.; recipient D.S.O., M.C. with 2 bars, French Croix de Guerre with Palm, U.S. Legion of Merit, Italian Gold Medal, Greek War Medal; Publisher North Hill News Ltd. 1954–73; Ald. City of Calgary 1961–71; Journalist, Calgary Herald 1950–54, 1979–88; Edmonton Journal 1979–83; CFAC 1969–71; Alta. M.L.A. 1971–79; Min. of Utilities & Telephones 1972–75; Solr. Gen. 1975–79; raises cattle near Black Diamond, Alta.; weekly Visiting Prof. in Pol. Sci., Univ. of Alta. 1984–89; author 'Winged Dagger' 1949; 'Jungle Chase' 1952; 'The Day After Tomorrow' 1955; 'The Search' 1958; 'History of the Calgary Highlanders' 1962; 'Operation Tombola' 1968; 'Never Had a Chance' 1972; mem. Un. Services Inst. Calgary; Hon. mem. Lord Strathcona's Horse (RC); R. Catholic; recreations: riding, fishing, shooting; Clubs: Glencoe; Cavalry & Guards (London, Eng.); Home: (PO Box 9) Site 30, R.R. 8, Calgary, Alta. T2J 2T9; Office: 507, 5920 1A St. S.W., Calgary, Alta. T2H 0G3.

**FARRAR, Geoffrey D.;** banker; b. Belfast, N. Ireland 7 Mar. 1935; e. Queen's Univ.; Univ. of W. Ont. Banking/Finance; m. Anne Louise Irwin Houston; children: Keith, Roger; PRES., C.E.O. AND DIR., BARCLAYS BANK OF CANADA and CHRMN., BARCLAYS CANADA LEASING CORPORATION; Dir. and Pres., Barclays de Zoete Wedd Asset Management Canada Ltd.; Dir., Barclays McConnell; with Canadian Imperial Bank of Commerce 1955–66; Vice Pres. First National City Bank 1966–75; Fellow, Inst. Candn. Bankers; Clubs: Toronto; R.C.Y.C.; Toronto; Royal Candn. Mil. Inst.; Home: 312 Douglas Dr., Toronto, Ont. M4W 2C3; Office: 304 Bay St., Box No. 1, Toronto, Ont. M5H 4A5.

**FARRAR, John L.,** B.Sc., M.Sc., Ph.D.; university professor emeritus; b. Hamilton, Ont. 31 Dec. 1913; s. Robert Watson and Sarah Wilson (Laird) F.; e. Delta Coll. Inst., Hamilton, Ont.; Univ. of Toronto, B.Sc., (Forestry) 1936; Yale Univ., M.Sc. (Forestry) 1939; Ph.D. 1955; b. Betty Joan, d. Walter May, Woking, Eng., 12 Oct. 1946; EMERITUS PROF. OF FORESTRY, UNIV. OF TORONTO; engaged in general woods work with Candn. Internat. Paper Co., Three Rivers, Que., 1936–37; with Forestry Br., Fed. Govt., 1937–41 and 1945–56 (site classification, tree breeding, silvicultural characteristics of tree species); apptd. Prof. of Forestry, Univ. of Toronto 1956–79; Editor, 'Canadian Journal of Forest Research' 1970–81; served in 2nd World War with R.C.A.F., 1941–45; Radar Offr. with R.A.F. in Middle East; mem., Candn. Inst. Forestry; Ont. Prof. Foresters Assn.; Candn. Bot. Assn.; Sigma Xi; Conservative; recreations: golf, bridge, square dancing; Home: 255 Bamburgh Circle, Unit 306, Scarborough, Ont. M1W 3T6.

**FARRELL, Alexander Patrick Seward,** B.A.; editor; b. New Glasgow, N.S. 19 Jan. 1933; s. Alexander Seward and Vivian (Pomeroy) F.; e. Amherst (N.S.) High Sch.; King's Coll. Halifax; Ludwig-Maximilian Univ. Munich; Concordia Univ. Montreal B.A. 1963; m. Mary Margaret d. Sylvester and Leona MacInnis 5 Sept. 1959; children: Brian, Cathleen, Sean, Mark, Patrick; ED.-IN-CHIEF (CAN.) READER'S DIGEST 1985– ; Founding mem., Candn. Soc. of Magazine Editors; journalist Amherst (N.S.) Daily News 1949–50; Moncton (N.B.) Times 1950–53; Halifax Chronicle-Herald 1954–56, 1958–59; Candn. Press Montreal, N.Y., UN and Ottawa offices 1959–69; The Montreal Gazette 1970–73; Asst. Ed. present mag. 1973, Sr. Ed. 1979; R. Catholic; recreations: books, chess, stamp-collecting; Home: 999, rue Montarville, St. Bruno, Que. J3V 3S9; Office: 215 Redfern Ave., Montreal, Que. H3Z 2V9.

**FARRELL, Mark,** B.Comm., C.A.; retired publisher; b. Montreal, Que. 22 Jan. 1913; s. Gerald William and Eileen (O'Meara) F.; e. Selwyn House Sch., Montreal, P.Q.; Ampleforth Coll., U.K.; McGill Univ., B. Com. 1934; Sociology Diploma, Moscow Univ. 1934; McGill Univ., C.A. 1937; m. Joanna Wright, 1939; one d. Sarah Vanessa; m. 2ndly, Florence Wall, 1952; two d. Fiona, Willa; Vice Pres., Southam Press, and Publisher, The Montreal Gazette 1972–76; Jr. Acct., with McDonald, Currie & Company, Chart. Accountants, Montreal 1934–36; Managing Editor, 'The Canadian Forum' 1936–38; Promotion Mgr., The Montreal Standard Publ. Co. Ltd. 1939–41; Internal Auditor, Brit. Air Comn. 1941–44; Gen. Mgr., Montreal Standard Publishing Co. Ltd. 1945–64; Mang. Dir. 1964–68; Publisher and Dir., Windsor Star, Ont. 1969–72; recreations: skiing, fishing; Clubs: Marden's; University; Home: P.O. Box 926, Stowe, Vermont USA.

**FARRELL, Ruby Violet Marilyn,** B.A., B.Ed., M.Ed.; author; b. Collins, Ont. (at father's trapline, Whitewater Lake) 24 Dec. 1952; d. Albert and Daisy (Patahoo) S.; e. Lakehead Univ. B.A. 1988, B.Ed. 1989, M.Ed. 1993; Ont. Teaching Cert. (primary/jr.) m. Patrick s. Ethel and Thomas Farrell 6 Feb. 1978; children: Rosanna,

Amy, Lindsay; COORDINATOR, NATIVE TEACHER EDUCATION PROGRAM, SCH. OF EDN., LAKEHEAD UNIV. 1993– ; Co-ord.-Counsellor, Native Support Serv., Lakehead Univ. 1989–90; Lecturer-Counsellor, Native Teachers Edn. Prog. 1990–92; Acting Coordinator 1992–93; Mem., Lakehead Univ. Fac. Assn.; Wm. A. West Edn. Medal, Lakehead Univ. 1993; City of Thunder Bay Citizenship Award for Cultural Achievement 1989; McAllan Monro Family Memorial Prize for Prose, Lakehead Univ. 1988; speaks fluent Ojibwa and can read and write in syllabics; author (Ruby Slipperjack): 'Silent Words' 1992, 'Honour the Sun' 1987; recreations: oil painting (art work appears on covers of her books), teaching native arts, camping, outdoor activities; Home: 587 Lansdowne Ct., Thunder Bay, Ont. P7C 1V2; Office: Thunder Bay, Ont. P7B 5E1.

**FARRIS, John Haig deBeque,** B.A., LL.B.; financial executive; b. Vancouver, B.C. 29 Nov. 1938; s. John L. and Dorothy (Colledge) F.; e. Univ. of B.C., B.A. 1960; Univ. of Pa. LL.B. 1963; m. Mary d. Jack and Elsie (Armstrong) Larsen 8 Aug. 1962; children: Jason Reynolds de Beque, Lara; PRESIDENT, FRACTAL CAPITAL CORP. 1973– ; Adjunct Prof., Dept. of Commerce, U.B.C.; Chair, Triumf Kaon Ventures Office; Dir., Gerle Gold Ltd.; Enertec Geophysical Services Inc., Fairfield Minerals Ltd.; Immune Network Rsch.; Ogy Petroleum Ltd.; Weir-Jones Automotive; Westley Technologies Ltd.; law practice Farris & Co. Vancouver 1963–68; recreations: golfing, boating; Clubs: Vancouver; Point Grey Golf; West Vancouver Yacht; Home: 102 – 7131 Granville St., Vancouver, BC V6P 4X6; Office: 904 – 675 W. Hastings St., Vancouver, B.C. V6B 1N2.

**FARROW, Gomer E.;** banker; b. Wiarton, Ont. 1 Sept. 1932; s. Gordon Edward and Mabel (Humphries) F.; e. Queen's Univ. assoc. course in banking, fellows course in banking; m. Orma Turner 14 Nov. 1959; children: Elizabeth, Blair; VICE-PRES., TREASURY & INVESTMENT BANKING – INSPECTION 1987– ; joined Royal Bank Wiarton 1950 and worked at several other branches; Jr. Inspector, Asst. Gen. Mgr. Dept. 1955; Chief Foreign Exchange Trader 1958; Chief Euro Dollar Trader 1966; Mgr., U.S. Dollar Money Markets N. Am. 1969; Mgr., Internat. Money Markets 1977; Asst. Gen. Mgr., Treas. 1979; Vice-Pres., Global Funds Management, Treasury 1982; Strategy & Finan., Treasury 1983; Global Finan. Risk Control 1987; Mem., The Canadian Club of Toronto; recreations: gardening, travel, handyman carpenter, reading; Home: 1440 Ivy Court, Oakville, Ont.; Office: 315 Front St. W., 16th Fl., Toronto, Ont. M5V 3A4.

**FARROW, Maureen A.,** B.Sc.; economist; b. Molesey, Eng. 20 July 1943; d. George Arthur and Winnifred Ivy (Gregory) Pickett; e. Hull Univ. UK, B.Sc. 1966; York Univ. post-grad. studies; m. John E.L. s. Eric Joseph and Lilly Elsie Farrow 24 July 1969; one s. Karl; PRESIDENT, ECONOMAP 1992– ; former Mkt. Rsch. Mgr. Ultra Electronics, London, Eng.; Econ. Cons. W.A. Beckett Associates 1969–74; Vice Pres. J.J. Singer Consulting Economists Ltd. 1974–80; Vice Pres. Singer Associates 1980–82; Partner & Chief Economist, The Coppers & Lybrand Consulting Group 1983–92; Pres. C.D. Howe Inst. 1987–89; Dir., National Trustco Inc. 1992– ; The Equitab le Life Insurance Co. of Can. 1993– ; Trustee of Imperial Oil's Pension & Savings Plans 1993– ; Public Gov., The Toronto Stock Exchange 1993– ; Dir., Candn. Chamber of Comm. 1990– ; Dir., The Nat. Ballet Sch. 1991– ; Judge, Candn. Bus. Writing Awards 1982–87; mem. Social Sci. & Humanities Rsch. Council Can. 1985–91; Pres., Toronto Assn. Bus. Econs. 1979–80; Fellow, Inst. of Mgmt. Consultants of Ont.; mem., Am. Econ. Assn.; Candn. Assn. Bus. Econs. (Pres. 1983–85); strategic economic adviser to business and govt.; author numerous publs.; frequent speaker on global trends, demographics, the environment, innovation and technology issues; recreations: current affairs, ballet, gardening; Club: RCYC; Home: 15 Douglas Dr., Toronto, Ont. M4W 2B2.

**FASICK, Adele Mongan,** B.A., M.A., M.L.S., Ph.D.; university professor; b. New York 18 March 1930; d. Stephen Leo and Florence Elizabeth (Geary) Mongan; e. Cornell Univ. B.A. 1951; Columbia Univ. M.A. 1954, M.L.S. 1956; Case Western Reserve Univ. Ph.D. 1970; m. 14 Aug. 1955; divorced; children: Pamela, Laura, Julia (Fasick); DEAN, FACULTY OF LIBRARY AND INFORMATION SCIENCE, UNIV. OF TORONTO 1990– ; Librarian, New York Public Lib. 1955–56; Long Island Univ. 1956–58; Asst. Prof., Rosary College 1970–71; Prof., Univ. of Toronto 1971– ; author: 'Ben Who Would Not Spin' (children's book) 1987, 'Managing Children's Services in Public Libraries' 1991; co-author: 'Childview: Reviewing Children's Books' 1987; editor: 'Lands of Pleasure: Essays in Honour of Lillian H. Smith' 1990; recreations: travel, swimming; Home: 4351 Bloor St. W., No. 40, Etobicoke, Ont. M9C 2A4; Office: 140 St. George St., Toronto, Ont. M5S 1A1.

**FATT, William R.,** B.A.; financial executive; b. Toronto, Ont. 11 Mar. 1951; s. William McCluer and Charlotte Kathleen Anne F.; e. York Univ., B.A.Econ. 1974; m. Teresa Lee 18 June 1976; children: Robert McCluer, Michael Patrick; VICE-PRES. FINAN. & ACCTG. & CHIEF FINAN. OFFR., CANADIAN PACIFIC LIMITED 1990– ; Auditor, Thorne Riddell 1973–75; Asst. Controller, Revenue Properties Co. Ltd. 1975–77; Acctg. Analyst, The Consumers Gas Co. 1977–78; Asst. Treas., Hiram Walker Resources Ltd. 1978–82; Treas. 1982–84; Vice-Pres. & Treas. 1984–86; Vice-Pres., Morgan Bank of Can. 1986–88; Treasurer, CP Limited 1988; Vice-Pres. & Treas. 1986–88; Dir., 17260 Canada Inc.; Canada Maritime Ltd.; CP Finance B.V.; CP Ships Inc.; CP Tel Inc.; Candn. Pacific Hotels (Internat.) B.V.; Candn. Pacific Hotels (U.S.) Inc.; Candn. Pacific Hotels & Resorts Inc.; Candn. Pacific Hotels Corp.; Candn. Pacific Securities Ltd.; Candn. Pacific (Bermuda) Ltd.; Candn. Pacific Enterprises Ltd.; Candn. Pacific (U.S.) Holdings Inc.; Candn. Pacific (U.K.) Ltd.; Candn. Pacific (U.S.) Finance Inc.; Candn. Pacific Securities (Ontario) Ltd.; Candn. Pacific Mgmt. Inc.; Centennial Shipping Ltd.; D & H Investments Inc.; Provident Properties Co.; Racine Terminal (Montreal) Ltd.; Rail Britannia Ltd.; Unitel Communications Holdings Inc.; Unitel Communications Inc.; mem., National Counc. of Financial Extves., Conf. Bd. of Can.; Home: 23 Aldershot Cres., Willowdale, Ont. M2P 1L7; Office: 123 Front St. W., Ste. 800, Toronto, Ont. M5J 2M8.

**FATTAH, Ezzat A.,** LL.L., M.A., Ph.D., F.R.S.C.; educator; criminologist; b. Assiout, Egypt 1 Jan. 1929; s. Abdel-Fattah and Nabawiya (Lotfi) Youssef; e. Univ. of Cairo LL.L. 1948; Univ. of Vienna Inst. of Criminol. grad. studies & rsch. 1961–64; Univ. de Montréal M.A. 1965, Ph.D. 1968; m. Jenny S. d. Iver and Johanna Juven 31 Dec. 1971; children: Sonia, Eric; PROF. OF CRIMINOLOGY, SIMON FRASER UNIV. 1974– , Founder and Chrmn. of Criminol. Dept. 1974–78; Dist. Atty., Pub. Prosecutor and Chief Prosecutor various Egyptian cities incl. Alexandria 1949–54 and Cairo 1958–61; Rsch. Asst. in Criminol. Univ. de Montréal 1965–68, Asst. and Assoc. Prof. of Criminol. there 1968–74; recipient Beccaria Prize Qué. Soc. Criminol. 1969; Presidential Citation Am. Soc. Criminol. 1975; Alex Edmison Award Candn. Assn. Prof. Criminols. 1977; Konrad Adenauer rsch. award in the Soc. Sciences and the Humanities 1992; Commemorative Medal, 125th Anniversary of Candn. Confedn.; author: 'A Study of the Deterrent Effect of Capital Punishment' 1972; 'La Victime est-elle coupable?' 1971; 'Understanding Criminal Victimization' 1991; co-author: 'L'alcool chez les jeunes Québecois' 1969; 'Le rôle de l'enseignement et de la recherche criminologique dans l'administration de la justice' 1969; 'Sondage d'opinion publique sur la justice criminelle au Québec' 1969; 'Fear of Punishment' 1976; ed.: 'From Crime Policy to Victim Policy' 1986; 'The Plight of Crime Victims in Modern Society' 1989; 'Towards a Critical Victimology' 1992; co-author: 'Crime and Victimization of the Elderly' 1989; author or co-author over 100 scholarly papers learned jours.; mem. various ed. bds.; Fellow, Royal Soc. of Can.; Consultant, Candn. Social Scis. & Humanities Rsch. Counc.; mem. Standards & Accreditation Devel. Ctte.; mem. Internat. Soc. Criminol. (Dir.); Am. Soc. Criminol.; Candn. Assn. Criminal Justice; Internat. Assn. Penal Law; recreations: swimming, tennis, fishing, hiking; Club: Jack & Sadie Diamond; Home: 1369 Lansdowne Dr., Port Coquitlam, B.C. V3E 1R3; Office: Burnaby, B.C. V5A 1S6.

**FAUCHER, François M.P.;** business executive; b. Bordeaux, France 6 July 1927; s. Henri and Madeleine (Perrier); e. Sch. of Commerce Bourdeaux France; m. Marie-Louise d. Gustave Cardon 7 May 1957; children: Jacques-Philippe, Damien, Renaud; Vice-Pres., Dumez North America Inc. 1975–92; Dumez S.A. 1951–61: Tunisia 1951–52, 1959–60; Tanganyica 1952–55; Irak 1955–59; Paris Head Office 1960–61; Asst. Mgr. & Dir., Dumez Canada Inc. 1961; Mgr. 1963; Vice-Pres. 1975; Vice-Pres., Atlas-Gest Inc. 1981– ; Dir., A.C.R.G.T.Q. Quebec 1987– ; French Govt. Trade Adviser 1983; Chevalier de l'Ordre Nat. du Mérite (Rép. Française); Dir., College Stanislas 1979– ; Mem., Franch C. of C. in Canada; recreations: skiing, sailing; Home: 55 Maplewood, Outremont, Que. H2V 2L9.

**FAUCHER, Jean-Guy,** C.A.; exécutif; né à Montréal, Qué. 14 septembre 1933; é. Hautes Etudes Commerciales comptable agréé 1957, C.A. 1958; ép. Thérèse Derome 11 oct. 1958; enfants: Martin, Julie, Nathalie; Président, J.G. Faucher Inc.; Dir., UniMedia Inc.; Groupe Coscient; Fondation Ressources-Jeunesse; Group Immaculée-Conception; récréations: ski, golf, tennis; Club: St-Denis; Adresse: 175, rue Somerville, Montréal, Qué. H3L 1A1; Bureau: 1130, Sherbrooke ouest, #1350, Montréal, Qué. H3A 2M8.

**FAULKNER, Hon. (James) Hugh,** P.C. (1972); politician; b. Montreal, Que. 9 March 1933; s. George V. and Elizabeth (Baird) F.; e. Lakefield (Ont.) Coll. Sch.; McGill Univ.; International Mgmt. Inst.; Carleton Univ.; Extve. in Residence, Internat. Management Inst., Geneva 1988–89; el. to H. of C. for Peterborough 1965–79; Depy. Speaker 1969; Parlty. Secy. to Secy. of State 1970; Secy. of State, Can. 1972–76; Min. of State for Science and Tech. 1976–77; Min of Indian Affairs and Northern Development 1977–79; Visiting Prof., Faculty of Administration, Ottawa Univ. 1979–80; Vice-Pres., Alcan Aluminium Ltd. 1981–83; Managing Dir., Indian Aluminum Co. 1983–86; Pres., Alcan Aluminium S.A., Geneva, Switzerland 1986–88; mem. Can. NATO Parlty. Assn.; Candn. Inter-Parlty. Union; Bd. of Gov., Trent Univ.; Candn. Arctic Resources Council; Bd. of Gov. Lakefield College School; Liberal; Address: 157 Cap. St. Jacques, Pierrefonds, Que.

**FAULKNER, Philippa Mary,** R.C.A., M.F.A., O.S.A., C.S.P.W.C., S.C.A.; artist; b. Belleville, Ont. 28 Feb. 1917; d. Sanford Rattray Burrows and Jessie Phillips Burrows; e. Bishop Strachan Sschool 1936 (Sr. Art Award); Parsons Sch. of Fine & Appl. Art, Instituto Allende 1946; San Miguel de Allende 1957–64, M.F.A. 1968; m. Dr. George Vermilyea Faulkner (dec'd.); children: Anne Burrows, George Sanford; studied with Hans Hofmann, New York and Provincetown 1946; studied with Fred Varley, Carl Schaefer, York Wilson, Clare Bice etc., Doon School 1948–60; Scholarship student, Instituto de Allende, San Miguel de Allende, Mexico 1957–64; painted with Sch. of Visual Arts in Tuscany 1987 and Barcelona 1990; many corp. collections incl.: Wallace Bond Partners Inc. 1990, Zurich Insur. 1990 Christmas card, Crown Life Insur. 1970 Collectors Choice, OSA, Bell Can., Stelco Co., Royal Bank; permanent coll.: Art Gall. of Hamilton, McLaughlin Gall. Oshawa, Royal Trust Co.; Diamond Jubilee Collection; Royal Library of Windsor Castle 1985; designed 900 lb. sculpture for Bata Internat. Ctr., Acapulco Mexico; 1st prize, Exhib. of Foreign Friends of Acapulco (silver cup by Pineda); long-time teacher at Schneider School of Art, Centennial Coll. etc.; Mem., R.C.A. 1990; The Arts & Letters Club 1990– ; (honoured with a retrospective exhibit of 50 paintings Nov. 21 1993); Colour & Form Soc. 1955– ; Life Mem., Soc. of Candn. Artists 1970; Ont. Soc. of Artists 1969; Can. Soc. of Painters in Watercolour 1963; presents slide show 'Travels With My Art' to schools, libr. & art assns.; Former home, 'Glanmore' (The Phillips-Burrows-Faulkner House, built 1883) together with the 'Faulkner Collection' of donated contents, is now the Hastings County Museum, Belleville, Ont.

**FAUTEUX, T.J. John,** B.A., B.Th., M.Ed.; public relations executive; b. Windsor, Ont. 7 June 1950; s. Louis Fauteux and Elizabeth Taylor; e. Univ. of Windsor Ont., B.A. 1974; Notre Dame Univ., B.Th. 1972; Univ. of Toronto (O.I.S.E.) M.Ed. 1991; m. Beth d. Winston and Dorothy Scharfe 15 Aug. 1970; children: Melissa Anne, Erin Michelle Mary; DIR., PUBLIC RELATIONS, METRO SEPARATE SCHOOL BD., Toronto; Teacher, St. Jules Elementary Sch., J.A. Rooney, Windsor, 1970–80; Consultant, Windsor 1970–80; Cons., Windsor Roman Catholic Separate Sch. Bd. 1980–82, 1982–83; Vice Pres., Ont. English Catholic Teachers' Assoc. (Pres. 1983–86); Cons., Dufferin-Peel R. Catholic Separate Sch. Bd. 1986–87; Pres. Ont. Teachers' Fedn. 1987–88; Pres., Metro Toronto Catholic Educ. Found.; Pres., Toronto-Parkdale Rotary Club; Dir., Redwood Shelter (for women and children of family violence); Dir., Catholic Children's Aid Found.; Student Teacher of the Year (Windsor Teachers' Coll.) 1969–70; named Teacher of the Year (Windsor 1978), Nativity of Our Lord R. Catholic Church 1975; recreations: tennis, raquetball; Home: 627 The West Mall, Apt. 507, Etobicoke, Ont. M9C 4X5; Office: 80 Sheppard Ave. E., Willowdale, Ont. M2N 6E8.

**FAWCETT, Eric,** M.A., Ph.D., F.A.P.S., F.Inst.P., F.A.A.A.S.; educator; b. Blackburn, Eng. 23 Aug. 1927; s. Harold and Florrie (Whittaker) F.; e. Queen Elizabeth's Grammar Sch. Blackburn 1946; Clare Coll. Cambridge, B.A. (Natural Sci's Tripos, 1st class hons.) 1951, M.A. 1952, Ph.D. 1954; m. Patricia d. Peter and Ethel Egan 9 Oct. 1954; children: Clare Priscilla, Andrew Peter, Ruth Margaret; PROFESSOR EMERITUS, UNIV. OF TORONTO 1993– ; Nat. Rsch. Council Post-Doctoral Fellow, Ottawa 1954–56; Fellow, Prin. Sci. Offr.

Royal Radar Est. Malvern, Eng. 1956–61; mem. Tech. Staff, Bell Telephone Labs. N.J. 1961–70; Prof. of Physics, Univ. of Toronto 1970–93; mem. Univ. Coll. 1984– ; mem. Scarborough Coll. 1988– ; ed. 'Physics of Transition Metals' 1978; 'The Name of the Chamber Was Peace' 1987; Founding Chrmn. Candn. Ctte. Sci's & Scholars 1980–83, Sec. 1983– ; Founding Pres. Sci. for Peace 1981–84; Pugwash 1982– ; convenor University College Lectures in Peace Studies 1983– ; mem., Council Internat. Network Engrs. and Scientists for Global Responsibility 1992– ; corresponding mem., World Federation of Scientific Workers 1986– ; recreations: swimming, languages, playing piano; Home: 7 Coldstream Ave., Toronto, Ont. M5N 1X5; Office: 60 St. George St., Toronto, Ont. M5S 1A7.

**FAZIO, Paul P.,** B.Sc., M.Sc., Ph.D., P.Eng., F.C.S.C.E.; university professor/administrator; b. Italy, 1 April 1939; s. Donato and Anna (Marini) F.; e. Assumption Univ. of Windsor, B.Sc. 1963; Univ. of Windsor, M.Sc. 1964, Ph.D. 1968; m. Lucy; children: Teena, Mark, Luke; PROF. & DIR., CTR. FOR BUILDING STUDIES, CONCORDIA UNIV. 1977– ; Chrmn., Civil Engr. Dept., Concordia Univ. 1972–77; Founder and Pres. SIRICON 1985– ; Founder and Pres., Quebec Bldg. Envelope Counc. 1989– ; Bd. Mem., Internat. Ctr. for Rsch. & Training in Major Projects Mngt. in Que.; Constr. Indus. Devel. Counc. of Can.; Past Vice-Chrmn., Candn. Constr. Rsch. Bd.; Vice-Pres., Que. Region, Candn. Soc. for Civil Engr.; mem., Le Cons. de la sci. et de la tech. du Qué.; elected fellow, Candn. Soc. for Civil Engr. 1984; Gzowski Medal for best paper in CSCE Journal 1979; Galbraith Prize for best paper in Engineering Inst. of Canada's transactions 1967; Mem., Am. Soc. for Engr. Edn.; Am. Soc. of Heating, Refrig. & Air-Cond. Engrs., Inc.; Am. Soc. of Civil Engr.; Air Pollution Control Assn.; Assn. of Profl. Engrs., Prov. of Ont.; co-editor of 3 symposium proceedings & author of over 150 tech. papers; recreations: jogging, reading, golf; Office: 1455 boul. de Maisonneuve W., Montreal, Que. H3G 1M8.

**FEARON, Blair,** B.A., M.D., F.R.C.S.(C), F.A.C.S., F.A.A.P.; physician and surgeon; b. Farnham, Que. 26 Jan. 1919; s. John William and Hattie Merrill (Hutchinson) F.; e. Mulgrave (N.S.) pub. and high schs.; Parrsboro (N.S.) High Sch.; Mt. Allison Univ. B.A. 1940; Univ. of Toronto M.D. 1944, U. of T. post-grad. course Otolaryngol. & Broncho-Esophagol. (also Univ. of Pa.) 1946–50; m. Joyce Doreen (dec.) d. Dr. Stanley S. Ball 1st June 1946; children: Merrill Ann, Judith Evalie (Mrs. Robert Sheepway), Dr. Stanley Blair; SR. SURGEON, HOSP. FOR SICK CHILDREN; Prof. Emeritus, Dept. Otolaryngol. Univ. of Toronto; First Chief of Otolaryngol. N. York Gen. Hosp.; Consultant Otolaryngol. & Broncho-Esophagol. Women's Coll. Hosp. and Oakville-Trafalgar Mem. Hosp.; served with R.C.A.M.C. 1942–46, rank Capt.; rec'd Chevalier Jackson Award in Broncho-Esophagol. 1976; Chevalier Jackson Award 1980, Philadelphia Laryngologic Soc.; 'Honour Award' from Am. Academy Otolarygnology, Head and Neck Surgery, 1981; Gabriel Tucker Medal from A.L.A. (Am. Laryngological Assoc.) 1989; author various book chapters and over 70 publs. in nat. and internat. med. journs.; mem. Acad. Med. Toronto; Ont. Med. Assn.; Royal Coll. Phys. & Surgs. (Ont.); Candn.Med. Assn.; Defence Med. Assn.; Candn. Otolaryngol. Soc.; Internat. Broncho-Esophagol. Assn. (Founding mem.); Am. Acad. Otolaryngol & Head & Neck Surg.; Am. Broncho-Esophagol. Assn. (Pres. 1966–67, only Candn.); Am. Triol. Soc. (Vice-Pres.; Chrmn. Eastern Sec. 1983–84); Am. Laryngol. Assn. (Vice Pres. 1973–74; Pres. 1987–88); Pan-Am. Assn. Oto-Rhino-Laryngol. & Broncho-esophagol. SENTAC; Am. Soc. Pediatric Otolaryngologists; Freemason; Alpha Kappa Kappa; P. Conservative; Protestant; recreation: photography; Clubs: Granite; Naval & Mil.; Rosedale Golf; Home: 13 Douglas Cres., Toronto, Ont. M4W 2E6; Office: 170 St. George St., Toronto, Ont. M5R 2M8.

**FEATHER, Frank;** consulting global business futurist and author; b. Yorkshire, Eng. 2 Apr. 1943; s. James and Susan Doris (Smith) F.; e. Keighley Sch., U.K., G.C.E. 1959; Inst. of Bankers U.K., A.I.B. 1966; Candn. Inst. of Bankers, A.I.B. 1974; York Univ., B.A. (Hons.) 1977; M.B.A. (1st Yr. Hons.) 1979; m. Tammie Min Tan; children by previous marriage: Alison Jane, Joanne Elizabeth; PRES. & C.E.O., GEODEVCO; Pres., Glocal Marketing Inc.; Chitech Agency Inc.; Special Adv., China State Counc. 1986– ; Asst. Chief Acct., Barclays Bank Ltd. U.K. 1959–68; Asst. Mgr., Internat. Div., Toronto-Dominion Bank 1968–73; Supt., Domestic Regions & Credit, Canadian Imperial Bank of Commerce 1974–81; Pres. & Co-founder, Global Futures Network 1981; Founding Pres., Global Management Bureau 1982; Chrmn. & Dir.-Gen., 1st Global Conf. on the Future 1980; Fellow, World Assn. for Social Psychiatry; mem., Am. Mktg. Assoc. & several other assns.; author: 'China Vision' 1994; 'The Future Consumer' 1993; 'G-FORCES: Reinventing the World' 1989; 'Canada's Best Careers Guide' 1989; 'Amexicana 2000: The Future of America, Mexico and Canada' 1986; 'The New Russia: Outlook to the Year 2000' 1985; Editor: 'Optimistic Outlooks' 1982; 'Through the 80s' 1980; Home: Aurora, Ont.

**FEDAK, The Honourable Mr. Justice Eugene B.,** B.A., LL.B., Q.C.; judge; b. Parkerview, Sask. 9 Dec. 1934; s. William and Pearl (Timoffee) F.; e. McMaster Univ. B.A. 1957; Osgoode Law School LL.B. 1961; m. Grace d. George and Anna Olynyk 13 Sept. 1958; children: Catherine, Mark; REGIONAL SENIOR JUSTICE, ONTARIO COURT OF JUSTICE (GEN. DIV.), CENTRAL SOUTH REGION 1992– ; Barrister and Solicitor 1963–86; Judge, District Court of Ont. 1986–90; Ont. Court of Justice (Gen. Div.) 1990–92; Q.C. 1975; Chair, Housing Authority, Hamilton-Wentworth 1985; Mem., Candn. Bar Assn.; Ont. Superior Court Judges Assn.; Hamilton Law Assn.; Candn. Judges Conf.; clubs: Canadian, Hamilton; Office: 50 Main St. E., Hamilton, Ont. L8N 1E9.

**FEDERER, Andrew H.;** real estate developer; b. Brockville, Ont. 19 June 1961; s. Henry Edward Charles and Frances Elizabeth Watson (Hardy) F.; e. Bishop's College School; Annex Village Campus (Toronto) 1980; m. Andrea d. Edmond and Gloria Odette, Toronto 24 June 1988; children: Jack Matthew McEwan, Henry Edward Charles; PRESIDENT, LAKEBURN LAND CAPITAL CORP., (DIVISION OF) BURNAC CORP. 1988; Burns Fry Limited 1980–83; Coldwell Banker Canada Inc. (now C.B. Commercial Realty Inc.) 1983; left as Partner & Dir., Real Estate Investment Division 1988; Protestant; recreations: golf, tennis; clubs: Rosedale Golf, Granite Club, Albany; Home: Bayview Wood (Lawrence Park), Toronto, Ont. M4N 1R7; Office: 48 St. Clair Ave. W., Suite 600, Toronto, Ont. M4V 3B6.

**FEDOROFF, Sergey,** B.A., M.A., Ph.D., D.Sc.; educator; b. Daugavpils, Latvia 20 Feb. 1925; e. Univ. of Sask. B.A. 1952 (Hons.) 1953, M.A. 1955, Ph.D. (Histol.) 1958, D.Sc. 1984; PROF. OF ANATOMY, UNIV. OF SASK.; Demonst. in Histol. Univ. of Sask. 1953, Instr. in Anat. 1955, Special Lectr. in Anat. 1957, Asst. Prof. of Anat. 1958, Adm. Asst. to Dean of Med. 1960–62, Assoc. Prof. 1962, Prof. 1964, Asst. Dean Undergrad. Educ. Coll. of Med. 1970–72, Head, Dept. of Anatomy 1964–87, Prof. Emeritus 1992; rec'd Lederle Med. Faculty Award 1957–60; Queen's Silver Jubilee Medal 1978; J.C.B. Grant Award 1987; New Frontiers Award (Jerusalem Mental Health Center) 1988; author or coauthor numerous scient. publs.; mem. Ed. Bd. 'In Vitro' 1975–87; Ed., 'Advances in Cellular Neurobiology' 1979–84; Ed. Bd. Intnl. J. Dev. Neuroscience 1983– ; Ed. Bd. J. Neurosc. Res. 1987– ; mem. Steering Comte. Study Basic Biol. Research Can., Science Secretariat 1966; mem. Med. Research Council Can. 1973–76 (served on various comtes.); Official Candn. Del. to Pan Amer. Cong. Anatomists Caracas 1969, New Orleans 1972, Pres. 4th Pan Amer. Cong. Montreal; mem. Bd. Govs., W. Alton Jones Cell Science Center, Lake Placid 1970–72, Vice Chrmn of the Bd., 1980–82; Chrmn. Internat. Comn. for Estab. Multinat. Training Centers for Anatomists Latin Am. countries 1973–87; Consultant, World Health Organ. in Israel 1977; Vice Chrmn. Candn. Council Animal Care 1979, Chrmn., 1980–81; mem. Candn. Assn. Anatomists (Pres. 1966–67); Am. Assn. Anatomists; Pan Am. Assn. Anat. (Pres. 1972–75, Hon. Pres. since 1975); Am. Soc. Cell Biol.; Candn. Soc. Cell Biol.; Tissue Culture Assn. (Pres. 1968–72); Soc. Exper. Biol. & Med.; Candn. Soc. Immunol. (Council 1966–71); Soc. for Neuroscience; Candn. Assoc. Neuroscience (Pres. 1986–87); Candn. Fed. Biol. Socs. (Pres. 1978–79); New York Academy of Sciences; Corr. mem. Mexican Assn. Anatomists; Hon. mem. Venezuelan Assn. Morphol.; Address: 36 Cantlon Cres., Saskatoon, Sask. S7J 2T3.

**FEDORUK, Sylvia O.,** O.C., S.O.M., B.A., M.A., D.Sc., LL.D., D.Hum.L., F.C.C.P.M.; physicist; educator; b. Canora, Sask. 5 May 1927; d. Theodore and Annie (Romaniuk) F.; e. Walkerville Coll. Inst., Windsor, Ont. 1942–46; Univ. of Sask., B.A. 1949 (Gov.-Gen.'s Gold Medal) M.A. 1951; D.Sc., Univ. of Windsor 1987; D.Sc., Univ. of Western Ont. 1990; LL.D., Univ. of Regina 1991; D.Hum.L., Mt. St. Vincent Univ. 1993; LIEUTENANT GOVERNOR, PROV. OF SASKATCHEWAN 1988– ; Chancellor, Sask. Order of Merit 1988– ; Prof. Emeritus Univ. of Sask.; Hon. Mem. Medical Staff, Univ. Hosp.; Dir. of Physics Services, Sask. Cancer Foundation 1966–86; Prof. Univ. of Sask., 1973–86; Chancellor, Univ. of Sask. 1986–89; Fellow of the Candn. Coll. of Physicists in Med., Jan. 1980; mem., Atomic Energy Control Bd. Can. (1973–88); past Chrmn. Saskatoon Centennial Auditorium Foundation 1978–79; past mem., Sci. Counc. of Can. 1971–74; Assistant Physicist, Saskatoon Cancer Clinic, 1951, Senior Physicist 1957; Assistant Prof., Univ. of Sask., 1956; mem., Adv. Comte. on Clin. Uses of Radioactive Isotopes in Humans to Min. of Nat. Health & Welfare, 1960; mem. Task Group on Scanning, Internat. Comn. on Radiation Units and Measurements, 1962; Consultant, Nuclear Medicine, Internat. Atomic Energy Agency, Vienna, 1966, 1968, 1969; Vice Chrmn., Nat. Forum on Post Secondary Education 1987; mem., Mayor's Committee Sport Participation Canada; author or co-author of over 38 scientific papers and book chapters; formerly Consulting Ed., The Curler Magazine; past Pres., Candn. Ladies Curling Assn.; Hon. mem., Peruvian Soc. Nuclear Medicine; Hon. mem., Hindu Soc. of Sask.; mem., Candn. Assn. Physicists (Past Chrmn. Med. & Biol. Phys. Div.); Candn. Assn. Radiols. (Council); Hosp. Physicists Assn.; Soc. Nuclear Med. (Past Trustee & Dir.); Health Physics Soc.; Candn. Radiation Protection Assn.; Past Dir., Sports Fed. of Canada; received Citation Saskatoon B&P Club, 1965; Queen's Jubilee Medal 1977; Century Saskatoon Medal 1982; Sask. Sports Hall of Fame; U. of S. Athletic Wall of Fame 1984; Candn. Curling Hall of Fame; Saskatoon Sports Hall of Fame; Y.W.C.A. Woman of the Year 1986; Officer, Order of Canada 1986; Sask. Order of Merit, 1986; Toastmasters Internat. Communications and Leadership Award 1991; Internat. Rotary Paul C. Harris Fellow 1992; Commemorative Medal, 125th Anniversary of Candn. Confedn. 1992; Toastmasters Internat. Award 1993; Ukrainian Greek Orthodox; recreations: curling, golf, fishing; Clubs: Faculty; Assiniboia; Wascana Golf & Country; Riverside Golf & Country; Home: 2 Lakeview Place, Regina, Sask. S4S 7B5; Office: Government House, 4607 Dewdney Ave., Regina, Sask. S4P 3V7.

**FEENEY, Gordon J.;** bank executive; b. Harvey Station, N.B. 4 Aug. 1941; SENIOR EXECUTIVE VICE-PRES., RETAIL BANKING, ROYAL BANK OF CANADA 1990– ; joined Royal Bank, Harvey Station N.B. 1959; various positions in Atlantic provinces, Ont. & Que. incl. Head Office; Asst. Gen. Mgr., Compensation 1979; Vice-Pres., Branch & Processing Opns. 1980; Sr. Vice-Pres., Personnel 1982; Sr. Vice-Pres. & Gen. Mgr., Atlantic Provinces 1986; Extve. Vice-Pres., Opns. & Service Delivery 1988; Chrmn., R.B.C. Insurance Holdings Inc.; Royal Bank Investor Trading Inc.; Royal Bank Mortgage Corp.; Royal Bank Group of Mutual Funds; Dir., Royal Trust Group of Companies; Royal Bank Realty Inc.; R.B.C. Bahamas Limited; R.B.C. Holdings (Bahamas) Limited; R.B.C. Investments Limited; Finance Corp. of the Bahamas Limited; Mem., Domestic Banking Policy Ctte.; Trustee, Candn. Figure Skating Hall of Fame; Mem., American Management Assn.'s General Management Council; Dir., Montreal Children's Hospital Found.; St. Mary's Hospital (Montreal); Office: 1 Place Ville Marie, P.O. Box 6001, Montreal, Que. H3C 3A9.

**FEENY, David Harold,** M.A., Ph.D.; educator; b. Wilmington, Del. 17 Sept. 1948; s. Harold Francis and Muriel Rebecca (Elliott) F.; e. N. Ill. Univ., B.A. 1970; Univ. of Wis., M.A. 1972, Ph.D. 1976; m. Darrell Joan d. Oliver and Maxine Tomkins 15 July 1977; children: Gwenneth Robin, Graham Tomkins; PROF. OF ECON. AND CLIN. EPIDEMIOL. & BIOSTATS., McMASTER UNIV. 1988– ; Asst. Prof. of Econ. McMaster Univ. 1976–82, Northeastern Univ. 1979–80; Assoc. Prof. of Econ. and Assoc. Prof. of Clin. Epidemiol. & Biostats. present univ. 1982–88; Visiting Fellow, Yale Univ. 1983–84; Visiting Scholar, Univ. of California, Berkeley 1990–91; Pres., Internat. Assn. for The Study of Common Property 1993–95; Cons. Candn. Internat. Devel. Agency, Agency for Internat. Devel., World Bank and several private-sector firms; mem. Panel on Common Property Resource Mgmt. Nat. Acad. Sci's (USA) 1983–86; recipient Woodrow Wilson Fellowship 1970; author 'The Political Economy of Productivity' 1982; co-ed. 'Health Care Technology' 1986; various papers acad. jours. and edited vols.; mem. Am. Agric. Econ. Assn.; Assn. Asian Studies. Am. Econ. Assn.; Candn. Health Econ. Rsch. Assn.; Econ. Hist. Assn.; Internat. Soc. Technol. Assessment Health Care; Alta. Wilderness Assn.; recreations: hiking, backpacking, travel; Club: Sierra; Home: 49 Haddon Ave. S., Hamilton, Ont. L8S 1X5; Office: Hamilton, Ont. L8S 4M4.

**FEFERMAN, Irving Jacob,** M.D.; physician; b. Toronto, Ont. 1 July 1947; s. Sol and Sarah (Lipkus) Pfeferman; e. Bathurst Hts. S.S. 1966; Univ. of Toronto M.D. 1972; Cert. Emerg. Med. Coll. Family Phys.

(Can.) 1983; m. Margot Renate d. Ralph and Isabella Snow 30 Dec. 1971; children: Teddy Jay, Sari Rachel, Noah Aaron; DIRECTOR OF EMERGENCY SERVICES, SCARBOROUGH GENERAL HOSPITAL 1980– ; med. practice Eglinton-Kennedy Med. Grp. 1977– ; Chrmn. Community Hospitals, Emergency Dept. Directors 1984– ; Vice Chrmn. Med. Adv. Bd., Dept. of Ambulance Services 1984– ; Consultant 'Science International' TV series 1980; Emergency Phys. Mt. Sinai Hosp. 1974; mem., Royal Coll. of Phys. & Surgeons; Am. Coll. of Emerg. Phys.; publ., 'Pica: A Review' 1976; 'Screening for Hypertension' 1973; 'Simple Method for Administering Endotracheal Medication' 1980; 'Use of Surgical Glove When Repairing Finger Injuries' 1985; recreations: jogging, piano; Office: 2432 Eglinton Ave. E., Scarborough, Ont. M1K 2P8.

**FEHLINGS, Michael George,** M.D., Ph.D., FRCS (C); neurosurgeon; neuroscientist; b. Toronto, Ont. 6 Nov. 1958; s. George John William and Ingrid Helga (Schnellhardt) F.; e. Richview C.I. 1977; Univ. of Toronto, M.D. (summa cum laude) 1983, Ph.D. 1989; FRCS (C) 1990; m. Darcy d. John and Joan Phillips 27 June 1981; children: Tara Kristen, Lauren Nicola, Nicholas Justin; ASST. PROF. OF NEUROSURGERY, UNIV. OF TORONTO; Staff Neurosurgeon, The Toronto Hosp.; Staff Scientist, Playfair Neuroscience Unit 1992– ; Internship, Gen. Surg., Kingston Gen. Hosp. 1983–84; Neurosurgery Residency, Univ. of Toronto 1984–90; Ph.D. training, Med. Sci., Univ. of Toronto; Postdoctoral training in Neuroscience and Spinal Surgery, New York Univ. Med. Ctr. 1991–92; Dr Mitchell Kohan Award 1983; MRC, post-doct. rsch. fellowship 1985–88; GM Neurotrauma Award, Am. Assn. of Neurol. Surg. (AANS) 1987; K.G. McKenzie Award, Royal Coll. of Physicians & Surg. (RCPS), for work on spinal cord regeneration 1987; also internat. awards from AANS & RCPS; Herbert Jasper Award in Neurophysiology 1988; Candn. Trauma Assoc. Award 1988; Laidlaw Award in Med. Sci. 1988; Career Scientist Award, Ont. Min. of Health 1992; mem., Candn. Med. Assn.; Clin. Rsch. Soc. of Toronto; Cong. of Neurol. Surg.; Candn. Soc. of Clin. Neurophysiol.; Internat. Soc. of Cerebral Blood Flow and Metabolism; Internat. Soc. for Neurotrauma; mem., Am. Acad. for Advancement of Sci.; Am. Assoc. of Neurological Surgeons; Candn. Neurosurgical Soc.; Royal Coll. of Physicians and Surgeons of Can.; author of sev. sci. papers; Home: 101 Constance St., Toronto, Ont. M6R 1S7.

**FEHR, Gordon John;** b. Montreal, Que. 6 May 1933; s. John Walter and Rosalie (Fischer) F.; e. Westmount (Que.) High Sch., 1950; McGill Univ., Chem. Engn. 1955; m. Marilyn, d. Larry P. McMahon, 22 June 1957; children: Michael, Kerry, Gary, Mary Clare, Carolyn; CHRMN., PFIZER CANADA INC., since 1992; Chem. Sales Rep., Shell Oil Co., 1955–56; Tech. Sales Rep., Canadian Analine & Extract, 1956–57; Asst. to Lubricants Mgr., BP Oil Ltd., 1957–58; Consumer Supvr. Que. 1958–59; Consumer Mgr. Can. (Indust. & Farm Sales) 1959–63; joined present Co. as Asst. to Pres. 1963–64; Operations Mgr.-Pharm. 1965–66; Materials & Distribution Mgr. 1966–67; Comptroller & Secy.-Treas. 1967–69; Gen. Mgr. Chem. Div. 1969–72; President 1972–92; mem. Adv. Bd., Extve. Programme, Univ. of Indiana; Pres., Montreal Bd. Trade; Dir. Forest & Stream Club; Corp. Prof. Engrs. Que.; R. Catholic; recreation: sports; Club: Nun's Island Tennis; Office: 17300 Trans Canada Hwy., Kirkland, Que. H9J 2M5.

**FEINDEL, William Howard,** O.C.(1982), B.A., M.Sc., M.D., C.M., D.Phil., D.Sc., LL.D., F.R.C.S.(C), F.A.C.S., F.R.S.C.; b. Bridgewater, N.S. 12 July 1918; s. Robert Ronald and Annie MacKay (Swansburg) F.; e. Acadia Univ. B.A. 1939, D.Sc. (Hon.) 1963; Dalhousie Univ. M.Sc.(Physiol.) 1942 (Banting Foundation Research Grant 1941); McGill Univ., M.D., C.M. 1945; Oxford Univ. D.Phil. (Neuroanat.) 1949 (Rhodes Scholar, Nova Scotia, Merton Coll. Oxford Univ., 1939); LL.D. (Hon.) Mt. Allison Univ. 1983; LL.D. (Hon.) Univ. of Sask. 1986; D.Sc. (Hon.) McGill Univ. 1984; Nat. Hosp. London grad. study in Neurol. 1949; m. Dorothy Faith Roswell d. late Lt. Col. Walter E. Lyman 28 July 1945; children: Christopher, Alexander, Patricia, Janet, Michael, Anna; SR. CONSULTANT IN NEUROSURGERY, M.N.I.; CHANCELLOR, ACADIA UNIV. 1991– ; Wm. Cone Prof. of Neurosurg. McGill Univ. 1959–88; Principal Investigator: MRC (Medical Rsch. Counc.) program on PET rsch., MNI 1981–87; USPH (U.S. Public Health Service) rsch. project on brain tumors 1986–90 (Co-investigator 1990– ;), also at MNI; Dir. of Professional Services, Montreal Neurological Hosp. 1972–84; Dir. Gen. Montreal Neurological Inst. and Montreal Neurological Hosp. 1972–84; Research Dir., Brain Imaging Centre, Montreal Neurological Inst. and Hosp. 1984–86; mem. Bd. Curators Osler Lib. McGill Univ. since 1963; Hon. Asst. Osler Librarian 1965–67; Founder and Dir. Cone Lab. for Neurosurg. Research 1960–89; Neurol. and Neurosurg.-in-Chief Royal Victoria Hosp. 1972–84 (Sr. Consultant 1984– ;); Neurosurg.-in-Chief Montreal Neurol. Hosp. 1963–72; Neurosurg. consultant, Sherbrooke Gen. Hosp., Montreal Gen. Hosp.; Nat. Research Council Grad. Fellowship 1949–50; Research Fellowship in Neuropath., Montreal Neurol. Inst. 1942–44; Research Fellowship in Neurophysiol. Montreal Neuro. Inst. 1951–52; R.C.A.M.C. 1941–45, War Research on brain and nerve injuries for Nat. Research Coun., Dalhousie Univ. and in M.N.I. under Dr. W. Penfield; Reford Postgrad. Fellowship 1953–55; Demonstr. in Biol. Acadia Univ. 1937–39, in Physiol. Dalhousie Univ. 1940–42; Research Asst. & Demonst. in Anat. Oxford Univ. 1946–49; Demonst. in Neurosurg. McGill Univ. 1951, Lectr. 1952–55, Chrmn. of Neurol. & Neurosurg. 1972–77; Prof. of Surg. (Neurosurg.) Univ. of Sask. and Univ. Hosp. Sasktoon 1955–59; Diplomate, Amer. Bd. Neurological Surg., 1955; Harvey (Yale, 1970), Elsberg (N.Y. Neurosurgery Soc. 1983), Penfield (Candn. Neurological Assn. 1984) and Hughlings Jackson (M.N.I. 1988); and various other lectureships and visiting professorships nat. and internat. insts.; Curator and Editor, Wilder Penfield Papers, 1976– ; estbld. (with T.B. Rasmussen) Neuro. Archives of MNI/MNH 1977; Dir. & Ed. of Neuro. History Project 1982– ; organized Penfield Centennial Symposium, MNI 1991; recipient of Grants-in-aid, Hannah Inst. for the History of Medicine, R.H.W. Found., Low-Beer Found. and Donner Candn. Found. for Neuro History Projects 1986– ; Hon. Lectr. in Hist. of Med. Univ. of B.C.; Editor, 'Memory, Learning and Language' 1959; Tercentary Edition Thomas Willis's 'Anatomy of the Brain' 1964; medical editorial and production Cons., National Film Bd. of Can.; played self in documentary on Wilder Penfield 1979; took role of neurosurgeon in NFB/Lavalin Imax film 'Urgence-Emergency' 1988; medical advisor, NFB film 'Princes in Exile' 1989; chief scientific adv., IMAX-NFB film 'Brain Works' 1991– ; author or co-author over 400 publs. on neurosurg. and neurosciences; ed. or co-ed. various med. publs.; mem. several med. journ. adv. bds.; Dir. Candn. Assn. Rhodes Scholars 1969–71, 1977; Consultant for Neurosciences, World Health Organ. 1974– ; mem. Neurosciences Comm., Med. Research Coun. of Can. (M.R.C.) 1975–79; Delegate on 1st Neurosciences Mission to China for World Health Org., 1979; Consul. Scient. to Alta. Heritage Found., Candn. Heart Found., Ont. Heart Found., Nat. Inst. of Health, U.S.A.; External examiner Univ. of Cambridge 1987; Scientific Council mem. Fondation pour l'Etude du systéme nerveux, Geneva 1982– ; Chrmn., Adv. Bd. Montreal Neurolog. Inst., 1979–84; Chrmn. Penfield Pavilion Fund & Bldg. Comte. 1972–84; Chrmn. Webster Pavilion Bldg. Comte. 1982–84; mem., Conseil de la politique scientifique, Gov. de Qué. 1975–78; Am. Assn. Neurol. Surgs.; Montreal Medico-Chirurgical Soc. (Pres. 1974); Am. Acad. Neurol. Surgs. (Pres. 1976); Soc. Neurol. Surgs. (Vice Pres. 1978); Am. Neurol. Assn. (Vice Pres. 1976); Candn. Med. Assn.; Montreal Neurol. Soc. (Pres. 1962); Assn. Neurochir. Prov. Qué. (Pres. 1964); Candn. Neurosurg. Soc. (Pres. 1968); Vancouver Med. Assn. (Hon.); Royal Soc. Med.; Osler Soc. McGill (Pres. 1945, Hon. Pres. 1978, 1988) Osler Club London (Hon.); Candn. & Am. Soc. Hist. Med.; Am. Osler Soc. Inc. and other med. assns.; Gov., Acadia Univ. 1980–90; Vice-Pres. Norman Bethune Found. 1984–92; Pres. Neuro-Foundation Toronto 1983–89; Ambassadeur, Palais des Congrès, Montreal 1986; Pres., Brain-87, (XIII Internat. Symposium for Cerebral Blood Flow and Metabolism) Montreal; Pres., Bluenose Bookworks Ltd. 1989– ; Distinguished Service Award, Acadia Univ. Alumni 1987; Alpha Omega Alpha; Anglican; recreations: music, history, tennis, book-binding; Club: University; Montreal Indoor Tennis; McGill Faculty; Home: 4021 Avenue de Vendôme, Montreal, Que. H4A 3N2; Office: 3801 University St., Montreal, Que. H3A 2B4.

**FELDBRILL, Victor,** O.C.; conductor and musical director; b. Toronto, Ont. 4 April 1924; s. Nathan and Helen (Lederman) F.; e. Harbord Coll. Inst., Toronto. Ont.; Royal Cons. of Music of Toronto (Artist's Dipl. 1949); studied conducting (under scholarship recommended by Sir Adrian Boult) at Royal Coll. of Music, and Royal Acad. of Music, London, Eng. (1945); also at Hiversum and Salzburg; studied under Pierre Monteux for two yrs.; m. Zelda, d. of M. Mann, Toronto, Ont., 30 Dec. 1945; children: Deborah Geraldine, Aviva Karen; at age 14 conducted sch. performances of Gilbert and Sullivan operas; age 18 apptd. Conductor, Univ. of Toronto Symphony Orchestra; invited (1943) by Sir Ernest MacMillan to conduct Toronto Symphony; on discharge from the Navy in 1946 apptd. Concert-master and Asst. Conductor, Royal Cons. Symphony and Opera till 1949 (when grad.); since 1949 has conducted regularly for C.B.C.; has made annual appearances with Toronto Philharmonic and Toronto Symphony Orchestras; appeared as Conductor for Candn. Ballet Festival 1952; Conductor for B.B.C. since 1957, Brussels World Fair 1958; Conductor, Winnipeg Symphony Orchestra 1958–68; has appeared as Conductor on TV a no. of times; rec'd (with Winnipeg Symphony Orchestra) The Concert Artists Guild of U.S. of Am. Award (first Candn. Conductor and Orchestra so honoured) at Am. Symphony Orchestra League Convention Awards Dinner, Detroit, July 1964; invited to conduct in U.S.S.R., 1963, 1967; conducted World Premiere of Harry Somers Opera 'Louis Riel' 1967; first recipient of Candn. League of Composers 'Canada Music Citation' 1967; rec'd. Can. Council Sr. Arts Award 1968; rec'd. City of Tokyo Medal 1978; Officer, Order of Canada 1985; invited by Japanese Ministry of Culture as Conductor at Tokyo Univ. of Fine Arts (Geidai) 1979 returning annually in addition to conduct. major Japanese Symphony Orchestras; named Professor Emeritus of Geidai 1987; 1st Candn. conductor invited to conduct Philippine Philharmonic Orch., Manila 1984; 1st Candn. conductor invited to conduct Chinese Orchs. in People's Republic of China 1987; apptd. Music Director & Principal Conductor, Hamilton Philharmonic Orch. 1989; rec'd LL.D. (hon. causa), Brock Univ. 1990; conducted trans Canada tour of National Arts Centre Orch. for 1992 celebration of Canada's 125th birthday; served in R.C.N.V.R. 1942–45; apptd. (1st) Conductor-in-Residence, Faculty of Music, Univ. of Toronto 1968–82; Resident Conductor, Toronto Symphony 1973–77; mem., Musicians Union (Toronto and Winnipeg); 1st recipient, Roy Thomson Hall Award 1985; Hebrew; recreations: reading, photography; Address: 170 Hillhurst Blvd., Toronto, Ont. M5N 1P2.

**FELDMAN, Seth Robert,** Ph.D.; university professor; b. New York, N.Y. 25 Oct. 1948; s. Carl Jacob and Anna (Reich) F.; e. The Johns Hopkins Univ., B.A. 1970; State Univ. of N.Y. at Buffalo, Ph.D. 1976; m. Renate Wickens 29 Apr. 1989; children: Shannon Morse Feldman, Dylan Paul Wickens; DEAN, FAC. OF FINE ARTS, YORK UNIV. 1992– ; T.A., Dept. of English, State Univ. of N.Y. at Buffalo 1970–75; Assoc. Dir., Media Study Buffalo, Buffalo, N.Y. 1974–75; Asst. Prof., English, Univ. of W. Ont. 1975–85; Assoc. Prof. (tenured) 1981–83; Dept. of Film & Video, York Univ. 1983–88; Assoc. Dean, Fac. of Fine Arts 1988–92; researcher, interviewer, writer, reviewer, announcer, & editor, CBC Radio 1982– ; (most recent work on CBC 'Ideas' programmes, 'Four Men and a Chair,' 'Operation RYAN,' 'The Rise and Falls of the Middle Class,' 'Frontiers, 1893'); author: 'Evolution of Style in the Early Work of Dziga Vertov' 1977 and several journal articles & newspaper reviews; Founder, Film Studies Assn. of Canada 1976; 'Dziga Vertov: A Guide to References and Resources' 1979; co-author: 'Canadian Film Reader' 1977; editor: 'Take Two' 1984; co-editor: 'Dialogue: Canadian and Quebec Cinema' 1987; recreations: canoeing, bicycling, swimming; Office: 4700 Keele St., North York, Ont. M3J 1P3.

**FELDTHUSEN, Bruce,** B.A., LL.B., LL.M., S.J.D.; professor of law; b. New York, N.Y. 7 Apr. 1949; s. Erik and Mildren (Kienitz) F.; e. Queen's Univ., B.A. (Hons.) 1972; Univ. of Western Ont., LL.B. 1976; Univ. of Michigan, LL.M. S.J.D. 1982; children: Diana Backhouse, Mark Feldthusen; PROF. OF LAW, UNIV. OF WESTERN ONT. 1977– ; Social Worker, Children's Aid Soc. Kingston 1970–71; author: 'Economic Negligence' 1989 and numerous articles & reports on personal injury comp., tort reform, urinalysis drug testing, equality rights; co-author: 'Cases and Materials on the Law of Torts' 1991; Home: 1017 Wellington St. N., London, Ont. N6A 3T5; Office: London, Ont. N6A 3K7.

**FELICITAS, Sister Mary,** R.N., M.Sc., LL.D.; b. Fife Lake, Sask. 18 Jan. 1916; d. the late Magdalena (Nickels) and Frank Wekel; e. St. Mary's High Sch., Edmonton, Alta. (Sr. Matric.); Providence Hosp., Moose Jaw, Sask., R.N., 1943; Univ. of Ottawa, B.Sc.; Cath. Univ. of Am., M.Sc. (Nursing Educ.) 1953; joined Sisters of Providence of St. Vincent de Paul, and made profession in Aug. 1934; apptd. Dir. of Nursing, St. Mary's Hosp., Montreal, and its Nursing Sch., 1945; subsequently (1957) Dir., Nursing Sch. only; President, Candn. Nurses' Assn., 1967–70; 1st Vice-Pres., Assn. of Nurses of P.Q. 1950–53; Chrmn., Ed. Bd., Candn. Nurses Journal, 1960–62; Regional Visitor, Special Project for Evaluation of Schs. of Nursing in Can., 1958–60; official del. to Cong. of Internat. Council of Nurses, Melbourne, 1961; attended cong., Germany, 1965; Chrmn., Candn. Conf. of Cath. Schs. of Nursing, 1960–64; served as Gen. Councillor of the Sisters of Providence of St. Vincent de Paul, 1971–77; frequent speaker on prof. and related topics; presently engaged in counselling and spiritual direction; LL.D. Queen's May 1974 (1st Sister and 1st Nurse so honoured); Pi Gamma Mu (U.S.A.), Sigma Theta Tau (Kappa Chapter, Washington, D.C.); recreations: music, crochet, crossword puzzles, reading; Address: Providence Mother House, Box 427, Kingston, Ont. K7L 4W4.

**FELL, Anthony Smithson;** investment dealer; b. Toronto, Ont. 23 Feb. 1939; s. Charles Percival and Grace (Matthews) F.; e. St. Andrews Coll., Aurora, Ont., 1959; m. Shari Helen, d. Dr. Allen F. Graham, 12 June 1965; children: Annabelle Elizabeth, Graham Charles, Geoffrey Allen; CHRMN. & C.E.O., RBC DOMINION SECURITIES INC.; Dir., Munich Reinsurance Co. of Canada & Subsidaries; Kellogg Can. Ltd.; Gov., St. Andrew's Coll.; Past Chrmn., Investment Dealers Assn. of Can. 1987–88; Past Campaign Chrmn., United Way of Greater Toronto 1989; Dir., Princess Margaret Hospital Foundation; Chrmn., Capital Campaign, Princess Margaret Hosp.; Baptist; Clubs: Toronto; York; Home: 52 Park Lane Circle, Don Mills, Ont. M3C 2N2; Office: P.O. Box 21, Commerce Court South, Toronto, Ont. M5L 1A7.

**FELL, Fraser M.,** Q.C.; executive; b. Toronto, Ont. 17 June 1928; s. Charles P. and Grace Elizabeth (Matthews) F.; e. Univ. of Toronto Schools; McMaster Univ., B.A., LL.D.; Osgoode Hall Law Sch., LL.B.; m. Margot Crossgrove 27 June 1953; children: David, Leslie, Susan, Martha, Mark; CHRMN., PRES. & C.E.O. GENTRA INC. 1993– ; read law with Fasken, Robertson, Aitchison, Pickup & Calvin 1951; called to Bar of Ont. 1953; apptd. Q.C. 1965; with Fasken, Robertson, Aitchison, Pickup & Calvin 1953–63; Partner, Fasken & Calvin and Fasken, Campbell, Godfrey 1963–93; Chrmn., Placer Dome Inc. 1987–93; Chrmn., Dir. and mem. Extve. Ctte., Aetna Life Insurance Co. of Canada 1988– ; Dir., The Toronto Symphony; Past Chrmn., World Gold Counc.; Chrmn., Bd. of Trustees, The Toronto Hosp.; Trustee and Past Chrmn., Toronto Western Hosp.; Past Chrmn., Bd. of Govs., McMaster Univ.; mem., Candn. Bar Assn.; Delta Chi; recreations: sailing; Clubs: Toronto; York; Home: 34 Glenorchy Rd., Don Mills, Ont. M3C 2P9; Office: 70 York St., Toronto, Ont. M5J 1S9.

**FELLEGI, Ivan P.,** C.M., B.Sc., M.Sc., Ph.D.; statistician; b. Szeged, Hungary 22 June 1935; s. Andor and Barbara (Partos) F.; e. Univ. of Budapest, B.Sc. 1956; Carleton Univ., M.Sc. 1958, Ph.D. 1961; m. Marika d. Istvan and Veronika Gulyas 27 Dec. 1958; children: Nicolette, Vivien; CHIEF STATISTICIAN OF CANADA 1985– ; joined Stats. Can. (then Dom. Bur. of Stats.) 1957; Statistician 1957–62; Chief, Sampling Rsch. & Consultation Sect. 1962–65; Dir., Sampling & Survey Rsch. Staff 1965–71; Dir. Gen., Methodology & Systems 1971–73; Asst. Chief Statistician, Statistical Services Field 1973–78; seconded to Pres. Carter's Comm. on the Reorgn. of the U.S. Statistical System 1978–79; Asst. Chief Statistician, Soc. Stats. Field 1979–84; Dep. Chief Statistician 1984–85; Hon. Fellow, Royal Statistical Soc.; Fellow, Am. Statistical Assn.; Am. Assn. for the Advancement of Sci.; Pres., Internat. Statistical Inst. 1987–89; mem. Internat. Assn. of Survey Statisticians (Pres. 1985–87); Statistical Soc. of Can. (Pres. 1982); Mem., Bd. of Govs., Carleton Univ. 1989–92; Member, Order of Canada 1992; Hon. Mem., Internat. Statistical Institute 1993; author or co-author of numerous sci. publs.; recreations: classical music, reading; Home: 16 Larchwood Ave., Ottawa, Ont. K1Y 2E3; Office: Tunney's Pasture, Ottawa, Ont. K1A 0T6.

**FELLOWS, Edward Spencer,** M.Sc.; forestry and forest products consultant; b. Pulham, Norfolk, Eng. 15 Feb. 1909; s. late Arthur Cecil (a Civil Engr.) and late Alice Margaret (Wallace) F.; e. London Polytech. Inst. 1925–26; Univ. of New Brunswick, B.Sc. (Forestry) 1930, M.Sc. 1935; D.Sc. (Hon.) 1980; m. late Annie Kathleen, d. late H.W. Woods 20 Apr. 1935; m. 2ndly Ersi, d. late E. Andreou, 14 Dec. 1967; children: David Michael, Peter Colin; engaged in research work at Forest Products Lab. (Chief of Wood Utilization Divn.) 1930–43; Supt. of Tech. Services, Maritime Lumber Bureau 1943–46; Specialist with Ont. Roy. Comn. on Forestry 1946–47; private consulting work in B.C., N.B. and Ont. 1947–48; Chief Forester, Eastern Rockies Forest Conservation Board 1948–55; mem., N.B. Forest Devel. Comn. 1955–57; practising as consultant throughout Can. and abroad 1957– ; Regd. Prof. Forester (N.B.); inducted in N.B. Forestry Hall of Fame 1986; formerly Gov. and mem. of Senate, Univ. of N.B.; former Chrmn., N.B. Water Authority; Past Pres. and Fellow, Candn. Inst. Forestry; mem. Am. Assn. Advance. Science; Soc. Am. Foresters; Forest Prod. Soc.; Commonwealth Forestry Assn.; Soil Conservation Soc. of Am.; Chrmn., Fredericton Area Pollution Control Comn.; Past-Pres., Associated Alumni, Univ. of N.B.; Anglican; recreations: music, photography; Home: 157 Parkhurst Dr., Fredericton, N.B. E3B 2J5; Office: P.O. Box 354, Fredericton, N.B. E3B 4Z9.

**FELLS, Anthony George,** M.A.; corporate director and consultant; b. Bristol, Eng. 11 July 1933; s. George Vincent and Dorothy Margaret (Cox) F.; e. St. Edward's Sch. Oxford, Eng.; Corpus Christi Coll. Oxford M.A. 1956; m. Kittie Marie Duncan d. Gordon and Marie Duncan McPhedran 1 June 1962; children: Emily Kathryn, Christopher Duncan; PRESIDENT, A. GEORGE FELLS CONSULTING INC.; Dir., Working Ventures Candn. Fund; Business Centurions; Horatio Enterprise Fund.; Inst. of Corporate Dirs.; held various mktg./market rsch. positions Lever Brothers 1956–60; Nestle (Canada Ltd.) 1960–64; Devel. Dept. T. Eaton Co. 1964–67; and in venture capital Investment Offr., Charterhouse Canada Ltd. 1967–73; Pres., SB Capital Corp. 1973–92; and North American Ventures Funds 1981–92; consulting assignments with Intl. Finance Corp. of World Bank, and others, including Spain, Kenya, Brazil, Argentina, Trinidad and Tobago, Hungary; Chrmn., Finance Ctte. Internat. Symposium on Small Business 1980; author various articles; Pres., Assn. Candn. Venture Capital Co's 1980–81; mem., Ministers' Small Business Adv. Ctte., Ottawa 1982–83; mem., Natl. Adv. Council, Candn. Advanced Technology Assoc., Ottawa 1986– ; mem., Candn. Adv. Counc., Internat. Fedn. of Insts. for Advanced Study; mem., Auditor General's Special Audit Ctte. on Crown Corporations 1993; Vice-Chrmn., The Quetico Found.; recreations: writing, farming; Club: The Bd. of Trade of Metro. Toronto; Home: 35 Nanton Ave., Toronto, Ont. M4W 2Y8; Office: Toronto, Ont.

**FELS, Sol Sidney,** M.Sc., B.A.Sc.; student; b. Kitchener, Ont. 5 July 1966; s. Morton and Juliet Erica (Sander) F.; e. Port Arthur C.I.; Univ. of Waterloo B.A.Sc. 1988; Univ. of Toronto M.Sc. 1990, Ph.D. in Computer Science in progress; m. Kirsty d. Pat and Paul Barclay-Estrup 8 July 1989; as co-op undergrad. 4 month work terms were alternated with 4 month school terms; work incl. (most recent to last): System Specialist, Abitibi Price Inc.; Researcher, Univ. of Victoria; Hardware Diagnostic Designer / Software Designer, Cadence Computer Corp.; Information Developer / Software Developer, IBM Toronto Lab.; Teaching Asst., Univ. of Toronto; Mem., Glove Input Device Panel, Human Factors Soc. conf. in San Francisco 1991; Guest Researcher & Lectr., Inst. of Perception Rsch. in Eindhoven 1990; NSERC scholarship; 2 undergrad. research assistantships & Upper Year Scholarship (Univ. of Waterloo); 3 times on Dean's Honour List; Thunder Bay Found. Scholarship; author of 4 articles; currently developing neural network models to build device which translates hand gestures to speech (an extension of the Glove-Talk pilot study); Office: Dept. of Computer Science, Univ. of Toronto, Toronto, Ont. M5S 1A4.

**FELSTINER, Hon. James P.,** B.A., J.D., M.S.W.; judge; b. New York City, N.Y., 28 May 1932; s. William and Nata (Purvin) F.; e. Phillips Exeter Acad. N.H. 1950; Haverford (Pa.) Coll. B.A. 1954; Harvard Law Sch. J.D. 1957; Univ. of Toronto Sch. of Social Work M.S.W. 1961; m. Barbara Jane d. Paul and Virginia Kartzke 4 Jan. 1964; three d. Katherine, Caroline, Laura; JUDGE, ONTARIO COURT OF JUSTICE (PROVINCIAL DIV.) 1990– ; Law Clk. Juvenile Court of Washington, D.C. 1958–59; admitted to the practise of law in New York State 1958, and the District of Columbia 1959; Detached Street Worker, Univ. Settlement Recreation Centre, Toronto 1961–65; Registrar and Clk. Juvenile Court of Metrop. Toronto 1967–70; Judge, Provincial Court (Family Div.) Ont. 1970–90; Hon. Trustee, Hosp. for Sick Children Toronto; recreations: tennis, photograpy, cooking; Club: Granite; Harvard Club of New York City; Office: 47 Sheppard Ave. E., Willowdale, Ont. M2N 5N1.

**FELTHAM, Ivan Reid,** Q.C., B.A., LL.B., B.C.L.; lawyer; b. Brandon, Man. 13 May 1930; s. Reginald Fairman and Ethel Lavina (Graham) F.; e. Univ. of B.C., B.A. 1951, LL.B. 1954; Oxford Univ. (Rhodes Scholar) B.C.L. 1956; m. Kristine d. Heinrich and Theodora Strombeck 30 May 1958; children: Derek Bruce, Andrea Lynn; LEGAL CONSULTANT AND ARBITRATOR; called to Bars of B.C. 1957, Ont. 1962; cr. Q.C. 1969; Asst. Prof. Univ. of B.C. 1957–61; Prof. and Co-Dir. Comm. Law Prog. Osgoode Hall Law Sch. 1961–65, Prof. and Dir. Business Law Prog. 1967–74; Cons. Baker & McKenzie, Chicago 1962–65, Assoc. 1965–67; Dir. York Univ. Transport Centre 1969–71, Gov. of Univ. 1969–71, Senator there 1968–74; First Chrmn. Univ. of Toronto-York Univ. Transp. Rsch. Prog.; cons. business law and econ. regulation 1957–74; Counsel Ont. Select Ctte. on Econ. Nationalism 1972–74; Counsel Fed.-Prov. Council, Motor Carrier Regulation 1971–72; Vice-Pres., Gen. Counsel and Secy., General Electric Canada Inc. 1974–87; Partner, McMillan Binch, Barristers and Solicitors 1988–91; Hyman Soloway Prof. of Business and Trade Law, Univ. of Ottawa 1991–92; Scholar Hague Acad. Internat. Law 1959; Fellow Internat. Legal Studies Univ. of Cal. Berkeley 1961; author numerous articles and speeches on legal business policy issues; Dir. Candn. Counc. for Internat. Business; Chrmn., Legislation Comte. and Dir., Candn. Mfrs.' Assn. 1986–88; Dir. Internat. Bus. Counc. of Can.; Pres., Inst. for Pol. Involvement 1985–88; mem. Candn. Bar Assn.; Internat. Bar Assn.; Internat. Law Assn.; Am. Bar Assn. (associate); Am. Soc. Internat. Law; Assn. Candn. Gen. Counsel; Candn. Counc. Internat. Law; Can. Exporters' Assoc. (Co-Chair Legal Ctte.); Inst. of Corp. Dirs.; recreation: tennis; Club: Granite; Home: 44 Hi Mount Dr., Willowdale, Ont. M2K 1X5; Office: Fac. of Law, Univ. of Ottawa, Ottawa, Ont. K1N 6N5.

**FENNELL, Stanley Elmer,** Q.C., L.S.M., LL.B., LL.D.; b. Marlborough Twp., Carleton Co., Ont. 6 Oct. 1909; s. Wm. Henry and Isabella (Macartney) F.; e. Brockville Coll. Inst.; Univ. of Toronto; Osgoode Hall, Toronto, Grad. 1937; Law Soc. Medal; m. Anna Isobel, d. James R. Cameron, 26 July 1941; children: Margaret Ann, John Robert; COUNSEL, FENNELL, RUDDEN, STEVENSON & LEVESQUE; hon. mem., Bd. of Govs., Cornwall Gen. Hosp. (Pres. 1946–55); Life Bencher, Law Soc. of Upper Canada; hon. mem., Candn. Bar Assn. (Pres. 1961–62); Clubs: Cornwall Golf & Country; The Moorings Country Club, Naples, Fla.; Home: 330 Sydney St., Cornwall, Ont. K6H 3H6; Office: 35 Second St. E., Cornwall, Ont. K6H 1Y2.

**FENNELL, Rev. William Oscar,** B.A., S.T.M., D.D. (Un. Ch.); retired educator; b. Brantford, Ont. 10 Jan. 1916; s. Harry Stark and Wilto Claire (Charters) F.; e. Bellvue Pub. Sch. and Brantford (Ont.) Coll. Inst. 1933; Victoria Coll. Univ. of Toronto B.A. 1939 (awarded the Blewett, Kennedy and Moss scholarships and the gold medal in philosophy); Emmanuel Coll. Dipl. in Theol. 1942 (awarded the Travelling Fellowship); Union Theol. Semy. N.Y. S.T.M. 1950; research leave Univs. of Strasbourg 1950–51, Freiburg 1961, London 1970–71; Univ. of Winnipeg D.D. 1963; Univ. of Trinity Coll. D.D. 1976; Victoria U. D.D., 1981; Knox College D.D., 1981; m. Jean Louise d. John Henry Birkenshaw, Toronto, Ont. 1 Sept. 1948; children: Paul William, Catherine Louise, Stephen Harry; PRINCIPAL-EMERITUS OF EMMANUEL COLL. 1987; o. 29 May 1942; Pastorate St. John's Un. Ch. Levack, Ont. 1942–44; Lectr. in Christian Doctrine Emmanuel Coll. and Sr. Tutor Victoria Univ. 1946, Prof. of Systematic Theol. 1957, Registrar of Coll. 1956–60, Dir. of Grad. Studies 1962–70, Acting Princ. of Coll. 1971–72; Principal, Emmanuel Coll. 1971–81; Prof. Em. of Systematic Theology and Past Principal of Emmanuel College, 1981; Principal-Emeritus of Emmanuel Coll. 1987; mem. Staff Internat. Students' Service Seminar Pontigny, France 1950; Chrmn. Nat. Extve. Student Christian Movement Can. 1951–54; Chrmn. Ch. & Univ. Comn. Candn. Council Chs. 1957–59; Un. Ch. Del. N. Am. Conf. on Faith and Order Oberlin, Ohio 1957; Candn. Del. Internat. Assembly World Univ. Service Nigeria (leader of del.) 1959, Germany 1960; rep. N. Am. Sec. World Alliance Reformed Chs. convs. with Lutheran World Fed. 1961–65; Un. Ch. Del. Fourth World Conf. on Faith & Order Montreal 1963; Chrmn. Faith & Order Comn. Candn. Council Chs. 1964–67; Chrmn., Comte. of Direction Toronto Grad. Sch. of Theol. Studies 1966–68; Chrmn., Comte. on Coop. in Theol. Educ. in Toronto 1967–70; Warfield Lectr. Princeton Theol. Semy. 1974; Principal, Emmanuel Coll. 1971–81; mem. Bd. Fund for Theol. Educ. 1972–75; served as Chaplain RCNVR 1953–57; author 'God's Intention for Man: Essays in Christian Anthropology' 1977; also book chapters, articles and reviews; Assoc. Ed. 'Canadian Journal of Theology' 1961–68; Fellow (1970), Am. Assn. Theol. Schs.; mem. Candn. Theol. Soc. (Pres. 1962–63, Hon. Mem. 1984); recreation: gardening, curling; Home: 71 Old Mill Rd., Apt. 306, Toronto, Ont. M8X 1G9; Summer home: Kingsett Rd., Lake Rosseau, R.R.#2, Port Carling, Ont.

**FENSOM, David S.,** B.A.Sc., C.Chem., FRSC(UK), F.R.S.A., LL.D.; university professor emeritus; b. Toronto, Ont. 10 Apr. 1916; s. Charles Joseph and Elizabeth Strathern (Keith) F.; e. Hillfield School, Hamilton; Westdale C.I.; Trinity Coll., Toronto, Sch. of Practical Science, B.A.Sc. 1938; Dalhousie Univ. LL.D. 1988; m. Kathleen d. Hugh and Fanny Robson 10 June 1944; children: Jean Nancy, Charles Hugh Robson; PROF. EMERITUS, MOUNT ALLISON UNIV. 1982– ; Consolidated Mining & Smelting Co. 1938–40; Asst., Chem. Supvr., Defence Indus. Ltd. 1940–42; Rsch. Chem., Imperial Chem. Indus. 1942–45; Candn. Armament Rsch. & Devel. Establishment 1945–46; Head of Sci. Dept., Ridley Coll. 1946–63; Prof. of Biology, Mount Allison Univ. 1963; Head of Dept. 1969–76; Ruggles Gates Prof. 1976–81; teaches plant physiol., biophysics & philos. of edn.; Nuffield Travel Scholarship 1960–61; Killam Sr. Rsch. Scholarship 1973–74; F.R.S.A. 1966 (Hon. Corr. Member for Atlantic Can. 1971–87; Silver medallist 1987); author: 'Geometric Form in ADAM Architecture' 1984; recreations: swimming, skiing, walking; Home: P.O. Box 1181, Sackville, N.B.; Office: Dept. of Biology, Mount Allison Univ., Sackville, N.B. E0A 3C0.

**FENTIE, Harvey Dwayne,** B.Sc.; engineering executive; b. Bancroft, Ont. 10 Oct. 1937; s. Harvey Alexander and Mary Marjorie (Milne) F.; e. Queen's Univ. B.Sc. (Hons.) (Medal of Honour for Highest Class Standing); m. Kathaline d. Hubert and Ruby Mountney 20 May 1961; children: John-David, Bradley, Jennifer; EXTVE. VICE PRES., HATCH ASSOC. LTD.; Metallurgist, Falconbridge Nickel Mines Ltd. 1959–62; Mill Metallurgist, Sociedad Minera & Gen. Supt., El Teniente, Santiago, Chile 1962–70; Gen. Supt. Concentrator, Lornex Mines 1970–73; Sr. Process Engr.-Extve. Vice Pres., present firm 1973– ; Home: 360 Bloor St. E., Apt. 1402, Toronto, Ont. M4W 3M3; Office: 2800 Speakman Dr., Mississauga, Ont. L5K 2R7.

**FENTON, Edward Warren,** M.Sc., Ph.D.; scientist; b. Lucky Lake, Sask. 5 March 1937; s. Edward Bruce and Marjorie Irene (Warren) F.; e. Univ. of Alta., B.Sc. 1959, M.Sc. 1962, Ph.D. 1965; m. Alice d. Rudolph and Pauline Jabs 2 July 1966; one s. Warren John; HEAD, CONDENSED MATTER SECT. NAT. RSCH. COUNCIL CAN. 1984– ; Geophysicist, Sun Oil of Canada 1959–61; Theoretical Physicist present Council, Asst. Rsch. Offr. to Principal Rsch. Offr. 1967–90; Lectr. rsch. instns., univs. and internat. confs. Can., USA, USSR, Eur. and Japan; USSR Acad. of Sci's Lectures 1975, 1987, 1989; Distinguished Lectr. Japanese Soc. Promotion Sci. 1978, 1989; Keynote and summary lectures at many internat. scientific conferences; author of approx. 90 physics papers; Home: 9 Rothwell Dr., Gloucester, Ont. K1J 7G3; Office: Ottawa, Ont. K1A 0R6.

**FENTON, Melville Brockett,** M.Sc., Ph.D.; educator; b. Mackenzie, Guyana 20 Oct. 1943; s. Paul Mortimer and Jean Melville (Tudhope) F.; e. Queen's Univ. B.Sc. 1965; Univ. of Toronto M.Sc. 1967, Ph.D. 1969; m. Eleanor Ruth d. M.R. and L.M. Feely 10 May 1969; PROF. OF BIOL. YORK UNIV. and Chrmn. of Dept. 1986– ; joined Carleton Univ. 1969–86, Asst. Prof. to Prof. of Biol.; recipient OCUFA Teaching Award 1986; 3M Teaching Award 1993; author 'Just Bats' 1983; 'Communication in the Chiroptera' 1985; co-ed. 'Recent Advances in the Study of Bats' 1987; 'Bats' 1992; mem. Natural Sci's & Eng. Rsch. Council (Animal Biol. Grant Selection Ctte. 1983–86, Chrmn. 1986); NSERC Life Sciences Group Chair 1992–95; Biol. Council Can.; Am. Soc. Mammalogists; Animal Behaviour Soc.; Am. Assn. Advanc. Sci.; Soc. Study Evolution; Assn. Tropical Biol. Inc.; Cooper Ornithol. Soc.; Home: 25 St. Georges Rd., Islington, Ont. M9A 3T2; Office: 4700 Keele St., North York, Ont. M3J 1P3.

**FENTON, Terry,** B.A.; artist, author, art consultant; b. Regina, Sask. 1 July 1940; s. John Albert and Gertrude Irene F.; e. Univ. of Sask. B.A. 1962; m. Sheila d. Marrett and Marjorie Cowie 1 Dec. 1962; one s. Mark; ARTISTIC DIR., THE LEIGHTON FOUND., Calgary 1988– ; Asst. to Dir. Norman MacKenzie Art Gallery Regina 1965–71; Dir. The Edmonton Art Gallery 1972–87; Visiting Critic, Emma Lake Artists Workshop 1977 and 1991; Co-Founder, Visiting Critic and Artistic Adv. Triangle Workshop 1982; author 'Jack Bush' 1976; 'Dorothy Knowles, Paintings 1964–82' 1983; 'Anthony Caro' 1987; 'Appreciating Noland' 1991; co-author 'Modern Painting in Canada' 1978; Home: #7, 64 Woodacres Cr. SW, Calgary, Alta. T2W 4V6; Office: Site 31, Box 9, R.R. 8, Calgary, Alta. T2J 2T9.

**FENWICK, D.K. Bruce,** B.Sc., M.Sc.; oil & gas industry executive; b. Gaspe, Que. 4 Oct. 1945; s. Donald Talmadge and Edna Muriel (Nonnenman) F.; e. Mount Allison Univ. B.Sc. 1965; Dalhousie Univ. M.Sc. 1967; m. Sheila G. d. F. Lindsay and Phyllis Miller 15 July 1972; children: Matthew A., Megan J., Shelley R.; SENIOR VICE-PRES., NORCEN ENERGY RESOURCES LIMITED 1993– ; Jr. through Sr. Geophysicist, Amoco Canada Ltd. 1967–73; Div. Geophysicist, Mesa Petroleums Ltd. 1973–79; Indep. Geophysical Cons., Fundy Explorations Ltd. 1979–80; Mgr., Internat. Explor., Mgr. Geophysics, Voyager Petroleums Ltd. 1980–85; Manager, Geoph., Norcen Energy Resources Limited 1985–86; Dist. Mgr. 1986–88; Gen. Mgr. Exploration 1989; Vice-Pres. Exploration 1989–92; Pres., Mid-West Gas Transmission; N.W. Transmission Co. Ltd.; Vancan Investments Ltd.; North Candn. Oils Ltd.; Coseka Resources Ltd.; Dir., Norwest Oil & Gas; Norcen Explorer Inc.; Norcen Mktg. Inc.; North Candn. Marketing, North Candn. Power Inc.; Sr. Vice-Pres. Prod., Prairie Oil Royalties; Vice-Pres., Labrador Mining & Exploration Co. Ltd.; C.S.E.G. Meritorious Serv. Award 1989; Jaycees Internat. Senatorship p1973; Pilot Offr., retired, RCAF 1966; Mem., Conf. Bd. of Can., Corp. Council on Edn.; Mem., St. Davids Un. Ch.; Rotary Club of Calgary; A.P.E.G.G.A.; C.S.E.G.; C.S.P.G.; recreations: golf, sailing, camping; clubs: Bearspaw Country, Calgary Winter; Office: 715 – 5 Ave. S.W., Calgary, Alta. T2P 2X7.

**FENWICK, Ian David,** B.A., Ph.D.; educator; consultant; b. Manchester, Eng. 30 Sept. 1949; s. John Hoole and Gertrude Mary (Robertson) F.; e. Nantwich & Acton Grammar Sch. Eng. 1967; Durham Univ. B.A. 1970; London Grad. Sch. of Bus. Ph.D. 1975; m. Gillian d. Patrick Royston and Joyce Manning 10 July 1971 (div. March 1991); one d. Virginia; m. Somjit Kamma d. Lee Kamma and Nun Kamma 24 Apr. 1991; PROF. OF MKTG. YORK UNIV. 1987– ; Lectr. in Econ. Durham Univ. 1970–72; Lectr. in Mktg. Bradford Univ. Mgmt. Centre Eng. 1974–77; Assoc. Prof. of Mktg. Dalhousie Univ. 1977–79; Visiting Assoc. Prof. of Mktg. Northeastern Univ. Boston 1979–80; Assoc. Prof. of Mktg. present Univ. 1981, Prof. 1985, Assoc. Dean of Adm. Studies 1983–85; cons. various bus. orgns. and govt. agencies Can., USA, Eur.; lectr. bus. progs. Eng., Can., USA, China, Poland, Thailand; recipient Operational Rsch. Soc. Pres.'s Medal 1980; author or co-author over 40 mktg. publs.; mem. Am. Mktg. Assn. (Dir. Toronto Chapter 1983–86); Profl. Mkt. Rsch. Soc. (Dir. 1987–88); Assn. Consumer Rsch.; Eur. Acad. Rsch. Mktg.; Inst. Mgmt. Sci.; Am. Assn. Pub. Opinion Rsch.; recreations: reading, writing, travel; Office: 4700 Keele St., North York, Ont. M3J 2R6.

**FENWICK, William Roland,** R.C.A.; artist; educator; b. Owen Sound, Ont. 4 Feb. 1932; s. Albert William and Marjorie (Patterson) F.; e. Owen Sound Coll. & Vocational Inst. 1950; Mount Allison Univ. 1952–55; m. Phyllis Ann Cregeen 30 June 1956; children: Graeme Scott, Jennifer Lea; PROF. EMERITUS; Assoc. Prof. of Visual Arts, Univ. of W. Ont. 1969–89; Art Dir. Simpsons-Sears Co. Ltd. Toronto 1956–66; rep. private and pub. colls.; extensive exhns. incl. restrospective London Regional Art Gallery 1975; designed 2 Candn. book covers publ. 1976; recreation: fishing; Home: 755 Maitland St., London, Ont. N5Y 2W4; Office: London, Ont. N5Y 2W4.

**FERCHAT, Robert A.,** F.C.A.; business executive; b. Toronto, Ont. 17 Nov. 1934; e. C.P.A. 1958; C.A. 1962; F.C.A. 1991; m. Gwenyth Gibson 14 May 1955; children: Craig Steven, Donna Gayle; CHAIRMAN, AECL 1990– ; Exec. Vice Pres. Finance & Adm., Northern Telecom 1980; Pres., Northern Telecom International Ltd. 1983; Pres., Northern Telecom Canada Ltd. 1985–90; Chrmn. Canada-Korea Bus. Counc.; Bd. mem., International Business Leadership Centre; mem., Policy Ctte. and Joint Ctte. on U.S.-Can. Relations; Candn. Chamber of Comm.; Dir., Nat. Adv. Ctte., Banff Centre Sch. of Mgmt.; Bd. mem., Coscan Limited; Hawker Siddeley Can. Inc.; TELUS Corp.; National Ballet of Can.; Chrmn., Candn. Coalition of Service Industries; Fellow, Ont. Inst. C.A.'s; Bd. of Govs., Jr. Achievement of Peel; recreation: golf; Clubs: Credit Valley Golf & Country (Mississauga); Office: 2251 Speakman Dr., Mississauga, Ont. L5K 1B2.

**FERDERBER, Peter;** prospector; b. Yugoslavia 2 Feb. 1927; s. Mark and Margaret (Baric) F.; e. Val d'Or H.S.; m. Dolores d. Jack Phippen 15 Aug. 1947; children: Randon, Rhonda, Angela, Harold, Daniel; OWNER, PROSPECTIVE GEOPHYSICS LTD.; 46 years of prospecting & geophysical; worked 10 years as party chief for Koulomzine & Geoffreon Geophysical Co.; Dir., Belmoral Mines Ltd. (discover of the mine); Aurizon Mines Ltd.; Hollinger North Shore Expl.; La Fosse Platinum Group Inc.; Arbor Resources Ltd.; Wealth Resources Ltd.; Prospect of the Year for Canada P.D.A.C.; Prospector of the Year Quebec Q.P.A.; Man of the Year for Town of Val d'Or, Que.; Mem., C.I.M.; Regional Dir. P.D.A.C.; Toronto Engineers Club; recreations: golf, fishing; clubs: Val d'Or Golf, Isla Del Sol Yacht & Country (Florida); Home: 114 Villeneuve St., Val d'or, Que. J9P 3L7; Office: 169 Perreault St., Val d'Or, Que. J9P 2H1.

**FERG, Hon. Patrick David,** B.A., LL.B.; justice; b. Glenboro, Man. 2 Nov. 1927; s. Francis Milton Q.C. and Helen Fleming (Paterson) F.; e. Glenboro H.S. 1945; Univ. of Man. B.A. 1948, LL.B. (Hons.) 1959; called to Bar of Man. 1959, Bar of Sask. 1969; children: Dr. Allison, Michael, John Paterson; JUSTICE, COURT OF QUEEN'S BENCH FOR MANITOBA 1984– ; Partner Wright, Ferg & Ferg, Flin Flon, Man. 1960–67; Partner Ferg & Singh, Flin Flon, Man. 1967–73; Sr. Partner Ferg, Cameron, Ginnell & Drapack, Flin Flon and Thompson, Man. 1973–75; apptd. County Ct. of Man. C.J.D. 1975; E.J.D. 1979; Q.C. 1969; el. Bencher, Law Soc. of Man. 1970–75; recreations: golf, hunting, fishing, curling, reading, French language studies; Home: 2501 - 11 Evergreen Pl., Winnipeg, Man. R3L 2T9; Office: Law Courts Complex, Broadway and Kennedy, Winnipeg, Man. R3C 0V8.

**FERGUSON, David,** B.Sc., M.B.A.; real estate executive; b. Quesnel, B.C.; s. William John and Dorothy Haynes (Petten) F.; e. Univ. of B.C. B.Sc. 1979, M.B.A. 1982; SENIOR VICE-PRESIDENT, COSCAN DEVELOPMENT CORPORATION 1991– ; Corp. Real Estate Dept., Citibank Canada 1982–86; Vice-Pres. Devel., Carena Developments Ltd. 1987– ; Sr. Vice-Pres., Corp. Devel., Brookfield Devel. Corp. 1989–91; recreations: skiing, running, travelling; clubs: Vancouver Club; Office: BCE Place, 181 Bay St., Suite 4500, P.O. Box 770, Toronto, Ont. M5J 2T3.

**FERGUSON, Frederick Drummond;** inventor; executive; b. Ottawa, Ont. 28 July 1949; s. John Keith and Dorothy Van Dusen (Hogg) F.; e. S. Carleton H.S. 1969; Sheridan Coll. Oakville, Ont. grad. Applied Design & Photography 1971; one d. Samantha Hamilton; CHRMN. & C.E.O., NORD-AM RESEARCH CORP. 1990– ; Dir., Northern Aerospace Industries, VT, U.S.A.; past Chrmn., Candn. Airworthiness Cttes., AIAC; Founder, Pres. & C.E.O., Van Dusen Commercial Development Corp. 1978– ; Founder and Dir., Magnus Aerospace Corp. 1982– ; Pres. and Dir. APH Ltd. 1972–78; Founder, Shareholder, Magnus Aerospace Mfg. Corp. (Supercomputer Facility), Sydney, N.S. 1986–88; Chrmn., Nord-Am Rsch. Corp. 1990–93; Chrmn. & C.E.O., Pan Atlantic Rsch. & Development Corp. 1993– ; recipient Can. Award for Excellence 1984 for invention of LTA 20–1 (lighter-than-air craft); Prime Design Award, U.S. Airforce S.D.I.O. 1987; Award of Merit, Aerospace Industries Assoc. Can.; Award for Surface Vehicle Design, Mars Outreach program, NASA 1990; holds maj. ind. patents under devel.; helicopter pilot, jet ranger and multi-engine; Past Dir. Aerospace Inds. Assn. Can.; recreations: flying, skiing, skating; Office: P.O. Box 599, Stn. B., Ottawa, Ont. K1P 5P7.

**FERGUSON, Gary Gilbert,** B.A., M.D., Ph.D., FRCS(C), FACS; neurosurgeon; educator; b. London, Ont. 30 Aug. 1941; s. Stephen Clement and Bethel Norine (Summers) F.; e. London Central Secondary Sch. 1959; Univ. of W. Ont. B.A. 1961, M.D. 1965, Ph.D. 1970; m. Mary d. Crosby and Marjorie Kirkpatrick 27 June 1964; children: Stephen, Heather, Sarah; PROF. OF NEUROSURGERY, UNIV. OF W. ONT. 1984– ; Chief of Neurosurgery, University Hosp. 1990– ; Asst. Prof. of Clin. Neurol. Sci's (Div. Neurosurgery) Dept. Med. Biophys. & Dept. Surgery present Univ. and mem. Active Staff Univ. Hosp. 1973, Assoc. Prof. 1981; cons. med. staff Victoria Hosp. and St. Joseph's Hosp. London, Ont. 1973– ; Visiting Professorships USA, UK, India, Japan and Israel; recipient Am. Acad. Neurol. Surgery Award 1970; author or co-author over 80 sci. publs. neurosurgery & cerebrovascular surgery; mem. Am. Assn. Neurol. Surgs. (Chrmn., Jt. Sect. Cerebrovascular Surgery 1992–94; Exec. Ctte. 1987–89); Candn. Med. Assn.; Candn. Neurosurg. Soc. (Sec.-Treas. 1981–84); Cong. Neurol. Surgs.; Internat. Soc. Cerebral Circulation & Metabolism; Ont. Med. Assn. (Chrmn. Sect. Neurosurg. 1977–80); Soc. for Neurosci.; Stroke Council Am. Heart Assn.; Anglican; recreations: tennis, golf, sailing; Club: London Hunt & Country; Home: 1013 Wellington St. N., London, Ont. N6A 3T5; Office: University Hospital, P.O. Box 5339, London, Ont. N6A 5A5.

**FERGUSON, George A.,** B.A., M.Ed., Ph.D., D.Sc.(Hon.), F.R.S.C., professor (emeritus); b. New Glasgow, N.S., 23 July 1914; s. Alexander McNaughton and Jean Smith-Pollock (Dennistoun) F.; e. Dalhousie Univ., B.A. 1936; Univ. of Edinburgh, M.Ed. 1938, Ph.D. 1940; m. Rowena Sheldon (dec.); children: Claudia, Leith; EMERITUS PROF. OF PSYCHOL., McGILL UNIV. 1981; Instr., Univ. of Edin., 1939–40; Indust. Consultant, Stevenson & Kellogg Ltd., 1945–47; Asst. Prof., Dept. of Psychol., McGill Univ., 1947–48, Assoc. Prof. 1948–49; Prof. 1949–81 (Chrmn. of the Dept. 1964–75; and Vice Dean for Biol. Sciences 1966–71); Consultant, Social Sciences, UNESCO, Paris, 1954–

55; served in 2nd World War with Candn. Army, 1941–45 (Overseas 1942–44); retired with rank of Major; Publications: author of 5 books and monographs and about 40 scient. papers; most recent book: 'Statistical Analysis in Psychology and Education' 6th ed. 1988; mem. Candn. Psychol. Assn. (Fellow and Past Pres., Hon. Pres., 1976–78); Am. Psychol. Assn.; Am. Stat. Assn.; Centennial Medal; Silver Jubilee Medal; Sigma Xi; Liberal; Anglican; recreations: art, gardening; Home: 3003 Cedar Ave., Montreal, Que. H3Y 1Y8.

**FERGUSON, George Ian,** B.A., LL.B.; financial executive; b. Port Arthur, Ont. 7 Oct. 1939; e. Univ. of N.B. B.A. 1962; Queen's Univ. LL.B. 1966; Canada Decoration; m. Sylvia; VICE-PRESIDENT, GENERAL COUNSEL & SECRETARY, MUNICIPAL FINANCIAL CORP., THE MUNICIPAL TRUST CO., THE MUNICIPAL SAVINGS & LOAN CORP. 1988– ; Solicitor, Canadian Pacific 1968–69; Harries, Houser 1969–74; Partner 1974–85; Gen. Counsel & Sec., Canada Deposit Insur. Corp. 1985–88; Dir., Barrie Press Inc.; Municipal Travel Consultants Inc.; Carswell Ferguson Health Resources Inc.; Mem., Candn. Bar Assn.; Law Soc. of Upper Canada; County of Simcoe Law Assn.; The Bd. of Trade of Metro. Toronto; clubs: Barrie Country, Toronto Ski; Office: 70 Collier St., P.O. Box 147, Barrie, Ont. L4M 4S9.

**FERGUSON, The Hon. Justice George Stephen Plow;** b. Montreal, Que. 23 Aug. 1923; s. William Brophy and Gladys Elizabeth (Plow) F.; e. Univ. of Toronto Schs., grad. 1941; Univ. of Toronto, (Pol. Science and Econ.), 1945; Osgoode Hall, Toronto, 1948; m. Diana, d. Roland C. Steven, Montreal, Que., 28 May 1949; children: George Steven Plow, Michael Taylor, Diana; Bd. of Govs., Wilfred Laurier Univ.; Adv. Counc., St. George's Coll., Toronto; mem., Candn. Bar Assn. (Past Pres., Ontario branch); Past Pres. Ont. March of Dimes; Past Pres. Goodwill Industries Toronto; called to Bar of Ont., 1948; cr. Q.C. 1959; Labour Arbitrator and Mediator 1972–76; Vice-Chrmn., Ont. Labour Relations Bd. 1973–76; First Chief Arbitrator for the Ont. Police Arbitration Comn. 1973–76; mem. Ont. Court of Justice (Gen. Div.); mem., County of York Law Assoc.; Candn. Bar Assoc.; Advocates Soc.; Candn. Judges Conf.; Candn. Inst. for the Admin. of Justice; Alpha Delta Phi (President, Toronto Chapter, 1945); Anglican; recreations; gardening, fishing; antique wooden boats; Clubs: Toronto Lawyers; Advocates Soc.; Toronto Hunt; Home: 1 Benvenuto Place, Apt. 405, Toronto, Ont. M4V 2L1.

**FERGUSON, Harry Stewart;** financial executive; b. Glasgow, Scotland Sept. 1933; e. Univ. of Strathclyde; Royal Coll. Science & Technol., Scotland; Univ. of Toronto post-grad. courses;. m. Kathleen Ruth Lowe Sept. 1959; children: Eileen, Evelyn, Kirsten; PRES., DO-SHIM CAPITAL INC. 1992– ; Pres., Glen Roy Resources Inc.; Gogama Resources Inc.; Chester Minerals; served as Comm. Offr., Ministry of Industry & Trade, Ont.; Pres., Forbes Campbell (Canada) Ltd. 1977–84; Pres., York Bay Capital Corp. 1987–92; Fellow, Internat. Bankers' Assn.; Past Pres., Sir Walter Scott Soc., Univ. of Toronto; Clubs: Oakville Yacht; Arts and Letters; Home: 1078 Cedar Grove Blvd., Oakville, Ont. L6J 2C4; Office: P.O. Box 78, Suite 2715, 401 Bay St., Toronto, Ont. M5H 2Y4.

**FERGUSON, Howard L.,** B.A., M.A.; public servant; b. Guelph, Ont. 14 July 1930; s. David Winter and Cora Jane (Kellar) F.; e. Univ. of West. Ont. B.A. (Hons.) 1952; Univ. of Toronto, M.A. 1955; m. Janet d. Howard and Marion Hugill 1952; children: David, Michael, Andrew, Christopher, Mark; Coordinator, Second World Climate Conf. (WMO, UNEP, UNESCO, ICSU) 1989–91; Dir., Air Quality & Inter-Envir. Rsch., AES 1979–81; Reg. Dir. Gen., Environ. Can. (Ont.) 1982–84; Dir. Gen., Candn. Climate Ctr. 1984–85; Asst. Dep. Min., Atmospheric Environment Serv. (AES) (Head, Canada's nat. weather service) 1986–89; Permanent Candn. Rep., World Meteorological Orgn. (WMO) 1986–89; Principal Candn. Del., WMO/UNEP Intergov. Panel on Climate Change 1988–89; Conf. Dir., World Conf. on the Changing Atmosphere, Toronto, June 1988; Public Serv. of Can. Merit Award for work on acid rain; Environment Can. Achievement Award for work on climate and atmospheric change; Mem., Candn. Meteorological & Oceanographic Soc.; Am. Meteorological Soc.; author of over 70 sci. pubs.; recreations: music, photography; Office: Bolton, Ont.

**FERGUSON, Ivan Graeme,** C.M., B.A., Hon. D. Univ. (Brad.), R.C.A.; film producer; b. Toronto, Ont. 7 Oct. 1929; s. Frank A. and Grace Irene (Warner) F.; e. Dickson Sch. and Galt (Ont.) Coll. Inst. 1947; Univ. of Toronto B.A. 1952; married first Betty June Ramsaur; children: James Norman Munro, Allison June; married second, Phyllis Marie Wilson; Pres., Imax Corp. 1967–90; Nat. Secy. World Univ. Service Can. 1953–55; films incl. 'The Legend of Rudolph Valentino' (Dir.); 'The Days of Dylan Thomas' (Dir.) First Prize, Bergamo Film Festival; 'The Love Goddesses' (Co-Producer); 'The Virgin President' (Co-Producer and Dir.-Cameraman); 'Polar Life,' multiscreen film Man and the Polar Regions Pavilion Expo '67 (Producer, Dir., Cameraman); 'North of Superior' in IMAX (Producer, Dir., Cameraman), Special Jury Prize Candn. Film Awards; 'The Question of TV Violence (Dir.) Chris Award, Best Documentary, Columbus Internat. Film Festival; 'Man Belongs to the Earth' in IMAX (Co-Producer, Dir., Cameraman) First Place Gold Camera Award, U.S. Industrial Film Festival, Chicago; 'Snow Job' in IMAX (Producer, Dir.); 'Ocean' in OMNIMAX (Producer, Dir., Co-Cameraman); 'Nishnawbe-aski' (Co-Producer, Cameraman); 'Hail Columbia' in IMAX and OMNIMAX (Co-producer, Dir., Co-cameraman); 'The Dream is Alive' filmed in space in IMAX and OMNIMAX (Producer, Dir., Co-cameraman) Special Jury Award, Candn. Film and Television Awards and Grand Prix du Public, 1st Festival Internat. de la Géode 1987; 'Blue Planet' filmed in space in IMAX and OMNIMAX (Producer, Co-Dir.) Grand Prix du Public, 3rd Festival Internat. de la Géode 1991; 'Journey to the Planets' (co-producer) EXPO 93; developed IMAX and OMNIMAX advanced motion picture systems; Member, Order of Canada 1993; Hon. Doctor, Univ. of Bradford 1993; Special Achievement Award, Acad. of Candn. Cinema & Television 1986 Genies; Royal Candn. Acad. of Arts Medal 1990; Aviation Week Laurel 1990; Candn. Govt. Environmental Achievement Award 1991; Hon. Lifetime Mem., Candn. Soc. of Cinematographers; Patron, Toronto Film Soc.; Home: Norway Point, R.R. #1, Baysville, Ont. P0B 1A0; Office: c/o Imax Corp., 45 Charles St. E., Toronto, Ont. M4Y 1S2.

**FERGUSON, James Kenneth Wallace,** M.B.E. (1945), M.D., F.R.S.C.; b. Tamsui, Formosa, 18 Mar. 1907; s. Dr. James Young and Harriet Arnold (Wallace) F.; e. George Watson's Coll., Edinburgh, Scot.; Malvern Coll. Inst., Toronto; Univ. of Toronto, B.A. 1928, M.A. 1929, M.D. 1932; m. Mary Frances, d. W.T. Wyndow, Toronto, 30 Aug. 1933; children: Ian, Anne, Brian, Shelagh; Dir., Connaught Med. Research Labs. 1955–72; Research Fellow, National Research Council, Washington, 1933–34; Assistant Professor of Physiol., University. of W. Ont. 1934–36; Ohio State Univ. 1936–38; Univ. of Toronto, Asst. Prof. of Pharm. 1938–41, and Prof. and Head of the Dept. 1945–55; served in World War 1941–45 with R.C.A.F. (Med. Br. Research); mem., Candn. Physiol. Soc. (Pres. 1950–51); Am. Physiol. Soc.; Am. Pharm. Soc.; co-author, 'Materia Medica,' 1948; has written some 50 papers on respiration, reproduction, and pharm. in scient. journs.; United Church; recreation: boating; Home: 56 Clarkehaven St., Thornhill, Ont. L4J 2B4.

**FERGUSON, James P.,** C.A.; business executive; b. Landis, Sask. 12 Aug. 1937; s. James and Gertrude (Schmit) F.; e. McGill Univ. C.A. 1971; m. Patricia Woodruff 27 Aug. 1960; children: James, Carolyn; PRES., LATIN AMERICA AND CORPORATE DEVELOPMENT DIR., THE HIRAM WALKER GROUP; Flight Lt., Royal Candn. Air Force; Audit Mgr., Tax Mgr., Clarkson Gordon & Co.; Controller & Treas., C.I. Power, Montreal; joined The Hiram Walker Group (previously Hiram Walker-Allied Vintners and Hiram Walker-Gooderham & Worts Limited) as Mgr. Taxation, became Vice Pres. & Treas., Sr. Vice Pres., Treas. & Chief Finan. Offr.; Extve. Vice Pres. & Corp. Devel. Dir.; Chrmn., Latin America & S. Europe Sector; recreations: golf, reading, nordic skiing; clubs: Essex Golf & Country; Office: 2072 Riverside Dr. E., Windsor, Ont. N8Y 4S5.

**FERGUSON, John Thomas,** B.Com., C.A.; executive; b. Edmonton, Alta. 21 Dec. 1941; s. Norman Robert and Dorothy Frances (Wigelsworth) F.; e. Univ. of Alta. B.Com. 1964; C.A. (Alta.) 1967; m. Bernice Evelyn McLean 23 July 1966; three s. Robert Brent, Bradley John, Douglas Gordon; PRESIDENT AND CHIEF EXTVE. OFFR., PRINCETON DEVELOPMENTS LTD. 1975– ; Dir., Royal Bank of Canada; Trans Alta Utilities Corp.; Bow Valley Energy Inc.; Barbican Properties Inc.; Acct., Price Waterhouse & Co. 1964–68; Comptroller, Oxford Development Group 1968– ; Vice Pres. and Treas. Numac Oil & Gas Ltd. 1969–75; Chrmn. Bus. Adv. Counc., Univ. of Alta.; mem. Alta. Inst. C.A.'s; Protestant; recreations: skiing, golf, squash; Clubs: Mayfair Golf & Country; Royal Glenora; Kappa Sigma; Home: 13011 – 65 Avenue, Edmonton, Alta. T6H 1W9; Office: #1400, 9945 – 108 St., Edmonton, Alta. T5K 2G6.

**FERGUSON, Jonathan Eric,** B.A., Diplôme, Nieman Fellow; journalist, writer; b. Halifax, N.S. 24 May 1957; s. Eric William and Joan Eloise (Hollett) F.; e. Dalhousie Univ. B.A. 1978 (Issac Killam Scholarship); Univ. of Paris, France dipl. en sci. écon. 1980 (Rotary Fellowship); Carleton Univ., journalism 1984; Harvard Univ., Nieman Fellow 1988–89; m. 31 Aug. 1991; FINANCIAL REPORTER, TORONTO STAR, TORSTAR 1994– ; Co-owned & managed a restaurant on Grand Manan Island, N.B. 1981–82; Analyst & Researcher, Transportation Canada 1982–83; Business Columnist & Finan. Inst. Reporter, Toronto Star 1985–88; Parliamentary Correspondent, Toronto Star, Torstar 1989–93; contbr.: 'Euromoney' mag. (U.K.), Curia's Publications (Chicago); Mem., Harvard Business Club (Ottawa); Nieman Found.; Harvard Univ. Alumni Assn.; Big Brothers; Carleton Univ. Alumni Assn.; recreations: squash, tennis, running; clubs: Westin Health, Lawn & Tennis; Home: 412 Besserer St., Ottawa, Ont. K1N 6C1; Office: One Yonge St., Toronto, Ont. M5E 1E6.

**FERGUSON, Marnie H.,** B.A.; business executive; b. Lindsay, Ont.; d. Noble William and Gladys Eileen (Smith-Emsley) Eberts; e. Lindsay Collegiate; Ryerson Polytech. Inst.; Waterloo Lutheran, Univ. of Waterloo B.A.; m. Garry S. s. Earl and Kathleen F. 23 Aug. 1969; children: Michael, Samuel, Christoper; VICE-PRESIDENT, PEOPLE, QUALITY AND EH & S, MONSANTO CANADA INC. 1991– ; various human resources management positions incl. Labour Relns., Organizational Devel. & Design. Organ. Transformation in Consumer Packaged Goods Indus.; Dir., Human Resources, Monsanto Canada Inc. 1989–91; Gen. Mgr., Monsanto Incite Consulting Div. 1991– ; Dir., Continuous Improvement, Monsanto Canada; Sr. Cons., Incite Div. of Monsanto; Mem., Personnel Assn. of Ontario; Chair, Council on Total Quality Management Conf. Bd. of Can.; Am. Management Assn.; Dir., Marriage Preparation/Marriage Enhancement, R.C. Diocese of Hamilton 1973– ; recreations: gardening, music, travel; Home: Kilbride, Ont.; Office: 2330 Argentia Rd., Mississauga, Ont. L5N 2G4.

**FERGUSON, Maynard;** musician; b. Montreal, Que. 4 May 1928; led own band Montreal area during 1940's; moved to USA 1948 performing in big bands of Boyd Raeburn, Jimmy Dorsey and Charlie Barnet; performed with Stan Kenton 1950–53 winning 'Down Beat' readers' polls for trumpet 1950, 1951, 1952; performed Hollywood studio orchestras 1953–56; formed Birdland Dreamland Band to perform at New York jazz club Birdland; performed and recorded at Expo 67 with a big band and a sextet; settled in Eng. 1968 performing with 17 piece band which made N. Am. debut 1971; returned to New York 1973 and reduced band to 13; recorded film themes 'Gonna Fly Now' ('Rocky') and 'Battlestar Galactica'; appearances in Can. incl. CBC TV 'Parade,' 'In the Mood'; Stratford Festival 1958, Massey Hall, Candn. Stage Band Festival; played solo trumpet opening ceremonies Montreal Olympics 1976; has made numerous recordings; cited various bibliogs.; designed the Firebird (combination slide and valve trumpet) and Superbone (combination slide and valve trombone).

**FERGUSON, Robert Bury,** M.A., Ph.D., F.R.S.C., F.M.S.A.; educator; b. Cambridge (Galt), Ont. 5 Feb. 1920; s. Alexander Galt and Harriet Henrietta (Bury) F.; e. Central Pub. Sch. and Galt Coll. Inst. 1937; Univ. of Toronto B.A. 1942, M.A. 1943, Ph.D. 1948; m. Margaret Irene Warren 29 Dec. 1948; children: Evelyn Bury, Robert Warren, Marion Galt; PROF. EMERITUS 1986– ; Asst. Prof. of Mineralogy Univ. of Manitoba 1947–50, Assoc. Prof. 1951–59; Prof. of Mineralogy 1959–85; Sr. Scholar, 1985–86; NRC Postdoctoral Fellow, Cambridge 1950–51; Visiting Scient. Oxford 1972–73; Adelaide Univ., 1979–80; Hawley Award, Mineralogical Assn. Canada, 1981; Distinguished Professor, Univ. of Man. 1983; author or co-author about 45 prof. papers mineralogical topics; mem. Mineral. Assn. Can. (Pres. 1977); Mineral. Soc. (London); Am. Crystallographic Assn.; served with RCAF 1945, Flying Offr. (Meteorol.); NDP; Unitarian; recreations: cross-country skiing, volleyball, photography, theatre; Home: 184 Wildwood Park, Winnipeg, Man. R3T 0E2; Office: Winnipeg, Man. R3T 2N2.

**FERGUSON, Robert John,** B.Comm.; insurance executive; b. Montreal, Que. 16 Apr. 1942; s. Arthur Donald and Dora Helen (Symons) F.; e. Concordia Univ. B.Comm. 1967; m. Glenna Marie d. Andy and Gertrude Wood 10 Apr. 1982; children: Christine, Colin, Robert, Andrew, Stephen; PRES. & CHIEF EXTVE. OFFR., ROYAL MACCABEES LIFE INSURANCE CO. 1991– ; Dir. and Extve. Vice Pres., Royal Financial Services, Inc.; Royal Investment Mgmt. Co. (all of Southfield, Mich.); Dir., Royal Life Ins. Co. of Am.,

Glastonbury Ct.; Bd. Chrmn. and C.E.O., Royal Life Ins. Co. of New York. Albany, NY; Dir., Personal Financial Assistant, Inc., Dover, Delaware; Bd. Chrmn., Royal Life and Annuity Co.; Bd. Chrmn. & C.E.O., Royal Institutional Investment Advisor Group, Inc.; Dir., Royal Associates, Inc. (the above three, Southfield, Mi.); Dir., Royal Life Canada, Oakville, Ont.; Dir., Roy Hold, Ltd., Oakville, Ont.; Vice-Pres., Equilease Can. Ltd. 1970–73; Vice-Pres., Mktg., Chem. Bank Affiliate (Can.) 1973–78); Dir., Mktg., East. Can., Bank of N.S. 1978–82; Vice-Pres., Bank of Boston 1983–84; Dir., Individual Mktg., London Life 1984–87; Dir., Royal Life Can.; Clubs: London Hunt; Oakville; Office: 26800 Northwestern Highway, Southfield, MI 48075.

**FERGUSON, (John) Trevor;** writer; b. Seaforth, Ont. 11 Nov. 1947; s. Percy Alexander and M.V. Joyce (Sanderson) F.; e. Barclay Sch. Montréal; Mount Royal High Sch.; m. Lynne d. Wentworth and Irene Hill 16 Dec. 1983; full-time novelist since 1983; Book Columnist, Montreal Gazette 1987–89; author (novels): 'High Water Chants' 1977; 'Onyx John' 1985, paperback 1988, Quebec French ed. 1990; 'The Kinkajou' 1989, paperback 1990; 'The True Life Adventures of Sparrow Drinkwater' 1993; new novel in progress; mem. Writers Union Can. (Nat. Council 1979–80, 1988–91, Chrmn. 1990–91); Writer-in-Residence, Univ. of Alta. 1992–93; P.E.N.; Elder, Ch. of St. Andrew & St. Paul (Presb.); Home: P.O. Box 597, Hudson Heights, Que. J0P 1J0.

**FERGUSON, William Bruce,** C.A., B.A.; manufacturing executive; b. Brockville, Ont. 24 June 1940; s. Bruce Hubert and Ethel Orpha (Poole) F.; e. Queen's Univ. B.A. 1965; C.A. 1968; m. Dr. L.L. Mickleborough; children: Christopher, Stephen, Jennifer, Lisa; PRESIDENT & DIR., TRITECH PRECISION INC.; Chrmn. & Dir., Grenville Castings Limited; President & C.E.O., Haley Industries Limited; Dir., The O.S. Kelly Company; Haley Industries Limited; various posns. incl. 2 years in Brazil and 1 year as Audit Mgr., Toronto, Clarkson Gordon & Co. 1965–72; Asst. Vice-Pres., fin. (Brazil), Brascan Ltd. 1972–76; Group Controller Elect. Utility 1976–77; Asst. to Pres. 1977–79; Dir. of Projects, Noranda Inc. 1979–82; Pres. & Dir., Orebed Inc.; Extve. Vice-Pres. and C.O.O., Noranda Metal Industries 1986–88; Pres. & Dir., Norcast Corp. 1982–89; Presbyterian; Home: 10 Whitney Ave., Toronto, Ont.; Office: Ste. 402, 60 Bloor St. W., Toronto, Ont. M4W 3B8.

**FERGUSSON, Hon. (Mrs.) Muriel McQueen,** O.C. (1976), P.C. (1974), Q.C., D.C.L., LL.D.; m. Aubrey S. Fergusson 1926 (d. 1941); has practised her prof. in Grand Falls, N.B.; long interested in Welfare work, and active in Business and Prof. Women's Club; first woman member of Fredericton City Council (former Depy. Mayor); Chairman of Internat. Relations Comte. of Candn. Fed. of Business & Prof. Women's Clubs, former Vice-President and former Educ. Secy. of Prov. Chapter, I.O.D.E.; Past Pres., Prov. Council of Women; apptd. Judge of Probate, Victoria County, N.B. 1935; Acting Clerk, Victoria County Court and Victoria Circuit Court, N.B. 1941; Clerk, Victoria County Court 1942; Clerk, Victoria Circuit Court 1943; Regional Dir. for N.B. for Dept. of Nat. Health & Welfare, 1947–53; during 2nd World War connected with W.P.T.B. as Enforcement Counsel for N.B.; summoned to the Senate of Can. 1953; apptd. first woman Speaker of the Senate of Canada 15 Dec. 1972–7 Nov. 1974; retired from Senate May 1975; Hon. D.C.L. Mount Allison 1953, LL.D., Univ. of N.B. 1969; D.C.L. Acadia 1974, St. Thomas 1974; LL.D. W. Ont. 1977; Hon. Chrmn., Candn. Conf. on Aging 1966; Hon. Chrmn., N.B. Conf. on Aging 1967; Hon. Chrmn., 2nd Candn. Conf. on Aging 1983; Hon. Vice Pres., Can. Council on Social Development; Hon. Pres., Can. Fed. of Business and Professional Women's Clubs; Trustee, Forum for Young Canadians; Patron, Lester B. Pearson College of the Pacific; Patroness, Women's Insts. of N.B.; N.B. Assoc. of Hospital Auxiliaries; mem. Candn. Bar Assn.; N.B. Barristers' Soc.; Life mem., N.B. Prov. Chapter I.O.D.E.; apptd. Queen's Counsel 1974; apptd. Officer Order of Canada 1976; Address: 102 Waterloo Row, Fredericton, N.B. E3B 1Z1.

**FERKO, Daryl Wayne,** B.Comm., C.M.A., C.A.; energy executive; b. Edmonton, Alta. 5 May 1954; e. Univ. of Alberta B.Comm. 1976; C.A. 1979; C.M.A. 1980; m. Renata C.; children: Michael W., Brooke K.; VICE-PRES., FINANCE, TREAS. & CHIEF FINANCIAL OFFICER, DRECO ENERGY SERVICES LTD. 1981– ; Manager, Collins Barrow 1976–79; Controller, Skytop Brewster 1979–80; Home: 11110-23 B Ave., Edmonton, Alta. T6J 4P2; Office: 3716 – 93 St., Edmonton, Alta. T6E 5N3.

**FERLEY, Paul Fredric,** B.E.S., B.A., M.A.; economist; b. Winnipeg, Man. 13 Oct. 1954; s. Boris Fredrick and Mary Isabel (McAnulty) F.; e. Silver Heights Collegiate 1972; Univ. of Manitoba B.E.S. 1975; Univ. of Manitoba B.A. (Hons.) 1981; Queen's Univ. M.A. 1982; ASSISTANT CHIEF ECONOMIST, ECONOMICS DEPT., BANK OF MONTREAL 1992– ; Economist, Research Dept., Bank of Canada 1982–87; Sr. Economist, Econ. Dept., Bank of Montreal 1987–92; Bd. of Dirs., Toronto Assn. for Business and Economics; recreations: skiing; Home: 20 Southport St., #402, Toronto, Ont. M6S 4Y8; Office: 21st floor, First Canadian Place, Toronto, Ont. M5X 1A1.

**FERNIE, Alastair Stewart,** M.A., F.F.A., F.C.I.A.; insurance executive; b. Edinburgh, Scotland 30 Aug. 1934; s. Alexander McLean and Mary Walker (Stewart) F.; e. George Heriot's Sch. Edinburgh 1945–52; Univ. of Edinburgh M.A. (Hons. in Math. & Nat. Philosophy) 1956; Faculty of Actuaries in Scotland F.F.A. 1963; children: Andrew, Keith, Alison; PRES., CANDN. OPNS., STANDARD LIFE ASSURANCE CO. 1980– ; Asst. Actuary, present firm 1964–67; Asst. Group Mgr. 1967–70; Assoc. Actuary 1970–72; Deputy Group Mgr. 1972–76; Sr. Vice Pres. (Group) 1976–79; Extve. Vice Pres. 1979–80; Dir., Monarch Devel. Corp.; Chairman, Candn. Life & Health Insur. Assn. Inc.; Pres., British Canadian Trade Assn.; Dir., Orchestre symphonique de Montréal; Presbyn.; recreations: golf, music; clubs: Mount Royal, Mount Bruno Country, National, Toronto, East India, London England; Home: 100 Berlioz, #302, Nun's Island, Que. H3E 1N4; Office: 1245 Sherbrooke St. W., #200, Montreal, Que. H3G 1G3

**FERNIE, John Donald,** M.Sc., Ph.D., F.R.S.C.; astronomer; educator; b. Pretoria, S. Africa 13 Nov. 1933; s. John Fernie Fernie; e. Univ. of Cape Town B.Sc. 1953; M.Sc. 1955; Ind. Univ. Ph.D. 1958; m. Yvonne Anne Chaney 23 Dec. 1955; two d. Kimberly Jan, Robyn Andrea; Chrmn. of Astronomy, Univ. of Toronto 1978–88, Affiliate Inst. Hist. and Philos. Science & Technol. since 1973, Dir. David Dunlap Observatory 1978–88; Lectr. in Physics and Astron. Univ. of Cape Town 1958–61; Asst. Prof. of Astron. Univ. Toronto 1961, Assoc. Prof. 1964, Prof. 1967; author 'The Whisper and the Vision' 1976; over 150 tech. papers astron.; mem. Royal Astron. Soc. Can. (Pres. 1974–76); Am. Astron. Soc.; Internat. Astron. Union; recreations: volleyball, swimming; Home: 12 Thornheights Rd., Thornhill, Ont. L3T 3M1; Office: David Dunlap Observatory, P.O. Box 360, Richmond Hill, Ont. L4C 4Y6.

**FERNS, William Paterson,** B.A., M.Soc. Sc.; television producer; b. Winnipeg, Man. 13 Jan. 1945; s. Henry Stanley and Helen Maureen (Jack) Ferns; e. King Edward's Sch.; Pembroke Coll., Cambridge, B.A. (Hons.) 1967 (Wrenbury Scholar); Birmingham Univ., M.Soc.Sc. 1968; m. Jenny d. Ronald and Vera Wills 3 Aug. 1968; children: Andrew Malcolm, Katharine Jane, Mark Richard; Chrmn., The Arts Network/Le Réseau des Arts; Pres., Primedia Inc.; Primedia Entertainment Inc.; Primedia Productions Ltd.; Primedia Releasing Inc.; Comedia Productions; Primedia-Héroux Productions; Vice Pres., Primedia Pictures; Soapbox Productions; Héroux-Primedia Productions; Extve. Dir., Bd. of Internat. Advisors, Banff Television Found.; Rsch. Dir., CBC, 'The Public Eye' 1968–69; Prod., 'CBC Weekend' 1969–71; Sr. Prod., 'CBC Weekend,' 'CBC Midweek' 1971–72; Vice Pres., Nielsen Ferns Ltd. & Dir., Intervideo Inc. 1972–76; Nielsen-Ferns Internat. 1976–81; Pres., Candn. Film & TV Assn. 1979–81; Co-Pres., Assn. of Cand. Film & TV Prods. 1984–85; Pres., Banff TV Found. 1984–89; TV Advr., Nat. Ballet of Can. 1981– ; TV Advr., Candn. Opera Co. 1989– ; First co-recipient, Chetwynd Award for Entrepreneurial Achievement; Winner of Que.-Alta. Prize for innovation in television 1987; CFTPA Personal Achievement Award 1990; plus num. nat. & internat. awards for TV prodn.; Dir., Desrosiers Dance Theatre 1983–88; Dir., National Ballet Sch.; Treas., Wildlife Preserv. Trust Can. 1985– ; Anglican; Mem., Royal Television Soc.; Alliance of Candn. TV & Radio Artists; Club: United Oxford & Cambridge Univs.; Home: 78 Manor Rd., E., Toronto, Ont. M4S 1P8; Office: Cinevillage, 65 Heward Ave., Suite A 109, Toronto, Ont. M4M 2T5.

**FERRABEE, Francis James,** B.A.; journalist; b. Montreal, Que. 20 Mar. 1937; s. Francis Gilbert and Roberta R. (Dunton) F.; e. Lower Can. Coll.; Bishop's Univ., B.A. 1957; Univ. of Toronto; m. Diane E., B.A., B.Ed.; d. Kathleen and Gavin b. Young 19 Dec. 1959; children: Jane W. (Mrs. James Pendergast), Michael J., F. David G.; BUSINESS EDITOR, THE GAZETTE, Montreal 1990– ; Police Reporter, Montreal Gazette 1958; covered prov. & fed. elections 1960, 62, 63; Reuters (U.K.) 1964–65; Pol. Writer, Montreal Gazette 1965–67; Massey Coll., Univ. of Toronto 1967–68 (Southam Journalism Fellowship); Assoc. Ed., Montreal Gazette 1968–72; Que. Bureau Chief, Southam News 1972; Ottawa Bur. Ch. 1973–76; opened African Bur. 1977; Eur. Bur. Ch. (Paris) 1979–83; Mng. Ed. (Ottawa) 1983–85; Bureau Chief (London, Eng.), Southam News 1985–89; Pres., Student's Counc., Bishop's Univ. 1956–57; Winner, Nat. Newspaper Award for Spot News Reporting 1987; Anglican; recreations: tennis, golf, postcard collecting; Clubs: Muthaiga Country (Nairobi), University (Montreal); Home: 58–1509 Sherbrooke St. W., Montréal, Qué. H3G 1M1; Office: 250 St. Antoine St. W., Montréal, Qué. H2Y 3R7.

**FERRETTI, Janine Helene,** B.A.; association executive; b. Washington, D.C. 26 June 1958; d. James Joseph and Irma Josephine (Priebe) F.; e. Bonn Am. H.S. (Germany) 1976; Univ. of Nairobi; Univ. of Calif. (Santa Cruz) B.A. 1983; York Univ.; m. Gary Thomas s. Thomas and Marilyn Gallon 15 April 1983; children: Kalifi Anna, Jenika Josephine; EXTVE. DIR., POLLUTION PROBE 1989– ; Rsch. Asst., Internat. Union for the Conservation of Nature & Natural Resources, Bonn, Germany 1977; Researcher, Environment Liaison Centre, Nairobi, Kenya 1980–82; Researcher, Pollution Probe 1984–87; Dir., Internat. Program, Pollution Probe 1987–89; Mem., Internat. Trade Advisory Ctte.; Advisory Ctte. on Environmental Protection; New Directions Group; Ont. Round Table on Environ. & Economy; Past Mem. Bd. of Dir., Candn. Council for Internat. Coop. 1985–88; author: 'International Directory of NGOs Working in the Field of Renewable Energy' 1981; assoc. editor: 'Common Futures, Exploring the Integration of the Global Economy and the Environment' 1988 (conf. proceedings); Home: 262 Willow Ave., Toronto, Ont. M4E 3K7; Office: 12 Madison Ave., Toronto, Ont. M5R 2S1.

**FERRIER, Andrew Alan,** B.B.A., M.B.A.; business executive; b. Montreal, Que. 29 March 1959; s. Ilay Charles and Elizabeth Jean (O'Brien) F.; e. Loyola H.S. 1976; Univ. of N.B. B.B.A. 1980; Concordia Univ. M.B.A. 1983; m. Danielle N. d. Arthur and Claudette Guitard 18 May 1985; children: Alexander, Nicole; VICE-PRESIDENT, SALES & MARKETING, LANTIC SUGAR LTD. 1991– ; Financial Analyst, Redpath Sugars 1983–85; Dir., Raw Sugar Purchasing, Refined Sugars Inc. 1986; Vice-Pres. Purchasing 1987–90; recreations: squash, tennis, skiing, rugby; clubs: Montreal Amateur Athletic Assn.; Brome Lake Boating Club; Home: 8 Grove Park, Westmount, Que. H3Y 3E7; Office: 1 Westmount Sq., Westmount, Que. H3Z 2P9.

**FERRIER, Donald Rolf,** B.Sc., P.Eng.; consulting engineer; b. Edmonton, Alta. 24 Jan. 1938; s. Richard Douglas and Ruby Alberta (Irish) F.; e. Victoria Comp. H.S. 1955; Univ. of Alta., B.Sc. 1959; Northwestern Univ., post-grad. courses 1963; m. Anne d. Les and Gladys Clark 26 Aug. 1961; children: Lynne, Brian, James; Vice Pres. & Gen. Mgr., Associated Engineering International Ltd. 1991–94, Retired; Project Engineer, Municipal, Edmonton, present firm 1959–61; Sr. Roadways Engr. 1962–65; Asst. Mgr., Sask. Opns., Regina 1966–70; Mgr., Bus. Devel. Alta., Edmonton 1971–74; Area Br. Mgr., Calgary 1975–79; Vice Pres., Bus. Devel. – Corp. 1980–85; Vice Pres., Mkgt., Assoc. Eng. Group Ltd. 1986–91; Founding Dir., Assoc. Engr. (Ont.) Ltd.; Kinsmen of the Year Award 1969–70; Past Sec., Timberidge Community Assn.; Mem., Assn. of Cons. Engrs. of Can. (Pres. 1988–89; Bd. Mem. 1986–90); Cons. Engrs. of Alta. (co-founder; Pres. 1983–84); Assn. of Profl. Engrs, Geol. & Geophys. of Alta. (Counc. 1975–78); Inst. of Traffic Engrs. (Assoc.); Roads & Transp. Assn. of Can. (Tech. Ctte. 1975–80); Regina Queen City Kinsmen Club (Dir. 1967–70; Delta Kappa Epsilon (Sec. 1958–59); author/co-author/editor of tech. papers; recreations: alpine skiing, cycling, sailboard, carpentry; club: Glencoe; Home: 18 Varsville Pl. N.W., Calgary, Alta. T3A 0A8.

**FERRIER, Ilay Charles;** b. 17 Aug. 1927; e. McGill Univ. B.Com., C.A.; m. Elizabeth Jean O'Brien; 6 children; Vice Pres., John Labatt Ltd. 1984–89 (retired); with Canron Ltd. 1953–75; with Dominion Textile Inc. 1975–84: Dir., Theatre Lac Brome; Brome Lake Land Found.; Past Chrmn. Financial Extves. Inst. (Can.); Past Pres. Montreal Chapter; Past Dir.: United Way of Gter. London; Candn. Red Cross, London Br.; Candn. Arthritis Soc., Que. Region; Montreal Symphony Orch.; University Club of Montreal; Sacred Heart School of Montreal; Clubs: Montreal Badminton & Squash; University (Montreal); Address: 20 Argyll Rd., Knowlton, Que. J0E 1V0.

**FERRIER, Lee Kenneth;** barrister; b. Toronto, Ont. 6 Feb. 1937; s. William Gladstone and Hazel Marguerite

(Box) F.; e. Cunningham & Mem. Pub. Schs. 1950, Delta Secondary Sch. 1955 Hamilton; McMaster Univ. B.A. 1959; Univ. of Ottawa LL.B. 1962; m. Shannon Miriam d. Ward Bruce Fawcett 11 Oct. 1958; two d. Allison Miriam, Tamara Lynn; apptd. JUSTICE, ONT. COURT OF JUSTICE (GEN. DIV.) 1991; called to Bar of Ont. 1964; cr. Q.C. 1976; former mem. COMSOC Ministry Comte. on Adoption Records; Ont. del. Uniform Law Conf. Can.; Past Bd. mem. Children's Aid Soc. Metrop. Toronto, Visiting Homemaker's Assn., Parkdale Community Legal Services; served as Project Consultant Clarke Inst. Psychiatry; Bar Admission Course Lectr. and Group Instr. 1968–80; Non-bencher Legal Aid Comte. 1972–79; mem. Clin. Funding Comte. 1975–79; Atty.-Gen.'s Comte. on Rep. of Children 1977–79; Trustee Foundation for Legal Research 1978–82; Vice Chrmn. Ont. Legal Aid Plan 1979–81; el. Bencher, Law Soc. Upper Can. 1979–81; Treas., Law Soc. of Upper Can. 1988–90; mem. Advocates Soc. (Founding); Candn. Bar Assn. (Past Chrmn. Family Law Sec.; mem. Council 1969–79); York Co. Law Assn.; Past Pres. Lawyers' Club; co-author 'MacDonald and Ferrier: Canadian Divorce Law and Practice' 1969; Ed. 'Infants and Children' Candn. Abridgement 1970; Protestant; recreations: skiing, sailing, photography, cooking; Home: 304 Keewatin Ave., Toronto, Ont. M4P 2A5; Office: Osgoode Hall, 130 Queen St. W., Toronto, Ont. M5H 2N5.

**FERRON, Claude,** M.Sc.Com., C.A.; insurance executive; b. Shawinigan, Que. 25 March 1937; s. Albert and Rose (Branchaud) F.; e. Coll. des Jesuites B.A. 1958; Laval Univ. M.Sc.Com. 1965; m. Ginette d. Jean-Paul Dore 1966; PRESIDENT & C.E.O., QUEBEC BLUE CROSS, CANASSURANCE LIFE, CANASSURANCE GENERAL and QUEBEC UNION GENERAL INSURANCE 1982– ; joined Clarkson, Gordon 1965; Treas. Groupe La Laurentienne 1966; Gen. Mgr. La Mutuelle-Vie Des Fonctionnaires and La Capitale, Cie Assurance Generale 1973; Vice Pres. Groupe Pret & Revenu 1980; Pres., Que. Diabetes Assn.; recreations: tennis, reading, travel; Club: St-Denis; Office: 550 Sherbrooke St. W., Montreal, Que. H3A 1B9.

**FERRON, Madeleine;** writer; b. Louiseville, Qué. 24 July 1922; d. Joseph-Alphonse and Adrienne (Caron) Ferron; e. Soeurs de Sainte-Anne, Lachine; Lettres à l'Univ. de Montréal (auditrice libre) et Ethnographie à l'Univ. Laval (auditrice libre); m. Robert s. Justice Léonce Cliche 22 Sept. 1945; children: Marie-Josée, Nicolas, David; author (short stories) 'Coeur de Sucre' 1966; 'Le Chemin des Dames' 1977; 'Histoires édifiantes' 1981; 'Un singulier amour' 1987; 'Le Grand Théâtre' 1989; (novels) 'La fin des loups-garous' 1966; 'Le baron écarlate' 1971; 'Sur le chemin Craig' 1983; co-author (essays) 'Quand le peuple fait la loi' 1972; 'Les Beaucerons, ces insoumis' 1974; 'Adrienne' 1993 (récit); recipient Prix des Editions La Presse 1982; Prix France-Québec (finalist 1966, 1987); Grand Prix littéraire de Montréal (finalist 1971, 1987); Chev., Ordre Nat. du Qué.; Chrmn. La Fondation Robert-Cliche pour la protection du patrimoine des Beaucerons 1979– ; mem. L'Union des écrivains québécois; Address: 1130 de la Tour, Québec City, Qué. G1R 2W7.

**FESSENDEN, Robert J.,** B.Sc.F., M.Sc., Ph.D.; research executive; b. Toronto, Ont. 26 May 1943; e. Univ. of Toronto B.Sc.F. 1965; Univ. of Guelph M.Sc. 1967; Macdonald Coll., McGill Univ. Ph.D. 1976; m. Doreen; children: Matthew, Daniel; VICE PRES., DEVELOPMENT AND PLANNING, ALBERTA RESEARCH COUNCIL 1992– ; Lectr., Fac. of Forestry, Univ. of Toronto 1967–76; Asst. Prof. 1976–78; Head, Terrestrial Environ. Section, Syncrude Can. Ltd. (Edmonton) 1978–82; Head, Soils Dept., Alta. Rsch. Counc. 1982–84; Head, Terrain Sci. Dept. 1984–88; Vice Pres., Natural Resources Div. 1988–89; Vice-Pres., Resource Technologies 1989–92; Office: 16 Greystone Cres., Sherwood Park, Alta.; Office: P.O. Box 8330, Postal Stn. F, Edmonton, Alta. T6H 5X2.

**FEVANG, Leroy,** B.Sc.Pharm., M.B.A.; pharmacist; b. High Prairie, Alta. 22 September 1936; s. Siguard David and Pearl (Wakefield) F.; e. Univ. of B.C., B.Sc. 1958, M.B.A. 1968; m. Patricia d. Stev and Reta Russell 31 Aug. 1957; children: Monte, Sharon; EXTVE. DIR., CANADIAN PHARMACEUTICAL ASSN. 1978– ; Pharm. empl., Glacier Drugs Ltd. 1958–61; Mgr. & Shareholder, Glacier Drugs (1961) Ltd. 1961–68; Pharm./Mgr., Cunningham Drug Stores Ltd. 1968–70; Shoppers Drug Mart 1970–71; Registrar, Sec.-Treas. (1971–78), Coll. of Pharmacists of B.C. (Ed. 'The Bulletin'); Lectr., Fac. of Pharm. Sci., Univ. of B.C.; Dir., Pharmacy Examining Bd. of Canada; Fedn. of Internat. Pharmacy (Vice Pres., Comn. of Administrative Pharmacy); Commonwealth Pharmaceutical Assoc.; B.C. Pharmacy Assoc.; mem., St. Thomas the Apostle Anglican Church; B.C. Pharm. Soc.; B.C. Coll. of Pharm.; Ont. Pharm. Assn.; Am. Soc. of Assn. Extves.; Publisher, 'Compendium of Pharamceuticals and Specialties,' 'Canadian Pharmaceutical Journal,' 'Canadian Self-medication'; recreations: tennis, hiking, skiing, jogging; Club: Ottawa Athletic; Home: 2475 Wyndale Cres., Ottawa, Ont. K1H 8J3; Office: 1785 Alta Vista Dr., Ottawa, Ont. K1G 3Y6.

**FEWSTER, Leo Blake;** actuary; insurance extve.; b. Tillsonburg, Ont. 3 Sept. 1924; s. Anson Oliver and Ada Belle (Sitts) F.; e. Tillsonburg (Ont.) elem. and high schs.; Univ. of W. Ont. 1942–46; m. Mary Josephine, d. late Herve Gerald Davies Humphreys, 27 May 1950; children: Andrea Jane, Mary Patricia, Peter Humphreys, Timothy John; Mem. Bd. of Dirs., London Life Insurance Co.; London Ins. Group Inc.; joined London Life Ins. Co. 1946, Asst. Actuary 1959, Actuary and Administrative Offr. 1970; Vice Pres. and Chief Actuary 1974; Vice Pres. Corporate Services and Chief Actuary 1988; Sr. Vice Pres. and Chief Actuary 1989–91; mem., Soc. Actuaries; Candn. Inst. Actuaries; Delta Upsilon; Anglican; recreations: walking, wine-making; Home: 70 Elmwood Ave. E., London, Ont. N6C 1J5; Office: 255 Dufferin Ave., London, Ont. N6A 4K1.

**FFOULKES-JONES, Peter S.,** B.Sc.; energy executive; b. Trinidad, W.I. 30 June 1939; s. Geoffrey Squire and Alice Eleanor (Purvis) F.; e. Cresent Heights H.S. 1956; Univ. of Alberta B.Sc. 1963; divorced; children: Shauna L., Trevalyn S.; PRESIDENT & CHIEF EXECUTIVE OFFICER, PETROREP RESOURCES LTD. 1988– ; Chief Engineer, Petrorep (Canada) Ltd. 1978–80; Vice-Pres. & Gen. Mgr. 1980–81; Vice-Pres. Production 1981–88; Dir., Petrorep Resources Ltd.; Ascentex Energy Inc.; Home: 7112 Bow Cres., NW, Calgary, Alta. T3B 2B9; Office: 1000, 630 – 6 Ave. SW, Calgary, Alta. T2P 0S8.

**FIELD, George Sydney,** M.B.E. (1946), D.Sc., F.R.S.C.; physicist; b. Wimbledon, Eng. 23 Oct. 1905; s. James and May Edith (Davies) F.; e. Waterville Academy, Que.; Univ. of Alta., B.Sc. 1929, M.Sc. 1930 (received Nat. Research Council Bursary), D.Sc. 1937; D.Sc. (Hon.), Royal Mil. Coll. 1972; m. Jean Olive, d. Jas. A. Richards, Edmonton, Alta., 19 May 1930; children: William James Robert, Gregory George, Marilyn Denise; Physicist, National Research Council, 1930–46; built up and directed NRC Acoustics Lab.; during World War II, spent three months in United Kingdom investigating anti-submarine and anti-mining devices for the National Research Council and the Royal Canadian Navy; also directed a number of researches in the field of underwater warfare and in acoustical aspects of telecommunication systems for the Canadian Armed Forces; mem. Canadian Del. to the Informal Commonwealth Conf. on Defence Science in London, Eng., 1946; Naval Research Adviser to the Defence Research Bd., 1947; Deputy Dir. General of Defence Research, 1948–52; Chief of Div. 'A,' Defence Research Bd. and Scientific Adv. to the Chief of the Naval Staff, 1952–54; Chief Scientist, Defence Research Bd., 1954–64, Vice Chrmn. 1964–66; Fellow, Acoustical Soc. Am.; has written numerous scient. articles on ultrasonics, vibrations in solids, short elect. waves; Fellow, Inst. of Elect. and Electronics Engrs.; Fellow, Royal Soc. of Can.; Presbyterian; recreations: gardening, oil painting; Home: 28285 Mango Dr. S.W., Bonita Springs, Fla. 33923.

**FIELD, Harris Gillespie,** B.A., LL.B., Q.C.; lawyer; b. Edmonton, Alta. 31 Jan. 1920; s. Sem W. and Jessie B. (Harris) G.; e. Univ. of Alberta B.A. 1942; LL.B. 1947; m. C. Primrose d. Charles and Helen Hyndman 15 July 1942; children: John (dec.), David, Catherine (Povaschak); SENIOR PARTNER & LAWYER, FIELD & FIELD PERRATON 1948– ; (presently semi-retired); also Chrmn., Mngt. Ctte. 1968–86; served as infantryman four-and-a-half years in World War II; Bencher, Law Soc. of Alta. 1964–74; Pres. 1972–73; Chrmn., Alberta Institute of Law Research and Reform 1968–72; Dir., Intensity Resources Ltd.; Former Dir., Edmonton Space & Science Ctr.; former Dir. & Chrmn., Sunshine Village Corp. (a private co.); recreations: golf, swimming, gardening; clubs: Edmonton, Mayfair Golf & Country; Home: 14018 – 100th Ave., Edmonton, Alta. T5N 0J3; Office: #2000, 10235 – 101st St., Edmonton, Alta. T5J 3G1.

**FIELD, Kenneth Arthur,** C.A.; investment dealer, real estate broker; b. Ficksburg, S. Africa 15 Sept. 1943; s. Arthur George and Stoffelina Issobel (Kriek) F.; e. Univ. of Natal, cert. in theory of accountancy; m. Gloriana d. Elsa Anisio; children: Shannon, Craig, Anthony, Annalisa; EXECUTIVE VICE-PRES., MCLEAN MCCARTHY INC. 1973– ; C.A., Arthur Hopewell & Co. 1960–66; Keur Uitgewers Bpk. 1967; Harris & Partners Inc. 1968–72; Dir., First Mercantile Currency Fund; recreations: golf, music, reading; clubs: National, Fitness Inst., St. Georges Golf, Wildcat Run Golf; Office: 222 Bay St., P.O. Box 64, Toronto-Dominion Centre, Toronto, Ont. M5K 1E7.

**FIELD, Kenneth E.,** LL.B.; business executive; b. Toronto, Ont. 17 Nov. 1943; s. Lewis E. and Susan F.; e. Univ. of Toronto B.A. 1965; Osgoode Hall Law Sch. LL.B. 1969; Univ. of Waterloo Bus. Adm.; York Univ. Advanced Mgmt. Acctg.; children: Lisa, Howard, Peter; Pres. & Dir., Invescorp Limited 1988–..; Pres. & Dir. K. Field Resources; Dir. Coseka Resources; Coho Resources; Budget Optical; Partner, Corvette Resources; Exec. Vice-Pres. and Dir., Bramalea Ltd. 1974–79, Pres. & Dir. 1979–88; mem. Young Pres.'s Orgn.; recreations: tennis, skiing, sailing; Clubs: York Racquets, Alpine Ski; Home: 14 Wilket Rd., Willowdale, Ont. M2L 1N6.

**FIELD, Maxwell John;** real estate consultant; b. London, Eng. 1 June 1934; s. Frederick John and Amelia Glasspool Dean (Allford) F.; e. Coll. of Estate Mang. (London) 1952–56; m. June Edith d. John and Edith Martin 2 Feb. 1957; divorced 1982; children: Guy William, Gillian Rosemary, Duncan Maxwell; m. 2ndly Alice H. (Pisquer) Morris 15 Apr. 1983; REAL ESTATE DEVELOPMENT AND CONSULTING 1984– ; Chrmn., C.E.O. and Dir., Marathon U.S. Holdings Inc. 1977–84; Dir. and mem. Extve. Comte. Marathon Realty Co. Ltd. Toronto 1970–84; articled Messrs. Howell & Brooks, Chart. Surveyors, London 1951–55; prof. Asst. Messrs. Gerald Eve & Co. London 1955–57; Messrs. W.H. Bosley & Co. Ltd. Toronto 1957–62; Property Mgr. MEPC Canadian Properties Ltd. Toronto 1963–65; Devel. Mgr. Monarch Investments Ltd. 1965–70; Fellow, Royal Inst. Chart. Surveyors; mem. Ont. Land Econs.; Clubs: Chicago; Home: 2066 North Ocean Boul., Apt. 2NE, Boca Raton, Fla. 33431 USA.

**FIELD, Paul M.,** B.Comm., C.A.; mutual funds management executive; b. Montreal, Que. 30 Aug. 1956; s. Michael F. and Jean M. (Rowinski) F.; e. Queen's Univ. B.Comm. 1978; Candn. Inst. of C.A.s C.A. 1980; m. Karen Anderson 23 Sept. 1983; children: Veronica, Casey; VICE PRES. CLIENT SERVICE & CHIEF FINAN. OFFICER, UNITED FINANCIAL MANAGEMENT LTD. 1988– ; Senior Auditor, Ernst & Whinney 1978–81; Mgr., Asset & Liability Mngt., Canada Permanent Mortgage Corp. 1981–86; Mgr., Internal Financial Reporting, Canada Trust 1986–88; Chair, Mississauga Block Parents Program Inc.; clubs: Millcroft Golf, Cambridge; Office: 200 King St. W., Toronto, Ont. M5H 3W8.

**FIELD, Richard Henning,** Ph.D.; material culture historian; curator; writer; b. Reading, Penn. 8 Aug. 1944; s. Richard Henning Sr. and Lila Virginia (Ritzman) F.; e. Eastern College, St. Davids, Penn., B.A. 1966; Univ. of Toronto, M.A. 1968; Dalhousie Univ. Grad. Fellowship 1984–88; Ph.D. in History (Material Culture), Dalhousie Univ. 1990; m. Deborah Mary d. William and Stella Kelly 20 Feb. 1981; DIR., DARTMOUTH HERITAGE MUSEUM; Candn. citizen 1972; various posns., Confederation Ctr. of the Arts 1973–79; Founding Ed. 'Arts Atlantic Magazine' 1977; 'Art Gallery of N.S. Journal & Calendar' 1983; Advtg. Mgr. 'Canadian Antiques & Art Review' 1979–81; Exhbn. Curator, 'Gameboards,' Art Gall. of N.S. 1980–81; 'Spirit of Nova Scotia' 1983–87; occasional Lectr., Atlantic Canada Inst.; Lectr., Mount Saint Vincent Univ. 1988–89; Dalhousie Univ., summer 1989; Mem., N.S. Provincial Adv. Counc. on Heritage 1989–94; Co-chair, Heritage Adv. Ctte., Lunenburg Town Counc. 1991 (Mem. 1989–94); Mem., City of Dartmouth Heritage Adv. Ctte. 1991–94; Mem., Bd. of Dirs., Musique Royale 1989–90; author: 'Canadian Gameboards of the 19th and 20th Centuries from Ontario, Quebec and Nova Scotia' 1981; author and editor 'Spirit of Nova Scotia: Traditional Decorative Folk Art, 1780–1930' (Exhbn. Catalogue) 1986; author numerous articles in arts/mus. magazines; recreations: nature studies, bird watching; Address: P.O. Box 1569, 125 Pelham St., Lunenburg, N.S. B0J 2C0.

**FIELDING, Joy,** B.A.; writer; b. Toronto, Ont. 18 March 1945; d. Leo and Anne Tepperman; e. Univ. of Toronto B.A. 1966; m. Warren 11 Jan. 1974; two d. Shannon, Annie; author (novels) 'The Best of Friends' 1972; 'The Transformation' 1976; 'Trance' 1978; 'Kiss Mommy Goodbye' 1980 (Book of Yr. Award Periodical Distributors Can.); 'The Other Woman' 1982; 'Life Penalty' 1984; 'The Deep End' 1986; 'Good Intentions' 1989; 'See Jane Run' 1991; 'Tell Me No Secrets' 1993; regular book reviews for 8 yrs. on 'The Radio Show' (now defunct), CBC Radio; former actress various TV progs. incl. 'Gunsmoke' and Candn. film 'Winter Kept

Us Warm' 1965; numerous mag. articles, short stories for Chatelaine and other magazines, 2 scripts CBC; film script: 'Dream Baby'; recreations: reading, tennis, golf, bridge, swimming, movies, travel; Office: c/o Stoddart Publishing, 30 Lesmill, Toronto, Ont. M3B 2T6.

**FIELDS, Anthony Lindsay Austin,** M.D., F.R.C.P.(C), F.A.C.P.; physician; b. Barbados 21 Oct. 1943; s. Vernon and Marjorie (Pilgrim) F.; e. Univ. of Cambridge M.A. 1969; Univ. of Alta. M.D. 1974; Univ. of Toronto, Post-Grad. Training 1975–80; m. Pat d. Charles and Irene Stewart 5 Aug. 1967; DIR., CROSS CANCER INST. 1988– ; and ASSOC. PROF., UNIV. OF ALTA. 1984– ; joined Cross Cancer Inst. as Sr. Specialist, Dept. of Med. 1980; Dir., Dept. of Med. 1985; joined Univ. of Alta. as Asst. Prof. 1980; Dir., Div. of Med. Oncology 1985–89; dir., Div. of Oncology 1988–93; mem. Candn. Med. Assn.; Candn. Soc. for Clinical Investigation; Am. Fedn of Clinical Rsch.; Am. Soc. of Clinical Oncology; recreation: photography; Home: 10414 – 127th St., Edmonton, Alta. T5N 1V7; Office: 11560 University Ave., Edmonton, Alta. T6G 1Z2.

**FIERHELLER, George A.,** B.A., LL.D.; company executive; b. Toronto, Ont. 26 Apr. 1933; s. Harold Parsons and Ruth Hathaway (Bauld) F.; e. Univ. of Toronto Schs.; Univ. of Toronto Trinity Coll. B.A. 1955, post-grad. work; Concordia Univ. LL.D. 1976; m. Glenna Elaine d. Dr. Walter R. Fletcher, Toronto, Ont. 17 Apr. 1957; two d. Vicki Elaine, Lori Ann; VICE CHAIR, ROGERS COMMUNICATIONS, INC.; Dir. GBC North America Fund Inc.; Crownx Inc.; Rogers Cantel; Teleglobe Inc.; Pacific Telecommunications Inc.; joined IBM 1955 holding various positions Toronto and Ottawa incl. Marketing Mgr. prior to founding Systems Dimensions Ltd.; Pres. & C.E.O., SDL 1968–79; Chrmn., Pres. & C.E.O., Premier Cablesystems Ltd. 1979–85; Pres., C.E.O. & Dir., Cantel Inc. 1985–89; Chrmn. Data Processing Adv. Comte. Algonquin Coll. Ottawa; Trustee and mem. Extve. Comte. Nat. Arts Centre 1973–79; held various positions Ottawa/Carleton Un. Way incl. Campaign Chrmn. 1972, Chrmn. Policy & Planning Comte., First Vice Pres. Bd. Dirs.; Campaign Chrmn. Carleton Univ., Chrmn. of Assoc's, Chrmn. Bd. Govs. 1977–79; Trustee, Roy. Ottawa Hosp. 1977–79; mem. Adv. Comte. Paterson Centre Internat. Affairs; has presented papers to many nat. and internat. confs. incl. Jerusalem Conf. 1971, CAN-AM Conf. 1972, OECD Paris 1974; OECD Vienna 1977; mem. Young Pres' Organ. 1972–83; Candn. Information Processing Soc. (Pres. Ottawa Br. 1967–78, Nat. Pres. 1970–71, Dir. 1972–74); Chief Executives Organ.; World Business Council; Founding Dir. Candn. Assn. Data Processing Service Organ's 1971; mem. Founding Comte. Inst. Cert. Computer Profs. 1973–74; Dir., Vancouver Opera 1979–84; Trustee, Vancouver Gen. Hosp. Foundation 1980–85; Chrmn. Council of the 80's 1980–83; Campaign Chrmn., United Way of the Lower Mainland 1981; Chrmn. Finance Comte., Bd. of Governors, Simon Fraser Univ. 1981–84; Dir. Vancouver Chamber Choir 1980; Trustee, Candn. Mediterranean Inst. 1983–85; Chrmn., Strategic Planning Comte., Candn. Cable T.V. Assn. 1980–84; Comm., Vancouver Centennial Commission 1983–84; Chrmn. Team B.C. 1982–83; Dir., Candn. Centre for Philanthropy 1987– ; Mem., Business Counc. on National Issues 1987– ; Chrmn., 1991 Campaign, Un. Way of Toronto; Dir. & Chair, Information Technology Assoc. of Canada 1993–94; Chrmn., Vision 2000 1989–91; Trustee, McMichael Cdn. Collection; Trustee, Sunnybrook Hosp. Found.; Dir., Metro Toronto Bd. of Trade; Sigma Chi; recreations: music, wine, travel; Clubs: Rideau; Vancouver; National (Dir.); Granite; Ontario; Shaughnessy Golf & Country; Vancouver Lawn Tennis; Rosedale Golf; Home: 24 Pearwood Cres., North York, Ont. M3B 2C2; Office: Suite 2600, Commercial Union Tower, T-D Centre, Toronto, Ont. M5K 1J5.

**FIFE, Edward H.,** B.Sc.L.A., M.L.A.; educator; b. Mass. 18 Oct. 1942; s. Edwin Kenneth and Yvonne Barbara (Bartlett) F.; e. Rhode Island Sch. of Design B.Sc.L.A. 1965; Harvard Grad. Sch. of Design M.L.A. 1967; Reg'd Landscape Arch. Commonwealth of Mass.; children: Sarah Rodman, Mike Malcolm; Chrmn. Prog. in Landscape Arch., Univ. of Toronto 1985–89, 1992– , Asst. Chrmn. 1983–85, Assoc. Prof. of Design 1975– ; Dir., Centre for Landscape Research, present univ. 1987–89; Instr. of Planting Design, & Ecol. Principles Planting Design Mgmt. 1973– ; Designer, Sasaki, Strong, Assoc. 1964–66; Instr. in Landscape Arch. Ohio State Univ. 1967–69; Prin. E.H. Fife Landscape Arch. 1979– ; Mem. Adv. Ctte. for Park Restoration of Monserrate Park, Portugal 1987–90; Mem. Bd. of Dir., Koffler Gallery 1985– ; Science & Educ. Ctte., Royal Bot. Gard. 1988–91; Property Ctte., Royal Botanical Gardens 1991– ; Bd. Mem., Landscape Architecture Canada Found. 1987–88; mem. Ont. Assn. Landscape Archs. (Pres. 1987–88, Exec. Council 1983–89, Treas. 1983–85); Roster of Visiting Educators in Landscape Arch., Am. Assn. Landscape Archs. 1984– ; mem., Candn. Soc. Landscape Archs. (Fellow, mem. Council, mem., Roster of Visiting Evaluators); Acad. Bd., Governing Counc., Univ. of Toronto 1988–89; recreations: painting, organic farming, canoeing; Home: 269 Waverley Rd., Toronto, Ont. M4L 3T5; Office: 230 College St., Toronto, Ont. M5S 1A1.

**FILER, Diana Mary Livingston,** B.A., N.D.C.; broadcasting consultant; b. Vancouver, B.C. 10 May 1933; d. David Alexander and Grace Evelyn (MacPherson) Livingston; e. Crofton House Sch. Vancouver 1950; Univ. of B.C. B.A. 1954; Nat. Defence Coll. Kingston Dip. 1982; m. Roderick George Filer 14 June 1956, div. 1963; one s. Roderick David; Dir. CBC Corp. Internat. Relations 1986–92; joined CBC 1961, Producer Radio Features and Current Affairs 1967–74; originated 'Quirks and Quarks'; Producer CBC TV ('24 Hours') 1975–77, Head Radio Variety 1977–81, Exec. Asst. to Asst. MD Eng. Networks 1982–83, Dir. CBC London 1984–86; recipient Commonwealth Relations Bursary 1972; Jury Chairwoman Prix Italia 1973, Premios Ondas Jury 1984; Pres., Music in the Morning Concert Soc. 1994– ; Bd. Mem., Michener Foundation 1989–93, Ottawa Ballet 1983–93, Writers' Development Trust 1992– , Ballet BC 1993– , Music in the Morning Concert Soc. 1993–94; Mem., Adv. Counc., North Am. Nat. Broadcasters' Assoc. 1988–93; Performing Arts Lodges of Canada 1992– ; Ctte. Mem., Ottawa Writers' Development Trust, Ottawa 1986–92; producer and writer numerous radio documentaries during 1970's incl. 'Tribute to Mahalia Jackson' 1972, 'David Livingston' 1973; organizer, Canada/Japan Television Extves. Conference (Toronto) 1987; mem. Internat. Inst. Communications; Royal Television Soc.; Candn. Inst. Internat. Affairs; Vancouver Institute; recreations: music, theatre, walking, reading; Clubs: Georgian; National Press; Home: Chancery Place Apartments, 301 - 847 Hornby St., Vancouver, B.C. V6Z 1T9.

**FILIATRAULT, Claude (Henri),** B.A., LL.L.; attorney; b. Val d'Or, Qué. 23 Oct 1942; s. Gaston and Laurence (Laurin) F.; e. Univ. of Ottawa B.A. 1964; Laval Univ. LL.L. 1968; m. Frances d. Gérard and Thérèse Higgins 29 Dec. 1982; VICE PRESIDENT, LEGAL AFFAIRS & CONTRACTS, SPAR AEROSPACE LIMITED, SPACE SYSTEMS DIV. 1992; Legal Counsel, Domtar Inc. 1969–73; Canadian Marconi Co. 1973–90: Legal Counsel 1973, Legal Counsel and Asst. Sec. 1976, Gen. Counsel and Sec. 1977–78, Vice Pres., Gen. Counsel and Secy. 1979–90; Consultant, International Contracts & Business Law 1990; Sr. Legal Counsel, BCE Telecom International Inc. 1991; Lectr. in Law, Univ. of Qué. 1971 and Concordia Univ. summer 1973 and 1973–74; mem. Montréal, Québec, Candn. and Internat. Bar Assns.; Club: St-Denis; Office: 20125 Trans-Canada Highway, Montréal, Qué. H9X 3R2.

**FILION, Gerard,** C.C.(1970), B.A., M.Com., F.R.S.C.; b. Isle Verte, Que. 18 Aug. 1909; s. Alfred and Philomène (Simard) F.; e. Laval Univ., B.A. 1931; Montreal Univ., M.Com. 1934; m. Françoise, d. Eugène Servêtre; 25 Jan. 1937; children: Nicole, Monique, Pierre, Jean, Marcel, Marc-André, Louise, Michel, Claudine; Pres., Conseil de Presse du Qué. 1983–87; Canadian Manufacturers Assn. 1971–72; Vice-Pres., Can. Council 1962–64; formerly Publisher of 'Le Devoir' (daily newspaper, estbd. 1910); rec'd. Nat. Newspaper Award for Edit. writing, 1951, 1959, 1961; Mayor, St. Bruno, Que. 1960–68; mem., Royal Comn. of Inquiry on Educ., Qué. 1961–66; named to Candn. News Hall of Fame by Toronto Men's Press Club 1966; Companion of the Order of Canada; Grand Officer of the National Order of Qué.; Doctor Honoris Causa, Univ. de Montréal; former Pres., Marine Industries Ltd.; Roman Catholic; recreations: hunting, fishing; Address: 1845, St-Laurent, St. Bruno de Montarville, Que. J3V 4Z2.

**FILLEUL, Francis Miles,** B.A.; foreign service officer; b. Tangier, Morocco 3 April 1938; s. Francis Edward and Mabel Mary Louise (Jenkins) F.; e. University School Victoria, B.A. 1953; Univ. of B.C. B.A. 1957; Oxford Univ. B.A. 1959; Univ. de Paris Sorbonne dipl. 1960; m. Elizabet d. Mario and Marjorie Rodriguez 30 Dec. 1963; children: Francisca, Sienna; AMBASSADOR TO HAITI 1993– ; joined Dept. of Northern Affairs & Nat. Resources 1960; Foreign Serv. Offr., Dept. of External Affairs 1962; Advr. to Candn. Del. to U.N. 1963; assignments to Candn. Embassy Ankara 1964–66; Candn. Embassy Dakar 1966–69; Ecole nat. d'Admin., Paris 1969; Candn. Embassy Rio de Janeiro (moved to Brasilia 1972) 1972–74; Consulate General N.Y. 1977–81; Dir. of Press Office & Official Spokesman, External Affairs Ottawa 1981–92; Ambassador to Costa Rica, Nicaragua, El Salvador, Panama 1982–86; Sr. Advr. for Fed.-Prov. Relns., External Affairs 1986–89; Ambassador to Ethiopia, the Sudan & Djibouti, External Affairs and International Trade Canada 1989–92; Dir. General of Personnel Admin., External Affairs, Ottawa 1992–93; Anglican; recreations: tennis, sailing; clubs: Rockcliffe Lawn Tennis; Home: 23 Braemar St., Ottawa, Ont. K1K 3C4; Office: 125 Sussex Dr., Ottawa, Ont. K1A 0H7.

**FILLION, Normand,** B.A., M.B.A.; marketing executive; b. Arvida, Que. 8 July 1950; s. Paul F.; e. York Univ. B.A. (Hons.) 1973; Univ. of Western Ont. M.B.A. 1977; m. Maria d. Joseph Chow; children: Genevieve, Louis Alexandre, Marie-Lyne; VICE-PRESIDENT, MARKETING, PORT OF MONTREAL 1991– ; Bank of Montreal (Toronto) 1973–75; Federal Business Development Bank (Montreal) 1977–84; Manager, Econ. Research & Analysis, Port of Montreal 1984–91; Mem., Chamber of Commerce; Pres., Port of Montreal Ctte. on competitiveness and Performance of the Port System; Office: Wing #1, Cité du Havre, Montreal, Que. H3C 3R5.

**FILLMORE, Peter Arthur,** B.Sc., M.A., Ph.D., F.R.S.C.; educator; b. Moncton, N.B. 28 Oct. 1936; s. Henry Arthur and Jeanne Margaret (Archibald) F.; e. Dalhousie Univ. Dipl. Engn., B.Sc. 1957; Univ. of Minn. M.A. 1960, Ph.D. 1962; m. Anne Ellen d. James W. Garvock, Berwick, N.S. 6 Aug. 1960; children: Jennifer Anne, Julia Margaret, Peter Alexander (Andy); PROF. OF MATH., DEPT. MATH., STATS. AND COMP. SCI., DALHOUSIE UNIV. 1976– , Chrmn. 1987–91; Instr. Univ. of Chicago 1962–64; Asst. Prof. to Prof. Ind. Univ. 1964–72; Killam Sr. Fellow, Dalhousie Univ. 1972–73, Killam Research Prof. 1973–78; Visiting Assoc. Prof. Univ. of Toronto 1970–71; Sr. Visiting Fellow, Univ. of Edinburgh 1977; Visiting Mem., Mathematical Sciences Rsch. Inst. (Berkeley) 1984–85; Visiting Prof., Univ. of Copenhagen 1990; Univ. Reserve Training Plan (RCAF) 1953–57; author 'Notes on Operator Theory' 1970; Ed. 'Proceedings of a Conference on Operator Theory' 1973; author various research articles functional analysis and operator theory; mem. ed. bds. several prof. journs.; mem. Candn. Math. Soc. (Vice Pres. 1973–75, Council 1975–79, Pres. 1994–96); Am. Math.Soc. (Council 1982–84); Home: 1348 Robie St., Halifax, N.S. B3H 3E2; Office: Halifax, N.S. B3H 3J5.

**FILMON, Gary Albert,** B.Sc.(C.E.), M.Sc., P.Eng.; politician; b. Winnipeg, Man. 24 Aug. 1942; s. Albert and Anastasia (Doskocz) F.; e. Sisler H.S. gr. 12 1960; Univ. of Man. B.Sc.(C.E.) 1964, M.Sc. 1967; m. Janice d. Harold and Marjorie Wainwright 1963; children: Allison, David, Gregg, Susanna; PREMIER OF MANITOBA, PRES. OF THE EXECUTIVE COUNCIL, MIN. OF FEDERAL-PROVINCIAL RELATIONS 1988– ; M.L.A. for Tuxedo Constituency 1981– ; Design Engr. and Area Mgr. Underwood McLellan and Assoc. 1964–69; Vice-Pres. and Pres. Success Bus. Coll. Winnipeg 1969–80; Winnipeg City Counc. 1975–79; M.L.A. River Heights Constituency 1979–81; Min. Consumer and Corp. Affairs and Environ. 1981; Min. of Housing; Leader of the Opposition, Manitoba Govt. 1983–88; Pres. Univ. of Man. Alumni Assn. 1974–75; Pres. Assn. of Candn. Career Colls. 1974–75; recipient, Award of Merit, B'Nai Brith Canada 1991; Meritorious Award for Community Services, Candn. Counc. of Profl. Engrs. 1992; Home: 36 Jaymorr Dr., Winnipeg, Man. R3R 1Y1; Office: Rm. 204, Legislative Bldg., Winnipeg, Man. R3C 0V8.

**FINCH, Robert Duer Claydon,** B.A., L.L.D., D.Litt., F.R.S.C.; professor emeritus; b. Freeport, Long Island, N.Y. 14 May 1900; s. Edward F.; e. Univ. of Toronto B.A. 1925; Univ. of Paris 1928; formerly Prof. of French, Univ. Coll., Univ. of Toronto; awarded Jardine Mem. Prize, 1924, for best Eng. verse; accepted by French Consul-Gen. for Bourse d'Etudes 1925; awarded Que. Bonne Entente Prize 1925; Hon. Pres., Univ. Coll. Players' Guild 1928; Hon. Pres., Univ. Coll. French Club 1939–40; author of 'Poems' (Gov. Gen.'s Awd. 1946); 'The Strength of the Hills' (poems) 1948; 'Dover Beach Revisited and Other Poems' 1961; 'Acis in Oxford' (Gov. Gen.'s Awd. 1961); 'Silverthorn Bush and Other Poems' 1966; 'The Sixth Sense: A Study of Individualism in French Poetry (1686–1760)' 1966; 'French Individualist Poetry' 1971; Saint-Evremond's 'Sir Politick Would-be' 1978; Saint-Evremond's 'Les Opéra' (Droz-Paris-Geneva) 1979; 'Variations & Theme' 1980; 'Has and Is' 1981; 'Twelve For Christmas' 1982; 'The Grand Duke of Moscow's Favourite Solo' 1983; 'Double Tuning' 1984; 'For the Back of a Likeness' 1986; 'Sailboat and Lake' 1988; 'Miracle at the Jetty' 1991; rec'd. Lorne Pierce Gold Medal Award 1968; held 13th public one-man show of pictures; represented in National Gallery, Ottawa, provincial museums of art and private collections in 5 countries; Address: 516 – 55 Belmont St., Toronto, Ont. M5R 1R1.

**FINCHAM, Kenneth C.,** B.Com., F.C.A., C.St.J.; association executive; b. Montréal 1928; e. McGill Univ. B.Com. 1950; C.A. Qué. 1953; rec'd Lt. Gov.'s Silver Medal; m. Alicia Baker; PRESIDENT EMERITUS, CANDN. INST. OF CHARTERED ACCOUNTANTS 1993– ; articled Coopers & Lybrand (formerly McDonald, Currie & Co.), Montréal; Asst. Comptroller, Canadian National Railways 1956–63; Partner, Deloitte & Touche (formerly Touche Ross & Co.) and P.S. Ross & Partners, Ottawa 1963–69; Dir. Gen. Audit Services Bureau, Dept. Supply & Services, Ottawa 1969–73; Pres., Candn. Inst. of Chartered Accountants 1973–92; mem. Ordre C.A. Qué.; Inst. C.A.'s Ont.; Inst. C.A.'s Y.T.; Inst. C.A.'s Bermuda; Past Hon. Treas., St. John Ambulance Can.; Past Treas. Nat. Council Boy Scouts Can.; Home: 1 River Oaks Court, Stittsville, Ont. K2S 1L3.

**FINDLAY, Craig Fraser,** B.A.; food industry executive; b. Toronto, Ont. 15 May 1953; s. Eric Fraser and the late Margaret E. (Shepherd) F.; e. Univ. of Western Ont. B.A. 1975; m. Deborah J. d. J. Trevor Eyton 20 June 1980; children: Katharine, Trevor, John, Hayley; Pres., Baskin-Robbins; Dir., Silcorp Limited; Silcorp Employee Holdings Limited; Execsil Limited; Frafin Corp.; Dir. & Pres., Silcorp Internat. Ltd.; Aylmer Street Ice Cream Co.; Trustee, Ontario Science Ctr.; Adv. Bd., Trent Univ.; Mem., Candn. Franchise Assn.; Internat. Franchise Assn.; Retail Counc. of Can., Candn. Restaurant & Foodservice Assn.; Nat. Dairy Counc. of Can.; recreations: tennis, skiing, swimming; club: Royal Candn. Yacht; Caledon Ski; Home: 11 Ridge Dr., Toronto, Ont. M4T 1B6.

**FINDLAY, Earl Charles;** B.Sc., M.Sc., Ph.D.; retired company executive; b. Toronto, Ont., 30 Dec. 1915; s. Charles H. and Ethel L. (Van Attan) F.; e. Public and High Schs., Toronto, Ont.; Sir Geo. Williams Univ.; Univ. of Toronto; Cal. Inst. Tech.; McGill Univ. and Univ. of Montreal (Extension); I.C.S.; Brit. Inst. Tech.; m. Norma W., d. William S. Lorenson, June 1939; three d. Willene, (Mrs. Albert James Benson), Sandra, (Mrs. Eugene Bernards), Trudi, (Mrs. Bruce Aston); Dir. of several Am. co's.; with Link Belt Co. Ltd. at Toronto, Montreal, Elmira, N.Y. and Chicago, Ill., 1937–46; Asst. Sales Mgr., United Steel Corp., Montreal, Que., 1946–52; Gen. Sales Mgr., Consol., Engineering & Machinery Co. Ltd., Montreal, 1953–62; joined Zurn Industries Canada Ltd. as Vice Pres. and Tech. Dir., 1962; Vice Pres. and Mang. Dir., 1963; joined Zurn Ind. Inc. U.S.A. as Vice-Pres., 1964; Vice Pres.-Regional Mgr., Mechanical Drives Div., Zurn Industries Inc. 1963–80; mem., Soc. for Advanc. of Management Engrs.; Soc. of Auto. Engrs.; Am. Soc. Tool & Mfg. Engrs.; Inst. of Power Engrs.; Candn. Inst. Mining & Metallurgy; Am. Soc. Mech. Engrs.; United Methodist; recreations: music, boating, photography, languages, foreign cruise travel; Clubs: Masonic; Shriners; Home: North Shore Drive, Isle La Motte, VT 05463.

**FINDLAY, Eric Fraser,** B.Com.; executive; b. Toronto, Ont. 16 July 1926; s. Hugh Fraser and Etta (MacPherson) F.; e. Univ. of Toronto B.Com. 1948; m. Ruth Bastedo 19 Oct. 1978; children by first marriage: Judy, Craig, Scott; CHRMN. & C.E.O., SILCORP LTD. 1982– ; Dir. Canada Trust; T.I. Industries Ltd.; Innopac Inc.; John Labatt Ltd.; I.A.I.C.M.-Washington; Dir., The John Robarts Research Institute; Past Pres. National Dairy Counc.; Vice Pres. Findlay Dairy Ltd. 1948–65; Pres. Findlay Kemp Dairies Ltd. 1965; joined present Co. 1966, E. Region Gen. Mgr. 1967, Extve. Vice Pres. 1969, Chrmn., Pres. and C.E.O. 1971; Clubs: London Hunt & Country; Granite; London; Address: 10 Commander Blvd., Scarborough, Ont. M1S 3T2.

**FINDLAY, The Hon. Glen Marshall,** M.L.A., B.S.A., M.Sc., Ph.D.; agrologist, politician; b. Shoal Lake, Man. 15 July 1940; s. Marshall Fredrick and Verna Bernice (Cochrane) F.; e. Univ. of Man. B.S.A. (Hon.) 1963; Univ. of Man. M.Sc. 1964; Univ. of Illinois Ph.D. 1968; m. Katherine d. Donald and Esther Kennedy 7 Oct. 1957; children: Carole, Keith, Gary, Jill; MINISTER RESP. FOR THE MANITOBA TELEPHONE SYSTEM, PROV. OF MANITOBA 1988– ; and MIN. OF HIGHWAYS AND TRANSPORTATION 1993– ; Pres., Edgehill Farms Ltd. 1977– ; Nat. Rsch. Counc. 1968–70; Assoc. Prof. of Entomol., Univ. of Man. 1970–77; M.L.A. for Virden Constituency 1986–90; for Springfield 1990– ; Dir., Labatt's (Man.) 1984–88; Grains Standards Ctte. 1984–88 (KAP 1984); Min. of Agriculture, Prov. of Manitoba 1988–93; Cons., Man. Herbicide Complaint Ctte.; Dir., Local Ctte., Man. Pool 1978–80; Pres., Shoal Lake Agric. Soc. 1983–84; Vice-Chrmn. then Chrmn., Natural Prod. Mktg. Counc. 1980–83; Lt. Gov. Gold Medal 1963; Nat. Acad. of Sci. Fellowship 1964; NRC post-doct. fellowship 1968; Un. Ch. of Can.; recreations: hockey, curling, family activities, sports coach for many years (ringette, soccer, baseball, hockey); Home: Box 429, Shoal Lake, Man. R0J 1Z0; Office: Room 203, Legislative Bldg., Winnipeg, Man. R3C 0V8.

**FINDLAY, Scott Fraser,** B.A.; convenience store executive; b. Toronto, Ont. 17 May 1956; s. Eric Fraser and Margaret Ethel (Shepherd) Gilfillan F.; e. Univ. of West. Ont., B.A. (Hons.) 1979; m. Sandra Lynn d. James and Mary Cameron 8 Sept. 1979; children: Brittany Anne, Cameron Fraser; VICE-PRES., MKTG. & DISTRIBUTION, SILCORP LTD. 1992– ; Sales/Budget Coord., Union Gas Ltd. 1979–81; Mktg. Prod. Mgr., Silverwood Dairies 1981–83; Dir., New Prod. & Serv., Mac's Convenience Stores 1983–86; Dir. of Merch., Convenience Serv. Ltd. 1986–87; Vice-Pres., Mktg. 1987–89; Pres., Convenience Services Limited (Mike's Mart; Northmar Distrib.) 1989–91; Vice-Pres., Ont. Div., Silcorp Ltd. 1991–92; Dir., Silcorp Employee Holdings Limited; Execsil Corp.; Home: 199 Fenn Ave., Toronto, Ont. M2P 1Y1; Office: 10 Commander Blvd., Scarborough, Ont. M1S 3T2.

**FINDLEY, Timothy;** writer; b. Toronto, Ont. 30 Oct. 1930; s. Allan Gilmour and Margaret M. (Bull) F.; e. Rosedale Pub. Sch. Toronto; St. Andrew's Coll. Aurora, Ont.; Jarvis Coll. Inst. Toronto; actor and charter mem. Stratford Shakespearean Festival, Stratford, Ont. 1953; extensive appearances in Can., UK and USA in theatre and television; Playwright-In-Residence, National Arts' Centre (1974–75); recipient Gov. Gen.'s Award 1977, ACTRA Award, Armstrong Award, Anik Award, Toronto Book Award (1977); Can. Council Award 1968; Sr. Arts 1978, 1983; Ont. Arts Council Award 1977–78; Periodical Distributor's Award (1978, 1983, 1984 and 1987); Candn. Booksellers' Award 1984; Candn. Authors Assn. Award 1985, 1991; CNIB Talking Book of the Year Award 1986; Western Magazine Award 1988; Trillium Award 1989; Mystery Writers of Am. Award ('Edgar') 1989; National Radio Award 1989, 1990; Writer-In-Residence, University of Toronto (1979–80); D.Litt. (Hon.) Trent University 1982; Univ. of Guelph 1984; York Univ. 1989; Writer-in-Residence, Trent Univ. 1984; Univ. of Winnipeg 1985; Officer, Order of Canada 1986; Order of Ont. 1991; author 'The Last of the Crazy People' 1967; 'Butterfly Plague' 1969; 'The Wars' 1977 (publ. in 9 langs.; screenplay 1981–82); 'Famous Last Words' 1981 (publ. in 5 langs.); 'Not Wanted on the Voyage' 1984 (publ. in 5 langs.); 'The Telling of Lies' 1986 (publ. in 5 langs.); 'Headhunter' 1993; 'Can You See Me Yet?' (play) 1977, performed Nat. Arts Center 1976; 'John A. Himself' (play) Theatre London 1979; 'The Stillborn Lover' (play) Grand Theatre, London and National Arts Centre 1993; co-writer (with William Whitehead) 'The National Dream' CBC TV (Actra Award 1975); 'Dieppe 1942' (Anik Award 1979); writer 'Newcomers, 1911'; 'Newcomers, 1832' (Nielsen/Ferns) (1977–78); short fiction 'New Canadian Stories, '74'; 'New Canadian Stories, '75'; 'Dinner Along the Amazon' (collection) 1984; 'Stones' (collection) 1988; Esquire, Cavalier, CBC Anthology, various lit. mags.; novellas include 'Hello Cheeverland, Goodbye' 1974; 'Harper's Bazaar' 1980; non-fiction 'Inside Memory: Pages from a Writer's Workbook' 1990; films incl. 5 film portraits (William Hutt, Kate Reid, Margaret Avison, Raymond Souster, Ulysses Comtois); 'The Paper People' 1968; 'Other People's Children' 1980; 'The Wars' 1983; interviewed in 'Eleven Canadian Novelists' 1973, 'Conversations with Canadian Novelists' 1973; subject of complete issue of 'Canadian Literature' Winter 1981; mem. Assn. Candn. TV & Radio Artists; Writers' Union Can. (Chrmn. 1977–78); PEN International (Pres. Candn. Eng./Speaking Ctr. 1986–87); recreations: gardening, music; Address: Box 419, Cannington, Ont. L0E 1E0.

**FINE, David;** film maker; b. Toronto, Ont. 13 Sept. 1960; s. Irving and Shirley (Chusid) F.; e. Nat. Film & TV Sch. (U.K.); m. Alison Snowden June 1984; Prod./Dir./Ed., 'One Man's Meat' 1976 (Gold Plaque, Chicago Internat. Film Fest.), 'The Only Game in Town' 1979 (Can. Counc. Short Film Showcase Award; 1983 Genie Award nom.), 'Viola' 1980 (Am. Film Fest. finalist; grand prize, Jacksonville Film Fest.); Dir., 'The Day After the End of the World,' 'The Man From Alde-beron' (half-hour live action dramas); co-author/co-animator, 'Second Class Mail' (Oscar nom. 1986); employed by Nat. Film Bd. of Can.; co-author/dir./anim., 'George and Rosemary' (Genie award for best short; Oscar nom. 1988; 1st prize, Zagreb Anim. Fest.); Co-author/dir., 'A Test of Time'; works primarily with partner, Alison Snowden.

**FINEBERG, Larry,** B.A.; playwright; b. Montréal, Qué. 22 Apr. 1948; s. Arnold Abraham and Ruth (Meyer) F.; e. Emerson Coll. Boston B.A. 1967; author (plays) 'Stonehenge' 1972; 'Hope' 1973; 'All the Ghosts' 1974; 'Death' 1974; 'Human Remains' 1975; 'Eve' 1976 (Chalmers Award Best Play); 'Medea' 1978 (Dom. Drama Festival Best Play 1978); 'Life on Mars' 1977; 'Montréal' 1981; 'Devotion' 1985; Playwrighting Instr. Humber Coll. 1985–86; Resident Playwright Stratford Festival 1976, 1978; Colonnades Theatre Lab. New York 1980–81; author 'Anthology' (4 plays) 1978; 'DrAmaturge' Buddies in Bad Times Theatre 1985–86; numerous radio and TV plays CBC and BBC; in preparation 'Other People's Lovers'; plays produced maj. Toronto theatres, Stratford and many regional theatres, Can., USA and UK; recipient numerous Can. Council & Ont. Arts Council Grants; Founding Chrmn. Playwrights Union Can. 1983–84; Founding mem. Guild Candn. Playwrights 1977; Chrmn. Playwrights Can. 1977–78; Office: c/o Playwrights Union, 2nd Flr., 54 Wolseley, Toronto, Ont. M5T 1A5.

**FINES, Eric G.,** B.A.Sc.; professional engineer, association executive; b. Bradford, Ont. 30 Nov. 1941; s. Lorne E. and Ona M. (Pinder) F.; e. Univ. of Toronto B.A.Sc. 1964; m. Loretta d. Joseph and Marie Soos 17 July 1965; children: Carie, Gregory; PRES., CANADIAN PORTLAND CEMENT ASSN. 1985– ; various positions involving the market development of cement and the design of transportation structures, Delcan 1965–71; Ont. Min. of Transp. & Communications 1971–73; joined Candn. Portland Cement Assn. 1973; also, currently Vice-Pres., Candn. Opns., Portland Cement Assn.; Chrmn. & Dir., Consulting Bd., Network of Centres of Excellence, High Performance Concrete; Past Chrmn., Masonry Counc. of Can.; Roads and Transp. Assn. of Can. (Bridge Deck Deterioration Ctte.); Mem., Assn. of Profl. Engrs. of Ont.; Candn. Soc. of Civil Engrs.; Am. Concrete Inst.; Candn. Prestressed Concrete Inst.; Candn. Standards Assn.; author: 'The Cement Industry's Contribution to Canada's Green Plan'; editor: 'Resource Recovery, The Cement Kiln Solution,' 'Concrete Bridge Decks, Guide to Construction, Maintenance and Repair; recreations: skiing, tennis, golf, bicycling; club: Bayview Golf & Country; Home: 74 Goldberry Sq., West Hill, Ont. M1C 3H7; Office: 1500 Don Mills Rd., Ste. 703, Toronto, Ont. M3B 3K4.

**FINESTONE, Bernard Julius,** B.A., B.Comm., F.I.I.C.; chartered insurance broker; b. Sacramento, Cal. 24 July 1920; s. Ab and Rosalie Naomi (Adalman) F.; e. West Hill and Strathcona High Schs. 1937; McGill Univ. B.Comm. 1941; Chart. Ins. Inst. London, Eng. 1951; Ins. Inst. Can. Assoc. 1955, Fellow 1967; Sir George Williams Univ. B.A. 1962; m. Rita d. Myer and Beatrice Shuchat 17 Oct. 1950; three s. Brian (dec.), Paul J., Neil R.; PRES., FINESTONE & SON LTD. 1956– ; Ins. Broker since 1947; served with 9th Armoured Regt. (BCD) 1941–45, wounded in Italy, rank Capt.; Lectr. in Ins. McGill Univ. Centre Cont. Edn. 1961–93; recipient Chancellor Gold Medal Econ. McGill Univ. 1941; Queen's Silver Jubilee Medal 1977; Rep. of the Life Mems., Counc., Royal Candn. Armoured Corps Assoc. (Cavalry); Hon. Lt.-Col., The British Columbia Dragoons; Past Pres., Sir Arthur Currie (Que. #1) Br., The Royal Cdn. Legion; Pres., Montreal Port Council 1972; Pres., Montreal Bd. Trade 1976, Chrmn. 1977–79; Pres., Jewish Gen. Hosp. 1979–82, currently Hon. Pres.; Chrmn., Qué. Candn. Jewish Cong. 1983–86, Nat. Vice Pres. 1986–89; Vice Chrmn., Montreal Port Corp. 1985–93; Chrmn. Candn. Unity Liaison Ctte. 1977–81; P. Cons. Cand. for St. Henri – Westmount Fed. g.e. 1978, 1979, Pres. Riding Assn. 1980–84; Vice-Pres. Cong. Shaar Hashomayim 1972–75; Pres., Jewish Vocational Services 1965–68; mem. Candn. Power Sqdn.; Mensa; recreations: skiing, yachting, golf; Clubs: Elm Ridge, Montefiore, Montreal J.B. Ski, Mt. Tremblant, Monterey Country (Palm Desert, Cal.); Home: 304, 3495 Ave. du Musée, Montréal, Qué. H3G 2C8; Office: 800, 1310 Greene Ave., Westmount, Qué. H3Z 2B2.

**FINESTONE, Sheila,** M.P., B.Sc.; politician; b. Montreal, Que. 28 Jan. 1927; d. Monroe and Minnie Cummings Abbey; e. McGill Univ.; Drake Univ., Des Moines, Iowa; m. Alan F. 9 June 1947; children: David, Peter, Maxwell, Stephen; SECRETARY OF STATE (Multiculturalism and the Status of Women) 1993– ; Dir. of Youth Protection, Social Service Ctr.; Mem., Nat. Counc. of Women; Nat. Counc. of Jewish Women; Orgn. for Rehab. and Training; Trustee, Jewish General Hosp. of Hope; Candn. Jewish Congress; Y.M./Y.W.H.A.; MATCH Internat.; el. to H. of C. for Mount Royal g.e. 1984; re-el. g.e. 1988, 1993; Critic for Communications and Culture 1985–93; Chair, Liberal Caucus Social Policy Ctte.; mem., Inter-Parlty. Union; Canada-Israel Friendship Group; Liberal; Jewish; Home:

4840 Roslyn Ave., Montreal, Que. H3W 2L2; Office: House of Commons, Ottawa, Ont. K1A 0A6.

**FINKBEINER, James Clark,** B.A., C.A.; financial executive; b. Hamiota, Manitoba 13 Sept. 1947; s. Syd James and Genevieve Louise F.; e. Simon Fraser Univ. B.A. (econ. & comm.) 1970, C.A. B.C. 1974; m. Ruby d. Bill and Noelle Katerenchuk 9 Oct. 1970; children: Jamie, Matthew, Paul; VICE-PRESIDENT, TAX PROPERTIES & RISK MANAGEMENT, MACMILLAN BLOEDEL 1983– ; articled with Price Waterhouse C.A. Jan. 1974; joined MacMillan Bloedel 1977; Mem., Tax Extve. Inst. (Past Pres.); Candn. Pulp & Paper Assn.; Dir., Trus Joist Macmillan; Marine Way Estates; North Shore Youth Ctr.; Past Gov., Candn. Tax Found.; recreations: golf, racquet sports; clubs: Capilano Golf & Country, Terminal City; Home: 2474 Berton Place, North Way, Vancouver, B.C. V7H 2W8; Office: 925 West Georgia St., Vancouver, B.C. V6C 3L2.

**FINKEL, Alvin,** B.A., M.A., Ph.D.; university professor; b. Winnipeg, Man. 17 May 1949; s. Leslie Simon and Rose (Piscun) F.; e. St. John's Tech. H.S. 1966; Univ. of Manitoba B.A. 1970, M.A. 1972; Univ. of Toronto Ph.D. 1976; m. Carol d. Ron and Winnifred Taylor 17 March 1984; children: Antony Delmore and Kieran Martin; PROFESSOR OF HISTORY, ATHABASCA UNIV. 1986– ; Lecturer, Univ. of Manitoba; Univ. of Brandon 1974; Visiting Lecturer, Queen's Univ. 1975–76; Lecturer, Dept. of History, Univ. of Alberta 1976–78; Asst. then Assoc. Prof., Dept. of History, Athabasca Univ. 1978–86; Founding Mem., History Program, Athabasca Univ.; Editor 'Prairie Forum'; Pubns. Bd. Mem., Canadian Plains Research Center; Mem., Candn. Historical Assn.; Activist, N.D.P.; author: 'Business and Social Reform in the Thirties' 1979, 'The Social Credit Phenomenon in Alberta' 1989; co-author: 'History of the Canadian Peoples' (Volumes 1 and 2) 1993; recreations: hiking, nordic skiing; Home: 15206 – 77 Avenue, Edmonton, Alta. T5R 3B6; Office: Box 10,000, Athabasca, Alta. T0G 2R0.

**FINKEL, Henry,** F.A.C.I.D., R.C.A., F.R.S.A.; industrial designer; b. London, Eng. 7 Nov. 1910; e. McGill Univ. Sch. of Arch.; m. Prof. Rose Goldblatt 28 Aug. 1937; estbd. HENRY FINKEL INDUSTRIAL DESIGN 1947; Pres., Thomfin Enterprises (1993) Inc.; consultant to many Candn. mfrs. most materials and processes incl. application plastic materials; successful products incl. first Candn.-made hand held calculator; lectr. in indust. design and related subjects McGill Univ., Univ. de Montréal, Univ. of Man., Concordia Univ.; TV and radio interviews; given papers internat. confs. on design; author various articles successful product designs, indust. design; rec'd Candn. Centennial Medal 1967; mem. Soc. Plastics Engrs. (past mem. Internat. Counc.); Assn. Candn. Industr. Designers (twice Pres.); Royal Canadian Acad. of Arts (mem. Counc.); Arts Westmount (Past Pres.); recreations: photography, music, drama, travel; Home: 342 Elm Ave., Westmount, Que. H3Z 1Z5; Office: P.O. Box 505, Westmount, Que. H3Z 2T6.

**FINKELMAN, Jacob,** O.C. (1976), Q.C., LL.D.; b. Poltava, Russia, 17 Jan. 1907; s. Rachmiel and Minnie (Seltser) F.; came to Can. 1907; e. Hamilton, Ont.; Univ. of Toronto, B.A. 1926; Osgoode Hall, Toronto, 1927–30; Univ. of Toronto, M.A. 1932, LL.B. 1933; York Univ. LL.D. (hon. causa) 1977; m. Dora, d. David Riskin, Edmonton, Alta., 30 June 1946; 3 sons: Michael, Barry Gordon, Steven Robert; Chrmn., Public Service Staff Relations Bd. 1967–76; read law with J. A. Sweet, K.C., Hamilton; called to Bar of Ont. 1930; cr. K.C. 1946; Lect., Sch. of Law, Univ. of Toronto, 1930–34; Asst. Prof. 1934–39; Assoc. Prof. 1939–44; Prof., 1944–54; Special Lect., Inst. Business Adm., Univ. of Toronto, 1954–67; Sessional Lect., Carleton Univ. School of Public Admin., 1977–79; McGill Univ. Faculty of Law 1977–79; Lect., Univ. of Ottawa Fac. of Law 1982; Editor, Univ. of Toronto Law Journal, 1949–53; Registrar, Labour Court of Ont., 1943–44; Advisor to Select Comte. of Leg. on Collective Bargaining 1943; Chrmn., Ont. Labour Relations Bd., 1944–47 and 1953–67; Public Service Staff Relations Bd. 1967–76; Nat. Acad. of Arbitrators; Assn.of Labour Relations Agencies; Society of Professionals in Dispute Resolution (Pres. 1976–7); author (with W.P.M. Kennedy) 'The Right to Trade' 1933; 'Report on Employer-Employee Relations in the Public Service of Canada: Proposals for Legislative Change' 1974; (with Shirley B. Goldenberg) 'Collective Bargaining in the Public Service: The Federal Experience in Canada' 1983; recipient, Human Rights Award, Candn. Conf. of Christians and Jews 1960; Annual Award, Candn. Industrial Relations Assoc. 1986; Hebrew; Home: 400 Laurier Ave. E., Apt. 9A, Ottawa, Ont. K1N 8Y2.

**FINKELSTEIN, Neil,** B.A., C.A., LL.B., LL.M.; lawyer; b. Montreal, Que. 5 Sept. 1951; s. E. Lawrence and Helene Joy (Crelinsten) F.; e. McGill Univ. B.A. 1973, LL.B. 1979; C.A. 1975; Harvard Law Sch. LL.M. 1980; m. Marie Alison d. Eric and Tilya Helfield 20 Aug. 1978; children: Jonathan, Emily, Sara; PARTNER, BLAKE, CASSELS & GRAYDON 1987; el. Bencher, Law Soc. of Upper Can. 1991; joined Touche, Ross & Co. Montreal 1973–76; Law Clk. Chief Justice Can. (Bora-Laskin) Ottawa 1980–81; joined present firm 1982, Sr. Policy Adv. Atty. Gen. Ont. (Ian G. Scott) (leave of absence) 1985–86; Lectr. in Constitutional Law, Univ. of Toronto 1987–90, Osgoode Hall Law Sch. 1981–83, 1988–89; Lectr. in Taxation McGill Univ. 1975–79; frequent speaker profl. assns. and groups; recipient Lazarus Phillips Prize 1979; Philip Meyerovitch, Q.C. Prize 1979; 'IME' Prize Comm. Law 1979; Chief Justice Greenshields Prize in Criminal Law 1979; Faculty Prize in Taxation 1978; Alexander Scholarship 1978; Thomas Shearer Stewart Travelling Fellowship 1979; McGill Univ. Scholarship 1977–79; author 'Laskin's Canadian Constitutional Law' 5th ed. 1986, 2 vols.; co-ed. 'New Developments in Administrative Law' 1987; 'The Canadian Charter of Rights and Freedoms: The Civil Side' 1988; co-author 'Constitutional Rights and Investigative Powers' forthcoming; numerous articles in professional journals and periodicals, Royal Comn. studies and other legal publs.; mem. Law Soc. Upper Can.; Candn. Bar Assn.; Inst. C.A.'s Ont.; Order C.A.'s Que.; Candn. Inst. C.A.'s; recreations: tennis, squash, running; Home: 12 Glenarden Rd., Toronto, Ont. M6C 3J9; Office: P.O. Box 25 Commerce Court West, Toronto, Ont. M5L 1A9.

**FINLAY, David C.,** B.A., C.A.; chartered accountant; b. Halifax, N.S. 22 Mar. 1940; s. Patrick C. and Margaret F.; e. Univ. of West. Ont. B.A. 1964; Inst. of C.A.'s of Ont. C.A. 1968; m. Marion MacDonald; children: John David, Matthew Thomas; EXECUTIVE PARTNER & REGIONAL MANAGING PARTNER, ERNST & YOUNG, Calgary; Partner, present firm 1975; Vice Chrmn., Calgary Philharmonic Soc.; Mngt. Adv. Counc., Univ. of Calgary; clubs: Willow Park Golf, Calgary Petroleum; Home: 15499 McKenzie Lake Way S.E., Calgary, Alta. T2Z 2J2; Office: 1300, 707 – 7th Ave. S.W., Calgary, Alta. T2P 3H6.

**FINLAY, Gordon T.,** F.C.G.A.; business executive; b. Honeywood, Ont. 6 Nov. 1934; s. William John and Martha Marie F.; e. C.G.A. 1958–63; FCGA Fellowship 1971; m. Elizabeth C. Wilson; PRESIDENT, A.C. NIELSEN COMPANY OF CANADA LTD. 1985– ; Area Dir., A.C. Nielsen Pacific, Latin America and Canada; Chief Acct., Southam-Maclean Publications 1954–62; Treasurer, present firm 1962, Vice-Pres. 1969, Dir. 1972, Gen. Mgr. Promotion Services Group 1977, Extve. Vice-Pres. 1980, Gen. Mgr. Mktg. Rsch. Group 1984; Past Pres., Cert. Gen. Accts. Toronto Chapter; Life Mem., CGA of Ont. (Past Pres.); Gen. Accts. Assn. of Canada (Life mem., former Dir.); mem., Metro Toronto Bd. of Trade; recreations: fishing, squash, tennis, classical & popular music, reading; Club: Bayview Country Club; Office: 160 McNabb St., Markham, Ont. L3R 4B8.

**FINLAY, James Campbell,** M.Sc.; museum director, retired; b. Russell, Man. 12 June 1931; s. William Hugh and Grace Muriel (Fleming) F.; e. Brandon (Man.) Coll. Inst. 1949; Univ. of Man. Brandon Campus B.Sc. 1952; Univ. of Alta. M.Sc. 1968; m. Audrey Joy d. Leonard Barton 18 June 1955; children: Barton Brett, Warren Hugh, Rhonda Marie; retired; Geophysicist 1952–53; Geol. becoming Dist. Geol. 1955–65; Chief Park Naturalist, Biol., Elk Island Nat. Park 1965–66; Dir. Hist. Devel. & Archives City of Edmonton 1967–71; Dir. Hist. & Science Services Edmonton 1971–75; Dir., John Janzen Nature Centre 1975–84; Dir., City Wide Program & Special Events 1984–92; Ed. 'A Nature Guide to Alberta' 1987; Compiler & Ed. 'A Bird Finding Guide to Canada' 1984; co-author (with wife) 'A Guide to Alberta Parks' 1987; 'Ocean to Alpine. A British Columbia Nature Guide' 1992; author booklet on outdoor museums, various ornithol. articles, several booklets on wildlife in a backyard; weekly Nature column in Edmonton Journal since 1985; Founding Dir. & Past Pres., Alta. Museums Assn.; Past Dir., Vice Pres. and Pres. Candn. Museums Assn.; Past Pres. Alta. Chapter Candn. Soc. Environmental Biols.; Founding Dir. Fed. Alta. Naturalists; Past Pres. Edmonton Bird Club & Natural Hist. Club; Life mem. Am. Ornothol. Union; Alta. Chrmn., Wildlife '87; Founding Extve. Dir., Alta. Wildlands Trust Found.; el. to Edmonton Hist. Hall of Fame (1st City Civil Servant); presented with Alta's Order of the Bighorn Award 1987; Canadian Parks Heritage Award, Envir. Canada 1990; Edmonton Natural History Conservation Award 1988; Loran Goulden Award, Fedn. of Alta. Naturalists 1991; Douglas Pimlot Award, Candn. Nature Fedn. 1991; awarded Commemorative Medal for 125th Anniversary of Candn. Confederation 1992; Protestant; recreations: nature in outdoors, canoeing, hiking; Home: 61 East Whitecroft 52313 Range Rd. 232, Sherwood Park, Alta. T8B 1B7.

**FINLAY, (Audrey) Joy,** C.M., B.A., M.Ed.; educator; naturalist; b. Davidson, Sask. 18 Sept. 1932; d. Leonard Noel and Vilhelmine Marie (Rossander) Barton (1905– ;); e. Dauphin Coll. Inst. 1951; Brandon Coll. Univ. of Man. B.A. 1954; Univ. of Alta. Dip. in Edn. 1974, M.Ed. 1978; m. James Campbell s. William Hugh and Grace Muriel Finlay 18 June 1954; children: Barton Brett, Warren Hugh, Rhonda Marie; National Chrmn. Wildlife '87, 1986–88; conducted first natural hist. interpretation & environmental edn. progs. schs., youth & family groups Edmonton 1965; apptd. Curriculum Cons. in Environmental & Outdoor Edn. Edmonton Pub. Sch. Bd. 6 yrs.; lectr. in environmental edn. & curriculum Univs. Alta., Calgary and Lethbridge during 1970's; Founding Pres. & Life mem. Environmental & Outdoor Edn. Council Alta. Teachers Assn.; former mem. Bd. Advs. Banff Sch. of Environment; Coordinator, Teacher's Centre Edmonton Pub. Sch. Bd. 4 yrs.; mem. Bd. N. Am. Assn. Environmental Edn.; Dir. Fedn. Alta. Naturalists and Chrmn. Environmental Edn. Ctte. during 1970's; mem. Alta Task Force on Environmental Edn.; Past Chrmn. Energy Conservation Study Group Pub. Adv. Ctte. Environmental Council Alta.; Dir. and Past Chrmn. Outdoors Unlittered Alta.; cons. and script writer various natural hist., environmental edn. & other topics ACCESS (prov. radio & TV); conducted numerous workshops and profl. devel. sessions local, prov. and nat. conventions and confs.; Vice Pres. Candn. Nature Fedn. and Chrmn. Edn. Ctte.; Dir., Sec., Pres. of Exec., Am. Nature Study Soc.; recipient Loran Goulden Award Fedn. Alta. Naturalists 1979; named Woman of Yr. Chatelaine Mag. 1975; recipient, Order of the Bighorn, Alta. 1987; Environment Canada presentation by H.R.H. Prince Philip 1987; Ralph D. Bird Award, Manitoba Naturalists Soc. 1988; Member, Order of Canada 1990; Candn. Parks Service Heritage Award, Environment Canada 1990; Reeve's Award of Distinction, County of Strathcona 1991; Douglas Pimlot Award, Candn. Nature Fedn. 1991; Commemorative Medal, 125th Anniversary of Candn. Confedn. 1992; author 'Winter Here and Now' 1982; co-author 'A Nature Guide to Alberta' 1980; 'A Guide to Alberta Parks' 1987; 'Ocean to Alpine. A British Columbia Nature Guide' 1992; contbr. 'Alberta Junior Atlas'; 'Elementary Science Curriculum Guide' Alta.; nature columnist Edmonton & Calgary newspapers; recreations: pottery, nature, photography; Address: 61 East Whitecroft, 52313 Range Rd. 232, Sherwood Park, Alta. T8B 1B7.

**FINLAY, Mary Louise;** broadcast journalist; b. Ottawa, Ont. 29 Mar. 1947; d. John Francis and Helen B. (Morriscey) F.; e. St. Joseph's H.S. (Ont. Scholar); Univ. of Ottawa, B.A. (cum laude) 1967; Harvard Univ., Nieman Fellow 1986; one s.: David Edan Alexander; HOST, 'Sunday Morning,' CBC, 1988– ; Hist. Rsch., Writing & Translation, Candn. War Mus. 1967–70; Current Affairs Interviewer & Prod., CBOT 1970–75; Host, 'Take 30' (Nat. CBC Prog.) 1975–77; Host/Writer 'Finlay and Company' CBC 1976; Contbr., 'As it Happens' CBC Radio 1977–78; '90 Minutes Live' CBC 1977–78; Host & Prod., 'Live it Up' CTV 1978–81; Co-Host 'The National Driving Test' CTV 1980; Co-Host & Prod., The Journal, CBC 1981–88; documentary writer for TV: 'The Railroad Show' 1974, 'The Mackenzie Valley Pipeline Inquiry' 1976, 'All is Calm' 1983, 'Timothy Findley's War' 1983, 'Taking a Chance on Faro' 1984; 'The Right to Die' 1984, 'The Death of Clarence Warren' 1985, 'Congress and the Contras' 1985; recreations: reading, skiing, tennis; Home: 100 Edith Dr., Toronto, Ont. M4R 1Z2; Office: Box 500, Stn. A, Toronto, Ont. M5W 1E6.

**FINLAY, Terence Edward,** B.A., B.Th., M.A., D.D.; Anglican bishop; b. London, Ont. 19 May 1937; s. Terence John and Sarah (McBryan) F.; e. Univ. of Western Ont. B.A. 1959; Huron College B.Th. 1962; Cambridge Univ. England B.A. 1964, M.A. 1967; Huron College D.D. (Hon. Causa) 1987; Wycliffe College D.D. (Hon. Causa) 1988; Trinity College D.D. (Hon. Causa) 1989; ordained Deacon 1961; Priest 1962; m. Alice-Jean Cracknell 20 June 1962; children: Sara-Jane, Rebecca; TENTH ANGLICAN BISHOP OF TORONTO 1989– ; Rector, All Saints Waterloo 1964–66; (Dean of Res., Renison College., Univ. of Waterloo; Angican Chaplain, Univ. of Waterloo & Wilfred Laurier); Incumbent, St. Aiden's (London, Ont.) 1966–68; Rector, St. John the Evangelist 1968–78; Grace Church (Brantford, Ont.) & Archdeacon of Brant 1978–82; Incumbent, St. Clement (Eglinton) 1982–86; consecrated Bishop in the Church of God & appt. Area Bishop, Trent-Durham 4 Dec. 1986; elected Coadjutor Bishop of Toronto 31 Oct. 1987; Chaplain, Metro. Aux. Police Force; Liaision Bishop for the Missions to Seamen in Canada; the Diocese of Toronto is Canada's largest diocese encompassing 215 parishes; recreations: music, skiing, travel; clubs: Albany, York; Home: 50 Castlefrank Rd., Toronto, Ont. M4W 2Z6; Office: 135 Adelaide St. E., Toronto, Ont. M5C 1L8.

**FINLAYSON, (Judith) Ann,** M.A.T., M.A.; writer; b. Burlington, Iowa 26 May 1941; d. John Ballard and Mary Elinor (Thompson) Lundgren; e. Smith Coll.; Univ. of Edinburgh; Boston Univ. B.A. 1964; Harvard Univ. M.A.T. 1965; Univ. of Toronto M.A. 1974; m. Edward Lazare Shorter 1962, div. 1974; children: Matthew Lundgren, Stephanie Caperton, Abigail Colby; m. Michael George Finlayson 10 June 1975; one s. John Michael Simon; freelance researcher sociol. and urban studies 1968–73; freelance ed. 1973–78; researcher, reporter, staff writer Maclean's mag. 1978–88; freelance writer since 1988; conducted writing workshops Atkinson Coll. York Univ. 1971–78; lectr. in mag. journalism prog. Ryerson Polytech. Inst. 1983–85; author: 'Whose Money Is It Anyway? The Showdown on Pensions' 1988; co-author: 'Card Tricks: Bankers, Boomers and the Explosion of Plastic Credit' 1993; author or co-author over 200 mag. articles; recreations: golf, tennis; Club: Rosedale Tennis; Address: 440 Markham St., Toronto, Ont. M6G 2L2.

**FINLAYSON, The Hon. Mr. Justice George Duncan,** Q.C., B.A., LL.D.; judge; b. Winnipeg, Man. 4 Nov. 1927; s. Roderick Kenneth and Jean (Duncan) F.; e. Univ. of Toronto, Univ. Coll. B.A. 1949; Osgoode Hall Law Sch.; called to the Bar 1953; LL.D. (hon. causa) 1981; m. Joan Helen d. Howard and Gertrude Twilley 23 Aug. 1953; children: Margot Elaine, Blair Roderick, Sheelah Amelia; JUDGE, COURT OF APPEAL FOR ONTARIO Sept. 1990– ; Couns. McCarthy & McCarthy 1953–84; practice restricted to trial and appellate advocacy in criminal and civil law; Judge of the Supreme Court of Ont. and a member, Court of Appeal for Ont. and Ex Officio Judge of the High Court of Justice for Ont. 1984–90; past mem. Bars of Alta., Nfld. and Labrador, the Yukon, and N.W.T.; Bencher 1970; Treas. Law Soc. of Upper Can. 1979–80; mem. Candn. Bar Assn.; Advocates' Soc.; Toronto Lawyers' Club; Medico-Legal Soc.; County of York Bar Assn.; Home: 166 Hudson Dr., Toronto, Ont. M4T 2K6; Office: Osgoode Hall, 130 Queen St. W., Toronto, Ont. M5H 2N5.

**FINLAYSON, Ian E.,** B.A., M.B.A.; business executive; b. Toronto, Ont. 29 Feb. 1948; s. Reginald William and Marjorie Jean (Winton) F.; e. Upper Canada College; Amherst Coll. B.A. (Hons.) 1971; Columbia Univ. M.B.A. 1973; m. Marlo d. George and Nila McLaughlin 12 April 1975; children: W. Campbell, Fraser M.; PRESIDENT, CHIEF EXECUTIVE OFFICER & OWNER, FINLAYSON ENTERPRISES LTD. 1979– ; joined Concern 1972; Executive Vice-Pres. 1976; Dir., Gerling Global Reinsur.; Gerling Global Investments; Han Holdings Ltd.; Chair, Springs Canada Ltd.; Pres., One Whitney Ltd.; Pres. & Chair, Suite 100 Ltd.; Governor, Roy Thomson Hall; Upper Canada College; Mem., Commanderie de Bordeaux; Chevaliers du Tastevin; recreations: golf, wine; clubs: York; Badminton & Raquet, Caledon Mountain Trout, Rosedale Golf, Union League; Home: 1 Whitney Ave., Toronto, Ont. M4W 1A7; Office: 1510 Caterpillar Rd., Mississauga, Ont. L4X 2W9.

**FINLAYSON, J(ock) K(inghorn);** executive; b. Nanaimo, B.C. 27 May 1921; s. John Archibald and Elizabeth (Lister) F.; m. Madeleine V. Coussement 7 Jan. 1976; 2 s. Daniel, Michel; 1 d. Janet; CHRMN. & DIR., ROYAL INSURANCE CO. OF CANADA; Dir., Canadian Reynolds Metals Co.; Group Acme Canada Inc.; R.J.R. MacDonald Inc.; Sun Life Assurance Co. of Can.; United Corp. Ltd.; Pres., Kinghorn Financial Corporation; joined Royal Bank of Can. in Nanaimo, B.C., 1939; served in various branches in that prov. and after mil. service was apptd. to the Bank's H.O. Montreal; served in managerial posts in Alta. and Man., returning to Montreal in 1960 as Mgr. of the Bank's Main Br.; Asst. Gen. Mgr., H.O. 1964; Gen. Mgr., Internat. 1967; Chief Gen. Mgr. 1969; Vice Pres. and Dir. 1970; Depy. Chrmn. and Extve. Vice Pres. 1972; Vice Chrmn. 1977; Pres. 1980–83 (ret.); Protestant; recreations: golf, fishing; Clubs: Mount Royal (Montreal); The Toronto; St. Andrews (Delray Beach).

**FINLAYSON, James Colin,** B.A.Sc.; aeronautical engineer; Canadian public service; b. Tignish, P.E.I. 12 Oct. 1918; s. Harold Alexander and Kate (Archer) F.; e. Univ. of Toronto, B.A.Sc. 1940 (Hons., Mech. Engn.; J.A. Findlay Scholar, in 3rd yr.); m. Jean Burwell, d. William F. Moore, Pembroke, Ont., 3 July 1943; children: Harold, Barbara, Judith; former Chief Control Div.; Aerospace Br., Dept. of Supply & Services, retired 1976; Asst. to Factory Supt., Dom. Ammunition Divn., Candn. Industries Ltd., Brownsburg, Que., 1940–41; Aero Engn. course R.C.A.F. Sch. of Aero. Engn., Montreal, Que., 1941–42; Research Aero. Engn. Offr., Test & Devel. Estab., R.C.A.F. Stn., Rockcliffe, Ont., 1942–45 with rank of Flight-Lieut.; Research Engr., Turbo Research Ltd., Leaside, Ont., 1945–46; Engr. in Charge (full scale) Test Plant, A.V. Roe Can. Ltd., Nobel, Ont., 1946–47; Research Aero. Engr., Air Transport Bd., Ottawa, Ont., 1948–49; Acting Chief, Research Aero. Engn. Br., 1949; Aero. Engr., Air Services Bd., Dept. of Transport, 1950–53; Sr. Production Offr., 1953–58; Tech. Adviser, Aircraft Br., 1959; Assoc. Fellow, Candn. Aero. & Space Inst.; mem. Assn. of Prof. Engrs. of Ont.; Anglican; recreations: amateur radio, photography, music; Home: 557 Edison Ave., Ottawa, Ont. K2A 1V6.

**FINLAYSON, Michael George,** M.A., Ph.D.; educator; b. Melbourne, Australia 20 Oct. 1938; s. George Stephen and Lillith (Martin) F.; e. Univ. of Melbourne B.A. 1959, M.A. 1964; Univ. of Toronto Ph.D. 1968; m. Judith Akehurst 1964; m. Ann Lundgren 1975; children: Brigid E., Joel, Simon; VICE PRES., (HUMAN RESOURCES) UNIV. OF TORONTO 1991– , Prof. of Hist. 1985– , Chrmn. of Hist. 1987–91; Tutor, Sr. Tutor Univ. of Melbourne 1960–64; Asst. Prof. present Univ. 1968, Assoc. Prof. 1974, Pres. Faculty Assn. 1979–81, 1985–87; Visiting Fellow, La Trobe Univ. Melbourne 1981, Corpus Christi Coll. Cambridge 1982, Clare Hall Cambridge 1989; Co-Chair Un. Way (Univ. Toronto) Appeal 1989; author 'Historians, Puritanism and the English Revolution' 1983; co-ed. 'The Struggle for Power' 1987; mem. Candn. Hist. Assn.; Conf. on Brit. Studies; recreations: squash, golf, tennis; Home: 440 Markham St., Toronto, Ont. M6G 2L2; Office: Toronto, Ont. M6S 1A1.

**FINLAYSON, William David,** M.A., Ph.D.; archaeologist; b. Toronto, Ont. 1 March 1946; s. William John Nimmo and Lois Ferguson (Lang) F.; e. Lorne Park Pub. & Secondary Schs.; Guelph Coll. Vocational Inst.; Univ. of Toronto, B.A. 1969, M.A. 1970, Ph.D. 1976; Visiting Grad. Student Northwestern Univ. 1971; m. Elizabeth d. William Booth and Joan Holmes 5 Dec. 1980; two s. W. Alexander, David A.; DIR.-GEN., LONDON MUSEUM OF ARCHAEOLOGY 1991– , Extve. Dir. 1976–91; mem. Dir. & Sec. Treas. 1978– ; Dir.-Gen., London and Middlesex Heritage Museum 1991– ; Lawson Prof. of Candn. Archaeol. Univ. of W. Ont. 1985– ; Special Lectr. Univ. of Toronto 1979–84, Visiting Assoc. Prof. (part-time) 1978–79, 1984–87; Adjunct Prof. Prog. in Jour. for Native People, Univ. of W. Ont. 1979–82; Lectr. in Anthrop. 1973–76, Visiting Asst. Prof. (part-time) 1976–79, Hon. Lectr. 1979–84; Adv. and Cons. Halton Region Conserv. Authority 1981–88; mem. Adv. Ctte. Fanshawe Pioneer Village, London, Ont. 1980–86; Adv. Ctte. R.C.R. Museum C.F.B. London 1981–83; Founding Pres. Ont. Council Archaeol. 1986–90; Dir. Ont. Heritage Found. 1987–89; mem. & Dir., Minnesing Heritage Soc., Christian Island, Ont.; named One of Five Outstanding Young Londoners, W. London Jaycees 1981; recipient, Milton Heritage Award 1992; author: 'The Saugeen Culture' 1976; 'The 1975 and 1978 Rescue Excavations at the Draper Site: Introduction and Settlement Patterns' 1985; co-author: 'What Columbus Missed!' 1987; author or co-author over 31 articles Ont. archaeol.; ed. Candn. Archaeol. Assn. Bulletin 1974–76; recreation: reading; Home: R.R. 2, Ilderton, Ont. N0M 2A0; Office: 1600 Attawandaron Rd., London, Ont. N6G 3M6.

**FINLEY, Gerald Eric,** Ph.D., R.C.A., F.R.S.C.; educator; author; b. Munich, Germany 17 July 1931; s. Frederick James and Winifred Margaret Mackenzie (Barker) F.; came to Can. 1931; e. Univ. of Toronto B.A. 1955, M.A. 1957; Johns Hopkins Univ. Ph.D. 1965; m. Helen Virginia d. Dr. Hawthorne Steele 1961; children: Christopher Frederick, Heath Christian; PROF. OF HIST. OF ART, QUEEN'S UNIV.; Lectr. in Art & Archaeol. Univ. of Toronto 1959–60; Lectr. in Art Univ. of Sask. Regina 1962–63; Acting Dir., Norman Mackenzie Art Gallery; estbd. Hist. of Art and Art Educ. Programs, Queen's Univ. while Head of Dept. Art Hist. 1963–72; Fellow, Inst. for Advanced Studies in Humanities Univ. of Edinburgh 1979–80; Fellow, Royal Soc. of Can. 1984; awards: Brit. Council; Can. Council; Social Sciences & Humanities Research Council Can.; Candn. Fed. Humanities; author 'In Praise of Older Buildings' 1976; 'George Heriot 1759–1839' 1979; 'Landscapes of Memory: Turner as Illustrator to Scott' 1980; 'Turner and George IV in Edinburgh , 1822' 1981; 'George Heriot: Postmaster – Painter of the Canadas' 1983; articles History of Ideas and various aspects of J.M.W. Turner's art and life; exhns. arranged: '3 Am. Painters: Olitski, Noland & Louis' Norman Mackenzie Art Gallery Regina 1963; 'Decline and Fall: the Arch. of Kingston & Frontenac Co.' Agnes Etherington Art Centre Kingston 1976; 'George Heriot: Painter of the Canadas' Agnes Etherington Art Centre Kingston; Nat. Gallery Can. Ottawa; McCord Museum Montreal; Sigmund Samuel Canadiana Gallery Toronto; 'Turner and George IV in Edinburgh' Tate Gallery London, Eng. 1978; Nat. Gallery Scot. Edinburgh 1981; mem. Turner Soc. Gt. Brit. (Vice Pres.); Protestant; Home: 'The Winston,' 52 Earl St. Kingston, Ont. K7L 2G6; Office: Dept. of Art, Queen's Univ., Kingston, Ont. K7L 3N6.

**FINLEY, John Powers,** M.Sc., M.D.,C.M., F.R.C.P.(C); pediatric cardiologist; b. Lunenburg, N.S. 2 Aug. 1945; s. John A. and Gretchen F. (Powers) F.; e. Saint John (N.B.) H.S. 1963; Dalhousie Univ. B.Sc. 1967, M.Sc. 1968; Magdalen Coll. Oxford (Rhodes Scholar) Physics 1968–69; McGill Univ. M.D.,C.M. 1973; Univ. of Toronto 1973–78; m. Carolyn d. Guy and Jean Slade 21 June 1975; children: Christine G., Ian A.; HEAD, DIVISION OF CARDIOLOGY, IZAAK WALTON KILLAM HOSP. FOR CHILDREN 1986– ; Prof. of Pediatrics Dalhousie Univ. 1992– ; mem. Sci. Review Ctte., Candn. Heart Found. 1978–81; Secy., Maritime Rhodes Scholar Selection Ctte. 1980–89; Chief Examiner, Pediatric Cardiology, Royal Coll. Phys. of Can. 1987–90; mem., Cardiology Nucleus Ctte. RCPC 1991– ; mem., Candn. Cardiovascular Soc.; Am. Physiol. Soc.; Office: 5850 University Ave., Halifax, N.S. B3J 3G9.

**FINLEY, John Robinson,** B.A., LL.B., Q.C.; lawyer; b. Oshawa, Ont. 23 April 1939; s. George Wolverton and Agnes Hamilton (Robinson) F.; e. Univ. of Toronto B.A. 1960; Osgoode Hall Law School LL.B. 1963; m. Freda K. d. Archibald and Audrey Dancey 6 June 1964; children: Karen Anne, Leanne Katherine; PARTNER, SMITH, LYONS, TORRANCE, STEVENSON & MAYER 1971– ; called to Bar of Ont. March 1965; joined Wahn McAlpine Mayer Smith Creber Lyons Torrance & Stevenson (predecessor of present firm) 1965; practices primarily in corp. & commercial law with particular emphasis on competition, franchising & mktg. law; Dir., Midas Canada Inc.; Yamaha Canada Music Ltd.; Hughes, King & Co. Limited; Capstone Group of Investment Funds; Roxton Furniture Ltd.; Anco Chem. Inc.; Q.C. 1980; Pres., Candn. Bar Assn. (Ont.) 1981–82; Pres., Ont. Div., Candn. Red Cross Soc. 1990–92 (Mem. National Bd. of Gov. 1990–92); Dir., Muskoka Heritage Foundation; recreations: golf, skiing; clubs: Muskoka Lakes Golf & Country (Dir.), Osler Bluff Ski, National; Home: 133 Alexandra Blvd., Toronto, Ont. M4R 1M3; Office: Suite 6200, Scotia Plaza, 40 King St. W., Toronto, Ont. M5H 3Z7.

**FINN, His Honour Gilbert,** O.C., B.A.; lieutenant governor; b. Inkerman Ferry, N.B. 3 Sept. 1920; s. Ephrem and Felicite F.; e. Séminaire de Chicoutimi; Laval Univ. B.A. 1947, C.L.U. 1958; St. Anne Univ. D.Adm. (Hon.) 1977; St. Thomas Univ. LL.D. (Hon.) 1981; Univ. de Moncton D.Adm. (Hon.) 1987; Mount Allison Univ. LL.D. (Hon.) 1993; m. Jeannine d. James and Victoria Boudreau 8 Sept. 1948; 9 children; LT. GOV. OF N.B. 1987– ; Fieldworker Credit Union and Co-ops. N.B. 1948–50; Conseil coopération du Qué. 1968–70; Vice Prés. Caisse populaire de St-Anselme 1961–63; Sales Dir. Assumption Mutual Life Assurance Co. 1950–62, Gen. Mgr. 1962–69, Pres. and Chief Exec. Offr. 1969–80 and Chrmn. Exec. Ctte., Chrmn. of Bd. and Chief Exec. Offr. 1975–80, Chrmn. 1980–87; Dir. Banque Nationale du Can.; Brunswick Mining and Smelting Corp. Ltd., also mem. Exec. Ctte.; Assumption Place Ltd., Chrmn. 1972–80, 1985–87; Carrefour Assomption Ltée, Chrmn. 1977–80, 1985–87; Pres., Atlantic Enterprise Prog. 1986–87; Chrmn. Dr. Georges L. Dumont Hosp. 1971–87, Pres. and Dir.; Pres. Univ. de Moncton 1980–85; Gov. 1965–71; mem. Atlantic Provs. Econ. Council 1962–68; Nat. Vice Pres. Lacordaire 1962–67; Pres. Union des Mutuelles-Vie françaises 1963–64; Chrmn. Atlantic Holdings Ltd. 1965–80; Chrmn. and Dir. Imprimerie Acadienne Ltée 1965–80; mem. N.B. Rsch. & Productivity Council 1966–72; Chrmn. Bonaccord Finance Corp. Ltd. 1970–80; mem. Econ. Council Can. 1973–76; Lebel Comn. 1974–75; Chrmn. Mother's Own Bakery Ltd. 1975–80, René's Bakery Ltd. 1975–80, Les Propriétés l'Assomption Ltée 1977–80, 1985–87; Hon. Pres. Féderation des Scouts de l'Atlantique 1975–85; Co-Chrmn. Task Force Amateur Sport N.B. 1979–81; Founding Chrmn. Conseil économique du Nouveau-Brunswick 1980–82; Trustee, Les Presses francophone du Nouveau-Brunswick 1984–87; Comité aviseur Fondation Donatien Frémont Inc. 1986–87; mem. Conseil économique du Nouveau-

Brunswick; R. Catholic; recreation: golf; Home: 238 Waterloo Rd., Fredericton, N.B. E3B 1Z3; Office: King St., P.O. Box 6000, Fredericton, N.B. E3B 5H1.

**FINN, Michael Raeburn,** B.A., M.A., Ph.D.; university professor and administrator; b. Sudbury, Ont. 14 Feb. 1941; s. Carroll Bernard and Clara Mary Elizabeth (Raeburn) F.; e. Univ. of Toronto B.A. 1963; Univ. de Paris Sorbonne 1963–64; Univ. of Toronto M.A. 1965; Harvard Univ. Ph.D. 1968; m. Elizabeth A. Park d. Matilda (Scully) and Cecil J. Park 26 March 1970; PROFESSOR AND CHAIR, DEPT. OF FRENCH, RYERSON POLYTECHNIC UNIV. 1984– ; Lecturer in French, Univ. of Manitoba 1968; Asst. Prof. of French, Univ. of N.B. 1969–71; Foreign Serv. Officer, Dept. of External Affairs (assignments in Bordeaux, Paris, San Francisco) 1971–80; Information Officer, Council of Ministers of Edn., Canada 1980–84; Past Pres., Assn. des Dép. d'études françaises des univs. de l'Ont.; author of articles on French lang. & lit., Marcel Proust, Balzac, language teaching methodologies; former member, Toronto Mendelssohn Choir; Mem., ACTRA; food writer; Office: 350 Victoria St., Toronto, Ont. M5B 2K3.

**FINN, Sheila May,** C.P.P.; purchasing, association executive; b. Montreal, Que. 21 July 1946; d. Joseph Wilcock and Violet Catherine (Hall) F.; e. McGill Univ., Mngt. Studies 1978; PMAC, Profl. Purch. Designation 1979; Dir. of Supply Mgmt. & Logistics, Consumers Glass, Consumers Packaging Inc. 1984–..; Bd. of Dirs., Ctr. for Environmental Training, Niagara Coll.; Purchasing Mgr., CIBA-GEIGY Can. Ltd. 1971–1980; Purchasing Mgr. McGaw Mfg. Div., Am. Hosp. Supply Corp. 1980–84; Teacher, Mohawk College 1980–84; Pres., Purchasing Mgmt. Assn. of Canada 1986–87; Sec., Trival Credit Union 1976–78; author: 'Purchasing in International Markets' seminar and vendor certification seminar; Home: 109 Warner Dr., Oakville, Ont. L6L 6G7.

**FINNEGAN, Cyril V.,** M.S., Ph.D.; educator; b. Dover, N.H. 17 July 1922; s. Cyril Vincent and Hilda Cecilia (McClintock) F.; e. Bates Coll. B.S. 1944; Univ. of Notre Dame M.S. 1948, Ph.D. 1951; Stanford Univ. postdoctoral studies 1952; children: Maureen A., Patrick S., Cathaleen C., Kevin S., Eileen D., Gormlaith R., Michaeleen S., Mairead B., Conal E.; DEAN EMERITUS, UNIV. OF B.C. 1988; Instr. & Asst. Prof. in Biol. St Louis Univ. 1952–56; Univ. of Notre Dame 1956–58; Asst. Prof. of Zool., Univ. of B.C. 1958, Assoc. Prof. 1960, Prof. 1964–88, Chrmn. Biol. Program 1969–74, Assoc. Dean of Science 1972–79, Dean of Science 1979–85, Assoc. Vice-Pres., Academic 1986–88; served with U.S. Army 1942–45; author various research publs. and review articles; mem., Soc. Devel. Biol.; Tissue Culture Assn.; Candn. Soc. Cell Biol.; Internat. Soc. Developmental Biol.; Office: Zoology, Univ. of B.C., 6270 Univ. Blvd., Vancouver, B.C. V6T 1Z4.

**FINNIGAN, Joan (Mrs. Joan MacKenzie),** B.A.; writer; b. Ottawa, Ont. 23 Nov. 1925; d. Frank and Maye (Horner) Finnigan; e. Lisgar Collegiate Sr. Matric. 1945; Queen's Univ. B.A. Eng., Hist. and Econ. 1967; m. late Dr. Charles Grant s. Belle and Charlie M. 23 May 1949; children: Jonathan, Roderick, Martha; teacher, one-room schoolhouse, Beechgrove, Que. 1945–46; Carleton Univ. studies in Journalism incomplete; Gen. Reporter, Ottawa Journal; 18 yrs. continuous occasional freelance writing for Chatelaine, St. Weekly, Globe & Mail, Ottawa Journal, Farmer's Advocate, Parents' Magazine, and contribs. to 'little mags' 1949–67; publicity, advtg., pub. relns. and special events, Kingston and Dist. United Way 1969–74; rsch., idea prodn., film outlines and scripts for NFB (incl. series 'Challenge for Change'; screenplay for 'The Best Damn Fiddler from Calabogie to Kaladar' 1969, winner of 9 out of 11 Etrogs [now Genies] incl. Best Screenplay, Candn. Film Awards) 1966–71; rsch., script and interviewing for CBC film 'Kingston: Celebrate This City' 1973; idea prodn., script-writing and interviewing for NFB film 'They're Putting Us Off the Map'; 'Home' (script for This Land, CBC) 1976; screenplay 'A Day in the Life of God's Country' 1982; CBC Radio scripts: 'Songs for the Bible Belt' (poetic documentary on Kitchener-Waterloo); 'May Day Rounds: Renfrew County' (anthologized in U.S. and Engl.); 'In the Brown Cottage on Loughborough Lake'; 'Children of the Shadows'; 'There's No Good Times Left – None at All' (poetic doc. on Ottawa Valley); 'Coming Over a Country of No Lights' (poetic doc. about N. Ont. Mining Belt) 1976; 'The Lakers' (doc.) 1977; 'Valley of the Outaouais' (poetic suite on Ottawa Valley) 1979; 'Poems from Pontiac Country' and 'The River' (suites of poems) 1984; author: 'Through the Glass, Darkly' (poetry) 1963; 'A Dream of Lilies' (poetry) 1965; 'Canada in Bed' (humour/sociology, under pseudonym Michelle Bedard) 1967; 'Entrance to the Greenhouse' (poetry; winner Centennial Prize for Poetry) 1968; 'It Was Warm and Sunny When We Set Out' (poetry) 1970; 'In the Brown Cottage on Loughborough Lake' (poetry) 1970; 'Kingston: Celebrate This City' (lit. hist.) 1976; 'Living Together' (poetry) 1976; 'I Come From the Valley' (lit. hist.) 1976; 'Canadian Colonial Cooking' (recipes from hist. sites of Ont.) 1976; 'A Reminder of Familiar Faces' (poetry) 1978; 'This Series Has Been Discontinued' (poetry) 1980; 'Some of the Stories I Told You Were True' (oral hist.) 1981; 'Giants of Canada's Ottawa Valley' (biography) 1981; 'Look! The Land is Growing Giants' (children's lit.) 1983; 'Laughing All the Way Home' (oral hist.) 1984; 'Legacies, Legends and Lies' (oral hist.) 1985; 'The Watershed Collection' (poetry) ed. & with an intro. by Robert Weaver 1988; 'Finnigan's Guide to the Ottawa Valley' 1988; 'Tell Me Another Story' (fourth oral history of the Ottawa Valley) 1988; 'The Dog That Wouldn't Be Left Behind' (children's lit.) 1989; 'Wintering Over' (poetry) 1992; 'Old Scores: New Goals' (history of the Ottawa Senators 1891–1992) 1992; 'A History of Ottawa's Lisgar Collegiate 1843–1993' 1993; plays: 'A Prince of Good Fellows' (based on the story of the last Laird Archibald MacNab; publ. in 'I Come from the Valley' 1976); 'Up the Vallee!' (Tarragon Theatre Workshop Prod., Toronto 1978); 'Songs from Both Sides of the River' (Nat. Arts Centre, Ottawa 1987); 'Wintering Over' (Museum of Civilization, Hull, Que. 1988–93); rep. Can. in Borestone Mountain Poetry Annuals (annual coll. of best in English-speaking world) 1959, 1961, 1963, 1967, 1969, 1971, 1973; recent anthologies: Atwood-Woodcock Poetry Anthology 'The Dry Wells of India' 1989; 'Canadian Childhoods' 1989; 'More than Words Can Say: Personal Perspectives on Literacy' 1990; writing anthologized in England, U.S., Australia, New Zealand; extensive guest lectr., instr., reader and pub. speaker incl. many radio and television appearances; First Writer-in-Residence, Ottawa Publ. Lib. 1987–88; photography incl. in 'Giants of Canada's Ottawa Valley'; 'Some of the Stories I Told You Were True'; 'Laughing All the Way Home'; 'Legacies, Legends and Lies'; Ottawa Magazine series on Ottawa Valley; showings of photographs: Upstairs Gallery Renfrew 1982; Gallery Café Pembroke 1982; opening of Petawawa Library 1983; Octagon Gallery Show, Calabogie 1986; other awards: Pres.'s Medal for Poetry, Univ. of W. Ont. 1969; five Can. Counc. Grants 1965–71, Sr. Can. Counc. Grants 1972–73 and 1977–78, Explorations Grant 1979–80; early literary papers purchased by Queen's Univ. 1969, 1974, 1977; set of lumbering papers and photographs, Queen's Univ. 1991; Sets of tapes of old-timers of Ottawa Valley deposited in National Archives, Ottawa 1989, 1990, 1992; Family hockey papers, National Archives; Original manuscript material and artwork for 'Look! The Land is Growing Giants' in Childrens' Coll., Nat. Lib. of Can.; Philemon Wright Award, Inst. for Rsch. and Hist. in the Outauoais, Que. Govt. 1983; 'Laughing All the Way Home' on short-list for Stephen Leacock Award for Humour 1984; first Ottawa-Carleton Literary Award for 'Legacies, Legends and Lies' 1985; 'The Watershed Collection' on short-list for League of Candn. Poets Pat Lowther Award 1988; 'Wintering Over' on short-list for Ont. Trillium Award 1993; Multiculturalism Grant for work on book on Opeongo Line 1987; Grants from Ont. Heritage Found. & Hist. Soc. of the Gatineau for work on fourth oral hist. of the Ottawa Valley 'Tell Me Another Story' 1988; Address: Hartington, Ont. K0H 1W0.

**FIORINI, Richard J.,** B.Sc., P.Eng.; mining executive; b. Durango, Colo. 02 Feb. 1938; s. Noel J. and Thelma F. (Rowe) F.; e. Univ. of Ariz. B.Sc. 1971; m. Karen d. Willard and Helen Howlett 8 Dec. 1962; one d.: Renée Ann; PRESIDENT & CHIEF EXECUTIVE OFFICER, ASAMERA MINERALS 1992– ; Mine Superintendent & Gen. Mgr., Northwood Mining 1961–69; Gen. Mgr. Opemiska Mine, Falconbridge Copper 1971–76; Quirke Mine, Rio Algom Ltd. 1976–78; Gen. Mgr., Opns., Gulf Minerals Corp. 1978–79; Pres., Noranda Mining Inc. 1979–84; Pres., Gold Division, Meridian Minerals 1984–90; Profl. Eng. Ont. & Que.; Honor Scholar; Mem., AIME; Soc. of Mining Eng.; recreations: skiing, golf; clubs: Denver, Elks, Masons; Home: 27 Quail Run, Wenatchee, Wash. 98807; Office: P.O. Box 398, Wenatchee, Wash. 98807.

**FIORITA, Dionigi (Dan) Mario,** B.Sc., B.C.L.; b. San Pietro in Guarano, Italy 14 Jan. 1947; s. Silvio Francesco and Filena Maria (Bruno) F.; e. Loyola Coll. Montréal B.Sc. 1969; McGill Univ. B.C.L. 1974; Inst. of Air & Space Law Dip. in Air & Space Law 1975; m. Jocelyne d. Jean-Yves and Agathe Lavoie 30 July 1977; LAVERY, de BILLY, Barristers & Solicitors, Montréal 1989– ; Candn. Rep. Council of Internat. Civil Aviation Orgn. and Head of Permanent Candn. Del. 1985–89; positions held 1977–85: Counsel Dept. of Justice Ottawa, Dir. Internat. Air Policy Dept. Transport Ottawa, Legal Counsel Nordair Ltée Montréal; guest lectr. Concordia Univ. 1984, 1985, 1986, 1988; McGill Univ./Air Canada, Profl. Aviation Mgmt. Course 1987–90; Internat. Aviation Mgmt. Training Inst. 1987–89 and 1991; Inst. of Air and Space Law, McGill Univ. 1989–94; Founding mem. Decision Canada 1977; awarded Cert. of Honour, Counc. for Candn. Unity 1980; mem., Inst. of Air & Space Law Assn. (Pres. 1985–89); Que Bar Assn.; Internat. Law Assn.; Candn. Inst. of Internat. Affairs 1986–89; Dir., Internat. Liaison, Chart. Inst. Transp. 1986–89; Vice Pres. & Dir., Ottawa Japan Karate Assn. 1979–90; Ont. Japan Karate Assn. 1979–90; recreations: squash, riding, skiing, tennis, classical guitar, reading; Home: 8050 Blvd. St. Laurent, Apt. 505, Brossard, Qué. J4X 2P1.

**FIRESTONE, Bruce Murray,** B.Eng. (Civil), M.Eng., Ph.D.; civil engineer; executive; b. Ottawa, Ont. 4 Dec. 1951; s. Otto Jack and Isobel (Torontow) F.; e. Ashbury Coll. Ottawa 1967; McGill Univ. B.Eng. (Civil) 1972; Univ. of New South Wales, Australia M.Eng.-Sci. 1976; Australian Nat. Univ. Ph.D. 1982; Univ. of Laval, French 1967; Univ. of W. Ont. Econ. 1969; Harvard Univ. Finance 1970; two s. Andrew Lawton, Matthew Pearce; three d. Rachel Jane, Miriam Rebecca, Jessica Hillary; CHRMN. & DIR., BRETTON WOODS ENTERTAINMENT INC., FIRESTONE HOLDINGS LTD. and TERRACE INVESTMENTS LIMITED 1982– ; Founder, Ottawa Senators Hockey Club; Part Owner, Ottawa Senators Hockey Club; The Palladium Co.; Consultant, Ottawa Senators Hockey Club; Former Publisher, Ottawa Business News; Former Cons., Rentalex Ltd.; Operations Rsch. Mgr. Metrop. Waste Disposal Authority, Sydney, Australia 1973–76; Rsch. Scholar, Australian Nat. Univ. Canberra 1976–79; Mgmt. Cons. Bureau of Mgmt. Consulting, Supply and Services Can. Ottawa 1980–82; author or co-author various reports, articles, papers; awarded Commemorative Medal for 125th Anniversary of Candn. Confederation 1993; CRTC Licensee Applicant, the Science Fiction Network 1993; Co-Chrmn., 'I'm a Free Trader' Campaign; Mem. BOMA; Chrmn., 'Bring Back the Senators Campaign'; Served on National Hockey League Bd. of Govs. and NHL Extve. Advisory Ctte.; Mem., Ottawa Internat. Airport Authority Planning Ctte.; Mem., Kanata Economic Development Task Force; Dir., Gall. of Arts Court; Firestone Group of Seven Art Collection; Chrmn., Bruce M. Firestone Atom Invitational Tournament; Vol., Minor Hockey, Eastern Ont. and Western Qué.; Candn. Cystic Fibrosis Found.; Fondation B3L; Scouts Canada; Salvation Army; Univ. of Ottawa Heart Inst. at Civic Hosp.; recreations: long distance running, volleyball, soccer, windsurfing, skiing, tennis, hockey; Clubs: Rockcliffe Lawn Tennis; The Country Club; Home: 22 Zokol Cres., Kanata, Ottawa, Ont.; Office: 3000–303 Moodie Dr., Nepean, Ont. K2H 9R4.

**FIRTH, J. Roy,** B.Comm., M.B.A.; banker; b. Winnipeg, Man. 1953; e. Concordia Univ. B.Comm. 1975; Columbia Univ. M.B.A. 1978; SENIOR VICE-PRESIDENT, MARKETING AND DEVELOPMENT, LAURENTIAN BANK OF CANADA; Office: 1981 McGill College Ave., 20th Floor, Montreal, Que. H3A 3K3.

**FISCH, Gerald Grant,** B.Sc., S.B., P.Eng., F.M.C.; executive consultant; b. Heidelberg, Germany 19 Apr. 1922; s. Arthur F.; e. Guelph (Ont.) Collegiate; McGill Univ., B.Sc. (Bio-Chem. and Econ.); Mass Inst. of Technol., S.B. (Indust. Mang. and Chem. Engn.); div.; children: Susan Eleanor, Emily Elizabeth, Michael Gerald; CHRMN. AND CHIEF EXTVE., HERMES GLOBAL CAPITAL CORP.; Sr. Assoc., Morrison Associates; engaged in Internat. Investment, Real Estate, Finance, Trade, Business Migration and Corporate Re-organization; formerly President, Access Canada International Corp.; Managing Partner: Peat, Marwick and Partners; P.S. Ross & Partners, and Principal and Dir. of Management Services, (also Chairman, International Mgmt. Consulting Ctte.), Touche, Ross, Bailey & Smart; for a no. of yrs., was Vice-Pres. and Dir. of a N.Y. management consulting firm; as a Mang. Consultant has lectured widely for prof. and educ. organ. incl. Am. Mang. Assn., Am. Marketing Assn. and Amos Tuck Sch. of Business Adm.; Publications: various articles to leading reviews and journs. on management organizations and promotion; author of 'Organization for Profit' 1964 (Am. Acad. of Mang. Award 1966); 'Modern Management' 1965; Pres., Management Consultants of Que. 1967; Founding Mem., Candn. Assoc. of Mgmt. Consultants; Que. Inst. of Mgmt. Consultants; mem., Soc. for Advanc. of Mang.; Assn. Prof. Engrs. Ont.; recreations: sailing, skiing; Club: Cercle Universitaire, Ottawa; Home: 24 Wellesley St. W., Toronto, Ont. M4Y 1G1;

Office: P.O. Box 97, 2 First Canadian Place, Toronto, Ont. M5X 1B1.

**FISCHER, James D.,** M.D., F.A.C.S., F.R.C.S.; physician; b. Calgary, Alta. 31 March 1943; s. Donald Francis and Fran Ann (Schmaltz) F.; e. Univ. of Alberta M.D. 1970; CLINICAL PROFESSOR, DEPT. OF SURGERY, UNIV. OF ALBERTA HOSPITAL 1977– ; General Surgery Resident, Univ. of Alta. 1971–75; Surgical Fellow, Children's Hosp. Seattle 1976–77; Dir., Div. of Gen. Surgery, Univ. of Alta. Hosp.; Acting Chair, Dept. of Surgery, Univ. of Alta. Hosp.; Bd. Mem., Univ. of Alta. Hosp. 1986–92; Mem., Candn. Assn. of Pediatric Surgeons; Pacific Assn. of Pediatric Surgeons; Candn. Assn. of Gen. Surgeons; Fellow, Am. Coll. of Surgeons; Alta. Assn. of Gen. Surgeons (Pres. 1989–90); Home: 9039 Saskatchewan Dr., Edmonton, Alta. T6G 2B2; Office: #602 – 8215 112 St., Edmonton, Alta. T6G 2C8.

**FISCHER, Joan Frances,** B.A.; business executive; b. Teeswater, Ont. 27 Dec. 1952; d. John Alexander and Anne Margaret (Baehr) F.; e. Univ. of Waterloo B.A. 1974; PRES., FISCHER BUSINESS SERVICES LTD. 1981– ; Counsellor, Waterloo Regional Rape Distress Centre 1974; Instr. Fanshaw Coll. London 1975; Office Mgr. Ont. Pub. Interest Rsch. Group 1976–78; Assoc. Simcar Ltd. (Financial Planners) 1978–81; mem. Extve. Ctte. Toronto Arts Awards; numerous articles and media appearances personal financial mgmt.; recreations: swimming, dance, theatre, skiing; Office: 50 Hillside Dr., Toronto, Ont. M4K 2M2.

**FISCHER, Thomas,** B.A., C.A.; financial executive; b. Budapest, Hungary 1 Sept. 1946; e. Univ. of Toronto, B.A. 1968; C.A. 1971; m. Helen 5 July 1970; children: Barry, Mark; VICE-PRES., C.F.O. & DIR., ST. CLAIR PAINT & WALLPAPER CORP. 1972– ; Student-in-accounts, Laventhol & Horwath (now Price Waterhouse) 1968–71; public practice 1971–72; Dir., Candn. Franchise Assn. 1974–82; Pres. 1982–83; Chrmn., Franchise Subctte., Retail Counc. of Can. 1983–85; Dir. 1984–85; speaker on franchising & finan. matters to var. groups; Home: 76 Aberfeldy Cres., Thornhill, Ont. L3T 4C4; Office: 2600 Steeles Ave. W., Concord, Ont. L4K 3C8.

**FISCHMAN, Sheila Leah,** M.A.; literary translator; b. Moose Jaw, Sask. 1 Dec. 1937; d. Samson and Anna (Adelkind) F.; e. Univ. of Toronto, M.A. 1959; translator of many French-Candn. books from French into English; authors incl. Roch Carrier, Anne Hébert, Jacques Poulin, Michel Tremblay, Naim Kattan, Jacques Savoie, André Major & others; Can. Counc. Translation Prize 1974 ('They Won't Demolish Me' by Roch Carrier & 'The Wolf' by Marie-Claire Blais), 1984 ('Lady With Chains' by Carrier & 'Thérèse and Pierrette and the Little Hanging Angel' by Michel Tremblay); First winner, Félix-Antoine Savard translation prize, Columbia Univ. 1989 and again in 1990; Founding Ed., 'Ellipse: Writers in Translation/Oeuvres en traduction'; Founding Mem., Lit. Translators Assoc. of Can.; Jewish; Home: 3640 Clark St., Montreal, Que. H2X 2S2.

**FISH, Edward B.,** M.D., F.R.C.S.(C); surgeon; educator; b. Toronto, Ont. 3 Mar. 1927; s. Edward Schooley and Nellie (Welstead) F.; e. Chefoo Schs. Shandung, China; Univ. of Toronto Schs.; Univ. of Toronto M.D. 1949; m. Joyce d. Dr. and Mrs. D.J. Bagshaw 29 Apr. 1950; children: Edward, Donald, Catherine, Mary; Principal Investigator N.S.A.B.P.; Surgeon, Women's Coll. Hosp. 1963–85; Dir., Henrietta Banting Breast Centre there 1977–85; Lectr., Asst. Prof. of Surgery Univ. of Toronto 1963–92, Fellow in Surgery 1961–62; internship: Toronto Gen. Hosp. & Hosp. for Sick Children 1949–50; Pathol. Inst. McGill Univ. 1950–51; Residency in Surgery N.Y. Univ. 4th Div. 1951–55, Instr. in Clin. Surgery 1955; Lectr. and Asst. Prof. in Surgery, Christian Med. Coll. Luhdiana, Punjab, India 1956–61; Consultant in Gen. Surgery Princess Margaret Hosp. Toronto; mem. Counc., Overseas Missy. Fellowship; Home: 404 Deloraine Ave., Toronto, Ont.; Office: 2 Carleton St., Ste. 721, Toronto, Ont. M5B 1J3.

**FISH, Hon. Mr. Justice Morris Jacob,** B.A., B.C.L.; court of appeal justice; b. Montreal, Que. 16 Nov. 1938; s. Aaron S. and Zlata (Grober) F.; e. McGill Univ., B.A. (with distinction) 1959, B.C.L. (1st class hons.) 1962; Univ. de Paris 1962–63; m. Judith d. Henry I. and Freda Chinks 25 Dec. 1966; children: Amy S., Laura A.; JUSTICE, QUEBEC COURT OF APPEAL 1989– ; Partner, Kaufman, Yarosky & Fish and successor firms 1968–89; read law with Joseph Cohen, Q.C. and Fred Kaufman, Q.C.; Bar of Que. 1964–89; Bar of P.E.I. 1968–73; Bar of Alta. 1974–89; Q.C. 1984; Lectr., Univ. de Montréal 1969–71; Univ. d'Ottawa 1971–74; Lectr. in Criminal Evidence and Procedure, 1973–80 and Advanced Criminal Law, 1986–89, McGill Univ.; Cons., Law Reform Comn. of Can.; Fed. Dept. of Justice; special counsel, various govt. inquiries; Edit. Dept., The Montreal Star 1959–63; mem., Hebrew Faith; recreations: photography, gardening; club: Mt. Royal Tennis; Home: 5090 Ponsard Ave., Montreal, Que. H3W 2A7; Office: Palais de Justice, 1 Notre Dame St. E., Montreal, Que. H2Y 1B6.

**FISHER, Alexander David,** B.A.Sc.; retired chemical engineer; industrial executive; b. Calgary, Alta. 24 Feb. 1915; s. Dr. Alexander and Sara Jane Vincent (Henderson) F.; e. Univ. of Toronto, B.A.Sc. (Chem. Engn.) 1937; Harvard Grad. Sch. of Business, 1953; m. Evelyn Ruth, d. John Edmund Pett, 30 Nov. 1940; children: John Robert, Katharine Ruth; Vice Pres., Planning, Engn. and Research, Steel Co. Of Canada Ltd., 1965–78; joined company as Metall. 1937; apptd. Foreman, Coke Plant, 1940; Gen. Foreman Coal Chems. Plant, 1941–42; Supt., Coke & Coal Chems. Dept., 1943–49; Asst. Gen. Supt., Hamilton Works, 1950, Gen. Supt., 1951; Mgr., Facilities Planning (corporate-wide), 1963; Vice Pres., Planning, Engr., Rsch. & Devel. 1965; Vice Pres. Corp. Planning, Rsch. & Devel. 1976; retired 1979; Past Pres., John Howard Soc. Hamilton; Hon. Dir., John Howard Soc. Ont.; Past Chrmn. & Hon. Dir., World Vision of Canada; Past Chrmn., World Vision International; Min. of Visitation, Boca Raton Community Ch.; mem., Assn. Prof. Engrs. Ont.; Conservative; Baptist; recreations: golf, swimming, painting, tennis, gardening; Home: 6530 Boca del Mar Dr., Apt. 438, Boca Raton, Florida 33433.

**FISHER, Arthur John;** professional engineer; b. London, Eng. 13 Sept. 1913; s. John Edward and Elizabeth (Dickinson) F.; e. Eltham Coll., London, Eng.; North Staffordshire Tech. Coll., Eng.; City and Guilds Cert. in Elect. Eng.; m. Dorothy Edith Hipkin, Dec. 1937, four children; formerly Chrmn. of Bd. Fiberglas Can. Inc.; began with Callenders Cable & Construction Co., Erith, Kent, and Johnson & Phillips Ltd., Charlton, Kent; prior to coming to Canada was Principal Experimental Offr., Atomic Research Estbl., Harwell, Eng.; apptd. Mgr. of Sarnia Plant of present firm in 1948, and Gen. Mgr., 1951; Vice Pres. (Mfg. & Devel.) and Dir., 1955; Pres., 1967, Chrmn. of the Bd. 1978; served in 2nd World War; Lieut.-Col., Royal Arty.; served at War Office, and Brit. Army Staff, Washington and 2nd Brit. Army on the Continent; Legion of Merit (U.S.A.); mem., Inst. of Elect. Engrs., Eng.; Assn. Prof. Engrs. Ont. (D.Eng. h.c.); Citizenship Award, Prof. Engrs. Ont.; Anglican; recreation: sailing; golf; Clubs: Granite; Rosedale Golf; Home: 8 Maytree Road, Willowdale, Ont. M2P 1V8.

**FISHER, Barry Michael,** M.A., LL.M.; lawyer; b. Montreal, Que. 12 Aug. 1949; s. Patrick John and Phyllis Elanor (Hiron) F.; e. Loyola Coll. Montreal B.Com. 1970, B.A. 1971; Univ. of Toronto M.A. 1973; Univ. of W. Ont. LL.B. 1976 (Law Review Prize 1976); Cleveland Marshall Coll. of Law Ohio LL.M. 1985; m. Rosemary d. Doug and Dorthy McCarney 25 Aug. 1979; children: D'Arcy Elzye, Courtney Consitt, Dylan Patrick; Foreign Legal Cons. Thompson, Hine and Flory 1990–..; Law Clk. to Chief Justice High Court of Justice Supreme Court of Ont. 1978–79; present firm 1979–84; Fasken & Calvin 1984–85; Goodman & Carr 1985–86; Gowling & Henderson 1986–88; Gen. Counsel and Corporate Sec. Dickenson Group of Co's 1988–90; ed. 'Legal Aspects of Doing Business in Canada' 1983; author various articles profl. jours.; Founding Chrmn. Ctte. Candn. Law Am. Bar Assn. 1981–86, mem. Council Internat. Law 1984–86, ed. Candn. Law Newsletter 1981–86; Vice Chrmn. Ctte. Trade & Invest. Candn. Bar Assn. 1985–89, Vice Chrmn. & Sec. Internat. Law Sect. 1986–88; Chrmn., Internat. Comm. Dispute Res. Ctte. 1991– ; recreations: running, skiing, chess; Club: Ontario; Home: 1 Nanton Ave., Toronto, Ont. M4W 2Y8.

**FISHER, Douglas Mason,** B.A., B.L.S., LL.D.; political columnist; b. Sioux Lookout, Ont. 19 Sept. 1919; s. late Roy Waldon and late Eva Pearl (Mason) W.; e. Sioux Lookout Pub. Sch., 1926–30; Fort William, Ont. Collegiate, 1931–37; Univ. of Toronto, B.A. 1949, B.L.S. 1950; Lakehead Univ., LL.D. 1987; former Librarian, Port Arthur Collegiate; Forest Library, Northwestern Ont.; served as Trooper, 18th Armoured Car Regt. (12th Man. Dragoons) 1941–45; el. to H. of C. for Port Arthur 1957; el. Deputy House Leader (N.D.P.) May 1963; def. cand., York Centre to H. of C., g.e. June 1968; former Pol. Columnist for 'Toronto Telegram' and now for 'Toronto Sun,' 'Legion Magazine'; Commentator and producer for CJOH-TV, Ottawa; author of provincial inquiry 'The Policy and Programs of the Ontario Government for Recreation, Sport and Fitness' 1980; former Chrmn. of Bd., Hockey Canada; mem. Ont. Comn. on the Legislature 1972–75; Unitarian; Address: c/o Parliamentary Press Gallery, Ottawa, Ont. K1A 0A8.

**FISHER, Edward Joseph,** M.A., D.Sc.; optometrist; b. Winnipeg, Man. 25 Nov. 1913; s. Joseph Thomas and Margaret (Cobean) F.; e. Malvern Coll. Inst., Toronto, Ont.; Coll. of Optometry of Ont. (Grad.) 1934; Univ. of Toronto, B.A. 1946 and M.A. (Psychology) 1948; D.Sc. Pennsylvania College of Optometry, 1969; m. Eleanor Jessie Cambridge, d. late Rev. Gordon M. Holmes, 28 Sept. 1936; children: Margaret Eleanor, Gordon Joseph (dec.), Barbara Marion; PROF. EMERITUS, SCH. OF OPTOMETRY, UNIV. OF WATERLOO; Curator, Museum of Visual Science and Optometry; practised as an optometrist in Lindsay, Ont., 1934–37, and in Toronto, Ont., 1937–45 and 1953–67; apptd. part-time Demonst. and Lectr. at the Coll. of Optometry of Ont. 1937 and full-time Lectr. 1945; apptd. Dean 1948–67; Dir., School of Optometry, Univ. of Waterloo 1967–1975; Prof., Univ. of Waterloo 1967–83; Prof. Emeritus 1987; Visiting Prof., Univ. of Benin, Nigeria 1976–84; Visting Prof., The City University, London 1976; mem., Optometrical Assn. of Ont.; Candn. Coll. of Organists; Fellow and Councillor and Past Pres. (1st non-resident), Am. Acad. of Optometry; rec'd Cert. of Merit, Univ. of Montreal 1961, Centennial Medal 1967; President's Award, Candn. Assn. of Optometrists 1971, James Cobean Mem. Award 1975; Phi Theta Upsilon; Freemason; Baptist; Address: Univ. of Waterloo, Waterloo, Ont. N2L 3G1.

**FISHER, Francis John Fulton,** M.Sc., Ph.D.; university professor; b. Roxburgh, New Zealand 31 Oct. 1926; s. Francis Vivian and Enid Fanny Hertzlet (Fulton) F.; e. Cathedral Grammar Sch. & Christ's Coll. (N.Z.) 1937–42; Canterbury Coll., Christchurch B.Sc., M.Sc. 1943–48; Univ. of N.Z. Ph.D. 1954; 1st m. Jocelyn d. George and Doris Purvis 8 May 1949; children: Paul, Hugh, Janis, Iona, John; 2nd m.: Patricia d. William and Joan McLeod 1 July 1984; one d.: Katherine; PROF., BIOLOGICAL SCIENCES, SIMON FRASER UNIV. 1967– ; Lectr., Univ. of Melbourne 1954–56; Sr. Lectr., Univ. of Tasmania 1957–58; Dir., Tasmanian Botanical Gardens 1957–58; Principal Sci. Offr., Dept. Sci. & Indus. Rsch., N.Z. 1959–65; Dep. Head, Biosciences, Simon Fraser Univ. 1965–66; Fac. Assoc., Dept. of Edn., SFU 1989–92; Univ. of N.Z. Rsch. Scholar 1949–59; Nuffield Found. Rsch. Scholar 1951–53; Carnegie Corp. Travel Scholarship 1955–56; Rsch. Fellow, Carnegie Inst. of Washington 1955–56; Brit. Counc. Schol. 1955–56; U.S. Public Health Serv. Scholar 1963–66; Fellow, Linnean Soc. of London 1954– ; Fellow, Soc. de Biogéographie Paris 1956– ; Simon Fraser Univ. Excellence in Teaching Award 1987; author: 'Variation and Evolution in the Alpine *Ranunculi* of New Zealand' 1965 & 44 papers in plant physiology, ecol., evolution, social change & values; Home: #27412, 104th Ave., Maple Ridge, B.C. V0M 1S0; Office: Burnaby, B.C. V5A 1S6.

**FISHER, Glen Thomas,** B.Eng., B.Comm.; executive, engineer; b. Montreal, Que. 8 July 1934; s. Frederick Sorley and Helena Millicent (Denovan) F.; e. McGill Univ. B.Eng. 1957; Concordia Univ. B.Comm. 1970; m. Susan d. Jack and Margaret Rachlis 30 March 1980; CHRMN. & CHIEF EXTVE. OFFR., CPCS LTD. 1993– ; var. positions with several telecommunications-related companies 1957–69; Dir., Tech. Rsch. & Devel., Candn. Pacific Limited 1969; Special Projects & Intermodal Devel. 1971; Vice-Pres. & Gen. Mgr., Candn. Pacific Cons. Serv. Limited 1974; Pres. 1981–82; Pres. & Chief Extve. Offr. 1982–89, company name changed to CPCS Ltd. 1989, Pres. & Chief Extve. Offr. 1989–93; worldwide experience in consulting field; Mem., Order of Engrs. of Que. (Dir. 1972–75; Vice-Pres., Finance 1974–75); Assn. of Profl. Engrs. of Ont.; Assn. of Profl. Engrs. of B.C.; Sr. Mem., Rsch. Ctte., Assn. of Am. Railroads 1972–74; Founding Mem., Inst. of Guided Ground Transport, Queen's Univ.; Gov., Vanier College 1975–82 (Chrmn. 1976–78); Concordia Univ. 1978–84 (Vice-Chrmn. 1979); author of several published papers & articles; recreations: sailing, photography, skiing; clubs: Rideau, Pointe Claire Yacht; Home: 142 Jasper Rd., Beaconsfield, Que. H9W 5S1; Office: 740 Notre-Dame St. W., Suite 760, Montreal, Que. H3C 3X6.

**FISHER, Harry K.,** B.A., B.Ed., M.Ed., Ph.D., LL.D.; public servant; b. Stratford, Ont. 23 Sept. 1930; s. Andrew K. and Mary C. (Fraser) F.; e. Univ. of W. Ont. B.A. 1953; Univ. of Toronto B.Ed. 1955, M.Ed. 1958, Ph.D. 1975; Lakehead Univ. LL.D. 1983; m. Lenore d. Percy and Ethel Radbourne 3 July 1954; two d. Kathryn Jane, Janet Mary; Dean, Fac. of Educ., Univ. of Western Ont. 1989–91; Dir. Gen. Council of Ministers of Education, Can. 1984–88; Insp. of Schs. Muskoka 1958–61;

Supt. of Schs. Welland 1961–66; Dir. Special Edn. Ont. Govt. 1969–72, Asst. Dep. Min. Adm. 1974–79, Dep. Min. of Colls. & Univs. and of Edn. 1979–84; Chrmn. Ctte. to Study Future Role of Univs. in Ont. 1980–81; first Candn. Rep. Internat. Bureau of Edn. 1986–89; mem. Exec. Bd. Candn. Comn. UNESCO 1985–88; mem. Bd. Idea Corp. Ont. 1982–84; Exec. Bd. Centre Ednl. Rsch. Innovation OECD 1979–81; Hon. Life mem. Candn. Edn. Assn. (1st Vice Pres. 1984–85); Home: 436 William St., Stratford, Ont. N5A 4Y6.

**FISHER, James D.,** B.A., M.B.A.; executive; b. Toronto, Ont. 18 March 1942; s. Frank Henry and Ruby (Roberts) F.; e. Univ. of Toronto, B.A. 1964; Harvard Bus. Sch., M.B.A. 1968; m. Mary d. Bruce and Elizabeth Charles; children: Kathryn, Charles, Amy; PRESIDENT, GEORGE WESTON NORTH AMERICAN BAKERIES 1993– ; Dir. Weston Foods Ltd. 1986– ; Chrmn., Stroehmann Bakeries Inc. 1991– ; joined The Toronto Dominion Bank 1968–70; McKinsey & Co. 1968–70; Co-Founder and Dir. The Canada Consulting Group Inc. 1970–86; Gov., Metro Central YMCA; Vice-Chrmn., ICAST (Internat. Ctr. for Agricultural Sci. & Technol.); Baker Scholar, Harvard Bus. Sch. 1968; recreations: tennis, triathlons, skiing, rowing, travel; Clubs: Osler Bluffs; Badminton & Racquet; Donalda; Office 501, 22 St. Clair Ave. E., Toronto, Ont. M4T 2S7.

**FISHER, John Philip,** B.E.; executive; b. Knowlton, Qué. 9 June 1927; s. Philip Sydney and Margaret Linton (Southam) F.; e. Royal Candn. Naval Coll. 1946; McGill Univ. B.E. 1951; m. Jean V. d. Malcolm S. and Grace MacKay 1978; children: Amanda, Elizabeth, Julia, Robert, Adam, Simon; joined Dominion Engineering Works Montréal 1951, Mktg. Mgr. Pulp & Paper 1971–75; Sr. Vice Pres. Devel. Fraser Inc. Edmundston, N.B. 1975, Extve. Vice Pres. 1975, Pres. 1976, Chrmn. and C.E.O. 1982; Pres. & C.E.O., Southam Inc. 1985–92; Chrmn., Counc. for Business and the Arts in Canada; National Community Tree Found.; Pres., Alva Found.; recreations: sailing, tennis, skiing; Clubs: Mount Royal; Toronto; York; Home: Ste. 1003, 175 Cumberland St., Toronto, Ont. M5R 3M9.

**FISHER, Murray M.,** B.A., M.D., Ph.D., F.R.C.P.(C); physician; educator; b. Gravenhurst, Ont. 15 Jan. 1934; s. Dr. Murray M. and Martha B. (Rome) F.; e. St. Andrew's Coll., Aurora, Ont., 1947–52 (Head Boy 1952); Univ. of W. Ont., B.A. 1957; Univ. of Toronto, M.D. 1958; Univ. of London, Ph.D. 1963; Diploma, Wine and Sarit Education Trust 1993; m. 2ndly Marion Ellen Paradine Britnell 5 May 1983; children: Mary Martha, David Malcolm, Suzanne Elizabeth; Assoc. Prof., Dept. of Pathol. and Dept. of Med., Univ. of Toronto; Co-Founder and Dir., Upper Canada Lower Bowel Clinic; Chrmn., Environment Protection Laboratories Inc.; Residency Program, Toronto Gen. Hosp., 1958–59, 1963–65; MRC Fellow, Univ. Coll. London and Royal Free Hosp., London, Eng., 1959–63; Res. Assoc., Dept. of Pathol., Univ. of Pittsburgh, 1965–68; Head, Div. of Gastroenterology, Sunnybrook Medical Center 1975–86; Vice Pres. (Rsch.), Sunnybrook Med. Ctr. 1985–87; Founding Mem. and Resource Ctte., Candn. Liver Foundation; rec'd Gold Medal Award, Royal Coll. Phys. & Surgs. 1972; Lectr., Royal Coll. of Phys. & Surgs. 1984; author of various papers relating to liver disease and bile acid metabolism; mem., Am. Assn. Advanc. Science; A.O.A.; Candn. Assn. Gastroenterol.; N.Y. Acad. Sciences; Zeta Psi; Protestant; recreation: gastronomy; Clubs: Granite; Caledon Mountain; Home: 76 Braeside Rd., Toronto, Ont. M4N 1X7.

**FISHER, Paul Taylor,** B.A., LL.B.; lawyer; b. Toronto, Ont. 15 Sept. 1946; s. James Taylor and Jean Mackenzie (Bauslaugh) F.; e. Univ. of Toronto, B.A. (Hons.) 1968; Osgoode Hall Law Sch., York Univ., LL.B. 1972; called to Ont. Bar 1974; m. Margaret d. James and Constance Barr 25 Apr. 1981; children: James Barr Fisher, Christopher Barr Fisher, Alexandra Barr Fisher; VICE PRES., CANADIAN IMPERIAL BANK OF COMMERCE 1989– , CORPORATE SECY. 1990– ; Student-at-accts., Clarkson & Gordon 1968–69; articled, Fraser & Beatty 1972–73; Solicitor 1974–77; Counsel, The Lummus Co. Can. Ltd. 1977–80; Gen. Couns. & Sec., Kellogg Salada Can. Inc. 1980–85, Vice Pres., Human Resources & Public Affairs & Secy. 1985–89; Dir. & Secy., Transportation & Communications Associates Ltd. 1989– ; Pres. & Dir., Imbank Nominees Ltd. 1990– ; Dir., Univ. of Toronto Schs. Alumni Assn. (Pres. 1989–91); mem., Law Soc. of Upper Can. 1974– ; Candn. Bar Assn. (Found. Chrmn., Ont. Corp. Couns. Section 1978–79; Ont. Counc. 1980–81, 1983–87; Membership Ctte., 1982–83; Fin. Review Ctte. 1984–87; Chrmn. 1986–87); Dir., Couchiching Inst. on Public Affairs (Pres. 1986–88); Public Affairs Assn. (Founding Dir.); Candn. Inst. of Internat. Affairs; recreations: sailing, skiing, squash; Clubs: Royal Candn. Yacht; Devils Glen Ski; Bd. of Trade of Metro Toronto; Home: 256 Cortleigh Blvd., Toronto, Ont. M5N 1P7; Office: Toronto, Ont.

**FISHER, Robin,** M.A., Ph.D.; educator; b. Palmerston North, N.Z. 24 Feb. 1946; s. Anthony Hornbrook and Miriel Abernethy (Hancox) F.; e. Palmerston N. Boys High Sch. 1964; Massey Univ., B.A. 1967; Univ. of Auckland, M.A. 1969; Univ. of B.C., Ph.D. 1974; two s. Manu Paul, Keri Anthony; CHAIR OF HISTORY, UNIV. OF NORTHERN BRITISH COLUMBIA 1993– ; Jr. Lectr. in Hist. Massey Univ. 1970; Asst. Prof., Simon Fraser Univ. 1974, Assoc. Prof. 1977, Prof. of Hist. 1983–93; recipient John A. Macdonald Prize, Candn. Hist. Assn. 1977; Dafoe Book Prize 1992; author: 'Contact and Conflict: Indian-European Relations in British Columbia 1774–1890' 1977; 'Duff Pattullo of British Columbia' 1991; 'Vancouver's Voyage: Charting the Northwest Coast, 1791-1795' 1993'; co-editor: 'Captain James Cook and His Times' 1979; 'An Account of a Voyage to the North West Coast of America in 1785 and 1786 by Alexander Walker' 1982; 'Candn. Hist. Review' 1984–87; 'Maps and Metaphors: The Pacific World of George Vancouver' 1993; Office: History Programme, Univ. of Northern B.C., P.O. Bag 1950, Stn. A, Prince George, B.C. V2L 5Y2.

**FISHER, (Frank) Ronald,** C.D., B.Sc., M.D., F.R.C.P.(C); physician; b. Kamloops, B.C. 1 Jan. 1945; s. Frank and Anne F.; e. Charles Bloom Jr.-Sr. High Sch. Lumby, B.C. 1962; Univ. of B.C., B.Sc. 1966, M.D. 1970, Specialty in Phys. Med. & Rehab. 1978; m. Mary Jane d. Carl and Evelyn Taylor 23 Apr. 1983; children: Julia Dawn, Jordan Ronald; STAFF PHYSIATRIST, GREATER VICTORIA HOSPITAL SOC., GORGE ROAD REHABILITATION CENTRE 1993– ; Chrmn. Med. Adv. Ctte., Bd. Trustees (Exec. & Admin. Cttes.), Bd. Dirs. Found., Royal Ottawa Health Care Group; mem. Univ./Hosp. Relations Ctte.; Adv. Bd. Dept. of Med. Univ. of Ottawa, Assoc. Prof. 1986–93, Chrmn. Div. of Phys. Med. & Rehab. 1985–93; mem. Jt. Chiefs of Staff; Physiatrist-in-Chief, Ottawa Rehabilitation Centre 1985–93; Program Dir., Chronic Pain Program, Rehab. Ctr. 1991–93, Chrmn. Rehab. Adv. Ctte.; Chrmn.: Associates in Rehab. Med. Ottawa, Chrmn. Exec. Ctte.; Cons. in Phys. Med. & Rehab. St. Vincent's Hosp., Ottawa Gen. Hosp., Chrmn., Peer Review Team Augmentative Communication Devices, Assistive Devices Prog., Govt. Ont. 1988–91; Mem., Adv. Ctte., Assistive Devices Prog., Govt. Ont. 1987–89; Mem., Fed. Govt. Task Force on Guidelines for Chronic Pain Facilities in Institutions 1987– ; Mem., Continuing Care Bd., Ottawa-Carleton District Health Counc. 1988– ; Chrmn., Task Force on Delivery of Assistive Devices Prog., Cont. Care Bd., D.H.C. 1988–89; mem. Orthotics & Prosthetics Subctte. Assistive Devices Prog. Govt. Ont. 1984–87; Health Adv. Services Ad Hoc Ctte. Fed. Govt. Can. 1983; mem. Dist. Health Council Ctte. Long Range Planning Special Rehab.; Med. Offr. 2nd Bn. P.P.C.L.I. Winnipeg 1971–72; Med. Offr. and Flight Surgeon CFB Moose Jaw, Sask. 1972–74; Head of Rehab. Med. Nat. Defence Med. Centre Ottawa and Cons. to Surgeon Gen. Candn. Forces 1979–84; recipient Residents' Rsch. Projects First Prize 1978; Leslie Trulove Meml. Award Outstanding Resident in Phys. Med. & Rehab. 1979; Fellow, Shaughnessy Hosp. Vancouver 1978–79; various rsch. grants Fitness Can., Univ. of Ottawa; co-author 'Handbook of Amputations and Prostheses' 1982; med. dir. 'A Higher Courage' Nat. Film Bd. Can. 1984; author or co-author various articles, abstracts; mem. Candn. Assn. Phys. Med. & Rehab.; Acupuncture Found. Can.; Internat. Soc. Prosthetics & Orthotics; Assn. Acad. Physiatrists; Ont. Med. Assn.; Candn. Med. Assn.; Candn. Pain Soc.; recreations: woodwork, antiques, art; Home: 111 – 3954 Cedar Hill Rd., Victoria, B.C. V8N 3B9; Office: Gorge Rd. Hosp., 63 Gorge Rd. E., Victoria, B.C. V9A 1L2.

**FISHER, S. Brian,** C.A., H.B.Math.; chartered accountant; b. Kitchener, Ont. 27 Feb. 1949; s. Stewart M. and Betty B. (King) F.; e. Univ. of Waterloo H.B.Math (Statistics) 1972; C.A. 1976; m. Christine d. Clarence Barrie and Janine Ilowski 22 Aug. 1974; children: Dianne, Darryl; PARTNER, PEAT MARWICK THORNE 1989– ; Mem., Partnership Board of Peat Marwick Thorne 1993– ; Partner, Thorne Riddell 1982, Nat. Dir. of Taxation 1985; Thorne Ernst & Whinney, Nat. Dir. of Taxation 1986, Partner in Charge of Taxation (Kitchener and Cambridge) 1988; Peat Marwick Thorne, Partner in Charge of Taxation, (Kitchener, Waterloo, Cambridge & Guelph) 1989; Nat. Commodity Tax Co-ord., Thorne Ernst & Whinney 1986–89; Business Taxation Course, Wilfrid Laurier 1978; Taxation Course, Conestoga College 1981; CICA & Ont. Inst. Tax Courses 1987, '89, '90, '94; Mem., Internat. Fiscal Assn.; Candn. Tax Found.; Peat Marwick Thorne Strategic Planning & Nat. Tax cttes.; editor: '1994 Canadian Personal Tax Planning Guide'; recreations: golf, curling; club: Westmount Golf & Country; Home: Waterloo, Ont.; Office: 180 Columbia St. W., Waterloo, Ont. N2L 3L3.

**FISHER, William Arthur,** B.A., M.S., Ph.D.; university professor; b. Brooklyn, N.Y. 23 Apr. 1952; s. Silvan and Helen (Friedberg) F.; e. Tel Aviv Univ., B.A. 1974; Purdue Univ., M.S. 1976, Ph.D. 1978; m. Randi d. Murray and Shirley Beckenstein 10 Aug. 1975; children: Benjamin, Daniel, Sarah; PROF. OF PSYCHOL., UNIV. OF WEST. ONT. 1991– , PROF. OF OBSTETRICS & GYN. 1992– ; Asst. Prof., present univ. 1978, Assoc. Prof. 1984; Chair, Social Psych. Prog. 1985–87; Vis. Prof., McMaster Univ. 1984; Sheba Med. Ctr. & Technion Fac. of Med. 1985; Tel Aviv Univ. 1989; Consultant 1980– ; Fellow, Soc. for the Sci. Study of Sex; Mem., Soc. of Exper. Soc. Psych.; Awards for Excellence in Teaching: The Dept. of Psych. 1982; U.W.O. 1989; Ont. Confed. of Univ. Fac. Assn. 1989; Cons., Health & Welfare Can., Expert Interdisciplinary Adv. Ctte. on Sexually Transmitted Disease; rsch. grants: SSHRCC, Health & Walfare Can., Nat. Inst. of Mental Health; Bd. of Dir., The Planned Parenthood Fed. of Can. 1986–92; of Ont. 1982–85; Adv. Bd., The Sex Info. & Edn. Counc. of Can.; co-editor: 'Adolescents, Sex and Contraception' 1983; author of over 60 scholarly papers; recreation: travel; Office: London, Ont. N6A 5C2.

**FISHER, William J.,** B.A., M.B.A.; executive; educator; b. Windsor, Ont. 27 Aug. 1928; s. George Lewis and Mary Alma (McCarthy) F.; e. Assumption High Sch. Windsor 1945; Assumption Coll. Windsor B.A. 1950; Univ. of Detroit M.B.A. 1952; m. Anna d. Wasil and Edna Belawetz 10 Sept. 1956; children: Mary, Bill, Anne, John; EXEC.-IN-RESIDENCE AND HONORARY PROFESSOR, SCH. OF BUS. ADM. UNIV. OF WINDSOR 1989– ; mem. Bd. Govs., Univ. of Windsor (Chrmn., Bd. of Govs. 1989–91); Ind. Relations Rsch. Analyst Ford Motor Co. of Canada Ltd. Windsor 1952; Mgmt. Devel. Coordinator/Staff Specialist/Labour Relations Coordinator Chrysler Canada Ltd. Windsor 1956, Personnel Dir. 1977, Vice Pres. Human Resources 1985–89; Supr. Employee Benefits-Corporate Chrysler Corp. Highland Park, Mich. 1959 and Mgr. 1966; mem. Adv. Bd. Brentwood (Alcohol & Drug Abuse Centre); Mem., Bd. of Regents, Assumption Univ.; Mem., Ont. Pension Bd.; Mem., Ont. Workplace Health and Safety Agency Bd.; Past Chrmn., Ind. Relations Ctte. Motor Vehicle Mfrs. Assn.; Past Dir. Windsor C. of C.; recreations: running, walking, golf; Club: Beach Grove Golf & Country (St. Clair Beach, Ont.); Home: 237 Burlington Rd., St. Clair Beach, Ont. N8N 1H3; Office: 401 Sunset Ave., Windsor, Ont. N9B 3P4.

**FISHWICK, Duncan,** M.A., D.Litt., F.R.S.C., F.S.A., F.R.H.S.; educator; b. Adlington, Lancs. UK 12 May 1929; s. Joseph and Elva (Lamb) F.; e. Preston Cath. Coll. 1947; Manchester Univ. B.A. 1950; Oxford Univ. B.A. 1953, M.A. 1956; Leiden Univ. D.Litt. 1976; m. Birgit d. Emil and Hanna Natanaellson 29 Dec. 1963; children: Birgitta, Peter, Steven; UNIVERSITY PROFESSOR, UNIV. OF ALTA. 1986– ; Lectr. McGill Univ. 1956–57; Asst. Prof. St. Michael's Coll. Univ. of Toronto 1957–64; Assoc. Prof. St. Francis Xavier Univ. 1964–71; Assoc. Prof. present Univ. 1971, Prof. of Classics 1975–86, University Prof. 1986– , Chrmn. of Classics 1987–92; recipient Univ. Alta. Rsch. Prize 1985, McCalla Rsch. Prof. 1985–86; numerous research awards; author 'Studies in Roman Imperial History' 1976; 'The Imperial Cult in the Latin West' Vol. I, 1–2, 1987; Vol. II, 1–2, 1991/1992; co-author 'The Foundations of the West' 1964; over 95 articles, numerous reviews internat. jours.; Associé correspondant étranger, Société Nationale des Antiquaires de France; Corr. der Koninklijke Nederlandse Akademie van Wetenschappen; Corr., Étranger Acad. des Inscr. et Belles-Lettres, Inst. de France; R. Catholic; recreations; golf; Home: 3615 – 114 A St., Edmonton, Alta. T0J 1N2; Office: Humanities Centre, Edmonton, Alta. T6G 2F6.

**FITCH, Brian Thomas,** B.A., Dr.de l'U., F.R.S.C.; professor; author; publisher; b. London, Eng. 19 Nov. 1935; s. Thomas Charles and Hilda (Parish) F.; e. Kings Coll. Univ. of Durham B.A. 1958; Univ. de Strasbourg Dr.de l'U. 1962; m. Josette d. late Aurélien François Jean Albert Ramel 29 Aug. 1959; children: Rafaëlla, Fabrice Julian, Sébastien Aïtor; UNIVERSITY PROFESSOR 1989– ; GERALD LARKIN PROF. OF FRENCH TRINITY COLL. UNIV. OF TORONTO 1966– ; Lecteur d'Anglais Univ. de Strasbourg 1960–62; Asst. Lectr. in French Manchester Univ. 1962–65; Visiting Assoc. Prof. of French present Coll. 1965–66, Head of French 1971–

75, Assoc. Chrmn. Grad. Studies in French present Univ. 1977–81; Visiting Sen. Research Fellow, Merton College, Oxford 1970; Visiting Prof. Bar-Ilan Univ. Israel 1983; Visiting Prof., Montpellier Univ. 1993; Can. Counc. Leave Fellowships 1970–71, 1976–77, 1982–83; Connaught Sr. Fellowship 1988–89; Founding Ed. 'Albert Camus' Journal 1968–87; Founding Co-Ed., 'Texte' 1982– ; Dir. Littéraire, Lettres Modernes, Paris 1969–90; Co-founder, Editions Paratexte 1985– ; author 'Narrateur et narration dans "L'Etranger" d'Albert Camus' 1960, 2nd ed. 1968; 'Les Deux Univers romanesques d'André Malraux' 1964; 'Le Sentiment d'étrangeté chez Malraux, Sartre, Camus et S. de Beauvoir' 1964, 2nd ed. 1983; 'Essai de bibliographie des études en langue française consacrées à Albert Camus 1937–62' 1965, 2nd ed. (1937–67) 1969, 3rd ed. (1937–70) 1972; 'Dimensions et structures chez Bernanos' 1969; '"L'Etranger" de Camus: un texte, ses lecteurs, leurs lectures' 1972; 'Dimensions, structures et textualité dans la trilogie romanesque de Samuel Beckett' 1977; 'The Narcissistic Text: A Reading of Camus' Fiction' 1982; 'Monde à l'envers/texte réversible: la fiction de Bataille' 1982; 'Beckett and Babel: an Investigation into the Status of the Bilingual Work' 1988; 'Reflections in the Mind's Eye: Reference and its Problematization in Twentieth-Century French Fiction' 1991; 'Lire les récits de Maurice Blanchot' 1992; '"The Fall": A Matter of Guilt' 1994; Ed. 'Configuration critique de Julien Green' 1964; 'Ecrivains de la Modernité' 1981; mem. Modern Lang. Assn. Am.; Candn. Assn. Univ. Teachers; Candn. Comp. Lit. Assoc.; Home: 71 Charles St. E., Ste. 1504, Toronto, Ont. M4Y 2T3; Office: Toronto, Ont. M5S 1H8.

**FITZGERALD, David Anthony,** F.C.A. financial executive; b. Brighton, England 15 May 1931; s. Edward Joseph and Marjorie Elizabeth (Richardson) F.; e. Xaverian Coll. Brighton Eng.; Brit. Coll. of Accountancy, Harpenden Eng.; m. Pauline d. Raymond and Ann Pitt 29 Aug. 1957; children: Andrew, John, Katherine, Stephen; Group Extve. Vice-Pres., Grosvenor Internat. Holdings 1989–90; various positions in England 1964; Sec./Treas., Ludlow Jute Co. Ltd., Calcutta India 1964–69; Treas., Grosvenor Internat. (Hawaii) Ltd. 1969–74; Chief Finan. Offr., present firm 1974–89; F.I.C.A. (England & Wales); Assoc., Chartered Inst. of Mngt. Accountants; recreations: tennis, swimming, walking, scuba; clubs: Hollyburn Country, Vancouver; Home: 3930 Marine Dr., W. Vancouver, B.C. V7V 1N4.

**FITZGERALD, The Hon. Gerald L.,** B.A., LL.B.; judge; b. Exeter, Ont. 10 Sept. 1942; s. John L. and Helen A. (Cameron) F.; e. St. Dunstan's, B.A. 1965; Dalhousie Univ., LL.B. 1969; Univ. d'Aix-Marseille (France), dipl. de Langue 1984; m. Lynda d. George and Rita Olscamp 10 July 1971; children: Bethanie, Garrett; JUDGE, PROVINCIAL COURT OF P.E.I. 1974– ; called to P.E.I. Bar 1970; law prac., Summerside, P.E.I. 1970–74; Judge, Provincial Court 1974– , Chief Judge 1990–91; labour arbitrator; active in home & sch. assn.; Mem., Candn. Assn. of Prov. Court Judges; Club: Pony; Home: 56 Ambrose St., Charlottetown, P.E.I. C1A 3P6; Office (Chambers): Law Courts Bldg., 42 Water St., Charlottetown, P.E.I. C1A 8B9.

**FITZGERALD, Judith Ariana,** B.A., M.A.; poet; literary critic; b. Toronto, Ont. 11 Nov. 1952; e. York Univ., B.A. (Hons.) 1976, M.A. 1977; writer for num. nat. & internat. mags. & periodicals; Writer-in-Residence, Univ. of Windsor 1993–94; syndicated columnist 'CountrySide' The Toronto Star (SouthamStar Network) 1991–93; Poetry Ed., Black Moss Press 1981–87; Poetry Critic, 'The Toronto Star' 1984–88; Toronto Lit. Corr., 'The Ottawa Citizen' 1985–86; In-house Ed., General Publishing 1985; Entertainment Jour., 'The Globe' 1983–84; Teacher, Erindale Coll. 1978–81; Prof., Laurentian Univ. 1981–83; part-time teaching, Glendon Coll. & Algoma Univ. Coll.; co-ord. sev. workshops; writer-in-res., sev. insts.; Ont. Grad. Scholarship; Fiona Mee Award for an outstanding contbr. to Eng.-lang. lit. journalism 1983; Arts Grant 'A' 1988, 1990, 1991 and 1994; Arts Grant 'B' 1983; Can. Counc. Explorations and External Affairs grants; Ont. Arts Counc. 'Works-in-Progress' & Toronto Arts Counc. grants; author: 'River' 1994; 'walkin' wounded' 1993; 'Habit of Blues' 1993; 'Ultimate Midnight' 1992; 'Rapturous Chronicles' 1991 (shortlisted for Governor General's Award in Poetry); 'Diary of Desire' 1987; 'Given Names' 1985 (Writers' Choice Award 1986), 'Beneath the Skin of Paradise' 1984, 'Heart Attacks' 1984, 'Split/Levels' 1983, 'Easy Over' 1981, 'Lacerating Heartwood' 1977, 'Victory' 1975, 'Journal Entries' 1975, 'City Park' 1972 (poetry); 'Whale Waddleby' 1986, 'My Orange Gorange' 1985 (children's poetry); editor: 'First Person Plural' 1988; 'Sp/Elles: Poetry by Canadian Women/Poésie de femmes canadiennes' 1986, 'Un Dozen: Thirteen Canadian Poets' 1982; anthols. incl. 'Canadian Poetry Now,' 'The New Canadian Poets,' 'Singularities,' 'Oxford Book of Poetry by Canadian Women'; columnist, 'Innings' 1985–87; 'Poetic Licence', 'Toronto Star' 1987; Address: Dept. of English, Univ. of Windsor, Windsor, Ont. N9B 3P4.

**FITZGERALD, Pamela R.;** health care executive; b. Montreal, Que. 8 Apl. 1954; d. George H. and Lorraine M. (Bruyere) F.; e. McGill Univ. D.C.S. 1974; Univ. of Cal. Berkeley grad. studies pub. health; m. Evert s. Adrian and Pearl Hoogers 3 Sept. 1989; two children: Nickolas F., Gabriel A.; EXEC. COORDINATOR CANDN. HEALTH COALITION 1989– ; Chief Exec. Offr. Operation Dismantle 1987–89; Project Coordinator Candn. Council Social Devel. 1986; Sr. Cons. Infolink Consultants 1985–86; Coordinator Ont. Pub. Interest Rsch. 1983–85; Jr. Pub. Health Chem. Cal. Dept. Health 1975–76; mem., Bob Hale Found.; author, ed. various publs.; recreations: bicycling, reading; Home: 5 Pansy Ave., Ottawa, Ont. K1S 2W5; Office: 2841 Riverside Dr., Ottawa, Ont. K1V 8X7.

**FITZGERALD, Richard P.,** B.Com.; business executive; b. Montreal, Que. 29 March 1952; s. Royden Patrick and Eleanor (Spry) F.; e. Concordia Univ. B.Com. 1978; m. Michèle d. Marie-France Bordeleau 15 March 1974; one d. Marie-France; PRES. AND CHIEF EXTVE. OFFICER, UNITED DISTILLERS CANADA 1992– ; joined Financial Publishing Co. of Canada Ltd. 1970–72; Reader's Digest (Association) of Canada Ltd. 1972–78; Benson & Hedges (Canada) Inc. 1978–84; Exec. Vice Pres., Sales and Mktg. Schenley Canada Inc. 1985–90; Pres. & C.E.O., United Distillers Canada Inc. 1991; Dir. Can. Safety Council; recreations: skiing, squash, cycling; Clubs: Mount Royal Club; M.A.A.A.; Home: 900 38th Ave., Lachine, Que. H8T 2C3; Office: 2200, 600 de Maisonneuve Blvd. W., Montreal, Que. H3A 3J2.

**FITZGERALD, William Raymond,** M.B.A., B.S.E.E.; aerospace industry executive; b. Chicago, Ill. 21 May 1937; s. William John and Ellen Bernadette (Cornfield) F.; e. Christian Brothers Univ. B.S.E.E. 1959; Univ. of Chicago M.B.A. 1968; m. Judith d. Rudolph and Anne Gawlik 17 Nov. 1962; children: William J., Michael P., John David; GROUP PRESIDENT, SPAR AEROSPACE LTD.; over thirty years in high tech. communications indus.; career began with ITT in US; spent over 15 years in US manned space and defence indus.; last 10 years devoted to domestic & internat. satellite communications systems; Pres., CITEC, R & D Ctte.; Trustee, Christian Brothers Univ.; Dir., RSI Inc.; CITR;Jaycee Man of the Year 1968; Home: Box 606, Hudson, Que. J0P 1H0; Office: 21025 Trans Canada Hwy., St. Anne de Bellevue, Que. H9X 3R2.

**FITZGIBBON, Gerald Michael,** C.M., O.M.M., O.St.J., C.D., L.R.C.P.&S.(Ireland), F.R.C.P.(C), F.A.C.C., F.A.C.P.; cardiologist; consultant; b. La Paz, Bolivia 24 Nov. 1926; s. Frederick Joseph and Hannah Elizabeth (Müller) F.; e. abroad; secondary edn. S.Africa; Royal Coll. Surgs. Ireland L.R.C.P.&S. 1952; postgrad. training Internal Med. & Cardiol. Toronto, London & Kingston, Ont. completed 1960; m. Maud Eileen d. Henry and Maud Stephens Rouse 21 Feb. 1947; two d. Hilary Jane, Gillian Ruth; served as M.O. RCAF and Candn. Forces 1952–70 incl. tour at RCAF Inst. Aviation Med. Toronto 1953–56; Specialist Phys. Fed. Pub. Service 1970–89; Dir. Cardio-Pulmonary Unit Nat. Defence Med. Centre Ottawa 1961–89, sometime Chief of Med. Staff, currently Cons. in Cardiol.; Assoc. Prof. of Med. (Cardiol.) Univ. of Ottawa; Past Chrmn. Adv. Ctte. Biomed. Eng. Nat. Rsch. Council Can.; author or co-author numerous papers Cardiol. various Med. Jours.; numerous presentations Learned Soc's; mem. Candn. Cardiovascular Soc.; Anglican; Liberal; recreations: music, history, gardening; Home: 1891 Florida Ave., Ottawa, Ont. K1H 6Y9; Office: Cardio-Pulmonary Unit, National Defence Medical Centre, Ottawa, Ont. K1A 0K6.

**FITZGIBBON, Pierre,** B.A.A., C.A.; chartered accountant; b. Montreal, Que. 10 Nov. 1954; s. Jacques and Yvette (Lauzon) F.; e. Univ. of Montreal, Hautes Etudes Commercials B.A.A. 1978; C.A. 1978; VICE-PRESIDENT CORP. DEVELOPMENT & TREASURER, DOMTAR INC. 1993– ; Senior Manager, Financial Services, Price Waterhouse 1978–88; Vice-Pres. Finance & Chief Financial Offr., Peerless Carpet Corp. 1988–93; Office: 395 de Maisonneuve Blvd. Ouest, Montreal, Que. H3A 1L6.

**FITZHARRIS, Tim,** B.A.; photographer/writer; b. Richmond, Indiana 23 Mar. 1948; s. Arthur Leonard and Erma Lois (Beckett) F.; e. Wilfrid Laurier Univ., B.A. 1969; grad., Stratford Teacher's Coll.; single; FREELANCE PHOTOGRAPHER / WRITER (B.C.) 1978– ; Public & H.S. Teacher, Ont. & Alta. 1970–76; Lectr. in Photography, S. Alta. Inst. of Technol. 1977–78; author/photographer: 'The Island' 1983, 'The Wild Prairie' 1983, 'The Adventure of Nature Photographer' 1983, 'British Columbia Wild' 1986, 'Wildflowers of Canada' 1987, 'Wild Birds of Canada' 1989; photographer: 'Canada: A Natural History' 1988; photographer/writer: 'The Audubon Society Guide to Nature Photography' 1990; 'Forest: A National Audubon Society Book' 1991; 'Wild Wings: An Introduction to Bird Watching' 1992; photographer: 'West Coast Wildlife' 1991.

**FITZHENRY, Robert E.;** business executive; b. Hamilton, Ont. 12 Feb. 1930; s. Charles and Margaret Frances (Regan) F.; e. McMaster Univ. B.A. (Hons.) 1954; m. Andrée d. Marguerite and Marcel Rhéaume 22 June 1984; children: Ann Elizabeth (Bedard), Mary Patricia (Shaw), Sean Robert, Michael Joseph, Alexandra Harvey; VICE CHRMN. & CHIEF OPERATING OFFICER, WOODBRIDGE GROUP OF COMPANIES 1978– ; Mktg., Paints Div., Can. Ind. Ltd. 1954–61, Merchandising Mgr. 1961–69; Mktg. Dir., Urethane Foam Div., Monsanto Can. Ltd. 1969–72, Bus. Dir. 1973–75, Consumer Prod. Div. 1975–78; Dir., Candn. Manoir Indus. Ltd.; Cartex Corp.; Delaware Seat Co.; Riverside Seat Co.; Woodbridge Foam Corp.; Woodbridge Corp.; Woodbridge-Inoac Inc.; Past Chrmn., Automotive Parts Manufacturers Assoc.; Past Pres., Polyurethane Foam Assoc.; Clubs: Nicholson Island; Bd. of Trade; Chaine des Rotisseurs; Granite; Internat. Wine & Food Soc.; Home: 83 Plymbridge Rd., Toronto, Ont. M2P 1A2; Office: 4240 Sherwoodtowne Blvd., Ste. 300, Mississauga, Ont. L4Z 2G6.

**FITZ-JAMES, (Denis) Michael,** B.A., LL.B., B.C.L.; lawyer; journalist; broadcaster; b. London, Ont. 18 Jan. 1951; s. Phillip Chester and Monica Mary (Allcut) F-J.; e. Carleton Univ. B.A. 1973; McGill Univ. LL.B. 1978, B.C.L. 1979; m. Ruth Ellen Gordon d. Stuart and Ellen 19 Dec. 1983; children: Aphra Megan, Charlotte Anthea, Harold Alexander; VICE-PRES., NEWSPAPER AND JOURNAL PUBLISHING, BUTTERWORTHS CANADA LTD. 1993– ; Publisher, 'The Lawyers Weekly'; 'The Bottom Line'; called to Bar of Que. 1982; law practice Mailhot, Fitz-James et associés Montreal 1985– ; journalist CBC TV 'Newswatch' 1982, weekly legal affairs columnist CBC 'Radio Noon' 1983–89, radio legal affairs commentator 'Basic Black' 1983–84, actor, commentator, summer host 'Basic Black' (character 'Harold Fiske') 1985– ; columnist, Medical-Legal Affairs, 'Medical Post' 1991– ; News Ed. 'National Examiner' Montreal 1978–81; Mng. Ed., The Lawyers Weekly 1983, Exec. Ed. 1984–87, Ed. and Pub. 1988–92; Publisher: 'The Lawyers Weekly' 1993– ; 'The Bottom Line' 1993– ; freelance writer numerous publs., orgns. since 1972; former mem. Assn. professionelle des journalistes du Québec; S.G.C.T.; Montréal Newspaper Guild; mem., ACTRA; YMCA; Montréal Bar Assn.; Candn. Soc. of Magazine Editors; Office: 204 Richmond St. W., Toronto, Ont. M5V 1V6.

**FITZPATRICK, Don F.,** B.A.; real estate executive; b. Toronto, Ont. 15 Aug. 1949; s. Allan and Mary (Acton) F.; e. Wilfrid Laurier Univ. B.A. (Hons.) 1974; m. Rhodelle d. Albert Byron 4 Oct. 1975; EXTVE. VICE PRES. & RESIDENT MGR., CB COMMERCIAL REAL ESTATE GROUP CANADA INC.; Salesman, Xerox Can. 1974; Nat. Acct. Mgr. 1977; Branch Prod. Mgr. 1977–79; Sales Planning Mgr. 1979–80; Sales Mgr. 1980–81; Salesman, major resp. Sun Life Centre, A.E. Lepage 1981–84; Sr. Vice Pres., Resident Mgr. & Dir., Coldwell Banker Can. Inc. 1984–..; recreations: golf, skiing; club: Donalda; Office: Suite 600, 145 King St. W., Toronto, Ont. M5H 1J8.

**FITZPATRICK, The Hon. Mr. Justice John J.,** B.A.; judge; b. Toronto, Ont. 1 Sept. 1914; s. John J. and Agnes (Wray) F.; e. De La Salle Coll.; Univ. of Toronto, B.A. 1939; Osgoode Hall Law Sch., Toronto, Ont.; m. Joan Elizabeth, d. late James Ratchford Cowie, 25 Aug. 1945; children: Kathleen, John, Margaret Ann, Moira, Janet, Sheila, James, Joan; Former Justice, Supreme Court of Ontario 1982–..; read law with Douglas Haines; practised law with Haines & Haines, Toronto, Ont. 1948–49; Phelan, O'Brien, Phelan & Fitzpatrick 1949–55; with Gardiner, Watson Ltd., stockbrokers, Toronto, Ont. 1955–60; Gardiner, Roberts, Anderson, Conlin, Fitzpatrick, O'Donohue & White 1960–74; Partner, Fitzpatrick & Poss 1974–82; served in 2nd World War; Pilot, Flight Lieut., R.C.A.F.; Fellow, Am. Coll. of Trial Lawyers; mem.: Canadian Bar Assn.; Int. Assn. of Insurance Counsel; past Pres., The Advocates' Soc.; Past Chrmn., The Advisory Bd., Sacred Heart Children's Village; Past Chrmn., Bd. of Trustees, Sir William

Campbell Foundation; Sigma Chi; Phi Delta Phi; R. Catholic; recreation: tennis; Clubs: Rosedale Golf; Queens; National; Osler Bluff Ski; Muskoka Lakes Golf & Country; Home: 407 Walmer Rd., Apt. 401, Toronto, Ont. M5R 3N2.

**FITZPATRICK, Peter J.,** M.B.,B.S., F.R.C.P.(C), F.R.C.R.; physician; educator; b. London, Eng. 13 May 1930; s. Sidney and Edith (Jeffries) F.; e. Kings Coll. London Univ. and Westminster Hosp. M.B.,B.S. 1954; m. Vivienne 16 Feb. 1963; children: Melanie, Claire, Simon; PHYS. IN CHIEF, CANCER TREATMENT AND RSCH. FOUND. OF N.S. 1989– ; Prof. and Chrmn. of Radiation Oncol. Dalhousie Univ. 1989– ; Adjunct Prof. of Oncol Ont. Veterinary Coll. Univ. of Guelph, mem. Bd. Govs. Grad. Studies 1985, estbd. radiation oncol. prog. 1983; joined Univ. of Toronto 1964–89, Prof. of Radiol. (Oncol.), Assoc. Faculty of Dentistry; served sr. med. staff OCI/PMH 1964–89; visiting radiation oncol. N.E. Ont. Sudbury 1964–88; visiting prof. 24 univs.; 195 publications incl. 14 book chapters; 285 lectures various profl. groups incl. 105 presentations at nat. and internat. meetings; Pres. Princess Margaret Hosp. Med. Staff Assn. 1985; Meml. Hosp. Sloan Kettering Radiation Therapy Alumni Assn. N.Y. 1986; Prin. Investig. and Clinic Dir. Collaborative Ocular Melanoma Study Group Toronto 1986–89, perm. mem. COMS/Nat. Eye Inst. Exec. 1986; mem. ASTRO Prog. Ctte. 1987, recipient Gold Plaque 1979; cons. mem. Soc. Head & Neck Surgs. 1988; recipient Premier Award XIII Cong. of Radiol. 1973; visiting lectr. Egypt and Israel 1982 & China 1993; John G. Maier Meml. Lectr. 1986; J.J. Nickson Meml. Lectr. 1988; Recognition of Excellence, Collaborative Ocular Melanoma Study 1987, '88, '89; el. Hon. Life mem., Acad. of Med., Toronto 1990; Vice Pres., Candn. Assoc. of Radiation Oncologists 1991–95; mem. Muskoka Lakes Assn.; Club: RCYC; Home: 162 Spinnaker Dr., Halifax, N.S. B3N 3C5; Office: 5820 University Ave., Halifax, N.S. B3H 1V7.

**FITZSIMMONS, Richard Graham,** B.A., M.A., LL.B.; lawyer; b. Moncton, N.B. 20 Dec. 1948; s. Thomas Richard and Edith Ethel (Wilson) F.; e. Bishop's Univ. B.A. 1970; L'Univ. de Strasbourg C.deS. 1969; Oxford Univ. B.A. 1972, M.A. 1977; Dalhousie Univ. LL.B. 1975; Rhodes Scholar (Que. and Exeter) 1970; Sir James Dunn Scholar, Dalhousie Law Sch.; called to the Bar 1977; m. Heather d. George and Jean Spear 17 Nov. 1982; two s. James Wilson Spear, Charles Richard; PARTNER, FITZSIMMONS, MACFARLANE & HARPUR 1980– ; Gowling & Henderson 1975–78; Goodman & Carr 1978–80; Instr., Bar Admission Course, Law Soc. of Upper Can.; mem. Candn. Bar Assn.; Candn. Tax Found.; Chief Fin. Offr. for June Rowland's Toronto Mayoralty Campaign 1991; Founder, Leonard Smithers Gastronomic Consortium; recreations: hockey, skiing, golf, tennis, painting; Clubs: University (Toronto); Cedar Springs; Home: 203 Byng Ave., Willowdale, Ont.; Office: 2500, 180 Dundas St. W., Toronto, Ont. M5G 1Z8.

**FJORDBOTTEN, The Hon. LeRoy;** politician; b. Claresholm, Alta. 4 Nov. 1938; e. Granum, Alta. schools; Camrose Lutheran Coll.; m. Deanne Marie d. John Perchinsky 16 Nov. 1962; children: Tracy, Karine; Min. of Forestry, Lands & Wildlife 1987–92; el. to provl. assembly 1979; Min. of Agriculture, Alta. 1982–86; Min. of Tourism, Alta. 1986–87; served on several Govt. and Legis. Cttes.; apptd. to Agric. Rsch. Counc.; mem., Planning, Priorities and Finance Cabinet Ctte., Treasury Bd., Agriculture and Rural Economy Cabinet Ctte., and Economic Planning Cabinet Ctte.; Alta. Flying Farmers (owned and operated farm for over 20 yrs.); P. Conservative; Lutheran; Home: P.O. Box 299, Granum, Alta. T0L 1A0.

**FLACK, Brian Leslie,** M.A.; educator; writer; b. Toronto, Ont. 2 Nov. 1948; s. Leslie Irwin and Phyllis Jean F.; e. Keys Pub. Sch. and MacKenzie High Sch. 1967, Deep River, Ont.; York Univ. B.A. 1970, Spec. Hon. B.A. 1971, M.A. 1975, Ph.D. studies 1976–78; Univ. of Alta. 1971–72; m. Laura d. Dr. Marvin and Rita Weintraub Nov. 1983; one child: Jesse; PROF. OF ENG. SENECA COLL. 1984– , Head of Dept. 1988–89, Co-ord. Candn. Authors King Campus Reading Series 1985– ; Teaching Asst., Sessional Lectr. in Eng. York Univ. 1974–78; Prog. Host 'Bookviews' Q107 Radio Toronto 1978–81; Dir. of Promotions & Pub. Relations Clarke Irwin & Co. Toronto 1980–82; Teaching Master in Eng. Humber Coll. Toronto 1982–84; workshop leader & reader Upper Can. Writers Workshop Kingston 1983–85; organizer & co-ord. First Mayworks Festival Reading Series The Rivoli Toronto 1986; participant Harbourfront Reading Series and other pub. readings univs. & libs.; recipient Ont. Arts Council Writing Awards 1978, 1982, 1983, 1985; Seneca Coll. Achievement Award Teaching Excellence 1990; author 'I Side Up' poems 1970; 'In Seed Time' novel 1978; 'With A Sudden & Terrible Clarity' novel 1985; 'Leave Them Laughing' and 'When Madmen Lead the Blind' forthcoming novels; 'Icicles and Stalagmites' forthcoming poems; ed. 'Do You Believe in Magic' 1987; 'Strange Things Done' 1988; 'A Freedom of Mind' 1989; 'Life on the Island' 1990; 'Who Will Tell the Children?' 1991; 'You Won't Hear the Bullet' 1992; numerous book reviews, poems, critical articles various newspapers, lit. mags.; recreations: opera, baseball; Home: 120 Riverdale Ave., Toronto, Ont. M4K 1C3; Office: Dufferin St. N., R.R.3, King City, Ont. L0G 1K0.

**FLADMARK, Knut Reidar,** B.A., Ph.D.; educator; b. Oslo, Norway 27 March 1946; s. Reidar and Dorothy (Claughton) F.; e. Univ. of B.C. B.A. 1964; Univ. of Calgary Ph.D. 1974; m. Sharon d. Lewis and Leah Johnson 25 Aug. 1972; children: Kristin Leah, Disa Dorothy; PROF. OF ARCHAEOL. SIMON FRASER UNIV. 1986– ; Asst. Prof. of Anthrop. Univ. of B.C. 1972; Instr. in Archaeol. present Univ. 1972, Asst. Prof. 1974, Assoc. Prof. 1979, Prof. 1986; Dir. Peace River Archaeol. Project 1974–76; Chrmn. Grant Adjudication Ctte. Social Sci. & Humanities Rsch. Council 1985–86; Vice Pres. Candn. Quarternary Assn. 1984–86; Pres.-Elect Candn. Archaeol. Assn. 1984–86; author 'The Prehistory of British Columbia' 1988, Can.'s Visual Hist. series; 'British Columbia Prehistory' 1986; 'Glass and Ice: The Archaeology of Mt. Edziza' 1985; ed. 'Fragments of the Past: B.C. Archaeology in the 1970's' 1981; recreations: site-seeing, photography; Office: Burnaby, B.C. V5A 1S6.

**FLAHERTY, David Harris,** M.A., Ph.D.; educator; b. Campbellton, N.B. 25 Feb. 1940; s. Edwin Benedict and Mary Monica (Harquail) F.; e. McGill Univ. B.A. 1962 (Gold Medal Hist. 1962); Columbia Univ. M.A. 1963, Ph.D. 1967; m. Kathryn d. Denis and Margaret Kindellan 15 Sept. 1962; div. 1988; children: Sean Terence, Michael David, Robert Denis; INFORMATION AND PRIVACY COMMISSIONER OF BRITISH COLUMBIA 1993– ; Dir. Centre for American Studies, Univ. of W. Ont. 1984–89, Prof. of Hist. and Law 1972– ; joined Princeton Univ. 1965–68; Univ. of Va. 1968–72; Lib. Arts Fellow Harvard Law Sch. 1971–72; Visiting Fellow Magdalen Coll. Oxford 1978–79; Visiting Scholar Stanford Law Sch. 1985–86; mem. Adv. Panel Office of Technol. Assessment US Cong. 1984–85; Adv. Council on Tax Adm. Min. of Nat. Revenue 1985–91; Fellow, Woodrow Wilson Internat. Ctr. for Scholars, Washington, DC 1992–93; Canada-U.S. Fulbright Scholar (Law) 1992–93; Visiting Scholar, Georgetown National Law Ctr. 1992–93; author: 'Privacy in Colonial New England' 1972; 'Privacy and Government Data Banks: An International Perspective' 1979; 'Protecting Privacy in Two-Way Electronic Services' 1985; 'Protecting Privacy in Surveillance Societies: The Federal Republic of Germany, Sweden, France, Canada, and the United States' 1989; editor: 'Privacy and Data Protection: An International Bibliography' 1984; 'Essays in the History of Canadian Law' 2 vols. 1981–83; 'Essays in the History of Early American Law' 1969; co-editor: 'Southern Exposure: Canadian Perspectives on the United States' 1986; 'Challenging Times: The Women's Movement in Canada and the United States' 1992; 'The Beaver Bites Back? American Popular Culture in Canada' 1993; mem. Ctte. on Can.-U.S. Relations Candn. C. of C. 1984–86; Dir. Am. Soc. Legal Hist. 1976–81; Home: 1939 Mayfair Dr., Victoria, B.C. V8P 1R1; Office: 4th Floor, 1675 Douglas St., Victoria, B.C. V8V 1X4.

**FLAMAND, Jacques,** Ph.D.; writer; publisher; b. Le Puy, France 12 July 1935; s. Augustin Gaston and Suzanne Marie (Duday) F.; e. Univ. of Caen, Hon.B.A. (French lit.; Eng. lang. & lit.); Univ. of Aix-en-Provence, Hon. B.A. (Philos.); Univ. of Paris, M.A. (Philos.); Strasbourg Univ., Hon.B.A. (Psych.), Ph.D. (Theol.) 1969; m. 1962; children: François, Pierre, Jean; PRES., LES EDITIONS DU VERMILLON PUBLISHERS 1982– ; Lectr., Fac. of Theol., Strasbourg Univ. 1964–66; Asst. Prof., Religious Studies, Univ. of Ottawa 1966–70; Reviser and Sect. Head, Transl. Bur., Sec. of State Dept. 1970–75; Lectr., Sch. of Transls. & Interpreters, Univ. of Ottawa 1972–82; Chief Transl., Writer & Ofcl. Langs. Offr., Can. Counc. 1975–87; Pres., Soc. des écrivains canadiens, Ottawa-Hull 1980–82, 1987–89; Co-Chrmn., Ottawa Valley Book Festival 1985–89; mem., Assn. of Transls. & Interpreters of Ont. (1st Vice-Pres. 1983–85); Founding mem. and Pres., Assoc. des auteurs de l'Ont. 1988–91; mem., Alliance cult. de l'Ont. 1990–92; author of more than 25 books since 1969, incl. poetry, children's literature, short stories and works on philos., theol., sexology, transl. and art; Address: 305 St. Patrick St., Ottawa, Ont. K1N 5K4.

**FLANAGAN, Thomas Eugene,** M.A., Ph.D.; educator; b. Ottawa, Ill. 5 March 1944; s. Thomas Eugene and Virginia Elizabeth (Lawniczak) F.; e. Univ. of Notre Dame B.A. 1965; Duke Univ. M.A. 1967, Ph.D. 1970; m. Marianne Stanford; three children; PROF. OF POL. SCI. UNIV. OF CALGARY and Head of Dept. 1982–87; joined present Univ. 1968; recipient Prix Champlain 1978; Univ. of B.C. Candn. Biog. Medal 1979; Margaret McWilliams Manitoba Hist. Medal 1993; author 'Louis "David" Riel: Prophet of the New World' 1979; 'Riel and the Rebellion: 1885 Reconsidered' 1983; 'Metis Lands in Manitoba' 1991; co-ed. 'Collected Writings of Louis Riel' 1985; co-author 'Introduction to Government and Politics' (with Mark O. Dickerson) 3rd ed. 1990; articles on aboriginal and human rights; Dir. of Rsch. for the Reform Party of Can. 1991–92; recreations: hiking, running, skiing; Home: 8307 Hawkview Manor Rd. N.W., Calgary, Alta. T3G 2Z6; Office: Calgary, Alta. T2N 1N4.

**FLANIGAN, The Hon. Keith Allan,** B.A., LL.B.; supernumerary justice; b. Cornwall, Ont. 19 Oct. 1924; s. Alex Michael and Rita (Colquhoun) F.; e. Queen's Univ., B.A. 1949; Osgoode Hall Law Sch., 1953; m. Shirley Mary; d. Theodore Joseph Miron, 6 Oct. 1945; children: Patricia, Michael, Ted, Sheila, Colleen, Gail, Maureen, Sean; SUPERNUMERARY JUSTICE OF ONT. COURT OF JUSTICE (GEN. DIV.); read law with Roberts, Archibald, Seagram & Cole; called to Bar of Ont. 1953; cr. Q.C. 1965; Partner, Gibson Sands & Flanigan, 1954–70; First Chrmn., Tax Review Bd., 1971–74; aptd. to Co. Court Bench, Ont. June 1970; Sr. District Court Judge, Judicial Dist. Ottawa-Carleton 1978–89; served with R.C.A.F. 1942–45; Chrmn., Capital Fund Campaign, Kingston Y.M.C.A., 1969–70; Pres., Kingston Red Cross; mem. Bd. of Govs., Hotel Dieu Hosp. and St. Mary's of the Lake Hosp., Kingston; mem., Canada Ports Corp. Police Ctte. 1987; Royal Candn. Mil. Inst. 1987; mem., Can. Judges Conference; R. Catholic; recreation: golf; Club: Rideau (Ottawa); Home: 852 Fairlawn Ave., Ottawa, Ont. K2A 4C2.

**FLECK, James Douglas,** B.A., D.B.A.; b. Toronto, Ont. 10 Feb. 1931; s. Robert Douglas and Norma Marie (Byrnes) F.; e. Whitney Pub. Sch. Toronto 1944; Univ. of Toronto Schs. 1949; Univ. of W. Ont. B.A. 1953; Harvard Univ. D.B.A. 1964; m. Margaret Evelyn d. late Robert Humphrys 6 June 1953; children: Robert J., A. Ellen, David A., Christopher C.; CHRMN. & C.E.O., FLECK MFG. INC.; ELECTRONIC INTERCONNECT SYSTEMS INC. (S. Hadley, Mass.); PROF., FACULTY OF MANAGEMENT, UNIV. OF TORONTO; Pres. Fleck Electrical Mfg. Ltd. Tillsonburg, Ont. 1953–60; Lectr. Harvard Business Sch. 1964–66; Prof. and Assoc. Dean Faculty of Adm. Studies and Dir. M.B.A. Program, York Univ. 1966–70; Extve. Dir. Comte. on Govt. Productivity 1970–71; Chief Extve. Offr. Office of the Premier 1972–73; Secy. to Cabinet 1974–75; Deputy Min. Ind. and Tourism 1976–78; William Lyon Mackenzie King Visiting Prof. Kennedy Sch. of Govt. Harvard Univ. 1978–79; Visiting Prof. Keio Sch. of Business Tokyo 1964; Univ. of W. Ont. Sch. of Business 1966; European Inst. Business Adm. Fontainebleau, France 1968; Chrmn., Alias Research Inc.; Tennis Canada; Dir., Zurich Insurance; Autrex Ltd.; Fleck Manufacturing Inc.; Multilingual Television Ltd.; Cable Utility Corp. Ltd.; Rogers Broadcasting Ltd.; The Power Plant at Harbourfront; Internat. Pres. Young Pres. Organ. 1972–73; served with RCAF Univ. Reserve 1949–53; author 'Life Insurance Investment Policy' 1969; 'Business Can Succeed!' 1984; 'Canada Can Compete!' 1985; 'Yankee Canadians in the Global Economy' 1988; various reports and articles on business and govt. mang.; Zeta Psi; Anglican; recreations: tennis, art collecting, travel, theatre; Clubs: Donalda; Queens; Home: 20 Wilket Rd., Willowdale, Ont. M2L 1N6; Office: 246 Bloor St. W., Ste. 709, Toronto, Ont. M5S 1V4.

**FLEGG, Keith Richard,** C.D., M.D., C.M., F.R.C.S.C; surgeon; b. Regina, Sask. 1 Jan. 1932; s. Herbert Carman and Gwendolyn Mae (Gill) F.; e. Regina Central C.I. 1950; Queen's Univ. 1956; m. Joan d. Robert William Alexander 6 Oct. 1956; children: Kathryn Mary, Douglas Alexander, Brian Keith; Chief, Dept. of Ophthalmology, Grace Gen. Hosp. 1982–91; Royal Candn. Navy 1952–74 (retired Surgeon Lt. Comdr.); exchange offr. with U.S. Navy (Philadelphia) 1962–65; qualified FRCSC 1965; private practice (Ophthal.) 1974– ; Anglican, Past Rectors Warden; Pres., Med. Staff, Grace Gen. Hosp. 1977–81; Chrmn., Med. Adv. Ctte. 1977–81; Mem. Bd. of Mgmt. Grace Gen. 1975–81; Bd. of Dirs., Ellwood House (Ottawa) Inc. 1990– (Chrmn. 1991–92); Candn. Ophthalmol. Soc. (Treas. 1984–86); recreations: sailing, skiing, singing; club: Soc. for the Preservation & Encouragement of Barber Shop Singing, Am.; Home: 19

Hacket St., Ottawa, Ont. K1V 0P9; Office: 500 – 1545 Carling Ave., Ottawa, Ont. K1Z 8P9.

**FLEISCHMANN, George;** association executive; b. Budapest, Hungary 31 Oct. 1935; s. Josef and Ella (Schwarcz) F.; e. Univ. of Toronto B.A. 1957, M.A. 1959, Ph.D. (Plant Pathol. & Genetics) 1962; m. Raizi d. Shamai Ogden, Toronto, 3 Sept. 1957; three d. Nira (dec.), Elana, Talya; PRES. & C.E.O., GROCERY PRODUCTS MANUFACTURERS OF CANADA 1981– ; Research Scientist, Cereal Diseases Lab., Winnipeg 1962–71; Adj. Prof., Sch. Grad. Studies, Univ. of Man. 1964–71; Director, Chem. & Biol. Research Inst., Ottawa 1972–73; Dir. Gen., Environment Can. 1974–75; Asst. Secy. Program Br. Treasury Bd. 1976–77; Sr. Asst. Depy. Min. (Operations) Agric. Can. 1978–79; Depy. Comptroller Gen (Mgmt. Practices) 1980; Chrmn, Reg. Reform, Privy Counc. Off. 1981; Adjunct Prof., Sch. of Business Admin., Univ. of Ottawa; C.D. Howe Mem. Fellow Hebrew Univ. of Jerusalem 1965–66; author over 50 scient. articles rust diseases cereals; CBC freelance commentator pub. affairs and science 1966–73; Home: 39 Chaplin Cres., Toronto, Ont. M5P 1A2; Office: 885 Don Mills Rd., Ste. 301, Toronto, Ont. M3C 1V9.

**FLEMING, Cecil Fredrick,** F.C.A.; chartered accountant; b. Winnipeg, Man. 1 Oct. 1936; s. John Fredrick and Kathleen Mabel (Nugent) F.; e. Toronto Sch. System, sr. matric.; Queen's Univ. C.A. & Mem., Inst. of C.A.s of Ont., 1960; Harvard Business Sch., Advanced Mngt. Prog. 1981; m. Barbara d. Norma and Bruce Syer 23 Sept. 1960; children: Heather, Leslie, Sean; NATIONAL MANAGING PARTNER, BDO DUNWOODY WARD MALLETTE, CHARTERED ACCOUNTANTS 1982– ; Mngt. Trainee, Shell Oil 1961–63; Audit Mgr., Dunwoody & Co. 1963; Partner 1966; elected to Extve. Ctte., Bd. of Dirs. 1970 & served seven consecutive years; Mng. Partner, Toronto Region 1976–81; Extve. Ctte., Dunwoody Robson McGladrey & Pullen (firm's internat. assn.); Mem., Policy Bd. of BDO Binder 1993– ; Mem., then Chrmn., Discipline Ctte., Inst. of C.A.s of Ont. (ICAO) 1983–90; previously Primary Audit Examiner & Special Ctte. on Practical Experience, ICAO; Lectr. & Instr., Univ. of Toronto, summer acctg. courses; participant, 1983 Human Resource Devel. Conf., CICA; F.C.A. 1985; Judge, Walter J. MacDonald Memorial Award, CA Magazine 1983; speaker, panelist, presentor at several CICA functions; Past Mem. & Chrmn., YMCA Task Force on Career Planning; Past Mem., Bd. of Gov.; Past Treas. & Dir., Dixon Hall; York Scarborough Fed. P.C. Assn.; author of two articles in CA Magazine; recreations: family, reading, gym; clubs: The National, The Granite; Home: 214 Timberbank Blvd., Agincourt, Ont. M1W 2A3; Office: P.O. Box 32, Royal Bank Plaza, Toronto, Ont. M5J 2J8.

**FLEMING, Christopher G.,** B.A.; b. Owen Sound, Ont. 1 Oct. 1928; s. George Donald and Alice Naomi (Beaton) F.; e. Univ. of Toronto B.A. 1951; m. 2ndly, Lois Sutherland Birkenshaw 1986; children (from previous marriage): Pamela, Andrew; Vice-Chrmn. & Dir., National Trustco; Dir., Premier Trust Co.; Equitable Life Ins. Co.; TASC Found.; recreations: skiing, tennis, sailing; Clubs: Queens; Craigleith; Badminton and Racquet; Home: 67 Heath St. W., Toronto, Ont. M4V 1T2.

**FLEMING, Everett R.;** investment executive; b. Pickering Twp., Ont. 16 Oct. 1928; s. Robert Russell and Doris Marjorie (Jenkins) F.; e. Whitby (Ont.) High Sch.; Univ. of Toronto; m. Frederica d. Frederick and Marjorie Bull 3 Nov. 1962; two d. Anne Victoria, Katherine Marjorie: VICE PRES., ROYAL BANK INVESTMENT MANAGEMENT; Dir. Westleigh Co. Ltd.; joined Burroughs Corp. 1948–55, Sales; volunteer with Moral Re-Armament Eur., Morocco, USA and Japan 1955–65; Asst. to Pres. for Devel. Mackinac Coll. Mich. 1965–68; Mgr. Invest. Mgmt. Dept. A.E. Ames and Co. 1969–82; Vice Pres. Invest. Mgmt. Pitfield MacKay Ross 1982; Vice Pres., RBC Dominion Securities Inc. 1984; Fellow, Financial Analyst Federation N.Y.; Asst. Organist Ch. of St. Augustine's of Canterbury (Ang.); Clubs: Toronto; Rosedale Golf: Home: 200 Dawlish Ave., Toronto, Ont. M4N 1H8; Office: P.O. Box 70, Royal Bank Plaza, Toronto, Ont. M5J 2J2.

**FLEMING, James MacLean,** M.A.; author/journalist; b. Haliburton, Ont. 19 Jan. 1951; s. Rev. Ian MacLean and Diana Kate (Arnold) F.; e. Preston H.S. 1970; Queen's Univ., B.A. (Hons.) 1974, M.A. 1980; m. Christine d. the late Donald Gillies and Evelyn Palmer 28 May 1977; children: Sarah Catherine, Iain Donald MacLean; EDITOR, 'FINANCIAL TIMES OF CANADA' 1993– ; Rsch. Asst., Queen's Univ., 1976–78; Assoc. Fgn. Ed., 'Maclean's Magazine' 1980–82, Bus. Ed. 1982–85; Sr. Ed., 'Report on Business Magazine' Globe and Mail 1985–87, Mng. Ed. 1987–89, Columnist 1989–91; joined Financial Times 1991; Mgr. Editor 1992–93; Winner, Nat. Magazine Award for business writing (Silver) 1990; Co-winner, Nat. Bus. Writing Award for Investigative Journalism 1983; Winner, Levy Award for best grad. paper in internat. relns., 1978 Candn. Pol. Sci. Assn. meeting; Univ. of Montreal, scholarship in Eur. Stud. 1975; mem., Un. Ch. of Can.; author: 'Circles of Power: The Most Influential People in Canada' 1991; 'Merchants of Fear: An Investigation of Canada's Insurance Industry' 1986; Home: 5 Evelyn Cres., Toronto, Ont. M6P 3C8; Office: 440 Front St. W., Toronto, Ont. M5V 3E6.

**FLEMING, John J.,** B.Comm., C.A.; oil and gas executive; b. Lashburn, Sask. 16 Oct. 1939; e. Univ. of Sask. B.Comm. 1960; C.A. 1963; m.; Chrmn. & Dir., Excel Energy Inc.; Dir., Poco Petroleums Ltd.; Newfoundland Capital Corp.; mem. Candn. Inst. C.A.'s; Alta. Inst. C.A.'s; Candn. Assn. Petrol. Landmen; Office: #1500, 340 – 12th Ave. S.W., Calgary, Alta. T2R 1L5.

**FLEMING, John Michael,** B.Sc., M.Sc.; geologist/public servant; b. St. John's, Nfld. 24 Sept. 1941; s. John Francis and Elinor (Jones) F.; e. St. Bonaventure's Coll.; St. Francis Xavier Univ. B.Sc. 1962; Mem. Univ. of Nfld. M.Sc. 1971; m. Roxanne; d. Edwin and Phyllis Press 21 May 1966; children: Michael, Stephen; DEP. MIN., DEPT. OF ENVIRONMENT & LANDS, GOVT. OF NFLD. 1989– ; Geol., Wabana Mines Div., Dominion Steel & Coal Corp. 1962–63; Sr. Geol., Min. Resources Div., Dept. of Mines, Agric. & Resources, Govt. of Nfld. 1966; Dir., Min. Devel., Dept. of Mines & Energy 1973; Asst. Dep. Min. of Mines 1976; of Energy 1981; of Mines 1984; Depy. Min., Dept. of Mines 1987–89; Mem., Adv. Counc., Ctr. for Resource Studies, Queen's Univ.; Fellow, Geol. Assn. of Can.; Mem., Candn. Inst. of Mining & Metallurgy; Assn. of Geosci. for Internat. Devel.; Amnesty Internat.; Office: Box 8700, St. John's, Nfld. A1B 4J6.

**FLEMING, Jonathan Adrian Ewing,** B.A., B.Ch., B.A.O., M.B., F.R.C.P.(C); physician, university professor; b. Dublin, Ireland 25 May 1948; s. John Browne and Jay (Fairweather) F.; e. Trinity College Dublin B.A., B.Ch., B.A.O., M.B. 1973; m. Carolyn d. Ernest and Lorna Montgomery 1 Feb. 1974; children: Ross, Rachel, Graham; CO-DIRECTOR, SLEEP DISORDERS PROGRAM, UNIVERSITY HOSPITAL & ASSOC. PROF., DEPT. OF PSYCHIATRY, UNIV. OF B.C.; Internship, Victoria Hosp. (London, Ont.) 1973–74; Residency, Psych., Univ. of B.C. 1974–78; Fellowship, Royal College of Physicians Canada 1978; Diplomate, Am. Bd. of Psych. & Neurol. 1981; Accredited Clinical Polysomnographer 1986; Diplomat, Am. Bd. of Sleep Disorders Med. 1991; elected Fellow, Am. Psych. Assn. 1989; B.C. Dir. & Extve. Mem., Candn. Psych. Assn.; Medical Consultant, Sleep-Wake Canada; author of 38 pubns. in medical journals, most recent: 'Insomnia: Assessment & Treatment' in 'Sleep Solutions' 1992; recreations: cooking, music, reading; clubs: B.C. Club; Home: 746 Millyard, Vancouver, B.C. V5Z 4A1; Office: 2211 Wesbrook Mall, Vancouver, B.C. V6T 2B5.

**FLEMING, Nancy Barbara;** arts administrator; b. Toronto, Ont. 23 June 1931; d. Gordon McCullough and Barbara Ellen (Needham) Chisholm; e. Western Tech. Comm. Sch. 1948; m. Allan Robb s. Allan S. and Isabella F. 17 Feb. 1951; children: Martha Ann, Peter Robb, Susannah Jane; EXTVE. DIR., BOOK & PERIODICAL COUNC. 1979– ; Secy., Candn. Give the Gift of Literacy Found. 1986–91; Constituency Asst., Hon. John Robarts, Sec. of State 1976–79; Mem., Rosedale Home & Sch. 1964–71 (Pres. 1971); Jarvis Coll. Home & Sch. 1972–76; Fellow, Candn. Copyright Inst.; Home: 12 South Dr., Toronto, Ont. M4W 1R1; Office: 35 Spadina Rd., Toronto, Ont. M5R 2S9.

**FLEMING, Patricia Lockhart,** Ph.D.; bibliographer; university professor; b. Hamilton, Ont. 27 Dec. 1939; d. Lisle Hastings and Marie Anne (Simard) Lockhart; e. McMaster Univ., B.A. 1960; Univ. of Toronto, B.L.S. 1964, M.L.S. 1970; Univ. of London, M.A. 1977, Ph.D. 1980; m. John Alexander s. Alexander and Alice Fleming 21 Sept. 1963; PROF., FAC. OF LIBRARY & INFORMATION SCIENCE, UNIV. OF TORONTO 1990– ; Metro. Toronto Lib. 1964–69; Teaching Asst., Univ. of Toronto, Fac. of Lib. & Infor. Sci. 1970; Lectr. 1971; Asst. Prof. 1980, Assoc. Prof. 1985; Adv. Bd., Nat. Lib. of Can. 1983–86; Ctte. on Bibliography & Infor. Serv. for Soc. Sci. & Humanities 1983–88; Bd. Mem., Candn. Inst. for Hist. Microreproductions 1988– , Vice Pres. 1989–92, Pres. 1992– ; Counc. Mem., Bibliographical Soc. of Can. 1982–85, Pres. 1986–89; Mem., Toronto Historical Bd. 1990– , Vice Chair 1991–93; author: 'Upper Canadian Imprints, 1801–1841: A Bibliography' 1988; 'Atlantic Canadian Imprints 1801–1820: A Bibliography' 1991; awarded Tremaine Medal 1992; Home: 39 Bernard Ave., Toronto, Ont. M5R 1R3; Office: Toronto, Ont. M5S 1A1.

**FLEMING, Robert John;** counsel to business and government; b. London, Eng. 5 Apr. 1925; s. Austin Lloyd and Helen (Hyde) F.; e. Appleby Coll. Oakville, Ont. 1936; Lakefield (Ont.) Coll. 1941; m. Patricia Carruthers Beeman 16 Dec. 1950; one s. Robert John Carruthers; PRESIDENT, ROBERT FLEMING INTERNATIONAL RESEARCH INC.; Founder and Ed.-in-Chief, Pace Programs Inc., Los Angeles 1964–70; Extve. Secy., Royal Comn. on Book Publishing, Toronto 1970–72; Extve. Secy., Ont. Comn. on Legislature, Toronto 1972–74; Princ. Secy. (Designate) to Hon. Robert L. Stanfield, Ottawa 1974; The Administrator, Ont. Legislature, Toronto 1974–87; Assoc., Hon. William E. Brock (The Brock Group), Washington, D.C.; Assoc., MultiState Associates Inc., Alexandria, Virginia; Founder & Editor, annual resource book 'Canadian Legislatures'; author various papers relating to govt.; Dir., Churchill Soc. for the Advancement of Parlty. Deomcracy, Toronto; Founding Chrmn. Youth Employment Skills, Canada Inc. (YES Canada); Founding Gov., Candn. Journalism Found.; Dir., Joseph B. MacInnis Found.; Internat. Adv. Bd., Up With People Inc. Tucson, Arizona; mem. Inst. Pub. Adm. Can.; Center for the Study of the Presidency, New York, N.Y.; Protestant; recreation: sailing; Clubs: York; RCYC; Empire; Office: 1 Clarendon Ave., Suite 304, Toronto, Ont. M4V 1H8.

**FLEMING, Rowland William;** executive; b. Dublin, Ireland 27 Aug. 1943; s. Charles and Dorothy F.; e. primary & sec. sch. Ireland; London Univ. & West. Ont. bus./adv. mngt. programs; m. Kate; children: Dawn, Mark; DEP. CHAIR, PRES., CHIEF EXTVE. OFFR. & DIR., NATIONAL TRUST CO. 1991– ; Bank of Ireland, Dublin 1962–67; Bank of Nova Scotia, Dublin 1967–70; Asst. Mgr., London, Eng. 1971–74; Credit Supvr., Toronto 1974–76; Sr. Rep., New York 1976–78; Mgr., Boston 1978–79; Asst. Gen. Mgr., U.S., Toronto 1979–81; Gen. Mgr. 1982–84; Sr. Vice-Pres., N. Am. 1984–86; Extve. Vice-Pres., Candn. Retail & Comm. Banking 1986–90; Pres., C.E.O. & Dir., Dominion of Canada Gen. Insur. Co. and Extve. Vice-Pres. & Dir., E-L Finan. Corp. Limited 1990–91; Pres., C.E.O. & Dir., National Trust Co., Chair, Pres. & Dir. The Premier Trust Co. and Victoria & Grey Mortgage Corp. 1991; Dir., Natrusco Investment Funds Limited; N.T. Insur. Mngt. Inc.; Nat. Trust & Banking Corp. (Caribbean) Limited; The Dominon of Can. Gen. Insur. Co.; Empire Life Insur. Co.; E-L Finan. Corp. Limited; United Corp. Limited; Blackburn Holdings Inc.; Blackburn Group Inc. Kilbyrne Investments Inc.; The Trust Companies Assn. of Can.; The Trust Companies Inst.; The Candn. C. of C.; The Ireland Fund of Can.; Metro. Y.M.C.A.; Stratford Shakespearean Fest.; Mem., Bus. Counc. on Nat. Issues; Ont. Bus. Adv. Counc.; The Metro Toronto YMCA; recreations: golf, photography; clubs: Islington Golf, Ontario, Mad River Golf, Toronto; Home: Mississauga, Ont.; Office: One Financial Place, 1 Adelaide St. E., Toronto, Ont. M5C 2W8.

**FLEMMING, Brian,** C.M., Q.C., D.C.L., B.Sc., LL.M., Dip. Internat. Law; barrister and solicitor; businessman; educator; b. Halifax, N.S. 19 Feb. 1939; s. late Everett Francis Joseph and Margaret Mary (Meagher) F.; e. primary and secondary schs., Halifax, N.S.; St. Mary's Univ. H.S.; St. Mary's Univ. B.Sc. 1959; Dalhousie Univ. LL.B. 1962; Univ. Coll. London, Eng. LL.M. 1964; Hague Dip. Internat. Law 1964; Univ. of King's Coll., Halifax, N.S. D.C.L. (hon. causa), 1991; m. Janice Jenifer d. late Dr. John W. Merritt 25 Aug. 1962; children: Ann Louise, Mark Alexander; CHRMN., C.E.O. & DIR., CanEast CAPITAL LTD. 1981– ; Pres., Shelburne Marine Ltd. 1986– ; Chrmn., C.E.O. & Dir., VGM Capital Corp. 1986– ; Hon. Dir., Noranda Inc.; Dir.: Brunswick Mining and Smelting Co. Ltd.; Counsel, Stewart, McKelvey, Stirling & Scales 1987–91 (Partner 1971–76, 1979–87); Chrmn. Bd. of Govs., Univ. of King's Coll.; Gov., Dalhousie Univ.; former Chrmn. Bd. of Govs. Internat. Centre for Ocean Devel.; read law with late G.S. Cowan Q.C. (later Chief Justice Cowan); called to Bar of N.S. 1963, Ont. 1981; Lectr. Dalhousie Law Sch. and St. Mary's Univ. 1965–76 and 1980–82; Asst. Princ. Secy. and Policy Advr. to Prime Min. of Can. 1976–79; Lib. cand. for Halifax in 1974, 1979 fed. els.; author numerous publs. in law, arts and pol.; mem. Brit. Inst. of Internat. and Comparative Law; Am. Soc. of Internat. Law; Candn. Bar Assn.; Internat. Bar Assn.; Dir. Scotia Chamber Players; former Pres. Symphony N.S.; past mem. and Vice-Chrmn. The Canada Counc. 1970–75; Dir., CBC 1975–76; Hon. Pres. Dalhousie Law Sch. Alumni Assn. of Can.; recreations: travel, reading, swimming, boating; Clubs: The Waegwoltic; Home: 2003 – 1470 Summer St., Halifax, N.S. B3H 3A3.

**FLEMMING, Hugh John Alexander (Ted),** Q.C., B.A., LL.B.; businessman, lawyer; b. Sussex, N.B. 13 June 1954; s. Hugh John and Millicent Florence (Esson) F.; e. Millidgeville North H.S. 1973; Univ. of N.B. B.A. 1976, LL.B. 1978; m. Nancy d. Edgar and Bertha Doucet 25 June 1977; children: Jonathan Alexander, Sarah Jane, Heather Anne; PRES., CALDWELL TRANSPORT LTD. 1985– ; Assoc., Clark, Drummie & Company Barristers & Solicitors 1978–83; Partner 1983–89; Mem., Gilbert, McGloan, Gillis, Barristers & Solicitors 1992– ; apptd. Q.C. 1992; Corp. Sec., present firm 1980–84; Pres., Provincial Lumber Ltd. 1984– ; Legal Counsel, Saint John Port Corp. 1986– ; Dir., Brunswick Timber Exports Inc. 1986–90; Federal Business Devel. Bank 1986– ; Market Square Corp. 1980–89; Corp. Sec., Saint John Port corp. 1986–88; Lord Beaverbrook Law Scholar, U.N.B. 1976, 1977; Rhodes Scholar Selection Ctte. 1984–88; Mem., Law Soc. of N.B.; Candn. Bar Assn.; Maritime Lumber Bur. (Corp.); Candn. Lumbermans Assn. (Corp.); editor: 'University of New Brunswick Law Review' 1977–78; recreations: golf, salmon fishing, skiing; clubs: Riverside Country, Union, Atlantic Salmon Fed.; Home: 90 Highland Ave., P.O. Box 132, Rothesay, N.B. E0G 2W0; Office: 152 Westmorland Rd., P.O. Box 278, Saint John, N.B. E2L 3Y2.

**FLETCHER, Frederick Ernest,** B.Arch., F.R.A.I.C., R.C.A.; architect; b. Toronto, Ont. 18 Jan. 1923; s. Edgar Storey and Ellen Isobella (Pritchard) F.; e. N. Toronto Coll. Inst. 1943; Univ. of Toronto B.Arch. 1948; m. Barbara d. Jacob and Jean Booth 22 Jan. 1954; children: Erin Ellen, Keith Malcom; joined Gordon S. Adamson, Arch. 1948, Partner 1960, retired 1988; retired as Pres. Design Group Consultants Ltd. 1988; Hon. Fellow, Ont. Coll. Art, Chrmn. Council 1969, Chrmn. Centennial Ctte. 1976, Chrmn. Found. 1988; Chrmn. Royal Candn. Acad. Arts Centennial Ctte. 1980; recreations: painting, swimming, travel, art; Home: 2 Valleyanna Dr., Toronto, Ont. M4N 1J8.

**FLETCHER, John Edward,** P.Eng.; retired mining executive; b. Windsor, Ont. 18 May 1931; s. Joseph Edward and Alice Gwendolyn (Poole) F.; e. Queen's Univ., B.Sc. Chem. Eng.; m. Philippa; children: Lee Anne (Paul), Loreen Patricia (Lloyd), John Edward Vernon; Sr. Vice-Pres. & C.O.O., Cominco Metals 1989–93, retired; Engr.-in-Training, Zinc Opns., Cominco Ltd. 1953; Devel. Engr. 1953–61; Asst. Supr., Staff & Training 1961–64; Asst. Supt., Phospate Plant 1964–66; C&F Opns. 1966–67; Spec. Duties, Budget Ctrl. 1967–68; Asst. Supt., Zinc Opns. 1968–70; Gen. Supt., Potash Div. 1970–75; Mgr. 1975–78; Gen. Mgr., Praire Group 1978–79; BC Group 1979–81; Vice-Pres. 1981–85; Chrmn. & Chief Extve. Offr., Cominco Engr. Services Ltd. 1982– ; Sr. Vice Pres., Cominco Metals 1985–89; Former Dir., Cominco Engr. Serv. Ltd.; Cominco American Inc.; Cominco Eur. Ltd.; Cominco Ltd.; Cominco QB Resources Ltd. (a holding company for the Quebrada Blanca operations); Exploration Minera Internacional Espana S.A.; Highland Valley Copper Corp.; Alternate Aberfoyle Pty Ltd.; Former Mem., Nat. Adv. Counc. and Mineral Processing Subctte.; Western Regional Adv. Ctte., Mem., Assn. of Profl. Engrs. of Sask.; Cand. Inst. of Mining & Metallurgy; Mining Assn. of B.C. (Mem. Extve. Ctte.); Mining Assn. of Can. (Dir., Sponsoring Dir., Trade Policy Ctte.); Nat. Technology Bd.; Dir., Mine Environment Neutral Drainage (MEND)); Club: Terminal City.

**FLETCHER, Joseph Francis,** Ph.D.; university professor; b. Philadelphia, Pa. 2 Aug. 1949; s. Joseph Francis and Dolores Mary (Bussone) F.; e. Wright State Univ., B.A. 1971; Univ. of Alberta, M.A. 1973; Univ. of Toronto, Ph.D. 1983; children: Logan Jarrett, Eden Elodie; POL. SCIENTIST, UNIV. TEACHER & SURVEY RESEARCHER, UNIV. OF TORONTO; Co-investigator, Charter Project, a landmark study of attitudes toward civil liberties in Can. following the Charter of Rights & Freedoms 1987; Co-investigator, The Australian Rights Project (the first nat. study of attitudes toward civil liberties in Australia) 1991; Co-investigator, The Constitutional Referendum Study 1992; Founding Partner, Arkelon Rsch.; Rsch. Fellow, Ctr. of Criminology, Univ. of Toronto & Inst. for Social Rsch., York Univ.; mem., Candn. Pol. Sci. Assn.; author of several influential & highly publicized reports related to Charter Project as well as other scholarly articles; Office: Dept. of Pol. Sci., Univ. of Toronto, Toronto, Ont. M5S 1A1.

**FLETCHER, Stephen Marshall,** C.M., B.A., C.L.U., LL.D.; annuity and insurance consultant; b. Binbrook Twp., Wentworth Co., Ont. 22 Feb. 1915; s. Niram Allen and Edna Viola (Marshall); e. Central C.I. Hamilton 1932; McMaster Univ. B.A. 1936; m. Dorothy Van Sickle d. Ethel and Frank Gage 15 June 1940; children: Neil, Eleanor, Philip; joined Canada Life H.Q. 1936; Branch Sec. Hamilton Branch 1937; Navigator Instructor, R.C.A.F. 1943–45; discharged as Flying Officer; Sales Rep. Hamilton Branch, Canada Llife 1945; Manager 1966; retired 1980; became a Pensioner Consultant and is still active in this capacity (Fletcher & Morrow Consultants); Charter Dir., Abstainer's Insur. Co. until 1984 (company sold); Dir., CHML/CKDS Radio 1979– ; C.L.U. 1948; Order of Canada 1984; Hamilton Gall. of Distinction 1988; Citizen of the Year, Hamilton 1983; Scottish Rite 33$ Mason; Trustee, St. Giles United Ch.; Hamilton Bd. of Edn. 1950–62 (Chair 1958); Pres., Hamilton C. of C. 1965; 31-year member, Hamilton Rotary Club (Pres. 1977); Past Pres., Royal Candn. Humane Assn.; Hemilton-Wentworth Children's Aid Soc.; McMaster Alumni Assn.; McMaster President's Club; Gov., Mohawk College 6 years (Chair 3 years); First Chair, Hamilton Psych. Hosp. Advisory Bd.; Past Chair, Salvation Army Adv. Bd.; Hamilton Conservation Found.; Mem., Bd. of Dir., Hamilton Found. 1987–91; Hon. Bd. Mem. Hamilton YMCA; Residence: 32 Edgewood Ave., Hamilton, Ont. L8T 1J9; Office: 1 King St. W., Hamilton, Ont. L8P 1A4.

**FLICHEL, Eugene A.,** B.A., B.Comm.; public servant; b. Gravelbourg, Sask. 30 May 1943; e. Univ. of Sask., B.A., B.Comm. 1964; m. Eileen Dumelie; children: Todd, Jeff, Tina, Shauna; PRES., CANADA MORTGAGE & HOUSING CORP., August 1990– ; Business Analyst, Dun & Bradstreet 1964–66; Dist. Econ., Manpower & Immigration, Sask. 1968–72; Reg. Econ., Prairie Region, CMHC 1972–73; Mgr., Regina Br. 1973–74; Asst. Reg. Dir., Prog., Ont. 1974–76; Extve. Dir. Housing 1977–79; Asst. Vice-Pres. Prog. Directorate 1979–81; Vice-Pres., Mngt. Infor. Systems 1981–82; Vice-Pres., Finan. & Mngt. Infor. Systems 1982–86; Sr. Vice Pres., Policy Research and Programs 1986– ; Mem., Bd. of Dir., CMHC; Club: Canadian; Home: R.R. 4, Osgoode, Ont. K0A 2W0; Office: 700 Montreal Rd., Ottawa, Ont. K1A 0P7.

**FLINN, Richard Jeffrey,** B.A., LL.B.; b. Halifax, N.S. 27 July 1929; s. Richard Jeffrey and Mary Agatha (Connors) F.; e. St. Mary's Univ. B.A. 1950; Dalhousie Univ. LL.B. 1953; m. Marilynn d. Robert and Carmen Johnston 29 Aug. 1958; children: Richard Jeffrey III, Mary Charlotte; JUSTICE, ONT. COURT OF JUSTICE (GEN. DIV.) 1990– ; articled with Dept. of Attorney Gen., Halifax; called to Bar of N.S. 1953; Bar of Ont. 1955; joined Jeffery & Jeffery; then Robarts, Betts, McLennan & Flinn; Q.C. 1971; Judge, District Court of Ont. 1981–90; Mem., Advocates Soc.; Candn. Bar Assn.; Candn. Assn. for Admin. of Justice; Chrmn., Bd. of Dir., Univ. Hospital; Dir., John P. Robarts Rsch. Institute; recreations: curling, golf, gardening, carpentry; clubs: London, London Curling, London Hunt & Country; Home: The Old Garlick Place, R.R. 6, London, Ont. N6A 4C1; Office: Court House, 80 Dundas St., London, Ont. N6A 2P3.

**FLINT, John Edgar,** M.A., Ph.D., F.R.Hist.S., F.R.S.C.; educator; b. Montréal, Qué. 17 May 1930; s. Alfred Edgar and Sarah (Pickup) F.; e. St. John's Coll. Cambridge B.A. 1952, M.A. 1954; Royal Holloway Coll. and Sch. of Oriental & African Studies Univ. of London Ph.D. 1957; m. Nezhat 19 Sept. 1975; children: Helen Sarah, Richard John James; EMERITUS PROFESSOR, DALHOUSIE UNIV. 1992– , Prof. of History 1967–92, Chrmn. of Hist. 1968–71, 1974–75, Dir., Centre for African Studies 1978–83; Asst. Lectr. in Hist., Univ. of London King's Coll. 1954–56, Lectr. 1956–64, Reader 1964–67; Visiting Prof., Univ. of California Santa Barbara and Fulbright Fellow 1960–61; Visiting Prof. and Head of Hist. Univ. of Nigeria Nsukka 1963–64; mem., Acad. Panel Can. Council 1976–78; Acad. Panel Social Sci's & Humanities Rsch. Council Can. 1978–79; author 'Sir George Goldie and the Making of Nigeria' 1960; 'Nigeria and Ghana' 1966; 'Cecil Rhodes' 1974; ed. 'Cambridge History of Africa' Vol. V 1977; Mary Kingsley's 'West Africa Studies' 1964 and 'Travels in West Africa' 1965; co-ed. 'Perspectives of Empire: Essays in Honour of Gerald Sandford Graham' 1973; contbr. chapters 'Oxford History of East Africa' Vols. I and II 1963, 1965; mem., Candn. Hist. Assn. (Council 1968–69); Candn. Assn. African Studies (Vice Pres. 1969–70, Council mem. 1977–79, 1982–83); Nigerian Hist. Soc. (Council mem. 1964–65); African Studies Assn. U.K.; recreations: chess, skiing; Home: 21 Erinlea Ct., Nepean, Ont. K2E 7C8; Office: Halifax, N.S. B3H 3J5.

**FLITTON, Robert Deane;** provincial civil servant; b. Port Alberni, B.C. 10 Feb. 1942; s. Francis William and Margaret Fay (Massey) F.; e. Woodrow Wilson High Sch. 1959; Caledonia Coll.; m. Jane d. Donald Morrison 1962; children: Robert Geoffrey, William Donald, Bradley David; Dep. Min. of Forests & Lands, B.C. 1984–..; former Vice Pres. and Gen. Mgr. Heights Land Development Co.; Div. Gen. Mgr. Dominion Construction, mem. Bentall Group, Vancouver 1979–84; Comnr. B.C. Internat. Skagit Environmental Comn.; Chrmn. Pacific Point Adv. Bd.; Past Chrmn. Cariboo Coll. Business Adv. Group; Past Pres.: Prince George Un. Way; Prince George Kinsmen; Nat. Pres. 1983 and Life Dir. Candn. Home Builders Assn.; recreations: bridge, fishing; Home: 3851 Epsom Dr., Victoria, B.C. V8P 3S8.

**FLOOD, A.L. (Al);** banker; b. Monkton, Ont. 22 Aug. 1935; e. Prog. for Mngt. Devel., Grad. Sch. of Bus., Harvard Univ. 1973; married; 4 children; CHAIRMAN & C.E.O., CIBC 1992– ; joined present bank 1951; held various mngt. positions in corp. credit & branch opns., Ont.; Area Extve., U.S.A. & Latin Am. 1974; Gen. Mgr. 1978; Vice-Pres., Corporate Banking 1979; U.S. Opns. 1980; Sr. Vice-Pres. 1983; Sr. Vice-Pres. & Head of Internat. Opns., Head Office 1984; Extve. Vice-Pres. 1984; Pres. Corporate Bank 1986; elected Dir. 1989; Mem., Bd. of Trustees, The Hosp. for Sick Children; Dir., Royal Ontario Museum Found.; Mem., Bd. of Gov., Ryerson Polytech. Inst.; clubs: The National; The Donalda; Ontario Club; Toronto Club; York Club; Office: Commerce Court, Toronto, Ont. M5L 1A2.

**FLOOD, John Michael,** Ph.D.; educator; publisher; poet; b. Hearst, Ont. 6 Sept. 1947; s. Thomas J. and Azilda (Deda) (Sigouin) F.; e. St. Dunstan's Univ. Charlottetown, B.A. 1969; Univ. of Calgary, M.A. 1973; Ph.D., OISE, Univ. of Toronto 1992; m. Eileen MacPherson 1969; children: Carmen, Michael, Thomas; PROF. OF ENGLISH, LE COLL. UNIVERSITAIRE DE HEARST 1971– ; Founder and Ed. Boreal (trilingual jour. of N.) 1974–79; Founder, Ed. and Publisher Penumbra Press 1979– , Northward Journal 1979– ; former Dir. Literary Press Group, Candn. Periodical Publishers' Assn., Kapuskasing Pub. Lib., OCUFA, present Coll.; recipient George Wittenborn Award Excellence Publ. in Visual Arts, Art Libs. Soc. N.Am. 1987; SSHRC Doctoral Fellowship 1989–91; author (poetry) 'The Land They Occupied' 1976; 'No Longer North' 1987; co-author (non-fiction) 'Educational Resource and Teacher's Guide to Selected Canadian Literary Titles for Secondary Schools' 1993; ed. 'Mooskek' (anthol.) 1977; 'D.C. Scott's Untitled Novel ca 1905' (fiction) 1979; 'Thoreau's MacDonald's Notebooks' (non fiction) 1980; Office: 435 Stillmeadow Circle, Waterloo, Ont. N2L 5M1.

**FLORIAN, Mary-Lou E.,** M.A.; conservation scientist, museum collections, emeritus retired; b. Vancouver, B.C. 28 Sept. 1925; d. Frederick Johnson and Marguerite Mary (Munn) Jeffery; e. Magee H.S. 1942; Univ. of B.C. B.A. 1948; Univ. of Texas M.A. 1950; m. Svatopluk Fred s. Mary Florianova 23 Sept. 1954; children: Jan Jeffery, Patrick Michael; Chief, Conservation Services, Royal British Columbia Museum 1988–91; Sessional Lectr., Carleton Univ. 1964–72; Contract Biol., Nat. Gall. of Can., Restoration & Conservation Lab. 1960–62, Edn. Serv. 1960–72; Can. Conservation Institute: var. positions ending as Sr. Conserv. Scientist, Environment & Deterioration 1972–78; Pres., Bd. of Dir., Victoria Natural Hist. Soc. 1982–84; Bd. of Dirs., Friends of Ecological Reserves 1983–84; Adv. Counc., Washington Archaeological Rsch., Washington St. Univ. 1984–90; Academic Adv. Counc., Univ. of Victoria 1982–90; Sci. Counc. of Can. 1980–83; B.C. Mus. Assn. Distinguished Serv. Award; awarded Commemorative Medal for 125th Anniversary of Candn. Confederation; 1st Lifetime Award, Soc. for Preservation of Natural History Collections; 40 pubns. related to conserv. mus. collections (rsch. papers, subject reviews, methodology & book chapters); recreations: gardening, fishing; Home: 129 Simcoe St., Victoria, B.C. V8V 1K5.

**FLOWER, George Edward,** B.A., M.A., Ed.D.; university professor; b. Montreal, P.Q. 15 Oct. 1919; s. Herbert William and Alice Gertrude (Tabb) F.; e. McGill Univ., B.A. 1940; Candn. War Staff Coll. R.M.C. 1944; McGill Univ., M.A. 1949; Harvard Univ., Ed.D. 1954; m. Muriel, d. Frederick M. and Leila E. Armstrong, 30 Nov. 1940; child: Judith Katherine (White); PROF. EMERITUS, MCGILL UNIV. 1983– ; Teacher, Montreal Protestant Sch. Bd. 1939–41, 46–49; Asst. Dir. Field Studies, Harvard Grad. Sch. Ed. 1950; Dir., Candn. Ed. Assn. (Kellogg Leadership Project) 1952; Prof., Ont. Coll. Ed. 1956–65; Chrmn. Grad. Dept. Ed. Theory, Univ. Toronto, 1963–75; Coordinator, Grad. Studies, Ont. Inst. for Studies in Ed. 1965–75; Prof. and Dean, Fac. of Educ., McGill Univ. 1975–83; author: 'How Big is Too Big? Problems of Organization and Size: The Quance Lectures' 1964; numerous papers and reports on aspects of education; editor: 'The Macmillan Spelling Series' 1960–78; co-ed. (with F.K. Stewart) 'Leadership in Action: The Superintendent of Schools in Canada' 1958; served Candn. Active Army, Canada and N.W. Europe 1941–46; Fellow, Candn. Coll. Teachers; Ont. Teachers' Federation; Mem. Bd. Govs., Ont. Inst. for Studies in Ed. 1965–75; McGill Univ. 1978–80; mem. Candn. Ed. Assn. (Pres. 1973–74); Candn. Assn. Profs. of Ed. (Pres. 1961–62); Candn. Foundation for Economic Ed. (Pres. 1980–81); recreation: music; Address: Terrace House, Cartwright Point, Kingston, Ont. K7K 5E2.

**FLOYD, Anthony,** B.Sc., M.Sc., F.G.A.C.; geologist; b. Clevedon, England 30 May 1950; s. Kenneth Francis and Kathleen Maud (Heritage) F.; e. Bristol Grammar School (U.K.) 1968; Nottingham Univ. B.Sc. (hons.) 1971; Leicester Univ. M.Sc. 1972; m. Katherine d. Pierre and Nicole Hanssens 31 Aug. 1985; children: Noelle, Sacha; PRESIDENT & CHIEF EXECUTIVE OFFR., BRIDGER RESOURCES & COMPANIA MINERA BRIDGER CHILE LTDA. 1988– ; independent geologist 1973–75; Project Geologist, McIntyre Mines 1975–78; Independent Exploration Management Consultant, Floyd Consultants 1978–85; Pres. & Chief Extve. Offr. 1985–88; Dir., Bridger Resources Inc.; Foundation Resources Inc.; Compania Minera Bridger Chile Ltda., Chile; recreations: skiing, cycling; Home: 3400 W. 2nd Ave., Vancouver, B.C. V6R 1J2; Office: #308 – 595 Howe St., Vancouver, B.C. V6C 2T5.

**FLOYD, Gordon Stirling,** B.A.; public affairs consultant; b. Montreal, Que. 23 June 1950; s. John Ellis and Margaret Alice (MacInnes) F.; e. Oakridge S.S.; Osgoode Hall Law Sch., Univ. of Toronto, B.A. 1971; DIRECTOR, PUBLIC AFFAIRS, CANADIAN CENTRE FOR PHILANTHROPY 1994– ; Pres., Great Lakes Schooner Co. Ltd. 1991– ; G Co. Corporation 1987– ; Dir. of Policy, Liberal Party of Can. 1973–74; Extve. Asst. to Leader, Ont. Liberal Party 1975–77; Principal Sec./Chief of Staff, Ont. Leader of the Opposition 1977–82; Pres., Public Affairs Mngt. Inc. 1981–94; Sr. Vice-Pres. & Dir., Ketchum Can. Inc. 1984–90; Pres., Nunsense Candn. Prod. Corp. 1985–86; Trustee, Un. Way of Greater Toronto; Past Chair, AIDS Ctte. of Toronto; Past Chrmn., Toronto Workshop Prodns.; Protestant; Liberal; Mem., Public Affairs Assn. of Can.; Candn. Council for the Americas; Candn. Civil Liberties Assn.; Amnesty Internat.; The Issue Exchange; recreations: squash, whitewater canoeing, theatre; Home: 41 Henning Ave., Toronto, Ont. M4R 1X6; Office: 1329 Bay St., Toronto, Ont. M5R 2C4.

**FLOYD, James C.,** C.Eng., P.Eng., F.R.Ae.S., F.C.A.S.I., F.A.I.A.A.; retired aviation consultant; b. England, 20 Oct. 1914; became Candn. Citizen 1951; early aero training at A.V. Roe Co. and the Hawker Aircraft Co. in Eng.; came to Canada 1946 as Chief Tech. Offr. with Avro Aircraft Ltd.; Chief Design Engr. in charge of the C-102 Jet Airliner project and CFIO5 Arrow Project; Vice-Pres. (Engn.), 1955–59; joined Hawker-Siddeley Aviation Ltd., Eng. to head up an Advance Projects Group 1959; formed J.C. Floyd & Assoc. (consulting co.) 1962; 1st non-American to be awarded Wright Bros. Medal (for meritorious contribution to Aero Engn.) by the U.S. in 1950; McCurdy Award, Candn. Aero Inst. 1958; Brit. Commonwealth Lectr., Royal Aero. Soc. 1958; George Taylor Gold Medal (Royal Aero. Soc.) for most valuable Aero. paper publ. in 1961; Lifetime of Achievement Award, Aerospace Industries Assoc. of Can. 1988; Dir., Internat. Hypersonic Rsch. Inst., U.S.A. 1989; Patron, Aerospace Heritage Found. of Can. 1990; Fellow, Roy. Aero. Soc.; Candn. Aero. and Space Inst.; Am. Inst. Aero. and Astronautics; Regd. Prof. Engr., Ont.; Chartered Engr. (U.K.); Award of Companion of the Order of Flight (Edmonton) 1993; inducted into 'Canada's Aviation Hall of Fame' 1993; recreations: photography; writing; Address: 288 Mill Rd., #B17, Etobicoke, Ont. M9C 4X7.

**FLYNN, Peter,** B.Sc., M.Sc., Ph.D.; executive; b. Plainfield, N.J. 1 Aug. 1946; s. John V. and Ellen Louise (Moran) F.; e. Univ. of Delaware B.Sc. 1967; Univ. of Calif. at Berkeley M.Sc. 1968; Univ. of Alta. Ph.D. 1974; children: Henry Charles, Morris; GENERAL MGR., BUSINESS DEVELOPMENT EDMONTON TELEPHONES and DIRECTOR, EDMONTON POWER; engineering & prod. position, Syncrude 6 yrs.; Nova 8 yrs.; G.E. Canada 3 yrs.; Dir., ExTerra Found.; Past Dir., CNG Fuel Systems; COROD Indus. Inc.; Theatre Network; Petroleum Serv. Assn. of Can.; Norwood Neighbourhood Assn.; Candn. Soc. of Chem. Engr.; Chem. Inst. of Can.; Past Chair, Hi Point Peat Ltd.; Past Gov., Univ. of Alta.; Past Mem., Fed. Min. of Energy's Nat. Adv. Ctte. on CANMET; Mem., Chem. Inst. of Canada; Candn. Soc. of Chem. Engrs.; Candn. Assn. of Oilwell Drillers & Contractors; Petroleum Serv. Assn. of Canada; Assn. of Petrol. Engrs., Geol. & Geophy. of Alta.; Candn. Chem. Prod. Assn., Bus. & Econ. Ctte.; Bd. of Gov., Univ. of Alta., Pres. Council; Home: 4904 – 154 St., Edmonton, Alta. T6H 5K7.

**FLYNN, Thomas P.;** construction executive; b. Glasgow, Scotland 23 July 1945; s. John Anthony and Catherine Veronica (Doherty) F.; e. St. Mungo's Acad. Glasgow 1961; m. Faye d. Mark and Joanne Dawson 27 Nov. 1982; children: Shelby Catherine, Stacy Anne; PRES. & CHIEF EXTVE. OFFR., THE STATE GROUP 1986– ; Vice-Pres., Lewis Energy Mngt. 1969–82; State Contractors 1982–86; Dir., Bracknell Corp.; Pres. & Dir., Dipro-Namur Inc.; Mem., Min. Adv. Ctte. on Construction, Govt. of Ont.; Construction Indus. Devel. Counc., Govt. of Canada; recreations: golfing, swimming; clubs: St. Georges Golf & Country, Fitness Inst., Beach Grove Golf & Country, Windsor; Home: 1585 Jalna Ave., Mississauga, Ont. L5J 1S8; Office: 2150 Islington Ave., Etobicoke, Ont. M9P 3V4.

**FODDEN, Simon Ritchie,** A.B., LL.B.; b. Leeds, Eng. 24 March 1944; s. John Henry and Jean (Brook) F.; e. Princeton Univ. A.B. 1965; Johns Hopkins Univ. Sch. of Advanced Internat. Studies 1966; Osgoode Hall Law Sch. LL.B. 1969; m. Christine d. Edelfried and Käte Koschmieder 23 May 1980; two d. Rebecca Jean, Jennifer Anne; ASSOC. PROF. OSGOODE HALL LAW SCH. YORK UNIV. 1971– , Asst. Prof. 1969–71, Asst. Dean 1987–88; author (as Simon Ritchie) novels 'The Hollow Woman' 1986; 'Work For A Dead Man' 1989; mem. Law Soc. Upper Can.; recreations: music, walking; Home: 9 Riverdale Ave., Toronto, Ont. M4K 1C2; Office: 4700 Keele St., North York, Ont. M3J 1P3.

**FOGEL, Stanley H.,** Ph.D.; university professor; writer; b. Montreal, Que. 15 July 1945; s. Jack Saul and Claire (Yaffe) F.; e. Carleton Univ., B.A. 1968; Univ. of B.C., M.A. 1970; Purdue Univ., Ph.D. 1973; PROF., UNIV. OF WATERLOO/ST. JEROME'S COLLEGE 1975– ; author: 'A Tale of Two Countries' 1984, 'The Postmodern University' 1988; co-author: 'Understanding John Barth' 1990; Office: Waterloo, Ont. N2L 3G3.

**FOGGIN, Peter Michael,** B.A., L-ès-L., Ph.D.; geographer; university professor; b. Changli (Hebei) China 1 July 1938; s. George Edward and Frieda Anne F.; e. Univ. of B.C. B.A. 1963; Univ. of Montreal L-ès-L. 1967; McGill Univ. Ph.D. 1970; m. Elizabeth d. Béatrice and James Stark 3 June 1967; children: Jonathan Marc, Timothy Michel; PROFESSOR, DEPT. OF GEOGRAPHY, UNIV. OF MONTREAL 1979– ; Elementary & Jr. High Teacher in B.C. 1958–63; Christian Radio Broadcaster 1961–70; joined Univ. of Quebec at Montreal 1969; Prof. of Geography, Univ. of Que. at Chicoutimi 1972–74; Field Dir.,Haiti, World Vision Internat. 1976–79; Chair, Dept. of Geography, Univ. of Montreal 1982–86, 1990–94; research: health status & risk factors of Inuit & Cree of N. Que. 1981–90; field research in East Asia (Mongolian Heath Status) 1990– ; urban geography in China 1988– ; 'Earthwatch' health rsch., Mongolia 1993; rsch. collaboration with Dept. of Geog., Peking Univ.; an urban as well as a medical geographer; Assoc., Sch. of Australian Environ. Studies, Griffith Univ. 1988; Doctoral Fellowship, CMHC 1966–70; rsch. grants, Nat. Health & Welfare (Canada) & SSHRCC; Dir., St. Stephens Univ.; World Relief of Canada; Candn. Bible Soc.; Communications La Foi Vivifiante; Mem., Groupe biblique de Ste-Julie (lay pastor); Candn. Assn. of Geographers; Assn. of Am. Geographers; author: 'Montréal: espace urbain' 1970 and scientific journal articles; recreations: travelling, reading, swimming; Home: 231, Bellevue, Ste-Julie, Que. J0L 2S0; Office: Box 6128, Station A, Montreal, Que. H3C 3J7.

**FOGH, Hans;** sailmaker; b. Copenhagen, Denmark 8 Mar. 1938; s. Carl Foldager and Anna Marie (Moeskaer) F.; e. Rodovre Sch.; m. Kirsten d. Knud and Lilly Andersen 17 Apl. 1965; two s. Morten, Thomas; PRES., NORTH SAILS FOGH LTD. 1981– ; has been sailing competitively for 35 yrs. participating numerous World Championships and 6 Olympic Games (winner Silver Medal 1960, Bronze Medal 1984); inducted into Sports Hall of Fame 1985; inducted into Amateur Sports Hall of Fame 1986; came to Can. 1969; Clubs: Royal Candn. Yacht; Boulevard; Office: 2242 Lakeshore Blvd. W., Toronto, Ont. M8V 1A5.

**FOGLER, Lloyd S.D.,** LL.B., Q.C.; lawyer; b. Toronto, Ont. 25 Jan. 1933; s. Harry L. and Gertrude (Greisman) F.; e. Univ. of Toronto B.Comm. 1954; Osgoode Hall Law Sch. LL.B. 1958; m. Gladys 20 Dec. 1955; children: Gary, Joanne, Elizabeth; SR. PARTNER, FOGLER, RUBINOFF; Instr., Bar Admission Course 1961–64; Lectr., var. pub. seminars 1980–89; Dir., Brampton Brick Limited; FCMI Finan. Corp.; First B Shares Inc.; First Marathon Inc.; First Mercantile Currency Fund; MDC Corp.; Mt. Sinai Hosp. (Chrmn.); St. Clair Paint & Wallpaper Corp.; Winchester Commodity Partnership; author of 1 article and 4 conf. papers; Office: Suite 4400, P.O. Box 95, Royal Trust Tower, Toronto-Dominion Centre, Toronto, Ont. M5K 1G8.

**FOLEY, Gerald Francis;** subsea engineering; b. Corner Brook, Nfld. 11 Oct. 1935; s. John Joseph and Mary Anne (Coleman) F.; e. St. Bernard's Acad. 1952; Radio Coll. of Can. (Hons.) 1958; McGill Univ., MTC grad. 1975; Univ. of West. Ont., MTC 1977; m. Dolores d. Ernest and Josephine Smith 14 Sept. 1957; children: Susan, Patricia, David, Anne-Marie; PRES. & CHIEF OF DIRECTION, TELEGLOBE MARINE INC. 1989– ; Supvr., Microwave Div., Avalon Telephone Co. 1958; joined Teleglobe Canada Inc. 1960 as a supervisor and progressed through several positions incl. Vice-Pres., Opns. before current appointment; Dir., Teleglobe Marine Inc. 1989; Mem., C.I.M. 1976– ; (Vice-Pres., Memberships); Assn. of Indus. Engrs. Am.; recreations: swimming, walking, hiking; clubs: Amateur Athletic Assn. of Montreal; Home: 15975 Perreault St. Pierrefonds, Que. H9H 1N4; Office: 1000 de la Gauchetière W., 24th Floor, Montréal, Qué. H3B 4X5.

**FOLEY, Joan Eleanor,** B.A., Ph.D.; educator; b. Sydney, Australia 31 May 1936; d. Alfred Joseph and Bessie Ridgway (Warden) Mason; e. Ravenswood Meth. Ladies Coll. Sydney 1952; Univ. of Sydney B.A. 1957, Ph.D. (Psychol.) 1960; two s. Brian Anthony, Colin Andrew; PROF. OF PSYCHOL., UNIV. OF TORONTO 1975– ; (on leave 1993–94); Scient. Offr. Defence Research Med. Labs. Downsview, Ont. 1960–62; Special Lectr. in Psychol. Univ. of Toronto 1963, Asst. Prof. 1963, Assoc. Prof. 1965, Prof. 1975, Acting Chrmn. Dept. of Psychol. 1969–70, Assoc. Dean Faculty of Arts & Science 1971–74, Chrmn. Div. of Life Science Scarborough Coll. 1975–77, Principal Scarborough Coll. 1976–84, Chrmn. Dept. of Psychology 1985; Vice-Pres. & Provost, Univ. of Toronto 1985–93; Dir. Donwood Inst. 1973–88 & Bd. Chrmn. 1986–88; Dir., Ont. Psychol. Found. 1987–92; Dir., Internat. Development Rsch. Centre 1989– ; & Vice-Chair 1992– ; author various articles and papers on learning, perception, and spatial orientation psychol. journs.; Fellow, Candn. Psychol. Assn.; recreations: gardening, tennis; skiing; Home: 168 Madison Ave., Toronto, Ont. M5R 2S5; Office: Div. of Life Sciences, Scarborough College, Univ. of Toronto, 1265 Military Trail, Scarborough, Ont. M1C 1A4.

**FOLINSBEE, Robert Edward,** O.C. (1973), B.Sc., M.S., Ph.D., LL.D. (Windsor 1972), D.Sc. (Alberta 1989); F.R.S.C., F.G.S.A.; professor emeritus; b. Edmonton, Alta. 16 Apr. 1917; s. Francis John and Elizabeth Irene (Woolverton) F.; e. Univ. of Alta., B.Sc. 1938; Univ. of Minnesota, M.S. 1940, Ph.D. 1942; Harvard Univ. 1945–46; Univ. of Calif. (Berkeley) 1954–55; m. Catherine Elizabeth, d. late Dr. N.L. Terwillegar, 6 July 1942; children: Robert A., John D., James T., Catherine D.; PROF. EMERITUS, UNIV. OF ALBERTA since 1978 (Chrmn. of Dept. of Geol. 1955–69); Asst. Geol., Geol. Survey of Can. 1941–43, Assoc. Geol. 1945–46; Asst. Prof., Univ. of Alta. 1946–50, Assoc. Prof. 1950–55, Prof. 1955–78; served in 2nd World War with R.C.A.F. as a Pilot, 1943–45; assisted with the devel. of Potassium argon method of dating rocks & minerals (Univ. of Cal.); Pres., 24th Internat. Geol. Cong., Montreal, 1972; Pres. Science Sec. Royal Soc. Can. 1969–70; mem., Candn. Inst. Mining & Metall.; Am. Assn. of Petroleum Geols.; Soc. of Econ. Geols.; Assn. Prof. Engrs., Geols. & Geophysicists, Alta.; Fellow, Geol. Assn. Can.; Pres. Geol. Soc. of Am. 1975–76; Pres. Royal Soc. of Can. 1977–78, Centenary Medal 1982; ; awarded Commemorative Medal for 125th Anniversary of Candn. Confederation 1992; Kappa Sigma; Conservative; Anglican; Club: Faculty Club; Home: 1703–11027 87 Ave., Edmonton, Alta. T6G 2P9.

**FOLLOWS, E.J. (Ted),** B.A.; actor/director; b. Ottawa, Ont. 30 Nov. 1926; s. Edward James and Isabella Douglas (Latimer) F.; e. Univ. of Man. (Broadway div.) 1944–46; Univ. of Toronto B.A. (Hons.) 1950; m. Dawn d. Laurence and Elizabeth Greenhalgh 4 Sept. 1958; div. 1988; m. Susan d. George and Thelma Trethewey 28 Dec. 1988; children: Edwina, Laurence, Samantha, Megan; grandchildren: Lyla, Aaron; founding mem., Everyman Theatre 1946–47; Straw Hat Players 1948–52; Neptune Theatre 1963–66; Mem., 'Spring Thaw' 1951, Candn. Repertory Theatre 1951–52; in England 1952–55: mem., Glasgow Citizen's Theatre; Chesterfield Repertory Theatre; Nottingham Playhouse; Oxford Playhouse; Arts Council Tour 'Merchant of Venice'; film 'Rob Roy'; Stratford Shakespearean Fest. 1955–59, 1972, 1978, 1979; Candn. Players 1956–59; Vancouver

Playhouse 1982, 1983; Muskoka Festival 1985, 1986, 1988, 1989, 1990; actor/dir., num. theatres, Can., U.S., U.K.; 100 TV dramas incl. Arnie Bateman in 'Wojek' and title role 'McQueen – the Actioneer'; latest, 'Patsy Mulkern' in mini series 'J.F.K.-Reckless Youth'; TV Dir., several mini-series & specials incl. 'Hooked on Reading' (winner, Internat. Reading Assn. Broadcast Media Award 1987 & finalist, other awards) and 'Family Matters' (award finalist); Best Actor, City of Winnipeg Drama Fest.; Banff Sch. of Fine Arts scholarship; Jr. Stick of Arts, U. of Man.; Queen Elizabeth 25th Anniv. Medal 1977; Mem., Candn. Actors Equity; Brit. Equity; Am. Equity; ACTRA; Acad. of Candn. Cinema & Television; Directors Guild of Canada; recreations: golf, cross country skiing, travel; Home: 7 Kilbirnie Court, Kitchener, Ont. N2R 1B7.

**FOLSTER, David,** B.A.; writer; b. Grand Falls, N.B. 7 Mar. 1937; s. Hugh Hammond and Clara Gertrude (Montgomery) F.; e. Grand Falls Composite H.S.; Univ. of N.B. B.A. 1960; m. Margot E. d. Thomas and Lillian Pond 10 Aug. 1963; separated; children: Tracy, Natalie, Andrea; worked briefly for 'The Daily Gleaner' (Fredericton) 1960; Technical Writer, Sprague Electric Co. (N. Adams, Mass.) 1961–66; began writing freelance mag. articles early 1960s; sold 2 articles to 'Sports Illustrated' and decided to take up full-time writing; has written hundreds of magazine & newspaper articles since for 'Maclean's,' 'The Globe and Mail,' 'Nature Canada,' 'Atlantic Insight,' etc.; broadcasts on CBC radio & TV: a New Brunswick writer, writing about its life and lore; author: 'The Great Trees of New Brunswick' 1987, 'The Chocolate Ganongs of St. Stephen, New Brunswick' 1990; editor: 'On with the Dance' 1986; Anglican; Mem., N.B. Museum; York-Sunbury Hist. Soc.; Pres., St. John River Soc.; Home: 11 Bremerhaven Ct., Island View, R.R. #6, Fredericton, N.B. E3B 4X7.

**FONG, Patrick,** higher diploma in design; advertising creative director; b. Hong Kong 29 Jan. 1955; s. Yuk Man and Luk Mui (Ng) F.; e. Hong Kong Polytechnic 1977; Wah Yan College, Hong Kong 1974; Ling Hai Art School, Cert. in Commercial Art 1974; m. Eva Lo; one d.: Dora; PRESIDENT & CREATIVE DIR., CAN-ASIAN ADVERTISING LTD. 1990– ; Designer, Amoy Canning Corp. Hong Kong 1977; Copywriter, Far East Advtg. 1978; SSC&B Lintas Advtg. 1979; Sr. Copywriter, Leo Burnett Advtg. 1980; Creative Supervisor, Grey Advtg. 1983; Creative Dir., Ted Bates Advtg. (now BSB) 1984–87; Creative Consultant, Ogilvy & Mather Direct Toronto & Lotus Internat. 1988–89; Founding Partner & Creative Cons., Storm Communications Hong Kong; winner of num. creative awards in advtg., industrial graphics & film, incl. the prestigious New York Film Festivals; actively engaged in cultural and economic contributions to Canada through advertising; in Chinese language served as judge/panelist for Hong Kong Advtg. Award & Clio Awards internationally; Mem., Soc. of Composers, Authors & Music Pubs. of Canada; author of numerous advertising essays in newspapers and magazines; host of radio talk shows; Home: 33 Dundalk Dr., House 8, Scarborough, Ont. M1P 4X6; Office: 57 Spadina Ave., Suite 208, Toronto, Ont. M5V 2J2.

**FONTAINE, Claude,** Q.C., B.A., LL.L.; lawyer; b. Montreal, Que. 12 May 1941; s. André and Juliette (Valois) F.; e. Coll. Jean de Brébeuf and Coll. des Jésuites B.A. 1958; Univ. de Montréal LL.L. 1963; admitted to Bar (Qué.) 1964; m. Michèle d. Florence and Paul-Emile Baillargeon 24 July 1965; one child: Anik;, MEM. EXTVE. CTTE., OGILVY RENAULT 1990– ; articled with present firm 1963; Assoc. 1964; Partner 1973; Sr. Partner 1989; Dir., Beneficial Canada Group of Companies; Benetton Sportsystem Canada Inc.; P. Bonhomme Enterprises Ltd.; Petro-Canada (Chrmn., Audit Ctte.); Pres., Montreal Jr. Bar Assn. 1968–69; Mem., Counc., Barreau du Qué. 1969–70; Candn. Bar Assn. 1978–86, 1990–92; Bd. Chrmn., Montreal Heart Inst. 1986–88; Dir., Montreal Heart Inst. Rsch. Fund; Council for Candn. Unity; Mem., Montreal Amateur Athletic Assn.; recreations: skiing, tennis, sailing, golf, reading; clubs: Club St. Denis, Knowlton Golf; Office: 1981 McGill College Ave., Montreal, Que. H3A 3C1.

**FONTAINE, Nicole;** curatrice publique; née. Montréal, Qué. 1 janvier 1946; f. Roland et Lucienne (Massicotte) Douville; e. Univ. d'Ottawa, maîtrise en gestion des serv. de santé boursière de M.S.S.S. (pendant deux ans); é. Pierre f. Alfred F. 10 octobre 1966; enfants: Karine, Thierry; CURATRICE PUBLIQUE, LE CURATEUR PUBLIC DU QUEBEC 1990– ; Prog. santé communautaire et du baccalauréat en sci. de la santé à l'Univ. du Qué. à Hull 1975–76; l'Union rég. de Montréal des caisses pop. Desjardins 1979; Coord. des serv. de santé mentale, Region de la Montérégie 1979–84; resp. successivement des secteurs des serv., Rég. de Montréal métro 1984–90; Mem., Conseil d'admin., Univ. de Montréal; Groupe Innovation; Groupes de femmes d'affaires; Corp. profl. des admin. agréés; Ordre des infirmières du Qué.; Conférence au niveau internat. et nat. (Paris, Barcelone, Vancouver, etc.); auteure de plusieurs articles; loisirs: voile, ski, lecture, vélo; rés.: 14, Place Cambrai, Outremont, Qué. H2V 1X5; bureau: 600, boul. René-Lévesque O., Montréal, Qué. H3B 4W9.

**FONTAINE, Phil,** B.A.; Grand Chief; b. Sagkeeng Ojibway First Nation, Fort Alexander Reserve, Manitoba 20 Sept. 1944; s. J.B. and Agnes F.; e. Powerview H.S. 1961; Univ. of Manitoba B.A. 1981; m. Janet Florence d. Ahab and Ruth Spence 23 March 1967; children: Michael, Maya; GRAND CHIEF, ASSEMBLY OF MANITOBA CHIEFS 1989– ; Band Administrator and various capacities in Manitoba Indian Brotherhood 1968–72 incl. Chief 1972–76; Deputy Fed. Coord., Native Economic Devel. Program & Yukon, Dept. of Indian Affairs 1977–81; during this time completed studies & served as Special Advisor to the South East Tribal Council in Manitoba; elected Vice-Chief, Assembly of First Nations, Manitoba 1977–89; recreations: running, jogging, reading, art, avid sports fan, hockey; Head Office: Scanterbury, Man. R0E 1W0.

**FOOT, David K.,** M.A., Ph.D.; educator; b. Eng. 9 May 1944; s. Raymond D. and D. Kerry (Theobald) F.; e. Univ. of W. Australia B.Econ. 1966; Harvard Univ. M.A. 1969, Ph.D. 1972; PROF. OF ECON. UNIV. OF TORONTO 1985– ; and mem. Inst. for Policy Analysis 1971–82; Pres. Footwork Consulting Inc.; Mem. of the Bd., CIBC Insurance; cons. to numerous private and pub. orgns., comns., task forces; Asst. Prof. of Econ. present Univ. 1971, Assoc. Prof. 1977; recipient, Teaching Award Social Sci's 1983, 1992; 3M Teaching Fellowship 1992; author: 'Provincial Public Finance in Ontario' 1977; 'Canada's Population Outlook: Demographic Futures and Economic Challenges' 1982; co-author: 'The Growth of Public Employment in Canada' 1979; 'The Compensation Decisions of the Anti-Inflation Board' 1980; 'The Over Forty Society' 1988; ed. 'Public Employment and Compensation in Canada: Myths and Realities' 1978; mem. Candn. Econ. Assn.; Candn. Population Soc.; Candn. Assn. Gerontol.; Am. Econ. Assn.; recreations: tennis, squash; Home: 391 Greer Rd., Toronto, Ont. M5M 3P8; Office: 150 St. George St., Toronto, Ont. M5S 1A1.

**FOOTE, John Benjamin;** merchant; b. Grand Bank, Nfld. 23 March 1918; s. Ambrose and Linda (Tibbo) F.; e. Grand Bank Un. Ch. Acad. 1936; m. Joan d. John G. Wilcox, Hearts Content, Nfld. 8 Aug. 1942; DIR. J.B. FOOTE & SONS LTD.; Mng. Dir., Foote Shipping Co. Ltd. 1963–80; Dir., Nfld. & Labrador Development Corp. Ltd. 1973–89; Newfoundland Light and Power Co. Ltd. 1978–90; mem. Atlantic Devel. Council 1969–74; former mem. Grand Bank Town Council; Notary Public since 1948; United Church; Club: Lions (Past Pres. Grand Bank-Fortune 1961–62); Home: Camp and Main St., Grand Bank, Nfld. A0E 1W0; Office: Water St., Grand Bank, Nfld. A0E 1W0.

**FORAN, Charles William,** B.A., M.A.; writer; b. North York, Ont. 2 Aug. 1960; s. David Lloyd and Muriel Marguerite (Fallu) F.; e. Univ. of Toronto B.A. 1983; Univ. Coll. Dublin M.A. 1984; m. Mary d. Frank and Jeanne Ladky 1 Aug. 1986; children: Anna Eileen, Claire Miriam; freelance writer and journalist since 1990; regular contbr., 'The Globe and Mail' and 'Montreal Gazette'; contbr. ed., 'Saturday Night' mag. 1993– ; Librarian & freelance journalist, N.Y. State 1985–88; Teacher, Beijing College 1988–90; Mem., P.E.N. Canada; Writers Union of Canada; author: 'Sketches in Winter' (non-fiction) 1992 ('Editor's Choice' Globe and Mail 1992), 'Kitchen Music' (novel) forthcoming; finalist QSpell Award and Nat. Mag. Award 1992), 'Coming Attractions 5' (short stories) 1987; recreations: sports, travel; Address: 4365 Marcil, Montreal, Que. H4A 2Z9.

**FORBES, James Dennis,** B.S., M.B.A., Ph.D.; educator and management consultant; b. Ancon, Canal Zone 19 Dec. 1932; s. (late) Raymond Earl and Erma Theo (Caswell) F.; came to Canada 1967 (Citizen 1975); e. Washington State Univ., B.S. (Highest Hons. Agric.) 1954; Harvard Business Sch., M.B.A. 1959; Univ. of Calif. (L.A.) Ph.D. 1967; m. Nancy Currie, d. late Thomas Penman 1 June 1963; children: Susan, Carol, James, Heather; PRES., FORBES ASSOCIATES, MANG. CONSULTANTS; PRES., FORBES FRASER WINES LTD.; PROF. OF COMM., UNIV. OF BRIT. COLUMBIA; joined present univ. 1967 as Asst. Prof., Assoc. Prof. 1970, Prof. 1988; served in U.S. Army Signal Corps 1955–57, rank 1st Lt.; Richard D. Irwin Doctoral Fellow 1967; mem. Am. Marketing Assn.; Inst. Mgmt. Sciences; Consumer's Assn. Can.; author of various articles on agriculture and food policy, distribution, consumer spatial behaviour, consumerism and marketing; author 'Institutions and Influence Groups in Canadian Farm and Food Policy' 1985; 'The Consumer Interest' 1987; co-author 'Economic Intervention and Regulation in Canadian Agriculture' 1982; 'Consumer Interest in Marketing Boards' 1974; Office: Fac. of Commerce, Univ. of B.C., Vancouver, B.C. V6T 1Z2.

**FORBES, L. Mackenzie,** B.Sc., M.Sc., P.Ag.; retired public servant; b. Berkeley, Calif. 22 Aug. 1932; s. Robin S.M. and Helen E. (Laundy) F.; e. Univ. of Alta., B.Sc. 1955; Utah State Univ., M.Sc. 1965; Alta. Inst. of Agrol., P.Ag. 1958; m. Dorothy d. Lars and Gertrude Lee 29 June 1957; children: Laura L., Cameron M.; Asst. Grazing Appraiser, Public Lands Div., Alta. Forestry, Lands & Wildlife 1955–62; Dist. Supvr. (Lethbridge) 1962–65; Range Survey Supvr. 1965; Head, Grazing Br. 1965–73; Asst. Dir. of Lands 1973–76; Dir., Prog. Support 1976–81; Asst. Dep. Min., Public Lands Div., Alta. Forestry, Lands & Wildlife 1981–87; Sr. Departmental Consultant, Alta. Forestry, Lands and Wildlife 1987–88; Mem., United Ch. of Can.; Alta. Inst. of Agrol. (Br. Pres. 1964); Soc. for Range Mgmt. (Section Pres. 1966); recreations: lake cabin, photography, golf; Home: 11139 – 50 Ave., Edmonton, Alta. T6H 0J1.

**FORBES, Ralph A.;** automotive executive; b. Tilbury, Ont. 3 Aug. 1924; s. Russell A. and Eileen Stuart (Ainslie) F.; e. Kitchener H.S.; RCAF; Univ. of Toronto, cert. course in business 1947; m. Phyllis J. d. J. Albert Smith 23 Aug. 1947; children: Russell Albert, Elaine Ainslie (Ormston); PRES., FORBES MOTORS LTD. 1985– ; Pilot Training & Graduation, RCAF 1943–45; Mercury Lincoln Dealer (Welland) 1948–55; Pontiac Buick Cadillac (Waterloo) 1955–85; Pres., Auto Dealers of Can. 1983–84; Dir., Waterloo Mutual Insur. Co. (Economical Insurance) 1963– ; Dir., R.A. Forbes Investments Ltd.; R.A. Villa Ltd.; Breslau Properties Ltd.; 43 years automobile dealer; Vice-Chrmn., Freeport Hosp. Found.; Mem., St. Andrews (Presbyn.) Ch.; recreations: golf, boating, fishing; clubs: Westmount Golf & Country, Muskoka Lakes Golf & Country, Atlantis Golf; Home: 'Westmount Mews' 671 - 7 Glasgow Rd., Kitchener, Ont.; Office: 165 Weber St. S., Waterloo, Ont. N2J 4A6.

**FORBES, Robert Earl,** B.A., LL.B., LL.M.; lawyer; b. Chesley, Ont. 1 Dec. 1948; s. Earl Alexander and Ethel Maryann (Redmond) F.; e. Univ. of West. Ont., B.A. 1970, LL.B. 1973; London Sch. of Econ., LL.M. 1974; m. Susan Jean d. Donald and Jean McCabe 12 Nov. 1983; children: Jacqueline, Justine, Brendan; PARTNER, McCARTHY TÉTRAULT, BARRISTERS & SOLICITORS 1983– ; Assoc. 1979; Asst. Prof., Fac. of Law, Univ. of West. Ont. 1974–79; Dir., Lawson Mardon Group Limited; Lectr., Contract Law, Osgoode Hall Law Sch., York Univ.; Bus. Law, Fac. of Mngt. Studies, MBA Prog., Univ. of Toronto; author: 'Taxation and Estate Planning' 1977, 'Canadian Companies and the Stock Exchanges' 1979, 'Canadian Business Organizations Law' 1984; Home: 7 Riverside Trail, Toronto, Ont. M6S 1G6; Office: Suite 4700, Toronto Dominion Bank Tower, Toronto-Dominion Centre, Toronto, Ont. M5K 1E6.

**FORBES, William Frederick,** Ph.D., D.Sc.; educator; e. Univ. of London, B.Sc. 1947, D.Sc. 1964, Imp. Coll. B.Sc. 1950, Ph.D. (Chem.) 1952, D.I.C.; m. Dr. Margaret Anne (nee Shadbolt); children: Christine Olivia, Alain James, Helena Vivienne; RESEARCH FELLOW, STATISTICS CANADA; Lectr., Univ. of Nottingham, Eng., 1952; Assoc. Prof., Memorial Univ. of Nfld., 1953, Prof. 1955; Princ. Research Offr., C.S.I.R.O., Australia, 1959; joined Univ. of Waterloo as Prof. of Gerontology and Statistics 1962; Dean, Faculty of Mathematics, Univ. of Waterloo 1972–80; Dir., Program in Gerontology, Univ. of Waterloo 1982–93; Prof. Emeritus, Univ. of Waterloo 1993– ; Visiting Prof., Univ. of Rochester, 1965–71; Head of WHO Centre for Reference on the Assessment of Smoking Habits; Consultant to U.S. Public Health Service (NICHD) 1965–69; mem., Candn. Counc. on Smoking and Health (Pres. 1983–85); WHO Expert Adv. Panel on Smoking & Health 1977–91; Bd. of Dirs., The Freeport Hosp. 1990–93; served with R.A.F. 1944–47; author of over 310 publs. in fields of gerontol., smoking & health, organic spectral chem.; Assoc., Royal Coll. Science; mem., Candn. Assn. Gerontol. (Pres. 1971–73) (rec. Assn. award for outstanding contributions to Gerontology, 1981); U.S. Gerontol. Soc. (Vice Pres. & Chrmn. Biol. Sciences Sec. 1971–72); mem., Ont. Gerontol. Assn. (Pres. 1981–84); awarded Queen's Jubilee Medal 1977; awarded Commemorative Medal for 125th Anniversary of Candn. Confederation

1993; recreations: military history, vegetarianism; Home: 2119 Black Friars Rd., Ottawa, Ont. K2A 3K7; Office: Ottawa, Ont. K1A 0T6.

**FORCESE, Dennis Philip,** M.A., Ph.D.; educator; b. Winnipeg, Man. 27 Sept. 1941; s. Ectore August and Eva Delima (Carriere) F.; e. St. Paul's High Sch. and St. James Coll. Winnipeg 1959; Univ. of Man. B.A. 1962, M.A. 1964; Wash. Univ. St. Louis Ph.D. 1968; m. Brenda d. George and Olive Roberton 24 Aug. 1963; children: Craig Stephen, Leah Kathleen; PROF. OF SOCIOL. CARLETON UNIV. 1980– , Asst. Prof. present Univ. 1967, Assoc. Prof. 1972, Grad. Supvr. Sociol. 1968, Asst. Chrmn. of Sociol. 1973–76, Chrmn. 1976–81, Dean of Social Sciences 1981–88, Vice Pres., Academic 1989–92; author 'Canadian Social Class Structure' 1975, rev. ed. 1980; 3rd ed. 1986; 'Policing Canadian Society' 1992; co-author 'Social Research Methods' 1973; co-ed. 'Stages of Social Research' 1970; 'Issues in Canadian Society' 1975; 'Social Issues' 1982; 'Issues in Canadian Society' rev. ed. 1988; Sociol. Ed., The Carleton Lib. Series 1972–81; Pres., Carleton Univ. Press 1985–86, 1989– ; Mem., Bd. of Dir., Carleton Univ. Press 1981– ; Mem., Bd. of Gov., Carleton Univ. 1983–86; Home: 190 Bourbon St., Ottawa, Ont. K1V 9K2; Office: Dept. of Sociology, Carleton Univ., Ottawa, Ont. K1S 5B6.

**FORD, Derek Clifford,** M.A., D.Phil., F.R.S.C.; educator; geomorphologist; b. Bath, Eng. 24 Apl. 1935; s. Clifford Sidney and Marjorie Alice (Branch) F.; e. City of Bath Sch.; Oxford Univ. B.A. 1958, M.A., D.Phil. 1963; m. Margaret d. William and Clare Rebbeck 5 Sept. 1958; children: Owen Derek Lagan, Piers Roger, Thomasin Sophia, William Toby; PROF. OF GEOG. McMASTER UNIV. 1973– ; Lectr. present Univ. 1959, Asst. Prof. 1964, Assoc. mem. Geol. 1965, Assoc. Prof. of Geog. 1968, Chrmn. 1973–79, mem. Bd. Govs. 1979–83; Asst. Prof. Cal. State Coll. Los Angeles 1963; recipient Gold Medal Union Internat. de Speleologie 1973; Award Scholarly Distinction Candn. Assn. Geogs. 1978; Cuthbert Peek Award Royal Geog. Soc. (London) 1984; Medal of Honour Geol. Soc. China 1984; Gold Medal Royal Geog. Soc. Can. 1986; G.K. Gilbert Award Am. Assn. Geogs. 1987; Medaille Dumont, Geol. Soc. Belge 1990; co-author 'Castleguard' 1985; 'Karst Geomorphology and Hydrology' 1989; co-ed. 'Paleokarst: A World Regional and Systematic Review' 1980; mem. Candn. Assn. Geogs. (Pres. 1982–83); Union Internat. de Speleologie (Pres. 1986–89); Geol. Assn. Can.; Brit. Geomorphol. Rsch. Group; recreations: mountaineering, caving, skiing, singing, garden; Home: 222 Martins Rd., Ancaster, Ont. L9G 3L2; Office: Hamilton, Ont. L8S 4K1.

**FORD, George Harry,** M.A., Ph.D.; university professor; author; b. Winnipeg, Man. 21 Dec. 1914; s. Harry and Emma Gertrude (Burgess) F.; e. Kelvin High Sch., Winnipeg, 1932; Univ. of Man., B.A. 1936; Univ. of Toronto, M.A. 1938; Yale Univ., Ph.D. 1942; m. Kathleen Patricia, d. late James Richard Murray, 4 May, 1942; children: Leslie Margaret, Harry Seymour; PROF. OF ENG., UNIV. OF ROCHESTER, since 1958 and Chrmn. of Dept. 1960–72; Lect., Univ. of Man., 1940–42, 1945–46; Assoc. Prof., Univ. of Cincinnati, 1946–55; Prof. 1955–58; Visiting Prof., Univ. of Chicago 1948, Johns Hopkins Univ., 1949, Univ. of B.C. 1953; served with RCA 1942–45; rank Capt.; rec'd John Addison Porter Prize, Yale Univ. 1942; Fellow, Am. Council Learned Socs. 1959; Guggenheim Fellow 1963–64; Huntington Library Fellow 1978; author: 'Keats and the Victorians' 1944 (repr. 1945, 1961); 'The Pickersgill Letters' 1948; 'Dickens and His Readers' 1955 (paperback 1961); 'Double Measure: A Study of D.H. Lawrence' 1965 (paperback 1968); Ed., 'Selected Poems of Keats' 1950; 'The Dickens Critics' 1961 (paperback 1966); 'David Copperfield' 1958; 'Hard Times' 1967, 1991; 'Vanity Fair' 1958; 'Bleak House' 1977; 'Victorian Fiction: A Second Guide to Research' 1978; 'The Making of a Secret Agent' 1978, 1983; Co-ed., 'The Norton Anthology of English Literature' 1962, 68, 74, 79, 85, 91; mem. Adv. Bd., 'Mosaic' (Univ. of Man. mag.) since 1967; Adv. Bd., 'Victorian Studies' 1964–67; Adv. Bd., 'Thalia' (University of Ottawa Mag.) 1978– ; mem., Eng. Inst. (Supvry. Bd. 1964–66); Modern Lang. Assn (Chrmn., Victorian Lit. Sec., 1965 and l985); Pres. (1973–74) Dickens Soc. Am.; Pres. (1975–77J The Dickens Fellowship (London); Pres. (1979–83) Int. Soc. for Study of Time (Extve. Council 1977); Vice Chrmn., New York Council for Humanities, 1978,79; Consultant, Ontario Council of Graduate Studies 1980–81; Am Acad. of Arts & Sci. 1980; mem., Int. Advisory Bd., Buckingham Univ., England; Wilbur Cross Medal, Yale Univ. 1983; Delta Upsilon; U.S. Citizen since 1954; Democrat; Anglican; recreation: riding; Clubs: Cincinnati Literary; Rochester Pundit; Home: 2230 Clover St., Rochester, NY 14618.

**FORD, John Edward,** B.A., A.R.C.T.; choral conductor; b. Toronto, Ont. 23 Sept. 1933; s. Ernest Algernon and Agnes Wylie (Berry) F.; e. Scarborough Collegiate 1952; Victoria College, Univ. of Toronto B.A. 1957; Royal Conservatory of Music of Toronto A.R.C.T. (singing – solo performer) 1978; ARTISTIC DIRECTOR, THE ORIANA SINGERS, TORONTO 1977– ; and CONDUCTOR, PAX CHRISTI CHORALE 1993– ; Teacher, Orono Dist. H.S. 1957–60; R.H. King C.I. 1960–65; Riverdale C.I. 1965–88; Lectr., Choral Techniques, Fac. of Music, Univ. of Toronto 1979–82; Dir. of Music, Washington Un. Ch. 1976–81; Eglinton Un. Ch. 1981– ; Conductor, Ontario Youth Choir 1983; Pres., Ont. Music Educators' Assn. 1975–76; Conductor, Summer School Choir, Fac. of Edn., Univ. of Toronto 1975–88, 1991; Hon. Life Mem., Ontario Music Educator's Assn. 1990; Mem., Warden Woods Mennonite Ch.; Royal Candn. Coll. of Organists; Ont. Choral Fed.; Assn. of Candn. Choral Conductors; Ont. Music Educators' Assn.; author of two articles for 'The Recorder' 1973, 1975; recreations: reading, walking, travel; Home: 10 Bayfield Cres., Toronto, Ont. M4K 2V4.

**FORD, John Kenneth Baker,** Ph.D.; zoologist; b. Victoria, B.C. 28 Jan. 1955; s. John Gordon and Suzette Mary Louie (Baker) F.; e. Univ. of B.C. B.Sc. 1976, Ph.D. 1985; m. Beverly d. George and Ethel Bluett 4 Nov. 1989; one s. Michael Kenneth Baker; MARINE MAMMAL SCIENTIST VANCOUVER AQUARIUM 1992– ; field rsch. behaviour & communication killer whales B.C., Alaska, Norway, Argentina discovering vocal dialects among different family groups; mem. jt. fed./prov. Johnstone Strait Killer Whale Ctte. 1990–92; field rsch. narwhals, belugas, bowhead whales Candn. Arctic 1975–86; Curator of Marine Mammals, Vancouver Aquarium 1988–92; Rsch. Assoc. in Zool. Univ. of B.C.; Adv. to U.S. Dept. of Justice impact 'Exxon Valdez' oil spill on killer whales 1990–92; rsch. expeditions Hawaii 1980, 1981, 1991 and Japan 1988 study humpback whales; NSERC Postdoctoral Fellow Pacific Biol. Stn. Dept. Fisheries & Oceans 1985–86; co-author 'Killer Whales: A Study of their Identification, Genealogy and Natural History in British Columbia and Washington State' 1987; author various sci. papers; Charter mem. Soc. Marine Mammalogy (Best Paper Award Boston 1983); mem. Vancouver Natural Hist. Soc.; recreations: scuba diving, photography; Home: 5454 Indian River Dr., North Vancouver, B.C. V7G 1L3; Office: P.O. Box 3232, Vancouver, B.C. V6B 3X8.

**FORD, Robert A.D.,** C.C. (1971), M.A., D.Litt., LL.D.; diplomat; b. Ottawa, Ont. 8 Jan. 1915; s. late Arthur R. and late Lavinia (Scott) F.; e. Univ. of W. Ont., B.A. 1938 (Hon. Soc. 1938); Cornell Univ., M.A. 1939; Univ. of W. Ont., D.Litt. 1965; Univ. of Toronto LL.D. 1987; m. (late) Maria Thereza Gomes, 1946; mem. Independent Commission on Disarmament and Security Issues (Palme Commission); Gov., Int. Inst. of Geopolitics 1980–88; mem., Counc. of Advisors, Candn. Centre for Arms Control and Disarmament; Hon. Pres., Canada-France Assoc. of the Bourbonnais; mem., Assoc. of Bourbonnais Writers; served on Staff of Cornell Univ., before joining the Dept. of External Affairs in 1940; held appts. in Rio de Janeiro and London before appt. as Second Secy., at Moscow in 1946; again served in London as Secy., later returning to Moscow as Chargé d'Affaires, 1951–54; subsequently Head of European Sec., Ottawa; Ambassador to Colombia, 1957–59; Ambassador to Yugoslavia, Jan. 1959–May 1961; Ambassador to Egypt 1961–63; Ambassador to U.S.S.R. 1964–80; Special Adviser on East-West Relations 1980–83; awarded Gold Medal, Prof. Inst. Pub. Service of Can. 1971; Award of Merit, Univ. of Western Ont. 1988; author of: 'A Window on the North' (poems), for which rec'd. Gov.-Gen. Award for Poetry (1956); 'The Solitary City' (poems); 'Holes in Space' (poems); 'Needle in the Eye' (poems); 'Russian Poetry: A Personal Anthology'; 'Doors, Words and Silence' (poems); 'Dostoyevsky and Other Poems'; 'Our Man in Moscow: Reflections on the The Soviet Union from Stalin to Brezhnev'; 'Coming from Afar: Selected Poems'; 'Diplomate et poète à Moscow: L'union sovietique de Stalin à Gorbatchev'; 'Literary Lions and Russians Bears: A Poet - Diplomat and the Great Russian Artist from Stalin to Gorbachev'; Address: La Poivrière, St-Sylvestre-Pragoulin, 63310 Randan, France.

**FORD, Robin John Christopher,** M.A., A.C.P.; public servant; b. England 10 May 1935; s. Walter Percy and Dorothy Laura (Clarke) F.; e. Oxford Univ. B.A. 1957, M.A. 1960; London Univ., Coll. of Preceptors, A.C.P. 1961; Univ. of B.C., teacher's cert. 1962; m. Muriel d. John and Edith Pollard 30 June 1958; children: Nicholas, Vicki Heather, Bryan, Cathey; DEP. MIN., ALTA. LABOUR 1990– ; H.S. & Univ. teacher 1957–62; Prod., CBC 1962–65; Mgr., Fed. Govt. of Can. 1965–69; Advr. on Rural Devel. & Employment for the U.N. in Africa 1970–75; Commonwealth Secretariat 1976; Cons., Mobil Oil & fed. govt. 1976–77; Advr. to Comnr. of N.W.T. on local govt. & const. devel. 1978–79; Dir. of Improvement Districts (I.D.'s), Govt. of Alta. 1979–80; Asst. Dep. Min., I.D.'s & Native Serv. 1980–87; Dep. Min., Consumer & Corporate Affairs, Alta. 1987–90; author/broadcaster for radio/TV; teacher; scholarships to Oxford 1953, 1954; Mem., ACTRA; Inst. of Pub. Admn.; author: 'The Indian Child and His Education' 1969, 'How to Start a Village Polytechnic' 1971, 'What Happens to Money in Rural Communities' 1973, 'Employment Oriented Training' 1976, 'Local Government – Direction for the 1980s'' 1980 and others; recreations: gardening, renovations; Office: 10th fl., 10808 – 99 Ave., Edmonton, Alta. T5K 0G5.

**FORD-JONES, Elizabeth Lee,** M.D., F.R.C.P.(C); pediatrician; b. Portland, Ore. 25 July 1950; d. John Warren and Shirley Lee (Parnum) Pearson; e. Queen's Univ. M.D. 1974; Montreal Children's Hosp. and McGill Univ. Pediatrics & Infectious Diseases 1974–79; m. Anthony s. Eric and Marcelle Ford-Jones 1 Dec. 1979; two d. Carrie, Polly; Assoc. Prof. of Pediatrics Univ. of Toronto 1990– ; Asst. Prof. of Pediatrics McGill Univ. 1980–81, Univ. of Toronto 1981–90; former Dir. of Infection Control Service Hosp. for Sick Children 1981–.; co-author 'Epidemiology and Public Health: Pretest Self Assessment and Review' 3rd ed. 1984; numerous sci. papers, reviews, book chapters; Project Dir. 'A Guide to the Physical Health, Safety and Emotional Well-being of Children in Child Care Centres and Family Day Care Homes,' 'Well Beings,' Candn. Pediatric Soc.; Candn. Infectious Diseases Soc.; Pediatric Infectious Diseases Soc.; Am. Soc. Microbiols.; Home: 359 McNichol Cres., Burlington, Ont. L7L 1E9; Office: 555 University Ave., Toronto, Ont. M5G 1X8.

**FORER, Arthur H.,** B.Sc., Ph.D.; educator; b. Trenton, N.J. 17 Dec. 1935; s. Bernard and Rose Ethel F.; e. Mass Inst. Technol. B. Sc. 1957; Univ. of Rochester 1957–59; Univ. of Wash. 1959; Dartmouth Coll. Med. Sch. Ph.D. 1964; m. Alexandra d. Frederik and Ellen Westengaard 18 Dec. 1964; two s. Michael, David; PROF. OF BIOL. YORK UNIV. 1975– ; Am. Cancer Soc. Rsch. Fellow Carlsberg Found. Biol. Inst. Copenhagen, Denmark 1964–66; Rsch. Fellow in Zool. Cambridge Univ. 1966–67, Helen Hay Whitney Found. Rsch. Fellow 1967–69; Helen Hay Whitney Found. Rsch. Fellow & Hargitt Rsch. Fellow in Zool. Duke Univ. 1969–70; Lektor, Odense (Denmark) Univ. 1970–72; Assoc. Prof. of Biol. Present Univ. 1972–75; external reviewer numerous sci. jours., granting agencies and publishers; author over 80 articles profl jours.; co-ed. 'Mitosis/Cytokinesis' 1981; assoc. ed. various cell biol. jours.; el. to Royal Soc. Can. 1984; mem., Sci. for Peace (Exec. 1984–86); Amnesty Internat.; Am. Soc. Cell Biol.; Am. Assoc. for Advancement of Sci.; Microscopical Soc. of Can.; former mem., Candn. Soc. Cell Biol. (Exec. 1981–83); Genetics Soc. Can.; mem. Grants Award Panel N.S.E.R.C. 1977–80; musician (single & double reeds) various local orchs. incl. Yorkminstrels, Scarborough Music Theatre, Broadway North, Etobicoke Music Theatre, Northdale Concert Band; recreations: cycling, hiking, gardening, music; Home: 17 Michigan Dr., Willowdale, Ont. M2M 3H9.; Office: 4700 Keele St., Downsview, Ont. M3J 1P3.

**FOREST, L'hon. Joseph-Isai-Yves;** judge; b. Sherbrooke, Que. 25 June 1921; s. Lionel, Q.C. and Marie-Alice (Deneault) F.; e. St. Charles Semy., Sherbrooke, Que.; Univ. of Montreal; m. Elizabeth, d. late Napoleon St. Martin, 11 Aug. 1947; children: Suzanne, Robert, Barbara, Pierre, Jean; JUSTICE SUPERIOR COURT, QUE.; called to Bar of Que. 1943; cr. Q.C. 1961; served as M.P. 1963–72; R. Catholic; recreations: skiing, golf, fishing; Home Merry St., Magog, Que.; Office: Court House, 1 Rue Notre-Dame E., Montreal, Que. H2Y 1B6.

**FOREST, Normand J.,** B.A., LL.B., LL.D.; lawyer; b. Verner, Ont. 2 Nov. 1937; s. Donat and Maria (Corriveau) F.; e. Univ. of Sudbury B.A. 1959; Osgoode Hall Law Sch. Toronto LL.B. 1962; m. Marie-Paule d. J. Lionel Lavallée 2 July 1962; children: Sylvie Palkovits, Josée Forest-Niesing, Dominique; PARTNER, LACROIX, FOREST & DEL FRATE 1966– ; Dir. Hebdo le Voyageur Inc. 1975–93; Gov. Laurentian Univ. of Sudbury (Past Chrmn.) 1976–91; Dir. L'Association des juristes d'expression française de l'Ontario (Past Pres.) 1982–92; Mem. of the Bench & Bar Counc. of Ont. 1984–85; Dir. La Fondation Franco-Ontarienne; Past Chrmn. Bd. Dirs. Sudbury Dist. Boys' Home Charitable Trust; mem. Bd. of Dirs. Ontario Educational Communications Authority (TV Ontario) 1986–92; mem. Bd. of Dirs., Council for Candn. Unity; Decoré de l'Ordre du Mérite de l'Association des Juristes d'Expression française de l'Ontario 1992; Agrégation de l'Université de Sudbury 1992; Récipiendaire de la Médaille Commémorative du 125e Anniversaire de la Confédération du Canada 1993; Doctor of Laws (LL.D. honoris causa) Laurentian Univ. 1993; recreations: golf, hunting, fishing, vocal music; Clubs: Richelieu; Idylwylde; R. Catholic; Home: Sudbury, Ont.; Office: 36 Elgin St., Sudbury, Ont. P3C 5B4.

**FORESTELL, Hon. Mr. Justice Michael Paul,** M.A.; judge; b. Bridgeberg, Ont. 22 July 1929; s. Tobias Frederick and Agnes Irene (O'Driscoll) F.; e. Phipps St. Pub. and Fort Erie High Schs. 1947; Univ. of Toronto, St. Michael's Coll. B.A. 1952, M.A. 1954; called to Bar of Ont. Osgoode Hall 1956; m. Dorothy Ethel d. William C. and Noami Gilchrist 6 Oct. 1956; children: Martha, Maureen, Susan, Paul; JUDGE, ONTARIO COURT (GEN. DIV.) 1990– ; law practice Raymond, Spencer, Law & MacInnes, Welland, Ont. 1956–58; M. Paul Forestell, Welland 1959–61; Kovacs, Forestell, Luciani (subsequently Forestell, Talmage, Stratton & Latinovich) 1961–85; Dist. Court Judge at Cayuga 1985–90; Chrmn. Legal & Legis. Ctte. Ont. Separate Sch. Trustees 1960–64; Bd. Govs. Niagara Coll. Applied Arts & Technol. 1966–72, First Chrmn. 1966–70; mem. Keiler McKay Ctte. Teaching Religion Pub. Schs. Ont. 1967–69; Dir. and Sec. Mahoney Silver Jubilee Dollhouse Found. until 1988; cr. Q.C. 1966; mem. Advocates Soc.; Candn. Bar Assn.; recreations: tennis, swimming, golf; Clubs: Albany, Peninsula Lakes Golf; Welland; Home: 6 First Ave., Welland, Ont. L3C 1X6; Office: P.O. Box 219, Cayuga, Ont. N0A 1E0.

**FORESTER, Andrew John,** B.Sc., Ph.D.; environmental scientist; b. London, England 15 June 1944; e. Univ. of London, B.Sc. (Hons.) 1965; Univ. of Reading, Ph.D. 1974; m. Elizabeth Mary Parker 1968; PROP., DARTSIDE CONSULTING/ASSOC., INST. FOR ENVIRON. STUDIES, UNIV. OF TORONTO 1984– ; Rsch. Fellow, Geology Dept., Univ. of Reading 1968–71; Zoology Dept., Univ. of Toronto 1974–77; Mem., Inst. for Environ. Studies, Univ. of Toronto 1978–84; Cand. Sci. Dir., Tri-Academy Ctte. on Acid Deposition (Nat. Acad. Sci., U.S.A./ Acad. Invest. Cient., Mexico/Roy. Soc. Can.) 1980–87; Sci. Offr., Royal Soc. of Can. review of Can./U.S. technical reports on the Long-Range Transport of Airborne Pollutants (LRTAP) 1982–83; Observer, Peer Review Can. Govt.'s LRTAP programme 1984; Sci. Dir., Roy. Soc. Can. study on Nuclear Winter & Environ. Impact of Nuclear War 1984–85; Coordinator Environment Canada study on Greenhouse Effect 1986 & Ozone Rsch. 1987; Consultant Author, U.N. Studies on the Climatic and Other Global Effects of Nuclear War 1987–88 and Use of Military Resources to Protect the Environment 1991–92; author, Environment Canada Study of the Effects of Halons on the Atmosphere 1988–89; 'Ozone' in 'State of the Environment, Canada 1992'; Cons. on Environmental Indicators, Govt. of Can. 1992–93; Research and teaching marine biology, zoology, environ. sci. & mgmt., environmental problems of indigenous peoples and developing countries, evolutionary biology & creationism, Univ. of Toronto; vol. tutor, Adult Literacy Movement; author various articles marine & environmental science, zoology, physiology; recreations: Prehist./Archeo. of Cent. & S. Am., canoeing, sailing, hunting; Office: 151 Yonge Blvd., Toronto, Ont. M5M 3H3.

**FORGET, Claude E.,** B.Sc., M.Sc., LL.B.; economist; consultant; b. Montreal, Que. 28 May 1936; s. Lucien and Isola (Nadeau) F.; e. Univ. of Montreal and Que. Bar, LL.B. 1959; Univ. of London, B.Sc. 1962, M.Sc. 1963; Johns Hopkins Univ., Doctoral work 1964–66; m. Monique Jerome 25 Mar. 1960; children: Elise, Nicolas; SR. VICE PRES., CORPORATE AFFAIRS, LAURENTIAN GROUP CORP. 1989– ; Researcher, Fed. Comn. on Taxation 1963–66; Comn. of Inquiry on Health & Welfare (Que. Govt.) 1968–70; Priv. Planning Assn. of Can. 1969–71; Min. of Soc. Affairs, Que. Lib. Govt. 1971–76; Quebec M.L.A. 1976–81; Lectr., McGill Univ. 1981–83; Sr. Partner, Secor Inc. 1983–89; Vice Pres., C.D. Howe Rsch. Inst. 1983–88; Chrmn., Comn. of Enquiry on Unemployment Insurance 1985–86; Pres., The Asbestos Inst. 1987–89; author: 'The Harmonization of Social Policies' 1984, 'Education Policy in Canada' 1985, 'La Caisse de Dépôt et de Placement du Québec' 1984; contrib.: 'Can. Pub. Admin.' 1973; Mem., Que. Bar; Home: 1227 Sherbrooke St. W., Apt. 82, Montreal, Que. H3G 1G1; Office: 1100 René-Lévesque Blvd. W., Montreal, Que. H3B 4N4.

**FORGET, Maurice A.,** B.A., B.C.L.; lawyer; b. Paris, France 9 Apr. 1947; s. Maurice E. and Catherine (Schulz) F.; e. Univ. of Montreal B.A. 1966; McGill Univ. B.C.L. 1969; PARTNER, MARTINEAU WALKER and FASKEN MARTINEAU, ADVOCATES 1978– ; admitted to Bar 1970; joined present firm 1970; practice concentrated in securities & corp. law; Dir., Martineau Walker 1981–92; Chrmn., Montreal Bar Library 1984–87; Mem., Que. Bar Disciplinary Ctte. 1990– ; Dir. & Mem. Extve. Ctte.: Cabano Transportation Group Inc.; Dir. & Mem. Ethics Ctte., Bonaventure Trust Co.; Dir., The Standard Life Assur. Co. of Can.; Harbour Indus. (Can.) Ltd.; Kingsway Transport of America Inc.; Cabano-Kingsway Inc.; American Express (Can.) Inc. 1982–86; Lectr., Securities Law, McGill Univ.; D.E.C. (honoris causa) Dawson Coll.; Gov. & Dir., Douglas Hosp.; Chrmn. & Dir., Ctr. d'Accueil Jean-Olivier-Chénier for the Intellectually Handicapped 1981–92; Chrmn., Heritage Montreal Found.; Found. of the Friends of the Musée d'art contemporain de Montréal; Dir., Ville Marie Found.; National Ballet Sch. of Can.; Montreal Chest Hosp. Found.; Musée d'art contemporain de Montréal; Montreal Chamber Orch. 1985–89; Dawson Coll. (Gov. 1983–88; Chrmn. 1984–88); Vice Pres. & Dir., Mus. of Decorative Arts; Dir. & Sec., Ctr. Internat. d'art contemporain de Montréal; Founding Dir., Corp. Art Collections Assn.; Mem., Acquisitions Ctte., Art Gall. of the Univ. du Qué.; Life Gov., Montreal Gen. Hosp.; Gov., Montreal Children's Hosp.; Roman Catholic; Liberal Party; Mem., Que., Candn. & Am. bar assns.; Montreal Bd. of Trade; Dir. & Sec., Montreal Better Business Bur. 1979–83; recreations: reading, travel, art collecting, philately; Home: 1700 Dr. Penfield Ave., Apt. 25, Montreal, Que. H3H 1B4; Office: 3400 The Stock Exchange Tower, 800 Victoria Sq., Montreal, Que. H4Z 1E9.

**FORGET, Nicolle,** c.r., B.en Sc. Com., L. ès D., Barreau, 1982 du Québec; née Saint-Liguori, Qué. 14 mai 1941; f. Léonard et Noella (Desmarais) F.; é. Ecole des H.E.C. Montréal B.en Sc. Com. 1970; Univ. de Montréal L. ès D. 1981; DESS en bioéthique 1993– ; mem. de l'institut d'arbitrage du Québec 1993– ; mem. de la corporation des conseillers au relations industrielles 1987– ; présidente du conseil d'administration de Nouveler Inc. 1981–85; mem. du conseil d'adm. de Hydro-Québec 1978–85; et de la Soc. d'énergie de la Baie James 1978–84; Hydro-Qué. Internat. 1978–82; mem. Conseil économique du Can. 1978–1981; Antofagasta, Chili, Colegio San José, enseignement du français et de la musique 1960; Séminaire de Joliette, bibliothèque 1961–62; CJLM, Joliette, Service des reportages et émissions féminines 1961–63; Coll. classique Joliette, enseignement du français littéraire 1963; Comn. scolaire régionale Lanaudière, service d'orientation, secrétaire 1963–65; Etoile du Nord, Joliette (Hebdomadaire) directrice des pages féminines et artistiques 1964–65; Union des Municipalités du Qué. Montréal, secrétaire 1965–67; Conseil de bien-être du Qué. Montréal, chef de secrétariat 1967–68, secrétaire générale intérimaire 1968–69, dir. gén. intérimaire 1970–71; Rédacteur d'une chronique sur la Consommation, Journal de l'Alimentation 1973; Inst. canadien d'éd. des adultes, chargée d'adm. 1973–77; fondateur et dir. de troupe de théâtre 'Les deux masques' Joliette 1961–66; mem. du comité des Jeunesses musicales du Can. Joliette 1963–66; dir., comité auxiliaire féminin de la Jeune Chambre de Comm. Joliette 1961–63; mem. Soc. des poètes canadiens-français 1961–66; mem. Conseil gén. de la Féd. des SSJB du Qué. 1964–67 (vice prés. 1966–67, trésorier 1967–69); secrétaire-trésorier de l'Agence Alerte Inc. 1967–69, mem. fondateur et secrétaire de la Féd. des Femmes du Qué. 1967–68; secrétaire francophone de la div. du Qué. de l'Assn. des consommateurs du Can. 1970–71, Vice Prés. 1971–72, trésorier 1972–73, prés. de l'Assn. des consommateurs du Qué. 1975–78; prés. Festival d'été de Lanaudière 1982–83; mem. du conseil d'admin. de l'Inst. Vanier pour la Famille 1982; Prés. des Ballets Eddy Toussaint de Montréal 1983–85; mem. du conseil d'admin. de l'Univ. de Montréal 1983–84; mem. du Conseil des services essentiels (Vice-Prés. 1985–88); mem. du conseil d'admin. de l'Agence québécoise de valorisation industrielle de la recherche (AQVIR) 1984–86; vice-présidente du Fonds de Solidarité des travailleurs du Qué. 1983–88; mem. du conseil d'administration de l'Ecole polytechnique de Montréal 1988–92; mem. de l'Office national des transports 1988–93; mem. du conseil d'admin. du Groupe Jean Coutu (PJC) inc. 1993– ; publié divers articles; Adresse: 1170 Maple, Longueuil, Qué. J4J 4N6.

**FORGUSON, Lynd Wilks,** B.A., M.A., Ph.D.; educator; b. Paducah, Kentucky 15 Jan. 1938; s. Iris Lynd and Alice Margarine (Wilks) F.; e. Fairmont H.S. 1956; Baldwin-Wallace Coll., B.A. 1960; Northwestern Univ., M.A. 1961, Ph.D. 1964; m. Georgiana d. Douglas and Helen Harris 23 Jan. 1960; children: Geoffrey Lynd, Christopher Reed; PRINCIPAL, UNIVERSITY COLLEGE, UNIV. OF TORONTO 1989– ; Fulbright-Hayes Fellowship, Oxford Univ. 1963–64; Asst. Prof. of Philos., State Univ. of N.Y. 1964–67; Nat. Endowment for the Humanities Fellowship, Oxford Univ. 1967–68; Prof. of Philos., Univ. of Toronto 1968– ; mem., Candn. Assn. Univ. Teachers; Candn. Philos. Assn.; Soc. for Philos. & Psychol.; Pres. & Chrmn., Lilian Fitzmaurice Found.; author: 'Common Sense' 1989 and numerous book chapters & learned journal articles; Home: Box 272, Collingwood, Ont. L9Y 3Z5; Office: 15 King's College Circle, Toronto, Ont. M5S 1A1.

**FORNER, Jane,** B.Mus.; performing arts administrator. b. St. Stephen, N.B.; d. Aubrey and Ethel (Williamson) Akerley; e. Saint John (N.B.) High Sch.; Mount Allison Univ. B.Mus. 1960; Acad. of Music & Dramatic Art Vienna, Austria postgrad. studies; DIR. OF MUSIC, MUSIC TORONTO 1987– ; pianist, coach, repetiteur, tutor Europe 1965–69; Asst. Ed. Opera Canada, Toronto 1969–71; Publicist CBC 1971–72; Producer Music CBC Ottawa 1972–79, Exec. Producer Music 1979–82; Dir. of Music, CentreStage Music 1982–87; Artistic Dir. BACH 300, Toronto 1985; Dir., Music Toronto 1987–89; Freelance writer 1989– ; Administrator, Threshold Theater, Kingston 1990; Gen. Mgr., BBSMF, Hamilton 1991– ; recreation: sailing; Club: Harbour City Yacht; Office: 518 Fruitland Rd., Stoney Creek, Ont. L8E 5A6.

**FORREST, Bob;** design marketing executive; b. Matatchewan, Ont. 4 May 1943; s. William Archie and Grace Adelaide (Moyer) F.; e. New Liskeard H.S. Grade XII; m. Nancy Sue d. Norman and Marjory Bernecker 4 June 1977; DESIGN & MARKETING SERVICES TO THE BUILDING INDUSTRY – L'IMAGE DESIGN and BOB FORREST CONSULTANTS; employed in funeral business New Liskeard 1962–64, Uxbridge 1964–67; Art Shoppe (Retail Furniture) 1967–69; estbd. present co. 1969 in Toronto; author 'Death Here is Thy Sting' (non-fiction) 1967; and various articles for building industry publs.; recreations: canoeing, squash; Address: 'Stonehearth,' 47 Aspenwood Dr., Willowdale, Ont. M2H 2E8.

**FORRESTALL, The Hon. John Michael William Curphey;** senator; b. Deep Brook, N.S. 23 Sept. 1932; s. Thomas Patrick and Esther Mary (Curphey) F.; widower; children: Mary Ellen, Daniel Patrick, Robert Arthur, Polly Sue, Michael Thornhill Matthews; SENATOR, THE SENATE OF CANADA 1990– ; Businessman / Journalist, Halifax Herald Limited; Member, House of Commons 1965–88; Past Mem., NATO Parly. Assn.; Past Rapporteur, N. Atlantic Assembly Military Ctte.; Past Mem., Inter-Parly. Union; Commonwealth Parly. Assn.; 1st elected to House of Commons 1965; re-elected general elections of 1968, '72, '74, '79, '80, '84; apptd. Parly. Sec. to Min. of Transport 1984; to Min. of Regional Industrial Expansion 1986; defeated general election 1988; presently serves as Mem., Standing Ctte. on Transport and Communications; Standing Senate Ctte. on Fisheries; Bd. Mem., Internal Economy; Bd. of Dir., Marine Atlantic Inc. 1989; apptd. Mem., Veterans Pension Appeal Bd. 1990; resigned Marine Atlantic Inc. & Veterans Pension Appeal Board upon appt. to Senate of Canada; Mem., Candn. Group, Inter-Parliamentary Union; Candn. Branch, Commonwealth Parliamentary Assn.; Canada-United States Inter-Parliamentary Group; Roman Catholic; Home: 21A Blink Bonnie Terrace, Dartmouth, N.S. B2Y 2C9; Office: Room 154-N, Centre Block, Ottawa, Ont. K1A 0A4.

**FORRESTALL, Thomas DeVany,** O.C., B.F.A., D.C.L., R.C.A.; artist; b. Middleton, N.S. 11 March 1936; s. Thomas Patrick and Esther Mary (Curphey) F.; e. elem. and high schs. Middleton and Dartmouth, N.S.; Mount Allison Univ. B.F.A.; travel and study Europe (Can. Council Grant) 1958–59; King's Coll. Halifax D.C.L. 1980; Mt. Allison Univ., D.F.A. (Hon.) 1987; m. Natalie Marie d. Frank LeBlanc, Atholville, N.B. 12 Sept. 1958; 7 children: William, Monica, Renee, John, Curphey, Francis, Colin (d.); Asst. Curator, Beaverbrook Art Gall., Fredericton 1959; self-employed artist since 1960; began experimenting with panels shaped other than rectangles 1961; completed Kennedy and Churchill Mem. Masks 1964, 1965; solo exhns. incl. Roberts Gall. Toronto 1965, 1970; Dartmouth Coll. Art Gall. Hannover, N.H. 1966; Large Outdoor Sculpture Atlantic Pavilion Expo '67 1967; Walter Klinkhoff Gall. Montreal 1967, 1969; Sir. George Williams Univ. Montreal 1968, 1975; Retrospective 'Forrestall High Realism' across Can. 1971 (organized by Beaverbrook Art Gall.); Mendel Art Gall., Saskatoon 1971, 1979; Art Gall. of Victoria 1971, 1979; Art Gall. of Windsor 1972, 1974; Montreal Museum of Fine Arts 1972; Winnipeg Art Gall. 1972; Candn. Cultural Center Paris, France 1972; Boston City Hall Art Gall. 1972; N.S. Museum of Fine Arts Centennial Gall. 1974; Hart House Univ. of Toronto 1975; Marlborough Godard Gall. Toronto 1975; Tom Thomson Mem. Gall. & Museum of Fine

Arts 1975; Robert McLaughlin Gall. 1975; London (Ont.) Pub. Lib. & Art Museum 1975; Marlborough Galleries London (Eng.), Zurich and Rome (individual pieces) 1975–76; Marlborough New York 1976; Mira Godard Gall. Montreal 1977, Toronto 1978; Art Gall. of N.S. tour 1977–78; W.End Gall. Edmonton 1978; Ownes Art Gall. Mount Allison Univ. tour 40 tempera paintings across Can. 1978–79; Evergreen Exhn. 1978; Saidye Bronfman Centre Montreal 1979; Hamilton Art Gall. 1979; Glenbow Inst. Calgary 1979; Beaverbrook Art Gall. Fredericton 1979; Liverpool (Eng.) Acad. 1980; Can. House Gall. London 1980; Cultural Museum Denant, Belgium 1980; Museum of Modern Art Belgrade 1980 and rep. Can. Beograde '80 Internat. Exhn. Plastic Arts; Nat. Museum of Art Sophia, Bulgaria 1980; Nat. Museum of Art of Romania Bucharest 1981; National Museum of Art, CLUJ, Transylvania; Nat. Museum of Art of Hungary, Budapest; Madison Gall., Toronto, 1981; Bayard Gall., N.Y., 1981; Gall. 32, Milan 1982; Candn. Academic Centre, Rome 1983; European travelling exhbn. of 25 Egg Tempera paintings 1983–84; Gall. 32, Milan 1984; solo exhbns. in Rome, Telaviv, Athens and Milan 1984–85, and Casablanca and Marrakesh 1987; Riverside Art Gall., Vero Beach Fla. 1989; Glendon Coll., York Univ. Toronto 1989; Beaverbrook Art Gall. Fredericton 1990; Robertson Gall. Ottawa 1991; Ring Gall., St. John. N.B. 1992; rep. Canada at 24th Internat. Art Exhbn., Monaco 1990; rep. various group exhbns. Can. and Europe; pub., corporate and private colls.; guest speaker, Harvard Univ. 1988; Beaverbrook Art Gall. 1991; painted official gift from nation to former P.M. Trudeau 1986; made a print for Epilepsy Canada 1985 and for l'Arche 1988; estbd. Three Oaks Corp. Ltd. 1972; Dir.: N.S. Museum of Fine Arts 1973–75; N.S. Talent Trust 1974–75; Dartmouth Acad. 1979–80; Art Gall. of N.S. 1986; co-judge Series V Olympic Coins '76; Advisor to Order of Canada on Arts 1988; rec'd Secy. of State's Citation Commonwealth of Mass. 1972; Royal Arch. Inst. Can. Allied Arts Medal 1975; Queen's Silver Jubilee Medal 1977; Officer, Order of Canada 1986; author 'This Good Looking Land' 1976; co-author 'Shaped By This Land' 1972; 'Returning the Favour Vision for Vision'; various catalogues; subject of numerous publs.; mem. St. Vincent de Paul Soc.; Candn. Artists Representation; Candn. Conf. of Arts; Heritage Advisary Council; P. Conservative; R. Catholic; recreations: swimming, outdoors, drawing; Address: 3 Albert St., Dartmouth, N.S. B2Y 3M1.

**FORRESTER, Maureen,** C.C. (1967), LL.D., D.Litt., D.Mus.; (contralto); b. Montreal, Que. 25 July 1930; d. Thomas and Mary Dumican (Arnold) F.; e. Wm. Dawson Sch., Montreal, Que.; private music study; LL.D., Sir George Williams Coll., McMaster Univ., Univ. of Victoria, Bishop's Univ., Wilfrid Laurier Univ., Carleton Univ., Dalhousie Univ., Univ. of P.E.I. 1986, Univ. of Windsor 1988, Univ. of Man. 1988; D.Litt., York Univ., St. Mary's Univ., Mt. Allison Univ., McGill Univ., Trent Univ., Lakehead Univ. 1988; D.Mus., Univ. of W. Ont.; m. Eugene Kash, 20 June 1957; separated; children: Paula (Mrs. Peter Burton), Gina (Mrs. Paul Dineen), Daniel, Linda, Susanna (Mrs. Bruce Whaley); Chrmn., Canada Council 1984–89; rec'd Banff Sch. Fine Arts, Nat. Award in Music 1967; Harriet Cohen Internat. Music Award 1968; Molson Prize 1971; Samuel Simons Sanford Award, Yale Sch. of Music 1983; Toronto Arts Award 1989; Fellow, Stong Coll., York Univ.; apptd. Trustee, Nat. Arts Centre Corp. 1973; Gov., Thomson Hall 1982; portrait painted by Miss Jean Primrose; Sigma Alpha Iota.

**FORST, Judith Doris,** B.Mus.; opera singer; b. New Westminster, B.C. 7 Nov. 1943; d. Gordon Stanley and Euna Jessie (Thompson) Lumb; e. Como Lake Secondary Sch. 1956; Univ. of B.C., B.Mus. 1964; m. Graham N. Forst 30 May 1964; children: Noel Graham, Paula Judith; performances incl. New York Metrop. Opera, New York City Opera, Munich State Opera, Symphony Orch. of Barcelona, Seattle Opera, San Francisco Opera, New Orleans Opera, Fort Worth Opera, Sante Fe Opera, Washington D.C. Opera, Candn. Opera Co. Toronto, Miami Opera, Vancouver Opera, Calgary Opera, Montreal Symphony, Vancouver Symphony, Hamilton Symphony, Baltimore Opera, L'Orchestre de la Radio France (Paris), San Diego Opera Soc., Orchestra of the Age of Enlightenment (London, UK); guest lectr. Univ. of B.C., Univ. of Mont.; winner Metrop. Opera Auditions 1968, CBC Cross-Can. Talent Contest 1968; named Candn. Woman of Yr. 1978; Greater Miami Opera Assn. Performer of Yr. 1980; named Distinguished Alumnus of the Year, Univ. of B.C. 1986; LL.D. (Hon.), U.B.C. 1992; invested into the Order of Canada 1992; Freeman, City of Port Moody 1992; inducted into Le Panthéon de l'Art Lyrique, Montreal 1992; mem. Actors' Equity; Am. Guild Musical Artists; Assn. Candn. TV & Radio Artists; Address: 428 Princeton Ave., Port Moody, B.C. V3H 3L3.

**FORSTER, Bruce Alexander,** B.A., Ph.D.; university professor; b. Toronto, Ont. 23 Sept. 1948; s. William Bruce and Anna May (Murray) F.; e. Beachville P.S. 1962; Woodstock Coll. Inst. 1967; Univ. of Guelph, B.A. 1970; Australian Nat. Univ., Ph.D. 1974; Jayes-Qantas Visiting Scholar, Univ. of Newcastle, Aust. 1983; children: Kelli, Jeremy, Jessica; DEAN, COLL. OF BUSINESS, UNIV. OF WYOMING, 1991– ; Prof., Dept. of Economics, Univ. of Wyoming 1987– ; (tenure granted 1989); Adjunct Prof., International Studies; Asst. Prof., Univ. of Guelph 1973–76; granted tenure 1976; Assoc. Prof. 1977–83; Prof. 1983–88 (on leave 1987–88); Visiting Assoc. Prof., Univ. of B.C. Jan.-July 1979; Vis. Fellow, Univ. of Wyoming 1979–80; Vis. Prof., 1983–84; Vis. Prof. Univ. of Wyoming Jan-July 1987; Vis. Scholar, Univ. of Newcastle, June-July 1983; Acting Chmn., Econ., Univ. of Guelph, May-Sept. 1985; Prof., Acad. of Internat. Economic Affairs, Professional Training Ctr., Min. of Economic Affairs, Taiwan, Republic of China, May-June 1990, June 1991, May 1992, May-June 1993, May 1994; Consultant, U.S. Environmental Protection Agency; Ont. Min. of Environment; Environment Canada; Agriculture Canada; Dept. of Fisheries & Oceans; Bd. mem. & Pres., Univ. of Guelph Faculty Club (Bd. mem. & Vice Pres. 1985–86) 1986–87; Acad. Assoc., Atlantic Counc. of the U.S.; mem., Am. Econ. Assn.; Assn. of Environmental & Resource Economists; 'The Acid Rain Debate: Science and Special Interests in Policy Formation' 1993; co-author: 'Economics in Canadian Society' 1986; mem. Ed. Bd., 'Journal of Environmental Economics and Management' 1989; Assoc. Ed. and mem. Ed. Bd., 'Journal of Applied Business Research' 1988 (mem. Ed. Bd. 1987, 1989); Assoc. Ed., 'Journal of Environmental Economics and Management' 1989–91; recreations: skiing (alpine & nordic), weightlifting, swimming, scuba, archery; Home: 3001 Sage Dr., Laramie, WY 82070; Office: Dept. of Economics, Univ. of Wyoming, Laramie, Wyoming 82071.

**FORSYTH, Adrian Bruce,** B.Sc., Ph.D.; writer; naturalist; b. Ottawa, Ont. 27 June 1951; s. William James and Barbara Rose (Temple) F.; e. Queen's Univ. B.Sc. 1974; Harvard Univ. Ph.D. 1978; m. Turid d. Wilhelm and Luise Fenzl 18 Jan. 1980; Rsch. Assoc. Entomol. Dept. Royal Ont. Museum; author 'Mammals of the Canadian Wild' 1985; 'A Natural History of Sex' 1986; co-author 'Tripical Nature' 1984; contbg. ed. 'Equinox' mag.; recipient 2 awards Candn. Sci. Writiers Assn.; 4 gold awards for sci. writing Nat. Mag. Awards; Office: Conservation International, 1015 18th St. N.W., Suite 1000, Washington, D.C. 20036.

**FORSYTH, Rev. Charles Harkness,** B.A., B.D., D.D. (Un. Ch.); b. Winnipeg, Man. 20 Apr. 1926; s. Charles Harkness and Hazel Margaret (Andison) F.; e. Robert H. Smith Jr. High and Kelvin High Schs., Winnipeg; Un. Coll. (Univ. of Man.), B.A. 1947; B.D. 1950; Univ. of Winnipeg, D.D. 1969; m. Myrna Lee, d. J.J. George, 28 June 1954; children: Charles, Janet Lee, Marcia Gail, Ian Lamont; CONSULTANT ON CHURCH AND URBAN DEVELOPMENT, HOUSING ORGANIZATIONS 1990– ; o. 1950; served at Sioux Lookout, Ont., 1950–54; John Black Mem. Ch., East Kildonan, Man., 1954–60; Supt., Central Winnipeg Parish, 1960–64; Sackville Un. Ch., N.B., 1964–66; Extve. Asst to Premier of N.B. 1966–68; mem., Can. Council 1965–66; Regent Un. Coll., 1963–64; served on various civic and philanthropic bds. 1954–66; Secy., Bd. of Evangelism & Social Service, United Church of Canada 1968–1970; Min., St. Andrew's Ch., Sudbury, Ont. 1970–78; Min., First Pilgrim United Ch., Hamilton 1978–90; mem. Sec. on Aging, Ont. Welfare Council; mem. Sudbury Regional Development Corporation; Hamilton City Central Area Planning Group; (Chrmn., Hamilton-Wentworth Region Food & Shelter Ctte.); Mem., Region of Hamilton-Wentworth Task Force on Affordable Housing; First Place, Hamilton; Founder & Dir., 'Renew' Community Projects, Hamilton; Chrmn., Corktown Cooperative Homes; recipient Centennial Medal 1967; Liberal; recreations: music, gardening; Adress: 175 Delaware Ave., Hamilton, Ont. L8M 1V9.

**FORSYTH, Hon. Gregory Rife,** B.A., LL.B; judge; b. Calgary, Alta. 15 June 1928; s. Thomas Dalgleish and Marjorie (Rife) F.; e. Univ. of Alta. B.A. 1950, LL.B. 1951; m. Elizabeth Anne d. late H. C. H. Brayfield, K.C. 8 Feb. 1958; children: Douglas, Jane; JUDGE, COURT OF QUEEN'S BENCH ALTA. since 1979; called to Bar of Alta. 1952; cr. Q.C. 1971; joined Canadian Pacific Railway Law Dept. Calgary 1952–55, Toronto 1955–57, Montreal 1957–59; Partner, Howard, Dixon, Mackie, Forsyth 1959–79; served with RCAF (Reserve) 403 City of Calgary Sqdn. 1951–55, 400 City of Toronto Sqdn. 1955, rank Flying Offr.; Anglican; recreations: golf, sailing; Clubs: Ranchmen's; Calgary Golf & Country; Glencoe; Office: Court House, 611 - 4th St. S.W., Calgary, Alta. T2P 1T5.

**FORSYTH, Joseph,** M.L.S.; manager; b. Washington, Co. Durham, Eng. 15 Aug. 1942; s. James Frederick and Maisie (Appleby) F.; e. Stockton Grammar Sch. 1960; Newcastle Sch. of Librarianship A.L.A. 1963; Univ. of London M.L.S. 1976; m. Kay Frances Appleby 3 Oct. 1964; two s. Julian Alastair, Andrew Stuart; ASST. DEPY. MIN., INDIVIDUAL RIGHTS & CITIZENSHIP, PROV. OF ALTA. 1993– ; Coll. Librarian, Easington Tech. Coll. 1963–64; Regional Librarian, N. Yorks. Co. Lib. 1964–66; Reference Librarian, Calgary Pub. Lib. 1960–70; Lib. Devel. Offr., Prov. Alta. 1970–77; Dir. of Library Services, Prov. of Alta. 1977–86, 1989–92; Regional Superintendent, Air Navigation Programming and Administration, Transport Canada 1986–87; Special Intergovernmental Advisor, Social & Constitutional Affairs, Alberta Federal and Intergovernmental Affairs 1988; Asst. Depy. Min., Cultural Development, Prov. of Alta. 1990–93; author 'Bibliography of Government Publications Relating to Alberta' 1971; various articles; Fellow, Lib. Assn. (U.K.); mem. Anglican; recreations: gardening, walking, cycling, reading, music, theatre, dog showing; Home: 15211 – 83 Ave., Edmonton, Alta. T5R 3T5.

**FORSYTH, Malcolm Denis,** D.Mus.; composer; conductor; musician; b. Pietermaritzburg, S. Africa 8 Dec. 1936; s. Claude McLean F. and Doris Bertha F.; e. Univ. of Cape Town B.Mus. 1963, M.Mus. 1966, D.Mus. 1972; Canford Summer Sch. of Music Conductors' class 1980–84; maj. areas of study incl. Trombone, Composition, Musicology, Conducting; m. Lesley Eales 1965, div. 1984; m. Constance Braun 1992; one d. (by 1st marriage) Amanda; PROF. OF MUSIC, UNIV. OF ALTA. 1977– ; Jr. Lectr., S.A. College of Music (Univ. of Cape Town) 1967; Asst. Prof. present Univ. 1968, Assoc. Prof. 1972; Chmn. Div. of Band & Orch. Studies and Asst. to Chmn. for Concert Activity 1984–86; Artistic Dir., Music Dept., Univ. of Alta. 1987–89; Visiting Prof.: Univ. of Cape Town 1976, Univ. of Witwatersrand 1983; Co-prin. Trombone CAPAB Symphony Orch. (S. Africa) 1971–72; Prin. Trombone, Edmonton Symphony 1973–80; Asst. Conductor, Univ. of Cape Town Orch. & Chamber Choir 1960–62; Guest Conductor: Cape Town Symphony Orch. 1967; CAPAB Symphony Orch. 1971; Edmonton Symphony Orch. 1971; Alta. Ballet Co. 1980; National Orch. of the SABC (Johannesburg) 1983; Conductor: St. Cecilia Orch. Edmonton 1977–86; Edmonton Wind Sinfonia 1978–79; West Wind Chamber Ensemble 1980–83; Chamber Choir, Univ. of Witwatersrand 1983; Host and Dir. '20th Century Music' CBC TV 1968; Broadcaster music Radio CKUA 1968–71; Program Annotator, Edmonton Symphony Orch. 1968–71; Artistic Dir. 'Explorations' Series, Edmonton 1973–74, 'Encounters' Concert Series 1985– ; Composer-in-Residence, Banff Centre 1975, '78; Juror: CBC Young Composers' Competition 1978; CAPAC (now SOCAN) Young Composers' Competition 1978, '89; Can. Council Composer Comns. 1983, '85, '86, 87, '88, '89, '90, '91, '92; original compositions for orch., brass, strings, woodwind, piano, voice have been performed in Eur., N.Am., S.Africa, UK, Ireland, USSR, China, Japan, Australasia; works incl. 3 symphs., 8 others for orch. 10 for soloist/s & orch. 3 for band, 47 for chamber ensembles, 2 for solo piano, 11 for vocalist/s; works commissioned by Can. Council, CBC, Univ. of Cape Town, Maureen Forrester, Judith Forst, Canadian Brass, Bläserensemble Mainz, and Symphony Orchs. of Cape Town, Montréal and Edmonton; Chamber Orchs. of Vancouver & Manitoba; recipient Pietermaritzburg Philharmonic Soc. John Carter Memorial Bursary 1958; Univ. of Cape Town Entrance Scholarship 1959; Sieger's Scholarship 1961–62; Emdin Composition Prize, Univ. of Cape Town 1962; Doctoral Fellowship, Can. Council 1971; Winner, Juno Award for Best Classical Composition 1987; named Candn. Composer of the Year, Candn. Music Counc. 1989; Edmonton Established Artist Award (Edmonton Ctte. for Bus. & the Arts) 1991; Fellow, Camargo Foundation, Cassis, France 1993; Assoc. Composer, Candn. Music Centre; Vice Pres., Alta. Composers' Assn. 1978–81; Counc. mem., Candn. League Composers 1986–90; mem. SOCAN (Soc. of Candn. Authors, Publishers, Composers); works published (by E.C. Kerby Ltd., G Ricordi, BMG Ariola, Candn. Brass Publications, Gordon V. Thompson, Waterloo Music); Home: 9259 Strathearn Dr., Edmonton, Alta. T6C 4E1; Office: Music Dept., Univ. of Alta., Edmonton, Alta T6G 2C9.

**FORTIER, André,** M.Sc., LL.D; retired Canadian public servant; b. Montreal, Que. 1927; e. Laval University; Univ. of Montreal, post-grad. math.; CONSULTANT,

ARTS & CULTURE and PUBLIC SERVICE MANAGEMENT 1983– ; upon grad. in 1952 joined Treasury Bd., Ottawa; in 1965 joined Can. Council as Financial Offr.; subsequently Treas.; Asst. Under Secy., Dept. Secy. of State 1969–72; Dir., Can. Council 1972–75; Under Secy. of State 1975–78; First Pres., Social Sciences & Humanities Research Counc. 1978–83; LL.D. Dalhousie Univ. 1983; Extve. Dir., Task Force on Funding of the Arts 1985–86; Professor, École des Hautes Études Commerciales, Univ. of Montreal; author 'Historique des Politiques fédérales dans le Domaine des Arts au Canada 1944–88', 'Review of Federal Policies for the Arts in Canada 1944–88' 1989; Diplôme d'Honneur, Candn. Conf. of the Arts, May 1990; R. Catholic; recreations: skiing, swimming, windsurfing; Address: 10 Perrot St., Hull, Que. J8Y 1R3.

**FORTIER, D'Iberville,** B.A., LL.B., Ph.D. (econ.); EXELCOM: conseiller de groupe parlementaire; consultant; né Montréal, P.Q. 5 fév. 1926; f. Carolus et Flore (Lanctôt) F.; é Coll. Jean-de-Brébeuf; Coll. Stanislas, B.A. 1945; Univ. de Montréal, Lic. en Sciences politiques, 1947, LL.B. 1948; London School of Econ.; Univ. de Paris, Dr. d'État, Sciences écon. 1952; ép. Marie-Thérèse, f. Robert Allegret, Paris, France, 15 oct. 1968; enfants: Sébastien, Valérie; Commissaire aux Langues Officielles, Ottawa 1984–91; reçu avocat (Montréal) 1948; collaboration à Esprit, Écrits du Canada français, Amérique française (journaux); entré au Ministère des Affaires extérieures, 1952; Washington, D.C. 1953; Conseiller des Commissaires canadiens à la CISC en Indochine, 1956; Direction des Affaires écon., Ottawa 1958; Commissaire canadien à la CISC au Cambodge, 1959; Détaché auprès du Secrétariat de l'OTAN, 1961; Dir. du Service de Presse et de Liaison du Ministère des Affaires extérieures, 1964; Professeur en communications sociales à l'Univ. d'Ottawa 1966–68; Prés. du Groupe de travail du Conseil privé sur l'information gouvernementale, 1968; Ambassadeur en Tunisie et en Libye, 1969; Conseil d'Adm. de l'Office national du Film, 1972–76, Sous-secrétaire d'État adjoint, Ministère des Affaires extérieures, Ottawa, 1972; Ambassadeur du Canada en Italie et Haut Comm. à Malte 1976–80; Ambassadeur du Canada en Belgique et au Luxembourg 1980–84; Médaille de la Fond. Montpetit 1985; Comdr. de l'Ordre des Chevaliers de Malte 1985; Doctorat (hon. causa), Univ. d'Ottawa 1987; Officier de l'Ordre de la Pléiade; Catholique; récréations: ski, littérature; Bureau: 29 Mackinnon, Vill. du Parc de Rockcliffe, Ont. K1M 0G4.

**FORTIER, Jean-Marie,** S.E. (R.C.); Archevêque de Sherbrooke, Que. depuis 1968; né Québec, Que. 1er juillet 1920; f. Joseph et Alberta (Jobin) F.; é. Petit Sém. de Québec, Faculté de Théologie, Univ. Laval 1940–45; Louvain University Grégorienne (Rome); Prof. histoire ecclésiastique, Univ. Laval, 1950–60; Evêque aux. La Pocatière, 1961–65; Evêque de Gaspé, 1965–68; Président assemblée des Evêques du Québec 1985–89; auteur: collab., 'Dictionnaire d'Histoire et de Géographie ecclésiastiques'; Chevalier de Colomb, Commandeur de l'Ordre du St-Sépulcre (1970); Résidence: 130 de la Cathédrale, Sherbrooke, Que. J1H 4M1.

**FORTIER, John Duncan;** information technology executive; b. Arvida, Que. 26 Jan. 1944; s. John Norman and Margaret (Meagher) F.; e. Thetford Acad. Vt. High Sch. 1963; Macdonald Coll. McGill Univ. Faculty of Edn. one yr.; Lyndon State Univ. Faculty of Edn. 2nd and 3rd yrs.; m. Shirley Louise d. Robert and Lillian Vaughan 6 May 1966; children: Jonathan Norman, James Duncan, Jessica Jane; PRES., JASCAN INVESTMENT CORPORATION 1991– ; IBM Mktg., Br. Mgr. Ottawa 1966–78; Sr. Mktg. AES Data 1978–82; Co-founder and Extve. Vice-Pres., Lease Corporation 1982–88; Dir., Westbridge Computer Corp. 1988–91; Pres. Westbridge Systems Corp. 1988–91; recreations: arts, golf; Club: Mississauga Golf & Country; Home: 48 Alexander Dr., Oakville, Ont. L6J 4B4 and North Hatley, QC; Office: 48 Alexander Dr., Oakville, Ont. L6J 4B4.

**FORTIER, L. Yves,** C.C., Q.C., B.A., B.C.L., B.Litt. (Oxon.), LL.D. (Hon.); b. Quebec City, Que. 11 Sept. 1935; s. François and Louise (Turgeon) F.; e. Univ. de Montréal, B.A. 1955; McGill Univ., B.C.L. 1958; Oxford Univ, (Rhodes Scholar), B.Litt. 1960; LL.D. (Hon.): Law Soc. of Upper Can. 1989, Acadia Univ. 1992, Univ. of British Columbia 1993; m. Cynthia Carol, d. John Wallace Eaton, Toronto, Ont., 26 Sept. 1959; children: Michel, Suzanne, Margot; formerly Canada's Ambassador and Permanent Representative to the United Nations, New York 1988, Pres., U.N. Security Council 1989, Vice Pres., U.N. General Assembly 1990; Chrmn. & Sr. Partner, Ogilvy, Renault, Montréal; Dir., Canadian Pacific Forest Products Limited; Dupont Canada Inc.; Hudson's Bay Company; Jannock Ltd.; Northern Telecom Limited; The Royal Bank of Canada; TransCanada PipeLines Limited and other Candn. cos.; read law with predecessor of present firm; called to Bar of Que. 1960; Dir., Candn. Assn. Rhodes Scholars (Prés. 1975–77); Gov., Hôpital Marie-Enfant; McGill Univ. (1970–85); Pres., Jr. Bar Assn. Montreal 1965–66; Pres., Jr. Bar Sec., Candn. Bar Assn. 1966–67; mem. Gen Council, Bar Prov. Que. 1966–67; Councillor, Bar of Montreal 1966–67; mem. Council, Candn. Sec., Internat. Comn. of Jurists 1967–87; Candn. Bar Assn. (Pres. Que. Br. 1975–76; Nat. Pres. 1982–83); Founding Dir., Candn. Bar Assoc. Law for the Future Fund; mem. Permanent Court of Arbitration, The Hague; Mem., Am. Arbitration Assoc. Panel of Arbitrators; Fellow, Am. Coll. of Trial Lawyers (Regent 1992– ;); Hon. Mem., Am. Bar Assn.; Dir., Candn. Inst. of Advanced Legal Studies; The Candn. Law Inst. of the Pacific Rim 1986–88; Mem., Internat. Trade Adv. Counc. (ITAC) Canada; Officer, Order of Canada 1984, Companion 1991; Liberal; R. Catholic; recreations: skiing, tennis, golf, squash; Clubs: University; The Hermitage Golf and Country (Prés. 1980–81); Mount Royal; Canadian; The Brook (New York); Rockaway Hunting (Long Island, N.Y.); Home: 19 Rosemount Ave., Westmount, Que. H3Y 3G6; Office: Suite 1100, 1981 McGill College Ave., Montreal, Que. H3A 3C1.

**FORTIER, Lévis,** C.M.A.; business executive; b. Robertsonville, Que. 11 Feb. 1938; s. Éphrem and Rose-Anna (Aubert) F.; e. Sherbrooke Univ. C.M.A. 1972; m. Micheline d. Edgar Tardif 28 June 1958; children: Manon, Christine, Stéphan; VICE-PRESIDENT AND CONTROLLER, PEERLESS CARPET CORP. 1980– ; Plant Acct., Solbec Copper Mines Ltd. 6 years; Chief Acct., Thor Mills Ltd. 7 years; Asst. to Vice-Pres. & Controller, Dennison Mfg. Co. of Can. 10 years; recreations: skiing, swimming, golf; Home: 430 Cockburn, Drummondville, Que. J2C 4L8; Office: 335 boul. Roxton, Acton Vale, Que. J0H 1A0.

**FORTIER, Peter Charles Hitchon,** C.D., B.A., Dip.Bus.Adm.; university administrator, retired naval officer; b. Buffalo, N.Y. 14 Aug. 1931; s. Wilfrid Allan and Alice Jean (Hitchon) F.; e. Royal Military College of Canada B.A. 1955; Univ. of W. Ont., Dip.Bus.Adm. 1969; m. Shirley Viola d. John Carol and Marion (Purcell) Lyons 16 July 1955; children: Philip Charles, Sandra Anne; REGISTRAR, ROYAL MILITARY COLLEGE OF CANADA 1981– ; Comnd. R.C.N. 1955; various positions in N.S., B.C., Calif. 1955–66; Dir., Costing & Financial Arrangements, NDHQ Ottawa 1969–72; Dir. of Admin., Royal Military Coll. of Can. 1972–77; Captain(N) 1977; Base Commander CFB Moncton & Commander, 5 Candn. Forces Supply Depot 1977–80; Dir., Procurement & Supply (Land) NDHQ 1980–81; several past extve. volunteer positions; Bd. of Gov. & Vice-Chair, Kingston Div., Candn. Corps. of Commissionaires 1991– ; Dir., Navy League of Can. 1982– ; Mem., Naval Officer's Assn.; Navy League; Royal Kingston United Serv. Inst.; Ont. Univ. Registrar's Assn.; Assn. of Registrars of Univs. & Colleges of Can.; Ont. Univs. Council on Admissions; recreations: gardening, boating, golf, reading; clubs: HMCS Bytown Wardroom, RMC Club of Can., RMC Senior Staff Mess; Home: Bateau Channel Estates, R.R. 1, Kingston, Ont. K7L 4V1 and 'Crowsnest' Portland-on-the-Rideau, Ont. K0G 1V0; Office: RMC, Kingston, Ont. K7K 5L0.

**FORTIN, Hon. Carrier,** B.A., LL.L., LL.D.; judge, retired; b. Beauceville, P.Q. 9 Sept. 1915; s. J. Edouard and Marie Blanche (Carrier) F.; e. Sacred Heart Coll., Beauceville; Semy. of Quebec, B.A. 1937; Laval Univ., LL.L. 1940; Univ. of Sherbrooke, LL.D. 1965; m. Solange, d. Albert Gobeil, Sherbrooke, P.Q., 9 Sept. 1943; children: Jean-Marie, Pierre, Claire; LEGAL COUNSELLOR, FONTAINE DÉSY FORTIN & ASSOCIÉS, Lawyers; called to Bar of Quebec, 1940; cr. Q.C. 1961; practised law in Asbestos, Que., 1940, moving to Sherbrooke with firm of Desruisseaux, Fortin, et al., 1942; Alderman, City of Sherbrooke and Leader of City Council, 1953–62; Secy., Law Faculty, Lectr., Univ. of Sherbrooke 1954–62; el. mem. for Sherbrooke, Nov. 1962; Min. of State Dec: 1962; Min. of Labour, Que., 1963–66; def. in Que. g.e. 1966; Justice Superior Court, Que. 1969; Supernumerary Judge Nov. 1984; Judge ad hoc Appeal Court Feb. to June 1988; retired 9 Sept. 1990; founded 'L'Asbestos' later known as 'Le Citoyen,' Asbestos, P.Q., 1941; founded, La Coopérative d'Habitation d'Asbestos (first such group in N. Am.) 1941; coestbd. summer colony for handicapped children of Sherbrooke, 1951; formed Legal Aid Bureau for needy persons, 1957; Assurance-Vie Desjardins (Dir. 1958–62); mem. Bd. Examiners, Que. Bar 1954–58; mem., Bar of St. Francis (Treas., 1950; Bâtonnier 1959); Rural Bar Assn. (Dir.); Candn. Bar Assn. (Dir. 1969); Sr. Chamber of Comm. (Sherbrooke) 1954–69; Sherbrooke Co. Liberal Assn. 1960–69; Prés., Assemblée Générale des Juges Cour Supérieure du Qué. 1973–75; Judge-Coordinator, Districts of St-Francis and Bedford 1975–84; mem., Club Richelieu (Pres. 1951); R. Catholic; recreations: swimming, yachting, skiing; Home: 2040 Vermont St., Sherbrooke, Que. J1J 1H1; Office: 2144 rue King Ouest, Bureau 220, Sherbrooke, Que. J1J 2E8.

**FORTIN, Célyne;** écrivain, peintre; née La Sarre, Abitibi, P.Q. 30 août 1943; f. Ernest et Bertha (Mercier) F.; é. Coll. Basile Moreau; Univ. de Montréal, lic. d'infirmière; ép. René Bonenfant 20 avril 1968; enfants: Marjolaine, Maude; 20 ans de codirection des Editions du Noroît depuis 1971; publie 6 recueils de poésie et 3 livres d'artiste; Bourse de type B du Min. des affaires culturelles 1990–92; mem., l'UNEQ; Conseil culturel de la Montérégie; auteure: 'Femme fragmentée' 1982, L'envers de la marche' 1982, 'L'ombre des cibles' 1984, 'Au coeur de l'instant' 1986, 'Secrète adhésion' 1987, 'D'Elle en elles' 1989, 'Une Tête' 1989, 'Voir' 1991, 'Les intrusions de l'oeil' 1993; résidence: 560 Mercier St., Lambert, Que. J4P 1Z5.

**FORTIN, Paul,** B.A., LL.B.; lawyer; b. Beauceville, Que. 22 Dec. 1938; s. Lauréat and Claire (Fortier) F.; e. Coll. des Jésuites B.A. 1958 (bronze & silver medals, Lt. Gov. of Que.); Laval Univ., LL.B. 1962; McGill Univ., bar admission course 1963; London Sch. of Econ. & Pol. Sci., post-grad. studies 1964; m. Huguette Perron; children: Marie-Laurence, Alexandre, David; LAWYER, PAUL FORTIN & ASSOC.; Lawyer, Ogilvy, Renault 1963–68; Asst. to Min. of Finance, to Min., Indus., Trade & Comm. & to Min. of Energy, Mines & Resources, Govt. of Can. 1968–71; Investment Advr. to Candn. cos. under control of Anglo-American & to Campeau Corp. 1971–75; Lawyer, Stikeman, Elliott 1976–85; Boisvert, Fortin 1985–90; part-time professor, Quebec Bar Sch. & Univ. of Montreal; invited expert to several seminars 1985– ; publication of courses & papers for var. seminars 1990; Dir., Corp. Persillier Lachapelle; Domaine Forestier Lemoyne Inc.; Euma Investment Ltd.; The Candn. Captioning Devel. Agency Inc.; Knitastiks (Can.) Inc.; Lac Minerals Ltd.; Les Investissments Sofortal Inc.; Parc Domiciliaire Boisbriand Inc.; 101430 Canada Inc.; Aristec Construction Inc., Corp. de Services Hainault-Deschamps; Mem., Candn. Bar Assn.; Qué. Bar; Internat. Bar Assn.; Union Internat. des Avocats; Former Pres., Soc. de Droit Internat. Econ.; Found & Pres., Ctr. Internat. de Rech. Juridiques, Econ. et Soc.; Office: 1 Westmount Square, Suite 1810, Westmount, Que. H3Z 2P9.

**FORTIN, Roch,** B.A., LL.B.; policy advisor and consultant (public affairs and communications); b. La Sarre, Que. 26 Nov. 1946; s. Joseph Arthur and Marie Flora (Labrecque) F.; e. Univ. of Sherbrooke B.A. Econ. 1968, LL.B. 1971; daughter, Erika; PARTNER, CABANA FORTIN, CONSEIL (PUBLIC AFFAIRS) (M&L); Sr. Policy Advisor to the Federal Min. Jean Charest 1986–89; Commr. Rail Passenger Action Force 1985–86; Regional Econ. Devel. Advr. and Lobbyist 1981–85; Proj. Coord. Internat. Aid 1976–81; recreations: trekking, golf, sailing, tennis; Home: 201 Court, Sherbrooke, Que. J1H 1G7; Office: 375 Av. du Mt-Royal, West, Apt. 304, Montreal, Que. H2V 2S4.

**FORTUGNO, Paul,** B.A., BCL, LLB, Q.C.; commission chairman, lawyer; b. Montreal, Que. 11 July 1946; e. Loyola Coll., B.A. 1968; Univ. of N.B., BCL (common law) 1973; Univ. Laval, LLC 1978; married with 2 children; CHAIRMAN, COMMISSION DES VALEURS MOBILIERES DU QUEBEC 1989– ; Partner, Crépeau, Fortugno & Beauregard 1978–80; Crown Prosecutor, Fed. Dept. of Justice in charge of crim. prosecution & fiscal frauds 1982–88; Vice-Chmn., present comn. 1988–89; Q.C. 1986; recreations: hunting, fishing, golf, skiing; Office: 800 Place Victoria, 17e etage, Montreal, Que. H4Z 1G3.

**FOSS, Jeffrey Ernest,** B.A., M.A., Ph.D.; university professor; b. Edmonton, Alta. 7 May 1948; s. Ernest William Ray and Loretta Marie (Dakin) F.; e. Univ. of Alta. B.A. (Hons.) 1969; Univ. of W. Ont. M.A. 1971, Ph.D. 1977; m. Christina d. Simeon and Teofila Gonzales 27 July 1986; children: Grace Pilar, Sylvie Loretta; ASSOCIATE PROF., UNIV. OF VICTORIA 1990– ; Lecturer, Univ. of Alta. 1974–75; Asst.prof. (with term), Univ. of Sask. 1975–77; Sessional Lectr., Univ. of Victoria 1977–78; Asst. Prof. (with term), Univ. of Regina 1979–80; Asst. Prof., Univ. of Winnipeg 1980–81; Sessional Lectr., Univ. of Man. 1981–84; Asst. Prof., Univ. of Victoria 1984–90; Chair, Philosophy 1991– ; Animal Care Ctte. 1985–88; Anglophone Programme Ctte., Candn. Philos. Assn. 1989–90; Canada Council Doctoral Fellowship 1972–73; Ont. Grad. Fellowship 1971–72; Pres. Special Bursary Univ. of W. Ont. 1969–70; Mem.,

Candn. Philos. Assn.; Philos. of Sci. Assn.; Assoc., Behavioral & Brain Sciences; Univ. of Victoria Faculty Assn.; author of scholarly articles in learned journals; recreations: skiing, motorcycling; clubs: Faculty; Home: 980 Eagle Rock Terrace, Victoria, B.C. V8X 3H9; Office: P.O. Box 3045, Victoria, B.C. V8W 3P4.

**FOSTER, William George Lewis 'Briar',** B.A.; portfolio manager; b. Pittsburgh, Pa. 28 Feb. 1935; s. George Vance and Eleanor (Lewis) F.; e. Bowdoin College B.A. (Hons.) 1957; m. Laura d. Fred and Simonne Hill 31 Oct. 1987; children (by prev. m.): Christopher, Eleanor, Charles, Morley; DIRECTOR, PORTFOLIO SERVICES, CANADIAN TAURUS CORPORATION 1993– ; emigrated to Canada 1958 and taught high school for 3 years; Investment Sales, Barclay & Crawford (Kingston) 1960–62; Branch Mgr. 1963–67; Branch Mgr., Walwyn, Stodgell (Kingston) 1967–82; (Calgary) 1982–83; Head Office Sales Mgr., Davidson Partners Ltd. 1984; Vice-Pres. & Dir., Portfolio Services 1985–88; Dir., Portfolio Services, Midland Capital 1988–90; Vice Pres. & Portfolio Manager, Stuart Investment Management Ltd. 1990–93; Financial Journalist for 4.5 years 'The Whig Standard'; work has also appeared in 'Calgary Herald' and 'Profile Kingston'; Guest Lectr., Queen's Univ.; Dir., Central Toronto Youth Services; Former Dir., Kingston Gen. Hosp.; Ongwanada Gen. Hosp.; Theatre Five; Former Mem., Kingston & The Islands P.C. Assn. (prov. & fed.) 1969–82; Chief Finan. Agent, Flora MacDonald's Leadership Campaign 1976; Campaign Mgr. 1979 fed. election; Pres., P.C. Assn. in Kingston 1979–81; author of one short story; recreations: baseball, live theatre, travel; clubs: The Dinosaur Club; Home: 1002 – 701 King St. W., Toronto, Ont. M5V 2W7; Office: Suite 2806, 79 Wellington St. W., Box 225, T.D. Centre, Toronto, Ont. M5K 1J3.

**FOSTER, Edward LeMarchand,** C.A.; pharmaceutical executive; b. Montreal, Que. 17 Aug. 1939; s. Russell Thomas Edward and Edna Elizabeth (Morrisson) F.; e. McGill Univ. C.A. 1962; Executive Development Institute 1971; m. Irene d. Ian and Tina Allan 28 Dec. 1991; children: Glen Edward, Shelagh Kathryn, Colin Andrew; VICE PRES. & CHIEF FINANCIAL OFFICER, DEPRENYL RESEARCH LIMITED 1990– ; Internat. Dir. of Finance & Dir. of Opns. & Planning, Syntex Corp./Syntex Canada Inc. 1976–82 (rec'd 10 years service award after only 7 years); Pres., LeMarchand Foster Consultants Inc. 1982–89; goal: to effect cost savings to cover the cost of my salary/fees (successfully achieved for 24 years); recreations: squash, tennis, jogging; club: Montreal Amateur Athletic Assn.; Home: 2083 Grosvenor St., Oakville, Ont. L6H 4N1; Office: 337 Roncesvalles Ave., Toronto, Ont. M6R 2M8.

**FOSTER, Harold Douglas,** B.Sc., Ph.D.; university professor; b. Tunstall, Yorks., Eng. 9 Jan. 1943; s. Arthur Frederick and Alison Skirving (Pratt) F.; e. Univ. Coll., London Univ., B.Sc.(Spl.) 1964, Ph.D. 1968; m. Lorelei Ann (dec. Nov. 1989) d. Winifred and Edwin Hairsine 21 July 1964; m. 2ndly, Sarah Lynn Davis d. Harry and Avis Boese 4 May 1990; PROF. OF GEOG., UNIV. OF VICTORIA 1981– ; joined Univ. of Victoria as Instr. 1967; Asst. Prof. 1968; Assoc. Prof. 1972; cons. to U.N., NATO, var. govt. depts.; rec'd Parry Award 1961; Sir Wm. Meyer Award 1964; Dixon Award 1966; formerly Dir., World Health Rsch. Found.; mem. Inst. of Brit. Geographers; Candn. Assn. of Geographers; Assn. of Am. Geographers; Am. Geophys. Union; New York Acad. of Sciences; The Royal Soc. of Literature; author: 'Disaster Planning: The Preservation of Life and Property' 1980; 'Health, Disease and the Environment' 1992; and numerous other books and articles; co-author: 'Water: The Emerging Crisis in Canada' 1981; ed. Western Geog. Series 1969– ; recreations: chess, hiking; Clubs: Arts; Union; Explorers; Home: 3085 Southdowne Rd., Victoria, B.C. V8R 6H3; Office: Victoria, B.C. V8W 2Y2.

**FOSTER, Herb;** actor; b. Winnipeg, Man. 14 May 1936; s. Herbert William and Dorothy (Miller) F.; e. King Edward H.S. 1954; Acting career (Canada): Red Barn at the Central Library Toronto 1962–63; National Arts Centre 1975; The Vancouver PlayHouse 1978; The Canadian Players Cross Country Tours 1959–62; Leading Player, The Shaw Festival 1981–91 (appeared as George Bernard Shaw); The Crest (Toronto); Manitoba Theatre Centre (Winnipeg); (USA): National Repertory Theatre (headed by Eva Le Gallienne) 1964–67; Old Globe Theatre (San Diego) 1971–73; Repertory Theatre of Lincoln Center 1970–71; A.C.T. (San Francisco) 1970, 1972–73; The Mark Taper Forum (Los Angeles) 1973–77; Broadway (8 prodns. incl. 'Noises Off,' 'Me and My Girl' 'Lettice and Lovage') 1967–90; day-time dramas on TV incl. 'As the World Turns,' 'Ryan's Hope,' 'Another World,' 'Days of Our Lives,' 'All My Children'; important roles include: Scrooge in 'A Christmas Carol,' The Fool in 'King Lear,' The Inquisitor in 'St. Joan,' Feste in 'Twelfth Night,' The Miser in 'The Miser, Tony Lumpkin in 'She Stoops to Conquer,' and Launce in 'Two Gentlemen of Verona'; Office: Box 774, Niagara-on-the-Lake, Ont. L0S 1J0.

**FOSTER, The Honourable Judge Hugh Derek,** B.A., LL.B.; judge; b. Toronto, Ont. 17 July 1920; s. Harold W.A. and Anna Helen Gowan (Strathy) F.; e. Upper Can. Coll. 1938; Univ. of Toronto B.A. 1941; Osgoode Hall Law Sch. 1947; JUDGE, ONTARIO COURT OF JUSTICE, PROVINCIAL DIVISION 1958– ; Solicitor, Ont. Securities Comn. 1948–53; Denison and Foster 1953–55; Legal Dept., Mun. of Metro. Toronto 1955–58; Lt., 2nd Candn. Armoured Brigade in Normandy from 'D-Day' until wounded 18 July 1944; recreations: golf, scuba diving, soaring (gliding); Clubs: Toronto Golf; Granite; Royal Candn. Military Inst.; Office: Old City Hall, 60 Queen St. W., Toronto, Ont. M5H 2M4.

**FOSTER, Jack C.,** B.Comm.; food industry executive; b. Winnipeg, Man. 6 Feb. 1943; s. Marjorie Lorrine (Scott) F.; e. Kelvin H.S. 1960; Univ. of Man., B.Comm. 1963; m. Arlene d. James and Irene Rowe 12 Feb. 1966; children: Marilyn, Gary; PRESIDENT & C.E.O., COBI FOODS INC. 1992– ; Canada Packers Ltd. 1963–74; Product Mgr., J.M. Schneider Inc. 1974–79; Dir. of Mktg. 1979–81; Gen. Mgr. (Natco) 1981–82; Vice-Pres., Sales & Mktg. 1982–84; Extve. Vice-Pres. 1984–85; Vice-Pres. & Gen. Mgr., General Printers 1986–88; Extve. Vice-Pres. & Chief Op. Offr., Melitta Canada Inc. 1988–91; recreations: sports, travel, reading; club: Curzons; Home: #701, 1700 The Collegeway, Mississauga, Ont. L5L 4M2.

**FOSTER, Janet Green,** B.A., M.A., Ph.D.; author; nature photographer; lecturer; television commentator; b.Ottawa, Ont. 8 Nov. 1940; d. John Joseph and Winifred Maud (Pascoe) Green; e. York Univ. B.A. 1969; Univ. of Toronto M.A. 1970; York Univ. Ph.D. 1976; m. John Gerald F., s. Gerald Foster and Nancy Stern 29 Aug. 1969; dancer, National Ballet Co. of Can. 1958–60; Script Asst. CFTO-TV 1960–61; Network Co-ordinator, CTV Television Network 1960–65; Co-host, nature and wildlife television specials, CBC and TVOntario 1972–88; Producer and cinematographer TVOntario and NHK Japan nature programming; professional still photographer (landscape and nature); author of books for children and adults: 'Working for Wildlife' 1978; 'A Cabin Full of Mice' 1980; 'Wilds of Whip-poor-will Farm' 1982; 'Journey to the Top of the World' 1987; co-author: 'To the Wild Country' 1975; 'Adventures in Wild Canada' 1984; mem., Fed. of Ont. Naturalists; Candn. Nature Fed.; recreations: wilderness travel, nature photography.

**FOSTER, John Bristol,** B.A., M.A., Ph.D.; ecologist; b. Toronto, Ont. 10 June 1932; s. Robert Leighton and Rita Middleton (Bristol) F.; e. Univ. of Toronto, B.A. 1955, M.A. 1957; Univ. of B.C., Ph.D. 1963; m. Annaliese d. Joseph and Agnes Urhahn 26 Apr. 1962; divorced; children: Eric Joseph, Mark Leighton; Prof., Wildlife Ecol., Univ. of Nairobi, Kenya 1963–68; Dir., Royal B.C. Museum 1969–74; Dir., Ecol. Reserves Unit, Prov. of B.C. 1974–84; writer on ecological subjects, ecol. activist, wildlife filmmaker & natural hist. guide to exotic places in world 1984– ; Dir., W. Can. Wilderness Ctte.; Pres., Friends of Ecol. Reserves; presently assoc. with CBC 'Nature of Things' and Special Expeditions (N.Y.); occasional lectr., univ. students & conservation groups; Mem., Assn. of Profl. Biol.; author: 'The Giraffe' 1976, 'Islands at the Edge' 1984, 'Endangered Spaces' 1989 & many sci. papers & articles incl. National Geographic & Equinox; recreations: kayaking, hiking, SCUBA diving, skiing, photography; clubs: W. Can. Wilderness Ctte., Sierra, Friends of Ecol. Reserves; Home: R.R. 4, Mansell Rd., C23, Ganges, B.C. V0S 1E0.

**FOSTER, John Elgin,** Ph.D.; professor; b. London, Ont. 19 Oct. 1938; s. Milton Ewart and Evelyn May (Dey) F.; e. Royal Rds. Mil. Coll. 1957; Univ. of Alta., B.A. 1959, M.A. 1966, Ph.D. 1973; m. Marie d. Wasyl and Anne Fedoruk 3 Mar. 1962; children: William Milton, Hanya Evelyn; PROF., DEPT. OF HIST., UNIV. OF ALTA. 1986– ; High Sch. Teacher, Edmonton P.S. Bd. 1962–70; Lectr., Dept. of Hist., Univ. of Alta. 1970; Asst. Prof. 1971; Assoc. Prof. 1977; occasional cons., Indian Assn. of Alta.; Native Counc. of Can.; Fed. of Métis Settlements; Mem., Candn. Hist. Assn.; Champlain Soc.; Royal Mil. Coll. Club; editor: 'The Developing West: Essays in Honour of Lewis H. Thomas' 1982; co-editor; 'The Métis: Past and Present' 1985; author of 15 articles & book chapters, 3 DCB/DBC entries, 8 Candn. Encycl. entries; Home: 12 Westridge Cres., Edmonton, Alta. T5T 1C6; Office: 2–56 H.M. Tory Bldg., Edmonton, Alta. T6G 2H4.

**FOSTER, John Gerald;** television producer; professional photographer; lecturer; author; b. London, England 4 Apl 1933; s. Gerald and Nancy Elizabeth Stern (Kirby) F.; e. Ont. Agric. Coll., dipl. Animal Husbandry 1954; m. Janet d. John and Winifred Green 29 Aug. 1969; Producer and cinematographer of nature specials for CBC, TVO, and Japan Broadcasting Corp.; host/writer TV series 'This Land'; Dir. & Co-host of 25 one-hour specials on Candn. wilderness; Co-Lectr. on Candn. wilderness; profl. still & film photography across Can. for 20 yrs.; co-author: 'To the Wild Country' 1975, 'Adventures in Wild Canada' 1984; Writer, consultant: wildlife scripts for public television.

**FOSTER, John William,** M.A., Ph.D.; agency director; b. Regina, Sask. 17 June 1942; s. William Henry and Hazel Margaret Mary Anne (Noble) F.; e. Abernethy, Sask.; Univ. of Sask. B.A. 1962; Univ. of Toronto M.A. 1973, Ph.D. 1977; Univ. of Paris, lang. studies; St. Andrew's Coll. Saskatoon, theol. studies; m. Sandra Sorensen 9 Sept. 1967 (divorced); one d. Johannah Nicole Amee Diette; NATIONAL SECRETARY, OXFAM – CANADA 1989– ; Trustee, Council Hemispheric Affairs Washington, D.C.; Bd. Mem., Candn. Counc. for Internat. Cooperation; Former Co-Chair, Coalition Against Free Trade (Ont.); former NDP Cand. Fed. Riding Toronto Spadina g.e. 1979, 1980; Co-founder, Inter Agency Coalition on AIDS and Development (ICAD); Chair, Common Frontiers; commentator, author or co-author numerous publs. internat. human rights, Candn. foreign relations Latin Am., domestic social & econ. justice; Home: 54 Delaware Ave., Toronto, Ont. M6H 2S7; Office: 301 – 251 Laurier Ave. W., Ottawa, Ont. K1P 5J6.

**FOSTER, Lt.-Gen. Kent Richard,** C.M.M., C.D., B.Sc.; Canadian forces; b. Coleman, Alta. 30 March 1938; s. Ross Neil and Eileen Doris (Richards) F.; e. Royal Roads Mil. Coll. Victoria 1958; Royal Mil. Coll. Kingston 1960; Univ. of Alta. B.Sc. (Chem. Eng.) 1960; Royal Mil. Coll. of Sci. Shrivenham, Eng. 1964; U.S. Armed Forces Staff Coll. Norfolk, Va. 1973; m. Del d. George Zinook 4 June 1960; one d. Terry Dawn; ASST. DEPUTY MIN., HEALTH PROTECTION BRANCH, HEALTH CANADA 1992; joined Candn. Army 1956 holding various inf. offr. positions incl. C.O. PPCLI 1st Btn. 1975–77; served 82nd Airborne Div. Fort Bragg, N.C. 1973–75; commanded Candn. Airborne Regt. 1978–80; Chief of Staff Candn. Forces NATO Lahr, FRG 1980–83, Dep. Chief of Staff Operations Central Army Group HQ Heidelberg 1983–86; Commdr. Special Service Force and Base Petawawa 1986–87; Dep. Commdr. Mobile Command 1987; Commdr., Mobile Command, Candn. Forces 1989–91; Asst. Deputy Min. (Personnel), National Defence HQ 1991; recipient Offr. U.S. Award of Legion of Merit 1987; Officier de l'Ordre national du mérite de France 1987; Order of St. John of Jerusalem 1990; Home: 518 Buchanan Crs., Gloucester, Ont. K1J 7X9; Office: Rm. 116, Bldg. #7, Tunney's Pasture, Ottawa, Ont. K1A 0L2.

**FOSTER, Maurice Brydon,** M.P., D.V.M.; veterinarian; politician; b. Bloomfield, Ont. 8 Sept. 1933; s. Dunam Noxon and Agnes Mary (Anderson) F.; e. Picton (Ont.) Coll. Inst. 1952; Ont. Veterinary Coll., Univ. of Toronto D.V.M. 1957; m. Janet Catherine, d. T. Herb Kerr, 20 Aug. 1955; children: Peter, Andrew, Peggy, James; estbd. veterinary practice Carnduff, Sask. 1957–59; Desbarats, Ont. 1959–68; el. to H. of C. g.e. 1968 as mem. for Algoma; re-el. to 1993; served as Chrmn. Veterans Affairs Comte.; Depy. Chief Govt. Whip; Parlty. Secy. Privy Council and Energy, Mines & Resources; Pres., Treasury Bd.; del. Inter-Parlty. Union, India 1969, UN (New York) 1971, Special Parlty. Del. to Cuba 1973; Chrmn., Commonwealth Parlty. Assn. of Can. 1977; leader Candn. Delegations to Int. Conf., Ottawa 1977; Jamaica 1978; N.Z. 1979; Regional Rep., Candn. Br., Commonwealth Parly. Assn. 1980; Vice Chrmn., Comn. Parl't Assoc. 1984–93; Vice Chrmn., External Affairs and Nat. Defence Comte., 1977; Chrmn., the Northern Gas Pipeline Comte. 1978; apptd. Chrmn., Standing Comte. on Privileges and Elections 1980; Chrmn., Ont. Liberal Caucus 1982–84; Vice Chrmn., Can.-U.S. Internat. Parl't Assoc. 1984–93; apptd. Official Opposition Critic Agriculture 1984–93; Deputy Critic for Energy; Critic for the Candn. Wheat Bd. 1987; apptd. Liberal Opposition Critic for Agriculture; Chrmn., Northern Ont. Caucus 1988–90; retired from House of Commons 1993; apptd. Special Advisor - Caucus to Prime Minister 1994; Chrmn. Johnson Twp. Sch. 1964–65; Chrmn. Algoma Dist. Sch. Area 1, 1966–68; Candn. Vet. Med. Assn.; Ont. Vet. Med. Assn. (Dir. 1967); Liberal; United Church; recreations: skiing, sailing; Home: Desbarats,

Ont. P0R 1E0 and 3011 Linton Rd., Ottawa, Ont. K1V 8H1.

**FOSTER, Patrick Henry Cunliffe,** B.Sc., M.Sc.; merchant banker; b. London, Eng. 8 May 1951; s. Douglas Cunliffe and Mary Patricia (Smith) F.; e. Charterhouse School 1969; St. Andrew's Univ. B.Sc. (Hons.) 1974; London Business Sch. M.Sc.(Econ.) 1979; m. Anne d. douglas Dryden 15 May 1982; children: James Alexander Cunliffe, Holly Sophie Scott Cunliffe; DIRECTOR, GLOBAL STRATEGY FINANCIAL INC. 1993– ; Geologist, De Beers 1974–77; Dir., Selincourt Limited 1979–81; Analyst, Scott Goff Hancock & Co. 1981–84; Dir., Rothschild Asset Management 1984–93; Farm Place Music Ltd.; Home: 17 Farm Pl., London W8, England; Office: Ste. 1600, 33 Bloor St. E., Toronto, Ont. M4W 3T8.

**FOSTER, Robert J.,** B.A., M.A., C.F.A.; merchant banker; b. Vancouver, B.C. 5 Sept. 1942; s. Robert and Jocelyn Lyle (Bonnycastle) F.; e. Univ. of B.C. 1962; Queen's Univ. Hons. B.A. Econ. 1965, M.A. Econ. 1966; Investment Dealers Assoc. Gold Medalist 1967; Chartered Financial Analyst 1975; m. Julia Elizabeth d. Walling and Julia Ruby 11 July 1968; children: Robert, Simon, Jessica, Joanna; PRESIDENT & C.E.O., CAPITAL CANADA LIMITED 1975– ; Mgr. Rsch., Dominion Securities 1966–73; Partner, Dominion Securities Ltd. 1968–73; Mgr., Institutional Sales 1973; Dir. and Princ. Thomson Kernaghan & Co. 1973–82; Past mem. Bd. of Regents Memorial Univ.; Art Gallery of Ontario; Past Dir., Toronto French Sch.; Past Pres., The Ticker Club; Past Chmn., Theatre Plus; Boy Scouts of Canada Haliburton Club Breakfast; Atlantic Salmon Fedn. Dinner; Chair, PC Canada Fund; Co-chair, Candn. Native Arts Found. National Ballet Tour; Dir., Dome Consortium Inc.; CHC Helicopter Corp.; Cabot Development Corp. Ltd.; Air Atlantic Ltd.; Signal Industries Ltd.; recreations: skiing, tennis, fishing; Clubs: Toronto; Badminton & Racquet; Osler Bluff Ski; Adlatok Fishing Camp; The Founders; Home: 102 Kilbarry Rd., Toronto, Ont. M5P 1K8; Office: Sunlife Centre Tower, Box 58, Ste. 2308, 150 King St. W., Toronto, Ont. M5H 1J9.

**FOSTER, Tony (James Anthony),** B.Economics; author; screenwriter; b. Winnipeg, Man. 3 Aug. 1932; s. Maj. Gen. Harry Wickwire and Margaret Ruth (Muir) F.; e. 6 univs. Can., UK, France, USA, Mexico; B.Economics 1962; m. Helen d. James and Marguerite Wickwire 10 Oct. 1964; children: Peter, Emily, Alice; FOUNDER AND DIR. SCREEN STAR GROUP INC. 1990– ; Dir. Thapex Resources Ltd.; various aviation and other careers Can., USA, Central & S. Am., Caribbean incl. Chief Pilot 'Operation Budworm' N.B. 1959, Exec. Pilot Trans Canada Pipe Lines 1960; Founder: Northcana Aviation Co. 1960; Provost Manufacturing 1964; Midair 1970; recipient Candn. Authors Award non-fiction 1987; Evelyn Richardson Meml. Award non-fiction 1987; author (fiction) 'Zig Zag to Armageddon' 1978; 'The Money Burn' 1983; 'Rue du Bac' 1988; 'Ransom for a God' 1990; 'Swansong' 1993; (non-fiction) 'By-Pass' 1982; 'Heart of Oak' 1984; 'Sea Wings' 1985; 'Meeting of Generals' 1986; 'Muskets to Missiles' 1987; 'The Bush Pilots' 1990; 'Sound & The Silence' 1993; screenplays incl. 'Green for the Grass', 'The Money Burn', 'Mona', 'Bell Ringers', 'Bordertown' 6 scripts, 'The Eagle and the Crown' mini-series, 'The Sound and the Silence' mini-series, 'Bluenose', 'Rue du Bac', Dir. Evelyn Richardson Meml. Found.; Past Pres. ACTRA Maritimes; Writers Fedn. N.S. (Exec.); Home: 67 Briarwood Cres., Halifax, N.S. B3M 1P2.

**FOULDS, Geoffrey A.;** public relations consultant; b. Toronto, Ont. 18 July 1957; s. Derek MacDonald and Barbara Anne (Matthew) F.; e. Burnhamthorpe Coll. Inst. grad. 1976; Univ. of Toronto; PRESIDENT, G.A. FOULDS ENTERPRISES INC.; Associate, The Impact Group; writer and cons. J.S. Anthony & Co. Ltd. Toronto 1980–85; Partner, Anthony, Jones, Foulds & Book Inc. 1985–88; mem. Candn. Ski Patrol (winning 3–mem. team 1987 Nat. First Aid Championship; Assoc. mem. and mem. of Extve. Candn. Sci. Writers' Assn.; recreation: skiing; Home: 150 Mountjoy Ave., Toronto, Ont. M4J 1K2; Office: Toronto, Ont.

**FOULKES, Frank Moulton,** B.Sc.(Eng.), M.I.E.E., P.Eng.; engineer; executive; b. Wolverhampton, Eng. 20 Jan. 1923; s. Harry and Lilian (Walker) F.; Univ. of Birmingham, U.K. B.Sc. (Eng.) 1950; m. Amber d. Harry and Gertrude Brown 12 Aug. 1950; children: Michael, Hilary, Rachel, Beth; PRESIDENT, FRAMEL CONSULTANTS INC. 1989– ; Clerical Officer, Br. Foreign Off. 1939–40; Royal Navy, Serv. in N. Atl. and Pac., Final Rank Lieut. Commander (Radar) R.N.V.R. 1941–46; Graduate Apprentice, Metrovick Manchester 1950–52; Montreal Engineering Co. Ltd. (MECO), Elect. Eng., Design and on Field Construction of Hydro, Fossil and Nuclear Generating Plants, on loan to Atomic Energy of Can. Ltd. (1958–64), Resident Elect. Engineer, Douglas Point Nuc. Station, Mgr., Nuclear Div. MECo 1952–69; transferred to MECo assoc. co., CANATOM Inc. successively Mgr., Engineering; Dir. and Vice-Pres., Engineering; Vice-Pres., Operations; Vice-Pres., Marketing; Chrmn., Pres. & C.E.O. 1969–83; Vice Pres., CANDU Opns., Atomic Energy of Canada Ltd. 1983–89; AECL Sr. Rep., Korea 1983–86; has published numerous papers relative to Nuclear Power; Chrmn., Org. of CANDU Industries 1980–81; mem., Queen's Univ., Engineering Adv. Council 1979–80; Vice-Chrmn., Canada Korea Business Counc. 1980–83; Dir., Canada Korea Soc. (Ont.) 1987– ; (Pres. 1992– ;); Chrmn. Candn. Nuclear Assn. 1982–83; Ian F. McRae Award, Candn. Nuclear Assn. 1983; Anglican; (Past Warden, Christ Ch., Beaurepaire); recreations: sailing, gardening, singing; Office: 1342 Birchcliff Dr., Oakville, Ont. L6M 2A4.

**FOULKES, Robert R.,** B.Sc., M.A., S.M.; petroleum executive; b. Taber, Alta. 6 March 1949; s. Maurice and Lillian Edna (Marose) F.; e. Univ. of Alta. B.Sc. 1970; Carleton Univ. M.A. 1972; Mass. Inst. Technol. S.M. 1981; m. Elaine d. Victor and Ruth Hourie 31 July 1971; children: Kristen Marie, Richard Blair; VICE PRES. PUBLIC & GOVT. AFFAIRS, PETRO-CANADA 1987– ; Dir.-Orgn. Lib. Party Can. 1972–74; Exec. Asst. Min. of Indian & N. Affairs 1974–76; Mgr. Pub. Affairs Petro-Canada 1974–83; Vice Pres. Pub. Affairs 1983–84; Pres. Bob Foulkes & Associates 1984–85; Sr. Dir. Pub. Affairs Petro-Canada 1985–86; Internat. Assn. Bus. Communicators; Home: 2904 Palliser Dr. S.W., Calgary, Alta. T2V 4G2; Office: P.O. Box 2844, Calgary, Alta. T2P 3E3.

**FOUND, William Charles,** M.A., Ph.D.; educator; b. Hamilton, Ont. 9 March 1940; s. William John and Melba Doris (Hall) F.; e. Ancaster (Ont.) Mem. Pub. Sch. 1953; Westdale Secondary Sch. Hamilton 1958; McMaster Univ. B.A. 1962; Univ. of Fla. M.A. 1964, Ph.D. 1966; Univ. of Umea, Sweden, Hon. Doctorate 1989; m. Jane G. Couchman; children: Trevor, Jeremy, Alison, Daniel; UNIVERSITY PROFESSOR, YORK UNIV. 1987– ; Prof. of Geog. and Env. Studies, York Univ. 1968– ; Prof., McMaster Univ. 1965–68; Chrmn. of Geog. York Univ. 1971–76, Acting Dir., York Transport Centre 1976–78, Dir., Office of Research Adm. 1976–78, Acting Dir., Inst. for Behavioural Research 1978–79, Dir., Office of Internat. Services 1978–82, Vice Pres. (Acad. Affairs) York Univ. 1979–85, Acting Pres. of Univ. Sept. 1 1984 – Jan. 1 1985; Visiting Scholar, Harvard Univ. Internat. Development Inst. 1986–87; Acad. Project Dir., ITB/FES Project in Environmental Management in Indonesia 1989– ; Consultant, Candn. Internat. Devel. Agency; recipient Woodrow Wilson Nat. Fellowship; Commonwealth Scholarship; author 'A Theoretical Approach to Rural Land Use Patterns' 1971; co-author 'Economic and Environmental Impacts of Land Drainage in Ontario' 1975; 'METRANS: Manual for A Simulation Game for Transportation/Land Use Planning in Metropolitan Toronto' 1978; numerous other books, book chapters, papers land use planning Can., Caribbean, E. Africa, Indonesia; mem., Candn. Assn. Geogs.; Toronto Chamber Soc.; United Church; recreations: squash, diving, cross-country skiing, music; Office: 326 Lumbers Bldg., 4700 Keele St., Downsview, Ont. M3J 1P3.

**FOURMY, Sally J.,** B.S.; fashion industry executive; b. Columbus, Ohio 24 June 1934; d. Joseph Howard and Dorothy Gertrude (Huston) Yearling; e. Northwestern U.; Ohio State Univ. B.S. 1956; post-grad. Univ. of Calif. at Berkeley 1959 & Columbia Univ. 1962–63; children: Patrick Rene, Christian Stephen; PRES., FOUNDER & OWNER, SALLY FOURMY & ASSOC. 1979– ; late 50s: Asst. Fashion Dr., Bloomingdale's; Public Sch. Teacher; Bilingual Flight Attendant, Pan Am. World Airways; 60s: founded company offering seminars to women in bus.; early 70s: Fashion Co-ord. Fac. Mem., LaSalle Coll.; her co. won 1st place award, Hotel & Restaurants Internat. competition 1983; former Ohio Beta Pres., Pi Beta Phi Sorority; Mem., Toronto Fashion Group; Adv. Ctte., Ryerson Polytechnical Inst.; Bd. of Dirs., Profit Sharing Council of Can.; winner, Candn. Woman Entrepreneur of the Year Award, Quality Plus Division 1992; Home: 10 Heather St., Toronto, Ont. M4R 1Y3; Office: 30 Duncan St., Toronto, Ont. M5V 2C2.

**FOURNIER, Guy,** C.M.; writer, TV host, producer; b. Waterloo, Qué. 23 July 1931; s. Joseph Omer and Juliette (Gagné) F.; e. Chambly and St-Hyacinthe, Qué. colls.; Univ. de Sherbrooke, Philos. & Econ. studies; children: Eric, Christian; PRIN., GUY FOURNIER & ASSOCIÉS INC.; Reporter, La Voix de l'Est, Granby; Financial Ed. La Tribune, Sherbrooke; News Ed. and Mng. Ed. Le Nouvelliste, Trois-Rivières 1953–58, Weekend Mag. and Perspectives 1959–61; Vice Pres. Prog. Télévision Quatre Saisons 1985–87; Chmn. Centenial Ctte. RCMP 1970–72; Vice Pres. J.V. Clyne Ctte. Telecommunications & Sovereignty 1978; Pres. Comn. d'étude sur le Cinéma et l'audiovisuel du Gouvernement du Qué. 1980–82; Pres. l'Institut Québécois du Cinéma 1976–80; mem. Bd. Ste-Justine Hosp. for Sick Children 1984–86; Chmn. Fund Raising Campaign; recipient Lauréat Union canadienne des Journalistes de Langue française 1960; Médaille Gérard Philippe Syndicat des Acteurs de France 1964; Toronto-Dominion Bank Gold Medal for Humour 1980; Special Award of Candn. Motion Picture Producers and Laboratories 1987; Gemini Award in 1991, 1992 and 1993 and Anik Award for best TV series 1991 and 1992; Award, Nat. Assoc. of Television Viewers 1991, 1992; writer over 200 hours drama Candn. and French TV incl. 'Pierre d'Iberville,' 'Jo Gaillard,' 'The Newcomers,' 'Jamais deux sans toi,' 'Peau de banane,' 'L'Or et le Papier' and 'Mount Royal'; several theatre plays incl. 'C'est maintenant qu'il faut boire' 1967; 'Sauve qui peut elle m'aime' 1982; 'L'amour ou la vie' 1984; 'Je t'aime clé en main' 1985 (co-author); 'Soleil! Maudit soleil' 1993; several books (mainly humour) incl. 'Guy Fournier 80 fois' 1974; 'Vivre avec ma femme' 1983; 'La mécanique du sexe' 1975; Mem. Order of Canada; mem., Société des Auteurs de France; Société des Auteurs du Can.; Union des Artistes du Can.; Alliance Candn. Cinema, TV & Radio Artists; Candn. Fedn. Authors & Artists (Pres. 1962–64); Candn. Acad. Cinema & TV; Home: 335 Mountain Rd., St-Paul d'Abbotsford, Qué. J0E 1A0; Office: 11 O'Reilly, Apt. 1209, Ile-des-Soeurs, Qué. H3E 1T6 and 1 de la Verrerie, Paris 75004, France.

**FOURNIER, Jacques,** B.S.S.; museum executive; b. Quebec, Que. 11 Oct. 1942; s. Paul-André and Thérèse (Bécotte) F.; e. Univ. of Ottawa B.S.S. 1968, M.S.S. studies 1970; children: Stéphane, Nadine, Élisabeth; m. Marion Tillstone-Rogers 1990; DEP. DIR. CANADIAN MUSEUM OF NATURE 1988– ; Dir. of Informathèque (Documentation Centre) Univ. of Ottawa 1968–73; Coordinator of Communications Univ. of Quebec 1973–76; Dir. of Communications Univ. of Quebec at Hull 1976–78; Dir. Gen. CEGEP de la Pocatière 1978–83; Dir. Gen. Coll. de l'outaouais 1983–88; mem. Council Sci. & Technol. 1981–87 (Pres. Ctte. Sci. & Tech. Culture 1983–86); mem. Bd. Trustees Fedn. of CEGEPs 1980–82; Sec. Assn. Dirs.-Gen. Colls. of Que. 1984–85, Pres. 1985–86; recreations: reading, music, philately, travel, languages, sports, fishing; Home: 22 Second Ave., Ottawa, Ont. K1S 2H3; Office: P.O. Box 3443, Stn. D, Ottawa, Ont. K1P 6P4.

**FOURNIER, Jean Arthur,** O.C., C.D., B.A., LL.L; b. Montreal, Que. 18 July 1914; s. Arthur and Emélie (Roy) F.; e. Laval Univ. B.A. 1935, LL.L. 1938; French Govt. Travelling Scholarship 1938; McGill Univ. Summer Sch. of Internat. Law 1939; 1st Candn. War Staff Coll. Ford Manor, Eng. p.s.c. 1941; Nat. Defence Coll. Kingston n.d.c. 1948; m. May d. late Dr. Patrick and Caroline (Taschereau) Coote 11 Apr. 1942; five s.; Mem., Metric Comn. of Can. 1981–85; Candn. Inst. Strategic Studies; Mem., Bd. of Dir., Candn. Inst. of Internat. Affairs, Toronto 1988–90; Vice Prés., Centre québecois de relations internationales, Qué. 1988– ; called to Bar of Que. 1939; joined Dept. External Affairs, Ottawa 1944, 2nd Secy. Buenos Aires 1945–48; seconded to Privy Council office 1948–51 and 1957–61 (Asst. Secy. to Cabinet); Prime Min.'s Office 1950–51; Counsellor, Paris 1951–54, Consul Gen. Boston 1954–57, Dir. Gen. European Affairs Ottawa 1961–64; Chrmn. Quebec Pub. Service Comn. 1964–71; Agt. Gen. for Que. London, Eng. 1971–78; Pres., Inst. Pub. Adm. Can. 1966–67; Chrmn. Consultative comte. Sch. Pub. Adm. York Univ.; served various regt'al and staff appts. Can. and Overseas 1939–44, rank Acting Lt. Col. 1944; returned to Reserve status at the request of the Dept. of External Affairs; Hon. Lt. Col. 6th Field Regt. RCA (M); rec'd. Freedom City of London 1976; Queen's Silver Jubilee Medal 1977; Pres., Candn. Veterans Assn. UK 1976–77; Clubs: Royal Candn. Military Inst. (Toronto); Address: #903, 201 Metcalfe Ave., Westmount, Que. H3Z 2H7.

**FOURNIER, Jean T.;** B.A., M.A.; public servant; b. Quebec, Que. 23 Dec. 1943; s. Jean and May (Coote) F.; e. Collège Stanislas, Montréal, B.A. 1961; Queen's Univ. B.A. 1964, Laval Univ., M.A. 1968; m. Lyse d. Paula Vermette Beaulieu 1 July 1967; children: Luc, Julie; SPECIAL ADVISOR, PRIVY COUNCIL OFFICE 1993– ; Rsch. Asst., Royal Comn. on Bilingual & Bicultural. 1964–66; Spec. Asst. then Extve. Asst. to Min of Indian and North. Affairs 1968–73; Assoc. Dir. then

Dir., Territorial & Social Devel. Branch 1973–76; Extve. Dir., Office of Native Claims 1976–78; Sr. Asst. Depy. Min., Dept. of Communications 1978–82; Asst. Depy. Min., Dept. of Fin. 1982–86; Under Sec. of State, Sec. of State of Can. 1986–91; Extve. Dir., Royal Commission on Aboriginal Peoples 1991–93; Dir., Telesat 1978–88; Candn. Mortage & Housing Corp. 1982–87; Candn. Arctic Prods. 1974–76; Fed. of Arctic Co-ops. 1974–76; Mem., Mgmt. Ctte., Candn. North. Studies Trust; Mem., Adv. Counc., Order of Canada 1986–91; Roman Catholic; author of var. articles & speeches; recreations: swimming, reading, nature; Club: Five Lakes Fishing; Home: 181 Marlborough, Ottawa, Ont. K1N 8G3; Office: P.O. Box 1993, Stn. B, Ottawa, Ont. K1P 1B2.

**FOURNIER, Léonard,** B.A., M.A.; executive; b. Amos, Que. 13 Oct. 1931; s. J. Albert and Maria (St-Onge) F.; e. Brébeuf and Ste-Marie Colls., Montreal, B.A. 1952; Montreal Univ., B.Sc. (Law and Social Sciences) 1954, M.A. (Industrial Relations) 1956; Univ. of Calif, (Berkeley), Doctoral residence in Indust. Sociology, 1956–58; m. Louise, d. late Alexandre Décarie, 7 May 1960; children: Hélène, Charles, Antoine, Francois; PRES. & C.E.O., DYNAME CORP. LTD. since 1971; Chrmn. and Pres., SOGRAMCAN (Ltée); Dir. of several other cos.; mem., Candn. Chamber Comm.; Board of Trade; Mem. of several other prof. associations; recreations: scientific research; Home: 838 Dollard Ave., Outremont, Montreal, Que. H2V 3G7; Office: 1155, boul. René-Lévesque ouest, Bureau 2500, Montréal, Qué. H3B 2K4.

**FOURNIER, Martin,** B.A.Sc., M.Sc., D.Sc.; business executive; b. Quebec, Que. 19 Feb. 1939; s. Lucien and Mona (Madden) F.; e. Laval Univ. B.A.Sc. 1961; Univ. of Illinois M.Sc. 1963; Laval Univ. D.Sc. 1966; m. Marjorie d. Rosaire and Emma Lou Baribault 21 Oct. 1961; children: Michèle, Richard, Nathalie, Brigitte; PRESIDENT AND CHIEF OPERATING OFFICER, TELEGLOBE INTERNATIONAL INC. 1992– ; Engr., Candn. General Electric Co. Ltd. 1963–65; Teaching Asst., Laval Univ. 1965–66; Research Engr., Syracuse Univ. Rsch. Corp. 1966–67; Assoc. Prof., Electrical Engr., Laval Univ. 1967–76; Dir. Gen., Radio & Radar R&D, DOC 1976–78; Dir. Gen., Technology & Systems R&D 1978–80; Vice-Pres., Engr. & System Devel., Teleglobe Canada Inc. 1980–91, Extve. Vice-Pres. & Chief Operating Offr. 1991; Chrmn. Bd. of Dirs., IDB-Mobile Communications Inc.; Mem. Bd. of Dirs., National Rsch. Council, Canada; Communications Rsch. Centre; Mem., Order of Engineers of Quebec; Inst. of Electrical & Electronics Engrs.; Clubs: St-Denis; Montreal Amateur Athletics Assn.; Home: 124 de Charente, St-Lambert, Que. J4S 1K3; Office: 1000 de la Gauchetière W., Montreal, Que. H3B 4X5.

**FOURNIER, Pierre,** B.Com., M.A., Ph.D.; b. Buenos Aires, Argentina 21 June 1947; s. Jean and May (Coote) F.; e. McGill Univ. B.Com. 1968, M.A. 1971, Ph.D. 1975; children: Nicole, Philippe, Mathieu, Julien; VICE PRES., RSCH. DIR., LÉVESQUE BEAUBIEN 1991– ; Prof. of Pol. Sci., Univ. of Québec at Montréal 1973–91, Chmn. of Pol. Sci. 1982–84; Visiting Prof. Institut d'Études Politiques Univ. de Bordeaux 1978–79; Dir. Rsch. Group Mil. Ind. in Can. 1985–91; cons. Royal Comn. Econ. Union & Can.'s Econ. Prospects; Office de Planification et de Développement du Québec; Comn. Consultative sur le Travail; Comn. d'Enquête sur le Système de Santé et les Services Sociaux au Québec; mem. Adv. Bd. Inst. Intergovt'al Relations Queen's Univ. 1981– ; author 'The Quebec Establishment' 1976; 'Les Sociétés d'Etat et les Objectifs Economiques du Québec' 1979; 'L'Entreprise Québécoise' 1987; 'Le Québec Militaire' 1989; 'Autopsie du lac Meech' 1990; co-author 'Le Capitalisme au Québec' 1979; 'Capitalisme et Politique au Québec' 1980; numerous articles Candn. mags. and newspapers; frequent contbns. radio and TV Candn. pub. affairs progs.; mem. Internat. Pol. Sci. Assn.; Candn. Pol. Sci. Assn.; recreations: tennis, swimming, skating; Home: 3906 Parc Lafontaine, Montréal, Qué. H2L 3M6; Office: 1155 Metcalfe, Montréal, Qué. H3B 4S9.

**FOWKE, Donald Vernon,** B.E., S.M., P.Eng., F.C.M.C.; management consultant; b. Saskatoon, Sask. 22 Sept. 1937; s. Vernon C. and Helen R.(Hilton) F.; e. High School and Univ. of Saskatchewan, B.E. 1959; Mass. Inst. of Tech., S.M. 1963; m. Bonnie McMillan 7 May 1960; children: Margaret, Barbara, Brian; MNG. DIR., THE NEW MANAGEMENT NETWORK, FOWKE LIMITED, Management Consultants, Toronto; Engineer with Bearing & Transmission Ltd., Saskatoon, 1960–62; Mang. Consultant, P. S. Ross & Partners, Toronto, Ont. 1963–64; Secy. and Dir. Research, Sask. Royal Comn. on Govt. Adm., Sask. 1964–65; Vice-Pres., Hillis & Partners (Mang. Consultants) Regina 1965–66; apptd. Vice-Pres., Hickling-Johnston Ltd. 1967, Sr. Partner 1971, Chrmn. & C.E.O. 1975–85; Mang. Dir., William M. Mercer Inc., N.Y. 1984–89; World Presidents' Organization; recreations: skin-diving; skiing; photography; personal computing; Address: 130 Carlton St., Ste. 605, Toronto, Ont. M5A 4K3.

**FOWKE, Edith Margaret Fulton,** C.M., M.A., LL.D., D.Litt., F.R.S.C.; folklorist; b. Lumsden, Sask. 30 Apr. 1913; d. William Marshall and Margaret (Fyffe) Fulton; e. Pub. and High Schs., Lumsden, Sask.; Regina Coll., Univ. of Sask., B.A. 1933, M.A. (Eng.) 1937; m. Franklin George Fowke, 1 Oct. 1938; prepared and wrote scripts for numerous CBC radio programs from 1950–72; series incl. 'Folk Song Time,' 'Folklore and Folk Music' and 'Folk Sounds'; items on 'Matinee,' 'Audio,' 'Assignment,' 'Ideas'; contrib. tapes of folksongs collected in Ont. and Que. to archives of Nat. Museum of Can. and Lib. of Congress; author: 'Traditional Singers and Songs from Ontario' 1965; 'Sally Go Round the Sun' 1969 (rec'd Medal for Candn. Lib. Assn.'s 'Book of the Year for Children' 1970); 'Lumbering Songs from the Northern Woods' 1970; 'Canadian Vibrations' (ed.) 1972; 'Penguin Book of Canadian Folk Songs' 1973; 'Folklore of Canada' 1976; 'Ring Around The Moon' 1977; 'Folktales of French Canada' 1979; 'Sea Songs and Ballads from Nineteenth Century Nova Scotia' 1982; 'Tales Told in Canada' 1986; 'Red Rover! Red Rover! Children's Games Played in Canada' 1988; 'Canadian' 1988; 'A Family Heritage: The Story and Songs of LaRena Clark' 1993; 'Legends Told in Canada' 1993; co-author: (with Richard Johnston) 'Folk Songs of Canada' 1954; (with Richard Johnston) 'Folk Songs of Quebec' 1957; (with Joe Glazer) 'Songs of Work and Freedom' 1960 (repr. as 'Songs of Work and Protest); (with Alan Mills) 'Canada's Story in Song' 1960 (new ed. 'Singing Our History' 1984); (with Richard Johnston) 'More Folk Songs of Canada' 1967 (repr. as 'Folk Songs of Canada II'); editor: 'Logging with Paul Bunyan' (by John D. Robins) 1957 (repr. as 'Paul Bunyan, Superhero'); 'Songs and Sayings of an Ulster Childhood' (by Alice Kane) 1983; co-editor: (with Carole H. Carpenter) 'Bibliography of Canadian Folkore in English' 1981; (with Carole H. Carpenter) 'Explorations in Canadian Folklore' 1985; other publs. incl. articles in various folklore and lit. mags.; 8 records of folk songs; pamphlets: 'They Made Democracy Work: The Story of the Cooperative Committee on Japanese Canadians' 1952; Ed., 'The Western Teacher' 1938–44; 'Food for Thought' 1950–51; 'Bulletin of the Indian-Eskimo Association' 1967–70; Assoc. Ed., 'Magazine Digest' 1944–49; joined Dept. of Eng., York Univ. as Assoc. Prof. to teach courses in folklore, 1971; Prof., 1977; Professor Emeritus 1984; Ed. 'Canadian Folk Music Journal' since 1973; Fellow, Am. Folklore Soc. 1974; LL.D., Brock Univ. 1974; D.Litt., Trent Univ. 1975; C.M. 1978; D.Litt., York Univ. 1982; LL.D., Regina Univ. 1986; Fellow, Royal Soc. of Can. 1983; Vicky Metcalf Award 1985; Lifetime Achievement Award, Children's Section, Am. Folklore Soc.; Hon. Life Mem., The Writers' Union of Can.; Candn. Folk Music Soc.; mem., Candn. Authors' Assn.; CANSCAIP; Am. Folklore Soc.; English Folk Dance and Song Soc.; Folklore Studies Assn. Can. (Pres. 1985–86); Mensa; ACUTE; recreations: reading mystery stories; bridge; theatre; cinema; travel; Home: 5 Notley Pl., Toronto, Ont. M4B 2M7.

**FOWKE, Helen Shirley,** B.A.; playwright; b. Oshawa, Ont. 5 Mar. 1914; d. Frederick Luther (former M.P. for S. Ont.) and Flora (Wheeler) F.; e. Bishop Bethune Coll.; Oshawa Coll. Inst.; Univ. Coll., Univ. of Toronto, B.A. (Modern Lang.; Gov. Gen. Medal for Modern Lang.) 1935; studied Ballet and Art for two seasons at Queen's Univ. Summer Sch.; won the Hermit Club Internat. Award in Playwriting, 1946 with a play 'Star in the Night'; another play 'Mistuh Job' was runner-up in this contest; both these plays were produced in Cleveland, Ohio; two plays have been produced by Dr. Wm. Angus, Dept. of Drama, Queen's Univ. ('Devil Take All' 1949; Lady in a Maze' 1951); won the Maxwell Anderson Award for a blank verse play in 1952 with 'Imperial Wife'; radio production for a one-act play, 'The Saving of Socrate Lebel' 1951, by the C.B.C.; 'Devil in the Heather' produced Dec. 1952 by St. Francis Xavier Univ. Drama group; author of one-act play 'A Wig for My Lady' publ. in 'Canadian One-Act Plays' series 1 and in 'Book Five Reader' for High Schools; (novel) 'Chase of the Black Swan' (publ. in serial form by 'Family Herald & Weekly Star' 1954–55); poems have appeared in 'Saturday Night'; 'Devil in the Heather' (full length radio play) produced on CBC-Stage 1963; children's TV series 1958; article in Illustrated London News 1961; stories read on John Drainie programs and publ. in collection; series of half hour plays produced by CBC Montreal; various stories read on CBC programs, etc.; publ. 'Joe, or A Pair of Corduroy Breeches' (a children's book, based on truth) 1971; 'Top-of-the-Stove Bakebook' 1984; Anglican; recreations: golf, gardening, painting, ballet; Address: 34A Broad St., Lunenburg, N.S. B0J 2C0

**FOWLER, Beverly Wayne,** C.I.P., C.A.; chartered accountant; b. Saint John, N.B. 4 March 1941; s. Winfield and Helen Marion (Flewelling) F.; e. Saint John High Sch. 1958; C.A. 1964; Trustee Licence 1978; m. Elizabeth d. James and Vera Wilson 18 Nov. 1961; children: Stephen Wayne, Suzanne Elizabeth; PRES., DOANE RAYMOND LTD. 1980; Partner, Reevey, Blackmore, Burnham, Laws & Page 1967 and Doane Raymond 1968 (by merger); Past Pres. Nat. Retriever Club Can.; Past Pres. Candn. Insolvency Practicioners Assn.; Dir. N.S. Insolvency Assn.; Home: 49 Forest Rd., Dartmouth, N.S. B3A 2M4; Office: P.O. Box 426, 1100 Cogswell Tower, Halifax, N.S. B3J 2P8.

**FOWLER, Charles Allison Eugene,** B.Sc., B.Eng., B.Arch., D.Eng. (Hon.), F.R.A.I.C., F.A.I.A.(Hon.); architect; engineer; b. Halifax, N.S. 24 Jan. 1921; s. Charles Allison De Witt and Mildred Allison (Crosby) F.; e. Dalhousie Univ., Dipl. in Engn., 1942, B.Sc. 1942; McGill Univ., B.Eng. (Mech.) 1944; Univ. of Manitoba, B.Arch. 1948; D.Eng. (Hon.) N.S. Tech. Coll. 1975; m. Dorothy Christine, d. George Graham, 30 Aug. 1947; children: Beverly Anne Louise, Graham Allison Douglas; PRES., C.A. FOWLER AND CO.; Past Chrmn., N.S. College Art and Design; mem. N.R.C. Standing Comte. on Energy Conservation in Building; served in 2nd World War as 2nd Lieutenant, R.C.O.C. and Lieutenant, R.C.E.M.E. in Canada and N.W. Europe; mem., Engn. Inst. Can.; Assn. Prof. Engrs. N.S.; N.S. Assn. Arch. (Past Pres.); Fellow, Royal Arch. Inst. Can. (Past Pres.); Fellow, Candn. Soc. for Civil Engn.; Hon. Fellow, Am. Institute of Architects; United Church; recreations: history, sailing, travel; Clubs: Saraguay; R.U.S.I.; R.N.S.Y.S.; Address: 2 Halls Road, Halifax, N.S. B3P 1P3.

**FOWLER, Edmund P.,** A.B., Ph.D.; university professor; b. Summit, N.J. 21 Dec. 1942; s. Edmund P. Jr. and Olivia Heather (Jarrett) F.; e. St. Paul's Sch. 1960; Dartmouth Coll. A.B. 1964; Univ. of N.C. at Chapel Hill Ph.D. 1969; m. Shelly d. David and Dorothy Dordick 22 Dec. 1971; children: Rebecca, Perry, Christopher; ASSOC. PROF., POL. SCI. & URBAN STUDIES, GLENDON COLL., YORK UNIV. 1967– ; Dir., Glendon Coll. Municipal Intern Program; active in promoting ecologically sensible urban planning; Mem., Candn. Pol. Sci. Assn.; Am. Pol. Sci. Assn.; author: numerous articles on urban public policy in books & jours.; co-author: 'Rites of Way: The Politics of Transportation in Boston and the US City' 1971; 'Building Cities That Work' 1992; Home: 61 Humewood Dr., Toronto, Ont. M6C 2W3; Office: 2275 Bayview Ave., Toronto, Ont. M4N 3M6.

**FOWLER, Graham,** B.F.A., M.A.; artist; b. Halifax, N.S. 15 Feb. 1952; e. N.S. Coll. of Art & Design B.F.A. 1975; Concordia Univ. M.A. 1980; McGill Univ. dipl. Ed. 1982; ASST. PROF. DEPT. ART & ART HISTORY, UNIV. OF SASK. 1989– ; Continuing Education, Art Gall. of N.S. 1978; part-time Faculty, Concordia Univ. 1979–80; Visual Arts Instr., Keyano Coll. 1982–89; visiting artist & guest lectr.: Art Gall. of N.S. 1985; Fine Arts Prog., North Peace Adult Educ. Consortium Grande Prairie Reg. Coll., Alta. 1985; Fine Arts Prog., Cariboo Coll., B.C. 1989; solo exhibitions: Woltjen/Udell Gall. Edmonton 'Recent Work' 1990, 'New Work' 1987, 1986; Nancy Poole's Studio 'Recent Paintings' 1988, 'Recent Paintings and Drawings' 1986, 'New Paintings' 1984, 'Paintings' 1982, 'New Works on Canvas' 1981; Art Gall of N.S. 'Recent Works' 1985; Prov. Bldg. Fort McMurray 1984; Concordia Univ. 'Master's Examination' 1980; Mt. St. Vincent Univ. 'Organic Life in Fluid Motion,' 1978–79; group exhibitions: Faculty Exhib., Univ. of Sask. 1990; Woltjen/Udell Gall. 'Big Picture Show' Vancouver 1989, and Fall & Spring Exhibs. of Gall. Artists, Vancouver & Edmonton 1989, 1987, 1986, 1985, 1984, 'Nocturn' 1988, Internat. Contemporary Los Angeles Art Fair 1987, 1986, Pacific Northwest Art Exposition 1987, Anniversary Gall. Exhib. 1984, 'American and Canadian Drawing' 1984, Gallery Opening 1984; 'Personal Vision in Landscape,' The Gallery Cambridge 1987; Nancy Poole's Studio 'Gallery Artists' 1987, 1984, 1983, 'Screens' 1986, 'Extensions' 1985; Art Gall. of Windsor 1982; 'Points de Vue,' La Chambre Blanche, Quebec City 1981; 'Art Through Nature' Man and His World Montreal 1980; Wiseman Gall. Concorida Univ. 1980; Art Gall. of N.S. reg. touring exhib. 1976–77; Centennial Gall. Halifax 1976; Murken Gall. Halifax 1974; Anna Leonowens Gall. Halifax 1974; numerous selected newspaper, catalogues & art journal reviews; selected collections: Paul Desmerais, Power Corp, Que.; York Downs, Unionville, Ont.; Dominion Securities, Toronto; Bish Corp., Toronto; Investors Group, Winnipeg; Pan Pacific Corp., Vancouver; Center 200, Sidney, N.S.; Art Gall. of N.S.; Alberta Art Found.; Hurtig Publishing, Edmonton; Keyano Coll., Alta; Texaco Canada; Kellner Jordan Ltd., Toronto; Maclean Hunter, Toronto; Pitfield, MacKay and Ross; Govt. of Ont.; Hudson Bay Corp. Collection; A.D.D., N.S.; N.S. Art Bank; awards: Alta. Art Found. Grant 1990, 1986; Profl. Development, Paris, France 1987–88 (grant provided by Keyano Coll.); Concordia Univ. Teaching Fellowship and Teaching Assistantship 1979–80; short term Can. Counc. grant 1977, 1978, 1979; N.S. Exhib. Grant 1978; Scholarship, Edinburgh Arts 73, Scotland 1973; mem. Visual and Performing Arts Ctte., Steering Ctte., Keyano Coll. 1983–88; The Art Ctte., Keyano Coll. 1982–87; The Gall. Ctte., The Bourget and Main Sprinkler Gall. 1979–80; Paintings used on stage set of film 'Model' 1982; Home: 734 9th Ave. N., Saskatoon, Sask. S7K 2Y9; Office: Saskatoon, Sask. S7N 0W0.

**FOWLER, John Douglas,** B.Sc.; company executive; b. Toronto, Ont. 5 Apr. 1931; s. Joseph and Elizabeth (Douglas) F.; e. Pub. and High Schs., Kingston, Ont.; Queen's Univ., B.Sc. 1955; m. Bette Gray, 8 Sept. 1956; children: Scott, Gray, Heather Ann; Pres., C.O.O. & Dir., Denison Mines Ltd. 1985–..; Vice Chrmn. Quintette Coal Ltd. 1990– ; (Vice Chrmn. & C.E.O. 1988–90; Dir. 1986– ;); Dir., The Lawson Marden Group 1988; Dir., Zemex Corp. 1988; commenced with Cominco Ltd. as Develop. Engr. Montreal and Toronto 1955; Sales Engr., Pennsalt Chemicals of Canada Ltd., Oakville, Ont. 1957; Sales Engr., Saskatchewan Cement Co. Ltd., Saskatoon, Sask. 1958; Sales and Develop. Engr., Inland Cement Industries Ltd., Edmonton, Alta. 1960; joined Lake Ontario Cement Ltd., Toronto 1962, Dir. 1971, Pres. & C.E.O. 1979, Vice Chrmn. 1985; Home: 22 Edenbridge Dr., Islington, Ont. M9A 3E9.

**FOWLER, Marian,** B.A., M.A., Ph.D.; b. Newmarket, Ont. 15 Oct. 1929; d. Robert Daniel and Dorothy Gertrude (Maconachie) Little; e. Univ. of Toronto, B.A. 1951, M.A. 1965, Ph.D. (Eng.) 1970; m. Rodney Fowler 19 Sept. 1953; divorced 1977; children: Timothy Evan, Caroline Jane; promotional work, Clarke, Irwin & Co. 1951–53; advt. copywriter, T. Eaton Co. 1953–54; part-time Course Dir. and Lectr., Atkinson Coll., York Univ. 1970–82; full-time writer since 1982; author: 'The Embroidered Tent: Five Gentlewomen in Early Canada' 1982; 'Redney: A Life of Sara Jeannette Duncan' 1983; 'Below the Peacock Fan: First Ladies of the Raj' 1987; 'Blenheim: Biography of a Palace' 1989; 'In a Gilded Cage: From Heiress to Duchess' 1993; Gov.-Gen.'s Gold Medal in Eng. 1951; Biog. Award, Assn. for Candn. Studies 1979; Anglican; mem. Writers' Union of Can.; Internat. P.E.N.; recreations: travel, bird-watching, antique collecting; Address: TH4, 70 Pleasant Blvd., Toronto, Ont. M4T 1J8.

**FOWLER, Hon. Richard S.,** Q.C., B.A., LL.B.; politician; b. Edson, Alta. 12 Apl. 1932; s. George Frederick and Adeline Alice (Gray) F.; e. Univ. of Alta. B.A. 1973, LL.B. 1976; m. Vera d. Stephen and Anna Bushko 28 July 1956; children: Cathy, James, Christine, Caroline, Stuart; Min. for Municipal Affairs and Min. Responsible for Native Affairs Alta. 1991–..; previously served Royal Bank of Canada and Dunham Bush (Canada) Ltd.; former Partner Rowand & Fowler; Councillor Town of St. Albert 1963–65, Mayor 1965–68, 1980–89; el. M.L.A. 1989, Solr. Gen., Min. Responsible for Alta. Liquor Control Bd. and for Professions & Occupations Bureau 1989; Chmn. Capital Region Sewage Comn. 1984–88; Dir. Fedn. Candn. Muns. 1986–89; Pres. Alta. Urban Muns. Assn. 1986–89; served as Dist. Comnr. and N. Alta. Comnr. Boy Scouts of Can.; Dir. and Chmn. Royal Candn. Air Cadets; mem. Bd. Govs. Athabasca Univ. 1968–71; Chmn. Alta. Summer Games 1978–79; Dir. Alta. 75th Anniversary Ctte. 1980; Hon. mem. St. Albert Lions Club, Progress Club Can.; mem. Law Soc. Alta.; Candn. Bar Assn.; K. of C.; recreations: golf, photography; Home: 56 Gresham Blvd., St. Albert, Alta. T8N 1A9.

**FOWLER, Robert R.;** federal civil servant; b. Ottawa, Ont. 18 Aug. 1944; s. Robert Maclaren and Sheila Gordon (Ramsay) F.; e. Queen's Univ. B.A. 1968; m. Mary d. John and Mary Stoker 13 June 1981; children: Linton, Ruth, Antonia, Justine; DEP. MIN., DEPT. OF NAT. DEFENCE 1989– ; joined Candn. Internat. Devel. Agency 1968–69; Dept. of External Affairs 1969, Candn. Embassy Paris 1971–74, Comm. Policy Div. 1974–76, Candn. Perm. Mission to UN, New York 1976, First Sec. and subsequently Counsellor, Security Council Affairs 1977–78; Exec. Asst. to Under Sec. of State for External Affairs 1978; seconded to Privy Council Office as Asst. Sec. to Cabinet (Foreign & Defence Policy) 1980, joined staff of PCO 1982; Asst. Dep. Min. (Policy), Dept. of Nat. Defence 1986–89; Deputy Min., Dept. of Nat. Defence 1989– ; Home: 216 Holmwood Ave., Ottawa, Ont. K1S 2P7; Office: MGen George R. Pearkes Bldg., 101 Colonel By Dr., Ottawa, Ont. K1A 0K2.

**FOWLER, Roderick Stanley;** investment executive; b. Halifax, N.S. 6 May 1949; s. Stanley W. and Irene A. (Shankle) F.; e. B.C. Silver H.S., Halifax; Dalhousie Univ.; m. Rowena M. d. Precila White 30 Dec. 1970; children: R. Sean, Adam J.; Dir. and Mgr., Foreign Exchange, Wood Gundy Inc. 1982–..; Mgmt. Training Prog. Bank of N.S. 1969–74; Sr. Asst. Acct. Bermuda National Bank 1974–76; Foreign Exchange Trader, Bank of N.S., Toronto 1976–78; Sr. Trader 1978, Chief Foreign Exchange Trader Vancouver 1978–80, Vice-Pres. and Mgr. Foreign Exchange Trading present firm 1980, Dir. 1988.

**FOWLIS, Allen M.,** C.A.; business executive; b. St. Boniface, Man. 20 Oct. 1934; s. John McQueen and Mary Ann (Allen) F.; e. Univ. of Man., C.A. 1956; Banff Sch. of Advanced Mgmt. 1969; m. Ruth d. George and Ellen James 14 June 1958; children: Lisa Ellen, John Allen, Sarah Ruth; PRES. & CHIEF EXEC. OFFR., SEASPAN INTERNAT. LTD. 1977– ; Staff C.A., Peat Marwick Mitchell & Co. 1957–59; var. pos., Vancouver Tug Boat Co./Vancouver Shipyards Co. 1959–69; Gen. Mgr., Vancouver Shipyards 1970–71; Dir., Admin., Seaspan Internat. 1971–72; Vice Pres., Admin. 1972–74; Pres., Vancouver Shipyards 1974–77; Gov., Bus. Counc. of B.C. 1977– ; Dir., Counc. of Marine Carriers 1977– ; Vancouver Bd. of Trade 1979– ; Candn. C. of C. 1987–93; Vancouver Public Aquarium 1989– ; Capilano College Found. 1991– ; Institute of Chartered Accountants of B.C. 1992– ; mem. Candn. Meml. Church; recreations: golf, curling; clubs: Point Grey Golf & Country; Vancouver; Office: 10 Pemberton Ave., North Vancouver, B.C. V7P 2R1.

**FOX, Allan J.,** B.Sc., M.D.C.M.; neuroradiologist; b. Montreal, Que. 26 July 1945; s. Nathan and Phyllis (Maron) F.; e. Monklands H.S. 1962; McGill Univ., B.Sc. 1968, M.D.C.M. 1970; m. Jennifer d. Alexander and Claire Laplante 30 Dec. 1971; one s.: Jason; DIRECTOR OF NEURORADIOLOGY, UNIVERSITY HOSPITAL, UNIV. OF WESTERN ONT. 1981– ; Internship, Royal Victoria Hospital 1970–71; Radiology Residency & Neuroradiology Fellowship, New York Univ. Med. Center 1971–75; cert. in diagnostic radiology, Am. Bd. of Radiology & R.C.P.S.C 1975; Neuroradiologist, Vancouver Gen. Hosp. 1975–76; Univ. Hosp., Univ. of W. Ont. 1976– ; Asst. Prof., Depts. of Diagnostic Radiology and Clin. Neurol. Sci. 1976; Assoc. Prof. 1981; Prof. 1986; Mem., Bd. of Dir., Univ. Hosp. 1990–93; Chair, Med. Adv. Ctte. 1992–93; active in var. neurorad. assns. with many ctte. contribs. to Am. Soc. of Neurorad.; Chair, Neurorad. Specialty Ctte., R.C.P.S.C.; author of 17 book chapters and 123 articles; Ed. Rev. Bd. for 9 journals incl. 'Am. J. of Neurorad.,' Can. Assoc. of Radiol. J.' and 'J. of Clin. Neuro-ophthal.'; research interests mainly in Neurovascular Diseases & Interventional Endovascular Therapy of Difficult Vascular Lesions of the Brain; recreations: running, cycling, theatre; Home: 84 Camden Rd., London, Ont. N5X 2K1; Office: P.O. Box 5339, 339 Windermere Rd., London, Ont. N6A 5A5.

**FOX, Beryl,** B.A., LL.D. (Hon.); film producer; director; writer; b. Winnipeg, Man. 10 Dec. 1931; d. Meyer and Sipora (Shliefman) F.; e. Univ. of Toronto, B.A. 1958; LL.D. (Hon.) Univ. of W. Ont. (1983); Dir., Writer, on camera interviewer 'This Hour Has Seven Days' 1962–65; Co-Dir., 'One More River' 1963 (winner Wilderness Award); 'Balance of Terror' 1963; 'The Chief' 1964 (winner Vancouver Film Festival); Producer/Dir., 'The Single Woman & the Double Standard' 1965; 'Summer in Mississippi' 1965 (winner, Candn. Film Award, Ohio Film Award Commonwealth Film Festival (Wales), Vancouver Film Festival, Oberhausen Film Award (Germany), Montreal Festival (Special Mention); 'The Mills of the Gods: Viet Nam' 1966 (winner George Polk Mem. Award U.S., Wilderness Award, Canadian Film Award, Cert. of Merit and Film of the Year, Vancouver Film Festival Award); 'The Honorable René Levesque' 1966; 'Youth: in Search of Morality' 1966; 'Saigon' 1967; 1967 Woman of the Year Award for Television; 'Last Reflections on a War: Bernard Fall' 1968 (winner Atlanta Film Festival Gold Medal for Peace Category 1969); 'A View from the 21st Century,' 'Martin Luther King Jr.: A Memorial' 1969; 'North With The Spring' 1970 (Silver Medal for Ecol., Atlanta Film Festival); 'Toward the Year 2000 – Jerusalem, Habitat 2000'; 'Travel and Leisure'; 'Walrus'; 'Man Into Superman'; 'Wild Refuge'; 'Fight Training'; 'Take My Hand'; 'The Visible Woman'; Co-Producer 'Here Come the 70's' documentary series 1970–71 (Dir. 'The Family,' 'Cinema,' 'Race,' and 'The Human Potential Movement' for this series); 'Take Five' (stage); NFB Producer 1976–78; Producer 'Surfacing' (feature film) 1979; 'I'm Getting My Act Together And Taking It On The Road' (stage musical; awarded Dora Mavor Moore Award for outstanding production of a musical 1980); 'By Design' (feature film) 1980; 'Key Exchange' (stage) 1981; Vice Pres. Mktg., Motion Picture Bond 1983– ; recreation: Arabian horses; Address: 14 Birch Ave., Toronto, Ont. M4V 1C8.

**FOX, Hon. Francis,** P.C., Q.C., B.A., LL.L., M.A., D.E.S., LL.M.; b. Montreal, Que. 2 Dec. 1939; s. Francis Moore and Pauline (Taschereau) F.; e. Jean-de-Brébeuf Coll. B.A. 1959; Univ. de Montréal LL.L 1962, D.E.S. 1965; Harvard Law Sch. LL.M. 1964; Oxford Univ. M.A. 1966; m.; three children; PARTNER, MARTINEAU, WALKER, Advocates 1985– ; Partner of the Nat. and Internat. law firm of Fasken Martineau, Toronto, Montreal, Quebec, London, Brussels; Chrmn., Rogers Cantel Inc.; Boards: Astral Communications Inc.; Diffulivre Inc.; Pelmorex Communications Inc.; called to the bar of Que. 1963, Ont. 1976; Lawyer, Tansey, de Grandpré, Montreal 1966–68; Special Asst. to Prime Min. of Can., Ottawa 1968–72; Mem. of Parliament, H. of C. for Argenteuil-Deux-Montagnes 1972–1984; Solicitor-General of Can., Govt. of Can. 1976–78; Secretary of State and Min. of Communications 1980–84; Min. of Internat. Trade 1984; mem., Candn. Bar Assoc.; Que. Bar Assn.; Law Soc. of Upper Can.; Candn. Assoc. of Rhodes Scholars; Dir., YMCA of Montreal; McGill Univ. Centre for Regulated Industries; Internat. Institute of Communications; Candn. Crafts Council Advisory Bd.; Centre D'Initiative Technologique de Montréal; Liberal; R. Catholic; recreations: skiing, tennis; Office: PO Box 242, 800 Victoria Sq., Ste. 3400, Montreal, Que. H4Z 1E9.

**FOX, George William;** singer; b. Cochrane, Alta. 23 March 1960; s. Herbert Charles and Anna Gertrude (Swalling) F.; e. Cochrane H.S. 1977; Juno Awards: Country Male Vocalist of the Year 1990, '91, '92; Canadian Country Music Assn. Awards: Vista Rising Star 1989, Country Male Vocalist 1990, '91, '93; RPM's Big Country Awards: Country Artist of the Year 1989; Male Vocalist of the Year 1989, '90, '91, '93; Single of the Year/Composer of the Year 'Angelina' 1989; Album of the Year 1991; Alta. Recording Industry Assn. Awards: Male Recording Artist of the Year 1989; Best Country Artist/Male Artist/Performer of the Year 1990; Calgary Country Music Assn. Awards: Album 'George Fox'/Single 'Angelina'/Male Artist/Song 'Angelina' of the Year 1989; Album 'With All My Might'/Single 'No Trespassing'/Calgary & Area Entertainer/Entertainer/Male Artist/Alberta Song 'No Trespassing' of the Year 1990; Entertainer of the Year 1991; SOCAN Song of the Year: 'Clearly Canadian' 1993; Cochrane C. of C., Ambassador of the Year 1990; Host, Canadian Country Music Awards 1991, '92, '93; over 35 television appearances incl. most recent: TNN's Crook & Chase 1993; Baton Broadcasting's 1993 'New Year's Eve Niagara'; Canada Day - Sevill, Spain 1992; Tommy Hunter Show April 1992, Juno Awards March 1992, Country Gold Feb. 1992, CBC Newsworld Jan. 1992, All About Country Jan. 1992, George Fox: Country on Campus Dec. 1991, Nashville Now Oct. 1991; CBC's 'George Fox's New Country' 1990; sang National Anthem at World Series 1993 in Toronto; Home: Cochrane, Alta.; c/o Balmur Ltd., Suite 2400, Madison Centre, 4950 Yonge St., Toronto, Ont. M2N 6K1.

**FOX, James William,** B.A., M.A.; executive; educator; b. Missoula, Montana 23 July 1946; s. William James and Blanche Ramona (Johnson) F.; e. Amherst Coll., Univ. of Montana, B.A. (cum laude) 1968; Univ. of Alta., M.A. 1970; m. Janna d. Edwin and Margaret Erlandson 8 June 1968; children: Shannon, Blanche; PRES., CANDN. BUREAU FOR INTERNAT. EDUCATION 1988– ; Asst. Lang. Advr. of Ont. 1972–75; Dir., Inter Univ. North of Man. 1975–76; Cont. Edn., Algonquin Coll. 1980–82; Commonwealth Advr. on Edn. to Seychelles 1982–86; Dir., Policy & Public Affairs, Candn. Bur. for Internat. Edn. 1986–88; Dir., Ottawa Bd. of Trade; Ottawa Small Bus. Corp. 1980; Mem., Ont. Task Force on the Edn. Needs of Native Peoples; Nat. Consortium of Edn. & Sci. Orgns.; Candn. Comn. for UNESCO; author: 'Telephone Gambits' 1980, 'Closing the Doors' 1986, 'Where to Now?' 1987; co-author: 'Teaching English as a Second Language' 1974, 1980; recreations: tennis, bicycling; Home: R.R. #1, Kingsmere, Que. J0X 1N0; Office: Ste. 1100, 220 Laurier Ave. W., Ottawa, Ont. K1P 5Z9.

**FOX, John Richard;** painter, university professor; b. Montreal, Que. 26 July 1927; s. James Wellman and Rosemary (Cunningham) F.; e. Sch. of Art & Design, Montreal Mus. of Fine Arts 1949; Slade Sch. of Art, Univ. of London (UK) 1953; m. Sandra d. Morton and Bess Paikowsky 11 Dec. 1982; children: Angelica, Marietta; ASSOC. PROF., DEPT. OF PAINTING & DRAWING, FAC. OF FINE ARTS, CONCORDIA UNIV.; regular participation since 1952 in solo & group exbns. in Montreal & Toronto & elsewhere in Canada; mural comn., Confederation Arts Ctr., Charlottetown P.E.I. 1964; circulating exhbn. of paintings to eastern & central Canada 1980–81; Mem., Candn. Group of Painters (Pres. 1965–66); Royal Candn. Academy (resigned); Address: 3621 University, #7, Montreal, Que. H3A 2B3.

**FOX, Lester L.,** M.Com., C.A.; executive; b. Montreal, Que. 8 Aug. 1920; s. Boris and Bess (Zudick) F.; e. Queen's Univ. B.Com. 1941; McGill Univ. M.Com. 1942; C.A. 1949; m. Zelda Lucille d. Israel and Ray Rothbart 15 March 1949; children: David Alan, Susan Barbara; Pres., Bankers Pen Co. 1972–91; Gen. Partner, Weinstein, Fox & Bessner, C.A.'s 1949–58; Vice Pres. present Co. 1958–72; served with Royal Canadian Artillery 1942–45; Pres., Accts. Study Group; Specialty Advertising Assn. Can. Inc. (mem. Hall of Fame); recreations: literature, music, hiking; Office: 5037 Ponsard Ave., Montreal, Que. H3W 2A6.

**FOX, Mark S.,** B.Sc., Ph.D.; university professor; b. 9 May 1952; s. Sollie and Ida (Socket) F.; e. Univ. of Toronto B.Sc. 1975; Carnegie Mellon Univ. Ph.D. 1983; m. Tressa d. Ronald and Donna Scott 11 Oct. 1984; children: Aaron, Jacob; PROFESSOR OF INDUSTRIAL ENGINEERING, UNIV. OF TORONTO 1991– ; Dir., Intelligent Systems Lab, Carnegie Mellon Univ. 1980–84; Co-Founder, Carnegie Group Inc. 1984; Vice-Pres., Engr. 1985; Pres. 1987; Assoc. Prof., Computer Sci. & Robotics, Carnegie Mellon Univ. 1987–91; NSERC Rsch. Chairholder in Enterprise Integration; Dir., Carnegie Group Inc.; Numetrix Ltd.; Cons., Digital Equipment Corp.; Ford Motor Co.; Am. Assn. for Artificial Intelligence (Fellow); Candn. Inst. for Advanced Rsch./PRECARN (Fellow); Home: 48 Admiral Rd., Toronto, Ont. M5R 2L5; Office: Dept. of Industrial Engineering, 4 Taddle Creek Rd., Toronto, Ont. M5S 1A4.

**FOX, Michael J.;** actor; b. Vancouver, B.C. 9 June 1961; s. Bill and Phyllis F.; TV series incl. Leo and Me (CBC) 1976; Palmerston USA 1980; Family Ties 1982– ; TV films incl. Letters from Frank 1979; Poison Ivy 1985; High School USA 1985; Feature films incl. Midnight Madness 1980; Class of '84 1981; Back to the Future 1985; Teen Wolf 1985; Light of Day 1986; The Secret of My Success 1987; Bright Lights, Big City 1988; Back to the Future II 1989; Office: c/o Philpott and Co., 16030 Bentara Blvd., Ste. 380, Encino, CA 91436.

**FOX, Paul Wesley,** O.C., M.A., Ph.D.; educator; b. Orillia, Ont. 22 Sept. 1921; s. Paul Hazelton and Ida Minnie (Meredith) F.; e. Univ. of Toronto B.A. 1944, M.A. 1947; Univ. of London Ph.D. 1959; m. Joan d. Samuel and Muriel Gladwin 20 June 1951; children: Rowley, Bruce, Nicholas; CHRMN., BD. OF REGENTS, VICTORIA UNIV. 1993– ; and SR. RSCH. ASSOC., VICTORIA UNIV., UNIV. OF TORONTO; Lectr. Carleton Coll. 1948–54; Asst. Prof. Univ. of Toronto 1954–60, Assoc. Prof. 1960–64; Prof. of Pol. Science Univ. of Toronto 1964–87; Principal, Erindale Coll., Univ. of Toronto 1976–86; Emeritus Prof., Univ. of Toronto 1987– ; Hon. Sr. Fellow, Renison Coll., Univ. of Waterloo 1988; Chrmn., Ont. Counc. on Univ. Affairs 1987–88; mem. Adv. Comte. on Research, Royal Comn. Bilingualism & Biculturalism 1964–68; Ont. Adv. Comte. on Confed. 1965–71; First Bilingual Dists. Adv. Bd. 1970–71; Chrmn. Second Bilingual Dists. Adv. Bd. 1972–75; served with Candn. Inf. Corps 1944–45, rank Lt.; author 'Canadian Government' 1964; 'Battlefront: The Fight for Liberty' 1965; 'Report of the Bilingual Districts Advisory Board' 1975; ed. 'Politics: Canada' 7 eds. 1962, 1966, 1970, 1977, 1982, 1987, 1991; Sr. Candn. Ed. 'The World Almanac' 1972–78; Gen. Ed. McGraw-Hill Ryerson Series in Candn. Politics (24 books) 1970– ; co-ed. 'Canadian Journal of Political Science' 1974–77; mem. Candn. Pol. Science Assn. (Dir. 1972–80; Pres. 1979–80); Soc. canadienne de Science politique (Bureau de direction 1974–77); recipient, Brit. Council Fellowship 1947–48; Can. Council Leave Fellowship 1970–71; Award for Faculty Excellence, Univ. of Toronto Alumni 1986; Paul Harris Fellow (Rotary Internat.) 1986; Officer, Order of Canada 1987; recreation: golf; Address: 262 Carlton St., Toronto Ont. M5A 2L3.

**FOX, Thomas Payne;** transportation executive; b. Vancouver, B.C. 24 Dec. 1909; s. late Thomas W. and late Sarah (Watson) F.; e. Vancouver, B.C.; m. Clara B. West 7 Sept. 1935; children: Mrs. S. Jean Limming, Thomas W., Barry D.; CHRMN., FOX INVESTMENTS LTD.; Pres. C.B. Holdings Ltd.; 309217 Alberta Ltd.; operated own fuel and trucking business in Vancouver, B.C. 1930–39; Pilot & Asst. Operations Mgr., No. 2 Air Observer Sch., Edmonton 1940–43; No. 45 Group R.A.F. Transport Command (Trans-Atlantic Ferry Pilot) 1944–45; formed Associated Airways Ltd., Edmonton 1945 (sold to Pacific Western Airlines 1956); formed Associated Helicopters Ltd. 1950 (sold to Neonex 1969); mem. Adv. Comte., United Community Fund; Vice-Chrmn., Pacific Western Airlines Ltd. 1961–68; Pres.: Alta. & Northwest Chamber of Mines & Resources 1955; Air Industries & Transport Assn. of Can. 1955–56; Edmonton Quarter Century Aviation Club (Charter Mem.) 1959; Edmonton Community Chest 1959–60 (General Campaign Chrmn. 1954–55); Candn. Cutting Horse Assn. 1961–63, 1971, 1978 (Secy-Treas. 1981–85); Quarter Horse Assn. of Alta. 1963–67 (Charter Mem.); Edmonton Chamber of Commerce 1964; Greater Edmonton Horsemen's Assn. 1969–74; Edmonton Speedway Motor Racing Assn. 1972–73; former Dir.: Edmonton Flying Club; Edmonton Airport Assn.; Candn. Quarter Horse Assn.; Y.M.C.A.; Edmonton Eskimo Football Club; Internat. Northwest Aviation Counc.; Edmonton Exhbn. Assn. (Chrmn., Finance Comte.); Alta. Northwest Chamber of Mines; Pacific Western Airlines Ltd.; Quarter Horse Assn. of Alta.; Edmonton Speedway Motor Racing Assn.; National Cutting Horse Assn.; Life Mem.: Air Transport Assn. of Canada; Quarter Horse Assn. of Alta.; Edmonton Flying Club; Northern Alta. Sports Car Club; Candn. Museum of Flight and Transportation; Edmonton and Area United Way (Hon. Life Mem.); Edmonton Northlands (Hon. Life Mem.); inducted into Canada's Aviation Hall of Fame 1983; Edmonton Klondike Days Hall of Fame 1987; Candn. Cutting Horse Assoc. Hall of Fame 1987; awarded Order of Polaris; Companion Order of Flight); mem. A.F. and A.M.; Past Master, Commercial Lodge #81; Al Shamal Temple (Charter Mem.); Edmonton Rotary Club; Edmonton Quarter Century Aviation Club; Royal Order of Jesters; Candn. Rodeo Historical Assn.; Fort Edmonton Hist. Found.; Western Heritage Ctr.; Protestant; recreations: training and showing Cutting Horses; (formerly) motor racing; Address: 14141 Fox Drive, Edmonton, Alta. T6H 4P3.

**FOX, Wayne Charles,** B.A., M.B.A.; investment executive; b. Toronto, Ont. 11 Aug. 1947; s. Charles Richard and Marion Theresa (Blainey) F.; e. Univ. of Waterloo B.A. 1971; McMaster Univ. M.B.A. 1973; m. Isabel d. John and Irene Campbell 14 Aug. 1971; children: Christopher, Elizabeth, Alexandra; DEPUTY CHAIRMAN, HEAD OF GLOBAL EQUITIES, WOOD GUNDY INC. 1989– ; joined Wood Gundy Inc. 1973; Financial Consultant 1975–80; Ontario Regional Mgr. 1980–83; Dir. of Capital Markets & Syndication 1983–86; of Fixed Income & Equities 1986–88; of Private Clients 1988–89; Bd. of Gov., The Toronto Stock Exchange; Past Dir., The CIBC Wood Gundy Corp.; CIBC Investment Management Corp.; clubs: Mississauga Golf & Country, The Fitness Inst.; Home: 3500 Sawmill Valley Dr., Mississauga, Ont. L3L 3A4; Office: BCE Place, P.O. Box 500, Toronto, Ont. M5J 2S8.

**FOXALL, Roger Arthur,** B.Sc., A.R.S.M., Ph.D.; research executive; b. Birmingham, Eng. 29 Jan. 1942; s. Arthur Oliver and Kathleen Ethel (Marsden) F.; e. Univ. of London B.Sc. 1962, A.R.S.M. 1962; Univ. of Cambridge Ph.D. 1966; Oxford Univ. postdoctoral research 1966–68; m. Marjorie d. James and Ethel Cox 31 March 1964; children: Michael James, Stephen William, Andrew Oliver; DIRECTOR GENERAL, INST. FOR MARINE BIOSCIENCES, NATIONAL RESEARCH COUNCIL CANADA 1984– ; Research Officer, Div. of Physics, National Research Council Can. 1968–75; various managerial support roles incl. 2-yr secondment to Treas. Bd. Secretariat; Dir., Candn. Centre for Fisheries Innovation; recreation: birding; clubs: Nova Scotia Bird Soc.; Home: 41 Chartwell Lane, Halifax, N.S. B3M 3S7; Office: 1411 Oxford St., Halifax, N.S. B3H 3Z1.

**FOXMAN, Stuart P.,** B.J.; communications executive; b. Montréal, Qué. 10 Sept. 1961; s. Hyman and Charna Lydia (Hahamovitch) F.; e. Herzliah High Sch. Montréal; Vanier Coll. Montréal 1980; Carleton Univ., B.J. 1984; m. Lisa Kleinberg; FOUNDER AND OWNER, FOXMAN COMMUNICATIONS INC. 1987– ; joined NIVA Inc. 1983–87, promotional writer 1983, Asst. to Pres. 1984–87; co-author: book and screenplay 'Time of Their Lives – The Dionne Tragedy' 1986 (Lit. Guild Can. Selection 1986, Lit. Guild USA Selection 1987, becoming feature film); Mem., Internat. Assn. of Business Communicators; Address: 28 Swinton Cres., Thornhill, Ont. L4J 2X1.

**FOY, David R.,** B.A., B.Comm.; business executive; b. Montreal, Que. 17 Jan. 1943; s. Albert J. and Dorothy (Fach) F.; e. Loyola Coll. B.A. 1963, B.Comm. 1964; m. Linda d. Edward and Jessica Laverty 17 Oct. 1964; children: Darren, Pamela, Bradley; Pres., Chief Extve. Offr. & Dir., Phillips Cables Ltd. 1985–..; Dir., Phillips-Fitel (Chrmn.) joint venture with Furukawa Electric Co. Japan; Dir., BICC Cables Corp. N.A.; Monsanto Canada Ltd. 1964–74; Steetley Indus. 1974–78; Dylex Ltd. 1978–85; recreation: golf; club: Donalda Golf & Country; Home: 22 Woodbridge Circle, Ashburn, Ont. L0B 1A0.

**FRAGASSO, Bruno M.,** B.A.; homme d'affaires; né. Québec, Qué. 1 mai 1938; f. Michel et Clara (Tache) F.; é. Univ. Laval, B.A. en psychologie 1959, en géographie 1960, Diplôme en gestion de l'entreprise 1967; ép. Diane Emond 18 mai 1963; enfants: Roberto, Marco; PRÉS. ET DIR. GÉNÉRAL, PALAIS DES CONGRÈS DE MONTRÉAL 1989– ; Agent passagers, Air Canada 1960–64; Surveillant au comptoir des billets 1965–68; Chef des ventes et serv., passagers et fret 1968–72; Chef des ventes, agences et intercompagnies & Chef de l'expansion marchés spéc. et ventes entreprises 1972–75; Dir. réservations et agences urbaines 1975–77; Dir. de dist., Qué. 1977–78; Dir., Marketing passages en gros 1978–79; Dir. gén., dist. de Montréal 1979–83; Dir. gén., Prov. de Qué. 1983–89; Gouverneur de la Jeune Chambre de Commerce de Mtl Inc.; Fondation Gérard Delage; Mem., Ass. Int. Palais des congrès; Ass. de l'Industrie touristique du Canada; Ass. Hôteliers de la Province de Québec; Ass. Restaurateurs du Québec; Organisation Mondiale du Tourisme; Conseil d'admin. de C. de C. de Montréal; Montreal Bd. of Trade; Conseil d'admin. de l'OCTGM; Prés. d'honneur de la campagne 1991; Div. Qué., Société Canadienne du Cancer; loisirs: voile; résidence: 370, Girouard, Oka, Qué. J0N 1E0; bureau: 201, ave Viger Ouest, Montréal, Qué. H2Z 1X7.

**FRAIKIN, Leon Arthur,** M.Sc., P.Eng.; company president; b. Brussels, Belgium 4 Feb. 1907; s. Joseph and Marie (Melotte) F.; e. Univ. of Ghent, C.E. 1929; Mass. Inst. Tech., M.Sc. (Civil Engn.) 1931; m. Mary, d. late Maurice Van Ysendyck, 20 Aug. 1930; children: Claire (Mrs. R. Bergman), Daniel, Eric; CHRMN., FRANKI CANADA LTD. 1964– ; (Hon. Chrmn. 1979–86; Pres. 1959–64; Foundation Engrs. and Contractors, estbd. 1932); Hon. Chrmn., Franki Foundation Co. Ltd., N.Y.; with Ste. des Pieux Franki, Liege, Belgium, 1931–35; Braithwaite & Co., London, Eng. for British India, 1935–37; McDonald Gibbs & Co., for Mohammed Ali Barrages, Cairo, Egypt, 1937–38; joined present firm in 1938 as Mgr.; served in 2nd World War, 1939–45; Capt. R.A., Belgian Army in Gr. Brit.; Mutual Aid Organ., Brussels; Chargé de Mission, Belgian Econ. Mission, Canada; Offr., Order of Leopold 1st, Belgium; Fellow, Am. Soc. Civil Engrs.; Life mem., Engn. Inst. Can.; Hon. Pres., Belg.-Am. Educational Foundation, New York; Christian Democrat; R. Catholic; recreations: golf, swimming, stamps; Home: Chateau Vincent d'Indy, 60 Ave. Willowdale, Ste. 611, Outremont, Que. H3T 2A3.

**FRAME, Clifford H.,** B.A.Sc., P.Eng.; company executive; b. Russell, Man. 28 May 1933; s. Hugh MacCallum and Thelma Jean (Setter) F.; e. J.L. Crowe High Sch. Trail, B.C.; Univ. of B.C., B.A.Sc. (Mining Engn.); m. Catherine d. David and Kathleen Graham; three d. Wendy A., Kathleen P., Jamie L.; four s. Clifford J., Geordie S., Cameron H., Mervyn J.; CHRMN., CHIEF EXEC. OFFR. AND DIR. CURRAGH INC. 1985– ; Dir., Curragh Investments Corp.; Curragh Mining Properties Inc.; Frame Mining Corp.; Curragh Resources Corp.; Westray Mining Corp.; formerly: Mine Capt., Consolidated Denison 1957; Chief Mines Planning Engr., International Nickel, Thompson, Man. 1960; Asst. Mgr. Denison Mines Ltd. 1966; Vice-Pres. Operations, International Nickel Australia and P.T. International Nickel Indonesia 1967–72; Vice-Pres. and Gen. Mgr. Tara Mines Ltd. Ireland 1972–75; Extve. V.P. Mining Oper. and Dir., Denison Mines Ltd., 1975–81; Pres. Mining Oper. and Dir. 1981–82; Pres., C.O.O. and Dir. 1982–85; mem. Candn. Inst. Mining & Metall.; Am. Inst. Mining and Metall.; Assn. Prof. Engrs. Ont.; Clubs: Toronto; York Downs Golf & Country; Cambridge; Office: 1900, 95 Wellington St. W., P.O. Box 12, Toronto, Ont. M5J 2N7.

**FRANCA, Celia (Mrs. James Morton),** O.C. (1967), C.C. (1985), O.Ont. (1987), D.C.L. (hon.), LL.D. (hon.); D. Litt. (hon.); director; choreographer; dancer; narrator; b. London, Eng., 25 June 1921; e. Guildhall School Music, London, England; Royal Academy of Dancing; LL.D. Univ. of Windsor 1959; Mt. Allison 1966; Univ. of

Toronto 1974; Dalhousie Univ. 1976; York Univ. 1976; Trent Univ. 1977; McGill Univ. 1986; D.C.L. Bishop's Univ. 1967; D. Litt. Guelph Univ. 1976; m. James Morton, 7 Dec. 1960; lends patronage to: Osteoporosis Soc. of Can.; Founder (1951) and Artistic Dir. (1951–74) Nat. Ballet of Canada; Co-founder (with Betty Oliphant) Nat. Ballet Sch., Toronto, 1959; Co-Artistic Dir., The Sch. of Dance, Ottawa 1978; made debut in corps de ballet in 'Mars' in 'The Planets' (Tudor), Mercury Theatre, London, Eng. 1936; Soloist, Ballet Rambert, London 1936–38, lead. dram. dancer 1938–39, guest artist 1950; dancer, Ballet des Trois Arts 1939, Arts Theatre Ballet and The Internat. Ballet, London 1941; leading dramatic dancer, Sadler's Wells Ballet 1941–46; guest artist and choreographer Sadler's Wells Theatre Ballet 1946–47; dancer and teacher, Ballets Jooss, Eng. 1947; ballet mistress and leading dancer, Metrop. Ballet, London 1947–49; dancer, Ballet Workshop, London 1949–51; a princ. dancer Nat. Ballet of Can. 1951–59; princ. roles incl. title role in 'Giselle'; Swanilda in 'Coppelia'; Young Girl in 'Spectre of the Rose'; Operetta Star in 'Offenbach in the Underworld'; Woman in His Past in 'Lilac Garden'; First Song in 'Dark Elegies'; Felice in 'Winter Night'; roles originated: Bird in 'Peter and the Wolf' (Staff) 1940; Queen in 'Hamlet' (Helpmann) 1942; Prostitute in 'Miracle in the Gorbals' (Helpmann) 1944; Spider in 'Le Festin de l'Araignée' (Howard) 1944; 'Lady from the Sea' (Leese) 1955; Black Queen in 'Swan Lake' (Bruhn) 1967; character roles inc. Madge the Witch in 'La Sylphide'; Lady Capulet in 'Romeo and Juliet'; Pianist in 'The Lesson'; Carabosse in 'Sleeping Beauty'; ballets choreographed inc. 'Midas' London 1939; 'Cancion' 1942; 'Khadra' 1946; 'Dance of Salome' BBC TV 1949; 'The Eve of St. Agnes' BBC 1950; 'Afternoon of a Faun' and 'Le Pommier' Toronto 1952; 'Casse Noisette' 1955; 'Princess Aurora' 1960; 'The Nutcracker' 1964; 'Cinderella' 1968; and choreography for CBC and Canadian Opera Co.; served on jury, 5th Internat. Ballet Competition, Varna, Bulgaria 1970, and 2nd Internat. Ballet Competition, Moscow 1973; 1st woman recipient, Gold Key to City of Washington (D.C.) 1955; rec'd Woman of Year Award, B'nai B'rith 1958; Toronto Telegram Award 'for the most outstanding contribution to the arts in Canada' 1965; Hadassah Award of Merit, Toronto 1967; Centennial Medal 1967; Molson Award 1974; Can. Counc. Senior Grants Award 1975; Int. Soc. of Performing Arts Admin.'s Award 1979; Invited by Chinese Govt. to teach & mount full-length 'Coppelia' 1980; honoured as one of the founders of Canada's major ballet cos., Alberta Ballet Co. 15th Anniv. 1981; Canada Dance Award 1984; Gold Card Recipient, IATSE Local 58, 1984; Candn. Conf. of the Arts Diplôme d'honneur 1986; Woman of the Year Award, The St. George's Soc. of Toronto 1987; author 'The National Ballet of Canada: A Celebration' 1978; Office: 250 Clemow Ave., Ottawa, Ont. K1S 2B6.

**FRANCEY, Jeannette Hanna,** B.A.; graphic designer; b. Rochester, N.Y. 10 Aug. 1952; d. John Russell and Jeanne Vivien (Kaufman) Hanna; e. Rutgers Univ. B.A. 1974; m. Peter s. Glenn and Iona Francey 25 Aug. 1979; two s. Blair Glenn, Russell Alexander; FOUNDING PARTNER, SPENCER FRANCEY PETERS (design & mktg. communicatons) 1977– ; Founder Macforum 1986– ; lectr., VICOM, MacWorld, Kent State Univ. Blossom Festival; 1992 Design Mgmt. Inst. Conf.; Univ. and Colleges Design Assoc.; rec'd various design awards New York Arts Dirs. Club; Toronto Art Dirs. Club; Home: 8 Juniper Ave., Toronto, Ont. M4L 1S2; Office: Ste. 200, 250 The Esplanade, Toronto, Ont. M5A 1J2.

**FRANCIS, Daniel Patrick,** M.A.; writer; b. Vancouver, B.C. 19 Apl. 1947; s. Gordon Herbert and Yvonne Blanche (Daniel) F.; e. Lord Byng High Sch. Vancouver; Univ. of B.C., B.A. 1969.; Carleton Univ. M.A. 1975; m. Maraquita d. Anthony and Dorothy Brealey 23 July 1971; children: Emily, Patrick; ed. writer Medicine Hat 'News' 1970–71; Reporter, 'Ottawa Journal' 1971–72; Historian, James Bay Hist. Project 1975–77; freelance hist. rsch. and writing 1977–84; ed. dir. 'Horizon Canada' 1984–87; contr. ed. 'The Junior Encyclopedia of Canada'; author 'Battle for the West: Fur Traders and the Birth of Western Canada' 1982; 'Arctic Chase: A History of Whaling in Canada's North' 1984; 'Discovery of the North' 1986; 'A History of World Whaling' 1990; 'The Imaginary Indian: The Image of the Indian in Canadian Culture' 1992; co-author 'New Beginnings: A Social History of Canada' 1981; 'Partners in Furs: The Indians and the Fur Trade in Eastern James Bay, 1670–1870' 1982; 'Our Canada: A Social and Political History' 1985; 'Transit in British Columbia: The First 100 Years' 1990; Address: 154 Windsor Rd. E., North Vancouver, B.C. V7N 1J8.

**FRANCIS, Diane Marie;** writer; b. Chicago, Ill. 14 Nov. 1946; d. Paul Marion and Mary Katherine (Egan) Davis; e. Niles East High Sch. Skokie, Ill.; Univ. of Ill.; Sheridan Coll. Oakville, Ont.; m. Frank s. Frank and Ada Francis 24 Apl. 1965; children: Eric Michael, Julie Marie; EDITOR, THE FINANCIAL POST; Columnist, Maclean's Magazine, The Sun 1987– ; Contbg. Ed. Candn. Business Mag. 1979–81; Columnist, Quest Mag. 1981–83; Financial Columnist, Toronto Star 1981–87; Commentator, CFRB; recipient Royal Bank Bus. Writing Award 1982; CPA Nat. Writing Awards 1984, 1985, 1987; Edward Dunlop feature Writing Award 1990; Woman of the Year, Chatelaine Magazine 1992; author 'Controlling Interest: Who Own Canada?' 1986; 'Contrepreneurs' 1988; 'The Diane Francis Inside Guide to Canada's 50 Best Stocks' 1990; 'A Matter of Survival' 1993; Vice Chrmn., Clarke Inst. of Psych. Found. Board; Dir., Candn. Found. for AIDS Rsch.; Adv. Bd., Financial Post Corp.; Office: 333 King St. E., Toronto, Ont. M5A 4N2.

**FRANCIS, Dorothy Delores;** artist; b. Dinsmore, Sask. 1 Jan. 1923; d. Remi Horace and Eva (Emard) Leonard; e. Nutana Coll. 1939; Vancouver Art Sch. 1957; m. Harold Reid s. Harry and Florence Francis 28 Nov. 1942; children: Kent (dec.), Randi, Timothy, Lisa, Mark; profl. artist since 1953; primarily portrays Candn. Native Indian and Inuit people; numerous solo exhns.; rep. private and corporate colls. Can. and abroad; perm. display Smithsonian Museum Washington, D.C.; Pacific Northwest Indian Centre Gonzaga Univ. Spokane, Wash.; published by Aaron Ashley Inc. New York 1959–72, Lawson Graphics Ltd. Vancouver 1966–78, Candn. Gallery Prints Ltd. Port Moody 1979–89, Arctic Art Gallery, Yellowknife, North West Territories 1990– , D.H. Ussher Ltd., Vancouver, B.C. 1992– ; Home: C–20, 885 Berwick Park, Qualicum Beach, B.C. V9K 1N7.

**FRANCIS, John Drummond,** B. Comm., M.S.; advertising executive; b. Calgary, Alta. 30 March 1932; s. the late Harry and the late Marjory (Drummond) F.; e. Univ. of Alta. B. Comm. 1953; Boston Univ. M.S. (Pub. Relations) 1958; m. Lois d. Norman McCutcheon 4 Dec. 1954; two d. Kathryn Joyce, Susan Ann; CHRMN. & C.E.O., FWJ COMMUNICATIONS LTD. (formerly Francis, Williams & Johnson Ltd.); active in pub. relations since 1954; estbd. present firm 1958; Chrmn., Calgary Parks Found. 1991–93; Chrmn., Partnerparks Endowment Council 1993– ; Past Pres., Candn. Public Relations Soc.; Alta. Theatre Projects; Calgary Philharmonic Soc.; past Vice Chrmn. Strathcona-Tweedsmuir Independent Sch.; recreations: golf, curling; Clubs: Earl Grey Golf; Glencoe; Home: 1424 Premier Way S.W., Calgary, Alta. T2T 1L9; Office: #500, 635 – 6 Ave. S.W., Calgary, Alta. T2P 0T5.

**FRANCIS, John Herbert,** Q.C., B.A., M.A., LL.B.; barrister & solicitor; b. Lindsay, Ont. 17 Nov. 1932; e. Univ. of Toronto, B.A. 1954, M.A. 1955, LL.B. 1960; Univ. of Chicago, grad. studies; SENIOR PARTNER, McCARTHY TETRAULT, BARRISTERS & SOLICITORS 1962– ; called to Bar of Ont. 1962; of Alta. 1982; of the State of New York 1982; of Saskatchewan 1984; Q.C. 1975; mem., Candn. Bar Assn.; Clubs: National; Oxford; Home: 4301–85 Thorncliffe Park Dr., Toronto, Ont. M4H 1L6; Office: Suite 4700, Toronto Dominion Bank Tower, Toronto-Dominion Centre, Toronto, Ont. M5K 1E6.

**FRANCIS, (Cyril) Lloyd,** P.C., M.A., Ph.D.; economist; b. Ottawa, Ont. 19 March 1920; s. Frederick Roland and Mary (Dyble) F.; e. Bayview Pub. Sch. and Glebe Coll. Inst. Ottawa 1936; Univ. of Toronto B.A. 1940; M.A. 1946; Univ. of Wis. Ph.D. 1955 (Econ.); m. Margery Elizabeth (dec.) d. late John Malcolm Miller 23 Dec. 1943; m. 2ndly Mary Barbara Penner 8 Oct. 1992; children (from previous marriage): John Paul, Donald Lyle, Mary Elaine; STATESMAN IN RESIDENCE, BABSON COLL., Wellesley, Mass. 1991; joined Gen. Chems. Div. C.I.L. 1940–41; Lectr. in Econ. and Indust. Relations Univ. of Buffalo 1948–51; Asst. Dir. Div. Research & Statistics, Nat. Health & Welfare 1951–60; Nat. Pres. Prof. Inst. Pub. Service of Can. 1958–59; Ald., Carleton Ward, City of Ottawa 1959–60, Depy. Mayor and Sr. Controller 1960–63, Ald. 1967–68; el. to H. of C. for Carleton 1963, Ottawa West 1968, 1974, 1980; Chrmn. Veterans' Affairs Comte. 1969–70; Chief Govt. Whip and Parlty. Secy. to Min. of Veterans' Affairs 1970–71; Parlty. Secy. to Pres. of Treasury Bd. 1975–76; Vice Chrmn. and Sr. Lib. mem. Pub. Accounts Comte. 1977–79; mem. Candn. Del. to Gen. Assembly U.N. 1967, 1975; Chrmn. Candn. Group Inter-Parlty. Union 1977–79; Dir., Parlty. Centre for Foreign Affairs and Foreign Trade 1980–84; Depy. Speaker of the House 1980–83; Speaker 1983–84; Canadian Ambassador to Portugal 1984–87; Visiting Prof. Sch. of Social Work McGill Univ. 1960–61; Dir. Candn. Fed. Mayors & Muns. 1962–63; mem. Extve. Ottawa Chapter Candn.Council Christians & Jews 1977–79; Trustee Ottawa Civic Hosp. 1960–63; Dir. Children's Aid Soc. 1961–63; served with RCAF 1941–45, Radar Mechanic & Air Navig., attached RAF 1942–43; author several articles on Candn. social welfare expenditures 1955–61; Liberal; Unitarian; recreations: amateur lapsmith, fishing, rock hunting; Clubs: Ottawa Lapsmith; Address: 94D Green Valley Cres., Ottawa, Ont. K2C 3K7.

**FRANCIS, Robert Douglas,** B.A., M.A., Ph.D.; professor; b. Fenwick, Ont. 2 Sept. 1944; s. Robert George and Vera Pauline (Barwell) F.; e. Pelham Dist. H.S. 1963; York Univ., B.A. (Hon.) 1967, Univ. of Toronto, M.A. 1968; York Univ. Ph.D. 1976; m. Barbara Lynne d. Edward and Norene Grant 21 July 1973; children; Marc Nathaniel, Myla Adelle, Michael Douglas Grant; PROF., UNIV. OF CALGARY 1988– ; Teacher, West Hill Collegiate 1968–69; Sessl. Instr., York Univ. 1974–75; Vis. Lectr., Univ. of B.C. 1975–76; Asst. Prof., Univ. of Calgary 1976–81, Assoc. Prof. 1981–88; Visiting Prof., Candn. Studies, Univ. of Tsukuba, Japan 1991–93; Adv. Ctte., Alta. Heritage Learning Resources Project, Govt. of Alta. 1980–81; Cons., Soc. Studies Curriculum, Dept. of Edn. Govt. of Alta. 1977–81; Chrmn. History Program Ctte., 1994 Learned Societies Meetings; recipient, Master Teacher Award, Univ. of Calgary 1982; winner of J.W. Dafoe Book Prize 1986; recipient, Award of Merit, Assoc. for Candn. Studies 1989; winner, Prime Minister's Award for publishing of a book about Canada in a foreign language (Japanese); Mem., Candn. Hist. Assn.; Alta. Hist. Assn.; Assoc. for Candn. Studies; Japanese Assoc. for Candn. Studies; author: 'Frank H. Underhill' 1986; 'Images of the West' 1989; co-author: 'Origins: Canadian History Before Confederation' and 'Destinies: Canadian History Since Confederation' 1988, 2nd ed. 1992; co-editor: 'The Dirty Thirties in Prairie Canada' 1980; 'Readings in Canadian History' 2 vols. 1982, 2nd ed. 1986, 3rd ed. 1989, 4th ed. 1994; 'The Prairie West' 1985, 2nd ed. 1992; 'The Regions and People of Canada: A Historical Approach' (in Japanese) 1993; recreations: squash, tennis, hiking, skiing; Home: 1432 – 5 St. N.W., Calgary, Alta.; Office: 2500 University Dr., Calgary, Alta. T2N 1N4.

**FRANCIS, Wm. Brent,** B.A.; petroleum wholesale-retail executive; b. Ottawa, Ont. 21 Aug. 1958; s. William J. and Gail C. (Aldus) F.; e. Univ. of Waterloo B.A. 1980; m. Sylvia d. Ray and Pauline MacFabe 10 Oct. 1981; children: Ben, Alex, Graham; VICE-PRES., FRANCIS FUELS 1980– ; H. Boehemers Petroleum Kitchener 1977–80; Dir., Candn. Assn. of Family Enterprise; Former Dir., Candn. Oil Heat Assn.; Soc. of Mngt. Accountants of Ont.; Univ. of Waterloo Alumni Assn.; recreations: multi-engine pilot; Office: 43 Auriga Dr., Ottawa, Ont. K2E 7Y8.

**FRANCISCO, Rolando C.,** B.B.A.; mining executive; b. Manila, Philippines 25 June 1950; s. Amado Cruz and Rosa (Cruz) F.; e. Univ. of the East, B.B.A. 1971; m. Teodora R. d. Gregorio and Lilim Soriano 21 Dec. 1974; children: Carol Lynne, Lucy Anne; concurrently SR. VICE-PRES. & CHIEF FINANCIAL OFFICER, DICKENSON MINES LIMITED, WHARF RESOURCES LTD., CSA MANAGEMENT LIMITED AND GOLDCORP INC. 1990–present; Lac Minerals Ltd.: Sr. Vice-Pres. Finance &
C.F.O. 1988–90, Sr. Vice-Pres. & Treas. 1987, Vice-Pres. & Treas. 1985–86, Treas. 1978–84; Faber-Castell Canada Ltd.: various acctg. positions 1976–77; Tilden Rent-A-Car: various acctg. positions 1975; Occidental Minerals (Philippines) INc.: various acctg. positions 1971–74; Dir., Dickenson Mines Limited; Wharf Resources Ltd.; Goldcorp Inc.; Goldquest Exploration Inc.; recreations: fishing, swimming, gardening, world history; club: Ontario; Home: 280 Gamma St., Etobicoke, Ont. M8W 4H1; Office: 145 King St. W., Ste. 2700, Toronto, Ont. M5H 1J8.

**FRANCOLINI, Geno F.,** H.B.A., F.C.A., LL.D.; b. Sault Ste. Marie, Ont. 31 Mar. 1931; s. Guiseppe and Argentina (Gianbartolemei) F.; e. Sault Coll. Inst. 1949; Univ. of W. Ont. Sch. of Bus. Adm. 1954; C.A. 1957; Fellow, Inst. of Chartered Accountants 1970; LL.D. Univ. of W. Ont. 1984; m. Joan Ann Barry 9 June 1956; children: Lezlie; Geoffrey; Sara; Anthony; James; Mark; PRES. & C.E.O., XENON CAPITAL CORP. 1984– ; Lonventure Capital Fund Ltd.; Joangeno Realty Inc. and 434891 Ontario Inc.; Limited Partner: Carlisle Partnership (Hydro Dams); Dir.: Algoma Steel Inc.; Algoma Finance Corp. (and Chrmn. Audit Ctte.); Bell Canada (and mem. Pension Fund Comte.); Continental Bank of Can. (and Chrmn. Audit Comte.); Harris Steel Group Inc. (and mem. Audit Comte.); International Innopac Inc. (and Chrmn. Audit Comte.); Advisor: Long Manufacturing Ltd.; Norfolk Resources Inc.; Westbury (Quebec) Securities Inc.; Univ. of Western Ont. Rsch. and Development Park Inc.; Bd., Lawson Rsch. Inst., St. Joseph's Health Ctr., London; Advisor, Schroders Canadian Buy-Out Fund; Mem. Advisory Comte., Sch. of Bus. Adm., Univ. of W. Ont.; Bd. of Govs., Algoma Univ. Coll., Sault Ste. Marie, Ont.; articled with Clarkson, Gordon & Co. 1954–57; Mgr. 1959–62; Partner 1962–69; Dir. and C.E.O., Livingston International Inc. (formerly Livingston Industries Ltd.) 1969–79; Vice-Chrmn. and C.E.O. 1979–83; formerly, Dir.: Air Canada and Interim Chrmn. 1983–84 (and mem. Extve. Comte., Strategic Planning Comte. and Chrmn. Audit Comte.) 1976–85; en Route Card Inc.; enRoute International Inc. (and Chrmn. Audit Comte. & mem. Human Resources / Compensation Comte.) 1990–92; Commonwealth Holiday Inns of Canada (and mem. Audit Comte.) 1978–79; Nordair Ltd. (and Chrmn. Audit Comte., mem. Extve. Comte., Compensation Comte.) 1980–84; Photochemical Research Associates Inc. (P.R.A.) 1976–86; Abbey Hill Vehicle Services Limited, United Kingdom (and Chrmn. of the Bd.) 1986–87; Laidlaw Inc. (and Chrmn. Audit Comte.) 1983–88; International Pathfinder Inc. (& Chrmn., Audit Ctte.) 1987–88; J.M. Schneider Inc. (and mem. Exec. Comte.; Compensation & Human Resources Comte.; Chrmn., Audit Comte.) 1979–89; Knowlton Realty Ltd. (Bd. of Mgmt.) 1985–89; Sovereign Life Insurance Co. (Chrmn. Audit Comte. ) 1985–92; Amertek Inc. (and mem. Audit Comte.) 1988–90; Ont. Development Corp. (Vice-Chrmn. 1973) 1974–75; Chrmn., Bd. of Govs., Univ. of Western Ont. (and mem. and Chrmn. various other comtes. there 1975–83) 1981–83; Trinity Coll. Sch., Port Hope (and mem. Budget and Scholarship Comte.) 1977–86; mem. Liberal Assns. of London (Vice Pres. London W. Assn.) 1962–72; R. Catholic; recreation: gardening; Clubs: London; London Hunt; Marconi; Home: 23 Tallwood Rd., London, Ont. N5X 2S1; Office: 400 - 248 Pall Mall St., London, Ont. N6A 5P6.

**FRANEY, Alan;** film festival director; b. London, Eng. 23 May 1957; s. Basil Victor and Helen Margaret (Simpson) F.; e. Simon Fraser Univ.; m. Donna d. Harold and Pearl Chisholm 1 Oct. 1983; two s. James Silvian, Evan Joseph; FESTIVAL DIR. VANCOUVER FILM FESTIVAL 1988– , Dir. of Prog. and Festival Co-ord. 1982–87; Theatre Mgr. Ridge Theatre Vancouver 1978–85; Adm. Dir. Olympic Film Festival Calgary 1987–88; Film Prog. Vancouver E. Cinema 1982–90; Home: 3550 W. 14th Ave., Vancouver, B.C. V6R 2W4; Office: 410, 1008 Beatty St., Vancouver, B.C. V6B 2X1.

**FRANK, John F.,** C.D., M.Sc.; retired business executive; b. Picton, Ont. 3 Mar. 1925; s. Reginald Wilson and Reta Eileen (Cavanah) F.; e. Royal Candn. Naval Coll. Esquimalt, B.C. 1944; Royal Naval Eng. Coll. Devonport, Eng. 1948; Cranfield Inst. of Technol. Bedford, Eng. M.Sc. 1948; m. Joan d. John and Mary Costain 28 Sept. 1946; children: Christopher, Timothy, Debbie; Bd. Chrmn., Pres. & C.E.O., R.L. Crain Inc. 1988–89; served with RCN 1958–62, D.N.D. Dir. Aircraft Design & Prodn., rank Commdr. (E); Eng. Cons. Dept. Trade & Comm. 1962–64; Sales Mgr. Ashton Press Mfg. Ltd. 1964–66; Plants Mgr. present co. 1966, Vice Pres. Mfg. 1973, Exec. Vice Pres. 1978–79, Pres. & C.E.O. 1979–90; mem. Internat. Business Forms Inds. Inc. (Chrmn. 1984–85); recreations: fishing, golf; Club: Royal Ottawa Golf; Home: 10, 215 Mackay St., Ottawa, Ont. K1M 2B6.

**FRANK, Roberta,** A.M., Ph.D.; university professor; b. New York City, N.Y. 9 Nov. 1941; d. Norman Burton and Doris (Birnbaum) F.; e. N.Y.U. A.B. 1962; Univ. Coll., Dublin 1962–63; Harvard Univ. A.M. 1964, Ph.D. 1968; m. Walter André s. Francis Léo and Andrée Goffart 31 Dec. 1977; PROF. OF MEDIEVAL ENGLISH & SCANDINAVIAN LIT., UNIV. OF TORONTO 1978– ; Asst. Prof., present Univ. 1968; Assoc. Prof. 1973; Vis. Sr. Fellow, Linacre Coll., Oxford 1979–80; Vis. Disting. Prof. of Med. Studies, U. of Cal., Berkeley 1992; Vis. Disting. Prof., Univ. of Rome, spring 1993; Assoc. Dir., Ctr. for Med. Studies 1988–89; Chair, Hum. & Soc. Sci. Ctte. of Rsch. Bd. 1988–89; Founding Mem., Internat. Soc. of Anglo-Saxonists 1981– ; (First Vice-Pres. 1982–85; Pres. 1986–88); Mem., Internat. Adv. Ctte., Dictionary of Old English 1987– ; Counc., Med. Acad. of Am. 1981–84; Gen. Ed., Toronto Old English Series 1976– ; Pubs. of the Dictionary of Old English 1985– ; Ed. Bd., 'Anglo-Saxon England' 1986– , 'Speculum' Anniv. Monographs 1984–87, 'Speculum' 1989– ; Bowdoin Prize in Humanities 1968; Elliott Prize 1972; fellowships: SSHRCC Rsch. 1990–93; Guggenheim 1986–87; SSHRCC Leave 1985–86; ACLS Leave 1973–74, 1979–80; Fellow, Med. Acad. of Am. 1989– ; Sec., Assn. for Advancement of Scan. Studies in Can. 1985–88; Extve. Ctte., Old English Group, MLA of Am. 1974–78; Div. on Comp. Studies in Med. Lit. 1989–93; author: 'Old Norse Court Poetry: The Dróttkvætt Stanza' 1978 and numerous articles; co-editor: 'Computers and Old English Concordances' 1970, 'A Plan for the Dictionary of Old English' 1973; Home: 171 Lowther Ave., Toronto, Ont. M5R 1E6; Office: Ctr. for Med. Studies, Univ. of Toronto, Toronto, Ont. M5S 1A1.

**FRANKLIN, Ben,** B.A.; mayor; b. Elgin, Ont. 15 Aug. 1942; s. Richard Ernest and Mary Anita (Patterson) F.; e. Ottawa Teachers Coll. 1964; Carleton Univ., B.A. 1971; m. Sherrell d. Clarence and Celeste Willman 17 Apr. 1965; children: Suzanne, Brent; MAYOR, CITY OF NEPEAN 1978– ; Teacher, Ottawa Bd. of Edn. 1967–78; elected City Councillor 1972–78; elected mayor 1978, '80, '82, '85, '88, 91; Mem., Ottawa Carleton Regional Counc. 1975– ; Nepean Police Comn. 1978– ; Nepean Hydro Comn. 1978– ; Ottawa-Carleton Transit Comn. 1978– ; Office: 101 Centrepointe Dr., Nepean, Ont. K2G 5K7.

**FRANKLIN, Cecil Hammond;** executive; b. Toronto, Ont. 5 April 1915; s. Harry Percy and Caroline Frances (Hammond) F.; e. Pub. Sch., Toronto, Ont.; High Sch. of Comm. (Toronto); Toronto Advertising and Sales Club; m. Phyllis Lorraine (d. 1983), d. late C.C. Tonkin, Toronto. 19 July 1939; children: Robert Michael; Sandra Anne (dec.); m. 2ndly Ingrid Elisabeth Fremerey 1984; Pres., Tintina Mines Ltd.; NSR Resources Inc.; Minaco Equipment Ltd.; Weiler Machine Co. Ltd.; founded Coupco Ltd. 1956 and purchased control of J.M.G. Manufacturing Ltd. 1961, later sold to Vascan Ltd. (now Teledyne Canada Ltd.) 1967; remained a Dir. until Dec. 1971; former controlling shareholder and Chrmn., Algonquin Mercantile Corp.; former Chrmn., Hardee Farms Internat.; Cobi Foods, etc.; Fellow, Univ. of Guelph; former Chrmn., Bd. of Govs., Univ. of Guelph; mem., Bd. of Trade of Metrop. Toronto; Candn. Inst. Mining; Prospectors and Developers Assn.; Anglican; recreations: curling, hunting; Clubs: Granite; Goodwood; Rosedale Golf; York; Ontario; Nicholson's Island; Home: R.R. 4, Stouffville, Ont. L4A 7X5; Office: Toronto, Ont.

**FRANKLIN, Robert Michael,** B.A.; business executive; b. Noranda, Qué. 6 Jan. 1947; s. Cecil Hammond and Phyllis Lorraine (Tonkin) F.; e. Hillsdale Coll., Michigan B.A. 1970; m. Lesley Taylor d. William and Mary Sheilds 20 Oct. 1973; children: Signy Virginia, Jordan Alexis, Robert Taylor; CHRMN. & DIR., PLACER DOME INC. 1993– ; and PRES., SIGNALTA CAPITAL CORPORATION 1989– ; Dir., Barrington Petroleum Ltd.; ClubLink Corporation; ELI Eco Logic International Inc.; N.S.R. Resources Ltd.; Tintina Mines Ltd.; Toromont Industries Ltd.; Gen. Mgr., Coupco Limited 1970–71; Gen. Mgr., Coupco Div., Algonquin Mercantile Corporation 1971–73; Vice Pres., Algonquin Mercantile Corporation 1971–77, Extve. Vice Pres. 1977–87, Vice Chrmn. & Chief Extve. Offr. 1987–89; Dir. & Chrmn. Investment Ctte., North York General Hosp. 1993– ; Alpha Tau Omega (Pres. Beta Kappa Chapter 1966–70); recreations: skiing, tennis, golf, hunting, reading; clubs: Osler Bluff Ski (Past Pres.), York, Granite, Goodwood, Cherry Downs Golf & Country, Bd. of Trade; Office: P.O. Box 350, Suite 2422, TD Centre, Toronto, Ont. M5K 1N3.

**FRANKLIN, Ursula,** O.C., C.C., O.Ont., Ph.D.; university professor emeritus; PROFESSOR EMERITUS, DEPT. OF METALLURGY & MATERIALS SCIENCE, UNIVERSITY OF TORONTO; Senior Resident & Associate Fellow, Massey College; recipient of numerous awards including the 1991 Governor-General's Award in Commemoration of the Person's Case; Order of Canada; Companion of the Order of Canada 1992; Order of Ontario; Office: Massey College, 4 Devonshire Place, Univ. of Toronto, Toronto, Ont. M5S 1A1.

**FRANKS, Christopher Ralph,** L.R.C.P.(Lond.), M.R.C.S.(Eng.), M.B., B.S.(Lond.), M.D. (Lond.), C. Biol., M.I.Biol., F.I.Biol., F.R.S.H., M.F.P.M., F.A.C.P., F.F.P.M.; medical oncologist; educator; b. Bombay, India 1 June 1937; s. Pehin Dato Dr. P. I. Franks, O.B.E.; e. Downside Sch. Somerset, UK; Guy's Hosp. Med. Sch. M.B., B.S. 1973, L.R.C.P., M.R.C.S. 1972; m. Angela Lucy d. M. Malleson, London, Eng. 31 July 1971; children: Timothy Ralph, Richard Christopher, Charlotte Angela; GENERAL MANAGER, QUINTILES (UK) LTD.; stage, TV and comm. film actor UK 1955–64; House Phys. and Surg. Guy's Hosp. London, Eng. 1972–73, Med. Registrar/Clin. Research Fellow I.C.R.F. Breast Unit, Guy's Hosp., 1973–76, Asst. Curator Gordon Museum 1974–76; Dir. Cancer Clinic, University Hosp. 1977–79; and Acting Head, Dept. Cancer Research, Univ. of Sask. 1977–79; Dir., Anti-Cancer Clinical Rsch., Europe, Middle-East, & Africa, Bristol-Myers Co. 1982–87; Hon. Consultant Physician in Med. Oncol. Westminster Hospital, London 1985–93 (Hospital closed Apr. 1993 - Medical School Rationalisation Programme); Speaker and Lectr. Guy's Hosp. Medical School and various scient. meetings Europe, U.S. and Can.; Astley Cooper Student and Greville Student Guy's Hosp. 1974–76; Laura DiSalicetto Student London Univ. 1976; Sask. Cancer Comn. Grant 1977–78; NCI Grant 1978; author over 100 publs.; Hon. Vice Pres. Candn. Cancer Soc. Saskatoon Div. 1978; mem. NCIC sub-comte on breast cancer 1978; Brit. Assn. Cancer Research; Brit. Soc. Immunology; Brit. Med. Assn.; Royal Soc. Health; Royal Soc. Medicine; Inst. of Biology; The Assn. of Cancer Physicians; Am. Soc. of Clinical Oncology; Europ. Soc. Med. Oncology; Br. Oncological Assoc.; New York Acad. of Sciences; Royal Coll. of Radiologists; R. Catholic; recreations: sailing, sculpting, music; Address: 79 High St., Bracknell, Berkshire RG12 1DZ, United Kingdom.

**FRANSSEN, Margot A.C.,** B.A.; entrepreneur; b. The Netherlands 21 March 1952; d. Guilliame G. and Rose J. (Ligtvoet) F.; e. York Univ. B.A. 1979; Invest. Dealers Assn. Courses I-III; m. Hall A. s. Hall and Betty Tingley 12 March 1983; 3 children: Philip Hall Franssen-Tingley, Ashley D. Franssen-Tingley, Jewell J. Franssen-Tingley; PRES. THE BODY SHOP 1979– ; Clk.-Typist, McLeod Young Weir & Co. 1970–72; Sec., United Funds Management 1972–73; Exec. Sec., Alfred Bunting & Co. 1973–75; Bd. Mem., C.I.B.C.; Toronto Salvation Army Advisory Bd.; York Univ. Trustee; Ont. Round Table on the Economy & Environment; Fellow, Ryerson Polytechnical Inst.; recipient Retail Council Mktg. & Communications Award 1987; 'Women Who Make a Difference' 1989; The Body Shop Canada named one of '50 Best Managed Private Companies' by Financial Post; awarded The Henry Singer Award, The Univ. of Alta. for Exceptional Leadership in Retailing and Services; Home: 52 Warren Rd., Toronto, Ont.; Office: 33 Kern Rd., Don Mills, Ont. M3B 1S9.

**FRAPPIER, Gilles,** B.A., B.Ph., B.L.S.; b. Papineauville, Que. 13 Feb. 1931; s. Roméo and Roma (Robinson) F.; e. Petit Séminaire d'Ottawa; Univ. of Ottawa, Faculty of Philos., Lib. Sch.; McGill Univ., Grad. Sch. Lib. Science; Degrees, B.A., B.Ph., B.L.S.; m. Gertrude, d. Alfred Mainville, Ottawa, Ont., 13 Oct. 1956; children: Raymond, Robert, Joanne; CHIEF LIBRARIAN & SEC.-TREAS. TO THE BOARD, OTTAWA PUBLIC LIBRARY, 1979– ; Assoc. Parlty. Librarian, Library of Parliament, 1970–79; Librarian, Baie Comeau (Que.) Community Assn., 1955–57; Founder, Woodlands Lib., Pulp and Paper Research Inst. Can., Pointe Claire, Que., 1957–59; Librarian, United Aircraft of Canada Ltd., Longueuil, Que., 1959–63; Supvr., Engn. Lib's, Canadair Ltd., St. Laurent, Que., 1963–69; Dir., Science Lib's, Univ. of Montreal, 1969–70; mem., Special Lib's Assn. (Pres. 1973; former Secy., Treas., Bull. Ed., Vice Pres. and Pres., Montreal Chapter; Observer, Internat. Fed. Lib. Assns. Conf., Grenoble, 1973; Sec., Org. Comtee., IFLA Conf. Montreal 1982); Corp. Prof. Librarians Que.; Candn. Lib. Assn.; Lib. Assn. Ottawa-Hull; former Dir., Community Info. Center, Ottawa; Former Chrmn., Adv. Comte. on French Library Services, Min. of Culture, Tourism and Recreation, Ont.; former mem., Adv. Comte. on French Language Services, Algonquin College, Ottawa; Council of Admrs. of Large Urban Public Libraries (Pres. 1982–84); Former Vice-Pres., Chief Extves. of Large Public Libraries, Ont.; L'alliance Française; Ont. Public Libraries Assn. Div. of Ont. Lib. Assn.; mem. & Dir. Candn. Writers Foundation; mem., Extve. Ctte., The Public Lending Right Comn.; former mem., Ont. Pub. Lib. Adv. Comte.; Adv. Comte. on Lib. Technicians, Algonquin Coll. Ottawa; Roman Catholic; recreations: fishing, camping, woodworking, golf, travel; Home: 423 Carillon St., Gatineau, Que. J8P 3P9; Office: 120 Metcalfe St., Ottawa, Ont. K1P 5M2.

**FRASER, Alistair Graeme,** B.A., LL.B.; Canadian public service; b. Toronto, Ont. 5 Jan. 1923; s. Jane Graeme (Ross) and the late Hon. Alistair F.; e. McGill Univ., B.A. 1946; Univ. of Brit. Columbia, LL.B. 1950; Clerk of the House of Commons, Aug. 1967–Sept. 1979; Lieut., Royal Candn. Artillery, 1942–45; read law with Davis & Co., Vancouver, B.C., 1950; called to Bar of B.C., 1951; engaged in practice of law, Prince Rupert, B.C., 1951–52; Extve. Asst. to Min. of Fisheries, 1952; to Leader of Opposition in Senate, 1959; to Secy. of State, 1963; to Min. of Transport, 1964; apptd. Clerk Asst., H. of C., Jan. 1966; mem., Candn. Bar Assn.; Protestant; Home: 124 Springfield Rd., Ottawa, Ont. K1M 2C8.

**FRASER, Brad;** playwright/director; b. Edmonton, Alta. 28 June 1959; s. Sharon Fraser; plays produced:

'Mutants' Walterdale Theatre Edmonton 1980; 'Wolfboy' 25th St. Theatre Sask. 1981, Theatre Network Edmonton 1983, Touchstone Theatre Vanc. 1983, Theatre Passe Muraille Toronto 1984; 'Rude Noises (For a Blank Generation)' 1982; 'Young Art' 1984; 'Chainsaw Love' 1985; 'Return of The Bride' 1986; 'Unidentified Human Remains and the True Nature of Love' ATP Calgary 1989, Workshop West Edmonton 1990, Crows' Theatre Toronto 1990, Halstead Theatre Chicago 1991, Theatre Quat'sous Montreal 1991, Orpheum Theatre N.Y. 1991, Hampstead Theatre, London 1993; 'Blood Buddies (with Jeffrey Hirschfield) 1988; 'Prom Night of the Living Dead' (with Darrin Hagen) 1989; 'The Ugly Man' ATP Calgary 1992; 'Outrageous' (with Darrin Hagen and Andy Northrup) Calgary 1994; 5 time winner, Alta. Culture Playwrighting Competition 1977, '78, '88 x 2, '90; The Laura May Kutney Stylings Award (best new Candn. play) Calgary 1990; The Floyd S. Chalmers Award 1991; The London Evening Standard Award, Most Promising Newcomer 1993; Time Out Award, London, Eng., Best New Play 1993; Home: 11605 97 St., Edmonton, Alta. T5G 1Y1.

**FRASER, Donald Alexander Stuart,** Ph.D., F.R.S.C., D.Math; statistician; mathematician; educator; b. Toronto, Ont. 29 Apr. 1925; s. Maxwell John and Ailie Jean (Stuart) F.; e. Univ. of Toronto B.A. 1946, M.A. 1947; Princeton Univ. A.M. 1948, Ph.D. 1949; Univ. of Waterloo D.Math (hon. causa) 1992; children: Julie, Danae, Maia, Andrea, Ailana, Cristin; PROF. OF MATHEMATICS, YORK UNIV. 1986– ; PROF. OF STATISTICS, UNIV. OF TORONTO since 1958; Asst. Prof. Univ. Toronto 1949, Assoc. Prof. 1953; Adjunct Prof. York Univ.; Adjunct Prof. Univ. Waterloo; Visiting Prof. Princeton Univ. 1955; Stanford Univ. 1961–62; Univ. of Copenhagen 1964; Univ. of Wis. 1965; Univ. of Hawaii 1969–70; Univ. of Geneva 1978–79; Stanford Univ. 1982; author 'Nonparametric Methods in Statistics' 1957; 'Statistics An Introduction' 1958; 'The Structure of Inference' 1968; 'Probability and Statistics' 1976; 'Inference and Linear Models' 1978; Fellow, Inst. Math. Stat.; Am. Stat. Soc.; Royal Stat. Soc.; Am. Assn. Advanc. Science; Internat. Stat. Inst.; Home: 4 Old George Pl., Toronto, Ont. M4W 1X9; Office: Toronto, Ont. M5S 1A1.

**FRASER, Duncan Grant Lovat,** C.D., M.A.; writer; retired university professor; b. Halifax, N.S., 3 March 1923; s. Simon McKay and Gladys Ruth (MacNamara) F.; e. New Glasgow (N.S.) High Sch.; Acadia Univ., B.A. (Hons. Hist.) 1948, M.A. (Hist.) 1949; Sidney Sussex Coll., Univ. of Cambridge (I.O.D.E. Scholar for N.S.) 1949–51; mem. Inst. Hist. Research and Inst. of Commonwealth Studies, Univ. London 1969–70; m. Iris, d. D.S. Watkins, 20 May 1946; children: Janet M., Kathryn E.; Prof., Dept. of Pol. Science, Acadia Univ. and Head of the Dept., 1961–78; Asst. Lectr. in Constitutional Hist., Univ. Coll. of the West Indies, 1951; promoted Lectr., 1952; apptd. Asst. Prof. of Hist. and Pol. Science, Acadia Univ., 1954, Assoc. Prof., 1956 visiting Prof. of Strategic Studies 1982–83; apptd. Univ. Fellow and retired June 1984; served in 2nd World War; commnd. in Cape Breton Highlanders, Nov. 1942; served as Lieut. and Capt. in Candn. Army in U.K., Italy (wounded in Liri Valley campaign) and Can.; served in Militia and C.O.T.C. as Maj., 1954–64; Hon. Lieut. Col. West Nova Scotia Regt. 1975–88; mem. Counc. of Colonels, Colonel Commandants and Hon. Colonels 1981–85; Pres., Nova Scotia Army Cadet League 1978–80; Dir., Army Museum, The Citadel, Halifax, N.S. 1975–89, 1991– ; Trustee, Canadian Museum of Civilization 1990– ; publs: articles, papers, and broadcasts on Candn. West Indian trade, evolution of Brit. Empire and Commonwealth, studies on the origins and functions of the Court of Vice-Admiralty in N.S. 1749–83; contrib. of weekly column 'Prejudiced View' to Halifax Chronicle-Herald; contrib. frequently to C.B.C. 1956–75; contrib. to The Candn. Annual Review 1963–78; mem., Royal Candn. Military Inst., Toronto; N.S. Adv. Comte. on Constitution; N.S. 1967–70 Del., Confed. of Tomorrow Conf., 1967 and Fed.-Prov. Constitutional Conf., 1968 and 1969; apptd. Special Consultant and Constitutional Adviser to the Office of the Premier of N.S., Oct. 1978; Special Consultant to the Exec. Coun. of N.S., Jan. 1979; Mem. of Delegation, First Ministers Constitutional Conf., 1978–82; apptd. Sec. of the N.S. House of Assembly Select Comm. on Constitutional Matters, May 1979–September 1981; Secy., N.S. Roy. Com. on Post Secondary Educ. 1983–85; Mem. Provincial Royal Visit Ctte. for six Royal Visits 1979–88; Presbyterian; awarded Commemorative Medal for 125th Anniversary of Candn. Confederation; Home: P.O. Box 46, Grand Pré, N.S. B0P 1M0.

**FRASER, Earl D.;** construction industry executive; b. New Glasgow, N.S. 26 Apr. 1933; s. Simon Carl and Rachel Katherine (MacQueen) F.; e. New Glasgow H.S.; arch. & constr. night courses; m. Bonnie d. Russell and Katherine Murdock 10 Aug. 1957; children: Katherine Anne, Sharon Bonnie; VICE-PRES. DEVEL. AND CONSTRUCTION, HALIFAX DEVEL. LTD.; Engr. Dept., Trenton Steel Works 1950–53; Northern Constr. Limited 1954; Est./Constr. Supt./Asst. Gen. Mgr. (Atlantic Concrete Ltd.); Mgr., (Twin City Sand & Gravel Ltd.), Cameron Contracting Ltd. 1955–65; Proj. Mgr., Durham Leaseholds Ltd. 1966–86; Devel. Offr., Halifax Developments Ltd. 1986; Dir., Park Lane Devel. Ltd.; Trustee, Iona Presbyn. Ch.; mem., Halifax Bd. of Trade; Masonic Lodge (25 yr.); Home: 35 Nova Terrace, Dartmouth, N.S. B2V 1B1; Office: P.O. Box 966, Halifax, N.S. B3J 2V9.

**FRASER, F. Murray,** Q.C., B.A., LL.B., LL.M., LL.D.; educator; b. Liverpool, UK 18 Apl. 1937; s. Frederick Murray and Sarah Audrey (Roulston) F.; e. Dalhousie Univ. B.A. 1957, LL.B. 1960; Univ. of London LL.M. 1962; Memorial Univ. LL.D. (hon. causa) 1993; Victoria Univ. LL.D. (hon. causa) 1993; m. Anne d. Gordon and Marion Archibald 20 Aug. 1960; three s. Scott, Andrew, Hugh; PRESIDENT, VICE CHANCELLOR AND PROFESSOR OF LAW, UNIVERSITY OF CALGARY 1988– ; Asst. Prof. of Law, Queen's Univ. 1963–64; law practice Halifax 1964–66; Assoc. Prof. of Law, Dalhousie Univ. 1966, Prof. of Law 1969–74, Assoc. Dean of Law 1971–73; Rsch. Assoc. Law Reform Comn. of Can. Ottawa 1973–74; Founding Dean of Law, Univ. of Victoria 1974–80; Vice-Pres. Acad. Univ. of Victoria 1983–88, Prof. of Law 1974–88; cr. Q.C. 1979; former Trustee, Lester B. Pearson Coll. of the Pacific; Trustee, Alta. Heritage Found. for Med. Rsch.; Mem., Premier's Counc. on Science & Technology; Dir., Assn. of Universities and Colleges of Can.; former Mem., Bd. of Dirs., Candn. Centre on Substance Abuse; Past Pres., Halifax YMCA; former Gov., Candn. Inst. Advanced Legal Studies; cons. to various prov. govts., Law Soc. B.C., Law Foundation B.C., Fed. Law Socs. Can.; contrib. various articles, book chapters family law, legal edn., legal prof.; mem., N.S. Barristers Soc.; Candn. Bar Assn.; Assn. Candn. Law Teachers; Office: 2500 University Dr., N.W., Calgary, Alta. T2N 1N4.

**FRASER, Frank Clarke,** O.C., B.Sc., M.Sc., Ph.D., M.D., D.Sc. (Acadia), F.R.S.C., F.R.C.P.S.(C.), F.C.C.M.G.; educator; b. Norwich, Conn. 29 Mar. 1920; s. Frank Wise and Annie Louise (Clarke) F.; family returned to Can. late 1920; e. Acadia Univ. B.Sc. 1940; McGill Univ. M.Sc. 1941, Ph.D. 1945, M.D., C.M. 1950; Acadia Univ. D.Sc. 1967; m. Marilyn Preus d. Reidar Preus; children: Norah, Noel, Alan, Scott; PROFESSOR EMERITUS, McGILL UNIV. 1985– ; joined McGill Univ. 1950 as Asst. Prof. of Genetics; Assoc. Prof. of Genetics 1955–60; Prof. of Genetics 1960–70; Molson Prof. of Genetics, Dept. of Biology 1970–82; Prof. of Paediatrics 1973–82; Prof., McGill Centre for Human Genetics 1979–82; Dir., Dept. of Medical Genetics, Montreal Children's Hosp. 1952–82; MRC Medical Genetics Group 1972–82; Montreal Children's Hosp.; Prof. of Clinical Genetics, Memorial Univ. of Newfoundland, 1982–85; Dir., Genetics Working Grp., Royal Comn. on New Reproductive Technologies 1990–92; Fellow, Royal Soc. of Can. 1966; Candn. Coll. of Medical Geneticists 1975; Royal Coll. Physicians & Surgeons 1976; Pres., Amer. Soc. of Human Genetics 1961–62; Teratology Soc. 1962–63; Chrmn., Med. Research Council Grant Comte. on Genetics 1971–74; Gen. Chrmn., Fourth Internat. Conference on Birth Defects, Vienna 1973; Vice-Pres., Internat. Birth Defects Congress Ltd. 1972–79; Scientific Officer, Med. Research Counc. Genetics Grants Comte. 1974–80; Vice-Pres., Candn. Coll. of Medical Geneticists, 1975–80; Honorary Pres., Fifth Internat. Conference on Birth Defects, Montreal 1978; Pres., Candn. Coll. of Med. Geneticists 1980–83; rec'd Blackader Award, Candn. Med. Assn. 1968; Honours of the Amer. Cleft Palate Assn. 1974; Medal of Honour, Amer. Assn. of Plastic Surgeons 1975; Allan Award, Amer. Soc. of Human Genetics 1979; Award of Excellence, Genetics Soc. of Can. 1980; Officer of the Order of Canada 1984; March of Dimes Award for contribution in field of birth defects 1987; Founder Award, Candn. College of Medican Geneticists 1991; Hon. Fellow, Am. College of Medical Genetics 1993; mem., Permanent Comte. for Internat. Conferences on Human Genetics 1967–75; Expert Comte. on Occurrence of Congenital Abnormalities, Dept. of Nat. Health & Welfare, Canada 1962–75; Nat. Inst. of Health, Genetics Study Section, U.S.A. 1961–65; Genetics Training Comte., Nat. Inst. of General Med. Sciences, U.S.A. 1971–74; World Health Org. Expert Advisory Comte. on Human Genetics 1963–80; Comte. on Mutagenic Hazards of Environmental Chemicals, Health & Welfare Can. 1977–83; Health and Welfare Grants Committee on Biology, Chemistry, Toxicology, 1982–89; Internat. Adv. Ctte., VIII Internat. Congress of Human Genetics 1991; Medical Rsch. Counc., Career Investigators Comte.; Ed. Bd. 'Amer. Journal of Med. Genetics'; 'Developmental Pharmacology & Therapeutics'; 'Brazilian Journal of Genetics'; 'Journal of Clinical Dysmorphology'; 'Human Genetics'; co-author (with J.J. Nora) 'Medical Genetics: Principles and Practice' 1974; 4th ed. 1993, 'Genetics of Man' 1975; 2nd ed. 1986; co-editor (with J.G. Wilson) 'Handbook of Teratology, Vols. 1–4' 1977; author of numerous scientific papers in Medical Genetics and Teratology; Liberal; Church of England; Clubs: Nu Sigma Nu; Alpha Psi Omega; served in R.C.A.F. 1942–45; recreations: tennis, photography; Home: 4168 Oxford Ave., Montreal, Que.; Office: McGill Centre for Human Genetics, 1205 rue Dr. Penfield, Montreal, Que. H3A 1B1.

**FRASER, Frank M.,** B.S.; executive; b. Montréal, Qué. 26 Oct. 1935; s. Felix Randolf and Marguerite Enid (Wiles) F.; e. Rose-Mount High Sch. Montréal 1954; Tenn. A&I Stn. Univ. Nashville B.S. (ME) 1964; m. T. Donna Coates 4 Oct. 1991; children: Gregory, Natalie, Wannita, Nathan; VICE PRES., MARKET DEVEL. DIV., NORDION INTERNATIONAL INC. 1985– ; Dir. Vindicator Inc., Fla.; played profl. football Montréal Als, Ottawa Rough Riders, Sask. Rough Riders, Winnipeg Blue Bombers 1954–63; Project Eng. Atomic Energy of Canada Ltd. 1964–74, Head Eng. Dept. 1975, Mktg. Mgr. 1978, Gen. Mgr. Ind. Irradiation Div. 1979, Vice Pres. Ind & Med. Sales & Service 1984; Gen. Chrmn. 6th Internat. Meeting Radiation Processing 1984–87; Vice Chrmn. 1984–86 and Can.'s Rep. IAEA Consultative Group on Food Irradiation; author various sci. papers; Beta Kappa Chi; recreations: hockey, golf, squash, coaching; Home: 51 Windeyer Cres., Kanata, Ont. K2K 2P7.

**FRASER, George Albert,** C.D., B.Sc., M.D., F.R.C.P.(C); psychiatrist; b. Charlottetown, P.E.I. 22 March 1941; s. George Vernon and Hilda Evelyn (Macdonald) F.; e. Prince of Wales Coll. P.E.I., Glebe Coll. Inst. Ottawa; St. Dunstan's Univ. P.E.I. B.Sc. 1962; Dalhousie Univ. M.D. 1967; Dalhousie Med. Sch. FRCP(C) Psychiatry 1975; m. Freda (J.W.) d. Thomas and Marcella Jones 18 Dec. 1965; children: Jane-Diane, Suzanne Marie, Sean George; DIR. ANXIETY AND PHOBIC DISORDERS CLINIC, ROYAL OTTAWA HOSP. 1983– ; Asst. Prof. of Psychiatry Univ. of Ottawa 1983– ; served with Candn. Forces (Med. Services) 1963–83, rank Lt. Col. (currently Candn. Supplementary Reserve); Chief of Psychiatry Candn. Forces Eur. 1975–78; Chief Psychiatry CFB Halifax 1978–82; Asst. Chief Psychiatry Nat. Defence Med. Centre Ottawa 1982–83; Pres., Atlantic Provinces Psychiatric Assoc. 1981–82; recipient Base Commdr. Eur. Commendation 1978; Pipe Sgt. Candn. Forces Eur. Pipe Band W. Germany 1976–78; Pipe Maj. Lovat Scots Pipe Band P.E.I. 1963–68 (solo record 1965, Internat. Artists); mem. Candn. Armed Forces Training Team Accra, Ghana 1970–72; author of anxiety, hypnosis and dissociation in various sci. publs., newspapers, mags.; Vice Pres (1989–91) and Fellow, Internat. Soc. Study Multiple Personality & Dissociation; mem. Black Watch Assoc. of Can., Upper Can. Br.; Ont. Soc. Clin. Hypnosis (Chrmn. Ottawa Sect. 1986–87); Candn. Med. Assn.; Candn. Psychiatric Assn.; Life Hon. mem. German Wine Soc. Halifax; Life mem. Phi Rho Sigma (Alpha Eta); recreations: squash, alpine skiing, windsurfing, bagpiping (currently mem., CFB Ottawa's Air Command Pipe Band); Club: R.A. Sports; Home: 84 Lillico Dr., Ottawa, Ont. K1V 9L8; Office: Royal Ottawa Hosp., 1145 Carling Ave., Ottawa, Ont. K1V 7K4.

**FRASER, Graham Blair,** B.A., M.A.; journalist; b. Ottawa, Ont. 22 Apr. 1946; s. Blair and Jean (MacLeod) F.; e. Univ. of Toronto B.A. 1964–68, M.A. Hist. 1972–73; m. Barbara d. Carl and JoAnne Uteck 12 Oct. 1968; children: Malcolm, Nicholas; WASHINGTON BUREAU CHIEF, THE GLOBE AND MAIL 1993– ; journalist for Toronto Star covering univ., entertainment and City Hall 1968–70; travelled to Europe, studied in Florence and worked as freelance broadcaster 1970–71; with Globe and Mail covering City Hall, regional planning and devel. 1973–76; Montreal Bur. Chief Maclean's 1976–79; Que. Bur. Chief The Gazette 1979–84; Quebec Bureau Chief, The Globe and Mail 1984–86; Parliamentary Correspondent, The Globe and Mail 1986–89; Ottawa Bureau Chief, The Globe and Mail 1989–93; author: 'Fighting Back: Urban Renewal in Trefann Court' 1972; 'PQ: René Lévesque and the Parti Québécois in Power' 1984 (nominated for Governor General's Award for Non-fiction 1984); 'Playing for Keeps: The Canadian Election of 1988' 1989; co-ed. 'Blair Fraser Reports' 1969; work incl. in following anthologies: 'Notes for a Native Land' 1969; 'Student Power and the Canadian Campus' 1969; 'The City: Attacking Modern Myths' 1972; 'Canada from the Newsstands: A Selection of the Best Canadian Journalism of the Past Thirty Years' 1978; wrote treatment for 'The Champions, Part III: The Final Battle' CBC-NFB 1986; founding mem. Centre for Investigative Journalism 1978–79, re-el. to Exec. 1980; guest lectr.: Candn. Studies Prog., Northwestern Univ. 1985–91; Convegno Internazionale di Studi Canadesi, Torre Canne, Italy; Americas Soc., N.Y.; Candn.-Am. Ctte., Ottawa 1990; Quebec Summer Seminar, State Univ. of New York, Plattsburgh 1986, 1987; Conf. on Canada in Transition, Universidad Nacional Autonoma de Mexico 1992; 1st recipient, Hyman Solomon Award for Excellence in Public Policy Journalism, Public Policy Forum 1992; Home: 2917 Cathedral Ave. N.W., Washington, D.C. 20008; Office: 1331 Pennsylvania Ave. N.W., Suite 524, Washington, D.C. 20004.

**FRASER, H. Ronald,** B.A., B.Econ., M.B.A.; executive; b. Durban, S. Africa 5 Oct. 1920; s. Andrew Gibson and Mary Margaret (Joyce) F.; e. Natal Univ. Coll., B.A. 1943; Univ. of S. Africa, B.Econ. 1947 (Hons. 1948); Univ. of Pretoria, M.B.A. 1951; m. Betty Wynne, d. late Herbert Barnes, Amberley, Sussex, 26 Dec. 1944; children: Michael, Mary, John, Peter, Elizabeth; DIR., ZAMBIA CONSOLIDATED INVESTMENTS, since 1970; Schoolmaster, Pretoria Boys High Sch., 1944–49; joined South African Iron & Steel Industrial Corp. Ltd. as Administrative Trainee 1949; subsequently Asst. to Chrmn. and Head of Organ. & Method Dept.; joined Anglo American Corp. of South Africa Ltd. 1954; trans. to London, Eng. 1961; became Mang. Dir., Anmercosa Sales Ltd. on its formation 1964; Mgr., Charter Consolidated Ltd. on formation 1965, Dir. 1970; trans. to New York 1970 as Extve. Vice Pres. and apptd. Pres., Anglo American Corp. of South Africa (N.A.) Inc.; apptd. C.E.O. of Anglo A. Corp. of Can. Ltd. 1973; Dir. of Hudson Bay Mining & Smelting Co. Ltd., Chrmn. 1976–80; Pres., Minerals & Resources Corp. Ltd., Bermuda 1979–85; R. Catholic; recreations: photography, reading, golf; Clubs: Mid Ocean; Riddell's Bay Wilderness; Address: Apt. 35, 19 Mizzentop, Warwick, Bermuda.

**FRASER, Lt. Cdr. James Ian,** C.D., B.A.; naval officer; b. Niagara Falls, Ont. 24 June 1959; s. Frank Rutherford and Rhoda Katharine (Lang) F.; e. E.L. Crossley S.S. 1977; Royal Roads Military College 1979; Royal Military Coll. of Canada B.A. 1981; Cert. of Competence, Level 1 1982, Level 2 1983; Naval Opns. Course 1982; Bridge Watchkeeping Ticket 1983; Ships Diving Offr., Mine Disposal Course 1983; Antisubmarine Warfare Dir. Course 1984; Tender Comnd. 1984; Candn. Forces Staff Sch. 1985; Ships Communications Officer Course 1985; CF OFficer Profl. Devel. Prog. completed 1987; qualified Command Part 1 1987; Combat Control Offricers Course 1989; m. Karen d. Gordon and Frances Stuart 13 July 1985; children: Stuart Alexander, Gordon Andrew; CHIEF OF STAFF MILITARY WING & STAFF OFFICER TRAINING, ROYAL MILITARY COLLEGE OF CANADA 1992– ; appts. Her Majesty's Candn. Ships: Assiniboine 1982–86; Cataraqui 1986–88 (Detachment Cmdr.); Qu'Appelle 1989–90 (combat & training officer); Command & Control, Communications, ASW & Human Engr. Operational Requirements, Candn. Patrol Frigate Project, ADM Materiel, NDHQ Ottawa 1990–93; Acting Sub-Lt. 1981; Sub-Lt. 1982; Lt. 1984; Lt. Cdr. 1991; Master Mariner, (Foreign Trade), Candn. Securities Course (CSI); involved in Kingston Dist. Scouting; recreations: antiques, home renovation; Home: 16 Ridout Row, Kingston, Ont. K7K 5L0; Office: Kingston, Ont. K7K 5L0.

**FRASER, Joan Thorne,** B.A.; journalist; b. Halifax, N.S. 12 Oct. 1944; d. John Norman and Mary Elisabeth (March) F.; e. Edgehill Sch. Windsor N.S.; Inst. Heubi, Lausanne, Switz.; McGill Univ. B.A. 1965; m. Michel Faure; 2 children; EDITOR-IN-CHIEF, THE GAZETTE 1993– ; general, women's & finan. reporting, The Gazette 1965–67; finan. reporting, editing, edit. writing, Que. bureau chief, Financial Times of Canada 1967–78; Editorial Page Editor, The Gazette 1978–93; host of French language radio prog. 'L'Econothèque,' Radio Canada 1970s & regular guest on PBS TV 'The Editors'; Nat. Newspaper Award for edit. writing: Award 1982, 1991; Citations 1986, '87, '90; Southam Newspaper Group prize for commentary: Prize 1987; Runner-up 1989; Southam Inc. Pres. Prize for outstanding contbn. to the co. 1990; co-author: 'Les journalistes' 1980; Office: 250 St. Antoine St. W., Montreal, Que. H2Y 3R7.

**FRASER, Hon. John Allen,** P.C., Q.C., M.P., LL.B.; politician; b. Yokohama, Japan 15 Dec. 1931; s. Clarence Rosswell and Lottie Livina Irene (Robinson) F.; e. Point Grey Jr. H.S., Prince of Wales H.S. Vancouver; Univ. of B.C., LL.B. 1954; m. Catherine Rose d. William Fraser Findlay 14 May 1960; three d. Sheena Catherine, Anna Rose, Mary Ellen; AMBASSADOR FOR THE ENVIRONMENT 1993– ; el. to. H. of C. for Vancouver S. g.e. 1972, re-el. since; Sworn of the Privy Counc. and apptd. Postmaster Gen. and Min. of the Environment 1979; Min. of Fisheries and Oceans, Can. 1984; resigned from Cabinet 1985; el. Speaker of the House of Commons 1986–93; P. Conservative; Anglican; Home: Vancouver, B.C.; Office: House of Commons, Ottawa, Ont. K1A 0A6.

**FRASER, John Anderson,** M.A.; journalist; b. Montreal, Que. 5 June 1944; s. John Ramsey and Catherine Margaret (Dickinson) F.; e. Upper Can. Coll. Toronto; Lakefield (Ont.) Coll. Sch.; Mem. Univ. of Nfld. B.A. 1969; Exeter Coll. Oxford Univ. Dipl. 1970; Univ. of E. Anglia M.A. 1971; Meml. Univ. of Nfld., D.Litt. (hon. causa) 1992; m. Elizabeth Scott d. Arthur R. MacCallum, Toronto, Ont. 8 March 1975; three d. Jessie, Kathleen, Clara; EDITOR, SATURDAY NIGHT 1987– ; Music and Dance Critic, Toronto Telegram 1971–72; Dance Critic and Feature Writer, The Globe and Mail 1972–75, Drama Critic 1975–77, Peking Corr. 1977–79, Nat. Columnist 1979–82, National Ed. 1982–84; European Bureau Chief 1984–87; Visiting Lectr. in Criticism York Univ. 1976–77; Mem., National Jury, Canada Pacific Found. 1988; Mem. Bd. of Dirs., Green College, U.B.C., Vancouver, el. 1993; Candn. Ctte. to Protect Journalists, el. 1991; Sch. of Journalism, Univ. of Western Ont., el. 1990; Nat. Youth Orchestra, el. 1988; Lakefield Coll. Sch. el. 1988; Nat. Magazine Awards Found. el. 1988; Friends of L'Arche el. 1988; Memorial Univ. of Nfld. Art Gallery el. 1988; Ryerson Sch. of Journalism el. 1988; Northrop Frye Centre, Victoria Coll., Univ. of Toronto el. 1988; Royal Sch. of Church Music 1984; rec'd Queen's Silver Jubilee Medal; rec'd Nat. Newspaper Awards for criticism (dance) 1974, (theatre) 1976, reporting (China coverage) 1978; rec'd Nat. Magazine Awards 1986, 1991; author 'Kain and Augustyn' 1977; 'The Chinese: Portrait of a People' 1980 (nominated Gov. Gen.'s Award Nonfiction 1980); 'Telling Tales' 1986; 'Private View' 1988; Mem., Hearing Panel: 'Ethical Reflections on the Economic Crisis' 1982, author of its report: 'Canada's Unemployed: The Crisis of our Times' 1983; el. Counc. mem., Champlain Soc., Toronto 1988; el. Founding Treas., Candn. Soc. of Magazine Editors 1990; Fellow, Massey Coll., Toronto 1991; Nat. Chair, annual fund-raising campaign, Memorial Univ. of Nfld. 1988–89; Mem., Commonwealth Journalists Assoc.; Candn. Authors' Assoc.; Writers' Union of Can.; The Candn. Ctr., Internat. PEN; Adv. Counc., St. Clement's (Eglinton) Ch., Toronto; Anglican; recreations: canoeing, piano, reading, tennis; Clubs: Badminton & Racquet (Toronto), Reform (London, Eng.); Home: 104 Bernard Ave., Toronto, Ont. M5R 1R9; Office: 184 Front St. E., Ste. 400, Toronto, Ont. M5A 4N3.

**FRASER, John Foster,** O.C., B.Com., LL.D.; executive; b. Saskatoon, Sask. 19 Sept. 1930; s. John Black F.; e. Victoria Sch. and Nutana Coll. Inst. Saskatoon; Univ. of Sask. B.Com. 1952; m. Valerie Georgina d. late George Ryder 21 June 1952; children: John F. Jr., Lisa; CHRMN., FEDERAL INDUSTRIES LTD. 1992– , Pres. and C.E.O. 1978–91, Chrmn. and C.E.O. 1991–92; Dir., Air Canada; Bank of Montreal; Canada Development Investment Corp.; Centra Gas Manitoba Inc.; Coca-Cola Beverages Ltd.; Continental Airlines Inc.; Ford Motor Co. of Canada, Limited; Inter-City Products Corp.; Investors Group Inc.; Shell Canada Ltd.; The Thomson Corp.; Past Pres., The Royal Winnipeg Ballet; Dir. and Past Chrmn., Counc. for Bus. and the Arts in Can.; Founding Chrmn., The Associates, Faculty of Management, Univ. of Manitoba; apptd. Officer of the Order of Canada 1990; Rec'd. Hon. Degree of Doctor of Laws 1993; Pres. Empire Freightways Ltd. 1953–62; Hanford Drewitt Ltd. 1962–68; Norcom Homes Ltd. 1968–78; Past Pres. Man. Theatre Centre; Past Gov. St. John's Ravenscourt Sch.; P. Conservative; Presbyterian; recreations: boating, reading; Clubs: Manitoba; Toronto; Royal Lake of the Woods Yacht; Home: 900, 237 Wellington Cres., Winnipeg, Man. R3M 0A1; Office: Suite 3100, 201 Portage Ave., Winnipeg, Man. R3B 3L7.

**FRASER, John Keith,** Ph.D.; geographer; b. Ottawa, Ont. 18 Feb. 1922; s. Robert James and Muriel Gordon (Campbell) F.; e. Univ. of Toronto B.A. 1949, M.A. 1955; Clark Univ. Worcester, Mass. Ph.D. 1964; m. Joyce Eileen Tate 1 Oct. 1949; children: Miriam Eileen, John Graeme; CONSULTANT; federal govt. Geog. Br. 1950, Research geog. 1950–62, Chief Toponymy Div. 1962–68; Exec. Sec. Candn. Perm. Ctte. on Geog. Names 1964–68, Exec. Sec. Nat. Adv. Ctte. on Geog. Research 1967–70, Mem. Candn. Ctte., Internat. Geog. Union 1967– ; (Exec. Sec. 1967–82, 1984–90); Sec.-Gen. 22nd Internat. Geog. Cong. 1969–73, Assoc. Sec. Candn. Environmental Adv. Council 1974–82, Sr. Adv. (Geog. Sciences) Office of Science Adv. 1976–82; served with RCAF 1942–45, radar tech., RAF Coastal Command Iceland, Azores, UK; del. numerous internat. geog. confs.; Sessional Lectr. in Geog. Carleton Univ. 1962–64; Pres., Rotary Club W. Ottawa 1967–68; mem., Environmental Adv. Ctte. City of Ottawa 1983–84; Dir.: Canyouth Pubs. 1983–88 (Chrmn. 1985–88); Arctic Inst. N. Am. 1989– ; Royal Candn. Geog. Soc. (Secy. 1967–82, Chrmn. Ed. Ctte. 1974–82, Publisher, 'Canadian Geographic' 1982–88, Gen. Mgr. and Exec. Dir. 1982–90); Charter mem., Candn. Assn. Geogs. (Archivist 1961– , Pres. 1981–82; rec'd. Award for Service 1975); mem. for Geog., Candn. Nat. Ctte. PanAm. Inst. Geog. & Hist. 1974–82; Fellow, Royal Candn. Geog. Soc.; Royal Geog. Soc.; A.I.N.A.; Paul Harris Fellow (Rotary Internat.); rec'd Camsell Award 1992; author or co-author numerous publs.; United Church; recreations: sketching and oils, travel, reading, canoeing, photography; Club: Laurentian; Home: 571 Fraser Ave., Ottawa, Ont. K2A 2R3.

**FRASER, John MacLeod;** foreign service officer; b. Montreal, Que. 12 Feb. 1935; s. Blair and Jean (MacLeod) F.; e. Ashbury Coll. 1952; McGill Univ., B.A. 1955; Magdalen Coll., Oxford Univ., B.A. 1958, M.A. 1983; m. Deborah, d. Richard and Ramona Wait, 12 Dec. 1974; Dept. of External Affairs, Ottawa since 1987; joined Dept. External Affairs 1958; Third, later Second Secy., Candn. Embassy, Belgrade 1959–62; Trade Commissioner, Hong Kong 1965–67; First Secy., Warsaw 1967–68; Chargé d'Affaires, then Counsellor, Peking 1971–72; Counsellor, Washington 1972–76; Dir., Middle East Div., Dept. Ext. Affairs 1976–80; Ambassador, Warsaw 1980–83; Ambassador, Belgrade 1983–87; Dir. Gen., Foreign Assessments Bureau (formerly Foreign Intelligence Bureau), Dept. External Affairs 1987–92; Foreign Service Visitor, Carleton Univ. 1992– ; co-author with Graham Fraser 'Blair Fraser Reports,' 1970; recreation: travel; Office: c/o Dept. External Affairs, Ottawa, Ont. K1A 0A6.

**FRASER, John William Donald (Jack),** B.Sc.; consultant; b. Cookshire, Que. 10 Nov. 1938; s. Donald A. and Alice E.M. (Hood) F.; e. Cookshire H.S.; Sir George Williams Univ. B.Sc. 1964; m. J. Merle d. Keith and Velma Dunn 28 May 1966; children: Shona, Daniel; PRESIDENT, CANADIAN AUTOMATED BUILDINGS ASSN. 1990– ; Asst. Vice-Pres., Commercial, Bell Canada 1976–77; Gen. Manager, Computer Communications Group 1977–79; Asst. Vice-Pres., Bus. Devel. 1979–83; Vice-Pres., Marketing, Telecom Canada 1983–88; Asst. Vice-Pres., Rates, Bell Canada 1988–90; Mem., Bd. of Dir., Center for Telecommunications Mngt., Univ. of S. Calif. Sch. of Bus. Admin. 1985–91 and Resident Dir. (Custom Programs) 1991– ; Founding Mem., Govt. of Canada's Candn. Videotext Consultative Ctte. 1979–82; Mem., Nat. Communications Ctte., Scouts Canada 1988–93; Chair, Div. of Communication, United Ch. of Canada 1986–90; Pres., Bureau of Municipal Research of Ont. 1972–75; Editor, CABA Newsletter 1990– ; club: YMCA Health Club; Office: 1200 Montreal Rd., Bldg. M-20, Ottawa, Ont. K1A 0R6.

**FRASER, Keath;** writer; b. Vancouver, B.C. 25 Dec. 1944; e. Univ. of B.C. B.A. 1966, M.A. 1969; Univ. of London Ph.D. 1973; m. Lorraine Horsman 31 May 1969; one s. Robin; Teacher, English Dept., Univ. of Calgary 1973–78; resigned with tenure to write full-time; Contbrs. prize 'Canadian Fiction Magazine' 1982; short-listed, Gov. Gen's Award for Fiction 1985; Ethel Wilson Fiction Prize 1986; Western Magazine Award for Fiction 1987; author: 'Taking Cover' 1982 (stories), 'Foreign Affairs' 1985 (stories & novellas); editor: 'Bad Trips' 1991, 'Worst Journeys: The Picador Book of Travel' 1992; Home: 3091 West 12th Ave., Vancouver, B.C. V6K 2R4.

**FRASER, Matthew William,** B.A., B.A.A., M.J., D.E.A.; journalist; b. Toronto, Ont. 3 July 1958; s. Matthew and Williamina (McLaughlin) F.; e. Univ. of Toronto (Victoria Coll.) B.A. 1981; Ryerson Polytech. Inst. B.A.A. 1983; Carleton Univ. M.J. 1987; Institut d'Études Politiques de Paris D.E.A. 1990; Université de Paris I (Sorbonne); London Sch. of Economics; Oxford Univ. (Nuffield Coll.); post-grad. studies in political sci. and public policy 1991–92; Institut d'Études Politiques de Paris, doctoral studies 1990– ; Copy editor, The Canadian Press 1982–83; National cultural affairs reporter, Globe and Mail 1983–85; Cultural Affairs Correspondant, Que. and East. Can., Globe and Mail 1985–88; Cultural Affairs Columnist, Montreal Gazette 1989–90; Editor-Translator, Agence France-Presse 1990; Paris Columnist for Montreal Gazette 1990–92; London Columnist for Montreal Gazette 1992– ; Maître de conférences, Inst. d'Études Politiques de Paris 1990–92; author: 'Quebec Inc.: French Canadian Entrepreneurs and the New Business Elite' 1987, French transl. 1987; recreations: squash, tennis, golf; Home: 24 Gunterstone Rd., London W14 9BU, England.

**FRASER, R. Graeme,** K.St.J.; film producer; b. Ottawa 7 Dec. 1914; s. Robert James and Muriel Gordon (Campbell) F.; m. June Isobel Ferguson; children: (Mrs.) Sonia Hennigar, Rhonda; CONSULTANT; Past Chrmn., Conf. on Candn. Information; Red Cross Nat. Pub. Relations Comte.; St. John Ambulance Assn. Nat. Public Relations Comte; Past Chrmn., Ottawa Civic Hosp.; Ottawa United Way; Past Pres., Candn. Adv. & Sales Fed.; Can. Film & Television Assoc; Canada's Capital Visitor's & Convention Bureau; Internat. Quorum of Motion Picture Producers; Ottawa Red Cross; Advertising & Sales Club of Ottawa; Past Vice-Pres., Candn. Pub. Relations Soc.; Former Dir., Ottawa Better Business Bureau; Central Volunteer Bureau; Candn. Film Inst.; Former Depy. Asst. Dir., Supplies & Transport, Candn. Army Overseas, rank Maj.; United Church; recreations: travel, public speaking; Clubs: Rotary (Past Dir.); Men's Canadian (Past Pres.); Home: 901, 370 Dominion Ave., Ottawa, Ont. K2A 3X4.

**FRASER, Rena Gail,** B.A., B.Ed.; educator; b. Wolfville, N.S. 22 Dec. 1935; d. Garth Longworth and Rena Coffin (Cox) Calkin; e. Acadia Univ. B.A. 1956, B.Ed. 1971; m. J. Roderick s. J. Archibald and Mary L. Fraser 5 July 1958; children: Rena Jo, Mary Suzan; Teacher, Remedial & Upper Form English London U.K. 1956–58; Teaching Substitute, Chester, N.S. 1970–80; presently or formerly active at committee, board and/or executive level of: Children's Aid Society, Chester Arts Guild, Home & School Assn., Chester Municipal School Bd., Lunenberg Co. Vocational School Bd., Church Memorial Park (Bd. Chair), Chester Curling Club, Chester Yacht Club, Chester Municipal C. of C.; South Shore Tourist Assn.; N.S. Govt. Advisory Voluntary Planning/Tourism & Culture Sector, Shoreham Village Sr. Citizens Assn. (Bd. Chair), Acadia Univ. Alumni Assn. (former Pres.), Bd. of Gov. & Extve. Ctte. Acadia Univ (2nd Vice-Pres. & Mem., Long-Term Planning, Investment, Labour Negotiations); active interest in two small businesses (restaurant, Dental Lab/Office); recreations: yachting, nordic skiing; Home: P.O. Box 350, Chester, N.S. B0J 1J0.

**FRASER, Robert C.,** B.Com., F.C.A.; b. Eureka, Pictou County, N.S. 27 Nov. 1929; e. Dalhousie Univ. B.Com. 1952; C.A. (Que.) 1959; F.C.A. (N.S.) 1984; m. Josephine Eaton 1953; children: Heather Jane, Allan Eaton; Vice Pres. & Chief Financial Offr., Nova Scotia Power Corp.; retired 1987; Treas., Tidal Power Corp. 1971–90; Eastern Light & Power Ltd. 1973–87; Nova Scotia Light & Power Co. Ltd. 1979–87; Adm. Asst. to Gen. Mgr. NSPC 1964, Secy.-Treas. 1965, Treas. & Chief Financial Offr. 1967, Vice Pres. Finance 1972; mem. Inst. C.A.'s N.S. (Past Pres.); Candn. Inst. C.A.'s; Financial Extves. Inst. (Past Pres. Maritime Chapter); N.S. Chapter, Candn. Bible Soc. (Pres. 1986–88); Mem., Nat. Extve. Ctte., Candn. Bible Soc.; Dir., Halifax Assistance Fund; Club: Halifax; Home: 80 Nightingale Dr., Halifax, N.S. B3M 1V6.

**FRASER, The Hon. Mr. Justice Robert Patrick,** B.A., LL.B.; judge; b. Saskatoon, Sask. 10 Oct. 1929; s. Isaac Matheson and Edith (Patrick) F.; e. Univ. of Sask. B.A. 1949, LL.B. 1952; m. Jean d. Winslow and Burness Robinson 6 June 1953; children: Kathryn, Mary, Elizabeth; JUSTICE OF COURT OF QUEEN'S BENCH OF ALBERTA 1991– ; admitted to Law Soc. of Alta. 1953; Barrister & Solicitor, Milner Fenerty and predecessor firms 1953–91 primarily in conveyancing & planning field; Calgary Bar Assn. (Dir. 1958–63); Pres. 1963; Alberta Branch, Candn. Bar Assn. (Extve. 1968–74, Prov. Pres. 1972–74); Dir., Alta. Inst. of Law Reform 1969–77; Bd. Mem., Calgary Ranchmen's Club 1974–80; Pres. 1979–80; Law Soc. of Alta. (Bencher 1978–87, Pres. 1986); Dir., Saddledome Found. 1987– ; recreations: golf, badminton; clubs: Calgary Ranchmen's, Calgary Glencoe, Calgary Golf & Country; Home: 56 Christie Cairn Sq. S.W., Calgary, Alta. T2T 0W9; Office: Judges Chambers, 611 – 4th St. S.W., Calgary, Alta. T2P 1T5.

**FRASER, Ronald Cleveland;** retired broadcasting official; b. Milton, Queens Co., N.S. 14 Mar. 1916; s. Allan Henry and Caroline Maud (Lloyd) F.; e. Pub.Sch., Yarmouth, N.S.; Yarmouth (N.S.) Acad., 1932; m. Gladys Florence, d. A. T. Dauphinee, Yarmouth, N.S., 23 Sept. 1942; has one s., Ronald Ian; SPECIAL ASST. TO THE PRES., C.B.C. 1981–82; Reporter and Columnist, Yarmouth (N.S.) papers and various pubs. in U.S. and Can., 1934–39; mem. of Staff, Radio Stn. CJLS, Yarmouth, 1939–43; joined C.B.C. 1943 in Halifax as Maritime Farm Broadcast Commentator and inaugurated CBC Fisherman's Broadcast; Producer, CBC Farm Broadcast (Nat. Office), Toronto, 1946–47; Asst. Supv., Press & Information Service, Toronto, 1947, and apptd. Supv. 1948; Nat. Dir. of Press and Information Services, 1949; trans. to Ottawa, 1953; Dir. of Public Relations, 1958; Vice Pres., Corp. Affairs, 1959–64; Vice-Pres. Corp. Affairs and Asst. to the Pres., 1964–81; involved in CHEO Development since 1964; Dir., Children's Hosp. of Eastern Ont. Foundation, 1981; Pres., CHEO Foundation 1982; retired 1986; apptd. Hon. mem. CHEO Bd. of Trustees 1987; apptd. Life Gov., CHEO Foundation 1989; Life Mem., National Press Club of Can.; United Church; Home: 544 Hillcrest Ave., Ottawa, Ont. K2A 2M9.

**FRASER, Hon. Russell Gordon,** M.L.A., B.A.Sc., F.E.I.C., P.Eng.; politician; b. Vancouver, B.C. 1 March 1934; s. W. Russell S. and Dorothy A. (Wilson) F.; e. Univ. of B.C. B.A.Sc. 1958; m. Jone 29 Apl. 1989; Attorney General of B.C. 1990–..; former pres. cons. eng. co.; Comnr. Vancouver Bd. Parks & Recreation 1976–82, Chrmn. of Bd. 2 yrs.; el. M.L.A. for Vancouver S. 1983, re-el. 1986; twice apptd. Min. of Post Secondary Edn.; Solr. Gen. of B.C. 1989–90; served as Chrmn. Mun. Affairs & Housing Ctte. and held other legis. positions; recipient R.A. McLaughlin Meml. Award Outstanding Eng. of Yr. 1980; Univ. of B.C. Eng. Alumni Award of Distinction 1986; Past Pres. Assn. Profl. Engs. B.C.; Past Dir. Candn. Council Profl. Engs.; Past Chrmn. Eng. Inst. Can. (Vancouver Br.); Past Vice Chrmn. CNIB B.C. & Y.T. Div.; Social Credit; Office: 232 Parliament Buildings, Victoria, B.C. V8V 1X4; Home: 3370 West 43rd Ave., Vancouver, B.C. V6N 3J7; Office: 1350 Willow St., Vancouver, B.C.

**FRASER, Sylvia Lois,** B.A.; author; b. Hamilton, Ont. 8 Mar. 1935; d. George Nicholas and Gladys Olive (Wilson) Meyers; e. Univ. of W. Ont. B.A.; divorced; writer, 'Toronto Star Weekly' 1957–68; mag. writing awards incl. Women Press Club Award 1967, 1968; President's Medal 1969; author 'Pandora' 1972 novel; 'The Candy Factory' 1975 novel; 'A Casual Affair' 1978 novel; 'The Emperor's Virgin' 1980 novel; 'Berlin Solstice' 1984 novel; 'My Father's House' 1987 memoir (winner of Candn. Authors' Assoc. Award for non-fiction book 1987); 'The Book of Strange' 1992; guest lectr., Banff Centre 1973–79, 85, 87 and 88; mem. Arts Adv. Panel to Can. Council 1977–81; Writer-in-Residence, Univ. of W. Ont. 1980; mem. of cultural delegation to China, 1985; Instr., Maritime Writers' Workshop 1986; Vice Pres., Writers' Development Trust; Home: 701 King St. W., #302, Toronto, Ont. M5V 2W7; Office: c/o Doubleday Canada, 105 Bond St., Toronto, Ont. M5B 1Y3.

**FRAZEE, Rowland Cardwell,** C.C.; retired banker; b. Halifax, N.S. 12 May 1921; s. Rowland Hill and Callie Jean (Cardwell) F.; e. St. Stephen, N.B.; King's Coll. and Dalhousie Univ.; m. Marie Eileen Tait, 11 June 1949; children: Stephen, Catherine; Chrmn., Royal Bank of Canada, Retired; Dir., Air Canada; IMC Fertilizer Group, Inc.; Continental Airlines Inc.; Ganong Bros., Ltd.; Newfoundland Capital Corp. Ltd.; served with Carleton & York Regt., 1st Candn. Inf. Div. in Can., UK and Europe during World War II; rank Maj. on retirement 1945; Vice Chrmn., Roosevelt Campobello Internat. Park Comm.; Montreal Children's Hosp. Found.; Chrmn. Advisory Bd., Huntsman Marine Science Centre; Officer, Order of Canada 1985; Companion, Order of Canada 1991; Phi Kappa Pi; Anglican; recreations: golf, swimming, reading; Clubs: The Toronto; Mount Royal; Algonquin (St. Andrews, N.B.); Lyford Cay (Nassau); Office: 1 Place Ville Marie, P.O. Box 6001, Montreal, Que. H3C 3A9.

**FRAZER, Gordon Francis,** B.A., M.A.; retired public servant; b. Toronto, Ont. 28 Apr. 1924; s. Clyde Ernest and Ida Agnes (Baker) F.; e. Shakespeare P.S. 1937; Stratford Coll. Voc. Inst. 1942; Univ. of Toronto B.A. 1947; Oxford Univ. B.A. 1949, M.A. 1953; Ont. Coll. of Educ. 1952; R.C.N.V.R. 1944–45; Lectr. Queen's Univ. 1949–51; teacher, Belleville Coll. 1952–54; Rsch. Offr., Royal Candn. Mounted Police 1954–58; Privy Council Office, Cabinet Secretariat 1958–83; R. Catholic; recreations: the arts, travel; Home: 867 Weston Dr., Ottawa, Ont. K1G 1W5.

**FRÉCHETTE, Sylvie;** olympic athlete, public relations executive; b. Montreal 27 June 1967; d. René (dec.) and Ginette (Charbonneau) F.; COMMUNICATIONS & MARKETING, NATIONAL BANK 1992– ; Gold Medal, Synchronized Swimming, Summer Olympics (Barcelona) 1992; Germany's Open Championship 1992 (1st position); Japan's Open Champ. 1992 (1st pos. solo); World Aquatic Champ. 1991 (1st pos.); Roma Sincro 1991–92 (1st pos.); FINA World Cup 1991 (Gold Medal), 1989 (2nd solo); Commonwealth Games 1990 (Gold Medal & 1st perfect note); 1st major corp. sponsor: Brita Water Filter Systems; coach for 18 years: Julie Sauvé; Sylvie Frechette Award created by Sports Fed. of Canada 1992; AICVS 'Per Lusos Fraternitas' Trophy 1992; Female Athlete of the Year, Aquatic Sports 1989, 90, 91, 92; Home: Ste-Dorothée, Laval, Que.; Office: 16th fl., 770 Sherbrooke St. W., Montreal, Que. H3A 1G1.

**FREDEMAN, William Evan,** M.A., Ph.D., F.R.S.C., F.R.S.L.; author; educator; b. Pine Bluff, Ark. 19 July 1928; s. Frank Henry and Lucille (Griffiths) Smith; e. Subiaco Acad. (Ark.) 1945; Hendrix Coll. Ark. B.A. 1948; Univ. of Okla. M.A. 1950, Ph.D. 1956; m. Elta Jane d. Robert J. Cowan, Vancouver, B.C. 25 Apr. 1964; one s. Robert Luke; PROF. OF ENGLISH, UNIV. OF B.C. since 1967; Teacher, Capitol Hill High Sch. Oklahoma City 1948–53; Instr. Univ. of B.C. 1956, Asst. Prof. 1958; Assoc. Prof. 1963; Can. Council/SSHRCC Leave Fellowships 1959–60, 1970–71, 1978–79, 1983–84; John Simon Guggenheim Mem. Foundation Fellow 1965–66, 1971–72; Killam Sr. Research Fellow 1970–71, 1978–79, 1983–84; S.W. Brooks Visiting Lectr. Univ. of Queensland 1978; served with US Naval Reserve (active) 1945–46, rank Lt., US Army Reserve (inactive) 1948–57; author 'Pre-Raphaelitism: A Bibliocritical Study' 1965; 'A Pre-Raphaelite Gazette: The Letters of Arthur Hughes' 1967; 'Prelude to the Last Decade: Dante Gabriel Rossetti in the Summer of 1872' 1971; 'The Letters of Pictor Ignotus: William Bell Scott's Correspondence with Alice Boyd 1859–1884' 1976; ed.: 'The P.R.B. Journal' 1975; double-numbers on William Morris and D.G. Rossetti, 'Victorian Poetry' 1975, 1982; (with Ira B. Nadel) 'Dictionary of Literary Biography' (4 vols.; on Victorian novelists and Victorian Poets) 1983–85; book chapters, articles bibliog., Rossettis, Pre-Raphaelites, Tennyson, Earle Birney; mem. Modern Lang. Assn. Am.; Bibliog. Soc. (London); Internat. Assn. Univ. Profs. Eng.; P. Conservative; recreation: book collecting; Home: 1649 Allison Rd., Vancouver, B.C. V6T 1S7; Office: 2075 Wesbrook Mall, Vancouver, B.C. V6T 1W5.

**FREDERICK, Dolliver H.;** merchant banker; b. Edmonton, Alta. 2 Apr. 1944; s. Henry and Gladys (Ganske) F.; e. Alta. Coll.; Univ. of Alta.; N. Alta. Inst. Technol. Business Adm. Grad.; m. Joan Beverly d. Lawrence and Luella Dickau 28 Aug. 1965; children: Blayne Jeffrey, Tamara Lea; CHRMN., PRES., & C.E.O., FREDERICK CAPITAL CORPORATION (CANADA) INC. 1981– ; Chrmn., Pres. & C.E.O., Frederick Capital Corporation, Newport Beach, Calif., U.S.A. 1989– ; Sales Rep. Imperial Oil Ltd. Edmonton 1966, Devel. Rep. Red Deer, Alta. 1968, Area Mgr. Regina 1969, Invest. Mgr. Edmonton 1971, Sr. Analyst-Marketing Toronto 1972–73; Corp. Devel. Mgr. Bovis-McNamara Corp. (Now Kesmark/Dexleigh) 1973, Corp. Vice Pres. 1975–78, Pres. and Chief Oper. Offr. General Supply Co. of Canada (1973) Ltd. 1975–78, Pres. and Chief Oper. Offr. Equipment Fédéral Quebec Ltée 1975–78; Pres., C.E.O. and Dir., CanWest Investment Corp. 1978–81; Dir. and Chrmn. Extve. Comte., Na-Churs Plant Food Co., Marion, Ohio 1979–81; Dir. & Chrmn. Extve. Comte., Macleod-Stedman Inc., Winnipeg, Toronto, Can. 1980–81; Chrmn., Pres. & C.E.O., Cochrane-Dunlop Ltd., Toronto 1982–87; Dir., Electrohome Ltd. 1984–86; Advisory Bd., Noram Capital Mgmnt. Inc. 1984– ; Dir. & Founder, Beacon Hall Golf & Residential 1986–88; Pres. & Dir., Comterm Inc., Montreal 1988–89; Dir.: Candn. Assn. for Corp. Growth 1982–85; Inst. of Corp. Dirs. in Canada 1984–87; Candn. Counc. of Christians and Jews 1984–88; P. Conservative; recreations: flying, golf, tennis, skiing; Clubs: Pacific Club (Newport Beach, Ca.); National; Canadian C. of New York; Young Presidents' Organ. 1981– ; (Calif. Chapter); Home: 24952 Catherine Way, Dana Point, Ca. 92629; Office: P.O. Box 77, Suite 2550, Toronto Dominion Bank Tower, Toronto, Ont. M5K 1E7 and Ste. 3000 West Tower, 5000 Birch St., Newport Beach, Calif. 92660.

**FREDETTE, André Ernest,** B.A., F.I.I.C.; insurance executive; b. East Orange, N.J. 26 July 1946; s. Ernest Alfred and Valentine (St. Jacques) F.; e. Loyola College B.A. 1968; Fellow, Insurance Inst. of Canada 1976; m. Elda d. Nicolas and Maria Monaco 26 Aug. 1972; children: Gabrielle, Marc; VICE-PRESIDENT, TREATY DIV., THE MERCANTILE & GENERAL INSURANCE, REINSURANCE CO. OF CANADA; Hartford Fire Insurance 1968–75; joined present firm 1975; prior positions incl. Property Underwriter, Regional Facultative Mgr., Property Mgr. for Canada, Assistant Vice-Pres. for Broker Unit; Mem., Reinsurance Research Council; Chair, Property Ctte. for Reinsurance Rsch. Council; Mem., Soc. of Fellows; mariner's Club; Casualty Property Underwriters Club; Ontario Club; author of articles on insurance and pollution; recreations: shortwave radio listening, photography, golf, music, swimming; club: Ontario D.X. Assn.; Home: 1487 Jasmine Cr., Oakville, Ont.; Office: 161 Bay St., Suite 3000, Toronto, Ont. M5J 2T6.

**FREDRICKSON, John Murray,** M.D., F.R.C.S.(C), F.A.C.S., Ph.D. (Hon.); surgeon-educator; b. Winnipeg, Man. 24 March 1931; s. Frank Sigurdur and Beatrice Sveinross (Peterson) F.; e. Univ. of B.C. B.A. 1953, M.D. 1957 (Surgery Award 1956); Linkoping Univ. Sweden Ph.D. 1975 (cited for excellence in vestibular research); m. Alix Louise d. late Rae Gordon 12 June 1956; children: Kristin, Lisa, Erik; PROF. AND CHRMN. OF OTOLARYNGOLOGY, WASHINGTON UNIV. 1982– ; Otolaryngologist-in-Chief, Barnes Hosp. and Children's Hosp., St. Louis; Research and Internship Univ. of B.C., Vancouver Gen. Hosp., Shaughnessy Hosp. Vancouver, Univ. of Chicago (Instr. in Surg. Otolaryngol. 1963–65); Research Fellow, Dept. Clin. Neurophysiol. Univ. of Freiburg (Visiting Investigator 1963–65); Asst. Prof. of Surg. Div. Otolaryngol. Stanford Med. Center 1965–68; Assoc. Prof. of Otolaryngol. Univ. of Toronto, Toronto Gen. Hosp. 1968–77, Asst. Prof. of Physiol. since 1969; Visiting Prof. Linkoping Univ. Sweden 1973; Professor of Otolaryngology, Univ. of Toronto 1977–1982; Dir., Clin. Sciences Div. there 1976–1982; Dir., Am. Board of Otolaryngology 1984; rec'd Medal for film 'Laryngeal and Pharyngeal Pouches' 49th Annual Clin. Cong. Am. Coll. Surgs. 1963; Research Award 1964 and Award of Merit 1976 Am. Acad. Ophthalmol. & Otolaryngol.; Hodge Mem. Award Candn. Otolaryngol. Soc. 1965; Graham Campbell Prize Univ. of Toronto 1970; served with RCAF Reserve 1956–60, Med. Offr.; Editor, Am. Journal of Otolaryngology 1987; Assoc. Ed. several prof. journs.; author or co-author numerous publs., scient. films; inventor of electromagnetic implantable voice box and hearing aid; Pres., Amer. Laryngological Assn. 1991–92; mem. Ba'ra'ny Soc.; B.C. and Ont. Coll. Phys. & Surgs.; Ont. Med. Assn.; Pan-Pacific Surg. Assn.; Candn. Otolaryngol. Soc.; Am. Soc. Head & Neck Surg.; Am. Acad. Ophthalmol. & Otolaryngol. Collegium Otolaryngologica and other prof. assns.; Protestant; recreations: racquet sports, skiing, golf, music; Home: 12 Carrswold, St. Louis, MO 63105; Office: School of Medicine, 517 S. Euclid, St. Louis, MO 63110.

**FREDRIKSSON, Borje J.G.,** M.Eng.; executive; b. Flen, Sweden 13 June 1949; s. Rune P.J. and Martha M. (Pettersson) F.; e. Royal Inst. of Technol. Stockholm M.Eng. 1974; m. Kerstin d. Rune and Lilly Jansson 10 June 1978; two d. Maria, Emma; VICE PRESIDENT, MINING & METALS, ASEA BROWN BOVERI INC.; Prodn. Eng. ASEA AB, Vasteras, Sweden 1974–76; Sales & Application Eng. ASEA INC. Montréal 1976, Product Mgr. 1978, Gen. Mgr. Ind. Div. 1982, Vice Pres. and Gen. Mgr. of Div. 1985 and of Central Operations (Toronto) 1986, Pres., Ind. Segment 1988–.; Dir. ABB Nordco Ltd.; mem. Candn. Inst. Mining & Metall.; recreations: tennis, squash, golf, skiing; clubs: Markvale Racket (Mississauga); Greystone Golf (Milton); Home: 619 Lyons Court, Milton, Ont. L9T 4R7; Office: 3 Robert Speck Parkway, Suite 650, Mississauga, Ont. L4Z 2G5.

**FREED, Josh,** B.Sc., B.A.; journalist; documentary film producer; b. Montréal, Qué. 6 Apr. 1949; s. Harry and Anne F.; e. McGill Univ., B.Sc., B.A. 1971; freelance writer 1970–73; feature writer Montreal Star 1973–78; TV Journalist & Producer CBC's 'The Journal' and other TV, radio progs. 1981–89; Urban Affairs Analyst & Commentary CBC radio 1981–89; Writer and Dir. 'North to Nowhere' internat. TV documentary 1987; Journalism Teacher, Dawson Coll. 1976–79, Concordia Univ. 1980–85; columnist, Montreal Gazette 1989–93; Host/Dir., 'Between Solitudes: the Anglos of Quebec' CBC/Radio-Quebec co-production; recipient Nat. Newspaper Award 1980, 1992; Nat. Bus. Writing Award 1976; author: 'Moonwebs' 1981; 'Sign Language and Other Tales of Montreal Wildlife' 1990; co-author and ed.: 'Anglo Guide to Survival in Québec' 1983; writer, NFB films: 'Song for Quebec'; 'Mile Zero' 1988–89; Dir.: PBS film 'Canada by Train' 1989; CBC film 'Turning Point' 1992–93 (all documentaries); Home: 4069 Esplanade, Montréal, Qué. H2W 7S9; Office: CBC, 1400 Dorchester W., Montréal, Qué. H3B 4N6.

**FREEDMAN, Benjamin,** M.A., Ph.D.; philosopher; bioethicist; b. Brooklyn, N.Y. 2 Aug. 1951; s. Manuel and Anne (Mauer) F.; e. Brooklyn Coll. B.A. 1972; Grad. Center City Univ. of New York M.A., Ph.D. 1975; m. Barbara d. Ludwig and Esther Lehrer 15 June 1971; children: Ariela, Orit, Avidan, Menachem; PROF. McGILL CENTRE FOR MED., ETHICS & LAW, McGILL UNIV. 1990– ; Clin. Ethicist, Sir Mortimer B. Davis-Jewish Gen. Hosp. 1987– ; Rsch. Intern, Hastings Inst. Hastings-on-Hudson, N.Y. 1973; Lectr. in Ethics & Jurisprudence Faculty of Law, Bar-Ilan Univ. Israel 1975–76; Lectr. in Philos. Yeshiva Univ. N.Y. 1978; Asst. Prof. of Bioethics Faculties of Med. & Humanities Univ. of Calgary 1979–81; Assoc. for Bioethics Westminster Inst. for Ethics & Human Values London, Ont. 1981–87; Assoc. Prof. present univ. 1987; Cons.: Law Reform Comn. Can. 1981–88; Candn. Nurses Assn. 1982–85; mem. Clark Comn. Min. Health Ont. 1984–85; Working Group Ethics Somatic Cell Gene Theraby in Humans Med. Rsch. Council Can. 1988; Task Force AIDS and Profl. Responsibility Hastings Center 1987–88; Inaugural Visiting Scholar Jakobovits Centre Jewish Med. Ethics, Israel 1986; recipient Matchette Award in Philos. 1973; Hintz Fellow in Philos. 1974; author: 'A Moral Theory of Informed Consent' 1975; 'Ethical Issues in Clinical Obstetrics and Gynecology' 1985; 'Equipoise and the Ethics of Clinical Research' 1987; 'On the Planet Grafool' 1985; 'Akiva: A Life in Two Acts' (midrashic fiction) 1987; co-ed.: 'Moral Responsibility and the Professions' 1984; mem. Human Context Sci. & Technol. Review Ctte., Social Sci's & Humanities Rsch. Council Can. 1985–86; Bnei Akiva (Maskirut 1973–75 NYC); Founder, Soc. Against Drunk Bioethics 1986; Phi Beta Kappa; Home: 5522 Westbourne Ave., Montréal, Qué. H4V 2H1; Office: Montréal, Qué. H3A 3A3.

**FREEDMAN, George A.,** D.C.S., B.Sc., D.D.S., F.A.A.C.D., F.A.D.I.; dentist; b. 5 May 1952; e. Outremont H.S. 1969; McGill Univ. D.C.S. 1971, B.Sc. 1975, D.D.S. 1978; m. Dr. Fay Goldstep; one daughter; SENIOR DENTAL PROFESSIONAL & CONSULTANT, ORVOSOK HOLDINGS INC. 1988– ; private dental practice 1978– ; Sr. Dental Profl. & Cons., D.A.C.A. Dental Group 1981–88; Accreditation, Am. Acad. of Cosmetic Dentistry 1986; Devel. Shofu Porcelain Veneer Kit 1986; Adjunct Assoc. Prof., Case Western Reserve Univ. (Cleveland, OH) & Dir., Post-grad. Prog. in Esthetic Dent. 1991– ; Course Dir., Post-grad. Prog. in Esthetic Dent., Baylor College of Dentistry (Dallas, TX) 1992– ; Consultant to Shofu Dental Corp.; Kerr Mfg. Co.; Caulk/Dentsply; Escan; Williams/Vivadent/Ivoclar; Matsushita, Weissman Technol. Internat. and several others; Mem., Esthetic Dentistry Rsch. Group 1988– ; Mem., Bd. of Dir., Am. Academy of Cosmetic Dentistry (Vice-Pres. 1987–90; Pres.-elect 1990; Pres. 1991–92; Fellow 1992– ;); Academy of Dentistry Internat. (Fellow); Candn. Dental Assn.; Royal Coll. of Dental Surgeons of Ont.; Ont. Dental Assn.; Acad. of Gen. Dent.; Fed. Dentaire Internat.; Alpha Omega Frat.; Mensa (Canada); Hon. Mem., Accademia di Estetica Dentale Italiana 1992– ; nom. Am. Dental Assn. Gold Medal Award for Excellence in Dental Research 1991; Chair of three symposia; extensive ctte. work; has delivered close to 100 scientific lectures worldwide; languages: English, French, Hungarian, Romanian, Hebrew; Bd. of Dir., Montreal Metro. 'Y' 1988–91; author: 'The Color Atlas of Porcelain Laminate Veneers' 1990, 'The Color Atlas of Tooth Whitening' 1991 (textbooks) and numerous scientific articles in professional journals; contbr.: 'Encyclopaedia Britannica Medical and Health Annual' 1990, 1991; Edit. Bd. Mem., 'Esthetic Dentistry Update' 1990– ; 'Dentistry Today'; 'Reality'; 'Current Opinion in Dentistry'; recreations: squash, scuba-diving, skiing, modern art collector; Home: 8 Marlborough St., Richmond Hill, Ont. L4B 2W7; Office: 675 Cochrane Dr., Suite 508, Markham, Ont. L3R 0B8.

**FREEDMAN, Harry;** O.C. composer; b. Lodz, Poland 5 Apr. 1922; s. Max and Rose (Nelken) F.; came to Can. 1925; e. St. Johns High Sch., Winnipeg, 1938; Winnipeg Sch. of Art, 1936–39; Royal Conserv. of Music, Toronto, 1945–50; m. Mary Louise, d. late Donald Morrison, 15 Sept. 1951; three d. Karen Liese, Cynthia Jane, Lori Ann; joined Toronto Symphony 1946 and remained playing mem. until appt. as Composer-in-Residence in 1970; won scholarship to study with Aaron Copland, 1949; Host of music segment of CBC's 'Junior Roundup,' 1960–61; apptd. to Ed. Bd. of 'Music Across Canada,' 1962; was one of 5 composers who organized Ten Centuries Concerts in Toronto, 1963; asked to rep. Can. at '2nd Festival of Music of the Americas and Spain,' Madrid, 1967; Host and Commentator on 'CBC Thursday Music,' 1968 and 1969; has been assoc. with several Toronto Sch. Bds. in field of educ. music; chosen by Ont. Arts Council to conduct research project on interdisciplinary arts educ.; winner of Canadian Film Awards 'ETROG' for best film score, 1970; Candn. Music Council award, 'Composer of the Year' 1979; Order of Canada 1985; princ. works incl.: '5 Pieces for String Quartet' 1948; 'Scherzo for Piano' 1949; 'Nocturne' (Orchestra) 1949; '2 Vocalises' 1953; 'Tableau' 1952; 'Images' 1957; 'Symphony No. 1' 1960 (premiered in Washington 1961); 'Wind Quintet' 1961; 'Fantasy and Allegro' 1962; 'The Tokaido' 1964; 'Chaconne' 1964; 'Little Symphony' 1966; 'Rose Latulippe' (ballet score) 1966; 'Anerca' (3 settings of Eskimo poems for soprano and piano) 1966; 'Tangents' 1967; 'Toccata' (flute and soprano) 1968; 'Poems of Young People' 1968; '5 Over 13' (ballet score) 1969; 'Scenario' 1970; 'Shining People of Leonard Cohen' 1970; 'Orchestration of Debussy's Preludes, Bk. 1' 1971; 'Graphic I (... Out of Silence)' 1971; 'Keewaydin' (SSA choir) 1971; 'Pan' (flute, sopr., piano) 1972; 'Graphic II' (string quartet) 1972; 'Tapestry' (orch.) 1973; 'Encounter' (violin and piano) 1974; 'Nocturne 2' (orch.) 1975; 'Alice in Wonderland' (quintet) 1976; 'Fragments of Alice' (chamber orch.) 1976; 'The Explainer' (narrator & chamber ensemble) 1976; 'Celebration' (concerto for Gerry Mulligan) 1977; 'Green ... Blue ... White ...' (choir) 1978; 'Abracadabra' (1–Act jazz opera) 1978–79; 'Chalumeau' (clar. & str. qt.) 1981; 'Royal Flush' (conc. grosso for br. qt. & orch., commissioned by Montreal Symph. Orch.) 1981; 'Concerto for Orchestra' (comm'd. by Toronto Symph.) 1982; 'Third Symphony' (comm'd. by Regina Symph. Orch.) 1983; 'Oiseaux Exotiques' (ballet) 1984; 'Contrasts' (The Web and the Wind) 1986; 'Breaks' (ballet) 1987; 'Fragments of Alice' (music theatre) 1987; 'A Dance on the Earth' (orch.) 1988; 'Sonata for Wind Orchestra' 1988; 'Touchings (Concerto for Percussion Ensemble) 1989; 'Bones' (marimba solo) 1990; 'Town' (orch.) 1991; 'Strands of Blue' (chamber orch.) 1992; 'Spirit Song' (sop. & str. qt.) 1993; Host of 'Music on a Sunday Afternoon' (CBC-TV) 1987; film and TV scores incl.: 'Shadow of the City' 1956; 'Where Will They Go' 1959; 'India' 1960; '20 Million Shoes' 1962; 'The Dark Did Not Conquer' 1963; '700 Million' 1964; 'Pale Horse, Pale Rider' 1965; 'Let Me Count the Ways' 1964; 'Spring Song' 1965; 'China: The Roots of Evil' 1966; 'Romeo and Jeanette' 1966; 'Isabel' (film) 1967; 'The Flame Within' (Cantata for film 'Act of the Heart') 1968; 'Night' 1970; music for 'Much Ado About Nothing' (stage, Stratford 1971); 'As You Like It' (stage, Stratford 1972); 'Twelfth Night' (stage, Toronto Arts Production 1972); The Pyx (film) 1973; 'Romeo and Juliet' (ballet) 1973; '1847' (CBC-TV) 1977; 'Pyramid of Roses' (1980); 'All That Glistens' (1983); 'Against Oblivion' (1983); served with RCAF 1942–45; mem. Adv. Bd., Pollution Probe (Univ. of Toronto); Advisor, Arts Educ., Ont. Arts Council; Founding mem. and Pres., (1975–78) Candn. League Composers, Ten Centuries Concerts; Founding mem. & Pres., Guild of Candn. Film Composers (1979–81); Music Officer, Toronto Arts Council 1985–90; N.D.P.; recreations: painting (Japanese Sumi), film-making, golf; Address: 35 St. Andrews Gdns., Toronto, Ont. M4W 2C9.

**FREEDMAN, Martin H.,** Q.C., B.A., LL.B.; lawyer; b. Winnipeg, Man. 12 Sept. 1937; s. Samuel and Claris (Udow) F.; e. Univ. of Man., B.A. 1958, LL.B. 1963; m. Roxy d. Max and Evelyn Berinstein 19 Aug. 1962; children: Jacqueline, Karyn, Lisa; MANAGING PARTNER, AIKINS, MACAULAY & THORVALDSON; called to Man. Bar 1963; law practice , Winnipeg 1963–69; Partner, Aikins, MacAulay & Thorvaldson 1969–75; Chief Couns., Royal Comn. on Corp. Concentration, Pub. Serv. of Can. 1975–77; returned to Aikins Firm 1977; Lectr., Univ. of Man. 1963–83; Dir., Fed. Indus. Ltd.; Dir., The Mutual Life Assurance Co. of Can.; Sec., Powell Equipment Ltd.; The Univ. of Manitoba Bus. Sch. Foundation Inc.; Gold Medallist, Fac. of Law, Univ. of Man. 1963; Mem., Can. Bar Assn.; Man. Bar Assn.; The Law Soc. of Man. (Pres. 1978–79; Life Bencher); Am. Bar Assn.; author: 'Tax Aspects of Home Ownership' 1974 and eight articles; editor: 'Casebook on Legal Institutions' 1970, 'Cases and Materials on Legal Aspects of Business Planning' 1971–76, 'Cases and Materials on Competition Law' 1982–83; contbr.: 'The Law Society of Manitoba 1877–1977' 1977; 'Lawyering and Legal Education into the 21st Century' 1989; published labour arbitration awards 1980–93; Regional Editor: 'Canadian Business Law Journal'; recreations: cycling, guitar; Home: 93 Ash St., Winnipeg, Man. R3N 0P4; Office: 3000–360 Main St., Winnipeg, Man. R3C 4G1.

**FREEDMAN, Melvin H.,** M.D., F.R.C.P.(C), F.A.A.P.; physician; professor; b. Saint John, N.B. 4 July 1939; s. Benjamin and Norma (Tanzman) F.; e. Saint John H.S. 1957; Dalhousie Univ., M.D. 1966; F.R.C.P.(C) 1971; m. Lila d. Nathan and Mary Oberman 18 Aug. 1963; children: Steven James, Monica Nora; CHIEF OF HEMATOLOGY AND CO-HEAD, DIV. OF HEMATOL.-ONCOL., HOSPITAL FOR SICK CHILDREN 1991– ; and SR. STAFF PHYSICIAN & HEMATOL.-ONCOL. 1979– ; PROF. OF PEDIAT., UNIV. OF TORONTO 1986– ; Res., Montreal Children Hosp. 1966–68; Fellow in Hematol.-Oncol., Childrens Hosp. of Los Angeles 1968–70; Montreal Gen. Hosp. 1970–71; Staff Phys. & Hematol.-Oncol., Hosp. for Sick Children 1971; Dir., Hematopoiesis Lab. & Project Dir., Rsch. Inst. 1972– ; Dir. of Transfusion & Iron Chelation Prog. 1981–88; Dir. of Clinical Hematology, H.S.C.

1988–91; Instr. in Pediat., Univ of S. Calif.; Clin. Teacher in Pediat., Univ of Toronto 1971–72; Asst. Prof. 1972–78; Assoc. Prof. 1978–86; Mem., Med. Adv. Counc., Candn. Red Cross, Toronto Transfusion Serv.; mem., Med. Adv. Ctte., Leukemia Rsch. Fund; Med. Advisor, Aplastic Anemia Family Assoc.; Bd. of Exam., R.C.P.S.C. 1975–89; mem., Specialty Ctte. in Hematology, Royal Coll. of Physicians and Surgeons of Can. 1987–92; Mem., Beth Tzedec Synagogue; Soc. for Pediat. Rsch.; Alpha Omega Alpha Hon. Soc.; Candn. Soc. for Clin. Investigation; Candn. Soc. of Hematol.; Am. Fed. for Clin. Rsch.; Am. Acad. of Pediat.; Am. Soc. of Hematol.; Am. Soc. of Pediat. Hemat./Oncol.; Internat. Soc. for Exp. Hematol.; Internat. Soc. of Hematol.; author of over 150 sci. pubs. in med. jours.; recreations: skiing, racquet sports, travel, music appreciation & participation, theatre; Office: 555 University Ave., Toronto, Ont. M5G 1X8.

**FREEDMAN, Morris,** B.Sc., M.D., F.R.C.P.(C); neurologist; b. Toronto, Ont. 25 May 1949; s. Myer and Henia F.; e. Univ. of Toronto B.Sc. 1971; Univ. of Ottawa M.D. 1975; F.R.C.P.(C) and cert. in neurol. 1980; m. Fay d. Aaron and Lydia Huppert 21 Aug. 1977; children: David Zev, Michael Howard, Lauren Fern; DIR. OF BEHAVIOURAL NEUROLOGY PROG., BAYCREST HOSP. 1986– ; STAFF NEUROLOGIST, MT SINAI HOSP. 1983– ; Staff Scientist, Rotman Rsch. Inst. of Baycrest Ctr. for Geriatric Care; Assoc. Scientist, Samuel Lunenfeld Rsch. Inst., Mt. Sinai Hosp.; Grad. Faculty, Inst. of Med. Sci., Univ. of Toronto; Assoc. Prof., Fac. of Med., Univ. of Toronto; John McMartin Award for highest standing in Ophthalmology, Fac. of Med., Univ. of Ottawa 1975; Francis McNaughton Prize, XIV Candn. Congress of Neurological Scis. 1979; Fellowship in Behav. Neurol., Boston Veterans Admin. Med. Ctr. 1981–83; Rsch. Scholarship, Gerontol. Rsch. Counc. of Ont. 1984–87; Career Sci. Award, Min. of Health of Ont. 1988–93; author of many scientific articles; Fellow, Am. Acad. of Neurology; Mem., Educ. Ctte., Div. of Neurology, Univ. of Toronto 1990– ; Mem., Rsch. Ctte., Div. of Neurology, Univ. of Toronto 1991– ; Bd. of Dirs., Candn. Soc. for the Weizmann Inst. of Sci. (Toronto Chapter) 1991– ; Mem., Scientific Prog. Ctte., Candn. Congress of Neurolog. Scis. 1992– ; Chrmn., Scientific Program Ctte., Candn. Congress of Neurological Sciences 1993; mem., Acad. of Aphasia; Alzheimer's Soc. for Metro. Toronto; Behavioural Neurology Soc.; Candn. Assoc. on Gerontology; Candn. Med. Assoc.; Candn. Neurological Soc.; Coll. of Physicians and Surgeons of Ont.; Internat. Neuropsycholog. Soc.; Medico-Legal Soc. of Toronto; Ont. Med. Assoc.; Royal Coll. of Physicians and Surgeons of Can.; World Federation of Neurology (Rsch. Group on Aphasia and Related Disorders); Office: 3560 Bathurst St., Toronto, Ont. M6A 2E1.

**FREEDMAN, Samuel Orkin,** O.C., B.Sc., D.Sc., M.D., C.M., F.R.C.P.(C), F.A.C.P., F.R.S.C.; educator; b. Montreal, Que. 8 May 1928; s. late Abraham Orkin Freedman; e. Westmount High Sch. 1945; McGill Univ. B.Sc. 1949, M.D., C.M. 1953; m. Norah Lee d. late Haim Maizel 28 Aug. 1955; children: David Orkin, Daniel Ari, Abraham Edward, Elizabeth Vera; DIR. OF RESEARCH, SIR MORTIMER B. DAVIS - JEWISH GEN. HOSP. since 1991, PROF. OF MED., McGILL UNIV. since 1968; Sr. Phys. Div. Clin. Immunology & Allergy, Dept. Med., Jewish Gen. Hosp. and Montreal Gen. Hosp.; Dir. Div. Clin. Immunology & Allergy, McGill Univ. 1968–77; Dean of Medicine, McGill Univ. 1977–81; Vice-Pres. (Academic) McGill Univ. 1981–91; co-discoverer CEA test for cancer; rec'd Queen's Silver Jubilee Medal; Gairdner Award Univ. of Toronto 1978; Officer, Order of Canada 1986; D.Sc. (honoris causa) McGill Univ. 1992; Commemorative Medal, 125th Anniversary of Candn. Confedn. 1992; co-author 'Clinical Immunology' 2nd ed. 1976; over 120 scient. articles on topics cancer immunology, clin. allergy and tuberculosis; Jewish; Club: University; Home: 658 Murray Hill Ave., Montreal, Que. H3Y 2W6; Office: 3755 Côte Ste-Catherine Rd., Montreal, Que. H3T 1E2.

**FREEDMAN, Theodore Jarrell,** B.Sc.Phm., D.H.A., C.H.E.; health care administrator; b. St. Boniface, Man. 13 Nov. 1943; s. Lou and Nydia (Omansky) F.; e. Univ. of Manitoba B.Sc.Phm. 1965; Univ. of Toronto D.H.A. 1970; m. A. Judy d. Elsie and Sol Hyman 16 June 1968; children: Lisa Gaye, Randal Asher; PRESIDENT & C.E.O., MOUNT SINAI HOSP. 1993– , Extve. Vice-Pres. & C.O.O. 1989–93; Hospital Pharm., Winnipeg Health Sci. Ctr. 1965–68; Admin. Asst., New Bldg. Co-ord., Mount Sinai Hosp. 1970–72; Asst. Admin. 1972–74; Asst. Extve. Dir. 1974–77; Assoc. Extve. Dir. 1977–82; Sr. Assoc. Extve. Dir. 1982–84; Sr. Vice-Pres. 1984–86; Extve. Vice-Pres. 1986–89; Assoc. Prof., Dept. of Health Admin., Univ. of Toronto 1993– ; Asst. Prof., Dept. of Health Admin., Univ. of Toronto 1988–93; Robert Wood Johnson Award, Univ. of Toronto 1970; Assn. of Young Health Extves. Article Publishing Award 1977, 1978; Univ. of Toronto, Soc. of Grads. in Health Admin., Graduate Literary Award 1989, '92; Univ. of Toronto, Dept. of Health Admin., Eugenie M. Stuart Award of Merit 1991; Pres., Soc. of Grads. in Health Admin. 1976–77; Mem., Am. Coll. of Health Care Extves.; Candn. Coll. of Health Serv. Extves.; author/co-author num. health care articles; recreations: sporting activities; clubs: Fitness Inst.; Mandarin; University; Home: 128 Aspenwood Dr., Willowdale, Ont. M2H 2G1; Office: Room 335, 600 University Ave., Toronto, Ont. M5G 1X5.

**FREEMAN, Barbara Marie,** B.J., M.A., A.B.D.; university professor; b. St. John's, Nfld. 7 July 1947; d. Thomas Sterry and Marie Loretta (Murphy) F.; e. Carleton Univ., B.J. 1969, M.A. 1988; ASST. PROF., CARLETON UNIV. 1988– ; Editor, Reporter, CBC Nfld. Region & freelance broadcast journalist 1972–74; Edn. & Community Affairs Reporter, CBC Radio, Ottawa 1974–78; Municipal Affairs Reporter, Newsreader with KEY Radio Ltd., Ottawa 1978–80; Instr., present univ. 1980–88; author: 'Kit's Kingdom: The Journalism of Kathleen Blake Coleman' 1989; Home: 6 Windsor Ave., Ottawa, Ont. K1S 0W4; Office: 332 SP, Carleton Univ., Ottawa, Ont. K1S 5B6.

**FREEMAN, Dennis H.,** B.A., C.A.; chartered accountant; b. Smiths Falls, Ont. 21 July 1949; s. Hubert P. and Leona C. (NcNamee) F.; e. Queen's Univ. B.A. 1970; C.A. 1977; m. Kathleen d. William and Sheila Wright 20 Sept. 1974; children: Matthew, Allison, Julia; PARTNER, PEAT MARWICK THORNE 1983– ; joined Thorne Riddell (predecessor firm of present firm) 1973; Dir., Federal Bus. Devel. Bank 1989; Past Dir., Ont. Place Corp. 1984–86; Friends of HMCS Haida 1986–90; Roman Catholic; recreations: tennis; clubs: Granite, Albany; Home: 5 Lombardy Lane, Thornhill, Ont. L3T 4W3; Office: 1 Toronto St., Toronto, Ont. M5C 2V5.

**FREEMAN, The Hon. Gerald Borden,** B.A., B.C.L., LL.B.; judge; b. Liverpool, N.S. 29 June 1931; s. George Weld and Helen Marie (Wentzell) F.; e. Univ. of N.B. Forestry 1950–51; Acadia Univ. B.A. 1953; McGill Univ. B.C.L. 1960; Dalhousie Univ. LL.B. 1961; m. Mary E. d. Eldon and Eileen Veinotte 30 June 1956; one s. James Andrew; JUDGE, NOVA SCOTIA COURT OF APPEAL 1990– ; joined Bank of Nova Scotia 1948–49; Mersey Paper Co. 1949–50; Halifax Chronicle Herald 1953, 1960–61; The Candn. Press Halifax, St. John.s, Montreal 1953–60; private law practice Liverpool, N.S. 1962–88; Judge, Co. Court Dist. No. 2 1988–90; Home: P.O. Box 479, Liverpool, N.S. B0T 1K0; Office: 1815 Upper Water St., Halifax, N.S. B3J 1S7.

**FREEMAN, Gordon Russel,** M.A., Ph.D., D.Phil.; university professor; b. Hoffer, Sask. 27 Aug. 1930; s. Winston Spencer Churchill and Aquila Maud (Chapman) F.; e. Sask. schs.: Lanigan; Sonningdale; Broadacres; Smeaton; Moose-Jaw; Salvador 1948; Univ. Sask., B.A. 1952; M.A. 1953; McGill Univ., Ph.D. 1955; Oxford Univ., D.Phil. 1957; m. Phyllis Joan, d. Charles and Anna Elson, 8 Sept. 1951; children: Michèle Leslie; Mark Russel; five grandchildren; PROF. OF CHEM., DIR., RADIATION RESEARCH CENTRE, UNIV. ALTA. since 1965; Chrmn., Radiation Control Comte. 1983–84; Stagiaire, Centre d'Etudes Nucléaires de Saclay (France) 1957; joined present univ. as Asst. Prof. 1958; Assoc. Prof. 1961; Prof. and Chrmn. Div. Physical and Theoretical Chemistry 1965–75; Sch. Library Sci. Counc. 1971–75; author of 370 articles in professional journals and contributions to books on chemistry and physics; ed./co-author: 'Kinetics of Nonhomogeneous Processes' 1987; 'Kinetics of Nonhomogeneous Processes and Nonlinear Dynamics' 1990; rec'd. many scholarships, Fellowships and prizes; Fellow, Chem. Inst. Can. (Chrmn. then Councillor, Physical Chem. Div. 1975–80); Candn. Nat. Comte., Internat. Union Pure and Applied Chem. (Chrmn. Awards 1982–84); mem., Candn. Assn. Physicists; Am. Physical Soc.; Epigraphic Soc. (U.S.); Candn. Archaeological Assn.; recreations: archaeology; music; badminton; languages and writing systems; Office: Chem. Dept., Univ. Alta., Edmonton, Alta. T6G 2G2.

**FREEMAN, Linda Alison Isobel,** M.A., Ph.D.; educator; b. Vernon, B.C.; d. Michael Stephen and Jean Lowden (Darling) F.; e. Univ. of B.C. B.A. 1965; Univ. of Toronto M.A. 1971, Ph.D. 1978; ASSOC. PROF. OF POL. SCI. CARLETON UNIV. 1980– ; Asst. Prof. of Pol. Studies Univ. of Guelph 1978–80; mem. Africa 2000 Consultative Group Min. External Relations 1987–91; testified to H. of C. Ctte. Human Rights S. Africa 1986, Jt. Ctte. Senate and H. of C. on Can. & Sanctions against S. Africa 1987, H. of C. Sub-ctte. on Internat. Development on 'South Africa Scenarios for the 1990s' 1992; mem. NGO Del. to observe Namibian els. 1989; mem., Program Ctte., Candn. Rsch. Consortium on Southern Africa 1992– ; internat. rsch. trips Africa, India since 1974; frequent commentator Candn. TV, Radio, Press on Africa and Third World Politics; author various articles, book chapters, reviews, presentations learned soc's.; mem. Candn. Assn. African Studies; Candn. Pol. Sci. Assn.; recreations: skiing, hiking, canoeing, music, cinema; Home: 3, 495 Percy St., Ottawa, Ont. K1S 4B2; Office: Dept. of Political Sci., Carleton Univ., 1125 Colonel By Dr., Ottawa, Ont. K1S 5B6.

**FREEZE, Roy Allan,** F.R.S.C., M.Sc., Ph.D.; hydrologist; educator; b. Edmonton, Alta. 23 May 1939; s. Donald Allan and Beatrice Isobel (Anderson) F.; e. Glebe Coll. Inst. Ottawa 1957; Queen's Univ. B.Sc. 1961; Univ. of Cal. Berkeley M.Sc. 1964, Ph.D. 1966; m. Donna Dorraine d. William B. Davis, Ottawa, Ont. 22 Dec. 1961; children: Geoffrey Allan, Donna Christine, Lori Sandra, Sean Davis; PRESIDENT, R.ALLAN FREEZE ENGINEERING, INC.; Prof. of Geol. Sciences, Univ. of B.C. 1973–91; rec'd Horton Award 1972, 1974 and MacElwane Award 1974, Am. Geophys. Union; Meinzer Award, Geol. Soc. Am. 1974; co-author 'Groundwater' 1979; author over 70 scient. papers hydrology; mem. Am. Geophys. Union (Pres., Hydrology Section 1984–86); Geol. Soc. Am.; Candn. Geotech. Soc.; Assn. Prof. Engrs. B.C.; recreations: golfing, camping, skiing, reading, duplicate bridge; Address: 3755 Nico Wynd Dr., White Rock, B.C. V4P 1J1.

**FREIFELD, Sidney,** B.Com.; diplomat (retired); writer; b. Toronto, Ont. 2 Sept. 1910; s. Louis and Jessie (Schipper) F.; e. Queen Victoria Pub. Sch., Parkdale Coll. Inst. Toronto; Univ. of Toronto B.Com. 1932; London Sch. of Econ. 1932–35; m. Crenia d. Moses and Sonia Sandler 25 Aug. 1939; two d. Riva, Miriam; Statistician & Economist Internat. Inst. Agric. Rome 1935–38; Corr. New York Herald Tribune and The Times (London), Rome 1936–38; Corr. Toronto Star, N.Y. 1938–39; mem. Profl. Staff Am. Jewish Ctte. N.Y. 1939–41; U.S. Office of War Info. N.Y. 1941–42; Wartime Info. Bd. Can. N.Y. 1942–45; Dept. of External Affairs 1946–75; Ambassador to Colombia and Ecuador 1970–75; author 'Undiplomatic Notes: Tales From The Canadian Foreign Service' 1990; numerous newspaper articles; ed. Dept. External Affairs Annual Review 1975–88; sr. ed. bd. 'Bout de Papier'; mem. Nat. Press Club; Overseas Press Club N.Y.; Retired Heads of Mission Assn; recreation: angling (world record holder for fly-rod caught sea trout); Clubs: Ottawa Fly Fishers; Hunt (Bogota); Address: 1403, 200 Rideau Terrace, Ottawa, Ont. K1M 0Z3.

**FREMES, Ruth,** B.A.; journalist; home economist; b. Toronto, Ont. 19 Jan. 1930; d. Frank and Bessie (Heller) Goldberg; e. Univ. of Toronto B.A. 1951; m. Dr. Z.I. Sabry 10 May 1984; children: Susan Fremes, Marjorie Fremes, Adam Shirriff, Jason Shirriff; Farm Broadcaster CBC Radio 1960–69, Nat. Consumer Affairs Broadcaster 1969–75; co-host CTV 'W5' 1975–77; Host 'What's Cooking with Ruth Fremes' CTV Network 1977– ; consulting home econ. Can. and U.S.A. 1960–85; mem. Adv. Bd. Consumer & Corp. Affairs Can. 1975–77; Nat. Advertising Stds. Counc., CAAB 1976–78; Task Force on Treatment of Obesity Health & Welfare Can. 1983– ; Instr. in Foods & Nutrition/Extension Univ. of Calif. Berkeley; Media Advisor, Expanded Food & Nutrition Program, Univ. of Calif. Cooperative Extension; Food & Nutrition Adv. Ctte. Baycrest Centre for Geriatrics 1983–85; frequent speaker Nat. and Internat. bodies; recipient ACTRA Award Best Pub. Affairs Broadcaster in TV 1978; author 'Ruth Fremes' "What's Cooking" Cookbook' Vol. 1 1980, Vol. 2 1981, Vol. 3 1982, Vol. 4 1983, Vol. 5 1984; 'Baby's First Year: One to Grow On' 1976, re-issued 1980; 'The Joy of Eating' 1977, re-issued 1978 & ea. yr. thereafter; 'The Nutritional Diet' 1977; 'The Canadian Woman's Almanac: A Guide to Coping in Canada' 1978; 'Eating Right' syndicated column maj. Candn. newspapers 1976–79; nutrition columnist 'Chatelaine Magazine' 1983–84; co-author 'Superwoman' 1978; 'Nutriscore: The Rate-Yourself Plan for Better Nutrition' 2nd ed. 1982; mem. Candn. Home Econ. Assn. (Past Extve. mem.); San Francisco Prof. Food Soc. (Chair, Liaison); Internat. Assn. Food Profs. (CM); ACTRA; Home: 4215 Lakeshore Ave., Oakland, CA 94610.

**FRENCH, Goldwin Sylvester,** B.A., M.A., Ph.D., D.S.Litt. (hon.), LLD. (hon.); historian; b. Camden Twp. (Dresden) Ont. 24 Jan. 1923; s. Owen Glen and Pearl Irene (Elliott) F.; e. Elem. Sch., Camden Twp.; Dresden Continuation Sch.; Univ. Toronto, B.A. 1944; M.A. 1947; Ph.D. 1958; m. Iris Thelma, d. Ira and Helena

Ivey, 9 Aug. 1946; children: Charles Andrew Ivey; Alison; PROFESSOR EMERITUS, VICTORIA UNIV.; Pres. & Vice-Chancellor, Victoria University 1973–87; Lectr., Dept. Hist., McMaster Univ. 1947; Assoc. Prof. 1958; Chrmn. Dept. 1964–70; Prof. 1964–72; author 'Parsons and Politics' 1962; ed. and contrib., Candn. Sect., 'Encyclopedia of World Methodism' 1974; contrib. 'The Shield of Achilles' 1968 (W.L. Morton, ed.); 'The Churches and the Canadian Experience' 1963 (J.W. Grant, ed.); rec'd. Can. Counc. Jr. Research Fellowship; Candn. Forces Decoration; served R.C.A.F. (Reserve) 1948–58, retiring as Squadron Leader; former Chrmn., Comte. Archives, United Church Can.; Ed., Candn. Studies in Hist. and Govt.; Ed.-in-Chief, Ont. Historical Studies Series 1971–93; mem., Candn. Hist. Assn.; Am. Hist. Assn.; C.I.I.A.; Soc. for French Hist. Studies; Candn. Methodist Hist. Soc.; Clubs: Arts & Letters; Faculty (Univ. of Toronto); University; recreations: gardening; walking; travel; Home: 65 Robinhood Dr., Dundas, Ont. L9H 4G2; Office: 73 Queens Park Cres., Toronto, Ont. M5S 1K7.

**FRENCH, John Barry,** B.A.Sc., M.Sc., Ph.D., F.R.S.C., F.R.S.A., F.C.A.S.I.; educator; b. Toronto, Ont. 22 Aug. 1931; s. John Edwin and Lilla (Hitchcox) F.; e. Mimico (Ont.) High Sch.; Univ. of Toronto B.A.Sc. (Chem. Engn.) 1955, Ph.D. 1961; Univ. of Birmingham M.Sc. (Thermodynamics) 1957; m. Gloria June Profit; 4 children: PROF. OF AEROSPACE ENGN. SCIENCE, INST. FOR AEROSPACE STUDIES, UNIV. OF TORONTO 1968– ; Asst. Dean, Sch. of Grad. Studies, Univ. of Toronto 1982–85; Corporate Scientific Advisor, Sciex Div., MDS Health Group; mem., Science Counc. of Can. 1987–92; Asst. Prof. present Inst. 1962, Assoc. Prof. 1964, Assoc. Dir. 1973–81; Pres. AERCOL 1969–71; holds several patents on Atmospheric Pressure Chem. Ionization Mass Spectroscopy; recipient Financial Post Best Business Venture Award 1979; Barringer Award in Applied Spectroscopy 1984; Bell Canada, Forum Award for excellence in furthering corporate-university cooperation in research 1990; Consultant to many U.S. and Candn. firms; author over 50 research papers rarefied gasdynamics, molecular beams, space simulation and instrumentation, trace gas analysis, mass spectroscopy; Fellow, Royal Soc. of Can.; Royal Soc. of Arts; Candn. Aeronautics and Space Inst.; mem., Assn. Prof. Engrs. Prov. Ont.; recreations: sailing, skiing; Office: 4925 Dufferin St., Downsview, Ont. M3H 5T6.

**FRENCH, John M.,** B.A., C.A.; executive; b. Toronto, Ont. 16 Aug. 1952; s. Stephen Charles and Margaret Jean (Millar) F.; e. Univ. of W. Ont. Hons. B.A. 1975; C.A. 1977; m. Louise d. Thérèse and Normand Perron 18 Aug. 1973; children: Véronique, Isabelle, David; PRES., CHIEF OPERATING OFFR. AND DIR. DUSTBANE ENTERPRISES LTD. 1986– ; joined Thorne Riddell C.A's 1975–79; Treas. present Co. 1979, Vice Pres. Finance 1980, Exec. Vice Pres. and Dir. 1982–86 and Pres. Modern Building Cleaning Inc. 1984–86; Pres. Ottawa Chapter, Financial Execs. Inst. Can. 1985, Dir. 1986–89; Chrmn., Ottawa-Carleton Economic Development Corp. 1993–94 (Dir. 1990– ;); recreations: golf, skiing, tennis; Clubs: Granite (Toronto); Rideau; Home: 35 Durham Private, Ottawa, Ont. K1M 2J1; Office: 25 Pickering Place, Ottawa, Ont. K1G 3K1.

**FRENCH, Stanley George,** M.A., Ph.D.; educator; b. Hamilton, Ont. 24 Sept. 1933; s. Reginald George and Marie (Lawson) F.; e. Carleton Univ. B.A. 1955; Univ. of Rochester M.A. 1957; Univ. of Va. Ph.D. 1959; Oxford Univ. 1961; Univ. de Nice Institut d'Etudes et de Recherches Interethniques et Interculturelles 1975–76; McGill Univ., Royal Victoria Hosp., Palliative Care Service 1987–88; The Hastings Ctr. 1992; children: Shona Renée, Sean Reginald, Lina, Garner Ewan; Prof. of Philosophy, Concordia Univ. 1974– ; Teaching Asst. Univ. of Rochester 1956–57, Univ. of Va. 1957–59; Asst. Prof. of Philos. Univ. of W. Ont. 1959–65, Assoc. Prof. 1965–68; Visiting Asst. Prof. Univ. of Man. summers 1963, 1964; Prof. of Philos. Sir George Williams Univ. 1968–74, Chrmn. of Philos. 1969–71; Dean of Grad. Studies, Concordia Univ. 1971–86, mem. Senate 1974–86; Research Assoc. Centre for Study of Candn. Philos. Univ. of Ottawa 1978; mem./offr. various comtes. Social Sciences & Humanities Research Council Can. 1980–82; Pres. London Council Adult Educ. 1965–66; Vice Chrmn. Bd. Educ. City of London 1967, Chrmn. 1968; Gov. Sir George Williams Univ. 1969–71; Chrmn. Westmount Sch. Comn. 1972; Tutor, Simone de Beauvoir Inst. 1978–80, 1982–84, Coordinator of Tutors 1979–80; author 'The North West Staging Route' 1957; 'Philosophers Look at Canadian Confederation/La Confédération canadienne: qu'en pensent les philosophes?' 1979; 'Interpersonal Violence, Health and Gender Politics' 1993; author or co-author various book chapters, monographs, articles, papers; mem. Comte. Publ. Standard Works in Candn. Philos., Univ. of Toronto Bibliog. project, Biographical Dictionary of Philosophers 1979– ; recipient Philip Francis du Pont Fellowship 1958–59; Can. Council Research Grant 1962; Humanities Research Council Can. Grant 1968; Brit. Council Visitorship 1972, 1984 and 1992; served with RCAF 1951–56, rank Flying Offr.; Pres. Humanities Assn. Can. London Br. 1965–66; Secy.-Treas. Candn. Assn. Grad. Schs. 1980–81; mem. Candn. Philos. Assn.; Candn. Bioethics Soc.; Am. Philos. Assn.; Mind Assn.; Am. Soc.; Office: 1455 de Maisonneuve Blvd. W., Montréal, Qué. H3G 1M8.

**FRENCH, William,** B.A., D.Litt.; retired literary editor; b. London, Ont. 21 March 1926; s. Harold Edward and Isabel Nimmo (Brash) F.; e. Sir Adam Beck Coll. Inst., London, Ont., 1944; Univ. of W. Ont., B.A. 1948; Harvard Univ. (Nieman Fellow 1955); m. Margaret Jean, d. William C. Rollo, London, Ont., 23 June 1951; children: Jane, Mark, Paul, Susan; Lit. Ed., 'Globe and Mail' 1960–90; Part-time Lectr. in Journalism, Ryerson Polytech. Inst. 1955–83; joined 'Globe and Mail' as Gen. Reporter, 1948; covered educ. and City Hall 1949–54; mem. Ed. Bd., 1956–57 and 1959–60; Staff Writer, 'The Globe Magazine,' 1957–59; author of 'A Most Unlikely Village: A Hist. of Forest Hill,' 1964; contrib. chapter on Sir Sam Hughes to 'The Flamboyant Canadians,' 1964; radio documentaries on CBC; awarded President's Medal, Univ. of W. Ont., for Best Gen. Mag. Article Pub. in Can., 1965; won Hon. Mention for ed. writing. Nat. Newspaper Awards, 1957; Winner Nat. Newspaper Award for Crit. Writing, 1977 and 1978; Winner President's Award, Candn. Booksellers Assoc. 1987; D.Litt. (Hon.), Univ. of W. Ont. 1991; Home: 78 North Hills Terrace, Don Mills, Ont. M3C 1M6.

**FRENETTE, The Hon. Thomas Roderick Orville,** B.A., B.C.L., D.S.L., LL.D., J.S.C.; superior court judge; b. Fort Francis, Ont. 2 May 1927; s. Edmond and Marie (Jeanbois) F.; e. Carleton Univ., B.A. 1949; McGill Univ., B.C.L. 1953; admitted Que. Bar 1954; Ottawa Univ., D.S.L. 1958; Ottawa Univ., LL.D. 1960; m. Jeannine Murray 31 Dec. 1949; children: Alain, Christiane, Lucie, Anne, Charles, Justin; JUDGE OF THE SUPERIOR COURT OF QUEBEC 1978– ; law prac. 1954–65; Part-time Lectr., Univ. of Ottawa 1960–68; Que. Bar Admission Course 1974–75; Asst. Crown Attorney, Hull 1960–63; Chief Crown Attorney 1963–65; Judge of Prov. Court 1965–78; Sec.-Treas., Hull Bar 1960; Trustee 1964–65; Extve. Mem., Que. Judge's Assn. 1973–75; Pres. 1974–75; Vice-Pres., Candn. Assn. of Prov. Court Judges 1977–78; Mem., Candn. Bar Assn.; Candn. Conf. of Fed. Judges; author: 'Quantum of Damages in Quebec' 1960, 'Assessment of Damages in Quebec ' 1966 (supplements 1973, 76, 79, 85); Home: 1045 Perry Rd., Aylmer, Que. J8V 6C2; Office: Court House, 17 Laurier St., Rm. 1.374, Hull, Que. J8X 4C1.

**FRENKEN, Hubert H.,** B.A.; statistician; b. Roggel, Netherlands 6 Aug. 1940; s. Wilhelmus Hubertus and Anna Maria (Manders) F.; e. St. Patrick's College, Univ. of Ottawa B.A. 1965; m. Paulette d. Jean-Paul and Berthe Lacasse 4 June 1966; children: Nathalie, Paul; SENIOR ANALYST, LABOUR & HOUSEHOLD SURVEYS ANALYSIS, STATISTICS CANADA 1990– ; joined Statistics Canada (then Dominion Bur. of Statistics) Nov. 1963; Technical Officer, var. divisions 1963–77; Asst. Chief, Pensions 1977–81; Chief 1981–87; Sr. Analyst, Population Studies 1987–90; Consultant, Privy Council Office and Health & Welfare Canada in devel. of pension policies; Trustee, Pension Plan, Boy Scouts of Canada 1981–87; Mem., Candn. Pensions & Benefits Conf. (formerly CPC); Ont. Council, CPC 1983–84; Ctte. of Supts. of Pensions 1977–87; co-author: 'Pension Plans in Canada' biennial 1978–86, 'Family and Friendship Ties among Canada's Seniors' 1988, 'Canada's Seniors' 1988; author of numerous articles on RRSPs, pension plans and retirement income; recreations: bicycling, baseball, nordic skiing; Home: 2689 Don St., Ottawa, Ont. K2B 6Y4; Office: 5th fl., Jean Talon Bldg., Ottawa, Ont. K1A 0T6.

**FRESCHI, Bruno Basilio,** O.C., B.Arch.(hon), R.C.A., F.R.A.I.C., A.I.B.C.; architect; b. Trail, B.C. 18 Apr. 1937; s. Giovanni and Irma (Pagotto) F.; e. J.L. Crown High Sch. Trail, B.C.; Univ. of B.C. B.Arch. 1961; Arch. Assn. London, Eng. postgrad. studies in arch.; m. Vaune Ainsworth 13 Dec. 1987; children: Dea Rachelle, Anna Nadine, Aaron Basilio, Reuben Alessandro; FOUNDER, BRUNO FRESCHI ARCHITECTURE, PLANNING, RESEARCH 1970– ; Bruno Freschi Architect Inc. (inc. 1986); Founder, Urbanisma Designs Ltd.; Assoc., Erickson Massey Archs. 1964–70; Assoc. Prof. Univ. of B.C. Sch. Arch. 1968–78, Head of Grad. Studies; Chief Arch. Expo '86; Guest Lectr. Simon Fraser Univ., N.S. Sch. Arch., Univ. of Man., Univ. of B.C. Sch. of Arch. & Centre Human Settlements, Bosman Mont. Sch. Arch.; Vice Pres. & Regional Chrmn. Can. Council Explorations Program 1973–75; Trustee, Vancouver Art Gallery 1973–74; Dir. and Vice Pres., Extve. of Civic Arts Council 1966–71; mem. Civic Design Panel Vancouver 1968–70; mem. Candn. Extve. Service Overseas (volunteer consultant arch. planning for B.C. Indians) 1971–80; mem. Heritage Adv. Comte. City of Vancouver 1980; Bd. of Dirs., Community Arts Counc. of B.C.; recipient Royal Arch. Inst. Can. Medal 1961; Pilkington Glass Travelling Fellowship in Arch. 1961; Can. Council Grant – Aspen Internat. Design Conf. 1967; AIBC Design Award 1968; Aspen Design Conf. IBM Fellow 1982; Confratellanza Italo-Canadese Man of the Year Award 1983; Gov. Gen.'s Medal 1983, RAIC Fellowship 1983; Sweney Award, Professional of the Year 1983; Merit Award, Canadian Wood Council 1984; Officer of the Order of Canada 1987; chosen as chief architect, planner, designer for a new town, requiring a master plan for a hotel, casino, villas and marina in Little Bay, Montserrat, West Indies; renovation of 19th century factory to fashion & design centre, 611 Alexander, Vancouver, B.C.; commercial and residential complex, 3033 Cambie, Vancouver, B.C.; maj. comns. incl. Master Plan and Design for Expo '86, 5 award homes 1964–82, MacMillan Bloedel Research Centre 1983, Burnaby Jamatkhana and Centre (first Ismaili Mosque in North Am.) 1983, Georgia Pl. 1980, Wickaninnish Interpretive Centre 1982, Cath. Sq. 1983, Burnaby Mun. Centre 1973–78, B.C. Place Design Consultant Stadium, Pier A Victoria 1982–83, Whistler Village Coordinating Arch. 1980; author numerous publs.; mem. Arch. Inst. B.C. (Council 1968–71 & Extve. Vancouver Chapter); Royal Arch. Inst. Can.; Royal Candn. Acad.; World Future Soc.; Downtown Vancouver Assn.; mem., Tarrytown 100 New York; recreations: painting, squash, mountain hiking, skiing.

**FREY, Gerrard (Gary) Rupert,** B.Comm., M.B.A.; education administrator; b. Medicine Hat, Alta. 7 June 1943; s. Walter and Margaret (Materi) F.; e. Univ. of Calgary B.Comm. (with distinction) 1970; Harvard Univ. M.B.A. 1972; m. Karen d. Andrew and Elizabeth Johnson 27 Aug. 1968; children: Samantha Elizabeth, Jonathan Edward; EXECUTIVE VICE-PRESIDENT, THE BANFF CENTRE FOR CONTINUING EDUCATION 1987– ; articled with Arthur Andersen & Co. 1970; Sr. Extve., Principal Group Ltd. & Dir. & Vice-Pres., Collective Securities Ltd. 1972–73; Program Mgr., TBC School of Mngt. 1974–75; Mgr., Financial Serv. 1976–81; Vice-Pres., Finance & Admin., The Banff Centre 1981–87 (concurrently Vice-Pres., Sch. of Mngt. 1981–83); Acting Pres. 1991–93; Former Dir., Chair & Chair, Extve. Ctte, Sunshine Village Corp. 1983–89; Former Dir., Koszec & Assoc. Ltd. 1974–84; Councillor, Canada West Foundation 1983– ; Comemorative Medal, 125th Anniversary of Candn. Confed.; several past executive positions in community and Banff Centre; Comn. Officer, RCAC (Militia), South Alberta Light Horse 1967–8; King's Own Calgary Regiment 1969–70; Chief Instructor, Mountain Training,Nat. Army Cadet Camp 1968–70; Mem., Candn. Assn. of Univ. Business Officer; Mem., Rotary Club of Banff; Candn. Ctte. for a Triple E Senate; recreations: golf, skiing, music; clubs: Banff Springs Golf, Riverside Golf & Country, Harvard Business School; Home: P.O. Box 698, 115 St. Julien Rd., Banff, Alta. T0L 0C0; Office: P.O. Box 1020, Banff, Alta. T0L 0C0.

**FREY, Paul B.;** performer, opera singer; b. Kitchener, Ont. 20 Apr. 1941; s. John H. and Lucinda B. (Brubacher) F.; e. Elmire Dist. H.S.; Univ. of Toronto, dipl. in music; m. Linda d. David and Elva Horst 19 June 1967; one s.: Benjamin; during the past six years has performed in the world's most reputed opera houses making him Canada's currently best known Helden Tenor: Bayreuth Fest., Munich, Bonn, Leipzig, Covent Garden (London), Barcelona, La Scala Milan, Berlin, Tokyo, Sydney, Moscow, Paris, The MET (N.Y.); previously house tenor at Basel, Switz. 1979–86; began opera career with tour group of Candn. Opera Co. 1977; recorded 'Ariadne auf Naxos' with J. Norman, E. Gruberova, J. Varady, D. Fischer-Dieskau, O. Bär, R. Asmus, 'Die Frau Ohne Schatten' with C. Struder, U. Vinzing, H. Schwarz, R. Kollo, A. Muff, et al., 'Lohengrin' with the company at Bayreuth Fest.; Home: Neugarten 22, 4117 Burgil, Switzerland.

**FRICK, Elizabeth Anne,** B.A., M.S.L.S.; educator; b. Ottawa, Ont. 3 Apl. 1936; d. Wilfrid (dec.) and Elizabeth Moffatt (Stewart) Sanders; e. Jarvis and Lawrence Park Coll. Insts. Toronto 1954; Univ. of Toronto Trinity Coll. B.A. (Hons.) 1958; Syracuse Univ. M.S.L.S. 1968; m. Stephen s. Ruth Ann Manning Frick 13 Sept. 1958; children: Kristin Elena, Rachel Alissa, Robin Stewart;

PROF. OF LIB. AND INFO. STUDIES, DALHOUSIE UNIV. 1985– ; Reference Lib. M.P. Catherwood Lib. N.Y. State School Ind. & Labour Relations, Cornell Univ. 1970–71; Assoc. Lib. Reference Colls. Cornell Univ., Olin Lib. 1972; Reference Lib. Earlham Coll. Richmond, IN 1972–76; Project Lib. for CLR, LSEP 1977–78; Head of User Services and Assoc. Prof. Lib. Univ. of Colorado, Colorado Springs 1976–83; Visiting Asst. Prof. present Univ. 1982, Asst. Prof. 1983; cons. various lib. and ednl. progs.; recipient: Council Lib. Resources Lib. Service Enhancement Prog. Grant 1977–78; British Council Grant 1986; author: 'Library Research Guide to History:Illustrated Search Strategy' 1980; ed. and contbr. 'A Place to Stand: User Education in Canadian Libraries' 1988; Mem. Ed. Bd. 'Research Strategies' 1992– ; author, numerous scholarly articles; consulting; Mem. Bd. of Dirs., Assoc. for Women's Residential Facilities, Halifax/Dartmouth 1992– ; mem. Am. Lib. Assn.; Assn. Coll. & Rsch. Libs.; Candn. Lib. Assn.; Candn. Assn. Coll. & Univ. Libs.; Candn. Assn. Grad. Edn. Lib., Archival & Info. Studies (Sec.-Treas. 1984–85); Assn. Lib. & Info. Sci. Edn.; Atlantic Provs. Library Assn.; awarded Commemorative Medal for 125th Anniversary of Candn. Confederation; Home: 6369 Coburg Rd., #906, Halifax, N.S. B3H 4J7; Office: Halifax, N.S. B3H 4H8.

**FRIDERES, James S.,** Ph.D.; university professor; associate dean research; b. Algona, Iowa 6 Aug. 1943; s. Prosper and Susan (Zeimet) F.; e. Montana State Univ. B.Sc. 1965; Washington State Univ., M.A. 1966; Ph.D. 1970; m. Carol, d. Carroll and Audrey Sinclair, 27 June 1965; children: Steffani; Jeréme; DIR., RESEARCH CENTRE FOR CANADIAN ETHNIC STUDIES, UNIV. CALGARY since 1982; Vice-Pres. consulting firm, HERA; Teacher, Univ. Man. 1969; Univ. Calgary 1971; Dalhousie Univ. 1981; Univ. Hawaii 1986; Assoc. Dean of Research, Univ. Calgary; author 'Canada's Indians,' 1974; 'Native Peoples in Canada' 1992; Editor 'A World of Communities' 1992; co-ed. Canadian Ethnic Studies; book review ed. Journal Comparative Family Studies 1976–87; mem. Canadian Assn. of Sociology & Anthropology; Home: 53 Hawkbury Close, N.W., Calgary, Alta. T3G 3N2; Office: Dept. Sociology, Univ. Calgary, Calgary, Alta. T2N 1N4.

**FRIDERICHSEN, Blanche Alexia,** B.A., B.L.Sc., M.Ed.; retired education consultant; b. Saskatoon, Sask. 21 March 1925; d. Alexander and Myrtle Jane (Henderson) Irvine; e. Univ. of Sask. B.A. 1948; Univ. of Toronto B.L.S. (on scholarship) 1949; Univ. of Alta. M.Ed. 1974; m. Matthias Godske Andreas Friderichsen, Denmark 28 Aug. 1956; Prov. Sch. Libraries Consultant, Alta. Educ. 1966–87; retired 1987; joined Edmonton Pub. Lib. Children's Services 1949–52; initiated children's services Bromley Pub. Lib., Kent, Eng. 1953–55; mem. Acquisitions Dept. Univ. of Toronto, Cataloging Dept. McGill Univ. 1955–56; Head of Circulation Edmonton Pub. Lib. 1957–59; Summer Session Lecturer, Univ. of Alta. 1959–61; Lib. Supvr. Co. of Strathcona, Sherwood Park, Alta. 1959–66; rec'd A.T.A. Learning Resources Council Award of Excellence 1978; Co-Chrmn., Internat. Assn. of School Librarianship Conf. 1982; Gov't Rep. on Sch. Library Network Technology Project 1983; rec'd. A.T.A. Greater Edmonton Learning Resource Counc. Award of Merit 1984; presenter at national and internat. confs.; Chairperson, Gov't. Task Force that developed 'Policies, Guidelines, Procedures and Standards for Alberta School Libraries' 1984 and 'Focus on Learning'; author numerous articles sch. lib. services; Assessor, Career Development & Assessment Centers for Librarians, Univ. of Washington, Seattle; recreations: golf, reading, writing, entertaining, crafts, world-wide travel; Home: 14703 – 51 Ave., Edmonton, Alta. T6H 5E6.

**FRIDHANDLER, Daryl S.,** B.A., LL.B.; b. Montreal, Que. 9 Oct. 1956; s. Louis Fridhandler and Ann Rose (Parleman) Gorber; e. Univ. de Moncton; McGill Univ. B.A. 1980 (Scarlet Key Award 1980); Dalhousie Univ. LL.B. 1983; m. Ellen d. Arnold and Geta Churgin 20 July 1986; children: Arnold, Rachel Sarah; PARTNER, BURNET, DUCKWORTH & PALMER 1990– ; called to Bar of Alta. 1984; Instr. in Comm. Law Alta. Bar Admission Course 1988– ; mem. Candn. Bar Assn. (Chrmn. Natural Resources Sect. Alta. 1987–88); Law Soc. Alta.; Calgary Bar Assn.; Federal Energy Bar (U.S.); Royal Philatelic Soc. Can.; Brit. N.Am. Philatelic Soc.; Am. Philatelic Soc.; Trustee & Vice-Chrmn., Calgary Public Library 1993– ; mem. Candn. Library Assn.; Jewish; Liberal; recreation: philatelics; Club: Calgary Petroleum; Home: 9924 Patton Rd. S.W., Calgary, Alta. T2V 5G2; Office: 1400, 350 – 7th Ave. S.W., Calgary, Alta. T2P 3N9.

**FRIDMAN, Gerald Henry Louis,** Q.C., M.A., B.C.L., LL.M., F.R.S.C.; barrister; educator; b. London, Eng. 24 Oct. 1928; s. Henry and Sarah (Cohen) F.; e. Oxford Univ., M.A. 1952, B.C.L. 1949; Univ. of Adelaide, LL.M. 1955; m. Janet Margaret, d. Ellis Blaskey, Sheffield, Eng., 4 Jan. 1959; children: Sara Jayne, Saul Benjamin David, Penelope Louise, Candida Helen; PROF. OF LAW, UNIV. OF WESTERN ONTARIO; Prof. and Dean, Faculty of Law, Univ. of Alta., 1969–75; read law with S. Lincoln; called to Bar of Eng. 1950, Bar of Alta. 1972; Bar of Ont. 1977; Q.C. 1985; Barrister-at-Law, Eng., 1950–53; Lectr. and Senior Lectr. in Law, Univ. of Adelaide, 1953–56; Lectr., Sr. Lectr. and Reader in Law, Univ. of Sheffield, 1957–69; author 'Law of Agency' (6th ed. 1990); 'Modern Law of Employment' 1963; 'Sale of Goods' 1966; 'Modern Tort Cases' 1968; 'Bankruptcy Law & Practice' 1970; 'Studies in Canadian Business Law' 1971; 'Sale of Goods in Canada' (3rd ed. 1986); 'Law of Contract in Canada' (2nd ed. 1986); 'Introduction to the Law of Torts' 1978; 'Restitution' (2nd ed. 1992); 'Law of Torts in Canada' vol. I, 1989, vol. II, 1990; 'Fridman on Torts' 1990; also numerous essays and articles in various prof. journs.; Fellow, Royal Soc. of Can. 1991; Walter Owen Book Prize 1991; mem., Soc. Pub. Teachers Law; Assn. Candn. Law Teachers; Law Soc. Upp. Can.; Jewish; recreations: music, theatre, travel; Clubs: Oxford Union Soc.; Wig and Pen; United Oxford and Cambridge; Home: Unit 3–1025, Brough St., London, ON; Offices: Faculty of Law, Univ. of Western Ont., London, Ont. N6A 3K7 and Cohen, Highley, Vogel and Dawson, One London Pl., 255 Queens Ave., 11th Floor, London, Ont. N6A 5R8.

**FRIDMAN, Josef Josel;** management holding company executive; b. Rubcousk, U.S.S.R. 24 Dec. 1945; came to Can. 1949; s. Moishe and Malka (Hersfeld) F.; e. McGill Univ. B.Comm. 1966, Lic. in Acctg. 1968, B.C.L. 1970; m. Georgette d. George and Anna (Kertesz) Weiss 23 Aug. 1970; children: Richard Samuel, Kenneth Howard, Michelle Sarah; SENIOR VICE-PRES., LAW, BCE INC. 1993– ; Solicitor, Bell Canada, Montreal, Que. 1971–74; Asst. Vice-Pres., Taxes, Bell Canada 1974–78; Asst. Vice-Pres., Corp. Performance Operations, Bell Canada 1978–79; Asst. Gen. Counsel, Bell Canada 1979–83; General Counsel, Bell Canada Enterprises Inc. (subsequently changed to BCE Inc. 1988), Montreal, Que. 1983–85; Vice-Pres. & Gen. Counsel, BCE Inc. 1985–90; Sr. Vice-Pres., Law and Corp. Services, BCE Inc. 1991–93; Bd. of Dirs., Telesat Canada, Ottawa; TMI Communications Inc., Ottawa; Alouette Telecommunications Inc., Montréal; Télébec ltée, Montréal; BCE Telecom Internat. Inc., Montreal; BCE Corporate Services Inc., Montréal; Past Pres., Jewish Family Services, Social Services Centre; Past Mem. Bd., United Talmud Torahs of Montreal; Allied Jewish Community Services; Baron de Hirsch Inst. and certain affiliated organizations; recipient, John W. Cook K.C. Prize; Minister of Edn. Gold Medal; I.M.E. Prize in Commercial Law; Lazarus Phillips Prize; Louis H. Rohrlick Prize (all from McGill Univ.) 1970; Mem. ABA; Candn. Inst. Chartered Accts.; Candn. Tax Found.; Inst. Chartered Accountants of Ont.; Candn. Chamber of Commerce; Order of Chartered Accountants of Que.; Candn. Bar Assn.; Internat. Bar Assn.; Montreal Bar Assn.; Quebec Bar Assn.; Jewish; Avocations: golf, skiing, tennis, reading; Clubs: University Club of Montreal; Saint James's Club of Montréal; Pinegrove Country Club; Home: 16 Malta Ave., Dollard des Ormeaux, Que. H9B 2J7; Office: 1000 de La Gauchetière St. West, Suite 3700, Montreal, Que. H3B 4Y7.

**FRIEDENBERG, Edgar Z.,** M.S., Ph.D.; educator; b. New York, N.Y. 18 March 1921; s. Edgar M. and Arline Rai (Zodiag) F.; e. Centenary Coll. Shreveport, La. B.S. 1938; Stanford Univ. M.A. 1939; Univ. of Chicago Ph.D. 1946; Prof. Dalhousie Univ. since 1970; Prof. Emeritus 1986; Asst. and Assoc. Prof. Brooklyn Coll. 1953–64; Prof. Univ. of Cal. (Davis) 1964–67; State Univ. of N.Y. Buffalo 1967–70; taught summer sch. Wash. Univ. St. Louis 1962, 1963; Cornell Univ. 1964; Harvard Univ. 1970; Visiting Prof. of Law, SUNY at Buffalo, fall 1986; served with USNR 1944–45; author 'The Vanishing Adolescent' 1959; 'Coming of Age in America' 1965; 'The Dignity of Youth and Other Atavisms' 1965; 'R.D. Laing' 1973; 'The Disposal of Liberty and Other Industrial Wastes' 1975; 'Deference to Authority: The Case of Canada,' 1980; frequent contrib. to various mags. and journs.; mem. Am. Civil Liberties Union; Candn. Civil Liberties Assn.; Soc. Study Social Problems; Candn. Soc. Study Educ.; Am. Assn. Univ. Profs.; Pres. Dalhousie Univ. Faculty Assn. 1980–81; Samuel Weiner Distinguished Visitor, University of Manitoba, 1982; Speaker, Conf. on the Educ. Legacy of Romanticism, Calgary Inst. for the Humanities 1988; Lectr., Stanford Coll. in Maine and Bay of Fundy 1991; Conf. Speaker, 'The Charter 10 Years Later' B.C. Civil Liberties Assoc. 1992; Zen Jewish; Home: Conrad's Rd., Hubbards, N.S. B0J 1T0; Office: Dalhousie University, Halifax, N.S. B3H 3J5.

**FRIEDENTHAL, Peter;** retail executive; b. Johannesburg, S.Africa 28 Aug. 1939; s. Hans F.; m. Roslyn d. Cyril and Gloria Hauser 31 Oct. 1989; PRES. AND OWNER YÜ FASHION LTD. 1989– ; mng. dir. largest fixture co. and dir. largest pub. co. S.Africa 1968–77; Owner and Founder House of Knives 1979–88; listed in 'Entrepreneurs' by Alan Gould; recreations: tennis, swimming, riding; Club: Toronto Lawn Tennis; Home: 277 Lytton Blvd., Toronto, Ont. M5N 1R7.

**FRIEDL, Maj. Gen. Maximilian Theodore,** C.D.; consultant; retired from Canadian armed forces; b. Germany, 28 Jan. 1923; s. Max Julius and Elizabeth (Schlemmer) F.; came to Can. 1928; e. Estevan (Sask.) Coll. Inst.; Univ. of Sask., B.Sc. 1949; Univ. of London, City & Guilds Coll., M.Sc. (Aeronautical Engn.) 1953; m. Ruth Margaret, d. late Lorne Billingsley, 5 Sept. 1947; children: Karen Elizabeth, Catherine Anne; PRESIDENT, MAX T. FRIEDL CONSULTANTS INC.; after a variety of staff and command appointments in Europe, Ottawa and Eastern Canada, promoted Maj. Gen. and apptd. Assoc. Adm. Materiel 1973; retired 1977; Chrmn. Aircraft Accident Review Bd. 1979–84; Advr. Candn. Aviation Safety Bd. 1985; mem., Candn. Aeronautics and Space Inst.; recreation: golf; Club: Rideau; Home: 1634 Amberdale Cres., Ottawa, Ont. K1H 7B3.

**FRIEDLAND, Martin Lawrence,** O.C., Q.C., B.Com., LL.B., Ph.D., F.R.S.C.; educator; b. Toronto, Ont. 21 Sept. 1932; s. Jack and Mina (Rogul) F.; e. Forest Hill Coll. Inst. Toronto 1951; Univ. of Toronto B.Com. 1955, LL.B. 1958; Cambridge Univ. Ph.D. 1967; m. Judith Fern d. Michael Pless, Toronto, Ont. 19 June 1958; children; Tom, Jenny, Nancy; PROF. OF LAW, UNIV. OF TORONTO; Dean, Faculty of Law 1972–79; Asst. and Assoc. Prof. Osgoode Hall Law Sch. 1961–65; Assoc. Prof. and Prof. Univ. of Toronto since 1965; University Prof., Univ. of Toronto since 1985; Sr. Fellow, Massey Coll. since 1985; Fellow, Candn. Inst. for Advanced Research since 1986; Visiting Prof., Hebrew Univ. and Tel Aviv Univ., 1979; Visiting Fellow, Clare Hall Cambridge Univ., 1980; assoc. with various Govt. Comtes. and Comns. incl. Atty.-Gen's Comte. on Enforcement of Law Relating to Gambling 1962, Jt. Comte. on Legal Aid 1965, Atty.-Gen's Comte. on Securities Leg. 1965, Min. of Reform Insts. Comte. on Regional Detention Centres 1967, Task Force on Can. Corps. Act 1968, Candn. Comte. on Corrections 1969, Solr.-Gen.'s Task Force on Gun Control Leg. 1975, Comn. of Inq. re Certain Activities of R.C.M.P., 1979; Criminal Code Review 1980– ; fulltime mem. of Law Reform Comm. of Canada 1971–72; Chrmn., Ont. Task Force on Inflation Protection for Employment Pension Plans 1986–87; part-time mem., Ont. Securities Comn. 1989–91; rec'd Angus MacMurchy Gold Medal Faculty of Law Univ. of Toronto; Treas.'s Medal Bar Admission Course Osgoode Hall; called to Bar of Ont. 1960; cr. Federal Q.C. 1975; Fellow, Royal Soc. of Can. 1983; Candn. Assoc. of Law Teachers/Law Reform Comm. of Canada Award for Outstanding Contribution to Legal Research and Law Reform 1985; U. of T. Alumni Faculty Award 1987; David W. Mundell Medal for Distinguished Contributions to Letters and Law 1990; apptd. Officer of the Order of Canada 1990; author 'Detention Before Trial' 1965; 'Double Jeopardy' 1969; 'Courts and Trials' 1975; 'Access to the Law' 1975; 'National Security: The Legal Dimensions' 1980; 'The Trials of Israel Lipski' 1984 (awarded Crime Writers of Canada Award for Non-fiction); 'A Century of Criminal Justice' 1984; 'The Case of Valentine Shortis' 1986; 'Sanctions and Rewards in the Legal System' 1989; (with Trebilcock and Roach) 'Regulating Traffic Safety' 1990; 'Securing Compliance' 1990; (with Kent Roach) 'Criminal Law and Procedure: Cases and Materials' 6th ed. 1991; 'Rough Justice: Essays on Crime in Literature' 1991; numerous articles; Office: Faculty of Law, Univ. of Toronto, Toronto, Ont. M5S 2C5.

**FRIEDLANDER, John Benjamin,** B.S., M.A., Ph.D., F.R.S.C.; b. Toronto, Ont. 4 Oct. 1941; s. Daniel Theodore and Beatrice Adele (Axler) F.; e. Univ. of Toronto B.S. 1965; Univ. of Waterloo M.A. 1966; Penn. State Univ. Ph.D. 1972; m. Cherryl d. Russell and Irene Koontz 1 Sept. 1974; children: Jonathan, Diana, Amanda, Keith; PROF. OF MATH. UNIV. OF TORONTO 1982– , Chrmn. of Math. 1987–91; studies at Princeton Inst. for Advanced Study 1972–74, 1983–84, 1990–91; Lectr. Mass. Inst. of Technol. 1974–76; Visiting Prof. Scuola Normale Pisa, Italy 1976–77; Rsch. Prof., MSRI Berkeley 1991–92; Asst. Prof. present Univ. 1977–79, Assoc. Prof. 1980–82; Asst. Prof. Univ.

of Ill. 1979–80; Trustee, Beatty, Blyth, and Fields Funds 1987–91; Dir., Fields Math. Rsch. Inst.; Candn. Number Theory Assn.; Math Discipline Rep. RSC; Div. Fellowship Rev. Comm. RSC 1990–93; Mem., NSERC Grant Comm. 1991–94; AMS Comm. 1991–94; author 10 book chapters in conference proceedings, 50 articles rsch. jours.; invited lectr. 35 univs., 40 confs.; referee for NSF, NSERC, Canada Council, 20 Rsch. J.; organizer or co-organizer 4 confs.; Fellow, Royal Soc. of Can. 1988; mem., Am. Math. Soc.; Am. Men and Women of Sci.; recreations: bridge, chess, sailing; Home: 22 Stonemanse Court, Scarborough, Ont. M1G 3V3; Office: Toronto, Ont. M5S 1A1.

**FRIEDMAN, Sydney M.,** M.D., C.M., M.Sc., Ph.D., F.R.S.C.; university professor; b. Montreal, Que. 17 Feb. 1916; s. Jack and Minnie (Signer) F.; e. McGill Univ., B.A. 1938, M.D., C.M. 1940, M.Sc. 1941, Ph.D. 1946; m. Constance A., d. I.F. Livingstone, Montreal, 23 Sept. 1940; PROF. EMERITUS, DEPT. OF ANATOMY, UNIV. OF BRIT. COLUMBIA 1985; Demonst. in Histol., McGill Univ., 1940–41; Teaching Fellow in Anat., 1941–43; apptd. Asst. Prof., 1944, Assoc. Prof., 1948; Chrmn., Dept. of Anat., U.B.C., 1950–81; Prof. 1950–85; served in 2nd World War 1943–44; Flight-Lieut., R.C.A.F. (Med.); rec'd. Ciba Award for Ageing Studies, 1955; Pfizer Trav. Fellow of Clin. Research Inst., Montreal 1971; J.C.B. Grant Award, Candn. Assn. of Anats. 1982; Outstanding Service Award of the Heart Foundations of Can. 1981; Distinguished Achievement Award, Candn. Hypertension Soc. 1987; awarded Commemorative Medal for 125th Anniversary of Candn. Confederation; founding mem. B.C. Heart Foundation; mem., Candn. Assn. of Anats. (Pres. 1965–66); Am. Assn. of Anats. (Extve.); Am. Physiol. Soc.; Candn. Physiol. Soc. (Council 1952–54); Am. Heart Assn.; A.O.A.; Council for High Blood Pressure Research; founding mem., Candn. Hypertension Soc.; author: 'Visual Anatomy,' Vols. I and II (Springfield, Ill.) 1950 and 1952; 'Visual Anatomy,' Vols. I, II and III (New York) 1970, 1971, 1972; and papers on salt and hypertension; Home: 4916 Chancellor Blvd., Vancouver, B.C. V6T 1Z3.

**FRIESEN, Albert David,** B.Sc., M.Sc., Ph.D.; administrator/scientist; b. Winnipeg, Man. 19 May 1947; s. Peter H. and Justina (Penner) F.; e. Univ. of Man., B.Sc. (Hons.) 1969, M.Sc. 1971, Ph.D. 1982; m. Leona M. d. Henry and Helen Wiebe 24 June 1967; children: Selena, Bonita, Tria; PRES., NOVOPHARM BIOTECH. 1991– ; Tech., Metro Waterworks Rsch. & Cont. Lab. (summer) 1967–69; Dir., Plasma Fract. & Rsch., Winnipeg Rh Inst. 1971–83 (Design Chrmn. & Project Mgr. for new facility 1981), Pres. & C.E.O. 1971–90; Cons., A.D. Friesen Enterprises Ltd. 1983– ; Founder, Chair, Pres. & C.E.O., ABI Biotechnology Inc. 1984–91; Founder, Chair, Pres & C.E.O., KAM Scientific Inc. 1989–92; Founder, Pres. & C.E.O., Genesys Pharma Inc.; 1991– ; Adjunct Prof., Dept. of Microbiol. and Faculty of Pharmacy, Univ. of Man. 1984– ; Founder & Bd. Chrmn., Indus. Biotechnol. Assn. of Can. 1986– ; Dir., MEOEC 1987– ; Mem., Candn. Biochem. Soc.; Sigma XI (Extve.) 1978– ; Parental Drug Assn. Inc. 1979– ; Nat. Biotechnol. Network 1983– ; Fin. & Budget Ctee., Man. Rsch. Counc. 1983; Young Pres. Orgn. 1986– ; Chrmn., Fort Garry Mennonite Fellowship 1993– ; (Vice Chrmn. 1987–90); author of 32 sci. paper & 21 abstracts; Home: 77 Shorecrest Dr., Winnipeg, Man.; Office: 147 Hamelin St., Winnipeg, Man. R3T 3Z1.

**FRIESEN, David,** Q.C., M.Sc., LL.B., Dr. Oec. (H.S.G.), LL.D.; b. Russia 16 Nov. 1911; s. David Abram and Aganeta (Driedger) F.; came to Canada 1924; became naturalized Candn., 1929; e. Univ. of Man., LL.B., 1939; Univ. of Minn., M.Sc. (Business Adm.), 1963; LIC. OEC.HSG Switzerland 1967; Ph.D. (Bus. Admin.) Grad. Sch. St. Gallen, Switzerland 1973; LL.D., Univ. of Winnipeg 1981; m. Katherine, d. Abraham J. Loewen, 30 Oct. 1943; three d. and one s.; Sr. Partner, David Friesen & Assoc.; read law with David Laird, Q.C.; called to the Bar of Manitoba, June 1941; cr. Q.C., 1956; mem., Canadian Bar Assn.; Man. Bar Assn.; German-Candn. Business & Prof. Men's Assn. of Man. (Past Pres.); Winnipeg Housebuilders Assn. (Past Pres.); Mennonite Benevolent Soc. (Past Pres.); Chrmn., Menno Simons Coll.; recreations: walking; Clubs: St. Charles Country; Home: 51 Colchester Bay, Winnipeg, Man. R3P 1W9; Office: 711 – 213 Notre Dame Ave., Winnipeg, Man. R3B 1N3.

**FRIESEN, David R.;** pharmaceutical distribution executive; b. Winnipeg, Man. 27 Dec. 1943; e. Univ. of Man. C.M.A. 1968; Stanford Extve. Program 1993; m. Colleen Wilford 26 June 1965; PRES., CHIEF OPERATING OFFR. AND DIR., MEDIS HEALTH AND PHARMACEUTICAL SERVICES INC. 1988– ; Dir., C.W.D.A.; joined National Drug and Chemical Co., Univa Group, Winnipeg 1965, various positions, Vice Pres. Finance and Planning, Treas. 1974; Corporate Dir. Fin. & Acctg., Provigo Group H.O. 1980, Vice Pres. Control and Info. 1984, Sr. Vice Pres. Control and Corporate Services 1985; Home: 67 Devon Rd., Baie d'Urfe, Que. H9X 2W8; Office: 101–3501 Saint- Charles Rd., Kirkland, Que. H9H 4S3.

**FRIESEN, Dawna Joy;** journalist; b. Winnipeg, Man. 31 Dec. 1963; d. Henry and Vivian Grace (Siemens) F.; e. Red River Comm. Coll., Communications dipl. 1984; SOUTHAM FELLOW, UNIVERSITY OF TORONTO 1993–94; Reporter-Anchor, CKX Brandon, Man. 1985–86; Reporter, CJLB Radio Thunder Bay 1986; Reporter-Anchor, CKPR-TV 1986–87; CKND-TV Winnipeg 1987–88; CFQC Saskatoon 1988–89; CBC-TV 1989–90; Reporter, CBC Toronto 1991–92; Documentary Reporter-Anchor, CBC Vancouver 1992–93; Bronze Plaque, Columbus Internat. Film & Video Festival 1992, '93; Office: 4 Devonshire Pl., Toronto, Ont. M5S 1A1.

**FRIESEN, Gerald Arnold,** B.A., M.A., Ph.D.; university professor; b. Prince Albert, Sask. 24 Sept. 1943; s. Arnold John and Jean Catherine (Stewart) F.; e. Prince Albert schools; Univ. of Sask. B.A. (Hons.) 1965; Univ. of Toronto M.A. 1966, Ph.D. 1974; m. Jean d. Prof. Reginald and Nancy Edwards 1974; children: Alexander Usher, Joseph Friesen; TEACHER, ST. PAUL'S COLLEGE, UNIV. OF MANITOBA 1970– ; active in adult education; Co-founder, Canada's Visual History series & Manitoba Studies in Native History series; Candn. Hist. Assn. Macdonald Prize & Regional History Awrd; Dir., Manitoba Labour Education Ctr.; Mem., Candn. Hist. Assn. (Council 1971–81); Manitoba Historical Soc. (Treas. 1976–79; Council 1976–85) Manitoba N.D.P. Provincial Council & Policy Cttes.; author: 'The Canadian Prairies: A History' 1984; co-author: 'Guide to the Study of Manitoba Local History' 1981; editor: 'Manitoba Studies in Native History' 6 vols. 1985–92, 'Canada's Visual History' 70 vols.; Home: 46 Home St., Winnipeg, Man. R3G 1W6; Office: Winnipeg, Man. R3T 2M6.

**FRIESEN, Henry George,** B.Sc., M.D., F.R.C.P.(C), F.R.S.C.; endocrinologist; educator; b. Morden, Man. 31 July 1934; s. Frank Henry and Agnes (Unger) F.; e. Univ. of Man. B.Sc. (Med.), M.D. 1958; m. Joyce Marylin d. Gordon MacKinnon, Halifax, N.S. 12 Oct. 1967; children: Mark Henry, Janet Elizabeth; PRES., MED. RSCH. COUNC. OF CANADA, Ottawa, Ont. 1992; Prof. and Head, Dept. of Physiol., Univ. of Man. 1973–92, Prof. of Med. since 1973; Intern, Winnipeg Gen. Hosp. 1958–59, Asst. Resident 1959–60 and Royal Victoria Hosp. Montreal 1961–62; Research Fellow Med. and Endocrinol. New England Centre Hosp. Boston 1960–61, 1962–63, Research Assoc. 1963–65; Asst. Prof. of Med. Tufts Univ. Sch. of Med. 1965–66; Asst. Prof. of Med. McGill Univ. 1965, Assoc. Prof. 1968–71, Prof. Exper. Med. 1972–73; Associateship, Med. Research Council Can., McGill Univ. 1965–73; mem. Organizing Comte. VI Internat. Endocrine Cong. Hamburg 1976; Breast Cancer Task Force Exper. Biol. Comte. Nat. Insts. Health Bethesda, Md. 1975–77; Task Force N.I.H. Comte. Evaluation Research Needs Endocrinol. and Metabolic Diseases 1978; Chrmn./mem. various comtes., Med. Research Council of Can. (Pres. 1991); rec'd Eli Lilly Award Endocrine Soc. 1974; Gairdner Foundation Award 1977; Sandoz Lectr. Candn. Soc. Endocrinol. & Metabolism 1978; Izaak Walton Killam Mem. Scholarship, 1979; Koch Award, Endocrine Soc. 1987; Officer of the Order of Canada 1987; McLaughlin Medal, Royal Soc. of Can.; Foreign Associate, Nat. Acad. of Sciences U.S.A. 1993; author or co-author numerous publs. endocrinol. and med.; mem. Am. Physiol. Soc.; Endocrine Soc. (Council 1973–76); Candn. Soc. Clin. Investigation (Council 1974–77, Pres. 1978); Candn. Physiol. Soc.; Am. Fed. Clin. Research; Am. Assn. Advanc. Science; Am. Soc. Clin. Investigation; Candn. Soc. Endocrinol. & Metabolism (Pres. 1974); Internat. Soc. Neuroendocrinol.; mem. various ed. bds. med. journs.; Assoc. Ed. 'Canadian Journal of Physiology and Pharmacology' 1974–78; Pres., Can. Soc. for Clinical Investigation, 1978; Mennonite; Office: 5th Flr., Holland Cross, Tower B, 1600 Scott St., Ottawa, Ont. K1A 0W9.

**FRIESEN, Patrick Franz,** B.A. (Hons.); freelance producer; writer; b. Steinbach, Man. 5 July 1945; s. Franz M. and Margaret (Sawatzky) F.; e. Univ. of Man. B.A. (Hons.) 1969; children: Marijke, Nikolaus; films, videos, plays and radio progs. incl. 'Esther Warkov: A Spy in the House' (Producer); 'Don Proch: The Spirit of Asessippi' (writer/dir./producer); 'Patrick Lane' (dir./producer); 'A Ritual of Horses: The Art of Michael Olito' (dir./producer); 'Amanda' (radio play written for CBC Man. 1986); 'Anna' (writer in a collaboration with choreographer Stephanie Ballard and guest artist Margie Gillis; work performed at Gas Station Theatre 1987); 'Noah' (script writer in multi-discipline project performed at Main/Access Gallery Winnipeg 1987); author (poetry) 'the lands i am' 1976; 'bluebottle' 1978; 'The Shunning' 1980, (play adaptation staged by Prairie Theatre Exchange 1985; anthologized in 'New Works' 1987; radio adaptation (CBC) 1990); 'Unearthly Horses' 1984; 'Flicker and Hawk' 1987; 'You Don't Get to be a Saint' (poetry) 1992; 'God's Blue Morris', Niels Hav A Selection of Poems, translated by Per Brask and Patrick Friesen 1993; 'The Raft' (play, staged at the Prairie Theatre Exchange 1992); 'Handful of Rain' (text writer for a multi-discipline collaboration with dance collective, performed at Gas Station Theatre, Winnipeg); 'Blasphemer's Wheel' (selected & new poems) 1994; Founding Pres. Man. Writers Guild; Man. Assn. Playwrights; Playwrights Union Can.; Home: Winnipeg, Man. R3J 3K2.

**FRIESEN, R.B.,** B.Sc.; business executive; b. St. Paul, Alta. 29 Sept. 1941; s. Leonard C. and Jeannette E. (Etiere) F.; e. Univ. of Alta. B.Sc. 1965; m. Jacenta d. Gillis and Malloney Maloney 7 Aug. 1987; children: Richard N., Roberta M.; VICE-PRES., OPNS., FIBERGLAS CANADA INC. 1991– ; Plant Engineering Mgr., present firm 1969–81; Process Engr. Mgr. 1981–82; Plant Mgr. Edmonton 1982–87; Corp. Mgr. H.R. 1987–88; Group Vice-Pres., Insulation 1988–91; Home: 3693 Price Court, Mississauga, Ont. L5L 4S6; Office: 4100 Yonge St., Willowdale, Ont. M2P 2B6.

**FRISQUE, Gilles,** ing.f., Ph.D.; university administrator; b. Brussels, Belgium 18 June 1943; s. Joseph Jean and Georgette Séverine (Versele) F.; e. Univ. de Louvain, agric. engr. 1965, M.Sc. Forestry 1967; Univ. Laval Ph.D. Forestry 1977; m. Cécile d. Jacques Ugeux 17 Oct. 1967; children: Catherine, Véronique; DIR., MULTIREGIONAL FOREST RSCH. CTR., UNIV. OF QUE. 1986– ; Rsch. Scientist, Laurentian Forest Rsch. Ctr. 1968–72; Project Leader, Silviculture & Forest Mngt., Candn. Forestry Serv. 1972–78; Program Mgr., Energy from Forest Biomass 1978–82; Rsch. Prog. Dir., Forest Resources & Protection 1982–85; Mem., Forest Rsch. Adv. Counc. of Can., Forestry Can.; Mem., Le Cons. de la rech. forestière du Qué. Inc.; Mem., James Bay Adv. Ctte. on the Environ.; Mem., Conseil d'Administration du Centre Québécois de Valorisation de la Biomasse; Assoc. Ed., 'Can. J. of Forest Res.'; Mem., Ordre des ing. forestiers du Qué.; Candn. Inst. of Forestry; Assn. forestière québécoise; Internat. Union of Forest Rsch. Orgn.; author of more than 60 sci. & tech. pubns.; Home: 2916, chemin du Foulon, Sillery, Que. G1T 1X4; Office: Institut Armand-Frappier, 531, boul. des Prairies, Laval, Que. H7N 4Z3.

**FRITH, Hon. Royce,** Q.C., B.A., LL.B., D.E.S.(D); senator; retired lawyer; b. Montreal, Que. 12 Nov. 1923; s. George Harry and Annie Beatrice (Royce) F.; e. Lachine (Que.) High Sch.; Parkdale Coll. Inst. Toronto; Univ. of Toronto Victoria Coll. B.A.; Osgoode Hall Law Sch. LL.B.; Univ. of Ottawa Dipl. d'études supérieures (droit); m. Elizabeth Mary (d. 1976) d. William E. Davison (dec.), Port Credit, Ont. 18 June 1948; children: Valerie Elizabeth, Gregory Royce, (d. 1980); Commissioner Royal Comn. on Bilingualism & Biculturalism; Legal Adviser to Commr. of Official Langs.; Lib. cand. Ont. prov. el. 1954; Past Pres. Ont. Lib. Assn. (1961–62); summoned to Senate 1977; Deputy Leader of Government 1980–84; Deputy Leader of Opposition 1984–91; Leader of Opposition 1991–93; Liberal; Protestant; recreations: music, theatre, golf, tennis, squash; Clubs: Links O'Tay Golf, Perth; Home: Apt. 1206, 151 Bay St., Ottawa, Ont. K1R 7T2; Offices: 10 Market Square, Perth, Ont. K7H 1V7 and The Senate, Parliament Bldgs., Ottawa, Ont. K1A 0A4.

**FRITZ, Irving Bamdas,** D.D.S., Ph.D.; cell biologist; scientist; b. Rocky Mount, N.C. 11 Feb. 1927; s. Henry Norman and Rose (Bamdas) F.; e. Univ. of Richmond 1943–47; Med. Coll. of Va., D.D.S. 1948; Univ. of Chicago, Ph.D. 1951; Univ. of Copenhagen, Post-doctoral fellowship 1953–55; m. 1st Helen (d. 1971), d. late Ralph Bridgman, N.C., 20 Aug. 1950; 2ndly Angela, d. late William McCourt, 21 Oct. 1972; children: Jonathan Bridgman, Winston Romaine, Rachel Bamdas, Zoë Benedicte McCourt, Daniel William; Sr. Rsh. Fellow, Dept. of Cell Physiology, Babraham Rsch. Institute, Babraham Hall, Cambridge, England 1991– ; Instr. Harvard Dental Sch. 1951; Asst. Dir. Dept. Metabolism & Endocrinol. Michael Reese Hosp. Chicago 1955; Asst. Prof. Dept. Physiol. Univ. of Mich. 1956, Assoc. Prof. 1960, Prof. 1964; Prof. Banting and Best Dept. Medical Research, Univ. of Toronto 1968–84 (Chrmn. and Prof. 1968–78) and University Professor, Univ. of Toronto, 1984–92, University Professor Emeritus 1992– ; Univ.

of Wash. Visiting Scholar Dept. of Biochem. 1963–64; Guggenheim Fellow, ARC Inst. of Animal Physiology, Babraham, Cambridge, 1978–79; Gairdner Award, 1980; AFRC, Dept. Molecular Embryology, Babraham, Cambridge 1988–89; served with US Army, Walter Reed Army Med. Service Grad. Sch. 1951–53; rank 1st Lt.; discovered action of carnitine on fatty acid metabolism and elucidated mechanisms of action; contrib. toward studies on hormone action (adrenal cortical steroids, insulin, gonadotropins, androgens); contrib. toward understanding of clusterin, spermatogenesis, and cell to cell interactions; author 'Insulin Action' 1972 and over 150 publs. and reviews in biol. journs.; mem. Am. Soc. Cell Biol.; Am. Soc. Biochem. and Molec. Biol.; Endocrine Soc.; Soc. for Study of Reproduction; recreations: squash, gardening, writing, hiking; Home: 79 Millway, Grantchester, Cambridge CB3 9ND England; Office: Dept. Cell Physiol., Babraham Rsch. Institute, Cambridge CB2 4AT England.

**FRIZE, Monique,** O.C., B.Sc.(EE), M.Phil., D.I.C., M.B.A., Doctorate, P.Eng., Hon. Doct.; educator; b. Montreal, Que. 7 Jan. 1942; d. Claude Bernard (Aubry) and Marie-Paule (Saint-Onge); e. Univ. d'Ottawa B.Sc.(EE) 1966; Imp. Coll. of Sci. & Technol. London, UK M.Phil, D.I.C. 1970; Univ. de Moncton M.B.A. 1986; Erasmus Universiteit Rotterdam Doctorate 1989; Hon. Doct., Univ. of Ottawa 1992; m. Robin David Peter s. Maurice and Maria Frize 10 Aug. 1968; one s. Patrick Nicholas; PROF. OF ELECT. ENG. AND NORTHERN TELECOM NSERC CHAIR IN WOMEN IN ENG. UNIV. OF N.B. 1989– ; Biomed. Eng. (CE) Hôpital Notre-Dame (1971) becoming Dir. Biomed. Services 7 hosps. S.E. N.B. (1979); cons. eng. Can. various projects Bangladesh and Morocco hosp. equipment maintenance; Chair first Internat. Clin. Eng. Div. Internat. Fedn. Med. & Biol. Eng.; Dir. CADMI/CADCAM and Incutech N.B.; mem. Comité Consultatif des Sciences et de la Technologie de Radio-Can. 1985–89; Nat. Advisory Bd. on Science and Technology 1990; Nat. Innovations Advisory Ctte. 1991; Athlone Fellow 1967–69; Affil. Sci. Staff Dr. Everett Chalmers Hosp. Fredericton; Chair, Candn. Ctte. on Women in Engineering 1990–92; mem. ed. bd. 2 internat. sci. jours.; author various papers, world-wide conf. presentations; mem. Inst. Elect. & Electronics Engs.; Biol. Eng. Soc. UK; Assn. Profl. Engs. N.B.; Officer, Order of Canada 1993; recreations: languages, skiing, gardening, music, Scottish country dancing, travel; Office: Fredericton, N.B. E3B 5A3.

**FROHLICH, Jiri J.,** M.D., F.R.C.P.(C); physician; educator; b. Nespeky, Czechoslovakia 12 Aug. 1942; s. Jan J. and Bozena Marie (Rihova) F.; e. Karlova Univ. Prague M.D. 1965; m. Milana d. Ivan and Stanislava Horska 27 June 1970; children: Teresa Alice, P. Thomas; DIR. LIPID CLINIC, UNIVERSITY HOSP. and Head of Med. Biochem. 1980– ; Prof. of Pathol. Univ. of B.C. 1987– ; internship and residency Montréal Gen. Hosp.; MRC Rsch. Fellow 1968–69, 1973–74; Med. Biochem. Vancouver Gen. Hosp. 1974–80; Asst. Prof. Univ. B.C. 1979, Assoc. Prof. 1985; mem. Orgn. Ctte. Candn. Consensus Conf. Cholestrol & Lipoproteins 1987; recipient B.C., Manitoba and Ontario Soc. Clin. Chems. Award 1985, 1988 and 1989; Dir. B.C. Heart Found. 1983–1988; co-ed. 'Lipoprotein Deficiency Syndromes' 1986; author over 100 rsch. papers lipoprotein biochem. & pathol.; mem. Candn. Soc. Clin. Chems.; Candn. Assn. Med. Biochems. (Council 1982–86); Candn. Lipoprotein Conf. (Council 1985–87); Candn. Atherosclerosis Soc. (Council 1984–86); Bd. Chrmn., Candn. Cholesterol Reference Found.; recreations: chess, tennis, ping pong; Home: 3011 W. 27th Ave., Vancouver, B.C. V6L 1W6; Office: 4500 Oak St., Vancouver, B.C. V6H 3N1.

**FROMBACH, Hannelore,** M.A.; psychologist, farmer; b. Falkenstein i.V., Germany 22 March 1941; d. Friedrich Ludwig Hinrichs and Annelotte (Messinger) Krull; e. College of Finance Nordkirchen dipl. 1961; Industrie und Handelskammer of Northrhine-Westphalia translator dipl. 1964; Univ. of Regina B.A. (High Hons.) 1988, M.A. 1992; m. Dale s. Hilda and Ernest Frombach 17 Dec. 1964; children: Kirsten, Inger, Britta; PSYCHOLOGIST, REGINA CHILD & YOUTH SERVICES 1990– ; Tax Inspector, Prov. Govt. of Northrhine-Westphalia, Düsseldorf, Germany 1959–64; involved in farming operation 1965– ; Counselling Services, Univ. of Regina 1989; special interest: group work with pregnant teens at Balfour Tutorial last 3 years, Step-Teen Group, psychoeducational & therapeutic groups for parents of teens, workshops on stress in rural Sask.; 1990 George W. Robertson Memorial Scholarship, Sask. Wheat Pool 1988; S.E. Stewart Award in Arts; Most Distinguished Grad., Fac. of Arts (Convocation); Mem., Bd. of Regents, Luther College; High School & Univ. Campus, Univ. of Regina 1990– ; member of several synodical cttes., Lutheran Ch. of Am. (LCA) 1979–85; Rep. at LCA conventions; Church Councillor, St. Paul's Lutheran Ch. Edenwold 1978–84; Mem., Psychological Soc. of Sask.; co-author: 'Where Aspens Whisper' 1981 (Edenwold History Book); Home: Box 148, Edenwold, Sask. S0G 1K0; Office: 1601 College Ave., Regina, Sask.

**FROST, Col. Charles Sydney,** C.D., Q.C., LL.B., LL.D.; b. St. John's, Nfld. 21 June 1922; s. Charles Sydney and Gertrude R. (Hains) F.; e. Nutana Coll. Saskatoon, Sask.; Saint John High Sch., N.B.; Royal Mil. Coll. Kingston, grad. 1942; Osgoode Hall grad. 1949; L.L.D., 1976; m. Margaret Alice, d. late Norman Cabeldu, 2 July 1947; one s. Norman, two d. Janet, Catherine; articled with Tilley, Carson, Morlock and McCrimmon; called to the Bar of Ont. 1949; practised law with Tilley, Carson Morlock and McCrimmon 1949–53; formed own firm 1953; cr. Q.C. 1960; Sr. Partner, Frost and Redway, 1966–84; served with P.P.C.L.I. in Italy and N.W. Europe 1942–45; Acting Second in Command 1945; apptd. P.P.C.L.I. Senate, 1978; Hon. Solicitor P.P.C.L.I. Assoc. 1988; twice wounded; Royal Regt. of Can. 1947–62, Commdr. 1959–62; Hon. Lt. Col. 1967–74, Hon. Col. 1974–82; awarded Can. Forces Decoration and two bars; awarded Candn. Silver Jubilee Medal, 1977; awarded Commemorative Medal for 125th Anniversary of Candn. Confederation 1992; Past Gov. Havergal Coll.; mem. Candn. Scholarship Trust Comte. 1964–77; Canadian Corps of Commissionaires 1981–87; Pres. Toronto Br. Royal Mil. Coll. Club of Can. 1969–70, Nat. Pres. 1971–72; Hon. Solicitor 1980–81; mem. Candn. Mil. Colls. Adv. Bd. 1975–78; Chrmn. Royal Regt. of Can. Foundation 1968–82; Trustee, Havergal College Foundation, 1966–69; Hon. Trustee, Havergal Coll. Foundation 1970–78; Soc. for Study of Egyptian Antiquities; Dir. (1965–72) Ft. York Br., Royal Candn. Legion; author: 'Once A Patricia' 1988; United Ch.; recreations: swimming, tennis, music; Clubs: Granite; Royal Candn. Mil. Inst.; Empire (Life mem. and Dir. 1958–62); Address: 50 Bayview Wood, Toronto, Ont. M4N 1R7.

**FROST, Peter John Charles,** Ph.D.; university professor; b. Johannesburg, S. Africa 30 Aug. 1939; s. Charles Felix and Mary Edith (Hancock) F.; e. Christian Brothers Coll. 1956; Univ. of Witwatersrand, B.Sc. (Hons.) 1960; Univ. of S. Africa, M.Sc. 1968; Univ. of Minnesota, Ph.D. 1973; m. Nola d. Edward and Aileen McMorran 31 Aug. 1963; children: Paul, Caitlin, Maeve; EDGAR F. KAISER PROF. OF ORGANIZATIONAL BEHAVIOUR, UNIV. OF B.C. 1975– , Assoc. Dean, Faculty Development and Professional Programs; Research Fellow, Indus. Relns. Ctr., Univ. of Minnesota 1970–72; Personnel Cons., S. African Breweries 1973–74; Senior Editor, 'Organization Science'; Extve. Dir., Org. Behaviour Teaching Soc. 1987–92; Mem., Bd. of Gov., Acad. of Mngt. 1987–89; Bd. of Advisors, Nat. Productivity Review; Canada Professor of the Year 1989 (Council for Support & Advancement of Education (CASE), Washington, DC; teaching excellence fellowship, 3M Can. 1988; Seagram Bus. Fac. Fellow; David L. Bradford Outstanding Educator Award 1993; co-author: 'Organizational Symbolism' 1983, 'Publishing in the Organizational Sciences' 1985; 'The Political Process of Innovation' 1990;'Reframing Organizational Culture' 1991, 'Organizational Reality' 4th ed. 1991; 'Management Live: The Video Book' 1991; 'Doing Exemplary Research' 1992; Ed. Bd. 'Academy of Management Review' 1983–87, 'J. of Management' 1983–86; recreations: movies, music, birding, travel, camping; clubs: W. Can. Wilderness Ctte., Animal Rescue Soc.; Home: 3869 West 38th Ave., Vancouver, B.C. V6N 2Y5; Office: 555 Henry Angus Bldg., Univ. of B.C. V6T 2Y5.

**FROST, Stanley Brice,** B.D., M.Th., Dr.Phil., D.D., D.Litt., LL.D.; b. London, Eng., 17 Feb. 1913; s. Henry George and Rosa (Goodbody) F.; e. Aske's Haberdashers' Sch., London, Eng. (1924–32); Richmond Coll., London Univ. (1932–36), B.D. 1936; Marburg Univ. (Dr. Williams' Scholar) Dr.Phil. 1938; M.Th. (London) 1943; D.D. Victoria, Univ. of Toronto 1963; D.D. Presbyterian Coll., Montreal 1967; D.Litt. Memorial Univ. 1967; LL.D. McGill Univ. 1990; m. Margaret Florence, d. George William Bradshaw, London, Eng., 29 July 1939; children: David Brice, Valerie Margaret; o. by Meth. Conference, Great Britain 1939; Min. of Un. Ch. of Can., 1957; held pastorates in London, 1939–42, Stoke on Trent, 1942–49; Professor of Old Testament Studies, Didsbury College, Bristol, 1949–56; Special Lect. in Hebrew, Bristol Univ., 1952; apptd. Prof. of Old Testament Lang. and Lit., McGill Univ., 1956, and Dean of Faculty of Divinity, 1957–63 when apptd. Dean of Grad. Faculty; Vice Principal, McGill Univ. 1969–74 since when Director, History of McGill Project; Gov. (1982) and Pres. (1984–89), Fraser-Hickson Inst. and Library; Publications: 'Die Authoritätslehre in den Werken John Wesleys' 1938; 'The Pattern of Methodism' 1948; 'Tutors Unto Christ' (Editor) 1949; 'Old Testament Apocalyptic' (Fernley-Hartley Lecture) 1952; 'The Beginning of the Promise: Eight Lectures on the Book of Genesis' 1960; 'Patriarchs and Prophets' 1964; 'Standing and Understanding: A Reappraisal of the Christian Faith' (Peake Lecture) 1969; 'McGill University: For the Advancement of Learning; Vol. I, 1801–1895' 1980, 'Vol. II, 1895–1971' 1984; 'The Man in the Ivory Tower, F. Cyril James of McGill' 1991; 'Something for My Friends, Poems Testament I' 1993; and various articles; Life Mem. Can. Soc. for Biblical Studies, 1983; Hon. Life Mem., McGill Graduates' Soc. 1986; Hon. Life Mem., James McGill Soc. 1991; Home: 5 Granville Rd., Hampstead, Que. H3X 3A9.

**FRUIN, Malcolm G.,** B.Sc.; management consultant; b. London, Eng. 15 Feb. 1933; e. City of London Freemen's Sch.; Univ. of London B.Sc. 1957; Brunel Coll. of Technol. Post-grad. Business Adm. 1957–58; m. Joan Gilling 20 July 1957; children: Russell, Neal, Sally; PRESIDENT, SOLVAY KINGSWOOD INC. 1991– ; and FRUIN CONSULTANTS INC.; Research Dir. International Surveys Ltd. Montreal 1957–64; Marketing Research Mgr., Eli Lilly Can. Inc., Toronto 1964, Dir. Marketing Planning 1965, Mgr. Marketing Research USA 1966 (Eli Lilly & Co.), Dir. Marketing Research Eli Lilly International Corp. Indianapolis1967, Gen. Mgr. Lilly Laboratories (S.A.) (Proprietary) Ltd. Johannesburg 1969–72, Pres. Eli Lilly Canada Inc. 1972–80; served with Royal Army Ordnance Corps 1956–57, rank 2–Lt.; Chrmn. Pharm. Mfrs. Assn. Can. 1977–78; Dir. Am. Marketing Assn. Montreal Chapter 1963–64; Dir., CDN Found. for Advancement Pharmacy 1978–82 Pres. Candn. Club Johannesburg 1971–72; recreations: golf, gardening; Club: Scarboro Golf & Country; Office: 50 Venture Dr. #4, Scarborough, Ont. M1B 3L6.

**FRUM, David,** M.A., J.D.; journalist; b. Toronto, Ont. 30 June 1960; s. Murray Bernard and Barbara Ruth (Rosberg) F.; e. Univ. of Toronto Schs. 1978; Yale Univ. B.A. 1982, M.A. 1982; Harvard Univ. J.D. 1987; m. Danielle d. Max and Yvonne Crittenden 26 June 1988; children: Miranda Ann, Nathaniel Saul; LAW EDITOR, FORBES MAGAZINE 1992– ; twice-weekly columnist, Financial Post and Toronto Sun; articles Saturday Night, Wall Street Jour., American Spectator, Spectator, Commentary, Harvard Jour. Law & Pub. Policy, Nat. Review; Visiting Lectr. Yale Univ. 1987; Assoc. Ed., Saturday Night mag. 1988–89; Asst. Features Editor, Wall Street Journal 1989–92; Home: 254 East 68th St., Apt. 6-D, New York, N.Y. 10021; Office: 60 Fifth Ave., New York, N.Y. 10011.

**FRUM, Linda,** B.A.; writer; b. Toronto, Ont. 13 Jan. 1963; d. Murray and Barbara (Rosberg) F.; e. Havergal Coll. 1981; McGill Univ. B.A. 1984; m. Timothy s. Helen and Allan O'Brien 15 May 1993; WRITER/HOST, LINDA FRUM'S VIDEO GUIDE TO CANADIAN UNIVERSITIES 1991– ; author 'Linda Frum's Guide to Canadian Universities' 1987; ed. 'The Newsmakers' 1990; articles, Chatelaine, Saturday Night mags., Toronto Sun newspaper; Address: 55 Prince Arthur Ave., Toronto, Ont. M5R 1B3.

**FRUM, Murray B.,** D.D.S.; executive; b. Toronto, Ont. 3 Sept. 1931; s. Saul and Rebecca (Ritz) F.; e. Univ of Toronto D.D.S. 1956; m. Barbara d. Harold and Florence Rosberg 3 Sept. 1957; children: David, Linda, Matthew; CHRMN. FRUM DEVELOPMENT GROUP 1987– ; practiced dentistry Toronto after grad.; simultaneously began property devel.; formed and became Pres. of Group R 1968, Chrmn., Toronto Internat. Festival; Vice Pres., Art Gallery of Ont. Found.; Dir.: Toronto Film Festival; Mount Sinai Hosp.; Past Pres., Stratford Festival; primitive art coll. exhibited various galleries incl.: Nat. Gallery, Ottawa; Art Gallery of Ont.; Museum of Modern Art, New York; Smithsonian Inst., Washington; Baltimore Museum of Art; Home: 25 Oxbow Rd., Don Mills, Ont. M3B 1Z9; Office: 720 Spadina Ave., Suite 220, Toronto, Ont. M5S 2T9.

**FRUTKIN, Mark Jamie,** B.A.; writer; editor; b. Cleveland, Ohio 2 Jan. 1948; s. Reynold Joseph and Anabel Elizabeth (Baigrie) F.; e. Loyola Univ. Chicago, Ill. and Rome, Italy B.A. 1969; Naropa Inst. Boulder, Colo. Studies in Creative Writing 1976; m. Faith d. Louis and Esther Seltzer 14 Dec. 1984; one s. Elliot William; Communications Dir., Candn. Artists' Representation and Ed. of ArtAction Magazine 1985–90; Asst. Ed. Ottawa Revue 1981; Coordinator, Marconi Amplified Project 1981; radio writer and researcher 1981–83; journalist/freelance writer over 250 publs. various mags. & lit. jours.; author 'The Growing Dawn' (fiction) 1984; 'Atmospheres Apollinaire' (fiction; nominated to Governor General's Award & Trillium Prize 1988) 1988; 'Invading Tibet' (fiction) 1991; 'The Alchemy of Clouds' (poetry) 1985; 'Acts of Light' (poetry) 1992; 'In the Time of the Angry Queen' (fiction) 1993; Co-Ed. Arc Mag. Ottawa 1988–90; various appearances performance art Candn. galleries; Teacher of Creative Writing: Naropa Inst., Halifax 1987 & 1989; Univ. of Ottawa; Univ. of Western Ont.; Univ. of New Brunswick; Dir. SAW Gallery Ottawa 1981–82; recipient numerous grants Can. Council, Dept. of Communications, Ont. Arts Council, Regional Mun. Ottawa-Carleton 1980–94; mem. Vajradhatu Internat. (mem. Exec. Ottawa Dharmadhatu 1980–92); Writers' Union Can.; PEN Internat.; recreations: reading, fine wines, films; Home: 874 Wingate Dr., Ottawa, Ont. K1G 1S5.

**FRY, Derek A.;** bank executive; b. Oxford, Eng. July 1944; m. Pamela; one s.: Matthew; SENIOR VICE-PRES., ELECTRONIC BANKING SERVICES, BANK OF MONTREAL 1988– ; Trade Fin., Computer Opns., Strategic Planning, Nat. Westminster Bank 1961–76; Mgr., Arch. & Design, Bank of Montreal 1977–82; Vice-Pres., Systems Devel. 1982–85; Sr. Vice-Pres., Information Systems 1985–88; Chair, Interac Assn. Canada; Vice-Pres., MasterCard Assn. of Can.; Mem., MasterCard Internat. Opns. Ctte.; recreations: cycling, squash, family, travel; club: Fitness Inst.; Home: R.R. #3, Stouffville, Ont. L4A 7X4; Office: 55 Bloor St. W., 15th fl., Toronto, Ont. M4W 3N5.

**FRY, Gary A.,** M.B.A.; vehicle leasing executive; b. Montréal, Qué. 14 Apr. 1946; s. Edward E. and Caroline M. (Smith) F.; e. Upper Can. Coll. Toronto 1964; York Univ. B.B.A. 1970, M.B.A. 1971; m. Joann B. d. Edward and Theresa Wickham 24 Dec. 1974; one s. Grant Andrew; DIRECTOR, OPERATIONS, BML LEASING LTD. 1988– ; joined City National Leasing Ltd. 1971–85, Vice Pres. and Gen. Mgr.; Pres., Foss National Leasing 1985–88; Office: 400 Carlingview Dr., Ste. 200, Etobicoke, Ont. M9W 6R8.

**FRY, Marion Golda,** M.A., B.Litt., D.C.L., D.Litt.; retired university administrator; professor; b. Halifax, N.S. 16 Apr. 1932; d. George W. and Marion I. (Publicover) F.; e. Queen Elizabeth H.S. 1950; Univ. of King's Coll., 1st class hon. & univ. medal in classics 1953; Dalhousie Univ., M.A. 1955; Oxford Univ., B.Litt. 1958; Univ. of King's Coll., D.C.L. 1985; Trent Univ., D.Litt. 1989; Pres., Univ. of King's Coll. 1987–93; Asst. Prof. of Phil. & Asst. Dean of Women, Bishop's Univ. 1958–64; Principal, Catharine Parr Traill Coll., Trent Univ. 1964–69; Assoc. Prof. of Phil. 1964–86; Vice-Pres. 1975–79; Acting Pres. Jan.-June 1978; Symons Award for Excellence in Teaching, Trent Univ. 1987; fields of interest are Greek and Mediaeval Philosophy, Philosophy of Lit.; Chrmn., Bd. of Dir., Arbor Theatre 1980–83; Mem., Bd. of Dir., United Way (Peterborough) 1984–87; Mem. of Senate, Dalhousie Univ. 1987–93; mem. Bd. of Dir., Halifax Found.; Dr. Helen Creighton Meml. Found.; University Scholarships of Can.; AUCC Rep., Nat. Lib. Bd. 1991–93; recreations: travel, classical music, walking; Home: 652 Walkerfield Ave., Peterborough, Ont. K9J 4W2.

**FRYER, John Leslie,** B.Sc.(Econ.), M.A.; visiting professor and consultant; b. London, Eng. 6 Oct. 1938; s. Leslie and Mollie (Steele) F.; e. Rutlish Grammar Sch.; London Sch. of Econ. & Pol. Science B.Sc. (Econ.) 1960; Univ. of Pittsburgh M.A. (Labour Econ.) 1962; m. Jeanne Crerar; three s. Darren, Blair, Andrew; three daughters Shelli, Lisa, Tanis; PRES., JOHN FRYER & ASSOCIATES (internat. consulting firm) and VISITING PROFESSOR, SCH. OF PUBLIC ADMIN., UNIV. OF VICTORIA; Managing Partner, Coastal Policy Planners, Victoria B.C.; President Emeritus, National Union of Public and General Employees (NUPGE) 1990– ; Special Adv. to NUPGE on Internat. Affairs 1990– , Pres. 1980–90; Rsch. Fellow, Candn. Ctr. for Mgmt. Development; Gen. Secy., B.C. Govt. Employees' Union 1969–83; Gen. Vice Pres., Candn. Labour Congress 1974–90; Research Dept. AFL/CIO, Washington, D.C. 1961–62; Dir. of Research, United Packinghouse Workers' Union 1962–65; Dir. of Research, Candn. Labour Congress 1965–69; mem. Public Services Int. World Extve. Comte.; Mem., Adv. Ctte., Norman Patterson Sch. of Internat. Affairs, Carleton Univ.; Mem., Bd. of Govs., Carleton Univ.1986–90; Labour Coll. of Can. 1982–90; mem., le Cercle Universitaire; Mem., Adv. Ctte., Sch. of Bus., Queen's Univ.; Mem., Bd. of Dirs., Inst. for Rsch. in Public Policy (I.R.P.P.); Extve. mem., Candn. Industrial Relations Assoc. (CIRA); former mem., Internat. Trade Adv. Ctte. (ITAC); Candn. Labour Market and Productivity Ctr. (CLMPC); mem. Candn. Consumer Council 1968–70; Duke of Edinburgh Fellow 1974; mem. Conf. Council, Duke of Edinburgh's Fifth Commonwealth Study Conf. 1980; rec'd Queen's Silver Jubilee Medal 1977; author numerous articles and presentations on industrial relations; mem. Internatl. Indust. Relations Research Assn.; London Sch. of Econ. Soc.; Univ. of London (Eng.) Convocation; recreations: cooking, reading, fishing, boating; Office: Saturna Island, B.C. V0N 2Y0.

**FUENTES-BERAIN, Her Excellency Sandra;** diplomat; b. Mexico City, Mex. 13 June 1950; d. M. Francisco and Ofelia (Villenave) F.; e. Natl. Autonomous Univ. 1971; London Sch. of Econ. postgrad. courses 1972; m. Henri s. Marcel and Marie Louise Robcis 9 Aug. 1974; children: Sebastien, Camille; AMBASSADOR OF MEXICO TO CANADA 1993– ; Multilateral Affairs Officer, Emb. of Mexico in Great Britain 1971–74; Pol. Affairs Offr., Emb. of Mex. in France 1974–79; Dir. Gen. for Western Eur., Fgn. Affairs Secretariat 1979–83; Deputy Chief of Mission, Emb. of Mex. in Italy 1983–86; Min. Pol. Affairs, Emb. of Mex. in USA 1986–88; Consul Gen. in Hong Kong 1988–91; Gen. Dir. for the Pacific, Fgn. Affairs Secretariat 1991–92; honours from govts. of Great Britain, Germany, France, Italy, Spain & Sweden; recreations: cycling, music, reading; club: Rideau; Office: 130 Albert St., Ste. 1800, Ottawa, Ont. K1P 5G4.

**FUJIWARA, David Ken,** B.Arch., OAA, MRAIC; architect; b. Toronto, Ont. 12 May 1952; s. Ozzie Osamu and Kay Kazue (Toyota) F.; e. Univ. of Toronto B.Arch. 1978; ARCHITECT, DAVID FUJIWARA ARCHITECT 1984– ; collaborated with architect Frank O. Gehry of Santa Monica, California on Chiat/Day Advtg. Toronto offices 1988–89; designed Into the Heart of Africa exbn. for curator Jeanne Cannizzo, R.O.M. 1988–89; designed Women's Detox Centre, Doctors Hosp. 1990–91; finalist, Cumberland Park Competition in collaboration with Garrison Creek Planting Co. 1991; work collected by the Candn. Centre for Architecture, Montreal - Chiat/Day Advertising, Toronto offices; Mem., Bd. of Trustees, McMichael Canadian Art Collection 1991– ; Pres., Nat. Assn. of Japanese Canadians, Toronto Chap. 1991– ; Bd. of Dir., Toronto Independent Dance Enterprise 1984–86; Mem., Toronto Soc. of Architects; Ontario Assn. of Arch. 1984; Royal Arch. Inst. of Canada 1984; Office: 20 Maud St., Ste. 203, Toronto, Ont. M5V 2M5.

**FULFORD, Patricia (Naomi),** (Mrs. R. Spiers), R.C.A.; sculptor; b. Toronto, Ont. 21 March 1935; d. Richard Turner and Muriel Lindsay Broughton (Parsons) Fulford; e. Branksome Hall Sch. Toronto 1953; Ont. Coll. Art. AOCA 1957; Edinburgh Coll. of Art D.A. (Edin.) 1960; m. Raymond Spiers 26 Jan. 1962; MEM. OF ARTIST'S COLONY, SAFED, ISRAEL; teacher, Ont. Coll. of Art 1960–63; Glendon Coll. York Univ. 1970–75; Cariboo Coll. Kamloops 1978–79; Langara College, Vancouver, B.C. 1985–86; solo exhns. incl. Mazelow Gallery Toronto 1972; N.B. Museum 1973; exhns. with R. Spiers incl. Mirvish Gallery 1964, Mazelow Gallery 1967, Toronto, Shalom Gallery, Vancouver 1984; worked at Harman Sculpture Foundry, Vancouver, B.C.; mem. Sculptors Soc. B.C.; Counc. mem. R.C.A. 1985–87; mem., Israel Assn. of Painters & Sculptors; recreations: music, gardening; Home: 92 Yod-Bet St., Artists' Quarter, Safed, Israel 13201.

**FULFORD, Robert Marshall Blount,** O.C., LL.D.; journalist; b. Ottawa, Ont., 13 Feb. 1932; s. Albert Edward and Frances Gertrude (Blount) F.; e. Malvern Collegiate, Toronto; m. Jocelyn Jean, d. late Jeffrey Dingman, 16 June 1956; children: James Marshall, Margaret Frances; divorced 1970; m. Geraldine Patricia Sherman, d. Philip and Helen Sherman, 28 Nov. 1970; children: Rachel Sherman, Sarah Helen; Reporter, The Globe and Mail, 1950–53, 1956–57; Asst. Editor, Canadian Homes and Gardens, 1955, Mayfair, 1956, Maclean's, 1962–64; Editor, Saturday Night, 1968–87; Host of This Is Robert Fulford (CBC radio) 1967–72; co-host, 'Realities,' TVOntario 1982–89; Literary Columnist, The Toronto Star, 1958–62, 1964–68; weekly arts columnist, Toronto Star 1971–87; Columnist and contributing editor, The Financial Times 1988–92; weekly arts columnist, The Globe and Mail 1992– ; Contrib. Ed., Toronto Life 1992– ; Barker Fairley Distinguished Visitor in Canadian Culture, University Coll., Univ. of Toronto 1987–88; Chair, Maclean Hunter program in communications ethics, Ryerson Polytechnical Inst., Toronto 1989–93; Chair, Banff Centre program in arts journalism, 1989–91; Mem. Bd. of Dirs., Candn. Civil Liberties Assoc.; Mem. Adv. Counc., Ont. Law Reform Comn.; contrib. to Canadian Art, Queen's Quarterly, New York Times Book Review, Saturday Night, Rotunda, Destinations, Canadian Geographic, Content; author 'This Was Expo' 1968; 'Crisis At The Victory Burlesk' 1968; 'Marshall Delaney at the Movies' 1974; 'An Introduction to the Arts in Canada' 1977; 'Canada: A Celebration' 1983; 'Best Seat in the House: Memoirs of a Lucky Man' 1988; Officer, Order of Canada, 1984; Prix d'Honneur, Candn. Conf. of the Arts, 1981; Hon. doctorates from McMaster Univ. 1986, York Univ. 1987; Univ. of Western Ont. 1988; Home: 19 Lynwood Ave., Toronto, Ont. M4V 1K3.

**FULLER, William Albert,** B.A., M.A., Ph.D.; professor emeritus (zoology); b. Moosomin, Sask. 10 May 1924; s. Albert Thomas and Helen Marguerite (Williams) F.; e. Univ. of Sask., B.A. 1946, M.A. 1947; Univ. of Wisconsin Ph.D. 1957; m. Marie d. Alfred and Kathleen Turtle 31 May 1947; children: Karen Jane, William James, Kathleen Marguerite, Gordon Albert; student mem. of party investigating fishery potential of L. Athabasca 1945; Great Slave L. 1946; Mammalogist, Govt. of Can., S. Mackenzie Dist., N.W.T. & Wood Buffalo Nat. Park 1947–56; Yukon Territory 1956–59; Asst. Prof., Assoc. Prof., Prof. of Zoology, Univ. of Alta. 1959–84; Dept. Chrmn. 1969–74; Nat. Chrmn., Subctte., Candn. Ctte. for the Internat. Biol. Prog. 1966–74; Mem., Sci. Adv. Bd. of N.W.T. 1976–82; Environ. Assessment & Review Panel on N. Diseased Bison 1989–90; Chrmn., Mammal., Internat. Union of Biol. Sci. 1985–89; Dir., Environ. Law Ctr. Edmonton; Mem., Am. Soc. of Mammal. 1948– ; Arctic Inst. of N. Am. 1948– (Fellow 1972–); Candn. Soc. of Zool. 1960– ; Candn. Soc. of Environ. Biol. 1960– ; elected Fgn. Mem., Finnish Biol. Soc. 1970; Corresp. Mem., All-Union Theriol. Soc., USSR 1986; co-author: 'Life of the Far North' 1972; co-editor: 'Productivity & Conservation in Northern Circumpolar Lands' 1970; recreations: wilderness travel, curling; Home: Box 672, Athabasca, Alta. T0G 0B0.

**FULLERTON, Douglas H.,** O.C., M.Com., LL.D., D.U.C.; economic and financial consultant; b. St. John's, Nfld. 3 Sept. 1917; s. Roy DeMille and Effie (Henderson) F.; e. McGill Univ. B.Com. 1939, M.Com. 1940; Hon. LL.D. Dalhousie 1969, Carleton 1974; Hon. D. Univ. Calgary 1975; m. Charlotte Maude Hickman 20 Nov. 1943; children: Mimi, John, Katherine; has served as adviser to federal, Newfoundland and Sask. govts. and on task forces for Que. Govt. incl. takeover of power cos. 1962–3, Financial Insts. 1966–69, Montreal Suburban Rail Transit, 1974–77; federal public service 1945–53; Asst. Dir. Research, Royal Comn. on Can.'s Econ. Prospects 1955–57; Treas. and later Investment Consultant, Can. Council 1957–68; Chrmn. Cape Breton Development Corp. 1967–69; syndicated newspaper columnist 1966–81; Chrmn. Nat. Capital Comn. 1969–73 and author 'The Capital of Canada: How Should It Be Governed?' 1974; Hon. Prof. Urbanism, Univ. of Calgary 1979–85; author of 'The Bond Market in Canada' 1962; 'The Dangerous Delusion: Quebec's Independence Obsession' 1978; 'Graham Towers and his Times,' biog. of 1st Gov. Bank of Canada 1986; Officer of the Order of Canada 1987; Home: 172 Clemow Ave., Ottawa, Ont. K1S 2B4.

**FULLERTON, R.D.,** B.A.; banker; b. Vancouver, B.C. 7 June 1931; s. late C. G. and late Muriel F.; e. Forest Hill Village High Sch., Toronto; Trinity Coll. Sch., Port Hope, Ont.; Univ. of Toronto, B.A. 1953; m.; CHRMN. & C.E.O., CIBC 1985– , a Dir. since 1974 and Chrmn. Extve. Ctte. since 1992; Dir.: AMOCO Canada Petroleum Co. Ltd.; IBM Canada Ltd.; T.C.C. Beverages Ltd.; George Weston Ltd.; Wellesley Hosp., Toronto; joined Bank in Vancouver 1953; Agt., New York 1964; Regional Gen. Mgr., Regina, 1966; Regional Gen. Mgr., Internat. 1967; Depy. Chief Gen. Mgr. 1968; Sr. Vice Pres. 1971; Exec. Vice Pres. and Chief Gen. Mgr. 1973; el. a Dir. 1974; Pres. & Chief Operating Officer 1976; C.E.O. 1984; Chrmn. & C.E.O. 1985; Chrmn. Extve. Ctte. 1992; recreations: golf, skiing; Office: Head Office, Commerce Court West, Toronto, Ont. M5L 1A2.

**FULTON, E(thel) Margaret,** O.C., B.A., M.A., Ph.D., Hon. F.R.P.I., D.S.E., D.L., LL.D.; educator; b. Birtle; d. Ernest Bain and Ethel Mary (Futers) F.; e. Winnipeg Normal Sch. 1942; Univ. of Minn. Phys. Educ. Dipl. 1946; Univ. of Man. B.A. 1955; Univ. of Toronto Ont. Coll. of Educ. Secondary Sch. Eng. Specialist 1956; Univ. of B.C. M.A. 1960; Univ. of Toronto Ph.D. 1968; Elementary & Secondary Sch. Teacher, Man. & Ont. 1942–61; Prof. of Eng., Wilfrid Laurier Univ. 1967–74; Dean of Women, Univ. of B.C. 1974–1978; Pres., Mount Saint Vincent Univ. 1978–86; Adjunct Prof. U.B.C. 1986–89; Education Consultant, Kinneuniversitetet, Norway 1987–88; Awards: rec'd Ont. Grad. Fellowships; named Hon. Class Pres. 1972, Wilfrid Laurier Univ.; William P. Huffman Scholar-in-Residence, Univ. of Miami, Oxford, Ohio 1979; Officer, Order of Canada; Hon. Fellow of Ryerson Polytech. Inst.; Hon. Degrees, D.Sc. de l'Educ., Univ. de Moncton; LL.D., Univ. of Winnipeg; LL.D., Dalhousie Univ.; D.L., York Univ.; LL.D., Concordia Univ.; D.L., Lakehead Univ.; Distinguished Educator Award, OISE 1991; Woman of Distinction Award, Vancouver YWCA 1991; Directorships held: Chairperson, Fed. Gov't, Task Force on Micro-Electronics and Employment; Dir. Wellington Insurance Co.; North-South Inst.; Elderhostel; Internat. Inst. for Peace & Security; National Advy. Comte. on Education Statistics; Prov. Gov't Com. of Inquiry on Rents, N.S.; Internat. Counc. for Adult Educ.; Fed. Govt. Ctte. on Learning Opportunities for Women; Assn. Univ. & Colleges of Can.; Assn. Candn. Univ. Teachers Eng.; Ed. Adv. Ctte., 'Atlantis' and 'Women's Studies Journal'; Candn. Council Teachers Eng.; Candn. Soc. Study Higher Educ.; Candn. Rsch. Inst. Advanc. Women; mem. United Church; recreations: international cultural, educational & environmental activities; Clubs: Voice of Women; University Women's; Group of '78; Science for Peace; Home: 207 – 5450 University Blvd., Vancouver, B.C. V6T 1K4.

**FULTON, Hon. Edmund Davie,** P.C. (Can.) 1957, O.C., Q.C., LL.D.; b. Kamloops, B.C. 10 Mar. 1916; s. Frederick John, K.C., and Winifred M. (Davie) F.; e. St. Michael's Sch., Victoria, B.C.; Kamloops High Sch.; Univ. of Brit. Columbia, B.A.; St. John's Coll., Oxford, 1937–39 (el. Rhodes Scholar 1937) B.A.; LL.D. Ottawa and Queen's; m. Patricia Mary, d. James M. Macrae, Winnipeg, Man., 7 Sept. 1946; three d., Catherine Mary, Patricia (Mrs. Richard G. Lockwood), Cynthia Ann (Mrs. Robert Y. Bonner); cr. Q.C. 1957; 1st el. to H. for Kamloops, g.e. 1945; re-el. g.e. 1949, 1953, 1957, 1958, 1962, 1965; Min. of Justice and Atty.-Gen. of Canada 21 June 1957 to 9 Aug. 1962 when appt. Min. of Public Works; Chrmn., Candn. del. which negotiated Columbia River Treaty with U.S. 1959–61; mem. of Senate, Univ. of B.C. 1948–57 and 1969–75; first Chrmn. The Law Reform Comn. of B.C. 1969–73; practised law in Kamloops, B.C. 1945–68 and Vancouver, B.C. 1968–73; apptd. Judge, Supreme Court of B.C. 1973, resigned 1981; resumed practice of law as Associate Counsel, Swinton & Co., Vancouver 1982; apptd. Comnr., Candn. Section, Internat. Joint Comn., Ottawa and Washington, D.C. 1986; re-apptd. and elected Chrmn., Candn. Sec. 1989–92; served in 2nd World War with Canadian Army overseas as Platoon and Company Commdr. with Seaforth Highlanders of Can., and as D.A.A.G. 1st Candn. Inf. Div., 1940–45 incl. both the Italian and N.W. Europe compaigns; Mentioned in Despatches; trans. to R.O. With rank of Maj. 1945; apptd. Hon. Col. 419 Tactical Fighter (Training) Squadron, R.C.A.F., (The Moose Squadron) 1st June 1993; Dir. Western Recovery Foundation, Vancouver; Physical Med. Rsch. Found., Vancouver; mem., Candn. Bar Assoc.; Law Soc. of B.C. (ret'd); Hon. Mem., Fellows of the Am. Bar Found.; Freeman, City of Kamloops, B.C. (apptd. 1969); Officer, Order of Canada 1992; R. Catholic; Clubs: Vancouver; Shaughnessy Golf & Country; Home: 1632 West 40th Ave., Vancouver, B.C. V6M 1V9.

**FULTON, Vice Admiral (Ret'd) James Andrew,** C.M.M., O.St.J., C.D.; b. Ottawa, Ont. 23 Jan. 1927; s. Andrew and Alice Romney (Hobden) F.; e. St. Joseph Coll. (London, England); Grimsby (Ont.) H.S.; Royal Candn. Naval Coll.; Royal Military Coll. of Sci. (England); Natl. Defence Coll. (Kingston, Ont.); m. Margaret, d. Percy and Marjory Coombs, 20 Oct. 1951; children: Elizabeth Anne; Heather Patricia; Dir., Halifax Herald Ltd., Halifax N.S.; joined Royal Candn. Navy 1946; promoted midshipman; served in Royal Navy 1946–49; returned to Canada 1949 as S/Lt., joined HMCS Haida; served in Korea in HMCS Huron 1951; HMS Excellent qualified in Gunnery 1952–53; post grad. course in Guided Weapons 1956; commanded HMCS Outrement 1961–62; HMCS Gatineau 1965–66; HMCS Provider 1969–72; Depy. Saclant Rep. Eur. (Capt.) 1966–69; promoted Commodore, Commdr. Northern Region 1973; Rear-Admiral, Chief of Personnel Careers and Sr. Appts. 1976; Vice-Admiral, NATO Candn. Mil. Rep. 1978; Commander Maritime Command, 1980–83; Colonel Commandant, Military Police, 1983–87; Order of Military Merit: Officer, 1972; Commander, 1981; Offr., Order of St. John; Candn. Forces Decoration; Chrmn., Candn. Naval Memorial Trust; Nova Scotia Tattoo Ctte.; Dir., N.S. Div., Candn. Corps of Commissionaires; Address: RR #1, Mahone Bay, N.S. B0J 2E0

**FULTON, M. Jane,** B.H.Ec., M.Sc., Ph.D.; university professor; b. Edmonton, Alta. 12 July 1947; d. James Blair and Margaret Anna (Massie) F.; e. Univ. of Brit. Columbia B.H.Ec. 1969, M.Sc. 1981, Ph.D. 1986; children: Jean, Amy, Sarah, Lila; ASSOC. PROF., STRATEGIC MANAGEMENT, ETHICS, UNIV. OF OTTAWA; Faculty Mem., Banff Sch. of Advance Mngt.; research focused on governance & mngt. of health care & evolution of health professions in Can.; Visitng Scholar, USC Sacramento 1991; Duke Univ. 1992; Dir. of Rsch. for Public Hosps. Act of Ont.; ctte. appts. on Science Council of Can.; MRCC; author: 'Health Care in Canada' 1988, 'Canada's Health System: Brodering on the Possible' 1993; Office: 136 Jean-Jacques Lussier, Ottawa, Ont. K1N 6N5.

**FULTON, Sandy Michael,** B.Sc., M.B.A.; forest products executive; b. Comox, B.C. 15 Nov. 1943; s. Russell Clyde and Muriel Maggie (Swan) F.; e. Univ. of B.C., B.Sc. 1966; Simon Fraser Univ. M.B.A. 1975; m. (Thelma) Diane Wiig 8 July 1967; children: Michael Colby, Kristen Wade, Treva Diane; PRES., C.E.O. & DIR., PACIFIC FOREST PRODUCTS LTD. and WOOD PRODUCTS 1993– ; Dir. and Pres., Burgoyne Bay Log Sorting Co. Ltd.; Chemainus Towing Co. Ltd.; Falt Towing Ltd.; Ladysmith Log Sorting Co. Ltd.; Lens Logging Ltd.; Mayo Forest Products Ltd.; Dir., Nanoose Log Supply Ltd.; Dir. and Pres., Nootka Transportation Co. Ltd.; Ucona Holdings Ltd.; Vanisle Land Development Ltd.; Dir., Forest Ind. Rlns.; P.P.I.R.B.; Forintek Canada Corp.; Vice Pres. Bldg. Material, MacMillan Bloedel, Pres. Atlantic Forest Products, Atlanta, Ga. 1979–81; Sr. Vice Pres. Bldg. Prodn. B.C. Timber Ltd., Vancouver 1981–83; Exec. Vice Pres. Operations 1983–84; Pres. & Dir., Westar Timber Ltd. 1984–87; Vice Pres., Candn. Pacific Forest Products Ltd., Vice Pres. Wood Products 1987–93; Office: Ste. 1000, 1040 West Georgia St., Vancouver, B.C. V6E 4K4.

**FULTON, Most Rev. Thomas,** D.J.C. (R.C.); b. St. Catharines, Ont. 13 Jan. 1918; s. Thomas Francis and Mary Catherine (Jones) F.; e. St. Nicholas Sch., St. Catharines, Ont.; St. Catharines Coll. Inst.; St. Augustine's Semy., Toronto, Ont., 1941; Catholic Univ. of America, D.J.C., 1948; named Domestic Prelate by Pope Pius XII, Nov. 1954; consecrated Aux. Bishop of the Archdiocese of Toronto 1969 by Pope Paul VI in Rome; apptd. Bishop of St. Catharines, 1978; Pres., Ont. Conf. of Cath. Bishops 1981–85; Treas., Candn. Conf. of Catholic Bishops 1985–89; Vice Pres., Candn. Conf. of Catholic Bishops 1989–91; publication: 'The Pre-Nuptial Investigation' (canonical study), 1948; Address: 122 Riverdale Avenue, St. Catharines, Ont. L2R 4C2.

**FUNASAKA, Shinichi;** executive; b. Kyoto, Japan 30 March 1918; s. Hamaichiro and Nobu (Hamaguchi) F.; e. Keio Univ. grad. in Econ. 1942; m. Mari d. Shuji Yamamoto 26 March 1948; children: Yutaka, Tom, Mako; PRES. FUNASAKA & ASSOCIATES LTD. 1980– ; Dir. Mitsui Taiyo Kobe Bank Canada; Gen. Mgr. Mitsui & Co. Hong Kong Br. 1967–71; Pres. Mitsui & Co. (Canada) Ltd. 1971–76; Pres. Candn Motor Industries Ltd. 1976–79; Chrmn. Toyota Canada Inc. 1979–80; served with Japanese Navy 1942–45, rank Lt.; recreations: fishing, golf; Club: National, Lambton; Office: 74 Bayview Ridge, Willowdale, Ont. M2L 1E6.

**FUNT, B(ruce) Lionel,** M.Sc., Ph.D., F.C.I.C.; university professor; b. Halifax, N.S., 20 Jan. 1924; s. Arthur and Rita (Rice) F.; e. Bloomfield High Sch., Halifax, N.S.; Dalhousie Univ., B.Sc. 1944, M.Sc. 1946; McGill Univ., Ph.D. 1949; m. Frances Margaret, d. Henry A. Russell, Amherst, N.S., 20 July 1947; children: Brian Vincent, Gordon Stanley, Warren Henry; PROF. EMERITUS, SIMON FRASER UNIV., Dir., Science Programs, Harbour Centre Campus 1989–92, Prof. of Chem. 1968–89, Dean of Science 1968–71, mem. Bd. of Govs. 1975–78; Dir., Nuclear Enterprises, Ltd.; Nuclear Enterprises (G.B.) Ltd., Edinburgh; Nuclear Enterprises Inc., San Carlos, Cal. 1956–76; Lectr., Dalhousie Univ., 1947; Asst. Prof., Univ. of Man., 1950–54, Assoc. Prof. 1954–59, Prof. of Chem. 1959–67, Dean of Grad. Studies 1964–67; author of about 100 publs. in field of polymer chem.; primarily interested in electro-chem. initiation and control of polymerization processes & also in nuclear radiation detection techniques; Chrmn. (1975–76) Chem. Educ., Chemical Institute of Can.; mem., Universities Grants Commission, Manitoba 1967–69; Vice-President, Canadian Assn. Graduate Studies, 1966–67; Nuffield Travelling Fellowship 1971–72; mem., Am. Chem. Soc.; United Church; recreations: photography, sailing; Home: 1545 Camelot Road, West Vancouver, B.C. V7S 2L9.

**FUREDY, Christine Philippa Margaret,** B.A., D.Phil.; educator; b. Colombo, Sri Lanka 9 Jan. 1940; d. William Joseph Berthon and Philippa Hume (Dale) Roche; e. North Sydney Girls High Sch. 1958; Univ. of Sydney B.A. 1964; Univ. of Sussex D.Phil. 1970; m. John J. s. Bela and Magda Furedy 30 June 1966; ASSOC. PROF. SOC. SCIENCE, YORK UNIV. 1976– , at Asian Inst. of Technology 1990; Associate, Environmental Studies, York Univ. 1981– ; Associate, Inst. Environmental Studies, Univ. of Toronto; Lectr., Div. of Social Science York Univ. 1969, Asst. Prof. 1971, Dir. Teaching Skills Programme 1973–76; recipient Commonwealth of Australia Scholarship 1958–63; Brit. Commonwealth Post-Grad. Scholarship 1964–66; Ont. Confed. Univ. Faculty Assns. Citation for Outstanding Contribution to Univ. Teaching 1977; Shastri Indo-Candn. Sr. Fellowship 1976–77, 1986; Social Sciences & Humanities Research Council Awards; author various articles: waste management, environmental issues, community orgns., Asia, hist. Calcutta, higher educ., urban studies; prof. journs.; recreations: skiing, tennis, swimming; Home: 24 Astley Ave., Toronto, Ont. M4W 3B4; Office: 331 Calumet Coll., 4700 Keele St., Downsview, Ont. M3J 1P3.

**FUREDY, John J.,** M.A., Ph.D.; educator; b. Budapest, Hungary 30 June 1940; s. Bela Furedy; e. Neutral Bay Boys Primary and North Sydney Boys High Schs. Australia 1957; Univ. of Sydney B.A. 1963 (Univ. Medal), M.A. 1964, Ph.D. 1966; m. Christine P.M. d. W.J. Roche 30 June 1966; PROF. OF PSYCHOL., UNIV. OF TORONTO 1975– ; Visiting Lectr. Ind. Univ. 1965, Visiting Asst. Prof. 1966; Asst. Prof. Univ. of Toronto 1967, Assoc. Prof. 1969–75; Fullbright Scholar; Fellowships Dept. External Affairs Can., Can.-Hungary and Canada-Japan Interchange Scheme and Social Science and Humanities Research Council of Canada Travel Grants; Award for Research Excellence, 1982, Pavlovian Soc. of North America; author book chapters, over 150 papers scient. journs.; Fellow, Australian Psychol. Soc.; Candn. Psychol. Assn.; Am. Psychol. Soc.; Internat. Coll. Psychosomatic Med.; Internat. Organ. Psychophysiol.; mem. Pavlovian Soc. (Vice-Pres. to Pres. 1986–89); mem. Society for Academic Freedom & Scholarship (Pres. 1993–95); Soc. for Psychophys. Research; recreations: tennis, skiing, bridge, scuba diving, body surfing; Clubs: Rosedale Tennis; Prince Arthur Bridge; Home: 24 Astley Ave., Toronto, Ont. M4W 3B4; Office: Dept. of Psychology, Toronto, Ont. M5S 1A6.

**FUREY, The Hon. Charles (Chuck) J.,** B.A., B.Ed.; teacher, politician; b. Avondale, Nfld. 6 Mar. 1954; s. Leo and Mary (Bruce) F.; e. Gonzaga H.S.; Memorial Univ. of Nfld., 2 yrs.; St. Francis Xavier Univ., 3 yrs.; MIN. OF INDUSTRY, TRADE & TECHNOLOGY, Govt. of Nfld. & Labrador 1992– ; High School Teacher 1976–81; Extve. Asst., M.P. 1981–85; M.H.A. 1985– ; Min. of Development 1989–92; Office: 4th floor, West Block, Confederation Bldg., St. John's, Nfld. A1B 4J6.

**FURLONG, Leon R.,** C.A.; health executive; b. Amherst, N.S. 18 Jan. 1938; s. Ross and Reta (Smith) F.; e. Amherst Reg. H.S. 1955; Inst. of C.A.s 1961; m. Catherine d. Ulric and Marie Anne Leger 28 Sept. 1979; children: Susan, Nancy, Patrick, Michelle; PRESIDENT, BLUE CROSS OF ATLANTIC CANADA 1977– ; Vice-Pres., Admin., Blue Cross of Atlantic Canada 1973–76; Extve. Vice-Pres. 1976–77; Mem., Candn. Assn. of Blue Cross Plans; Internat. Fed. of Health Funds; N.B. Inst. of C.A.s; Moncton Rotary Club; Home: One Havenwood Court, Moncton, N.B. E1A 5W4; Office: Box 220, Moncton, N.B. E1C 8L3.

**FURLONG, Patrick Garret,** Q.C., L.S.M., B.A., LL.B.; barrister; b. Riverside, Ont. 7 Sept. 1926; s. William Henry and Beatrix Elizabeth (Green) F.; e. elem. separate schs.: St. Clair, Notre Dame de Bon Secours, Windsor, Ont.; St. John the Baptist Amherstburg, Ont.; Assumption High Sch. Windsor; Assumption Coll. B.A. 1948; Univ. of W. Ont. Summer Session 1946; Osgoode Hall Law Sch. LL.B. 1952; m. Shirley Day d. John Frederick Waterhouse 20 Aug. 1954; children: Ann Elizabeth, John Garret, Andrew Patrick, Diana Louise, David William; SR. PARTNER, FURLONG, CHODOLA, REYNOLDS; Dir. The Lake Erie and Detroit River Railway Co.; Dir., Chrmn. Lawyer's Professional Indemnity Co. 1990–91; read law with Hon. J. Frank Hughes; called to Bar of Ont. 1952; cr. Q.C. 1969; Mem. Bd. of Govs., Univ. of Windsor 1978–89, Chrmn., Bd. of Govs. 1986–88; Former Dir., Pre-paid Legal Services Program Can.; mem. Essex Co. Dist. Health Council Task Force 1978; Past Dir. former Fed. Co. & Dist. Law Assns. Ont.; Fellow, Foundation for Legal Research Can.; mem. Candn. Inst. Adm. Justice; Windsor Jr. Chamber Comm. 1953–58, Chrmn. Legal Sub-Comtes. Windsor Harbour Devel. and Legal Sub-Comte. Implementation Jr. Achievement Business Program Windsor; Del. Can. Dept. Justice Nat. Conf. on Law Ottawa 1972; Nat. Conf. on Quality of Legal Services Can. 1978; author various papers; Life Bencher, Law Soc. Upper Can.; Former mem., Editorial Bd. Ont. Lawyers Weekly; mem. Candn. Bar Assn. (Pres. Ont. Br. 1968–69, mem. Nat. Extve. Comte. 1972–74); Essex Co. Law Assn. (Pres. 1973–74); Essex Co. Med.-Legal Soc. (Pres. 1970–72); Nat. Assn. Rr. Trial Counsel; Defense Research Inst. Advisory Bd. Windsor-Essex Mediation Centre; Liberal; R. Catholic; recreations: sailing, golfing;

Clubs: Detroit Good Guys; University (Toronto); Windsor Yacht; Windsor; Faculty (Univ. of Windsor); Essex Golf & Country; Home: 2035 Willistead Cres., Windsor, Ont. N9A 1K6; Office: Suite 1010, 100 Ouellette Ave., Windsor, Ont. N9A 6T3.

**FURNIVAL, George Mitchell,** C.M., B.Sc., M.A., Ph.D., F.R.S.C., F.G.S.A., F.S.E.G., F.G.A.C.; petroleum and mining consultant; b. Winnipeg, Man. 25 July 1908; s. William George and Grace Una (Rothwell) F.; e. Carleton & Alexander Schs., Kelvin Tech. High Sch. Winnipeg; Univ. of Man. B.Sc. 1929; Queen's Univ. M.A. 1933; Mass. Inst. Technol. Ph.D. 1935; m. Marion Marguerite d. Alexander Dickie Fraser, 8 March 1937; children: William George Fraser F., Dr. Sharon Grace (Roscoe), Patricia Marion F., Bruce Alexander F; PETROLEUM & MINING CONSULTANT 1985– ; employed by mining companies, 1928–39; Asst. Mine Supt., O'Brien Mining Ltd., 1935–38; Geol. Surv., Canada, 1939–42; for 28 years served Standard Oil Co. of California Inc. (Chevron Corp. Inc.) 1942–70, teams under his direction making significant petroleum discoveries in Alberta, Manitoba, Trinidad, Columbia and Australia, while holding various positions incl.: Vice Pres. and Dir. California Standard Co. Alta. 1950–55, Pres. and Dir. Dominion Oil Ltd. Trinidad, 1952–60; Dir. and Vice Pres. Exploration, Chevron Overseas Petroleum Inc. (San Francisco), 1955–63; Asst., Land, to Vice Pres. Exploration and Land, Standard Oil Co. of California San Francisco 1958–63; Chrmn. Bd. and Mang. Dir. West Australian Petroleum Pty. Ltd. (Chevron operated) Perth W.A., 1963–70, and incl., from 1953–70 (as Vice-Pres. Exploration, and Dir. of various subsidiaries), directing numerous offshore seismic and drilling programs in Trinidad, Bahamas, Guatemala, Br. Guyana, Cuba, Belize, Ecuador, Peru and Australia; Dir. of Mines, Prov. of Man. 1946–47; estbd. consulting practice Calgary 1971–72; Vice Pres. Operations Dir., Brascan Resources Ltd. 1973, mem. Extve. Comte., Sr. Vice Pres. 1975 also Pres. and Dir. Coalition Mining Ltd., Sr. Consultant 1977; Pres., CEO and Dir., Western Mines Ltd. (Brascan), 1978–80 developing a geological concept and initiating a program that led to the discovery of a major base metal/precious metal orebody at its Vancouver Island, Myra Falls Mine; Extve. Vice Pres., Gen. Mgr. and Dir., Westmin Resources Ltd. 1981–82; Petroleum & Mining Consultant 1982–83; Pres. and Dir. Western Coal Holdings Inc.; Pres., Chief Oper. Offr. & Dir., Lathwell Resources Ltd. 1983–85; Secy., Interprovincial Mines Ministers' Winnipeg Conf. 1947; mem. Policy and Mang. Comte. Earth Resources Data Systems Project; in 1953 conceived a new principle, 'Progressive Displacement,' to explain the accumulation of oil and gas fields in sequential traps on the updip margins of basins, that occur in reverse order of their specific gravities; recipient: Distinguished Service Award, Petroleum Soc., Candn. Inst. Mining & Metall. 1974; Selwyn G. Blaylock Gold Medal, Candn. Inst. of Mining & Metall. (for contribs. to petroleum and mining industries in field of geology) 1979; Centennial Award, Assn. of Profl. Engrs., Geologists & Geophysicists of Alta. 1985; author numerous tech. papers and govt. reports mining and petroleum fields incl. Geol. Surv. of Can. Memoir 242 (a standard univ. reference text); in 1947, when Dir. of Mines for Manitoba, he founded the Manitoba Geological Survey, employing a staff of 6 geologists, for the first time on a permanent basis, to serve the mining, petroleum and industrial minerals industries of Man.; Fellow, Royal Soc. of Canada since 1947; Geol. Assn. Can.; Geol. Soc. of Am.; Soc. of Economic Geologists; Hon. Life mem. Candn. Inst. Mining & Metall. (Past Vice Pres.; Chrmn. Petroleum Division); Engn. Inst. of Canada; Alta. Assn. Prof. Engrs., Geols. & Geophysicists; Australian Petroleum Exploration Assn. (Past State Chrmn. MBR National Counc.); mem., Am. Assn. Petroleum Geols.; Scholarship established in his name in mining geology at U.B.C. 1982; mem., Order of Canada 1982; Clubs: Ranchmen's; Calgary Petroleum; Calgary Golf & Country; Home: 1315 Baldwin Cr. S.W., Calgary, Alta. T2V 2B7.

**FURTER, William Frederick,** B.A.Sc., S.M., Ph.D., F.C.I.C.; P.Eng.; educator; consulting engineer; b. North Bay, Ont. 5 Apr. 1931; s. Alfred Frederick and Eva Margaret (Stinson) F.; e. Royal Mil. Coll., 1949–53; Univ. of Toronto, B.A.Sc. 1954, Ph.D. 1958; Mass. Inst. of Technol., S.M. 1955; Nat. Defence Coll., 1969–70; m. Pamela Margaret, d. H.C. Cooper, Kingston, Ont., 6 Aug. 1966; three d., Lesley Margaret, Jane Elizabeth, Pamela Catharine; DEAN OF GRAD. STUDIES AND RESEARCH, ROYAL MILITARY COLL. 1984– ; Secy., Grad. Sch. there 1967–80, and Professor-in-Charge, Chem. Engn. Div., Dept. of Chem. & Chem. Engn. there 1960–80, Acting Dean of Grad. Studies & Research 1978–79 and 1982, Dean of Candn. Forces Military Coll. and Chrmn. Extension Div. Royal Mil. Coll. 1980–84; Teaching Asst., Mass. Inst. of Technol., 1954–55; Univ. of Toronto 1955–58; Research Engr., Research & Devel. Dept., Du Pont of Canada Ltd., 1958–59; Sr. Tech. Investigator of Dept. 1959–60; joined present Coll. as Special Lectr. in Chem. Engn. (part-time) 1958–60; Asst. Prof. 1960–61; Assoc. Prof. 1961–66; Prof. since 1966; Consulting Engr. to Hexcel Corp., San Francisco, to Union Carbide Corpn., Charleston, W. Va. and to Air Liquide Canada Ltée, Montreal; served with RCE (COTC) 1950–53; militia service with 2nd Field Engr. Regt. RCE, Toronto, 1953–57; rank Capt.; rec'd. Dom. Scholarship, Gov. Gen. of Can. Bronze and Silver Medals; Lt. Gov. of Ont. Silver Medal; Engn. Inst. Can. Prize; Royal Candn. Sch. Mil. Engn. Prize; 2 M.I.T. Scholarships; 2 N.R.C. Studentships; Dept. of Nat. Defence research grants annually since 1963; Research Grants from Nat. Science Foundation and Petroleum Research Fund; rec'd the Distinguished Professor Award, Royal Mil. Coll. 1981–82, 1986–87, 1989–90, 1991–92; Fellow, Chem. Inst. of Can.; mem., Assn. Prof. Engrs. Prov. Ont.; Candn. Soc. Chem. Engn. (Dir. 1979–82; Chrmn. Intersociety Rlns. Comte. 1985– ;); Candn. Nuclear Assn.; Interam. Confed. Chem. Engn.; RMC Club of Can. (Pres., Kingston Br. 1967–68; Extve. Comte. 1972–75; Foundation 1972– , Dir. of the Found. 1991– ;); author of over 100 scient. papers and book contribs.; listed in Who's Who in America, 40th to 47th edns.; United Church; recreations: hunting, New Orleans jazz; Home: 406 Elmwood St., Kingston, Ont. K7M 2Z3.

**FURTWANGLER, Virginia,** B.A., M.A., Ph.D. (pseud. Ann Copeland); fiction writer, teacher; b. Hartford, Conn.; d. William Michael and Agnes Catherine (Bresnahan) Walsh; e. Coll. of New Rochelle, B.A. 1954; Catholic Univ. of Am., M.A. 1959; Cornell Univ., Ph.D. 1970; m. Albert J. s. Albert E. and Laurice F. 17 Aug. 1968; children: Thomas Gavin, Andrew Edward; Teacher of Engl. Lit. & Fiction Writing, Coll. of New Rochelle 1963–66; Indiana Univ. N.W. 1970–71; Mt. Allison Univ. 1975–76; Dorchester Penitentiary 1976–77; Distinguished Visiting Fiction Writer, Coll. of Idaho 1980; Linfield Coll. 1980–81; Univ. of Idaho Winter 1986, Spring 1982; Bemidji State Univ. Spring 1987; Wichita State Univ. Oct. 1988; Writer-in-Residence, Mt. Allison Univ. 1990–91; St. Mary's Univ. Jan. 1993; leader of various writers' workshops in Can. & U.S.; Cornell-Kent Fellowship; Can. Counc. Arts Grant B 1980, 1988; Nat. Endowment for the Arts Writing Fellowship 1978 and 1994; Can. Counc. Short Term Grants 1977, 1988; Ingram Merrill Award 1990; Nominated for Gov.-Gen.'s Award in Fiction 1990; Mem., Writers' Union of Can.; The Authors Guild; Assoc. Writing Progs.; N.B. Fed. of Writers; Internat. Women's Writing Guild; N.S. Dance Fed. (Bd. Mem. 1986–87; Organist, St. Vincent's Ch., Sackville; author: 'The Golden Thread' 1989 (linked stories); 'Earthen Vessels' 1984, 'The Back Room' 1979, 'At Peace' 1978 (short fiction); stories pub. in num. jours. in U.S. & Can.; widely anthologized incl. 'Best Canadian Stories' & 'Best American Short Stories'; recreations: piano, ballroom dancing; Home: P.O. Box 1450, Sackville, N.B. E0A 3C0; Agent: Barbara Kouts, P.O. Box 558, Bellport, N.Y. 11713.

**FUSÉ, Toyomasa,** B.A., M.A., Ph.D.; university professor; b. Sapporo, Japan 20 Jan. 1931; s. Norimasa and Shizué F.; e. Missouri Valley Coll., B.A. 1954; Univ. of Calif. at Berkeley, M.A. 1956, Ph.D. 1962; m. Lois d. Emile and Shirley Prochaska 23 Dec. 1961; children: Megimi, Kenji; PROF., YORK UNIV. 1972– ; Antioch Univ. 1961–64; Carleton Coll. 1964–66; Cornell Univ. 1966–68; Univ. de Montréal 1968–72; H.H. Humphrey Fellow (Israel) 1987; Award for Multicultural Suicide Research 1992; rsch. fellowships in France, Germany, Italy, Hungary, the Netherlands, Japan; Mem., Candn. Assn. of Suicide Prevention; Internat. Assn. of Suicide Prevention; author: 'Suicide and Culture' 1985; 'Introduction to Suicidology' 1990; 'Profiles of Death' 1991; 'Personal Crisis and Ethnotherapy' 1992; editor: 'Modernization and Stress' 1975; Home: 8 Nina St., Toronto, Ont. M5R 1Z3; Office: S728 Ross, Div. of Soc. Sci., Fac. of Arts, York Univ., Downsview, Ont. M3J 1P3.

**FUSS, Melvyn Alan,** B.Sc., M.A., Ph.D.; professor; b. Kitchener, Ont. 29 Mar. 1940; s. Abraham Bernard and Florence (Rosenberg) F.; e. Univ. of Toronto, B.Sc. 1963; M.A. 1965; Univ. of Calif. at Berkeley, Ph.D. 1970; m. Susan d. Fred and Erna Kaufman 10 Oct. 1974; one d.: Adina; PROF. OF ECON., UNIV. OF TORONTO 1979– ; Asst. Econ Prof., Harvard Univ. 1970–72; Assoc. Econ. Prof., Univ. of Toronto 1972–79; Chrmn., Dept. of Econ. 1985–90; Rsch. Assoc., Nat. Bur. of Econ. Rsch. 1983– ; author of num. scholarly articles; author: 'Costs and Productivity in Automobile Production' 1992; editor: 'Production Economics' 1978, 'The Econometrics of Temporary Equilibrium' 1986; recreations: golf, tennis; Home: 66 Otter Cres., Toronto, Ont. M5N 2W5.

**FYFE, W.S.,** C.C., M.Sc., Ph.D., F.R.S., F.R.S.C.; geochemist; educator; b. Ashburton, N.Z. 4 June 1927; s. Colin Alexander and Isabella (Pullar) F.; e. Otago (N.Z.) Univ., B.Sc. 1948, M.Sc. 1949, Ph.D. 1952; m. Patricia Jacqueline (Walker), children: Christopher David, Catherine Mary, Stefan Scott; PROFESSOR EMERITUS, DEPT. OF GEOLOGY, UNIV. OF WESTERN ONT., Prof. 1972–90, Dean of Science there 1986–90; Fulbright Fellow, U.S.A., 1952–55; Prof. of Chem. in N.Z. 1955–58; Prof. of Geol., Univ. of Cal. Berkeley, 1959–66; Guggenheim Fellow, Cambridge 1964; Royal Soc. Research Prof., Univ. of Manchester, 1966–72; author 5 text books and over 400 research papers; Chrmn. Roy. Soc. Can. Ctte. on Global Change 1985–88; Chrmn., I.C.S.U. committee (continental storage of nuclear waste); mem., I.C.S.U. Ctte. for The Internat. Geosphere Biosphere Program 1987–90; Pres., Internat. Union of Geological Sciences 1992– ; I.C.S.U. Ctte. for the International Space Year 1988–90; Companion of the Order of Canada 1989; Logan Medal, Geological Asoc. of Can.; Willet G. Miller Medal, Royal Soc. of Can.; Arthur Homes Medal, Euorpean Union of Geosciences; Arthur Day Medal, Geological Soc. of Am.; Canada Gold Medal for Science and Engr., NSERC 1991; The New Zealand 1990 Commemoration Medal; Canada 1992 Commemoration Medal; D.Sc. (Hon.) Memorial Univ. of Nfld. 1989; D.Sc. (Hon.) Lisbon Univ., Portugal 1990; D.Sc. (Hon.) Lakehead Univ. 1990; D.Sc. (Hon.) Guelph 1992; Hon. Fellow, Royal Soc. N.Z.; Geol. Soc. Am.; Hon. Fellow, Geological Soc. of London (U.K.); Life Fellow, Mineral. Soc. Am.; Fellow, Guggenheim 1964–65 and 1983–84; Hon. mem., Acad. Science Brazil; Hon. Life Mem., Mineralogical Soc., Gt. Britain & Ireland; Fellow, Am. Assoc. for the Advancement of Sci.; mem., Am. Chem. Soc.; Brit. Chem. Soc.; Geol. Assn. Can.; Mineral. Soc. U.K.; recreations: travel, swimming; Home: 1197 Richmond St., London, Ont. N6A 3L3; Office: Dept. of Geology, Univ. of Western Ont., London, Ont. N6A 5B7.

**FYFFE, Gregory George,** B.A., M.A.; public servant; b. 21 June 1946; e. Queen's Univ. B.A. (Hons. 1st Class) 1969; Univ. of B.C. M.A. 1970; Parliamentary Internship 1970–71; m. Alison Ann Hare 23 June 1984; one s.: Duncan George; EXECUTIVE DIRECTOR, IMMIGRATION AND REFUGEE BOARD 1993– ; Asst. to Opposition (P.C.) House Leader 1973–82; Extve. Asst. to Hon. Walter Baker, Pres. of the Privy Council & Min. of Nat. Revenue 1979–80; Special Adviser to Dep. Premier, Prov. of Sask. 1982–83; Asst. Principal Sec. to Premier 1983–84; Chief of Staff to Hon. Bill McKnight 1984–89; Asst. Dep. Solicitor General, Corrections Branch, Solicitor Gen. Secretariat 1989–92; Bd. of Dir., CMHC; recreations: tennis, cycling; Office: 240 Bank St., 6th floor, Ottawa, Ont. K1A 0K1.

# G

**GAASENBEEK, Matthew,** B.A.; corporate finance specialist; b. Bloemendaal, Holland 27 Feb. 1930; s. Matthew and Hendrina Barbara (Scheeres) G.; e. Univ. of W. Ont. Hons. B.A. 1956; m. Mary Hilda d. late Steven and Mary Smella 3 June 1955; children: Karen Barbara, Joanna Elizabeth, Matthew; Pres., Northern Crown Capital Corp.; Dir.: Royal Oak Mines Ltd.; Lagash Internat. Development Corp.; Cannistra Capital Corp.; joined Woods Gordon & Co. 1956–59; Dir. Corporate Finance Annett & Co. 1959–66; Sr. Advr. Candn. Internat. Devel. Agency Ottawa 1966–68; Sr. Corporate Finance Offr. A.E. Ames & Co. 1968–72; Sr. Vice Pres. Corporate Finance Midland Doherty Ltd. 1972–83; Dir. and Past Pres. Fedn. Ont. Naturalists; Past Chrmn. Save Our Streams; former Trustee Candn. Sportsmen's Funds; Past mem. Ont. Council Univ. Affairs; Chrmn., Quetico Park Found.; Protestant; recreations: reading, farming, skiing, boating; Clubs: National; Royal Military Inst.; Beaver Valley Ski; Home: Suite 1502, 30 Wellington St. E., Toronto, Ont. M5E 1S3; Office: Suite 605, 55 University Ave., Toronto, Ont. M5J 2H7.

**GABEL, Brian Paul,** B.B.A., C.A.; financial executive; b. Parry Sound, Ont. 18 Feb. 1956; s. Jarvis MacDonald and Miriam (Selkirk) G.; e. Wilfrid Laurier Univ. B.B.A. (Hons.) 1979; C.A. (Clarkson, Gordon, London, Ont.) 1981; m. Janine d. Dr. Fabien and Norma Curry 18 Aug. 1979; children: Brandon, Ian, Graham; VICE PRESIDENT, MARKETING, STORAGE & TRANSPORTATION, UNION GAS LTD. 1993– ; Staff Accountant, Clarkson Gordon (London, Ont.) 1977–81; Client Mgr.

1981–85; Mgr., Financial Forecasts, Union Gas Limited 1985–86; Regulatory Proceedings 1986–1988; Financial Planning 1988–90; Controller 1990–92; Vice Pres., Human Resources 1992–93; Pres. & Dir., Family Services Kent; Chrmn. & Dir., Chatham-Kent Small Business Support Corp.; Mem., Ont. Natural Gas Assn.; Candn. Gas Assn.; Financial Extves. Inst.; Ont. Inst. of C.A.s; Candn. Inst. of C.A.s; recreations: golf, curling, hockey, baseball; clubs: Chatham Granite, Maple City Country; Home: 60 Hedge Maple Path, Chatham, Ont.; Office: 50 Keil Dr. N., Chatham, Ont. N7M 5M1.

**GABEREAU, Vicki Frances;** broadcaster; b. 31 May 1946; d. Harry Francis and Veryl Allison (Strickland) Filion; divorced; children: Morgan, Eve; CBC RADIO 'GABEREAU' 1988– ; Talk Show Host, CHIC Radio Brampton 1975–76; Researcher, Story Ed., Prod., On-Air Contbr., CBC Radio 1976–80; Assoc. Prod. 'Real Story' with Jim Laxer, TV Ont. 1978; Host, 'Edmonton A.M.' CBC Radio 1980–81; Assoc. Prod., 'Thrill of a Lifetime' CTV 1981; Host, 'Variety Tonight' CBC Radio 1981–86; Bd. Mem., Vancouver East Cultural Ctr. 1984– ; Hon. Fundraising Chair, Central City Mission 1990; 'This Won't Hurt a Bit' 1987; Home: 3550 St. Georges Ave., N. Vancouver, B.C. V7N 1V9; Office: P.O. Box 4600, Vancouver, B.C. V6B 4A2.

**GABOURY, Etienne J.,** B.A., B.Arch., R.C.A., F.R.A.I.C.; architect; b. Bruxelles, Man. 24 Apr. 1930; s. late Napoleon Joseph and late Valentine (Lafreniere) G.; e. St. Boniface Coll. B.A. 1953; Univ. of Man. B.Arch. 1958; Ecole des Beaux-Arts Paris 1958–59; Univ. of Man. LL.D. (hon. causa) 1987; m. Claire Marie Therese d. late Alberic Breton 1 Sept. 1956; children: Lise Jeanne, Pierre Maurice, Jacques Gabriel, François Adrien; PRINC., GABOURY ASSOCIATES – ARCHITECTS; guest speaker and conf. chrmn. several occasions Can. and USA; mem. Expo '67 Arch. Adv. Comte.; Candn. Housing Design Council 1970–73; Gov., Univ. of Man. 1970–73, Vice Chrmn. 1973; Adv. Comte. Winnipeg Symphony Orchestra Ltd. 1970–72; Adv. Comte. Royal Winnipeg Ballet; Pres. Soc. Franco-Manitobaine 1969–70; Founding Gov. Heritage Can. 1973–74; Prov. Adv. Comte. on Transport. 1973–74; Man. Arts Council (Chrmn. 1977–78); Candn. Nat. Comte. Habitat 1976 UN Conf.; mem. N.C.C. Arts Adv. Comte. 1982– ; Studio critiques Sch. of Arch. Univ. of Man. 1965– ; rec'd 5 awards arch. composition Univ. of Man.; French Govt. Scholarship 1958; Massey Awards 1964, 4 bldgs. nominated; Candn. Arch. Yearbook Significant Bldg. Awards 1964, 1966, 1968; Candn. Home Journ. Home of the Yr. 1966; Candn. Housing Council Awards 1967, 1970; Man. Hist. Soc. Centennial Medal of Honor 1970; Man. Assn. Archs. Award 1964; Vincent Massey Awards for Excellence in Urban Environment Special Mention 1971; Heritage Canada Architectural Preservation Award for St. Boniface Cathedral 1985; Heritage Winnipeg Award 1988; Two MAA Awards of Excellence 1989; competition juror on various occasions; author numerous articles, papers; work cited various publs.; major projects, Candn. Embassy in Mexico, 1981; Lycée professionnel hôtelier, Abidjan, 1980; Royal Candn. Mint, Winnipeg, 1973; St. Boniface Cathedral, 1972; St. Boniface Civic Centre, 1963; Precious Blood Church, 1967; E. J. Gaboury residence, 1968; Berney Residence, 1974; Drake Center for Management 1988; Nelson House Sch. & Teacherage 1987; mem. Man. Assn. Archs.; recreations: squash, tennis, golf, reading, music, art; Office: 62 Roslyn Rd., Winnipeg, Man. R3L 0G6.

**GABRIEL, Gary K.;** corporate executive; b. Montreal, Que. 14 Dec. 1955; s. Rudolf and Eleonore (Brauckhoff) G.; e. McGill Univ. management cert. program 1983; m. Jennifer Sprenger 7 May 1988; one s.: Jeffrey; EXTVE. VICE-PRESIDENT & CHIEF FINANCIAL OFFICER, SIEMENS ELECTRIC LTD. 1990– ; various positions incl. mngt. training programs, Siemens AG Berlin/Munich & Siemens Electric Ltd. 1975–84; Gen. Mgr. & Controller, Standard Products Group, Siemens Electric Ltd. 1984–90; Dir., Osram Canada Ltd.; Siemens Nixdorf Information Systems Ltd.; Siemens Automotive Ltd.; Governor General's Study Conf. 1987– ; recreations: golf, tennis, skiing; clubs: Hamilton Golf & Country; Office: 1180 Courtney Park Dr. E., Mississauga, Ont. L5T 1P2.

**GABRIELSE, Hubert,** M.A.Sc., Ph.D.; geologist; b. Golden, B.C. 1 March 1926; s. Christian and Lena (Van Hoepen) G.; e. Univ. of B.C., B.A.Sc. 1948, M.A.Sc. 1950; Columbia Univ. Ph.D. 1955; m. Jean Whitehouse d. George C. Freeman, Millington, N.J. 1 Jan. 1955; children: Peter Christian; Nancy Elizabeth; RESEARCH SCIENT., GEOL. SURVEY OF CAN. 1979– ; Geol., Geol. Survey Can. 1953, Head of Cordilleran Subdiv. 1971–79; author various publs.; mem. Geol. Soc. Am. (Councilor 1981–83); Royal Soc. Can.; N.Y. Acad. Sciences; Geol. Assn. Can.; Candn. Soc. Petrol. Geols.; Am. Assn. Advanc. Science; United Church; recreations: skiing, hiking, golf, photography; Home: 693 Alpine Court, North Vancouver, B.C. V7R 2L7; Office: 100 W. Pender St., Vancouver, B.C. V6B 1R8.

**GADBOIS, André E.,** Q.C., B.C.L.; barrister and solicitor; b. Montréal, P.Q. 14th Apr. 1920; s. Emilien, Q.C. and Louise (Landry) G.; e. Coll. Montréal (Classical course); Séminaire de philosophie, Montréal, B.A. 1941 (Univ. Montréal); McGill Univ., B.C.L. 1949; m. Margaret (Babs), d. Frederick and Marie Drumm, 11 Sept. 1948; children: Anne; Louise; Marie; Frédéric and Josée; COUNSEL, DESJARDINS DUCHARME STEIN MONAST 1986– ; admitted to Quebec Bar 1949; joined Brais & Campbell (Montreal); Gatineau Power Co.; Sec'y. 1953; Vice-Pres. and Sec'y. 1961; mem. Law Dept., Hydro-Québec 1963; cr. Q.C. 1968; Asst. Chief Counsel 1969; Chief Counsel 1979–85; served in Royal Candn. Artillery as Capt. 1941–45; mem. and Past Pres., Montreal Children's Hosp.; mem. Candn. Bar Assn.; Montreal Children's Hosp. Foundation; Alderman, City of Beaconsfield, P.Q. 1969–70; Roman Catholic; clubs: St. Laurent Tennis; recreations: tennis; golf; Home: 4998 de Maisonneuve St. W., Apt. 1422, Westmount, P.Q. H3Z 1N2; Office: 600 de la Gauchetière St. W., Ste. 2400, Montréal, P.Q. H3B 4L8.

**GADBOIS, Ronald,** B.A.; insurance executive; b. London, Ont. Aug. 1940; e. Univ. of West. Ont. B.A. 1962, managers training course 1978; Fellow, Life Office Mngt. Assn. 1972; Chartered Financial Analyst 1988; m. Marilyn Hartleib May 1963; children: Steven Daniel, David Scott; Vice-Pres. & Chief Finan. Offr., Equitable Life Insur. Co. 1988–92; Asst. Vice-Pres., Corp. Planning 1985; Vice-Chrmn., Life Insur. Inst. (Bd. Mem. 1988– ;); Mem., Assn. for Investment Mngt. & Rsch.; recreations: tennis; club: Waterloo Tennis; Home: 30 Glenwood Dr., Kitchener, Ont. N2A 1H7.

**GAFFIELD, Chad,** M.A., Ph.D.; educator; b. New York City, N.Y. 5 July 1951; s. Charles Mitchell and Harriett Aileen (Mathias) G.; e. McGill Univ. B.A. 1973, M.A. 1974; Univ. of Toronto, O.I.S.E. Ph.D. 1978; m. Pamela d. Harry and Hortense Stevenson 19 June 1971; children: Johanna, Scott, Julia; VICE-DEAN, SCHOOL OF GRADUATE STUDIES AND RESEARCH & PROF. OF HIST., UNIV. OF OTTAWA 1988– , Chrmn. Grad. Studies Ctte. 1987–89; Assoc. mem. Sch. of Grad. Studies, Univ. of Toronto 1982– ; Visiting Asst. Prof. of Hist. McGill Univ. 1978–79; Asst. Prof. of Hist. Univ. of Victoria 1979, Assoc. Prof. 1983–85; Assoc. Prof. of Hist., Univ. of Ottawa 1985–88; Co-Prin. Investig., Candn. Social Hist. Project Toronto 1977–78, Vancouver Is. Project 1982–85; Directeur scientifique, Projet d'histoire de l'Outaouais 1987– ; Chair, History Adjudication Ctte., Social Sciences & Humanities Rsch. Counc. 1990; Vice-prés., Comité d'évaluation, Fonds pour la Formation de Chercheurs et l'aide à la Recherche 1991–92; mem., Minnesota Social History Project 1988– ; Pres., Candn. Hist. of Educ. Assoc. 1988–90; Vice-Pres., Science Policy and Rsch., Social Science Federation of Can. 1993–95; various media interviews; acad. conf. orgn.; recipient McGill Scholarship 1974; Can. Council Doctoral Fellowship 1976–77; Univ. of Victoria Rsch. Grants; Social Sci. & Humanities Rsch. Council Can. grants and others; awarded Certificate of Merit, Candn. Historical Assn. 1988; awarded Founders' Prize, Candn. Hist. of Educ. Assn. 1988; awarded Post-Secondary Curriculum Award of Excellence, Minnesota Historical Soc. 1992; recipient, Riddell Award, Ont. Historical Soc. 1992; author: 'Language Schooling and Cultural Conflict: The Origins of the French-Language Controversy in Ontario' 1987; 'Aux origines de l'identité franco-ontariene: education, économie, et culture' 1993; co-ed. 'Children's Rights: Legal and Educational Issues' 1978; 'Universities in Crisis: The Future of a Medieval Institution in the Twenty-First Century' 1986; 'Archives, Automation and Access' 1985; various book chapters, articles scholarly jours., reviews and papers; mem. ed. bd. 'Historical Atlas of Canada' Vol. III, 1979–90; mem. Adv. Bd., Centre de recherche sur la civilisation canadienne-française 1988–89; ed. 'Histoire sociale/Social History' 1985–91; Principal Investigator, 'Family Reproduction in 19th Century Canada' 1991–94; mem. Adv. Bd., Univ. of Ottawa Press 1987–90; Mem., Bd. of Govs., Univ. of Ottawa 1992–95; mem. Candn. Hist. Assn.; Social Sci. Hist. Assn.; Assn. Candn. Studies; Candn. Ethnic Studies Assn.; recreations: basketball, tennis; Home: 65 Ella St., Ottawa, Ont. K1S 2S3; Office: 155 Séraphin-Marion, Ottawa, Ont. K1N 6N5.

**GAFFNEY, George Franklin;** bank executive; b. 9 Nov. 1942; m. Annabelle McCarthy; one d.: Meredith; SR. VICE-PRES. & GENERAL MANAGER, B.C. & YUKON, ROYAL BANK OF CANADA 1989– ; joined Royal Bank of Canada 1964; has had assignments in Halifax, Toronto, Montreal, Calgary & Vanc.; Vice-Pres., Nat. Accounts, B.C. 1982; Vice-Pres. & Mgr., Vanc. Main Branch 1984; Vice-Pres., Independent Business, H.O. Montreal 1988; Community Leadership Award, Vanc. Jr. Bd. of Trade Jaycees; Dir., B.C. Children's Hosp. Found.; Jr. Achievement; Bd. Mem., Fraser Inst.; Senior Vice-Chrmn., Vanc. Bd. of Trade; Business Council of B.C.; Sr. Adv. Bd. Mem., YMCA; Chair, Open Learning Agency Found.; recreations: hockey, fishing; clubs: Hollyburn Country, The Vancouver; Office: P.O. Box 11141, 1055 W. Georgia St., Vancouver, B.C. V6E 3S5.

**GAGAN, David Paul,** M.A., Ph.D.; educator; b. Toronto, Ont. 11 Apl. 1940; s. Charlie B. and Lena M. (Morrow) G.; e. Univ. of W. Ont. B.A. 1963, M.A. 1964; Duke Univ. Ph.D. 1969; m. Rosemary d. Henry and Eleanor Ball 17 May 1963; children: Sarah, James, Rebecca, Abigail; VICE-PRES. (ACADEMIC), THE UNIV. OF WINNIPEG 1992– ; Asst. Prof. of Hist Univ. of Calgary 1966; Asst. Prof. of Hist. McMaster Univ. 1970, Assoc. Prof. 1973, Prof. 1980–92; Dean of Humanities 1981–91; author 'The Denison Family of Toronto' 1973; 'Hopeful Travellers' 1981; 'A Necessity Among Us' 1990; ed. 'Prairie Perspectives' 1970; 'Canada: An Historical Magazine' 1976–79; co-ed. 'Canadian History Through the Press' 10 vols. 1970–76; various articles learned journs.; mem., Candn. Hist. Assn.; Office: 515 Portage Ave., Winnipeg, Man. R3B 2E9.

**GAGE, Frances Marie,** R.C.A.; sculptor; b. Windsor, Ont. 22 Aug. 1924; d. Russell and Jean Mildred (Collver) G.; e. Oshawa (Ont.) Coll. & Vocational Inst. 1943; Ont. Coll. of Art (Sculpture) 1951; Art Students League New York 2 yrs. (scholarship); Ecole des Beaux-Arts Paris 2 yrs. (Royal Soc. Scholarship); maj. sculptures incl. twice-life statue and 4 walnut reliefs Fanshaw Coll. London, Ont. 1962; Dr. Bertram Collip portrait relief Univ. of W. Ont. 1963; Kitchener-Waterloo Art Gallery life sized torso 1964; life sized walnut torso Univ. of Guelph 1966; 'Bear' ciment fondu Wiszniewski, Newmarket 1965; bronze bust Dr. Andrew Smith Univ. Guelph 1967; 4 bronze portrait reliefs A.Y. Jackson, Fred Varley, Healy Willen, Sir Ernest MacMillan 1967; 'Rosamund' twice-life bronze statue Toronto 1968; mem. 'Song in the Wind' Music Bldg. Mount Allison Univ. 1968; 'Woman' marble statue Women's Coll. Hosp. Toronto 1969; bronze relief mem. Robert Meredith Janes Univ. of Toronto 1969; Memorial, Charles Lake Gundy, Mt. Pleasant Cemetery; commemorative medal Samuel Bronfman 1971, Dr. Jason Hannah Royal Soc. Can. 1973 (also 5 commemorative busts); medal for Jean P. Carriere Award, Standards Council of Canada; Dr. Gordon Nikiforuk bust, Univ. of Toronto 1975; bronze 'Baby' Mem. Kew Gardens Toronto 1975; portrait bust, Elmer Iseler, Roy Thompson Hall 1990; portrait head, late Co. R.S. McLaughlin, for Ottawa HQ, Royal Coll. of Physicians, Surgeons (Can.), S. McLaughlin Found.; Guelph Arts Counc. Heritage Award Plaques (ongoing); 'Mindemoya' bronze dog L/S, Donald Forster Sculpture Park, Guelph, Ont. 1990; rec'd Rothman Purchase Award 1965; exhibitor, Internat. Congress of Medallic Arts, Florence 1984, Colorado 1987, Helsinki 1990, Fidem London 1992; served with W.R.C.N.S. during World War II; mem. Council Royal Candn. Acad. Art; recreations: music, conservation; Address: Roseneath Landing, P.O. Box 7, R.R. 2, Roseneath, Ont. K0K 2X0.

**GAGE, Ronald Gordon,** B.Comm., F.C.A.; chartered accountant; b. Brantford, Ont. 7 Feb. 1939; s. Gordon Ross and Maudie (Thompson) G.; e. Brantford Coll. Inst. 1957; Univ. of Toronto B.Comm. 1961; C.A. 1964; F.C.A. 1976; m. Judith Ann d. John and Lillian Wintrip 21 May 1961; children: James David, Christopher Gordon; CHRMN. & C.E.O., ERNST & YOUNG 1993– ; joined present firm (formerly Clarkson Gordon) 1961, Partner 1970, Nat. Dir. of Auditing 1974–76, Office Mng. Partner Kitchener Office 1976–80, Victoria Office 1980–81; Pres., Inst. C.A.'s Ont. 1990–91 (Counc. Mem. 1983–91; Extve. 1986–91); 2nd Vice-Chrmn., Candn. Inst. C.A.'s; Mem., Pub. Accts. Council of Ont.1985–90; Campaign Chrmn., Un. Way of Kitchener 1979; Mem. Bd. of Gov., Wilfrid Laurier; Dir., National Ballet of Canada; recreations: skiing, sailing; Clubs: Toronto; York; Granite; Home: 127 Stratford Cres., Toronto, Ont. M4N 1C9; Office: P.O. Box 251 Ernst & Young Tower, Toronto-Dominion Centre, Toronto, Ont. M5K 1J7.

**GAGLARDI, Philip Arthur;** b. Mission City, B.C. 13 Jan. 1913; s. John and Dominica G.; e. Pub. School, Mission City, B.C.; Northwest Bible Coll., Seattle, Wash.;

m. Jennie Margurette, d. John Sandin, 8 Dec. 1938; two s.: Robert, William; Mayor, City of Kamloops 1988–90; o. Pentecostal Min.; Master Mech., A.R. Williams Machinery Company, Vancouver, B.C. and Bloedel, Stewart and Welch, Victoria, B.C.; 1st elected to Brit. Columbia leg. for Kamloops, in g.e. June 1952; Min. of Public Works 1952–55, Min. of Highways 1955 till resignation from Cabinet, March 1968; apptd. Min. of Rehabilitation & Social Improvement 1969; def. in g.e. 1972; Chrmn., Provincial Alliance of Businessmen; as Min. of Highways was responsible for establishment of B.C. Ferry Service and construction of many highways; built one of first sawdust highways in world, constructed Deas Island Tunnel and Rogers Pass on the TCH #1, first suspension bridge of its kind in Can. at Hudson Hope, first orthotropic deck used in bridge constr. and first jet engine powered snow plow in the world; founder of 'Beautiful British Columbia' publ.; originator of communication system for Dept. of Highways; has travelled extensively in Europe, Asia, Africa, Australia and S. Am.; conducted three-month speaking tour 1949; prominent child and youth worker; Chrmn. & Pres., American Westwater Technology Group Ltd.; Westwater Investment Corp.; Pres., Silverthreads Apt. Soc.; Dir., Northland Properties Ltd.; Mem., Balch Coll. of over 2000 World Leaders, Seattle, Wash. Lib.; Hon. Citizen (and former High Sheriff), City of Palm Springs; Social Credit; Pentecostal; Clubs: Rotary (Hon. mem.); Kiwanis; Lions; recreations: youth work; ranching; raising and showing horses; Home: 514 Strathcona Terrace, Kamloops, B.C. V2C 1B9.

**GAGLIANO, Alfonso;** politician; b. Siculiana, Italy 25 Jan. 1942; s. Vincenzo and Maria (Augello) G.; e. Sir George Williams Univ., Courses in Acctg.; Cert. Gen. Acct. (C.G.A.); m. Ersilia d. Immacolata and Amatore Gidaro 3 July 1965; children: Vincenzo, Maria, Immacolata; MEM. OF PARLIAMENT FOR ST.-LÉONARD 1984– ; (re-el. 1988); practicing Gen. Acct. since 1969; joined Que. Liberal Party 1978; Official Party Agent for Jeanne-Mance 1981; apptd. Liberal Assn. Exec. for Viger 1984; mem. Liberal Party of Can. 1978– ; Opposition Critic for Min. of Small Bus. 1984–90; Revenue Canada 1985–86 and Canada Post Corp. 1987–89; Immigration 1990–91; el. Chrmn., Que. Liberal Caucus 1988–91; apptd. Official Opposition Whip 1991; Pres. Gagliano and Co. Mgmt. Cons.; elec. sch. Trustee 1977; Comnr. (1977) and Chrmn. (1983–84) Jerome-Leroyer Regional Sch. Bd., Montreal; past Dir. Fed. des Commissions Scolaires Catholiques du Que.; past mem. Assn. des Commissions Scolaires; Dir. Trinacria Assn.; Treas. Italexporama 84; founding Pres. Siculiana Assn.; founding mem. St.-Gilbert Optimist Club, St. Leonard; mem. St. Leonard C. of C.; Assn. of Italian-Candn. Businessmen; Dir. Raphael Iadeluca Found.; past Pres. Sub-Ctte. on Personnel Devel. and past mem. Exec., Assn. of Sch. Bds. of Montreal; recreations: golf, gourmet cooking, wine making; Home: 6275 Place St. Zotique, St. Leonard, Que.

**GAGLIANO, Tony;** printing executive; b. Toronto, Ont. 13 June 1958; s. Gaetano and Guiseppina (Arcuri) G.; e. Ryerson Inst. of Technol., bus. degree; m. Lina d. John and Teresa DiPietrantonio 2 May 1987; PRES., ST. JOSEPH PRINTING 1987– ; joined St. Joseph Printing as Gen. Mgr. 1980 (then a 10-employee, family-run business with annual sales of $500,000; now $50.7 million annual sales); planned & started a $25 million expansion in 1989 incl. new facility & equipment; currently fastest growing printing company independently owned; Bd. of Dir., Candn. Printing Indus. Assn.; Mem., Young Pres. Orgn.; Environ. Ctte., Candn. Printing Indus.; Bd. of Dir., The Boy Scouts of Can.; Home: 5 Rosewood Court, Stouffville, Ont.; Office: 50 MacIntosh Boulevard, Concord, Ont.

**GAGNÉ, Gaston R.,** B.comm., M.B.A.; credit manager; b. Sherbrooke, Qué. 2 Oct. 1932; s. Rosario and Aline (Dubreuil) G.; e. Laval Univ., B.Comm. 1956, M.B.A. 1957; m. Louise d. Antonio and Rita Bégin 31 May 1956; children: Alain, Jacques, Michel; CREDIT MGR., ICI CANADA INC. 1974– ; Banking & Fgn. Exch., C.I.L. Inc. 1957; Credit Supr. 1960; Sales & Mktg. 1962; Sec. Asst. 1965; Mktg. Planning 1966; Reg. Mgr., Agric. Group, E. Can. 1969; Area Mgr., Agric. Group, E. Can. 1970; Dir., Creditel of Can. Ltd. 1983–90; Dir. & Vice-Pres., Les Explosifs Chretien Ltée; Explonitrate Ltée; mem., CIREM (Group Pres.); recreations: golf, bridge, travel; Club: Sherbrooke Golf & Country; Home: 182 Westcliffe, Pointe Claire, Qué. H9R 1M9; Office: Box 10, Montréal, Qué. H3C 2R3.

**GAGNÉ, Paul E.;** executive; b. Hearst, Ont. 17 Sept. 1946; e. Queen's Univ. M.B.A. 1975; Ont. Inst. of Chartered Accts. C.A. 1974; Univ. of Ottawa B.Comm. 1972; m. Shari Mayer; one d. Sara Anne; PRES. & C.E.O., AVENOR INC. (formerly Canadian Pacific Forest Products Ltd.) 1991– ; Public Acct., Normandin, Séguin 1972–74, 1975–76; various positions present firm 1976–79, Asst. To Comptroller 1979–80, Vice-Pres. Finance (Dominion Cellulose) 1980–81, Chief Internal Auditor 1981–82, Treasr. 1983–84, Vice-Pres. Finance 1984–86, Vice-Pres., Finance, Accounting and Logistics 1986–88, Extve. Vice-Pres., Finance, Accounting and Logistics 1988–90, Pres., C.O.O. & Dir. 1990–91; Dir., NBIP Forest Products Ltd.; Chrmn., Pacific Forest Products; Office: 1250 René Lévesque Blvd., 20th Floor, Montréal, Qué. H3B 4Y3.

**GAGNE, Raymond,** B.Comm., C.G.A.; business executive; b. Quebec 29 July 1936; e. Univ. of Laval B.Comm.; Insead, France; m. Raymonde Lachance 1960; children: France, Mario, Yves; PRES. & CHIEF OPERATING OFFR., SOC. D'INVETISSEMENT DESJARDINS 1989– ; Auditor, Raymond, Chabot, Martin, Paré 1958; Conf. des Caisses Populaires et d'econ. Desjardins du Qué. 1960; Accountant & Treas., Les Placements Collectifs 1965; Treas., Fiducie du Qué. 1969; Vice-Pres., Claurémiand; Sr. Vice-Pres., present firm 1979; Pres., Soc. d'Investissements Tremplin 2000 Inc. 1987; Chrmn., Culinar Inc.; Chrmn. & Chief. Extve. Offr., Soc. d'Investissement Trempin 2000 Inc.; Dir., Groupe Canam Manac Inc.; Gestion Placement Desjardins; Office: 1717, 2 Complexe Desjardins, Montreal, Que. H5B 1C2.

**GAGNIER, Daniel,** B.A., M.A.; g. Montreal, Que. 11 May 1946; s. Carl and Gisèle (Morin) G.; e. Loyola Coll. B.A. (Hons.) 1968; McGill Univ. M.A. (Hons.) 1990; Australian Nat. Univ.; m. Rose Simpson 28 Aug. 1987; children: Laurie, Daniel, Nicholas, Stefan, Marissa; PRESIDENT, BREWERS ASSN. OF CANADA 1992– ; Profl. Serv. Rep., Proctor & Gamble 1969–70; Liaison Offr., Cult. Affairs, UNESCO then Project Offr., Training & Devel., Dept. of External Affairs 1971–72; various diplomatic positions, Dept. of External Affairs 1972–82; Extve. Dir., Candn. Unity Information Office, Dept. of Justice then Asst. Sec. to Cabinet (Commun.), Privy Council Office 1982–85; Dep. Min., Econ. Devel. & Trade, Govt. of Sask. 1985–87; Asst. Sec. to Cabinet, Econ. Policy & programs, Fed.-Prov. Relns. Office 1987–88; Dep. Min., Min. of Energy & Min. of Intergovt. Affairs & Spec. Advr. to Cabinet, seconded to Premier's Office as Chief of Staff, Govt. of Ont. 1988–90; Depy. Sec. to the Cabinet (Communications), & Consultations Privy Council Office, Govt. of Canada 1990–92; Office: 155 Queen St., Ste. 1200, Ottawa, Ont. K1P 6L1.

**GAGNON, Alain-G.,** B.A., M.A., Ph.D.; university professor, author; b. Saint-Gabriel de Rimouski, Que. 13 Jan. 1954; s. François and Éliane (Normand) G.; e. Univ. du Qué. à Rimouski B.A. 1974; Simon Fraser Univ. M.A. 1978; Carleton Univ. Ph.D. 1983; PROFESSOR, DEPT. OF POLITICAL SCIENCE, MCGILL UNIV. 1992– ; Asst. Prof., Dept. of Pol. Sci., Queen's Univ. 1982–83; Research Branch, Federal-Prov. Relns. Office, Govt. of Canada 1983–84; Asst. Prof., Dept. of Pol. Sci., Carleton Univ. 1984–87; Assoc. Chair, Dept. of Pol. Sci., Carleton Univ. 1986–89; Assoc. Prof. 1987–89; Assoc. Prof., Dept. of Political Science, McGill Univ. 1989–92; Director, Québec Studies Programme, McGill Univ. 1992– ; Stein Rokkan Fellowship, International Political Science Assn. 1982; Vice-Pres., Soc. Qué. de sci. pol. 1990–91; Pres. 1991–92; Mem., Candn. Pol. Sci. Assn.; Soc. qué. de sci. pol.; Internat. Pol. Sci. Assn. Rsch. Ctte. on Comparative Federalism & Federations; Am. Pol. Sci. Assn.; author: 'Le développement régional, l'État et les groupes populaires 1985; co-author: 'Social Scientists and Politics in Canada' 1988; 'Quebec: Beyond the Quiet Revolution' 1990; 'Allaire, Bélanger, Campeau et les autres: Les Québécois s'interrogent sur leur avenir' 1991; 'The Almanac of Canadian Politics' 1991; 'Québec: au - delà de la Révolution tranquille' 1992; editor: 'Quebec State and Society' 1984, 2nd ed. 1993; co-editor: 'Canadian Parties in Transition' 1990; 'Canadian Politics: An Introduction to the Discipline' 1990; 'Democracy with Justice: Essays in Honour of Khayyam Zev Paltiel' 1992; 'Répliques aux détracteurs de la souveraineté du Québec' 1992; 'Le référendum du 26 octobre 1992' 1992; 'Comparative Federalism and Federation' 1993; TV and radio commentator; Home: 3639 Coloniale St., Montreal, Que. H2X 2Y7; Office: 855 Sherbrooke W., Montreal, Que. H3A 2T7.

**GAGNON, André,** O.C.; musician; b. St-Pacôme-de-Kamouraska, Qué. 1 Aug. 1942; e. theory lessons with Léon Destroismaisons 1952–53, 1957; CMM 1957–61, piano, composition, solfège (rec'd premier prix harmony 1961); studied in Paris with Yvonne Loriod and took courses in accompanying and conducting 1961 (Que. Govt. Grant); accompanist for Claude Léveillée also music dir., arranger and pianist for most of his recordings 1962–69; sometime accompanist and arranger for Monique Leyrac and others; soloist Mozart concert Place des Arts 1967; recorded his 4 concertos in the style of Vivaldi 'Mes Quartre Saison' with London Baroque Orchestra 1969; performed Expo 70 Osaka and toured with Québec Symphony Orchestra in Qué. 1970; recorded 'Les Turluteries' with Hamburg Philharmonic Orchestra 1972; other recordings incl. 'Let It Be Me' and 'Projection' 1971, 'Saga' 1974, 'Neiges' 1975 (Juno Award 1976 best selling LP), 'Le Saint-Laurent' (selected instrumental record of yr, ADISQ 1979), 'Mouvements' 1979, 'Virage à gauche' (best instrumental record of yr. ADISQ 1981); rec'd Juno Award for instrumental artist of 1977, and the Order of Canada for his outstanding contribution to Canadian Music in 1979; performed in France 1975, 1976, Mexico 1976, 1982, Venezuela, Greece and Roumania in 1982, toured USA 1979, and Canada 1978, 1979, 1980, 1981 and 1982; wrote music for Ann Ditchburn's ballet 'Mad Shadows' premiered by Nat. Ballet of Can. O'Keefe Centre Toronto 1977; composed music for pas de deux 'Nelligan' and for ballet 'Adage' performed by Compagnie de Danse Eddy Toussaint at Place des Arts 1977; performed in concert at Massey Hall 1978, and Place des arts 1974, 1976, 1978, 1980; wrote music for NFB film 'Games of the XXI Olympiad' 1977, CBS TV movie 'Night Flight' 1978, and feature films 'Running' 1979, 'Phobia' 1980 and 'Hot Touch' 1982; host and accompanist CBC TV 'Cri-Cri' 1962–64 and Music Dir. 'Moi et l'autre' 1966–70; composed music several series incl. 'Vivre en ce pays' 1967–71, 'Les Forges du St-Maurice' 1972–75 and 'Techno-Flash'; wrote and performed music children's program 'La souris verte' 1967–76; guest artist 'Zoom,' 'Vedettes en direct,' 'Dimanshowsoir,' 'Superspecial' with Karen Kain 1978, with Ann Ditchburn 1979, 'The Perry Como Christmas Special' 1981; composition 'Petit Concerto pour Carignan et orchestre (1976) performed by Carignan & Yehudi Menuhin on CBC TV 'The Music of Man' 1978; played for Queen Elizabeth II at the National Art Center in Ottawa, 1977; wrote the score for 'Phobia' a John Huston film and performed with London Symphonic Orchestra in 1980; in 1981 wrote the score for 'Hot Touch,' directed by Roger Vadim; at the end of 1982 'André Gagnon Greatest Hits' released, including a new single 'Beau et chaud'; mem. SOCAN; Home: 2686 Laval St., Montreal, Que. H2X 3C9; Office: c/o Great Artists Mgmt., 1501 Jeanne-Mance, Place des Arts, Montreal, Que. H2X 1C9.

**GAGNON, Ann,** R.N.; volunteer management and former fund raising consultant; b. Montreal, Que. 4 Nov. 1925; d. Adhémard and Kathleen (Hull) G.; e. Acad. St-Urbain, Couvent d'Outremont; Univ. of Montreal R.N.; 1st m. Jean s. Alexandre and Imelda Trudel 13 May 1950; 2nd m. Bruno s. Pierre and Claire Messier 2 July 1984; children: Jean, Laurent, Marie, François, and Ann Trudel; CHAIRMAN, NAT. COUNCIL OF WELFARE 1990–94; registered nurse; insurance underwriter; volunteer fund raiser for Candn. Cancer, Soc. & Multiple Sclerosis; director of volunteer serv. for the disabled; Mem., citizens adv. ctte., Leclerc Prison; Mem., Conseil de l'admin. de l'Assn. Québecoise des droits des retraités; Mem., Comité d'admin. du Comité aux services des collectivités de l'Univ. du Qué. à Montréal; Dir., Devel., Montreal Children's Hosp. Found. 1988–91; author of articles on volunteer mngt., pub. in newspaper; speaker on self-esteem, stress/mngt. & volunteering; recreations: reading, writing, photography; Address: Rm. 1876, Jeanne Mance Bldg., Tunney's Pasture, Ottawa, Ont. K1A 0K9.

**GAGNON, Claude;** réalisateur; né. St-Hyacinthe, Qué. 18 déc. 1949; f. Lucien et Rita (Pépin) G.; é. Séminaire St-Hyacinthe; ép. Yuri f. Tatsuji et Kumiko Yoshimura 14 fév. 1973; enfants: Samuel, Angèle, Marilou; réside Japon 1970–79; Comédien, 'Satsujin Ken II' 1974, 'Onna Hitsatsu Godan Ken' 1976, 'Rashamen Oyuki' 1977; Scénariste / réalisateur, 'Essai filmique sur musique Japonaise' 1974, 'The Kid Brother' 1987 (sept prix inclus Grand Prix des Ameriques, Fest. des Films du Monde, Montréal 1987); participation numbreux festivals des films); Réalisateur/ monteur:'Geinin' 1974, 'Yui to hi' 1977; Réal. / scén. / prod. / monteur: 'Keiko' 1978 (quatre prix), 'Larose, Pierrot et la Luce' 1982, 'Visae Pale' 1985 (numbreux prix inclus Prix de la presse internat., Fest. des Films du Monde 1985; participation numbreux festivals des films); Monteur: 'L'Homme d'Ailleurs' 1979; Prod., 'Rafales' 1990, 'La Postière' 1991; Prod. / réalisateur, 'The Pianist' 1991; Prés., Yoshimura-Gagnon Inc. 1979; Co-fond. et vice-prés., Aska Film Internat. Inc. 1987– ; rés.: 824, rue Des Colibris, Longueuil, Qué. J4G 2C1; bureau: 1600, av. De Lorimier, bureau 211, Montréal, Qué. H2K 3W5.

**GAGNON, Denis J.,** B.A., B.Pharm., M.Sc., Ph.D.; pharmacologist; educator; b. Quebec City, Que. 3 Sept. 1939; s. Jean-Paul and Alphonsine (Hallé) G.; e. St-Louis Coll. Edmunston, N.B. B.A. 1959; Laval Univ. B.Pharm. 1963; McGill Univ. M.Sc. 1965, Ph.D. 1967; m. Jeannine d. late Louis-Philippe Rheault 26 May 1962; children: François, Josée, Michèle; VICE-RECTOR, RESEARCH, LAVAL UNIV.; Assoc. Prof. and Chrmn. of Pharmacol. 1975–80, Prof. 1980, Assoc. Dean of Rsch. & Grad. Studies, Fac. of Med., present univ. 1977–86; Post doctorate Fellow, Stockholm Univ., Karolinska Inst. 1967–68; Visiting Scient. Royal Coll. Surgs. Eng. 1968; Assoc. Prof. of Pharmacol. Univ. of Sherbrooke 1968, Asst. Prof. 1971–75; co-author 'Introduction to Neurological Sciences' (in French) 1978; author or co-author of numerous articles and scient. papers; mem. Natural Sciences and Engrg. Rsch. Counc. of Can.; Pharmacol. Soc. Can.; recreations: skiing, biking, sailing; Home: 1401 Gaspard Fauteux, Sillery, Que. G1T 2T7; Office: Quebec City, Que. G1K 7P4.

**GAGNON, Emile;** industrialist; b. Montreal, Que. 18 Apr. 1928; s. Wilfrid and Yvonne (Senecale) G.; e. Brébeuf Coll., Montreal; Babson Inst. Business Adm., Boston, Mass.; m. Mireille, d. Jacques Fortier, 10 June 1960; two s. Emile Jr., E. Philippe; Extve., Studio Wallace Inc.; past Dir.: Champlain Oil Products Ltd.; Hôpital de la Miséricorde; Soc. des Alcools du Qué.; past Pres. and Dir., Shoe Mfrs. Assn. Can.; past mem. Adv. Counc., Min. of Industry & Comm., Can.; R. Catholic; recreation: sports; Clubs: St. Denis; Laval-sur-le-Lac; Home: 31 Les Sorbiers, Laval-sur-le-Lac, Cité Laval, Que. H7R 1E5.

**GAGNON, Jean-Louis,** O.C., F.R.S.C. (1971); né Québec, 21 fév. 1913; f. Adhémar et Marie-Elise (Nadeau) G.; é. coll. Ste-Marie et Bréboeuf, Montréal; Univ. d'Ottawa; Univ. Laval, Québec, (sc. sociales); ép. Hélène Jobidou, Château d'Eau, Qué., 12 sept. 1936; fondateur, magazine littéraire 'Vivre,' Qué., 1933, rédact. en chef: 'La Voix de l'Est,' Granby, Qué., 1935; 'L'Evénement-Journal,' Qué., 1940; corres. de guerre 'Le Soleil,' Londres, Angl., 1941; Dir., West African Broadcasting Unit, Accra, Gold Coast, Afrique, 1942; Dir., Agence France-Afrique, Canada, 1943; chef du bureau, Agence France-Presse, Wash., D.C., 1944; Dir. service d'information et relat. publiques, Brazilian Traction Light and Power Co. Ltd., Rio de Janeiro, Brésil, 1946; Editorialiste, CKAC Montréal, 1949; a lancé 'Les Ecrits du Canada Français,' Montréal, 1953; Rédact. en chef 'Le Canada' Montréal 1953; a lancé l'hebdo 'La Réforme' Montréal, 1955; Rédact. en chef 'La Presse' Montréal 1958; a lancé 'Le Nouveau Journal' Montréal 1961; co-prés., Comm. Royale d'enquête sur le Bilinguisme et le Biculturalisme; trophée Laflèche 'pour la plus grande contribution à la radio canadienne' 1957; Le Grand Prix du Journalisme de l'union can. des journalistes de langue fr. 1962; Trophée des commentaires (p. programme 'Choc') du Congrès du Spectacle, Union des Artistes 1963; 'Journaliste de l'Année' National Press Club of Can. 1970; mem. Soc. Royale du Canada 1970; doctorat d'honneur en Droit, Univ. Laurentienne 1972; auteur: 'Vent du Large' 1944; 'La Fin des Haricots' 1955; 'La Mort d'un Nègre' 1961; préface d'album de caricatures de Robert Lapalme 1950; préface de 'Un Monde Fou' de Berthio 1960; en collaboration: 'A Century of Reporting/Un siècle de reportage' 1967; 'Le Canada au seuil du siècle de l'abondance' 1969 (avec Prof. R. Mandrou, Paris, France); Dir.-Gen. Information Canada 1970; Ambassadeur UNESCO, Paris 1972; nommé mem. du Conseil de la radio diffusion et des telecommunications canadiennes; mem. Acad. canad.-fr.; Conseil des Arts du Qué.; Officier de l'Ordre du Canada 1980.

**GAGNON, Jean-Marie,** M.Sc., M.B.A., Ph.D., F.R.S.C.; university professor; b. Fabre 16 July 1933; s. Pierre and Yvette (Langlois) G.; e. Univ. Laval, M.Sc. 1957; Univ. of Chicago, M.B.A. 1966; Univ. of Chicago, Ph.D. 1970; m. Rachel 15 Aug. 1959; children: Jean-Pierre, Denys, Eric; PROF. OF FINANCE, LAVAL UNIV. 1959– ; Auditor, Clarkson, Gordon & Co., Montreal 1957–59; Vis. Prof., Fac. Univ. Catholique a Mons (Belgium) 1972–74; Vis. Prof. of Finan., Nankai Univ. (China) summer 1984; Rsch. Assoc., Econ. Counc. of Can. 1981–82; Dir., Serv. de Santé du Qué.; Mutuelle d'Assur.; F.R.S.C.; Mem., Ordre des comptables agréés du Qué.; author: 'Risque financier, taux de rendement des entreprises canadiennes et intervention de l'état' 1984; 'Taxes and Dividends'; co-author (with N. Khoury) 'Traite de gestion financière' 1987; Office: Ste. Foy, Que. G1K 7P4.

**GAGNON, Michel A.,** B.A., LL.L.; lawyer; b. Montreal, Que. 6 July 1939; s. Adrien and Ninon (Charbonneau) G.; e. Coll. de Montréal B.A. 1957; Séminaire de Philosophie 1959; Univ. de Montréal LL.L. 1962; m. Colette d. Marguerite and Albert A. Gagné 25 Sept. 1965; children: Brigitte, Eric, Marc-André; SENIOR PARTNER, OGILVY RENAULT 1988– ; articling student, Ogilvy Renault 1962; Lawyer 1963; Partner 1973; Dir. & Sec., Canoptec Inc.; Dafran Sport Inc.; Essilor Canada Ltd.; Scoa Canada Inc.; SMS Rolling Mills Inc.; Dir., Concast Canada Inc.; Donohue Inc. & subsidiaries; Lectr., Que. Bar Sch.; Mem. Bd. of Examiners Que. Bar; Sec., Féd. Internat. des Patrouilles de Ski; Dir., Orchestre Métropolitain du Grand Montréal; Mem., Assn. des Anciens du Coll. de Montréal; Diplômés de l'Univ. de Montréal; Candn. Bar Assn.; Que. Bar; recreations: skiing, golf, travel, reading; clubs: Club de Golf Val Morin; Home: 795 Muir, #1604, St-Laurent, Que. H4L 5H8; Office: 1981 McGill College Ave., Montreal, Que. H3A 3C1.

**GAGNON, Patrick C.,** M.P.; politician; s. Dr. Alban J. and Lili (Duguay) G.; e. McGill Univ. and Univ. of Paris; PARLIAMENTARY SECRETARY TO THE SOLICITOR GENERAL 1993– ; Govt. Affairs Consultant, S.A. Murray Consulting (Ottawa) 1988; Asst. Ed., 'The Financial Post' Dir. of Government' (Hicks Media, Ottawa) 1988–92; Public Relations Dir., Candn. Inst. of Mining, Metallurgy & Petroleum (Montreal) 1989–90; Special Projects Co-ord., Nippon Industries (Japan) 1990–92; Vice-Pres. & Pres. (Qué.), OAI Inc. (Montreal) 1992; Journalist 'United Press Internat.' & Assoc. Ed. 'The Financial Post' Dir. of Government (Hicks Media, Ottawa) 1992–93; Member of Parliament (Bonaventure-Îles-de-la-Madeline) 1993; Gov. & Corp. Sec., Bruce M. Hicks Education Foundation; Liberal; recreations: fly fishing, skiing; Address: 468 West Block, House of Commons, Ottawa, Ont. K1A 0A6.

**GAGNON, Paul Martin,** B.E., P.Eng.; petroleum executive; b. Moose Jaw, Sask. 17 Sept. 1937; s. Wilfred Joseph and Adelaide Beatrice (Cotter) G.; e. Univ. of Sask. B.E. 1959; m. Maureen d. Bert and Genoa Walsh 3 June 1961; children: Deanna, Yvonne, Paul, Jennifer, Lisa; el. to H. of C. for Calgary North g.e. 1984; did not run in g.e. 1988; Geol. Pan American Petroleum 1959–64; Prodn. Mgr. to Vice Pres. International Petro Data Inc. 1964–69; Candn. Mgr. Panoil 1970; Voyager Petroleums 1971; Pres. and Chief Exec. Offr.: Joli Fou Petroleums Ltd. 1972– ; Liberty Petroleums Inc. 1979–81; Dir. Calpetro Resources Inc. 1981–83; mem. Candn. Assn. Petrol. Geols. (Bus. Mgr. 1976, Treas. 1980); Am. Assn. Petrol. Geols.; recreations: skiing, jogging, tennis, fishing, bridge, carpentry; Home: 59 Coleridge Cres. N.W., Calgary, Alta. T2K 1X8.

**GAGNON, William Norman,** B.A., B.C.L.; textile executive; b. Montreal, Que. 4 May 1933; s. William Oliver and Freda May (Black) G.; e. St. Patrick's High Sch. Arvida, Que. 1950; St. Francis Xavier Univ. B.A. 1954; McGill Univ. B.C.L. 1957; PRESIDENT INTERNAT. OPERATIONS, DOMINION TEXTILE INC. 1982– ; Dir., Dominion Textile Intnl. B.V. (Switzerland); DHJ Industries A.G. (Switzerland); DHJ Industries Europe S.A. (France); Entretelas DHJ-Novamerica S.A. (Brazil); DHJ Industries (Hong Kong) Ltd.; DHJ Industries S.A. (Pty.) Ltd. (S. Africa); Swift Textiles S.A. (France); Solr., Bell Canada 1959–61; Vice Pres., Law Canadair Ltd. 1961–70; Solr., Duquet, Mackay, Weldon, Bronstetter, Johnson 1970–71; Treas., present Co. 1971, Vice Pres. Adm. 1973, Pres. DHJ Industries Europe S.A. 1976, Vice Pres. and Gen. Mgr. Internat. Div. 1980, Sr. Vice Pres. Human Resources and Internat. 1981; recipient Prix d'Argent République française; Gov. Que. Blue Cross; Clubs: St-Denis (Montreal); Baur au Lac (Zurich); Home: Rosenbergweg 10A, CH-6300 Zug, Switzerland; Office Industriestrasse 40, CH-6301 Zug, Switzerland.

**GAGNON-TREMBLAY, Monique,** M.N.A., B.A., LL.B.; politician; b. Plessisville, Qué. 26 May 1940; d. Joseph and Antoinette (Provencher) Gagnon; e. elem. and high schs. Plessisville; Quirion Bus. Sch. Thetford Mines 1958; Univ. Laval B.A. 1969; Law Licence at Univ. de Sherbrooke 1972, Degree in Notarial Law 1973; m. Jacques s. Adrien Tremblay 23 May 1970; DEPUTY PREMIER, TREASURY BOARD PRESIDENT and Min. responsible for Administration and the Public Service 1994– ; Exec. Sec. notary's office 1958–69; opened own notary office Ascot Corner and became Teaching Asst. in Notarial Law Univ. de Sherbrooke 1973; Lib. Can. Qué. g.e. 1981, def.; el. M.N.A. for Saint-François 1985, re-el. 1989; Min. responsible for status of women, Que. 1985–89; Min. Cultural Communities and Immigration, Vice-pres. Qué. Treasury Bd. 1989–94; former Vice Pres. Produits chimiques Shefford Inc. Granby; mem. mgmt. office Sherbrooke's Corp. de l'hôpital d'Youville; Dir. Centre Communautaire juridique de l'Estrie; Dir. Fondation Mieux-Vivre; mem. Club de Réforme de Sherbrooke; mem. Mun. Council Ascot Corner 1979–85; Founding mem. Québec-Can. 1979; mem. Qué. Lib. Party Nat. Exec., Chairperson Lib. Assn. Saint-François and Regional Adv. Qué. Lib. Party 1981–84; Chairperson sub-ctte. Status of Women QLP 1984–85; mem. Chamber Notaries Qué.; Fédération des notaires de la prov. de Qué.; Soc. Saint-Jean-Baptiste du diocèse de Sherbrooke; Assn. québécoise de planification fiscale et successorale; Home: 360, rue McGill, Montréal, Qué. H2Y 2E9; Office: 935 King St. E., Sherbrooke, Qué. J1G 1E3.

**GAGOSZ, Bernard Arthur,** B.A.; dipolmat; b. Val D'or, Que. 4 Apl. 1940; s. John and Emilie (Kostek) G.; e. Weston (Ont.) Coll. Inst. 1958; Sir Wilfrid Laurier Univ. B.A. 1964; Banff Sch. Advanced Mgmt. Dip. 1974; m. Mary-Lou d. Maurice and Leone Wanamaker 9 May 1964; children: Nathalie Monique, Christopher Bernard; CONSUL GENERAL OF CANADA, SEATTLE 1992– ; 3rd Sec. Vienna 1965; 1st Sec. Brussels 1965–69; Consul and Sr. Trade Comnr. Manila 1969–70, Detroit 1970–71; Counsellor Athens 1971–76; Dir. Personnel Trade Comnr. Service Ottawa 1976–79; Consul Gen. Melbourne 1979–83, Minneapolis 1983–87; Dir. Gen. Personnel Dept. of External Affairs and Internat. Trade Ottawa 1987–89; High Comnr. for Can. to Singapore and Brunei 1989–92; Consul General, San Francisco 1992; author numerous articles internat. trade various publs.; mem. Profl. Assn. Foreign Service Offrs.; Rotary; World Affair Council; Seattle Chamber of Commerce; Vancouver Bd. of Trade; City Club; Candn. Bus. Assn. Singapore; recreations: sailing, scuba diving, skiing, tennis, golf, music, literature; Clubs: Singapore Cricket; Tanglin; New Edinburgh Tennis (Ottawa); Rainier Club; Seattle Yacht; Home: 128 Lake Washington Blvd. E., Seattle, Washington 98112; Office: Candn. Consulate General, 412 Plaza 600, Sixth and Stewart, Seattle, Washington 98101–1286.

**GAIRDNER, James Robert;** real estate executive; b. Oakville, Ont. 22 Nov. 1938; s. James Harland and Ruthann (Johnston) G.; e. Appleby Coll.; Univ. of B.C.; Univ. of W. Ont.; m. Stephanie Jane d. Arthur William Leggett 19 Feb. 1983; children: James Michael, Molly Ruth; PRES. & CHRMN., JOHNSTON & DANIEL LTD. 1984– ; Trainee, Davis Leather, Newmarket 1961; Mngt. Cons., De Marco & Co., Connecticut 1962; Vice-Pres. & Gen. Mgr., Ford Smith Machine Co. Ltd., Hamilton 1963; Asst. to Pres., Internat. Helium, Toronto 1967; Vice-Pres. & Gen. Mgr., Castle Glen Estates, Toronto 1968; Pres., Johnston & Daniel Ltd. 1970–84; Dir., The Gairdner Found.; Lac Bleu Holdings Limited; D'Or Noir Resources; Lloyd's of London; Candn. Real Estate Assn.; Ont. Real Estate Assn.; Toronto Real Estate Bd.; Royal Agricultural Winter Fair; Conservative; Anglican; recreations: scuba diving, tennis; clubs: Chief Executives Orgn., XPO, World Bus. Counc., Toronto Club, Caughnawana Fishing & Hunt, Caledon Riding & Hunt, Badminton & Racquet, Fed. of Ont. Naturalists, World Wildlife, East Hill, Ont. Equestrian Fed., Muskoka Lakes Golf & Country; Home: 257 Warren Rd., Toronto, Ont. M4V 2S7; Office: 477 Mount Pleasant Rd., Toronto, Ont. M4S 2L9.

**GAIRDNER, John Smith;** industrialist; b. Toronto, Ont. 25 July 1925; s. late James Arthur and Norma Ecclestone (Smith) G.; e. Appleby Coll., Oakville, Ont.; Univ. of Toronto 1942–43; m. Ivy Jane, d. Lewis Brothwell, Smiths Falls, Ont., 30 Nov. 1946; two s., John Lewis (dec.), Robert Donald; one d., Brenda Leigh; PRES., JORONDA RESOURCES LTD. (formerly Gairdner & Co. Ltd.); Pres. & Dir., Gairdner International Ltd.; Vice Chrmn., The Gairdner Foundation; Life Mem., Bd. of Govs., Appleby Coll., Oakville, Ont.; served in 2nd World War with R.C.A.F. 1943–45; Anglican; recreations: golf, fishing, gardening; Clubs: Toronto Golf; National; Caughnawana Fishing & Hunting; La Jolla Country; La Jolla Beach & Tennis; Homes: 2 Ennisclare Dr. W., Oakville, Ont. L6J 4N2 and 1080 Muirlands Drive, La Jolla, CA 92037; Office: 2 Toronto St., Suite 404, Toronto, Ont. M5C 2B6.

**GÁL, László,** RCA; illustrator; b. Budapest 18 Feb. 1933; s. István and Anna (Gémes) G.; e. Széchény Gimnázium Budapest 1943–51; Superior School of Pedagogy Budapest, Art Teacher 1951–54; m. Armida d. Mary and Nicola Romano-Gargarella 20 Jan. 1962; children: Anna Maria (Marika), Raffaella; GRAPHIC DESIGNER, CANADIAN BROADCASTING CENTRE TORONTO 1975– ; Graphic Designer, CBC Toronto 1958–65; Illustrator of Children's Books, Arnoldo Mondadori Verona Italy 1965–69; freelance illustrator 1970–74; IODE Book Award 1978; Canada Council Award 1979, 1983; Amelia Frances Howard-Gibbon Award 1979; illustrator: 'Nibelungenlied' 1966, 'El Cid' 1967, 'Chancon de Rolland' 1968, 'The Twelve Dancing Princesses'

1979, 'Illiad & Odyssey' 1981, 'Little Mermaid' 1983, 'Canadian Fairytales' 1984, 'Willow Maiden' 1985, 'Goodman of Ballengiech' 1987, 'The Enchanted Tapestry' 1987, Iduna and the Magic Apples' 1988, 'Flask of Seawater' 1989, 'Spirit of the Blue Light' 1990, 'Pome and Peel' 1990, 'The Firebird' 1991, 'Seawitches' 1991, 'The Moon and The Oyster' 1992; recreations: classical music, photography; Home: 86 Franklin Ave., Willowdale, Ont. M2N 1B9; Office: 25 John St., Toronto, Ont. M5V 3G6.

**GALAVARIS, George,** F.R.S.C., M.A., M.F.A., Ph.D.; university professor, art historian; b. Greece 17 Oct. 1926; s. Panos and Olympia (Garibaldi) G.; e. Athens M.A. 1951; Princeton Univ., M.F.A. 1957, Ph.D. 1958; also studies in painting, music, contemporary European lit.; single; PROF., DEPT. OF ART HISTORY, McGILL UNIV. 1965– ; Vis. Fellow, Dumbarton Oaks, Ctr. for Byzantine Studies, Harvard Univ. 1957–59; Asst. Prof., present univ. 1959; Vis. Prof., Univ. of Wisconsin at Madison Fall 1967; Vis. Fellow, Princeton Univ. Fall 1977; Inst. for the Study of Icon Art 'De Wijenburg,' Echteld, Holland 1978–81; Vis. Prof., Univ. of Crete Spring 1987; hon. advr., reader & assessor of mss. for var. acad. presses & journs. & mem., ed. bds. incl. 'RACAR' 1975–83; F.R.S.C.; Corresponding Mem., Acad. of Athens; Fellow, Greek Christian Arch. Soc.; Founder & First Pres., Candn. Nat. Ctte. of Byzantine Studies; Mem., Med. Acad. of Am.; Am. Numismatic Soc.; Soc. of Nubian Studies and others; author: 'The Illustrations of the Liturgical Homilies of Gregory Nazianzenus' 1969, 'Bread and the Liturgy' 1970, 'Icons from the Elvehjem Centre' 1973, 'The Illustrations of the Prefaces in Byzantine Gospels' 1979, 'The Icon in the Life of the Church' 1981, 'Invocation to a Pagan Divinity' (short stories) 1971; co-author: 'The Monastery of St. Catherine at Sinai, The Illuminated Manuscripts' vol. 1, 1990 (Acad. of Athens Award); 'Treasures at Sinai' 1990; profl. practising painter exhibiting works regularly in Can. & Eur.; his pictures are found in private & public collections incl. the Vorrés Mus. of Modern Art, Athens, Greece; Office: 853 Sherbrooke St. W., Montreal, Que. H3A 2T6.

**GALBRAITH, David Ian,** B.A., M.A.; curator; b. Trenton, Ont. 10 Feb. 1953; s. James and Doris (Maukonen) G.; e. Univ. of Toronto B.A. 1975; Carleton Univ. M.A. 1978; Univ. of Toronto Ph.D. (in progress); m. Heather d. Eunice and Donald Murray 1 May 1991; CURATOR, CENTRE FOR REFORMATION AND RENAISSANCE STUDIES, VICTORIA UNIV., UNIV. OF TORONTO 1990– ; Mem., Bibliographical Soc.; Candn. Soc. for Renaissance Studies; Renaissance Soc. of Am.; Pres., Marxist Literary Group, Univ. of Toronto; Office: 71 Queen's Park Cres., Toronto, Ont. M5S 1K7.

**GALBRAITH, John Kenneth,** M.S., Ph.D., LL.D.; economist; b. Iona Station, Ont. 15 Oct. 1908; s. William Archibald and Catherine (Kendall) G.; e. Univ. of Toronto (Ont. Agric. Coll.), B.S.A. 1931; Univ. of California, M.S. 1933 and Ph.D. 1934; Cambridge Univ.; LL.D. Univ. of Toronto, Univ. of Western Ont., Queen's, McMaster, Saskatchewan, Guelph, Harvard, Oxford and other universities; m. Catherine Merriam, d. Charles Atwater of New York, 17 Sept. 1937, three children; Consultant, U.S. Govt. Agencies, Nat. Resources Planning Board; Instr., Harvard Univ., 1934–39; Asst. Prof., Princeton Univ., 1939–40; Depy. Adm., Office of Price Adm. (U.S), 1941–43; Editor of 'Fortune' mag., 1943–48 (subject to leaves of absence); Dir., U.S. Strategic Bombing Survey, 1945; Dir., Econ. Security Policy, U.S. Dept. of State, 1946; other govt. posts; Lectr., Harvard Univ., 1948 and Paul M. Warburg Prof. of Econ. 1949–75; Warburg Professor Emeritus 1975– ; U.S. Ambassador to India, 1961–63; Visiting Fellow, Trinity Coll., Cambridge Univ., Eng. 1970–71, Hon. Fellow 1987– ; awarded U.S. Medal of Freedom and President's Cert. of Merit; author: 'Modern Competition and Business Policy' 1938; 'American Capitalism' 1952; 'A Theory of Price Control' 1952; 'The Affluent Society' 1958; 'The Liberal Hour' (essays) 1960; 'The Scotch' 1964; 'The New Industrial State' 1967; 'The Triumph' (novel) 1968; 'Ambassador's Journal' 1969; 'Economics and the Public Purpose' 1973; 'Money' 1975; 'The Age of Uncertainty' 1975; 'A Life in Our Times' (memoirs) 1981; 'The Anatomy of Power' 1983; 'A Tenured Professor' (novel) 1990; 'The Culture of Contentment' 1992; and numerous tech., scient. and popular monographs and articles; mem. and past pres., Am. Econ. Assn.; Amer. Acad. of Arts and Letters 1982; mem. and past Chrmn., Americans for Democratic Action; mem., Am. Ag. Econ. Assn.; Democrat; Home: 30 Francis Ave., Cambridge, Mass. 02138.

**GALE, David C.;** banker; b. Wallaceburg, Ont. 1942; m. Joan; one child; e. Northeastern Univ. Extve. Devel. prog. 1988; VICE-PRES., BAHAMAS & CAYMAN ISLANDS, ROYAL BANK OF CANADA 1991– ; joined Royal Bank of Canada Wallaceburg, Ont. 1960; various branches, S.W. Ont. until 1978; Sr. Acct. Mgr., Toronto 1978; Mgr. Halifax 1982; Vice-Pres., Mktg. & Serv. Delivery Halifax 1987; Vice-Pres., Corporate Banking Toronto 1989; recreations: golf; club: St. George's Golf & Country Toronto, Lyford Cay Club & Royal Nassau Sailing Club Nassau, Bahamas; Office: East Hill Street, P.O. Box N 7549, Nassau, Bahamas.

**GALE, Diana Bennett,** M.A.; association executive; b. Toronto, Ont. 19 Sept. 1943; d. John A.E. and Dorothy H. (Gurofsky) Bennett; e. York Mills C.I. 1961; Univ. of Toronto B.A. 1965, Fac. of Edn., H.S.A. – Type A 1967; Univ. of Toronto M.A. 1968; children: Matthew, Cameron, Jay, Loron; 3rdly m. Garry Gordon Gale; MANAGING DIR., CORPORATE AFFAIRS, TVONTARIO 1993– ; Dept. Head of Visual Arts, North York Bd. of Edn. 1965–80 (Dir., Summer Studio 1972–75); Mgr., Bus. Relns., TV Ontario 1980–81; Dir., Revenue Devel. 1981–87; Extve. Dir., Metro Toronto Zoological Soc. 1987–91; Dir., Community Development and Liaison, TVOntario 1991–93; Adjunct Prof., York Univ., Fac. of Edn. Teaching Assoc. 1975–76; Fac. of Edn., Univ. of Toronto 1976–79; Team Mem., Nat. Defence Sch., West Germany, Min. of Edn., Ont. 1974; Cons. to voluntary and profl. assns., spec. in devel. & planning; academic awards in curricular design & mktg. 1961, 1965, 1968, 1970, 1982, 1983; Mem. Bd. of Dirs., Granite Club 1989; Canada Publishing Corp. 1989; Mem., Art Gall. of Ont.; Visual Arts Ont.; Guild of Crafts, Ont., Metro Toronto Zool. Soc.; artist: fabric collage & stitchery; solo exhibs.: 'Fabricated Ladies,' Gallery 'O' 1978, 'Stitched Collage,' Baas Gall. 1987; represented in a number of juried shows, tours & pubs.; recreations: fitness, gardening, reading, film going, travel; club: Granite; Home: 28 Glengrove Ave. W., Toronto, Ont.; Office: P.O. Box 200, Stn. Q, Toronto, Ont. M4T 2T1.

**GALEF, Bennett G.,** A.B., M.A., Ph.D.; university professor; b. New York 23 May 1941; s. Bennett G. and Susan (Hochstadter) Galef; e. Princeton Univ. A.B. 1962; Univ. of Pennsylvania M.A. 1964, Ph.D. 1968; m. Mertice d. Harold and Harriet Matthews 7 Feb. 1991; PROFESSOR, PSYCHOLOGY, MCMASTER UNIV. 1978– ; Asst. Prof., Psychol., McMaster Univ. 1968–72; Assoc. prof. 1972–78; Visiting Scientist, Smithsonian Tropical Rsch. Inst. 1974; Affiliated Scientist, Monell Chem. Senses Ctr. 1987–96; Visiting Prof., Univ. of Colorado 1981, '84, '87, '93; Univ. of Tel Aviv 1986; Dir., J.L. Galef & Son Inc. 1975–85; Consultant, Union Carbide Corp.; CSIRO (Australia); Monell Chem. Senses Ctr.; U.S. Dept. of the Interior; Fellow, Am. Psychol. Assn.; Candn. Psychol. Assn.; Am. Assn. for the Adv. of Sci.; Bd. of Dir., Internat. Soc. for Devel. Psychobiol.; Mem., Animal Behavior Soc.; Extve. Ctte., Psychonomic Soc.; author of more than 150 pub. sci. papers; co-editor: 'Social Learning' 1988, 'Ontogeny and Social Transmission of Food Preferences' 1993; recreations: skiing, fly fishing, travel; Home: 7 Turnbull Rd., Dundas, Ont. L9H 3W4; Office: Hamilton, Ont. L8S 4K1.

**GALIPEAULT, André Jacques,** B.A., B.C.L.; executive; b. Quebec City, Que. 10 July 1937; s. late Jacques and Jacqueline (Dessaint) G.; e. Jesuits Coll., Quebec City B.L. 1953; Laval Univ. B.A. 1955; McGill Univ. B.C.L. 1959; m. Suzanne d. Charles Valiquette, Montreal, Que. 26 Aug. 1961; children: Nathalie, Eric; PRESIDENT, FASKEN MARTINEAU DAVIS 1990– ; Dir., Provincial Construction Co.; read law with Lucien Beauregard, Q.C.; called to Bar of Que. 1960; Assoc. Beauregard Brisset, Reycraft & Chauvin 1960–64; joined Texaco Canada Inc. as Solr. 1964, Assoc. Gen. Counsel 1971, Gen. Solr. 1973, Gen. Counsel 1975; Vice Pres. and Gen. Counsel 1977–89; Past Pres. of the Nat. Ballet of Can.; Past Chrmn., Bd. of Govs., Nat. Theatre Sch. of Can.; Past Pres. Chambre de Comm. Française au Can. (Ont.); Dir., Ballet Opera House Corp.; 1989 Toronto Internat. Choral Festival; Opera Hamilton; Power Plant; Council for Candn. Unity; Swiss Candn. Chamber of Commerce (Ont.); Cercle Candn. (Toronto); Past Pres., Assn. Candn. Gen. Counsel; mem., Bar Prov. Que.; Bar Montreal; Candn. Bar Assn.; Liberal; R. Catholic; recreations: tennis, squash; Clubs: Univ. Club of Toronto; Toronto Cricket Skating & Curling; Montreal Racket; Home: 21 Harlington Rd., Don Mills, Ont. M3B 3G3.

**GALLAGHER, David R.,** B.A., M.B.A., C.M.A.; financial executive; b. Cadillac, Que. 20 Sept. 1948; s. John David and Martha Washington (Cummings) G.; e. Univ. of Windsor B.A. 1969, M.B.A. 1973; Soc. of Mngt. Accountants C.M.A. 1983; m. Joan d. Wallace and Jeraldine Buchanan 1 Dec. 1979; children: John Wallace, Stephanie Joan, Mackenzie David; VICE-PRES. FINANCE & ADMIN., CARLSON MARKETING GROUP LTD. 1977– ; Industrial Engineer, Falconbridge Copper 1971–73; Audit & Tax, Arthur Anderson & Co. 1973–77; various assn. memberships; recreations: fitness, skiing, cycling; club: Knights of Columbua; Home: 35 Closs Sq., Aurora, Ont. L4G 5H6; Office: 3300 Bloor St. W., 14th Floor, Center Court, Toronto, Ont. M8X 2Y2.

**GALLAGHER, Donald McKenzie,** B.Sc.; company executive; b. Saskatoon, Sask. 1915; e. Pub. Sch., Saskatoon, Sask.; High Sch., Sydenham, Ont.; Queen's Univ., B.Sc. (Mining Engn.); m. Margaret Johnston, 1939 (dec.); children: David, Andrew, Katherine (Mrs. M. Boyes); Extve. Vice President ICI U.S. (ret.), 1972–78 and a Dir. since 1972; Pres. and Dir., ICI America Inc. 1969–72; joined Defence Industries Ltd., subsidiary of Canadian Industries Ltd., and served in engn. and supervisory capacities 1943–46; held Supv. and Mang. positions in explosives mfg. with Candn. Industries Ltd., 1946–64; apptd. Prod. Mgr., Explosives, 1964–66; Gen. Mgr., Plastic Div., 1966–68, Vice-Pres. 1968; Pres., ICI America Inc. 1969–71 (Extve. Vice Pres., 1972–78); Dir. Delaware State Chamber of Comm.; mem., Soc. Plastics Indust.; Soc. Chem. Industs.; Assoc. mem., Chem. Inst. Can.; Club: Canadian (N.Y.); Home: 47 Cache Cay Dr., Vero Beach, Fla. 32963.

**GALLAGHER, James S.,** B.A., M.B.A.; stock exchange executive; b. New York, N.Y. 7 March 1943; s. John J. and Catherine M. (Morrissey) G.; e. Regis High Sch. New York 1961; Fordham Univ. B.A. 1965; St. John's Univ. New York M.B.A. 1977; m. Veronica d. Joseph and Catherine Redding 13 May 1967; three s. Sean, Geoffrey, Marc; EXEC. VICE PRES. TORONTO STOCK EXCHANGE 1988– ; Dir. Trans Canada Options; Pres. The Toronto Futures Exchange; Pres. The Canadian Dealing Network Inc.; Vice Pres. DuPont Glore Forgon 1971–74; mem. New York Stock Exchange 1972–74, held various positions 1974–78, Vice Pres. 1979; Vice Pres. New York Futures Exchange 1980; Pres. and Chief Operating Offr. Pacific Stock Exchange 1981–88; Dir. Options Clearing Corp. Chicago 1981–88; mem. Am. Stock Exchange 1971–72; Omicron Delta Epsilon; Beta Gamma Sigma; Home: 169 Claxton Dr., Oakville, Ont. L6J 4N8; Office: 2 First Canadian Place, Toronto, Ont. M5X 1J2.

**GALLAGHER, John Patrick,** B.Sc., geologist and executive; b. Winnipeg, Man. 16 July 1916; s. James and Constance Mary (Burdett) G.; e. Univ. of Manitoba, B.Sc. 1937; Harvard Univ. (Advanced Management) 1948; m. Kathleen Marjorie, d. Norman Stewart, Penhold, Alta., 20 Aug. 1949; children: James Stewart, Thomas Patrick, Frederick Michael; CHRMN., PRIME ENERGY INC. 1984– ; Chrmn., Galtannia Investmets Ltd.; Arctic Methanol Ltd.; Asst. Geol., Candn. Geol. Survey N. Manitoba and N.W.T. 1936–37; Field Geol., Shell Oil Co. in Calif. and Egypt 1938–39; Standard Oil Co. (N.J.) rising from field geologist to Exploration Mgr. in Africa, Middle East, Central & South America 1940–50; Extve. Vice-Pres. and Gen. Mgr., Dome Petroleum Ltd. Calgary 1950–53, Pres. 1953–74, Chrmn. & C.E.O. 1974–83; Pres., Independent Petroleum Assn. of Canada 1966; recreations: golf, skiing; Clubs: Calgary Petroleum; Calgary Golf & Country; Office: 500 – 407 2nd St. S.W., Calgary, Alta. T2P 2Y3.

**GALLAGHER, Paul,** C.M., B.A., M.Ed., D.C.L.; education consultant; b. Montreal, Que. 26 Sept. 1929; s. Charles Edward and Edna Josephine (Guilfoyle) G.; e. Univ. de Montréal (Loyola Coll.) B.A. 1950; Bishop's Univ. Lennoxville M.Ed. 1957; m. Grace Maude d. Neil Beaton 1 July 1955; children: Katherine, Stephen, Edward, Peter; High Sch. Teacher and Prof. St. Joseph Teachers Coll. Montreal 1951–60, Dean of Studies 1962–67, Founding Dean Quebec 1961–62; Dir. Gen.: Baldwin Cartier Sch. Comn. Pointe Claire 1967–69; Dawson Coll. Montreal 1969–75; Exec. Dir. Can. Studies Found. Toronto 1975–79, Chrmn. of Bd. 1979–80; Prin. Capilano Coll. N. Vancouver 1977–85; Pres. Vancouver Community Coll. 1985–91; Dir., The B.C. Human Resource Development Project 1991–93; Founding mem. Conseil superieure de l'edn. Que. 1964–68; cons. and mem. adv. ctte. Edn. Stats. Br. Stats. Can.; Dir.: Un. Way Lower Mainland 1980–85; Pacific Rim Inst. Tourism 1988–92; Vancouver Bd. Trade 1985–88; Assn. Candn. Community Colls. 1984–88; mem. Premier's Council Native Affairs 1989–90; Chrmn.: Provl. Adv. Ctte. Internat. Edn. Policy; Provl. Literacy Adv. Ctte. 1988–89; Pres. Candn. Soc. Study Higher Edn. 1988–89; author 'Community Colleges in Canada: A Profile' 1990; co-author 'Canada's Story For Young Canadians'

Vols. I, II 1964, 1965; 'Dawson College: A Case Study in Democratic Education' 1977; 'Teaching Canada For The Eighties' 1978; 'Canada's Community Colleges: A Critical Analysis' 1986; Fellow, Candn. Coll. Teachers 1963; Sir George Williams Univ. D.C.L. 1970; Member, Order of Canada 1986; Master Teacher Univ. of Texas Austin 1990; Hall of Merit Loyola High Sch. Montreal 1990; Commemorative Medal, 125th Anniversary of Candn. Confedn. 1992; recreation: golf; Home: 2011 Arroyo Court, North Vancouver, B.C. V7H 2A3; Office: 2011 Arroyo Court, N. Vancouver, B.C. V7H 2A3.

**GALLAGHER, Richard Paul,** B.Sc., M.A.; epidemiologist; b. Barking, Eng. 3 Dec. 1944; s. Paul Anthony and Doris Regina (Hamilton) G.; e. Univ. of B.C. B.Sc. 1967; Univ. of W. Wash. M.A. 1973; m. Deberah d. John and Luella Dueckman 31 Aug. 1968; children: Emerson, Noelle; HEAD OF SECTION EPIDEMIOL. B.C. CANCER AGENCY 1986– ; Assoc. Prof. of Health Care & Epidemiol. Univ. of B.C. 1989– , Assoc. mem. Div. Dermatol. 1990– ; and Dept. Ophthalmol. 1989– ; Dir. Iowa Cancer Surveillance Prog. Univ. of Iowa 1977–79; Epidemiol. present Agency 1980–85; author over 100 sci. publs.; ed. Epidemiol. of Malignant Melanoma 1986; Fellow, Am. College Epidemiol.; mem. Candn. Soc. Epidemiol. & Biostats. (Bd.); Internat. Epidemiol. Assn.; Soc. Epidemiol. Rsch.; Am. Soc. Preventive Oncology; R. Catholic; recreations: skiing, mountaineering; Office: 600 W. 10 Ave., Vancouver, B.C. V5Z 4E6.

**GALLAGHER, Stephen Bernard,** B.Comm., F.C.A.; chartered accountant; b. Ottwa, Ont. 12 Sept. 1945; s. Lawrence Roy and Frances Mary (Bertrand) G.; e. Univ. of Ottawa B.Comm. 1966; C.A. Ontario 1969; F.C.A. Nfld. 1984; F.C.A. Ont. 1991; m. Margaret Lee d. Walter and Margaret Souchen 25 May 1973; children: Heather, Robyn, David; OFFICE MANAGING PARTNER, ERNST & YOUNG OTTAWA 1985– ; joined Ernst & Young (formerly Clarkson, Gordon) 1966; Manager 1971; transferred to Halifax N.S. 1973; to St. John's, Nfld. 1975; promoted to Partner; Office Managing Partner 1978; Prof. (part-time), Carleton Univ. 1972–73; St. Mary's Univ. 1973–74; Memorial Univ. 1976–80; Chair, Ottawa-Carleton Econ. Devel. Corp. 1991–92; Chair, The School of Dance; Dir., Ottawa-Carleton Bd. of Trade 1989–91; recreations: skiing, squash, tennis, hockey, fishing; club: Rideau 1986– ; Home: 2 Wren Rd., Gloucester, Ont.; Office: Suite 1600, 55 Metcalfe St., Ottawa, Ont. K1P 6L5.

**GALLAHER, Patrick William;** early childhood educator; small businessman; b. Tacoma, Wash. 30 July 1949; s. Ernest Eugene and Joanne (Gregorak) G.; e. Univ. of B.C. 1967–68; Capilano Coll. 1969–71, dipl. Early Childhood Edn. 1973–75; m. Hermila d. Jose and Maria Quintanar 12 May 1979; children: Emily Rebekah, Mischa Morningstar, Breelana Sasha; FOUNDER & OP. OWNER, B.C. PLAYTHINGS 1976– ; Bookstore Asst./Mgr., Capilano Coll. 1973–79; Cons., & Guest Lectr. 'Children's Play' for radio, TV, parents groups, teachers & preschool teaching students; Playthings Mag. 1985 internat. Award of Merit for Store Promotion; past Pres. and Duty Parent, Norgate Parent Participation Preschool 1983–90; Mem., Brio Scanditoy's Product Devel. Adv. Ctte.; Vancouver Aquarium Assn. 1976– ; Counc. of Parent Participation Preschools (Past Bd. Extve.; Ed., Monthly Newsletter); Early Childhood Educators' of B.C. Assoc. (Past Branch Extve.) 1975– ; Nat. Assoc. for the Educ. of Young Children 1975– ; Candn. Child Day Care Fedn. 1986– ; Candn. Day Care Advocacy Assoc. 1987–90; Candn. Assoc. of Toy Libraries and Parent Resource Centres 1986–90; author: 'B.C. Playthings annual catalogue'; regular columnist, 'Early Childhood Educator' J. of ECEBC; 'Co-operatively Speaking' J. of Parent Co-operative Preschools Internat.; winner, First Award for Department Promotion, Internat. Merchandising Achievement Competition, Playthings Magazine 1988; Candn. Acad. of Recording Arts & Sciences JUNO Awards judge (Best Children's Album category) 1994; recreations: swimming, skiing, violin, dulcimer; Home: 1090 Handsworth Rd., N. Vancouver, B.C. V7R 2A6; Office: 1065 Marine Dr., N. Vancouver, B.C. V7P 1S6.

**GALLANT, Edgar,** O.C., M.A.; b. Egmont Bay, P.E.I. 19 Sept. 1924; s. Cyrus P. and Edna (Arsenault) G.; e. Seminaire de Joliette, B.A. 1946; Laval Univ., M.A. (Social Science-Econ.) 1949; m. Annette Louise, d. Wilfrid and Asyiva (Roy) Perras, Joliette, Que., 3 June 1949; children: Pierre, Louise, Marie, Christel; PRESIDENT, EDGAR GALLANT CONSULTANT; 1949–64: served with Federal Treasury Bd. and the Depts. of Finance and Defence Production as well as with NATO International Secretariat in Paris and Canada's Mission to the European Communities in Brussels; Secy., Economic Council of Can. 1964–65; Dir., Fed.-Prov. Relations Div., Dept. of Finance, Ottawa 1965–68; Secy. of Constitutional Conf. 1968–69; Depy. Secy. to the Cabinet 1969–71; Secy. to Council of Maritime Premiers 1971–73; Chrmn., National Captial Comn. 1973–76; Chrmn., Public Service Comn. 1976–85; Fellow-in-Residence, I.R.P.P. 1985–88; Sr. Advisor, Correlation Secretariat Services Inc. 1988–91; mem., Inst. Pub. Adm. Can.; Officier, Ordre de la Pleiade, Assn. des Parlementaires de Langue Française; Vanier Medal, Inst. of Public Admin. of Canada 1978; LL.D. (hon. causa) Univ. of P.E.I. 1981; Univ. of Moncton 1983; Univ. Sainte Anne, N.S. 1992; Médaille du Mérite Acadien, Société Nationale des Acadiens 1986; Officer, Order of Canada 1987; Commemorative Medal, 125th Anniversary, Candn. Confedn. 1992; mem., Ordre de la fidélité française 1987; R. Catholic; Address: 2257 Bowman Road, Ottawa, Ont. K1H 6V4.

**GALLANT, Mavis;** writer; b. Montreal 1922; worked at the National Film Bd. of Canada and the 'Montreal Standard'; moved to France 1950; Short stories published in 'The New Yorker' from 1951; Reviews and essays, 'New York Review of Books' and 'The New York Times Book Review'; Books published: (Short stories) 'The Other Paris' 1956; 'My Heart is Broken' 1964; 'The Pegnitz Junction' 1973; 'The End of the World' 1974; 'From the Fifteenth District' 1978; 'Home Truths' 1981 (Gov. Gen. Award); 'Overhead in a Balloon' 1985; 'In Transit' 1988; (Novels) 'Green Water, Green Sky' 1969; 'A Fairly Good Time' 1970; (Play) 'What Is To Be Done?' 1984; (Non-fiction) 'Paris Journals; Selected Reviews and Essays' 1986; Writer-in-Residence, Univ. of Toronto 1983–84; Officer of the Order of Canada 1981; Hon. Mem., Am. Acad. and Inst. of Arts and Letters 1989; Fellow, Royal Soc. of Lit. 1989; LL.D. (hon. causa), Queen's Univ. 1991; Address: c/o McLelland & Stewart, 481 University Ave., Toronto, Ont. M4Y 2W8.

**GALLERY, Brian O'Neill,** B.A.; publisher; b. Montreal, Que. 11 Oct. 1934; s. the late John O'Neill and Katherine (Hingston) G.; e. Loyola Coll. Montreal B.A. 1957; m. Nancy d. Malcolm and Dorcas MacNaughton 3 June 1967; three d. Ann, Mary, Elizabeth; PRES. AND OWNER, GALLERY PUBLICATIONS LTD. 1969– ; Publisher & Editor-in-Chief 'Canadian Sailings' (weekly, national, marine publication); Sr. Marine Editor in Can.; Vice Chrmn., Canada Space Technologies Inc.; Dir., Donalco (Quebec) Inc.; Export Development Corp.; St. Mary's Hosp. Foundation; began career as Sales Rep., Texaco Canada Ltd. 1957–59; Sales Mgr. present company 1959, Pres. 1964, Owner 1969; Alderman and Commnr. of Public Services of the City of Westmount 1975–83; Mayor 1983–87; Chief Reviewing Offr., St. Patrick's Parade in Montreal 1993; Past Dir., PC Can. Fund, Chief Agent, PC Party of Canada (1983–93) and Past Chrmn., The '500' (1983–93) a special project of PC Canada Fund; Past Dir., Ireland Fund of Can. and Past Chrmn., Montreal Chapter (1988–92); Past Dir., Canadian National (1986–90), Acting Chrmn. (1987–89) and Vice Chrmn. (1989–90); Past Chrmn. & Dir.: Canac Internat. Inc. 1986–90; CN (France) 1986–90; CN Hotels 1987–88; CN Tower 1988–90; Past Quebec Dir., Candn. Council of Christians and Jews; Past Pres., Loyola College Alumni Assn.; Past Vice-Pres.: PC Assn. of Westmount; Montreal Candn. Club; Mem., McGill Assocs.; Whiff of Grape (Past Chrmn.); PC Assn. of St. Henri-Westmount; Traffic Club of Montreal; Toronto Marine Club; Grunt Club (Past Pres.); St. Patrick's Soc.; Montreal Museum Fine Arts; Royal Commonwealth Soc.; Assoc's of Concordia Univ.; Candn. Maritime Law Assn.; Affiliate, Chartered Institute of Transport; Awarded: Medal of Merit, Candn. Port and Harbour Assn. (for contribution of over 25 yrs. to the shipping/marine industry in Canada) 1983; Commemorative Medal for 125th Anniversary of Candn. Confederation 1993; recreations: tennis, golf; Clubs: Hillside Tennis; Knowlton Golf; Montreal Press; Montreal Indoor Tennis; Albany (Toronto); Coral Beach (Bermuda); Home: 627 Belmont Ave., Westmount, Qué. H3Y 2W3.

**GALLIMORE, Michael J.,** B.Comm., M.B.A., C.F.A.; business executive; b. U.K. 1957; e. Concordia Univ. B.Comm. (cum laude) 1977, M.B.A. 1982; PRESIDENT, DIVERSIFIED FUND MANAGEMENT INC. 1988– ; Sr. Investment Analyst, Sun Life of Canada 1977–81; Pension Fund Mgr., IBM Canada Ltd. 1981–87; Consultant, Towers Perrin Forster & Crosby 1987–88; Dir., RCB Internat. Inc.; Fellow, Life Mngt. Inst. 1980; Toronto Soc. of Fian. Analysts 1980; C.F.A. 1983; Mem., Pension Investment Assn. of Can. (former Pres.); Benefits Can. (Adv. Ctte.); Toronto Soc. of Finan. Analysts; Inst. of Chartered Finan. Analysts; author: 'Mixed Portfolio Investment Strategies' 1982, 'Managing Global Portfolios' 1989; Office: 20 Toronto St., Suite 440, Toronto, Ont. M5C 2B8.

**GALLON, Gary T.,** A.A., B.A.; environmental expert; b. California 1 Oct. 1945; naturalized Canadian 1973; s. Tommy Fulton and Marilyn Rae (Moon) G.; e. Bakersfield H.S. 1963; Bakersfield College A.A. 1965; Calif. State Univ., Northridge B.A. 1968; m. Janine d. Irma and James Ferretti 15 April 1983; children: Kalifi, Jenika; PRES., CANADIAN ENVIRONMENT INDUSTRY ASSN., ONTARIO; Past Pres., Candn. Environmental Co.; Environmental Economics Internat.; helped establish the environmental movement in Canada; Founding Mem., Friends of the Earth Canada 1976; Greenpeace Internat. (Bd. of Dir.) 1972; Founding Mem., Candn. Assn. for the Human Environment (CAHE) 1971–73; Candn.-U.S. Environ. Council (CUSEC) 1973–80; Extve. Dir., B.C. Environ. Group, Soc. for the Promotion of Environ. Conserv. (SPEC) 1974–77; Candn. Environmentalist of the Year 1976; Extve. Dir., Environ. Liaison Ctr. Internat. Nairobi Kenya 1977–81; Co-ordinator, Probe Internat. 1981; Sr. Policy Advr., Ont. Minister of the Environ. 1985–90; Chair, Earthroots Environmental Assn. 1991–93; Candn. Investment Dealers Assn. Courses I & II (Hons.); Nat. Record Holder, Masters Swimming (competitive), Etobicoke Olumpium Masters Swim Club; Co-Founder, Ont. Coalition for a Green Econ. Recovery 1992; Chair, Earthroots Canada 1991– ; helped create & participated in Berger Inquiry into the proposed Mackenzie Valley Natural Gas Pipeline 1973–76; Mem., Wingspread U.S.-Canada Environ. Think Tank; Mem. Candn. Environmental Industries Assn. (CEIA); author: 'A Trip North: Views of an Environmentalist' 1976; 'A Short History: The Environment Liaison Centre International' 1992, 20 reports, 35 articles & 1 book chapter; co-author: 'Workplace Guide: Practical Action for the Environment' 1991; Home: 262 Willow Ave., Toronto, Ont. M4E 3K7; Office: Ste. 300, 9 Sultan St., Toronto, Ont. M5G 1L6.

**GALLOP, David,** M.A.; educator; b. London, Eng. 9 March 1928; s. Constantine and Irene (Klaber) G.; Tonbridge Sch. 1946; Magdalen Coll. Oxford B.A. 1951, M.A. 1955; m. Catharine d. Leslie and Marjorie Trist 1 Aug. 1956; children: Frances, Paul, Martin, Timothy; PROFESSOR EMERITUS, TRENT UNIV. 1989– , Prof. of Philos. 1969–89, Chrmn. of Philos. 1973–78; Lectr. in Philos., Univ. of Toronto 1955, Asst. Prof. 1960, Assoc. Prof. 1964, Prof. 1966; Dean of Arts and Science, Trent Univ. 1979–84; Rsch. Fellow, Australian National Univ. 1985; transl. with notes Plato's 'Phaedo' 1975; transl. with introduction 'Parmenides of Elea, Fragments' 1984; transl. with introduction and notes 'Aristotle on Sleep and Dreams' 1991; revised transl. with introd. and notes Plato's 'Phaedo' (World's Classics ed.) 1993; mem., Candn. Philos. Assn.; Soc. Ancient Greek Philos.; Am. Philos. Assn.; Country Dance & Song Soc. Am.; recreations: music, folk dancing; Home: 12 Bruce St., Peterborough, Ont. K9H 1A7.

**GALLOP, Richard Kerry Bruce,** M.A.; public relations executive; b. U.K. 1 Jan. 1939; s. Kingsley Malcolm Gallop; e. Magdalen Coll. Sch. Oxford 1958; Merton Coll. Oxford M.A. 1961; m. Ruth Margaret d. late Harold Joffre Amiel 1976; three s. Michael Joffre, Stephen Amiel, David Bruce; EXTVE. DIR., HEART & STROKE FOUND. OF ONT. 1986– ; joined J. Walter Thompson Ltd. 1970–73, Dir. W. Candn. Operations; Gen. Mgr., Cockfield Brown, Toronto 1975, Extve. Vice Pres. 1979, Pres. & Chief Oper. Offr. 1980, Pres. 1981; C.E.O., Burson-Marsteller Inc. 1985; Dir., Candn. Mental Health Assn.; Inst. Candn. Advertising; Anglican; recreations: running; photography, sailing; Club: Leander; Home: 71 Castle Frank Cres., Toronto, Ont. M4W 3A2.

**GALLOWAY, Col. Andrew Strome Ayers Carmichael-,** E.D., C.D.; b. Humboldt, Sask. 29 Nov. 1915; s. Andrew Scott Jubilee and Bertha Maude (Strome) G.; e. High Schs. Que. and Ont.; m. Jean Caroline d. George Alexander Love, Aylmer West, Ont. 29 May 1948; two d, Jean Caroline (Mrs. R. W. Blackburn), Rosemary Dawn (Mrs. M.G. Armstrong); HON. ED. EMERITUS, HERALDRY IN CANADA (Hon. Ed. 1970–87); Colonel of the Regiment, The Royal Candn. Regiment 7 1989–93; comnd. 2nd Lt. Candn. Militia (The Elgin Regt.) 1934, trans. to Royal Candn. Regt. 1939 serving Overseas 5 yrs. UK, Tunisia, Sicily and Italy, N.W. Europe; apptd. to Regular Army 1946 rank Maj., Lt. Col. 1951, Col. 1962, retired 1969; mem. Directing Staff Candn. Army Staff Coll. 1951–54, C.O. 4th Bn. Candn. Guards 1955–57, GSO1 HQ 1 Candn. Inf. Div. 1957–58, mem. Nat. Defence Coll. 1961–62, Commdr. Fort Churchill 1962–64, Mil. Naval and Air Attaché Germany 1965–68; Hon. Lt. Col. Gov. Gen.'s Foot Guards 1969–79;

Commandant RCAC Bisley Team 1974–76; mem. Fed. Dist. Council St. John Ambulance 1976–86; Pres. Ottawa Un. Services Inst. 1978; Officer, Most Venerable Order of St. John of Jerusalem; Chevalier Commandeur, Ordre Militaire et Hospitalier de St. Lazare de Jérusalem 1976; Grand Officer 1991; rec'd Centennial Medal 1967; Queen's Jubilee Medal, 1977; awarded Commemorative Medal for 125th Anniversary of Candn. Confederation 1992; Boy Scouts Assn. Can. 'Thanks Badge' 1964; 'Medaglio d'Argento' of the City of Rimini, Italy 1979; Past Pres. P. Cons. Assn. Ottawa-Carleton and def. cand. g.e. 1972; Columnist, Legion Magazine 1974–86; author various articles Candn., Brit., Am. and foreign books, periodicals and newspapers; Hon. Life mem. RCR Assn. London, Ont.; Gov. Gen.'s Foot Guards Assn. Ottawa; Hon. Pres. Ottawa and District Garrison Sgts' Assoc.; Former Hon. Vice Pres. N. Am. Br. Grenadier Guards Assn.; Hon. Chrmn., Ottawa Br. Monarchist League 1986; Life Mem. Royal Candn. Legion (Past Pres. Ottawa Br.); life mem. RCMI (Toronto); mem. Cavalry and Guards Club (London Eng.); Fellow, Heraldry Soc. Can. 1975; Distinguished Fellow, Am. Coll. of Heraldry 1986; Fellow, Candn. Guild of Authors 1988; Hon. Commander, Pinellas Co. Post (U.S.A.) 144, Royal Candn. Legion 1991; pubs: 'A Regiment at War' 1979; 'The General Who Never Was' 1981; 'Beddoe's Canadian Heraldry' 1981; 'The White Cross in Canada' 1983; 'Some Died at Ortona' 1983; 'With The Irish Against Rommel' 1985; 'Bravely into Battle' 1988; contrib. to: 'Loyal She Remains' (2 chapters) 1984; 'Canadian Encyclopedia' 1985; 'Allegiance' (1 chapter) 1991; under Scottish law officially recognized by the nobiliary name of Carmichael-Galloway, which name is also recognized in Canada under Ont. Vital Statistics Act; Bannerman to the 30th Chief of the Name and Arms of Carmichael; listed in Debrett's 'Canadian Establishment' among 'Debrett's 600'; Anglican; Address: 'Redstones,' 1922 Alta Vista Dr., Ottawa, Ont. K1H 7K6.

**GALLOWAY, Bruce Cameron,** B.Com.; banker; b. Montréal, Qué. 27 Aug. 1947; s. George Cameron and Margaret Ellen (Cully) G.; e. Acadia Univ. B.Com. 1968; m. Sheila d. Clyde and Ruth Nickerson 28 June 1969; children: Mark, Andrea, Carolyn; SR. EXTVE. VICE PRES., CORPORATE BANKING, ROYAL BANK OF CANADA 1990– ; joined present Bank 1968, Br. Acct. 1969, Rsch. Offr. H.O. Invest. Dept. 1970, Asst. Mgr. Pension Fund 1973, Mgr. H.O. Govt. Bond Portfolio 1977, Mgr. Money Mkt. Assets 1980, Asst. Gen. Mgr. Candn. Money Mkts. 1981 becoming Vice Pres. 1982, Vice Pres., Trading-Canada, Foreign Exchange and Internat. and Candn. Money Market groups 1984; Sr. Vice Pres., Invest. Banking & Treasury Operations-Can. 1986–88; Exec. Vice Pres. Treasury, Invest. Banking & Treasury Div. 1988–90; Bd. of Govs., Acadia Univ.; Mt. Sinai Hosp.; Office: Royal Bank Plaza, Toronto, Ont. M5J 2J5.

**GALLOWAY, Charles Thomas Peffers,** B.A., F.S.A., F.C.I.A., M.A.A.A.; retired insurance executive; b. Buckingham, P.Q. 26 Apr. 1927; s. Andrew Scott Jubilee and Bertha Maude (Strome) G.; e. University College (Toronto), B.A. 1950; m. Frances Alice, d. David Mackey, 26 Oct. 1956; children: Charlene Angela, Pamela Frances, Deborah Sue; VICE-CHRMN., THE NATIONAL LIFE ASSURANCE CO. OF CANADA 1985– ; joined present Company as Actuarial Clerk 1950, Asst. Actuary 1953, Associate Actuary 1955, Actuary 1957, Vice-Pres. and Actuary 1963, a Dir. 1973, Pres. 1975, Pres. & C.E.O. 1976; Dir., Gen. Am. Life Reinsurance Co. of Can. 1992– ; Pres. Candn. Inst. of Actuaries 1980–81; Protestant; Home: 27 Keily Cres., Bolton, Ont. L7E 5S1; Office: 522 University Ave., Toronto, Ont. M5G 1Y7.

**GALLOWAY, David A.,** B.A., M.B.A.; publishing executive; b. Toronto, Ont. 1 Nov. 1943; s. Robert and Dorothy Elizabeth (Kennedy) G.; e. Univ. of Toronto Schs.; Univ. of Toronto B.A. 1966; Harvard Univ. M.B.A. 1968; m. Judy K. d. Roger Curran Clarkson 10 June 1966; children: Andrew, Stephanie; OFFICE OF THE CHIEF EXECUTIVE, TORSTAR CORP. 1988– ; Marketing, General Foods 1968–71; Partner, Canada Consulting Group 1971–80; Vice Pres. Corp. Devel. Torstar Corp. 1980–81, Exec. Vice. Pres. 1981–82; Pres. & C.E.O., Harlequin Enterprises Ltd. 1983–88, Chrmn. 1990; Bd. mem., Trent Univ.; Candn. Film Centre; Hospital for Sick Children; Ont. Arts Council Found.; Chrmn. Delegate, Connaught Ctte., Univ. of Toronto; Mem. Adv. Counc., Fac. of Admin. Studies, York Univ.; recreations: running, tennis, golf; Clubs: Badminton & Racquet; Devil's Pulpit Golf (Caledon); Toronto; Home: Suite 801, 561 Avenue Rd., Toronto, Ont. M4V 2J8; Office: One Yonge St., Toronto, Ont. M5E 1P9.

**GALLOWAY, Joan Patricia (Pat);** actress; b. Kent, Eng. 13 May 1933; d. Bertram George W. and Mildred Alice (Berry) G.; e. Royal Acad. Dramatic Art London, Eng. Dip. 1954; Conservatoire d'Art Dramatique Paris Dip. 1955; m. Dr. Bernhard A. s. John and Else Frischke 28 July 1966; began acting career Eng. Repertory Theatres; came to Can. 1957 performing in CBC TV series Montreal and appearing at Comedie Canadienne; joined Man. Theatre Centre Winnipeg 1963–66 and 1974–75 seasons performing various title roles; Shaw Festival 1966 and 1978–79 seasons; Stratford Shakespearean Festival 1960–62, 1968–76, 1980–87, 1989–92 seasons, various title roles, participated internat. tours Eur. 1973, Australia 1974, USA 1981; appearances various CBC TV Specials, MGM TV Special; co-produced and appeared various topical revues Theatre-in-the-Dell Toronto; dir. student prodns. Nat. Theatre Sch. Montreal 1975–76; Artist-in-Residence Alfred (N.Y.) Univ. 1988; recreations: riding, golf, gardening; Address: Fishfolds Farm, R.R.7, St. Mary's, Ont. N0M 2V0.

**GALLOWAY, John Herbert,** B.A., M.A., Ph.D.; university professor; b. Stranraer, Scotland 22 Jan. 1940; s. James Lloyd and Hylda Mary (Dixon) G.; e. Internat. Sch. of Geneva; McGill Univ., B.A. 1960; The Univ. of Calif., Berkeley, M.A. 1961; Univ. of London, Ph.D. 1965; PROF., VICTORIA COLL., UNIV. OF TORONTO 1977– ; joined present univ. 1964; rsch. interests: Brazil, The Sugar Cane Indus.; Fellow, Victoria Coll., Univ. of Toronto; McGill Univ. Moyse Travelling Scholarship; Woodrow Wilson Fellowship, Guggenheim Fellowship 1970; Vis. Fellow, Emmanuel Coll., Cambridge 1977–78; Mem., Gov. Counc., Univ. of Toronto 1985–90 (Chrmn., Acad. Bd. 1989–90); mem., Candn. & Am. Assns. of Geographers; Am. Geographical Soc.; Fellow, The Royal Geog. Soc.; author: 'The Sugar Cane Industry: An Historical Geography from Its Origins to 1914' 1989 and papers in acad. jours.; editor: 'The Canadian Geographer' 1969–73; Ed. Bd., 'Journal of Historical Geography' 1974– ; recreations: skiing, squash, travel, reading; club: Univ. of Toronto Faculty Club; Home: 50 Quebec Ave., Apt. 1908, Toronto, Ont. M6P 4B4; Office: 73 Queen's Park Cres., Toronto, Ont. M5S 1K7.

**GALT, Thomas M.,** F.S.A., F.C.I.A.; company director and executive committee chairman; b. Winnipeg, Man. 1 Aug. 1921; s. George F. (deceased) and Muriel Julyan (Maunsell) Galt (Mrs. R.M. Gemmel) (deceased); e. Ashbury Coll., Ottawa; Lakefield (Ont.) Prep. Sch.; Arnprior (Ontario) High School; Queen's University; University of Manitoba, B.Comm. 1948; m. Helen W., d. late George Duncan Hyndman, Southboro, Mass., 15 June 1942; children: Lesley Maunsell (Mrs. S.R. Brown), George Hyndman; DIR. & CHRMN. OF THE EXTVE. CTTE., SUN LIFE ASSURANCE CO. OF CAN.; Dir.: Sun Life Assur. Co. of Canada (U.K.) Ltd.; Stelco Inc.; Textron Canada Ltd.; joined Sun Life Math. Dept. 1948, Asst. Actuary 1954, Vice-Pres. and Chief Actuary 1963, Extve. Vice-Pres. 1968; el. a Dir. 1970; Pres. and Chief Oper. Offr., 1972; Chrmn. & C.E.O. 1978–88; served in 2nd World War; Flight Lieut., R.C.A.F. 1941–45; Clubs: Toronto, York, Toronto Golf; Mt. Royal; Office: Sun Life Centre, 150 King St. W., Toronto, Ont. M5H 1J9.

**GALVIN, Edward Anthony,** B.S.; industrialist; b. Richmond, Cal. 10 Jan. 1913; s. William Joseph and Gertrude Anna (Planz) G.; e. Long Beach (Cal.) Polytechnic High Sch.; Univ. of S. Cal., B.S. 1938; m. Frances Esther, d. Percival Merton Bell, 20 Sept. 1938; children: Edward Anthony, Nancy Kathryn Peters; BOARD OF DIRS., POCO PETROLEUMS LTD. (Chrmn. 1982–..); Dir., Bonanza Oil & Gas Ltd.; Central Explorers Inc.; Dominion Equity Resource Fund Inc.; Domequity Growth Fund; Prairie Oil Royalties Co. Ltd.; Plant Foreman, The Texas Co., Long Beach, Cal. 1933; Supt. Gas Operations, DelValle Gasoline Co. California 1940; Natural Gas and Natural Gasoline Analyst, Petroleum Adm. for War, Los Angeles 1942; Chief Petroleum Engr., Western Gulf, Los Angeles 1945; Canadian Gulf Oil Ltd. 1954; Gen. Mgr., Pathfinder Petroleums Ltd. 1955–59; subsequently Medallion Petroleums Ltd. where apptd. Pres. and Gen. Mgr. 1959; Pres. of Can. Ind. Gas & Oil Ltd. (formed by amalg. Medallion Petroleums) 1965; Vice Chrmn. of Bd., Norcen 1972–78; Pres. Poco Petroleum Ltd. 1978–82; Chrmn., Poco Petroleums 1982– ; reg'd Prof. Engr. State. of Cal.; Life mem., Candn. Petrol. Assn. (Chrmn. 1972); Life mem., I.P.A.C.; Life mem., Assn. Prof. Engrs. & Geols. Alta.; Sigma Gamma Epsilon; Protestant; recreations: golf, fishing; Clubs: Calgary Golf & Country (Pres. 1973–74); Ranchmen's; Calgary Petroleum; Home: 4103 Crestview Rd. S.W., Calgary, Alta. T2T 2L5; Office: 3510, 205 - 5th Ave. S.W., Calgary, Alta. T2P 2B7.

**GAMEY, Ronald Kenneth,** B.A., M.B.A.; transportation executive; b. Victoria, B.C. 6 Aug. 1945; s. Kenneth J. and Helga I. (Franzen) G.; e. Victoria High Sch. 1963; Univ. of Victoria B.A. 1967; Univ. of B.C., M.B.A. 1969; m. Nancye d. Arnold J. Walker 17 May 1969; one child: Tyler; EXTVE. VICE PRES. CANADIAN PACIFIC LTD. 1988– ; Dir. Canada Maritime Agencies Ltd.; Canadian Pacific Enterprises; Canadian Pacific Hotels; Canadian Pacific Securities Limited; CP (US) Holdings Inc.; Canadian Pacific Express & Transport; CanPac International Freight Services Inc.; Fording Coal Limited; Laidlaw Inc.; Marathon Realty Co. Ltd.; Unitel; mem., C.D. Howe Inst.; Rsch. Analyst CP Ltd. 1969; Operations Analyst CP Rail Vancouver 1971, Mgr. Analysis & Planning Projects 1973; Dir. Special Projects Office of Chrmn. & Pres., CP Ltd. Montréal 1974; Mgr. Mktg. Planning & Econ. Analysis CP (Bermuda) Ltd. 1975, Gen Mgr. 1976; Mng. Dir. Ship Mgmt. Services Div. CP Steamships Ltd. London, Eng. 1979; Vice Pres. CP (Bermuda) Ltd. and Mng. Dir. above Services Div. London 1983; Pres. and Chief Exec. Offr. CP Bulkships, London and Vice Pres. CP (Bermuda) Ltd. 1984; Group Vice Pres., CP Ltd. 1985; recreation: squash; Club: Donalda; Home: 86 Glen Rd., Toronto, Ont. M4W 2V6; Office: Suite 800, Citibank Place, 123 Front St. W., Toronto, Ont. M5J 2M8.

**GAMPEL, Morison [prof. known as C.M. Gampel];** actor; stage director; b. Montreal, P.Q. 19 Feb. 1921; s. late Abraham and late Sofie (Matorin) G.; div.; m. Fran Herald; one d. Abigail; began acting career with Little Theatre in Niagara Falls, Ont.; played in two amateur plays, and num. radio shows over CKTB, St. Catharines, Ont.; joined three prof. cos. in Niagara Falls, N.Y., Buffalo, and Rochester N.Y., playing about 30 rôles within first year; proceeded to N.Y. and scholarship with Neighbourhood Playhouse Sch. of Theatre and then returned to Can. when he joined the Candn. Army; leaving the Army, played stock in Jennerstown, Pa., Milford, Pa., Boston, Newport, East Hampton, Atlantic City, and has played on approx. 2000 TV shows orig. from N.Y.; Broadway debut in Shaw's 'Captain Brassbound's Conversion' in support of Edna Best; followed by 'Richard II' in support of Maurice Evans; then Tabori's 'Flight into Egypt' dir. by Elia Kazan; Arthur Miller's 'The Crucible'; Shaw's 'Saint Joan'; 'Compulsion'; in 1956 was engaged as 'standby' for Sir Ralph Richardson in 'Waltz of the Toreadors' by Jean Anouilh, subsequently taking over the rôle of Gen. St. Pé for one third of its Broadway run; in Christopher Fry's 'The Firstborn,' played on Broadway opposite Katharine Cornell and Anthony Quayle as the Pharaoh and later when the Co. was invited to Israel (10th anniversary of the State); toured 50 cities in leading male role of Gibson's 'The Miracle Worker' 1962; featured on Broadway in 'Girl Who Came to Supper' musical by Noel Coward; revival of 'Front Page'; featured opposite Shirley MacLaine in film 'Desperate Characters'; was the Commandant of U.S. Marine Corps in 'Hail'; featured as Charles Bronson's boss in 'Death Wish,' the Doctor in 'Annie Hall'; film roles in 'Fire Power,' 'The Changeling' (filmed in Vancouver), 'The Promise of Love,' 'The Ultimate Being,' 'Personal Effects,' 'Beyond the Universe'; played in over 300 commercials; played on TV soap operas 'Guiding Light,' 'All My Children,' 'General Hospital'; toured in support of Ethel Merman in revival of 'Call Me Madam'; played Dr. Chumley opposite Shirley Booth in 'Harvey'; played in several off-Broadway productions; Internat. tour (16 countries S. Amer. and Europe, one yr. duration) of 'West Side Story'; served in 2nd World War with Candn. Army, rank of Sgt.; mem. The Players; Actors Equity Assn.; Am. Fed. of TV & Radio Artists; Screen Actors Guild; well known as drama coach with own studio; Hebrew; recreations: chess, golf; Address: 3 Peter Cooper Rd., New York, N.Y. 10010 and c/o S. Gampel, 5986 Main St., Niagara Falls, Ont. L2G 5Z8.

**GANDZ, Jeffrey,** M.B.A., Ph.D.; university professor; b. Leeds, Eng. 21 July 1944; s. Barnet and Rhoda (Joseph) G.; e. York Univ., M.B.A. 1975, Ph.D. 1977; PROF. AND DIR., MBA PROGRAM, WESTERN BUSINESS SCHOOL, UNIV. OF W. ONT. 1977– ; held var. sales and mktg. positions in Europe before moving to Can. 1969; Candn. experience incl. positions with Warner-Lambert, Grey Advt., Cheeseborough-Ponds; joined Univ. of W. Ont. 1977; Pres. Gandz Consulting Network Inc.; guest lectr., var. N. Am. and European univs.; Comnr., Colls. Collective Bargaining Comm.; mem. Acad. of Mgmt.; author 'Managing Absenteeism' 1977; 'Changing Relationships in Educational Bargaining' 1981; 'Effective Managerial Action' 1988; 'Good Management: Business Ethics in Action' 1991; numerous articles in fields of orgnl. behaviour, human resource mgmt., bus. ethics; recreations: golf, music; Office: London, Ont. N6A 3K7.

**GANNON, Robert P.J.,** B.A., M.B.A., C.A., F.L.M.I.; financial executive; b. Timmins, Ont. 25 Aug. 1942; s. Patrick J. and Kathleen M. (Nolan) G.; e. Univ. of Toronto B.A. 1964; Univ. of Manitoba M.B.A. 1974; m. Judee d. Joseph and Anne Regan 25 June 1966; children: Maureen Louise, Angela Marlene, Steven Brian; VICE-PRESIDENT FINANCE & TREASURER, JAMES RICHARDSON & SONS, LIMITED 1990– ; various admin. positions, Great West Life Assur. Co. 1964–74; Arthur Anderson 1974–76; Controller, K-Tel Music 1976–79; Divisional Controller, Inter-City Gas 1979–80; Vice-Pres. Finance 1980–83; Vice-Pres. Finance & Admin., Keeprite Inc. 1983–86; Vice-Pres. & Gen. Mgr., Candn. Opn. 1986–88; Pres. 1988–90; Dir., Richardson Greenshields Limited; Richardson Oil & Gas Limited; Extve. Ctte., Health Sciences Centre Found. (Winnipeg, Man.); Campaign Cabinet, United Way 1992 & 1993; Past Chrmn. & Past Dir., St. Joseph's Hosp. (Brantford, Ont.); Extve. Mem., Financial Executives Inst. (Manitoba Chapter); Mem., Inst. of C.A.s; recreations: golf, tennis; clubs: St. Charles Golf & Country, Manitoba; Manitoba Club; Home: 7 Bardsley Place, Winnipeg, Man. R3P 2B8; Office: 30th Floor, One Lombard Place, Winnipeg, Man. R3B 0Y1.

**GANONG, David A.,** B.B.A., M.B.A.; manufacturer; b. St. Stephen, N.B. 14 Sept. 1943; s. Philip D. and Margaret (Alison) G.; e. High Sch. St. Stephen, N.B. 1961; Univ. of N.B. B.B.A. 1965; Univ. of W. Ont. M.B.A. 1970; m. Diane d. Eugene Simpson, St. Stephen, N.B. 8 July 1972; children: Bryana, Aaron, Nicholas; PRES. & DIR., GANONG BROS. LTD.; Ganong Chocolatiere Inc.; Dir. Ganong Ltd. (Thailand); New Brunswick and Candn. Railway Co.; L.E. Shaw Ltd.; Air Canada; Mutual Life of Canada; Dalhousie Medical Rsch. Found.; Past Chrmn. APEC; mem. YPO; Bd. of Govs., Univ. of N.B.; Confectionery Mfg. Assn. Can. (Past Chrmn.); Baptist; recreations: skiing, tennis, travel; Home: 44 Union St., St. Stephen, N.B. E3L 2B1; Office: Chocolate Dr., St. Stephen, N.B. E3L 2X5.

**GANONG, Rendol Whidden, C.M.;** company executive; b. St. Stephen, N.B. 2 Oct., 1906; s. Arthur D. and Berla Frances (Whidden) G.; e. Royal Mil. Coll., Ont., 1924–26; m. Eleanor Katherine Deacon of St. Stephen, N.B., 11 Oct. 1941; CHRMN. GANONG BROS. LTD.; Past Pres., Atlantic Prov. Econ. Council; mem., Bd. of Dirs., C.B.C. 1958–61; Mayor, Town of St. Stephen 1956; entered family firm 1926; served in 2nd World War overseas with R.C.A.F.; mem., Confect. Chocolate and Coca Indust. Can. (Pres. 1947); D.C.L., Univ. of N.B. 1982; Member of the Order of Canada 1990; recreations: farming; Home: 2 St. Croix St., St. Stephen, N.B. E3L 2X5.

**GANOZA, M. Clelia,** B.Sc., Ph.D., F.R.S.C.; university professor; b. Lima, Peru 24 Oct. 1937; d. Julio Augusto and Clelia Hortensia (Finney) G.;e. Rollins College B.Sc. 1959; Duke Univ. Ph.D. 1964; m. Andrew John Becker 6 Sept. 1968; one d.: Monica Anne Becker; PROFESSOR, BANTING & BEST DEPT. OF MED. RESEARCH, UNIV. OF TORONTO 1974– ; Postdoctoral fellow, Rockefeller Univ. 1963–66; Rsch. Assoc. 1966–68; Assoc. Prof., Univ. of Toronto 1968–74; Assoc. & Career Investigator, Medical Research Council of Canada 1969– ; Assoc. Ed., 'Mol. Biology Reports' 1974–90; Grant Referee, MRC, NCI, NIH (Canada, USA, the Netherlands) 1968– ; Prof., Microbiol., Univ. of Toronto 1979– ; NIH Pre & Postdoctoral Fellowships, Duke & Rockefeller Univs. 1959–66; Ayerst Award, Biochem. Soc. of Canada 1976; Fellow, Royal Soc. of Canada 1983; Tenure, Univ. of Toronto 1977; research grants: MRC 1968– , Nat. Cancer Inst. of Canada 1969–73, Bickel & Connaught foundations 1969– ; Royal Academy of Sciences 1983; Mem., Am. Fed. of Biol. Chem. 1982– ; Mem., The Candn. Fed. of Biol. Chem. 1985– ; Sigma XI 1964– ; author of several journal articles, symposia, lectures & book chapters; recreations: oil painting, classical music; Home: 208 Douglas Dr., Toronto, Ont. M4W 2B8; Office: 112 College St., Toronto, Ont. M5G 1L6.

**GANSNER, Hon. Leo Simeon,** Q.C.; retired judge; b. Nelson, B.C. 3 Jan. 1909; s. Christian Gansner; e. Univ. of B.C., B.A., B.Com. 1935; m. Margaret Annette (Netta) d. late John Harvey; 28 Dec. 1939; children: Rosemary Oberheide, Harvey L.; Judge, Co. Court of Kootenay, B.C. 1978–83; called to Bar of B.C. 1938; cr. Q.C. 1964; apptd. Judge, Co. Court of West Kootenay 1965; Chancellor, Notre Dame Univ. of Nelson 1978–84; mem. Pub. Adv. Bd. B.C. Habitat Conserv. Fund 1981–89; mem. W. Kootenay Naturalists; B.C. Wildlife Fedn.; W. Can. Wilderness Ctte.; E. Kootenay Historical Soc.; Hon. Mem., Kootenay Mountaineering Club; United Church; recreation: reading, gardening; Home: 2004 – 7th St. S., Cranbrook, B.C. V1C 4L4.

**GANT, William George Bruce;** retired executive; b. Vancouver, B.C., 20 Oct. 1927; s. late Alfred George and Emily (Bruce) G.; e. Pub. and High Schs., Medicine Hat, Alta.; Mont. Sch. of Mines; m. Jean Louise, d. late Frank Redmond, 28 Dec. 1950; children: Patricia Lea, Sharon Elizabeth, Nancy Lynn; Gen. Mgr., Calgary Chamber of Commerce 1984–88; Engn. Asst., Clk., Office Mgr., Sparling Davis Ltd., Edmonton 1948–52; Acct. and Office Mgr., Northwest Industries Ltd. and Western Propeller Ltd., Edmonton 1952–56; Office Mgr., H.C. Price of Can. Ltd. 1957–60; Adm. Mgr. 1961–64; Vice Pres. 1964; Pres. 1968–75; Project Mgr., Price, Potashnik, Codell, Oman, J.V., Alyeska Pipeline 1974–75; Construction Mgr., Beafort Delta Oil Project 1975–76; Sen. Construction Mngr., Cdn. Arctic Gas 1977; Vice-Pres., Operations, Lorcan Co. Ltd. 1977–79; Vice Pres. Project Mgmt. Services, Loram Internat. Ltd. 1979; Asst. Gen. Mgr. Mancal Ltd. 1980–84; Past Dir., Calgary Philharmonic Soc.; Dir., United Way of Calgary 1985–91; Hon. Life Dir. (Dir. 1973–85) Calgary Exhn. & Stampede; Pres., Pipe Line Contractors Assn. Can., 1964 and 1970 (Dir. 1961–75); mem. Labour Comte. 1958–72, Chrmn 1965–68); Chrmn., Candn. Gas Assn., Contractors Sec., 1964 and 1971; Chrmn., Candn. Standards Assn. Z183 and Z184 Jt. Welding Sub-Comte. 1965–75; Pipeline Jt. Adv. Council; Freemason; United Church; recreations: hiking, genealogy; Clubs: Rotary of Calgary (Pres. 1986–87); R.I. District 5360 Governor 1993/94; Calgary Golf & Country; Commerce; Home: 1416 Craig Rd. S.W., Calgary, Alta. T2V 2S8.

**GARBUTT, Jeremy,** C.A.; company president; b. Yorkshire, England 11 April 1950; s. Jerry and Mary G.; e. Kings School Pontefract; Howardian H.S.; Maidstone Grammar School; Chartered Accountants C.A. 1974; m. Jane d. Andrew and Lois Greenhalgh 9 June 1977; children: Kate Mary, Jeremy Andrew; PRES., THE HORSHAM CORP. & CLARK OIL & REFINING CORP.; C.A., Coopers & Lybrand, Liverpool & Toronto; Group Controller, Barrick Group; Extve. Vice-Pres., Am. Barrick Resources Corp.; Dir., Am. Barrick Resources, The Horsham Corp., Clark Oil & Refining Corp.; Queen Elizabeth Hosp. Capital Campaign; recreations: tennis, skiing; clubs: St. Louis Racquet; Office: 24 Hazelton Ave., Toronto, Ont. M5R 2E2.

**GARCEAU, Gaston;** association executive; b. Hull, Que. 1 Jan. 1920; m. Rita; children: Murray, Marlene; PAST DOMINION PRES., ROYAL CANDN. LEGION 1990– ; (Pres. 1988–90); Mem., Veterans Appeal Bd.; served with RCAF 1940–44; Civil Serv. Vet. Affairs 1944–47; Que. Prov. Police 1947–58; Min. of Justice Bailiff Section 1958–89; Life Mem., Hull Br., Royal Candn. Legion (joined 1944; former branch & Que. Command Pres., 2 terms); Dominion Vice-Pres. 1976–86; 1st Vice-Pres. 1986–88; Chrmn., Legion Ritual & Awards Ctte., Nat. Ceremonies Ctte., BCEL (Can.) Ctte.; Past Chrmn., Legion Leadership & Devel. & Dominion Convention cttes.; Hon. Pres., Que. Memorial Housing Corp.; Pres., Canvet Pubs. Ltd.; Candn. Centennial Medal; Jubilee Medal; LMSM; Palm Leaf (branch & dist.); recreations: golf, community service; club: Royal Candn. Legion; Office: 359 Kent St., Ottawa, Ont. K2P 0R7.

**GARCEAU, Yvan,** B.A., M.Sc.; business executive; b. Shawinigan, Que. 7 June 1934; s. Louis Arthur and Cecile (Vandal) G.; e. Séminaire Sainte-Marie B.A. 1957; Univ. of Laval M.Sc. 1960; m. Louise d. Aurèle and Anne-Marie (Rioux) Paré 1 Oct. 1960; children: José, Louis; VICE-PRES., ADVERTISING, DAIRY BUREAU OF CANADA 1982– ; various sales & advtg. positions 1960–73; General Manager, Communications PNMD 1973–78; Allard Lesiège Advtg. 1978–79; Vice-Pres. & Group Head, Cockfield Brown Ltd. 1979–82; Candn. del., Internat. Dairy Fed.; Bd. Mem., IDF Canada; Mem., Internat. Milk Promotion; Bd. Mem., Audit Bur. of Circulation; Bd. Mem., Association of Canadian Advertisers (ACA); AMA 'Montreal Chapter' 1993 Personality of the Year (packaged goods, less than 100 employees); Board Sec., Qué. Paraplegic Assn.; Mem., Corp. of Ch. Administrators; Publicité Club of Montréal; recreations: skiing, gardening; Home: 3530 Kent St., Montreal, Que. H3S 1W2; Office: 1981 McGill College Ave., Ste. 1330, Montreal, Que. H3A 2X9.

**GARCIA, Claude A.,** B.A., B.Comm., F.S.A., F.C.I.A.; insurance executive; b. Lévis, Qué. 12 Nov. 1940; s. Antonio and Jacqueline (Ethier) G.; e. Coll. Univ. Laval B.A (Hons.) 1960, B.Comm. (Hons.) 1963; F.S.A. 1968; F.C.I.A. 1970; m. Danielle d. René and Germaine Grégoire 13 Sept. 1966; children: Bernard, Stéphane; PRESIDENT, CANADIAN OPERATIONS, THE STANDARD LIFE ASSURANCE CO. 1993– , Sr. Vice-Pres. & Actuary 1983–88, Extve. Vice-Pres. Operations 1988–90; Extve. Vice-Pres. & C.O.O. 1990–93; Pres. & Dir., Bonaventure Trust 1990– ; The Standard Life Mutual Funds Limited 1992– ; Vice-Pres., Hébert, Le-Houillier et Associés Inc. 1978–82; Bd. Chair & Dir., The Standard Life Portfolio Management Limited 1991– ; Univ. du Qué. à Montréal 1990– ; Dir., The Standard Life Assur. Co. of Canada 1989– ; Les Grands Ballets Canadiens 1986– ; Internat. Financial Centres Orgn. of Montreal 1988– ; Montreal Heart Inst. Rsch. Fund 1992– ; QUNO Corp. 1993– ; recreations: skiing, swimming; clubs: Saint-Denis; Mount Royal; Home: 19 Hazelwood Ave., Outremont, Que. H3T 1R2; Office: 200, 1245 Sherbrooke St. W., Montreal, Que. H3G 1G3.

**GARDAM, John Alan Robert,** OMM, C.D., B.A.; retired armed forces officer, writer; b. Conington, England 20 June 1931; s. Vaughan Newman and Ellen Rebecca (Jex) G.; e. Univ. of Manitoba, B.A. 1979; m. Elaine d. Edith and Joe Wood 27 Aug. 1955; children: John, Robert, David, Michael; DND PROJECT DIRECTOR, 50TH ANNIVERSARY CANADA REMEMBERS 1993– ; Reserve army 1947–51; Trooper, Cdn. Army 1951; Officer, Canadian Army 1952–84 (2 Lt to Col); Asst. Sec. Gen., Candn. Agency, Commonwealth War Graves Comn. 1984–89; Project Dir., Peacekeeping Monument Project 1989–92; Bd. of Dir., Canadian Forces Personnel Assistance Fund 1992– ; Order of Military Merit 1980; 3rd clasp to Candn. Forces Decoration 28 Feb. 1990 (42 yrs. serv.); CDS Commendation 1993; Mem., Royal Candn. Dragoons Assn.; Royal Candn. Legion Br. 517; Nat. Pres., Cdn. Assoc. of UN Peacekeepers 1993– ; author: 'Canadian War Memorial' 1982, '70 Years After 1914–1918' 1983, 'The Legacy' 1988, '50 Years After' 1990; 'Ordinary Heroes' 1992; 'The Canadian Peacekeeper' 1992; contb. author: 'The Gate: History of Fort Garry Horse' 1971; 'Korea - Oral history from those who were there 1950–1954' forthcoming; recreations: sailing; Address: 18 Canter Blvd., Nepean, Ont. K2G 2M2.

**GARDINER, George Ryerson,** O.C., O.Ont., B.Com., M.B.A.; stockbroker; b. Toronto, Ont. 25 Apr. 1917; s. Percy Ryerson and Gertrude Margaret (Corcoran) G.; e. Univ. of Toronto Schs.; Univ. of Toronto, B.Com. 1939; Harvard Business Sch., M.B.A. 1941; children: Judith, Michael, Christine, Chrmn., Green Line Investor Services Inc.; Garbell Holdings Limited; Gardiner Group Capital Ltd.; Gardiner Oil & Gas Ltd.; Trustee, The George R. Gardiner Museum of Ceramic Art; Home: 4 Old Forest Hill Rd., Toronto, Ont. M5P 2P7.

**GARDINER, J. Robert,** B.A., LL.B.; barrister and solicitor; b. Toronto, Ont. 15 Sept. 1947; s. Percy MacDonald and Mary (Sowdon) G.; e. Univ. of Toronto B.A. 1969; Osgoode Hall, York Univ. LL.B. 1972; called to Bar 1974; m. Janet d. Wilfred and Pearl Leek 1967; PARTNER, MESSRS. GARDINER, BLUMBERG 1986– ; articled & practised at Harries Houser 1972–75; Lee Fireman, Regan 1975–79; established own firm 1979; Partnership, Gardiner, Somer 1983; present practice: Business / Condominium / Entertainment / Commercial Real Estate; Editor, 'Osgoode Hall Law J.' 1972; Instr., Business Law, Ryerson Poly. Inst. 1978; Moderator & Lectr. 1979– ; Founding Pres., SCRAP! (ratepayers assn.); Mem., Law Soc. of U.C.; Candn. Bar Assn.; originated & worked with trappers & govts. to enact over 118 humane trapping laws across Canada; helped to devel. trapper edn. courses, trap research & internat. trap standards; initiated internationally-adopted humane concepts pertaining to wildlife, incl. 'Use of wildlife must be sustainable & humane'; drafted proposed Criminal Code Amendments pertaining to cruelty to animals & other animal welfare legis.; monthly review of exper. med. rsch. protocols; involvement in environ., nuclear disarmament & third world issues; Chair: Wildlife, Humane Trapping, Status of Animals & Resolution Cttes. & Dir. & Mem., Extve. & Policy Cttes., Candn. Fed. of Humane Soc.; Pres. & Dir., Candn. Assn. for Humane Trapping; Founding Pres., LEGHOLD!; Dir., Fur Inst. of Canada; past Mem., Animal Care Ctte., Sick Children's Hosp.; Mem., Internat. Standards Orgn., Trap Standards Working Group 2; Candn. Standards Bd., Trap Standards Ctte.; author of over 30 business law articles, 40 briefs, resolutions, speeches, articles & presentations to legis. cttes., promoting num. humane improvements pertaining to wildlife or trapping, 'Come on In' (poetry) 1990, 'The Riddle of Reality' (non-fiction) 1992, 14 classical guitar compositions and 20 songs; awarded Commemorative Medal for 125th Anniversary of Candn. Confederation; recreations: white-water canoeing, skiing, windsurfing, the wilderness, photography; Home: 130-year-old farm house, Gormley, Ont.; Office: 1202, 390 Bay St., Toronto, Ont. M5H 2Y2.

**GARDINER, James Allan,** B.Sc.; executive; b. Victoria, B.C. 26 May 1944; s. John Douglas and Muriel Jean (Hanbidge) G.; e. Univ. of Waterloo; York Univ. B.Sc. 1968; m. Iris d. Hans and Renate Heydenreich 6 June 1980; children: Shawn, Amanda; PRES., CONSUMERS DISTRIBUTING (U.S.); Mgr. MIS Ford Motor Co. 1970–82; Corporate Dir. MIS Canron Inc. 1982–84; Exec. Dir. Workers Compensation Bd. Ont. 1984–86, Vice Pres. Client Services 1986–87; Vice Pres. Operations Semi-Tech Microelectronics Inc. 1988–90; Pres. STM Systems Corp. 1990–91; Extve. Vice Pres., Field Optns., ISM Information Systems Mgmt. Corp 1991–93; Dir.: CADAPSO; Can.-USSR Bus. Council; Lake Muskoka Cottagers Assn.; recreations: cottage, sailing, snowbiling; Clubs: South Muskoka Sailing; Milford Bay Snowmobile; Home: 12 Viamede Cres., North York, Ont.; Office: 215 Consumers Rd., North York, Ont. M2J 4R3.

**GARDINER, Janet C.,** B.Comm., F.C.A.; accountant; b. St. John's, Nfld. 28 May 1933; d. Chester E. and Phyllis M. (Carson) Dawe; e. Holloway Sch.; Prince of Wales Coll. (St. John's); Trafalgar Sch. for Girls (Montreal); Dalhousie Univ., B.Comm. 1954; m. late Peter J., s. A.J. and Dorothy Gardiner, 27 May 1961; children: Dr. Jane; Susan; Steven; TREASURER, CHESTER DAWE LTD.; Pres., Cavendish Café Inc.; Dir., Chester Dawe Ltd. & Assoc. Cos.; Fishery Products Internat. Ltd. (Extve. & Nominating Comte.); WHIN Publications Ltd.; chartered accountant, Lee & Martin (Halifax) 1956; joined present firm in 1957; Chrmn., Bd. of Regents, Memorial Univ. of Nfld.; Mem., Citizen's Adv. Bd., Salvation Army; Chrmn. Finance Ctte., St. Thomas' Anglican Church; Chrmn., Grace Communities Advisory Bd.; recreations: piano playing; needlework; Home: 19 Winter Place, St. John's, Nfld. A1B 1J5 & Hogan's Pond; Office: P.O. Box 8280, St. John's, Nfld. A1B 3N4.

**GARDINER, John Muir,** B.Sc., P.Eng.; consulting engineer; b. Madras, India 16 March 1929; s. John Muir and Norah Violet (Reynolds) G.; e. Univ. of Glasgow B.Sc. (Civil) 1950; m. Gladys Goodall Apl. 1955; two s. John Michael, Neil Reynolds; PRES. & C.E.O., ACRES INCORPORATED AND ACRES INTERNATIONAL LTD. 1987– ; joined Sir William Halcrow & Partners, London, Eng. 1950–51; RAF 1951–53; Aberdeen County Engineers, Scot. 1953–58; present firm 1957; recreations: tennis, sailing; Clubs: Royal Candn. Mil. Inst.; Home: 1273 Catchacoma Court, Mississauga, Ont. L5H 2X5; Office: 480 University Ave., Toronto, Ont. M5G 1V2.

**GARDINER, Michael R.,** M.B.A., LL.B.; executive; b. Wilmington, Delaware 18 Aug. 1945; s. George Ryerson and Anne (Dumstrey) G.; e. Univ. of Toronto B.A. 1967, LL.B. 1970; Harvard Univ. M.B.A. 1974; m. Heather d. Gordon and Jean Warren 9 June 1973; children: Scott, Rebecca, Mark; PRES. & C.E.O., FAIRWATER CAPITAL CORP. & SONOR INVESTMENTS LIMITED 1991– ; articling student, McCarthy & McCarthy 1970–71; Spec. Asst., Cabinet Office, Govt. of Ont. 1974; Corp./Comm. Lawyer, McCarthy & McCarthy 1975–80; Pres., Fairwater Capital Corp. & Sonor Investments Ltd. 1981–87, Chrmn. & C.E.O. 1987–91; Bd. Vice Chrmn., Scott's Hosp. Inc. (Chrmn., Extve. Ctte. and Manpower Resources Ctte.; Mem., Nominations Ctte.); Vice-Pres. & Dir., The Sonor Found.; Mem., Harvard Bus. Sch. Club of Toronto (Past Pres.); Young Pres. Orgn.; Law Soc. of U.C.; Clubs: Toronto; The Badminton & Racquet; Toronto Lawn Tennis; Oxford; Office: Suite 1500, BCE Place, 181 Bay St., Box 810, Toronto, Ont. M5J 2T3.

**GARDINER, W. Douglas H.,** C.M.; retired banker; b. Chatham, Ont. 21 Apr. 1917; s. William Henry and Elsie (Armstrong) G.; e. Kennedy Coll. Inst., Windsor, Ont. (Hon. Matric.); m. Jean Elizabeth, d. Dr. Franklin A. Blatchford, Fort William, Ont. 5 Sept. 1945; 3 s.: Donald, Campbell, Gregory; Pres., W.D.H.G. Financial Assoc. Ltd.; Bd. Chrmn., Reed Stenhouse Companies Ltd.; served in R.C.N.V.R. 1940–46 (discharged with rank Lt. Com.); joined The Royal Bank of Canada 1935; retired as Vice-Chrmn. 1980; mem., Order of Canada 1982; Protestant; recreations; golf, fishing, shooting, Clubs: Toronto; York (Toronto); The Vancouver; Shaughnessy Golf & Country; Home: 3115 W. 49th Ave., Vancouver, B.C. V6N 3T3.

**GARDNER, David Emmett,** M.A., Ph.D.; actor; director; adjudicator; teacher and historian of Canadian theatre; b. Toronto, Ont. 4 May 1928; s. David and Madeleine Vera (Cunningham) G.; e. Public Schs., Lawrence Park Coll. Inst. (Valedictorian), Toronto, Ont.; Victoria Coll., Univ. of Toronto, B.A. (Art & Archaeol.) 1950, Graduate Centre for Study of Drama, M.A. 1974 (Drama), Ph.D. 1983 (Drama); m. Dorothy Rosemary Wood (née Kerr) 1965; one d., Jennifer Kathleen; mem., A.C.T.R.A.; Actors' Equity; Acad. of Candn. Cinema and Television; Am. Soc. for Theatre Research; Hon. Mem., Assn. Canadian Theatre Research 1993; Gov., National Theatre School; Chrmn., Candn. Theatre Centre Comte., which estbd. National Theatre Sch. of Canada (Montreal-Stratford) in 1960, and co-author of the blueprint of sch. aims, curriculum, etc.; Bd. of Dirs., Red Barn Theatre, Jackson's Point; Past Vice-Pres., Candn. Theatre Centre; former Gov., Dom. Drama Festival; former mem. T.V. Producers Assn.; Actor with original post-war Hart House Theatre group under Robert Gill, performing as Othello, Macbeth, Marc Antony; Asst. to Warden of Hart House, Univ. of Toronto 1951–52; 1949–90: profl. acting career with Straw Hat Players (4 seasons), Crest Theatre, New Play Society, Jupiter Theatre, Canadian Repertory Theatre (Ottawa), Brae Manor Theatre (Quebec), 'Spring Thaw,' 'Clap Hands'; 1956–57, Canadian Players tour of 'Hamlet' (Horatio) and 'Peer Gynt' (8 roles); Stratford Shakespearean Festival 1955, 1956 and 1986 seasons; 'Tamburlaine the Great' (N.Y.C.); Edinburgh Festival (winner, Tyrone Guthrie Award 1956); 1957–58: London, Eng., 'Requiem for a Nun' at Royal Court Theatre, and leading role in 'Hunter's Moon' by Marc Connelly; with Old Vic Co., played London, Edin. Festival and the 1957–58 N. Am. tour of 'Henry V' (Capt. Gower); 'Twelfth Night' (Sea Capt.) and 'Hamlet' (Fortinbras), CentreStage 'The Philadelphia Story' (1982), Tarragon Theatre 'Tower' (1983); Necessary Angel 'The Castle' (1987); Neptune Theatre (Halifax) 'Deathtrap' (1989); created Candn. roles of John Serang in 'Marsh Hay' (1974), Robert Rogers in 'Pontiac and the Green Man' (1977), Paul in 'Tower' (1983); since 1950, over 900 TV and radio roles with CBC, CTV, Global, BBC, Granada, ITV Networks (London), and CBS (NYC) including roles of: Bellamy in CBC's 'Bethune' (1977); Wes McClung in CBC's 'Nellie McClung' (1978); Gibson McFarland in CBC's 'Artichoke' (1979); Brian Webster in CBC's 'One of Our Own' (1979); Larry Greene in 'Home Fires' (1980–83); C.D. Howe in 'Empire Inc.' (1983); Ilsley in 'The King Chronicle' (1988); the Chairman in 'Robocop' TV Series (1994); plus appearances in 'Adderley,' 'Night Heat,' 'Seeing Things,' 'The Campbells,' 'Mount Royal,' 'War of the Worlds,' 'Street Legal,' 'Katts and Dog,' 'Alfred Hitchcock Presents,' 'Starting from Scratch,' 'In Opposition,' 'My Secret Identity,' 'Scales of Justice,' 'Counterstrike,' 'E.N.G.,' 'Missing Teasures,' etc.; films incl.: 'Family Circles' (NFB 1950); 'Oedipus Rex' (Stratford 1956); lead in 'The Field' (U.S. 'Navy Log' TV series 1958); role of Reverend Powelly in 'Who Has Seen The Wind' (1977); psychologist in 'Prom Night I' (1979); health minister in 'Virus' (1979); Dr. Steffen in 'If You Could See What I Hear' (1981); school principal in 'The Class of 1984' (1982); Dr. Lorstrum in 'When Angels Fly' (1983); Barney in 'Heartsounds' (1984); Trial Judge in 'The Good Mother' (1988); Rev. Roach in 'Glory Enough For All' (1988); Dr. Lett in 'Beautiful Dreamers' (1990); Padre in 'White Light' (1990); Father in 'The World's Oldest Living Bridesmaid' (1990); Geo. Lukacs in 'The Making of Monsters' 1991; Judge in 'Trial and Error' 1993; Henry Luce in 'JFK' 1993; Candn. Film Award, Best Sup. Actor, for 'The Insurance Man from Ingersoll' (1976); Stage Director of a number of plays in Toronto, Halifax, Ottawa and Vancouver; Crest Theatre, 'King Lear' 1960; Candn. Players Ltd. 1961, controversial Arctic 'King Lear,' 'The Lady's Not For Burning' 1961 and 'Masterpieces of Comedy' 1962; 'No Sex Please, We're British' (Variety Dinner Theatre) 1985; Hart House productions 'Look Back in Anger' 1964, 'The Father' 1967; 'Rosmersholm' 1972; 'Sweet Bird of Youth' 1977; 'Major Barbara' 1983; 'The Trojan War' 1985; U.C. Playhouse 'Can You See Me Yet?' 1984; 'Uncle Vanya' 1985; 'Places Please' 1986; 'Under Milk Wood' (Neptune Theatre, Halifax) 1966; George Brown Coll. 'Cry of the Loon' (1988); 'The Ecstasy of Rita Joe' (1st Eng. Prod. at Nat. Arts Centre 1969); Vancouver 'Royal Hunt of the Sun,' 'Che Guevara,' (1969) 'Rosencrantz and Guildenstern are Dead' (1970) and 'Othello' (1971); in 1959–69 joined CBC as contract television Drama Producer for such series as 'Festival' ('The Applecart' 1962; 'Doctor's Dilemma' 1963; 'Uncle Vanya' and 'Resounding Tinkle' 1964; 'Yesterday the Children Were Dancing' 1968; 'The Paper People' 1967 (winner of 1968 Wilderness Award for direction and design); 'The Three Musketeers' 1969); 'Playdate' ('Village Wooing' 1962; 'Dear Liar' 1964); 'The Serial' ('Jake and the Kid,' 'Train of Murder,' 'Reluctant Agent,' 'Mr. Member of Parl.' 1965); Producer/Dir. of 'Quentin Durgens, M.P.' series 1966–67–68; 'Judge' 1984; Artistic Dir., Vancouver Playhouse 1969–71; Theatre Arts Offr., Canada Council 1971–72; has written many articles for journs. and contrib. chapter on Drama in English-Speaking Canada for 'Canadian Annual Review' for 1961, 1962, 1963 and sections on Canada and Canadians in 4th Ed. of 'The Oxford Companion to the Theatre' 1983, 'The Canadian Encyclopedia' 1985 and (2nd ed.) 1988, 'The Oxford Companion to Canadian Theatre' 1989, 'The World Encyclopedia of Contemporary Theatre' (N.D.), 'Dictionary of Canadian Biography' vols. XIII, XII and VII; chapter on variety entertainment in Ont. for 'Later Stages' 1993; Work in Progress: Concise History of the Theatre in Canada; Dom. Festival Regional Adjudicator Maritimes (1961), Alta., B.C. (1962), CODL (1965 and 1973), WODL (1968), Simpson's Festival (1963 and 1968); teaching: Univ. of Toronto, York Univ., National Theatre Sch., Seneca Coll., George Brown Coll.; Liberal; Agency: The Characters; Home: 25381 Kennedy Rd., R.R. #1, Sutton West, Ont. L0E 1R0.

**GARDNER, J.A.F.,** C.M., M.A., Ph.D., F.C.I.C., F.I.A.W.S.; educator; b. Nakusp, B.C. 17 Aug. 1919; s. George Hunter and Maude (Williams) G.; e. Univ. of B.C. B.A. 1940, M.A. 1942; McGill Univ. Ph.D. 1944; m. Hilda Joyce d. William Harper 3 June 1944; children: Joseph William, Mary Lee Woodworth; DEAN EMERITUS, FAC. OF FORESTRY, UNIV. OF B.C. 1984– ; Research Assoc. McGill Univ. 1944–45; Research Chem. Howard Smith Paper Mills 1945–47; Head Wood Chem. Forest Products Lab. Vancouver 1947–63; Dir. Western Forest Products Lab. 1963–65; Dean, Faculty of Forestry, Univ. of B.C. 1965–83; author over 50 publs. mainly in chem. and utilization of wood fields; Fellow, Internat. Acad. Wood Science; Fellow, Chem. Inst. of Canada; mem. Candn. Inst. Forestry; Tech. Assn. Pulp & Paper Indust. (U.S.A.); Tech. Sect. Candn. Pulp & Paper Assoc.; Reg'd. Prof. Forester (Hon.); Member of the Order of Canada 1994; Protestant; recreations: fishing, golf, skiing, tennis; Home: 5537 Wallace St., Vancouver, B.C. V6N 2A1.

**GARDNER, John R.,** F.S.A., F.C.I.A., M.A.A.A.; insurance executive; b. Evanston, Ill. 9 Oct. 1937; s. John and Margaret C. G.; e. Univ. of Toronto Schs. 1955 (Prince of Wales Scholarship); Univ. of Toronto B.A. 1959 (Gov.-Gen.'s Medal); Oxford Univ. B.A. 1961, M.A. 1965 (Commonwealth Universities Scholarship); m. Maria Encarnacion (Encarnita) Seco de Lucena Vasquez, Ph.D. 14 Oct. 1964; children: Maria Luisa, John Anthony, Sara Margaret; PRES. AND DIR., SUN LIFE ASSURANCE CO. OF CANADA 1987– ; Sun Life Assurance Co. of Can. (U.S.); Sun Life Insurance and Annuity Co. of New York; Sun Benefit Services Co.; Chrmn. and Dir., Sun Investment Services Co.; Dir.: Sun Life of Canada Home Loans Ltd.; Massachusetts Financial Services Co.; Spectrum Mutual Fund Operations Corp.; Spectrum Mutual Fund Services Inc.; Sun Life Assurance Co. of Canada (U.K.) Limited; Sun Life of Canada Unit Managers Limited; Sun Life of Canada Investment Management Limited; Sun Life Trust Co.; Massachusetts Casualty Ins. Co.; Dir., Sun Life Financial Holdings Inc.; Sun Life Savings and Mortgage Corp.; joined firm 1961, Asst. Actuary 1965, Assoc. Actuary 1968, Vice-Pres. and Actuary United States Head Office 1973, Vice-Pres. Marketing, U.S. 1974, Vice-Pres. Group for Canada 1978, Sr. Vice-Pres. and Gen. Mgr. for Can. 1982; Sr. Vice Pres. and Extve. Offr. 1985–87; Lt., Royal Candn. Navy Reserve (Ret'd); mem., Am. Acad. of Actuaries; Fellow, Soc. of Actuaries; Fellow, Candn. Inst. of Actuaries; Chrmn. Bus. Bd., Governing Counc., Univ. of Toronto; Bd. of Trustees, Sunnybrook Med. Centre; Dir., Candn. Life and Health Ins. Compensation Corp. (CompCorp); Dir., Toronto Symphony; Mem., CLHIA (Task Force on Retirement Income Plans and Standing Ctte. on Public Relations); recreations: classical music, hiking, travel; Clubs: Donalda; Toronto; Office: Sun Life Centre, 150 King St. W., Toronto, Ont. M5H 1J9.

**GARDOM, Garde Basil,** Q.C., B.A., LL.B.; b. Banff, Alta. 17 July 1924; s. Basil and Gabrielle Gwladys (Bell) G.; e. Univ. of B.C., B.A., LL.B.; m. Theresa Helen Eileen Mackenzie 11 Feb. 1956; children: Kim, Karen, Edward, Brione, Brita; Dir., Crown Life Insurance Co.; called to Bar of B.C. 1949; el. M.L.A. for Vancouver-Point Grey prov. g.e. 1966; re-el. 1969, '72, '75, '79, '83; Govt. House Leader 1977–86; Atty. Gen. B.C. 1975–79; Min. of Intergovernmental Relations, B.C. 1979–86; Chrmn., Constitution Ctte. 1975–86; Legislation Ctte. 1975–86; Mem., Treasury Bd. and Planning and Priorities Ctte. 1983–86; Min. responsible, Official Visits to Expo '86; Policy Cons. Office of the Premier 1986–87; Agent General for British Columbia in the U.K. and Europe 1987–92; Mem., Candn. Bar Assoc. 1949– ; Vancouver Bar Assoc. 1949– ; B.C. Sports Hall of Fame; Phi Delta Theta 1943; Anglican; recreations: tennis, fishing, skiing; Clubs: Union Club of BC; Vancouver Lawn Tennis and Badminton; Home: 1738 Angus Dr., Vancouver B.C. V6J 4H5.

**GAREBIAN, Keith Stephen James,** B.Ed., M.A., Ph.D.; writer; b. Bombay, India 15 July 1943; s. Adam Stephen and Lorna Constance (Alimo) G.; e. Univ. of Montreal B.Ed. 1964 (Lt. Gov.'s Medal); Sir George Williams Univ. M.A. 1971; Queen's Univ. Ph.D. 1973; m. Caryl d. Francis and Ethel Taugher 23 Dec. 1972, div. 1991; one s. Michael Ian; Discussion Leader and Lectr. Thomas More Inst. Montreal 1969–70, 1981, 1987; Asst. Prof. McGill Univ. 1974; Instr. Concordia Univ. 1975–77, 1981; Instr. Trent Univ. 1990–91; Judge Eng. Entries Grand Prix de la Ville de Montréal 1978; Dir. Candn. Theatre Critics Assn. 1981, Co-organizer Fall Conf. 1982; cited various lit. reference books; author 'Hugh Hood' 1983; 'Hugh Hood and His Works' 1985; 'William Hutt: A Theatre Portrait' 1988; 'Leon Rooke and His Works' 1989; 'A Well-Bred Muse: Selected Theatre Writings 1978–1988' 1991; 'Shaw and Newton: Explorations of Shavian Theatre' 1992; 'The Making of "My Fair Lady"' 1993; 'The Making of "Gypsy"' 1994; contbr. to various lit. publs. incl. 'The Oxford Companion to Canadian Literature' 1983; 'Dictionary of Literary Biography' 1986; 'The Oxford Companion to Canadian Theatre' 1989; 'Das Moderne Englisch-Kanadische Drama' 1991; recreations: swimming, tennis; Home: c/o 1006, 3375 Pony Trail Dr., Mississauga, Ont. L4X 1V8.

**GARFINKEL, Hon. Marvin Franklin,** B.A., LL.B.; judge; b. Winnipeg, Man. 7 Feb. 1943; s. Saul and Jennie (Cohen) G.; e. Univ. of Man. B.A. 1964, LL.B. 1967; m. Merle Rochelle d. Arthur and Betty Vinsky 25 May 1970; children: Ara Beth, Jeffrey Hayden, Sadira Marnie; JUDGE, PROVINCIAL COURT OF MAN. 1979– ; articled with Walsh Micay and Co. 1967–68; called to Bar of Man. 1968; law practice Pollock and Conner 1970–76; Partner, Conner and Garfinkel 1976–78; operated own firm 1978–79; part-time Prov. Judge 1977–79; Dir. Schizophrenia Treatment & Rsch. Found. Man. Inc. 1986– ; Presenting Faculty mem. W. Judicial Edn. Centre; mem. Exec. Ctte. Prov. Judges Assn.; Pres. Vaad Ha-Ir 1986–89; Pres. Rosh Pina Cong. 1981–83; Office: 5th Flr., 408 York Ave., Winnipeg, Man. R3C 0P9.

**GARFINKEL, Paul E.,** M.D., F.R.C.P.(C); university professor / psychiatrist; b. Winnipeg, Man. 21 Jan. 1946; e. medical training Univ. of Manitoba; internship Toronto Western Hospital; psychiatric residency Univ. of Toronto; m. Dorothy; 3 children; PROFESSOR & CHAIR, DEPT. OF PSYCHIATRY, UNIV. OF TORONTO AND DIR. & PSYCHIATRIST-IN-CHIEF, CLARKE INST. OF PSYCHIATRY 1990– ; Psychiatrist-in-Chief, Toronto Gen. Hosp. 1982; Toronto Hosp. 1989; Home: 210 Vesta Dr., Toronto, Ont. M5P 2Z9; Office: 250 College St., Suite #835, Toronto, Ont. M5T 1R8.

**GARIEPY, (Joseph Harry) André,** B.Sc., P.Eng.; b. Detroit, Mich. 29 Oct. 1927; s. Joseph Alphonse Honoré and Ernestine (Mathurin) G.; e. Queen's Univ. B.Sc. (Mech. Eng.) 1952; m. Pauline d. René and Dorina Ouellette 26 Sept. 1953; children: Marc, Yves, Jean; EXTVE. DIR., CANDN. INTELLECTUAL PROPERTY OFFICE (CIPO); Project Eng. E.B. Eddy Co. 1952–53; Patent Examiner Mech. Div. Patent Office 1953, Special Projects Offr. Planning & Special Duties Div. Patent Office 1969, mem. Rsch. & Internat. Affairs Br. 1973, Dir. Tech. Adv. Services Br. Bureau Intellectual Property 1974, Comnr. of Patents 1976, Registrar of Trade Marks 1981, Dir. Gen. Patents, T.M. Copyright & Ind. Design; Comnr. of Patents, Registrar of Trademarks & Dir. Gen. Intellectual Property, Consumer & Corporate Affairs Can. 1981–..; mem. Assn. Prof. Engs. Prov. Ont.; recreations; swimming, skiing; Home: 4 Place Belisle, Hull, Qué. J9A 1L3; Office: 50 Victoria St., Place du Portage, 5th Floor, Zone 8, Hull, Qué. K1A 0C9.

**GARIGUE, Philippe,** O.C., B.Sc., Ph.D., F.R.S.C. (1963); professor; b. Manchester, England 13 Oct. 1917; s. Joseph and Giselle (Burke) G.; e. London Sch. of Econ., B.Sc. (Econ.) 1951; Univ. of London, Ph.D. 1953; Diploma of Defense Studies, Nat. Defence College, Kingston, 1973; m. Amalia Maria, d. Giuseppe Porcheddu, 11 Oct. 1946; three children: PROFESSOR EMERITUS and SENIOR SCHOLAR, GLENDON COLLEGE and SR. RSCH. FELLOW, CENTRE FOR INTERNATIONAL AND STRATEGIC STUDIES, YORK UNIV.; Chrmn., Family Superior Council of Que. Govt. 1964–71; Pres., Adm. Bd., Inst. of Urban Studies, Univ. of Montreal 1959–67; mem. Bd. Govs., Univ. of Moncton 1967–70; mem. Scient. Comn., Ecole Internat. de Bordeaux, Agence de Cooperation Culturelle et Technique 1971; Pres., Internat. Union of Family Organs. 1969–73; Mem., Ctte. for Mil. and Strategic Studies, Min. of Defence 1970–82; Vice-Chrmn. Consultative Council, Environment Canada, 1975–80; mem., Counc. of Franco-Ontarian Affairs, Prov. of Ont. 1983–87; Council of Franco-Ontarian Education, 1984–87; Mem. Adv. Ctte., Law Reform Comn., Govt. of Ont. 1989; Lect., National Defence Coll., 1968; Staff School and College, Toronto, 1975; Research Assist., Univ. of Edinburgh 1951–53; Research Fellow, Univ. of London, 1953–54; Asst. Prof., McGill Univ., 1955–57; Full Prof., Pol. Sci., Univ. of Montreal, 1957–80, formerly Dean of Soc. Sci. 1957–72; Pres., Adm. Council, Inst. for Urbanism, Univ. of Montreal, 1959–67; Comte on Acad. Status 1965–72; mem. Joint Commis. of Univ. Council of Univ. Assembly for the reorgan. of the Univ. of Montreal, 1968–70; mem. Consultative Comte, Centre of Eur. Stu. & Doc. 1975–77; Principal, Glendon Coll., York Univ. 1980–87; Assoc. Prof. Institut de Droit de la Paix et du Developpement, Université de Nice, France since 1987; served in 2nd World War; joined Brit. Army, 1939; Sandhurst Royal Mil. Acad.; Commnd. in Royal Fusiliers; Special Air Service (African Campaign, Italy and Austria); attained rank of Captain; Publications: 'Changing Political Leadership in West Africa' (thesis) 1953); 'A Bibliographical Introduction to the Study of French Canada' 1956; 'Etudes sur le Canada Français' 1958; 'La Vie Familiale des Canadiens Français' 1962, re-ed. 1970; 'L'Option politiques des Canadiens Français' 1963; 'Analyse du comportement familial' 1967; 'Bibliographie de Quebec (1955–65)' 1967; 'Science Policy in Canada' 1972; 'Famille, Science et Politique,' 'Famille et Humanisme,' 'Le temps vivant' all 1973; 'L'Humaine Demeure' 1974; 'Guerres, Metastrategies et Societes' 1987; 'Introduction to the metastrategy of War and Peace 1987; 'Questions de strategie et de metastrategie' 1991; articles on pol. leadership in W. Africa, studies on coloured students in Gt. Brit., on the European family system, Defence Policy, Strategic Studies, International Relations, European Community, Francophone affairs, etc.; Am. Sociol. Soc.; mem. Can. Econ. & Pol. Assn. (Vice Pres. 1959–60); Soc. Intern. des soc. de langue française; Am. Pol. Sci. Assn.; Soc. Candn. de Sci. Pol.; Royal Soc. of Can. (mem. of Council, Sect. I., 1975–76; of Comte. of Internat. Rel. 1977–); Acad. des Sci. Morales et Pol.; U.S. Strategic Inst.; Candn. Inst. of Strategic Studies; Royal United Services Inst. for Defense Studies (U.K.); Fellow, Internat. Inst. of Strategic Studies (London); Founding Dir. & Vice-Pres. (1965–69), Vanier Inst. of the Family; mem. of Counsel, Internat. Union of Family Org., 1965–75 (Pres. 1969–73); Secty, Council for Social Action, Conf. of Candn. Bishops (1966–70); Officer of the Order of Canada 1986; Officer of the Legion of Honour of France 1987; awarded Knight Grand Cross. and Grand Officer 1972, 1978 and 1979; Hosp. and Mil. Order of St. John of Jerusalem, Rhodes and Malta; Grand Croix, Orden de Cicernos 1971; Commemorative Medal, 125th Anniversary of Candn. Confedn. 1992; plus 5 other military medals and 2 hon. citizenships; Literary Prize Prov. Quebec 1968; Catholic.

**GARLAND, George David,** B.A.Sc., M.A., Ph.D., F.R.S.C. (1959); university professor; b. Toronto, Ont. 29 June 1926; s. Nicholas Lowrie and Jean Irene (McPherson) G.; e. Univ. of Toronto Schs. (1937–43); Univ. of Toronto, B.A.Sc. (Engn. Physics) 1947; M.A. 1948; St. Louis Univ., Ph.D. 1951; m. Elizabeth Peat, d. A.S. MacMillan, Schumacher, Ont., 10 June 1949; children: Mary Isabelle, Nicholas, George David, Jr.; PROF. OF GEOPHYSICS, UNIV. OF TORONTO, since 1963; Secy. Gen., Internat. Union of Geodesy & Geophysics since 1963–73; Pres. International Union of Geodesy & Geophys 1979– ; Vice-Pres., Acad. of Sci., Royal Soc. of Can. 1980– ; Lectr., Physics, Univ. of Toronto, 1949–52; Geophysicist, Dom. Observatory, Ottawa, 1952–54; Prof. of Geophysics, Univ. of Alberta, 1954–63; Fields of Research: structure of the earth's crust, gravity, magnetic variations, geophysical exploration; mem., Assn. Prof. Engrs. Ont.; Am. Geophysical Union; Conservative; Protestant; recreations: camping, photography, collecting of Canadiana.

**GARNEAU, Brig.-Gen. André,** O.St.J., C.D.; army officer (ret.); b. Quebec, Que. 18 Feb. 1921; s. late Col. Gérard O.B.E., E.D. and late Andrée de Varennes G.; e. Univ. of Ottawa; m. Jean Richardson 1946; four s. (incl. Marc, Canada's first astronaut); joined Gov. Gen.'s Footguards as Guardsman 1937; Regtl. Sgt. Maj. and Lt., Univ. of Ottawa COTC 1940; trans. C.A. (Active) as Lt., Sept. 1942; served in 2nd World War, Can., U.K., N.W. Europe, with Regt. de Maisonneuve, rank Capt.; Candn. War Staff Course 1945–46; Staff Capt., Mil. H.Q., Montreal 1946, Quebec City 1947; Gen. Staff Offr. 3, H.Q. Central Command, Oakville, Ont. 1951; promoted Maj. and apptd. Gen. Staff Offr. 2 1952; with 2nd Bn. Royal 22e Regt. in Can. and W. Germany 1953; Dir. Mil. Studies, Coll. Mil. Royal, Saint-Jean, Que. 1957; Secy. Army Bd., Mil. Agency for Standardization. NATO, London, Eng. 1961; promoted Lt.-Col. 1962; Comd. 3rd Bn. Royal 22e Regt. 1964; Head, Combat Arms Sec., Dir. Postings and Careers, Ottawa, Ont. 1966; promoted Col. and apptd. Candn. Forces Attaché, Yugoslavia and Greece 1968; Depy. Comd. and C.O. Regular Support Staff, Central Mil. Area, Downsview, Ont. 1971; promoted Brig-Gen. 1972; Administrative Secy. to the Gov. Gen. of Can. 1972–75; Commissioner, Canadian Pension Commission 1976–84; Past Pres., Ottawa-Carleton Br., Red Cross; R. Catholic; recreations: skiing, curling, tennis, swimming, reading, gardening; Home: 470 Oakhill Rd., Rockcliffe, Ont. K1M 1J6.

**GARNEAU, Captain (N) (Retired) Marc,** O.C., C.D., Ph.D., P.Eng.; Joseph Charles André and Jean Armstrong (Richardson) G.; e. Coll. Militaire Royal de St-Jean 1968; Roy. Mil. Coll. B.Eng. 1968–70; Imperial Coll. (U.K.) Ph.D. 1973; Hon. Doctorates: Laval Univ.; Royal Mil. College; Technical Univ. of N.S.; Coll. Militaire Royal de St-Jean; children: Yves, Simone; ASTRONAUT, CANADIAN ASTRONAUT PROGRAM 1984– , currently seconded to NASA to train as a Mission Specialist Astronaut 1992– ; First Candn. Astronaut to fly in space aboard Challenger on mission 41G, 5–13 Oct. 1984; retired from Candn. Navy 5 Apr. 1989; apptd. Depy. Dir., Candn. Astronaut Program 1988; seconded by Candn. Navy to National Rsch. Counc. 1984–89; Combat Systems Engr. (Halifax), Dept. of National Defence 1973–74; HMCS Algonquin 1974–76; Naval Weapons Instr. Fleet Sch. (Halifax) 1976–77; Project Engr. Naval Weapons (Ottawa) 1977–80; Naval Engr. Resp. for Surface and Air Weapons (Halifax) 1980–82; attended Candn. Forces Command and Staff Coll. (Toronto 1982–83); Design Auth. for Comm. and Electronic Warfare Equipment, Candn. Navy (Ottawa) 1983–84; recipient, Athlone Fellowship 1970; Nat. Rsch. Council Bursary 1972; awarded, Candn. Decoration CD (military) 1980; NASA Space Flight Medal 1984; apptd. Officer, Order of Canada 1984; co-recipient, F.W. (Casey) Baldwin Award (best paper in the Candn. Aeronautics and Space Journal) 1985; mem. Candn. Aeronautics and Space Inst. (Hon. Fellow, May 1993);Assn. of Professional Engrs. of N.S.; Navy League of Canada; Hon. Mem., Candn. Soc. of Aviation Medicine 1988– ; Mem., Acad. of Engineering 1992; recreations: squash, tennis, swimming, car mechanics, flying, scuba diving; Office: Canadian Space Agency, 6767 Route de l'Aéroport, St-Hubert, Qué. J3Y 8Y9.

**GARNEAU, Raymond,** L.Econ.Sc., M.Com.Sc.; company executive; former politician; b. Plessisville, Que. 3 Jan. 1935; s. Daniel and Valérie (Gosselin) G.; e. Laval Univ. M.Com.Sc. 1958; Geneva Univ. Licence Econ. Sciences, 1963; m. Pauline d. Eusèbe and Simone Roy 7 May 1960; children: Jean-François, Véronique; PRESIDENT AND CHIEF EXECUTIVE OFFICER, INDUSTRIAL-ALLIANCE LIFE INSURANCE CO. 1988– ; Chrmn. & C.E.O., National Life; Chrmn., The North West of Canada and North West of America; Dir., Sodarcan; Québec-Téléphone; Phillips Cables Limited; Dir., Laval Univ.; Extve. Secy. and later Extve. Asst. to the Hon. Jean Lesage, Premier and Leader of Opposition Que. 1965–70; mem. Nat. Assembly for Jean-Talon, Que. 1970–78; Min. of Finance and Pres. Treasury Bd. 1970–76 (and Min. of Educ. 1975–76); Vice Pres. Devel. Laurentian Group 1979–80; Chrmn. & C.E.O., Montreal City & District Savings Bank and Credit Foncier 1980–84; M.P. for Laval-des-Rapides and Opposition Critic for Matters Related to Finance 1984–88; Chrmn., Canada-France Comte. 1982–84; Pres., Que. Liberal Caucus 1984–86; awarded medal 'Gloire de l'Escolle' by Laval Univ. Alumni in Quebec City 1984; Pres., Fondation Raymond Garneau; Liberal; R. Catholic; recreations: tennis, golf; Clubs: Mount Royal; Mont Bruno Golf; Home: 4700 St. Catherine St. W., app. 104, Montreal, P.Q. H3Z 1S6; Office: 1080 St. Louis Rd., Sillery, P.Q. G1K 7M3.

**GARNER, Joseph Edwin;** entrepreneur, author; b. Saltspring Island, B.C. 11 Feb. 1909; s. Olander Joseph and Lona Beatrice (Edwards) G.; e. Saltspring Is. H.S. 1926; 2 years night school; m. Patricia d. Robert and Harriet English 26 Feb. 1938; children: Virginia, Dana, Joanne, Thomas, Edwin, Gerry; founded Garner Brothers with brother Tom in 1929; Past Pres. & Gen. Mgr. (subsidiaries): Cowichan Housing Ltd., Garner Builder's Supplies Ltd., Duncan Flying Club, G. & T. Tree Farm Ltd., Foulger Creek Logging Ltd., Garner Bros. Cariboo Ltd., G.B. West. Pulp Ltd. Dir., Pacific Helicopter Ltd.; B.C. Truck Loggers Assn.; B.C. C. of C.; Duncan C. of C. (also Pres.); Dir. & Pres., 52 C. of C.s of Vanc. Is.; Mem., Aircraft Owner & Pilots Assn. (pilot lic. no. P-1799); Dir., B.C. Aviation Council; Mem., Writers' Union of Can.; Mem., Union Club of B.C. 1955– ; Rotary Internat. 1948– ; Vice-Pres., Duncan Rotary Club; Dir., Victoria & Nanaimo clubs (20 years); a qualified Rotary pioneer; Pres. & Owner, Cinnabar Press Ltd.; author: 'Never Fly Over an Eagle's Nest' 1980, 'Never a Time to Trust' 1984, 'Never Chop Your Rope' 1988; 'Never Under The Table' 1991; recreations: fishing, hunting, flying, sports; clubs: Cowichan Golf & Country (Pres. & Life Mem.), Pacific Indians (Dir. & Past Chief), Royal Victoria Yacht, Nanaimo Yacht, Maple Bay Yacht, Duncan Gun (Pres. & Founder), B.C. Fish & Wildlife, Nanaimo Fish & Game; Office: Box 392, Nanaimo, B.C. V9R 5L3.

**GARON, Roger D.;** executive; b. Sherbrooke, Que. 19 May 1930; s. Antoine and Irène (Letarte) G.; m. Thérèsa, d. Joseph Morin, Welland, Ont. 16 Nov. 1952; children: Richard, Michel, Mark; PRES. & CHIEF EXTVE. OFFR., VETOQUINOL N.A. INC.; Dir., Hees International Bancorp Inc.; Les Vins Andrès Inc. (Que.); I A F Biovac Inc.; Domco Inc.; Hydrotel Inc.; R. Catholic; Home: Le Champlain, 120 Ferland, Apt. 11B, Nun's Island, Que. H3E 1L1.

**GARRAMONE, Jack,** B.A., C.L.U., C.H.F.C.; insurance executive; b. Montreal, Que. 29 Aug. 1950; s. Francis P. and Marion G. (Lynch) G.; e. Concordia (Sir George Williams Univ.) B.A. 1973; C.L.U. 1978; C.H.F.C. 1985; m. Martha d. Rev. Arthur and Elizabeth Reynolds 17 Aug. 1973; children: Patrick, Glenna, Jason; VICE-PRES. SALES/TRAINING/DISTRIBUTION, METROPOLITAN LIFE INS. CO. 1991– ; Sales Rep., Metropolitan Life 1973; Sales Mgr. (Toronto) 1974; Regional Training Consultant 1976; Dist. Mgr. 1977–81; Mgr. Winnipeg Monarch Life 1981–84; Dir. of Planning, Metropolitan Life 1985; of Supplemental Mktg. 1987; Mng. Dir., Suppl. Mktg. & Training 1988; Reg. Mgr., Western Canada 1989–91; Canadian Council, Agency Mngt. Training Course; past Bd. of Dir., YMCA (Winipeg); Womens Employment Counselling Serv. (Winnipeg); Jr. Achievement (Ottawa-Carleton); Mem., Life Underwriters Assn. of Can.; Life Insur. Mgrs. Assn. of Can.; recreations: jogging, theatre art, music, literature; Home: 61 Shaugnessy Cres., Kanata, Ont.; Office: 99 Bank St., Ottawa, Ont. K1P 5A3.

**GARRETT, J. Gordon,** B.Elec.Eng., Prof.Eng.; information technology industry executive; b. Montreal, Que. 28 Sept. 1939; m. Diane; children: Margo, David, Michael; CHAIRMAN & CHIEF EXECUTIVE OFFICER, ISM INFORMATION SYSTEMS MNGT. CORP. 1990– ; Vice-Pres., General Systems Div., IBM Canada 1974–76; Gen. Mgr., General Business Group, IBM Northern Area, Paris, France 1977; Vice-Pres. & Gen. Mgr., Gen. Business Group, IBM Canada Toronto 1978–81; Vice-Pres., Marketing, National Distribution Div.; Gen. Mgr. Distbn. Channels Business Unit, IBM N.Y. 1981–87; Pres., I.I.I., Information Supplies Co. Meriden, CT 1989; Pres., Gestetner U.S.A. 1989–91; United Way Campaign Chrmn., Greenwich, CT 1991; Chrmn., Technology and Telecommunications Sector, United Way of Greater Toronto 1992; Bd. Memberships: ISM-BC Corp., Vancouver, B.C.; Datacor/ISM Corp., Moncton, N.B.; ISM Alberta Corp., Edmonton/Calgary, Alta.; NULOGIX Technical Services Inc., Toronto; Office: One Research Drive, Regina, Sask. S4S 7H1 or 251 Consumers Rd., North York, Ont. M2J 4R3.

**GARRETT, John Frederick,** B.A., Ph.D.; physical oceanographer; b. Yonkers, N.Y. 15 June 1942; s. John Rollin and Louise Katherine (Young) G.; e. Mansfield H.S. 1959; Harvard Coll., B.A. 1963; Univ. of B.C., Ph.D. 1970; m. Verena d. Philip and Patricia Tunnicliffe 8 May 1987; children: Christopher, Susanna, Benjamin, Arielle; DIR., PHYSICAL & CHEMICAL SCIENCES, INST. OF OCEAN SCI. 1986– ; Engr., Buoy Group, Woods Hole Oceanographic Inst. 1963–64; Grad. Stud., Nonlinear Interaction in Ocean Waves, Univ. of B.C. 1964–70; Head, Offshore Oceanography Group, Inst. of Ocean Sci. 1970–80; Head, Ocean Physics, Inst. of Ocean Sci. 1980–89; Pres., Internat. Theatre Inconnu Soc.; Office: P.O. Box 6000, Sidney, B.C. V8L 4B2.

**GARRICK, David Elwood,** B.A.; b. Toronto, Ont. 20 Aug. 1939; s. James Marshall and Marjorie Elizabeth (Binkley) G.; e. Swansea Pub. Sch. and Runnymede Coll. Inst., Toronto; Waterloo Univ., B.A.; m. Joy, d. Owen W. Fonger, Etobicoke, Ont., 27 June 1964; children: Kimberley, David James; VICE PRES., CORPORATE AFFAIRS, STADIUM CORP. OF ONT.; joined Candn. National Exhbn. as Stadium Mgr. 1962, Secy. and Concessions Mgr. 1967, Asst. Gen. Mgr. 1969, Gen. Mgr. 1972, Dir. of Operations 1975; Gen. Mgr., CN Tower 1978–82; Pres., CN Tower 1983–87; Trustee, Toronto Bd. of Educ.; Candn. Nat. Exhn. Assn.; Chrmn. Toronto Sesquicentennial Bd.; Freemason; Shriner; Presbyterian; recreations: skiing, curling; Home: 8 Grenadier Hts. Toronto, Ont. M6S 2W6; Office: 1 Blue Jays Way, Toronto, Ont. M5V 1J3.

**GARRIGAN, John William,** B.Com.; executive; b. Kingston, Ont. 6 May 1934; s. William Joseph and Evelyn Margaret (Jeroy) G.; e. Queen's Univ., B.Com. 1958; m. Marielle, d. Joseph McKenzie, Cap de La Madelaine, Que., 19 June 1962; children: Bruce, Brian, Michelle; PRES. & C.E.O., INTERNATIONAL CELLULOSE CORP. 1990– ; with Canadian Industries Ltd. in various mang. positions 1958–65; with Consolidated-Bathurst Ltd. in various posts incl. Vice-Pres. and Gen. Mgr., Concel Inc. (U.S. subsidiary) 1965–71; Pres. and CEO, Price and Pierce Int. Inc. 1971–79; Chrmn., 1979–83; Pres. & C.E.O., International Fibers Corp. 1983–89; Vice-Pres., TKM (U.S.A.) Holdings Inc.; R. Catholic; recreations: astronomy, skiing, swimming; Office: 60 Pine Brook Rd., Chestnut Ridge Village, N.Y. 10952.

**GARRIOCK, William C.,** B.Com., M.B.A.; b. N. Vancouver, B.C. 11 Aug. 1938; s. Robert and Charlotte (Weeks) G.; e. N. Vancouver High Sch. 1956; Univ. of B.C. B.Com. 1961; Northwestern Univ. M.B.A. 1963; children: Janice, Jeffrey, David, Robert; VICE PRESIDENT & MANAGING PARTNER, PHARMACEUTICALS AND DIAGNOSTICS, MDS HEALTH VENTURES INC. 1993– ; Pres. & C.E.O., Miles Canada Inc. 1975–93; Product/Sales Mgr. Household Products Div. of Miles Canada Inc. 1969, also held positions of Business Planning Mgr. and Group Marketing Mgr.; served 6 yrs. in Marketing and Mfg. positions General Foods; mem. Faculty of Business Adm. Univ. of B.C. 1963–64, 1984; Faculty of Commerce & Business Admin., Fac. Advis. Counc., Univ. of Toronto; Pres. and Dir., Household Cleansers Ltd. & The S.O.S. Manufacturing Co. of Canada Ltd. 1975–92; Dir., Cameco Inc. 1992– ; Chrmn. of Bd., Drug Royalty Corp. Inc. 1993– ; Dir., GSW Viewstar 1984–86; GSW Inc. 1984–85 and 1991; GSW Building Products Co.; Chrmn. of Bd. Proprietary Assn. Can. 1977–78; mem., Grocery Products Manufacturers of Canada, Exec. Ctte. 1979–83; Dir., Pharmaceutical Mfrs. Assoc. of Can. (Chrmn. 1988–90 and 1991); mem. Candn.-Am. Ctte.; Young Pres's Organ.; Protestant; recreations: squash, golf; Home: 1 St. Ives Cres., North York, Ont. M4N 3B3; Office: 100 International Blvd., Etobicoke, Ont. M9W 6J6.

**GARRISON, Robert Frederick,** Ph.D.; astronomer/professor; b. Aurora, Ill. 9 May 1936; s. Robert Wilkins and Dorothy Ione (Rydquist) G.; e. Earlham Coll., B.A. 1960; Univ. of Wisc. 1960–61; Univ. of Chicago, Ph.D. 1966; m. Ada Virginia d. Albert and Dorothy Mighell 7 June 1957; div. 1980; children: Forest Lee, Alexandra, David Charles; PROF. OF ASTRONOMY, UNIV. OF TORONTO 1978– ; Assoc. Dir., David Dunlap Observ. for Chile Operations; Rsch. Assoc., Mt. Wilson & Palomar Observ. 1966–68 (Calif.); Asst. Prof., Univ. of Toronto 1968–74; Assoc. Prof. 1974–78; Vice-Pres., Sci. Adv. Counc., Can.-France-Hawaii Telescope 1979–80; Discovery of Pure Helium Star 1973, Brightest-known Cataclysmic Variable Star 1983; Mem., Internat. Astron. Union (Vice-Pres., Comn. on Stellar Classification 1982–85; Pres. 1985–88); Candn. Astron. Soc. (Counc. 1978–81); Am. Astron. Soc.; Royal Astron. Soc. of Can.; Astron. Soc. of the Pacific; Am. Assoc. Variable Star Observers; Bd. of Dir., Bruce Trail Club 1977–78; Vice-Pres., Univ. of Chicago Club of Can. 1982–88 (Pres. 1988–90); Royal Candn. Inst. (Counc. 1988–94, Vice Pres. 1991–93, Pres. 1993–94); editor: 'MK Process and Stellar Classification' 1984; recreations: singing opera, hiking, wilderness canoeing, photography; Home: DDO Box 360, Richmond Hill, Ont. L4C 4Y6; Office: Astronomy Dept., Univ. of Toronto, Toronto, Ont. M5S 1A7.

**GARWOOD, Audrey,** R.C.A.; painter; printmaker; b. Toronto, Ont. 7 July 1927; d. John H. and Minnie (Robertson) Carwood; e. N. Vocational High Sch. and N. Toronto Coll. Inst.; Ont. Coll. of Art; Rijks Academie Amsterdam; La Grande Chaumiere Paris; m. 5 Feb. 1953; children: Evan Hosie, Spencer Hosie, Graham, Cameron; solo exhns. incl. York Univ. Toronto 1968; Univ. of San Francisco 1974; Lafayette Bank Gallery Uniontown, Pa. 1974; Berkeley (Cal.) City Hall 1975; Lafayette (Cal.) Lib. 1976; Univ. of Cal. Hayward 1978; rep. in various group exhns. incl. Nat. Gallery Can. Drawing & Print Show 1966; Internat. Exhn. Montreal 1971; Candn. Consulate Washington 1971; Contemporary Prints Pratt Inst. 1972; Internat. Print Exhn. Los Angeles 1977; San Francisco Art Festival (invitational) 1974; Palo Alto (Cal.) Invitational 1975; rep. in pub., corporate and private colls. incl. Art Gallery Ont., La Jolla Museum of Contemporary Art Cal.; recipient Print Award Candn. Soc. Printmakers; Sterling Trust Award Candn. Painters & Engravers; Forester Award Ont. Soc. Artists; Purchase Award San Francisco Art Festival; illustrator 'Flavors of Southeast Asia' 19..; '101 Productions San Francisco' 19..; mem. Ont. Soc. Artists; Royal Candn. Academy of Arts; Artists Equity Assn.; represented by: Geraldine Davis Gall., 225 Richmond St. W., Toronto, Ont.; NDP; recreations: dancing, travel; Home: 97 Dixon Ave., Toronto, Ont. M4L 1N8.

**GASCON, France,** M.A., M.B.A.; museologist; b. Montreal, Que. 4 Aug. 1952; s. Gérard and Luce (Séguin) G.; e.Univ. d'Aix-en-Provence, France D.E.S. Semiotics 1976; Univ. de Montréal M.A. 1977; Ecole des Hautes Commerciales Montréal M.B.A. 1987; CHIEF CURATOR, McCORD MUSEUM OF CANADIAN HISTORY 1988– ; Curator, Travelling Exhns. Dept. Musée d'art contemporain Montréal 1978, Curator and Asst. Head of Dept. 1980–83, Curator and Head of Exhibitions Dept. 1983–88; Comnr. Candn. participation 43rd Venice Biennial 1988; Prés., Société des musées québécois 1990–92; Office: 690 Sherbrooke St. W., Montreal, Que. H3A 1E9.

**GASKELL, Jane S.,** B.A., Ed.D.; university professor; b. London, England 9 Oct. 1946; d. John Stobo and Joan Suzanne (Webber) Prichard; e. St. Clement's School 1964; Swarthmore Coll., B.A. (Hons.) 1968; Harvard Univ., Ed.D. 1973; m. P. James s. Peter and Kathleen G. 14 June 1969; children: David James, Joanne Catherine; ASSOC. DEAN FOR GRADUATE PROGRAMS AND RESEARCH, UNIV. OF B.C. 1993– ; apptd. Fac. of Edn., Queen's Univ. 1972; moved to present univ. 1974; Chrmn. & Prof., Dept. of Social & Educational Studies 1988–93; Pres., Candn. Soc. for the Study of Edn.; Vice-Pres., Soc. Sci. Fedn. of Can.; Killam Fellowship 1988–89; author: 'Women and Education: Canadian Perspectives' 1987, 'Claiming an Education: Feminism and Canadian Schools' 1989; 'Gender Matters from School to Work' 1991; Home: 4585 West 6th Ave., Vancouver, B.C.; Office: Vancouver, B.C. V6T 1W5.

**GASKEY, William S.,** B.A.; advertising executive; b. Port Colborne, Ont. 16 July 1932; e. Univ. of Western Ontario, Sch. of Business B.A. (Hons.) 1955; m. Barbara; children: William Jr., Thomas, Jennifer Dobell; Chairman & Chief Extve. Offr., FCB/Ronalds-Reynolds, Ltd. 1990–93, Retired; Acct. Mgr., E.W. Reynolds 1959; Acct. Supervisor, Ronalds-Reynolds & Co. Ltd. 1964; Dir. 1970; Extve. Vice-Pres. 1975; Pres. & Chief Operating Offr. 1987; recreations: golf, tennis, curling, skiing; clubs: Granite, Bayview Golf & Country; Home: 222 Blythwood Rd., Toronto, Ont. M4N 1A6.

**GASKIN, David Edward,** B.Sc., Ph.D., F.R.E.S.; university professor; b. Croydon, England 21 June 1939; s. Edward Thomas and Daisy (Lobb) G.; e. John Ruskin School; Univ. of Bristol B.Sc. (Special Hons.) 1961; Massey Univ. (N.Z.) Ph.D. 1968; m. Maureen d. Thomas and Joyce Wood 18 Aug. 1962; children: Ross Edward, Paul Thomas; PROFESSOR, DEPT. OF ZOOLOGY, UNIV. OF GUELPH 1981– ; Biologist-MAAF (UK), whaling factory ship 'Southern Venturer,' Antarctic Ocean 1961; Exp. Offr., MAAF, Lowestoft U.K. 1962; Scientific Offr., Well. N.Z. 1962–65; Lectr. Massey Univ. 1965–68; Asst. Prof., Zool., Univ. of Guelph 1969–72; Assoc. Prof. 1972–81; Extve. Dir., Whale & Seabird Rsch. Stn., North Head, N.B.; Chief Consultant, Environ. Programme Assessment Serv.; Mem., Internat. Union for Conserv. of Nature Species Survival Ctte. (Switz.); Internat. Whaling Comn. Sci. Ctte.; U.S. Nat. Marine Fisheries Serv., Nat. Right Whale Recovery Task Force; Sci. Adv. Bd., Mystic Aquarium (U.S.); Inst. for Ecotoxicology (Que.); Ministerial Adv. Ctte., Fisheries & Oceans on whales and whaling; Cons., World Bank Chinese Univ. Project; U.N. Environ. Prog.; Educansult Ltd Saudi Arabia Univ. Project; Fellow, Royal Entomol. Soc. of London; Mem., Soc. for Marine Mammalogy (Charter Mem.); Lepidoptera Rsch. Found.; Lepidopterist Soc.; Michigan Entomol. Soc.; N.Z. Entomol. Soc.; Modern Greek Studies Assn.; author: 'The Butterflies and Common Moths of New Zealand' 1966, 'Whales, Dolphins and Seals' 1972, 'The Ecology of Whales and Dolphins' 1982, '85 (N. Am. Univ. & Coll. Library Assn. Award for best text of 1983); co-author: 'Kujira to Iruka no Seitai'; author/co-author of 115 articles in sci. journals; recreations: languages, music, photography, travel, hiking; Home: 49 Albert St., Guelph, Ont. N1G 1C7; Office: Guelph, Ont. N1G 2W1.

**GASTON, Bill,** B.A., M.A., M.F.A.; writer, teacher; b. Oslo, Norway 14 Jan. 1953; s. Robert A. and Mary Jean (Michel) G.; e. Univ. of B.C., B.A. 1975, M.A. 1978, M.F.A. 1981; m. Edythe d. Thomas and Millicent Crane 1986; children: Lise, Connor; Teacher of Literature, Writing: Univ. of British Columbia, Seneca Coll., St. Mary's Univ., Mt. St. Vincent Univ. (current), Naropa Inst. (current); Writer-in-Residence, Univ. New Brunswick 1990–91; author: 'Deep Cove Stories' 1989 (short fiction collection); 'Tall Lives' 1990 (novel); 'Inviting Blindness' 1990 (poetry collection); Past Fiction Ed., 'Prism International'; recreations: wine tasting, polo; Address: 18 Brighton Court, Fredericton, N.B. E3B 4N6.

**GATENBY, Gregory Francis,** B.A.; author; b. Toronto, Ont. 5 May 1950; s. Gregory Roy and Margaret Helen (O'Connor) G.; e. Glendon Coll. York Univ. B.A. 1972; author 'Adrienne's Blessing' (poetry) 1976; 'Rondeaus for Erica' (poetry) 1976; 'The Salmon Country' (poetry) 1978; 'Growing Still' (poetry) 1981; ed. '52 Pickup' (poetry anthol.) 1976; 'Whale Sound' (poetry and visual art) 1977; 'Whales: A Celebration' (poetry, fiction, music, art) 1983; 'The Definitive Notes (essays) 1992; 'How Others See Us' vol. one (literary hist. and anthol.) 1993; rep. in over 150 nat. and internat. lit. periodicals; readings of own work and lectr. on Candn. lit. at over 50 univs. and lit. festivals Europe; Artistic Dir. Harbourfront Reading Series 1975– ; winner, Toronto Arts Award 1989; consultant several foreign arts council on authors and devel. Candn. letters; recreations: travel, squash, reading, book collecting; Home: 420 Bloor St. W., Toronto, Ont. M5S 1X5; Office: Harbourfront, 410 Queen's Quay W., Toronto, Ont. M5V 2Z3.

**GATENBY, William Arthur,** M.Sc.; energy and mining executive; b. Leader, Sask. 27 Nov. 1925; s. William E. and Vera (Mahaffy) G.; e. Univ. of Okla. B.Sc. 1949; Pa. State Univ. M.Sc. (Petrol. Eng.) 1956; m. Eileen d. Ernest and Lorena Speers 7 Sept. 1955; two s. William H., Patrick T.; Chairman, Cameco Corporation 1991–..; Eng., Mene Grande Oil Co. Venezuela 1949–53; Eng., Canadian Gulf Oil Co. Ltd. 1954–55; dist. Eng., Chief Petrol. Eng. Asst. Dist. Supt. Texaco Petroleum Co. Venezuela 1956–64; Staff Eng., Chief Petrol. Eng. Texaco Exploration Co. (Can.) 1964–69; Chief Petrol. Eng. Producing W., Texaco U.S., Denver 1969–70; Asst. Gen. Mgr. Texaco Latin Am., Coral Gables 1971–73; Asst. Mgr. Texaco Exploration Canada Ltd. 1973–77; Asst. to Sr. Vice Pres. Texaco Inc. Harrison N.Y. 1977–79; Vice Pres. and Asst. to Pres., Texaco Canada Resources Ltd. 1979–81, Pres. and C.E.O. 1981–88; Chrmn., Pres. & C.E.O., Cameco Corp. 1988–91; inducted into Saskatchewan Petroleum Industry Hall of Fame 1991; Dir., Ranger Oil Company Ltd.; Texaco Canada Petroleum Inc.; mem., A.P.E.G.G.A.; recreations: farming, baseball, hockey; Club: Saskatoon; Address: Sceptre Farms, Sceptre, Sask. S0N 2H0.

**GAUDAUR, Jacob Gill;** sports manager; b. Orillia, Ont. 5 Oct. 1920; s. Jacob Gill and Alice (Hemming) G.; e. Orillia (Ont.) Coll. Inst., Sr. Matric. 1939; m. Isobel Grace, d. late Joseph Scott, 16 Apl. 1943; three d. Jacqueline, Diane, Janice; Exec. Consultant to Candn. Football League 1984–85; with Burns Bros. & Co., Toronto 1946; joined White Motor Co. of Canada as Salesman 1947–51, Mgr. Hamilton Br. 1952–53, Mgr. Toronto Br. and Ont. Wholesale Mgr. 1954–55; Founder and Pres., Gaudaur Motor Co. 1956 and Jaygil Ltd. 1966– ; Pres. Hamilton Tiger-Cat Football Club 1954, Pres. and Gen. Mgr. 1956–68, principal shareholder 1961, sold interest 1968; Comnr. Candn. Football League 1968–84; Pres., Eastern Football Conf. 1959; Candn. Football League 1962; served with RCAF as Pilot 1942–45; Chrmn., Downtown Div., Hamilton Un. Appeal 1967; Chrmn. Selection Ctte., Lou Marsh Award; Gov., Canada's Sports Hall of Fame; Gov., Variety Village; Officer, Order of Canada 1985; Commemorative Medal, 125th Anniversary of Candn. Confedn. 1992; inducted into Candn. Football Hall of Fame 1985; inducted into Candn. Sports Hall of Fame 1990; Freemason; Anglican; recreations: golf, oil painting, skiing; Clubs: Albany; Scottish Rite; Variety; Home: 3082 Balmoral Ave., Burlington, Ont. L7N 1E4.

**GAUDIERI, Alexander V.J.,** B.A., M.B.A., M.A.; art historian; b. Columbus, Ohio 23 Apr. 1940; s. Alexander Vincent and Olga A. (Orsini-d'Ascanio) G.; e. Ohio State Univ. B.A. 1962; Colgate Univ.; Am. Grad. Sch. of Internat. Comm. M.B.A. 1965; La Sorbonne, L'Univ. de Paris; Inst. of Fine Arts, N.Y. Univ. M.A. 1976; m. Millicent E. Hall d. John Thompson and Sara Pollock H. 10 June 1967; one child: Alexandre Barclay Everson; Internat. Banking Offr. Marine Midland Bank, N.Y. 1965–72; Dir. Telfair Acad. of Arts & Sci., Savannah, GA 1977–83; Dir., Montreal Museum of Fine Arts 1983–86; Dir., Memphis Brooks Museum of Art, Memphis, Tenn. 1992; Adjunct Prof., New York Univ., Graduate School of Arts & Science, N.Y.; Bd. Mem., Young Concert Artists, N.Y.; Am. Assn. of Museums; Candn. Museum Assn.; listed in Who's Who in Am., Who's Who in Am. Art; recreations: riding, tennis; Clubs: Mount Royal, Montreal; River, N.Y.; Rockaway Hunting, N.Y.; Hurlingham, London; Home: 444 Central Park West, New York, N.Y. 10025.

**GAUDREAULT LABRECQUE, Madeleine,** B.A., M.A.; writer, journalist; b. La Malbaie, Que. 25 April 1936; d. Edouard and Georgette (Lavoie) Gaudreault; e. B.A. (Literature & Journalism); Laval Univ. M.A. (Creative Writing) 1984; m. Victor Labrecque 3 Sept. 1955; children: Michel, Ann; Classical ballet teacher; Journalist & literary critic, Radio-Canada; Teacher of Creative Writing, Laval Univ. fall 1984; Lectr. to adults & children at libraries & schools; Honours, Radio-Canada Soc. 1946; French Canadian Poets Soc. 1963; Memberships: Quebec Writers Fed.; Union of Writers for the Youth; Que. Prof. Journalists Fed.; Internat. Authors and Writers Who's Who; author: 'Vol à bord du Concordia' 1979, 'Alerte ce soir à 22 heures' 1979, 'Gueule-de-loup' 1985, 'Sur la piste du dragon' 1986, 'Le secret de la pierre magique' 1987, 'Panique dans les Rocheuses' 1988 (Michel Labre collection of adventure novels for teenagers); 'Le mystère du grenier' 1982 (for teenagers); 'Les aventures d'un manuscrit' 1989, 'La dame de pique' 1988 (for adults); 'La girafe' 1982, 'Dents-de-lions' 1981, 'Le merle odieux' 1983, 'Flocons de rêve' 1990 (for children); also author of dramatic & poetic texts for Radio-Canada; Home: 4887 Saint Félix, Cap-Rouge, Qué. G1Y 3C7.

**GAUDRY, Marc J.I.,** B.A., M.A., B.Th., Ph.D., F.R.S.C.; professor of economics; b. Quebec City, Que. 13 Apr. 1942; s. Roger and Madeleine V. (Vallée) G.; e. Univ. of Montreal, B.A. 1961; Oxford Univ., M.A. 1964; Inst. Cathol. de Paris, B.Th. 1967; Princeton Univ., Ph.D. 1973; one d.: Catherine; PROFESSOR, UNIV. OF MONTREAL 1981– ; Asst. Prof., Univ. of Montreal 1972–67; Assoc. Prof. 1978–80; Founding Mem. & Assoc. Dir., Centre for Research on Transp., Univ. of Montreal 1978–92 (Occasional Dir. 1978–79, 1985–86); Mem., Royal Comn. on Nat. Passenger Transp. 1989–92; Invited Prof., Ecole Nationale des Ponts et Chaussées (Paris), Univ. Louis-Pasteur (Strasbourg) and Univ. of Karlsruhe 1993; Mem., INSPIRIT 95 Rsch. Prize Jury (Initiativkreis Ruhrgebiet); Mem. Advisory Ctte. on Nuclear Safety, Atomic Energy Control Bd.; occasional cons., Montreal & Toronto Transit Comn., Société de l'Assur. Auto. du Qué.; Inst. Nat. de la Rch. sur les Transp. et leur Sécurité, Paris, France; German Min. of Transp.; Rhodes Scholar 1961–64; Alexander von Humboldt rsch. fellow 1985–89, rsch. award 1990; Prix 1990 du Conseil de la recherche et du développement en transport du Québec; author/co-author 62 sci. articles, 50 tech. pubs. 1974– ; 500 citations in sci. jours.; Home: 600 Carlyle, Mont-Royal, Que. H3R 1T7; Office: B.P. 6128, Succ. A., Montreal, Que. H3C 3J7.

**GAUDRY, Roger,** C.C. (1968), B.A., B.Sc., D.Sc., D.C.L., LL.D., F.R.S.C. (1954), F.C.I.C.; chemist; company director; b. Quebec City, P.Q. 15 Dec. 1913; s. Marc and Marie-Ange (Frenette) G.; e. Laval Univ., B.A. 1933. B.Sc. (Chemistry), 1937, D.Sc. (Chemistry) 1940; Oxford Univ. (Rhodes Scholar) 1937–39; (hon.) D.Sc. Royal Mil. Coll. 1966; (hon.) D.Sc. British Columbia 1967; (hon.) Doctorate Clermont-Ferrand (France); (hon.) LL.D. McGill 1967; (hon.) D.C.L. Brock 1969; (hon.) LL.D., Toronto, (1966) Bishop's (1969), Fredericton (1968); LL.D., Concordia (1980); (hon.) D.Sc., Sask. (1970), Western (1976); m. Madeleine, d. Ivan E. Vallée, Quebec City, P.Q., 19 June 1941; children: Marc, Jean, Hélène, Thérèse, Denise; RECTOR, UNIV. OF MONTREAL 1965–75; Vice Chrmn., Science Council of Can. 1966–72; Chrmn. 1972–75; Pres., Internat. Assn. of Univs. 1975–80; Mem. of Council, United Nations Univ. (Toyko) 1974–80; Chrmn. of Council., U.N. Univ. (Tokyo) 1974–76; Asst. Prof. of Chem., Fac. of Med., Laval Univ. 1940–45, Assoc. Prof. 1945–50; Prof. 1950–54; Guest Lectr., the Sorbonne, Paris 1954; Asst. Dir. of Research, Ayerst, McKenna & Harrison Ltd., Montreal 1954–57, Dir. Ayerst, McKenna and Harrison Ltd. and Ayerst Laboratories, N.Y. 1957–65, Vice-pres. 1963–65; three-time recipient of P.Q. Scient. Prize (1942, 1946, 1950) for publ. work; awarded Pariseau Medal, Assn. Candn.-française pour l'Avanc. des Sciences' 1958; Medal of Centenary of Can. 1967; Montreal Medal, Chem. Inst. of Can. 1974; Knight of the Order of Malta 1976; Queen's Jubilee Medal 1977; Grand Officer of the Order of Qué. 1991; author or co-author of some 90 papers dealing with the chem. or metabolism of amino acids; Chrmn., Nordic Inc. 1975–91; Bd. Mem., Connaught Laboratories Ltd. 1975–84; CDC Life Sciences Inc. 1975–84, Chrmn. 1977–84; Bank of Montreal 1975–84; Alcan Aluminium Ltée. 1976–86; Hoechst du Can. Ltée 1978–87; S.K.W. Canada Ltd. 1978–88; Bio-Recherche Ltée 1978–88; Corby Distilleries Ltd. 1975–88; St. Lawrence Starch Co. Ltd. 1983–89; mem. Econ. Council of Can. 1970–73; Pres., The Chem. Inst. of Can. 1955–56; Prés. Fondation Jules et Paul-Emile Léger 1983– ; Bd. Chrmn., Network for Neural Regeneration and Functional Recovery 1990– ; R. Catholic; Office: Univ. de Montréal, Montréal, P.Q. H3C 3J7.

**GAULD, Thomas,** B.A.; business executive; b. Welland, Ont. 6 Oct. 1949; s. Lawrence M. and Frances J. (Hay) G.; e. Univ. of Windsor B.A. 1971; m. Jane d. Alexander and Mary Gray 12 Dec. 1975; children: Scotty, Christina; MANAGING DIR., SPALDING SPORTS EUROPE 1990– ; Asst. Product Mgr. Unilever, S. Africa 1971–72 and General Foods, Can. 1972–73; Product Mgr. Bristol Myers Can. and U.S.A. 1973–77; Mktg. Mgr. Beecham Products Inc. Can. 1978–80, Dir. Mktg. 1982–85; Gen. Mgr. Beecham Products, Santiago, Chile 1980–82; Vice Pres. Mktg., Beecham Canada Inc. 1985–87; Pres., Spalding Sprots Canada 1987–90; Mem. Bd. of Dirs., Spalding and Evenflo Canada 1987–90; recreations: skiing, golf.

**GAUNCE, Harry P.,** F.I.I.C.; executive; b. Carleton Co., N.B. 15 July 1934; s. Basil F. and Clara A. (Purinton) G.; e. Saint John High Sch. 1952; Ins. Inst. Can. F.I.I.C. 1963; m. Glenna F. d. Gordon and Grace Henderson 22 Sept. 1956; children: Stephen F., Phillip H., Andrew B.; CHRMN., SAINT JOHN PORT CORP. 1987– ; Pres., Armstrong & Bruce Insurance Ltd. 1987– ; began ins. career 1953; Past Pres., Saint John Jaycees; N.B. Jaycees; Past Nat. Prog. Chrmn. Can. Jaycees; Senatorship Jaycee Internat. 1967; Past Pres., Saint John Un. Way; mem. and Past Campaign Chrmn. Un. Way Greater Saint John; Past Nat. Dir., Un. Way Can.; Dir. & Vice Pres., N.B. Prot. Orphans Home; Gov., Jr. Achievement Saint John; Dir., Saint John Jeux Can. Games Found. Inc.; Family Services Saint John Inc.; Past mem. Area Adv. Bd., Central Trust Co.; mem. Saint John Bd. Trade; Soc. Fellows Can.; mem. and Past Pres. Ins. Inst. N.B.; Ins. Agts. Assn. N.B.; Past Pres. Candn. Fedn. Ins. Agts. & Brokers Assn.; recipient Jean Charles D'Auteil Meml. Award of Merit 1979; Saint John's Sportsperson of Yr. Award 1987; Transportation Person of the Year, Transportation Club of St. John 1992; Past Gov., Nat. Sports Hall of Fame; Dir., Family Services Inc.; Dir., Atlantic National Exhbn. Assoc.; Chrmn., Greater St. John Economic Development Commission; Baptist; recreations: waterskiing, minor hockey, minor baseball; Home: 946 Manawagonish Rd., Saint John, N.B. E2M 3X1; Office: 133 Prince William St., P.O. Box 6429 Station A, Saint John, N.B. E2L 4R8.

**GAUTHIER, Gilles;** administrateur; né Palmarolle, Qué. 28 mars 1935; f. Henri et Adéline (Grenon) G.; é. Primaire Ecole St-Paul 1947; Séminaire D'Amos (classique) 1949; Académie Commerciale de Québec 1952; Univ. Laval (cours corr. Finance et Placements) 1964; ép. Léonne, f. Nérée Aubé, La Sarre, Qué. 19 nov. 1955; enfants: Michelle, Louise, Murielle, Claude; REPRÉSENTANT ASSOCIÉ, LA LAURENTIENNE VIE, depuis 1991; Directeur Régional, Autobus Auger Inc., 1989–90; Commissaire Industriel, Directeur Général, Société de developpement Economique de Rouyn-Noranda, 1987–89; Courtier-Analyste, Gauthier, Giroux et Associés Inc. 1986–87; Président, Automobile du Cuivre Inc., Gestion Financiere R.N. Inc. 1976–86; Vice-Président et directeur, Canadian Financial Corporation; Dir., Canadian Affiliated Financial Corp. 1972–76; Comptable div., Min. de la Voirie, Prov. Qué. 1952–55; Premier employé fondateur de Continental Discount Corp., à titre de gérant 1955, de dir. gén. adjoint 1960, de vice prés. exécutif 1972, Prés. and Chef de la dir., 1974–76; Commissaire, Comm. des Loisirs de la Ville de LaSarre; mem. Chambre de Comm. de la Prov. Qué.; ex-prés., Jeune Chambre de Comm. de La Sarre; Catholique r.; récréations: golf, chasse, pêche; Clubs: Richelieu (Prés. 1970); Beattie Golf (Prés. 1968–70); Kiwanis Club of Rouyn, Prés. 1980; Résidence: 570 Guertin, Rouyn-Noranda, Qué. J9X 5S7.

**GAUTHIER, Jacques,** F.C.A.; financial executive; b. Montreal, Que. 25 July 1943; s. Antonio and Thérèse (Décary) G.; e. Ecole des Hautes Etudes Commerciales, Univ. de Montréal C.A. 1968; m. Suzanne Leroux 21 Sept. 1968; children: Marie-Josée, Annie; AREA MANAGING PARTNER, QUEBEC REGION, PEAT MARWICK, THORNE 1989– ; C.A. 1968; Audit Partner 1973–84; Office Mng. Partner 1984–89; Extve. Partner, Que. Region 1989; Mem., Nat. Mngt. Ctte., Partnershp Bd., Peat Marwick Thorne; Nat. Extve. Ctte., Thorne Ernst & Whinney; Mem., Ordre de comptables agréés du Qué. 1968– ; (Mem., Public Information Ctte. 1983–84; Recruiting Ctte. 1970–71); Candn. Inst. of C.A.s' 1968– ; Montreal Bd. of Trade; C. de C. de Montréal; Candn. C. of C.; C. de C. Française au Can.; Pres., Que. C.A.'s Student Soc. 1968–69 (Bd. of Dir. 1964–69); Mem., Bd. of Dir. & Audit Ctte., Maisonneuve-Rosemont Hosp. 1989– ; Bd. of Dir. & Treas., Que. Paraplegic Assn. 1984–89; Bd. of Dir., Jr. Achievement of Que. 1986; recreations: golf, tennis, skiing;

clubs: St. Denis, Le Sanctuaire Sporting, Val-Morin, Rosemère; Home: 141 Morrison Ave., Town of Mount-Royal, Que. H3R 1K5; Office: Suite 1900, 2000 McGill College Ave., Montreal, Que. H3A 3H8.

**GAUTHIER, Jacques,** B.Sc.; pharmaceutical executive; b. Montreal, P.Q. 5 Jan. 1928; s. Antoinette (Morin) and late Henri H. S.; e. Univ. of Montreal, B.Sc. (Chem.), 1949; Univ. of Western Ont., grad., Mang. Adm., 1964; m. Louise, d. late J.A. Lapointe, 30 May 1953; one s. Yves; two d. Danielle, Christiane; PRES. & GEN. MGR., BIO-MÉGA / BOEHRINGER INGELHEIM RESEARCH INC. 1984– ; joined The Upjohn Co. of Canada as prof. Sales Representative, Sherbrooke and Montreal, P.Q., 1949; Dist. Sales Mgr. for P.Q. 1956; Gen. Sales Mgr., 1964; Gen. Mgr., 1968; Pres. and Gen. Mgr. 1969; Gen. Mgr., Labs. Upjohn S.A.R.L., Paris 1971; Vice Pres., Upjohn International 1974–1984; Group Vice-Pres. Upjohn International Inc. Sept. 1979–84; Roman Catholic; recreations: golf, travelling; Office: 2100 Cunard, Laval, Que. H7S 2G5.

**GAUTHIER, Hon. Paule,** P.C., O.C., Q.C.; lawyer; b. Joliette, Qué. 3 Nov. 1943; d. Gaétan and Mariette (Marchand) Gauthier; e. Coll. Jésus-Marie B.A. 1963; Laval Univ. LL.B. 1966, LL.M. 1969; m. Gilbert J. Cashman s. H. William Cashman 6 Apr. 1974; PARTNER, DESJARDINS DUCHARME STEIN MONAST; Dir., Royal Bank of Canada; Royal Trust Corp. of Can.; The Royal Trust Co.; The Bankers' Trust Co.; The Royal Trust Co. Mortgage Corp.; Celanese Canada Inc.; Laval Univ. Found., The Found. for Legal Rsch.; Corporate Secy., Radio Saguenay Ltée; called to Bar of Que. 1967; Chrmn. Counc. of Arbitration; Business Law Teacher, Prof. Training Sch. Bar. Prov. Qué.; mem. Security Intelligence Review Comte.; Pres. Candn. Bar Assn. (Que. Br.) 1984–1985; Pres. Candn. Bar Assoc. (Nat.) 1992–93; Mem. of Council, Internat. Bar Assn.; R. Catholic; recreations: swimming, tennis, skiing; Home: Le Montmorency, 165, Grande-Allée Est, app. P-6, Québec, Qué. G1R 2L1; Office: 1150 Claire-Fontaine, Québec City, Qué. G1R 5G4.

**GAUTHIER, Robert,** C.M., D.Paed., B.A., Ph.B., Ph.L., F.R.S.C.; educator; b. Cap Chat, P.Q., 10 Apr. 1902; s. Dr. L. P. and Antoinette (Thibault) G.; e. Ottawa Univ., B.A., Ph.B., Ph.L., 1925; Univ. of Toronto Faculty of Educ. 1926; Univ. of Montreal, B.Paed., 1940; Laval D.Paed. 1942; D.Sc.Ed. Montreal, 1958; m. Juliette Roy, 1932; four children; Insp., Elem. Schs., Cochrane, Ont., 1927, Windsor, 1928; Master, Univ. of Ottawa Normal Sch., 1935; Dir. of French Instruction, Ont. Dept. of Educ., 1937–64; mem. of Comm. of Inquiry into Textbooks used by French-speaking pupils; conducted survey of systems of educ., Europe, 1949; UNESCO educ. mission, Burma, 1954; Candn. del., Internat. Conf. on Educ., Geneva, 1959; Lectr. in French Lit., Univ. of W. Indies, Trinidad 1964–65, Barbados 1965–66 for Candn. External Aid; Head of Inspection Br. Sch. of Lang., Public Service of Can. 1966–67; mem., Assn. Candn. des Educ. de Langue française (Past Pres.); Past Pres., Soc. de Confs. of Univ. of Ottawa; mem., Candn. Educ. Assn.; Nat. Adv. Comte. on Educ. Research; Assn. d'Educ. d'Ont.; Hon. mem., Assn. acadienne d'Educ.; awarded Ordre du Mérite scolaire franco-ontarien. 1947; Offr. d'Acad. République française 1948; de l'Ordre 'Honneur et Mérite' 1952; Coronation Medal 1953; Confederation Centenary Medal 1967; author of: 'Frou-Frou et Fin-Fin' (primer) 1939 and its workbook 1941: 'Chez Nous' 1949; 'Notre Famille' (guide pédagogique) 1950; 'Tan-Gau' (a natural method of learning a second lang.); Clubs: Richelieu (Toronto); Canadian (Ottawa); Home: 2011 - 400 Stewart, Ottawa, Ont. K1N 6L2.

**GAUTHIER, Serge,** M.D., FRCP(C); university professor, physician; b. Montreal, Que. 18 Sept. 1950; s. Gaston and Suzanne (Tremblay) G.; e. Coll. Ste-Marie, B.A. 1969; Univ. of Montreal, M.D. 1973; McGill Univ., FRCP(C) Neurology 1977; m. Louise d. Pierre and Thérèse Lacasse 8 Sept. 1973; children: Eric, Judith; DIR., MCGILL CTR. FOR STUDIES IN AGING 1987– ; Fellow, Med. Rsch. Counc. of Can. 1976–78; full-time staff, Montreal Neurological Hosp. & Inst. 1978–86; Carex Chair for Studies in Aging, McGill 1989– ; Prof., Dept. of Med.; Dept. of Psych.; Dept. of Neurology & Neurosurg.; author of 135 articles; Home: 93 Maple, P.O. 715, Hudson Heights, Que. J0P 1J0; Office: St. Mary's Hosp., Annex Bldg., 1st Flr., 3830 Lacombe Ave., Montreal, Que. H3T 1M5.

**GAUTRIN, Henri F.,** B.A., C.E., L.Sc., F.C.A.E.; construction executive; HON. PRES., A. JANIN & CO. LTD.; Chrmn. of the Bd., Fabrital Group Inc.; Dir., Ciments Quebec Ltd.; Structal (82) Inc.; Truscon Inc.; Aciers Transbec; Famec Inc.; Allmark Steel Buildings (1991) Inc.; Chrmn. Candian Foundation Co. Ltd. 1968–80; mem., Candn. Inst. Mining and Metall.; Engn. Inst. Can.; Corp. Prof. Engrs. Que.; Assn. of Prof. Engrs., Ont. & N.B.; Quebec Road Builders Assn. (Pres. 1966–68); Chrmn., Bd. of Governors, Candn. Assn. for Latin America & Caribbean (CALA) 1979–83; Chrmn., Que. Sect. of CCRB (NRC); Dir. CIDC; Catholic; recreation: fishing; Clubs: St. Denis; Home: 1117, Route 138, Neuville, Que. G0A 2R0; Office: P.O. Box 128, Neuville, Que.

**GAUVIN, Michel;** C.V.O. (1976), O.C. (1973), D.S.O., B.A.; retired diplomat; b. Quebec, Que. 7 April 1919; s. Stella (MacLean) and late Raymond G.; e. Coll. St. Charles Garnier, Quebec, Que., B.L. 1939; Laval Univ., 1939–40: Carleton Univ., B.A. 1948; m. Nguyen Thi Minh Huong; two s. Jean, Marc; one d. Kim; Dir.: Canada-China Trade Council; on loan from Candn. Army and Dept. of External Affairs to Prime Minister's Office 1946–50; Extve. Asst. to Undersecretary of State for External Affairs 1950–51; postings: Ankara 1951–53; Lisbon 1953–55; Saigon 1955–56; Caracas 1958–59; Buenos Aires 1959–60; Leopoldville 1961–63; Nat. Defence Coll., Kingston, Ont. 1963–64; special assignments: special mission to Kenya, Ethiopia, Congo during Stanleyville crisis Nov. 1964 and to Dominican Republic, May-June 1965; Ambassador to Ethiopia 1966–69, to Portugal 1969–70, to Greece 1970–75; special assignment: Head of Candn. Delegation to ICCS at Saigon-Vietnam 1973; Consul General of Can., Strasbourg, Fr. 1976–78; Ambassador to Morocco 1978–80, to People's Rep. of China 1980–84; retired from public service July 1984; special assignment: Candn. Secy. to Queen and Coordinator of Royal Visits on Occasion of Montreal Olympics 1976 and of Her Majesty's Jubilee, Oct. 1977; apptd. Special rep. of the U.N. Comn. on Human Rights to Haiti Aug. 1986– Mar. 1987; Annual Award of Candn. Inst. of Internat. Affairs (Que. Section) 1978; served with Candn. Army in U.K., France, Belgium, Holland and Germany during 2nd World War; commd. 2nd Lt., 1940; discharged as Major, 1947; wounded once; author 'La Geste du Régiment de la Chaudière' (war hist. of Regt.); mem., Prof. Inst. Pub. Service Can.; L'Assn. des Anciens du Coll. des Jésuites de Qué.; L'Amicale du Régt. de la Chaudière; Carleton Univ. Alumni Assn.; R. Catholic; recreations: golf, hunting; Clubs: Royal Ottawa Golf; Cercle Universitaire; Address: 706 Echo Dr., Ottawa, Ont. K1S 1P3.

**GAUVIN, William Henry,** C.C. (1975), Ph.D., D.Eng., FRSC, FAICHE, FCIC, FIChemE; chemical engineer; b. Paris, France 30 March 1913; s. Hector Gustave and Albertine Marie (Van Halle) G.; e. Paris, Brussels, London schs.; McGill Univ. B.Eng. 1941, M.Eng. 1942, Ph.D. 1945; Univ. of Waterloo D.Eng. 1967; D.Sc. (h.c.): McGill Univ. 1983, Queen's Univ. 1984, McMaster Univ. 1986; m. Dorothy Edna, d. late Horace F. Strong, 23 Aug. 1966; one d. Suzanne (Mrs. S. Schutt); PRES., WILLIAM H. GAUVIN TECHNOLOGIES, INC.; Sci. Adv. to Vice Pres., Hydro-Québec Research Inst.; Pres., Advis. Comte., Industrial Materials Research Inst. (Nat'l. Research Council) since 1978; Past Pres., Interamer. Confed. of Chem. Engineering; Past Pres., Assoc. des Directeurs de Recherche Industrielle du Qué. 1980– ; Hon. Pres. II World Congress of Chem. Eng., Montreal (1981); Chrmn. Candn. Research Mgmt. Assn. (1982–84); Sr. Research Assoc. and Dir. Plasma Technol. Group Dept. Chem. Engn. McGill Univ. since 1972; Lectr. Dept. Chem. Engn. McGill Univ. 1942–44, Assoc. Prof. 1947–62, Research Assoc. 1961–72, Auxiliary Prof. 1983– ; Plant Supt. F.W. Horner Ltd. Montreal 1944–46; Consultant, Pulp and Paper Research Inst. Can., Montreal 1951–57, Head Chem. Engn. Div. 1957–61; Research Mgr. Noranda Research Centre 1961–70; Dir. of Research and Development, Noranda Mines Limited (1970–82); Délégué-Général, Nat. Research Council Can. 1970–71 (Council 1964–70); mem. Science Council Can. 1966–70, and 1973–76; mem. Adv. Com. on Nuclear Safety (AECB) 1981–88; Candn. Council Weizman Inst. Science; Conseil de la Politique Scientifique du Qué.; Emeritus Gov. McGill Univ. 1982– ; Award for Innov. in Drying, Versailles, France 1988; Izaac Walton Killam Mem. Prize in Eng. 1988; Julian C. Smith Medal, Eng. Inst. of Can. 1986; Thomas W. Eadie Medal, R.S.C. 1986; Quebec Scientific Marie-Victoria Prize 1984; Montreal Medal, Chem. Inst. of Can. 1983; recipient of Gold Medal of the Société d'Encouragement pour la Recherche et l'Invention (France) 1979; rec'd Distinguished Lectr. Award Candn. Inst. Mining & Metall. 1972; Decorated Companion, Order of Canada 1975; Alcan Award 1970; Candn. Soc. Chem. Engn. Award 1968, R. S. Jane Mem. Lecture Award 1963; Médaille Archambault ACFAS 1966; Palladium Medal Chem. Inst. Can. 1966 (Awards for best papers Candn. Journal Chem. Engn. 1960, 1961 and 1981); Sr. Moulton Medal Inst. Chem. Engrs. 1964; I. H. Weldon Medal Candn. Pulp & Paper Assn. 1958; holds patents in high-temperature chem. processing; author over 190 papers in fields of electrochem., high temperature heat and mass transfer, fluid mech. and particle dynamics; Foreign Mem., Acad. of Eng., U.S.A.; mem. Candn. Soc. Chem. Engn. (Pres. 1966–67); Cand. Acad. of Eng.; Engn. Inst. Can.; Candn. Nuclear Assn.; Internat. Centre Heat & Mass Transfer (Yugoslavia); Candn. Pulp & Paper Assn. (Tech. Sec.); Order Engrs. Que.; Candn. Inst. Mining & Metall.; Am. Inst. Mining & Metall. Engrs.; Candn. Research Mang. Assn.; Indust. Research Inst. (USA); Brit. Non-Ferrous Metals Research Assn. (UK); Dechema (Germany); La Soc. de Chimie Industrielle (France); La Soc. des Ingenieurs Civils de France; Soc. Chem. Indust. (UK); Am. Mang. Assn. (Research & Devel. Planning Council); Am. Assn. Advanc. Science; Corp. Prof. Engrs. Que.; Sigma Xi and other assns.; Montreal Bd. Trade; recreations: tennis, sailing, chess, piano; Clubs: Royal St. Lawrence Yacht; University; Home: 7 Harrow Pl., Beaconsfield, Que. H9W 5C7.

**GAUVREAU, Denis,** Ph.D.; university professor, research scientist; b. Jersey City, N.J. 23 Apr. 1951; s. Adrien and Elizabeth (McBrearty) G.; e. Univ. of Montreal, B.Sc. 1973, M.Sc. 1975; Univ. of Cambridge, Ph.D. 1980; m. Claire d. Charles-Henri and Jacqueline (Nolet) Beaucage; children: Sarah, Erica, David, François; DEPT. OF PATHOLOGY, UNIVERSITY OF MONTRÉAL and DIR., UNITÉ INTERDISCIPLINAIRE DU PROJET IMAGE, CENTRE DE RECHERCHE DU CENTRE HOSPITALIER CÔTE-DES-NEIGES 1990– ; Institut National de la Recherche Scientifique-Santé 1981–90; Dir. Coord. of the IMAGE Project, interinstitutional studies on the causes of Alzheimer disease, a multidisciplinary approach and a rsch. model founded on a population-based registry; Assoc. Mem., McGill Ctr. for Studies in Aging; Pres., Project IMAGE / IMAGE Project, a non-profit orgn.; mem., Cambridge Philos. Soc. 1976– ; Assn. can.-française pour l'avancement des sciences 1983– ; N.Y. Acad. of Sciences 1983– ; Gerontol. Soc. of Am. 1985– ; author of sci. articles & book chapters; recreations: music, photography, reading; Home: 4810 de Mobile, Montreal, Que. H1T 2C2; Office: 4565, Queen Mary, Montreal, Que. H3W 1W5.

**GAVIN, Jos. B.,** B.A., Ph.L., M.A., S.T.L., Ph.D.; b. Lansdowne Ont. 30 Aug. 1935; s. Charles W. and E. Leona (Leeder) G.; e. Gonzaga Univ. B.A. 1960. Ph.L. 1961; Columbia Univ. M.A. 1966; Regis Coll. M.A. 1968, S.T.L. 1968; McGill Univ. Ph.D. 1972; DIR., LOYOLA PEACE INST., CONCORDIA UNIV., MONTREAL; Sessional Lecturer, History, Ignatius Coll. Guelph, Ont. 1965–68; Ordained a Priest 1968; Sessional Lecturer 1971–73, Asst. Prof. 1975–79, Historical Theology, Regis Coll., Toronto; Visiting Prof., Ecclesiastical Hist., Università Gregoriana, Rome 1973–75; Final Vows in Soc. of Jesus 1975; Pres., Campion Coll. 1979–86; published numerous articles in scholarly journals on historical and theological topics; Gen. Ed., 'Tradition and Innovation, Belief and Consent' 1983; Ed. 'Friends in Heaven' 1984; mem., Candn. Hist. Assn.; Inst. of Historical Research, Univ. of London; Candn. Soc. of Church Hist.; Intl. Comm. of Comparative Ecclesiastical Hist.; The Friends of Reformation Research, The Renaissance Soc. of Am.; Can. Council Fell. 1969–72; British Council Grant 1972; recreations: singing, water skiing, skating, travelling; Office: 2480, West Broadway, Montreal, Que. H4B 2A5.

**GAVORA, Jan Samuel,** D.Sc.; research scientist; b. Brezova pod Br., Czechoslovakia 14 July 1933; s. Miloslav and Zuzanna (Bendova) G.; e. Univ. of Agric. Sci.'s Nitra, Czechoslovakia M.Sc. 1957, C.Sc. (Ph.D.) 1967, D.Sc. 1991; m. Eva d. Dr. Ferdinand and Margareta Valachova 29 June 1959; PRIN. SCI., CENTRE FOR FOOD AND ANIMAL RESEARCH 1971– ; agric. rsch. Czechoslovakia 1957–68; Postdoctoral Fellow in Animal Sci. Univ. of Man. 1969–71; Rsch. Sci. present Centre 1971– , Sci. Adv. Biotechnol.; Auxiliary Prof. of Animal Sci. Macdonald Coll. McGill Univ. 1981–86; recipient Pub. Service of Can. Merit Award 1984; Tom Newman Internat. Award (UK) 1985; Japan Soc. Promotion Sci. Travel Award 1988; Cert. Merit Candn. Soc. Animal Sci. 1989; co-author 'Animal Breeding: Recent Advances and Future Prospects' 1989; co-ed. 'Biotechnology Research and Applications' 1988; Assoc. Ed. 'Poultry Science' 1980; Assoc. Ed., 'Canadian Journal of Animal Science' 1991– ; over 150 sci. articles, book chapters and tech. publs. primarily disease resistance in chickens; mem. Candn. Soc. Animal Sci.; Genetics Soc. Can.; Poultry Sci. Assn.; World's Poultry Sci. Assn.; Internat. Soc. Animal Genetics; Czechoslovak Soc. Arts & Sci.'s ; Agric. Inst. Can.; recreations: tennis, travel; Home: 51 Forest Hill Ave., Ottawa, Ont. K2C 1P7; Office: Ottawa, Ont. K1A 0C6.

**GAVREL, Paul Alexander,** B.A., M.S.W., LL.B., N.D.C.; lawyer; federal prosecutor; b. Shanghai, China 11 Aug. 1947; s. Alexander Francis and Monica Iovna (Borisova) G.; e. Univ. of Winnipeg B.A. 1968; Univ. of Man. M.S.W. 1970; Univ. of Toronto LL.B. 1974; Nat. Defence Coll. Can. 1985; PROJECT OFFICER, OFFICE OF ENFORCEMENT, ENVIRONMENT CANADA, Hull, Qué. 1991– ; Parole Offr. Nat. Parole Service Guelph, Ont. 1970–71; Jr. Fellow Massey Coll. Univ. of Toronto 1972–74; called to Bar of Ont. 1976, Alta. 1984; law practice Evans, Bragagnolo, Sullivan & Levesque Timmins, Ont. 1976–79; Asst. Crown Atty., Atty. Gen. Ont., Sault Ste. Marie 1980–83; Asst. Dir. Family & Youth Br. Alta. Atty. Gen. Edmonton 1983–84; Sr. Policy Analyst Criminal Justice Policy, Solr. Gen. Can. Ottawa 1985–86; Legal Counsel, Intnl. Assistance Group, Criminal Prosecutions Sect., Dept. of Justice, Ottawa 1986–88; Drug Prosecutor, Criminal Prosecutions Sect., Dept. of Justice, Canada, Ottawa 1986–91; mem. Continuing & Adult Edn. Adv. Ctte. Ottawa Bd. Edn. 1985–88; Mem., Bd. of Dirs., Children's Aid Soc. of Ottawa-Carleton 1986–91 (Pres. 1988–89); Counsellor, Candn. Inst. Internat. Affairs, National Capital Br. 1986–90, 1992–93 (and Program Secy. 1989–90; Membership Secy. 1992–93); mem. Couchiching Inst. Pub. Affairs (Dir. 1971–76, 1979–84); mem., Cochrane Dist. Health Council 1976–79; Pres. Algoma Dist. Health Fair Inc. 1981–83; mem. Religious Adv. Ctte. Programming CBC 1980–85; mem., Bd. of Mgmt., Candn. Red Cross Soc. (Ottawa-Carleton Br.) 1990– , Chair, Internat. Awareness Ctte. 1991–93 (Vice-Chair 1990); Eastern Ont. Area Rep., Internat. Services Ctte., Ont. Div., Candn. Red Cross Soc. 1992– , Vice-Chair 1993– ; Mem., Extve., Eastern Ont. Environmental Sec., Candn. Bar Assoc. Ont. (CBAO) 1992– ; mem., Candn. Bar Assoc.; Candn. Inst. Strategic Studies; Nat. Defence Coll. Assn.; Candn. Council Internat. Law; Internat. Law Assoc.; Law Soc. Alta.; Law Soc. Upper Can.; Candn. Environmental Law Assn.; co-author: 'The Arctic Environment and Canada's International Relations' 1991; United Church; recreations: swimming, cycling, tai chi; Clubs: Massey Coll.; RCAF Mess Ottawa; Office: Office of Enforcement, Environment Canada, 351 St. Joseph Blvd., Hull, Qué. K1A 0H3.

**GAVSIE, David C.,** B.A., B.C.L.; lawyer; b. Montréal, Qué. 18 Sept. 1940; s. Charles and Sara (Halparin) G.; e. Sir George Williams Univ. B.A. 1963; McGill Univ. B.C.L. 1967; m. Ronnie d. Bernard and Queenie Leibel 5 Nov. 1967; children: C.J., Jamie, Lorne; MANAGING PARTNER, OGILVY, RENAULT, Ottawa Office 1992– ; called to Bar of Qué. 1968, Ont. 1975; Assoc. Lawyer, Ogilvy Renault, Montréal 1968–70; Rulings Offr. Revenue Can. Taxation, Sr. Tax Policy Offr. Finance, Ottawa 1971–74; Partner, Gowling, Strathy & Henderson 1978–92; Sr. Instr. Income Tax Sect. Ont. Bar Admission Course Ottawa 1975–85; Contractee income tax matters Publishing, Arts & Culture, Sec. of State 1983; Lectr. in Income Tax Continuing Edn. Law Soc. Upper Can. 1975–87; Gov. Candn. Football League 1987; Chrmn. Ottawa Football Club (Rough Riders) 1987; Counsel, Dir. & Mem. Extve. Ctte., Candn. Red Cross Soc. 1986–89; Chrmn. Ottawa Civic Hosp. Found. 1987–89, Dir. 1978–91; Dir. and Vice-Chrmn., Ottawa-Carleton Bd. of Trade 1990– ; (mem. Extve. Ctte. 1992– ;); Chrmn., Planning Ctte., Ottawa Internat. Airport Authority 1992– ; mem. Candn. Tax Found.; Candn. Bar Assn.; Internat. Bar Assn.; Qué. Bar Assn.; Law Soc. Upper Can.; Office: 1600, 45 O'Connor St., Ottawa, Ont. K1P 1A4.

**GAWNE, Roger E.,** B. Comm.; business executive; b. Saffron Walden, Essex, England 24 Mar. 1938; s. Murray Eden and Jean (Henderson) G.; e. Lancing Coll. cert of edn. 1957; McGill Univ., B. Comm. 1963; Harvard Bus. Sch., Mgmt. Devel. Prog. 1978; m. Diana d. Boleslaw and Katarzyna Korzep 12 July 1969; children: Leslie, Eden; PRES. & C.O.O., SCHERING-PLOUGH HEALTHCARE PRODUCTS CANADA INC. 1984– ; Lt., Brit. Army 1957–59; Sr. Brand Mgr., Colgate-Palmolive of Can. Ltd. 1963–70; Group Brand Mgr, Pharm. Div., Pennwalt Corp. 1970–76; Mgr., Frame Mktg., Shuron Div., Textron Inc. 1977–79; Vice-Pres. & Gen. Mgr., Mitchum-Thayer Ltd., Revlon Inc. 1979–84; Chrmn., Non Prescription Drug Manufacturers Assn. 1986; Candn. Cosmetics, Toiletries & Fragrances Assn.; Extve. Mem., Candn. Drug Wholesale Assn.; recreations: jogging, old cars, classical music; Club: Lambton Golf and Country; Home: 170 Humbervale Blvd., Toronto, Ont. M8Y 3P8.

**GAY, Marie-Louise;** author; illustrator; b. Québec City, Qué. 17 June 1952; d. Bernard Roland and Colette (Fontaine) G.; e. Institut des Arts Graphiques de Montréal 1970–71; Montréal Museum of Fine Arts Sch. grad. 1973; Acad. of Art Coll. San Francisco 1977–79; m. David Toby s. Irving and Bernice Homel; children: Gabriel Reuben, Jacob Paul; ed. illus. Candn. and Am. mags. since 1972; Graphic Designer, Perspectives and Décormag mags. 1974–76; Art Dir. La Courte Echelle publishing house 1980; Lectr. in Illus. Univ. du Québec à Montréal since 1981, Ahuntsic Coll. 1984–85; workshops, confs. schs., univs. & libs. since 1981; Illus. 'Hou Ilva' 1976; 'Dou Ilvien' 1978; 'Hébert Luée' 1980; 'Lizzy's Lion' 1984; 'The Last Piece of Sky' 1993; author & illus. 'De Zéro à Minuit' 1981; 'La Soeur de Robert' 1983; 'La Drôle d'Ecole' 1984; 'Moonbeam on a Cat's Ear' 1986; 'Rainy Day Magic' 1987; 'Angel and the Polar Bear' 1988; 'Fat Charlie's Circus' 1989; 'Willy Nilly' 1990; 'Mademoiselle Moon' 1992; 'Rabbit Blue' 1993 (all children's books); author and designer 'Bonne Fête Willy' (children's puppet play) opening 1989; set designer 'La Boîte' (NFB animated film) 1989; author and designer 'Qui a peur de Loulou?' (children's puppet play) opening 1993; recipient 1st Prize Claude Neon Nat. Billboard Award 1972; Western Art Dirs. Club Award San Francisco 1978; Soc. Illus. Los Angeles Award 1979; Toronto Art Dirs. Club Merit Award 1983, 1985; Alvine Bélisle Award 1984; Can. Council Prize (2) 1985; Candn. Librairians Assoc. (CLA) Amelia Frances Howard Gibbon Award 1987; Amelia Frances Howard Gibbon Award 1988; Governor General's Award 1988; mem. Assn. des Illustrateurs et Illustratrices du Qué.; Soc. Children's Book Writers USA; recreations: cycling, canoeing; Address: 773 Davaar, Montréal, Qué. H2V 3B3.

**GAYLORD, Monica,** B.Mus., M.Mus.; concert pianist, teacher; b. New York City 6 Feb. 1948; d. Donald I. and Daphne M. G.; e. Eastman Sch. of Music (Rochester, N.Y.) B.Mus. 1968, M.Mus. 1969; has performed on television & radio; piano soloist: Toronto Symphony, Hamilton Philharmonic, National Arts Ctr. Orch., Calgary Philharmonic, London Symphony, Victoria Symphony; solo & chamber music recitals in all Candn. provinces as well as the U.S.; Consultant, Frederick Harris Music Publishing Co.; faculty, Royal Conservatory of Music 1986– ; initiated Pi Kappa Lambda hon. music society 1970; recreations: gardening; Address: 318 Robert St., Toronto, Ont. M5S 2K8.

**GAYNER, Robert H.,** B.A.; international aid executive; b. Lethbridge, Alta. 13 March 1930; s. Percival H. and Pearle M. (Clarke) G.; e. St. Paul's College, Winnipeg; Univ. of Manitoba; Univ. of B.C. B.A. 1952; m. Helen d. Algernon Purchase 3 May 1958; children: William, Michael, Mary; EXECUTIVE DIRECTOR, TRADE FACILITATION OFFICE CANADA 1990– ; Candn. Govt. Trade Comnr. Service 1957–78; Ambassador to Iraq 1978–80; Consul General in Chicago 1980–84; retired from External Affairs 1986; Extve. Dir., Business Fund for Candn. Studies in the U.S.A. 1986–90; Pres., Catholic Family Serv. of Ottawa-Carleton; Mem., Order of Malta; Clubs: River Mead Golf; Home: One Elmdale Lane, Ottawa, Ont.; Office: 56 Sparks St., Ste. 500, Ottawa, Ont. K1P 5A9.

**GAYNOR, C. William,** B.Sc., M.B.A.; forest industry executive; b. Buffalo, N.Y. 24 Aug. 1940; s. Cornelius W. and Gertrude V. (Hess) G.; e. Iowa State Univ. B.Sc. 1962; Arizona State Univ. M.B.A. 1973; m. Barbara d. Eugene and Jean Dees 16 July 1967; children: Katherine, M.L., Janet; VICE-PRES. & GEN. MGR., SASKATCHEWAN DIV., WEYERHAEUSER CANADA 1986– ; U.S. Naval Officer (Lt. Comdr.) 1962–71; Weyerhaeuser Co. 1974–80; Mgr., Planning & Devel., Weyerhaeuser Can. 1980–84; Vice-Pres., Timberland & Planning 1984–86; Dir., Sask. C. of C.; Provincial Action Ctte. on the Economy; Sask. Chap. Candn. Counc. on Native Business; Home: 931 University Dr., Saskatoon, Sask. S7N 0J9; Office: P.O. Box 1900, Prince Albert, Sask. S6V 4W1.

**GAYNOR, Kimberley J.,** B.A., M.B.A.; arts manager, administrator; b. Hamilton, Ont. 3 Dec. 1961; d. Hugo Gaynor and Patricia Lynn Greening (Jackson) G.; e. Univ. of Toronto B.A. (Hons.) 1983; York Univ. M.B.A. 1989; SENIOR MARKETING OFFICER, NATIONAL ARTS CENTRE 1992– ; Market Devel. Coord., Canada Council Touring Office 1986–89; Dir. of Admin., Les Grands Ballets Canadiens 1989–91; Acting Dir. Gen. 1991–92; Assoc. Dir. Gen. 1992; Award for 'Outstanding Progress and Achievement,' York Univ. M.B.A. prog. 1992; recreations: cycling; Home: 5 – 413 Elgin St., Ottawa, Ont. K2P 1N4; Office: P.O. Box 1534, Stn. B, Ottawa, Ont. K1P 5W1.

**GEATROS, The Hon. Mr. Justice Theodore Leonidas,** LL.B.; court of queen's bench judge; b. Weyburn, Sask. 29 Apr. 1925; s. Aristotle Leonidas and Evangeline G.; e. Weyburn C.I.; Univ. of Sask., LL.B., cum laude 1948; divorced; children: Timothy, Gregory, Theodore; JUDGE, COURT OF QUEEN'S BENCH OF SASK. 1981; Prov. Pres., Sask. Jr.C. of C. 1954; Past Br. Pres., Royal Candn. Legion; Mason; Shriner; Office: Court House, Melville, Sask. S0A 2P0.

**GEDDES, Carol,** B.A.; film/video producer, writer; b. Teslin, Yukon 17 Nov. 1945; d. Edward and Anne (Johns) G.; e. Carleton Univ. B.A. 1978; Concordia Univ., grad. dipl. in communications 1981; PRODUCER, STUDIO ONE, NATIONAL FILM BOARD; Econ. Devel. Offr. then Extve. Asst. to Chairperson, Council for Yukon Indians 1979–81; 1st major film 'Doctor, Lawyer, Indian Chief' won an award at the National Educational Film & Video Festival 1988; 1st documentary 'Place for Our People' centred on Montreal's Native Friendship Centre; currently working on film, 'George Johnston, Tlingit Photographer'; produced 20 videos on the lives of aboriginal people in Canada, their customs & arts, and other current issues 1986–90; Dir., Canada Council (1st Northerner and 1st Aboriginal person); National Magazine Awards Found. Silver Award 1991 (for article 'Growing Up Native'); Dir., Yukon Human Rights Comn.; Banff Television Festival Bd.; author: 'Community Profiles: The Native Community' (NFB report) 1986; recreations: wilderness hiking and fishing, reading; Home: 61 Green Cres., Whitehorse, Yukon Y1A 4R8.

**GEDDES, Eric A.,** C.M., B.Com., F.C.A., L.L.D.; chartered accountant; b. Victoria, B.C. 28 Sept. 1926; s. George and Florrie (Court) G.; e. Edmonton Public Schools; Edmonton Univ. of Alta. B.Com. 1947; C.A. 1950; LL.D. 1980; m. Frances Jean d. late Russell Stanley 29 Aug. 1947; children: Catherine, Elaine, David, Sheila; Chrmn., Edmonton Region Health Facilities Planning Counc. 1991– ; Chrmn., Bd. of Dirs., Candn. Bacterial Disease Network 1991– ; Chrmn., Bd. of Dirs., Protein Engrg. Network of Centres of Excellence 1991– ; Member, Premier's Council on Science and Technology, Alta. 1990–92; Bd. Mem., Candn. Inst. for Advanced Rsch. 1991–93; Sr. External Advisor, Office of Intellectual Property and Contracts, Univ. of Alta.; Chrmn., Advanced Technology Project 1986–91; Consulting Partner Edmonton Office, Price Waterhouse; joined present firm 1959; Chrmn., Alta. Heritage Foundation for Medical Research 1980–90; Past Chrmn. Bd. of Govs. Univ. Alta.; Founding Chrmn. Old Strathcona Foundation 1975; mem. Council Inst. C.A.'s Alta. 1959–65 and Pres. 1964–65; Past Treas. Alta. P. Cons. Assn.; Past Nat. Vice Pres. for Alta. P. Cons. Assn. Can.; Past Treas. Edmonton Symphony Soc.; Pres. (1981) Edmonton Chamber of Commerce; Mem., Nat. Counc., Duke of Edinburgh's Award in Can. 1980–85; mem. Business Adv. Council, Fac. of Bus., Univ. of Alta. (Chrmn., 1983–84); former Dir., Edmonton Research and Devel. Park Authority; Chrmn., Winspear Found. 1983–93; Bd. Mem., Edmonton Community Found. 1989–93; Pres. Can.-German Cham. of Comm. Inc. 1983–85; Alberta Achievement Award 1979; Univ. of Alta. Alumni Golden Jubilee Award 1984; first recipient, Distinguished Alumnus Award, Fac. of Bus., Univ. of Alta.; Mem., Order of Canada 1989; recipient Alta. Science and Technology Leadership Award 1990; Phi Delta Theta; P. Conservative, Protestant; recreation: golf; Clubs: Edmonton; Mayfair Golf & Country; Faculty Club, Univ. of Alta.; Home: 6631 – 123 St., Edmonton, Alta. T6H 3T3; Office: 2401 Toronto-Dominion Tower, Edmonton Centre, Edmonton, Alta. T5J 2Z1.

**GEDRUJ, Mel,** O.A.A., M.R.A.I.C.; architect; b. Casablanca, Morocco 29 April 1959; s. M. and S. (Dali) G.; e. Ecole d'arch. et d'urbanisme (Algiers) degree in arch. 1983; post-grad. studies in Arch. Eng., Bath Univ. (U.K.); m. Helena d. G. and W. Koja 3 Aug. 1982; one d.: Sandra Kim; ASSOCIATE, TORSNEY-GRAFF ARCHITECTS INC. 1992– ; moved to Canada 1986; joined Petroff Partnership Arch. & Stone Kohn McGuire Vogt Arch. Toronto designing mostly commercial bldgs.; joined Torsney Graff Arch. Inc. designing inst. & community projects 1991; Licenced Mem., Ont. Assn. of Architects 1990; Royal Arch. Inst. of Can. 1992; Mem., Dirigeants & Intervenants Francophones; Hamilton Soc. of Architects; Home: 165 Ferrie St. E., Hamilton, Ont. L8L 3T4; Office: 144 James St. S., Hamilton, Ont. L8P 3A2.

**GEDYE, Richard Neville,** Ph.D., F.C.I.C.; university professor; b. Morecombe, Lancashire, England 10 Oct. 1938; s. Rupert and Barbara Margaret (Osborne) G.; e. Kingswood Sch., Bath, England; Univ. of St. Andrews, Queen's Coll., Scotland, B.Sc. (Hons.) 1961; Ph.D. 1965; m. Cynthia Whitehouse 19 May 1979; children: Alison, Adrian; PROF., DEPT. OF CHEMISTRY, LAURENTIAN UNIV. 1987– ; Sr. Demonstrator, Chem. Dept., Univ. of Durham 1964–65; post-doct. fellow, Chem., Univ. of Waterloo 1965–66; Asst. Prof., present univ.

1966; Assoc. Prof. 1972; co-discover of a method for carrying out rapid organic reactions using a microwave oven; Fellow, Chemical Inst. of Can. 1987; Mem., Chem. Inst. of Can. 1966– ; (served several extve. posts; incl. Chrmn. 1980–81, 1985–87; Counsellor Elect, Eastern Region 1989– ;); author of 15 journal articles; recreations: running, cycling; club: Sudbury Fitness Challeng (Extve.), Sudbury Multiple Sclerosis Soc. (Vice-Chair); Sudbury Philatelic Soc.; Home: 38 Boland Ave., Sudbury, Ont. P3E 1X7; Office: Sudbury, Ont. P3E 2C6.

**GEE, David M.,** B.Sc., M.B.A.; manufacturer; b. Toronto, Ont. 19 July 1947; s. Arthur M. and Margaret Z. (Williams) G.; e. Univ. of Toronto B.Sc. 1969, M.B.A. 1971; m. Nancy d. Lorne and Nancy Millar 6 June 1970; two s. Stephen, Christopher; PRES. & C.E.O., DERLAN AEROSPACE CANADA LTD. 1985– ; Dir., S-S Technologies Inc.; Brand Financial Mgr. General Foods Ltd. 1971–72; Mgr. Financial Analysis Toronto Dominion Bank 1972, Mgr. Project Lending 1975–76; Gen. Mgr. Custom Div. 1976, Vice Pres. Mktg. 1978, Exec. Vice Pres. 1980; Pres. & Chief Oper. Offr., C&C Yachts Ltd. 1981–85; mem., Young Pres.' Orgn.; Clubs: RCYC; Home: 70 Blair Rd., Cambridge, Ont. N1S 2J1; Office: 180 Market Dr., Milton, Ont. L9T 3H5.

**GEE, Ellen M.,** Ph.D.; educator; b. Vancouver, B.C. 29 Jan. 1950; d. John Anton and Margaret (Redfern) Thomas; e. Univ. of B.C. B.A. 1971, Ph.D. 1978; m. Gordon K.W. s. Hing Shing and Sue Fong Gee 21 June 1974; one d. Adrienne; PROF. OF SOCIOL. SIMON FRASER UNIV. 1992– , Assoc. Dean of Arts 1988–92, Acting Dean of Grad. Studies 1992; awarded Commemorative Medal for 125th Anniversary of Candn. Confederation; cons. various govt. depts.; co-author 'Women and Aging' 1987; co-ed. 'Canadian Gerontological Collection: The Challenge of Time' 1985; author various sci. publs., papers; recipient rsch. grants & contracts; Assoc. Ed., Candn. Public Policy 1990– ; mem. Candn. Assn. Gerontol. (Chair Social Sci's Div., Rsch. Ctte. 1987–91); Candn. Sociol. & Anthrop. Assn. (Status of Women Ctte. 1990–93); Candn. Population Soc. (Council 1984–86); Am. Sociol. Assn.; Population Assn. Am.; Gerontol. Soc. Am.; Ctte. Family Rsch. (Div. Internat. Sociol. Assn.); Home: 637 Elmwood St., Coquitlam, B.C. V3J 3W9; Office: Burnaby, B.C. V5A 1S6.

**GEE, Gregory Williams,** B.A., LL.B.; lawyer, financial institution executive; b. Toronto, Ont. 31 Dec. 1948; s. Arthur Melburn and Margaret Zillah (Williams) G.; e. Univ. of Toronto B.A. 1970; Univ. of Western Ont. 1971; Osgoode Hall Law Sch. LL.B. 1973; m. Valerie Jean Fizzell 23 Sept. 1977; children: Carolyn Elaine, Lisa Jean, Brian Gregory; VICE-PRES., GENERAL COUNSEL & SEC., SUN LIFE ASSURANCE CO. OF CANADA 1988– ; articled with Blake, Cassels & Graydon 1973–74; Corp. Lawyer 1975–78; Dir. of Corp. Affairs, Gen. Counsel & Sec., American Motors (Can.) Inc. 1978–88; Instr. of Bus. Law, Univ. of Toronto 1981–87; Candn. Corp. Counsel Assn. (Director 1987– ; Chairman 1993–95; Mem., Candn. Bar Assn. (Chair, Ont. Corp. Counsel Section 1983–85); Am. Bar Assn.; Internat. Bar Assn.; Am. Corp. Counsel Assn.; Assn. of Life Insur. Counsel; Chairman, Legal Section, Candn. Life & Health Insurance Assn. 1993–94; contbg. ed., 'Canadian Financial Services Alert'; recreations: photography, music; clubs: Fitness Inst., Ontario, Bd. of Trade; Home: 2081 Stonehouse Cres., Mississauga, Ont. L5H 3H9; Office: 150 King St. W., Ste. 1400, Toronto, Ont. M5H 1J9.

**GEHRY, Frank Owen,** B.Arch.; architect; b. Toronto, Ont. 29 Feb. 1929; s. Irving and Thelma (Caplan) G.; e. Univ. of S. Calif. B.Arch. 1954; Harvard Univ. postgrad. 1956–57; children from 1st m.: Leslie, Brina; 2nd m. Berta Aguilera 11 Sept. 1975; children: Alejandro, Sami; PRINCIPAL, FRANK O. GEHRY & ASSOC. 1962– ; registered profl. architect, Calif.; Designer, Victor Gruen Assn. 1953–54; Planning, Design & Project Dir. 1958–61; Project Designer, Planner, Pereira & Luckman L.A. 1957–58; Architect, Calif. Aerospace Mus. 1984, Loyola Law Sch. 1981–84, Mus. of Contemporary Art 1983, Frances Howard Goldwyn Regional Br. Lib. 1986, Info & Computer Sci. Engr. Rsch. Facility, Univ. of Calif. at Levine 1986, Vitra Furniture Mfg. Facility & Design Mus., Germany 1989, Chiat/Day H.Q. Venice, Calif. 1991, Am. Ctr. in Paris 1992; Trustee, Hereditary Disease Found. 1970– ; recipient Arnold W. Brunner Memorial Arch. Prize 1983; Pritzker Arch. Prize 1989; (Praemium imperiale Award in Arch, 1992) Wolf Prize in Arts 1992; Fellow, AIA; Office: 1520B Cloverfield Blvd., Santa Monica, Ca. 90404-3543.

**GEIGER, John Grigsby,** B.A.; writer / journalist; b. Ithaca, N.Y. 20 Jan. 1960; s. Dr. Kenneth Warren and Shirley Frances (Gilchrist) G.; e. Concordia Coll., cert. of achievement 1979; Univ. of Alta., B.A. 1982; CITY COLUMNIST, EDMONTON JOURNAL 1987– ; Weekly columnist, Edmonton Sun 1981–83; Reporter, Edmonton Sun 1983–86; Edmonton Journal 1986–87; City Hall Reporter 1987; articles published in Candn. & fgn. mags. & newspapers including News of the World, Stern, 23, and The Beaver; Edward Dunlop Award of Excellence (Spot News) 1984; Mem., Un. Ch.; The Candn. Ctr. Internat. P.E.N.; co-author: 'Frozen in Time: The Fate of the Franklin Expedition' 1987 (Candn., U.K., U.S., Dutch & German eds.; nat. bestseller, repr. 5 times); 'Buried in Ice' 1992 (Candn., U.K., U.S., Danish, German, Spanish, Italian eds.); 'Dead Silence' 1993 (Canada, U.K. & German eds.; Nat. Bestseller); editor: 'Empire of the Bay' 1989; Assoc. prod., award-winning TV documentary 'Buried in Ice' CBC (Nature of Things), PBS (Nova) and BBC-TV (The Wide World); recreations: travelling, hiking, art; Office: Box 2421, Edmonton, Alta. T5J 2S6.

**GEIST, Valerius,** B.Sc., Ph.D.; educator; b. Nikolajew, USSR 2 Feb. 1938; s. Alexej Shutov and Olga Geist; e. Univ. of B.C., B.Sc. 1960, Ph.D. 1966; post-doctoral study Max-Planck Inst. Behaviour & Physiology, Germany 1967; m. Renate d. Karl and Irmgard Brall 20 May 1961; children: Rosemarie, Karl-Alexander, Harold; PROF. OF ENVIRONMENTAL SCIENCES, UNIV. OF CALGARY 1977– , Adjunct Prof. of Biol. 1982– ; Asst. Prof. Environmental Sci's Centre present Univ. 1968, Prog. Dir. of Environmental Sci's in Faculty of Environmental Design 1971–75 and 1991–94; Assoc. Dean of Faculty 1977–80, part-time lectr. in Biol. 1974–82 and 1989– ; Dir. Wildlife Heritage Ltd. Calgary; recipient Book of Yr. Award Wildlife Soc. 1972; Alta. Achievement Award 1972; Wildlife Soc. Group Award 1980; author 'Mountain Sheep' 1971, Japanese ed. 1975; 'Life Strategies, Human Evolution, Evironmental Design' 1978; 'Mountain Sheep and Man in the Northern Wilds' 1975; co-ed. 'The Behaviour of Ungulates and its Relation to Management' 1974; with M.H. Francis 'Mule Deer Country' 1991; 'Elk Country' 1991; 'Wild Sheep Country' 1993; Fellow, Am. Assn. Advanc. Sci.; Dir. Alta. Soc. Prof. Biols. 1981–83; co-chrmn. Panel 10 Candn. Ctte. Internat. Biol. Prog. 1968–78; Councillor Candn. Soc. Zools. 1983–86; Survival Comn. mem. IUCNC 1977– ; Sci. Adv. Ctte. World Wildlife Fund 1982–86; Pres. Calgary Chapter Sigma Xi 1985–86; recreations: hunting, fishing, gardening; Home: 6140 Dalmarnock Cres. N.W., Calgary, Alta. T3A 1H2; Office: Calgary, Alta. T2N 1N4.

**GELBART, Daniel,** B.Sc., M.Sc.; engineer; b. Germany 10 Feb. 1947; s. Mordechai and Regina G.; e. Technion, Israel, B.Sc. 1968, M.Sc. 1972; m. Daphne d. Adek and Stella Sherakoviak 1988; children: David, Daphna, Michael; CO-FOUNDER (1983) AND PRESIDENT, CREO ELECTRONICS CORP.; came to Canada 1973; Engr., then Principal Engr., MacDonald, Dettwiler & Assoc. 1973–83; devel. mobile data terminal & FIRE line of film recorders; awarded B.C. Sci. Gold Medal 1986; awarded 10 patents; recreation: reading; Home: 4987 Marguerite St., Vancouver, B.C. V6M 3J9; Office: 3700 Gilmore Way, Burnaby, B.C. V5G 4M1.

**GELBER, Arthur,** O.C.(1972); b. Toronto, Ont. 22 June 1915; s. Louis and Sara Leah (Morris) G.; e. Upper Canada College, Toronto, Ont. (1934); m. (late) Esther d. late Joseph Salomon, Montreal, P.Q., 17 June 1941; children: Nancy Joan Bjarnason, Patricia Susan Rubin, Judith Ann Wintrob, Sara Beth Charney; Pres., Argel Holdings Ltd.; Trustee: Glen Gould Memorial Found.; Sir Ernest Macmillan Memorial Found.; Art Gallery of Ont.; Life Gov., National Theatre School; Montreal; Bd. mem.: Nat. Ballet of Canada; Toronto Internat. Festival; Canada Israel Cultural Found.; Hon. Vice-Pres., Candn. Soc. for Weizmann Inst. of Sci.; Pres., Lionel Gelber Foundation and The Lionel Gelber Book Prize; mem., Americas Soc., New York; former Bd. mem., Esprit Orchestra; Past Pres., Candn. Conf. of the Arts; National Ballet; St. Lawrence Centre; Toronto Arts Productions; former Chrmn. of Bd. of Trustees, Nat. Arts Centre Corp., Ottawa 1977–81; Chrmn. Ont. Arts Counc. 1979–82; former Chrmn. Adv. Comn., Ont. Cabinet Bi-Centenary Ctte.; former Gov. York Univ.; former Dir., Am. Counc. for the Arts (N.Y.); former Bd. mem., Stratford Shakespearean Festival; mem., Chrmns. Internat. Adv. Counc., Americas Soc., N.Y. (former mem. Candn. Affairs Advisory Ctte.); Candn. Jewish Cong.; Centennial Medal 1967; Diplome d'Honneur 1978; City of Toronto Award of Merit; Queen's Jubilee Medal; LL.D. (h.c.) Brock Univ. 1982; Lifetime Achievement Award, Toronto Arts Awards 1988; Clubs: Arts & Letters; University; Home: 166 Roxborough Dr., Toronto, Ont. M4W 1X8; Office: 203 Richmond St. W., Toronto, Ont. M5V 1V3.

**GELBER, Sylva M.,** O.C.; Canadian Government officer (retired); b. Toronto, Ont. 4 Dec. 1910; d. Louis and Sara (Morris) G.; e. Havergal Coll. Toronto; Univ. of Toronto; Columbia University; LL.D. (Hon.), Queen's Univ. 1976; LL.D. (Hon.), Memorial Univ. Nfld. 1976; D.Hum.L. (Hon.), Mount St. Vincent Univ. 1976; LL.D. (Hon.), Univ. of Guelph 1977; Jewish Community Office (Kehillah), Jerusalem, Palestine, Social Work Bureau 1932–37; Hadassah Medical Orgn., Jerusalem 1937–42; Govt. of Palestine Dept. of Labour, 1942–48; Govt. of Can., Dept. of Nat. Health and Welfare, Consultant, Health Insur. 1950–68; Can. Dept. of Labour, Dir. Women's Bureau, 1968–75; Special Advisor to Dep. Min. of Labour, 1975–78; mem., Can. Delegation to UN General Assembly 1976, 78; Can. Delegations to ILO Conferences 1969, 1971, 1975, 1976; Can. Rep. UN Commission on Status of Women 1970–1974; Chrmn., Working Party of OECD 1973–8; mem. (Hon.), Bd. of Governors, Trent Univ., Peterborough; Dir., Sylva Gelber Music Foundation; mem. Candn. Inst. Internat. Affairs; U.N. Assoc. of Canada; Publications: reports, papers, articles on labour, health ins., human rights; author 'No Balm in Gilead: A Personal Retrospective of Mandate Days in Palestine' 1989; Officer of the Order of Canada 1975; recreations: music; Home: 77 Placel Rd., Rockcliffe Park, Ottawa, Ont. K1L 5B9.

**GELDART, Donald James Wallace,** B.Sc., Ph.D., F.R.S.C.; university professor; b. Havelock, N.B. 6 July 1938; s. Austin Freeze and Nettie Louise (Corey) G.; e. Horton Acad. 1955; Acadia Univ., B.Sc. (Hons.) 1959; McMaster Univ., Ph.D. 1964; PROF., PHYSICS DEPT., DALHOUSIE UNIV. 1978– ; NRC postdoct. fellow, CEN-Saclay, France 1964–65; Vis. Asst. Prof., McGill Univ. 1965–67; Asst. Prof., present univ. 1967–79; Assoc. Prof. 1969–78; Chair of Physics Dept. 1985–89; Vis. Prof., KTH, Stockholm, Sweden 1973; Chalmers Inst., Goteborg, Sweden 1974; Univ. Paris 1980–81; Univ. New South Wales 1990–91; A.C. Fales Prof. of Theoretical Physics 1986– ; F.R.S.C. 1986; author/co-author of over 100 sci. articles, reviews & book chapters; recreations: hiking, swimming, cycling; Home: Herring Cove, N.S. B0J 1S0; Office: Halifax, N.S. B3H 3J5.

**GELFAND, Erwin W.,** B.Sc., M.D., F.R.C.P.(C); immunologist; educator; b. Montréal, Qué. 10 March 1941; s. Samuel and Sylvia (Nadler) G.; e. McGill Univ. B.Sc. 1962, M.D.C.M. 1966; m. Adele d. Reuben and Fanny Zilbert 22 June 1967; children: Lauren, Allison; CHRMN., DEPT. OF PEDIATRICS, NAT. JEWISH CENTER FOR IMMUNOLOGY AND RESPIRATORY MEDICINE and PROFESSOR OF PEDIATRICS, MICROBIOLOGY AND IMMUNOLOGY, UNIV. OF COLORADO, Denver, CO 1987; Prof. of Pediatrics and Immunology Univ. of Toronto 1979–87; Fellow in Med. (Immunol.) Children's Hosp. Med. Centre, Boston 1969–72; Rsch. Fellow in Immunol. Harvard Med. Sch. 1969–71; Rsch. Assoc. Max Planck Inst. for Immunobiol. Freiburg, W. Germany 1971–72; Asst. Prof. of Pediatrics Univ. of Toronto 1972, Assoc. Prof. 1976; Sci., Rsch. Inst. present Hosp. 1972–78, Chief of Immunol. and Sr. Sci. Rsch. Inst. 1978; Chief of Immunol. and Rheumatol., The Hosp. for Sick Children 1979–87; recipient Med. Rsch. Council Can. Post-doctoral Fellowship 1969–72; Queen Elizabeth II Rsch. Sci. Award 1975–81; Mead Johnson Award Rsch. Pediatrics 1981; McLaughlin-Gallie Visiting Prof. Royal Coll. Phys. & Surgs. Can. 1986; Raymond and Beverly Sackler Foundation Scholar 1987– ; Visiting Prof. of Immunol. Japan, Canada, Israel, The Netherlands, USA; author or co-author over 370 publs.; mem. Candn. Med. Assn.; Candn. Soc. Immunol.; Candn. Soc. Clin. Investig.; Ont. Med. Assn.; Am. Acad. Advanc. Sci.; Am. Soc. Clin. Investig.; Am. Fedn. Clin. Rsch.; Am. Assn. Immunols.; Home: 4275 S. Bellaire Circle, Englewood, CO 80110; Office: 1400 Jackson St., Denver, CO 80206.

**GELGOOT, Arthur,** C.A.; chartered accountant; b. Toronto, Ont. 17 March 1937; s. Benjamin Harold and Thelma (Isenberg) G.; e. Forest Hill Collegiate; C.A. Designation 1961; children: Daryl, Jeffery; FOUNDER, ARTHUR GELGOOT AND ASSOCIATES 1978– ; established private practice, Adelman Gelgoot and Company 1964; as senior partner of Arthur Gelgoot & Assoc. has devoted most of his time to servicing & negotiating in the cultural, communications and entertainment industries; Dir. and/or Bd. Mem., Opportunity House; Skylight Theatre, Ethos Magazine; Treas., National Advertising Benevolent Soc. of Canada; Extve. Bd. Mem., The Arts Foundation of Greater Toronto; The Internat. Reading Series at Harbourfront' Arts and the Cities; Internal Audit Ctte. of the United Way; Investment Ctte., The Canada Council; Extve. Consultant on CTV series 'Peter Ustinov's Russia'; Asoc. Prod., Michael Maclear's 'The Greatest Journey'; Office: 1075 Bay St., Suite 505, Toronto, Ont. M5S 2B1.

**GELHORN, Carolyn,** B.Ed.; business executive; inventor; b. Winnipeg, Man. 3 March 1944; d. George John (dec.) and Elsie Bertha (Kreger) G.; e. West Kildonan C.I.; Univ. of Man. B.Ed. 1976; children: Shawna Carol Pachal, Michael Stanley Pachal; PRES., CARSHAW INC. 1984– ; probably the only woman in Can. in field of Auto. Electronics; Teacher, River E. Sch. Div. 1970–79; Mktg. Rep., Pitney Bowes 1980; Mgr., Court Lodge Hotel (U.K.) 1981 (working holiday); Mktg. Rep., Pitney Bowes 1981–82; Sales Mgr. 1982–86; Mktg. Adv. Bd. 1983; developed in-house training ctr. for mktg. reps. in Can.; Mem., Women Inventors Project 1987– ; Seminar leader and facilitator, Manitoba Women Inventors 1992– ; author: 'Street Smarts' forthcoming; editor: 'Individual Instruction in Music Through Learning Centres' 1977; Address: Box 652, Ile des Chenes, Man. R0A 0T0.

**GÉLINAS, Gaetan,** B.A., B.A.A.; nursing home executive; b. Montreal, Que. 5 Apr. 1948; s. Henri Paul and Laurette (Tousignant) G.; e. Univ. de Montréal B.A. 1969; Hautes Etudes Comm. B.A.A. 1973; m. Louise d. Jacques and Jacqueline Normandin 19 July 1972; children: Philippe, Simon; FIRST VICE-PRES. GROUPE CHAMPLAIN INC. 1990– ; Vice-Pres. Finan. Cable TV 1976–82; Sr. Coord., Petro Can. 1982–83; Vice-Pres. Finan., Videotron Inc. 1983–84; Vice-Pres. Opns. 1984–85; Pres., Mode Mirage Inc. 1985–87; Vice-Pres., Finan. & Admin., present firm 1987–88; C.A. 1975; Dir., Fond. Champlain; recreations: skiing, tennis, wind surfing, golf; Home: 388 Olivier, Apt. 16, Westmount, Que. H3Z 2C9; Office: 7150 Marie Victorin, Montreal, Que. H1G 2J5.

**GELINAS, Gratien,** O.C. (1967), D.Litt., LL.D., F.R.S.C. (1959); producer; author; director; actor; b. St. Tite (near Three Rivers) P.Q. 1909; father a French-Candn. and mother (née Davidson) of Scots-Irish descent; e. Coll. of Brothers, St. Jerome, P.Q.; Coll. de Montreal (Sr. Matric); Sch. of Higher Comm. Studies, Montreal; Hon. D. Litt.: Univs. of Montreal 1949, New Brunswick 1969, Toronto 1951, McGill 1968; LL.D.: Sask. 1966; Trent 1970; Mount Allison 1973; Ottawa 1987; named 'one of 25 great Canadians whose achievements stand out above all others in the Century since Confederation' by Candn. Centennial Lib. 1966; m. 1stly Simone Lalonde 1935 (d.1967); six children; 2ndly Huguette Oligny Jan. 1973; began career in designing with Dupuis Freres (Dept. Store) Montreal 1929; two months later joined La Sauvegarde Ins. Co. as acct., remaining with them for nine years, during which period indulged in casual radio and stage acting; at the cabaret 'Mon Paris,' Montreal, developed the character of 'Fridolin' in a series of monologues about Le Bon Petit Garcon and Le Mauvais Petit Garcon; given first opportunity to act his monologues on the stage in 'Televise-moi-ça' at St. Denis Theatre, Montreal, 1936, and was an immediate success; resigned from insurance business in 1937 and made radio debut with 'Fridolin' (wrote whole show) in 'Carrousel de la Gaité' (re-named Le Train de Plaisir following year), 1937; staged his first 'Fridolinons Revue' 1938, which extended a one-week engagement to 25 performances, establishing a new record for theatre in Can.; discontinued radio performances in 1941 and engaged in full-time theatre; during 1940–46 wrote, directed, produced and starred in annual reviews playing 75 performances in Montreal and Quebec City, playing to nearly 105,000 theatre-goers per year; scored a hit in 'St. Lazare's Pharmacy' (played in Chicago) 1945; sometime called the 'Charlie Chaplin' of French Canada; awarded Grand Prix of Dramatists Soc.; his play 'Tit-Coq' (1949) mentioned by Prime Min. Hon. St. Laurent in H. of C. as an example of first-rate Candn. art, the Montreal première (May 1948) running for two yrs. to break all Candn. box office records; signed contract to produce Eng. version for N.Y. stage 1959; filmed version rec'd 'Film of the Year Award' 1952; wrote and starred in T.V. serial 'Les Quat'Fers en l'Air' 1954–55; 'Fridolinades' (revue) at Orpheum Theatre, Montreal, 1956; appeared as Chas. VI in 1956 presentation of Henry V at Stratford Shakespearean Festival; as Pres. and Dir. founded 'La Comedie-Canadienne' in Montreal 1 June 1957, after taking over the former Radio City Theatre; dir. 1st production 'L'Alouette' Feb. 1958 and played part of Charles VII in its English adaptation, 'The Lark'; Gov., Nat. Film Bd. of Can. 1950–52; Chrmn. Candn. Film Devel. Corp. 1969–78; author 'Bousille et les Justes' (Montreal première 16 Aug. 1959); wrote, produced and starred in 'Le Diable à quatre' (satirical revue, opening Feb. 1964); author and dir. of play 'Hier les enfants dansaient' (Montreal premiere 15 April 1966, and Eng. trans. by Mavor Moore 1967); wrote and starred in 'La Passion de Narcisse Mondoux' 1986 (playing at Le Théâtre du P'tit Bonheur, Toronto 1986, Le Théâtre du Rideau-Vert, Montreal 1987); Founding mem. Nat. Theatre Sch. of Can. 1960; Pres., Candn. Theatre Inst. 1959–60; Vice-Pres., Greater Montreal Arts Council, 1957–62; el. Pres., Assn. Canadienne du Theatre Amateur 1950–6l; awarded the Victor-Morin Prize for 1967 ('exceptional theatrical talents'), by St. Jean Baptiste Soc., Oct. 1967; Award, Candn. Conf. of the Arts 1987; makes frequent visits to Candn., European and Am. drama centres; recreations: classical music, boating, tennis, skating, travel; Address: Box 207, 316 Girouard St., Oka, Que. J0N 1E0.

**GELLATLY, Allan Bruce,** B.A., LL.D., F.C.G.A.; university administrator; b. Kitchener, Ont. 31 Dec. 1931; s. Harold John and Pearl Irene (Eagle) G.; e. Univ. of West. Ont., B.A. 1952; certified general accountant 1964; m. Audrey May d. Esther and Louis Guenther 25 Sept. 1953; children: Barbara, Anne, Mary, Sean; VICE-PRES., ADMIN. & FINANCE, UNIV. OF B.C. 1984– ; Candn. Offr. Training Corps. 1950–52; Dominion Electrohome Indus. 1952–57; Comptroller, Univ. of Waterloo 1957–66; Treas. & Chief Finan. Offr. 1966–70; Vice-Pres., Finan. & Opns. 1970–83; Dir., WESTECH Information Systems 1989–91; Sec.-Treas., UBC Real Estate Corp.; Doctor of Laws, Univ. of Waterloo 1984; F.C.G.A. 1983; Pres., Candn. Assn. of Univ. Bus. Offrs. 1989–90; Mem., Western Univ. Finan. & Admin. Vice-Presidents 1984– ; Chair, Richmond Hospital Found. 1992– ; Past Bd. Mem., Peoples Warden, & Rectors Warden, St. Columba's Anglican Ch.; Past Bd. Mem., St. Monica House (Treas. & Chrmn. 10 yrs.); Past Bd., K-W Philharmonic Choir (Treas. & Chrmn.); Mem., Cert. Gen. Accountants Assn., B.C.; club: Quilchena Golf & Country; Home: 5351 Opal Pl., Richmond, B.C. V7C 5B4; Office: 6328 Memorial Rd., Vancouver, B.C. V6T 1Z2.

**GELLER, John Arthur,** Q.C., B.A., LL.B.; solicitor; b. Toronto, Ont. 22 June 1930; s. Kalman and Katy (Ladowsky) G.; e. Forest Hill Coll. Inst. 1948; Univ. of Toronto B.A. 1951; Osgoode Hall Law Sch. (hons.) 1955; m. Sybil d. Phillip and Sarah Gangbar 1 July 1951; children: Lawrence Ian, Dana Sue Lampe, Janet Anne Babins, Harold Leslie; VICE-CHRMN., ONTARIO SECURITIES COMMISSION 1993– ; joined predecessor firm of Fasken Campbell Godfrey 1955, Partner 1962–93; called to Bar of Ont. 1955; cr. Q.C. 1966; Dir., Upper Lakes Group Inc.; Past Pres. Holy Blossom Temple Toronto; Past Vice Chrmn. Union Am. Hebrew Congs.; Clubs: National; Cambridge; Home: 7 Silverwood Ave., Toronto, Ont. M5P 1W3; Office: 20 Queen St. W., Suite 800, Toronto, Ont. M5H 3S8.

**GELLER, Michael Arthur,** B.Arch., MAIBC, MCIP; architect, planner, real estate executive; b. Blackpool, U.K. 6 Oct. 1947; s. Samuel and Naomi Louise (Abbott) G.; e. Univ. of Toronto B.Arch. 1971; m. Sally d. William and Marjorie Pethybridge 3 Dec. 1981; children: Claire, Georgia; FOUNDER & PRES., THE GELLER GROUP 1983– ; architect in private practice, Toronto 1971–72; Architect / Planner / Executive, Canada Mortgage & Housing Corp. 1972–81; Vice Pres., Narod Development Ltd. 1981–83; active in property devel. & real estate consulting; nat. recognized as expert in housing & urban devel. issues; Past Pres., Urban Devel. Inst. of Canada (UDI); Past Mem., Candn. Housing Design Council; Mem., Candn. Inst. of Planners; Mem., Arch. Inst. of B.C.; Dir., B.C. Buildings Corp. 1992– ; Award of Excellence UDI 1989; Dir., Bldg. Ctte., Louis Brier Home & Hospital 1989–91; Jewish Family Service Agency 1990–92; Dir., Vanc. Volunteer Centre 1983–88; frequent speaker & commentator on housing & devel. issues; Mem., Lambda Alpha Internat. author of num. reports & pubns. on housing issues in Canada; recreations: golf, tennis; clubs: Arbutus; University GC; Home: 3366 Deering Island Place, Vancouver, B.C. V6N 4H9; Office: 270 – 601 West Cordova St., Vancouver, B.C. V6B 1G1.

**GELLER, Sybil,** B.A.; professional volunteer; b. Toronto, Ont. 10 May 1931; d. Philip and Sarah (Miller) Gangbar; e. Univ. of Toronto B.A. 1951; m. John Arthur s. Kalman and Katy Geller 1 July 1951; children: Lawrence Ian, Dana Sue Lampe, Janet Anne Babins, Harold Leslie; Pres. Ont. Div., Candn. Red Cross Soc. 1984–86, Chrmn. Metro Toronto 1976, mem. Adv. Ctte. Blood Transfusion Service 1986– , Capital Campaign-Mgmt. Ctte. 1984– ; Dir. Un. Way Metro Toronto 1977–82; Dir., Ont. Cancer Treatment and Research Found. 1987– ; Chrmn., Ont. Breast Screening Coalition 1989–91; Pres. Pomegranate Guild Judaic Needlework 1986–88; Pres. Forest Hill Home & Sch. Council 1967; el. mem. Order of Red Cross 1986; Home: 7 Silverwood Ave., Toronto, Ont. M5P 1W3.

**GELLERT, James Herbert,** B.A., M.A., Ph.D.; university professor and administrator; b. Montreal, P.Q. 31 May 1945; s. Herbert William and Juanita Jane G.; e. Schreiber P.S. & H.S.; Lakehead Univ. B.A. 1968, M.A. 1975; Univ. of Birmingham Ph.D. 1975; m. Mary Carol d. John and Verona Zuback 31 Aug. 1973; one d.: Jennifer Alexandra; ASSOCIATE PROFESSOR OF ENGLISH, LAKEHEAD UNIV. 1986– ; Asst. Prof. of English, Lakehead Univ. 1976–85; Dean of Arts & Science 1991– ; Visiting Prof. of English, San Diego State Univ. 1985–86; Co-editor / Field Editor, British Children's Literature, G.K. Hall Inc. 1987– ; Assistant Editor, Children's Literature Association Quarterly 1984–87; Internat. Rsch. Soc. for Children's Lit. 1986– ; Western Social Science Assn. 1985– ; Children's Lit. Assn. 1981– ; (Awards Ctte. 1989–91); Assn. of Candn. Univ. Teachers of English 1975– ; editor: 'P.L. Travers' by Patricia Demers 1991, 'Hugh Leftwig' by Gary Schmidt and 'Roald Dahl' by Maria West forthcoming; author of num. articles; recreations: golf, squash, reading; Home: 106 Herrick Place, Thunder Bay, Ont. P7C 4V1; Office: Thunder Bay, Ont. P7B 5E1.

**GELLMAN, Harvey S.,** B.A., M.A., Ph.D.; company executive; b. Radom, Poland 28 June 1924; s. Max and Gertrude (Hacker) G.; e. Univ. of Toronto B.A. 1947, M.A. 1949, Ph.D. 1951; m. Lily d. Chaim and Sarah Applebaum 30 June 1946; children: Steven, Paul; SR. VICE PRESIDENT, THE CGI GROUP INC. 1992– ; Staff Mathematician, Univ. of Toronto 1948–52; Head Electronic Computing Section, AECL, Toronto 1952–55; Pres. H.S. Gellman & Co. Ltd., Toronto 1955–64; Vice-Pres. DCF Systems Ltd., Toronto 1964–74; Chrmn., Gellman, Hayward & Partners Ltd. 1974–92; author of several articles on information technology and related topics; Pres., Candn. Information Processing Soc. 1965; Pres. Candn. Operational Rsch. Soc. 1971; Pres. Inst. of Mgmt. Consulting of Ont. 1968; mem. Bd. of Educ. Forest Hill Village 1958–65; Internat. Systems Man of the Year, ASM, Cleveland, OH 1966; Home: 40 Ridge Hill Dr., Toronto, Ont. M6C 2J4; Office: 33 Yonge St., 8th Flr., Toronto, Ont. M5E 1G4.

**GELLMAN, Steven David;** composer; pianist; educator; b. Toronto, Ont. 16 Sept. 1947; s. Harvey S. and Lil (Applebaum) G.; e. Forest Hill Coll. Inst. 1965 (Ont. Scholar); Royal Conserv. Music Toronto 1959–65; Juilliard Sch. NYC 1968; Conservatoire de Paris 1976 (Premier Prix); m. Cheryl d. Harold and Sylvia Reitapple 18 Oct. 1970; children: Dana, Misha; ASSOC. PROF. OF MUSIC, UNIV. OF OTTAWA 1984– ; Asst. Prof. 1976–84; composer many works for orch., chamber ensembles, instrumental & vocal solos; performed throughout Can. and other countries incl. USA, Eur., S. Am., Japan; performed as soloist own piano concerto opening ceremony Univ. of Toronto Edward Johnson Bldg. 1964; many comns. from orchs. & soloists incl. Toronto Symphony, CBC, NAC, Hamilton Phil., Angela Hewitt, Jon Kimura Parker; recipient BMI Prize 1964 (1st Candn.); 1st Prize Aspen Music Festival 1966; Unesco Award 1970; named Composer of the Year, Candn. Music Counc. 1987; composer many musical works incl. 'Mythos' 1968; 'Symphony in Two Movements' 1970; 'Odyssey' 1971; 'Pieces of Dāna' 1973; 'CHORI' 'Sonate pour Sept.' 1975; 'Deux Tapisseries' 1978, French Govt. comn. to commemorate Olivier Messiaen's 70th birthday; 'Trikāya' 1981; 'Awakening' 1982, performed by TSO during Eur. tour 1983; 'Fantasia on a Theme of Schumann' 1983; 'The Bride's Reception' 1983; 'Universe Symphony' 1984–85, opened Internat. Yr. Candn. Music (Andrew Davis conducting TSO & Candn. Electronic Ensemble); 'Triptych' 1986, keyboard (piano/synthesizer); 'Love's Garden' 1987, soprano & orchestra; 'Chiaroscuro' 1988; 'Piano Concerto' 1988; 'Canticles' of St. Francis of Assisi, choir & orchestra 1989; 'Burnt Offerings' 1990; 'Red Shoes' 1990; 'Musica Eterna' 1991; discography incls.: 'Mythos' Robert Aitken & SMCQ Ensemble CBC RCI 301; 'Symphony in Two Movements' Hamilton Phil. CBC SM 295; 'Poème: The Warrior' Angela Hewitt CBC RCI 496; 'Wind Music' Composers' Brass Group, Music Gallery; 'Psalm 121' Joanne Dorenfeld CBC RCI 569; 'Fantasia on a theme of Schumann' Christina Petrowska CBC SM 5000; mem. Candn. League Composers; Candn. Music Centre; SOCAN; Home: 25 Elmdale Ave., Ottawa, Ont. K1M 1A1; Office: Music Dept., Univ. of Ottawa, Ottawa, Ont. K1N 6N5.

**GELLNER, John,** C.M., D.F.C., C.D., D.L., D.M.S.(h.c.); author; educator; b. Trieste 18 May 1907; s. Dr. Gustav and Maria (Tomasi) G.; e. Masaryk Univ. Brno, Czechoslovakia D.L. (Doctor of Law) 1930; D.M.S. (h.c.) Royal Roads Military Coll. 1983; m. Lilo d. Wilhelm Mattheis, Essen, Germany 14 March 1978; came to Can. 1939; Jr. Partner law firm Brno, Czechoslovakia 1935–39; served with R.C.A.F. 1940–58, Pilot, rank Wing Commdr.; Ed. 'Commentator' (Toronto pol. monthly now defunct) 1964–70; Ed. 'Canadian Defence Quarterly/Revue canadienne de défense' 1971–87; Visiting Prof. of Pol. Science York Univ. 1970–82; Dir. Atlantic Council Can.; rec'd Czechoslovak Mil. Cross; Czechoslovak Medal for Valour; author 'Canada in NATO' 1970; 'Bayonets in the Streets: Urban Guerilla at Home and Abroad' 1974; co-author 'Climbers' Guide Through the High Tatras' 4 vols. 1936–38; 'The Czechs and Slovaks in Canada' 1968; author over 500 publs. incl. articles on internat. relations and defence issues, book chapters; apptd. Mem., Order of Canada 1983; mem. Candn. Inst. Internat. Affairs; Candn. Inst. Strategic Studies; Internat. Inst. Strategic Studies (UK); R. Catholic; Clubs: Royal Candn. Mil. Inst.; Home: R.R. 3, Caledon East, Ont. L0N 1E0.

**GEMMELL, Robert Joseph,** B.A., LL.B., M.B.A.; investment banker; b. Toronto, Ont. 28 Feb. 1957; s. Robert Joseph and Catherine Lamb Harper (McFarlane) G.; e. Cornell Univ. B.A. 1979; Osgoode Hall Law Sch. LL.B. 1983; York Univ. M.B.A. 1983; m. Cynthia H. d. Harry and Marina Cholakis 28 Feb. 1987; two d. Jennifer Anne, Laura Christine; SR. VICE PRES., DIR., HEAD OF CORPORATE FINANCE ONT. and HEAD OF MERGERS AND ACQUISITIONS CANADA, MERRILL LYNCH CANADA INC. 1990– ; Mng. Dir., Merrill Lynch & Co. (N.Y.); joined Wood Gundy Inc. 1983, Asst. Vice Pres. 1985, Vice Pres. 1986; Morgan Stanley & Co. Inc. 1986, Vice Pres. 1987, Prin. 1989–90; recreation: golf; Clubs: Beacon Hall Golf (Toronto); St. George's Golf & Country (Toronto); Cornell (N.Y.); Glencoe (Calgary); Glencoe Golf & Country (Calgary); Office: 200 King St. W., Toronto, Ont. M5H 3W3.

**GENDREAU, Hon. Paul-Arthur,** B.A., LL.L.; court of appeal judge; b. Rimouski, Qué. 19 Aug. 1939; s. Hon. Arthur and Lucie (Labrie) G.; e. Laval Univ. B.A. 1960, LL.L. 1963; London Sch. of Econ. & Pol. Sci. (Commonwealth Scholar) 1964–65; m. Micheline d. Henri-A. and Virginie Martin 28 May 1966; JUDGE, COURT OF APPEAL QUE. 1986– ; law practice Gendreau, Pelletier & Associés, Rimouski 1965–80, Sr. Partner; Assoc. Dep. Min. of Justice Prov. Qué. 1980–82; Partner, Clarkson, Tétrault, Montréal, Québec and Ottawa 1982–86; Home: 1345 Teillet, Ste-Foy, Qué. G1W 3C1; Office: 300 blvd. Jean-Lesage, Québec, Qué. G1K 8K6.

**GENDRON, Jean-Denis,** B.A., L. ès L., doctorat phonétique; ne St-Antoine-sur-Richelieu, P. Q. 1er Janv. 1925; f. Antonio et Aldina Langevin; é. Univ. Montréal, B.A. 1946; Univ. Laval, L. ès. L. 1950; Univ. Strasbourg, doc. phon. 1958; ép. Gisèle, f. Dr. Eugène Blouin, 23 âout 1952; enfants: Christiane, Yves, Dominique, Michel; professeur retraité 1990; Dir. du Centre International de recherche sur le bilinguisme (Univ. Laval) de 1979 à 1986; Professeur Université Laval 1950–74 et depuis 1979; professeur aux. langue française 1950–55; professeur aux. puis agrégé et titulaire-phonétique 1958–64; secr. Dép. Linguistique 1964–67 dir. adjoint 1967–68; vice-doyen, fac. lettres 1968–69; prés. Comn. Royale d'Enquête sur la situation de la langue française et sur les droits linguistiques au Québec déc. 1968–72; Vice-prés. de la Régie de la langue française du Qué. 1974–77; Prés. du Conseil de la langue française du Qué., 1977–79; auteur 'Tendances phonétiques du français parlé au Canada' 1966; 'Phonétique orthophonique à l'usage des Canadiens-Français' 1968; co-auteur: 'Etudes de linguistiques franco-canadienne' 1967; 'Rapport de la Commission royale d'enquête: vol. I La langue de travail, 1973; 'La situation du français comme langue d'usage au Québec' 1974; 'Statut des langues et statut des hommes' 1975; 'La définition d'une norme de langue parlée au Québec' 1975; 'Rapport annuel de la Régie de la langue française' 1975 et 1976; 'La situation de la langue française et des francophones au Québec et au Canada' 1977; 'Fluctuation des frontières ethniques et recrudescence des tensions au Canada' 1979; 'Une conception institutionnelle des rapports entre langues en contact' 1982; 'La norme et les critères de normalisation du langage au Québec' 1983; 'Langue et société au Canada' 1984; 'Evolution de la conscience linguistique des Québécois depuis la Révolution tranquille' 1986; 'L'autonomie linguistique dans le cadre de l'aménagement linguistique du Nouveau-Brunswick' 1991; de divers ouvrages et articles sur la phonétique; membre: assn. can. de ling.; assn. internat. de phonétique; soc. de ling. & philologie romanes; conseil internal. langue frse; mem. Soc. royale du Can.; Ordre des francophones d'Amérique; Officier de l'Ordre des Palmes Académiques de France 1991; Officier de l'Ordre National du Québec 1992; Professeur émérite, Université Laval 1992; Prix Marcel-Vincent (sciences sociales) de l'Assn. canadienne-française pour l'avancement des sciences (ACFAS); Catholique; Résidence: 1470 Av du Maire-Beaulieu, App 107, Sillery, Qué. G1S 4T9.

**GENDRON, Jean-Louis,** B.A., M.S.W., Ph.D.; university professor; b. Amos, Que. 1 April 1944; s. Edouard and Angélina (Ricard) G.; e. Séminaire d'Amos B.A. 1965; Laval Univ. M.S.W. 1969, Ph.D. 1980; children: Marie-Eve, Jean Philippe, Pierre-Marc; PROFESSOR, LAVAL UNIVERSITY 1988– ; Community Organizer 1970–72; Prof., Sherbrooke Univ. 1972–88; specializes in social policies analysis and social work with communities; recreations: hiking (mountains); Home: 1406 Gaspard-Fauteux, Sillery, Que. G1T 2T6; Office: School of Social Work, Laval Univ., Quebec, Que. G1K 7P4.

**GENEST, Jacques,** C.C. (1967), M.D., LL.D., D.Sc., C.S.P.Q., F.R.C.P., F.R.S.C., M.A.C.P.; b. Montreal, Que. 29 May 1919; s. Rosario and Annette (Girouard) G.; e. Coll. Jean de Brébeuf, Montreal B.A. 1937; Univ. of Montreal, M.D. 1942; Harvard Med. Sch. (Surg. Anat.) 1938, (Physiol.) 1939; Harvard Sch. of Chem., 1948; Johns Hopkins Hospital 1945–1948; Rockefeller Inst. 1948–1951; LL.D Queen's 1966, Toronto 1970; D.Med.Sc., Laval; Memorial Univ.; McGill; Sherbrooke; Ottawa; St. Francis Xavier Univ.; N.Y. State Univ.; Rockefeller Univ.; Concordia Univ.; Montpellier Univ.; m. Estelle, d. Albert Deschamps, 3 Oct. 1953; children: Paul, Suzanne, Jacques Jr., Marie, Hélène; CONSULTANT, CLINICAL RESEARCH INST. OF MONTREAL; Prof. of Med., University of Montreal; rec'd Gairdner Award 1963; Soc. Médicale de Montréal Awards, 1956 and 1959; Assn. Canadienne française pour l'Avanc. des Sciences, Parizeau Award 1965; Flavelle Award, Royal Soc. of Canada; Stouffer award 1969; Marie-Victorin Prize of Quebec 1977; Loyola Medal 1978; Royal Bank of Canada Award 1980; Scientific Prize, Assn. Med. Langue Française du Canada 1980; F.N.G. Starr Award of the Candn. Med. Assn. 1982; Killam Memorial Prize 1986; R.V. Christie Award, Candn. Assoc. Professors of Med. 1988; J.H. Graham Prize, Roy. Coll. Phys. Surg. Canada 1993; Master, Amer. Coll. of Phys.; mem., Peripatetic Club; Am. Clin. & Climatol, Assn.; Assn. Am. Phys.; R. Catholic; Home: 5955 Wilderton Ave., Montreal Que. H3S 2V1; Office: 110 Pine Ave. West, Montreal, Que. H2W 1R7.

**GENN, Robert Douglas;** artist; b. Victoria, B.C. 15 May 1936; s. Hugh Douglas and Florence (Caton) G.; e. Univ. of Victoria; Art Ctr. Sch. Los Angeles; m. Carol d. Kohei and Kimei Shimozawa 29 Aug. 1964; children: David, Sara, James; Candn. artist; oil, acrylic, watercolour, serigraphy, painted in most prov. of Can., U.S.A., Europe, the Orient; exhibits in Europe & N. Am.; work incl. landscape & people in environ. with romantic, classical quality; author: 'In Praise of Painting' 1981; 'The Dreamway' 1986; 'The Painter's Keys' 1994; Dir., Emily Carr College of Art and Design; Federation of Candn. Artists; Arena Theatre Company; Ivanhoe Heritage Foundation; Home: 12711 Beckett Rd., Surrey, B.C. V4A 2W9.

**GENNO, Charles N.,** B.A., M.A., Ph.D.; university professor; b. Toronto, Ont. 19 Nov. 1934; s. Lorne and Amy (Webb) G.; e. Univ. of Toronto B.A. 1957, M.A. 1959, Ph.D. 1961; m. Marianne d. John and Christine Engels 30 May 1960; one s.: Charles Ian; PROFESSOR, GERMAN, UNIV. OF TORONTO 1987– ; Alexander von Humboldt Rsch. Fellow (Tübingen, Germany) 1960–61; Lectr., Victoria Coll., Univ. of Toronto 1961–63; Asst. Prof. 1963–68; Assoc. Prof. 1968–87; Chair, Dept. of German 1989– ; Visiting Prof., Univ. of B.C. 1967; Guest Prof., Univ. of Trier, Germany 1973; author: 'Structured Language Practice and Grammatical Review' 2nd ed. 1990, 'German for Advanced Intermediates' 3rd ed. 1992; editor: 'The First World War in German Narrative Prose' 1980; recreations: tennis, travel, gardening; club: Bayview Country; Home: 32 Delair Cres., Thornhill, Ont. L3T 2M4; Office: 97 St. George St., Toronto, Ont. M5S 1A1.

**GENT, Michael,** D.Sc., F.S.S., F.I.S., F.I.M.A., educator; b. Stanley, Co. Durham, Eng. 4 May 1934; s. John and Winifred Elizabeth (Gibbon) G.; e. Henry VIII Grammar Sch. Coventry 1952; Univ. of Durham B.Sc., M.Sc. 1957; m. Betty d. William Purvis, Co. Durham, Eng. 20 July 1957; children: Steven Michael, Heather Margaret; PROF. OF CLIN. EPIDEMIOL. AND BIOSTAT., McMASTER UNIV.; mem. Scient. Comte. Candn. Heart Foundation 1971–1980; Vice Chrmn. of Comte. 1975–77 and Chrmn. Scient. Review Comte. 1977–80; mem. Med. Research Council Comte. for Assessment Diagnostic & Treatment Procedures 1972–75, mem. Grants Panel C D1 Clin. Investigation and Epidemiol. Nat. Cancer Inst. Can. 1973–74; mem. Petch Task Force on Health Research Requirements 1974–75; mem. of Exec. of Council on Thrombosis, Amer. Heart Assn. 1975–77; Co-Chrmn. Subcomte. on Clin. Trials, Internat. Comte. on Haemostasis & Thrombosis 1978–82; Chrmn. Subcomte. on Clin. Trials 1982–84; mem. Exec. Comte. Internat. Soc. of Clinical Biostatistics 1978–80; mem. Comte. for Clin. Trials, Med. Research Council 1979–86 (Chrmn. of Comte. 1982–86); Chrmn. Research Comte., Council of Ont. Faculties of Med. 1980–82; Chrmn., Health Research Personnel Development Ctte., Ont. Min. of Health 1981–88; mem., Med. Research Counc. 1982–89 (Vice Pres. 1987–89); mem., Bd. of Dirs., Soc. for Clinical Trials 1984–88; mem., Bd. of Dirs. of Heart and Stroke Found. of Ont. 1985–87 (mem., Rsch. Policy Ctte. 1985–87); author several book chapters and over 180 scient. articles methodology clin. trials and reports of studies relating to thrombosis; Fellow, Am. Statistical Assn., 1981; mem. Editorial Bd. of Applied Stat. (J.R.S.S. Series C) 1967–69, Review Ed. of Applied Stat 1968; Ed. Bd. of Stroke 1982–87, 1992– ; Secty. Leeds/Bradford Sectn. of Royal Stat. Soc. 1968–69; mem. Biometric Soc.; Am. Stat. Assn.; Candn. Soc. Clin. Investigation; Am. Heart Assn.; Internat. Epidemiol. Assn.; Candn. Cardiovascular Soc.; Internat. Soc. Clin. Biostatistics; Internat. Soc. on Thrombosis & Haemostasis; P. Conservative; R. Catholic; recreations: travel, golf; Home: 11 Ridgeview Court, Ancaster, Ont. L9G 3X9; Office: Hamilton Civic Hosps. Rsch. Centre, Henderson Gen. Hosp., 711 Concession St., Hamilton, Ont. L8V 1C3.

**GENTLES, Ian,** B.A., M.A., Ph.D.; university professor; b. Kingston, Jamaica 25 Oct. 1941; s. John and Margaret Jane (Ellison) G.; e. Univ. of Toronto B.A. (Hons.) 1963, M.A. 1965; Univ. of London Ph.D. 1969; m. Sandra d. Gordon and Carol Jack 31 Aug. 1963; children: Stephen, Peter; PROFESSOR & CHAIR, DEPT. OF HISTORY, GLENDON COLLEGE YORK UNIV. 1993– ; Asst. Prof., Glendon Coll., York Univ. 1969; Dean of Students & Master of Residence 1970–75; Assoc. Prof. 1974; Assoc. Principal, Academic Affairs 1985–87; Fellow, Royal Historical Soc. 1978– ; Visiting Scholar, Corpus Christi College Cambridge 1982–83; Visiting Fellow, Clare Hall Cambridge 1993; Vice-Pres. & Rsch. Dir., Human Life Rsch. Inst. 1983–93; Chairman, London House Assn. of Can. 1984–87; Anglican; Rector's Warden, St. Bartholomew's Ch. 1990–92; Mem., Toronto Chamber Soc. 1991– ; author: 'The New Model Army in England, Ireland and Scotland, 1645–1653' 1992; co-author: 'Public Policy, Private Voices: the Euthanasia Debate' 1992; editor: 'A Time to Choose Life' 1990, 'Care of the Dying and the Bereaved' 1982; recreations: tennis, squash, canoeing, music; Home: 428 Roselawn Ave., Toronto, Ont. M5N 1J8; Office: 2275 Bayview Ave., Toronto, Ont. M4N 3M6.

**GEORGANAS, Nicolas D.,** Ph.D., P.Eng.; educator; b. Athens, Greece 15 June 1943; s. Demetrios N. and Athanasia (Kotsovou) G.; e. Nat. Tech. Univ. of Athens Dipl.Ing. 1966; Univ. of Ottawa Ph.D. 1970; m. Jacynthe Savard 1972; two s. Nikita, Emmanuel; PROF. OF ELECT. ENG., UNIV. OF OTTAWA 1980– ; Lectr. present Univ. 1970, Asst. Prof. 1971, Assoc. Prof. 1976, Chrmn. of Elect. Eng. 1981–84, Dean of Eng. 1986–93; Visiting Prof. IBM Centre of Studies & Rsch. La Gaude, France 1977–78; Invited Prof. Bull Transac, Paris and Institut Nat. de Recherche en Info. et Automatique, Paris 1984–85; Visiting Prof., BNR, Ottawa 1993–94; Cons. Can. Dept. of Communications 1978–83; Bell Canada 1986– ; mem. and subsequently Chrmn. Elect. Eng. Grants Selection Ctte. NSERC 1983–86; recipient Greek Govt. Scholarship 1966; NRC Postgrad. Scholarship 1967–70; author numerous publs. and rsch. reports; Fellow, Inst. Elect. & Electronic Engs.; mem., New York Acad. of Science; mem. Assn. Profl. Engs. Prov. Ont.; recreations: swimming, reading; Home: 1915 Montereau Ave., Orleans, Ont. K1C 5W9; Office: Ottawa, Ont. K1N 6N5.

**GEORGE, David Lewis,** M.B.A., C.E.T; communications executive; b. Corner Brook, Nfld. 6 Jan. 1940; s. Reuben Apsey and Stella Mae (Hodder) G.; e. Horton Acad. of Acadia Univ., Wolfville, N.S., Sr. Matric. 1955; Univ. of N.B., Bus. Admin. 1955–57; Ryerson Poly. Inst., Toronto, Grad. Electronic Technol. 1960; Univ. of Toronto, Faculty Mgmt. Studies, Grad. M.B.A. 1985; m. Clara, d. George and Katie Cater, 22 June 1963; children: Lynne, Lisa, Mark; PRES. & CHIEF OPER. OFFR., IMAGINEERING LTD. (a Candn. communications consulting and project mgmt. co.); Chief Eng., Nfld. Broadcasting Co. 1961–68, 1970–72; Communications Design and Planning Eng., Nfld. Hydro 1968–70; Pres., Inc. Engs.(U.S. subs. of Imagineering Ltd.; Pres.and Dir., Ontel Communications; Editorial Vice Pres. & Fellow, Soc. of Motion Picture and Television Engineers (past Secy. and Chrmn., Toronto Section); author and co-author of sev. communications ind. papers, articles in learned soc. jours., etc.; recreations: flying, sailing, amateur radio, photography; clubs: Toronto Hydroplane and Sailing Club; North York Power Squadron; Toronto Repeater Orgn.; Home: 20 Rondeau Dr., Willowdale, Ont. M2H 1R4; Office: Suite 112, 95 Barber Greene Rd., Don Mills, Ont. M3C 3E9.

**GEORGE, David V.,** B.Sc., Ph.D.; educator; b. Cardiff, Wales 14 Feb. 1938; s. David Lewis and Elizabeth Jane (Poole) G.; e. Cathays Grammar Sch., Cardiff, 1955; Univ. of Wales, B.Sc. 1958, Ph.D. 1961; m. Eila Mae, B.A., d. Maurice Connor and Agnes Schommer, Victoria B.C., 13 May 1967; children: Rhiannon Elizabeth, David Maurice, Glenys Myfanwy; CONSULTANT, MIN. OF ADVANCED EDUC. & JOB TRAINING; Head of Chem. Dept., Notre Dame Univ. of Nelson, 1964–69, Dean of Studies, 1969–75; Vice-Pres., Notre Dame Univ. of Nelson, 1975, Pres., 1976; Pres., Northwest Community Coll., B.C., 1976–90; Post-doctoral Research Fellow Univ. of B.C. 1961, Teaching Fellow 1963; mem. Extve. Comte. B.C. Educ. Research Council; Dir. Educ. Research Inst. B.C.; B.C. Council for Leadership in Educ.; mem., Selkirk Coll. Bd.; Royal Inst. Chem.; Pro-Life Society of B.C.; Pres., Nelson and Dist. United Way; Pres. Terrace and Dist. Arts Council; Pres. Northwest Regional Arts Council; Pres. Terrace Concert Soc.; School Trustee, Nelson, Sci. Counc. of B.C.; Alderman, City of Terrace; author 'Principles of Quantum Chemistry' 1972 and various papers and articles in prof. journs. & outdoors mags.; R. Catholic; recreations: hunting, fishing, choral singing; natural history; Address: 4904 Gair Avenue, Terrace, B.C. V8G 2K2.

**GEORGE, Denis Richard John,** F.I.A., F.C.I.A., A.S.A.; actuary; b. Ruspidge, England 13 May 1921; s. William and Bessie (Brain) G.; e. Monmouth School, England 1931–40; m. Eileen d. Frank and Alice Nash 1951; children: Lesley, Hilary, Andrew, Amanda; DIRECTOR EMERITUS, WILLIAM M. MERCER LTD. 1988– ; Dir., William M. Mercer Limited 1957–66; Vice-Pres. & Gen. Mgr., Westmount Life Insur. Co. 1966–69; Dir. 1967–70; Pres. & Dir., Westmount American Life INsur. Co. 1969–70; Dir., William M. Mercer Ltd. 1970–88; Managing Dir. New York 1982–88; Vice-Chair, William M. Mercer Ltd. 1984–88; Mem., Inst. of Actuaries Students' Soc. (Journal Ed.) 1953–54; Inst. of Actuaries (U.K.) (Fellow 1951); Candn. Inst. of Actuaries (Fellow 1965); Soc. of Actuaries (Assoc. 1955); Chair, Anglican Diocesan Pension Ctte. Montreal; Trustee M.D. Realty Fund; Councillor, City of Beaconsfield; author: 'Experience Rating Unemployment Insurance,' 'A Simple Computer Model to Forecast Income and Outgo of Unemployment Insurance Programmes'; co-author: 'The Use of Computerized Cash Flow Models of U.S. Unemployment Insurance Programmes'; recreations: photography, sailing; clubs: St-James's, Royal St-Lawrence Yacht, Summerlea Golf & Country; Home: 19 East Gables Court, Beaconsfield, Que. H9W 4G9; Office: 600 de Maisonneuve W., Room 1100, Montreal, Que. H3A 2N4.

**GEORGE, Donald A.,** M.S., Sc.D., P.Eng.; university professor and administrator; b. Cambridge (Galt), Ont. 24 Apr. 1932; s. Roy Abbott and Florence Margaret G.; e. McGill Univ. B.Eng. 1955; Stanford Univ. M.S. 1956; M.I.T. Sc.D. 1959; m. June d. Percy Coates-Baxendale 13 Dec. 1987; children: Douglas & Patricia (George), Mark, Sandra, & Andrea (Landsburg); PROF., ELECTRICAL & ELECTRONIC ENGR. & ASSOC. PRO-VICE-CHANCELLOR FOR ACADEMIC AFFAIRS, HONG KONG UNIV. OF SCI. & TECHNOL. 1991– ; Asst. Prof., Univ. of N.B.; Asst., Assoc., Full Prof., Carleton Univ. (Dean of Engr. 1969–75; Dir., Sch. of Cont. Edn. 1977–79); Prof., Simon Fraser Univ. (Dean of Applied Sci. & Dir., Sch. of Engr. Sci. 1982–91); research: nonlinear systems late 1950s; adaptive equalizers for communications 1960s; human factors in communications 1970s; num. pubns. & consultancies; Pres., Donald A. George & Assoc. 1975–81; Dir., B.C. Rsch. Corp. 1984–91; Mem., I.E.E.E.; Assn. of Profl. Engrs. of B.C.; recreations: nordic skiing, bicycling; Office: School of Engineering Science, Simon Fraser Univ., Burnaby, B.C. V5A 1S6.

**GEORGE, James,** B.A.; retired diplomat; foundation executive; b. Toronto, Ont. 14 Sept. 1918; s. Ruggles Kerr and Helen (Heaton) G.; e. Upper Can. Coll. 1936; Univ. of Grenoble 1938; Univ. of Toronto Trinity Coll. B.A. 1940 (Rhodes Scholar); m. Caroline d. C.D. and Caroline Parfitt 7 Nov. 1942; children: Daniel, Graham, Caroline Randolph (Dolphi); served with RCNVR 1940–45, rank Lt. Commdr., Head Candn. Naval Hist. Overseas London 1943–45; joined Dept. External Affairs 1945–77 serving Athens 1945–48, UN New York 1951–55 (Dep. Perm. Rep.), Disarmament Ctte. New York & Geneva; Min. and Dep. Rep. NATO Paris 1957–60; High Comnr. to Ceylon (Sri Lanka) 1960–64; Head of Eur. Div. Ottawa 1964–66; Min. Paris 1966–67; High Comnr. to India and Ambassador to Nepal 1967–72; Ambassador to Iran, Kuwait, Oman, Bahrain, UAE, Qatar 1972–77; Founder and Pres. Threshold Found. London 1977–82, Sec.-Treas. New York 1982–84; Pres., Sadat Peace Found., New York 1984–92; Chrmn. Harmonic Arts Soc., Cath. St. John the Divine, New York 1984– ; Founding mem. Rainforest Action Network San Francisco 1987; Chrmn. Asian NGO Conf. Tropical Forests New Delhi 1987; Leader, Friends of the Earth Internat. scientific mission to Kuwait and the Gulf to assess post-war environmental damage 1991; subject one hr. Candn. TV Special Toronto 'James George Leaves India' 1974; author various articles; mem. Soc. Traditional Studies; Asian Arts Soc.; recreations: skiing, sailing; Home: 270 Forest Hill Rd., Toronto, Ont. M5P 2N6; Office: 129 Stephensburg Rd., Port Murray, N.J. 07865.

**GEORGE, John Alan,** M.Sc., Ph.D.; educator; b. Lloydminster, Sask. 9 Nov. 1943; s. late John Edward and Margaret Anne (Brown) G.; e. elem. and high schs. Alta. and Sask.; Univ. of Alta. B.Sc. 1964, M.Sc. 1966; Stanford Univ. Ph.D. 1971; two s. Geoffrey Alan, David Edward; PROFESSOR, UNIV. OF WATERLOO 1993– ; Instr. Univ. of Alta. 1966–67; Research Asst. Stanford Univ. 1967–71; Asst. Prof. of Computer Science Univ. of Waterloo 1971; Assoc. Prof. 1973; Prof. 1977–86, 1993– ; Dean of Mathematics Univ. of Waterloo 1980–86; Vice-Pres., Academic and Provost, Univ. of Waterloo 1988–93; Distinguished Prof., Univ. of Tennessee and Distinguished Scientist, Oak Ridge National Laboratory, Oak Ridge TN 1986–88; Consultant to various co's and govt. agencies Can., U.S.A. and U.K. incl. IBM (U.S.), U.S. Atomic Energy Comn. 1972–74, NASA Langley Research Centre 1974–90, Can. Centre for Inland Waters 1977–79, U.S. Dept. Energy 1980– , Atomic Energy Research Estab. (U.K.); recipient IBM Grad. Fellowship 1969–70; G.E. Forsythe Mem. Award for leadership in numerical mathematics, Assn. Computing Machinery 1982; co-author 'Computer Solution of Large Sparse Positive Definite Systems' 1981; author or co-author over 80 research articles scient. computation and math. software; mem. various ed. bds.; mem. Assn. Computing Machinery; Soc. Indust. & Applied Math. (Counc. Mem. 1987–90); ACM Special Interest Group on Numerical Math. (Chrmn. 1980–83); Fellow: Royal Soc. of Can.; IEEE; Inst. Math. & Its Applications (UK); Inst. Combinatories & Its Applications; recreations: squash, skiing, reading; Home: 595 Wingrove Court, Waterloo, Ont. N2T 2C1; Office: DC 3124, Davis Centre, Univ. of Waterloo, Waterloo, Ont. N2L 3G1.

**GEORGE, Peter James,** M.A., Ph.D.; educator; b. Toronto, Ont. 12 Sept. 1941; s. Ralph Langlois and Kathleen May (Larder) G.; e. Univ. of Toronto Schs. 1958; Univ. of Toronto B.A. 1962, M.A. 1963, Ph.D. 1967; m. Gwendolyn Jean d. Evan and Christine Scharf 19 Oct. 1962; children: Michael James, Katherine Jane; PRES., COUNCIL OF ONTARIO UNIVERSITIES 1991– ; PROF. OF ECON., McMASTER UNIV. 1980– , mem. Bd. Govs. 1981–84, 1986–89; apptd. Mem., Ont. Counc. on University Affairs 1987–91; Lectr. McMaster Univ. 1965, Asst. Prof. 1967, Assoc. Prof. 1971, Assoc. Dean of Grad. Studies 1974–79, Dean of Social Sciences 1980–89; Special Lectr. Univ. of Toronto 1967; Visiting Lectr. Univ. of Cambridge 1974; Econ., Govt. of Ont. 1963; Project Mgr. Tanzania Tourist Corp. 1970–71; author 'Government Subsidies and the Construction of the Canadian Pacific Railway' 1981; 'The Emergence of Industrial America: Strategic Factors in American Economic Growth since 1870' 1982; many articles; Chrmn., Counc. of Deans of Arts and Science of Ont. 1988–89; Dir. Great Lakes Anglers' Assn. 1978–80; Dir., Burlington Hamilton-Wentworth Un. Way 1990– ; Queen Elizabeth Hosp. 1992– ; Dir., Ont. Chamber of Commerce 1994– ; mem. Candn. Econ. Assn. (Extve. Council 1974–77; Chrmn. Econ. Hist. Comte. 1974–80); Candn. Hist. Assn.; Am. Econ. Assn.; Econ. Hist. Assn.; recreations: angling, canoe-tripping, squash; Home: 91 South St. W., Dundas, Ont. L9H 4C7; Office: 444 Yonge St., Ste. 203, Toronto, Ont. M5B 2H4.

**GEORGE, Richard Lee,** B.Sc., J.D.; oil and gas executive; b. Colorado 16 May 1950; s. Albert H. and Betty Lou (McDill) G.; e. Colorado State Univ. B.Sc. 1973; Univ. of Houston J.D. 1977; Harvard Business Sch., P.M.D. Program 1984; m. Julie G. d. George and Corinne White 4 June 1972; children: Zachary Ryan, Matthew Shane, Emily Christine; CHRMN., PRES. & C.E.O., SUNCOR INC. 1993– ; Dep. Mng. Dir., Sun Oil Britain (London) 1982–86; Dis. Mgr. (Aberdeen, Scotland) 1986–87; Vice-Pres. Internat. E. & P., Sun Exploration & Prod. (Dallas, Texas) 1987–88; Mng. Dir. (London, England) 1988–91; Pres. & C.O.O., Suncor Inc. 1991, Pres. & C.E.O. 1991–93; Mem., State Bar of Texas; Registered Profl. Engineer, Texas; recreations: skiing, tennis, fitness; Office: 36 York Mills Rd., North York, Ont. M2P 2C5.

**GEORGE, Vice-Admiral Robert E.,** CMM, CD, B.Sc.; naval officer; b. Prince Albert, Sask. 6 Oct. 1940; s. Douglas E. and Mabel G. (Stanley) G.; e. North Vanc. H.S. 1958; Univ. of B.C., B.Sc. 1962; m. Lois d. Gwen and Henry Elwood 6 Feb. 1965; children: Haydn, Craig, Ryan; CANADIAN MILITARY REPRESENTATIVE TO NATO 1992– ; joined RCN 1961 serving on var. ships based on Pacific & Atlantic coasts; comdr., HMCS Margaree 1974–75, Iroquois 1978–79 (destroyers); Defence Attache, Candn. Embassy in Tokyo 1980–82; comdr., destroyer squadron, Esquimalt 1982–84; naval staff, Defence H.Q., Ottawa 1984–87; Commander Maritime Command, Commander Atlantic Region, Canadian Navy 1989–91; Depy. Chief of Defence Staff, Ottawa 1991–92; Anglican; recreations: skiing, squash; Office: NATO HQ, 1110 Brussels, Belgium.

**GEORGE, Roger M.;** farm lobbyist; b. England 28 March 1946; s. Leslie James and Eva Mary (Bainbridge) G.; e. Worcester Royal Grammar Sch. 1963; Pershore Horticultural Inst. 1965; m. Rosemary d. John and Georgina Dixon 10 Nov. 1973; one s.: Michael; PRESIDENT, ONT. FEDERATION OF AGRICULTURE 1990– ; immigrated to Canada from England 1972; livestock & grain farmer, Northern Ont. 1972– ; Founder, East Nipissing Fed. of Agric. 1981; elected to Ont. Fed. of Agric. Bd. of Dir. 1981; Extve. Ctte. 1987–90 1st Vice-Pres.; Bd. Mem., Candn. Fed. of Agric. 1990– ; Chair, Agricultural Publishing Co.; Mem., Premier's Round Table on Envir. & Econ. 1993– ; Don Mazankowski's Agric. Policy Review Task Force 1990–92; Ont. Crop Insur. Review Ctte. 1986–87; Ont. Farm Income Stabilization Comn. 1985– ; Co-chair, Farm Envir. Coalition 1992– ; farm rep. on several internat. trade missions regarding GATT talks in Geneva; Advanced Agric. Leadership Prog. graduate 1985–86; Dir., Foundation for Rural Living; recreations: sports, reading; Home: R.R. 4, Powassan, Ont. P0H 1Z0; Office: 491 Eglinton Ave. W., Ste. 500, Toronto, Ont. M5N 3A2.

**GEORGE, Roy Edwin,** B.Sc., M.A., Ph.D.; educator (retired) and business consultant; b. Liverpool, Eng. 17 Feb. 1923; s. Frederick Williamson and Minnie (Crabtree) G.; e. Bootle Grammar Sch. 1934–39; Univ. of London, B.Sc. 1949, Ph.D. 1967; Bristol Univ. M.A. 1957; m. Jean d. Clifford and Lillian Morgan 10 Sept. 1949; two d. Michele, Karen; Professor Emeritus, Dalhousie Univ. 1988– , Dean of Mgmt. Studies 1986–88, and William A. Black Prof. 1974–88; served with RAF 1941–46; Asst. Personnel Mgr. South Western Gas Bd. Eng. 1949–56; Area Staff Mgr. Nat. Coal Bd. 1956–60; Asst. Prof. Saint Mary's Univ. Halifax 1960–63; Assoc. Prof. present Univ. 1963–65, Prof. 1965–88; Vice Pres. BGI Management Consultants Ltd. 1964–86; econ. cons. various govts. and bus.; Dir. Maritime Provs. C. of C. 1973–74; author: 'Technological Redundancy in a Small Isolated Society' 1969; 'A Leader and a Laggard' 1970; 'The Life and Times of Industrial Estates Limited' 1974; 'Targeting High-Growth Industry' 1983; 'Understanding the Canadian Economy' 1988; mem. Candn. Assn. Univ. Teachers (Vice Pres. 1965–66, Treas. 1966–67); Candn. Econ. Assn.; Home: 208 – 1350 Oxford St., Halifax, N.S. B3H 3Y8; Office: Dalhousie Univ., Halifax, N.S. B3H 3J5.

**GEORGETTI, Kenneth V.;** labour executive; b. Trail, B.C. 12 May 1952; PRES. AND CHIEF EXTVE. OFFR., B.C. FEDN. OF LABOUR 1986– , re-el. 1992, Vice-Pres. 1984–86; Pres., Local 480, United Steelworkers of Am. 1981; Provincial Vice-Pres., Candn. Labour Congress 1986– ; (& mem. Extve. Counc.); mem., Bd. of Dirs., VLC Properties; Bd. Mem., Public Policy Forum; Chair, B.C. Federation of Retired Union Members; Mem. of the Bd., B.C. Transit Authority; ABC Canada; Mem. of Dean's Advisory Council, UBC Faculty of Commerce and Business Admin.; mem. Bd. of Govs., Labour College of Canada; Chrmn., Pacific Region Labour Educ. Studies Ctr.; Bd. of Dirs., Molson Indy; Hon. Chair, Assoc. of Learning Disabled Adults; Chair, Working Opportunities Fund, Working Enterprises; Office: 4279 Canada Way, Burnaby, B.C. V5G 1H1.

**GERACI, Daniel T.;** financial executive; b. New Britain, Conn. 12 June 1957; s. Benedict J. and Constance M. (Ciarcia) G.; e. Lafayette College; m. Paulina d. Filippo and Teresa Fortuna 11 April 1992; EXECUTIVE VICE-PRES. & DIRECTOR, MIDLAND WALWYN CAPITAL, INC. 1991– ; & CHAIRMAN, HERCULES INTERNATIONAL MANAGEMENT, LLC 1993– ; var. positions, E.F. Hutton & Co. 1980–86; Vice-Pres. &

Dir., National Sales Dev. 1986–88; Extve. Vice-Pres. & Dir., Retail Div., Walwyn Stodgell Ltd. 1988–90; owner of brokerage industry sales devel. cons. firm (Connecticut)1990–91; Guest Lecturer, Securities Industry Inst.; recreations: astronomy, the Sciences, writing Science Fiction; Home: 69 John St., Thornhill, Ont. L3T 1Y3; Office: 40 King St. W., Suite 3500, Toronto, Ont. M5H 4A1.

**GERAD, Peter,** B.Sc., M.B.A., F.C.I.S.; banker; b. Dresden, Germany; e. Sir George Williams Univ. B.Sc. 1964; Univ. of Western Ont. M.B.A. 1968; SENIOR VICE PRES. & SECRETARY, THE BANK OF NOVA SCOTIA 1986– ; Production Process Designer, Northern Electric Co. 1964–66; joined The Bank of N.S. King & Victoria Br. Toronto 1968; Supvr., Special Projects, Internat. Gen. Admin. 1970; Asst. Comptroller 1971; Comptroller 1972; Mgr., Frankfurt Br., W. Germany 1973; Asst. Gen. Mgr., subs. cos., Admin., Internat. 1976; Extve. Asst. to Pres. 1978; Sr. Vice-Pres., Finance & Admin. 1983; Sr. Vice-Pres. & Extve. Asst. to Chairman 1985; Chrmn. & Pres., Scotia Realty Antilles N.V.; Senior Vice-Pres. & Dir., Brunswick Square Ltd.; Pres. & Dir., Tour Scotia Ltd.; Scotia Factors (1985) Limited; Scotia Ventures Limited; First Vice-Pres. & Dir., Scotia Centre Limited; Vice-Pres. & Dir., Fredericton Devel. Limited; Kings Place Opns. Limited; Dir., Scotia Leasing Limited; Scotia Realty Limited; Scotia-Toronto Dominion Leasing Limited; The Bank of N.S. Properties Inc.; Kings Place II Limited; Spring Garden Devel. Corp.; Market Sq. Leaseholds Ltd.; NOVA Corp. of Alberta; Internat. Monetary Conference; Scotia Properties Quebec Inc.; Office: 44 King St. W., Toronto, Ont. M5H 1H1.

**GERAETS, Theodore F.,** L.Ph., L.Th., Ph.D.; educator; b. The Hague, Netherlands 12 March 1926; s. Francis J. and Cecilia M. (Schlick) G.; e. Heythrop Coll., Berchmanianum L.Ph. 1951, Canisianum L.Th. 1957; Gregorianum, Sorbonne, Paris Ph.D. 1969; m. Heidi d. Otto and Christine Keim 26 Feb. 1967; two d. Isabelle, Stéphanie; PROF. OF PHILOS., UNIV. OF OTTAWA 1974– ; Lectr. Berchmanianum Nijmegen 1957–59; Univ. of Ottawa 1966, Asst. Prof. 1967, Assoc. Prof. 1971, Prof. 1974; Dean and Chrmn. of Philos. 1976–80; Pres. Nat. Capital Region Chapter Council of Candns. 1985–89; Exec. Dir. and Chair 'Network on the Constitution' 1991– ; author: 'Vers une nouvelle philosophie transcendantale' 1971; 'Lo Spirito Assoluto Come Apertura del Sistema Hegeliano' 1985; ed. proceedings 5 internat. confs.; transl. (with W.A. Suchting and H.S. Harris) of Hegel: 'The Encyclopaedia Logic' 1991; mem. Candn. Philosophical Assoc.; Hegel Soc. Am; Internat. Hegel Vereinigung; Internat. Hegel Gesellschaft; Internat. Gesellschaft fur Dialektische Philosophie; Soc. Phenomenology & Exist. Philos.; Merleau-Ponty Circle; Home: 2018 Rideau River Dr., Ottawa, Ont. K1S 1V2; Office: 65 University St., Ottawa, Ont. K1N 6N5.

**GERBER, Douglas E.,** M.A., Ph.D.; educator; b. North Bay, Ont. 14 Sept. 1933; s. Earl Jacob and Bertha Thelma (Cox) G.; e. Univ. of W. Ont. B.A. 1955, M.A. 1956; Univ. of Toronto Ph.D. 1959; one d. Allison Suzanne; PROF. AND CHRMN. OF CLASSICAL STUDIES, UNIV. OF W. ONT. 1969– ; (presently holds William Sherwood Fox Chair of Classics); author 'A Bibliography of Pindar 1513–1966' 1969; 'Euterpe: An Anthology of Early Greek Lyric, Elegiac and Iambic Poetry' 1970; 'Emendations in Pindar 1513–1972' 1976; 'Pindar's Olympian One: A Commentary' 1982; 'Lexicon in Bacchylidem' 1984; ed. 'Greek Poetry and Philosophy. Studies in Honour of Leonard Woodbury' 1984; over 40 articles ancient Greek poetry; mem. Ed. Bd. 'Phoenix' 1972–74, 1979–81; mem. Ont. Classical Assn. (Pres. 1968–70); Classical Assn. Can. (Treas. 1960–62, Vice Pres. 1986–88, Pres. 1988–90); Am. Philol. Assn. (Ed. Transactions 1974–82; mem. Ed. Bd. of Assn. 1974–82, Chrmn. 1978); Corr. mem. Quaderni Urbinati di Cultura Classica; served with RCN (Reserve), rank Lt.; Anglican; Home: 2 Grosvenor St., London, Ont. N6A 1Y4; Office: London, Ont. N6A 3K7.

**GEREIN, Hon. William Frank,** B.A., LL.B.; judge; b. Regina, Sask. 16 Apr. 1939; s. Anthony Benedict and Mary Frances (Molloy) G.; e. Univ. of Sask. B.A. 1960, LL.B. 1963; m. Eileen d. Michael and Wilhelmina Bihler 5 Sept. 1964; children: Anthony, Michelle, Katherine; JUDGE, COURT OF QUEEN'S BENCH, SASK. 1980– ; law practice Gerrand, Gerein, McLellan & Mulatz, Regina 1964–80; Home: 2809 Louise St., Saskatoon, Sask. S7J 3L2; Office: 520 Spadina Cres. E., Saskatoon, Sask. S7K 3G7.

**GERICH, John E.;** politician; farmer; b. Leask, Sask. 13 Jan. 1947; s. John and Paula Bernadette (Fortier) G.; e. Leask H.S. 1965; Bus. Admin. course 1965–66; Royal Candn. Mounted Police Acad. 1966–67; m. Judy d. Robert and Alice Renaud 30 Nov. 1968; children: John Jr., Judd; Assoc. Min. of Econ. Diversification & Trade 1989–.. & Min. Resp. for Sask. Liquor Bd., Govt. of Saskatchewan 1990–..; RCMP Officer 1967–72; farmer 1972– ; Grain Buyer & Asst. Mgr., Cargill Grain Co. 1972–82; 1st elected M.L.A. Saskatchewan for Redberry Constituency 1982; re-elected & apptd. Govt. Whip 1986; Mem., Sask. Round Table on the Environ.; Order-in-Council Review Ctte.; Agriculture Caucus; Dir., Sask. Property Mngt. Corp.; recreations: hockey, fastball, big game hunting, snowmobiling, dirt biking, flying (working towards pilot's licence); Home: Box 337, Blaine Lake, Sask. S0J 0J0.

**GERIN, Jacques;** consulting engineer; b. Montréal, Qué. 19 Feb. 1938; s. Maurice and Marcelle (Mercier) G.; e. Coll. Jean-de-Brébeuf B.A. 1956; Ecole Polytechnique, Univ. de Montréal B.Sc.A. and Civil Eng. degree 1962; Univ. of North Carolina Master's Degree in Regional Planning 1968; m. Odile Pelletier 5 May 1962; children: Michel, Marc, Anne-Marie; PRÉS., HATCH & ASSOCIÉS INC.; Exec. Sec. Internat. Student Conf. Leiden, Holland 1962–64, Planning Eng. and Project Dir. Surveyer Nenniger & Chênevert Inc. 1964–70; Dir. Gen. Sorès Ltée, Montréal and Lectr. in Regional Planning Univ. de Montréal 1970–71; Vice Pres. CIDA Bilateral Progs. 1971–74; Asst. Sec. to Cabinet (Priorities & Planning) Privy Council Office 1975–77; Sr. Asst. Dep. Min. Environment Can. 1977–82, Dep. Min. 1982–85; Assoc. Dep. Min. (North) Indian & Northern Affairs Can. 1985–89; Home: 4150 Avenue Old Orchard, Montréal, Qué. H4A 3B2; Office: 5, Place Ville Marie, Ste. 100, Montréal, Qué. H3B 2G2.

**GERIN-LAJOIE, Jean;** university professor; b. Montreal, Que. 16 Mar. 1928; s. Alexandre and Madeleine (Beaudry) G.; e. St.-Louis Univ. M.A. 1947; Rhodes Scholar, Oxford Univ.; McGill Univ. Ph.D. 1953; m. Micheline Letellier d. Edouard and Simone Letellier de Saint Just 26 Aug. 1969; children: Michèle, José, Isabelle; PROFESSOR, ECOLE DES HAUTES ETUDES COMMERCIALES 1984– ; Staff Rep., United Steelworkers of Am. 1952–65; Dist. Dir. 1965–81; Vice-Pres. Que. Fed. of Labour 1959–81; mem. Comm. Consultative du Travail 1984–85; Chevalier, Ordre Nat. du Qué. 1985; author: 'La lutte syndicale chez les Métallos' 1976; 'Les Métallos, 1936–1981' 1983; 'Les Relations du Travail au Québec' 1991; recreations: walking, skiing, tennis; Home: 571 Champagneur, Outremont, Que. H2V 3P4; Office: 5255 Decelles, Montreal, Que. H3T 1V6.

**GERIN-LAJOIE, Paul;** b. Montreal, P.Q. 23 Feb. 1920; s. Henri and Pauline (Dorion) G-L.; e. Jean-de-Brebeuf Coll.; Univ. of Montreal; Ph.D. (Oxford); m. Andrée Papineau, 1944; children, François, Bernard, Sylvie, Dominique; COUNSEL, GÉRIN-LAJOIE LABERGE, BARRISTERS & SOLICITORS; Pres. Projecto Internacional Inc.; el. to Que. Leg. for Vaudreuil-Soulanges in g.e. 1960; Min. of Youth, 5 July 1960–64; Min. of Educ. (1st) May 1964–66; re-el. g.e. 1966 (govt. def.); apptd. Vice Chrmn. of Fed. Prices & Incomes Comn. 1969–70; Pres., Candn. Inter. Development Agency (CIDA), 1970–77; Roman Catholic.

**GERMAIN, Claude,** M.A., Ph.D.; educator; b. St-Tite, Que. 27 June 194l; s. Maurice and Rose (Cossette) G.; e. St-Viateur Coll. Outremont, Que. B.A. 1962; Univ. de Montréal L.ès L. 1965, C.A.P.E.S. (Edn.) 1967, M.A. 1968; Univ. of Aix-Marseille, France Ph.D. (Linguistics) 1970; Univ. of Ottawa Ph.D. (Philos.) 1989; m. Louise d. Venance and Valéda Latour 29 July 1972; children: Todd Massey, François, David; PROF. OF LINGUISTICS, UNIV. DU QUEBEC A MONTREAL 1987– ; Lang. teacher Royal Mil. Coll. St-Jean, Que. 1965–67; Prof. of Gen. & Applied Linguistics, Head of French\Eng. & Rsch. Sectors, Second Language Inst., Univ. of Ottawa 1970–79; Prof. of Edn. Univ. de Montréal 1979–87, Visiting Prof. of Edn. 1973–74; Visiting Scholar and Visiting Researcher Stanford Univ. 1985–87; recipient Candn. Modern Lang. Review Best Article Award 1980; Ghyslaine Coutu-Vaillancourt Award 1985; author 'La notion de situation en linguistique' 1973, Eng. transl. 1979; 'La sémantique fonctionnelle' 1981, Spanish transl. 1986; 'Le Point sur l'Approche communicative' 1991; 'Évolution de l'Enseignement des Langues: 5000 Ans d'Histoire' 1993; co-author 'Le Français International' 1972–74, 'Introduction à la linguistique générale' (6 Vols.) 1981–85; 'L'évaluation de la communication écrite au primaire' (2 Vols.) 1985; ed. 'Etudes de linguistique appliquée' No. 56 1984, No. 75 1989; Sec. and Adm. Dir. Candn. Assn. Applied Linguistics 1971–76; Founding Dir. Centre d'étude sur la pédagogie de la communication en langue seconde 1983–85; Home: 2790 Belcourt, Longueuil, Que. J4M 1Y7; Office: C.P. 8888 Succ. A, Montreal, Que. H3C 3P8.

**GERMAIN, Doric,** B.A., M.A.; university professor, writer; b. Hearst, Ont. 14 April 1946; s. Ubald and Marie (Cantin) G.; e. Coll. Univ. de Hearst B.A. 1967; Univ. d'Ottawa M.A. 1971; m. Louise d. Aurèle and Marie Emard 22 Aug. 1970; children: Mylène, Nicolas, Andréanne; PROF., COLLEGE UNIVERSITAIRE DE HEARST 1990– ; Secondary School Teacher, Hearst 1969–70; Prof., Coll. de Hearst 1970–84; Pres., Senate 1978–80; Sec., Bd. of Gov. 1972–82; freelance translator 1984–90; Head, Council Serv. & Public Relns., Ottawa Separate Sch. Bd. 1987–88; Writer-in-Residence, Timmins Public Library 1989; Sec., Bourdeau Comn. of Inquiry on French-Language Serv. in Ont. (C.A.A.T.s); 3 Ontario Arts Council awards; rep. Ontario at 'Les Vingt-quatre heures du livre' Le Mans, France 1990; Trustee, Hearst Bd. of Edn. 1977–81; Mem., Assn. des auteurs de l'Ont.; Assn. des Traducteurs et Interprètes de l'Ont.; author: 'La Vengeance de l'orignal' 1980, 'Le Trappeur du Kabi' 1982, 'Poison' 1985, 'Le Soleil se lève au Nord' 1991 (novels); recreations: hunting, fishing; Home: Val-Côté, Box 1252, Hearst, Ont. P0L 1N0; Office: Box 580, Hearst, Ont. P0L 1N0.

**GERMAIN, Jean-Claude;** playwright, actor, director; b. Montréal, Qué. 18 June 1939; s. Jean and Mercedes (Cloutier) G.; e. Coll. Sainte-Marie 1957; Univ. de Montréal 1957–59; children: Christine, Renaud; Journalist & Drama Critic Petit Journal 1965–69; Exec. Sec. Centre d'Essai des auteurs dramatiques 1968–71; Co. Dir. Les Enfants de Chénier 1969–71 and Les petits enfants Laliberté 1971–73; Artistic Dir. Théâtre d'Aujourd'hui 1972–82; Dir. Playwrighting Dept. Ecole nationale de théâtre du Can. 1973–86; radio and TV commentator, raconteur 'Trouvez l'erreur', 'Faut voir ça', 'L'aventure'; actor 'L'Héritage'; conférencier; mem. Can. Council 1990– ; recipient Prix Victor Morin, Soc. Saint-Jean Baptiste 1977; author (plays) 'Diguidi diguidi Ha! Ha!' 1972; 'Les hauts et les bas de la vie d'une diva' 1976; 'Un pays dont la devise est je m'oublie' 1979; 'L'école des rêves' 1979; 'Les nuits de l'Indiva' 1983; 'Mamours et conjugat' 1983; 'A Canadian Play; une plaie canadienne' 1983; Sec. Assn. des directeurs de théâtre 1974–82; Radio series for CBC 1991–92; Series of 16 on history of Montréal, Théâtre d'Aujourd'hui 1993–94; recreations: pipe smoking, book collecting; Address: c/o Agence Goodwin, 2, 839 Sherbrooke est, Montréal, Qué. H2L 1K4.

**GERMAN, Andrew Barry (Tony);** writer; b. Ottawa, Ont. 28 Sept. 1924; s. P. Barry and Dorothy (Schofield) G.; e. Trinity College Sch. 1942; Royal Candn. Naval Coll., Royal Roads, B.C. 1943; Royal Naval Staff Coll., Greenwich, Eng. 1956; m. Sage d. Richard H. and Thérèse J. Ley 27 Mar. 1948; children: Richard B., Kiloran S., Sarah G., Andrew J.; Royal Candn. Navy 1942–66; commanded H.M.C.S. 'Sioux,' 'Micmac,' and 'Mackenzie'; retired as Commander; Pres., Hoverwork Canada Ltd. 1966–70; Dir. of Devel., Ashbury Coll. 1972–78; Founder & Extve. Dir., Forum for Young Canadians 1975–78; author of 6 books, writer/researcher of 6 films & radio scripts 1977–90; Cons., Nat. Rsch. Counc.; Transport Can.; Candn. Coast Guard 1967–70; Senate Ctte. on Nat. Finan. 1972; Counc. for Candn. Unity (Youth) 1978–79; Dept. of Nat. Defence 1980–83; Co-Pres., Ottawa Valley Book Fest.; Founding Pres., Wentworth Valley (N.S.) Ski Club; Past Dir., Candn. Ski Mus.; Hist. Soc. of the Gatineau; Mem., The Writer's Union of Can.; Candn. Soc. of Children's Authors, Illustrators and Performers; The Writers Devel. Trust; Naval Officers Assn. of Can.; author: 'Tom Penny' 1977, 'River Race' 1979, 'The Grand Canal' 1982, 'A Breed Apart' 1985 (novels); 'The Sea is at Our Gates: The History of the Canadian Navy' 1990; 'A Character of its Own: Ashbury College 1891–91,' 1991; recreations: skiing, sailing, wilderness canoeing; Home: Kingsmere, Old Chelsea, Que. J0X 2N0.

**GERMAN, The Hon. Judge Patricia Riley;** b. St. Catharines, Ont. 2 Jan. 1929; d. George Wilfrid and Mildred K. (Houston) Riley; e. Jarvis Coll. Inst. Toronto; Univ. of Toronto B.A. 1949; Osgoode Hall Law Sch. LL.B. 1966; York Univ. LL.M.; m. John B. German 9 Sept. 1950; children: John Bruce, Jacqueline Green, Timothy R., William M.; JUDGE, DISTRICT COURT ONT.; Alpha Gamma Delta; Anglican; Home: 62 Wellesley St. W., Toronto, Ont. M5S 2X3; Office: 361 University Ave., Toronto, Ont. M5G 1T3.

**GERRARD, John Watson,** B.A., B.Ch., D.M., F.R.C.P.(C); F.R.C.P. (L); pediatrician; b. N. Rhodesia 14 Apr. 1916; s. Herbert Shaw and Doris (Watson) G.; e. Oxford Univ. B.A. 1938; B.M., B.Ch. 1941, D.M. 1951; M.R.C.P. (London) 1947; F.R.C.P. (London) 1968;

F.R.C.P. (Canada) 1956; m. Lilian Elisabeth Whitehead, 28 Aug. 1941; children: Jonathan Michael, Peter, Christopher David; PROF. EMERITUS OF PEDIATRICS, UNIV. OF SASK.; served overseas in 2nd World War with R.A.M.C., in N. Africa, Italy, Palestine, 1941–45; John Scott Award, 1962; Ross Award of Canadian Paediatric Society 1985; United Church; recreation: ornithology; Home: 809 Colony St., Saskatoon, Sask. S7N 0S2.

**GERRY, Thomas Martin Farr,** B.A., M.A., B.Ed., Ph.D.; university professor; b. Toronto, Ont. 31 Jan. 1948; s. Thomas Martin Farr and Erma Frances (Rennick) G.; e. Lawrence Park C.I. 1967; Univ. of Toronto B.A. 1971, B.Ed. 1975; York Univ. M.A. 1973; Univ. of Western Ont. Ph.D. 1983; m. Linda d. Edith and William Lockridge 20 July 1985; children: Natalie Jane, Kathleen Alexandra; ASSOC. PROF. & DIR., CANDN. STUDIES PROGRAM, LAURENTIAN UNIV. 1988– ; Teacher, Grades 2 and 3, Hastings Co. Bd. of Edn. 1975–78; Asst. Prof. of English (limited-term appts.) Trent Univ. 1985–87, Acadia Univ. 1987–88; Juror, The Gabrielle Roy Prize in Candn. Lit. Criticism, Assn. for Candn. & Que. Literatures; Laurentian Univ. Rsch. Fund Awards 1990, 1992; Mem., Assn. for Candn. Studies; Assn. for Candn. Studies in the US; Assn. of Candn. College and Univ. Teachers of English; MLA; NEMLA (Chair, English Candn. Poetry Section 1990–91); Project Ploughshares; author: 'Contemporary Canadian and US Women of Letters'; editor: 'The York Pioneer' 1985; recreations: swimming, canoeing; Home: 1227 Belmont Dr., Sudbury, Ont. P3E 2T7; Office: Ramsey Lake Rd., Sudbury, Ont. P3E 2C6.

**GERSHATER, Raziel,** M.B., CL.B., FRCP(C), DABR; radiologist; b. Pretoria, South Africa 30 April 1939; s. Morris and Eva (Green) G.; e. Univ. of Pretoria M.B., CL.B. 1962; m. Jeanne d. Corrie and Tom Adelaar 1967; children: Tal Hannah, David Hirsch, Elize; CHIEF DIAGNOSTIC IMAGING, NORTH YORK GENERAL HOSP. 1981– ; Internship, Univ. of Witwatersrand 1963; Res., Internal Med. 1964; Michael Reese Hosp. Chicago 1965; Res., D.Radiology, Downstate Med. Ctr. and New York Univ. 1965–69; Instr., Radiology, N.Y. School of Med. 1969–70 immigrated to Can. 1970; Staff Radiologist, North York Gen. Hosp. 1970– ; Diplomate, Am. Bd. of Radiology; Fellow, Royal Coll. of Physicians & Surgeons; Mem., Ont. & Candn. med. assns. (Sec., Vice-Chair, Chair, section on Radiology, Ont. Med. Assn. 1977–800; Ont. Assn. Radiologists; author of articles on angiography and a book chapter; Home: 9 Montclair Ave., Toronto, Ont. M4V 1W2; Office: 401 Leslie St., Toronto, Ont. M2K 1E1.

**GERSON, Lloyd Phillip,** M.A., Ph.D.; educator; b. Chicago, Ill. 23 Dec. 1948; s. Solomon and Pearly (Adler) G.; e. Grinnell Coll. B.A. 1970; Univ. of Toronto M.A. 1971, Ph.D. 1975; m. Theresa d. John and Margaret Krystyniak 30 Aug. 1975; children: David, Elizabeth, Jonathan, Catherine, Veronica; PROF. OF PHILOS., ST. MICHAEL'S COLL., UNIV. OF TORONTO 1990– , Asst. Prof. 1974, Assoc. Prof. 1979; recipient Woodrow Wilson Fellowship 1970; Univ. Toronto Open Fellowship 1972; Woodrow Wilson Doctoral Dissertation Fellowship 1973; Phi Beta Kappa; author: 'God and Greek Philosophy' 1989; 'Plotinus' 1994; co-author: 'Aristotle. Selected Works' 1986; 'Aristotle's Politics' 1987; 'Hellenistic Philosophy' 1988; ed.: 'Graceful Reason' 1985; Home: 33 Lauder Ave., Toronto, Ont. M6H 3E2; Office: 81 St. Mary St., Toronto, Ont. M5S 1J4.

**GERSOVITZ, Sarah Valerie,** R.C.A.; artist; playwright; b. Montreal, Que.; d. Solomon and Eva (Gampel) Gamer; e. Macdonald Coll. Sch. for Teachers grad. 1939; Concordia Univ. Dipl. in Communication Studies 1978, M.A. in Creative Writing, Concordia Univ. 1982; Art Courses; Montreal Museum of Fine Arts Drawing, Design, Etching, Sculpture; L'Ecole des Arts appliqués Sculpture; Univ. of Alta. Japanese Wood-block Printing; Visual Arts Centre Rochester, N.Y. Photography; m. Benjamin Gersovitz 22 June 1944; children: Mark, Julia, Jeremy; has taught painting, drawing, printmaking, art history at Saidye Bronfman Centre as well as at Visual Arts Centre (Montreal), Pointe Claire Cultural Centre and Sir Sandford Fleming Coll.; solo exhns. incl. Montreal Museum of Fine Arts (twice); Universitat Kaiserslautern, West-Germany; Art Gall. of Greater Victoria; Burnaby Art Gall.; Art Gall. of Hamilton; Mount Saint-Vincent Univ.; Univ. of Alta.; Coll. Saint-Louis; l'Univ. de Sherbrooke (twice); Saint-Mary's Univ.; Confed. Art Gall.; London Regional Art Gall.; Peter Whyte Gall.; Holland College; Stewart Hall Art Gallery; l'Instituto Culturel Peruano, Lima; comm. galleries Bogota, Lima, Montreal, Toronto, Winnipeg, Calgary, Halifax, Hamilton, Stratford; participated in over 64 internat. exhns. France, Spain, Korea, Norway, Switzerland, Yugoslavia, Eng., Scot., Chile, Australia, Italy, Germany, Brazil, Peru, Colombia, Venezuela, Bulgaria, Czechoslovakia, Hong Kong, Taiwan, Hungary, U.S.A., Can.; rep. in various perm. colls. incl. Lib. of Cong., N.Y. Pub. Lib., Nat. Gall. S. Australia, Instituto Culturel Peruano Lima, American Embassy, House of Humor & Satire, Gabrovo, Bulgaria, The Israel Museum, Jerusalem, more than 37 Candn. museums, univs. and embassies, 55 corporate collections as well as other pub. and private colls. Europe, S.Am., U.S.A., Can.; Art critic, 'ARTSATLANTIC' (and others) since 1984; has acted on numerous art juries; Travel Award, House of Humour & Satire, Bulgaria 1991; First Prize, Internat. Jury, 9th Internat. Biennale, Gabrovo, Bulgaria 1989; First Prize Concours Graphique l'Univ. de Sherbrooke; Hon. Mention Miniature Painters, Sculptors & Gravers, Washington, D.C.; First Prize and Gold Medal Seagram Fine Arts Exhn.; Graphic Art Prize First Winnipeg Show Biennial; Anaconda Award Candn. Painter-Etchers & Engravers (twice); Third Prize Windmill Point Competition; Purchase Awards Dawson Coll., Le Musée du Qué., Thomas More Inst., Nat. Gall. S. Australia, Univ. de Sherbrooke; First Prize, Nat. Playwriting Competition, Ottawa, 1982, Performances for invited audiences, Ottawa Little Theatre 1983; Hon. Mention Nat. Playwriting Competition Ottawa 1979 and 1980; Finalist, Short Story Competition, CBC 1983; Special Mention, Nat. Playwriting Comp. 1984; Finalist, 16th Annual Playwriting Competition, Jacksonville University, Florida, for 2 plays 1985; staged reading (2 plays), N.Y. City 1985; Winner, Country Playhouse Playwriting Competition, Houston, Texas 1985; Contender for Honours, Nat. Playwriting Competition 1985; Staged readings, 2 plays, 53rd St. YWCA, New York City 1985; Hon. Mention, Dubuque, Iowa One-Act Play Competition 1987; Finalist, Wo/Man's Showcase, Ft. Lauderdale 1987; Semi-Finalist, Drury Coll., Springfield, Missouri 1987; Finalist, 17th Annual Playwriting Competition, Jacksonville Univ., Fla. 1987; Finalist, West Coast Ensemble Competition, Los Angeles 1987; Staged Reading, New York Univ. 1987; Semi-Finalist, Texas Woman's Univ. 1987; Radio production of one-act play by Radio McGill; Fully staged readings of full-length play, The Maxwell Anderson Playwrights Series, Stamford, Conn. 1987; Finalist, Kernodle Competition, Univ. of Arkansas, for 2 plays 1987; Hon. Mention and Finalist Standing for 3 plays, SETC New Play Project, Clemson Univ., South Carolina 1987; Co-winner, 18th Annual Playwriting Contest, Jacksonville Univ., Fla. 1988; Finalist, West Coast Ensemble Playwriting Competition, Los Angeles, for 2 plays, 1988; Staging of a one-act play by Stamford Community Arts Counc., Stamford, CT 1988; Publication of one-act play, 1989; Finalist, CBC Radio Drama Competition 1989; Finalist, John Gassner Playwriting Competition, Waltham, MA 1989; Fully-staged readings of one-act play, The Maxwell Anderson Playwrights Series, Stamford, Conn. 1991; Staging of one-act play at Nate Horne Theatre, Off Broadway, New York City 1991; Commissioned by City of Westmount to present full-length play in annual Arts Festival 1991; staged reading of one-act play by Solar Theatre, Toronto 1992; Finalist, Playformers Playwriting Competition, New York City 1992; Finalist, Drury College Biennial, Missouri, for one-act play 1993; Semi-Finalist, Playwrights Theatre of Baltimore, for full-length play 1993; Founder-Pres., Assoc. for the Protection of the Environment of Trout Lake, Que.; Mem. Council, Royal Candn. Acad. Arts; Jewish; recreation: gardening; Address: 4360 Montrose Ave., Westmount, Que. H3Y 2B1.

**GERSTEIN, Bertrand,** B.A., L.L.D.; merchant; b. Boston, Mass., 11 Feb. 1918; s. Frank and Etta (Wein) G.; came to Canada 1918; e. Univ. of Toronto, B.A. (Pol. Science and Econ.) 1938; m. children: Irving Russell, Ira Mitchael; Former Chrmn., Peoples Jewellers Limited (Estbd. 1919); former Chrmn., Bd. of Govs., York Univ., Toronto; former Chrmn. of Bd., Mount Sinai Hosp., Toronto; Past Pres., Ont. Div., Candn. Mental Health Assn.; Candn. Jewellers Assn.; Dir., Candn. Imperial Bank of Commerce; mem., Toronto Bd. Trade; City of Toronto Redevel. Adv. Council: Jewish; recreations: tennis, golf, sailing; Clubs: Albany; Ontario; Primrose; Oakdale Golf & Country; Queen's; Home: 175 Cumberland St., #1404, Toronto, Ont. M5R 3M9.

**GERSTEIN, Irving Russell,** B.S.; merchant; b. Toronto, Ont. 10 Feb. 1941; s. Bertrand and Reva (Appleby) G.; e. London Sch. of Econ. 1961; Univ. of Pa. Wharton Sch. of Finance & Comm. B.S. 1962; m. Gail d. Samuel and Beatrice Smith 6 Feb. 1964; children: Marcy, Frank, Anthony, Carrie Lynn; Dir., Peoples Jewellers Ltd. 1974–..; Dir., Baton Broadcasting Inc.; Confederation Life Insurance; Economic Investment Trust Ltd.; Chrmn. Emeritus of Bd., Mt. Sinai Hosp.; Dir., Hosp. Council Metrop. Toronto 1980–84; Baycrest Home for Aged; Young Pres. Orgn. 1977–81; Gov., Olympic Trust of Canada; Upper Can. Coll. 1982–84; Ont. Inst. Studies in Edn. 1972–75; Bishop Strachan Sch. 1976–79; mem., Adv. Council Faculty of Admin. Studies York Univ.; Vice Chrmn. (Ont.) P. Conservative Can. Fund; Clubs: Albany; Alpine Ski; Granite; Griffith Island; National; Oakdale Golf & Country; Primrose; Queens; Toronto; Home: 78 The Bridle Path, Don Mills, Ont. M3B 2B1.

**GERSTEIN, Reva,** C.M. (1974), O.C. (1979), O.Ont. (1988), M.A., Ph.D., LL.D., D.Litt.; registered psychologist; b. Ont.; d. David and Diana (Kraus) Appleby; e. Fern Ave. Sch. and Parkdale Coll. Inst., Toronto; Univ. of Toronto, B.A. 1938; M.A. 1939, Ph.D. 1945; Univ. of W. Ont., LL.D. 1972; Lakehead Univ. D.Litt. 1974; Univ. of Guelph LL.D. 1975; Queen's Univ. LL.D. 1981; York Univ. LL.D. 1993; m. Bertrand Gerstein 1939; div. 1971; children: Irving Russell, Ira Michael; m. David Raitblat 1979; CHANCELLOR, UNIV. OF WESTERN ONT. 1992–95; Dir. McGraw-Hill Ryerson Ltd. 1974–87; INCO Ltd. (Extve. mem.) 1976–89; Avon Products Ltd. 1975– ; Maritime Life Assnce. Co. 1977–87 (Hon. Bd. Mem. 1987– ;); Stratford Shakespearean Festival Inc. 1977 (Hon. Secty. 1979, Senator 1980); Niagara Inst. 1978; Inst. for Rsch. and Public Policy 1978; Fellow Founders Coll., York Univ.; mem. and Chrmn., Univ. Affairs Comte. 1962–78; Hall-Dennis Comte.; mem. and Ed. Chrmn., Comn. on Post-Secondary Educ.; mem., University Affairs Counc. 1975–79; mem. Cardinal Emmett Carter's Panel on the Economy 1983; Chrmn. Mayor's Task Force on Discharged Psychiatric Patients 1983; mem. Mental Health Care Comn. District Health Counc. 1983–87; Founder, Chrmn. of Bd., Gerstein Crisis Centre 1988– ; Bd. & Extve. Mem., Nat. Arts Centre 1988–91; Mem., Premier's Health Strategy Counc. 1988–91; Bd. of Dirs. & Chrmn., Candn. Inst. for Advanced Rsch. 1989– ; Lectr., Dept. of Psychol., Univ. of Toronto 1939–49; York Univ. 1965–73; Nat. Dir. of Program, Candn. Mental Health Assn.; Bd., Royal Conservatory of Music 1990– ; Psychol. (first), E. York-Leaside Health Unit; mem. Clinical Education Comm. (Ont. Council on Health) 1979; mem. Task Force of Council of Health 1971 and Arts Council 1972; Chrmn. Co-ordinator, Social Plan. Council Youth Proj. 1969–71; Chrmn., Adv. Council on Policy to Leader of Opposition, Ottawa 1977; mem., Prime Minister's Transitional Task Force 1979; Cons. Metro. Toronto Police; Chrmn. Solicitor-General's Task force on Policing (Dec. 1979–June 1980); mem., Ont. Police Commn. 1982–88; Chrmn., Hospital Counc. Metro Toronto 1984–87; Pres., Ontario Psych. Foundation 1987– ; Hon. Life Fellow, Can. Psychol. Assoc.; Founder & Past Pres., Hincks Treatment Centre; Nat. Pres., Can. Council on Children & Youth 1957–65; Nat. Pres., Nat. Council Jewish Women 1955–59 (Internat. Vice Pres. 1955–59); Vice-Chrmn., & Chrmn. of Capital Campaign, Hosp. for Sick Children 1975–93; mem. of Foundation, Trustee, Hosp. for Sick Children 1975– ; Mem. of Bd., Nat. Assn. of Children's Hosps. & Related Institutions, Inc. U.S.A. (NACHRI); mem., Candn. Opera Comte.; Art Gall. of Ont.; Royal Ont. Museum; bd. mem., Cdn. Council of Christians and Jews; founder, Toronto Friends of Stratford; Nat. Council of Human Rights Foundation; Albert Einstein Coll. of Med. Award 1956; named B'nai Brith Woman of the Year 1961; Hon. Life Mem. Ontario Psychiatric Assn. 1967; Centennial Medal 1967; Outstanding Woman Awards of Ont. 1975; mem. Order of Canada 1974; Officer of Order of Canada 1979; C.M. Hincks National Award for Mental Health 1987; recipient of Order of Ontario 1988; mem., hon. mem. of Ont. Chiefs of Police Assn.; registered pyschologist in Ont.; Hon. Mem., Ont. Psychol. Assn. 1984– ; Candn. Psychol. Assn.; Am. Psychol. Assn.; Address: 625 Avenue Rd., Apt. 703, Toronto, Ont. M4V 2K7.

**GERSTUNG, Manfred H.;** banker; b. Germany 25 Dec. 1938; s. Otto Karl and Elisabeth Amalia (Sprengel) G.; e. High School, Germany 1954; Business College, Germany 1957; Undergrad. Studies, Canada 1958–62, 1976–79; m. Regina M. d. Georg and Johanna Gehrmann, 31 March 1969; children: Katja, Stephanie; VICE-PRESIDENT, ISRAEL DISCOUNT BANK OF CANADA 1989– ; Controller & Mgr., Admin., Dresser Industries Inc. (Dallas, Texas) 1965–75; Vice-Pres., Opns., Morgan Bank of Canada 1975–89; teaching positions (languages) in Japan & Germany 1962–65; volunteer engagements, Metro. Toronto Zoo; Mem., Zoological Soc.; Uxbridge Horsemen's Assn.; Audubon Soc.; Toronto Symphony Soc.; author of travel articles in various German & Candn. papers; recreations: horses, gardening, literature, music; Home: 10 Shalom St., R.R. #4, Stouffville, Ont. L4A 7X5; Office: 150 Bloor St. W., Toronto, Ont. M5S 2Y5.

**GERVAIS, Charles Henry Martin,** B.A., M.A.; writer; b. Windsor, Ont. 20 Oct. 1946; s. Albert Ted and Marion (Mineau) G.; e. Univ. of Guelph, B.A. 1971; Univ. of Windsor, M.A. 1972; m. Donna d. Virgil Wright 7 Nov. 1968; children: Elise, André, Stéphane, Gabriel; PUBLISHER, BLACK MOSS PRESS 1969– ; Book Ed., Windsor Star 1980– ; Contbg. Ed., 'Where to Eat in Canada'; Contbg. Writer, CBC 'Morningside'; Dir., Theatre Alive 1988–89; Teacher, St. Clair Coll., Canadore Coll., Univ. of Windsor; Cons., Hiram Walkers, St. Clair Coll.; winner of 10 'Western Ontario Newspaper Awards' and 2 'Ontario Reporters Assn. Awards; twice runner-up, Milton Acorn Memorial People's Poetry Award; Roman Catholic; author: 'The Border Police: 125 Years of Policing in Windsor' 1992; 'Scenes from the Present: New Selected Poems' 1991, 'People in Struggle: The Art of Bill Stapleton' 1991; 'Autobiographies' 1989, 'Letters from the Equator' 1986, 'Public Fantasy' 1983, Into a Blue Morning' 1982 and six earlier poetry books; 'The Fighting Parson' 1983, 'Baldoon' 1976 (plays); 'If I Had a Birthday Every Day' 1983, 'How Bruises Lost His Secret' 1976 (children's lit.); 'The Pope in Canada' 1984, 'Voices Like Thunder' 1984, 'The Rumrunners' 1980, 'Northern Calamities' 1976 (non-fiction); work incl. in anthologies: 'Storm Warning' 1971, 'Soundings' 1970, 'The Poets of Canada' 1978; Office: Box 143, Stn. A, Windsor, Ont. N9A 6K1.

**GERVAIS, (Ret'd) Lieutenant-General James Cyril,** CMM, CD; army officer; b. Noranda, Que. 5 March 1938; s. Anthime Alexandre and Juliette Marie (Mongrain) G.; e. Ottawa Univ. H.S. 1955; Royal Military College of Canada B.Sc. 1962; m. Sandra M. d. Ernest and Agnes Hall 12 Oct. 1963; children: Lisa, Sue Anna, Jocelyne; DEPUTY SECRETARY AND DEPUTY HERALD CHANCELLOR, CHANCELLERY, GOVERNMENT HOUSE; Home: 2043 Cabot St., Ottawa, Ont. K1H 6J7.

**GERVAIS, (Rev.) Marc,** S.J., Ph.D., M.A., M.F.A., L.Ph., L.Th. (R.C.); university professor; film specialist and critic; international peace worker; b. Sherbrooke, Que., 3 Dec. 1929; s. Césaire and Sylvia (Mullins) G.; e. Loyola Coll., B.A. 1950; L'Immaculée Conception, Montreal, L.Ph. 1956; Cath. Univ. of Am., Washington, M.F.A. (drama) 1960; Regis Coll., Toronto, L.Th. 1964; St. Mary's Univ., M.A. (Theol.) 1964; Sorbonne Univ., Ph.D. (film aesthetics) 1973; PROF. OF FILM, AESTHETICS, ETC., DEPT. OF COMMUNICATION STUDIES, CONCORDIA UNIV., Loyola Campus; Founding Dir. (1988) & Bd. Chrmn., The Loyola Inst. for Studies in Internat. Peace 1988– ; Commissioner, C.R.T.C. 1981–86; Bd. of Dirs., Canadian Film Inst. 1986–89; mem., Institut National de l'Image et du Son 1990– ; mem., Bd. of Judges, Candn. Film Awards; mem. film juries (Cannes, Venice, Oxford, etc.); TV and radio work including TV Specials on Ingmar Bergman for CBC, CTV and VISION; received Canada Council Fellowship 1966–67; author 'Pasolini' 1972; other writings incl. film articles in journals and newspapers in Eng., France, USA, Can., Spain, Sweden, Norway, Italy, and Australia; recreations: sports, arts; Address: 7141 Sherbrooke St. W., Montreal, Que. H4B 1R6.

**GERVAIS, Marcel André,** D.D.; archbishop; b. Elie, Man. 1931; e. Sparta and St. Thomas, Ont.; e. Pontificum Athenaeum Angelicum and Pontificium Institutum Biblicum Rome, Ecole Biblique et Archéoligique Française Jerusalem, L.S.Th. 1959, L.S.Sc. 1961, D.D. 1980; ARCHBISHOP OF OTTAWA 1989– ; Chancellor, St. Paul's Univ., Ottawa; Pres., Candn. Conf. of Catholic Bishops 1991–93; o. London, Ont. 1958; Prof. of Sacred Scripture St. Peter's Semy. London 1962–79; Dir. of Divine Word Internat. Centre Religious Edn. London, Ont. 1974–79; served Adv. Comn. Internat. Comn. for Eng. in Liturgy 1974–78; mem. Edn. Ctte. Candn. Cath. Orgn. for Devel. & Peace 1975–80; Auxiliary Bishop of London 1980; Bishop of Sault Ste-Marie 1985; Chrmn. Episcopal Comn. Christian Edn.; Chrmn. Family Life Curriculum Ctte. Ont. Conf. Cath. Bishops; former Chrmn. Bd. Dirs. Cardinal Carter Centre for Bioethics Toronto; former mem. Episcopal Comns. Theol. and Liturgy; Ang.-R.Catholic Dialogue Can.; Office: 1247 Kilborn Place, Ottawa, Ont. K1H 6K9.

**GERVAIS, Michel,** O.C., B.A., B.Th., L.Th., L.Ph., D.Th.; university rector; b. Lévis, Qué. 27 May 1944; s. Paul and Ghislaine (Gosselin) G.; e. Collège de Lévis B.A. 1961; Laval Univ. B.Th. 1964, L.Th. 1966, L.Ph. 1968; Pontifical Univ. of St. Thomas Aquinas (Rome) D.Th. 1973; Bishop's Univ. D.C.L. (Hon.) 1993; McGill Univ. D.D. (Hon.) 1993; m. Ghislaine d. Henri-Louis and Carmen Breton 17 April 1977; children: Justin, Rachel, Marie-Claire, Paul, Guillaume, Françoise; RECTOR, LAVAL UNIVERSITY 1987– ; teaching & research at Laval Univ., from Asst. 1969 to Prof. 1979; Dir., Project Laval 1979–82; Vice-Rector (Academic & Research) 1982–87; acad. fields of interest: logic, theol. anthropology, eschatology; Pres., World Univ. Serv. of Canada 1989–92; Conf. of Rectors & Principals of Univs. in Que. 1991–93; Chrmn. of the Bd., Assn. of Univs. & Colleges of Can. 1993– ; Bd. of Dirs. & Extve. Ctte., Assn. of Partly and Fully-French Language Univs. (AUPELF) 1993– ; Mem., Post-Secondary Edn. Comn., Que. High Council for Edn. 1981–82; Council of Univs. of Que. 1984–88; SSHRCC 1987–93; Assn. of Univ. & Colleges of Canada 1987– ; Assn. of Commonwealth Univs. 1987– ; Adv. Ctte. on Centres of Excellence, Min. of Sci. & Tech. Canada 1989– ; Nat. Adv. Ctte. on Advanced Tech. 1989– ; Rsch. Council, Candn. Inst. for Adv. Rsch. 1991– ; Bd. of Dir. & Extve. Ctte., Assn. of Partly & Fully-French Lang. Univs. (AUPELF) 1991– ; National Counc. on Educ., Conf. Bd. of Can. 1992– ; Pres., United Way (Que.) Funding Drive 1991; Mem., Bd. of Dir., Saint-Sacrement Hosp. 1982–87; Groupe d'action pour l'avancement tech. et indus. de la région de Qué. 1987– ; Que. Metro High Tech Park 1987– ; Que. Commercial & Internat. Arbitration Ctr. 1989– ; René Richard Found. 1987– ; Sponsoring Ctte., Employment Forum 1989– ; Corp. of Maison Michel-Sarrazin 1990– ; Officer, Order of Canada; Officer of l'Ordre nat. du mérite (France); Mem., Candn. Theol. Soc.; Candn. Assn. for French-Lang. Edn.; co-editor: 'Le Christ, hier, aujourd'hui et demain' 1976; author of num. research papers, edn. policy reports & pub. talks; club: The Quebec Garrison; Home: 2136, Bourbonnière, Sillery, Que. G1T 1B1; Office: Quebec, Que. G1K 7P4.

**GERVAIS, P. André,** Q.C., B.A., LL.L.; lawyer; b. Sherbrooke, Que. 27 Sept. 1932; s. Césaire and Sylvia (Mullins) G.; e. Concordia Univ., B.A. 1954; Univ. of Sherbrooke, LL.L. 1957; McGill Univ., cert. profl. competence 1958; called to Qué. Bar 1958; apptd. Queen's Counsel 1974; children: Marc, Nathalie, Robert; PARTNER, MACKENZIE GERVAIS 1968– ; Lawyer, Bronstetter, Wilkie, Penhale, Donovan, Giroux & Charbonneau 1957–66; Doheny Mackenzie 1966–68; Dir. & Sec., Marks & Spencer Canada Inc.; Marks & Spencer Holdings Canada Inc.; D'Allaird's Stores Inc.; Dir., Ciro Inc.; Dir., World Satellite SA; Secy., Hilton Canada Inc.; Co-Secy., Hilton-Place Québec Ltd.; Gov. & Past Chrmn., Bd. of Gov., Concordia Univ.; Dir. & Mem. and Past Extve. Vice-Pres., Orch. symphonique de Montréal; Co-Pres., Governors Circle, Montreal Children's Hosp. Found.; Mem., Qué Bar 1958– ; Montreal Bar 1958– ; Candn. Bar Assn. 1958– (Gen. Counc. 1973–85); Alderman, City of Westmount 1977–83; Lt., Royal Candn. Armoured Corp 1954–57; recreations: tennis, squash, ski; Clubs: Club Saint-Denis; Hillside Tennis; Mount-Royal; Home: 427 Mount Stephen Ave., Westmount, Que. H3Y 2X8; Office: 770 Sherbrooke St. W., Ste. 1300, Montreal, Que. H3A 1G1.

**GERVAIS, Hon. Paul M.,** B.A., LL.L.; superior court justice; b. Sherbrooke, Que. 8 Dec. 1925; s. Hon. Justice Césaire and Sylvia (Mullins) G.; e. St. Charles Semy.; Loyola Coll.; Laval Univ.; m. Hélène Cannon, Quebec City, 14 Nov. 1953; children: Edouard, Charles, Carolyne; JUSTICE, SUPERIOR COURT OF QUE. 1972– ; cr. Q.C. 1968; Ald., City of Sherbrooke. 1955–67; Batonnier, Bar of St. Francis, 1967–68 (Past Secy.); mem. Gen. Council, Que. Bar (Extve. Council); mem. Nat. Council, Candn. Bar Assn., since 1966; Pres., Indust. Comn. Assn. Que., 1965–67; first el. to H. of C. g.e. 1968–72; Vice Chrmn. Standing Comte. on Justice & Legal Affairs 1968–70 (Chrmn. 1970–72); Home: 453 Fréchette St., Sherbrooke, Que. J1J 2V5.

**GERVAIS, Richard G.,** M.A.; public relations and government relations executive; b. Montréal, Qué. 20 Feb. 1942; s. J.G. Gervais and A. Piquette; e. Coll. Stanislas, Outremont; Loyola Coll., Montréal, B.A. Pol. Sci. 1963; Fordham Univ., New York, M.A. Pol. Sci. 1965; Inst. d'Études Politiques de Paris, Scolarité de Doctorat 1967; m. Marie Elizabeth (advocate and régisseure) d. the late Lucienne (Brûlé) and the late Hon. Lionel Chevrier 14 June 1975; PRESIDENT & C.E.O., GERVAIS GAGNON & ASSOCIATES INC./GGA COMMUNICATIONS, PUBLIC AND GOVERNMENT RELATIONS CONSULTANTS; Special Asst. to Hon. Jean Marchand, Min. of Manpower and Immigration & Qué. Leader, Ottawa 1967; Candn. Del. to 20th Anniversary of NATO, Washington 1968; P.E. Trudeau Ctte. for Leadership of Liberal Party, Ottawa 1968; Special Asst. to Hon. Mitchell Sharp, Secy. of State for External Affairs 1968–70; mem. Candn. Del. for State Visits to Finland, Norway, Sweden, Iceland, Denmark 1970; Ex-officio mem., Candn. Delegation to United Nations General Assembly 1968–70; Exec. Asst. to Special Joint Ctte. of Senate and H. of C. on the Constitution 1970; mem., Hughessen Comn. 1972; Exec. Secy. to Comn. of Inquiry on Security in Penitentiaries 1974; Dir. External Affairs, Imperial Oil Ltd. 1975–81; Vice-Pres. PIR Public and Industrial Relations Ltd. 1981; Dir. 1983; Sr. Vice-Pres. & Gen. Mgr. 1982–85; Bd. mem., Renault Canada Ltd.; former Bd. mem., Continental Pharma Cryosan; Chrmn., les Ballets Jazz de Montréal; Vice-Chrmn. Maison des Étudiants Canadiens, Paris; Mem., Bd. of Dirs., Counc. for Business and the Arts in Can.; The Canadiana Fund, Ottawa; Confederation Centre of the Arts, P.E.I.; Hon. Ctte., Cercle International de Montréal; Gov., le Théâtre du Nouveau Monde (former Pres.); Mem., Founder's Circle, Candn. Centre for Architecture; Hon. Mem., Order of St. John's (Qué. Counc.); Honorary Consul in Québec, Republic of Mauritius; Mem., Museum of Contemporary Art of Montreal; McCord Museum of Candn. History; International Ctr. for Candn. Art; Maeght Found., France; Lionel-Groulx Found.; World Wildlife Fund Canada; Club Français de la médaille; Friends of The Banff Centre; Amnesty Internat.; Loyola Alumni Assn.; Life mem., The Montréal Museum of Fine Arts; Benefactor, Héritage Montréal; Candn. Associate, Ben-Gurion Univ. of Negev; Associate, The Montreal Opera Guild; mem., several nat. and internat. profl. assocs.: Candn. Public Relns. Soc.; Société des Relationnistes du Qué.; Bd. of Trade of Metro. Montreal; Candn. Club of Montreal; Political Sci. Soc. of Am.; Formerly: Vice-Pres. International Theater/La Poudrière; Dir., France-Canada Chamber of Commerce; Vie des Arts Governor, La Quinzaine Internationale de Théâtre (Qué.) and of de Lanaudière Arts Festival; Hon. Ctte., McGill Open-House 1989; Mem. of the Bd.: Association Française pour la Communauté Atlantique (NATO); Candn. Inst. for Internat. Affairs; The Univ. Club of Montréal; The Qué. Found. for South East Asia Refugees; Numerous fundraising activities for various orgns. incl.: The Arthritis Soc. (Co-Chrmn. 1990 Gala); Friends of the Candn. Museum of Civilization (Gala Chrmn. 1988); The Gazette Christmas Fund 1987–89; Le Théâtre de la Licorne (Gala Chrmn. 1987); Fundraising Ctte., Montreal Symphony Orch. (Bd. mem. 1975–83); La Maison Marguerite; The Montreal Museum of Fine Arts; L'Institut de Réadaptation de Montréal; Héritage Montréal; Sport Scolaire; Found. for Women Journalists; Fondation du Patrimoine des Beaucerons; frequent panelist and guest speaker on the arts and on the Candn. political system; Societies: Commanderie de Bordeaux, Montreal, Great Master 1979–83; Club Prosper-Montagné; Mousquetaire d'Armagnac; Honours: Commemorative Medal, 125th Anniversary of Candn. Confedn. (1992); Comdr., Mil. and Hospitaller Order of St. Lazarus of Jerusalem (1980); Order of St. John's (1986); Recreations: wine tasting, collecting of political memorabilia; Clubs: Mount Royal (Mem. Bd. of Dirs.); The Beaver Club, Montréal; Cercle de St-Germain-des-Prés et de St-Sulpice, Paris; Home: Westmount, Que.; Office: Canada Cement Bldg., Phillips Square, 606 Cathcart St., Montréal, Que. H3B 1K9.

**GERWIN, Martin Edgar,** B.A., M.A., Ph.D.; university professor and administrator; b. Redruth, Cornwall, U.K. 11 Jan. 1940; s. Edgar Erich Wilhelm Max and Elsie Lilian (Davis) G.; e. Michael Hall Sch. 1958; Queen's Univ. B.A. (Hons.) 1962; Princeton Univ. M.A. 1964, Ph.D. 1985; m. Elma d. Herbert and Mary Beall 12 Sept. 1964; children: John Robert Davis, Elisabeth Mara, James Douglas; DEAN OF STUDIES, ST. JOHN'S COLLEGE, UNIV. OF MANITOBA 1991– ; City Reporter, The Calgary Herald summer 1961; Editor-in-Chief, The Queen's Journal 1961–62; Lecturer in Philos., Univ. of Man. 1965–67; Asst. Prof. of Philos. 1967–87; Assoc. Prof. of Philos. 1987– ; Acting Head, Dept. of German 1977–79; Program Co-ord., St. John's Coll. 1983–88; Instr. in Philos., Stony Mountain Penitentiary 1974, '77; Winnipeg Edn. Ctr. 1979; Inter-Universities North 1990– ; Woodrow Wilson Fellow 1962; Mem., Anglican Ch. of Canada; Science for Peace; Candn. Philos. Assn. (Mem. Bd. of Dir. 1986–88); Candn. Soc. for the Study of Practical Ethics; Candn. Peace Research & Edn. Assn.; Am. Assn. of Philos. Teachers; author of articles in 'Dialogue,' 'Can. J. of Philos.' & 'Can. Philos. Rev.'; recreations: choral singing; Home: 654 Centennial St., Winnipeg, Man. R3N 1R2; Office: 400 Dysart Rd., Winnipeg, Man. R3T 2M5.

**GERWING, Henry Carl,** B.A., LL.B.; lawyer; b. Lake Lenore, Sask. 29 May 1927; s. John Henry and Amalia Elizabeth (Schulte) G.; e. Univ. of Sask. B.A. 1951, LL.B. 1954; m. Rita d. Louis and Rosanna Peltier 19 July 1958; children: Miriam, Carolyn, Anita, Steven; PRIN. H. CARL GERWING PROFESSIONAL CORP. 1958– ; articled Regina 1955, Edmonton and Calgary 1957; called to Bar of Sask. 1956, Alta. 1958; Dir. Calgary Opera Assn. since 1975, currently Pres.; mem. K. of C. since 1954 holding various exec. positions; Co-founder

1988 and Dir. St. Thomas More Lawyers Guild; R. Catholic; recreations: curling, gardening, choir; Home: 190 Shannon Hill S.W., Calgary, Alta. T2Y 2Y8.

**GESTRIN, Bengt V.,** M.A., Ph.D.; banking executive; b. Helsinki, Finland 12 Jan. 1935; s. Emil Victor and Naimi (Osterberg) G.; e. Univ. of Toronto, M.A. 1963, Ph.D.(Econ.) 1966; m. Carita, d. Edwin George Erlin, March 1957; two s., Michael Victor, Philip George; EXTVE. VICE-PRES. & ECON. ADVISER, CANADIAN IMPERIAL BANK OF COMMERCE 1986– ; joined the Bank 1957 serving in various capacities; Econ., Bank for Internat. Settlements, Basle, Switzerland, 1966; Monetary Div., OECD, Paris, France, 1967–68; responsible for Econ. Briefings for Prime Min., Privy Counc. Office, Ottawa 1968–71; Head of N. Am. Sec., O.E.C.D. 1971–73; Vice-Pres. Econ. C.I.B.C. 1973–83; Sr. Vice-Pres. 1983–86; author various financial articles for banking journs.; mem. Am. Econ. Assn.; Candn. Econ. Assm.; Home: 1B Rosedale Rd., Toronto, Ont. M4W 2P1; Office: Head Office, Commerce Court West, Toronto, Ont. M5L 1A2.

**GETTER, Ruth,** B.Sc., M.A., Ph.D.; economist; b. Tel Aviv, Israel 10 Nov. 1942; d. Solomon and Betty (Hermann) G.; e. McGill Univ. B.Sc. 1964; Ohio Univ. M.A. 1973; Boston Univ. Ph.D. 1983; children: Aaron Jay, Rebecca Shoshana; VICE PRES., ECONOMIC RESEARCH, DEPT. OF ECON. RSCH., TORONTO DOMINION BANK 1992– ; Econ. and Mgr. Product Devel. and Special Studies Interind. Group Data Resources Inc. Lexington, Mass. 1978–84; Sr. Econ. and Dir. Product Devel. Economica Inc. Cambridge, Mass. 1984–87; Sr. Econ. Ind. and Regional Econ. Dept. of Econ. Rsch., present bank 1987–92; mem. Bd. Visitors Ohio Univ. Coll. Arts & Sci.; co-author 'Modeling The U.S. Economy' 1987; various articles profl. jours.; mem. Candn. Assn. Bus. Econs.; Toronto Assn. Bus. Econs.; Am. Econ. Assn.; Mem., National Statistics Council 1992– ; recreations: music, travel, books; Home: PH2, 250 Heath St. W., Toronto, Ont. M5P 3L4; Office: Box 1, T-D Centre, Toronto, Ont. M5K 1A2.

**GETTY, Donald R.,** M.L.A., B.A.; businessman; politician; b. Westmount, Que. 30 Aug. 1933; s. Charles Ross and Beatrice (Hampton) G.; e. pub. schs. Montreal, Ottawa and Toronto; high schs. Toronto and London, Ont.; Univ. of W. Ont., B.A. (Honours Business Adm.); m. Margaret Inez Mitchell, 18 Aug. 1955; children: Dale, David, Darin, Derek; Premier, Province of Alberta 1985–92; Partner, Doherty, Roadhouse & McCuaig Ltd., 1967–71; el. M.L.A. for Stratchcona W. prov. g.e. 1967; re-el. M.L.A. for Edmonton Whitemud 1971, 1975 and at a by-election 1985; re-el. in a prov. g.e. 1986 & in a by-el. 1989; former Min. of Fed. and Intergovernmental Affairs 1971; former Min. of Energy and Natural Resources 1975, Gov. of Alta.; First recipient, 'Order of the Sash,' Metis Nation of Alberta; mem. Edmonton Eskimo Football Team for 10 yrs. (quarterback); named 'Outstanding Canadian in Western Canada Football League' 1959; advisor, fundraiser, Alberta Northern Lights Wheelchair Basketball Team; Kappa Alpha; P. Conservative; United Church; recreations: golf, horseracing; hunting; Clubs: Petroleum (former Gov.); Derrick Golf & Winter (Past Dir.); Home: Box 300, Erskine, Alta. T0C 1G0.

**GHADIALLY, Feroze Novroji,** M.B., B.S., M.D., Ph.D., D.Sc., F.R.C.P.(C); pathologist; educator; b. Bombay, India 13 Nov. 1920; s. Novroji Bomanji Ghadially; e. Univ. of London M.B., B.S. 1947, M.D. 1949, Ph.D. 1955, D.Sc. 1962; Hon.D.Sc. Univ. of Guelph 1986; m. Edna May d. late Edward Thomas Bryant 15 Aug. 1950; 4 children; author 'Ultrastructural Pathology of the Cell' 1975; co-author 'Ultrastructure of Synovial Joints in Health and Disease' 1969; author 'Diagnostic Electron Microscopy of Tumours' 1980, 2nd ed. 1985; 'Ultrastructural Pathology of the Cell and Matrix' 1982, 3rd ed. 1988; 'Fine Structure of Synovial Joints' 1983; 'Diagnostic Ultrastructural Pathology: A Self-Evaluation Manual' 1984; author or co-author over 250 med. publs.; author over 50 non-med. papers and books; principal writing on electron microscopy and electron probe x-ray analysis; Fellow, Royal Coll. Pathols.; Royal Soc. of Arts; Emeritus Prof., Univ. of Sask.; Adjunct Prof., Univ. of Ottawa; Izaak Walton Killam Laureate of the Canada Council 1981; recipient, William Boyd Lectureship Award 1993; recreations: aquariums, music, photography, marquetry, sculpture; Office: Candn. Reference Ctr. for Cancer Pathology, Clinical Studies Unit Bldg., Ottawa Civic Hosp., Ottawa, Ont. K1Y 4M9.

**GHENT, Cameron Neil,** M.D., F.R.C.P.(C); physician; educator; b. Mount Forest, Ont. 9 May 1945; s. Robert Sidney and Clara (McLennan) G.; e. Univ. of W. Ont. M.D. 1970; Teaching and Rsch Hepatol. (Liver Transplantation Prog.) University Hosp. 1977– ; Assoc. Prof. of Med. Univ. of W. Ont. 1984– ; training in Internal Med. and Gastroenterol. Univ. of W. Ont. 1970–74; Hepatol. Fellowship Training Yale Univ. 1974–77; Dir. Univ. Hosp. 1986–88, Chrmn. Med. Adv. Ctte. 1987–88; numerous sci. papers; mem. Candn. Assn. Gastroenterol.; Candn. Assn. Study Liver; Candn. Assn. Med. Teachers; Candn. Phys. Prevention Nuclear War; Am. Assn. Study Liver Disease; Office: P.O. Box 5339, London, Ont. N6A 5A5.

**GHITTER, Ron,** B.A., LL.B., Q.C.; lawyer; b. Calgary, Alta. 22 Aug. 1935; s. Louis and Etta (Kronick) G.; e. Univ. of Alta. B.A. 1956, LL.B. 1959; m. Myrna d. David and Diana Naimark 11 July 1993; one d.: Corinne; PRESIDENT, RON GHITTER PROPERTY CONSULTANTS LTD.; commenced law practice as Partner, Ghitter & Co. 1960–87; 1st elected as MLA, Calgary, Alta. Prov. Legislature 1971; re-elected 1975; Past Extve. V.P. of Devel., Trizec Corp. Ltd.; Q.C. 1978; Dir., Calgary Beautification Found.; Past Dir., Calgary C. of C.; Candn. Council of Christians & Jews; Calgary Jr. Achievement Calgary Found.; Chair, Arts Festival Ctte., 1988 Winter Olympics Calgary; Min. Consultative Ctte. on Tolerance & Understanding for Alta.'s Min. of Edn.; Mayor's Task Force on Community & Family Violence Calgary; Candn. Human Relations Award, Candn. Council of Christians & Jews 1985; Alta. Human Rights Award, Alta. Human Rights Comn. 1990; Mem., Federal Adv. Ctte. on Violence against Women; Dir., Internat. Centre for Human Rights & Democratic Devel.; Dignity Found.; co-author (as Chairman): 'Report of the Minister's Consultative Committee on Tolerance and Understanding,' 'Report of the Task Force on Community and Family Violence'; recreations: tennis, biking, golf; clubs: Glencoe Golf & Country; Home: 1701, 318 – 26th Ave. S.W., Calgary, Alta. T2S 2T9; Office: 346 – 23rd Ave. S.W., Calgary, Alta. T2S 0J2.

**GHIZ, Joseph A.,** B.Com., LL.B., LL.M., LL.D., M.L.A., Q.C.; b. Charlottetown, PEI 27 Jan. 1945; s. Atallah J. and Marguerite Farah (McKarris) G.; e. Prince of Wales Coll., Dalhousie Univ. B.Com. 1966, LL.B. 1969; Harvard Univ. LL.M. 1981; LL.D. (hon.) Univ. of Prince Edward Island 1987; m. Rose Ellen d. Douglas and Elizabeth McGowan 16 Dec. 1972; children: Robert, Joanne; DEAN, FACULTY OF LAW, DALHOUSIE UNIV. 1993– ; Chair, Bd. of Advisors to Anderson Consulting Canada; Mem. Bd. of Trustees, McGill Institute for the Study of Canada; Sr. Partner, Scales, Ghiz, Jenkins & McQuaid 1970–81; Crown Prosecutor, Queens Co. 1970–72; Fed. Narcotics Drug Prosecutor 1970–79; Counsel to Comm. of Inquiry into Charlottetown Police Force 1977; e. Leader, Liberal Party of PEI 1981; private practice 1981–86; el. M.L.A. 1982; Leader, Her Majesty's Loyal Opposition in PEI 1982–86; Premier of PEI 1986–93; former Lectr., Univ. of PEI; apptd. Q.C. 1984; former Gov., Frontier Coll.; Founding Mem., Montague Boys & Girls Club; mem. and Past Regional Chrmn., Candn. Counc. of Multiculturalism; Pres., Liberal Party of PEI 1977–78; Mem., St. Andrew's United Church; co-author: 'Towards a New Canada' 1978; author: 'Constitutional Impasse over Oil and Gas' unpubl. thesis (final chapter publ. Univ. of N.B. Law Jour. 1982); Clubs: The Charlottetown; Halifax; Home: 933 Greenwood Ave., Halifax, N.S. B3H 3L1; Office: Weldon Law Bldg., 6061 University Ave., Halifax, N.S. B3H 4H9.

**GHOSE, Tarunendu,** M.B., B.S., Ph.D., F.R.C.Path. (UK); b. Begusarai, India 5 May 1928; s. Promodendu and Nalini G.; e. Calcutta Univ. M.B., B.S. 1950, Ph.D. 1959; PROF. OF PATHOL. & ASSOC. PROF. OF MICROBIOL. DALHOUSIE UNIV. 1977– ; Assoc. Pathol. and Head Section of Immunopathology, Victoria Gen. Hosp. Halifax 1969– ; Dir. Pathology Scientific Research Ltd. Halifax; Resident several hosps. Calcutta 1950–54; Med. Offr. and Rsch. Offr. Dept. Atomic Energy Govt. of India 1954–61; on deputation to labs. Atomic Bomb Casualty Comn. Hiroshima and Nagasaki, Japan 1958–59; Sr. Rsch. Fellow and Lectr. in Pathol. Univs. of Aberdeen and Leeds 1961–64; Sr. Lectr. in Pathol. Monash Univ. Melbourne, Australia 1964–68; Assoc. Prof. of Pathol. present Univ. 1969–77; recipient Col. Amirchand Prize Indian Council Med. Rsch. 1958; Visiting Sci. Award Med. Rsch. Council Can. 1978–79; Fellowships World Health Orgn. 1955, Internat. Union Against Cancer 1962, Internat. Agency Rsch. Cancer 1968; author or co-author approx. 200 sci. publs. profl. jours.; mem. Am. Assn. Cancer Rsch. Pathol. Soc. Gt. Brit. & Ireland; Mem., Grants Rev. Cttes., Med. Research Counc. of Can. and Cancer Rsch. Soc. Inc., Montreal; invited as the principal lectr. in workshop 'Design and Development of Drug-Antibody Conjugates' Inst. of Hematology, Chinese Acad. of Med. Scis., Tianjin, People's Republic of China Nov. 1988; Invited guest lectr., 17th Internat. Meeting of the Controlled Release Soc., Reno, 1990; Chrmn., Workshop on Drug Conjugates and Immunotoxins, Sixth Internat. Conf. on Monoclonal Antibody Immunoconjugates for Cancer, San Diego, CA 1991; recreations: classical music, experimental plays, contemporary history; Home: 444 Franklyn St., Halifax, N.S. B3H 1A9; Office: Sir Charles Tupper Medical Bldg., Halifax, N.S. B3H 4H7.

**GHOSH, Sanjib K.,** Ph.D.; educator; b. Calcutta, India 9 Sept. 1925; s. Sasanka K. and Suniti B. (Mojumder) G.; e. Calcutta Univ. B.Sc. 1945, postgrad. studies 1945–46; Offrs. Training Sch. Survey of India 1946–48; ITC The Netherlands Photogrammetric Eng. 1957, UN Fellow in Eur. 1956–57; Ohio State Univ. Ph.D. 1964; m. Tapati d. Charuchandra and Snehalata Bose 16 Aug. 1951; two s. Sanjoy, Sujoy; PROFESSEUR ASSOCIÉ, DEPT. OF PHOTOGRAMMETRY LAVAL UNIV. 1992– , Prof. 1979–92, retired; Surveyor 1948–60; Prin. Instr. in Photogrammetry Survey of India 1957–60; Rsch. Assoc. in Photogrammetry Ohio State Univ. 1960, Instr. 1961, Asst. Prof. 1964, Assoc. Prof. & Rsch. Supvr. 1967–79, Faculty Adv. India Assn. 1970–76; served Am. Soc. Photogrammetry & Remote Sensing various capacities, latterly as Pres. Great Lakes Region and Dir. Photog. Survey Div. 1965–82 and Internat. Soc. Photog. & Rem. Sensing various positions 1970– ; UN Cons. World Cartography 1980– ; Distinguished Visiting Prof. several internat. univs. 1974– ; recipient Citation and Ford Bartlett Award ASPRS 1971; Cert. of Commendation Ohio House of Reps. 1978; Prize of Excellence Can. finalist Invention cat. 1986; el. Fellow ACSM 1989; originator New Method Determining Latitude & Azimuth in Astronomy 1953; co-holder US-Can. patent Simulator Allowing Spatial Viewing Cerebral Probes using Floating Line Concept 1985–86; author 'Stereophotogrammetry' 2 edns. 1968, 1972; 'Phototriangulation' 1975; 'Analytical Photogrammetry' 2 edns. 1980, 1988; co-author 'Methods in Cell Biology' Vol. 22 1981; 'Perspectives in Agricultural Geography' 2 editions 1981, 1990; 'Non-topographic Photogrammetry' 2 edns. 1979, 1989; 'Space Commercialization: Satellite Technology' Vol. 128, 1990; over 160 other publs., rsch. reports, jour. articles; Hindu; recreations: photography, travel, reading; Home: 5330 Bressler Dr., Columbus, Ohio 43026, USA; Office: 1355 Pavillon Casault, Laval Univ., Québec, Qué. G1K 7P4.

**GIANGRANDE, Carole,** M.A.; author; b. Mount Vernon, N.Y. 20 Jan. 1945; d. Vincent James and Antonia Giovanina (Tedesco) G.; e. Univ. of Toronto, B.A. 1966, M.A. 1968; m. Brian s. late Henry Louis and late Eileen Gibson 15 July 1983; teacher Pol. Sci. Seneca Coll. Applied Arts & Technol. 1968–73; freelance broadcaster, writer and researcher CBC Radio 1973–79, progs. incl. 'Ideas,' 'Quirks and Quarks,' 'Metro Morning'; co-host CBC 'Radio Noon' 1979–84; full-time freelance author, broadcaster and pub. speaker since 1984; Writer-in-Residence Cobourg, Ont. Pub. Lib. 1987; daily contributor, CBC 'Radio Noon' 1989; Writer-in-Residence, North York (Ont.) Public Lib., fall 1990; Media Writing Instr., Ryerson Polytechnical Inst., Toronto 1991–92; recipient Can. Council Arts Grant Non-Fiction Writing 1985, Explorations Grant Writing 1983; Ont. Arts Council Writers Grants 1982, 1984, 1992, 1993; Prov. Ont. Writers-in-Libs. Grant 1987; Scholarship, May Writing Studios, Banff Ctr. for the Arts 1992; author: 'The Nuclear North: The People, The Regions and The Arms Race' 1983; 'Down to Earth: The Crisis in Canadian Farming' 1985; 'Missing Persons' (short fiction collection) 1994; short fiction published in 'Grain,' 'New Quarterly,' 'Matrix,' 'Canadian Forum' and 'Descant'; mem. ACTRA; Writers Union Can. (Ont. Rep 1993–94); recreations: music, gardening; Home: 18 Glenaden Ave. W., Etobicoke, Ont. M8Y 2L7.

**GIANNOU, Chris Paul,** C.M., M.B., B.Ch., M.Ch.; surgeon; b. Toronto, Ont. 16 Sept. 1949; s. Paul Chris and Anastasia (Sulla) (Fotinos) G.; e. Univ. of Toronto Schs.; McGill Univ.; Algiers Univ.; Cairo Univ., Fac. of Med., M.B., B.Ch. 1975; Cairo Univ., Nat Cancer Inst., M.Ch. 1979; m. Saïda d. Arzki and Dania Belas 1971; div. 1984; Surgeon, Palestine Red Cres. Soc. 1980–89; left Can. 1968; Teacher, Bamako, Mali 1968–69; Algiers 1969–71; Cairo 1971–80; Chief Res., Gaza Hosp., Palestine Red Cres. Soc. (PRCS) 1980; Establ. & dir., PRCS hosp., Nabatieh, S. Lebanon 1981; Tripoli, N. Lebanon 1983; Sanaa, N. Yemen 1985; Shatila Refugee Camp, Beirut 1985–88; Dir., PRCS hosp., Cairo 1984; prisoner of war, Israeli Army, released after Candn. govt. intervention 1982; delegate of Candn. Red Cross, surgeon with Internat. Ctte. of Red Cross, Somalia 1990, Cambodia 1991, Somalia 1992–93, Afghanistan 1993, Burundi 1993–94; Hum. Award, Assn. of Arab-Am. Univ. Grad. 1982; Velan Foundation, Montreal Rotary Internat. Hum. Award 1987; Star of Palestine, Extve. Ctte., P.L.O. 1987; Mem., Extve. Ctte., PRCS 1987–89; Member of the Order of Canada 1990; author of several med. jour. articles; publ. 'Besieged: A Doctor's Story of Life and Death in Beirut' 1990; 'Vie et Mort au Camp de Chatila' 1993; Home: c/o Janetos, 1 Revlis Cres., Scarborough, Ont. M1V 1E8.

**GIARD, Alphonse,** Q.C., B.A., L.LL.; lawyer; b. 1937; e. Sém. de Phil. B.A. 1958; Univ. of Montreal L.LL. 1961; post-grad. study 1962–65; VICE-PRES., LAW & SECY., CANADIAN NATIONAL RAILWAYS 1983– ; Pres., Bd. of Dir., Montreal Chest Hosp. 1981– ; Gov., Montreal Chest Hosp. Found. 1981; mem. Que Bar; Candn. Bar Assn. (mem. Extve. Ctte.; Pres. Que. Air Law Section 1975–77); Montreal C. of C.; recreations: fitness, golf, boating; Home: 42 Barwick St., Pierrefonds, Que. H8Z 2W8; Office: Box 8100, Montreal, Que. H3C 3N4.

**GIARRUSSO, Giovanni,** B.Com., C.A.; b. Montreal, Que. 22 March 1939; s. Michele and Marie (Ciarlo) G.; e. Ecole St-Philippe-de-Benizi 1953; Ecole Supérieure St-Viateur 1957; Sir George Williams Univ. B. Com. 1961; McGill Univ. Accounting 1961–63; C.A. 1967; Harvard Bus. Sch. AMP 1990; m. Suzanne d. Lucien l'Ecuyer, Montreal, Que. 1 Sept.1962; children: Nathalie, Gian Carlo; EXTVE. VICE PRES. AND CHIEF OPERATING OFFICER, MONTREAL EXCHANGE 1974– ; Student in Accounts 1961–63 Touche, Ross, Bailey & Smart; joined Exchange as Asst. to Secy. 1963, Dir. of Listings 1964, Vice Pres. and Secy. 1969, Extve. Vice Pres. Adm. 1973; mem. Ordre des Comptables Agréés du Qué.; Mem.: Chambre de Comm. Française au Can.; Montreal Bd. Trade; Chambre de Commerce du District de Montréal; Candn. Italian Business & Professional Assn.; Italian Chamber of Comm.; Dir., Candn. Depository for Securities Ltd.; Office: B.P. 61, 800 Victoria Sq., Montreal, Que. H4Z 1A9.

**GIBARA, Germaine,** B.A., M.A., C.F.A.; business executive; b. Cairo Egypt 20 Sept. 1944; d. Michel Antoine and Odette (Turcomani) G.; e. American Univ. in Cairo (High Hons.) B.A. 1966; Dalhousie Univ. M.A. 1968; C.F.A.; Harvard Univ. PM.D. 1984; Pres., Alcan Automotive Structures 1988–92; Investment Analyst & Portfolio Mgr., Lombard Odier Canada 1970–75; Dir., Investor Relns., Alcan Aluminum Ltd. 1975–84; leader of a diversification study for Alcan's C.E.O. with Profs. Porter & Monitor 1985–86; Project Mgr., Automotive Technol. Dept., Alcan Internat. 1986–88; Fed. Govt. SAGIT (Indus.) 1987– ; Financial Analysts Soc.; occasional guest teacher on transfer of technol. at M.I.T. & McGill; voted Woman of the Year (Business) 1990; Dir., Theatre du Nouveau Monde; Centraide; recreations: tennis, skiing, flute; clubs: MAAA, Hillside; Home: Habitat 67, #517, Montreal, Que. H3C 3R6; Office: 630 Réné Levesque Ouest, Montreal, Que.

**GIBB, Robert Duncan,** B.Sc., M.B.A.; business executive; b. Manitoba 15 May 1945; s. the late James and Lavina Mary (Milne) G.; e. Univ. of Manitoba B.Sc. 1966; Harvard Business Sch. M.B.A. 1970; m. Sally-Anne d. Arnie and Olive Gillis 6 Apr. 1968; children: Christy, Matthew; Senior Vice Pres., Canadian Liquid Air 1993– ; Principal, The Cypress Group 1992– ; Business Analyst & Sales Engr., Imperial Oil Limited Toronto & Winnipeg 1966–68, 1969; Sales Engr. & Area Mgr., Raychem Corp. San Francisco & Chicago 1970–75; Pres., Gibb Farms Limited Winnipeg 1975–83; Pres., Raychem Can. Limited Toronto & Mgr., Raychem Corp.'s Caribbean opns. 1983–90; Pres. & C.E.O., Canadian Oxygen Limited 1990–92; Dir., Agrico Canada Ltd.; Dir., MKS Inc. of Waterloo; Jr. Achievement of Toronto; Harvard Bus. Sch. Club of Toronto; recreations: golf, tennis, skiing; clubs: Founders Club; St. Charles Country; The Manitoba, Man.; St. Georges Golf (Dir.); The Boulevard; The Fitness Inst.; Heights of Horseshoe Ski, Ont.; Home: 107 Ravensbourne Cres., Islington, Ont. M9A 2B3.

**GIBBARD, Harold Allan,** Ph.D.; retired university professor: b. Mission City, B.C. 25 Jan. 1912; s. George and Clara Gertrude (Cox) G.; e. Pub. and High Schs., Mission City B.C., 1918–27; Univ. of B.C., B.A. (Econ.) 1932; McGill Univ., M.A. (Sociol.) 1934; Univ. of Mich., Ph.D. (Sociol.) 1938; m. Eleanor Elizabeth. d. late J. Addison Reid, 8 Sept. 1938; children: Allan Fletcher, Sarah Eleanor (Mrs. A.M. Cook); Instr. and Rsch. Asst. in Sociol., Mich. State Univ. 1937–38; Instr. and Asst. Prof. of Sociol., Brown Univ. 1938–46; Asst. Prof. of Sociol., Univ. of Kansas 1946–48; Visiting Assoc. Prof. of Sociol., Univ. of Missouri, summer 1947; Prof. of Sociol., West Virginia Univ. 1948–77, Chrmn. Dept. of Sociol. and Anthrop. 1948–69 and 1975–77; Acting Dean, Coll. of Arts and Sciences 1969–70, Asst. to Provost for Instr. 1970–76, Assoc. Provost for Instr. 1976–77, Professor Emeritus 1977; Rsch. Assoc., Makerere Univ. Coll., Kampala, Uganda 1968; co-author; 'Fundamentals of Sociology' 1950; 'A Survey of the Educational Programs of the West Virginia Public Schools' 1957; 'The Southern Appalachian Region, A Survey' 1962, 'Poverty Amid Affluence' 1966; 'Retraining the Unemployed' 1968; other writings incl. articles and book reviews; mem., Am. Sociol. Assn.; North Central Sociol. Assn. (Pres. 1960–61); Democrat; Unitarian; Home: 741 Augusta Ave., Morgantown, W. Va. 26505.

**GIBBINS, Roger,** B.A., M.A., Ph.D.; university professor; b. Prince George, B.C. 17 Apr. 1947; s. Louis George and Frances Eugene (Olds) G.; e. Prince George Sr. S.S. 1965; Univ. of B.C. B.A. (Hons.) 1969; Stanford Univ. M.A. 1970, Ph.D. 1974; m. Isabel d. William and Margaret King 24 Aug. 1968; children: Christopher, Daniel; PROF. & HEAD, DEPT. OF POLITICAL SCIENCE, UNIVERSITY OF CALGARY; joined present univ. 1973; Former Co-editor (English language) 'Canadian Journal of Political Science'; author: 'Conflict and Unity: An Introduction to Canadian Political Life' 1990, 'Regionalism: Territorial Politics in Canada and the United States' 1982, 'Prairie Politics and Society' 1980; co-author: 'New Elites in Old States' 1990, 'Canadian Political Life: An Alberta Perspective' 1990; Home: 145 Hawkdale Circle N.W., Calgary, Alta. T3G 2W9; Office: Calgary, Alta. T2N 1N4.

**GIBBS, Leonard James;** artist; b. Cranbrook, B.C. 5 May 1929; s. Alex James and Roberta Charlotte (Butcher) G.; e. Brandon, Man. and Edmonton, Alta.; m. Elizabeth d. Andrew and May Ballantine 3 Oct. 1953; children: Brandy Elizabeth, Michael Kenneth; former Vice Pres. and Creative Dir. James Lovick Advertising; self-employed artist over 25 yrs.; named Hon. Alta. Artist 1983, Hon. Citizen City of Victoria 1985; exhns. incl. Travelling Exhn. to Peking, Shanghai, Szchewan 1981; Prairie Art Gallery Grande Prairie 1981; West End Gallery Edmonton 1981, 1983, 1985, 1988, 1992; Hollander York Gallery Toronto 1984, 1986, 1987, 1989, 1993; Candn. Soc. Marine Artists Vancouver & Victoria 1984, 1986, 1987, 1993; Royal Inst. Painters in Watercolour London, Eng. 1984, 1985, 1986, 1987, 1988; Runnings Gall., Seattle, WA 1992; Art Gall. of Greater Victoria 1993; numerous exhns. Can., USA, Eng. and Denmark prior to 1980; rep. maj. corporate colls. Can.; co-author 'The Art of Len Gibbs' 1981; 'Yacht Portraits' 1987; 'Images' 1988; articles various mags. & art jours.; half hour TV film 'Len Gibbs, The Artist' prod. 1989; mem., Union Club of B.C.; recreations: sailing, miniatures; Home: 1, 416 Dallas Rd., Victoria, B.C. V8V 1A9.

**GIBBS, Ronald Darnley,** M.Sc., Ph.D., F.R.S.C., F.L.S.; botanist; emeritus professor; b. Ryde, Isle of Wight, Engl. 30 June 1904; s. late Frank Ernest and Edith Beatrice (Wills) G.; e. Univ. Coll., Southampton, Eng.; Univ. of London, B.Sc. 1925, Ph.D. 1933; McGill Univ., M.Sc. 1926; Bd. of Educ. Cert. in Teaching 1923; m. Dr. Avis Patricia Cook 1961; one s.; Macdonald Prof. of Botany, McGill Univ., 1965–71, (Prof. of Botany there 1955–65), Prof. Emeritus, 1971; Pres., Fraser Inst., Montreal, 1955–58; Bio-chemist, Am. Rubber Producers, Salinas, Cal., 1927–28; Fellow, Roy. Soc. Can., 1939 (Pres., Sect. 5, 1953–54); Fellow, Linnean Society of London, 1949; emeritus mem., Am. Soc. Plant Physiol.; author (with E.J. Holmes) 'A Modern Biology' 1937; 'Botany: An Evolutionary Approach' 1950; 'Chemotaxonomy of Flowering Plants' 1974; has also contrib. about 30 papers and articles to scient. journs.; Sigma Xi (Pres. McGill Chapter 1944); recreations: gardening; Home: 32 Orchards Way, Southampton SO2 1RD, England.

**GIBEAULT, André,** LL.L., M.B.A.; lawyer; b. Montreal, Que. 31 Oct. 1936; s. Hervé and Germaine (Prévost) G.; e. Univ. of Montreal LL.L. 1961; Columbia Univ. M.B.A. 1963; m. Michèle d. Adalbert Jarry 15 July 1961; one s.: Eric; SR. VICE-PRES., LEGAL AFFAIRS, LEVESQUE BEAUBIEN GEOFFRION INC. 1992– ; began career in 1963 with Credit Interprov. Inc. which through mergers & acquisitions, etc. became Lévesque Beaubien Geoffrion Inc.; Corp. Sec. & Legal Counsel 1975–92; Director or Officer of various privately held companies; Trustee or Fiduciary of various estates; Treas., Lower Canada Arms Collectors Assn. Inc.; Mem., Military Vehicle Preservation Assn. U.S.A.; Candn. Charolais Assn.; recreations: Charolais breeder, arms collector, Candn. Army vehicles of World War II restoration; Home: 4590 Stanley Weir, Montreal, Que.; Office: 1155 Metcalfe St., Montreal, Que. H3B 4S9.

**GIBSON, Donald Armstrong,** M.D., F.R.C.S.(C); orthopaedic surgeon; retired; b. Kaifeng, Honan, China 15 June 1924; s. Douglas Medlicott and Janet Paterson (Nelson) G.; e. Chefoo Sch., China; Univ. of B.C., pre-med.; Univ. of Toronto M.D. 1946; m. Elizabeth d. Thomas and Eva Hutchings 1950; children: Ian, Joy, Robin; Medical Dir., The Hugh MacMillan Medical Centre 1977–89; Assoc. Prof. of Surg. and of Rehab. Med. Univ. of Toronto 1977–89; surgical training 1946–52; Missionary surg., Kampala, Uganda 1952–59; Orthopaedic training 1959–62; apptd. to surgical staff Hosp. for Sick Children, Toronto 1962; leave of absence to serve CIDA teaching orthopaedics at Makerere Coll., Uganda 1969–71; Chief, Orthopaedic Div., Hosp. for Sick Children 1971–77; Bd. Mem., Leprosy Mission Can.; contbr. 'Care of the Injured Child' 1975; 'Rehabilitation Management of Amputees' 1982; mem., Ont. Med. Assn.; Dewar Orthopaedic Soc.; Candn. Orthopaedic Assn.; recreations: bonsai, carpentry, photography; Home: R.R. #1, Kirkfield, Ont. K0M 2B0.

**GIBSON, Douglas Maitland,** M.A.; book publisher; b. Kilmarnock, Scot. 4 Dec. 1943; s. Thomas Young, O.B.E. and Janet Thomson (Maitland) G.; e. Dunlop Pub. Sch.; Glasgow Acad.; Univ. of St. Andrews M.A. (Sloan Prize) 1966; Yale Univ. M.A. 1967; two d. Meg, Katie; PUBLISHER, McCLELLAND & STEWART 1988– ; came. to Can. 1967; Adm. Asst. to Registrar, McMaster Univ. 1967–68; Ed. Trainee, Doubleday Canada, Toronto and N.Y. 1968, Mng. Ed. 1969; Ed. Dir., Macmillan of Canada 1974; Publisher 1979–86; Publisher, Douglas Gibson Books 1986–88; Teacher, Book Publishers' Profl. Assn. Course on Editing 1979–80; Faculty Advr. Banff Publishing Workshop Prog. 1980–83, Prog. Co-Dir. 1984–88; Mem., Working Ctte., Candn. Centre for Studies in Publishing, Simon Fraser Univ. 1986–87; Mem., Adv. Bd. 1987– , Chrmn. 1988–93; Mem. Bd., Assoc. of Candn. Publishers 1989–90; Judge: Nat. Mag. Awards Humour 1982, Fiction 1984–85; CBC Lit. Competition 1985; The Financial Post Award For Business In The Arts 1987, Jury Chrmn. 1988; Dir. Candn. Conf. Arts 1984–85, Extve. Ctte. 1986–88; Chrmn., Awards Ctte. 1986–88; weekly film reviewer CBC Radio 'Sunday Morning' 1981–84; nominated Nat. Mag. Award for Humour 1979; Guest Speaker 1983, Learned Soc.'s Conf. to Candn. Oral Hist. Assn.; Guest Speaker, Internat. Publishers' Assoc. Congress, London 1988; rec'd President's Award, Candn. Booksellers' Assoc. 1991; frequent invited speaker various groups, writers' confs. and univ. classes; co-author: 'Author and Editor: A Working Guide' 1983; 'The Bumper Book' 1986; ed. 'Hugh MacLennan's Best' (anthology) 1991; author various articles mags and journs.; mem. Internat. PEN; Past Pres. St. Andrews Univ. Club Toronto; mem. Leacock Associates; recreations: sports, art, films, theatre, reading; Clubs: Rosedale Tennis; Mooredale Swimming Pool; Home: 15 Pine Hill Rd., Toronto, Ont. M4W 1P5; Office: Suite 900, 481 University Ave., Toronto, Ont. M5G 2E9.

**GIBSON, Graeme C.,** C.M., B.A.; author; b. London, Ont. 9 Aug. 1934; s. Brig. Thomas Graeme and Mary B. (Cameron) G.; e. Univ. of Waterloo 1953–54; Univ. of W. Ont. 1954–55, 1956–58 B.A.; Univ. of Edinburgh 1955–56; children: Thomas Matthew Mann, Graeme Charles Alexander, Eleanor Jess Atwood; author 'Five Legs' 1969; 'Communion' 1971; 'Eleven Canadian Novelists' 1973; 'Perpetual Motion' 1982; 'Gentleman Death' 1993; Founding mem. Writers' Union of Can. (Chrmn. 1974–75); Chrmn. Book & Periodical Devel. Council 1976; Chrmn. Writers' Devel. Trust 1977–78; Pres., Candn. Centre, Internat. P.E.N. 1987–89; apptd. Member, Order of Canada 1992; recreations: birding, travel, nature; Address: c/o Writers Union, 24 Ryerson Ave., Toronto, Ont. M5T 2P3.

**GIBSON, J. Kerr,** B.Com., F.C.A.; b. Hamilton Ont., 12 Aug. 1924; s. Hon. Colin William George and Florence (Kerr) G.; e. Hillfield Sch. Hamilton, Ont. 1941; Upper Can. Coll. Toronto, Ont. 1942; Univ. of Toronto B. Com. 1948; m. Marion Alison d. Brig. G. R. D. Farmer, Ancaster, Ont., 31 May 1952; children: Marian, Jane, Nancy, James; joined Clarkson Gordon firm 1948, partner 1956–84; served with Candn. Army 1944–45, rank Pte.; Chrmn. Candn. Tax Foundation, 1975–76 (Gov. 1968–71 and 1973–77); Pres. Bd. Trade Metrop. Toronto 1977–78, (mem. Council 1970–79), Dir., Amex Bank of Canada 1990– ; 1993 Internat. Choral Festival (1987– ;); The Glory of Mozart Festival Inc. 1990– ; Preview Concerts for Young Candn. Musicians 1990– ; Kappa Alpha; Liberal; Presbyterian; recreation: tennis; Clubs: University; Queens; Tamahaac; Home: 164 Sulphur Springs Rd., Ancaster, Ont. L9G 4T7; Office: Ste. 1510, 1 First Canadian Place, P.O. Box 19, Toronto, Ont. M5K 1A9.

**GIBSON, James Alexander,** C.M., M.A., M.Litt., D. Phil. (Oxon.); LL.D.; president emeritus; b. Ottawa, Ont., 29 Jan. 1912; s. John Wesley, M.A., D.Paed., & Belle Crawford (Magee) G.; e. Public and High Schs. and Victoria Coll., Victoria, B.C.; Univ. of B.C., B.A. 1931; New Coll. Oxford (Rhodes Scholar from B.C. 1931), B.A. 1933, M.Litt. 1934, D.Phil. (Modern History) 1938, M.A. 1953; Carleton Univ., LL.D. 1964; Brock University, LL.D. 1984; m. Caroline Rauch, d. late Rev. J.R. Stein, D.D., Philadelphia, Pa., 29 Dec. 1938; children: Mrs. Julia C. Matthews, Peter James, Mrs. Gérald Joly; Emeritus Pres., Brock Univ. 1974 (apptd. Pres. 1963); Lecturer, University of British Columbia, 1937–38; Foreign Service Offr., Dept. of External Affairs, 1938–47 (seconded to office of Prime Min.); mem. Candn. del. to U.N. Conf. on Internat. Organ., San Francisco (1945); Secy to Prime Min. at meeting of Commonwealth Prime Mins., London (1946); mem. Candn. del. Conf. on Peace Treaties, Paris (1946); joined Carleton Univ. as Assoc. Prof. of Hist., 1947; Prof. 1949; Dean, Faculty of Arts & Science, 1951–63; Dean of Arts and Deputy to the Pres., 1963; resigned 1963; Guggenheim Fellow 1953; Visiting Fellow, Princeton Univ., 1953–54; Visiting Scholar, Univ. of Kent at Canterbury, 1972; Visiting Prof. of Candn. Studies, Univ. of Edinburgh, 1976–77; Jules & Gabrielle Léger Fellowship, 1980; Publications: 'Sir Edmund Head: A Scholarly Governor' (with D.G.G. Kerr), 1954; 'A Governor General looks at Canada' 1978; contrib. to learned journs.; mem. Bd. Govs. Ridley Coll. 1964–1982; Pres., Candn. Assn. Rhodes Scholars, 1963–65, Secy.-Treas. 1977–87 and Ed., 1975– ; Chrmn. Niagara District Health Council 1982–84; mem., Canadian Hist. Association; Candn. Inst. Internat. Affairs; Pres., Canadian Writers Foundation, Inc., 1960–63; Vice-Pres., UN Assn. in Can. 1970–72; awarded Medal of Hellenic Red Cross, 1953; Coronation Medal, 1953; Centennial Medal, 1967; Queen Elizabeth II Silver Jubilee Medal, 1977; Prix du Mérite, Canadien Jeunesse Education, 1990; C.M. 1992; Unitarian; recreation: gardening; Home: R.R.1, Vineland Stn., Ont. L0R 2E0.

**GIBSON, John Desmond,** B.A., LL.B., C.D., A.D.C.; barrister & solicitor; b. Hamilton, Ont. 6 Nov. 1949; s. Desmond Hope and Margaret Howard (Ambrose) G.; e. Trinity College School 1967; Royal Military College of Canada B.A. (1st Class Hons.) 1971; Univ. of Toronto LL.B. 1974; m. Gail S. d. John and Dorothy Spencer 19 June 1971; children: Heather, Jennifer; BARRISTER & SOLICITOR, RICKETTS, HARRIS 1976– ; Mem., Candn. Bar Assn.; County of York Law Assn.; Toronto Lawyers' Club; Fort York Br., Royal Candn. Legion; Commanding Officer, 7th Toronto Regiment, Royal Candn. Artillery 1985–88; Sec., Toronto Artillery Found. 1978– ; Dir., Royal Candn. Military Inst. 1988– ; (Vice-Pres. 1991– ;); Aide-de-Camp to Lieutent Gov. of Ont. 1975– ; Past Pres., Toronto Br., Royal Military College Club 1984–85; Pres., Royal Candn. Artillery Assn. 1992; Mem., Extve. Ctte., St. John Ambulance Toronto Br. 1988–93; Mem., Bd. of Dir., St. John Ambulance Ont. Council 1992; Hon. Solicitor, Dominion of Canada Rifle Assn.; Ont. Rifle Assn.; Pres., Last Post Fund, Ont. Br.; Anglican; recreations: squash, running, riding; clubs: Royal Candn. Military Inst.; Home: 16 Glengrove Ave. E., Toronto, Ont. M4N 1E7; Office: 181 University Ave., Suite 816, Toronto, Ont. M5H 2X7.

**GIBSON, John Edward Guy,** B.A.; foreign service officer; b. Hamilton, Ont. 26 Dec. 1937; s. John Stephenson and Dorothy Verna (Shaver) G.; e. Univ. of West. Ont., B.A. 1958; Univ. of London; m. Jayne E. d. Kenneth R. and Jessie MacGregor 18 May 1963; children: Deborah Jayne, Julia Lynn, Jennifer Elizabeth; CONSUL-GENERAL OF CANADA, DALLAS, TEXAS; joined Trade Comnr. Serv. 1962; overseas assignments: Mexico City 1963–66; Canberra, Austr. 1966–68, Islamabad, Pakistan 1968–70, Caracas, Venezuela 1972–76; The Hague, NL 1976–79; Dir. Gen., Eur. Bur., Dept. of Indus., Trade & Comm. 1979–81; Asst. Under Sec., Eur. Trade Devel., Dept. of External Affairs 1982–83; Ambassador of Can. to Colombia 1983–87; Dir. Gen., Internat. Mktg. Bureau, Dept. of External Affairs 1987–92; Anglican; author of var. articles on internat. mktg.; recreations: golf, swimming; Clubs: Royal Oaks C.C.; City Club, Dallas; Home: P.O. Box 72, Portland, Ont.; Office: Candn. Consulate General, 750 N. St. Paul, Suite 1700, Dallas, Texas 75201.

**GIBSON, Neville Ernest;** retired real estate executive; b. Liverpool, Eng. 26 Jan. 1929; DIR., GROSVENOR INTERNATIONAL HOLDINGS LTD. 1970– ; Dir., Barclays Bank of Canada; Fellow, Royal Inst. Chart. Surveyors; Past Pres., Candn. Inst. of Public Real Estate Cos.; recreations: sailing, tennis; Clubs: Vancouver; Royal Vancouver Yacht; Royal Victoria Yacht; Australia Club (Sydney); Victoria Golf; Office: 21st Fl., The Grosvenor Bldg., 1040 W. Georgia St., Vancouver, B.C. V6E 4H1.

**GIBSON, Robert Orford,** B.Comm., M.B.A.; marketing executive; b. Ottawa, Ont. 3 Nov. 1939; s. Judge Clarence Cecil and Mildred Louise (Burn) G.; e. Glebe Coll. 1959; Carleton Univ. B.Comm. 1964; York Univ. M.B.A. 1970; m. Ann P. d. Air Commodore Joseph and Helene Hurley 18 July 1970; children: Robin, Maggie, Graham; PRES., CONTACTS TARGET MARKETING INC. 1990– ; Extve. Asst. to Dep. Min. of Revenue, Govt. of Ont. 1970–79; Mgr. of Admin. & Finan., Wood Gundy Ltd. 1979–84; Mgr., Syndication Control, McLeod Young Weir Ltd. 1984–85; Asst. Vice-Pres., Merrill Lynch Canada Inc. 1985–88; Vice-Pres., Pemberton Securities Inc. 1988–89; Mem., Vancouver Bd. of Trade; Victoria C. of C.; Vancouver Extves. Assn.; Executive Network; Sales & Mktg. Extves. Assn.; Candn. Direct Mktg. Assn.; recreations: skiing, hiking; Club Sierra; Home: 5837 Angus Dr., Vancouver, B.C. V6M 3N7; Office: 1260 E. Georgia, Vancouver, B.C. V6A 2B1.

**GIBSON, Ronald Dale,** B.A., LL.M., F.R.S.C.; educator; b. Winnipeg, Man. 17 May 1933; s. Benjamin Boright and Anna Sarah (Johnston) G.; e. Univ. of Man. B.A. 1954, LL.B. 1958; Harvard Univ. LL.M. 1959; m. Lee d. George and Evelyn Patterson 18 May 1956; children: Kristin Lee, Allan Scott; m. Sandra Anderson d. Ellsworth and Geraldine Mosher 26 June 1993; BELZBERG FELLOW OF LAW, UNIV. OF ALBERTA 1993–94; Asst. Prof. of Law, Univ. of Man. 1959, Assoc. Prof. 1964, Prof. 1968, Distinguished Prof. 1984, Chrmn. Legal Rsch. Inst. 1968–82; Belzberg Prof. of Constitutional Studies, Univ. of Alberta 1988–90, Bowker Prof. of Law 1991–93; Dir. Archives W. Candn. Legal Hist. 1970–80; mem. Man. Law Reform Comn. 1970–79; Chairperson, Man. Human Rights Comn. 1982–84; recipient Univ. of Man. and Law Soc. Man. Gold Medals in Law 1958; Man. Rh Inst. Grant for Contributions to Scholarship & Rsch. 1975; Law Reform Comn. Can. Award for Legal Rsch. & Reform 1986; author 'The Law of the Charter: Equality Rights' 1989; 'The Law of the Charter: General Principles' 1986; co-author 'Substantial Justice: Law and Lawyers in Manitoba 1670–1970' 1972; 'Attorney for the Frontier: Enos Stutsman' 1983; 'The Bear That Wouldn't Dance: Failed Attempts to Reform the Soviet Constitution' 1992; ed. and contbr. 'Aspects of Privacy Law' 1980; co-ed. and contbr. 'Law in Cynical Society: Law and Public Opinion in the 1980s' 1985, 'Glimpses of Canadian Legal History' 1991; Home: 11018 – 125 St., Edmonton, Alta. T5M 0M1; Office: Fac. of Law, Univ. of Alberta, Edmonton, Alta. T6G 2H5.

**GIBSON, Russell Gordon;** publisher; s. Gordon Russell and Elaine Rosemary (Herrick) G.; e. Univ. of Ottawa; Univ. of W. Ont.; PRESIDENT, DIRECTOR & CORP. SEC., GIDNEY NEWS & PUBLISHING LIMITED 1993– ; Researcher & Writer, The Financial Post 'Directory of Government' 1988–89; Asst. Ed. 1991–93; Assoc. Ed. 1993; Placement Officer, Employment & Immigration Canada 1990; Consultant, E.R. Fisher Ltd. 1990–92; Researcher (Air Investigations Br.), Transportation Safety Bd. 1992; Co-Founder & Vice-Pres., Candn. Parly. Serv. 1991–93; Reporter, 'United Press International' 1992–93; Pres. & Gov., Bruce M. Hicks Edn. Found. 1993– ; Mem., Candn. Bar Assn.; Phi Delta Phi; Candn. Parly. Press Gallery; Vice-Chair, Nat. Liberal Advisory Team 1993 Gen. Election; Liberal; club: National Press; Office: 2408, 221 Lyon St. N., Ottawa, Ont. K1R 7X5.

**GIBSON, Shirley Mann;** writer; broadcaster; arts administrator; b. Toronto, Ont. 28 Dec. 1927; d. Charles Stuart and Ivy Grace (Mann) White; e. Howard Park Public School and W. Tech. & Comm. High Sch., Toronto; m. Graeme Cameron Gibson, 1959; two s., Thomas Matthew Mann, Graeme Charles Alexander; divorced 1976; EXTVE. PROD., OPEN COLLEGE, CJRT/FM 1989– ; joined Radio Stn. CHUM, Toronto, 1944–45; Asst. to Curator, London (Ont.) Art Museum, 1946–52; founded and managed own retail business 1953–59; Asst. to Ed., 'Arts/Canada' mag. 1967–69; joined House of Anansi Press as Mang. Ed. 1970; Pres. Mang. Ed. and Dir. 1972–74; Extve. Dir., Playwrights Canada 1977–83; apptd. to Bd. of Dirs., 'Dying With Dignity' 1993; apptd. to Curriculum Ctte., Ryerson P.I. Publishing Prog. 1989; Vice-Pres. Can. Centre of Internat. Theatre Inst. 1980–83; Pres., Assn. of Cultural Executives, 1981–83; apptd. Dir., Internat. Theatre Congress, Canada/1985, 1983–84; mem. Nat. Joint-Parl. Comte. on Cult. Policy; former mem. Bd. of Govs., Candn. Conf. of the Arts; Past Chrmn. League Candn. Poets; author, 'I am Watching' (poetry) 1973; 'Bloodline and other Poems' 1982; awarded Queen's Jubilee Medal 1977; Can. Council Senior Arts Grant (Writing) 1979; Explorations Grant 1984; Ont. Govt. Volunteer Service Award 1986; Protestant; recreations: books, music; Clubs: Bookmen's; Home: 314 Sumach St., Toronto, Ont. M5A 3K5.

**GIBSON, Terence R.,** B.Com., M.B.A., C.F.A.; investment executive; b. Essex, England 4 Dec. 1939; s. Jack A. and Elizabeth (Gill) G.; e. Univ. of B.C., B.Com. 1962; Univ. of Cal. Berkeley M.B.A. 1964; Univ. of Va. C.F.A. 1971; m. Sandy Howard 17 Aug. 1985; children: Susan, Wendy, David, Andrea, Tom Howard, David Howard; PRES., EMERGING ALBERTA RESOURCE CORP.; Pres., TRG Management Ltd.; CWM Investment Management Inc.; Dir., Beaufort Exploration Ltd.; Pelorus Navigation Systems Inc.; joined Wood Gundy Ltd. 1962–80 becoming Vice Pres. and Dir., Corporate Finance Alta.; Partner, GT Management 1981–87; Clubs: Glencoe; Calgary Petroleum; Home: G301, 500 Eau Claire Ave. S.W., Calgary, Alta. T2P 3R8; Office: 500, 635 8th Ave. S.W., Calgary, Alta. T2P 3M3.

**GIBSON, Thomas H.;** b. Beaupre, Que. 8 Nov. 1929; s. Thomas Ayton and Dorothy Elizabeth (Armstrong) G.; e. Jarvis C.I. 1950; m. Betty Anne d. Roy and Lillian Shields 3 Oct. 1952; children: Judith, Thomas, Shelley, John, Catherine; Volunteer Consultant, Candn. Extve. Service Orgn. (C.E.S.O.); with Lever Bros Ltd. 1950; Advtg. Mgr. Exquisite Form Brassiere Can. Ltd. 1957; Advtg. and Sales Promotion Mgr. Traders Group Ltd. 1959; Dir. of Tourism Advtg., Dept. of Tourism Info. 1971; Dir. Tourism Mktg., Min. of Industry and Tourism 1974; Gen. Mgr. Ontario Place 1982; Depy Min., Min. of Tourism & Recreation 1984–85; Dean, Sch. of Tourism and Hospitality, Georgian Coll. of Applied Arts and Technology 1985–90; Partner, A Tisket A Tasket 1990–92, retired; Treasr. Attractions Ont. 1982; Dir. Tourism Ind. Assn. of Canada 1983; Co-Chrmn. T.I.A.C. Education Ctte. 1986–89; mem. Marketing Ctte., Art Gallery of Ontario 1986–89; Co-Chrmn., C.H.R.I.E. Industry Govt. Liaison 1987–89; Dir., Georgian Lakelands Travel Assoc. 1987–89; mem., Candn. Tourism Mgmt. Centre Adv. Ctte. 1987–90; Club; Albany (Toronto); Scouting Long Service Medal and Medal of Merit; Home: Box 220, Coboconk, Ont. K0M 1K0.

**GIBSON, William Boyd,** B.A., B.Comm., C.A.; financial executive; b. Brandon, Man. 25 June 1947; s. Walter Bury and Marion Isobel (Boyd) G.; e. Univ. of Sask. B.A. 1968, B.Comm. 1970; C.A. 1973; m. Karen d. Armand and Berneice Donais 1 May 1982; children: David, Amy; Pres. & C.E.O., Crown Management Bd. of Sask. 1986–..; Arthur Andersen & Co. 1970–76; Nu-West Group Ltd. 1976–85; recreations: golf, curling; clubs: Wascana Golf & Country, Assiniboia, Derrick Golf & Country.

**GIBSON, William Carleton,** M.D., D.Phil.; b. Ottawa, Ont. 4 Sept. 1913; s. John Wesley and Belle Crawford G.; e. Univ. of B.C. B.A. 1933; McGill Univ. M.Sc. 1936, M.D. 1941; Oxford Univ. D.Phil. 1938; LL.D. (Hon.) McGill Univ. 1986; D.Sc. (Hon.) Victoria Univ. 1991; D.Sc. (Hon.) Univ. of B.C. 1993; m. Barbara Catherine (dec.) d. late Dr. Walter Stewart Baird 28 Dec. 1946; children: David Baird Penfield, Ian Kenneth, Catherine Ann; m. Ruth Elizabeth Pyper Bourne 1984 (dec.); m. Clotilde Southgate 1989; Chancellor, Univ. of Victoria, 1985–90; Chrmn., Terry Fox Med. Res. Fdn.; B.C.; Kinsmen Prof. of Neurol. Research Univ. of B.C. 1950–60, Prof. Hist. of Med. & Science 1960–78; Dir. of Research, Mental Hosps. of New S. Wales, Sydney 1948–49; Visiting Prof. Neurol. Univ. of Cal. San Francisco 1949, Hist. of Med. Yale 1960; Ald. City of Vancouver 1972–74, 1976–78, Parks Commr. 1974–76; Chrmn. Univs. Council of B.C. (adv. to Govt. of B.C. on univ. affairs) 1979–84; served with RCAF 1941–45, Clin. Investigation Units, Depy. Dir. Med. Research AFHQ 1945; Sr. Med. Offr. 19 Wing (Auxiliary) Vancouver; Wing Commdr. 1950–60; rec'd Centennial Medal 1967; Queen's Silver Jubilee Medal 1977; author 'Young Endeavour' and 'Creative Minds in Medicine' 1959; co-author 'The World of Ramon y Cajal' 1962; 'Sherrington: His Life and Thought' 1978; 150 scient. articles on brain research and med. hist.; Hon. Fellow, Green College, Oxford and Green College, U.B.C.; Bot. Gdns. Assn. (Past Pres.); Past Pres. UBC Alumni Assn.; UBC Faculty Assn.; Past Pres. Am. Osler Soc.; mem., Council of the Rockefeller Univ. in New York; Hon. mem. Osler Club London; Med. Soc. London; Hon. Fellow, Royal Society of Medicine; Past Vice-Pres., Muscular Dystrophy, N.Y., 1987; Mayor's Cttee., Jerusalem; United Church; recreation: music; Home: 123, 2345 Cedar Hill Cross Road, Victoria B.C. V8P 5M8.

**GIDMARK, David;** writer; b. Chippewa Falls, Wis. 28 Nov. 1947; s. Vernon and Irene (Hughes) G.; e. Moorpark Coll. Cal.; Univ. of Wis.; Univ. de Grenoble, France; m. Ernestine d. Jonas and Florence Caibaiosai 23 July 1988; author 'Journey Across A Continent' 1977; 'The Indian Crafts of William and Mary Commanda' 1980; 'The Algonquin Birchbark Canoe' 1988; 'Birchbark Canoe' 1989; numerous articles Candn. and Am. mags., newspapers, legal jours.; cons. British Museum, Nat. Museums Can.; Co-founder The Maranda Found.; recreation: splitting wood; Address: Box 26, Maniwaki, Que. J9E 3B3.

**GIERUSZCZAK, Thaddeus Edward,** B.Sc.; P.Eng.; b. Sulkowice, Krakow, Poland 25 Sept. 1923; s. late Albert Wojciech and Anna (Marek) G.; came to Canada 1929; e. Holy Rosary Separate Sch. Hamilton, Ont. 1936; Cathedral High Sch. 1941; McMaster Univ. B.Sc. (Hons.) Chem. and Physics 1945; Univ. of Toronto, M.B.A. course; m. Alda Isabelle, d. late John Torrey 26 July 1958; children: John Albert, Lori Jean, Marianne; Vice-Pres. Administrative Services, Consumers' Gas Co. 1980–85 (ret'd 1986); joined the Co. as Lab. Asst. Works Div. 1947, Chief Chem. Works Div. 1952, Staff Asst. to Gen. Supt. Works 1955, Asst. Gen. Supt. Gas Supply 1957, Asst. to Vice-Pres. Gas Supply 1966, Staff Asst. to Pres. and Mgr. Research and Devel. 1968, Asst. to Pres. 1970; Vice-Pres. Research and Special Projects, 1973; First Chrmn. Bd. Dirs. Candn. Gas Research Inst.; Past Pres., Ont. Natural Gas Assn.; Dir., Watusa Investments Ltd.; mem., Chem. Inst. Can. (Past Treas. Econ. and Business Mang. Div.); recipient: Am. Gas Assn. Award of Merit 1965; Queen Elizabeth II Silver Jubilee Medal 1977 for contributions to Candn. gas industry; Hon. Life Mem., Ont. Natural Gas Assoc., Candn. Gas Assoc., Candn. Gas Rsch. Inst.; Assn. Prof. Engrs. Ont.; United Church; recreations: gardening, fishing, philately, skiing, golfing, curling; Clubs: Canadian; Toronto Bd. of Trade; Home: 57 Doonaree Dr., Don Mills, Ont. M3A 1M5.

**GIFFEN, John A.,** B.Sc., M.B.A.; executive; b. Ingersoll, Ont. 17 Dec. 1938; s. John and Kathleen Marion (McQuinn) G.; e. Univ. of Windsor B.Sc. 1962, M.B.A. 1972; m. Joan E. d. Walter and Marion Rothwell 20 Jan. 1962; children: John Walter, Janis Beth, Julie Michelle; CHRMN., CORBY DISTILLERIES LTD. 1992– , Dir. 1980– ; Regional Chrmn.-The Americas, Allied-Lyons PLC 1992–93, Dir. 1988–93; Dir., Hiram Walker-Gooderham & Worts Ltd. 1982–86 and 1988–93, mem. Mgmt. Bd. 1987–88; Depy. Chrmn., The Hiram Walker Group 1992–93; mem. Windsor Adv. Bd. Royal Trustco; joined Hiram Walker as Plant Foreman 1962, Project Eng. 1965, Div. Supt. 1972, Inventory Mgr. 1973, N. Am. Distbn. Mgr. 1977, Asst. to Pres. 1979, Vice Pres.- Worldwide Prodn. 1980; Pres., Hiram Walker & Sons Ltd. 1987–88; Chrmn. and C.E.O., Hiram Walker – Allied Vintners (Canada) Ltd. 1988–89; & Sons Ltd. 1987–89; Mng. Dir., Hiram Walker - Allied Vintners Ltd. 1989–91; Chrmn. & Chief Extve., The Hiram Walker Group 1991–92; Pres., Hiram Walker-Gooderham & Worts Ltd. 1989–92; Dir. and Vice Pres. Windsor C. of C. 1979–83; mem. Can.-UK Ctte. Candn. C. of C. 1983–91; Gov. Metrop. Gen. Hosp., Windsor 1979–85; Dir. Inst. Candn.-Am. Studies 1983–86; recreations: golf, curling; Clubs: Beach Grove & Country; St. Clair Beach; Windsor; Office: Walkerville P.O. Box 2518, Windsor, Ont.

**GIFFIN, Hon. Ronald Chapman,** LL.B., Q.C.; former politician; b. Windsor, N.S. 1 Dec. 1942; s. Reginald Manning Giffin; e. Windsor Acad. 1959; Acadia Univ. B.A. 1963; Dalhousie Univ. Law Sch. LL.B. 1966; Q.C. 1982; m. Patricia Wade 11 July 1970; two s. Gregory Bennett, Christopher Reginald; ARCHIBALD & LEDERMAN, Truro, N.S.; called to Bar of N.S. 1966; Partner, Burchell, MacDougall & Gruchy, Truro, N.S. 1966–78; el. M.L.A. for Truro-Bible Hill prov. g.e. 1978, re-elected 1981, 1984, 1988, did not re-offer prov. g.e. 1993; Min. of Mun. Affairs and Min. responsible adm. Human Rights Act 1978–79; Chrmn., Management Bd. N.S. 1979–81; Pres., Treasury Bd.; Min. responsible for Adm. of Civil Service Act 1979–81, mem. Exec. Council; N.S.; Pres. Colchester Barristers Soc. 1978; Min. of Transportation & Min. Responsible for Comm. Policy, N.S. 1981–83; Attorney General and Provincial Secy. N.S. 1983–87; Min. of Vocational and Technical Training 1987; Min. of Educ. 1987–92; mem. N.S. Barristers Soc. (Council 1976–78); Candn. Bar Assn.; P. Conservative; Baptist; recreations: curling, swimming, movies, reading, cooking; Club: Truro Men's; Home: 34 Broad St., Truro N.S. B2N 3G2; Office: 43 Walker St., P.O. Box 1100, Truro N.S. B2N 5G9.

**GIFFORD, Anthony Marston,** M.A.; management consultant; b. Kingston, Ont. 22 July 1944; s. John M. and Barbara A. (Macnee) G.; e. Univ. of Toronto B.A. 1965; Queen's Univ. M.A. 1967; m. Nancy Lee d. Edwin and Elizabeth Mooers 8 June 1968; children: Lee, Sally, Kathleen; Teacher of Eng. & Drama, North Toronto C.I. 1968–71; Acting Head & Asst. Prof., Dramatic Arts. Dept., Faculty of Ed., Univ. of Toronto 1971–74; Utilization Officer & Directing Ed. of Educational Pubs., Ont. Educational Communications Authority 1974–77; Dean, Applied Arts, Ryerson Polytech. Inst. 1977–80, Vice-Pres., Academic 1980–83; Prof. 1983–84; Sr. Consultant, William M. Mercer Ltd., 1984–86; Pres., Wilson Learning (Canada) Ltd. 1986–88; Pres., Gifford Services Inc., 1988– ; Partner, Peat, Marwick, Stevenson and Kellogg 1990–93; Partner, KPMG Management Consulting 1994– ; editor 'The Play's The Thing,' 1976; ed. 'Making Television Educational,' 1977; Bd. of Trade of Metro. Toronto 1981–86; Bd. of Dir., CJRT-FM Inc. 1980–83; mem., Council of Ont. Universities 1980–83; The Delta Seminar, GAMMA 1978–82; Intl. Inst. of Communications 1977–83; Dir., St. Philips Community School 1980–81; Chrmn., Education Div.; United Way of Metro Tor. 1981 and 1982 campaigns; National Task Force on Youth Employment 1983; Chrmn., Bd. of Triune Acting Ensemble 1984–85; Mem. Bd. of Dir., Toronto Internat. Jazz Festival 1986– ; Mem., Bd. of Dirs., Ont. Music Arts Centre 1989– ; recreations: squash, skiing, jogging; Club: Dunfield Squash; Home: 234 Glengrove Ave., Toronto, Ont. M4R 1P4.

**GIFFORD, Hilda Gorham,** B.A., B.L.S., D.Litt; retired librarian; b. Montreal, P.Q. 22 Sept. 1915; d. William Alva and Charlotte Elsie (Hitcham) G.; e. McGill Univ. B.A. 1937, B.L.S. 1938; D.Litt. (Hon. causa), Carleton Univ. 1982; with Dalhousie Univ. Library, Halifax, N.S., 1938–43; Postal Censorship, German P.O.W., 1943–45; Internat. Labour Office Lib., 1945–46; Dartmouth Coll. Lib., Hanover, N.H., 1947–48; Chief Lib., Carleton Univ. 1948–69; Collections Librarian there 1969–81; United Church; recreation: travelling; Clubs: Cercle Universitaire (Ottawa); Royal Overseas League (London); Home: 150 Queen Elizabeth Driveway, Apt. 109, Ottawa, Ont. K2P 1E7.

**GIGANTES, Hon. Philippe Deane,** M.A., Ph.D.; senator; b. Greece 16 Aug. 1923; s. General Christodoulos, K.C.B., D.S.O., M.C. and Mary (Dracouli) G.; e. Lycée Janson de Sailly Paris; Athens Coll. (Greece); Royal Naval Coll. (Dartmouth, Eng.); Univ. of Toronto Trinity Coll. M.A., Ph.D.; Carleton Univ. Econ.; m. Sylvie Bedard 1974; children: Eleni, Claire, Eve-Marie; Foreign Corr. The Observer, London and The Observer Foreign News Service 1950–56, Washington Corr. 1956–61; Dir. U.N. Office Washington, D.C. 1961–64; Sec. Gen. to the King of Greece, 1964; Min. of Culture, Greece 1964–65; writer and host CBC TV 'The Public Eye'; also wrote and produced various CBC TV specials 1965–66; Columnist Thomson newspapers 1967–70; Prof. of Classics and Dean 1970–72; Sr. Exec. Offr., Candn. Pub. Service 1972–79 serving as Dir. Gen. Lang. Bureau, Special Asst. to Prime Min.; Columnist and ed. writer Ottawa Journal 1979–80; mem. Ed. Bd. and ed. writer The Gazette, Montreal 1981–84; summoned to the Senate of Can. 1984; served with Britain's Royal Navy WW II; author 11 books on urban planning, the UN, hist., full employment and training, trade and travel; winner, Bowater award for journalism 1960; Office: The Senate, 202, 140 Wellington St., Ottawa, Ont. K1A 0A4.

**GIGNAC, Jacques,** B.A., TH.L., L.ScS., L. Lettres; diplomate; né Shawinigan, Qué. 24 Juil. 1928; f. James (décédé) et Jeanne (Gigaire) G. (décédée); é. Collège Jean-de-Brébeuf, Montréal, Institut des Sciences Politiques, Paris; Institut Catholique de Paris; La Sorbonne; Etudes post graduées (Sociologie) Univ. de Montréal; ép. Françoise, f. Guilhem Teisserenc (décédé) et Elisabeth Coste (décédée), Lodève, France, 19 Juil. 1958; enfants: Guillaume, Sébastien, Emmanuel, Marie-Félicité, Marie-Flore; Ambassadeur du Canada aux Pays-Bas 1987–92; Professeur d'économie au Collège Ste.-Marie, Montréal 1957–58; entre au Ministère des Affaires extérieures comme agent du service extérieur, Ottawa 1958; Direction de l'Information 1958; Direction des Affaires d'Asie 1959; Vice-Consul, Boston, Mass. 1960; Deuxième Secrétaire, Paris 1962–65; Adjoint, Direction des Affaires culturelles, Ottawa 1965, puis Chef, 1967–70; Ambassadeur du Canada au Liban, 1970–74, et concurremment en Syrie, 1970, en Jordanie 1970, ainsi qu'en Iraq en 1972 et en Arabie Saoudite en 1973; Ambassadeur en Tunisie 1974–77; Dir. général des Affaires d'Amérique Latine et des Antilles, 1977; Sous-Secrétaire d'Etat adjoint aux Affaires extérieures 1978; Sous-secrétaire d'Etat suppléant, 1981; Sous-Ministre adjoint 1982; Ambassadeur et Chef de la Mission du Canada près les Communautés écon. européennes (C.E.E.) 1982–86; Ambassadeur, Représentant Permanent du Canada aupès des Organisations Internationales à Vienne 1986–87; Cath. romain; récréations: ski, natation, golf, lecture; Bureau: Ministere des Affaires Extérieures (A/S APE), Promenade Sussex 125, Ottawa, Ont. K1A 0G2.

**GIGNAC, Jean-Paul,** O.C. (1976), B.A., B.Sc.A., P.Eng.; industrial executive; b. Shawinigan, Que. 7 Feb. 1922; s. James and Jeanne (Giguère) G.; e. Coll. Jean-de-Brébeuf, B.A. 1942; Ecole Polytechnique B.Sc.A. (Engn.) 1947; m. Joan Hébert, Shawinigan, Que. 11 Dec. 1947; 7 children; Bd. Chrmn., Roctest Ltée; Special Consultant, Hatch & Associates; mem. Extve. Comte. (1967–70) and mem. Bd. of Govs. (1967–73) Univ. of Montréal; former Dir., B.G. Checo International (1984–93); Hydrogenal Inc. (1983–87); Hydro Quebec (1983–87); Power Corporation (1969–92); Pratt and Whitney, Canada, Inc. (1975–80); former Dir., Conf. Bd. Can.; Dir. and mem., Extve. Comte., Candn. Standards Assn. 1963–69; mem., Natl. Research Counc. 1968–72; began as Engn. Supvr., Dufresne Engineering 1947–51; Extve. Vice Pres. & Gen. Mgr. of Albert Gigaire Co. Ltd., Shawinigan, 1951–69; Commr., Hydro-Québec 1961–69; Pres. & C.E.O. Sidbec & Sidbec-Dosco Ltd. 1966–79; Pres. & C.E.O. Iron and Steel Co. Trinidad & Tobago, Pt. of Spain, Trinidad, W.I. 1979–83; Awards: Dr. Applied Science, Univ. Sherbrooke (1968), Montreal (1973); Hon. Life Dir., Bd. of Govs., Univ. de Montréal 1978; Prix Mérite annuel de l'Assoc. des Diplômés de Polytechnique 1978; Mérite d'Or, Univ. Montreal (1947); 'Man of the Year' York Univ. (1968); Archambault Medal for Advanc. of Sciences (1971); Officer, Order of Canada 1976; recreations: tennis, golf, skiing; R. Catholic; Home: 3400 rue de la Montagne, Shawinigan, Que. G9N 6V4.

**GIGUÈRE, Diane;** writer; b. Montréal, Qué.; d. Louis G. and Carmen Liliane (Harvey) G.; e. Coll. Marie de France; Conserv. Dramatic Arts (First Prize 1956); stage and TV actress in French and Eng.; announcer CBC French network 25 yrs.; author 'Le temps des jeux' 1961, Eng. transl. 'Innocence' (Prix du Cercle du livre de France 1961); 'L'eau est profonde' 1965, Eng. transl. 'Whirlpool'; 'Dans les ailes du vent' 1975, Eng. transl. 'Wings in the Wind' (Prix France-Québec 1976); 'L'Abandon' 1993; recipient Guggenheim Fellowship Award 1969; recreation: outdoor sports; Address: 304, 60 William Paul, Nun's Island, Que. H3E 1M6.

**GIGUERE, Hon. Louis de G.;** senator; retired administrator; b. Hébertville, Qué., 18 Dec. 1911; s. Joseph and Alexina (Michaud) G.; e. Chicoutimi (Qué.) Coll.; Sherbrooke (Qué.) Coll.; Laval Univ., Law, Social Sciences and Pol. Econ. 1934–37; Secy. Gen., Institut Canadien des Affaires publiques 1954–61; Dir. and mem. Extve. Comte., Central Mortgage & Housing Corp. 1963–68; mem. Candn. NATO Parlty. Assn. and Candn. World Federalists Parlty. Assn.; Canada U.S. Inter-Parliamentary Group; mem. Standing Senate Comte. on Foreign Affairs; Nat. Finance Comte.; Candn. Observer to U.N. 1984; summoned to Senate of Can. Sept. 1968; Liberal; recreation: golf; Clubs: Laval sur le Lac Golf; Indian Creek Country (Fla.); Home: 1455 Sherbrooke West, Montreal, Que. H3G 1L2.

**GILBERT, Most Rev. Arthur Joseph,** D.D., B.A., B.D. (R.C.); bishop emeritus; b. Hedley, B.C. 26 Oct. 1915; s. George Miles and Ethel May (Carter) G.; e. St. Joseph's (N.B.) Coll.; St. Francis Xavier Univ. B.A.; Holy Heart Semy. B.D.; BISHOP EMERITUS OF SAINT JOHN, N.B. since 1986; o. Priest 1943; served as Curate St. Andrews Parish N.B.; Secy. to Bishop and Chancellor of Diocese Saint John 1943–49; Dir. Silver Falls Orphanage 1949–55; Pastor St. Pius X Parish 1955–69; St. Joseph's Loch Lomond 1969–71, St. Joachim's Saint John 1974; Bishop of Saint John, N.B. 1974–86; Former Chancellor & Chrmn. Bd. of Governors, St. Thomas Univ. Fredericton, N.B.; Former Chrmn. Bd. Dirs. (diocesan newspaper) 'The New Freeman'; K. of C.; Home: 100 Villa Madonna Road, Renforth, Saint John, N.B. E2H 2T2.

**GILBERT, Guy,** Q.C., B.A., LL.L.; b. Alma, Qué. 19 June 1929; s. Jules and Adrienne (Desjardins) G.; e. St. Charles Garnier Coll. Qué. 1947; Brébeuf Coll. Montréal 1948; Loyola Coll. Montréal B.A. 1951; Univ. of Montréal LL.L. 1955; Univ. of W. Ont. Sch. of Business Adm. 1955–56; m. Lise d. Paul Dufresne, St-Hilaire, Qué. 1 Oct. 1960 children: Frédéric, Philippe, Clément, Bernard; COUNSEL, GUY & GILBERT, BARRISTERS & SOLICITORS 1983– ; Pierre Gauthier & Fils Ltée; called to Bar of Qué. 1955; cr. Q.C. 1972; law practice Tansey, de Grandpré, Bergeron & Monet 1955–62; Sr. Partner, Gilbert, Magnan, Marcotte, Simard, Tremblay & Forget 1962–83; Pres. Goodholme Investments 1960–

61; Pres. Disciplinary Comte. Prof. Corp. Phys. Que. 1974–76; offr. various assns. Brébeuf Coll. 1973–76; Pres. déjeuners-causerie Chambre de Comm. du dist. de Montréal 1974–75; Councillor, Bar of Montreal 1984–85; Bâtonnier, Bar of Montreal 1985–86; Vice Pres., Bar of Que. 1987–88; Bâtonnier, Bar of Quebec 1988–89; Coroner, Inquest on the causes and circumstances surrounding the death of Corporal Marcel Lemay of the Sûreté du Québec; Bd. of Dirs., Foundation du Théâtre du Rideau Vert; Pres., Que. Bar Found.; Pres., Profl. Liability of the Dentists Insur. Fund; Comnr., MacDonald Comn.; served with UNTD 1950–52, rec'd Strathcona Medal; awarded Bronze Medal Competition Order of Forestry Merit Dept. Lands & Forests Qué. 1975; author various articles; del. legal confs.; Counsel Jr. Bar 1960–62; mem. Montréal Bar (offr. various comtes.; prof. to articling students); Qué. Bar Assn. (Secy. 1964–65); Candn. Bar Assn.; R. Catholic; recreations: arts, agriculture, education; politics; Home: 1515 Doctor Penfield Ave., Apt. 504, Montréal, Que. H3G 2R8; Office: 2200, 770 Sherbrooke St. W., Montréal, Que. H3A 1G1.

**GILBERT, Martin (John),** C.B.E., M.A., F.R.S.L.; historian; b. 25 Oct. 1936; s. Peter and Miriam G.; e. Highgate Sch.; Magdalen Coll., Oxford Nat. Serv. (Army) 1955–57; Sr. Rsch. Schol., St. Antony's Coll., Oxford 1960–62; 1st m. Helen d. Joseph Robinson, CBE 1963; one d.; 2nd m. Susan d. Michael Sacher; two s.; OFFICIAL BIOGRAPHER, SIR WINSTON CHURCHILL 1968– ; Res./Sr. Res. Asst. to Hon. R.S. Churchill 1962–67; Recent Hist. Corr., 'Sunday Times' 1967; Res. Asst., BBC 1968; Hist. Adv., Thames TV 1977–78; Script des. & co-author: 'Genocide' 1981; Hist., Cons., Southern Pictures 'Winston Churchill: The Wilderness Years' 1980–81; Hist. Adv., BBC TV 'Auschwitz and the Allies' 1981–82; Hist. Cons. 'Yalta 1942' 1982–83; 'Churchill, A Film Biography' 1989–91; Vis. Lectr., Budapest Univ. 1961; Hebrew Univ. of Jerusalem 1975 (Gov. 1978– ;); Univ. of Cape Town 1984; Soviet Acad. of Sciences, Moscow 1985; Ukrainian Acad. of Sciences, Kiev 1991; and other Eur. & U.S. univs.; Vis. Prof., Univ. of S. Carolina 1965; Tel-Aviv Univ. 1979; Hebrew Univ. 1980; Hon. D.Litt., Westminster Coll. 1981; author: 'Winston S. Churchill' volumes 3–8 1971–88, and nine companion volumes of Churchill documents (the most recent, 'The Churchill War Papers' volume 1, September 1939 - May 1940), and over 30 books (many of them transl.), most recent: 'Churchill, A Life' 1991, 'Second World War' 1989, 'Shcharansky, Portrait of a Hero' 1986, 'The Holocaust: The Jewish Tragedy' 1986, 'Jerusalem: rebirth of a city' 1985, 'The Jews of Hope: the plight of Soviet Jewry today' 1984, 'Atlas of the Holocaust' 1983 (and twelve other atlases), 'Churchill's Political Philosophy' 1981, 'Auschwitz and the Allies' 1981; contbr., hist. articles & reviews to jours.; recreations: drawing maps; Club: Athenaeum; Office: Merton Coll., Oxford, England.

**GILBERT, Robert L.,** M.Sc.; manufacturer; b. Tillsonburg, Ont. 17 Aug. 1945; s. Thomas Leighton and Pearl (Balzer) G.; e. Univ. of Waterloo B.A.Sc. 1969; Univ. of Birmingham M.Sc. (Mech. Eng.) 1970; City Univ. (UK) M.Sc. (Business Adm.) 1971; m. Jean d. Stan and Ruth Colven 28 Aug. 1970; children: Gregory, Carolyn, Brian; PRESIDENT, VME CANADA LTD. 1985– ; Gen. Mgmt. Cons. N.B. Rsch. and Productivity Council 1971–73; Production Mgr. SMI Industries 1973–77; Mgr. Mfg., GSW (Water Heater Div.) 1977–79; Vice Pres., Clark Equipment of Canada Ltd. 1979–82; Pres. 1982–85; Athlone Fellow 1969; recreations: golf, squash, bridge; Club: Highland Golf and Country; Home: 31 Elmgrove Cres., London, Ont. N6J 3X4; Office: 25 Michigan Blvd., St. Thomas, Ont. N5P 1H2.

**GILCHRIST, William McKenzie,** B.Sc.; company president; b. Weyburn. Sask. 29 July 1909; s. William A. and Mary Elizabeth (Scott) G.; e. High Schs., Kelvington, Sask., and Chatham, Ont.; Univ. of Manitoba; Queen's Univ., B.Sc. (Mining and Metall.) 1936; PRES., W.M. GILCHRIST & ASSOC. LTD. since 1975; Director, Madawaska Mines Ltd.; Royal Candn. Geographical Society; Westfield Minerals Ltd.; Candn. Inst. of Mining & Metallurgy (Pres. 1974–75); Candn. Nuclear Assn. (Pres. 1971–72); engaged in various mining operations in Central Man. and N.W. Quebec, 1936–39; Engn. Staff, Preston East Dome Mines Ltd., 1939–41; Efficiency Engr. there, 1945–46; exploration and devel. in N.W. Terr. for Trans American Mining Co. Ltd., 1946–50; Chief Engr. and Underground Supt., Giant Yellowknife Gold Mines Ltd., 1950–51; Vice-Pres. and Mgr. of Mines, Transcontinental Resources Ltd., 1951–52; joined Eldorado Nuclear Ltd. in 1952; Asst. Mgr. of Beaverlodge Operation, 1952–1955, Mgr. 1955–58; Vice-Pres. in charge of Western Operations, 1958; Pres. and Chrmn. of Bd. of Eldorado Nuclear Ltd. and subsidiaries, 1958–74; retired as Pres. of Eldorado Nuclear Ltd., remaining Chrmn. of Bd.; remained as Pres. of all subsidiaries, 1974; retired from all companies 1975; served in 2nd World War, 1941–45 with Royal Canadian Engrs.; discharged with rank of Staff Capt.; awarded Massey Medal, 1975; Clubs: Engineers (Toronto); Rideau; Royal Ottawa Golf; United Church; Address: 2005, 71 Somerset St. W., Ottawa, Ont. K2P 2G2.

**GILES, Philip Douglas,** B.Sc.; survey methodologist; b. Brantford, Ont. 26 Sept. 1955; s. James Mervyn and Irene Miriam (Clair) G.; e. McMaster Univ. B.Sc. (Hons.) 1977; m. Susan Lois d. Herbert and Iris McCooeye 4 July 1987; children: Steven Thomas, Lisa Holly; MANAGER, ANALYSIS AND DISSEMINATION, SURVEY OF LABOUR AND INCOME DYNAMICS, STATISTICS CAN. 1992– ; author or co-author numerous publs. methodology for surveying homeless persons and devel. generalized edit and imputation system; mem. Statistical Soc. Can.; Am. Statistical Assn.; recreations: basketball, baseball, bowling; Home: 6 Rockcress Gardens, Nepean, Ont. K2G 5A3; Office: 11-D8 Jean Talon Bldg., Tunneys Pasture, Ottawa, Ont. K1A 0T6.

**GILES, William Henry,** C.M., Q.C., B.A., LL.B., M.Ed.; educator; lawyer; economist; b. Windsor, Ont. 1 Sept. 1930; s. George Burt and Hazel Viola (Barwick) G.; e. Univ. of Toronto B.A. 1952, grad. studies in Eng. 1954–57; Osgoode Hall LL.B. 1956; Univ. of Toronto M.Ed. 1970, studies towards M.B.A. 1972; m. Anna d. Geza and Katherine Por May 1954 (dec. 1975); children: David, Katherine, Christa; FOUNDER, THE MARKHAM SCH. FOR HUMAN DEVELOPMENT 1989– ; Founder, Dir., The Toronto French Sch. 1962–86; Founder, Dir., Candn. Chemistry & Physics Olympiad; Barrister and Solr. for internat. real estate investors in Can., internat. airlines and hotel co's, mfg. operations; Econ. in Ont. and Kuwait; Dir. various private and pub. corps.; adv. maj. Kuwait corps.; former Dir., Coast to Coast Opera (Opera Can.); Browndale Ont.; Candn. Children's Opera Chorus; recipient C.M. 1973; Queen's Silver Jubilee Medal 1977; cr. Q.C. 1971; author 'A Paean For Love' (poetry) 1985; 'Mazaryk' (3 act play); 'Schools and Students' (legal text on liability in schools and universities) 1988; articles various jours., Toronto Star, Globe and Mail, Ottawa Citizen; mem. Candn. Tax Found.; Candn. Bar Assn.; Am. Bar Assn.; Lawyers & Pilots Bar Assn.; United Church; Home: Apt. 1904, 1501 Woodbine Ave., Toronto, Ont. M4C 4H1; Office: 6075 Kestrel Rd., Mississauga, Ont.

**GILHOOLY, David James, III,** M.A., R.C.A.; artist; b. Auburn, Cal. 15 Apr. 1943; s. Dr. David James, Jr. and Gladys Catherine (Schulte) G.; e. Univ. of Cal. Davis B.A. 1965, M.A. 1967; m. 1stly Sheila Anne d. late Rodney Allée 10 Oct. 1963; children: David James IV, Andrea Elizabeth, Abigail Margaret, Peter Rodney; m. 2ndly Camille, d. Kenne Chang 23 Aug. 1983; children: Hakan Yutatsu; Teacher, San Jose State Coll. 1967–69; Univ. of Sask. 1969–71; York Univ. Toronto 1971–75, 1976–77; Univ. of Cal. Davis 1975–76, summers 1971, 1975, 1976; Cal. State Univ. Sacramento summers 1978–79; maj. solo exhns. incl.: San Francisco Museum of Art 1967; M.H. deYoung Mem. Museum San Francisco 1968; Matrix Gallery Wadswarth Atheneum Hartford, Conn. 1976; Museum of Contemporary Art Chicago 1976; Vancouver Art Gallery 1976; ARCO Center for Visual Arts Los Angeles 1977; Traveling Exhn. Candn. maritimes and Ont. 1978–79; St. Louis Ms. of Art 1981 rep. in numerous group exhns. incl.: Berkeley (Cal.) Art Museum, Inst. Contemporary Art Boston 1967; Musée d'art de la Ville Paris 1973; Art. Gallery Ont. and N.Y. Cultural Center 1973; Whitney Museum of Am. Art N.Y. 1974, 1982; San Francisco Museum of Modern Art 1982, 1983; San Francisco Museum of Art and Nat. Coll. of Fine Art and Nat. Coll. of Fine Art Washington, D.C. 1976–77; Stedelijk Museum Amsterdam 1979; Whitney Mus. of Am. Art, N.Y. 1981; comns. incl. 'Merfrog Family Fountain' Stanford Univ.; 'Seattle's Own Ark' Woodland Park Zoo Seattle; 'Bread Wall' Govt. Can. Bldg. Calgary; 'Performing Frogs' Eugene (Ore.) Center for Performing Arts; rep. in various perm. colls. incl. Nat. Gallery Can.; Can. Council Art Bank; Stedelijk Museum Amsterdam; Whitney Museum of Am. Art and other colls. Can., USA and Australia; work cited various publs.; came to Can. 1969; Candn. citizen 1976; recreations: collecting; Address: c/o Smith-Anderson Gallery, 200 Homer, Palo Alto, CA.

**GILL, Charles F.,** B.Comm., C.A.; jewellery industry executive; b. Toronto, Ont. May 1949; e. Univ. of Toronto B.Comm. 1971; m. Mary Elizabeth; four children; CHIEF FINANCIAL OFFR., THE W.G. YOUNG CO., LTD. 1993– ; Clarkson Gordon 1971–73; Asst. to Vice-Pres., Finance, Peoples Jewellers Limited 1973–75; Asst. to Extve. Vice-Pres. 1975–82; Vice-Pres. Finance & Admin. 1982–86; Sr. Vice-Pres., Finance & Admin. 1986–90; Extve. Vice-Pres. Finance 1990–91; Pres., Peoples Jewellers Limited 1991–93; Mem., C.A. profl. societies; Office: 277 Adelaide St. S., London, Ont. N5Z 3K7.

**GILL, Gwyneth;** banker; b. Calgary, Alta.; divorced; one d.: Diana; EXTVE. VICE PRES., CUSTOMER SEGMENTS, CANADIAN IMPERIAL BANK OF COMMERCE; joined The Royal Bank of Can. 1964; Vice-Pres., Orgn. Planning & Devel., Montreal 1984; Vice-Pres., Retail Banking, Metro Toronto 1987; Sr. Vice-Pres., Mktg. & Planning, Retail, Royal Bank of Canada 1990–..; Office: Commerce Court West, 4th Flr., Toronto, Ont. M5L 1A2.

**GILL, Stephen Matthew,** B.A., M.A.; writer, novelist, literary critic, poet, editor; b. Sialkot, Panjab 25 June 1932; s. Sohan Lal Matthew and Christina G.; e. Panjab Univ. B.A. 1956; Meerut College, Agra Univ. M.A. 1963; Univ. of Ottawa, doctoral prog. 1967–70; Exeter College, Oxford Univ. 1971; m. Sarala d. Subhkti and Baburao 17 Feb. 1970; children: Rekha, Ajay, Sarita; taught in India, Ethiopia & Canada; editor, 'Canadian World Federalist' 1971–73, 1977–79; 'Writer's Lifeline' 1982– ; Chief Delegate, Rep., World University for Can.; Mem., Cornwall Arts Bd. 1992; Pres., Vesta Publications Ltd. 1974–90; Mem., Candn. Authors Assn. (Pres., Cornwall Br. 1977–78); PEN; Internat. Acad. of Poets (Fellow); World Federalists of Can. (Vice-Pres. 1979–81); Indo-Asian Assn. of Cornwall (Vice-Pres. 1986); Multicultural Council of Stormont and Dundas (Vice-Pres. 1987); Edn. Press Assn. of Am.; World Acad. of Arts & Culture; Ont. Grad. Fellowship 1968, '69, '70; Plaque from Biographical Centre, Cambridge, England for distinguished achievement 1982; Fellowship of the Celtic Chair, Univ. of Ottawa 1984; Hon. Doctorate in Lit., World Univ. 1986; World Acad. of Arts & Lit. 1990; Volunteer Serv. Award, Min. of Citizenship & Min. of Culture & Communication 1989 and 1993; Sohan Singh Gill Memorial shiromani Sahitkar Purskar, Candn. Internat. Punjabi Sahit Assn. 1990; Doctorate in Literature, World Acad. of Arts & Culture 1990; Hon. Life Mem., Texas State Poetry Soc. 1991; Fellow Membership and award of Internat. Eminent Poet, Internat. Poets Academy, Madras, India 1991; Pegasus Internat. Poetry for Peace Award, Poetry in the Arts (Inc.), Austin, Texas 1991; Laureate Man of Letters, World Congress of Poets, 1992; Certificate of Appreciation, Asian Biographical Ctr., Toronto 1992; Vice-King of Olympoetry, The Olympoetry Movement, N.Y. 1992; Best Poet of Peace in the World, Rogers Community Cable for the year 1993; author: 'English Grammar for Beginners' 1977; 'Simon and the Snow King' 1981, 'The Blessings of a Bird' 1983 (children's stories); 'Six Symbolist Plays of Yeats' 1974, 'Scientific Romances of H.G. Wells' 1975, 'Political Convictions of G.B. Shaw' 1980 (criticism); 'Life's Vagaries' 1974 (short stories); 'Discovery of Bangladesh' 1975 (history); 'Why' 1976, 'The Loyalist City' 1979, 'Immigrant' 1982 (novels); 'Reflections & Wounds' 1978, 'Moans & Waves' 1989, 'The Dove of Peace' 1989, 'The Flowers of Thirst' 1991, 'Songs for Harmony' 1992 (poems); 'Shrine' 1994 (poems); 'Flashes' (Haiku poems) 1994; ('Immigrant' and poems have been transl. in Punjabi lang.;) 'Sketches of India' 1980 (essays, illus.); 'Aman Di Ghuggi (poems in Panjabi) 1994; anthology editor: 'Tales from Canada for Children Everywhere' 1979, 'Green Snow' 1976, 'Anti-War Poems' vol. 1 1984, vol. 2 1986; 'Asian Poets of North America; anthology co-editor: 'Poets of the Capital' 1974, 'Seaway Valley Poets' 1975; Editor-in-Chief, 'Who's Who of North American Poets'; mem., United Poets Laureate International; The Doctorate Assn. (N.Y., USA); recreations: to promote world peace and make friends; Mailing address: P.O. Box 32, Cornwall, Ont. K6H 5R9.

**GILLAM, Heath,** C.M.A.; financial executive; b. London, Ont. 4 July 1992; s. Ronald Heath and Eleanor Elizabeth (Hiscox) G.; e. Soc. of Mngt. Accountants of Ont. C.M.A. 1974; m. Donna M. d. Cliff and Annie Wright 19 Oct. 1963; children: Gregory H., Laura L.; ASST. TREASURER, EMCO LIMITED; joined Emco 1958; Mem., Soc. of Managment Accountants of Ont.; recreations: fishing, hunting; Home: 160 Stanley St., South Thamesford, Ont. N0M 2M0; Office: 620 Richmond St., London, Ont. N6A 4L6.

**GILLESE, Eileen Elizabeth,** B.Com. & Business Adm., B.A. (Honors Jurisprudence), B.C.L. (Oxon.); lawyer; educator; b. Edmonton, Alta. 8 July 1954; d. John Patrick and Thelma Elizabeth G.; e. Univ. of Alta. B.Com. & Business Adm. 1977; Oxford Univ. (Rhodes Scholar) B.A. 1979, B.C.L. (Oxon.) First Class 1980

(Wadham Coll. Prize Acad. Distinction); m. Robert Donald s. Walter and Jean Badun 14 Aug. 1982; children: Meghan Elizabeth Badun, David Robert Badun, Amy Evelyn Badun, Sarah Jean Badun; PROF. OF LAW, UNIV. OF W. ONT. 1983– , Assoc. Dean (Administration) 1992– ; on leave to practice law with McCarthy Tétrault, London, Ont. 1989–91; Assoc. Dean (Academic), Fac. of Law 1988–89; articled with Reynolds, Mirth & Cote, Edmonton; called to Bar of Alta. 1981; called to Ont. Bar 1988; law practice with above firm 1980–83; Sessional Lectr. in Law Univ. of Alta. 1983 and in Business 1981; Charter mem., Associates Program Faculty of Business, mem., Senate 1976, Exec. mem. Alumni Assn. 1981–83; Dir., Nat. Rhodes Scholar Assn. Can. 1982–85; Ont. Rhodes Scholar Selection Ctte. 1986–93 (Secy. 1989–93); Ont. Pension Comn. 1988– ; (Vice Chrmn. 1989– ;); Ont. Municipal Police Authorities 1987; Comnr., London Municipal Police Comn. 1986–88; Conf. on Access to Civil Justice, Attorney-Gen., Prov. of Ont. 1988: 'The Role of Paralegals in the Provision of Legal Services'; publ. rsch. paper for Task Force on Paralegals, Attorney-Gen. Prov. of Ont.: 'Potential Regulatory Mechanisms for Independent Paralegals'; Author of 'Case Note Re Kowbel'; 'The Rights of a Beneficiary in an Unadministered Estate'; 'Workbook on the Fundamentals of Canadian Law' (3rd ed. 1991); 'Case Note Re Purpur'; 'Greymac Trust Company: A Comment'; 'Legal Research, Writing and Moot Court Materials' 5th ed.; 'Study Guide to The Law and Business Administration in Canada' 6th ed.; 'The Rights of an Adopted Child on a Natural Parent's Intestacy'; 'Case Note "Mernickle v. Westaway"'; Case Note Re Levy (The Philanthropist); 'Vehicle Operational Safety and Insurance, Learning Workbook' 1985; 'Property Law Cases, Text and Materials' 2nd ed. 1990; Co-author (with R. Solomon) 'An Introduction to the Law Governing Physicians' 4th ed. 1991; (with A.H. Oosterhoff) 'Text, Commentary and Cases on the Law of Trusts' 4th ed. 1992; 'OSC v. Greymac Credit Corp.' a case note in 1985 and a subsequent one in 1987; publ. papers: 'Employee Rights Under Bill 170' 1987; 'Fiduciary Relations and Their Impact on Business and Commerce' 1988; Ed. Bd. (Assoc. Ed.), 'The Dominion Law Reports,' 'The All Weekly Canada Summaries' (1988– ;); Ed. Bd., 'The Estates and Trusts Journals'; mem., Law Faculty Bd. Oxford 1980; recipient Prov. Alta. Scholarship 1976; Comm. Cup for Outstanding Comm. Student 1976; 2 awards Pres. Univ. Alta. for Outstanding Contrib. to Students 1976; Escheated Estates Award Bd. Govs. Univ. Alta. 1976; named Outstanding Candn. Woman (Fed. Govt. Award) 1978; Award for Faculty Excellence in Teaching 1985–86 and again 1991–92; inaugural award from 3M for excellence in teaching; Univ. of Western Ont. Edward G. Pleva Award for Excellence in Teaching 1993; recreations: squash, hiking, cycling, reading, public speaking; Home: 77 Green Acres Dr., London, Ont. N6G 2S4; Office: Fac. of Law, Univ. of Western Ont., London, Ont. N6K 3M7.

**GILLESHAMMER, Hon. Harold,** M.L.A., B.A., B.Ed.; cabinet minister; b. Winnipeg, Man. 8 April 1942; s. Olaf M. and Karly (Mosti) G.; e. Univ. of Manitoba B.A. 1967; Brandon Univ. B.Ed. 1969; m. Diana d. Carman and Helen Poole 8 July 1967; children: Susan, Barbra; MINISTER OF CULTURE, HERITAGE & CITIZENSHIP, GOVT. OF MANITOBA 1993– ; High School Teacher; Principal; 1st elected to the Man. Leg. g.e. 1988 as member for Minnedosa; Min. of Family Services, Govt. of Manitoba 1990–93; Life Mem., Kinsmen Clubs of Can.; P.C.; Protestant; recreations: skiing, golf; clubs: Minnedosa Alpine, Minnedosa Golf; Home: 367 – 2nd Ave. S.W., Minnedosa, Man. R0J 1E0; Office: Rm. 118, Legislative Bldg., Winnipeg, Man. R3C 0V8.

**GILLESPIE, Hon. Alastair William,** P.C., M.A., M.Com.; b. Victoria, B.C. 1 May 1922; s. Erroll Pilkington and Catherine Beatrice (Oliver) G.; e. Brentwood Coll. Inst., 1937, 1941; Univ. of B.C. 1941; McGill Univ., B.Com. 1947; Oxford Univ., M.A. 1949; Univ. of Toronto, M.Com.; m. Diana Christie, d. Christie T. Clark, 17 June 1947; children: Cynthia, Ian; CHRMN., NATIONAL WESTMINSTER BANK OF CANADA LTD.; currently: Pres., Scotia Synfuels Limited; Alastair Gillespie & Assoc.; formerly: Vice Pres. and Dir., Canadian Corporate Mgmt. Co. Ltd.; Dir. and Vice Pres. Operations, W.J. Gage Ltd.; Dir., Richardson, Bond and Wright Ltd.; International Equipment Co. Ltd.; Mechanics for Electronics Inc.; The Larkin Lumber Co.; Rothmans Internat. PLC; Uniroyal-Goodrich Inc.; Former Chrmn., Scotia Coal Synfuels Project; Carling O'Keefe Ltd.; Point Tupper Terminals Co. 1992–93; Former Pres., Welmet Industries Ltd.; Canadian Chromalox Co. 1965–68; Extve. Lib. Party in Ont. 1965–68; el. to H. of C. for Etobicoke in g.e. 1968, 1972, 1974; defeated g.e. 1979; Partly. Secy. to Pres. of Treasury Bd. 1970; Min. of State for Sci. & Technology 1971–72; Min. of Ind. Trade & Commerce 1972–75; Min. of Energy Mines & Resources 1975–79; mem. Med. Policy Comte. and Budget Comte. Hosp. for Sick Children 1965–68; Dir., Nat. Ballet Sch.; Gage Research Inst.; Chrmn., Candn. Inst. Pub. Affairs 1962–64 (Dir. 1954–65); Pres., Candn. Opera Co. 1986–88; Dir., Ballet Opera House Corp.; Bd. of Govs., Lyndhurst Hospital; served with RCNVR Air Arm 1941–45; rank Lt. (Pilot); Anglican; recreations: skiing, squash, tennis, golf; Clubs: Toronto; Badminton & Racquet; Toronto Golf; Osler Bluff Ski; Home: 175 Heath St. W., Toronto, Ont. M4V 1V1.

**GILLESPIE, John Bedford,** Q.C., B.A.; lawyer; b. Toronto, Ont. 21 Sept. 1926; s. late John K. (M.C.) and late Mary (Simpson) G.; e. Upper Canada Coll.; Trinity Coll., Univ. of Toronto B.A. 1948; Osgoode Hall Law Sch.; articled with McMillan, Binch, Toronto; called to Bar of Ont. 1951; apptd. Q.C. 1970; m. Harriet Louise d. late W. Douglas Morton 28 Aug. 1948; children: John Douglas Howland, Patricia Joan, Barbara Jill, Susan Louise; retired Partner, Fraser & Beatty, Barristers and Solicitors; associated with present firm since 1953; Instr., Corporation Law Sect., Bar Admission Course of Ont. 1960–64; mem.: Law Soc. of Upper Can.; Candn. Bar Assn.; mem. of Council, Bd. of Trade of Metrop. Toronto 1988–92; Trustee Upper Canada Coll. Found. 1978–85; Kappa Alpha; Anglican; recreations: golf, tennis, squash; Clubs: Toronto Golf; The University, Toronto (Dir.); Badminton and Racquet; Muskoka Lakes Golf and Country (Dir. 1978–84); Homes: 55 St. Edmunds Dr., Toronto, Ont. M4N 2P8; (summer) Helen Island, Lake Rosseau, Muskoka, Ont.; Office: P.O. Box 100, First Canadian Place, Toronto, Ont. M5X 1B2.

**GILLESPIE, John H.;** business executive; b. Kitchener, Ont. 24 Mar. 1950; s. Harry J. and Gwendolyn Elgie (Hanna) G.; e. Ryerson Polytech Inst.; Wilfrid Laurier; m. Linda Jean d. James and Ann Yule 18 June 1973; children: Ewan Yule, Elizabeth Jean, Rachel Linda; CHRMN./OWNER, GOLIGER'S TRAVEL (INTERNAT.) LTD. 1988– ; President/Owner, Ryan's Pet Food Inc. (Ont. retail chain) 1992– ; Co-owner/founder, Yule Inc. (franchising & bldg. Pizza Delight outlets in Ont.) 1970–78; Pres./Shareholder, Pizza Pizza Limited (130 franchised outlets in Ont.) 1978–88; Chrmn./Past Pres., Assn. of Candn. Franchisors 1985–89 (designated 'Executive of the Year' 1987); club: Granite; Home: 5 Doncliffe Dr., Toronto, Ont. M4N 2E5; Office: 5230 South Service Rd., Burlington, Ont. L7L 5K2.

**GILLESPIE, Robert Douglas (Sid),** B.A.Sc., M.B.A.; engineering and consulting executive; b. Colborne, Ont. 10 Nov. 1931; s. William Stanley and Ruby Mary (Grant) G.; e. Royal Mil. Coll. Kingston 1955; Univ. of Toronto B.A.Sc. (Mech. Engn.) 1956, M.B.A. 1961; m. Marion Elaine d. Robert Erle MacMurdo 23 May 1955; two d. Susan Elizabeth, Cynthia Margaret; PRES. & C.E.O., MACVIRO CONSULTANTS INC.; joined James F. MacLaren Ltd. 1956 serving as Mech. Engr.; apptd. Dir. and Secy.-Treas. 1962, Extve. Vice Pres. 1971; Consultant to World Health Organ. (water & sewerage) Kabul, Afghanistan and Nassau 1966; dir. various studies incl. Toronto dist. heating study; Project Dir., site selection for Lepreau Nuclear Generating Stn. N.B. Electric Power Comn.; site selection Atomic Energy Organization of Iran nuclear generating stn., Eldorado Nuclear Ltd. uranium hexafluoride plant, Water & Agric. Devel. Studies – Arabian Shield South in Saudi Arabia; qualified as Navig. RCAF; author or co-author various tech. papers; mem. Assn. Consulting Engrs. of Can. (Chrmn. Research & Develop. Comte. 1971–75; Dir. 1979–82); Candn. Nuclear Assn. (Dir. 1979–82); Assn. Prof. Engrs. Ont. (Consulting Practice Comte. 1975–81; Chrmn. 1979–80); Am. Soc. Mech. Engrs.; Am. Water Works Assn.; Water Environment Assn. of Ont.; Water Environment Fed.; United Church; recreations: golf, curling; Club: Thornhill Country (Pres. 1975–76); Home: 12 King Maple Place, Willowdale, Ont. M2K 1X6; Office: 7270 Woodbine Ave., 3rd Flr., Markham, Ont. L3R 4B9.

**GILLESPIE, Robert James,** B.Sc., B.Eng., M.S.I.A.; executive; b. Halifax, N.S. 16 July 1942; s. Robert Leo and Pearl (Wincek) G.; e. Royal Candn. Elect. & Mech. Engrs. Sch. 1961–62; St. Mary's Univ. B.Sc. 1962; N.S. Tech. Coll. B.Eng. (Mech.) 1964; Purdue Univ. M.S.I.A. 1965; m. Carol Ann d. Frank M. Caliendo, Bronxville, N.Y. 16 Nov. 1968; children: Erica Christine, Brooke Caroline, Grant Robert; PRESIDENT, BEST FOODS 1988– ; (A Division of CPC Internat. Inc.) and SENIOR VICE-PRES., CPC INTERNAT. INC. 1991– ; Dir., CPC International, Inc.; Mgr. Facilities Planning, CPC International Inc., Englewood Cliffs, N.J. 1967, Asst. to Vice Pres. Finance Devel. Div. 1969, Product Mgr. Indust. Div. 1970, Group Product Mgr. Indust. Div. 1972, Vice Pres. Business Mang. Indust. Div. 1973; Pres. Canada Starch Co. 1976–80; Pres., Corn Products 1980–84; Extve. Vice-Pres., Best Foods 1984–88; Pres., Best Foods 1988– ; Sr. Vice-Pres., CPC Internat. Inc. 1991– ; served with Candn. Army 1960–64, W. Germany 1963, Halifax 1964; author 'Selection of Engineering Materials and Their Use in A Marine Environment' 1966; 'Merger and Acquisition Factbook' 1970; Bd. of Advisors, Sarah W. Stedman Center for Nutritional Studies, Duke Univ.; recreations: tennis, squash, skiing; Clubs: Montreal Badminton & Squash; St. James's; Upper Ridgewood.

**GILLESPIE, Robert Thomas Ellis,** P.Eng.; executive; b. Edinburgh, Scot. 9 June 1931; e. Heriot-Watt Univ. Edinburgh, Elect. Engn. 1952; Harvard Business Sch., Boston 1976–77; m. Norma Irene; children: Margaret, Susan, Robert; CHRMN. AND CHIEF EXECUTIVE OFFR., GENERAL ELECTRIC CANADA INC.; Dir., General Electric Canada; General Electric Trading Co., New York; GE Fanuc Automation Canada Inc.; GE Plastics Canada Ltd.; Valmet Canada; Bramalea Ltd.; Pres. & Dir., GE Capital Canada; Communications Equipment Design Engr. present Co. Toronto 1952; held various management positions in Designing, Development Engineering & Rsch. and then General Mngmt. in 1967; Vice-Pres., Consumer Products Business Div. 1974; Vice-Pres., Consumer and Construction Products 1977; Extve. Vice-Pres. 1983; Dir. 1991; Vice-Chrmn. 1992; Member, Candn. Council for Internat. Business (Chrmn.); Candn. Standards Assn. (Dir.); Elect. & Electronic Mfrs. Assn. of Canada (Past Chrmn.); Candn. Appliance Mfrs. Assn. (Past Pres.); Fellow, Candn. Acad. of Engrg.; Pres.-Elect, Professional Engrs. of Ont.; Chrmn., Toronto Symphony Orch.; Vice Chrmn., Credit Valley Hospital; Office: 2300 Meadowvale Blvd., Mississauga, Ont. L5N 5P9.

**GILLESPIE, Ronald James,** B.Sc., Ph.D., D.Sc., F.R.S., F.R.S.C., F.C.I.C.; educator; b. London, Eng. 21 Aug. 1924; s. James Andrew and Miriam Grace (Kirk) G.; e. Harrow Co. Sch. Middlesex, UK 1937–42; Univ. Coll. London B.Sc. 1944, Ph.D. 1949; m. Madge Ena d. William Garner 24 June 1951; two d. Ann Hilary, Lynn Judith; PROF. EMERITUS, McMASTER UNIV. 1989– , Prof. of Chemistry 1958–89; author 'Molecular Geometry' 1972; 'Chemistry' 1986, 2nd ed. 1989; 'The VSEPR Model of Molecular Geometry' 1991; 'Atoms, Molecules and Reactions: An Introduction to Chemistry'; over 300 articles inorganic chem. and chem. educ. prof. journs.; recipient Ramsay Medal Univ. Coll. London 1949; Commonwealth Fund Fellowship Brown Univ. 1953–54; Harrison Mem. Medal Chem. Soc. 1954; Noranda Award Chem. Inst. Can. 1966; Candn. Centennial Medal 1967; Am. Chem. Soc. N.E. Region Award Phys. Chem. 1971; Mfg. Chems. Assn. Coll. Chem. Teacher Award 1972; Prof. Associé, Univ. des Sciences et Techniques de Languedoc, Montpellier, France 1972–73; Am. Chem. Soc. Award Distinguished Service Advanc. Inorganic Chem. 1973; Chem. Inst. Can. Union Carbide Award Chem. Educ. 1976; Chem. Inst. Can. Medal 1977; Chem. Soc. Nyholm Lectureship 1978–79; Am. Chem. Soc. Award Creative Work Fluorine Chem. 1981; Henry Marshall Tory Medal, Royal Soc. of Can. 1982; Izaak Walton Killam Memorial Prize 1987; LL.D. (hon. causa), Concordia Univ. 1988; LL.D. (hon. causa), Dalhousie Univ. 1988; Doctorat (hon. causa) Univ. of Mont-pellier, France 1991; recreations: sailing, skiing, travel; Home: 150 Wilson St. W., Apt. 315, Ancaster, Ont. L9G 4E7; Office: Dept. of Chem., McMaster Univ., Hamilton, Ont. L8S 4M1.

**GILLESPIE, Thomas Stuart,** B.A., B.C.L.; advocate; b. Montreal, Que. 18 July 1938; s. Alexander Robert and Lois Tully (O'Brien) G.; e. McGill Univ. B.A. 1959, B.C.L. 1963; m. Caroline Pierce d. William George Herbert Doyle, Boca Grande, Fla. 28 June 1963; children: Caroline Alexandra, Alexandra Olivia, Vanessa Margaret, Joshua William; SENIOR PARTNER, OGILVY RENAULT 1989– ; (Partner 1973–88); Vice Chrmn. & Dir., Montreal YMCA; Dir. H. H. Brown Shoe Co. (Canada) Ltd.; Guerlain Canada Ltd.; Bouverie Investments Ltd.; Carnegie Institution of Can.; Charlottetown Trust Co.; YMCA Canada; Montreal YMCA Found.; called to Bar of Que. 1964; mem., Candn. Bar Assn.; Que. Bar Assn.; Candn. Tax Foundation; Internat. Fiscal Assn.; Assn. de Planification Fiscale et Financière; R. Catholic; recreations: skiing, fishing, golf, reading; Clubs: University; Orleans Fish & Game (Dir.); Mount Bruno Country (Dir.); Tarratine; Home: 48 Aberdeen Ave., Westmount, Que. H3Y 3A4; Office: 1981 McGill College Ave., Montreal, Que. H3A 3C1.

**GILLETT, Margaret,** B.A., Dip.Ed., M.A., Ed.D., LL.D.; university professor; b. Wingham, N.S.W., Australia, 1 Feb. 1930; d. Leslie Frank and Janet Alene (Vickers) G.; e. Univ. of Sydney, B.A. (Eng., Hist., Anthrop.) 1950, Dipl. Educ. 1951; Univ. of Copenhagen, summer 1953; Russell Sage Coll., M.A. (Eng., Sociol.) 1958; Columbia Univ., Ed.D. (Social & Philos. Foundations of Educ.) 1961; Univ. of Saskatchewan, LL.D. 1988; MACDONALD PROF. OF EDUC., MCGILL UNIV., 1982– ; High Sch. Teacher, N.S.W., Aust. 1951–53; Educ. Offr. (Research & Adm.), Commonwealth Office of Educ., Sydney 1954–57; Asst. Prof. of Educ., Dalhousie Univ. 1961–62 and Visiting Prof. there 1967; Registrar, Haile Selaissie I Univ., Addis Ababa, Ethiopia 1962–64; Assoc. Prof. of Educ., McGill Univ. 1964, Prof. 1967, and Chrmn., Dept. of Hist. & Philos. of Educ. 1965–69; Chrmn., Dept. Social Found. of Educ. 1979–80; Founding Ed., 'McGill Journal of Education' 1966–77; author 'A History of Education: Thought and Practice' 1966; 'Readings in the History of Education' 1968; 'Educational Technology: Toward Demystification' 1973; 'We Walked Very Warily: A History of Women at McGill' 1981; 'A Fair Shake: Autobiographical Essays by McGill Women' (co-ed. with Kay Sibbald) 1984; 'Dear Grace: A Romance of History' 1986; 'Aspects of Education' (co-ed. with Ann Beer) 1991; 'Our Own Agendas: A Second Volume of Autobiographies by McGill Women' (co-ed. with Ann Beer) work in progress; co-author 'The Laurel and the Poppy' 1967 (chosen by Catholic Digest Book Club as selection for March '68); contributor, 'Plot Outlines' 1962; Consulting Ed., 'Educational Studies,' (Journ. of Am. Educ. Studies Assn.); co-ed. 'Foundation Studies in Education: Justifications and New Directions' 1973; Ed. Bd., Journal of International Education; Vitae Scholasticae; Fontanus; has written numerous articles for learned journs. and read papers at many prof. conferences; active in Women's Studies; Founding Dir., McGill Centre for Research and Teaching on Women 1988; first chairperson of McGill Senate Comte. on Women; Mem., Bd. of Govs., McGill Univ. 1990–92; mem., Pres., Sub. Comm. on the Status of Women, Candn. Nat. Comm. for Unesco; Bd. mem., Women's Information and Referral Centre, Montreal; rec'd. Canada Council grants for research and writing; recipient, Sage Medal (for contrib. to higher education) 1991; Hon. Life Mem., James McGill Soc. (for contrib. to higher education) 1993; mem., Canadian Association University Teachers; Candn. Assn. Profs. of Educ.; Comparative Educ. Soc. (U.S.): Comparative & Internat. Educ. Soc. Can. (Founding Secy., Pres., 1977–79); Hist. of Educ. Soc.; Foundations of Educ. Soc.; Australian Coll. of Educ.; recreations: tennis, skiing, theatre; Home: 2480 Chemin du Club, Ste. Adele, P.Q. J0R 1L0; Office: 3724 McTavish St., Montreal, Que. H3A 1Y2.

**GILLETT, Robert Charles,** B.A., M.Ed.; educator; b. Ottawa, Ont. 9 Sept. 1943; s. William and Eleanor (Armstrong) G.; e. Carleton Univ. B.A. 1967; Univ. of Ottawa M.Ed. 1978; m. Anne d. Reginald and Evelyn Baker 3 Sept. 1966; children: Stephanie, Dianne; DIR. OF EDN., OTTAWA BD. OF EDN. 1988– ; teacher, Sir John A. MacDonald High Sch. 1969–73; Vice-Prin., Cont. Edn. Dept., Ottawa Bd. of Edn. 1973–77; Vice-Prin., Glebe Collegiate 1977–79; Prin., Cont. Edn. Dept., Ottawa Bd. of Edn. 1979–81; Supt. of Cont. Edn. 1981–83; Supt. of Schools 1983–85; Supt. of Acad. Affairs 1985–87; Asst. Dir. of Edn. 1987–88; Lectr., Univ. of Ottawa 1983–86; Trustee, Children's Hosp. of E. Ont. 1983–86; Mem., Bd. of Govs., Algonquin Coll.; Bd. of Dirs., International Students' Exchange; Dir., Ottawa-Carleton Learning Found.; Am. Mgmt. Assoc.; The Presidents Assoc.; mem. Am. Assn. of Sch. Administrators; Anglican; recreations: Tae Kwon Do, woodworking; Home: 9 Knoll Terr., Nepean, Ont. K2J 2P3; Office: 330 Gilmour St., Ottawa, Ont. K2P 0P9.

**GILLHAM, P. Michael,** B.E., P.Eng.; executive; consulting engineer; b. Montreal, Que. 3 Dec. 1934; s. the late Harry and Emily Avernia (Hinton) G.; e. West Hill High Sch. Montreal 1952; Mount Allison Univ. Dipl. in Engn. 1957; Tech. Univ. of N.S. B.E. 1959, post-grad. courses; m. Ann, d. late Leonard Crane, 27 Aug. 1966; children: Liseanne Kathryn, Jeffrey Michael, Andrew James; PRES., WHITMAN, BENN LTD.; WHITMAN, BENN GROUP INC.; Core Design Group; Dir., Keltic Inc.; mem. Assn. Prof. Engrs. N.S. & Nfld.; Perm. Assn. Navig. Cong's; N.S. Consulting Engrs. Assn. (Past Pres.); Design Constr. Inst. N.S. (Past Dir.); Assn. Consulting Engrs. Can., (Past Pres.); recreations: sailing, skiing; Clubs: R.N.S. Yacht Sqdn. (Past Commodore); Home: 5758 Inglis St., Halifax, N.S. B3H 1K6; Office: 1874 Brunswick St., Halifax, N.S. B3J 2G7.

**GILLIATT, Brig.-Gen. Courtney Spurr S.,** D.F.C., C.D., B.Sc., (AGR), M.A.; b. Annapolis Royal, N.S., 19 Aug. 1921; s. Frederick Courtney and Hortense (Spurr) G.; e. Annapolis Acad. 1938; N.S. Agric. Coll., grad. 1941; Macdonald Coll., McGill Univ., B.Sc. (AGR) 1947; M.A. (International Affairs) Carleton Univ., 1978; m. Helen Wilhelmina, d. W. F. L. Edwards, 1 May 1948; children: Victoria, Christopher, Catherine; joined RCAF 1941; grad. as Pilot 1942; completed tour of operations in Europe on Mosquito Fighter Bomber Aircraft (107 Sqdn. RAF); awarded Distinguished Flying Cross and Mentioned in Dispatches; retired 1945; rejoined 1947; promoted to Brigadier General 1971 and apptd. Dir. Gen. Air Forces; retired 1976; Anglican; recreations: skiing, swimming; Home: 618 Denbury Ave., Ottawa, Ont. K2A 2P1.

**GILLICK, Pat;** sports executive; VICE-PRESIDENT, THE TORONTO BLUE JAYS (WORLD SERIES CHAMPIONS 1992, 1993); Office: 3200, 300 Bremner Blvd., Toronto, Ont. M5V 3B3.

**GILLIES, James,** M.A., Ph.D., LL.D.; educator; b. Teeswater, Ont. 2 Nov. 1924; s. John Midford and Gladys Irene (Macpherson) G.; e. Univ. of W. Ont., B.A. (Econ.); Brown Univ., M.A. (Econ.); Indiana Univ., Ph.D. (Econ.); m. Elizabeth Louise, d. Harry Etienne Matson, 30 Dec. 1953; children: David, Catherine, James, Edward; PROFESSOR EMERITUS OF POLICY, AND DIRECTOR, MAX BELL BUSINESS GOV'T STUDIES PROGRAM FAC. OF ADM. STUDIES, YORK UNIV.; former Dean, Fac. of Adm. Studies 1965–72; Dir. of a no. of important industrial and comm. companies; former mem., Hellyer Task Force; Dir., Senate Comte. on Growth Employment & Price Stability; Prof., Univ. of Calif., 1951–65; served with R.C.A.F. during 2nd World War; former mem. Candn. Civil Libs. Assn.; Humber Mem. Hos.; Export Adv. Counc.; served as Vice Chrmn., Redevel. Agency of City of Los Angeles and Adviser to Calif. Comn. on Metrop. Problems; author of 'Management in the Light Construction Industry' 1962; 'Metropolis: Values in Conflict' 1964; 'Where Business Fails' 1981; contrib. to 'Federal Credit Programs in the Housing Sector of the Economy' 1963; 'Essays in Urban Land Economics' 1966; 'Facing Reality: Consultation, Consensus and Making Economic Policy for the 21st Century' 1986; 'Boardroom Renaissance: Power, Morality, and Performance in the Modern Corporation' 1992; el. M.P. for Don Valley 1972, re-el. 1974; Sr. Policy Adviser to Prime Min. 1979–80; Protestant; Home: 73 Fairway Heights Dr., Thornhill, Ont. L3T 3A7.

**GILLIES, John Frederick,** C.M.A.; financial executive; b. Vancouver, B.C. 8 Nov. 1938; e. C.M.A. 1967; m. Betty Germaine Jeannotte; Sr. Vice-Pres., Mktg., Sales & Admin., Falconbridge Limited 1989–..; worked for Noranda Mines Limited in various positions in opns. & acctg.; joined Falconbridge Group in 1964, Controller various units until 1983; Vice Pres., Controller & Chief Finan. Offr. 1983–86; Vice-Pres., Mktg. & Sales 1986–89; Offr. and/or Dir.: Falconbridge Gold Corp.; Falconbridge (Japan) Ltd.; Falconbridge Limited; Kidd Creek Mines Ltd.; New Pascalis Mines Limited; Ventures Limited; Zeballos Iron Mines Limited; Address: 2458 Deerrun Ave., Oakville, Ont. L6J 6K9.

**GILLIN, Mark Patrick,** B.Sc.Eng., D.Sc.(Hon.); civil engineer; b. Ottawa, Ont. 20 June 1925; s. Col. Mark C. and Marie Lucienne (Desbarats) G.; e. St. Patrick's Coll., Ottawa B.Sc. 1946; Univ. of N.B., B.Sc.Eng. 1949, D.Sc.(Hon.) 1981; m. 1stly Constance d. Falconio and Juliette Choquette 17 Oct. 1952 (dec.); children: Janet (Campbell), Louise, Mark, Andrée (Desjardins); m. 2ndly Heather d. Dr. C.B. and Ruth Petrie 5 Feb. 1971; children: Jeffrey, Christopher; FOUNDER, PRES. & GEN. MGR., GILLIN ENGINEERING & CONSTRUCTION LTD. 1950– ; Pres., Boys & Girls Clubs of Ottawa-Carleton; Chrmn., Bd. of Dirs., Ashbury College; Vice-Pres., Rideau Club; Dir., Elizabeth Bruyère Hosp.; Past Pres., Building Owners & Mgrs. Assn. of Can. 1985–87; recreations: jogging, golf, tennis; Clubs: Rideau; Royal Ottawa Golf; Home: 480 Manor Ave., Rockcliffe, Ont. K1M 0H9; Office: 141 Laurier Ave. W., Ottawa, Ont. K1P 5J3.

**GILLIN, R. Peter,** B.A., C.F.A.; investment banker; b. London, Ont. 3 Feb. 1949; s. Charles H. and Madeleine G.; e. Univ. of Western Ont. B.A. (Hons.); Inst. of Chartered Finan. Analysts, Charlottesville, N.C. C.F.A.; m. Dianne J. d. Douglas and Louise Sloan 4 Nov. 1978; children: Sarah, Andrew, Elizabeth, Claire; SENIOR VICE-PRES., SCOTIAMcLEOD INC. 1988– ; joined present firm 1973; Dir. 1981– ; Gov., Toronto East General Hosp.; recreations: skiing, boating; clubs: Granite, Toronto Hunt; Home: 57 Kingswood Rd., Toronto, Ont. M4E 3N4; Office: P.O. Box 433, Toronto Dominion Ctr., Toronto, Ont. M5K 1M2.

**GILLIS, Daniel Alexander,** M.D., F.R.C.S.(C); surgeon/university professor; b. Point Tupper, N.S. 26 June 1928; s. Alexander and Hilda (Chisholm) G.; e. St. Francis Xavier Univ. B.Sc. (magna cum laude) 1948; Dalhousie Univ. M.D. 1953; Univ. of Minn. M.S. (Surg.) 1959; m. Rose d. Thomas and Rose Langley 1 Sept. 1952; children: Jane, Sandy, Mark, Colin, Lorna; CHIEF OF SURG., I.K. KILLAM HOSP., PROF. OF SURG. & PROF. OF PEDIATRICS, DALHOUSIE UNIV. 1984– , HEAD, DEPT. OF SURGERY 1989– ; Res. in Pathol., Victoria Gen. Hosp., Dalhousie Univ. 1953–55; Fellow in Surg., Mayo Clinic 1955–59; Res. in Surg., Children's Mem. Hosp. (Chicago) 1959–61 (McLaughlin Travelling Fellowship); Pres., Candn. Assn. of Pediatric Surg. 1987–89; Cons. in surg., Halifax Infirmary; Grace Maternity Hosp.; mem., multiple med. & surg. assns.; author/co-author of 50 med.-surg. pubs.; recreations: golf, curling; clubs: Ashburn Golf (Bd. of Dir. 1973–84; Pres. 1980–81), Halifax Curling; Home: 1612 Cambridge St., Halifax, N.S. B3H 4A6; Office: 5850 University Ave., Halifax, N.S. B3J 3G9.

**GILLIS, Duncan Hugh,** B.A., Ph.D.; educator; b. Glen Alpine, Antigonish Co., N.S. 11 Aug. 1918; s. John J. and Catherine Ann G.; e. St. Francis Xavier Univ., B.A. 1939; London Sch. of Econ., Ph.D. 1948; post-doctoral studies Fribourg and Laval Univs.; m. Celia Antoinette, d. late Alfred Hamilton, Edinburgh and London, 21 June 1952; children: Rosemary, Anthony, Paulina; Asst. Prof., St. Francis Xavier Univ. 1948–50; Research Writer Encyclopedia Canadiana and Ed., Labour Journal, Cape Breton 1952; Assoc. Prof., Marymount Coll., N.Y. 1953–55; Program Organizer and Asst. Nat. Supvr. Pub. Affairs Dept., CBC 1955–59; Prof. and Div. Chrmn., Boston Univ. 1959–70; Dir., Sch. of Adult Learning, Univ. of Botswana, Lesotho and Swaziland 1968–70; Extve. Dir., Coady Internat. Inst., Antigonish, 1970–72; Academic Vice Pres., Saint Mary's Univ. 1972–76, Prof. there 1980–83; Advisor to Govt. of Swaziland 1976–80; currently preparing political history of Swaziland; served with RCA Italy and N.W. Europe during World War II; RCHA Korean War; militia 1957–59; rank Lt. Col.; Mentioned in Despatches (Korea); P. Conservative cand. g.e. 1965, 1968; author 'Democracy in the Canadas,' 1951; Progressive Conservative: R. Catholic; recreations: walking, travel; Home: 1766 Cambridge St., Halifax, N.S. B3H 4A9 and 2730 SE 7th Place, Homestead, Fla. 33033.

**GILLIS, Robert Vincent (Vince),** CAE; association executive; b. New Waterford, N.S. 20 Dec. 1941; s. Alexander A. and Ada (Grant) G.; e. Mt. Carmel High Sch. New Waterford 1960, Central High Sch. 1961; Univ. of Guelph 1965; m. Maria (dec. 21 Nov. 1989) d. Michael and Janina Bunko 19 Aug. 1967; two d. Michelle Marie, Kristen Melanie; EXTVE. DIR., CANDN. GOLF SUPERINTENDENTS ASSN. 1989– ; Appt. by Order-in-Council March 1989 as mem., Dist. Health Counc. for Metro. Toronto; Apptd. Acting Sec.-Gen. Alzheimer Disease Internat. 1986; el. Vice Pres., Bd. of Dirs., Alzheimer Soc. of Metro Toronto 1991; Chrmn., Alzheimer's Disease Internat. Conf., Toronto 1993; elected Bd. of Dirs., Alzheimer Assn. of Ont. 1993; Sec. and Founding Dir. Leisurability Publications Inc.; Asst. Dir. of Recreation, Petrolia, Ont. 1964, Exec. Dir. Fairbank Adult Edn. Centre 1965; Dir. of Recreation Children's Psychiatric Rsch. Inst. London, Ont. 1965; Dir. Recreation, Camping Services & Youth, Metrop. Toronto Assn. for Mentally Retarded (MTAMR) 1966, Asst. Exec. Dir. MTAMR 1971, Sr. Asst. Exec. Dir. 1977, Exec. Dir. 1979–84; Nat. Exec. Dir. Alzheimer Soc. of Can. 1984–88; Past mem. Mental Retardation Co-Ordinating Ctte. Metrop. Toronto, Chrmn. Proposal Review Sub-Ctte.; mem. Speakers' Bureau Un. Way Greater Toronto; Chrmn. Ont. Exec. Dirs. Co-ordinating Ctte. (Mental Retardation); Fellow, Am. Assn. Mental Deficiency (Chrmn.: Ont. Chapter, Recreation Subdiv. (Internat.). Nat. Examining Bd.); Pres, Ont. Recreation Soc.; mem. World Cong. Ctte. Internat. Assn. Sci. Study Mental Deficiency; recreations: family activities, reading, community affairs; Address: 32 Garden Pl., Toronto, Ont. M8W 1M3.

**GILLMORE, Allan K.,** B.A., D.U., LL.D., O.L.M.; university administrator; b. London, Ont. 20 Aug. 1923; s. John Joseph and Ruby Florence (Gregory) G.; e. Sir Adam Beck Coll. Inst. London, Ont. 1939; McMaster Univ. B.A. 1943; Univ. of Ottawa D.U. 1982; Univ. of Regina LL.D. 1985; McMaster Univ. LL.D. 1988; m. Hilda Jean, d. late William Adams, 20 May 1944; children: Donald Allan, Marilyn Jean (Mrs. J. Cavill); RETIRED – EXECUTIVE DIRECTOR EMERITUS, ASSOC. OF UNIVERSITIES AND COLLEGES OF CANADA 1988– ; Vice-Rector, Univ. of Ottawa 1966–1980; Extve. Dir., Assn. Colleges and Universities of Canada, 1980–88; Special Adv. to the Pres., Univ. of

Victoria 1988–90; Mem., Implementation Planning Group, B.C. Govt. for Creation of Northern Univ. 1989–90; Chrmn., Ottawa Adv. Bd. Guaranty Trust Co. 1980–88; mem. Council of Trustees, Inst. for Research on Public Policy 1982–88; Mem. of Faculty Review Comte., Candn. Military Colleges; Dept. of National Defense 1980–94; mem. Univ. Advisory Comte. for Internat. Development 1980–88; mem., Bd. of Dirs., Candn. Bureau for Internat. Education 1968–78; Extve. Dir. Sarnia Y.M.-Y.W.C.A. 1948; Dir. Sask. House, Centre for Continuing Educ. Regina, 1960; Asst. to Min. of Educ. Sask. 1961; Extve. Dir. Wascana Centre Authority, Regina, 1962; rec'd Candn. Parks and Recreation Assn. National Citation for outstanding Achievement, 1974; Anglican; recreations: gardening, wood carving, painting; Home: 4029 White Rock St., Victoria, B.C. V8N 4M4.

**GILMORE, John Norman,** B.F.A.; writer; b. Montréal, Qué. 10 Nov. 1951; s. John Frederick and Grace Meek (Young) G.; e. Concordia Univ. B.F.A. 1981; author 'Swinging in Paradise: The Story of Jazz in Montreal' 1988; 'Who's Who of Jazz in Montreal: Ragtime to 1970' 1989; journalist The Glamorgan Gazette, Bridgend, Wales 1974–76; The Gazette, Montreal 1977–78; The Candn. Press Montreal Bureau 1984; Radio Can. Internat. 1986–91; freelance ed. scholarly, trade and govt. publs. since 1981; staff ed. Social Problems 1981–84; Lectr. in Jazz Hist. Concordia Univ. 1984–85, co-creator jazz hist. archival colls. incl. John Gilmore Jazz Hist. Coll.; host weekly jazz prog. radio stn. CINQ-FM Montreal 1979–81; recipient Can. Council Explorations Grant 1981; recreations: tai-chi, outdoors; Office: c/o Véhicule Press, Box 125, Pl. du Parc Stn., Montréal, Qué. H2W 2M9.

**GILMOUR, Clyde,** C.M., LL.D.; broadcaster; journalist; b. Calgary, Alta. 8 June 1912; s. John Milton and Theresa Olive (McCabe) G.; e. Alexandra High Sch. Medicine Hat, Alta. 1929; McMaster Univ., Hon. LL.D. 1976; m. Barbara d. William and Florence Donald 27 May 1950; children: Jane, Paul; HOST 'GILMOUR'S ALBUMS' CBC RADIO 1956– ; free-lance magazine writer; Reporter and Columnist Medicine Hat News, Edmonton Journal, Vancouver Province; Movie Critic Vancouver Sun 1949–54, Toronto Telegram 1954–71, Toronto Star 1971–80; Movie Critic 'Critically Speaking' CBC Radio 1947–64, TV Host 'Folio' CBC 1958–59; Movie Critic Maclean's Magazine 1950–64; Record Columnist Audio Canada mag. 1977–83; Contractual Columnist Toronto Star 1980–83; Record Columnist Leisure Ways mag. 1983–85; Press Offr. RCNVR 1942–45; Mem. Order of Canada 1975; inducted into Candn. News Hall of Fame 1990; recreations: reading, music, jokes; Office: CBC Radio Music, PO Box 500, Stn. A, Toronto, Ont. M5W 1E6.

**GILMOUR, Gordon Hugh,** B.A., LL.B.; provincial court judge; b. Vancouver, B.C. 9 June 1925; s. Stuart Hugh and Hazel Victoria Hilbert (Scott) G.; e. Univ. of B.C., B.A. 1948, LL.B. 1949; m. Jean d. David and Nelly McKenzie 28 Dec. 1948; children: David Hugh, Marilyn Victoria, Stuart Gordon, Robert Scott, Katherine Anne; JUDGE, PROVINCIAL COURT OF B.C. 1976– ; barrister & solicitor, Vancouver, B.C. 1949–76 – last partnership, Swinton & Company; recreations: skiing, golf; club: Kelowna, Kelowna Golf & Country; Home: 1532 Ayre Court, Kelowna, B.C.; Office: 1456 St. Paul St., Kelowna, B.C. V1Y 2E6.

**GILMOUR, Gordon 'Harvey',** B.A., J.D.; university administrator; b. Kingston,Ont. 29 June 1944; s. Samuel Maclean and Mary Elizabeth (Young) G.; e. Wilbraham Academy 1961; Acadia Univ. B.A. 1966; Boston University School of Law J.D. 1969; Boston Univ. Tax Program 1970–71; m. Judith d. Winslow and Marjorie Shaw 22 June 1968; children: Christopher, Darren; DIRECTOR OF DEVELOPMENT, MOUNT ALLISON UNIVERSITY 1977– ; Legal Aid Attorney, Zuni N.M. Legal Aid & Defender Soc. 1969–70; Executive Asst. to the Pres., Mount Allison Univ. 1972–77; Sec. to the Board of Regents, Mount Allison Univ.; Dir., Cape Cod Sea Camps Inc.; Partner: Block Investments-Holdings Limited; private consulting, fund raising, executive search; Past Bd. Chair, Sackville Memorial Hosp.; Past Sec., Sackville & Area C. of C.; Trustee, Dr. L.A. Goodridge Trust; Mount Allison Univ. Found.; Mem., Council for Advancement/Support of Education; Candn. Council for Advancement of Edn.; Mass. Bar Assn.; N.B. Hockey Officials Assn.; recreations: golf, minor hockey; clubs: Amherst N.S. Golf & Country; Home: 48 E. Main St., Sackville, N.B. E0A 3C0; Office: 64 York St., Sackville, N.B. E0A 3C0.

**GILROY, R. Malcolm,** F.C.S.I.; banker; b. Johannesburg, Rep. of S. Africa 2 March 1949; s. James Campbell, M.D., O.B.E. and Aileen Moira (Howard) G.; e. St. Davids Coll., Johannesburg; m. Cheryl A. d. Johnson and Elizabeth Mont; children: Derek Scott Malcolm; Jonathon Alistair Mont; LAKETON INVESTMENT MANAGEMENT 1993– ; Whinney Murray C.A. S.A., Johannesburg 1967–70; Finan. Controller, Cochran Murray Ltd. 1971–74; Money Market Trader, Pitfield Mackay Ross 1975–78; Treas., Chemco Equipment Finan. 1978–80; Vice-Pres. & Head of Money Markets, Midland Doherty Ltd. 1980–83; Vice-Pres. & Treas., Chem. Bank of Canada 1983–86; First Chicago Canada 1986–88; Co. Head of Fixed Income, First Boston Canada 1988–90; Senior Vice-Pres. & Treas., Union Bank of Switzerland (Canada) 1991–92; Alternate, Candn. Fgn. Exchange Ctte.; Past Bd. Pres., Amyotrophic Lateral Sclerosis Soc. of Canada (Lou Gehrig's Disease); recreations: golf, skiing, squash; clubs: Adelaide; Cambridge; Home: 3456 Mulcaster Rd., Mississauga, Ont. L5L 5B3.

**GILSIG, Toby,** Ph.D., Eng.; computer software executive; b. Montreal, Que. 18 March 1940; s. David and Mary (Dwarkin) G.; e. McGill Univ. B.Eng. (Elec.), 1961; Imperial Coll., Univ. of London, Ph.D. 1966; m. Clare d. Babs and Phil Johnstone 25 Sept. 1965; children: Deborah Elizabeth, Jessalyn Sarah; PRESIDENT, M3i SYSTEMS INC. 1991– ; Engr., Montreal Engineering Co. 1961–63; Development Engr., Westinghouse Electrical Corp. 1967–68; Sr. Researcher, High Voltage Lab., then Dir., Systems Engineering Lab., Hydro Québec Inst. of Rsch. (IREQ) 1968–74; Dir., Electrotechnical Projects, then Generating Station Design, Hydro-Québec 1975–81; Asst. Dir., IREQ 1981–82; Vice-Pres., Rsch., Hydro Quebec 1983–86; Vice-Pres., Technol. Innovation 1986–91; Mem. of the Bd., Eicon Technologies Inc.; Computer Rsch. Institute of Montreal; Mem.: Candn. Advanced Technology Assoc.; Candn. Rsch. Mgmt. Assoc.; Order of Engrs. of Qué.; Qué. Counc. of Sci. & Technol.; Athlone Fellow 1963; Home: Mount Royal, Qué.; Office: 1111 St-Charles W., Ste. 135, East Tower, Longueuil, Qué. J4K 5G4.

**GILSON, (James) Clayton,** B.S.A., M.Sc., Ph.D., LL.D., F.A.I.C.; educator; b. Deloraine, Man. 7 Feb. 1926; s. George Edward and Ellen Rose (Kerrison) G.; e. Univ. of Man. B.S.A. 1950, M.Sc. 1951; Iowa State Univ. Ph.D. 1954; Univ. of Guelph LL.D. 19..; m. Jean d. John and Mary Rudy 16 July 1955; children: Stuart, Garth, David, Brian; DISTINGUISHED PROF. UNIV. OF MAN., Prof. of Agric. Econ. 1954– ; Head of Agric. Econ. present Univ. 1967–70, Dean of Grad. Studies 1968–70, Vice Pres. (Acad.) 1970–77; Chrmn. Bd. Dirs. Manitoba Crop Insurance Corp. 1960–70, 1977–81, 1988– ; mem. Sci. Council Can. 1963–67, 1984– ; Dir. Rh Inst. 1970–87; mem. Can. West Found. 1972– ; recipient City of Winnipeg Service Award 1983; Order of Canada 1993; author 'World Agricultural Changes: Implications for Canada' 1989; over 345 reports, tech. publs., jour. articles, conf. & seminar presentations; United Church; recreation: farming; Home: 745 Townsend Ave., Winnipeg, Man.; Office: Winnipeg, Man. R3T 2N2.

**GIMBERT, Richard (Rick) D.,** B.S., C.P.A.; tax partner; b. Norfolk, Va. 19 Jan. 1949; s. John D. and Carol A. G.; e. Univ. of Tampa, Fla. B.S. Acctg. 1975; m. Mary d. Andrew and Eleanor Beck 12 Apl. 1974; children: Alaina Michele, Daniel Alan; TAX PARTNER PRICE WATERHOUSE 1989– ; joined Price Waterhouse Houston, Texas 1979, Mgr. 1981, Sr. Mgr. 1984, trans. to Tokyo 1986 and Toronto 1987; served with U.S. Army 1966–79, rank Maj.; mem. U.S. Inst. Cert. Pub. Accts.; Texas Soc. Cert. Pub. Accts.; U.S. C. of C. Tokyo and Toronto; Campaign Ctte. 1991 Un. Way; recreations: fishing, racquetball, travel; Home: 15 Boxbury Rd., Etobicoke, Ont. M2C 5W1; Office: 3300, 1 First Canadian Place, Toronto, Ont. M5X 1H7.

**GINGRAS, Gustave,** C.C., K.St.J., Q.H.P., M.D., D.M., LL.D. D.C.L., D.Sc., F.R.S.A., F.R.C.P.(C); physician; b. Montreal, Que. 18 Jan. 1918; e. Coll. Bourget, Rigaud, Que. B.A. 1938; Univ. de Montréal M.D. 1941; Sir George Williams Univ., Univ. of Winnipeg and Univ. of W. Ont. LL.D. 1967, 1970, 1971; Univ. de Sherbrooke D.M. 1973; Bishop's Univ. D.C.L. 1974; McMaster Univ. D.Sc. 1982; St. Mary's Univ., D.Sc. 1983; Univ. of P.E.I., LL.D. 1987; D.M., D.Sc., Doctor Honoris Causa, Univ. of Paris, France 1988; CHANCELLOR EMERITUS, UNIV. OF P.E.I. 1993– ; Chancellor, Univ. of P.E.I. 1974–82; Chrmn. Candn. Hosp. Assn. 1984–85; Hon. Pres. Nat. Council Candn. Human Rights Foundation 1978– ; mem. Candn. Forces Med. Counc. 1973– , Chrmn. 1984, Consultant 1954–59, 1968–71; Hon. Vice Pres. Candn. Nat. Inst. Blind 1975– , mem. Bd. Mang. Que. Div. 1965–67; Dir. Abbott Laboratories Ltd. 1975–90; Comnr., Internat. Comn. of Health Professionals (Geneva) 1988; Hon. Vice Pres., Defence Medical Assoc. of Can. 1988; mem. Social Sciences & Humanities Research Council 1978–83, Extve. 1981–83; Extve. Dir. Rehabilitation Inst. Montreal 1949–76; Prof. of Phys. Med. & Rehabilitation Univ. de Montréal 1954–76, Dir. Sch. Rehabilitation 1954–76, Chrmn. Extve. Council Geriatric Inst. 1961–65, Prof. Emeritus 1976– ; Chief of Service, Phys. Med. & Rehabilitation, Queen Mary Veterans Hosp. and D.V.A. Montreal Dist. 1945–76; Consultant, World Health Organ. on Med. Rehabilitation 1955–80; Chief Med. Consultant, War Amputations Can.; Centre de reéduc. des Handicapés de Yaoundé, Cardinal Léger and His Endeavours Organ.; UN. Tech. Assistance Div. 1953–59; mem. Nat. Adv. Bd. Rehabilitation. Disabled Persons 1954–65; Dir. Ecole de Réadaptation Univ. Laval 1964–69; Head, Dept. Phys. Med. & Rehabilitation Pasteur Hosp. Montreal 1947–57; mem. Nat. Med. Adv. Comte. Candn. Rehabilitation Council Disabled 1960–68; Dir. Rehabilitation Services Dept. Health P.E.I. 1977–80 and Med. Dir. Rehabilitation Centre; recipient Royal Bank of Can. Award 1972; Medal of Honour Pharm. Mfrs. Assn. Can. 1973; Albert Lasker Award Internat. Soc. Rehabilitation Disabled 1969; Can. Centennial Medal 1967; Silver Medal Internat. Coop. 1965; Rabbi Dr. Harry J. Stern Award 1974 (co-recipient); Outstanding Citizen Award Montreal Citizenship Council 1970; B'nai B'rith Humanitarian Award 1966; Cavaliere Order St. Agatha Repub. San Marino 1968; Order Cedar of Lebanon 1972; Chuong My Medal Repub. S. Viet Nam 1973; Medal of Merit Veterans Ministry S. Viet Nam 1969; Order of Ouissam Alaouite, Morocco 1990; F.N.G. Starr Award Candn. Med. Assn.; 1978; Que. Hosp. Assn. Award 1980; George Findlay Stephens Mem. Award of Merit Candn. Hosp. Assn. 1981; Queen's Hon. Physician 1982; Knight of Grace, the Order of St. John of Jerusalem of Rhodes and Malta 1986; Order of the Keepers of Compassion (1st recipient) 1987; Canada Volunteer Certificate of Merit, Min. of National Health and Welfare 1989; Hon. Col. of 35 (Sydney) Medical Co. 1990, Ret'd 1993; Angus 'Gus' MacFarlane Scroll of Honour, Candn. Paraplegic Assn. P.E.I. Div. 1993– ; the author 'Combats pour la survie' 1975, Eng. transl. 'Feet Was I To The Lame' 1977; co-author 'Human Rights for the Physically Handicapped and Aged' 1977; numerous articles; Pres., P.E.I. Hosp. Assn. 1980–88; Pres., St. John Council P.E.I. 1981–90; Candn. Med. Assn. 1972–73; Internat. Fed. Phys. Med. 1968–72; Que. Pres. Corp. Phys. 1966–72; Candn. Assn. Phys. Med. & Rehabilitation 2 terms; Que. Physiatrists Assn. 1959–60; Hon. Pres. Candn. Physiotherapy Assn. 1973–75: Hon. Vice Pres. Order St. John Que. Council; Fellow, Am. Acad. Phys. Med. & Rehabilitation; Internat. Coll. Surgs.; Am. Geriatric Soc.; Hon. mem. Que. Med. Assn.; Am. Med. Assn. and various internat. med. scient. assns.; Candn. Red Cross Soc.; mem. Royal Soc. Med.; Internat. Med. Soc. Paraplegia; Internat. Rehabilitation Med. Assn.; Heraldry Soc. Can.; Candn. Railroad Hist. Assn.; UN in Can.; Steamship Hist. Assn. Can.; served with R.C.A.M.C. Can. and Overseas 1942–46; Address: Glen Green, Monticello R.R. 5, Souris, P.E.I. C0A 2B0.

**GINN, Robert McGunegal,** M.Sc., Ph.D., P.Eng.; consulting geologist; b. Toronto, Ont. 20 Aug. 1930; s. George Ryce and Muriel Elizabeth (McGunegal) G.; e. Lawrence Park Coll. Inst. Toronto 1949; Queen's Univ. B.Sc., M.Sc. 1958; Univ. of Toronto Ph.D. 1960; m. Dorothy d. Roy and Myrel Shadlock 11 May 1957; children: Kathleen, David, Caroline, Nancy; ASSOC., WATTS, GRIFFIS & McQUAT LTD. 1987– ; Resident Geol. Ont. Dept Mines 1959–62; Rsch. & Planning Geol. Hollinger Gold Mines Ltd. 1962–65; Sr. Geol. Texas Gulf Sulphur Inc. 1965–70; Exploration Mgr. Vangulf Exploration Co. 1970–72; Vice Pres. St. Joseph Explorations Ltd., Canadaka Mines Ltd., Canadian Smelting & Refining Ltd. 1972–81; Pres. Sulpetro Minerals Ltd., Novamin Resources Inc. 1981–87; cons. to mining ind., govts. N.Am., Eur., Asia 1987– ; mem. Prospectors & Developers Assn. Can. (Pres. 1989–91); Assn. Prof. Eng. Prov. Ont. (Councillor 1988–89); United Church (Elder 1961–89); recreations: tennis, sailing; Clubs: Granite (Hon. Dir.; Pres. 1986–87); Ontario; Home: 84 Glencairn Ave., Toronto, Ont. M4R 1M8; Office: 400, 8 King St. E., Toronto, Ont. M5C 1B5.

**GIRARD, Alice M.,** O.C. (1968), R.N., B.Sc.N., M.A., D.Sc., LL.D., O.St.J.; administrateur, professeur émérite; née. Waterbury, Conn., 11 Nov. 1907; f: Philippe et Rose (Joyal) G.; venue au Canada avril 1918; éduc. école normale, brevet superieur en pédagogie 1925; diplôme d'infirmière l'Hôpital St. Vincent de Paul, Sherbrooke, P.Q. 1931; diplôme en hygiène publique, Univ. of Toronto 1939; B.Sc.N. Catholic Univ. of America, Washington, D.C. 1942; M.A. Columbia Univ. 1944; cours d'adm. hospitalière (Fellow de la Fondation

Kellogg) Johns Hopkins Univ. 1954; LL.D. (hon. causa) Univ. of Toronto 1968; D.Sc. (hon. causa) Univ. de Montréal 1975; DOYENNE FONDATRICE DE LA FACULTÉ DES SCIENCES INFIRMIÈRES DE L'UNIV. DE MONTRÉAL depuis 1962; doyenne 1962–73 (fondatrice de la faculté et première femme doyen de l'Univ. de Montréal); infirmière hygiéniste 1931–38; dir. l'Ecole d'infirmières hygiénistes de l'Univ. de Montréal 1942–48; dir. nat. du nursing la Cie. d'assurance-vie Metropolitan 1949–53; dir. et asst. admn. l'Hôpital St. Luc à Montréal 1956–62; mem. la Commission Royale d'Enquête sur les services de santé au Can. 1961–64; nommée mem. hon. de la Registered Nurses Assn. of Ont., Sask. Registered Nurses Assn.; citoyenne hon. de la Ville de Montréal; reçue la médaille du Centenaire; la médaille Florence Nightingale (la Ligue de la Croix Rouge Internat.); prés., l'Assn. des Infirmières Candnnes. (1958–60); Prés. la Fondation des Infirmières Candnnes.; Prés. Nat. du Victorian Order of Nurses (1975–77); Première prés. canadienne, Conseil Internat. des Infirmières (1965–69); Comité Rélations Publiques P.E.M.P. (1974); mem. bureau des govs. du Conseil Candn. du Bien-être; Fed. internat. des Hôpitaux; American Coll. of Hospital Administrators; recue Commandeur de l'Ordre de St. Jean (1977); dame commandant de l'Ordre de Saint Lazare en 1980; Membre du Club du Recteur, Univ. de Montréal; résidence: 4911 Côte des Neiges Rd., Montréal, P.Q. H3V 1H7.

**GIRARD, Camil,** B.A., M.A., Dr.; historien, professeur chercheur universitaire; né. Chicoutimi, Qué. 18 juillet 1950; f. Valmore et Emma (Maltais) G.; é. Univ. du Qué. à Chicoutimi B.A. 1973; Univ. of Western Ont. M.A. 1975; Sorbonne Doctorat, histoire contemporaine 1982; ép. Wendy Lee Williams f. K.J. Williams 1977; enfant: Daniel; PROFESSEUR-CHERCHEUR, HISTOIRE, UNIV. DU QUÉ. À CHICOUTIMI 1977– ; Prof.-chercheur, Univ. du Qué. à Rimouski 1982–83; IQRC 1986–90; membre, Commission Études, UQAC 1987–89; Conseil d'admin. 1989–96; Direction, Groupe de rech. sur l'hist. 1983–93; Vice-prés. syndicat chargés de cours 1989–94; Cert. de mérite, Soc. historique du Canada 1990 pour l'ouvrage 'Histoire du Saguenay-Lac-St-Jean' IQRC 1989; membre, Soc. historique du Canada; Inst. d'hist. de l'Amérique; Assn. des Études can.-française; auteur: 'Question d'Empire' 1988, 'Le Saguenay en 1850' 1988, 'Histoire du Saguenay-Lac-St-Jean' 1989, 'Mémoires d'un village' 1992, 'Un pays fragile: Le times de Londres et l'image du Canada 1908–1922' 1994, 'Culture et dynamique interculture' 1994; résidence: 167 Chauvin, Chicoutimi, Qué. G7J 1Z6; bureau: 555 Blvd. Université, Chicoutimi, Qué. G7H 2B1.

**GIRARD, Claude,** R.C.A.; painter; stage designer; b. Chicoutimi, Que. 30 Nov. 1938; s. Armand and Yvette (Tremblay) G.; e. Ecole des Beaux-Arts du Qué.; Academia of Venice, Italy; Dean of Art Dept. Coll. Brébeuf, Montréal; collab. with over 50 theatrical groups incl. Les Grands Ballets Canadiens, Nat. Ballet of Can., Alberta Ballet Co., Banff Festival of the Arts, Opera de Nancy (France), Opera de Wallonie (Liège), Palais des Congrès, Paris (France), Opera de Montréal, Opera of Philadelphia, Portland Opera (Oregon), Seattle Opera, Edmonton Opera, Tulsa Opera, Theatre du nouveau monde; paintings in colls. maj. Candn. galleries; Address: 4077 St. Hubert, Montreal, Que. H2L 4A7.

**GIROUARD, Fernand E.,** B.Sc., Ph.D.; university professor; b. Ste Marie de Kent, N.B. 19 Sept. 1938; s. Prosper and Irene (LeBlanc) G.; e. Univ. St Joseph B.Sc. 1959; Univ. of Notre Dame Ph.D. 1965; m. Emerise d. Edmond and Exelda Léger 15 Aug. 1960; children: Gisele, Jacqueline, Daniel; PHYSICS PROF., UNIV. DE MONCTON 1964– ; Chair, Physics & Math. 1967–73; Math., Physics & Computer Science 1985–91; Visiting Fellow, Univ. of W. Ont. 1973–74; Visiting Scientist, Physics, CNRC Ottawa 1985; Pres., N.B. Science Fair 1975–79; Mem., Bd. of Gov., Univ. de Moncton 1970–72; Mem., Academic Senate 1967–73, 1977–81, 1991–94; Trustee, Candn. Mus. of Nature 1992; Roman Catholic; Mem., Candn. Assn. of Physicists (Councillor 1970–72, 1968–88); American Assn. of Physics Teachers; author/co-author of over 40 sci. papers; recreations: skiing, snowmobiling, windsurfing, golfing, swimming; Home: 65 Marquette Ave., Moncton, N.B. E1A 6H7; Office: Univ. de Moncton, Dept. of Physics, Moncton, N.B. E1A 3E9.

**GIROUX, Pierre A.,** B.Comm., M.B.A.; financial executive; b. Rouyn-Noranda, Que. 4 Nov. 1938; s. Cecil A. and Inez M. (FitzJohn) G.; e. Carleton Univ. B.Comm. 1961; Univ. of Toronto M.B.A. 1963; children: Larissa Danièle, Adrienne Clare; MANAGING PARTNER, FINANCIAL INSTITUTIONS, ROYAL TRUST CORP. OF CANADA 1989– ; Regional Rep., Paris, Royal Bank of Canada 1981–84; Mgr., Govt. Business Ottawa 1984–87; Vice-Pres., Govt. Finance, Pemberton Securities 1987–89; recreations: tennis, squash; clubs: Toronto Lawn Tennis; Home: 16 Ames Circle, Toronto, Ont. M3B 3B8; Office: 77 King St. W., Toronto, Ont. M5W 1P9.

**GIROUX, Robert Jean Yvon,** B.Com., M.Sc.; Canadian public service; b. Rockland, Ont. 1 March 1939; s. Leo Romeo and Cecile Marie (Brunet) G.; e. Univ. of Ottawa B.Com. 1961, M.Sc. 1970; m. Therese A. d. Ernest and Catherine Briand 31 Aug. 1963; children: Benoit, André, Jean-Pierre; two grandchildren; PRESIDENT, PUBLIC SERVICE COMN. OF CANADA 1990– ; Pay Research Offr. Civil Service Comn. Can. 1963–65; Asst. Research Dir., Public Service Alliance of Can. 1965–70; Dir., Dept. of Regional Econ. Expansion 1970–73; Asst. Depy. Min. Fitness & Amateur Sport, Nat. Health & Welfare 1973–75; Dir. Gen. Public Service Comn. Can. 1975–78; Administrator, Surface Transport Adm., Transport Can. 1978–82; lectr. in Statistics & Pub. Adm. Univ. of Ottawa 1964–65, 1979–82; Depy. Min. Customs & Excise, Nat. Revenue Canada 1982–86; Depy. Min., Public Works Canada 1986–90; Mem., Candn. Pub. Personal Mang. Assn. (Dir. 1976–78); National Film Board 1989– ; Mem. Bd. of Dirs., Institute of Public Admin. of Canada 1990– ; Univ. du Québec 1993– ; recreation: sports organizations; Home: 438 Cannes, Gatineau, Que.; Office: L'Esplanade Laurier, West Tower, Ottawa, Ont. K1A 0M7.

**GIRVAN, Garth Malcolm,** B.A., LL.B.; lawyer; b. Toronto, Ont. 14 April 1949; s. John Fraser and Joyce Eleanor (Booth) G.; e. Univ. of Toronto B.A. (Hons.) 1972; Univ. of Western Ont. LL.B. 1976; common law spouse: Sue d. Charles and Betty McKenzie; one s.: Samuel Fraser McKenzie Girvan; PARTNER, BUSINESS LAW GROUP, McCARTHY TÉTRAULT 1984– ; Assoc., McCarthy Tétrault 1977–84; specializes in mergers and acquisitions, corp. finance, financial institution regulation; called to Bar of Ont. 1978; of Alta. 1981; of New York 1986; spent 1985 in New York with Wall St. firm of Cleary Gottlieb, Steen & Hamilton; Dir., Silcorp Limited; Past Chair & Dir., Goodwill Indus. of Toronto; Dir., Casey House; clubs: Toronto; Office: Box 48, Toronto-Dominion Bank Tower, Toronto, Ont. M5K 1E6.

**GIRVAN, Marilyn Ann (Marnie),** B.A.; b. Toronto, Ont. 12 Dec. 1939; d. Archiebald Middleton and Beatrice Ann (Christmas) G.; e. Port Hope H.S.; Toronto Teacher's Coll. 1958; Carleton Univ. B.A. Pol. Sci. 1971; div.; children: David Kheri Duchesne, Scott Kesi Duchesne; SENIOR ADVISOR, WOMEN IN DEVELOPMENT POLICY BRANCH, CANADIAN INTERNATIONAL DEVELOPMENT AGENCY 1988– ; teacher, Toronto Bd. of Educ. 1959–65; CUSO Volunteer Butimba Teachers' Coll., Tanzania 1965–67; Dar Es Salaam Internat. Sch. 1967–69; Remedial Reading Prog., Kingston, Jamaica 1971–75; Dir. Prog. Funding CUSO Ottawa 1975–78; Exec. Dir. Match Internat. Centre 1978–81; Exec. Dir. Candn. Adv. Counc. Status of Women 1981–84; Extve. Dir., Candn. Bureau for Internat. Education 1985–88; Mem. Adv. Bd., Inst. for Study of Women, Halifax; mem. First Unitarian Congregation, Ottawa; recreation: travel, films; Home: 615 Burn St., Ottawa, Ont. K1K 1B4; Office: 200 Promenade du Portage, 7th Flr., Hull, Qué. K1A 0G4.

**GIRVIN, John P.,** M.D., Ph.D., FRCS(C); neurosurgeon; b. Detroit, Mich. 5 Feb. 1934; s. Patterson and Sally (Hawkins) G.; e. Univ. of Western Ontario M.D. 1958; McGill Univ. Ph.D. 1965; m. Bettye; children: Douglas, Michael, Jane; CHAIR & PROGRAM DIR., DIV. OF NEUROSURGERY, DEPT. OF CLIN. NEUROLOGICAL SCIENCES, UNIV. OF W. ONT. 1990– ; Chair, Dept. of Clin. Neurol. Sci., Univ. of W. Ont. 1984–89; Senate 1989–93; Bd. of Gov. 1989–93; Chair, Royal Coll. of Surgeons of Can. Specialty Ctte. of Neurosurgery 1991; Assoc. Ed., 'Can. J. of Neurol. Sci.' 1991– ; Editorial Boards, 'J. of Neurosurgery' 1990– , 'J. of Epilepsy' 1988– ; recreations: canoeing, cooking; Home: 4 Linksgate Rd., London, Ont. N6G 2A7; Office: 339 Windermere Rd., London, Ont. N6A 5A5.

**GISH, Norman Richard,** B.A., LL.B.; executive; b. Eckville, Alta. 13 Oct. 1935; s. Robert Bruce and Lillian Barbara (Foster) G.; e. Red Deer Composite High Sch. 1954; Univ. of Alta. B.A. 1957; Univ. of B.C. LL.B. 1960; Banff Sch. of Advanced Mgmt., Mgmt. Cert. 1967; m. Joan d. Reg and Irene Thompson 5 Sept. 1959; children: David, Carolyn, Graeme; BUSINESS CONSULTANT; Dir., Hees International Bancorp Inc.; Northstar Energy Corp.; Queenston Gold Mines Ltd.; Conf. Bd. of Can.; read law with Ladner Downs Vancouver; called to Bar of B.C. 1961; Foreign Trade Service Can., Ottawa and Hong Kong 1961–65; B.C. Forest Products 1965–77, latterly Vice Pres., Gen. Counsel and Secy.; Chrmn. B.C. Energy Comn. 1977–80; Turbo Resources Ltd. 1980–86, latterly Dir., Chrmn., Pres. & C.E.O.; Pres. C.E.O. & Dir., North Candn. Oils Ltd. 1986–93; recreations: golf, tennis, badminton, skiing; Clubs: Calgary Petroleum; Glencoe Golf; Vancouver Lawn Tennis; Home & Office: 8940 Bayridge Dr. S.W., Calgary, Alta. T2V 3M8.

**GITTINGS, Edward Horace;** communications executive; b. Toronto, Ont. 16 June 1928; s. William Horace and Bertha Gertrude (Blinn) G.; e. Toronto (Ont.) Coll. Inst. 1947; Univ. of Toronto 1947–48; Northern Vocational Sch. Toronto 1948–49; Ryerson Inst. 1949–50; Univ. of Montreal 1956–57; m. Joyce Kettlehut 27 Sept. 1952; children: Linda Parrot, Janice Lewin, David, Sandra Keane, and Gregory; PRES., AD PLANNER CORP.; formerly Pres. & C.E.O., Comac Communications Ltd. 1974–85; Publisher, Homemaker's Magazine/Madame Au Foyer 1967–85; Asst. Advertising Mgr. Eaton's College St. Toronto 1947–50; Supvr. Dealer Advertising, Goodyear Tire & Rubber Co., 1950–52; Promotion & Merchandising Mgr. Chatelaine Magazine 1952–54; Montreal Mgr. Chatelaine Magazine, Maclean Hunter 1955–59, Sales Mgr. Toronto 1960–67; United Church; recreation: golf; Club: Mississaugua Golf & Country; Home: 1638 Ruscombe Close, Mississauga, Ont. L5J 1Y3.

**GIVEN, Brian J.,** B.A., M.A., Ph.D.; university professor; b. Halifax, N.S. 5 Jan. 1952; s. James Arnold and Phyllis Ada (Ashby) G.; e. Carleton Univ. B.A. 1976, M.A. 1978; Univ. of Alberta Ph.D. 1986; m. Dr. Heather R. Bissonette d. Claude and Ena Bissonette 18 Jan. 1979; one d.: Alexis Persephone; PROF., SOCIOLOGY & ANTHROPOLOGY, CARLETON UNIV. 1990– ; Postdoctoral Fellowship, SSHRCC; has conducted rsch. in Canada on ethnohist. of early Eur./Native contact period & in Can. & India on anthropology of religion; presently working on a nat. study of cultural survival issues with the Tibetan-Candn. refugee community; active researcher in ethnohistory, the anthropol. of ritual, esoteric pedagogies & epistemologies, cross-cultural communication; author: 'A Most Pernicious Thing: Gun Trading and Native Culture in the Early Contact Period' 1994 and journal articles; recreations: all year bicycling, sailing; clubs: Britannia Yacht; Office: Carleton Univ., Ottawa, Ont. K1S 5B6.

**GIVNER, Joan Mary,** B.A., M.A., Ph.D.; university professor, editor, writer; b. Manchester, England 5 Sept. 1936; d. Thomas and Elizabeth Parker Short; e. Univ. of London, B.A. 1958, Ph.D. 1972; Washington Univ., M.A. 1962; m. David s. Ann and Nathan G. 15 Apr. 1965; children: Emily Jane, Jessie Louise; PROF. OF ENGLISH, UNIV. OF REGINA 1965– ; Fellow, Bunting Inst., Radcliffe Coll. 1978–79; Editor, 'Wascana Review' 1984– ; mem., Sask. Writers' Guild; author: 'Katherine Anne Porter: A Life' 1982; 'Tentacles of Unreason (short stories) 1985; 'Unfortunate Incidents' (short stories) 1988; 'Mazo de la Roche: The Hidden Life' 1989; 'Scenes from Provincial Life' (short stories); 'The Self-Portrait of a Literary Biographer' (autobiography); editor: 'Katherine Anne Porter: Conversations' 1987; Home: 2587 Seaview Rd., R.R. 1, Mill Bay, B.C. V0R 2P0.

**GLASCO, Kimberly Ann;** ballerina; b. Eugene, Oregon 27 Nov. 1960; PRINCIPAL BALLET DANCER, NAT. BALLET OF CANADA 1987– ; Nat. Ballet School 1974–79; Nat. Ballet of Canada, Corps de Ballet 1979, 2nd soloist 1981–83, 1st soloist 1985–86; Am. Ballet Theatre 1983–84; Guest, Australian Spoleto Festival 1987; World Ballet Festival Japan; Verona Italy Festival; Guest, Kitchener, Syracuse and Vancouver Symphonies; created role of Alice in 'Alice' by Glen Tetley; lead roles: Snow Queen/Sugar Plum Fairy in 'The Nutcracker' by Franca, Hanna in 'The Merry Widow,' Kitri in 'Don Quixote,' Swan Queen/Black Swan in 'Swan Lake,' Princess Aurora in 'Sleeping Beauty'; title roles in 'Raymonda Act III,' 'Giselle'; danced in 'Etudes' by Harald Lander; 'Symphony in C,' 'Serenade,' 'The Four Temperaments,' 'Divertimento No. 15' by Balanchine; 'Forgotten Land,' 'Dream Dances' by Jiri Kylian; 'Voluntaries,' 'Daphnis and Chloë,' 'La Ronde' by Tetley; 'Les Sylphides' by Bruhn; 'Romeo and Juliet' by Cranko; 'Paquita Act III,' by Makarova; 'La Bayadere Act III'; 'Transfigured Night'; 'Elite Syncopations'; Silver Medal, Moscow Internat. Comp. 1981; Office: c/o National Ballet of Can., 157 King St. E., Toronto, Ont. M5C 1G9.

**GLASS, Charles Lapslie Ogden,** M.A., D.C.L., D.d'U.; b. Montreal, P.Q. 26 July 1913; s. Louis Gordon and Sallie (Judah) G.; e. Bishop's Coll. Sch.; Bishop's Univ., B.A. 1935 (Rhodes Schol., Prov. of Que.); Oxford

Univ., B.A. 1938, M.A. 1941; D.C.L. Bishop's 1960; D.d'U., Univ. of Sherbrooke 1967; m. Janet Wright, d. H.F. McNeil, Boston, Mass., 9 Sept. 1939; children: Nancy Ogden, Janet Diana, Charles Philip Gordon, Richard Ogden; Reporter, Montreal 'Gazette,' 1938–39; Asst. Master, Bishop's Coll. Sch., Lennoxville, P.Q., 1939–41; Headmaster, Ashbury Coll., Ottawa, Ont., 1945–50; Headmaster, Bishop's Coll. Sch. 1950–60; Principal and Vice Chancellor Bishop's Univ. 1960–69; served in World War 1941–45 with R.C.N.V.R. ashore and at sea; Hon. mem., Headmasters Assn. Can. (Pres. 1949–50; Recording Secy., 1947); Hon. Life Trustee, Corp. of Bishop's Univ.; Anglican; recreations: golf; Address: 13749 W.M. Davis Parkway W., Jacksonville, Fla. 32224, U.S.A.

**GLASS, Irvine Israel,** M.A.Sc., Ph.D., F.R.S.C.; professor; b. Poland 23 Feb. 1918; s. Samuel Solomon and Gitel (Helfand) G.; came to Canada 1930; e: Ogden Pub. Sch. and Central Tech. Sch., Toronto, Ont.; Univ. of Toronto, B.A.Sc. (Engn. Physics), M.A.Sc. (Aero. Engn.) Ph.D. (Aerophysics) 1950; m. late Anne, d. Israel Medres, Montreal, P.Q., 30 Aug. 1942; children: Vivian Judith (Mrs. Shimon Felsen), Ruth Miriam (Mrs. Robt. Moses), Susan Hinda; m. 2ndly Alfreda (Potok) Gryn, 19 Aug. 1983; WITH INST. FOR AEROSPACE STUDIES, UNIV. OF TORONTO since 1950, FULL PROF. OF AEROSPACE SCIENCE & ENGINEERING since 1960 and Asst. Dir. (Education); Consultant for Candn. and U.S. industry; held positions as Stress Analyst and Aerodynamicist with Canadair, Canadian Car & Foundry, A. V. Roe and Canadian Armament Research and Devel. Establishment; Chrm., Dept. of Aerospace Studies, Sch. of Grad. Studies, Univ. of Toronto 1961–66; served in 2nd World War with R.C.A.F. rank Fl. Lt. 1942–45; spent sabbatical leave at the Imp. Coll. of Science and Tech., research in high-temperature gas flows 1957–58; invited by Soviet Acad. of Sciences to lect. on high-temperature gas flows at Moscow Univ. and other Insts. 1961 and 1969; Chrmn., Astronautics Sec. (CASI) 1961; mem. Assoc. Comte. on Space Research, Nat. Research Council 1962–65; mem. Assoc. Comte. on Aerodynamics and Chrmn., Standing Subcomte. on High Speed Aerodynamics, Nat. Research Council 1968–71; mem., NASA Basic Research Adv. Subcomte., on Fluid Mech. 1965–69; mem., Extve. Comte., Div. of Fluid Dynamics Am. Phys. Soc.; Assoc. Ed. 'Physics of Fluids' 1967–70; mem. Bd. of Editors, 'Progress in Aerospace Sciences' 1973–90; mem., AIAA Honors and Awards Comte. 1978–85; mem., U.S. Comte. of Concerned Scientists 1978–90; mem., Candn. Profs. for Peace in the Middle East; mem. Adv. Bd., Sino-Judaic Inst. 1987–91; mem., Assn. Prof. Engrs. Ontario; Fellow, Am. Inst. of Aero. and Astronautics; Am. Assn. Advanc. Science; Candn. Aeronautics and Space Inst.; Am. Phys. Soc.; author and editor of books and over 200 scient. papers on gasdynamics, shock-wave phenomena and aerophysics; W. Rupert Turnbull Lectr. for 1967; 1st G.N. Patterson Lecturer (1974); Royal Candn. Inst. Lect. 1965 and 1976; premier Paul Vieille Lecturer at 13th International Symposium on Shock Tubes and Waves Niagara Falls, N.Y. 1981; gave invited lectures in many countries; Chrmn., 7th Internat. Shock Tube Symposium, June 1969, Toronto; Lady Davis Fellow, Technion-Israel Inst. of Technology, Haifa, sabbatical leave, 1974–75; Visiting Prof., Japan Soc. for Promotion of Science, Kyoto Univ., 1975; supervised 126 Master's, Ph.D.'s, Postdoctoral Fellows and visiting Professors on research problems in unique facilities conceived by him; rec'd about 4 1/2 million dollars in support of his rsch. programs from U.S. and Candn. agencies and industries; recent book, 'Shock Waves and Man' transl. into Russian, Moscow 1977, Polish ed. Warsaw 1980, Chinese ed. Peking 1984, Hindi ed. 1983 and Japanese ed. 1987; U. of T. Sesquicentennial Long Service Honour Award 1977; invited by Chinese Acad. of Sciences to lecture in a number of institutions 1980; named distinguished 'University Professor,' University of Toronto 1981; awarded 'Honorary Professorship' by Nanjing Aeronautical Inst., Nanjing, China 1985 (highest honour for an academic; first to be awarded to a foreign visitor); awarded prestigious Dryden Lectureship in Rsch., Am. Inst. of Aeronautics and Astronautics (AIAA), incl. medal, certificate and rosette; lecture 'Some Aspects of Shock Wave Research' delivered at AIAA 24th Aerospace Sciences Mtg., Reno, Nevada 7 Jan. 1986; Testimonial from 8th Internat. Mach Reflection Symposium 'for seminal contributions to theoretical and experimental shock-wave phenomena' July, 1988; awarded Einstein Fellowship, Israel Acad. of Sciences and Humanities 1990; Ed.-in-Chief of new internat. journal 'Shock Waves' (Springer Verlag) 1990; Hall of Distinction, Engr. Alumni, Univ. of Toronto 1992; Hebrew; recreations: walking, photography, literature, art, music; Home: 131 Torresdale Ave., #1107, Willowdale, Ont. M2R 3T1.

**GLASS, Leon Mark,** B.Sc., Ph.D.; university professor; b. Brooklyn, N.Y. 29 March 1943; s. Samuel and Jennie (Kahn) G.; e. Erasmus Hall H.S. 1959; Brooklyn Coll. (N.Y.) B.Sc. (cum laude) 1963; Univ. of Chicago Ph.D. 1968; m. Kathleen d. Edward P. Cranley 8 Feb. 1969; children: Hannah, Paul; PROF., DEPT. OF PHYSIOLOGY, McGILL UNIV. 1984– ; Postdoctoral Fellow, Machine Intelligence and Perception, Univ. of Edinburgh 1968–69; Postdoctoral Fellow, Theoretical Biology, Univ. of Chicago 1969–71; Rsch. Assoc., Asst. Prof. (part-time), Physics & Astronomy, Univ. of Rochester 1971–75; Asst. Prof., present univ. 1975–76; Assoc. Prof. 1976–84; Visting Prof., Inst. for Nonlinear Science, Univ. of Calif. at San Diego 1984–85; Ed. Bd., 'J. of Theoretical Biol.,' 'Internat. J. of Bifurcation and Chaos,' 'Chaos: An Interdisciplinary J. of Nonlinear Science'; Sci. Ctte., Field Inst. for Rsch. in Mathematics; Mem., Soc. for Mathematical Biology; Am. Physical Soc.; Candn. Physiological Soc.; co-author: 'From Clocks to Chaos: The Rhythms of Life' 1988; co-editor: 'Theory of Heart' 1991; recreations: playing the French Horn, hiking; Home: 4006 Harvard Ave., Montreal, Que. H4A 2W7; Office: 3655 Drummond St., Montreal, Que. H3G 1Y6.

**GLASS, Susan Jane,** B.Comm.; community volunteer; b. Vancouver, B.C. 8 July 1945; d. Floyd Robert Jr. and Helen (Preston) Glass; e. Univ. of Manitoba B.Comm. 1967; m. Arni Clayton s. Johann and Mayme Thorsteinson 28 Oct. 1984; Board of Governors, University of Manitoba; Computer Systems Management & Marketing, Air Canada 1970–86; Bd. of Dir., Royal Winnipeg Ballet (President-elect 1994), St. Boniface Hospital, St. Boniface Hosp. Research Fdn., Canadian Club of Winnipeg, Univ. of Man. Alumni Assn.; Protestant; Progressive Conservative; Gamma Phi Beta Sorority; Junior League of Wininpeg; recreations: travel, theatre, ballet, fishing, motorcycling; Home: 12D – 221 Wellington Crescent, Winnipeg, Man. R3M 0A1.

**GLAVIN, Gary Bertrun,** Ph.D.; university professor; b. Winnipeg, Man. 2 Feb. 1949; s. Bertrun Elwood and Viola Harriet (Mallows) G.; e. Univ. of Man., Ph.D. 1975; m. Karen d. Thomas and Elizabeth Dooley 9 June 1973; one s.: Matthew; PROF., PHARMACOLOGY & THERAPEUTICS, UNIV. OF MAN. and ASSOC. PROF. SEC. OF NEUROSURG. DEPT. SURGERY 1986– ; Asst./Assoc. Prof., Brock Univ. 1976–81; Assoc. Prof., Univ. of Winnipeg 1981–86; Vis. Assoc. Prof., Univ. of Man. 1984–85; Ed. Bd. 'Digestive Diseases and Sciences'; Internat. J. of Experimental and Clinical Gastroenterology'; Vice-Pres., Internat. Brain-Gut Soc.; Cons., Dept. of Justice (Man. & Sask.); Best Teacher Award, Fac. of Med. 1984, honourable mention 1985, '86, '87, '88, '89, '90, '91, '92; Matsumae Internat. Fellowship (Japan) 1982; NRC post-doct. fellow, Johns Hopkins Univ. 1975–76; Harvard Univ., Sch. of Med. Fellowship (vis. sci.) 1989; Consultant, European Center for Digestive Diesases (Zagreb, Croatia); Consultant, Laboratorios Dr., Esteve, S.A., Barcelona, Spain 1992– ; Office: Winnipeg, Man. R3E 0W3.

**GLEAVE, Alfred Pullen;** farmer; politician; b. West Zorra Twp., Ont. 6 June 1911; s. Robert Pennell and Mary Ann (Pullen) G.; e. elem. schs. Sask.; Perdue (Sask.) High Sch. 1929; m. Mary d. Evan and Ethel Rees 6 Apl. 1961; one s. Sheldon Wayne (by former marriage); worked on family farm 1930–38; owner/operator farm Sask. 1938–73; Dir. Un. Farmers' Can. (Sask. Sect.), Sask. Farmers' Union 1948–54 (Pres. 1957–62); Chrmn. Interprov. Farm Union Council, Pres. Nat. Farmers' Union 1961–64 (Hon. Life mem.); apptd. to Econ. Council Can. 1964; el. to H. of C. for Saskatoon-Biggar 1968, re-el. 1972, def. 1974; Chrmn. NDP Fed. Caucus 1968–72; served Sask. Prov. & Fed. Exec. NDP; mem. Adv. Ctte. Farm Credit Corp., Candn. Wheat Bd.; Del. Internat. Wheat Agreement Negotiations Geneva 1959, 1962; Dir. Candn. Fedn. Agric.; Sask. Power Corp.; author 'United We Stand: Prairie Farmers 1901–1975' 1991; articles agric. affairs 'Report' 1979–80; commentaries agric. Saskatoon 'Star-Phoenix' 1974–78, 1982–85; mem., Assn. Former Parliamentarians; Candn. Centre Policy Alternatives; Unitarian; recreations: writing on agric. & current affairs, collecting books & art by W. Candns.; Club: National Press; Address: 81 Park Ave., Ottawa, Ont. K2P 1B1.

**GLEBE, Heather Jean,** B.Ed.; writer; b. Edmonton, Alta. 15 Sept. 1946; d. James Davidson and Elizabeth Martin (Herd) Bowman; e. Univ. of Victoria, B.Ed. 1971; m. Allan Nicholas Soldan 1992; Freelance author / editor for Province of Alta. etc.; Pres., Fed. of B.C. Writers 1989–90; Vice-Pres. 1988–1989, Regional Rep. (Okanagan) 1986–88; Teacher, Merritt and Penticton, B.C. 1971–79; Journalist, Penticton Herald 1979–89; Creative Writing Instr., Okanagan Coll. 1988–90 and Vegreville Family and Community Support Services 1991; Bd. Mem. Okanagan Summer School of the Arts 1989–90; Author: 'Now That's an Egg! The Story of the Vegreville Pysanka' 1991; 'All Things Considered' (essays) 1989 and numerous articles in periodicals; Editor: 'Pens in Motion Anthology' 1986; 'Pulse to Pen, Remembering When' (anthology of seniors' anecdotal stories) 1992; Mem. & Founding Pres., Okanagan Writers League; Grad. with distinction, Naramata Christian Leadership Training Centre 1965; recreations: playing and teaching violin, reading, outdoor activities; Address: P.O. Box 29, Two Hills, Alta. T0B 4K0.

**GLEED, Douglas H.,** C.L.U., CHFC; insurance executive; b. Toronto, Ont. 22 March 1957; s. William Hubert and Joan Ellen (Pettit) G.; e. Stephen Leacock C.I. 1976; C.L.U. 1988; separated; children: Jodi, William; VICE PRESIDENT, DISTRICT SALES, PRUDENTIAL INSURANCE CO. OF AMERICA 1991– ; Professional & Gen. Mgr., Cedarhurst Golf Club 1976–78; Sales Rep., Richmond Hill, London Life Insurance Co. 1979–80; Manager Orillia 1980–86; Regional Mgr. Guelph 1986–88; Mississauga Regional Mgr. 1988–91; Dir., Life Underwriters Assn. 1984–88; Anglican; recreations: golf, coaching hockey, squash, baseball; club: Granite; Home: 280 Randall Crescent, Milton, Ont.; Office: 880 Upper Wentworth, Unit #2, Hamilton, Ont. L9A 4W4.

**GLEED, William Hubert;** insurance executive; b. Toronto, Ont. 13 Nov. 1933; s. Wallace H. and Doris M. (Moss) G.; e. Riverdale Coll. Inst. Toronto; m. Joan d. Charles J. and Lettie Pettit 29 May 1954; children: Donald, Douglas, Derrick, Darlene; PRES., C.E.O. AND DIR., WINTERTHUR CANADA CORP., THE CITADEL GENERAL ASSURANCE CO. AND THE CITADEL CAPITAL CORP.; Pres. Canadian Premier Properties Inc. 1984–91; Claims Adjuster, Mutual Omaha, Toronto 1953–55; Sales Agt., London Life, Toronto 1955–58; Supervisor 1958–61; Home Office Training, London 1961; Br. Mgr., Oshawa 1961–67; Br. Mgr., Toronto 1967–69; Assoc. Dir. Mktg. & Co. Officer, London 1969–71; Area Dir. 1971–80; Pres. & C.E.O., Colonia Life Insurance Co., Toronto and Pres., Colonia Life Holdings Ltd. 1981–84; Pres. & C.E.O., The Citadel Group of Companies 1984– ; Dir., Life Office Mgmt. Assoc. (LOMA) 1984–91, Chrmn. 1989; Founding mem., Alliance for Drug Free Canada; Dir.: The Ont. Safety League; Policy Mgmt. Systems Canada Ltd.; Gov., The Candn. Baseball Hall of Fame and Museum; Past Chrmn. Extve. Ctte., LIMRA Combined Companies; Past Bd. Chrmn. & Dir., Candn. Palliative Care Found. of Can.; Past Pres., St. David's Non-Profit Housing Corp.; Mem., Governors' Council, North York General Hosp.; Pres., Granite Club Ltd. 1993; Anglican; recreations: boating, curling, tennis; Clubs: Granite (Dir.); Cedarhurst Golf & Country; National; Rotary (of Toronto); Home: 345 Banbury Rd., Willowdale, Ont. M2L 2V2; Office: 1075 Bay St., Toronto, Ont. M5S 2W5.

**GLEESON, Timothy P.,** C.F.A.; investment executive; b. Toronto, Ont. 3 July 1957; s. Richard A. and Mary Jane (Oulahen) G.; e. Univ. of Toronto; m. Theresa d. Tom and Lois Kalyn 27 June 1980; children: Kimberly, Kathleen, David, Stephen; VICE-PRESIDENT, MACKENZIE FINANCIAL CORP. 1989– ; Bond Trader, Merrill Lynch Canada 1979–81; Sr. Trader, Burns Fry Ltd. 1981–87; Sr. Trader & Dir., Richardson Greenshields Ltd. 1987–89; C.F.A.; recreations: golf, skiing; club: York Downs Golf; Office: 150 Bloor St. W., Toronto, Ont. M5S 3B5.

**GLEGG, Robert,** B.Eng., M.B.A.; business executive; b. Montreal, Que. 1 June 1951; s. Keith Cecil and Olga Tessa (Lanyi) G.; e. McGill Univ. B.Eng. 1973, M.B.A. 1976; PRESIDENT & CHIEF EXECUTIVE OFFICER, GLEGG WATER CONDITIONING, INC. 1977– ; recreations: sailing, tennis, reading; clubs: Port Credit Yacht, Cutten; Home: 250 Boland Cres., Campbellville, Ont. L0P 1B0; Office: 29 Royal Rd., Guelph, Ont. N1H 1G2.

**GLEN, Ian Fraser,** RCNC, C.Eng., P.Eng.; professional naval architect/executive; b. Glasgow, Scotland 28 Apr. 1944; s. John Fraser and Anne (Craig) G.; e. Jordanhill Coll. Sc. 1962; Royal Naval Engr. Coll. 1962–64; Royal Naval Coll., M.Sc. (RCNC, 1st Class Hon) 1967; children: Nicola Frances, Leslie-Ann; PRES., FLEET TECHNOLOGY 1983– ; Offr., Royal Corps of Naval Constr., Brit. Admiralty Ship Design Group 1971–74; Secondment to Candn. Def. HQ as Lt. Comndr. 1971–74; Adv. ship design tasks, Bath, England 1974/75; Civilian Engr., Nat. Def. HQ 1975–79; Head, Naval Architecture 1979–80; Prog. Mgr., Arctec Can. Limited 1980; Vice-Pres. 1981; Pres. 1983; Mem., profl. soc. incl. Past

Chrmn., E. Candn. section, Soc. of Naval Arch. & Marine Engrs. 1984, ASNE, CI Mar E, RINA, APEO; recreations: sailing, tennis; Home: 960 Teron Rd., Kanata, Ont. K2K 2B6; Office: 311 Legget Dr., Kanata, Ont. K2K 1Z8.

**GLENNY, Robert G.,** B.Comm., C.A.; chartered accountant; b. Fort Erie, Ont. 3 April 1950; s. Donald H. and Ivy J. (Brown) G.; e. McMaster Univ. B.Comm. (Hons.) 1973; divorced; children: Heather, Christine; MANAGING PARTNER, COOPERS & LYBRAND HAMILTON 1991– ; joined Coopers & Lybrand Hamilton 1973; Audit Mgr. 1976–81; Audit Partner 1981–91; Dir. & Treas., Mohawk College Foundation; Hamilton Civic Hospitals Foundation; Dir., Chedoke-McMaster Hospital; recreations: sailing; clubs: Hamilton, Tamahaac; Home: 6 Kinnel St., Hamilton, Ont.; Office: 21 King St. W., Hamilton, Ont. L8P 4W7.

**GLEZOS, Matthews,** B.Com.; business executive; b. Montreal, Que. 27 Aug. 1927; s. George and Ekaterina (Bakalos) G.; e. McGill Univ. B.Com. 1952; m. Sophia d. John Protonotarios 23 Sept. 1952; children: George, Mary; Pres. Imasco B.V. 1984–89, retired 1989; joined Imasco Ltd. 1955, Treas. 1967, Vice Pres. and Treas. 1978; Club: Royal Montreal Golf; Home: 366 Kindersley Ave., Town of Mount Royal, Que. H3R 1R9.

**GLICK, Srul Irving,** Mus.Bac., Mus.M.; composer, conductor, teacher, producer; b. Toronto, Ont. 8 Sept. 1934; s. David and Ida (Chaplick) G.; e. Univ. of Toronto Mus.Bac. 1955, Mus.M. 1958; m. Reva Dorothy d. Michael and Lillian Sandler 1957; now separated; children: Julie, Stefan, Paula; COMPOSER-IN-RESIDENCE & CHOIR DIR., BETH TIKVAH SYNAGOGUE 1969– ; Producer with CBC 1962–85 (winner of 7 Grand Prix du Disques Canada and a Juno Award); Program Dir., Musica Beth Tikvah 1986– ; one of Canada's prominent composers; music performed by most major orchestras & chamber ensembles in Canada and is widely performed worldwide; devotes his time to composing, conducting, teaching and lecturing on his music at home and abroad; Mem., Candn. League of Composers (Pres. 1966–69); SOCAN; J.I. Segal Award for Contbn. to Jewish Music 1972; Kavod Award, Cantor's Assembly of Am. 1982; Solomon Schechter Internat. Award for best annual mus. prog. for a synagogue 1985; one of Canada's most prolific composers and author of 25 recordings and 23 published compositions plus two published volumes of liturgical music; recreations: painter, photographer; Home: 140 Farnham Ave., Toronto, Ont. M4V 1H4.

**GLICKMAN, Barry,** M.Sc., Ph.D.; educator; scientist; b. Montréal, Qué. 6 July 1946; s. Ralph S. and Isabelle E. (Speyer) G.; e. McGill Univ. B.Sc. 1968, M.Sc. 1969; Rijksuniversiteit te Leiden Ph.D. 1972; children: Natasha, Roanna, Daniel; PROF. OF BIOL., UNIV. OF VICTORIA 1984– ; Dir., Centre for Environmental Health; Assoc. Dir. for Molecular Genetics, Fundaçao Neves das Ledes Ferreira, Goiania, Brazil; Pres., Glickman Consulting Inc.; mem. Sci. Adv. Panel Chem. Industries Inst. of Toxicology; Assoc. Prof. of Biochem. Univ. of Leiden 1972–80; Expert on Mutagenesis, Nat. Inst. Environmental Health Sci's USA 1980–84; Adjunct Prof. of Pathol. Univ. of N.C. 1980–84; Prof. of Biology, York Univ. 1984–91; Fellow, Soc. Promotion Sci. in in Japan 1974–75; Steacie Fellow 1986–88; author numerous publs.; assoc. ed. Mutation Rsch.; mem. various ed. bds.; recreation: sailing; Office: Dept. of Biology, Univ. of Victoria, Victoria, B.C. V8W 2Y2.

**GLOCKNER, Peter G.,** B.Eng., M.Sc., Ph.D., P.Eng., F.C.S.M.E., F.A.A.M., F.A.S.C.E., F.E.I.C.; university professor; b. Moragy, Hungary 26 Jan. 1929; s. Peter and Elisabeth (Biel) G.; e. McGill Univ. B.Eng. 1955; M.I.T. M.Sc. 1956; Univ. of Michigan Ph.D. 1964; m. Sarah d. Frederick and Martha Kraft 18 June 1955; one d.: Marilyn Elizabeth Veronica; PROF. OF CIVIL ENGINEERING, UNIV. OF CALGARY 1968– ; Design Engr., C.C. Parker, Whittaker & Co. 1956–58; Asst. Prof. of Civil Eng., Univ. of Alta. 1958–62; Assoc. Prof. 1962–68; Prof. of Mechanical Engineering, Univ. of Calgary 1976– ; EIC's Gzowski Gold Medal 1971; ASCE's Moisseiff Medal & Prize 1983; Cancam Medal & Prize 1993; author: 'A Place of Ingenuity' 1994; recreations: accordion, tennis, swimming; Home: 2536 Charlebois Dr. NW, Calgary, Alta. T2L 0T6; Office: Calgary, Alta. T2N 1N4.

**GLOOR, Pierre,** M.D., Ph.D., F.R.C.P.(C); physician; educator; b. Basel, Switzerland 5 Apr. 1923; s. Fritz and Marie (Meier) G.; e. Humanistisches Gymnasium, Basel, Matura 1942; Univ. of Basel M.D. 1949; McGill Univ. Ph.D. 1957; m. Luba d. Leonid Genush 30 Sept. 1954; children: Irene Mary, Daniel Victor; Prof. of Clin. and Exper. Neurophysiol., McGill Univ. 1968–88; Chief of Lab. Electroencephalography & Clin. Neurophysiol. Montreal Neurol. Inst. and Hosp. 1961–84, Asst. Dir. (Research) 1965–85, Neurophysiologist and Chief of Neurophysiol. Labs. 1966–88; Phys.-in-Charge of Electroencephalography Royal Victoria Hosp. 1962–84, Assoc. Electroencephalographer 1960–62; Electroencephalographer, Montreal Neurol. Inst. and Hosp. 1968– ; Med. Consultant, Montreal Children's Hosp. 1972– ; Consultant Dept. Neurosciences Jewish Gen. Hosp. 1974– ; Consultant in Neurophysiol. Douglas Hosp. 1975– ; Lectr. in Electroencephalography McGill Univ. 1954–57, Asst. Prof. of Exper. Neurol. 1957–62, Assoc. Prof. of Clin. & Exper. Neurophysiol. 1962–68, Prof. 1968– ; Assoc. Electroencephalographer Montreal Neurol. Inst. 1955–61, Asst. Neurophysiol. 1957–66; Electroencephalographer Jewish Gen. Hosp. 1956–61; William G. Lennox Lectr. Am. Epilepsy Soc. 1977; Hans Berger Lectr. Med. Coll. Va. 1978; Preston Robb Pediatric Neurol. Lectr. Montreal Children's Hosp. 1978; 1st Penfield Mem. Lectr. Western EEG Soc. 1981; Jerome K. Merlis Lectr. in Neuroscience, Dept. Neurology, Univ. of Maryland 1989; Internat. Lectr., British Br., Internat. League against Epilepsy 1989; First hon. lectr., Oregon Comprehensive Epilepsy Program 1990; recipient Robert Bing Prize Swiss Acad. Med. Sciences 1962; Michael Prize (W. Germany) 1980; William G. Lennox Award Am. Epilepsy Soc. 1981; Fellow, Amer. Electroencephalographic Soc. 1982, Jasper Award (AES) 1988; Hon. Pres., XII Internat. Congress of Electroencephalography and Clinical Neurophysiology, Rio de Janeiro 1990; Wilder Penfield Award of Candn. League against Epilepsy 1990; served with Swiss Army 1943–45; author, ed. various scient. publs.; Candn. Del. Internat. Fed. Socs. Electroencephalography & Neurophysiol. 1966–69; Fellow, N.Y. Acad. Sciences; Hon. mem. Deutsche EEG Gesellschaft; Assn. des Techniciens(nes) et Technologistes en EEG du Qué.; Corresponding mem., Swiss Assoc. for Electroencephalography and Clin. Neurophysiol.; Swiss Neurologic. Soc.; Cuban Neurosci. Soc. (Epilepsy Sect.); mem. Internat. Brain Research Organ.; Candn. Soc. Clin. Neurophysiols. (Secy. 1962–63, Pres. 1964–65); Candn. Physiol. Soc.; Candn. Neurol. Soc.; Candn. Med. Assn.; Am. Electroencephalographic Soc. (mem. Council 1965–66, 1980–81; Pres. 1978–79); Am. Epilepsy Soc. (Pres. 1976); Soc. Neuroscience; E. Assn. Electroencephalographers (Pres. 1965); Am. Assn. Advanc. Science; Sigma Xi; Montreal Physiol. Soc.; Candn. League Against Epilepsy; Montreal Neuroscience Group; Protestant; Recreations: music (piano and harpischord), gardening, hiking; Home: 17 Strathcona Dr., Montréal, Qué. H3R 1E3; Office: 3801 University St., Montréal, Qué. H3A 2B4.

**GLOSSOP, Robert Glenn,** B.A., Ph.D.; program director; b. Orange, N.J. 7 Dec. 1947; s. Glenn A. and Helen J. (Abraham) G.; e. Trent Univ. B.A. (Hons.) 1971; Univ. of Birmingham Ph.D. 1977; m. Margaret d. Ross and Gwendolyn Edmison 26 June 1971; children: Emily Anne, Owen Glenn; DIRECTOR OF PROGRAMS & RESEARCH, VANIER INST. 1991– ; Lectr., Extramural studies, Univ. of Birmingham 1972–73; Program Asst., Vanier Inst. 1975–77; Program Offr. 1977–83; Co-ord. of Programs & Rsch. 1983–91; Mem., Adv. Ctte. to the Chief Statistician, Statistics Canada 1987–93 (Chair 1989–91); Social Policy Project Ctte., Econ. Council of Canada 1989–93; Child & Family adv. ctte., Laidlaw Found. 1991– ; (Chair 1993– ;); Dir., Nat. Forum on Family Security 1991– ; Canada Council Doctoral Fellowship 1973–75; Dir., Family & Patient Communication Centre of Ottawa 1983–87; Vice-Chair, Westboro Community Assn. 1985–86; Dir., Candn. Assn. for the Treatment & Study of Families 1987–92; Mem., Candn. Sociology & Anthrol. Assn.; author of numerous journal articles, book chapters, parly. briefs & reports; recreations: skiing, bicycling; Home: 677 Edison Ave., Ottawa, Ont. K2A 1W2; Office: 300, 120 Holland Ave., Ottawa, Ont. K1Y 0X6.

**GLOVER, Douglas Herschel,** B.A., M.Litt., M.F.A.; author; b. Simcoe, Ont. 14 Nov. 1948; s. Murray Pettit and Jean Montrose (Ross) G.; e. York Univ. B.A. 1969; Univ. of Edinburgh M.Litt. 1971; Univ. of Iowa M.F.A. 1982; Iowa Writers Workshop grad.; Fiction Ed. 'The Iowa Review' 1980–81; First Novels Columnist 'Books in Canada' 1985–86; Co-editor 'Coming Attractions' 1991, 1992 and 1993; Writer-in-Residence: Univ. of N.B. 1987–88; Univ. of Lethbridge, fall 1988; St. Thomas Univ., winter 1992; New York State Writers Inst., State Univ. of N.Y. at Albany, fall 1992 and fall 1993; Lectr., Dept. of Eng., Skidmore Coll., Saratoga Springs N.Y., fall 1992 and spring 1993; recipient 'Canadian Fiction Magazine' Contbrs. Prize 1985; Lit. Press Group Writers Choice Award 1986; Nat. Magazine Award for fiction 1990; nominated for Gov. General's Award 1991; author (short stories): 'The Mad River' 1981; 'Dog Attempts to Drown Man in Saskatoon' 1985; 'A Guide to Animal Behaviour' 1991; (novels): 'Precious' 1984; 'The South Will Rise at Noon' 1988; 'The Life and Times of Captain N.' 1993; fiction selected for 'Best Canadian Stories' 1985, 1987, 1988; 'Best American Stories' 1989; contbr. to various mags. and lit. jours.; mem. Writers Union Can.; PEN Internat.; recreation: running (winner Candn. 20–kilometre road race championship 1979, Bronze Medal Candn. Marathon Championship 1967); Home: 2 Deer Run, Gansevoort, N.Y. 12831 and R.R. 1, Waterford, Ont. N0E 1Y0.

**GLUBE, Hon. Constance R.,** B.A., LL.B., LL.D.; b. Ottawa, Ont. 23 Nov. 1931; d. Samuel, Q.C. and Pearl (Slonemsky) Lepofsky; e. Mutchmore and Hopewell Ave. Pub. Schs., Glebe Coll. Inst. 1948 Ottawa; McGill Univ. B.A. 1952; Dalhousie Univ. LL.B. 1955; LL.D. (Hon. Degree) Dalhousie Univ. (Law Sch. Centennial Convocation) 1983; m. Richard H. Glube 6 July 1952; children: John B., Erica D., Harry S., B. Joseph CHIEF JUSTICE, TRIAL DIV. SUPREME COURT OF N.S. since 1982; called to Bar of N.S. 1956; cr. Q.C. 1974; Award of Merit, City of Halifax 1977; Solr. Kitz & Matheson, Halifax 1964–66; Partner Fitzgerald & Glube 1966–68; Solr. Legal Dept. City of Halifax 1969–74; City Mgr. City of Halifax 1974–77; mem. Court House Comn. 1972–74; Metro Centre Bd. 1975–77; appt'd. Judge, Trial Division, (ex officio Appeal Div.) Supreme Court of N.S. 1977; Halifax Grammar Sch. Bd. Trustees 2 terms; mem. Extve. and Bd. Candn. Council Christians & Jews (Atlantic Provs.) 1977–79, Co-chrmn. 1980–81; mem. Bd. of Dir. Candn. Judges Conference 1979, 2nd Vice-Chrmn. 1980–82; mem. Bd. of Dir. Candn. Inst. for the Adm. of Justice, 1979–83; Extve. and Bd. Candn. Assn. Mun. Adm. 1975–77; Inst. Pub. Adm. Can. Extve. 1975–77; Internat. City Mgrs. Assn.; N.S. Bar Soc.; Candn. Bar Assn.; Hon. Chrmn., Candn. Mental Health Assn. N.S. Div.; mem. Bd. Halifax Heritage Found. 1983– ; mem. Bd. Candn. Judicial Counc. 1982– ; (Exec. 1985–88); Adv. Counc., Family Mediation of Canada; Hebrew; recreations: gardening, swimming; Clubs: RNSYS; Home: 5920 Inglewood Dr., Halifax, N.S. B3H 1B1; Office: Law Courts, 1815 Upper Water St., Halifax, N.S. B3J 3C8.

**GLYNN, Peter Alexander Richard,** B.Eng., M.A.Sc., Ph.D.; hospital executive; b. Toronto, Ont. 14 Oct. 1944; s. John Richard Lewis and Jessie Mackenzie (Dalziel) G.; e. Royal Mil. Coll. B.Eng. 1965; Univ. of Waterloo M.A.Sc. 1967, Ph.D. 1972; m. Arlene d. Margaret and Henry Whalen 13 Aug. 1966; children: Jennifer, Jeffrey; PRES. AND C.E.O., KINGSTON GENERAL HOSPITAL 1991– ; Offr., Candn. Army, R.C.E.M.E. 1961–69; var. policy posns., Dept. of Coll. & Univ., Govt. of Ont. 1972–75; Dir., Policy Planning & Mgmt. Infor. Systems Br., Govt. of Sask. 1975–80; Assoc. Depy. Min., Dept. of Health 1981–84; Asst. Depy. Min., Health Services & Promotion Br., Health & Welfare Canada 1984–91; former trustee of three Sask. hosps.; Sask. Cancer Found.; Sask. Alcoholism Comn.; currently mem. Bd. of Dirs., National Cancer Inst. of Can.; Kingston Gen. Hosp.; recreations: sailing, skiing, hiking; Office: 76 Stuart St., Kington, Ont. K7L 2V7.

**GNAROWSKI, Michael,** M.A., Ph.D.; educator; editor; b. Shanghai, China 27 Sept. 1934; s. Daniel and Nina G.; e. McGill Univ. B.A. 1956; Univ. de Montréal M.A. 1960; Univ. of Ottawa Ph.D. 1967; m. Diana d. Earl and Françoise Paquet 21 Oct. 1961; children: Franceska, Sybille, Daniel; PROF. OF ENGLISH, CARLETON UNIV. 1972– , Vice Pres., Gen. Ed. and Dir. Carleton University Press Inc. 1981– ; Lectr. in Eng. Univ. de Sherbrooke 1961–62; Asst. Prof. Lakehead Univ. 1962–65; Asst. and Assoc. Prof. Sir George Williams Univ. 1966–72; Visiting Prof. Univ. of Ottawa 1970–72; Exchange Scholar, Univ. of Leningrad 1977, Univ. of Warsaw 1979; Guest Lectr. McGill Univ., Univ de Montréal, State Univ. of N.Y., Univs. of Paderborn, Siegen and Bonn 1986; Univ. of Mainz and Tübingen 1987; Université Canadienne en France 1989; Visiting Prof., Univ. of Siegen 1989; ed. 'Three Early Poems From Lower Canada' 1969; 'Archibald Lampman' 1970; 'Selected Stories of Raymond Knister' 1972; 'New Provinces' 1976; 'Leonard Cohen: The Artist and His Critics' 1976; co-ed. 'The Making of Modern Poetry in Canada' 1967; Compiler 'A Concise Bibliography of English-Canadian Literature' 1973, revised 1978; 'Selected Poetry of Archibald Lampman' 1990; recreations; book collecting; Home: 409 Oxford St. E., Kemptville, Ont. K0G 1J0; Office: c/o Carleton Univ. Press, PA 160, 1125 Colonel-by-Drive, Ottawa, Ont. K1S 5B6.

**GOAR, Carol,** B.J.; journalist; b. Hamilton, Ont. 30 Nov. 1951; d. John Hamilton and Thone Adeline (Wyman) G.; e. Carleton Univ. B.J. 1974; NAT. AFFAIRS

COLUMNIST, THE TORONTO STAR 1985– ; Reporter, Ottawa Citizen 1974–76; Candn. Press 1977–79; FP News Service 1980–81; Ottawa Bureau Chief, Maclean's mag. 1982–84; recipient Nat. Newspaper Award 1986; Office: 903, 150 Wellington St., Ottawa, Ont. K1P 5A4.

**GODARD, Barbara Jane,** M.A., Doctorat; educator; critic; translator; b. Toronto, Ont. 24 Dec. 1941; d. William Franklin and Margaret Jean (Platten) Thompson; e. St. Clement's Sch. Toronto 1960; Univ. of Toronto Trinity Coll. B.A. 1964; Univ. de Montréal M.A. 1967; Univ. de Paris VIII Maîtrise 1969; Univ. de Bordeaux Doctorat 3e cycle 1971; one child: Alexis; ASSOC. PROF. OF ENG., YORK UNIV. 1981– ; lectr. Univs. Montréal (1964–67) and Paris (1968–70); Asst. Prof. present Univ. 1971; mem. Adv. Ctte. Hist. Lit. Instn. in Can./Histoire de l'instn. littéraire au Can.; recipient Gabrielle Roy Prize Assn. Candn. & Que. Lits. 1988; author 'Talking About Ourselves: The Literary Productions of Native Women of Canada' 1985; 'Bibliography of Feminist Criticism/Bibliographie de la critique féministe' 1987; 'Audrey Thomas: Her Life and Work' 1989; over 80 essays; ed. 'Gynocritics/Gynocritiques: Feminist Approaches to the Writing of Canadian and Quebec Women' 1987; 'Collaboration in the Feminine: Writing on "Women" and "Culture" from *Tessera*' 1994; Founding Co-ed. 'Tessera'; Co-ed. 'Open Letter'; mem. various ed. bds.; Transl., Antoinine Maillet's 'The Tale of Don L'Orignal' 1978; Nicole Brossard's 'These Our Mothers' 1983, 'Lovhers' 1986, 'Picture Theory' 1991; France Théoret's 'The Tangible Word' 1991; mem. P.E.N. Internat.; Assn. Candn. & Que. Lits.; Assn. Candn. Univ. Profs. Eng.; Candn. Comparative Lit. Assn.; Assn. Lit. Translators; Candn. Semiotic Assn.; Toronto Semiotic Circle; Candn. Women's Studies Assn.; Candn. Rsch. Inst. Advanc. Women; Modern Lang. Assn.; Candn. Amateur Music Assn.; Toronto Museum Childhood; Home: 217 Major St., Toronto, Ont. M5S 2L4; Office: 350 Stong Coll., 4700 Keele St., North York, Ont. M3J 1P3.

**GODARD, Gilles A.,** B.A.; songwriter, producer; b. Cornwall, Ont. 13 July 1957; s. Guillaume B. and Marie-Rose (Rouselle) G.; e. St. Laurence H.S.; La Citadelle, Ottawa Univ. B.A. 1977; m. Susan d. Douglas and Lynn Lascelle 6 Oct. 1979; children: Chloé Lane, Jazz Marie; worked for family business as supervisor of 9 card & gift shops while writing & performing as an artist 1975–82; moved to Nashville, Tennessee to pursue career as writer, producer, performer 1983; Mng. Dir., Marbleworks Music; Signed Writer to BMG Music Pub. Canada Inc.; 4 SOCAN awards (Writer, Publisher); Big Country RPM Award (Prod.) 1986; Félix Award for best country album on RCA 1987; Record Industry Person of the Year, Candn. Country Music Assn. 1990; Mem., CMA, CCMA, AFofM, AFTRA, CARAS; has written over 200 songs recorded by artists such as Anne Murray, Lisa Brokop, Susan Jacks, Colleen Peterson, Dan Seals, Tommy Hunter, Ronnie Prophet, Kelita, Eddie Eastman, Janie Fricke, etc.; recreations: cooking, travel, exercise; Home: 2258 Lebanon Rd., Unit 13, Nashville, TN 37214; Office: 1030 17th Ave. S., Nashville, TN 37212.

**GODARD-BENNETT, Mira Marina,** C.M., B.Sc., M.B.A.; historian/publisher/art dealer; b. Bucarest, Roumania 31 Jan. 1932; d. Emile John and Madeleine Mally (Marian) Godard; e. Ecole du Louvre, Art History 1949; Sorbonne Univ., Sci.dipl. 1950; Concordia Univ., B.Sc. 1954; McGill Univ., M.B.A. 1960; m. Reginald Sydney Bennett 30 June 1962; OWNER, MIRA GODARD GALLERY 1981– ; Metrology Engr., aircraft indus., Mtl. 1955–61; Founding Sec., Candn. Standards Assn.; Owner, Godard-Lefort Gallery 1961– ; Marlborough-Godard Gallery 1971– ; Founding Mem. & First Pres., Candn. Profl. Art Dealers Assn.; Mem., Arts Adv. Counc., Fed. Dept. of Public Works; Can. Counc. Travelling Juries; Sectoral Adv. Ctte., Free Trade (Arts & Cultural Indus.); Patron, Montreal Mus. of Fine Arts; Trustee, Art Gallery of Ont. Found.; Member of the Order of Canada 1988; Office: 22 Hazelton Ave., Toronto, Ont. M5R 2E2.

**GODBOUT, André D.,** B.A., B.C.L., M.B.A.; investment dealer; b. Montreal, Que. 19 Dec. 1949; s. Maurice D. G.; e. College Jean de Brébeuf B.A. 1969; McGill Univ. B.C.L. (Law) 1972; Barreau du Qué. 1975; Univ. of Western Ont. M.B.A. 1975; m. Francine De Grandpré 25 May 1977; children: Charles, Marie-Jeanne, Dominique, Laurent; SENIOR EXTVE. VICE-PRESIDENT, RETAIL SERVICES, INSTITUTIONAL FIXED INCOME, OPERATIONS, LEVESQUE BEAUBIEN GEOFFRION INC. 1976– ; Analyst & Legal Counsel, Dir. of Registration Q.S.C. 1975–76; Dir., I.D.A.; Gov., V.S.E.; Pres., Que. Univ. Sports Found.; recreations: skiing, tennis; clubs: St-Denis, St-James; Home: 222 Geneva Cres., Town of Mont-Royal, Que. H3R 2A8; Office: 1155 Metcalfe St., Montreal, Que. H3B 4S9.

**GODBOUT, Jacques,** M.A.; écrivain, cinéaste; né Montréal 27 nov. 1933; f. Fernand et Mariette (Daoust) G.; é. Univ. de Montréal, B.A., M.A., 1954; ép. Ghislaine, f. Henri Reiher, 31 juil. 1954; enfants: Alain, Sylvie: SCENARISTE ET REALISATEUR, OFFICE NATIONAL DU FILM; Prof. asst., Univ. Coll. d'Addis Abeba, Ethiopie 1954; Publicitaire, McLaren Advertising Agency, Montréal 1957; Réalisateur aux versions françaises, Office National du Film, Montréal 1958; scénariste, réalisateur et monteur 1961; Dir. de la prod. française 1969; scénariste et réalisateur 1970; chargé de cours a l'Univ. de Montréal 1969; invited lectr., U. Cal. in Berkeley 1985; écrivain en résidence, Univ. de Montréal 1991–92; films: 'Les Dieux' 1961; 'Pour quelques Arpents de Neige' 1962 (1er prix. 17e Festival internat. du Film documentaire, Salernes, Italie); 'A Saint-Henri' 1962; 'Rose et Landry' 1963 (Prix du Centre de la Culture et de la Civilisation, de La Fondation G. Cini, Venise 1963; Plaque du Lion de St-Marc, Expn. intern. du film documentaire, Venise 1963; ler prix, Festival du film du Mid-West, Chicago 1964; Mention, Festival du film documentaire, Cordoba, Argentine 1964); 'Paul-Emile Borduas' 1963; 'Le Monde va nous prendre pour des Sauvages' 1964 (diplôme, 16e Palmarès du film canadien, Toronto 1965); 'Fabien ne sans son Jules' 1964 (Grand prix, 2e semaine internat. du film 16mm, Evian, France 1964); 'Huit Témoins' 1965 (Prix, Palmarès du film canadien, Toronto); 'Yul 871' 1966 (Meilleure réalisation, 2e Festival internat. du film Chicago 1966); 'Kid Sentiment' 1968; 'Les vrais Cousins' 1970; 'Le Roman d'Ixe-13' 1972; 'Les Troubbes de Johny' 1973; 'La Gammick' 1974; 'Aimez-vous Les Chiens?' 1975; 'Arsenal' 1976; 'L'Invasion' 1977; 'Derrière L'Image' 1978; 'Feu L'objectivité' 1978; 'Deux Épisodes dans la vie d'Hubert Aquin' 1979; 'Distorsions' 1981 (Prix du Publique, Nyon, Suisse); 'Un Monologue Nord-Sud' 1982; 'Comme en Californie' 1983; 'Québec Soft' 1984; 'En Dernier Recours' 1987; 'Alias Will James' 1988; 'Pour l'Amour du Stress' 1990; 'Le Mouton Noir' 1992; littérature: 'Carton-Pâte' (poèmes) 1956; 'Les Pavés secs' (poèmes) 1958; 'La chair est un commencement' (poèmes) 1959; 'C'est la chaude Loi des Hommes' (poèmes) 1960; 'l'Aquarium' (roman) 1962 (Prix France-Canada 1962); 'le Couteau sur la Table' (roman) 1965 (prix de l'Acad. française 1965); 'le Mouvement du 8 avril' (pamphlet) 1966; 'Salut Galarneau!' (roman) 1967 (Prix du Gouverneur-Général 1968); 'la grande Muraille de Chine' (poèmes, en collab. avec J.R. Colombo) 1969); 'd'Amour P.Q.' (roman) 1972; 'L'Interview' (théâtre) 1973; 'Le Réformiste' (essai) 1975; 'L'Isle au Dragon' (roman) 1976; 'Les Têtes à Papineau' (Roman) 1981; 'Le Murmure Marchand' (essai) 1984; 'Souvenirs Shop' (poésie) 1985; 'Une Histoire Américaine' (roman) 1986; 'Un Coeur de Rockeur' (biographie) 1988; 'L'Écran du bonheur' (essai) 1990; 'L'Écrivain de Province' (journal) 1991; 'Le Temps des Galarneau (Roman)' 1993; Résidence: 815 Pratt, (Outremont), Montréal, P.Q. H2V 2T7; Bureau: C.P. 6100, Montréal, P.Q. H4N 2N4.

**GODDARD, Merritt Henry,** B.A.(Hons.), F.R.I., C.F.P.; financial executive; b. Hamilton, Ont. 25 April 1950; s. Charles Henry and Hilda May (Genoe) G.; e. Port Dover H.S. 1969; Univ. of Western Ont. 1970 grad. & mem., honour society of business school, B.A. (Hons.) 1974; m. Liz d. Adrian and Marie Sietses 1 Sept. 1979; children: Meredith, Hillary, Samuel; EXECUTIVE VICE-PRES. & SENIOR FINANCIAL ADVISOR, THE EQUION GROUP; worked in real estate industry 1974–80; joined The Equion Group 1980 and assisted in developing it into one of the premier comprehensive personal financial planning companies in Canada; Past Pres., Central Ontario Chapter, Candn. Assn. of Financial Planners; Dir., The Equion Group; F.R.I., Real Estate Inst. of Canada; C.F.P., Candn. Inst. of Financial Planning; clubs: Western's Business School Alumni Club, The Fitness Institute, The Oakville Club; Home: 300 Balsam Dr., Oakville, Ont. L6J 3X6; Offices: 212 King St. W., Ste. 300, Toronto, Ont. M5H 1K5 and 150 Lakeshore Rd. E., Oakville, Ont.

**GODEL, Jean-Claude;** engineering/manufacturing executive; b. Surpierre (Fribourg) Switz. 14 Apr. 1937; s. Arthur Joseph and Mathilde (Badoud) G.; e. (all in Switz.) Swiss Engr. Coll. of Fribourg; Inter-Cadres-Corede (bus. sch.) 1970; Internat. Mngt. Inst. 1981; IMEDE Bus. Sch. 1985; m. Françoise d. Michel and Marguerite Huwiler 29 Aug. 1964; children: Nicolas, Laurent; DIR. & PRES., SULZER CAN. INC. 1984– ; Dir., FuelMaker; Sulzer Bingham; Swiss Army Officer; Tech. Dept. Mgr., Cardinal Brewery S.A., Switz. 1963–70; Sales Eng., Sulzer Bros. Limited, Switz. 1970–72; Dept. Mgr., Sulzer Hermanos Buenos-Aires, Argentina 1972–76; Sulzer del., W. Africa & Mng. Dir., Sulzer Nigeria 1976–81; Dir. & Vice-Pres., Sulzer do Brasil, Rio de Janeiro 1981–84; Pres., Swiss Can. C. of C. 1987–90; Mem., Rotary Club Ville Marie, Montreal; Home: 6150 ave. du Boisé, 7B, Montréal, Qué. H3S 2V2; Office: 295 Hymus Blvd., Pointe Claire, Qué. H9R 1G6.

**GODFREY, Bert;** company president; b. Toronto, Ont., 1 June 1908; s. Solomon and Minnie (Reisman) G.; e. Pub. and High Schs., Toronto, Ont.; m. Ruth Grossman, 26 Jan. 1934; children: Corinne (m. Prof. Baruch Levine), Sheldon J. (m. Judy Cole); PRESIDENT, S. GODFREY CO. LTD., Wool Importers; mem., Toronto Citizens' Centenary Comte. 1965–67; Pres., Jewish Pub. Library of Toronto 1959–64; Pres., Goel Tzedec Synagogue 1948–52; Bureau of Jewish Educ. of Toronto 1960–62; Founding Pres: Beth Tzedec Synagogue (amalg.) 1952–56 (Hon. Pres. since 1956); Ont. Region, Un. Synagogue of Am. (now Hon. Pres.) 1956; United Synagogue Day Sch. 1961–62; Gen. Campaign Chrmn., Israel Bond Campaign 1964–65; Nat. Vice-Pres., Un. Synagogue of Am. 1957–61, 1965–69; mem. Extve. Ctte., Candn. Counc. of Christians and Jews (Chrmn., Awards Ctte.; Toronto Co-Chrmn., Brotherhood Week) 1954; 1954: mem. Bd. of Gov.: Mount Sinai Hosp.; Baycrest Centre for Geriatric Care; mem. Bd. of Dir.: United Jewish Welfare Found.; Candn. Found. for Jewish Culture; Vice Pres., World Council of Synagogues 1964; 1960–64: mem. Bd. of Overseers, Jewish Theol. Seminary of Am.; original mem. Candn. Camp Ramah; Bd. mem., Associated Hebrew Schs.; mem., Extve. Comte., Candn. Jewish Cong. (Central); Chrmn., Conventions World Counc. of Synagogues (Mexico City) 1964; Chrmn., Bd. of Govs., Israel Bond Orgn., Toronto 1966; Mem., Social Planning Counc., Metro. Toronto 1966; Chrmn., Israel Histadrut Campaign (Fundraising Soroka Med. Centre (Beer-Sheva Israel) 1986; recipient, Louis Marshall Award, Jewish Theol. Semy. of Am. 1961; Human Relations Award, Candn. Council Christians & Jews 1964; Honored at Jewish Nat. Fund – Negev Dinner 1966; 'Tower of David' award for participation in Israel Bond effort 1983; Hebrew: Clubs: Canadian; Primrose; Oakdale; B'nai Brith; Office: 49 Front St. E., Toronto, Ont. M5E 1B3.

**GODFREY, Charles Morris,** C.M., B.A., M.A., M.D., F.R.C.P.(C); physician; b. Philadelphia, Pa. 24 Sept. 1917; s. Charles and Martha (McKitterick) G.; e. Jarvis Coll.; Univ. of Toronto M.D. 1953; McLaughlin Fellowship 1956–57; specialist 1958; m. Margaret Ethel d. Alexander and Ethel Gemmell 25 Oct. 1941; children: Mark, Kristen, Adam; CONSULTANT, DEPT. OF REHABILITATION, THE WELLESLEY HOSP. 1990, Dir. 1970–90; Prof. Emeritus, Fac. of Med.; Archivist, Fac. of Med., Univ. of Toronto 1986–90; Med. Dir., Dept. of Rehab., Toronto East Gen. Hosp. 1958–60; Toronto Gen. Hosp. 1958–62; Sunnybrook Hosp. 1960–70; Toronto Rehab. Ctr. 1967–70; five years serv. R.C.A.F.; Red Cross Service Medal 1960; Centennial Medal 1967; CARE Outstanding Serv. Award 1971; Assn. for Children with Learning Disabilities Cert of Recognition 1974; Hon. Life Mem., Ont. Med. Assn. 1983; Queen's Silver Jubilee Medal 1977; Sr. Mem., Candn. Med. Assn. 1985; Pres. Xth Cong. of Internat. Fed. PM&R 1988; Member of the Order of Canada; Founding Mem., Assn. of Neurologically Disabled 1983–84; Chrmn., CARE/Canada; CARE/Internat.; CARE/MEDICO (Chrmn.); Integra (Founding Mem.); Non-Smokers Rights Assn.; Physicians for Social Responsibility; author: 'A Handbook for Laryngectomy' 1964; 'The Cholera Epidemics in Upper Canada 1832–1865' 1966; 'Selected Readings in Aphasia' 1974; 'People or Planes' 1974; 'Medicine for Ontario' 1979; 'The Ageless Exercise Plan' 1982; co-author (with Charles Templeton) 'End Back Attacks' 1991; 'John Rolph: Rebel With Causes' 1993; contrib. author: 'A Handbook for Family and Community Medicine' 1986; John B. Neilson Award, Hanna Inst. of Hist. of Med. 1987; Office: 484 Church St., Ste. 107, Toronto, Ont. M4Y 2C7.

**GODFREY, Ellen Rachel,** B.A.; author; businesswoman; b. Chicago, Ill. 15 Sept. 1942; d. William Maurice and Mary (Rosen) Swartz; e. Stanford Univ. B.A. Hist. 1963; m. William David s. Marguerite and Richmond G. 25 Aug. 1963; children: John (dec.), Rebecca, Sam; PRESIDENT, SOFTWORDS RESEARCH INTERNATIONAL LTD. 1979– ; Pres., Vancouver Island Advanced Technology Centre; Vice Pres., Software Productivity Ctr.; has worked in advtg., promotion, editing, publishing and software; author: (novels) 'The Case of the Cold Murderer'; 'Murder Among the Well-to-Do'; 'Murder behind locked Doors' 1988; 'Georgia Disappeared' 1992; (non-fiction) 'By Reason of Doubt' (winner Edgar Allan Poe Special Award for true crime,

Mystery Writers of Am. 1982); (short story) 'Common or Garden Murder'; speaker across Can. on electronic publ., publ. and new technol., project mgmt. in computer based training; Bd. of Dirs., B.C. Trade Develop. Corp.; Premier's Adv. Counc. on Science & Technol.; Univ. of Victoria Co-op; Office: 4252 Commerce Circle, Victoria, B.C. V8Z 4M2.

**GODFREY, John Ferguson,** D. Phil., D.Litt.S.; b. Toronto, Ont. 1942; s. John Morrow and Mary (Burwell) G.; e. Upper Can. Coll. Toronto 1960; Neuchatel Jr. Coll. Switzerland 1961; Trinity Coll. Univ. of Toronto B.A. 1965; Balliol Coll. Oxford Univ. M.Phil. 1967, St. Antony's Coll. D.Phil. 1975; m. Patricia Ann Bongard 1991; MEMBER OF PARLIAMENT, DON VALLEY WEST (TORONTO) 1993– ; Can. Council Doctoral Fellowship 1968–69 (Nat. Archives Paris 1 yr.); Asst. Prof. of Hist. Dalhousie Univ. 1970–75, Assoc. Prof. 1980–87; Asst. Prof. Univ. of King's Coll. 1975–76, Pres. and Vice Chancellor 1977–87; Ed., The Financial Post 1987–91; Vice-Pres., The Candn. Inst. for Advanced Rsch. 1992–93; Hon. Mem., Prayer Book Soc. of Canada; Mem. of Bd., Pollution Probe; Chrmn. Advisory Bd., Royal Soc. of Canada; Mem., Gov. Gen.'s Study Conf.; Pres., Council for Candn. Unity; Bd. mem., Canadian Club of Toronto; Ballet Jorgen; Internat. Fed. of Institutes for Advanced Studies; Westminster Inst. for Ethics and Human Values; Mem., Friends Group, UNICEF Canada; Dir. and Co-founder, Ethiopia Airlift and Adopt-a-Village' St. Antony's Coll. Trust; Ctte. Concerned Nova Scotians for Justice; numerous book reviews, commentaries on hist. events, educ. matters and current events CBC radio and TV; author 'Capitalism at War' 1987 and various publs. prof. journs. and mags., ednl., pol., internat., social & econ. affairs; N. Brit. Soc.; St. George's Soc. Halifax; Amnesty International; Soc. French Hist. Studies; Chrmn., N.S. Comm., HRH Duke of Edinburgh's 1980 study conference; Queen's Jubilee Medal, 1977; Vanier Award, 1981; First Honorary Member, Friends of the Citadel, 1983; D.Litt.S. (hon. causa), Trinity Coll., Toronto 1987; Hon. Vice Pres., Gilbert and Sullivan Society of Nova Scotia; recreations: squash, running, tennis, golf, skiing, sailing, wilderness canoeing; Clubs: Toronto; Badminton and Racquet; Osler Bluff Ski; Home: 379 Markham St., Toronto, Ont. M6G 2K8; Offices: 562 Eglinton Ave. E., Suite 105, Toronto, Ont. M4P 1B9 and House of Commons, Ottawa, Ont. K1A 0A6.

**GODFREY, Martyn,** B.A., B.Ed.; writer of books for young people; b. Birmingham, England 17 Apr. 1949; s. Sidney and Helen (Brown) G.; e. Univ. of Toronto, B.A. 1973, B.Ed. 1974; children: Marcus, Selby; elementary & jr. high teacher in Alta. & Ont. 1974–85; Mem., Writers Guild of Alta. (Vice-Pres. 1986; Pres. 1987); The Writers Union of Can.; Candn. Soc. of Children's Authors, Illustrators & Performers; best children's short story 'Ms Teeny-Wonderful' 1985; Univ. of Lethbridge, best children's book award 'Here She is – Ms Teeny-Wonderful' 1987; Candn. Children's Book Centre, Our Choice Award 19 titles; winner, Geoffrey Bilson Award for Hist. Fiction for Young People 1989; Manitoba Young Readers Award 1993; author (books for young people): 'Please Remove Your Elbow from My Ear'; 'They Call Me Boom Boom'; 'Meet You In The Sewer' 1993; 'Mystery in the Frozen Lands'; 'Don't Worry About Me, I'm Just Crazy'; 'Is It O.K. If This Monster Stays for Lunch,' 'Wally Stutzgummer, Super Bad Dude' 1992, 'There's a Cow in My Swimming Pool' (with Frank O'Keeffe), 'Monsters in the School' 1991, 'The Great Science Fair Disaster,' 'I Spent my Summer Vacation Kidnapped into Space,' 'Can You Teach Me to Pick My Nose?' 1990; 'Why Just Me?' 1989; and 19 earlier books; Office: c/o Joanne Kellock, Literary Agent, 11017 – 80 Avenue, Edmonton, Alta. T6G 0R2.

**GODFREY, Paul Victor,** B.A.Sc., P.Eng.; b. Toronto, Ont. 12 Jan. 1939; s. Philip and Bess (Greenbaum) G.; e. Univ. of Toronto B.A.Sc. (Chem. Engn.) 1962; m. Regina, d. Irving Bowman, Willowdale, Ont., 19 Nov. 1967; three s. Robin James, Noah Adam, Joshua Jay; PRES. & C.E.O., THE TORONTO SUN PUBLISHING CORP. 1992– ; Ald. and Controller, Borough N. York 1965–73; Commr., Toronto Transit Comn. 1973–84; Chrmn., Metrop. Toronto Council 1973–84; Publisher, The Toronto Sun 1984–91; Leader in crusade to bring major league baseball to Toronto, resulting in the Toronto Blue Jays; leading proponent of a new dome stadium for Metro Toronto; Commr. Metro Board of Commissioners of Police 1973–84; Comnr., Toronto Transit Comn. 1973–84; Bd. of Trustees, Hospital for Sick Children 1984– ; Bd. of Govs., Crescent Boys Sch.; Chrmn., Molson Indy Bd. of Trustees; Dir., Bowes Publishers Limited; Counsel Corp.; Delcan Ltd.; The Financial Post (Company Dir.); Florida Sun Publications Inc.; Stadium Acquisition Inc.; Founder of The Herbie Fund 1979; mem. Assn. Prof. Engrs. Ont.; B'nai B'rith; P. Conservative; Jewish; Home: 44 Arjay Cres., Willowdale, Ont. M2L 1C7; Office: 333 King St. E., Toronto, Ont. M5A 3X5.

**GODIN, Jean Cléo,** B.A., L.Lett., Dr. de l'U.; professeur; né Petit-Rocher, N.B. 13 août 1936; f. Nicolas et Anastasie (Doucet) G.; é. Coll. Ste. Marie, 1949–55; Boston Coll., B.A., 1961; Univ. de Montréal, L.Lett., 1964; Dr. de l'U. d'Aix-Marseille, 1966; ép. Michèle, f. Hermann Gervais, 3 août, 1963; enfants: François, Christian, Isabelle, Nicolas; PROF. TITULAIRE, DEPT. D'ETUDES FRANCAISES, Université de Montréal; Boursier du Conseil des Arts, 1962 et 1964; Boursier du Ministère de l'Education de Qué. 1963 et 1965; mem., Association Canadienne d'histoire du théâtre; Société d'histoire du Théâtre du Québec; Fédération internat. de la recherche théatrale; l'auteur du livre 'Henri Bosco: une poétique du mystère' 1968 (Prix littéraire du Québec 1969) et de l'édition critique de 'Visages du monde' d'Alain Grandbois 1990; l'auteur en collaboration avec Laurent Mailhot, des livres 'Le Théâtre québécois' 1970; 'Théâtre québécois II' 1980; l'auteur de nombreux articles; Catholique; récréations: ski, natation; Résidence: 3769 avenue Melrose, Montréal, Qué. H4A 2S3; Bureau: C.P. 6128, Succ. A., Montréal, Qué. H3C 3J7.

**GODKIN, Celia,** M.Sc.; educator; writer; illustrator; b. London, Eng. 15 Apl. 1948; d. Geoffrey Maxwell and Olive Mary (Oakey) G.; e. London Univ. B.Sc. 1969; Univ. of Toronto M.Sc. 1983; Ont. Coll. of Art A.O.C.A. 1983; Asst. Prof. of Biomedical Communications, Univ. of Toronto 1987– , Prog. Supr. 1988–89, Teaching Asst. in Comparative Anatomy 1979–83, Instr. in Bot. Drawing & Watercolour, Nat. Sci. Illus., Drawing in the Park, Drawing from Nature & Wildlife Drawing Sch. of Continuing Edn. 1988– , Instr. in Nat. Sci. Illus. 1981–82; Herpetol. Reptile Breeding Found. Picton, Ont. 1974–76; Fisheries Biol. Glenora Fisheries Stn. Ont. Min. of Natural Resources summers 1976–81; Biol. Cons. Min. of Environment 1985–86; Teaching Asst. Toronto Bd. Edn. devel. and taught ecol. prog. 1972; Instr. in Drawing from Nature Network for Learning 1985; Instr. in Creative Arts prog. Royal Ont. Museum 1985–90; art exhns. incl. Gallery 76 Toronto 1976; Slusser Gallery Univ. of Mich. 1983; Taiwan Museum Taipei 1986; R.O.M. 1984, 1989, 1990; Harbourfront 1992; Academy of Spherical Arts 1993; high sch. text book illus. since 1985; illus. acad. publs. comnd. by curators, profs. since 1977; various poster illus.; ltd. ed. print comnd. by Linn-Tarn Prints 1985; author and illus. 'Wolf Island' juvenile 1989, winner of the 1990 Roundtable Information Book Award (shortlisted for Mr. Christies Children's Book Awards 1990); author and illus. 'Ladybug Garden' juvenile 1994; designed and illus. 'Endangered Species: Canada's Disappearing Wildlife' 1987; book cover design 'Conserving Sea Turtles' 1983; Founder (1985) and Dir. Guild of Natural Sci. Illus. Can., ed. Newsletter; Address: 1155A Dundas St. W., Toronto, Ont. M6J 1X3.

**GODSOE, (Joseph) Gerald, Jr.,** Q.C., B.Sc., M.A., LL.B.; lawyer; b. Toronto, Ont. 28 Feb. 1942; s. Joseph Gerald and Margaret (Cowperthwaite) G.; e. Upper Can. Coll.; Univ. of Toronto B.Sc. 1963; Oxford Univ. (Rhodes Scholar Ont. 1963) B.A., M.A. 1965; Dalhousie Univ. LL.B. 1968; m. Dale Anne d. J. D'Arcy and Gertrude Sullivan 4 July 1969; three d. Suzanne, Stacey, Laura; PARTNER, STEWART McKELVEY STIRLING SCALES 1974– ; Dir., Eastern Telephone and Telegraph Co.; Candn. Inst. of Resource Law; Chrmn., Ocean Inst. of Can. 1986– ; External Reviewer, Dalhousie Law Sch.; Chrmn., N.S. Bar Soc. Ctte. on Fac. of Law Review; Exec. Dir., Royal Comn. on the Economic Union & Development Prospects for Can. (Macdonald Comn.) 1982–85; mem., N.S. Law Reform Adv. Comn. 1972–79; Chrmn. Co-ordinating Ctte. Maritime Provs. on Offshore Mineral Rights 1977–78; Advr. to Govt. of Can. on Constitutional Negotiations 1980–82; Chrmn. Halifax Br., Candn. Inst. Internat. Affairs 1974–76; Gov. Mount St. Vincent Univ. 1975–81 (and Chrmn. Finance Ctte. 1978–81); Sec., Rhodes Scholarship Selection Ctte. Maritime Provs. 1975–82; mem. Candn. Bar Assn.; Internat. Bar Assoc.; N.S. Barristers' Soc. (Counc. Mem. 1987–88); Liberal; Home: 6560 Geldert St., Halifax, N.S. B3H 2C8; Office: P.O. Box 997, Halifax, N.S. B3J 2X2.

**GODSOE, Peter C.,** B.Sc., M.B.A., F.C.A.; banker; b. Toronto, Ont. 2 May 1938; s. Joseph Gerald and Margaret Graham (Cowperthwaite) G.; e. Univ. of Toronto Schs. 1956; Univ. of Toronto B.Sc. 1961; C.A. 1964; Harvard Univ. M.B.A. 1966; m. Shelagh Cathleen Reburn 30 Nov. 1963; children: Craig, Eden, Cynthia; DEPUTY CHRMN., PRES. AND C.E.O., THE BANK OF NOVA SCOTIA; Dir. of various Bank of Nova Scotia subsidiaries and affiliates; joined Price Waterhouse & Co. 1961–64; The Bank of Nova Scotia, Ottawa 1966, Asst. Mgr. Montreal 1967, Agt. New York 1969, Asst. Gen. Mgr. Toronto 1971, Gen. Mgr. 1974, Sr. Vice Pres. 1979, Extve. Vice Pres. 1980, Vice Chrmn. 1982, Pres. & C.O.O. 1992, Pres. & C.E.O. 1993; Dir., Alexander & Alexander Services Inc.; Reed Stenhouse Companies Ltd.; Empire Co. Ltd.; Mt. Sinai Hosp.; Dir., Candn. Council Christians & Jews; Trustee, The Hugh MacMillan Medical Centre; Fellow, Inst. of Chartered Accountants of Ont.; Past Pres., The Canadian Club; Past Pres., Bd. of Trade Metrop. Candn. Bankers Assn., Toronto; recreations: golf, squash, tennis; Clubs: Granite; Cambridge; Toronto Golf; Toronto; York; Office: Scotia Plaza, 44 King St. W., Toronto, Ont. M5H 1H1.

**GODSON, Warren Lehman,** M.A., Ph.D., F.R.S.C.; atmospheric physicist; b. Victoria, B.C. 4 May 1920; s. Walter Ernest Henry and Mary Edna (Lehman) G.; e. Victoria, B.C. pub., high schs. and coll. 1937; Univ. of B.C. B.A. 1939, M.A. 1941; Univ. of Toronto M.A. 1944, Ph.D. 1948; Univ. of Victoria, D.Sc. (Hon.) 1992; m. 1stly Merl Ellen Hotson (d.) Dec. 1942; m. 2ndly Ruth Margaret Clarke Sept. 1967; m. thirdly Harriet Rosalie Burke Dec. 1977; children: Elliott, Marilyn Henderson, Murray, Ralph, Ellen; step-children: Alan Bloom, Alison Bloom, Stephen Bloom; EMERITUS RESEARCH SCIENTIST, ATMOSPHERIC ENVIRONMENT SERVICE 1991– ; Gen. Research and Lecturing post, Candn. Meteorological Service (became Atmospheric Environment Service) 1943–54, Supt. Atmospheric Research Sec. 1954–71, Dir. Atmospheric Processes Research Br. 1971–73; Dir. Gen., Atmospheric Res. Directorate 1973–84; Sr. Science Advisor 1984–91; Pres. Comn. for Atmospheric Sciences (UN) 1973–77; rec'd IMO Prize 1975, Patterson Medal 1968; Buchan Prize 1964; Ministerial Medal for 50 yrs. of service, AES 1992; co-author 'Atmospheric Thermodynamics' 1974 and 1981; over 100 scient. articles meteorol. research; Fellow, Am. Meteorol. Soc. (former Councillor); mem., Candn. Meteorol. & Oceanographic Soc. (Pres. 1957–59); Internat. Assn. Meteorol. & Atmospheric Physics (Secy. 1960–75, Vice Pres. 1975–79, Pres. 1979–1983,); Anglican; recreation: colour photography; Home: 39 Dove Hawkway, City of North York, Ont. M2R 3M8.

**GODWIN, Ted,** R.C.A.; artist; educator; b. Calgary, Alta. 13 Aug. 1933; s. John Griffin and Hilda (Sirett) G.; e. S. Alta. Inst. of Technol. & Art Calgary 1951–55; m. Phyllis Wanda d. Walter Goota, Prince Albert, Sask. 24 Dec. 1955; children: Teddi Ruth (Driediger), Tammi Lynn; granddaughter: Jessie Lynn; PROF. OF ART, UNIV. OF REGINA; art dir.-TV, Ad Agency work, store display, sign writer, neon sign designer 1955–61, 1963–64; solo exhns. incl. Allied Arts Centre Calgary 1958, 1967; Norman MacKenzie Art Gallery Regina 1965; Univ. of Man. 1966; Ont. Art Circuit 1966; Atlantic Art Circuit 1967; Blue Barn Gallery 1967 Ottawa (2 man show 1962); Dunlop Art Gallery 1968, 1976; York Univ. Toronto 1971; Bau-Xi Gallery Vancouver 1971, 1979, 1980, Victoria 1974, Toronto 1977, 1978, 1979; Edmonton Art Gallery 1971; Perry's Art Centre Regina 1974; Moose Jaw Art Museum, Mendel Art Gallery Saskatoon, Art Gallery of Greater Victoria 1975 (Recent Landscapes); Subway Art Gallery Winnipeg 1976 (Survey 1964–74; Rocks, Flowers, Scissors), 1977; Candn. Art Galleries Calgary 1977 (2 exhns.), 1978, 1980; Lefebvre Gallery Edmonton 1977; Glenbow Art Museum Calgary 1980; rep. in various group shows incl. Young Contemporaries (nat. tour) 1955; 3rd Biennial Candn. Art Nat. Gallery (nat. tour) 1959; 5 Painters from Regina (nat. tour) 1961; 4th Biennial Candn. Art 1961, 6th Biennial 1965; Candn. Pavillion Expo '67; Painting 68 Art Gallery Ont.; Selected Sask. Painters Waddington Art Galleries Montreal 1968; 2 man exhn. Kenny's Art Gallery Galway, Eire 1972; 9 out of 10 (nat. tour) 1974; Survey of Candn. Painting since 1776 Art Gallery Ont. 1975; Hist. Suvey of Watercolour Alta. Glenbow Art Museum, Calgary 1980 and other exhns.; rep. in various pub., corporate and private colls. incl. Nat. Gallery Can., Art Gallery Ont., Can. Council Art Bank; recipient 2nd Prize Internat. Neon Design Competition 1958; Merit Award Winnipeg Biennial 1964; Winnipeg Show Purchase Award 1968; Can. Council Grant (Greece) 1962–63; Queen's Silver Jubilee Medal 1978; featured various bibliogs.; Home: 1012 – 73rd Ave. S.W., Calgary, Alta. T2V 0R8; Office: Regina, Sask. S4S 0A2.

**GOEDE, William,** Ph.D.; writer, lecturer, musician, college professor; b. Eau Claire, Wisc. 29 Aug. 1932; s. William Carl and Myrtle Elvira (McLellan) G.; e. Univ. of Wisconsin, B.A. 1958; Univ. of Edinburgh, M.A. 1959; Univ. of Calif., Ph.D. 1968; m. Marilyn M. Brulhart; PROF., ENGLISH DEPT., CAPILANO COLLEGE

1986– ; Prof., Univ. of Victoria 1966–72; Assoc. Exec. Sec., Candn. Assn. of Univ. Teachers 1972–73, 1977–78; Chrmn., Engl. Dept., Cariboo College 1973–75; Language Expert in People's Republic of China 1982–86; Mem., 'Beijing Underground' China's 'official' rock-and-roll band; toured China 1984–85; Language Expert, Jakarta, Indonesia, W.U.S.C.-C.I.D.A. 1988; B.C. Booksellers Book Prize 1988; author: 'Quantrill' 1982 (novel), 'Love in Beijing & other stories' 1988 (short story collection), 'The Man from Vancouver' 1986 (a radio play in 52 parts: Central China Broadcasting Corp.); recreations: musician: jazz, rock; Home: 8–4149 Sophia St., Vancouver, B.C.; Office: North Vancouver, B.C. V7J 3H5.

**GOETZ, Peter,** artist; b. Slavgorod, Russia 8 Sept. 1917; s. Henry Peter and Justina (Friesen) G.; came to Can., 1929; e. grad Kitchener-Waterloo Collegiate, 1938; studied art with F.H. Varley (1947); Waterloo Coll. (1944); Doon Sch. Fine Art, (1946); m. Helena Warkentin, 9 Aug. 1941; children: Jean Margot, Peter Andrew; paints and travels full time; has exhibited with Royal Candn. Acad., Ont. Soc. of Artists, Candn. Soc. of Painters in Watercolour, Montreal Museum of Fine Arts, National Gallery, Winnipeg Show, Western Art League; exhibited one-man shows annually since 1957; Fellow, International Institute Arts and Letters; International Platform Association; Centro Studie Scambi Internat., Rome; mem. Ont. Soc. Artists; Candn. Soc. Painters in Watercolour; Candn. Soc. of Artists; Address: 784 Avondale Ave., Kitchener, Ont. N2M 2W8.

**GOFFART, Walter André,** A.M., Ph.D.; educator; b. Berlin, Germany (Belgian citizen by birth) 22 Feb. 1934; s. late Francis Léo and late Andrée (Steinberg) G.; e. Phillips Acad. Andover, Mass. 1951; Harvard Univ. A.B. 1955, A.M. 1956, Ph.D. 1961; Ecole normale supérieure, Paris 1957–58 (concurrently Ecole pratique des Hautes études, sciences historiques); m. Roberta d. Norman Frank, St. James, L.I., N.Y. 31 Dec. 1977; children (by first marriage): Vivian (Mrs. Lewis Humphrey), Andrea Judith; PROF. OF MEDIEVAL HIST., UNIV. OF TORONTO 1971– ; Lectr. present Univ. 1960, Asst. Prof. 1963, Assoc. Prof. 1966–71, Acting Dir. Centre for Medieval Studies 1971–72; Visiting Asst. Prof. Univ. of Calif. Berkeley 1965–66; Visiting Fellow, Inst. Advanced Study, Princeton 1967–68; Dumbarton Oaks Center for Byzantine Studies, Washington, D.C. 1973–74; Connaught Sr. Fellow in the Humanities, Univ. of Toronto 1983–84; recipient Can. Council Leave Fellowship 1967–68; Am. Council Learned Socs. Fellowship 1973–74; Guggenheim Fellowship 1979–80; S.S.H.R.C. Leave Fellowship 1985–86; S.S.H.R.C. Research Grant 1990–92; Haskins Medal, Medieval Acad. Amer. 1991; author 'The Le Mans Forgeries' 1966; 'Caput and Colonate' 1974; 'Barbarians and Romans A.D. 418–584' 1980; 'The Narrators of Barbarian History (A.D. 550–800)' 1988; 'Rome's Fall and After' 1989; co-translator 'The Origin of the Idea of Crusade' 1978; numerous articles late Roman & early medieval subjects; mem., Am. Hist. Assn.; Internat. Soc. of Anglo-Saxonists; Haskins Soc.; Fellow, Medieval Acad. Am. (Councillor 1978–80); Fellow, Royal Historical Soc.; Home: 171 Lowther Ave., Toronto, Ont. M5R 1E6; Office: Dept. of History, Univ. of Toronto, Toronto, Ont. M5S 1A1.

**GOGAN, Lt. Col. Dorothy Jean,** R.N., O.M.M., O.St.J., C.D.; commissioner; b. N.S. 19 Apr. 1926; d. James and Mary Evangeline (McManaman) G.; e. Amherst Sr. H.S. 1944; St. Charles Comml. Sch. 1945; R.N., Highland View Hosp. 1947–50; Dalhousie Univ., Nursing Serv. Admin. dip.; Commissioner, Canadian Pension Comn. 1985; Night Supvr., Amherst Hosp. 1950–53; various sr. nursing appts. in Canada and abroad (3 tours of duty in Eur.), Candn. Forces 1953–81 (ret. as Lt. Col.); Chief Nursing Offr. & Mem., Priory Counc., St. John Ambulance Brigade in Canada 1980–85; Past Pres., Altrusa Club of Ottawa; Mem., St. Paul's Anglic Ch.; Registered Nurses Assn. of N.S., of Ont.; Coll. of Nurses of Ont.; Order of St. John of Jerusalem; P.E.I. Branch, Nursing Sisters' Assn. of Can.; Royal Candn. Legion; Candn. Bible Soc.; recreations: painting watercolours, walking, swimming; Club: Charlottetown Fitness; Home: PO Box 1118, Charlottetown, P.E.I. C1A 7M8; Office: c/o Daniel J. MacDonald Bldg., Grafton St., Charlottetown, P.E.I. C1A 7M8.

**GOGAN, James Wilson,** B.Comm.; business executive; b. Springhill, N.S. 19 May 1938; s. James and Jean Elizabeth (Wilson) G.; e. Dalhousie Univ. B.Comm. 1959; articles for C.A. 1959–62; McGill Summer Sch. of Bus. 1961; m. Maureen d. John and Muriel Richard 26 Oct. 1963; children: James Richard, Mary Monique, John Paul, Susanne Maureen; PRESIDENT, EMPIRE COMPANY LTD. 1985– ; Chief Fin. Offr., Empire Group 1962–74; Extve. Vice-Pres. 1975–85; Chrmn., Halifax Developments Ltd.; Dir., Atlantic Shopping Centres Ltd.; Crombie Insurance (U.K.) Ltd.; Sobey Leased Properties Ltd.; Sobey Inc.; Lawton's Drug Stores Ltd.; Barclays Bank of Can.; Hannaford Bros. Co. (U.S.A.); Wajax Ltd.; Offr. & Dir. of over 25 other cos.; recipient, Order of Malta 1992; mem., Lloyds of London; Internat. Inst. of Dirs.; Bd. of Govs., Saint Francis Xavier Univ.; Aberdeen Hosp. Found.; R. Catholic; Past Extve. Dir., United Way of Pictou Co.; Charter Mem., Pictou Co. YM-YWCA; Past Pres., Gyro Club of New Glasgow; Club: Abercrombie Golf & Country; recreations: golf, fishing, travel, gardening, investing; Home: 183 High St., New Glasgow, N.S.; Office: 115 King St., Stellarton, N.S. B0K 1S0.

**GOHEEN, Duncan S.,** B.A., M.S., Ph.D.; financial and development executive; e. Graceland Coll. Iowa B.A. 1966; Univ. of Mo. M.S. 1968; Ryokan Coll., California Ph.D. 1988; PRESIDENT AND CHIEF EXTVE. OFFR., SUN FINANCIAL CORP. LTD.; Coordinator, Global Inst.; recreations: sailing, skiing, travel, singing; Address: 430 St. Patrick St., Victoria, B.C. V8S 4X3.

**GOLBERG, Thomas H.,** B.Sc., F.S.A., F.C.I.A.; insurance executive; b. Montreal, Que. 20 Aug. 1943; s. William E. and Sarah (Rosenbloom) G.; e. McGill Univ. B.Sc. 1964; m. Nancy d. Jack and Sade Hausner 21 Aug. 1966; children: Daniel, Deborah; SENIOR VICE-PRESIDENT, CUSTOMER SERVICES, STANDARD LIFE ASSURANCE CO. 1988– ; joined Standard Life Montreal 1964; Vice-Pres., Admin. 1978; Vice-Pres., Group 1980; Member, Executive Ctte. 1990; Fellow, Candn. Inst.of Actuaries; Soc. of Actuaries; Dir., Que. Heart Found.; Immediate Past Chair, CLHIA Sub-Ctte. on Retirement Income Programs; recreations: harness racing, golf, cycling, gardening; clubs: Curling, Fitness; Home: 157 Bexhill Dr., Beaconsfield, Que. H9W 3A6; Office: 300, 1245 Sherbrooke St. W., Montreal, Que. H3G 1G3.

**GOLD, Hon. Alan B.,** O.Q., Q.C., B.A., LL.L., LL.D.; barrister and solicitor; b. Montreal, Que. 21 July 1917; s. Samuel and Leah (Stein) G.; e. pub. and h.s., Montreal; Queen's Univ. B.A. 1938; Univ. of Montreal LL.L. cum laude 1941; called to Bar of Que. 1941; m. Lynn d. Terri and Meyer Lubin 14 Aug. 1949; children: Marc, Nora, Daniel; SR. COUNSEL, PHILLIPS & VINEBERG 1992– ; read law with Marcus Sperber, Q.C.; Lectr. Fac. of Law McGill Univ. 1957–71; Dist. Judge and Vice-Chrmn. Que. Labour Relations Bd. 1961–65; Assoc. Chief Judge, Prov. Ct. of Que. 1965–70, Chief Judge 1970–83; Chrmn., Conseil du Referendum 1980; Pres. Jr. Bar Assn. of Montreal 1951–52; mem. Counc. of the Bar of Montreal 1952–53; Bd. of Examiners, Bar of Que. 1952–61; Ctte. for revision of by-laws, Bar of Que.; Founding Dir. and Offr. Legal Aid Bureau of Montreal 1956–60; Pres. Judicial Counc. Prov. of Que. 1978–83; Chief Arbitrator under the collective labour agreements between Govt. of the Prov. of Que. and its employees 1966–83; Chief Justice, Superior Ct., P.Q. 1983–92; Gov. McGill Univ. 1974–83, Chrmn. Bd. of Govs. 1978–82, Gov. Emeritus 1984– ; Chancellor, Concordia Univ. 1987–92; Chancellor Emeritus, Concordia Univ. 1992– ; Dir. and mem. Exec. Counc. Place des Arts 1973–82, Vice-Chrmn. 1982– ; mem. Conf. des Juges du Que.; Assn. Candn. des Juges des Cours Provinciales; Candn. Judicial Council; Candn. Judges Conference; Candn. Bar Assn.; Soc. of Professionals in Dispute Resolution U.S.A. (recipient Special Award for Excellence 1981); Hon. Life Mem., Nat. Acad. of Arbitrators U.S.A.; Hon. mem. Corp. Professionelle des Conseillers en Relations Industrielles de la Prov. de Que.; mem. Phi Delta Phi (internat. legal frat.); Scholar in Residence, McGill Univ. Fac. of Law 1982; LL.D. (h.c.) Univ. of Montreal 1978, Queen's Univ. 1982, McGill Univ. 1984, Yeshiva Univ. 1987; Officer, Ordre national du Québec 1985; Pres., Conseil de l'Ordre national du Québec 1985–87 and 1989–91; Recipient, Human Relations Award, Candn. Counc. of Christians and Jews 1985; Distinguished Bora Laskin Award, Yeshiva Univ. 1987; Médaille du Premier ministre du Québec 1987; Bar of Québec Medal 1990–91; National Assembly of Quebec Medal 1992; Université de Montréal Medal 1992; Samuel Bronfman Medal, Candn. Jewish Congress 1992; Commemorative Medal, 125th Anniversary of Candn. Confedn. 1992; Distinguished Friend of Education Award, CASE District 1, 1993; Clubs: Univ. of Montreal; Canadien; McGill Univ. Fac.; Home: 3071 Cedar Ave., Montreal, Que. H3Y 1Y8; Office: 5 Place Ville Marie, 17th Flr., Montreal, Que. H3B 2G2.

**GOLD, Charles C.,** M.D., F.R.C.S.(C), F.S.O.G.C., F.A.C.O.G.; physician, obstetrician and gynecologist; executive; b. Toronto, Ont. 26 May 1940; s. Harry and Sally (Zeiden) G.; e. Univ. of Toronto M.D. 1964; m. Marilyn d. Saul and Rae Saltzman 19 June 1962; children: James, Barbara Taerk, Paul; Pres., Whitland Construction Co. Ltd. - The Glen Group; Dir., Candn. Inst. for Advanced Rsch. 1991– ; Dir., Candn. Psychiatric Rsch. Found. 1991– ; Dir., The Baycrest Center Found. 1992– ; Bd. of Govs., Baycrest Ctr. for Geriatric Care 1992– ; Dir., Mature Woman's Clinic, Toronto General Hospital 1981–89, staff Obstetrician-Gynecol. 1970–89; Asst. Prof. of Obstetrics & Gynecol. Univ. of Toronto 1977–89; Dir. Genesis Rsch. Found. 1985–87; Dir., United Israel Appeal, Can. 1978–92; Vice Pres., Candn. Friends of the Hebrew Univ. of Jerusalem 1989– ; Assoc. Gov., Internat. Bd., Hebrew Univ. of Jerusalem; Founding mem., The Candn. Menopause Found.; Past Pres., Toronto Chapt. Candn. Friends of the Hebrew Univ. of Jerusalem; Office: 100 Scarsdale Rd., Don Mills, Ont. M3B 2R8.

**GOLD, Edgar,** B.A., LL.B., Ph.D., MCIT, ACIArb., FNI, FOI, MRIN; university professor; lawyer; master mariner; b. Hamburg, Germany 5 Mar. 1934; s. Josef and Anne Marie (Kuenn) G.; e. Melbourne H.S. 1951; Austr. Citizen 1952; Merchant Marine Cadetship 1952–55; Sydney Tech. Univ., 2nd Mate Cert. 1957; Univ. of Southampton, 1st Mate 1961, Master (FG) 1964; Dalhousie Univ. B.A. 1970, LL.B. 1972; Univ. of Wales Ph.D. 1980; m. Judith d. James and Anne Hammerling 27 June 1965; Candn. citizen 1972; ASSOC. & MEM. BD. OF DIRS., OCEANS INST. OF CAN.; Cadet to Master, Merchant Marine 1952–68; called to N.S. Bar 1973; Assoc. Prof., Faculty of Law, Dalhousie Univ. 1975–79; Prof., Maritime Law, Dalhousie Univ. 1979– ; Prof., Resource & Environmental Studies, Dalhousie Univ. 1985– ; Dir., Ocean Studies Programme, Dalhousie Univ. 1979–87; Exec. Dir., Oceans Inst. of Can. 1988–90; Associate, Huestis Holm, Barristers & Solicitors 1980– ; Hon. Consul, Fed. Republic of Germany for N.S. and P.E.I. 1986– ; Visiting Prof., Maritime Law, World Maritime Univ., Malmo, Sweden 1983– ; Consultant, UNCTAD; IMO; World Wildlife Fund; Club of Rome; Internat. Ocean Inst.; IDRC Rsch. Assoc. Award 1973–75; Albert Lilar Prize in Maritime Law 1984; Hon. degree, Can. Coast Guard Coll. 1992; Fellow, Nautical Inst. 1978; Fellow, Offshore Inst. 1990; Fellow, World Acad. of Arts & Science 1990; Titulary Mem., Comité Maritime International 1987; Assoc. Mem., Chartered Inst. of Arbitrators; Mem., Chartered Inst. of Transp.; Royal Inst. of Navigation; Co. of Master Mariners of Can.; Hon. Co. of Master Mariners of London, Eng.; Candn. Bar Assn. (Nat. Counc. 1979–82); Candn. Maritime Law Assn. (Pres. 1992– ;); Internat. Law Assn.; Internat. Bar Assn.; Candn. Counc. on Internat. Law (Extve. Bd. 1979–82); author: 'Maritime Transport' 1981; 'Handbook on Marine Pollution' 1985; editor: 'Oil Pollution' 1971; 'Canadian Admiralty Law' 1975; plus numerous monographs, reports, articles, etc.; recreations: sailing, swimming, maritime history; Club: Saraguay; Home: 1465 Brenton St., #605, Halifax, N.S. B3J 2K6; Offices: 1236 Henry St., 5th Flr., Halifax, N.S. B3H 3J5 and 708/1609 Barrington St., Halifax, N.S. B3J 3K8.

**GOLD, Joseph,** B.A., Ph.D., university professor; b. London, Eng. 30 June 1933; e. Univ. of Birmingham, Eng. B.A. 1955; Univ. of Wisconsin, Ph.D. 1959; PROF. OF ENGLISH, UNIV. OF WATERLOO; Univ. of Wisconsin, Dept. of Eng., 1955–59; Whitewater State Coll, Wis., Dept. of Eng., 1959–60; Univ. of Man., Dept. of Eng., 1960–70; El. to Senate, Univ. of Man., 1968–71; El. Pres., Assn. of Chrmn. of Eng. of Ont. 1971–72; Re-el. 1972–73; Chrmn. & Prof. Eng., Univ. of Waterloo, 1970–73; Chrmn. ACUTE Cmte. on Professional concerns, 1974–76; author of 'William Faulkner: A Study in Humanism from Metaphor to Discourse' 1966; ed., 'King of Beasts and Other Stories' 1967; author 'The Stature of Dickens: A Centenary Bibliography' 1971; 'Charles Dickens: Radical Moralist' 1972; ed., 'In the Name of Language' 1975; 'Read For Your Life' 1990; Trustee, Dickens Soc. of Amer. 1971–73; apptd. to Man. Censor Appeal Bd. 1969; Bd. of Gov. Man. Theatre Centre 1969; Pres., Temple Shalom Reform Congreg. 1978; Extve. Mem. Candn. Assn. for Amer. Studies 1964–73; el. Pres., Assoc. for Bibliotherapy in Canada 1992–93; mem., ACUTE, ACTRA, IAUPE; Clin. mem., A.A.M.F.T.; Marriage and Family Therapist; Dir., Southern Ontario Counselling Centre; Jewish; recreations: Nordic skiing, cooking, canoeing; Home: RR #2, Baden, Ont. N0B 1G0; Office: Univ. of Waterloo, Waterloo, Ont. N2L 3G1.

**GOLD, Lorne W.,** B.Sc., M.Sc., Ph.D., F.R.S.C., F.E.I.C.; physicist; b. Saskatoon, Sask. 7 June 1928; s. Alexander Stewart and Grace Dora (Davis) G.; e. Univ. of Sask., B.Sc. (Eng. Physics) 1950; McGill Univ., M.Sc.(Physics) 1952, Ph.D. 1970; m. Joan, d. Cecil and Elsie L'Ami, 8 Sept. 1951; children: Catherine Anne, Patricia Ellen, Judith Sharon, Kenneth Robert; Nat. Rsch. Counc.: Rsch. Officer, Div. Building Rsch.

(D.B.R.) 1950–52; Head, Snow and Ice Sect., D.B.R. 1953–69; Head, Geotech. Sect., D.B.R. 1969–74; Asst. Dir., D.B.R. 1974–79; Assoc. Dir., D.B.R. 1979–86; Guest worker, Inst. for Rsch. in Construction, NRC 1987; Sr. Visiting Scientist, Center for Cold Oceans Resources Engineering (C-CORE), Memorial Univ. of Nfld. 1987–88; Researcher Emeritus, Nat. Rsch. Counc. of Can. 1988– ; Chrmn., Assoc. Ctte. on Geotechnical Rsch., Nat. Rsch. Counc. 1976–83; Candn. Del. to RILEM 1982–87; Mem. Bd., Conseil Internat. du Batiment 1983–86; Mem.: Royal Soc. of Can.; Internat. Glaciological Soc. (Pres. 1978–81); Assn. of Prof. Engineers of Ont.; Engrg. Inst. of Can. (Hon. Treas. 1991– ;); Candn. Geotech. Soc.; Candn. Soc. of Civil Eng.; Arctic Inst. of N. Amer.; Fellow, Engineering Inst. of Canada 1985; Fellow, Candn. Soc. of Civil Engr. 1989; United Ch. of Can.; Home: 1903 Illinois Ave., Ottawa, Ont. K1H 6W5; Office: National Research Council, Ottawa, Ont. K1A 0R6.

**GOLD, Phil,** C.C., O.Q., M.D., C.M., Ph.D., M.Sc., F.R.C.P.(C), F.R.S.C., F.A.C.P.; medical scientist; educator; b. Montreal, Que. 17 Sept. 1936; s. Jack Gold; e. McGill Univ. B.Sc. 1957, M.Sc. 1961, M.D., C.M. 1961, Ph.D. (Physiol.) 1965; m. Evelyn Katz 21 Aug. 1960; children: Ian Jeffrey, Joselyn Sue, Joel Todd; DOUGLAS G. CAMERON PROF., DEPT. OF MED., McGILL UNIV. 1987– , Prof. of Oncology there 1989– , Prof. of Physiol. there 1974– ; and Chrmn. 1985–90; Physician-in-Chief Montreal Gen. Hosp. 1980– ; Dir. McGill Univ. Med. Clinic, Mont. Gen. Hosp. 1980– ; Sr. Investigator Montreal Gen. Hosp. Research Inst. 1972– ; Consultant in Medicine, Royal Victoria Hosp., Montreal, Que.; internship and residency Montreal Gen. Hosp. 1961–62, 1965–66; Career Investigator, Med. Research Council Can. 1968–80 (Fellow 1963–65, Chrmn. Grants Panel for Cancer Research 1972–77, 1981–83; Mem. of Counc. 1986–92; Mem. Exec. Ctte. 1986–92); Mem. Comm. on Ethics and Med. Rsch. 1989; Chrmn., Ctte. on Membership of Cttes. 1991– ; Panel Am. Cancer Soc. 1968–73; Pres. Med. Adv. Bd. Cancer Research Soc. Inc. Montreal 1975–77; Dir. McGill Cancer Centre 1977–80; Founding mem. and mem. Constitution Comte. Internat. Research Group for Carcinoembryonic Proteins since 1976; Pres. Scient. Adv. Bd. Israel Cancer Research Fund 1980–85; mem. Cancer Grants Panel B, Nat. Cancer Inst. Can.; Mem., Adv. Ctte., on Rsch. 1984–87; Bd. of Dirs., Mount Sinai Inst. Toronto; mem., Med. Adv. Bd., Gairdner Foundation, 1979–91, Pres. Med. Chi Soc. (Montreal) 1986–88; Pres. Ninth Ann. Meeting of International Soc. for Oncodevelopment Biology and Medicine, Alta. 1981; Chrmn. Medical Research Council Grants Cmtee. for Cancer 1981–82; Inaugural Terry Fox Lectr. 1981; Visiting Scient. Pub. Health Research Inst. N.Y. City 1967–68; rec'd numerous univ. scholarships and awards; Royal Coll. Phys. & Surgs. Can. Medal in Med. 1965; E.W.R. Steacie Prize for Science, NRC 1973; Outstanding Scientist Award (Inaugural) Internat. Research Group Carcinoembryonic Proteins 1976; Queen's Silver Jubilee Medal 1977; Award Internat. Conf. on Clin. Uses Carcinoembryonic Antigen 1977; Johann-Georg-Zimmermann Prize for Cancer Research, Medizinische Hochschule, Hannover 1978; Gairdner Foundation Annual Award 1978; Officer, Order of Canada 1978; Gold Medal Award of Merit, Grad. Soc. McGill Univ. 1979; Heath Mem. Award, M.D. Anderson Hosp. & Texas Inst. of the Univ. of Texas Cancer Centre, 1980; 1981 Chair in Science, Weizmann Inst. of Sc., Israel; first recipient Terry Fox Medal, B.C. Medical Assn.; Ernest C. Manning Found. Award (Inaugural) 1982; Candn. Assn. of Mfrs. of Medical Devices Award 1983; F.N.G. Starr Award, Candn. Med. Assn. 1983; Isaak Walton Killam Prize, Canada Council 1985; Tower of Hope Award, Israel Cancer Research Fund 1985; Squires Visiting Prof., Univ. of Toronto 1983; Companion, Order of Canada 1985 (Investiture 1986); Academy of Great Montrealers, Montreal, Que. 1986–87; Douglas G. Cameron Prof. of Med. (inaugural) McGill Univ. 1987– ; Hon. Dr. of Science, McMaster Univ.; L'Ordre Nationale du Québec 1989; Scientific Achievement Medal, Govt. of Italy 1991; Candn. Soc. for Clinical Investigation 1992; Distinguished Service Award 1992; ISOBM Internat. Abbott Award 1992; R.M. Taylor Award, Nat. Cancer Inst. of Can. 1992; Mem., Sigma XI; mem. various med. journ. ed. bds., Assoc. Ed. 'Cancer Research' 1973; co-ed. and co-author 'Clinical Immunology' 2nd ed. 1975; over 110 papers scient. journs.; mem. Am. Acad. Allergy; Am. Assn. Advanc. Science; Am. Assn. Cancer Research; Am. Assn. Immunols.; Assn. of Am. Physicians; Am. Fed. Clin. Research; Am. and Candn. Soc. Clin. Investigation; Candn. Fed. Biol. Sciences; Candn. Med. Assn.; Candn. Oncology Soc. (Founding mem.); Candn. Soc. Allergy & Clin. Immunol.; Candn. Soc. Immunol. (Pres. 1975–77) and other med. and scient. socs.; Alpha Omega Alpha; recreations: photography, music, lapidary, sailing, cross-country skiing; Club: Explorers; University (Montreal); Office: Room D6-237, Montreal Gen. Hosp., 1650 Cedar Ave., Montreal, Que. H3G 1A4.

**GOLD, Sylvia,** B.A., M.A.; executive civil servant; b. Montreal, Que.; e. McGill Univ., B.A. 1967, M.A. 1981; Ont. Inst. for Studies in Edn. 1984–85; m. Jack Gold; DIR., MNGMT. TRAINEE PROGRAM and FACULTY MEM., CANADIAN CENTRE FOR MANAGEMENT DEVELOPMENT 1993– ; Extve. Asst., Montreal Teachers' Assn. 1971–75; Dir., Profl. Devel. Serv., Candn. Teachers' Fed. 1975–85; Pres., Candn. Adv. Counc. on the Status of Women 1985–89; Dir. of Rsch. and Evaluation, Royal Comm. on New Reproductive Technologies 1990–92; Fac. Mem., Candn. Ctr. for Mgmt. Devel. 1989–90, 1992–93; Office: 646 rue Principale, Touraine, Qué. K1N 8V4.

**GOLDBERG, Benjamin,** B.Sc., M.D.,C.M., FRCP(C); educator; b. Saint John, N.B. 24 July 1929; s. Abraham Haskell and Esther G.; e. Saint John Grammar Schs.; Univ. of N.B., B.Sc. 1949; Univ. Coll. London (Fellow in Genetics) 1950; Dalhousie Univ. M.D.,C.M. 1955; Menninger Sch. of Psychiatry 1960; m. Judith Insky 9 Oct. 1977; children: Cathy Ellen Solomon, Joel, Mark, Brian, Adele; DIR. DEVELOPMENTAL DISABILITIES PROG. AND PROF. OF DEVELOPMENTAL NEUROPSYCHIATRY, UNIV. OF W. ONT. 1988– , Cons. to affiliated Gen. Hosp. Psychiatric Units 1960– ; Intern Saint John Gen. Hosp. 1954–55; Resident in Psychiatry Menninger Sch. of Psychiatry 1955–60; Supt., Dir. of Edn., Med. Dir. Children's Psychiatric Rsch. Inst. London, Ont. 1960–88; UN Tech. Adv. Mental Retardation Govt. Guatemala 1965; W.H.O. Visiting Fellow, Australia 1992; Acting Adm. Huronia Regional Centre 1976; Visiting Prof. Dalhousie Univ.; McMaster Univ.; Queen's Univ.; Univ. of Toronto; Lectr. Fanshawe Colle.; Gold Medalist Sr. Matric. 1945; Beaverbrook Scholar; Overseas Scholar; Distinguished Contbr. Award Ont. Assn. Children's Mental Health Centres 1981; Citation, Candn. Assn. of Occupational Therapists, 1988; co-author: 'One Million Children' 1970; ed. 'Intrusive Procedures' 1987; columnist: 'On Being a Teenager' London Free Press 1984–87; author or co-author over 32 articles profl. jours.; Fellow, Am. Orthopsychiatric Assn.; Am. Assn. Mental Retardation (Chrmn. Great Lakes Region); mem. Candn. Psychiatric Assn. (Council 1966–68); Ont. Psychiatric Assn. (Council 1982–87); Ont. Mental Health Found. (Adv. Ctte. 1980–85); Chrmn. Coordinating Ctte. Children & Youth London 1980–82; Cubmaster 1962–66; Pres. Or Shalom Synagogue 1973–75, Choir Leader 1965– ; recreations: vocalist, tennis, bridge; Home: 33–30 Doon Dr., London, Ont. N5X 3P1; Office: London, Ont. N6A 5C1.

**GOLDBERG, David Myer,** M.B., Ch.B., Ph.D., M.D.; educator; b. Glasgow, Scot. 30 Aug. 1933; e. Univ. of Glasgow B.Sc. 1958, M.B., Ch.B. 1959, Ph.D. 1965, M.R.C. Path. 1970, F.R.I.Ç. 1972, M.D. 1974, F.R.C. Path. 1979; F.R.C.P.(C) 1987; m. 9 March 1964; children: Susan, Tanya; came to Can. 1975; PROF. AND FORMER CHRMN., DEPT. OF CLINICAL BIOCHEMISTRY, UNIV. OF TORONTO; Head of Biochem., Hosp. for Sick Children 1975–89; mem. World Health Organ. Expert Panel on Biochem. Indicators of Radiation Damage, Paris; 1970, and Expert Panel on Enzymes in Clinical Diagnosis, Tutzing, Bavaria 1973 and Munich 1974; Organ. Comte. 6th (1974), 7th (1976), 8th (1978), 9th (1980), 10th (1982), 11th (1984), 12th (1986), 13th (1988), 14th (1990) and 15th (1992) Internat. Cong. on Clin. Enzymol.; Foundation Comte. Internat. Soc. Clin. Enzymol. 1974–76, Extve. 1976–84, Vice Pres. 1978–83; mem. Candn. Soc. Clin. Chems.; Candn. Assn. Med. Biochem.; Candn. Soc. Clin. Invest.; Candn. Atherosclerosis Soc.; author over 190 scient. Papers and reviews, 100 abstracts diagnostic enzymol., gastroenterol. and biochem. of cancer; Editor of 'Clinical Biochemistry Reviews' and 'Progress in Clinical Enzymology'; Joint Editor-in-Chief of 'Clinical Biochemistry' and 'Critical Reviews in Clinical Laboratory Sciences'; recipient, Van Slyke Award, Amer. Assn. for Clinical Chem. 1982; Roman Award, Australian Assn. of Clinical Biochemists 1984; Nova Idea Internat. Prize in Laboratory Medicine 1985; Ames Award, Candn. Soc. of Clinical Chem. 1991; recreations: wine, music, theatre; Home: 9 Harrison Rd., Willowdale, Ont. M2L 1V3; Office: Banting Inst., 100 College St., Univ. of Toronto, Toronto, Ont. M5G 1L5.

**GOLDBERG, Michael Arthur,** M.A., Ph.D.; educator; b. Brooklyn, N.Y. 30 Aug. 1941; s. Harold Irving and Ruth (Abelson) G.; e. Brooklyn Coll. B.A. 1962; Univ. of Cal. Berkeley, M.A. 1965, Ph.D. 1968; m. Rhoda d. Louis and Hilda Zacker 22 Dec. 1963 (div. 1987); m. Deborah Nelson 7 Sept. 1991; two d. (from previous marriage) Betsy Anne, Jennifer Heli; THE HERBERT R. FULLERTON PROF. OF URBAN LAND POLICY, UNIV. OF B.C. 1981– , Prof. of Urban Land Econ. 1976– ; Asst. Prof. present Univ. 1968, Assoc. Prof. 1971, Chrmn. Urban Land Econ. Div. 1975–79, Acting Assoc. Dean of Comm. 1978–79, Assoc. Dean 1980–84, Dir. of Devel. Faculty Comm. and mem. Senate 1985–88, Dean 1991– ; Extve. Dir., IFC Vancouver 1988–91; Dir.: Brink Hudson & Lefever Ltd.; Imperial Parking Ltd.; Chair, Candn. Fedn. of Deans of Mgmt. and Admin. Scis. 1992–94 (Vice-Chair 1991–92); cons. to Govt. Can., Prov. B.C., federal & state agencies USA; Fellow, Urban Land Inst.; Fellow, Homer Hoyt Inst.; author 'The Housing Problem: A Prices Crisis?' 1983; 'The Chinese Connection: Getting Plugged into Pacific Rim Trade and Capital Markets' 1985; 'On Balance' 1988; co-author 'Zoning in the '80s' 1980; 'The Future of North American Housing Markets' 1983; 'Urban Land Economics: An Introductory Textbook' 1984; 'The Myth of the North American City: Continentalism Challenged' 1986; 'The Rites and Wrongs of Land Policy: A Canadian/American Comparative Analysis' 1987; Comnr., B.C. Housing Mgmt. Comn. 1989–92; Gov., B.C. Real Estate Found. 1985–92 (Chrmn. 1985–91); Dir. Vancouver Chapter, Hong Kong Can. Bus. Assn. (Dir. 1986–93); Gov., Vancouver Maritime Museum 1992– ; Gov., Inst. for the Study of Internat. Cities 1989– ; mem. Am. Real Estate & Urban Econ. Assn. (Dir. & Past Pres.); Candn. Econ. Assn.; Am. Econ. Assn.; Candn. Regional Sci. Assn.; Regional Sci. Assn.; W. Regional Sci. Assn.; Candn. Assn. Housing & Renewal Officials; Am. Planning Assn.; Vancouver Bd. Trade; recreations: swimming, tennis, windsurfing, travel; Home: #119 - 6505 3rd Avenue, Delta, B.C. V4L 2N1; Office: Fac. of Comm. and Bus. Admin., Univ. of B.C., 2053 Main Mall, Vancouver, B.C. V6T 1Z2.

**GOLDBLATT, Rose,** ARCM; university professor; b. Montreal 1913; e. Royal College of Music (U.K.) with Kendall Taylor, ARCM (Montreal Strathcona Scholarship), McGill Univ. 1930; postgrad. extension, 2 yrs.; studied further with Egon Petri, distinguished Busoni disciple; m. Henry Finkel 1937; Professor, McGill Univ., retired; began career as concert pianist at age six & continued for over 50 years; among 1st musical artists on CBC TV; has concertized in Canada, the U.S., England & Ireland; Past Pres., Que. Music Teachers' Assn.; also headed Que. Prov. Counc., Candn. Fed. of Music Teachers' Assns. (currently Prov. Vice Pres. for Que.); Past Pres., Candn. Competitive Festival of Music in Que.; Music Consultant, Arts Westmount Fest.; Artistic Dir., Montreal Classical Music Fest.; Candn. Correspondent for Journal of the European Piano Teachers' Assn. & has delivered a number of papers in England at its annual confs. concerning music in Can.; Fellow, Royal Soc. of Arts of Great Britain; Home: 342 Elm Ave., Westmount, Que. H3Z 1Z5.

**GOLDBLOOM, Richard B.,** O.C., B.Sc., M.D., C.M., F.R.C.P.C.; physician; university professor; b. Montreal, Que. 16 Dec. 1924; s. Alton, M.D. and Annie E. (Ballon) G.; e. Selwyn House Sch. and Lower Can. Coll., Montreal; McGill Univ., B.Sc. 1945, M.D., C.M. 1949; postgrad. med. educ. Royal Victoria Hosp., Montreal, Montreal Children's Hosp. and Children's Med. Center, Boston; m. Ruth Miriam, d. Abraham Schwartz, New Waterford, N.S., 25 June 1946; children: Dr. Alan, Barbara, Dr. David; PROFESSOR OF PAEDIATRICS, DALHOUSIE UNIVERSITY; Dir. of Ambulatory Services, Izaak Walton Killam Hospital for Children, Halifax; Teaching Fellow, Dept. of Pediatrics, Harvard Med. Sch. 1951–52; Hosmer Teaching Fellow in Paediatrics, McGill Univ. 1953–56; Assoc. Prof. McGill and Phys., Montreal Children's Hosp. 1964–67; Head of Pediatrics, present Univ., and Physician-in-Chief & Director of Research, The Izaak Walton Killam Hospital for Children, Halifax 1967–85; rec'd Lederle Med. Faculty Award 1962; el. mem., Med. Research Council 1970–72; Pres., Atlantic Symphony Orchestra 1976–79; Vice Pres., Assn. of Candn. Orchestras 1978–79; Dir., Atlantic Trust Co. 1977–79; Atlantic Research Centre for Mental Retardation; Trustee, Queen Elizabeth II Fund for Research in Diseases of Children; mem., Candn. Pediatric Soc. (Past Pres.); Soc. Pediatric Research; Am. Pediatric Soc.; Am. Acad. Pediatrics; Assn. Med. Sch. Pediatric Dept. Chrmn. 1967–85; Comte. on Areas of National Concern, Medical Research Council; Founding Trustee & Extve., Nat. Inst. of Nutrition; Past Chrmn., Extendicare Award Committee; Candn. Assn. of Health Service Execs.; Mem. Ed. Bd., 'Pediatrics'; Ed., International Abstracts in Pediatrics; Killam Awards Comte. Canada Council 1977–80; Chrmn., Waterfront Devel. Corp., Halifax 1976–80; Chrmn., Rhodes Scholar Selection Comte. 1983–85; Chrmn., Rhodes Scholar Selection Comte. (Maritimes) 1989– ; mem. Silver Medal Selection Comte., Royal Soc. for the Arts; mem. Selection Ctte., Prix d'Excellence en Recherche pédiatrique 1986– ; mem. Selection Ctte., Candn. Medical Hall of Fame 1993– ; Chrmn., Evaluation Ctte., Science-Culture Canada 1990–93; Vice Pres., Symphony Nova Scotia 1986–87; Editorial Bd.: 'Encyclopedia of Music in Canada' 1989–91; 'Pediatrics in Review' 1990– ; Co-editor: (with Robert S. Lawrence) 'Preventing Disease: Beyond the Rhetoric' 1990; Editor: 'Pediatric Clinical Skills' 1992; Contbr. ed., 'Pediatric Notes' 1980– ; Officer, Order of Canada 1987; Alpha Omega Alpha; Liberal; Jewish; recreations: music, sailing; Clubs: Bluenose Golf; Lunenburg Yacht; Royal Nova Scotia Yacht Squadron; Saraguay; Home: 324 Purcell's Cove Rd., Boulderwood, Halifax, N.S. B3P 1C7.

**GOLDBLOOM, Ruth Miriam,** C.M.; volunteer worker; b. New Waterford, N.S. 5 Dec. 1924; d. Abraham Lloyd and Rose (Claener) Schwartz; e. Mt. Allison Sch. for Girls (Sackville) 1940; McGill Univ., Diploma in Phys. Ed. 1944; m. Richard B., s. Alton and Annie Goldbloom, 25 June 1946; children: Alan Lloyd; Barbara Jill; David Samuel; Dir.: Simpsons Ltd. 1982–85; Nova Scotia Savings & Loan Co. 1984–87; St. George's Sch., Montreal 1948–67; Women's Auxiliary Montreal Children's Hosp.; Montreal Symphony Orchestra; Founding Chrmn. & Buyer, The Gift Shop, Izaak Walton Killam Hosp. for Children, Halifax 1967–74; Mt. St. Vincent Univ., Chrmn. Bd. Govs. 1974–77, Mem. Bd. Govs. 1977–80, Dir., Voluntary Planning Assn. 1978; Bd. Mem., Halifax Sch. Commission; Bd. Mem., Vocational Sch. Bd., Halifax; Life Mem., Halifax Hadassah Wizo; Regent, Mount Allison Univ. 1971–77, 1987– ; Dir., Industrial Estates Ltd. 1977–79; Chrmn., Project One, Futures for Women (1st Major Fund Drive for Mt. St. Vincent Univ.) 1979; Chairperson, Metro United Way 1989; Adv. Bd., IMAGINE, Toronto 1989; Nat. Adv. Bd., L.E.A.F. 1990; Mem., Postal Service Customer Counc., Atlantic Div., Canada Post; Chrmn., Women's Recognition Dinner, Y.W.C.A. 1982; Humanitarian Award, Candn. Counc. of Christians & Jews 1978; D.Hum.Litt. (hon. causa) Mt. St. Vincent Univ. 1985; LL.D. (hon. causa) Dalhousie Univ. 1987; Member, Order of Canada 1992; apptd. mem. Canadiana Fund 1993; mem. Shaar Shalom Synagogue, Halifax; Home: 324 Purcell's Cove Rd., Halifax, N.S. B3P 1C7.

**GOLDBLOOM, Victor Charles,** O.C., O.Q., LL.D., Litt.D., M.D.; former legislator, pediatrician; b. Montreal, Que., 31 July 1923; s. Dr. Alton and Annie (Ballon) G.; e. Selwyn House and Lower Can. Coll., Montreal; McGill Univ., M.D. 1945; m. Sheila, d. late Jacob Saul Barshay, New York, 15 June 1948; children: Susan, Michael, Jonathan; COMMISSIONER OF OFFICIAL LANGUAGES 1991– ; Exec. Dir., Fonds de la Recherche en Santé du Qué. 1990–91; former Pres., Candn. Counc. of Christians and Jews; Pres., Internat. Council of Christians and Jews, 1982–90; Bd. mem.: Jules and Paul-Emile Léger Found.; Jean Lesage Found.; Hon. Patron, Quebec Bar Found.; former Min. of Environment and of Municipal Affairs, Quebec; Candn. Delegate to U.N. Environment Conf. Stockholm, 1972, and U.N. Habitat Conf. Vancouver, 1976; Hon. LL.D., Univ. of Toronto, 1980; Hon. Litt.D., McGill Univ. 1992; Hon. LL.D., Concordia Univ. 1993; Officer of Order of Canada, 1983; Officer of Order of Quebec 1991; served with RCAMC 1944–46; Hebrew; recreations: opera, lieder singing; Home: 5 Grove Park, Montreal, Que. H3Y 3E6; Office: 110 O'Connor St., Ottawa, Ont. K1A 0T8.

**GOLDEN, Anne,** B.A., M.A., Ph.D.; fundraising executive; b. Toronto, Ont. 21 May 1941; d. Theodore D. and Florence (Golden) Richmond); e. Univ. of Toronto B.A. 1962; Columbia Univ. M.A. 1964; Univ. of Toronto Ph.D. 1970; m. Ronald s. Harry and Gertrude Golden 27 June 1960; children: Beth, Karen; PRES., UNITED WAY OF GREATER TORONTO 1987– ; Teacher, Am. Pol. Hist., Newark Coll. of English, Univ. of Toronto, York Univ., Scarborough College, Erindale College 1964–74; Rsch. Co-ord., Bureau of Municipal Rsch., Govt. of Ont. 1973–78; Special Advisor to Leader of Opposition 1978–81; Dir., Liberal Policy Rsch. Office 1981–82; Dir. of Allocations, United Way of Greater Toronto 1982–86; Campaign Dir. 1986–87; Dir., Sceptre Investment Counsel Limited; Mem., Governing Council, Univ. of Toronto; Candn. Council of Christians and Jews Award for United Way of Greater Toronto 1993; Office: 26 Wellington St. E., Toronto, Ont. M5E 1W9.

**GOLDEN, Aubrey Edward,** B.A., LL.M.; barrister-at-law; b. Toronto, Ont. 9 Aug. 1934; s. Harry and Gertrude G.; e. Univ. Coll., Univ. of Toronto, B.A. 1955; Osgoode Hall Law Sch., barrister-at-law; grad. studies; York Univ., LL.M. 1990; m. Judith Carol d. Samuel and Pearl Freedhoff 9 July 1957; children: Marshall Adam, Alysa Miriam, Amelia Gayle; BARRISTER-AT-LAW, GOLDEN, GREEN & CHERCOVER 1959– ; practises constitutional, civil liberties, labour & admin. law; Mem., Bar of Ont. 1959, P.E.I. 1971, Alta. 1972, N.W.T. 1981; has represented labour, farmer & native orgns. throughout Can. before prov. & fed. courts & the Supreme Court of Can.; Nat. Chrmn., Civil Liberties Section, Candn. Bar Assn. 1967–69; Chrmn., Nat. Lawyers Ctte., Coalition Against the Return of the Death Penalty 1987; Chrmn. & Dir., Canadian Forum Limited 1988– ; Dir., Home Again 1982–87; Q.C. 1980; cert. by Law Soc. of U.C. as a specialist in civil litigation 1989; Hebrew; Mem., Beth Tzedec Cong. Toronto (Dir. 1973–75); Advocates Soc. 1966– ; Coach Advocates Soc. Training Inst.; Mem., Writers' Union of Can.; Internat. P.E.N. (Candn. Section); author: 'Rumours of War' 1971, 2nd ed. 1976; frequent guest lectr. & speaker; recreations: flying, scuba diving, skiing; Home: 400 Glengrove Ave. W., Toronto, Ont. M5N 1W9; Office: Suite 200, 101 Yorkville Ave. W., Toronto, Ont. M5R 1C1.

**GOLDEN, David A.,** O.C., LL.B., LL.D.; executive; b. 1920; e. University of Manitoba (Law); Rhodes Scholar 1941, Oxford Univ.; m. Molly Berger, Winnipeg, Man., Sept. 1946; two s.; mem. Ottawa Adv. Bd., Royal Trust Co.; Chrmn.: Parliamentary Centre for Foreign Affairs and Foreign Trade; Centre for Legislative Exchange; Parliament, Business and Labour Trust; Trustee: Ottawa General Hosp.; Inst. for the Future; Depy. Min. Dept. of Defence Production 1954–62; Depy. Min., Dept. of Industry, 1963–64; Pres., Air Industries Assn. Can. 1964–69; Pres., Telesat Canada 1969–80, Chrmn. 1980–92; enlisted in Candn. Army in 1941 and served overseas; prisoner of war in Hong Kong 1941–45; discharged Dec. 1945 with rank of Capt.; named an Offr. of Order of Canada, 1977; Home: Apt. 2001, 400 Stewart St., Ottawa, Ont. K1N 6L2; Office: Parliamentary Centre, 5th Floor, 275 Slater St., Ottawa, Ont. K1P 5H9.

**GOLDENBERG, Andrew A.,** B.Sc., M.A.Sc., Ph.D., P.Eng.; educator; b. Bucharest, Romania 14 Aug. 1945; s. Dionis N. and Charlotte T.(Grosu) G.; e. Technion, Israel Inst. of Technol. B.Sc. 1969, M.A.Sc. 1972; Univ. of Toronto Ph.D. 1976; m. Aviva d. Joseph and Edith Abramovich 1970; two d. Maya Joy, Keren Eve; PROFESSOR OF MECH., ELECT. AND BIOMEDICAL ENG. UNIV OF TORONTO 1982– ; Dir. Robotics & Automation Lab.; Staff Eng. Spar Aerospace Ltd. 1975–81; Rsch. Asst. Prof., Univ. Rsch. Fellow in Elect. Eng. present Univ. 1981–82; Assoc. Prof. 1982–87; Prof. 1987– ; Pres. Engineering Services Inc.; author over 97 jour. papers and 150 conf. papers; Sr. mem. Soc. Mfg. Eng.; mem. Am. Soc. Mech. Engs.; Sr. Mem., Internat. Elect. & Electronic Engs. Soc.; Assoc. Editor of IEEE Transactions on Robotics & Automation; recreation: sports; Office: 5 King's College Rd., Toronto, Ont. M5S 1A4.

**GOLDENBERG, Gerald Joseph,** M.D., Ph.D., F.R.C.P.(C), F.A.C.P.; educator; b. Brandon, Man. 27 Nov. 1933; s. Jacob and Fanny (Walker) G.; e. Univ. of Man. M.D. 1957; Univ. of Minn. Ph.D. 1965; m. Sheila Claire d. Henry Melmed, Winnipeg, Man. 4 Jan. 1959; children: Lesley Peace, Jacob Alan, Suzanne Elise, Ellen Rachel; PROF. OF MED. AND PHARMACOLOGY, UNIV. OF TORONTO, DIR., INTER-DEPARTMENTAL DIV. OF ONCOLOGY, ASST. DEAN (ONCOLOGY), UNIV. OF TORONTO 1990– ; Staff, Dept. of Med., Ont. Cancer Inst. / Princess Margaret Hosp. 1990– ; Mem., Bd. of Dirs., Ont. Cancer Inst. / Princess Margaret Hosp. 1992– ; Lectr. in Med., Univ. of Man. 1964, Asst. Prof. 1966, Assoc. Prof. 1970–75, Prof. 1975–90; Research Asst. Man. Cancer Foundation 1964–73; Dir., Manitoba Inst. of Cell Biol. 1973–88; Physician to Winnipeg Munc. Hosps. 1964–67 and to Winnipeg Gen. Hosp. 1965–90; Consultant in Oncology Winnipeg Children's Hosp. 1967–90; recipient Univ. of Man. Gold Medal Faculty Med., Dr. Charlotte Ross Gold Medal 1957; Fellow, Am. Cancer Soc. 1959–61; McEachern Fellow Candn. Cancer Soc. 1961–62; Fellow, Nat. Cancer Inst. 1962–63, Clin. Research Assoc. 1967–73, Candn. Hadassah Cancer Research Fellow 1963–64; author over 90 scient. publs.; mem. Am. Assn. Cancer Research; Am. Assn. of Pathol.; Candn. Soc. Clin. Investigation; Candn. Oncology Soc.; Sigma Alpha Mu; Y.M.H.A.; Freemason; Jewish; recreations: golf, tennis, swimming, skiing, chess; Home: 34 Duggan Ave., Toronto, Ont. M4V 1Y2; Office: 92 College St., Toronto, Ont. M5G 1L4.

**GOLDENBERG, Hon. H. Carl,** O.C. (1967), O.B.E., Q.C., M.A., B.C.L., LL.D.; lawyer; b. Montreal, Que. 20 Oct. 1907; s. Maurice and Adela (Gradinger) G.; e. McGill Univ., B.A. 1928, M.A. 1929, B.C.L. 1932; Gold Medal in Econ. amd Pol. Science 1928, in Law 1932; LL.D. (Hon.) of McGill, Montréal, Toronto, B.C., York and Queen's Univs.; m. Shirley Claire, d. Myer Block, Montreal, Que., Feb. 1945; children: Edward Stephen, Ann Helen Bergman; Special Counsel on the Constitution to the Prime Minister of Canada 1968–71; summoned to the Senate of Canada 4 Nov. 1971 (Chrmn. Standing Senate Comte. on Legal and Const. Affairs); mem. Joint Senate-House of Commons Comm. on the Constitution of Canada, 1980–81; retired from Senate, 20 Oct. 1982; called to the Bar of Que. 1932; Q.C. 1952; Sessional Lecturer in Economics and Political science, McGill University 1932–36; Adviser to Royal Commission on Dominion-Prov. Relations 1937–38; Chairman, Royal Comn. on Finances and Adm. of Winnipeg 1938–39; Commr., Man. Govt. Comm. Enterprises Inquiry 1939–40; Adviser to Que. Tax Revision Bd. (Montpetit Comn.) 1940; Chrmn., Prov. Bd. of Arbitration, Women's Apparel Indust. in Que. 1940; apptd. to Can's. War Organ., Sept. 1940 and occupied posts: Dir.-Gen., Econ. and Stat. Br. and mem. of Production Bd., Dept. of Mun. and Supply; Chrmn., Indust. Production Co-operation Bd.; mem., Nat. Selective Service Advisory Bd.; Extve. Asst. to Chrmn., Joint War Production Comte. of Can. and U.S.A. (Candn. Sec.); as a special Fed. Commr., settled Montreal Tramways Co. employees strike, 1943 and Great Lakes Shipping Strike, 1956; Rept. Min. of Mun. & Supply at War Production meetings in London, Eng., 1943; Adviser to Candn. Govt. Del. to Internat. Labour Organization Conf., Philadelphia, 1944; Labour Adviser, Dept. of Reconstruction, 1945–46; Roy. Commr. on Prov.-Mun. Relations in B.C., 1946–47; Special Commr. under Combines Act to investigate alleged combine in Baking Indust. in W. Can. 1948; Special Counsel for B.C. (1950–56), N.B. (1960–61) and Nfld. 1957–65, at Fed.-Prov. Confs.; Special Commr. under Combines Act to investigate alleged combine in Wire & Cable Industry 1952–53; Counsel for Nfld. on Revision of Financial Terms of Union with Canada, 1954–58; Commr. on Mun. Taxation in Winnipeg, 1957–58; Chrmn. Comn. of Enquiry into the strikes in the sugar industry of Jamaica, 1959 and of Trinidad, 1960 and 1962; Chrmn., Industrial Inquiry Comn. on constr. indust. strikes in Vancouver, 1958; Royal Commr. on Labour-Mang. Relations in Constr. Industry Ont., 1961–62; settled year old Royal York Hotel strike in Toronto, 1962; Vice-Chrmn., Prov. Que. Royal Comn. of Enquiry into Prov., Mun. and Sch. Bd. sources of Revenue, 1963–65; Vice-Chrmn., Quebec Econ. Adv. Council, 1962–68; Royal Comn. on Metropolitan Saint John, N.B., 1963, on Greater Fredericton, N.B. 1970–71, on Greater Moncton, N.B. 1970–71; Royal Comn. on Metrop. Toronto, 1963–65; Royal Commr. on Mail Transport in Montreal 1970; Impartial Chrmn. and Arbitrator, Men's Clothing Industry, Montreal; Impartial Umpire of Juris. Disputes, Candn. Labour Cong.; Arbitrator, Ont. Hydro Employees' Dispute 1962; Federal Mediator in national railway strike 1966; settled nat. strike in meat-packing industry 1966, and strike at Sydney Steel Corp., N.S. 1972; Mediator in Man. Hydro Employees' dispute 1973; Arbitrator, Nfld. Hosp. Employees' strike 1973; Chrmn. Bd. of Arbitration, Windsor, Ont. separate sch. teachers' dispute 1974; Arbitrator, Toronto Transit Comn. Employees' strike 1974; Arbitrator, Univ. of Man. Faculty Assoc. disputes 1976; settled Vanier College Teachers' strike, 1978; Arbitrator, Acadia University Faculty Assoc. Salaries 1979; Arbitrator, Metrop. Toronto Police Force Salaries 1984; Chrmn., Tri-Level Confs. of Fed., Prov. and Mun. govts. 1972 and 1973; Chrmn. First Nat. Conf. on Multiculturalism, 1973; Special Counsel, Royal Comn. on the Economic Union and Develop. Prospects of Can. 1983–85; Conciliation Comnr., Air Canada and Machinists Negotiations 1985; Concilicia-tion Comnr., Candn. Broadcasting Corp. & Nat. Assoc. of Broadcast Employees and Technicians Negotiations 1986; Chrmn., Conciliation Bd. under Govt. Services Resumption Act re Hospital Services Group, Public Service Alliance and Treasury Bd. of Can. 1990; Gov. Emeritus McGill Univ.; Mem. Adv. Comm. Centre de Recherche en Droit Public, Univ. de Montréal; Hon. mem. Bd. Adm. Montreal Jewish General Hospital; author: 'The Law of Delicts Under the Quebec Civil Code' 1935; 'Municipal Finance in Canada' 1939; Co-Editor 'Construction Labour Relations' 1969; mem., Candn. Historical Soc.; Hon. mem., Candn. Bar Assn.; recreations: reading, music; Club: McGill Faculty; Home: 18 Lower Village Gate, Toronto, Ont. M5P 3L7; Office: 70 Bond St., Toronto, Ont. M5P 3L7.

**GOLDFARB, Leo;** real estate executive, financier; b. Warsaw, Poland 8 May 1925; s. Max and Helen (Haberman) G.; e. Baron Byng H.S.; Sir George Williams Univ.; m. Rita (d.), d. Sam Steinberg, 19 Nov. 1950; children: Eileen, Robert, Gail; m. 2ndly Shirley Greenfeld Hitzig 26 Jan. 1973; one d. Susan Hitzig; Pres., Ringold Enterprises Ltd.; Dir., MD Realty Fund 1993– ; Mem. Bd. of Governors and the Corp. of Concordia Univ. 1993– ; with Steinberg Ltd. 1954–68 as Mgr.-

Real Estate, Vice-Pres. Develop., then Dir. and Extve. Vice Pres. Corp. Affairs; Trizec Corp. 1969–80: Sr. Vice Pres. Retail Operations, then Extve. Vice-Pres. and Chief Oper. Offr.; Pres. & C.E.O., Place Bonaventure Inc. 1969–93; Dir. and Past Pres., Jewish Gen. Hosp. Bd.; Past Pres., Jewish Gen. Hosp. Med. Rsch. Found.; Dir., Montreal Symphony Orch.; Clubs: Elm Ridge Golf and Country; Mount Royal Tennis; Montefiore; Home: 3 Westmount Square, Montreal, Que. H3Z 2S5; Office: PO Box 1045, Place Bonaventure, Montreal, Que. H5A 1G2.

**GOLDFARB, Martin,** B.A., M.A.; sociologist; marketing consultant; b. Toronto, Ont. 6 May 1938; s. David and Sonia (Silverstein) G.; e. Univ. of Toronto B.A. 1963, M.A. 1965; m. Joan d. Ida and Laz Freedman 7 June 1961; children: Alonna, Baila, Rebecca, Daniel, Avi; CHAIRMAN, THE GOLDFARB CORP. 1966– ; teacher 1964–65; key pollster to Federal Liberal Party 1973–92; Dir., Candn. Counc. of Christians and Jews; Toronto Symphony Orch.; former Dir., Canadian Opera Co.; Shaw Festival; mem. Bd. of Govs., York Univ.; Trustee, The Martin Wise Goodman Trust for Candn. Nieman Fellows; author: 'Goldfarb Report'; 'Marching to a Different Drummer' 1988; recreations: tennis, skiing, sailing; Club: Alpine Ski; Home: 17 Misty Cres., Don Mills, Ont. M3B 1T2; Office: 4950 Yonge St., Suite 1700, Toronto, Ont. M2N 6K1.

**GOLDIE, David Michael Mills,** B. Com., LL.B., Q.C. (1972); b. Toronto, Ont. 1 July 1924; s. Edward Crosby and Margaret Mostyn (Mills) G.; e. Pub. and High Schs. Bowen Island, Vancouver and Westmount, Que.; Univ. of B.C., B.Com. 1946; Harvard Law Sch., LL.B. 1949; m. Lorraine Catherine, d. J.J. Conway, 27 March 1948; children: Diana, David, Mary, Christopher; JUSTICE OF APPEAL, COURT OF APPEAL FOR B.C. and COURT OF APPEAL YUKON TERRITORY 1991– ; called to Bar of B.C. 1950 and of Yukon Territory 1986; Assoc., MacDougall, Morrison & Jestley, 1950–52; Partner, Jestley, Morrison, Eckardt & Goldie, 1952–56; Solr., British Columbia Electric Co. Ltd., 1956–59; Gen. Solr., 1959–61; Vice Pres. and Secy., British Columbia Power Corp. Ltd., 1961–64; Partner, Russell & DuMoulin 1964–91; Candn. Army 1943–45 and 1952–62 (reserve); mem. B.C. Cancer Foundation; Cdn. Inst. for Advanced Legal Studies; Internat. Law Assn.; Am. Coll. Trial Lawyers; recreations: reading, walking, sailing; Clubs: Vancouver; Royal Vancouver Yacht; Home: #4, 5389 Vine St., Vancouver, B.C. V6M 3Z7; Office: Law Courts, Vancouver, B.C. V6Z 2E1.

**GOLDIE, Gordon L.;** CFRE(Ret.); fund raising consultant; b. Montréal, Qué. 12 Aug. 1925; s. John Alexander and Charlotte (LeRoy) G.; e. elem. and high schs. Toronto; m. Kathleen Ann d. David and Agnes Williams 27 Dec. 1954; two d. Carol, Jill; Chrmn. and Chief Exec. Offr., Gordon L. Goldie Co. Ltd. 1986–92; mem. Ed. Dept. Toronto Daily Star 1942–43, 1945–46; served with RCNVR 1943–45, N. Atlantic Convoy Duty; Ed. and Co-Owner Geraldton (Ont.) Times-Star 1946–51; Fund Raising Acct. Exec. John Price Jones Co. (Canada) Ltd. 1951, Vice Pres. successor co. G.A. Brakeley Co. 1953–64; estbd. present Co. 1965; as fund raising counsel has served numerous non-profit institutions from B.C. to Nfld., managing capital campaigns for Brock Univ., Lester B. Pearson Coll. of the Pacific, Roy Thomson Hall, Hamilton Place, Kitchener Centre in the Square, St. Lawrence Centre, Toronto Gen. Hosp., Univ. of Waterloo, Carleton Univ., the Stratford Shakespearean Festival, Art Gallery of Ont., The Candn. Red Cross Soc. Nat. Centre, Ridley Coll., St. Andrews Coll. and the Inst. for Rsch. on Public Policy; Founder and first Pres. Communications & Pub. Relations Found.; Dir., York Co. Hosp. Found. 1982–86; Walter Perry DeiterFound.; Hon. Dir., Candn. Council for Native Bus.; Patron, Lester B. Pearson Coll. of the Pacific; author 'Paying the Piper' (fund raising manual) 1969, re-issued 1990; Nat. Soc. Fund Raising Execs.; Home: 3865 Kimatouche Rd., R.R. 3, Kelowna, B.C. V1Y 7R2.

**GOLDIE, James Hugh,** M.D., F.R.C.P.(C); physician; b. Windsor, Ont. 16 Jan. 1937; s. James Smith and Anne (Humeniuk) G.; e. Humberside Coll. Inst. Toronto 1955; Univ. of Toronto M.D. 1961; m. Enid d. Joseph and Hilda Sartor 20 March 1970; one s. Ian S.; HEAD, DIV. OF MED. ONCOLOGY, B.C. CANCER AGENCY and Clin. Prof. Med. Univ. of B.C. 1984– ; Asst. Prof. (Med.) Univ. of Toronto 1970–76; Med. Oncol. present Agency 1976– , Head, Sect. Advanced Therapeutics 1977–84; mem. Bd. Sci. Counsellor, US Nat. Cancer Inst. 1981–85; Adv. Council on Rsch. Nat. Cancer Inst. Can. 1986–89; Terry Fox Medallist 1982; ed. 'Drug and Hormone Resistance in Neoplasia' Vols. I and II 1982–83; 'Neoadjuvant Chemotherapy' 1986; author or co-author over 100 sci. articles; recreations: reading, hiking, astronomy, hist. of cinema; Home: 2558 W. 7th Ave., Vancouver, B.C. V6K 1Y9; Office: 600 W. 10th Ave., Vancouver, B.C. V52 4E6.

**GOLDIE, Raymond J.,** B.Sc., M.Sc., Ph.D.; financial analyst; b. New Zealand 10 Aug. 1948; s. John and Norma (Reid) G.; e. Victoria Univ. N.Z. B.Sc. 1972; McGill Univ. M.Sc. 1972; Queen's Univ. Ph.D. 1976; Univ. of Toronto Dip.Bus.Admin. 1979; m. Jo-Anne d. Graham and PJ Raynes 19 Sept. 1971; children: Katie, Alexandra; MINING ANALYST, RICHARDSON GREENSHIELDS OF CANADA 1980– ; applications of Modern Portfolio Theory, Canavest House Ltd. 1977–80; Dir., Prospectors & Developers Assn. of Canada; author of numerous pubns. on geology and finan. theory in academic journals; recreations: photography, volcanoes, hot springs; clubs: Engineers; Office: 130 Adelaide St. W., Ste. 1400, Toronto, Ont. M5H 1T8.

**GOLDIE, Terry (Terence William),** B.A., M.A., Ph.D.; university professor; b. Regina, Sask. 17 July 1950; s. Angus Maclean and Dorothy Florence (Little) G.; e. Sheldon-Williams C.I. 1968; Univ. of Sask., B.A. (Hons.) 1972; Carleton Univ., M.A. 1975; Queen's Univ., Ph.D. 1978; m. Robyn d. Derek and Jill (Leir) Salter 29 Aug. 1970 (separated 1990); children: Norah Jill, Alexander Angus; ASSOC. PROF., YORK UNIV. 1988– ; Lectr., Meml. Univ. of Nfld. 1977–78; Asst. Prof. 1978–83; Assoc. Prof. 1983–88; Theatre Critic, CBC Radio (St. John's) 1980–85; for the 'Sunday Express' 1986–88; Contrb. Ed., 'Books in Canada' 1983–88; Ed. Bd., 'English Studies in Canada' 1985– , 'Open Letter' 1989– , 'Studies in Canadian Literature' 1989– ; 'Essays in Theatre' 1991– ; adjudication juries for SSHRCC & Ont. Arts Counc.; Can. Counc. doct. fellowship; various SSHRCC grants; The Pres. Award for Outstanding Rsch. (Meml. Univ.) 1986; Anglican; N.D.P.; Mem., Assn. of Candn. Univ. and Coll. Teachers of English; Candn. Assn. for Commonwealth Language & Lit. Studies; Assn. for the Study of Austral. Lit.; Assn. for Candn. & Que. Lits.; author: 'Louis Dudek' 1985 (lit crit.), 'Fear and Temptation: The Image of the Indigene in Canadian, Australian and New Zealand Literatures' 1989; co-editor: 'Violence in the Canadian Novel since 1960' 1981; 'An Anthology of Canadian Native Literature in English' 1992; recreations: folk music, tennis, hockey; Home: 383 Willard Ave., Toronto, Ont. M6S 3R4; Office: 4700 Keele St., North York, Ont. M3J 1P3.

**GOLDING, Mark Alan Frederick;** business executive; b. Bombay, India 12 Feb. 1937; s. Cyril Frederick and Yvonne Simone (Bunnetat) G.; e. Salesian Coll., Farnborough, Eng. 1955; m. Louise d. Herbert and Mildred Warren 31 Aug. 1962; children: Christopher, Nicholas, Andrew; VICE-CHAIRMAN, CORPORATE DEVEL., GUARDIAN CAPITAL GROUP LIMTED 1987– ; Chrmn. & C.E.O. Guardian Capital Advisors, Guardian Capital Inc., The Guardian Group of Funds Limited 1987– ; Chrmn., Guardian Capital Inc. Strategic Investment Cttee. 1987– ; Maclean Hunter Ltd. 1960–66; Pitfield Mackay Ross & Co. Ltd. 1966–70; Loewen, Ondaatje, McCutcheon & Co. Limited 1970–87; Home: 182 Crescent Rd., Toronto, Ont. M4W 1V3; Office: 110 Yonge St., Toronto, Ont. M5C 1T4.

**GOLDIN ROSENBERG, Dorothy,** M.Environ.Studies, dipl. Physiotherapy; educator, consultant, researcher on global issues; b. Montreal, Que. 1 Oct. 1937; s. Azar and Ray (Nadel) Goldin; e. McGill Univ., dipl. physical therapy; York Univ., Masters in Environ. Studies; children: Pamela, Matthew; Doctoral Candidate, Ont. Institute of Studies in Education (OISE), Univ. of Toronto; Cons., Nat. Film Bd. of Canada, Challenge for Change & Studio D, The Women's Unit 1978–86; Mem., Consultative Ctte. on Arms Control & Disarmament 1984–86; Devel. & Disarmament Coord., Candn. Council for Internat. Coop. 1986–88; Dir., Women's Directory Project which produced 'Les femmes s'en melent, Making a World of Difference: A Directory of Women in Canada Specializing in Global Issues' 1988–90; Workshop Coord., Militarism and Alternatives Towards Peace and Development; Coord., Energy Environ. Education Program, NFB; Candn. Coord., Internat. Coalition on Energy for Devel. 1986–87; U.N. Environ. Program Award for environmental stewardship; Dir., Third Biennial Conf. on the Fate of the Earth 1985–86; Montreal Safe Water Coalition; Green Energy Conf. 1989; Cons., Candn. Environ. Network on Internat. Environ. & Devel. Issues 1988; Cons. & Mem., Program Ctte., 'Healing the Planet: A Prescription for Survival' 1988 (annual congress of Internat. Physicians for the Prevention of Nuclear War); Founding & present Bd. Mem., Candn. Coaliton for Nuclear Responsibility; Advisor & Dir., Internat. Youth for Peace and Justice Tour 1984–89; Advisor, Students against Global Extermination 1985–88; Dir., Student Action for a Viable Environment Tour 1990; Bd. Mem., Women Environments and Education (WEED) Found. 1991; Coord., Fac. of Environ. Studies Peace & Global Studies Group, York Univ. 1991; Women for a Just and Healthy Planet (Toronto); mem., Energy Environment Caucus of the Ont. Environment Network; recipient, Commemorative Medal for 125th Anniversary of Candn. Confederation; author: 'The New Alchemists,' 'If You Love This Planet: Dr. Helen Caldicott on Nuclear War' (books to accompany films); collaborator & contributor of three chapters in book, 'Collateral Damage: Environmental and other Considerations of the War in the Gulf' by the Working Group on the Environmental Implications of the Gulf War, Inst. of Environmental Studies, Univ. of Toronto; recreations: folk dancing, bicycling, walking, swimming; Home: 44 Walmer Rd., Ste. 1006, Toronto, Ont. M5R 2X5.

**GOLDMAN, Gary Warren,** B.A., M.E.S.; trust company executive; b. Toronto, Ont. 13 July 1953; s. Murray and Rae (Shaefer) G.; e. Acadia Univ. B.A. 1975; York Univ. M.E.S. (Environ. Studies) 1978; m. Wendy d. Kalman Cohen 21 June 1977; children: Jonathan, Jacqueline, Melanie; Pres. & C.E.O., The Dominion Trust Co. 1983–..; Pres. Dominion Trustco Corp.; joined A.E. LePage 1977–78; Cadillac-Fairview Corp. 1978–80; Pres., Meadows Homes Ltd. 1980–83; Regd. Real Estate Broker; Clubs: York Racquets; Alpine Ski; Fitness Inst.; Home: 25 Alderbrook Dr., Don Mills, Ont. M3B 1E3.

**GOLDRING, Charles Warren,** B.A.; financial executive; b. Toronto, Ont. 21 Oct. 1927; s. Dr. Cecil Charles and Helen Beatrice (Mitchell) G.; e. Blyth-wood; Lawrence Park Coll. Inst.; Univ. of Toronto, B.A. (Pol. Science & Econ.) 1949; London Sch. of Econ., 1953–54; m. Dorothy Barbara, d. Dr. Kenneth Eardley and Dorothy Agnes (Brock) Dowd, Montreal, Que. 10 Sept. 1953; children: Blake, Bryce, Jill, Jane, Judy; CHRMN., C.E.O. & DIR., AGF MANAGEMENT LTD. and AGF TRUST COMPANY (asset managment); Dir. or Gov., AGF American Growth Fund; AGF Special Fund; AGF Canadian Bond Fund; AGF Growth Equity Fund; AGF Global Government Bond Fund; AGF Canadian Resources Fund; AGF Japan Fund; AGF Asian Growth Fund; AGF High Income Fund; AGF Canadian Equity Fund; Corporate Investors Limited; Corporate Investors Stock Fund; AGF Convertible Income Fund; AGF U.S. Dollar Money Market Fund; AGF Money Market Fund; Analyst, Sun Life Assurance Co. of Canada, Montreal, 1949–53; Fry & Co. Ltd., Toronto, 1954; author, 'How to Invest for Bigger Profits' 1957; 'Your Guide to Investing for Bigger Profits' 1975; Past Pres., Toronto Soc. Financial Analysts; recreation: fishing; Clubs: Granite; National; Empire; Ticker; Rosedale; Home: 41 Montressor Dr., Willowdale, Ont. M2P 1Y9; Office: Toronto-Dominion Centre, 31st Flr., Toronto, Ont. M5K 1E9.

**GOLDRING, Gvirol,** M.Sc., Ph.D.; nuclear physicist; b. 6 Feb. 1926; s. Pessach and Dora (Seligman) G.; e. Gymnasia Ivrit, Jerusalem 1944; Hebrew Univ. Jerusalem, M.Sc. 1949; Imperial Coll. Science & Tech., Ph.D., D.I.C. 1953; m. Hanna, d. Rafael Kohn, 16 March 1950; children: Alon Pessach, Noa; LADY DAVIS PROFESSOR OF EXPER. PHYSICS, CANDN. CENTRE OF NUCLEAR PHYSICS, WEIZMANN INST. OF SCIENCE; at Hebrew Univ., Jerusalem 1953; joined present Inst. 1954 and Head, Heineman Accelerator Lab. there 1964–84, Head of Dept. of Nuclear Physics 1984–87; Chrmn., Bd. of Nuclear Physics, European Physical Soc. 1985–92; mem. Israel Physical Soc.; Am. Physical Soc.; Co-Ed. (with R. Kalish) 'Hyperfine Interactions in Excited Nuclei' (Proceedings of Rehovot Conf.) 1970; author of numerous papers on nuclear structure, nuclear electromagnetic moments and transition probabilities; awarded Landau Prize 1973; Jewish; Address: Rehovot, Israel.

**GOLDSACK, Douglas Eugene,** B.Sc., Ph.D.; physical chemist; b. Can. 17 July 1939; s. Charles and Marjorie Ruby (Mitchell) G.; e. Sir Adam Beck Coll. Inst. 1957; Univ. of W. Ont. B.Sc. 1961; Mass. Inst. of Tech. 1961–62; Univ. of Wis. Ph.D. 1966; m. Maria Elena d. Richard and Madelene Squire 22 Aug. 1964; children: Sondee, Charles; PROF. OF CHEM., LAURENTIAN UNIV. 1983– ; Post-Doctoral Fellow Univ. of Wis. 1966–67; Rsch. Sci. Fisheries Rsch. Bd. 1967–68; Asst. Prof. of Chem. present Univ. 1968, Assoc. Prof. 1972, Chrmn. of Chem. 1976–80, Acting Dean of Sci. summers 1978, 1979, Dean of Science & Engineering, Laurentian Univ. 1980–92; mem., Can. Inst.; Assoc. Chem. Inst. Ont.; Sigma Xi; recreations: cross-country skiing, fishing, reading; Home: 13 Aspenwood Ct., Sudbury, Ont. P3E 5T6; Office: Sudbury, Ont. P3E 2C6.

**GOLDSTEIN, Allan A.,** B.A., M.A.; film writer, director; b. Montreal, Que. 23 May 1951; s. Saul and Anne (Cofsky) G.; e. Sir George Williams Univ., B.A. (Hons.) 1972; York Univ., M.A. 1974; m. Gabrielle d. Gabriel and Nora Kelly 30 May 1986; children: Fiona, Eamon; independent film maker of 3 award winning documentaries 1975–77; Dir., Nat. Film Bd. 1978; Directors Atelier, B.B.C. 1979; Dir., 'True West' (Best Dir. 1987) 1980–84; 'Outside Chance of Maximillian Glick' (winner, Toronto (best Candn. feature) & Vanc. (most popular picture) Film Festivals & Alberta/Que. award for Innovation in Film) 1987; Writer/Co-Prod., 'Rooftops' 1988; 'In The Skin of the Lion' 1989; Dir., 'The Phone Call' 1989; Dir., 'Chaindance' 1990; Writer/Dir. 'Death Wish V' 1992; Writer/Dir. 'No Return' 1993; Monitor Award, Best Dir. 1986; Am. Film Fest., blue ribbon; Mem., Dir. Guilds of Can. & Am.; ACTRA; Candn. Acad. of Motion Pictures; feature film writer: 'Whispers,' 'Everyman's Christmas,' 'In the Skin of a Lion,' 'The Lesson'; recreations: skiing, diving, climbing, poetry; Home: 2509 Greenvalley Rd., Los Angeles, CA 90046.

**GOLDSTEIN, Richard Alan,** LL.M., LL.B., B.B.A.; company executive; b. Boston, Mass. 16 Feb. 1942; s. Harold Matthew and Effie Grace (Klayman) G.; e. Harvard Law Sch., Boston Univ., Univ. of Mass. B.B.A. 1963; m. Linda Joan d. Paul Freedman 31 July 1966; children: Laura Beth, David; CHAIRMAN AND CHIEF EXEC. OFFICER, UNILEVER CANADA; Jewish; recreations: tennis, golf; Home: 24 Hilltop Dr., Chappaqua, N.Y. 10514; Office: 160 Bloor St. E., Toronto, Ont. M4W 3R2.

**GOLDSTEIN, Sol J.,** M.D., F.R.C.P.(C), F.A.P.A., F.R.S.H.; child & adolescent psychiatrist/psychoanalyst; b. Medicine Hat, Alta. 13 May 1938; s. David Leib and Masha (Kazimiro) G.; e. Dalhousie Med. Sch., M.D. 1963; Menninger Sch. of Psychiatry, Adult Psych. 1966, Child Psych. 1967; Candn. Psychoanalytic Inst., Psychoanalysis 1974; m. Ruhama d. Aba and Freda Gefen 15 Feb. 1971; children: Benjamin Israel, Rachel Malka, David Amihai; Proctor to Dr. Karl Menninger, Loyola Univ. Med. Sch. (Chicago) & Lectr., Chicago Med. Sch. 1967–68; Fac. of Med., Dept. of Psych. (presently Asst. Prof.), & Lectr., Fact. of Dentistry, Univ. of Toronto 1968– ; Fac. Mem., Assn. of Psychoanal. Psychotherap. for Children; Toronto Psychoanal. Inst.; Staff Mem. & Cons., I.C.U., Hosp. for Sick Children; Cons., West End Creche, Toronto 1968–74; Jewish Famuly & Child Serv. 1974–81; Mem., Candn., Am. & Internat. Psych. Assns. and Psychoanalytic Socs.; Charter Mem., Candn. Acad. of Child Psych; Candn. Assn. of Psychoanal. Psychotherap. for Children; F.R.C.P.(C), F.A.P.A., F.R.S.H.; author: 'Divorced Parenting – How to Make it Work' 1982, 'Michael's Ship' 1986; contbr.: 'Psychological Problems of the Child' 1977; Home: 690 Briar Hill Ave., Toronto, Ont. M6B 1L3; Office: 362 Spadina Rd., Toronto, Ont. M5P 2V4.

**GOLTZMAN, David,** B.Sc., M.D.C.M., F.R.C.P.(C); physician, scientist,educator; b. Montreal, Que. 22 Sept. 1944; s. Jack and Lily (Roth) G.; e. McGill Univ. B.Sc. 1966, M.D.C.M. 1968; m. Naomi d. Herbert and Molly Lyon 29 Dec. 1968; children: Jonathan, Rebecca, Daniel; PHYSICIAN-IN-CHIEF, ROYAL VICTORIA HOSP. 1994– ; Intern, Royal Victoria Hosp. 1968–69; Medical Resident, Columbia Univ. Coll. of Physicians & Surgeons New York 1969–71; Clin. & Rsch. Fellow in Endocrinology, Mass. Gen. Hosp. Boston 1971–75; Instructor in Med., Harvard Med. Sch. 1974–75; Asst. Prof. of Med., McGill Univ. 1976–78; Assoc. Prof. 1978–83; Prof. 1983– ; Prof. & Chair, Physiology 1988–93; Hosmer Prof. of Physiology 1992–93; Massabki Prof. of Med. 1994– ; Dir., Calcium Rsch. Lab., Royal Victoria Hosp. 1981– ; Sr. Physician 1987– ; Chair, Experimental Med. Ctte., MRC Canada 1984–88; Adv. Ctte. on Sci. 1993– ; Mem., Extve. Ctte. 1993– ; Medical Adv. Bd., Osteoporosis Soc. of Can. 1985– ; Gen. Med. B Study Section, Nat. Insts. of Health Bethesda MD 1987–91; Sci. Adv. Ctte., Loeb Rsch. Inst. 1990– ; Adv. Ctte. on Rsch., Nat. Cancer Inst. of Can. 1993– ; MRC Canada Scholarship 1975–83; Chercheur Boursier (Scholar) Award, Fonds de la rech. en santé du Qué. 1980–83; Scientist Award, MRC of Canada 1983–88; André Lichtwitz Prize, Nat. Inst. for Med. Rsch. 1987; Mem., Candn. Soc. of Endocrinology & Metabolism (Pres. 1990–92); Candn. Soc. of Clin. Investigation (Council Mem. 1986–89); The Endocrine Soc. U.S. (Program Ctte. Mem. 1989–91); Am. Soc. for Bone & Mineral Rsch. (Council Mem. 1985–88; Chair, Program Ctte. 1989–90); Am. Soc. for Clin. Investigation; Am. Physiol. Soc.; Candn. Physiol. Soc.; Am. Assn. of Physicians; Charter Mem., Candn. Soc. of Acad. Med.; co-author: 'Metabolic Basis of Endocrinology' 1979, 'Pediatric Endocrinology' 1989, 'Principles and Practice of Endocrinology and Metabolism' 1990, 'The Parathyroids' 1994 and num. articles on clin. & basic biomed. research 1975– ; Edit. Bd. Mem., 'Bone and Mineral' 1991–94, 'Osteoporosis International' 1991–94; Assoc. Ed., 'Bone' 1989– ; recreations: classical music, tennis; Home: 667 Belmont Ave., Westmount, Que. H3Y 2W3; Office: Room A3.09, 687 Pine Avenue W., Montreal, Que. H3A 1A1.

**GOM, Leona,** B.Ed., M.A.; writer; b. Fairview, Alta. 29 Aug. 1946; d. Tony and Mary (Baron) G.; e. Univ. of Alta., B.Ed. 1968, M.A. 1971; taught in English Dept., Univ. of Alta. 1971–73; taught at Columbia College, Douglas College and Kwantlen College in B.C. 1974–92; currently teaching in Creative Writing Dept., Univ. of B.C.; Ed., 'Event' 1979–85; Writer-in-Res., Univ. of Alta. 1987–88; Univ. of Lethbridge 1989; Univ. of Winnipeg 1990; author of books of poetry: 'Kindling' 1972; 'The Singletree' 1975; 'Land of the Peace' 1980; 'North-Bound' 1984; 'Private Properties' 1986; 'The Collected Poems' 1991; novels: 'Housebroken' 1986; 'Zero Avenue' 1989; 'The Y Chromosome' 1990; radio plays: 'The Inheritance' 1973; 'Sour Air' 1974; rec'd Candn. Authors' Assn. Award for Best Book of Poetry 1980; Ethel Wilson Award for Fiction 1986; Address: 15534 Semiahmoo Ave., White Rock, B.C. V4B 1V1.

**GOMERY, Hon. John Howard,** B.A., B.C.L.; judge; b. Montreal, Que. 9 Aug. 1932; s. Walter Bertram and Jean Elizabeth (Brook) G.; e. Montreal W. High Sch.; McGill Univ. B.A. 1953, B.C.L. 1956; m. Pierrette d. Joseph and Colette Rayle 18 Aug. 1973; children: (by previous marriage) Geoffrey, Cymry, Sally, (present marriage) Elizabeth; JUDGE, SUPERIOR COURT OF QUE. (APPEAL DIV. MONTREAL) 1982– ; called to Bar of Que. 1957; cr. Q.C. 1972; joined law firm now known as Martineau Walker 1957, Partner 1966; mem., Council Candn. Bar Assn. 1965–69, Bar of Montreal 1969–70; Anglican; Club: Montreal Badminton and Squash; Home: 695 Aberdeen Ave., Westmount, Que. H3Y 3A9; Office: Court House, 1 Notre Dame E., Montreal, Que. H2Y 1B6.

**GONTHIER, Hon. Charles Joseph Doherty,** B.C.L; judge; b. Montreal, Que. 1 Aug. 1928; s. Georges and Kathleen (Doherty) G.; e. Ecole Garneau, Ottawa, 1939; Coll. Stanislas, Montreal, B.A. Paris, 1947; McGill Univ. B.C.L. 1951; McGill Univ. LL.D. (hon. causa) 1990; m. Mariette Morin, M.D., M.Sc., F.R.C.S.(c), F.A.C.O.G.; children: Georges, François, Pierre, Jean-Charles, Yves; JUSTICE, SUPREME COURT OF CANADA 1 Feb. 1989; called to Bar of Que. 1952; Q.C. 1971; read law with Senator John T. Hackett, Q.C.; practised law Hackett, Mulvena & Laverty, Montreal 1952–57; Laing, Weldon, Courtois, Clarkson, Gonthier & Tetrault 1957–74 (formerly known as Hugessen, Macklaier, Chisholm, Smith & Davis); Justice, Que. Superior Court 17 Oct. 1974; Justice, Que. Court of Appeal 24 May 1988; Mem., Cdn. Bar Assn. (Pres. Junior Bar Sect. 1961–62; Secy. Que. Div. 1963–64); Pres., Candn. Inst. for Admin. of Justice 1986–87; Pres., Cdn. Judges Conf. 1988–89; Mem., Internat. Comn. of Jurists; Assn. Henri Capitant; Que. Assn. of Comparative Law; Bd. of Coll. Stanislas; Bd. of Gov., Société Pro Musica; formerly: Secy., Montreal Br., Cdn. Inst. of Internat. Affairs 1957–58; Bd. of Dirs., Montreal Legal Aid Bureau 1959–69; Pres., Junior Bar of Montreal 1960–61; Bd. of Dirs., Montreal Bar 1961–62; Comm. on Building Contracts, Que. Civil Code Revision 1969–72; Discipline Comm. of Que. Bar 1973–74; Chrmn., Comn. for National Judges of the First World Conf. on the Independence of Justice in Montreal 1983; Hon. Secy., Montreal Museum of Fine Arts 1961–76; Dir., McCord Museum of Cdn. History, Montreal 1976–89; Chrmn., Assn. des Anciens du Coll. Stanislas 1954–55; Chrmn. of Bd., College Stanislas of Montreal 1984–90; decorated Knight, L'Ordre des palmes académiques (France) 1988; R. Catholic; Club: University (of Montreal); Home: 221 Outremont Ave., Outremont, Que. H2V 3L9; Office: Supreme Court of Canada, Supreme Court Bldg., Ottawa, Ont. K1A 0J1.

**GOOCH, Bryan Niel Shirley,** M.A., Ph.D., A.R.C.T., F.T.C.L.; educator, administrator, performing artist (pianist and conductor); b. Vancouver, B.C., 31 Dec. 1937; s. Commdr. Niel Cyril Shirley and Mary Adeline Bryan (Williams) G.; e. (external) Roy. Conservatory of Music, Toronto, A.R.C.T. 1957; Trinity Coll. of Music, London, Engl. L.T.C.L. 1959; F.T.C.L. 1961; e. (internal) Univ. of B.C., B.A., 1959, M.A. 1962; Univ. of London, Ph.D. 1968; m. Dr. Jane Lytton Tryon, 1974; two sons: Arthur Bryan Shirley, Robert Edward Lytton; FACULTY MEM., UNIV. OF VICTORIA and Asst. Dean from 1972 to 1975; Instr., Dept. of English, Univ. of Victoria, 1964; Asst. Prof., 1968; Assoc. Prof., 1976; Prof., 1986; Res. Fellow, Craigdarroch Coll., 1968–69; Master of Lansdowne Coll. 1969–72; Faculty, Victoria Conservatory of Music, 1967–70; Musical Dir. and Conductor, Nanaimo Symphony, 1968–71; New Westminster Symphony, 1975–77; served with R.C.S.C., 1957–62 as Div. Offr. and Instr., rank Lt.; numerous awards and scholarships, including IODE Second War Memorial Post-Grad. 1962–64; co-holder Can. Council Research Grant, 1973, 1974, 1975–78, SSHRCC Research Grant, 1978–80, 1980–81, and SSHRCC Negotiated Grant 1982–1988; Can. Council Leave Fellowship, 1976–77; co-editor 'Poetry is for People'; 'Musical Settings of Late Victorian and Modern British Literature: A Catalogue'; 'Musical Settings of Early and Mid-Victorian Lit.: A Catalogue'; 'Musical Settings of British Romantic Literature: A Catalogue'; 'A Shakespeare Music Catalogue'; 'The Emergence of the Muse: Major Canadian Poets from Crawford to Pratt'; and author of reviews and of articles in 'Encyclopedia of Music in Canada' and learned journs.; frequent concerts, recitals, and broadcasts; mem., Advisory Academic Panel, SSHRCC, 1978–81; Chrmn. Leave and Postdoctoral Fellowships Cttee. (Eng. Lit. and Linguistics), SSHRCC, 1983–85; mem. Specialized Rsrch. Collections Cttee., SSHRCC, 1984–87 (Vice Chrmn. 1985, Chrmn. 1985–87); mem., Am. Musicological Soc.; Renaissance Soc. of Am.; Shakespeare Assn. of Am.; Candn. Assn. of Music Libraries (Chrmn. Publications Ctte. 1989–92, Programme Ctte. 1990–91, Vice-Pres. 1991–92); mem. Bd. of Dirs., 'Encyclopedia of Music in Canada' 1988– ; Voting Member, Candn. Music Centre 1991– ; former mem., Modern Lang. Assn. (to 1986) (mem., Delegate Assembly 1983–86); Life Fellow of Roy. Commonwealth Soc.; Anglican; recreations: climbing, hiking, tennis, sailing, model railways, watercolours; Home: 2791 W. 43 Ave., Vancouver, B.C. V6N 3H8; Office: Univ. of Victoria, P.O. Box 3045, Victoria, B.C. V8W 3P4.

**GOOCH, Paul William,** B.A., M.A., Ph.D.; university professor; b. Toronto, Ont. 24 June 1941; s. George Frederick and Evelyn Ruth (Lovering) G.; e. Bishop's Univ. B.A. 1963; Univ. of Toronto M.A. 1965, Ph.D. 1970; M. Pauline Ann d. J. Samuel and Kathleen Thompson 5 May 1976; VICE-DEAN, SCHOOL OF GRADUATE STUDIES, UNIV. OF TORONTO 1994– ; Lectr., Philosophy, Scarborough Coll., Univ. of Toronto 1967; Asst. Prof. 1970; Assoc. Prof. 1973; Prof. 1988; Chair, Div. of Humanities 1977–82; Dir., Grad. Ctr. for Religious Studies, Univ. of Toronto 1986–88; Assoc. Dean, Humanities, Sch. of Grad. Studies 1988–90; Asst. Dean, School of Grad. Studies 1990–92; Acting Dean 1992–93; Commonwealth Fellow, St. John's Coll. Cambridge 1982–83; Anglican; Mem., Candn. Philos. Assn.; Classical Assn. of Can.; Candn. Soc. for the Study of Religion; Candn. Soc. of Biblical Studies; Soc. of Christian Philos.; author: 'Partial Knowledge: Philosophical Studies in Paul' 1987 and num. articles on Greek Phil., Biblical Studies & Phil. of Religion; recreations: cooking; Home: 116 Sutherland Dr., Toronto, Ont. M4G 1H9; Office: 65 St. George St., Toronto, Ont. M5S 2Z9.

**GOOD, Cynthia A.,** B.A., M.A.; editor; b. Toronto, Ont. 11 Apr. 1951; d. Philip M. and Charlotte S. (Dawson) G.; e. Univ. of Toronto, B.A. 1973, M.A. 1974; VICE-PRES. & PUBLISHER, PENGUIN BOOKS CANADA LIMITED 1989– ; Co-founder & mem., Menagerie Players 1969–73; Student, Univ. of Toronto 1973–77; Editor, Dorset Pub. 1978–80; Mktg. Mgr., Doubleday Book Clubs 1980–82; Ed. Dir., present firm 1982– ; Bd. Mem., Cdn. Ctr. for Studies in Pub.; Canadian Stage Company; The Gerstein Centre; recipient, Rueben Wells Leonard Award; has edited works of Mordecai Richler, John le Carré, Peter C. Newman, Katherine Govier, Rohinton Mistry, Eric McCormack, Timothy Findley and others; Office: 10 Alcorn Ave., Ste. 300, Toronto, Ont. M4V 3B2.

**GOODALE, Hon. Ralph E.,** B.A., LL.B.; business executive; b. Regina, Sask. 5 Oct. 1949; s. Thomas Henry and Winnifred Claire (Myers) G.; e. Milestone (Sask.) High Sch. 1967; Univ. of Regina B.A. 1971; Univ. of Sask. LL.B. 1972; m. Pamela Jean d. Willard and Lois Kendel 8 Feb. 1986; MINISTER OF AGRICULTURE and AGRI-FOOD, GOVT. OF CANADA 1993– ; Leader, Saskatchewan Liberal Party 1981–88; family farm operation prior to 1975; CBC (Sask.) News & Pub. Affairs 1968–72; law practice 1972–73; Fed. Pub. Service 1973–74, 1979–81; el. M.P. for Assiniboia 1974–79; former Parlty. Sec. to Min. of Transport, Min. responsible for Candn. Wheat Bd. and to Pres. of Privy Council; el. Leader Sask. Liberal Party 198–88; el. M.L.A. for Assiniboia-Gravelbourg 1986, resigned 1988; Liberal Candidate for Regina Wascana, fed. el. 1988, defeated; Corp. Secy., Pioneer Lifeco Inc. and Pioneer Life Assurance Co. 1989–90; Corp. Secy., Sovereign Life Insurance Co. 1990–..; mem. Law Soc. Sask.; Lutheran; recreation:

sports; Clubs: Eau Claire YMCA; Calgary Curling; Office: Rm. 175, East Block, House of Commons, Ottawa, Ont. K1A 0A6.

**GOODALL, Nigel,** M.A., M.C.Inst.M.; b. Watford, U.K. 29 Mar. 1945; s. Kenneth and Muriel (Barratt) G.; e. Merchant Taylors' Sch. 1956–64; St. John's Coll., Oxford Univ., M.A. (Hons.) 1968; m. Savi; children: Glynn, Sean; PRES. & C.E.O., STRATEGICOS INC. 1990– ; Pres., Barramundi (U.S.A.) Inc. 1991– ; Vice Chrmn., St. John's Rehabilitation Hosp. 1992– ; Sales & Mktg. Mngt., Unilever Ltd. (U.K. & Can.) 1968–80; Extve. Vice Pres., Corby Distilleries 1980–83; Extve. Vice-Pres., Gilbey Canada Inc. 1983–86, C.O.O. 1986–87, Pres. & C.E.O. 1988–90; Past Pres., Candn. Meat Counc. 1979; Chrmn., Chartered Inst. of Mktg. Mgt. of Ont.; clubs: National (Toronto); Home: R.R. 3, 19 Bartley Dr., Caledon E., Ont. L0N 1E0.

**GOODALL, Robert G.,** H.B.A., C.G.A., M.B.A.; real estate finance executive; b. London, England 18 Dec. 1957; s. Robert G. and Helen A. (Ayer) G.; e. Univ. of Western Ont. B.A. (Hons.); York Univ. M.B.A.; m. Susan I. d. Barry G. Finan 12 July 1987; MANAGING PARTNER, REAL ESTATE FINANCE GROUP, ROYAL TRUST 1986– ; financial consultant to independent dealer network in Canada, John Deere Limited 1980–82; Commercial Account Mgr., Bank of Montreal 1984–86; Mem., Investment Ctte., Royal LePage Commercial Real Estate Fund; recreations: squash, tennis, golf, skiing; club: Ontario Racquet; Home: 1485 Petrie Way, Mississauga, Ont. L5J 4A5; Office: Suite 3700, Royal Trust Tower, P.O. Box 7500, Stn. A, Toronto, Ont. M5W 1P9.

**GOODFELLOW, Byron B. (Ike),** M.A.Sc., P.Eng.; educator; executive; b. Toronto, Ont. 5 March 1931; s. late Lawrence Byron and late Mary (Beaton) G.; e. Univ. of Toronto B.A.Sc. 1953, M.A.Sc. 1954; children: Jane, Sharon, Nancy, Keith; ASST. VICE PRES., GLOBAL ACCOUNTS, NORTHERN TELECOM CANADA LTD., Mississauga, Ont.; joined IBM Canada 1955, Adm. Asst. to Pres. 1964, Mgr. Systems Eng. 1966, Dir IBM's Toronto Lab. 1967, Dir. Orgn. IBM World Trade Corp., New York 1972, Dir. Data Processing Operations IBM Canada Ltd. (Ottawa Div.) 1976–85; Mng. Dir., Centre for Advanced Technol. Edn., Ryerson Polytech. Inst. 1985–87 (on secondment from IBM); Corporate Div., Un. Way Campaign, Ottawa 1980–81; Corporate Donations Div., Univ. of Ottawa Achievement Fund 1981–83; mem. Exec. Ctte. Ottawa Carleton Econ. Devel. Corp. 1982–85; Past Pres. Candn. Info. Processing Soc. 1968; mem. Assn. Prof. Engs. Prov. Ont.; Past Pres. Candn. Club Ottawa 1983–84; Clubs: Cercle Universitaire (Ottawa); Rideau (Ottawa); Engineers' (Toronto); Home: 451 Balliol St., Toronto, Ont. M4S 1E1; Office: 2920 Matheson Blvd. E., Mississauga, Ont. L4W 2M7.

**GOODFELLOW, C. Richard,** B.B.A., M.B.A.; lumber merchant; b. Montreal, Que. 24 Aug. 1944; s. Charles William and Ann Martha (Treglown) G.; e. Bishops College Sch. 1961; Univ. of N.B. B.B.A. 1965; Univ. of Western Ont. M.B.A. 1967; m. Louise d. Yvette and Louis Roy 15 Sept. 1973; children: Patrick, Vincent, Gabrielle, William; PRESIDENT & C.E.O., GOODFELLOW INC. 1989– ; Sales Engineer, Canadair 1967–68; Sales Rep., IBM Canada 1968–73; Vice-Pres., Operations, Goodfellow INC. 1973–89; Home: 1020 Lakeshore, Dorval, Que. H9S 2C5; Office: 225 Goodfellow St., Delson, Que. J0L 1G0.

**GOODFELLOW, George Douglas,** B.Eng.; executive; b. Montreal, Que. 6 Aug. 1915; s. George Clarke and Caroline Elizabeth (Jones) G.; e. Selwyn House Sch. Montreal; Trinity Coll. Sch. Port Hope; McGill Univ. B.E. 1936; m. Hildegarde G. d. Jim and constance Brown 28 Dec. 1940; two s. G. Douglas, David Allan; CHRMN. OF THE BD., GOODFELLOW INC. 1970– ; Mining Eng., Geol. and Mine Mgr. 1936–40; Pres., Candn. Plywoods Ltd. Montreal 1946–54; Vice Pres., Weldwood of Canada Ltd. Montreal 1954–65; Gen. Mgr. Bldg. Materials Group CIP Ltd. 1965–69; served with RCE 1941–45, rank Capt.; recipient Candn. Centennial Medal 1967; Queen's Silver Jubilee Medal 1977; mem., McGill Fund Council; Past Pres., Candn. Yachting Assn.; mem., Candn. Olympic Assn.; recreations: skiing, sailing; Clubs: Royal St. Lawrence Yacht; Woodlands Yacht; Khandahar Ski; Home: 480 Chemin du Lac, Ville de Lery, Que. J6N 1A3; Office: 225 Rue Goodfellow, Delson, Que. J0L 1G0.

**GOODFELLOW, The Hon. Mr. Justice Walter R.E.,** C.D., LL.B., Q.C.; supreme court justice; b. Ottawa, Ont. 5 Nov. 1934; s. Norman Edward and Thelma Hanna (Creen) G.; e. Queen's Univ.; Dalhousie Univ. Law Sch.; m. Sandra d. Edward and Marion (both dec.) Burt 24 May 1968; children: Alan, Steven, Heather, Geoffrey; SUPREME COURT JUSTICE, NOVA SCOTIA SUPREME COURT 1990– ; admitted to Bar of Prov. of N.S. 1960; Lawyer, Hart, Cox, Donahoe, Palmeter Rogers & MacKinnon 1960–65; joined Cox, Downie & Goodfellow 1965 and left as Senior Partner; Part-time Teacher, Dalhousie Law School for several years; Pres., N.S. Barristers' Soc. Digby 1990; Q.C. 1975; Hon. Life Mem., Wardroom, HMCS Scotian; President of a Standing Court Martial, Captain (N) and Sr. Reserve Legal Advisor in Canada to the Chief of Reserves and Cadets, Candn. Armed Forces 1988; Hon. Life Mem., Candn. Paraplegic Assn. (N.S. Div.); Mem. of Advisory Bd., Candn. Journal of Family Law 1977– ; awarded Commemorative Medal for 125th Anniversary of Candn. Confederation 1993; Office: The Law Courts, Box 2314, Halifax, N.S. B3J 1S7.

**GOODLAD, John Inkster,** Ph.D., L.H.D., LL.D., D.Ed., Litt.D.; educator; dean; b. N. Vancouver, B.C. 19 Aug. 1920; s. William James and Mary (Inkster) G.; e. Vancouver Normal Sch., Teaching Cert. 1939; Univ. of B.C., B.A. 1945, M.A. 1946; Univ. of Chicago, Ph.D. 1949; Nat. Coll. of Educ., L.H.D. 1967; Univ. of Louisville, L.H.D. 1968; Kent State Univ., L.L.D. 1974; Pepperdine Univ., L.L.D. 1976; Eastern Mich. Univ., D.Ed. 1982; Southern Ill. Univ., L.H.D. 1982; Simon Fraser Univ., LL.D. 1983; Bank Street Coll. L.H.D. 1984; Niagara Univ., L.H.D. 1989; State Univ. of New York, Coll. at Brockport, L.H.D. 1991; Miami Univ., L.H.D. 1991; Univ. of Manitoba, LL.D. 1992; Montclair State Coll., Litt. D. 1992; Linfield College L.H.D. 1993; m. Evalene M. d. Harry and Edith Pearson 23 Aug. 1945; children: Stephen John, Mary Paula; PROF. OF EDUC., UNIV. OF WASHINGTON 1985– ; Prof. of Educ., Univ. of California, Los Angeles 1960–85 and Dean Grad. Sch. of Educ. there 1967–83; also Dir., Univ. Elem. Sch. of Univ. 1960–84; Distinguished Visiting Prof., Brigham Young Univ. 1983–85; Dir., Research Div. Inst. for Devel. of Educ. Activities Inc. 1966–82; former Teacher and Princ., Surrey Schs., B.C.; Past Dir. of Educ. Prov. Indust. Sch. for (Delinquent) Boys, B.C.; Consultant in Curriculum, Atlanta (Ga.) Area Teacher Educ. Service, 1947–49; Assoc. Prof., Emory Univ. and Agnes Scott Coll., 1949–50; Dir., Teacher Educ. Program there and Prof. and Dir., Div. of Teacher Educ., Emory Univ., 1950–56; Professor and Dir. Center for Teacher Educ., Univ. of Chicago, 1956–60; Chrmn., Bd. of Dirs., Council for Study of Mankind (Bd. of Dirs. 1965–69); mem., Curriculum Theory Network, Ont. Inst. for Studies in Educ., Toronto; also mem. of numerous bds. and comtes. in field of educ. in U.S. incl. mem. Pres. Task Force on Early Educ. 1966–67 and on Educ. of the Gifted 1967–68; survey participant and educ. consultant to schs. and colls. in most states and consultant to educ. foundations; author: 'Planning and Organizing for Teaching' 1963; 'School Curriculum Reform in the United States' 1964; 'School Curriculum and the Individual' 1966; 'The Changing School Curriculum' 1966; 'The Dynamics of Educational Change' 1975; 'Facing the Future: Issues in Education and Schooling' 1975; 'What Schools Are For' 1979; 'A Place Called School' 1984; 'Teachers for Our Nation's Schools' 1990; 'Educational Renewal: Better Teachers, Better Schools' 1994; co-author: 'The Elementary School' 1956; 'Educational Leadership and the Elementary School Principal' 1956; 'The Nongraded Elementary School' 1959, revised ed. 1963 and 1987; 'Computers and Information Systems in Education' 1966; 'The Development of a Conceptual System for Dealing with Problems of Curriculum and Instruction' 1966; 'Behind the Classroom Door' 1970; 'Early Schooling in the United States' 1973; 'Early Schooling in England & Israel' 1973; 'Toward a Mankind School: An Adventure in Humanistic Education' 1974; 'The Conventional and the Alternative in Education' 1975; 'Curriculum Inquiry: The Study of Curriculum Practice' 1979; ed., 'The Changing American School' 1966; 'The Ecology of School Renewal' 1987; co-ed.: 'The Elementary School in the United States' 1973; 'Individual Differences and the Common Curriculum' 1983; 'School-University Partnerships in Action' 1988; 'The Moral Dimensions of Teaching' 1990; 'Access to Knowledge: An Agenda for Our Nation's Schools' 1990; 'Places Where Teachers Are Taught' 1990; 'Integrating General and Special Education' 1992; Chrmn. Ed. Adv. Bd. 'New Standard Encyclopedia' since 1953; mem. Ed. Adv. Bd. 'Child's World'; 'The Education Digest'; Editorial consultant, 'Journ. of Curriculum Studies' Univ. of Birmingham (Engl.); mem. Ed. Bd. 'The Educational Forum' 1969–71; 'Internat. Review of Education' 1972–79; past mem. of numerous other ed. bds. of prof. journs.; other writings incl. chapters and papers in over 80 books and yearbooks, numerous articles in prof. journs. and encyclopedias: Kappa Phi Kappa Fellow 1946–47; Ford Foundation Fellow 1952–53; Fellow, Internat. Inst. Arts & Letters; Charter mem., Nat.

Acad. Educ., Sec.-Treas. 1972–5; Past Pres. (1962–63) Nat. Soc. Coll. Teachers of Educ.; Am. Educ. Research Assn. (1967–68); Past Pres., Am. Assn. of Colleges for Teacher Educ. 1989–90; mem. Gov. Bd., UNESCO Instit. for Educ., Hamburg, Germany 1968–79; Chrmn. Prof. Advis. Council, Internat. Learning Cooperative, Oslo, Norway 1978–86; Teachers Coll., Columbia Univ., Distinguished Service Medal 1983; Office: Coll. of Education, DQ 12, Univ. of Washington, Seattle, WA 98195.

**GOODMAN, Hon. Allan,** B.A.; b. Hamilton, Ont. 22 Feb. 1921; s. Samuel and Fanny (Swircz) G.; e. Delta Coll. Inst., Hamilton 1937; McMaster Univ. B.A. 1940; Osgoode Hall Law Sch.; Gold Medalist, Osgoode Hall, 1943; m. Rhoda Katzman 24 Dec. 1950; children: Frances, Susanne, Daniel; JUSTICE SUPREME COURT OF ONT. 1973; apptd. to Court of Appeal, Ont. 1979; called to the Bar of Ont. 1944, cr. Q.C. 1963; Sr. Partner, Goodman, Gowan and Fleury, Welland, Ont. 1946–73; Ald., City of Welland 1953–60, Water Commr. 1961–66, Chrmn., Bd. of Water Commrs. 1964–65; served in R.C.A.F. 1943–45; mem. Candn. Bar Assn.; Jewish; Home: 33 Protea Gardens, Willowdale, Ont. M2L 1T4; Office: Osgoode Hall, Toronto, Ont. M5H 2N5.

**GOODMAN, Edwin A.,** O.C., Q.C., D.U., B.A.; b. Toronto, Ont. 1918; s. David Bertram and Dorothy (Soble) G.; e. Harbord Coll. Inst., Toronto, Ont.; Univ. of Toronto (Hon. Law) B.A.; Osgoode Hall Law Sch., Toronto, Ont.; m. Suzanne Dorothy, d. late Selig Gross, 21 Dec. 1953; two d. Joanne Ruth (dec.), Diane Selena; PARTNER, GOODMAN & GOODMAN, Estbd. 1917; Hon. Dir., John Labatt Ltd.; Dir., Brascan Ltd.; Central Capital Corp.; BGH Central Investment Management Ltd.; Central Guaranty Trustco Ltd.; Stelworth Investments Ltd.; Suvretta Entertainments Ltd.; Chrmn. Emeritus, Bd. of Trustees, Royal Ont. Museum; Trustee, Quetico Found.; Dir., The Edward Dunlop Foundn.; Past Pres. and Dir., National Ballet Guild of Canada; Trustee, Ont. Jockey Club; Past Dir., Shaw Festival; Hon. Counsel, Baycrest Geriatric Hosp.; Past President, Toronto Chapter, Canadian Friends of the Hebrew Univ.; Dir., Toronto Y.M.H.A.; New Mount Sinai Hosp.; Hon. Pres., Boy Scouts of Gter. Toronto; Past Pres., Univ. Coll. Alumni Assn. of Univ. of Toronto; P. Cons. Cand. in St. Andrew's Riding, Toronto, Prov. g.e. 1945; former Chrmn. of Organ. and Vice Pres. of P. Conservative Party of Canada; Former Vice Pres. of P. Conservative Party of Ont.; Former Chairman of Comte. for an Independent Canada; read law with David B. Goodman, Q.C.; called to the Bar of Ont., June 1947; cr. Q.C. Dec. 1954; Life Bencher, Law Soc. of Upper Can.; mem., Candn. Bar Assn. (mem. of Council); served in 2nd World War on active service 1940–45: Major, Fort Garry Horse; twice wounded in N.W. Europe; Mentioned in Despatches; Past Pres., Gen. Wingate Chapter, Royal Candn. Legion; Officer, Order of Canada; Doctor of the Univ. (hon. causa), Univ. of Ottawa; Tau Epsilon Rho; Pi Lambda Phi (Rex); P. Conservative; Hebrew; recreations: tennis, riding; Clubs: Queen's; Empire; Albany; Primrose; Home: 402 Glenayr Road, Toronto, Ont. M5P 3C7; Office: Suite 2400, 250 Yonge St., P.O. Box 24, Toronto, Ont. M5B 2M6.

**GOODMAN, Evelyn,** B.A.; fashion industry executive; b. Toronto, Ont. 2 Jan. 1929; d. Jack and Sonia Louise (Rodd) Lipton; e. Univ. of Toronto, B.A. 1950; m. Marvin s. S. Goodman 29 June 1949; children: Stephen, Barbara; CO-FOUNDER, MERCHANDISER & PRES., LIPTONS INTERNAT. LIMITED; Dir., Ont. Devel. Bd.; Festival of Fashion; recreations: bicycling, hiking, reading, arts (music, literature, theatre); club: Primrose; Home: 57 Old Park Rd., Toronto, Ont.; Office: 29 Connell Court, Toronto, Ont. M8Z 5T7.

**GOODMAN, Jeffrey Mark,** B.A.; corporate communications executive; b. Toronto, Ont. 21 March 1952; s. Sidney and Mary (Rotman) G.; e. Forest Hill Coll. Inst. 1971; York Univ. B.A. 1974; m. Ruth Nash 10 Aug. 1976; children: Jordan Matthew, Michele Caryn; PRES. & C.E.O., GOODMAN COMMUNICATIONS INC. 1986– ; Reporter, Columnist, Feature Writer 'The Globe and Mail' 1973–80; Sr. Communications Adv. to Prime Min. of Can. 1980–82; Vice Pres. Corporate Affairs RJR-Macdonald Inc. 1982–85; Prin. Communications Adv. to Mr. Charles R. Bronfman 1985–86; mem. Nat. Adv. Council on Fitness & Amateur Sports 1983; mem. Dean's Adv. Council Faculty Mgmt. Studies Univ. of Toronto 1988–89; author 'Huddling Up: The Inside Story of the Canadian Football League' 1981, soft cover 1982 (non-fiction); Liberal; recreations: reading, baseball, art, tennis; club: Bayview Golf & Country; Office: 160 Bloor St. E., Toronto, Ont. M4W 1B9.

**GOODMAN, Marvin;** retail executive; venture capitalist; b. Toronto, Ont. 22 May 1925; s. Samuel and Tobe G.; e. Harbord, C.I. 1945; Univ. of West. Ont. 1948; m. Evelyn P. d. Jack Lipton June 1949; children: Stephen, Barbara; CHRMN. & CHIEF EXTVE. OFFR., LIPTONS INTERNATIONAL LTD. 1984– ; Co-founder 1950; Dir., Kee Group Inc.; Pres., Marvin Goodman Holdings; Barstev Developments Inc.; Barstev Holdings; GrandQuantum Inc.; Matarra Ltd.; Marvin Fin. Corp.; Masae Ltd.; Fashion Can.; recreations: bicycling, swimming, theatre; Clubs: Island Yacht; Primrose; B'nai B'rith-Masons; Home: 57 Old Park Rd., Toronto, Ont. M6B 3E5; Office: 29 Connell Ct., #2, Toronto, Ont. M8Z 5T7.

**GOODMAN, Ned,** B.Sc., M.B.A., C.F.A.; investment counsel; b. Montréal, Qué. 8 Nov. 1937; e. McGill Univ. B.Sc. 1960; Univ. of Toronto M.B.A. 1962; Univ. of Va. C.F.A. 1967; m. Anita Silver 18 Oct. 1960; four children: Jonathan, David, Mark, Daniel; CHRMN. AND CHIEF EXEC. OFFR., GOODMAN & COMPANY, Investment Counsel; Chrmn. & Chief Exec. Offr., Dundee Bancorp Inc.; Dynamic Fund Management Ltd.; Dir., BGR Precious Metals Inc.; The Dynamic Group of Mutual Funds; Securities Analyst, Portfolio Mgmt., Edper Investments 1962–67; Dir. and Co-founding Partner, Beutel, Goodman & Co. Ltd. 1967–90; Gov., Trent Univ. Peterborough; Pres., Candn. Counc. of Christians and Jews; Dir., Jr. Achievement of Can.; recreations: squash, tennis, skiing; Club: Cambridge; Office: 6 Adelaide St E., Toronto, Ont. M5C 1H6.

**GOODMAN, Paul Gene,** B.Comm., FCA; chartered accountant; insolvency specialist; b. New Glasgow, N.S. 30 July 1946; s. Hyman J. and Mary (Levitin) G.; e. New Glasgow H.S.; Saint Mary's Univ. B.Comm. 1969; Inst. of C.A.s of N.S., C.A. 1973; Trustee in Bankruptcy 1977; m. Mary d. Joe and Ellen Hodgins 5 Oct. 1972; one s.: Joel Harry; PARTNER, PEAT MARWICK THORNE 1980– ; joined Thorne Gunn 1969; Supvr., Thorne Riddell 1975; Manager 1977; Partner 1980; Vice-Pres., Thorne Riddell Inc. 1980; Extve. Vice-Pres. & Dir. 1984; Thorne Ernst & Whinney Inc. 1986; Sr. Vice Pres., Peat Marwick Thorne Inc. 1989, Mem. Partnership Bd. 1991–93; Teacher, Saint Mary's Univ. and Tech. Univ. of N.S.; Dir., N.S. Special Olympics; Treas., N.S. Special Olympics Summer Games 1984–92; Treas., Candn. Special Olympics 1994 Summer Games Soc.; Extve. Mem., Saint Mary's Alumni Assn.; Bd. of Gov. and Extve. Ctte., Saint Mary's Univ.; Mem. Counc., Inst. of C.A.s of N.S. 1981–90 (Sec. 1981–82, 1986–87; Treas. 1987–88; Vice-Pres. 1988–89; Pres. 1989–90); Mem., Bd. of Govs., CICA 1989–90; Candn. Insolvency Practitioners Assn. (Sec. 1982–88, 1987–88; Mem. of Counc. 1979–85, 1987–88); Candn. Rep., Counc. Insol International 1989–93; Mem., Superintendents Joint Ctte. on Bankruptcy 1985–88; N.S. Insolvency Assn. (Extve. 1979–89); Insolvency Inst. of Can.; Candn. Progress Club of Halifax (Past Pres. & Past Zone Gov.); author of num. papers presented to various orgns.; recreations: boating, curling, hockey (Coach, Halifax Minor Hockey); Clubs: Halifax; Waegwoltic; Saint Mary's Varsity; Home: 940 Robie St., Halifax, N.S. B3H 3C4; Office: Ste. 1505, Purdy's Wharf Tower I, 1959 Upper Water St., Halifax, N.S. B3J 3N2.

**GOODRIDGE, The Hon. Noel Herbert Alan,** B.A., LL.B.; judge; b. St. John's, Nfld. 18 Dec. 1930; s. William Prout and Freda Dorothy (Hayward) G.; e. Rockford Sch., Bishop Feild Coll., St. John's, Nfld.; King's Coll. Sch. Windsor, N.S.; Bishop's Coll. Sch. Lennoxville, Que.; Dalhousie Univ. B.A. 1951, LL.B. 1953; m. Isabelle Galway, 23 April 1956; four children, Alan, William, Douglas, Maria; apptd. CHIEF JUSTICE OF NFLD. Nov. 17, 1986; apptd. mem. of the Trial Div., Supreme Court of Nfld. Nov. 14, 1975; Justice of the Court. Martial Appeal Court of Can. July 22 1981; mem., Candn. Judicial Counc. and Candn. Judges Conf.; called to Bar of Nfld. 1953; Q.C. 1974; practiced law with Stirling Ryan and Goodridge; Past Gov. and Life mem. Kinsmen Clubs Can.; Past Councillor, Nfld. Bd. Trade; Past Secy. Nfld. Law Soc.; Past exec. mem., Nfld. Assn. Help Retarded Children; past. exec. mem. Candn. Bar Assn. (Past Pres. Nfld. Br.); Past Chrmn., St. John's Transportation Commission; Past Vice-Chrmn., Gen. Hosp. Corp.; Can. Bar Assoc.; Candn. Judges Conf.; Zeta Psi; Anglican; recreations: golf, tennis, skiing, bridge, walking; Home: 71 Rennies Mill Rd., St. John's, Nfld. A1C 3P9; Office: P.O. Box 937, St. John's, Nfld. A1C 5M3.

**GOODWILL, Dan Z.,** B.A., M.B.A.; transportation executive; b. Montreal, Que. 7 Oct. 1946; s. Leon and Ethel G.; e. McGill Univ. B.A. (Hons.) 1967; McMaster Univ. M.B.A. 1969, cert. of proficiency in French 1975; m. Gail d. Manuel Leder 23 June 1991; VICE-PRES., EASTERN REGION, CLARKE TRANSPORT 1990– ; Sales Rep., Product Mgr., Supvr., Mktg. Rsch. & Supvr., Long-Term Planning to Staff Supvr., Product Mngt. & Dir., Marketing, Ont. Region, Bell Canada 1969–82; Dir. of Sales & later Vice-Pres., Sales, TNT Overland Express 1982–85; Gen. Mgr., TNT Railfast 1985–90 (firm sold to Clarke Transport 1990); Past Pres., Candn. Pool Car Operators Assn.; past lectr., Concordia Univ.; recreations: jogging, tennis, skiing; Home: 105 Hillhurst Blvd., Toronto, Ont. M5N 1N7; Office: P.O. Box 32, Bowes Rd., Concord, Ont. L4K 1B2.

**GOODWIN, Betty;** artist; b. Montreal, Que. 19 May 1923; d. Abraham and Claire Edith (Rudich) Roodish; m. Martin s. Saul and Gertrude Goodwin 30 Apl. 1945; one s. Paul (dec. 1976); solo exhns. incl. Penthouse Gallery Montreal 1962; Galerie Pascal Toronto 1971; Bau-XI Gallery Vancouver 1972; Galerie B Montreal 1974; 'Betty Goodwin 1969–76' Musée d'art contemporain Montreal 1976; Galerie France Morin Montreal 1981, 1982 (Betty Goodwin Works on Paper 1963–1982), 1983 (Recent Drawings from 'Swimmers' series Part II); Univ. of Vt. 1984; Sable-Castelli Gallery Toronto 1985, 1987, 1988, 1989, 1991, 1993; Concordia (Univ.) Art Gallery 1986; Galerie René Blouin Montreal 1986, 1989, 1990, 1991, 1992, 1993; 'Betty Goodwin Works 1971–1987' Art Gallery of Ont., Vancouver Art Gallery, New Museum N.Y., 1987; 49th Parallel N.Y. 1988; Musée des Beaux-Arts Montreal 1988; Kunstmuseum Bern 1989; Sao Paulo Biennale 1989; Edmonton Art Gallery 1990; 'Centric 46: Betty Goodwin' University Art Museum, Long Beach, C.A. 1992; rep. numerous nat. and internat. group exhns. since 1955 incl. Brit. Internat. Print Show (3), 9th Internat. Biennial Exhn. Prints Tokyo, Internat. Exhn. Graphic Art Yugoslavia, Bologna Art Fair, Nat. Gallery Can., Akademie der Kunste W. Berlin, Art Cologne, Museum Van Hedendaagse Kunst Gent, Belgium, 20th Internat. Biennial at São Paulo, Brazil; Rose Art Museum, Mass.; Musée du Québec; Musée d'art contemporain de Montréal; rep. various pub. and corporate colls. incl. Nat. Gallery Can., Art Gallery Ont., Musée du Québec, Vancouver Art Gallery, Nat. Museum Women in the Arts Washington, D.C., Musée des beaux-arts de Berne; private colls. Can. and USA; recipient Lynch-Stauton Award of Distinction 1983; Banff Centre Nat. Award Visual Arts 1984; Prix Borduas 1986; Guggenheim Found. Fellowship 1988; Docteur (honoris causa), Université de Montréal 1992; Fellowship at Ont. College of Art, Toronto 1993; Doctorate (honoris causa) Guelph Univ. 1993; cited numerous nat. and internat. catalogues; recreations: friends, travel, reading, films; Address: 4270 Coloniale Ave., Montreal, Que. H2W 2C4.

**GOOLD, Susan Rae;** artist; b. San Diego, Calif. 11 Aug. 1939 (Candn. citizen); d. Harold Raymond and Laburna Jean (Mackenzie) Foottit; e. Ottawa Teachers' College 1959; Univ. of B.C.; Ottawa Sch. of Art; m. David s. Nyda and Ralph Goold 16 July 1960; children: Donna, Jeffrey, Karen; art instructor 1980– ; num. group exbns since 1973, most recent: Ottawa Watercolour Soc. 27th Juried Exbn & fall Show, Gallery on the Lake, Buckhorn, Ont. 1993; 4 solo exbns Ottawa area1984–92; subject of TV program 'Germotte Studio' CKWS Kingston 1990; rep. by Raymer Gallery Nepean and Gallery on the Lake Buckhorn; 3 paintings hang perm. at Queensway Carleton Hosp.; Partnership with 'Friends by Design' for 'Petals' (designs by Susan Goold) 1993; Watercolour Teacher, Buckhorn Sch. of Fine Art 1992, '93; Art Cons., Parkview Gall. 1985–90; num. awards since 1977, most recent: 1993 cover design, Kanata Parks & Rec. Fall Brochure; Ont. Volunteer Serv. Award 1989; Volunteer Recognition Cert., City of Kanata 1993; Bd. of Dir., Kanata Civic Art Gall. (Founding Mem. 1992); Treas., Ottawa Watercolour Soc. 1992, '93; Pres., Art Lending of Ottawa 1991; Fellow, Ottawa Watercolour Soc. 1985; recreations: cottaging; clubs: Kanata Art Club, Bells Corner Art League, Manotick Art Assn.; Home: 8 Carr Cres., Kanata, Ont. K2K 1K4.

**GORDON, Alison Ruth;** writer; b. New York, N.Y. 19 Jan. 1943; d. the late (John) King and Ruth (Anderson) G.; e. Queen's Univ. 1960–65; m. Paul s. Avie and Beverly Bennett 2 Oct. 1982; Prog. Asst., 'The Way It Is,' CBC TV 1968; Prod., CJOH-Ottawa 1969–70 (freelance – 74); Host, 'Here Today,' CBC Halifax 1974 (freelance – 76); Prod., 'As It Happens,' CBC Radio 1976–78; Sportswriter, The Toronto Star 1979–85 (1979–83 covered baseball); Runner-up, Nat. Mag. Awards, Humour 1978 for 'Margaret's Diary' in Weekend Magazine; Citation of Merit, Sportswriting, Nat. Newspaper Awards 1979; author: 'Foul Balls' 1984, 'The Dead Pull Hitter' 1988; 'Safe at Home' 1990; 'Night Game' 1992; mem., Pres., The Candn. Centre, Internat. PEN; North Am. Vice-Pres., Internat. Assoc. of Crime Writers; recreations: reading, bird watching, gardening, baseball; Home: 58 Playter Blvd., Toronto, Ont. M4K 2W3.

**GORDON, Donald Harold,** B.A., LL.B.; logistics management services executive, lawyer; b. Thunder Bay, Ont. 28 June 1940; s. Asbjorn H. and Aileen M. (Luthala) G.; e. Queen's Univ. B.A. 1962, LL.B. 1965 (Gold Medallist); Osgoode Hall Law Soc., Bar Admission Course 1966–67; called to Bar Apr. 1967; Univ. of Western Ont., Mngt. Training Course 1975; m. Ann d. Charles and Dorothy Parish 20 June 1964; children: Julie Ann, Michael John; PRES. & CHIEF EXTVE. OFFR., LIVINGSTON GROUP INC. 1987– ; Associate, Ivey & Dowler (London, Ont.) 1967–70; Partner 1971–74; Vice Pres. & Sec., Ivest Corp. 1974–78; Vice Pres., Corp. Devel. 1979–80; Extve. Vice Pres. 1980–87; Acting Pres., present firm 1986–87; Dir., Livingston Group Inc. former dir. of 6 companies; Lectr., Securities Law, Univ. of West. Ont. Law Sch. 1972–73; Founding Mem., London Fitness Found. 1975; Governor, Etobicoke Gen. Hosp. 1989–; Founding Mem. & Dir., Canada-U.S. Business Assn. 1989– , Chrmn. 1991– ; several previous non-business directorships & positions; Mem., Metro. Toronto Bd. of Trade; Candn. Assn. of Logistics Mngt.; Counc. of Logistics Mngt.; Candn. Bar Assn.; Assn. for Corp. Growth (Toronto Chap.); Western Bus. Sch. Club of Toronto; Law Soc. of U.C.; The Bus. Counc. on Nat. Issues; recreations: golf, skiing, photography, flying & boating; clubs: London, London Hunt & Country, Port Credit Yacht; Home: 7 Windrush Rd., Kleinburg, Ont. L0J 1C0; Office: 405 The West Mall, Toronto, Ont. M9C 5K7.

**GORDON, Harold P.,** B.Comm., B.A., B.C.L., Q.C.; lawyer; b. Montreal, Que. 19 Apr. 1937; s. Isaac and Rebecca (Bregman) G; e. McGill Univ. B.Comm. 1958; Sir George Williams Univ. B.A. 1961; McGill Univ. B.C.L. 1964; PARTNER, STIKEMAN, ELLIOTT 1975– ; Directorships: Alliance Communications Corp.; Anglo American Clays Ltd.; Ariola-Eurodisc Inc.; Auscan Closures Canada Inc.; BMG Music Publishing Canada Inc.; BMG Music Canada Inc.; Burns, Philp Canada Inc.; Burns Philp Closures Canada Inc.; Casimcan Holdings Inc.; DWS/Hines Holdings Ltd.; Dersingham Holdings Ltd.; Doubleday Canada Limited; Fleischmann's Yeast Ltd.; Fondation pour l'Etude et la Recherche sur le Federalisme Canadien; Fonorola Inc.; G.T.C. Transcontinental Group Ltd.; Hasbro Inc.; Hayes Microcomputer Products (Canada) Limited; Henry J. Kaiser Co. (Can.) Ltd.; The Jeanne Sauvé Youth Found.; Kleinwort Benson (Canada) Limited; LIG Canada Inc.; Lombard Odier Trust Company; Louis Dreyfus Canada Ltd.; Luxottica Canada Inc.; Regentor IC Holdings Inc.; Rentokil (Canada) Limited; Rotorcraft Atlantic Inc.; Toyoda Gosei Holdings Co. Ltd.; Warburg Asset Management Canada Ltd.; Waterville (TG) Inc.; Canadian Guild of Crafts, Que.; Hon. Dir., Centaur Theatre Co.; Mem.: Que. Bar Assn.; Yukon Bar; Que. Bar Found.; Candn. Bar Assn.; Internat. Bar Assn.; Internat. Fiscal Assn.; Inst. of Corporate Directors in Can.; Assoc. of Am. Bar Association; Candn. Inst. for Administration of Justice; Home: 345 Redfern, Westmount, Que. H3Z 2G4; Office: 1155 René Levesque Blvd. W., Suite 3900, Montreal, Que. H3B 3V2.

**GORDON, Howard Scott,** B.A., A.M., Ph.D.; university professor; b. Halifax, N.S. 14 Aug. 1924; s. Ely and Dorothy (Shabbes) G.; e. Dalhousie Univ., B.A. 1944; Columbia Univ., A.M. 1947; McGill Univ., Ph.D. 1964; Cambridge Univ., 1954–55; m. Barbara, d. late William Rowe, Coaticook, Que., 27 Aug. 1945; children: Geoffrey William, Paul Maxwell Ivan, James Marshall; PROF. OF ECON., INDIANA UNIV. 1966– ; Distinguished Professor 1981–89; jointly, Distinguished Prof. of Econ. and Prof. of the History and Philos. of Science 1984–89; Distinguished Prof. Emeritus since 1989; Prof. of Econ., Queen's Univ., Kingston 1970–89, Adjunct Prof. since 1989; Lectr., McGill Univ., 1947–48; Asst. Prof., Carleton Univ., 1948–53, Assoc. Prof. 1953–57, Prof. 1957–66; Visiting Prof., Univ. of Chicago, 1956–57; Guggenheim Foundation Fellow, 1965; LL.D., Carleton Univ. 1992; Pres., Candn. Economics Assn. 1976–77; Pres., Western Economics Assn. 1976–77; Home: 314 Arbutus Ave., Bloomington, Ind. 47401.

**GORDON, Hugh Allan,** B.A., C.A., R.M.C.; chartered accountant; b. Winnipeg, Man. 10 Feb. 1942; s. William Gilbert and Helen Hughena (McNairnay) G.; e. Royal Military College of Canada B.A. (Hons.) 1965; C.A. Alta. 1974; m. Elisabeth d. Joseph and Cynthia Flint 23 Apr. 1988; children: Victoria Jean, Allison Leigh; TAX PARTNER, THORNE RIDDELL, THORNE ERNST & WHINNEY, PEAT MARWICK THORNE 1978– ; Officer, Royal Candn. Corps of Signals, Canada and Germany 1965–71; Student in accounts, supvr. & mgr., Thorne Riddell Calgary 1971–78; National Dir. of

Tax, Thorne Riddell 1984–85; Chair, National Tax Ctte., Thorne Ernst & Whinney 1986–88; National Tax Ctte., Peat Marwick Thorne 1986–93; Comn. to review indus. property taxation for B.C. Govt. 1985; Ctte. to Privatize a B.C. Crown Corp. 1987; Consultant to govt. on various revenue & other strategic issues; Nisga'a Land Claim Negotiations, Govt. of B.C. 1992– ; Lecturer, Income Tax Practice Course, Candn. Inst. of C.A.s 1980– ; Mem., Candn. Tax Found.; Chair, Greater Victoria Econ. Devel. Comn.; Mem., Arts Comn. of Greater Victoria; Dir., B.C. & Yukon Council, The Duke of Edinburgh's Award in Canada 1993– ; author of various papers on taxation presented at national and regional confs., Candn. Tax Found.; recreations: boating, tennis; clubs: Union Club of B.C.; Home: 8833 Forest Park Dr., Sidney, B.C. V8L 4E8; Office: 3rd floor, 707 Fort St., Victoria, B.C. V8W 3G3.

**GORDON, J. Lindsay,** B.A., M.B.A.; banking executive; b. Shetland Islands, U.K. 26 March 1952; s. George and Rosemary G.; e. Univ. of B.C. B.A. 1973, M.B.A. 1976; m. Elizabeth d. Bill and Alena Ross 22 June 1974; children: Katherine, Ian, Alexandra, Andrew; SENIOR VICE-PRES., HONGKONG BANK OF CANADA 1987– ; T.D. Bank 1973–74; Export Devel. Corp. 1976–87; Office: 885 W. Georgia St., Vancouver, B.C. V6C 3E9.

**GORDON, John Mitchell,** B.Sc., P.Eng.; mining executive; b. Sydney, N.S. 31 Oct. 1929; s. Harold Cowan Morton and Dorothy Elizabeth (Ross) G.; e. Westville (N.S.) Pub. and High Schs. and Argyle Pub. Sch. Sydney, N.S. (1941–42) 1946; Queen's Univ. B.Sc. (Mining) 1952; m. Irene Meriam d. late John Nieminen 16 May 1959; children: Dorothy Lynn, Stephen Harold; Extve. Vice Pres., Mining Opns., Noranda Minerals Inc. 1991–92, retired; Pres. and Dir., Brenda Mines Ltd.; Mattabi Mines Limited; Vice Pres. & Dir., Hemlo Gold Mines Inc.; Dir., Sask. Potash Producers Assn., Inc.; Canpotex Limited; Ont. Mining Assn.; Potash and Phosphate Inst.; Mining Industry Technology Counc. of Can. (MITEC); Westmin Resources Ltd.; Chrmn., John T. Ryan Trophies Comte. (CIM); MRD Mining Research Directorate Inc.; Mining Engr. Dominion Steel and Coal Corp. 1952–56 (Nova Scotian Coal Mines 1952–54 and 1956, on loan to Nat. Coal Bd. Eng. 1955); Mine Supvr. Horne Mine, Noranda Mines, Noranda, Que. 1956–58; Mine Supt. Hallnor Mines Ltd. Timmins, Ont. 1959–62, Mine Mgr. 1962–65; Mine Mgr. Aunor Gold Mines Ltd. Timmins 1965–67; Mine Supt. Potash Div. Noranda Mines Ltd. Saskatoon 1967–70; Gen. Supt. Central Canada Potash, Saskatoon 1970–71, Mine Mgr. 1971–76; Gen. Mgr. Mines, Noranda Mines Ltd. 1976; Vice Pres., Mines, Central Can. 1981; Group Vice Pres., Noranda Inc. 1982–86; Vice Pres., Noranda Minerals Inc., Sr. Vice Pres. 1986–90; mem. Assn. Prof. Engrs. Prov. Ont.; Candn. Inst. Mining & Metall.; Club: The Ontario; recreations: tennis, swimming, skiing, reading, gardening; Home: 1346 Ravine Dr., Mississauga, Ont. L5J 3E5.

**GORDON, John Peter George,** OC, B.Sc., LL.D., P.Eng.; engineer, steel executive; b. Toronto, Ont. 14 Nov. 1920; s. Peter William and Lolita (Craig) G.; e. Univ. of Toronto B.Sc. 1943; Harvard Univ. 49th AMP 1966; m. Muriel Joan d. Wm. James MacPherson 24 Sept. 1943; children: Peter Douglas and Susan Alexandra; joined RCEME May 1942 (served in Canada, U.K. & N.W.E.; discharged as Captain March 1946); joined Steel Co. of Canada & worked in engr. & operating divisions as expeditor, foreman & gen. foreman; Asst. Supt. 1956; Supt. of Cold Mills, Tin Mills & Galvanizing depts. 1961; Gen. Supt., Flat Roll Div. 1964; Vice-Pres., Finishing Plants 1964; Vice-Pres., Opns. 1966; Sr. Vice-Pres. 1970; Dir. 1970; Pres. 1971; Chief Extve. Offr. 1973; Chrmn. 1976; retired as chairman 1985; Dir., Stelco; Loram Group; Interam Holdings; Alumni Bd. of Harvard Business School; retired Dir., Bank of Montreal; Inco; Encor CGE; Fed. Indus.; Molson Cos.; Canada Systems; Northern Telecom; Gulf Canada; Gulf Oil Corp. (Pittsburgh); Sun Life Assur.; BCE; Bell Canada; RKW; Hon. Dir., Molson Companies; Inco Ltd.; Past Chrmn., McMaster Univ.; retired Vice-Chrmn., BCNI & Wellesley Hosp.; Winner, Fairless Award AIMM&PE; elected Distinguished Life Mem., ASME; Gold Medal, Am. Soc. of Mfg. Engrs.; Distinguished Alumnae Medal, Univ. of Toronto; Elected to the Univ. of Toronto's 'Engineering Hall of Distinction' 1991; LL.D.s from York & McMaster univs.; recreations: golf, curling; clubs: Hamilton, Hamilton Golf & Country, Tamahaac, Mississauga Golf & Country; Home: 'Stone Crest,' 1343 Blythe Rd., Mississauga, Ont. L5H 2C2.

**GORDON, John R.M.,** B.A.Sc., M.B.A., Ph.D.; educator; b. Toronto, Ont. 3 Feb. 1935; s. late Russell Charles Gordon; e. Trinity Coll. Sch. Port Hope, Ont. 1953; Univ. of B.C. B.A.Sc. 1958; Queen's Univ. M.B.A. 1963; Mass. Inst. Technol. Ph.D. 1966; m. Virginia d. late Walter E. Huckvale, Lethbridge, Alta. 3 Jan. 1959; children: Jane, Charles, Ian; ALCAN/NSERC/SSHRC CHAIR IN MANAGEMENT AND TECHNOLOGY 1991– ; and PROF., SCH. OF BUSINESS, QUEEN'S UNIV. 1978– ; Dean 1978–88; Visiting Prof. of Mgmt., Grad. Sch. of Business, Stanford, Univ., Stanford, Calif. 1988–89; mem. Adv. Comte. Institut pour l'Etude des Methodes de Direction de l'Enterprise, Lausanne, Switzerland 1976–89, Chrmn. MBA Program 1973–75, Dir. of Research 1973–74, Prof. 1970–75; Past Chrmn. Can. Fed. of Deans of Mang. & Adm. Studies; Dir. KGH Found.; Can. Labour Market & Productivity Centre; Lectr. in Mech. Engn. Royal Mil. Coll. 1959–63; Lectr. Sloan Sch. of Mang. Mass. Inst. Technol. 1965–66; Asst. Prof. Sch. of Business Adm. Univ. of W. Ont. 1966–68, Assoc. Prof. 1968–73, Dir. Production/Operations Mang. Course 1970–72, Chrmn. Undergrad. Program in Business Adm. 1968–69; Assoc. Prof. Sch. of Business Queen's Univ. 1975–78, Chrmn. Continuing Educ. 1976–78, Dir. Small Business Consulting Program 1976–78; Drug Pricing Comnr. Prov. of Ont. 1984; Chrmn., Fee Negotiating Ctte. (Ont. Min. of Health/Ont. Pharmacists Assoc.) 1987; Gov., Inst. of Cndn. Bankers (ICB) 1981–88; Pilot Offr. Aircrew Training RCAF 1954–57; Design Offr. Canadian Pacific Airlines Repairs Ltd. Calgary 1957; Engn. Offr. Dept. Nat. Defence Ottawa 1958–59; Gen. Mgr. Vicom Ltd. Kingston 1976–77; rec'd various research grants and fellowships incl. Ford Foundation Doctoral Fellowship 1963–66; consulting and seminar mang. devel. activities various univ., govt. and business programs; author various publs.; mem. Inst. Mgmt. Sciences; Am. Inst. Indust. Engrs.; Am. Inst. Decisions Sciences; Acad. Mgmt.; Candn. Assn. Adm. Studies; Am. Production & Inventory Control Soc.; Kingston Branch Adv. Bd., Royal Trust; Dir. Junior Achievement (Kingston & Dist.); P. Conservative; Anglican; recreations: tennis, skiing, sailing; Club: Kingston Tennis; Office: Sch. of Business, Queen's Univ., Kingston, Ont. K7L 3N6.

**GORDON, Kenneth Stewart;** business executive; b. Rosetown, Sask. 21 Sept. 1947; s. Stewart Douglas and Mary Elizabeth (Smith) G.; e. Univ. of Sask. B.A. 1969, M.A. 1975; New Sch. for Soc. Rsch. 1975–78; m. Ruth R. d. Samuel and Mary Wolfe 17 Apr. 1972; two sons: Adam Benjamin Wolfe, Eric Geoffrey Wolfe; PRESIDENT, JADE SIMULATIONS INTERNATIONAL CORP. 1993– ; Pres., Precise Systems Corp. 1991– ; Asst. Prof., Univ. of Sask. 1979–82; Visiting Asst. Prof., Univ. of Alta. 1982–84; Pres., Myrias Research Corp. 1983–88, Dir., Business Development 1988–90, Vice-Pres., Corporate Development 1990; Office: 380, One Thornton Court, Edmonton, Alta. T5J 2E7.

**GORDON, L. Lamont,** B.A.; investment banker; b. Harriston, Ont. 29 April 1932; s. Ernest Francis and Katharine Walker (Brown) G.; e. Univ. of Western Ont. B.A. (Hons.) 1955; m. Denise d. Joan and Stylianos Goulimis 31 Dec. 1991; children: Katherine, Deborah, James, Pamela, Jennifer; CHAIRMAN, SPROTT SECURITIES LTD. 1987– ; Dir. & Manager, Equities, Nesbitt Thomson 1957–68; Founder & Pres., Gordon Securities Limited 1969–79; Founder & Chair, Gordon-Lloyd Price Investments Ltd. 1979–87; Dir., Bioniche Inc.; Zoom Telephonics Inc.; T/A Pacific Select Investment; Investment Bankers Cert., Wharton Sch. of Finance 1963; recreations: skiing, tennis, cresta; clubs: St. Moritz Toboganning, Montreal Racket, St. James, Candn. Club of New York; Home: 1177 Yonge St., Suite 402, Toronto, Ont. M4T 2Y4; Office: Suite 2300, Royal Bank Plaza, South Tower, Toronto, Ont. M5J 2J2.

**GORDON, Lorne Bertram,** C.A.; executive; b. Edmonton, Alta. 9 May 1945; children: Joelle, Jason, Kira, Candice; PRESIDENT, C.O.O. AND DIR., LORAM CORP. 1993– ; Dir., Pembina Corp.; Manalta Coal Ltd.; Loram Maintenance of Way Inc.; Vice-Pres. and Gen. Mgr. Mancal Ltd. 1979–85; Pres., C.E.O. & Dir., Pembina Corp. 1985–93; Bd. of Govs., Candn. Assoc. of Petroleum Producers; Dir., The Royfund Group; Dir., Candn. Energy Rsch. Institute; mem. Inst. of Chartered Accts. of Alta.; Inst. of Chartered Accts. of Can.; Home: Box O, Site 6, R.R. 2, Cochrane, Alta. T0L 0W0; Office: P.O. Box 2550, 707 – 8th Ave. S.W., Calgary, Alta. T2P 2M7.

**GORDON, Lynne,** B.A.; broadcaster; actress; b. New York City, N.Y.; d. Louis and Blanche (Lewis) Smith; e. Columbia Univ. B.A. (journalism) 1945; children: Frank, Johanna, Evelyn Faulk; PRIN. LYNNE GORDON MANAGEMENT LTD. 1975– ; Dir. of Communication, Senior Care, Independence for Elderly (non-profit agency) 1988– ; full-time radio and TV broadcaster and actress various radio and TV channels since 1968; Instr., Media Writing, Ryerson Polytech. Inst 1988– ; Lectr. Radio, Television Arts 1986– ; Instructor, Interviewing Skills, Continuing Education, Ryerson Polytech Inst. 1989– ; Ont. Correspond. for CBC TV, 'The 50 Up Show' (national show, formerly 'The Best Years'; cons. in mktg. and merchandising Candn. Exec. Service Orgn.; Chair, Ont. Status Women Council 1976–82; Vice Chrmn. Pension Comn. Ont.; mem. Transit Adv. Group Barker Variety; named Woman of Yr. Ont. Gov. 1975; served Un. Way, Red Cross Soc., Variety Village, Multiple Sclerosis Soc. (Hon. mem.), Juvenile Diabetes Soc.; author (autobiog.) 'Working Without a Net' 1986; 2 consumer handbooks; recreations: tennis, horseback riding, water skiing, acting, travel; Address: 71 McGill St., Toronto, Ont. M5B 1H3.

**GORDON, Michael,** M.B., Ch.B., F.R.C.P.(C), F.A.C.P.; physician; educator; b. New York, N.Y. 7 May 1941; s. Max and Roslyn G.; e. Brooklyn Coll. B.A. 1962; Univ. of St. Andrews, Scot. M.B., Ch.B. 1966; m. Gilda d. Shimon and Naomi Berger 24 Oct. 1982; children: Neta, Amir, Talia, Eytan; VICE PRES., MEDICAL SERVICES, BAYCREST CENTRE FOR GERIATRIC CARE 1992– , Med. Dir. 1989–92; Assoc. Prof. of Med. 1985–93; Prof. of Med., Univ. of Toronto 1993– ; Med. Dir. Baycrest Terrace 1983–89; Head, Div. of Geriatrics, Mount Sinai Hosp. 1985– ; mem. Adv. Bd. Hume Publs.; Mem., Pharmaceutical Inquiry of Ont. 1988–90; internship Aberdeen City Hosp. 1966, Rambam Hosp. Haifa 1967, Boston Univ. Hosp. 1967–68; med. residency Royal Victoria Hosp. Montréal 1968–69; Shaare Zedek Hosp. Jerusalem 1971–73; Resident in Pathol. Hadassah Hosp. Jerusalem 1969–70; Med. Offr. Israel Defence Forces 1970–71; Resident in Nuclear Med. Toronto Gen. Hosp. 1973–74; Chief Med. Resident Mount Sinai Hosp. 1974–75; Staff Phys., Baycrest Centre 1975– ; joined Univ. of Toronto 1975; author 'Old Enough to Feel Better' Med. Guide for Srs. 1981; 'An Ounce of Prevention – The Canadian Guide to a Healthy and Successful Retirement' 1984; Fellow, Am. Geriatrics Soc.; mem. Ont. Med. Assn.; Gerontol. Soc. Am.; Candn. Soc. Geriatric Med.; recreations: music, writing; Home: 62 Appian Dr., Willowdale, Ont. M2J 2P9; Office: 3560 Bathurst St., Toronto, Ont. M6A 2E1.

**GORDON, Myron J.,** M.A., Ph.D., LL.D., F.R.S.C.; educator; b. New York, N.Y. 15 Oct. 1920; s. Joseph G.; e. Univ. of Wis. B.A. 1941; Harvard Univ. M.A. 1947, Ph.D. 1952; m. Helen Elizabeth Taylor 14 March 1945; children: Joseph, David; PROF. OF FINANCE, FACULTY OF MGMT. STUDIES, UNIV. OF TORONTO; served with US Army World War II, rank 2nd Lt.; author 'Finance Investment and Macroeconomics' 1994; 'The Drug Industry: A Case Study in Foreign Control' 1981; 'Accounting: A Management Approach' 6th ed. 1979; 'The Cost of Capital to a Public Utility' 1974; 'The Investment Financing and Valuation of the Corporation' 1962; Pres. Am. Finance Assn. 1975; recreation: tennis; Home: 33 Elmhurst Ave, Apt. #1009, Willowdale, Ont. M2N 6G8; Office: 246 Bloor St. W., Toronto, Ont. M5S 1V4.

**GORDON, Nancy Margaret Thain,** B.A.; public servant; b. Belleville, Ont. 23 Nov. 1939; d. Grant Linn and Catherine Ellis (Burch) Thain; e. Queen's Univ. B.A. (Hons.) 1962, grad. sch. 1962–63; m. Charles William s. J. King and Ruth Gordon 30 Jan. 1965; children: John Grant and Mary Alison; UNIT LEADER, MARKETING & COMMUNICATIONS, CARE CANADA 1992– ; Foreign Serv. Officer, Dept. of External Affairs, Ottawa 1963–65; Political Science Teacher, Brandon Univ. 1965–67; joined Nat. Office, U.N. Assn. in Canada 1976; Extve. Dir. 1977–78; Information Offr., 1980–84; joined newly-created Candn. Inst. for Internat. Peace & Security 1985, Dir. Public Programmes 1986–92; co-author: (with Bernard Wood) Canada and the Reshaping of the United Nations in 'International Journal' 1992; (with Geoffrey Pearson) Shooting Oneself in the Head: The Demise of CIIPS in 'Global Jeopardy Canada Among Nations 1993–1994' 1993; Mem., United Ch.; Home: 2046 Blackfriars Rd., Ottawa, Ont. K2A 3K8; Office: Box 9000, Ottawa, Ont. K1G 4X6.

**GORDON, Philip,** P.Eng.; company director and Industrial Consultant; b. Montreal, Que. 7 Nov. 1917; e. McGill Univ. B.Eng. (Chem. Engn.) 1939; m. Rachel Winer; children: David, Penny; Sr. Vice-Pres., and Dir., Shell Can. Ltd.; (ret. 1977); Dir., Saskferco Products, Inc.; New Grade Energy Inc.; mem. Fed. Gov't Energy Supply Allocation Bd.; Medallist, Brit. Assn. for Advance. Science; Assn. Prof. Eng. Ont.; Club: Donalda; Home: No. 3 Royal Oak Dr., Don Mills, Ont. M3C 2M1.

**GORDON, Robert Alan,** B.A.Sc., P.Eng.; commissioner; b. Toronto, Ont. 28 Aug. 1932; s. Alan and Eveleen (Carson) G.; e. Parkdale Coll. Inst. 1952; Univ. of Toronto B.A.Sc. 1956; m. Joan d. Walter and Norma Nelson 24 May 1957; children: Lynn, Ian; COMNR. (part-time) CANDN. RADIO-TV AND TELECOMMUNICATIONS COMN. 1990– ; joined Treasury Bd. Secretariat Govt. Can. 1969–74; Dir. Gen. Fed.-Prov. Relations Dept. of Communications 1974–76; Exec. Sec. Ctte. on Fed. Ombudsman Privy Council Office 1976–78; Dir. Gen. Edn. Progs. Sec. of State 1978–81; Dir. of Operations Privy Council Office 1981–83; Asst. Dep. Min. of Communications 1983–90; Office: Ottawa, Ont. K1A 0N2.

**GORDON, Robert Douglas,** B.Eng.Sc.; software industry executive; b. Brantford, Ont. 19 May 1946; e. Université Laval B.Eng.Sc. 1969; PRESIDENT AND CHIEF EXECUTIVE OFFICER, ORACLE CORPORATION CANADA INC.; held a variety of systems engineering, sales, marketing & general mngt. positions with IBM, Datapoint, Northern Telecom, Bell Atlantic, Stratus Computer (Can. & Latin Am.) and Oracle Corp.; Oracle is the world's leading supplier of integrated software products and professional services incl. relational database management, development tools, financial, manufacturing, distribution and human resources applications; Mem., Assn. of Prof. Engineers of Ont.; Bd. of Trade of Metro Toronto; Extve. Dir. & Treas., Information Technology Assn. of Canada; Extve. Council, Candn. Business Telecommunications Alliance; Office: 110 Matheson Blvd. W., Mississauga, Ont. L5R 3P4.

**GORDON, Robert Macaire,** B.A., M.A., Ph.D.; university professor; b. Potters Bar, Hertfordshire, Eng. 1 Jan. 1947; s. George Henry and Eva May (Lacey) G.; e. La Trobe Univ., B.A. (Hons.) 1979; Simon Fraser Univ., M.A. 1981; Univ. of B.C., Ph.D. 1988; DIR., UNDERGRADUATE PROGRAMME, SCH. OF CRIMINOLOGY, SIMON FRASER UNIV. 1992– , Assoc. Prof. Sch. of Criminology 1990– ; Staff Mem., Fitzroy Legal Serv. & Tutor in Legal Studies, La Trobe Univ. 1977–79; Rsch. Assoc. & Sess. Instr., Crim. Rsch. Ctr. & Dept. of Crim., Simon Fraser Univ. 1980–84; Asst. Prof., Sch. of Criminology, Simon Fraser Univ. 1985–90; Cons., Yukon Govt. on mental health & adult guardianship law 1984–92; City of Vanc. on elder abuse & neglect & adult guardianship matters 1985–87; Nfld. Govt. on adult guardianship law 1989–92; Min.of Health (B.C.), Mental Health Act Review Ctte. 1991–93; Cons., B.C. Attorney-General 1992– ; B.C. Joint Ctte. on Adult Guardianship 1991–93; Office of the Public Trustee (B.C.) Ctte. on Incapability 1991–93; B.C. Youth Adv. Counc. 1991–92; Commonwealth Scholar 1979–80; Killam Doct. Fellow (U.B.C.) 1983–85; Founding Mem. & Dir., The Lower Mainland Purpose Soc. 1983– ; The Bur-West Opportunity Soc. 1983– ; Mem., Psychology and Law Inst. 1988–91; Mem., Internat. Acad. on Law and Mental Health 1989– ; Mem., Inst. for Mental Health, Law, and Policy 1992– ; Mem., The B.C. Project to Review Adult Guardianship 1989–93; Dir., Community Legal Assistance Soc. (Vancouver) 1991– ; co-author: 'Practising Poverty Law' 1979, 'Adult Guardianship Law in Canada' 1992; author of num. articles in scholarly jours. and book chapters in fields of mental health law, adult guardianship law, adult protection law, elder abuse and neglect, and corporate crime; recreations: sailing, mountaineering, hiking, scuba diving; Home: 611 Queen's Ave., New Westminster, B.C. V3M 1L1; Office: Burnaby, B.C. V5A 1A6.

**GORDON, Roderick Angus,** C.D., B.Sc., M.D., FRCPC, FRCA, FWACS, Hon. FFARCS; physician; educator; b. Watrous, Sask. 2 Aug. 1911; s. Alexander James, Q.C. and Mabel Margaret (Richardson) G.; e. Toronto Conservatory of Music, L.T.C.M. 1929; Univ. of Sask., B.Sc. 1934; Univ. of Toronto, M.D. 1937, postgrad. training Anaesthesia 1937–39; Dipl. in Anaesthesia, Conjoint Bd., London, Eng. 1940; Cert. R.C.P. & S. Can. 1944; Dipl. Am. Bd. Anaesthesiol. 1948; FRCPC 1952; m. Ruth Anna Catherine, d. Albert L. Breithaupt, Kitchener, Ont. 30 June 1939; children: Catherine Anne (Mrs. E. L. Wilson), Janet Elizabeth, Roderick Arthur James; PROF. EMERITUS, DEPT. OF ANAESTHESIA, UNIV. OF TORONTO since 1977; Prof. and Chrmn. of Anaesthesia, U. of T., 1961–77; Anaesthetist in Chief, Toronto Gen. Hosp. 1961–77; Pres. and Dir., Candn. Anaesthetists' Mutual Accumulating Fund 1957–92; Intern, Toronto Gen. Hosp. 1937, Resident Anaesthetist 1938–39, Anaesthetist 1945; joined present Univ. as Clin. Teacher, Faculty of Med. 1945, Asst. Prof. 1954: served with RCAMC (Active Force) 1939–45; 15 Candn. Gen. Hosp. and Basingstoke Neurol. & Plastic Surg. Hosp.; Candn. Rep., Inter-allied consultants Comte. in Anaesthesia, UK 1944–45; rank Maj.; Anaesthetist, Special Treatment Unit, Christie St. Hosp., Toronto 1945; Lt.-Col. O.C. 7 Field Ambulance (Reserve) 1945–49; Col., A.D.M.S., Med. Adv. Staff 1949–52; mem. Defence Med. Assn. Can. Council 1946–59 (Pres. 1959–61); Cons. in Anaesthesia: Dir.-Gen. of Med. Services, Cdn. Army 1951–54; Cdn. Emergency Measures Orgn. 1956–61; Cdn. Forces Med. Counc. 1957–61; Vice Pres., World Fed. Soc's Anaesthesiologists, 1968–72 (Extve. Comte. 1955–68; former Trustee and Co-Chrmn. Educ. & Relief Fund); rec'd Cdn. Forces Decoration 1949; Coronation Medal 1953; Centennial Medal 1967; Candn. Anaesthetists' Soc. Medal 1969; Queen's Jubilee Medal 1977; U. of T. Hon. Sesquicentennial Award, 1977; Citation of Merit, Acad. of Anaesthesiology 1978; Kt. Cmdr. St. Lazarus of Jerusalem; The R.A. Gordon Career Rsch. Award estbd. in his honour by Candn. Anaesthetists' Soc. 1990; ed. 'Anaesthesia for Thoracic Surgery' 1963; 'Anaesthesia and Resuscitation: A Manual for Medical Students' 1967, 2nd ed. 1973; co-ed. 'Malignant Hyperthermia' 1973; Hon. Fellow, W. African Coll. Surgs.; mem. Candn. and Ont. Med. Assns.; Candn. Anaesthetists' Soc. (Trustee & Chrmn. Anaesthesia Training Fund (1965–87); Council 1945–82; Secy. 1946–61; Vice Pres. 1961–63; Pres. 1963–64; Ed. of Journ. 1954–82); Acad. Med. Toronto; Acad. Anaesthesiol. (Pres. 1961–62); Assn. Anaesthetists Gt. Brit. & Ireland; Assn. Anaesthetists W. Africa (Hon Pres. 1965–67); United Church; recreations: boating, music; Club: Aesculapian; Home: 44 Charles St. W., Apt. 4009, Toronto, Ont. M4Y 1R8.

**GORDON, Steven H.,** B.Sc., C.P.M., F.R.I., C.R.A., P.L.E., C.R.E.; real estate executive; b. Ottawa, Ont. 13 July 1951; s. Harold and Miriam (Lurie) G.; e. Univ. of Ottawa, B.Sc. 1973; m. Laurie d. Leonard and Mary Potechin 20 May 1973; children: Erin, Nina, Shanon, Alexander, Aliza; PRES. & C.E.O., REGIONAL GROUP OF COMPANIES 1982– ; Chrmn., Regional Capital Properties; Pres., Regional Realty Ltd.; Len Potechin Holdings Ltd.; R.V. Capital Corp.; Dir., Regional Constn. (Ottawa) Ltd.; Gemini Capital Corp.; Ottawa Boys & Girls Club; Governor, Candn. Institute of Conflict Resolution; Bd. of Govs., Jr. Achievement of Canada; Vice-Chrmn., Ottawa Airport Economic Development Bd.; Past Chrmn., Ottawa-Carleton Bd. of Trade; Past Pres., Real Estate Inst. of Can., E. Ont. Chapter; Inst. of Real Estate Property Mgmt., Ottawa; Housing & Urban Devel. Assn. of Can., Ottawa; Past Nat. Dir., Real Estate Inst. of Can.; Man of the Year Award, HUDAC 1984; Nat. Presidential Award of Honour, Candn. Home Builders Assn.; Past Pres., West Ottawa Rotary Club; mem., Inst. of Real Estate Mgmt.; Appraisal Inst. of Can.; Can. Home Builders Assn.; Lambda Alpha Internatl. (hon. land economics soc.); Assn. of Ont. Land Economists; Internat. Real Estate Inst.; Am. Soc. of Real Estate Counsellors; A.F. & A.M.; recreations: walking, swimming, mountain hiking; Clubs: Rideau; Canadian; Home: 32 Cedarhill Dr., Nepean, Ont.; Office: 200 Catherine St., 6th Floor, Ottawa, Ont. K2P 2K9.

**GORDON, Wilferd,** Q.C., B.A., LL.B., Ph.B., M.H.L.; b. Toronto, Ont. 21 Aug. 1909; s. late Rabbi Jacob and Lena (Sobol) G.; e. McMaster Univ., B.A. 1931; Univ. of Chicago, Ph.B. 1931; Osgoode Hall, Toronto, Ont. (1935); M.H.L. 1963; o. Rabbi by Rabbi Saul Silber, Pres. of Hebrew Theol. Coll., Chicago, Ill.; Dr. of Rabbinic Studies, Ner Israel Rabbinical Coll., Baltimore, 1972; LL.B., Osgoode Hall, Toronto 1991; m. Balfoura, d. late Dr. Joseph Feldman 30 June 1952; children: Jared, Daniel T.; Counsel, Gordon, Traub; Twenty-Seven Wellington West Ltd.; Cloverdale Park Ltd.; Vice-Pres., Yorkville Financiers Ltd.; Martingrove Homes Ltd.; Torlease Properties Ltd.; mem. Toronto Adv. Bd., Metropolitan Trust Co.; read law with Roebuck & Bagwell, Toronto, Ont.; called to Bar of Ont. 1935; cr. Q.C. 1954; Rabbi, McCaul St. Synagogue, Toronto 1935–36 and 1942–44; Chaplain (part-time civilian) Camp Borden, Ont. 1942–43; Chaplain, R.C.A.F. 1944–46; Pres. Camp Massad of Ont. 1954–61; Pres. Hebrew Day Sch. of Toronto 1962; Past Pres., Assoc Hebrew Schs. of Toronto; Nat. Vice-Pres., Candn. Friends Bar-Ilan Univ., Natl. Vice Pres., 1961; Chrmn. Negev Dinner 1962; Chrmn. Ner Israel Yeshiva Coll. of Toronto; Extve. Mem. Central Fund for Traditional Insts. 1961–62; United Jewish Welfare of Toronto; Keren Hatarbut of Canada; mem. Nat. Extve. Counc., Zionist Organization of Can.; Jewish Nat. Fund; Candn. Jewish Cong.; mem. Ont. Housing Adv. Comte. 1962; Advisory Comm., Metro. Trust Co. 1962; mem. Exec. Ont. Men's ORT; Exec. Mem. Cdn. Friends of Boys Town Jerusalem 1974– ; Gov., State of Israel Bonds (Canada-Israel Securities Ltd.); Candn. Friends of Yeshiva Univ.; Trustee, Emet Rabbi Herzog World Acad. 1966; Regional Vice Pres., Nat. Comm. on Torah Educ. 1970; mem. Nat. Extve., Mizrachi Orgn. of Can. 1970; Dir. Candn. Friends of Bar. Ilan Univ. since 1975; Home: 10 Prue Dr., #801, Toronto, Ont. M6B 1R4.

**GORHAM, Paul Raymond,** B.A., M.S., PhD., F.R.S.C. (1961); biologist; educator; b. Fredericton, N.B., 16 April 1918; s. Raymond Paddock and Marie Jeanette (Tanner) G.; e. Univ. of New Brunsick, B.A. 1938; Univ. of Maine, M.S. 1940; Cal. Inst. of Tech., Ph.D. 1943; Univ. N.B., D.Sc., 1973; m. Evelyn Ruth, d. late Lewis Greene Woods, 8 July 1943; children: John Henry, Arthur Raymond, Harriet Ruth; PROFESSOR EMERITUS OF BOTANY, UNIV. OF ALBERTA 1983– ; formerly Princ. Research Offr., Div. of Biol., Nat. Research Council; Agric. Assistant, Div. Botany and Plant Path., Dept. of Agric., Ottawa, Ont., 1943–45; joined N.R.C. as Jr. Research Offr., Div. of Applied Biol., 1945; Asst. Research Offr., 1946–50, Assoc., 1950–57; Sr., 1957–65 Princ. Research Officer 1965–69; Prof. of Botany, Univ. of Alta. 1969–83; Chrmn., Dept. Botany, Univ. of Alberta, 1971–79; Assoc. Dir., U. of A. Devonian Botanic Garden 1976–83; Adjunct Prof., W.K. Kellogg Bio. Sta., Mich. State U. 1976; Visiting Scientist, Agr. Can. Res. Sta., Lethbridge, Alta. 1977; Academic Relations Lecturer, Can. Embassy to Japan, 1977; Publications: author or co-author of some 70 papers in the field of plant physiol. and aquatic ecology; mem. Canadian Society Plant Physiologists (first Pres., 1958–59); Am. Soc. Plant Physiols. Emeritus (Edit. Bd. Plant Physiology 1973–83); Candn. Biochem. Soc. (emeritus); Candn. Botanical Assn. (pres. 1977–78); Phycological Soc. Am. (retired) (Vice-Pres. 1966, Ed. Bd. Journ. Phycology 1967–69); Soc. Internat. Limnologiae; Am. Assn. Adv. Science; Secy., Candn. Comte. for Internat. Biol. Programme 1968–69; received Centennial Medal (1967); Silver Jubilee Medal (1978); Candn. Bot. Assoc., Mary E. Elliot Award (1979); George Lawson Medal (1988); Candn. Soc. Plant Physiol. Gold Medal (1987); Certificate of Commendation, Min. of Foreign Affairs of Japan (1991); Fellow, Rawson Acad. Aquat. Sci. (1979–91); mem., Bd. of Trustees, Friends of Univ. of Alta. Devonian Bot. Garden 1972– ; Bd. of Dirs., Edmonton Art Gallery 1980–92 (secy. 1981–90); recreations: hiking, skiing; Office: 12408 - 49 Ave. Edmonton, Alta. T6H 0H2.

**GORHAM, Richard Vessot,** B.A., M.A., LL.D.; retired diplomat; b. Fredericton, N.B. 18 May 1927; s. Raymond P. and Marie J. (Tanner) G.; e. Univ. of N.B. B.A. 1950; Clark Univ. Worcester, Mass. M.A. 1951; LL.D., Univ. of New Brunswick 1988; m. Doris d. George and Lydia Landry 22 Oct. 1951; children: George (dec.), Patricia, Timothy, Robert, Andrew; ADJUNCT PROF., UNIV. OF NEW BRUNSWICK; joined Dept. External Affairs 1952, Second Sec. Tokyo 1954–60, First Sec. New Delhi 1963–66, Comnr. Pnom Penh 1968–70, Dir. Press Office External Affairs 1971–74, Min. Tokyo 1974–79, Asst. Under Sec. Latin Am. & Caribbean Affairs 1979–83; Ambassador to People's Republic of China 1984–87; Roving Ambassador for Latin Am. and Ambassador and Permanent Observer of Canada to the Orgn. of Am. States (OAS) 1987–90; Special Adv. to the Secy. of State for External Affairs on Implementing Policy regarding Lat. Am. 1990; Foreign Service Visitor, Univ. of New Brunswick 1990–91; retired from govt. service 1991; recreations: music, reading, history; Home: Gorham's Bluff, R.R. 2, Clifton Royal, N.B. E0G 1N0; Office: c/o Univ. of N.B., Saint John Campus, St. John, N.B.

**GORING, David Arthur Ingham,** B.Sc., Ph.D., F.C.I.C., F.R.S.C.; scientist; b. Toronto, Ont. 26 Nov. 1920; s. late George Ingham and Susan Edna Hill (Jones) G.; e. Queen's Coll. Brit. Guiana 1939; Univ. Coll. London B.Sc. 1942; McGill Univ. Ph.D. 1949; Cambridge Univ. Ph.D. 1953 (Merck Postdoctoral Fellow 1949–51); Univ. of W. Ont. Business Mang. 1976; m. Elizabeth Dodds d. late William Rochester Haswell 24 Aug. 1948; children: James Haswell Ingham, Rosemary Jane Erskine, Christopher David Gowland; PROF., DEPT. CHEM. ENGN. AND APPLIED CHEM., UNIV. OF TORONTO 1986– ; Pulp and Paper Rsch. Inst. of Can., Pointe Claire 1955–85; Chem. Dept. McGill Univ., Montreal 1955–86; Maritime Regional Lab. Nat. Research Council, Halifax 1951–55; rec'd Anselme Payen Award 1973 Am. Chem. Soc.; rec'd Gunnar Nicholson TAPPI Gold Medal, Tech. Assoc. Pulp Paper Indus. 1986; rec'd Certificate of Appreciation, Tech. Sec. Candn. Pulp & Paper Assn. 1986; rec'd Le Sueur Memorial Lectr. Award, Soc. of Chem. Industry, Candn. Sect. 1988; author or co-author over 200 scient. publs.; Fellow, Internat. Acad. Wood Science; Fellow, Tech. Assn. Pulp & Paper Industry; mem. Tech. Sec. Candn. Pulp & Paper Assn.; Cellulose, Paper & Textile Div. Am. Chem. Soc.; Anglican; recreations: fishing, music; Home: 141/2 Ottawa St., Toronto, Ont. M4T 2B6; Office: 200 College St., Toronto, Ont. M5S 1A4.

**GORING, Peter A.,** B.Com., C.A.; real estate executive; b. Sudbury, Ont. 3 Jan. 1943; s. Allan Elliott and

H. Marie (Legrow) G.; e. Laurentian Univ. B.Com. 1967, C.A. 1970; m. Erica d. James G. Pratt 16 Dec. 1972; children: Simon, Sarah; PRES., BENNINGTON ADVISORS 1992– ; Staff Acct. Clarkson Gordon & Co. 1967–70; Vice Pres. Canmort Consultants Ltd. 1970–80; Vice Pres. Wood Gundy (Parent) 1978–80; Vice Pres. and Treas. Bramalea Ltd. 1980, Sr. Vice Pres. Corporate Finance & Treasury 1985–86, Exec. Vice Pres. and Treas. 1986–90, Exec. Vice Pres., Corporate Development 1990–93; Dir., Alliance for Ont. Universities; Gov. Laurentian Univ. 1987–93; Dir., Urban Devel. Inst. Ont. 1981–83; Dir. and Treas., Ont. New Home Warranty Bd. 1987–90; mem. Inst. C.A.'s Ont.; Clubs: National; Toronto Hunt; Home: 50 Bennington Hts. Dr., Toronto, Ont. M4G 1A9; Office: 130 Bloor St. W., Suite 1200, Toronto, Ont. M5S 1N5.

**GORMAN, David John,** B.Sc., Ph.D., D.I.H.; university administrator; b. Hamilton, Ont. 15 May 1941; s. Joseph Patrick and Mabel Irene (Smith) G.; e. McMaster Univ. B.Sc. 1963, Ph.D. 1967; Univ. of Toronto D.I.H. 1990; m. Amy d. Xiao-Wen and Doris Kung 6 Dec. 1986; children: Michael Andrew, Erin Elizabeth; DIR. OF ENVIRONMENTAL HEALTH & SAFETY, UNIV. OF TORONTO 1986– ; and Adjunct Prof. of Chem. Eng. & Applied Chem.; Rsch. Lawrence Berkeley Lab. Univ. of Cal. 1968–70; Staff Sci. Bureau Internat. des Poids et Mesures, Sèvres, France 1971–73; Asst. Health Phys. Bruce Nuclear Generating Stn. A, Ont. Hydro 1974, Health Phys. Environmental & Internal Dosimetry of Health & Safety Div. 1975–82, Dept. Services Mgr. of Div. 1982–83 and Ind. Hygiene Services Mgr. 1984–86; mem. Adv. Ctte. Radiol. Protection, Atomic Energy Control Bd.; mem. Candn. Standards Assn. (Tech. Ctte. Environmental Radiation Protection); Health Phys. Soc.; Am. Ind. Hygiene Assn.; Candn. Radiation Protection Assn. (Dir. 1982–84); Office: 215 Huron St., Rm. 702, Toronto, Ont. M5S 1A1.

**GORMAN, Eugene Michael,** B.A.; Consultant Sea Fisheries; b. Welland, Ont. 21 Feb. 1914; s. George Earl and Mary (McKenna) G.; e. St. John Evangelist High Sch., N. Cambridge, Mass.; Boston Coll.; St. Dunstans Univ., B.A.; Business Mang. Courses; m. Vera Ruby, d. Joseph Barnett, Sept. 1945; children: Ian Earl, Mary Teresa, Eugene Michael; Dir. Extension Services, St. Dunstans Univ. 1947–50; Chrmn. (1st) Fishermen's Loan Bd. P.E.I. 1949–57; Dir. (1st) Fisheries Div. Dept. Indust. and Natural Resources 1950–57; Depy. Min. P.E.I. Dept. Mun. Affairs 1965–66 and Depy. Min. (1st) P.E.I. Dept. of Fisheries 1957–74; Special Asst. To Dir. Gen. Atlantic Region, Fisheries and Marine Service, Environment Canada 1974–78; served in 2nd World War U.K., Italy and N.W. Europe, citation from Field Marshal Montgomery; mem. Internat. Oceanog. Soc.; Candn. Inst. Food Science Technol.; R. Catholic; recreation: boating; Home: 191 Mt. Edward Rd., Charlottetown, P.E.I. C1A 5T1.

**GORMAN, Ruth,** O.C. (1968), B.A., LL.B., LL.D., lawyer and writer; b. Calgary, Alta. 14 Feb. 1914; d. late Col. M.B. (K.C.) Peacock and Fleda (Pattyson) P.; e. Calgary Pub. Sch.; Strathcona Lodge Sch., B.C.; Univ. of Alberta; m. (Judge) John C. (Q.C.), 14 Sept. 1940 (dec. 1991); one d., Linda I.F. Gorman B.A. LL.B., called to Bar 1940; Publisher 'Golden West' mag. 1965–70, editor until 1975; named Calgary's 'Woman of the Year' by Local Council of Women 1960; 'Citizen of the Year' by Calgary Jr. Chamber of Comm. 1961; awarded 'Alberta Woman of the Century Medal,' Nat. Council of Jewish Women 1968; Legal Humanities Award 1988; Lifetime Achievement Award, Calgary Access Awareness 1991; Confederation Medal 1993; Past Hon. Convenor of Laws to Canada's Nat. Council of Women; mem. and on Founding Bd. Tweedsmuir Sch., Calgary; past Chrmn. Civil Liberties Sec. of Candn. Bar on Indian Law; Queen Mother of Cree and Princess of the Stony Indian Tribe of Alberta; winner of three Calgary Br., Candn. Women's Press Club Award, 1966 and 1968; Anglican; Pi Beta Phi; Home: 203 Roxboro Rd. S.W., Calgary, Alta. T2S 0R2.

**GORNALL, Allan Godfrey,** B.A., Ph.D., D.Sc., F.C.A.C.B., F.R.S.C. (1966); university professor (emeritus); b. River Hebert, N.S. 28 Aug. 1914; s. late Rev. Dr. Herbert Thomas and Lucy Amy (Markham) G.; e. High Sch., Saint John, N.B.; Mount Allison Univ. B.A. (cum laude) (Hon. Chem.) 1936, D.Sc. (Hon.) 1978; Univ. of Toronto, Ph.D. 1941; m. Mary Elizabeth Sheila, d. late Dr. Herbert Leslie Stewart, 27 Dec. 1941; children: William Stewart, Douglas Allan, Thomas Herbert, Catherine Anne; Asst. Prof., Dept. of Pathol. Chem., Univ. of Toronto 1946–52; Assoc. Prof., 1952–63; Prof. of Clin. Biochem., Univ. of Toronto 1963–80 and Chrmn. of Dept. 1966–76; Nuffield Scholar, Edinburgh, Scot. and London, Eng., 1949; served with R.C.N.V.R. (Special Br.), 1942–46; retired as Lt. Commdr.; author or co-author of 85 scient. articles; awarded Reeve Prize 1941; MDS Award 1975 and The Ames Award, Candn. Soc. Clin. Chem. 1977; Lectureship Award, Man. Soc. Clin. Chem. 1982; Somogyi-Sendroy Award, N.Y. State Clin. Chem. 1982; Award for Outstanding Contributions in Education, Amer. Assoc. for Clin. Chem. 1984; Award for Outstanding Contribution to Educ., Can. Soc. of Clin. Chemists 1989; mem., Toronto Biochem. Biophys. Soc. (Pres. 1954); Am. Chem. Soc.; Am. Physiol. Soc.; Candn. Physiol. Soc. (Treas. 1954–57); Biochem Soc. (Gt. Brit.); Endocrine Soc.; Candn. Soc. Clin. Investigation; Candn. Biochem. Soc.; Candn. Fed. Biol. Socs. (Hon. Treas. 1957–62); Candn. Soc. Clin. Chem. (certified, 1964); Candn. Soc. Endocr. Metab.; Academy Clin. Labor. Physicians and Scientists; Roy. Soc. of Can.; United Church; recreations: sailing, skating, tennis, gemstone faceting; Clubs: Toronto Cricket Skating & Curling; Lunenburg (N.S.) Yacht; Home: 135 Hanna Rd., Toronto, Ont. M4G 3N6.

**GORSHENIN, Nick,** Dip.Bus.(NSWIT), CPA; pharmaceutical executive; b. Newcastle, Australia 7 Feb. 1952; s. Nick and Joan (Sturrock) G.; e. North Sydney Tech. H.S. 1969; New South Wales Inst. of Tech. Dip.Bus. 1974; m. Catherine d. Walter and Ellen O'Shea 25 April 1981; children: Nicholas Louis, Daniel John; GENERAL MANAGER, ALCON CANADA INC. 1993– ; audited with Peat Marwick & Price Waterhouse in Sydney, Jakarta, Indonesia and Port Vila, Vanuatu; Chief Accountant, Blue Circle Cement Nigeria 1982–84; Commercial Manager, Indonesia 1985–86; Gen. Mgr., Coopervision Australia 1988–89; Divisional Mgr., Alcon Australia 1990–93; moved to Canada 1993; rep. Indonesia in Rugby Union at Hong Kong Sevens 1977; Grand Master, Medan Hash House Harriers 1985–86; Sec., Manly Vikings Junior Rugby Club 1992–93; recreations: rugby union, squash, skiing, chess, reading; club: Oakville Crusaders Rugby; Home: Oakville, Ontario; Office: 2145 Meadowpine Blvd., Mississauga, Ont. L5N 6R8.

**GOSE, Elliott Bickley,** M.A., Ph.D.; educator; b. Nogales, Ariz. 3 May 1926; s. Elliott Bickley and Eleanor (Paulding) G.; e. Univ. of Colo. B.A. 1949, A.M. 1950; Cornell Univ. Ph.D. 1954; m. Kathleen Kavanaugh Brittain 1950; children: Peter C., Sarah E.; PROF. EMERITUS, UNIV. OF B.C. 1991, Prof. of English 1967–91; rec'd Can. Council Travel Grants research Dublin 1970–71 and Sr. Fellowship 1971–72; grant-in-aid of publ. 1972, 1978, 1982, 1986; Founding mem. New Sch. 1960–62, Pres. of Bd. 1962–63, 1965–66, Vancouver; Trustee, Vancouver Sch. Bd. 1973–76, Vice Chrmn. 1975–76; author 'Imagination Indulged: The Irrational in the Nineteenth-Century Novel' 1972; 'The Transformation Process in Joyce's "Ulysses"' 1980; 'The World of the Irish Wonder Tale' 1985; 'Mere Creatures: Modern Fantasy Tales for Children' 1988; Home: Box 20, R.R. 5, Durrance Rd., Victoria B.C. V8X 4M6.

**GOSEWICH, Arnold,** B.B.A.; literary agent; b. Ottawa, Ont. 23 Feb. 1934; s. Samuel and Rae (Rosen) G.; e. Lisgar Coll. Inst. and H.S. of Comm. Ottawa 1950; Clarkson Coll. B.B.A. 1956; m. Jackee d. Sam and Sybil Spunt 17 Mar. 1957; children: Robin-Joy, Stephen; CHAIRMAN, McNIGHT GOSEWICH ASSOCIATES AGENCY INC. 1989– ; Pres. & C.O.O., Gordon V. Thompson Music Co.; Pres. Cover to Cover Inc. 1981– ; Advtg. Mgr. Wholesale Food Supply Co. Ottawa 1957; Partner Treble Clef Record Store Ottawa 1958; Partner Sherman Enterprises Ltd. 1959; Vice Pres. Group Mktg. Capitol Records of Canada Ltd. 1969, Pres. and Chief Oper. Offr. 1970; Chrmn. and Chief Exec. Offr., CBS Records of Canada Ltd. 1977; Pres. & C.E.O., Macmillan of Canada 1982–89; Pres. and Dir.: Candn. Recording Ind. Asn. 1972; Maple Music Inc. 1974; Dir.: Candn. Acad. Recording Arts & Sci's. 1984; Candn. Book Publishers Counc. 1984; Treas. Canadian Telebook Agency (Pres. 1985); Bd. of Trustees, Candn. Acad. Recording Arts & Sciences 1986; mem. Adv. Ctte. Recording Course Fanshawe Coll. 1979; named to Candn. Recording Ind. Hall of Fame 1978; recipient Billboard Trendsetter Award 1973; Juno Award 1973; mem. B'nai B'rith (Pres. Ottawa Chapter 1967); Beth Tzedec; Karma Frat.; Phalanx Hon. Soc.; Pi Delta Epsilon; recreations: running, travelling; Clubs: Fitness Inst.; Variety; Home: 155 Banbury Rd., Don Mills, Ont. M3B 2C7; Office: 10 St. Mary St., Ste. 510, Toronto, Ont. M4Y 1P9.

**GOSS, Dawn Elaine,** B.A.Sc.; freelance photojouranlist, writer; b. St. Catharines, Ont. 27 June 1961; d. Douglas William and Marjorie Jane (Morgan) G.; e. E.L. Crossley S.S. 1980; Brock Univ.; Univ. of Guelph B.A.Sc. 1984; co-ordinated & co-author 'Trans-Canada Country' 1986, an 18-month photographic journey along the Trans-Canada Hwy.; photography featured in Candn. Pavilion, Expo '86; Consultant & Contbg. Photographer/Writer 'Share the Flame' Olympic Torch Relay 1987; has travelled extensively throughout Canada & internationally for several other books & mags. incl. Equinox, Harrowsmith, Canadian Geographic, Internat. Wildlife, Maclean's, Signature, This Country Canada, Newsweek, Canada Wide Magazines, Garsduinen, and for Globe and Mail and L.A. Times newspaper; Mem. & rep. by First Light Assoc. Photographers; nom. for photojournalism, Nat. Magazine Awards for 'Der Wild Westen' Equinox Mag.; Mem., Greenpeace; Friends of Clayoquot Sound; The Pollution Probe Found.; recreations: cross-country skiing, piano playing; Home: 561 Erickson, Man. R0J 0P0; Office: First Light, 1 Atlantic Ave., Suite 204, Toronto, Ont. M6K 3E7.

**GOSS, Maj. Gen. (Ret.) Denys William,** C.D., B.A.Sc., M.Sc. FCASI, P. Eng.; b. Hamilton, Ont., 18 June 1922; e. Queen's Univ., B.A.Sc. (Mech. Engn.) 1949; Univ. of Michigan, M.Sc. (Aeronaut.) 1955 and M.Sc. (Instrumentation Engn.) 1956; Air Force Coll., Toronto 1962; Bd. Chrmn., Mechron Energy Ltd.; joined R.C.A.F. 1941 and trained as a pilot; served as Flying Instructor in Canada until 1944 when assigned to a Mosquito sqdn.; was selected to attend guided missile course in U.S.A., 1949; seconded to Defence Research Bd., 1950; apptd. to staff duties with directorate of armament engn., AFHQ, 1952; attended special armament course with R.A.F. in Eng., 1953; apptd. to directorate of aircraft engn., AFHQ, 1956; posted to No. 3 Fighter Wing, Zweibrucken, Germany as Chief Tech. Services Offr., 1963; apptd. Sr. Tech. Staff Offr., Air Defence Command HQ, St. Hubert, Que., 1964; posted to Material Command HQ as Sr. Staff Offr., Aircraft, 1965; Depy. Chief of Staff, Logistics Materiel Command, 1966; Dir. Gen., Maintenance 1968–69; Depy. Chief of Staff, Logistics & Adm. NATO, Fourth Tactical Air Force HQ, Ramstein, Germany, 1969–71; Dir. Gen. Aerospace Systems 1971; Chief of Logistics 1972; Chief of Eng. and Maint. 1973; Ret. Can. Forces 1976; Vice Pres. ONEX Holdings 1976–78; Assist. Dean and Registrar, Fac. of Eng., Sch. of Indust. Design, Sch. of Archit., Carleton Univ., 1978–80; CEO, D.S. Fraser & Co. Ltd. 1981–82; Pres., Hovey Industries Ltd. 1980–86; C.E.O. Tech 5 Ltd. 1986–89; Bd. Chrmn. & C.E.O., Hovey Industries Ltd. 1986–92; Bd. Chrmn., Piesographics Inc., Seprotech Systems Inc., Moreguard Windows & Doors Ltd. and Hovey Manufacturing (Canada) Ltd. 1985–92; Address: 2378 Holly Lane, Ottawa, Ont. K1V 7P1.

**GOSS, Paul Edward,** MB.BCH, MRCP (UK), FRCP(C), Ph.D.; medical oncologist; b. South Africa 17 Feb. 1955; s. Dillon Edward and Diane Juliette (Bernhard) G.; e. Univ. of Witwatersrand MB.BCH 1978; Univ. of London Ph.D. 1986; m. Susan d. Robert and Betty Lindsay (Simmonds) 31 Aug. 1985; children: Caroline Olivia, Edward James; MEDICAL ONCOLOGIST, THE TORONTO HOSPITAL & ASST. PROF. OF MED., UNIV. OF TORONTO; cancer training, The Royal Marsden and Princess Margaret Hosp.; mem., local and national breast cancer cttes.; author of numerous peer-reviewed articles in sci. journals; recreations: tennis, skiing; Office: The Toronto Hosp., Gen. Div., 200 Elizabeth St., MLW 2-022, Toronto, Ont. M5G 2C4.

**GOSSAGE, Stevenson Milne,** M.Sc.; b. London, Eng. 6 Dec. 1905; s. Alfred Milne, C.B.E., M.D., and Bertha Pillans (Stevenson) G.; e. Hilderham House, Broadstairs, Eng.; Rugby Sch., Eng. (1923); Univ. Coll., Univ. of London, B.Sc., (Engn.) 1926; Yale Univ., M.Sc. (Transportation), 1934; m. Edith, d. Frederick Chatfield, New Haven, Conn., 6 May 1935; children: Jonathan Frederick Milne, Edith Abigail; 2ndly, Eva Maria, d. Kurt Huldschinsky, M.D., Berlin, Germany, 19 April 1958; PRINCIPAL CONSULTANT, CANADIAN PACIFIC CONSULTING SERVICES, since 1977; Chrmn., Metric Comn. Can. 1971–76; (Sr. Extve. Offr. CP Rail, 1969–71); came to Can. 1926; Trucker, Clerk, Steno., Freight Office, Three Rivers, Que., 1926–28 (Candn. Pac. Rly. Co.); Steno, Supts. Office, Montreal, 1929–30; Steno-Clerk, Vice-Pres. and Gen. Mgrs. Office, Montreal, 1930–34; Statistician, Vice-Pres. and Gen. Mgrs. Office, Montreal, 1935–37, and at Toronto, 1937–41; Asst. to the Vice-Pres. and Gen. Mgr., Toronto, 1941–45; Asst. Mgr. of Personnel, Montreal, 1945–56; Mgr., Labour Relations, 1956–58; Vice-Pres., E. Region, Toronto, 1958–62, and of Prairie Region, Winnipeg, Man., 1962–64; Vice Pres., Co. Services, Montréal, 1964–66, Vice-Pres., Dir., and mem. Extve. Comte., 1966–71; Anglican; Clubs: University: Canadian Railway; Home: 6 Hilltop Cres., P.O. Box 248, Sutton, Que. J0E 2K0.

**GOSSE, Richard Fraser,** Q.C., B.A., LL.B., D.Phil.; justice affairs consultant; professor; b. Vancouver, B.C. 25 Mar. 1924; s. Richard Josiah and Annabelle Maude (Fraser) G.; e. McGill Univ. B.A. 1947; Univ. of B.C. LL.B. 1950; Oxford Univ. D.Phil. 1960; m. Jean d. Dr. Arthur Milne 14 Dec. 1957; children: Richard, Gisela, Alexandra; LAW FOUNDATION PROFESSOR, UNIV. OF SASK. 1993– ; Adjunct Prof. of Law, McGill Univ. 1991– ; Partner, Gosse & Wright, Kitimat, B.C. 1954–60; Prof. of Law, Queen's Univ. 1960–69, McLaughlin Fellow 1966–67, mem. Senate 1965–67, Pres. Faculty Assn. 1965–66; Counsel, Ont. Law Reform Comn. 1967–69; first full-time mem. B.C. Law Reform Comn. 1970–72; Prof. of Law, Univ. of B.C. 1972–77; Dep. Atty. Gen. of Sask. 1977–85; Inspector Gen., Candn. Security Intelligence Service 1985–88; Chrmn., RCMP Public Complaints Comn. 1988–91; Special Consultant to Law Reform Comn. Can. on custody children divorcing spouses 1973–75; conducted study for Min. of Consumer Services on need regulation funeral & cemetary services B.C. 1975–76; mem. Regulated Inds. Prog. Consumers Assn. Can. 1976–77; Chrmn. Pub. Legal Edn. & Info. Ctte. Candn. Law Info. Counc. 1978–82; Sask. Comnr. to Candn. Uniform Law Conf. 1977–84; Treas., Candn. Counc. of Administrative Tribunals 1988–90; served as pilot RCAF 1943–45, rank Flying Offr.; mem. Law Soc.'s B.C., Ont. and Sask.; Candn. Bar Assn.; Office: P.O. Box 1661, Saskatoon, Sask. S7K 3R8.

**GOSSELIN, Claude Alphonse,** B.A.; curator; arts administrator; b. Valleyfield, Que. 5 June 1944; s. Sauveur and Georgette (Bélair) G.; e. Coll. Bourget, Rigaud, Que. 1962; Coll. St-Thomas, Valleyfield 1966; Univ. de Montréal B.A. 1969; Univ. du Qué. à Montréal B.A. (hist. art) 1971; FOUNDING DIR., CENTRE INTERNAT. D'ART CONTEMPORAIN DE MONTREAL (CIAC) 1983– ; Dir., 'Les Cent Jours d'Art Contemporain de Montréal' (an annual internat. event on contemporary art) from 1985– ; Co-ordinator, Que. Prof. Artists Soc. 1972–74; Art Critic, Le Devoir, Montreal 1974–75; Visual Arts Offr. Can. Council for the Arts 1975–79; Curator, Musée d'art Contemporain de Montréal 1979–83; jury mem. for visual arts; lectr. Candn. Cultural Program Organ. 1982; jury mem. Qué. Biennial of Painting 1981; author various exhn. catalogues; mem. Bd. of Dirs., O'Vertigo Dance Co.; mem. Adv. Bd., Gall. at the Saidye Bronfman Center, Montréal 1989–91; Conseil du Module, Animation et recherche culturelle, UQAM 1990–91; Voting mem., ICOM CIMAM; ICOM Canada; Qué. Museums Soc.; Adresse: 3651 ave. Laval, Montréal, Qué. H2X 3E1.

**GOSSELIN, Howard J.,** B.A., M.B.A., F.I.C.B.; b. Ottawa, Ont. 28 Feb. 1948; e. St. Patrick's College, Carleton Univ. B.A. 1969; Queen's Univ. M.B.A. 1978; Fellow, Inst. of Canadian Banking; m. Susan Callan 21 Sept. 1974; children: Cindy, Jay, Grant; SENIOR VICE-PRES., BARCLAYS BANK OF CANADA; recreations: golf, coach & play hockey; clubs: University, Summerlea Golf; Office: 1 Place Ville Marie, Ste. 3625, Montreal, Que. H3B 3P2.

**GOSSELIN, Léo,** B.Sc.Pharm., L.Pharm.; pharmacist; b. Amos, Abitibi, Qué. 4 Apr. 1924; s. Joseph Elie and Maria (Tremblay) G.; e. Coll. de Montréal; Coll. de St-Laurent 1945; Univ. de Montréal B.Sc.Pharm. 1949 (Gold Medal); m. Micheline d. George and Aline Desrosiers 20 Aug. 1949; children: Marie, Jean, Paul, François; estbd. own pharmacy Montéal 1949–53; Founding mem. Geigy Pharmaceutical (now Ciba-Geigy) 1954–71, Dir. Mktg.; Vice Pres. Sci. Affairs, Franca Laboratories and Octo Laboratories 1971–85 (became Nordic Laboratories Inc. 1978), Asst. to Pres. of Nordic 1985–88; retired 1989; monthly columnist 'Le Pharmacien'; author: 'Nordic Laboratories – A Success Story' 1989; mem. Order Pharms. Qué.; Candn. Pharm. Assn.; Candn. Ind. Pharms. Assn.; Gov. Coll. Pharms. Qué. 1968–70; recreations: fishing, hunting, skiing, reading; Home: 12465 Grenet St., Montréal, Qué. H4J 2K4.

**GOTH, Lynn H.,** B.A.; business executive; b. Brandon, Man. 10 May 1938; s. George William and Marjorie Isabelle (Blackburn) G.; e. Univ. of Western Ont. B.A. 1960; m. Patricia d. James and Dorothy Cobain 13 Oct. 1962; children: Susan, Peter, Christopher; DIR., GORDON CAPITAL CORP. 1988– ; A.E. Ames & Co. Toronto 1960–66; N.Y. 1966–76; Pres. 1974–76; Vice-Pres. & Dir., A.E. Ames, then Dominion Securities Inc. (Montreal) 1976–87; Dir., MPL Communications Inc.; Dir., Montreal Gen. Hosp.; recreations: golf, tennis, fishing; clubs: Mount Bruno Country, Metropolitan, Tuxedo, Mount Royal, Knowlton Golf & Country, Country Club of Florida; Home: 22 Rosemount, Westmount, Que. H3Y 3G7; Office: 1 Pl. Ville Marie, Ste. 4130, Montreal, Que. H3B 3P9.

**GOTLIB, Lorraine, The Honourable Madam Justice;** judge; b. Toronto, Ont. 13 May 1931; d. Abraham and Esther (Kerbel) G.; e. Harbord C.I., Toronto; Univ. Coll. Univ. of Toronto B.A. 1952; Osgoode Hall Law Sch., Toronto; called to Bar of Ont. 1959; m. Christopher B. s. Dr. Donald and Dorothy (Blaikie) Paterson 19 Apr. 1975; JUSTICE, ONTARIO COURT OF JUSTICE (GEN. DIV.) at Toronto 1990– ; apptd. to Bench of District Court of Ont. 3 Dec. 1985; practised as assoc. with Mssrs. Lorenzetti, Mariani & Wolfe; Phillips & Phillips; Croll, Borins & Shiff; McMillan, Binch 1963–69; Partner McMillan, Binch 1969–81; Partner, Kingsmill, Jennings 1981–85; Dir. Bd. of Trade Metrop. Toronto 1979–83; Group Seminar Instr. Bar Admission Course (Real Estate) 1968–72; mem. Medico-Legal Soc of Toronto (Dir. 1975–77); mem. Candn. Bar Assn. (Nat. Exec. 1976–78, Pres. Ont. Br. 1983–84); former Mem., Ont. District Court Judges Assoc. (Extve. 1988–90); mem., Candn. Judges Conf.; mem., Ont. Superior Court Judges' Assoc.; mem., Candn. Assoc. for the Admin. of Justice; County of York Law Assn.; Women's Law Assn. of Ont.; Lawyers' Club of Toronto; Counc., Ont. Coll. of art 1976–79; apptd. Q.C. 1973; awarded Jubilee Medal 1977; LL.B., Osgood Hall Law Sch. at York Univ. 1991; recreations: visual and performing arts, music, skiing; Clubs: Empire (Dir. 1981–86); Royal Candn. Yacht; Royal Candn. Mil. Inst.; Home: 51 Rosedale Rd., Toronto, Ont. M4W 2P5; Office: The Court House, 361 University Ave., Toronto, Ont. M5G 1T3.

**GOTLIEB, Allan E.,** C.C., LL.B., M.A., B.C.L., LL.D.; public servant; b. Winnipeg, Man. 28 Feb. 1928; s. David Phillip and Sarah (Schiller) G.; e. Univ. of Cal., B.A. 1949; Harvard Law Sch., LL.B 1954 (Ed., 'Harvard Law Review,' 1950–51); Oxford Univ., M.A., B.C.L. (Vinerian Law Scholar, 1954–56); LL.D., Univ. of Windsor 1982; State Univ. of N.Y. 1983; Univ. of Central Florida 1984; LL.D. (Hon.) Univ. of Winnipeg; Univ. of New Brunswick 1985; m. Sondra, d. David Kaufman, 20 Dec. 1955; children: Rebecca, Marcus, Rachel; CHRMN., CANADA COUNCIL; CHRMN., BURSON-MARSTELLER, Canada; Chrmn., Executive Consultants Ltd., Ottawa; Dir., Alcan; Hollinger Corp.; Champion Int. Corp.; Peoples Jewellers Limited; Bd. Vice-Chrmn., Saturday Night Magazine Inc.; Adv. Bd., Bank of Montreal; The Inv. Co. of America; Hollinger Corp.; Nestlé Enterprises Ltd.; Arbitrator, Canada-France Tribunal on East Coast Waters; Consultant, Stikeman, Elliott, Toronto; Wilmer Cutler & Pickering, Washington, D.C.; Called to the Bar of Eng. (Inner Temple) 1956; former Fellow, Wadham Coll. and Univ. Lectr. in Law, Oxford Univ., 1954–56; Asst. Under Secy of State for External Affairs and Legal Adviser, 1967–68; Depy. Min. of Communications, 1968–73; Depy. Min. of Manpower & Immigration, 1973–77; Under-Sec. of State for External Affairs, 1977–81; Ambassador of Canada to the United States 1981–89; Visiting Fellow, All Souls Coll., Oxford, 1975–76; William Lyon Mackenzie King Visiting Prof., Harvard Univ. 1989; Claude Bissell Visiting Prof., Univ. of Toronto 1989; former Gov. Internat. Development Research Centre; Nat. Film Bd.; Export Development Corp.; author 'Disarmament and International Law' 1965; 'Canadian Treaty-Making' 1968; 'Impact of Technology on International Law' 1982; 'I'll be with you in a minute, Mr. Ambassador' 1991; Ed., 'Human Rights Federalism and Minorities' 1970; Recipient Addison-Browne prize in pvt. Internat. Law, Harvard Law Sch., 1954; Deak prize Am. Soc. Internat. Law, 1974; Outstanding Achievement Award, Govt. of Canada 1983; Haas Internat. Award, Univ. of California Regents, 1985; Companion, Order of Canada; Companion, Order of Canada; Jewish; Address: Ste. 5300, P.O. Box 85, Commerce Court W., Toronto, Ont. M5L 1B9.

**GOTLIEB, Calvin Carl,** M.A., Ph.D., D.M., D.Eng., F.R.S.C.; computer scientist; univ. professor; b. Toronto, Ont. 27 March 1921; s. late Israel and Jennie (Sherman) G.; e. Harbord Coll. Inst., Toronto, Ont. (1933–38); Univ. of Toronto, B.A. (Physics and Chem.) 1942, M.A. (Physics) 1944, Ph.D. (Physics) 1947; D.M. Waterloo 1968; m. Phyllis Fay, d. late Leo Bloom, 12 June 1949; children: Leo, Margaret, Jane; PROF. EMERITUS, COMPUTER SCIENCE, UNIV. OF TORONTO; worked with proximity fuse group in Can., U.S. and U.K.; involved with electronic computers since 1948; appointed Lecturer in Physics, Univ. of Toronto, 1949; Candn. Rep. to Internat. Fed. Information Processing (known as IFIP) 1960–65; Chrmn. IFIP Technical Comte., (Relationships between Computer and Society), 1975–81; Pres., C.C. Gotlieb Consulting Ltd.; Consultant to UN, Can. and other govts., industry; Publications: 'High Speed Data Processing' (with J. N. P. Hume) 1958, 'Social Issues in Computing' (with A. Borodin) 1973, 'Data Types and Structures' (with L. R. Gotlieb) 1978, 'Economics of Computers' 1985, over 100 articles on all phases of electronic digital computers; mem. Candn. Information Processing Society (which helped organize in 1958; Pres. 1960–61; Hon. Mem. 1987); Assn. for Computing Machinery (ACM); Fellow, Brit. Computer Soc.; Editor-in-chief Communications of ACM 1962–65, Journ. 1966–68; Editor, Annals of History of Computing 1977– ; Univ. of Toronto Faculty Alumni Award 1988; Jewish; recreations: sailing, swimming, chess; Address: University of Toronto, Toronto, Ont. M5S 1A4.

**GOTLIEB, Leo Ronald,** B.Sc., M.Sc., Ph.D.; management consùltant; b. Toronto, Ont. 8 March 1950; s. Calvin Carl and Phyllis Fay (Bloom) G.; e. Univ. of Toronto B.Sc. 1972; Brown Univ. M.Sc. 1974; Univ. of Toronto Ph.D. 1978; m. Marion Dorothea Levi 1992; DIRECTOR, CGI GROUP 1992– ; Asst. Prof. of Computer Science, Univ. of Toronto 1978–79; private consultant 1979; joined Gellman, Hayward & Partners Ltd. & co-founded Calgary office 1980, Principal 1986, Partner 1989–92; 3-month assignment for the Govt. of Colombia 1990; Certified Management Consultant 1985; Vice-Pres., Inst. of Cert. Mngt. Consultants of Alta. 1988–89; Mem., Candn. Information Processing Soc.; Pres., Inst. of Certified Mngt. Consultants of Ont. 1993–94; co-author: 'Data Types and Structures' 1978; columnist, 'CMA Magazine' 1992– ; recreations: skiing, sailing, cycling, classical music; Office: 33 Yonge St., Toronto, Ont. M5E 1G4.

**GOTLIEB, Phyllis Fay Bloom,** M.A.; writer; b. Toronto, Ont. 25 May 1926; d. Leo and Mary (Kates) Bloom; e. Public Schs., Toronto, Ont.; Victoria and Univ. Colls., Univ. of Toronto B.A. 1948, M.A. 1950; m. Calvin Carl. s. Israel G. 12 June 1949; children: Leo, Margaret, Jane; author of 'Within the Zodiac' (poems) 1964; 'Sunburst' (science fiction novel) 1964; 'Why Should I have all the Grief?' (novel) 1969; 'Ordinary Moving' (poems) 1969; 'Doctor Umlaut's Earthly Kingdom' (poems) 1974; 'O Master Caliban!' (science fiction novel) 1976; 'The Works' (collected poems) 1978; 'A Judgement of Dragons' (science fiction novel) 1980; 'Emperor, Swords, Pentacles' (science fiction novel) 1982; 'Son of the Morning and Other Stories' (science fiction collection) 1983; 'The Kingdom of the Cats' (science fiction novel) 1985; 'O Master Caliban' (science fiction novel) 1989; 'Heart of Red Iron' (science fiction novel) 1989; poems and stories publ. in mags. and anthologies in Can. and U.S.; poetry-dramas broadcast on CBC; mem. Science Fiction Writers of Am.; Writers Union of Canada; Jewish; Home: 19 Lower Village Gate, Apt. 706, Toronto, Ont. M5P 3L9.

**GOTLIEB, Sondra;** writer; b. Winnipeg, Man. 30 Dec. 1936; d. David Samson and Fanny Clare (Rossen) Kaufman; e. Univ. of Manitoba 1 yr.; Carleton Univ. 2 yrs.; m. Allan Ezra (Candn. Ambassador to U.S.) s. David and Sarah G. 20 Dec. 1955; children: Rebecca, Marcus, Rachel; former Columnist, Washington Post; Toronto Sun; Financial Post; author 'Washington Rollercoaster' 1990; ''Wife of' An Irreverant Account of Life in Washington' 1985; 'First Lady Last Lady' (novel) 1981; 'The Gourmet's Canada' 1972; 'Cross Canada Cooking' 1976; 'True Confections (novel) 1978; ed. 'Where to Eat in Canada' 1972; articles publ. in Macleans, New York Times, Vanity Fair, Chatelaine, Homemakers; winner, also finalist Stephen Leacock Prize for Humour; Address: Ste. 5300, P.O. Box 85, Commerce Ct. W., Toronto, Ont. M5L 1B9.

**GOTTDANK, Michael Kim;** business executive; b. Ottawa, Ont. 4 July 1953; s. Arthur J. and Violet K. (Fisher) G.; e. Gloucester High Sch. 1972; Carleton Univ. 1973–74; R.I.A. Prog. 1974–78; m. Barbara d. James and Madeline Barnard 21 Nov. 1977; one child Kayla Leigh; Co-Founder, Pres. & Chief Extve. Offr., COM/MIT Leasing 1983– ; financial cons. 1976–83; Dir. Gottdank Holdings Corp.; recreations: squash, hunting, fishing; Club: Country (Aylmer, Qué.); Home: R.R. 1 Kemptville, Ont. K0G 1J0.

**GOUDGE, T.A.,** M.A., Ph.D., LL.D., F.R.S.C. (1955); university professor; b. Halifax, N.S. 19 Jan. 1910; s. Thomas Norman and Effie (Anderson) G.; e. Halifax (N.S.) Acad., Grad. 1927; Dalhousie Univ., B.A. 1931 and M.A. 1932; Univ. of Toronto, Ph.D. 1937; Harvard Univ., 1936–37; m. Helen Beryl, d. H. B. Christilaw, Blind River, Ont., 23 June 1936; one s. Stephen T.; PROF. EMERITUS OF PHILOSOPHY, UNIV. OF TORONTO, since 1976; Interim Lect. in Philos., Waterloo Coll., Ont., 1934; Fellow and Tutor in Philos. and later Lect., Queen's Univ., 1935–38; Lect. in Philos., Univ., of Toronto, 1938–40; Asst. Prof. 1940–45, Assoc. Prof. 1945–49; Prof. 1949–75 and Chrmn. of Dept. 1963–69; Special Lect. 1975–76; mem. of Editorial Comte., 'University of Toronto Quarterly' 1951–76

(Acting Editor, 1955); served in 2nd World War; joined R.C.N.V.R., 1943, with rank of Sub-Lieut. (S.B.); discharged 1945, Lieut.-Commdr. (S.B.); author of 'Bergson's Introduction to Metaphysics' 1949; 'The Thought of C.S. Peirce' 1950; 'The Ascent of Life' 1961 (Governor General's award winner, 1961); more than 50 articles on philos. subjects, logic, epistemology, philos. of science, etc. in learned journs.; Pres., Candn. Philos. Assn. (1964); mem. Editorial Board, Ency. of Phil.; mem. Editorial Board, The Monist; mem., Am. Philos Assn.; Mind Assn.; Humanities Assn. of Can.; Pres., Charles S. Peirce Soc., 1957–59; mem. Acad. Panel, Can. Council 1965–68; received Centennial Medal, 1967; Canada Council Sr. Fellowship, 1970–71; 'Pragmatism and Purpose: Essays Presented to Thomas A. Goudge' 1981; recreation: oil painting; Home: 244 Glenrose Ave., Toronto, Ont. M4T 1K9.

**GOUDIE, John E.,** CMA, FCMA; b. Calgary, Alta. 3 March 1924; m. Audrey E., 1948; Dir., Alberta Natural Gas Co. Ltd.; mem., Soc. of Mgmt. Accountants; Clubs: The Calgary Golf and Country; Ranchmen's; Calgary Petroleum; Calgary Professional; Glencoe; Address: 2900, 240 – 4th Ave. S.W., Calgary, Alta. T2P 4L7.

**GOUDIE, Scott William;** visual artist; musician; b. St. John's, Nfld. 1 Nov. 1955; s. Herbert William and Joan Elizabeth (Hibbs) G.; e. private art and music studies 1967–72; Vancouver Sch. of Art 1972–74; apprentice Open Studio Toronto 1979–82; m. Ingrid A. Fraser 7 June 1986; freelance artist since 1977, exhns. incl. Gallery Pascal, Geraldine Davis Gallery Toronto and Christina Parker Fine Art, St. John's, Nfld.; studied blues guitar performing various clubs and concerts; recorded music progs. CBC Radio both acoustic and with band since 1977; released album 'Renata' 1982; recipient 4 grants Nfld. Arts Council 1978–86; Can. Council Materials Grant 1978; 2 grants Elizabeth Greenshields Found. 1981, 1985; 1st Prize Nfld. Arts & Letters Competition 1980, 1989; 1st Prize Cognac, France for 2 mezzotints and 2 water colours of Baffin Is.; recreation: fly fishing (salmon); Office: Phoenix Press, P.O. Box 2627 Station C, St. John's, Nfld. A1C 6K1.

**GOUDREAULT, Henri,** O.M.I., B.A. L.Ph., L.S.Sc., D.Th.; educator; b. Casey Twp., Ont. 30 Apr. 1928; s. Alfred and Marie-Anna (Labonté) G.; e. Belle-Vallée, Case Twp. 1942; Univ. of Ottawa High Sch. 1946; Coll. Univ. of Ottawa 1946–48; Univ. of Ottawa B.A., B.Ph. 1951, L.Ph. 1952, L.Th. 1957; Pontifical Biblical Inst. Rome L.S.Sc. 1965; Institut Catholique de Paris D.Th. 1969; BISHOP OF LABRADOR CITY-SCHEFFERVILLE 1987– ; Prof. of Theol. Univ. of Ottawa (now St. Paul Univ.) 1957–62, 1965–66, 1968–71; Dir. Inst. of Mission Studies, Saint Paul Univ. 1971–77; Rector, same univ. 1977–85; Superior Provincial of the Oblates Saint Joseph's Province 1985–87; mem. Extve. Pastoral Council Archdiocese of Ottawa 1970–72, Vice Pres. Priests' Synod 1972–73; mem. Council Adm., L'Entraide Missionnaire Montréal 1971–77; Nat. Missy. Council 1972–75; Council Adm., Assn. canadienne d'éduc. des adultes dans les univs. de langue française 1979–82; Le Centre Saint Pierre Apôtre Montréal 1979–82; Prov. Council, O.M.I. (Saint Joseph's Prov.) 1973–79, 1982–85; Observer, Holy See 5th meeting World Food Council 1979; Delegate of Holy See Centennial Forum (100th session of Internat. Wheat Council) 1984; Del. of R.C. Ch. at Ang. Nat. Meeting 'Partners in Mission Consultation' 1979; Mem., Congregation for the Evangelization of Peoples, Rome 1989– ; mem. Candn. Oblate Conf. of Mission 1976–80; Council Adm., Le Centre Missionnaire Oblat Montréal 1974–77; co-founder and mem. Council Adm., Med. Aid Foundation Can. 1981–84; Official Preacher Ecumenical Service Can. Week 1978; Vice-Pres., Oblate Conference of Canada (1985–87); teaching resource person in Lesotho, Malawi, Liberia, Haiti, U.S.A.; Delegate to the 1990 Roman Synod on the formation of future priests and ongoing formation of priests; mem. L'Assn. Jacques Maritain 1979– ; Soc. Canadienne de Théologie et Assn. catholique des études bibliques au Can. 1970–1985; author numerous articles; mem. ed. bd. 'Vie Oblate Life' (learned journal); recreations: swimming, volley-ball, billiards; Address: Bishop's Residence, EE 318 Elizabeth Ave., Box 545, Labrador City, Labrador, Nfld. A2V 2K7.

**GOUGEON, Guy,** B.Eng.; television executive; b. Montreal, Que. 17 Aug. 1938; s. Azellus and Aurore Loyer G.; e. McGill Univ. B.Sc. 1962; children: Diann, Robert; VICE-PRES., FRENCH TELEVISION, CANADIAN BROADCASTING CORP. 1990– ; Vice-Pres., Engineering, CBC 1982–90; Chrmn., Extve. Ctte., Broadcast Ctr. Devel. Project in Toronto 1986–90; has represented Canada at several symposiums & internat. meetings; Internat. Broadcasting Convention; Symposium Ctte., Montreux; active mem., Soc. of Motion Picture & TV Engineers (Presidential Proclamation 1986; Fellow of the Society 1990); Mem., Bd. of Dirs.: Montreal Opera Guild; Telesat Canada; Candn. Women in Radio and Television; Pres., Conseil international des radio-télévisions d'expression française (CIRTEF); author: 'Canadian Space Communications and the CBC' address at Dakar, Senegal, 28 June 1979; recreations: tennis, skiing, swimming, golf, music, reading; Office: 1400 east, René-Lévesque, 12th floor, #1233, Montréal, Qué. H2L 2M2.

**GOUGH, Barry Morton,** B.Ed., M.A., Ph.D., D.Lit., F.R.Hist.S.; educator and historian; b. Victoria, B.C. 17 Sept. 1938; e. Victoria Public Schools; Univ. of Victoria; Univ. of BC, B.Ed. 1962; Univ. of Mont. M.A. 1966; King's Coll. Univ. of London Ph.D. 1969; D.Lit. 1991; m. Barbara Louise Kerr (dis.); 2ndly Marilyn Joy Morris 1981; children: Melinda Jane, Jason Jeremy, Spencer John, Zachary Samuel Morris; PROF. OF HISTORY, WILFRID LAURIER UNIV. 1978– ; Pres., Clio Research Associates Ltd. 1986– ; Convocation founder, Univ. of Victoria 1964; taught high sch. B.C. 3 yrs.; lectr. in hist. Western Wash. Univ., co-founder Candn. Studies Program; co-dir. and archivist Pacific Northwest Studies Centre; teacher Northwest Interinstitutional Council on Study Abroad 1968–72 (Financial Dir. London, Eng. program 1970); Adjunct Prof. of Hist. Univ. of Waterloo 1972–77; joined present univ. as Assoc. Prof. 1972, Founding Coordinator Candn. Studies 1973–79, served as mem. Senate and Senate Extve. also Univ. Rep. to Humanities Council Can. and Social Science Fedn. of Can.; mem. ed. bd. Wilfrid Laurier Univ. Press 1973–80 and 1985–88; visiting lectr.: Duke Univ., Univ. of Victoria, Univ. of Me., Simon Fraser Univ., Univ. of B.C.; Visiting Fellowship, European Comn. and European Parlt. 1980; William Evans Visiting Professor, University of Otago, Dunedin, New Zealand 1982; NATO Visiting Scholar 1984; Visiting Scholar, St. Edmunds Coll. and Clare Hall, Scott Polar Rsch. Inst., Cambridge 1984–85; Distinguished Lecturer on seapower and maritime strategy to the Candn. Forces Coll. 1984–88; Visiting Scholar, Inst. of Commonwealth Studies, London Univ. and Scott Polar Rsch. Inst., Cambridge Univ. 1991–92; Archives Fellow, Churchill Coll. 1991–92; author 'The Royal Navy and the Northwest Coast of North America 1810–1914: A Study of British Maritime Ascendancy' 1971; 'To the Pacific and Arctic with Beechey: Lieutenant George Peard's Journal of the Voyage of H.M.S. Blossom 1825–8' 1973; 'Canada' 1975; 'Distant Dominion: Britain and the Northwest Coast of North America 1579–1809' 1980; 'Gold Rush!' 1983; 'Gunboat Frontier: British Maritime Authority and Northwest Coast Indians, 1846–1890' 1984; 'The Journal of Alexander Henry the Younger' 1988, 1992; 'The Northwest Coast' 1992; 'British Mercantile Interests in the Making of the Peace of Paris, 1763' 1992; 'Falklands/Malvinas' 1992; various articles and reviews in learned journals; recipient Can. Council, Koerner Foundation and other awards for research; John Lyman Prize N. American Soc. for Oceanic Hist. 1980 and 1985; B.C. Lieutenant-Governor's Medal 1984; B.C. Historical Federation Certificate of Merit 1985; Keith Matthews Prize, Candn. Nautical Research Soc. 1985; Roderick Haig-Brown Prize, B.C. Books 1985; Candn. Historical Assn. Regional History Award 1985; Chrmn., Jt. Comte., Candn. Hist. Assn.-Am. Hist. Assn. 1972–73; Life mem., Assoc. of Candn. Studies 1985– ; mem. Council Champlain Soc. 1975–89, Vice Pres. 1984–89; Chrmn. Kitchener-Waterloo Br., Candn. Inst. Internat. Affairs 1978; Pres., Kitchener Civic Centre Neighbourhood Assn. 1982– ; Foundation mem. and Pres., Candn. Friends of Kings College, London 1984–92; Charter Mem. and Pres., Candn. Nautical Rsch. Soc. 1987–90; Vice Pres., Wilfrid Laurier Univ. Faculty Assoc. 1987–88; Dir. & Extve. Mem., Ont. Confed. of Univ. Faculty Assocs. 1987–89; Bd. Mem., and Chrmn. of Publications, Ont. Historical Soc. 1988; Pres., N. Am. Soc. for Oceanic History 1988–92; mem. Nat. Council Candn. Human Rights Foundation 1980– ; Foundation mem., Friends of the Inst. of Commonwealth Studies, London Univ. 1989; Official U.S. Delegate to Internat. Comn. on Maritime Hist. 1990– ; Vice Pres. for Rsch. Communication, Social Science Fedn. of Can. 1990–92; NATO Research Fellow 1990–91; Chair, Acad. Restructuring Ctte., Wilfrid Laurier Univ. 1992– ; recreations: flyfishing, collecting benefactions; Clubs: The Athenaeum (London); Royal Commonwealth Soc. (Toronto and London); University (Waterloo); Kitchener Rotary; Home: 37 Ahrens St. W., Kitchener, Ont. N2H 4B6; Office: Waterloo, Ont. N2L 3C5.

**GOUGH, Denis Ian,** M.Sc., Ph.D., D.Sc., F.R.S.C., F.R.A.S.; geophysicist; educator; b. Port Elizabeth, S. Africa 20 June 1922; s. Frederick William and Ivy Catherine (Hingle) G.; e. Selborne Coll. East London, S. Africa 1938; Rhodes Univ. B.Sc. 1943, M.Sc. 1947; Univ. of Witwatersrand Ph.D. 1953; m. Winifred Irving d. late William Irving Nelson 1 June 1945; children: Catherine Veronica, Stephen William Cyprian; PROFESSOR EMERITUS 1988– ; Prof. of Physics, Univ. of Alta. 1966–87 and Dir. Inst. Earth & Planetary Physics 1975–80; Research Offr. and Sr. Research Offr. S. African Council for Scient. and Indust. Research 1947–58; Lectr. and Sr. Lectr. Univ. Coll. of Rhodesia and Nyasaland 1958–63; Assoc. Prof. Southwest Center for Advanced Studies Dallas, Texas 1964–66; served with S. African Corps of Signals 1943–45; Hugh Kelly Fellow, Rhodes Univ. 1977; Visiting Fellow, Churchill Coll. Cambridge 1978; author numerous papers geophys. research; Past Pres., Internat. Assn. of Geomagnetism and Aeronomy; Fellow, Royal Soc. of Can.; Am. Geophys. Union; Geol. Assn. of Can.; Roy. Astr. Soc., Chapman Medal 1988; mem., Candn. Geophys. Union (Past Pres.; awarded J. Tuzo Wilson Medal, C.G.U. 1983); awarded Rudolf Krahmann Medal, S. African Geophys. Assn. 1989; D.Sc. (hon. causa) 1990; Anglican Catholic; recreations: reading, gardening, poetry, music; Home: 11747 – 83 Ave., Edmonton, Alta. T6G 0V2; Office: Edmonton, Alta. T6G 2J1.

**GOUGH, Douglas W.,** B.B.A. (Hon.), M.B.A.; banker; b. Montreal, Que. 14 Oct. 1947; e. York Univ. M.B.A. 1973; m. Karen 8 Dec. 1978; children: Laura; Ashleigh; PRES., MOSS, LAWSON MORTGAGE BANKING & INVESTMENT CORP.; Pres., First Business Finance Corporation; previously Financial Analyst, Confederation Life; Account Mgr., Internat. Banking Group, Citicorp Ltd.; Sr. Vice Pres., Commercial Banking, Bank of Montreal; Clubs: Granite; Hunt; Home: 135 Balmoral Ave., Toronto, Ont. M4V 1J5; Office: One Toronto St., Ste. 410, Toronto, Ont. M5C 2W3.

**GOUGH, William John;** writer; producer; director; b. Halifax, N.S. 24 Aug. 1945; s. Drs. James and Ruby (Case) G.; e. John Burke Reg. H.S.; Meml. Univ. of Nfld., var. courses; m. Anna Sandor d. Agnes and Paul Sandor 31 July 1981; children: Rachel Alice Sandor-Gough (2nd m.), James, Sarah (1st m.); joined CBC Radio (Nfld.) 1965; Host, then Extve. Prod. & Dir. (50 documentaries), 'Here & Now' CBNT 1972–78; Prod., (CBC) 'For the Record' 1979–82, 'One of our Own' 1979, 'Certain Practices' 1979, 'A Question of the Sixth' 1980, 'The Winnings of Frankie Walls' 1980, 'War Brides' 1980, 'Running Man' 1981, 'Cop' 1981, 'An Honorable Member' 1982, 'High Card' 1982 (also Dir.), 'Anne's Story' 1984, 'Charlie Grant's War' 1985, 'The Suicide Murders' 1986, 'The Marriage Bed' 1986; Producer 'Mama's Going to Buy You a Mockingbird' 1987–88; Producer, 'Two Men' 1988; Dir., 'Take Thirty' 'Access' etc. 1972–78 (CBC); 'Media Outport' 1974, 'The Brothers Byrne' 1974, 'A Figgy Duff Christmas' 1978 (NFB); Series Writer, 'The Campbells' (Sweetest Song), 1 episode 1986; Writer, 'The Campbells' (Face of a Stranger) 1987; Series Co-Writers, 'Seeing Things' 9 episodes 1983–86 & co-story cons. 1985–86; Writer & Prod., 'The Accident' (tv movie) 1983; Co-writer, 'A Far Cry from Home' (tv movie) 1981; (with Anna Sandor) 'Tarzan in Manhattan' (tv movie & pilot) Am. First Run/CBS 1989; (with Anna Sandor) 'Stolen One Husband' CBS 1990; Creative Producer, 'Tarzan' syndicated series (U.S., Canada, Europe), Writer 4 scripts for 'Tarzan' series 1991–92; Co-writer & Prod., 'Family of Strangers' CBS, Alliance, 1992–93; awards incl. Gemini Award, ACTRA, Prix Anik (three times), Genie, Bijou, Blue Ribbon Award, Am. Film Fest., Amerfest, Columbus Film Fest., Chris Plaque (twice), Chris Statuette, John Muir Med. Film Fest.; Mem., WGA West; Acad. of TV Arts & Sciences; ACTRA; Writer's Union of Can.; Acad. of Candn. Cinema & TV; Crimewriters of Can. (Immed. Past Co-Chair); PAND; author: 'The Proper Lover' 1986 (poetry); 'Maud's House' 1984 (novel); 'The Last White Man in Panama' 1987 (novel); 'The Art of David Blackwood' 1988 (art book); 'Chips & Gravey' 1991 (novel); co-author: 'Fingerprints' 1984 (short story); works widely anthologized; recreations: computer studies; Office: c/o Steve Weiss, William Morris Agency, Los Angeles, CA 90212.

**GOUIN, Serge,** B.A., M.B.A.; executive; b. Montreal, Que. 6 March 1943; s. Jean-Marie and Mariette (Champoux) G.; e. Coll. Mont Saint-Louis B.A. 1963; Univ. of W. Ont. B.A. 1965, M.B.A. 1966; m. Ginette d. G.H. Dupuy 22 Aug. 1964; children: Sophie, Philippe, Simon; PRESIDENT AND CHIEF OPERATING OFFICER, LE GROUPE VIDÉOTRON LTÉE 1991– ; Chrmn. of Bd., Télé-Métropole Inc. 1991– ; Asst. to Pres. J.E. Fournier Ltd. Montreal 1966–68; Mang. Consultant, Currie, Cooper & Lybrand 1968–73; Gen. Mgr. National Cablevision Ltd. 1973–76; Extve. Vice Pres., Canada Development Corp. 1976–83; Chrmn. of Bd., Savin Corp. 1983–86; Pres. & C.E.O., Télé-Métropole Inc.

1987–91; Bd. of Dirs., Le Groupe Vidéotron Ltée 1985– ; Cott Corp. 1986– ; Corp. du Groupe La Laurentienne 1991– ; Onex Corp. 1991– ; Mem., World Presidents' Organ. (WPO); recreations: cross-country skiing, hunting, tennis; Club: Mount Royal; Home: 740 Pratt Ave., Outremont, Que. H2V 2T6; Office: 300 Viger Ave. E., Montreal, Que. H2X 2W4.

**GOULANDRIS, Niki,** B.A., Ph.D.; trade executive; b. Athens, Greece 9 Jan. 1925; d. Minas and Eleni (Marketou) Kefalas; e. Univ. of Athens B.A. 1954; Univ. of Frankfort postgrad. studies 1956–60; m. Angelos N. s. Nicholas and Sofia G. 1944; BOARD MEMBER, INTERNAT. DEVELOPMENT RESEARCH CENTRE 1992– ; Co-founder, Goulandris Natural History Museum 1964; Dep. Min. for Social Services 1974–75; Dept. Pres., Nat. Radio-TV Orgn. of Greece 1975–81; Dept. Pres., Nat. Tourism Orgn. of Greece 1989–91; Mem., World Comn. for Culture & Devel. 1992– ; Officer, Légion d'Honneur; Doctor Honoris Causa, Aristotalian Univ. of Thesaloniki, Greece; recipient, Academy of Greece Award; Pres., Save the Children Assn. in Greece 1980– ; Mem., Brit. Linnean Academy; botanical painter with exhibits in major museums in U.S., London, Cyprus, Africa, etc.; illustrator of 2 books: 'Wild Flowers of Greece' 1968 'Peonies of Greece' 1984; Home: 45 Deligianni St., 145 62 Kifissia, Greece; Office: 13 Levidou St., 145 62 Kifissia, Greece.

**GOULD, Allan Mendel,** B.Ph., M.A., Ph.D.; writer / broadcaster; b. Detroit, Mich. (Candn. citizen) 22 Apr. 1944; s. Earl and Anne Helen (Zaldin) G.; e. Monteith Coll., Wayne State Univ., B.Ph. 1965; New York Univ., M.A. 1967; York Univ., Ph.D. 1977; m. Merle d. Harry and Rose Benjamin 30 May 1968; children: Judah Jonathan, Elisheva Sarit; civil rights work Miss. 1964; social work Newark, N.J. 1965–67; H.S. teacher, Toronto 1968–72; Lectr., Drama, York Univ. 1973–75; Candn. Drama, Univ. of Guelph 1976–78; Humanities, Univ. of Toronto 1978–81; Ont. Coll. of Art 1977–82; comedy & pol. satire writer & sometime performer var. TV & radio progs. incl. 'King of Kensington,' 'Shh! It's the News,' 'Canada AM,' 'Don Harron's Morningside,' 'Anybody Home?,' 'Thrill of a Lifetime'; author num. mag. articles; profiled columnist, 'Chatelaine' 1982–84; bus. columnist 'enRoute' 1986–87; bus./hum. columnist 'Report on Business Magazine' The Globe and Mail 1988–89; monthly columnist 'Financial Times' 1988–90; monthly book reviews Thomson Newspaper chain 1977– ; regular humour column and profiles, 'Canadian Magazine'; Pres., Osher Inc.; Vice-Pres., Ziv; recipient Author's Award Humour Found. for Advanc. Candn. Letters 1980; Brascan Award for Culture (Hon. Mention), Nat. Mag. Award 1981; author: 'The Toronto Book' 1983 (travel guide), 'Air Fare' 1984, 'The New Entrepreneurs' 1986, rev. paper ed. 1987 and 1990, 'Straight from the Lip' (under pseud. Jean Deau) 1986, rev. 1987, 'The Great Wiped Out North, or When Sacred Cows Come Home to Roost' 1988 (paper ed. 1989), 'Scarborough' 1988, 'Fodor's Toronto 1989, 1990, 1991, 1992, 1993' 'Canned Lit' 1990; 'What Did They Think of The Jews' 1991; co-author: 'The Unorthodox Book of Jewish Records and Lists' 1982, 'The Top Secret Tory Handbook' 1984, 'Introduction "The Holocaust"' 1985, 'Letters I've Been Meaning to Write' 1986, 'First Stage' 1987, 'The Violent Years of Maggie MacDonald' 1987, paper ed. 1988, 'Child Finder' 1989, 'Creating the Service Culture' 1990; 'Ghosts and Other Scary Stories' 1992; var. entries 'A Toronto Lampoon' 1984, 'Unsportsmanlike Conduct' 1985, 'The Canadian Encyclopedia' 1985, 1988; editor and anthologizer 'The Great Big Book of Canadian Humour' 1992; mem. Periodical Writers Assn. Can.; Writers Union Can.; ACTRA; Candn. Civil Liberties; Amnesty Internat.; P.E.N.; Beth Ha-Minyan; recreations: swimming, reading, theatre, music; Address: 31 Glen Rush Blvd., Toronto, Ont. M5N 2T4.

**GOULD, John Howard,** R.C.A.; artist; filmmaker; jazz musician; b. Toronto, Ont. 14 Aug. 1929; s. Graham and Mona (MacTavish) G.; e. Ont. Coll. Art A.O.C.A. 1952; m. Ingi Bergman; children: Maria, Ellen, Melissa; solo exhns. incl.: Here and Now Gallery 1961; Agnes Lefort Gallery Montreal 1962; Dorothy Cameron Gallery Toronto 1963; Arwin Gallery Detroit 1963, '64, '66, '68, '70, '72, '75; Hart House Univ. of Toronto 1965; Roberts Gallery Toronto 1966, '68, '70, '71, '72, '74, '76, '78, '81, '82, '84, '86, '88, '90, 92; Galerie Sherbrooke Montreal 1969; Art Gallery of Ont.; Whitby Art Centre; Tom Thomson Gallery Owen Sound; Algoma Festival Sault Ste. Marie; Art Gallery of Brant; Lynwood Arts Centre Simcoe; Masters Gallery Calgary 1983, 1987, 1993; Preston Burke Galleries Detroit 1988; Stratford Festival retrospective 1992; rep. nat. and internat. group exhns.; filmmaker since 1965; pioneered technique of drawn documentary for TV; works incl. 'Pikangikum' 1968 (Nat. Film Bd.); 'Marceau on Mime' 1971; 'Waubaushene Faces' 1975; rep. Can. Venice Biennale 1966 (short films); Instr. in Life Drawing Ont. Coll. of Art; author 'The Drawn Image' 1978; 'What a Piece of Work is Man' (litho portfolio) 1980; work incl. in 'The Nude in Canadian Painting'; 'One Hundred Years of Canadian Drawings'; 'Great Canadian Painting: A Century of Art'; 'Art in Architecture'; mem. Toronto Musicians Assn.; Jazz Albums: 'Fig Leaf Rising' 1979'; 'Gone to the Onion Room' '82; 'Good Tunes' '86; recreations: cross-country skiing, biking, swimming; Address: P.O. Box 132, Moonstone, Ont. L0K 1N0.

**GOULET, Lorette**; public servant; b. Hull, Que. 2 Feb. 1939; DEPUTY MINISTER, FEDERAL OFFICE OF REGIONAL DEVELOPMENT (QUEBEC) 1992– ; ten years, mngt. experience in private sector; Dir., Canada Mortgage & Housing Corp. 1976–81; Dir. Gen., Management Services, Indian and Northern Affairs Canada 1981–83; Dir., Health, Envir. & Housing, Min. of State for Social Devel. 1983–84; Special Advisor to ADM, Environment Canada 1984–85; Asst. Dep. Min., Conservation 7 Protection 1985–90; Assoc. Dep. Min., Environment Canada 1990–92; francophone, fluently bilingual; Office: 800 Place Victoria, P.O. Box 247, Montreal, Que. H4Z 1E8.

**GOULET, Robert Gerard;** singer, actor; b. Lawrence, Mass. 26 Nov. 1933; s. Joseph and Jeanette (Gauthier) G.; e. Royal Conservatory of Music, Toronto, Ont.; m. Louise Longmore 1956 (div.); one d. Nicolette; m. Carol Lawrence 1963 (div.); children: Christopher, Michael; m. Vera Chochrovska Novak 1982; made Broadway debut in 'Camelot' 1960; numerous stage appearances incl. 'Carousel' 1995; 'Finian's Rainbow' 1956; 'Gentlemen Prefer Blondes' 1956; 'The Pajama Game' 1957; 'The Beggar's Opera' 1958; 'Bells Are Ringing' 1959; 'Meet Me In St. Louis' 1960; 'The Happy Time' 1968; 'I Do I Do' 1970; 'Carousel' 1979; 'On A Clear Day' 1980; 'Kiss Me Kate' 1981; 'South Pacific' 1986/87/88; 'The Fantasticks' 1990; 'Camelot' (as King Arthur) 1990, 1992, 1993, 1994; star in ABC-TV series 'Blue Light' 1966; numerous television specials and guest TV appearances incl. 'The Big Valley' 1967; 'Police Story' 1970; 'Mission Impossible' 1972; 'Police Woman' 1975; 'Cannon' 1976; 'Dream Merchants' 1980; 'Matt Houston' 1983; 'Glitter' 1984; 'Murder She Wrote' 1985; 'Finder Of Lost Love' 1985; 'Mr Belvedere' 1986/88/89/90; 'Make My Day' (CBS Pilot) 1991; 'In the Heat of the Night' 1992; 'Based on a Untrue Story' 1992; star films 'Honeymoon Hotel' 1964, 'I'd Rather be Rich' 1964, 'I Deal in Danger' 1966, 'Underground' 1970, 'Atlantic City' 1981; 'Beetle Juice' 1988; 'Scrooged' 1989; 'Naked Gun II 1/2' 1991; has recorded over 60 albums; recipient numerous awards incl. World Theater Award; Tony Award; Grammy Award; Gold Album 'My Love Forgive Me' 1964; Hon. Fellow, Royal Conservatory of Music 1993; Address: c/o Rogo & Rove, 2700 E. Sunset Rd., Suite C-27, Las Vegas, Nevada 89120.

**GOURD, Alain,** B.Ph., M.A., LL.L.; federal civil servant; b. Amos, Qué. 17 Apr. 1946; s. David Armand and Anne G.; e. St. Paul's Univ. B.Ph. 1966; Univ. of Ottawa, M.A. 1968, LL.L. 1970; m. Jacinthe Théberge 8 Aug. 1987; children: Frédéric, Catherine; Associate Secretary to the Cabinet and Deputy Clerk of the Privy Council, Canada 1992–93; former Dep. Min. of the Dept. of Communications, Can.; former Prof. of Law & Philos. Univ. of Ottawa; law practice; Pres. and Dir. Gen. Radio-Nord Inc.; Pres. Radio-mutuel; Vice Pres. Civitas; Dir. Candn. Museums Constrn. Corp.; Pres., Internat. Inst. of Communications; Extve. Ctte. Mem., Assoc. of Professional Extves., Public Service of Can.; author or co-author various publs.; Home: 22 rue Cochrane, Aylmer, Qué. J9H 2G2.

**GOURLAY, Douglas MacLeod,** B.Sc.A.; former politician; agrologist; b. Brandon, Man. 1 Dec. 1929; s. late Andrew Judson and Catherine MacLeod (Rammage) G.; e. White Bank Lea Elem. Sch. 1943; Cardale High Sch. 1947; Univ. of Man. B.Sc.A. 1952; m. Audrey May d. late William Thomas Porter 27 Sept. 1952; children: Diane, Joan, Gerald, Robert; PRESIDENT & CHIEF EXTVE. OFFR., MANTEX HOLDING COMPANY INC. 1993– ; Settlement Offr. Fed. Dept. Immigration 1952–56; Agric. Rep. Prov. Man. Pilot Mound 1956–63, The Pas 1963–66, Swan River 1966–77; Councillor Town of Swan River 1972–75, Mayor 1975–77; el. M.L.A. for Swan River 1977; Re-el. 1981; former Min. of Municipal Affairs, Min. of Northern Affairs, Min. Responsible for Comm. Econ. Devel. Fund 1987–90; Gen. Mgr., Farm Debt Review Bd. (Manitoba); P. Conservative; Home: P.O. Box 387, Swan River, MB R0L 1Z0 and Winter Address: 210 Melton Place, Pine to Palm Resort Park, Weslaco, Texas 78596.

**GOVIER, George W.,** O.C.(1982), P.Eng., Sc.D., LL.D., D.Sc., D.Eng.; professional engineer; b. Nanton, Alta. 15 June 1917; s. George Arthur and Gertrude (Wheeler) G.; e. Univ. of British Columbia, B.A.Sc. (Chem. Engn.) 1939; Univ. of Alberta, M.Sc. (Phys. Chem.) 1945; Univ. of Michigan, Sc.D. (Chem. Engn.) 1949; LL.D. (hon. causa) Univ. of Calgary 1976; D.Sc. (hon. causa) McGill Univ. 1981; D.Eng., (hon. causa) Univ. of Waterloo; m. Doris Eda, d. Henry Kemp, 23 Feb. 1940; children: Gertrude Rose, Katherine Mary, Susan Elizabeth; PRES., GOVIER CONSULTING SERVICES LTD. since 1978; Chrmn. and Dir., International Permeation Inc. 1986– ; Dir. Candn. Foremost Ltd. 1979– ; Texaco Canada Petroleum Inc. 1985– ; Candn.-Montana Gas Co. Ltd. 1980– ; Candn.-Montana Pipeline Co. 1980– ; Roan Resources Ltd. 1980– ; Stone Webster Can. Ltd. 1980– ; Cooperative Energy Develop. Corp. (now Co-enerco Resources Ltd.) 1982– ; Western Gas Marketing Ltd. 1986– ; former Dir., Alberta Helium Ltd. 1973–86; Combustion Engineering-Superheater Ltd. 1980–87; Bow Valley Resource Servs. Ltd. 1981–87; Texaco Canada Inc. 1979–85; Instr., Lectr., Asst. Prof., Assoc. Prof. of Chem. Engn., Univ. of Alta. 1940–48; Prof. of Chem. Engn., 1948–54; Head of the Dept. of Chem. and Petroleum Engn., 1948–59; Dean of Faculty of Engn. and Prof. of Chem. Engn. 1959–1978 (except 1975–77); Chrmn., Energy Resources Conservation Bd., Alta. 1962–78 (mem. since 1948; Depy. Chrmn. 1959–62); Chief Deputy Minister of Energy and Natural Resources, Gov't of Alta. 1975–77; Publications: over 60 scient. and tech. papers; Fellow, Chem. Inst. Can. (Chrmn., Chem. Engn. Div., 1948–49, and Vice-Chrmn., 1959–60; Councillor, 1951–52); Foreign Assoc., Nat. Acad. of Eng. of U.S.; Chrmn., Sci. Programme Comm., World Petroleum Congresses 1975–83; Fellow, Engn. Inst. Can. (Chrmn., Chem. Engn. Div., 1961–63); mem. Candn. Nat. Comte. for World Petroleum Cong.; Candn. Inst. Mining & Metall. (Chrmn., Petroleum and Natural Gas Div. 1950–51; Pres. 1966); Assn. Prof. Engrs. Alta. (Pres., 1958–59; mem. Council, 1959–60); Fellow, Am. Inst. Chem. Engrs.; Dir. 1966–79, Vice Pres., 1976–79, Petroleum Recovery Inst.; Chrmn. Policy Comte 1977–78; Vice Pres. 1978–79 Coal Mining Research Centre; recipient: R.S. Jane Meml. Award, Chem. Inst. of Can. 1964; Award of Merit, Candn. Natural Gas Processing Assoc. 1964; Sesquicentennial Award, Univ. of Mich. 1967; Candn. Centennial Medal 1967; Centennial Award, Assoc. of Profl. Engrs., Geologists and Geophysicists of Alta. 1970; Selwyn G. Blaylock Medal, Candn. Inst. of Mining and Metallurgy 1971; Gold Medal, Candn. Counc. of Profl. Engrs. 1976; Achievement Award, Govt. of Alta. 1976; Sir John Kennedy Medal, Engr. Inst. of Can. 1987; Anthony F. Lucas Gold Medal, Soc. of Petroleum Engrs., AIME 1989; named 1978 'Oil Man of the Year' Oilweek Magazine; Member, Order of Canada 1976; Officer of the Order of Canada 1982; recreations: fishing, skiing, dancing; Club: Calgary Petroleum; Glencoe; Glencoe Golf & Country; Home: 1507 Cavanaugh Pl., Calgary, Alta. T2L 0M8; Office: 1507 Cavanaugh Pl., N.W., Calgary, Alta. T2L 0M8.

**GOVIER, Katherine Mary,** B.A., M.A.; writer; b. Edmonton, Alta. 4 July 1948; d. George Wheeler and Doris Eda (Kemp) G.; e. Univ. of Alta., B.A. (Hons.) 1970; York Univ., M.A. 1972; m. John Allen s. Beland and Florence Honderich 27 Feb. 1981; children: Robin, Emily Rose; first published pieces of journalism & fiction 1972; wrote fiction & non-fiction for major Candn. & Eng. mags. 1973–81; short fiction anthologized 'The Oxford Book of Canadian Short Stories'; 'Canadian Short Stories' ed. R. Weaver 1985; 'More Stories by Canadian Women' ed. Rosemary Sullivan 1987; 'Celebrating Canadian Women' ed. Greta Hofmann Nemiroff 1989; 'Essential Essays' ed. David Jackel and Maurice Legris 1990; 'Short Fiction' ed. Gerald Lynch and David Lampton 1991; 'Canadian Short Stories: Fifth Series' ed. R. Weaver 1991; Visiting Lectr., Prog. in Creative Writing, York Univ. 1982–86; Rsch. Fellow, Leeds Univ. 1986; Lectr. in Eng., Ryerson Polytech. 1973–74; Contbr. Ed., 'Toronto Life Magazine' 1975–77; recipient Nat. Mag. Award 1979; Authors Award Found. Advanc. Candn. Letters 1979; author: 'Random Descent' 1979, 1980, 1987, 'Going Through the Motions' 1981, U.S. ed. 1982, 'Fables of Brunswick Avenue' (short stories); 1985, UK ed. 1985; 'Between Men' (novel) 1987, UK ed. 1988; 'Before and After' (short stories) 1989, 1990; 'Hearts of Flame' (novel) 1991 (winner, 1992 City of Toronto Book Award); Mem., P.E.N. Can.; The Writers Union of Can.; Chrmn., The Writers Development Trust 1990–91; Chair, Writers in Electronic Residence (W.D.T.) 1991– ; recreations: skiing, travel; Home: 54 Farnham Ave., Toronto, Ont. M4V 1H4; Office: c/o Writers Union of Canada, 24 Ryerson Ave., Toronto, Ont. M5T 2P3

**GOW, David M.**; benefits consultant executive; b. Toronto, Ont. 25 Nov. 1930; s. James Taylor, Q.C. and Lesley Ford (Tudhope) G.; e. North Toronto C.I. 1950; Univ. of West. Ont.; m. Gail d. Murry and Vivien (Robinson) Frances 2 Oct. 1981; children: James Campbell, Lesley Janet, Valerie Jean; VICE-PRES. & GENERAL MGR., MLH+A INC. / K.G. BROWN ASSOC. LIMITED 1987– ; Estate Serv. Div., Can. Life 1954–61; Partner, Kenneth G. Brown Assoc. 1961–87; Part-time Lectr., Mohawk Coll.; Former Pres., Hamilton Estate Planners Counc.; Past Pres., Hamilton Philharmonic Soc.; Theatre Aquarius; Big Brothers Assn. of Hamilton; Hamilton Humane Soc.; Dir., McMaster Univ. Art Gall.; The Hamilton Found.; Hope Haven Homes and Family Rehabilitation Centre; Former Dir., United Way; Social Planning & Rsch. Counc.; Candn. Club of Hamilton; Elizabeth Fry Soc.; Dundas Valley Sch. of Art; Past Chrmn., The Hamilton Club; Mem., Hamilton C. of C.; Candn. Pension Conf.; Assn. of Candn. Pension Mngt.; Candn. Assn. of Pre-retirement planners; clubs: Toronto Badminton & Racquet, The Hamilton Golf & Country; Tamahaac; Home: 279 Bay St. S., Hamilton, Ont. L8P 3J5; Office: 1 Hughson St. N., Hamilton, Ont. L8R 3L5.

**GOW, Hon. James John,** B.L., Ph.D., LL.D.; retired judge; b. Aberdeen, Scot. 24 July 1918; B.L. 1947; Ph.D. 1950; LL.D. 1964; Judge, Supreme Court of B.C. 1987–93, Retired; called to Bar of B.C. 1968; cr. Q.C. 1983; Judge, County Court Vancouver Island 1985; served with Brit. Army 1939–46, 5th Bn. Gordon Highlanders, 51st Highland Div.; Life Bencher, Law Soc. B.C.; Home: 1377 Hampshire Rd., Victoria, B.C. V8S 4T4.

**GOWAN, Charles Walter;** personnel consultant; b. Winnipeg, Man. 12 Apr. 1910; e. Kelvin High Sch. Winnipeg; Univ. of Man. 2 yrs.; m. Georgina Steuart Hubie (dec.); children: Robert Fraser, Charles Edward, Janet Alice, Marjory Frances; Pres. and Gen. Mgr. Gowan Personnel Service 1958–78, 1982–91; City of Winnipeg 1941–50, Audit Dept., Asst. Mgmt. Personnel Dept.; Sanatorium Bd. of Man. 1950–52, Asst. to Exec. Dir.; MacLeod's Ltd. 1952–55, Personnel Mgr.; Federated Co-operatives Ltd. 1955–58, Br. Personnel Mgr.; served Gen. Curriculum Ctte. Man. Dept. Edn. 1947–49; Offr. and Lectr. Adult Edn. Group 1935–39; Personnel Assn. Winnipeg mem. 1948–83; Social Service Audit Prov. Man.; mem. Chaplains' Volunteers Stony Mountain Correctional Instn. 1967–72; mem. Bd. Opportunities for Independence 1983–90; Anglican; recreations: summer cottage, canoeing, swimming; Home: 305, 71 Roslyn Rd., Winnipeg, Man. R3L 0G2.

**GOWDEY, Charles Willis,** B.A., M.Sc., D.Phil.; educator; b. St. Thomas, Ont. 3 Sept. 1920; s. William Charles and Myrtle (Craford) G.; e. St. Thomas Coll. Inst. 1940; Univ. of W. Ont. B.A. 1944, M.Sc. 1946; Oxford Univ. D.Phil. 1948; m. Madelon Craig d. late Clarence E. Gilmour, London, Ont. Sept. 1946; children: David, Katherine, Kevin, Sheila; PROF. EMERITUS, PHARMACOL. UNIV. OF W. ONT. (Head 1960–81); Demonst. Oxford Univ. 1946–48; Lectr. present Univ. 1948, Asst. Prof. 1950, Assoc. Prof. 1952–60, Prof. 1960–86; served with RCAF Auxiliary 1951–64; mem. Defence Research Bd. Panel on Aviation Med. 1955–68; Candn. Drug Adv. Comte. to Min. of Nat. Health & Welfare 1962–69; Special Comte. on Compulsory Licensing 1965; Nat. Research Council, Assoc. Comte. on Dental Research 1965–68, Assoc. Comte. on Space Research 1967–69; author various research papers; mem. Pharmacol. Soc. Can. (Pres. 1964–65); Brit. Pharmacol. Soc.; Am. Soc. Pharmacol. & Exper. Therapeutics; Alpha Omega Alpha; Club: Harvey; Home: 428 Wortley Rd., London, Ont. N6C 3S8; Office: London, Ont. N6A 5C1.

**GOYER, Hon. Jean-Pierre,** P.C., Q.C. (1976); lawyer; corporate director; b. St. Laurent, Que., 17 Jan. 1932; s. Gilbert and Marie-Ange G.; e. Notre Dame des Neiges and Beaudet Schs.; St. Laurent (Que.) Coll.; Ste-Marie Coll.; Univ. of Montreal; children: Christine, Sophie, Julie; 1st el. to H. of C. for Dollard, g.e. 1965; re-el. 1968, 72, 74; apptd. Parlty. Secy. to Secy. of State for External Affairs 1968–70; Mem. of cabinet and Solr. Gen. of Can. 1970–72; Min. of Supply and Services and Receiver General for Can. 1972–78 and Min. responsible for Canada's relations with francophone countries 1976–78; resigned seat in House of Commons, Dec. 1978; Bd. of Dirs.: Bombardier Inc.; and of private investment corps.; Mem., Bd. of Trustees, Heritage Montreal Found.; Chrmn.: Montreal Cancer Inst.; Montreal Urban Community Arts Counc. 1982–89; recreations: tennis, skiing, squash; Liberal; Clubs: Forest & Stream; Dorval; Home: 30 Berlioz, Apt. 1105, Montreal, Que. H3E 1L3.

**GOYER, Robert,** B.Sc., Ph.D.; university professor; b. Montreal, Que. 13 May 1938; s. Charles E. and Cécile (Cousineau) G.; e. Univ. of Montreal B.Sc. 1962; Sorbonne, Paris Ph.D. 1965; children: Charles, Lysanne; PROF., FAC. OF PHARMACY, UNIV. OF MONTREAL 1987– ; Asst. Prof. 1965–69, Assoc. Prof. 1969–87; Rsch. Dir., Desbergers-Nadeau 1971–77; Pres., Clinipharm 1977–87; Pres., Jouveinal Can. 1983–87; Vice-Pres., Patented Med. Price Review Bd. 1987– ; Mem., Eastman's Comm./Enquiry on Pharm. Indus.; Nat. Rsch. Counc.; Med. Rsch. Counc.; Candn., Am., European and internat. assns., esp. in pharm., clinical studies & in regulatory affairs; author/co-author of over 75 sci. pubs. & communications; Home: 2911 Douglas, Montreal, Que. H3R 2C7; Office: Montreal, Que. H3C 3J7.

**GRACE, David Michael,** M.D., D.Phil., F.R.C.S.(C), F.A.C.S.; surgeon; educator; b. London, Ont. 7 May 1940; s. Archibald John and Mary Kathleen G.; e. Ridley Coll., St. Catharines 1953–58; Univ. of W. Ont. M.D. 1964; Oxford Univ. D.Phil. 1968 (Rhodes Scholar 1965); m. Linda d. Leonard and Phyllis Hutton 3 Apr. 1971; children: Gillian Claire, Michael John; PROFESSOR OF SURGERY, UNIVERSITY OF WESTERN ONTARIO 1990– ; Rotating Intern, Victoria Hosp. (London, Ont.) 1964–65; Resident, General Surg., Royal Victoria Hosp. (Montreal) 1968–72; Asst. Prof. of Surgery and Attending Surgeon present Univ. 1972, Assoc. Prof. 1978, Prof. 1990; Pres., London & Dist. Acad. of Medicine 1981–82; mem. Ont. Medical Assn.; Assn. for Academic Surgery; Candn. Assn. of Clinical Surgeons; Candn. Assn. of General Surgeons; author several articles in medical journals; recreations: tennis, skiing; Clubs: London Hunt; Devil's Glen Ski; Home: 151 Windermere Rd., London, Ont. N6G 2J4; Office: Univ. Hospital, London, Ont. N6A 5A5.

**GRACE, John Ross,** B.E.Sc., Ph.D.; university professor and administrator, professional engineer; b. London, Ont. 8 June 1943; s. Archibald John and Mary Kathleen (Disney) G.; e. Ridley College; Univ. of Western Ont. B.E.Sc. 1965; Cambridge Univ. Ph.D. 1968; m. Sherrill d. Alfred and Elizabeth Perley 20 Dec. 1964; children: Elizabeth, Malcolm; PROF. OF CHEM. ENGINEERING, UNIV. OF B.C. 1979– ; student summer work: Ellis-Don Ltd. 1962, Operation Crossroads (Africa) 1963, Atomic Energy of Can. 1964, Dupont of Can. 1965; during PhD studies at Cambridge did supervisions for King's, Fitzwilliams & St. Catherines colls.; Asst. Prof., Engr., McGill Univ. 1968–71; Assoc. Prof. 1971–78; Prof. 1978–79; Head, Chem. Engr. at UBC 1979–87; Dean of Grad. Studies, present univ. 1990– ; private consultant; profl. engr.; chartered engr. (U.K.); Faculty Affiliate, Pulp & Paper Centre; ERCO award, Candn. Soc. for Chem. Engr.; Lauchland Alumni Award, UWO; Killam Leave Fellowship & Killam Rsch. Prize, UBC; NRC Sr. Industrial fellowship working as Sr. Project Engr., S.N.C. Inc. 1974–75; mem., var. cttes., NSERC; Chrmn., Internat. Fluidization confs. 1980, 1989; Candn. Chem. Engr. Conf. 1991; Candn. Soc. for Chem. Engr. (Pres. 1989–90); Candn. Engr. Accred. Bd. 1988–92; Inst. of Chem. Engrs.; Assn. of Profl. Engrs. of B.C.; author of approx. 150 articles, books chaps., etc.; co-author: 'Bubbles, Drops and Particles' 1978; editor, 'Fluidization' 1980, 'Fluidization VI' 1989; recreations: jogging, classical music, contemporary art; Home: 7308 Angus Dr., Vancouver, B.C. V6P 5J9; Office: 235 – 2075 Wesbrook Mall, Vancouver, B.C. V6T 1Z1.

**GRACE, John William,** M.A., Ph.D.; journalist; b. Ottawa, Ont. 6 Jan. 1927; s. Archibald William and Beatrice (O'Connor) G.; e. Holy Cross Convent, Ottawa, Ont. 1934; Corpus Christi Sch., Ottawa, 1939; St. Patrick's Coll. High Sch., Ottawa 1941; St. Patrick's Coll., Ottawa, B.A. 1949; Catholic Univ. of Am., M.A. 1952; Univ. of Mich., Ph.D. 1958; m. Ruth Ellen, d. John Allen Herbert, Newport, Md., 8 Sept. 1954; children: James, Ellen, John, Christopher, Elizabeth, Anne; INFORMATION COMMISSIONER OF CANADA 1990– , Privacy Comnr. 1983–90; Instr., Dept. of English, Univ. of Mich. 1956–59; Ottawa Journal 1959–80 (Assoc. Editor 1959–79, Editor-in-chief and Vice-President 1979–80); Commissioner, C.R.T.C. 1980–83; Gov., Univ. of Ottawa 1968–81; mem. Canada Council 1971–77; mem. Coll. Inst. Bd. of Ottawa 1963–69 (Chrmn. 1967); R. Catholic; recreations: gardening, skiing, boating; Club: Gatineau Fish & Game; Home: 291 Clemow Ave., Ottawa, Ont. K1S 2B7.

**GRACE, Sherrill Elizabeth,** B.A., M.A., Ph.D., F.R.S.C.; university professor; b. Ormstown, Que. 18 Aug. 1944; d. Alfred Arnold and Elizabeth Frances (Cribbs) Perley; e. Univ. of Western Ont. B.A. 1965; McGill Univ. M.A. 1970, Ph.D. 1975; m. John R. G.; children: Elizabeth, Malcolm; PROFESSOR, ENGLISH, UNIV. OF B.C. 1987– ; Lecturer, McGill Univ. 1974–77; Asst. Prof., English, U.B.C. 1977; Assoc. Prof. 1981; Assoc. Dean, Fac. of Arts 1991–94; Senator 9 years; frequent guest lecturer, consultant, referee, conf. organizer; Edit. Bd. Mem., 'Studies in Can. Lit.,' 'Can. Rev. of Am. Studies,' 'Theatre History in Canada,' 'Zeitschrift für Anglistik u. Amerikanistik,' etc.; Canada Council Doctoral Fellow 1971–74; DAAD Rsch. Fellow 1985; Killam Fac. Rsch. Fellow 1990–91; Fellow, Royal Soc. of Can. 1991; Killam Research Prize 1990; F.E.L. Priestley Prize 1993; Mem., SSHRC Doctoral Ctte. 1986–88 (Chair 1988–89); Candn. Fed. for the Humanities Adjudication Ctte. 1993–96; held major rsch. grants; Mem., Candn. Comp. Lit. Assn.; ACUTE; Assn. of Candn. Studies; Assn. of Candn. Theatre History; Candn. Assn. of Am. Studies (Pres. 1990–92; Modern Language Assn.; author: 'Violent Duality' 1980, 'The Voyage that Never Ends' 1982, 'Regression and Apocalypse' 1989 and over 100 articles, book chapters & reviews; editor: 'Swinging the Maelstrom' 1992, 'Sursum Corda' 1994; co-editor: 'Margaret Atwood: Language, Text, and System' 1983; Office: 397 – 1873 East Mall, Vancouver, B.C. V6T 1W5.

**GRACEY, Donald P.,** M.A., M.Sc.; consultant; b. Woodstock, Ont. 15 Sept. 1948; s. William Garfield and Edith Elizabeth (Down) G.; e. Univ. of W. Ont. B.A. 1970; Carleton Univ. M.A. 1971; London Sch. of Econ. M.Sc. 1972; m. Nancy d. Bruce W. and Lora K. Coldham 5 Aug. 1978; children: Jordan Alexandra, Jaklin Anastasia; PRES. C.G. MANAGEMENT & COMMUNICATIONS 1982– ; Bd. Chrmn., ENPRODEMEX, S.A. de C.V. (Mexico) 1992– ; Asst. to Min. of Agric. 1972–74, Sr. Offr. Privy Council Office Govt. Can. 1974–79; Asst. Sec. Dept. of Prime Min. and Cabinet Canberra, Australia 1979–82; sessional lectr. Sch. of Adm. Studies York Univ., Sch. of Pub. Adm. Carleton Univ.; cons. World Bank/IMF; Exec. Dir. Senate Ctte. Terrorism & Pub. Safety; mem. Chancellor's Circle Univ. of W. Ont., Patron Gilbert & Sullivan Soc.; mem. Laurier Club; author various articles acad. publs.; United Church; recreations: reading, music; Clubs: Wellington; L.S.E. Soc.; Home: 8 Hunt Club Court, Thornhill, Ont. L3T 7L4; Office: 780, First Canadian Place, Toronto, Ont. M5X 1A9.

**GRADY, Albert Wayne;** editor; writer; translator; b. Windsor, Ont. 1 Aug. 1948; s. Albert and Zoe (Goodridge) G.; e. Carleton Univ., B.A. (English) 1972; children: Morgan, Claire; Ed., Harrowsmith Mag. 1987–89; Assoc. Ed., Weekend Mag. 1978–79; Managing Ed., Books in Can. 1979–84; Contbg. Ed., Sat. Night Mag. 1983–85; Managing Ed., Harrowsmith Mag. 1985–87; John Glassco Prize for Lit. Transl. 1984; Governor-General's Award for Translation 1989; mem. Lit. Translators Assn.; ed.: 'Penguin Book of Canadian Short Stories' 1980; 'Penguin Book of Modern Canadian Short Stories' 1982; co-ed. (with Matt Cohen) 'Intimate Strangers: New Stories from Quebec' 1986; ed. 'From the Country: Writings About Rural Canada' 1991; transl. 'Christopher Cartier of Hazelnut, Also Known as Bear' by Antonine Maillet, 1984; 'On the Eighth Day' by Antonine Maillet, 1989; 'Obomsawin of Sioux Junction' by Daniel Poliquin, 1991; Home: 142 Patrick St., Kingston, Ont. K7K 3P5.

**GRADY, Patrick Michael,** A.B., Ph.D.; economist; b. New York, N.Y. 29 Dec. 1947; s. Dr. Wm. F. and Norah (McClintock) G.; e. Schlarman H.S. (Ill.) 1965; Univ. of Illinois A.B. 1968; Univ. of Toronto Ph.D. 1973; m. Jean d. Mark and Ruth Fitzgerald 15 June 1968; children: Heather, Meghan, Mark; PRES., GLOBAL ECONOMICS LTD. 1988– ; Bank of Canada 1972–76; Dept. of Finance 1976–81; Dir., Fiscal Policy 1979–81; Principal, Grady Economics Ltd. 1981–86; Dir., Econ. Analysis & Forecasting, Dept. of Finance 1986–88; Phi Beta Kappa; Woodrow Wilson Fellow; Mem., Candn. Assn. for Business Economics; Candn. Econ. Assn.; co-editor, Candn. Business Economics; author: 'The Economic Consequences of Quebec Sovereignty' 1991, 'The State of the Art in Canadian Macroeconomic Modelling' 1985; editor: 'Peering under the Inflationary Veil' 1982; Home: 36 Granville Ave., Ottawa, Ont. K1Y 0M4; Office: 403 – 22 Metcalfe St., P.O. Box 927, Stn. B, Ottawa, Ont. K1P 5S6.

**GRADY, Wayne J.,** B.Com., M.Health Adm.; provincial civil servant; b. Halifax, N.S. 15 Dec. 1943; s. Joseph Myles and Helen Virginia (McNeil) G.; e. St. Mary's Univ. B.Com. 1973; Univ. of Alta. M.Health Adm. 1975; m. Sharon d. Richard and Mary Walsh 16 Aug. 1968; DEP. MIN. OF ENVIRONMENT 1991– ; joined Victoria Gen. Hosp. Halifax 1963–68; Izaak Walton Killam Hosp. for Children Halifax 1968–73; N.S. Health Services & Ins. Comn. 1975–76; Asst. to Dep. Min. of Health, N.S. 1977–87; Dep. Min. of Health & Fitness,

N.S. 1987–91; recreations: golf, skiing, fitness; Club: Ashburn Golf; Home: P.O. Box 38, Site 8, R.R. 1, Halifax Co., N.S. B0N 2S0; Office: P.O. Box 2107, Halifax, N.S. B3J 3B7.

**GRAEFE, Christian Wilhelm Arnold,** CM, FVR RI; investment consultant; consul of Finland; b. Helsinki, Finland 29 Nov. 1932; s. David Andreas Herman Arnold and Astrid Margareta Sunniva (Sandroos) G.; e. Finland and Germany; came to Can. 1952; m. Cynthia Jeanetta nee. Day; children: Mathias Maximilian Arnold, Victoria Sunniva Alexandra; PRES., CHRISTIAN GRAEFE AND CO. INVESTMENT CONSULTANTS LTD.; Pres., Internat. Candn. Petroleum Exhn. & Conf. Ltd. 1978–80; Internat. Candn. Trade Fair Mgmt. Corp. Ltd., 1979– ; Hon. Consul of Finland for Alta. 1975– ; joined Agric. Can. and Ford Motor Co. Oakville 1952–54; served with Royal Candn. Dragoons 1954–56; W. Command H.Q. Edmonton 1956–57; Weber Bros. Real Estate Co. Edmonton 1957–69, Dir. Internat. Div. 1967–69; Founding Pres. and Past Dir., German Candn. Business & Prof. Assn. Alta.; Past Chrmn. W. Comm., Candn. German Chamber Indust. & Comm. Inc.; Past Dir. Edmonton Real Estate Bd.; Scandinavian Centre Edmonton and Edmonton Exhn. Assn.; Member, Order of Canada 1979; Edmonton Ambassador Award for community service 1989; Knight in the Order of the White Rose of Finland 1987; Commemorative Medal, 125th Anniversary of Candn. Confedn. 1992; Knight-Commander, Military and Hospitaller Order of St. Lazarus of Jerusalem 1982; Co-Chrmn., The Governor General's 1992 Celebrations, Northern Alberta; mem. City of Edmonton Brit. Commonwealth Games Del. to Olympics, Munich 1972; Sponsor, Scandinavian Businessmen's Club; Home: #1207, 11135 – 83 Ave., Edmonton, Alta. T6G 2C6; Office: Lower Flr., Westin Hotel, Edmonton, Alta.

**GRAFF, Elyse,** B.A., P/IR; association executive; b. Toronto, Ont. 18 March 1945; d. Max and Bess (Resnick) Gelberg; e. Univ. of Toronto B.A. 1966; Cert. in Personnel & Indus. Relations 1982; one s.: Jonathan Edward Graff; NATIONAL EXECUTIVE DIRECTOR, CANADIAN COUNCIL OF CHRISTIANS & JEWS 1991– ; Mgr., Personnel Devel., Peoples Jewellers Ltd. 1980–82; Dir., Human Resources, Embassy Cleaners 1982–84; Cadet Cleaners 1984–86; Owner/Mgr., Elyse Graff & Assoc. 1986–88; Sr. Mgr., Orgn. Consulting, Laventhol & Horwath/Price Waterhouse 1988–91; Bd. Mem., Christian Jewish Dialogue of Toronto; Past Vice-Pres., YWCA of Metro. Toronto & Chair, Social Justice Ctte.; Past Pres., Young Women's Ctte., Metro. Toronto Assn. for the Mentally Retarded (Assn. for Community Living); Home: 701 King St. W., Suite 405, Toronto, Ont. M5V 2W7; Office: 44 Victoria St., Suite 600, Toronto, Ont. M5C 1Y2.

**GRAFFTEY, Heward,** B.A., B.C.L., P.C.Q.C.; b. Montreal, Que. 5 Aug. 1928; s. William A. and H. R. (Heward) G.; e. Mount Allison Univ., B.A.; McGill Univ., B.C.L.; m. Alida Grace, d. Mattheus Visser, San Francisco, Cal. 28 Dec. 1961; children: Arthur Heward, Clement Tai Yong, Leah; CHRMN., SAFETY SENSE ENTERPRISES AND PUBLICATIONS; Chrmn. of Bd., Montreal Lumber Co. Ltd.; Dir., Steamship Supply Lumber Co. Ltd.; Pres., Missisquoi Realties Ltd.; Past Dir., John Howard Soc. (1958); read law with Heward, Holden & Co.; called to the Bar of Que., 1955; 1st el. to H. of C. for Brome-Missisquoi in g.e. 1958; Parlty. Secy. to Min. of Finance, 1962–63; re-el. in g.e. 1962, 63, 65, 72, 74, 79; Min. of State (Social Programs); Min. of Sci. and Technol. Can.; Candn. Delegate to U.N., 1958 and 1966; author: 'The Senseless Sacrifice: A Black Paper on Medicine'; 'Lessons From the Past: From Dief to Mulroney'; 'Why Canadians Get the Politicians and Governments They Don't Want'; 'Safety Sense on the Road'; 'Safety Sense in the Home'; 'Safety Sense at Play'; P. Conservative; Anglican; Address: 317 Metcalfe St., Ste. 304, Ottawa, Ont. K2P 1S3.

**GRAFSTEIN, Hon. Jerahmiel (Jerry) S.,** Q.C., LL.B.; senator; b. London, Ont. 2 Jan. 1935; s. Solomon and Helen (Bleeman) G.; e. Univ. of W. Ont. B.A.; Univ. of Toronto Law Sch. LL.B.; admitted to Bar of Ont. 1960; m. Carole d. Harry and Molly Sniderman 4 June 1958; children: Laurence Stephen, Michael Kevin; SENATOR 1984– ; Chrmn., Bd. & Extve. Ctte., CUC Broadcasting Ltd.; Chrmn., Extve. Ctte., CITYTV; Muchmusic; Bd. Mem., MTV-Channel 47; Bd. Mem., Toronto Life Magazine; former mem., World Film Festival of Toronto, Inc.; Toronto Arts Awards; Canada/China Toronto Found.; Co-Chrmn., Adv. Ctte. to the 1988 Toronto Economic Summit; Chrmn., City of Toronto Asia/Pacific Ctte.; Mem., Metro World 1990; Exec. Asst. to Registrar-Gen. of Can. 1966; Special Advr., Dept. of Consumer and Corp. Affairs 1967–68; mem. Adv. Ctte., Dept. of Justice 1968–72; apptd. Q.C. 1973; Counsel, Minden, Gross, Grafstein and Greenstein; former Chrmn., Mgmt. Ctte., O'Keefe Ctr.; mem. Beth Tzedec Congregation; B'nai Brith; The Weizmann Inst.; Jewish; Liberal; founded and edited 'Journal of Liberal Thought' 1965–66; mem. Senate Foreign Affairs Ctte.; Senate Ctte. of Peace and Security; Special Jt. Senate & Commons Ctte. on External Affairs; Senate Constitutional & Legal Affairs Ctte.; mem., Ont. Bar Assn.; Candn. Bar Assn.; Am. Bar Assoc. (Assoc. mem.); York County Law Soc.; Law Soc. of Upper Canada; Broadcast Executive Soc.; mem., Canada-France, Canada-Europe Interparliamentary Assoc.; Canada-Japanese Friendship Assn.; Candn. Inst. of Internat. Affairs; Soc. of the Americas; recreations: tennis, squash; Clubs: University; Cambridge; Primrose; Oakdale; Turnberry (Fla.); Home: 499 Spadina Rd., Toronto, Ont. M5P 2W6; Office: Ste. 600, 111 Richmond St. W., Toronto, Ont. M5H 2H5.

**GRAHAM, Hon. (Bernard Alasdair) Al,** B.A.; senator; b. Dominion, N.S., 21 May 1929; s. the late Dr. John A. Graham and Genevieve MacDonald; e. schs. in Dominion and Glace Bay, N.S.; St. Francis Xavier Univ. B.A. 1950, post-grad. studies in English and Educ.; m. Jean Elizabeth MacDonald 30 June 1952; ten children: Patricia, Alasdair, John, David, Eileen, William, Daniel, Mary, Jean, Anne Marie; appointed to the Senate of Canada 1972; teacher, journalist, broadcaster, corporation executive; Special Asst., Federal Min. of Labour; Extve. Asst., Min. of Nat. Health & Welfare; Vice Pres. and Gen. Mgr., Middlesex Broadcasters, London, Ont.; Extve. Vice Pres. and Extve. Secy., Cape Breton Development Corp.; Pres. Liberal Party of Can. 1975–80; Mem. Internat. Observer Delegations to the Philippine Presidential and Congressional Elections 1986 and 1987; apptd. Nat. Campaign Co-Chair, Liberal Party of Can. 1987; Chrmn., Lib. Internat. Congress on Human Rights 1987; el. Vice Pres., Liberal Internat. 1989; Co-Leader, Internat. Observer Delegation to Paraguay Election, May 1989; Leader, Internat. Observer Delegation to Namibia, June 1989; Mem., Internat. Observer Delegations to Nicaragua, Feb. 1990, to Hungary, March 1990; R. Catholic; Club: Royal Cape Breton Yacht; Home: 93 Whitney Ave., Sydney, N.S. B1P 4Z8; Office: The Senate, Ottawa, Ont. K1A 0A4.

**GRAHAM, The Hon. Alan R.;** politician; b. Main River, N.B. 20 June 1942; s. Harrison Michael and Nellie Harris (Ross) G.; m.: 1st Sharon Crothers May 1964, 2nd Constance; d. Millard Tramley Jan. 1973; children: Shawn, Andrew, Patricia, Peter, Ashley; MINISTER OF NATURAL RESOURCES & ENERGY 1991– ; self-employed, operating companies involved in bldg. supplies, construction, lumber, farming, transp., export sales to U.S. & Christmas trees (25 yrs.); elected to N.B. Legislature, Riding of Kent Ctr. for the Liberal Party 1967, 1970, 1974, 1978, 1982, 1987, 1991 (youngest person ever elected to N.B. Leg.); Min. of Agriculture, Prov. of New Brunswick 1987–91; Dir., various cos.; Anglican; Mem., Spec. Task Force on Agric. to Liberal Party of Can.; Nat. Task Force on Mental Retardation; Normalization study for C.A.M.R.; recreation: fly fisherman; clubs: Rexton Curling, Boston Fly Casters & others; Home: Rexton, N.B. E0A 2L0; Office: P.O. Box 6000, Fredericton, N.B. E3B 5H1.

**GRAHAM, Angus Frederick,** M.A.Sc., Ph.D., D.Sc., F.R.S.C.; scientist; educator; b. Toronto, Ont. 28 March 1916; s. Frederick James and Mary Ann (Ball) G.; e. Univ. of Toronto B.A.Sc. 1938, M.A.Sc. 1939; Univ. of Edinburgh Ph.D. 1942, D.Sc. 1952; m. Jacqueline Françoise d. Joseph Poirier 3 July 1954; three s. Robert James, Andrew Donald, Paul Frederick (dec.); PROFESSOR EMERITUS, McGILL UNIV. 1986; Mem. of Bd. of Dirs., W. Alton Jones Cell Science Centre, Lake Placid, N.Y. 1980– ; Rsch. Assoc., Connaught Med. Rsch. Labs. 1947–58; Assoc. Prof. of Microbiol. Univ. of Toronto 1956–58; mem. Wistar Inst. of Anat. & Biol. Philadelphia and Wistar Prof. of Microbiol. Univ. of Pa. 1958–70; Gilman Cheney Prof. of Biochem., McGill Univ. 1970–86, Chrmn. of Biochem. 1970–80; mem. Scient. Adv. Bd. Inst. for Cancer Research Philadelphia 1974–82; ENS Biologicals, Inc., Toronto 1979–84; Mem., Virus and Rickettsiology Study Section, U.S. Public Service 1964–69; Eleanor Roosevelt Internat. Cancer Fellow, l'Institut du Radium, Paris 1964–65; Mem., MRC of Canada Comte. on Recombinant DNA, Animal Cells and Viruses 1975–77; Josiah Macy Jr. Foundation Faculty Scholar, Imp. Cancer Research Fund Labs.; London, Eng. 1977; Mem. of various grants comtes., Medical Research Council of Canada 1971–83; author over 100 research papers aspects cell biol. and virology various scient. journs.; Ed.-in-Chief 'Journal of Cellular Physiology' 1965–70; mem. various scient. journ. adv. bds.; mem. Am. Assn. Advanc. Science; Am. Soc. Microbiols.; Fellow, Royal Society of Canada 1978; recreations: skiing, sailing, tennis; Home: 4300 de Maisonneuve Blvd. W., Apt. 616, Westmount, Que. H3Z 3C7; Office: McIntyre Medical Sciences Bldg., 3655 Drummond St., Montreal, Que.

**GRAHAM, Anthony F.,** M.D., F.R.C.P.(C), F.A.C.P., F.A.C.C.; physician; educator; b. Ottawa, Ont. 9 June 1941; s. John and Susanne C. (Hill) G.; e. Queen's Univ. M.D. 1966; post-grad. training McGill Univ.; Royal Victoria Hosp. 1966–70; Stanford (Calif.) Univ. 1970–72; m. Shannon d. Douglas and Margorie Butt 24 June 1970; children: Mark, Heather, Suzanne; CHIEF, CARDIOLOGY DIV., WELLESLEY HOSP. 1980– ; Lectr., Dept. of Med., Stanford Univ. Med. Ctr. 1972–73; Cardiologist, present hosp. 1973– ; Assoc. Physician, The Toronto Hosp. 1973– ; Assoc. Prof. of Med., Univ. of Toronto 1973– ; mem. Bd. of Dirs., Wellesley Hosp. 1980–85; Pres., Heart and Stroke Found. of Ont. 1986–88 (mem. Bd. of Dirs. 1978– ;); Chrmn., Emergency Cardiac Care Ctte., Candn. Heart Found. 1983–85 (founding member of Ctte. 1976–89); Pres., Heart and Stroke Found. of Canada 1991–93 (mem. Bd. of Dirs. 1986– ;); Lifestyle Award and Medal, Health and Welfare Canada 1985; annual Tony Graham Award estbld. in his name by Heart and Stroke Found. of Ont. to honour Found.'s Outstanding Volunteer 1988; Canada Volunteer Award, Health and Welfare Can. 1992; involved in developing improved early care for heart attack victims through Emergency Cardiac Care Programs at the community level; author of 25 medical articles; recreations: sailing, skiing; Home: 10 Edgar Ave., Toronto, Ont. M4W 2A9; Office: 160 Wellesley St. E., Toronto, Ont. M4Y 1J3.

**GRAHAM, Anthony Richard;** investment dealer; b. Montreal, Que. 8 Jan. 1957; s. Francis Ronald and Renee Beatrice (Moncel) G.; e. Selwyn House Sch.; Bishop's College Sch.; Univ. of Western Ont.; m. Helen d. C.J. Chisholm 16 Sept. 1978; children: Laura, Diana, Marina; SENIOR VICE-PRES. & MNG. DIR., LEVESQUE BEAUBIEN GEOFFRION INC. 1983– ; Account Extve. Wood Gundy Ltd. to 1976–79; Vice-Pres. (Eur.), Levesque, Beaubien Inc., London Eng. 1979–83; Pres. & C.E.O., Sumarria Inc.; Dir., Continental Lime Ltd.; Energex Inc.; Graymont Ltd.; Graystone Materials Inc.; G.U.S. Holdings Inc.; Levesque Beaubien Geoffrion Inc.; Levesque, Beaubien & Co. Inc.; Power Broadcasting Inc.; Ronbec Holdings Inc.; Scott's Hospitality Inc.; Sulconam Inc.; Sumarria Inc.; Vice-Chrmn., & Gov., Wellesley Hosp. Found.; Gov., Bishop's College Sch.; Branksome Hall Sch.; The Wellesley Hosp.; The Shaw Festival; Trustee, The Art Gallery of Ont.; Ont. Coll. of Art Found.; former Gov., The Toronto Stock Exchange; The Canadian Securities Inst.; Mem. YPO; Clubs: The Toronto, National, Royal Candn. Yacht, Granite, Toronto Hunt, Founders, Caledon Ski, Montreal Racket; Home: 12 Edgar Ave., Toronto, Ont. M4W 2A9; Office: 121 King St. W., Suite 600, Toronto, Ont. M5H 3T9.

**GRAHAM, Charles Paul,** F.I.I.C.; reinsurance executive; b. Belfast, N. Ireland 4 Apr. 1934; s. Herbert and Lilian Elisabeth (Paul) G.; e. Royal Belfast Academical Instn. 1952; PRESIDENT AND CHIEF EXECUTIVE OFFICER, CDN. REINS. CO. 1988– ; sch. teacher, Belfast 1953; held positions with Phoenix Ins. Co., Candn. Surety Co. 1961–68; joined Candn. Reins. Co. 1968; Ins. Inst. of Can., Fellow 1968 (Past Pres., Toronto Chapt. Soc. of Fellows); Clubs: Albany, Toronto Cricket; Home: 41 Kimbark Cres., Markham, Ont. L3R 5Y9; Office: 99 Yorkville Ave., Toronto, Ont. M5R 3K5.

**GRAHAM, (Hugh Frederick) Colin,** B.Com., M.B.A., F.C.A., F.R.P.I.; chartered accountant; b. Ottawa, Ont. 2 May 1934; s. Frederick Wesley and Jessie Elizabeth Dulmage (Conn) G.; e. Glebe Coll. Inst. Ottawa 1952; Univ. of Toronto B.Com. 1956; C.A. 1959; Univ. of W. Ont. M.B.A. 1962; F.C.A. 1979; F.R.P.I. 1985; m. Sherrill 16 June 1990; children: David, Beth, Andrew Walker, Tyler Walker; PARTNER AND NAT. DIR., EDUC. INSTITUTIONS & NON-PROFIT ORGANIZATIONS, ERNST & YOUNG; joined present firm 1956, Partner 1967; Dir. Internat. Standing Conf. on Philanthropy, Geneva 1978– ; Chrmn. of Bd. Ryerson Polytech. Inst. 1979–83; Chrmn. of Bd. Havergal Coll. 1980–83, Chrmn. Rowing Comte. Upper Can. Coll. 1978–81; Treasurer, Timothy Eaton Mem. Ch. 1987–91, Recording Steward 1993– ; co-author 'Guide to Accounting Principles, Practices and Standards of Disclosure for Colleges and Universities of Ontario' 1977; 'Financial Reporting for Non-Profit Organizations' 1980; national distance education course 'Financial Management in the Non-Profit Sector'; author various articles; Chrmn. Comte. Colls. & Univs. Inst. C.A.'s Ont. 1972–76, Chrmn. Research Study on Financial Reporting for Non-Profit Organizations, Candn.

Inst. C.A.'s 1976–80; mem., Accounting Standards Comte. Candn. Inst. C.A.'s 1985–90 (Chrmn. 1989–90); mem. Editorial Bd. 'The Philanthropist' magazine 1987– ; mem. Ont. Counc. on Univ. Affairs 1987–93, Interim Chair 1992; Chrmn., Trust Companies Auditors Adv. Ctte., Office of the Superintendent of Financial Institutions 1988–94; United Church; recreation: curling; Clubs: University; Granite; Muskoka Lakes Golf & Country; Home: 172 Strathallan Blvd., Toronto, Ont. M5N 1T1; Office: P.O. Box 251, Royal Trust Tower, Toronto, Ont. M5K 1J7.

**GRAHAM, Colin C.,** B.A., Ph.D.; university professor; b. China 16 Jan. 1942; s. Walter G.C. and Alice (Swan) G.; e. Harvard College B.A. 1964; Massachusetts Inst. of Technology Ph.D. 1968; m. Rev Mary K. (Weir) d. Ruth and Donald Williams 26 March 1987; children: Jennifer and Alison Graham, Robert and David Weir; PROFESSOR, LAKEHEAD UNIV. 1989– ; Asst. to Full Prof., Northwestern Univ. 1968–91; Sigma Xi 1968; co-author: 'Essays in Commutative Harmonic Analysis' 1979; Office: Thunder Bay, Ont. P7B 5E1.

**GRAHAM, Hon. Donald Ferguson,** B.A., LL.B.; judge; b. Toronto, Ont. 31 Jan. 1921; s. Kingsley and Eileen G.; e. Upper Can. Coll. 1939; Univ. of Toronto Victoria Coll. B.A. 1942; Osgoode Hall Law Sch. 1948; one. s. Kingsley; JUDGE, ONTARIO COURT OF JUSTICE 1957– ; Chrmn., Metrop. Licensing Comn.; Chrmn., City of Toronto Housing Appeal Bd.; served with RCNVR 1942–45, rank Lt.; mem. YMCA; Clubs: Osler Bluff Ski; Toronto Lawn Tennis; Home: 102 Castlefield Ave., Toronto, Ont. M4R 1G4; Office: Old City Hall, 60 Queen St., Toronto, Ont. M5H 2M4.

**GRAHAM, Donald Ralph,** M.A.; lighthouse keeper; writer; b. Regina, Sask. 3 Aug. 1947; s. James Arthur and Marjorie Irene (Anderson) G.; e. Univ. of Sask. B.A. 1968, M.A. 1971; m. Elaine d. Michael and Rose Quinn 4 Jan. 1969; children: David Michael, Jonathan Zak; LIGHTHOUSE KEEPER, CANDN. COAST GUARD 1977– ; Econ., Sask. Econ. Devel. Bd. 1967–69; Cultural Conserv. Co-ordinator, Govt. Sask. 1970–76; recipient Roderick Haig-Brown Regional Prize, B.C. Book Awards 1987; author: 'Keepers of the Light: A History of British Columbia's Lighthouses and Their Keepers' 1985; 'Lights of the Inside Passage: A History of British Columbia's Lighthouses and Their Keepers' 1986; Address: Pt. Atkinson Lighthouse, P.O. Box 91338, West Vancouver, B.C. V7V 3N9.

**GRAHAM, Eric Stanley,** M.Sc., Ph.D., F.O.A.S., F.C.S., D.Mil.Sci., O.L.M.; retired university administrator; b. Kingston, Ont. 31 Dec. 1921; s. Stanley Newlands and Beatrice Deacon (Birch) G.; e. Queen's Univ. B.Sc. 1942, M.Sc. 1946; Mass. Inst. Technol. Ph.D. 1950; m. Barbara Frances d. late Laurence G. Herchmer 5 Sept. 1945; two s. Ian Stanley, David Laurence; Assoc. Prof. Kenyon Coll. Gambier, Ohio 1950, Prof. 1956, Head Chem. Dept. 1957–61; Research Assoc. Univ. of London (Ford Foundation Faculty Fellow) 1954–55; Coll. Entrance Exam. Bd. Advanced Placement Program (Chief Reader 1959–61) 1958–61; Am. Chem. Soc. Visiting Scientists Program 1958–64 (Visiting Scient. 1958–64; Dir. H.S. Visits 1959–61); Principal, Royal Roads Millitary Coll. 1961–83; Asia Foundation Visiting Prof. Univ. of Dacca 1961 (summer); Visiting Prof. Univ. of Redlands (Cal.) summers 1962, 1963, 1965; Honourary Visiting Fellow, Royal Military College, Duntroon, Australia, 1982; served with Royal Cdn. Corps Signals 1942–45 Eng.; N.W. Europe; Past Dir. Service for Admission to Coll. and Univ.; Fellow, Ohio Acad. Sciences; D.Mil.Sci., Royal Roads Mil. Coll. 1988; Sigma Xi; Anglican; recreations: fishing, golf, gardening; Home: 2864 Seapoint Dr., Victoria, B.C. V8N 1S8.

**GRAHAM, Francis Ronald;** business executive; b. Toronto, Ont. 6 May 1920; s. Francis Ronald and Helen Marguerite (Phelan) G.; e. St. Michael's Coll. Sch., Toronto, Ont. (1938); m. Renee Beatrice, d. Rene Moncel, Montreal, P.Q., 10 Mar. 1942; children: Susan (Mrs. David Wild), Ronald, Robert, Margot (Mrs. Peter Heyerhoff), Anthony, Ian; Chrmn., Sumarria Inc.; Pres. and Dir., Ronmount Holdings Ltd.; Dir., Sulconam Inc.; Pres. & Dir., Ronbec Holdings Inc.; Dir., Energex Pellet Fuel Corp.; with Bank of Nova Scotia, 1939–41; served in 2nd World War, 1941–46, with 14th Candn. Armoured Regt.; R. Catholic; Clubs: St. James's; Montreal; Royal Canadian Yacht; Toronto; Home: 34 South Dr., Toronto, Ont. M4W 1R1; Office: Suite 1020, 11 King St. W., Toronto, Ont. M5H 1A7.

**GRAHAM, Gary Duncan,** B.A., LL.B.; lawyer; b. Toronto, Ont. 2 Apr. 1955; s. Gordon Nelson and Reta Jessie (Cameron) G.; e. York Univ. B.A. 1977; Osgoode Hall Law Sch. LL.B. 1980; Mem., L.S.U.C.; m. Sandra d. William and Shirley Stephenson 30 Aug. 1980; children: Mark, Michael; PRESIDENT, WESTINGHOUSE CANADA 1991– ; Assoc. Lawyer, Blake, Cassels & Graydon 1980–83; Solicitor present firm 1983–85, Asst. Gen. Couns. 1985–88, Mgr. Radar Programs 1988–90, Vice-Pres., Sec. & General Counsel 1990–91; Lectr., Bar Admission Course; Dir., var. Westinghouse Electric Corp. subs. in Can.; Sir James Dunn Scholarship; Gov., Hamilton-Wentworth Jr. Achievement; Dir., Candn. Manufacturers Assn. 1993– ; Hamilton-Wentworth Chamber of Commerce 1993; Mem., Law Soc. of Upper Canada; Bar of Ontario; Hamilton Law Assn.; Hamilton-Wentworth Renaissance Ctte.; Dir., Energy Council of Can.; recreations: hockey, baseball, golf, tennis; clubs: Burlington, Golf & Country; Home: 3168 Trailwood Dr., Burlington, Ont. L7M 2B8; Office: 120 King St. W., P.O. Box 2510, Hamilton, Ont. L8N 3K2.

**GRAHAM, James Edmund;** executive; b. Coboconk, Ont. 24 Dec. 1933; s. Henry Archibald Roy and Etta Isobel (Jackson) G.; e. Lindsay (Ont.) Coll. Inst. Sr. Matric.; m. Lorna Margaret; children: Deborah Louise, Catherine, Jeffrey Edmund, Stephanie, Meredith; PRES., C.E.O. AND DIR., VERSA SERVICES LTD.; Bd. Vice Chrmn., Modern Building Cleaning Inc.; Chrmn. & C.E.O., Versabec Inc.; Chrmn., Major Foods Ltd.; joined Northern Electric 1953–61; Procter & Gamble (Sales rep., Supervisor, District Mgr.) 1961–75; Shopsy's Ltd., Div. of Lever Bros. (Gen. Sales Mgr.) 1976–78; Versa Services Ltd., Toronto (Vice Pres., Sales; Vice Pres., Mktg. 1979; Pres. & C.E.O. 1980) 1978– ; Mem., Ont. Business Adv. Counc.; Chrmn., President's Counc., 'We Care' Campaign for Easter Seals; Past Chrmn. and founding mem., Advanced Mgmt. Program for Hospitality Industry (AMPHI), Univ. of Guelph; mem., President's Ctte., Children's Aid Soc. Found.; Anglican; recreations: squash, tennis; Home: Mississauga Ont.; Office: Box 950, Stn. U, Toronto, Ont. M8Z 5Y7.

**GRAHAM, James Lee,** F.T.I.; bank executive; b. North Vancouver, B.C. 8 Sept. 1932; m. Sheila 1954; 3 children; CHAIRMAN AND CHIEF EXECUTIVE OFFICER, MANULIFE BANK OF CANADA 1993– ; joined Bank of Montreal 1951; various posts ending as Sr. Branch Mgr., Orillia 1977; Co-founder, Managing Dir. & C.E.O., Huronia Trust Co. 1977; Pres. & C.E.O., Huronia Trust, Cabot Trust, and Regional Trust 1991 (the 3 companies merged in 1993); Dir., Georgian College Found.; Pres., Helping Hands Orillia; Past Chair, Orilia Area Community Futures Corp.; Former Trustee, Trust Companies Inst. of Can.; Former Chair, City of Orillia Econ. Devel. Comn.; Orillia Devel. Corp.; Former Pres., Orillia & Dist. C. of C.; Bicentennial Medal for Community Service in Ont. 1984; Govt. of Can. Cert. of Merit for Community Contribution 1988; Citizen of the Year Orillia 1992; Office: 2 Mississaga St. E., Orillia, Ont. L3V 6H9.

**GRAHAM, John Jr.;** asset manager; b. Ottawa, Ont. 4 Feb. 1935; s. John and Susanne Clare (Hill) G.; e. Loyal Coll., Carleton Univ., Candn. Securities Courses, Stanford Univ.; children: John R., Alex E.; PRES., JOHN GRAHAM & COMPANY LTD. 1965– ; Pres., John Graham Realty Investors Ltd.; Jock River Farms Ltd.; Nat. Gov., Shaw Festival; former Dir., Investment Dealers Assn. of Can.; Ottawa Bd. of Trade; Artscourt Ottawa; co-author: 'Mayor's Task Force on Housing, City of Ottawa'; recreations: skiing, tennis; Clubs: Rideau, Rockcliffe Tennis; Home: 193 Lansdowne Rd., Rockcliffe Park, Ottawa, Ont.; Office: 130 Albert St., Ottawa, Ont. K1P 5G4.

**GRAHAM, John Richard,** B.A.; aid administrator; b. Calgary, Alta. 18 June 1957; s. Henry Irvine and Muriel Martha (Adams) G.; e. Univ. of Calgary B.A. (Hons.) 1979; Univ. of Victoria; m. Gillian d. John and Gretchen Brewin 29 Dec. 1983; children: Danielle, Iain; PROGRAMME OFFICER, OXFAM CANADA 1988– ; Co-ordinator, Arusha Cross Cultural Ctr. 1979–81; Vancouver Island Coord., Oxfam 1985–86; B.C. Coord. 1986–88; Mem., Group of 78 1985–92; Chair, Inter-Agency Working Group in S. Africa 1991–92; Cooperation Canada Mozambique 1989–91; Pres., N.D.P. Constituency Assn. Victoria 1985–86; recreations: nordic skiing, running, skating; Home: Box 50295, Windhock, Namibia; Office: 251 Laurier Ave. W., #301, Ottawa, Ont. K1P 5J6.

**GRAHAM, John Webb,** E.D., Q.C., B.A., LL.B., D.S. Litt.; b. Toronto, Ont. 10 Sept. 1912; s. George Wilbur and Rosaline Campbell (Webb) G.; e. Upper Canada Coll., Toronto; Univ. of Toronto; Osgoode Hall Law Sch.; m. Velma Melissa, d. William J. Taylor, 19 June 1941 (deceased 1971); m. Natalia Nikolaevna, d. Nikolaj A. Popov, 15 July 1976; one step-s. Edward Samuel Rogers, one d. Ann Taylor Calderisi; COUNSEL, CASSELS, BROCK & BLACKWELL since 1988; Chrmn. Emeritus, Rogers Communications Inc.; Rogers Broadcasting Limited; Rogers Telecommunications Ltd.; Rogers Cable T.V. Limited; Rogers Cantel Inc.; Dir. Scorfin Inc.; read law with Peter White, K.C. 1933–36; called to Bar of Ont. 1936; cr. Q.C. 1956; with Toronto General Trusts Corp. as Corporate Trust Offr. 1936–39; Solr., Daly, Thistle, Judson & McTaggart 1946–48; Gen. Counsel, Imperial Life Assurance Co. of Canada 1949–58; Partner, Payton, Biggs & Graham 1958–77; Cassels, Brock 1977–84; Cassels, Brock & Blackwell 1984–88; served with Gov. Gen.'s Body Guard 1930–36, Gov. Gen.'s Horse Guards 1936–39; 2nd World War in Can., U.K., and N.W. Europe with R.C.A.C. 1939–46; retired with rank Maj.; Hon. Lt. Col., Gov. Gen.'s Horse Guards 1970–75; Registrar, Inc. Synod, Diocese Toronto; Chrmn., Extve. Comte., Corp. of Trinity Coll. 1966–69; Pres. (1957–61) St. Paul's P. Conservative Assn.; Vice-Pres. (1966–69) P. Conservative Business Men's Club Toronto; mem. Candn. Bar Assn.; County of York Law Assn.; Assn. Life Ins. Counsel; Candn. Tax Foundation; Estate Planning Council Toronto; Sigma Chi (Internat. Pres. 1971–73); Conservative; Anglican; Clubs: Empire Club of Canada; The Toronto Hunt; The York; Albany; Royal Canadian Military Institute (Hon. Pres. 1988–94); Home: 2 Wood Ave., Toronto, Ont. M4N 1P4; Office: 40 King St. W., Suite 2100, Toronto, Ont. M5H 3C2.

**GRAHAM, Kathleen Margaret (K.M.),** B.A., R.C.A.; painter; b. Hamilton, Ont. 13 Sept. 1913; d. Charles and Blanche (Leitch) Howitt; e. Trinity Coll. Univ. of Toronto B.A., Hon. Fellow 1988; m. Dr. J. Wallace Graham 17 Dec. 1938; children: Dr. John Wallace, Janet Howitt; Solo exhns. incl.: Carmen Lamanna Gall. Toronto 1967; York Univ. Founders Coll. Toronto 1970; Pollock Gall. Toronto 1971, 1973, 1975; Art Gall. of Cobourg 1972; City Hall Toronto 1974; David Mirvish Gall. Toronto 1976; Klonaridis Inc. Toronto 1979, 1981, 1982, 1983, 1985, 1987, 1990; Frans Wynans Gall. Vancouver 1979; Watson Willour Gall., Houston, Texas 1980; Downstairs Gall., Edmonton, 1980, 1982; Lillian Heidenberg Gall. New York 1981, 1986; Elca London Gall. Montreal 1983, 1984; Survey Exhibition – Solo – originating at MacDonald Stewart Art Centre, Guelph, and touring 1984 – Glenbow Gallery, Calgary, Alta, Agnes Etherington Gallery, Kingston, Concordia University Gallery, Montreal, 1985 – Art Gallery, Windsor, Ont., Hart House, Toronto; The Douglas Udell Gallery, Vancouver 1993; maj. Group exhns. incl. 'Canada X Ten' 1974–75, 'The Canadian Canvas' 1975, 'Changing Visions, The Canadian Landscape' 1976–77 (all toured maj. pub. galleries Can.); 'Four Toronto Painters' Washington 1977; '14 Canadians' Hirshhorn Museum Washington 1977; 'Certain Traditions' toured Can. and Gt. Brit. 1978–80; 'Recent Paintings Bolduc, Fournier, Graham' London (Eng.), Paris, Brussels, Liverpool, 1982–83; Associated American Artists, New York, U.S.A. 1986–87; The Woltjen-Udell Gall., Edmonton 1989; The Woltjen-Udell Gall., Vancouver 1990; The Emma Butler Gall., St. Johns, Nfld.; Anglican; Home: 26 Boswell Ave., Toronto, Ont. M5R 1M4.

**GRAHAM, Laura Sara Emelia;** professional ballet dancer (modern, jazz, tap); b. Philadelphia, Pa. 6 Sept. 1964; d. Charles Richard and Edith Helena (Andreas) G.; e. National Ballet of New Jersey 1972–77; Joffrey Ballet School, full scholarship 1979–83; coaching from Laura Alonso (daughter of Alicia Alonso) in Habana, Cuba, Jacqueline Fynaert in Paris, France & David Howard in New York City; constantly learning & experiencing different perspectives, techniques & styles; PRINCIPAL, ROYAL WINNIPEG BALLET 1990– ; Principal Dancer, Nat. Ballet of N.J. 1977–80; Dancer, Joffrey III 1980–83; Royal Winnipeg Ballet Sch. 1983–85; Corps de ballet 1985–88; 2nd Soloist Jan. 1989; 1st Soloist July 1989; Top Prize, Varna Internat. Ballet Competition July 1990; performs a variety of roles from classical ballet, contemporary, jazz to modern ballets all over the world; major roles performed: Titania in 'The Dream,' and lead in 'Ballo Della Regina'; Tchaikovsky pas de deux; Louise in Neumiers' 'Nutcracker'; Kitri in 'Don Q'; Odette & Odile in 'Swan Lake'; Aurora in 'Sleeping Beauty'; Giselle & Queen of the Willis in 'Giselle'; Juliet in Van Dantzigs' 'Romeo & Juliet'; 'Firebird' title role; lead couple: 5 Tangos, Le Jazz Hot pas deux, Myth modern pas deux (created for her by Mark Godden), Concerto Barrocco; num. contemporary roles created for her incl. 'Anne' in ballet, 'Anne of Green Gables'; travelled extensively with Royal Winnipeg Ballet to Hong Kong, Taiwan, Thailand, Singapore, Malaysia, Japan, China, Germany, Holland, Russia, Hungary, Mexico, Peru, Argentina, Venezuela, France, etc.; TV appearances incl. 'Big Top' (snakes, black cat ...), Le Jazz Hot with Jacques Lemay for CBC; has appeared in commercials & music videos; recreations: travel, psychology, singing & acting, photography, seeking different coaches; Home: 29C – 626 Wardlaw Ave., Winnipeg, Man. R3L 0M2; Office: 380 Graham Ave., Winnipeg, Man. R3C 4K2.

**GRAHAM, Mark Stephen,** B.Sc., Ph.D.; curator; b. Hamilton, Ont. 8 Nov. 1958; s. Donald Frederick and Helen Patricia (Matricardi) G.; e. Univ. of Guelph B.Sc. 1980; Meml. Univ. of Nfld. Ph.D. 1985; m. Linda Marie d. Denis and Marita Ullyett 10 Oct. 1986; one d. Kate Marita; CURATOR OF FISHES VANCOUVER PUBLIC AQUARIUM 1987– ; Adjunct Prof. of Biol. Sci's Simon Fraser Univ. (NSERC Postdoctoral Rsch. Fellowship 1986–87); Co-founder Resolute Bay Aquarium, Cornwallis Island; author or co-author various sci. papers; mem. Candn. Soc. Zools.; Am. Soc. Zools.; Candn. Assn. Icthyols; Am. Soc. Icthyols. & Herpatols.; B.C. Assn. Profl. Biols.; Am. Assn. Zool. Pk's & Aquariums; Candn. Assn. Zool. Pk's & Aquariums; Am. Elasmobranch Soc.; Internat. Assn. Aquatic Animal Med.; recreations: scuba, fly fishing, running; Home: R.R.1 S-8, C-53 Gibsons, B.C., V0N 1V0; Office: P.O. Box 3232 Vancouver, B.C. V6B 3X8.

**GRAHAM, Philip David,** B.Sc. (Agr.); business executive; b. Toronto, Ont. 12 Nov. 1925; s. Francis Ronald and Helen Marguerite (Phelan) G.; e. Univ. of B.C. B.Sc. (Agr.) 1947; married; CHAIRMAN, GRAYMONT LIMITED; Chrmn., WestMount Press Limited; Dir.: Continental Lime Ltd.; Ecowaste Industries Ltd.; Graymar Industries Limited; Graybec Calc. Inc.; G.U.S. Holdings Inc.; Pres., Jopac Investments 1992 Limited, Hornfluh Holdings Limited; clubs: Vancouver, Royal Vancouver Yacht, Shaughnessy Golf & Country, Vancouver Lawn Tennis and Badminton; Office: 1160, 999 W. Hastings St., Vancouver, B.C. V6C 2W2.

**GRAHAM, Robert Grant,** B.Com.; b. Ottawa, Ont. 8 Apr. 1931; s. Wilmer A. and Lylian (Wiltsie) G.; e. McGill Univ. B.Comm.; m. L. Robin; d. Susan Diane; s. Bruce Wilson; CHRMN. & C.E.O., INTER-CITY PRODUCTS CORPORATION; Bd. Chrmn., Inter-City Products (U.S.); Dir., Canadian General Insurance Co.; Federal Industries Ltd.; The Great-West Life Assurance Co.; Investors Group Ltd.; MICC Investments Ltd.; Moffat Communications Ltd.; Mortgage Insurance Co. of Can.; Traders Group Ltd.; United Church; Clubs: Granite; Manitoba; National; Office: 20 Queen St. W., Toronto, Ont. M5H 3R3.

**GRAHAM, Robert James,** A.M.A.; executive; b. Toronto, Ont. 13 June 1936; s. Gawn and Mary E. (Stephenson) G.; e. Toronto Public Sch.; Leaside High Sch.; Meisterschaft Coll.; Univ. of Toronto A.M.A.; Harvard Univ. Sr. Financial Mgmnt.; m. Evelyn E., d. W.H. Ferguson, Hudson, Que. 21 Sept. 1963; children: Sean W., Joel T., Toby H.; VICE PRES., R.J. GRAHAM & ASSOC. 1991– ; Mgr. 1967; Vice Pres. Sales 1971, Sr. Vice Pres. 1973, Pres. and Dir. 1976, Canadian Dominion Leasing Corp.; Extve. Vice Pres., First City Trust 1978; Pres. & Chrmn., FidMor Investors Corp. 1981–84; Pres., First City Capital 1982–87; Dir., First City Trust 1985–87; Pres., Industrial Leasing Corp., Portland, Oregon 1986, Vice-Chrmn., Financial Trust 1989–90; Pres. & C.E.O., Morgan Leasing Inc. 1987–90; Home: 22 Gibson Ave., Toronto, Ont. M5R 1T5.

**GRAHAM, Stephen Douglas Andrews,** B.Comm.; business executive; b. Peterborough, Ont. 22 Dec. 1955; s. Douglas Charles and Marilyn Yvonne (Andrews) G.; e. Centre Hastings S.S.; Queen's Univ., B.Comm. (Hons.) 1979; m. Gillian d. Mary and Archibald Grace 25 June 1983; children: Nicholas, Joshua, Jake; PRES., SCALI, McCABE, SLOVES (CANADA) 1988– ; Mktg., Procter & Gamble (Can.) 1979–82; Group Mktg. Mgr., Coca-Cola Ltd. (Can.) 1982–86; Sr. Mngt. Cons., CMA Consulting 1986–88; Dir., Scali, McCabe, Sloves (Can.); Inst. of Candn. Advtg. (ICA); Candn. Children's Found.; mem., ICA; AMA; recreations: golf, tennis, skiing; clubs: Bd. of Trade, Donalda; Home: 63 Fairmeadow Ave., North York, Ont. M2P 1W8; Office: 2 St. Clair Ave. E., 8th fl., Toronto, Ont. M4T 2T5.

**GRAHAM, Victor Ernest,** M.A., D.Litt., Ph.D., F.R.S.C.; educator; author; musician; b. Calgary, Alta. 31 May 1920; s. William John and Mary Ethel (Wark) G.; e. Univ. of Alta. B.A. 1946; Oxford Univ. (Rhodes Scholar) B.A. 1948, M.A. 1952, D.Litt. 1968; Columbia Univ. (Open Fellowship) Ph.D. 1953; m. Mary Helena d. late Joseph Michael Faunt 1 Aug. 1946; children: Ian Robert, Gordon Keith, Miriam Elizabeth, Ross William; Prof. of French, Univ. Coll. Univ. of Toronto 1960–85; Asst. Prof. of French and Eng. Univ. Alta. 1948, Assoc. Prof. of French 1953, Prof. 1958; Assoc. Prof. of French present univ. 1958, Prof. 1961, Chrmn. Grad. Dept. French 1965–67, Assoc. Dean Sch. of Grad. Studies 1967–69, Vice Princ. Univ. Coll. 1969–70; mem. Gov. Council 1973–76; Can. Council Sr. Fellow 1963; Guggenheim Fellow 1970; Connaught Sr. Fellowship in Humanities 1978; Organist & Choirmaster, First Bapt. Ch. Calgary 1948–49, Grace Presb. Ch. Calgary 1950–58, Park Rd. Bapt. Ch. Toronto 1959–61, Yorkminster Park Bapt. Ch. Toronto 1961–62; Organist, First Ch. of Christ Scientist Toronto 1964–74; pub. recitals and concerts Calgary, Edmonton, Ottawa, Toronto, CBC; editor, Philippe Desportes, 'Cartels et Masquarades, Epitaphes' 1958; 'Les Amours de Diane' I 1959; 'Les Amours de Diane' II 1959; 'Les Amours d'Hippolyte' 1960; 'Les Elégies' 1961; 'Cléonice Dernières Amours' 1962; 'Diverses Amours' 1963; editor, 'Representative French Poetry' 1962, 2nd ed. 1965; 'Sixteenth Century French Poetry' 1964; author 'How to Learn French in Canada' 1965; editor, André Chamson, 'Le Chiffre de nos jours' 1965; author 'The Imagery of Proust' 1966; editor, Pernette du Guillet, 'Rymes' 1968; author 'Bibliographie des études sur Marcel Proust et son oeuvre' 1976; co-author 'Etienne Jodelle: Le Recueil des Inscriptions 1558' 1972; 'The Paris Entries of Charles IX and Elisabeth of Austria 1571' 1974; 'The Royal Tour of France by Charles IX and Catherine de Medici 1564–1566' 1979; author 'Chinese Snuff Bottles: A Critical Bibliography' 1983; co-author 'The Art of the Chinese Snuff Bottle: The J&J Collection' 1993; numerous articles prof. journs. and newspapers, book reviews; Presbyterian; Home: 100 Glenview Ave., Toronto, Ont. M4R 1P8.

**GRAHAM, William Carvel,** Q.C., B.A., LL.B., D. de l'Univ., (Paris); professor; b. Montreal, Que. 17 Mar. 1939; s. Francis Ronald and Helen Payne (White) G.; e. Univ. Hill Sch. 1951; Upper Can. Coll. 1958; Univ. of Toronto, B.A. 1961, LL.B. 1964; Univ. de Paris, D. de l' Univ. 1970; m. Catherine Elizabeth d. Hugh and Elizabeth Curry 1962; children: Katherine Helen, Patrick William; PROF., FAC. OF LAW, UNIV. OF TORONTO 1980– ; Dir., Ctr. for Internat. Studies, Univ. of Toronto 1986–88; Barrister & Solicitor, Fasken and Calvin 1967–80; Couns., Spanish Govt. Barcelona Traction Case 1966–70; Comn. of Enquiry into Bilingual Air Traffic Serv. in Que. 1976–77; Candn. Rep., UNCITRAL Conf. on Internat. Comml. Arbitr. (Vienna) 1985; Mem., Ont. Bar; Ont. Attorney Gens. Ctte. on the use of French in the courts of Ont.; Dir., Scott's Hosp. Inc.; Credit Lyonnais (Can.) Ltd.; Graymont Ltd.; Chair, Candn. Bar Assoc. Internat. Trade & Commercial Arbitration Ctte. 1986–88; Vice-Pres., Union Internat. des Avocats 1974–78; Vis. Lectr., Univ. de Montréal; McGill Univ.; Chevalier de la Legion d' Honneur 1985; Med. d'Or de l' Alliance Francaise 1980; Med. d'Argent de la ville de Paris 1983; Pres., Alliance Francaise de Toronto 1977–87; Candidate, Lib. Party of Can., 1984 Fed. election (Rosedale); Candidate (Rosedale) 1988 Fed. election; contbr.; 'New Dimensions in International Trade Law' 1982, 'International Business Transactions and Economic Relations' 1986; 'L'Arbitrage Commercial International' 1986; 'The Legal Framework for Canada-United States Trade' 1987; 'International Law Chiefly as Interpreted and Applied in Canada' 1987; 'The Canadian Law & Practice of International Trade' 1991; author of numerous legal articles; recreations: riding, cross-country skiing; Clubs: York; Rideau; Lansdowne; Home: 35 Sherbourne St. N., Toronto, Ont.; Office: 78 Queen's Park Cres., Toronto, Ont. M5S 2C5.

**GRAHAM, William Hugh,** B.A.; b. Winnipeg, Man., 18 May 1912; s. Robert Blackwood Whidden and Louisa (Ramwell) G.; e. St. John's Coll. Sch. 1929; Univ. of Manitoba, B.A. 1934; m. Catherine Eleanor Godfrey, 29 March 1940; child: William Hugh; Chrmn., Tarragan Theatre 1974–79; mem. extve. Nat. Theatre School of Can. (Pres. 1971–74); formerly Extve. Vice Pres. and Dir., MacLaren Advertising Co. Ltd.; served in 2nd World War 1940–45; Toronto Scot. 2nd Bn.; Queen's Own Cameron Highlanders of Can.; Staff, 6th Candn. Inf. Bgde.; II Candn. Inf. Div.; II Candn. Corps; author: 'The Tiger of Canada West,' biog. of Dr. William Dunlop, (Univ. of B.C. Award for Popular Biog.); 'Greenbank: Country Matters in 19th Century Ontario' (regional history awards: Cdn. Hist. Assn.; Ont. Hist. Soc.); publisher: 'Whittaker's Theatre'; Home: 56 Perry St., Port Perry, Ont. L9L 1J4.

**GRAN, Hon. Caroline Mary,** M.L.A.; politician; b. Saskatoon, Sask. 18 Nov. 1941; d. Charles and Hilda Irene (Handbury) Millard; e. Winfield High Sch.; m. John s. Levi and Margaret Gran 13 Oct. 1970; children: Blair, Corinne; Min. of Govt. Mgmt. Services and Min. Responsible for Women's Progs. 1989–..; served 17 yrs. radio advt.; Ald. Mun. Council Twp. of Langley 5 yrs.; Exec. Asst. to former Cabinet Min. 4 els.; el. M.L.A. for Langley 1986 and served 2 terms as Govt. Caucus Chrmn.; mem. various Cabinet Cttes. incl. Cultural Heritage, Social Policy, Legis. and Regulations; Min. Responsible for B.C. Bldgs. Corp., B.C. Systems Corp., Purchasing Comn., Superannuation Comn.

**GRANATSTEIN, Jack Lawrence,** M.A., Ph.D., F.R.S.C., D.Litt.; historian, author; b. Toronto, Ont. 21 May 1939; s. Benjamin and Shirley (Geller) G.; e. Coll. Militaire Royal de St-Jean 1959; Royal Mil. Coll. Kingston B.A. 1961; Univ. of Toronto M.A. 1962; Duke Univ. Ph.D. 1966; Memorial Univ. D.Litt. 1993; m. Elaine d. Percy Hitchcock 29 Nov. 1961; children: Carole, Michael (d. 1985); PROF. OF HIST., YORK UNIV. 1966– ; Director, Grad. Programme in History 1984–87; Historian, Directorate of Hist., Nat. Defence HQ Ottawa 1964–66; Ed. 'Canadian Historical Review' 1981–84; author 'The Politics of Survival' 1967; 'Peacekeeping: International Challenge and Canadian Response' 1968; 'Marlborough Marathon' 1971; Co-ed. 'Forum: Canadian Life and Letters 1920–70' 1972; 'Canada's War' 1975; 'Ties that Bind' 1975; 'Broken Promises: A History of Conscription in Canada' 1977; 'Mackenzie King: His Life and World' 1977; 'American Dollars-Canadian Prosperity' 1978; 'A Man of Influence' 1981; Co-ed 'The Gouzenko Transcripts' 1982; 'The Ottawa Men' 1982; 'A Reader's Guide to Canadian History' 1982; 'Twentieth Century Canada' 1983; 'Bloody Victory: Canadians and the D-Day Campaign 1944' 1984; 'The Great Brain Robbery' 1984; 'Canada 1957–67' 1986; 'Canadian Foreign Policy: Historical Readings' 1986; 'Sacred Trust? Brian Mulroney and the Conservatives in Power' 1986; 'The Collins Dictionary of Canadian History' 1988; 'How Britain's Weakness Forced Canada into the Arms of the United States' 1989; 'Marching to Armageddon' 1989; 'A Nation Forged in Fire' 1989; 'Mutual Hostages' 1990; 'Pirouette: Pierre Trudeau and Canadian Foreign Policy' 1990; 'Spy Wars: Espionage and Canada From Gouzenko to Glasnost' 1990; 'For Better or For Worse: A History of Canadian-American Relations' 1991; 'War and Peacekeeping' 1991; co-ed. '"English Canada" Speaks Out' 1991; 'Oxford Dictionary of Canadian Military History' 1992; 'The Generals: The Canadian Army's Senior Commanders in the Second World War' 1993, etc.; various articles pol. hist., defence and foreign policy in scholarly and popular journs.; Killam Research Fellow 1982–84, 1991–93; Fellow, Royal Soc. of Can.; Tyrrell Medal for Canadian History 1992; Joanne Goodman Lectr., Univ. of Western Ont. 1988; served with Candn. Army 1956–66; mem. Candn. Inst. Internat. Affairs; Home: 53 Marlborough Ave., Toronto, Ont. M5R 1X5; Office: 4700 Keele St., North York, Ont. M3J 1P3.

**GRANDMAÎTRE, Bernard;** Liberal MPP for Ottawa East; politician; b. Vanier, Ont. 24 June 1934; s. Léon Zotique and Rhéa Marie Louise (St-Louis) G.; e. Eastview High Sch. 1951; Cdn. Inst. of Sci. & Tech. (Bus. Admin.) 1956; m. Mariette d. Léon and Elzire Daoust 21 July 1957; two sons Denis, Marc; Official Opposition Critic for the Min. of Francophone Affairs and Municipal Affairs 1992– ; Alderman, City of Vanier 1969–74, Mayor 1974–80, 1982–84; Owner, Pharma-Plus 1970–83; el. Liberal MPP for Ottawa East in by-election 1984, re-elected 1985, 1987; Minister of Municipal Affairs 1985–87; Min. responsible for Francophone Affairs 1985–89 and Min. of Revenue 1987–89; Mem., Standing Ctte. on Govt. Agencies; former member of Cabinet Committees on Economic Policy and Northern Development; former trustee Ottawa General Hospital; named Ontario Outstanding Young Man 1970; Hon. mem. Royal Canadian Legion; mem. Institut canadien français; Institut culturel et social de Vanier; le Club Richelieu; le Club optimiste de Vanier, Knights of Columbus; mem. & Past Pres. Vanier Chamber of Commerce; Founder & Chrmn., Vanier Arena (renamed Arena Bernard Grandmaître in his honour 1985); recreation: golf; Club: Outaouais Golf; Home: 257 Lavergne St., Vanier, Ont. K1L 5E4; Office: Rm. 1414, Whitney Block, 99 Wellesley St. W., Queen's Park, Toronto, Ont. M7A 1A4.

**GRANDY, James Frederick,** B.A., M.Phil.; retired company director and former public servant; b. Ft. William, Ont. 24 Nov. 1919; s. Clarence Wood and Anne (Adams) G.; e. Univ. of Western Ont. (Econ. & Pol. Science), B.A. 1941; Oxford Univ. (Rhodes Scholar Christ Church), M.Phil. 1948; m. Alexandra, d. late Norman Shaw, 18 Aug. 1945; children: David, John, Kathleen; Chrmn., Candn. Marconi Co. 1981–91; Pres., Reisman and Grandy Ltd. 1975–85; sometime director various Candn. corporations and charities; joined Dept. of External Affairs, Sept. 1948; trans. to Dept. of Finance 1957; Asst. Secy. to the Cabinet, Privy Council Office 1963–64; Asst. Depy. Min. of Finance 1964–67; Depy. Min. Consumer and Corporate Affairs Dec. 1967–Sept. 1971; Depy. Min., Dept. of Industry, Trade and Comm. 1971–75; attended various internat. conferences and meetings of General Agreement on Tariffs and Trade; served in 2nd World War 1941–1946; Maj., R.C.A.; United Church; Home: 920 Muskoka Ave., Ottawa, Ont. K2A 3H9.

**GRANDY, Robert Duke,** LL.B., M.B.A.; investment banker; b. Toronto, Ont. 13 July 1951; s. Frank Stoodley and Myrtle (Johnson) G.; e. Univ. of Toronto LL.B. 1974; Harvard Univ. M.B.A. 1976; Osgoode Hall 1978; m. Joanne d. William and Frances Collins 25 Sept. 1976; children: Meghann Collins, Kathleen Margaret, Michael Richard; VICE CHRMN. MERRILL LYNCH CANADA INC. 1990– , Head of Invest. Banking 1989; called to Bar of Ont. 1978; joined Wood Gundy Ltd. 1978–81, Mgr. Prairie Region 1985–88; Vice Pres. Hatleigh Corp. 1981–82; mem. Mensa Can.; Fitness Inst.; R.Catholic; recreations: reading, golf, swimming, skiing; Clubs: Granite; Beacon Hall; Founders; Glencoe; Glencoe Golf & Country; Ranchmen's; Calgary Petroleum; St. George's Golf Club; Office: 200 King St. W., Toronto, Ont. M5H 3W3.

**GRANGE, Hon. Samuel George McDougall;** judge; b. London, Ont. 19 March 1920; s. Edward Wilkinson and Marion Osborne (McDougall) G.; e. Univ. of Toronto 1937–39; Osgoode Hall 1946–48; LL.D. (York) 1990; children: Alice Alexandra, Robert Morris McDougall; JUDGE, COURT OF APPEAL FOR ONT., and ex-officio Judge of the Ont. Court of Justice (General Div.) Sept. 1990– ; Judge, Supreme Court of Ont. 1974–90, Court of Appeal 1982–90; read law with T. H. Wickett, Q.C. and A. C. Heighington, Q.C.; called to the Bar of Ont. 1948; cr. Q.C. 1963; practised law with Heighington, Symons & Grange 1948–61; McMillan, Binch 1961–74; Chrmn., Min. Comte. on Franchising 1969–70; Chrmn., Min. Comte. on Hosp. Privileges 1970–71; Chrmn. Inq. into Legal Aid Clinical Funding, 1978; Commissioner, Mississauga Railway Accident Inq. 1980; Commr., Royal Comn. inquiring into certain deaths at Hosp. for Sick Children 1983–84; served in 4th Candn. Field Regt. R.C.A. 1940–45, rec'd. Croix de Guerre avec Etoile de Vermeille, France 1944; Bencher, Law Soc. of Upper Can. 1971–75 (Vice Chrmn., Legal Educ. Comte. 1973–75); Clubs: University; Lawyers (Pres. 1967; Hon. Pres. 1987–90); Home: 120 Rosedale Valley Rd., Suite 511, Toronto, Ont. M4W 1P8; Office: Osgoode Hall, 130 Queen St. W., Toronto, Ont. M5H 2N5.

**GRANIRER, Edmond Ernest,** M.Sc., Ph.D., F.R.S.C.; mathematician; b. Constanza, Romania 19 Feb. 1935; s. Jacob and Mina G.; e. Hebrew Univ. of Jerusalem M.Sc. 1959, Ph.D. 1962 (under H. Kesten); m. Pnina 10 Aug. 1954; children: Dan M., David E.; PROF. OF MATH. UNIV. OF B.C. 1970– ; Instr., Univ. of Ill. 1962–64; Asst. Prof., Cornell Univ. 1964–65; Asst. Prof., present Univ. 1965–66, Assoc. Prof. 1967–70; Visiting Assoc. Prof., Univ. Montréal 1966–67; author numerous rsch. articles various internat. math. jours.; mem., Candn. Math. Soc.; Am. Math. Soc.; Address: Dept. of Math, Univ. of B.C., 2075 Westbrook Pl., Vancouver, B.C. V6T 1W5.

**GRANSOW, Helmut Wilhelm,** R.C.A.; artist; b. Rottluff/Chemnitz, Germany 10 Jan. 1921; s. Wilhelm Johann and Frieda (Rempel) G.; e. Akademie der Bilden Kuenste Berlin 1945–47, Karlsruhe 1947–49; m. Pia Victorine (dec'd. 1960) d. Alexander and Emilie Scherf children: Alice Victorine, Ralph Hermann (dec. 1989); 2ndly m. Marguerite d. Milton and Adela Eaton 1962; came to Can. 1949; freelance artist since 1950; solo exhns. incl. Montreal Museum of Fine Arts 1953, 1958; Argenteul Art Assn. 1958; Galerie Moos Montreal 1967; Four Winds Gallery Ferrisburgh, Vt. 1973; Galerie Bernard Desroches Montreal 1974, 1976, 1978, 1980, 1983, 1986, 1989; Galerie L'Apogée St-Sauveur, Que. 1976; Galerie Michel Bigue St-Sauveur 1978, 1990; Kaspar Gallery Toronto 1981; Wallack Gallery Ottawa 1984; Yaneff Gallery Toronto 1989; 'Mexican Debut' Galeria L. Temple San Miguel D.A. GTO 1992; 'The Mexican Decade' Candn. Embassy, Mexico City 1993; group exhns. incl. Art Gallery London, Ont. 1951, 1952, annual exhns. Soc. Candn. Etchers & Engravers Toronto 1952–59; retrospective Candn. Printmaking Univ. of Toronto 1958; Fourth, Fifth and Sixth Winnipeg Show 1958, 1959, 1961; Exposition Provinciale Québec 1958, 1967; Art Gallery of Hamilton 1959, 1960, 1961; annual exhns. Candn. Soc. Graphic Art Toronto & Hamilton 1959, 1961; teacher Fine & Applied Art Chomedy Polevalent High Sch. Laval, Que. 1968–72; art classes Morin Hts. Sch. Bd. 1960–61; rep. various pub., corporate and private colls.; recipient Painting Prize Exposition Provinciale Qué. 1958, Graphic Prize 1977; Purchase Award Art Gallery Hamilton 1959; Hon. Mention Fourth Winnipeg Show 1959; subject numerous publs.; mem. Candn. Soc. Painters Etchers & Engravers 1956; Royal Candn. Acad. of Arts 1983; Address: 955 Village Rd., Morin Heights, Que. J0R 1H0.

**GRANT, Allison Jean,** B.Mus.; actor/singer/dancer; b. Vancouver, B.C. 23 Nov. 1958; d. Ian Van Felson and Antoinette (Toni) Suzanne (Grimm) G.; e. Banff Sch. of Fine Arts 1976; Univ. of West. Ont. B.Mus. (Hon.) 1980; Morley Coll. (U.K.); The Dance Centre (U.K.); voice teachers incl. A. Reimer, G. Little, M. Morrison, J. Mammon; performed with various choirs & appeared as soloist, Wigmore Hall (U.K.); five seasons, Stratford Fest. 1982–85 and starred as Julie Jordan in 'Carousel' 1991; toured across Can., U.S. & at the Old Vic (U.K.) in Gilbert & Sullivan operettas; created the role of 'Marie' in the World Premiere of Leslie Arden's 'The House of Martin Guerre' (Theatre Plus, Toronto) 1993; Cast Mem. (Toronto), 'Cats'; theatre roles incl. Mary in 'The Drunkard,' Susan in 'Desert Song,' Papagena in 'The Magic Flute,' Billie in 'Heat,' Fiona in 'Brigadoon,' Donna in the premiere prod. of 'Not Available in Stores,' Sarah in 'Guys & Dolls' and Sonia Walsk in 'They're Playing Our Song'; has appeared with symphonies across Can. in 'Gershwin and Gershwin'; taught Children's Drama, Alma Coll.; winner, 1986 Dora Mavor Moore Award for best actress in a musical for role as Mary Lennox in world prem. of 'The Secret Garden'; Tyrone Guthrie Award, Stratford 1982, 1983; co-author of a musical revue featuring Gilbert & Sullivan favourites; recreations: travel – Burma, Thailand, Egypt, Greece, Turkey.

**GRANT, The Honourable Campbell,** O.C., LL.D., Q.C.; retired supreme court justice; b. Norman By Twp. Grey Co., Ont. 3 Jan. 1902; s. William and Robena (Watson) G.; e. grad. Osgoode Hall Law Sch. 1925; m. Margaret Grace d. Charles and Louise Kyle 10 Sept. 1932; law prac., Walkerton 1925–62; Reeve & Mayor, Walkerton 1927–36; Warden, Bruce Co. 1933; apptd. Trial Div., Supreme Court of Ont. 1962; ret. 1977; Deputy Judge, Fed. Court of Can. 1977– ; (when requested); Dir., Victoria & Grey Trust Co. 1957–62; Prov. of Ont. Bicentennial Medal for Serv. to the Community 1984; Law Soc. of Upper Can., LL.D. 1985; Officer, Order of Canada 1986; Paul Harris Fellow, Rotary Club 1992; Chrmn., Blue Water Div., Arthritis Soc. (Ont.) 1979– ; mem., United Ch. of Can.; Univ. Club of Toronto 1962– ; mem. Rotary Club of Walkerton; recreations: golf, fishing; Clubs: Walkerton Golf; Hepworth Angler's; Address: 620 Gibson St., Walkerton, Ont. N0G 2V0.

**GRANT, Carl T.,** Q.C.; b. Ottawa, Ont. 20 June 1933; s. Archibald Joseph and Patricia (Cormier) G.; e. Lisgar Coll. Inst., 1951; Carleton Coll., B.A. 1955; Osgoode Hall Law Sch., 1959; m. Valerie Price 6 Sept. 1990; children (from previous marriage): Michèle, Gregory, Nadine; PARTNER, AIRD & BERLIS; President & Dir. no. of real estate devel. and invest. co.'s; called to Bar of Ont. 1959; cr. Q.C. 1971; has practised law in Toronto since 1959; Lectr., Osgoode Hall Law Sch.; legal editor, 'Business and Securities Valuations' 1972; also several articles on business valuation; legal; Founding Dir., Candn. Liver Foundation; Fellow, Candn. Institute of Business Valuators; mem. Law Soc. Upper Can.; Delta Chi; Liberal; Anglican; recreation: golf; Home: 2 McKenzie Ave., Toronto, Ont. M4W 1J9; Office: B.C.E. Place, Ste. 1800, Box 754, 181 Bay St., Toronto, Ont. M5J 2T9.

**GRANT, David Robert,** M.D., F.R.C.S.(C); surgical scientist-clinician; b. Windsor, Ont. 2 Nov. 1953; s. Robert Henry and Jean Olive (Henneberg) G.; e. Univ. of Toronto Schools 1967–72; Univ. of West. Ont. 1972–78; rotating Intern, Holy Cross Hosp. 1978–79; Res., Gen. Surg., U.W.O. 1979–83; Fellow, Colorectal Surg., Univ. of Toronto 1984; MRC Rsch. Fellow (Immun.) U.W.O. 1985–86; m. Carol d. John and Marie F. Robinson 18 June 1983; children: Robert, Jeffery; ASSOC. PROF., DEPT. OF SURG., UNIV. OF WEST. ONT. 1990– ; Asst. Prof., present univ. 1987–89; Med. Staff & Dir., Transplant Unit, Univ. Hosp. (London, Ont.) 1987– ; Scientist, Robarts Rsch. Inst. 1987– ; Career Sci., Ont. Min. of Health 1988; Hon. Lectr., Dept. of Microbiol. & Immun., U.W.O. 1988– ; Medalist in Surgery, Royal Coll. of Physicians and Surgeons, Can. 1991; performed world's first succesful human liver–small intestine transplant 1989; Mem., Alpha Omega Alpha Soc.; Am. Soc. of Transplant Surg.; Candn. Assn. of Gen. Surg.; Candn. Med. Assn.; Candn. Soc. of Colon & Rectal Surg.; Candn. Transplantation Soc.; London & Dist. Acad. of Med.; F.R.C.S.(C); S.W. Surg. Assn.; The Transplantation Soc.; author/co-author of 70 papers 1984–93; recreations: squash, birdwatching, hiking; Office: 339 Windermere Rd., London, Ont. N6A 5A5.

**GRANT, Elizabeth Jane McCurdy,** B.Mus., M.Mus., A.R.C.T., A.M.C.M.; university / conservatory teacher, choral conductor; b. Sydney, Cape Breton, N.S. 10 July 1947; d. Margaret Elizabeth (Kinsman) McCurdy and the late Archibald Campbell McCurdy; e. Maritime Conservatory of Music Assoc. Dipl. (piano perf.) 1966; Royal Cons. of Music Assoc. dipl. (piano perf.) 1966; Brandon Univ. B.Mus. 1969, Kodaly Music Edn. Cert. 1984, M.Mus. 1988; m. Dwight Cordell s. Donald and Eileen (both dec.) G. 24 Aug. 1968; children: Margaret Elizabeth, Deborah Christine; founded Brandon Univ. Conservatory Chorale 1981; began as 14 voice chorale ensemble which has grown to 110 boys & girls from grades 2–12 in 4 ensembles; the most select & experienced form a 32 voice SSA Chamber Choir which rec. Gold Achievement Award, Can. Musicfest 1989 & appeared at other nat. events such as Cdn. Choral Conductor's Conf. 1990 and Carnegie Hall N.Y. 1991; Chamber Choir invited to 92 Olympics but declined in order to accept an invitation to Kathaumixw Internat. Choral Comp. in Powell River, B.C.; accepted a return invitation to Carnegie Hall May 1993; Adjudicator, Clinician, Guest Conductor at prov. & nat. events; Pres., Kodaly in Man. 1990–93; Past Pres., Brandon Fest. of the Arts; Brandon Reg. Music Teachers; Bd. Mem., Kodaly Soc. of Canada; Mem., Man. Choral Assn.; Cdn. & Am. Choral Conductor's Assns.; Cdn. Music Fest. Adjudicators Assn.; Home: 7 Patmore Dr., Brandon, Man. R7B 0V5; Office: Brandon Univ. Sch. of Music, 260 – 18th St., Brandon, Man. R7A 6A9.

**GRANT, Fred B.,** CMA, FCMA; financial executive; b. Calgary, Alta. 2 Jan. 1931; CHRMN., THE SOCIETY OF MANAGEMENT ACCOUNTANTS OF CANADA; joined Pacific Petroleums Ltd. 1956; Asst. Controller 1971; Controller 1975; Treasurer 1977; upon acquisiton of Pacific Petroleums by Petro-Canada apptd. Treas., Petro-Canada 1979; Vice-Pres. & Treas. 1981; retired 1989; Chair, Income Tax Ctte., Candn. Petroleum Assn. 1972; Pres., Candn. Petroleum Tax Soc. 1972–73; Pres., Soc. of Management Accountants of Alberta 1985–86; Extve. Ctte., Soc. of Management Accountants of Canada 1989– ; Fellow, The Soc. of Management Accountants of Canada FMCA 1988; Volunteer Venue Administrator, Calgary Winter Olympics 1988; Office: 120 King St. W., Hamilton, Ont. L8N 3C3.

**GRANT, Hunter S.;** b. Brockville, Ont. 25 July 1942; s. Malcolm Seafield and Helen Lois (Graham) G.; e. Brockville C.I.; Sir George Williams Univ.; m. Betty d. Dwight and Elsie Ogilvie 18 Sept. 1964; children: Meredith, Kingsley; CO-PUBLISHER, PRESIDENT & GENERAL MANAGER, THE RECORDER AND TIMES LIMITED 1977– ; Asst. Gen. Mgr., The Recorder and Times Limited 1968; Vice-Pres. & Asst. Gen. Mgr. 1976; Bd. Mem., Newspaper Mktg. Bureau (Past Chair); Vice-Chair, Treas. & Extve. Ctte. Mem., Candn. Daily Newspaper Assn. (Past Chair, Telecommunications Ctte.); Past Bd. Mem., Candn. Press; Mem., Candn. Press Advisory Bd.; Bd. of Dir., Audit Ctte., Corel Corp.; Chair, Brockville Found.; Chair, Brockville Gen. Hosp. Found.; Hon. Chair, Dickens of A Festival; weekly columnist of 'From This Corner' (6 years); recreations: squash, golf, fishing, hunting; clubs: Brockville Yacht, Thousand Islands, Brockville Country, Grenadier Island Country, Military Inst.; Home: 1 Granite St., Brockville, Ont. K6V 3P2; Office: 23 King St. W., Brockville, Ont. K6V 5T8.

**GRANT, James Andrews,** B.A., B.C.L., Q.C.; lawyer; b. Montreal, Que. 31 May 1937; s. William Kenneth and Jean (Andrews) G.; e. McGill Univ., B.A. 1958, B.C.L. 1961; m. Nancy d. Alfred and Jean (Roland) Pierce 25 Oct. 1962; children: Katherine, Jennifer, Christy; LAWYER, STIKEMAN, ELLIOTT 1961– ; Chrmn., Extve. Ctte., present firm 1988– ; practices Commercial, Banking and Securities Law; Dir., Canadian Imperial Bank of Commerce; CAE Industries Ltd.; United Dominion Industries Limited; Biochem Pharma Inc.; Youth Horizons; Youth Horizons Found.; Montreal Symphony Orchestra; Care Canada; Gov., Montreal Gen. Hosp.; Montreal Children's Hosp.; former editor, Que. Corp. Manual; lectr., Univ. & Bar Assn.; recreations: golf, skiing, cycling; clubs: Mount Royal, University Club of Montreal, Royal Montreal Golf, Mount Bruno Country, Toronto Golf, Lost Tree, Red Birds Ski; Home: 41 Thornhill Ave., Westmount, Que. H3Y 2E3; Office: 1155 Blvd. René-Lévesque W., Montreal, Que. H3B 3V2.

**GRANT, James C.;** business executive; b. Antigonish, N.S. 24 Jan. 1937; s. John D. and Isabel (Chisholm) G.; e. St. Francis Xavier Univ. dipl. Eng. 1957; Tech. Univ. of N.S. elect. eng. 1959; m. Sonia d. Walter Chicorli 5 July 1965; one d.: Allison Lee-Anne; PRESIDENT, C.G. JAMES & ASSOC. INTERNAT. ADVISORY SERVICE

1992– ; Engineer, Federal Govt. 1959–64; Mgr., Computer Support, Gulf Oil 1964–68; Mgr., Tech. Services, Royal Bank of Canada 1968–72; Dir., Computer Opns. 1972–76; Vice-Pres., Systems 1976–81; Strategic Planning 1981–84; Sr. Vice-Pres., Opns. 1984–87; Extve. Vice-Pres. Systems & Technology 1987–92 Dir., Roger Cantel Mobile Communications; Consultant, United Nations T.N.C.; Guest Lectr., Univ. of Toronto; Mem., Telecom & Computer Serv. Sectoral Adv. Group on Internat. Trade, Govt. of Canada; Carnegie Mellon Univ. in conjunction with the Am. Mngt. Systems Award for Achievement in Systems 1989; C.I.O. 100 award 'Quality Systems' 1991; Candn. Business Telecommunications Alliance 1992 Presidents Award for contribution to the application & use of telecommunications in Canada; recipient, Candn. Information Processing Soc. Award (outstanding achievements in information processing) 1993; Mem., Profl. Engrs. of Ont.; Candn. Information Processing Soc.; Address: 9 Birch Hill Lane, Oakville, Ont. L6K 2P1.

**GRANT, John,** B.A. Ph.D.; economist; b. Thunder Bay, Ont. 23 May 1938; s. Norman Stewart and Margaret Glenn (Stevenson) G.; e. Kapuskasing (Ont.) High Sch. 1955; Univ. of Toronto B.A. 1959; Univ. of London (London Sch. of Econ.) Ph.D. 1964; m. Judith Ann, d. Sydney R. Skelton 27 Sept. 1963; children: Adam, Hamish; began as Lectr. Monetary Econ., London Sch. of Econ. 1960; Asst. Prof. of Econ., Univ. of Toronto 1964; Dir. & Chief Econ., Wood Gundy Inc. 1973; Home: 17 Admiral Rd., Toronto, Ont. M5R 2L4; Office: BCE Place, Box 500, Toronto, Ont. M5J 2S8.

**GRANT, John Stuart,** Q.C., B.A.; lawyer; b. Ottawa, Ont. 29 Sept. 1919; s. George Sydney and Genevieve Mary (O'Neill) G.; e. Lisgar Coll. Inst.; Univ. of Toronto B.A. 1946; Osgoode Hall Law Sch. 1949; m. Yvonne d. W.S. and Jessie Rumfeldt 5 Sept. 1942; children: Mary-Ann McCloskey, John S. Jr., Steven A.; PARTNER, GOWLING, STRATHY & HENDERSON (and of its predecessor firm Strathy, Archibald and Seagram) 1986– ; Chrmn. Toronto Sun Publishing Corp.; Dir. Roman Corp. Ltd.; Agnico-Eagle Mines Ltd.; Dumagami Mines Ltd.; Canarchon Holdings Ltd.; law practice since 1949 successively with Manley and Grant, Manley, Grant and Camisso and present firm; Past Chrmn. and Dir. Emmanuel Convalescent Found. (Southdown); Past Dir. Coaching Assn. Can.; Masters Athletics (Track & Field); Kt. of Malta; R.Catholic; recreation: golf; Clubs: Lambton Golf & Country; Engineers; Home: 302, 77 Clarendon Ave., Toronto, Ont. M4V 1J2; Office: P.O. Box 438, Commerce Court W., Toronto, Ont. M5L 1J3.

**GRANT, Rev. John Webster,** M.A. D.Phil., D.D., LL.D.; retired university professor; b. Truro, N.S. 27 June 1919; s. late Rev. William P. and Margaret Dorothy (Waddell) G.; e. Dalhousie Univ., B.A. (Eric Dennis Scholarship in Pol. Science) 1938 and M.A. 1941; Rhodes Scholar from N.S., 1941; Princeton Univ. (Grad. Sch., Dept. of Politics) 1938–39; Pine Hill Divinity Hall, Halifax, N.S., Cert. in Theol. (Travelling Scholarship) 1943; Oxford Univ., D.Phil. 1948; m. Gwendolen Margaret, d. late John S. Irwin, 3 June 1944; Pres., Pacific Coast Theol. Conf., 1951–52; o. 1943; Minister, West Bay, N.S., 1943; Director of Religious Information to non-R.C. Churches, Wartime Information Bd. 1943–45; Lectr. in Systematic Theol. Pine Hill Divinity Hall, N.S., 1945–46; Woodward Foundation Prof. of Ch. Hist., Union Coll. of B.C., 1949–59; Editor-in-Chief, The Ryerson Press, 1960–63; Professor of Church History, Emmanuel College, University of Toronto, 1963–84; Editor, 'Dalhousie Gazette,' 1941–42 and 'Canadian Churches and the War,' 1943–45; managing editor SR. 1972–77; Publications: 'Free Churchmanship in England, 1870–1940,' 1955; 'God Speaks XXX We Answer,' 1965; 'The Canadian Experience of Church Union,' 1967; Ed. 'Salvation! O the Joyful Sound: the Selected Writings of John Carroll,' 1967; Ed. 'Die Unierten Kirchen,' 1973; author 'God's People in India' 1959; 'George Pidgeon: a Biography' 1962, 'The Church in the Canadian Era' 1972; 'Moon of Wintertime' 1984; 'A Profusion of Spires' 1988; joint editor 'The Contribution of Methodism to Atlantic Canada' 1992; served in 2nd World War as Chaplain with R.C.N.; United Ch.; Address: Apt. 1002, 86 Gloucester St., Toronto, Ont. M4Y 2S2.

**GRANT, Jon King,** B.B.A., LL.D. (Hons.); executive; b. Toronto, Ont. 25 Apr. 1935; s. John King (dec.) and Rita May (Loney) G. (dec.); e. Humberside Coll. Inst. Toronto 1954; Univ. of W. Ont. Sch. of Business Adm. 1959; m. Shelagh Dawn d. late Donald I. Adams, 10 June 1960; children: Susan Whitney Thorne, Deborah Lynne Aben, David Adams Grant; CHAIRMAN OF THE BOARD, THE QUAKER OATS COMPANY OF CANADA LIMITED since 1992; Chrmn., Ont. Round Table on the Environment and Economy; Dir., Consumer's Gas Ltd.; Laurentian Bank of Canada Ltd.; Boreal Insur. Inc.; Scott Paper Ltd.; United Grain Growers Ltd.; Genstar Capital Corp.; held sr. mgmt. positions in the food industry; joined Quaker Oats as Vice Pres. of Mktg. 1974; Vice Pres. and Gen. Mgr. 1975; Pres. and C.E.O. 1976; Chairman 1993; Past Gov., Lakefield Coll. Sch.; Past Chrmn., Bd. of Govs., Trent Univ.; Mem. Adv. Comte., Sch. of Bus. Admin., Univ. of W. Ont.; Bus. Counc. on National Issues; Candn./CUBC Business Counc.; Ont. Science Centre; past affil.: The Private Sector '6 & 5' Ctte.; Nat. Finance Ctte., U.N. Assoc. of Can.; Founding Chrmn., Greater Peterborough Economic Counc.; Nat. Chrmn., Trent Univ. Fund Raising Campaign; Adv. Bd., Arbor Theatre Co.; Jr. Achievement of Peterborough; former lectr., Sch. of Bus. Admin., Univ. of W. Ont.; York Univ.; public speaker; Past Chrmn., Grocery Products Mfrs. Can.; Ont. Agriculture Council; author of articles and book chapters on education, government and the environment; recipient, Corporate Humanist Award, Candn. Fedn. of Humanities 1990; Knight of the Golden Pencil Award 1990; LL.D., Trent Univ. 1991; Zeta Psi; Protestant; recreations: skiing, tennis, squash, whitewater canoeing; Clubs: Granite (Toronto); Toronto; Peterborough; Residences: Peterborough, Ont.; Les Pentes-Nord, Mont Tremblant, Qué.; Heart's Content Islands, Pointe au Baril, Ont.; Office: Quaker Park, Peterborough, Ont. K9B 7B2.

**GRANT, Jonathan Windsor;** executive; b. Southampton, Eng. 6 June 1934; s. John Walker and Catherine Ann (Smith) G.; various Brit. instns.; creative writing Clyde Bedell 1960–62; Univ. of W. Ont. Creative Writing 1965; PRES. & C.E.O., G & D ADVERTISING CONSULTANTS INC. 1981– ; Advt. Exec. London Free Press 1958–68; joined James Lovick Ltd. 1968 becoming Vice Pres. of subsequent firm Baker, Lovick, BBDO Ltd. 1975–78; Creative Dir. McConnell Advertising 1978–81; Guest Lectr. Ryerson Polytech. Inst.; Conestoga Coll.; internationally pub. wildlife photog.; 115 nat. and internat. awards TV, Radio, Print and outdoor advertising; Home: R.R. #3, 230 Upper Ganges Rd., S16 – B6 Ganges, B.C. V0S 1E0.

**GRANT, Jordan Blake,** B.A.; real estate executive; b. Toronto, Ont. 9 Aug. 1953; s. Jack Sheldon and Sylvia Doreen (Shapiro) Fair; e. Univ. of Toronto B.A. 1976; m. Meg d. the late John and Margaret Floyd 20 July 1984; children: Gabriel MacInnes, Alicia Beth Jacqueline; PRES., SEATON GROUP 1990– ; Project Mgr. & Asst. to Vice-Pres., Devel., Imbrook Properties Ltd. 1979–85; Principal, Jordan Grant & Assoc. Ltd. 1985–88; Vice-Pres., Devel., present firm 1988; Dir., CMS Group Inc.; Caribbean Investments Ltd.; Exec. Mem., Ctte. on Monetary & Econ. Reform; Mem., Amnesty International; Canadian Civil Liberties Assn.; World Federalists; Chrmn., Bank of Canada for Canadians Coalition; recreations: hockey, snow and water skiing, golf, swimming; Home: 54 Fulton Ave., Toronto, Ont. M4K 1X5; Office: 8077 Islington Ave., Suite 206, Woodbridge, Ont. L4L 7X7.

**GRANT, Kenneth Andrew,** B.A., M.B.A., C.M.C.; management consultant; b. Paisley, Scotland, 2 Sept. 1946; s. Andrew and Mabel (Rothnie) G.; e. Allan Glen's Sch., Glasgow 1964; Open Univ. (U.K.), B.A. 1976; York Univ., M.B.A. 1981; m. Candace d. Gordon and Eugenia Ingram 21 Aug. 1971; children: Stuart, Iain; SENIOR DIRECTOR, MANAGEMENT ADVISORY SERVICES PRACTICE, LGS GROUP INC.; Brit. Min. of Nat. Defence to 1968; B.M.W., U.K. to 1974; Coopers & Lybrand, U.K. to 1978; Candn. Oxygen to 1979; Partner, Peat Marwick Stevenson & Kellogg 1979–92; part-time faculty, York Univ.; mem., Ont. Inst. of Cert. Mngt. Cons.; Candn. Infor. Processing Soc.; co-author: 'A Practical Guide to Law Office Automation' 1988; frequent mag. author & interviewee on infor.-technol. related subjects; clubs: Argonaut Rowing, Lambton Golf & Country; Address: 59 Glenwood Ave., Toronto, Ont. M6P 3C7.

**GRANT, Kit Ross,** B.A., B.Ed., M.Ed.; management training and development consultant; b. Winnipeg, Man. 24 July 1947; e. Univ. of Manitoba B.A. 1968, B.Ed. 1970, M.Ed. 1975; m. Susan Brydges 16 Oct. 1970; children: Scott, Kathryne; PRESIDENT GRANT TRAINING SYSTEMS INC. Palo Alto, California 1985– ; President, Learning Dynamics (Canada) Ltd. 1976–..; Sch. Couns. Gimli, Man. 1970–71; Virden, Man. 1971–72; Clinical Psychologist, Australia 1972–73; Sch. Couns. Souris, Man. 1974–76; Exhibits Mgr., Show Mgr. Southex Exhbn., Winnipeg and Calgary 1977–80; Pres., Professional Speakers Alta. 1989–90; mem. Nat. Speakers Assoc.; Calgary C. of C.; Edmonton C. of C.; Am. Soc. of Training & Development; mem., Internat. Platform Assoc.; recreations: golf, tennis; Clubs: Shawnee Slopes Golf (Gov. 1984–88, Pres. 1985–86); Southwood Golf and Country (Gov. 1978); Home: 272 Sunmills Dr., S.E., Calgary, Alta. T2X 3E7.

**GRANT, Thomas Jeffrey,** B.A., LL.B.; lawyer; b. Toronto, Ont. 8 June 1950; s. late Thomas Charles and Gladys (Ferguson) G.; e. McGill Univ. B.A. (Hons.) 1971; Osgoode Hall Law Sch., York Univ. LL.B. 1974; Law Soc. of U.C., Bar Admission Course 1975–76; m. Carmen d. Laurier and Rhea Lachance 27 Dec. 1980; VICE-PRES., GENERAL COUNSEL & SECY., CHRYSLER CANADA LTD. 1990– ; Solicitor, John Deere Limited & its subsidiaries 1976–90 (left as Vice-Pres., Gen. Counsel, Sec. & Dir.); Dir., Chrysler Canada Ltd.; Chrysler Life Insur. Co. of Can.; Mem., Candn. Mfrs. Assn. (Legislative Ctte.); Motor Vehicle Mfrs. Assn. (Sr. Legal Offrs. Ctte.); Candn. Corp. Couns. Assn.; Candn. Bar Assn.; author of 1 conference paper; recreations: golf, tennis, raquetball, skiing; club: Pointe West Golf; Home: 118 Golfwood Dr., Amherstburg, Ont. N9V 3T4; Office: 2450 Chrysler Center, Windsor, Ont. N8W 3X7.

**GRANT, William Frederick,** M.A., Ph.D., F.L.S. (1962), F.R.S.C. (1989); university professor; b. Hamilton, Ont. 20 Oct. 1924; s. William Aitken and Myrtle Irene (Taylor) G.; e. McMaster Univ., B.A. (Science) 1947, M.A. (Botany) 1949; Univ. of Virginia, Ph.D. (Biol.) 1953; m. Phyllis Kemp, d. William John Harshaw, 23 July 1949; one s., William Taylor; EMERITUS PROF. OF GENETICS, McGILL UNIV., 1990; Blandy Research Fellow. Univ. of Virginia, 1949–53 (awarded Andrew Fleming Prize, 1953); Botanist to Dept. of Agric., Kuala Lumpur, Malaya, 1953–55 under tech. co-op. prog. of Colombo Plan; Asst. Prof. Genetics, McGill Univ., 1955–61, Assoc. Prof. 1961–66, Prof. 1967– ; Adjunct Prof. Biology, York Univ. 1983– ; appointed Hon. mem. of Morgan Aboretum and Woodlot Devel. Assn. of Macdonald Coll. of McGill Univ., 1960; Specialist in plants of genus 'Lotus'; mem., Am. Soc. Plant Taxonomists; Genetics Soc. Can. (Pres. 1974–75, Life member 1979, Archivist 1983– , Presidential citation 1991); Crop Science Soc. of Am.; Environmental Mutagen Soc.; Bot. Soc. Am.; Candn. Bot. Assn. (George Lawson Medal 1989); Pres., Internat. Organ. Plant Biosystematics, 1981–86 (Past Pres. 1986–89; Life Member 1989); Treas., Biol. Council Can. 1974–78; Fellow, Royal Soc. of Can. 1989; Am. Assn. Advanc. Science; Linnean Soc. London; awarded, The McMaster Univ. Distinguished Alumni/Alumnae Scholar Award 1990; Consultant to UN Environmental Program; Adviser to WHO Internat. Prog. on Chemical Safety Collaborative Study on Higher Plant Short-Term Tests for Genotoxicity and Carcinogenicity (Chrmn., Steering Ctte. 1987– ;); Rec'd. Silver Jubilee medal; awarded Sr. Rsch. Fellowship, Japan Soc. for the Promotion of Science 1984, 1989; Sigma Xi (Pres., McGill Chapter 1975–76); Soc. Study Evolution (Vice-Pres. 1972); mem. Environmental Contaminants Adv. Comte. on Mutagenesis to the Ministers of Nat. Health and Welfare and the Environment, Ottawa, 1978–86; Editor, Candn. Journ. of Genetics and Cytology 1974–82, Lotus Newsletter 1970–84 and Hon. Editor-in-Chief, Plant Species Biology 1993– ; Home: 43 St. Andrews Rd., Baie d'Urfe, Que. H9X 2T9; Office: Dept. of Plant Science, Box 4000 Macdonald Campus, McGill Univ., Ste. Anne de Bellevue, Que. H9X 3V9.

**GRANT, Hon. William Johnston,** LL.B.; judge; b. Weymouth, N.S. 17 Sept. 1925; s. H.B. and Annie (O'Brien) G.; e. Kings Coll. Sch. 1943; Acadia Univ. Pre Law 1946–47; Dalhousie Law Sch. LL.B. 1950; m. Marie d. John F. Whebby 7 May 1957; children: John O'Brien, Anne Marie, Andrew MacGregor; JUDGE, SUPREME COURT OF N.S. 1977– ; called to Bar of N.S. 1951; cr. Q.C. 1965; Assoc., Patterson & Smith, Truro, N.S. 1951–56; Partner, Patterson, Smith, Matthews & Grant 1956–77; Chrmn., N.S. Civil Service Arbitration Bd. 1973–77; Candn. Bar Assn. 1955; Internat. Assn. of Jurists; Dir., Candn. Judges Conf. 1982–84; Continuing Legal Educ. Soc. 1983–86; Colchester Children's Aid Soc. 1955–79; Candn. Nat. Inst. Blind 1960–82; Pres., Boy Scouts Council Colchester 1970–75, mem. 1946–75; mem., Candn. Inst. for Adm. Justice; Candn. Comn. Prevention Crime; mem., Extve. Council N.S. Barristers Soc.; Lectr., N.S. Bar Admission Course 1972–77; Pres., Colchester Co. Bar 1960–64; Pres., Maritime Rugby Union 1949–53; served at sea with RCN 1944–45; N.S. Highlanders Militia 1947–70, rank Maj.; Home: 24 Parker St., Truro, N.S. B2N 3R1; Office: Halifax, N.S. B3J 3C8.

**GRANT, William Neil,** B.Ed.; venture management and financing; b. New Westminster, B.C. 13 July 1942;

s. William Albert and Dorothy Patricia (Nielson) G.; e. Como Lake High Sch. 1960; Univ. of B.C., B.Ed. 1967; m. Sue J. (Spicer) 19 June 1970; three children: William Douglas, Robert Brian, Cheryl Ann; PRES. & C.E.O., CONSOLIDATED FIRSTFUND CAPITAL CORP.; Chrmn. & Dir., Vitality Products Inc.; Pres. & C.E.O., FraserFund Venture Capital (VCC) Corp.; Guardian Knight Financial Corp.; Costar Marketing Corp.; Gold Star Resorts, Inc.; Dist. Field Asst., Procter & Gamble, Vancouver 1967–70; Gen. Mgr., Hygrade Packers 1971–72; Div. Mgr., Standard Brands 1972–74; Vice Pres. and Gen. Mgr., Standard Brands Food Co. (now RJR Nabisco, Toronto), Montreal 1975; Pres. Standard Brands Food Service, Toronto 1976; Pres., Nabob Foods Ltd., Vancouver 1976–78; Pres., Vitality Products Ltd. 1979–81; Pres., Newtec Industries Ltd. 1983–85; Pres., Consolidated Firstfund Capital Corp. 1983– ; Nat. Dir., Candn. Mfrs. Assn. 1987–91 (Dir. 1978–88; Chrmn., B.C. Div. 1989–90); Mem., Assoc. of Candn. Advertisers (Dir. 1975); Grocery Products Mfrs. of Can. (Dir. 1974–78); Vice Pres. & Dir. YMCA 1982–85; Dir., Banff Sch. of Mgmt. 1977–79; Candidate, P. Cons. Party, Federal Riding New Westminster/Coquitlam 1984; mem., Young President's Org.; Depy. Chrmn., B.C. Div., Candn. Mfrs. Assn. (Chrmn. Legislation Comte.); Delta Kappa Epsilon; Protestant; recreations: golf, cycling, photography, reading; Clubs: Vancouver Golf; Arbutus; Blue Mountain Racquet; Terminal City; Home: 4701 Drummond Dr., Vancouver, B.C. V6T 1B3; Office: Ste. 1730, 999 West Hastings St., Vancouver, B.C. V6C 2W2.

**GRANTHAM, Robert G.,** B.Sc., F.G.A.C.; museum curator; b. Halifax, N.S. 19 Apr. 1947; s. Arnold George and Helen Lorraine (Little) G.; e. St. Mary's Univ., B.Sc. 1970; m. Barbara Ann d. James and Julia Nickerson 9 May 1970; children: Heather Ann, Andrew Robert; CURATOR OF GEOL., NOVA SCOTIA MUSEUM 1974– ; Geol., Internat. Nickel Co. Ltd. 1970–73; Lab Instr. & Occasional Lectr., St. Francis Xavier Univ. 1973–74; Owner, Earth Science Interpreters 1975–78; Creative Computer Mart 1980–83; rec'd Candn. Mus. Assn. Study Tour grant for dinosaur trackway rsch. in the S.W. U.S. 1986; Founder, Atlantic Can. Aviation Mus. 1978; R. Catholic; Fellow, Geol. Assn. of Can.; mem. Atlantic Geosci. Soc.; Nova Scotian Inst. of Sci.; author of var. sci. abstracts and papers; recreations: golf, flying, aviation archeol.; Home: 2 Carnation Cres., Halifax, N.S. B3R 2E9; Office: 1747 Summer St., Halifax, N.S. B3H 3A6.

**GRANTHAM, Ronald Douglas,** B.A.Sc., P.Eng.; consulting engineer; b. Vancouver, B.C. 8 Aug. 1925; s. Douglas Charles and Dora Isabel (Harrald) G.; e. grad. H.S. in Vancouver 1943; Univ. of B.C. B.A.Sc. 1948; M.I.T. post-grad. studies in advanced structures 1953; m. June d. Franklin Kay and Vera Edith Collins 6 July 1951; children: Susan Vera (Hobkirk), David John Harrald, Laura Isabel, Nancy June; PRESIDENT, GRANTHAM PROJECT MANAGEMENT 1992– ; Project & Design Engr., B.C. Electric Co. Ltd. (now B.C. Hydro) 1948–55 (seconded to Severud Elstad & Kruger N.Y. & The Public Service Co. Newark, N.J. 1954); Mgr., Dominion Construction Co. Ltd. 1955–74; Sr. Vice-Pres. & Partner, Reid Crowther & Partners Ltd. 1974–87; Chrmn., Chembiomed Limited 1987–92; Mem., Science Council of Canada 1990–92; Dir., Atomic Energy of Canada Limited 1993– ; mem., Federal Justice Ctte. for selecting judges to Federal Courts 1993– ; Founding Dir., Consulting Engineers of Alta. 1978; Recipient 1981 Charlesworth Award, Assn. of Profl. Engrs., Geol. & Geophysicists of Alta. (APEGGA); Chrmn., Winspear Found. 1974; Founder & Pres., Canterbury Found. 1970–84; Pres., The Edmonton Club 1965; Pres., The Rotary Club of Edmonton 1964; Dir., Edmonton Opera; Edmonton Symphony Soc. 1959–64; Mem., Anglican Parish of Christ Ch. (Bishop's Extve. Ctte. 1962–66); Dir., Candn. Bible Soc. 1963–67; Edmonton C. of C. 1974–76 (Vice-Pres. 1977); Life Mem., APEGGA; Chrmn., Task Force to study students' contbns. to post-secondary edn. (Govt. of Alta.) 1976; recreations: power boating, cycling, big game hunting; clubs: Mayfair Golf & Country, The Edmonton, Royal Glenora, Rotary; Home: 13811 – 90th Ave., Edmonton, Alta. T5R 4T3.

**GRAPKO, Michael Frederic,** M.A., Ph.D.; educator; b. Stuartburn, Man. 4 Feb. 1921; s. Gregory and Helen (Morell) G.; e. St. Paul's Coll. Winnipeg; United Coll. Winnipeg, Univ. of Man. B.A. 1944; Univ. of Toronto M.A. 1947, Ph.D. 1953; m. Tillie d. late Nicholas Stefanik 18 Sept. 1948; two d. Deborah Anne, Janice Ellen; PROF. OF EDUC. ADM., FACULTY OF EDUC. & INST. OF CHILD STUDY, UNIV. OF TORONTO 1980– ; Asst. Prof. of Psychol. and Inst. of Child Study present Univ. 1960–64, Assoc. Prof. 1964–71, Prof. and Dir. 1971–80; Co-ordinator of Educ. Services Thistletown Regional Centre 1964–71; Psychol. Consultant, Kenora Bd. Educ. 1965–72, Grey Co. Bd. Educ. 1968–76; Faculty Rep. Governing Council Univ. Toronto 1971–75, mem. Planning & Resources Sub-comte. 1979–80; Chrmn. Faculty Assn. 1967–69; Candn. Rep. to White House Conf. 1971; Dir. Internat. Fed. Parent Educ. 1967–84; Dir. Toronto YMCA; recipient grants Ont. Mental Health Foundation and Ministry of Educ. Ont. 1962–79; author numerous publs., papers, addresses; mem. Ont. Psychol. Assn. (Dir. and Secy. Treas. 1978–80); Candn. Psychol. Assn.; Am. Psychol. Assn.; Soc. Research Child Devel.; served with RCNVR 1944–45; R. Catholic; Home: 1864 Mississauga Rd., Missisauga, Ont. L5H 4C8.

**GRATIAS, Orvald Arthur,** B.Sc., M.Sc., Ph.D., M.B.A., C.F.A.; financial analyst; b. Pekin, N.D. 25 Jan. 1909; s. Otto and Ingeborg (Bjorlie) G.; e. pub. and high schs. Sask.; Univ. of Sask. B.Sc. 1928, M.Sc. 1930; Oxford Univ. (Rhodes Scholar) Ph.D. 1932; London Sch. of Econ. 1933; McGill Univ. M.B.A. 1975, Dip. in Mgmt. 1965; Chart. Financial Analyst 1970; m. Elizabeth d. François and Mary Plaunt 4 June 1938; children: Mary, Alan, Paul; FINANCIAL ANALYST, PENSION FUND TRUSTEE, MACDOUGALL, MACDOUGALL & MACTIER INC. 1964– ; joined J. & P. Coats, Glasgow 1934; J. & P. Coats (Canada) Montreal 1935, Vice Pres. and Mng. Dir. 1940, Pres. 1950–60; Pres. Atlas Asbestos Co. (subsidiary Turner & Newall, UK) 1960–64; Gov. Montreal Gen. Hosp. Found.; author various sci. publs. on radioactive branching in uranium; mem. Inst. of Chartered Financial Analysts; Montreal Soc. of Financial Analysts; Planetary Soc.; Oxford Soc.; Inducted Univ. of Sask. Athletic Wall of Fame 1984; Protestant; recreations: archaeology, astronomy, outdoor sports, reading; Club: University; Home: #503, 3468 Drummond St., Montreal, Que. H3G 1Y4; Office: Ste. 2000, Place du Canada, Montreal, Que. H3B 4J1.

**GRATTAN, Patricia Elizabeth,** B.A., B.F.A.; art gallery director; b. Sault Ste. Marie, Ont. 19 Sept. 1944; d. David Andrew and Virginia Gwendolyn (Graham) G.; e. Univ. of W. Ont. B.A. 1966 (Univ. Gold Medal); Sir George Williams Univ. B.F.A. 1974; m. M. Ian s. Ron and Doreen Bowmer 28 June 1968; DIR.-CURATOR, MEML. UNIV. OF NFLD. ART GALLERY 1982– ; joined Toronto Telegram 1966–67; pub. relations Montreal 1968–71; special projects present Gallery 1976, exhns. co-ordinator 1978, Acting Curator and Head Visual & Performing Arts Sect. 1980; Acting Chief Curator Nfld. Museum Govt. Nfld. (secondment) 1981–82; Chair, City of St. John's Art Purchase Program; Adv. Ctte. The Nfld. Sound Symposium; Adv. Ctte. Textile Studies Program, Cabot Institute; Juror grant progs. Can. Council, Nat. Museums Can.; author various articles and mem. ed. bd. Arts Atlantic mag.; exhn. catalogues incl. 'Flights of Fancy: Newfoundland Yard Art' 1983; 'Twenty-five Years of Art in Newfoundland' 1986; 'Painting the Past: Carl Barbour, Folk Artist' 1992; mem. Candn. Museums Assn. (Councillor and 1989 Annual Conf. Chair); Candn. Art Museums Dirs. Orgn. (Pres.); Atlantic Provs. Art Gallery Assn. (Pres.); recreations: travel, swimming, kayaking, theatre; Home: 7 Winter Place, St. John's, Nfld. A1B 1J5; Office: St. John's, Nfld. A1C 5S7.

**GRATTON, Paul L.M.,** M.Ps.; communications executive; b. Ottawa, Ont. 21 June 1952; s. Gerard and Mary Helen (Pilon) G.; e. Univ. of Ottawa, B.A. 1967, B.Ps. 1968, M.Ps. 1971; SENIOR PROGRAM EXECUTIVE, CHUM/CITY TELEVISION 1994– ; Psychol. Cons. Prescott Russell Sch. Bd. 1977–79; Programmer, Toronto Festival of Festivals 1979; Ed. Film Sect. Ottawa Revue Mag. 1979–80; Film Critic, CHEZ-FM Ottawa 1980–81; Mgr. and Booker, Towne Cinema, Ottawa 1980–82; Film Booker and Buyer, Cineplex Theatres 1982; Prog. Mgr. Superchannel Pay TV 1982–85; Vice Pres., Programming, First Choice Canadian Communications 1985–91; Chief Extve. Officer, Ontario Film Development Corp. 1991–94; mem., Banff Television Festival Bd.; Home: 809, 360 Bloor St., Toronto, Ont. M4W 3M3; Office: 300, 175 Bloor St. E., Toronto, Ont. M4W 3R8.

**GRATTON, Robert,** LL.L., LL.M., M.B.A.; financial executive; b. Montreal, Que. 23 Oct. 1943; s. Dr. Bernard and Judith (Dufour) Gratton; e. Univ. of Montreal LL.L.; London Sch. of Econ. & Pol. Science LL.M.; Harvard Grad. Sch. of Bus. Admin. M.B.A.; m. Nicole Marcil, Aug. 1966; three children; PRES. & C.E.O., POWER FINANCIAL CORP.; Chrmn., Great-West Life & Annuity (U.S.); Investors Group Inc.; Dir., Power Corporation of Can.; Power Financial Corp.; Great-West Life; Parfinance (France); Pargesa Holding S.A.; Pratt & Whitney Canada Inc.; called to Bar of Que. 1967; Asst. to Hon. Paul Gérin-Lajoie, Quebec City 2 yrs.; joined Credit Foncier 1971, C.O.O. 1975, Pres. and C.E.O. 1979; joined Montreal Trust as Chrmn., Pres. and C.E.O. 1982; apptd. Pres. and C.E.O., Power Financial Corp. 1989; Clubs: Mount Royal; St-James's; St-Denis; Office: 751 Victoria Square, Montréal, Qué. H2Y 2J3.

**GRATWICK, John,** B.Sc.; transportation consultant and writer; b. Langley, Eng. 2 March 1923; s. Ernest Frank and Doris Hilda (Shepherd) G.; e. St. Clement Danes Grammar Sch., London, Eng., 1941; King's Coll., Univ. of London, B.Sc. 1948; Northwestern Univ., ATMP 1968; m. Gwendoline S., d. Percy Johnston, 23 Mar. 1957; one s. Adrian; PARTNER, HICKLING CORPORATION; served with RAF Tech. Sigs. (Radar) Br. 1942–46; Scient. Offr., Brit. Colonial Office, Gambia, 1948–50; Exper. Offr. and subsequently Sr. Scient. Offr., UK Dept. of Scient. Adv. to Air Ministry, 1950–57; Depy. Dir. of Mang. Engn. RCAF 1957–60; joined CNR as Sr. Operational Research Analyst, Research & Devel., 1960–63; Sr. Tech. Adv. to Head Express Services 1963–70; Co-Chrmn., Ministry of Transport Task Force on Objectives and Structure for fed. transport., 1969; Chrmn., Transport. Devel. Agency, Montreal (Fed. Govt.) 1970–72; Vice-Pres., Research and Devel., CN, 1972–76; Pres. and CEO, CN Marine, 1976–79; Vice Pres. Corporate Policy and Development 1979–80; Vice Pres., Extve. 1981–82; Dir., Can. Marine Transport Centre, Dalhousie Univ. 1983–86; Exec. Dir., Internat. Inst. for Transport and Ocean Policy Studies 1986–88; Assoc., Oceans Inst. of Can.; Gov., Mount Saint Vincent Univ.; Chrmn. Halifax-Dartmouth Port Development Comn.; Comnr., National Transport Act Review Comn. 1992–93; Candn. Organ. for Simplification Trade Procedures (Chrmn. 1971–77); Fellow, Chartered Inst. Transport.; Fellow, Royal Stat. Soc. (Cert. 1954); Candn. Operational Research Soc. (Nat. Pres. 1969–70); Operations Research Soc. Am.; Candn. Transport. Research Forum (Pres. 1971–72, Hon. Life Mem. 1993); Sigma Xi; recreations: flying, puppetry, food, theatre; Address: 984 Bellevue Ave., Halifax, N.S. B3H 3L7.

**GRATZER, George A.,** Ph.D.; educator; b. Hungary 2 Aug. 1936; s. Jozsef and Maria (Herzog) G.; e. L. Eötvös Univ. Budapest Bachelor's Degree 1959, Master's Degree 1960; Hungarian Acad. of Sciences Ph.D. 1960; m. Catherine Zahony 25 Jan. 1961; children: Thomas, David; PROF. OF MATH. UNIV. OF MAN. since 1967; Postdoctoral Fellow, Queen's Univ. 1961; Visiting Asst. Prof., Assoc. Prof. and Prof., Pa. State Univ. 1963–67; rec'd Steacie Prize in Natural Sciences 1971; Zubek Mem. Award for Excellence in Research and Scholarship 1974; Distinguished Professor, Univ. of Manitoba 1985; Killam Research Fellowship 1986–88; author 'Universal Algebra' 1968; 'Lattice Theory: First Concepts and Distributive Lattices' 1971; 'General Lattice Theory' 1978 (rev. and expanded ed., Russian, 1982); 'Universal Algebra,' 2nd expanded ed., 1979; 'Fast BASIC: Beyond TRS-80 BASIC,' 1982 (with Thomas Gratzer); 'Math into Tex. A simple introduction to AMS-Latex' 1993; over 150 papers on algebra, especially universal algebra and lattice theory; mem. Royal Soc. Can.; Am. Math. Soc.; Candn. Math. Soc.; Home: 416 Lamont Blvd., Winnipeg, Man. R3P 0G3; Office: Dept. of Mathematics, Univ. of Manitoba, Winnipeg, Man. R3T 2N2.

**GRAUER, Sherry,** B.F.A., R.C.A.; artist; b. Toronto, Ont. 20 Feb. 1939; d. Albert Edward and Shirley (Woodward) Grauer; e. York House Sch. Vancouver 1955; Wellesley (Mass.) Coll. 3 yrs., 3rd yr. as exchange student Ecole du Louvre, Ecole de Science Politique, Paris; Atelier Ziegler Paris 1958–59; San Francisco Art Inst. B.F.A. 1964; m. John Keith-King 12 Feb 1971; children: Callum, Jonathan, Max; solo exhns. incl.: Mary Frazee Gallery West Vancouver 1964; Bau-Xi Gallery 1965, '67, '68, '70, '75, '76, '78, '80, '83, '85, '87, '89, '90, '92; Loyola Bonsecours Centre Montreal 1968; Jerrold Morris Gallery Toronto 1969; Véhicule Art Inc. Montreal 1973; Surrey (B.C.) Art Gallery (retrospective) 1980; Vancouver: Women in Focus Gallery 1987; Art Gallery of the Southern Okanagan 1987; rep. in various group exhns. since 1964 incl. The Candn. Group of Painters Travelling Exhn. 1965–68; Montreal Museum of Fine Arts and Candn. Pavilion Expo '67 1967; Nine out of Ten Hamilton Art Gallery 1973; Nat. Gallery Can. Some Candn. Women Artists 1975; B.C. Prov. Coll. Travelling Exhn. Europe 1978–79; Making History, Vancouver Art Gall. 1986; Still Life, Snakes & Ladders, & Bogeymen: 2 man show, installations, Charles H. Scott Gallery, Vancouver 1985; ARTROPOLIS, Vancouver 1993; comns. incl. World Wide Internat. Travel Office Vancouver wall mural 1969; Univ. of B.C. sculpture 'Swimmers' 1972; Dept. Pub. Works Ottawa for Fed. Bldg. Powell River, B.C. ceiling sculpture 1976; Habitat Banners for Burrard Bridge Vancouver 1976; Candn. Training Inst. Cornwall sculpture 'Brave Birdmen' 1978–80; New Play Centre, Du Maurier Festival: set for 'Knitequest' by Peter Eliot Weiss 1985; set for 'Time Out of Mind' by Brian McDonald, for B.C. Ballet; set for 'Song of this Place' by Joy Coghill 1988; 'Constellation of Cygnus' Steel Relief for Wesgar Industries, Vancouver 1990; 'Sockeye' for Foreshore Projects, Vancouver 1993; rep. in various pub. and private colls. incl. Vancouver Art Gall., Can. Council Art Bank, Musée d'Art Contemporain Montreal, Nat. Gallery Can.; cited numerous articles, reviews; Founding Bd. mem., Arts, Sciences, and Technology Centre Vancouver 1980–83; Trustee Vancouver Art Gallery 1974–76 (Hon. Secy. 1975–76); mem., Candn. Conf. Arts; C.A.R.S.; recreations: sailing, reading; Clubs: Royal Vancouver Yacht; Address: 106 - 8828 Heather St., Vancouver, B.C. V6P 3S8.

**GRAVEL, Claude,** B.A., Lic.ADM., F.S.A., F.C.I.A.; insurance company executive; b. Quebec, Que. 18 Oct. 1944; s. Robert and Charlotte (Larochelle) G.; e. Sem. de Qué., B.A. 1964; Laval Univ., Lic.ADM. 1968; Soc. of Actuaries, Chicago, F.S.A. 1972; Cdn. Inst. of Actuaries, F.C.I.A. 1972; m. Nicole d. Moïse and Yvette Dionne 1968; children: Martin, Nicolas, Alain; PRES. AND C.E.O., DESJARDINS LIFE ASSURANCE CO. INC. 1990– ; Asst. Dir., Actuarial Dept., Que. Govt. 1970; Chief Actuary, Mutuelle des Fonctionnaires du Que. 1973; Asst. Gen. Mgr., MFQ & La Capitale Que. 1976; Gen. Mgr., La Capitale Casualty Insur. Co. 1981; Mutuelle des Fonctionnaires du Que. 1983; Exec. Vice-Pres. 1985; Pres. & C.E.O., Safeguard Life Assur. Co. 1989–90; Bd. Chrmn., Laurier Life; Chrmn. Bd. of Trustees, Musée de l'Amérique française; Mem. Bd. of Dirs., Candn. Life and Health Insur. Compensation Corp. (CompCorp); clubs: Quebec Garrison, Royal Quebec Golf; The Geneva Assoc.; Home: 1395 de Lantagnac, Sillery, Que. G1T 2E5; Office: 200 Ave. des Commandeurs, Lévis, Que. G6V 6R2.

**GRAVEL, François,** B.S.E.; writer; b. Montreal, Que. 4 Oct. 1951; s. Gérard and Martine (Robillard) G.; e. Univ. of Que. at Montreal, B.S.E. 1975; m. Murielle Grégoire 28 Oct. 1971; children: Elise, Simon; ECONOMICS TEACHER, CEGEP SAINT-JEAN-SUR RICHELIEU 1975– ; author: 'La Note de Passage' 1985, 'Benito' 1987 (transl. by Sheila Fischman 1989), 'L'Effet Summerhill' 1988, 'Bonheur Fou' 1990 (transl. as 'Felicity's Fool' 1990), 'Les Black Stones vous Renviendront dans Quelques Instants' 1991 (novels); 'Corneilles' 1989, 'Zamboni' (Prix du Livre M. Christie 1990) 1990 (transl. as 'Mr Zamboni's Dream Machine' 1991), 'Deux Heures et Demie avant Jasmine' (Prix du Gouverneur Général 1991) 1991, 'Granulite' 1992 (children's novels); Home: 3185 Beauclerk, Montreal, Que. H1N 3J9.

**GRAVEL, Gilbert;** stock broker; b. Chicoutimi, Que. 30 March 1932; s. Charles and Estelle (Lespérance) G.; m. Denise d. Joseph and Josette (Tremblay) Desbiens 30 Jan. 1957; children: Véronique, Nathalie, Catherin; VICE-PRESIDENT, LÉVESQUE BEAUBIEN GEOFFRION INC.; stockbroker for last 40 years; Chair & Pres., Veronat Inc.; Mem., Military & Hospitaller Order of Saint Lazarus Jerusalem Grand Priory in Canada; Dir., Hopital de Chicoutimi Inc.; Vice-Pres. & Dir., Fond. Sagamie Inc.; Fond. de l'Univ. du Qué. à Chicoutimi; Inst. scientifique du Saguenay Lac St Jean; Fond. Monseigneur Victor Tremblay; Ctr. Nat. d'expositon de Jonquière; MC[2] Extase Inc.; Margie Gillis Dance Found.; Marie Chouinard Dance Co.; Fond. Roméo Vachon Inc.; Governor, Coll. de Chicoutimi; Soc. historique du Saguenay; recreations: skiing, golf, salmon fishing; clubs: Club de Golf de Chicoutimi, Club des '21' Chicoutimi; Home: 575 Chabanel Ave., Chicoutimi, Que. G7H 5C2; Office: 206 Racine St. E., Chicoutimi, Que. G7H 1R9.

**GRAVEL, Roy Andre,** M.Sc., Ph.D.; scientist; educator; b. Montreal, Que. 10 Dec. 1946; s. Guy Jacques and Lavinia (Craig) G.; e. McGill Univ. B.Sc. 1967, M.Sc. 1969; Yale Univ. M.Phil. 1970, Ph.D. 1972; m. Ying-Lin d. Ta-Ming and Mung-Ha Tso 10 June 1972; one s. Christopher; ASSOC. PROF. FACULTY OF MED., MCGILL UNIV.; SCIENTIFIC DIR., MCGILL UNIV. and MONTREAL CHILDREN'S HOSP. RESEARCH INST. 1989– ; Genetics Dept. Hosp. for Sick Children 1974–89; Prof. of Med. Genetics and of Med. Biophysics Univ. of Toronto 1987–89, Asst. Prof. 1974, Assoc. Prof. 1981; Postdoctoral Fellow Dept. Human Genetics and Biol. Yale Univ. 1972–74; author or co-author various sci. publs.; recreation: astronomy; Home: 383 Roslyn Ave., Westmount, Que. H3Z 2L7; Office: Montreal Children's Hosp., Research Inst., Room 202, 4060 St. Catherine St. W., Montreal, Que. H3Z 2Z3.

**GRAVELLE, Pierre,** Q.C., B.A., B.Ph., LL.L.; federal civil servant; b. Ottawa, Ont.; e. Univ. of Ottawa B.A. 1963, B.Ph. 1963, LL.L. 1966; m. Marguerite Labbé; children: Louis-Pierre, Kristian, Chloé; DEPY. MIN., DEPT. OF NATIONAL REVENUE, CUSTOMS, EXCISE AND TAXATION 1992– and SECRETARY GENERAL TO MULTILATERAL CONSTITUTIONAL DISCUSSIONS 1992– ; called to Bar of Que. 1967; cr. Q.C. 1981; Asst. Sec. to Bd. Canada Mortgage and Housing Corp. 1965–67; Sec. and Legal Counsel Nat. Arts Centre Corp. Ottawa 1967–72; various positions Privy Council Office, Asst. Sec. to Cabinet (Fed.-Prov. Relations) 1971–75; Asst. Dep. Min. Health & Welfare 1975–78, Asst. Dep. Min. Dept. of Justice 1978–83; Deputy Secy. to the Cabinet responsible for Office of Aboriginal Constitutional Affairs F.P.R.O. 1983–85; Assoc. Sec. Treasury Bd. 1985–87; Dep. Min. Dept. of National Revenue (Taxation) 1987–92; Office: 123 Slater St., Ottawa, Ont. K1A 0L8.

**GRAVES, Charles Frederick;** executive; b. Victoria, B.C. 21 Aug. 1933; s. Percy Frederick and Evelyn A. (Midgley) G.; e. Victoria High Sch. 1950; Victoria Coll. 1951; Inst. Chartered Accountants Prov. B.C., admitted to membership 1957; m. Mary E., d. James Rogers, 9 May 1959; children: Peter; John; Anne; Dir., Zellers Inc. (Montreal) 1978–83; articled student, Bailey Monteith & Holmes (Victoria) 1951; Chartered Accountant, McIntosh McVicar & Dinsley (Vancouver) 1957; Comptroller, Ritnet Consolidated (Victoria) 1958; Partner, Irving G. Chertow & Co. (Vancouver) 1959; Partner, C.F. Graves & Co. 1964; Vice-Pres., Fields Stores Ltd. 1969–78; Pres. 1978–83; Past mem., Advisory Counc. to the Dean of Commerce, Univ. B.C.; Past mem., Vancouver Kiwanis Club; Uptown Kiwanis Club (Past Pres.); Vancouver area Kiwanis Clubs (Past Lt. Gov. 1969); recreation: Y.M.C.A.; Club: Terminal City; Home: 614 Lowry Lane, N. Vancouver, B.C. V6B 4J9.

**GRAVES, Frank J.,** B.B.A.; pulp & paper industry executive; b. Toronto, Ont. 9 Sept. 1955; s. James Gary and Kathleen Gertrude (Campbell) G.; e. St. Francis Xavier Univ. B.B.A. 1976; m. Manon d. Clément and Carmen Seguin 26 April 1981; children: Marie France, Steven James; Vice-Pres. & General Mgr., Pulp, Lumber & Recycled Fibre, Abitibi-Price 1991–93; Sales Mgr. – Export, Consolidated-Bathurst Inc. 1981–87; Admin. Delegue et Dir. Général, Consolidated-Bathurst (Europe) S.A. 1987–89; Division Vice-Pres., Internat. Pulp Marketing, Canadian Pacific Forest Products Ltd. 1989–91; clubs: Royal St. Lawrence Yacht, Confrèrie des Chevaliers du Tastevin, Summer Lea Inc.; Home: 60 Ashburton Cres., Dorval, Que. H9S 5K2.

**GRAY, (Alexander) Earle;** writer, publisher; b. Medicine Hat, Alta. 24 May 1931; s. Alexander Ronald and Mary Edith Rachel (Johnson) g.; e. public & high schools Sechelt, B.C.; m. Joan d. Clement and Edith Barraclough 13 Sept. 1952; children: Glen, Mary, Carol, Gordon; PUBLISHER AND EDITOR, CANADIAN SPEECHES: ISSUES OF THE DAY 1987– ; News Reporter, Vancouver Sun, Calgary Albertan, Myers Oil News Serv. 1949–54; Publisher, Columbia Valley Echo 1954–55; Editor, Oilweek Magazine 1955–71; Dir. of Public Affairs, Candn. Arctic Gas Pipeline 1971–77; Writer & Editorial Consultant 1977–87; numerous business writing awards; Agnostic; Independent; Mem., Candn. Magazine Pub. Assn.; Pres., Canadian Club (Lindsay, Ont.) 1993; author: 'The Impact of Oil' 1969, 'The Great Canadian Oil Patch' 1970, 'Super Pipe' 1979, 'The Great Uranium Cartel' 1982, 'The Wildcatters' 1982; editor: 'Free Trade, Free Canada, Canadian Speeches' 1988; recreations: nordic skiing; Home: 194 King St., P.O. Box 250, Woodville, Ont. K0M 2T0.

**GRAY, Bill,** LL.B.; film executive and executive producer; b. Selkirk, Man. 12 July 1949; s. William and Margaret Marie (Keating) G.; e. Univ. of Alta. Drama Dept. 1972–75; Univ. of Calgary LL.B. 1986; m. Valerie d. Dexter and Marion Pennington 1 Apl. 1978; children: Whitney, Julian, Theresa; Pres., Sojourn Pictures Ltd. 1993; joined broadcast ind. CBC Winnipeg 1967; after law sch. practiced with Bennett Jones Calgary; Dir.-Operations, Telefilm Canada 1988–91; Vice Pres., Western Operations, Atlantis Films Limited 1991– ; nominee various ACTRA Awards for Producer and as Writer; mem. CFTPA; ACTRA (Vice Pres. Edmonton 1976); Actors Equity; Candn. Bar Assn.; Nat. Radio Producers Assn. (Pres. 1980–81); Home: 4601 Wickenden Rd., North Vancouver, B.C. V7G 1H3.

**GRAY, Charlotte Judith,** B.A.; writer; political columnist; b. Sheffield, UK 3 Jan. 1948; d. Robert and Elizabeth (Beckett) G.; e. Cheltenham Ladies Coll. 1965; Oxford Unv. B.A. 1969; London Sch. of Econ. & Pol. Sci. Dip. Social Adm. 1970; m. George s. Reginald and Alice Anderson 27 Oct. 1979; three s. Alexander, Nicholas, Oliver; teacher 1970–71; hist. rsch. UK Foreign Office 1971–73; Daily Express, Fleet St. London 1973–74; Asst. Ed. Psychology Today (UK) becoming Ed. 1974–78; freelance writer various Candn. mags. and profl. jours. since 1978; Ottawa Ed. Saturday Night 1986–93; recipient Pakenham Award for 'most promising young woman journalist' UK 1978 and several Candn. journalism awards, incl. Asia Pacific Found. Fellowship 1991; Trustee Ont. Sci. Centre 1986–92; mem. Bd. Children's Hosp. E. Ont. 1986–92, 1993– ; mem. ed. bd., Peace & Security magazine 1989–92; mem. Parlty. Press Gallery; Address: 183 MacKay St., Ottawa, Ont. K1M 2B5.

**GRAY, Gordon C.,** F.C.A.; real estate broker; b. Copper Cliff, Ont. 24 Oct. 1927; s. Robin and Corinne (Muir) G.; e. Pub. and High Schs., Copper Cliff, Ont.; Queen's Univ., B.Com.; m. Patricia d. R. G. Godson; children: Donald, David, Diane, Douglas, Deborah; Chrmn. & Dir., Rio Algom Limited; Dir., Markborough Properties Inc., CGC Inc., The Toronto-Dominion Bank, Rogers Communications Inc., McDonald's Corporation, OMERS Realty Corp., Stone-Consolidated Corp.; Fellow, Real Estate Inst. of Can.; Gov., Olympic Trust of Canada; Bd. of Dirs., Atlantic Salmon Fedn. of Can.; with Price, Waterhouse & Co., 1950–55; joined A.E. LePage Ltd., 1955; Apptd. Pres., Chrmn. & C.E.O. 1970; Hon. Chrmn., Royal LePage Ltd. 1993– ; Chrmn., A.E. LePage Investments Ltd.; Fellow, Inst. C.As. Ont.; Roman Catholic; recreations: golf, fishing, travel; Clubs: Toronto Golf; Toronto; Rosedale Golf & Country; York; Granite; Muirfield (Ohio); Loxahatchee (Jupiter, Fla.); Home: 300 Jefferson Sideroad, Richmond Hill, Ont. L4E 3M4; Office: Suite 1000, 33 Yonge St., Toronto, Ont. M5E 1S9.

**GRAY, Hon. Herbert Eser,** P.C., Q.C., M.P.; b. Windsor, Ont. 25 May 1931; s. the late Harry and Fannie G.; e. Victoria Sch. and Kennedy Coll. Inst., Windsor; McGill Univ., Grad. Sch. of Comm.; Osgoode Hall Law Sch., Toronto; m. Sharon, Sholzberg, Ville St. Laurent, Que. 23 July 1967; children: Jonathan, Elizabeth; el. to H. of C. for Windsor W. in g.e. 1962; re-el. since; SOLICITOR-GENERAL and LEADER OF THE GOVERNMENT IN THE HOUSE OF COMMONS 1993– ; (Opposition House Leader 1984–90, Depy. Leader of the Opposition 1989–90, Leader of the Opposition 1990–91, Opposition Finance Critic 1991–93); Chrmn., House of Commons Standing Committee on Finance, Trade and Economic Affairs, 1966–68; served as Parlty. Secy. to Min. of Finance, 1968–69; named Min. Without Portfolio 1969; Min. of National Revenue 1970–72; Min. of Consumer & Corporate Affairs 1972–74; Appointed Critic on Finance, Chrmn., Comm. on Fiscal and Monetary Affairs for Official Opposition, 1979; Sr. Minister for Ont. (apptd. by Prime Minister) 1980–84; Minister of Industry. Trade and Commerce 1980–82; Min. of Regional Economic Expansion (1982); Pres. of the Treasury Bd. 1982–84; has served as mem. of Candn. dels. to various internat. confs. on econ. and other matters; Del. Internat. Monetary Fund and World Bank meetings 1967, 69, 70; Co-Chrmn., Candn. Del to OECD Ministerial meeting 1970; Leader, Candn. Del. to Commonwealth Finance Mins. meeting 1970; Windsor Pres., Jaycees, 1961–62; Home: 1504 – 75 Riverside Dr. E., Windsor, Ont. N9A 2S4; Office: House of Commons, Ottawa, Ont. K1A 0A6.

**GRAY, Jack;** playwright; author; b. Detroit, Mich. 7 Dec. 1927; s. John Russell and Jessie Parsons (Paterson) G.; e. Queen's Univ.; Univ. of Toronto; m. Araby, d. James W. Lockhart 4 Dec. 1952; children: John, Nicholas, Rebecca, Susannah, Felix; Asst. Ed. 'Maclean's Magazine' 1953–57; freelance writer since 1957; Pres., John Gray Productions Ltd.; Secy. Gen., Candn. Theatre Centre 1971–73; Prof., Dept. of Integrated Studies, Univ. of Waterloo 1969–71; Special Consultant on Cultural Policy, Dept. of Communications, Ottawa 1982–83; Pres., League for Candn. Communications 1984; plays produced incl.: 'Bright Sun at Midnight' (Crest Theatre, Toronto) 1957; 'Ride a Pink Horse' (musical with Louis Applebaum, Crest Theatre) 1958; 'The Teacher' (Stratford, Ont.) 1960; 'Chevalier Johnstone' (Neptune Theatre, Halifax) 1964; 'Emmanuel Xoc' (Crest Theatre) 1965; 'Godiva!' (Belgrade Theatre, Coventry) 1967; 'Striker Schneiderman' (St. Lawrence Centre, Toronto) 1970; 'And I, Mayakovsky?' (Rock Garden, London, Eng.) 1977; extensive work in radio, TV, film and journalism; Chrmn. Candn. Film Awards 1976; Council of Candn. Filmmakers 1977; Vice-Chrmn. Acad. of Candn. Cinema 1979–80; mem., Writers Guild Gt. Brit.; Alliance Candn. Cinema, TV & Radio Artists (Pres. 1978–82); Writers Guild of Canada (Pres. 1991–94); Pres., Internat. Writers Guild; Address: 155 Hopewell Ave., Ottawa, Ont. K1S 2Z4.

**GRAY, James Henry,** C.M., LL.D., D.Lit.; author; b. Whitemouth, Man. 31 Aug. 1906; s. Harry and Maria (Sargent) G.; e. Winnipeg, Man. 1921; Univ. of Man. LL.D. (hon.) 1974; Univ. of Brandon D.Lit. (hon.) 1974; Univ. of Calgary LL.D. (hon.) 1975; m. Kathleen Burns 28 Dec. 1926; children: Patricia, Alan, Linda; Office Boy, Winnipeg Grain Exchange 1922, Margin Clk. 1925–29; Mgr., Stockbroker's Office Lethbridge 1930; on relief Winnipeg 1931–33; Reporter, 'Winnipeg Free Press' 1935–42, Ed. Writer 1942–46, Ottawa Corr. 1947; Ed., 'Farm and Ranch Review' Calgary 1947–55; 'Western Oil Examiner' 1955–58; Pub. Relations Mgr. Home Oil Co. 1958–64; author 'The Winter Years' 1966; 'Men Against the Desert' 1967; 'The Boy From Winnipeg' 1970; 'Red Lights on the Prairies' 1971; 'Booze' 1972; 'The Roar of the Twenties' 1975; 'Troublemaker!' 1978; 'Boomtime' 1979; 'Bacchanalia Revisited' 1982; 'A Brand of its Own' 1985; 'Talk to My Lawyer' 1987; 'R.B. Bennett, the Calgary Years' 1991; rec'd Candn. Hist. Soc. Award 1967; Alta. Hist. Soc. Award 1968, 1975; Margaret McWilliams Medal 1967; Univ. of B.C. Silver Medal 1971; Alberta Order of Excellence 1987; Order of Canada 1988; Club: Calgary Petroleum; Address: 11 Strandell Cres. S.W. Calgary Alta. T3H 1K8.

**GRAY, John,** B.A.; journalist; b. Toronto, Ont. 28 April 1937; s. John Morgan and Frances Antoinette (Lalonde) G.; e. Univ. of Toronto B.A.; London School of Economics; m. Elizabeth d. George and Enid Binks 21 May 1960; children: Colin, Rachel, Joshua; MOSCOW CORRESPONDENT, THE GLOBE AND MAIL 1991– ; various newspapers in Canada incl. Montreal Gazette, Que. Chronicle-Telegraph, Montreal Star, Toronto Star, Ottawa Citizen, Ottawa Journal and United Press Internat. (London); Ottawa Bureau Chief, The Globe and Mail 1980–84; Nat. Editor 1984–85; Foreign Ed. 1985–87; European Correspondent 1987–91; Nat. Newspaper Award for feature writing 1990, 1991; Home: 1 Kaluzhskaya Ploshad, Kv. 229, Moscow, Russia; Office: Kutuzovsky Prospect, 7/4, Kv. 60, Moscow, Russia.

**GRAY, John Howard,** M.A., LL.D.; playwright; author; composer; director; b. Ottawa, Ont. 26 Sept. 1946; s. Howard Newell and Marion Louise (MacLachlan) G.; e. elem. and high schs. Truro, N.S.; Mount Allison Univ. B.A. 1968; Univ. of B.C., M.A. 1972; LL.D. (Hon.), Mount Allison Univ. 1989; m. Beverlee Miller Larsen d. Nathan and Esther Miller; children: two s. Zachary Miller, Ezra Wolf Miller; founded Tamahnous Theatre Vancouver 1972, Dir. until 1974; composed and directed with Theatre Passe Muraille Toronto 1974–76; writer, composer '18 Wheels' 1976; 'Billy Bishop Goes To War' 1978 (Gov. Gen.'s Award Drama 1983; Los Angeles Drama Critics Award Best Play, Best Prodn., Best Direction 1981; Golden Globe Award Boston, Best Musical 1983; ACTRA Award Best TV Program 1982); 'Rock and Roll' 1981 (Dora Mavor Moore Award Best Musical, Best Direction Musical 1981); 'The King of Friday Night' 1984 (Best Performance Special Banff Festival 1985; Best Feature-Length Video New York Film & TV Festival 1985); feature-length video of 'Rock and Roll'; Regular contributor music videos 'The Journal' TV; 'Balthazaar and the Mojo Star' and 'Bongo From the Congo' (children's musicals) 1982; 'Better Watch Out, You Better Not Die' 1983; 'Don Messer's Jubilee' 1984; author (novel) 'Dazzled' 1984; 'Health, The Musical' 1989; Vancouver Award for excellence in writing 1988; various articles and stories mags. & anthols.; frequent spokesman, lectr. Candn. cultural politics; Address: 3392 West 37th Ave., Vancouver, B.C. V6N 2V6.

**GRAY, Nigel George Davidson,** B.Sc., LL.B.; b. Chakrata, U.P., India 16 June 1935; s. Dr. James D. Gray; e. St. Paul's Sch. London, Eng. 1952; Coll. Militaire Royal, St. Jean, Que. 1955; Dalhousie Univ. B.Sc. 1959, LL.B. 1964; Lincoln Coll. Oxford Univ. post-grad. studies Comparative Law 1964–65; Advanced Mgmt. Program, Harvard Univ. 1986; m. Barbara Johnston d. Allan A. Ferguson, Pictou, N.S. 22 Aug. 1964; two s. Nicholas, Christopher; CONSULTANT 1988 to present; Geol., Canadian Pacific Rly. 1959–61; read law with Stewart, McKeen & Covert; called to Bar of N.S. 1966; Asst. Secy. and Asst. Counsel, Petrofina Canada Ltd. 1966–69; Legal Counsel and Secy., Capital Management Ltd. 1969–72; Asst. Gen. Counsel, Brinco Ltd. 1972–75, Assoc. Gen. Counsel 1975–78; Assoc. Gen. Counsel, Polysar Energy & Chemical Corp. 1975, Vice Pres. and Gen. Counsel 1978–88; mem. N.S. Barristers Soc.; Candn. Bar Assn.; Assn. Prof. Engrs., Geologists & Geophysicists of Alberta; Phi Delta Theta; Anglican; Club: University (Toronto); Home: 506 Lakeshore E., Oakville, Ont. L6J 1K5.

**GRAY, Parker Totten,** B.A.; public servant; b. Louisville, Kentucky 14 Oct. 1946; s. Judson Clark and Claire (Totten) G.; e. Ecole d'Humanité & Ecole Internat. (Switz.); Verde Valley School (Arizona); Rollins Coll. (Florida); Universidad de los Andes (Colombia); Friends World Coll. (N.Y.) B.A. 1968; Univ. Aix-Marseille (France) 1987; m. Elaine d. Harold and Josephine Bulmer 14 Nov. 1977; children: Kai, Belknap, Taylor, Ashley; SENIOR POLICY ADVR., DEPT. OF THE ENVIRONMENT, PROV. OF N.B. 1989– ; Owner/operator, cow/calf farming opn. (Glassville, N.B.) 1970–79; Extve. Dir., Reg. Br., Candn. Assn. for the Mentally Retarded 1979–81; Mgr., Community Adjustment Prog., Community Improvement Corp. 1981–85; Internal Consultant to N.B. on Productivity Improvement 1985–86; Mgr., Information Systems, Bd. of Mngt., Prov. of N.B. 1987–89; Dir., N.B. Reg., Inst. of Public Admin. of Can. (Sec.) 1989–92; initiated designation & co-ord. mngt., St. Croix Waterway Internat. Recreation Area (St. Croix is now a Canadian Heritage River); principal architect 1991 N.B. Beverage Containers Act; on Secretariate to N.B. Round Table on Environment & Economy; recreations: skiing, swimming, tennis, camping; Home: 236 Eglinton St., Fredericton, N.B. E3B 2W1; Office: P.O. Box 6000, Fredericton, N.B. E3B 5H1.

**GRAY, Patrick Trevor Robert,** B.A., S.T.B., S.T.M., Th.D.; professor; b. Toronto, Ont. 16 Oct. 1940; s. Robert Holt Roberts and Margaret Derwyn (Owen) G.; e. Univ. of Toronto Schs. 1958; Univ. of Toronto, B.A. 1962; Trinity Coll., S.T.B. 1965, Th.D. 1973; Yale Univ., S.T.M. 1966; m. Allison d. Kenneth and Beverley McNaught 19 June 1976; children: Trevor, Benjamin, Timothy, Geoffrey; ASSOC. PROF., HUMANITIES DEPT., ATKINSON COLL., YORK UNIV. 1984– ; Divinity Tutor, Trinity Coll. 1967–69; Assoc. Rector, Church of St. Simon-the-Apostle 1969–71; Instr. & Vis. Asst. Prof., York Univ. 1972–75; Sr. Tutor, Stong Coll., York Univ. 1973–76; Res. Tutor 1974–76; Rsch. Assoc., Pontifical Inst. of Med. Studies 1976–78; Asst. & Assoc. Prof. of Hist. & Philos. Theol., McMaster Divinity Coll. 1978–84; Killam Post-doct. Rsch. Scholarship 1976–78; Dir., Candn. Fed. for the Humanities 1984–87; Convenor, 'Outside the Nuclear Club' Conf., York Univ. 1987; Priest, Anglican Ch. of Can.; NDP; Vice-Pres., Candn. Soc. of Patristic Studies (Pres. 1977–79; Hon. Pres. 1979–83); Candn. Ctte., Assn. Internat. des Etudes Byzantines 1976– ; Science for Peace; author: 'The Defense of Chalcedon in the East (451–553)' 1979; recreations: music, gardening, winemaking; Home: 'The Cedars,' R.R. 1, Stella, Ont. K0H 2S0; Office: 724 Atkinson, York Univ., 4700 Keele St., North York, Ont. M3J 1P3.

**GRAY, Viviane Alice,** B.A.; art administrator, professor, curator, writer; contemporary native arts & culture; fibre artist; b. Restigouche, Qué. 1 Apr. 1947; d. Joseph and Alice (Dionne) G.; e. Coady Internat. Inst. St. Francis Xavier Univ. Dip. Social Leadership & Community Devel. 1965; Carleton Univ. B.A. (Anthr. & French) 1973; N.S. Coll. of Art & Design, Halifax textile, design & art edn. 1976–77; m. John Charles s. William and Agnes Clifford; children: Ruby Agnes, Seamus John; PARTNER, CLIFFORD GRAY ASSOCIATES 1983– ; mem., Restigouche Band, Que.; apprenticeship with Curatorial Interpretation Sect. Parks Can. Atlantic Region, Halifax, N.S. (17th century Acadian sites) 1979–80; Exhibit Planner and Curator First Native Artist Competition & Exhn. Ottawa 1983; Cons., to Restigouche Band for proposed Micmac Museum 1985– ; 'Federal Presences' exhbn. on Candn. exports for Candn. Govt. 1986; 'L'Oeil Amerindien: Regards sur l'Animal' travelling exhbn. for Musée de la Civilisation, Que. 1991–92; 'Pe'l A'tukwey' Seventeen Mi'Kmag and Maliseet Artists of the East Coast, Art Gallery of Nova Scotia 1993; Sr. Land Claims Analyst, Indian & N. Affairs 1987–88; Mgr., Indian Arts Centre, Indian & N. Affairs 1988– ; sessional Lectr., Contemporary Native Art at Univ. Ottawa 1982– ; author, ed., art dir. various publs.; rep. group art exhnbs. since 1981; Founding mem. Ottawa Indian & Inuit Art Study Group; founding mem., C.A.N.E. (Ctte. for the Advancement of Native Employment, Indian & N. Affairs, Ottawa/Hull Chapter); recipient Explorations Grant Can. Council 1975; Jean Chalmers Award 1986; recreations: cycling, walking, tennis, piano, reading, textile arts; Address: 166 Marlborough Ave., Ottawa, Ont. K1N 8G4.

**GRAY, Hon. Wesley Gibson,** B.A., LL.B., LL.D.; judge; b. Toronto, Ont. 19 Mar. 1917; s. Ernest D. and Elsie E. (Gibson) G.; e. Jarvis Coll. Inst. 1930–35; Univ. of Toronto B.A. (Hons. Law) 1935–39; Osgoode Hall Law Sch. 1939–42; m. Nancy Elizabeth d. R.B.S. and Ida Burton 14 Sept. 1942; children: Patsy (Mrs. T.M. Porter), Katy (Rev. Catherine Waugh), Barbara (Mrs. J.D. Coyle); JUSTICE, SUPREME COURT OF ONTARIO AND ONTARIO COURT OF JUSTICE 1979–92, retired; read law with Mason, Foulds, Davidson and Kellock 1939–42; apptd. Q.C. 1958; practiced law with Tilley, Carson, Morlock & McCrimmon, Toronto 1945–49; Partner Borden & Elliot 1949–79; Bencher Law Soc. of Upper Can. 1964–79 (Treas. & C.E.O. 1976–78); Life Bencher 1976; LL.D., Law Soc. of Upper Can. 1981; Comnr. Ont. Law Reform Comn. 1964–79; served in Royal Canadian Navy (Lieut. (N)) 1942–45; mem. Un. Ch. of Can.; Phi Delta Theta (Pres.); recreations: historical reading, fishing; Clubs: Royal Candn. Mil. Inst.; The Badminton & Racquet of Toronto; Home: 66 Highland Ave., Toronto, Ont. M4W 2A3; summer residence: Smoke Lake, Algonquin Park.

**GRAYDON, Kenneth Rubert,** M.S.A.; association executive; b. Toronto, Ont. 23 Sept. 1934; s. Rubert and Helen (Eland) G.; e. Public and High Schs. Toronto; Univ. of Toronto, B.S.A. (Agric.) 1956, M.S.A. (Agric.) 1958; m. Phyllis, d. Kenneth MacDougall 8 June 1957; children: Catherine, Sheila; EXTVE. VICE-PRES., FEDERATION OF AUTOMOBILE DEALER ASSNS. OF CAN., since 1977; Pres. Rubber Assn. of Can. 1973–76; joined C.B.C. Radio and TV Broadcasting 1957; advertising Dept. Massey Ferguson Industries Ltd. 1959; Dir. Public Relations, Meat Packers Council of Can. 1960–66; Gen. Mgr. Cdn. Farm and Industrial Equipment Inst. 1966–72; past Gov., George Brown Coll.; past Chair, Candn. Soc. of Assoc. Extves.; Dir., Candn. Automotive Inst.; CARS Counc.; Traffic Injury Rsch. Foundation; mem., Metrop. Toronto Bd. Trade; Presbyterian; recreations: music, boating, fishing, curling, photography; Home: R.R. #5, Bolton, Ont. L7E 5S1; Office: 85 Renfrew Dr., Markham, Ont. L3R 0N9.

**GRAYDON, William Frederick,** M.A.Sc., Ph.D., F.C.I.C.; engineer; educator; b. Toronto, Ont., 27 June 1919; s. Walter and Josephine (Hamilton) G.; e. Univ. of Toronto, B.A.Sc. (Chem. Engn.) 1942, M.A.Sc. 1945; Univ. of Minnesota, Ph.D. 1949; m. Evelyn Crouch, 28 May 1945; children: John William, Mary Evelyn, Jane Hamilton, Elizabeth Ann, Catherine Ruth; PROFESSOR OF CHEMICAL ENGINEERING, UNIV. OF TORONTO since 1960; Pres., Chemical Engineering Research Consultants Ltd.; Asst. Prof. of Chem. Engn., Univ. of Toronto, 1949; Prof. 1960; Assoc. Dean, Faculty of Applied Science and Engn. 1966–70; el. to Etobicoke Bd. of Educ. since 1958 (Chrmn. 1963, 1966); mem. Bd. of Govs., Humber Coll. of Applied Arts and Tech.; author of over 50 research publs. in field of applied surface chem.; Conservative; Presbyterian; recreation: sailing; Club: T.S. & C.C.; Home: 3 Mossom Pl., Toronto, Ont. M6S 1G4; Office: Room 217, Wallberg Bldg., 200 College St., Toronto, Ont. M5S 1A4.

**GRAY-DONALD, Katherine,** B.Sc., Ph.D.; university professor; b. Quebec, Que. 22 Dec. 1947; d. E. Donald and Osla Margaret (Hingston) G.; e. McGill Univ. B.Sc. 1969, Ph.D. 1984; m. Robert L. s. D. Lorne and Isabel Gales 3 June 1977; children: Sarah Hingston, Geoffrey Donald, Margaret Osla; PROF., SCHOOL OF DIETETICS & HUMAN NUTRITION, MACDONALD CAMPUS, MCGILL UNIV. 1989– ; Professional Dietitian working in community orgns. providing profl. training & direct service to improve the nutritional intake of the population 1973–80; teaching and research in depts. of Epidemiology and Biostatistics, McGill Unvi. 1985– ; Mem., Candn. Dietetic Assn. 1973– ; co-author of 15 research articles; recreations: skiing, hiking, canoeing; clubs: Brome Lake Boat; Home: 316 Grosvenor Ave., Westmount, Que. H3Z 2M2; Office: 21, 111 Lakeshore Rd., Ste. Anne de Bellevue, Que. H9X 3V9.

**GRAYSON, A(lbert) Kirk,** M.A., Ph.D., F.R.S.C.; educator; b. Windsor, Ont. 1 Apl. 1935; s. Albert Kirk and Helen (Smith) G.; e. Univ. of Toronto B.A. 1955, M.A. 1958; Univ. of Vienna 1959–60; John Hopkins Univ. Ph.D. 1962; m. Eunice Marie d. John and Lillian Service 3 Aug. 1956; two d. Vera Lorraine, Sally Frances; grandd. Rachel Anne Mariek, Melaena Janine; PROF. OF NEAR EASTERN STUDIES, UNIV. OF TORONTO 1972– , Dir. The Royal Inscriptions of Mesopotamia Project 1981– ; Research Asst., Chicago Assyrian Dictionary Project Oriental Inst. Univ. of Chicago 1962–63; Asst. Prof. of Hist. Temple Univ. 1963–64; Asst. Prof. of Near E. Studies present Univ. 1964, Assoc. Prof. 1967, Prof. 1972; Visiting Lectr. in Oriental Langs. Univ. of Pa. 1963–64; Special Asst. Dept. W. Asiatic Antiquities Brit. Museum 1967–76; Invited Lectr. Univ. of Chicago, John Hopkins Univ., Brit. Museum, Univ. of Heidelberg, Univ. of Vienna, Cetona (Italy), Iraq Museum (Baghdad) and other instns.; recipient Can. Council Pre-doctoral Fellowship 1959–61; Samuel S. Fels Fund Fellowship 1961–62; various grants research N.Am., Europe & Asia 1965–80; Maj. Editorial Grant Social Sciences & Humanities Research Council

Can. 1981–2001; author 'Assyrian and Babylonian Chronicles – Texts from Cuneiform Sources' V 1975; 'Assyrian Royal Inscriptions' I 1972, II 1976; 'Babylonian Historical – Literary Texts – Toronto Semitic Texts and Studies' III 1975; co-author 'Papyrus and Tablet' 1973; 'Cambridge Ancient History' III 1992; 'Assyrian Rulers of the Third and Second Millennia BC – Royal Inscriptions of Mesopotamia: Assyrian Periods I' 1987; 'Assyrian Rulers of the Early First Millennium BC I - Royal Inscriptions of Mesopotomia: Assyrian Periods II' 1991; 'Royal Inscriptions on Clay Cones from Ashur Now in Istanbul' 1984; over 30 articles scholarly journs.; Pres., Soc. Mesopotamian Studies 1980–92; Hon. Secy., Acad. II, The Royal Soc. of Can. 1989–92; mem., Brit. Sch. Archeol. in Iraq; Fondation Assyriologique Georges Dossin (Belgium); Oriental Club Toronto (Sec. 1969–70, Pres. 1979–80); Rencontre Assyriologique Internationale (sessional chrmn. meetings, Berlin, Vienna, Leiden); Am. Oriental Soc.; Anglican; recreations: family, bird watching, music, reading; Home: 56 Rathnelly Ave., Toronto, Ont. M4V 2M3; Office: 4 Bancroft Ave., Toronto, Ont. M5S 1A1.

**GRAYSON, J. Paul,** B.A., M.A., Ph.D.; university administrator; professor; b. England 15 Apr. 1944; s. Adam Joseph and Joy Alice (Watson) G.; e. York Univ. B.A. 1967, M.A. 1968; Univ. of Toronto Ph.D. 1972; m. Linda d. James and Mary Forrest 1970; one s.: Kyle Andrew; Dir., Inst. for Social Rsch.; former Associate Dean Academic and Prof. of Sociology, Atkinson College, York University 1981–84; Asst. Prof. Univ. of W. Ont. 1972–73; Asst. and Assoc. Prof. present Univ. 1973–76, and Chrmn. Dept. of Sociology 1976–79; mem. Gov. Gen.'s First Candn. Study Conf. 1983; author various books and articles on Candn. phenomena; Former Ed. 'Atkinson Review of Canadian Studies'; consultant various agencies incl. Sci. Counc. of Can., Ont. Min. of Labour, Labour Can., Ont. Min. of Municip. Affairs and Housing; mem. Adv. Bd. 'Our Times'; past Chrmn. Adv. Bd. Inst. for Social Rsch.; mem. various profl. assns. incl. Candn. Sociology and Anthropology Assn., Assn. for Candn. Studies, Candn. Pol. Sci. Assn.; recipient various rsch. grants from sources incl. Can. Counc., Social Sci. & Humanities Counc., Labour Can.; rsch. interest in corp. strategies and ind. re-structuring, plant closures and unemployment; Home: 274 Douglas Dr., Toronto, Ont. M4W 2C1; Office: 4700 Keele St., Downsview, Ont. M3J 1P3.

**GREANEY, James M.;** insurance executive; b. Houlton, Maine 13 Oct. 1941; s. John C. and Winnifred M. (Murphy) G.; e. St. Francis Xavier Univ. B.A. (Hons.) 1964; McGill Univ. M.A. 1965; Chartered Fin. Analyst 1972; Univ. of W. Ont. Mgmt. Dipl. 1978; m. Pamela d. Philip and Pauline Quinn 15 May 1963; children: John, Heather, Michael; SR. VICE PRES., INVESTMENTS & TREASURER, AETNA LIFE INSURANCE CO. OF CAN. 1989– ; Chrmn., Aetna Capital Management; Pres., Aetna Acceptance; Mount Battan Properties; Lanex Properties; Dir., Aetna Trust; Sr. Investment Analyst, Sun Life Assurance Co. of Can. 1965–70; Investment Mgr. for S. Africa 1970–75; Chief Property Investments Offr. for Can. 1975–80; Vice-Pres., Property Investments for Can. 1981; Vice Pres., Investments for Canada 1982–86; Vice Pres. & Treas., present co. 1986–88; R. Catholic; mem., Toronto Soc. of Fin. Analysts; Chart. Fin. Analyst Soc.; recreations: golf, tennis, squash; Clubs: Ontario; Waterfront; Home: 14 Ravensbourne Cres., Islington, Ont. M9A 2A6.

**GREAVES, Lorraine J.,** M.A.; educator; sociologist; b. Manchester, Eng. 14 June 1950; d. Alec and Rene (Price) G.; e. Univ. of W. Ont. B.A. 1970, M.A. 1974; London Teachers Coll. 1971; Monash Univ. Melbourne, Australia Ph.D. courses; two s.: Lucas, Simon; PROF. OF HUMAN SERVICES, FANSHAWE COLL. OF APPLIED ARTS AND TECHNOL. 1974– and DIR., CENTRE FOR RESEARCH ON VIOLENCE AGAINST WOMEN AND CHILDREN (London); Community Cons. Addiction Rsch. Found. Ont. 1982–83; Dir. Women's Edn. & Rsch. Found. Ont.; Founder and Dir. London Battered Women's Advocacy Clinic; Vice Pres. London Status of Women Action Group 1980–81; Exec. mem. Nat. Action Ctte. Status of Women 1985–88, Vice Pres. 1987–88; recipient Augusta Stowe-Gullen Award 1986; Outstanding Young Londoner Award 1986; author: 'Background Paper on Women & Tobacco' 1987, 1990; 'Taking Control: An Action Handbook on Women and Tobacco' 1989; various articles, papers women's movement, health and addictions; mem. YWCA; recreations: swimming, skiing; Home: 946 Wellington St. N., London, Ont. N6A 3S9; Office: Univ. of W. Ont. Rsch. Park, Suite 240, London, Ont. N6G 4X8.

**GREB, Charles Erwin;** business consultant; b. Kitchener, Ont. 2 Sept. 1929; s. Erwin Charles and Clara Mina (Miller) G.; e. high school; business courses at var. schools; m. Fern I. d. Ruth and Lloyd McEwing 20 April 1991; children: Ross, John, Paul, Lori Janice; PRESIDENT, GREBCO HOLDINGS LTD. & GENERAL PARTNER, WOODSIDE FUND 1983– ; DIR. & CONSULTANT, SKYJACK INC. 1992– ; var. positions incl. Extve. Vice-Pres. Greb Shoes Limited, Greb Industries Limited, Greb Realty Ltd., Bauer Candn. Skate Inc. 1948–76; Dir., Logisticon Inc. 1972–78; Pres., Musitron-Danning Inc. 1978–88; Musitron Communications Inc. 1978–90; Canada 125 Medal; Paul Harris Fellow, Rotary Internat.; Companion, Fellowship of Hon., YMCA Canada 1986; Prov. of Ont. Bicentennial Medal 1984; Citizen of the Year Kitchener-Waterloo 1978; Mem., Extve. Ctte., Jr. Achievement of Canada 1990– (Dir. 1970–87, 1990– ); Dir., Jr. Achievement of the Waterloo Region 1970–81, 1988– (Pres. 1971, 1989–93); Dir., C.A.A. Mid-Western Ont. Auto Club 1977– (Pres. 1990–92); Bd. of Regents, Luther College 1988– ; Bd. of Dir. YMCA of Kitchener-Waterloo 1945– (Pres. 1969–71); Life Mem., Nat. Council of YMCAs of Canada 1978– (Chair 1982–84); Mem., Advisory Council of K.W. Oktoberfest Inc. 1978– (Pres. 1977–78); Founding Dir. & Life Mem., C. of C. of Kitchener and Waterloo 1992; clubs: Kitchener-Conestoga Rotary K.W. Gyro, Westmount Golf & Country, Concordia, Confrère de la chaine des rotisseurs; Address: R.R. 1, Ayr, Ont. N0B 1E0.

**GREB, Harry D.,** LL.D.; industrialist; b. Kitchener, Ont. 4 Oct. 1915; s. Erwin C. and Clara M. (Miller) G.; e. Pub. and High Schs., Kitchener, Ont.; LL.D. Waterloo Lutheran 1971; m. Dorothy M., d. John C. Spain, Galt, Ont., 10 Sept. 1938; Hon. Dir., Equitable Life Ins. Co. of Can.; Clk., Greb Shoe Co. Ltd. 1933; Dir. and Vice-Pres. 1936, Pres. 1954, retired 1975; Freemason; Lutheran; recreation: yachting; Clubs: Royal Canadian Yacht (Toronto); Scottish Rite (Hamilton); Royal Hamilton Yacht; Bronte Harbour Yacht (Oakville); Westmount Golf & Country (Kitchener) Rotary; Home: 292 Pilgrim Circle, Waterloo, Ont. N2K 1Y4.

**GREBEN, Stanley Edward,** B.A., M.D., FRCP(C), DABPN, FAPA, FRCPsych., FACPsych.; physician, author, editor, university professor; b. Toronto, Ont. 6 Aug. 1927; s. Abraham and Kitty (Goodman) G.; e. Univ. of Toronto B.A. 1949,M.D. 1953; m. Marilyn d. Stanford and Eva Scher 3 April 1955; children: Daniel Howard, Jan Elizabeth; PROFESSOR EMERITUS, UNIV. OF TORONTO 1993– ; Founding Psych.-in-Chief, Mount Sinai Hosp. 1966–85; Prof. of Psych., Univ. of Toronto 1973–93; of Psychotherapy 1985–93; Cons., Toronto Hosp., Clarke Inst. of Psych., Baycrest Ctr.; Examiner in Psych., Royal Coll. of Physicians & Surg. of Can. 1976–86; Am. Bd. of Psych. & Neur. 1979– ; Chief Cons. Psych. & Health Cons., Nat. Ballet School 1980– ; Vice-Pres. & Chief Cons. Psych., Dancer Transition Center 1984– ; Lifetime Special Adviser, Albert & Temmy Latner Inst. for Rsch. in Soc. Psych. & Psychotherapy (Israel) 1990– ; Visiting Prof., Univ. of Calif. 1981–82; Hebrew Univ. of Jerusalem 1982; Fellowhsip, Laidlaw Found. 1979; Mem., Candn. Psych. Assn. (Chair, Bd. of Dir. 1975–85; Pres. 1986–87); Candn. Psychoanalytic Soc. (Pres. 1975–77); Canadian Psychoanalytic Institute; Mem., Bd. of Dir., Carmel Inst. for the Advancement of Society; Authors Guild & Authors League of Am.; Am. Soc. of Composers, Authors & Pubs.; author: 'Love's Labor' 1984 and over 80 articles in sci. journals; co-editor & co-author: 'A Method of Psychiatry' 1980, 'Office Treatment of Schizophrenia' 1990, 'Clinical Perspectives on Psychotherapy Supervision' 1994; recreations: skiing, swimming; Home: 148 Dunvegan Rd., Toronto, Ont. M5P 2N9; Office: Room 933, Mount Sinai Hosp., 600 University Ave., Toronto, Ont. M5G 1X5.

**GREEN, Donald Mackenzie,** C.M. (1980); executive; b. Hamilton, Ont. 8 Oct. 1932; s. Victor and Isabelle G.; e. Westdale Secondary Sch. Hamilton; Ryerson Inst. Technol. Toronto; McMaster Univ., Hamilton; Univ. of Western Ont., London; m. Sandra Little 13 July 1957; children: Stephen, Sharon; CHRMN. & C.E.O., TRIDON LIMITED; Chrmn. Innovation Ontario Corp.; Dir.: Laidlaw Transportation Ltd.; Thermadyne Welding Prodcuts (Can.) Ltd.; Devtek Corp.; Union Gas Ltd.; Commercial Union of Can. Holdings Ltd.; National Bank of Canada; Gov., Ortech International; Hon. Life Dir. Candn. Nat. Sportsmen's Shows; mem. Bd. of Govs., Hamilton/Burlington YMCA; former Chrmn. and Dir. Hamilton Civic Hosps., former Chrmn. Sch. Nursing; former Chrmn. Hamilton-Wentworth Dist. Health Council; former Pres.: Burlington Chamber Comm.; Greater Hamilton YMCA; Candn. Cancer Soc. Hamilton Unit; former Dir.: Jr. Achievement Hamilton; Thomson Gordon Ltd.; North Sails Fogh Ltd.; former Gov., Olympic Trust of Canada; rec'd Admin. Man. of the Year Award 1986; Ursaki Sales & Mktg. Exec. of the Year Award 1983; Order of Canada 1980; Ryerson Fellowship 1979; named Young Man of Yr. Burlington 1969; One of Ten Outstanding Men Ont. 1969; author 'White Wings Around the World' 1953; winner Can.'s Cup races Bayview, Mich. as owner racing yacht 'Evergreen' 1978; Chrmn. & C.E.O., True North, Canada's Challenge '87 for the America's Cup; Young Pres. Organ. '49ers'; Clubs: Hamilton Yacht (Past Commodore); mem. Royal Nova Scotia Yacht Squadron; Burlington Golf & Country; Hamilton Club; Home: 364 North Shore Blvd. E., Burlington, Ont. L7T 1W9; Office: 1150 Corporate Dr., P.O. Box 5029, Burlington, Ont. L7R 4A2.

**GREEN, Gordon R.A.,** B.A., C.A.; utility executive; b. Marathon, Ont. 16 Aug. 1949; s. Jack Allan and Viola A.G. (Johnson); e. Lakehead Univ. B.A. 1972; Inst. of C.A.'s of B.C. C.A. 1979; m. Celia d. Cecil and Gwendolyn Wheeler 6 Aug. 1976; children: Neal, Emily; VICE PRESIDENT, EDMONTON POWER; articled Peat Marwick Thorne Vernon B.C. 1977–79; Nassau, Bahamas 1980–82; Mgr., Soligo Koide & John (Castlegar, B.C.) 1982–83; Mgr., Peat Marwick Thorne (Kamloops) 1984–85; Mgr., Dept. of Finan., Govt. of the N.W.T. 1985–88 (Dir., Govt. Acct.; Treas. Serv.); Vice-Pres., Finan., present firm 1988–89; Sr. Vice Pres., Northwest Territories Power Corp. 1989; Mem., Bd. of Dir., N.W.T. Power Corp.; Bd. of Trustees, N.W. Public Power Assn.; Past Pres., Inst. of C.A.'s of the N.W.T.; Past Gov., Candn. Inst. of C.A.s; 1st Vice-Pres., Hay River C. of C.; Mem., Counc. of Inst. of C.A.s of N.W.T.; recreations: oldtimers hockey, skiing, golf; club: Hay River Golf; Home: 703 Hendra Cres., Edmonton, Alta. T6R 1S1.

**GREEN, (Dorothy) Jane Stuart,** B.Sc., M.Sc.; medical geneticist, university professor; b. Vancouver, B.C. 13 Sept. 1943; d. Gordon Stuart and Dorothy Alice (Buchanan) Scholefield; e. Lord Byng S.S. 1960; Univ. of B.C. B.Sc. 1964, M.Sc. 1966; Memorial Univ. of Nfld. Ph.D. expected 1994; m. John s. Joseph and Elinor G. 19 Nov. 1966; children: Teresa, Timothy, Valerie; work in genetics inspired by David Suzuki; Rsch. Asst., Genetics, Fac. of Medicine, Memorial Univ. of Nfld. 1978; Lecturer 1988; Asst. Prof. 1991; research focus: hereditary eye diseases and hereditary cancers; has collaborated on mapping and cloning a gene for colorectal cancer 1993; teaches, provides genetic counselling, development & monitoring of screening programs; invited collaborator, Candn. Genetics Diseases Network for recent submission to Fed. Govt. Network of Centres of Excellence Program; Mem., Am. Soc. of Human Genetics; Internat. Collaborative Group on Hereditary Non-Polyposis Colon Cancer; Internat. Soc. for Genetic Eye Diseases; N.Y. Acad. of Sciences; Candn. Assn. of Genetic Counsellors; recreations: sports (softball, squash, nordic skiing), travel; Home: Box 60, R.R. 1, Torbay, Nfld. A0A 3Z0; Office: Medical Genetics, Health Sciences Centre, St. John's, Nfld. A1B 3V6.

**GREEN, Joan M.,** B.A., B.Ed., M.Ed.; educational executive; b. Windsor, Ont. 26 June 1946; d. Gerald William and Eleanore Ursula (Payne) Cronk; e. Univ. of Toronto B.A. (Hons.) 1969, B.Ed. 1970, M.Ed. 1977; children: Erin Elizabeth, Caitlin Eleanore; DIRECTOR, SEC.-TREAS. & CHIEF EXECUTIVE OFFICER, TORONTO BOARD OF EDUCATION 1990– ; Teacher, Consultant Lecturer, Co-ordinator Instructor, Vice-Principal, Principal, various institutions 1970–84; School Supt. (Elementary & Secondary Schools), Toronto Bd. of Edn. 1984; Supt. (Secondary Schools) 1986; Co-ord. Supt. 1986; Chief Supt. of Field Serv. 1989; international speaker; Bd. of Dir., Candn. Edn. Assn. (Extve. Ctte.); Founding Mem., Metro Toronto Learning Partnership; Extve. Ctte. Mem., Council of Ont. Dir. of Edn.; Founding Mem. & Extve. Mem., Women in Edn. Admin. in Ont.; Theology Award, Univ. of Toronto 1969; Nominee, Woman of the Year, Toronto Sun 1991; Woman of the Year, Orgn. for Women in Leadership 1990; Extve. Ctte. Mem., Gov. Council, Univ. of Toronto 1993; Mem. 1992; Chair, Edn. Ctte., United Way of Greater Toronto 1992; several past directorships; Mem., Phi Delta Kappa; Ont. Public Supervisory Officers' Assn.; Subject Matter Expert on Edn. Law Text for School Admin.; Council Voter Edn. S. Africa Canada; co-author: 'The Interactive Classroom' 1989, 'Your Voice and Mine' I 1986, II 1987, 'In Your Own Words' I 1981, II 1982 and var. articles & profl. development materials; recreations: symphony, theatre, canoeing, cottaging, travel; Home: 46 Bemersyde Dr., Islington, Ont. M9A 2T2; Office: 155 College St., Toronto, Ont. M5T 1P6.

**GREEN, Joseph G.,** M.A., Ph.D.; educator; b. Philadelphia, Pa. 24 June 1934; s. late Herman I. and Anna M. (Brantz) G.; e. Temple Univ., B.A. 1956; Ind. Univ., M.A. 1959, Ph.D. 1964; m. Rhoda Arlene, d. Morris Rabinowitz, Camden, N.J., 23 Dec. 1956; two s., Michael, Marc; DIR., PROG. IN ARTS ADMIN., YORK UNIV. 1982– ; Mgr., Louisville Little Theatre, 1959–60; Dir. of Theatre, Ind. Univ., and Asst. Prof. of Theatre 1961–65; Theatre Co-ordinator and Asst. Prof., Hunter Coll., 1965–68; Visiting Prof. of Theatre, Columbia Univ. Teachers Coll., 1967; joined present Univ. as Asst. Dean of Fine Arts and Dir. of Theatre 1968–71, Dean of Fine Arts and Prof. of Theatre 1973–80; writings incl. numerous book reviews and articles; CBC radio critic for Summer 1970; Lectr., Stratford Shakespeare Seminar Summer 1971; Producer, Gemstone (Film & Theatre) Productions Ltd.; 'The Dining Room' (theatrical production 1984); 'Glory Enough For All' (television mini-series for CBC & Thames TV 1988; Masterpiece Theatre, PBS, 1989); 'Sullivan & Gilbert' (theatrical production 1988); Producer, Fundamentally Film Inc.; Jewish; Office: 4700 Keele St., Downsview, Ont. M3J 1P3.

**GREEN, Kenneth Gordon,** B.S.F., M.B.A.; financial consultant; b. London, Eng. 27 Oct. 1934; s. John Kenneth and Miriam Agnes (Lehmann-Haupt) G.; e. Univ. of B.C., B.S.F. 1961; Harvard Business Sch. M.B.A. (Baker Scholar) 1967; m. Diana d. Fenner and Stephanie Douglas 7 July 1962; children: Douglas, Andrea; DIRECTOR, AINSWORTH LUMBER CO. LTD. 1993– ; Vice Pres. and Dir., RBC Dominion Securities Inc. 1980–92; Mng. Dir. Morgan Stanley Canada Ltd. 1975–80; Vice Pres. Slater Walker Canada Ltd. 1974–75; Vice Pres. and Dir. Nesbitt Thomson Securities Ltd. 1968–73; Lumber Trader, Rayonier Canada Ltd. 1961–65; Dir., Candn. Psychiatric Rsch. Found.; Dir., Strings Across The Sky Found.; Anglican; recreations: music, theatre, reading, tennis, hunting, fishing; Club: York; Home: 895 Towner Park Rd., Sidney, B.C. V8L 3R9.

**GREEN, Leslie Claude,** C.M., LL.B., LL.D., F.R.S.C.(1980); educator; b. London, England 6 Nov. 1920; s. Willie and Raie (Goldberg) G.; came to Can. 1965; e. Univ. Coll., London LL.B. 1941; LL.D. 1976; m. Lilian Denise, d. Sasun Meyer 1 Sept. 1945; one d.: Anne Roslyn; University Professor, Univ. of Alberta 1969–91, Emeritus 1992– ; Asst. Lectr. in Laws, London Univ. 1946–49; Lectr. in Internat. Law, Univ. Coll. (London) 1949–60; Prof. of Internat. Law, Univ. of Singapore 1960–65; Dir., Inst. of Advanced Legal Studies, Univ. of Singapore 1962–65; Dean, Faculty of Law there 1964–65; Prof. of Pol. Sci., Univ. of Alta. 1965–69; Hon. Prof. of Law 1982– ; awarded Cecil Peace Prize 1941; Hume Scholarship in Jurisprudence 1941; Grotius Medal 1954; F.R.S.C. 1980; Univ. of Alta. Research Prize 1982; Mem., Order of Canada 1993; author: 'International Law Through the Cases' 4th ed. 1978; 'Law and Society' 1975; 'Superior Orders in National and International Law' 1976; 'International Law: A Candian Perspective' 2nd ed. 1988; 'Essays on the Modern Law of War' 1985; (with O.P. Dickason) 'The Law of Nations and the New World' 1989; 'The Contemporary Law of Armed Conflict' 1993; ed.: Chen's 'International Law of Recognition' 1951; 'Conference Reports of the International Law Association' 1952–60, 1966–70; papers in learned journals; Academic in Residence, Dept. Ext. Affairs 1974–75; Special Consultant on Armed Conflict Law to JAG, 1974–88; Consultant to U.S. Dept. of Justice; author of numerous articles on War Law, International Law, Human Rights, Sociology of Law, Terrorism etc.; many visiting professorships and lectureships in universities in this country and abroad; delegate or speaker to various conferences on aspects of International Law; mem., Ctte. of Experts, Naval Warfare Law 1989– ; mem. Ctte. of Experts on Intl. Crim. Ct.; consultant in field (to Royal Commn. on R.C.M.P. 1979–80; to Att. Gen., Alta. and Solicitor Gen., Ottawa 1978); Cdn. Dept. of Justice 1992– ; mem. Constitutional Consultative Comte. for Liberia 1982; Internat. Commn. for Constitutional Reform in S. Africa 1982; London Inst. of World Affairs (Vice Pres.); Candn. Soc. of Internat. Law (Vice Pres.); Candn. Human Rights Found. (Council mem.); Amer. Soc. of Internat. Law (Ctte., Certificate of Merit); Brit. Inst. Comparative and Internat. Law; Candn. Council Internat. Law; Internat. Law Assn.; Candn. Assn. Law Teachers; Soc. of Public Teachers of Law, etc.; served with British Army 1941–46 (Japanese Translator, G.H.Q., India 1942–44; Deputy Military Prosecutor there 1944–46); discharged with rank of Major, Depy. Asst. Adjutant Gen.; Jewish; recreations: reading, speaking, cross-country skiing; Club: Athenaeum (London); Home: 7911 – 119 St., Edmonton, Alta. T6G 1W6; Office: Univ. of Alberta, Edmonton, Alta. T6G 2H4.

**GREEN, Robert,** B.Sc., Ph.D.; research executive; b. Newcastle on Tyne, England; e. Univ. of Newcastle, B.Sc., Ph.D. 1948–54; Yale Univ., postdoctoral rsch. 1954–56; VICE-PRES., OPERATIONS, ALBERTA RESEARCH COUNCIL 1983– ; Geologist, Alta. Research Council spec. in stratigraphy & micropaleontology 1956–59; Head, Geol. Survey Dept. 1959–65; Vice-Pres., Natural Resources Div. 1965–79; Dir., Policy Devel. & Program Evaluation 1980–83; currently resp. for all support service depts. & the staff safety, occupational health & financial integrity of the Rsch. Council; Office: P.O. Box 8330, Stn. F, Edmonton, Alta. T6H 5X2.

**GREEN, Stewart Edward,** B.Com., LL.B.; executive; b. Toronto, Ont. 1 Aug. 1944; s. Robert Edward Stewart Green; e. Univ. of Toronto B.Com., LL.B.; VICE PRES., SECY., & GEN. COUNS. GEORGE WESTON LTD.; Sr. Vice Pres. & Secy., Loblaw Companies Ltd.; recreations: sailing, skiing; Office: 22 St. Clair Ave. E., Suite 1500, Toronto, Ont. M4T 2S7.

**GREEN, Terence Michael,** B.A., B.Ed., M.A.; writer; educator; b. Toronto, Ont. 2 Feb. 1947; s. Thomas Matthew and Margaret Mary (Radey) G.; e. Univ. of Toronto B.A. 1967, B.Ed. 1973; Univ. Coll. Dublin M.A. 1972; two s. Conor, Owen; Eng. Teacher East York Coll. Inst. 1968– ; author: 'The Woman Who is the Midnight Wind' (short story coll.) 1987; 'Barking Dogs' (novel) 1988; 'Children of the Rainbow' (novel) 1992; numerous articles, interviews, reviews, poetry, short stories; reader/ lectr. 3rd, 4th and 5th Internat. Conf. on Fantastic in Arts; invited reader Internat. Festival Authors Toronto 1985; lectr., workshop conductor Edn. Conf. Laurentian Univ. 1984; guest instr. 1st Candn. SF Writers Workshop Trent Univ. 1986; lectr. SF writing Toronto 'Skills Exchange'; Judge, Ont. Sci. Centre 'Invent an Alien' contest 1988; Guest of Honour Wilfcon 5 Wilfrid Laurier Univ. 1989; interviewee, 'Books in Canada' 1988; instructor in SF writing, Humber Coll., Toronto 1990; mem. Sci. Fiction Writers Am.; recreations: reading, sons, movies; Home: 32 Brooklyn Ave., Toronto, Ont. M4M 2X5.

**GREEN, William John,** F.I.I.C.; insurance executive; b. Montreal, Que. 26 Oct. 1936; s. William Thomas and Emma (Leblanc) G.; e. Le Plateau 1951; Fellow Ins. Inst. of Can. 1974; Concordia Univ. post-grad. studies 1980; m. Pierrette d. Emile Girard 2 May 1959; children: Johanne, Pierre, Daniel, Michel, Marie Helene; PRESIDENT FEDERATION INSURANCE CO. OF CANADA 1983– ; joined Dominion of Can. 1959, Mgr. Que. Operations 1972–81; Sr. Vice-Pres. present firm 1981–83; Chrmn., Personal Property Ctte., Insur. Bur. of Can.; Mem., Bd. of Dir., Insurers' Adv. Orgn. (1989) Inc.; Insur. Crime Prevention Bur.; R. Catholic; recreations: sports, reading; Home: 200 Pinkerton Cre., Rosemère, Qué. J7A 4L6; Office: 1080 Côte du Beaver Hall, 20th Floor, Montréal, Qué. H2Z 1S8.

**GREENBERG, The Hon. Mr. Justice Benjamin Joseph,** B.A., B.C.L.; judge; b. Montréal, Qué. 2 Dec. 1933; s. Max and Ida (Ballon) G.; e. McGill Univ. B.A. 1954, B.C.L. 1957 (First Class Honours; Elizabeth Torrance Gold Medal Highest Standing; Macdonald Travelling Scholarship; Montréal Bar Assn. Prize Civil Law; Jr. Bar Assn. Prize Civil Procedure; Chief Justice R.A.E. Greenshields Prize Criminal Law; I.M.E. Prize Comm. Law; Univ. Scholar); Univ. of Paris Comparative Civil Law studies 1957–58; m. Linda d. Adam and Lena Gold 4 Nov. 1979; children: Stephen D., Deborah R., Andrea Z.; PUISNE JUDGE, QUE. SUPERIOR COURT 1976– ; called to Bar of Qué. 1959; law partnership with late Louis H. Rohrlick, Q.C. becoming head of firm upon death of partner 1969; cr. Q.C. 1976; Gov. many yrs. YM-YMHA and Camp B'Nai Brith; Vice Pres. and Dir. Centre D'Accueil Miriam; Dir. Miriam Home Found.; mem. Legal Aid Ctte. Baron de Hirsch Inst. 8 yrs.; mem. McGill Univ. Alumni Soc., Faculty Law Bldg. Fund. Alma Mater Fund; Pres. Japan Soc. Can. 1970–71, Dir. 1969–72; Dir. Dickanwise Sch. Special Edn. (now Summit Sch.) 1965–72, Pres. 1970–72; mem. Shaare Zion Cong. (Trustee 1975–77); recreations: golf, tennis, skiing; Home: 3269 Cedar Ave., Westmount, Qué. H3Y 1Z6; Office: 12.40 Palais de Justice, 1 est Notre Dame, Montréal, Qué. H2Y 1B6.

**GREENBERG, Bruce M.,** B.Sc., Ph.D.; university professor; b. Oakland, Ca. 7 Feb. 1956; s. Aaron M. and Frances M. (Pierce) G.; e. Univ. of California B.Sc. 1980; Univ. of Colorado Ph.D. 1985; m. Lorelei F. d. Joan K. and Walter Zeiler 3 Nov. 1984; children: Sean, Johanna, Isaac; PROFESSOR, DEPT. OF BIOLOGY, UNIV. OF WATERLOO; research for past 14 years in photobiology of plants incl. the influence of light on plant devel., the effects of UV-B irradiation & the impact of photoactive pollutants on plants; Mem., Extve. Ctte., Dept. of Biology, Univ. of Waterloo; Candn. & Am. societies for Plant Physiology; Am. Soc. for Photobiol.; Soc. of Environ. Toxicology & Chem.; Am. Soc. of Testing & Materials; Fellow, Nat. Inst. of Health (U.S.) 1985–88; Mem., Vice Pres., Congregation Beth Jacob Kitchener; author/co-author of 40 scholarly publications; recreations: golf, skiing; clubs: American Coaster Enthusiasts; Office: Waterloo, Ont. N2L 3G1.

**GREENBERG, Harold;** communications executive; b. Montréal, Qué. 11 Jan. 1930; s. Abraham and Annie (Kirschner) G.; e. Devonshire Elem. Sch.; Baron Byng High Sch.; m. Edith Freedman 1954; children: Stephen, Joel, Anna-Sue; CHRMN. OF THE BD. AND C.E.O., ASTRAL COMMUNICATIONS INC. (formerly Astral Inc.); Bd. Chrmn., Astral Film Enterprises Inc.; Astral Broadcasting Group Inc.; First Choice Canadian Communications Corp.; Premier Choix: TVEC (operates Super Écran and Canal Famille); started Park Photo with brothers in 1953; Angreen Photo 1961; Bellevue Photo Labs 1964; purchased Pathé-Humphries Ltd. and changed name to Bellevue Pathé Limited 1967; merged with Astral Communications Limited 1973 to form Astral Bellevue Pathé Inc.; name changed to Astral Communications Inc. 1992; Chrmn., Candn. Culture/Communications Industries Ctte.; Mem., Sectoral Adv. Group in Internat. Trade (SAGIT); Candn. Friends of Tel Aviv Univ., Hon. Fellow (for support of Fac. of Visual Arts) 1985; Past Pres., Davis Lodge, B'Nai B'rith; Past Chrmn., E. region, Can.-Israel C. of C.; Chrmn., Camp B'nai B'rith Sr. Citizens Centre Bldg. Fund; mem. Assn. Candn. Movie Prodn. Co's; Candn. Film & TV Assn.; Brit. Kinematog. Sound and Television Soc. (Fellow 1992); Soc. Motion Picture & TV Engs. (Internat. Relations Ctte.; Presidential Proclamation Award 1985); Past mem. Adv. Bd., Candn. Film Devel. Corp.; Past Pres., Master Photo Dealers & Finishers Assn.; recipient, Concordia Univ. Faculty of Commerce and Admin. Award of Distinction 1993; Ordre National du Québec 1992; Légion d'Honneur of France 1991; Air Canada Award, Acad. of Candn. Cinema and TV 1990; Achievement Award, Montreal Film Festival 1989; 'Man of the Year' Camp B'Nai Brith 1989; Home: Westmount, Qué.; Office: Ste. 900, 2100 Ste. Catherine St. W., Montréal, Qué. H3H 2T3

**GREENBERG, Shirley Elizabeth,** B.A., LL.B.; lawyer; b. Ottawa, Ont. 6 Oct. 1931; d. Jacob George and Elizabeth Bertha (Welke) Schnell; e. Carleton Univ. B.A. 1970; Univ. of Ottawa LL.B. 1976; m. Irving s. Roger and Rose Greenberg 23 Nov. 1959 (dec. 1991); children: Daniel, Phoebe, Martha; PRIN. GREENBERG & ASSOCIATES 1988– ; Co-founder, Aitken, Greenberg 1978–88; Chair Adv. Bd. Women in Candn. Forces 1990–93; founding mem. Nat. Assn. Women & Law, Ottawa Women's Lobby, Ottawa Women's Centre; mem. Exec. Candn. Fedn. Univ. Women 1978; Vice Pres. (Policy) P. Cons. Women's Caucus 1988; Treas. Le Cercle Ottawa 1988–90; Legal Edn. Action Fund; mem., Law Soc. of Upper Canada; Candn. Bar Assn.; County of Carleton Law Assn.; author various pamphlets, articles; Clubs: Le Cercle Universitaire; Rideau; Home: Apt. 202, 15 Murray St., Ottawa, Ont. K1N 9M5; Office: 330, 440 Laurier Ave. W., Ottawa, Ont. K1R 7X6.

**GREENE, Barbara,** M.P., B.A., M.P.A.; politician; b. Pembroke, Ont. 1 Sept. 1945; d. Alfred and Mary (Hutchinson) G.; e. St. Michael's Coll., Univ. of Toronto; Ont. Coll. of Education; Harvard Univ.; John F. Kennedy Sch. of Govt.; one d.: Caroline; Secondary School Teacher; Controller, City of North York Council, mem. Metropolitan Toronto Council 1972–80, 1982–85; Exec. mem., Metropolitan Toronto Council 1974–80, 1982–85; Dep. Mayor, North York 1974–80; el. to H. of C. for Don Valley North g.e. 1988; P.C.; Roman Catholic; Home: 255 Johnston Ave., Willowdale, Ont. M2N 1H5.

**GREENE, Charles Ian George,** M.A., Ph.D.; educator; b. Innisfail, Alta. 28 Jan. 1948; s. Charles Joseph and Helen Fenwick (Hodge) G.; e. Innisfail High Sch. 1966; Royal Conserv. Music A.R.C.T. 1967; Univ. of Alta. B.A. 1970; Univ. of Toronto M.A. 1972; Ph.D. 1983; m. Eilonwy d. Dr. John and Helen Morgan 30 July 1982; children: Christina, Philip; ASSOC. PROF. OF POL. SCI., YORK UNIV. 1990– , Undergraduate Dir., Pol. Sci., York Univ. 1992– ; Visiting Fellow, Clare Hall, Univ. of Cambridge 1992; Exec. Asst. to Min. of Consumer Affairs Alta. 1972–73; Instr. E. Kootenay Community Coll. Golden and Invermere, B.C. 1980; Lectr. Univ. of Lethbridge 1981–82; Asst. to S. Regional Dir. Alta. Social Services & Community Health 1982–85; part-time Lectr. Univ. of Lethbridge (Pol. Sci.) and Univ. of Calgary Lethbridge Div. (Social Welfare); Dir. John Howard Soc. Lethbridge 1984–85; Asst. Prof., York Univ. 1985–90; Co-ordinator, Public Policy and

Administration Program, York Univ. 1989–91; author 'The Charter of Rights' 1989; co-author 'Judges and Judging: Inside the Canadian Judicial System' 1990; various articles profl. jours. and newspapers; mem. Candn. Pol. Sci. Assn.; Candn. Law & Soc. Assn. (Secy.-Treas. 1990–91); Candn. Evaluation Soc.; Anglican; recreations: mountain climbing, skiing; Home: 361 Indian Grove, Toronto, Ont. M6P 2H6; Office: 4700 Keele St., North York, Ont. M3J 1P3.

**GREENE, Donald Johnson,** B.A., M.A., Ph.D., D.Litt.,F.R.S.C.; university professor; b. Moose Jaw, Sask. 21 Nov. 1916; s. Waldron Joseph and Katharine Annie (Beaton) G.; e. Univ. of Sask., B.A. 1941; Univ. College, London: M.A. 1948, D.Litt. 1973; Columbia Univ., Ph.D. 1954; Litt.D. (h.c.), McMaster Univ., 1985; Leo S. Bing Professor Of English, Univ. of S. California, 1968–85, Prof. Emeritus 1985; taught in pub. elementary and high schs. in Sask. and Alta. 1933–40; active service, Royal Can. Artillery 1941–45; I.O.D.E.Overseas Grad. Fellowship 1946–48; instructor in Engl., Univ. of Sask. 1948–52; Asst. Prof. of Engl., Univ. of California, Riverside 1954–57; Guggenheim Fellowship 1957–58; Brandeis Univ. 1958–60; Assoc. Prof. of Engl., Univ. of New Mexico 1960–62; Prof. of Engl., Victoria Coll., Univ. of Toronto 1962–65; Can. Counc. Sr. Rsch. Fellowship 1965–66; Vilas Rsch. Prof. of Engl., Univ. of Wisconsin 1967–68; Guggenheim Fellowship 1979–80; Fellow, Nat. Humanities Center, N. Carolina 1984–85; Mod. Langs. Assn. of Am.: ed. ctte. 1968–73, nominating ctte. 1973–74; founding sec., Am. Soc. for Eighteenth-Century Studies 1968–73; Internat. Soc. for Eighteenth-Century Studies: exec. ctte. 1967–73, Vice-pres. 1975–78; Bd. of Dirs., Jane Austen Soc. of N. Am. 1979–83; Hon. Mem., Johnson Club, England 1974; Pres., The Johnson Society (Lichfield) and the Johnson Society of Southern California 1985–86; author of 'The Politics of Samuel Johnson' 1960, 'The Age of Exuberance' 1970, 'Samuel Johnson' (Twayne's English Authors) 1970, 'Samuel Johnson's Library, an Annotated Guide' 1975, 'Samuel Johnson, Political Writings' (Vol. X of Yale Ed. of Works of Samuel Johnson) 1977; co-author of 'Samuel Johnson: A Survey and Bibliography of Critical Studies' 1970; editor of 'Samuel Johnson: A Collection of Critical Essays' 1965; ed. 'Samuel Johnson' (The Oxford Authors) 1984; (with John A. Vance) 'A Bibliography of Johnsonian Studies 1970–85' 1987; Clubs: Athenaeum, Royal Commonwealth Society (London); Home: 3001 Fernwood Ave., Los Angeles, Calif. 90039; Office: Dept. of English, Univ. of Southern California, Los Angeles, Calif. 90089.

**GREENE, Gordon K.,** A. Mus., B.A., B.Ed., M.A., Ph.D.; educator; b. Cardston, Alta. 27 Dec. 1927; s. Edwin Kent and Julia L. (Leavitt) G.; e. Univ. of Alta. A. Mus. 1952, B.A. 1954, B.Ed. 1955, M.A. 1961; Ind. Univ. Ph.D. 1971; PROF. EMERITUS OF MUSIC HIST., WILFRID LAURIER UNIV.; Prof. of Music Hist. 1978–93, Dean of Music 1979–89; lectr. Extension Dept. and Music Dept. Univ. of Alta. 1955–63; Music Hist. Dept. Univ. of W. Ont. 1966–78, Chrmn. 1966–75; ed./author of 5 vols. French secular music in series 'Polyphonic Music of the Fourteenth Century' 1980–87; author articles medieval music 'Grove's Dictionary of Music and Musicians' and 'Dictionary of the Middle Ages'; mem. Candn. Univ. Music Soc. (Pres. 1985–87); Am. Musicol. Soc.; Internat. Musicol. Soc.; recreations: skiing, swimming, philately; Home: 230 Forsyth Dr., Waterloo, Ont. N2L 1A5; Office: Wilfrid Laurier Univ., Waterloo, Ont. N2L 3C5.

**GREENE, John George,** B.Com., F.C.A.; chartered accountant; b. Arnprior, Ont. 1 March 1937; s. George Mancel and Jean (Cambell) G.; e. Queen's Univ. B.Com. 1958, C.A. 1961; m. Joan d. Charles and Olive Moseley 29 June 1963; children: Jane, David, Jeffrey; Nat. Dir. of Tax, Clarkson Gordon 1984–88; joined present firm 1958, Partner 1968, Winnipeg; Dir. Victorian Order Nurses Can., Past Pres. Winnipeg Br.; Vice Pres., Winnipeg Art Gallery; co-ed. 'Income Taxation in Canada'; United Church; recreations: tennis, hunting, fishing, skiing; Clubs: St. Charles Country; Manitoba; Winnipeg Winter; Waterhen Lodge; Home: 1201 Handsart Blvd., Winnipeg, Man. R3P 0C6; Office: 2700 – 360 Main St., Winnipeg, Man. R3C 4G9.

**GREENE, Nancy Catherine (Mrs. Al Raine),** O.C. (1968); ski champion; b. Ottawa, Ont. 11 May 1943; d. Robert Kenneth Wollaston and Helen Catherine (Sutherland) G.; e. Rossland (B.C.) Pub. and High Schs.; Trail (B.C.) Business Coll.; Notre Dame Univ. of Nelson; m. Al Raine, Apl. 1969; twin s. Charles, William; Proprietor, Nancy Greene's Olympic Lodge; mem. Nat. Ski Team 1959–68; Olympic Team 1960, 1964 and 1968; World Championship Team 1962 and 1966; winner of Gold Medal for Giant Slalom and Silver Medal for Slalom, Olympic Games 1968; winner of 1967 and 1968 World Cup for Skiing; named Canada's Woman Athlete of the Year 1967; Lou Marsh Trophy for Athlete of the Year (twice) 1967, 1968; mem. Candn. Ski Assn.; Candn. Ski Instrs. Alliance; Beta Sigma Phi (Hon.); recreations: skiing, reading, music, tennis; Clubs: Blackcomb Ski; Soroptomist (Hon.); Office: 4154 Village Green, Box 280, Whistler, B.C. V0N 1B0.

**GREENE, Peter A.,** B.A., M.B.A.; advertising executive; b. New York, N.Y. 25 June 1946; s. Richard C. and Marion P. (Bader) G.; e. Mamaroneck (N.Y.) High Sch. 1964; Trinity Coll. Hartford, Conn. B.A. 1968; Columbia Univ. Sch. of Business M.B.A. 1969; m. Rosemarie C. d. Edward and Christine Gambale 19 July 1970; Pres. and C.E.O., Saatchi and Saatchi Compton Hayhurst Ltd. 1986; Acct. Exec. SSC&B Inc. New York 1969–71 and Ted Bates & Co. New York 1971–72; Acct. Supr. Case & McGrath Inc. New York 1972–74; Mgmt. Supr., Sr. Vice Pres. Benton & Bowles Inc. New York 1974–83; Pres. & C.E.O., Scali, McCabe, Sloves (Canada) Ltd. 1983–86; mem. Bd. of Dirs., Alliance for a Drug Free Canada; Chrmn., Inst. Candn. Advertising; Home: 1132 Bay St., Toronto, Ont. M5S 2B4.

**GREENE, Ronald G.,** B.Sc.; petroleum executive; b. Calgary, Alta. 1 Nov. 1948; e. Univ. of Calgary B.Sc. 1969; m.; 3 children; CHRMN., RENAISSANCE ENERGY LTD. 1987– ; Jr. Landman Sun Oil Co. Ltd. Calgary 1969; Asst. Landman, Voyager Petroleums Ltd. 1971, Land. Mgr. 1971; Vice Pres. & Dir. Concept Resources Ltd. 1973; estbd. present Co. 1974; Pres. & Chrmn. Renaissance Energy Ltd. 1974–87; Dir., Skywest Resources Corp.; De Havilland Aircraft of Canada Ltd. 1985–86; De Havilland Aircraft Transition Adv. Bd. to Boeing of Canada Ltd. 1986–87; InterProvincial Steel Co. 1988–93; Bd., Calgary Petroleum Club 1989–93; Strathcona Tweedsmuir Sch. 1989–93; mem. Independent Petrol. Assn. Can. (Dir. & mem. Exec. Ctte. 1985–87); Candn. & Am. Assn. Petrol. Landmen; Office: 3300, 400 Third Ave. S.W., Calgary, Alta. T2P 4H2.

**GREENER, Brian H.;** business executive; b. Toronto, Ont. 1 May 1942; m. Jane Nickerson 31 Aug. 1963; children: David, Jacqueline; PRESIDENT, NARCO CANADA INC.; Office: P.O. Box 910, Burlington, Ont. L7R 3Y7.

**GREENGLASS, Esther Ruth,** B.A., M.A., Ph.D.; university professor; b. Toronto, Ont.; d. David and Betty (Schwartz) G.; e. Univ. of Toronto, B.A. 1962, M.A. 1963, Ph.D. 1967; m. George Hiraki; children: Linda Hiraki, Susan Hiraki; PROF. OF PSYCH., YORK UNIV. 1985– ; postdoctoral fellow, present univ. 1967–68; Asst. Prof. 1968–72; Assoc. Prof. 1972–84; Mem., Am. Psychol. Assn.; Candn. Rsch. Inst. for the Advancement of Women; Internat. Assn. for Applied Psychol.; Acad. of Management; Fellow, Candn. Psychol. Assn.; member of numerous edit. bds. in Can. & abroad; has served on numerous govt. bds. & panels dealing with status of women issues in Canada; author: 'After Abortion' 1976, 'A World of Difference: Gender Roles in Perspective' 1982 and several articles on stress & coping in psychology journals; recreations: aerobics, jogging, cooking, movie buff, reading biographies; Office: 4700 Keele St., North York, Ont. M3J 1P3.

**GREENHALGH, William F.,** B.Sc., M.B.A.; publishing executive; b. Londonderry, N. Ireland 24 Dec. 1946; s. Charles and Philomena (Cassidy) Greenhalgh; e. Southampton Univ. B.Sc. 1969; Reading Coll. of Technology HNC 1970; London Business Sch. M.B.A. 1972; PRESIDENT & CHIEF OPERATING OFFICER, THE GLOBE & MAIL 1991– ; Project Engineer, UKAEA 1968–70; Mgr., Financial Planning, Gulf Oil 1972–75; Div. Controller, Northern Telecom 1975–76; Dir., Mktg. 1976–78; Mfg. 1978–80; Asst. Vice-Pres., Mfg. 1980–85; Div. Gen. Mgr. 1985–90; General Mgr., Globe & Mail 1990–91; Bd. of Dir., Newspaper Mktg. Bureau; Bd. Mem., Toronto Symphony; Chairman, Exec Forum, IMDQ; Vice-Pres., Help Other People Everywhere 1990–92; recreations: sports, music, theatre; clubs: Fitness Inst., Toronto Scottish R.F.C., Dunfield Squash, Old Reading Alumni Assn.; Business Grad. Assn.; London Bus. Sch. Alumni Assn.; Office: 444 Front St. W., Toronto, Ont. M5V 2S9.

**GREENHOUGH, John H.,** B.A.; printing executive; b. London, Eng. 6 Aug. 1939; s. Thomas Chaplin and Rena (Pilling) G.; e. Wilfrid Laurier Univ. B.A. 1962; m. Georgina 8 Sept. 1962; GROUP PRES. PRINTING MACLEAN HUNTER LIMITED 1990– ; Chrmn. and Chief Exec. Offr. Data Business Forms Ltd. 1983– , Vice Pres. & Gen. Mgr. 1972–80; Chrmn. Davis & Henderson Ltd. Toronto; Dir. General Business Forms Ltd. Edmonton; Transkrit Corp. Brewster, N.Y.; Sales and Mktg. positions Bus. Publs. Div. present Co. 1962–68, Group Pub. of Div. 1969–72, Vice Pres. Printing 1981–82; Founding Pub. CDN DATA Systems Mag. 1969; Dir. and Vice Pres. Candn. Bus. Forms Assn. 1982–88; recreations: tennis, skiing; Office: 2 Shaftsbury Lane, Brampton, Ont. L6T 3X7.

**GREENLEE, James Grant Christopher,** B.A., M.A., Ph.D.; university professor; b. Hamilton, Ont. 4 July 1945; s. Francis and Grace (Presnail) G.; e. McMaster Univ. B.A. 1968, M.A. 1969, Ph.D. 1975; m. Joanne d. John and Merle Swan 27 Dec. 1969; PROF. OF HISTORY, GRENFELL COLL., MEMORIAL UNIV. 1989– ; Asst. Prof., Univ. of Windsor, Summer 1977; Asst. Prof., McMaster Univ. 1973–77; Asst. Prof., Grenfell Coll., Meml. Univ. 1977, Assoc. Prof. 1983, Prof. 1989; 4 seasons as judge on CBC's 'Reach for the Top'; mem. Humanities Assn. of Can.; Assn. of Atlantic Historians; author: 'Education and Imperial Unity' 1988; 'Sir Robert Falconer: A Biography' 1988; recreations: squash, baseball, skiing; Home: 1 Stuart St., Corner Brook, Nfld. A2H 6R8; Office: Corner Brook, Nfld. A2H 6P9.

**GREENSHIELDS, Duncan S.,** H.B.A.; b. St. Catharines, Ont. 18 Nov. 1948; s. Colin A. and Dorothy M. (Hodgson) G.; e. Univ. of W. Ont. Sch. of Bus. Adm. H.B.A. 1972; PRES., FOREKNOWLEDGE LTD. 1990– ; Restaurant Mgr. Controlled Foods Corp. Ltd. 1972–75; Client Service Asst., A.C. Nielsen Co. of Canada Ltd. 1975, Analyst 1976, Exec. 1977, Acct. Mgr. 1979, Gen. Mgr. Inspeck Services 1980, Vice Pres. Group Head 1984, Vice Pres. Mgr. Toronto Sales/Service 1985, Vice-Pres. Marketing 1987, Vice Pres. Mktg. and Business Develop. 1987–90; mem. Am. Mktg. Assn.; recreations: distance running, competitive touch football, skiing, history, internat. affairs; Club: London (Ont.) Hillside; Home: 114 Kenilworth Ave., Toronto, Ont. M4L 3S6; Office: 1450 O'Connor Dr., Suite 219, Toronto, Ont. M4B 2V2.

**GREENSLADE, Brian;** insurance executive; b. Croyden, England 19 Jan. 1930; s. William (dec.) and Helen Victoria G.; e. Whitgift Sch. (Croydon); m. Monique Anne d. Thomas Cullinane 23 Feb. 1952; children: Christopher Paul, Gillian Anne, Janine Elizabeth; PRES., CHIEF EXTVE. OFFR. & VICE CHRMN., PILOT INSURANCE CO.; National Service, Royal Signals 1948–51; Underwriter, Commercial Union Insur. Toronto 1955–59; Pilot Insur. Co. Toronto 1954–64; Mgr., Property Dept. 1964–70; Sec. 1970–73; Vice Pres. 1976; Dir., Underwriters Labs. of Canada; Insurance Crime Prevention Bureau; Anglican; recreations: photography; Mem., Ontario Club; Bd. of Trade; Home: 11 South Marine Dr., Scarborough, Ont. M1E 1A1; Office: 90 Eglinton Ave. W., Toronto, Ont. M4R 2E4.

**GREENSPAN, David B.,** Q.C., B.A., LL.B.; lawyer; b. Toronto, Ont. 23 May 1937; s. Max and Rose (Kirshenblatt) G.; e. Univ. of Toronto B.A. (Hons.) 1958; Osgoode Hall Law Sch. LL.B. 1962; children: Naomi, Rebecca, Rachel; PARTNER, THOMSON, ROGERS 1981– ; Couns. to Spec. Parliamentary Ctte. on Election Expenses 1971; Chrmn., Fed./Prov. Task Force on Land Prices 1978; Chrmn., Ont. Housing Corp. 1986–89; Adjunct Prof., Sch. of Urban and Regional Planning, Univ. of Waterloo 1971–76; Lectr., Urban Planning Prog., Ryerson Polytech. Inst. 1973–75; Mem., Panel of Arbitrators, Am. Arbitration Assoc. 1988– ; Mem., Lambda Alpha Internat., Hon. Land Economics Soc. 1990– ; Mem., The Advocates' Soc.; Beth Radom Cong.; Candn. Bar Assn.; Liberal; author: 'Down to Earth' 1978 and num. articles on planning law, zoning, the politics of affordable housing, topical political issues; Speaker, U.S. & Candn. forums on land devel., etc.; recreations: collecting antiquities, reading archaeology & hist., hiking, swimming, cross-country skiing; Home: Ste. 1201, 131 Bloor St. W., Toronto, Ont. M5S 1S3; Office: Ste. 3100, 390 Bay St., Toronto, Ont. M5H 1W2.

**GREENSPAN, Edward Leonard,** B.A., LL.B., Q.C.; lawyer; b. Niagara Falls, Ont. 28 Feb. 1944; s. Joseph and Emma (Mercel) G.; e. Univ. of Toronto B.A. 1965; Osgoode Hall Law Sch. LL.B. 1968; m. Suzy, d. Mimon and Rachel Dahan, 18 Aug. 1968; children: Julianna; Samantha; SENIOR PARTNER, GREENSPAN, ROSENBERG AND BUHR; co-author 'Greenspan: The Case for the Defence' (autobiog.) 1987; Assoc. Ed., Dominion Law Reports 1971– ; Assoc. Ed., Ontario Reports 1971–91; Assoc. Ed., Criminal Law Quarterly 1971– ; Ed.-in-Chief, Candn. Criminal Cases 1975– (Assoc. Ed. 1971–75); Ed., Criminal Appeal Rules Annotations 1976– ; Ed. Martin's Annual Criminal Code 1978– ; Ed. Martin's Related Statutes 1980– ; Ed. Martin's Ont. Crim. Practice 1992– ; co-editor Perspectives in Criminal Law 1986; mem. Ed. Bd., Canadian Charter of Rights Annotated 1982– ; mem., Ed., Bd., The Canadian Lawyer 1986– ; Mem., Ed. Bd., The Law Times 1990– ; Lectr., Criminal Law, Univ. of Toronto Law Sch. 1972– ; Lectr., Bar Admission Course in Criminal Law, Law Soc. of Upper Canada 1971–82; Lectr., Criminal Procedure, Osgood Hall Law Sch., York Univ. 1972–81 and 1987–90; apptd. Queen's Counsel 1981; Milvain Chair of Advocacy, Univ. of Calgary Law Sch. 1982; Distinguished Lectr., Univ. of W. Ont., Law Sch. 1983; Culliton Lectr., Univ. of Sask. Law Sch. 1986; Maclean Visiting Lecturer in Criminal Law, Univ. of Victoria Law Sch. 1989; Uniformity Commissioner for Canada at Uniform Law Conf. 1978–84; mem. Adv. Counc., Centre of Criminology, Univ. of Toronto 1977–82; Dir. Candn. Civil Liberties Assn. 1981– ; Vice Pres., Candn. Civil Liberties Assoc. 1989– ; Dir. Theatre Plus 1982–91; Dir. Toronto Arts Awards Found. 1985–90; Bd. mem., Cdn. Shaare Zedek Hosp. Found. 1988– ; mem. Adv. Bd., Toronto Lung Transplant Team 1989– ; mem. Cdn. Bar Assn. [Chrmn., Criminal Justice Subsection (Ont.) 1973; Chrmn., Criminal Justice Subsection (National) 1983–85]; Criminal Lawyers Assn. (Vice Pres. 1977–81); Advocates' Soc. (Dir. 1982–84); Lawyers Club; Medico-Legal Soc. (Dir. 1982–83); Amer. Coll. of Trial Lawyers (el. 1991); Amer. Bar Assn.; Amer. Natl. Assn. of Criminal Defence Lawyers; York County Law Assn.; Host/Narrator, 'The Scales of Justice' CBC Docu-Drama (Actra Award 1983 & 1986 – Best Radio Show; Gemini Award 1993 - Best Television Show); awarded Commemorative Medal for 125th Anniversary of Candn. Confederation 1992; Home: 43 Kimbark Blvd., Toronto, Ont. Office: 401 Bay St., 32nd Flr., Toronto, Ont. M5H 2Y4.

**GREENSPON, Edward Brian,** B.J., M.Sc.; journalist; b. Montreal, Que. 26 March 1957; s. Mortimer and N.R. Rosalie (Rapoport) G.; e. Wagar H.S.; Dawson Coll.; Carleton Univ. B.J. (Hons.) 1979; London School of Economics M.Sc. (with distinction) 1985; m. Janice d. Allan and Mary Neil 21 May 1983; children: Bailey Liza, Joshua Ethan, Jacob Neil; OTTAWA BUREAU CHIEF, GLOBE & MAIL 1993– ; Lloydminster Times 1979–80; Regina Leader-Post 1980–82; Prairie Bureau Chief, Financial Post 1982–84; joined Globe & Mail 1986; European Business Correspondent 1987–91; Managing Editor, Report on Business 1991–92; Depy. Managing Editor 1992–93; Commonwealth Scholar 1984–85; Office: 165 Sparks St., 3rd Floor, Ottawa, Ont. K1P 5B9.

**GREENSTEIN, Michael,** M.A., Ph.D.; educator; b. Toronto, Ont. 27 June 1945; s. Syd and Jean (Mandel) G.; e. SUNY Stony Brook M.A. 1969; York Univ. Ph.D. 1974; m. Anita d. Harry and Adele Weinstock 31 May 1970; children: Jordana, Daniel; ADJUNCT PROF. OF ENGLISH, UNIV. DE SHERBROOKE 1990– ; asst. associé Univ. de Bordeaux 1976–77; Asst. Prof. present Univ. 1979–83, Assoc. Prof. 1983–90; Visiting Lectr. Trent Univ. 1985 and 1991– , Univ. of Toronto Sch. Continuing Edn. 1989– ; recipient Toronto Jewish Cong. Book Award 1990; author 'Adele Wiseman and Her Works' 1985; 'Third Solitudes: Tradition and Discontinuity in Jewish-Canadian Literature' 1989; Contributing Ed., 'Viewpoints'; Fiction Ed. 'Parchment'; mem. Modern Lang. Assn.; ACUTE; PEN; Home: 15 West Grove Cres., Toronto, Ont. M5N 2S9; Office: Sherbrooke, Que. J1K 2R1.

**GREENSTOCK, Clive Lewis,** B.Sc., M.Sc., Ph.D., F.Inst. P., C. Phys.; research officer; b. High Wycombe, Eng. 14 Aug. 1939; s. George Henry and Clarice Irene (Lewis) G.; e. Univ. of Leeds B.Sc. 1960; Univ. of London M.Sc. 1963; Univ. of Toronto Ph.D. 1968; m. Gwen d. Harold and Sybil Johns 17 July 1965; two d. Erica Jane, Andrea Gail; RADIATION BIOLOGY BRANCH, AECL RESEARCH 1988– ; Adjunct Professor, Univ. of Man. 1977– , Univ. of Ottawa 1988– , Carleton Univ. 1992– ; Med. Physicist, Cardiff Radiotherapy Centre, UK 1960–61; Scientific Offr. Nat. Physical Lab. UK 1963–64; Nat. Cancer Inst. Postdoctoral Fellow, Rsch. Unit in Radiobiol. Mount Vernon Hosp. UK 1968–70; Visiting Scientist Nat. Rsch. Counc. Ottawa 1982; Sabbatical Fellow, Heineman Found. Award, Royal Soc. Fellowship, Paterson Labs., Christie Hosp. and Holt Radium Inst. UK 1983–84; Visiting Scientist, Internat. Union against Cancer Award, Wallac Oy, Finland 1987; Part-time Lectr. St. Bart's Hosp. Med. Coll. London, UK 1961–63; Depts. of Physics & Med. Biophysics Univ. of Toronto 1966–68; Dept. of Physics Univ. of Man. 1971–75; Radiation Oncology Center, Wayne State Univ. 1986; Man. Cancer Foundation 1987; Supr. undergrad. & grad. students 1970– ; Lectr. WNRE 1970– , mem. Sci. in Schs. Prog. and Visiting Speakers Bureau 1978– ; Rsch. Officer, Medical Biophysics Br., Atomic Energy of Can. Ltd., Pinawa, Man. 1970–88; Consultant: Cancer Special Prog. Adv. Ctte. Nat. Cancer Inst. USA; Nat. Cancer Prog. Radiation Oncology, US Dept. Health, Edn. & Welfare; Fed. Strategy for Rsch. Biol. Effects Ionizing Radiation, Nat. Insts. Health USA; Prov. Cancer Hosp. Bd. Alta.; Man. Dept. Edn. Sci. Prog. Devel.; Candn. Cancer Soc. Man. Div.; US Dept. Health & Human Services; mem. Radiation Chem. Data Centre Adv. Ctte. Notre Dame USA 1975–80; Radiosensitizer/Radioprotector working group, Radiation Oncology Coordination Ctte. Dept. Cancer Treatment NCI 1982– ; Cancer in Workplace Ctte. Candn. Cancer Soc. Winnipeg 1985– ; People to People Cancer Rsch. & Treatment Del. to S. Africa 1985; Environmental Protection Service Winnipeg 1986; Councillor, Candn. Biophysical Soc.; Assoc. Ed. 'Radiation Research' 1977–80; Guest Lectr., Soviet Acad. of Sciences, USSR 1987; Chrmn., Radiation Protection Course, Chalk River Labs 1989–90; Visiting speaker, Univs. and Research Insts. in Argentina, Brazil and Chile 1991; Invited speaker, Saudi Arabia, India and Int. Atom. Energy Agency, Vienna, Austria 1993; co-editor various publs.; author or co-author over 90 papers; mem. Am. Assn. Cancer Rsch.; Assn. Radiation Rsch.; Biophys. Soc. Can. (Councillor); Candn. Assn. Physicists; Chem. Inst. of Can.; Inst. Phys.; Inst. Risk Research; Radiation Rsch. Soc.; Oxygen Soc. (Councillor); Sigma Xi; Anglican; recreations: cycling, sculling, skiing, wind-surfing; Club: Mensa; Home: 9 Country Lane, Petawawa, Ont. K8H 3E2; Office: Chalk River Labs., Chalk River, Ont. K0J 1J0.

**GREENWALD, Roger Gordon,** B.A., M.A., Ph.D.; writer; translator; university teacher; b. Neptune N.J.; s. Lewis and Sylvia (Halpern) G.; e. City Coll. of N.Y., B.A. 1966; N.Y. Univ.; Univ. of Toronto, M.A. 1969, Ph.D. 1978; Poetry Workshop, St. Marks in the Bouwerie Poetry Project, N.Y. 1966–67; TUTOR & SR. TUTOR, CREATIVE WRITING & COMP., UNIV. OF TORONTO 1969– ; Guest Instr., Poetry Workshop, Norwegian Authors Ctr., Oslo 1984–85; Readings in Toronto; London, Eng.; N.Y.C.; Hilversum; Oslo; Stavanger; Oslo Internat. Poetry Fest.; World Poetry Fest., Toronto; Arts Court, Ottawa; Juror, Ont. Arts Counc. (Works-in-Progress) 1986; Am.-Scandinavian Found. (trans. prize) 1986; Amer. Lit. Trans. Assn. (Richard Wilbur Trans. Prize) 1987; Teacher, Pub. Serv. Comn. of Can.; Fed. Dept. of Commun.; Alcohol & Drug Addiction Rsch. Found.; Cons., Norwegian Univ. Press; Norsemen's Fed., Oslo; Kopinor, Oslo; Wesleyan Univ. Press; Univ. of Texas at Dallas; recipient, Toronto Arts Council Grant for poetry 1991; Thord-Gray Meml. Fund Grant 1991; American-Scandinavian Found. Translation Prize 1990; Works-in-Progress Grant for poetry (Ont. Arts Counc.) 1990; F.R. Scott Trans. Prize, Richard Wilbur Trans. Prize 1986; Alice & Corrin Strong Fund Grant 1984; Columbia Univ. Trans. Ctr. Award 1983; Norma Epstein National Creative Writing Comp. (poetry) 1977; Samuel G. Colby Meml. Award 1966; Riggs Medal 1965; Pres., Cloudberry Found.; Mem., Assn. for the Advancement of Scand. Studies in Can.; PEN Am. Ctr.; Am. Lit. Trans. Assn.; co-editor: 'Promethean' 1964–66; editor: WRIT magazine 1970– ; co-author: 'A Mustard Sandwich' 1980 (poetry); author: 'Connecting Flight' 1993 (poetry); trans./ed.: 'The Silence Afterwards: Selected Poems of Rolf Jacobsen' 1985 (poetry); co-trans.: 'Stone Fences' by Paal-Helge Haugen 1986 (poetry); trans.: 'The Time in Malmö on the Earth' by Jacques Werup 1989 (poetry); ed.: 'Our Lives As Dogs: Scandinavian Literature in the Marketplace' 1989 (proceedings); Office: Innis Coll., Univ. of Toronto, 2 Sussex Ave., Toronto, Ont. M5S 1J5.

**GREENWOOD, Arthur Alexander,** Ph.D., F.C.I.S., F.R.S.A., F.R.Econ.S., P.Adm.; writer, retired army officer; b. Corby Glen, Eng. 8 March 1920; s. Dr. Augustus Charles and Constance Elfrida Thomson (Dick) G.; e. Oakham Sch. & Sidney Sussex Coll., Cambridge Univ. Ph.D. 1939; m. 2ndly Shirley d. Wing Comdr. Alec Knowles-Fitton 16 Sept. 1976; children: Jane Alexandra, Nicholas Alexander; 2nd Lt. Royal Lincolnshire Regt. 1939; Capt. 1942; Major 1953; served in WW2 in Norway, Iceland, India & Burma; A.D.C. to Field-Marshal Sir Claude Auchinleck 1943–44; 13th Frontier Force Rifles (Indian Army) 1942–45; G.S.O.2 (Int.) Middle East 1951–52; Chief Instr., Sch. of Military Intelligence, U.K. 1954–56; Mem., London Stock Exchange 1959–75; emigrated to Canada 1980; Candn. citizen 1983; Founder Dir., Allied City Share Trust PLC 1964–73; Chair, Lincolnshire Chickens Ltd. 1963–87; Alderney Offshore Serv. Ltd. 1976–80; Brit. North Channel Co. Ltd. 1976–80; Dir., Longy Investment Trust Ltd. & other companies 1976–80; Lectr. in Genealogy, Malaspina Coll. 1984– ; Pres., Old Oakhamian Club 1960–61; Freeman of the City of London 11 April 1960; Liveryman Worshipful Co. of Pattenmakers 1965; Founder Mem., Alderney Rotary Club, Channel Islands 1979; Riding Dir., Reform Party of Canada 1992– ; Anglican; Mem., Authors Soc.; Soc. of Genealogists; Heraldry Soc.; Heraldry Soc. of Can.; Assn. of Profl. Genealogists (US); Reform Party of Can.; author: 'A Brief History of the 4th Battn. The Royal Lincolnshire Regt.' 1949, 'The Greenwood Tree in Three Continents' 1988, 'Field-Marshal Auchinleck' 1990 and many articles on genealogy; recreations: golf, shooting, genealogy; clubs: Carlton, Union, The Pilgrims; Address: R.R. 1, Box 40, Madrona Dr., Nanoose Bay, B.C. V0R 2R0.

**GREENWOOD, Hugh John,** B.A.Sc., M.A.Sc., Ph.D., F.M.S.A., F.R.S.C., P.Eng.; geologist; educator, retired; b. Vancouver, B.C. 17 March 1931; s. John Marshall and Joan (Sampson) G.; e. N. Vancouver High Sch. 1949; Univ. of B.C. B.A.Sc. 1954 (F.J. Nicholson Scholarship 1954), M.A.Sc. 1956; Princeton Univ. Ph.D. 1960 (Siscoe Fellowship 1959, Porter Ogden Jacobus Fellowship 1958); Carnegie Inst. of Washington Predoctoral Fellow (Geophys. Lab. 1959); m. Mary Sylvia d. late John Proudfoot Ledingham 5 Oct. 1955; children: Stuart Bruce, Kelly Louise, Barbara Lynn; PROF., GEOL. SCIENCES, UNIV. OF B.C. (Retired); Geol. Ventures Ltd. Lake Dufault Mines, Que. 1956–57; Phys. Chem., Geophys. Lab. Carnegie Inst. of Washington 1960–63; Assoc. Prof. of Geol. Princeton Univ. 1963–67; Assoc. Prof. Univ. of B.C. 1967, Prof. 1969; Head, Dept. Geol. Sciences, Univ. of B.C. 1977–85; rec'd Steacie Prize Nat. Research Council; author or co-author numerous publs. petrology, metamorphism, phys. chem., thermodynamics; mem. Geochem. Soc. (Pres. 1978); Geol. Assn. Can.; Mineral. Assn. Can. (Pres. 1986, 1987); Assn. Prof. Engrs. B.C.; recreations: skiing, sailing, mountain climbing, music; Home: 241 Saltspring Way, R.R. 2, S-12, B-9, Ganges, B.C. V0S 1E0.

**GREENWOOD, Lawrence George,** L.L.D.; banker; b. Briercrest, Sask. 16 June 1921; s. late George Tuckfield and Mildred Jane (Greenwood) G.; e. Regina Central Collegiate, grad. 1938; m. Margaret, d. Wm. Purser, Winnipeg, Man., 28 June 1947; Chrmn., Cdn. Reinsurance Co. and Cdn. Reassurance Co; Chrmn., Swissre Mngmt. Ltd.; Pres. Swissre Holding (Canada) Ltd.; Mem. Finance Ctte., Swissre Corp., New York; Dir. Emeritus, Candn. Imp. Bank of Commerce; mem., Candn. Adv. Bd., Liberty Mutual Ins. Co.; joined Candn. Bank of Commerce, 1938; Asst. Mgr., Toronto Br., 1953; Mgr., Seattle (Wash.) Br. 1956; Supt. H. O. Toronto, March, 1958; Mgr., Toronto Br., Sept. 1958; Asst. Gen. Mgr., H.O., 1962; Regional Gen. Mgr., Internat., 1963; Depy. Chief Gen. Mgr., H.O., 1964, and Chief Gen. Mgr., Dec. 1964; el. a Dir., Nov. 1967, Pres. 1968–71; Vice-Chrmn. of Bd., 1971–76; retired from active service with bank 1981; served in 2nd World War overseas in North Africa and Europe with R.C.A.F., 1941–45; Hon. Trustee, Hospital for Sick Children; mem., Nat. Trust for Scotland; United Church; recreations: tennis, fishing; Clubs: York; Home: 7 Tudor Gate, Willowdale Ont. M2L 1N3 Office: Ste. 2601, Commerce Court North, P.O. Box 63, Commerce Court Postal Stn., Toronto, Ont. M5L 1B9.

**GREER, Allan Robert,** M.A., Ph.D.; educator; b. New Westminster, B.C. 4 June 1950; s. Ralph Albert and Ethel (Heaton) G.; Univ. of B.C., B.A. 1972; Carleton Univ. M.A. 1975; York Univ. Ph.D. 1980; m. Brenda d. Walter and Jean Gainer 19 March 1976; ASSOC. PROF. OF HIST., UNIV. OF TORONTO 1986– , Asst. Prof. 1983; Asst. Prof. of Hist., Univ. of Me. 1980–83; Assoc. Prof. of Hist., Univ. of B.C. 1989–91; recipient John A. Macdonald Award Candn. Hist. Assn. 1985; Alan Sharlin Prize, Soc. Sci. Hist. Assn. 1985; author 'Peasant, Lord and Merchant: Rural Society in Three Quebec Parishes 1740–1840' 1985; 'The Patriots and the People: The Rebellion of 1837 in Rural Lower Canada' 1993; various jour. articles; Gen. Ed., Social History of Canada Series; mem. Candn. Hist. Assn.; Institut d'histoire de l'Amerique française; Amnesty Internat.; Office: Univ. of Toronto, Toronto, Ont. M5S 1A1.

**GREER, Brian Harold,** B.A., LL.B., Dip. (Leg. Drafting); lawyer, civil servant; b. Trochu, Alta. 14 Jan. 1948; s. Harold Joseph and Julia Hope G.; e. Univ. of Alberta B.A. 1969, LL.B. 1973; Univ. of Ottawa Dip. Leg.Drafting 1979; m. Nancy Henwood d. Geoffrey and Vivian Henwood 8 Aug. 1971; children: Geoffrey, Suzanne, Eric; CHIEF LEGISLATIVE COUNSEL FOR BRITISH COLUMBIA 1992– ; admitted to Alberta Bar 1974; Crown Counsel, Gen. & Special Prosecutions 1974–75; joined Alta. Legis. Counsel Office 1975; Asst. Chief Legis. Counsel for Alta. 1981–88; joined B.C. Legis. Counsel Office 1988; admitted to B.C. Bar 1989; Home: 2082 Haultain St., Victoria, B.C. V8R 2L7; Office: 5th fl., 1070 Douglas St., Victoria, B.C. V8V 1X4.

**GREER, William Newton,** B.Arch., M.S., O.A.A., F.R.A.I.C.; R.C.A.; architect; b. Kingston, Ont. 21 Feb. 1925; s. Lt. Col. George Garnet and Mamie Louisa (Garrett) G.; e. Crescent Sch. Toronto 1937; Trinity Coll. Sch. Port Hope 1943; Univ. of Toronto B.Arch. 1948; Ill. Inst. of Technol. M.S. (Product Design) 1951 (Nat. Indust. Design Council Scholarship); m. Rina Claire d. Sydney Sussman, Long Island, New York 17 Nov. 1973; children: Jonathan Newton, Simon Garnet; ARCHITECTURAL HERITAGE CONSULTANT 1992– ; joined Shore & Moffat, Archs. 1950, Assoc. 1955, Partner of Shore & Moffat and Partners, Archs., Engrs., Site Planners 1962–72; Sole Princ., William N. Greer, Arch. 1972–76; Arch., Toronto Historical Bd. 1976–91; mem. Corp. of Trinity College 1958– ; Adv. Bd. St. James Cemetary 1968– ; served with RCN 1944–45; mem. Ont. Assn. Archs.; Toronto Soc. Archs.; Arch. Conservancy Ont.; Soc. Study Arch. Can.; Can. Assn. Prof. Heritage Consultants; Kappa Alpha; P. Clubs: R.C.Y.C.; Osler Bluff Ski; Home: 155 Hudson Dr., Toronto, Ont. M4T 2K4.

**GRÉGOIRE, Bernard;** business executive; b. Montréal, Qué. 12 March 1932; s. Wilfrid and Gertrude G.; e. Collège Stanislas; École des Hautes Etudes Commerciales C.P.A.; m. Denise Céline Fiset 4 August 1956; children: Nicole, Martine, Geneviève, Simon; Pres., Rescope Inc. 1981– ; Vice-Pres., Pierre Des Marais Inc. 1964–81; Asst. Vice-Pres., Public Affairs, Fed. Business Devel. Bank 1982–84; Vice-Pres. 1984–87; Vice-Rector, Public Affairs, Univ. de Montréal 1987–91; Vice Pres., Corporate Affairs, BCE Inc. 1991–93; recreations: tennis, skiing; clubs: Mount Royal, Saint-Denis, Saint Laurent Tennis; Home: 875, cr. du Ruisseau, #G2, Saint-Laurent, Qué. H4L 5E2.

**GREGOIRE, Pierre P.,** B.A., B.C.L.; insurance executive; b. Berthierville, Que. 30 Aug. 1947; s. Bernard B. and Madeleine (Rochette) G.; e. Univ. of Montréal, B.A. 1968; McGill Univ., B.C.L. 1971; children: two sons; Pres., Parapet Underwriters Inc. 1992; Pres., Samaantree Consultants Inc. 1992; Chief Operating Offr., Townson & Alexander Inc. 1993; Sr. Vice-Pres., ENCON Group 1980; Lawyer, Lavery, O'Brien 1972; Partner 1978; Mem., Que. & Candn. Bar Assn. 1972– ; Property Casualty Underwriters' Club; Nat. Assoc. of Corp. Dirs., Que. Soc. of Med. and Law; Inst. of Corporate Dirs. in Can.; Practising Law Inst.; author of 5 articles on profl. liability and directors' and officers' liability; Clubs: Le Cercle Univ.; Rideau Tennis & Squash; Home: 33 Hime Cres., Ottawa, Ont. K1G 4R9; Office: 201 – 2150 Thurston Dr., Ottawa, Ont. K1G 5T9.

**GREGORY, Gordon F.,** Q.C., B.C.L., LL.M.; lawyer; b. Saint John, N.B. 25 Nov. 1938; s. Robert Alexander and Gertrude B. (Deakin) G.; e. Univ. of N.B., B.B.A. 196l, B.C.L. 1963; Harvard Univ. LL.M. 1965; m. Carol A., d. Elston L. Reid, Fredericton, N.B., 8 Aug. 1964; children: Andrew R., Kathryn A.; Deputy Min. of Justice, N.B., 1971–87; read law with Benjamin R. Guss, Q.C.; called to Bar of N.B. 1963; mem., Candn. Bar Assn.; Barristers Soc. N.B.; Fredericton Law Soc,; United Church; Home: 365 Wright St., Fredericton N.B. E3B 2E3; Office: 206 Rookwood Ave., Fredericton, N.B. E3B 2M2.

**GREGORY, Michael Joseph Patrick,** B.A. M.A., P.G.C.E.; university professor/theatre director; b. Great Crosby, Lancs., England 7 April 1935; s. Thomas and Lillian (Connellan) G.; e. St. Edward's Coll. 1954; Balliol Coll., Oxford Univ. (Goldsmith Scholar), B.A. (1st class hons.) 1958, M.A. 1963; Leeds Univ., P.G.C.E. with distinction 1959; m. Caroline d. Revd. Russell & Mariana Woolley 16 Nov. 1957; divorced 1988; children: Patrick, Catherine, Richard, David; PROF., GRAD. FAC. & GLENDON COLL., YORK UNIV. 1970– ; Master, Oratory Sch. 1959–61; Lectr., Royal Coll. of Sci. & Technol., Glasgow 1961–62; Sch. of English, Leeds Univ. 1961–66; Assoc. Prof., Grad. Faculty & Glendon Coll. of York Univ. 1966–70; Chrmn., English Dept. 1966–71, 1973–74; Dir., Dramatic Arts Prog. 1967–80; Co-ord., Linguistics & Language Studies 1983– ; Vis. Prof., Cornell-Fulbright Nat. Ling. Project in Italy 1964, 1965; Ibadan Univ., Nigeria 1972–73; Univ. of Internat. Bus. & Econ., Beijing, China 1985–86; Courant Inst. of Maths., New York Univ. 1992–93; Artistic Dir., Aquarius Prodns., Toronto 1973–77; GP Prodns., Toronto 1981–83; Guest Artistic Dir., Arts Theatre, Ibadan 1973; author: 'What Is Good English?' 1969, 'English Patterns' 1972; co-author: 'Linguistics and Style' 1964, 'Language and Situation' 1978; editor: Linguistic Series for Canadians, Book Soc. of Can. 1969– ; Ed. Adv., 'Language and Style, an International Journal' 1970– ; 'Functions of Language' 1993; 'International Journal of Forensic Linguistics' 1993; recreations: running, terrier breeding, fishing, travel; Home: RR #2, Little Britain, Toronto, Ont. K0M 2C0; Office: Bayview Ave., Toronto, Ont. M4N 3M6.

**GREIG, Paul David,** B.Math., M.D., F.R.C.S.(C), F.A.C.S.; surgeon; researcher; educator; b. Toronto, Ont. 24 May 1949; s. George Durham and Jean Patterson (Gallow) G.; e. Univ. of Waterloo B.Math. 1972; Univ. of Toronto M.D. 1976; m. Anne L. d. Robert A. and Rita C. McAlear 9 Oct. 1976; children: Kevin Scott, David James, Julia Suzanne; STAFF SURG., THE TORONTO HOSP., TORONTO GEN. DIV. 1984– ; Assoc. Prof. of Surg. Univ. of Toronto 1990– , Dir., Adult Liver Transplant Prog. 1989– ; Dir., Multiple Organ Retrieval & Exchange (MORE) Programme at Toronto 1992– ; Assoc. Staff Mount Sinai Hosp. 1987– ; Cons. Hosp. for Sick Children 1987– ; Irving Heward Cameron Rsch. Fellow Toronto Gen. Hosp. 1981; Med. Rsch. Council Can. Fellow in Surg. Metabolism Prog. Columbia Univ. N.Y. 1982–83; TGH Award for teaching excellence undergrad. surg. 1987, 1991; author of over 75 scientific papers and chapters in books; Pres., Candn. Transplant Soc. 1993–94 (Pres.-elect 1992–93); mem., Candn. Assn. Gen. Surgs.; Assn. Acad. Surg.; Am. Soc. Transplant Surgs.; The Transplant Soc.; World Assn. of HPB Surgery; Candn. Transplantation Soc.; Soc. of University Surgeons; recreation: music; Home: 31 Alexandra Blvd., Toronto, Ont. M4R 1L8; Office: Norman Urquhart Wing 10-152, 200 Elizabeth St., Toronto, Ont. M5G 2C4.

**GREINER, Peter Charles,** B.Sc., M.A., Ph.D., F.R.S.C.; educator; b. Budapest, Hungary 1 Nov. 1938; Dr. Anthony Charles and Ildiko (Willoner) G.; e. Univ. of B.C. B.Sc. 1960; Yale Univ. M.A. 1962, Ph.D. 1964; m. Kathryn Suzanne d. Dr. Wayne S. Dewald, Watertown, Conn. 3 July 1965; children: Michael Anthony, Melissa Suzanne; PROF. OF MATH. UNIV. OF TORONTO since 1977; Instr. Princeton Univ. 1964–65; Asst. Prof. Univ. of Toronto 1965, Assoc. Prof. 1970; mem. Inst. for Advanced Study, Princeton, N.J. 1973–74; Visiting Prof., Université de Paris VI, 1980–81; rec'd Steacie Prize in Natural Sciences 1977; co-author 'Estimates for the $\bar{\partial}$-Neumann Problem' 1977; various math. articles; mem. Candn. Math. Soc.; Am. Math. Soc.; R. Catholic; Office: Toronto, Ont. M5S 1A1.

**GRENDLER, Paul Frederick,** M.A., Ph.D.; educator; b. Armstrong, Iowa 24 May 1936; s. late August and Josephine (Girres) G.; e. Oberlin Coll. A.B. 1959; Univ. of Wisc. M.A. 1961, Ph.D. 1964; m. Marcella T. d. late Peter J. McCann, Chicago, Ill. 16 June 1962; children: Peter, Jean; PROF. OF HISTORY, UNIV. OF TORONTO 1973– ; Instr. in Hist. Univ. of Pittsburgh 1963–64; Lectr. in Hist. present Univ. 1964, Asst. Prof. 1965–69, Assoc. Prof. 1969–73; Postdoctoral Fellow, Inst. Research in Humanities Univ. of Wisc. 1967–68; Can. Council Leave Fellowship 1970–71; Am. Council Learned Socs. Fellowship 1971–72; I Tatti Fellow (Harvard Univ. Center for Italian Renaissance Studies) Florence, Italy 1970–72; Sr. Fellow, Soc. for Humanities Cornell Univ. 1973–74; Guggenheim Mem. Fellowship 1978–79; Social Sciences & Humanities Research Council Can. Leave Fellowship 1979–80; Fellow, Woodrow Wilson Internat. Center for Scholars, Washington, D.C. 1982–83; Social Sciences & Humanities Research Council Can. Leave Fellowship 1985–86; SSHRCC Rsch. Time Stipend 1988–89; Nat. Endowment for the Humanities Interpretive Rsch. Grant 1989–90, 1992; author 'Critics of the Italian World 1530–1560' 1969; 'The Roman Inquisition and the Venetian Press 1540–1605' 1977 (Howard R. Marraro Prize, Am. Cath. Hist. Assn. 1978); 'L'Inquisizione Romana e l'editoria a Venezia 1540–1605' rev. Italian ed. 1983; 'Culture and Censorship in Late Renaissance Italy and France' 1981; ed. 'An Italian Renaissance Reader' 1987, 2nd ed. 1992; 'Schooling in Renaissance Italy' 1989 (Howard R. Marraro Prize, Am. Hist. Assoc. 1989), paperback reprint 1991, Italian transl. 1991; editor, John D'Amico, 'Roman and German Humanism 1450-1550' 1993; numerous articles and reviews learned journs.; mem. Ed. Bd. and Extve. Comte. 'Collected Works of Erasmus' 1976– ; mem. Renaissance Soc. Am. (Vice-Pres. 1991–92, Pres. 1992–94); Am. Cath. Hist. Assn. (Vice-Pres. 1983, Pres. 1984); Am. Hist. Assoc.; Soc. Italian Hist. Studies (Adv. Counc. 1986–90); Sixteenth Century Studies (Counc. 1987–90); recreations: piano playing, golf; Office: Dept. of History, University of Toronto, Toronto, Ont. M5S 1A1.

**GRENVILLE-WOOD, Geoffrey,** LL.B.; barrister and solicitor; b. Cario, Egypt 2 Nov. 1943; s. Alan C. and Catherine Minerva (Hawawini) G.; e. Univ. of Ottawa LL.B. 1982; m. Jacqueline d. Georges and Harriet Léger 30 Nov. 1979; children: Emma, Simon; BARRISTER AND SOLICITOR, GRENVILLE-WOOD AND ASSOC. 1982– ; Supervisor, Prudential Assur. Co. Ltd. 1965–71; Dir. of Publication, Candn. Council for Internat. Coop. 1971–74; Extve. Dir., United Nations Assn. in Canada 1974–77; Law School & Bar Admission 1977–82; Vice-Pres. & Dir., Candn. Office, Environmental Mediation Internat. 1980–90; Sessional Lectr., Law Dept., Carleton Univ. 1980–87; Occasional Lectr., Dalhousie Univ. Law School 1986–90; Queen's Jubilee Medal 1977; Red Cross Service Award 1990; Vice-Pres., Candn. Council for Internat. Coop. 1974–72; Candn. Red Cross Soc. Ottawa-Carleton Br. & Hon. Legal Counsel 1982–86; Vice-Pres. & Hon. Legal Counsel, Candn. Red Cross Soc. Ont. Div. 1986–90; Hon. Legal Counsel, United Nations Assn. in Canada 1990– ; Chair, Extve. Ctte., World Fed. of United Nations Assns. 1991– ; Mem., Candn. Del. to UN Conf. on Human Settlement 1976; to UN Conf. on Environ. & Devel. 1992; Mem., Candn. Bar Assn.; Law Soc. of U.C.; Candn. Red Cross Soc.; author of several articles, conference papers, lectures, etc.; Home: 377 Huron Ave. S., Ottawa, Ont. K1Y 0W9; Office: 43 Florence St., Ottawa, Ont. K2P 0W6.

**GRETZKY, Wayne,** O.C. (1984); hockey player; b. Brantford, Ont. 26 Jan 1961; s. Walter and Phyllis G.; coached from childhood by his father and widely publicized as a ten-year-old scoring sensation; played Jr. hockey with Sault Ste. Marie Greyhounds; WHA, Indianapolis Racers 1978–79; scored 110 points in WHA at age seventeen; Edmonton Oilers (WHA) and then in NHL in 1979–80 season; tied Marcel Dionne for scoring championship 1st season (51 goals, 86 assists, 137 points); 2nd NHL season captured records: most points (164, breaking Phil Esposito's 1970–71 record of 152); most points in one season incl. playoffs (185, again breaking Esposito's 1970–71 record of 162); most assists in one season (109, breaking Bobby Orr's 1970–71 record of 102); most assists in one season incl. playoffs (123, again breaking Orr's 1970–71 record of 109); youngest player in league history to win scoring championship; in 1981–82 season demolished all his own records (scoring a phenomenal 92 goals and 120 assists for a total of 212 points in regular season play, and reaching 50–goal plateau in 39 games); holds NHL Records career: highest aver. goals per game (.905); highest aver. assists per game (1.41); highest aver. points per game (2.325); most 100 point seasons (13); most consecutive 100 point seasons (13); single season: most goals (92, 1981–82); most assists (120, 1981–82); most points (212, 1981–82); most 3–or-more goal games (10, 1981–82); most short-handed goals (12, 1983–84); most goals incl. playoffs (97, 1981–82); most assists incl. playoffs (151, 1982–83); most points incl. playoffs (234, 1982–83); most goals by centre (92, 1981–82); most assists by centre (125, 1981–82); most points by centre (212, 1981–82); most goals in first 50 games of season (60, 1981–82); most consecutive games, one or more assists (17, 1983–84); most consecutive games, one or more points (51, 1983–84); most assists, one game, first NHL season (7, 1980); playoffs: most points, one playoff yr. (38, 1982–83); most assists, one playoff yr. (26, 1982–83); most points, one playoff game (7, 1983); All-Star: most goals, one All-Star game (4, 1983); most goals, one All-Star period (4, 1983); most points, one All-Star period (4, 1983); shares NHL records for: most assists, one game (7, with Billy Taylor 1946–47 Detroit Red Wings); most goals, one period (4, with six others); most assists, one period (4, with 19 others); most short-handed goals, one playoff year (3, 1982–83, with three others); most shorthanded goals, one game (2, 1983, with two others); most goals, one playoff period (3, with 16 others); most assists, one playoff period (3, with 29 others); fastest goal from start of period other than 1st (9 sec., 1983, with six others); most points, one All-Star game (4, 1983, with four others); holds or shares 57 NHL records; by achieving 1050 points in only 9 yrs. in NHL, surpassed Gordie Howe's career points total record, March 1988; reg. winner many hockey awards incl. Hart Memorial Trophy (NHL Most Valuable Player to Team), Art Ross Trophy (Leading Scorer, Regular Season), Lady Byng Trophy (Sportsmanship and Gentlemanly Conduct), Lester B. Pearson Award (Most Valuable Player, voted by players); The Hockey News Award Player of the Year, 8 times 1979–87; NHL Second All-Star Team 1980, 1987, First All-Star Team 1981, 1982, 1983, 1984, 1985, 1986; Player of the Year for 7 seasons; Team Canada Helsinki 1982 (Bronze Medal); numerous other awards incl.: Charlie Conacher Award (humanitarianism and community service) 1981; Victor Award (excellence in American sport) 7 times 1980–87; Candn. Male Athlete of Year 1980, 1981, 1982, 1983, 1985; Amer. Acad. of Achievement Award (world-wide excellence in chosen field) 1982; Sports Illustrated Sportsman of the Year 1982; Sport Magazine MVP Trophy 1985 and 1988; Seagram Sports Award (statistical superiority in chosen sport) 6 consecutive times; Sporting News Player of the Year, 7 times; traded to the Los Angeles Kings, Aug. 9, 1988; Officer Order of Can. 1984; recreations: tennis, baseball, golf; Address:

c/o Mr. M. Barnett, IMG Agency, 11755 Wilshire Blvd., Ste. 850, Los Angeles, Calif. 90025.

**GRICE, John Lloyd,** B.A.; transportation executive; b. New Glasgow, N.S. 16 Dec. 1942; s. Elizabeth S. G.; e. Univ. of N.B., B.A. (Econ.) 1966; m. Judith A. Ross 3 Oct. 1987; Chrmn., Halifax-Dartmouth Port Comn. 1984–90; Extve. Dir., Halifax-Dartmouth Port Comn. 1970–74; Pres., Analytic Serv. Limited 1974–79; Gen. Mgr., Nfld. Container Lines 1977–82; Pres., Halifax Offshore Terminal Serv. Limited 1982– ; recreations: diving; club: Halifax; Address: P.O. Box 2452, Halifax, N.S. B3J 3E8.

**GRIER, David Denham Eyre,** B.A., APR., AP; public affairs / public relations executive; b. Johannesburg, S. Africa 12 April 1932 s. Charles Denham and Ruby Stephènie G.; e. King Edward VII School; Univ. of the Witwatersrand; McGill Univ. B.A. 1953; 1st m. Deena Stern 24 May 1955; 2nd m. Annette d. Marion and Lawrence Hebb 3 March 1984; children (from 1st m.): John Denham, Wendy Ruth, Robin Anne; VICE-PRES., CORPORATE AFFAIRS, ROYAL BANK OF CANADA 1989– ; Dir., Corp. Program, IMAGINE, Candn. Centre for Philanthropy (part-time secondment) 1990– ; Extve. Dir., Royal Bank of Canada Charitable Found. 1993– ; Radio Tech., CFCF Montreal 1952–54; Reporter, Montreal Gazette 1954; Editor, Grad. Soc., McGill Univ. & Wallace Pubns. 1954–56; Editor, WEEKEND Magazine 1959–61; Public Relations, DuPont of Canada Ltd. 1961–67; Head, Public Relations, Royal Bank of Canada, Montreal 1967–84; Head, Public Affairs, Royal Bank of Canada, Toronto 1984–89; Editor-in-Chief McGill Daily 1952–53; Winner, John Bracken Award, Candn. Univ. Press (Editorials); Accredited in Public Relations (APR); Advanced Pilot (AP), Candn. Power and Sail Squadron; serves or has served on boards of Candn. Public Relns. Soc.; Candn. Ctr. for Ethics & Corp. Policy; Area Selection Ctte., Candn. Merit Scholarship Found.; Policy Rsch. Ctr. on Children, Youth & Family; Adv. Ctte., Human Devel. Program, Candn. Inst. for Advanced Rsch.; frequent public speaker on public affairs issues, corp. ethics, social responsibilites of business, corp. philanthropy; recreations: photography, sailing, woodworking, scuba; Home: 272 Millwood Rd., Toronto, Ont. M4S 1J8; Office: 9th Floor, South Tower, Royal Bank Plaza, Toronto, Ont. M5J 2J5.

**GRIER, Hon. Ruth Anna,** B.A., M.P.P.; politician; b. Dublin, Ireland 2 Oct. 1936; d. Alexander Earls and Gertrude (Sykes) Dowds; e. Trinity College Dublin, dipl. in Pub. Admin.; Univ. of Toronto B.A. (Hons.) 1958; m. Terence s. Crawforth and Ruth G. 5 Dec. 1958; children: David Terence, Timothy Alexander, Patrick Wyly; MIN. OF HEALTH, ONT. 1993– ; Alderman, City of Etobicoke 1970–85; 1st elected to the Ont. Leg. (Etobicoke-Lakeshore) g.e. 1985; re-elected g.e. 1987, 1990; formerly Deputy Whip & Environ. Critic; Min. of the Environment & Min. Resp. for The Greater Toronto Area 1990–93; mem., num. community & social serv. orgns.; N.D.P.; Anglican; Home: 74 Arcadian Circle, Toronto, Ont. M8W 2T9; Office: 135 St. Clair Ave. W., 15th Flr., Toronto, Ont. M4V 1P5; Riding Office: 2800 Lakeshore Blvd. W., Etobicoke, Ont. M8V 1H5.

**GRIERSON, David Alan;** broadcaster; b. Toronto, Ont. 19 Feb. 1955; s. Charles William and Marjorie Catherine (Collins); e. Richmond Sr. S.S.; Univ. of B.C.; Simon Fraser Univ.; B.C. Inst. of Technology, broadcasting; m. Sheri d. Arthur and Margaret Hambrook 20 May 1978; one s.: Patrick Hambrook; ANNOUNCER/PRODUCER, CBC RADIO BRITISH COLUMBIA; Host, Stereo Morning, CBC Stereo, CBC; Program Producer, CHQM AM/FM Vancouver; Program Dir.; Programming Consultant – Independent Vancouver & Calgary; Program Dir., CJAZ-FM Vancouver; Exec. Prod. CKKS-FM Vancouver; Host, The Arts Report, CBC Stereo; Columnist, Sunday Arts Entertainment, CBC TV; Dir., B.C. Chapter, Cdn. Acad. of Recording Arts & Sciences; Mem., A.C.T.R.A.; Founding Mem., Writers Guild of Canada; author: 'The Expo Celebration' (official retrospective of EXPO '86); recreations: oenophile, cook, fisherman; Office: P.O. Box 4600, Vancouver, B.C. V6B 4A2.

**GRIEVE, Brig.-Gen. Patrick V.B.,** C.D.; b. Montreal, Que. 9 June 1921; s. John and Isabel Helen (MacCarthy) G.; e. Univ. of Toronto Schs.; Candn. Army Staff Coll.; U.S. Marine Corps Sr. Sch.; Candn. and Brit. Army Staff Colls., Directing Staff; m. Muriel L.E. Veitch 5 Sept. 1942 (dec.); children: Susan Elizabeth (dec.); James Patrick; Peter Michael, Robert John; enlisted Armoured Corps 1940; comnd. RCAC 1942; served 22 Candn. Armd. Regt. UK and N.W. Eur.; post-war regt'al and staff appts. incl. Command Royal Candn. Dragoons, Sr. Staff NDHQ, Command 4 CMBG (NATO), Commandant Candn. Land Forces Staff Coll.; Sec.-Gen. Candn. Agency Commonwealth War Graves Comn. 1976–84; Bd. mem. Army Benevolent Fund 1984– ; Past Col. of Regt. Royal Candn. Dragoons; Vice-Pres., Kingston-Frontenac Council on Aging; Life mem. RCAC (Cavalry) Assn.; RCD Assn.; Army Navy and Air Force Veterans Can. (Past Hon. Dom. Pres.); mem. Royal Candn. Legion; recreations: fishing, skiing; Home: 'Loch Hame' R.R.2, Sharbot Lake, Ont. K0H 2P0.

**GRIEVE, Richard Andrew Francis,** Ph.D., D.Sc.; research scientist; b. Aberdeen, Scot. 15 Sept. 1943; s. Thomas Gray and Isabella Mennie (Simpson) G.; e. Aberdeen Grammar Sch. 1961; Univ. of Aberdeen B.Sc. 1965, D.Sc. 1985; Univ. of Toronto M.Sc. 1967, Ph.D. 1970; Brown Univ. M.A. 1983; m. Parise 4 Sept. 1989; children: Patrick, Malcolm, Misha; RSCH. SCI. ENERGY, MINES & RESOURCES CAN. 1974– ; Rsch. Assoc. Univ. of Ore. 1970–72; Post-Doctoral Fellow Nat. Rsch. Council Can. 1972–74; Rsch. Sci., Dept. Energy, Mines and Resources 1974– ; Visiting Prof. Brown Univ. 1980–81, Prof. 1983–84; Visiting Sci. NASA Johnson Space Center 1985–88; Visiting Prof., Univ. Münster 1993–94; mem. Lunar Sci. Council, Univ. Space Rsch. Assn. 1985–88; mem. Lunar & Planetary Geol. Review Panel NASA 1981–83, 1992– ; mem., Ctte.on Meteorites, Nat. Res. Coun. Assoc. 1990–92; sec. Meteorites and Impacts Adv. Ctte., Can. Space Agency 1992– ; mem., Ctte. on Astrogeology, Am. Assoc. Petrl. Geol. 1985– ; author or co-author over 140 sci. papers impact phenomena, terrestrial crustal evolution & planetary geol.; Assoc. Ed. Jour. Geophys. Rsch. 1983–85; Meteoritics 1987– ; Proceedings Lunar & Planetary Sci. Conf.; recipient Distinguished Tech. Writing Award Soc. Tech. Communications Can. 1982; Fellow, Meteoritical Soc.; Barringer Medal, Meteoritical Soc. 1990; Alexander von Humbolt Rsch. Award 1993; namesake to Mars-crossing asteroid; Fellow, Royal Soc. Canada 1992; mem. Internat. Union Geol. Sci's Comn. Comparative Planetol. (Vice-Chrmn.); Am. Geophys. Union; Geol. Assn. Can.; Candn. Geophys. Union; Am. Assn. Advanc. Sci.; Sigma Xi; Home: 3990 River Rd., Gloucester, Ont. K1G 3N3; Office: 1 Observatory Cres., Ottawa, Ont. K1A 0Y3.

**GRIFFIN, Anthony George Scott;** semi-retired company director; b. Lovehill, Langley, Bucks, England, l5 Aug. 1911; s. (Edward) Scott and Mabel Hannora (Mackenzie) G.; e. Appleby Sch., Oakville, Ont. 1922–29; Univ. of Toronto (Arts) 1929–30; Royal Mil. Coll., Kingston, Ont. 1930–31; m. Kathleen Lockhart, d. Col. H.D. Lockhart Gordon, Toronto, Ont. 12 June 1937; children: Scott, Ian Gordon, Margaret Ann (McCall), Peter Mackenzie Gordon, Timothy Kirkfield; 15 grandchildren; 1 great-grandchild; Chrmn. & Dir., Guardian Capital Group Ltd.; Guardian Pacific Rim Corp.; Bunting Warburg Limited; Hon. Dir. and former Dir. (1966–86) & former Chrmn. (1975–85) St. Michael's Hosp.; Internat. Adviser and former Dir., S.G. Warburg Group plc, London, Eng.; former Dir., Nat. Film Bd.; former Gov. Nat. Theatre School; former Gov. Royal Life Saving Soc.; Patron, Pearson Coll. of the Pacific; mem. Adv. Council Nat. Ballet Can. (Pres. 1955–58); Secy., Wartime Prices & Trade Board 1945–47; Dept. of Ext. Affrs. 1948–51; Secy., Royal Comn. on Prices 1948–49; Secy., Dollar-Sterling Trade Bd. 1949–51; retired Chrmn., Triarch Corp., Home Oil, Scurry-Rainbow Oil, Halifax Ins. and retired director 25 companies in Canada, the U.S. and U.K.; served in 2nd World War in R.C.N. 1940–45; Commanded Corvette and Frigate; Staff Offr. (operations), to Flag Offr., Nfld., rank Cdr.; Mentioned in Despatches; mem., Candn. Inst. of Internat. Affairs; Adv. Group, Bilderberg Meetings; keen sailor; Mgr., Cdn. Olympic Yachting Team 1976; Commodore (1972–3) Canadian Albacore Assoc.; Pres. (1975–77) Internat. Albacore Assn.; R. Catholic; recreations: tennis, golf, sailing, skiing, history; Clubs: Toronto; Toronto Racquet; Badminton & Racquet; Royal Cruising; Royal Canadian Yacht; Osler Bluff Ski; Home: 2l Dunvegan Road, Toronto, Ont. M4V 2P5; Office: 110 Yonge St., 19th Flr., Toronto, Ont. M5C 1T4.

**GRIFFIN, Diane F.,** M.Sc., B.Ed., B.Sc.; conservation executive; b. Summerside, P.E.I. 18 Mar. 1947; d. Thomas Errol and Margaret Catherine (Murphy) Laughlin; e. St. Dunstan's Univ. B.Sc. 1969; Univ. of P.E.I. B.Ed. 1973; Acadia Univ. M.Sc. 1973; m. Kevin s. James and Margaret G. 14 Aug. 1970; one d.: Sharleen Margaret; EXECUTIVE DIRECTOR, ISLAND NATURE TRUST 1986– ; Supervisor of Interpretation, P.E.I. Dept. of Tourism, Parks & Conservation 1973–77; Natural Areas Co-ord., Alta. Dept. of Forestry, Lands & Wildlife 1977–86; Nat. Parks Centennial Award 1985; Canadian Outdoorsman of the Year Award 1986; Governor General's Conservation Award (Tourism Indus. Assn. of Canada) 1989; Merit Award, Atlantic Soc. of Fish & Wildlife Biol. 1990; Distinguished Alumna Award, Univ. of P.E.I. 1992; Douglas H. Pimlott Conservation Award, Candn. Nature Fed. 1992; Dir., Adv. Bd., Sch. for Resource & Environ. Studies, Dalhousie Univ.; Mem., Nat. Round Table on the Environ. & the Economy 1989– ; P.E.I. Round Table on the Environ. & the Economy 1989– ; Candn. Ctte. for the Unesco Prog. on Man & the Biosphere 1990– ; Roman Catholic; Mem., Candn. Nature Fed. (Pres. 1979–81); Alta. Soc. of Profl. Biol. (Dir. 1979–81); Atlantic Soc. of Fish & Wildlife Biol. (Vice-Pres. 1987–89); Wildlife Habitat Canada (Vice-Chrmn. 1987–90); Candn. Environ. Adv. Council 1986–92; author: 'Atlantic Wildflowers' 1984; Home: Charlottetown, P.E.I. C1A 3R7; Office: Box 265, Charlottetown, P.E.I. C1A 1M6.

**GRIFFIN, Ian Gordon,** B.A.; investment dealer; b. Hamilton, Ont. 7 Jan. 1940; s. Anthony George Scott and Kathleen Lockhart (Gordon) G.; e. Sedberg School 1952–55; Upper Canada College 1955–59; Bishop's Univ. B.A. 1963; m. Judith d. William D. Robb 11 June 1966; children: Alastair, Emily, Willa; VICE CHAIRMAN, RESEARCH CAPITAL CORP. 1986– ; S.G. Warburg & Co., London 1963–65; Vice-Pres., Wood Gundy Ltd. 1965–80 (Toronto 1965–67, Peterborough 1967–70, Toronto 1970–73, Tokyo 1973–76, Vancouver 1976–80); Sr. Vice Pres., F.H. Deacon Hodgson Inc. 1980–86; Trustee, N. Am. Wildlife Found. 1982– ; Knight Officer, St. Hubertis Soc.; recreations: skiing, tennis, golf, fishing, hunting; clubs: Toronto, Badminton & Racquet, Osler Bluff Ski (Ont.), Vancouver (B.C.), Bow Valley, Executive Breakfast (Alta.); Home: 1014 Prospect Ave. S.W., Calgary, Alta. T2T 0W7; Office: Suite 1330, 140 – 4 Ave. S.W., Calgary, Alta. T2P 3N3.

**GRIFFIN, John Douglas Morecroft,** M.A., M.D., F.R.C.P.(C); psychiatric specialist; b. Hamilton, Ont. 3 June 1906; s. Herbert Spohn Griffin and Edith Moore (Robinson) G.; e. Hamilton Coll. Inst. 1924; Univ. of Toronto B.A. 1929, M.A. 1933, M.D. 1932; Dipl. in Psychol. Med. (Eng.) 1936; m. 1stly Erica Maude Withrow 22 Sept. 1934 (d. 1981); children: Charles Peter Morecroft, John David Anthony; m. 2ndly Barbara Mary Solandt 12 March 1982; Consultant, Candn. Mental Health Assn. 1972– ; post-grad. training Hosp. for Sick Children Toronto; Butler Hosp. Providence, R.I.; Nat. Hosp. Queens Square, London, Eng. (Rockefeller Fellow) 1934–36; Dir. of Educ. Candn. Mental Health Assn. 1936–41, Med. Dir. 1945–52, Gen. Dir. 1952–72; served with RCAMC 1941–45, rank Col.; Special lectr. in psychiatry at Sch. of Social Work, Univ. of Toronto 1948–58; mem. Extve. Comte. Ont. Mental Health Foundation 1975–81; rec'd Bowis Award Am. Coll. Psychiatry 1974; rec'd first annual Hincks award 1986; The Neilson Award, The Hannah Inst. for the Hist. of Med. 1988; Hon. mem. Ont. Sch. Counsellors Assn.; Candn. Coll. Family Physicians; Sr. mem. Candn. Med. Assn.; Life mem. Ont. Med. Assn.; Toronto Acad. of Med.; Am. Psychiatric Assn.; Candn. Psychiatric Assn. (Pres. 1967–68); Ont. Psychiatric Assn.; Hon. Mem., Candn. Psychiat. Assn. 1986; Hon. Mem., Ont. Psychiat. Assn. 1987; author 'In Search of Sanity': A Chronicle of the Canadian Mental Health Association 1918–1988, 1989; author or co-author numerous publs.; Liberal; recreations: sailing, woodwork, travel; Clubs: National Yacht; U of T Faculty Club; Home: Westclair Apts. #1204, 47 St. Clair Ave. W., Toronto, Ont. M4V 3A5.

**GRIFFIN, Scott,** B.A.; technology executive; b. Hamilton, Ont. 30 Nov. 1938; s. Anthony George Scott and Kathleen Lockhart (Gordon) G.; e. Sedbergh Sch. Jr. Matric. 1956; Bishops Univ., B.A. Engl. and Phil. 1960; m. Krystyne d. Edward and Krystyne Romer 7 July 1977; children: Anthony, Christian, Tessa, Chloe; PRESIDENT AND C.E.O. MERIDIAN TECHNOLOGIES INC. 1979– ; Chrmn. & Dir. Canadian Education Microprocessor Co. Ltd.; Clemmer Industries Ltd.; General Kinetics Engineering Corporation; Jutras Die Casting Ltd.; Richmond Die Casting Ltd.; Accurcast Ltd.; Magnesium Products Ltd.; Microdesign Ltd.; Dir., Magnesium Products of Am. Inc.; Stackpole Ltd.; mgmt. positions in Mktg., Corp. Planning & Supply, BP Canada Ltd. 1961–73; seconded to British Petroleum Ltd., London, Eng.; Pres. & C.E.O., Les Breuvages Innopop Ltee (a subs. of Innocan Ltd.) Montreal 1973–76; Exec. Vice-Pres. Pop Shoppes Internat. Inc. 1976–79; Dir., Candn. Psychiatric Rsch. Found.; Chrmn., Bd. of Trustees, Sedbergh Sch. Assoc., Montebello, Que.; Dir., St. Michael's Hosp.; R. Catholic; recreations: sailing, flying; Clubs: Toronto Club, Badminton & Racquet of Toronto; Home: 36 St. Andrews Gardens, Toronto, Ont. M4W 2E1; Office: 2 St. Clair Ave. W., Ste. 1700, Toronto, Ont. M4V 1L5.

**GRIFFIN, Stanley Ivan,** B.A., M.A., A.I.I.C.; insurance executive; b. Leamington, Ont. 31 May 1949; s. Donald Ivan and Marion Isabel (Dewhirst) G.; e. Univ. of Toronto B.A. 1972; Univ. of Chicago M.A. 1973; VICE-PRESIDENT, ONT., INSURANCE BUREAU OF CANADA 1992– ; Lectr. in Geography, Ryerson Polytechnical Inst. 1973–75; Research Officer, Insurance Bureau of Canada 1975; Manager, Econ. Research 1984; Vice-Pres., Insurance & Econ. Services 1990; Dir., Ont. Safety League; Mem., Insurance Inst. of Ont.; Empire Club; recreations: travel, arts; club: Ontario; Home: 2 Sultan St., #405, Toronto, Ont. M5S 1L7; Office: 181 University Ave., Toronto, Ont. M5H 3M7.

**GRIFFITH, Rev. A. Leonard,** D.D. (Ang. Ch.); b. Preston, Lancs., Eng. 19 Mar. 1920; s. Thomas Mostyn and Sarah Jane (Taylor) G.; both parents were prof. opera singers with companies touring the Brit. Isles; e. Wesley Coll., Dublin, Ireland; Brockville (Ont.) Coll. Inst.; McGill Univ., B.A. 1942; United Theol. Coll., B.D. 1945, D.D. 1962, Wycliffe Coll. D.D. (Hon.) 1985; ordained U.C. of Can. 1945; Ang. Church, 1975; m. Anne Merelie, d. Stanley B. Cayford of Montreal, Que., 17 June 1947; two d.; Associate Minister St. Paul's Church 1975–86 (retired); Asst. Min., St. Andrew's-Westmount Ch., Montreal, Que. 1941–44; Dominion-Douglas Ch., Montreal, Que. 1944–45; Min., Arden-Mountain Grove (Ont.) 1945–47; Trinity Ch., Grimsby, Ont. 1947–50; Chalmers Ch. Ottawa, Ont. 1950–60; City Temple, London, Eng. 1960–66; Deer Park United Church, Toronto 1966–75; Lectr. in Homiletics, Toronto School of Theology; Organist when at Divinity Hall, McGill Univ.; has been interested in theatre as actor and organizer with Brockville Theatre Guild, McGill Players, Montreal Repertory Theatre, C.B.C., Montreal and Grimsby Players' Guilds; author: 'From Sunday to Sunday'; 'Take Hold of the Treasure'; 'Reactions to God'; 'Gospel Characters'; 'We Have This Ministry'; 'Ephesians: A Positive Affirmation'; 'Hang on to the Lord's Prayer'; 'The Need to Preach'; and others; recreations: cottage life, gardening, walking, reading, adult education; Address: 91 Old Mill Rd., Etobicoke, Ont. M8X 1G9.

**GRIFFITH, Gwyneth P.,** B.A., M.S.W., Ed.D.; adult educator; b. Toronto, Ont. 30 June 1932; d. John Edward and Bona Mildred (Mills) G.; e. Univ. of Toronto B.A. (Hons.) 1953; Sch. of Social Work, Univ. of Toronto M.S.W. 1956; Union Theol. Sem., N.Y., Fellow, Prog., Adv. Religious Studies 1964–65; Ont. Inst. for Studies in Edn., Ed.D. 1982; EDUCATIONAL CONSULTANT (freelance); Social caseworker, Children's Aid Soc. of Ont. Co. 1953–58; Hamilton Children's Aid Soc. 1958–62; Dir. of Individual Serv., YWCA of Metro Toronto 1962–64; Branch Dir. 1965–67; Area Dir. 1967–69; Extve. Dir. 1971–77; Cons. for Leadership & Prog. Devel., YWCA of Can. 1969–71; Acad. Staff, Ctr. for Christian Studies 1980–82; Principal, Ctr. for Christian Studies 1982–91; Queen's Jubilee Medal 1977; active lay person, Un. Ch. of Can. holding various offices; author of articles & book chapters; Address: 154 Davisville Ave., Toronto, Ont. M4S 1E8.

**GRIFFITH, Julius,** R.C.A.; artist; b. Vancouver, B.C. 21 Apl. 1912; s. Julius Henry and Katharine Ada (Lindsay) G.; e. elem. & high schs. B.C.; L.C.C. Central Sch. of Arts & Crafts London, Eng. wood engraving tech.; Vancouver Sch. of Art studies with F.H. Varley & J.W.G. Macdonald 1928; B.C. Coll. Art; Royal Coll. of Art London, Eng. mural techniques 1935; Ont. Coll. Art etching, aquatint; m. Rachile d. Ilya and Sonya Orelovs 24 March 1944; children: David Julius, Lorne Michael, Ian Henry (dec.), Andrew Lindsay; part-time teaching positions incl. W. Tech. Comm. Sch., Artists Workshop, Central Tech. Sch. and Ryerson Polytech Inst. Toronto during 1950's and '60's; served with Air Raid Precautions Depot London and Red Cross 1939–42; RNVR (Sp.) 1942–46; over 90 works (drawings, paintings & wood engravings) Candn. War Museum; exhns. incl. Picture Loan Soc. Toronto (solo exhn. water colours 1954; others later); 20th Brooklyn Museum Show 1959; Art Gallery of Hamilton Retrospective Exhn. 1970; Rodman Hall Art Gallery Retrospective 1983; solo exhn. 1992 Libby's of Toronto '80 years'; rep. Nat. Gallery Can., British War Artists Coll., Art Gallery Ont., Art Gallery Hamilton, Glenbow Museum and other pub. and private colls.; author 'Watercolour' 1966; illus. 'River for My Sidewalk' 1953; recipient Centennial Medal 1967; Queen's Silver Jubilee Medal; mem. and Past Pres. Candn. Soc. Painters in Water Colour; mem. Ont. Soc. Artists; recreations: hiking, walking; Home: 102 Hillsdale Ave. W., Toronto, Ont. M5P 1G3.

**GRIFFITHS, Alison,** B.A.; writer; b. Summerside, PEI 23 Jan. 1953; d. Peter Gilbert and Patricia Margaret G.; e. Dalhousie Univ. B.A.; Univ. of Alta. 2 yrs. postgrad.; m. David Cruise; two d. Claudia, Quinn; writer primarily mag. articles 1979–86; writer non-fiction books 1986– ; co-author 'Fleecing the Lamb' 1987; 'Lords of the Line' 1988; 'Net Worth' 1991; Creator and co-host, 'The Score' a CBC-TV Sports Magazine show 1994– ; recipient Nat. Bus. Writing Award 1987; Silver Medal Nat. Mag. Awards 1986; Hon. Mention Candn. Investig. Jour. Award 1986; Address: 738 Selkirk Ave., Victoria, B.C. V9A 2T7.

**GRIFFITHS, Bryan P.;** bank executive; b. Toronto, Ont. 30 Dec. 1942; s. Victor Brian and Catherine Higgins (Brawley) G.; m. Wendy Yan 5 Nov. 1989; children: Lori-Anne, Corinna; SR. VICE-PRES., TREASURY OPERATIONS, ROYAL BANK OF CANADA 1991– ; various posts, Royal Bank of Canada (Montreal and area) 1960–68; Trainee Trader, Head Office & Jr. Fgn. Exchange Trader (UK) 1968; Sr. Fgn. Exchange Trader, H.O. 1970; Chief Trader, Fgn. Exchange 1972; various internat. money market trading mngt. positions incl. Vice-Pres., Global Trading 1976–82; Vice-Pres., Trading & Treas. Serv. 1982–87; Sr. Vice-Pres., Fgn. Exchange 1987–90; Dir., Royal Bank Mortgage Corp.; Past Pres., Forex Assn. of Can.; Office: 16th fl., South Tower Royal Bank Plaza, Toronto, Ont. M5J 2J5.

**GRIFFITHS, Donald John;** retired banker; b. Dudley, Eng. 24 Aug. 1920; s. Donald Cecil and Doris Rosalind (Purnell) G.; e. Dudley (Eng.) Grammar Sch., 1937; Oxford Univ., Honours Dipl. Econ. Studies, 1945; Carnegie Mellon Univ., Extve. course, 1970; m. Celia Doreen, d. James Carpenter, 15 March 1952; children: Peter John, Elaine, Joan Margaret; Consultant to Superintendent Financial Institutions; joined Barclays Bank Ltd. 1937; Barclays Bank (Can.), Montreal 1947–56; Imperial Bank of Can. 1956–62; Candn. Imperial Bank of Commerce Asst. Mgr. Montreal Br. 1962–66, Regional Gen. Mgr. Que. 1969, Vice Pres. and Regional Gen. Mgr. Que. 1970, Vice-Pres. Europe, Africa, Middle East 1973–80, Extve. Vice Pres. 1982–83, retired 1984; served with RAF 1940–45; attached RCAF 419 Sqdn. 1943–45; Fellow, Inst. Candn. Bankers; Fellow, Chartered Inst. Bankers, Eng.; Anglican; recreations: golf, skiing; Home: 1284 Minaki Rd., Mississauga, Ont. L5G 2X4.

**GRIFFITHS, Franklyn John Charles,** Ph.D.; educator; b. Edinburgh, Scot. 8 Sept. 1935; s. John Francis and Tamara Juliana (Wender) G.; e. Ridley Coll. St. Catharines, Ont. 1953; Trinity Coll. Univ. of Toronto B.A. 1958; Columbia Univ. Sch. of Internat. Affairs M.I.A. 1962, Dept. Pub. Law & Govt. Ph.D. 1972; m. Margaret Reva d. late James Hogarth 18 Oct. 1958; children: Tamara Juliana, Rudyard John Francis; PROF. OF POL. SCI., UNIV. OF TORONTO 1973– ; Visiting Prof., Stanford Univ., Palo Alto, Ca. 1987–88; Sr. Policy Adv., Office of the Sec. of State for External Affairs 1986–87; Ed., Pergamon Inst., London and Oxford 1958–60; Researcher, Candn. Peace Rsch. Inst. Toronto 1962–63 and M.I.T. Center for Internat. Studies Cambridge, Mass. 1963–64; Asst. Prof. of Pol. Econ. Univ. Toronto 1966, Dir. Centre for Russian & E. European Studies 1975–79; recipient Ford Foundation Award arms control 1976; Fellow, Woodrow Wilson Internat. Center, Smithsonian Inst. 1979; commentator on pub. affairs incl. Candn. foreign policy, internat. security affairs, arctic internat. relations; author 'Khrushchev and the Arms Race' 1966; Ed., 'Politics of the Northwest Passage' 1987; 'Arctic Alternatives: Civility or Militarism in the Circumpolar North' 1992; co-ed. and contrib. 'Interest Groups in Soviet Politics' 1971; 'The Dangers of Nuclear War' 1979: author various articles, short studies; Co-Chair, Working Group on Arctic Internat. Relations 1988–91; Co-chair, Arctic Council Panel 1990– ; Mem. of Adv. Counc., Centre for Arms Control and Disarmament; Candn. Assn. Slavists (Pres. 1978–79); mem. Council, Comite Arctique International; recreations: squash, guitar; Home: 360 Brunswick Ave., Toronto, Ont. M5R 2Y9; Office: 100 St. George St., Toronto, Ont. M5S 1A1.

**GRIFFITHS, James C.,** C.A.; financial executive; b. Long Island, NY 21 Aug. 1946; m. Helen Robinson; children: Katherine, Leigh, Christine; PRESIDENT, REALFUND; C.A.; Bd. of Dir., Branksome; Office: 151 Yonge St., Toronto, Ont. M5C 2W7.

**GRIFFITHS, Naomi E.S.,** M.A., Ph.D.; b. Hove, England 20 Apr. 1934; d. Robert Lewis and Agnes Mary (Saunders) G.; e. Lewes Co. Grammar Sch. for Girls; London Univ. Bedford Coll. B.A. 1956, Ph.D. 1969; Univ. of N.B., M.A. 1957; Dean, Faculty of Arts, Carleton Univ. 1979–87 and Prof. of Hist. since 1978; Lectr. Coll. Maillet 1957–58; joined present Univ. as Instr. in Hist. 1961, Lectr. 1962, Asst. Prof. 1964, Pres. Acad. Staff Assn. 1971–72; rec'd State Scholarship 1953–56, Goldsmith Travelling Scholarship 1956, Univ. N.B. Grad. Fellowship 1956–57, Lord Beaverbrook Overseas Travelling Fellowship 1958–60, Can. Council post-doctoral research grant 1971, 1972, 1973; Shastri Fellowship to visit India 1987; Winthrop Pickard Bell Chair in Maritime Studies, Mount Allison Univ. July-Dec. 1988; Chairwoman CAUT Comte. on Status Acad. Women in Can. 1973; author 'The Acadian Deportation: Deliberate Perfidy or Cruel Necessity' 1969, 'The Acadians: Creation of a People' 1973, 'Penelope's Web, Some Perceptions of Women in European and Canadian Society' 1976; 'Contexts of Acadian History' 1991; (with G. Rawlyk) 'Mason Wade Quebec and Acadia: The Perception of an Outsider' 1991; 'The Splendid Vision: The History of the National Council of Women of Canada' 1993; also pamphlets, articles and reviews; TV programmes various topics and script for ETV '1755'; hon. mem. Candn. Research Inst. for Advanc. Women (mem. Bd. of Dirs.) 1975–78; apptd. mem., Ontario Press Counc. 1987; awarded hon. doctorate in hist., Univ. de Moncton 1988 and Univ. de St. Anne 1990; el. F.R.S.C. 1990; NDP; R. Catholic; recreations: music, science fiction, cooking, cross-country skiing; Home: 38 Glencairn, Ottawa, Ont. K1S 1M6.

**GRIFFITHS, Hon. Wilson David;** b. Owen Sound, Ont. 28 May 1925; s. Leonard Whitney and Jean Mearns (Davidson) G.; e. Pub. and High Schs., Owen Sound; Univ. of Toronto, Victoria Coll. B.A. Law (Hons.) 1948, Post Grad. LL.B. 1950; Gold Key, Osgoode Hall 1951; Upper Canada Law Soc. Hon. LL.D. 1983; m. Doris Jean, d. late Aylmer Plowright 4 Sept. 1948; children: Pamela Read, Brenda, Bradley, Wilson; apptd. JUSTICE TO THE COURT OF APPEAL FOR ONT. 1987– ; JUSTICE, SUPREME COURT OF ONT.; appt'd. Deputy Judge N.W.T. 9 June 1983, of Yukon Territory 2 Dec. 1982; read law with Haines and Haines 1948–49 and Fraser Beatty Tucker & McIntosh 1950–51; called to the Bar of Ont. 1951; cr. Q.C. 1962; Jr. Solr. J. Donald Bell, Toronto 1951–53; Partner, Bell Keith Ganong & Griffiths, Toronto 1953–56; Bell Griffiths Temple & Genest 1956–66; Sr. Partner, Cassels Brock 1966–75; served as Wireless Navig. 1943–44, with Candn. Army 1944–45, rank Lt.; Past Bencher, Law Soc. Upper Can. (Lectr. and Instr., Head of Civil Procedure, Bar Admission Course 1959–75; Lectr., panelist, sometime Chrmn. 16 Cont. Legal Educ. series; Vice Chrmn., Ont. Legal Aid Plan 1971–75; Chrmn., Prepaid Legal Services Comte.; Errors & Omissions Ins. Comte. 1971–75); Chrmn., (1960–71) Civil Justice Sec., Co. of York Law Assn.; Chrmn. (1963–74) Ins. Sec., Candn. Bar Assn.; mem. Council (1972–75) Medico-Legal Soc. of Toronto; Hon. mem. Am. Trial Lawyer Assn.; Dir. (1968–71. Pres. 1971–72) The Advocates' Soc.; LL.D. (hon.), Law Soc. of Upper Can. 1983; Chrmn. (1956–57) Building Comte., W. Ellesmere United Ch.; Hon. Life Mem., Guildwood Community Assn.; United Ch.; recreations: flying, skiing, fishing, sailing, golf; Clubs: Toronto Hunt; Ontario; Home: 19 Somerdale Square, Scarborough, Ont. M1E 1M9; Office: Osgoode Hall, Toronto, Ont. M5H 2N5.

**GRIGGS, Terry,** B.A., M.A.; writer; b. Little Current, Manitoulin Is. 20 Dec. 1951; d. John Joseph and Janet Marshall (Scott) G.; e. Univ. of West. Ont. B.A. 1977, M.A. 1979; m. David s. George and Patricia Burr 17 Nov. 1978; one s.: Alexander Galen Griggs-Burr; stories published in a number of lit. mags. & the following anthologies: 'The New Press Anthology: Best Canadian Short Fiction #1' 1984, 'The Macmillan Anthology 1' 1988, 'The Journey Prize Anthology 2' 1990, 'The Third Macmillan Anthology' 1990, 'Street Songs 1: New Voices in Fiction' 1990; 'The New Story Writers' 1992; Teaching Asst., U.W.O. 1977–78; Book Reviewer, 'The London Free Press' 1980–84; Readings co-ord., Forest City Gall. London Ont. 1987–88, 1989–90; Mem., Forest City Gall. 1986–91; author: 'Harrier' 1982 (chapbook), 'Quickening' 1990 (short stories; Finalist 1991 Governor General's Awards (Fiction)); Home: 272 Grosvenor St., London, Ont. N6A 1Y8.

**GRILLER, David,** B.Sc., Ph.D., F.C.I.C., F.R.S.C.; science and technology consultant; research chemist; b. London, Eng. 29 May 1948; s. Lewis and Renee (Kellinger) G.; e. Univ. Coll., London B.Sc. 1969, Ph.D. 1972; m. Alexis Myers 22 Aug. 1971; children: Hannah, Mark, Nadia; PRINCIPAL, GROUPE SECOR; Salters Co. fellow, London 1973; postdoct. fellow, NRC 1973–75; mngt. cons., Deloitte, Haskins & Sells, London 1975–77; Head, Organic Chem., Nat. Rsch. Counc. of Can. 1977–91; author of over 180 sci. papers & books; Recipient CNC-Iupac award, Internat. Union Pure & App. Chem. 1984; Fellow, Candn. Inst. Chem. (Merck Sharp & Dohme award 1985); Royal Soc. of Can., Rutherford Medal 1986, Fellow 1988; recreations:

squash, skiing; Home: 2026 Delmar Ct., Ottawa, Ont. K1H 5R6; Office: 155 Queen St., Ottawa, Ont. K1P 6L1.

**GRIMARD, Hon. Normand,** B.A., LL.L., Q.C.; senator, lawyer; b. Rigaud, Que. 16 June 1925; s. Emile and Antoinette (Le Sieur Désaulniers) G.; e. St. Joseph's Seminary B.A. 1946; Laval Univ. LL.L. 1949; m. Dorothy d. Techon and Lizaveta Kurus; children: Marc, Louise, Monique; SENATOR, SENATE OF CANADA 1990– ; called to Barreau du Québec 1949; Q.C. 1959; served as Bâtonnier of the Barreau d'Abitibi-Témiscamingue; Sr. Partner, Grimard Gagné TRUDEL (Rouyn-Noranda, Ville-Marie (Témiscamingue), Val-d'Or & La Sarre (Abitibi); specialist in insurance law; Pres., Que. Mining Comn. formed by Prov. of Que. to formulate a new Mining & Natural Gas Act 1957; Pres., African Chamber of Commerce and Industry of Can. 1992– ; Cttes. Mem., Joint Chrmn. of Standing Ctte. for the Scrutiny of Regulations; Ctte. Mem. and Acting Chrmn., Privileges, Standing Rules and Orders; P.C.; Bd. Mem., C. de C. de Qué. 1957–60; Pres., La Soc. Richelieu Internat. 1954; recreations: golf, reading, clubs: Le Club Laval-sur-le-Lac, Club Saint-Denis; Home: 77 Tremoy, Rouyn-Noranda, Que. J9X 1W2; Office: Rm. 503, Victoria Bldg., Ottawa, Ont. K1A 0A4.

**GRIMES, Douglas Robert,** B.Eng., M.Sc., P.Eng.; consulting engineer/executive; b. Montreal, Que. 22 June 1932; s. James Duncan and Anna Louise (McCullough) G.; e. McGill Univ. B.Eng. (Hons.) 1954; Queen's Univ. M.Sc. 1956; m. Elizabeth d. John and May Clements 21 Aug. 1954; children: Bruce Robert, Michael John, Wendy Elizabeth, Douglas James; PRES., WARDROP ENGINEERING INC. 1987– ; Lectr., Civil Engr., Royal Military Coll. 1954–56; Bridge Engr., Public Works Can. 1956–59; Cons. Engr., Winnipeg 1959–62; joined Wardrop Engr. Inc. 1962 (Dir. 1964, Vice-Pres. 1975); Dir., Ancast Indus. Limited; Acres Wardrop; Dir., Tetres Consultants Inc.; Past Pres., Assn. of Profl. Engrs. of Man.; Assn. of Cons. Engr. of Man.; Winnipeg Boys & Girls Clubs; club: Manitoba; Home: 191 Victoria Cres., Winnipeg, Man. R2M 1X6; Office: 386 Broadway, Winnipeg, Man. R3C 4M8.

**GRIMES, Hon. Roger D.,** B.Sc., B.Ed., M.Ed.; politician; b. Grand Falls, Nfld. 2 May 1950; s. Fred and Winnie Pearl (Rideout) G.; e. Memorial Univ. B.Sc., B.Ed. 1972, M.Ed. 1988; one d.: Victoria Carol; MINISTEROF EMPLOYMENT & LABOUR RELATIONS, GOVT. OF NEWFOUNDLAND 1991– ; High School Teacher 1972–88; Pres. & Dir., Nfld. Teachers' Assn. 1985–87; 1st elected as Member of Nfld. House of Assembly 20 Apr. 1989; apptd. Parl. Asst. to the Premier 1989; re-elected M.H.A. (Exploits) 1993; Mem. (player category), Nfld. Baseball Hall of Fame; recreations: golf, softball, hockey, reading; Home: 41 Baird Pl., St. John's, Nfld. A1B 2A7; Office: P.O. Box 8700, St. John's, Nfld. A1B 4J6.

**GRIMLEY, Peter H.,** B.Sc., Ph.D.; exploration geologist; b. Blackpool, England 18 Oct. 1933; s. Hugh & Ruth (Greenwood) G.; e. Royal Sch. of Mines, B.Sc. (Min. Geol.) 1955, ARSM 1955; Imp. Coll. Dipl. (DIC) 1958; Univ. of London, Ph.D. (Mining Geol.) 1958; m. Patricia Harriet, d. Stephen William Still, 29 Sept. 1961; children: Simon Jonathon, Judith Sarah; COOPERS AND LYBRAND CONSULTING GROUP since 1986; field work E. Africa 1955–58; Geol. on expdn. to Karakoram Himalayas, W. Pakistan, 1957; exploration activities in Can. 1959; geol. & topographical exploration in Antarctica 1959–61; Exploration Mgr. various exploration activities, Argentina, 1961–66; joined Brinco Ltd. 1966; Vice-Pres. and Exploration Mgr., Brinex 1972–81; Vice-Pres., Brinco Ltd.; Vice Pres., Corporate Banking, Bank of Montreal 1981–86; awarded Polar Medal; Fellow, Inst. Mining & Metall., London; mem., Candn. Inst. Mining & Metall.; Anglican; recreation: fishing; Clubs: Antarctic, Engineers; Home: R.R. #2, Orton, Ont. L0N 1N0; Office: Coopers and Lybrand, 145 King St. W., Toronto, Ont. M5H 1J8.

**GRISÉ, Yolande,** B.A., L.èsL., M.èsL., D.èsL. de 3e cycle; professeure d'université; née. Montréal, Qué. 5 août 1944; f. Arthur et Gertrude (Tougas) G.; é. Univ. de Montréal B.A. 1965, Univ. Laval L.èsL. 1971; Univ. de la Sorbonne M.èsL. 1972, D.èsL. de 3e cycle 1977; PROFESSEURE DE LITTÉRATURE AU DÉPARTEMENT DES LETTRES FRANÇAISES DE L'UNIV. D'OTTAWA 1980– ; Prof. d'hist. romaine, Dép. d'Hist., l'Univ. Laval 1978–79; Prof. adjointe, Dép. des lettres françaises, l'Univ. d'Ottawa 1980; Prof. agrégée 1983; Directrice, Ctr. de rech. en civilisation canadienne-française, Univ. d'Ottawa 1985–88, 1989–91, 1991–94; Boursière, Gouv. du Qué. 1971–72, 1972–75; Conseil des arts du Can. 1972–75; Prés., jury du Prix litt. du Gouv. gén., catégorie 'Études et essais' 1989; Groupe de travail min. pour l'élaboration de la prem. pol. culturelle des francophones de l'Ont. Toronto 1991; mem., Cercle Horace-Viau, Fond. Richelieu Internat. 1992; Bureau de dir., Fed. can. des études humaines 1991–93; Conseil des arts de l'Ont. 1991–94 (Prés. 1991–94); Com. pour le français dans les comm. francophones et acadienne du Can., Conseil de la langue française du Qué. 1992–93; Soc. des études latines (Paris); l'Union des écrivains québécois; l'Assoc. des études canadiennes; l'Assoc. des litt. can. et québécoise; auteure: 'Le suicide dans la Rome antique' 1982, 'Textes littéraires de l'Ontario français' (anthologie en 4 vols) 1982, 'Le Monde des dieux' 1985, 'Les Arts visuels en Ontario français' 1990, 'Émile Nelligan, Cinquante ans après sa mort' 1993 (Co-dir.); auteure de nombreux articles spécialisés en études anciennes au Canada et en Europe et a participé à des jurys academ. et litt.; Directrice et co-auteure: 'Les Textes poétiques du Canada français, 1606–1867' (12 vols; à date, six vols ont paru) 1987– ; rés.: 196, rue Cobourg, Ottawa, Ont. K1N 8H6; bureau: 145, rue Jean-Jacques-Lussier, Ottawa, Ont. K1N 6N5.

**GROGONO, Peter David,** Ph.D.; educator; b. London, Eng. 24 May 1944; s. Noel Desmond and Moira Katharine (Gladstone) G.; e. Forest Sch. Walthamstow, London 1961; Queens' Coll. Cambridge, B.A. 1965, M.A. 1973; Concordia Univ. Montréal, M.C.S. 1980, Ph.D. (Computer Sci.) 1984; m. Sharon d. Rubie and Brenda Nelson 8 Jan. 1972; ASST. PROF. OF COMPUTER SCI., CONCORDIA UNIV. 1984– ; Pres. Metonymy Productions (Canada 96616 Inc.); Dir. Film Festival Cardiff Commonwealth Arts Festival 1965; Dir. Electronic Music Studios London; author 'Programming in Pascal' 1978, 1980, 1984; 'MOUSE: A Language for Microcomputers' 1983; co-author 'Problem Solving and Computer Programming' 1982; Dir. Sci. for Peace 1981–84; mem. Adv. Bd. 1986– ; mem. Assn. Computing Machinery; Inst. Elect. & Electronic Engs.; recreation: photography; Office: 1455 de Maisonneuve Blvd. W., Montréal, Qué. H3G 1M8.

**GRONDIN, C.R.,** B.Ed., M.Ed., Ph.D.; university professor; b. St. Jacques, N.B. 23 Aug. 1938; e. Coll. Saint-Louis 1955; R.C.A.F. Cold Lake, Alta. Sr. Matric. 1963; Univ. of Alta. B.Ed. 1967, M.Ed. 1969, Ph.D. 1975; m. Dr. Deirdre Thomas-Grondin 16 Sept. 1963; children: Sheila, Sean, Tanya; PROFESSOR, DEPT. OF POLITICAL SCIENCE, UNIV. OF NEW BRUNSWICK 1970– ; Mem., R.C.A.F. 1955–63; Extve. Asst., Leader of the Opposition, Prov. of N.B. (on special leave from U.N.B.) 1983; Guest, Political Analyst & Commentator on Prov. & Fed. Political Affairs for CBC French & English Prov. & Nat. Networks & ATV Networks 1975– ; Interviews for the N.B. Prov. Cable Network on 'Opposition Forum,' 'Government Forum,' 'Provincial Prospectus,' and 'Survol Provincial' 1989– ; Mem., Adv. Bd., The Dushkin Publishing Groups, Inc. for 'Canadian Politics'; Roman Catholic; Mem., Candn. Pol. Sci. Assn. (Ctte. for Teaching Pol. Sci. in Community Colleges & High Schools 1972–74; Research Policy Ctte. 1976–78; resp. for devel. of a research 'Code of Ethics'); author: 'Concerns of New Brunswickers' 1984, 'Personal Attributes and Political Leadership' 1989, 'Redistricting' (research project for Royal Comn. on Electoral Reform & Party Financing) 1990, one book chapter: 'The Export Orientation of Female Entrepreneurs in New Brunswick' in 'Proceedings of the Academic of International Business' 1991 (best paper award); also author/co-author of several journal articles and of a collection of 58 statistical profiles of N.B. electoral districts (1991); recreations: fishing, fly tyer, woodworking; Home: Mary Ellen Dr., Comp. 34, Site 19, RR #6, Fredericton, N.B. E3B 4X7; Office: P.O. Box 4400, Fredericton, N.B. E3B 5A3.

**GRONDIN, Pierre,** O.C. (1968), M.D., F.R.C.S.(C), F.A.C.S.; né Québec, 18 août 1925, f. G. Antoine et Germaine (Fortier) G.; é. Univ. Laval, Québec, B.A., magna cum laude, 1945; M.D., magna cum laude, 1951; Conseil Nat. de. Méd. du Canada, L.M.C.C., 1951; Univ. de Pennsylvanie, chirurgie, 1955; Calif. Board of Med. Examiners, licence, 1956; Coll. Royal du Canada, F.R.C.S. (chirurgie); Coll. des Méd. et Chirurgiens du Qué., C.S.P.Q., 1959; F.A.C.S., 1960; Univ. Baylor, Houston, Texas, chirurgie thoracique cardiaque, 1961–62; enfants: Louis, Jean; MEDECIN-CHIRURGIEN, HÔPITAL LAVAL DE QUÉBEC; méd. gén., Trois-Rivières, Qué., 1951; pratique chirurgie gén., Trois-Rivières, 1960–61; consultant, Hôpital Ste-Marie, Trois Rivières et Cloutier, Cap de la Madeleine; Prof. associé de chirurgie clinique, Univ. Laval, Qué., 1961; Chef résident, chirurgie cardiaque et vasculaire, Children et St. Lukes Hospitals, Houston, Texas, 1962; Chef du départ. de chirurgie cardiaque et vasculaire et du départ. de chirurgie expérimentale, Inst. de Cardiologie de Montréal, 1963; Consultant en chirurgie cariovasculaire, Hôpital Jean-Talon, Montreal et Hôpital St-Joseph, Trois-Rivières, 1963; Medecin-Chirurgien, Institut de Cardiologie de Montreal 1963; Membre associé, chirurgie cardio-vasculaire, Hôpital Jean-Talon, Montréal, 1965; Consultant chirurgie thoracique et cardio vasculaire, Hôpital Fleury, Montréal, 1966; et Hôpital, Bellechasse, Montréal, 1967; Membre fondateur, The Society of Thoracic Surgery, 1966; Membre: Soc. Can. de Cardiologie; Soc. de Cardiologie de Montréal, Assoc. des Méd. de Langue Fr., Soc. Méd. Can., Assoc. de Chirurgie Thoraciques et Cardio-vasculaire de la Prov. de Qué.; Soc. Française de Chirurgie Thoracique; Soc. Espagnole de Cardiologie; decoré de Lords de Christophe Colomb (Republique Dominicainne); Auteur de plus de 125 articles sur la chirurgie cardio-vasculaire et la greffe du coeur humain; Prix Bergeron, Univ. Laval et le Laval Méd., 1961; Médaille Bene Merenti de Patria, Soc. St-Jean Baptiste, 1968; Personalité de l'Année 1968, Assoc. des Hommes d'Affaires et Prof. Can.-Italiens Inc.; Catholique; Loisirs: sports d'hiver et d'été; Office: 2725 Ste-Foy, Québec, Qué. G1V 4G5.

**GROOME, Reginald K.;** O.C.; hotel executive; b. Montreal, Que. 18 Dec. 1927; s. late Muriel Harbord (Forbes-Toby) and Cyril Thomas G.; e. Willingdon Elem. Sch., Montreal; Montreal High Sch.; McGill Univ., Montreal; Cornell Univ., Ithaca, N.Y.; m. Christina Marie Florence, d. Alfred George Walker, 20 June 1953; SPECIAL ADVISOR TO PRESIDENT, CANADIAN PACIFIC HOTELS & RESORTS 1991– ; Dir., Industrial-Alliance Life Insurance Co.; Impact Corp.; Groupe Trans-A.T. Inc.; Voyageur Insurance Co.; Assured Assistance Inc.; started career as journalist with Montreal Publishing Co., served as overseas correspondent 1951; joined Hilton Canada Inc. at Queen Elizabeth Hotel 1957; Chrmn. and Pres., Hilton Canada Inc. 1972–90; invested with Silver Acorn 1964 (Boy Scouts of Can.) by Gov. Gen. Vanier; Outstanding Citizen Award by Montreal Citizenship Council, 1976; Queen's Jubilee Medal 1977; B'nai B'rith Inaugural Award of Merit 1978; Invested with Silver Wolf (Boy Scouts of Can.) by Gov. Gen. Léger 1978; Meritorious Citizen's Award from Lt. Gov. Jean-Pierre Coté, Quebec 1980; invested as Officer. Order of Can. by Gov. Gen. Schreyer, 1980; free lance broadcaster since 1946, now with CIQC (Montreal); Chrmn., Hotel Assn. of Canada 1991–93; Past Pres. Montreal Bd. of Trade; Past Chrmn., United Way of Can.; Chrmn. Bd. of Govs., Concordia Univ., Life Gov. Montreal Gen. Hosp.; Hon. Vice Pres. & Past Pres. & Past Internat. Commis., Boy Scouts of Can.; recreations: water skiing, boating; Club: Mount Royal; Address: 3577 Atwater Ave., Apt. 207, Montreal, Que. H3H 2R2.

**GROSMAIRE, Jean-Louis,** Ph.D.; professeur; né à Abidjan, Côte- d'Ivoire, 27 mai 1944; f. Pierre et Suzanne (Parisot) G.; é. Sorbonne, Licence en Histoire et Géographie 1966, Maîtrise en Géographie 1967; Univ. de Montréal, Ph.D. 1981; PROFESSEUR, COLL. DE L'OUTAOUAIS 1975– ; Prof. à Londres 1965–66, à Paris 1967–68; à Montréal 1969–74; un des initiateurs et responsable du jumelage entre la Franche-Comté et l'Outaouais; auteur 'L'Attrape-Mouche' 1985, 'Un Clown en Hiver' 1988: Prix Littéraire du Journal 'Le Droit' Ottawa 1989; 'Paris-Québec' 1992: Prix Littéraire du Journal 'Le Droit' Ottawa 1993; 'Rendez-Vous à Hong Kong' 1993; co-auteur 'Initiation à la géographie générale' 1974; réalisateur du film: 'Momotombo' (Nicaragua) 1991; nombreux articles; Catholique; membre de l'union des écrivains du Qué.; L'Assn. des auteurs de l'Outaouais; honoré par l'Assoc. Québec-France pour sa contribution exceptionnelle à l'essor des relations franco-québécoises 1990; récréations: ski, planche à voile, course, natation; Adresse: 43 Ch. Fraser, Aylmer, Qué. J9H 2H1; Bureau: 333 Cité des Jeunes, Hull, Qué.

**GROSMAN, Brian Allen,** Q.C. B.A., LL.B., LL.M.; b. Toronto, Ont. 20 May 1935; s. Morris and Bessie Celia (Benson) G.; e. Forest Hill Coll. Inst. Toronto 1954; Univ. of Toronto B.A. 1957, LL.B. 1960; Osgoode Hall 1961; McGill Univ. LL.M. 1967; m. Penny-Lynn d. Arthur George Cookson, Calgary, Alta. Verna Cookson, Saskatoon, Sask. 1 Sept. 1967; one s. John Shain; SR. PARTNER, GROSMAN, GROSMAN & GALE; read law with Harries, Houser, Brown & Houlden, Toronto; called to Bar of Ont. 1962, Bar of Sask. 1971; private law practice Toronto 1962–66 in assn. with Burrell M. Singer; assoc. with firm Greenberg, Gorsky & Greenberg, Ottawa 1966; Special Prosecutor to Ministry of Justice (part-time) 1964–65; Teaching Fellow McGill Univ. 1966; Fellow N.Y. Univ. Inst. Comparative Criminal Law 1966; Asst. Prof. McGill Univ. 1966–68, Assoc. Prof. 1969–71; Prof. of Law, Coll. of Law, Univ. of Sask., 1971–79; Founding Chrmn. Law Reform Comn.

Sask. 1974–1978; Partner, Greenglass & Grosman 1979–82; Lawyer in Private Practice 1982–90; Visiting Prof. Univ. of Free Berlin 1968; Russell Sage Fellow Univ. of Denver 1969; Consultant: Royal Comn. on Status of Women in Can. 1970; Law Reform Comn. of Can. Project on Criminal Procedure 1972–73; Canadian Wildlife Service, A Survey of Resource Sharing Agreements (3 Vols.); Ont. Task Force on Policing 1972; City of Winnipeg Comte. Studying Unification Police Forces Greater Winnipeg 1972; Nat. Adv. Comte. Task Force on Disorders and Terrorism Washington 1976; apptd. one-man Comn. Inquiry into Police Organ. and Structure P.E.I. 1974; Candn. del. Conf. Centre Internat. de Criminologie Comparee Versailles, France 1971; Candn. Rep. l'Indice Penale Internat. Criminol. Quarterly Univ. of Milan; Sask. Commr. Uniformity Conf. Can. 1974–77; Chrmn. Conf. Natives and the Law McGill Univ. 1970 and Que. Conf. on Crime and Delinquency 1969; Moderator Unitel Univ. of Sask. Educ. TV 1972–73; Chrmn. Senate Comte. Discrimination as to Sex at Univ. McGill 1970; Chrmn. Conf. on Human Rights and the Adm. of Justice, 1980–81; Host-Moderator 'The Law Belongs to You,' C.J.R.T. 1987–88; rec'd. Candn. Bar Foundation Award for Legal Research 1966; author 'The Prosecutor, An Inquiry into the Exercise of Discretion' 1969; 'Police Command: Decisions and Discretion' 1975; 'New Directions in Sentencing' 1980; 'The Executive Firing Line: Wrongful Dismissal and the Law' 1982; 'Fire Power' 1985; 'Corporate Loyalty' 1988; 'Employment Law in Ontario' 1991; 'Fire Proofing, Job Protection for the Nineties' 1992; Ed.-in-Chief, The Employment Bulletin' 1991–94; contrib. to 'Canadian Bar Review' 1982 and 'Conflict Quarterly' 1980–82; also various articles, book chapters, booklets, surveys and reports including 'The Grosman Report on Policing in PEI' 1974, 'New Developments in Wrongful Dismissal' 1983 and video 'Corporate Loyalty' 1990; Assoc. Secy. Gen., Que. Soc. Criminol. 1968–69 (Vice Pres. 1969–70); Life mem. Internat. Soc. Study Comparative Law: mem. Am. Judicature Soc.; Internat. Assn. De Droit Penale; Internat. Conf. Criminal Law; Am. Soc. Criminol. (Extve. 1973; rec'd Presidential Citation 1975); Am. Law Inst.; Advocate's Soc. of Ont. (Dir. 1982–85); Candn. Assn. Law Teachers; mem. Adv. Council, Candn. Human Rights Foundation (1975–81); mem., Metropolitan Toronto Police Complaints Bd. (1982–86); Law Soc. Upper Can.; Ont. Bar Assn.; Law Soc. Sask.; Sask. Bar Assn.; Candn. Bar Assn. (Council 1974–76); Delegate, U.S./China Joint Session on Trade and Economic Law 1987; Chrmn. of Bd., Metro Cond. #692 1989–90; Jewish; recreations: riding, travel; Club: Cambridge; Home: 4 Lowther Ave., Apt. 309, Toronto, Ont. M5R 1C6; Office: One Queen St. E., Ste. 1410, Toronto, Ont. M5C 2W5.

**GROSS, Michael Robert,** P.Eng.; executive; b. Toronto, Ont. 10 Sept. 1940; s. Harold and Roslyn (Abrams) G.; e. Forest Hill Coll. Inst. Toronto 1959; Rensselaer Polytechnic Inst. Troy, N.Y. B.Mgt.Eng. 1964; m. Jo-Anne d. Roy and Yvette Hacquard 30 June 1976; two s. David Charles, Jeffrey Ross; PRES. GROSS MACHINERY GROUP 1978– ; joined present co. 1964; Gov. Mount Sinai Hosp.; mem. Assn. Prof. Engs. Prov. Ont.; Young Pres.' Orgn. (XPO); Variety Club; recreations: boating, tennis; Clubs: Oakdale Golf & Country; York Racquets; Home: 482 Russell Hill Rd., Toronto, Ont. M5P 2S7; Office: 18 Lower Jarvis St., Toronto, Ont. M5E 1N1.

**GROSS, Hon. Reginald John,** M.L.A.; politician; b. Vanguard, Sask. 3 Oct. 1948; s. Edward W. and Emilia T. (Biesek) G.; e. Glen Bain (Sask.) Elem. Sch.; Kincaid (Sask.) Central High Sch.; children: Jeffrey, Theodore, Taylore, Alexis; MIN. OF GOVT. SERVICES AND MIN. OF TOURISM & RENEWABLE RESOURCES, SASK. 1979– ; el. M.L.A. for Gravelbourg 1971, def. 1974, re-el. 1978; Chrmn. of Bd., Sask. Minerals; Sask. Fur Marketing Service; Secy.-Treas. Glenwood Co-op; Dir., Phoenix Group; mem. Nat. Farmers Union; NDP; R. Catholic; recreation: skiing; Home: 279 Reed Ave., Regina, Sask. S4T 7H2; Office: 1106 – 2500 Victoria Ave., Regina, Sask. S4P 3X2.

**GROSSBERG, Frederick Alan,** Ph.D.; educator; b. Toronto, Ont. 16 May 1946; s. Benjamin and Elise Hart (Green) G.; e. Forest Hill Coll. Inst. 1964; Univ. of Toronto B.A. 1968; Oxford Univ. (Rhodes Scholar) 1968–70; Harvard Univ. Ph.D. 1975; m. Laurie Smith 20 Oct. 1985; Asst. Prof. of Eng., George Mason Univ. 1974–83, Assoc. Prof. 1983–88; Project Dir. 'Televised Models of Teaching Writing' (fed. grant Edn. Div. Nat. Endowment for Humanities) 1978–83; Producer, Dir. and Co-author 'Teachers Teaching Writing' (6 videotapes and workshop guides for teacher edn.) 1984; Dir., Robert F. Kennedy Memorial 1990–91; Internat. Educ. Cons., Acad. for Educ. Development 1992–93; recipient Gov. Gen.'s Gold Medal in English 1968; Gov. Gen.'s Medal for Best Degree any Honours Course Univ. Coll. 1968; Woodrow Wilson Hon. Fellowship 1968; Imperial Oil of Canada Grad. Rsch. Fellowship 1970–73; Harvard Grad. Sch. of Arts & Sci. Grad. Prize Fellowship 1970–74; Can. Counc. Doctoral Fellowship 1972–74; mem. YMCA; Candn. Assn. of Rhodes Scholars 1970– ; recreations: racquetball, body surfing, skiing; Home: #405, 2456 20th St. N.W., Washington, D.C. 20009.

**GROSSKURTH, Phyllis,** M.A., Ph.D.; educator; author; b. Toronto, Ont. 16 March 1924; d. Milton Palmer and Winifred Agnes (Owen) Langstaff; e. St. Clement's Sch., Toronto, Ont.; Univ. of Toronto, B.A. 1946; Univ. of Ottawa, M.A. 1960; Univ. of London, Ph.D. 1962; m.; children: Christopher, Brian, Ann; author of 'John Addington Symonds' (biography) 1964 (Gov. Gen. Lit. Award for 1965; University of B.C. Award for Biography 1965); 'Havelock Ellis' 1980; ed. 'Memoirs of John Addington Symonds' 1984; 'Melanie Klein: Her World and Her Work' 1986; 'Margaret Mead: A Life of Controversy' 1989; 'The Secret Ring: Freud's Inner Circle and Politics of Psychoanalysis' 1991; articles in 'Review of English Literature,' 'Review of English Studies,' 'Modern Language Review,' 'University of Toronto Quarterly,' 'The New York Review of Books,' 'The Times Literary Supplement,' etc.; Prof. Emeritus, Dept. of English, Univ. of Toronto; Prof., Humanities and Psychoanalytic Thought program, Univ. of Toronto 1986– ; mem., Nat. Film Bd. Can. 1968–74; Book Ed., 'The Canadian Forum' 1975–76; Short list for National Book Award (U.K.), 1981; Canada Council Leave Fellowship 1969–70; 1976–77; John Simon Guggenheim Memorial Fellowship, 1977–78; Killam Fellowship, 1978–80; Laidlaw Fellowship, 1980–82; Rockefeller Fellowship, 1982; Fellow, Univ. of Kent; Social Sciences and Humanities Rsch. Grant 1989–92; Hon. Research Fellow, University College, London, 1978–82; John Simon Guggenheim Memorial Fellowship, 1983; Finalist, Governor General's Award 1987; Canada Counc. Arts Award 1989–90; D.S.L., Trinity Coll., Univ. of Toronto 1992; Anglican; Address: New College, University of Toronto, Toronto, Ont. M5S 1A1.

**GROSSMAN, Emanuel;** executive; b. Toronto, Ont. 29 May 1918; s. late Annie (Applebaum) and late Samuel Grossman; e. Ryerson Pub. Sch., Toronto; Harbord Coll. Inst., Toronto; Central Tech. Sch., Toronto; Univ. of Toronto (Extension), m. Dorothy, d. late Samuel Kerzner, 16 June 1940; one d. Elisa Ellen (Mrs. Jeffrey E. Friedman); PRESIDENT, MANDOR RESEARCH AND MARKETING SERVICES LTD. since 1972; with Reliable Toy Company Limited 1934–51; joined Dee & Cee Toy Co. Ltd., 1951; apptd. Treas. 1954–56; Vice-Pres. and Treas. 1957–58; Pres. and Gen. Mgr., 1959–61 (Co. sold to Mattel, Inc., Calif., 1962); apptd. Pres. and Gen. Mgr., Dee & Cee Toy Co. Ltd. (Div. of Mattel, Inc.), 1962; resigned 1963; Man. Consultant 1964; Dir. of Marketing, Noma Lites Canada Ltd., 1965–66; Pres., Reliable Toy Co. Ltd. 1966–72; Charter mem. N. Toronto Y.M.H.A.; member, Society of Mfg. Engrs.; Hebrew; recreations: fishing, golf, curling, photography, reading; Club: Maple Downs Golf & Country; Home: 1555 Finch Ave. E. Apt. 1105, Willowdale, Ont. M2J 4X9; Office: 1210 Sheppard Ave E., Suite 304, Willowdale, Ont. M2K 1E3.

**GROSSMAN, Irving,** B.Arch., F.R.A.I.C., R.C.A.; b. Toronto, Ont. 7 Dec. 1926; s. Benny and Jenny (Appel) G.; e. Harbord Coll. Inst., Toronto, 1945; Sch. of Arch., Univ. of Toronto, B.Arch. 1950; m. Helena Derwinger, 28 Feb. 1970; two s.; arch. practice, Toronto, since 1954; Academician of Royal Candn. Academy; Ont. Assn. Arch.; Fellow, Royal Architectural Inst. of Can.; arch.-planner for several large scale residential communities such as Flemingdon Pk. and Edgeley Village and Crombie Park mixed use building, in St. Lawrence neighbourhood, Toronto; maj. urban renewal, pub. housing, condominiums, pub. schs., private residences, several synagogues, and the Admin. Building for Expo '67, Montreal; lectr., Univ. of Toronto Sch. of Arch. for 8 yrs. and other Candn. & U.S. Schools; recently Visiting Prof. at Univ. of Toronto and Past Pres., Architectural Alumni Assoc.; Visiting Prof. at Nova Scotia Tech.; papers at numerous confs. in Can. and U.S.; wrote and presented 13 weeks radio series on 'Streetscene' for CBC; numerous articles for Candn. and foreign publs.; TV appearances; numerous Design awards include Pilkington Glass Travel Fellowship to Europe for three years, housing design awards, and a Massey Medal; Canada Centennial Medal 1967; Mem., Can. Architectural Mission to China, continuing to India, Nepal on study of art/architecture; Jewish, recreations: music, sailing, tennis, skiing; Home: 21 Chestnut Park, Toronto, Ont. M4W 1W4; Office: 9 Sultan St., Toronto, Ont. M5S 1L6.

**GROSSMAN, Hon. Lawrence S. (Larry),** Q.C., B.A., LL.B.; lawyer; b. Toronto, Ont. 2 Dec. 1943; s. Allan and Ethel (Starkman) G.; e. McMurrich Pub. Sch.; Forest Hill Jr. High and Coll. Inst.; Univ. of Toronto B.A. 1964; Osgoode Hall Law Sch. LL.B. 1967; called to Bar of Ont. 1969; PARTNER, CHUSID & FRIEDMAN; Barker Fairley Distinguished Visitor (Candn. Culture), Univ. Coll., Univ. of Toronto 1993; columnist, Obiter Dicta (Osgoode Hall Law Sch. newspaper); cr. Q.C. 1977; el. M.P.P. for St. Andrew-St. Patrick Sept. 1975; Parlty. Asst. to Atty. Gen. Oct. 1976; re-el. June 1977; Min. of Consumer and Comm. Relations Ont. 1977–78; Min. of Industry and Tourism 1978–82; Min. of Health 1982–83; Treasurer of Ont. and Min. of Economics 1983–85; Min. of Education 1985; Min. of Colleges and Universities 1985; Prov. Sec. for Social Development 1985; Govt. House Leader 1985; Leader of the Official Opposition and Leader of P.C. Party of Ont. 1985–87; Dir. and Mem. of Extve. Ctte., Canada Post Corp.; Dir., CFMT (Channel 47); Bd. of Advisors of Med.-Emerg Inc.; Pres., The Grossman Group Internat. Inc.; Chrmn., Rosedale Health Services Inc.; Vice Pres., B'Nai Brith Canada; founding Chrmn., SkyDome Corporation; mem. Bd. Dir., Mount Sinai Hosp.; Hon. Chrmn., Candn. Mental Health Assoc.; mem. Bd. of Dirs., Baycrest Found.; Outreach Abuse Found.; Palliative Care Work Group; Haemophilia Soc.; Patron's Counc. for Alzheimer Soc. of Metropolitan Toronto; Amyotrophic Lateral Sclerosis (ALS) Soc. of Ont.; former Vice Chrmn., mem. Bd. Govs. Doctors Hosp.; former Dir., Lonvest Corp.; Diversicare Corp.; Toronto Arts Awards; Ont. Assn. Corrections & Criminology; former Dir. and mem. Extve. Comte., Metro Toronto Zool. Soc.; mem. Family Service Assn.; hon. mem., Alumni Federation, George Brown College; Candn. Technion Soc.; Hon. Dir., Kidney Fndn. of Can.; Founding mem. Forest Hill Residents' Assn.; former mem. Extve. Comte. Candn.-Jewish Cong. Central Region and Toronto Jewish Cong.; mem. B'Nai Brith, Toronto Freedom Lodge; Holy Blossom Temple Brotherhood; Teacher of Eng. to new Candns.; Mun. Law Lecturer, Candn. Bar Assn.; P. Conservative; Jewish; recreations: baseball, folk music, hockey, tennis, squash, skiing; Address: 30 St. Clair Ave. W., Ste. 900, Toronto, Ont. M4V 3A1.

**GROSSMAN, Robert Jay,** B.A.; computer systems executive; b. Montreal, Que. 9 Sept. 1955; s. the late David and Eileen G.; e. Loyola H.S. 1972; Sir George Williams Univ. B.A. 1976; m. Barbara d. Seymour and the late Roslyn Rosen 15 Oct. 1978; children: Ryan Steven, Ali Stephanie; VICE-PRESIDENT AND GENERAL MANAGER, TOSHIBA INFORMATION SYSTEMS GROUP 1991– ; Sales Rep., Xerox Ottawa; Sales Mgr., AES Data Ottawa; Internat. Sales Mgr. Asia; Corp. Sales Mgr. Montreal; Regional Mgr. Toronto; Nat. Sales Mgr., ITT; Compaq Computer Corp.; Pres., Univ. Students Assn. Mtl.; recreations: hockey coach; Home: 53 Tangreen Circle, Thornhill, Ont. L4J 5E3; Office: 191 McNabb St., Markham, Ont. L3R 8H2.

**GROTSKY, Hon. Isadore;** judge; b. Regina, Sask. 6 Apr. 1925; s. William and Molly (Cohen); G.; e. Univ. Sask., LL.B. 1949; m. Hazel (Gunderson) 22 Dec. 1984; children: Kenneth Mitchell; Garry Steven; JUSTICE, SASKATCHEWAN COURT OF QUEEN'S BENCH; Home: 12 – 3415 Calder Cres., Saskatoon, Sask. S7J 5A1; Office: Court House, 520 Spadina Cres. E., Saskatoon, Sask. S7K 3G7.

**GROTTEROD, Knut;** B.Eng.; retired pulp and paper executive; b. Sarpsborg, Norway 12 Feb. 1922; s. Klaus and Maria Magdelena (Thoresen-Tveter) G.; e. Sarpsborg (Norway) High Sch. 1941; Horten (Norway) Tech. Sch. 1945; McGill Univ. B.Eng. 1949; post-grad. work 1951; m. Isabel Edwina d. late Donald G. and Isabella MacMaster 25 Feb. 1950; children: Ingrid, Christopher, Karen; Pres., Incutech Brunswick 1988– ; held various mgmt. positions incl. Asst. to Vice Pres.-Mfg. 1951–70 Consolidated-Bathurst and predecessor Co's; Vice Pres. and Gen. Mgr. Nova Scotia Forest Industries 1970–73; joined Fraser Companies Ltd. as Vice Pres. Mfg. 1973, Sr. Vice Pres. Operations 1975, Dir. 1976; Exec. Vice Pres. present Co. 1980, Pres. and C.O.O. 1982; Dir. mem. Local Adv. Bd., Central Trust Co. (N.B.) 1982–87; Chrmn., C.E.O. and Dir., Fraser Inc. 1985; retired 1987; Chrmn., Island Paper Mills Limited, New Westminster, B.C. 1985–87; Atlantic Waferboard Inc. Chatham, N.B. 1985–87; Dir. (1983) & Pres. (1985–87) New Brunswick Forest Products Assn., Inc., Fredericton, N.B.; Dir., Alberta Newsprint Co. Ltd. 1988–92; Chrmn., Potato Development and Marketing Counc. N.B. 1989–91; Chrmn., Alberta Newsprint Co. 1988–90; mem. Norwegian Underground Army 1941–45; Dir. (1985) & Chrmn. (1986– ), Research and Productivity Counc. (N.B.); mem. Candn./Scandinavian Foundation (Pres. 1977–78); Candn. Pulp & Paper Assn.

(Technical Sect.); Tech. Assn., Pulp & Paper Industry; N.B. Forest Products Assn. (Pres. 1986–87); Corp. of Profl. Engrs., Prov. of Que. and New Brunswick; Mem. Bd. of Govs., Univ. of New Brunswick 1984–93; mem. (Past Pres.) Rotary Club; Hon. Dr. of Sci., Univ. of Maine; Extve. in Residence (hon.), Univ. of N.B. 1989; Protestant; recreations: flying, skiing, sailing, carpentry, photography, electronics, music; Home: 67 Castleton Court, Fredericton, N.B. E3B 6H3; Office: Research and Productivity Counc., 921 College Hill Rd., Fredericton, N.B. E3B 6Z9.

**GROVES, John Currie,** B.Sc., B.A., M.B.A.; business executive; b. Toronto, Ont. 22 May 1940; s. James and Helen (Currie) G.; e. Northview Hts. High Sch. 1959; Mich. Technol. Univ. B.Sc., B.A. 1963; York Univ. M.B.A. 1966; m. Patricia d. Dr. and Mrs. W.L. Donohue 29 Oct. 1966; two s. Michael William, Christopher James; PRES., OWNER AND DIR. WATT & WALLACE LTD. 1977– ; Pres., Owner and Dir. Rockrimmon Investment Corp. 1983– ; Founder, Chief Exec. Offr. and Dir. Laser Data Systems Inc. 1983– ; C.E.O., Data Card Canada 1987– ; Dir. Andaurex Resources Inc.; Sales Mgr. Xerox Toronto 1958–59; Vice Pres. and Partner Kencom Systems Toronto and Ottawa 1959–70; Pres. Cellulose Products Corp. Los Angeles 1970–72; Vice Pres. Mktg. Rapid Data Systems Toronto 1972–74; Founder and Pres. Tradecom Inc. 1974–77; Capt. Mich. Huskies Football Team 1963; mem. E. York Argonauts 4 time Candn. Champions 1964–68; ORFU Scoring champ 1967; Protestant; recreations: golf, tennis, jogging, football; Clubs; Mississauga Golf & Country; Beaumaris Golf; Ontario Racquet; Caledon Ski; Home: 2259 Chancery Lane, Oakville, Ont. L6J 6C1; Office: 4275 Village Centre Court, Misssissauga, Ont. L4Z 1V3.

**GRUBEL, Herbert G.,** M.P., B.A., Ph.D.; politician; economist; educator; b. Frankfurt, Germany, 26 Feb. 1934; s. Ernst and Elisabeth (Hessler) G.; e. Abitur 1954, Germany; Rutgers Univ., B.A. 1958; Yale Univ., Ph.D. 1962; m. Dr. Hélène Bertrand; children: Eric, Heidi; MEMBER OF PARLIAMENT FOR CAPILANO-HOWE SOUND, REFORM PARTY OF CANADA 1993– ; Prof. of Economics, Simon Fraser Univ. since 1971; Instr., Yale Univ. 1961–62; Asst. Prof., Stanford Univ. 1962–63 and Univ. of Chicago 1963–66; Visiting Fellow, Australian Nat. Univ. 1969; Asoc. Prof. of Econ., Univ. of Pa. 1967–70; Sr. Policy Adviser, US Treasury, Washington, D.C. 1970–71; Visiting Fellow, Nuffield Coll., Oxford 1974–75; Visiting Prof., Univ. of Nairobi, Kenya 1978–79; Visiting Prof., Univ. of Cape Town 1984; Distinguished Fellow, Inst. Southeast Asian Studies, Singapore 1985; Deutsche Bundesbank Visiting Prof. of Internat. Finance, Free Univ. of Berlin, summer 1990; author: 'Forward Exchange' 1966; 'The International Monetary System' 1985; 'International Economics' 1981; 'Free Economic Zones' 1983; co-author: 'Intra-Industry Trade' 1975; 'The Brain Drain'; 'The Canadian Service Industries' 1989; 'The Economics of Cross-Border Shopping' 1992; editor: 'International Monetary Reform' 1964; co-editor: 'Effective Protection' 1971; 'Exchange Rate Policies in South East Asia' 1973; 'The European Community after 1992' 1992; other writings incl. over 200 papers and notes in prof. journs. and colls.; mem., Candn. Econ. Assn.; Am. Econ. Assn.; recreations: skiing, tennis, hiking; Home: PH2–125 West Second Str., N. Vancouver, B.C. V7M 1C5; Offices: 215 - 1571 Bellevue Ave., West Vancouver, B.C. V7V 1A6 and Room 648 D, Centre Block, House of Parliament, Ottawa, Ont. K1A 0A6.

**GRUCHY, Charles George,** B.Sc.A., M.Sc.A.; public servant; b. Rainy River, Ont. 9 March 1939; s. George and Annie Adelaide (Irving) G.; e. Ontario Agricultural College B.Sc.A. 1962, M.Sc.A. 1964; m. Ann d. John and Margaret Sutherland 10 Aug. 1974; children: Megan, Andrew; DIRECTOR GENERAL, CANADIAN CONSERVATION INST. 1987– ; Asst. Curator of Fishes, National Museum of Natural Sciences 1970–75; Chief, Invertebrate Zoology Division 1975–80; Asst. Dir., Collections and Research 1980–87; Acting Dir. 1985–86; Mem. of Council, Internat. Centre for Convervation (ICCROM) Rome Italy 1988– ; Chairman 1980–92; reelected Chairman 1992–94; Pres., ICCROM General Assembly (82 member States) 1990; Mem., Internat. Trust for Zoological Nomenclature 1983–87; Anglican; Mem., Internat. Inst. for Conservation; author of 30 scientific papers; recreations: woodworking, gardening; clubs: Royal Overseas League; Home: Box 35, North Gower, Ont. K0A 2T0; Office: 1030 Innes Rd., Ottawa, Ont. K1A 0C8.

**GRUCHY, The Hon. David W.;** supreme court justice; b. Bishop's Falls, Nfld. 17 March 1932; s. Philip and Evelyn Jean (Baird) G., C.B.E.; e. Dalhousie Law School 1957; m. H. Elizabeth d. Charles and Esther Stayner 4 July 1958; children: Philip Stayner, Stephen Charles, Richard Baird, Sarah Louise; JUSTICE, SUPREME COURT OF NOVA SCOTIA, TRIAL DIV. 1990– ; Founding Partner, Burchell, MacDougall & Gruchy; Town Solicitor for Town of Truro 25 years; Founding Mem., Truro Industrial Comn.; Past Pres., Candn. Transportation Lawyers Assn.; recreations: various community activities esp. Youth Symphonic Band; clubs: Kinsmen; Office: The Law Courts, 1815 Upper Water St., Halifax, N.S. B3J 1S7.

**GRUEL, Daniel;** distillery executive; b. Rennes, France 4 Nov. 1940; s. Henri and Yvonne (Fayer) G.; e. Ecole des hautes études commerciales, Paris 1962; m. Réjeanne d. Paul-Emile Bergeron 1971; EXEC. VICE PRES., CORBY DISTILLERY LTD. 1989– ; Shipping Exec. San Francisco 1964–66 and Montréal 1967–71; Dir. Transport. and Vice Pres. Purchasing Société des Alcools du Qué. Montréal 1972, Vice Pres. Mktg. 1976–84; Vice Pres. Meaghers Distillery 1985–87, Exec. Vice Pres. 1988–89; Office: 1002 Sherbrooke St. W., Suite 2300, Montréal, Qué. H3A 3L6.

**GRYSKI, Camilla Milton,** B.A., M.L.S.; librarian, writer; b. Bristol, England 2 March 1948; d. Denis Claude and Eileen Margaret (Morgan) Milton; e. Loretto Abbey 1962–67; Univ. of Toronto B.A. (Hons.) 1971; Toronto Montessori Inst. primary teaching cert. 1972; Univ. of Toronto M.L.S. 1976; m. Chester s. Mary and Walter G. 29 July 1973; children: Mark, Damian; CHILDREN'S LIBRARIAN, HOSPITAL FOR SICK CHILDREN, TORONTO PUBLIC LIBRARY 1977– ; Teacher 1972–74; has toured Canada and visited England & the U.S. sharing cat's cradle games & their traditions with children & adults; frequent speaker at workshops and confs; Mem., Candn. Soc. of Children's Authors, Illustrators & Performers (Treas. 1985–87; Vice-Pres. 1991–93, Pres. 1993–95); Internat. Bd. on Books for Young People (Councillor 1984–87); Writers' Union of Canada; Candn. Children's Book Centre; author: 'Cat's Cradle, Owl's Eyes: A Book of String Games' 1983 (Am. Lib. Assn. Notable Book 1984), 'Many Stars and More String Games' 1985, 'Super String Games' 1987, 'Hands On, Thumbs Up' 1990 (1991 Information Book Award, Children's Literature Roundtables of Canada), 'Friendship Bracelets' 1992; 'Boondoggle: Making Bracelets With Plastic Lace' 1993'; recreations: jewellery making, juggling; clubs: Toronto Jugglers, Internat. Jugglers Assn.; Address: 76 Glenholme Ave., Toronto, Ont. M6H 3B1.

**GRZYBOWSKI, Stefan,** O.C., M.D., F.R.C.P., F.R.C.P(C), F.A.C.C.P.; physician; professor emeritus; b. Warsaw, Poland 13 Jan. 1920; s. Czeslaw and Jadwiga (Kopytowska) G.; e. Warsaw Univ. 1937–39; Edinburgh Univ. Polish Sch. of Med. M.B.,Ch.B. 1944, M.D. 1949; m. Betty Jean d. George and Jean Poland 25 Mar. 1949; children: Stefan, Julian, Jane, Alexander; Prof. Emeritus of Med. Univ. of B.C. 1985– ; mem. Staff Vancouver Gen. Hosp.; B.C. Cancer Inst.; rsch. childhood tuberculosis Highwood Hosp. Brentwood, Essex, Eng. 1949–54; joined Div. of Tuberculosis Prevention Ont. Dept. Health 1954 becoming Head of Epidemiol. and Rsch. Sect. 1957; Chair of Respiratory Diseases Dept. of Med. Univ. of B.C. 1964; maj. rsch. project tuberclosis in Eskimos 1965–74; Cons. World Health Orgn. Geneva and various developing countries; mem. World Bank Mission to Haiti; world-wide teaching assignments tuberculosis; author 'Tuberculosis in Childhood and Adolescence' 1954; 'Tuberculosis and its Prevention' 1983; author or co-author over 137 sci. papers and reports; Hon. mem. Candn. Thoracic Soc.; B.C. Lung Assn.; Latin Am. Med. Assn.; Polish Pneumonology Soc.; Chrmn. Ctte. Epidemiol. Internat. Union Against Tuberculosis; Pres. W. Vancouver NDP Riding Assn. 1989; recreations: skiing, fishing, hunting; Office: Respiratory Clinic, 2775 Heather St., Vancouver, B.C. V5Z 3Y5.

**GRZYMSKI, Krzysztof Adam,** M.A., Ph.D.; archaeologist/museum curator; b. Kalisz, Poland 19 May 1951; s. Adam and Janina (Stasiak) G.; e. Kosciuszko Liceum, Kalisz; Lodz Univ. 1970–71; Warsaw Univ. M.A. 1976; Univ. of Calgary Ph.D. 1981; m. Iwona d. Stefan and Albina Morawska 26 June 1977; one d.: Anna; one s.: Martin; ASSOC. CURATOR, EGYPTIAN DEPT., R.O.M. & ASSOC. PROF., DEPT. OF NEAR EASTERN STUDIES, UNIV. OF TORONTO 1984– ; Arch. Cons., PIW Pub., Warsaw 1976–77; Rsch. & Teaching Asst., Univ. of Calgary 1977–81; Lifeways of Can. Ltd.; Project Arch. 1981–82; Univ. of Calgary post-doct. rsch. fellowship 1982–84; Rsch. Fellow, Univ. of Calgary 1982–84; Asst. Dir., Dongola Reach Survey 1982–84, Dir. 1984–86; Dir., ROM Expedition to Nubia 1986– ; Pres., R.O.M. Curatorial Assoc. 1992– ; author: 'Archaeological Reconnaissance in Upper Nubia' 1987; Club: Sudan (Khartoum); Home: 8 Ladner Dr., Toronto, Ont. M2J 3Z7; Office: 100 Queen's Park, Toronto, Ont. M5S 2C6.

**GUALTIERI, Roberto Domenico;** public servant; b. Niagara Falls, Ont. 5 Dec. 1936; s. Domenico Roberto and Theresa (Omodeo) G.; e. McGill Univ. Hons. B.A. 1957 (Prince of Wales Gold Medal); Oxford Univ. M.A. 1960 (Rhodes Scholar); m. Margot d. Jean, Lady Brinckman and Paul Peters 15 Oct. 1963; children: Eric Whist, Inger Whist, Dominic Gualtieri; VISITING PROF. IN PUBLIC ADMIN., CARLETON UNIV.; with Dept. of External Affairs 1960–67; Head, GATT Div., Ind., Trade & Comm. 1967–70; Assoc. Coordr. Working Grp. on Foreign Investment 1970–72; Advr. to Depy. Min., Foreign Direct Investment 1972–73; Reader, St. John's Coll., Cambridge Univ. 1974; Sr. Adv., TAP Program, Treasury Bd. 1975–77: projects included Adv., Anti-Inflation Bd., Coordinator, Working Group on Gun Control and Chrmn., Task Force on Federal Role in Law Enforcement; Asst. Secy. to Cabinet, Social and Native Affairs 1978–81; Exec. Dir. Task Force on Pensions 1981–84; Sr. Advr. Privy Counc. Office (Reform of Cabinet Paper System) 1983–84; Depy. Secy., Govt. and Univs. Sector, Min. of State for Sci. and Technology 1984–88; Asst. Depy. Min. (Science and Technology), Industry, Science and Technology, Canada 1988–92; Secy. to the Minister's Adv. Bd. on the Networks of Centres of Excellence Program; Past Pres., Candn. Assoc. of Rhodes Scholars 1989–91; Chrmn., Ottawa Cycling Adv. Grp.; Past Chrmn. Le Groupe de la Place Royale; author articles on foreign investment and wine; recreations: trekking in the Himalayas, wine consulting and making, skiing, bicycling, arts and culture; Home: 108 Acacia Ave., Ottawa, Ont. K1M 0P9; Office: Rm. 847–F, 240 Sparks St., Ottawa, Ont. K1A 0H5.

**GUDERLEY, Helga,** B.A., Ph.D.; educator; b. Dayton, Ohio 24 Sept. 1949; d. Karl Gottfried and Irmgard (Delius) G.; e. Beavercreek (Ohio) Sch.; Earlham Coll. Richmond, Ind. B.A. 1971; Univ. of British Columbia Ph.D. 1976; m. John s. Henry and Phyllis Himmelman 29 Aug. 1973; two s. Nicholas, Tristan; PROF. OF BIOL., LAVAL UNIV. 1989– , Post-Doctoral Assoc. in Pharmacol. 1978–79, Asst. Prof. of Biol. 1979–83, Assoc. Prof. 1984–89, Full Prof. 1989– ; mem. Amazon Expdn. Alpha Helix 1976; Post-Doctoral Fellow in Biochem. & Biophys. Ore. State Univ. 1977–78; Dir. Sci. for Peace, Asst. Rsch. Dir.; author or co-author over 50 sci. papers; mem., Am. Soc. Physiol.; Candn. Soc. Zool.; Phi Betta Kappa; Science for Peace; recreations: camping, biking, squash; Office: Dép. de biologie, Québec, Qué. G1K 7P4.

**GUELPA, Robert Keith,** B.Com.; business executive; b. Victoria, B.C. 1 March 1947; s. Oscar A. and Lydia E. (Pettenuzzo) G.; e. St. Louis Coll. Victoria, B.C.; Univ. of B.C., B.Com. 1970; m. Sue E. d. Jack and Bette Allan 1975; two s. Michael, Christopher; PRES., WESTERN PRO IMAGING LABS LTD. 1991– ; Bus. Devel. Mgr. Warner Lambert 1970–75; Dir. of Mktg. Laura Secord 1975–79; Co-owner Consulting Group, Management Resource Group 1979–81; N. Am. Vice Pres. Mktg./Sales Fisons Western Corp. 1981–84; Pres. & C.E.O., A.E. McKenzie Co. Ltd. 1984–87; Chrmn. of Bd., The Westarc Group 1985–87; Pres. & C.E.O., Kingsgrange, Inc. 1987–90; guest speaker various confs.; author various publs.; mem. Am. Mktg. Assn.; recreations: skiing, tennis, squash; Club: Hazelmere Golf & Tennis; Home: 1400 Kerfoot Rd., White Rock, B.C. V4B 3L6.

**GUÉRARD, Yves,** B.A., B.Sc., F.S.A., F.C.I.A., F.C.A.; actuary; executive; b. St-Félix-de-Valois, Qué. 7 June 1934; s. Jean-Paul and Augustine (Charbonneau) G.; e. Séminaire de Joliette; Coll. Jean-de-Brébeuf; Coll. Saint-Laurent; Univ. de Montréal, B.A. 1954, B.Sc. 1956; SOA, Fellow 1963; Laurentian Univ., Ph.D. Bus. Admin. (hon. causa) 1990; two s. Vincent, Bastien; BD. CHRMN. & C.E.O., SOBECO ERNST & YOUNG INC.; Sr. Assoc., Sobeco Ernst & Young 1964– ; Extve. Partner, Ernst & Young 1992– ; Chrmn., Candn. Chamber of Commerce 1988–89, (Bd. Mem. 1981–90, Mem. Extve. Ctte. 1986–90, Mem. Internat. Affairs Ctte. 1990– ); with Manufacturers Life Insurance Co. 1956–60; Alliance Mutual Life 1960–64; Teaching Fellow in Actuarial Sciences, Univ. de Montréal 1970–86; Pres. Candn. Inst. Actuaries 1982–83; Pres. Chambre de Comm. du Montréal Metropolitain 1978–79, mem. Bd. 1972–80; mem. Bd., Montréal Fine Arts Museum & Co-Chrmn., Friends Comte. 1983–93; Pres., Bd. of Dirs., Corim (Conseil des relations internationales de Montréal 1990– ); Pres., Univ. de Montréal Alumni Assn. 1970–72; mem. Bd., Honeywell Canada Ltd.; Bd. mem., Société Générale de Financement du Québec; Mem., Economic Council of Canada 1984–90; Mem. Adv. Ctte.,

Econ. Counc. of Can. for the Reference on Governments' Impact on Competitiveness 1991– ; Mem. Sr. Adv. Ctte., National Round Table on the Environment and the Economy (NRTEE) 1991– ; mem. Council, Pension Section, Soc. of Actuaries 1984–87; Bd. Mem., Conf. of Consulting Actuaries 1985–87; Mem., Gov.'s Office, Soc. of Actuaries 1987–90; Charter mem. and Pres., Assn. Québec-France 1973–78; Charter Mem. & Pres., Centre for Continuing Studies in Employee Benefits of HEC-Montréal Sch. of Business Adm. 1977–79; Pres., CEGEP Maisonneuve 1974–77; Bd. mem., Candn. Labour Market and Productivity Centre 1984–85; Bd. mem., Internat. Assoc. of Actuaries and Chair, Scientific Ctte. of the 1992 Internat. Congress; Mem., 1992 Triennal Comn. on Judges, Salaries and Benefits; Mem., ASEAN-Canada Bus. Counc., Candn. Chamb. of Comm.; recreations: travel, squash, tennis; Club: St-Denis; Home: 702 Hartland, Outremont, Qué. H2V 2X6; Office: 505 René-Levesque Blvd. W., Immeuble Sobeco, 7th Floor, Montréal, Qué. H2Z 1Y7.

**GUÉRETTE, Rachel Vandandaigue,** C.M.; editor; b. Sherbrooke, Que. 26 Oct. 1918; d. Arthur Georges and Léona (Comtois) Vandandaigue; e. Holy Names Business Coll. 1937; m. Fernand s. Nérée G. 12 July 1947; children: Serge, Nicole, Claudine, Martin, Laurent, Bruno; Founder, 'L'AVIRON (a francophone minority) newspaper 1962; incorporated 1967; Pres. of the Bd. and Principal Manager until 1978 when the paper was sold to Acadian interests (remained Dir. 1978–80); paper continues as important instrument of cultural & econ. devel. in Campbellton & Restigouche Co. N.B.; Founding Mem., Le Cercle des Dames D'Acadie 1968 (became Féd. des Dames D'Acadie 1978); Gen. Sec. & Coord., Féd. des Dames D'Acadie 1980–84; reactivated Campbellton C. of C. (inactive for 15 years) 1985 and acted as Pres. 1985–88; Mem., Campbellton Econ. Devel. Comn. 1988; Co-founder, Assn. de la Presse francophone hors Qué.; active in several orgns. and community involvement incl. Home & School Assn., Girl Guides of Canada, Soc. cult. de la Baie-des-Chaleurs, Soc. des Acadiens et Acadiennes du N.-B., la Féd. des Dames D'Acadie, etc.; Mem., 'One Hundred People Who Made the Difference,' Campbellton centennial 1989; Order of Canada 1990; recreations: music, golf, reading, walking; clubs: Alliance Culturelle Inc., L'Assn. des Familles Vandandaigue-Gadbois Inc. (initiated 1990); Home: 12,480 Odette-Oligny, Montreal, Que. H4J 9Z7.

**GUERIN, Hon. Claude;** judge; b. Montreal, Que. 23 March 1930; s. Judge Charles Edouard and Antoinette (Foucreault) G.; e. Coll. Stanislas, Outremont, Que.; Univ. de Montréal; Univ. of Toronto; m. Henriette d. Arthur Clement 11 Aug. 1967; children: Charles Edouard, Michel, Julie; JUDGE, SUPERIOR COURT OF QUE. 1980– ; called to Bar of Que. 1954; cr. Q.C. 1972; Partner, Johnson & Tormey 1954–64; Sr. Partner, Bruneau, Dulude, Guerin 1964–80; Crown Prosecutor 1957–60, 1966–70 (Special Cases); P. Conservative; R. Catholic; recreations: golf, tennis, skiing, jogging, fishing; Club: Laval-sur-le-Lac Golf & Country; Home: 25 Beloeil Ave., Outremont, Que. Office: Court House, 1 rue Notre-Dame E., Montreal, Que. H2Y 1B6.

**GUÉRIN, Gladys M.M.,** B.Admin., B.Comm., C.A.; trésorière; née. Pétion-Ville, Haiti 23 août 1950; f. René et Janine (Drouin) G.; é. Univ. d'Ottawa B.Admin. 1971, B.Comm. 1972, C.A. 1975; ép. Serge Monette 6 septembre 1980; une enfant: Caroline; TRÉSORIÈRE À LA COMMUNAUTÉ URBAINE DE L'OUTAOUAIS 1987– ; Stagiaire chez Normandin Séguin à Ottawa 1972–75; Expert comptable chez Géo Welch & Co. à Hull 1975–79; Dir. des serv. finan. à la Comm. scolaire Champlain à Gatineau 1979–80; Consultante en systèmes comptables 1980–84; Analyste finan. à la Comm. scolaire des Draveurs à Gatineau 1984–87; Mem. du Conseil d'Admin. et Prés. du Com. de Vérification interne de l'Univ. du Québec à Hull; Mem. de l'Inst. of C.A.s of Ont.; L'Ordres des C.A. du Qué.; Réseau des femmes d'affaires et professionnelles de l'Outaouais; loisirs: lecture, natation, tennis; rés.: 54, rue Bernier, Hull, Qué. J8Z 3B1; bureau: 25, rue Laurier, bureau 500, Hull, Qué. J8X 4C8.

**GUERRIERE, Michael Robert John,** M.D.; physician, hospital administrator; b. Toronto, Ont. 2 June 1963 s. Robert Anthony and Rosalee Ann (Hewlett) G.; e. Univ. of Toronto M.D. 1986; VICE PRES., UTILIZATION MGMNT. & CHIEF INFORMATION OFFR., TORONTO GENERAL HOSPITAL; specialty training in internal med. 1986–90; Dir. of Information Systems, St. Michael's Hosp. 1990–91; Vice Pres., Clinical Affairs and Planning, St. Michael's Hosp. & Chief Information Offr. 1991; Pres., Distributed Medical Systems Inc.; Mem., Ont. Med. Assn.; Candn. Med. Assn.; Am. Coll. of Physicians; recreations: pilot; Home: 127 Underhill Dr., Don Mills, Ont. M3A 2K3; Office: College Wing, 1-207, 101 College St., Toronto, Ont. M5G 1L7.

**GUERTIN, Jean,** B.A., L.Sc.Comm., D.B.A.; educational executive; e. Collège Saint-Viateur B.A. 1962; Ecole des Hautes Commerciales L.Sc.Comm. 1965; Harvard Univ. D.B.A. 1974; m. Christiane Robert, children: Geneviève, Catherine; DIRECTOR, ECOLE DES HAUTES ETUDES COMMERCIALES 1987– ; owner of a small mfr. firm 1975–77 Rsch. Asst., Ecole des Hautes Etudes Commerciales 1965–69; Lectr. 1969–70; Asst. Prof. 1970–74; Assoc. Prof. 1974– ; Guest Prof., INSEAD, Fontainebleau, France 1976–78; Ecole Sup. de Gestion des Entreprises, Sénégal Dakar 1983–84; Guest Researcher, Ecole Sup. de Commerce de Lyon, France 1978; Mem., Investment Ctte., Soc. d'investissements Desjardins; Adv. Council on Financial Insts.; Bd. Mem., Montreal Stock Exchange; Cercle des chefs mailleurs du Qué.; Internat. Training Inst. in Civil Aeronautics Mngt.; Productivity Council; Bd. of Gov., Inno-Centre Qué.; co-author: 'Le management de la P.M.E.' 1985, 'Chartered Bank Financing of Small Business in Canada' 1982, 'Réussir en affaires' (How to Make it in Business) 1982, 'L'économie démystifiée' 1981; Office: 5255 avenue Decelles, Montreal, Que. H3T 1V6.

**GUEST, Gowan T.,** Q.C.; investor; businessman; b. Toronto, Ont. 8 Feb. 1929; s. Edmund T. and Gwen (Ferguson) G.; e. Univ. of Toronto B.A. 1950; Univ. of B.C. LL.B. 1954; m. Michele d. Norman and Jenni Shaw 6 May 1978; children: Martin, Alexandra, Marni, Douglas, Arthur; PRES., GUEST HOLDINGS LTD. 1970– ; Dir.: Cundill Value Fund; Versa Services; Wajax Limited; Exec. Asst. to Prime Min. of Can. 1958–60; Partner: Alexander Guest 1961–83; Owen, Bird 1983–86; Chrmn., Cundill Value Fund Ltd. 1976–93; Northwest Drug Co. Ltd. 1988–93; Investment Funds Inst. of Can. 1987–88; mem. Exec., Candn. Bar Assn. 1965–66, 1975–76; Chrmn., York House Sch. 1974; Pres.: B.C. Conservative Assn. 1957; World Fed. Mental Health 1979–81; recipient Centennial Medal 1967; Commemorative Medal 1992; Anglican; Conservative; Clubs: Vancouver; Royal Vancouver Yacht; Albany; Home: 1390 W. King Edward, Vancouver, B.C. V6H 1Z9; Office: 3030, 700 W. Georgia St., Vancouver, B.C. V7Y 1A1.

**GUEST, John Terence Moulton,** B.A., Dip. Ed.; headmaster; b. St. Catharines, Ont. 23 Sept. 1939; s. John Sherratt and Ruth Welland (Rigby) G.; e. Ridley Coll. St. Catharines, Ont. 1959; Bishop's Univ. Lennoxville, Qué. B.A. 1964, Dip.Ed. 1968, Cert. in Studies in Advanced Educ. 1970; m. Susan d. Dr. J.W. McCubbin 10 Aug. 1963; two s.: John David Walker, Thomas Alexander; HEADMASTER, BAYVIEW GLEN 1990– ; Ex-Dir., The Round Square (Internat. Schools Assn.) 1992– ; Housemaster, Bishop's Coll. Sch. Lennoxville 1964, Master-in-Charge Prep. Sch. 1968–70; Math. Teacher Lakefield Coll. Sch. 1970–71, Headmaster 1971–85; Cons. Candn. Exec. Service Overseas 1985–86; Headmaster, Sedbergh Sch. 1986–89; Educational Cons., J.T.M. Guest Consulting 1989– ; Founding mem. Bd., Bethany Hills Sch. 1980, mem. Bd. of Gov. 1980– ; Exec. Ctte., National Counc., Duke of Edinburgh's Award 1978–92; mem. Bd. Peterborough Symphony Orch. 1980–85; Anglican; Clubs: University (Toronto); Seigniury (Montebello); Empire (Toronto); Address: 460 Douglas Rd., R.R. #2, Warsaw, Ont. K0L 3A0; Office: 275 Duncan Mill Rd., Don Mills, Ont.

**GUEST (McLOUGHLIN), Michele Ida-Jane,** B.I.D., R.C.A.; interior designer; b. Calgary, Alta. 18 Jan. 1944; d. Norman Ridley and Jenni (Apponen) Shaw; e. Univ. of Man. Bachelor of Interior Design 1965; m. Gowan Thomas Guest 6 May 1978; children: Marni Michele McLoughlin, Douglas Gowan Guest, Arthur Norman Guest; PROP., SPECIALIZED PLANNING & CREATIVE ENVIRONMENT LTD. 1972–85; Consultant, National Council for Interior Design Qualification; Bd. Mem. of Design Exchange; Instr. and Co-ordinator Interior Design Program Kwantlen Coll. 1979–85; Fellow, Interior Designers Can.; Fellow, Interior Designers Inst. B.C.; Extve. mem., Canadiana Fund; Chrmn., Design British Columbia; Anglican; Address: 1390 W. King Edward, Vancouver, B.C. V6H 1Z9.

**GUEVREMONT, Jacques,** B.Eng.; utilities executive; b. Cap de la Madeleine, Qué. 16 Sept. 1932; s. Olivier and Juliette (Doucet) G.; e. McGill Univ. B.Eng. 1955; Hydro-Québec Representative to the U.S. 1992–94; Mem., Order of Professional Engineers of Qué.; Mem., Americas Society; Bd. Mem., Canada-United States Business Counc.; New England-Canada Business Council, Inc.; The Inst. for North Am. Trade and Economics (INATE); Mem. Bd. of Dirs., Public Television Assn. of Qué.; Former Mem., Vermont-Québec Joint Comn.; Dir. Control & Communications, Hydro-Québec 1971–79; Dir. System Operations 1979–81; Dir. Production & Systems Operations 1981–82; Vice Pres. External Markets 1982–86; Consultant 1991–92; frequent confs. USA and Can. elect. trade; Home: 8855 Roussin, Brossard, Qué.; Office: 230 Park Ave. S., New York, N.Y. 10003.

**GUIDOIN, Robert G.,** M.Sc., D.Sc., Ph.D.; university professor; b. Le Guédeniau, France 11 Nov. 1945; s. Jules A. and Marie E. (Angot) G.; e. Nantes, France M.Sc. 1968, Ph.D. 1970; Compiègne, France D.Sc. 1982; m. Raymonde d. Raymond and Bertille Sylvain 4 May 1974; children: Marie-France, Philippe, Claudine, Mireille; PROF. OF SURGERY, LAVAL UNIV. 1986– , Asst Prof. 1976, Assoc. Prof. 1981; Chrmn., Biomaterials Program; main area of rsch.: medical devices with particular interest in membrane oxygenators, heart valves, blood conduits, breast implants; Sci. Dir., Biomaterials Inst., St.-François d'Assise Hosp.; Cons., more than 30 firms and agencies worldwide 1975– ; referee, grant cttes. incl. MRC, FRSQ, CHSF, NSERC: Internat. Ed. Bd., journals of biomat. and/or artific. organs; Mem., Science Council of Canada 1987–92; Chrmn., 4th Ann. Meet. Can. Biomat. Soc. 1983; author of more than 200 refereed papers in biomaterials field; Invited conf. speaker worldwide; R. Catholic; Home: 1622 Route de l'Eglise, Ste-Foy, Qué. G1W 3P9; Office: Lab. Experimental Surgery, Rm. 1701, Services Bldg., Laval Univ., Quebec, Qué. G1K 7P4.

**GUIDOTTI, Tee Lamont,** M.D., M.P.H., F.R.C.P.(C), C.C.B.O.M., F.A.C.P., F.A.C.O.M., F.C.C.P., F.A.C.P.M.; physician; educator; b. Glendale, Calif. 14 May 1949; s. Anthony James and Jackie Marcine (Lamont) G.; e. Univ. of S. Calif. B.S. 1971; Univ. of Calif. at San Diego Sch. of Med. M.D. 1975; fellowships in pulmonary and occupational med. 1979–81; The Johns Hopkins Hosp. internship and residency in med. 1975–77, Sch. of Hygiene and Pub. Health M.P.H. 1981; PROFESSOR OF OCCUPATIONAL MEDICINE, UNIVERSITY OF ALBERTA 1984– ; Acting Chair, Dept. of Health Services Admin. and Community Medicine 1993– ; Clinical Assoc. Nat. Inst. of Health, Bethesda 1977–79; Consultant Occupational Med., The Rees-Stealy Med. Group, San Diego 1981–84; Prof. and Head, Div. of Occupational and Environ. Health, Grad. Sch. of Pub. Health, San Diego State Univ. 1980–84; Clinical Assoc. Prof., Univ. of Calif. at San Diego, Sch. of Medicine 1981–85; Acting Med. Dir. Univ. of Alta. Hospitals Occupat. Health Service 1985–87; Pres. and Sr. Assoc. Environ. and Occupational Health Assn. 1977–81; Bd. Cert. in Internal Med., Pulmonary Med., Occupational Med.; licensed to practice med. in Alta., Calif., Maryland and D.C.; author 90 sci. papers and 2 books; past Regent for Occ. Med., Am. Coll. Prev. Med.; Past Pres., Alberta Occupational Health Soc.; Past Dir. Western Occupational Med. Assn.; Overseas Fellow, Royal Soc. Med. (London); past Dir., UCSD Alumni Assn.; mem. The Johns Hopkins, NIH, UCSD and USC Alumni Assns.; Siemens Award for Occupational Health from Alta. Occupational Health Assoc. 1989; recipient Resolution of Commendation, Calif. State Assembly 1984; Jean Spencer Felton Award for Occupational Med. 1981; Award for Rsch. and election to hon. soc. Phi Sigma (USC Chapter) 1971; Fellow Am. Coll. of Physicians 1982, Am. Coll. of Chest Physicians, Royal Soc. of Med. 1982, Am. Coll. of Occupational Med. 1982, Am. Coll. of Preventive Med. 1980; mem. principal profl. assns. and internat. bodies; Office: Dept. of Health Servs. Admin. and Community Med., 13–103 Clincial Sciences Bldg., Univ. of Alta., Edmonton, Alta. T6G 2G3.

**GUILBAULT, Jacques,** B.Ph., M.Sc.Soc.; b. St-Jacques de Montcalm, Que. 1 Nov. 1928; s. Rolland and Madeleine (Dugas) G., e. St. Viateur (Que.) High Sch., 1946; Laval Univ., B.Ph. 1947, M.Sc.Soc. 1950; Columbia Univ., Sch. of Business Adm., 195l; m. Andrée, d. late Roger Valiquette, 15 June 1958; children: Jean, Bernard; VICE PRES. OF HUMAN RESOURCES, VISA DESJARDINS 1982– ; Invited Prof., School of Indus Relations, Laval Univ.; Lecturer at Sch. of Indust. Rel., Montréal Univ.; co-author: 'Les Relations patronales syndicales au Québec' (ed. Gaetan Morin) 1982; Employer Rep., Can. Labour Relations Board, July 1966–73; Pub. Staff Relations Bd., Apl. 1967–Oct. 1970; joined Que. Dept. of Labour as a Conciliator, 1951 and also worked for Fed. Dept. of Labour as Indust. Relations Offr.; joined Candn. British Aluminium Co. Ltd., Baie Comeau, Que., as Mgr., Indust. Relations, 1962; Dir. of Indust. Relations, Montreal Urban Community Transit Comn. 1966–82; R. Catholic; recreations: golf, fishing, curling; Home: 5505 Cavendish, Apt. 304, Cote St. Luc, Que. H4V 2Y6; Office: 425 Viger St. W., Montreal, Que. H2Z 1W5.

**GUILBEAULT, Jean L.,** B.A., L.L.L., C.R., Q.C.; public servant; b. Montreal, Que. 10 July 1936; s. Albert and Esther B. G.; e. Coll. Jean de Brébeuf, B.A. Rhetho. 1953; Coll. Pères de Saint Viateur B.A. Philo. 1957; Univ. de Montréal B.A., L.L.L. 1963; VICE-CHAIRMAN, CANADA LABOUR RELATIONS BOARD 1992– ; called to Bar of Que. 1964; Partner, Villeneuve Pigeon Clement Guilbeault 1964–87; Partner, McDougall Caron 1987–92; Q.C. 1984; Former Dir., Via Rail 1987–90; Former Chair, Caisse pop. Sacre Coeur de Montréal 1976–90; Fond. Félix Leclerc Inc. 1985–92; Fond. Saint Laurent Kiwanis de Montréal; Former Gov., Frontier College; Pres., 1980–81, Club Saint Laurent; Kiwanis de Montréal; Dir., Fond. du Barreau du Qué.; Les amis des compagnons du Devoir; recreations: seaplane pilot, gardening, beekeeping; clubs: Kiwanis; Home: 1505-110 Chemin du Chateau, Hull, Que. J9A 1T4; Office: 240 Sparks St. W., 4th fl., Ottawa, Ont. K1A 0X8.

**GUILLEMETTE, Michel,** M.D., C.C.B.O.M.; medical executive; b. La Tuque, Que. 9 Sept. 1945 s. Léo and Laurence (Gagnon) G.; e. Laval Univ. M.D. 1970; Séminaire de Trois-Rivières B.A. 1966; m. Nicole d. Bruno and Emilienne Pelletier 13 Aug. 1966; children: Michel Jr., François, Julie; Corporate Manager, Medical Services, Canadian Pacific Forest Products Ltd. & CIP Inc. 1982; practiced family medicine in Grand'Mère and Shawinigan, Que. 1971–79; Pres., Laflèche Hosp. Bd. of Physicians, Dentists & Pharmacists 1974; Consultant in occupational medicine for several companies in the area; Medical Dir., Quebec Region, Candn. General Electric 1979–82; Bd. of Dir., Que. Occupational Physicians Assn. (Dir. & Past Pres. 1979–83); Joint Assn. for Prevention of Occupational Diseases (Dir. 1981–83); Occupational Med. Assn. of Canada (Dir. & Vice-Pres. 1980–89; currently Dir.-at-large); Mem., Ad Hoc Ctte., Prov. Govt. on the Occupational Health & Safety & Compensation System 1987– ; Bd. of Dir., Comn. de la santé et la sécurité du travail du Qué. 1987– ; Bd. of Gov., Candn. Ctr. for Occupational Health & Safety 1990– ; Mem., Mensa 1975– ; author of several articles & conf. papers on occupational health & safety; recreations: reading books, enjoying sunshine in the summer; Home: 1029 Nicaise, Repentigny, Que. J5Y 2B8.

**GUILLET, James Edwin,** Ph.D., Sc.D., F.R.S.C.; educator; inventor; b. Toronto, Ont. 14 Jan. 1927; s. Edwin Clarence and Mary Elizabeth (Scott) G.; e. Univ. of Toronto Schs.; Univ. of Toronto B.A. 1948; Cambridge Univ. Ph.D. 1955, Sc.D. 1974; m. Helen Ann d. Louis and Mathilde Bircher 4 July 1953; children: Edwin Louis, Barbara Lynn, Patricia Ann, Carolyn Jean; EMERITUS PROF. OF CHEM., UNIV. OF TORONTO 1991– , Assoc. Prof. 1963–69, Prof. 1969–91, Assoc. Dean (Rsch. & Planning) Scarborough Coll. 1983–84; Rsch. Chem. Eastman Kodak Co. Rochester 1948–50, Tennessee Eastman Co. 1950–52, 1955–62; Chrmn., EcoPlastics Ltd. 1975–88, Pres. 1973–83; Pres., Solarchem Corp. 1984–85; Chrmn. & C.E.O., MediPro Sciences Ltd. 1989–93, Pres. 1985–89; Dir., VP-Research, Pharmapatch PLC 1993– ; Visiting Prof. of Polymer Chem. Vanderbilt Univ. summers 1964, 1966; Visiting Prof. Macromolecular Inst. Strasbourg, France 1970–71; Kyoto Univ. summer 1973; Univ. of Cal. La Jolla 1978–79; Visiting Sci. IBM Rsch. Labs. San Jose, Cal. 1980; Guggenheim Fellow Univ. of Mainz, W. Germany and Univ. of Cal. Berkeley 1981–82; Visiting Fellow Univ. of St. Andrews, Scot. 1983; Overseas Visiting Scholarship, St. John's College, Cambridge 1985–86; holds Gold Medal and Can.'s patent no. 1,000,000 for invention of photodegradable plastics 1977; Dunlop Lecture Award Chem. Inst. Can. 1979; author 'Polymer Photophysics and Photochemistry' 1985; ed. 'Polymers and Ecological Problems' 1973; author or co-author approx. 250 sci. articles; 76 inventions plastics and chems.; Fellow, Royal Soc. of Can.; mem., Am. Chem. Soc.; Chem. Inst. Can.; Royal Soc. Chem.; Home: 31 Sagebrush Lane, Don Mills, Ont. M3A 1X4; Office: Dept. of Chem., Univ. of Toronto, Toronto, Ont. M5S 1A1.

**GUINDON, Hubert,** B.A., B.Ph., L.Ph., M.A.; sociologist; educator; b. Bourget, Ont. 10 Oct. 1929; s. Pascal and Josephine (Lalonde) G.; e. Ottawa Univ. B.A., B.Ph. 1949, L.Ph. 1950, M.A. 1951; Univ. of Chicago 1951–54; PROF. OF SOCIOL. CONCORDIA UNIV. since 1970; Asst. Prof. of Sociol. Univ. de Montréal 1954–60; Assoc. Prof. of Sociol. Sir George Williams Univ. 1964–67, Prof. 1967–69; Prof. of Sociol. and Visiting Prof. Inst. Candn. Studies, Carleton Univ. 1969–70; co-ed. 'Modernization and the Canadian State' 1978; 'Quebec Society: Tradition, Modernity, and Nationhood' 1988; author various articles, book chapters; mem. Royal Soc. Can.; Candn. Assn. Sociol. & Anthrop. (Pres. 1971); Internat. Sociol. Assn. (Extve. 1970–74); mem. Task Force on Urbanization, Que. 1974–77; Research Sociol., Task Force on Candn. Unity 1978; R. Catholic; Office: Dept. of Sociology, Concordia University, Sir George Williams Campus, 1455 de Maisonneuve Boul. W., Montreal, Que. H3G 1M8.

**GUINDON, Rev. Roger,** O.M.I., C.C., B.A., L.Ph., D.Th. (Frib), LL.D. (Trent, Laur, W.O., RMC, York, Carleton), D.U. (MTL, Laval, Ottawa), Fellow (Ryerson, O.I.S.E.); retired university administrator; b. Ville-Marie, P.Q. 26 Sept. 1920; s. Aldéric and Germaine (Morisset) G.; e. Juniorat du Sacré-Coeur; Scolasticat St.-Joseph; Univ. Ottawa, B.A., B.Ph., L.Ph., B.Th., L.Th.; Univ. Angelicum, Univ. Gregoriana (Rome); Univ. Fribourg (Switz.) D.Th.; ordained priest (O.M.I.) 1946; joined Univ. Ottawa as Prof., Secy. and Dean, Faculty Theology 1947–51, 1954–64; Rector, Univ. Ottawa 1964–84; mem. Assn. des Univs. & Colls. Can. (Pres. 1967–68); Conseil des Univs. Ont.; Assn. Commonwealth Univs.; Assn. Internat. Univs.; Soc. Candnne. l'Enseignement Supérieur; Assn. Univs. Partiellement ou Entièrement de Langue Française; Assn. Can. Educateurs de Langue Française; Commercial & Industrial Development Corp. Ottawa-Carleton; Bd. Trade, CIDC High Tech., Steering Comte.; Health Sciences Complex, Co-ordinating Counc. Chrmn. 1971–84; Ont. Cancer Treatment & Research Foundation; Companion, Order Canada; Order of Ontario; Ordre de la Pléiade; Pres. Hon., United Way-Centraide; mem. Forum pour Jeunes Canadiens; Inst. Vanier de la Famille; Coll. Candn. des Travailleurs; Vice-Pres., Inst. Internat. Jacques-Maritain; Prés., Foundation franco-ontarienne; recreations: fishing; bridge; Clubs: Cercle Universitaire d'Ottawa; Home: 305, Rue Nelson, Ottawa, Ont. K1N 7S5.

**GUINSBURG, Thomas Nathan,** B.A., M.A., Ph.D.; university professor; b. New York, N.Y. 2 Feb. 1938; s. Theodore and Elena (Fried) G.; e. Woodmere High Sch., (New York) 1955; Columbia Coll., B.A. 1959; Columbia Univ., M.A. 1961; Ph.D. 1969; m. Marie-Julie (Krebs) 1989; children: Heather; Laura; PROFESSOR OF HISTORY, UNIV. OF WESTERN ONT. 1977– ; Lectr., Hist., Hunter Coll. C.U.N.Y. 1964–67; joined present univ. as Lectr., Hist., 1967; progressed to Prof.; Asst. Dean of Social Sci. 1972–75; Asst. Provost 1975–77; Dean, Faculty of Part-Time and Continuing Education 1979–93; author 'The Pursuit of Isolationism in the United States Senate from Versailles to Pearl Harbor' 1982; editor 'The Dimensions of History' 1971; co-ed. (with G.L. Reuber) 'Perspectives on the Social Sciences in Canada' 1974; Consulting Ed., Candn. Journal of University Continuing Education; mem. Organization of American Historians; Ont. Counc. for Univ. Continuing Education (Extve. Bd. 1980–85; Pres. 1984); Candn. Assn. for Univ. Continuing Education (Extve. Bd. 1983–91; Pres. 1988–90); Assn. for Continuing Higher Education; Jewish; Office: Social Science Centre, Univ. of W. Ontario, London, Ont. N6A 3K7.

**GUIRY, James Duncan,** B.Sc., P.Eng.; industrial executive; b. Chatham, Ont. 11 Oct. 1933; s. Emmett David and Beatrice Mary (Duncan) G.; e. St. Joseph's Chatham 1946; Assumption High Sch. Windsor 1951; Univ. of Windsor 1951–52; Univ. of Detroit B.Sc. (Civil Engr.) 1955; m. Barbara Jane d. late Ernest Hector Predhomme 1 Oct. 1954; children: Shawne Marie Pehar, James Paul, Timothy David; VICE PRES. HUMAN RESOURCES INCO LIMITED 1986– ; PRES. & MANAGING DIR., P.T. INCO INDONESIA, 1989– ; Pres., Inco Tech 1979– ; Vice Pres. responsible for Engineering, Environment, Energy, Inco Metals, 1980– ; Dir. Engn., Inco Metals 1972– ; Engr. Trainee, Westinghouse Canada Ltd., Hamilton 1955–56; Design Engr. Steep Rock Iron Mines 1956–63; Project Engr. Fenco, Toronto 1963–65; Mgr. Project Engn. Rio Algom Mines 1965–71; Asst. to Vice Pres. Engn., Inco Metals 1971–72; mem. Assn. Prof. Engrs. Prov. Ont.; Candn. Inst. Mining & Metall.; P. Conservative; R. Catholic; Home: 714 The West Mall, Apt. 1612, Etobicoke, Ont. M9C 4X1; Office: Royal Trust Tower, Toronto Dominion Centre, Toronto, Ont. M5K 1N4.

**GUISSO, Richard William Louis,** B.A., D.Phil.; university professor; b. Cambridge (Galt), Ont. 1 May 1943; s. Joseph F. and Phyllis Eleanor (Schaller) G.; e. St. Patrick's Grammar Sch. 1959; Galt C.I. 1962; Univ. of Toronto, St. Michael's Coll., B.A. 1966; Oxford Univ., D.Phil. 1972; single; PROF., DEPT. OF EAST ASIAN STUDIES, UNIV. OF TORONTO 1989– ; Vis. Fgn. Scholar, Univ. of Kyoto 1968–71; Asst. Prof., Univ. of Waterloo (Hist.) 1972–79; Assoc. Prof., present univ. 1979–89; Departmental Chair 1980–84; Ed. Bd., 'Historical Reflections' 1974–82; Sec. & Vice-Pres., T'ang Soc., Am. Assn. for Asian Studies 1983–88; Bd. of Dir., Joint Ctr. for Asia-Pacific Studies 1980–84; Mem. of Senate, Univ. of St. Michael's Coll. 1980–90; Bd. of Dir., Ctr. for Religious Studies, Univ. of Toronto 1980–85; Assessor, China Prog., Am. Counc. of Learned Soc. 1980–90; Rhodes Scholar; Woodrow Wilson Fellow; Dir., Can.-Korea Soc. 1981–87; Adv. Ctte., Big Brothers (Kitchener-Waterloo) 1973–79; mem., Candn. Asian Studies Assn.; Am. Assn. for Asian Studies; Am. Oriental Soc.; author: 'Wu Tse-t'ien and the Politics of Legitimation in China' 1978, 'The First Emperor of China' 1989; editor: 'Women in China' 1981, 'Shamanism: The Spirit World of Korea' 1987; co-editor: 'Sages and Filial Sons: Studies in Early Chinese History' 1989; recreations: theatre, tennis, gourmet cooking; Home: 33 Keele St., Toronto, Ont. M6P 2J8; Office: Dept. of East Asian Studies, Rm. 14207, Robarts Library, 130 St. George St., Toronto, Ont. M5S 1A5.

**GUITE, Harold Frederick,** M.A.; educator; b. Clayworth, Notts. Eng. 12 March 1920; s. Frederick William and Amy Hetty Eliza (White) G.; e. Abbeydale Council Sch. Sheffield, Eng. 1925–1931; Scholar, King Edward VII Sch. Sheffield 1931–1939; Open Exhibitioner in Classics, St. Catharine's Coll. Cambridge 1939–40; B.A. (London External) 1946; Arthur Platt Student in Classics, univ. of London (held at St. Catharine's Coll. Cambridge) 1946–47; M.A. (London External) 1952; m. Janetta Inglis Keith d. late John Hay Murray 26 March 1951; children: Candace Jane Elizabeth, Ayodeji Malcolm; PROF. EMERITUS OF CLASSICS, McMASTER UNIV. 1985– ; Mem., Senior Common Room of St. John's College, Durham 1993– ; Coll. Supvr. in Classics, King's and other colleges, Cambridge 1987–92; Hon. Secy., Epworth Press, Cambridge 1989–91; Coll. Supvr. in Classics St. Catharine's and Downing Colls. Cambridge 1946–47; Asst. Lectr. in Latin and Lectr. in Classics Univ. of Manchester 1947–56, Gov. Hartley Victoria Coll. 1952–56; Lectr. and Sr. Lectr. in Classics Univ. of Ibadan, Nigeria 1956–63; Her Majesty's Inspr. of Educ. (Hon.) W. Region, Nigeria 1958–63; Prof. and Head of Classics, Univ. of Zimbabwe 1963–67, Dean of Arts and mem. Bd. Govs. Extve. 1964–66; Prof. of Classics, McMaster Univ. 1967–85; mem. Bd. of Govs. there 1983–85; Local Preacher Meth. Ch. Eng. since 1943; Sr. Friend, Student Christian Movement 1947–67; Chrmn. Youth Comte. Internat. Fellowship of Reconciliation 1951–56; mem. Nigerian Comte. World Univ. Service 1957–63; Rhodesian Govt. Adv. Comte. on Teacher Training Colls. 1964–67; Co-Chrmn. Un. Way Campaign 1978; Gov. Waddilove Training Inst. Zimbabwe 1964–67; author various publs.; Life mem. Youth Hostels Assn.; U.N.A.; Counc. of Christians and Jews; Sir Walter Scott Club Toronto; Methodist; recreations: theatre, walking, gardening; Home: 4 Dinsdale Dr., Durham, U.K. DH1 2TS.

**GULAY, Bohdan Wsevolod,** B.Sc., P.Eng.; professional engineer; b. Cory, Sask. 31 March 1938; s. Ivan and Mary (Jumaga) G.; e. St. John's H.S.; Univ. of Man., B.Sc. 1962; m. Beverley d. Samuel and Gladys Calder 17 Feb. 1962; children: Charles Graham, Sheri Dawn; VICE PRES. AND GENERAL MANAGER, MANITOBA DIVISION, WARDROP ENGINEERING INC. 1993– ; Struct. Designer, Crosier, Greenberg & Partners 1955–65; Struct. Des. & Project Engr., W.L. Wardrop & Assoc. 1965–70; Sr. Project Mgr. 1970–80; Dir. & Manager of Structural Engineering, Wardrop Engineering Inc. 1980–93; major projects incl. K-1 Mill, Internat. Minerals & Chem. Corp. (Esterhazy); building envelope, New Children's Hosp. (Winnipeg); Provencher Bridge (Winnipeg); Chrmn. (1987–89) & Extve. Mem. (1986– ), Manitoba Chap., Candn. Construction Rsch. Bd.; Extve. Mem., Man. Bldg. Envelope Counc. Inc. 1986– (Founding Chrmn. 1986–87); and other previous extve. posts; Mem., Assn. of Profl. Engr., Prov. of Man. 1967– (Safety Ctte. 1985– ; shop drawing ctte. 1985–88); Assn. of Profl. Engr., Ont. 1967– ; licensed to practice Sask. 1981–90; Alta. 1982–91; N.W.T. 1986– ; Mem., Candn. Inst. of Mining & Metal.; Am. Soc. of Civil Engr.; Am. Concrete Inst.; Candn. Prestressed Concrete Inst.; recreation: photography; Home: 43 River Heights Dr., La Salle, Man. R0G 1B0; Office: 400 – 386 Broadway Ave., Winnipeg, Man. R3C 4M8.

**GULDEN, Simon,** B.A., LL.L., P. Adm.; executive; lawyer; b. Montreal, Que. 7 Jan. 1938; s. Zelda (Long) G. and late David; e. High Sch. of Montreal 1955; McGill Univ. B.A. 1959; Univ. de Rennes, St. Malo, France Cert. 1961; Univ. de Montréal LL.L. (cum laude) 1962; m. Ellen Lee Barbour d. late Samuel Alexander Barbour Jr. and late Ellen (Pente) B. 12 June 1977; VICE PRES., GEN. COUNSEL AND SECY., NABISCO BRANDS LTD. 1975– ; Dir., Freezer Queen Foods (Canada) Limited; Hervin Holdings Inc.; The Hervin Co.; Lowney Inc.; Nabisco Brands Ltd.; RJR Nabisco Securities Ltd.; called to Bar of Que. 1963; Law Partner,

Genser, Phillips, Friedman & Gulden, Montreal 1963–68; Secy. and Legal Counsel, Place Bonaventure Inc. Montreal 1969–72; Legal Counsel Real Estate, Steinberg Inc. Montreal 1972–74; Legal Counsel and Prime Atty., Bell Canada, Montreal HQ 1975; mem., Am. Bar Assn.; Am. Corp. Couns. Assoc.; Bar of Quebec; Candn. Bar Assn.; Internat. Bar Assn.; Internat. Assn. Jewish Lawyers & Jurists; Internat. Fiscal Assn.; Inst. of Chartered Secretaries and Administrators; Lord Reading Law Soc.; Osgoode Law Soc.; Assn. des conseils en francisation du Qué.; Advertising & Sales Extve. Club of Toronto; Am. Mang. Assn.; Bd. Trade Metrop. Toronto; B'Nai B'Rith; Liberal; Jewish; recreations: sailing, skiing, horseback riding, karate, physical fitness; numismatics, philately, music, literature, theatre, travel, politics, community organs; Clubs: Cambridge; Canadian Power and Sail Squadrons; Canadian (Toronto); Founders; Hot Stove; Island Yacht; Ontario Club; Home: 23 Danbury Ct., Unionville, Ont. L3R 7S1; Office: 10 Park Lawn Rd., Suite 101, Etobicoke, Ont. M8Y 3H8.

**GULKIN, Harry;** film producer; arts administrator; b. Montréal, Qué. 14 Nov. 1927; s. Peter Oliver and Raya (Shinderman) G.; e. Baron Byng High Sch. Montréal 1942; children: Cathy, James Peter; DIR. OF PROJECTS, SOCIÉTÉ GÉNÉRALE DES INDUSTRIES CULTURELLES QUEBEC; Film Producer, Jape Film Services Inc.; Merchant Seaman and trade union organizer 1944–49; labour journalist, entertainment and arts critic labour publs. 1950–56; Marketing Consultant, Market Researcher, Business Extve. 1957–70; Executive & Artistic Dir., Saidye Bronfman Centre 1983–87; films incl. 'Penny and Ann' (2nd Prize Film Festival Internat. Cong. Rehab Centres 1976; Red Ribbon Award Am. Film Festival 1977; Award AMTEC Film Festival 1977); 'Lies My Father Told Me' (Hollywood Foreign Critics Award Golden Globe 1975; Academy Award nomination best screenplay 1975; Best Film Candn. Film Awards 1976; Grand Prize Virgin Islands Internat. Film Festival 1975; Christopher Awards (U.S.) best writing, direction and production 1975; ACTRA Award best screenplay 1976; Candn. Motion Picture Distributors Golden Reel Award 1976); 'Jacob Two Two Meets the Hooded Fang' (Gold Medallion Special Jury Award Miami Internat. Film Festival 1976; Special Jury Award 8th Internat. Children's Film Festival Los Angeles 1979); 'Two Solitudes' 1977; 'Challenger' (For Nat. Film Bd. Can.) 1979; 'Bayo' 1984; Lectr. (part-time) in Screenwriting, Concordia Univ.; author various articles film publs.; served with Candn. Army Reserve 1942–44; Candn. Merchant Marine 1944–49; Past Chrmn., Past Pres., Candn. Film Inst.; Founding Pres. Motion Picture Inst. Can. 1977–79; Past Vice Pres. Candn. Assn. Motion Picture Producers; Past Pres. Montreal Chapter Am. Marketing Assn.; mem. Assn. Que. Film Producers; Cinematheque Québecoise; Acad. of Candn. Cinema and Television; Address: 111 Boul. St. Joseph O., Montréal, Qué. H2T 2P7.

**GULLIVER, Philip Hugh,** Ph.D., F.R.S.C.; educator; b. Eng. 2 Sept. 1921; e. Univ. of London Ph.D. 1952; DISTINGUISHED RESEARCH PROF. OF ANTHROP. YORK UNIV. 1984– ; Govt. Sociol. Tanganyika 1952–58; Visiting Lectr. Harvard Univ. 1958–59; Prof., Boston Univ. 1959–62; Prof. Sch. of Oriental & African Studies, London 1962–71; Prof., Univ. of Calgary 1971–72; Prof., York Univ. 1972–84; author 'The Family Herds' 1955; 'Social Control in an African Society' 1963; 'Neighbours and Networks' 1971; 'Disputes and Negotiations' 1979; 'In the Valley of the Nore' 1986; ed. 'The Family Estate in Africa' 1964; 'Tradition and Transition in East Africa' 1969; 'Cross-Examinations' 1978; Office: Room 2042, Vari Hall, 4700 Keele St., North York, Ont. M3J 1P3.

**GULOIEN, Donald Arthur,** B.Comm., FLMI; financial services executive; b. Parry Sound, Ont. 27 April 1957; s. Edward Perry and Elizabeth Marjorie (Pay) G.; e. Univ. of Toronto B.Comm. 1980; Candn. Securities Course, Candn. Securities Inst. 1980; FLMI, Life Office Mngt. Assn. 1982; m. Irene d. Pauline and William Boychuk; VICE-PRESIDENT, U.S. INDIVIDUAL BUSINESS, MANULIFE FINANCIAL 1990– ; Pres., Manufacturers Life of America; Chrmn. & Pres., Manulife Series Fund; Dir., Manulife U.S.A.; Pres., Household Finance Corp. of Canada 1977–81; joined Manulife Financial 1981; Dir., Market/Product Development, Candn. Div. 1983; Dir., Insurance Marketing, U.S. Individual 1985; Asst. Vice-Pres., Insurance Products, U.S. Individual 1986; Marketing Vice-Pres., U.S. Individual 1988; active with Children's Aid Soc. Found.; Former Mem., Governing Council, Univ. of Toronto; Hart House Board of Stewards; recreations: sailing, skiing, tennis, saxophone; clubs: Cottingham Tennis, Eight Mile Point Cottagers Assn.; Home: 84 Highland Ave., Toronto, Ont. M4W 2A5; Office: 200 Bloor St. E., NT-M, Toronto, Ont. M4W 1E5.

**GULSOY, Joseph,** M.A., Ph.D., F.R.S.C.; educator; b. Ordu, Turkey 15 Aug. 1925; s. Murat and Gul (Bugday) G.; e. Univ. of B.C., B.A. 1953; Univ. of Toronto M.A. 1955; Univ. of Chicago Ph.D. 1961; m. Hilde d. Martin and Milla Schmid 1959; children: Andrea, Angela, Christopher; EMERITUS PROF. OF SPANISH, UNIV. OF TORONTO 1991– ; Instr. in Spanish present Univ. 1953–55, 1958–60, Lectr. 1960–62, Asst. Prof. 1962–66, Assoc. Prof. 1966–70, Prof. 1970-91; Dir. and Organizer III Colloquium Catalan Studies N. Am. 1982; author 'El Diccionario Valenciano-Castellano de M.J. Sanelo' 1964; 'Catalan' (Philology & Linguistics) 1979; collaborator 'Diccionari etimologic i complementari de la llengua catalana' Vols. I 1980, II 1981, III 1982, IV 1983, V 1985, VI 1986, VII 1987, VIII 1988, IX 1991; ed. 'Catalan Studies Volume in Memory of Josephine de Boer' 1977; author over 35 monograph articles; recipient Premi Catalònia of Inst. Estudis Catalans 1988; Premi Ramon Llull of Fund. Congr. Cult. Cat. 1989; mem., Société de Linguistique Romane; Associacio Internacional de la Llengua i Literatura Catalanes (Exec. Bd.); N.Am. Catalan Soc. (Pres. 1980–82); Home: 150 Newton Dr., Willowdale, Ont. M2M 2N3; Office: Toronto, Ont. M5S 1A1.

**GUNDERSEN, Sonja J.,** LL.B.; lawyer; b. Miami, Florida 8 June 1947; d. Oscar O. and Muriel (Hanson) G.; e. Miami-Dade College; Univ. of Western Ont. LL.B. 1983; called to the Bar, Ont. 1985; one s.: Charles Thomas Kaighin; VICE PRESIDENT, LAW & CORPORATE DEVELOPMENT, APPLE CANADA INC. 1987– ; Asst. Counsel, IBM Canada Ltd. 1985–87; Mem., Canadian Corporate Counsel Assn. (of the Candn. Bar Assn.); Computer Law Assn.; Bd. of Gov., George Brown College 1987– (finance & audit cttes.); Office: 7495 Birchmount Rd., Markham, Ont. L3R 5G2.

**GUNDERSON, Morley,** Ph.D.; educator; b. Fort Frances, Ont. 29 Apr. 1945; s. Magnus and Ann (Person) G.; e. Queen's Univ. B.A. 1967; Univ. of Wis. Ph.D. 1971; m. Melanie Brady d. Jack and Lorraine Brady 19 Oct. 1970; children: Brady, Jessica, Rory, Brendan; DIRECTOR, CENTRE FOR INDUSTRIAL RELATIONS AND PROFESSOR OF ECONOMICS, UNIVERSITY OF TORONTO 1985– ; joined present univ. as Asst. Prof. of Economics 1971, Assoc. Prof. 1975, Full Prof. 1980; Visiting Scholar: Internat. Inst. for Labour Studies Geneva 1977–78; Nat. Bureau of Econ. Rsch. Stanford 1984–85, 1991–93; Advr./Consultant: Ont. Dept. Labour; Stats Can.; Howe Rsch. Inst.; Rsch Br. Anti-Inflation Bd.; Candn. Inst. Rsch. Pub. Policy; Ont. Law Reform Comn.; Royal Comn. Distribution Wealth in U.K.; Ont. Econ. Counc.; Ont. Royal Comn. on Asbestos; Labour Can.; Internat. Labour Orgn.; Ont. Manpower Comn.; Abella Comn. on Equality in Employment; Macdonald Comn. on Econ. Union; Ianni Task Force on Mandatory Retirement; Donner Task Force on Hours of Work and Overtime; Pay Equity Comn.; Human Rights Comn.; Candn. Labour Market and Productivity Ctr.; Ont. Premier's Council Health Panel; B.C. Task Force on Employment and Training; B.C. Task Force on Health Care and Costs; Ont. Workers' Compensation Bd.; author 'Labour Market Economics: Theory, Evidence and Policy in Canada' (3rd ed. with C. Riddell) 1993; 'The Political Economy of Corporate Bailouts' (with M. Trebilcock, M. Chandler, P. Halpern and J. Quinn) 1985; 'Economics of Poverty and Income Distribution' 1983; 'Women and Labour Market Poverty' (with L. Muszynski) 1990; 'Pay Equity: Issues, Options and Experiences' (with N. Weiner) 1990; some 30 book chapters and 40 articles acad. jours.; ed. 'Collective Bargaining in the Essential and Public Service Sectors' 1975; 'Union-Management Relations in Canada' (2nd ed. with John Anderson and Allen Ponak) 1989; 'Labour Arbitration Yearbook' (with W. Kaplan and J. Sack) 1991, 1992, 1993; mem. various ed. bds.; recreations: tennis, skiing, jogging; Home: 97 Whitehall Rd., Toronto, Ont. M4W 2C8; Office: 121 St. George St., Toronto, Ont. M5S 1A1.

**GUNDY, Henry Pearson,** M.A.; professor emeritus; b. Toronto, Ont. 1 June 1905; s. Henry Wentworth & Gracey (Mackay) G.; e. Univ. of Toronto Schs.; Univ. of Toronto, B.A. 1928, M.A. 1930; Univ. of Chicago; Columbia Univ. Library Sch. (summer session) 1944; m. Dorothy Diamond (dec. 28 Dec. 1967), d. Very Rev. Dr. James Endicott, 31 Aug. 1929; children: Joyce, Carolyn; Fellow in Eng., Victoria Coll., Toronto, 1929–31; Lectr. in Eng., McMaster Univ., 1931–35; Instr. in Eng., Univ. of Chicago, 1936–37; Asst. and Assoc. Prof. Mt. Allison Univ., 1937–42; Joseph Allison Prof. of Eng., Head of Dept., and Dir. of Library Service, 1942–47; Librarian, Queen's Univ., 1947–65; Prof. of Eng. Lang. and Lit. 1966–70; Editor 'Queen's Quarterly' 1967–72; Assoc. Dir. and Sr. Ed. McGill-Queen's Univ. Press 1969–71; Ed., 'Historic Kingston' 1959–75; Ed. 'Letters of Bliss Carman' 1981; 'Queen's University at Kingston' 1967; 'The Spread of Printing, Western Hemisphere, Canada' 1972; other monographs on printing and publishing in Canada; mem., Candn. Hist. Ass.; Bibliographical Society of Can.; United Church; amateur artist; Home and Studio: 3017 Queen St. E., Apt. G3, Scarborough, Ont. M1N 1A5.

**GUNDY, Peter V.,** B.A., B.C.L., M.Sc.; financial executive; b. Montréal, Qué. 17 Oct. 1939; s. Harry Fountain and Jean Clary (Paterson) G.; e. Lower Can. Coll. 1951; Univ. of W. Ont. B.A. 1960; McGill Univ. B.C.L. 1963; London Sch. of Econ. M.Sc. 1971; children: Andrew, Harry, Benson, Samuel; CHRMN., ADVANCED MATERIAL RESOURCES LIMITED and CHRMN., RENAISSANCE SECURITIES INC.; Dir., NPC Inc.; Mohawk Canada Ltd.; called to Bar of Qué. 1964; Lawyer, Doheny & McKenzie, Montréal 1964–69; Staff mem. Ctte. on Govt. Productivity, Ont. 1971; Corporate Finance Harris & Partners, later Dominion Securities 1972–75; Exec. Vice Pres. Finance Potash Corp. of Sask., Chrmn. Potash Corp. of Sask. Sales Corp. 1976–78; Vice Pres. Brascan 1978–79; Home: 130 South Dr., Toronto, Ont. M4W 1R9; Office: 121 King St. W., Standard Life Centre, Ste. 810, Toronto, Ont. M5H 3T9.

**GUNN, G. Stuart E.,** B.A.; trust company executive; b. Toronto, Ont. 8 May 1951; s. Geoffrey Bunnel and Jocelyn Bamford (Harley) G.; e. McMaster Univ. Hon. B.A. 1975; m. Patricia d. Peter and Christina Les 22 June 1974; children: Geoffrey, Michael; SENIOR VICE-PRES., INCOME PROPERTY LENDING, MONTREAL TRUST CO. OF CANADA 1992– ; Asst. Vice-Pres., The Mercantile Bank of Canada 1981–86; Vice-Pres., Chemical Bank of Can. 1986–87; Vice-Pres., Montreal Trust 1987–92; club: Credit Valley Golf and Country; Office: 15 King St. W., 5th fl., Toronto, Ont. M5H 1B4.

**GUNN, John Alexander Wilson,** M.A., D.Phil., F.R.S.C.; educator; b. Quebec City, Que. 17 Aug. 1937; s. Hector Fraser and Jean Matheson (Taylor) G.; e. Quebec High Sch. 1955; Queen's Univ. B.A. 1959; Univ. of Toronto M.A. 1961; Nuffield Coll. Oxford D. Phil. 1966; children: James Hector Fraser, Andrea Jean Taylor; PROF. OF POL. STUDIES, QUEEN'S UNIV. 1970– ; sessional lectr. present Univ. 1960, Head of Pol. Studies 1975–83; mem. Bd. Lib. Co-ordination, Council Ont. Univs. 1973–77; Publs. Ctte. Social Sci. Rsch. Council Can. 1970–76; Gen. Assembly Social Sci. Fedn. Can. 1979–83; various orgns. Can. Council and SSHRCC; mem. Adv. Ed. Bds. Russell Project (McMaster) and Disraeli Project (Queen's); author 'Politics and the Public Interest' 1969; 'Factions No More' 1972; 'Beyond Liberty and Property' 1983; co-ed. 'Benjamin Disraeli, Letters 1815–1834, 1835–1837' 2 vols. 1982; recreations: book-collecting, hiking, running; Home: 69 L. Union St., Kingston, Ont. K7L 2N2; Office: Kingston, Ont. K7L 3N6.

**GUNN, Nigel Hamilton;** investment dealer (retired); b. Edinburgh, Scotland 19 July 1910; s. James Hamilton and Agnes Cecilia (Mackenzie) g.; e. Pub. and High Schs., British Columbia; grad. 1925 Brentwood Coll., Victoria, B.C.; m. Eleanor Jessie, 8 Oct. 1938; children: Patricia H., Neil H.; retired 1985; Pres., Invest. Dealers' Assn. of Can. 1956–57; Vice-Pres., Ont. Dist. Extve. Comte., Invest. Dealers' Assn. of Can. 1954–56; Chrmn., Toronto East General & Orthopaedic Hosp. 1982–88; Pres., Visiting Homemakers Assn. 1981–83; joined Bell, Gouinlock Ltd. (Toronto) 1932; Vice-Pres. 1951; Pres. 1957; Chrmn. 1972; Hon. Chrmn. 1979; recreation: golf; Clubs: National; Rosedale Golf; Home: 255 Glencairn Ave., Toronto, Ont. M5N 1T8.

**GUNNARS, Kristjana,** M.A.; professor; writer; editor; b. Reykjavik, Iceland 19 Mar. 1948; s. Gunnar and Tove (Christensen) Bodvarsson; e. Ore. State Univ. B.A. 1972; Univ. of Regina, M.A. 1977; one child: Eyvindur Kang; ASSOC. PROF. OF ENGLISH, UNIV. OF ALBERTA, Edmonton 1991– ; Asst. Ed. 'Iceland Review' Iceland 1980–81; freelance writer, translator, ed. since 1981; Writer in Residence, Regina Public Library, Regina 1988–89; Writer in Residence, Univ. of Alta., Edmonton 1989–90; Instructor, Okanagan College, Kelowna 1990–91; author 'Settlement Poems' I and II 1980, 1981; 'One-Eyed Moon Maps' 1981; 'Wake-Pick Poems' 1982; 'The Axe's Edge' 1983; 'The Night Workers of Ragnarök' 1985; 'The Prowler' 1989; 'Carnival of Longing' 1989; 'Zero Hour' 1991, 'The Guest House and Other Stories' 1992, 'The Substance of Forgetting' 1992; co-author 'The Papers of Dorothy Livesay' 1985; editor 'Crossing the River, Essays in Honor of Margaret Laurence' 1988; 'Unexpected Fictions, New Icelandic

Canadian Writing'; transl. 'Stephan G. Stephansson, In Retrospect' 1982; 'Stephan G. Stephansson, Selected prose and Poetry' 1988; mem. P.E.N.; Writers Union Can.; League Candn. Poets; Composers Authors & Publishers Assn. Can.; Alliance Candn. Cinema TV & Radio Artists; Address: Dept. of English, Univ. of Alta., Edmonton, Alta. T6G 2E2.

**GUNNING, Kenneth Samuel,** B.A., F.C.A.; b. Vancouver, B.C. 6 Apr. 1930; s. Basil Hewitt and Olive May (Laffere) G.; e. Pub. and High Schs. Vancouver 1948; Univ. of B.C. B.A. 1952; Brandon Coll. Univ. of Man. 1952–53; Assoc. Royal Conserv. of Music Toronto; m. Flora Marie d. Hans Johnson 2 July 1954; children: Laureen Elizabeth, Lynda Marie, Karen Jane, Kevin John; CONSULTING ASSOC. AND RETIRED PARTNER, DOANE RAYMOND; Dir., Canada Trust and affiliated corps.; Mem., Standards Adv. Bd., Candn. Inst. of C.A.'s (CICA); Chrmn., CICA Rsch. Studies Advisory Ctte.; Chrmn., CICA Federal Legislation Ctte.; articled Helliwell Maclachlan & Co. Vancouver 1953, C.A. 1957, Partner 1966; Dir. of Research and Training Thorne Gunn Helliwell & Christenson, Toronto 1970; Adm. Partner Thorne Gunn & Co. 1972, Nat'l Extve. Partner 1973; Nat'l Extve. Partner, Thorne Riddell 1977–83; Nat. Extve. Partner, Pannell Kerr MacGillivray 1986–91; Chrmn. of Policy Bd., Doane Raymond 1991–93; mem. Int'l. Counc. Pannell Kerr Forster (Internat. Firm) 1986–91; former mem., Central Mgmt. Comte. and past Chrmn., Region II, Klynveld Main Goerdeler (KMG); former mem., Accounting Adv. Comte. to Supt. of Brokers of B.C.; former mem. Bd. of Govs. and past Chrmn. Research & Prof. Practices Comte., the Can. Comprehensive Auditing Found.; past Chrmn. CICA Auditing Standards Comte; mem. CICA Special Comte to Examine the Role of the Auditor (1977–78); author numerous articles in prof. and other accounting journs.; rec'd Queen's Silver Jubilee Medal 1978; Fellow, Inst. C.A.'s Ont. (1976) and B.C. (1977); Beta Theta Pi; Protestant; recreations: golf, tennis, fishing, music; Clubs: Vancouver; Vancouver Lawn Tennis & Badminton; Vancouver Racquets; Sechelt Golf & Country; Home: Box 69, Mission Site, R.R. 1, Sechelt, B.C. V0N 3A0; Office: c/o Doane Raymond, Suite 2000, 1066 West Hastings St., Vancouver, B.C. V6E 3X1.

**GUOLLA, Louis,** Q.C., B.A.; b. Sault Ste. Marie, Ont. 2 Feb. 1917; s. Vincent and Elvira (Ceccol) G.; e. High Sch. Timmins, Ont; Univ. of Toronto, Ont. B.A. (Hon. Law) 1939; Osgoode Hall Law Sch., Toronto, 1943; m. Eleanor, d. John Pariselli 29 June 1944; PARTNER, DALE & DINGWALL; Dir., ITT Canada Limited; ITT Industries of Canada Ltd.; Stoffel Seals of Canada Ltd.; read law with Wilfred Wolman, Q.C., Toronto, Ont.; called to the Bar of Ont. 1943; created Q.C. 1962; practised with Daly, Hamilton and Thistle and successor firms since 1943; mem., Candn. Bar Assn.; Bd. Trade Metrop. Toronto; Golf Assn. of Toronto Bar (Past Pres.); Roman Catholic; recreations: golf, fishing, hunting; Club: St. George's Golf & Country (Past Pres.); Home: 70 Prince George Drive, Islington, Ont. M9A 1Y6; Office: Box 65, Toronto-Dominion Centre, Toronto, Ont. M5K 1E7.

**GURD, Fraser Newman,** M.D., C.M., M.Sc., D.A.B.S.; surgeon (retired, 1979); b. Montreal, Que. 19 Mar. 1914; s. Jessie Gibson (Newman) and Fraser Baillie G., M.D.; e. Selwyn House, Montreal, 1920–27; Westmount High Sch., Montreal, 1927–29; Inst. Sillig, Vevey, Switzerland, 1929–30; McGill Univ., B.A. 1934, M.D., C.M., 1934–36 and 1937–39; Univ. of Munich, 1936–37; Jr. Intern, Johns Hopkins Hosp., 1939–40; Asst. Res., Montreal Gen. Hosp., 1940–41; Research Fellow, Univ. of Penna., M.Sc. (Med.) 1946–47; Res., Royal Victoria & Montreal Gen. Hosps., 1947–48; m. Mary Louise, d. Harold Willis Moore, Denver, Colo., 19 Dec. 1938; children: Patricia Pryde, Katharine Chaplin, Mary Goss, Susan Bexton, Deborah Gregorash; consultant; Gov., Un. Theol. Coll., Montreal 1958–72; Jr. Asst., Montreal Gen. Hosp., 1948, Sr. Surg. 1959; Surg.-in-Chief, Reddy Mem. Hosp., 1952–59, Consultant 1959; Hon. Consultant in Surg., Jewish Gen. Hosp., 1964; Consultant in Surg., Queen Elizabeth Hospital, 1964; (all Montreal); Demonstrator in Surg., McGill Univ., 1948; Research Asst. Dept. Exper. Surg., 1948–52; Asst. Prof., Surg., 1955, Assoc. Prof. 1959; Prof. and Chrmn. of the Dept. 1963–71; Emeritus Prof., McGill Univ., 1980– ; Surgeon-in-Chief, Montreal Gen. Hosp. 1963–71; Assoc. Dir., McGill-Montreal Gen. Hosp. Univ. Surg. Clinic, 1959–63, Dir., 1963–71; Assoc. Secy., R.C.P. & S. of Can., 1972–75, Consultant to that body 1976–82; has lectured at many N. Am. univs.; served as Capt., R.C.A.M.C. in Can., U.K., Italy and Holland, 1941–46; rec'd Duncan Graham Award, Royal Coll. of Phys. & Surgs. of Can. 1985; Surgeon's Award for Service to Safety, Nat. Safety Counc. 1985; F.N.R. Starr Award, Candn. Med. Assoc. 1990; Publications: Chapter on shock in 'Complications in Surgery and Their Management' by Artz and Hardy, 1967; over 80 articles in prof. journs.; Assoc. Ed., 'Journal of Trauma'; Ed. Comte., 'British Journal of Surgery'; Ed. Bd. 'Canadian Journal of Surgery'; 'Annals of Surgery'; F.R.C.S.(C); mem., Council and Comtes.; F.A.C.S.; mem., Board of Regents and Comtes.; mem., American Association Surg Trauma (Pres.); Central Surg. Assn. (Pres.); Canadian Assn. Clin. Surgs. (Pres.); Am. Surg. Assn. (Vice Pres.); Assn. Surgs. Que.; C.M.A.; Candn. Physiol. Soc.; Candn. Soc. Clin. Investigation; Internat. Fed. Surg. Colls. (Research Comte.); James IV Assn. Surgs. Inc. (Pres.); Montreal Medico-Chirurgical Soc.; Montreal Physiol. Soc.; Surg. Travel Club; Soc. Univ. Surgs.; Internat. Surg. Group (Treas.); Soc. for Surg. of the Alimentary Tract (Trustee); Candn. Assoc. of Gen. Surgeons (Hon. Mem.); Univ. Assoc. for Emergency Med. (Hon. Mem.); Delta Upsilon; Alpha Kappa Kappa; Alpha Omega Alpha; Un. Ch.; recreations: history, writing, travel; Home: 85 Range Road, Apt. 801, Ottawa, Ont. K1N 8J6.

**GURD, James W.,** B.A., Ph.D.; b. Montreal, Que. 23 June 1943; s. David Slessor and Catherine (Wood) G.; e. Mount Allison Univ. B.A. 1964; McGill Univ. Ph.D. 1969; m. Linda d. Edward and Betty Johnson Sept. 1968; children: Sean A., Brendon J.; CHAIR, DIVISION OF LIFE SCIENCE, SCARBOROUGH CAMPUS, UNIV. OF TORONTO 1989– ; MRC Postdoctoral Fellow, Nat. Inst. for Med. Rsch. 1969–72; Rsch. Assoc., Brain Research Group, Indiana Univ. 1972–74; Prof. of Biochem., Univ. of Toronto 1974– ; Office: Toronto, Ont. M1C 1A4.

**GURNEY, David John,** B.A.; business executive; b. Toronto, Ont. 18 Dec. 1956; s. John Morley and Norma Mae (Bulmer) G.; e. York Univ., B.A. 1979; m. Lori d. John and Doris Gibson 5 Sept. 1981; CHRMN. AND C.E.O., SOFTQUAD INTERNATIONAL INC. 1993– and PRES., CAROLIAN SYSTEMS 1987– ; Bd. Chrmn., Information Technology Rsch. Centre 1991– (Bd. Chrmn., Industrial Adv. Counc. 1988–91); Vice Pres., Chief Financial Offr. & Dir., Carolian Systems 1983–86, Vice Pres. & Dir. 1986–87; Secy. Treas. & Dir., Delrina Corp. 1989–92; Office: 5 – 3397 American Dr., Mississauga, Ont. L4V 1T8.

**GURR, David Hugh Courtney,** C.D., B.Sc.; writer; b. London, Eng. 5 Feb. 1936; s. James Hugh Courtney and Janet Isolde (Harvey) G.; e. Sherborne Prep. 1946; Univ. Coll. Sch. London 1947; Belmont High Sch. Victoria 1954; Royal Candn. Naval Coll. 'Venture' 1954–56; Univ. of Victoria, B.Sc. 1965; m. Judith d. Alan and Marion Deverell 30 Aug. 1958 (separated 1989); children: Anthony, Gregory, Nicola; served with RCN 1954–70, HMCS 'Ontario,' 'James Bay,' 'Fraser,' 'Beacon Hill,' 'Yukon'; served as computer systems analyst hydrofoil project 'Bras d'Or' with Canadian Westinghouse Hamilton 1966–68, Iroquois Destroyer Class 280 with Litton Industries Ottawa 1968–70, Computing Devices of Canada (Project Leader) 1970; house designer and builder Vancouver Island 1971–80; writer since 1976; author: (novels) 'Troika' 1979; 'A Woman Called Scylla' 1981; 'The Action of the Tiger' 1984; 'An American Spy Story' 1984; 'On the Endangered List' 1985; 'The Ring Master' 1987 (nominated for the Gov. General's Award); 'The Voice of the Crane' 1989 (short-listed for Commonwealth Prize, Candn.-Caribbean Div.); (stage plays) 'Leonora' 1984; 'The Ring Play: An Evening with Hitler' 1991; co-author 2 screen plays (with George Cosmatos); mem., P.E.N., Writers' Union of Can.; Authors' Guild; recreations: landscape design, music; Address: 239E Argyle Ave., Ottawa, Ont. K2P 1B8.

**GUSELLA, Mary Margaret,** B.A., LL.B.; lawyer, public servant; b. Ottawa, Ont. 15 Nov. 1948; d. Frank and Helen (Noel) G.; e. Univ. of Toronto B.A. 1970; Univ. of Ottawa LL.B. 1977; Candn. Securities Inst. Certificate; PRESIDENT, ATLANTIC CANADA OPPORTUNITIES AGENCY (ACOA) 1993– ; Energy, Mines & Resources and Canada Oil & Gas Lands Admin. 1980–82; Dept. of Finance 1982–83; Crown Corps., Treasury Bd. 1983–86; Asst. Sec. to the Cabinet (Communications), Privy Council Office 1986–90; Assoc. Under Sec. of State, Sec. of State 1990–91; Deputy Minister, Multiculturalism and Citizenship Canada 1991–93; Mem. Bar of Ontario; Office: 644 Main St., P.O. Box 6051, Moncton, N.B. E1C 9J8.

**GUSELLA, Richard A.,** M.A.; executive; b. Drumheller, Alta. 26 March 1944; s. Henry Ernest and Margaret Beryl (McCrackin) G.; e. Univ. of Calgary B.A. 1966, M.A. (Econ.) 1969; m. Margaret Isabel McLeod 19 May 1967; children: Jennifer, Michael; PRES., GUSELLA OIL INVESTMENTS LIMITED 1991– ; Dir., North Canadian Oils Limited; Past Chrmn., Independent Petroleum Assn. of Canada (IPAC); Dir. & Past Pres., Calgary Petroleum Club; Landman, Texaco Exploration, Calgary 1966–67, 1969–70; Analyst, Greenshields Inc., Calgary 1970, Research Mgr. Toronto 1973, Mgr. Edmonton 1974, Div. Vice Pres. Calgary 1976; Partner, Peters & Co., Calgary 1977–79; Pres. & C.E.O., Sceptre Resources Limited 1979–91; recreations: golf, skiing; Clubs: Glencoe Golf & Country; Calgary Golf & Country; Calgary Petroleum; Ranchmen's; Home: 107 Oakside Close S.W., Calgary, Alta. T2V 4T9.

**GUSHUE, Hon. James Randell,** M.A.; judge; b. St. John's, Nfld. 4 June 1933; s. Raymond and Phyllis (Randell) G.; e. Prince of Wales Coll. St. John's 1950; Mem. Univ. of Nfld. B.A. 1955; Oxford Univ. (Rhodes Scholar Nfld.) M.A. (Jurisprudence) 1959; m. Gail Allison d. Hubert C. Herder, Topsail, Conception Bay, Nfld. 11 June 1970; one s. Jonathan; JUDGE, COURT OF APPEAL, SUPREME COURT OF NFLD. since 1976; called to Bar of Nfld. 1960; practiced law with Hon. P. J. Lewis, Q.C., St. John's 1960–61; joined Food & Agric. Organ. of UN, Rome 1961–62; practiced law St. John's 1963–76; Partner, Stirling, Ryan & Goodridge; apptd. Q.C. 1975; Commr., Royal Comn. on Health & Safety Standards and Standard of Care in Nursing Homes and Homes for Special Care in Prov. Nfld. 1977–78; recreations: tennis, fishing, walking; Home: 144 Elizabeth Ave., St. John's, Nfld. A1B 1S3; Office: St. John's, Nfld. A1C 5P5.

**GUSSOW, William Carruthers,** M.Sc., Ph.D., F.R.S.C. (1955), F.G.S., F.G.S.A.; consulting geologist and engineer; b. London, Eng., 25 April 1908; s. Hans Theodor and Jenny Maria (Hitzigrath) G.; e. Pub. and High Schs., Ottawa, Ont.; Queen's Univ., B.Sc. 1933, M.Sc., 1935; Mass. Inst. of Tech., Ph.D. 1938; m. Margaret Blackett, d. late Christopher Blackett Robinson, 24 Sept. 1936; children: Christopher H., David William, James Frederick Robinson; Map Draughtsman, Geological Survey of Can., 1927–29; ten field seasons on geol. mapping with Fed. and Prov. Geol. Surveys in Ont., Que., and N.W.T., 1930–39; travelled extensively in U.S., Mexico, Panama, Japan, Philippines, Malay, Burma, India, Ceylon, N. Africa, Italy, Sicily, Austria, Germany, Holland, England 1937–38; Geol. Royal Mil. Coll. staff, Kingston, Ont., 1938–39; Cost Engr., Office Engr. and Resident Engr. on Shipshaw Hydro-Elect. Power Devel. and Arvida Works Que. 1939–44; Chief Geol. and Exploration Mgr., Shell Oil Co. of Can. Ltd., and Shell Inc. in Okla. and Texas, 1945–52; Consulting Geol. and Engr., 1953–55; Staff Geol., Union Oil Co. of Calif. 1956–62, Sr. Research Assoc., 1962–71; Consultant, Japan Petroleum Development Corp., 1972–74; awarded Royal Soc. of Can. Research Fellowship, 1936; discovered principle of differential entrapment of oil and gas; has publ. numerous articles on geol. and related subjects; discovered Gussow Method of enhanced oil recovery 1985 (patents approved 1986) a method that promises to recover all the oil left in the ground and double or triple recoverable oil reserves world-wide (U.S. patent issued 1987, Candn. patent 1989; USSR patent 1990); named Mt. Lipalian (near Lake Louise); Fellow, Geol. Assn. Can.; Soc. of Econ. Geols.; Life Mem., Am. Assn. of Petroleum Geols. (mem. Pacific Sect. 1962–72), (Distinguished lectr. 1955); Internat. Assoc. Sedimentol.; Life Mem., Candn. Inst. Mining & Metall. (Chrmn., Calgary Br. 1954–55); rec'd 'Dr. W. J. Wright Award' for pioneering geological mapping in N.B., Candn. Inst. Mining & Metallurgy 1986; Engn. Inst. Can. (Program Chrmn., Calgary Br. 1953–54); Alta. Soc. of Petroleum Geols. (Pres. 1959); Assn. Prof. Engrs. Alta. (mem. Council 1955–56); Fellow, Am. Assn. Advanc. Science; Charter mem., Am. Inst. Prof. Geol. (Secy.-Treas., Calif. Sec., 1967–68, Emeritous Mem.); mem., Nat. Adv. Comte. on Research in Geol. Sciences, Ottawa, 1957–59; House of Soc. Reps., Am. Geol. Inst., (1963–65); Nat. Acad. of Sciences Subcomte. on Geol. Comte. on Space Programs for Earth Observationss Adv. to U.S. Geol. Survey, 1966–72; Hon. mem. Candn. Soc. of Petroleum Geol., 1980; Guest, Accademia Nazionale dei Lincei, Italy, 1957; Guest Lectr., Lomonosov Univ., Moscow, USSR, 1960; U.N. Expert to Research & Training Inst., Oil & Natural Gas Comn., Dehra Dun, India, 1967; Guest, People's Republic of China, to discuss Taching oilfield, Oct. 1977; recreations: geological field work; Home: 1005 - 1510 Riverside Dr., Ottawa, Ont. K1G 4X5.

**GUSTAFSON, Leonard Joe;** senator; politician; farmer; b. Macoun, Sask. 10 Nov. 1933; s. Clarence Arthur and Theresa G.; e. Macoun (Sask.) Sch.; m. Alice Snider 9 Jan. 1952; children: Jerry, Terry, Bonna Jean, Bentley; APPOINTED TO THE SENATE 1993– ; Farmer, cattleman, contractor, businessman; el. to H. of

C. G.E. 1979, re-el. 1980, Sept. 1984, Nov. 1988; mem., Standing Ctte. on Agric. 1983; named Shadow Cabinet Critic to Candn. Wheat Bd.; appt'd. Parl. Secty. to Prime Minister Nov. 1984; re-appt'd. Nov. 1985, Oct. 1986, Oct. 1987, Apr. 1989, Apr. 1990, Sept. 1990 and again in Jan. 1991; Dir., Macoun Co-op Assn. 12 yrs.; lay leader Evangelical Ch. of Can. 25 yrs.; Pres., Estevan Crusade for Christ 4 yrs.; mem., Bd. Evangelical China Fellowship (Orphanages) 1967– ; mem., Bd. Hillcrest Christian Coll.; Councillor, R.M. of Cymri 36, 1973–79; recreations: curling, hockey; Home: P.O. Box 100, Macoun, Sask. S0C 1P0; Office: 603 Victoria Bldg., Ottawa, Ont. K1A 0A4.

**GUSTAFSON, Ralph Barker,** C.M., M.A., D. Litt., D.C.L.; poet; b. Lime Ridge, Que. 16 Aug. 1909; s. Carl Otto and Gertrude Ella (Barker) G.; e. Bishop's Univ., B.A. 1929 (1st Class Hons. in Hist. and Eng., winner of Gov.-Gen's. Medal, Chancellor's Prize, Ven. Archdeacon Scott's Prize for Poetry, Mackie Eng. Essay, and 1st Class Aggregate Prize), M.A. 1930 (Thesis on 'Sensuous Imagery in Shelley and Keats,' winner of Ven. Archdeacon Scott's Prize for Poetry again); Oxford Univ., B.A. 1933 (Hons. in Eng. Lit. and Lang.), M.A. 1963; D.Litt. Mt. Allison 1973; D.C.L. Bishop's Univ. 1977; D.Litt. York Univ. 1991; m. Elisabeth, d. Francis X. Renninger, 1958; Prof. and Poet in Residence, Bishop's Univ. 1963–1979; Prof. Emeritus 1993; Univ. Award of Merit 1992; music critic, C.B.C. since 1960; Mus. Master, Bishop's Coll. Sch. 1930; Master St. Alban's Sch., Brockville, Ont., 1934; thereafter lived in London, Eng., until return to Can. 1938; with Brit. Inf. Servs. 1942–46; author of following books of poems: 'The Golden Chalice' 1935 (awarded Prix David by Que. Govt. 1935); 'Alfred the Great' (a play in blank verse) 1937; 'Epithalamium in Time of War' 1941; 'Lyrics Unromantic' 1942; 'Flight into Darkness' 1944; 'Rivers Among Rocks' 1960; 'Rocky Mountain Poems' 1960; 'Sift in an Hourglass' 1966; 'Ixion's Wheel' 1969; 'Selected Poems' 1972; 'Theme & Variations for Sounding Brass' 1972; 'Fire on Stone' 1974 (winner of Gov. Gen.'s Award for poetry 1974, and winner of A.J.M. Smith Award of Internat. Studies Program, Michigan State Univ. 1974); 'Corners in the Glass' 1977; 'Soviet Poems' 1978; 'Sequences' 1979; 'Gradations of Grandeur' 1982; 'Landscape with Rain' 1980; 'Conflicts of Spring' 1981; 'At the Ocean's Verge' (selected poems U.S.) 1984; 'The Moment is All: Selected Poems 1944 to 1983' 1983; 'Solidarnosc: Prelude' 1983; 'Manipulations on Greek Themes' 1988; 'Impromptus' 1984; 'Directives of Autumn' 1984; 'Twelve Landscapes' 1985; 'Collected Poems' Vol. I & Vol. II 1987; 'Winter Prophecies' 1987; 'The Celestial Corkscrew' 1989; 'Shadows in the Grass' 1991; 'Configurations at Midnight' 1992; 'Tracks in the Snow' 1994; 'The Brazen Tower' (short stories) 1974; 'The Vivid Air' (short stories) 1980; 'Plummets and Other Partialities' (essays) 1987; wrote 'Poetry and Canada' for Candn. Legion Educ. Services 1945; his short stories and crit. articles have appeared in foremost lit. journs. in Can. and abroad, incl. 'The Best American Short Stories' 1948, 1950; 'Canadian Short Stories' 1960; 'A Book of Canadian Stories' 1962; and in foremost poetry anthologies up to the present; Ed. of 'Anthology of Canadian Poetry' 1942; 'Canadian Accent' 1944 (contemporary Candn. poetry and prose); 'A Little Anthology of Canadian Poets' 1943; Candn. poetry issue of 'Voices' 1943; 'Penguin Book of Candn. Verse' 1958, rev. ed. 1967, 1975, 1984; 'A Literary Friendship: The Correspondence of Ralph Gustafson and W.W.E. Ross' (ed. Bruce Whiteman) 1984; 'A Poetics of Place; the Poetry of Ralph Gustafson' by Dermot McCarthy 1991; awarded Queen's Silver Jubilee Medal 1978; Member of the Order of Canada 1992; Commemorative Medal, 125th Anniversary of Candn. Confedn. 1992; Poetry Award, The Quebec Soc. for the Promotion of English Language Literature 1993; readings recorded by Library of Congress, Washington, D.C. 1977 & 1993; poetry delegate to U.K. 1972, to U.S.S.R. 1976, to Washington, D.C. 1977, to Italy 1981 and 1982; 'Winter Prophecies: The Poetry of Ralph Gustafson' prod. by the National Film Bd. of Can., premiered at Bishop's Univ. and at Montreal and Toronto, 1989, 1990; Founding and Life Mem., League of Candn. Poets; Writers' Union of Can.; Keble Coll. Assn., Oxford (Life); Home: North Hatley, Que. J0B 2C0.

**GUTELIUS, John Robert,** B.A., M.D., C.M., F.R.C.S.(C), F.A.C.S.; surgeon; educator; b. Montreal, Que. 18 Jan. 1929; s. Nelson Edward and Gertrude (Regina) G.; e. Univ. of Montreal (Loyola Coll.) B.A. 1950; McGill Univ. M.D., C.M. 1955, Dipl. Surg. 1961; m. Elizabeth Ann Timmins 23 July 1955; children: Charles, Julie, Ann, John, Joan, Peter, Matthew, Kathryn; PROF. OF SURGERY, QUEEN'S UNIV. 1973– ; Intern Royal Victoria Hosp. Montreal 1955–56; Resident McGill Univ. Teaching Hosp. 1956–61, Assoc. Prof. of Surgery McGill Univ. 1965–69, Assoc. Dean 1968–69; Prof. and Head of Surgery Univ. of Saskatchewan 1969–73, Dean Coll. of Med. 1970–73; practice specializing in Surgery Kingston, Ont. 1973– ; Surgeon-in-Chief, Kingston Gen. Hosp., Prof. and Head of Surgery present univ. 1973–83; James IV Traveller in Surgery 1973; Markle Scholar in Acad. Med. 1963–68; mem. Assn. Candn. Med. Colls. (Pres. 1973–74); Am. Surg. Assn.; Candn. Assn. Clin. Surgs. (Pres. 1979–80); Candn. Soc. Vascular Surg. (Pres. 1980–81); Dir., Heart and Stroke Found. of Ont. 1981–87; R. Catholic; Home: R.R. #1, Kingston, Ont. K7L 4V1; Office: Kingston, Ont. K7L 3N6.

**GUTH, DeLloyd J.,** B.A., M.A., Ph.D., F.R.H.S.; legal historian, university teacher; b. Stevens Point, Wisc. 7 Nov. 1938; s. Frank L. and Angeline F. (Glodowski) G.; e. Marquette Univ. B.A. 1960; Creighton Univ. M.A. 1962; Clare Coll., Cambridge Univ., B.A. status 1964; Univ. of Pittsburgh Ph.D. 1967; m. Katherine Ann d. Dr. Rigdon and Maureen Ratliff 23 Jan. 1971; children: Geoffrey John, Martha Angeline; PROFESSOR OF LAW AND DIR., CANADIAN LEGAL HISTORY PROJECT, UNIV. OF MANITOBA 1993– ; Univ. Teacher of ancient, med., modern history with emphasis on English common law and Candn. legal-judicial hist.: Clare Coll., Cambridge 1964–66; Queen Mary Coll. London 1965–66; Univ. of Michigan 1966–73; Univ. of Bristol 1974–75; Univ. of Lancaster 1975–77; Univ. of Missouri-St. Louis 1978–79; Univ. of Wisconsin-Stevens Point 1978–81; Univ. of Illinois 1981–82; Univ. of Victoria Law School 1983; Univ. of B.C., Fac. of Law 1982–93; Consultant Curator, Supreme Court of Canada & Founder & Extve. Ed., Supreme Court of Can. Hist. Soc. 1987– ; Consultant & Activist for legal-judicial archives & records mngt., as well as Cons. for legal his. rsch. in present-day litigation; designer & builder of displays in Supreme Court of Can.; Andrew Mellon Pre-doct. Fellow 1963–66; Frederic W. Maitland Bursary 1965–66; Fellow, Royal Hist. Soc.; Treas., Selden Soc. (Canada); Occasional Guest, Vicki Gabereau Show, CBC-AM; Mem., Am. Hist. Soc.; Candn. Hist. Soc.; The Osgoode Soc.; Selden Soc.; Supreme Court of Can. Hist. Soc.; Am. Soc. for Legal Hist.; N. Am. Conf. on British Studies; author: 'Late-Medieval England 1377–1485' 1976, 'The Assassination of John F. Kennedy ... Historical and Legal Bibliography' 1980, 'Tudor Rule and Revolution' 1982 and num. articles & book reviews; editor of annual vols for Supreme Court of Can. Hist. Soc 1991– , 'Late-Medieval Family Law 1250–1500' 1994; recreations: opera, mystery, travel; Office: Faculty of Law, Univ. of Manitoba, Winnipeg, Man. R3T 2N2.

**GUTHRIE, Arthur Derek, The Hon. Mr. Justice,** B.A., B.C.L.; judge; b. Montreal, Que. 16 Dec. 1935; s. Arthur Weeks and Sheila Frances (Saunderson) G.; e. Lower Can. Coll. 1953; McGill Univ. B.A. 1957, B.C.L. 1960; m. Monique d. Jean-Robert and Marie-Aimée Piette 20 Aug. 1960; children: Albert Christopher, Julie Anna; JUDGE, SUPERIOR COURT 1987– ; Partner, Ogilvy, Renault 1961–87; Past Lectr., Fac. of Law, McGill Univ.; Environ. Law, MacDonald Coll.; Past Editor-in-Chief, McGill Law Journal; Past Pres., Reddy Mem. Hosp. Ctr.; Victorian Order of Nurses, Montreal; Mem., Candn. Inst. for the Admin. of Justice; Bar of Que. 1961–87; Sec., Bar of Montreal 1968–69; Mem., Candn. Bar Assn.; Assoc. Mem., Am. Bar Assn.; Past Pres., McGill Kappa Alpha Soc.; recreations: 'week-end' farming, hiking, hunting, photography, philately; Club: Shahwandahgooze; Home: 174 Melbourne, Mount Royal, Que. H3P 1G4; Office: Palais de Justice, 1 rue Notre-Dame est, Montreal, Qué. H2Y 1B6.

**GUTHRIE, H(ugh) Donald,** Q.C., B.A., LL.B.; lawyer; b. Toronto, Ont. 20 March 1929; s. late Donald, Q.C. and late Mary Louise (Telfer) G.; e. Univ. of Toronto Schs. 1946 (Maurice Cody Prize Hist.); Trinity Coll., Univ. of Toronto, B.A. (Hons.) 1950 (F.H. Cosgrave Scholarship Social & Philos. Studies, Urwick Prize Pol. Sci. & Econ.); Osgoode Hall Law Sch. grad. 1954 (Bronze Medal, Christopher Robinson Meml. Scholarship); m. Ann Lambert 3 Sept. 1953; children: Gay, Barbara, Neil; Sr. Partner, Cassels, Brock & Blackwell, Barr. & Sol., Chrmn. of Partnership 1987–92; gen. law practice Toronto since 1954; cr. Q.C. 1968; mem. Exec. Ctte. present firm 1980–87; Dir., Candn. National Railway Co. and member, Real Estate and Environmental & Social Policy Cttes. 1993– ; Dir., C.N. Tower Ltd.; Grand Trunk Corp.; Central Vermont Railway Inc. 1993– ; Dir., Travcan Ltd., Travelers Indemnity Co. of Can. & Travelers Life Ins. Co. of Can. 1987–88; Chief Agent for Canada of Travelers Ins. Co., Travelers Indemnity Co. and Phoenix Ins. Co. of Hartford 1988– ; Dir. & Sec., Brockhouse Canada Ltd.; Internat. Flavors & Fragrances (Canada) Ltd.; Trustee, Law Found. Ont. rep. Atty. Gen. Ont. 1974– , Chrmn. 1983– ; mem. Can. Council 1986–92, Audit & Evaluation Ctte. 1987–92 (Chrmn. 1990–92), Exec. Ctte. 1988–92, Compensation Ctte. 1990–92; Comnr. & Chrmn. 1986 Comn. Judges' Salaries & Benefits; mem. Comn. El. Finances Ont. 1980–90; Life mem. Art Gallery Ont.; Hon. Life & Benefactor mem. & Hon. Trustee, Royal Ont. Museum, Trustee & mem. Exec. Ctte., Chrmn. Property Ctte. 1973–79, Project Control Group Renovation & Expansion Project 1974–79, Vice Chrmn. of Bd. 1975–79, Acting Chrmn. 1979, mem. Gallery Devel. Ctte. 1983–89; Gov. Branksome Hall Sch. 1973–83, Vice Chrmn. 1980–82, Chrmn. Property Ctte., Hon. Trustee of Found. 1983– ; mem. Gen. Ctte. Leonard Found. 1982– and Charities Ctte. 1990– ; Candn. Inst. Advanced Rsch. 1986– ; Dir., Toronto Internat. Festival 1981– ; active every Ont. and fed. g.e. 1948–90; various riding exec. & campaign positions 1957–74; Founding Dir. P.C. Can. Fund – Le Fonds P.C. du Can. 1974, Sec. 1974–93, Dir. 1989–93; mem. Pres.' Ctte. Univ. of Toronto; Candn. Museums Assn.; Ont. Hist. Soc.; York Pioneer & Hist. Soc.; Simcoe Co. Museum; Huronia Woodland Owners Assn.; Founding mem. Candn. Assn. Univ. Solrs., Pres. 1982–83, Exec. Ctte. 1978–84; mem. Nat. Assn. Coll. & Univ. Attys. (rep. Univ. Toronto) 1977– ; Nat. Health Lawyers Assn.; Delta Kappa Epsilon; Trustee Bd., Presb. Ch. in Can. 1986–92; Elder & mem. of Session, mem. Bd. Mgrs. St. Andrew's Ch. Toronto; P. Conservative; Clubs: Empire; Canadian; University; Badminton & Racquet; Albany (Dir. 1968–82, 1984– ); Home: 305 Russell Hill Rd., Toronto, Ont. M4V 2T7; Office: 2200, 40 King St. W., Toronto, Ont. M5H 3C2.

**GUTHRIE, Hugh,** Q.C., B.Com.; solicitor; b. Toronto, Ont. 3 Feb. 1931; s. Hugh Comyn and Margaret (Murray) G.; e. elem. and high schs. Guelph; Univ. of Toronto B.Com. 1952; Osgoode Hall Law Sch. 1956; m. Lorna Jean Ellen d. Harold A. Knight, Guelph, Ont. 4 Aug. 1961; two d. Lorna Margaret, Patricia Ann; PROPRIETOR, HUNGERFORD, GUTHRIE & BERRY; Dir. The Homewood Sanitarium of Guelph Ltd.; Blount Canada Ltd.; Linamar Corp.; called to Bar of Ont. 1956; cr. Q.C. 1968; sometime lectr. Univ. of Guelph; mem. Dental Technols. Adv. Comte. 1972; Past Pres. Guelph Y.M.-Y.W.C.A.; served with C.O.T.C. 1950–52; Fellow, Foundation for Legal Research; Past Pres. Wellington Law Assn.; mem. Waverley Lodge Guelph; Delta Kappa Epsilon; P. Conservative; Presbyterian; recreation: golf; Clubs: Albany (Toronto); University (Toronto); Home: 49 Edinburgh Rd., Guelph, Ont. N1H 5P2; Office: 59 Woolwich St., Guelph, Ont. N1H 6J9.

**GUTHRIE, Richard Hamilton,** B.Sc.; b. London, Ont. 15 Nov. 1916; s. Hamilton and Bernice J. (Meldrum) G.; e. London Central Collegiate, Sr. Matric., 1934; McGill Univ., Sch. of Arch., 1934–36; Mass. Inst. Tech., B.Sc. (Aero Engn.) 1939; m. Isobelle Ruth, d. Brainard Carlyle, Oshawa, Ont., Dec. 1942; children: Richard, Barbara, Susan, Carolyn, JoAnn; began career with National Research Council, Ottawa, 1940–42; Turbo Research Ltd., 1945; DeHavilland Aircraft, 1946–50; Hussman Refrigerator Co. Ltd., 1951; joined United Aircraft of Canada Ltd. 1951; Engn. Mgr. until 1962; Planning Mgr. until 1966 when apptd. Vice Pres., Indust. & Marine Div.; Pres. and Dir., Scan Marine Inc., and Vice Pres., Pratt and Whitney Aircraft of Canada Ltd. 1980–84 (ret.); served as Flt. Lieut., R.C.A.F., 1942–45; AFHQ Engineering Officer; Fellow, Candn. Aero. & Space Inst. (Founding mem. and Chrmn., Planning Comte.); mem., Corp. Prof. Engrs. Que.; United Church; recreations: swimming, canoeing, tennis, gardening, skiing, sailing; Clubs: Lake Brulé Country; Royal St. Lawrence Yacht; Homes: 123 Beacon Hill Rd., Beaconsfield, Que. H9W 1S8; Lac Brulé, Terrebonne, Que.

**GUTHRIE, Roderick Ian Lawrence,** Ph.D., B.Sc.(Eng.), A.R.S.M., D.I.C., F.C.I.M., P.Eng.; educator; b. Sutton Coldfield, Eng. 12 Sept. 1941; s. Lawrence Carr and Norah Gertrude (Smith) G.; e. Sessions's Sch. Cyprus 1950; Durham Cath. Choristers Sch. 1954 (Head Chorister 1953–54); Nottingham High Sch. 1959; Royal Sch. of Mines, Imp. Coll. London 1960–67 B.Sc.(Eng.) 1963, A.R.S.M. 1963, Ph.D. 1967, D.I.C. 1967; m. Margaret d. Arthur and Olive Skinner 22 Oct. 1966; children: Alexandra, Jason; MACDONALD PROF. OF METALL. ENG. McGILL UNIV. 1980– and DIR. AND FOUND., McGILL METALS PROCESSING CENTRE 1989– , Pres., Metallurgical Soc. of CIM 1992–93; Asst. Prof. of Metall. Eng. present Univ. 1967, Assoc. Prof. 1970, Prof. 1979; seconded for rsch. studies 1979–81; recipient numerous awards incl. Steacie Fellowship Sci. & Eng. Rsch. Council 1979–81 (1st Candn. Eng.); Light Metals & Tenenbaum Awards AIME 1988 and Extractive Metall. Awards 1984, 1988; Alcan Award 1987; Plummer Gold Medal Eng. Inst. Can. 1976; Henry Marion Howe Awards AIME, ASM 1976, 1982; John Chipman Awards Iron & Steel Soc. AIME 1975,

1983; holds some 50 patents: detection of inclusions in liquid metals and metal delivery techniques for high speed thin strip metal casting machines; Cons. to many steel and non-ferrous nat. and internat. co's; presented courses process metall. and steelmaking some 15 univs.; author 'The Physical Properties of Liquid Metals' 1988; 'Engineering in Process Metallurgy' 1989; author or co-author over 175 rsch. papers; Fellow, Candn. Inst. of Metallurgy; mem. C.I.M.; A.I.M.E.; A.S.M.; Sigma Xi; recreations: running, cycling; Home: 328 Roslyn Ave., Westmount, Que. H3Z 2L6; Office: McGill Metals Processing Centre, 3450 University St., Montreal, Que. H3A 2A7.

**GUTKNECHT, Lt.-Gen. (RTD) René Gutknecht,** CMM, OStJ, CD; organization executive; b. Montréal, Qué. 23 July 1930; s. Herman and Germaine (Bernier) G.; e. Coll. Notre Dame; McGill Univ. B.A. 1953; m. Claire d. George and Leona Forget 7 Aug. 1954; one s.: Eric; GENTLEMAN USHER OF THE BLACK ROD, THE SENATE OF CANADA 1989– ; Nat. Extve. Secy., Cdn. Corps of Commissionaires 1991– ; 35 years of service in Candn. Army; Regimental Serv., Royal Candn. Dragoons & Lord Strathcona Horse (RC) & command & staff appts. in Can., Vietnam, India, Pakistan, U.S. & Fed. Rep. of Germany; last appt., Candn. Military Rep., NATO Military Ctte. in Brussels; 3 years as Commandant, Ottawa Div., Candn. Corps. of Comnrs.; Col. Commandant Royal Candn. Armoured Corps.; Life mem., Royal Candn. Armoured Corps. Assn.; Mem., Bd. of Dir., Conf. of Defence Assn. Inst.; Extve. Mem., Det Assn. Network; Mem. Editorial Bd., Forum Magazine; recreations: jogging, skiing; Home: 21 Ramsgate Private, Ottawa, Ont. K1V 8M4; Office: Rm. 503, 100 Gloucester, Ottawa, Ont. K2P 0A4.

**GUTTERIDGE, Donald George,** B.A.; educator; writer; b. Sarnia, Ont. 30 Sept. 1937; s. William Ernest Charles and Margaret Grace (McWatters) G.; e. Chatham (Ont.) Coll. Inst. 1956; Univ. of W. Ont. B.A. 1960; m. Anne D. John and Margaret Barnett 30 June 1961; children: John, Kate; PROFESSOR EMERITUS OF EDUCATION, UNIV. OF WESTERN ONT.; High Sch. Eng. Teacher Elmira, Ingersoll and London (Ont.) 1960–68; Asst. Prof. of Edn. present Univ. 1969; author (poetry) 'Riel' 1968; 'The Village Within' 1970; 'Death at Quebec' 1971; 'Saying Grace: An Elegy' 1972; 'Coppermine: The Quest For North' 1973; 'Borderlands' 1975; 'Tecumseh' 1976; 'A True History of Lambton County' 1977; 'God's Geography' 1981; 'The Exiled Heart' 1986; 'Love in the Wintertime' 1990; (fiction) 'Bus-Ride' 1974; 'All In Good Time' 1980; 'St. Vitus Dance' 1987; 'Shaman's Ground' 1988; 'How the World Began' 1991; 'Summer's Idyll' 1993; (Pedagogy) 'Incredible Journeys' 1986, rev. 1990; 'Brave Season' 1983; 'The Country of the Young' 1977; ed. 'Language and Expression' 1970 (textbook); 'Mountain and Plain' 1978, 'Rites of Passage' 1979 (high sch. anthols.); 'The Dimension of Delight' (pedagogy) 1988; recipient Pres.' Medal Univ. of W. Ont. Best Poem 1972; recreations: golf, racquetball; Home: 114 Victoria St., London, Ont. N6A 2B5.

**GUTTMAN, Irving Allen;** C.M.; artistic/stage director; b. Chatham, Ont. 27 oct. 1928; s. Shea and Bernetta (Schaffer) G.; e. Guy Drummond Sch., Strathcona Acad. 1941–46; Royal Cons. of Music 1947–52; ARTISTIC DIR., EDMONTON OPERA 1966– ; Artistic Dir., L'Atelier Lyrique de l'Opéra de Montréal 1989– ; Asst. Dir. to Herman Geiger-Torel, Candn. Opera Co. 1947–52; Asst. Dir., New Orleans 1951–52; Dir., Opera Guild of Montreal 1959–68; Montreal Symphony 1963–68; Montreal Fests.; Dir., Prodns. for Baltimore Opera, New Orleans, Phil., San Francisco, Seattle, Toronto, Gran Teatro Liceo Barcelona, Spain, Rio de Janero, Puerto Rico, Hawaii, Radio-Canada-TV, Montreal, Taiwan; Founding Artistic Dir., Vancouver Opera 1960–74; 1981–84; Artistic Dir., Manitoba Opera 1972– ; Artistic Dir., Edmonton Opera 1966– ; Courteney Youth Music CYMC 1974–84; Centennial Medal 1967; Queen's Jubilee Medal 1977; Order of Canada 1989; Edmonton Cultural Hall of Fame 1989; The Alberta Achievement Award 1989; Commemorative Medal, 125th Anniversary of Candn. Confedn. 1992; Home: 50 - 1386 Nicola St., Vancouver, B.C. V6G 2G2.

**GUTTMAN, Naomi Ellen,** B.F.A., M.A.; writer; b. Montreal, Que. 10 July 1960; d. Frank Myron and Herta Ann (Hofmann) G.; e. Concordia Univ. B.F.A. 1985; Univ. of Southern Calif. at Los Angeles, Ph.D. studies 1993– ; m. Jonathan T. s. James and Sharon Mead 6 July 1986; teacher of creative writing, literature, and composition; Bliss Carman Award for Lyric Poetry 1989; QSpell (A.M. Klein Award) for Poetry 1992; author: 'Reasons for Winter' (poetry) 1991; Home: 1303 Acacia Ave., Torrance, CA 90501; Office: c/o Brick Books, P.O. Box 38, Stn. B., London, Ont. M6A 4V3.

**GUY, Claude;** stockbroker; b. Montreal, Que. 15 May 1930; s. Roméo and Marguerite (Lapointe) G.; e. St. Charles Garnier Coll., Quebec City; coll. Ste. Marie and Loyola Coll. (Comm.), Montreal; children: Geneviève, Charles, Sylvain; VICE PRES., DOMINION SECURITIES INC. (RBC); Clk., Montreal Refrigerating and Storage, The Sun Life Assurance Co. and Canadian Alliance Corp. for 1 yr. each; Salesman, W.C. Pitfield & Co. Ltd. for 8 yrs.; Partner, Brault & Chaput, 1959; Extve. Vice-Pres. and Dir., Brault, Guy, Chaput Inc.; mem. Bd. of Mang., Candn. Stock Exchange, 1963 (Chrmn. 1968); Dir., Montreal Br., Jr. Invest. Dealers' Assn. Can., 1954–55 (Pres. 1957–58; Hon. Pres. 1958–59); Gov., Montreal Stock Exchange 1969; R. Catholic; recreations: skiing, swimming, golf; Clubs: St-Denis; Home: 1550 Dr. Penfield St., Montreal, Que. H3G 1C2; Office: 2000 McGill College, Suite 300, Montréal, Que. H3A 3H5.

**GUY, Donald Byron,** B.S.I.E., P.Eng.; professional industrial engineer; b. Chelsea, Mass. 11 Oct. 1914; s. John and Leotta A. (McPhee) G.; e. Northeastern Univ. B.S.I.E. 1937; Univ. of Pennsylvania & Yale Univ., grad. studies in indus. mgmt.; m. Frances d. Hedwig and Nils Carlson 29 July 1939; children: Bonnie Lee, Cheryl Lynne, Wendy Jo; Indus. Engr., U.S. Steel Corp., Asst. Chief Ind. Engr., Johnson & Johnson, Field Engr., The Bellows Co. 1937–52 (U.S.); Pres., Bellows Internat. Ltd. Toronto (& Internat. Vice-Pres. parent co.) 1952–78; Mgmt. Engr. Consultant, priv. pract. & with Fed. Bus. Devel. Bank 1978– ; mem. & former Dir., Candn. Indus. Mgmt. Assn.; Candn. Mfg. Assn. (Pub. Chrmn. 1966–72); Toronto Indus. Comn.; mem., Pacific Basin Econ. Counc. (del. Japan-U.S.-Canada) 1966–71; Bd. of Govs., Queensway Gen. Hosp. 1969– (former Sec.; Chrmn. 1985– ); Bd., Lakeshore Psychiatric Hosp. 1973–79; Oakville Transit for Handicap 1983– ; Volunteer, Red Cross, United Appeal, Cancer Fund, various hospitals; rec'd Citizenship Award, A.P.E.O. 1987; Dir., Candn. Hosp. Assn. 1978–82 (Finance Chrmn. 1979–82); Peel Abilities Ltd. 1981–83; Trustee, Northeastern Univ. 1962– ; Chrmn., Acad. Affairs 1970–80; Hon. Trustee, Internat. Student Ctr., Univ. of Toronto 1980– (Co-Founder & Former Dir., 1962–72); mem., Pres. Adv. Ctte., Ohio Univ. 1965–68; Oakville Rotary Club (Paul Harris Fellow 1992); Masons; Am. Club (Pres. 1965–66); Soc. of Mgmt. (Pres. 1950–51); Assn. Profl. Engrs.; Address: 139 Elton Park, Oakville, Ont. L6J 4C2.

**GUY, Geoffrey Ivan,** B.Sc., F.C.I.A., F.I.A., A.S.A., M.A.A.A.; insurance executive; b. Saxmundham, U.K. 3 Jan. 1947; s. Ivan George and Gladys Mabel (Etheridge) G.; e. Leiston Grammar Sch. 1965; Univ. of London B.Sc. 1968 (Hons. Math); m. Jo Ann Martin 1981; children: Andrea, Mireille; VICE-PRES. & CHIEF ACTUARY, U.S. OPERATIONS, THE MANUFACTURERS LIFE INSURANCE CO. 1987– ; Prudential Assurance 1968–87 (left as Sr. Vice-Pres. & Actuary); Mem., Candn. Inst. of Actuaries; Soc. of Actuaries; Acad. of Actuaries; U.K. Inst. of Actuaries; recreations: golf, skiing, fitness, reading; Home: R.R. #1, Elora, Ont. N0B 1S0; Office: 200 Bloor St. E., Toronto, Ont. M4W 1E5.

**GUY, Paul,** M.B.A.; b. 11 May 1935; s. Philippe and Gerardine R.; e. Univ. Laval L.Comm. 1971, M.B.A. Fin. 1972; m. Huguette d. Jean-Charles Larose 23 June 1956; children: Joyce, Richard; SECY. GEN., INTERNAT. ORGANIZATION OF SECURITIES COMMISSIONS 1990; served 17 yrs. with Candn. Armed Forces; various positions in Que. civil service incl. Chmrn., Commission des Valeurs Mobilières du Qué. 1981, Dir. de l'enregistrement, Dir. de la Surveillance, Dir. Gen.; while with Comn., involved with preparation of new Securities Act; also 1 yr. as Dir. of Operations at the Montreal Exchange; recreations: tennis, skiing, hockey; Home: 60, rue de Bresoles, apt. 409, Montreal, Que. H2Y 1V5; Office: P.O. Box 171, Stock Exchange Tower, 45th Flr., 800, Square Victoria, Montreal, Que. H4Z 1C8.

**GUYATT, Doris Elsie,** C.D., A-de-C, B.A., B.S.W., M.S.W., Ph.D.; civil servant; b. New Glasgow, N.S. 29 April 1929; d. Joseph and Margaret Shield (Roberts) Woolcott; e. Guelph Coll. Voc. Inst. 1946 (Hons.); Univ. of W. Ont., B.A. 1949; Univ. of Toronto, B.S.W. 1950; M.S.W. 1967, Ph.D. 1976; m. Richard Glenn s. Richard and Florence Guyatt 25 December 1950; children; Richard John, Margaret Leslie, Joseph Neil, Donald Alan; ACTING MANAGER, ONT. MIN. OF HEALTH 1990–94; Social Worker, Children's Aid Soc. of Hamilton, York County, Metro Toronto 1950–54; Workers' Compensation Board 1966–69; Lecturer, Ryerson Polytech. Inst. 1968–69; Teaching Asst., Fac. of S.W., Univ. of Toronto 1971–74; Researcher, Vanier Inst. of Family, 1970–71; Prog. Developer, Project Coordin., Sr. Prog. Analyst, Sr. Policy Analyst, Sr. Policy Adv., Ont. Min. of Comm. & Soc. Serv. 1973–91; Pres., Toronto Business & Prof. Women's Club 1983–85; Dir., Cradleship Creche 1979–83; Gov., Toronto Dist. Candn. Corps of Commissionaires 1983–94; Dir., Royal Candn. Military Inst. 1985–86; Dir., Queen's Park Child Care Ctr. 1985–86; Aide de Camp to Lieut. Gov. of Ont. 1975–94; Candn. Forces Decoration 1972; Queen's Silver Jubilee Medal 1977; Commemorative Medal, 125th Anniversary of Candn. Confedn. 1992; Woman of Distinction Award, Toronto YWCA 1985; Dir., Alumni Assn., Fac. of S.W., Univ. of Toronto 1976–79; Mem., Fac. Council, 1976–80; Mem., Adv. Ctte., Sch. of S.W., Ryerson Polytch. Inst. 1983–87; Pres., Metro Br. Ont. Assn. of Prof. Soc. Workers 1979–80; Prof. Advisor, Parents without Partners Int. 1973–87; Vice Pres., Business and Prof. Women's Clubs of Ont. 1986–87; Chair Public Affairs, Candn. Fed. of Business and Prof. Women's Clubs 1992–94 (First Vice Pres. 1988–90, Pres. 1990–92); 2nd Vice Pres., Candn. Intelligence and Security Assn. 1992–94 (Dir. 1988–92); Chair, United Way Campaign, Ont. Min. of Health 1993; Mem., Vanier Inst.; Candn. Coun. on Social Devel.; Candn. Population Soc.; Candn. Assn. of Sociologists and Anthropologists; Candn. Assoc. on Gerontology; Family Serv. Canada; Candn. Assn. of S.W.; author: 'The One-Parent Family in Canada' 1972; recreations: theatre, music; Clubs; Toronto Bus. & Prof. Women's; R.C.M. Inst.; Home: 47 Vradenberg Dr., Agincourt, Ont. M1T 1M5.

**GUYATT, Gordon Henry,** B.Sc., M.D., F.R.C.P.(C), F.A.C.P.; b. Hamilton, Ont. 11 Nov. 1953; s. Gordon and Charlotte (Bergman) G.; e. Univ. of Toronto, Victoria Coll. B.Sc. 1974; McMaster Univ. M.D. 1977; PROF. OF MED. AND OF CLIN. EPIDEMIOL. McMASTER UNIV. 1991– ; Dir., Fellowship Programme in Academic Internal Med., McMaster Univ. 1987–90; Dir., Internal Med. Clinical Teaching Unit, McMaster Univ. Health Sciences Ctr. 1987–90; Dir., Dept. of Med. Residency Program 1990– ; internship and residency Women's Coll. Hosp., Toronto Western Hosp. and McMaster Univ. 1977–82; Med. Rsch. Council Fellowship present Univ. 1982–83, Ont. Min. of Health Career Sci. Award 1983–93, Asst. Prof. of Med. and of Clin. Epidemiol. 1983, Dir. Masters Prog. Design Measurement & Evaluation Dept. Clin. Epidemiol. & Biostats. 1985–87, Assoc. Prof. Med. and of Clin. Epidemiol. 1987–91; Prof., Dept. Clin. Epidemiol. & Biostats & Med. 1991– ; Founding mem. Med. Reform Group Ont. 1979, mem. Steering Ctte. 1982–87, 1990– , Pub. Spokesperson 1984–88, 1990– ; cons. various pharm. firms; mem. Ont. Min. Health Review Ctte. 1983– , Vice Chrmn., 1986–88, Chrmn. 1988–90; author or co-author numerous publs. rsch. areas incl. measurement quality of life in clin. trials, assessment diagnostic & therapeutic technols., scientific overviews, medical education; Fellow, Am. Coll. of Physicians; Am. Coll. Chest Phys.; Candn. Med. Protective Assn.; Home: 495 Aberdeen Ave., Hamilton, Ont. L8P 2S5; Office: 2C12 Health Sciences Centre, 1200 Main St. W., Hamilton, Ont. L8S 4J9.

**GUZMAN, Carole Ann,** B.A., M.Sc., M.D., F.R.C.P.(C); physician; b. Toronto, Ont. 31 Oct. 1933; d. Thomas and Mary Agnes (Shea) Broadhurst; e. Loretto Abbey; St. Michael's Coll., Univ. of Toronto B.A. 1954; Univ. of Toronto, Fac. of Med. M.D. 1958; McGill Univ. M.Sc. 1965; Royal Coll. of Physicians & Surgeons FRCP(C); m. Danilo Antonio G. 22 June 1963; children: Douglas Antony, Andrew Thomas; ASSOC. SECRETARY GENERAL, CANADIAN MEDICAL ASSOCIATION 1992– ; Assoc. Prof., Faculty of Med., Univ. of Ottawa 1971– ; Dir., Respiratory Rehab. Prog. & Cystic Fibrosis Prog., Rehab Ctr. Ottawa 1974–92; Consultant, Nat. Defence Med. Ctr. & Ottawa Gen. Hosp. 1971–90; Pres., Ont. Thoracic Soc. 1978–80; Fed. of Medical Women Canada 1981–82; Ont. Med. Assn. 1989–90; Candn. Medical Assn. 1991–92; Dir., Workers Comp. Appeals Tribunal 1988–94; Candn. Forces Medical Council 1992–93; Candn. Thoracic Soc. (Med. Dir.) 1992– ; A.O.A. Medical Society; Award of Excellence, Fac. of Med., Univ. of Ottawa 1990; Mem., Royal Coll. of Physicians & Surgeons of Can.; Candn. Lung Assn.; Am. Thoracic Soc.; Ont. Lung Assn.; ALS Soc. Ottawa; Home: 1913 Camborne Crescent, Ottawa, Ont. K1H 7B6; Office: Box 8650, 1867 Alta Vista Dr., Ottawa, Ont. K1G 0G8.

**GWARTZ, Jack,** B.Sc.Phm.; business executive; b. Toronto, Ont. 28 June 1932; s. Sam and Sarah G.; e. Harbord C.I.; Univ. of Toronto B.Sc.Phm. 1956; m. Judith Pearl d. Frank and Mollie Gold 11 June 1957; children: Shelley Beth, Franklin Stuart, Daniel Michael; CHAIRMAN, G.S. DUNN 1988– ; Store Owner, Shoppers Drug Mart 1962; Extve. Vice-Pres., Koffler Stores Ltd. 1965–71; Pres., Shoppers Drug Mart 1983;

various business investments to 1988; Dir., Pennington Stores Ltd.; Bank Hapoalim; O.C.P.; recreations: var. activities incl. squash, tennis, skiing; club: York Racquets; Home: 2 Lynwood Ave., #602, Toronto, Ont. M4V 1K2; Office: 80 Park St. N., Hamilton, Ont. L8R 2M9.

**GWYN, Richard John Philip Jermy;** journalist; author; b. Bury St. Edmunds, Eng. 26 May 1934; s. Philip Jermy and Elizabeth (Tilley) G.; e. Stonyhurst Coll.; Royal Mil. Acad. Sandhurst; m. Alexandra d. Claude and Ruth Fraser 12 Apl. 1958; COLUMNIST, TORONTO STAR 1982– ; Parlty. Corr. United Press International 1957–59; Thomson Newspapers 1959–60; Ottawa Ed. Maclean-Hunter Business Publications 1960–62; Parlty. Corr. Time Canada 1962–65, Contrib. Ed. Montreal 1966–68; Exec. Asst. to Min. of Communications Can. 1968–70; Dir.-Gen. Socio-Econ. Planning, Dept. Communications 1970–73; Nat. Affairs Columnist, Toronto Star 1973–85; International Affairs Columnist 1985–92; recipient Nat. Newspaper Awards 1980, 1985; Nat. Magazine Award 1985; named Author of the Yr., Foundation for Advanc. Candn. Letters 1982; author 'The Shape of Scandal: A Study of Government in Crisis' 1965; 'Smallwood: The Unlikely Revolutionary' 1968, rev. 1972; 'The Northern Magus: Pierre Trudeau and Canadians' 1980; 'The 49th Paradox: Canada in North America' 1985; R. Catholic; LL.D. (hon. causa), Univ. of King's College 1987; Home: 300 Carlton St., Toronto, Ont. M5A 2L5; Office: 1 Yonge St., Toronto, Ont. M5E 1E6.

**GWYN, Sandra (Alexandra) Jean Fraser;** journalist/author; b. St. John's, Nfld. 17 may 1935; d. Claude Alexander and Ruth Margaret (Taylor) Fraser; e. Convent of the Sacred Heart 1951; Dalhousie Univ. B.A. 1955; m. Richard s. Philip and Elizabeth G. 12 Apr. 1958; Info. Offr., Nat. Gall. of Can. 1957–60; freelance journalist 1960–75; Ottawa Ed., Saturday Night Magazine 1975–80; Contbr. Ed. 1980–87; Nat. Magazine Awards: Silver Medal 1978, Gold Medal 1979, 1985; Authors Awards, Found. for Advancement of Arts and Letters 1977, 1978, 1984 (joint authorship); author: 'The Private Capital' 1984; 'Tapestry of War' 1992; Governor General's Award for Non-Fiction 1984; Canadian Author's Assn. Prize 1984; LL.D. (hon. causa), Memorial Univ. 1991; Address: 300 Carlton St., Toronto, Ont. M5A 2L5.

**GYLES, Carlton LLoyd,** D.V.M., M.Sc., Ph.D.; educator; b. Guy's Hill, Jamaica 15 May 1940; s. John and Myrtle Mae (Powell) G.; e. Univ. of Toronto D.V.M. 1964; Univ. of Guelph M.Sc. 1966, Ph.D. 1968; m. Kaye d. Jane and Morton Scott 8 Aug. 1964; children: Carla, Curtis; CHAIR, DEPT. VET. MICROBIOL. IMMUNOL., UNIV. OF GUELPH 1992– , Dean of Grad. Studies 1981–86, Asst. Prof. to Prof. 1969–81; mem., Ont. Council on Univ. Affairs; mem. Bd. Scient. Advisors Merck & Co.; Gold Medalist Ont. Vet. Coll. 1964; MRC Post-doctoral Fellow, Eng. and Denmark 1968–69; author or co-author over 80 articles journs. and books; mem., various prof. journ. ed. bds.; mem., Ont. Vet. Assn.; Candn. Vet. Med. Assn.; Candn. Soc. Microbiol.; Am. Soc. Microbiol.; recreations: tennis, soccer, cricket; Office: Guelph, Ont. N1G 2W1.

**GYLES, Cedric G.E.;** insurance executive; b. Vancouver, B.C. 23 Dec. 1926; s. Cedric Harold and Vera (Rider) G.; e. Public and High Schs., Vancouver, B.C.; m. Barbara I. Martin, 18 Feb. 1949; children: Cedric James, Patricia Catherine, Marti Ann, John Phillip, George Edward, Peter David; CHRMN., ALEXANDER & ALEXANDER / REED STENHOUSE LTD. 1983– ; Dir., Alexander & Alexander / Reed Stenhouse Companies Ltd.; with Price Waterhouse, Vancouver, B.C. 1947–50; Prof. Football Player with Calgary Stampeders 1948–51; Godfrey Investments Ltd., Calgary, 1950–53; Reed Stenhouse Ltd. & predecessor Companies Calgary and Edmonton 1953–61, Winnipeg Mgr. 1961–71; Sr. Vice-Pres. Toronto 1971–74; Extve. Vice-Pres. 1974–75; Pres. & C.E.O. 1975–82; Clubs: Royal Canadian Yacht; Royal Vancouver Yacht; Ontario; Griffith Is.; The Toronto Hunt; Winnipeg Football (Life mem., Pres. 1968–69); Home: 401 Queen's Quay W., Apt. 712, Toronto, Ont. M5V 2Y2; Office: Reed Stenhouse Tower, 20 Bay St., Suite 2200, Toronto, Ont. M5J 2N9.

# H

**HAAN, David Henry,** B.A., M.A.; advertising executive; b. Battle Creek, Mich. 31 May 1953; s. Henry E. and Helen Isadora (Lasalle) H.; e. Wayne State Univ. B.A. 1975; Michigan State Univ. M.A. 1977; m. Andrea d. Arthur and Shirley Warren 13 June 1981; children: David henry Jr., Katherine Elizabeth, Meredith Claire; PRES. & C.E.O., FOOTE CONE AND BELDING/RONALDS-REYNOLDS ADVERTISING (TORONTO) 1989– ; Advtg. Mgr. & Dir. of Mktg., Faygo Beverages Detroit 1975–83; Dir. of Strategic Planning, Tupperware Orlando, Fl. 1983–84; Management Dir. / Group Mngt. Dir. / Dir. of Client Services / Gen. Mgr. (Toronto) / Pres. (Candn. Opns.), Foote Cone and Belding Advertising Chicago 1984–89; Dir., Inst. of Candn. Advertising 1991– ; Guest Instructor, Am. Mngt. Assn.; Am. Mktg. Assn.; Michigan State Univ.; Univ. of Illinois; Phi Kappa Phi Hon. Scholastic Soc.; author: 'Key Visuals as an Aid in Copytesting' 1978; recreations: tennis, basketball, swimming; clubs: The Granite; Home: 132 Alexandra, Toronto, Ont. M4R 1L6; Office: 245 Eglinton Ave. E., Toronto, Ont. M4P 3C2.

**HAANAPPEL, Peter P.C.,** B.C.L., D.E.S., LL.M., D.C.L.; university professor; b. Bloemendaal, Netherlands 7 Jan. 1949; s. Piet A.M. and Mathilde A.K.F. (Reyners) H.; e. Free Univ. (Amsterdam), B.C.L. 1972; Internat. Comp. Law Faculty (Strasbourg), D.E.S. 1972; McGill Univ., LL.M. 1974; D.C.L. 1976; single; PROF., SCHOOL OF LAW, MCGILL UNIVERSITY 1989–90; on leave 1990–93; Asst. Prof. 1976–79; Assoc. Prof. 1979–89; Assoc. Dean (Academic, Law) 1985–87; Assoc. Dean (Grad. Studies & Rsch. in Law) 1988–90; Mem., Bd. of Dir., Internat. Inst. of Air & Space Law, State Univ. of Leyden; Dir., European Affairs, Internat. Air Transport Assoc., Geneva; Mem., Royal Dutch Acad. of Sciences: Mem., Russian Acad. of Transport; author: 'Ratemaking in International Air Transport' 1978, 'Pricing and Capacity Determination in International Air Transport' 1984; co-author: 'Civil Law Dictionary' 1988; 'Translation of New Dutch Civil Code' 1991; Home: 2775 Darling St., Montreal, Que. H1W 2X6.

**HABER, David;** impresario; theatre manager and producer; b. Montreal, Que. 15 July 1927; s. Louis and Molly (Nahamovitz) H.; e. Bancroft Sch. and Baron Byng High Sch., Montreal; Quebec (Que.) High Sch., 1945; various theatre, dance and music schs.; PRESIDENT, DAVID HABER ARTISTS MANAGEMENT INC. founded 1975, inc. 1976, represents Canadian performing artists internationally, also tour direction and touring productions, consultancy; Production, Stage and General Mgr.; Brae Manor (summer) Theatre, Knowlton, Que., 1948–56; Production Stage Mgr.; Candn. Repertory Theatre, Ottawa, 1949–51; Nat. Ballet of Can., Toronto, 1951–56; Indust. productions in Can. and U.S.A., Nat. Film Bd., Montreal, 1956–58, Assoc. Producer 'The Drylanders' 1961; personal and tour mgr. to various performers incl.: Sir John Gielgud 'Ages of Man,' Stanley Holloway 'Laughs and Other Events,' Mahalia Jackson World Tour, 1958–61; Personal Agt. and Mgr., William Morris Agency, N.Y. (incl. Mahalia Jackson, Basil Rathbone, Celeste Holm); Producer of Theatre Presentations for World Festival of Expo 67, Montreal, 1964–67; Dir. of Programming, Nat. Arts Centre, Ottawa 1968–73; Artistic Dir., Nat. Ballet of Can. 1973–75; rec'd Centennial Medal 1967; Queen's Jubilee Medal, 1976; organizes tours abroad for Dept. of External Affairs and tours in Can. for Candn. and foreign co.'s; mem., Internat. Soc. Performing Arts Administrators, Vice Pres. of Entertainment, Consultant & Producer of World Festival for 1982 World's Fair, Knoxville Tenn.; Consultant, Southwest Arts Foundation, Houston; Tel-Pro Prods., L.A.; Jubilee Festival, Toronto; mem. Bd., Internat. Soc. of Performing Arts Administrators; mem. Assn. of Coll., Univ. and Community Arts Adm.; Candn. Assn. of Artists Managements (Past Pres.); Candn. Music Council; Candn. Conf. of the Arts (Bd. Govs.); Assn. of Theatrical Press Agents and Mgrs.; Dance Can. Assn.; Can.-Israel Cultural Fdns. (Adv. Bd.); Hebrew; recreation: swimming.

**HABER, Stephen Michael,** B.Sc., M.Sc., Ph.D.; research scientist; b. Vancouver, B.C. 20 Nov. 1954; e. Univ. of B.C. B.Sc. 1975, M.Sc. 1979; Univ. of Illinois Ph.D. 1983; m. Dr. Ma Luo; children: Lee, Darren; RESEARCH SCIENTIST, WINNIPEG RESEARCH STATION, AGRICULTURE CANADA 1983– ; Grad. Science Teacher, CUSO, Oyo, Nigeria 1975–77; research: co-devel. of new disease-resistant cereal varieties; Gordon Green Award, Candn. Phytopathological Soc. 1993; Best Student Paper, Sigma Xi, Univ. of Illinois 1981, 1983; Bd. Mem., Man. Alliance for a Democratic China; Mem., Candn. & Am. Phytopathological socs.; co-author: 'Diseases of Oat' in Oat Science and Technology; Office: 195 Dafoe Rd., Winnipeg, Man. R3T 2M9.

**HABIB, Pierre,** B.Comm., C.A.; business executive; b. Cairo, Egypt 18 Sept. 1946; s. Joseph and Yvonne (Badra) H.; e. Univ. of Montreal B.Comm. 1972, C.A. 1973; m. Nimette d. Charles Shenouda 25 Dec. 1971; children: José-Christian, Alain-Michel, Julien-Charles; PRESIDENT & CHIEF EXECUTIVE OFFICER, LEADER INDUSTRIES INC. 1991– ; Teacher (part-time), Univ. of Que. in Montreal 1974–75, '76; S. Schwartz, C.A. 1971–74; Mgr., Gen. Acctg., Pfizer Pharm. 1974–75; Price Waterhouse (France) 1975–76; Regional Mgr. & Asst. Gen. Mgr., Avis Canada 1976–81; Pres. & Country Mgr., Avis Canada 1981–84; Pres. & C.E.O., Visway Transport Inc. 1984–88; Pres., Residev Monaco Inc. 1988–91; Treas., St. Vincent de Paul 1991–93; recreations: skiing, tennis, swimming; Home: 620 Pl. Stewart, St. Laurent, Que. H4M 2W9; Office: 1280 Nobel St., Boucherville, Que. J4B 5H1.

**HACCOUN, David,** B.Sc.Ap.,Eng., S.M., Ph.D.; educator; b. Bizerte, Tunisia 4 July 1937; s. late Charles Shalom and Emma (Melloul) H.; e. École Polytechnique de Montréal B.Sc.Ap. (Eng. Phys.) 1965; Mass. Inst. of Technol. S.M. (Elect. Eng.) 1966; McGill Univ. Ph.D. (Elect. Eng.) 1974; m. Lyson d. late Armand and Claire Tobaly 26 Dec. 1971; children: Nathalie, Laurent; PROF. OF ELECT. ENG. AND COMP. ÉCOLE POLYTECHNIQUE DE MONTRÉAL 1980– , Head of Communications Sect. 1988– ; Communications Eng. City of Montréal 1965; Rsch. Asst. Rsch. Lab. Electronics M.I.T. 1965–66; Asst. Prof. present École 1966, Assoc. Prof. 1974; Rsch. Asst. Communications Rsch. Centre Ottawa 1970; Visiting Rsch. Prof. Concordia Univ. Montréal 1984–85; Project Leader Candn. Inst. Telecom. Rsch. Nat. Centres of Excellence Govt. Can. 1990– ; Visiting Rsch. Fellow, Advanced Systems Inst., Univ. of Brit. Columbia 1992; govt., univ. and corporate cons. Can., USA, France; Commonwealth Fellow London 1965; Grass Fellowship M.I.T. 1966; M.I.T. Scholarship 1965–66; Hydro-Qué. Fellowship 1969–72; Fellow, Inst. of Electrical & Electronics Engrs., N.Y. 1993; co-author 'Digital Communications by Satellite' 1981, transl. Japanese 1984, Chinese 1988; over 100 articles sci. jours. & internat. confs.; recreations: swimming, skiing, photography; Home: 57 Strathcona Dr., Town of Mount Royal, Qué. H3R 1E5; Office: P.O. Box 6079, Succ. Centre Ville, Montréal, Qué. H3C 3A7.

**HACHBORN, Walter J.;** business executive; b. Conestogo, Ont. 24 July 1921; s. William Walter and Florence Elizabeth (Ritter) H.; e. Elmira Dist. Secondary Sch. 1938; m. Jean Marie d. Mr. and Mrs. W.C. Brown 20 Sept. 1947; children: Susan Jean Heard, Elizabeth Ann Huehn, William Walter; PRESIDENT, HOME HARDWARE STORES LTD. 1964– ; Pres., Alliance Ro-Na Home Inc.; joined Hollinger Hardware 1938–43, 1946–63; served with RCOC 1943–46; named Citizen of Yr. Woolwich Twp. 1976; mem. Bd. Govs., Wilfrid Laurier Univ. 1971–81, Financial Cabinet 1981–86; Woolwich Twp. Arena Bd. Chrmn. 1971–80; Pres., Luther League of Can. 1949–54; mem., Exec. and Ctte. Lutheran Ch. of Am. Can. Synod 1965–71; LL.D. (h.c.) Wilfrid Laurier Univ., Waterloo, Ont. 1985; designated for Annual Distinguished Retailing Award, Retail Council 1988; inducted into the Candn. Hardware Hall of Fame 1989; Life Mem., Candn. Retail Hardware Assoc.; recreations: swimming, skiing; Home: 18 Northside Dr., St. Jacobs, Ont. N0B 2N0; Office: 34 Henry St., St. Jacobs, Ont. N0B 2N0.

**HACHINSKI, Vladimir,** B.A., M.Sc.(D.M.E.), M.D., F.R.C.P.(C), D.Sc.(Med.); neurologist/medical scientist/educator; b. Zhitomir, Ukraine 13 Aug. 1941; s. Stanley and Vera (Mostowitsch) H.; e. Port Perry H.S. 1960; Univ. of Toronto M.D. 1966 (Bronze T Athletic Award, Students Admin. Counc.); F.R.C.P.(C) 1972; Univ. of London B.A. 1977; McMaster Univ. M.Sc.(D.M.E.) 1987; Univ. of London D.Sc.(Med.) 1988; m. Mary Ann d. Michael and Katherine Demianiuk 1967; children: Vladimir, Larissa, Eric; RICHARD AND BERYL IVEY PROF. AND CHRMN., DEPT. OF CLINICAL NEUROLOGICAL SCIENCES, UNIV. OF WEST. ONT. 1990– ; Lectr. to Assoc. Prof. Neurol. Univ. of Toronto 1974–80; Assoc. Prof. of Neurol., U.W.O. 1980–83; Prof. Neurology, Physiology, Epidemiology and Med., U.W.O.; Dir., Invest. Stroke Unit, Univ. Hosp. 1983– ; Dir., Stroke & Aging Rsch., The John P. Robarts Rsch. Inst.; Chrmn., Sci. Prog. Ctte., Internat. Joint Conf. on Stroke & Cerebral Circ., Am. Heart Assn. 1986–91; Pres., Candn. Stroke Soc. 1981–85; Extve. Ctte., Stroke Counc., Am. Heart Assoc.; Bd. of Dirs., Heart and Stroke Found. of Ont. 1989– ; Dir. Internat. Soc. for Cerebral Blood Flow and Metabolism 1985–89, Chrmn., Steering Ctte. World Fed. of Neurology 1985– ; Extve., International Stroke Soc. 1989– ; Extve. Bd., Am. Acad. of Neurology 1990– ; Extve. Bd., Am. Neurological Assoc. 1990–92; several past extve./ctte. posts; Founding mem., Candn. Atherosclerosis Soc.; Migraine Found. of Can.; Foster Ont.; Mem., Candn. Neurological Soc.; Bd. of Dirs.,

Candn. Heart and Stroke Found., Royal Soc. of Med.; Mem., Am., Brit. & Candn. Hist. Assns.; Internat. Brain Rsch. Orgn.; N.Y. Acad. of Sci.; Am. Assn. for the Adv. of Sci.; Ukrainian Acad. of Med. Sciences; Hon. mem., Neurological Societies of Argentina, Bolivia, Colombia, Ecuador, Spain, Venezuela & Neurological and Neurosurgical Soc. of Uruguay; Hon. Mem., Venezuelan Soc. of Internal Med.; Canada's delegate, Panamerican Congresses of Neurology; Lectr. and/or Visiting Prof. in Canada, U.S.A., Puerto Rico, Argentina, Bolivia, Brazil, Colombia, Cuba, Ecuador, Mexico, Peru, Uruguay, Venezuela, Austria, Denmark, Finland, France, Germany, Hungary, Italy, Spain, Sweden, Switzerland, U.K., Ukraine, Israel, India, Japan & China; Murray Robertson Lectr., Heart and Stroke Found. of Ont.; Bruce S. Schoenberg Memorial Lectr., Panamerican Neuroepidemiological Soc.; Pan Am. Congress of Neurology; First Decade of the Brain, Bertha Meml. Lecture, World Stroke Congress; Milton Shy Lecturer, Columbia Univ., Univ. of Pennsylvania and National Institute of Health; author/co-author: 'The Acute Stroke,' and over 200 sci. and 30 educ. papers on migraine, stroke, dementia, and brain-heart relationships; originated the term, concept and method of diagnosis of multi-infarct dementia; has served as an expert witness in landmark medico-legal cases; Ed., 'Challenges in Neurology'; Co-ed.: 'Prevention of Stroke'; 'Cerebral Ischemia: Treatment and Prevention'; Ed. Bd. Mem., 'Acta Neurologica Scandinavica,' 'Circulation et Metabolism du Cerveau,' 'Alzheimer's Disease: an International Journal,' 'Journal of Cerebral Blood Flow and Metabolism,' 'Cerebrovascular and Brain Metabolism Reviews'; Consulting Ed. 'Stroke' 1992– (Assoc. Ed. 1985–86); Assoc. Ed. 'Archives of Neurology' 1985– ; 'Journal of Neurological Sciences' 1990– ; First Trillium Clinical Scientist Award for 'outstanding research accomplishments and contributions to Ont. health care'; recreations: swordsmanship, early XIX cent. Latin Am. History; clubs: London Med. Hist. Club (founding pres.); Office: Univ. Hosp., Clin. Neurol. Sci., P.O. Box 5339, Stn. A, London, Ont. N6A 5A5.

**HACKETT, Barbara J.,** B.B.A., M.B.A., C.M.A.; financial executive; b. Welland, Ont. 22 May 1954; d. Donald Jackman and Dorothy Yvonne (Phillips) H.; e. York Univ. B.B.A. 1979, M.B.A. 1980; C.M.A. 1984; m. John H. s. John and Liz Tory 27 May 1978; children: John, Christopher, Susan, George; VICE-PRES., FINANCE & ADMIN., BELL & HOWELL 1991– ; Bd. of Dirs., YTV Canada Inc.; Financial Analyst, Finan. Planning Dept., Ont. Hydro 1980–85; Mgr. Finance, MDS Health Group Limited 1985–88; Dir., Finan. Serv., MDS Health Ventures Inc. 1989–91; Gold Medalist; MBA thesis 1980; Chair, Bd. of Dir., Toronto French School 1991; Treas. & Bd. of Dir. Women's Legal Edn. & Action Fund (LEAF) 1987–90; Pres. & Co-Founder, MBA Women's Assn. 1982; recreations: skiing, golf tennis; clubs: Craigleith Ski, Rosedale Golf; Home: 37 Stratheden Rd., Toronto, Ont. M4N 1E5; Office: 230 Barmac Dr., Toronto, Ont. M9L 2X5.

**HACKING, Ian MacDougall,** Ph.D., F.R.S.C.; university professor; b. Vancouver, B.C. 18 Feb. 1936; s. Harold Eldridch and Margaret Elinore (MacDougall) H.; e. Univ. of B.C. B.A. 1956; Cambridge Univ. B.A. 1958, Ph.D. 1962; 1st m. Laura Anne d. Darrell and Walter Leach 4 Jan. 1962; 2nd m. Judith d. Ruth and Samuel Polsky 14 Aug. 1983; children: Jane Frances, Daniel, Rachel; UNIVERSITY PROFESSOR, INST. FOR HIST. & PHILOSOPHY OF SCI. & TECHNOL., UNIV. OF TORONTO 1991– , Prof. 1983; Asst. then Assoc. Prof. of Philos., Univ. of B.C. 1964–69 (seconded by External Aid Can. to Makerere Univ. Coll., Kampala, Uganda 1967–69); Univ. Lectr., Cambridge Univ. 1969–74; Ctr. for Adv. Study in Behav. Sci., Stanford Univ. 1974–75; H.W. Stuart Prof. of Philos. 1975–82; Zentrum fur Interdisziplinäre Forschung, Bielefeld, W. Germany 1982–83; Killam Fellowship 1986–88; Mem., Inst. for Adv. Study Princeton 1986–87; Tarner Lectr., Trinity College Cambridge 1988–91; Guggenheim Fellowship 1990–91; author: 'The Emergence of Probability' 1975, 'Why Does Language Matter to Philosophy?' 1975, 'Representing & Intervening' 1983, 'The Taming of Chance' 1990 and 2 earlier books; editor: 'Scientific Revolutions' 1981, 'Exercises in Analysis' 1985; Fellow, Am. Acad. of Arts & Sciences; Home: 391 Markham St., Toronto, Ont. M6G 2K8; Office: Victoria Coll., Univ. of Toronto, Toronto, Ont. M5S 1K7.

**HADDAD, Hon. William Joseph,** B.A., LL.B.; judge (retired); b. Meyronne, Sask. 26 Nov. 1915; s. late Abdelnour Farhat and Sophia Mary (Ead) H.; e. Univ. of Alta. B.A., LL.B. 1941; m. Frances Margaret d. late Peter Assaly 24 May 1944; children: Gail Frances Blake, Ronald William, Kenneth Peter; Judge, Court of Appeal, Alta. 1974–90; read law with Nelles V. Buchanan, K.C.; called to Bar of Alta. 1942; cr. Q.C. 1957; law practice Marks and Haddad 1946–51; Partner, Wood, Haddad, Moir & Hope 1952; Lectr., Bar Admission Course 1959–66; Partner, Haddad, Cavanagh & Buchanan 1961, merged with Simpson, Henning & Co. 1962 under name Simpson, Haddad, Cavanagh, Henning, Buchanan & Kerr; apptd. to Dist. Court, Dist. of N. Alta. 1965; apptd. to Appellate Div. Supreme Court of Alta. 1974 (became present Court 1979); served with RCN 1942–46, rank Lt. (SB), legal offr. Staff C.O. Pacific Coast 1943–46; Dir., Vice Pres. and mem. Mang. Comte. Edmonton Eskimo Football Club 1958–64, Dir. and Secy. Touchdown Club 1956–57; Secy.-Treas. Edmonton Lib. Assn. 1962–63; Chrmn. Edmonton Bd. Police Commrs. 1966–72; mem. Alta. Securities Comn. 1966–74, Vice Chrmn. 1972–75; Pres., Men's Candn. Club Edmonton 1954; Pres., Edmonton Kinsmen Club 1955–56; Pres. Edmonton Bar Assn. 1955; mem. Royal Candn. Legion; Anglican; recreation: golf; Clubs: Mayfair Golf & Country (Pres. 1973); Royal Glenora; Home: 6507 Grandview Dr., Edmonton, Alta. T6H 4K2; Office: Law Courts, 1A Sir Winston Churchill Sq., Edmonton, Alta. T5J 0R2.

**HADFIELD, Major Chris A.,** B.M.E., M.A.; Canadian astronaut; b. Sarnia, Ont. 29 Aug. 1959; e. Royal Military College B.M.E. (Hons.) 1982; U.S. Air Force Test Pilot School grad. 1988; Univ. of Tennessee, Masters of Aviation Systems 1992; m. Helena Walter; children: Kyle, Evan, Kristin; CANADIAN ASTRONAUT; Research Engr., Univ. of Waterloo summer 1982; Fighter Pilot, 425 Tactical Fighter Squadron, Candn. Forces Base Bagotville 1985–88; Canadian Exchange Officer, U.S. Naval Air Test Center 1989–92; selected for Canadian Astronaut Program 1992; enrolled in Mission Specialist training, Johnson Space Center (1st yr completed Aug. 1993); it is expected that he will receive a flight assignment within 3–4 years; NSERC Summer Rsch. Scholarship and Duncan Sayre MacInnes Mem. Scholarship 1982; Golden Centennaire Trophy, Prov. of Sask. Award, City of Moose Jaw Award, Base Commander's Award 1983; Liethen-Tittle Award, USAF Test Pilot School 1988; Rey E. Tenhoff Award 1991; U.S. Navy Test Pilot of the Year 1991–92; NASA Group Achivement Award for High Angle-of-Attack Flight Research 1992; Ronaasen Award for Best Paper 1992; Mem., Soc. of Experimental Test Pilots; Candn. Aeronautics and Space Inst.; Royal Military College Ex-Cadet Club; Mensa; recreations: alpine and water skiing, squash, SCUBA diving, horseback riding, sailing, writing, singing and playing the guitar, men's & co-ed volleyball leagues, coaches soccer at 6–8-year-old level; Office: 6767, Route de l'aéroport, Saint-Hubert, Qué. J3Y 8Y9.

**HADLEY, Michael L.,** CD., B.A., M.A., Ph.D.; university professor; b. Campbell River, B.C. 6 April 1936; s. Norman and Winnifred (Sheppard) H.; e. Lord Byng High 1954; Univ. of B.C. B.A. 1959; Univ. of Manitoba M.A. 1964; Queen's Univ. Ph.D. 1971; m. Anita d. Osmund Hudson & Christiane Lippens Borradile 30 May 1959; children: Pauline Christiane, David Llewellyn, Michèle Anita, Norman Borradaile; PROFESSOR, NAVAL HISTORY AND GERMAN LITERATURE, UNIV. OF VICTORIA 1986– ; joined Univ. Naval Training Div. 1954; comnd. Royal Candn. Navy 1957; subsequent shore & seagoing commands; Foreign Service Offr. 1959–62; Captain (N) 1980; Lectr., St. John's Coll. 1962–64; Asst. Prof., Univ. of Winnipeg 1964–71; Assoc. Prof., Univ. of Victoria 1974–86; Professor 1986– ; Ready Reserve (Navy); Chair & Past Chair, Defence Min. Acad. Adv. Bd. to Military Colleges 1986–90 (Extve. Bd. Mem. 1981–90); Past-Pres., Maritime Defence Assn. of Can.; Mem., Candn. Ctte. for History of Second World War; Maritime Awards Soc.; Naval Officers Assn. of Can.; Candn. Nautical Rsch. Soc.; Candn. Assoc. of Univ. Teachers of German (Past Pres.); Founding Mem., Pacific & Maritime Strategic Studies Group; Ctr. for Studies in Religion and Soc., Univ. of Victoria; Candn. Forces Decoration & Clasp 1983; Queen's Jubilee Medal 1977; Hon. Ad C to Gov.-Gen. Jules Léger; to Lt-Gov. of Man. 1969–71; Keith Mathews Prize, Candn. Nautical Rsch. Soc. 1986, '92; John Lyman Prize, N.-Am. Soc. for Oceanic History 1986, '92; Anglican; author/co-author of num. sci. articles & books incl. 'UBoats against Canada' 1985, '90 (German ed. 1990), 'Tin-Pots and Pirate Ships' 1991, 'Count Not the Dead: The Popular Image of the German Submarine in Literature and Film' forthcoming; commentator on TV, radio and press on nat. defence issues; recreation: sailing; Office: P.O. Box 3045, Victoria, B.C. V8W 3P4.

**HADWEN, John Gaylard,** M.A.; retired public servant; b. Ottawa, Ont. 18 Apr. 1923; s. Dr. Seymour and Estelle Alden (Godwin) H.; e. Brown Pub. Sch., Toronto 1935; Univ. of Toronto Schs. 1941; Trinity Coll., Univ. of Toronto, B.A. 1948, M.A. 1949; London Sch. of Econ. 1950; Inst. Universitaire des Hautes Etudes Internats., Genève, Switzerland, 1971; m. Shirley V. Brown 1955; children: Timothy, Peter, Matthew (twins), Anthony; Lectr. and Consultant; joined Dept. External Affairs as Foreign Service Offr., 1950 Ottawa; Pakistan 1952–54, New York 1956–59, Oslo 1961–64; Special Asst. to SSEA and to P.M. 1964–67; High Commr., Malaysia and Singapore and Ambassador to Burma 1967–71; Ambassador to Pakistan and Afghanistan, 1972–74; High Commr. to India and Ambassador to Nepal 1979–83; Dir. Gen., East Asia Bureau 1983–85; Director General, Bureau for Security Services, Dept. of External Affairs 1985–86; served in R.C.A., enlisted Cadet, discharged Lance Sgt.; perm. rank Lt.; Candn. Rep., Fifth Ctte. (Finan. Admin.), 41st Gen. Assembly, UN 1986; Adv. (at seminars for U.N. diplomats), Internat. Peace Acad., N.Y., June 1987 and 1988; rapporteur for seminar in Bangkok and New Delhi on 'Peace and Security in South East Asia and the South West Pacific' Dec., 1987; Adviser to Auditor-Gen. of Canada 1989–90; mem. Extve., Shastri Indo-Candn. Inst.; Ghurka Welfare Trust (Can.); co-author of 'How United Nations Decisions are Made' 2nd ed. 1962 (French, Arabic translations); 'The Future of Aid and the Colombo Plan' forthcoming; and other works; United Church; recreations: golf, tennis, philately; Clubs: East India and Sports (London, Eng.); Royal Selangor Golf (Kuala Lumpur); Royal Candn. Mil. Inst.; Office: 331 Elmwood Ave., Rockcliffe Park, Ottawa, Ont. K1M 0C5.

**HAEHLING von LANZENAUER, Christoph,** Ph.D.; educator; b. Wiesbaden, W. Germany 11 May 1939; s. Alois and Josepha (von Stockhausen) H. von L.; e. Univ. of Bonn, Dip. Volkswirt 1963, Ph.D. 1966; M. Gabriele d. Gerhard and Ursula von Schuckmann 20 March 1964; children: Konstantin, Hubertus, Andreas; PROF. OF BUS. ADMIN., UNIV. OF WESTERN ONT. 1976– ; staff mem. Inst. for Econometrics & Operations Rsch., Univ. of Bonn 1963–66; Asst. Prof. of Bus., Univ. of Wis. 1967–69; Asst. and Assoc. Prof. of Bus. Admin. present Univ. 1969–75, Prof. 1976– , Dir. Ph.D. Program 1987–92; Visiting Assoc. Prof. 1975–76 and Visiting Prof. 1977–78 Sloan Sch. of Mgmt., Mass. Inst. of Technol.; Visiting Prof., Univ. of Kaiserslautern, Germany 1991; Visiting Prof., Univ. of Heidelberg, Germany 1992–93; Visiting Prof., Hochschule St. Gallen, Switzerland 1993; recipient Karl Guth Award 1976; author 'Operations Research and Managerial Decision Problems' 1972; 'Cases in Operations Research' 1975; co-author 'Retirement Income Provisions in Canada's Independent Business Sector' 1981; contbr. 'The Canadian Encyclopedia' 1985; over 60 articles acad. and profl. jours.; mem. Inst. Mgmt. Sci.; Am. Risk & Ins. Assn.; Inst. for Risk Rsch.; Internat. Soc. for Inventory Rsch.; Candn Soc. Operational Rsch.; Assn. Candn. Pension Mgmt.; Pres., Risk Analyses Group; recreations: tennis, horseback riding, travel, photography; Home: 93 Fox Mill Cres., London, Ont. N6J 2B6; Office: London, Ont. N6A 3K7.

**HAERING, Rudolph Roland,** O.C. (1976), M.A., Ph.D., FRSC; educator; b. Basle, Switzerland, 27 Feb. 1934; s. Rudolph and Selma (Tschudin) H.; e. Univ. of B.C., B.A. 1954, M.A. 1955; McGill Univ. Ph.D. 1957; Memorial Univ. D.Sc. 1986; McMaster Univ. D.Sc. 1989; Univ. of Waterloo, D.Sc. 1990; m. Mary Patricia, d. late Edward Peatfield 6 Aug. 1954; two d. Susan Jane, Linda Jean; Dir., Moli Energy Ltd. 1977–90; Prof. and Head of Physics, Univ. of Brit. Columbia 1973–76, Prof. of Physics 1976–86; post-doctoral Fellow Univ. of Birmingham 1957–58 (NRC Fellowship); Asst. Prof. of Theoretical Physics McMaster Univ. 1958–60; Research Staff mem. IBM Research Center, Yorktown Heights, N.Y. 1960, Group Leader 1961–63; Prof. of Physics Univ. of Waterloo 1963–64; Prof. and Head Dept. of Physics Simon Fraser Univ. 1964–69, Acting Acad. Vice Pres. 1968–69, Prof. of Physics 1969–72; Visiting Prof. Univ. of B.C. 1964–65; Consultant IBM Research Labs. Poughkeepsie 1959–66; United Mineral and Chemical Corp. N.Y. 1963–64; Lear Siegler Corp. Grand Rapids 1964–65; Editor, Can. Journal of Physics, 1968–73; Pres. Candn. Thin Films Ltd. 1970–73; Pres., Can. Assn. Physicists, 1978; mem. Nat. Research Council 1974–77; Adv. Council B.C. Inst. Technol. 1965–72; Bd. of Mgmt. B.C. Research Council 1968–74; Adv. Comte. for Physics Defence Research Bd. 1969–75; Bd. of Mgmt. TRIUMF 1973–76; Centennial Medal 1967; C.A.P. Herzberg Medal 1970; Queen's Jubilee Medal 1978; C.A.P. Medal, Achievement in Physics 1982; Gold Medal, B.C. Sci. and Engn. 1984; Ed. 'Canadian Journal of Physics' 1968–72; Chrmn. Theoretical Physics Div. Candn. Assn. Physicists 1965–67; recreation: outdoor sports; Home: Box 6, Alec Meadow Site, R.R. #5, Quesnel, B.C. V2J 3H9.

**HAFEMAN, Michael Joseph,** B.A., F.S.A.; insurance executive; b. St. Paul, Minn. 26 Aug. 1952; s. Eugene Earl and Mildred (Sova) H.; e. Univ. of Minn. B.A. 1974; F.S.A. 1977; m. Rita d. Michael and Elizabeth Zubrzycki 28 June 1974; children: Scott, Eric, Laura; EXTVE. VICE PRES., CHIEF FINANCIAL AND ADMINISTRATIVE OFFICER AND DIR., NN LIFE INSURANCE CO. OF CANADA 1988– ; Vice Pres. and Actuary Nationale- Nederlanden U.S. Corp. 1983–85; Pres., C.O.O. and Dir., The Halifax Life Insurance Co. 1985–89; mem. Am. Acad. Actuaries; Bd. Trade Metrop. Toronto; Bayview Country Club; Parkview Club; United Church; recreations: skiing, tennis, squash, golf, travel; Home: 14 Hashbury Pl., Thornhill, Ont. L3T 7H3; Office: One Concorde Gate, Don Mills, Ont. M3C 3N6.

**HAFTING, Robin L.;** business executive; b. Kristiansand, Norway 13 May 1937; s. Otto Christian and Winnifred Helga (Olsen) H.; e. Oslo Comm. Coll. 1955; m. Judith Lynne d. Walter Samuel and Gwendolyne Mabel (Kirkham) Jackson 11 May 1962; children: Stephen Michael, Tammy Lynne, Jennifer Denise, Jeffrey Todd; PRES., JANTZEN CAN. INC. 1988– ; Indus. Engr., Jantzen Can. Inc. 1955–58; Head Engr. 1958–65; Prod. Mgr. & Head Engr. 1965–75; Mfg. Mgr. 1975–80; Plant Mgr. 1980–88; V.V.I., Adv. Bd. for Power Sewing 1975–83; Dryclean Arbitration Panel, Better Bus. Bur. 1975–80; Vice Pres., B.C. Apparel Mfrs. Assoc. 1989–92; Pres., B.C. Apparel Mfrs. Assn. 1993– ; Vice Pres., Apparel B.C. 1993– ; Dir., Candn. Apparel Federation 1994; recreations: soccer coach, Coquitlam Womens; coached soccer teams to prov. title 1980, 1987, 1988; Candn. title 1987; Clubs: Burnaby YMCA (Dir. 1970–72); Cliff Avenue Soccer (Secy. 1982–86); Office: 196 Kingsway, Vancouver, B.C. V5T 3J3.

**HAGAN, John,** M.A., Ph.D., F.R.S.C.; educator; b. U.S.A. 15 Feb. 1946; s. Charles Banner and Dorthy Debra (Vinus) H.; e. Univ. of Ill. B.A. 1968; Univ. of Alta. M.A. 1971, Ph.D. 1974; m. Linda d. Marshal and Jeanette Weber 1972; two s. Jeremy, Joshua; PROF. OF SOCIOL. AND LAW UNIV. OF TORONTO 1982– ; Editor, Annual Review of Sociology 1993– ; Killam Rsch. Fellow 1991–93; joined present Univ. 1974; Fellow Candn. Inst. Advanced Rsch. 1987–90; also served faculties Ind. Univ. and Univ. of Wis.; recipient Distinguished Scholar Award Am. Sociol. Assn. 1989; Outstanding Scholarship Award Soc. Study Social Problems 1989; author 6 books incl. 'Victims Before the Law' 1983; 'Modern Criminology' 1985; 'Structural Criminology' 1989; 'The Disreputable Pleasures' 3rd ed. 1990; over 100 articles books and jours.; mem. various ed. bds.; Fellow, Am. Soc. Criminol. (Pres. 1990–91); Stats. Can.; mem. Sociol. Rsch. Assn.; Nat. Acad. Sci's (mem. Panel High Risk Youth); Am. Sociol. Assn.; Law & Soc. Assn.; Candn. Law & Soc. Assn.; recreation: running; Home: 287 Lytton Ave., Toronto, Ont. M5N 2N2; Office: Toronto, Ont. M5S 2C5.

**HAGAN, Jon Nairn,** B.Sc., C.A.; financial executive; b. Moose Jaw, Sask. 8 Apr. 1947; s. Nairn and Joyce H.; e. Univ. of Sask. B.Sc. 1970; Inst. of C.A.s of B.C. 1971; Univ. of Alta. M.B.A. program 1975; children: Sean, Adele; EXECUTIVE VICE PRESIDENT, EMPIRE COMPANY LIMITED; Coopers & Lybrand Vancouver 1969–72; Imperial Oil Limited Edmonton/Toronto 1973–77; Oxford Devel. Group Limited 1977–79; Cambridge Shopping Centres Limited 1979–92; Mem., N.S., Ont. & B.C. Institutes of C.A.s; Finan. Extves. Inst.; Candn. Inst. of Public Real Estate Cos.; Internat. Counc. of Shopping Centres; Conference Bd. of Canada; Office: 115 King St., Stellarton, N.S. B0K 1S0

**HAGE, Keith Donald,** B.A., M.A., Ph.D.; university professor; b. Kandahar, Sask. 15 March 1926; s. Clarence and Alma (Frederickson) H.; e. Univ. of B.C. B.A. 1949; Univ. of Toronto M.A. 1950; Univ. of Chicago Ph.D. 1957; m. Olive d. Joseph and Elva Piggott 16 Aug. 1952; children: Karen, Cameron, Dawn; PROF. EMERITUS, UNIV. OF ALTA.; Meteorologist, Meteorol. Serv. of Can. 1950–57; Rsch. Meteorologist, Suffield Exper. Stn., Ralston, Alta. 1957–60; Dir., Micrometeorol. Div., Travelers Rsch. Center, Hartford, Ct. 1960–67; Prof., Dept. of Geog., Univ. of Alta. 1967–85; Assoc. Dir., Inst. of Earth & Planetary Phys., Univ. of Alta. 1975–80; Nat. Corr., Internat. Assn. for Meteorol. & Atmospheric Phys. 1980–83; Cons., Electric Power Rsch. Inst., Palo Alto, Calif. 1982–86; elected Fellow, Am. Meteorol. Soc. 1982; awarded Patterson Medal 1989; mem. Candn. Meteorol. & Oceanographic Soc.; Am. Meteorol. Soc.; Royal Meteorol. Soc.; co-ed.: 'Essays on Meteorology and Climatology: In Honour of Richmond W. Longley' 1978; author or co-author of more than 70 sci. papers and tech. reports; recreations: cross-country skiing, gardening; Address: Box 6, Site 15, R.R. 2, Winterburn, Alta. T0E 2N0.

**HAGEN, George Leon,** B.S.; chemical engineer; b. Bancroft, Idaho 8 Sept. 1924; s. George William and Mabel (Waddell) H.; e. Boise (Idaho) High Sch.; Boise Jr. Coll.; Montana Sch. of Mines, Butte, Mon.; Univ. of Washington, B.S. (Chem. and Indust. Engn.); m. Anita Louise, d. Arthur O. Rowe, 31 Aug. 1946; three s., one d.; PRES., G.L. HAGEN ASSOC. INC., BUSINESS CONSULTANT 1981– ; Pres. & C.E.O., Reichhold Ltd. 1966–81; Indust. Engr., Methods, Boeing Airplane Company, Seattle, Wash., 1948–51; Plant Engr., Reichhold Chemicals Inc., 1951–56, Sales Representative 1956–61; Division Manager, Western Division, Reichhold Chemicals (Canada) Ltd., Vancouver, B.C., 1961–63; Vice-Pres. and Gen. Mgr., 1963–64, Extve. Vice-Pres., 1964–66; el. Dir. 1963, el. Pres. 1966, el. C.E.O. 1968, el. Chrmn. 1968; served as Lt. with U.S. Naval Reserve, Aviation Br.; private airplane Pilot; former Prof. Engr., State of Washington and B.C.; Am. Mang. Assn.; Toronto Bd. of Trade; Pres. Assn.; author of: 'Patent on Formaldehyde Manufacturing'; Phi Kappa Psi; recreations: skiing, swimming, tennis, fishing, hunting, reading, golf, photography; Home: 4848 Palm Aire Dir., Sarasota, FL 34243 USA.

**HAGEN, Paul Beo,** M.B., B.S., F.C.I.C.; educator; chemist; physician; b. Sydney, Australia 15 Feb. 1920; s. Conrad and Mary (McFadzean) von Hagen; e. North Sydney Boys' High Sch. 1938; Univ. of Sydney M.B., B.S. 1945; m. Jean d. Frederick Himms, Oxford, Eng. 1956; two d. Anna, Nina; PROF. OF PHARMACOLOGY, UNIV. OF OTTAWA 1969– ; Lectr., Sr. Lectr. in Physiol. Univ. of Sydney 1948–51; Sr. Lectr. in Physiol. Univ. of Queensland 1951–52; Research Fellow in Pharmacol. Oxford Univ. 1952–54; Asst. Prof. of Pharmacol. Yale Univ. 1954–56, Harvard Univ. 1956–59; Prof. and Head of Biochem. Univ. of Man. 1959–64; Craine Prof. and Head of Biochem. Queen's Univ. 1964–67; Dir. Nat. Research Council Ottawa 1967–68; Dean, Grad. Studies and Research, Univ. of Ottawa 1968–83; Trustee, Ottawa Gen. Hosp. 1984– ; Lycée Claudel Ottawa 1978–80; Candn. Inst. Particle Physics 1971–79; Candn. Legal Aid Research Inst. Inc. 1980–82; mem. Med. Research Council 1965–67, Vice Chrmn. 1967; mem. various M.R.C. cttes. 1960–75; mem. Research Bd. Ont. Heart Foundation 1971–75; Ont. Bd. for Lib. Coordination 1971–74, Chrmn. 1971–73; Med. Adv. Bd. Muscular Dystrophy Assn. Can. 1960–88 (Chrmn. 1977–88; Nat. Pres. of Assn. 1980–83); Candn. Assn. Grad. Schs. 1969–83, Vice Pres. 1971–75, Pres. 1975–76; Regional Devel. Comte. Nat. Science & Engn. Research Council 1979–83; C.J. Martin Fellow 1952; Fulbright Fellow 1954; recipient Lederle Faculty Award (Yale) 1956; Candn. Centennial Medal 1967; Queen's Silver Jubilee Medal 1977; author or co-author various book chapters, scient. articles; former mem. ed. bds. various scient. journs.; mem. Physiol. Soc.; Brit. Pharmacol. Soc.; Am. Pharmacol. Soc.; Fellow, Chem. Inst. of Can.; Home: 233 Tudor Pl., Ottawa, Ont. K1L 7Y1; Office: 451 Smyth Rd., Ottawa, Ont. K1H 8M5.

**HAGERMAN, Allen R.,** B.Comm., C.A., M.B.A.; financial executive; b. Calgary, Alta. 11 May 1951; s. Douglas R. and Isobel A. (Allen) H.; e. Univ. of Alta. B.Comm. 1973; C.A. 1975; Harvard Univ. M.B.A. 1977; m. Patricia H. d. Robert and Margaret Race 11 May 1974; children: Allison, Christine; VICE-PRES. & CHIEF FINANCIAL OFFICER, HOME OIL COMPANY LIMITED 1991– ; articling student & staff accountant, Arthur Andersen & Co. 1973–75; Finan. Analyst, Hudson's Bay Oil & Gas Co. Ltd. 1977–79; Dir., Project Analysis 1979–80; Mgr., Treas. Div. 1980–82; Corp. Sec. & Extve. Asst. to C.E.O., Home Oil Company Limited 1982–84; Treas. 1984–87; Treas., Interhome Energy Inc. 1987–88; Vice-Pres. & Treas. 1988–90; Vice-Pres. Finance 1990–91; Dir. & Vice-Pres., Scurry-Rainbow Oil Limited; Dir. & Vice-Pres. Finance, Federated Pipe Lines Ltd.; Dir., Alta. Children's Hosp. Found.; Fin. Extve. Inst.; Inst. of C.A.s; clubs: Calgary Golf & Country; Calgary Petroleum; Harvard Club of Calgary; Office: 3200, 324 – 8th Ave. S.W., Calgary, Alta. T2P 2Z5.

**HAGERMAN, Barbara Oliver;** classical musician; e. Mount Allison Univ. music 1965; voice teacher; soloist; adjudicator, P.E.I. & N.B. music festivals; Bd. Mem., Assn. of Candn. Choral Conductors; Dir., Summerside Community Choir; Past Member for P.E.I., Canada Council; former public school music teacher; Former Mem., Bd. & Extve., Fed. of Candn. Music Festivals; Mem., Charlottetown First Baptist Ch.; P.E.I. Music Festival Assn.; Friends of Confederation Centre; P.E.I. Council of the Arts; Home: 41 Ellen Creek Dr., Charlottetown, P.E.I. C1E 1C3.

**HAGERMAN, John D.,** B.Sc., P.Eng.; business executive; b. Belleville, Ont. 22 Jan. 1934; s. Stanley Denike and Edythe Campbell (Moore) H.; e. Belleville Collegiate Queen's Univ. Dipl. Indust. Rel. 1956, B.Sc. 1957; m. Barbra Leacock 12 Dec. 1959; children: Fred, Joan, John, Jennifer; PRESIDENT & DIRECTOR, CANADA CUP INC. A JAMES RIVER CORPORATION CO. 1988– ; President & Dir., Wilkinson Sword/Eddy Match 1983–86; Dir., Extve. Ctte., Environmental Plastics Inst. of Canada; recreations: skiing, sailing, curling; clubs: Boulevard, Etobicoke Yacht; Home: 49 Strath Ave., Etobicoke, Ont. M8X 1R2; Office: 137 Bentworth Ave., Toronto, Ont. M6A 1P6.

**HAGGERTY, Daniel William,** B.Comm.; consulting executive; b. Regina, Sask. 16 March 1933; s. Daniel and Elda Lenoma (Nixon) H.; e. Regina Coll., Assoc. in Arts 1952; Univ. of Sask., B.Comm. 1955; Sr. Extve. Prog., London Sch. of Bus. Admin. 1972; m. Diana Mary d. Harry E. Henderson 1 Sept. 1962; children: Catherine Melissa, Melanie Jane; PRES. & CHIEF EXTVE. OFFR., CANDN. EXTVE. SERV. ORGN. 1984– ; various internat. mktg. pos., Colgate Palmolive 1959–69; Mng. Dir., Beecham (Far East) Sdn. Bhd. 1969–72; Vice-Pres., Mktg., Libby, McNeill & Libby 1973–76; Corp. Devel., The BCP Group 1977–81; Mktg. Serv., Joseph E. Seagram and Sons 1981–84; Pres., Advt. & Sales Extve. Club of Montreal 1980–82; Vice-Chrmn., Assn. of Candn. Advertisers 1983–84; Mem., Nat. Extve. Candn. Counc. of Christians and Jews; Bd. of Dir., Trade Facilitation Office; Anglican; Clubs: Granite; Laurentian Lodge Ski; Home: 358 Davisville Ave., Toronto, Ont. M4S 1H3; Office: Ste. 2000, 415 Yonge St., Toronto, Ont. M5B 2E7.

**HAGGERTY, Terry R.,** B.A., B.P.H.E., M.A., Dip.Ed., Ph.D.; university professor and administrator; b. Port Colborne, Ont. 10 Dec. 1945; s. William O. and Mae (Davis) Haggerty; e. Queen's Univ. B.A. 1968, B.P.H.E. 1969; Univ. of W. Ont. M.A. 1973; Althouse College Dip.Ed. 1973; State Univ. of New York at Buffalo Ph.D. 1988; m. Julia C. d. John and Jesse Forde 31 May 1969; children: Jeffery, Leeann; PROFESSOR, PHYSICAL EDUCATION AND RECREATION, UNIV. OF N.B. 1991– ; involved in the field of sport & physical activity as a univ. varsity athlete, high school & college coach, univ. athletic business manager and Prof., Univ. of W. Ont. 1982–88; Penn State Univ. 1988–91; Dean, Fac. of Phys. Ed. & Recreation, Univ. of N.B.; author of over 50 pubs. & scholarly presentations in the area of sport admin.; Founding Mem., N. Am. Soc. for Sport Management (Sec. 1987–89); Mem., Acad. of Management; Am. Alliance for Health, Phys. Ed., Recreation & Dance; Candn. Assn. for Health, Phys. Ed. & Recreation; Internat. Soc. of Comparative Phys. Ed. & Sport; author: 'Developing Microcomputer Literacy' 1985; co-author: 'Financial Management of Sport-Related Organizations' 1984; recreations: fly fishing, golf; Home: 63 Bromley Ave., Starlight Village, Fredericton, N.B. E3C 1M8; Office: P.O. Box 4400, Fredericton, N.B. E3B 5A3.

**HAGGIS, Paul George,** B.A.; trust company executive; b. Belleville, Ont. 27 Feb. 1952; s. George Paul and Octavia E. (Ingram) H.; e. Trinity Coll. Sch. Port Hope; Univ. of W. Ont. B.A. 1977; m. Bonnie d. Colin and Ruth Lawrence 24 Sept. 1977; three s. George Paul, Philip Lawrence, Ian Parkinson; PRES. & C.E.O., METROPOLITAN TRUST CO. 1990– ; Pres.: Metropolitan Trustco Limited; Metropolitan Trust Co. of Canada; Metropolitan Financial Advisors Ltd.; comnd. Candn. Forces 1971; Mgr. Cash Mgmt. Corporate & Govt. Banking Bank of Montreal 1984; Asst. Treas. Traders Group Ltd. 1987; Vice Pres. Corporate Finance Citibank Canada 1988; Vice Pres. and Treas. Met Life Candn. Operations 1989; mem. Candn. Inst. Strategic Studies; Club: Royal Candn. Mil. Inst. (Toronto); Royal Glenora (Edmonton); Hon. Col., 435 (T) Sqn. CFB Edmonton; Home: 170 Roy St., Edmonton, Alta. T6R 2A8; Office: 2700, 10303 Jasper Ave., Edmonton, Alta. T5J 3N6.

**HAGON, Garrick,** B.A.; actor; b. London, Eng. 27 Sept. 1939; s. William Albert and Corinne (Young) H.; e. Univ. of Toronto Schs. 1958; Univ. of Toronto Trinity Coll. B.A. 1963; m. Jane (Liza) d. Romaine K. and Mary Ross 16 Aug. 1965; children: Nicholas Christopher, Alison Jane; first profl. theatre apperance as Prince of Wales in 'Richard III' Stratford Festival 1953; mem. Stratford Festival co. 1959–63; played King of Navarre in 'Love's Labour Lost' and Don John in 'Much Ado About Nothing' Stratford's Young Co. 1983; played season with Man. Theatre Centre 1964; toured Eng. with Prospect Prodns. 1965; played numerous roles Brit. theatre since 1966 incl. Chris Keller 'All My Sons' London's West End 1983; 'After The Fall' National Theatre 1990; first feature film role Eros 'Antony and Cleopatra' dir. Charlton Heston 1971; lead role 'Some Kind of Hero' 1972; numerous other roles dir. by Robert Aldrich, George Lucas, Richard Attenborough, Tim Burton incl. 'Twilight's Last Gleaming' 1974, 'Star Wars' 1976, 'A Bridge Too Far' 1977, 'War and Remembrance' 1986, 'The Great Escape, Final Chapter' 1987; ' Cry Freedom' 1987; 'Batman' 1988; Ed Murrow 'The Nightmare Years' 1989; numerous CBC TV dramas since 1956 and BBC TV (London) since 1981 incl. Frank Oppenheimer 'Oppenheimer' series 1981 and 'A Talent for Murder' with Laurence Olivier 1983; other work incls. US Steel Hour 1962, series 'The Adventurer' 1977, Dumas Fils 'The Lady of the Camellias,' episodes of 'Colditz,' 'Lily Langtry,' 'The Duchess of Duke Street,' 'The Sun Also Rises,' 'The Bretts,' 'London Embassy,' 'Revolver' (CBS) 1992; numerous CBC and BBC radio presentations incl. Duke of Windsor in 'Famous Last Words' by Timothy Findley and 'Mourning Becomes Electra' 1986; recipient Tyrone Guthrie Award Stratford Festival 1963; ACTRA Award Best Supporting Performance TV 1985; mem. ACTRA; AFTRA; Candn. and Brit. Equity; recreations: swimming, riding; Home: 24 Rodenhurst Rd., London SW4 8AR, England; Office: c/o Rex Hagon, 19 Playter Blvd., Toronto, Ont. M4K 2W1.

**HAHN, Jack,** F.E.I.C.; P.Eng.; B.Eng.; electrical engineer; b. Hersfeld, Germany 21 June 1920; s. Adolph and Rosa (Nussbaum) H.; e. McMaster Univ., pre-engn. 1941–42; McGill, B.Eng. (Elect.) 1947; m. Freda, d. Max Handman, 14 Dec. 1947; children: Alan, Norman, Rosanne; CONSULTANT, PRES., JACK HAHN ASSOCIATES; Dir., S.N.C. Group, 1966–80; Chrmn., SNC/GECO Can. Inc. (Toronto) 1977–80; joined S.N.C. 1946; Project Engr., 1952; Dir. of Engn., 1956; Partner 1959; mem., Corp. Engrs. of Que.; Assoc. Prof. Eng. of Ont.; Fellow & Past Pres., Engn. Inst. of Can.; Candn. Soc. of Mech. Engrs.; Conservative; Jewish; recreations: gardening, sailing, tennis; Club: Montefiore; Address: 10 Shallmar Blvd., Toronto, Ont. M5N 1J4.

**HAHN, Murray Marc,** C.Bus., CA, CIP, F.C.A.M.; financial consultant; b. Russia; s. Irving Bleistift and Anna (Gurevitch) H.; e. Univ. of Toronto Cert. in Bus. Admin. 1946; CA 1962; F.C.A.M. 1989; CIP (Chartered Insolvency Practitioner) 1992; m. Marilyn d. Sol and Rose Patchen; children: Harley (Bruce), Randolph, Melissa, Hilary, Mitchell; stared Hahn & Co. 1962, public acctg. firm and licensed trustee in bankruptcy; in 1979 founded and was 1st Pres. of Clarke Henning & Hahn Ltd. until 1992, insolvency practitioners specializing in financial restructuring; introduced several innovations in the insolvency and bankruptcy field; in 1978 initiated the interim proposal (referred to as the holding proposal) which for the first time provided an understandable stay for debtors requiring time to organize an acceptable financial arrangement with creditors and subsequently in 1982 introduced and pioneered the consumer proposal, both of which are now an integral part of the Bankruptcy and Insolvency Act (BIA 1992); recipient Appreciation Award from Supt. of Bankruptcy 1989; enlisted in R.C.A.F. and served for 3½ yrs. before attending Univ. of Toronto; Special Lectr., Bar Admission Course Ont.; Guest Lectr., Univ. of Toronto, York Univ., Seneca Coll.; Past Treas. Harold King Farm (halfway house); author 'Understanding Proposals' 1986; 'The Family Budget' 1989, revised 1990; various articles profl. jours.; Fellow, Candn. Inst. Cert. Adm. Mgrs. (Past Treas.); recreation: swimming, cross-country skiing, cycling, reading, writing; Club: Cambridge; Home: 309 Richview Ave., Toronto, Ont. M5P 3G4; Office: 350 Bay St., Suite 1000, Toronto, Ont. M5H 2S6.

**HAIDASZ, Hon. Stanley,** P.C. (1972), Senator, M.D.; b. Toronto, Ont. 4 Mar. 1923; s. Peter and Josephine (Justynski) H.; e. St. Mary's Sch., Toronto, Ont. 1929–36; St. Michael's Coll. Sch., Toronto, 1936–41; Univ. of Ottawa, B.Ph. 1944, L.Ph. 1945; Univ. of Toronto, M.D. 1951; Course in Electro-cardiog., Cook Co. Post Grad. Sch. of Medicine (Chicago) 1955; Course in Geriatric Med., Univ. of Sask. 1976; m. Natalie, d. Stanley Gugala, Toronto, 26 Aug. 1950; children: Marie, Walter, Barbara, Joanne; el. to H. of C. for Trinity g.e. 1957; re-el. 1962, 63, 65, 68, 72 and 1974 g.e.'s for Parkdale; Ont. Vice Pres., Nat. Liberal Federation, 1958–61; Parlty. Secy. to Min. of Health & Welfare, 1963; Parlty. Secy. to Secretary of State for External Affairs, 1964 & 65; Parlty. Secy., to Min. of Indian Affairs and Northern Development, 1966 & 67; Parlty. Secy., to Minister Consumer & Corporate Affairs, 1968; to Min. Nat. Health and Welfare 1969–70; appt'd first Min. of State for Multiculturalism 1972–74; Head, Candn. Del., World Food Program, Geneva 1964; Del., U.N. Gen. Assembly 1964, 1965; mem. Candn. Parl. Del. to Poland's Millenium, Warsaw 1966; mem. Candn. Del., WHO, Geneva 1970 and 1972; Head of Candn. del. to Inter-Am. Health Social Security Congress, Santo Domingo 1969 and Bogota 1970; accompanied Prime Minister, Pierre E. Trudeau on official visit to U.S.S.R., 1971; Queen's Privy Council, 1972; Candn. Delegation to U.N. World Population Conf., Bucharest 1974; Candn. Parly. Delegation, North Atlantic Assembly, Venice 1981, Madeira 1982, Hague 1983 & Istanbul; Candn. Del., Inter-Parliamentary Union meetings on Human Rights, Belgrade, 1976, Vienna, 1978, Brussels 1980, Budapest & Madrid 1983; Head, Candn. Del., WHO-UNESCO Conf., Primary Health Care, Almata, USSR 1977; Head, Candn. Del., Canada-Poland Med. Exchange Mtg., Krakow 1977; apptd. to Senate 1978; mem., Senate Standing Comtes. on Foreign Rel., Soc. Affairs, Sci. & Technol.; Past Dir., Council on Drug Abuse; Assoc. in Surgery, Shouldice Clinic, Toronto, 1952–55; Staff, St. Joseph's Health Centre, Toronto; Past Pres., Toronto Br., Candn. Polish Cong.; former Nat. Chrmn., Candn. Polish Millenium Fund; Bd. Dirs., Copernicus Sen. Citizens Lodge; Noram Capital; Pro merito medal citations of Polish Combattants Assn., Polish Army Veterans of Amer., Latvian Fed. of Can., Estonian Nat. Counc., Candn. Polish Congress; Assoc., Soviet & E. European Studies, Carleton Univ., Ottawa 1964–72; Hon. citizen of Winnipeg; Hon Life Mem., Lithuanian Nat. Fed., Ethnic Press Fed., Polish Alliance of Can.; Merit Award, Catholic Univ. of Lublin, Poland 1984; Knight Commander Grand Cross of the Sovereign Order of St. John of Jerusalem, (Knights of Malta), Chancellor of its Priory in Canada and 4th degree Knight of Columbus; D.Adm. (hon. causa), Northland Univ. 1988; decorated Commander of the Order of Merit of Poland 1989; Ph.D. (hon. causa), Catholic Univ. of Poland, Lublin 1991; Commander of the Order, Polonia Restituta 1991; Nat. Co-Chrmn., Financial Campaign, John Paul II Collegium, Catholic Univ. of Poland; Campaign Chrmn., Penederecki String Quartet, Wilfrid Laurier Univ., Waterloo, Ont.; Liberal; R. Catholic; Home: 77 Sir William's Lane, Islington, Ont. M9A 1V2.

**HAIG, Graeme Thomson,** M.C., C.M., C.D., Q.C.; b. Moose Jaw, Sask. 7 Aug. 1923; s. Gordon Stuart and Catherine Margaret (Thomson) H.; e. elem. and high schs. Moose Jaw (Sask.) 1931 and Winnipeg (Man.) 1940; Univ. of Man. 1940–42; Man. Law Sch. LL.B. 1949; m. Patricia Evelyn 3 Oct. 1992; children: Gordon, Briony, Margot, Angela; PARTNER, D'ARCY & DEACON; Dir.: Granville Savings & Mortgage Corp.; Wawanesa Mutual Life Insurance Co.; Wawanesa Mutual Insurance Co.; called to Bar of Man. 1949; cr. Q.C. 1964; Vice Chrmn., Found. for Legal Rsch.; Mem., RCMP Public Complaints Comn.; Trustee, Candn. Inst. for Advanced Legal Studies; Pres. Man. P. Cons. Assns. 1970–74; Pres. Un. Way of Winnipeg 1977–78; served in N.W. Europe 1943–46; Fort Garry Horse Militia 1949–61, Hon. Lt. Col.; mem. Winnipeg Chamber Comm. (Past Pres.); Man. Bar Assn. (Past Pres.); Candn. Bar Assn. (Past Vice Pres.; Nat. Council); Candn. Foundation on Alcohol & Drug Dependencies (Past Pres. and Hon. Life mem.); Hon. Dir., Knowles Centre Inc.; Member, Order of Canada; Presbyterian; P. Conservative; recreations: golf, curling, music, reading; Clubs: Cavalry and Guards (London, U.K.); Manitoba; St. Charles Country; Home: 355 Lyndale Dr., Winnipeg, Man. R2H 1M3; Office: 1200, 330 St. Mary Ave., Winnipeg, Man. R3C 4E1.

**HAIG, Susan E.,** M.M., M.M., D.M.A.; orchestral conductor; b. Summit, N.J. 14 April 1954; d. E. Hawley and Elizabeth F. (Myers) H.; e. Princeton Univ. B.A. 1976; State Univ. of N.Y. at Stony Brook M.M. 1979, M.M. 1980, D.M.A. 1983; MUSIC DIRECTOR, WINDSOR SYMPHONY ORCHESTRA 1991– ; Coaching/Conducting Fellow, Juilliard 1981–83; Asst. Conductor, Minnesota Opera 1983–84; N.Y. City Opera 1984–86; Resident Coach, Canadian Opera Co. 1986–88; Resident Staff Conductor, Calgary Philharmonic Orchestra 1988–91; Adjunct Faculty, Univ. of Windsor; 1992 Heinz Unger Conducting Award; Mem., St. John's Anglican Church, Sandwich; Office: 174 – 198 Pitt St. W., Windsor, Ont. N9A 5K4.

**HAIGHT, James S.J.,** M.D., Ph.D., F.R.C.S., F.A.C.S.; surgeon; otolaryngologist; b. Capetown, S. Africa 28 May 1944; s. Frank Arnold and Maybelle Violet (Jackson) H. (forebears in N. Am. in 1628); e. French Switz. 1950–53; Winchester Coll. & Oxford Univ., BM, B.Ch. 1973, M.A. 1966, D.Phil. 1971; University of Toronto, F.R.C.S.(C) 1979; dipl.Am.Bd. of Otolaryngology 1979; F.A.C.S. 1984; m. Lynn d. Joy and Alfred Schofield 11 July 1970; children: Emma, Adrian; FOUNDER NOSE, SINUS, SLEEP CLINIC, ST. MICHAEL'S HOSP. 1984– (a multidisciplinary clinic for investigation and treatment of airway problems in sleep); Med. Rsch. Counc. Scholar U.K. 1967–71; doctorate rsch. in labs. of Sir Hans Krebs & Sir George Pickering; part-time tutor, Oxford Univ. Med. Sch. 1969–70; Lectr., Physiol., London Hosp. 1970–71; Rsch. Assoc., Gage Rsch. Inst. 1981– ; Asst. Prof., Univ. of Toronto 1980– ; attending physician, Sunnybrook Med. Ctr. 1980– ; Northwestern Hosp. 1980– ; Branson Hosp. 1982– ; St. Michael's Hosp. 1984– ; invited speaker, Joseph Soc. (UK); Am. Rhinol. Soc.; Pan Am. Cong. of Otolaryngology, Head & Neck Surgery; Univ. of Toronto external rhinoplasty course; numerous rsch. presentations; Project Mgr., Internat. Biol. Rsch. Prog. (UK Royal Soc.) in Phys. Anthropol. in Peru 1966; Hodge Award Winner (Candn. Otol. Soc.) 1986; author of numerous pubs. in orig. rsch.; recreations: sports, reading; Club: Athenaeum (UK); Home: 197 Strathgowan Ave., Toronto, Ont. M4N 1C4; Office: 250 Lawrence Ave. W., Ste. 308, Toronto, Ont. M5M 1B2.

**HAIGHT, Lynn J.,** M.A., C.A., C.M.C.; b. Bournemouth, England 13 Jan. 1947; d. Alfred and the late Joy Schofield; e. Oxford Univ. M.A. 1970; A.C.A. (England & Wales) 1973, F.C.A. 1978; C.A. 1976, C.M.C. 1979; m. Dr. James S.J. s. Frank and Mabel H. 1970; children: Emma, Adrian; VICE-PRES., INTERNATIONAL INSTITUTE OF CERTIFIED MANAGEMENT CONSULTANTS OF CANADA 1993– ; Price Waterhouse Assoc. 1975–82; U.N. Consultant for UNDTCD, World Bank and UNDP in a number of countries, Price Waterhouse Limited 1982–85; Vice-Pres., Scotiabank 1986–93; Pres., Inst. of Certified Mngt. Consultants of Ont. 1991–92; Women's Internat. Scholarship to London Business School Extve. Program; Univ. of Jerusalem Educational Trust Scholar; Dir., Tafelmusik Baroque Orch. (Treas. 1983–87); recreations: playing the flute, running; club: Oxford & Cambridge (U.K.); Home: 197 Strathgowan Ave., Toronto, Ont. M4N 1C4; Office: 121 Bloor St. E., Toronto, Ont. M4W 3M5.

**HAILEY, Arthur;** author; b. Luton, England 5 Apr. 1920; immigrant to Canada 1947; became Candn. citizen 1952; s. (late) George Wellington and (late) Elsie Mary (Wright) H.; e. British Elem. Sch. until age 14; m. 2ndly Sheila Marjorie d. (late) James Watt Dunlop 28 July 1951; children: Jane, Steven, Diane (and by previous m.) Roger, John, Mark; author of novels: 'Runway Zero-Eight' (with John Castle) 1958; 'The Final Diagnosis' 1959; 'In High Places' 1962; 'Hotel' 1965; 'Airport' 1968; 'Wheels' 1971; 'The Moneychangers' 1975; 'Overload' 1979; 'Strong Medicine' 1984; 'The Evening News' 1990; novel in progress (untitled); (collected plays) 'Close-Up on Writing for Television' 1960; motion pictures 'Zero Hour' 1956; 'Time Lock' 1957; 'The Young Doctors' 1961: 'Hotel' 1966; 'Airport' 1970; 'The Moneychangers' 1976; 'Wheels' 1978; 'Strong Medicine' 1986; 'A Last Request' (poem); television plays include: 'Flight into Danger' 1956 and 11 others; U.S. TV Series 'Arthur Hailey's Hotel' based on novel; novels publ. in 38 languages, est. 150 million copies in print; served as Pilot with RAF 1939–47, rank Flight Lieut., Air Efficiency Award (A.E.); subject TV program 'This Is Your Life' (England) 1991; mem. Alliance of Candn. Cinema, Tel. and Radio Artists (hon. life member); Authors League of Am.; Writers Guild of America; Independent Conservative; Clubs: Lyford Cay, Bahamas; recreations: boating, fishing, enology, music; Home: Lyford Cay, P.O. Box N-7776, Nassau, Bahamas; Office: Seaway Authors Ltd., 3400 First Canadian Place, P.O. Box 130, Toronto, Ont. M5X 1A4.

**HAINEY, Alex,** B.Comm., M.B.A.; business executive; e. McGill Univ. and Univ. of Western Ont.; PRESIDENT, DRAKE BEAM MORIN-CANADA INC.; formerly Sr. Vice-Pres. & Dir., Union Carbide Canada Limited; Dir., Union Carbide Can. Limited; Drake Beam Morin-Can. Inc.; Intermetco Limited; Timminco Limited; Beaumaris Minerals Inc.; Granite Club; Candn. Council of Christians and Jews; Lectr. in Bus., Univ. of Toronto, York Univ.; Co-Chair, McGill Devel. Fund; Special Gifts, Univ. of Montreal, Share the Vision Campaign; Mem., Am. Soc. for Metals; Am. Inst. of Mining, Metal. and Petroleum Engrs.; Conseil d'Industrie, Quebec; Adv. Ctte., Industrial Accident Prevention Assn. Ont. (Past Chair & Life Mem.); Internat. Brotherhood of Magicians; recreations: skiing, sailing, amateur theatre, politics; clubs: Rotary (Past Pres.) Royal Canadian Yacht, Granite, Mount Royal; Office: 77 Bloor St. W., Toronto, Ont. M5S 1M2.

**HAIRFORD, Warren James,** B.S., M.B.A.; oil and gas industry executive; b. Dupont, Louisiana 6 Feb. 1949; s. Nealson Joseph and Sadie Mary (Ducote) H.; e. Louisiana State Univ. B.S. 1971; Univ. of Texas of the Permian Basin M.B.A. 1982; m. Paula G.; d. Gilroy and Mary Lee Guilbeau 12 Sept. 1970; one s.: Jason Anthony; PRESIDENT & GENERAL MANAGER,

CONOCO CANADA LIMITED 1990– ; 1st Lt., U.S. Army 1971–73; 22 years with Conoco; a U.S. expatriate with various mngt. positions in Texas 1971–84, Alaska 1984–86, Dubai–United Arab Emirates 1986–89, Maplethorpe England 1989, Aberdeen Scotland 1989–90; The Extve. Program, Darden Grad. Sch. of Business Admin., Univ. of Virginia; Mem., Soc. of Petroleum Engrs. of AIME; Soc. of Profl. Well Log Analysts; recreations: golf, reading; clubs: Glencoe Golf & Country; Home: 355 Canterville Dr., S.W., Calgary, Alta. T2W 4R1; Office: 3900, 205 – 5th Ave. S.W., Calgary, Alta. T2P 2V7.

**HALAMANDARIS, Pandelis G.,** M.S., Ph.D.; educator; b. Suez, Egypt 9 Jan. 1932; s. George P. and Georgina G. (Argyridou) H.; e. Am. Univ. of Cairo B.A. 1958; Ind. Univ. M.S., Ph.D. 1968; m. Helga d. Frederick and Anna Kretschmann 15 July 1961; children: Yorgo, Petros; PROF. OF EDN. BRANDON UNIV. 1975– , Dir. of Internat. Devel. Projects 1987– , Internat. Liaison Offr. 1975– ; Dean of Student Services, Am. Univ. of Cairo 1958–61; Visiting Prof. Va. State Univ. 1967; Rsch. Assoc. Ind. Univ. 1967–68, Rsch. Assoc. 1983; Dir. of Reading Comn. Man. Teachers Soc. 1968–69; Lectr. Univ. of Man. 1969; Visiting Scholar London Univ. Inst. of Edn. 1975–76 and Min. of Edn. Guyana 1973; Assoc. Prof. present Univ. 1969–74; Lectr. Univ. of Swaziland summers 1980–84, Malawi Inst. of Edn. summers 1984–88; Pres. Westman Multicultural Council Man.; Man. Ednl. Rsch. Council; recipient US Office of Edn. Grant 1967–68; various Grants for Internat. Develop., Teacher Educ., Staff Develop.; author 'Reading in Manitoba Schools – A Survey Book' 1971; various edn. articles, evaluation reports; mem. Am. Ednl. Rsch. Assn.; Linguistic Soc. Am.; Candn. Edn. Rschers. Ednl. Assn.; Comparative & Internat. Edn. Soc. Can.; Candn. Assn. Ednl. Psychol.; Phi Delta Kappa; recreation: stamp collecting; Home: 44 Buttercup Bay, Brandon, Man. R7B 1G3; Office: Brandon, Man. R7A 6A9.

**HALDE, Jean-R.,** M.A., M.B.A.; b. Montreal, Que. 15 Apr. 1948; s. Jean L. and Florida L. (Legault) H.; e. Univ. of Montreal B.A. 1967; Univ. of W. Ont. M.A. 1969; Harvard Business Sch. M.B.A. 1972; m. Hélène d. Rosa and Jean-Baptiste Lévesque 16 Oct. 1987; children: Julie, Marie-Renée, Patrick; PRES. & C.E.O., CULINAR INC. 1987– ; Unigesco Inc.; Le Groupe Vidéotron Ltée; Vice Pres. and Gen. Mgr. Peoples Jewellers Ltd. Guild Div. 1973–76, Peoples Stores Div. 1976–77; Sr. Vice Pres. E. Can. Carling O'Keefe Breweries of Canada Ltd. and Vice Pres. and Gen. Mgr. La Brasserie O'Keefe Ltée 1977–79; Pres. & C.E.O., Métro-Richelieu Inc. 1979–83; Pres. & C.E.O., Atlantique Video & Sound Inc. 1984–87; mem. Young Pres. Organ.; Assn. des M.B.A. du Qué.; G.P.M.C.; BCNI; recreations: skiing, golf; Clubs: Club de Golf Balmoral; Saint-Denis; Home: 1160 Mistral St., Montréal, Que. H2P 2Z1; Office: 2 Complexe Desjardins, Ste. 2700, Montreal, Que. H5B 1B2.

**HALDENBY, Eric Ross Macdonald,** B.Arch.; educator; b. Toronto, 7 Apr. 1951; s. Douglas Charles and Muriel Ross (Macdonald) H.; e. Univ. of Waterloo B. Arch. 1975; m. Rosemary Josephine Aicher; children: Adrian Douglas, Julian Charles; DIR., SCH. OF ARCH., UNIV. OF WATERLOO and Assoc. Prof. of Arch. 1988– ; Chair, Candn. Counc. of University Schools of Arch. 1990–93; Vice-Chair, Local Architectural Conservation Adv. Ctte., City of Kitchener, 1989; joined present univ. 1976; founded the Waterloo Rome Studies Program 1979; mem. Bd. of Dirs., Royal Architectural Inst. of Can. 1990–93; Bd. of Dirs., Assoc. of Collegiate Schs. of Architecture; mem., Candn. Architectural Certification Bd.; mem., Program Ctte., Candn. Academic Centre in Italy; special Arch. Adv. Ctte. to the Candn. Counc. for the Arts; Soc. of Arch. Historians; Classics Assn. of Can.; Club: Osler Bluff Ski; Home: 134 David St., Kitchener, Ont. N2G 1Y2; Office: Univ. of Waterloo, Waterloo, Ont. N2L 3G1.

**HALE, Grete (Marguerite),** B.J., G.C.L.J.; food company executive; b. Ottawa, Ont. 1929; e. Carleton Univ. B.J. 1954; m. Reginald B. Hale 1957; CHAIRMAN, MORRISON LAMOTHE INC.; Dir., North American Life Assurance Co.; Key Radio Ltd.; Nation's Capital Television Inc.; Consumer Gas; Beechwood Cemetary; former Mem., Agriculture, Food & Beverage SAGIT; Vice Senechale de la Chaîne des Rôtisseurs; Immed. Past Pres., Cdn. Club of Ottawa; Heraldry Soc. of Can.; Chrmn., MacDonald Cartier Lib.; mem. Bd. Govs., Ottawa Univ.; Hon. Col., 78th Fraser Highlanders; Chair, Community Found. of Ottawa-Carleton; Adv. Bd., Salvation Army; Vice Chancellor, Registrar-General, Hospitaler Order St. Lazarus Jerusalem; Sec., Royal Candn. Geog. Soc.; after grad. rec'd 10 yrs. catering experience Eng., France, Scandinavia, Switzerland and U.S.A.; Vice Pres., Canada World Youth; Dir., Foundn. for Internat. Training; Chrmn., Ellen Fairclough Found.; first woman Pres., Bakery Council Can.; Chrmn., Hospital Food Services, Ont. Inc.; formerly Chrmn. Algonquin Coll.; mem. Ont. Counc. of Regents; Vice Pres. Ottawa Council Women; Corr. Secy. Nat. Council Women in Can.; Dir. P.C. Canada Fund; Dir. Alliance for Bilingualism in Can.'s Capital Region; Women's Adv. Council (5 yrs.) Ministry of Industry & Tourism; Councillor Ottawa Bd. Trade; Home: 40 Fuller St., Ottawa, Ont. K1Y 3R8; Office: Ste. 1603, 275 Slater St., Ottawa, Ont. K1P 5H9.

**HALL, Agnez,** M.L.S.; retired librarian; b. Tracadie, N.B. 25 Nov. 1933; s. allen and Judith (Arseneault) H.; e. Coll. de Bathurst (N.B.) B.A. 1957; Univ. de Montréal B.L.S. 1963; Univ. of B.C. M.L.S. 1974; Univ. of Moncton M.A. (not completed); m. Doria d. Lucien Noel 1 July 1966; one s. Serge; SCHOOL LIBRARIES AND MEDIA CONSULTANT, N.B. DEPT. OF EDUCATION 1987–1991; Cataloguer, Univ. Larentian Sudbury, Ont. 1963–64; French Sect. N.B. Teachers' Coll. Lib. Fredericton 1964–66; Dir., Tech. Services Univ. de Moncton Lib. 1966–67, Univ. Lib. 1967–73; Asst. to Dir. N.B. Lib. Service 1974–79, Acting Dir. 1979–80; Dir., N.B. Library Service 1980–83; Co-ordinator, N.B. Governmental Libraries 1984–87; mem., Task Force on Nat. Union Catalogue Nat. Lib. of Can. 1972–75; Chrmn., Communauté Chrétienne Universitaire, Univ. de Moncton 1969–71; Foyer Ecole (Home & Sch. Assn.) 1983–84; Club Richelieu (Fredericton) 1986–88; author various publs.; mem., Atlantic Provs. Lib. Assn. (Past mem. Exec. Council); Candn. Lib. Assn. (Past mem. Exec. Council); ASTED; K. of C.; Club Richelieu; Home: 22 Dahlia Dr., Fredericton, N.B. E3A 1N3.

**HALL, Alan Harold,** B.Arch., C.I.T.; retired distribution executive and educator; b. London, England 8 Nov. 1924; s. Harold George and Adelaide (Partridge) H.; e. Rutlish 1935–40; Queen's Univ. 1941–43; McGill Univ. 1946–50, B.Arch. 1950; York Univ. 1975–76; m. Carmel d. Rupert and Kathleen Millan 22 June 1946; children: Christopher, Pamela, Anthony, Kathleen; Lecturer, McMaster Univ. 1989–90; Distbn. Mgr., AFG Glass Inc. (and predecessors Pilkington Brothers Canada Ltd. and Ford Glass Ltd.) 1967–89; Candn. Army Serv. 1943–46; Reserve Serv., Black Watch of Can. 1949–53 (Lieut.); Archit./Engr., Tower Co. Ltd. 1948–53; Pres., Toohall Ltd. 1953–65; Gen. Mgr., Shannon Glass Ltd. 1965–67; Guest Lectr., McMaster Univ., Waterloo Univ., George Brown Coll.; Chrmn., Candn. Shippers' Counc. 1982–89; Dir., Progress Place 1987–89; Mem., Transportation Ctte., Internat. Bus. Counc. of Can. 1984–89; Mem., Transport. Ctte., Candn. Manufacturers' Assoc. 1982–89; Chrmn., Ont. Plywood Dist. Assn. 1960–61; Chrmn., Kingston Br., Candn. Inst. of Internat. Affairs 1961–63; Pres., Candn. Assn. of Phys. Dist. Mgmt. 1973–74; Dir., Candn. Glass Fed. 1965–67; Adv. Bd., Hotel Dieu Hosp. 1962–64; Assoc. Mem., Chartered Inst. of Transp.; Silver Award, McGill Univ. 1949 (Pres. Arch. Undergrad. Soc.); Roman Catholic; Mem., McGill Grad. Soc.; Queen's Univ. Alumni Assn.; Old Rutlishians' Assn.; author: 'Canadian Distribution is Different' 1971; recreations: sailing, tennis, skiing; Home: 6880 Wallace Dr., Apt. 724, Brentwood Bay, B.C. V0S 1A0.

**HALL, Anthony James,** B.A., M.A., Ph.D.; university professor; b. Toronto, Ont. 4 April 1951; s. James Jamison and Nancy Blair Fergusson H.; e. York Univ., B.A. (Hons.) 1975, M.A. 1976; Univ. of Toronto, Ph.D. 1984; m. Lena d. Bertha Nabigon; children: Sampson James Hall Nabigon, Riley George Hall Nabigon; ASSOC. PROF., DEPT. OF NATIVE AM. STUDIES, THE UNIV. OF LETHBRIDGE 1989– ; Asst. Prof., Dept. of Native Studies, Laurentian Univ. of Sudbury 1982–89; films photographed and directed: 'Flight Plan' 1971, 'Sky Surfers' 1975, 'Serpent River Paddlers' 1976, 'Seasons of the Mind' 1982; Rsch. Ed., 'The Canadian Journal of Native Studies' 1987– ; Dir., The Candn. Indian/Native Studies Assn. 1985– ; The Candn. Alliance in Solidarity with the Native Peoples 1982–83 (Vice-Pres. 1983–85; Pres. 1985–86 and 1991– ); Mem., ACTRA 1965–82; Candn. Hist. Assn.; author: 'The Nungosuk Report: A Study in Aboriginal Language Renewal' 1987; acad. articles incl. 'Native Limited Identities and Newcomer Metropolitanism in Upper Canada, 1814–1867' in Keane and Read, eds., 'Old Ontario: Essays in Honour of J.M.S. Careless' 1990; 'The St. Catherine's Milling and Lumber Company versus the Queen' in Abel and Friesen, eds., 'Aboriginal Resource Use in Canada' 1991; 'Aboriginal Issues and the New Political Map of Canada' in Granatstein and McNaught, eds., '"English Canada" Speaks Out' 1991; 'Indian Summer, Canadian Winter' 25 (3) 'Report on the Americas' 1991; 'Blockades and Bannock: Aboriginal Protests and Politics in Northern Ontario 1980–90' 1991; 'The Politics of Aboriginality: Political Fault Lines in Indian Country' 1993; journalism, especially opinion pieces in The Globe and Mail; regular columnist 'The Canadian Forum'; frequent presentations to govts. on constitutional issues, incl. the Beaudoin-Dobbie Parlty. Ctte. on behalf of Assembly of First Nations (Jan. 1992); recreations: book collecting, downhill skiing; Club: Craigleith Ski; Office: 4401 University Dr., Lethbridge, Alta. T1K 3M4.

**HALL, Sir Arnold A.,** M.A., F.R.S., F.Eng., F.R.Ae.S.; engineer and administrator; b. Liverpool, Eng. 23 Apr. 1915; s. Robert and Ellen (Parkinson) H.; e. Alsop High Sch., Liverpool, Eng.; Cambridge Univ. M.A. 1936; m. Dione Sykes (dec.); m. Iola Nealon; Dir., Rolls-Royce Ltd. 1983–88; Royal Ordnance PLC 1984–87; Lloyds Bank PLC 1966–85; Phoenix Assurance Co. PLC 1969–85; I.C.I. PLC 1970–85; Prof. of Aeronautics, Univ. of London 1945–51; Dir. Royal Aircraft Estab., Farnborough, Eng. 1951–55; Tech. Dir., Hawker Siddeley Group PLC 1955–58; Mng. Dir., 1963–68; Chrmn. & Managing Dir. 1968–81; Chrmn. 1981–86; Bristol Siddeley Engines Ltd. 1958–63; Mang. Dir., 1959–63; Chrmn., Hawker Siddeley Canada Inc. 1968–86; Pres., Brit. Elect. and Allied Mfrs. Assn. 1967–68; Locomotive and Allied Mfrs. Assn. 1968–71; Soc. Brit. Aerospace Cos. 1972–73; Hon. Fellow, Inst. Mech. Engrs. (U.K.); Inst. Elec. Engrs. (U.K.); Royal Aeronautical Soc. (U.K.); U.S. Academy of Eng.; Foreign Assoc., Am. Inst. Aeronautics & Astronautics; Hon. Mem., Am. Soc. Mech. Eng.; Hon. Fellow, Clare Coll., Cambridge; Fellow, Imp. Coll. of Science & Tch., London Univ.; Chancellor, Loughborough Univ. 1980–89; Freeman, City of London 1988; Chrmn., Fasco Industries Inc. 1980–81 (U.S.A.); Anglican; recreation: sailing; Address: Wakehams Dorney, Windsor, England.

**HALL, Brian Keith,** Ph.D., D.Sc., F.R.S.C.; educator; author; b. Port Kembla, Australia 28 Oct. 1941; s. Harry James and Doris Grace (Garrad) H.; e. Univ. of New Eng. Armidale, N.S.W., Australia B.Sc. 1963, B.Sc. (Hons.) 1965, Ph.D. 1968, D.Sc. 1977; m. June d. John and Nancie Priestley 21 May 1966; children: Derek Andrew, Imogen Elizabeth; KILLAM RESEARCH PROF., DALHOUSIE UNIV. 1990– , PROF. OF BIOL., DALHOUSIE UNIV. 1975– , Prof. of Physiotherapy 1989–92; Fellow, Inst. Human Biology, Univ. of W. Australia 1993; Teaching Fellow in Zool. Univ. of New Eng. 1965–68; Asst. Prof. of Biol. present Univ. 1968, Assoc. Prof. 1972, Chrmn. of Biol. 1978–85; Visiting Prof.: Univ. of Guelph 1975; Univ. of Queensland 1981; Southampton Univ. 1982; Turner-Newall Lectr. Univ. of Manchester 1985; Warwick James Fellow, Univ. of London 1989; Raine Meml. Visiting Prof., Univ. of W. Australia 1993; von Hofsten Lectr., Uppsala Univ. 1993; mem. Adv. Ctte. Life Sci's NSERC 1985–87; mem. Dental Sciences Ctte., M.R.C. 1988–90; mem. Council, Biol. Council Can. 1978–80; Fellow, Royal Soc. of Can. (FRSC) 1985; Nuffield Commonwealth Fellow 1982; APICS Young Sci. of Yr. 1974; 25th Anniversary Lectr. 1987; Fry Medal, Candn. Soc. of Zoology 1994; Plenary Lectr., Internat. Congress Vert. Morphol. 1994; Alta. Heritage Found. for Med. Rsch. Visiting Lectr. 1985, 1990, 1992; mem. World Univ. Service (Can.) Scholarship Ctte. 1985–88; mem., Candn. Nat. Ctte., Internat. Union of Biological Sciences 1987– ; mem. Univ. Rsch. Adv. Bd. 1986–88; guest lectr. Can., USA, Australia, N.Z., UK, Israel, Russia, Austria, Switzerland, Germany, Belgium, Spain, Finland, Sweden; author 'Developmental and Cellular Skeletal Biology' 1978; (with N. Maclean) 'Cell Commitment and Differentiation' 1987; 'The Neural Crest' 1988; 'Evolutionary Developmental Biology' 1992; ed. 'Cartilage' Vols. 1–3, 1983; 'Bone' Vols. 1–9, 1990–94; 'Homology' 1994; co-ed. 'The Vertebrate Skull' Vols. 1–3, 1993; 'Cartilage: molecular aspects' 1991; author or co-author over 160 sci. papers; mem. various jours. ed. bds.; Ed. 'Anatomy and Embryology' 1987– ; Jour. of Craniofacial Genetics and Developmental Biology; mem. Nat. Exec. Can. Ctte. Univ. Biol. Chrmn. 1978–80; Internat. Dir., Craniofacial Biology Group, Inter. Assoc. Dental Rsch. 1989– ; recreations: gardening, music, tennis, walking, reading; Home: 2384 Armcrescent E., Halifax, N.S. B3L 3C7; Office: Halifax, N.S. B3H 4S1.

**HALL, Budd Lionel,** M.A., Ph.D.; educator; b. Long Beach, Cal. 16 Oct. 1943; s. George Lyman and Wynona May (Eslow) H.; e. Mich. State Univ. B.A. 1965, M.A. 1968; UCLA Ph.D. 1972; two s. Shawn Richard, Dana Lionel; PROF. OF ADULT EDUC., ONT. INST. FOR STUDIES IN EDUC.; Sec.-Gen. Internat. Council for Adult Edn. 1979–91; Extra-mural Prof. of Adult Edn. Ont. Inst. Studies in Edn. Univ. of Toronto 1980–91; Extra-mural Prof. of Environmental Studies York Univ. 1989– ; Asst. Prof. of Edn. Cal. State Univ. San Fernando, Los Angeles 1969–70; Head of Rsch. Inst. Adult Edn. Univ. of Dar es Salaam, Tanzania 1970–74; Fellow, Inst. Devel. Studies Univ. of Sussex, Eng. 1974–75; Rsch. Offr. ICAE 1975–79; Co-ordinator, Ctr. for Community and Global Transformation Studies; Hon. Gov. Frontier Coll. Toronto; Internat. Adv. Council Inst. Devel. Rsch. Cambridge, Mass.; Chair, Doris Marshall Inst., Toronto; Founder, Participatory Rsch. Group Toronto; Treas. Peacefund Can. 1986–90; author 'Adult Education and the Development of Socialism in Tanzania' 1975; 'Mtu ni Afya: Tanzania's Health Campaign' 1978; 'Voices for Change: Participatory Research in North America' 1993; co-author 'Adult Learning: A Design For Action' 1978; numerous articles; recreations: poetry, bicycling, out-of-doors, music; Office: 252 Bloor St. W., Toronto, Ont. M5S 1V6.

**HALL, (Charles) Denis,** B.Eng., M.Sc., Ph.D.; management consultant; b. Sherbrooke, Que. 1 July 1938; s. Charles Wayne and Grace Elizabeth (Hall) H.; e. Macdonald H.S. 1955; McGill Univ. B.Eng. 1960; Univ. of Saskatchewan M.Sc. 1961, Ph.D. 1964; m. Florence d. Herbert and Refa Falkingham 23 Nov. 1963; one s.: Jeffrey Wayne; PRES., TECH TEAM MANAGEMENT INC. (Consulting, corporate tech. strategies) 1992– ; various managerial positions resp. for telecommunications product design (resp. for design of world's 1st commercially viable digital voice switch), Bell Northern Research Ltd. 1964–76; Pres. & Chrmn. (U.S. subs.) 1976–81; Extve. Vice-Pres., Mktg. & Technol, Northern Telecom Canada 1981–83; Senior Vice-Pres., Technol. 1983–86; Partner, Manufacturing & Logistics Practice, Coopers & Lybrand Consulting Group 1986–92; 1st Managing Dir., Ctr. for Advanced Technol. Edn., Ryerson Polytech. 1984–85; Chrmn., Steering Ctte. on Telecommunications, Candn. Standards Assn.; author of many articles & talks on communication switching, computing in mfg. & post secondary edn. (in constant demand as a speaker); Office: 7 Darlingbrook Cres., Etobicoke, Ont. M9A 3H4.

**HALL, The Hon. Donald M.,** LL.B., Q.C.; judge; b. Berwick, N.S. 22 Oct. 1931; s. John Henry and Elizabeth (Palmer) H.; e. Dalhousie Univ. LL.B. 1958; m. Irene d. Eugene and Leona Charlton; 2 Feb. 1955; children: Katherine, Heather, Janice, Alyson; JUSTICE OF THE SUPREME COURT OF NOVA SCOTIA 1993– ; law practice Berwick, N.S. 1959–82; Crown Prosecutor, County of Kings 1972–79; Judge of the County Court and Local Judge, Supreme Court of N.S. (Trial Div.) 1982–93; cr. Q.C. 1974; Home: 165 Cottage St., Berwick, N.S.; Office: P.O. Box 747, 1270 Commercial St., Berwick, N.S. B0P 1E0.

**HALL, Douglas John,** B.A., M.Div., S.T.M., Th.D., D.D., LL.D.; educator; b. Ingersoll, Ont. 23 March 1928; s. John Darius and Louisa Irene (Sandick) H.; e. Univ. of W. Ont. B.A. 1953; Union Semy. New York City M.Div. 1956, S.T.M. 1957, Th.D. 1963; Queen's Univ. D.D. 1988; Univ. of Waterloo LL.D. 1992; m. Rhoda d. James Ernest and Rhoda Palfrey 28 May 1960; children: Mary Kate, Christopher, Sara, Lucia; PROF. OF CHRISTIAN THEOL. McGILL UNIV. 1975– ; o. Un. Ch. of Can. 1956; Min. St. Andrew's Ch. Blind River, Ont. 1960–62; Prin. St. Paul's Un. Coll. Univ. of Waterloo 1962–65; McDougald Prof. of Systemic Theol. St. Andrew's Coll. Saskatoon 1965–75; Visiting Prof. Universität-Gesamthochschule Siegen, Germany 1980; Visiting Scholar Doshisha Univ. Kyoto, Japan 1989; Theol. Adv. World Alliance of Reformed Chs.; World Council Chs.; author 15 books incl. 'Lighten Our Darkness' 1976; 'The Canada Crisis' 1980; 'Has The Church A Future?' 1980; 'The Steward: A Biblical Symbol Come of Age' 1983, revised ed. 1990; 'Thinking The Faith: Christian Theology In A North American Context' 1989; 'The Future Of The Church: Where Are We Headed?' 1989; 'Professing the Faith' 1993; numerous articles; recreation: music; Home: 5562 av. Notre-Dame-de-Grace, Montreal, Que. H4A 1L7; Office: 3520 University St., Montreal, Que. H3A 2A7.

**HALL, Emmett M.,** C.C., Q.C., LL.B., D.C.L., LL.D., D.M., D.Sc.; retired justice Supreme Court of Canada; b. St. Columban, Que. 29 Nov. 1898; s. James and Alice (Shea) H.; e. St. Canute, Que.; Saskatoon, Sask.; Univ. of Sask. LL.B., D.C.L. 1964; Univ. of Ottawa D.M.; LL.D.: Univ. of Windsor 1968, Univ. of Man. 1968, Queen's Univ. 1974, Dalhousie Univ. 1975, York Univ. 1977, UNiv. of Regina 1979; St. Francis Xavier Univ. D.Sc. 1974; m. Isabel Mary Parker, Humboldt, Sask. 26 June 1922; children: Marian Wedge, John E.; CHANCELLOR, UNIV. OF SASK. 1980–86; Lectr. in Law 1948–58, mem. Senate 1942–54; Hon. Prof. Univ. of Calgary 1977– ; Chancellor Univ. of Guelph 1971–77; called to Bar of Sask. 1922; cr. K.C. 1935; Chief Justice Queen's Bench Court Sask. 1957; Chief Justice of Sask. 1961; Justice Supreme Court of Can. 1962–73; Chrmn., Royal comn. on Health Services 1961; Chrmn., Comte. on Aims & Objectives for Educ. in Ont., report tabled 1968; Arbitrator, Railway Dispute 1974; Conciliation Commr. railway dispute 1976; arbitrated disputes between Terminal operators and Grain Handlers Union Vancouver; Chrmn., Sask. Royal Comn. on Univ. Structure & Organ.; Commr. Study Judicial System Prov. Sask.; Chief Commr. Grain Handling and Transport Comn. 1975–77; arbitrated dispute Air Operators and Treasury Bd. 1979; Special Commr. study for Govt. Can. on state of health services in Can. 1979; Chrmn. Bd. Trustees, St. Paul's Separate Sch. Dist. Saskatoon 1949–57; Pres., Can. Sch. Trustees Sask. 1945–52; mem., Exec. Sask. Sch. Trustees Assn. 1952–57; Chrmn., St. Paul's Hosp. Bd. 1947–63; Legal Advisor Cath. Hosp. Conf. many yrs.; active Candn. Red Cross Soc.; recipient Bronfman Award Am. Pub. Health Assn. 1966; Wilder Penfield Award Vanier Inst. Family 1980; Performance Citation Award Cath. Health Assn. Can. 1983; named Goodman Lectr. Univ. of Toronto Law Sch. 1975; Nat. Hon. Pres. Candn. Civil Liberties Assn.; Dir., Candn. Inst. Adm. Justice; Pres., Candn. Sec. Intnl. Comn. Jurists 1976–77; K. of C.; Bencher, Law Soc. Sask. 1945–57, Pres. 1952; Vice Pres. Sask. Candn. Bar Assn. 1943–45; Clubs: Rideau (Ottawa); Saskatoon.

**HALL, Frederick Albert,** Assoc. Dipl., B.Mus., M.A., Ph.D.; university professor; b. Niagara-on-the-Lake, Ont. 2 July 1944; s. Albert Gerrish and Marjorie Mae (Irvine) H.; e. Niagara Dis. S.S.; McGill Univ., Assoc. Dipl. 1966, B. Mus. 1969; Univ. of Toronto, M.A. 1970, Ph.D. 1978; m. Sharyn d. Arthur and Mary Hall 19 June 1971; children: Matthew, Elliott; ASSOC. PROF., MUSIC DEPT., MCMASTER UNIV. 1972– ; Chrmn. 1980–86; Assoc. Dean of Humanities (Studies) 1988– ; editor: 'Songs I to English Texts' 1985; co-editor: 'The Romantic Tradition' 1992; 'Musical Canada: Words and Music Honouring Helmut Kallmann' 1988; Contrib.: 'Encyclopedia of Music in Canada,' 'The Canadian Encyclopedia'; 'Symphony Orchestras of the World: Selected Profiles'; 'Studies in Eighteenth-Century Culture'; author of articles in music periodicals; Home: 1 Melville St., Dundas, Ont. L9H 1Z7; Office: Dept. of Music, McMaster Univ., Hamilton, Ont. L8S 4M2.

**HALL, Gordon McCamus,** B.Sc., F.S.A., F.C.I.A., M.A.A.A.; financial executive; b. Peterborough, Ont. 15 Jan. 1941; s. Willis Stewart and Margaret Isobel (McCamus) H.; e. Kenner C.V.I.; Queen's Univ. B.Sc. (Hon.) 1963; m. Wendy V. d. Gerald and Barbara Quart 9 Oct. 1971; children: Deborah Christine, Darren Stewart, Derek Timothy; VICE CHRMN. & DIR. OF PRACTICE DEVELOPMENT, WILLIAM M. MERCER LIMITED 1973– ; Asst. Actuary, Crown Life Insur. Co. 1963–73; Chrmn., Internat. Bus. Devel. Group, William M. Mercer Companies Inc.; Dir., William M. Mercer Limited; Mng. Dir., William M. Mercer Companies; Mem., Candn. Inst. of Actuaries; Soc. of Actuaries; Toronto Bd. of Trade; ACPM; Office: BCE Place, 161 Bay St., P.O. Box 501, Toronto, Ont. M5J 2S5.

**HALL, Hamilton,** M.D., F.R.C.S.(C); orthopaedic surgeon; educator; b. Seattle, Wash. 25 Oct. 1938; s. Eric and Dorothy (Higday) H.; e. Port Credit (Ont.) Secondary Sch. 1957; Univ. of Toronto M.D. 1963; m. Geraldine d. Michael and Vera Volpe 27 June 1964; children: Deborah, Michael, Joanne; FOUNDER & MEDICAL DIRECTOR, CANADIAN BACK INSTITUTE 1974– and ORTHOPAEDIC SURGEON, ORTHOPAEDIC & ARTHRITIC HOSP. 1985– ; served Care/Medico, Malaysia 1964–66; Duncan Fellow in Orthopaedics, Toronto Gen. Hosp. 1971–72, Orthopaedic Surgeon 1973–85; Sr. Lectr. in Med. Edn. in Orthopaedics Univ. of Dundee, Scot. 1972–73; Orthopaedic Surgeon, Women's Coll. Hosp. 1973; Assoc. Prof. of Surgery Univ. of Toronto, Lectr. in Anatomy 1974–79, Co-ordinator Con. Med. Edn. 1975–77; Assoc. Staff Orthopaedic Surgeon Mount Sinai Hosp. Toronto 1982–85; Dir. Cand. Back Inst. 1978; Med. Dir. Personal Injury Clinic Toronto 1985; Cons. to Behavioural Health Inc. Toronto 1981– ; Internat. Adv. Nat. Back Found. Inc. Little Rock, Ark. 1982– ; author 'The Back Doctor' 1980; co-author 'Talking Back in Class' 1983; contbg. author 'Disorders of the Foot' Vol. 1, 1982; 'Recent Advances in Rheumatology' Vol. 2, 1981; ed. 'The New Medicine' Vol. 1, 1983; mem. Ed. Adv. Bd. Back Pain Monitor, Am. Health Cons. Atlanta, Ba. 1983– ; ed. bd. Spine 1984– ; mem. Back Assn. Can. (Vice Pres., Chrmn. Med. Adv. Bd. 1981– ); Candn. Med. Assn.; Ont. Med. Assn.; Ont. Orthopaedic Assn.; N. Am Spine Soc.; Internat. Soc. Study Lumbar Spine; Alpha Omega Alpha; recreations: skiing, scuba, basketball; Home: 36 Mellowood Dr., Willowdale, Ont. M2L 2E3; Office: 330 Front St. W., Suite 1200, Toronto, Ont. M5V 3B7.

**HALL, J. Robert,** B.A., M.B.A.; biscuit and cracker manufacturing executive; b. Tadcaster, Yorkshire, England 14 Aug. 1952; s. Robert R. and Elizabeth G. (Smith) H.; e. Oglethorpe Grammar Sch. 1963–70; Oxford Univ. B.A. 1974; Wharton Sch., Univ. of Penn. M.B.A. 1974–76 (Beta Gamma Sigma, top 8% of class); m. Elizabeth d. William and Doris Sayers 7 April 1979; children: Emma, Alistair, Duncan; PRESIDENT, CHRISTIE BROWN & CO., NABISCO BRANDS LTD. 1992– ; R&D Lab. Technician, Procter & Gamble 1971; Brand Asst. 1975; Product Asst., Salesperson, Product Mgr., Group Product Mgr., Bus. Dir., Nestle 1976–85; Dir., Strategic Planning & Business Devel., Vice-Pres., Cheese; Vice-Pres. & Bus. Unit Mgr., Refrigerated Products; Grocery Products, Kraft General Foods Canada 1985–92; Vice-Pres. Strategy, Kraft USA; Chair, Grocery Product Mfrs. of Can. Marketing Council 1992; Vice-Chair 1991–92; Research Ctte. Chair 1990–91; Adv. Bd. Mem., Coppley Apparel Group 1993– ; Actt. Extve., United way of Metro Toronto 1993– ; Treas. & Extve. Ctte. Mem., Internat. Cheese Council of Can. 1987–89; Adv. Bd. Mem., Food in Canada Mag. 1991–92; Open Exbn. to Oxford Univ. 1971–72; Open Scholarship 1972–74; Thouron Scholarship, Wharton Sch. 1974–76; author: 'Generic vs. Brand Av.' 1990; recreations: sports, investing; clubs: Nat. Golf, Toronto Cricket, Skating & Curling, Toronto Racquet; Home: 12 Wanless Cres., Toronto, Ont. M4N 3B7; Office: 2150 Lakeshore Blvd. W., Etobicoke, Ont. M8V 1A3.

**HALL, John Alexander;** artist; teacher; designer; illustrator; typographer; b. Toronto, Ont. 10 Oct. 1914; s. Alexander G. and Dorothy B. (Hughes) H.; e. Upper Canada Coll.; Ont. Coll. of Art, 1937; m. 1stly, Joan Margaret, d. Barker Fairley, Toronto, 29 May 1937; children: Susan Jane, Margaret Gillian, Rebecca Ann, Jennifer Ruth; 2ndly Pauline Hooton, 27 April 1968; Assoc. Prof. in Drawing & Colour, Faculty of Architecture and Landscape Architecture, Univ. of Toronto 1946–80; Teacher, Upper Can. Coll. Preparatory Sch. (Art and acad. subjects) 1936–43 and 1945–46; Sat. morning classes, Art Gallery of Toronto, 1936–37; York Twp. Schs., 1938–42; teachers' summer courses in art, Ont. Dept. of Educ., 1938–39, 1946–52, and 1958–73; rec'd. Canada Council award (1 yr.) 1963; instr. in Art and Campcraft, Taylor Statten Camps, for 11 summers; has exhibited with Ont. Soc. of Artists, Roy. Candn. Acad., Candn. Soc. of Graphic Art, Contemp. Art Soc., Candn. Group of Painters, Montreal Art Assn.; Nat. Gallery of Can., Candn. Soc. of Painters in Watercolour, and in the U.S.A. and S. Am.; works purchased by Nat. Gallery, Ottawa, Art Gallery of Ont., McLaughlin Gall., Oshawa; mem., Candn. Soc. of Graphic Art, Pres. 1947–48 and 1959; Ont. Soc. of Artists; Hon. Mem., Ont. Assn. of Architects, 1982; Anglican; Home: Glencroft, R.R. 2, Newmarket, Ont. L3Y 4V9.

**HALL, John E.,** B.A., LL.B.; judge; b. London, Ont. 15 May 1939; s. John A. and Mary M. (McCormick) H.; e. Univ. of Western Ontario B.A. 1959, LL.B. 1963; JUDGE, SUPREME COURT OF B.C. 1991– ; called to B.C. Bar 1964; Yukon Bar 1971; Q.C. 1982; Fellow, Am. College of Trial Lawyers 1985; Pres., Vancouver Bar 1978; Federal Royal Commissioner 1987; Office: The Law Courts, 800 Smithe St., Vancouver, B.C. V6Z 2E1.

**HALL, Judith G.,** B.A., M.S., M.D., FRCP(C), FAAP, FCCMG, FABMG; medical doctor, university professor; b. Boston, Mass. 3 July 1939; d. Martin Leland and Margaret Louise (Jayne) Goslin; e. Wellesley Coll. B.A. 1961; Univ. of Washigton M.S. 1965, M.D. 1966; Johns Hopkins Hosp. Res. in Ped. 1969–71; divorced; children: Hilary, Sarah, Benjamin; PROFESSOR & DEPT. HEAD, UNIV. OF B.C. SCHOOL OF MEDICINE; Asst., Assoc. & Full Prof., Med. & Peds., Div. of Med. Genetics, Univ. of Washington Sch. of Med.; Prof., Med. Genetics, Univ. of B.C.; Asst. Ed., 'Am. J. of Med. Genetics'; Edit. Bd., 'Growth, Genetics, Hormones,' 'Am. J. of Human Gen.,' 'Eur. J. of Ped.,' J. of Gen./Gen. Counselling,' 'J. of Med. Gen.,' 'Eur. J. of Human Gen.,' 'Clin. Dysmorphology; Consulant, 'Growth, Genetics and Hormones,' 'Gene Screen'; FRCPS; FAAP; FCCMP; FABMG; RCPS, Ped. & Med. Gen. Study Leave, Oxford Univ. 1988–89; Founding Bd., Am. Bd. of Med. Gen.; UBC Killam Rsch. Prize; nom., YWCA Woman of Distinction Award; Disting. Med. Alumn, Univ. of Wash.; March of Dimes Award; B.C. Who's Who; Pres., Western Soc. for Ped. Rsch.; Am. Soc. of Human Genetics; Mem., Hastings Inst. of Ethics & Life Sci.; N. Pacific Ped. Soc.; Teratology Soc.; Soc. for Ped. Rsch.; Birth Defects & Clin. Genetics Soc.; Physicians for Social Resp.; Genetics Soc. of Can.; Candn. & Am. Ped. socs.; Soc. of Craniofacial Gen.; Skeletal Dysplasia Group; Clin. Gen. Soc.; Eur. Soc. of Human Gen.; Internat. Soc. for Twin Studies; Internat. Neurofibromatosis Assn.; author of over 230 peer-reviewed articles, 35 chapters & 3 books; recreations: hiking, camping; Home: 4024 W. 31st Ave., Vancouver, B.C. V6S 1Y6; Office: 4480 Oak St., Room 2D19, Vancouver, B.C. V6H 3V4.

**HALL, Kevin Willis,** B.Sc., Pharm.D., C.I.M.; hospital pharmacy administrator and university professor; b. Halifax, N.S. 18 Oct. 1954; s. Willis Murdoch and Carol Evelyn (Wagner) H.; e. Dalhousie Univ. B.Sc. 1976; State Univ. of N.Y. at Buffalo Pharm.D. 1978; Univ. of Man. C.I.M. 1987; m. Gayle d. Harry and Geraldine Gray 30 Dec. 1976; DIRECTOR OF PHARMACEUTICAL SERVICES, WINNIPEG HEALTH SCIENCES CENTRE 1992– ; Clinical Pharmacist, Critical Care, Winnipeg Health Sci. Ctr. 1978–82; Coord., Critical Care Pharm. Services 1982–86; Asst. Dir., Pharmacy Operations 1986–91; Asst. Prof., Fac. of Pharm., Univ. of Manitoba 1992– ; Sec.-Treas., Beryllus Corp.; Pharm. Serv. Consultant, Kevin Hall & Assoc.; Course Devel. Coord., Assn. of Pharm. Mfrs. Assn. of Canada; Baxter Award 1993; Burroughs-Wellcome Award 1983; Roche Award 1985; Winthrop Award 1986, '88, '90; Pres., Candn. Pharm. Assn.; Chair, Bd. of Trustees, Candn. Soc. of Hosp. Pharm. Rsch. & Edn. Found.; Mem., Candn. Soc. of Hosp. Pharm., (Manitoba Br. Pres. 1980–81; Nat. Pres. 1986–87); Am. Soc. of Hosp. Pharm.; Man. Pharm. Assn.; Man. Soc. of Pharm.; Dalhousie Alumni Assn.; author/co-author of 31 research or review articles in scientific journals, 18 abstracts, letters, editorials or book reviews and 5 full-length course texts; recreations: canoeing, fishing, computers; clubs: Amnesty Internat., Greenpeace; Home: 1555 - 400 Webb Place, Winnipeg, Man. R3B 3J3; Office: 820 Sherbrook St., Winnipeg, Man. R3A 1R9.

**HALL, Laurance David,** B.Sc., Ph.D., M.A. (Cantab.), C.Chem., F.R.S.C., F.R.S.(Can.), F.C.I.C.; educator; b. London, U.K. 18 March 1938; s. Daniel William and Elsie Ivy (Beard) H.; e. Univ. of Bristol B.Sc. 1959, Ph.D. 1962; m. Winifred Margaret d. Arthur and Winifred Golding 1 Aug. 1962; children: Gwendolen, Juliet, Dominic, D'Arcy; apptd. first HERCHEL SMITH PROF. OF MEDICINAL CHEMISTRY, CAMBRIDGE UNIV., U.K. 1984– ; Prof. of Chem., Univ. of B.C. 1973–91, Instr. in Chem. 1963, Asst. Prof. 1964, Assoc. Prof. 1969; Royal Soc. and Nuffield Foundation Commonwealth Bursary 1967; Alfred P. Sloan Foundation Rsch. Fellow 1971–73; Jacob Biely Faculty Rsch. Prize U.B.C. 1974; Carbohydrate Chem. Award, The Chemical Soc. (UK) 1974; Merck, Sharp and Dohme Award, Chem. Inst. Can. 1975; Corday-Morgan Medal and Prize, The Chemical Soc. (UK) 1976; Killam Sr. Rsch. Fellow U.B.C. 1979; Barringer Award, Spectroscopy Soc. Can. 1982; Killam Rsch. Fellow Can. Council 1982–84; Cecil Green Scholar Univ. of Texas Galveston 1983; Van Cleve Lectr. Univ. of Regina 1983; summer Prof. Northwestern Univ. 1983; Brotherton Visiting Prof. Univ. of Leeds 1985; Roy. Soc. of Med. Lederle Visiting Prof., USA 1984; Cavendish Laboratory, Cambridge, 1986 Scott Lectures; Philosophical Soc. Cambridge, Larmor Lecture 1986; Interdisciplinary Award, Royal Soc. of Chem. 1988; Marconi Lecture, Royal Inst. 1989; Eduard Faber Lecture for Medical Physics, Univ. of Chicago and Argonne National Laboratory 1990; 1990 Award for Chemical Analysis and Instrumentation, Royal Society of Chemistry; author or co-author over 350 rsch. publs.; mem., Royal Soc. Chem.; Am. Chem. Soc.; Spectroscopy Soc. Can.; Chem. Inst. of Can.; recreations: skiing, sailing, music, woodwork; Address: c/o Herchel Smith Laboratory for Medicinal Chemistry, Cambridge Univ. Clinical School, University Forvie Site, Robinson Way, Cambridge CB2 2PZ, U.K.

**HALL, Monty,** O.C., B.Sc.; television performer and producer; b. Winnipeg, Man.; s. late Maurice and late Rose (Rusen) Halparin; e. Univ. of Man., B.Sc. 1944 (Pres. Student Body 1944); m. Marilyn Doreen, d. Joseph Plottel, Vancouver, B.C. 28 Sept. 1947; children: Joanna, Richard, Sharon; producer and performer on TV and radio in Can. and U.S. for over 40 yrs.; singer-actor-sportscaster-M.C. on nationally broadcast programs in Can. 1940–55 and in U.S. from 1955; TV show, 'Let's Make a Deal' (Producer-M.C.), ran for 22 years; has received over 500 awards in U.S. and Canada for charitable and philanthropic contributions; read into United States Cong.-Record by Congressman Thos. Rees, Feb. 1971 'for outstanding humanitarianism'; also several awards for TV performances; rec'd Variety Club 'Heart' Award, Toronto, 1954; Variety Club 'Star of the Year,' Hollywood, Cal. 1971; Winner, International Humanitarian Award, Variety Clubs International 1983; Officer of the Order of Canada 1987; LL.D. (Hon.) Univ. of Manitoba 1987; LL.D. (Hon.) Hanneman Med. Sch. 1988; LL.D. (Hon.) Haifa Univ. 1989; Dir., UCLA Monty Hall Children's Centre; Monty Hall Pavilion at Hahnemann Hospital, Philadelphia; Spon., Monty Hall Celebrity Tennis for Diabetes; author 'Emcee Monty Hall'; mem., Am. TV & Radio Artists; Screen Actors Guild; Alumni Gold Medal, Univ. of Manitoba 1987; el. Internat. Pres. of Variety Clubs in London, Eng. 1975; el. Lifetime Internat. Chrmn., Variety Clubs Internat. 1981; honoured by 'Hollywood Walk of Fame' star in cement 1973; recreations: golf, tennis; Clubs: Variety International; Hillcrest Country; Office: Monty Hall Enterprises, 519 N. Arden Dr., Beverly Hills, CA USA.

**HALL, Peter M.,** B.Sc., C.M.A.; financial executive; b. Jamaica (Candn. born abroad) 1950; married; two children; VICE-PRES., FINANCE & ADMINS., HUSKY INJECTION MOLDING SYSTEMS LTD. 1981– (Dir.); Accountant, Sunbeam Applicance Serv. 1972–74; Husky Injection Molding Systems Ltd. 1974–76; Controller 1976–81; Mem., Candn. Soc. of the Plastics Industry; Soc. of Management Accountants; Financial Extves. Inst.; recreations: business, sailing, skiing; clubs: Port Credit Yacht; Office: 500 Queen St. S., Bolton, Ont. L7E 5S5.

**HALL, Philip Frederick,** M.D., B.Sc.Med., F.R.C.S.C.; perinatologist; b. Toronto, Ont. 28 Oct. 1948; s. Frederick Henry Robert and the late Wanda Ruth H.; e. McMaster Univ., B.Sc.Med. 1970, M.D. 1973; m. Judith Barbara d. Dr. David and Joan Leslie 20 Dec. 1975; children: Nicholas Leslie, Ashleigh Ruth; PROF. AND HEAD OBSTETRICS, GYNAECOLOGY AND REPRODUCTIVE SCIENCES, ST. BONIFACE GEN. HOSP., UNIV. OF MANITOBA 1989– ; Intern/Resident in Obstetrics & Gynaecol. McMaster Univ. Hosps. Hamilton 1973–78; Rsch. Fellow, Prenatal Diagnosis Univ. of Toronto, Toronto Gen. Hosp. 1978–80; Asst. and Assoc. Prof. of Obstetrics & Gynaecol., Univ. of Ottawa 1980–89; editor: 'Maternal Mortality in Ontario' 1985, 1986, 1987; Ont. Med. Assn.; Editor-in-Chief 'Contemporary Ob/Gyn Canada' 1992– ; Bd of Govs., St John's Ravenscourt 1992– ; Senator, U. of Manitoba 1993– ; recreations: musician (keyboard), antiquarian print/book collecting, canoeing, camping, cross-country skiing; Home: 86 McNulty Cres., Winnipeg, Man. R2M 5H4; Office: St. Boniface Gen. Hosp., 409 Taché Ave., Winnipeg, Man. R2H 2A6.

**HALL, Ronald Henry,** B.Eng.; M.A.Sc.; P.Eng.; retired; b. Regina, Sask. 7 Nov. 1920; s. Cedric L. and Hilda M. (Shepherd) H.; e. Univ. Sask.; B.Eng. 1941; Univ. Toronto, M.A.Sc. 1946; McGill Univ., Diploma Bus. Admin. 1960; m. Anne I., d. Neil and Sarah MacNeil, 26 June, 1954; children: Andrew; Margaret; self employed consultant 1981–89; Nat. Research Counc. 1943–44; Research Eng., Shawinigan Chemicals Ltd. 1941–43; 46–50; Project Eng., B.A. Shawinigan Ltd. 1950; Plant Mgr. 1954; Gen. Mgr. 1956; Petrochem. Proj. Mgr., Shawinigan Chemicals Ltd. 1961; Vice-Pres., Mfg. 1964; Mgr. Operations, Ref. Dept., Gulf Can. (acquired Shawinigan when parent co. nationalized) 1969; Mgr. Engineering, Ref. Dept., 1972; Advisor to Sr. Extve. (Environmental Affairs) 1975–81; Retired 1989; rec'd Gov. Gen.'s Gold Medal (Univ. Sask.) 1941; served in Paratroops, Canadian Army 1944–45; Vice-Pres. & Dir. Petrol. Assn. for Conserv. Candn. Environ. (PACE) 1980–81; mem., Candn. Soc. for Chem. Engineering: Assn. Prof. Eng. of Ont.; Clubs: Mississauga Golf & Country; Probus Club of Oakville; recreations: golf; tennis; skiing; Home: 320 Dalewood Dr., Oakville, Ont. L6J 4P5.

**HALL, Thomas Jack,** B.Sc.; petroleum executive; b. Minitonas, Man. 26 Sept. 1923; s. Walter Henderson and Mary Hunter (Marr) H.; e. Univ. of Alta. B.Sc. (Chem. Eng. 1950; m. E. Violet d. Victor and Esther Young 11 Sept. 1946; children: Dennis E., Dawn Browne, Bonnie C. Hall-Staples, Robbin Shandel; CHAIRMAN, C.E.O. AND DIR., OMEGA HYDROCARBONS LTD. 1990– ; Pres. & Dir. Omega Oil & Gas Ltd.; Omega Oil & Gas Inc.; Alberta Gas Products Ltd.; New North Oil & Gas Ltd.; Past Dir. Midland Bank Canada; served with RCAF 1941–45; estbd. consulting practice 1972–74; Pres. & Dir. (and major shareholder) Omega Hydrocarbons Ltd. 1974–90; mem. Assn. Profl. Engs., Geols. & Geophys. Alta.; Calgary Chamber Comm. recreations: golf, fishing; Clubs: Earl Grey Golf; Calgary Petroleum; Home: 6926 Livingstone Dr. S.W., Calgary, Alta. T3E 6J5; Office: #1300, 112 – 4 Ave. S.W., Calgary, Alta. T2P 0H3.

**HALL, Thomas R.,** B.A.Sc.; pulp and paper executive; b. St. Catharines, Ont. 24 July 1929; s. Robert Abbott and Hilda Annetta (Warner) H.; e. Univ. of Toronto B.A.Sc. (Chem. Eng.) 1952; m. Angela d. Hans and Helene Knauer 26 Nov. 1977; children: Susan, Karen, Brian, Bruce; PRES., STORA FOREST INDUSTRIES 1985– ; Q & O Paper 1952–60; Spaulding Fibre 1960–64; Kimberly-Clark 1964–67; several positions ending as General Mgr., Domtar 1967–80; Vice-Pres., Abitibi-Price 1980–85; Dir., Stora Forest Indus.; Canso Chem.; Nova Scotia Power Inc.; Nova Scotia Ctr. for Environmentally Sustainable Economic Develop. (CESED); Mem., CPPA (Bd. & Extve. Ctte.), TAPPI, PIMA (Past Chrmn., N.Y.-Candn. Div.); Former mem., Candn. Labour Force Devel. Bd.; recreations: boating, video photography, sketching, painting, public speaking; Home: P.O. Box 118, Port Hawkesbury, N.S. B0E 2V0; Office: P.O. Box 59, Port Hawkesbury, N.S. B0E 2V0.

**HALL, Vicki,** B.Sc., M.A.; information systems executive; b. Dayton, Ohio 1 Apr. 1947; d. Carey D. and C. Maxine H.; e. Ohio State Univ. B.Sc. 1969; York Univ. M.A. 1972; m. Michael E. s. Eitel and Florence Woeller 13 May 1988; children: Michael Zinszer, Kate Zinszer, Jill Zinszer; VICE PRES., INFORMATION SERVICES, CANDN. DEPOSITORY FOR SECURITIES 1992– ; D.P. Mgr., Hurst Equipment 1981–82; M.I.S. Dir. 1982–83; Lectr. in Computer Sci., Univ. of Wterloo 1983–87; Sr. Consultant, Woods Gordon Cons. Group 1988; Sr. Mgr., KMPG, Peat Marwick Cons. Group 1988–89; Dir., Customer Serv., Dun & Bradstreet Software 1989–92; author: 'Information Systems Analysis with an Introduction to Fourth-Generation Technologies' 1988; recreations: architectural history of Ont.; clubs: Kitchener Horticultural Soc., L.A.C.A.C.; Office: 85 Richmond St. W., Toronto, Ont. M5H 2C9.

**HALL, (Charles) Wayne,** M.A., D.C.L. (Bishop's Univ. 1978); educator; b. Lennoxville, Que. 1 March 1910; s. Charles Loring and Sadie Jane (McMurray) H.; e. Lennoxville High Sch.; Bishop's Coll., B.A. 1931 and M.A., 1932; Ont. Coll. of Educ. post-grad. work in Psychol., 1933; m. Grace Elizabeth, d. A.A. Hall, Coaticook, P.Q., 1936; children: Denis, Mary, Jane, Christopher; PROF. EMERITUS, McGILL UNIV. since 1975; Dean, Fac. of Educ. 1965–75; Dir., Inst. of Education, McGill Univ. since 1964; Teacher, Sherbrooke High Sch. 1932–34; Principal, Coaticook High Sch. 1934–36 and St. Francis Coll. High Sch., 1936–37; Inspector of Schs. for Dept. of Educ. (Que.) 1937–40; Supervisor of English in Prot. Schs. of Que. 1940–49; Assoc. Prof., Macdonald Coll. 1949–52; Pres., Prov. Assn. of Prot. Teachers 1946; Tech. Adv. to Nigerian Gov. in teacher training 1960–61; Secy., UNESCO Comn. on the Univ. of Lagos 1961; Dir., Nat. Council of Teachers of English (Am.); Fellow, Candn. Coll. of Teachers; Publication: 'Growth Through the Language Arts' 1955; Order of Scholastic Merit (3rd Degree) 1956; Anglican; recreations: gardening, camping; Home: 12 Belvidere St., Lennoxville, Que. J1M 1T9.

**HALLAM, Robert John,** B.Mus., M.B.A.; opera director; b. Edmonton, Alta. 24 Oct. 1952; s. Donald Robert and Mary (Dutton) H.; e. Univ. of Alberta, B.Mus. 1976, M.B.A. 1983; m. Sydney d. Philip and Geraldine Scott 6 Oct. 1984; one s.: Robert Ian Scott-Hallam; GENERAL DIRECTOR, VANCOUVER OPERA 1991– ; Administrative Mgr., Edmonton Opera 1983–85; General Manager 1985–89; General Director 1989–91; Treasurer & Dir., Opera America; Office: 1132 Hamilton St., Vancouver, B.C. V0B 2S2.

**HALLBAUER, Robert Edward,** B.A.Sc.; mining executive; b. Nakusp, B.C. 19 May 1930; s. Edward F. and Lillian E. (Kendrick) H.; e. Univ. of B.C., B.A.Sc. (Mining Engn.) 1954; m. Joan d. Roy and Sarah Hunter 6 Sept. 1952; children: Russell, Catherine, Thomas; PRES., C.E.O. & DIR., COMINCO LTD. 1986– ; Sr. Vice Pres. & Dir., Teck Corp. 1979– ; held various engn. and supervisory positions Placer's Candn. exploration operation Salmo, B.C. 1954–60; Mine Supt. Craigmont Mines Ltd. 1960, Mine Mgr. 1964; Vice Pres. Mining Teck Corp. 1968–79; Home: 6026 Glenwynd Pl., West Vancouver, B.C. V7W 2W5; Office: 500 - 200 Burrard St., Vancouver, B.C. V6C 3L7.

**HALLETT, Archibald Cameron Hollis,** O.B.E., B.A., Ph.D.; b. Paget Parish, Bermuda 5 Feb. 1927; s. late Hon. Rupert Carlyle Hollis, D.C.L., and Jessie Wales (Cameron) H.; e. Saltus Grammar Sch., Bermuda, 1931–44; Univ. of Toronto, B.A. 1948, King's Coll., Univ. of Cambridge, Ph.D. 1951; m. Clara Frances Edith, d. late Rev. Charles Langton Gilbert, Gravenhurst, Ont. 5 Sept. 1950; children: William Langton Hollis, Mary Frances Hollis, James Archibald Hollis; Consultant 1992– ; joined Univ. of Toronto as a Lectr., Dept. of Physics 1951; apptd. Asst. Prof. 1952; Assoc. Prof. 1958; Prof. 1963; Assoc. Dean, Faculty of Arts & Science 1966–70; Principal, Univ. Coll., Univ. of Toronto 1970–77; Pres., Bermuda College 1977–92; mem., Am. Physical Soc.; Candn. Assn. Physicists; Comm. 1, Institut. Internat. du Froid; Anglican; recreations: music, cabinet-making; Office: Bermuda College, P.O. Box 356, Devonshire DVBX, Bermuda.

**HALLETT, Hon. James Doane,** B.Comm., LL.B.; supreme court justice; b. Halifax, N.S. 5 July 1932; s. Edward Forbes and Helen Josephine (Scriven) H.; e. Halifax public schools; Saint Mary's Univ. B.Comm. 1952; Dalhousie Univ. LL.B. 1955; m. Marjorie d. Hayward Archibald 4 Aug. 1956; children: Cynthia Jane, Joseph Edward Forbes, Helen, Scriven, Mary Elizabeth; JUSTICE, APPEAL DIVISION, SUPREME COURT OF NOVA SCOTIA 28 Mar. 1990– ; practised law with Wickwire, MacInnes & Wilson; MacInnes, Wilson & Hallett 1956–77 (area of practice: property, commercial & corp.); appt. to Trial Div., Supreme Court of N.S. 1 March 1977; activities 1956–90: Mem., Bd. of Gov., Saint Mary's Univ. & Hon. Sec., N.S. Div., Candn. Cancer Soc.; Extve. Mem., Candn. Judges Conf. & Chrmn., Independence of the Judiciary Ctte.; Gov., Royal Candn. Golf Assn.; Pres., Ashburn Golf Club; Halifax Club; Council Mem., N.S. Barristers' Soc.; recreations: golf; clubs: Ashburn Golf Club; Home: 935 Young Ave., Halifax, N.S. B3H 2V9; Office: The Law Courts, P.O. Box 2314, Halifax, N.S. B3J 3C8.

**HALLIDAY, Ian,** M.A., Ph.D., F.R.S.C.; astronomer; b. Lloydminster, Sask. 10 Nov. 1928; s. Clarence Peter and Edith Victoria (Phillips) H.; e. elem. schs. Saskatoon, Montreal; secondary schs. Toronto, Sherbrooke, Ottawa; Univ. of Toronto B.A. 1949, M.A. 1950, Ph.D. 1954; Univ. of Cal. Berkeley 1950–51; m. Norma d. John and Isabelle Mobley 7 July 1951; children: John Douglas, Janet Elizabeth; GUEST WORKER, NAT. RESEARCH COUNCIL OF CAN. 1990– , Research Offr. 1970–90; research interests incl. positional astron., spectroscopy of meteors, studies of terrestrial meteorite craters (West Hawk Lake, Man.), determination of size of planet Pluto; est. network 12 camera stns. w. Can. to study astron. properties of bright meteors and aid in recovery of assoc. meteorites; studies of comets; recipient Royal Astron. Soc. Can. Gold Medal 1949, Service Award 1974; Medal of Merit Poland 1976; Queen's Silver Jubilee Medal 1977; minor planet 3944 named Halliday 1989; author or co-author over 80 scient. research papers; co-ed. 'Solid Particles in the Solar System' 1980; mem., Internat. Astron. Union (Pres. comn. 22 Meteors & Interplanetary Dust 1976–79); Royal Astron. Soc. Can. (Journ. ed. 1970–75, Asst. ed. 1964–69; Pres. 1980–82; Hon. Pres. 1989–93); Meteoritical Soc. (Councilor 1968–72); Am. Astron. Soc.; Planetary Soc.; Candn. Astron. Soc.; Steering Grp., Internat. Halley Watch 1981–90 (Chrmn. 1985–90); recreations: photography, canoeing; Home: 825 Killeen Ave., Ottawa, Ont. K2A 2X8; Office: Herzberg Inst. of Astrophysics, National Research Council, Ottawa, Ont. K1A 0R6.

**HALLIWELL, Dean Wright,** M.A., B.L.S.; librarian, b. Estevan, Sask. 26 July 1924; s. late John and Gladys May (Wright) H.; e. Univ. of Sask. B.A. 1943, M.A. 1948; Univ. of Toronto B.L.S. 1949; m. Marjory Allen d. late George Lawson Robertson, Wapella, Sask. 29 Oct. 1949; children: Kathryn Allen, John Robertson; Univ. Librarian, Univ. of Victoria 1960–88; Bookmobile Librarian, Cuyahoga Co. Pub. Lib. Cleveland, Ohio 1949–52, Coordinator of Reference Services 1952–55; Canadiana Librarian, Univ. of Sask. 1955–57, Asst. Librarian 1957–60; Dir., Un. Way Greater Victoria 1978–87 (Pres. 1985–1986); served with RCAF 1943–45, Pilot Offr. (Navig.), Reserve 1957–60, 1961–64, rank Flight Lt.; rec'd Queen's Silver Jubilee Medal 1977; mem. Candn. Lib. Assn. (Pres. 1971–72); Candn. Assn. Coll. & Univ. Libs. (Pres. 1967–68); B.C. Lib. Assn. (Pres. 1965–66); Am. Lib. Assn. (Dir. 1980–83; 1985–88); United Church; recreations: golf, travel; Club: Uplands Golf (Dir. 1978–81); Home: 1828 St. Ann St., Victoria, B.C. V8R 5W1.

**HALLIWELL, Janet E.,** B.Sc., M.Sc.; senior federal government executive; b. Quebec, Que. 2 Dec. 1945; d. Walter MacFarlane and Frances Kathleen (Bailey) Smith; e. Queen's Univ., B.Sc. (Hons. 1967); Univ. of B.C., M.Sc. 1970; m. Robin E. s. William and Ivy H. 15 June 1968; Chrmn., Science Counc. of Can. 1990; Acad. Rsch. Assoc., Microbiol., Univ. of B.C. 1969–74; Sess. Lectr., Chem., Queen's Univ. 1974–75; Tech. Ed., 'Canadian Journal of Chemistry,' NRC 1975–77; Officer, Grants & Scholarships (devel. & implemented prog. of Strategic Grants) 1977–78; Mgr., Strategic Grants Prog., NSERC 1978–80; Mngt. & Coord., Operating Grants Progs. 1980–83; various posts, NSERC Rsch. Base Progs. 1984–88; Dir. Gen., Research Grants, NSERC 1988–90; Mem., Bd. of Dir., Fields Institute; scholarships: Ont. 1963; Queen's Univ. 1966; NRC 1967–69; Medal in Chem., Queen's Univ. 1967; CIC Golden Key of Merit 1967; U.B.C. Teaching Asst. Award 1968; D.Sc. (Honoris causa) Memorial 1991; D.Sc. (Honoris causa) York Univ. 1991; D.laws (Honoris causa) Brock Univ. 1991; Walter Hitschfeld Prize, Research Administration 1991; mem., Candn. Chem. Soc.; Candn. Assn. of Physicists; Candn. Assn. of Univ. Rsch. Admin.; Internat. Sci. Policy Found.; recreations: gourmet cooking, bird watching.

**HALLIWELL, John Clayton;** retired association executive; b. Shellbrook, Sask. 27 June 1932; s. John Henry and Edith Wilma (Clark) H.; e. Shellbrook H.S.; m. Eunice d. Harvey and Jennie Wood 30 June 1952; children: Boyd Clark, Dawn Wynn; Past Pres., Canadian Construction Assn. 1990–93 Retired; Saskatoon Police Force 1954–57; Hardware Merchant 1957–63; Brandon, Manitoba Police 1963–66; Extve. Dir., Manitoba Govt. Employees Assn. 1966–76; Ont. Prov. Police Assn. 1978–79; Candn. Construction Assn. 1979– ; Chrmn., Infrastructure Ctte., Construction Indus. Counc.; Pres., Candn. Internat. Employers Counc.; Chief Employer Delegate, Internat. Labor Orgn., Geneva, Switz. 1985–86; Home: P.O. Box 195, Sandy Hook, Man. R0C 2W0.

**HALLWARD, Hugh Graham,** B.A.; construction executive; b. Montreal, Que. 14 Aug. 1926; s. Bernard M. and Alice H. (Graham) H.; e. Selwyn House Sch.; Bishop's Coll. Sch.; McGill Univ. B.A. 1951; m. Martha d. Philip S. Fisher 21 Jan. 1955; children: Graham, Margaret, Faith, John, Annabel; PRESIDENT, ARGO CONSTRUCTION INC.; Chrmn., Atlas Copco Canada Inc.; Dir., Southam Inc.; Avon Canada Inc.; Beauward Shopping Centres Ltd.; Identicard Ltd.; Helix Investments Ltd.; Schokbeton Quebec Inc.; Co-Founder, Argo Construction Ltd. 1952, Schokbeton Quebec Inc. 1961, Beauward Shopping Centres Ltd. 1963; Past Chrmn. Bd. Govs. McGill Univ. (Chrmn. 1982–90); past Chrmn. Bd. Dirs. Bishop's Coll. Sch.; Dir., Candn. Inst. for Advanced Resch.; Past Pres. Candn. Squash Racquets Assn.; Past Pres., Royal Candn. Golf Assn.; Dir., Montreal Children's Hosp.; mem. Candn. Constr. Assn. (Past Dir.); recreations: golf, cross-country skiing; Clubs: Mount Royal; University; Montreal Badminton & Squash; Royal Montreal Golf; Mount Bruno Country; Toronto Golf; Royal & Ancient Golf (Scot.); Hon. Co. Edinburgh Golfers; Seminole Golf (Fla.); Lost Tree (Fla.); Home: 637 Carleton Ave., Westmount, Que. H3Y 2Y3; Office: 4300 Jean Talon St. W., Ste. 300, Montreal, Que. H4P 1V5.

**HALLWARD, John Marsham,** B.A., M.A.; business executive; b. Montreal, Que. 2 Mar. 1929; s. Bernard Marsham and Alice Hamilton (Graham) H.; e. Selwyn House Sch. 1943; Trinity Coll. Sch. 1946; McGill Univ. B.A. 1950; Oxford Univ. M.A. 1953; m. Clare d. Everard and Rose Meynell 28 Dec. 1956; children: Jennifer, Anne, Mary, Peter, Kate, Christopher; PRESIDENT, MARSHAMITE LIMITED; Publisher, PACE Magazine 1965–69; Editor, Mid-Canada Development Report 1970; Extve. Dir., Exporama Ltd. 1970–71; Chrmn., J.J.C.T. Fine Arts Ltd. 1973–91; Vice-Pres., Bell Molybdenum Mines Limited; Candn. Endowment Mngt. Limited; Dir., Identicard Limited; Elan Energy; Okanagan Radio Limited; Waddington and Gorce Inc.; Dep. Chair, Bd. of Gov., McGill Univ.; Vice-Pres., Montreal Neurol. Hosp.; Red Feather Found.; Chrmn., Canada-Poland Chamber of Commerce 1991–93; Pres., Candn. Club of Montreal 1980–81; Bd. Chrmn., The Study School 1980–81; Pres., McGill Grad. Soc. 1980–81; Bd. Chrmn., Centraide Montreal 1977–79; Rachel Ship Found.; Rector's Warden, Christ Ch. Cathedral (Anglican) 1975–76; Founding Mem., Positive Action Ctte. 1976–83; Chrmn. Ad Hoc Quebec-Canada Ctte.; recreations: nordic skiing, hiking; clubs: McGill Faculty; Hillside Tennis; Laurentian Lodge Ski; Home: 1745 Cedar Ave., P4, Montreal, Que. H3G 1A7; Office: 4300 Jean Talon St. W., Ste. 300, Montreal, Que. H4P 1V5.

**HALPENNY, Francess Georgina,** C.C., M.A., LL.D., D.Litt., D.ès l., F.R.S.C.; editor, professor; b. Ottawa, Ont. 27 May 1919; d. James Leroy and Viola Gertrude (Westman) H.; e. Oakwood Coll. Inst., Toronto, 1936; Univ. of Toronto, B.A. 1940, M.A. 1941; LL.D.: Univ. of Guelph 1968, Dalhousie Univ. 1978; D.Litt: Memorial Univ. 1982, York Univ. 1982, Univ. of N.B. (Saint John) 1983, Queen's Univ. 1984, McMaster Univ. 1987, Carleton Univ. 1991, Univ. of Windsor 1992; D.ès l.: Laval Univ. 1986; Associate, Massey College, Univ. of Toronto 1989– ; Dean, Faculty of Library Science, Univ. of Toronto 1972–78, Prof. of Library Sci. 1972–84, Prof. Emeritus 1984– ; Gen. Ed., 'Dictionary of Canadian Biography' 1969–88; Gen. Ed. Emeritus 1988– ; joined Ed. Dept., Univ. of Toronto Press 1941, Ed. 1957–65, Mang. Ed. 1965–69; Assoc. Dir. (Academic), Univ. of Toronto Press 1979–84; served with Womens Div., RCAF, as Meteorol. Observer in Nfld. and P.E.I., 1942–45; author: 'Canadian Collections in Public Libraries' 1985; 'Catalogue to Reader' 1991; and articles on biography, publishing and editing in various collections and journals; Nat. Lib. Adv. Bd., 1976–82 (Chrmn. 1979–82); mem. Comte. on Bibliog. Services for Can. 1976–85, Chrmn. 1977–79; mem., Comte. on Library Info., Book and Periodical Devel. Council 1974–89 (Chrmn. 1979–83, 1985–86); mem. Counc. 1983–86 and Chrmn. 1984–85; Univ. of Toronto Research Bd. (Chrmn., Humanities and Social Sciences Res. Comte 1979–84); Fellow, Royal Soc. of Canada, 1977 (Chrmn., Awards Comte. 1980–82; Vice-Pres. Academy II 1982–84, Pres. 1984–86; mem. Comte. for Advancement of Women in Scholarship 1988–93); Officer, Order of Canada, 1979, Companion 1984; Molson Prize 1983; Faculty Award, Univ. of Toronto 1985; U.B.C. Medal for Candn. Biography 1986; Adv. Bd., Centre for Editing Early Canadian Texts; Ed. Bd., 'Journal of Canadian Studies'; Adv. Bd., Candn. Centre for Studies in Publishing, Simon Fraser Univ.; recreation: theatre and travel; Clubs: Univ. Alumnae Dramatic Club (Past Pres.); Heliconian (Past Pres.); Home: 32 Glenbrae Ave., Toronto, Ont. M4G 3R5; Office: Faculty of Library and Information Science, University of Toronto, Toronto, Ont. M5S 1A1.

**HALPERIN, Hon. Irving J.,** B.A., B.C.L.; judge; b. Montréal, Qué. 9 July 1927; s. Elie and Hannah (Schlaer) H.; e. Dalhousie Univ. B.A. 1949; McGill Univ. B.C.L. 1952; m. Grace d. Sidney and Lillian Feil 6 Nov. 1955; children: Vivian, Elliot; JUDGE, SUPERIOR COURT OF QUEBEC 1983– ; called to Bar of Qué. 1953; cr. Q.C. 1972; Partner: Halperin & Morris 1955–72; Halperin, Ashenmil, Kotler & Shuster 1972–76; Phillips, Halperin 1976–83; Mun. Judge, Town of Hampstead, Qué. 1973–83; Vice Pres. Counc. Jewish Fedns. (USA) 1985; Pres.: Allied Jewish Community Services Montréal 1979–81; Neighbourhood House 1964; Trustee, YM-YWHA Montréal 1980– ; mem. Bd. Prof. Corp. Chems. Prov. Qué. 1973; mem. La Conference des juges municipaux de la prov. de Qué. 1973–83; Lord Reading Law Soc.; recreations: skiing, tennis; Club: Montefiore; Home: 58 Holtham Rd., Hampstead, Qué. H3X 3N4; Office: Palais de Justice, 1 rue Notre-Dame est, Montréal, Qué. H2Y 1B6.

**HALPERIN, Maurice,** A.M., D. de l'Un., LL.D.; educator; b. Boston, Mass. 3 March 1906; s. Philip and Ethel (Summer) H.; e. Harvard Univ., A.B. 1927; Univ. of Okla., A.M. 1929; Sorbonne, D. de l'Un. 1931; LL.D. (hon. causa) Simon Fraser Univ. 1992; m. Edith (dec. 1988), d. late Herman Frisch, 5 Sept. 1926; children: David, Judith (Mrs. Hillel Gamoran); PROF. OF POL. SCIENCE, SIMON FRASER UNIV. since 1968; Prof. Emeritus since 1979; univ. teaching in various insts. in N.Am., Europe and Latin Am. since 1931; Visiting Prof., Govt. Dept., Harvard Univ., summer 1988; served with U.S. Office of Strategic Services 1942–45; rec'd. Order of the S. Cross, Brazil 1952; author of various publications since 1931, including 'The Rise and Decline of Fidel Castro' 1972; 'The Taming of Fidel Castro' 1981; 'Return to Havana: The Decline of Cuban Society Under Castro' 1994; also numerous articles in acad. journs.; Home: 385 – 1142 Dufferin St., Coquitlam, B.C. V3B 6V4; Office: Burnaby, B.C. V5A 1S6.

**HALPERIN, Stephen,** M.Sc., Ph.D., F.R.S.C.; educator; b. Kingston, Ont. 1 Feb. 1942; s. Israel and Mary Esther (Sawdey) H.; e. Univ. of Toronto B.Sc. 1965, M.Sc. 1966; Cornell Univ. Ph.D. 1970; m. Janet d. Thor and Pamela Thorgrimsson 14 Apl. 1979; children: Nicole Esther, Adam Hugh; CHAIR, DEPT. OF MATH, UNIV. OF TORONTO 1991–95, PROF. OF MATH. 1979– ; Asst. Prof. present Univ. 1970, Assoc. Prof. 1974; Visiting Prof. Univ. de Lille, France 1976–77, 1981, 1982, 1989; Univ. de Nice 1982, 1986; Univ. Catholique de Louvain 1979, 1988, 1990; Visiting Sci. Univ. of Stockholm 1985; Univ. of Bonn. 1981; co-author 'Connections, Curvature and Cohomology' Vol. I 1972, Vol. II 1974, Vol. III 1976; mem. Candn. Math. Soc.; Am. Math. Soc.; Home: 75 Wembley Rd., Toronto, Ont. M6C 2G3; Office: Scarborough, Ont. M1C 1A4.

**HALPIN, Charles Aime,** B.A., B.Th., J.C.L.; archbishop; b. St. Eustache, Man. 30 Aug. 1930; s. John S. and Marie Anne (Gervais) H.; e. Univ. of Man., B.A. (Hons.) 1950; Univ. of Montreal, B.Th. 1956; Gregorian Univ., Licentiate Canon Law 1960; ARCHBISHOP OF REGINA 1973– ; ordained priest, Roman Cath. Ch. 1956; named Monsignor 1969; consecrated bishop 1973; Asst., St. Mary's Cathedral 1956; Vice-Chancellor, Archdiocese of Winnipeg 1960; Officialis Archdiocesan Matrimonial Tribunal 1962, Vice-Offic. Reg. Matrim. Trib. 1971; Mem., Candn. Conf. of Cath. Bishops (Dir. until 1993); Mem., Comn. for Canon Law and Inter-Rite; Home: 2522 Retallack St., Regina, Sask. S4T 2L3; Office: 445 Broad St. N., Regina, Sask. S4R 2X8.

**HALPIN, Gerard Brian,** B.Sc.; publisher; b. Ottawa, 8 Aug. 1928; s. David Joseph and Winifred Mary (Driscoll) H.; e. Univ. of Ottawa, B.Sc. 1949; m. Jeannette, d. Valmore and Emma Jane Gougeon, 5 Oct. 1953; children: David, Nancy, Matthew, Susan, Kathryn, Andrew; Pres., Richard de Boo Publishers 1984–93, retired; Extve. Vice Pres., Thomson Professional Publishing Canada 1990– ; Sales, Wm. S. Merrell Co. (pharmaceuticals) 1952–57; Sales, Prentice Hall Canada Inc. (publishers) 1957–61, Editor 1961–66, Ed.-in-Chief 1966–81, Dir. 1968–81; Vice-Pres. present firm 1982–84; recreations: violinist with York Symphony Orchestra, tennis, swimming, riding; Home: 3 Rayneswood Cres., Thornhill, Ont. L3T 2N5.

**HALSALL, Robert,** B.Sc.; consulting engineer; b. Preston, England 2 Jan. 1928; s. Harry and Lucy (Richardson) H.; e. Manchester Grammar Sch.; Daniel Stewart's Coll.; Glasgow Univ. B.Sc. (Hons.) 1947; m. Anne d. Robert and Helen Tennent 23 June 1951; children: Robert John Tennent, Alan Peter, Dexter George; PRES., HALSALL ASSOC. LIMITED 1960– ; 2nd Lt., Royal Engineers (U.K. & Jordan) 1947–49; Engr., Steelwork Contractors Glasgow 1949–51; Calcutta 1952–53; Structural Consultants Toronto 1954–56; estab. priv. practice 1956; Bd. Mem., Ortech Internat.; Fellow, Candn. Soc. for Civil Engr.; Engr. Inst. of Can.; Inst. of Civil Engrs.; Inst. of Structural Engrs.; clubs: Royal Candn. Yacht; Office: 188 Eglinton Ave. E., 6th Floor, Toronto, Ont. M4P 2X7.

**HALSTEAD, John G.H.,** B.A., B.Sc.; consultant and educator; b. Vancouver, B.C. 27 Jan. 1922; s. Frank Henry and Minnie Williams (Horler) H.; e. Prince of Wales High Sch. Vancouver 1939, John Oliver High Sch. 1940; Univ. of B.C. B.A. 1943; London Sch. of Econ. B.Sc. 1950; m. Jean McAllister, d. late Paul Gemmill 20 June 1953; children: Ian (dec.), Christopher; ADJUNCT RESEARCH PROF., PATERSON SCH. OF INTERNAT. AFFAIRS, CARLETON UNIV., Ottawa 1990– ; Lectr., Sch. of Public Admin., Carleton Univ. 1993– ; Lectr., Candn. Foreign Service Inst. 1992–93; served with RCNVR 1943–46, rank Lt. (S.B.); Dept. of External Affairs 1946–82: Asst. Under Secy. 1971–74; Depy. Under Secy. of State for External Affairs, Ottawa 1974–75; Ambassador to Fed. Republic of Germany 1975–80; Amb. and Permanent Rep. of Can. to NATO 1980–82; Visiting Prof., Inst. for Study of Diplomacy, Georgetown Univ., Washington, D.C. 1983; Distinguished Research Prof., Sch. of Foreign Service, Georgetown Univ., Washington, D.C. 1984–89; Internat. Counselor, Inst. for Study of Diplomacy 1987– ; Paul Martin Prof. of Internat. Affairs and Law, Univ. of Windsor 1987–88; awarded Peace Prize by the Assoc. of German Veterans 1989; Hon. Ph.D., Univ. of Augsburg 1994; author 'Labour of Love: a Review of Canadian Studies Programs in the United States'; 'A New Germany in a New Europe'; co-author 'The Troubled Partnership in Transition'; mem. Candn. Inst. of Strategic Studies; Internat. Inst. for Strategic Studies; UN Assoc. of Can.; Assoc. of Candn. Studies in Germany; Assoc. of Candn. Studies in the U.S.; Assoc. of Candn. Studies (Can.); Past Chrmn., Candn. Counc. for European Affairs; Ed. Bd., 'NATO's Sixteen Nations'; Dir.: Candn. Inst. for Internat. Peace & Security 1988–90; Dir., Candn. Inst. Internat. Affairs 1990– ; Atlantic Council of Canada; Zeta Psi; United Church; recreations: tennis, swimming, sailing; Home: 187 Billings Ave., Ottawa, Ont. K1H 5K8.

**HALTON, David Campbell,** B.A.; broadcast journalist; b. Beaconsfield, U.K. 28 May 1940; s. Mathew Henry and Jean Joslin (Campbell) H.; e. King's Sch. Canterbury, U.K. 1957; Sorbonne, Paris, Dipl. D'Etudes De Civilisation Française 1958; Trinity Coll. Univ. of Toronto B.A. 1962; Inst. D'Etudes Politiques, Paris Cert. d'Etudes Politiques 1963; m. Zoia Titova 12 Sept. 1968; two s. Julian Alexander, Daniel Andrew; SR. WASHINGTON CORR., CBC 1991– ; contrib. ed. Time Magazine (Candn. Ed.) 1964–65; Paris Corr. CBC 1965–67, 1969–71; Moscow Corr. 1967–68; Que. Nat. Reporter CBC TV News 1971–73; London Corr. 1974–78; Chief Pol. Corr. Ottawa, CBC TV 1978–91; rec'd Anik Award Host-Narration documentary 'The October Crisis' 1975; Anglican; recreations: tennis, sailing; Club: National Press; Home: 5070 Macomb St., N.W., Washington, D.C. 20016; Office: National Press Bldg., Ste. 500, 529 – 14th St. N.W., Washington, D.C. 20045.

**HALVORSON, Hon. Kenneth R.,** B.A., LL.B.; judge; b. Sask. 28 Nov. 1937; s. late Melvin Halvorson; e. Flin Flon (Man.) Coll. Inst. 1956; Univ. of Sask. B.A., LL.B. 1962; m. Carol Ann d. late Joseph Harrison 6 Oct. 1962; children: Bonnie, Becky, Peter; JUDGE, COURT OF QUEEN'S BENCH SASK.; called to Bar of Sask. 1963; Dir., Can. W. Agribition Assn.; Vice Pres., Royal Agricultural Soc. of the Commonwealth; recreation: athletics; Home: 77 Calder Cres., Regina, Sask. S4S 4A5; Office: 2425 Victoria Ave., Regina, Sask. S4P 0S8.

**HALVORSON, Marilyn E.,** B.Ed.; writer; b. Olds, Alta. 17 Jan. 1948; d. Trygve and Irene G. (McConnell) H.; e. Bergen Elem. Sch. 1958; Sundre High Sch. 1964; Univ. of Calgary, B.Ed. 1981; author 'Cowboys Don't Cry' 1984 (winner Alta. Culture/Clarke Irwin Writing for Youth Competition 1982; filmed 1987); 'Let It Go' 1985; 'Nobody Said It Would Be Easy' 1987 (winner Children's Lit. Award, Writers' Guild of Alta. 1987); 'Dare' 1988; 'Bull Rider' 1989; 'Brothers and Strangers' 1991; 'To Everything A Season' 1991; 'Stranger on the Run' 1992; 'But Cows Can't Fly and Other Stories' 1993; recipient Short Poem Award Alta. Poetry Yearbook 1977; author various short stories, articles children's mags. and lit. jours.; sch. teacher various levels Co. of Mountain View for 18 yrs.; recreations: horseback riding, photography, gardening; Home: P.O. Box 364, Sundre, Alta. T0M 1X0.

**HAM, James Milton,** O.C., O.Ont., B.A.Sc., S.M., ScD.; b. Coboconk, Ont. 21 Sept. 1920; s. James Arthur and Harriet Boomer (Gandier) H.; e. Runnymede Coll. Inst., Toronto, Ont., 1936–39; Univ. of Toronto, B.A.Sc. 1943; Mass. Inst. of Tech., S.M. 1947, ScD. 1952; D.èsSc.A., Montreal 1973; D.Sc., Queen's 1974; New Brunswick 1979; McGill 1979; McMaster 1980; N.S. Tech Univ. 1980; Guelph 1992; Dr.Eng., Memorial Univ. 1981; Univ. of Toronto 1991; LL.D. Man. 1980; Hanyang (Korea) 1981; Concordia 1983; D.S.L. Wycliffe College 1983; m. Mary Caroline, d. Albert William Augustine, Kitchener, Ont., 4 June 1955; children: Peter Stace, Mary Martha, Jane Elizabeth (d.); PRESIDENT EMERITUS, UNIV. OF TORONTO 1988; Adv. to Pres., Candn. Inst. for Advanced Rsch. 1988–90; Dean, Faculty of Applied Sc. & Engn., Univ. of Toronto 1966–73; Chrmn. Research Bd., 1974–76; Chrmn., Royal Comn. on Health and Safety of Workers in Mines, Ont., 1974–76; Dean, Grad. Studies, Univ. of Toronto 1976–78; Pres., Univ. of Toronto 1978–83; Brookings Fellow in Sci. & Public Policy, Washington D.C. 1983–84; Prof. of Sci., Technology & Public Policy, Univ. of Toronto 1983–88; Chrmn., Industrial Disease Standards Panel, Ont. 1986–88; mem. Nat. Research Council 1969–75; Bd. of Govs., Ont. Research Foundation 1971–86; Dir. Shell Canada; Lectr. & Housemaster, Ajax Div., Univ. of Toronto, 1945–46; Research Assoc., Mass. Inst. of Tech., 1949–51; Asst. Prof. of Elect. Engn. 1951–52; Assoc. Prof. of Elect. Engn., Univ. of Toronto 1952–59; Prof. since 1959; Chrmn., Assoc. Comte. on Automatic Control, Nat. Research Council, 1959–65; Visiting Scientist, Cambridge Univ., and U.S.S.R., 1960–61; Head, Dept. of Elect. Engn., Univ. of Toronto, 1964–66; served with R.C.N.V.R. as Elect. Lt., 1944–45; awarded Brit. Assn. for Advanc. of Science Medal, 1943; Research Fellowship in Electronics, Mass. Inst. Tech. 1950; Fellow of New Coll., Univ. of Toronto, 1963; Chrmn. of Comte. on Engn. Educ. of World Fed. of Engn. Organs. 1970–74; author of 'Scientific Basis of Electrical Engineering' (with G. R. Slemon), 1961 and some 20 papers for scient. journs.; patented (U.S.) 'Apparatus for Electronic Integration,' 1955; Fellow, Inst. Elect. & Electronic Engrs.; mem., Assn. Prof. Engineers Ontario; F.E.I.C.; awarded Centennial Medal; Engn. Medal, Assn. Prof. Engrs. Ont. 1974; Engr. Alumni Medal, Univ. of Toronto, 1974; McNaughton Medal, I.E.E.E. 1977; Silver Jubilee Medal, 1977; Officer of the Order of Canada, 1980; Sir John Kennedy Medal, E.I.C. 1983; Gold Medal, Assn. Prof. Engrs. Ont. 1984; Order of Ontario 1989; Confederation Medal 1992; Founding Fellow, Candn. Acad. of Engr. 1987 (Vice Pres. 1988–89; Pres. 1990–91); Sigma Xi; Anglican; recreations: photography, fractals; Home: 135 Glencairn Ave., Toronto, Ont. M4R 1N1.

**HAM, Leslie Gilmer,** B.A., B.Comm., M.B.A., C.A.; beverage company executive; b. Winnipeg, Man. 3 March 1930; s. Arthur Leslie and Frances Irene (Gilmer) H.; e. McGill Univ. B.A. 1951, B.Comm. 1953; Univ. of W. Ont. M.B.A. 1956; m. Anne Corris d. Charles Adrian Dinsmore, Toronto, Ont. 12 June 1954; children: Charles Keith, Susan Lesley, Cynthia Anne; PRESIDENT, EAST EUROPE/ASIA, PEPSI-COLA INTERNATIONAL 1989– ; Auditor, Peat Marwick Mitchell, Montreal 1953–55; Brand Mgr. Proctor & Gamble Co. of Canada, Toronto 1956–58; Extve. Vice Pres. Seven Up Montreal Ltd. 1958–70; Vice Pres. Operations Pepsi-Cola Canada Ltd., Toronto 1970–74; Pres., Soc. Internationale de Produits Alimentaires, Paris 1974–75; Extve. Vice Pres. Sales, Pepsi-Cola Bottling Group, Purchase, N.Y. 1975–78; Pres., C.E.O., and Dir., Pepsi-Cola Can. Ltd. 1978–81; Sr. Vice Pres., Can./Europe, Pepsico Internat. 1981–86; Pres., Seven Up International 1986–89; Pres. Theta Delta Chi 1951; Anglican; Clubs: Mississauga Golf; Royal Montreal Golf; Red Birds Ski (Montreal); Darien (Conn.) Country; Clearwater Golf; Aberdeen Marina (Hong Kong); Home: 784 Smith Ridge Rd., New Canaan, CT 06840 USA; Office: 1255 Bay St., Toronto, Ont. M5R 2A9.

**HAMACHER, Vincent Carl,** Ph.D., P.Eng.; university professor; b. London, Ont. 28 Sept. 1939; s. Vincent and Evelett Mae (Levie) H.; e. Univ. of Waterloo B.A.Sc. 1963; Queen's Univ. M.Sc. 1965; Syracuse Univ. Ph.D. 1968; m. Elizabeth d. Jack and Helen Orgill 19 June 1965; children: Jeffrey David, Janis Aileen; DEAN, FACULTY OF APPLIED SCIENCE, QUEEN'S UNIV. 1991– ; Asst. Prof. 1968; Assoc. Prof. 1972; Assoc. Chrmn. 1976–78; Div. of Engr. Sci. 1981–84; Prof., Dept. of Elect. Engr., Univ. of Toronto 1982–90; Dir., Computer Systems Rsch. Inst. 1984–88; Chrmn., Div. of Engr. Sci. 1988–90; Vis. Sci., IBM Rsch. Lab., San Jose, CA 1978–79; Rsch. Vis., LCS Lab., INPG Grenoble, France 1986; Mem., Assn. of Profl. Engrs. of Ont.; Assn. for Computing Machinery; Sigma XI; Sr. Mem., Inst. of Electrical & Electronics Engrs.; co-author: 'Computer Organization' 1978, 2nd ed. 1984, 3rd ed. 1990; author/co-author of over 50 sci. papers in jours. & conf. proceedings and 3 book chapters; Home: 2 Beverley St., Kingston, Ont. K7L 3Y4; Office: Fac. of Applied Sci., Ellis Hall, Queen's Univ., Kingston, Ont. K7L 3N6.

**HAMBLETON, George Robert,** B.A.Sc., M.B.A.; engineer; horticulturalist; b. Vineland, Ont. 7 Dec. 1921; s. George Samuel and Evelyn Eola (Butler) H.; e. Univ. of Toronto B.A.Sc. 1950; McMaster Univ. M.B.A. 1966; m. M. Kathleen, d. James and Alice Collins, 15 June 1946; children: Elizabeth Ann; Margaret Catherine; Lillian May; William Harold; Sr. Equipment Specialist, Candn. Comstock Ltd. 1950; Sr. Design Engr. (Transformers), Ferranti-Packard Ltd. 1952–72; Farmer (Fruit and Nuts), Niagara-on-the-Lake 1973; Mgr., Technical Services, Penzer Products 1976; Design Engineer, Ferranti Packard Transformers Ltd. 1978–87; served overseas with R.C.A.F. (Radar Mechanic 1941–43; Pilot 1943–44); mem. Central Assembly, Niagara Falls (Dir. 1971–90; Usher 1975– ; Treas., Christian Educ. Dept. 1974–93); Jordan Vineland Branch, Candn. Bible Soc. (Treas. 1954–62; Pres. 1963–70); Assn. of Profl. Engrs. of Ont.; Northern Nut Growers Assn.; one of 3 organizing members of Soc. of Ont. Nut Growers (SONG); involved in breeding and research on nuts and fruits; Home: R.R. #2, 1540 Conc. 6 Rd., Niagara-on-the-Lake, Ont. L0S 1J0.

**HAMBLEY, David Carr;** human resources executive; b. North Bay, Ont. 24 April 1943; s. Robert B. and Isabel H. (Carr) H.; e. Ryerson; m. Susan d. Arthur Smith and Ellen Keay Aug. 1981; one s.: Robert; VICE-PRES., HUMAN RESOURCES, NORANDA MINERALS INC. 1991– ; Human Resources Professional, Falconbridge Limited, Sudbury 1969–80; Director, Human Resources, Toronto 1980–89; Vice-Pres., Human Resources 1989–91; Office: Suite 2700, 1 Adelaide St. E., Toronto, Ont. M5C 2Z6.

**HAMBLEY, J. Mervyn,** B.Sc., D.Eng., D.Sc.; retired consultant; b. Copper Cliff, Ont. 26 May 1905; s. William John and Ella (Harris) H.; e. Public Sch., Copper Cliff, Ont.; High Sch., Sudbury, Ont.; Queen's Univ., B.Sc. (Elect. Engn.) 1929, D.Sc. 1967; Univ. of W. Ont. (Mang. Training) 1952; Waterloo Univ., D.Eng. 1965; m. Leonia Jule, d. Edward Joyner, Kingston, Ont., 26 Dec. 1933; one s.: Dr. E. John; joined Ont. Hydro in 1930 as Asst. Dist. Operating Engr., Georgian Bay Divn. and N. Ont. properties; Dir. of Operations, Toronto, Ont., 1947–53; Deputy Asst. Gen. Mgr. (Adm.), 1953–55; Asst. Gen. Mgr.-Adm., 1955–59; Depy. Gen. Mgr. 1959; Gen. Mgr. 1960–70; mem., Assn. of Prof. Engrs. of Ont.; Candn. Elect. Assn. (Pres. 1964–65); Fellow Engn. Inst. of Can. (Pres., 1966–67); Fellow, Inst. of Elect. & Electronic Engrs.; United Church; recreations: gardening, fishing; Clubs: Granite; Electric; Home: 943 Weller St., Peterborough, Ont. K9J 4Y1.

**HAMEL, J. Patrick Réginald,** M.A., Ph.D.; historien; éducateur; né à Frampton, Qué. 14 fevrier 1931; f. Côme et Helena (Welch-Chevalier) H.; é. Coll. Sainte-Marie-de-Beauce 1943; Coll. de Lévis 1946; Coll. de Saint-Laurent 1951; Univ. d'Ottawa B.A. 1956, M.A. 1961; Univ. de Montréal Ph.D. 1971; Univ. of Mich. 1957–58; ép. Pierrette f. J.A. Méthé 26 octobre 1957; enfants: Julie, Sonia; PROF. EMERITUS, UNIV. DE MONTRÉAL 1994– ; Officier d'Artillerie 1953–55; Conseiller, Musée Nat. de Can. 1956, Expédition Archéologique et géodésique Groenland, Yukon et Alaska 1956–57; Conservateur, Public Archives of Can. 1957–58; Sec. Cabinet Min. of Transp. Can. 1961–62; Lectr. in Social Sci's Univ. d'Ottawa 1959–61, Prof. invité 1973–74; Dir.-fondateur du Centre de documentation des lettres Canadiennes Univ. de Montréal 1964–69, Chargé sénior d'ens. Fac. des Arts 1964–71, Prof. adjoint Études Fran. 1971–75, Prof. agrégé 1975, Prof. de littérature canadienne et francophone 1983, Prof. Emeritus 1994; Prof. invité: Lakehead Univ. 1971–75; Sorbonne IV et VII et fondateur d'un Centre de Recherche Sorbonne VII 1972; Univ. of Birmingham 1972; Haïfa, Tel Aviv, Beercheva, Jérusalem 1978; Nanjing (China) 1992; Radio et TV: Colls. au Micro (CKAC) 1951; CJLX Thunder Bay 1972; Canal 10 TV 1975; Radio-Can. TV 1976; Unv. Montréal Canal 23 TV 1985–91 (Tour à Tour); bourses: Soc. du Bon parler Français 1951; Univ. d'Ottawa 1959–61; Min. de l'édn. du Qué. 1962–64; Affaires culturelles du Qué. 1964, 1976, 1986; Candn. Jewish Council 1979; C.R.S.H. 1985–86; Chevalier des Palmes Acad. de France 1992; auteur (Essais et histoire littétaire): 'Préromantisme au Canada-français' 1965; 'Bibliographie des lettres Can-Fran. '1966; 'Cahiers bibliographiques des lettres québécoises' 1966–69; 'La littérature et l'érotisme' 1967; 'La Correspondance de Charles Gill' 1969; 'Introduction à la Littérature Québécoise' 1970; 'Une de Perdue, deux de trouvées de Boucherville' 1972; 'Procès Verbaux de l'École Littéraire de Montréal' 1974; 'Bibliographie de l'écriture féminine' 1974; 'Analyse de la documentation (France, Belgique, Israel) 1975, 1977, 1978; 'Gaétane de Montreuil' 1976; 'Dictionnaire des Auteurs québécois' en Collab. 1976; 'La Louisiane Creole' 1984; 'L'Habitation St-Ybars de Mercier' 1981–89; 'Répertoire pratique' en Collab. (avec E. Bessette et L. Mailhot) 1982; 'Dumas Insolite' 1988; 'Dictionnaire des auteurs de langue française en Amérique de Nord' en Collab. (avec J.E. Hare et P. Wyczynski) 1989; 'Dictionnaire Dumas' en Collab. (avec Pierrette Méthé) 1990; 'Introduction à la francophonie' 1989; 'Jules Faubert, roi du papier de Paquin' 1991; 'Histoire du Devoir' (en collaboration) 1994; récreations: musique, Arts martiaux; Adresse: 219 Springdale, Pointe-Claire, Qué. H9R 2R4; Bureau: C.P. 6128 Succ. A, Montréal, Qué. H3C 3J7.

**HAMEL, Jean-Marc,** O.C., M.Com., M.P.A.; b. Lotbinière, Que. 19 Feb. 1925; s. Lorenzo and Hermine (Leclerc) H.; e. Lotbinière and Ste-Croix, Que., Pub. Schs.; La Pointe de Lac, Que., High Sch.; Laval Univ., B.Com. 1948, M.Com. 1949; Syracuse Univ., M.P.A. 1956; m. Jacqueline, d. late Emile Lapointe, 11 July 1953; children: Pierre, Denis; with Industrial Life Ins. Co. as Asst. Chief, Selection of Risks Dept., 1949–50; joined Civil Service Comn. 1950, Regional Rep. in Quebec City, 1950–53; Asst. Regional Dir. for Prov. of Que., 1953–57; Personnel Selection Offr., 1957–58; Organ. and Classification Offr., 1958–60; Asst. Secy. to Comn. 1960; Secy. 1960–63; Co-ordinator of Lang. Training for Pub. Service, 1963–64; apptd. Dir. of Adm., H. of C. 1964–65; Asst. to Under-Secy. of State, 1965–66; Chief Electoral Offr., Canada, 1966–90; Royal Comm. on Electoral Reform and Party Financing 1990–92; Privy Council Office 1992–93; sec. Can.-Fr. Interpartly. Assn. 1965–66; Mem. Coll. d'Enseignement Gen. et Prof., Hull, Que. 1967–72; v.p. 1971; medal of merit, Fr. Nat. Assembly 1965; Centennial Medal 1967; Silver Jubilee Medal 1977; Chevalier de la Légion d'Honneur 1981; Personnalité Richelieu 1984; Public Service Outstanding Achievement Award 1989; Commander of the Order of Bernardo O'Higgins (Chile) 1990; Officer of the Order of Canada 1990; awarded Commemorative Medal for 125th Anniversary of Candn. Confederation 1992; R. Catholic; recreations: music, swimming, travel; Club: Cercle universitaire d'Ottawa; Home: 2376 Wyndale Cres., Ottawa, Ont. K1H 7A6.

**HAMEL, Roger de Beaufort,** B.Sc., B.A., B.Eng., M.E.I.C.; b. Ottawa, Ont. 15 Feb. 1929; e. Univ. of Ottawa B.Sc. 1950, B.A. 1950; McGill Univ. B. Eng. (Mech.) 1954; Hon. doctorate: Univ. of Ottawa 1990; Pres. Candn. Chamber of Comm. 1985–89; Bd. of Dirs., Sun Life Trust Co.; Sun Life Savings & Mortgage Co.; Mem. Adv. Bd., International Golf Partners Inc.; joined Imperial Oil serving various positions Qué., H.O. Toronto, Esso Petroleum London, Eng. becoming Pres. Champlain Oil Products Ltd. (subsidiary), retired as Sr. Exec. Prov. Qué. 1984; joined C. of C. 1973 serving as Dir., Chrmn. Nat. Exec. Ctte., Vice Chrmn. Bd., Pres. Qué. Prov. Chamber; Past Pres. Qué. Petrol Assn.; mem., Engrn. Inst. of Can.; Clubs: Royal Ottawa Golf; Landings (Savannah, Georgia); Residence: 2202 – 1510 Riverside Dr., Ottawa, Ont. K1G 4X5.

**HAMELIN, Mt. Rev. Jean-Guy,** B.A., L.Th., L.Sc.Soc.; R. Catholic bishop; b. St-Severin, Qué. 8 Oct. 1925; s. Bernard and Gertrude (Bordeleau) H.; e. Laval Univ. B.A. 1945; Angelicum Univ. Rome L.Th. 1953; Gregorianum Univ. Rome. L.Sc.Soc. 1955; BISHOP, DIOCESE OF ROUYN-NORANDA 1974– ; Teacher in Theol. and Social Sci's Semy. Trois-Rivières, Qué. 1955–58; Chaplain for Social Movements Diocese of Trois-Rivières 1958–64; Dir. Social Action Dept. Candn. Conf. Cath. Bishops 1964–68; Gen. Sec. Conf. Bishops of Qué. 1968–74; mem. of Bd. and Vice Pres. of Conf. 1975–85; Ecclesiastical Adv., CIDSE (cooperation internationale pour le développement et la solidarité) Bruxelles 1988–94; Pres., Candn. Conf. of Bishops 1993– (Vice-Pres. 1991–93); Address: 515 Cuddihy, Rouyn, Qué. J9X 5W9.

**HAMELIN, Louis-Edmond,** Ordre du Can. (1974), M.S.R.C., doctorat en géographie; prof. d'univ.; ses ancêtres sont arrivés de France au Can. au 17e siècle; né St-Didace, Comté de Maskinongé, Qué.; f. Antonio et Maria (Désy) H.; 21 mars 1923; e. Séminaire de Joliette, P.Q. B.A. 1945; Univ. Laval M.A. (Econ.) 1948; Univ. de Grenoble, France, Cert. d'études supérieures en géographie, histoire, économie politique, 1949–50; D. en Géog. 1951; Univ. de Paris, recherches 1956–57; Scott Polar Research Institute, Cambridge, 1964; Doctorat d'Etat (France), 1975; Univ. Laval M.A. (ling.) 1989; ép. Colette, prof., fille de Gaston Lafay, Grenoble, France, 11 août 1951; enfants: Philippe, Anne-Marie; mem. N.W. Terr. Council 1971–75; prof. de géographie, 1951; premier directeur de l'Institut de Géographie, 1955; dir. jusqu'en 1962; dir.-fondateur du Centre d'Etudes Nordiques, Univ. Laval 1961–72; Recteur, Univ. du Quebec, Trois-Rivières 1978–83; participation à des congrès internat. de geographie et du Quaternaire; voyages d'études dans les zones arctiques et subarctiques; professeur invité à Montréal, Ottawa, Toulouse, Abidjan; Publications: 'Sables et Mer aux Iles-de-la Madeleine' 1959; 'Périglaciaire par l'image: Illus. Glossary of Periglacial Phenomena' 1967 (avec Frank A. Cook); 'Le Canada' 1969; 'Canada: a geographical perspective' 1973; 'Nordicité canadienne' 1975; 'Le Nord et son Langage' 1977; 'Canadian Nordicity' 1979; 'Chemins de l'université' 1985; 'Obiou' 1990; 'Le rang d'habitat' 1993; Gouv., Centre de Recherches pour le développement international, Ottawa 1984–88; Assn. Canadienne des Géographes, Ottawa (Pres. 1972); Soc. de Géographie de Qué. (Pres. 1952–56); Arctic Inst. of N. Am. (Gouv. 1964–68); Prix littéraire du Québec 1969; Prix du Gouverneur Géneral 1975; Prix Scientifique du Québec 1976; Prix Fondation Molson 1982; Quatre Doctorats d'honneur; Northern Science Award 1986; correspondant Institut de France 1989; Catholique R.; récréation: voyage; photographie; Résidence: 1244, rue Albert-Lozeau, Sillery, Que. G1T 1H4.

**HAMELIN, Marcel,** D.ès L.; educator; b. Saint-Narcisse, Que. 18 Sept. 1937; e. Séminaire Ste-Marie, Shawinigan 1958; Univ. Laval L.és L. 1961, D.ès L. 1972; m. Judith Purcell 18 Aug. 1962; children: Danielle, Christine, Marc; RECTOR AND VICE-CHANCELLOR, UNIV. OF OTTAWA 1990– , Prof. of Hist. 1966– ; Chrmn. of Hist. 1968–70, Vice Dean Sch. of Grad. Studies 1972–74, Dean of Arts 1974–90; author 'Les premières années du parlementarisme québécois: 1867–1878' 1975; co-author 'Les élections provinciales dans le Québec' 1969; 'Les moeurs électorales dans le Québec, de 1791 à nos jours' 1962; 'Aperçu de la politique canadienne au XIX$^{e}$ siècle' 1965; 'Confédération 1867' 1966; éd. 'Les mémoires de l'honorable Raoul Dandurand' 1967; 'Les débats de l'Assemblée legislative de la province de Québec 1867–1870' 1974; (vol. I-IV); 'Les débats de l'Assemblée législative de la province de Québec 1871–1875' 1976 (vol. V-VIII); 'Les débats de l'Assemblée législative de la province de Québec 1875–1878' 1977; (vol. IX-XI); mem. Assn. canadienne-française pour l'avancement des Sciences; Candn. Hist. Assn.; Royal Soc. Can.; Home: 7 Crescent Heights, Ottawa, Ont. K1S 3G7; Office: 550 Cumberland, Ottawa, Ont. K1N 6N5.

**HAMER, Ian M.,** B.A.Sc., F.R.Ae.S., F.C.A.S.I.; professional engineer; consultant; b. Ottawa, Ont. 1914; s. late Roy Stokes (C.B.E.) and Mary Isabel (Hope) H.; e. Public and High Schs., Ottawa, Ont.; Univ. of Toronto. B.A.Sc. (Mech. Engn. and one year teaching fellowship in Aeronautics), 1937; m. Gladys Gertrude, d. H.S. Johnston, Lindsay, Ont., 1941; children: Kathryn Eryl (Mrs. P.J. Edwards), Mary Margot (Mrs. L.S. Turner), David Ian Wallace; mem. Staff, Univ. of Toronto, 1937–38; Design Office, Handley Page Ltd., London, England, 1938–40; Stress Office, and Staff Assistant to Managing Director, Dowty Equipment Limited, Cheltenham, England, 1940–41; Chief Engineer, Dowty Equipment of Canada Limited, Montreal and Ajax, 1941–51; Tech. Dir., 1951–56; Dir., Vice-Pres. and Gen. Mgr., 1956–60; Pres., Cametoid Ltd., 1956–60; Consultant to Roy. Comn. on Govt. Organ. (Glassco), 1961–62; Co-ordinator, External Aid/CIDA Student Services, Univ. of Toronto 1968–69; mem., A.P.E.O.; C.Eng. (U.K.); mem. Steering Comte. and Interim Council leading to founding of Candn. Aero Inst. 1954; mem. Indust. Council and Chrmn., Assoc. Mfrs. Comte., Air. Indust. & Transport Assn. 1958–60; C.A.S.I. del. at Anglo-American Aero. Conference, London, England 1973; United Church; recreations: reading, photography, gardening, woodworking; Clubs: Univ. (Toronto); Home: 'Westlea,' 701 King St., Whitby, Ont. L1N 5A2.

**HAMERTON, John Laurence,** D.Sc., F.C.C.M.G.; professor; administrator; b. Brighton, England 23 Sept. 1929; s. Bernard John and Nora (Casey) H.; e. London Univ., B.Sc. 1951; London Univ., D.Sc. 1968; m. Irene d. Keith and Irene Tuck 13 Sept. 1967; children: Susan, Michael, Katharine, Sarah; Distinguished (1987) Prof. & Head, Dept. of Human Genetics, Univ. of Man. 1984–93; Sci. Staff., M.R.C. Radiobiol. Rsch. Unit 1951–56; Sr. Sci. Offr., Brit. Mus. 1956–59; Sci. Staff. Brit. Empire Cancer Campaign, Univ. of London 1959–60; Lectr. & Head, Cytogenetics Sect., Guy's Hosp. Med. Sch. 1962–69; Sr. Lectr. & Head 1962–69; Assoc. Prof., Head, Genet. Sect. & Dir., Dept. of Genet., Children's Hosp. of Winnipeg; Vis. Prof., Hebrew Univ. 1974 (summer); Head, Genet. Sect, Pediat., Univ. of Man. & Dir., Dept. of Genet., Health Sci. Ctr. Winnipeg 1972–79; Prof. & Med. Staff Sci. Category 1972–87; Assoc. Dean, Grad Studies & Rsch., Fac. of Med., Univ. of Man. 1977–81; Dept. of Pediat., St. Boniface Gen. Hosp.; University Distinguished Professor, Univ. of Manitoba 1987– ; Chrmn., Manitoba Health Rsch. Counc. 1990– (Vice Chrmn. 1989–90); Robert Roessler de Villiers Award, Leukemia Soc. of Am. 1956; Huxley Meml. Medal, Imperial Coll. of Sci. & Technol. 1958; Rsch. Prof., Med. Rsch. Counc. of Can. 1981–82; Fellow, Candn. College of Medical Geneticists 1975 (Pres. 1991–94); Mem., Am. Soc. of Human Genet. (Pres. 1975); Genet. Soc. of Can. (Pres. 1977); Linnean Soc. (Fellow); Candn. Soc. for Clin. Investigation; Genet. Soc. of Am.; Royal Soc. of Med. (Fellow); Soc. for Pediatric Rsch.; author; 'Human Cytogenetics' 2 vols. 1971; editor: 'Chromosomes in Medicine' 1962; recreation: sheep farming (Pres., Manitoba Sheep Assoc. 1987–89; Chrmn., Can. Sheep Counc. 1988–90); Home: Box 27, Group 7, RR #1, Dugald, Man.; Office: 250 - 770 Bannatyne Ave., Winnipeg, Man. R3E 0W3.

**HAMET, Pavel,** M.D., Ph.D., C.S.P.Q., F.R.C.P.(C); research executive; b. Klatovv, Czech. 13 June 1943; s. Vaclav and Ruzena H.; e. College of Prague, Univ. Charles grad. 1967; McGill Univ. Ph.D. 1972; Univ. of Montreal C.S.P.Q. 1974; m. Johanne d. Louis Tremblay 21 Feb. 1987; children: Sharka, Cléo, Mallory, Mirek; DIRECTOR, CENTRE DE RECHERCHE, HôTEL-DIEU DE MONTRÉAL, UNIV. OF MONTREAL 1990– AND CHIEF OF MOLECULAR MEDICINE; completed training as endocrinologist specialist, Univ. of Montreal 1972–74; spent two years at Vanderbilt Univ., Nashville, TN; Lab. Dir., Clinical Rsch. Inst. of Montreal 1975–90; Edit. Bd. Mem., 'Am. J. of Hypertension,' 'J. of Cardiovascular Pharm.,' 'Current Medicine,' 'High Blood Pressure & Cardiovascular Prevention,' Knight, Order of Malta; Great Montrealer of the Future (Medicine); Goldblatt Award, Am. Heart Assn.; Honorific Cert., Heart & Stroke Found. (Que.); member of 26 societies including Past-Pres., Candn. Hyptertension of Canada; Secy., Internat. Soc. of Hypertension; author of 252 publications and 325 abstracts; recreations: skiing, tennis; Home: 325, Ellerton, Ville Mont-Royal Que. H3P 1E1; Office: 3850 Saint-Urbain St., Pav. Marie de la Ferre, Montreal, Que. H2W 1T8.

**HAMILTON, Albert Charles,** M.A., Ph.D., F.R.S.C.; educator; b. Winnipeg, Man. 20 July 1921; s. Clifford and Mary (Briggs) Goddard; e. Univ. of Man. B.A. 1945; Univ. of Toronto M.A. 1948; Cambridge Univ. Ph.D. 1953; m. Mary McFarlane 1950; four s. Ian, Malcolm, Peter, Ross; PROF. OF ENGLISH, QUEEN'S UNIV. since 1968; Prof. of Eng. Univ. of Wash. 1952–68; Fellow, Huntington Lib. 1959–60; Fellow, St. John's Coll. Cambridge 1974–75; Fellow, Humanities Rsch. Centre, Canberra Apr.-July 1985; Excellence in Research Award, Queen's Univ. 1981; apptd. Cappon Prof. of English 1982; Visiting Prof., Kumamoto Univ. Apr.-July 1988; author 'The Structure of Allegory in "The Faerie Queene"' 1961; 'The Early Shakespeare' 1967; 'Sir Philip Sidney: A Study of His Life and Works' 1977; 'Edmund Spenser's "Faerie Queene"' 1977, 'Northrop Frye: Anatomy of his Criticism' 1990; Gen. Ed., 'The Spenser Encyclopedia' 1990, critical studies in Renaissance lit.; mem. Ed. Bd. 'English Literary Renaissance'; Duquesne Studies in English; mem. Modern Langs. Assn. Am.; Renaissance Soc. Am.; Assn. Candn. Univ. Teachers Eng.; Spenser Soc. Am.; Protestant; recreations: canoeing, hiking; Home: 50 Edgehill St., Kingston, Ont. K7L 2T5; Office: Kingston, Ont. K7L 3N6.

**HAMILTON, Hon. Alvin Chown,** LL.B.; retired judge; b. Winnipeg, Man. 14 Aug. 1926; s. Judge Frank A.E. and Mary Aleda (Chown) H.; e. Kelvin High

School, Winnipeg; Un. Coll.; University of Man., LL.B. 1950; m. Lorna, d. late Charles Hasselfield, Deloraine, Man. 24 Oct. 1951; one d., three s.; Associate Chief Justice, Man. Court of Queen's Bench, Family Division 1983–93, retired; read law with B.C. Parker, K.C., C.T. Wyrzykowski, K.C. and E.N. McGirr, K.C.; called to Bar of Man. 1951; cr. Q.C. 1968; private law practice Roblin, Man. 1951–54; Winnipeg 1954–55; Melita, Man. 1955–58; Brandon, Man. 1958–72; apptd. Judge, Man. Court of Queen's Bench 1971; served with Candn. Army during World War II; Commissioner, Aboriginal Justice Inquiry 1988–91; Past Pres., Man. Assn. Sch. Trustees; John Howard Soc. (Brandon Br.); former sch. bd. mem. and Chrmn.; Lib. cand. in Brandon-Souris 1963; Past Pres., Brandon Chamber Comm.; Bencher, Law Soc. of Man.; mem., Candn. Bar Assn.; Man. Bar Assn.; United Church; Home: 4585 Roblin Blvd., Winnipeg, Man. R3R 0G2.

**HAMILTON, The Rt. Hon. (Francis) Alvin George,** P.C. (Can.) 1957; LL.D. (Hon.) 1989; b. Kenora, Ont. 30 Mar. 1912; s. Francis Robert and Alice May (Jamieson) H; e. Public Sch., Kenora, Ont.; High Sch., Delisle, Sask. (Grad. 1930); Normal Sch., Saskatoon, Sask., 1930–31; taught school 1931–34; Univ. of Saskatchewan, B.A. 1937, B.A. (Hons. in Hist. and Econ.) 1938; m. Constance Beulah Florence (d. Sept. 1979), d. late William John Major, 14 Nov. 1936; two s. Robert Alexander, William Alvin; Chrmn., Resources and Industries Associates, an Internat. Trading Co., New York and now Vancouver 1975– ; Partner, Baker Trading Co, Houston, Texas 1972–79; def. cand. for Rosetown-Biggar g.e. 1945 and 1949; Prov. cand. for Rosetown (def.) 1948, and for Lumsden, 1952; def. cand. for Qu'Appelle 1953; Prov. cand. (def.) for Saskatoon, 1956; 1st el. to H. of C. for Qu'Appelle, g.e. June 1957; re-el. 1958, 1962, 1962, 1965; apptd. Min. of Northern Affairs & Nat. Resources, 22 Aug. 1957; Min. of Agric. 11 Oct. 1960–Apl. 1963; def. cand. for Regina E. g.e. June 1968; el. for Qu'Appelle-Moose Mt. g.e. Oct. 1972; re-el. 1974, 1979, 1980, 1984; rec'd title Rt. Honourable 1992; Prov. Organizer for Conservative Party in Sask., 1948–57; Prov. Ldr. of Conservative Party in Sask., 1949–57; served in 2nd World War with R.C.A.F., 1941–45, Navigator, Flight-Lieut. (Burma Star Decoration); biography 'Alvin' written in his honour by Patrick Kyba; mem., Royal Canadian Legion; R.C.A.F. Assn.; Conservative; Protestant; recreations: outdoor activities, historical reading; Home: 4 Kitoman Crescent, Manotick, Ont. K0A 2N0.

**HAMILTON, Donald G.,** B.Sc., M.S., Ph.D.; Canadian public service, retired; b. Fredericton, N.B. 22 July 1917; s. Charles and Mary Jane (Scott) H.; e. McGill Univ., B.Sc., 1938; Univ. of Wisconsin, M.S. 1940, Ph.D. 1947; m. Helen Easley, d. James K. Hewett, Omaha, Neb., 22 March 1947; children: James Hewett, Douglas Scott; Consultant, Agric. Research Council, Agriculture Canada, and internat. development agencies 1978–86; Dir.-Gen. (Planning and Eval.) Research Br., Dept. of Agric., 1975–77; Asst. Dir.-Gen., 1964–75; joined service in 1938; Asst. in Oat-breeding, 1938–42 and 1945–49; Offr. in Charge of Barley Breeding Unit, 1949–55; Chief, Cereal Crops Div., Exper. Farms Service, 1955–59; Dir. of Program (Crops) Research Br., 1959–64; served in 2nd World War Overseas with Royal Candn. Arty., 1942–45; demobilized with rank of Capt.; Fellow Agric. Inst. Can. (Pres., Eastern Ont. Br., 1950–51; Hon. Sec. 1951–53; Vice Pres., 1953–54); Fellow, Am. Assn. Advanc. Science; Sigma Xi; Gamma Alpha; Anglican; Home: 1701 – 1195 Richmond Rd., Ottawa, Ont. K2B 8E4.

**HAMILTON, Gavin Francis,** D.V.M., Ph.D., D.D.; veterinarian; educator; b. Nokomis, Sask. 6 Aug. 1930; s. William and Elizabeth Ross Illingworth (Cunningham) H.; e. Ont. Vet. Coll. Univ. of Toronto D.V.M. 1952; Colo. State Univ. Ph.D. 1970; St. Andrews Coll. Saskatoon D.D. 1982; m. Jean d. Ralph and Sara Haight 6 July 1956; children: Lyle, Heather, Bruce, Nancy, Gavin, Brent; DEAN EMERITUS, WESTERN COLL. OF VET. MED., UNIV. OF SASK. 1993– , Prof. of Vet. Surgery 1973–93, Dean 1982–92; private vet. practice 1952–66; Asst. Clin. Prof. present Univ. 1966–67, Assoc. Prof. 1970–73, Dir. Large Animal Clinic Dept. of Vet. Clin. Studies 1970–75, Chrmn., Surgery Sec. 1974–79, Head of Vet. Clin. Studies 1980–82, Chrmn. Univ. Planning Ctte. 1975–78; Chrmn., Coordinating Ctte.-Faculty Council 1978–81; Pres., Sask. Livestock Assoc. 1988–89 (Vice Pres. 1987–88); Chrmn., Animal Health Technician Ctte., Commonwealth Veterinary Assn. 1985–90; Vice Pres., Confed. of Candn. Faculties of Agric. and Vet. Med. 1989–91; Fellow, Med. Research Council Can. 1967–70; Consultant, Pitman-Moore Co. 1972–74; Chrmn., Kelsey Inst. of Applied Arts & Science Adv. Bd. 1976–85; mem., Bd. Regent St. Andrews Theol. Coll. Saskatoon 1960–68, 1971–79, Chrmn. 1963–68, 1971–79; Chrmn. of Council St. Thomas Wesley UN. Ch. 1971–80, Clk. of Session 1959–67; Ch. Extension Ctte. Sask. Conf. Un. Ch. of Can. Chrmn. 1964–67, Finance Ctte. Chrmn. 1963–67; Commr. Gen. Council Un. Ch. of Can. 1958, 1964; Area Commr. Saskatoon Hockey Assn. 1973–75; Pres., Caledonian Soc. Saskatoon 1964–65; author or co-author various publs.; mem., Am. Assn. Bovine Practitioners; Am. Assn. Vet. Clinicians; Am. Coll. Vet. Surgs.; Candn. Assn. Faculties Vet. Med. (Pres. 1972–73); Candn. Vet. Med. Assn. (mem. Council 1963–67, Vice Pres. 1965–66, Pres. 1966–67); Sask. Vet. Med. Assn. (Pres. 1962–63); Am. Vet. Med. Assn.; recreations: hockey, golf, badminton; Home: 219 Tacoma Ave. N., Tacoma, WA 98403 USA.

**HAMILTON, George Stanley,** B.Comm., C.A.; consultant; b. Hamilton, Ont. 21 Nov. 1936; s. Stanley George and Anne Elizabeth (McGee) H.; e. McMaster Univ., B.Com. 1959; C.A. 1962; Certified Mgmt. Cons. 1978; m. Irene d. Steven and Nellie Sloka 28 May 1961; children: Karen, James, Stephen; PARTNER, ERNST & YOUNG 1972– ; joined firm in 1959; Dir. and Treas., Wiarton Marina Ltd.; Chrmn., Candn. Opera Found.; mem. Bd. of Dirs., Candn. Opera Co.; Mem., Church of St. Bride, Clarkson; recreations: sailing, opera, music; Club: Bd. of Trade of Metrop. Toronto; Home: 1713 Valentine Gdns., Mississauga, Ont. L5J 1H4; Office: P.O. Box 251, Royal Trust Tower, Toronto, Ont. M5K 1J7.

**HAMILTON, John Drenan,** M.D., D.Sc. (Hon.), F.R.C.P.(C); pathologist, retired; b. Revelstoke, B.C. 22 Sept. 1911; s. James Henry and Mary Stearns (Edwards) H.; e. Univ. of B.C.; Univ. of Toronto, M.D. 1935; Cambridge Univ. 1937–39; Johns Hopkins Univ., 1939–40; m. Frances Doone, d. Maj.-Gen. C. F. Constantine, Kingston, Ont., 6 Sept. 1947; children: John Charles Douglas, Suzanne Margery, Alice Jane, Maria Doone; Vice Provost, Univ. of Toronto, 1972–76; Dean, Faculty of Med. there 1961–66, Vice-Pres., Health Sciences 1966–72; former Dir., Connlab Holdings; and Connaught Laboratories Ltd. 1972–79; former Trustee, Toronto General Hosp., Sunnybrook Med. Centre, Clarke Inst. of Psychiatry, Princess Margaret Hosp., Addiction Research Foundation; Prof. of Pathol. & Head of Dept., Univ. of Toronto & Pathologist-in-Chief, Toronto Gen. Hosp., 1951–61; Asst. Prof. of Path., McGill Univ. 1945–46; Prof. of Path. and Head of Dept., Queen's Univ. 1946–51; served in 2nd World War with R.C.A.M.C., No. 1 Research Lab., 1940–45; mem. of Ont., Candn. Assns. of Path.; has published articles on arteriosclerosis, immunology, wound infection experimental glomerulo-nephritis; Home: 305 - 2050 Nelson St., Vancouver, B.C. V6G 1N6.

**HAMILTON, Peter Williamson,** M.Arch., M.R.A.I.C., O.A.A., R.C.A.; architect; b. Toronto, Ont. 15 July 1941; s. John Williamson and Dorothy Clarkson (Hogg) H.; e. Upper Can. Coll. Toronto 1958; Univ. of Toronto B.Arch. 1963; Harvard Univ. Grad. Sch. of Design M.Arch. 1969; m. Linda Deb Kasen, d. George Kasen, N.Y.C., 8 Jan. 1967; two d. Jennifer Kara, Alissa Anne; SOLE PROPRIETOR, PETER HAMILTON ARCHITECTS; rec'd Jyväskyla, Finland New Town First Prize with Bengt Lundsten Arch. 1964; Candn. Housing Design Council Award 1974; Ont. Assn. Archs. Design Prize 1978, Heritage Can. Nat. Award of Honour 1979 with Hamilton Ridgely & Bennett Archs.; EDEE Award Nomination for Cantelevered Child's High Chair; Award of Merit, Toronto Historic Bd. 1985; Ont. Clay Masonry Design Awards for Malvern Coll. 1987; Ont. Assoc. of Archs. Design Award 1991; work exhibited in 'Le Nouveau Nouveau Monde' Exhbn., Paris, Barcelona, Milan 1987, Toronto 1988; Minaki Lodge Resort in Joint Venture with R.V.B. Burgoyne & Hamilton Kemp Architects; mem., Ont. Assn. Archs.; Royal Arch. Inst. Can.; Royal Canadian Academy of Arts; recreations: sailing, skiing, squash; Clubs: Toronto Lawn Tennis; Harvard; Home: 67 Roxborough St. W., Toronto, Ont. M5R 1T9; Office: 21 Price St., Toronto, Ont. M4W 1Z1.

**HAMILTON, Richard Frederick,** M.A., Ph.D.; educator; b. Kenmore, N.Y. 18 Jan. 1930; s. Delmer Vernon and Ethelwyn Gertrude (Stevenson) H.; e. Univ. of Chicago A.B. 1950; Columbia Univ. M.A. 1953, Ph.D. 1963; m. Irene Maria Elisabeth Wagner 12 Aug. 1957; two s. Carl Thomas, Tilman Michael; PROF. OF SOCIOLOGY AND POLITICAL SCIENCE, OHIO STATE UNIV., Columbus, Ohio 1986– ; Instr., Skidmore Coll., Saratoga Springs, N.Y. 1957–59; State Univ. of N.Y. Binghamton 1959–64; Asst. Prof. Princeton Univ. 1964–66; Assoc. Prof. Univ. of Wisc. 1966–69, Prof. 1969–70; Prof. of Sociology, McGill Univ. 1970–86; served with U.S. Army 1954–56; author 'Affluence and the French Worker' 1967; 'Class and Politics in the United States' 1972; 'Restraining Myths' 1975; 'Who Voted for Hitler?' 1982; (with James Wright) 'The State of the Masses' 1986; 'The Bourgeois Epoch' 1991; over 50 articles aspects of politics U.S.A., Can. and Germany; mem. Steering Comte. Council for European Studies 1975–78; Council mem. Inter-Univ. Consortium Pol. & Social Research 1975–79; mem. Pol. Sociol. Comte. Internat. Sociol. Assn.; recipient, Distinguished Scholar Award, Ohio State Univ. 1993; recreation: music; Home: 1354 London Dr., Columbus, Ohio 43221; Office: 392 Bricker Hall, 190 North Oval Mall, Columbus, Ohio 43210-1353.

**HAMILTON, Robert Morris,** B.A., B.L.S.; librarian, retired; b. Lachine, Que. 25 March 1912; s. Andrew McWhirter and Agnes (Morris) H.; e. McGill Univ., B.A. 1934, B.L.S. 1935; Columbia Univ. (Carnegie Fellow, 1936–37); m. Anne Louise, d. late John H. Harrington, 30 July 1938; children: John, Robert, Louise; Asst. Univ. Librarian, Univ. of Brit. Columbia, 1964–77; entered the Civil Services of Can. 1937; apptd. Asst. Librarian (English), Library of Parliament, Ottawa, 1946; Assoc. Prof. Sch. of Librarianship, Univ. of B.C., 1961–64; Pres. (1961–62), Canadian Lib. Association; author 'Canadian Quotations and Phrases' 1952; 'Canadian Book-prices Current 1950–58' 1957–59; 'Orchid Flower Index 1736–1979' 1979; 'Dictionary of Canadian Quotations' (with D. Shields), 2nd ed. rev. 1982; 'The Orchid Doctor' 2 vols. 1980–88; Home: 9211 Beckwith Rd., Richmond, B.C. V6X 1V7.

**HAMILTON, Stanley William,** B. Comm., M.B.A., Ph.D.; university professor; b. Moose Jaw, Sask. 10 Apr. 1939; s. Gordon F. and Kathleen (McCormick) H.; e. Univ. of Sask., B.Comm. 1960; Univ. of B.C., M.B.A. 1965; Univ. of Calif. at Berkeley, Ph.D. 1970; m. Kathryn d. A.C. McEown 5 May 1962; children: Heather M., Keith W.; PROF., FAC. OF COMMERCE & BUSINESS ADMIN., UNIV. OF B.C. 1968– ; Proctor & Gamble Co. 1960–62; Student 1962–68; Dir., Exec. Programmes, present univ. 1973–75; Assoc. Dean, Profl. Progs. 1975–76; Acting Dean 1976–77; Assoc. Dean 1977–78 and 1986–89; Hon. Life Mem., Kootenay, Vancouver Island, and Fraser Valley Real Estate Boards; Real Estate Inst. of Can.; Real Estate Inst. of B.C.; Dir., B.C. Assessment Authority 1989– ; Public Gov., Vancouver Stock Exchange 1980–86; co-author: 'Housing: It's Your Move' vol. 1 1976, 'Condominiums: A Decade of Experience in B.C.' 1978, 'Regulation and Other Forms of Government Intervention Regarding Real Property' 1981, 'Foundations of Real Estate Financing' 1983; Home: 3854 W. 37th Ave., Vancouver, B.C.; Office: Vancouver, B.C. V6T 1W5.

**HAMILTON HARDING, Robin A.,** F.C.A.; financial executive; b. Sri Lanka 12 July 1939; s. G. Trevor and Anne Gregg (Waterhouse) H.; e. King's College School (U.K.); Inst. of C.A.s of Scotland C.A. 1965; m. Marjorie Curtis 22 Sept. 1971; children: Kate, Helen, Jenny, James; VICE-PRES. (FINANCE) & CHIEF FINANCIAL OFFICER, BELL CANADA 1992– ; Staff Supvr., Accounting Research, Bell Canada 1972; General Accountant, Corp. Reporting 1973; Asst. Vice-Pres. (Corp. Accounts) 1974; Controller, Northern Telecom 1976; Asst. Vice-Pres., Regulatory Matters, Bell Canada 1977; Asst. Vice-Pres. (Finance) & Corp. Comptroller 1983; Vice-Pres. & Comptroller 1985; Dir., Bell Sygma; Bimcor Inc.; Tele-Direct (Publications) Inc.; Pres., The Quest Foundation; Dir., Les Grands Ballets Canadiens; Dir., Cancer Research Soc.; Mem. Ctte. on Corp. Reporting, Financial Executives Inst. of Canada; Chrmn., St. James's Club of Montreal; author: 'The Comptroller of the '90s' in 'Business Quarterly' spring 1990 and other articles; recreations: skiing, gardening, fishing, reading; clubs: St. James's Club of Montreal, Royal St. Lawrence Yacht; Home: 10 Claremont Ave., Pointe Claire, Que. H9S 5C5; Office: 1050 Beaver Hall Hill, Floor 18, Montreal, Que. H2Z 1S4.

**HAMLYN, His Honour Peter Dean,** B.A., LL.B.; tax court judge; b. Oshawa, Ont. 21 Apr. 1939; e. Carleton Univ. B.A. 1964; Univ. of Ottawa LL.B. 1967; JUDGE OF THE TAX COURT OF CANADA 1990– ; appt. Provincial Court Judge, Prov. of Ont. 1973; appt. Sr. Prov. Court Judge 1979; appt. Deputy Judge, Tax Court of Canada 1988; appt. Judge Tax Court of Canada 1990; Office: 200 Kent St., Ottawa, Ont. K1A 0M1.

**HAMM, Abram Bernard,** C.L.U.; employee benefits consultant; b. Neville, Sask. 23 Nov. 1930; s. Jacob K. and Helena (Bergman) H.; e. Neville H.S. 1949; Univ. of Calgary 1968–73; C.L.U. 1963; m. June Elizabeth d. Dennis and Phyllis McAlear 26 Nov. 1982; children (prev. m.); Kevin Scott, Shauna Lee; PRINCIPAL, WM. M. MERCER LTD. 1980– ; Mngt. Trainee, Eaton's

1949–50; Sec.-Treas., Arthur Powell Investments Ltd. 1951–53; Mgr., Med. Serv. Inc. 1953–58; Group Rep., London Life 1958; Group Supvr. 1959; Group Benefits Mgr. 1964; Brokerage Mgr. 1978–80; Founder & Pres., Motivation Rsch. Inst. Ltd. 1962; Vis. Lectr., Banff Sch. of Fine Arts 1970–71; Pres., Lethbridge Jr. C. of C. 1958; Pres. Calgary Chapt. Life Underwriters 1973; cert. of appreciation, Life Underwriters' of Can. (for teaching); Chrmn., Calgary United Way 1971; Dir., Calgary Little League; Mem., Life Underwriters Assn. of Can. 1958– ; Bd. of Trade Toronto 1984–87; Bd. of Trade Vancouver 1987–89; North York Chamber of Comm. 1990– ; Candn. Pension Conf. 1985– ; Protestant; recreations: skiing, golf, squash, badminton, tennis; Clubs: The Boulevard (Toronto); Glencoe; Calgary; Home: PH4, 211 St. Patrick St., Toronto, Ont. M5T 2Y9.

**HAMMILL, Tim David,** LL.B.; business executive; b. Australia 1 April 1946; s. Colin N. and Nancy Kathleen (Robson) H.; e. Univ. of Western Ont. LL.B. 1970; m. Mary Jeanne d. Bill and Jeanne Hewitt 28 June 1969; children: Amanda Jeanne, Anthony Colin, Kathleen Joanne; PRES., A.T. & T. CAPITAL CANADA INC. 1992– ; private legal practice 1972–76; Sr. Legal Advisor, Bank of Montreal 1976–80; Dep. Supt., Insurance & Real Estate, Prov. of B.C. 1980–83; Legal Counsel, First City Trust 1983–91; Office: 900 - 3650 Victoria Park Ave., Willowdale, Ont. M2H 3P7.

**HAMMOND, John Allan;** administrator; b. St. Lambert, Que. 13 Oct. 1920; s. Frederick Peter and Mary Anne Elizabeth (Callan) H.; e. St. Lambert (Que.) High Sch. 1938; m. Elizabeth Grace, d. Arthur Douglas Cooke, 15 Sept. 1945; two s. Peter Wallace, Michael Douglas; PRES., FOCUS CONSULTANTS INC., Vancouver, 1985; Radio Announcer, CFCF, Montreal, 1945; Mgr., CFCF, 1950; Broadcasting Mgr., Canadian Marconi Co., 1953; Gen. Sales Mgr., Comm. Products Div., 1956; Mgr., CKRC, Winnipeg, 1959; Dir. of Adm., St. John's-Ravenscourt Sch., Winnipeg, 1962; Extve. Vice Pres., Glenbow Alberta Inst., Calgary, 1970; Extve. Dir., Granville Island 1978; served with RCAF 1941–45; Past Dir., Royal Winnipeg Ballet; Candn. Assn. Broadcasters; Central Can. Assn. Broadcasters; Bureau Broadcast Measurement; former mem., Adv. Comte. on Broadcasting, Ryerson Inst. Technol.; former mem. of Senate, Univ. of Calgary; Past Pres., Museum Directors Assoc. Can.; mem., Candn. Museums Assn.; Past Pres., Alta. Museums Assoc.; past Chrmn., Candn. Comte., Internat. Council of Museums: Protestant; Home: 4888 Headland Dr., West Vancouver, B.C. V7W 2Z3.

**HAMMOND, Ruth Bunting,** B.A., A.B.C., A.P.R.; public relations consultant; b. Toronto, Ont. 6 July 1920; d. William Herbert and Ella Elizabeth (Fawns) Andrew; e. Queen Victoria Sch., Toronto 1934; Parkdale Collegiate Inst. 1939; Univ. of Toronto Victoria Coll. B.A. Hons. Engl. Lang. and Lit. 1943; Ont. Coll. of Edn. 1944; m. Lawrence John H. (dec. 1985) 7 Oct. 1950; children: Gillian Elizabeth, John Andrew; m. David Wall Bunting (dec. 1988) 10 July 1988; Teacher of Engl. and Hist. Ripley, Ont. 1943–44, Oakville Ont. 1945, Queen's Coll. Nassau 1945–46; Reporter and Women's Ed., Toronto Star 1946–50; Pres., Mgr., Owner Ruth Hammond Public Relations 1951–76; Publ. Relns. Dir. North Am., Drake Internat. Ltd. 1976–77; Dir. Publ. Relns. and Alumni Affairs Ont. Coll. of Art 1977–84; Vice-Pres. and Gen. Mgr. Publ. Relns. Sect., Vickers and Benson Advertising 1984–85; Instr. Publ. Relns. Ryerson Polytech. Inst., York Univ. and Univ. of Toronto Sch. of Continuing Studies 1970–85; co-author 'Public Relations for Small Business' 1979; numerous articles in consumer and bus. jours.; monograph on Publ. Relns. and Publ. Affairs Careers 1980, 1983; Dir. Candn. Publ. Relns. Soc. Toronto Inc. 1969–74; Pres. Candn. Women's Press Club, Toronto 1966–67; Dir., Toronto Press Club 1980–94; numerous national & internat. awards in public relations; named Woman of Distinction (Communications), YWCA of Metro Toronto 1985; mem. United Ch. of Can.; Liberal; recreations: reading, writing, travel; Club: Toronto Press; Women's Press Club of Toronto; Heliconian; Address: 33 Elmhurst Ave., Suite 2410, Willowdale, Ont. M2N 6G8.

**HAMOWY, Ronald,** B.A., Ph.D.; educator; b. Shanghai, China 17 Apr. 1937; s. Elias and Marie (Rofe) H.; e. City Coll. of N.Y. B.A. in Hist. and Econ. 1960; Balliol Coll. Oxford 1963–64; Univ. of Chicago Ph.D. in Social Thought 1969; PROFESSOR OF INTELLECTUAL HISTORY, UNIVERSITY OF ALBERTA 1983– ; Lectr. in Modern European Hist. Brooklyn Coll. City Univ. of N.Y. 1964–65; Asst. Prof. and Asst. Dir. Western Civilization Prog., Stanford Univ. 1968–69; Asst. Prof. Dept. of Hist. present Univ. 1969, Assoc. Prof. 1972; Visiting Assoc. Prof. Dept. of Pol. Sci., Simon Fraser Univ. 1975–77; author 'Canadian Medicine: A Study in Restricted Entry' 1984; 'The Scottish Enlightenment and the Theory of Spontaneous Order' 1987; Ed. 'Dealing With Drugs: Consequences of Government Control' 1987; author of numerous articles on Am. and Candn. legis. hist., pol. and social theory of the Augustan Age, and jurisprudential theory; Office: Dept. of Hist., Univ. of Alta., Edmonton, Alta. T6G 2H4.

**HAMPSON, Mary 'Elizabeth' Anne,** B.A., M.A., Ph.D., C.Psych.; university professor, researcher, b. Kamsack, Sask. 3 Feb. 1957; d. John and M.J. Margaret (Ranford) H.; e. Univ. of Saskatchewan B.A. (Hons.) 1980; Univ. of Western Ont. M.A. 1982, Ph.D. 1989; m. Richard A. s. Allan and Louise Harshman 3 July 1991; ASST. PROF. OF PSYCHOLOGY & CORE MEM., NEUROSCIENCE PROG., UNIV. OF W. ONT. 1991– ; Neuropsych. intern, Univ. Hosp. 1983–84; St. Joseph's Hosp. 1984–85; Montreal Neurol. Inst. 1985; Lectr., Univ. of W. Ont. 1986; Neuropsych. Cons., Univ. Hosp. 1986–88; Rsch. Assoc., U.W.O. 1988; Rsch. Fellow, Hosp. for Sick Children 1989–91; Scientist (Adjunct), Rsch. Inst. 1991– ; Asst. Prof. (Status), Psychol., Univ. of Toronto 1990– ; Curt P. Richter Prize for rsch. in behav. neuroendocrinology 1989; Mem., Soc. for Neurosci.; Internat. Soc. of Psychoneuroendocrinology; Internat. Soc. for Behav. Neurosci.; Internat. Neuropsychol. Soc.; author of sci. papers; recreations: gardening, gourmet cooking; Home: 75 Chesham Ave., London, Ont. N6G 3V1; Office: London, Ont. N6A 5C2.

**HAMPSON, H. Anthony,** M.A. (Econ.); corporate executive; investor; b. Montreal, Que. 18 Aug. 1930; s. Harold Ralph and Geraldine Mary (Smith) H.; e. Selwyn House Sch., Montreal; Westmount (Que.) Pub. Schs.; Bishops Coll. Sch., Lennoxville, Que.; McGill Univ., B.A. 1950; Cambridge Univ., M.A. (Econ.) 1952; m. Wendy Kathleen Dobson; children: Terence, Greville, Hilary, Alexandra; Chrmn., Novocon International Inc.; Intera Information Technologies; Microhydraulics, Inc.; Vice Chrmn. & Chrmn., Finance & Development Ctte., Telemedia Inc.; Dir., Trimac Ltd.; with Bank of Montreal, Credit Analyst, H.O. 1952; Department of Finance, Ottawa, Econ. Policy Div. on loan for 2 years to Royal Comn. on Can.'s Econ. Prospects (The Gordon Comn.) and co-authored study on Can.'s Secondary Mfg. Indust. 1953–57; Dir., Burns Bros. & Denton, Toronto 1957–64; Secy., Royal Comn. on Banking and Finance (The Porter Comm.) 1961–64; Vice-Pres., Power Corp. of Canada Ltd. 1964–68; Pres., Capital Management Ltd. 1965, (full time) 1968–72; Pres. & C.E.O., Canada Development Corp. 1972–87; Past Chrmn., Gen. Adjustment Assistance Bd., Dept. of Industry, Ottawa; Pharm. Industry Devel. Adv. Comte.; Office: Suite 300, 8 King St. E., Toronto, Ont. M5C 1B5.

**HANBIDGE, R. Walter D.,** B.S.A.; agriculturalist; retired corporate executive; b. Peterborough, Ont. 5 Apr. 1925; s. the late Hazel Elizabeth (Dawson) and the late George Burnham H.; e. Peterborough Coll. Inst., 1939–44; Ont. Agric. Coll., Univ. of Toronto, B.S.A. (Econ.) 1948; m. the late Mary Elizabeth, d. late Dr. H. J. Vallentyne of Brantford, Ont., 25 July 1946; children: Catherine Anne, Robert John, Val Elizabeth (deceased), Mary Ellen; OWNER/OPERATOR, TINNAHINCH FARMS; Advertising Supervisor, Product Accounts, Candn. Industries Ltd., 1948–53; Advertising Promotion Manager, Reader's Digest Assn. (Can.) Ltd., Toronto, 1953–54; Advertising Supvr., Gen. Co. and Merchandising Mgr. of Textile Fibres, Candn. Industries (1954) Ltd. 1954–58; Dir. of Marketing Services, Leetham Simpson Ltd., 1958–61; Offr., Royal Comn. on Govt. Organ., 1961; joined BP Canada Inc. as Comm. Mgr., 1961; apptd. Gen. Mgr., Marketing, 1963; Vice-Pres., Marketing, 1964; Extve. Vice Pres., 1966; Pres., 1977; Pres. and C.E.O. 1981–83; recreations: photography; restoration of Canadian antiques; Club: Granite; Home: 14 Salvi Court, Toronto, Ont M4A 1P7; Office: Tinnahinch Farms, R.R. 2, Napanee, Ont. K7R 3K7.

**HANCOCK, Beryl Lynette (Lyn),** B.Ed., M.A.; writer; lecturer; photographer; b. East Fremantle, Western Australia 5 Jan. 1938; d. Arthur Edward George and Doris Jean (Williams) Taylor; e. Univ. of W. Australia, A.S.D.A. 1955, Teacher's Dip. in Edn. 1956; L.S.D.A. 1957; Trinity Coll., London, Eng., L.T.C.L. 1959; Royal Acad. of Music, London, Eng. L.R.A.M. 1961; Simon Fraser Univ., B.Ed. 1977, M.A. 1980; m. Frank Schober 14 Sept. 1991; teacher 1956–70; lecturer 1963– ; filmmaker 1963–80; 13 books, multitudinous articles pub. 1964– ; specializes in nature, outdoors, adventure, travel, history, the far north (Yukon/N.W.T.); author: 'Pacific Wilderness' 1970; 'There's a Seal in my Sleeping Bag' 1972, 1992; 'The Mighty Mackenzie' 1974; 'There's a Raccoon in my Parka' 1977; 'Love Affair with a Cougar' 1978; 'An Ape Came Out of my Hatbox (or Gypsy in the Classroom)' 1979, 1980; 'Tell Me, Grandmother' 1985; 'Northwest Territories' 1986; 'Looking for the Wild' 1986; 'Alaska Highway' 1988; 'The Predator Hunters' in Our Wildlife Heritage 1988; 'The Northwest Territories: Canada's Outback' 1993; 'Nunavert' (forthcoming); 'Tabasco, the Saucy Raccoon' (forthcoming); ed. 'Vanderhoof: The Town that Wouldn't Wait' 1979; Francis J. Kortright Award for Excellence in Outdoor Writing 1978, 1987; American Express Travel Writing Award 1981, 1983; Pacific Northwest Booksellers Award 1973; mem. Writers' Union of Can.; Friends of the Sea Otter; Candn. Nature Fedn.; Outdoor Writers of Can.; Northwest Writers' Assn.; Periodical Writers' Assoc. of Can.; Address: R.R. 1, 2457 Baker View Rd., Mill Bay, B.C. V0R 2P0 and (1991–94) Box 244, Fort Simpson, N.W.T. X0E 0N0.

**HANCOCK, David Graeme,** B.A., LL.B.; lawyer; b. Fort Resolution, N.W.T. 10 Aug. 1955; s. Richard Harwood and Kathleen Elizabeth (Porter) H.; e. La Crete Public; Univ. of Alberta B.A. 1975, LL.B. 1979; m. Janet Ellen d. Marjorie and David Crawford 4 Aug. 1979; children: Ian, Janis, Janine; PARTNER, MATHESON & COMPANY 1985– ; admitted to Bar of Alberta 16 June 1980; Queen's Counsel 1994; specializes in corp. commercial, corp. finance, intellectual property & gen. solicitor's practice; Dir., Credit Union Deposit Guarantee Corp. 1990– ; Mem., Univ. of Alberta Hosp. Bd. 1992; Bd. Mem., Phi Gamma Delta Education Found. of Canada 1992– ; Pres., South Edmonton Business Assn.; Alberta Student Finance Bd. 1985–92; Past Mem. Bd. of Mgrs., Strathcona Presbyn. Ch.; Candidate - P.C. Party 1993 Prov. Election - Edmonton-Whitemud; Past Pres., P.C. Assn. of Alta. (Pres. 1990–92; Past Northern Vice-Pres. & Reg. Dir.); Mem., Alta. Fiji Soc.; Fraternity of Phi Gamma Delta incl. Past Pres., Fiji Soc.; Bd. Mem. & Past Chair, Phi Gamma Delta Housing Corp.; Mem., Kiwanis Club of S. Edmonton (Pres. 1986, '87); recreations: politics, Citadel Theatre, reading, swimming; Home: 10607 – 10th Ave., Edmonton, Alta. T6J 6G7; Office: 10410 – 81st Ave., Edmonton, Alta. T6E 1X5.

**HANCOCK, Geoffrey White,** M.F.A.; editor; writer; b. New Westminster, B.C. 14 Apr. 1946; s. Jonas White and Margaret Eileen (Ramsbottom) H.; e. Vincent Massey Jr. High and Lester Pearson Sr. High Schs. New Westminster; Univ. of B.C., B.F.A. 1973, M.F.A. 1975; m. Gay Allison d. Isaac and Julia Hanson Aug. 1983; one d. Meagan Julia b. 1985; ED.-IN-CHIEF, CANADIAN FICTION MAGAZINE 1974– ; Lectr. in Creative Writing Univ. of B.C. 1974–76 and Simon Fraser Univ. 1976–77; Treas. Nat. Mag. Awards Found. 1976–77; Cons. to Multiculturalism Directorate Ottawa, Lit. Cons. to CBC Radio Prog. 'Anthology,' freelance radio journalist; regular book reviewer Toronto Star 1979– ; book reviewer, Globe & Mail 1988– ; Contbg. Ed. Writer's Quarterly 1980–89; Fiction Ed. Canadian Author and Bookman 1979–91; Publications Co-ordinator, Stratford Festival 1992; recipient Fiona Mee Award Quill & Quire 1979; Grant Redford Prize for Playwrighting 1973; Russell Bankson Prize for fiction 1975; ed. 'Magic Realism' 1980; 'Illusion: Fables, Fantasies and Metafictions' 1983; 'Metavisions' 1983; 'Shoes and Shit: Stories for Pedestrians' 1984; 'Moving Off the Map' 1986; 'Invisible Fictions: Contemporary Stories from Quebec' 1987; 'Canadian Writers at Work: Interviews' 1987; 'Fast Travelling' 1990; 'Singularities' 1990; 'Fire Beneath the Cauldron' 1991; 'The Prehistoric Art of Canadian Writing' 1993; 'The Future of Fiction' 1994; 'Published in Canada: The Small Presses' 1994; author various book chapters; mem. Candn. Magazine Publishers Assn. (Dir. 1974–78); Periodical Writers Assn. Can.; ACTRA; recreations: travel, movies, tai chi, mythopoetic men's movement; Office: P.O. Box 946 Station F, Toronto, Ont. M4Y 2N9.

**HANCOCK, Robert Ernest William,** Ph.D.; university professor; b. Merton, England 23 Mar. 1949; s. Robert Valentine and Sonya (Swatisky) H.; e. Univ. of Adelaide, B.Sc. 1970, B.Sc. (Hons.) 1971, Ph.D. 1975; m. Elizabeth d. Ian and Joan Hunter 8 Dec. 1973; children: David Graeme, Lynn Marissa; PROF., UNIV. OF B.C. 1978– ; SCIENTIFIC DIR., CANDN. BACTERIAL DISEASES NETWORK; Alexander Von Humboldt Scholar, Tübingen, West Germany 1975–7; Lectr. of ASM, Found. for Microbiol. 1985–6; Candn. Soc. of Microbiol. Award 1987; UBC Killam Rsch. Prize 1988; CSM/New England Biolabs Lectr. 1992; awarded Commemorative Medal for 125th Anniversary of Candn. Confederation 1993; Am. Men & Women in Science 1989; Mem. of edit. bd. 1982– ; Cons., Centocor 1983–86; Bristol Myers-Squibb Ltd. 1984–91; Oncogen 1988–91; Dir., Micrologix Biotechnology Inc. 1993– ; Scientific Advisory Bd., ID Biomedical 1993– ; Chrmn. & Extve. Mem., Sci. Adv. Bd., Candn. Cystic Fibrosis Found. 1990–93, (Extve. Mem. 1987–93); Sci. Adv. Bd.,

Vaccine Evaluation Ctr. 1988–93; Pres., N.W. Br. of Am. Soc. for Microbiol. 1985–86; Scientific Dir., Candn. Bacterial Diseases Network 1990– ; author of 160 rsch. papers; editor: 'Antibiotics and Chemotherapy' 36, 'Pseudomonas aeruginosa: new therapeutic approaches from basic research'; recreations: water polo, volleyball; Office: Dept. of Microbiology, Univ. of B.C., Vancouver, B.C. V6T 1W5.

**HANCOCK, Trevor,** B.Sc., M.B., B.S., M.H.Sc.; public health consultant; b. London, Eng. 6 Oct. 1948; e. St. Bartholomews Hosp. London B.Sc. 1970, M.B., B.S. 1973; Univ. of Toronto M.H.Sc. 1980; m. the lovely Fran; PUBLIC HEALTH CONS. 1986– ; Cons. to World Health Orgn., Health & Welfare Can., Ont. Min. of Health, City of Toronto, Canadian Healthy Comunities project, various cities and hospitals in Canada, USA & Europe; Assoc. Prof. of Environmental Studies, York Univ.; Family Phys. 1975–78; Health Planner, Health Advocacy Unit City of Toronto 1980–82, Assoc. Med. Offr. of Health Toronto 1982–86; Chair, Ont. Healthy Communities Coalition 1987– ; Founding mem. Paradigm Health, Green Party Can.; author numerous articles, several book chapters pub. health; Hon. Life Mem., Candn. Pub. Health Assn. 1990 (Bd. 1986–88); mem., Ont. Pub. Health Assn. (Pres. 1986–87); World Futures Studies Fedn.; Address: 28 Napier St., Kleinburg, Ont. L0J 1C0.

**HANCOX, Ralph;** business executive; b. Hampstead, Eng. 23 Aug. 1929; s. Harold Barnsley and Ada Frances (Smith) H.; e. Harrow Co. Grammar Sch. for Boys; R.A.F. Flying Coll.; Heany, S. Rhodesia; Sch. of Modern Languages; Regent St. Polytech., grad. 1954; m. Margaret Gilmour, d. George Chisholm Frier, 5 June 1954; children: Linda Elaine, Kenrick Guy, Alison Janet (Niles), Julian Roderick Rufus; Chrmn., Reader's Digest Magazines Ltd.; Chrmn. & Pres., Reader's Digest Foundation of Canada; Chrmn., Pres. & C.E.O., The Reader's Digest Association (Canada) Ltd.; Chrmn., Nat. Assn. of Major Mail Users; immediate past Chrmn., Magazines Canada; Gov., Conseil du Patronat du Qué.; Chrmn., Adv. Ctte., The Candn. Ctr. for Studies in Publishing, Simon Fraser Univ.; former Consigliere delegato Selezione dal Reader's Digest, S.P.A. Milano 1990–92; former Ed., Cdn. edition, The Reader's Digest; Peterborough (Ontario) 'Examiner'; former Vice-Pres., Op.-Customer Serv., Book Pubs., Produc., Readers Digest Assn. (Can.); sometime News Editor, Weekly Post, London, Eng.; Daily Columnist, Kingston (Ont.) 'Whig-Standard'; Correspondent Candn. Affairs, Observer Foreign News Service, London; articles in numerous papers incl. 'The Scotsman' (Edinburgh), 'The Jerusalem Post' (Israel) and many papers in U.S.A.; served with R.A.F., 1947–52; discharged with rank of Sgt. Pilot; Trustee, Peterborough Bd. Educ. 1964–66; Nieman Fellow, Harvard Univ. 1965–66; winner Nat. Newspaper Award for Edit. Writing 1966; recreations: reading, anthropology, writing, travel, photography; Office: 215 Redfern Ave., Montreal, Que. H3Z 2V9.

**HANDELMAN, David E.,** B.Sc., M.Sc., Ph.D., F.R.S.C.; mathematician; b. Toronto, Ont. 22 Nov. 1950; s. Morris and Goldie (Gorlitzky) H.; e. Univ. of Toronto B.Sc. 1972; McGill Univ. M.Sc. 1973, Ph.D. 1975; m. Rochelle Ann d. Max and Evelyn Gold 3 Aug. 1975; two s.: Michael, Daniel; PROFESSOR OF MATHEMATICS, UNIVERSITY OF OTTAWA 1984– ; Nato Postdoctoral Fellow, Giessen, W. Germany 1975–76; Instr. Univ. of Utah, Salt Lake City 1976–77; Asst. Prof. Math. present Univ. 1977, Assoc. Prof. 1980; Steacie Meml. Rsch. Fellow 1985; co-winner quinquennial Israel Halperin Award, Operators and Operator Algebra 1985; author over 60 jour. articles and several monographs; recreation: badminton; Address: (E-mail: dehsg @ uottawa.bitnet) University of Ottawa, Ottawa, Ont. K1N 6N5.

**HANDLEY, Chris,** B.A., M.Ed.; information systems executive; b. Birmingham, Eng. 25 Feb. 1947; s. Denis Charles and Barbara Audrey (Richardson) H.; e. Univ. of Toronto B.A. 1969, M.Ed. 1982; m. Gail d. Sigmund and Lucy Mazur 17 Oct. 1983; one s.: Isaac Christopher; DIR.OF BUSINESS RE-ENGINEERING, UNIV. OF TORONTO 1993– ; Instr., Psychol., Univ. of Toronto 1971–86; Information Systems Cons., Computing Serv. 1986–89; Dir. of Information Systems, Devel. & Univ. Relations 1989–93; Information Systems Cons. for health care and private sectors; Gov., Women's Coll. Hosp. 1990– ; Bd. Sec. & Extve. Ctte. Mem. 1992– ; Bd. of Dir., Women's Coll. Hosp. Found. 1991–93; Mem., IEEE, ACM, CAUSE; recreations: reading, gardening, carpentry; Home: 64 Jackman Ave., Toronto, Ont. M4K 2X6; Office: 21 King's College Circle, Toronto, Ont. M5S 1A1.

**HANES, Ursula Ann, (Ursula Hanes Guthrie),** R.C.A., S.S.C.; sculptor; b. Toronto, Ont. 18 Jan. 1932; d. Prof. Charles Samuel, Ph.D., F.R.S. F.R.S.C., and Theodora Burleigh (Auret) H., Ph.D.; e. Perse Sch. for girls, Cambridge, U.K., 1949. Cambridge Sch. of Art, 1951; Art Student's League, N.Y.C., 1953 (studied under Wm. Zorach, John Hovannes); Dept. of Fine Arts, Columbia Univ., N.Y.C., 1953 (studied under Oronzio Malderelli); Inst. of Child Study, Univ. of Toronto, (Dipl.) 1954; m. David John Fry, C.D., M.A. s. Harold Fry, Toronto, Ont., 30 Aug. 1956; divorced 1968; m. Daniel P. Guthrie 1976; divorced 1981; children: Rachel Sabina, Simon David, Tanya Amanda, Timothy Jeremy John; has exhibited at Columbia Univ., 1953, New Eng. Soc. Artists, 1953, O.S.A., 1954–62, R.C.A., 1955, 1957, 1959–62, Stratford Festival, 1955, Young Candn. Contemporaries, 1957, Candn. Nat. Ex., 1956, 1959–60; several sculpture and batik exhibitions in Lanzarote, Canary Islands, Spain 1969–75; Audio-Visual Consultant for I.D.R.C. (Ottawa) in Rep. Du Mali, West Africa 1971–72; Exhibition, Saxe Gallery, Toronto, 1980; also various civic art galleries in Can.; Commissions incl.; bust of Dr. Tyrone Guthrie, Evan McCowan, Dr. Margaret McCready, Dr. Dorothy Corbett & Buffalo Dog, Signora Anty Renzi, Signori Celso Bianchini, Francesco Orsetti, Mme. Marietta Bottequin & Son Ezra 1989, Dr. Cyla Mandel 1992; and various murals and fountains; commissioned to paint 4ft. x 16in. wooden panels of the 21 California Mission Saints for the town of San Juan Bautista, Calif. Aug. 1983 – completed Dec. 1983; 1984 completed 5 bronze maquettes, Encounter Series to be executed in bronze 8 ft. tall; concluded 6 abstract figures, inspired by Tuscan Mtns. first in bronze, then in large size in marble Aug. 1986, which formed major part of her exhbn. in Geneva Switzerland, Sept. 1986; marble abstract two figure composition 1986; architectural comns. in 1987 incl. bronze bas relief 75 cms high x 60 wide 'Bathers'; cast stone bas relief 85 cm high x 76 wide 'Dragon in Arch'; completed several bronze maquettes 'Abstractions on Mountain Forms' subsequently carved in marble 1988; exhbd. in 2 group shows in France simultaneously, as guest of honour at Tréguier and La Rochelle 1988; new works in bronze & marble 'Towards a New Balance' prepared in 1989 for one-woman exhbn., Musée du Nouveau Monde, La Rochelle, France, Apr.-Sept. 1990; Bronze bust of Vincent Van Gogh commissioned for B.N.P. (National Bank of Paris) Arles, completed Sept. 1991; 'Arles' inauguration, Arles 1991; one woman show, Arles May-July 1991; 1992 exhbn. for Aix-en-Provence; one woman show, large works in marble and bronze and smaller works, 'The Gallery' Fontvieille May-June 1993; winter 1993/94 working on 4 metre high figure in local stone for local quarry and reclining figure in limestone 4 meters long, 170 centimeters high; currently preparing an exhbn. for Paris; mem., Sculptors' Soc. Can. (Pres. 1964–65); Ont. Soc. Artists; Royal Candn. Acad. of Arts; recreations: reading, theatre, dance arts; Address: La Juliere, 13930 Aureille, France.

**HANIGAN, Lawrence;** transportation executive; b. Notre-dame de Stanbridge, Que. 3 Apr. 1925; s. John Henry and Alice (Lareau) H.; m. Anita d. Joseph O. Martin 20 July 1946; children: Carmen, Doris, Guy, Patricia, Michael; CHRMN. VIA RAIL CANADA INC. 1985– ; Vice-Pres. Cooper-Widman (Que.) Ltd. 1950–70; mem. City of Montreal Counc. 1960–78, Exec. Ctte. 1970–78; Chrmn. Exec. Ctte. Montreal Urban Community 1972–78; Chrmn. & Gen. Mgr. Comn. de Transp. de la Communaute Urbain de Montreal 1974–85; R. Catholic; Club: Saint-Denis; Home: 358 du Baron St., Saint-Sauveur-des-Monts, Que. J0R 1R4; Office: P.O. Box 8116, Station A, Montreal, Que. H3C 3N3.

**HANINGTON, Rear Admiral Daniel Lionel,** D.S.C., C.D.; marine consultant; b. London, England 10 July 1921; s. Charles Lionel and Mary Arbuthnot (Willet) H.; e. Rothesay (N.B.) Coll. Sch., 1940; Royal Naval Staff Coll., psc 1961; m. Margot Rita, d. H. V. Wallace, Halifax, N.S. 1 Mar. 1943; children: Gillian, Mark, Brian, Felicity; joined RCNVR as Midshipman, 1940; sunk in HMS 'Rajputana,' Denmark Strait, 1941; trans. to RCN 1944; promoted Cdr. 1955; C.O., HMCS 'Iroquois,' 1955–57; Offr.-in-Charge, Navig.-Direction Sch., 1958; promoted Capt. 1961; Cdr., 3rd Candn. Escort Sqdn. 1965–66; promoted Commodore 1966 and apptd. Commandant, Candn. Maritime Warfare Sch.; subsequently Depy. Commdr., Candn. Defence Educ. Estab., Ottawa; Dir.-Gen. Program Vice Chief of Defence Staff Br.; promoted Rear Adm. 1973 as Chief of Program; trans. to staff of Supreme Allied Command Atlantic 1974 as D/COS (Support) (ret. 1976); spec. marine navig. offr. & fighter control; qual. Clearance Diving Offr. (ships); Master Foreign Going Steamships; Clubs: Chesapeake (founding mem.); Naval Officers Assoc.; Union Club of B.C.; Bytown Seagull; Anglican; recreations: history, philately; Home: 3452 Sunheights Dr., Victoria, B.C. V9C 3P7.

**HANKINSON, James F.,** B.Com., M.B.A., C.A.; executive; b. Weymouth, N.S. 21 Sept. 1943; s. J. Scott and Edith Ann (Journeay) H.; e. Weymouth (N.S.) Sch. sr. matric. 1961; Mt. Allison Univ. B.Com. 1964; C.A. 1969; McMaster Univ. M.B.A. 1970; m. Grace Mary d. Elmer and Grace Buck 16 July 1966; children: Mary Grace, John Scott; PRES. & C.O.O., CANADIAN PACIFIC LTD. 1990– ; Dir., Canadian Pacific Enterprises Limited; Canadian Pacific Express and Transport; Canadian Pacific Forest Products Limited; Canadian Pacific Hotels Corporation; Canadian Pacific Limited; Canadian Pacific Securities Limited; Canadian Pacific Securities (Ont.) Ltd.; Fording Coal Ltd.; Laidlaw Inc.; Marathon Realty Company Ltd.; PanCanadian Petroleum Ltd.; United Dominion Industries Inc.; United Dominion Industries Ltd.; Asst. to Dir. of Acctg., CP Rail, Montreal 1973, Asst. Dir. of Acctg. 1974, Dir. of Acctg. 1975, Comptroller, Canadian Pacific Ltd., Montreal 1979; Vice Pres. Fin. and Acctg., Canadian Pacific Enterprises Ltd., Calgary 1981–85; Chrmn. and C.E.O., Canadian Pacific Securities Ltd., Calgary 1981–85; Group Vice-Pres., Canadian Pacific Ltd. 1985–88, Extve. Vice-Pres. 1988–90; mem., Ont. Inst. C.A.'s; Chrmn., Bd. of Regents, Mount Allison Univ.; Candn.-Am. Ctte. sponsored by C.D. Howe Inst. (Can.); Nat. Planning Assoc. (U.S.A.); Club: The Toronto (Dir.); Canadian Club of Toronto; Home: 33 Strathallan Blvd., Toronto, Ont. M5N 1S8; Office: Ste. 800, 123 Front St. W., Toronto, Ont. M5J 2M8.

**HANLEY, Rev. Msgr. John Gerald,** B.A., D.D.; priest; b. Read, Ont. 21 Feb. 1907; s. Denis and Jessie Elizabeth (Bryson) H.; e. Regiopolis Coll. Kingston; St. Michael's Coll. Univ. of Toronto B.A. 1927; Queen's Univ. D.D. 1973; Msgr. Archdiocese of Kingston; Dir. Hotel Dieu Hosp. Kingston 1977–88; mem. Bd. Mgmt. Queen's Theol. Coll. Kingston 1972–85; Ed. The Canadian Register 1942–70; Teacher, Jr. Semy. Christ the King, Ladner, B.C. 1932–34; named Prelate of Honor 1955; Protonotary Apostolic 1976; author 'Across Canada with Newman' 1953; mem. Cath. Press Assn. U.S. & Can. (Secy. 1962–68); Candn. Fed. Newman Clubs (Nat. Chaplain 1944–45, 1952–55); Vic. Gen., Archd. of Kingston (R.C.) 1969–83; Hon. Canon Diocese of Ont. (Anglican) 1983; Address: 279 Johnson St., Kingston, Ont. K7L 1Y5.

**HANLON, Carl Patrick,** B.A.; television correspondent; b. Ottawa, Ont. 5 Nov. 1957; s. James Desmond and Mona Bán (Blake-Kelly) H.; e. Carleton Univ. B.A. (Hons.) 1980; m. Mary d. Robert Russell and Janet Lenore Bliss 20 July 1984; children: Patrick Russell, Bliss Erin, Taylor Gabriel; WASHINGTON CORRESPONDENT, GLOBAL TELEVISION NETWORK 1991– ; TV Anchor Radio Reporter, CJDC Dawson Creek 1980; Reporter, CJOH TV Ottawa 1980–84; CFTO TV Toronto 1984–87; Senior Correspondent, Ottawa Parly. Bureau, Global TV Network 1987–91; Home: 8512 Irvington Ave., Bethesda, Maryland 20817.

**HANLON, Theodore M.,** C.A., B.Comm.; energy industry executive; Extve. Chair, Wascana Energy Inc.; Dir., Computalog Ltd.; Grant Geophysical Inc.; Saskferco Products Inc.; Pres., The Sage Group Inc.; Sec., Shawnee Oils Ltd.; Past Co-Chair, New Grade Energy Inc.; Past Chair, Sask. Economic Development Corp.; Swift Current Sask. School Bd.; Swift Current Local Housing Authority; Past Councillor, Inst. of C.A.s of Sask.; Past Acting Pres., Crown Investment Corp. of Sask.; clubs: Calgary Petroleum, Willow Park Golf and Country, Calgary Professional; Home: 311 Parkview Cres., Calgary, Alta. T2J 4N8.

**HANNA, Charles G.,** B.Sc., M.B.A.; computer executive; b. Alexandria, Egypt 15 July 1952; s. George B. and Mary (Tannoss) H.; e. Univ. of Toronto Hons. B.Sc. Physiology 1975; York Univ. studies toward M.B.A. 1976; one d.: Darcy; FOUNDER AND PRESIDENT, BRAINS II, INC./CANADIAN USED COMPUTERS LTD. 1980– , CANADIAN SYSTEMS MAINTENANCE 1983 and UC AMERICA INC. 1986; Publisher of 'Action Bulletin' and 'Executive Summary' computer review publications; Mktg. Rep. IBM Canada Ltd. 1976–79; Vice-Pres. Mktg. Annex Holdings Ltd. 1979–80; author 'Canadian Federation of Biological Societies' 1975; awarded Ross S. Lang scholarship 1975; Top Sales Performer, IBM Canada Ltd. 1977; recreations: art, travel, racquetball, swimming, music; Club: Brains II Fitness Ctr., Toronto; Home: 128 Burbank Dr., Willowdale, Ont. M2K 1N8; Office: 165 Konrad Cres., Markham, Ont. L3R 9T9.

**HANNA, David Scott,** B.Sc., A.M., Ph.D.; university professor; b. Deep River, Ont. 22 Dec. 1953; s. Geoffrey Chalmers and Barbara Helen (Scott) H.; e. McGill Univ. B.Sc. 1975; Harvard Univ. A.M. 1976, Ph.D. 1980; m. Paula d. Joseph and Adeline Stone 19 July 1980; children: Derek, Trevor; ASSOCIATE PROF., MCGILL UNIV. 1990– ; Scientific Assoc., CERN (Geneva Switz.) 1980–81; Rsch. Assoc., Rockefeller Univ. 1982; Asst. Rsch. Offr., Nat. Rsch. Council 1983–84; Asst. Prof., McGill Univ. 1985–90; Alexander von Humboldt Fellow 1992–93; Mem., Candn. Assn. of Physicists; Inst. of Particle Physics; Am. Physical Soc.; recreations: music, long distance running; Home: 4196 Beaconsfield Ave., Montreal, Que. H4A 2H3; Office: 3600 University St., Montreal, Que. H3A 2T8.

**HANNA, Geoffrey Chalmers,** M.A., F.R.S.C.; physicist; b. Stretford, Lancs., England, 5 Oct. 1920; s. Walter and Dorothy (Cross) H.; e. Manchester Grammar Sch. 1931–38; Trinity Coll., Cambridge, B.A., M.A. 1938–41; m. the late Barbara Helen, d. late Harry Scott, 7 April 1951; three s. Christopher Scott, David Scott, Jeremy Scott; Rsch. Dir., Chalk River Nuclear Labs., Atomic Energy of Canada Ltd. until retired 1985; with British Min. of Supply, radar research and devel., 1940–45; Nat. Research Council of Can., Montreal and Chalk River, nuclear physics research, 1945–52; mem., Candn. Assn. Physicists; fellow, Royal Soc. of Can.; Anglican; Home: 5 Tweedsmuir Place, Deep River, Ont. K0J 1P0.

**HANNA, John A.,** B.Comm., FCGA; finance and administration executive; b. Montreal, Que. 26 Nov. 1942; s. Abraham and Marie H.; e. Loyola Univ. B.Comm. 1967; cert. in gen. acctg. 1974; m. Carol-Anne Newton 1967; children: Robert, David; SR. VICE-PRES., FINANCE AND ADMIN., AND CHIEF FINANCIAL OFFR., UNITED WESTBURNE INC. 1992– ; Business Analyst, CGE Co. Ltd. Montreal 1968–72; Vice-Pres., Finance, Canada Port Corp. Montreal 1971–81; Vice-Pres. Finance & Admin., VIA Rail Canada Inc. Montreal 1981–87; Extve. Vice-Pres., Finance & Administration, Hydro-Quebec 1987–92; Dir., YMCA; Fellow CGA, 1990; recreations: skiing; Home: 1148 Pierre-Mallet St., Dorval, Que. H9S 5V9; Office: 6333 Décarie Blvd., Ste. 400, Montreal, Que. H3W 3E1.

**HANNAFORD, Derek Crawford;** investment dealer; b. Montreal, Que. 2 NOv. 1930; s. Harold J. and Marjorie S. (Davie) H.; e. Westmount H.S.; Sir George Williams Univ.; m. Merle d. Lida and Charles Shields 15 May 1954; children: Harold Charles, Craig Shields, Karen Marilyn; CHAIRMAN & FOUNDER, FIRST CANADA SECURITIES 1982– and FIRST CANADIAN PROPERTIES INVESTMENTS 1986– ; Chairman & Chief Extve. Offr., Mead & Co. Ltd. 1961–78; Pres., Derhan Ltd. 1978– ; Founder & Dir., Avline Trading Corp. 1985– ; Chair, Govt. of Canada Privatization Ctte. 1979–80; Vice-Pres., Boy Scouts of Canada; Dir., Y.M.C.A. Found.; Youth Horizons Found.; Gov., Montreal Gen. Hosp.; Mem., Un. Ch. of Canada; recreations: skiing, squash, golf; clubs: National, Montreal Badminton & Squash, Mount Bruno Golf; Home: 52 St. Sulpice Rd., Westmount, Que. H3Y 2B7; Office: 1155 Rene Levesque Blvd. W., Suite 816, Montreal, Que. H3B 2H7.

**HANNAH, John Charles,** B.A.Sc., P.Eng.; mining executive; b. New Westminster, B.C. 15 March 1939; s. Charles Hamilton and Elsie May Kuoppala (Szkilnyk) H.; e. Univ. of B.C. B.A.Sc. 1961; m. Doreen Faye Danard 24 Sept. 1960; children: Charles Gordon, Cheryl Glenda May; PRESIDENT & CHIEF EXECUTIVE OFFICER, MINERA ESCONDIDA LTDA. 1992– ; Engineer, B.C. Forest Serv. 1961–66; Field Engr., Bregoliss Construction Ltd. 1966–68; Project Engr., McElhanney Surveying Engr. 1969–70; Project Mgr., McCarter & Nairne 1970–72; Project Engr., Island Copper Mine 1972–75; Admin. Mgr. 1975–77; Maintenance Mgr. 1977–79; Production Mgr. 1979–82; Mine Mgr. 1982–88; Vice-Pres. Operations, Minera Escondida Ltda. 1988–91; Dir, Mining Assn. of B.C. 1987–88 (Chair, Mine Mgrs. Ctte. 1988–89); Dir., Rupert Arm Mines 1988–89; Bd. of Gov. Dir., SONAMI (Santiago, Chile) 1992– ; Mem., Am. C. of C. (Santiago) 1992– ; Chair, Econ. Devel. Comn. 1985–86; Hospital Bd. Port Hardy, B.C. 1974–76; Profl. Engr., Prov. of B.C.; recreations: military history, gunnery, riflemanship, fishing; clubs: Prince of Wales (Santiago) 1992– ; Offices: 3200 Apoquindo, Piso 7, Santiago, Chile, S.A. and (Canadian Office) BHP-Utah Mines Ltd., 1600 - 1050 West Pender St., Vancouver, B.C. V6E 3S7.

**HANNAH, Richard Stanley,** M.Sc., Ph.D.; educator; b. Brantford, Ont. 29 March 1946; s. Richard H. and R. Bernice (Richards) H.; elem. and high schs. Brandon, Man.; Brandon Coll. B.Sc. 1967; Univ. of Man. M.Sc. 1970, Ph.D. 1973; m. Kathryn J. d. Robert and Elda Nightingale 5 Aug. 1966; two s. Richard R., Sean M.; PROF. OF ANAT. UNIV. OF CALGARY 1979– , Dir. of Gross Anat. 1986– ; Dir. Triple I Productions Ltd.; Lectr. in Zool. Brandon Univ. 1970; Asst. Prof. of Anat. Med. Coll. of Ga. 1973–75; Asst. Prof. present Univ. 1976, Asst. Dean (Rsch.) Faculty of Med. 1978–80; served with RCAF (R) 1963–67; recipient Rsch. Excellence Award Imperial Oil Ltd. 1990; author over 60 publs. sci. jours.; Troop Scouter Scouts Can. 1979–84; mem. Candn. Assn. Anats. (Exec. Bd.); recreations: wood carving, skiing; Home: Unit 252, 4037 - 42 St. N.W., Calgary, Alta. T3A 2M9; Office: 3330 Hospital Dr. N.W., Calgary, Alta. T2N 4N1.

**HANNINGTON, Frederick Gilmore,** C.D., B.A.psac,pfsc, Col. (ret'd); association executive; b. Glassville, N.B. 31 May 1930; s. Fred F. and Christeen (McBrine) H.; e. Bath H.S. 1947; Teacher's Coll., N.B. 1948; RCAF Staff Coll. 1964; York Univ. B.A. 1974; CF Coll. 1972; Carleton Univ. Grad. Studies 1974–76; var. tech., language & mngt. schools; m. Shirley d. James and Jean McDonald 22 May 1954; children: Frederick, Steven, Mark; DOMINION SEC., THE ROYAL CANDN. LEGION 1985– ; School teacher 1948–49; enrolled RCAF 1949; comnd. Air Navigator 1950; served in Maritime Air, Air Def. & Air Transp.; instr., Maritime & Air Transp. Units & C.F. Coll.; commanded Air Def. & Air Transp. units; extensive staff duties esp. in manpower; served in Germany, Belgium, U.S. and Candn. Arctic; participated in aircraft opns. in Middle East, Africa, S. Am. & Eur.; NDHQ Dir. of Establishment Requirements then Dir. Gen. Orgn. & Manpower 1983–85; Dir. & Sec.-Treas., Canvet Pub. Ltd.; Colonel Candn. Forces Suppl. Reserve; Candn. Forces Decoration; Centennial Medal; awarded Commemorative Medal for 125th Anniversary of Candn. Confederation 1992; Hon. Mem., Chilean Air Force 1960; Legion Meritorious Service Award (LMSM); Mem., Royal Candn. Legion; RCAF Assn.; recreations: golf, skiing, cottage; Clubs: RCAF Officers, Legion; Home: 18 Archer Sq., Ottawa, Ont. K1V 9Y8; Office: 359 Kent St., Ottawa, Ont. K2P 0R7.

**HANSEN, Herman P.,** CD, pfsc, B.Comm.; public servant; b. Carragana, Sask. 21 Feb. 1938; s. Clifford P. and Agnes L. (McLean) H.; e. H.S., Minitonas, Man. 1956; St. Mary's Univ., B.Comm. 1972; m. Olive d. Edwin and Pauline Cleveland 19 Sept. 1956; children: Maren, Kirsten, Edwin; ASST. DEP. MINISTER, OPERATIONS, LABOUR CANADA 1986– ; served with Royal Candn. Navy 1956–74; Asst. Dir. in Mngt. Cons. Serv., Dir. of Internal Audit, Dept. of Health & Welfare 1974–79; Dir. Gen., Personnel Admin. Branch 1979–82; Asst. Sec., Orgn. & Classification, Personnel Policy Branch, Treas. Bd. Sec. 1982–83; Asst. Sec., Program Branch 1983–86; Chrmn., Merchant Seamen Compensation Bd.; Hazardous Material Information Review Comn., CCOHS Counc. of Govs.; recreations: skiing, motor cycling; Home: 1952 Fairbanks Ave., Ottawa, Ont. K1H 5Y4; Office: Ottawa, Ont. K1A 0J2.

**HANSEN, Inger,** Q.C., LL.B.; provincial court judge; b. Copenhagen, Denmark 11 May 1929; d. Marius and Agnes (Jorgensen) H.; e. Univ. of Copenhagen 1952; Univ. of B.C., LL.B. 1960; Carleton Univ. LL.D. (hon.) 1990; Trent Univ. LL.D. (hon.) 1993; PROVINCIAL COURT JUDGE (ONT.); apptd. Chair, inquiry into allegations of sexual misconduct at Bell Cairn Staff Development Ctr., Hamilton (Min. of Correctional Services, Ont.); Information Commissioner of Canada (Canada's First) 1983–90; called to Bar of B.C. 1961; private litigation practice in B.C.; joined federal Dept. of Justice as Legal Couns. to Solicitor Gen.'s Dept. 1969; Correctional Investigator (Canada's First), Penitentiary Ombudsman 1973–77; Candn. Human Rights Comn. and Canada's first Privacy Comn. 1977–83; Guest Lectr. various Facs. of Law and Pol. Sci.; Ed. Bd., Transnational Data Report; Law Soc. of B.C.; Candn. Bar Assn.; Internat. Bar Assn. (Mem. of Counc., Section on Gen. Practice); Internat. Comn. of Jurists; Candn. Assn. for the Prevention of Crime; Zonta Internat.; John Howard Soc.; Elizabeth Fry Society; recreations: theatre, dance, swimming, literature; Home: Ottawa, Ont.

**HANSEN, Poul;** executive; b. Denmark 9 Nov. 1931; s. Svend Jorgen and Lilly (Jacobsen) H.; e. Schneekloth's Gymnasium & Mercantile Sch. Copenhagen B.Com equivalent; m. Judith d. George and Nell Sellers 30 Dec. 1960; children: Tani Victoria, Sian Elizabeth, John Poul; PRES. HIGHLAND VALLEY COPPER 1986– ; Mgr. The East Asiatic Co. Tokyo 1962, Vice Pres. Vancouver 1965, Pres. 1968–74; Pres. & Chief Exec. Offr. West Kootenay Power, Trail, B.C. 1975–78; Group Vice Pres. Cominco, Calgary 1977–78, Chrmn. and Mng. Dir. Cominco Europe, London, Eng. 1978–86; Clubs: Vancouver; Shaughnessy Golf; Home: 3589 Pine Cres., Vancouver, B.C. V6J 4K2; Office: P.O. Box 10024 Pacific Centre, 3000, 700 West Georgia St., Vancouver, B.C. V7Y 1A1.

**HANSEN, Rick,** C.C., O.B.C., B.P.E., LL.D. (Hon.); athlete; b. Port Alberni, B.C. 26 Aug. 1957; e. Univ. of B.C., B.P.E.; Hon. LL.D., Univ. of B.C. 1987; Hon. LL.D., Univ. of Calgary 1989; Hon. LL.D. St. Mary's Univ., N.S. 1993; Hon. LL.D. Univ. of Victoria 1994; m. Amanda Reid 10 Oct. 1987; children: Emma Kathleen, Alana Victoria; Pres., Rick Hansen Enterprises Inc. 1990– , a motivation and public relations co.; paraplegic as result of truck accident 1973; winner of 19 internat. wheelchair marathons; 3-time world wheelchair marathon champion; began 'Man in Motion World Tour' 21 March 1985; main goal was to create a greater awareness of the potential of persons with disabilities; raised over 23 million dollars for persons with spinal cord injuries to be used in the areas of research, rehabilitation, wheelchair sports and awareness; completed journey 22 May 1987, having travelled over 40,000 km (the circumference of the earth) on 4 continents, through 34 countries; made Freeman of the City of Vancouver, 24 March 1987; awarded Companion, Order of Canada 1987; initiated National Access Awareness Week in 1987; apptd. Commissioner General to Canadian Pavilion at Expo '88; apptd. Consultant to the President (Disabilities) to plan and implement the Univ. of B.C. Disability Resource Centre, 1 Mar. 1989; Order of B.C. 1990; apptd. Chair, INDEPENDENCE '92, internat. congress and exposition on disability, Vancouver, B.C., Apr. 1992; apptd. Canadian Secretary to the Queen for Her Majesty's visit to Ottawa 1 Jul. 1992; Chair, Commission for the Inclusion of Athletes with a Disability; quote: '...It is important to strive to be the best you can be. Don't be afraid to reach for your dreams.' Univ. Office: The Rick Hansen National Fellow Programme, U.B.C., Disability Resource Centre, 1874 East Mall, Vancouver, B.C. V6T 1Z1.

**HANSON, Arthur John,** B.Sc., M.Sc., Ph.D.; environment executive; b. New Westminster, B.C. 12 Sept. 1943; s. Hans and Gladys Bonar (Breen) H.; e. Univ. of B.C. B.Sc. 1965, M.Sc. 1969; Univ. of Michigan Ph.D. 1972; m. Ellen d. Harry and Harriett Jomini 24 Sept. 1966; children: Jordan, David, Laura; PRESIDENT AND C.E.O., INTERNATIONAL INST. FOR SUSTAINABLE DEVELOPMENT (IISD) 1992– ; Ed. Bd., 'Ecodecisions'; Asst. Research Prof., Univ. of Mich. 1972–74; Project Specialist, Ford Found. 1974–77; Dir. (1978–87) and Prof. (1978–91), School for Resource and Environmental Studies, Dalhousie Univ. Programme Dir., Dalhousie Ocean Studies Programme 1979–85; Chairperson, CEARC (Candn. Environmental Assessment Research Counc.) 1983–86; experience in environmental studies: B.C. salmon fisheries ecol., West Ind. marine biol., S.E. Asia Ecol. & resource management, Maritime Can./N.E. U.S.A. marine problems; environmental education-action programs U.S.A. 1968–72, incl. first major Teach-In on Environ., Mich. 1970; Consultant, World Bank; U.N. Devel. Program; U.S. Agency for Intl. Devel., CIDA, in Resource & Environ. problems; Leader World Bank/UNDP and CIDA Proj. for Environmental Management Development Indonesia 1980–88; mem., British Ecol. Soc.; Internat. Assoc. for Ecological Economics; co-author 'Recycle this Book: Ecology, Society and Man' 1972; 'CIDA and the Environment' 1981; co-ed. 'Atlantic Fisheries and Coastal Communities' 1984; H.R. MacMillan Family Fellowship U.B.C.; Distinguished Teaching Fell., Univ. of Mich; recreations: hiking, jogging, swimming, canoeing; Home: 30 Roslyn Cres., Winnipeg, Man. R3L 0H7; Office: 161 Portage Ave. E., 6th Flr., Winnipeg, Man. R3B 0Y4.

**HANSON, George S.,** M.B.E.; food executive; b. Drinkwater, Sask. 31 May 1921; s. Henry and Freida H.; e. Western Sch. of Commerce; m. Donna d. George and Eirene Duns 17 June 1944; children: Peter George, M.D.; Penny Ann, B.A., LL.D.; Food Processing Extve., Canada Packers Inc. 1941–68; Vice Pres. & Sales Mgr., Vaunclair Purveyors Ltd. 1968–70; Vice Pres. & Mgr., Candn. Opns., The Meat Export Development Co. (N.Z.) Ltd. 1970–73, Extve. Vice Pres., Opns. in N.A. 1973–76; Pres. & Dir., The New Zealand Lamb Co. Ltd. 1975–80, Depy. Chrmn., Pres. & Dir. 1980–86, Depy. Chrmn. & Dir. 1986–87; Pres. & Dir., George S. Hanson International Marketing Inc. 1986–93; Extve. Vice Pres., Hanson Stress International Inc. 1988–90; served with RCAF 3 yrs.; mem. Royal Commonwealth Soc.; Clubs: Lambton Golf & Country; Empire; Home: 42 Farningham Cres., Islington, Ont. M9B 3B6.

**HANSON, Peter George,** M.D.; physician; public speaker; author; b. Vancouver, B.C. 4 April 1947; s. George and Donna (Duns) H.; e. Univ. of Toronto, M.D.

1971; m. Sharilyn d. Robert and Janet Smith 6 Nov. 1976; children: Kimberley Anne, Trevor George, Kelly Christine; PRACTICES MEDICAL ACUPUNCTURE, AT PORTER HOSPITAL, DENVER CO.; author and pub. 'The Joy of Stress' 1985; 'Stress for Success' 1989; syndicated radio feature 'The Stress Doctor'; Team Dr., Toronto Argonauts 1972–73; family practice, Newmarket, Ont. 1973–87; United Church; mem. Candn. Med. Assn.; recreations: skiing, tennis; Address: 7917 S. Fairfax Ct., Littleton, Colorado 80122.

**HANSON, Tennys McDonald,** B.Sc.; foundation executive; b. Winnipeg, Man. 7 Dec. 1951; d. Andrew Crosbie and Fern Louisa (Strachan) McDonald; e. Univ. of Toronto B.Sc. 1973; m. Douglas Hanson 4 Oct. 1989; VICE PRES. MOUNT SINAI HOSP. FOUND. 1989– ; Co-ord. Secondary Sch. Liaison Erindale Campus, Univ. of Toronto 1974, Co-ord. Community & Sch. Liaison 1976, Dir. Campus Relations 1981, Exec. Dir. Campus Devel. & Pub. Affairs 1984–89; Dir., Univ. of Toronto Alumni Assn.; Gov., St. Mildred Lightbourn Sch.; mem. Assn. Healthcare Philanthropy; Mississauga Bd. Trade; Centre for Philanthropy; Coll. of Electors Univ. of Toronto; Past Pres., Mississauga Bd. of Trade; Mississauga Symphonic Assoc.; Office: 332, 600 University Ave., Toronto, Ont. M5G 1X5.

**HANSSEN, Kenneth Ralph,** Q.C., B.A., LL.B.; judge; b. St. Boniface, Man. 5 Jan. 1945; s. Henning Osvald and Lillian Elvera (Timrose) H.; e. Inwood (Man.) Collegiate 1962; Univ. of Manitoba (United Coll.) B.A. 1965, LL.B. 1968; m. Elizabeth d. John and Caroline Larter 26 Apr. 1969; children: Mark Gregory, Corey Andrew, Kendra Elizabeth; JUDGE, COURT OF QUEEN'S BENCH, MANITOBA 1984– ; articled with Duncan & Co., Morden, Man. 1968–69, Assoc. 1969–71, Partner 1971–84; called to Bar. of Man. 1969; author 'The Constitutionality of Conditional Grant Legislation' in Man. Law Jour. 1967; 'Federal Declaratory Power under the British North America Act' in Man. Law Jour. 1968; Pres. Sun Valley Radio Inc. 1979–84; Instr. Man. Bar Admission Course 1983–84; Trustee Evangelical Lutheran Ch. of Can. 1974–80 (and Secy. Bd. of Trustees 1976–80); Secy., Pension Comte., Evangelical Lutheran Ch. in Canada 1986–93 (mem. 1985–93); Dir., Winnipeg Football Club (Blue Bombers) 1975–89; Candn. C. of C. 1974–76; Man. C. of C. 1981–83; Pres. Morden and Dist. C. of C. 1971–72; 1st Vice-Pres. Man. Bar Assn. 1984; Dean's Hon. List United Coll. 1964–65; Can. Law Book Prize 1966, 1968; Mr. Justice I. Nitikman Prize 1966; Man. Law Soc. Prize 1968; Univ. of Man. Law Class Valedictorian 1968; cr. Q.C. 1983; recreations: sports, football; Home: 5930 Southboine Dr., Winnipeg, Man. R3R 0B6; Office: Law Courts Bldg., 411 Broadway Ave., Winnipeg, Man. R3C 0V8.

**HANSULD, John Alexander,** B.Sc., M.Sc., Ph.D.; mining executive; b. Port Arthur, Ont. 16 Oct. 1931; s. Alvin F. and Effie J. (Agnew) H.; e. McMaster Univ., B.Sc. (Hons.) 1954; Univ. of B.C., M.Sc. 1956; McGill Univ., Ph.D. 1961; Harvard Bus. Sch., PMD 1968; m. Jane d. Thomas and Rosalind Rutherford 24 Sept. 1955; children: Cameron, Conrad, Stephanie; PRES., PROSPECTORS & DEVELOPERS ASSN. OF CANADA and VENCON GOLD CORP. 1991– ; Pres., Int. Platinium Corp. 1990–91; Pres. & C.E.O., Canamax Resources Inc. 1983–89; named Developer of the Year, Prospectors & Developers Assoc. 1988; Mining Man of 1988, Northern Miner; inducted into Alumni Hall of Fame, McMaster Univ. 1990; Dir. and Pres., Prospectors & Devel. Assn. of Can.; Mem., Candn. Inst. of Mining & Metallurgy; Ont. Profl. Engrs.; Assn. of Expl. Geochem. (founding mem. & former pres.); Dir., Mississauga Golf & Country; recreations: golf, curling, skiing; Club: Bd. of Trade of Metro. Toronto; Home: 1115 Algonquin Dr., Mississauga, Ont. L5H 1P3; Office: Ste. 1215, 111 Richmond St. W., Toronto, Ont. M5H 2G4.

**HANTHO, Charles Harold,** B.Sc.; company executive; b. Lethbridge, Alta. 1931; e. Univ. of Alta., B.Sc. (Chem. Engn.) 1953; m. Phyllis Mae Weir 1957; children: Karl Alan, Mark Albert, Jon Andrew, Heather Gale; CHRMN., PRES., CHIEF EXECUTIVE OFFR. & DIR., DOMINION TEXTILE INC.; Dir.: Dofasco Inc.; Inco Ltd.; TransAlta Corp.; Imasco Limited; joined C-I-L as Technical Asst., Plastics, Edmonton 1953; held various positions in production and marketing – Gen. Mgr., Plastics 1968–71; Vice-Pres., C-I-L 1971; was seconded to Imperial Chemical Industries, England, as Depy. Chrmn. of ICI Petrochemicals Division 1976; Pres. & C.E.O., C-I-L Inc. 1982; Chrmn. & C.E.O. 1984; retired 1988; joined Dominion Textile Inc. as Pres. & C.O.O. Jan. 1989; apptd. C.E.O. July 1989; apptd. Chrmn. Oct. 1990; Past Chrmn.: Soc. of Chemical Industry; Candn. Manfacturers' Assoc.; Candn. Chemical Producers' Assoc.; Mem. Policy Ctte., Business Counc. on Nat. Issues; Fellow, Cdn. Acad. of Engineering; Dir., Montreal YMCA Found.; Dir., Canadian Club of Montreal; Clubs: Mount Royal; Toronto; St. George's Golf & Country; Mont Bruno Country; recreations: golf, skiing, squash, scuba diving; Office: 1950 Sherbrooke St. W., Montreal, Que. H3H 1E7.

**HARA, Arthur S.,** C.M., B.Sc.; executive; b. Vancouver, B.C. 3 Apr. 1927; s. Takeo and Ryu (Koki) H.; e. Kobe Univ. Japan B.Sc. 1951; Harvard Grad. Bus Sch. Advanced Mgmt. Prog. 1980; Shizue d. Kokichi and Yae Horii 30 Jan. 1948; children: George, Elaine; CHRMN. MITSUBISHI CANADA LTD. 1983– ; Chrmn. United Oilseed Products Ltd.; Dir., Lakeside Farm Industries; The Molson Companies; joined present Co. 1962, Mgr. Grains Dept. 1968, Asst. to Pres. 1972, Vice Pres. 1975, Exec. Vice Pres. 1979; Past Chrmn. Vancouver Bd. Trade; Vice Chrmn. Candn. Ctte. Pacific Basin Econ. Council; Chrmn., Asia Pacific Found. of Can.; Gov., Bus. Counc. of B.C.; Dean's Adv. Ctte., Fac. of Comm., Univ. of B.C.; Patron, Vancouver Pub. Aquarium; Dir. Council Candn. Unity; recreations: swimming, reading; Clubs: Vancouver; Vancouver Lawn Tennis.

**HARBRON, John Davison,** M.A., C.D., F.R.S.A.; b. Toronto, Ont. 15 Sept. 1924; s. Tom and Sara Lillian (Peace) H.; e. Lawrence Park Coll. Inst., Toronto; Univ. of Toronto, B.A. 1946, M.A. 1948; post graduate studies, University of Havana 1947–48; m. Sheila Elizabeth. d. late Egerton Lester, 20 Sept. 1950; children: Patrick John, Christopher Thomas, Ann Kathryn; SENIOR RESEARCH ASSOCIATE, CANADIAN INSTITUTE OF STRATEGIC STUDIES 1990– , A founder and the first Vice-Pres. 1976–90; Chrmn., Dept. of Hist. and Econ., Canadian Services College, Royal Roads, Victoria, B.C. 1948–51; Candn, Ed. 'Business Week,' N.Y. 1956–60; Ed., 'Executive' Magazine 1961–66; Assoc. Ed., 'The Toronto Telegram' 1966–71; Mem., Mgmt. Review Group Task Force (MRG), Dept. of National Defence, Ottawa 1971–72; Foreign Affairs Analyst, Thomson Newspapers, Toronto 1972–90; Candn. Correspondent 'The Miami Herald', Miami, Fla. 1972– ; Candn. Ed. 'North South Magazine of the Americas' Miami, Fla. 1990– ; served in Royal Canadian Navy during Korean War 1950–53; Lieutenant-Commander RCN(R) retired; Gov., St. George's Coll., Toronto 1962–84; Pres., Couchiching Inst. on Public Affairs 1978–80; author 'Communist Ships and Shipping' 1963; 'This is Trudeau,' 'C.D. Howe,' 'Canada Without Québec,' 'Spanish Foreign Policy Since Franco' 1984; 'Trafalgar and the Spanish Navy' 1988; 'The Longest Battle: The RCN in the Battle of the Atlantic, 1939-1945' 1993; Commdr., Order of Isabella the Catholic (Spain); presented with Maria Moors Cabot Medal, Columbia Univ., N.Y. 1970; awarded Silver Jubilee Medal 1977; Fellow, Royal Soc. of Arts, London; Candn. Assoc. for Latin Am. and Caribbean Studies (CALACS), Ottawa; The Naval Reserve Assoc., Alexandria, Va.; Nat. Dir., Naval Officers' Assoc. of Canada (NOAC); recreations: sailing, philately; Clubs: Royal Canadian Military Institute; Barrie Yacht; Home: 4 Elstree Rd., Etobicoke, Ont. M9A 3Z1.

**HARCOURT, John Peter,** M.A.; professor; writer; b. Toronto, Ont. 26 July 1931; s. John Adam Alexander and Constance Aileen Gordon (Watson) H.; e. Bloor Coll.; Etobicoke H.S.; Univ. of Toronto; Cambridge Univ. M.A. 1958; children: John Adam, Jennifer Elizabeth; PROF., CARLETON UNIV. 1978– ; worked at British Film Inst. 1962–65; founded, Film Studies Dept., Queen's Univ. 1967; taught at York Univ. 1974–78; regular jury mem., Can. Counc.; Ont. Arts Counc.; Gov. Gen. Commemoration Medal 1978; Mem., Soc. for Cinema Studies (U.S.); Film Studies Assn. of Can.; author: 'Jean Pierre Lefebvre' 1981, 'Movies & Mythologies' 1977, 'Six European Directors' 1974; recreation: swimming; Home: 28 Marco Lane, Ottawa, Ont. K1S 5A2; Office: Carleton Univ., Ottawa, Ont. K1S 5B6.

**HARCOURT, Michael Franklin,** B.A., LL.B., M.L.A.; lawyer; politician; b. Edmonton, Alta. 6 Jan. 1943; s. Frank Norman Vernon and Stella Louise (Good) H.; e. Univ. of B.C., B.A. 1965, LL.B. 1968; m. Mai-Gret Wibecke d. Irene Pedersen 26 June 1971; one s.: Justen Michael; PREMIER OF THE PROVINCE OF BRITISH COLUMBIA 1991– ; Exec. Dir. Vancouver Community Legal Assistance Soc. 1969–71; Partner Lew & Co. 1971–79; Alderman City of Vancouver 1972–80; Mayor City of Vancouver 1980–86; el. M.L.A., Vancouver Centre 1986; el. M.L.A., Vancouver-Mount Pleasant 1991; Leader of the B.C. New Democratic Party 12 Apr. 1987; Leader of the Official Opposition in B.C. 1987–91; recreations: tennis, golf, skiing, jogging, basketball; Club: Jericho Tennis; Office: Parliament Bldgs., Victoria, B.C. V8V 1X4.

**HARDAKER, Roy Warren,** B.Sc., M.B.A., F.C.S.I.; stockbroker; b. Winnipeg, Man. 21 July 1929; s. George and Phyllis Jessie (Sellwood) H.; e. Univ. of Man. B.Sc. 1951; Univ. of W. Ont. M.B.A. 1956; m. Sharon Judith d. Reuben and Mary Levy 8 Feb. 1973; children (by first marriage): Bernadette Ann, Susanne Joan, John William, Matthew Warren; adopted daughter: Shelly Gaye; VICE PRES., RBC SECURITIES INC. 1989– ; served with Lord Strathcona's Horse 1951–54, rank Lt.; Tank Troop Leader Korea 1953–54; joined invest. bus. 1956; held various positions in various firms becoming Vice Pres. RBC Dominion Securities Inc.; contbg. ed. 'The MoneyLetter' 1978– ; Fellow, Founder and 1st Pres. Assn Fellows Candn. Securities Inst. 1976; Club: Royal Candn. Mil. Inst.; Home: 1270 Bryn Mawr Lane, R.R. #3, Campbellville, Ont. L0P 1B0; Office: Suite 300, 2 Bloor St. E., Toronto, Ont. M4W 1A8.

**HARDER, Rolf,** R.C.A.; graphic designer, painter; b. Hamburg, Germany 10 July 1929; s. Henry and Henriette (Loeffler) H.; e. Christianeum (High Sch.) Hamburg 1948; Hamburg Acad. of Fine Arts 1948–52; m. Maria-Inger d. Karl Rumberg 3 May 1958; children: Christopher, Vivian; self-employed ROLF HARDER & ASSOC.; travelling exhn. with Ernst Roch sponsored by Candn. Govt. in Can., U.S.A., Germany and Yugoslavia; rep. in group exhns. Can., U.S.A., Europe, S.Am., Japan, Russia; One of two Candn. representatives at 36th Venice Biennale Exper. Graphic Design Sec. 1973; rec'd over 100 nat. and internat. design awards; work publ. in prof. publications Can., U.S.A., Eng., Austria, Germany, Switzerland, Italy, France, Japan, Korea; mem. Alliance Graphique Internationale (Pres. Candn. Group); Royal Candn. Acad. of Arts; Internat. Centre for Typographic Arts; Fellow, Soc. Graphic Designers Can.; Am. Inst. Graphic Arts; recreations: tennis, music; Home: 43 Lakeshore Rd., Beaconsfield, Que. H9W 4H6; Office: 273-A Bord du Lac, Pointe-Claire, Que. H9S 4L1.

**HARDER, Vernon Peter,** B.A., M.A.; public servant; b. Winnipeg, Man. 25 Aug. 1952; s. John Norman and Mary (Tiessen) H.; e. Univ. of Waterloo, B.A. (Hons.) 1975; Queen's Univ., M.A. 1977; one s.: Andrew Peter Burnett; DEPUTY MINISTER, CITIZENSHIP AND IMMIGRATION CANADA and DEPUTY SOLICITOR GENERAL OF CANADA 1993– ; Parliamentary Intern 1976–77; Fgn. Serv. Offr. 1977–80; Chief of Staff to Rt. Hon. Joe Clark, Leader of the Opposition 1980–83; to Hon. Erik Nielsen, Depy. Prime Minister 1984–86; Extve. Dir., Immigration & Refugee Bd., Govt. of Can. 1986–91; Assoc. Depy. Min. (Immigration) 1991–93; Mennonite; recreations: tennis; club: Ottawa Tennis; Home: 20 Grove Ave., Ottawa, Ont. K1S 3A6; Office: Phase I, 23rd Floor, 50 Victoria St., Ottawa, Ont. K1A 1L1.

**HARDIN, Herschel R.,** B.A.; author, consultant; b. Vegreville, Alta. 17 Aug. 1936; s. Samuel H. and Marie (Goorevitch) H.; e. Queen's Univ. B.A. 1958; m. Marguerite d. Stewart and Evelyn McRae 14 Oct. 1961; children: Lisa, Kelsey; author: (non-fiction) 'A Nation Aware: The Canadian Economic Culture' 1974, 'Closed Circuits: The Sellout of Canadian Television' 1985, 'The Privatization Putsch' 1989, 'The New Bureaucracy: Waste and Folly in the Private Sector' 1992; (drama) 'Esker Mike and his Wife, Agiluk' 1973, 'The Great Wave of Civilization' 1976; assorted magazine and newspaper articles; radio broadcaster and commentator, CBC and Radio-Canada (public affairs, talks, the arts, books) 1966–73; Founder and Pres., Assn. for Public Broadcasting in BC. 1972–84; Gen. Mgr., Capital Cable Co-op. (advocacy) 1975–83; Newspaper Columnist, Toronto Star 1977–79; Public Policy Consultant 1978– ; Principal, Herschel Hardin Associates; lecturer; Dir., Candn. Broadcasting League 1974–79; Insur. Corp. of B.C. 1992– ; Mem., Writers' Union of Canada; B.C. Civil Liberties Assn. (Dir. 1965–74); Soc. Promoting Environmental Conservation (SPEC); Amnesty Internat.; B.C. Schizophrenia Soc.; Council of Canadians; recreations: tennis, badminton; clubs: West Vancouver Tennis, Hollyburn Badminton, West Vancouver Badminton; Home: 3498 Marine Dr., West Vancouver, B.C. V7V 1N2.

**HARDING, David James (Jim),** B.A. (Hons.), M.A., Ph.D.; professor of human justice; b. Swift Current, Sask. 28 June 1941; s. William Fredrick and Beatrice Louise (Lewis) H.; e. Regina Cent. Coll. 1959; Univ. of Sask., B.A. (Hons.) 1963, M.A. 1964; Simon Fraser Univ., Ph.D. 1970; m. Janet d. Vera and William Stoody; children: Reece Eugene, Joel Mica, Dagan Gabriel; PROF. OF HUMAN JUSTICE, UNIV. OF REGINA 1987– ; Mem., Univ. of Regina (Regina College), Cougar basketball team 1959–60, Univ. of Sask. Pups basketball team 1960–61; NDP federal candidate, 1964; Saskatoon by-election; Chrmn., Fed. Counc., Student

Union for Peace Action (SUPA) 1964–66; ind. environ. ('green') prov. candidate, 1982 (Regina-East); Pres., Regina's Core Community Group 1986–88 & 1989–90; Candidate for Regina City Council 1991; Rsch. Asst., Ctr. for Community Studies 1964; Teaching Asst./Sess. Lectr. in Psychol., Univ. of Sask. 1964–65; Lectr. in Psychol., Lakehead Univ. 1966; Asst. Prof. of Integrated Studies 1970–72 and Envir. Studies 1972–76, Univ. of Waterloo; Teaching Master, Confed. Coll. 1976; Dir. of Rsch., Sask. Alcoholism Comn. 1977–79; Assoc. Prof. of Soc. Work, Univ. of Regina 1980; Human Justice 1981–87; Dir., Prairie Justice Rsch., Univ. of Regina 1982–85, 1987–91; Acting Coordinator, Sch. of Human Justice 1989–90; Dir., Sch. of Human Justice 1990–93; Bd. of Listeners, World Uranium Hearings, Austria 1992; awards: Can. Counc. Fellowships 1968–70, Non-Medical Use of Drugs Directorate grants 1977–78; Health & Welfare Rsch. on Drug abuse (RODA) grant 1978; Sask. Health Rsch. Bd. socio-health grant 1982; Soc. Sci. & Humanities Rsch. Counc. Human Context of Science & Technology Strategic Grant 1984–87, Univ. of Regina Presidents Fund 1990, 1993; Consultant, National Film Board award winning film 'Uranium'; author and narrator: 'Pharmaceutical Control' CBC Ideas Series 1983; editor: 'Social Justice and Social Policy: The NDP Government During the Blakeney Years' 1994; articles or book reviews in 'Alternatives,' 'The Ecologist,' 'J. of Impact Assessment,' 'Can. J. of Criminology,' 'J. of Can. Family Physician,' 'Can. Rev. of Sociology and Anthropology,' 'Prairie Forum,' as well as other journals and magazines and several research reports on pharmaceutical drugs; a Rsch. Series on Aboriginal Justice and one on Uranium Mining Inquiries; chapters in several Sociology & other books on educational reform, environmental health, alcohol & drugs, social change, aboriginal justice and public inquiries; Presentations at many professional & academic bodies including: Western Assn. of Sociology & Anthropology (WASA); Candn. Sociology & Anthropology Assn. (CSAA); Candn. Addictions Foundation, Socialist Studies; Candn. Assn. of Schools of Social Work; Am. Criminology Soc.; Candn. Peace Rsch.; German Ethnology Soc. and at hundreds of community workshops and conferences throughout Canada; recreations: organic farming; Home: 1909 Toronto St., Regina, Sask. S4P 1M9; Office: Univ. of Regina, Regina, Sask. S4S 0A2.

**HARDING, Keith John,** F.C.I.A., F.I.A., M.A.A.A., A.S.A.; b. London, Engl. 8 Apr. 1933; s. Ernest John and Constance Grace (Stone) H.; e. Harrow County Grammar Sch., Harrow, Middlesex 1948; m. Carol d. George and Victoria Goodburn 21 Dec. 1957; children: Graham Michael, Sylvia Frances, Christine Andrea; Consulting Actuary, The Alexander Consulting Group, Calgary, Alta. 1990–91; Retired 1991; Cons. Actuary 1971–74; Gen. Mgr. Wananesa Mutual Life Ins. Co. 1974–81; Pres. & C.E.O., Royal Life Canada 1981–87; Pres. and Dir. Royal Life Ins. Co. of Can. 1983–87; Vice-Pres., Johnson & Higgins Willis Faber Ltd., Calgary, Alta. 1987–90; mem., City of Calgary Taxi Commission; Vice Pres., & Dir., Chinook Trail Assoc.; past Dir., Candn. Centre for Creative Tech. 1982–89; past Dir. & Chrmn. Land Acquisition Ctte., Bruce Trail Assn. 1984–87; past Dir. and Treas. Social Planning Counc. of Winnipeg 1978–81; past Chrmn. Winnipeg Presbytery United Ch. of Can. 1979–81; Past Dir. Peel Career Assessment Services Inc. 1982–85; mem. Southminster United Ch. Calgary, Alta.; recreations: hiking, bridge; Home: 3405 – 10th St. S.W., Calgary, Alta. T2G 3H7.

**HARDSTAFF, William J.,** B.Sc., P.Eng.; business executive; b. Sask. 21 Apr. 1926; e. Univ. of Sask. B.Sc. (Civil Eng.) 1950; 4 children; Dir.: Altafund Investment Corp.; Marks Work Wearhouse Ltd.; Tiverton Petroleums Ltd.; Pres., Seabreaker Resources Ltd.; Refinery Sales Mgr. Royalite Oil Co. Ltd. 1951–56; Sr. Vice Pres. Trimac Ltd. 1956–76; Pres. Sultran Ltd. 1976–78; Pres. GenEnergy Resources Ltd. 1980–82; Pres., American Eagle Petroleums Ltd. 1982–89; mem. Assn. Prof. Engs., Geols. & Geophys. Alta.; recreations: boating, fishing; Clubs: Calgary Petroleum; Home: 1005 – 80 Point McKay Cres. N.W., Calgary, Alta. T3B 4W1.

**HARDWICK, David Francis,** M.D.; educator; b. Vancouver, B.C. 24 Jan. 1934; s. late Walter Henry Wilmot and Iris Lillian (Hyndman) H.; e. Univ. of B.C. M.D. 1957; Cert. Pathol. 1965; m. Margaret McArthur d. late Robert Lang, Vancouver, B.C. 22 Aug. 1956; children: Margaret Frances, Heather Iris, David James; ASSOC. DEAN, RSCH. & PLANNING, FACULTY OF MED., UNIV. OF B.C. since 1990; residencies Montreal Gen., Vancouver Gen., Children's Los Angeles 1957–65; Clin. Instr. Univ. S. Cal. and Univ. of B.C. 1960–64; Asst. Prof. Univ. of B.C. 1965, Assoc. Prof. 1969, Prof. of Pathol. 1974, Prof. and Head of Pathol. 1976–90; Pediatric Pathol. Vancouver Gen. Hosp. and Children's Hosp. 1965–69; Chrmn. Med. Adv. Ctte., Children's Hosp. 1969–86; Dir. Children's Hosp. and Pediatric Pathol. Vancouver Gen. Hosp. 1969–90; Dir. Labs. Vancouver Gen. Hosp. 1976–90; rec'd Queen's Silver Jubilee Medal 1978; Alumni Award, Univ. of B.C. 1987; Wallace Wilson Leadership Award 1990; publisher B.C. Geog. Series, Candn. Culture Series, Tantalus Research Ltd.; co-ed. 'Intermediary Metabolism of the Liver' 1973; 'Directing the Clinical Laboratory' 1990; author or co-author numerous articles prof. journs.; Past Pres. Soc. for Pediatric Pathol.; Pres., Internat. Acad. of Pathology 1992–94; Past Pres., U.S. & Candn. Acad. of Pathology; mem. Candn. Med. Assn.; B.C. Med. Assn. and other med. assns.; Home: 727 W. 23rd Ave., Vancouver, B.C. V5Z 2A7; Office: #317 – 2194 Health Sciences Mall, Vancouver, B.C. V6T 1W5.

**HARDY, John C.,** B.Sc., F.C.A.; investment; b. S. Africa 4 Nov. 1941; s. George and Ethel (Goss) H.; e. Sutton Valence, Kent 1959; St. Andrews Univ. B.Sc. 1963; m. Patricia Lewis 3 May 1969; children: Rupert, Jessica; Dir., Hendron Financial Group 1986; Leitch Video Ltd.; SHL Systemhouse Ltd.; joined Price Waterhouse, London, Eng. 1963–68; Charterhouse Development Ltd. London, Eng. 1968–79, served as Acct., Invest. Extve., Dir.; Pres. Charterhouse Canada Ltd. 1979–86; Clubs: Walton Heath Golf (UK); St. Enodoc Golf (UK); Home: 48 Rathnelly Ave., Toronto, Ont. M4V 2M3.

**HARDY, John Christopher,** B.Sc., M.Sc., Ph.D., FRSC; physicist, science communicator; b. Montreal, Que. 10 July 1941; s. Noel Woodburn and Ethel May (Collins) H.; e. McGill Univ. B.Sc. 1961, M.Sc. 1963, Ph.D. 1965; m. Lynn Helen d. Annette and Bruce Frederick 3 June 1964; children: Ericka, Kirsten, Bruce, Alana; DIR., TASCC DIV., ATOMIC ENERGY OF CANADA, CHALK RIVER and CHRMN., BD. OF DIR., DEEP RIVER SCIENCE ACADEMY 1986– ; NRC post-doctoral fellow, Oxford Univ. 1965–67; Miller Rsch. Fellow, Lawrence Radiation Lab., Berkeley, Calif. 1967–69; Staff Physicist 1969–70; Assoc. Rsch. Offr., Atomic Energy of Canada, Chalk River 1970–74; Sr. Rsch. Offr. 1975– ; Head, Nuclear Physics Branch 1983–86; Scientific Assoc., Cern, Geneva (sabbatical leave) 1976–77; Editor, 'North Renfrew Times' 1972– ; D.W. Ambridge Prize (outstanding McGill Grad. with science Ph.D.) 1965; Herzberg Medal (Candn. Assn. of Physicists) 1976; FRSC 1979; Rutherford Medal in Physics (Royal Soc. of Can.) 1981; Fellowship, Am. Physical Soc. 1983; Mem., Candn. Assn. of Physicists; author/co-author of over 180 sci. articles in refereed profl. jours. & over 200 articles & editorials pub. in newspapers; recreations: reading, writing, skiing, swimming; Home: 108 Bessborough St., Deep River, Ont. K0J 1P0; Office: AECL Research, Chalk River Labs, Chalk River, Ont. K0J 1J0.

**HARDY, Kenneth George,** B.A., M.B.A., Ph.D.; educator; b. Sarnia, Ont. 13 Nov. 1941; s. George Williams and Alice Idell (Jardine) H.; e. Univ. of W. Ont. B.A. 1963; Univ. of Mich. M.B.A. 1966, Ph.D. 1969; m. Rosemary d. George and Viola Harris 26 Oct. 1963; children: Stephen Andrew, Suzanne Kathleen; R.A. BARFORD PROF. IN MARKETING COMMUNICATIONS, UNIV. OF W. ONT. 1992– , Assoc. Dean, Research 1993 & Director, National Centre for Management Rsch. and Development 1993; Prof. of Bus. Adm., Univ. of W. Ont. 1988– ; Dir., Hons. Bus. Adm. Prog.; Pres. K.G. Hardy Associates Ltd.; Dir. G.F. Sterne and Sons Ltd. Brantford; Asst. Prof. present Univ. 1968, Assoc. Prof. 1972 and 1974–86; Counsel, Special Ctte. Investig. Trends Food Prices Govt. Can. 1973; Visiting Prof. North Eur. Mgmt. Inst. Oslo, Norway 1973–74; Visiting Prof. INSEAD Fontainebleau, France 1987; cons. various studies, seminars govts. Can., Ont., N.B., N.S. and bus. corps.; nat. and internat. lectr. execs.; Pres. London N. Lib. Assn. 1975–78, Mgr. London N. El. Campaign 1975; community service incls. London Goodwill Inds. Assn. (Dir. 1971), Un. Way Campaign 1979, London C. of C. (various cttes.); recipient Touche Ross Award mgmt. publs. 1989; sr. author 'Canadian Marketing: Cases and Concepts' four eds. 1978, '85, '88, '94; 'Marketing Channel Management: Strategic Planning and Tactics' 1988; author numerous publs.; mem. Am. Mktg. Assn.; London Hunt and Country Club; recreations: polo, hunt to hounds, skiing, music; Home: 32 Sprucedale Court, London, Ont. N5X 2N9; Office: London, Ont. N6A 3K7.

**HARDY, Walter Newbold,** B.Sc., Ph.D., F.R.S.C.; educator; physicist; b. Vancouver, B.C. 25 March 1940; s. Walter Thomas and Julia Marguerite (Mulroy) H.; e. Burnaby N. High Sch.; Univ. of B.C. B.Sc. 1961, Ph.D. 1965; m. Sheila Lorraine d. Ernest and Elizabeth Hughes 10 July 1959; two s. Kevin James, Steven Wayne; PROF. OF PHYSICS, UNIV. OF B.C. 1976– ; Consultant, CTF Systems; Powertech; Rutherford Meml. Fellow Centre d'Etudes Nucleaires de Saclay, France 1964–66; mem., tech. staff Spectroscopy Group, North American Rockwell Science Center, Cal. 1966–71; Assoc. Prof. of Physics present Univ. 1971; Visiting Prof., École Normale Superiéure, Paris, 1980–81, 1985, 1988; Alfred P. Sloan Fellow 1972–74; Herzberg Medal Candn. Assn. Phys. 1978; Stacie Prize Nat. Rsch. Council Can. 1978; Canada Council Killam Fellowship 1984–86; Killam Research Prize 1986–88; B.C. Science Council Gold Medal 1989; Gold Medal for Achievement, Candn. Assn. Phys. 1993; holds two patents precision microwave instrumentation; author over 90 publs. condensed matter phys.; mem., Candn. Assn. Phys.; Am. Phys. Soc.; recreations: hiking, piano; Home: 3076 W. 34th St., Vancouver, B.C. V6N 2K2; Office: Vancouver, B.C. V6T 1Z1.

**HARDY, Yvan J.,** B.Sc.A., M.Sc., Ph.D.; forest engineer; b. Québec City, Qué. 11 Aug. 1941; s. Maurice A. and Fernande J. (Gagnon) H.; e. Univ. Laval B.Sc.A. 1965, M.Sc. 1968; N.Y. State Univ. Ph.D. 1971; m. Thérèse d. Yvette and Paul-Emile Poirier 12 Aug. 1967; children: Mireille, Vincent; ASST. DEPY. MIN., FORESTRY CANADA, Ottawa 1991– ; Asst. Prof. Univ. Laval 1970, Prof. 1978–85; Chrmn. of Forest Mgmt. and Silviculture 1975–78, Vice Dean 1979–80, Dean of Foresterie et Geodesie 1980–85; Dir. Gen., Forestry Canada, Quebec Region 1985–91; Cons. to govts. and forest ind. in forest entom.; Comnr. ad hoc Bureau of Pub. Hearings on Environment Govt. Qué.; author or co-author 18 scient. publs., over 30 tech. reports and articles; Invited Lectr., Entom. Soc. Can. 1978–82; IUFRO Dornoch, Scot. 1980; Pacific Science Assn. Dunedin, N.Z. 1983; Soc. of Amer. Foresters, Burlington, VT 1984; International Congress of Forestry, Qué. 1984; World Forestry Congresses, Mexico 1985 and Paris 1991; ACFAS, Montréal 1986; Assn. des Entomologistes de langue francaise, Trois-Rivières 1986; FAO, Fredericton, N.B. 1987; Assoc. forestière québecoise 1987–88; Dir., Conseil de la Recherche forestière du Québec; Pres., Ordre des ingénieurs forestiers du Qué. 1980 (Dir. 1979–80); Assn. forestière quebecoise; Candn. Inst. Forestry; Knight of Malta 1985; Sigma Xi; recreations: jogging, fishing, philately, sailing; Home: 1739 Autumnridge Dr., Gloucester, Ont. K1C 6Z1; Office: 351, boul. St. Joseph, Hull, Qué. K1A 1G5.

**HARE, Ewan Nigel Christian,** B.A., D.P.A.; diplomat; b. Southport, U.K. 11 May 1939; s. Ewan John and Muriel Jeanette (Jones) H.; e. Coll. Cévenole, Le Chambon sur Lignon, Haute Loire, France 1956; Earlham Coll. B.A. 1961; Carleton Univ. D.P.A. 1964; m. Raina Ho d. Yu Lin and Marguerite Ho 10 June 1985; children: Penny, Jonathan, Alexa; COMMONWEALTH DEPUTY SECRETARY-GENERAL (DEVELOPMENT COOPERATION) 1993– ; Treas. Bd. Sec. 1962–64; CUSO Teacher, Sarawak 1964–66; Prog. Offr., C.I.D.A. 1966–69; 1st Sec., Candn. High Comn., Accra, Ghana 1969–72; Reg. Dir., Asia S.E., C.I.D.A. 1972–76; Reg. Dir., Cent. & S. Africa 1976–78; Dir. Gen., Resources Branch 1978–80; Dir.-Gen., U.N. Programs 1980–84; Candn. Ambassador to Zaire, Rwanda, Burundi, Congo 1984–87; Dir., Africa Trade Develop. Div., Dept. of External Affairs, Ottawa 1987–88; Dir-Gen., Industrial Cooperation Program, C.I.D.A. 1988–91; Canadian High Commissioner to Nigeria and Canadian Ambassador to Benin 1991–93; Office: Commonwealth Secretariat, Marlborough House, Pall Mall, London SW1Y 5HX, U.K.

**HARE, Frederick Kenneth,** C.C., O.Ont., B.Sc., Ph.D., F.K.C., F.R.S.C., LL.D., D.Litt., D.S.Litt., D.Sc.; b. Wylye, England, 5 Feb. 1919; s. Frederick Eli and Irene (Smith) H.; e. Windsor Grammar Sch., Eng.; King's Coll., Univ. of London, B.Sc. (Special) (1st Class Hons. in Geog.) 1939; Univ. of Montréal, Ph.D. (Geog.) 1950; m. Helen Morrill d. Cliffe Alvin and Margaret Neilson; two s., Christopher, Robin; one d. Elissa Beatrice; CHANCELLOR, TRENT UNIV. 1988– ; UNIVERSITY PROFESSOR EMERITUS IN GEOGRAPHY, UNIV. OF TORONTO 1984– , and Chair Adv. Bd., Inst. of Internat. Programs 1990– ; Chair, Technical Adv. Panel on Nuclear Safety, Ont. Hydro 1991– ; Mem., Advisory Panel on Research & Development, AECL Research 1991– ; Mem. Bd. of Dirs., Candn. Institute for Rsch. in Atmospheric Chemistry 1990–93; Lectr. Univ. of Manchester 1940–41; Operational Meteorologist in Air Min. 1941–45; Asst. Prof. of Geog., McGill Univ. 1945, and subsequently Prof. and Chrmn., Dept. of Geog.; Warden of Peterson Residences 1946–50; Dean, Faculty of Arts & Science 1962–64; Prof. of Geog., King's Coll., Univ. of London 1964–66; Master of Birkbeck Coll. there 1966–68; Pres., Univ. of B.C. 1968, resigned 1969; Univ. Prof. of Geography and Physics, Univ. of Toronto 1976–84 and Provost of Trinity Coll.

1979–86; Dir., Resources for the Future Inc. 1968–80; Mem. of Corporation 1989– ; Dir.-Gen. of Research Coordination, Environment-Canada (on leave from U. of T.) 1972–73; Dir., Inst. for Environmental Studies, Univ. of Toronto 1974–79; Chrmn., Candn. Climate Program Planning Bd. 1979–90; author of 'The Restless Atmosphere' (textbook on climatology) 1953; 'On University Freedom' 1967; co-author of 'Climate Canada' (1974, 2nd ed. 1979); many articles on climatol., meteorol, and geog. in scient. journs.; Co-Chrmn., Nat. Acad. of Sci. (U.S.A.)/Roy. Soc. Can., Study of Acid Precipitation 1980–82; Chrmn., Peer Review of Federal Candn. Govt.'s LRTAP (Long-Range Transport of Airborne Pollutants) Program, Roy. Soc. of Can. 1983–84; Study of Nuclear Winter Phenomenon, Roy. Soc. of Can. 1984; Comn. on Lead in Candn. Environment, Roy. Soc. of Can. 1984–86; Comnr., Ont. Nuclear Safety Review 1987–88; Chair, Candn. Global Change Program Bd., Royal Soc. of Can. 1989; Chair, Special Ctte. on the Environment, City of Toronto 1989–90; Gov., Trinity Coll. Sch. 1979–86; Mem. of Corp., Trinity Coll. 1979– ; mem., Nat. Research Council of Can., 1962–64; Am. Meteorol. Soc. (Council); Chrmn. of Bd., Arctic Inst. of N. Am., 1963; Hon. Fellow, Am. Geog. Soc., 1962; Councillor, Assn. of Am. Geogs. and Candn. Assn. of Geogs., 1964; Chrmn. Adv. Comte. on Canadian Urban Demonstration Program 1976; Special Program Panel on the Ecosciences, NATO, 1975; Pres. Sigma Xi 1986–87; awards: Hon. LL.D. (Queen's Univ. 1964, Univ. of Western Ont. 1968, Trent Univ. 1979, Univ. of Toronto 1987); Hon. D.Litt. (Memorial Univ., Nfld. 1985); Hon. D.S.Litt. (Thorneloe Coll., Sudbury 1984); Hon. D.Sc. (McGill 1969, Adelaide 1974, York Univ. 1978, Windsor 1988); Hon. Certificate of Grad., Nat. Defence Coll., Can. 1986; Fellow, King's Coll. 1967; Fellow, Royal Soc. of Can. 1968; Patterson Medal, Canadian Meteorological Service 1973; Massey Medal, Roy. Candn. Geog. Soc. 1974; Patron's Medal of Royal Geog. Soc. of U.K. 1977; U. of T. Alumni Award 1982; R.S.C. Centenary Medal 1982; Co-recipient, first award of Dawson Medal, Royal Soc. of Can. 1987; IMO Prize, World Meteorological Orgn. 1988; Cullum Medal, Am. Geog. Soc. 1987; Hon. Fellow, Woodsworth Coll., Univ. of Toronto 1987; Hon. Fellow, Trinity Coll., Univ. of Toronto 1991; Officer, Order of Canada 1978; Companion, Order of Canada 1987; Order of Ontario 1989; Anglican; recreations: music, gardening; Address: 301 Lakeshore Rd. W., Oakville, Ont. L6K 1G2.

**HAREL, Hubert,** M.B.A.; business executive; b. Montreal, Que. 13 Aug. 1944; s. René and Germaine H.; e. Univ. of Houston M.B.A. 1967; m. Madeleine Fortier 5 Oct. 1974; children: Marc-André, Jean-Nicholas; Extve. Vice-Pres., Le Groupe Juste pour Rire Inc. 1991; Sales Representative, Candn. General Electric (Data Processing) 1968; Mgr. Marketing Rsch., Pfizer 1969–70; Asst. Dir., Marketing Research / Director, Master Charge / Vice-Pres., Marketing, Provincial & National Bank of Canada 1970–84; Pres. & C.E.O., Premier Choix: TVEC Inc. 1984–91; Home: 7800 Sartre Ave., Brossard, Qué. J4X 1K2.

**HAREL, Louise,** B.A., LL.L.; avocate, députée; née Ste-Thérèse de Blainville 22 avril 1946; f. Roger et Mignonne (Laroche) H.; é. Séminaire Ste-Thérèse B.A. 1967; Univ. de Montréal LL.L. 1979; enfant: Catherine; DEPUTEE DU COMTE, HOCHELAGA-MAISONNEUVE, L'ASSEMBLEE NAT. DU QUE. 1981– ; elue députée du comte Hochelaga-Maisonneuve, L'Assemblée nat. du Qué. 13 avril 1981,réelue déc. 1985; sept. 1989; Min. de l'Immigration et des communautes culturelles du Qué. 1984; Prés., Comn. parlementaire de l'Education 1989– ; bureau: Hôtel du Parlement, Québec, Qué. G1A 1A4.

**HAREL GIASSON, Francine,** B.A., B.Ped., L.Ped., M.B.A., Ph.D.; university professor; b. Montreal, Que. 28 Oct. 1940; d. Theobald and Lucille (Cadieux) Harel; e. Univ. of Montreal B.A. 1959, B.Ped. 1960, L.Ped. 1961; Ecole des Hautes Etudes Commerciales de Montréal M.B.A. 1972, Ph.D. 1981; m. Bertin s. Gerard Giasson 23 June 1962; children: Isabelle, Benoit; PROFESSOR, ECOLE DES HAUTES ETUDES COMMERCIALES; Teacher, Coll. Marguerite-Bourgeoys 1960–63; Teacher, Comn. des Ecoles Catholiques de Montréal 1963–70; Prof., Royal Military College of St. Jean; joined Ecole des Hautes Commerciales 1976; Dir. of Programs 1985–91; Dir., John Labatt Ltd.; General Trustco of Canada; Trust Général du Canada; John Labatt Foundation; author of several scientific & professional articles & lectures; Office: 5255 avenue Decelles, Montreal, Que. H3T 1V6.

**HARGREAVES, Andrew,** Ph.D.; university professor; b. Accrington, Lancashire, England 13 Feb. 1951; s. Albert and Doris (Kenyon) H.; e. Accrington Grammar Sch. 1969; Univ. of Sheffield, B.A. 1972; Univ. of Leeds, Ph.D. 1985; m. Pauline d. William and Louise Beales 1973; children: Stuart Andrew, Lucy Gemma; PROF., ONT. INST. FOR STUDIES IN EDUCATION 1987– ; Teacher, Hartshorne Primary Sch. 1973–74; Rsch. Student, Univ. of Leeds 1974–77; Lectr., Trinity & All Saints Coll., Leeds 1977–79; Open Univ. 1979–80; Oxford Univ. 1981–85; Warwick Univ. 1985–87; author: 'Two Cultures of Schooling' 1986, 'Curriculum and Assessment Reform' 1989; 'Changing Teachers, Changing Times' 1994; co-author: 'Personal and Social Education' 1988; 'What's Worth Fighting For: Working Together For Your School' 1991; co-editor: 'Curriculum Practice' 1983; 'Classrooms and Staffrooms' 1984; 'Educational Policies' 1989; 'Understanding Teacher Development' 1992; 'Teacher Development and Educational Change' 1992; recreations: hiking, travel, snooker, bowling, family activities; Home: 2189 Hixon St., Oakville, Ont. L6L 1T6; Office: 252 Bloor St. W., Toronto, Ont. M5S 1V6.

**HARGREAVES, Terence Albert;** broadcast executive; b. Glastonbury, England 14 July 1936; s. Albert and Mary Agatha (Bonsall) H.; e. Jodi d. Norman and Shirley White 19 April 1975; children: Tyler, Blake; EXECUTIVE DIRECTOR, RADIO CANADA INTERNATIONAL 1991– ; Reporter, Windsor Star, Hamilton Spectator; private Radio & TV, CBC Radio & TV for 25 years in Toronto, Ottawa, Montreal; Extve. Producer, National TV News 1970–71; Parliamentary Bureau Chief 1972–80; Government Relations Mgr., Dome Petroleum & Senior Political Writer Macleans 1980–85; Senior Advisor to Pres., CBC 1985–91; Grad., National Defence College; Mem., CIIA, CISS; recreations: tennis, cooking, piano; clubs: Rideau, Albany; Office: 1055 René Levesque Blvd. E., Montréal, Qué. H2L 4S5

**HARGROVE, Clifford Kingston,** B.A., B.Sc., M.Sc., Ph.D.; elementary particle physicist; b. Saint John, N.B. 22 Nov. 1928; s. James William and the late Olive Amelia (Kingston) H.; e. Saint John High Sch. 1945; Univ. of N.B. B.A. 1949; Univ. of Ottawa 1952–53; McGill Univ. B.Sc. 1955, M.Sc. 1957, Ph.D. 1961; one s. Ian Kingston; RESEARCH OFFICER, CRPP, CARLETON UNIV. 1990– ; Adjunct Prof. Carleton Univ. 1977– ; Hosp. Physicist, Royal Victoria Hosp. 1961; Asst. Rsch. Offr. NRC 1961, Assoc. Rsch. Offr. 1965, Sr. Rsch. Offr. 1973–84; Prin. Rsch. Offr., Nat. Rsch. Council of Canada 1984–90, Sect. Head High Energy Physics Div. 1979–90; co-editor: 'High Energy Physics and Nuclear Structure' 1975; author or co-author over 100 publs. profl. jours.; mem. LAMPF Users Group 1976–79; Council IPP 1970–74; CAP; APS (Fellow, 1992); Inst. of Particle Physics; recreations: tennis, bridge, sailing; Club: RA Tennis & ACBL; Home: 121 Starwood Rd., Nepean, Ont. K2G 1Z6; Office: Colonel By Drive, Ottawa, Ont. K1S 5B6.

**HARKER, William Clinton,** B.E.; commodity broker; b. Regina, Sask. 18 Dec. 1938; s. late Gordon and Mary (Brady) H.; e. McGill Univ. B.E. 1962; m. Anne Kathryn d. late Herbert and late Kathryn Hughes 1962; children: David, Stacey; Mng. Director, Dir. & C.E.O., Rudolf Wolff & Co. Ltd. 1991– ; Dir., Rudolf Wolff Fund Management; Rudolf Wolff & Co.; joined IBM 1962–72; Datacrown 1972–75; Bank of Montreal 1975–84; Royal Trust 1984–91; Rudolf Wolff & Co. 1992– ; mem., Institute of Dirs., Capital Club, Broadgate; Home: 88 Hermitage Court, Knighten St., London E1 9PW England.

**HARLAND, Harry Edward,** B.Sc.(Hons.), F.S.A.; retired insurance executive; b. Minnedosa, Man. 24 Sept. 1927; s. Thomas Edward and Florence Mabel (Millward) H.; e. Moorepark (Man.) High Sch.; Univ. of Man., B.Sc.(Hons.) 1951; m. Edith Phyllis Catherine, d. Herbert Budgen, Winnipeg, Man., 20 Jan. 1953; children: Carol Louise, Shelley Ruth, Mary Edith, Thomas Edward; joined Great-West Life Assurance Co. 1952, retired as Exec. Vice Pres., Corporate Resources 1987; Dir. and Treas., Health Sciences Centre, Winnipeg; Pres., Manitoba Chamber Orch. 1988–91; Fellow, Soc. of Actuaries; Cdn. Inst. of Actuaries; mem. Internat. Actuarial Assoc.; Anglican; recreations: tennis, skiing, canoeing; Clubs: Unicity Racquet; Manitoba; Home: 501 Bower Blvd., Winnipeg, Man. R3P 0L7.

**HARLEY, Calvin B.,** Ph.D.; associate professor; b. Moncton, N.B. 9 June 1952; s. Ralph H. and Mabel E. (Gartley) H.; e. Univ. of Waterloo B.Sc. 1975; McMaster Univ. Ph.D. 1980; m. Deborah d. J. Barry and Gloria French 8 Oct. 1972; children: Leyenda, Gabriel, Jason; ASSOC. PROF., DEPT. OF BIOCHEM., MCMASTER UNIV. 1989– , Asst. Prof. 1982–89; post-doct. with J.M. Smith, Univ. of Sussex on evolution of learning 1980–81 and H. Boyer, Univ. of Calif. on promoter structure-function in prokaryotes 1981–82; current rsch. on molecular biol. of aging and terminal differentiation; telomere structure and function; op. support from MRC, NIA; Mem., Candn. Assn. of Gerontol.; Gerontological Soc. of Am.; Home: 1730 University Ave., Palo Alto, CA 94301 USA; Office: Geron Corp., 200 Constitution Dr., Menlo Park, CA 94025 USA.

**HARLEY, David Murray,** Q.C., M.A.; lawyer; b. Saint John, N.B. 1 May 1931; s. Edward Burnett and Constance Aileen (Murray) H.; e. Rothesay Coll. Sch. 1948; Univ. of Toronto, B.A. 1952, MA. 1953; Rhodes Scholar, N.B. 1953; Oxford Univ., B.A. 1955, B.C.L. 1956, M.A. 1959; m. Birgitta d. Frederick and Gertrud Capps 27 May 1961; children: Robert Adam, Anne Margareta; PARTNER, BORDEN & ELLIOT 1967– ; called to Bar of N.B. 1957; Ontario 1962; apptd. Queen's Counsel 1972; practiced with Carter, Taylor & Ryan 1956–62; Borden & Elliot 1962– ; Mem., Law Soc. of Upper Canada; Candn. Bar Assn.; Internat. Bar Assn.; New York State Bar Assn.; Chrmn., CBA Legis. & Law Reform Ctte. 1984–85; CBAO Extve. Mem. 1979–83, 1985–87; Chrmn., CBAO Cont. Legal Edn. Ctte. 1979–81; Counsel to Ont. Legis. Assembly Select Ctte. On Company law 1973–75; Chair, U.S.-Canada Sub. Ctte., Internat. Law and Practice Sect., New York State Bar Assoc.; Dir., Sony of Canada Ltd.; Austin Knight Canada Inc.; Corrosion Serv. Co. Ltd.; Anglican Ch. of Can.; Delta Kappa Epsilon Frat.; recreations: squash, tennis, skiing, gardening; Clubs: University Club of Toronto; Ontario; Vincent's Club; Oxford; Home: 8 Maple Ave., Toronto, Ont. M4W 2T6; Office: 44th Flr., Scotia Plaza, 40 King St. W., Toronto, Ont. M5H 3Y4.

**HARLEY, Graham David,** M.A., D.Phil.; actor; director; b. Willenhall, Staffs. Eng. 20 Oct. 1942; s. Harry and Minnie (Russell) H.; e. Queen Mary's Grammar Sch. Walsall 1961; Brasenose Coll. Oxford B.A. 1964, M.A. 1967, D.Phil. 1971; Asst. Lectr. in Eng. Univ. of Aberdeen 1965–69; Visiting Prof. Univ. of W. Ill. 1969–70; Asst. Prof. of Eng. Dartmouth Coll. N.H. 1970–72, Univ. of Toronto 1972–74; Founding Artistic Dir. Phoenix Theatre Toronto 1974–83; mem., Stratford Festival Co. 1981–82; Shaw Festival Co. 1989–90; Actor (stage, TV, radio), Dir. Man. Theatre Centre, Candn. Opera Co. 1983– ; Chrmn. Adv. Ctte. George Brown Coll. Theatre Dept.; mem. Can. Council Theatre Adv. Ctte.; Ont. Arts Council Programme Evaluation, Theatre Training; Founding Gov. Dora Mavor Moore Theatre Awards; nominated outstanding performance by male in leading role, Dora Awards 1987; lectr. Nat. Theatre Sch. Montréal, Univ. of Ottawa Theatre Dept., Equity Showcase; recreations: piano, squash, theatre, opera, tennis, reading, gardening; Address: 714 Adelaide St. W., Toronto, Ont. M6J 1B1.

**HARLEY, James Ian,** D.Mus.; composer; b. Vernon, B.C. 23 Sept. 1959; m. Norman David and Audrey Joan (Copperthwaite) H.; e. Vernon Sr. S.S. 1977; Western Washington Univ. B.Mus. 1982; Royal Academy of Music (London) 1983–85; Univ. de Paris 1985–87; Chopin Academy of Music (Warsaw) 1987–88; McGill Univ. D.Mus. 1994; m. Maria d. Aleksy and Henryka Trochimczyk 28 June 1987; children: Marcin, Ania, Ian; commissions: Soc. de musique contemporaine du Qué.; Polish Ctr. of Art for Young People; Polish Soc. for Contemp. Music; Vancouver Bach Choir; Western Washington Univ.; Kelowna Internat. Festival of the Arts; Huddersfield Fest.; prizes: C.A.P.A.C. Young Composers Competition; CBC Young Composers Comp.; Lutoslawski Internat. Composer Comp. Poland; Irino Prize Japan; Lloyd's Bank Comp. England; MC2 Assn. Comp. France; broadcasts: CBC/Radio Canada, Great Britian, Ireland, Denmark, Poland; Instructor, Fac. of Music, McGill Univ.; McConnell Doct. Fellowship, McGill Univ.; Polish Govt. Scholarship; Mendelssohn Scholarship G.B.; Canada Council grants; Member-at-Large, Admin. Council, Codes d'accès 1992–93; recreations: cycling, walking, films; Home: 6105 28th Ave., Apt. 19, Montreal, Que. H1T 3H7.

**HARLOW, Robert Grant,** D.F.C., B.A., M.F.A.; author; educator; b. Prince Rupert, B.C. 19 Nov. 1923; s. Roland Alden and Kathleen (Grant) H.; e. Baron Byng High Sch. Prince George, B.C. 1941; Univ. of B.C. B.A. 1948; Univ. of Iowa M.F.A. 1950; four d.: Gretchen, Roseanne, Genevieve, Kathleen; Regional Producer Pub. Affairs CBC Vancouver 1951–53; Stn. Mgr. CBU Vancouver 1953–55; Dir. of Radio B.C. Region 1955–65; Head of Creative Writing Univ. B.C. 1965–77; Prof. of Creative Writing, Univ. of B.C. 1977–88; Prof. Emeritus 1988; author 'Royal Murdoch' 1962; 'A Gift of Echoes' 1964; 'Scann' 1972; 'Making Arrangements' 1978; 'Paul Nolan' 1983; 'Felice: A Travelogue' 1985; 'The Saxophone Winter' 1988; papers and mss to date acquired by The National Library, Ottawa 1984; various reviews, criticism, mag. articles; Founding mem. Writers' Union of Can. (former mem. Nat. Council, 2nd Vice Chrmn. 1975–76); served with RCAF 1941–45, Sgt.-Pilot Lancaster and Halifax aircraft, discharged Flying Offr., DFC; recreation: amateur jazz musician; Home: C-9 Bluffway, R.R. #1, Mayne Island, B.C. V0N 2J0.

**HARMAN, Chris Paul;** composer; b. Toronto, Ont. 19 Nov. 1970; s. John Joseph Paul and Anne Carol (Norrington) H.; e. private studies, cello, classical guitar, electronic music at the Royal Conservatory of Music, Toronto 1982–89; the works of Chris Paul Harman have been performed across Canada by the UART MIDI Ensemble, the Evergreen Club Gamelan Ensemble, the Batterie Park Percussion Ensemble, the St. Lawrence String Quartet, the Orch. de Chambre de Radio-Canada, the Composers' Orch., the Esprit Orch., the Edmonton Symphony, the Winnipeg Symphony, the National Youth Orch. & the C.B.C. Vancouver Orch.; has composed on comn. for the C.B.C., guitarists William Beauvais and Sylvie Proulx, the Fest. of the Sound in Parry Sound, percussionist Beverley Johnston, and Continuum; Finalist, C.B.C. National Radio Competition for Young Composers 1986, Grand Prize Winner 1990; 'Iridescence,' the piece which earned him the Grand Prize was subsequently awarded First Prize in the 'under-30' category at the 1991 International Rostrum of Composers in Paris and has since been recorded by the Espirit Orch. for compact disc release on CBC's SM5000 series label; Mem., Soc. of Composers, Authors and Music Publishers of Canada 1987– ; Associate Mem., Candn. Music Centre 1991– ; Address: 91 Beaconsfield Ave., Toronto, Ont. M6J 3J3.

**HARMER, Robert William (Herb),** B.A., B.Sc., P.Eng.; engineering executive; b. Southampton, Ont. 23 Jan. 1933; s. Herbert Wellington and Jessie Margaret H.; e. Univ. of W. Ont. B.A. 1954; Queen's Univ. B.Sc. (Civil Eng.) 1958; m. Mary d. Henry and Agnes Droeske 28 Feb. 1959; children: Robert, Alexandra, Lesley; CHRMN., CANDN. ENVIRONMENTAL ENERGY CO. 1991– ; Asst. Engr. to Mgr. of Engn. Hamilton (Ont.) Harbour Comnrs. 1958–65; Sr. Engr. to Project Supt. Canadian Bechtel Ltd. Montréal 1965–72, Bus. Devel. Mgr. 1972–75, Vice Pres. and Mgr. Candn. Operations Canadian Bechtel Ltd., Montreal/Toronto 1975–77, Mgr. of Operations (Domestic) Mining & Metals Div. Bechtel Corp., San Francisco 1977–79, Vice Pres. of Corp. 1979, Depy. Gen. Mgr. Mining & Metals 1980–82; Vice Pres. & Gen. Mgr. Mining & Metals, Bechtel Civil & Minerals Inc. 1982–84; Pres. & Dir., Bechtel Canada Engineers Ltd.; Bechtel Québec Ltée 1985–87; Pres. & Dir., Bechtel Canada Ltd. 1987; Sr. Vice Pres. & Dir., Bechtel Canada Inc. 1988–89, Consultant & Dir. 1990–91; mem. Assn. Prof. Engrs. Prov. Ont.; Order Engrs. Qué.; Candn. Inst. Mining & Metall.; Soc. Mining Engrs. AIME; recreations: golf, hunting, fishing; Clubs: Granite (Toronto); Toronto; Thornhill Country; Goodwood (Toronto); Ranchmen's (Calgary); Vancouver; Home: 121 Rochester Ave., Toronto, Ont. M4N 1N9; Office: 200, 10 Gateway Blvd., Don Mills, Ont. M3C 3N8.

**HARNETT, Hubert G.,** C.A.; bakery executive; b. Lamaline, Nfld. 4 Sept. 1932; s. Basil and Clarissa (Strickland) H.; e. Mem. Univ. of Nfld. 1952; m. Emma d. William and Martha Raymond 7 Aug. 1954; children: Christine, Paul, David, Michelle; CHAIRMAN, WEST COAST BAKERY LTD. 1979– ; Dir., Resource Can. Ltd.; Harnett Group Ltd.; Dir., Conpak Seafoods Inc.; American BOA Inc.; Dir., A.C.O.A.; Special Investigator Revenue Can. 1952–57; Treas. Hann Brothers Ltd. 1957–66; Comptroller Corner Brook Garage Ltd. 1966–69; Partner Harnett, Kean Power & Co. (C.A.'s) 1969–78; Past Pres. Corner Brook Chamber Comm.; mem. Corner Brook City Council 1967–74; Pres. Nfld. Fed. of Muns. 1970–72; recreation: golf; boating; Club: Blomidon Country; Home: Humber Arm South, Nfld.; Office: 19 Union St., Corner Brook, Nfld. A2H 5P9.

**HARNETTY, Peter,** A.M., Ph.D.; educator; b. Eng. 6 June 1927; s. Edward and Anita (McKeon) H.; e. Univ. of B.C., B.A. 1953; Harvard Univ. A.M. 1954, Ph.D. 1958; m. Claire d. Ovide Demers 5 Sept. 1956; one s. Richard; PROFESSOR EMERITUS OF ASIAN STUDIES, UNIV. OF B.C.; Instr. in Hist. and Internat. Studies present Univ. 1958–61, Asst. Prof. 1961, Asst. Prof. of Asian Studies & Hist. 1962–65, Assoc. Prof. 1965–71, Prof. 1971–92, Head of Asian Studies 1975–80; Author 'Imperialism and Free Trade: Lancashire and India in the Mid-Nineteenth Century' 1972; numerous articles learned journs.; served with Brit. and Indian Armies 1944–49; mem. Assn. Asian Studies; Econ. Hist. Assn.; Hist. Assn.; Shastri Indo-Candn. Inst. (Pres. 1970–71); Assoc. Ed., 'Pacific Affairs' 1966–87; Fellow, Royal Historical Soc. 1988; recreations: hiking (climbed Mount Kilimanjaro Sept. 1992), skiing; Home: 3026 W. 34th Ave., Vancouver, B.C. V6N 2K2.

**HARNOY, Ofra;** cellist; b. Hadera, Israel 31 Jan. 1965; d. Jacob and Carmen Carmela H.; e. studied with William Pleeth, London; with Vladimir Orloff, Toronto; in master classes with Mstislav Rostropovich, Pierre Fournier and Jacqueline Du Pre; Royal Conservatory of Music, Toronto; began cello instr. from her father at age 6; made profl. debut as soloist with Dr. Boyd Neel and his orch. 1975; has since appeared as soloist with numerous major orchestras and in solo recitals in U.S.A., Can., France, Germany, Austria, Belgium, England, Japan, Israel, Holland, Denmark, Australia, Italy, Czechoslavakia, Taiwan, Hungary, Korea, Venezuela, Spain, Portugal, Hong Kong, Rumania, Poland, Turkey, Yugoslavia and Luxemburg; solo orchestral and recital debut Carnegie Hall N.Y. 1982; soloist in world prem. performance and commercial recording of Cello Concerto by Jacques Offenbach w. Cincinnati Symphony Orch. 1983; presented the N. Am. prem. of Sir. Arthur Bliss' Cello Concerto and world premiere recording of Cello Concertos by Viotti, Myslivecek and several of Vivaldi's Cello Concertos; winner First Prize Montreal Symphony Competition 1978; First Prize Candn. Mus. Competition 1979; International Concert Artists Guild Award (youngest recipient in 42 yrs.) 1982; Young Musician of the Yr., Musical Am. Magazine 1983; The Maclean's 1987 Honor Roll; 5 Juno Awards for 'Best Classical Soloist' 1987–1988, 1989 and 1991, 1992 and 1993; Grand Prix du Disque 1988; 35 Classical Solo Albums for RCA Victor, London, EMI, Pro Arte; Address: 122 Alfred Ave., Willowdale, Ont. M2N 3H9.

**HARNUM, Bill,** B.A., M.A.; book publisher; b. Sault Ste. Marie, Ont. 28 Nov. 1950; s. Percy Elwood and Christine (McArthur) H.; e. St. James Collegiate Winnipeg 1967; Univ. of Winnipeg B.A. (Hons.) 1973; Univ. of Manitoba M.A. 1976; m. Janice Handford 8 July 1977; children: Alan, James; VICE-PRES., SCHOLARLY PUBLISHING, UNIVERSITY OF TORONTO PRESS INCORPORATED 1992– ; Sales Mgr., Western Producer Prairie Books 1979–84; Univ. of Toronto Press 1984–90; Marketing Manager 1990–92; Teacher, various courses in marketing; Consultant (Publishing), Man. Govt.; recreations: golf, squash; clubs: Univ. of Toronto Faculty; Home: 511 Kingston Rd., Toronto, Ont. M4L 1V5; Office: 10 St. Mary St., Suite 700, Toronto, Ont. M4Y 2W8.

**HARPER, Alex M.,** B.Sc., M.Sc., Ph.D.; retired; b. Lethbridge, Alta. 10 March 1926; e. Lethbridge (Alta.) Coll. Inst.; Univ. of Alta. (Gold Ring Extve. A Award 1948); Wash. State Univ.; m. Georgean Hirst; children: Bradley, Shawna, Paula, Liana; Scientist Emeritus, Research Br. Agric. Can. 1987–88; Research Officer, Sc. Service, Agric. Can. 1948–59; Research Scient., Research Br. Agric. Can. 1959–86; Dir. Lethbridge YMCA 1967–68; Lethbridge Boy Scout Comte. 1972–74; author numerous scient. and tech. papers; mem. S. Alta. Br., Prof. Inst. Pub. Service of Can. (Secy.-Treas. 1966–67; Pres. 1967–68); mem. Entomol. Soc. Can.; Entomol. Soc. Am.; Entomol. Soc. Alta. (Secy. 1960, Dir. 1963, Treas. 1966, Secy. Treas. 1972–73, Vice Pres. 1974, Pres. 1975); Lethbridge Naturalist Soc.; Chinook Outdoor Club; Southern Alta. Art Gallery Assoc.; Writers' Guild of Alta.; Lethbridge and District Japanese Garden Soc. (Dir. 1981, 1985–91; Vice-Pres. 1982; Pres. 1983–84); World Future Soc.; Friend Glenbow Museum; Kiwanis; Alta. Assn. Bright Children (Dir. 1984–87); Senate, Univ. of Lethbridge (Chrmn. Extve. Ctte.); Univ. of Lethbridge Planning Ctte. 1993–94; recreations: skiing, hiking, writing, reading; Home: 1654 Scenic Heights South, Lethbridge, Alta. T1K 1N5.

**HARPER, Elijah,** M.P.; politician; b. Red Sucker Lake, Man.; s. Allen B. and Ethel C. H.; e. Winnipeg H.S.; Univ. of Man.; m. Elizabeth Ann Ross 23 Sept. 1972; children: Marcel George, Holly Juliette, Bruce Allen, Tanya Catherine; MEMBER OF PARLIAMENT FOR CHURCHILL, GOVT. OF CANADA 1993– ; first elected to the Man. Leg. g.e. 1981; relected g.e. 1986, '88, '90; Community Development Worker & Researcher, Manitoba Indian Brotherhood; Program Analyst, Dept. of Northern Affairs 1975–77; Chief, Red Sucker Lake Indian Band (now Red Sucker Lake First Nation) 1978–81; elected M.L.A. Rupertsland, Govt. of Manitoba 1981–92; apptd. to cabinet as Min. Without Portfolio Responsible for Native Affairs 1986; Min. of Northern Affairs, Manitoba 1987; nominated as Liberal Candidate for federal riding of Churchill in northern Manitoba April 1993; Mem., Working Group, Northern Hydro Dev.; Protestant; Home: Red Sucker Lake, Man.; Office: Room 331, Confederation Bldg., Ottawa Ont. K1A 0A6.

**HARPER, Frank Berryman Wilson,** M.A., Ph.D.; professor emeritus; b. Scotland 29 Mar. 1927; s. Craig and Annie (Berryman) H.; e. Univ. of Glasgow M.A. 1952; Univ. of Calif. (Berkeley) Ph.D. 1961; m. Ethel d. Hugh John Cook 23 Aug. 1956; children: Craig, Stephanie; PROFESSOR EMERITUS 1992– ; Consultant, Computers in Special and General Education; Mem., Bd. of Dirs., Victoria Hosp., London 1990– ; Mem. Bd. of Govs., Westminster Institute for Ethics and Human Values 1993– ; Asst. Prof., Univ. of Minnesota 1961; Assoc. Prof., Univ. of West. Ont. 1965; Prof. 1971; Acting Dean, Fac. of Edn. 1986–88; Dir., Ctr. for Communicative and Cognitive Disabilities, Univ. of West. Ont. 1985–92; Mem., Bd. of Govs., Univ. of West. Ont. 1986–92; Mem., Soc. for Study of Edn. in Can.; Am. Edn. Rsch. Assoc.; Soc. of Sigma XI; recreations: golf, badminton; Home: 73 Bloomfield Dr., London, Ont. N6G 1P4; Office: Fac. of Edn., Univ. of West. Ont., London, Ont. N6G 1G7.

**HARPER, Gerald,** Ph.D., P.Eng.; mining executive; b. Southampton, England 16 May 1945; s. Stanley Hugh and Muriel Elford (Hubble) H.; e. Univ. of London B.Sc. (Geol. & Chem.) 1965, (Geol. Hons.) 1966, Ph.D. 1970; emigrated to Canada 1970; m. Maureen Anne Williams 11 Jan. 1975; children: Katherine, Helen; Pres., Gamah Internat. Ltd. 1992– ; Sci. Offr., Counc. for Sci. & Indus. Rsch. Capetown, S. Africa 1967; Rsch. Fellow, Anglo Am. Corp. Zimbabwe 1967–70; Project Geol., Falconbridge Limited Vancouver 1970–75; Sr. Geol. Sudbury 1975–76; Reg. Geol., Brinco Limited Montreal 1977–80; Chief Geol., Northgate Exploration Ltd. 1980–88; Vice Pres., 1988–92; Pres., C.E.O. & Dir., Geddes Resources Limited 1988–92; Dir., Orofino Resources Limited 1983–91; Prof. Engr., Ont.; Mem., Soc. of Econ. Geol.; Candn. Inst. of Mining; Fellow, Geol. Soc. of London; Geol. Soc. of S. Africa; Mem., N.W. Mining Assn.; Soc. Mining, Metallurgy & Exploration; Dir., Prospectors & Developers Assn. of Canada; recreations: skiing; Home: 26 Orchard Cres., Etobicoke, Ont. M8Z 3E1.

**HARPER, His Hon. James D.,** U.E., Q.C., B.Sc., B.C.L.; judge; b. Saint John, N.B. 23 Nov. 1925; s. Dufferin Wolsely and Alyce Mary (Byrne) H.; e. St. Vincent's Boys H.S. and Saint John H.S. 1943; Saint Francis Xavier Univ. B.Sc. 1946; Univ. of N.B. Law Sch. B.C.L. 1951; m. Gloria Hazel d. Roy and Hazel Seely 10 Aug. 1957; children: Dr. Byrne Donal, Dufferin Roy, Seely Lyn; JUDGE, CRIMINAL DIV., PROV. COURT OF N.B. 1976– ; articled with B.R. Guss, Q.C. 1951; awarded Q.C. 1973; private practice Saint John 1952–55; Partner, Atkinson & Harper 1956–66; estbd. firms Harper & Fenton; and Harper D'Arcy & Fenton; served with RCAF 1943–44; Dir. Candn. Bridge Fedn. 5 yrs. (Pres. 1980–82); Life Master A.C.B.L. 1979; Pres. Fredericton Law Soc. 1973; Pres. N.B. Assn. Prov. Court Judges 1984–85; R. Catholic; hobbies: duplicate bridge, photography; Home: 29 Talisman Cres., Site 20, Comp. 19, RR #3, Fredericton, N.B. E3B 4X4; Office: P.O. Box 6000, Justice Building, Fredericton, N.B. E3B 5H1.

**HARPER, John M.,** Q.C., B.A., LL.B.; lawyer; b. Toronto, Ont. 26 June 1917; e. Univ. of W. Ont. B.A. 1939; Osgoode Hall Law Sch. 1948; m. Mary E. Jamieson 1943; children: William J., Susan E. Palmer, George H.; PAST CHRMN., THE EQUITABLE LIFE INSURANCE CO. OF CANADA 1987– ; Counsel, Gowling Strathy & Henderson, Ottawa, Toronto, Kitchener and Cambridge; Former Dir. & Vice Chrmn., Economical Mutual Insurance Co.; Pres. & Dir., K-W Community Foundation; Dir., Lincoln Village Ltd.; 1061 Queens Blvd. Ltd.; Comtran Investments Ltd.; called to Bar of Ont. 1948; cr. Q.C. 1958; law practice since 1948; served with Argyll & Sutherland Highlanders Can. 1940–45, Can., Caribbean, Eng. N.W. Eur. (4th Div.), rank Maj.; H/Colonel Highland Fusiliers of Canada; recipient Centennial Medal 1967; awarded Commemorative Medal for 125th Anniversary of Candn. Confederation 1992; named Citizen of Yr. Kitchener-Waterloo 1975; Hon. Dir. K-W United Way (Past Chrmn.); recipient Paul Harris Award (Rotary); Former mem. of Bd. of Govs. Wilfrid Laurier Univ. (mem. Chancellor's Club); former Dir. Kitchener-Waterloo YMCA; Past Pres. Kitchener and Waterloo Cons. Assns.; former Dir. and Co-Founder Cons. Bus. Assn. Kitchener-Waterloo; mem. Waterloo C. of C. (Past Pres.); Pres.'s Ctte. Univ. of Waterloo; Trustee, First United Ch. Waterloo; Clubs: Lions (Past Pres. Waterloo); Westmount Golf & Country (Hon. Life Mem. & Past Pres.); Albany (Toronto); Home: 595 Deer Run Dr., Waterloo, Ont. N2K 3A2; Office: 1 Westmount Rd. N., Waterloo, Ont. N2J 4C7.

**HARPER, Merry Deirdre,** B.A., M.L.S., LL.B.; lawyer; b. Regina, Sask. 25 Nov. 1948; d. Wilson James and

Helen Jane (Clarke) H.; e. Sarnia (Ont.) N. Coll. Inst. 1967; Univ. of W. Ont. B.A. 1971, M.L.S. 1976; Univ. of Sask. grad. teaching fellowship in pol. science 1972; Univ. of Man. LL.B. 1986; m. Robert Eric Harbottle 1 Sept. 1972; one d. Anne Deirdre; Consultant, Manitoba Telephone System; Asst. Clk. Leg. Assembly Sask. 1972–74; Prov. Librarian of Sask. 1981–82; Bd. of Govs., Winnipeg YM-YWCA; mem. Parlty. Assn. Clks.-at-the-Table (Secy. for Can.); Candn. Bar Assn.; Pi Beta Phi (Secy.); Home: 126 Lake Grove Bay, Winnipeg, Man. R3T 4Y2.

**HARPER, Robert J.C.,** M.A., Ph.D.; educator; b. Greenock, Scotland 29 Mar. 1927; s. Abram Craig and Anne (Berryman) H.; e. Holmscroft Sch. and Greenock High Sch., 1945; St. Andrews Univ., M.A. 1951; Edinburgh Univ., M.A. 1953, Ph.D. 1964; m. late Margaret Everilde, d. late Thomas Kirk, 22 Dec. 1953 four s., Paul, Alan, David, Michael; EMERITUS PROFESSOR, SIMON FRASER UNIV.; Prof., Div. of Interdisciplinary Studies, Simon Fraser Univ. since 1973 and Senator there 1966–71; Clin. Psychol., Prov. Mental Hosp., Alta., 1953–54, Lectr. and Dir., Educ. Clinic, Univ. of Alt., 1954, Asst. Prof. 1956, Assoc. Prof. 1962; Consulting Clin. Psychol., Dept. of Veterans' Affairs, Univ. Hosp., Edmonton, 1954; Prof. and Dir. of Studies, Behavioral Science Foundations, Simon Fraser Univ., 1965, Chrmn. of Dept. 1965 till resigned 1972; Hon. Lectr. and Examiner in Psychol. and Ethics, Royal Coll. of Nursing, London and Edinburgh, 1959–60; served with R.A.F. 1945–48; R.A.F.V.R. St. Andrews Univ. Air Sqdn. 1949–51, Edinburgh Univ. Air Sqdn, 1951–53; author, 'Cognitive Processes,' 1964; also numerous prof. papers, articles and addresses; mem. Candn. Assn. Univ. Teachers; Presbyterian; recreations: skiing, fishing, golf; Office: Div. of Interdisciplinary Studies, Faculty of Arts, Simon Fraser Univ., Burnaby, B.C. V5A 1S6.

**HARPER, Robert Ray,** B.A.; public relations executive; b. Detroit, Mich. 26 July 1930; s. William Lee and Pauline (Brown) H.; e. Stanford Univ. B.A. 1957; m. Gwendolyn d. James and Lenore Waterfield 29 May 1959; children: Lynne, Geoffrey; Founder, Harper & Harper Public Relations Ltd. 1972; Reporter, The Los Angeles Times 1958–61; Vice Pres. The Phillips Group, Los Angeles 1961–66; emigrated to Can. 1966; Vice Pres. Petlock Ruder & Finn, Toronto 1966–70; Dir. of Publ. Relations Ogilvy & Mather Inc. New York 1970–72; recipient Charles Kendrick Warren Meml. Honours Fellowship Stanford Univ. 1955–57; Dir. The Candn. Opera Co. 1969–70; author 'International Public Relations Handbook' 1971; contrbr. The Financial Post, The Financial Times, The Toronto Star, AutoWorld; recreation: jogging, auto racing; Club: Fitness Inst.; Address: 35 Lynch Rd., Willowdale, Ont. M2J 2V6.

**HARPER, William H.,** B.Sc., P.Eng.; management consultant; b. Eatonia, Sask. 20 July 1924; s. William R. and Susan N. (Tucker) H.; e. Univ. of Sask. B.Sc. (Mech. Engn.) 1946; m. Isobel B. d. Charles E. Daw 18 Aug. 1947; children: Catherine R. Estey, Joyce L. Whidden, William R., Heather L. Riel; PROP., W.H. HARPER INC. 1978– ; Chrmn./C.E.O., Lovell & Christmas (Canada) Inc.; Lovell & Christmas (O) Ltd., Montreal; Topimex Inc. (Montreal); Dir., Sakura Bank (Can.); Transatlantic General Development Ltd.; held various positions with Carrier Air Conditioning (Canada) Limited in Engn., Procurement and Sales becoming Regional Mgr. Sales, Constr. & Service (Que. border to W. Coast) 1947–53; Chrmn. and Pres. Beaver Engineering Ltd. 1953–78; Hon. Gov., Queen Elizabeth Hosp.; Trustee, Humber Valley Un. Ch.; Past Dir., Jr. Achievement Metrop. Toronto; Harp House; Past Pres. Kiwanis Humber Valley; recreations: golf, tennis; Clubs: St. George's Golf & Country; Riomar Golf, Beach & Yacht (Vero Beach); Home: 10 The Kingsway, Toronto, Ont. M8X 2T1.

**HARPP, David Noble,** A.B., M.A., Ph.D.; university professor; b. Albany, N.Y. 20 Jan. 1937; s. Noble H. and Nina S. (Swanson) H.; e. Middlebury College B.A. 1959; Wesleyan Univ. M.A. 1962; Univ. of North Carolina Ph.D. 1965; Cornell Univ., postdoctoral fellow 1965–66; m. Susan d. Jean and Robert Benham 5 June 1961; divorced 1981; children: Karen, Emily; PROF. OF CHEMISTRY, MCGILL UNIVERSITY 1975– ; Asst. / Assoc. Prof. of Chemistry, McGill Univ. 1966–74; Union Carbide Award, Chem. Inst. of Canada 1982; Leo Yaffe Award for Excellence in Teaching, McGill Univ. 1982; Catalyst Award, Chem. Mfrs. Assn. 1988; The McNeil Medal for the Public Awareness of Sci., Royal Soc. of Can. 1992; author of over 160 scientific articles; Home: 290 Walnut Ave., St. Lambert, Que. J4P 2T1; Office: 801 Sherbrooke St. W., Montreal, Que. H3A 2K6.

**HARPUR, Thomas William,** M.A. (Oxon), M.Div.; journalist; broadcaster; educator; author; b. Toronto, Ont. 14 Apr. 1929; s. William Wallace and Elizabeth (Hoey) H.; e. Univ. Coll. Univ. of Toronto B.A. (Classics) 1951; Oriel Coll. Oxford Univ. M.A. 1954; Wycliffe Coll. M.Div. 1956; Rhodes Scholar, Ont. 1951; Gold Medal in Classics, Univ. of Toronto 1951; o. Anglican priest 1956; m. Mary W. Clark 1956; children: Elizabeth, Margaret, Mary Catharine; m. 2ndly Susan Bette Anne d. Clifford and Joan (Campbell) Coles 7 Apr. 1984; SYNDICATED COLUMNIST, TORONTO STAR 1984– ; Host, 'Harpur's Heaven and Hell' new hourly interview show on Vision-TV, the national religion channel 1988– ; Curate St. John's York Mills 1956–57; Rector St. Margaret's-in-the-Pines 1957–64; Lectr. Ancient Philosophy, Trinity and Wycliffe Colls. 1960–62; Prof. New Testament and Greek, Wycliffe Coll. 1964–71; Religion Editor Toronto Star 1971–83; Host CFTO-TV 'Paradox' 1979–84; Lectr., Toronto Sch. of Theology 1983–87; recipient Internat. Award of Merit for Religious Journalism 1974; Fellow Religious Public Relations Council 1974; Silver Medal for Outstanding Journalism, State of Israel 1976; author: 'Road to Bethlehem: 2000 Years Later' 1977; 'Harpur's Heaven and Hell' 1983; 'For Christ's Sake' 1986; 'Communicating the Good News Today' 1987; 'Always on Sunday' 1988; 'The Mouse that Couldn't Squeak' 1988; 'The Terrible Finn MacCoul' 1990; 'Life after Death' 1991; 'God Help Us' 1992; 'The God Question' 1993; 'The Uncommon Touch' An Investigation of Spiritual Healing 1994; commentator on various television and radio programs; recreations: hiking, canoeing, travel; Address: 5 Willowbank Ave., Station B, Richmond Hill, Ont. L4E 3B4.

**HARRIGAN, Kenneth William James,** B.A. (Hons.); executive; b. Chatham, Ont. 27 Sept. 1927; s. Charles Angus and Olga Jean (Wallace) H.; e. Univ. of W. Ont. B.A. 1951; m. Margaret Jean Macpherson 18 June 1955; children: Tara Lynne Tomlinson, Stephen Charles; Past Chrmn. & C.E.O., Ford Motor Co. of Canada 1990–92; Dir. Camco Inc.; London Insurance Group; London Life Insurance Co.; Noranda Forest Inc.; Ontario Jockey Club; Samuel Manu-Tech Inc.; Versa Services Ltd.; joined Ford Motor Co. of Canada 1951; Gen. Field Mgr. Edmonton 1962, Regional City Mgr. Vancouver 1963, Asst. Regional Mgr. Toronto 1964, Regional Mgr. Toronto 1965, Gen. Sales Mgr. Central Office Oakville 1968, Staff Dir. Sales & Marketing Ford Asia-Pacific Inc. Australia 1972–73, Group Dir. S. European Sales Ford of Europe, Eng. 1973–76, Vice Pres. Truck Sales & Marketing Ford of Europe 1977–78, Vice Pres., Gen. Mgr. Sales, Ford of Canada, Oakville 1978–81; Pres. & C.E.O., Ford of Canada 1981–90, Chrmn & C.E.O. 1990–92; mem. Policy Comte., Business Counc. on Nat. Issues 1986–92; Former Chrmn. & Dir., Motor Vehicle Mfrs.' Assn.; Past Dir., Dome Consortium Investments Inc.; Co-Chrmn., Automotive Adv. Ctte., Federal Govt. 1988–92; Dir., Conference Bd.; mem., Candn. Labour Market and Productivity Centre Steering Ctte. of the Economic Restructuring Project; National Adv. Counc. (NAC), World Energy Conference; Fed. Govt. Chrmn. Sectoral Adv. Group on Internat. Trade (SAGIT) 1988– ; Mem., Federal Internat. Trade Advisory Ctte. 1991– ; Chrmn., Candn. Delegation to IMS (Intelligence Manufacturing Systems) Internat. Steering Ctte.; Dir., Canada/U.S. Business Assn. 1989–92; Dir., Western Business School Club of Toronto; mem. Adv. Comte., Univ. of Western Ont. Bus. Sch.; Dir., Forum for Internat. Trade Training Inc. (FITT); Chrmn., Royal Ont. Museum; Chrmn. ROM Foundation; Clubs: York; Founders; Mississauga Golf & Country; Office: The Canadian Rd., Oakville, Ont. L6J 5E4.

**HARRINGTON, Arthur Russell,** B.Eng., D.Eng., D.C.L.; b. Sydney, N.S. 28 June 1914; s. Arthur Lloyd and Ethel Tryphena (Cunningham) H.; e. Halifax (N.S.) Acad., grad. 1931; Dalhousie Univ., (Engn.), 1934; N.S. Tech. Coll., B.Eng., 1936, D.Eng. 1968; m. Beatrice Marian, d. late Harry Dean, Halifax, N.S., 17 Sept. 1938; one s. Arthur Gordon; Vice Pres. and Dir., Halifax Developments Ltd.; joined Nova Scotia Light and Power Company Limited as Jr. Engr., 1936; apptd. Asst. Mgr., 1951, Mgr., 1958; apptd. to Bd. of Dir., 1960; Vice Pres., 1961; Pres. and Gen. Mgr. 1962–72; Halifax Adv. Council, Salvation Army; Past Pres. Halifax Y.M.C.A. (now Trustee); Dir., N.S. Labour Relations Bd.; mem. Assn. Prof. Engrs. N.S.; Fellow, Engn. Inst. Can.; D.C.L. Acadia 1969; Baptist; recreations: fishing, swimming; Clubs: Halifax; Waegwoltic; Home: 2350 Armcrescent West, Halifax, N.S. B3L 3E3.

**HARRINGTON, Conrad F.,** C.M., KStJ, C.D., B.A., B.C.L., LL.D. (Hon.), C.T.C.I.; retired; former company director; b. Montreal, Que. 8 Aug. 1912; s. late Conrad Dawson and Muriel Theodora (Fetherstonhaugh) H.; e. Selwyn House, Montreal; Trinity Coll. Sch., Port Hope, Ont.; McGill Univ., B.A. 1933, B.C.L. 1936; Univ. of Besancon (France) 1936–37; Hon. LL.D., McGill Univ. 1984; m. Joan Roy, d. late John O. Hastings, Montreal, Que., 6 Aug. 1940; one s. Conrad; two d., Jill, Susan; HON. DIR., THE ROYAL TRUST CO. (and former Chrmn. of Bd. & Extve. Comte.); former Chrmn., Glaxo Canada Ltd., former Chrmn., Redpath Industries Ltd.; Dir., Gerling Global Gen. Ins. Co.; Gerling Global Reins. Co.; Gerling Global Life Insurance Co.; former Dir., R.L. Crain Ltd.; Consumers Glass Co. Ltd.; MPG Investment Corp. Ltd.; Stone and Webster Canada Ltd.; practised law in Montreal with Phelan, Fleet, Robertson & Abbott, 1937–39; called to the Bar of Que. 1936; joined Estates Dept. of Royal Trust Co. 1945; Asst. to Gen. Mgr., 1951–52; Mgr., Toronto Br., 1952; Asst. Gen. Mgr. at Toronto, 1954; Supvr. of Ont. Brs., 1955; Vice Pres. 1957; el. a Dir. 1960; Vice-Pres. and Gen. Mgr. 1963; Extve. Vice-Pres. 1964; Pres. 1965; served in 2nd World War with R.C.A., 1940–45; U.K., Italy, N.W. Europe, with 5, 2, 17 Candn. Field Regts., twice Mentioned in Despatches; Centennial Medal, 1967; Reserve Army, 1945–80; O.C. 37 Candn. Field Regt.; Hon. Lt. Col., and Col., 2nd Field Regt. RCA (M); Life Gov., Trinity Coll. Sch., Port Hope, Ont.; former Chrmn., Salvation Army, Mtl. Adv. Bd.; Chancellor of McGill Univ. 1976–83; Emeritus Gov., McGill Univ. 1984; Hon. Dir., Que. Council, St. John Ambulance; Hon. Vice-Pres., Montreal Regional Council, Boy Scouts of Can.; Past Pres., McGill Grads. Soc.; Trustee, Montreal Museum of Fine Arts; former Chrmn., McCord Museum; Chrmn. Toronto United Appeal Campaign, 1958; Pres., Trust Co.'s Assn. Can. 1958–59, 1970–71; recipient Human Relations Award, Candn. Council of Christians and Jews 1981; Distinguished Friend of Education Award, Council for Advancement and Support of Education (CASE) 1984; Order of Distinguished Auxiliary Service Award, Salvation Army 1984; Member, Order of Canada 1986; Zeta Psi; Anglican; recreations: golf, reading, painting; Clubs: York (Toronto); Toronto Golf; University (Montreal); St. James's; Mt. Bruno Golf; Home: 556 Lansdowne Ave., Westmount, Que. H3Y 2V6; Office: 630 René-Lévesque Blvd. W., Montreal, Que. H3B 1S6.

**HARRINGTON, Conrad H.,** B.A.; private banker; b. Montreal, Que. 19 Oct. 1946; s. Conrad F. and Joan Roy (Hastings) H.; e. Trinity College School 1964; Bishop's Univ. B.A. 1967; m. Sally St Clair 7 April 1979; children: Clare, Conrad, George; PRIVATE BANKER, LOMBARD ODIER TRUST COMPANY 1991– ; Bank of Montreal 1967–68; Wood Gundy (Montreal, Toronto, New York & London); Dir., The Jean Coutu Group; Knightsbridge Integrated Holdings; Chair, Bishop's Univ. Found.; Pres., Mackay Centre; Trustee, McCord Museum; Selwyn House School; Trinity College Sch.; Vice-Pres., Duke of Edinburgh Award; Montreal Adv. Bd., Salvation Army; clubs: Toronto Golf, Mount Bruno Golf, Montreal Badminton & Squash, Hillside Tennis, University Club of Montreal; Home: 609 Clarke Ave., Montreal, Que. H3Y 3E5; Office: Suite 1500, 1155 Sherbrooke St. W., Montreal, Que. H3A 2W1.

**HARRINGTON, John Maurice,** M.A., M.Sc. (Econ.); retired diplomat; b. Cromer, England 14 March 1924; s. late Maurice Joseph and Dorothy Deacon (Hollyman) H.; e. St. Illtyd's Coll., Cardiff, Wales; Central Coll., London, Ont.; Univ. of W. Ont., B.A. 1946, M.A. 1947; London Sch. of Econ. and Pol. Science, M.Sc. (Econ.) 1949 (IODE Scholarship); m. Dorothy Irene, d. late Sylvester Pocock 1950; one s. Douglas John; Asst. Prof. Econ., St. Francis Xavier Univ. 1949; joined Dept. External Affairs 1950, served in Belgrade 1952–55; Econ. Div., Ottawa 1955–57; attended ICAO Assembly, Caracas 1956 (Adviser); London 1958–62; Candn. Observer, First Session U.N. Econ. Comn. for Africa, Tangier 1960, Second Session, Addis Ababa 1961; Econ. Div., Ottawa 1962–65; Adviser, 18th U.N. Gen. Assembly, N.Y. 1962; Counsellor, Candn. Embassy Tokyo 1965–68; mem. Del. to Inaugural Meeting, Asian Development Bank, Tokyo 1966 and to ECAFE Sept. 1966; Special Ambassador, Inauguration of Pres. Park, Republic of Korea, Seoul 1967; Depy. Head, Far E. Div., Ottawa 1968, Dir. Pacific Div. 1970; mem. Science and Tech. Mission to Japan, Feb. 1972; High Commr. to Jamaica, Bahamas and Belize 1972–76; Foreign Service Visitor, Univ. of Toronto (Trinity Coll.) 1976–77; Depy. Cmdt., Nat. Defence, Coll., 1977–79; Dir., Academic Relations, External Affairs 1979–80; Dir. Internat. Economic Relations, Dept. of Finance 1980–81; Dir-Gen., Internat. Div., Min. of State for Sci. and Technology 1981–83; Dir., Social Policy & Programs, Dept. of External Affairs 1983–84; Ambassador to Norway and Iceland 1985–88; Extve. Co-ordinator, Task Force on Europe 1992, Jan-Apr. 1989; retired Apr. 30, 1989; varied consulting assignments 1989–92; current activities: CIIA, Canada-Korea Soc.; Retired Heads of Mission Assoc.; R. Catholic; recreations: photography, swimming, gardening, cross-country skiing, cycling; Home: 37 Belvedere Cres., Ottawa, Ont. K1M 0E5.

**HARRIS, Charles Alexander,** B.A.; retired public affairs consultant; b. Toronto, Ont. 10 Mar. 1920; s. Charles Alexander and Arline (Rouget) H.; e. University of Toronto, B.A. (Modern History) 1947; m. Bernice, d. G.L. Adam, Toronto, Ont., 9 Oct. 1942; children: David, Robert, Reed; Reporter, Toronto 'Globe & Mail' 1937–41; joined C.B.C. as a Producer in Talks and Public Affairs Dept., May 1947; apptd. Asst. to Dir. of Television, C.B.C. Toronto 1950; joined Candn. Mfrs. Assn. as Public Relations Offr. 1951; Asst. to Dir. of Public Relations, Candn. Nat. Railways, Montreal 1952, Asst. Dir. 1956, Dir. 1959, Vice-Pres. 1970; joined Bell Canada as Vice-Pres., Public Relations, Montreal 1972; Vice-Pres., Public and Environmental Affairs 1973–80; Pres., Harris Heal Ltd. 1980–85; served in R.C.A.F., 1941–45, rank Flying Offr.; Past Pres., Candn. Public Relations Soc. (rec'd. Nat. Award of Attainment 1966); recreations: sailing, computer music; Clubs: Toronto Press; Home: 2251 Constance Dr., Oakville, Ont. L6J 5L8.

**HARRIS, Claire Kathleen Patricia,** B.A., Dip.Ed., Dip.Media; b. Port of Spain, Trinidad 13 June 1937; d. Conrad Arthur Knowlton and Gladys Claire (Cardinal) H.; e. Nat. Univ. of Ireland, B.A. (Hons.) 1961; Univ. of W. Indies, Dip.Ed. 1963; Univ. of Lagos, Dip.Media 1975; author: 'Fables from the Women's Quarters' 1984, 'Translation into Fiction' 1984, 'Travelling to Find a Remedy' 1986, 'The Conception of Winter' 1989, 'Drawing Down a Daughter' 1992 (poetry), 'Under Black Light/New and Selected Poems' forthcoming and short stories & essays; first poems were pub. in Nigeria; co-pub., 'Poetry Goes Public' (poster series) 1979; Poet Ed., 'Dandelion' 1981–89; Co-founder: 'blue buffalo, a magazine of AB' 1982, Mng. Ed. 1982–84; co-editor: 'Kitchen Talk: An Anthology of Writings by Canadian Women' 1992; Secondary Sch. Teacher, Sep. Sch. Bd., Calgary; Commonwealth Award for Best 1st time Pub. Poet in Am. Area 1985; Writer's Guild of Alta. S.G. Stephansson Award 1987 & Alta. Culture Poetry Prize 1987 for 'Travelling'; Dragonfly Award for Haiku 1978, 1983; Alta. Achievement Award 1987; Alta. Culture Special Award for poetry 1990 for 'Conception'; 'Drawing Down a Daughter' nominated for G.G. Award in poetry 1993; Mem., Writers' Guild of Alta.; Dandelion Mag. Soc.; Amnesty Internat.; Inter Pares; Assoc. League of Candn. Poets; Roman Catholic; recreations: crime fiction, travel, photography; Home: 701, 300 Meredith Rd. N.E., Calgary, Alta. T2E 7A8.

**HARRIS, Daniel Gibson,** B.A., CD; writer; b. Missenden, England 10 Dec. 1915; s. James Gibson and Betty (Miles) H.; e. Sherborne England; Carleton Univ., B.A. 1989; C.A. (England & Wales) 1940; m. Marianne d. Robert and Anna Syk 28 Aug. 1943; children: Madeleine Callway, Michael (dec'd.); HISTORIAN, 'MARITIME AFFAIRS' 1985– ; Asst. Naval Attaché, Brit. Legation Stockholm 1940–46; Lt. Cmdr. RCNR 1955; oil & gas industry 1949–59; Asst. Finan. Advr., Nat. Energy Bd. 1960–77; Dir., Finan. Regulatory Br. 1977–80; Sr. Adviser 1980–82; Consultant for Den Norske Veritas Soc. 1982–85; author 'F.H. Chapman First Naval Architect' 1989; articles on Canadian & Swedish maritime history for 'Inland Seas' & 'The Mariner's Mirror'; and of 3 chapters for 'World Warships' 1990, 1991 & 1992 edns.; Founder, Candn. Nordic Soc., Ottawa 1963; Co-founder, Candn. Nautical Rsch. Soc.; Elected mem., Swedish Royal Soc. of Naval Sciences 1989; Candn. Forces Decoration (CD) Officer First Class; Netherlands Order of Oranje Nassau; Knight first class Swedish Order of the North Star; Swedish Wasa Rediviva Medal; Medal of Merit, Swedish Royal Soc. of Naval Sciences 1991; Office: c/o Vanwell Publishing, Box 2131, Stn. B., St. Catharines, Ont. L2M 6P5.

**HARRIS, David John,** L.R.C.P., M.R.C.S., L.M.C.C., F.R.C.P.C., M.R.C.Psych.; university professor; b. Bath, Eng. 13 May 1944; s. Dr. David and Anne (Gill) H.; e. Bradford Grammar Sch., Yorkshire; Leeds Univ. Sch. of Med. 1962–68; m. Ceridwen d. Leslie and Gwyneth James 30 Dec. 1972; children: Aubrey, Sian, Owain, Rhys; ASSOC. PROF. (GERIATRIC PSYCH.), UNIV. OF W. ONT. 1987– ; House Offr. and Sr. House Offr. Med., Leeds Gen. Infirmary 1968–71; Sr. House Offr. Med., Chapel Allerton Hosp., Leeds 1971; Registrar, Psych., Graylingwell Hosp., Chichester 1971–72; Registrar and Rsch. Fellow, Psych., London Hosp. 1972–76; Asst. Prof., Univ. of Ottawa and Dir., Psychogeriatric Clinic, Ottawa Gen. Hosp. 1976–80; Asst. Prof., Univ. of W. Ont. 1980–87; Dir., Psychogeriatric Community Clinic, Victoria Hosp., London 1980– ; Cons. Psych., London Psych. Hosp., Parkwood Hosp.; mem. Candn. Psych. Assn. (Chrmn., Geriatrics Sect. 1987–89); Ont. Psych. Assn. (Chrmn., Geriatrics Sec. 1983–87, 1990–91); Candn. Soc. for Geriatric Med.; Candn. Assn. of Gerontology; Candn. Academy Geriatric Psychiatry; Am. Assoc. for Geriatric Psychiatry; Brit. Med. Assn.; Hon. Soc. of Cymmrodorion; London (Ont.) Welsh Soc. (Pres. 1991–94); Glamorgan Hist. Soc.; Royal Archaeol. Inst.; recreations: history, genealogy, archeology; Office: Victoria Hosp., P.O. Box 5375, London, Ont. N6A 4G5.

**HARRIS, Geoffrey Thomas;** b. Edmonton, Alta., 16 Sept. 1912; s. Thomas and Florence A. (Young) H.; e. Queen Alexandra Elem. and Strathcona High Schs., Edmonton, Alta.; Candn. Army Staff Coll., 1945; Univ. of W. Ont., Marketing 1957, Mang. Training Course 1967; m. Norma Amelia, d. Verner Winfield Smith, 15 Aug. 1947; children: Thomas Claude, Leslie Margaret, Beverly Ann, Terry Kathleen, Nancy Elizabeth; Clerk-Salesman, Edmonton Wholesale Grocers 1929–37; Rep. of Mutual Life of Can. 1937–40; Mgr. 1947–50; Supt. of Field Training 1951–52; Supt. of Agencies 1953–64; Sr. Supt. Agency Operations 1965–68; Vice-Pres., I/C Agencies 1968; Sr. Vice Pres. and Dir. of Marketing, Mutual Life of Can. 1969–78 (ret.); Re-estbl. VP Agencies, Lutheran Life Insur. 1980–82; Dir., Life Insurance Mktg. and Rsch. Assn. 1968–72; Life Dir., Kitchener-Waterloo Symphony Orchestra 1988; enlisted as Private in Inf. 1940; joined Loyal Edmn. Regt. (Lieut.) Oct. 1942; assault landing Sicily July 1943, W I. Action; re-joined L.Edmn.R. in Italy 1943, Adjutant Oct. 1943; attached S. Alta. Regt. May 1944 (Capt.); N.W. Europe campaign, staff Capt. 'A' 10 Cdn. Inf. Bde. (4th Cdn. Div.); Canadian Army Staff College (RMC) 1945. GSO II (Maj.) Cdn. Army, Ottawa, Dir. Mil. Training July 1945 – May 1946; P. Conservative; Anglican; recreations: golf, curling, swimming, photography; Club: Westmount Golf & Country; Home: 266 Stanley Dr., Waterloo, Ont. N2L 1J1.

**HARRIS, Henry Silton,** M.A., Ph.D., F.R.S.C.; university professor; b. Brighton, England 11 Apr. 1926; s. Henry and Amy Adelaide (Sampson) H.; e. Hove (Sussex) Co. Sch.; Lancing Coll., Shoreham, Sussex; St. Edmund Hall, Oxford, B.A. 1949, M.A. 1952; Northwestern Univ.; Univ. of Illinois, Ph.D. 1954; m. Ruth Evalene, d. Henry A. Koski, Chassell, Mich., 20 June 1952; children: Carol Elizabeth, David Neville Silton, Peter Geoffrey, Anne Cassandra; DISTINGUISHED RESEARCH PROF. OF PHILOS., GLENDON COLL., YORK UNIV. 1984– ; Instr. in Philos., Ohio State Univ., 1954–57; Asst. and Assoc. Prof. of Philos., Univ. of Illinois, 1957–62; Assoc. Prof. of Philos., York Univ., 1962, Prof. of Philos. 1965– ; served in 2nd World War with Brit. Army; Signalman, Royal Signals, 1944–45; Publications: 'The Social Philosophy of Giovanni Gentile' 1960; 'Hegel's Development I-II' 1972, 1983; mem., Candn. Philos. Assn.; Hegel Soc. of Am. (former Pres.); Hegel Soc. of G.B. (Hon. Pres.); Int. Hegel Vereinigung; Hume Soc.; Peirce Soc.; Home: 2527 Graham St., Victoria, B.C. V8T 3Y6.

**HARRIS, John Richard,** B.Sc., M.A.; geologist; b. McAllen, Texas 5 March 1931; s. John Richard and Helen (Francis) H.; m. Roelle Missal d. Adalbert and Eleonore Missal 1 Sept. 1981; children: Rick, Charles, David, Helen; OIL & GAS CONS., HARRIS CONSULTANTS 1985– ; Dir., Anderson Exploration Ltd.; Grad & Walker Energy Corp.; oil & gas cons., Houston and Calgary 1957–66; Pres., Syracuse Oils Ltd. 1966–71; Sr. Vice Pres., Bow Valley Inds. Ltd. 1971–76, Pres. 1976–81; Pres., Corrida Oils Ltd. 1981–82, Chrmn. 1982–85; Cert. Petroleum Geol. #169 (USA); Cert. Profl. Geol. Sci. #3179 (USA); Profl. Geol. #13783 (Can.); Life Mem., Sigma Gamma Epsilon, the Nat. Honour Soc. of the Earth Sciences; Office: Suite 820, 717 – 7th Ave. S.W., Calgary, Alta. T2P 0Z3.

**HARRIS, Leslie,** O.C., B.A.(Ed.), M.A., Ph.D.; university president, retired; b. St. Joseph's, Placentia Bay, Nfld. 24 Oct. 1929; s. James William and Rachel (Bishop) H.; e. St. Joseph's All Grade Sch.; Memorial Univ. of Nfld. B.A.(Ed.) 1956, M.A.(Hist.) 1959; Sch. of Oriental and African Studies, Univ. of London Ph.D.(Asian Hist.) 1960; m. Mary, d. William and Mary Ann Hewitt 22 Aug. 1951; Pres. and Vice-Chancellor, Memorial Univ. of Newfoundland 1981–90; Teacher, Nfld. 1945–58; Dir. Tri-coll. Co-op. Prog. (Asian Studies) Sweet Briar Coll., Randolph-Macon Women's Coll., Lynchburg Coll., Virginia, U.S.A. 1960–62; Dir. Summer Inst. (Asian Studies) Univ. of Virginia 1962; Memorial Univ. of Nfld.: Asst. Prof. of Hist. 1963, Assoc. Prof. and Head (pro tem.) Dept. of Hist. 1964, Head Dept. of Hist. 1965, Prof. of Hist. and Acting Dean of Arts and Sci. 1966, Dean of Arts and Sci. 1967, Vice-Pres. (Academic) and Pro Vice-chancellor 1974; recipient: Can. Counc. Pre-doctoral Fellowship to S.O.A.S., Univ. of London 1958–60; Am. Counc. of Learned Socs. and Social Sci. Rsch. Counc. Combined Travel Fellowship for travel and study in India and Pakistan 1962–63; mem. and office-bearer of sev. cttes. and learned socs. incl. (currently) Dir. Assn. of Univs. and Colls. of Can. 1970–73, 1981–86; Social Sci. and Humanities Rsch. Counc. of Can. 1978– ; Petroleum Training Coordinating Ctte. (Dept. of Edn., Govt. of Nfld. and Lab.) 1979– ; Chrmn., Advisory Counc. on Edn. & Tng. and Rsch. & Devel. (Dept. of Mines and Energy, Govt. of Nfld. and Lab.) 1980– ; Exec. Counc., Assn. of Atlantic Univs. 1981– , Chrmn. 1987– ; Atlantic Can. Counc. of Chief Exec. Officers, Conf. Bd. of Can. 1981– ; Nfld. and Lab. Award for Bravery Review Panel 1982– ; Bd. of Trustees, Ocean Ranger Disaster Fund 1982– ; Chrmn. Historic Sites and Monuments Bd. of Can.; mem. Prov. Panel of Arbitration Chrmn.; Chrmn. and Dir. Nfld. and Labrador Computer Services Ltd.; Chrmn. Nfld. and Labrador Heritage Found. 1984– ; mem. Bd. of Dir., Huntsman Marine Laboratory 1985– ; Chrmn., Battle Hr. Hist. Trust 1990– ; Chrmn., Panel to Review State of Northern Cod 1989–90; Mem., Nat. Round Table on the Environment and the Economy; Cons. Ed., Can. Jour. of Higher Edn. 1980– ; Ed. 'Aspects' 1966– ; author 'Newfoundland and Labrador: A Brief History' 1968; of numerous scholarly works on Asian hist. and the hist. and people of Nfld. and Lab.; Officer of the Order of Canada 1987; recreation: fishing, bridge, reading gardening; Home: 8 Ellis Place, St. John's, Nfld. A1B 3G1; Office: Memorial Univ. of Newfoundland, St. John's, Nfld. A1C 5S7.

**HARRIS, Leslie Philip,** B.A.; film/tv producer/director; b. Essex, England 4 Jan. 1947; s. Herbert Philip and Marie (Solden) H.; e. King's Coll.; Sheffield Univ. B.A. (Hons.); m. Jane d. Robert and Dorothy Pearson 22 May 1976; children: Brett, Lee, Sean; PRES., CANAMEDIA PROD. LTD. 1979– ; Film Ed., BBC TV 1968–71; Film Dir., Leshar Films 1972–74; Mng. Dir., Leshar Film Sales Ltd. 1974–76; Prod., CBC TV 1976–78; 'W5,' CTV Network 1978–80; 'Escape from Iran' (CBS TV/CTV) 1981; Chief Extve. Offr., Offnonline Video Post Prodn. 1983–88; Dir., YTV; Friday St. Prod.; Servington Corp.; 2 Gemini Awards; Banff Rockie Award for 'King of Friday Night' 1985; Children's Broadcast Inst. Award of Excellence and Japan Maeda Prize for 'Take Off' 1991 & '92; Peabody Award 1992 for 'Threads of Hope'; Office: 125 Dupont St., Toronto, Ont. M5R 1V4.

**HARRIS, Marjorie Kathleen,** B.A.; writer; b. Shaunovon, Sask. 15 Sept. 1937; d. Bernard George and Kathleen Amelia (Frazer) Stibbards; e. McMaster Univ., B.A. (Hons.) 1959; m. Jack s. Jack and Kathleen Batten 20 April 1968; children: Christopher Harris, Jennifer, Harris; writer/curator, art shows 1964–66; writer/senior writer, Maclean's 1966–70; numerous freelance articles for every major Candn. mag.; regular commentator, writer/prod. of documentaries, CBC radio; Assoc. Ed., Chatelaine 1973–77; co-developer, The Sunday Star; Goodage; columnist, Cityspan (The Canadian); National gardening columnist, The Globe & Mail 1991– ; mem., Ont. Rock Garden Soc.; Alpine Club of B.C.; Candn. Wildflower Soc.; Am. Rock Garden Soc.; Mem., Bd. of Dirs., Civic Garden Ctr., Toronto; author: 'Toronto: City of Neighbourhoods' 1984; 'The Canadian Gardener' 1990; 'Ecological Gardening' 1991; 'The Canadian Gardener's Year' 1992; 'The Canadian Gardener's Guide to Foliage & Garden Design' 1993; 'Marjorie Harris' Favorite Garden Tips' (Flowering Shrubs; Shade Plants; Perennials; Annuals) 1994; ghost writer: 'The Bare Facts: The Autobiography of Annie Ample' 1988; co-author: 'Sciencescape' 1986 (with David Suzuki), 'Everyday Law' 1987 (with Jack Batten), 'How to Make Love to a Lobster' 1988 (with Peter Taylor); co-author/ed.: 'Historic Canada' 1984; co-editor: 'Farewell to the Seventies' 1979 (with Anna Porter); photo-ed.: 'Times to Remember' 1986; recreations: gardening; Home: 199 Albany Ave., Toronto, Ont. M5R 3C7.

**HARRIS, Michael D.,** M.P.P.; provincial party leader; politician; b. Toronto, Ont. 23 Jan. 1945; s. Sidney Deane and Hope Gooding (Robinson) H.; E. Algonguin H.S.; North Bay Teachers' Coll., teacher's cert.; courses, Laurentian & Nipissing univs.; m. Janet Ina d. Doug and Ina Harrison 19 Apr. 1947; children: Michael Stewart, Jeffrey Deane; LEADER, ONTARIO PROGRESSIVE CONSERVATIVE PARTY 1990– ; M.P.P., Legislative Assembly of Ont. 1981– ; former teacher / businessman (family-owned tourist & ski resorts); Trustee, Nipissing Bd. of Ed. 1975–81 (Chrmn. 1977–81); Pres., North. Ont. Trustees' Assn. 1980–81; served as Parlty. Asst. to Envir. Min.; Chrmn. of Public Accounts; Gen. Govt. & Resources Devel. Cttes.; apptd. Min. of Natural Resources & Min. of Energy 1985; P.C. House Leader

1986–89; Housing Critic & North. Devel. Critic for Ont. P.C. Party; devel. Party fiscal policy 1988 as Finan. Critic; el. Ont. P.C. Party Leader 12 May 1990; Bd. of Dir., PC Ont. Fund; Mem., Ont. Profl. Golfing Assn.; Ont. Ski Instr. Alliance; Anglican; P.C.; recreations: golf, skiing, hunting & fishing, bridge; club: Albany (Dir.); Home: North Bay, Ont.; Offices: Rm. 116 M.B., Queen's Park, Toronto, Ont. M7A 1A8 and Ste. 1, 374 Fraser St., North Bay, Ont. P1B 3W7.

**HARRIS, Michael Terry,** B.A.; author; journalist; b. Toronto, Ont. 11 Mar. 1948; s. Charles Arthur and Audrey Eleanor (Tilley) H.; e. York Univ., B.A. (Hons.) 1971; Univ. Coll. (Dublin) 1972; m. Lynda d. Gwendolyn and William Smith 31 August 1970; children: (Sarah) Peyton, Emily Kathleen; author; Regular panelist, CTV's Sunday Edition; Co-host, PBS series 'Literatti'; Host, 'The Harris Report,' CBC 1979–80; 'The Harris/Lorimer' Report 1980–81; Bureau Chief, Atlantic Reg., Globe & Mail 1981–85; Parl. Corr. 1985–86; Pub. & Editor-in-Chief, 'The Sunday Express', St. John's, Nfld. 1986–90; Extve. Dir., News & Current Affairs, Nfld. Television 1990–92; Mem. Bd. of Dirs., The Michener Found. 1991; Woodrow Wilson Scholar; Radio & TV News Dirs. Award; Hon. Mention, Michener Award for Journalism 1989; Centre for Investigative Journalism Award 1989; Silver Medal, Best News Documentary for 'Unholy Orders', The New York Festivals 1991; author: 'Justice Denied: The Law Versus Donald Marshall' 1986; 'Unholy Orders: The Mount Cashel Tragedy' 1990 (named Book of the Year, Found. for the Advancement of Candn. Letters 1991); 'Rare Ambition' a history of the Crosbie family, 1992 (non-fiction); Home: Box 189, Lunenburg, N.S. B0J 2C0.

**HARRIS, Milton E.,** O.C., B.Com.; construction executive; b. Detroit, Mich. 26 July 1927; s. Sam Harris; e. St. George's Sch. and Central Coll. Inst. London, Ont. 1945; Univ. of Toronto B.Com. 1949; m. Ethel, d. of Joseph Brody 4 Sept. 1949; children: Judith Rachel, Naomi Ruth, David Eli; CHRMN. & PRES., HARRIS STEEL GROUP INC.; former Dir., Livingston Industries Ltd.; Canadair Ltd.; former Dir. Air Canada; Past Pres. London Liberal Assn.; Past Chrmn., Finance Comte., Liberal Party of Can.; past mem. London Bd. Educ.; past mem. Senate, Univ. of W. Ont.; Past Pres. London Jewish Community Counc.; founding Pres., Toronto Jewish Cong.; Hon. Officer, Nat. Officers' Ctte., Candn. Jewish Congress; Past Pres. Candn. Jewish Cong. (and Past Chrmn. for Ont.); Past Dir. Bank Hapoalim; Mount Sinai Hosp.; Past Bd mem., Canadian Opera Co.; Mem., Metals and Minerals Ctte., Sectoral Adv. Group on Internat. Trade (SAGIT); mem., Internat. Bd. of Govs., Tel-Aviv Univ.; Officer, Order of Canada 1986; Conservative; Jewish; recreations: bicycling, sailing, reading, history; Home: 28 Fifeshire Rd., Toronto, Ont. M2L 2G5.

**HARRIS, The Hon. Raymond Hamilton,** B.A., LL.B.; provincial court judge; b. Wilferforce, Ohio 14 Mar. 1926; s. Raymond Hamilton and Marjorie Vera (Gideon) H.; e. St. Johns H.S.; United Coll.; Univ. of Man., B.A. 1952; LL.B. 1956; m. Mimi Beth d. Robert and Marjory Brennand 13 Aug. 1960; JUDGE, PROV. COURT OF MAN. 1974– ; law prac., Levin & Harris 1956–71; Levin, Soronow & Harris 1971–74; Univ. of Winnipeg Bd. of Regents; Mem., Man. Bar Counc.; Candn. Bar Counc.; Past Pres., Man. Assn. of Prov. Court Judges 1980, 1981; Univ. of Winnipeg Alumni Assn. 1978; recreations: golf, skating; Home: 1311–65 Swindon Way, Winnipeg, Man. R3P 0T8; Office: 408 York Ave., Winnipeg, Man. R3C 0P9.

**HARRIS, Richard Colebrook,** B.A., M.Sc., Ph.D., F.R.S.C.; educator; b. Vancouver, B.C. 4 July 1936; s. Richard Colebrook and Ellen Gertrude (Code) H.; e. Univ. of B.C. B.A. 1958; Univ. of Wis. M.Sc. 1962, Ph.D. 1964; m. Muriel Joyce d. Douglas and Gertrude Watney, Vancouver, B.C. 6 June 1964; children: Douglas, Colin, Rachel; PROF. OF GEOG., UNIV. OF B.C.; Prof. of Historical Geography, Univ. of Toronto until 1971; Guggenheim Fellow; Sr. Killam Fellow; author 'The Seigneurial System in Early Canada: A Geographical Study' 1966, republished 1984; co-author 'Canada Before Confederation: A Study in Historical Geography' 1974; Ed. 'Letters from Windermere, 1912–1914' 1984; 'Historical Atlas of Canada vol. I From the Beginning to 1800' 1987; numerous articles on European settlement in early Can. particularly Que. and B.C.; Home: 6660 Wiltshire St., Vancouver, B.C. V6P 5G7; Office: Univ. of B.C., 1984 West Mall, Vancouver, B.C. V6T 1Z2.

**HARRIS, Robert Garfield;** business executive; b. Montreal, Que. 6 Aug. 1941; s. William James and Ruth Mary (Buchanan) H.; e. Sir George Williams Univ.; m. Ann d. Kennin and Marjory Hamilton 27 Oct. 1962; children: Elizabeth Alison, Robert Gregory; PRESIDENT, CANADA BUSINESS CENTERS LTD. 1969– ; Mktg. Dept., BP Canada 1959–63; Sales Rep. then Regional Sales Mgr., Facelle Co. Ltd. 1964–66; Consultant, E Plus Ltd. 1967– ; Owner/Pres., Canada Business Interiors Ltd. 1975– ; Cambrian Travel Ltd. 1980– ; Execuspace Inc. 1992– ; Past Dir., West Island Coll.; recreations: hockey, squash, tennis; Clubs: Dorval Golf; Office: 705, 6600 Trans Canada Hwy., Pointe Claire, Que. H9R 4S2.

**HARRIS, Robin Sutton,** B.A., M.A., Ph.D., D.Litt.; educator; b. Toronto, Ont. 27 Oct. 1919; s. George Henry Ronalds and Lorna Craig (Gibbons) H.; e. Univ. of Toronto B.A. 1941, M.A. 1947; Univ. of Michigan Ph.D. 1952; m. Mary Patricia d. John Gunn 22 June 1946 (div.); m. 2ndly Terry Gonçalves 5 July 1988; children (from previous marriage): Catherine A., David R., Mary M. Shaw-Rimmington; Professor of Higher Education, Univ. of Toronto 1964–85, now emeritus; Jr. Master, Ridley Coll., St. Catharines, Ont. 1941, 1945–46; Lt., Captain, Royal Cdn. Artillery 1941–45; Lectr. Dept. of Eng., Univ. of W. Ont. 1947–49; Lectr., Asst. Prof., Assoc. Prof., Dept. of Eng., Univ. of Toronto 1952–64 (and Principal Innis Coll. 1964–71); author (with R.L. McDougall) 'The Undergraduate Essay' 1960; 'Quiet Evolution: A Study of the Ontario Educational System' 1967; 'A History of Higher Education in Canada 1663–1960' 1976; 'English Studies at Toronto: a history' 1988; Sch. Trustee Toronto Bd. of Educ. 1959–62; recreations: golf, squash; Club: Toronto Golf; Home: 9 Dennis Dr., King City, Ont. L0G 1K0.

**HARRIS, Roland Allen,** O.B.E., B.A.; b. Toronto, Ont. 20 Nov. 1906; s. Roland Caldwell and Alice Mary (Ingram) H.; e. Univ. of Toronto Schs., Sr. Matric. 1923; Univ. Coll., Univ. of Toronto, B.A. (Pol. Sci.) 1928; Imperial Staff Coll., Camberley, Eng., 1943; m. Dae, d. late F.H.B. Lyon, 23 Sept. 1933; children: Molly Dae, John Roland; joined A. McKim Ltd. as Asst. Acct. Extve., 1928; Salesman, Pub. Dir. & Adv. Mgr., DeForest Crosley Ltd., Toronto, 1929; Asst. to Sales Mgr., Woods Underwear Co. (Toronto), 1933; Sales Mgr., Dent. Allcroft & Co. Ltd. (Eng.), 1937; Gen. Mgr., C. H. Smith Co. Ltd., Windsor, 1945, Mang. Dir. 1949; Dir., Gordon Mackay and Stores Ltd., 1949 and Dir. i/c Retail Divs., 1954; Vice Pres., 1955; Pres., Walker Stores Ltd., 1957; Pres., Canada Cycle & Motor Co. Ltd. 1959–61; Vice-Pres., Marketing B.F. Goodrich Canada Ltd., 1961–67; served with Q.O.R. of C., 1940–45; held staff appts. with HQ 8th Candn. Inf. Bgde., HQ 1st Candn. Corps, HQ 1st Candn. Army, HQ S.E. Command and Candn. Planning Staff; Mil. Asst. to Lt. Gen. Sir Frederick E. Morgan (planned Normandy Invasion); returned to HQ 1st Candn. Army 1945 and attached to HQ 30th Brit. Corps; discharged Oct. 1945 with rank Lt. Col.; awarded O.B.E.; Mentioned in Despatches; Pres., Ont. Chamber Comm., 1957–58; ad hoc Magistrate and Police Commr., Windsor, Ont., 1950; Phi Delta Theta; Conservative; Anglican; recreations: fishing, golf; Clubs: University (Toronto); Toronto Racquet; Westmount Golf & Country; Home: 10 Westgate Walk, Kitchener, Ont. N2M 2T8.

**HARRIS, Stuart Arthur,** B.Sc., M.Sc., Ph.D.; university professor; b. Cheltenham, Eng. 14 Jan. 1931; s. Samuel and Dorothy Edith Irene (Kirk) H.; e. Univ. of London B.Sc. (Hons.) 1952, M.Sc. 1955, Ph.D. 1968; m. Pamela d. Leslie and Gwendolyn Payne 20 July 1957; children: Stephen Clive, Kevin Peter, Fiona Clare; PROFESSOR, GEOGRAPHY, UNIV. OF CALGARY 1973– ; Chief Engineers Branch, Royal Engineers Egypt 1952–56 (incl. a spell with Arab Legion under Col. Glubb); Rsch. Sci., Hunting Tech. Services 1955–59; Soil Surveyor, Brit. Guiana 1959–62; Visiting Asst. Prof., Geog., Univ. of Chicago 1962; Asst. Prof., Wilfrid Laurier Univ. 1962–66; Assoc. Prof., Univ. of Kansas 1966–69; Assoc. Prof., Univ. of Calgary 1969–73; Sec., Internat. Correlation Prog. Project 297, Geocryology of the Americas 1989–94; Mem., Internat. Permafrost Assn. Working Group on Mountain Permafrost 1988–93; Assoc. Ctte. on Permafrost Rsch., NRC 1976–84; IPA Working Group Workshop & Field Trips 1983, 1992; IGU Workshop 1972; First recipient, Westmark Klondike Inn Sci. Award 1989; Mem., Parks & Rec. Bd., City of Calgary 1983–89 (Vice Chair 1985–89); Rsch. Assoc., Arctic Inst. of N. Am. 1982– ; author: 'The Permafrost Environment' 1986 and over 140 pubns.; co-author 'Glossary of Permafrost & Related Ground-Ice Terms' 1988; Home: 6316 Dalton Dr. NW, Calgary, Alta. T3A 1E4; Office: Calgary, Alta. T2N 1N4.

**HARRIS, Hon. Sydney Malcolm,** Q.C., B.A., LL.B.; judge, retired; b. Toronto, Ont. 23 June 1917; s. Samuel Aaron and Rose (Geldzaeler) H.; e. Jesse Ketchum Pub. Sch. and Jarvis Coll. Inst. Toronto 1935; Univ. of Toronto, B.A. 1939; Osgoode Hall Law Sch. grad. 1942, LL.B. 1991; m. Enid d. Louis and Emma Perlman 9 Nov. 1949; two s. S. Mark, David K.; cr. Q.C. 1962; Judge, Prov. Court of Ont. (Criminal Div.) 1976–90; Judge, Ont. Court of Justice (Prov. Div.) 1990–92; Deputy Judge, Ont. Court of Justice (Small Claims) 1993– ; Nat. Pres. Candn. Jewish Cong. 1973–76; Home: 2006, 3303 Don Mills Rd., Willowdale, Ont. M2J 4T6.

**HARRIS, Walter Edgar,** M.Sc., Ph.D., FCIC, F.R.S.C. 1977, FAAAS 1980; retired educator; b. Wetaskiwin, Alta., 9 June 1915; s. Ernest William and Emma Louise (Humbke) H.; e. Wetaskiwin (Alta.) High Sch., 1934; Univ. of Alta., B.Sc. 1938, M.Sc. 1939; Univ. of Minn., Ph.D. 1944; Univ. of Waterloo, D.Sc. (Hon.) 1987; Univ. of Alta., D.Sc. (Hon.) 1991; m. Phyllis, d. Samuel Pangburn, Northwood, Iowa, 14 June 1942; children: Margaret Anne, William Edgar; Chrmn., Pres.'s Adv. Comte. on Campus Reviews, 1982–90; Prof. of Analytical Chem., Univ. of Alberta, 1946–80; Chrmn. Dept. of Chem. there 1974–80 (ret.); rec'd Fisher Scient. Lecture Award, Chem. Inst. Can., 1969; Outstanding Achievement Award for Univ. of Minn. Alumni, 1973; Chem. Educ. Award, Chem. Inst. of Can. 1975; co-author: 'Programmed Temperature Gas Chromatography' 1966; 'Chemical Separations and Measurements' 1974; 'Chemical Analysis' 1975; 'An Introduction to Chemical Analysis' 1981; author over 100 articles in scient. journs.; Ed., Candn. Journ. Chem.; Advisory Board, Anal. Chem.; Councillor, Chem. Inst. Canada; mem., Am. Chem. Soc.; Fellow, Royal Soc. of Can., 1977; Fellow, Am. Assoc. for the Advancement of Sci., 1980; rec'd Alberta Outstanding Achievement Award 1974; Sigma Xi; Protestant; recreations: curling, bridge, ballroom dancing; Home: 9212 – 118 St., Edmonton, Alta. T6G 1T9.

**HARRIS, Hon. Walter Edward,** P.C. (Can.), Q.C., D.C.L.; b. Kimberley, Ont. 14 Jan. 1904; s. Melvin and Helen (Carruthers) H.; m. Grace Elma, d. J.J. Morrison, Toronto, Ont.; children: Fern, Margaret Helen, Robert Walter; member, firm of Harris, Willis, Barristers, Markdale, Ont.; 1st el. to H. of C. for Grey-Bruce, g.e. 1940; apptd. Parlty. Asst. to Secy. of State for External Affairs (Hon. L.S. St. Laurent) 1947, and Parlty. Asst. to the Prime Min. 1948; Min. of Citizenship & Immigration 1950–54; Min. of Finance 1954–57; served in 2nd World War; Freemason (P.M.); Liberal; Baptist; Clubs: Ontario (Toronto); Home: 32 Wellington St., Markdale, Ont. N0C 1H0; Office: Main St., Markdale, Ont. N0C 1H0.

**HARRIS, William Bowles,** M.A., LL.D. (Hon.); financier; b. Toronto, Ont. 17 Aug. 1930; s. William Cranfield and Ethel Mary (Bowles) H.; e. Upper Can. Coll.; Univ. of Toronto, B.A. 1953, Oxford Univ. (Christ Ch.), M.A. 1955; m. M. Patricia, d. the late Rev. Canon F. Arthur Smith, 22 May 1957; children: Diana, Virginia; William A.; Chrmn., Mercantile & General Reinsurance Co. of Can.; Chrmn. Barclays Bank of Canada; Dir., E-L Financial Corp. Ltd.; Key Publishers Ltd.; Consumer's Gas; Prudasco Inc.; joined Harris & Partners Ltd. 1955; apptd. Dir., 1960; Vice-President, 1964; Pres. 1966–73; Co-Chrmn., Dominion Securities Harris 1973–74; former Chrmn. World Wildlife Fund Canada; mem. Candn. Econ. Policy Comte.; former Chrmn. Exec. Comm., Trinity Coll., Univ. of Toronto; former Chrmn. Bd. Govs., Univ. of Toronto; Alpha Delta Phi; Anglican; recreations: farming; Clubs: Toronto; York; Mount Royal (Montreal); Home: 56 Cluny Drive, Toronto, Ont. M4W 2R2.

**HARRIS, William Edgar,** M.Sc., Ph.D.; astronomer; educator; b. Edmonton, Alta. 28 Nov. 1947; s. Walter Edgar and Phyllis June (Pangburn) H.; e. Univ. of Alta. B.Sc. 1969; Univ. of Toronto M.Sc. 1970, Ph.D. 1974; m. Gretchen L. Hagen 24 Aug. 1974; two d. Glenna, Martha; PROF. OF PHYSICS McMASTER UNIV. 1984– ; Postdoctoral Fellow Yale Univ. 1974–76; Asst. Prof. present Univ. 1976, Assoc. Prof. 1980; Office: Hamilton, Ont. L8S 4M1.

**HARRISON, Alexander George,** M.Sc., Ph.D., F.C.I.C.; b. Peterborough, Ont. 1 Apl. 1931; s. Charles Leslie and Grace Fleming (Edwards) H.; e. Univ. of W. Ont. B.Sc. 1952, M.Sc. 1953; McMaster Univ. Ph.D. 1956; m. Barbara d. Douglas and Mabel Smith 20 Aug. 1955; two d. Jane E., Ann P.; PROF. OF CHEM. UNIV. OF TORONTO 1967– ; Lectr. in Chem. present Univ. 1959, Asst. Prof. 1960, Assoc. Prof. 1962, Assoc. Chrmn. of Chem. 1971–74; Visiting Prof. of Chem. Univ. of Warwick 1975; Professeur Invité Inst. Chim. Phys. EPFL Lausanne 1982; Visiting Prof. of Chem., Univ. of Colorado 1989; Alfred P. Sloan Fellow 1962–64; Noranda Lecture Award Chem. Inst. Can. 1971; Killam Rsch. Fellow 1985–87; author 'Chemical Ionization Mass Spectrometry' 1983 (2nd ed. 1992); author or co-author over 200 sci. publs.; mem. Am. Soc. Mass Spectrometry (Dir. 1976–79); Chem. Inst. Can. (Chrmn. Phys. Chem. Div. 1979–81, mem. Council 1980–83); Home: 225 Ranleigh Ave., Toronto, Ont. M4N 1X3; Office: Toronto, Ont. M5S 1A1.

**HARRISON, Brian George;** politician; b. Toronto, Ont. 7 Sept. 1931; s. Ernest Edwin and Lillian Jane (Keefe) H.; e. East York C.I. 1949; children: Scott, Karen, Cindy, Sean; METRO. TORONTO COUNCILLOR, SCARBOROUGH CITY CENTRE 1988– ; el. (Scarborough) School Trustee Ward 7 1964–65; Councillor, Ward 5 1965–66; Controller 1967–82; Mem. of Metro Council 1967–82; Comnr., Toronto Transit Comn.; Chrmn., Metro. Toronto Coach Terminal Inc.; Chrmn., Bd. of Mgmt., Metro Toronto Zoo; Mem., Metro. Toronto Parks & Property Ctte.; Metro. Toronto Council Striking Ctte.; Metro. Toronto Region & Conservation Authority; Candn. Nat. Exhibition Assn.; Pitman Ctte., Task Force on Human Relations; Exhibition Task Force; Dir., Pauline McGibbon Cultural Centre; Founding Pres., North Bendale Community Assn.; Charter Extve. Mem., North Bendale Home and School Assn.; Founding Mem. & Hon. Mem., Scarborough Business Assn.; Past Mem., Canadian National Exhibition; Police Comn. of Metro. Toronto; Past Pres., Ont. Chapter, Am. Public Works Assn.; Dir., Candn. Public Works Assn.; Past Pres. & Secy.-Treas., Ont. Traffic Conference; Dir., Scarborough Chamber of Commerce; Bd. Mem., Scarborough Gen. Hosp.; Scarborough Centenary Hosp.; East Scarborough Boys' Club; Mem., Am. Right-of-Way Assn.; Inst. of Solid Wastes; Inst. for Equip. Services; Royal Candn. Legion (258); Metro. Bd. of Trade; Metro. Toronto Traffic Conf.; Rameses Shrine Temple; Anglican; Office: Metro Hall, Stn. 1020, 55 John St., Ste. 215, Toronto, Ont. M5V 3C6.

**HARRISON, David Archibald,** B.Comm., C.A.; financial executive; b. Trail, B.C. 28 March 1943; e. Univ. of B.C. B.Comm. 1967; B.C. C.A. 1970; COMPTROLLER/TREASURER, B.C. HYDRO 1988– ; Collins & Barrow, C.A.s 1967–72; Dir., Special Projects, Dart Enterprises 1972–78; Mgr., Corp. Acctg., B.C. Hydro 1978–79; Group Comtroller, Eng. Group 1979–80; Comptroller 1981–86; Dir., Information Systems 1986–88; recreations: sailing, golfing, skiing; clubs: Burrard Yacht (Rear-Commodore); Home: 3090 Discovery St., Vancouver, B.C. V6R 3Y7; Office: 12th Floor, 333 Dunsmuir St., Vancouver, B.C. V6B 5R3.

**HARRISON, Edward Hardy (Ted),** C.M., A.T.D., B.Ed.; b. Wingate, Co. Durham, UK 28 Aug. 1926; s. Charles Edward and Martha (Thirlaway) H.; e. Wellfield Grammar Sch. Wingate 1943; Hartlepool Coll. of Art, Cleveland, UK Nat. Dip. in Design 1950; Kings Coll. Univ. of Durham Art Teacher's Dip. 1951; Univ. of Alta. B.Ed. 1977; Athabasca Univ., Alta., hon. doctorate 1991; m. Robina d. Alexander and Annie McNicol 12 Nov. 1960; one s. Charles Edward; sch. teacher Tech. Sch. for Boys Middlesborough, UK 1951–57; Slim Sch. Cameron Highlands, Malaysia 1958–62; Te Kauwhata Dist. High Sch. N.Z. 1963–65; Wingate (UK) Jr. Sch. 1965–66; Dene House Sch. Peterlee, UK 1966–67; Wabasca Elem. Sch. N. Alta. 1967–68; Carcross (Y.T.) Elem. Sch. 1968–71; Yukon Vocational Sch. 1971–75; F.H. Collins Secondary Sch. Whitehorse 1975–80; served with Brit. Army Intelligence Corps Field Security Sect. India, Egypt, Kenya, Uganda & Somaliland 1945–48, rank Sgt.; Fire Chief Carcross, Y.T. 1968–71; author & illus. 'Children of the Yukon' 1977; 'The Last Horizon' (autobiog.) 1980; 'A Northern Alphabet' (children) 1982; 'The Blue Raven' 1989; illus. 'The Cremation of Sam McGee' by Robt. Service 1986; 'The Shooting of Dan McGrew' (also by R.W. Service) 1988; 'O Canada' 1992; paintings hung many private & pub. colls. incl. Festival Theatre Stratford, Ont., City of Ushiku, Japan, Alta. House London, UK, Great Ormond St. Children's Hosp. London, UK, Govt. of Y.T., Hosp. for Sick Children Toronto; mem. Can. Council Explorations Ctte. 1978–80; Dir. Nat. Parks Citizens Centennial Ctte. Y.T. 1983–86; subject NFB film 'Harrison's Yukon' 1978; recipient Medal of Merit Boy Scouts Assn. N.Z.; Cert. of Honour Award for Illus. Internat. Bd. Books for Youth, Cyprus 1984; 'New York Times' Certificate of excellence for one of the year's best illustrated children's books 1987; Mem., Order of Canada 1987; Commemorative Medal, 125th Anniversary of Candn. Confedn. 1992; Life mem. Yukon Teachers Assn.; mem., Vancouver Art Gallery; Writers Union Can.; Candn. IBBY (Internat. Bd. of Books for Youth); recreations: travel, walking, fishing; Club: Edmonton; Home: 2029 Romney Place, Victoria, B.C. V8S 4J6.

**HARRISON, J.B. (Ben);** consultant; insurance executive; b. Detroit, Mich. 5 Sept. 1935; s. Joseph C. and Helen Anita (Nobles) H.: e. Univ. of Windsor; Univ. of Michigan; Walden Univ. Inst. for Adv. Studies (Ph.D. Candidate); m. Dr. Sheila d. Charles and Marion (Catto) Pennington 24 June 1974; children: Michael, Timothy (Harrison); step-children: Ann, Alex (Pennington); Consultant to business and not-for-profit sector; Pres., Board Governance Inc.; Sales Mgr., Allstate Insur. 1957–68; Vice-Pres. & Chief Agent, Wausau Insur. Cos. 1968–86; Pres., Metropolitan Insur. Co. 1986–90; Bd. Canada Ctte., Internat. Year of Family; Former Bd. Chrmn., Family Serv. Can.; Dir., Family Serv. Am.; Past Pres., Family Serv. Metro. Toronto; frequent contbr. of articles and extensive public speaker; awarded Commemorative Medal for 125th Anniversary of Candn. Confederation 1992; recreation: running; Club: Cambridge; Home: 14 Thurloe Ave., Toronto, Ont. M4S 2K2.

**HARRISON, James Ernest,** B.A., M.Litt.; educator; writer; b. Trincomalee, Sri Lanka 15 Jan. 1927; s. George William and Jane Elizabeth (Bell) H.; e. Woodhouse Grove Sch., Yorks.; Durham Univ., U.K., B.A. 1951, M.Litt. 1968; m. Vivienne d. Oswald and Jane Denton; children (by a previous marriage): Adam, Simon, Katharine, Naomi; PROFESSOR EMERITUS, UNIV. OF GUELPH 1992– ; various sch. & colleges in the U.K. 1952–69; Asst. Prof., present univ. 1969, Assoc. Prof. 1972, Prof. 1982; prizewinner, C.B.C. Literary Competition, Poetry, 1979; N.D.P.; author: 'Catchment Area' (poems) 1959, 'Rudyard Kipling' 1982, 'Flying Dutchmen' (poems) 1983; 'Salman Rushdie' 1991; editor: 'Scientists as Writers' 1965; Home: 18 Wolfrey Ave., Toronto, Ont. M4K 1K8; Office: Guelph, Ont. N1G 2W1.

**HARRISON, Joan Elizabeth,** M.D., F.R.C.P.(C); retired medical scientist and educator; b. Toronto, Ont. 29 July 1926; d. Almon Andrew and Helen (Mowat) Fletcher; e. Bishop Strachan Sch.; Univ. of Toronto M.D. 1951; m. Donald Christopher s. Fredrick and Gladys Harrison 17 June 1950; children: Michael, Christopher, David, Helen; Prof. of Medicine, Univ. of Toronto 1987–92 (Retired), Chrmn. Bone & Mineral Group 1978–86; Dir. Med. Phys. Lab. Toronto Gen. Hosp. 1974–92, Staff Phys. 1961–92 (Retired); recipient Nutrition Rsch. Award 1984; Annual Lecture Award Clin. Rsch. Soc. Toronto 1985; author or co-author 113 rsch. publs. osteoporosis; 4 book chapters; book ed.; ed. bd. Calcified Tissue Internat. 1983–88; mem. Osteoporisis Soc. Can. (Dir. 1982–86; Med. Adv. Bd. 1982–87); Am. Soc. Bone & Mineral Rsch.; Internat. Conf. Calcium Regulating Hormones; Candn. Soc. Clin. Investig.; Candn. Soc. Endocrinol. & Metabolism; recreations: sailing, skiing; Home: 28 Wychwood Park, Toronto, Ont. M6G 2V5; Office: Toronto Gen. Hosp., Toronto, Ont. M5G 2C4.

**HARRISON, John H.,** B.Com.; retired insurance executive; b. Winnipeg, Man. 20 Aug. 1928; s. J.D.B. and Mary B. (Smithers) H.; e. Glebe Coll. Inst. Ottawa 1946; Queen's Univ. B.Com. 1949; m. M. Elizabeth MacRae 28 Dec. 1957; two s. Ian, Donald; Sr. Vice Pres. Invests., Sun Life Assurance Co. of Canada 1988–91; retired; Dir.: Sun Life Trust Co.; Sun Life Savings & Mortgage Corp.; Maritime Electric Co. Ltd.; Fortis Inc.; Century 21 Real Estate Canada Ltd.; joined Invest. Dept., Sun Life 1949, Asst. Treas. 1959, Assoc. Treas. 1961, Treas. 1969, Financial Vice Pres. Securities 1973 and Property Invests. 1974, Vice Pres. Property Invests. 1976 and Invests. 1985; mem. Endowment Invest. Ctte. Queen's Univ.; Past Chrmn. Invest. Sect. Candn. Life & Health Ins. Assn.; Club: Toronto Cricket Skating & Curling; Home: 5 Green Valley Rd., Willowdale, Ont. M2P 1A4.

**HARRISON, Mark,** B.A.; newspaper editor; b. 10 Aug. 1924; s. late Harry and late Sonia (Doduck) H.; e. Univ. of Toronto B.A. 1948, one yr. grad. studies Pol. Science & Econ.; m. Isabel Cliften d. late Frederick George and Zaidee Maude (Smith) Hay-Roe, Toronto, Ont. 24 Feb. 1950; children: Steven, Timothy, Judith, Nancy; Editor, Montreal Gazette 1977–89; joined Toronto Star 1949, Ottawa Bureau Chief 1958–59, European Corr. 1963–66, Ed. Page Ed. 1959–63 and 1966–69, Extve. Ed. 1969–77; Canada's 1st newspaper Ombudsman 1972–74; served with R.C.A.F. 1943–46, Flying Offr. (Navig.), RAF No. 78 Bomber Sqdn. U.K.; recreations: sailing, alpine skiing, golf, reading; Office: 5B-300 Driveway, Ottawa, Ont. K1S 3M6.

**HARRISON, Michael A.,** B.A.Sc., D.B.A., F.I.C.B., F. Inst. D.; executive; b. Toronto, Ont. 24 Apr. 1930; s. James Arthur and Thekla Rothschild (Pineo) H.; e. Univ. of Toronto, B.A.Sc. 1952; London Sch. Econs., Dipl. in Business Adm. 1958; Inst. of Cdn. Bankers, F.I.C.B., 1981; m. Elizabeth Marshall (Ramsden), 2 June 1956; children: Michael Scott, Mark Marshall, Nancy Elizabeth; DEAN, SCHOOL OF BUSINESS, BRITISH COLUMBIA INSTITUTE OF TECHNOLOGY; with C.B.C. 1952–56 (Toronto) as TV Tech., Indust. Relations Asst., Adm. Asst. to Regional Dir.; 1958–65 (Ottawa) Asst. Mgr., Indust. Relations and Mgr. Indust. Relations 1958–61; Extve. Asst. to Pres. 1962–64; Project Offr., Royal Comn. on Govt. Organ. 1961; Planning Offr., Royal Comn. Implementation, Treas. Bd. 1965; Extve. Asst. to Pres. and Marketing Offr., Denison Mines Ltd., 1965–67; Vice Pres. Computers/Communications, Southam Press Ltd. 1967–75; Exec. Dir., Canadian Bankers Assn. 1975–80; Pres., Mgt. Consultants Internat., Inc. 1980–89; Dir. and Past Pres., Council on Drug Abuse; Huguenot Soc. of Canada; Dir., B.C. Chamber of Commerce; Rotary Club of Burnaby; Awards: Athlone Fellow 1956–58; Fellow, Inst. of Directors 1981; Fellow, Inst. of Candn. Bankers (honours) 1981; Fellow, Huguenot Soc. of London; Mem.: Inst. of Directors (U.K.); Vancouver Bd. of Trade; Burnaby Chamber of Comm.; Candn. Ski Instructors Alliance; Publications: Cdn. Business Mgt. Devel., CCH Cdn. Ltd.; 'Canada's Huguenot Heritage' (Ed.), Huguenot Soc. of Can. 1987; recreations: swimming, tennis, skiing, golf, bridge, theatre, films; Office: 3700 Willingdon Ave., Burnaby, B.C. V5G 3H2.

**HARRISON, Michael St. B.;** investment banker; b. Montreal, Que. 12 Nov. 1934; s. Francis Sladen and Nelo Carlotta (Ballantyne) H.; e. Lower Can. Coll. 1952; PRES., MACDOUGALL, MACDOUGALL & MACTIER; var. posts ending as Sr. Bond Trader, Head Office, Bank of Montreal 1954–65; joined Walwyn Stodgell Cochran Murray 1965, Vice Chrmn. 1987; Dir., First Mercantile Currency Fund; Municipal Finance Corp.; Clubs: Royal Candn. Yacht; Mt. Bruno G.C.; University Club, Montreal; Address: 2000 Place du Canada, Montreal, Que. H3B 4J1.

**HARRISON, Norman A.,** C.G.A.; business executive; b. Toronto, Ont. 21 Aug. 1941; s. Howard Thomas and Emma (St Croix) H.; e. Victoria Park H.S.; Ryerson Polytech.; C.G.A. 1971; m. Dale d. Charles and Grace Steine 2 Oct. 1965; children: Laura, Heather; EXTVE. VICE-PRES., BANISTER INC. and CHRMN. & C.E.O., BANISTER MAJESTIC INC. 1993– ; Chrmn., The Foundation Company Inc. 1993– ; Office Mgr. on various projects, Pitts Engineering Construction Ltd. 1961–67; Asst. Treas. / Asst. Controller / Treas. & Controller 1967–80; Vice-Pres. Finance, Banister (parent co. of Pitts) 1980–81; Sr. Vice-Pres., Finance & Admin. & C.F.O., Majestic Contractors Ltd. 1981–91; Extve. Vice-Pres., Finance & Admin., Monenco Group Ltd. 1988–92; Pres., C.E.O. & C.F.O., Majestic Contractors Ltd. 1992–93 (company sold to Banister Inc.); Mem., F.E.I. Canada; recreations: golf, antique cars; Home: 5 Hodgkinson Cres., Aurora, Ont. L4G 6K4; Office: 3660 Midland Ave., Scarborough, Ont. M1V 4V3.

**HARRISON, Paul Garth,** B.Sc., Ph.D., RPBio; university professor; b. Alert Bay, B.C. 10 Sept. 1949; s. Brian Stuart and Marion Audrey (Watkins) H.; e. Lord Byng H.S. 1966; Univ. of B.C. B.Sc. 1970; Dalhousie Univ. Ph.D. 1974; m. Brenda d. Keith and Betty Thompson 24 May 1975; children: Julia Wynne, Brian Edward Keith; ASSOC. PROF., DEPT. OF BOTANY, UNIV. OF B.C. 1984– ; NATO postdoctoral fellowship, Aarhus Univ., Denmark 1974–75; Asst. Prof., present univ. 1975–84; Visiting Scientist, Delta Inst. for Hydrobiol. Rsch., Yerseke, The Netherlands 1989–90; consultant to num. govt. & private agencies on matters of coastal resource mngt.; Sec., Candn. Botanical Assn. 1984–86; Mem., Ecological Soc. of Am.; Estuarine Rsch. Fed.; Soc. for Conservation Biol.; Science for Peace; Registered Profl. Biol. of B.C.; Ed. 'Can. J. of Botany' 1992–93; author: 'Marine Habitat Compensation: Understanding the Habitat' 1988 & several articles & book chapters; recreations: gardening, swimming; Home: 3818 West 15th Ave., Vancouver, B.C. V6R 2Z9; Office: Rm. 3529 – 6270 University Blvd., Vancouver, B.C. V6T 1Z4.

**HARRISON, Rowland John Hill,** LL.B., LL.M.; barrister and solicitor; educator; consultant; b. Hobart, Australia 25 Sept. 1943; s. Colin Darrell Hill and Beryl Mary (Sibley) H.; e. St. Virgil's Coll. Hobart; Univ. of Tasmania LL.B. 1968; Univ. of Alta. LL.M. 1975; m. Alexandra d. Edmund and Robina Baker 30 June 1972; two s. Stewart, Edward (Teddy); PARTNER, STIKEMAN, ELLIOTT, Barristers and Solicitors, Calgary; mem. Bars of Tasmania, N.S., Ont. and Alta.; professorial appts. in law Univ. of Alta., Dalhousie Univ., Univ. of Calgary, Univ. of Ottawa; Visiting Prof., World Maritime Univ., Malmö, Sweden 1986–93; Assoc., Oceans Institute of Canada 1992– ; Council mem., Section on Energy and Resources Law, Internat. Bar Assoc. 1986– , Secy. 1990– ; Founding Exec. Dir., Candn. Inst. Resources Law 1979; Dir.-Gen. Land Mgmt. Br. Canada Oil and Gas Lands Adm. 1981–84; natural resources mgmt. cons. various govts. and ind.; author articles energy regulation & constitutional law various jours.; recreations: music, sailing; Clubs: Royal Nova Scotia Yacht Squadron; Rideau; Calgary Petroleum; Home: 97 Woodpath Terrace S.W., Calgary, Alta. T2W 5Z6; Office: 1500 Bankers Hall, Calgary, Alta.

**HARRISON, Russell Edward;** banker; b. Grandview, Man. 31 May 1921; s. Edward Smith and Annie L. (Purvis) H.; m. Nancy Doreen Bell, 18 Oct. 1944; one s., one d.; former Chrmn., Canadian Imperial Bank of Commerce; Dir., Can. Life Assnce. Co.; served in W.W.II; Clubs: Toronto; Rosedale Golf; Ontario; York (Toronto); Address: P.O. Box 235, Commerce Court Postal Stn., Toronto, Ont. M5L 1E8

**HARROD, Brian C.;** advertising executive; b. Capetown, S. Africa 23 May 1933; s. Clifford Arthur and Valerie (Parnell) H.; e. St. Andrews Coll. Grahamstown, S. Africa; Gen. Botha Nautical Coll., Gordon's Bay, S. Africa; London Sch. of Printing (U.K.); m. Sheila Ann d. Leslie and Mary Harvey May 1964; children: Justine, Jessica; CREATIVE DIRECTOR, HARROD & MIRLIN ADVERTISING 1987– ; Masius E. Wynne Williams (U.K.) 1957; Afamal Advtg. (S. Africa) 1960; Vanzijl & Schultz 1963; J.W. Thompson 1966; MarLaren Advtg. (Canada) 1967; McCann Erickson 1968; Miller, Myers, Bruce, Dalla Costa, Harrod & Mirlin 1985; Harrod & Mirlin 1987; Home: 71 Albany Ave., Toronto, Ont.; Office: 151 Bloor St. W., Toronto, Ont. M5S 1S4.

**HARRON, Donald,** B.A.; actor; writer; b. Toronto, Ont. 19 Sept. 1924; s. Lionel William and Delsia Ada (Hunter) H.; e. Univ. of Toronto, B.A. 1948 (Sanford Gold Medal in Philos. 1948; Regent's Silver Medal 1948); m. Catherine McKinnon 12 Mar. 1969; children: Martha, Mary (both by previous marriage), Kelley; as an actor has starred on Broadway ('Tenth Man'), London, Eng. ('Mary, Mary'); first 3 seasons with Stratford, Ont. Festival; one season with Bristol Old Vic, one with New York Shakespeare Festival; 6 shows on Broadway, 4 in London's W. End; T.V. appearances in Can., U.S. and Eng. incl. guest star on most U.S. drama series, comedy star role in CBS series 'Hee Haw'; played title role in 2 TV specials 'Reddick I' and 'Reddick II' now sold to Am. and Brit. TV; has appeared opposite such actresses as Katherine Hepburn, Catherine Cornell, Maggie Smith, Irene Worth, Zoe Caldwell, Joanne Woodward, Rosemary Harris, Ann Todd; helped create first ed. of 'Spring Thaw,' 1948 and wrote and performed in subsequent yrs. culminating in writing entire show for 'Spring Thaw '67'; has written for BBC radio and TV incl. regular writing assignment on 'Bedtime with Braden'; wrote musical comedy 'Anne of Green Gables' with Norman Campbell (20 seasons in Charlottetown Summer Festival; 1967 tour of Can.; productions in Kenya and Sweden; 10 months at New Theatre, London; rec'd London Theatre Critics' Award 'Best Musical of 1969'); also wrote 'Private Turvey's War' (musical comedy), 'Broken Jug' (farce, played in New York Phoenix Theatre 1959), 'Once' (original screenplay), 'Here Lies Sarah Binks' (musical comedy), 'And That's the News Good Night' (TV special 1969); Host of CBC Radio's 'Morningside'; author of 'Charlie Farquharson's History of Canada' 1972; 'Charlie Farquharson's Jogfree of Canada, the Wild and Other Places' 1974; 'Charlie Farquharson's Korn Almanac' 1976; 'Olde Charlie Farquharson's Testament' 1978; 'Wonder of It All' (stage musical on life of Emily Carr) 1980; 'Once' (film, CBC TV) 1981; 'Yer Last Decadent' (book) 1982; host of Don Harron Show (CTV Network, 1983–85); 'Cum by the Farm' (book) 1987; 'Olde Charlie Farquharson's Testament and Magic Lantern Show' (musical comedy) 1988; 'Charlie Farquharson's Universe' 1990; served as Pilot Offr. with RCAF 1943–45; recreation: football; Address: c/o Paul Simmons, 261 Davenport Rd., Ste. 301, Toronto, Ont. M5R 1K3.

**HART, Alexander H.,** Q.C., LL.B.; b. Regina, Sask. 17 July 1918; s. Alexander and Mary (Davidson) H.; e. Dalhousie Law Sch., LL.B.; m. Janet MacMillan, d. Colin Mackay, Rothesay, N.B., 5 June 1948; children: Mary, Colin, Sandy, John; Agent General for Prov. of B.C. in London, Eng. 1981–87; Sr. Vice-President, Canadian Nat. RLYS., 1971–81 previously Vice Pres., Marketing 1967–71; Past Pres., Vancouver Bd. Trade; Past Pres., Can.-Japan Soc.; Past Pres., Canada-United Kingdom Chamber of Commerce (London) 1983; called to Bar of N.S. 1947; served in 2nd World War with Royal Canadian Artillery, 1939–45; retired with rank of Major; mem., N.S. Barristers Soc.; Phi Kappa Pi; Presbyterian; Clubs: Shaughnessy Golf & Country; Royal and Ancient Golf Club of St. Andrews (Fife); Home: Ste. 3B, 1568 W. 12th Ave., Vancouver, B.C. V6J 2E1.

**HART, Douglas Robinson Sanford,** M.Sc.; energy research executive; b. Ottawa, Ont. 29 June 1948; s. Jackson Sanford (Ph.D., F.R.S.C.) and Eleanor Marie (Street) H.; e. Lisgar Coll. Inst. Ottawa 1965; Queen's Univ. B.Sc. 1969; Univ. of Toronto M.Sc. 1972; m. Sarah d. Martin and Judith Hunter, Aug. 1991; Marilynne d. Saul and Frances Glick July 1978; two d. Rebecca, Naomi; PRESIDENT, WATERSHED ENERGY SYSTEMS LTD. 1977– ; Project Mgr. and Dir. MacDonald Construction, Ottawa 1974–75; estbd. present co. 1977; 578144 Ontario Inc. 1984; Canoe Sailors Ltd. 1985; Frozen Sun Inc. 1985; holds four patents energy field: HeatMaze window 1977, diagnostic thermostat 1983, solid state tritium lighting system 1988, automatic termination device for electric clothes dryers 1991; lectr. in solar energy and bldg. design Ryerson Polytech. Inst. and Seneca Coll. 1978–82; present co. recipient numerous awards and grants solar energy rsch.; co-author 'Renewable Energy Handbook' 1978; various sci. papers solar energy heat transfer; mem. Assoc. Ctte., National Rsch. Counc.; Candn. Solar Inds. Assn.; recreations: tennis, cross-country skiing, piano; Home: 94 Yarmouth Rd., Toronto, Ont. M6G 1W9; Office: 481 N. Service Rd. W., Ste. A9, Oakville, Ont. L6H 2V6.

**HART, George Arnold,** M.B.E., C.M., D.C.L., LL.D., D.C.Sc.; retired banker; b. Toronto, Ont. 2 Apr. 1913; s. George Sanderson and Laura Mary (Harrison) H.; e. Pub. Schools and Oakwood Coll. Inst., Toronto, Ont.; Fellow, The Canadian Inst. of Bankers, 1936; LL.D., Univ. of Sask. 1961; Univ. of Montreal 1962; D.C.L., Bishop's Univ. 1963; Acadia Univ. 1970; D.C.Sc., Univ. of Sherbrooke 1965; m. late Jean C. Gilbert, 2 Sept. 1939; one d., Diane (Mrs. Edwin S. Keeling); m. 2ndly Patricia I. Plant, 8 Dec. 1961; joined Bank of Montreal, Toronto 1931; Chrmn. of the Exec. Comte. 1964–77; Chrmn. of the Bd. 1964–75; C.E.O. 1959–74; Pres. 1959–67; served with Canadian Army 1941–46; discharged with rank Major; Anglican; Clubs: Mount Royal; Forest and Stream; Mount Bruno Country; Home: R.R. 2, Mountain, Ont. K0E 1S0 Office: 129 St. James St. West, Montreal, Que. H2Y 1L6.

**HART, Hon. Gordon Leavitt Shaw,** LL.B.; judge; b. Halifax, N.S. 23 Dec. 1924; s. Gilbert Shaw and Jean Thompson (Leavitt) H.; e. Halifax (N.S.) Co. Acad. 1942; King's Univ. B.A. 1946; Dalhousie Law Sch., LL.B. 1948; m. Catherine, d. Dr. Hugh MacKinnon, 1 Jan. 1949; children: Christine Ellen, Thomas E., Norah, Gordon G., Hugh A., Jonathan L.; SUPERNUMERARY JUDGE, COURT OF APPEAL, SUPREME COURT OF N.S. 1993– ; called to the Bar of N.S. 1948; cr. Q.C. 1963; Ald., City of Dartmouth 1956–60; M.L.A. 1960–63, 1967–68; apptd. to Trial Div., Supreme Court of N.S. 1968; apptd. Royal Comn. to conduct inquiry into pollution of Candn. waters by steam tanker 'Arrow' 1970; apptd. a Mem. of Court Martial Appeal Court, 1972; apptd. to Appeal Div. of Supreme Court of N.S., 1978; apptd. Supernumerary Judge, Appeal Div. 1989; served in R.C.N. 1944–45, rank Sub. Lt.; Pres., N.S. Assn. Urban & Mun. Sch. Bds. 1958–59; mem. and Chrmn., Dartmouth Sch. Bd. 1954–60; Vice-Pres., Candn. Sch. Trustees Assn. 1959; mem. Bd. Govs., Dartmouth Acad. 1968–70; United Church; Home: 18 Clearview Cres., Dartmouth, N.S. B3A 2M8; Office: Court House, Halifax, N.S. B3J 1S7.

**HART, Howard,** B.Com.; association executive; b. Montreal, Que. 12 July 1930; s. William Henry and Alice (Howard) H.; e. Queen's Univ., B.Com., 1953; m. Elinor Diane, d. C. E. Goodwin, Picton, Ont., 1954; children: William, Peter, Suzanne, Caroline; PRES., CANDN. PULP AND PAPER ASSN. 1972– ; joined present Assn. 1954; Secy. of the Assn. and Asst. to Pres., 1962–67; Vice Pres. 1967; Extve. Vice Pres. 1970–72; Home: 18 Kirkwood Ave., Beaconsfield, Que. H9W 5L2; Office: 1155 Metcalfe St., 19th Floor, Montreal, Que. H3B 4T6.

**HART, Ian C.,** Q.C., B.A.; b. Toronto, Ont. 28 Sept. 1925; s. Alfred Purvis and Katherine (Crichton) H.; e. Univ. of Toronto Schs., Toronto; Univ. of Toronto, B.A. 1946; Osgoode Hall Law Sch.; m. Patricia Ann, d. late Avery Clifton Turner, 29 Aug. 1951; children: Stephen Peter, Sheila Ann Sisley, Derek Alfred; PARTNER, COATSWORTH, RICHARDSON & HART; read law with H. A. Coon, Q.C.; called to Bar of Ont., 1949; cr. Q.C., 1961; served with R.C.N.V.R.; Councillor, Toronto Twp., 1953–54; mem., Toronto Twp. Pub. Utilities Comn., 1955–57; mem., Metrop. Toronto Bd. of Trade; Alpha Delta Phi; Protestant; recreations: golf,; Club: Toronto Golf; Home: 1 Darlingbrook Cres., Islington, Ont. M9A 3H4; Office: 4195 Dundas St. W., Suite 305, Toronto, Ont. M8X 1Y4.

**HART, Ian Ritchie,** MB, ChB, MSc, FRCP, FACP, FRCP(Glas); professor of medicine; b. Dalmuir, Scotland 11 May 1937; s. John and Margaret (Ritchie) H.; e. Clydebank H.S.; Univ. of Glasgow MB, ChB 1960; McGill Univ. MSc 1973; m. Catherine d. Joseph and Josephine Ferns 7 Jan. 1961; children: Roderick Iain, Gordon Ritchie; PROFESSOR OF MEDICINE, DIVISION OF ENDOCRINOLOGY, UNIVERSITY OF OTTAWA, OTTAWA CIVIC HOSPITAL 1982– ; Internship, Victoria Infirmary Glasgow; Jr. Medical Officer, Bonne Bay and Grand Bank Nfld. 1961–63; Resident in Med., Ottawa Civic Hosp. 1963–65; Resident in Med., MRC Fellow in Endocrinology 1965–69; Asst. then Assoc. Prof., Univ. of Ottawa 1969–82; Assoc. Dean 1986–90; Chief, Dept. of Med. & Physician in Chief, Ottawa Civic Hosp. 1979–87; Dir., The McLaughlin Centre Ottawa 1986–89; Mem. of Council, Medical Research Council (current); Royal Coll. of Physicians & Surgeons 1984–88; Gov., Am. Coll. of Physicians 1987–91; Mem., Nat. Bd. of Med. Examiners of the U.S. 1987– ; Editor & Chair, Edit. Bd., 'Medicine North America' 1980– ; Hon. Prof. of Med., Univ. of Dundee 1991–92; 1987 Award for Outstanding Contbn. to Univ. Teaching, Ont. Confed. of Univ. Faculty Assns.; 1993 Award, Candn. Assn. for Med. Edn. for Contbns. to Medical Edn.; FRCP; FACP (Gov. 1987–91); FRCP(Glasgow); Mem., Royal Soc. of London; co-author: 'Endocrinology: The New Medicine' 1983; senior editor: 'Newer Developments in Assessing Clinical Competence' 1986, 'Further Developments in Assessing Clinical Competence' 1988, 'Current Developments in Assessing Clinical Competence' 1992; co-editor: 'Approaches to the Assessment of Clinical Competence' 1993; recreations: fishing, travel; clubs: Rideau, Maganassipi Fish and Game, St. Sixte Fish and Game; Home: 44 Kenilworth St., Ottawa, Ont. K1Y 3Y1; Office: Ottawa, Ont. K1Y 4E9.

**HART, Matthew;** writer; b. Ottawa, Ont. 14 April 1945; s. John Garton and Theresa (Turner) H.; e. St. Patrick's Coll., Ottawa; Univ. of Ottawa Preparatory Sch., St. Dunstan's Univ.; m. Sylvia Alden d. Peter and Priscilla Morley 28 March 1985; Staff Reporter, Ottawa Citizen and stringer, Montreal Star 1968–70; reporter and producer, CBC and CTV 1970–80; travelled extensively throughout N. Am., Africa & the Middle East; freelance writer 1980–90; pub. articles in various Candn. and American publs.; regular columnist, Toronto Mag. 1987–90; Writer-in-Residence, Richmond Hill Pub. Lib. 1987–88; author: 'Death Train' (novel) 1981; 'A Viewer's Guide to Halley's Comet' 1985; 'Golden Giant: Hemlo and the Rush for Canada's Gold' 1985; Address: c/o Features Editor, The Globe and Mail, 444 Front St. W., Toronto, Ont. M5V 2S9 and c/o Douglas & McIntyre, 1615 Venables St., Vancouver, B.C. V5L 2H1.

**HART, Michael D.,** B.A.; bond trader/arbitrager; b. Toronto, Ont. 21 Dec. 1959; s. Manfred Emil Erich and Penina (Urkovitch) H.; e. Northview H.S. 1979; York Univ., B.A. (Hon.) 1985; Candn. Securities Inst., cert. 1984; m. Mahra (Dranov); children: Willem Manfred; CHIEF BOND-TRADER/ARBITRAGE, FRIEDBERG MERCANTILE GROUP 1985– ; resp. for trading in Euro-, Yankee, and convertible bonds, LDC debt, in addition to gold and all currencies; Candn. Nat. Railway Express 1978–80; Teacher, Ryerson, Fac. of Bus., 'Financial Instruments' 1989–91; freelance financial consultant; Jewish; co-author: 'Currency and Commodity Comments' a monthly pub.; freelance writer, 'Excalibur' York Univ.; Bd. of Dirs., J.C.C., Toronto 1991– ; Koffler Gallery, Toronto; recreations: squash, amateur filmmaking; club: Imperial; Office: 347 Bay St., Ste. 207, Toronto, Ont. M5H 2R7.

**HART, Michael Marten,** M.A.; federal civil servant; b. Velp, The Netherlands 26 March 1944; s. Klaas and Wilhelmiena (Fonds) H.; e. Calvin Coll. Grand Rapids, Mich. B.A. 1965; Univ. of Va. postgrad. studies 1965–67; Univ. of Toronto M.A. 1968, doctoral studies 1967–74; m. Mary Virginia d. William Edward and Mary Pauline Terry 4 Aug. 1967; children: Elinor Meredith, Michael Edward; SENIOR ADVISOR, TRADE POLICY STUDIES, EXTERNAL AFFAIRS AND INTERNAT. TRADE LAW 1992– ; Adjunct Prof. of Internat. Affairs Carleton Univ. 1989– ; various teaching positions Univ. of Toronto Scarborough Coll., McMaster Univ., Brock Univ., Univ. of P.E.I. 1967–74; various assignments Dept. External Affairs and Geneva 1974–82; project leader Can.'s trade policy review and ed. review publs. 1982; Rsch. Visitor Internat. Econ. Prog. Inst. for Rsch. Pub. Policy 1983, Sr. Rsch. Fellow 1988; Dir. Domestic Policy Candn. Air Transport. Adm. Transport

Can. and concurrently cons. Royal Comn. Econ. Union & Devel. Prospects for Can. 1984; Special Adv. Can.-U.S. Trade Liberalization Dept. External Affairs 1985; Sr. Adv. to Chief Trade Negotiator for Can. 1986; Visiting Prof. Univ. of W. Ont., Norman Paterson Sch. Internat. Affairs Carleton Univ., Univ. of Ottawa 1988; Dir. & Founder Centre for Trade Policy and Law 1989; Dir. Trade and Econ. Analysis, External Affairs and Internat. Trade Canada 1990–92; author various trade policy publs.; elder & mem. Bd. Mgrs. St. Timothy's Presb. Ch. Ottawa; Home: 27 Saddle Cres., Ottawa, Ont. K1G 5L4; Office: 125 Sussex Dr., Ottawa, Ont. K1A 0G2.

**HARTAL, Paul,** M.A., Ph.D.; artist; writer; b. Szeged, Hungary 25 Apr. 1936; e. Concordia Univ. Montréal M.A. 1977; Univ. de Montréal; Columbia Pacific Univ. San Rafael Ph.D. 1986; m. Penina Fromm 14 Aug. 1958; 3 children; DIR. CENTRE FOR ART, SCI. & TECHNOL. 1987– ; Cons. McGill Univ.; Urban Planner 1964–66; solo exhns. incl. Jacquie Gallery Montréal 1975; Galerie J. Yahouda Meir Montréal 1983; Centre Psycho-Social Univ. of Lausanne Montreux 1984; Micro Hall Art Center, Edewecht (Oldenburg), West Germany 1989; group exhns. incl. Colbert Gallery Montréal 1975; Internat. Art Fair Washington, D.C. 1976; Belknap Meml. Invitational Print Exhns. Columbia Greene Community Coll. Hudson, N.Y. 1978; Salon des Surindependants Musée du Luxembourg Paris 1978; Academie Internationale de Lutece Paris 1978; Festival Internat. de Peinture et d'Art Graphico-plastique de Saint Germain-des Prés Paris 1978; Artistes USA Galeries Raymond Duncan Paris 1978; Ligoa Duncan Gallery New York 1978; Le Festival Internat. des Arts Olympic Velodrome Montréal 1979; Vehicule Living Art Museum Montréal 1980; Brain Cell Osaka 1985–88; Art Festival Seoul 1988; Studio Dieci, Vercelli, Italy 1989; La Rose Des Vents, Villeneuve d'Ascq, France 1989; Contemporary Gallery Aono, Matsuyama City, Ehime 790, Japan 1989; Eco Museum, Savona, Italy 1991; The Archeology of the Future, Bergamo, Italy 1991; Lo Straneiro International Show, Oxford, Engl. 1991; Centro Culturale, Firenze (Florence) Italy 1991; Space and Humanity, Montreux, Switzerland 1992; Ward Nasse Gall., New York. 1992; Soc. of Experimental Artists: Longboat Key Art Center, Fla. 1992; Musée de la Poste, Paris Sept. 1993–Jan. 1994; La Galerie Fokus, Montreal Dec. 1993–Jan. 1994; comns. incl. Seoul Olympic Graphics project 1988 (selected as one of 10 artists); recipient Rubens Award and Prix de Paris 1978; Academia Italia Award 1984; author: 'A History of Architecture' 1972; 'Windfall' poetry anthol. 1975; 'A Manifesto on Lyrical Conceptualism' 1975; 'George Lukacs: Aesthetics and History' 1977; 'Ode to a Skyscraper' concrete poems 1979; 'Vernissage' essay 1979; 'Painted Melodies' essay 1983; 'Black and White' images 1984; 'The Brush and the Compass: The Interface Dynamics of Art and Science' 1988; 'Rain Drop' 1994; author of the Foreword in 'Communication and Rural Development' by B. Ambekar (New Delhi, India) 1993; contbr., 'Un Segno di Pace' ed. by F. Vallone 1989; 'Kostar Kravat Numero Special, Art Postal,' Troyes, France 1989; 'Encyclopedia of Living Artists' vols. 5, 6 & 7, and other journals and publications; contbr., Art Montréal TV prog.; lecturer; Adv. Mem., Forum for Environmental Conservation and Development in South Asia, Inst. of Sci. and Technology, Tribhuvan Univ., Nepal; Orbiting Unification Ring Satellite: OURS; Space Art, Switzerland; Co-Founder Lyrical Conceptualist Soc.; mem. Internat. Soc. Art, Sci. & Technol.; Inst. Advanced Philosophic Rsch.; Internat. Soc. Ecological Psychol.; Inst. Earth Edn.; Internat. Soc. Artists; recreations: fencing, bicycling, cinema; Office: P.O. Box 1012, St. Laurent, Qué. H4L 4W3.

**HARTFORD, Douglas Wayne,** B.A.; business executive; b. Calgary, Alta. 25 May 1945; s. Donald Harold and Ruth Vivian (Vernon) H.; e. Viscount Bennett H.S. 1963; Whitworth College Spokane WA B.A. 1967; m. Bonita Ann d. Don and Mary Phanenhour 7 July 1972; Founder, Battery Technologies Inc. and BTI Group of Cos. 1986– ; Product Mngt., Warner Lambert 1967–68; Marketing Mgr., Feminine Hygiene Div., Kimberly Clark 1968–71; Cdn. Vice-Pres., Helena Rubenstein 1972; founded D.W. Hartford & Assoc. Mktg. Cons. firm 1973– ; Exclusive Marketer for Battery Technologies Inc. which develops & licenses rechargeable alkaline mngt. technology (invented by Dr. Karl Kordesch); current licences incl. Canada, US, Hungary, Russia, India & China with numerous additional territories under investigation; Vice Chair, Candn. Nat. Sportsmen Show (1989) Limited; Pres., Real Radio; Dir., Candn. Nat. Sportsman Show Fund; recreations: boating, hunting, fishing, skiing, tennis; clubs: The Mt. St. Patrick, Mayfair Tennis, The Goodwood; Home: 43 Fairmeadow Ave., Willowdale, Ont. M2P 1W8; Office: 35 Pollard St., Richmond Hill, Ont. L4B 1A8.

**HARTFORD, Donald Harold;** executive, b. Edmonton, Alta. 24 Jan. 1919; s. Harold Hunter and Mabel Irene (Younge) H.; e. W. Canada Schs.; m. Jean Emilie Skogland, 1973; children from previous marriage: Donald Leigh, Douglas Wayne, Diane Leslie; stepchildren: Fred, Kari Skogland; Past Pres., Radio Div., Standard Broadcasting Corp. Ltd.; CJAD Inc.; St. Clair Prod. Ltd.; Eastern Sound Co. Ltd.; Past Dir., and Vice-Pres., Standard Broadcast Productions; Sr. Vice-Pres., Standard Broadcasting Corp. Ltd.; Standard Sound Systems Co. Ltd.; served with Calgary Regt. Tanks, later with R.C.A.F.; discharged with rank of Flying Offr.; Past Pres. Western Assn. of Broadcasters; Ont. Safety League; Advtsg. and Sales Club, Calgary; Co-Chrmn., Toronto Waterfront Counc.; Asst. Exec. Dir., Seaquarian Corp.; Vice-Chrmn., Candn. Assn. of Broadcasters; Dir., and mem., Candn. Nat. Sportsmen's Show; Past Vice-Chrmn., Ontario Place; Past Chrmn., Variety Village; Fndg. Dir., Radio Bur. of Can.; Fndg. mem., Broadcast Extve. Soc.; Past Council mem. Bd. Trade Metrop. Toronto; Past Dir., Can. Nat. Exhibition; Past Pres., CFRB Limited (retired Dec. 1983); Chrmn., Real Radio Corp. Ltd.; Mem., Candn. team, Internat. Tuna Cup Match, 1970; Advis. Bd., Salvation Army; Past Dir., Alta. Heart Foundation, Clarke Instit. of Psychiatry; Past Assoc. Dir., Calgary Stampede; Past Vice-Chrmn., United Appeal, Calgary; Past Zone Chrmn., United Appeal, Toronto; Dir., Whaler's Group; Awards: Centennial Medal; Candn. Music Hall of Fame; Humanitarian Award of International B'nai B'rith, 1978; 'Broadcaster of Yr.' Award, Central Can. Broadcasters Assn., 1981; recreations: fishing, hunting, boating; Clubs: Variety; Yacht & Country C. of Stuart, Florida; Home: T.H. 14 The Hammersmith, 2112 Queen St. E., Toronto, Ont. M4E 1E2.

**HARTLE, Douglas Graham,** M.A., Ph.D., F.R.S.C.; economist and educator; b. Winnipeg, Man. 10 Mar. 1927; s. Francis Stewart and Elsie (Perry) H.; e. Pub. and High Schs., Winnipeg, Ottawa and Montreal; Carleton Univ., B.A. (Hon.); Duke Univ., M.A., Ph.D., F.R.S.C.; m. Lexia Weir, d. late Harry J. Clark, 5 Sept. 1955; children: Sandra, Paul, Martha, Geoffrey; EMERITUS PROF. OF ECONOMICS, UNIV. OF TORONTO and Dir., Govt. of Botswana/Univ. of Toronto Programme; Dir., National Bureau of Econ. Research, N.Y. City 1960–62; Prof. of Econ., Univ. of Toronto, 1957–62 and Dir., Inst. for Quantitative Analysis of Social and Econ. Policy, 1967–69; Research Dir., Royal Comn. on Taxation, 1962–67; Depy. Secy. – Planning, Treasury Bd. 1969–73; Research Dir., Extve. Secy., Ont. Econ. Council 1980–81; Economic Adv., Govt. of Botswana 1985–88; former mem. Bd. of Govs., Carleton Univ.; mem., Candn. Econ. Assn.; (Pres. 1980–81); Anglican; Home: 14 South Drive, Toronto, Ont. M4W 1R1; Office: University Coll., Univ. of Toronto, Toronto, Ont. M5S 1A1.

**HARTLEY, Stuart Leslie,** C.A., F.C.A.; business executive; b. Luton, Eng. 3 Apl. 1938; s. Leslie and Isobel (Buchan) H.; e. Royal Liberty Sch. London Gen. Cert. Edn. 1955; C.A. 1960 (Ont.); F.C.A. (Eng., Wales); m. Patricia Holmes 27 Dec. 1960; children: Stephen, Caroline, Susan; EXEC. VICE PRES. AND CHIEF FINANCIAL OFFR. THE MOLSON COMPANIES LTD. 1979– ; Dir.: Canada Malting Co. Ltd.; Groupe Val Royal Inc.; Vice Chrmn., National Ballet Sch.; Controller IBM Canada Ltd. Toronto 1971–73; Dir. Finance Latin Am. IBM American Far East Corp. 1973–74; Vice Pres. Finance & Planning Gen. Bus. Group IBM Canada 1975–79; Co-Chrmn. Financial Execs. Council Conf. Bd. Can. 1989–92; Chrmn., Financial Exec. Inst. 1990–91 (Pres. Toronto Chapter 1983–85); Home: 1 Meadow Height Court, Thornhill, Ont. L4J 1V5; Office: 3600 Scotia Plaza, 40 King St. W., Toronto, Ont. M5H 3Z5.

**HARTMANN, E. George,** CMA, F.C.M.A.; transportation executive; b. Berlin, West Germany 31 Aug. 1929; e. R.I.A. 1970; m. Irmgard; one d.; EXTVE. VICE PRES. FINAN. & SEC., LOOMIS CAN. (Mayne Nickless Canada) 1985– ; Opns.-Merchandise Mgr., Taylor & Drury Dept. Stores; Corp. Controller, White Pass and Yukon Corp.; Dir., Admin., Flecto Coatings Ltd.; Mem., Soc. of Mngt. Accountants, B.C. (Past Pres.); Finan. Extve. Inst.; Fellow, Soc. of Mngt. Accts. of Can. 1983; recreations: travel, community service; Office: 300, 1290 Hornby St., Vancouver, B.C. V6Z 2G4.

**HARTNETT, William J.,** B.A., LL.B.; lawyer; b. Syracuse, N.Y. 1 July 1949; s. John Richard and Mildred Helen (Fahl) H.; e. Cazenovia (N.Y.) Central Sch.; Providence (R.I.) Coll. B.A. 1971; Univ. of Fribourg, Switzerland; Univ. of W. Ont. LL.B. 1976; m. Elizabeth d. Dennis and Ann Newton 29 July 1978; two s. William Justin, Christopher John; GENERAL COUNSEL, IMPERIAL OIL RESOURCES LIMITED (a subsidiary of Imperial Oil Ltd.) 1991– ; Private Practice, Hamilton 1978–79; Solr., Imperial Oil Ltd. Toronto 1980–84; Mgr. Exec. Compensation, Imperial Oil Ltd. 1984–86; Counsel, Imperial Oil Ltd., Toronto 1986–88; Gen. Counsel, Esso Chemical Canada (a div. of Imperial Oil Ltd.) 1989–90; Asst. Gen. Counsel, Esso Resources Canada Ltd. 1991; Chrmn./Pres. Oakville Childrens Centre and Onstage Productions 1984–90; mem. Law Soc. Upper Can. (Legal Aid Ctte. 1987–89); Candn. Bar Assn. (Ont./Exec. Ctte. 1988–90; Council 1983–91; Ont./Chrmn. Legal Aid Ctte. 1985–88; Ont./Chrmn. Q.C. Ctte. 1987–90; Ont./Chrmn. Access to Justice Inquiry 1985–86; Nat. Legal Aid Ctte. 1986–88; Nat. Communications Ctte. 1989– ; Ed. Bd., Candn. Bar Review 1989– ); mem. Am. Bar Assn.; Candn. Corporate Council Assn.; recreations: sailing, skiing; Club: Calgary Petroleum Club; Home: Calgary, Alta.; Office: 237 – 4th Ave. S.W., Calgary, Alta. T2P 0H6.

**HARTOG, Diana Maria,** B.A., M.A.; writer; b. Palo Alto, Calif. 1946; d. Charles William and Mary Robin (Hannibal) Lane; e. San Francisco St. Univ. B.A. 1965, M.A. 1974; m. Mathew s. Henry Lea Hudson 16 Sept. 1967; divorced 1982; one d. Selena; author of books of poetry 'Matinee Light' 1983; 'Candy from Strangers' 1986; 'Polite To Bees' 1992 (short-listed for 1992 BC Poetry Prize); Gerald Lampert Award, League of Candn. Poets 1983; 2nd place for poetry, CBC Lit. Competition 1983; B.C. Poetry Prize 1986; short-listed for the Journey Prize 1991; Address: c/o Coach House Press, 401 Huron St., Toronto, Ont. M5S 2G5.

**HARTOG, Robbert,** CM; M.A.; manufacturer; b. Nijmegen, Netherlands 28 Jan. 1919; s. Arthur and J. S. E. (Catz) H.; e. Secondary Sch. The Hague; Dipl. Ecole Libre des Sciences Politiques, Paris; Univ. of Toronto M.A. 1942; PRESIDENT, ROBHAR INVESTMENTS LIMITED; Pres. and Dir. Foreign Investment Trust Inc.; Dir. Dalex Co. Ltd.; Fairfax Financial Co. Ltd.; Morden & Helwig Ltd.; Hughes, Leitz Co. Ltd.; Padinox Inc.; served with Royal Netherlands Army during World War II, rank Captain; author 'De L'Utilite du Controle de Change en Temps du Guerre'; mem. Candn. Pol. Science Assn.; United Church; recreations: canoeing, boating; Club: Granite; Home: R.R. 1, Perkinsfield, Ont. L0L 2J0.

**HARTSFIELD, Carla Jean,** M.Mus.; pianist; poet; music teacher; b. Waxahachie, Texas 29 Aug. 1956; d. Thomas Eugene and Mary Katherine (Milam) H.; e. Univ. of Texas Austin B.Mus. (piano) 1978, M.Mus. (piano) 1981; m. Kenneth s. Ron and Marie Ross 18 May 1990; one s. Alexander Milam; began piano studies at 4 yrs. winning local and state-wide honours incl. Sid Richardson Found. Scholarship; teaching fellowships held at Univ. of Houston and Univ. of Texas 1979–81; immigrated to Can. 1982; mem. Piano Faculty Royal Conserv. of Music 1987– ; recipient Piano Guild Paderewski Medal 1974; author: 'The Invisible Moon' poetry 1988 (short-listed LCP Gerald Lampert Meml. Award); 'The Signal Anthology' 1993; poetry pub. various lit. mags.; mem. Phi Kappa Phi; Univ. Scholastic Honor Soc. (Am.); Address: 488 Strathmore Blvd., Toronto, Ont. M4C 1N7.

**HARTT, Andrew Douglas,** B.A., B.Comm., C.M.A., F.C.M.A.; financial executive; b. Halifax, N.S. 1 Sept. 1947; s. Leo Alexander and Kathleen Rose (Carter) H.; e. Saint Mary's Univ., B.A. 1968, B.Comm. 1969; Soc. of Mngt. Accountans of Can., C.M.A. 1973; m. Gisele d. John and Nettie LeBlanc 31 Dec. 1981; children: Megan, Nicola, Annette, Carmen, Max, Brigitte; TREAS., MARITIME TELEGRAPH & TELEPHONE CO.; Vice-Pres. & Treas., MT&T Mobile Inc.; Vice-Pres., Finan., MT&T Leasing Inc.; MT&T Technologies; Maritime Telecom Holdings Inc.; The Island Telephone Co. Ltd.; various finan. mngt. positions, current firm 1969– ; Fellow, Soc. of Mngt. Accountants of Can. (SMAC) 1986; Vice-Pres. & Dir., Finan. Extves. Inst. of Can.; Past Dir., Assn. of Candn. Pension Management; Mem., SMAC (Past Dir., Past Ctte. Chrmn.); Candn. Pension Conf. (Past Dir.); Chrmn., Review Ctte., SMAC Research Pubns.; mem., City of Dartmouth Industrial Commission; recreations: family, swimming, hockey; Office: 1505 Barrington St., Halifax, N.S. B3J 2W3.

**HARTT, Stanley Herbert,** B.A., M.A., B.C.L., Q.C.; executive; b. Montreal, Que. 11 Nov. 1937; s. Maurice and Rose (Gallay) H.; e. McGill Univ. B.A. 1958, M.A. 1961, B.C.L. 1963; m. Beverly Maureen Brooks 31 March 1990; children: Heather, Michael, James, Douglas; CHAIRMAN, PRES. & CHIEF EXECUTIVE OFFICER, CAMDEV CORP. 1990– ; called to Bar. of Que. 1965; Lawyer & Partner, Stikeman Elliott 1965–85, 1988–89, 1990; Dep. Min., Dept. of Finance 1985–88; Chief of Staff, Office of the P.M. 1989–90; Chair,

Nat. Econ. Conf. Private Sector Adv. Ctte. 1984–85; Lectr., Sir George Williams Univ. 1962–63; McGill Univ. 1965–67, 1972–81; Labour Coll. of Can. 1963, '64, '66; Mem., Que. Bar Assn.; Dir., Camdev Corp., Hong Kong Bank of Canada; Quaker Oats Co. of Canada Limited; Ultramar Corp.; Gulf Canada Resources Ltd.; Abitibi-Price Inc.; Sun Life Assurance Co. of Canada; Finreal Properties Inc., Castlefield Realty Inc.; A & G Resources Corp. Dir., Montreal Symphony Orch.; Toronto Symphony; Canada/U.S. Fulbright Program; Mem., P.C. Party; recreations: skiing, tennis, classical music; Clubs: Mount Royal, Rideau, Cercle Universitaire; Home: Toronto, Ont.; Office: 40 King St. W., Ste. 2700, Toronto, Ont. M5H 3Y2.

**HARTWICK, John Martin,** B.A., Ph.D.; university professor; b. Arvida, Que. 8 Dec. 1944; s. E. Frederick and Grace L. (Day) H.; e. Carleton Univ. B.A. (Hons.) 1966; Johns Hopkins Univ. Ph.D. 1969; children: Jennifer L., Adam J., Andrea D.; PROF., DEPT. OF ECONOMICS, QUEEN'S UNIV. 1980– ; Dept. of Econ., Queen's Univ. 1969–71; Min. of State for Urban Affairs 1971–72; leaves: M.I.T. 1974–75; Stanford Univ. 1980–81; Oxford Univ. 1985–86; author: 'Non-renewable Resources: Programs and Markets' 1989; 'A Brief History of Price' 1993; co-author: 'The Economics of Natural Resource Use' 1986; Home: 176 College St., Kingston, Ont. K7L 4L8; Office: Kingston, Ont. K7L 3N6.

**HARTY, Christopher John,** C.A.; chartered accountant; b. Jamaica W.I. 14 Jan. 1939; s. Robert Claude and Poppie Kathleen (Watson) H.; e. Bishops Stortford Coll. (U.K.) 1953–57; A.C.A. (U.K.) 1962; F.C.A. (U.K.) 1971; C.A. (Ont.) 1978; Trustee in Bankruptcy 1982; m. Jill d. Allan and Freda Harvey 28 Sept. 1963; children: Jonathan James, David Neil; INSOLVENCY PARTNER & SENIOR VICE-PRES., PRICE WATERHOUSE 1980– ; joined Price Waterhouse, Kingston, Jamaica 1962; Audit Partner 1968–76; transferred to Price Waterhouse Canada 1976; Mem., Candn. Insolvency Assn.; Dir. & Treas., Advocacy Rescource Centre for the Handicapped; lecturer; recreations: swimming, travel; clubs: Ontario; Home: 235 Livingston Rd., Scarborough, Ont. M1E 1L8; Office: Box 33, 1 First Canadian Place, Toronto, Ont. M5X 1H7.

**HARTY, Dwayne John;** artist/painter/sculptor; b. Shaunavon, Sask. 23 May 1957; s. John Henry and Henriette (Beauchesne) H.; e. Art Student's League 1977–78; m. Carolyn Elizabeth; daughters: Eden, MacKenzie Rose; apprentice with Clarence Tillenius 1973–83; with Robert Lougheed 1978–82; Bob Kuhn Invit. Workshop 1984; 3 wk. field trip to Sweden 1981; Commissioned painting as Internat. Artist for Oklahoma Wildlife Art Festival, Tulsa, Oklahoma 1994; Commissioned for four natural history murals for new Wye Marsh Interpretive Centre 1993; Commissioned for five natural history dioramas and one decorative mural for new Algonquin Park Museum 1991–93; Cons., Tucker Communications Inc. for Stonewall Quarry Mus. 1984; contract employment to design & execute dioramas, Royal Ont. Mus. 1983–84, 1985–86; Chief Dioramist, Sask. Mus. of Nat. History 1987–90; leave of absence (one year commn.) to design & execute Ont. Wetlands Waterfowl diorama, Royal Ont. Museum 1989–90; Comnd. by Sask. Dept. of Parks for series of 5 big game paintings; by Ducks Unlimited for paintings for head office; by World Wildlife Fund for design of 4 postage stamps & cachet paintings for countries of Kampuchea and Botswana, Africa 1986, Columbia, South Am. 1989; 2–week expedition with Dr. Robert Wrigley 1983; work displayed on CBC, 'Take 30'; interview, 'Canada A.M.'; comnd. paintings in corp. & priv. collections; Sask./Manitoba/N. Ontario official commission for Panda Bear painting for Panda visit to Winnipeg Zoo (summer '89) – Safeways Canada and Candn. Air Intn'l. sponsors; accompanying trip to National Zoo (Dec. '88) Washington D.C. to study pandas on permanent display; commissioned to paint Saskatchewan Wildlife Habitat Trust Fund 1989 stamp and print; corporate comn. work on-going for U.K.H.M. and private collectors 1991; exhibited in several galleries & travelling shows; exhibited 'Art and the Animal', S.A.A., Tacoma, Washington 1993 (Award of Excellence) and Jamestown, N.Y. 1992; 'Wildlife: The Artist's View' Leigh Yawkey Woodson Art Museum, Wausau, Wisconsin 1993; one-man show Loch/Mayberry Fine Art (Dec. '88); instructor; judge; lecturer; Candn. Nature Fed. Scholarship 1977; Can. Counc. Grant 1978; Sask. Arts Bd. Scholarship 1981; listed (International Biographical Centre, Cambridge England): 'Dictionary of Internat. Biographies,' 1991– ; 'International Who's Who of Intellectuals' 1992– ; 'First Five Hundred' 1992– ; illustrator: 'The Squirrels of Canada' 1980; 'Manitoba's Big Cat' 1982; 'Large Mammals' Vol. I & II 1983, 1986; 'Mammals in North America' 1986, 'An Atlas of Endangered Species of Canada' 1988 and others; Mem., Soc. of Animal Artists (US) 1980– ; Mem., Royal Ontario Museum; recreations: hunting, fishing, birdwatching; Clubs: Sask. Nat. Hist. Soc.; Salmagundi Club, NYC 1992; Home: R.R. 1, Dunchurch, Ont. P0A 1G0.

**HARVARD, John,** M.P.; politician; b. Glenboro, Man. 4 June 1938; s. Harry and Mabel (Johnson) Heidman; e. Glenboro Coll. Inst.; m. Lenore d. Irvine and Bernice Berscheid; children: Sasha, Stephanie; radio and TV broadcast journalist 31 yrs. speciliazing in pol. reporting; host open-line prog. 1960's and early 1970's; host several CBC radio and TV news and pub. affairs progs. incl. '24 Hours' for 7 yrs.; served as journalist regional and network CBC documentaries; el. Lib. M.P. for Winnipeg St. James g.e. 1988; Critic, Grains & Oilseeds; Mem. Standing Ctte. on Agriculture; recipient ACTRA Award Best Pub. Affairs Broadcaster 1976; Home: 257 Wharton Blvd., Winnipeg, Man. R2Y 0T3; Office: House of Commons, Ottawa, Ont. K1A 0A6.

**HARVEY, Andrew Sydney,** B.A., M.A., Ph.D.; university professor; b. St Stephen, N.B. 21 Sept. 1939; s. Sydney Herbert and Elizabeth Peters (Martin) H.; e. Univ. of Maine B.A. 1961; Clark Univ. M.A. 1967, Ph.D. 1971; m. Dawn d. James and Laura Daly 17 June 1961; children: Kathryn Anne, Heidi Lynne; CHRMN., DEPT. OF ECON., SAINT MARY'S UNIV., Prof. 1983– ; Dir., Time-Use Rsch. Program, Saint Mary's Univ.; Teaching Fellow, Clark Univ. 1963–65; Asst. Prof., Ricker College 1965–66; Rsch. Assoc., Dalhousie Univ. 1966–79; Sr. Econ., N.S. Prog. Devel. Agency 1968–70; Guest Prof., Univ. Karlshrue 1975; Vis. Prof., Univ. of Ottawa 1979–81; Prof. (Rsch.), Dalhousie Univ. 1981–86; Adjunct Prof. 1987– ; Vis. Scholar, Radcliffe Coll. 1989–90; Statistics Can. Fellow 1990; Past mem./Chrmn. of numerous cttes. U.S. & Can.; Cons., Stats Can., U.N. Food & Agric. Orgn., Korean Broadcasting Corp., NHK (Japanese Broadcasting Co.) & other fed., prov. & munic. agencies; internat. lectr.; U.N. Statistical Office; UN-INSTRAW; Eur. Found. on Living & Working Conditions; Pres., Temporal-Spatial Res. Incorp.; Mem., Anglican Ch. of Can. Long Range Planning Ctte. 1983–89; Life mem., Order of Demolay; mem. several Masonic lodges; Sec., Internat. Assoc. for Time Use Research; Mem., Am. Econ. Assn.; Mem./Past Pres., N.E. Regl. Sci. Assn.; Charter Pres., Candn. Regl. Sci. Assn.; mem., Atl. Can. Econ. Assn. (Past Pres.); Atlantic Assoc. of Applied Economists; Candn. Population Assn.; Carribean Studies Assn.; North Brit. Soc.; Lay Reader, St. James Anglican Ch. (Past Warden); Past mem., Anglican Synod of N.S.; co-author: 'Time Budget Research' 1984; 'Where Does Time Go' 1991; author of num. monographs & articles; Mem., Ed. Bd., 'Social Indicators Research' 1983– ; 'Occupational Sciences' 1993– ; Founding co-editor 'Canadian Journal of Regional Science'; editor: 'It's About Time'; recreations: computing, theatre; club: Queen Scout (1955); Lt. Gov. Key Club Internat. 1955–57; Home: 19 Balcome Dr., Halifax, N.S. B3N 1H9; Office: Halifax, N.S. B3H 3C3.

**HARVEY, Anne,** B.A.; feminist, writer, trade union organizer; b. Stockport, England 10 Jan. 1947; d. Joseph Jeffrie and Constance (Jackson) H.; e. Manchester Polytechnic B.A. (Hons.) Sociology; journalism apprenticeship, Nat. Union of Journalists; m. Gary s. Patrick and Clara Murray 1982; children: Nicholas Watts, Emma Watts, Helen Murray; CHIEF OPERATING OFFICER, B.C. NURSES UNION 1992– ; journalist in West Midlands (Birmingham), England; emigrated to Vancouver 1975; Reporter, 'Vancouver Sun' 1978; Communications Ed., B.C. Hydro 1979; Pres., Internat. Assn. of Business Communicators in B.C. 1979–81; Pres., Office & Technical Employees Union (OTEU) Local 378 1984–90; Vice-Pres., B.C. Fed. of Labour 1984; Vice-Pres., Western Canada, Office & Profl. Employees' Internat. Union (OPEIU) 1986, Candn. Dir. 1989–90; raised in Salvation Army; Home: 7330 Jubilee Ave., Burnaby, B.C. V5J 4B6; Office: 4740 Imperial St., Burnaby, B.C. V5J 4B6.

**HARVEY, Dallace Jane;** lawyer; b. Toronto, Ont. 17 Nov. 1951; d. William Case and Evelyn May (Fullerton) H.; e. Univ. of West. Ont., B.A. 1971; Univ. of Toronto, LL.B. 1974; called to Ont. Bar 1976; m. Donald E. O'Born 8 Sept. 1978; two children; OWNER, JANE HARVEY ASSOCIATES, LAWYERS & JANE HARVEY PREPAID LEGAL INC. 1979– ; Legal Offr., Torstar Corp. 1976–78; opened first storefront law office in Ont. 1980; Bencher, Law Soc. Upper Canada 1988–91; Ed. Bd., 'Canadian Lawyer'; Club: Royal Candn. Yacht; Home: Toronto; Office: Richmond Adelaide Centre Concourse, Ste. C-12A, 120 Adelaide St. W., Toronto, Ont. M5H 1T1.

**HARVEY, Donald,** R.C.A.; artist; educator; b. Walthamston, Eng. 14 June 1930; s. Henry and Annie Dorothy (Sawell) H.; e. Worthing (Eng.) High Sch. 1946; W. Sussex Coll. of Art Worthing, Eng. Nat. Dipl. of Design, Nat. Dipl. of Painting 1950; Brighton Coll. of Art Eng., Art Teachers Dipl. 1952; m. Elizabeth d. Albert James Clark 9 Aug. 1952; children: David Jonathon, Shan Mary; PROF. OF FINE ARTS, UNIV. OF VICTORIA 1961– ; Art Master, Ardwyn Grammar Sch. Wales 1952–56; Extve. Secy. to Sask. Arts Bd. 1958–61; rep. in various pub. and private colls. incl. Nat. Gallery Can., Montreal Museum Fine Arts, Charlottetown Confed. Gallery, Art Gallery Greater Victoria, Albert Knox Gallery Chicago, Seattle Art Museum; rec'd Sr. Can. Council Fellowship 1966; mem. Royal Canadian Academy; Candn. Group Painters; Candn. Painters & Etchers; recreations: movies, music, tennis; Home: 1025 Joan Cres., Victoria, B.C. V8S 3L3; Office: PO Box 1700, Victoria, B.C. V8W 2Y2.

**HARVEY, The Right Reverend Donald Frederick,** B.A., M.A., M.Div.; bishop; b. St. John's, Nfld. 13 Sept. 1939; s. Robert Joseph and Elsie May (Vaters) H.; e. St. Michael's Sch. 1956; Memorial Univ. B.A. 1985, M.A. 1987; Queen's Theological Coll. M.Div. 1986; m. Gertrude d. George and Jessie Hiscock 31 Oct. 1964; BISHOP, DIOCESE OF EASTERN NEWFOUNDLAND & LABRADOR, ANGLICAN CH. OF CAN. 1993– ; School Teacher 1956–57; Parish of Portugal Cove 1963–64, 1973–76; of Twillingate 1965; of King's Cove 1965–68; of Happy Valley Labrador 1968–73; of St. Michael & All Angels 1976–83; Anglican Chaplain, Memorial Univ. of Nfld. 1984–87; Rector, Cathedral of St. Jhn the Baptist 1989–92; Lectr. in Pastoral Theol., Queen's Coll. 1984– ; Sessional Lectr., English, M.U.N. 1985–89; Rural Dean of Labrador 1968–73; Dean of St. John's 1989–92; clubs: Rotary; Home: 22 Church Hill, St. John's, Nfld. A1C 3Z9; Office: 19 King's Bridge Rd., St. John's, Nfld. A1C 3K4.

**HARVEY, Earle Hugh,** B.E., P.Eng., R.I.A.; pulp and paper executive; b. S. Porcupine, Ont. 18 July 1942; s. Hugh A. and Rita M. (Lacombe) H.; e. Technical Univ. of N.S., B.E. (Chem.) 1967; McMaster Univ. R.I.A. 1975; m. Alma d. Thomas Standing 10 Sept. 1966; children: Heather, Kim; VICE PRES. OPERATIONS, QUEBEC AND ONTARIO PAPER COMPANY LTD. 1984– ; Process Engr. Abitibi Pper Co. 1967–71; Asst. Pulping Supt. Nova Scotia Forest Industries 1971–74; Asst. to Mill Mgr. Fraser Inc. 1974, Mill Mgr. 1976, Asst. to Vice Pres. Operations 1981–83; Gen. Mgr. Pulp and Paper present co. 1983–84; recipient Chrmn. Ind. Award 1967; Office: P.O. Box 1040, Allanburg Rd., Thorold, Ont. L2V 3Z5.

**HARVEY, George E.,** B.A.; communications executive; b. Cheshire, Eng. 10 June 1938; s. Donald J. and Catherine (Abbott) H.; e. Leeds Univ. B.A. 1959; m. Janet Christine d. Herbert and Dorothy Moore 10 Aug. 1963; children: Gavin Anthony, Rachel Josselyn; CHAIRMAN OF THE BOARD, UNITEL COMMUNICATIONS INC. 1987– ; Sales Rep. Burroughs Corp. Manchester, UK 1961–66, Acct. Mgr. London 1966–71, Br. Mgr. 1971–74; Dir. Financial Mktg. Detroit 1974–79; Pres. Burroughs Canada Toronto 1979–82; Pres. ROLM Canada Toronto 1982–86; Vice Pres. World-Wide Mktg. ROLM Corp. Santa Clara, Cal. 1986–87; Vice-Chrmn., Junior Achievement of Canada; Dir., Unitel Comm. Inc.; Royal Insurance Can.; Info. Tech. Assoc.; Toronto Symphony; Candn. Club of Toronto; Museum of Science & Technology; served with Royal Army Service Corps 1959–61, rank Lt.; Mem., Business Council on National Issues; Ont. Business Advisory Council; Ont. Opposition Leader's Business Advisory Council; Info. Technol. Assn. Can. (Dir.); Candn. Bus. Equipment Mfrs. Assn. (Dir. 1979–82, Treas. 1982–85, Chrmn. 1985–86); Internat. Bus. Council Can. (Dir. 1985–86); mem. Lodge of Fortitude and Old Cumberland No. 12 London, Eng.; Bd. Trade Metrop. Toronto; recreations: golf, squash; Clubs: St. George's Golf; Granite; Home: 310 Oriole Parkway, Toronto, Ont. M5P 2H5; Office: 200 Wellington St. W., Toronto, Ont. M5V 3G2.

**HARVEY, Janice Estelle,** B.Ed.; environment/development practitioner; b. Grand Manan, N.B. 25 Sept. 1955; d. Mansell R. and Estella C. (Brown) H.; e. Grand Manan High Sch. 1973; Univ. of N.B. B.Ed. 1977; St. Francis Xavier Univ. Master Adult Edn. in progress; m. David Coon s. Charles Coon and Iris Page 4 June 1988; PRINCIPAL, INSTITUTE FOR SUSTAINABLE COMMUNITIES; jr./sr. high sch. teacher 1977–80; mgr. small graphic art & design bus. 1980–83; Exec. Dir. Conservation Council 1983–89; Pres., Conserv. Council of N.B. 1989–93; Mem., Public Adv. Ctte. on State of the Environment Reporting 1990–92; Dir., The Bay of

Fundy: A Case for Community Action (project of Huntsman Marine Science Center and Conservation Counc. of N.B. 1990–93); mem. Fed. Task Forces on Mgmt. of Chemicals 1985–86 and Consultation Etiquette & Protocol 1985; Atlantic Co-ordinator Heritage for Tomorrow project Nat. Parks Centennial celebrations 1985; mem., Nat. Adv. Bd. Candn. Environ. Defence Fund 1986–88; Candn. Environmental Network (N.B. Rep. Nat. Steering Ctte. 1984–87, 1993–95, Chair 1987); Dir., Environmental Choice Prog. Mgmt. Bd. 1988–90; Vice Pres., Friends of the Earth Can. 1983–91; Pres., Fundy Community Found. 1993– ; Steering Ctte., Charlotte County Heritage Region 1992–93; Steering Ctte., Maritime Area Leadership Training 1992–93; author: 'Protecting the Bay of Fundy: A Citizen's Guide' 1993; Co-ed.: 'Voices of the Bay: Reflections on Changing Times along Fundy Shores' 1992; publication: 'The New Power Relations: Government, Communities and Sustainable Development' presented to Aylmer Conference, Nov. 1991, published in Chretien, J (ed.) Finding Common Ground 1992; Fredericton Voice Women for Peace; Home: Waweig, R.R. #6, St. Stephen, N.B. E3L 2Y3; Office: 180 St. John St., Fredericton, N.B. E3B 4A9.

**HARVEY, Jocelyn G.,** M.A., Ph.D.; arts executive; b. Eau Claire, Wis. 16 Dec. 1936; d. Julius Charles and Dorothy M. (Barrington) Gilbertson; e. Wis. State Univ. B.A. 1958; Ohio State Univ. M.A. 1959; Cornell Univ. Ph.D. 1964; m. David Dow (dec.) s. Lashley G. and Ernestine Harvey 3 Sept. 1966; children: Kerridwen, John Blake; SPECIAL ADVISOR TO THE DIRECTOR, THE CANADA COUNCIL 1993– ; Instr. in Eng. Lit. Westbrook Jr. Coll. 1959–60; Instr., Asst. Prof. of Eng. Lit. Univ. of Wash. 1963–66; Asst. Prof. Union Coll. 1967–69; Sr. Writer present Council 1978, Asst. to Dir. 1982, Asst. Dir. and Corporate Sec. 1985–92, Asst. Dir. & Dir. of the Arts Division 1992–93; Home: 9 Harvard Ave., Ottawa, Ont. K1S 4Y9; Office: 350 Albert St., Ottawa, Ont. K1P 5V8.

**HARVEY, John Dennis,** B.Sc., P. Eng.; exploration geologist; b. Toronto, Ont. 23 Feb. 1936; s. Dennis and Rosina (Cisterna) H.; e. Malvern Coll. Inst. Toronto; Univ. of N.B. B.Sc. 1959; (separated); children: Cheryl Anne, Susan Marie, David Gordon; Pres. & C.E.O., Hemlo Gold Mines Inc. 1988– ; Pres., Noranda Exploration Co. Ltd. 1982– ; Exploration Geol. Noranda Mines Ltd. 1959–60; Mine Geol. Aunor Gold Mines Ltd. 1960–64; Exploration Geol., Cadesky Assoc. Ltd. 1964–66; Renzy Mines Ltd. 1966; Systems Engr. I.B.M. 1966–67; Exploration Mgr. – Vice Pres. Mattagami Lake Exploration Ltd. 1967–82; Home: #915 – 55 Harbour Square, Toronto, Ont. M5J 2L1; Office: P.O. Box 45, Commerce Court W., Toronto, Ont. M5L 1B6.

**HARVEY, John S.;** marketing executive; b. Montreal, Que. 30 Sept. 1955; s. John S. and Catherine D. (Scott) H.; e. Kings College, England; Univ. of N.B.; m. Rita d. Angela Budinsky 5 Nov. 1988; children: Laura, Scott; GROUP DIRECTOR, GM MARKETING, HOUSEHOLD CREDIT SERVICES (Salinas, Ca.) 1993– ; joined Household Finance Corp. 1978; Br. Mgr. 1980; held various br. assignments 1980–85; promoted to Head Office, Corp. Planning 1985 & subsequent assignments to Mktg. until 1987; Asst. to Pres. 1987; Vice Pres. Opns. (U.S.) then Vice Prs. Mktg., Household Retail Services 1988; Sr. Vice Pres. of Marketing, Household Financial Corp. Limited 1991–93; Mem., Internat. Credit Assn. (CCEC Designation); Alumni Gold Medal, Univ. of N.B. (oldest academic award in Canada); Office: Salinas, Ca. USA.

**HARVEY, Malcolm,** B.Sc., Ph.D., F.A.P.S., F.R.S.C.; scientist; b. London, Eng. 9 Oct. 1936; s. Charles William and Winifred Alice (Tranter) H.; e. Spring Grove Grammar Sch. Eng. 1955; Southampton Univ. B.Sc. 1958, Ph.D. 1961; m. Patricia d. John and Elsie Jarman 21 Aug. 1959; children: Michael John, Deborah Ann, Rebecca Ellen; DIR., PHYSICS DIVISION, CHALK RIVER LABS. 1989– , Chrmn. Sci. for Educators Seminar (Annual) 1987– ; Postdoctoral Rsch. Fellow Nat. Rsch. Council Can. 1961, Asst. Rsch. Offr. 1962, Assoc. Rsch. Offr. 1964, Sr. Rsch. Offr. I 1970, Sr. Rsch. Offr. II 1980–89; Acting Dir. of Physics present Labs. 1985–86, Speakers Bureau 1984– ; Visiting Fellow Niels Bohr Inst. Copenhagen 1964–65; Visiting Lectr. Japanese Univs. 1970; Sr. Visiting Fellow Manchester Univ. 1978; Visiting Prof. State Univ. of N.Y. 1981; Visiting Sr. Sci. Institut fur Kernphysik, Kernforschungsanlage, Julich, W.Germany 1986; Fellow Am. Phys. Soc.; Royal Soc. of Can.; mem. Grant Selection Ctte. Natural Sci's & Eng. Rsch. Council 1989–90; Ford Found. Fellow 1964–65; mem. Candn. Assn. Physicists; Candn. Nuclear Soc.; recreations: singing, skiing, sailing, tennis; Home: 2 Mountain View Cres., Deep River, Ont. K0J 1P0; Office: Chalk River, Ont. K0J 1J0.

**HARVIE, Donald Southam,** O.C., LL.D.; professional engineer; charitable foundation executive; b. Calgary, Alta. 16 March 1924; s. Eric Lafferty and Dorothy Janet (Southam) H.; m. Mary, d. J.J. Soper, Victoria, B.C., 10 Sept. 1949; children: Dorothy Janet, Ian Soper, Patrick Neil, Mary Ann; Dir., The Molson Companies; Bank of Montreal; Northern Telecom Ltd.; Chrmn., Devonian Foundation; Hon. LL.D., Univ. of Alta. 1985; Hon. LL.D. Univ. of Lethbridge 1990; Anglican; Clubs: Ranchmen's; Calgary Golf and Country; Home: 4119 Crestview Rd. S.W., Calgary, Alberta T2T 2L5; Office: 770, 999 Eighth St. S.W., Calgary, Alta. T2R 1J5.

**HARVIE, James Duncan,** B.Sc.; government executive; b. Glasgow, Scotland 21 Jan. 1945; s. George Stein and Jessie McLennan (McLeod) H.; e. Hutcheson Boys' Grammar Sch.; Univ. of Glasgow B.Sc. (Hons.) 1966; m. Marion d. Alexander and Helen Cunningham 16 Oct. 1967; children: Derek, Lisa, Amber; DIRECTOR GENERAL, DIRECTORATE OF RESEARCH AND SAFEGUARDS, ATOMIC ENERGY CONTROL BD. 1990– ; Researcher in Thermal Hydraulics, Atomic Energy of Canada Ltd. 1966–74; Project Offr. & Sr. Project Offr., Bruce Nuclear Generating Station 1974–79; Mgr., Power Reactor Div. 1979–90; Mgr., Safety Evaluation Div. 1984–86; Vice-Pres. Cumbrae Sch. of Dancing; recreations: sailing, cycling, soccer, golf; Home: 16 Amberly Court, Gloucester, Ont. K1J 8A3; Office: 280 Slater St., Ottawa, Ont. K1P 5S9.

**HARVOR, (Erica) Elisabeth (Arendt),** M.A.; author; teacher; b. Saint John, N.B. 26 June 1936; d. Lauritz Kjeld and Erica Louise (Matthiesen) Deichmann; e. Macdonald Coll. Sch. Kingston Peninsula, N.B. 1953; Saint John High Sch. 1954; Concordia Univ. Montréal M.A. 1986; m. Stig Harvor s. Lisbeth and Halvor Haraldsen 16 Nov. 1957 (div.); children: Finn, Richard; former teacher of Creative Writing Concordia Univ.; currently teaching writing prog. York Univ.; organized and led workshops, women and Candn. writers, Algonquin Coll. Ottawa; participated Artists-in-Schs. progs. Ottawa; recipient various grants Can. Council and Ont. Arts Council; Writer-in-Residence, Ottawa Public Library and Carleton Univ. 1993–94; stories have appeared in many magazines and journals, inc. Grain, The Hudson Review, The New Yorker, Saturday Night and Quarry; poetry has appeared in The American Voice, Arc, The Antigonish Review, The Canadian Forum, Event, The Fiddlehead, The Malahat Review, The Medical Post, Prairie Fire, Poetry Canada Review, Prism International, The New Quarterly, The New Yorker, Ontario Review, Quarry and Saturday Night; First prize, CBC New Canadian Writing Series, 1965; first prize (co-winner) League of Canadian Poets' National Poetry Prize 1989; Malahat Long Poem Prize 1990; first prize, League of Canadian Poets' National Poetry Prize 1991; Confederation Poets' Prize for the best poem published in Arc 1991; National Magazine Award, poetry (Silver Medal) 1991; Confederation Poets Prize, Arc 1992; The Gerald Lampert Memorial Award for 'Fortress of Chairs' 1992; stories chosen prize-winning anthols. incl. 'Best American Short Stories' 1971; 'Best Canadian Stories,' 'Stories from Atlantic Canada,' 'The Penguin Book of Canadian Short Stories,' 'The Penguin Book of Modern Short Stories,' 'Canada Foreteller' (Norwegian transl.), 'More Stories By Canadian Women'; 'From Ink Lake'; 'The Possibilities of Story'; 'Frictions II'; poems chosen prize-winning anthols. incl. 'More Garden Varieties'; 'Vintage 91'; 'Sudden Miracles'; 'The Signal Anthology'; author: 'Women and Children' 1973, 'If Only We Could Drive Like This Forever' 1988, 'Our Lady of All the Distances' (slightly rev. ed. of the first story collection) 1991, 'Fortress of Chairs' 1992; Address: c/o The League of Candn. Poets, 24 Ryerson Ave., Toronto, Ont. M5T 2P3.

**HARWOOD, Brian Dennis;** securities industry executive; b. London, Eng 3 Feb. 1932; s. William and Catherine (O'Brien) H.; e. Shene Grammar School, London, Eng.; PRES., CANACCORD CAPITAL CORP. (formerly L.O.M. Western Securities) 1987– ; var. positions, Bk. of Montreal 1953–70; Lending Offr., Security First Nat. Bk., Los Angeles 1963–64; joined Canarim as Credit Mgr. 1970; Corp. Sec. 1973; Exec. Vice Pres. 1975; Dir. & Past, Chrmn., Canadian Investor Protection Fund; Gov. (Past Chrmn.) & Mem. Extve. Ctte., Vancouver Stock Exchange; Past Dir., Investment Dealers Assn. of Can. & Past Chrmn. of its Pacific Dist.; Dir., West Canada Depository Trust Co.; Exec. Vice Pres. & Dir., Intercan Holdings Ltd.; recreations: boating, walking, reading; Clubs: Royal Vancouver Yacht; Vancouver Lawn Tennis & Badminton; Terminal City; Home: 6066 Blink Bonnie Rd., West Vancouver, B.C. V7W 1V8; Office: P.O. Box 10337, Pacific Centre, Vancouver, B.C. V7Y 1H2.

**HARWOOD, Vanessa Clare,** O.C.; ballerina; b. Cheltenham, Eng. 14 June 1947; d. Peter Griffiths and Hazel Marian (Smith) Harwood; e. Bendale Pub. Sch. 1959; Nat. Ballet Sch. Toronto 1964; m. Dr. Hugh E., s. Hugh and Joyce Scully 14 June 1980; step-children: Laura, Alexa; children: Shannon Harwood; VICE PRES., ACTOR'S FUND OF CANADA 1991– ; Arts Found. of Toronto 1991– ; Theatre Plus Toronto 1989–90; mem., Dancer Transition Center; joined Corps de Ballet Nat. Ballet of Can. 1965, Soloist 1967; Principal Dancer, Nat. Ballet of Can. 1970–87; Master Class Univ. of S. Fla. 1977; Guest Ballerina, Australian Ballet 1977, Detroit Symphony 1977, Chicago Ballet 1978, Norfolk, Va. 1978, Jacobs Pillow 50th Anniversary 1981, Dutch Nat. Ballet 1979, Munich Opera Ballet 1981, Godunov and Stars Tour U.S.A. 1982; staged full-length prodn. of 'Giselle' for Universal Ballet, Seoul, Korea 1985; Guest teacher, Parksville Ballet Sch. (Vancouver Island) B.C. July 1986; 'Encore Encore!' Dancer & Actress at Candn. Pavillon, EXPO 86 Aug.; choreographed & staged 'Stars on Parade' Variety Club Convention, Toronto May 1986; TV appearances incl. 'Newcomers' 1982, 'Magic Planet' 1982; Olympia Dale in 'Road to Avonlea' 1992; ballerina role in 'Stepping Out' (film); roles danced incl.: Swan Queen, 'Swan Lake' The Dying Swan; Corsaire 'Pas de Deux'; Lise 'La Fille Mal Gardee'; title role 'Giselle'; Aurora 'Sleeping Beauty'; Juliet 'Romeo and Juliet'; Swanhilda 'Coppelia'; 'Cinderella'; 'Nutcracker'; 'Allure' and 'Locatelli Sonata' created for her by Matthew Nash; male dance partners: Rudolf Nureyev (dec.); Fernando Bujones (ABT); Wayne Eagling, Stephen Jeffries (Royal Ballet); Gary Norman, Kelvin Coe (dec.) (Australian Ballet); Patrick Bissell (dec.) (ABT); Georges Pilleta (Paris Opera); Vladamir Gelvan (Berlin Opera); Stylist Coach, Olympic Bronze Medal Winners (Tracy Wilson & Robert McCall, Candn. Ice Dancers) Calgary 1988 and World Bronze Medalists, Budapest 1988; debut as an actress: Mollie Ralston in 'The Mousetrap' Kingston Grand Theatre, Kingston, Ont. 1989; staged & performed 'Merry Widow' for Dallas Opera (starring Joan Sutherland) 1989; Artistic Dir., Balletto Classico, debut with Kitchener Symphony 1989; Officer, Order of Canada 1984; mem. ACTRA; mem. Candn. Actors' Equity Assn.; Home: 316 Spadina Ave., Toronto, Ont. M5R 2V6.

**HARWOOD-NASH, Derek Clive,** M.B., Ch.B., FRCPC; physician; educator; b. Bulawayo, S. Rhodesia 11 Feb. 1936; s. Dudley and Madeline Anne H-N; e. Univ. of Cape Town M.B., Ch.B. 1960; m. Barbara d. Kitchener and Marion Jordan 9 March 1963; three d. Heather, Marianne, Louise; RADIOLOGIST-IN-CHIEF, HOSP. FOR SICK CHILDREN 1978– , Head Pediatric Neuroradiol. 1968– ; Prof. of Radiol. Univ. of Toronto 1976– , Assoc. Chrmn. Radiol. 1991– ; Assoc. Staff Toronto Gen. Hosp., Hugh McMillan Rehabilitation Center; Distinguished Lectr. for 22 named Lectrs. USA and Eur.; 65 worldwide Visiting Professorships; Sir Alfred Beit Scholar; recipient: Presidential Medal Brazil; Indian Society of Radiology Medal; author: 'Neuroradiology in Infants and Children' 1976; co-author 'CT and Myelography of the Spine and Cord' 1982; 'Anomalies of the Central Nervous System' 1985; over 200 sci. articles and chapters; 750 sci. presentations and lectures various univ. and soc. meetings; Hon. Mem.: Swedish Soc. Med. Radiol. and Medalist; Soc. for Pediatric Radiology; Australasian Soc. Paediatric Imaging; Europ. Soc. of Paed. Radiol.; Europ. Congress of Europ. Assn. Radiol. 1991; Fellow: Royal Coll. of Physicians of Can. 1967; American Coll. of Radiology 1991; Hon. Fellow, Fac. of Radiology, Coll. of Med., S. Africa 1991; mem.: Radiol. Soc. N. Am. (Program Chrmn. 1987–90, 1st Vice Pres. 1991–92); Candn. Assn. Radiols.; Am. Soc. Neuroradiols. (Vice Pres. 1984, Pres. 1986); Soc. Pediatric Radiol. (Dir. 1981–84, Pres. 1986, Bd. Chrmn. 1987); Co-Pres., Internat. Paed. Radiol. Congress 1987; recreations: cross-country skiing, classical music and opera; Club: Granite; Home: 73 George Henry Blvd., Willowdale, Ont. M2J 1E8; Office: 555 University Ave., Toronto, Ont. M5G 1X8.

**HASKAYNE, Richard Francis,** B.Com., F.C.A.; petroleum executive; b. Calgary, Alta. 18 Dec. 1934; s. Robert S. and Bertha (Hesketh) H.; e. Univ. of Alta. B.Com. 1956; C.A. 1959; Univ. of W. Ont. Mang. Training Program 1968; m. Lee Mary d. Matthew W. Murray, Gleichen, Alta. 25 June 1958; CHRMN. & DIR., NOVA CORP. OF ALTA. 1992– ; Dir., Alberta Energy Company Ltd.; TransAlta Utilites; Crestar Energy Inc.; ManuLife Financial; Fording Coal Limited; Home Oil Company Ltd.; Canadian Imperial Bank of Commerce; Articling Student and Staff Acct. Riddell, Stead, Graham & Hutchison, Calgary 1956–60; Corporate Accounting Supvr. to Vice Pres. Finance, Hudson's Bay Oil and Gas Co. Ltd. 1960–73; Comptroller, Canadian Arctic Gas Study Ltd. Calgary 1973–75; Sr. Vice Pres. to Pres., Hudson's Bay Oil and Gas Co. Ltd. 1975–81; Chrmn., Pres., C.E.O. & Dir., Interhome Energy Inc. 1988–91; Pres. & C.E.O., Interprovincial Pipe Line Co. 1987–91 and Home Oil Co. Ltd. 1981–91; Life Mem., Alta. Children's Hosp. Foundation; Dir. and Past Pres., Calgary Petroleum Club; Chrmn., Bd. of Govs., Univ. of Calgary; mem. Financial Extve. Inst.; Fellow, Inst. C.A.'s; C. D. Howe Research Inst.; Kappa Sigma; P. Conservative; Anglican; recreations: golf, weekend farming; Clubs: Calgary Petroleum; Ranchmen's; Calgary Golf & Country; Earl Grey Golf; Home: 6942 Leaside Dr. S.W., Calgary, Alta. T3E 6H5; Office: 2030 Bankers Hall, 855 - 2nd St. S.W., Calgary, Alta. T2P 4J8.

**HASLAM, Robert H.A.,** M.D., F.A.A.P., F.R.C.P.(C); pediatrician; b. Saskatoon, Sask. 11 Sept. 1936; s. Robert N.H. and Elizabeth O. (Schmeiser) H.; e. Univ. of Sask. B.A. 1958, M.D. 1960; m. Barbara d. Dr. & Mrs. Archie E. McGregor 4 July 1959; three s. Robert, David, Christopher; PEDIATRICIAN-IN-CHIEF, THE HOSP. FOR SICK CHILDREN 1986– ; Prof. and Chrmn. of Pediatrics, Univ. of Toronto 1986– ; Pediatric Resident, Johns Hopkins Univ. Sch. of Med. 1962–67, Asst. Prof. of Pediatrics & Neurol. 1970–72, Assoc. Prof. 1972–75; Pediatric Neurol. Fellow, Univ. of Ky. 1967–70; Dir. John F. Kennedy Inst. Baltimore, Md. 1970–75; Prof. & Head of Pediatrics, Univ. of Calgary 1975–86; Dir. of Pediatrics, Foothills Hosp. 1975–86; Phys.-in-Chief, Alta. Children's Hosp. 1975–86, Dir. of Rsch. Dept. Pediatrics 1975–86; Dir., Ronald McDonald House Calgary 1984–86; Bd. of Dirs., Wycliffe Coll. 1986– ; Pres., Candn. Pediatric Soc. 1992–93; co-author 'Medical Problems in the Classroom – The Teacher's Role in Diagnosis and Management' 1985; author over 100 publs. med. jours.; recreations: jogging, hiking, skiing; Home: 364 Davisville Ave., Toronto, Ont. M4S 1H3; Office: 555 University Ave., Toronto, Ont. M5G 1X8.

**HASLEY, Michael A.,** B.A., M.B.A.; insurance executive; b. Montreal, Que. 22 Oct. 1941; s. Alexander and Dorothy H.; e. McGill Univ. B.A. (Hons.) 1962; Columbia Univ. M.B.A. 1964; Samuel Bronfman and James Talcot fellowships; m. Diane 20 Feb. 1965; children: two daughters; SENIOR VICE-PRESIDENT, FINANCE, SUN LIFE ASSURANCE CO. OF CANADA 1988– ; various, ending as Asst. Mgr., New York, Montreal, Toronto, Mercantile Bank of Canada 1964–66; various, ending as Asst. Treasurer, T. Eaton Co. Ltd. 1966–72; Vice-Pres. Finance & Admin., Rapid Data Systems & Equipment Ltd. 1973–74; various, ending as Exec. Vice-Pres. & Chief Operating Offr., Guaranty Trust 1974–88; Dir., Sun Life Trust Co.; Sun Life Savings & Mortgage Corp.; Pres. & Dir., Sun Life Financial Holdings Inc.; Dir., Sun Life of Canada Home Loans Limited; Century 21 Real Estate Canada Ltd.; Senior Advisory Bd. Mem., C.M. Hincks Inst.; Past Pres., Bd. of Trustees, Art Gallery of Ont.; Pres., AGO Foundation; recreations: running, skiing, reading, contemporary art; clubs: National, Cambridge; Office: Sun Life Centre, 150 King St. W., Toronto, Ont. M5H 1J9.

**HASSAN, Marwan Assaf;** writer; b. London, Ont. 9 May 1950; s. Alex and Ayshi (Shousher) H. (Hussein Assaf); single; friend and mother of children: Catherine Shepherd; children: Baalqis, Qays; author: 'The Confusion of Stones: Two Novellas' 1989, 'The Memory Garden of Miguel Carranza' 1991 (novel); mem. PEN; The Writers Union of Canada; Home: 99 Holmwood Ave., Ottawa, Ont. K1S 2P1.

**HASSELBACK, Richard,** B.A., M.D., C.M., FRCP(C); retired physician, medical oncologist; b. Winnipeg, Man. 3 Dec. 1928; s. Richard Charles and Myriene Alberta H.; e. Univ. of Saskatchewan B.A. 1949; McGill Univ. M.D., C.M. 1953; FRCP(C); m. Betty Jane d. Kate and Joseph Lahay 13 July 1978; children: Angela Day, Martin Julian, Mark Richard Hasselback, Michael Julian, Dr. Paul Douglas Hasselback, Alexandra Julian; Medical Oncologist, Ontario Cancer Institute 1962–94, retired; Intern / Resident, Vancouver 1953–58; Asst. Hematologist, Vancouver Gen. Hosp. 1958–62; Chrmn., Med. Adv. Ctte., Ont. Div., Candn. Cancer Soc. 1977–79; Candn. Breast Cancer Foundation 1987–91; Asst. Prof., Dept. of Med., Univ. of Toronto; recreations: tennis, bridge; clubs: Waterfront Racquet; Home: 80 Front St. E., Toronto, Ont. M5E 1T4.

**HASSELL, Hilton MacDonald,** R.C.A.; artist; b. Lachine, Que. 14 March 1910; s. Hilton George Samuel and Elizabeth (Cooper) H.; e. Ont. Coll. of Art; Heatherly's Sch. of Fine Art, Eng.; m. Valerie Ariel Richardson 2 Aug. 1914; children: Dr. Christopher Hilton, Laurel Ann; solo exhns. annually Eaton's Gallery 1961–71; Mem. Univ. of Nfld. 1963; Univ. of Toronto 1964; Laurentian Univ. 1971; Kensington Fine Art Gallery Calgary 1973, 1979; Wallack Galleries Ottawa 1978; Kaspar Gallery Toronto 1980; mem. Ont. Soc. Artists; Club: Arts & Letters; Address: 32 Inglewood Drive, Toronto, Ont. M4T 1G8.

**HASSEN, Philip Charles,** B.Sc., M.P.H.; hospital administrator; b. Detroit, Mich. 13 Aug. 1943; s. Philip and Helen H.; e. Wayne State Univ. B.Sc. 1968; Univ. of Mich. M.P.H. 1971; m. Nancy Lake 21 Jan. 1967; children: Keith Philip, Michelle Marie; PRES. & CHIEF EXTVE. OFFR. ST. JOSEPH'S HEALTH CENTRE OF LONDON 1988– ; Asst. Adm. Holy Cross Hosp. Calgary 1976–78; Exec. Vice Pres. Foothills Provincial Gen. Hosp. Calgary 1978–87; Sr. Vice Pres. and Chief Op. Offr. Toronto Western Hosp. 1987–88; mem. Bd. Alta. Blue Cross 1981–86; author or co-author various profl. publs.; Dir., Alta. Hosp. Assn. 1981–87; Fellow, Candn. Coll. Health Service Execs.; mem., MENSA; Am. Coll. Health Care Execs.; Office: P.O. Box 5777, London, Ont. N6A 4L6.

**HASSON, Reuben Alex,** B.A., LL.B., LL.M.; professor of law; b. Southern Rhodesia (now Zimbabwe) 20 August 1938; s. Moise Reuben and Rachel (Sevim); e. Prince Edward Sch. 1955; Univ. of Cape Town, B.A. 1958; Univ. of London, LL.B. 1962; Yale Univ., LL.M. 1968; PROF., OSGOODE HALL LAW SCHOOL 1975– ; Lecturer, Sch. of Oriental & African Stud. 1962–66; Teaching Fellow, Stanford Law Sch. 1970–71; Lect., Queen Mary Coll. 1971–75; Visiting Fellow, London Sch. of Econ. 1983–84; author of numerous articles in Candn. & U.K. law journals; recreations: walking, theatre; Home: 75 Gilgorm Toronto, Ont. M5N 2M4; Office: 4700 Keele St., Downsview, Ont. M3J 1P3.

**HASTINGS, Hon. Earl Adam;** senator; b. Regina, Sask., 7 Jan. 1924; s. Clarence Beverly and Eva Pearl (Winter) H.; e. Wetmore & Strathcona Pub. Schs., Regina; Balfour Tech. Sch., Regina; Regina Coll.; m. Evelyn Audrey, d. late John Andrew Kain, 19 Apl. 1952; children: David Telfer, Donald Earl, Leslie-Lynn; MEMBER, THE SENATE OF CANADA; Asst. to Leader of Opposition and Leader of Sask. Lib. Party, 1948–52; also Asst. Secy., Sask. Lib. Assn.; Land Adm., Dept. of Agric., Sask., 1952–57; Petroleum Landman, Sun Oil Co., Calgary, 1957–66; summoned to the Senate of Can., 1966; served with RCAF, 1942–45; Pres., Calgary Lib. Assn., 1958 and 1959 and Alta. Lib. Assn., 1960, 1961 and 1962; Chrmn., Senate Comte. Northern Pipeline 1979–83; Chrmn., Senate Energy Comte. 1983–89; Special Rapporteur and Chrmn., various cttes., NATO North Atlantic Assembly 1979–89; named Distinguished Humanitarian, John Howard Soc. of Can. 1985; Liberal; United Church; recreations: swimming, curling, hunting; Home: 3419 Utah Crescent, Calgary, Alta. T2N 4A9; Office: Rm. 225, East Block, The Senate, Ottawa, Ont. K1A 0A4.

**HATCH, Gerald Gordon,** B.Eng., Sc.D.; consulting engineer; b. Brockville, Ont., 30 July 1922; s. Earle Clifton and Ethel Helen (Goodfellow) H.; e. McGill Univ., B.Eng. 1944; Mass. Inst. Of Technol., Sc.D. 1948; m. Sheila Pamela, d. John S. Baillie, 4 Sept. 1946; children: Linda, Douglas, Christopher, Joan; CHRMN., HATCH ASSOCIATES LTD.; Research Engr., Shawinigan Water & Power Co. Ltd., 1944–45; Research Engr., Armour Research Foundation, Chicago, Ill., 1948–52, engaged on devel. of processes for prod. of titanium metal; joined Quebec Iron & Titanium Corp., Sorel, Que., as Dir. of Research & Devel., 1952–54; apptd. Works Mgr., 1954–58; became Pres., W. S. Atkins & Associates Ltd., 1958–65; awarded 1st President's Gold Medal in 1961, the Airey Medal in 1986, and the INCO Medal in 1988 by Candn. Inst. Mining & Metal.; D.Sc. (hon.), McGill Univ. 1990; mem., Am. Inst. Mining & Metall. Engrs.; Ordre des Ingrs. du Que.; Sigma Xi; Anglican; recreation: golf, tennis; Clubs: National (Toronto); St. George's Golf & Country; Home: 421 The Kingsway, Islington, Ont. M9A 3W1; Office: Toronto, Ont.

**HATCH, H. Clifford;** executive; b. Toronto, Ont. 30 Apr. 1916; s. Harry Clifford and Elizabeth (Carr) H.; m. Joan, d. late E. G. Ferriss, 1 May 1940; children: Henry Clifford, Gail Elizabeth, Sheila M., Richard F.; Dir., Hiram Walker Resources Ltd. 1980–86, Chrmn. and C.E.O. 1980–84; Chrmn. and CEO Hiram Walker-Gooderham & Worts Ltd. 1978–80; Pres., 1964–78; Dir. & Offr. of subsidiary companies; Commdr., Royal Candn. Navy, 1940–45; Roman Catholic; Clubs: Essex Golf & Country (Windsor); Rosedale Golf (Toronto); York (Toronto); Detroit Athletic (Detroit, Mich.); Lost Tree (N. Palm Beach, Fla.); Home: 7130 Riverside Drive East, Windsor, Ont. N8S 1C3; Office: 1304 Bank of Commerce Bldg., 100 Ouellette Ave., Windsor, Ont. N9A 6T3.

**HATCH, Roger Eugene,** B.Sc.; consultant; b. Strasbourg, France 11 June 1919; s. Eugene and Amandine H.; e. Mount Allison Univ., B.Sc. (Hons. Chem.; Eng. Cert.) 1941; McGill Univ. 1942; Harvard Univ. (Adv. Mgt.) 1959; m. Betsy (Gay) G., d. Graham Wanless, Sarnia, Ont., 5 May 1945; one d. Barbara; CONSULTANT 1985– ; Dir., Dresdner Bank; Chrmn., Diffracto Ltd.; Past Chrmn., Candn. Export Assn.; Past Chrmn., Export Trade Dev. Bd.; Dir. and past Pres., La Chambre de Commerce Française au Canada (Ont. Section); past mem. Extve. Comte. and Bd. of Regents, Mount Allison Univ.; joined Polysar Ltd. (formerly Polymer Corp.) as Chem. Engr., 1942; Mgr., Sales & Tech. Service Div., 1948; Gen. Sales Mgr., 1954; Vice-Pres., Marketing, 1957; Dir. and C.E.O. of numerous subsidiary companies, including Pres. of Polymer Corp. (France) and Polysar Internat. (Switzerland) 1960–69; Extve. Vice-Pres. 1969–71; Group Vice Pres. 1971–72; Pres. & C.E.O., Canpotex Ltd. 1972–84; Pres., Canpotex Shipping Services Ltd. 1972–84; Lieut., R.C.E. (inactive); Protestant; Clubs: Harvard Business School Club of Toronto & Naples, Florida; Granite; Rosedale; Home: 9 Bayview Ridge Crescent, Willowdale, Ont. M2L 1E8.

**HATCH, Thomas Bradley Lawrence;** industrial food service executive; b. Toronto, Ont. 26 Sept. 1924; s. Herbert Earl and Jennie Todd (Jamieson) H.; e. Frankland P.S.; Jarvis Coll.; Mont Ste. Louis Coll.; m. Beryl d. Edwin and Florence Wratten, 17 Oct. 1947; children: Bradley, Cheryl, Mark; BD. CHRMN., CANADA CATERING CO. 1973– ; R.C.A.F. 1943–46; Acct. Extve., R.C. Smith & Son 1946–47; Asst. Treas., Canada Catering 1952; Sec. Treas. 1958; Vice-Pres. 1960; Past Pres., Granite Club; recreations: golf, curling; Clubs: Rosedale Golf; Granite; Home: 6 Glenallan Rd., Toronto, Ont.; Office: 5 Southvale Dr., Toronto, Ont. M4G 1G2.

**HATCH, William McLaren Jr.;** business executive; b. Hamilton, Ont. 21 June 1951; s. William McLaren and Diane Franklin (Jones) H.; e. Upper Canada Coll. 1969; Univ. of W. Ont., B.A. 1973; m. Linda d. Bruce and Audrey Ritchie 6 Sept. 1985; OWNER & PRES., WILL TOOLS INC., Mississauga 1988– and B.N.T. PRODUCTS 1981– ; Vice-Pres., Redlaw Indus. 1977–80; Pres., Hatch Resources Limited 1980– ; Anglican; Clubs: Rosedale Golf; Home: 200 Chartwell Rd., Oakville, Ont.; Office: 2444 Haines Rd., Mississauga, Ont. L4Y 1Y6.

**HATCH-DINEL, Heather Ann,** B.A.; curator; arts administrator; b. Hamilton, Ont. 5 Jan. 1955; d. William McLaren and Diane Franklin (Jones) H.; e. Chatham Hall H.S., Virgina, U.S.A. 1972; Univ. of Guelph, B.A. (Hons.) 1975; PRESIDENT, THE HALEY GROUP 1991– ; Asst. Curator, Univ. of Guelph Art Gall. 1976–78; Admin. Asst. to Dir., The Winnipeg Art Gall. 1978; Devel. Offr. 1979; Asst. to Chief Curator 1981; Curator/Arts Administrator, City of Toronto 1982–90; Curator of the Market Gallery, City of Toronto Archives 1982–87; Staff Liaison, Pub. Art Comn., City of Toronto 1985– ; Admin., Toronto/Amsterdam Artists Exch. Prog. 1984– ; U.S. Embassy grant to tour Am. Art Mus. 1979; Co-ordinator, Olympic Arts Adv. Ctte., Toronto Ont. Olympic Counc. 1989; Chrmn., Toronto Outdoor Art Exhib. 1986–89; Pres., 4th Internat. Ceramics Conf. 1985; Dir., Toronto Arts Awards Found. 1988– ; Ont. Assn. of Art Galls. 1983; Mem., Assn. of Cultural Extves; Art Gall. of Ont.; The Corp. Art Collectors Group; The Power Plant; author & co-author of five exhib. catalogues; recreations: tennis, sailing, bicycling; Club: Metro. Toronto Central YMCA Women's Health Club; Address: 70 Pricefield Rd., Toronto, Ont. M4W 1Z9.

**HATCHER, Stanley Ronald,** M.Sc., Ph.D., F.C.A.E., F.C.I.C., P.Eng.; b. Downton, Wilts., Eng. 20 Aug. 1932; s. Reginald and Nellie Evelyn (Weeks) H.; e. Univ. of Birmingham B.Sc. 1953, M.Sc. 1954; Univ. of Toronto Ph.D. 1958; m. Gladys Mary d. Frank and Gladys Robinson 17 Sept. 1955; children: Adrian David, Kevin Lloyd, Michael Francis, David Scott; Pres. & C.E.O., Atomic Energy of Canada Ltd. (AECL) 1989–92; Asst./Assoc. Rsch. Offr. Chem. Eng. Br. AECL Chalk River 1958–63; Head, Chem. Eng. Sect. AECL Whiteshell Nuclear Rsch. Est. (WNRE) 1963–65, Br. Head Chem. Technol. Br., WNRE 1965–74; UK Liaison Offr. for AECL 1968–69; on loan to Bruce Heavy Water Plant 1973–74; Dir. Applied Sci. Div. WNRE 1974–77, Asst. to Exec. Vice Pres. AECL H.O. 1977–78; Vice Pres. & Gen. Mgr. WNRE 1978–81; Vice Pres., Mktg. & Sales, AECL CANDU Operations 1981–85; Pres. AECL

Research Co. 1986–89; Dir., Am. Nuclear Soc.; Fellow, Candn. Acad. of Engrg.; Chem. Inst. Can.; mem. Cdn. Nuclear Soc.; Cdn. Soc. for Chem. Engrg.; Assn. Profl. Engrs. Ont.; recreations: canoeing, fishing, squash, theatre, travel, woodwork, computers; Home: R.R. 1, Terra Cotta, Ont. L0P 1N0.

**HATCHER, William Spottswood,** Docteur ès Sciences; educator; b. Charlotte, N.C. 20 Sept. 1935; s. Albert Spottswood and Helen (Hardman) H.; e. Vanderbilt Univ. B.A. 1957, M.A.T. 1958; Univ. de Neuchâtel Docteur ès Sciences 1963; m. Judith Ann d. Philip and Genevieve Bernstein 6 June 1959; children: Sharon Nur, Carmel Lynne, Benjamin Faizi; PROFESSEUR TITULAIRE DEPT. DE MATHEMATIQUES, UNIV. LAVAL 1972– ; Professeur Chargé de Cours Dépt. de Mathématiques Univ. de Neuchâtel 1964–65; Assoc. Prof. of Math. Univ. of Toledo, Ohio 1965–68; Prof. Agrégé present Univ. 1968–72; Prof. Invité Ecole Polytechnique Fédérale Suisse, Lausanne 1972–73; recipient NSERC Grant 1969–91; Que. Ministry Educ. Grant 1970–74, 1982–88; IBM Corp. Grant 1973–74; Hon. Mention Westinghouse Science Talent Search 1953; DuPont Fellowship 1957–58; Swiss Nat. Fund for Scientific Research Grant 1962–64; author or co-author 'Foundations of Mathematics' 1968; 'The Science of Religion' 1977; 'Absolute Algebra' 1978; 'The Logical Foundations of Mathematics' 1982; 'The Baha'i Faith' 1985; 'Logic and Logos' 1990; various articles math. sciences and philos.; mem.,Candn. Math. Soc.; Am. Math. Soc.; Math. Assn. Am.; Assn. Symbolic Logic (mem. Council 1979–82); recreations: chess, tennis, swimming, running; Home: 1060 Brown Ave., Quebec City, Que. G1S 2Z9; Office: Quebec City, Que. G1K 7P4.

**HATFIELD, Rt. Rev. Leonard Fraser,** M.A., D.D.; retired bishop; b. Port Greville, N.S. 1 Oct. 1919; s. Otto Albert and Ada (Tower) H.; e. Port Greville and Amherst High Sch.; Univ. of King's Coll. and Dalhousie Univ. B.A. 1940, M.A. (Sociol.) 1943; Hon. D.D., King's Coll. 1956; Atlantic Sch. of Theol. 1985; o. Deacon 1942; o. Priest 1943; Priest Asst. All Saints' Cath. Halifax 1942–46; Rector of Antigonish, N.S. 1946–51; Asst. Secy. Council for Social Service Ang. Ch. Can. 1951–54, Gen. Secy. 1955–61; Rector, Christ Ch. Dartmouth 1961–71; St. John's Ch. Truro 1971–76; Canon of All Saints' Cath. 1969; consecrated Bishop Suffragan Diocese of N.S. 1976; Bishop of N.S., Ang. Ch. of Canada 1980–84; ret. 1984; author 'He Cares' 1958; 'Simon Gibbons – First Eskimo Priest in the World' 1987; "Sammy the Prince' S.H. Prince, one of Canada's Pioneering Sociologists" 1990; recreations: fishing, gardening, travel, bridge; Home: Site #31, Box #0, R.R. #3, Parrsboro, N.S., B0M 1S0.

**HATHAWAY, Donald B.,** B.Eng., B.Sc., M.B.A., C.M.C., O.C.M., U.E.L.; management consultant; b. Deloraine, Man. 26 Sept. 1936; s. Thomas McCullough and Evelyn Mary (Hamblin) H.; e. Sir George Williams Univ. B.Eng. 1965, B.Sc. 1968; York Univ. MBA 1973; Certified Management Consultant 1978; m. Mary-Ann d. George and Kathleen Lark; children: Michael, Patrick, Andrew, Katherine, Sarah; PRESIDENT, PEOPLETECH, CONSULTING INC. 1992; Pres. Hathaway Consulting Group 1978–92; joined RCAF 1956; Product Eng. Sperry Gyroscope 1966; Asst. Dean Sir George William Univ. 1968; Asst. Dean of Business York Univ. 1970–73; Cons. Urwick Currie 1973; Hathaway Consulting Group 1978–81; Partner, Towers, Perrin, Forster & Crosby 1981–85; guest Lectr. Univs. W. Ont., Queen's, York, Toronto and B.C., various community colls. and service clubs; recipient Order of Constantine 1981; Gov. Gen.'s Warrant (Scout Leader) 1961; mem. Bd.: Uxmal Holdings Ltd., Cornerstone Strategic Holdings, Comac Communications Ltd.; Keystone Enterprizes inc. 1993; Wordwrap Associates Inc.; author numerous jour. articles; Fellow, Inst. of Certified Mgmt. Consultants of Ont. (Pres. 1985–86, Dir. 1981–86) 1987; Mem., Extve. Ctte., Inst. of Certified Mgmt. Consultants of Can. 1986–92 (Pres. 1990–91); recreations: reading, cooking, painting, gardening, home renovations; Club: Toronto Racquet; Home: Keystone House, R.R. #1, Erin, Ont. N0B 1T0.

**HATHAWAY, James Curtis,** LL.M., J.S.D.; educator; b. Calgary, Alta. 14 Apl. 1956; s. Charles Curtis and Bernice Elizabeth (Stoddart) H.; e. McGill Univ.; Osgoode Hall Law Sch. Toronto LL.B. 1979; Columbia Univ. LL.M., J.S.D. 1982; ASSOC. PROF. OF LAW, OSGOODE HALL LAW SCH. 1984– ; Assoc Dir. (Law) Ctr. for Refugee Studies; articled Fasken & Calvin, Toronto 1979–80; Professeur adjoint de droit Univ. de Moncton 1980–83; Cons. Special Legal Assistance for Disadvantaged Dept. of Justice Can. 1983–84; Barrister & Solr., Ont. & N.B.; author: 'The Law of Refugee Status' 1991 and various publs. internat. human rights law, refugee and asylum law, poverty law, clin. legal edn.; mem. Internat. Comn. Jurists (Can.); Candn. Council Internat. Law; Am. Soc. Internat. Law; Candn. Assn. Law Teachers; Office: 4700 Keele St., North York, Ont. M3J 2R5.

**HATHAWAY, Norman Blasdell;** executive; educator; b. New Hamburg, Ont. 18 Aug. 1924; s. George Blasdell and Rolena Violet (Roos) H.; e. New Hamburg, Stratford, Elmira and Kitchener schs.; Ont. Coll. of Art 1949 AOCA; PRES., HATHAWAY & ASSOC. INC.; Advt. and Sales Promotion Mgr., Office Specialty Ltd. Newmarket 1949; Mgr., Direct Mail and Promotion Rolph Clark Stone Ltd., Toronto 1957; Sales Mgr., Art Dept., Bomac Ltd. Toronto 1960; Exec. Vice Pres., Hathaway-Templeton Ltd. 1961; Exec. Vice Pres., Sebert Productions Ltd. 1966; Chrmn., Canac Communications 1968; Pres., Ont. Coll. of Art 1983–87; Hon. Col., The 78th Fraser Highlanders; Chevalier, NIADH NASK; Kt. Cmdr., Mil. & Hospitaller Order St. Lazarus Jerusalem; Kt. Intnl. Constantinian Order; Knight, The Sovereign Military Order of the Temple of Jerusalem; Knight Grand Commander, the Order of the Noble Companions of the Swan; mem., Intnl. Council Fine Arts Deans; Heraldry Soc. Can.; Monarchist League; Royal Commonwealth Soc.; Anglican; P. Conservative; recreations: saxophone, clarinet, antique & classic car collecting, antique boating; Clubs: Arts & Letters; Antique & Classic Car Can.; Antique Boat Soc.; Rolls Royce Owner's; RCYC; Royal Candn. Mil. Inst.; West Point Officers'; Home: 22 Sunset Place, North Salem, N.Y. 10560; Offices: 36 Mill Plain Rd., Ste. 310, Danbury, CT 06813.

**HATTERSLEY, (Rev.) John Martin,** Q.C., M.A., LL.B., A.Th.; b. Swinton, Yorkshire, Eng., 10 Nov. 1932; s. Charles Marshall and Ethel Vera (Chambers) H.; e. Repton Sch., Derbyshire, Eng. 1946–50; Clare Coll., Cambridge 1952–56, B.A. (Econ. and Law) 1955, LL.B. (Pub. and Adm. Law) 1956, M.A. 1959; Thorneloe Univ. A.Th. 1992; m. Florence Anne, d. Frederick William Stilwell, 14 Sept. 1957; three d. Catherine Rose (dec. 1988), Nancy Jane, Janet Marie; PARTNER, HATTERSLEY & PERRY; emigrated to Can. 1956; articled with Milner & Steer, Edmonton, Alta.; read law with Ronald Martland, Q.C.; called to Bar of Alta. 1957; 1962–64 served as Personal Secy. to Robert Thompson, M.P., Nat. Leader of Social Credit Party, becoming also Dir. of Research and Editor of 'Focus' for S.C. Assn. of Can.; served as Offr. in Royal Arty. 1951–56, rank on discharge Lieut.; Nat. Pres., Social Credit Party of Can. 1973–78, Nat'l Leader 1980–83; Vice-Pres. (Policy), Alberta Social Credit Party 1983–85, Interim Leader 1985–88; former Vice Pres., Sorrento Centre for Human Devel.; former mem. Doctrine & Worship Comte., Gen. Synod, Ang. Ch. Can.; Hon. Asst. Priest, St. Peter's Anglican Ch., Edmonton, 1974–88; Mem., Interim Ministry Team, Diocese of Edmonton 1988– ; mem. Edmonton Chamber Comm. (Vice Pres., Gov't. Dept., 1977, 1979–82, Dir. 1989–92); Law Soc. Alta.; Edmonton and Candn. Bar Assns.; Mensa; Economics Soc. of Northern Alta. (Pres. 1986); Alberta Human Rights & Civil Liberties Assoc. (Pres. 1991–92); Prison Fellowship; Alternate to Violence·Project; Mem., City of Edmonton Charitable Appeals Ctte. 1990–92; Publications: 'Human Rights-The New Political Direction' and 'Monetary Reform for Canada' 1980; Social Credit; Reform; Anglican; recreations: reading, music, criminology; Club: The Edmonton; Home: 8112 - 144A St., Edmonton, Alta. T5R 0S2; Office: 2240 Sun Life Place, 10123 - 99 St., Edmonton, Alta. T5J 3H1.

**HATTERSLEY-SMITH, Geoffrey Francis,** M.A., D.Phil., F.R.S.C., F.R.G.S.; glaciologist; toponymist; b. London, Eng. 22 Apl. 1923; s. Maj. Wilfrid Percy, D.S.O. and Ethel Mary (Willcocks) H-S.; e. Winchester Coll.; New Coll. Oxford B.A. 1948, M.A. 1951, D.Phil. 1956; m. Maria d. Dionysios and Anastasia Kefallinos 12 May 1955; children: Kara Mary, Fiona Anastasia; Principal Scientific Offr., British Antarctic Survey 1973–91, Secy. Antarctic Place-names Ctte. Foreign & Commonwealth Office 1975–91; served with RNVR N. Atlantic, Arctic, Eng. Channel, Indian Ocean 1943–46, rank Sub-Lt.; Base leader and Glaciol. King George Island, S. Shetland Islands, Falkland Islands Dependencies Survey 1948–50; Defence Research Bd. Can. 1951–73, Defence Sci. Staff Offr., Head Geotech. Sec. Defence Research Est. Ottawa 1971–73; mem., Assoc. Ctte. on Geodesy & Geophysics (Chrmn. Sub-Ctte. on Glaciers) Nat. Research Council Can. 1960–66; awarded Founder's Gold Medal Royal Geog. Soc. 1966; author 'North of Latitude Eighty' 1974; 'Present Arctic Ice Cover' in 'Arctic and Alpine Environments' 1974; 'The History of Place-names in the Falkland Islands Dependencies (South Georgia and the South Sandwich Islands)' 1980; ed., 'The Norwegian with Scott: Tryggve Gran's Antarctic Diary 1910–1913' 1984; 'The History of Place-names in the British Antarctic Territory' 1991; Fellow, Arctic Inst. N.Am. (Gov. 1963–66); Intnl. Glaciol. Soc. (Council 1962–64); Pres., Arctic Circle Club Ottawa 1967–69; Arctic Club UK 1976; mem., Ctte. Antarctic Club UK 1983–86; recreations: polar and mountaineering history, gardening; Home: The Crossways, Cranbrook, Kent, England TN17 2AG.

**HATZIS, Christos P.,** M.Mus., Ph.D.; composer; b. Volos, Greece 21 March 1953; s. Panagiotis C. and Maria P. H.; e. Eastman Sch. of Music Rochester B.Mus. 1976, M.Mus. 1977; State Univ. of N.Y. Buffalo Ph.D. 1982; m. Rania d. George and Sophia Xiarchos 3 Dec. 1984; children: George, Maria; emigrated to Can. 1982, Candn. Citizen 1985; composer over 20 maj. works comnd. various media incl. symphonic and electroacoustic; participant various internat. festivals; compositions performed by Montreal Symphony Orch., the viola section of the Toronto Symphony Orchestra, and soloists such as Steven Dann and Robert Aitken; frequently broadcast by CBC and foreign networks; Home: 184 Fulton Ave., Toronto, Ont. M4K 1Y3; Mailing Address: Box 307, Suite 100, 2 Bloor St. W., Toronto, Ont. M4W 3E2.

**HAUST, M. Daria,** M.D., M.Sc., FRCPS(C); university professor, physician; e. Univ. of Heidelberg M.D. 1951; Queen's Univ. M.Sc.(Med) 1959; Queen's Univ. & Kingston Gen. Hosp. grad. residency 1952–59; FRCPS(C) 1959; Postdoct. Fellow, Cincinnati Children's Hosp. 1959–60; m. Heinz L. H.; children: Bill M.H., Jan H.; PROF. UNIV. OF WESTERN ONT. 1968– ; Asst. Prof., Pathology, Queen's Univ. 1960–65; Assoc. Prof. 1965–67; Univ. of West. Ont. 1967–68; Prof. of Paediatrics, present univ. 1972– ; of Obstetrics & Gynaecol. 1978– ; Dir. of Pathology, Childr. Psychiatr. Rsch. Inst. 1967– ; Visiting Sci., Oxford Univ. 1972–73; Consultant in Pathol., Sick Children's Hosp. Toronto 1978– ; Paediatric Pathol. (in charge), Kingston Gen. Hosp. 1960–67; Cons. in Paed. Pathol., Victoria Hosp. London 1967–73; Staff Pathologist, Univ. Hosp. London 1973– ; invited lectr. on over 400 occasions worldwide; reviewer of grants, MRC 1960– , Candn. Heart Found. 1963– , Heart & Stroke Found. of Ont. 1960–87, Nat. Inst. of Health Bethesda, U.S.A. 1967– and others; serves on several edit. bds.; Hon. Mem., Hungarian & Eur. Atherosclerosis socs.; Hungarian, Chilean, & Cuban assns. of Pathol.; Brit. Atherosclerosis Discussion Group; Latin Am. Soc. for Paed. Pathol.; Heidelberg Acad. of Sciences; Special Distinguished Colleague Award, Soc. for Paed. Pathol. 1987; Hon. Fellowship, Internat. Paed. Pathol. Assn. 1988; Alexander von Humboldt Distinguished Serv. Award, Internat. Atherosclerosis Soc. 1982; Gold Medal Outstanding Serv. Award, Internat. Atherosclerosis Soc. 1988; Dist. Serv. Award, Am. Heart Assn. 1986; 'An Appreciation Award to First Pres.' Candn. Atherosclerosis Soc. 1986; Hon. Guest, 1st Altschul Symposium Sask. 1990; William Boyd Lectr., Candn. Assn. of Pathol. Nfld. 1990; I.W. Killam Award, Can. Counc. 1990; Medal of Andreas Vesalius Bruxellensis, Univ. of Padova (Italy) 1993; Special Recognition Award, Am. Heart Assn., Council on Arteriosclerosis 1993; elected 7 consecutive years as best teacher, Queen's Univ. 1960–67; Award in Basic Sciences, 1978, 1984 and Class-62-Award 1982, Univ. of Western Ont.; and several other honours; Secy./Treas., Internat. Atherosclerosis Soc. 1978–85; Treas. 1985– ; Past Pres., Internat. Paediatric Pathology Assn.; Soc. for Pediatric Pathology; Candn. Atherosclerosis Soc.; and other past presidency and extve. positions in med. societies; author/co-author of 262 pubns. in sci. journs.; recreations: music (classical), reading, hiking, walking; Office: London, Ont. N6A 5G1.

**HAVEL, Jean Eugène Martial,** Dr. ès L.; writer; retired university professor; b. Le Havre, France 16 June 1928; s. the late Marc Louis Gustave and the late Suzanne Céline Marie (Doré) H.; e. Univ. de Paris, Faculté de Droit, Lic. 1950; Institut des Etudes Politiques, Diplôme, 1952; Institut des Etudes Scandinaves 1953, Faculté des Lettres Dr. ès L. 1956; Univ. of Oslo Sch. of Law 1953–54; m. late Anne Marie, d. Georg Robert Mauritz Luhr, Djursholm, Sweden 22 Aug. 1955; children: Jean Guillaume, Frédérik, Mathilde Sophie, Ingrid Lucie; Part-time Teacher of French, Univ. of Stockholm, 1956–59; Asst. Prof. of Pol. Science, Univ. de Montréal, 1959–62; Asst. Prof. of Pol. Science, Laurentian Univ., 1962, Assoc. Prof. 1964, Acting Head of Dept. 1967–70, Prof. of Political Science 1969–93, retired; ; rec'd Norwegian and Finnish Govts., Swedish Inst. and Council of Europe Scholarships; author of 'La Finlande et la Suède' 1978; 'Les états scandinaves et l'intégration européenne' 1970; 'Les citoyens de Sudbury et la politique' 1966 (Eng. transl. 1966); 'La condition de la femme' 1961 (Italian transl. 1962, Spanish transl. 1965); 'Habitat et Logement' 1957, 1964, 1967, 1974 and 1985 (Spanish transl. 1961, Chinese transl. 1990); 'La fabrication du journal' 1957; 'Cours de journalisme: la rédaction' 1957; 5 pamphlets and numerous articles and reviews for learned journs.; mem. Canadian Political Science Association; scholarship from Salzburg Seminar on Am. Studies 1957; grants from Can. Council, 1968, 1969 and 1975–76 and Social Science Research Council of Can. 1979–80; awarded Centennial Medal; Can. Council Fellowship Award 1968 and 1975; Home: 175 Boland Ave., Sudbury, Ont. P3E 1Y1.

**HAVERSTOCK, Lynda Maureen,** B.Ed., M.Ed., Ph.D., M.L.A.; politician, clinical psychologist; b. Swift Current, Sask. 16 Sept. 1948; d. Thomas Edward and O'Nita Abbey (McCaskill) Ham; e. Univ. of Sask. B.Ed. 1972, post-grad. dipl. 1975, M.Ed. 1977, Ph.D. 1985; reg. as psychologist 1987; m. Harley s. William and Irene Olsen 26 July 1991; one child: Dani Lee Hay; LEADER, SASKATCHEWAN LIBERAL PARTY (FIRST WOMAN) 1989– and M.L.A. FOR SASKATOON GREYSTONE 1991– ; Special Ed. Teacher & Cons., Saskatoon Public Bd. of Edn. & Sask. Catholic Schools 1972–80; Doctoral Intern, Clarke Inst. of Psych. 1984–85; Asst. Prof. with term, Univ. of Sask., Dept. of Psych. 1985–86; Rsch. Assoc., Ctr. for Agricultural Med. (part-time), Sessional Lectr., Univ. of Sask. (part-time), and Psychologist, Saskatoon Mental Health Clinic 1986–89; Sessional, Part-time & Full-time Lectr., Dept. for the Edn. of Exceptional Children, Univ. of Sask. 1972, '73 (summers), 1973–76; Visiting Lectr., Fac. d'Ed., Moncton N.B. 1977; Triple 'E' Award of Excellence, Sask. Mental Health Serv. Br., Prov. of Sask. 1987; Music Scholarships 1960–67; SSHRCC grants 1981–85 (4); has presented hundreds of seminars to rural families in crisis & workshops for profls.; Pres., Sask. Fed. of Exceptional Children 1976; Sask. Women's Agric. Network 1988–92; Sask. Women's Network 1991–92; Persephone Theatre (Bd. of Dir.) 1981–85, 1986–87; Sask. Psych. Assn. 1987–92; author: 'Alternative Education for Truant High School Students' 1980, 'An Experimental Team Approach to Diagnostic-Prescriptive Teaching 1977 and 2 book chapters on stress; recreations: musical theatre, swimming, foreign films; Home: 1201 Elliott St., Saskatoon, Sask. S7N 0V5; Office: Rm. 140, Legislative Bldg., Regina, Sask. S4S 0B3.

**HAWEY, Ghislain,** M.Com., C.M.C., F.C.A.; b. Quebec, Que. 16 Aug. 1931; s. Arthur and Juliette (Lajeunesse) H.; e. Laval Univ., B.Com. 1952, M.Com. 1953, C.A. 1955; m. Yolande Baril; children: Steven, Douglas, Michaël; PARTNER, DELOITTE TOUCHE since 1962 and Vice Pres. of the Quebec Practice Unit also called Samson Belair; Prof. of Accounting, Faculty Adm. Sciences, Laval Univ. 1961–63; Pres., Que. Chamber Comm. 1971–72; Pres., Que. Planning and Develop. Counc. 1974–80; Dir. Que. Industrial Development Corp. 1973–78; Pres., Quebec E. Rotary Club 1967–68; Gov., Laval Univ. Found.; mem. Que. Order Chart. Accts.; Inst. Mgmt. Consultants of Que.; The Prof. Corp. of Chart. Administrators of Que.; recreations; swimming, fishing, tennis, golf; Clubs: Garnison; Royal Quebec Golf; Avantage Tennis; St-Marc Fishing; Home: 3336 Arthur Grenier St., Beauport, Qué. G1E 1G8; Offices: Suite 600, 5600 boul. des Galeries, Québec, Qué. G2K 2H6.

**HAWKE, John Howard,** B.A.; company chairman; b. St. Catharines, Ont. 14 Apr. 1926; s. late Charles W. and late Edith Moore (Magee) H.; e. St. Catharines Coll. Inst.; Univ. of Toronto B.A. 1949; m. Aileen Gwendolyn Demont Jan. 1960; children: Laurien, Martha, Charles, Gordon, Kelly; CHRMN., & DIR., FLETCHER LEISURE GROUP INC.; Pres., Hawke-Lea Holdings Ltd.; Dir. and mem. Exec. Ctte.: Canadian Occidental Petroleum Ltd.; Jannock Ltd.; Dir.: Fishery Products International Inc.; Brick Brewing Co. Ltd.; with Gairdner & Co. Ltd. (investment dealers) 1949–70; Pres., Jannock Ltd. 1970–73, Vice-Chrmn. 1973–75; Pres. & C.E.O. Bache & Co. Canada Limited (now Prudential-Bache Securities Canada Ltd.) 1975–79; Chrmn. & C.E.O. 1979–87; served overseas during 2nd World War with R.C.N.V.R.; Delta Upsilon; United Church; recreations: golf, tennis; Clubs: Ontario; Rosedale Golf; Fiddlesticks Country (Fort Myers, Fla.); The Crowsnest (St. John's, Nfld.); Homes: 159 Lyndhurst Ave., Toronto, Ont. M5R 3A1; Office: Ste. 3910, 40 King St. W., Box 201, Scotia Plaza, Toronto, Ont. M5H 3Y2.

**HAWKES, David Craig,** M.A.; educator; consultant; b. Estevan, Sask. 11 Apl. 1947; s. Archie David and Beatrice (Smyth) H.; e. Univ. of Sask. B.A. 1970; Queen's Univ. M.A. 1972; Carleton Univ. Doctoral Studies 1973–75; m. Pauline d. Joseph Lemieux 24 May 1969; children: Craig Cordon, Andrea Dawn; CO-DIR. OF RESEARCH, ROYAL COMMISSION ON ABORIGINAL PEOPLES 1992– ; Faculty mem. Candn. Centre for Mgmt. Devel. 1990–92; Govt. of Sask. 1975–82, Dir. Social Planning Secretariat, Exec. Dir. becoming Dep. Min. of Intergovt'al Affairs; Assoc. Dir. Inst. Intergovt'al Relations Queen's Univ. 1983–87; Visiting Prof. of Pub. Adm., Carleton Univ. 1987–89; Prof. School of Public Admin., Carleton Univ. 1989– ; author: 'The Search for Accommodation' 1987; 'Aboriginal Peoples and Constitutional Reform: What Have We Learned?' 1989; co-author: 'The Medicare Debate in Canada' 1988; 'Canada's North: A Profile' 1990; 'Alternative Methods for Aboriginal Participation in Processes of Constitutional Reform' 1991; 'Meech Lake and Elijah Harper: Native-State Relations in the 1990s' 1991; ed. 'Aboriginal Peoples and Government Responsibility: Exploring Federal and Provincial Roles' 1989; Chair, Selection Ctte. Aboriginal Affairs SSHRC and DIAND 1990–93; Rsch. Sub-ctte. Special Ctte. Native Issues CBA 1986–88; mem. Candn. Pol. Sci. Assn.; Inst. of Public Admin. of Can.; recreation: swimming, theatre, curling; Home: 177 Second Ave., Ottawa, Ont. K1J 2H6; Office: Ottawa, Ont. K1S 5B6.

**HAWKES, Donald Frederick,** B.A.A.; b. Toronto, Ont. 29 March 1934; s. Frederick Benjamin and Elsie Lillian (Tilley) H.; e. Ryerson Polytechnical Inst. B.A.A. 1958; m. Suzanne d. Gaston and Yvette Maurice 27 Feb. 1980; children: Alex, Martin (by previous marriage); Adrienne, Jonathan; SENIOR EDITOR, TORONTO SUN 1992– ; Reporter, Cartoonist Windsor Star 1958; News Writer CBC Nat. News; Entertainment Ed. Globe and Mail; Prof. of Journalism Ryerson Polytech. Inst. 1969; rtn'd to CBC 1980; Assoc. Ed. Toronto Sun 1985; Editor, Ottawa Sun 1989–91; recreations: cartooning, painting; Club: Nat. Press; Home: 41 Grant St., Toronto, Ont. M4M 2H6; Office: 333 King St. E., Toronto, Ont. M5A 3X5.

**HAWKES, Jim,** B.A., M.Sc., Ph.D.; b. Calgary, Alta. 21 June 1934; s. Frederick John and Amy Mary Kathleen (O'Hanlon) H.; e. Sir George Williams Coll. (Concordia) B.A. 1957; Univ. of Calgary M.Sc. 1968; Colorado State Univ. Ph.D. 1970; m. Joanne Christine d. Christine and Harold Herriot 31 Aug. 1957; children: Teresa, Robert; Chief Government Whip, House of Commons 1988–93; Counsellor, Univ. of Calgary 1964–71; Asst. Prof. 1971–75; Prof. 1975– ; 1st elected Member of Parliament for Calgary West 1979; re-elected 1980, 1984, 1988; Parliamentary Secretary to Deputy Prime Minister & Pres. of the Privy Council 1987–88; Pres., Evalucan Ltd. (social science rsch. firm) 1972–77; Pres., Hawkes Coffee Services Ltd. 1978–83; Birks-Beaton Memorial Scholarship 1955; Canada Council Doctoral Fellow 1969–70; Clubs: YMCA; Mount Royal; Home: 2 Varmoor Place N.W., Calgary, Alta. T3A 0A1.

**HAWKES, Robert H.,** Q.C., B.A., LL.B., F.Inst. D.; lawyer; b. Toronto, Ont. 9 March 1930; s. Agnes (Howie) and late Robert Kelvin H.; e. Univ. of Toronto, B.A.; Osgoode Hall Law Sch. LL.B.; m. Joan May, d. late Earl Lepard, 6 May 1960; one s. Robert Scott; Former Pres., Rothmans Inc.; Former Superintendent, Pension Commission of Ontario; read law with J. Harold Wood, 1953–55; called to Bar, 1955; cr. Q.C., 1969; Secretary, Mary Lake Assn.; Vice Chrmn. & Treas., Huntsville District Memorial Hospital Foundation; recreations: sailing; snowmobiling; tennis; skiing; Clubs: The National (Past Pres.); Hidden Valley Highlands Ski; Huntsville Curling; Port Sydney Yacht; Home: Port Sydney, Ont. P0B 1L0.

**HAWKINS, Dallas Euel;** petroleum executive; b. Houston, Texas 29 May 1923; s. Dallas Euel and Loretta (O'Reilly) H.; e. Rice Univ.; Univ. of Mich.; m. Mary Ann, d. Franklin Pierce Wood, Dallas, Texas, 27 Apl. 1951; children: Kathleen, Dallas O'Reilly, Robert Pierce; DIR., PIPER PETROLEUMS LTD. (estbl. 1987) and its subsidiaries; Extve. Chrmn., Hydromet Environmental Recovery Ltd.; Pres., Linden Holdings Inc.; Dir., Loumic Resources Ltd.; Hydromet Corp. (Canada) Ltd.; Roustabout, Illinois Oil Fields, 1936–40: Field Engr., Magnolia Petroleum Co., Victoria, Texas 1944; Chief Engr., Comanche Corp., Dallas, Tex., 1947–50; came to Can., 1951; Supt. i/c Operations, Candn. Delhi Oil & Gas Ltd., Calgary, Alta., 1951; Gen. Mgr., Scandia Drilling Co. Ltd. 1952–53; Asst. Supt., Sun Oil Co., 1954–56; Vice Pres. Gen. Mgr. and Dir., Fargo Oils Ltd., 1956–62; Dir., British Columbia Oil Transmission Co. Ltd., 1960–62; Chrmn., Am. Eagle Petroleums Ltd. 1975–80; Chrmn., Oakwood Petroleums Ltd. 1984–87; mem., Assn. Prof. Engrs. Alta., Man., Texas; Am. Inst. Mech. Engrs.; Am. Inst. Chem. Engrs; Alta. Oil Field Tech. Soc.; Am. Petroleum Inst.; served overseas in 2nd World War with U.S.N. in Pacific with Underwater Demolition Team 12, Jt. Intell. Command, Tokyo, Japan, Iwo Jima, Okinawa invasions; Tau Beta Pi; Sigma Xi; Phi Lambda Upsilon; Anglican; recreations: sailing, golf; Clubs: Bow Valley (Calgary); Calgary Golf & Country; Calgary Petroleum; Ranchmens (Calgary); Silver Beach Yacht (Coeur D'Alene, Ill.); The Spokane (Spokane); Club: Spokane Golf & Country; The Wailea Golf; Home: 16, 3203 Rideau Place S.W., Calgary Alta. T2S 2T1 Office: 2850, Bow Valley 2, 250 – 5th Ave. S.W., Calgary, Alta. T2P 2V7.

**HAWKINS, Hon. John,** M.L.A., M.A.; politician; b. Halifax, N.S. 5 May 1932; s. Walter John and Dorothy M. H.; e. E. H. Horne Sch., Enfield, N.S.; Dalhousie Univ.; St. Mary's Univ. B.A. (Lit. Award, French Grad. Award); Univ. of N.B., M.A.; m. Monique Marie Roach, May 1956; children: John, Eleanor, Mary Ann; former Min. of Agric. & Marketing, N.S.; Min. of the Environment & Min. for Emergency Measures Organ. 1976; Chrmn., Treasury Bd. 1976–78; N.S. Liberal Caucus 1981–84; served with Candn. Army Halifax, Germany 1954–60, rank Lt.; Dir. of Recreation Mun. of E. Hants 1961–63; Prof. of English, St. Mary's Univ., and Nova Scotia Agricult. Coll., Truro, 1963–70; el. M.L.A. 1970, re-el. since; did not re-offer for 1993 election; rec'd N.S. Playwriting Award 1960, 1962; author 'Life and Times of Angus L. Macdonald,' 1969, 'Deer Hunting in Eastern Canada' 1981, 'Recollections of the Regan Years (N.S. Government 1970–78)' 1990, 'Hunting Deer and Rabbits in Eastern Canada' 1993 and various articles in learned journs.; mem. Royal Commonwealth Assn., Halifax; St. George's Soc., Halifax; Royal Candn. Legion; Cambridge Military Library; Royal Artillery Park Officers Mess, Halifax; Liberal; recreations: hunting, fishing; Home: Horne Settlement, Enfield, Hants Co., N.S. B0N 1N0.

**HAWKINS, O. John,** B.P.A.; visual artist; b. Oregon City, Ore. 18 Dec. 1935; s. John and Helen (Kennedy) H.; e. Art Center Coll. of Design Pasadena, Cal. B.P.A. (Profl. Arts) 1960; m. Alaine d. Alan and Myra Lishman 8 Sept. 1962; children: Alicia, Zilla, Gwyneth; Candn. citizen 1972; devel. style and interest in realism during periods in Los Angeles, New York City, Greece, Ont. and B.C., the latter becoming maj. landscape subject; exhns. The Kaspar Gallery Toronto; rep. pub., corporate and private colls.; Quaker; recreations: swimming, travel; Home: 601, 680 Queens Quay W., Toronto, Ont. M5V 2Y9; Studio: Argenta, B.C. V0G 1B0.

**HAWKRIGG, Melvin Michael,** B.A., C.A., F.C.A.; financial services executive; b. Toronto, Ont. 26 Aug. 1930; s. Harry and Ida May (Cornish) H.; e. McMaster Univ., B.A. (Hist. & Pol. Economy); C.A. 1956; m. Marilyn Jane, d. Jack Field, 4 June 1954; children: Elizabeth Jane, Michael John, Peter Alan, Mary Ann, John Richard; CHRMN. & DIR., TRILON FINANCIAL CORP. 1989– (Chrmn., Extve. Ctte. and Investment Cttes.); Chrmn. and Dir., Holden Group, Inc. (Los Angeles, CA); Depy. Chrmn. & Dir., London Life Insurance Co. (Chrmn., Extve. Ctte.; Mem.: Audit, Management Development & Compensation and Investment Cttes.); London Insurance Group (Chrmn., Extve. Ctte.; Mem.: Audit, Management Development & Compensation and Investment Cttes.); Royal LePage Ltd. (Chrmn.: Extve. Ctte.); Dir.: Gentra Inc. (Mem., Credit & Extve. Cttes.; Human Resources & Compensation Ctte.); Triathlon Leasing Inc.; Trilon Bancorp Inc.; Trivest Insurance Network Limited; Wellington Insurance Co.; The T.E.A.M. Corp. (non-extve. Chrmn.); Career: Ernst and Young (last position, Manager) 1952–59; Fuller Brush Co. Ltd. 1959 (Comptroller, 1961; Comptroller and Gen. Mgr., 1963 and subsequently Pres. to 1971); Vice-Chrmn., Central Ont. Region, Canada Trustco 1972–81; Extve. Vice-Pres., Brascan Financial Services 1981–82; Sr. Vice-Pres., Brascan Ltd. 1982–83; Pres. & C.E.O., Trilon Financial Corp. 1982–88, Chrmn. & C.E.O. 1988–89; former Chrmn. and C.E.O., Candn. Depository for Securities; former Chrmn., Bd. of Trade of Metro Toronto Country Club; former Vice Pres., Candn. Club of Toronto; Former Mem., Bd. of Govs., McMaster Univ.; Former Mem., Hamilton Tiger Cats Professional Football Team; inducted into McMaster Univ. Sports Hall of Fame 1984; Fellow, Inst. C.A.s 1985; mem., Inst. of Chart Accts. of Ont.; Anglican; recreations: golf, skiing, horses, community activities; Clubs: Toronto; Toronto Golf; Canadian; Bd. of Trade of Metro Toronto; Office: Suite 4420, PO Box 771, BCE Place, Toronto, Ont. M5J 2T3.

**HAWN, Paul Ross,** B.A., M.B.A., CHRP; professional human resources manager; b. Cornwall, Ont. 4 April 1949; s. Ross and Mary Olive (McDonald) H.; e. St. Lawrence Coll. Dipl.Pub.Admin. 1974; Univ. of Waterloo B.A. 1990; Lake Superior State Univ. M.B.A. 1993; m. Hélène Faubert 6 June 1970; MANAGER, HUMAN RESOURCES, ONTARIO LOTTERY CORP. 1990– ; Clerk's Dept., Town of Oakville then Human Resources

Dept., City of Kingston 1974–80; Asst. Executive Dir., Human Resources, Gen. Hospital Sault Ste. Marie, Ont. 1980–90 13 years of active involvement in Human Resources Profl. Assn. of Ont. at local & prov. level (served on Bd. for 4 years); recreations: equestrian sports, sailing, travel; Home: R.R. #2, Water Cres., Goulais River, Ont. P0S 1E0; Office: 70 Foster Dr., Suite 800, Sault Ste. Marie, Ont. P6A 6V2.

**HAWORTH, Lawrence Lindley,** M.A., Ph.D., F.R.S.C.; educator; b. Chicago, Ill. 14 Dec. 1926; s. Lawrence and Ruth (Johnson) H.; e. Rollins Coll. Fla. B.A. 1949; Univ. of Ill. M.A. 1950, Ph.D. 1952; m. Alison Mindea d. Graham Pedlar, Bourne, Eng. 24 Dec. 1977; children: Lawrence III, Ruth; PROF. OF PHILOS., UNIV. OF WATERLOO 1965– , Assoc. Dean Computing and Research 1991– ; Assoc. Dean Grad. Studies 1975–81, 1984–86; Chrmn. of Philos. 1967–70, 1988–89; Dir., Centre for Society, Technology and Values 1984–86; served with U.S. Army 1945–46; author 'The Good City' 1963; 'Decadence and Objectivity' 1977; 'Autonomy' 1986; co-author 'Value Assumptions in Risk Assessment' 1991; numerous papers prof. journs.; mem. Candn. Philos. Assn.; Phi Beta Kappa; Fellow, Royal Soc. of Can.; recreations: cross-country skiing, jogging; Home: R.R. 1, St. Agatha, Ont. N0B 2L0; Office: Dept. of Philosophy, Univ. of Waterloo, Waterloo, Ont. N2L 3G1.

**HAWTHORN, Harry Bertram,** O.C. (1972), B.A., M.Sc., Ph.D., F.R.S.C. (1956); retired univ. prof.; b. Wellington, N.Z. 15 Oct. 1910; s. Henry Josiah and Henrietta Louisa (Hansen) M.; e. Wellington Coll. 1924–27; Victoria Univ. Coll. B.Sc. 1931, M.Sc. 1934; Univ. of N.Z. B.A. 1937; Univ. of Hawaii 1938–39; Yale Univ., Ph.D. 1941; LL.D.(Hon.) Univ. of B.C., Brandon Univ. and McMaster Univ.; m. Audrey Genevieve, d. Dr. E.T. and Mirth Engle, New York, N.Y. 1941; children: Margaret Louise, Henry Gilbert John; PROFESSOR EMERITUS, UNIVERSITY OF BRITISH COLUMBIA; primary sch. teacher 1934–38; Fellowships: Univ. of Hawaii, Carnegie Corp., Yale Univ. 1938–42; Research Asst., Inst. of Human Relations, Yale Univ. 1939–42; Resch. Fellowship, Yale Univ. (Bolivia) 1941–42; Fac. Mem., Sarah Lawrence Coll. 1942–47; Prof. of Anthropol., Univ. of B.C., 1947–76 (and Head of Dept. 1956–68; Dir. Museum of Anthropology 1948–74); Dir., Doukhobor Rsch. Comte. 1950–51; Dir., B.C. Indian Rsch. Comte. 1954–56; Dir., Study of the Indians of Can. 1966–68; O.C. 1972; former Dir., Leon and Thea Koerner Found.; Chrmn., Western Region, Woodrow Wilson Found.; Chrmn. and mem. various Can. Council comtes.; author: 'The Maori: A Study in Acculturation' (memoir) 1944; ed. and co-author 'The Doukhobors of British Columbia' 1956; 'The Indians of British Columbia' 1957; ed., 'A Survey of the Contemporary Indians Of Canada' 1967–68; Home: 4575 W. 15th Ave., Vancouver, B.C. V6R 3B3.

**HAWTHORN, Pamela,** B.A., M.F.A.; artistic director; b. Trail, B.C. 15 Dec. 1939; d. George Palmer and Eileen Alberta Rebecca (Simpson) Rutledge; e. Univ. of B.C., B.A. 1961; Yale Univ. M.F.A. 1965; m. Tom s. Robert and Gladys McBeath 22 Oct. 1981; one d. Laura Hawthorn; CREATIVE MANAGER, TELEFILM CANADA 1989– ; Artistic Dir., New Play Centre 1972–89; Assoc. Dir. McCarter Theatre Princeton, N.J. 1967–68; Playhouse Holiday Vancouver, B.C. 1969–70; Lectr. in Theatre, Earlham Coll. Richmond, Ind. 1966–67; Lectr. in Theatre, Univ. of B.C. 1974–75, Lectr. in Creative Writing 1985–86; Acting Teacher, Vancouver City Coll. 1985, 1987; Past Chrmn. Vancouver Profl. Theatre Alliance 1978–89; Past Vice Chrmn. Profl. Assn. Candn. Theatres 1979–83; mem., Waterfront Theatre Bd.; recipient Sam Payne Award ACTRA/CBC Award 1984; Vancouver Award 1988; Home: 811 E. 15th, Vancouver, B.C. V5T 2S1; Office: #350, 375 Water St., Vancouver, B.C. V6B 5C6.

**HAY, Donald Robert,** B.Eng., M.S., Ph.D.; executive; b. Ottawa, Ont. 1 Apr. 1939; s. Donald MacPherson and Elinor Mary (McCoy) H.; e. McGill Univ. B.Eng. 1961; Cornell Univ. M.S. 1964, Ph.D. 1966; m. Claudette d. Paul and Flora Roy 20 Jan. 1961; children: John, Andrew, Joel, Peter, Thomas; Pres., Tektrend International Inc. 1973; Pres. Tektrend Ventures Inc. 1983– ; Adjunct Prof. of Computer Science, Concordia Univ. 1982– ; Adjunct Prof. of Mining Eng., McGill Univ. 1990– ; Tech. Dir. Hydrogen Industry Council 1982–86; Asst. Prof. Drexel Univ. 1966–69, Assoc. Prof. 1969–72; Invited Prof. Univ. of Montreal 1972–74; Dir., Technology Development Center, Montreal 1974–79; Dir., Montreal Industrial Innovation Center, Montreal 1979–81; Pres., ADRIQ (Assoc. des Dirs. de Recherche Industrielle du Québec) 1988–89; mem. Bd. of Dirs., Hydrogen Industry Council, Montreal 1993– ; author over 70 tech. publs.; Tau Beta Pi; Sigma Xi; ASM; ASTM; ASNT; recreations: golf, skiing, music, maple syrup; Club: Dunany Country; Home: R.R. 6, Lachute, Que. J8H 3W8.

**HAY, George Edward,** Ph.D.; mathematician; b. Durham, Ont. 11 June 1914; s. Edward Alexander and Frances Annetta (Scarr) H.; e. Durham (Ont.) Pub. and High Schs., 1919–28; Brampton (Ont.) High Sch., 1928–31; Univ. of Toronto, B.A. 1935, M.A. 1936, Ph.D. 1939; m. Lillian Edith Parker, d. late Thomas Herbert Howl. 28 May 1943; children: Edward James, John Robert, Kathryn Ann; PROF. OF MATH., UNIV. OF MICHIGAN since 1955 and Assoc. Dean Grad. Sch. 1967–76; Instr., Ill. Inst. of Technol., 1939–40; joined present Univ. as Instr., 1940–42; Asst. Prof. 1942–47; Assoc. Prof. 1947–55; Chrmn., Math. Dept., 1957–67; Assoc. Dean Grad. School, 1967–76; Consultant, U.S. Health, Educ. and Welfare, since 1964; during World War II Research Assoc., U.S. Govt. Office of Scient. Research and Devel., 1944–45; author: 'Vector and Tensor Analysis,' 1953; other writings incl. several scient. papers on Mech. of a Continuum; mem., London Math. Soc.; Am. Math. Soc.; Math. Assn. Am.; Soc. Indust. & Applied Math.; Indust. Math. Soc.; Sigma Xi; Democrat; Protestant; recreation: golf; Club: Rotary; Home: 1714 Morton Ave., Ann Arbor, Mich. 48104.

**HAY, James Miller,** B.E., M.P.E., Ph.D., F.C.I.C.; retired chemical executive; b. Regina, Sask. 9 July 1929; s. Charles Cecil Hay; e. Univ. of Sask. B.E. (Chem. Engn.) 1950; Univ. of Tulsa M.P.E. 1954; Univ. of Toronto Ph.D. 1957; m. d. of Ralph M. Cantlon 28 Oct. 1950; Vice-Chrmn., Dow Chemical Canada Inc. 1988–93, retired; Dir., Mutual Life of Canada; Dir. Dow Chemical Canada Inc.; joined Refinery Engineering Co. Tulsa, Okla. and Toronto 1950–54; Process Engn. and Devel. in various supervisory positions Dow Chemical of Canada Ltd., Sarnia 1957–65, Mgr. Devel. Sarnia 1965–68; Business Mgr., Corporate Planning, Dir. Information Systems & Technol. Adm. The Dow Chemical Co. Midland, Mich. 1968–73; Vice Pres. Operations and Dir. Dow Chemical Canada Inc. 1973–80; Pres., C.E.O. and Dir. 1980–83, Chrmn. 1983–85; Vice Pres. Materials Mgmt. and Hydrocarbons & Energy, The Dow Chemical Co. 1985–88; mem. Assn. Prof. Engrs. Prov. Ont.; Candn. Chem. Producers Assn. (past Chrmn.); Dir., Inst. Chemical Sci. & Technol. (ICST); Fellow, C.I.C.; Distinguished Engineering Graduate, Univ. of Sask. 1986; Canada Medal, Soc. of Chem. Industry (SCI) 1986; United Church; recreations: sports, music.

**HAYCOCK, Kenneth Roy,** A.M.L.S., M.Ed., Ed.D.; educator; b. Hamilton, Ont. 15 Feb. 1948; s. Bruce Frederick Travis and Doris Marion Page (Downham) H.; e. Univ. of W. Ont. B.A. 1968, Dipl. in Educ. 1969; Univ. of Toronto Specialist Cert. in Sch. Librarianship 1971; Univ. of Ottawa M.Ed. 1973; Univ. of Mich. M.A. (Lib. Science) 1974; Brigham Young Univ. Ed.D. 1991; Director of Program Services, Vancouver Sch. Bd. 1985; Teacher and Dept. Head, Glebe Coll. Inst. Ottawa 1969–70; Teacher and Dept. Head, Colonel By Secondary Sch. Ottawa 1970–72; Educ. Media Consultant (K-13), Wellington Co. Bd. Educ. Guelph 1972–76; Supervisor of Instruction and Coord. of Lib. Services, Vancouver Sch. Bd. 1976–84; Acting Manager, Elementary/Secondary Education, Vancouver Sch. Bd. 1984–85; special assignment as principal, Waverley Sch. 1989–91; mem. Cultural Services Br. Publishing Assistance Comte., B.C. Ministry of Prov. Secy. and Govt. Services 1979–82; B.C. Arts Bd. Lit. Arts Comte., 1980–82; Can. Council Book and Periodicals Promotion Comte., 1980–82; Lib. Tech. Program Adv. Comte., Vancouver Community Coll. 1979–81; Council, Sch. of Library, Archival and Information Studies, Univ. of B.C. 1978–85; Trustee, Guelph Pub. Lib. 1975–76; sometime sessional instr. in Librarianship, Educ., Univs. of Toronto, West. Ont., Windsor and B.C. 1975– ; guest lectr., workshops, addresses; author 'Free Magazines for Teachers and Libraries' 1974, 2nd ed. 1977; 'Index to the Contents of Moccasin Telegraph' 1975; 'Security – Secondary School Resource Centres' 1975; 'Sears List of Subject Headings: Canadian Companion' 1978, 2nd ed. 1983, 3rd ed. 1985; book chapters, pamphlets, articles, reports; Publisher, 'Free Materials for Schools and Libraries' 1979– ; 'Emergency Librarian' 1979– ; Co-Ed. 'Kids and Libraries' 1984; Ed., 'School Library Program in the Curriculum' 1990; Ed. 'Program Advocacy' 1990; mem. various advisory and ed. bds.; rec'd Wilson Lib. Bulletin 'Front-Liner' 1974; Beta Phi Mu Award Univ. of Mich. 1976; Queen's Silver Jubilee Medal 1977; Margaret B. Scott Award of Merit, Candn. Sch. Lib. Assn. 1979; Phi Delta Kappa Leaders in Education Award, 1980; Ken Haycock Professional Development Award estbld. in his honour, B.C. Teacher-Librarians Assn. 1988; Distinguished Service Award, B.C. Teacher-Librarians' Assoc. 1989; Distinguished School Admin. Award, Candn. Sch. Lib. Assoc. 1989; Outstanding Service to Librarianship in Canada, Candn. Lib. Assn. 1991; mem. Am. Lib. Assn.; Am. Assn. Sch. Librarians (Dir. 1974–75); Assn. for Media & Technol. in Educ. Can.; Assn. for Library & Info. Science Educ.; Assn. for Supervision and Curriculm Devel.; Assn. of B.C. School Superintendents; B.C. Council for Leadership Educ. Adm.; B.C. Lib. Assn. (Extve. 1981–82); B.C. Teachers' Fed.; B.C. Primary Teachers' Assn.; B.C. Teacher-Librarians Assn. (Exec. Council 1980–86); B.C. Assn. for Supervision and Curriculum Development; Candn. Lib. Assn. (Pres. 1977–78, Dir. 1974–75, 1976–79, Council 1974–81); Candn. Lib. Trustees Assn.; Candn. Sch. Lib. Assn. (Pres. 1974–75, mem. Council 1973–76); Ont. Sch. Lib. Assn.; Ont. Lib. Assn.; Pacific Instructional Media Assn.; Vancouver Schs. Administration Assn. Coordinators (Treas. 1978–79, Pres. 1979–80); Internat. Assn. Sch. Librarianship; Candn. Coll. Teachers (Pres., Gter. Vancouver Chapter 1985–87); Bd. of Dirs., Information Services Vancouver 1987–90; Beta Phi Mu; Phi Delta Kappa (Exec., UBC Chapter 1982–84); Home: 5118 Meadfield Rd., West Vancouver, B.C. V7W 3G2.

**HAYDEN, Gerald Francis,** Q.C., LL.B.; b. Toronto, Ont. 14 Dec. 1924; s. Hon. Salter Adrian and Ethel Gwendolyn (Connolly) H.; e. Allenby Pub. Sch. and De La Salle Coll., Toronto, Ont.; Univ. of Toronto; Osgoode Hall Law Sch., Toronto, Ont.; m. Mary Louise, d. Lauren Drake Mayer, Toronto, Ont., 19 Aug. 1953; children: Gerald Francis, Judith Louise, Richard Drake Laird, Andrew Crashley; President and Director, Nelson Arthur Hyland Foundation; Salden Foundation; Pres. & Dir., T. Donald Miller Foundn.; Chrmn. and Dir., Orthopaedic and Arthritic Hospital Foundn.; mem., Nat. Council of Boy Scouts; read law with Beaton, Bell & Pond, Toronto, Ont.; called to Bar of Ont., June 1950; cr. Q.C., 1 Jan. 1965; Liberal; R. Catholic; recreations: golf, swimming; Club: Rosedale Golf; Home: 29 Oriole Road, Toronto, Ont. M4V 2E6 and 607 Old Stouffville Rd., P.O. Box 1151, Uxbridge, Ont. L9P 1N4.

**HAYDEN, Michael Reuben,** MB, ChB, PhD, DCh, FRCP(C); medical genetics professor; b. Cape Town, S. Africa 21 Nov. 1951; s. Roger Randolph and Ann Joyce H.; e. Univ. of Cape Town M.B., ChB (Hons.) 1980; Res. in Internal Med., Groote Schuur Hosp. Cape Town 1976–78; Univ. of Cape Town Ph.D. 1979; Res. Fellow, Children's Hosp. Harvard Med. Sch. 1980–81; Dipl., Am. Bd. of Int. Med. 1982; Am. Bd. of Med. Gen. 1982; m. Sandra Ferera 30 March 1980; children: Sarah, Anna, Jessica, Gideon; PROFESSOR OF MEDICAL GENETICS, UNIV. OF B.C. 1991– ; Asst. Prof., Univ. of B.C. 1983; Sci. Dir., Networks of Centres of Excellence, Human Genetic Diseases Network; Dir., Adult Genetics Clinic, Univ. Hosp., UBC; Physician & Dir., Lipid Clin, Univ. Hosp.; Sec.-Gen. (1st geneticist), World Fed. of Neurology Rsch. Group of Huntington's Disease; Killam Rsch. Award 1987; Henry Christian Meml. Award 1991; Dir., Lipid Clinic Outreach Prog.; Hemochromatosis Soc. of Can.; Ctr. for Preventative & Predictive Med.; Sci. Adv. Bd., Huntington's Soc. of Canada; extensive lecturer; TV and radio interviews; Mem., B.C. Task Force on Lipids; Policy Adv. Bd., Regress Study Inter-Univ. Cardiology Inst.; SPARK Ctte., Sci. Council of B.C.; SAB, Merck Frosst; Res. Eval. Com. Heart & Stroke Fdn. of BC & Yukon; Internat. Lipid Council; author/co-author of over 300 pubs., book chapters & abstracts; most outstanding: 'Huntington's Chorea in S. Africa' (PhD thesis) 1979, 'Huntington's Chorea' (2nd prtg.) 1981, 'Huntington's Disease' (co-author of chapter in 'Metabolic Basis of Inherited Diseases') 1992; recreations: travel, collection of antique art and artefacts; num. clubs incl. Vancouver Aquarium; Home: 4484 W. 7th Ave., Vancouver, B.C. V6R 1W9; Office: NCE Bldg., 416 – 2125 East Mall, Univ. of B.C., Vancouver, B.C. V6T 1Z4.

**HAYES, Alan Lauffer;** theological educator; b. Oakland, Calif. 29 Sept. 1946; s. Lauffer Truby and Margaret (Fair) H.; e. Pomona Coll. B.A. 1967; Brown Univ.; McGill Univ. B.D. 1971, Ph.D. 1975; two d.: Jessica, Alexandra; PROFESSOR OF CHURCH HISTORY, WYCLIFFE COLLEGE, UNIV. OF TORONTO 1989– ; Asst. Prof., Wycliffe Coll., Toronto Sch. of Theology 1975–79; Assoc. Prof. 1979–89; Bps. Wilkinson Prof. 1989– ; Registrar 1979– ; Can. Counc. Doct. Fellowship 1972–75; Anglican Ch. of Can.; Ed. & Contbr. 'By Grace Co-Workers' 1989; author of articles in profl. jours.; Home: 346 Maple Grove Dr., Oakville, Ont. L6J 4V5; Office: Toronto, Ont. M5S 1H7.

**HAYES, Dale T.,** M.A., Ed.D.; educator; b. E. St. Louis, Ill. 2 Aug. 1937; s. L. Thomas and Cecil Susan (Miller) H.; e. Bob Jones Univ. Greenville, S.C., B.A. 1959; Ariz.

State Univ. M.A. 1968, Ed.D. 1977; m. Eva M. d. Otis and Martha Lilley 18 Aug. 1961; children: Teryll Anne, Lorinda Kaye, Heather, Jason, Justin; PROF. OF SPECIAL EDUC./READING, BRANDON UNIV. 1988– , and Dean of Educ., 1978–87; Owner, Cedar Haven Custom Homes; Dir., I.C.F. Enterprises; classroom teacher, special educ. teacher program developer 1962–68; Coordinator of Learning Assistance Programs, Mt. Royal Coll. Calgary 1968–70; Doctoral Fellow U.S. Office of Educ. Leadership Devel. Program, Ariz. State Univ. 1971–72; U.S. Office of Educ. Title VIII Dir. South Dakota 1972–73 (Prog. selected as U.S. National Model 1973); Grad. Prof. (Reading/Special Educ.) Sch. of Advanced Studies, Coll. of Educ., Univ. of S. Maine 1973–75, Dir. of Upward Bound and Bridge Programs 1975; Div. Chrmn. Univ. of N.B. 1975–78; co-devel. reading/lang. arts methods system used throughout Canada and the U.S., consultant to numerous sch. dists., community colls. and univs. since 1970; speaker, workshop leader, seminar dir. numerous internat., nat., prov., state and regional confs. since 1970; served as Chrmn. and Program Convenor 2 nat. confs. incl. First Nat. Candn. Community Educ. Conf.; Dean of the Faculty receiving the 1983 Distinguished Teacher Education Program Award from Assn. of Teacher Educators; author (poetry), 'Cinderella Was a Fat Old Lady' 1975; 'Dr. Fossil's More Fun Than Earth People' 1980; 'Willie Peter Suntan' 1981; 'Hoots of Derision' 1982; ed. 'Reach Them-Teach Them: Using Performance Reading to Reach the Reading Disabled'; contrib. various prof. journs.; Freemason; mem. Board of Dirs., Miramonte Foundation; Internat. Platform Assn.; Candn. Assn. Studies Educ.; Assn. Teacher Educators; Pres. 1981–82 of W. Candn. Assn. Student Teaching; Council for Exceptional Children; Internat. Reading Assn.; Phi Delta Kappa; recreations: martial arts, old books, military history, poetry; Home: Delton Rd., Oakland, Man.; Office: Dept. of Humanities, Brandon Univ., Brandon, Man. R7A 6A9.

**HAYES, Derek Cumberland,** LL.M.; lawyer; executive; b. Toronto, Ont. 27 Sept. 1936; s. Charles Walter and Phyllis (Cumberland) H.; e. Upper Can. Coll. Toronto 1950; Trinity Coll. Sch. Port Hope, Ont. 1954; Univ. of Toronto, Trinity Coll. B.A. 1958, LL.B. 1961; Univ. Coll. Univ. of London LL.M. 1966; m. Susan Howard Bennett 15 July 1963; children: Sean, Kate, Stewart; SR. VICE PRES. AND GEN. COUNSEL, CANADIAN IMPERIAL BANK OF COMMERCE 1984– ; called to Bar of Ont. 1963; Solr., McCarthy & McCarthy 1963–67; Solr., Massey-Ferguson Ltd. 1967–71; Sr. Solr., The T. Eaton Co. Ltd. 1971–73; Legal Advisor, Atty. Gen.'s Chambers, Republic of Tanzania 1973–74; Asst. Secy. Massey-Ferguson Ltd. 1974–77, Secy. 1977–80; Vice Pres., Secy. and Gen. Counsel Shell Canada Ltd. 1980–1984; mem. Law Soc. Upper Can.; Candn. Bar Assn.; Club: University; Office: Commerce Court W., Toronto, Ont. M5L 1A2.

**HAYES, Lawrence Joseph,** Q.C., B.A., LL.B.; lawyer; b. Halifax, N.S. 1 Apr. 1939; s. William Arthur and Marjorie Geraldine (LaPierre) H.; e. St. Mary's Univ., B.A. 1959; Dalhousie Univ., LL.B. 1962; m. Sharon L. Nicolle 14 July 1988; Mng. Partner, McInnes Cooper & Robertson 1983–93; Partner 1971; cr. Q.C. 1977; Dir. Maritime Life Assurance Co.; Halifax Dance; Chrmn. Mount Saint Vincent Univ. 1983–86, mem. Bd. 1978–86; Gov. St. Mary's Univ. 1970–73; former Gov. Candn. Tax Found.; former mem. N.S. Law Reform Adv. Comn.; Past Vice Pres. and Dir. Atlantic Symphony Orch.; Past Treas. N.S. Lib. Assn.; mem. Halifax Bd. Trade; Club: Halifax; Home: 967 Beaufort Ave., Halifax, N.S. B3H 3X9; Office: 1601 Lower Water St., Halifax, N.S. B3J 2V1.

**HAYES, Meredith S.;** retired executive; b. New York, N.Y. 10 Sept. 1914; s. Meredith and Roberta (Rajotte) H.; e. Lower Can. Coll. 1933; m. Marjorie Ella, d. late Harry Hall, 7 March 1941; three children; Dir., Seaway International Bridge Corp. Ltd.; Past Pres. Canadian Machine Tool Distributors Assn.; mem.: Soc. Mech. Engrs.; Numerical Control Soc.; Dir., Que. Soc. for Disabled Children; Past Chrmn., Internat. Material Mang. Soc.; Protestant; recreations: fishing, photography; Clubs: Mount Stephen; Montreal St. George Kiwanis; Home: 514 Stanstead Ave. Montreal, Que. H3R 1X7.

**HAYHURST, Douglas Palmer,** B.A., C.A.; chartered accountant; b. Toronto, Ont. 26 Jan. 1947; s. William Palmer and Jean Eleanor (Hunnisett) H.; e. Upper Canada College 1965; Univ. of Western Ont. B.A. (Hons.) 1969; m. Natalie d. Hughson and Allaneen Murray; children: Greyson, Daniel, Jillian; DEPUTY MANAGING PARTNER, PRICE WATERHOUSE 1991– ; Price Waterhouse Toronto 1970–73; Peat Marwick Thorne Vanc. 1973–75; Special Asst. to Min. of Nat. Revenue Ottawa 1976; Consultant, Tax Policy Div., Dept. of Finance Ottawa 1977; Price Waterhouse Vanc. 1977–84, Mng. Tax Partner 1985–91; Hon. Prof., Banff Centre Sch. of Management; Past Pres. & Dir., Children's Family House Soc. of B.C. (Ronald McDonald House); Past Trustee, Vanc. Gen. Hosp.; Gov., Cdn. Tax Found.; clubs: Badminton and Racquet Club of Toronto, Toronto Golf, The Vancouver Club, Hollyburn Golf & Country; Office: Box 190, 1 First Canadian Pl., Toronto, Ont. M5X 1H7.

**HAYHURST, James Frederick Palmer,** H.B.A.; business executive; b. Toronto, Ont. 24 May 1941; s. William Palmer and Jean Eleanor (Hunnisett) H.; e. Upper Can. Coll. 1959; Univ. of Western Ont. Sch. Bus. Adm. H.B.A. 1963; m. Susan d. Dr. Harry and Adele Ebbs 17 Oct. 1964; children: Cynthia Susan, James Taylor Palmer, Barbara Jean; Pres., The Hayhurst Career Centre; Pres., Wyldwyn Holdings Limited; with Procter & Gamble 1963–67; Principal, Hayhurst Advertising 1967–86; Chrmn., Saatchi, Saatchi, Compton Hayhurst 1984–86; Chrmn., Public Information: Candn. Red Cross National Bldg. Centre Fund; Past Chrmn., Outward Bound Can.; former Trustee, Un. Way Toronto; Dir., Street Kids International; Founder and Co-Chrmn., Trails Youth Initiatives Inc.; recreations: family, fishing, golf; Clubs: Toronto Golf; Olde Florida Golf; The Caledon Mountain Trout; Office: 378 Fairlawn Ave., Toronto, Ont. M5M 1T8.

**HAYNE, David M.,** M.A., Ph.D., D.U., F.R.S.C. (1970); retired university professor; b. Toronto, Ont. 12 Aug. 1921; s. Herbert George and Elizabeth (Mackness) H.; e. Norway Public Sch. and Malvern Coll. Inst., Toronto, Ont.; Univ. Coll., Univ. of Toronto, B.A. 1942; Univ. of Ottawa, M.A. 1944, Ph.D. 1945; m. Madge Hood Robertson, d. David P. Niven, St. Andrews, Scotland, 20 Dec. 1955; one d. Heather Elizabeth; two s., Frederick Steven, Bruce Jonathan; PROFESSOR EMERITUS OF FRENCH, UNIV. OF TORONTO 1985– ; Rsch. Offr., National Rsch. Counc., Ottawa 1942–45; attached to Directorate of Mil. Intelligence, N.D.H.Q. 1943–45; joined Univ. Coll., Univ. of Toronto as Lectr. in French, 1945; Asst. Prof. 1950, Assoc. Prof. 1956, Prof. 1961–85; Registrar of University Coll., 1956–61; Visiting Prof. of Fr., U.B.C. 1970–71; D.U. (h.c.), Univ. of Ottawa 1985; mem., Pres., Bibliographical Soc. Can.; Candn. Assn. Univ. Teachers; Internat. Comparative Lit. Assn., etc.; Anglican; Home: R.R. 5, Claremont, Ont. L1Y 1A2.

**HAYNES, Arden R.,** O.C., B.Com.; retired petroleum executive; b. Sask. 1927; e. Univ. of Manitoba, B.Com. 1951; retired Chrmn. and C.E.O., Imperial Oil Ltd., Toronto; joined Imperial Oil at Winnipeg 1951, held various positions in Canada and the United States; Vice Pres. & Gen. Mgr., Mktg. Dept. 1973, Dir. and Sr. Vice Pres. 1974; Pres. & C.E.O., Esso Resources Canada Ltd., a wholly owned subsidiary of Imperial 1978–81; Bd. Chrmn. 1981–85; Exec. Vice Pres. Imperial Oil Ltd. Jan.-Oct. 1982, Pres. & C.O.O., Oct. 1982, Chrmn. & C.E.O. Apr. 1985–92; Dir.: Power Corp. of Canada; Royal Bank of Canada; Moore Corporation Ltd.; Rio Algoma Ltd.; McCain Foods Ltd.; Paige Manufacturing Inc.; Gov., the Olympic Trust; Dir., Alzheimer Soc. of Canada; Centre for Research in Neurodegenerative Diseases, Univ. of Toronto; Gov., North York Hospital, Governor Portage; Officer, Order of Canada 1989; D.C.L. Acadia Univ., N.S. 1990; LL.D. Univ. of Manitoba 1990; recreations: golf, fishing; Clubs: Calgary Ranchmen's; Granite; York; Toronto; Rosedale Golf; York Downs Golf and Country; Office: 26 Glenorchy Rd., Don Mills, Ont. M3C 2P9.

**HAYNES, Robert Hall,** O.C., B.Sc., Ph.D., F.R.S.C.; educator and biophysicist; b. London, Ont. 27 Aug. 1931; s. James Wilson McKenzie and Lillian May (Hall) H.; e. Univ. W. Ont. B.Sc. 1953, Ph.D. 1957; m. 1stly Nancy Joanne May; children: Mark Douglas, Geoffrey Alexander, Paul Robert; m. 2ndly Charlotte Jane d. Orson and Beatrice Banfield 2 June 1966; DISTINGUISHED RESEARCH PROF. EMERITUS, YORK UNIV. 1992– , Prof. of Biol. 1968, Chrmn. 1968–73, Distinguished Research Prof. 1986; Brit. Empire Cancer Campaign Fellow Phys. Dept. St. Bartholomew's Hosp. Med. Coll. Univ. of London 1957–58; Asst. Prof. of Biophys., Univ. of Chicago 1958–64; Assoc. Prof. of Biophys., Univ. of Cal. Berkeley and Biophys., Lawrence Radiation Lab. Berkeley 1964–68; Visiting Fellow Molecular Biophys. Yale Univ. 1974–75; Assoc. Fellow, Candn. Inst. for Advanced Rsch. 1987– ; Walter L. Gordon Research Fellow, York Univ. 1987–88; Fellow, Inst. for Advanced Study (Wissenschaftskolleg), Berlin 1988–89; Exchange Visitor USSR Acad. of Sci's. Moscow 1972, 1978; Brit. Council Exchange Visitor Oxford Univ. 1973; Exchange Visitor Japan Soc. Promotion Sci. Kyoto Univ. 1979; Visiting Lectr. Academia Sinica, Beijing, China 1980; Visiting Prof. Fudan Univ., Shanghai, China 1981; Visiting Prof. King Faisal Hosp. Cancer Therapy Inst. Riyadh, Saudi Arabia 1982; mem., Subctte. Radiobiol. U.S. Nat. Acad. Sci's. 1963–73; Mem., Nat. Rsch. Council Can. Grant Selection Ctte. on Cell Biology & Genetics 1971–74; Mem., Biology Adv. Ctte., Nat. Rsch. Council Can. 1971–75; Mem., Council Ont. Universities (Exec. Ctte.) 1973–74; Vice Pres., Biol. Council Can. 1975–80; Mem., Nat. Rsch. Council Can. 1975–82 (Exec. Ctte. and others); Mem., Med. Sch. Admissions Ctte., Univ. of Toronto 1978–83; Chrmn., Adv. Ctte. Mutagenesis, Depts. Nat. Health & Welfare and of Environment 1978–86; Tech. Adv. Ctte. Nuclear Fuel Waste Mgmt. Program, Atomic Energy of Canada Ltd. 1979–83; Mem., Rsch. Council (Exec. Ctte.) Candn. Inst. Advanced Rsch. 1982–87; Chrmn., Adv. Ctte. Life Sciences, Nat. Scis. Eng. Rsch. Council Can. 1985–87; Adv. Panel, Ont. Nuclear Safety Review 1987–88; Mem., Internat. Comn. on Protection Against Environmental Mutagens and Carcinogens 1988–93; Pres., XVI Internat. Congress of Genetics, Toronto, 1988; Pres., Internat. Assoc. of Environmental Mutagen Societies 1989–93; Pres. & Editor-in-Chief, *Annual Reviews* 1992–93; recipient Queen's Silver Jubilee Medal 1977; Annual Research Award U.S. Environ. Mutagen Society 1984; Gold Medal of the Biological Council of Canada 1984; Flavelle Medal, Royal Soc. of Can. 1988; Presidential Citation 1989, Award of Excellence 1993, Genetics Soc. of Can.; Annual Rsch. Lectr., Amer. Soc. Photobiology, Los Angeles 1986; James S. McDonnell Memorial Lectr., Washington Univ., St. Louis, MO 1986; Sigma Lectr., NASA Langley Research Ctr., Hampton, VA 1991; Distinguished Scientist Lectr., Trinity Univ., San Antonio, TX 1992; ed. 'The Molecular Basis of Life' 1968; 'The Chemical Basis of Life' 1973; 'Man and the Biological Revolution' 1975; 'Prevention of a Biological and Toxin Arms Race and the Responsibility of Scientists'; author about 120 sci. papers; Fellow, Royal Soc. of Can. 1982; Fellow, Am. Assoc. for the Advancement of Sci. 1988; Assoc. Fellow, Third World Acad. of Sciences 1990; Officer, Order of Canada 1990; mem., Genetics Soc. Can. (Pres. 1983–85); Genetics Soc. America; Environmental Mutagen Soc. (Councillor 1978–81, 1985–88); Radiation Rsch. Soc.; Indian Science Congress Assn. (Life mem.); Hon. Mem., Chinese Soc. of Genetics (Taiwan) 1989; Sigma Xi; Beta Theta Pi; recreation: antiquarian book collector; Clubs: University; Home: 15 Queen Mary's Dr., Toronto, Ont. M8X 1S1; Office: Dept. of Biology, York University, 4700 Keele St., North York, Ont. M3J 1P3.

**HAYOS, Andrew Robert,** C.A.; corporate executive; b. Budapest Hungary 22 Dec. 1929; s. Jeno and Klara (Lakos) Hajos; e. Hungarian Econ. Univ., Budapest diplomaed economist 1952; Inst. of C.A.s of Ont. C.A. 1961; m. Vera A. d. Dr. Andrew and Frederika Sandor 3 July 1951; children: Gabriel James, Catherine Audrey; EXTVE. VICE-PRES., POLARIS REALTY (CANADA) LIMITED 1990– ; Founder, Andrew Hayos & Assoc. C.A.s (Toronto, Kitchener, Calgary & Vancouver) 1962–80; Mng. Partner, Samson Belair C.A.s Toronto office & Mem., Nat. Extve. Ctte. 1980–87; Deputy Mng. Partner, Ont. Reg. & Chrmn., Real Estate Adv. Group, Deloitte & Touche (formerly Deloitte Haskins & Sells) 1987–90; Dir., Lord Realty Holdings Limited; Tchibo International Ltd.; Ahorn Properties Limited; Eaglewood Investments Limited; Urban Devel. Inst. Ont. 1988–90; Inst. of C.A.s of Ont.; articles & lecturer on fgn. investment in Candn. Real Estate & the Candn. tax system; recreations: tennis, skiing, golf, travel; clubs: Albany, Mayfair Lakeshore Raquet, Bd. of Trade – Golf Section, Hot Stove Club; Home: 20 Chelford Rd., Don Mills, Ont. M3B 2E5; Office: 150 King St. W., Ste. 2307, Toronto, Ont. M5H 1J9.

**HAYS, Hon. Daniel P.,** B.A., LL.B.; senator; lawyer; livestock breeder; b. Calgary, Alta. 24 Apr. 1939; s. Hon. H. W. Hays, P.C.; e. Univ. of Alta. B.A. 1962; Univ. of Toronto LL.B. 1965; called to Bar of Alta. 1966; three d. Carol E., Janet M., Sarah L.; PARTNER, MACLEOD DIXON 1966– ; summoned to the Senate June 1984; Chrmn., Standing Senate Comte. on Agriculture and Forestry; Past Chrmn., Standing Senate Comte. on Energy, the Environment and Natural Resources; former Dir. Canadian Broadcasting Corp.; Calgary YMCA; Calgary & Dist. Foundation; mem. Alta. Law Soc.; Candn. Bar Assn.; Law Society of Alberta; Clubs: Rotary; Calgary Golf & Country; Office: 3700 Canterra Tower, 400 Third Ave. S.W., Calgary, Alta. T2P 4H2 and The Senate, Ottawa, Ont. K1A 0A4.

**HAZELL, Stephen Donald,** B.Sc., M.Sc., LL.B.; environmental lawyer; b. Toronto, Ont. 18 Sept. 1953; s. Donald Norman and Shirley (Hamilton) H.; e. Univ. of Toronto, B.Sc. 1976, M.Sc. 1979; Queen's Univ., LL.B.

1981; m. Mary Zella d. Larry and Edith Osberg 14 Sept. 1985; children: Elspeth Anne Osberg, Duncan Lars Osberg; DIRECTOR, REGULATORY AFFAIRS, FEDERAL ENVIRONMENTAL ASSESSMENT REVIEW OFFICE; admitted to Bar, Law Soc. of U.C. 1983; Sr. Cons., J. Phillips Nicholson Policy & Mngt. Consultants 1982–84; Gen. Counsel, Candn. Wildlife Fed. 1984–89; Extve. Dir., Candn. Arctic Resources Ctte. 1989–92; Dir., Ecovision, an environmental orgn.; recreations: nordic skiing, canoeing, botanizing; Home: 21 Lindenlea Rd., Ottawa, Ont. K1M 1A9; Office: 200 Sacre-Coeur Blvd., 14th Flr., Hull, Que. K1A 0H3.

**HAZELWOOD, Gaylord;** executive; b. Mattawa, Ont. 24 June 1934; s. Charles Edward and Imilda (Regimbald) H.; m. Miriam d. Percy and Juanita Toole 21 June 1955; children: Gaylord, Gwen, Megan, Judy, Derek; DIR., INTERNATIONAL DEVELOPMENT, TCG INTERNATIONAL INC. 1988– ; Pres., Millcreek Properties Ltd.; Nelgay Holdings Ltd.; Dir., Autostock Inc.; Glentel Inc.; business founder and Pres. Standard Auto Glass Ltd.; Pres. Vanfax Corp. 1960–82; Pres. Gaylord Farms Ltd. 1972–89; Pres. and Chief Oper. Offr. CNG Fuel Systems Ltd. 1982–83; Pres. and Dir., Trans Canada Glass Ltd. 1983–88; Vice Pres. & Dir., present co. 1988; mem. Bd. Trade Metrop. Toronto; recreations: hunting, fishing; Home: R.R. 4, Cookstown, Ont. L0L 1L0; Office: 5915 Airport Rd., Ste. 522, Mississauga, Ont. L4V 1T1.

**HEAD, (George) Bruce,** R.C.A.; artist; b. St. Boniface, Man. 14 Feb. 1931; s. George Melborne and Ellen (Ingram) H.; e. Univ. of Man. Dipl. in Fine Arts 1953; m. Verona Sadella Orchard; divorced; children: Glenn Roland, Grant Coleman, Ian Bruce, Toni Eileen, Tara Nadine; paintings, designs, sculptures rep. in numerous group and solo exhns. incl. Nat. Gallery Can.; Art Gallery of Ont.; Montreal Museum of Fine Arts; Commonwealth Arts Festival Cardiff, Wales; Dirs. Choice Traveling Exhn. 1967–68; 150 yrs. of Art in Man.; Spectrum Can. RCA 1976 Olympic Exhn.; one-man show, Univ. of Winnipeg 1987, '88, '89; 'Achieving the Modern: Canadian Abstract Painting Design in the 1950' Winnipeg, Charlottetown, Windsor, Edmonton 1993, '94; and other maj. exhns. Can. and USA; rep. in various pub., corporate and private colls. incl. Nat. Gallery Can., Montreal Museum of Fine Arts, Can. Council Art Bank, Govt. Man. Dept. Pub. Works; work cited maj. publs.; awards incl.: Monsanto Candn. Art Exhn. 1957; 5th, 6th and 7th Winnipeg Shows; 20th W. Ont. Exhn.; Eaton Graphics Award Manisphere 1969; Haddassah Art Exhibit 1st 1973; CBC Banner Competition Vancouver 1975; comns. incl. Man. Teachers' Coll. Mural 1959; Benson & Hedges Art Walls Winnipeg 1972; Woodsworth Bldg. Main Wall Man. Govt. 1976; City of Winnipeg Portage & Main Concourse 1980; D.M.C.I. Alumni Commission 1983; Address: 19 Woodlawn Ave., Winnipeg, Man. R2M 2P3.

**HEAD, Ivan Leigh,** O.C., Q.C., B.A., LL.M., LL.D.; b. Calgary, Alta. 28 July 1930; e. Elem. and High Schs., Calgary and Edmonton, Alta.; Univ. of Alta., B.A. 1951, LL.B. 1952; Harvard Law Sch., LL.M. 1960 (Frank Knox Mem. Fellow); LL.D. (hon. causa): Univ. of Alberta 1987; Univ. of West Indies 1987; Univ. of Western Ont. 1988; Univ. of Ottawa 1988; Univ. of Calgary 1989; Beijing Forestry Univ. 1990; St. Francis Xavier Univ. 1990; Univ. of Manitoba 1991; Univ. of Notre Dame 1991; Officer, Order of Canada 1990; m. Ann Marie Price; four children; PROF. OF LAW AND POLITICAL SCIENCE, UNIV. OF B.C. 1991– ; called to Bar of Alta. 1953; cr. Q.C. (Can.) 1974; practised law in partnership with S. J. Helman, Q.C. and R. H. Barron, Q.C., Calgary 1953–59; Foreign Service Offr., Dept. of External Affairs serving in Ottawa and Kuala Lumpur 1960–63; Assoc. Prof. of Law, Univ. of Alta. 1963, Prof. 1967 (on leave 1967–1973); Assoc. Counsel to Min. of Justice Can. for constitutional matters 1967; Leg. Asst. to Prime Min. of Can. 1968; named Special Asst. 1970 (special responsibility for advice on foreign policy and conduct of foreign relations); mem. Candn. Dels. to Commonwealth Heads of Govt. meetings London 1969, Singapore 1971, Ottawa 1973, Kingston 1975, London 1977; Sr. Advisor to Prime Min. on official visits to UN 1968, 1969; USA 1969, 1971, 1974, 1977; Britain 1969, 1972, 1975; Soviet Union 1971; People's Republic of China 1973 and other countries; Special emissary of Prime Minister in consultations with Heads of numerous countries including Nigeria, Britain, India, Japan; Prime Minister's Personal Representative to Economic Summits 1976, 1977; Organizer and Chrmn., Banff Conf. on Law & Order in Internat. Community 1965; Secy. to Fed. Electoral Boundaries Comn. for Alta. 1965–66; Extve. mem. Banff Conf. On World Affairs 1964–68; Extve. Comte. The Atlantic Conference 1971–90; author, 'On a Hinge of History' 1991; co-author, 'International Law, National Tribunals and the Rights of Aliens' 1971; Ed. and Contrib., 'This Fire-Proof House' 1966; Ed. 'Pierre Elliott Trudeau, Conversation with Canadians' 1972; mem. Bd. of Eds., 'Canadian Yearbook of International Law' since 1965; Adv. Comte., 'University of Toronto Law Journal' 1966–70; mem. Can. Council on Internat. Law; Law Soc. Alta. (Secy. to Benchers' Special Comte. on Mineral Titles 1955–56); Candn. Bar Assn. (Extve. Comte. Internat. & Constitutional Law Sec. 1968–74; Candn. Br. Internat. Law Assn. (Nat. Council 1966–68, Vice Pres. 1968–90); Candn. Inst. Internat. Affairs (Bd. Mem., 1993– ); National Defence College (Bd. Mem. 1993– ); Am. Soc. Internat. Law (Extve. Council 1968–71); Pres. and Gov., Internat. Dev. Rsch. Centre 1978–91; Trustee, Internat. Food Policy Rsch. Inst. 1979–88; mem., Independent Comn. on Internat. Humanitarian Issues 1983–87; Internat. Aviation Mgmt. Training Inst. (Extve. Ctte. 1984–93); mem., High Level Review Comte., Inter-American Development Bank 1988; Chrmn. of V International Conf. on AIDS 1989; Fellow, World Acad. of Art and Sci.; mem., Inter-Am. Dialogue (Extve. Comte. 1985– ); Soc. for Internat. Development, Rome (Extve. Ctte. 1991– ); Internat. Ocean Inst., Malta (Bd. Mem. 1992– ); Salzburg Seminar (Bd. Mem. 1992– ); Home: 2343 Bellevue Ave., West Vancouver, B.C. V7V 1C9; Office: Fac. of Law, Univ. of B.C., 1822 East Mall, Vancouver, B.C. V6T 1Z1.

**HEAD, Jim,** B.A., F.O.T.F.; educator; association executive; b. East York, Ont. 2 Feb. 1940; s. James William and Margaret (McKay) Graham H.; e. McMaster Univ. B.A. 1966; Univ. of Toronto Faculty of Edn. 1969; York Univ. M.B.A. studies 1972; Niagara Univ. M.Ed. studies; m. Andrea d. Don and Muriel (Brown) Rose 1962 (div.); two d. Nicole, Natasha; Pres., Ontario Teachers' Fedn. (OTF) Aug. 1993–94, 3rd Vice Pres. 1990–91, 2nd Vice Pres. 1991–92, 1st Vice Pres. 1992–93; Dir., Candn. Teachers' Fedn. (CTF) 1990– (Chair of Finance Ctte. 1991–94); Bd. of Dirs.: Cert. Gen. Accts. Assoc. of Ont. (CGA) 1990– ; Ont. Inst. for Studies in Educ. (OISE) 1992–94 (Chair of Finance & Audit Ctte. 1993–94); Candn. Inst. for Reading Recovery (C.I.R.R.) 1992– (and Secretary Treasurer 1993– ); TVOntario 1991– (and Chair, Finance Ctte. 1992– ); Eng. Teacher W.A. Porter Coll. Inst. 1966 becoming Asst. Head of Eng.; Assoc. Head of Eng. Midland Ave. Coll. Inst. 1969; Dept. Head Sir Wilfrid Laurier Coll. Inst. 1970–74, Vice-Prin. 1975; Vice-Prin. Maplewood Vocational Sch. and Eng. Teacher 1975; seconded to present Fedn. rsch. study role Secondary Sch. 1974–75, OTF Gov. 1977–83 and 1984– , Pres. Dist. 16 1978–80 and Chief Negotiator 1982–83, Exec. Offr. of Fedn. 1983–85, Vice-Pres. 1985–88, Pres. 1988–91; Pres., Ont. Secondary Sch. Teachers' Fedn. (OSSTF) 1988–91; Vice Prin. Borden Secondary Sch. 1980–82; Vice Prin. Scarborough Ctr. for Adult Studies (S.C.A.S.) 1992–93; recipient S.G.B. Robinson Meml. Award; Mem., Ont. Fair Tax Comn. Property Tax Subctte. 1992– and OSSTF Writer of Fair Tax Brief 1992; Co-Founder Coasters (Toronto Wheelchair Sports) and First Coach; co-author 'English '70' 1970; 'Man and Myth' 1972; 'Myth and Meaning' 1973; 'Signatures' 3 vol. poetry anthol. 1976; Chief Rscher. & Prin. Writer 'At What Cost?: The Role of the Secondary School' 1974; recreations: weight lifter, hiking, bicycling, squash; Clubs: Bruce Trail; Ganaraska; Home: 428 Cranbrooke Ave., North York, Ont. M5M 1N5; Offices: S.C.A.S., 39 Highbrook Dr., Scarborough, Ont. and 1260 Bay St., Toronto, Ont. M5R 2B5.

**HEAGLE, Douglas Evans,** B.A.; executive; b. Hamilton, Ont. 7 Nov. 1930; s. Walter Donald and Elizabeth Albright (Evans) H.; e. Univ. of Western Ont. B.A. (Hon) 1953; m. Marylyn d. Clendon and Elizabeth Colbert 20 June 1953; children: Marnie, Janice, Bruce, Barbara, Brian; CHRMN., NATIONAL SYSTEM OF BAKING LTD.; Dir. Central Fund of Canada Ltd.; All Canadian Resources Corp.; joined present firm in 1953; Former Gov., Hon. Life Mem. Bd. of Govs., Hillfield-Strathallan Coll., Hamilton (Chrmn. 1977–78, 1978–79); mem., Bakery Council of Can.; (Pres., 1976–77); A.O.P.A.; C.O.P.A.; Retail Bakers of America; Chamber of Commerce; Delta Upsilon Frat.; 18$ Mason; United Church; recreations: flying, scuba, swimming; Club: Hamilton; Home: 38 Woodside Dr., Hamilton, Ont. L8T 1C3; Office: 596 Upper Sherman Ave., Hamilton, Ont. L8V 3M2.

**HEALD, Hon. Darrel Verner,** B.A., LL.B.; judge; b. Regina, Sask. 27 Aug. 1919; s. Herbert Verner and Lottie (Knudson) H.; e. Univ. of Sask., B.A. 1938, LL.B. 1940; m. Doris Rose, d. A. P. Hessey, Regina, Sask., 30 June 1951; children: Lynn Doris, Brian Darrel; JUSTICE, APPEAL DIV., FEDERAL COURT OF CANADA since 1975; Co-Commr. re. bilingual IFR Air Traffic Services in Que. 1976; formerly Atty. Gen. and Prov. Secy. of Sask.; el. to Sask. Leg. for Lumsden, g.e. 22 April 1964; Dir. for 16 yrs. of Sask. Roughrider Football Club; Past Pres., Regina Bonspiel Assn.; read law with A. B. Gerein; called to Bar of Sask. 1941; cr. Q.C. Dec. 1964; apptd. Justice, Trial Div., Fed. Court of Can. 1971; served in 2nd World War as Radar Tech. with R.C.A.F., 1941–45; Freemason; United Church; recreation: curling; Home: 44 Aleutian Rd., Ottawa, Ont. K2H 7C8; Office: Supreme Court Bldg., Ottawa, Ont. K1A 0H9.

**HEALEY, Eldon James,** C.M.M., C.D., P.Eng.; consultant; b. Owen Sound, Ont. 11 Aug. 1934; s. late James and Hazel Mary (Acheson) H.; e. Royal Roads Mil. Coll. Victoria Eng. Dip. 1955; Royal Naval Eng. Coll. Plymouth, Eng. Mech. Eng. Cert. 1959, Marine Eng. Cert. 1961; m. Beverly Anne d. Harvey and Anne Doane 24 March 1962; children: David Alan, Anne Margaret, Christopher James; PARTNER, CFN CONSULTING; joined RCN as Naval Cadet 1953, retired as Chief Eng. Cdn. Forces 1985, rank Rear Admiral; retired as Asst. Dep. Min. (Material) Dept. of Nat. Defence 1990; Mem., Assoc. of Profl. Engrs. of N.S. (APENS); Mem., Inst. of Marine Engrs. of Canada (I Mar E); Defence Assocs. Nat. Network (DANN); Naval Officers Assoc. of Can. (NOAC); recreations: sailing, skiing; Clubs: Kiwanis; Rideau (both Ottawa); Home: 6 Sioux Cres., Nepean, Ont. K2H 7E5; Office: 222 Queen St., Ottawa, Ont. K1P 5V9.

**HEALEY, Robert J.,** B.Comm., F.C.A.; chartered accountant; b. St. John's, Nfld. 31 Oct. 1943; s. Joseph F. and Catherine M. (O'Keefe) H.; e. Memorial Univ. of Newfoundland B.Comm. (Hons.) 1965; C.A. 1971; F.C.A. 1991; m. Sylvia d. Randell and Rose Turpin 12 April 1971; children: Karen,Lynn; OFFICE MANAGING PARTNER, ERNST & YOUNG ST. JOHN'S; joined Ernst & Young (formerly Clarkson Gordon) 1968; Bd. Chair, Hoyles Escasoni Sr. Citizens Complex; Past Pres. & Hon. Mem., St. John's Regatta Ctte.; Mem., Adv. Bd., Sch. of Business, Memorial Univ.; Inst. of C.A.s of Nfld. F.C.A. 1991; mem. Bd. of Govs., Nfld. and Labrador Business Hall of Fame; Home: 72 Carpasian Rd., St. John's, Nfld. A1B 2R4; Office: Baine Johnston Ctr., 7th Floor, 10 Fort William Place, St. John's, Nfld. A1C 1K4.

**HEAP, Rev. Daniel James Macdonnell,** M.P., B.A., B.D.; politician; b. Winnipeg, Man. 24 Sept. 1925; s. Frederick and Margaret L. (Macdonnell); e. Upper Can. Coll.; Queen's Univ.; Univ. of Chicago; Montreal Diocesan Theol. Coll.; McGill Faculty of Divinity; m. Alice d. Rev. W.A. and Mrs. Boomhour 2 Sept. 1950; children: Margaret, Eleanor, Susan, Harold, Daniel, Andrew, David; priest; printer/slotter operator; Alderman, City of Toronto 1972–81; Alderman, Counc. of Metro. Toronto 1974–78; Fed. cand. ge. 1968 and def.; Prov. cand. g.e. 1971 and def.; el. to H. of C. for Spadina by-election 1981; re-el. g.e. for Trinity-Spadina 1984 and 1988; N.D.P.; Anglican; Home: 211 College St., #111, Toronto, Ont. M5T 1R1.

**HEAPS, Frank N.,** B.Sc., M.Sc., P. Eng., M.T.P.I.C.; brewery executive; b. Toronto, Ont. 26 Apr. 1941; s. Gerrard Denis and Pauline Gertrude (Hukish) H.; e. Haileybury Sch. of Mines; Michigan Tech. Univ., B.Sc. 1965; Univ. of Toronto, M.Sc. 1967; m. Heather E. d. John T. and Elizabeth M. Maclean 10 Sept. 1966; children: Ian, Angus, Cameron, Cailey; PRES., UPPER CANADA BREWING CO. 1984– ; Sr. Planner, Project Planning Assocs. Ltd. 1966–69; Planning Dr., Parkin Architects, Engrs. & Planners 1969–72; Pres., Devel. Planners Collaborative Ltd. 1972–74; Econ. Devel. Planning, Un. Nations, West Indies 1974–75; Policy Adv., Cabinet Ctte. of Ont. Govt. 1975–80; Princ., Currie, Coopers & Lybrand 1980–83; Dir., Castcailian Mgmt. Cons. Ltd.; Mem., Vancouver Art Gallery; R.O.M., Toronto; Art Gallery of Ont.; Pres., The Rosedale-Moore Park Assoc. 1989–90; Mem., United Way of Toronto Campaign Cabinet 1993; Mem. of Council, Toronto Bd. of Trade 1992–94; recipient, Canada Award for Business Excellence 1987; Financial Post 50 Best Managed Private Companies 1993; recreations: tennis, golf, music, oil painting; Clubs: Shaughnessy Golf & Country; Donalda Club; Home: 7 Inglewood Dr., Toronto, Ont. M4T 1G7; Office: 2 Atlantic Ave., Toronto, Ont. M6K 1X8.

**HEAPS, Leo J.,** M.C.; author; b. Winnipeg, Man. 7 July 1923; s. Abraham Albert and Bessie Elisabeth (Morris) H.; e. Univ. of S. Cal.; Queen's Univ.; Concordia Univ.; McGill Univ.; m. Tamar Szell Schnitlander Sept. 1948; children: Karen, Gill, Adrian, Wendy; served as paratrooper and mem. M15, M16; organised Dutch Resistance; Head, Internat. Rescue Ctte. Team during Hungarian Revolution 1956; organized Israeli Army Units War of Independence; Head, U.N. Rescue

Mission, S.E. Asia 1979–80; discovered some of North America's historical treasures for the National Archives and the Museum of Man in Ottawa 1965–80; opened first gallery of Candn. art (which first exhbd. many of today's foremost artists), The Gallery, Ottawa 1949; recipient runner-up Gov. Gen.'s Award 1946; author: 'Escape from Arnhem' 1947; 'Rebel in the House' 1968 and 1986; 'High Rise' 1972; 'Log of the Centurion' 1974; 'Grey Goose Arnhem' 1978; 'Operation Morning Light' 1979; 'Quebec Plot' 1980; 'Boy Called Nam' 1986; 'Hugh Hambleton Spy' 1983; 'The Cyclops Auction' 1990; 'Our Canada' 1991; The A.A. Heaps scholarship given annually by the Candn. Labour Congress and the A.A. Heaps Bldg. in Winnipeg (commemorated by the Man. Govt. in 1987) are tributes to his father as a pioneer in Canada's social legislation; Address: 56 Soho Sq., Toronto, Ont. M5T 2Z4.

**HEARD, Raymond E.,** B.A.; communications executive; b. Johannesburg, S. Africa 18 Dec. 1935; s. George A. and Vida (Stodden) H.; e. Durban H.S.; Univ. of Witwatersrand B.A. (Hons.) 1960; Harvard Univ. Frank Knox Fellow 1961–62; m. Gillian d. Dr. J.B.R. and Alison Cosgrove; children: Josephine, Antony, Jennifer; SENIOR ADVISOR, GOVT. AND CORPORATE AFFAIRS, THE ROYAL BANK OF CANADA, Toronto 1991– ; Reporter The Friend, Bloemfontein 1954–55; Reporter, Rand Daily Mail, Johannesburg 1954–60; Reporter, Art Critic and Ed. Writer The Montreal Star 1961–64, Washington Corr. 1964–73; Ed. Observer Foreign News Service, The Observer, London 1973–76; Managing Ed. The Montreal Star 1976–79; Dir. T.V. News, Global Television Network 1979–80, Gen. Mgr. News and Current Affairs 1980–81, Vice-President News and Current Affairs 1981–88; Dir., Communications, Office of the Leader of the Opposition, Ottawa 1988–90; co-creator and Host The Editors (weekly TV show) Montreal 1977–79; Broadcast commentaries for CBC news from Washington 1964–73; author articles for London Observer, Financial Times 1964– ; mem. Radio-TV News Dirs. Assn.; Pres. Candn. Correspondents Assn., Washington 1971–72; Anglican; winner Press Award, The Hudson Inst. 1969; Royal Humane Soc. Award for Bravery (rescue of bather) 1975; recreations: tennis, skiing, surfing; Home: 92 Binscarth Rd., Toronto, Ont. M4W 1Y4.

**HEARN, John R.,** C.A.; b. London, Eng. 22 Feb. 1930; s. Jackson and Elizabeth (Potter) H.; came to Canada 1957; e. Grammar Sch., Bucks. Eng.; London Sch. of Econ., Post-Grad. Studies; m. Agnes, d. John Young Boyd, May 1953; children: Steven, Deborah, Jackson; Francis F. King & Son, C.A.'s, London Eng. 1947–52; Extve. Asst. to Mang. Dir., Suntex Safety Glass Industries Ltd. 1952–54; Consultant, R.F. Fraser, Mgmt. Consultants (London) 1954–56; joined Peat, Marwick, Mitchell & Co. as Consultant, Toronto 1957, Regional Dir. – W. Can. 1958–63, Partner 1963–75; Canadian Managing Partner, Peat Marwick & Partners 1969–75; Chrmn. & C.E.O., Elco Fine Foods Inc.; Equity Investments Inc., Equity Leasing Ltd., Equity International Inc.; Equity (USA) Inc.; Dir., Long Range Invest.; Euroclean Can. Ltd.; Euroclean Holdings Ltd.; Infinitum Growth Fund Inc.; Environment II Inc.; Kroy Wools Inc.; mem. Insts. Chart. Accts., Eng. and Wales; Anglican: recreations: golf, squash, bridge; Clubs: Rosedale Golf; Beacon Hall; Gator Creek, Florida; Homes: 29 Swansdown Dr., Willowdale, Ont. M2L 2N2 and Lake of Bays, Muskoka, Ont.

**HEARNDEN, Kenneth W.,** B.Sc.F.; professional forester; b. Toronto, Ont. 11 May 1923; s. Arthur William and Elsie Hutchinson (Monk) H.; e. Parkdale Coll. Inst., Toronto, Ont.; Univ. of Toronto, B.Sc.F. (1st Class Hons.); m. Sheilagh Jean, d. Rev. E. C. McCullagh, Dunnville, Ont., 7 Oct. 1950; children: James Stanley, John; Prof. & Dir. Sch. of Forestry, Lakehead Univ. 1971–80; Dean of Students 1980–85; Prof. Emeritus of Forestry 1986– ; Chrmn., Lakehead Region Conservation Authority 1968–73; Chrmn., Local Architectural Conservation Adv. Ctte., Township of Delhi 1988–91; mem., Candn. Inst. Forestry (Pres. 1964–65); Ont. Prof. Foresters Assn. (Pres. 1969–71); Freemason (Scot. Rite); mem., Bd. of Dir., Thunder Bay Temple Bldgs. Ltd., (Pres., 1974–77); Vice-Chrmn., Municipality of Shuniah Planning Bd. 1981–83; Secy-Treas., Assn. of University Forestry School of Can. 1973–80; mem., Haldimand-Norfolk District Health Counc. 1990– (Chrmn. 1993– ); Chrmn., Ont. Independent Forest Audit Ctte. 1991–92; recreations: photography, carpentry, music listening; Address: Box 31, R.R. #1, Vittoria, Ont. N0E 1W0.

**HEASLIP, W. David,** B.E.S.; business executive; b. Toronto, Ont. 6 Nov. 1948; s. William T. and Jean P. (Myatt) H.; e. Univ. of Waterloo B.E.S. 1971; m. Rebecca d. Jack and Eilleen Fulcher 22 Jan. 1977; children: Alexander, Burton, Luke; VICE-PRES., CORP. MKTG., ORTECH CORPORATION 1987– ; mngt. consultant in strategic planning & mktg. 1972–80; Dir., Mkt. Planning, Genstar Structures 1980–84; Mktg. & Bus. Devel. Mgr., W.R. Grace of Can. Ltd. 1984–87; Dir., Planning Forum (Toronto Chap.); Sheridan Park Rsch. Community Assn.; Home: 372 River Oaks Blvd. W., Oakville, Ont. L6H 5E7; Office: 2395 Speakman Dr., Mississauga, Ont. L5K 1B3.

**HEASLIP, William Thomas,** B.A.Sc.; aeronautical consultant; professional engineer; b. Toronto 13 Oct. 1920; s. William Henry and Eva Louise (Moody) H.; e. W. Tech. Sch., Toronto, 1933–38; Univ. of Toronto, 1938–40 and 1945–47, B.A.Sc. (Aero. Engn.); m. Jean Phyllis d. L. G. Myatt of Hamilton, 13 Sept. 1947; children: William David, James Edward, Anne Marie, John Leonard, Patricia Jean, Robert Vernon, Kathleen Carol, Paul Douglas; joined de Havilland Aircraft of Canada in May 1947; employed in various capacities in aerodynamics, stress analysis and design; spent 3 yrs. with Parent Co. in Hatfield, Eng.; apptd. Depy. Chief, Design Engr., 1955; Chrmn., Engn. Directorate, 1961; Chief Engr. (Product) 1962; Depy. Vice-Pres., Engn., 1965, Vice Pres., Engn. 1966, Dir. 1970, Vice Pres., Special Project, 1977, retired Dec. 1983; Cons., A.B. Schwartz and Associates; Volunteer Consultant, Candn. Extve. Services Orgn. (CESO); served with R.N. & R.C.N. 1941–45 as Radar Offr. in Mediterranean & N. Atlantic with rank of Elect. Lt. RCNVR; Trustee, King (Ont.) School Bd., 1962–65 (Chrmn., 1964–65); mem. Assn. Prof. Engrs. Ont.; Fellow, Candn. Aero & Space Inst. (Pres. 1972–73); Conservative; United Church; recreations: golf, woodworking, travel; Home: 108 Confederation Way, Thornhill, Ont. L3T 5R5.

**HEASMAN, George Robert,** O.B.E., B.Com.; b. Ottawa, Ont. 22 Dec. 1898; s. George and Rose (Cawdron) H.; e. Queen's Univ., B.Com. 1925; m. Audrey Beatrice, d. Charles Cooke, New Carlisle, Que., 18 Sept. 1930; children: Robert George, Rosemary Louise; Wayagamack Pulp & Qaper Co., Three Rivers, Que., 1923–27; Asst. Trade Commr. to Batavia, Java, N.E.I., 1928; Trade Commr. 1930; Trade Commr. in S. Africa, London and Chicago; Chief, Export Permit Br., Trade & Commerce and Asst. Dir. of Mutual Aid Adm., Ottawa, 1941–45; Director, Trade Commissioner Service, 1946–53; Candn. Ambassador to Indonesia, 1953–57; Candn. High Commr. to New Zealand, 1958–63; retired 1964; Anglican; recreations: golf, fishing; Club: Royal Ottawa; Address: Rideau Place, 550 Wilbrod St., Ottawa, Ont. K1N 6N2.

**HEATH, David Gordon,** C.S.B., B.A., S.T.B., M.S., D.Ed.; educator; b. Detroit, Mich. 20 Feb. 1930; s. Gordon Charles and Florence Irene (McGowan) H.; e. Univ. of W. Ont. B.A. 1953; Univ. of St. Michael's Coll. S.T.B. 1958; Ind. Univ. M.S. 1961, D.Ed. 1967; TREASURER-GENERAL, BASILIAN FATHERS OF TORONTO 1991– ; High Sch. Teacher and Adm. 1953–65; Univ. Prof. and Adm. 1965–79; Pres., Assumption Univ. 1979–91; former Chrmn. Bd. Govs., Mem. Senate, Univ. of Windsor; Chrmn., Finance Comte., Basilian Fathers of Toronto; mem. Cong. of St. Basil (C.S.B.) Toronto; Address: Cardinal Flahiff Centre, 95 St. Joseph St., Toronto, Ont. M5S 3C2.

**HEATH, Francus Edward,** C.D.; manufacturer; b. Toronto, Ont. 26 Dec. 1944; s. Gordon Edward and Sarah Anne (Gallagher) H.; e. Central Tech. High Sch. 1964; Ryerson Polytech. Inst., York Univ. various tech., sales & mgmt. courses; m. Donna Smith 30 Apl. 1966; one s. Ian Stuart; PRES., DIR. AND CHIEF EXECUTIVE OFFR. HOUGHTON CANADA INC. 1989– ; joined present Co. as lab. tech. 1964, sales trainee 1965, Tech. Sales Rep. S.W. Ont. 1967 and Area Sales Mgr. 1981, Div. Sales Mgr. Ont. 1983, Nat. Sales Mgr. 1984, Gen. Mgr. 1988; served with Candn. Armed Forces (R) 1961–81, commissioned 1971, currently on Supplementary Ready Reserve List, rank Capt.; mem. The Bd. of Trade of Metrop. Toronto; Cdn. Mfrs. Assn.; N. Am. Die Casting Assn.; Soc. Tribologists & Lubrication Engs. (Past Dir. Hamilton Sect.); Am. Soc. Metals; Cdn. Pulp & Paper Assn.; Queen's Own Rifles Offrs. Mess; Royal Cdn. Legion; recreations: golf, downhill skiing; Club: Royal Cdn. Military Institute; Board of Trade Golf and C.C.; Home: 1130 Falgarwood Dr., Oakville, Ont. L6H Office: 100 Symes Rd., P.O. Box 113, Stn. D, Toronto, Ont. M6P 3J5.

**HEATH, Michele Christine,** B.Sc., Ph.D., D.I.C.; university professor; b. Bournemouth, England 22 Sept. 1945; d. Percy and Winifred Iris Lily (Downes) Roy; e. Westfield Coll., Univ. of London (U.K.), B.Sc. (1st class hons.) 1966; Imperial Coll., Univ. of London, Ph.D., D.I.C. 1969; m. Ian Brent s. Eileen and Archibald Heath 23 Sept. 1967; one d.: Lorraine; PROF., BOTANY DEPT., UNIV. OF TORONTO 1981– ; post-doctoral fellow, Univ. of Georgia 1969–71; Lectr., Asst. Prof., Assoc. Prof., Univ. of Toronto 1972–81; Huxley Meml. Medal for Rsch. Achievement 1979 (Imperial Coll.); one of the youngest people designated a fellow of the Am. Phytopathological Soc. 1982; first woman recipient, Steacie Meml. Fellowship, NSERC 1982; 1st recipient of Gordon Green Award, Candn. Phytopathol. Soc. 1984; Fellow, Candn. Phytopathological Soc. 1993; Sr. Ed., APS Press 1988–91; 'Physiological and Molecular Plant Pathology' 1982–89; Chair, Programme Ctte., 6th Internat. Congress of Plant Pathology 1993; mem., Candn. & Am. Phytopathol. Societies; Mycological Soc. of Am.; Am. Soc. of Plant Physiol.; co-author (with L.J. Littlefield) 'Ultrastructure of Rust Fungi' 1979; recreations: lapidary, painting, horse riding; Home: R.R. 1, Acton, Ont. L7J 2L7; Office: 25 Willcocks St., Toronto, Ont. M5S 3B2.

**HEATH, Terrence,** M.A., D.Phil.; museum director; author; b. Regina, Sask. 25 Aug. 1936; s. Harold Frost and Mary (Kelly) H.; e. Univ. of Sask. B.A. 1961; Univ. of Munich, Germany 1960; Univ. of Ore. M.A. 1962; Oxford Univ. D.Phil. 1966; children: Paul James, Joseph Mark, Simon Andrew; Assoc. Prof. of Hist. Univ. of Sask. 1967–72; freelance writer/curator 1972–77, 1980–83; Dir., Winnipeg Art Gallery 1983–85; Exec. Dir. W. Devel. Museums 1977–80; curator, writer, consultant 1985– ; Chrmn. Heritage Property Review Bd. Sask.; Chair, Taskforce on the Art Gall. of Ont. 1992; author: 'The Truth and Other Stories' (prose) 1972; 'Interstices of Night' (poetry) 1979; 'The Last Hiding Place' (novel) 1982; 'Uprooted: The Life and Art of Ernest Lindner' (biog.) 1983; co-author: 'Journey/Journée' (poetry) 1988; 'Wild Man's Butte' (poetry) 1979; mem. Ed. Bd. 'Vanguard' mag.; Man. Writers Guild; Candn. Museums Assn.; founding mem and mem. Counc., Writers Union Can.; Home: Box 499, Niagara-on-the-Lake Ont. L0S 1J0.

**HEATH, William Ronald,** B.S.A.; university administrator; b. Belleville, Ont. 21 March 1943; s. William Norris and Frances Marian (McKeown) H.; e. Univ. of Guelph B.S.A. 1965; REGISTRAR & SECRETARY OF SENATE, SIMON FRASER UNIV. 1984– ; Asst. then Assoc. Registrar, Univ. of Guelph 1966–84; 125th Canada Commemorative Medal; Pres., Assn. of Registrars of Universities & Colleges of Canada 1992–94; Ont. Univ. Registrars Assn.; Extve. PACRAO 1991–92; recreations: skiing, gardening; Home: 1765 Westover Rd., North Vancouver, B.C. V7J 1X7; Office: Burnaby, B.C. V5A 1S6.

**HEATHCOTE, Isobel Winnifred,** B.Sc., M.S., Ph.D.; university professor; b. Boston, Mass. 24 Nov. 1952; d. Eric Thomas Blake and Barbara Jessie (MacAskill) H.; e. Univ. of Toronto B.Sc. 1974; Yale Univ. M.S. 1975, Ph.D. 1978; m. Alan Frederick s. George and Patricia Belk 19 Oct. 1988; children: Elspeth Alicia Anne, Zoe Charlotte Erica, Edward Alexander George; ASSOC. PROF., ENVIRON. ENGINEERING (AND ENVIRON. SCI.), UNIV. OF GUELPH 1991– ; Physical/Chem. Limnologist, Acres Cons. Serv. 1978–79; Ont. Min. of Environ. 1979–80; Chief, Water Quality Systems 1980–84; Supvr., Great Lakes Investigations and Surveillance 1984–85; Dir., Environ. Studies & Environ. Sci., Univ. of Toronto 1985–91; Dean of Women, Univ. College 1986–90; Pres., Wyndham Rsch. Inc.; Mem., Bd. of Dir., Candn. Inst. for Environ. Law & Policy; Knowledge of the Environ. for Youth; Candn. Environ. Law Assn. 1986–90; Pollution Control Assn. of Ont. 1989–92; Chair, MISA Adv. Ctte., Ont. Min. of Environ. & Energy; Mem., Great Lakes Sci. Adv. Bd., Internat. Joint Comn.; author of dozens of tech. papers, policy analyses & commentaries; noted teacher and researcher; recreations: gardening, travel; Home: 2 Hunter's Lane, Guelph, Ont. N1C 1B1; Office: Guelph, Ont. N1G 2W1.

**HEATHCOTE, Lesley Muriel,** B.S., M.A.; librarian (retired); b. Edmonton, Alta. (formerly N.W.T.) 12 May 1904; d. Henry Walter and Annie Selina (Hilton) H.; e. Westmount Grade Sch. and Victoria High Sch., 1921, Edmonton, Alta.; Univ. of Alta., B.A. 1924, M.A. 1928; Univ. of Wash., B.S. (Lib. Science) 1929, grad. work in hist. 1939–51; D.Hum.Litt. (Hon.), Montana State Univ. 1981; Asst. to Registrar, Univ. of Alta., 1924–28; Serials Librarian, Univ. of Wash., 1929–44; Research Asst., Internat. Labour Office, Montreal, 1945–46; Lib. Asst., Montana State Univ. (then Mont. State Coll.), 1946–47; Assoc. Prof. and Librarian, 1947–52; Prof. and Librarian, 1952–65; Prof. and Dir. of Libraries 1965–70 (during tenure of Office at Univ. Lib. has grown from some 75,000 vols. to nearly 500,000 and two lib. bldgs. have been erected); one of founders & incorporators,

Bozeman Symphony Soc. Inc.; Secy. 1968–70; author of numerous articles for prof. periodicals in lib. field; mem., Pacific N.W. Lib. Assn. (Pres. 1951–52); Mont. Lib. Assn. (Pres. 1953–54); Am. Lib. Assn.; chosen Librarian of the Year for Montana 1969; Montana State Univ. Blue and Gold Award, 1978; recreations: hiking, riding, gardening, flute playing; Club: Alpine of Can.; Home: 9236 SE 33rd St., Mercer Island, Wash. 98040 USA.

**HEATLEY, Stephen Naylor,** B.A., M.F.A.; theatre director; b. Brampton, Ont. 4 May 1951; s. Herbert Allan and Hazel Marion (Sproule) H.; e. Brampton Cent. S.S. 1970; Brock Univ., B.A. (Hons.) 1974; Candn. Mime Sch. 1976; Univ. of Alta., M.F.A. 1979; Artistic Dir., Theatre Network 1981–92; Res. Ensemble Mem., Carousel Players, St Catharines 1974–75; Asst. Dir., Magnus Theatre North-West, Thunder Bay 1976–77; Chrmn., Assn. of Touring Profl. Theatres of Alta. 1984– ; Jury Mem. (var.), Can. Counc.; Lectr., Drama Dept., Univ. of Alta. (sessional) 1977– ; Team Mem. & Planning Ctte., Arts Trek, Summer Drama Prog. 1982, 1983, 1985–89; Founding Mem., Alta. Playwrights' Network; Mem., Candn. Actors' Equity Assn., ACTRA, Playwrights' Union of Can.; Vice-Pres., Profl. Assoc. of Cdn. Theatres 1989–93; co-author: 'The Other Side of the Pole' (with M. Heatley & E. Connell) in 'Eight Plays for Young People' 1984, 'Working Title' (with E. Connell) prod. at Theatre Network 1984; 'Welcome to Theatre Fabulous' (with E. Connell and C. Massing) prod. at Theatre Network 1989; recipient, Alta. Achievement Award for Excellence in Chosen Profession 1990; recreations: gardening; Home: 9314 – 110 Avenue, Edmonton, Alta. T5H 1H1.

**HEATON, Donald Harold;** retired police officer; b. Coalhurst, Alta. 13 Jan. 1934; s. Harold and Kathleen (Neidig) H.; e. Lethbridge (Alta.) Collegiate Inst. 1951; Candn. Police Coll. Advanced Course in Police Admin. and Investigation 1968, Exec. Devel. Course 1979; m. Norleen d. Ferdinand and Ada Koch 18 May 1957; children: Douglas, Laurel, Diane & Debra (twins), Jeffrey; Mgr., Corporate Security, Transcanada Pipelines Ltd. 1988–90; joined R.C.M.P. 1952; served in Regina, Indian Head, Weyburn, Estevan (Sask.); Ottawa, Niagara Falls, London, Toronto (Ont.); promoted to Offr. Rank 1970, and to Asst. Comnr. 1985; served as Offr. Co-ordinator 'O' Div. C.I.B. Investigations, Toronto 1970–73; Asst. Commanding Offr. Saskatoon Sub-Div. 1973–76; Offr. in Ch. Drug Enforcement for S.W. Ont. Div. 1976–82; Offr. in Ch. of of Criminal Operations for Southwestern Ont. Div., R.C.M.P. 1982–85; Commanding Offr. 'F' Div., Prov. of Saskatchewan, R.C.M.P. 1985–88; retired assistant commissioner, R.C.M.P.; Past Chrmn. Zone 3 Ont. Assn. of Chiefs of Police; mem. and past Chrmn. Drug Ctte. Ont. Assn. of Chiefs of Police; founding mem. Drug Educ. Co-ordinating Counc.; Past mem. Prov. Adv. Counc. Alcohol and Drug Concerns Inc.; variety of offices incl. Pres. and Chrmn. St. Matthew's Lutheran Ch., Scarborough, Ont. 1965–85; recipient R.C.M.P. Long Service Medal with bronze, silver and gold clasps; Ont. Assn. of Chiefs of Police Service Award in recognition of exceptional service in the interests of Law Enforcement 1982; recreations: golf, photography; Home: 9 Wheeling Dr., Scarborough, Ont. M1C 3X2.

**HEBB, Laurence Dingman,** Q.C., B.A., LL.B.; lawyer; b. Toronto, Ont. 11 Jan. 1937; s. Andrew Olding and Ruth Gordon (Dingman) H.; e. Deer Park Pub. Sch. and N. Toronto Coll. Inst. 1955; Univ. of Toronto Victoria Coll. B.A. 1959; Dalhousie Univ. LL.B. 1962; m. Margaret Ann McIntosh d. John and Anna McIntosh 19 March 1977; children: Katherine Ann, Christopher John; MNG. PARTNER, OSLER, HOSKIN & HARCOURT 1989– ; called to Bar of N.S. 1963, Ont. 1964; cr. Q.C. 1983; joined present firm 1964, Partner 1971, Chrmn. Mgmt. Ctte. 1986–91; Pres. Social Planning Council Metrop. Toronto 1975–78, Dir. and Chrmn. various cttes. 1971–78; Trustee, Un. Way Greater Toronto, Chrmn. various cttes. 1980–86; Dir. Ont. Welfare Council 1978–81; Past Dir. Volunteer Centre Metrop. Toronto, Founding Dir. N. York Br.; Instr. in Corps. & Comm. Law Bar Admission Course Law Soc. Upper Can. 1969–73; participation continuing edn. progs.; author various articles; mem. Candn. Bar Assn. (Chrmn. various cttes.); Candn. Civil Liberties Assn.; Candn. Council Social Devel.; Amnesty Internat.; The National Club; recreations: public affairs, travel, tennis, swimming, sailing; Home: 83 Glenview Ave., Toronto, Ont. M4R 1P9; Office: 66F, 1 First Canadian Place, Toronto, Ont. M5X 1B8.

**HEBENTON, G. Sholto,** Q.C.; lawyer; b. Quesnel, B.C. 29 May 1935; s. William and Mona H.; e. Penticton High Sch. 1953; Univ. of B.C., B.A. 1957; Oxford Univ. (Rhodes Scholar) B.A. 1959, B.C.L. 1960; Harvard Law Sch. LL.M. 1961; m. Shirley d. Hugh and Florence Lynch 3 Sept. 1960; children: Barbara, Jeffrey; PARTNER, McCARTHY TÉTRAULT 1989– ; Assoc., Dewey, Ballantine, Bushby, Palmer & Wood N.Y.C. 1961–63; articled clk. Russell & Du Moulin Vancouver 1964; Partner, Shrum, Liddle & Hebenton 1965–89; Visiting Lectr. in Law, Univ. of Toronto and Osgoode Hall Law Sch., York Univ. 1974; Pres., Candn. Assn. Rhodes Scholars 1985–87; provincial editor, Candn. Bar Review, 1986– ; mem., Vancouver Police Bd. 1978–83; Dir., Can. Inst. Admin. Justice, 1978–1982; Pres., Univ. of B.C. Alumni Assn. 1969–70, mem. Exec. 1967–71; Pres., Candn. Club of Vancouver 1988–89, Dir. 1984–90; Dir., IFC Vancouver 1988–91; ed. 'British Columbia Corporation Manual' 1975–92; Club: University (Pres. 1979–80, Dir. 1974–81); Home: 1488 W. 32 Ave., Vancouver, B.C. V6H 2J3; Office: 1300, 777 Dunsmuir St., Vancouver, B.C. V7Y 1K2.

**HEBERT, Gérard,** Ph.D.; university professor; b. Verdun (Montréal), Qué., 13 Dec. 1921; s. Jean-Jacques and Mériza (Bédard) H.; e. Collège Ste-Marie, Univ. de Montréal, B.A. 1942; Fac. de la Cie de Jésus, Montréal, L.Ph. 1947, L.Th. 1954; McGill Univ., Ph.D. 1963; m. Frances, d. John B. and Laure Woods, 19 Jan. 1974; children: Francis, Josée, Edmond, Sylvie Maltais; PROFESSOR OF INDUSTRIAL RELATIONS, UNIV. DE MONTREAL 1965– ; Prof. of Greek Lang. and Lit., Montreal 1947–48; Prof. of French Lit. and Can. Hist., Coll. Ste-Marie, 1948–50; lectr., Dept. of Economics (Ind. Rels), McGill Univ. 1957–65; editor (part-time) of 'Relations' (monthly review) 1963–68; dir.(part-time), Institut Social Populaire, Montréal 1965–68; contract researcher, Can. Constrn. Assn. 1965–67 and 1979–81; mem. of Review Ctte. on Public Service Staff Relations Act (Fed. Govt.) 1970; contract rschr., Econ. Counc. of Can. (labour rels. in constrn.) 1973–78; pres., Review Ctte. on Constrn. Ind. Labour Rels. Act (Quebec) 1977–78; contract rschr. for Kent Comn. (labour rels. in Can. daily newspapers), for Task Force on Broadcasting Policy (labour rels. in Can. broadcasting ind.), for Task Force on Deregulation in Que. (Dereg. the construction ind.) 1986; Coordr., State of the Art in Ind. Rels. (Can. Ind. Rels. Assn.) 1980–88; Gen. rapporteur on public and private pension plans at Madrid World Congress of the Internat. Soc. for Labour Law and Social Security 1987–88; mem.: Royal Soc. of Can. (elected 1979); Can. Ind. Rels. Assn. (Pres. 1980–81); Social Sci. Fed. of Can. (Pres. 1984–85); author, 'Traité de négociation collective' 1992; several other books, chapters and scholarly articles on industrial relations and on collective bargaining, labour standards and working conditions, especially in the construction industry and in the public sector, in Quebec and other Can. provinces; recreations: historic sites, rare books; Home: 825 rue Brunet, Ville St-Laurent, Qué. H4M 1Y4; Office: Ecole de relations industrielles, Univ. de Montréal, Case postale 6128, Succursale 'A,' Montréal, Qué. H3C 3J7.

**HÉBERT, Guy,** B.Sc., M.B.A.; mining executive; b. St-Hilaire, Que. 4 Dec. 1949; s. Joseph A. and Huguette (Hubert) H.; e. Univ. of Montreal B.Sc. 1973; Univ. of Sherbrooke M.B.A. 1977; m. Carmen d. Léo and Rose Nolet 13 Aug. 1977; children: Maude, Jean-Philippe, Audrey, Charles-Antoine; PRESIDENT & CHIEF EXECUTIVE OFFICER, LYON LAKE MINES LTD. 1986– ; DIR., BD. OF DIRS., AUDREY RESOURCES INC. 1985– ; Student employment in cartography, prospection & drilling programs, Québec Energy & Resources 1966–72; Geologist, Soquem 1973–75; Project Manager 1975–78; President Advisor 1978–80; Pres. & Chief Extve. Offr., Aiguebelle Resources Inc. 1980–85; Pres. & Chief Extve. Offr., Audrey Resources Inc. 1985–92; Mem., Consulting Ctte., National Bank of Canada; named Man of the Month, 'Commerce' mag. Jan. 1984; Govt. of Que., 'Award of Excellence' for the mining industry 1988; 1st recipient 'Developer of the Year,' Quebec Prospectors Assn. 1989; Pres. & Founder, Univ. of Quebec Foundation, Rouyn-Noranda; Mem., Candn. Inst. of Mines; Prospectors & Developers Assn. of Canada; Quebec Prospectors Assn.; MBA Assn.; recreations: boating, hunting, fishing; clubs: Mount Stephen; Office: 1010 Sherbrooke West, Suite 2320, Montréal, Qué. H3A 2R7.

**HEBERT, Jacques,** O.C.; senator; b. Montreal, Que. 21 June 1923; s. Dr. Louis-Philippe and Denise (Saint-Onge) H.; e. Coll. Ste-Marie, Montreal; St. Dunstan's Coll, Charlottetown, P.E.I.; Ecole des Hautes Etudes Commerciales, M.Com. 1945; m. Thérèse, d. Dr. Desjardins, Beloeil, Que., 21 Oct. 1951; children: Michel, Pascale, Isabelle, Bruno, Sophie; Founder & Pres., Canada World Youth; Founder & Pres., Katimavik; Opposition Whip in Senate; Vice-Chrmn., National Liberal Caucus; Chief Whip of the Govt.; Founder and Publisher, VRAI (weekly newspaper), 1954–59; Founder and Gen. Mgr., Editions de l'Homme, 1959–61; Founder, Pres. and Gen. Mgr., Editions du Jour, 1961–74; Co-Chrmn. Fed. Cultural Policy Review Comte. 1980–82; Chrmn., Special Senate Ctte. on Youth 1985–86; author: 'Autour des trois Amériques' 1948; 'Autour de l'Afrique' 1950; 'Aicha l'Africaine' 1950; 'Aventure autour du Monde' 1952; 'Nouvelle aventure en Afrique' 1953; 'Coffin était innocent' 1958; 'Scandale à Bordeaux' 1959; 'Deux innocents en Chine rouge' (with Pierre Elliott Trudeau) 1960; 'J'accuse les assassins de Coffin' 1963; 'Trois jours en prison' 1965; 'Les Ecoeurants' 1966; 'Ah! mes Aieux!' 1968; 'Obscénité et Liberté' 1970; 'BlaBlaBla du Bout du Monde' 1971; 'La terre est ronde' 1976; 'Faites-leur bâtir une tour ensemble' 1979; 'Le grand branle-bas' 1980; 'L'Affaire Coffin' 1980; 'La jeunesse des années 80: Etat d'urgence' 1982; 'Voyager en pays tropical' 1984; 'Trois semaines dans le hall du Sénat' 1986; 'Yémen: Invitation au voyage en Arabie heureuse' 1989; 'Deux innocents dans un igloo' 1990; 'Deux innocents au Mexique' 1990; 'Deux innocents au Guatemala' 1990; 'Deux innocents en Amérique centrale' 1991; books published in English: 'I Accuse the Assassins of Coffin ' 1963; 'The Temple on the River' 1967; 'Two Innocents in Red China' (with Pierre Elliott Trudeau) 1968; 'The World is Round' 1977; 'Have Them Build a Tower Together' 1979; 'The Great Building Bee' (with Maurice Strong) 1980; 'The Coffin Affair' 1982; '21 Days – One Man's Fight for Canada's Youth' 1986; 'Travelling in Tropical Countries' 1986; 'Yémen: Invitation to a Voyage in Arabia Felix' 1989; Officer, Order of Can.; R. Catholic; Home: 3480 Prud'Homme, Montréal, Qué. H4A 3H4; Office: The Senate, Ottawa, Ont. K1A 0A4.

**HEBERT, Norman D.;** automotive dealership & leasing executive; b. Montreal, Que. 15 Nov. 1925; s. Henri and Merilda (Morency) H.; e. secondary level dipl.; extension courses in bus. admin.; Hon. dipl., Ecole des Hautes Etudes Comm.; m. Johanne Capra 3 Feb. 1951; children: Norman E., Louise; PRES., ENTREPRISES NORMAN HEBERT INC. & CHRMN. & CHIEF EXTVE. OFFR., GROUPE PARK AVENUE INC. (includes Park Ave. Chev. Oldsmobile Cadillac Inc., Park Ave. Leasing Inc., Brossard Nissan Inc., Brossard Honda, Brossard Toyota Inc., Park Ave. BMW, Park Avenue Volks/Audi); Bd. Mem., l'Indus. Alliance Insur. Co.; Triathlon Leasing Inc.; Past Pres., The Arthritis Soc. (Que.); Founder & Chrmn., Montreal Internat. Auto Salon; Past Pres., Montreal Auto. Dealer Assn.; General Motors Montreal Assn.; Prov. Auto Dealers Assn. of Que.; Past Pres., Fond. Hop. Notre Dame; Past Pres., Special Names Ctte., CENTRAIDE; several other past business & community executive positions; Man of the Month (Revue Commerce) Feb. 1976; First Winner, Time Magazine Quality Dealer Award 1972; recreations: golf, tennis, skiing, boating; clubs: Laval Sur-le-Lac Golf, Saint-Denis, Mont Tremblant Ski, Mont Royal, Montreal Indoor Tennis, Mayacoo Golf (Palm Beach, Florida); Home: 3430, Peel St., Apt. 17D, Montreal, Que. H3A 3K8; Office: 5000 Jean-Talon St. E., St-Leonard, Que. H1S 1K6.

**HEBERT, Paul D.N.,** B.Sc., Ph.D.; educator; b. Kingston, Ont. 6 May 1947; s. Neil Asquith and Evelyn Elizabeth H.; e. Kingston Coll. & Vocational Inst. 1965; Queen's Univ. B.Sc. 1969; Cambridge Univ. Ph.D. 1973 (Commonwealth & Rutherford Scholar); m. Judith Ann d. Russell and Virginia Clay 6 June 1970; one child: Brianne Cara; CHAIR AND PROF., DEPT. OF ZOOLOGY, UNIV. OF GUELPH 1990– ; former Rsch. Assoc. Univ. of Sydney, Australia; Asst. Prof. of Biol., Univ. of Windsor 1976, Assoc. Prof. 1977, Prof. 1980–90, Dir. Great Lakes Inst. 1987–89; Chrmn. NSERC Population Biol. Panel 1988–89; mem. MISA Adv. Ctte.; Fellow, Royal Soc. of Can.; author over 125 sci. papers, 4 book chapters; Home: R.R. #1, Puslinch, Ont. N0B 2J0; Office: Guelph, Ont. N1G 2W1.

**HEBERT, Pierre,** B.Sc., B.A.; filmmaker; b. Montréal, Qué. 19 Jan. 1944; s. Marcel and Carmel (Messier) H.; e. Coll. St. Viateur, B.A. 1962; Univ. of Montréal, B.Sc. 1964; children: Etienne Noreau-Hébert; ANIMATION FILMMAKER, NAT. FILM BD. 1965– ; films most recently directed incl. 'La lettre d'amour' 1988; 'Adieu bipède' 1987; 'O Picasso – Tableaux d'une surexposition' 1985, 'Songs and dances from the inanimate world – the subway' 1984, 'Etienne et Sara' 1984, 'Memories of War' 1982; also involved in many multidisciplinary works involving live music & films and dance & films incl. 'La symphonie interminable' 1986; 'Adieu Leonardo' 1987; 'In Memory' 1989; Teacher, Univ. of Montréal and Univ Laval; Melkweg Cinema Award for Reality Rsch. (Amsterdam, Holland) 1985; Bessy Award (New York dance and performance award) for films in 'The technology of tears' (Rosalind Newman and dancers) 1987; Norman McLaren Heritage Award 1988; Home: 4465 rue de Bordeaux, Montréal, Qué. H2H 1Z6; Office: C.P. 6100, Montreal, Que. H3C 3H5.

**HÉBERT, Raymond-Marc,** B.A., M.A., Ph.D.; educator; b. Victoria, B.C. 13 Apl. 1944; s. Georges Roland and Juliette Marie (Couture) H.; e. St. Boniface Coll. B.A. 1964; Univ. of Man. M.A. 1968, Ph.D. 1991; Cert. Translator 1983; div.; children: Marc-Yvan, Francine Andréa; ASSOC. PROF. OF POL. SCI. ST. BONIFACE COLL. UNIV. OF MAN. 1989– (Asst. Prof. 1980); Pres. Trans-Excel Inc. Winnipeg; ed. Lance Publications 1964–65; Cons. M.D.T. Associates Winnipeg and Fredericton 1968–70; Rsch. Dir. N.B. Task Force Social Devel. 1970–71; Regional Dir. (Bathurst, N.B.) Community Improvement Corp. 1972–74; Dir. St. Boniface Coll. Rsch. Centre 1975–76; Asst. Dep. Min. of Edn. Man. 1976–79; Visiting Associate Professor: Univ. of Man., winter 1993; Univ. of Washington, summer 1992, 1993; Federal Electoral Boundaries Commission (Manitoba) 1993–94; Vice-Pres., Assoc. of Translators and Interpreters of Manitoba 1992– ; Mem., Nat. Conference Program Ctte., Inst. Pub. Adm. Can. 1991–92; mem. National Council, Network on the Constitution 1991–92; mem. Winnipeg Core Area Initiative Community Services & Facilities Adv. Council 1987–91, Chrmn. 1988–89; Dir. Festival du Voyageur Inc. Winnipeg 1988–91, 1st Vice Pres. 1990–91; mem. General Assembly, Social Sci. Federation of Can. 1986–89; mem. Man. Arts Council 1982–86, Exec. 1983–86, Chrmn. Music Ctte. 1983–86; Founding Chrmn. Man. Arts Gaming Fund Comn. 1984–86; Dir. Winnipeg Symphony Orch. 1981–82, Co-Chrmn. Prog. & Audience Devel. Ctte.; ed. and co-author 'Rendement académique et langue d'enseignement chez les élèves franco-manitobains' 1976; ed. 'Le Français au Manitoba: une histoire inachevée' in press; numerous articles various jours. and other publs.; pol. commentaries various newspapers and other media; mem. Canadian Club (Winnipeg); Inst. of Public Admin. of Can.; Candn. Pol. Sci. Assn.; Société québécoise de science politique; Assn. Translators & Interpreters Man.; recreations: hiking, swimming, bridge; Home: 397 Gaboury Place, Winnipeg, Man. R2H 0L5; Office: 200 ave. de la Cathédrale, St. Boniface, Man. R2H 0H7.

**HÉBERT, Roger,** B.Com., M.A.; pulp and paper executive; b. St-Hyacinthe, Que. 20 Nov. 1940; s. Adrien and Angela H.; e. Univ. de Montréal B.A. 1960, M.A. 1969; Concordia Univ. B.Com. 1963; Univ. of W. Ont. Mgmt. Devel. Prog. 1979; VICE PRES. ADMINISTRATION, CANADIAN PACIFIC FOREST PRODUCTS LTD. 1990– ; Office: 1250 René Lévesque Blvd. W., Montréal, Qué. H3B 4Y3.

**HECHT, Alfred,** B.Sc., M.A., Ph.d.; university professor; b. Steinfeld, Ukraine 26 Feb. 1942; s. Leonidas and Susanne (Krause) H.; e. Univ. of Manitoba B.Sc. 1964, M.A. 1968; Clark Univ. (Worcester, Mass.) Ph.D. 1972; m. Linda A. d. John and Tina Huebert 26 June 1965; children: Marvin A., Melinda M.; PROFESSOR, WILFRID LAURIER UNIV. 1982– ; High School Teacher 1964–65, 1968–69; Counsellor, Dept. of Manpower & Immigration 1967–68; Asst. Prof., Wilfrid Laurier Univ. 1972–76; Assoc. Prof. 1976–82; has taught various courses at other institutions; Visiting Prof., John F. Kennedy Inst. of N. Am. Studies Freie Univ. Berlin 1976, '79; Philips Univ. Marburg Germany, 1979, '90; Justus-Liebeg Universitat Giessen 1987; Canada Council Doctoral Fellow 1971–72; Clark Univ. Fellow 1969–72; Alexander von Humboldt Fellow 1980, '83, '86; Conrad Grebel College Fellow, Univ. of Waterloo 1985– ; consultant, shopping centre location; importer of Paraguayan Native Indian crafts; Pres., Candn. Assn. of Geographers (Ont. Div.) 1992–94; Mem., Assn. of Am. Geographers; Glencairn MB. Ch.; Former Moderator, Waterloo M.B. Ch. 1983–86; Bd. Mem., M.B. Conf. 1983–86; Eden Christian College Bd. Mem. 1980–83; editor: 'Regional Development in the Peripheries of Canada and Europe' 1983; co-author: 'Ethnicity and Well-Being in Ontario and Toronto' 1983, 'Regional Development in Ontario'; author/co-author of numerous articles; Home: 117 Ralston Pl., Waterloo, Ont. N2T 1C7; Office: Waterloo, Ont. N2L 3C5.

**HECKMAN, Gerald (Gerry) R.,** B.Eng.; bank executive; b. Montreal, Que. 6 May 1934; s. George F. and Gwen (Burdock) H.; e. McGill Univ. B.Eng. (Hons.) 1956; m. Therese d. Victor and Antoinette La Rue 8 Oct. 1966; one d.: Heidi Anne; VICE-PRES., TECHNOLOGY PLANNING & DEVEL., SYSTEMS & TECHNOLOGY, ROYAL BANK OF CANADA TORONTO 1985– ; Engineer, Bell Canada 1956; Bell Telephone Labs. N.J. 1962; Supervising Engr., Bell Canada 1961; Chief, Communication Systems, Royal Bank Montreal 1968; Head, Technical Support Systems 1972; Manager, Processing Systems 1976; Asst. General Mgr. 1980; Vice-Pres., Processing Systems Devel. 1982; Pres., Waterloo Adv. Council, Univ. of Waterloo; Mem. Bd. of Dirs., Candn. Business Telecommunications Alliance; Dir., Extve. Liaison, CBTA; Mem. Extve. Council, CBTA; Mem. Gandalf Advisory Council; Mem., Fac. of Environ. Studies Standing Ctte., Univ. of Waterloo; Assn. of Profl. Engrs. of Ont.; Pres., Catch the Canada Wave; recreations: tennis, skiing; Home: 516 Pipers Green, Oakville, Ont. L6M 1H2; Office: 315 Front St. W., Toronto, Ont. M5V 3A4.

**HEDDLE, John A.,** B.Sc., Ph.D.; biologist; b. Oakville, Ont. 9 Nov. 1938; s. Dunbar Moodie and Flora (McLaren) H.; e. Oakville Trafalgar High Sch. 1957; Univ. of Toronto, B.Sc. 1961; Univ. of Tenn. Ph.D. 1964; m. Judith Gail d. Jack and Olive McArthur 16 June 1962; children: Robert Moodie, Catharine Moodie; PROF. OF BIOL. AND SCIENCE STUDIES, YORK UNIV. 1976– ; Pres. Bio-Mutatech Inc. 1986–91; Pres., Mutatech Inc. 1992– ; James Picker Fellow, Oak Ridge Nat. Lab. 1964–65, Med. Rsch. Council Radiobiol. Rsch. Unit., Harwell, U.K. 1965–66; Asst. Rsch. Prof. Univ. of Cal. San Francisco 1966–70, Assoc. Prof. 1970–71; Assoc. Prof. present univ. 1971–76; Head of Genetics, Ludwig Inst. for Cancer Rsch. Toronto Br. 1980–84; Prof. of Med. Biophys. Univ. of Toronto 1981–84; mem. Min. Adv. Ctte. Mutagenesis Health & Welfare Can. & Environment Can.; Rep. Fedn. Biol. Soc's Can. on Tech. Adv. Ctte. to Atomic Energy of Canada Ltd. Nuclear Fuel Waste Mgmt. Prog. 1984– ; ed. 'New Horisons in Mutagenesis' 1981; N. Am. ed. 'Mutagenesis' 1985– ; mem. various ed. bds.; mem. Candn. Fedn. of Biological Socs.; Genetics Soc. Can.; Soc. Toxicol. Can.; Environmental Mutagen Soc. (Councillor 1974–77, Vice Pres. & Prog. Chrmn. 1985–86, Pres. 1986–87); Chrmn., Local Ctte., Internat. Congress Genetics, Toronto 1988; Past Pres., Genetics Soc. of Canada 1993–95 (Vice Pres. 1989–91; Pres. 1991–93); recreations: squash, gardening; Home: R.R. 1, Kleinburg, Ont. L0J 1C0; Office: 4700 Keele St., Toronto, Ont. M3J 1P3.

**HEDDON, Kenneth Frederick,** B.A.Sc.; retired company executive; b. Columbus, Ont. 27 Aug. 1912; s. Frederick John and Elsie (Orchard) H.; e. Oshawa Collegiate, Oshawa, Ont.; Univ. of Toronto, B.A.Sc., 1933; m. Doris B., d. Luther Bone, July 1939; Asst. Chassis Engr., General Motors Ltd., 1933–36; financial interest in Chrysler-Plymouth Dealership, 1936–38; Rep. Indust. & Wholesale Products, Sun Oil Co. Ltd. 1938–40; Tech. Rep., 1940–44; Mgr., Indust. Products & Wholesale Div., 1944–58; Dist. Mgr., London, Ont., 1958–59; Asst. Regional Mgr. (Western Region U.S.) Detroit, 1959–62; General Sales Manager, 1962–64; Pres., 1964; Vice Pres., Great Candn. Oil Sands Ltd. 1967; Pres., Great Can. Oil Sands Ltd., 1967; Chrm. of Bd. of Dir., Great Can. Oil Sands Ltd., 1977; Chrmn. of Bd. of Dirs., Sun Oil Ltd. 1972; retired from Sun Oil Co. Ltd., Aug. 1977; retired as Chrm., Great Can. Oil Sands Ltd., Aug. 1979; mem., Association Prof. Engineers Ontario; United Ch.; recreations: fishing, photography, music; Clubs: Granite; The Franklin; Home: 900 Wilson Rd. North, Suite 304, Oshawa, Ont. L1G 7T2.

**HEENAN, Roy Lacaud,** B.A., B.C.L.; lawyer; b. Mexico City 28 Sept. 1935; s. Ernest and Yvonne Mable (Lacaud) H.; e. Trinity Coll. Sch. 1953; McGill Univ. B.A. (Hons. Hist. and Pol. Sci.) 1957; McGill Univ. B.C.L. 1960; m. Rae d. Charles and Wynn MacCulloch 9 Oct. 1965; children: Louise, Charles, Anne, Julie-Claire; CHRMN. & SR. PARTNER, HEENAN BLAIKIE 1972– ; Dir. Candn. Bar Financial Corp.; called to Bar of Que. 1961; practiced with McMaster Meighen 1961–68; McCarthy, Monet, Johnston and Heenan 1968–72; Adjunct Prof., Labour Law McGill Univ. Fac. of Law 1972– , Lectr., Labour Law McGill Fac. of Mgmt. 1982–88, Laval Univ. 1979 and Univ. of Ottawa 1978–79, 1980–81, 1985; Lectr. on Arbitration, Queen's Industrial Relations Ctr. 1974– ; Mem., Consultative Ctte. of Justice to the Quebec Min. of Justice 1976–80; author various articles on labour law; Mem., Editorial Adv. Bd., Canada Law Book 'Labour Times' 1991– ; Mem. Ed. Adv. Bd., Carswell Publication 'Hiring and Firing' Newsletter 1990– ; Trustee, Queen's Univ.; Gov. Montreal Diocesan Coll.; Trinity Coll. Sch.; Chrmn., Adv. Bd., McGill Law Faculty 1990– ; past Pres. and Life Gov. Martlet Found.; K.C.L.J.; Montreal Mus. of Fine Arts (mem. Acquisition Ctte. Candn. Art); Anglican; recreations: skiing, tennis, squash, Canadian art; Clubs: Mount Royal; University; Montreal Indoor Tennis; Montreal Badminton & Squash; Montreal Racquet; The Hillside Tennis; Home: 3044 St. Sulpice, Montréal, Qué. H3H 1B5; Office: 1250 René-Lévesque Blvd. W., Ste. 2500, Montréal, Qué. H3B 4Y1.

**HEENAN, Terence F.,** B.Sc., B.E., Hon. D.Eng., Hon. D.Sc., P.Eng.; retired executive; b. Halifax, N.S. 3 Dec. 1926; s. late Joseph Gregory and late Margaret Lilian (Cable) H.; e. St. Mary's Univ., B.Sc. 1947; Hon. D.Sc. St. Mary's Univ. 1985; N.S. Tech. Coll. B.E. (Elect.) 1949; Tech. Univ. of N.S., Hon.D.Eng. 1980; children: Catherine Mary, Richard Gregory, Robert Michael, Martha Anne; joined Maritime Telegraph & Telephone Co. Ltd. 1949–65; Chrmn. Adv. Group to Bd. of Mgmt. & Exec. Asst. to Chrmn. of Bd., TransCanada Telephone System 1965–67; Vice Pres. Staff (Operations) B.C. Telephone Co. 1967, Vice Pres. Operations 1971–75, Vice Pres. Adm. and Chief Financial Offr. 1976–77; Pres., TransCanada Telephone System 1978–81; Pres. & C.E.O., AEL Microtel Ltd. 1982; Pres. & C.O.O., B.C. Telephone Co. 1983–87; former Dir. Telesat Can.; Past Chrmn. Candn. Telecommunication Carriers Assn.; former mem. Adv. Council B.C.I.T.; Past Chrmn., Bd. of Trustees, St. Paul's Hosp.; Past Dir., St. Paul's Hosp. Found.; Past Vice-Chrmn., Vancouver Bd. of Trade; Past Dir., Candn. Club of Vancouver; Past Bus. Gov., Vancouver Stock Exchange; mem. Assn. Prof. Engrs. Provs. B.C. and Ont.; Sr. mem. IEEE; Clubs: Royal Ottawa Golf; Vancouver; Shaughnessy Golf; Home: 10, 4900 Cartier St., Vancouver, B.C. V6M 4H2.

**HEERSINK, Ewout Reinald,** B.A., M.B.A., C.A.; financial executive; b. Netherlands 11 July 1950; s. the late Jan and Grada Willemena (Hillen) H.; e. Univ. of Western Ont. B.A. (Hons. Bus.) 1973; Queen's Univ. M.B.A. 1974; m. Lynn d. Orville and Kathleen Wilson 17 May 1980; children: Alysa, Kelsey, Benjamin, Jordan, Jeremy; CHIEF FINANCIAL OFFICER & VICE-PRES., ONEX CORPORATION 1983– ; Auditing, Cons. & Business Valuations, Peat Marwick Mitchell 1974–79; Extve. Asst. to Pres., CanWest Capital Corp. 1979–83; Dir., Dayton Superior; Delfield; Sky Chefs; Protestant; Mem., Candn. Inst. of C.A.s; recreations: tennis, golf; club: Boulevard; Credit Valley Country & Golf; Home: 31 Colonial Cres., Oakville, Ont.; Office: P.O. Box 700, 161 Bay St., Toronto, Ont. M5J 2S1.

**HEES, Hon. George Harris,** O.C., P.C. (1957); b. Toronto, Ont. 17 June 1910; s. Harris Lincoln and Mabel Mills (Good) H.; e. Trinity Coll. Sch., Port Hope, Ont.; Roy. Mil. Coll., 1927–31; Univ. of Toronto, 1931–33; Cambridge Univ., Eng., 1933–34; m. Mabel Ferguson, d. Hon. E. A. Dunlop, 30 June 1934; children: Katherine Mabel, Martha Ann, Roslyn Georgia; def. cand. for Spadina to H. of C. at g.e. 1945; 1st el. to H. of C. for Toronto-Broadview, by-el., May 1950; not a cand. in g.e. Apr. 1963; apptd. Min. of Transport, 22 June 1957, Min. of Trade & Comm. 11 Oct. 1960; resigned from Diefenbaker Cabinet 9 Feb. 1963; former Pres., P. Cons. Assn. of Canada (el. 1954); apptd. Pres., Montreal and Canadian Stock Exchanges, Apl. 1964, resigning to re-enter active politics, Sept. 1965; el. to 16th H. of C. for Northumberland, g.e. 8 Nov. 1965 and for Prince Edward-Hastings in g.e. June 1968, 1972, 1974; and for Northumberland (formerly Prince Edward Hastings) 1979, 1980 and 1984; Chrmn. of Candn. Sect. of Can.-U.S. Permanent Joint Bd. on Defense, Oct. 1979 – Dec. 1983; Min. of Veterans Affairs 1984–88; Canada's first Minister of State for Seniors 1987–88; apptd. Ambassador at Large, Nov. 1988; served in World War, 1939–45; Bgde. Maj., 5th Inf. Bgde.; wounded in Holland, Nov. 1944; LL.D. (Hon.), Waterloo Univ. Coll. 1961; Dr. of Mil. Sci. (Hon.), Royal Mil. Coll., Kingston, Ont. 1988; Officer of the Order of Canada 1989; Zeta Psi; P. Conservative; Anglican; Clubs: Badminton & Racquet; Home: 55 Belmont St., Toronto, Ont. M5R 1R1.

**HEFFELFINGER, George,** B.A.; company officer; b. Minneapolis, Minn. 15 Oct. 1926; s. George W.P. and Ruth J. H.; e. Blake Sch., Minneapolis; Univ. of Minn., B.A.; m. Jane, d. Henry Glenn Sayler, Fargo, N. Dakota, 22 July 1949; children: Totton, Park, Adam, Lisa, Amanda; PRES., HIGHCROFT ENTERPRISES LTD.; Chrmn., Monday Publications Ltd.; Dir., Mega Enterprises Ltd.; N. American Life Assurance Co.; began as Elevator Helper, National Grain Co., Grenfell, Sask. 1949, Div. Mgr. 1955, Pres. 1960, Chrmn. 1974; served with U.S. Navy as Seaman 1944–45; S. Pacific Theatre; Dir., Pacific Opera Assn.; American Bonsai Assn.; Home: 3155 Rutland Rd., Victoria, B.C. V8R 3R7 Office: 1609 Blanshard St., Victoria, B.C. V8W 2J5.

**HEFFERNAN, Peter F.J.;** bank executive; b. Toronto, Ont.; m. Christine Hosegood; one s.: Gavin Barclay; SENIOR VICE-PRESIDENT, BANK OF NOVA SCOTIA 1983– ; various positions to sr. mngt., Bank of Montreal 1966–77; various positions in Canada & Paris leaving as Vice-Pres., Banque Nat. de Paris 1977–83; Fellow, Inst. of Candn. Bankers; Jr. Master, Am. Contract Bridge League; recreations: fishing, skiing, windsurfing; clubs: Annabel's, Fitness Inst.: Office: 44 King St. W., 8th fl., Toronto, Ont. M5H 1H1.

**HEIDEBRECHT, Arthur Cornelius,** B.Sc., M.S., Ph.D., P.Eng., F.C.S.C.E.; educator; b. Camrose, Alta. 13 Aug. 1939; s. Cornelius Kornelius and Neta Aganeta (Tjart) H.; e. Univ. of Alta. B.Sc. (Civil Engn.) 1960; Northwestern Univ. M.S. 1961, Ph.D. 1963; m. 1stly Ruth Bertha d. Ludwig and Emma Moltzahn 20 Dec. 1960 (d.); m. 2ndly Margaret Elinor d. Earle and Kaye Haase 14 July 1978; children: by 1st marriage, Douglas Arthur, Allan James, Joanne Carol; by 2nd marriage, Christine Louise, David William; PROVOST AND VICE-PRESIDENT (ACADEMIC), McMASTER UNIV. 1989–94, Prof. of Civil Engn. & Engn. Mechanics 1974– ; Asst. Prof. present Univ. 1963, Assoc. Prof. 1968, Chrmn. of Civil Engn. & Engn. Mechanics 1968–71, 1974–77; Dean of Engineering 1981–89; Visiting Prof. Univ. of Southampton 1971–72; Visiting Prof. Univ. of Bristol 1986–87; mem. and Vice Pres., Candn. Assoc. for Earthquake Engn.; mem. Candn. Nat. Comte. on Earthquake Engn. (Chrmn. 1975–81); Candn. Soc. Civil Engrs.; Am. Soc. Engn. Educ.; Seismol. Soc. Am.; Earthquake Engn. Research Inst.; Assn. Prof. Engrs. Prov. Ont.; Fellow, Candn. Academy of Engineering; Fellow, Candn. Soc. for Civil Engn.; Presbyterian; recreations: tennis, badminton, cross-country skiing; Club: Hamilton; Home: 7 Soble Place, Dundas, Ont.; Office: McMaster Univ., 1280 Main St. W., Hamilton, Ont. L8S 4K1.

**HEIDECKER, Brian Richard;** farmer, businessman, corporate director; b. Coronation, Alta. 29 Oct. 1944; s. Arthur R. and Muriel A. (Hood) H.; e. Coronation Sch., sr. matric. 1961; Camrose Lutheran College, interdisciplinary studies 1988; m. Gail d. Dick and Fran Davies 9 April 1966; children: Shelley Lynn, William Arthur, Brenda Jean, Lee Allisson; OWNER, DRYLANDER RANCH LTD. 1966– and CAMROSE RESTAURANTS LTD. 1990– ; Drylander Ranch Ltd. now consists of 9,760 acres sustaining a 750 cow-calf operation & 4,000 acres of grain (started from scratch in 1966); Dir., Bank of Canada (Alta.) 1986– ; Alta. Agric. Devel. Corp. 1985–90; Alta. Securities Comn. 1988– ; Small Business Person of the Year, Alta. C. of C. 1983; Outstanding Young Farmer Award, Second 1982; Dir., Canada West Found. 1987– ; Camrose Internat. Inst. 1989– ; Senate, Univ. of Alta. 1991– ; Mem., Finance Policy Task Force, Agriculture Canada 1989–91; Dir., Prairie Assn. for Water Mngt. 1983–89; Dir., Candn. Cattlemen's Assn. 1979–83; Alta. Cattle Comn. 1976–87; Southern Vice-Pres., P.C. Party of Alta. 1987–90; Pres., Crowfoot P.C. (Fed.) Assn. 1989–91; Treas., Chinook P.C. (Prov.) Assn. 1985–89; Candidate, Alta. P.C. Senatorial Selection 1989; author of 1 book chapter; recreations: skiing, golf; Address: Box 549, Coronation, Alta. T0C 1C0.

**HEIDENREICH, Rosmarin,** M.A., Ph.D.; educator; b. Winkler, Man. 14 Sept. 1943; d. Dr. Victor and Elisabeth (Dyck) Peters; e. Moorhead State Univ. B.A. 1964; Univ. of Man. M.A. 1966; Univ. of Toronto Ph.D. 1983; children: Stephanie Andrea, Jacob Philip Sebastian; PROF. OF ENG. AND OF TRANSL. SAINT-BONIFACE COLL. UNIV. OF MAN. 1983– ; Lectr. in Eng. Univs. of Tübingen and Freiburg, Germany 1969–74; Visiting Prof. Inst. Candn. Studies Univ. of Augsburg, Germany 1990 and Univ. canadienne en France, Villefranche-sur-mer 1991; radio author and cons. Südwestfunk, Freiburg, Germany 1972; TV Moderator 'Telekolleg Englisch' series Südwestfunk, Baden-Baden, Germany 1972; interviewer and researcher 'The Battle of Mons' BBC-TV London 1972; freelance transl.; past mem. Man. Arts Council and Prix La Liberté Juries; Dir. Westgate Mennonite Coll. Inst. 1989–92; author 'The Postwar Novel in Canada. Narrative Strategies and Reader Response' 1989; numerous essays, articles & reviews various Candn. and Eur. jours. & colls.; Dir. 'Les Editions du Blé' 1986–89; contbg. ed. 'Prairie Fire' since 1986; Publ. Ctte. Man. Writers Guild 1985–87; mem. editoral ctte., several journals; mem., various profl. assocs.; recreations: swimming, music, theatre; Home: 226 Elm St., Winnipeg, Man. R3M 3P2; Office: 200 ave. de la Cathédrale, Saint-Boniface, Man. R2H 0H7.

**HEIGHTON, John Steven,** M.A.; editor; writer; b. Toronto, Ont. 14 Aug. 1961; s. John McEwen and Lambie George (Stephanopoulos) H.; e. Silverthorn Coll. Inst. 1980; Queen's Univ. B.A. 1985, M.A. 1986; m. Mary d. Robert and Susan Huggard 26 Aug. 1988; ED. QUARRY MAG. 1988– ; contbr. poetry, fiction and critical articles nat. and internat. periodicals and anthols. since 1984; author 'Stalin's Carnival' (poetry) 1989; 'Foreign Ghosts' (travelogue/poetry) 1989; 'Flight Paths of the Emperor' (fiction) 1992; Home: 675 Johnson St., Kingston, Ont. K7L 2A7; Office: P.O. Box 1061, Kingston, Ont. K7L 4Y5.

**HEIMBECKER, Herbert Charles,** B.S.A.; grain company executive; b. Elmira, Ont. 24 Oct. 1921; s. Clayton William and Hilda Marie (Fischer) H.; e. Runnymede Coll. Inst. 1939; Univ. of Guelph B.S.A. 1943; three s. David Murray, Donald John, Alan Ray; CHRMN. & C.E.O., PARRISH & HEIMBECKER LTD. 1962– ; Dir. Goderich Elevators Ltd.; Dover Industries Ltd.; Chrmn., New-Life Mills Ltd.; Smith Brokerage Ltd., Saint John, N.B.; mem. Agric. Inst. Can.; recreation: golf; Clubs: Islington Golf; Home: HC 1, 88 Erskine Ave., Toronto, Ont. M4P 1Y3.

**HEIMBECKER, Raymond,** M.D., M.A., M. Surg., F.R.C.S.(C.), F.A.C.S.; b. Calgary, Alta. 29 Nov. 1922; s. Harry O. and Dorothy A. (Turner) H.; e. Univ. of Sask., B.A. 1944; Univ. of Toronto, M.D. 1947, M.A. 1950, M. Surg. 1957; m. Kathleen Jensen, 18 Nov. 1950; children: Kathleen, Raymond, Harry, Anita, Constance; PROF. EMERITUS, UNIV. OF WEST. ONT.; former Chief Surgeon Cardiovasc. and Thoracic Surg., Univ. Hosp., London, Ont. 1973–86; formerly Asst. Professor, Dept. of Surgery, Univ. Toronto & Surgeon, Toronto Gen. Hosp.; Visiting Prof. in more than 40 med. centres in N. Am. as well as India, Beijing, Jerusalem, Great Britain, Paris, Saudi Arabia, Brazil, and Tokyo; helped perform the first heart valve transplant in 1956 and carried out world's 1st mitral valve transplant 1967; initiated Canada's first modern heart transplant (cyclosporin) program 1981; Volunteer Physician, Bahama Wilderness (winters); mem., Bishop Strachan Sch. Foundation; served in C.O.T.C., 1941–45; Assoc. ed., 'European Surg. Research' and Candn. Journ. Cardiology; Publications: over 160 book chapters and med. articles incl. most recent 'The History of Heart Valve Surgery' and 'Medical Aid in Southern Waters' 1991; former Examiner Royal Coll. Phys. & Surgeons; former Gov. for Ont., Am. Coll. of Chest Phys. and member presidential committee; mem., Soc. Univ. Surgs.; Internat. Cardiovascular Soc.; Soc. for Vascular Surg.; Am. Assn. Thoracic Surg.; Soc. for Thoracic Surg.; Candn. Cardiovascular Soc.; Am. Heart Assn.; Candn. Soc. Microcirculation (Former Pres.); Am. Surg. Assn.; rec'd George Armstrong Peters Award (Exper. Surg.) 1950, Lister Award (Exper. Surg.) 1957; Gold Medal, Royal Coll. of Phys. and Surg. 1967; Special Award from Rose Fndn. of India 1976; First Gordon Murray Memorial Lectureship, Univ. of Toronto 1981; The Medal of Jeddah, Saudi Arabia March 1984; Hon. Mem., College of Medicine Alumni Assn., Univ. of Sask. 1984; First P.K. Sen Meml. Lectr., King Edward Memorial Med. School, Bombay, India 1985; Hon. Mem., Beijing Heart Inst. 1985; 2nd W.G. Bigelow Annual Lectr., Royal Coll. of Physicians & Surgeons of Can. 1985; 3rd Conrad Lam Annual Lectr., Henry Ford Hosp., Detroit 1986; Mem., A.O.A. Honor Med. Soc. 1986; Special Mem., Soc. Cardiovascular and Thoracic Surgeon, Gt. Britain and Ireland 1987; Sr. Hon. Mem., Candn. Med. Assn. 1989; el. Assoc. Mem., Am. Watercolor Soc. 1990; Hon. Mem., Candn. Soc. Cardiovascular & Thoracic Surgeons 1992; Anglican; recreations: sailing, fishing, farming, flying; Clubs: Badminton & Racquet (Toronto); Hunt (London); Royal Canadian Yacht; Nut Island Shooting; Hopetown Sailing; Address: (summer) R.R. #1, Collingwood, Ont. L9Y 3Y9 and (winter) Toad Hall, Hopetown Abaco, The Bahamas.

**HEINBECKER, Paul,** B.A.; diplomat; b. Kitchener, Ont. 18 Sept. 1941; s. Earl William and Shirley Frieda (Baty) H.; e. Wilfrid Laurier Univ. B.A. (Hons.) 1965; m. Ayse d. Sabahat Köymen 8 Feb. 1969; children: Yasemin, Céline; AMBASSADOR, CANADIAN EMBASSY, BONN, GERMANY 1992– ; joined Foreign Affairs & Internat. Trade Canada 1965; various positions Canada and abroad 1965–85; Minister, Candn. Embassy, Washington 1985–89; Sr. Policy Advisor & Speech Writer for the Prime Minister Ottawa 1989–91; Foreign Policy Advisor for the P.M. & Asst. Sec. to the Cabinet (Fgn. & Defence Policy), Privy Council Office 1991–92; Hon. Doctorate, Wilfrid Laurier Univ.; num. speeches and articles on Candn. fgn. policy on behalf of Candn. govt. leaders 1983–93; recreation: tennis; Home: Fasanenstrasse 25, 53179 Bonn, Germany; Office: Friedrich-Wilhelm-Str. 18, 53113 Bonn, Germany.

**HEINE-BAUX, Manfred,** M.F.A., Ph.D.; artist, painter and printmaker; b. Munich, W. Germany 24 Dec. 1940; s. Dr. Helmut and Inge (Schmidt) H.; e. Acad. of Fine Arts, Munich, M.F.A., Ph.D. in Art Hist. 1965; Candn. citizen; Assoc. Prof., Acad. of Fine Arts, Munich (Stone Lithography and Aquatint-Etching) 1965–66; travelled extensively, painting and exhibiting 1967–77; first exhbn., Thomson Gall., New York City 1974; portrait commissioned by King Faisal 1974; exhbn., Goethe Inst. of Teheran, Iran 1975; Living Arts Biennale, Johannesburg, 1st prize in Painting 1976; group exhbn., Le Grand Palais, Paris 1977; Maxwell Gall. San Francisco 1980; exhbn. (with Dali, Chagall), Munich 1983; exhbns. in New York, Montreal, Toronto 1984–88; exhbns. in Ont., Philadelphia, Detroit 1988–91; represented in many public and corporate collections in Europe, USA, Canada and Japan incl.: Univ. of Kyoto, Univ. of Toronto, Museum of Fine Arts in Munich; various television appearances in Canada; Friend, Royal Candn. Acad.; Soc. of Candn. Artists; recreation: travel; Address: 641 Queenston Rd., Cambridge, Ont. N3H 3K2.

**HEINKE, Gary W.,** M.A.Sc., Ph.D., P.Eng.; educator; b. Austria 11 Dec. 1932; s. Erich and Maria (Schwabe) H.; e. Univ. of Toronto B.A.Sc. 1956, M.A.Sc. 1961; McMaster Univ. Ph.D. 1969; m. 1989; children: Elizabeth Hibberd, Richard Heinke; PROF. OF CIVIL ENGN., UNIV. OF TORONTO 1974– ; Cons. Eng. G.E. Hanson Associates Toronto 1956–61; Fischer & Porter Ltd. Philadelphia and W. Germany 1961–62; Partner, Urban Engineering Consultants Toronto 1962–65; joined Univ. of Toronto 1962, full-time 1968, Chrmn. of Civil Engn. 1974–84, Dean of Applied Sci. and Engn. 1986–93; cons. to govts., ind. and bus. specializing in northern environmental eng.; co-author 'Environmental Science and Engineering' 1989; recreation: tennis; Home: Upper 6, 2 Airdrie Rd., Toronto, Ont. M4G 1L7; Office: 35 St. George St., Toronto, Ont. M5S 1A4.

**HEINRICH, Charles G.,** B.Sc., M.B.A.; business executive; consultant; b. Budapest, Hungary 31 March 1941; s. Gabor A. and Louise M. (de Erney) de Heinrich; e. Loyola Coll. 1957; Mass. Inst. Technol. B.Sc. 1964; McGill Univ. M.B.A. 1966; m. Louise E. d. John Henry Richardson 8 Apl. 1968; two d. Christina, Susan; various tech. positions Northern Electric 1957–66; Royal Comn. Bilingualism & Biculturalism 1964–66; Lectr. McGill and Loyola Univs. 1967–68; Alcan Smelters & Chemicals, Econ. Analyst 1966, Mgr. Info. & Planning Arvida 1968, Mgr. Smelting Div. 1970, Smelter Rsch. & Devel. Dir. 1971, Chief Financial Offr. 1974; Alcan Products Ltd., Vice Pres. and Dir. Corporate Services 1976, Vice Pres. & Gen. Mgr. 1980–85; Alcan Aluminium Ltd., Pres. Wire & Cable Div. 1985–89, Pres. Alcan Pacific 1988–89; Pres. & C.E.O., Sherritt Gordon Ltd. 1990; Extve. in residence, Fac. of Commerce and Bus. Admin., Univ. of B.C., spring 1991; mem. Vancouver Art Gallery; Vancouver Bd. Trade; Can.-Japan Soc.; recreations: golf, tennis, skiing, music; Clubs: Canadian; Montreal Badminton & Squash; Mount Royal Tennis (Montreal); Granite (Toronto); Shaughnessy Golf & Country (Vancouver); Home: #37, 5760 Hampton Place, Vancouver, B.C. V6T 2G1.

**HEINRICHS, Elfrieda Elizabeth,** B.A., A.Music; full time volunteer; b. Kitchener, Ont. 1 Jan. 1936; d. Peter George and Anna Petrovna (Becker) Dick; e. Univ. of Toronto B.A. (Hons.) 1959; Univ. of Western Ont. A.Music (piano, 1st class hons.) 1954 (Gold Medalist); m. Vern s. Julius and Mary H. 26 Dec. 1959; children: Debra Cecile, Anne Marie; Secondary School Teacher 1959–64 (History & German language); Bd. of Dir., Ceci Heinrichs Found. for Developmentally Handicapped Children (Pres.) 1975– ; The Bayview Glen Found. 1979–82; The Heinrichs Found. (Pres.) 1987– ; Schoolhouse Concerts 1965–69; Ceci's Homes for Children 1979–84 (Pres. 1979–84); Oriana Singers 1985–89; Ont. Choral Fed. 1985–92 (Pres. 1988–90); Assn. of Candn. Choral Conductors 1990– ; Steering Ctte., Podium '92 1990–92; 150th Anniversary Ctte., Little Trinity Ch. Toronto 1991–92; Mem. Advisory Council, Ont. Choral Federation 1993– ; Dir., University of Toronto Foundation 1994; Mem., Art Gall. of Ont.; Royal Ont. Mus.; McMichael Gall.; Stratford Festival; Shaw Festival; Elora Festival; Guelph Spring Festival; National Ballet of Canada; Maestro Club (TSO); President's Ctte., Univ. of Toronto; Art Institute of Chicago; Metro. Mus. of Art N.Y.C.; Metro. Opera Guild; English Speaking Union, London, U.K.; The Assn. for the Severely Handicapped (International); Canadian Women's Club, London, U.K.; Royal Acad. of Arts, U.K.; active in promoting peace & conflict resolution studies, Univ. of Toronto; Anglican; recreations: extensive foreign travel, Iyengar Yoga, collecting Mennonite quilts; Home: One Upper Brook Street, London W1Y 1PA, United Kingdom.

**HEISEY, Wm. Lawrence,** M.B.A.; b. Toronto, Ont. 29 May 1930; s. Karl Brooks and Alice Isobel (Smith) H.; e. Lawrence Park Coll. Inst. Toronto 1948; Univ. of Toronto Trinity Coll. B.A. 1952; Harvard Business Sch. M.B.A. 1954; m. Barclay Ann d. Norval and Llewellyn Smith 24 July 1973; children: Janet Elizabeth, Mark Alexander; PRES., MARKFIELD HOLDINGS LIMITED 1990– ; Dir., Aetna Life Insurance Co. of Canada 1988– ; Gov., FINSCO Services Ltd. 1985– ; Dir., The Business Depot Ltd.; joined Procter & Gamble 1954–67 serving as Asst. Product Mgr., Mgr. of Advertising Prodns. Div.; Exec. Vice Pres., Standard Broadcast Sales 1967; Pres. and Dir., Harlequin Enterprises Ltd. 1971–82, Chrmn. 1982–90, Chrmn. Emeritus 1991– ; Dir.: Torstar Corp. 1980–90, and mem. Exec. Ctte. 1982–88; Mills & Boon Ltd. (London, Eng.) and other Harlequin subsidiaries 1972–90; Unicorp Canada Corp. 1988–90; recipient Donald B. McCaskill Award for Marketing Excellence, Am. Marketing Assn. Toronto 1981; Dir., Toronto French Sch. 1966–73, Chrmn. 1967–71, Hon. Dir. 1973– , Foundation Trustee 1978–82; Gov., Banff Centre 1982–88; Mem., Bd. of Govs., York Univ.; Bd. of Dirs., Candn. Film Centre; The National Ballet of Canada; Dir., Toronto Chamber Players 1983–84; Dir., Canadian Opera Company 1984–86; Chrmn., Comm. Div. Un. Way Toronto 1983–84; Dir., Bureau Broadcast Measurement 1963–69; Assn. Candn. Advertisers 1964–66; Zeta Psi; P. Conservative; Clubs: Granite; Badminton & Racquet; Home: 9 Highland Ave., Toronto, Ont. M4W 2A2.

**HEITNER, Philip,** B.E., M.B.A.; investment executive; b. Montreal, Que. 19 March 1942; s. Michael and Jeannine (Sauriol) H.; e. McGill Univ. B.E. 1965, M.B.A. 1969; m. Sandra d. Hyman and Rose Dubrofsky 3 July 1966; children: Danna Stacey, Stuart Howard; PRESIDENT, BANK OF MONTREAL INVESTMENT COUNSEL LTD. 1993– ; Sales Rep. Union Carbide 1965–67; Mgr. Mortgages & R.E. Invests. Royal Trust 1969–74; Portfolio Mgr. Capital Dynamics 1974–75; Extve. Vice Pres. & Dir. of Rsch., Nesbitt Thomson Inc. 1975–93; Lectr. McGill Univ. M.B.A. Evening Prog. 1969–79; Trustee Financial Analysts Fedn., Invest. Workshop; Past Chrmn. Edn. Prog. Toronto Soc. Financial Analysts, Chrmn. Award Ctte.; Trustee Candn. Council Financial Analysts; mem. Assn. Investment Mgmt. & Rsch. Council of Examiners; Home: 1 Lafayette Pl., Thornhill, Ont. L3T 1G4; Office: 21F, 150 King St. W., Toronto, Ont. M5H 3W2.

**HELD, Peter E.,** F.C.A.; chartered accountant; b. Cape Town, S. Africa 23 Dec. 1937; s. Herbert and Hilda (Falkenstein) H.; e. elem. and high schs. S. Africa; Univ. of Witwatersrand C.T.A. 1959; C.A. 1960; m. Gyneth d. Louis and Gladys Gordon 20 Oct. 1965; children: Heather E., Michael S.; MNG. PARTNER TORONTO REGION, BDO DUNWOODY WARD MALLETTE 1981– , Exec. Ctte. 1984–90, Partner 1964– , Nat. Chrmn. 1986–87, Executive Partner 1988–89, Nat. Chrmn., 1989–90; articled Leveton Boner & Co. Johannesburg 1955–60; C.A., Andrew W. Barr & Co. London, Eng. 1960–61; joined present Co. 1961; Dir. Kiwanis Club Trenton 1964–65; Un. Way Metrop. Toronto (Div. Chrmn. 1976); Parents Assn. Gifted Children's Edn. 1980–82; Candn. Paraplegic Assn. (Div. Chrmn. 1984); The Toronto Mendelssohn Choir 1987–89; C.O.I.N. 1987–88; Mem. Adv. Counc., Financial Admin. Services, York Univ. 1987–89; Mem., Acctg. Adv. Counc., Univ. of Waterloo 1992– ; ed. 'Check Mark' 1980–84, ed. adv. bd. 1980–87 (Chrmn. 1985–86); mem. German-Candn. Bus. & Profl. Assn.; Candn.-German Chamber Ind. & Comm.; Toronto Bd. Trade; mem. Council, Inst. C.A.'s Ont. 1978–87, Exec. Ctte. 1981–87, Pres. 1986–87; Bd. of Govs., Candn. Inst. C.A.'s 1984–88 and 1989–92, Exec. Ctte. 1985–87 and 1989–92, 2nd Vice Pres. 1989–90, 1st Vice Chrmn. 1990–91, Chrmn. 1991–92; Pres. Toronto C.A.'s Assn. 1974–75, Bd. of Govs., Candn. Comprehensive Auditing Found. 1990–92; Dir., C.A.A. Toronto 1987–89; Inst. of Corp. Dirs. 1992– ; Bd. of Dirs., Ont. Chamber of Commerce 1994– ; N. York YMCA; recreations: golf, reading, music; Clubs: Donalda (Dir. 1979–82); Ontario (Dir. 1984– , Pres. 1988–89, 1st Vice Pres. 1987–88, 2nd Vice Pres. 1986–87); Home: 47 Foxwarren Dr., Willowdale, Ont. M2K 1L1; Office: (P.O. Box 32) Royal Bank Plaza, Toronto, Ont. M5J 2J8.

**HELLEINER, Christopher Walter,** B.A., Ph.D.; educator; b. Vienna, Austria 21 March 1930; s. late Karl Ferdinand Maria and Grethe (Deutsch) H.; e. Brown Sch. and Oakwood Coll. Inst. Toronto 1948; Univ. of Toronto B.A. 1952, Ph.D. 1955; Oxford Univ. postdoctoral 1955–57; m. Mary Margaret d. late Frederick Harold Burbidge, Toronto, Ont. 20 May 1955; children: Edith Caroline, Margaret Hope; PROF. OF BIOCHEM., FACULTY MED. DALHOUSIE UNIV. since 1965; Research Scient. Princess Margaret Hosp. Toronto 1957–63; Asst. Prof. of Med. Biophysics Univ. of Toronto 1959–63; Asst. Prof. of Biochem. Dalhousie Univ. 1963, Assoc. Prof. 1964–65; Prof. and Head of Biochem. 1965–1979; former mem. Bd. Halifax Grammar Sch.; mem. N.S. Bird Soc.; Orchid Soc. of N.S.; Candn. Biochem. Soc.; numerous articles in scient. journs.; Home: 834 Marlborough Ave., Halifax, N.S. B3H 3G6; Office: Sir Charles Tupper Med. Bldg., Halifax, N.S. B3H 4H7.

**HELLEINER, Gerald Karl,** Ph.D., F.R.S.C., LL.D. (Hon.); educator; b. St. Polten, Austria 9 Oct. 1936; s. Karl Ferdinand and Grethe (Deutsch) H.; e. Univ. of Toronto B.A. 1958; Yale Univ. Ph.D. 1962; LL.D. (Hon.), Dalhousie Univ. 1988; m. Georgia d. George and Vera Stirrett 16 Aug. 1958; children: Jane Leslie, Eric Noel, Peter David; PROF. OF ECON., UNIV. OF TORONTO 1971– ; Asst. Prof., Yale Univ. 1961–65; Assoc. Prof. present Univ. 1965; Assoc. Rsch. Fellow, Nigerian Inst. Social & Econ. Rsch. 1962–63; Dir., Econ. Rsch. Bureau Dar es Salaam, Tanzania 1966–68; Visiting Fellow, Inst. Devel. Studies, Sussex 1971–72, 1975; Queen Elizabeth House, Oxford 1979; Chrmn., North-South Inst. 1990–92; Dir., Friends of l'Arche 1980–92; Internat. Development Research Centre 1985–91; Internat. Food Policy Rsch. Inst., Chrmn. 1990– ; West Toronto Special Needs Support Group; mem., U.N. Ctte. for Develop. Planning 1984–89; North-South Roundtable; cons. various world orgns.; author 'Peasant Agriculture, Government and Economic Growth in Nigeria' 1966; 'International Trade and Economic Development' 1972; 'International Economic Disorder' 1980; 'Intra-firm Trade and the Developing Countries' 1981; 'The New Global Economy and the Developing Countries' 1990; ed. 'Agricultural Planning in East Africa' 1968; 'A World Divided' 1976; 'For Good or Evil' 1982; 'Africa and the International Monetary Fund' 1986; 'The Other Side of International Development Policy' 1989; 'Trade Policy, Industrialization and Development: New Perspectives' 1992; mem., Candn. Econ. Assn.; Royal Econ. Soc.; Am. Econ. Assn.; African Studies Assn.; Candn. Assn. for Studies in Internat. Development; Royal African Soc.; Pres., Candn. Assn. African Studies 1969; recreations: hiking; Office: Toronto, Ont. M5S 1A1.

**HELLEINER, Mary Burbidge,** B.A., LL.B.; legal executive; b. Toronto, Ont. 30 Apr. 1933; d. Frederick Harold and Helen Hope (Heggie) Burbidge; e. Oriole Park Sch. 1946; Havergal Coll. 1951; Univ. of Toronto B.A. (Hons.) 1955; Dalhousie Law Sch. LL.B. 1974; m. Dr. Christopher s. Karl and Grethe H. 20 May 1955; children: Edith Caroline Fisher, Margaret Hope Bennett; EXTVE. DIR., LAW FOUNDATION OF N.S. 1977– ; articled clerk, Stewart, MacKeen & Covert, Halifax 1974–75; Admin. Asst., Dalhousie Law Sch. 1975–77; Editor, N.S. Law News 1974–89; Mem., N.S. Barristers' Soc.; Candn. Bar Assn.; Orchid Soc. of N.S. (Founding Mem. & Pres. 1989–90); author: 'Case Law Indexing in Canada' 1980, 'Standards for Case Identification' 1984 as well as gardening articles esp. on orchid growing; recreations: gardening, playing recorder; Home: 834 Marlborough Ave., Halifax, N.S. B3H 3G6; Office: Box 325, Halifax, N.S. B3J 2N7.

**HELLER, Susanna,** B.F.A.; painter; b. New York, N.Y. 13 Mar. 1956; d. Irving Israel and Zelda Sara (Cohen) H.; e. Westmount H.S. Montrea; N.S. Coll. of Art & Design B.F.A. 1978; teacher, N.S. Coll. of Art & Design; Parsons Sch. of Art N.Y.; State Univ. of N.Y.; Sara Lawrence Coll. N.Y.; McMaster Univ.; solo exhibitions: Concordia Univ. Montreal 1991; Tomoko Liguori Gallery 1988, '90; Grunwald Gall. Toronto 1989; Mount St. Vincent Univ. Art Gall. 1989; Grunwald and Watterson Toronto 1986, '87; Galerie Paul Andriesse Amsterdam 1986; Anna Leonowens Gall. Halifax 1977, '85; Embassy Cultural House London 1985; Saidye Bronfman Ctr. Montreal 1978; The Shooting Gall. Halifax 1976; group exhibitions incl.: Jack Tilton Gall. N.Y. 1991; 'Small Works,' Tomoko Liguori Gall. 1990; Chicago Internat. Art Exposition 1990; '49th Parallel,' N.Y. 1989; 'Art on Paper,' Weatherspoon Art Gall. 1989; 'Gallery Artists,' Tomoko Liguori Gall. and over 20 others; selected collections: Air Canada Corp.; Candn. Art Bank; Concordia Univ. Art Gall.; Osler, Hoskin and Harcourt Toronto; Toronto Dominion Bank; Weatherspoon Art Gall. Greensboro, NC and numerous corp., public & private collections in U.S. and abroad; Olga Korper Gall. Toronto, rep.; recipient, Canada Council B Grants (1 yr Paris Studio; Guggenheim Fellowship 1988; National Endowment for the Arts 1991–92 and other awards; subject of many reviews; Home: 262 Franklin St., Brooklyn, N.Y. 11222.

**HELLIKER, John,** B.A., M.A.; film director, producer; b. Toronto, Ont. 16 July 1951; s. John Alexander and Margaret Elizabeth (Gibson) H.; e. Syracuse Univ. B.A. 1972; Beijing Univ., philosophy dipl. 1976; York Univ. M.A. 1978, Ph.D. (all but dissertation) 1979; m. Denise d. Tom and Cecile O'Rourke 10 Apr. 1986; PRES., LAVA PICTURES LIMITED; Resident, Candn. Film Centre 1991; films: Writer/Co-Prod., 'Don't Call me Stupid' 1983 (winner of Columbus & Am. Film Festivals); Prod., 'Killing Time' 1988; 'Beach Story'1991; Dir./Co-Prod., 'Norha and the Microbabe' 1991; TV series: Writer, 'Indonesia: A Generation of Change' 1986; Production Mgr., 'OWL-TV' 1986–87; Home: 184 Wright Ave., Toronto, Ont. M6R 1L2.

**HELLIWELL, David Leedom,** B.A., C.A., F.C.A.; b. Vancouver, B.C. 26 July 1935; s. late John Leedom and Kathleen B. (Kerby) H.; e. Prince of Wales High Sch. Vancouver 1953; Univ. of B.C., B.A. 1957, 1st yr. Law 1958; C.A. 1962; F.C.A. 1979; m. Margaret Jeanette d. late J. Cowan Adam 2 June 1961; children: Kerby C., Wendy J., Catherine J., Marnie L., John A.; PRESIDENT, D.L. HELLIWELL & ASSOCIATES LTD. 1986– ; Dir., GWIL Industries Ltd.; Mark Anthony Group Ltd.; Seaboard Life Insurance; joined Thorne Riddell & Co. as C.A. 1962–65; Div. Mgr. Steel Brothers Canada Ltd. 1965, Vice Pres. and Gen. Mgr. for B.C. 1967, for Alta. 1969, Extve. Vice Pres. 1971, Pres. 1973; Pres., B.C. Resources 1978; Chrmn. 1980; Pres. Marin Invest 1980; Pres. D.L. Helliwell & Assoc. 1985; Anglican; Clubs: Vancouver; Home: 8580 Caversham Crt., Vancouver, B.C. V6P 6R8; Office: 500 – 1525 Robson St., Vancouver, B.C. V6G 1C3.

**HELLIWELL, John Forbes,** O.C., B.Com., M.A., D.Phil., F.R.S.C.; educator; b. Vancouver, B.C. 15 Aug. 1937; s. John Leedom and Kathleen Birnie (Kerby) H.; e. Prince of Wales High Sch. Vancouver 1954; Univ. of B.C. B.Com. 1959; Oxford Univ. (Rhodes Scholar) St. John's Coll. B.A. 1961, Nuffield Coll. D.Phil. 1966; m. Judith Isobel d. late E. A. Millsap, London, Ont. Oct. 1969; children: David Forbes, James Allen; PROF. OF ECON., UNIV. OF B.C. 1971– , and Head of Dept. 1989–91; Econ. Research Consultant Bank of Can. 1965–80; mem. Research Staff Royal Comn. on Banking & Finance 1962–63, Royal Comn. on Taxation 1963–64; Lectr. in Econ. St. Peter's Coll. Oxford Univ. 1964–65, Research Fellow Nuffield Coll. 1965–67; Assoc. Prof. of Econ. Univ. of B.C. 1967–71; Managing Ed., Canadian Journal of Economics 1979–82; Rsch. Assoc., Nat. Bureau of Economic Research 1980– ; mem. Adv. Com. on Taxation of Personal Invest. Income 1982, Chrmn., Econ. Adv. Panel to Fed. Min. of Finance 1982–84; Sr. Consultant, OECD, Paris 1983–84; Vice-Pres., Pres.-Elect, and Pres., Canadian Economics Assn. 1983–86; Clifford Clark Visiting Economist, Fed. Dept. of Finance 1987–89; Mem., Social Sciences and Humanities Rsch. Counc. of Can. 1989–93; mem., Royal Comn. on National Passenger Transportation 1989–92; Mackenzie King Prof. of Candn. Studies, Harvard 1991–94; author 'Public Policies and Private Investment' 1968; co-author 'The Structure of RDX2' 1971; 'Oil and Gas in Canada' 1989; Ed. and contrib. 'Aggregate Investment' 1976; contrib. 'The Australian Economy: A View from the North' 1984; 'Progress in Natural Resource Economics' 1985; 'Handbook of International Economics' 1985; 'Handbook of Public Economics' 1985; various articles incl. 'Supply-side Macroeconomics' Candn. Journal of Economics 1986; 'Supply-oriented Macroeconomics: The MACE Model of Canada' (with others) Economic Modelling 1987; 'Comparative Macroeconomics of Stagflation' Journal Economic Literature 1988; 'Reducing International Imbalances: Evidence from Multicountry Models' Am. Econ. Review 1989; 'Macroeconometrics in a Global Economy' Am. Econ. Rev. 1993; 'Empirical Linkages Between Democracy and Economic Growth' (Brit. Journal of Pol. Sci.) 1994; Anglican; Home: 4659 Simpson Ave., Vancouver, B.C. V6R 1C2; Office: Dept. of Econ., Rm 997, 1873 East Mall, Vancouver, B.C. V6T 1Y2.

**HELLSTROM, Brig.-Gen. Sheila Anne,** C.D., B.Sc., LL.D.; Canadian armed forces (retired); b. Bridgewater, N.S. 15 Jan. 1935; d. Albinus Fardinand and Dorothy Margaret (Zinck) H.; e. Lunenburg (N.S.) Co. Acad. 1953; Mount Allison Univ. Sackville B.Sc. 1956, LL.D. 1989; Candn. Forces Staff Coll. Toronto pfsc 1974; Nat. Defence Coll. Kingston ndc 1987; joined Candn. Armed Forces serving Gimli, Man., Metz, France, Winnipeg and Rivers, Man., Montreal, North Bay, Ottawa and Toronto 1956–80; Adv. and Cons. plans and policies relating to employment, training and profl. devel. women in Candn. Forces, Nat. Defence HQ Ottawa 1980–86; Dir. Gen. Personnel Careers Offrs. HQ Ottawa 1987–89; Candn. del. to Ctte. on Women in NATO Forces Brussels 1983–86, Chrmn. of Ctte. 1987–89; mem. Minister's Adv. Bd. on Women in the Candn. Forces 1990– ; mem. Adv. Ctte. on Women in Police Services 1990–92; mem. Race Relations and Employment Equity Adv. Ctte., Ottawa Police Services Bd. 1992– ; mem. Bd. Govs. Ottawa Div. Candn. Corps Commissionaires; named Can.'s first woman gen. 1987; Woman of Yr. Zonta Club Charlottetown 1988; mem. Mount Allison Univ. Fed. Alumni; Assn. Nat. Defence Coll. Can.; Air

Force Offrs. Adv. Group; Friends of the Candn. War Museum; Lutheran; recreations: reading, travel, tai chi; Address: 2048 Valley Dr., Ottawa, Ont. K1G 2P4.

**HELLYER, Paul T.,** P.C. (Can.) 1957, B.A., F.R.S.A.; b. Waterford, Ont. 6 August 1923; s. Audrey Samuel and Lulla Maud (Anderson) H.; e. High Schs., Waterford; Curtiss-Wright Tech. Inst. of Aeronautics, Glendale, Cal., Dipl. in Aeronautical Engn., 1941; Univ. of Toronto, B.A. 1949; m. Ellen Jean, d. late Henry Ralph, 1 June 1945; children: Mary Elizabeth, Peter Lawrence, David Ralph; with Fleet Aircraft Ltd., Fort Erie, Ont., 1942–44, commencing as Jr. Draughtsman, later becoming Group Leader in Engn. Dept.; estbd. Mari-Jane Fashions in 1945; became Pres. of Curran Hall Ltd., Bldrs. & Contractors, and of Trepil Realty Ltd.; served in 2nd World War 1944–46; Aircrew R.C.A.F., 1944; R.C.A. Active, 1945–46; 1st el. to H. of C. for Toronto Davenport in e. 1949; re-el. g.e. 1953; appt. Parlty. Asst. to Min. of Nat. Defence, 9 Feb. 1956; Assoc. Min. of Nat. Defence, 26 April 1957; def. in g.e. June 1957 and March 1958; el. for Toronto Trinity in by-el. Dec. 1958 and G.E.'s of 1962, 63, 65, 68 and 72; Min. of Nat. Defence, 1963–67; apptd. Min. of Transport, Sept. 1967; Min. responsible for Central Mortgage & Housing Corp., Apl. 1968; Chrmn., Task Force on Housing and Urban Devel., 1968–69; resigned from Cabinet 1969; joined Canadian Parlty. Press Gallery as syndicated Columnist for the Toronto Sun, 1974–84; Distinguished visitor, Grad. Faculty of Environmental Studies, York University 1969–70; Chrmn. Chimo Media Ltd. 1985–89; Extve. Dir., The Canada UNI Assn. 1991– ; author of 'AGENDA: A Plan for Action' 1971; 'Exit Inflation' 1981; 'Jobs for All – Capitalism on Trial' 1984; 'Canada at the Crossroads' 1990; 'Damn the Torpedoes' 1990; United Church; recreations: singing, gardening, stamp collecting; Address: Ste. 506, 65 Harbour Sq., Toronto, Ont. M5J 2L4.

**HELPER, Hon. Bonnie Merilyn,** LL.B.; judge; b. Winnipeg, Man. 20 Aug. 1943; d. Samuel L. and Pauline (Shell) Zinman; e. Univ. of Man. LL.B. 1966; m. Michael s. Manual and Yetta Helper 28 July 1966; children: Jeffrey, Cara, Steven; JUDGE, COURT OF APPEAL, MAN. 1989– ; lectr. Man. Law Sch. 1966–67; private law practice 1967–78; Prov. Judges Court (Family Div.) part-time 1978–80, full-time 1980–83; Judge, Court of Queen's Bench (Family Div.) Man. 1983–89; Office: Main Flr., Law Courts Bldg., Broadway and Kennedy, Winnipeg, Man. R3C 0P9.

**HELWIG, David Gordon,** M.A.; author, educator; b. Toronto, Ont. 5 Apr. 1938; s. William Gordon and Ivy Lorraine (Abbott) H.; e. Stamford Coll. Inst. 1956; Univ. of Toronto B.A. 1960; Univ. of Liverpool M.A. 1962; m. Nancy Mary d. James Henry Keeling 19 Sept. 1959; two d. Sarah Magdalen, Kathleen Rebecca; educ. in Eng. Queen's Univ. 1962–80; author 'Figures in a Landscape' 1968; 'The Sign of the Gunman' 1969; 'The Streets of Summer' 1969; 'The Day Before Tomorrow' 1971; 'A Book About Billie' 1972; 'The Best Name of Silence' 1972; 'Atlantic Crossings' 1974; 'The Glass Knight' 1976; 'A Book of the Hours' 1979; 'Jennifer' 1979; 'The King's Evil, 1981; 'It Is Always Summer' 1982; 'The Rain Falls Like Rain' 1982; 'A Sound Like Laughter' 1983; 'Catchpenny Poems' 1983; 'The Only Son' 1984; 'The Bishop' 1986; 'A Postcard from Rome' 1988; 'Old Wars' 1989; 'The Beloved' 1992; mem. ACTRA; Writers' Union Can.

**HEMBROFF, Hon. W. Vaughan;** Court of Queen's Bench Justice; b. Moose Jaw, Sask. 9 May 1937; s. Edwin Frank and Gladys Hesther (Ennis) H.; e. Univ. of B.C. B.A., LL.B. 1962; m. Marilyn d. Owen and Crilla Richards 7 Sept. 1957; children: Brad, Tracy, Scott, Lisa; JUSTICE OF THE COURT OF QUEEN'S BENCH OF ALBERTA 1991– ; articled at Virtue & Co. & called to Alberta Bar 1963; Lawyer, Virtue & Co. 1963–91; Q.C. 1980; Alderman, City of Lethbridge (3 terms/9 yrs.); Mem., Attorney Gen. Task Force to review Legal Aid in Alta. 1987–88; Bencher, Law Soc. of Alta. 1991; Mem., Candn. Bar Assn.; Candn. Assn. of Univ. Solicitors; Past Pres., Lethbridge Bar Assn.; Chair, Legal Aid Soc. of Alta. 1984–87; Former Senate Mem., Univ. of Calgary; Past Bd. Mem. & Pres., Lethbridge YMCA; Lethbridge Musical Theatre; Hon. Solicitor, Lethbridge Symphony Assn.; One of Jaycees Three Outstanding Young Men for Alta. 1970; recreations: golf, skiing, racquet sports; clubs: Y's Men Club of Lethbridge; Home: 3414 South Parkside Dr., Lethbridge, Alta. T1K 0E3; Office: Court, House 340 4th St. S., Lethbridge, Alta. T1J 1Z8.

**HEMLOW, Joyce,** M.A., Ph.D., LL.D., F.R.S.C. (1960); professor; author; b. 30 July 1906; d. William and Rosalinda (Redmond) H.; e. Queen's Univ., B.A. 1941, M.A. 1942, LL.D. 1967; Radcliffe Coll., A.M. 1944, Ph.D. 1948; Marty Travelling Fellow, Queen's, 1942–43; Candn. Fed. of Univ. Women Fellow, 1943–44; Guggenheim Mem. Foundation Fellow, 1951, 1967; Nuffield Fellow (summer), 1954; Greenshields Professor, McGill Univ. 1965; Emeritus 1975; LL.D. Dalhousie Univ., 1972; mem. of Humanities Research Council of Canada, 1957–61; Publications: 'The History of Fanny Burney,' 1958 (rec'd. Gov-Gen. Award for Acad. Non-fiction 1958, Rose Mary Crawshay Prize, and James Tait Black memorial book prize for the best biography in the U.K. in 1958;); 'A Catalogue of the Burney Family Correspondence, 1749–1878,' (1971); 12 volumes of an edition 'The Journals and Letters of Fanny Burney (Madame d'Arblay) 1791–1840,' 1972–84; 'Selected Letters and Journals' 1986 (paperbook ed. 1987); and various articles about the Burney's and about John Umlach; awarded Grad. Achievement Medal by Radcliffe Grad. Soc. 1969; Phi Beta Kappa; mem. IAUPE; Protestant; Address: Liscomb, Nova Scotia B0J 2A0 or 1521 LeMarchant St., Apt.3–G, Halifax, N.S. B3H 3R2.

**HEMMANS, George E. W.;** retired banking executive; b. Regina, Sask. 19 July 1914; s. George W. and Mary (Carthew) H.; e. Public Sch. Regina, Sask.; High Sch. Vancouver, B.C.; Harvard Univ. Advanced Mang. Program; m. Gwendolyn F., d. Lawrence Haskins 2 Sept. 1942; children: Gayden A., Barbara P.; joined Toronto-Dominion Bank (then Bank of Toronto) 1934, Sr. Offr. in various capacities Div. and H.O. Vancouver and Toronto 1949–57, Br. Mgr. Toronto 1957, Vancouver Supt. Pacific Div. 1963 and Vice-Pres. Pacific Div. 1965, Vice-Pres. Corp. Credit, H.O. 1970 Pres. T.D. Realty Inv. 1972; served in 2nd World War, Candn. Armed Forces 1941–46, rank on discharge Lt.; Anglican; recreation: golf; Club: St. George's Golf and Country; Home 26 Ridgevalley Cres., Islington, Ont. M9A 3J6.

**HEMPHILL, Hon. Maureen Lucille,** M.L.A., R.N.; politician; b. Grand Forks, B.C. 26 Jan. 1937; d. Jim Leroy and Elaine Agnes (McParlon) Miller; e. Vancouver Gen. Hosp. R.N. 1958; children: Carol, Jim, Ross, Susan; nurse Vancouver Gen. Hosp., North Vancouver Hosp.; Min. of Education, Man. 1981–86; Min. of Housing, Business Development & Tourism Man. 1986–87; Min. of Community Services and Corrections 1987–88; Chairperson Assiniboine S. Sch. Bd.; Pres. Man. Assn. Sch. Trustees; Exec. Dir., Hemophilia Soc.; Dir., Man. Heart Foundation; United Way Man.; el. M.L.A. for Logan prov. g.e. 1981, 1986; Vice Pres., NDP Man; Address: Group 4, Box 40, RR 1, Anola, Winnipeg, Man. R0E 0A0.

**HENDERSON, Anne,** B.A.; film director; producer; b. Westmount, Que. 28 May 1948; d. William Charles and Mary McQueen (Gray) H.; e. McGill Univ. B.A. 1967; Co-Dir./Ed. 'The Right Candidate for Rosedale' 1978; Dir./Ed. 'Attention: Women at Work!' 1982 (Blue Ribbon Am. Film Festival); Assoc. Dir./Ed. 'Not A Love Story' 1983; Dir. 'The Impossible Takes A Little Longer' one hr. documentary on disabled women 1985 (Cum Laude Medikinale Internat. Parma 1987); Producer/Dir. 'Holding Our Ground' one hr. documentary women's movement Philippines 1988, all above prodns. Nat. Film Bd.; Producer/Dir. 'A Song for Tibet' (People's Choice Award, Hawaii International Film Festival 1991; Blue Ribbon, Am. Film & Video Festival 1992; Genie Award, Best Short Documentary, Acad. of Candn. Cinema & Television 1992) one hr. documentary on struggle by Tibetans-in-exile for self-determination & cultural survival, co-produced by Arcady Films, D.L.I. Productions, and the National Film Bd. 1991; Dir. 'The Gods of Our Fathers' episode 3 from 'The Human Race' series (written & hosted by Gwynne Dyer, on the roots of the 'Patriachal Revolution') 1994; recreations: hiking, gardening; Address: 4121 Esplanade, Montreal, Que. H2W 1S9.

**HENDERSON, Brad J.,** B.A.; real estate executive; b. Toronto, Ont. 30 Sept. 1958; s. Douglas James and Bunty Brown (Findleton) H.; e. York Univ. B.A. 1983; m. Laurie d. George and Anne Bingham April 1987; children: Brandon, Austin; VICE-PRESIDENT & SALES MANAGER, ROYAL LEPAGE COMMERCIAL REAL ESTATE SERVICES; joined Royal LePage 1980 and is key member of the management team, Head of Office Leasing in Toronto; Mem., Bd. of Dir., Junior Achievement of Metro Toronto; Mem., Internat. Devel. Research Council; Soc. of Industrial & Office Realtors; Internat. Assn. of Corp. Real Estate Executives; Building Owners & Managers Assn.; Metro Toronto Bd. of Trade; French Chamber of Commerce; Office: 33 Yonge St., Suite 1000, Toronto, Ont. M5E 1S9.

**HENDERSON, Christopher Frederick,** B.A.; health care and environment executive and entrepreneur; b. Bombay, India 20 Oct. 1956; s. Ernest Charles and Colleen Moira H.; e. Sir Robert Borden H.S. (Hons.) 1975; Carleton Univ. B.A. (Hons.) 1979; Candn. Coll. of Health Service Execs., C.H.E.; m. Andrea d. Les and Millie Prazmowski 15 June 1990; CHIEF EXECUTIVE OFFICER, THE DELPHI GROUP 1991– ; Assoc. Extve. Dir., Royal Ottawa Hosp. 1985–91; Cons., Candn. Pub. Health Assn., Carleton Univ., Fedn. of Assns. on the Candn. Environ., Credit Valley Hosp. 1980–83; Fin. Cons., Ont. Min. of Health 1982–85; Assn. of Young Health Extves. 1983– ; mem. Bd., African Med. & Rsch. Found.; Prov. Appointee, Fed./Prov. Ctte. on Productivity; Prof., Candn. Sch. of Mgmt.; Mentor in Candn. Hosp. Assn. Mgmt. Training Program; Vice-Chrmn., Pax Humana Group 1985– ; Pres., Royal Commonwealth Soc. 1987–90; Alumni Counc., Carleton Univ. 1981–84; mem. Bd., St. Clair Meals on Wheels 1983–85; Chrmn., Candn. Coll. of Health Service Execs., Nat. Capital Chapt. 1988–90, Fellowship 1990– ; Summit Chairperson, Commonwealth Conf. for Young Leaders 1987; Fellowship, Commonwealth Foundation 1991; Dir., Commonwealth Liaison Unit (Canada) 1991– ; Chrmn., The Delphi Group 1988–91; co-contbr.: Journal Mental Health Admin. 1991; 'Dimensions' 1982; recreations: active sports, classical & jazz music, literature; Club: Carleton University; Home: 332 Clifton Rd., Ottawa, Ont. K1Z 5T9; Office: 1145 Carling Ave., Ottawa, Ont. K1Z 7K4.

**HENDERSON, Donald B.,** B.Sc., M.B.A.; plastics industry executive; b. Montreal, Que. 22 Sept. 1939; s. John Verte and Eileen Isabel (Baxter) H.; e. Univ. of New Brunswick, B.Sc. 1963; Univ. of West. Ont., M.B.A. 1967; children: Michael, Scott; OWNER, MANAGER, TUCKER PLASTICS INC. 1982– ; Mfg. Engr., Ford Motor Co. 1963–65; Logistics Mgr., Benson & Hedges Tobacco 1967–69; Plant Mgr. 1969–72; Gen. Mgr., J.R. Short Candn. Mills 1972–74; Pres., Tucker Plastic Prod. Ltd. 1975–82; BSR (Can.) Ltd. 1978–82; recreations: squash, tennis; Clubs: Albany of Toronto; Toronto Athletic; Office: 1255 Yonge St., Toronto, Ont. M4T 1W6.

**HENDERSON, Keith,** B.A., M.A., M.A.; writer, college professor; b. Montreal, Que. 4 Apr. 1945; s. George Melville and Mildred Rachel (Batty) H.; e. McGill Univ. B.A. 1969, M.A. 1971; Concordia Univ. M.A. (Creative Writing) 1985; one d.: Veronica; LEADER, THE EQUALITY PARTY 1993– ; Chrmn., Dept. of English, Vanier Coll. 1980–85; Que./Can. Studies Prog. 1986–88; Chrmn., Acad. Counc., Vanier Coll. 1987–91; Vice-Pres., Equality Party of Que. 1991–93 (Chrmn., Ctte. on the Constitution of Can. 1990–93); author: 'The Restoration: The referendum years' 1987, 'The Beekeeper' 1990 (novels); recreations: tennis; Home: 4384 Sherbrooke St. W., #4, Westmount, Qué. H3Z 1E4; Offices: 821 Ste.-Croix Blvd., Montréal, Qué. H4L 3X9 and 6600 Cote des Neiges, Suite 302, Montréal, Qué. H3S 2A9.

**HENDERSON, Lorne Charles;** former politician; farmer; b. Enniskillen Twp. Lambton Co. Ont. 31 Oct. 1920; s. David Howard and Elizabeth Lomena (Robinson) H.; m. Reta Pearl d. late Floyd Sackrider, Norwich, Ont. and the late Lula Maw, Petrolia, Ont. 21 Aug. 1947; children: Shirley Durance, David, Marian Redford; M.P.P. 1963–85; Min. of Agriculture and Food, Ont. 1979–82; Prov. Sec. for Resources Development, Ont. 1982–83; Min. of Govt. Services Ont. 1978–79; mem. Enniskillen Twp. Council 1946–49; Depy. Reeve 1950–51; Reeve 1952–57; Warden Lambton Co. 1957; Assessor Enniskillen Twp. 1958–63; el. to Ont. Leg. g.e. 1963, re-el. until 1981 (did not run in 1985 el.); Chrmn. Select Comte. on Land Drainage; served on all Standing Comtes., Chrmn. of several; Min. without Portfolio 1975; Chrmn. of Cabinet 1977; has operated gen. mixed farming operation Enniskillen Twp.; Past Pres. St. Clair Dist. Boy Scout Assn.; Five Co.'s Trustees & Ratepayers Assn.; Lambton Rural Game Conserv. Assn.; Lambton Trustees & Ratepayers Assn.; Petrolia & Enniskillen Agric. Soc.; Past Dir. Ont. Mun. Assn.; Bd. of Dirs., Union Gas 1985–91; Bd., CEE Hospital 1986; named Hon. mem. Walpole Island Indian Band 1968; P. Conservative; United Church; Home: R.R. 3, Oil Springs, Ont. N0N 1P0.

**HENDERSON, Lyman George,** B.A.; retired company executive, prof. consultant, speaker and writer; b. Toronto, Ont. 12 Aug. 1920; s. late Marion Joy (Ryan) and the late Lyman Abraham H.; e. Whitney Pub. Sch., and Univ. of Toronto Schs., Toronto, Ont.; Trinity Coll., Univ. of Toronto, B.A. 1942; m. Ann Elizabeth L.M.Z., d. late Capt. E. W. Buchanan, R.N. and late Countess Elfrida Zamoyska, London, Eng., 3 March 1945; children: Buchanan Lyman M., Victoria Ann Z., Antonia Joy Z.; HON. CHRMN., DAVIS AND HENDERSON LTD. (Graphic Communications., Estbd.

1875, now a Div. of Maclean Hunter Limited) since 1986 (joined 1942); served in 2nd World War, 1942–46; Captain, R.C.A. (Overseas 1943–46); Hon. Life mem. Candn. Cancer Soc. (Past Pres. Toronto Branch and Ont. Div.); Past Chrmn., Good Neighbour Club; Past Pres. (1972–73) Graphic Arts Industries Assn. (Distinguished Service to Industry Award 1984); Hon. Fellow, Ryerson Polytechnic Inst.; Past Vice Chrmn., Art Gallery at Harbourfront; Past Pres. & mem. Bd. of Govs., Nat. Ballet of Canada (Celia Award 1972); Past Treas.: Visual Arts Ont.; Open Studio; Chrmn., Adv. Bd., First Canadian Printing Source; mem. Adv. Bd.: Desrosiers Dance Theatre; Danny Grossman Dance Co.; Dancers in Transition; Famous People Players; Past mem. Bd., Counc. for Business and the Arts in Can.; Pres., Arts & Letters Club of Toronto; Trustee, McMichael Canadian Art Collection; Bd. of Gov., The Banff Centre; originator, The Young in Art programme; Bd. The National Ballet Found.; Alpha Delta Phi (Past Pres.); Presb. (Elder, Woodbridge Ch.); pub., 'The Ten Lost Commandments of Fund Raising' 1984; 'Sam, Sam, The Printer's Man' 1989; 'How to Make a Business Plan that Works' 1994; recreations: home computer, arts consumption, skiing, travel, tennis; Clubs: University; Arts & Letters; Address: Windborne, 6421 Rutherford Rd., R.R. No. 3, Woodbridge, Ont. L4L 1A7.

**HENDERSON, Marc C.,** B.A., C.F.A.; mining executive; b. Toronto, Ont. 25 April 1959; s. Paul and Shelagh H.; e. Middlebury College (Vermont) 1977–79; Univ. of Colorado B.A. 1981; PRESIDENT, REPUBLIC GOLDFIELDS 1988– ; Pitfield Mackay Ross (now RBC Dominion Securities) 1982–84; Vice-Pres., Republic Goldfields 1984–88; C.F.A.; Dir., Minefinders Corporation Ltd.; Office: 2401, 1 Dundas St. W., Toronto, Ont. M5G 1Z3.

**HENDERSON, Mary Elizabeth Park,** B.L.S.; M.A., LL.D.; b. Kindersley, Sask. 12 Apr. 1921; d. James Archibald and Elizabeth Jane (Park) H.; e. Elem. Schs. rural Sask 1933; Airdrie (Scot.) Acad. 1938; Univ. of B.C., B.A. 1941, M.A. 1943; Univ. of Toronto B.L.S. 1944; LL.D. Univ. of P.E.I. 1975; PROF. EMERITUS, UNIV. OF ALTA. 1982– ; Jr. Cataloguer and Reference Lib., Univ. of B.C. Lib., 1944–49; Cataloguer, Univ. of Wales Lib. Aberystwyth 1950–51; Tech. Services Lib., Govt. of Sask. Prov. Lib., Regina 1952–59; Chief Lib. Regina Campus, Univ. of Sask. 1960–66; Asst. Lib. i.c. tech. services – experiments in lib. technol., Prince of Wales Coll., Charlottetown, P.E.I. 1967–69; Assoc. Prof. Fac. of Lib. Science, Univ. of Alta. 1970–74 and Acting Dir. 1971–72; Prof., Faculty of Library Sci., Univ. of Alta. 1974–82; Dir./Dean, 1972–76; mem. Univ. Senate, 1975–77; Nat. Lib. Adv. Bd., 1975–78; Candn. Lib. Assn. (Pres. 1974–75); Can. Research Inst. for the Advancement of Women; author of 'Planning the Future by the Past' 1969; Ed. Sask. Lib. Bull. 1954–57; judge for Leacock Medal for Humour from 1978–80; Bd. of Dir., P.E.I. Women's Network 1986–88; has contrib. numerous articles and book reviews to various newspapers, learned and prof. journs.; Recipient of Candn. Library Assoc. Outstanding Service to Librarianship Award 1985; recreations: books, art, record collecting, travel; Home: R.R. 2, Cornwall, P.E.I. C0A 1H0.

**HENDERSON, (Andrew) Maxwell,** O.B.E., F.C.A., L.L.D.; chartered accountant; b. Carshalton, Surrey, Eng. 24 March 1908; s. Andrew Louis and Eva Gertrude H.; e. Mill Hill Sch., London, Eng.; Rollins Coll., Fla.; m. Beatrice Johnstone, d. Charles L. Maltby, Toronto, Ont. 1 June 1935; one s., David J.; Auditor Gen. of Can., 1960–73; joined Harvey E. Crowell, F.C.A., Halifax, 1924–29; Price Waterhouse & Co., Toronto, 1929–36; Comptroller, Hiram Walker-Gooderham and Worts Ltd., Walkerville, Ont., 1936–40; Foreign Exchange Control Bd. and Asst. to Chrmn. and Comptroller of W.P.T.B., Ottawa, 1940–46; Secy.-Treas., Distillers Corp.-Seagrams Ltd., Montreal, 1946–56; Comptroller, Candn. Broadcasting Corp., Ottawa, 1957–60; mem. Inst. C.A.'s Que. and Ont.; Club: Arts & Letters, Toronto; Anglican; Home: 41 Alcina Ave., Toronto, Ont. M6G 2E7.

**HENDERSON, Robert J.,** B.Comm., C.A., AMPHI; food industry executive; b. Seaforth, Ont. 24 Aug. 1943; s. Reginald Robert and Elizabeth Ann (Ethier) H.; e. Univ. of Windsor B.Comm. (Hons.) 1966; Clarkson Gordon (London) C.A.; Univ. of Guelph AMPHI (Adv. Mngt. Course); children: Derek, Kim; PRES., BEAVER FOODS LTD. 1985– ; Clarkson Gordon 1966–70; joined present firm as Controller, Treas. 1970; Vice Pres. Finan. 1975; Vice Pres. Beaver Foods Ltd. 1979; Bd. of Dir., Candn. Restaurant & Foodservices Assn.; Dir., Orchestra London; Rotary Club; Candn. Assn. of C.A.s; Candn. Hosp. Found.; actively involved in fundraising activities, most recent: Huron College, Fanshawe College, & Orchestra London; recreations: sailing, skiing, tennis, swimming; club: London; Home: 56 Hillsmount, London, Ont. N6K 1W2; Office: 493 Dundas St., P.O. Box 5644, Stn. A., London, Ont. N6A 5M9.

**HENDERSON, Hon. William J.,** M.B.E.; retired S.C.O. judge; b. Empress, Alta. 13 Oct. 1916; s. late John Albert and late Leita (Davey) H.; e. Queen's Univ., B.A. 1938; Osgoode Hall Law Sch., Toronto 1942; LL.B. York Univ. 1991; LL.D. Queen's Univ. 1983; m. late Helen MacDougall; three d., Margaret Rose, Judith, Anne; read law with late J.M. Hickey, Q.C., Kingston, Ont.; called to Bar of Ont. 1942; cr. Q.C., 1961; Justice, Supreme Court of Ont. 1965–79 (ret.); estbd. law firm 1945, later known as Henderson & Woods, engaged in general practice; estbd. and became Pres. of Loyalist Farms Ltd. for dairy products and reg'd. Holstein cattle; Pres., Fronpress Realty Ltd.; Loyalist Farms (Alta.) Ltd.; served with Candn. Army 1942–45 in Eng., Italy, France, Belgium, Holland and Germany; Member, Order of the British Empire; el. M.P. for Kingston, 1949–58; Pres., Ont. Lib. Assn., 1958–60; mem., Candn. Bar Assn.; Judicial Conf. of Can.; Dir., Candn. Inst. for the Adm. of Justice; mem. of Bd. Hotel Dieu Hospital, 1947– ; Bd. of St. Mary's on the Lake Hospital, 1954– ; Gen. Chrmn., Hotel Dieu Hospital-Kingston General Hospital Capital Appeal Fund Raising Campaign; Life Gov., Kingston General Hospital; mem., Le Royer Circle of the Bd. of Dir. of Hotel Dieu Hospital, Kingston; Chrmn., local Capital Appeal Campaign, CNIB; Paul Harris Fellow, Rotary; Melvin Jones Fellow, Lions; apptd. Honorary Lieutenant-Colonel, The Reserve Electronic Warfare Squadron 1994; United Church; recreations: farming, golf, curling, sailing; Clubs: University; Cataraqui Golf & Country; Brockville Golf & Country; Home: Box 127, Stn. A, Kingston, Ont. K7M 6P9.

**HENDRICK, Keith Coleman,** B.A.Sc., M.A.; executive; b. Toronto, Ont. 20 May 1926; s. Ross Edward and Irene Emma (Coleman) H.; e. Univ. of Toronto B.A.Sc. 1947; Oxford Univ. (Rhodes Scholar) B.A. 1948, M.A. 1954; m. Mary Frances d. Carman and Verna Stothers 5 May 1951; children: Peter, Mark, Susan, Jane; Dir., Brenda Mines Ltd.; Brunswick Mining and Smelting Corp. Ltd.; Chemical Bank of Canada; The Council for Business and the Arts in Canada; The General Accident Assur. Co. of Can.; Hemlo Gold Mines Inc.; Kerr Addison Mines Ltd.; Prudential Corporation Canada; began career as Engr., Union Carbide Corp.; joined Noranda Mines Ltd. 1953; Mang. Dir., Noranda Sales Corp. of Canada Ltd. London, Eng. 1962–65; Vice Pres. Noranda Sales Corp. Ltd. 1965–68; Exec. Vice Pres. 1968–72; Pres. 1972–86; Pres., Noranda Minerals Inc. 1986–90, Chrmn. 1991–92; Past Chrmn., Candn. Export Assn.; The Gold Inst.; Intnl. Counc. on Metals and the Environment; Intnl. Lead Zinc Research Org. Inc.; The Mining Assoc. of Canada; Zinc Inst.; Zinc Develop. and Lead Develop. Assns.; Past Pres., Art Gallery of Ont.; Mem., Am. Inst. Mining Engrs.; Assn. Prof. Engrs. Ont.; Candn. Inst. Mining & Metall.; recreations; skiing, golf; Clubs: Toronto Golf; Granite; Craigleith Ski; Home: 169 Rosedale Heights Dr., Toronto, Ont. M4T 1C7; Office: 1 Adelaide St. E., Suite 2700, Toronto, Ont. M5C 2Z6.

**HENDRICKS, Suzanne,** B.Sc.; b. Montréal, Qué. 3 Nov. 1937; d. Arthur and Médora (Cloutier) Filion; e. Univ. de Montréal B.Sc. 1958; Cornell Univ. grad. studies; m. Martin I. Hendricks 1966; children: Simon, Justine; PRES. NAT. INST. OF NUTRITION 1990– ; Cons. Health Protection Br. 1969–79; Mgr. Nutrition Services Ross Labs. Montréal 1979–90; mem. CDA (Past Chair Strategic Planning & Rsch. Ctte.); CPDQ (Past Chair Pub. Affairs); Home: 28 – 635 Richmond Rd., Ottawa, Ont. K2A 0G6; Office: 302, 265 Carling Ave., Ottawa, Ont. K1S 2E1.

**HENDRY, Thomas Best,** F.C.A.; playwright; producer; b. Winnipeg, Man. 7 June 1929; s. Donald and Martha (Best) H.; e. Bishop Taché Sch. and Norwood Coll. Inst. St. Boniface, Man. 1945; Kelvin High Sch. Winnipeg 1947; C.A. (Man.) 1955; m. Judith d. late George Hubert Sherriff Carr 22 Nov. 1963; children: Thomas John, Christopher Stefan Carr, Ashleigh Elizabeth Jane; Consultant, Toronto Arts Counc. 1984–85, Policy Dir. 1985– ; Chrmn., Task Force on the National Arts Centre 1986; co-founder Hendry & Evans, C.A.'s 1955–61; co-founder Theatre 77 Winnipeg 1957; co-founder Man. Theatre Centre 1958 (Gen. Mgr. 1958–63); re-organized Rainbow Stage 1958 (Gen. Mgr. 1958–61); Candn. Players Foundation 1964; Candn. Centre Internat. Theatre Inst. 1964 (Secy.-Gen. 1964–68); Literary Mgr. Stratford Festival 1969–70; co-founder Playwrights Can. 1971 (Chrmn. and Treas. 1972–82); co-founder Toronto Free Theatre 1971 (Pres./Prod. 1971–82; Past Pres. 1983–84); co-founder Banff Playwrights Colony 1974 (Head 1974–76); Co-Founder, Arts and the Cities/Les Arts et la Ville, and Cons. thereto 1986– ; Treas., Writers Guild of Canada 1993– ; Fellow, Bethune Coll. York Univ.; MacDowell Colony Peterborough, N.H.; Candn. del. World Theatre Congs. 1965, 1967, 1981; Audit Officer, Dept. of National Revenue 1982–85; author: '15 Miles of Broken Glass' (comedy/drama) 1965; (with composer Stanley Silverman) 'Satyricon' (musical) 1969; 'How are Things with the Walking Wounded' (drama) 1972; (with composer Steven Jack) 'Gravediggers of 1942' (musical) 1973; lyricist 'Dr. Selavy's Magic Theatre' (musical; original cast LP United Artists) 1972; (with Paul Hoffert) 'Hogtown' (musical) 1981; 'Cultural Capital: The Care and Feeding of Toronto's Artistic Assets' 1985; 'East of the Sun and West of the Moon' (drama for young audiences) 1987; 'Financial Trends: Toronto's Non-Profit Arts and Culture Community: 1981–87' (with projections to 1994) 1987; 'Trends Update: 1981–92' (with projections to 2000) 1994; Co-editor: 'The School/L'Ecole 25' 1986; 'Accent on Access' Report on Nat. Arts Centre 1986; various book chapters, articles; rec'd Centennial Medal 1967; Lt. Gov. of Ont's Medal 1969; Queen Elizabeth's Silver Jubilee Medal 1977; Award for Distinguished Contribution to Cdn. Theatre, Toronto Drama Bench 1982; Chrmn. Elgin-Lowther Ratepayers Assn. 1977–89; Hon. Mem., Assoc. for Candn. Theatre History 1986; Barker Fairley Distinguished Visitor in Candn. Culture, Univ. College, Univ. of Toronto 1986; Fellow, Man. Inst. C.A.'s 1987; mem., Ont. Inst. C.A.'s; Playwrights Union of Can.; Candn. Actors Equity Assn.; Toronto Arts Council (1983–84); Anglican; recreations: building World War I and II model aircraft, reading, collecting Canadian prints; Home: 34 Elgin Ave., Toronto, Ont. M5R 1G6.

**HENDY, Robert Ian,** V.R.D., C.D., Q.C., D.Sc.Mil., LL.B.; b. Toronto, Ont., 4 Dec. 1916; s. Harold Robert and Isabel (Reid) H.; e. Upper Canada Coll., Toronto, 1930–35; Trinity Coll., Univ. of Toronto, B.A. 1939; Osgoode Hall Law Sch., Toronto, 1945–48; m. Margaret Elizabeth, d. Cecil M. Corkett, 26 Oct. 1940; children: Thomas C., Beverly Joan, Julia M., Susan I; COUNSEL, BIGELOW, HENDY; read law with Maxwell C. Purvis, Q.C.; called to Bar of Ont. 1948; cr. Q.C. 1959; joined Sommerville, Purvis & Bigelow, 1949 (predecessor firm); served with RCNVR and RCNR, 1936–62, on active service 1939–45; Chrmn., Conf. of Defence Assns., 1962; former C.O., HMCS York, Sr. Naval Offr., Toronto; retired as Commodore; Hon. ADC to Gov. Gen. of Can., 1952–67; Chrmn., Comte. on Naval Reserve, 1964; Gov., Candn. Corps Commissionaires (E. Can.) since 1951 (Chrmn. of Bd. 1965–66); mem. Bd. Govs., Upper Canada Coll., 1960–64; Nat. Council, Navy League of Can. (Pres., 1976–78) and mem. Ont. Mang. Comte. 1951–74; mem., Law Society Upper Can.; Co. of York Law Assn.; Royal Candn. Legion (Past Pres., Fort York Br.); St. George's Soc.; St.Andrews Soc.; Naval Offrs. Assn. Can.; Royal Candn. Naval Assn. (Hon. Pres. 1959–74); Toronto Brigantine Inc.; Haida Inc. (mem. Adv. Comte.); Candn. Inst. of Strategic Studies (Council 1976–84); Zeta Psi; awarded Admiral's Medal 1985; Conservative; Protestant; recreations: tennis, skiing; Clubs: Badminton & Racquet; Caledon Ski; Empire; Royal Candn. Mil. Inst.; Naval; Home: 179 Dunvegan Rd., Toronto, Ont. M5P 2P1; Office: 789 Don Mills Rd., Don Mills, Ont. M3C 1T5.

**HENIGHAN, Thomas Joseph,** M.Litt., Ph.D.; educator; writer; b. New York, N.Y. 15 Oct. 1934; s. Thomas Augustus and Helen Patricia (Smith) H.; e. St. John's Coll. N.Y. 1956; Columbia Univ. 1956–57; Durham Univ. M.Litt. 1963; Univ. of Newcastle-Upon-Tyne, Ph.D. 1977; m. Marilyn d. John and Vera Carson 26 Aug. 1970; children: Michael, Stephen, Phoebe; ASSOC. PROF. OF ENG., CARLETON UNIV. 1969– ; served U.S. Foreign Service 1957–61; Am. Vice Counsul S. Arabia 1957–59, Hamburg, Germany 1959–61; Instr. in Eng. Central Mich. Univ. 1963–65; Lectr. present Univ. 1965, Asst. Prof. 1966; writer/broadcaster CTV and ITV 1977–81; Arts Cons. Can. Council Selection Cttes. 1978–79, 1982–83, 1987, 1989; Nat. Arts Centre 1981–82; Ottawa-Carleton Region 1979–80; Prov. Ont. 1983; National Gallery of Canada 1991; recipient Can. Council Fellowship 1969–70, Explorations Grant 1983; Ont. Arts Council Grants 1970, 1972; Candn. Fedn. Humanities Grant 1981; author 'Natural Space in Literature' (scholarly/critical) 1982; 'Tourists From Algol' (stories) 1983; 'The Well of Time' (novel) 1988; 'Knut Hamsun' (play) 1990; 'Strange Attractors' (stories) 1991; various econ. reports, scholarly reviews, articles, poetry & stories lit. mags.; Contbr., Assoc. Ed. 'Ottawa Revue' 1976–79; Co-Founding Ed. 'Arc' 1977–79; Ed., Contbr. 'Brave New Universe' 1980; recreations: music, fishing; Home: 469 Tweedsmuir Ave., Ottawa, Ont.

K1Z 5P1; Office: Colonel By Dr., Ottawa, Ont. K1S 5B6.

**HENNEN, Brian Kenneth Edward,** M.D., M.A.; family physician; educator; b. Hamilton, Ont. 14 June 1937; s. Albert Victor Hennen and Violet M. Russell; e. Queen's Univ. M.D. 1962; Mich. State Univ. M.A. 1969; m. Mary Margaret d. Fred R. Barnum and Ida M. Waddle 20 Aug. 1960; children: Albert, Leslie, Nancy; PROF. OF FAMILY MED., UNIV. OF WESTERN ONT. 1987– ; internship and residency Kingston Gen. Hosp.; Teaching Fellow in Family Med. McMaster Univ. 1967–68; Fellow in Med. Educ. and Instr. in Med. Mich. State Univ. 1968–69; Family Practitioner, Harvie Clinic, Orillia, Ont. 1963–65; Lectr. in Community Med. Univ. of W. Ont. 1969, Asst. Prof. of Family Med. 1970, Assoc. Prof. 1973; Prof., Dept. of Family Med. Dalhousie Univ. 1974; Visiting Prof., Univ. of Newcastle 1981–82; Prof. & Chrmn., Dept. of Family Med., Univ. of Western Ont.; co-author 'Family Medicine – A Guidebook for Practitioners of the Art' 1986; author or co-author numerous articles med. journs.; Pres., Coll. Family Phys. Can. 1989–90; mem. Med. Soc. N.S.; Ont. Med. Assoc.; Alpha Omega Alpha; Protestant; recreation: music; Home: 363 St. James St., London, Ont. N6A 1X8; Office: Dept. of Family Med., Univ. of Western Ont., London, Ont. N6A 5C1.

**HENNESSEY, Frank M.,** B.Sc.; business executive; b. Lynn, Mass. 30 April 1938; e. North Eastern Univ. B.Sc. 1964; m. Carol; children: Caytlin, Frank, Michael; PRESIDENT AND CHIEF EXECUTIVE OFFICER, EMCO LIMITED 1990– ; Group Managing Partner, Coopers & Lybrand 1977–81; C.E.O., Handleman Co. 1981–90; Vice-Pres., Strategic Planning, Masco Corp. 1990– ; Adv. Bd., United Way of S.E. Michigan; Trustee & Treas., Hudson-Webber Found.; Dir. & Treas., Greater Detroit & Windsor Japan-America Soc.; Dir. & Trustee, Citizens Rsch. Council of Michigan; Dir., Habitat for Humanity Canada; Dir., MCN Corp.; Director at Large, Northeastern Univ.; clubs: Detroit, London; Home: 236 Cloverly Rd., Grosse Pointe Farms, MI 48236 USA; Office: 620 Richmond St., P.O. Box 5252, London, Ont. N6A 4L6.

**HENNESSY, Vice-Admiral Ralph L.,** D.S.C. (1942), C.D.; b. Edinburgh, Scot., 5 Sept. 1918; s. Col. Patrick and Ellen Dorothy (Robb) H.; e. George Watsons, Edinburgh; Pub. Sch., Winnipeg, Man. and Esquimalt, B.C.; Univ. of Toronto Schs.; RCAF Staff Coll., 1947; Nat. Defence Coll., 1954; m. Mary Constance d. J.T. O'Neil, Ottawa, 9 May 1944; children: Diana, Michael, Terence, Timothy; m. Diana Eloise d. J.A.D. Falkner 18 Dec. 1991; former Extve. Dir., Standards Council of Canada 1971–82; retired; joined RCN 1936; service afloat in World War II and subsequently; Senior Staff appointments Canada and abroad; Vice-Admiral June 1966; Comptroller-General, Candn. Forces 1966–68; Chief of Personnel, 1969–70; Vice Pres. of Internat. Organ. for Standardization from 1976–81; Fellow, Standards Eng. Soc.; Hon. Life Gov., Ottawa Div., Can. Corps of Commissionaires; Past Pres., Royal Ottawa Golf Club; mem., Can. Nav. Memorial Trust; Anglican: recreations: golf, swimming; Home: 271 Glenforest Rd., Toronto, Ont. M4N 2A5.

**HENNIG, Frederick E.;** company executive; b. Kitchener, Ont. 13 Aug. 1932; s. Siegfried and Elsie (Reeck) H.; e. Kitchener/Waterloo Coll. Inst.; Univ. of W. Ont. Exec. Mgmt. Courses; m. D. Margaret d. Frank and Isobel Jones 9 July 1955; children: Brian, Cathy, Richard, Grant; PRES. AND CHIEF OPERATING OFFR. WOOLWORTH CORP. 1987– ; various managerial positions 1949–71; Vice Pres. and Asst. Gen. Mgr., Vice Pres. Operations, Sr. Vice Pres. Operations and Gen. Mgr. 1971–78; Sr. Vice Pres. and Gen. Mgr. 1978–83; Exec. Vice Pres. Corporate Operations 1983; Corp. Sr. Vice Pres. Worldwide Gen. Merchandise Operations Woolworth U.S. 1984; mem. Bd. of Dirs., Borden, Inc. 1990– ; mem. Candn.-Am. Soc.; Candn.-Am. Ctte.; Boy Scouts of Am. Chrmns. Club; recreations: tennis, swimming; Home: 3 Trevino Court, Florham Park, N.Y. 07932; Office: 233 Broadway, New York, N.Y. 10279.

**HENNIGAR, David J.,** M.B.A., B.Comm.; business executive; b. Windsor, N.S. 5 July 1939; s. Dean S. and Jean B. (Jodrey) H.; e. Mt. Allison Univ., B.Comm. (Hons.) 1960; Queen's Univ. M.B.A. 1962; m. Carolyn d. Frances and Glenn MacMillan 8 June 1964; children: Brian, Jan; CHRMN., CROWNX INC. 1985– ; Security Analyst, Burns Bros. & Denton Ltd. 1963; Br. Mgr., Halifax 1967; Atlantic Regional Dir. 1972–92; Chrmn., Aquarius Coatings Inc.; Annapolis Basin Pulp & Power Co. Ltd.; Dir., Atlantic Shopping Centers Ltd.; Ben's Holdings Ltd.; Cobi Food Inc.; Crown Life Ins. Co. (Vice-Chrmn.); Halifax Devel. Ltd. (Vice-Chrmn.); National Sea Products Ltd. (Vice-Chrmn.); Scotia Investments Ltd.; The Montserrat Co. Ltd.; Cougar Helicopters Inc. (Chairman); Crombie Insurance (UK) Ltd.; Maritime Paper Products Ltd.; Minas Investments Ltd.; Minas Basin Pulp & Power Co. Ltd.; Oceans Inst. of Can.; Missionair Transportation Network; Landmark Inc.; Club; Halifax; Home: 51 Forest Lane, Bedford, N.S. B4A 1H8; Office: 3 Bedford Hills Rd., Bedford, N.S. B4A 1J5.

**HENNING, Doug;** illusionist; b. Ft. Garry, Man. 1947; grad. in Physiol. Psychology, McMaster Univ.; m. Barbara De Angelis, Dec. 1977; Candidate fed. el., Natural Law Party 1993; creator/star of rock magic musical 'Spellbound' Toronto 1973–74; co-creator/star rock magic musical 'The Magi-Show' N.Y.C. 1974–75; TV specials 'Doug Henning's World of Magic' 1975, 76, 77, 78; lecture tour on magic and consciousness expansion, univs. U.S. and Canada, 1977–78; appeared casino shows, Las Vegas and Lake Tahoe; recipient Las Vegas best spl. attraction of yr. award 1978; appeared on 'Night of a Hundred Stars' 1982; co-author (with Charles Reynolds) 'Houdini, His Legend and His Magic' 1977.

**HENRIE, Maurice,** B.A., M.A., Ph.D.; consultant and writer; b. Rockland, Ont. 19 Dec. 1936; s. Yvain and Lucille (Labrèche) H.; e. Ottawa Univ. B.A. 1959, M.A. 1962, Ph.D. 1969; Univ. of Toronto Teacher's Cert. H.S. 1960–61; Sorbonne Univ. research on thesis 1965–66; m. Anne-Marie d. René and Eve (Fournier) Grenier 15 Aug. 1959; children: François, Pierre-Paul, Dominique, Isabelle; H.S. Teacher & Univ. Prof., Univ. of Ottawa and Carleton Univ. 1958–67; Language Specialist & Advisor on Bilingualism, Public Serv. Comn., External Affairs, Sec. of State Dept. & Comnr. of Official Languages 1967–75; Sr. Extve., Fed.-Prov. Relns., Privy Council Office 1975–80; Sr. Advisor on econ. & reg. devel. 1980–81; Sr. Policy Advr., Treasury Bd. Sec. 1981–88; Sr. Advisor, Nat. Librarian 1988–91; active involvement in Soc. d'hist. et de gén. d'Ottawa; Jury Mem., Ont. Trillium Award; Mem., L'Assn. des écrivains de l'Outaouais; author: 'La Chambre à mourir' 1988 (Finalist, Trillium Award 1989), 'Le Pont sur le temps' 1992 (short stories), 'La Vie secrète des grands bureaucrates' 1989 (Finalist for best book of humour pub. in Canada 1991 for this book & trans.), 'The Mandarin Syndrome' 1991 (translation of La Vie ...), 'Le Petit Monde des grands bureaucrates' 1992 (satires of bureaucracies); Home: 1957 Oakdean Cres., Gloucester, Ont. K1J 6H6.

**HENRIKSEN, Sheila P.,** M.A., B.A., R.N.; civil servant; b. Trinidad; d. Preston St. Clair and Josephine Adelina (Moses) Shepherd; e. Queen's Univ. M.A. 1972 (Fed. Corr. Scholarship); Univ. of Toronto B.A. 1965; Ryerson Polytech. Inst., dipl. 1963; Port of Spain Gen. Hosp., lic. midwife 1954; R.N. 1953; m. Alan s. Hans and Grethe H. 20 June 1964; SPECIAL ADVISOR TO THE COMMISSIONER OF CORRECTIONS 1992– ; RN, Trinidad & Can.; var. posts beginning as Recreation & Hobbycraft Offr. and leaving as Acting Dep. Comnr. of Commun., Federal Corrections 1965–86; Chair, Ont. Bd. of Parole 1986–92; extve. exchange, Perth Australia 1978; extensive career and personal travel; Presentor, Internat. Corrections Conf. (Australia) 1988; Mem., Candn. Crim. Justice Assn.; Ont. Assn. of Crim. Justice; Candn. Assn. of Paroling Authy.; Am. Assn. of Paroling Authy. Internat.; Am. Prob. & Parole Assn.; Am. Correctional Assn.; The Soc. for the Reform of Criminal Law; author of proceedings & papers; recreations: travel, reading, sailing, playing saxophone, listening to music; Home: 9 Barker Dr., Kingston, Ont. K7K 6J7; Office: 440 King St. W., Kingston, Ont. K7L 4Y8.

**HENRIPIN, Jacques,** L. ès Sc., Dr. de l'U. (Paris); éducateur; né Lachine, Qué. 31 août 1926; f. Gérard et Gertrude (Poitras) H.; é. Univ. de Montréal, L. ès Sc. (sociales économiques et politiques) 1951; Dr. de l'U. (Paris) sciences économiques 1953; ép. Marthe f. Albert Pinel 1951–83; enfants: Catherine, Natalie, Sophie; ép. Michèle f. Maurice Gervais 20 juillet 1983; enfants: Alexis, Olivier, Miakim; PROF. DE DEMOGRAPHIE, UNIV. DE MONTREAL; enseigne et fait de la recherche à l'Univ. de Montréal depuis 1954; a fondé et dirigé le Dépt. de démographie de cette univ. 1964–73; Médaille Innis-Gérin de la Soc. royale du Can.; Prix Léon-Gérin de la prov. de Qué.; prix Esdras Minville de la Société St-Jean-Baptiste; prix Vincent de l'A.C.F.A.S.; membre de l'Ordre du Canada; officier de l'Ordre national du Québec; auteur, 'La population canadienne au début du XVIIIes' 1954; 'Tendances et facteurs de la fécondité au Canada' 1968; 'Le coût de la croissance démographique' 1968; co-auteur, 'Perspectives d'accroissement de la population de la province de Québec et de ses régions et prévision des effectifs scolaires 1961–1981' 1962; 'La population du Québec et de ses régions 1961–1981' 1964; 'Evolution démographique du Québec et de ses régions 1966–1986' 1969; 'La fin de la revanche des berceaux: qu'en pensent les Québécoises?' 1974; 'La Situation demolinguistique au Canada' 1980; 'Les Enfants qu'on n'a plus au Québec' 1981; 'Naître ou ne pas être' 1989; a écrit une cinquantaine d'articles scientifiques et de nombreux autres articles de vulgarisation dans divers journaux et revues; auteur de plusieurs rapports pour divers gouvernements; mem. Féd. canadienne de démographie (prés. 1978–82); Assn. des démographes du Qué.; Population Assn. Am.; Union internat. pour l'étude scientifique de la population; Assn. internat. des démographes de langue française (vice-prés. 1977–84); Soc. royale du Can.; Inst. canadien des affaires publiques (prés. 1966–67); récreations: sports, musique; adresse: 435 ave. Greenock, Mont-Royal, Qué. H3P 2H3; bureau: C.P. 6128, Succursale A, Montréal, Qué. H3C 3J7.

**HENRIQUEZ, Richard G.,** M.Arch., R.C.A., M.A.I.B.C., O.A.A., A.A.A., F.R.A.I.C.; architect; b. Jamaica, W.I. 5 Feb. 1941; s. Alfred George and Essie (Silvera) H.; e. Calabar High Sch. Kingston, Jamaica 1956; Univ. of Man. B.Arch. 1964; Mass. Inst. of Technol. M.Arch. (Urban Design) 1967; m. Carol Gail d. Isidor and Bella Aaron, Vancouver, B.C. 3 Sept. 1962; children: Alfred Gregory, Alisa Ruth Gay; PARTNER, HENRIQUEZ & PARTNERS 1979– ; Pres., Henriquez Production Ltd.; Partner, Henriquez & Todd 1969–1977; Henriquez Associates 1977–79; Lectr. in Design Univ. of B.C. Sch. of Arch. 1968–70; former mem. Vancouver Urban Design Panel; Past Vice Chrmn. Vancouver Heritage Adv. Bd.; alternate mem. Gastown Hist. Area Adv. Comte.; rec'd various undergrad. scholarships and prizes incl. Royal Arch. Inst. Can. Gold Medal 1964; Avalon Foundation Post Grad. Fellowship 1966; R.A.I.C. Festival of Arch. 2 Honour Awards, 2 Awards of Merit 1980; C.H.D.C. Award 1981; Candn. Architect Awards of Excellence 1970, 1972, 1976, 1985, 1990; AIBC 2 Honour Awards 1988; City of Vancouver Heritage Awards 1987 and two in 1988; Gov. Gen.'s Award for Architecture 1990; Lt. Gov.'s Award of Merit for Arch. 1990 and 1992; Competition Winner (with Jack Harmon), U.N. Peacekeeping Monument in Ottawa 1990; 'Richard Henriquez: Memory Theatre' Exhibition at the Vancouver Art Gallery and Candn. Centre for Architecture in Montreal 1994; author various articles relating to arch.; Fellow, Royal Arch. Inst. Can.; mem. Council, Arch. Inst. B.C. 1983–85; Jewish; other pursuits: sculpture; Home: 4344 Jericho Circle, Vancouver, B.C. V6R 1E9; Office: 402 West Pender St., Vancouver, B.C. V6B 1T6.

**HENRY, Hon. David (Howard Woodhouse),** Q.C.; judge (retired); b. London, England 30 October 1916; s. Howard Robert Lawrence and Mabel Marion Josephine (Woodhouse) H.; came to Canada, 1921; e. Ottawa Normal Model Sch.; Lisgar Coll. Inst., Ottawa; Queen's Univ., B.A. 1939 (Econ. and Hist.); Osgoode Hall Law Sch., Toronto, Ont.; m. Elizabeth Elaine, d. Emile A. Pequegnat, Stratford, Ont., 24 March 1945; one d. Janice Elizabeth; DEPUTY JUDGE, FEDERAL COURT OF APPEAL 1992– ; read law with Mason, Foulds, Davidson and Kellock, Toronto, Ontario, called to the Bar of Ont., June 1942; cr. Q.C. (Dom.) 1955; practised law with Fleming, Smoke & Mulholland (Toronto) June 1942; apptd. Jr. Advisory Counsel, Dept. Of Justice, Oct. 1945; Solr. to the Treas., Nov. 1949; Dir., Advisory Sec., July 1953; Acting Dir. Criminal Law Section, 1958; Dir. of Investig. and Research, Combines Investig. Act, Ottawa 1960; Lectr. in Adm. Law, Univ. of Ottawa 1961–73; Visiting Lectr. in Law, McGill Univ., 1962–73; Chrmn., Comte. of Experts on Restrictive Business Practices, O.E.C.D., Paris, 1966–72; Justice, Supreme Court of Ont. and its successor Ont. Court of Justice 1973–1991 (retired); apptd. Chrmn. of Federal Electoral Boundaries Commission for Ont. 1982 (report laid before House of Commons June 2 1983); conducted judicial enquiry regarding a Sr. Judge of Prov. Court (Criminal Div.) of Ont. 1986–87; served as member and alternate Chrmn. Lt. Gov.'s Bd. of Review (now Ont. Criminal Code Review Bd.) 1991–92; currently a member of The Private Court commercial panel (alternate dispute resolution under the Arbitration Act 1991); served in 2nd World War; Commissioned, 1941 in 2nd Bn., Royal Regiment of Canada; Overseas, 1943–44 with 1st Bn. (England and Normandy); wounded at Falaise; transferred to Judge Advocate General Branch, Ottawa, with rank of Captain, Nov. 1944; Past Pres., Fed. Lawyers' Club; Life Mem., Law Soc. of Upper Can.; Clubs: Rideau Club, Ottawa; University Club of Toronto; Faculty Club, McGill Univ.; Anglican; recreations: wood-working, photography, clock repairing; Address: The Private Court, 150 King St. W., Suite 2512, Toronto, Ont. M5H 1J9.

**HENRY, John Chester,** B.A.Sc. (Aero); business executive; b. Kirkland Lake, Ont. 14 July 1927; s. Joseph Nathan and Mary Doris (Mason) H.; e. Univ. of Toronto B.A.Sc.(Aero) 1949; Empire Test Pilot Sch. 1953; Nat. Defence College 1970; m. Eilleen d. Eldon and Betty Anderson 28 Aug. 1949; children: Christine Burke, Susan Rollins, Wendy, Robert, Jill Talbot; CONSULTANT, 1992– ; joined RCAF as Pilot Offr. 1949; served USAF Space Prog. DYNA-SOAR 1961–63; commanded 416 AW(F) Sqdn. 1964–67, CFB Trenton 1974–78, rank Col.; Dep. Commdr. 25 NR Tacoma, Wash. 1978–80, rank Brig. Gen.; Vice Pres. Flight Operations Canadair 1981–84; Dir. Business Devel. Paramax Electronics 1984–92; Consultant 1992– ; Candn. Defence Preparedness Assn.; Candn. Aeronautics & Space Inst.; RCAF Assn.; recreation: golf; Club: Vaudreuil Golf; Home & Office: 206 Lorraine Dr., Baie d'Urfé, Que. H9X 2P7.

**HENRY, Keith Austen,** B.Sc., P.Eng.; consulting engineer; b. Winnipeg, Man. 18 Oct. 1923; s. Austen Percival and Greta Madgeline (Humphries) H.; e. Consort (Alta.) High Sch., 1943; Univ. of Alta., B.Sc. 1948; m. Marguerite Irene, d. James A. Hayes, 2 June 1945; children: Margaret Jeanne (Keegan-Henry), Kathleen Elizabeth (Corrigan), James Patrick, William Keith; CONSULTANT 1983– ; Commr., Internat. Jt. Comn. 1972–78; Special Commr., B.C. Utilities Comn. (Chrmn., Peace River Site 'C' Review Panel) 1981–83; Chrmn., Counc. of Westwater Research Ctr., Univ. of B.C. 1977–92; joined Ontario Hydro 1948, Design Engr. 1948–51, Hydraulic Model Engr., 1951–56, River Control Engr., St. Lawrence Power Project, 1956–61; joined CBA Engineering Ltd. as Chief Mech. and Hydraulic Engr., Hugh Keenleyside Dam, 1961–63, Extve. Vice Pres., Operations and Project Mgr. there 1963–69; Pres., C.E.O. and Dir. 1969–83; Dir. and Vice Pres., Crippen Consultants 1981–83; Proj. Mgr., Lower Mainland Refuse Project 1983–85; served with Candn. Army 1943–45; rank Lt.; Fellow, Am. Soc. Civil Engrs.; Recipient of ASCE Can-Am Amity Award 1983; Fellow, Engn. Inst. Can.; Recipient of Can. Council of Prof. Eng. Meritorious Service Award 1983; mem. B.C., Alta. & Ont. Assns. Professional Engrs.; Assn. Consulting Engrs. Can.; Consulting Engrs. of B.C.; recreations: reading, writing, walking, birding; Clubs: Vancouver; Terminal City; Hollyburn Country; Address: 1110 Millstream Rd., W. Vancouver, B.C. V7S 2C7.

**HENRY, Martha,** O.C.; actress; b. Detroit, Mich. 17 Feb. 1938; d. Lloyd H. and Kathleen (Hatch) Buhs; e. Kingswood Sch. Cranbrook; Carnegie Mellon Univ. B.F.A.; Nat. Theatre Sch. of Can.; one d.: Emma Rain; ARTISTIC DIR., GRAND THEATRE, London 1988– ; performed with The Crest Theatre, Toronto 1959–60: 'You Can't Take It with You'; 'Epitaph for George Dillon'; 'Macbeth'; 'The Seagull'; 'Matchmaker'; 'Under Milkwood'; with Stratford Festival, Stratford, Ont. 1961–80, incl.: 'The Tempest' (Miranda); 'Macbeth' (Lady Macduff); 'Troilus and Cressida' (Cressida); 'A Midsummer Night's Dream' (Titania, Helena); 'King Lear' (Cordelia, Goneril); 'Timon of Athens' (Phrynia); 'Twelfth Night' (Viola); 'Pericles' (Thaisa); 'All's Well That Ends Well' (Helena); 'Much Ado about Nothing' (Beatrice); 'Othello' (Desdemona); 'Comedy of Errors' (Luciana); 'A Winter's Tale' (Paulina); 'Henry IV Part I' (Lady Percy); 'Henry IV Part II' (Doll Tearsheet); 'Henry VI' (Jeanne La Pucelle); 'King John' (Constance); 'Richard III' (Lady Anne); 'Love's Labours Lost' (Rosaline, Princess of France); 'Measure for Measure' (Isabella); 'Le Bourgeois Gentilhomme'; 'Cyrano de Bergerac'; 'The Country Wife'; 'Tartuffe'; 'The Devils'; 'Uncle Vanya'; 'The Cherry Orchard'; 'Three Sisters'; 'The Crucible'; 'The Woman'; 'Colours in the Dark'; 'There's One in Every Marriage'; with Shaw Festival 1965: 'Arms and the Man' (Raina); Manitoba Theatre Centre 1961–72: 'The Lady's Not for Burning' (Jennet Jourdemayne); 'A Midsummer Night's Dream' (Titania); 'The Hostage' (Teresa); 'Mother Courage' (Yvette); 'Threepenny Opera' (Jenny); 'Heartbreak House' (Ellie Dunn); 'Three Sisters' (Masha); 'Hedda Gabbler' (Hedda); Theatre Calgary 1983: 'Farther West' (May Buchanan); Canadian Players 1966: 'Playboy of the Western World' (Pegeen Mike); Centaur Theatre, Montreal 1976: 'Affairs of Anatol' (his 6 women); Theatre London, London, Ont. 1979: 'The Lady of the Camellias (Marguarite); The Grand Theatre, London, Ont. 1983–84: 'Waiting for the Parade' (Margaret); 'The Doctor's Dilemma' (Jennifer Dubedat); 'Hamlet' (Gertrude); 'The Club' (Freddie); 'Dear Antoine' (Carlotta); Theatre Plus, Toronto 1983: 'The Crucible' (Elizabeth Proctor); 1986 'Happy Days' (Winnie); National Arts Centre, Ottawa 1983: 'New World' (Carla); Centre-Stage, Toronto 1984–85: 'Tonight at 8:30' (Mable Grace, Laura); 'New World' (Carla); Tarragon, Toronto 1986: 'Pal Joey' (Mrs. Simpson); Grand Theatre, London 1989: 'Pal Joey' (Mrs. Simpson); 'Warm Wind in China' (Mother); 1990: 'The Cocktail Hour' (Ann); 1993: 'The Stillborn Lover' (Marian); television appearances incl.: CBC: 'Venus Observed'; 'Orpheus and Eurydice';
'Lord Arthur Saville's Crime'; 'Talking to a Stranger'; 'The Master Builder'; 'Ladies in Retirement'; 'Waiting for the Parade'; 'The Newcomers'; 'Empire, Inc.'; 'Glory Enough for All'; 'Adrienne Clarkson Presents'; CBC Radio: 'St. Joan'; 'The Deptford Trilogy'; 'Children's Hour'; 'A Month in the Country'; 'Memoir'; film: 'The Wars'; 'Dancing in the Dark'; 'White Light'; in U.S.A. Arena Stage, Washington 1967: 'The Crucible' (Abigail); 'The Government Inspector' (Peasant); 'Look Back in Anger' (Alison); Lincoln Centre, N.Y. 1970–72: 'Playboy of the Western World' (Pegeen Mike); 'Antigone'; 'Narrow Road to the Deep North' (Georgina); 'Scenes from American Life'; 'The Crucible' (Elizabeth); 'Twelfth Night' (Olivia); in London, England 1968–70: 'Who Killed Santa Claus?'; BBC-TV 'Daniel Deronda' (Gwendolyn Harleth); Toronto Symphony: narration to 'A Midsummer Night's Dream'; 'Façade'; Great Hall, Hart House, Toronto: Schönberg's 'Pierrot Lunaire' with Camerata; Stratford Summer Music: Sitwell's 'Façade'; Roy Thomson Hall: Bernstein's 'Kaddish' with Toronto Mendelssohn Choir; 'Tales of the Netsilik' Calgary Philharmonic; Third Stage, Stratford, Ont.: Dir. 'Brief Lives'; McManus Theatre, London, Ont.: Dir. ''night Mother'; 'Cecil and Cleopaytra'; 'Miss Julie'; Tarragon Theatre, Toronto: Dir. 'Moon for the Misbegotten,' 'All Other Destinations Are Cancelled,' 'The Colored Museum'; The Grand Theatre, London: Dir. 'Brighton Beach Memoirs,' 'Filthy Rich,' 'Biloxi Blues,' 'Blood Relations,' 'Toronto, Mississippi,' 'Bordertown Cafe,' 'The Girls in the Gang,' 'Woman in Mind,' 'Fire'; 'The Odd Couple'; 'A Walk in the Woods'; 'The Dining Room'; 'Moon for the Misbegotten'; 'Love Letters'; 'The Miracle Worker'; Toronto Free Theatre, Toronto: Dir. 'The Grace of Mary Traverse'; Globe Theatre, Regina: Dir. 'Top Girls'; Avon Theatre, Stratford: Dir. 'An Enemy of the People'; mem. Adv. Ctte. Theatre Section, Canada Counc. 1985–87, Bd. of Canada Counc. 1988–93; Instr., National Theatre Sch.; Maggie Bassett Studio; Univ. of Windsor; recipient Theatre World Award, N.Y. 1970; Genie Award Best Performance Television (for 'The Newcomers') 1979; Genie Award Best Performance Film (for 'The Wars') 1983; Genie Award Best Perf. Film (for 'Dancing in the Dark') 1986; Gemini Award Best Perf. TV 'Mount Royal' 1988 and 'Glory Enough for All' 1989; Hon. LL.D., Univ. of Toronto 1986; Hon. D.F.A.: Lawrence Univ., Wisconsin; York Univ.; Univ. of Guelph and Univ. of Windsor; Toronto Drama Bench Award for Outstanding Contribution to Canadian Theatre 1989; Officer, Order of Canada; Companion, Order of Canada; Address: 90 Mornington St., Stratford, Ont. N5A 5E8.

**HENRY, Roderick L.;** business executive; b. Montreal, Que. 15 Dec. 1929; e. Hudson H.S.; Lower Canada Coll.; m. Jill (dec.); children: Willa, Diana, Jane; m. Josephine G. Massey; CHAIRMAN, PRESIDENT C.E.O. & DIR., WIRE ROPE INDUSTRIES LTD. 1977– ; Chrmn. & Dir., Standard Chartered Bank of Can.; Pres. & Dir., Henco Holdings Inc.; Noranda Metal Industries Inc. (U.S.A.); Noranda Metal Industries Ltd.; Dir., CAE Industries Ltd.; BioChem Pharma; Brome Lake Ducks Inc.; Atlas Copco Canada Inc.; Grupo Industrial Camesa S.A. de C.V. (Mexico); Price & Markle Equipment Ltd.; Westroc Industries Ltd.; Mktg. Trainee, Dominion Wire Rope 1952, Time Study Engr. 1954, Asst. to sales Mgr. 1956, Sales Mgr. 1960; Gen. Sales Mgr. Wire Rope Industries 1963, Asst. to Exec. Vice-Pres. 1966, Vice-Pres. 1967, Vice-Pres. & Gen. Mgr. 1969, Exec. Vice-Pres. 1971, Dir. 1972, Pres. 1973, Chrmn. 1977; mem. Candn. Inst. of Mining and Metallurgy; Am. Mgmt. Assn.; Candn. C. of C.; recreations: golf, tennis, skiing; Clubs: Mount Royal; Mount Bruno Country; Montreal Badminton & Squash; Toronto; Home: 602 Clarke Ave., Westmount, Que. H3Y 3E4; Office: 1800 McGill College Ave., Ste. 2400, Montreal, Que. H3A 3J6.

**HENRY, Stuart Ward,** B.A., M.B.A., C.A.; financial executive; b. Montreal, Que. 20 Feb. 1942; e. Bishop's Univ. B.A. 1963; C.A. 1968; Wharton, Univ. of Pa. M.B.A. 1970; m. Marie Elise Vaillancourt; VICE PRES. & CHIEF FINANCIAL OFFICER, FIRST MARATHON SECURITIES LTD.; Dir., First Marathon Inc.; Samoth Capital Corp.; First B Shares Inc.; First V Shares Inc.; Price Waterhouse 1963–69; Vice Pres. Bank of America (N.Y.) 1971–73; Asst. Treas. Crown Zellerbach Corp. San Francisco 1973–75; Treas. Northern Telecom Ltd. 1975–78; Sr. Vice Pres., Bank of Montreal 1978–84; Sr. Vice Pres., Midland Doherty, Ltd. 1984–89; mem. Financial Extves. Inst.; Clubs: Cambridge (Toronto); Montreal Badminton & Squash; Home: R.R. #2, Baltimore, Ont. K0K 1C0; Office: The Exchange Tower, Toronto, Ont. M5X 1J9.

**HENRY, Victoria,** M.A.; visual arts curator/writer; b. Hamilton, Ont. 18 Feb. 1945; d. William Roy and Elinor Frances (Kimber) Smith; e. Univ. of Toronto B.F.A. 1967; Carleton Univ. M.A. 1993; m. David Henry 20 Apr. 1968; children: Andrew William Sidney, Angus David, Catherine Darlene; Owner and Dir., Ufundi Gallery 1976–92; Art Teacher Zambia 1971–75, Can. 1984–86; author: 'A Slice of Life: Betty Davison' 1987; 'The Big 3 0, Mark Marsters' 1991; Writer, Canadian Forum 1989; Curator, 'Why Do You Call Us Indians...?' travelling exhbn. U.S.A. 1989–91; 'From Icebergs to Iced Tea' travelling exhbn. 1994; Mem., Profl. Art Dealers Assoc. of Can. 1991– ; Home: 139 Stanley Ave., Ottawa, Ont. K1M 1P2; Office: Box 52068 (41 York), Ottawa, Ont. K1N 5S0.

**HENSON, Michael Lennox,** B.S., M.B.A.; mining executive; b. Georgetown, Guyana, S.A. 23 Oct. 1948; s. Augustus Anthony and Cleo Beryl (Luther) H.; e. Queen's Univ., B.Sc. (Hons.) 1971; Univ. of West. Ont., M.B.A. 1977; m. Migan d. Whittington and Emily Fung 15 Aug. 1970; children: Dayan Michael, Davin John, Drew Elliott; PRES. & CHIEF EXEC. OFFR., SMOKY RIVER HOLDINGS LTD. 1987– ; Alcan (Guyana Bauxite Co. Ltd.), Prod. & Planning Engr., 1971–75; B.C. Hydro & Power Auth., Project Engr., 1977–80; McIntyre Mines Ltd. 1980–87: Mgr., Corp. Planning 1980–82; Dir., Engr. & Planning 1982–83; Gen. Mgr., Smoky River Coal Ltd. 1983–85; Vice Pres., Opns. 1985; Pres. & Chief Op. Offr. 1986–87; Dir., Neptune Bulk Terminals (Can.) Ltd.; Smoky River Holdings Ltd.; Smoky River Coal Ltd.; The Coal Assoc. of Can.; Alcan Scholarship 1967–71; Mem., Assn. of Profl. Engrs.; Candn. Inst. of Mining & Mettalurgy; recreations: golf, skiing; Clubs: Pinebrook Golf & Country, Bow Valley; Office: 2020, 335 - 8 Ave. S.W., Calgary, Alta. T2P 1C9.

**HENTHORN, George Leslie,** B.Com.; retired telephone executive; b. Montreal, Que. 22 Jan. 1923; e. Huntingdon, Que.; McGill Univ., B.Com. 1949; Vice Pres. and Comptroller, Bell Canada 1969–85; Vice-Pres., Bell Canada 1973–85; former Dir., Tele-Direct Publications Ltd.; Newfoundland Telephone Co.; FEI Can.; joined Bell Canada 1941; various mang. positions in Treasury Dept., Montreal, 1945–58; Am. Telephone & Telegraph Co., N.Y. 1958–60; returned to Bell Canada 1960; named Gen. Supvr. – Financial Studies, 1964; Regional Accounting Mgr. 1967; served with RCN in N. Atlantic 1942–45; former mem., Montreal Soc. of Financial Analysts; Dir., Lakeshore Gen. Hosp.; mem., Frederick Johnson Council, Telephone Pioneers Amer.; Past Chrmn., Financial Extves. Inst. Canada; Home: 115 Charnwood Rd., Beaurepaire, Que. H9W 4Z5.

**HEPBURN, G. Gordon;** executive; b. Inverurie, Scotland 8 Feb. 1925; s. Robert and Mary Helen (Duguid) H.; e. Inverurie Acad.; Dundee Sch. Economics; m. Lillian, d. Ralph and Lilly Hetherington, 1965; children: Stuart, Joan, Lisa, Craig; ASSOC. DIR., THE RMR GROUP INC. and REP., THE PLAYER CLUB (a new internat. golf assn. formed by Gary Player); Dir., Council Travel Services, USA; Chrmn. Managing Dir., Edenvale Travel Group (U.K.) 1950; Marketing & Sales Dir., Nairn Travel Group (U.K.) 1971; Gen. Mgr., Retail Travel Services, Thomas Cook Ltd. (U.K.) 1977–81; Pres., Thomas Cook Canada 1981–88; Brit. Can. Trade Assoc.; Club: Summit Golf and Country; recreations: golf; gardening; cross-country skiing; travel; Home: 3 King's Inn Trail, Thornhill, Ont. L3T 1T6; Office: Toronto, Ont.

**HEPBURN, Victor C.,** C.A.; business executive; b. Glasgow, Scot. 17 Jan 1944; s. Simon Smith and Eleanor (Smith) H.; e. Hutcheson's Boys' Grammar Sch. 1961; Univ. of Glasgow C.A. 1966; m. Marion d. James and Mary McLean 13 July 1968; children: Neil, Claire; PRES. JANNOCK BRICK GROUP 1985– ; Dir., Jannock Limited; joined French & Cowan, C.A.'s 1961–66; Canadian Pacific, Canadian National 1967–70; Reed Inc. 1970–76; Jannock Ltd. 1977– ; mem. Brick Inst. Am.; Bd. Trade Metrop. Toronto; Fitness Inst.; recreations: running, tennis; Home: 279 Elmwood Ave., Willowdale, Ont. M2N 3M9; Office: P.O. Box 668, Streetsville, Ont. L5M 2C3.

**HEPPELL, Clarence Leslie;** business executive; b. Cloverdale, B.C. 15 Jan. 1929; s. David Leslie and Eva Ruth (Griffith) H.; e. Lord Tweedsmuir H.S.; m. Mary Lou d. Bert and Margaret Lipp 5 Dec. 1953; children: James Leslie, Kennth Leonard; Pres., Overwaitea Foods Ltd. 1972–89; part-time after school, Overwaitea Foods 1946; full-time var. locations 1946–64; Dist. Mgr., Hd. Office 1964, then Br. Opns. Mgr. and later Gen. Mgr.;

Chrmn., United Grocer Wholesale Ltd.; 1987 Winner of the Knight of the Golden Pencil Award; Home: 12791 Beckett Rd., Surrey B.C. V4A 2W9.

**HEPWORTH, The Hon. Lorne Henry,** D.V.M.; former minister of the crown; veterinarian; b. Assiniboia, Sask. 20 Dec. 1947; s. Henry Bramall and Eileen (Malesh) H.; e. Univ. of Regina, Arts & Sci. 1965–67; Univ. of Sask. D.V.M. 1971; m. Fern Dianne d. Adolph and Violet Marguerite Presber 23 Dec. 1969; children: Graeme, Alana; Min. of Finance, Govt. of Sask. 1989 and Min. in Charge of Sask. Energy Corp. 1991; Veterinarian, Hepworth/Pulfer Vet. Serv. 1982; Min. of Agric., Govt. of Sask. 1983–85; Min. of Energy & Mines 1985–86; Min. of Edn. and Min. responsible for the Public Service Comn. 1986–89; Min. of Finance and Min. responsible for Sask. Property Mgmt. Corp. and Public Participation 1989; Min. of Finance and Min. responsible for Crown Investment Corp. 1990; Progressive Conservative Party of Sask.; Home: 4349 Castle Rd., Regina, Sask. S4S 4W2.

**HERBER, Robert W.;** executive; b. Eng. 7 May 1935; s. Somah and Phyllis (Levine) H.; e. elem. sch. U.S.A.; Marist Brothers Coll. Johannesburg, S. Africa; Univ. of Witwatersrand, partial B.Com.; Mahler Advanced Mgmt. Skills; m. J. Catherine (dec.) d. William and Vera Sinclair 20 Dec. 1962; children: Gary, Sandra Lea; PRES., HERBER ASSOCIATES 1991– ; Dir., Paradigm Consulting Ltd. 1993– ; Candn. National Sportsmen's Show (1989) Ltd. 1993; International U.N.P. 1990; Shirmax Fashions Ltd. 1992; Instr., Univ. of Toronto M.B.A. Programme Retailing 1993; Mem., Retail Extve. Council of Canada 1983–87; joined Greatermans, S.A. 1954–69 serving as Asst. to Mgr., Div. Mgr., Regional Mgr., Gen. Mgr. Vice Pres./Gen. Mgr., Dir.; Jt. Mng. Dir. Gresham Industries, S.A. 1969–72; Extve. Asst. to Dep. Mng. Dir. Hudson's Bay Co. Toronto 1972, Gen. Merchandise Mgr. Toronto Region 1973, Group Merchandise Mgr. 1978–80; Pres., C.E.O., Dir. and Mem. of Extve. Bd., Holt Renfrew & Co. Ltd. 1980–86; Pres., Glemby Canada 1987–90; recreations: tennis, swimming, travelling; Clubs: RCYC; Waterfront Racquet Club; Office: 89 Montclair Ave., Toronto, Ont. M5P 1P5.

**HERBERT, John (John Herbert Brundage);** author; educator; b. Toronto, Ont. 13 Oct. 1926; s. Claude Herbert and Gladys Rebecca (Kirk) Brundage; e. York Mem. Coll. Inst. Toronto 1944; Ont. Coll. Art 1948–50; Nat. Ballet Sch. 1954–57; Boris Volkoff Ballet Sch. 1953–57; New Play Soc. Theatre Sch. 1956–59; WRITER-IN-RESIDENCE AND ASSOCIATE DIR., THE SMILE COMPANY, TORONTO 1984– ; Artistic Dir.: Adventure Theatre Co. Toronto 1960–62; New Venture Players Toronto 1963–65; Garret Theatre Studio 1965–71; Medusa Theatre Co. Toronto 1972–74; Teacher of Drama and Writing, Three Schs. of Art 1975–81; Tappa Sch. of Art 1982–83; Assoc. Ed. Arteditorial Co. Toronto 1975–82; Guest Lectr. Ryerson Inst., York Univ., Univ. of Waterloo and others 1969–82; Artistic Dir., Maverick Theatre, 519 Community Centre, Toronto 1984–93; Teacher of writing classes, Northern Secondary Sch., Toronto Bd. of Educ. 1985–91; rec'd Chalmers Award 1975 (Best Candn. Play Performed on Stage); named Life mem. Actors Studio New York 1967; author 'Fortune and Men's Eyes' play 1967 (rec'd Special Honour Lib. of Cong. USA 1969); 'Some Angry Summer Songs' 4 plays 1976; 'Omphale and the Hero' play 1974; various book chapters, articles, essays and critiques since 1967; John Herbert papers purchased by Univ. of Waterloo Archives; Hon. mem. Bd. Fortune Soc. Am. (prison reform organ. founded 1967 as result of play 'Fortune and Men's Eyes'); Dir. Comte. Candn. Playwrights Co-op 1974–75; mem. Dramatists Guild Am.; Soc. des Auteurs et Compositeurs Dramatiques (France); NDP; Address: Suite 614, 550 Jarvis St., Massey House, Toronto, Ont. M4Y 1N6.

**HERBERT, Stephen W.,** B.Sc., M.Hosp.Adm.; health and social service executive; b. Montreal, Que. 18 Aug. 1941; s. Theodore and Mary (Rothstein) H.; e. McGill Univ. B.Sc. 1963; Univ. of Ottawa M.Hosp.Adm. 1968; m. Marcia d. Sydney and Reva Maislin 7 Feb. 1982; children: Michele, Robbie; PRES., CHIEF EXEC. OFFR. AND DIR. BAYCREST CENTRE FOR GERIATRIC CARE 1990– ; Assoc. Prof. of Health Adm. Univ. of Toronto 1991– ; served Adm. and Paramed. Depts. Hosp. d l'Est Montréal 1960–62; Bus. Mgr. Bayview Enterprises Inc. Montreal 1963–64; Personnel Dir. Lakeshore Gen. Hosp. Pointe Claire, Que. 1964–66; Assoc. Exec. Dir. Diagnostic & Support Services McMaster Univ. Med. Centre Hamilton 1968–77; Dir. Patient, Diagnostic, Therapeutic & Support Services Royal Victoria Hosp. Montreal 1977–78; Pres., Royal Victoria Hosp. 1978–88; Pres., Royal Victoria Hosp. Found. 1978–88; Dir. AMI Advanc. Fund; Pres. Meditron Corp. and Progressive Products Ltd. 1988–90; part-time Faculty mem. Sch. Health Adm. Univ. of Ottawa 1969–77, Adjunct Prof. of Adm. 1984–88; Asst. Prof. of Epidemiol. & Biostats. McGill Univ. 1981, Assoc. Prof. 1986–88, Adjunct Prof. 1988– , Assoc. Dean Health Care Planning 1986–88; recipient Robert Wood Johnson Award 1969; Extendicare Award Candn. Coll. Health Service Execs. 1981; Governor Gen.'s Special Medal; Internat. Fellow King's Fund Coll. London, Eng. 1988– ; Dir. Baycrest Centre Found.; Canabec Health Services Consulting; Meditron Corp.; Montreal Gen. Hosp. Found. (Gov.); Produits Progressif Ltée; N. Am. Assn. of Jewish Homes and Housing for the Aged; memberships: Am. Acad. of Medical Administrators; Am. Public Health Assn.; Candn. Coll. of Health Service Extves.; Candn. Health Economics Assn.; Candn. Public Health Assn.; Centre for Med., Ethics and Law, McGill Univ.; Expert Working Group - Economy, Costs and Funding, Candn. Hosp. Assn.; Hosp. Council of Metro Toronto (Strategic Issues Ctte.); Internat. Health Economics and Managements Assn.; Internal. Health Policy and Management Institute; Internat. Hosp. Fed.; Institute of Health Services Management; Metro Toronto District Health Council (Priorities & Planning Ctte., Long Term Care Ctte. and Rsch., Education and Health Care Industry Sub-Ctte.); Mount Sinai Hosp. (Bd. of Govs.); Northeast Candn./Am. Health Council; Royal Soc. of Health; Toronto Jewish Fed., Council; Young President's Orgn.; World President's Orgn.; Home: 504, 1166 Bay St., Toronto, Ont. Office: 3560 Bathurst St., North York, Ont. M6A 2E1.

**HERBIG, Gunther;** conductor; e. Franz Liszt Academy Weimar; studied with Herbert von Karajan for 2 years; m. Jutta Czapski; children: Beate, Thomas; Music Director, The Toronto Symphony 1988–94; General Music Dir., Dresden Philharmonic Orch. 1977–83; East Berlin Symphony Orch. 1983–84; Music Dir., Detroit Symphony Orch. 1984–90; career in Western Europe was launched when invited to become Principal Guest Conductor of the BBC Philharmonic Orchestra in 1982; has appeared with the orchestras of London, Paris and Rome and with the Monte Carlo and Rotterdam philharmonics; toured Japan and is a regular visitor to the Israel Philharmonic Orch.; has appeared with all major North American orchestras; toured U.S. with Detroit Symphony, and in 1989 led the orchestras on its first European tour; toured extensively with The Toronto Symphony, including appearances in New York, Montreal, Vancouver, San Francisco, Australia, Japan, Singapore and Taiwan; European tour 1991; Guest Conductor, Minnesota Orchestra, Seattle Symphony, Baltimore Symphony, Houston Symphony, Orchestre symphonique de Montréal, Royal Philharmonic, Halle Orchestra, BBC Philharmonic, Royal Liverpool Philharmonic, Orchestre de Paris, Orchestre de la Suisse Romande and the Dresden Philharmonic; Prof. of Conducting, Yale Univ. 1990.

**HERDER, Stephen Rendell;** retired newspaper publisher; b. St. John's Nfld., 15 July 1928; s. Ralph Barnes and Mary (Rendell) H.; e. King's Coll. Sch., Windsor, N.S. 1938–44; Mount Allison Acad., Sackville, N.B. 1944–45; m. Lillian Joan, d. late W. J. and Marion Bursey, 9 Sept. 1949; children: Arthur Daniel, R.I.A., Stephanie Lynn, M.D., F.R.C.S. (neurosurgery); Publisher, Canadian Newspapers Ltd., 1970–91; Retired; publisher of The Evening Telegram, founded April 3, 1879 by his grandfather W.J. Herder; Vice Pres., Dir., Gen. Mgr. and Chief Extve. Offr., St. John's Publishing Co. Ltd., 1967–70; joined the Evening Telegram, St. John's, Nfld., as apprentice, 1945; reporter daily newspapers Sarnia and Woodstock, Ont. 1949; rejoined the Evening Telegram 1950, Mang. Ed. 1954, Dir. 1958, Vice Pres. and Gen. Mgr. 1967, till assets bought by St. John's Publishing Co., later Canadian Newspapers Ltd., 1970; Dir. Western Printing and Publishing Co. Ltd. 1954–70; Gen. Chrmn., Candn. Sch.; Curling Championships, St. John's Nfld. 1966; mem. St. John's Comte. Candn. Curling Championships 1972; Charter mem. Nfld. Curling Assoc. Hall of Fame 1986; Gold Stick Award, Nfld. Amateur Hockey Assn.; Happy Fraser Conservation Award, Atlantic Salmon Fed. 1986; Gunter Behr Conservation Award, Salmon Assn. Eastern Nfld. 1986; Tuck Walters Conservation Award, Nfld. Natural History Soc. 1992; Canada 125 Medal 1992; Dir., Nfld. Historic Parks Assn. 1984–89; Dir., Quidi Vidi Rennies River Devel. Found. 1985– ; Chrmn. Murphy Cancer Clinic Campaign, Nfld. Cancer Found. 1993–94; Hon. Patron, Candn. Sr. Men's Softball Championships 1989; Hon. Patron, Candn. Jr. Men's Softball Championships 1991; recreations: fly fishing; Home: 5 Pringle Pl., St. John's, Nfld. A1B 1A2.

**HERIE, J.A. Euclid,** M.S.W., LL.D.; association executive; b. St. Jean Baptiste, Man. 14 Oct. 1939; s. Leo H.; e. Univ. of Man. B.A. 1962, B.S.W. 1963, M.S.W. 1965, LL.D. 1981; m. Ellen d. Serge and Sarah Richer 2 June 1962; children: Marilyn, Neil; PRES., C.E.O. AND GEN. SEC., CANADIAN NATIONAL INSTITUTE FOR THE BLIND 1983– ; Supr. in Protection Service and subsequently Dir. of Adoption & Unmarried Parents Services Children's Aid Soc. Winnipeg 1967–77; Exec. Dir. Man. Div. CNIB 1977–79, Asst. to Mng. Dir. and Exec. Dir. Ont. Div. CNIB 1980–83; Treas., World Blind Union 1988– ; author various articles; featured guest speaker nat. and intnl. forums on child welfare and disabilities; Office: 1929 Bayview Ave., North York, Ont. M4G 3E8.

**HERING, Günther E.,** M.B.A.; business executive; b. Munich 22 Sept. 1936; s. Erwin and Wera (Binder) H.; e. Univ. of Hamburg M.B.A. 1959; divorced; children: John, Gunther, Bren, Elizabeth; CHRMN., KLÖCKNER INDUS.-ANLAGEN GmbH 1990– ; McKinsey & Co. N.Y. 1971–75; Vice Pres., Fluor Corp. (Irvine, CA) 1975–85; Sr. Vice Pres., Shearson Lehman Bros., N.Y. 1986–87; Pres. & Chief Extve. Offr., Harpener Ag, Dortmund, Germany 1987–89; Mem., Bd. of Mngt., Klöckner & Co AG, Duisburg, Germany; Chrmn., Klöckner Stadler Hurter Ltd. Montreal; Office: 1400 rue du Fort, Suite 900, Montreal, Que. H3H 2T1.

**HERLING, Michael,** B.Comm., Ph.D.; steel industry executive; b. Cernauti; s. David and Amalia (Gottesman) H.; e. Vienna Univ. B.Comm.; Univ. of Florence, Ph.D. (Economics); m. Marta d. Abraham and Berta Klein; children: Dorothy, Joyce; SENIOR VICE-PRES., IVACO INC., MONTREAL 1967– ; Sivaco Wire & Nail Co. 1950–67; Governor, Ben Gurion University, Israel; Vice Pres., H.I.A.S., New York; Office: 770 Sherbrooke West, Montreal, Que. H3A 1G1.

**HERMAN, Michael John;** real estate executive; s. Murray Morris and Ruby Sylvia H.; e. Osgoode Hall Law Sch.; married; children: Jacob, Rebecca, Elizabeth; PRES. & CHIEF EXTVE. OFFR., CITICOM INC. 1989– ; Law Clerk to Chief Justice Bora Laskin 1974–75; practised law in Toronto for 13 years until 1988, latterly as a senior litigation partner & counsel with Goodman and Carr; active with Citicom for several years initially as legal counsel & then Dir. & Extve. Bd. Mem.; former Editor-in-Chief, Osgoode Hall Law Journal; has written & lectured widely; special lectr., Osgoode Hall Law Sch., 4 years; Office: One Toronto St., Suite 810, Toronto, Ont. M5C 2V7.

**HERMAN, Thomas Bruce,** B.A., M.Sc., Ph.D.; university professor; b. Baltimore, U.S.A. 26 Oct. 1949; s. Bruce Alfred and Evenden Ellsworth (Daley) H.; e. Loyola High School Baltimore 1967; Antioch College B.A. 1972; Univ. of Alta. M.Sc. 1975, Ph.D. 1979; m. Kathleen d. William and Marie Fuller 27 Sept. 1974; children: Tobias Kent, Giles Patrick; PROF., BIOLOGY DEPT., ACADIA UNIV. & CO-DIR., ACADIA CENTRE FOR WILDLIFE & CONSERVATION BIOLOGY 1992– ; Asst. Prof., Acadia Univ. 1980; Assoc. Prof. 1984; awarded tenure 1985; teaches and conducts research in population ecology & conservation biology; Fac. Rep., Bd. of Gov., Acadia Univ. 1992–95; N.S. Adv. Ctte. on the Protection of Special Places 1992–95; Teacher, ElderHostel courses in tropical ecology & conservation, Universidad Para La Paz, Costa Rica 1989–90; Councillor, Candn. Soc. of Zoologists 1992–95; Vice-Chair, Science and Protected Areas Assn. 1992– ; Pres., Blomidon Naturalists Soc. 1990–94; Mem., Orgn. Ctte., N.S. Nature Trust 1993–94; co-editor: 'Science and Management of Protected Areas' 1992; author/co-author of 27 refereed scholarly articles; recreations: canoeing, dragonfly-watching; Home: 40 Elm Ave., Kentville, N.S. B4N 1Y9; Office: Wolfville, N.S. B0P 1X0.

**HERMAN, William Bernard,** Q.C.; barrister; executive; b. Toronto, Ont. 31 March 1911; s. Joseph and Rose (Scop) H.; e. Grace St. Pub. Sch., Harbord & Oakwood Coll. Insts. Toronto; Univ. of Toronto Univ. Coll. B.A. 1931; Osgoode Hall Law Sch. Toronto grad. with honours 1934; m. Alice Blanche Suroff 6 July 1933; two d.; Secy. Wilson Century Theatres Ltd. 1952– ; called to Bar of Ont. 1934; cr. Q.C. 1962; Chrmn., Citicom Inc.; Past Gov. Univ. of Toronto; Dir. and Past Chrmn. York-Finch Gen. Hosp. Toronto; Dir. and Past Chrmn. York-Finch Hospital Found.; winner Class A, S. Ocean Racing Conf. 1972 with yacht Bonaventure IV; repeatedly winner Freeman Cup Lake Ont. Internat. with yachts Inishfree, Bonaventure II and V; Yacht of the Yr. between 1962 and 1980; mem. Pi Lamda Phi; P. Conservative; Hebrew; recreations: yacht racing, golf, tennis, squash; Clubs: Albany; Oakdale Golf & Country (Past

Pres.); Island Yacht Club, Toronto, Past Commodore; Palm Beach Country (Fla.); Home: 34 High Point Rd., Don Mills, Ont. M3C 2R3; Office: 1 Toronto St., Toronto, Ont. M5C 2V7.

**HERMANIUK, Mt. Rev. Maxim,** C.SS.R., O.C. (1982), D.D.; theologian (Ukrainian Cath.); b. Nove Selo, W. Ukraine 30 Oct. 1911; s. Mykyta and Anna (Monczuk) H.; e. Louvain, Belgium, Philos. 1933–35, Dr. Theol. 1943, Maitre Agregé Theol. 1947; Beauplateau, Belgium, Theol. 1935–39; came to Can. 1948; ARCHBISHOP METROPOLITAN EMERITUS OF UKRAINIAN CATHOLICS OF CANADA 1993– ; joined Redemptorist Cong. 1933; o. Priest 1938; Superior Vice-Prov. of Can. and U.S.A. 1948–51; consecrated Bishop 1951; Auxiliary Bishop Winnipeg 1951; Apostolic Adm. 1956; Archbishop-Metrop. of Ukrainian Catholics of Canada 1956–92; mem. Vatican II Council 1962–65; mem. Secretariat for Promoting Christian Unity, Rome, 1963; mem. Jt. Working Group (World Council Chs.) 1969; mem. Council to the Secretariat of the Synod of Bishops, Rome, 1977 and 1983; Officer, Order of Canada, 1982; D.D. (hon. causa), Univ. of St. Michael's, Toronto 1988; Prof. of Moral Theol., Sociol. and Hebrew, Beauplateau, Belgium, 1943–45; Prof. Moral Theol. and Holy Scripture, Redemptor Semy., Waterford, Ont., 1949–51, Co-founder mem. Ukrainian Relief Comte., Belgium, 1942–48; Co-founder and first Pres., Ukrainian Cultural Soc., Belgium, 1947; Organizer Ukrainian Univ. Students Organ., Obnova, Belgium 1946–48 and Can. 1953; mem. World Congress of Free Ukrainians since 1967; Taras Shevchenko Scient. Soc. 1951; Pontifical Commission for the Revision of the Kodex of Oriental Canon Law, 1983; Hon. mem. Mark Twain Soc. 1972; mem. Ukrainian Hist. Assn.; author: 'La Parabole Evangélique' 1947; 'Our Duty' 1960; First Ed., Logos Ukrainian Theol. Review, 1950–51; Editor, Logos 1993– ; K. of C.; Address: 235 Scotia St., Winnipeg, Man. R2V 1V7.

**HERMANT, Adam B.T.,** O.S.T.J., C.D.; business executive; b. Toronto, Ont. 5 June 1946; s. Sydney M. and Margret L. (Shaw) H.; e. Upper Can. Coll.; m. Jill D. d. Col. W.W. Etches 11 Sept. 1976; children: Elizabeth Jane, Simon Charles Percy; CHIEF EXEC. OFFR., SAFETY SUPPLY CO. 1985– ; joined present Co. 1967; Dir. The PAJA Group of Companies; Ont. Safety League; Ont. Special Olympics; Past Pres. The Duke of Edinburgh Awards (Ont.); O.St.J.; Dir. Ont. Council St. John Ambulance; Dir., Safety Equipment Distributors Assn. (Dir.); Young Pres. Orgn. (Upper Can. Chapter Exec.); Chrmn. & Pres., 'The Sports Festival' in favour of Special Olympics in Canada; Bd. Trade Metrop. Toronto; recreations: golf, tennis, skiing; Clubs: Albany; Board of Trade Metrop. Toronto; Empire & Canadian; RCYC; Toronto Golf; Office: 90 West Beaver Creek Rd., Richmond Hill, Ont. L4B 1E7.

**HERMANT, Peter Morris;** optical executive; b. Toronto, Ont. 30 Sept. 1939; s. Sydney M. and Margaret Lewis Marshall (Shaw) H.; e. Brown Sch.; Upper Can. Coll.; Univ. of B.C.; m. Kathleen (Katie) d. Edwin and Pauline Norman 7 July 1962; children: Margaret (Maggie) Lewis Marshall; Norman Warren; Mary Kathleen; Chrmn., C.E.O., Imperial Optical Canada; Dir., Inst. of Corp. Dir.; Toronto Economic Development Corp.; Vision Indus. Counc. of Am.; Mem., Bd. of Trustees, Hosp. for Sick Children; Chrmn., Variety Village; Past Mem., Expo 2000 Can. Nat. Bid Steering Ctte.; Past Pres., Bd. of Trade Metrop. Toronto; Empire Club of Can.; past Candn. Chrmn., Optical Lab. Assn.; Past Chrmn. Rotary Creche Ctte.; Past mem., Special Olympics Breakfast Adv. Bd.; mem., Optician's Assn. of Canada; Ont. Assn. of Dispensing Opticians; Royal Commonwealth Soc.; Civic Awards Ctte., City of Toronto; Master, Ordre Internat. des Anysetiers; Fellow, Nat. Acad. of Opticianry; Freeman of City of London, Engl.; Liveried of the Worshipful Co. of Spectacle Makers; Beta Theta Pi; Clubs: Arts & Letters; Queen's (Toronto, and London, England); Royal Candn. Yacht; CEO; New York Athletic; Mandarin Club; Chelsea Arts Club (London, Eng.); Royal Automobile.

**HERNDL, Kurt,** LL.D.; diplomat; b. Villach, Austria 8 Nov. 1932; s. Egon and Inge (Schmeger) H.; e. Gymnasium Innsbruck, baccalauréat 1950; Univ. of Innsbruck, LL.D. 1956; m. Erika d. Franz and Frieda Robl 11 Oct. 1965; AMBASSADOR OF AUSTRIA IN CANADA 1989– ; Asst. Lectr., Law Fac., Univ. of Innsbruck 1956–62; joined Austrian Diplomatic Serv. 1962; Dep. Permanent Rep. to U.N. in Geneva 1965–69; Chief Legal Advr., Fgn. Ministry 1977–82; Dir., Fgn. Min. U.N. Dept. 1987–89; seconded to U.N. Secretariat 1969–77, 1982–87 where he served as Dir., Security Counc. Div., as Dir., Sec.-Gen.'s Extve. Office and as U.N. Asst. Sec.-Gen. for Human Rights; el. Mem., Human Rights Ctte. (U.N.) 1990–94; Lectr., Vienna Diplomatic Acad.; Salzburg Seminar for Diplomats; Vienna Seminar of the Internat. Peace Acad.; holds several decorations (Austria, Fed. Rep. of Germany, Spain); mem., Internat. Law Assn. (Austrian Br.); Am. Soc. of Internat. Law; UNA-Austria; Austrian Assn. for Eur. Law; author of numerous articles on internat. law & the law of internat. orgns. in various languages; recreations: swimming, nordic skiing; Home: 9 Crescent Rd., Rockcliffe Park, Ont. K1M 0N1; Office: 445 Wilbrod St., Ottawa, Ont. K1N 6M7.

**HÉROUX, Denis,** O.C.; film producer; b. Montréal, Qué. 15 July 1940; s. Laurent and Marie-Ange (Desmarais) H.; e. Univ. de Montréal, Lic. ès lettres; m. Justine Bouchard 25 March 1972; one s. Marc-Antoine; Director & Producer: 'Jacques Brel is Well and Alive and Living in Paris' 1974, 'Violette Nozière' 1977, 'Atlantic City' 1979, 'Les Plouffe' 1980, 'Quest for Fire' 1981, 'Louisiana,' 'Blood of Others,' 'The Bay Boy' 1983, 'Le Matou,' 'Hold Up' 1985, 'Vengeance,' 'Control' 1986, 'The Jeweller's Shop,' 'Bordertown' 1988, 'French Revolution' 1989; 'Black Robe' 1991; Prix du Mérite, Univ. de Montréal 1982; Order of Canada 1984; Mem., Applebaum-Hébert Ctte. 1980–82; Film Rep., Cinévidéo U.K.; Home: 8 Vestry Court, 5 Monck St., London SW1, England; Contact in Canada: Cinévidéo Plus, 2100 rue Ste-Catherine ouest, Bureau 810, Montréal, Qué. H3H 2T3.

**HÉROUX, Justine;** film producer; b. Montréal, Qué. 25 May 1942; d. Philémon Bouchard and Cécile Hamelin; e. Graduate Radiology Technician at Maisonneuve Hosp.; m. Denis Héroux 25 March 1972; one s.: Marc-Antoine; first AD and Production Manager from 1969 to 1979 on a large number of films; Assoc. Producer: 'Atlantic City,' 1979; Producer: 'Les Plouffe' 1980, 'Little Gloria... Happy at Last,' 1982, 'Le Crime d'Ovide Plouffe,' 1983, 'L'Adolescente Sucre d'Amour,' 1984, 'Le Matou' 1985; Exec. Producer: 'Les Fous de Bassan' 1986, 'Flag,' 1987; Co-Prod. 'Dames Galantes' 1990, 'A Star for Two,' 'Sous le Signe du Poisson' 1990, 'Miss Moscou' 1991, 'Monsieur Ripois' 1991 (first of the series 'La Grande Collection II'), 'La Fenêtre' 1991, 'L'Homme de ma Vie' 1991; 'Connections' 1992, 'Flight From Justice' 1992; 'Meurtre en Musique' 1993; 'Crosswinds' 1993; Pres. Cinévidéo Plus and Cinéroux Films since 1990; Mem., A.P.F.T.Q.; Home: 28 Roskilde, Outremont, Qué. H2V 2N5; Office: Cinévidéo Plus, 2100 rue Ste-Catherine ouest, Bureau 810, Montréal, Qué. H3H 2T3.

**HÉROUX, Paul,** Ph.D.; university professor; b. Trois-Rivières, P.Q. 9 Jan. 1951; s. Georges and Thérèse (Cloutier) Héroux; e. Univ. Laval, B.Sc. 1972; Inst. Nat. de la Rech. Scientifique, univ. du Qué., M.Sc. 1975, Ph.D. 1981; ASSOC. PROF., OCCUPATIONAL HEALTH, FACULTY OF MEDICINE, McGILL UNIV. 1987– ; main rsch. interest: interactions between electromagnetism and life; started rsch. in labs of Inst. de Rech. d'Hydro Qué.; contrib. in electrical corona, pathophysiol. of electrical burns & for designing an electromagnetic dosimeter used in epidemiol. studies on reln. between magnetic fields & leukemia; developed 'Electrical Impedance Spectroscopy' a med. diagnostic tool to assess living tissue through electrical impedance, useable in measurement of edema and burn severity (other applications are under development); Med. Sci., Dept. of Plastic Surg., Royal Victoria Hosp.; Dir., Electropathol. Lab., RVH; Mem., Bioelectromagnetics Soc.; Bioelect. Repair & Growth Soc.; Internat. Comn. on Occup. Health; Am. Aging Assn.; Bioelectrochem. Soc.; Prix Mica, Conseil de l'Indus. Electr. du Qué. 1988; 1st Award, Plast Surg. Edn. Found. 1986; author: 'Electrical Shock Safety Criteria' 1985, 'Electromagnetics in Medicine and Biology' 1991; 'Electrical Trauma' 1992; recreations: badminton, riding, fencing, sailing; Home: 921 J.P. Vincent, #6, Longueuil, Qué. J4G 1V1; Office: 1140 Pine Ave. W., Montreal, Qué. H3A 1A3.

**HERRERO, Stephen Matthew,** B.A., Ph.D.; educator; b. San Francisco, Ca. 31 Dec. 1939; s. Edward Peter and Queena Vivian (Stroup) H.; e. Univ. of Calif. at Berkeley, B.A. 1961 (with great distinction), Ph.D. 1967; Univ. of Calgary, post-doct. fellow in Animal Ecol. 1968–69; children: Blaine, Jacob, Hilary, Mia; PROF. OF ENVIRONMENTAL SCI. & BIOL., UNIV. OF CALGARY 1981– ; Prog. Dir., Environ. Sci., Univ. Calgary 1989–91; Pres. BIOS Envir. Rsch. & Planning Assoc. Ltd. 1981– ; Asst. Prof. of Psychol. & Biol. present Univ. 1970, Asst. Prof., Envir. Sci. & Biol. 1972, Assoc. Prof. 1974; invited speaker Candn., Brit., Am. & Mexican univs.; guest speaker numerous orgns.; nat. & local radio/TV appearances related to bear mngt., wildlife; special adv. group design Calgary Zoo; prin. script writer & sci. ed. award-winning NFB film 'Bears and Man' 1979; recipient Woodrow Wilson Fellowship 1963; Nat. Inst. Mental Health 1964–67; Alta. Achievement Award 1985; Killam Fellowship 1981; exhibited rsch. grizzly bear ecol. & mgnt., Alta. Prov. Exhibit Sci. & Technol. 1980–85; speaker, Internat. Cong. Mammalogy Moscow 1974; Am. Inst. Biol. Sci's Plenary Session 1970; author: 'Bear Attacks' 1985; author/co-author num. publs.; ed. 'Bears: Their Biology and Management' 1972; Chrmn., World Wildlife Fund's Wild West Prog. 1986–89; mem., IUCN Specialist Group on Bears 1976– ; Exec. Ctte. Internat. Bear Biol. Assn. 1974– ; Sec. 1977–80; Nat. Vice-Pres. (1971–76) & Calgary/Banff Chap. Chair (1968–70, 1978–83), Nat. & Prov. Parks Assn.; Dir., Candn. Himalayan Found. 1982–85; Soc., Envir. & Energy Devel. Studies 1979–81; Founding mem., Envir. Counc. Alta. 1970–72; Phi Beta Kappa; Sigma Xi; Chrmn. Species Survival Comn. Bear Group 1988– ; Pres., Internat. Assn. Bear Rsch. & Mngt. 1986–89; Office: Calgary, Alta. T2N 1N4.

**HERRICK, John Dennis,** KCHS, B.A.; consultant; b. St. Paul, Minn. 8 Oct. 1932; s. late Willard R. and Gertrude (O'Connor) H.; e. Cretin High Sch., St. Paul, Minn.; Univ. of St. Thomas, B.A. 1954; Chief Operating Offr., Borden & Elliot, Barristers & Solicitors 1986–89; retired Chrmn., General Mills Canada Inc. 1971–87; Field Auditor, General Mills, Minneapolis, 1954–59; Accounting Supvr., Chem. Div., Kankakee, Ill., 1959–61; Adm. Mgr., S. Chicago Plant, 1961–62; Mgr. of Auditing, Minneapolis, 1962–65; Mgr., New Business Devel., 1965–66; Dir. of Adm. and Controller, Smiths Food Group (subsidiary), London, Eng., 1966–68; Pres., General Mills Cereals Ltd., Toronto, 1969–71; Dir. CP Express and Transport; Dir., Catholic Charities of Palm Beach; Past Chrmn. Grocery Products Mfrs. of Can.; mem., World Presidents' Orgn.; Past Chrmn., Junior Achievement of Can. 1974–75; Past Pres. Jr. Achievement of Toronto 1971–72; mem. Pres. Council, Coll. of St. Thomas, 1971– ; Past Pres. Toronto Area Industrial Develop. Bd.; Past Chrmn., Emmanuel Convalescent Foundation; Past Pres. Bd. of Trade of Metrop. Toronto; Past Pres., Amer. Club; past mem., Young Pres.'s Org.; Accademia Italiana Della Cucina; Dir. CentreStage Co.; Gov. Nat. Theatre Sch. of Can.; Past Chrmn., Candn. Chamber of Comm.; Past Chrmn., The Toronto Harbour Comnrs.; served with USAF 1954–57; rank Capt.; Queen's Silver Jubilee Medal, 1978; Distinguished Alumnus Award, College of St. Thomas, 1984; K. of C.; Knight Commander, Order of The Holy Sepulchre of Jerusalem; Sovereign Order of Saint John of Jerusalem; Knight Cmdr., Order Polinitzia Restituti; Roman Catholic; recreations: boating, golf, flying, tennis squash; Clubs: Royal Canadian Yacht; Lambton Golf & Country; Old Port Yacht; Bd. of Trade of Metrop. Toronto; Bd. of Trade; Beefeater; The Loxahatchee; NYAC; RCMI; Empire; Home: 15100 Palmwood Rd., Palm Beach Gardens, FL 33410 and New York, N.Y.

**HERRNDORF, Peter A.,** O.C., B.A., LL.B., M.B.A., LL.D. (Hon.); b. Amsterdam, The Netherlands 27 Oct. 1940; s. late Bob and late Anna Marie H.; e. Ridley Coll. 1958; Univ. of Manitoba B.A. 1962; Dalhousie Univ. LL.B. 1965; Harvard Univ. M.B.A. 1970; LL.D. (Hon.): York Univ. 1989, Univ. of Winnipeg 1993; Offr., Order of Canada 1993; m. Eva d. Stephen and Magda Czigler 6 June 1979; two children: Katherine Alexandra, Matthew Alexander Nicholas; CHAIRMAN, TVONTARIO 1992– ; Television Producer, CBC 1965–68; Head of Television Current Affairs CBC 1974–77, Vice Pres. Planning CBC 1977–79, Vice Pres. and Gen. Mgr. CBC Eng. Network 1979–83; Publisher Toronto Life Magazine 1983–92; Chrmn. of the Bd., Candn. Museum of Civilization and Candn. War Museum; Pres., The Gov. General's Performing Arts Awards; Past Pres., The Canadian Stage Co.; Past Pres., Bd. of Govs., Stratford Shakespearean Festival; Past Pres., Toronto Arts Awards Found.; Past Pres., American City and Regional Magazine Assn.; co-founder, Kidsummer; Mem., Premier's Council on Economic Renewal 1991– ; Mem., Governing Council, Univ. of Toronto; Dir.: Key Publishers; Festival of Festivals; Ontario Film Development Corporation; Toronto International Festival; International Choral Festival; The Glory of Mozart Festival; Friends of Candn. Broadcasting; Print Measurement Bureau; National Magazine Awards; Adv. Counc., Ont. Law Reform Commn.; Adv. Ctte., Sch. of Bus., York Univ.; Adv. Ctte., Sch. of Journ., Univ. of Kansas; Adv. Counc., Elgin-Wintergarden Theatre; Banff Television Festival; Candn. Journalism Found.; Home: 379 Walmer Rd., Toronto, Ont. M5R 2Y5; Office: 2180 Yonge St., Toronto, Ont. M4T 2T1.

**HERSOM, Naomi Louisa,** M.Ed., Ph.D.; educator; b. Winnipeg, Man. 4 Feb. 1927; d. Frederick Harvey and Anna Sophia H.; e. Univ. of Man. B.A. 1947, B.Ed.

1955, M.Ed. 1962; Univ. of Alta. Ph.D. 1969; LL.D. (Hon.): McGill Univ. 1988; York Univ. 1988; Univ. of Manitoba 1989; Saint Mary's Univ. 1991; Univ. of Victoria 1991; Univ. of Alberta 1992; D.U., Univ. of Ottawa 1990; Teacher and Prin. Winnipeg 1954–67; Prof. of Curriculum Studies, Univ. of Alta. 1969–75; Dir. of Undergrad. Progs. and Assoc. Dean (Acad.) Univ. of B.C. 1975–79, Prof. of Edn. Adm. 1979–81; Dean, College of Education, Univ. of Sask. 1981–86; Pres., Mount Saint Vincent Univ. 1986–91; Dir. and Vice Pres., Social Sci. Fed. Can. 1979–82; Rep. to UNESCO Can. Comn.; Accreditation Ctte. for R.N.'s of B.C. 1978–80; Co-sponsor Rsch. Seminar on Women & the Work Force, Social Scis. & Humanities Rsch. Council Can.; mem., Task Force Rsch. in Edn. 1982–83; Dir., Bapt. Union of W. Can. 1972–75; Inter-Varsity Christian Fellowship of Can. 1973–76; Regent Coll. 1979–81; Vice Pres., Internat. Fellowship of Evangelical Students 1991– ; Candn. Comm. on Women in Engr. 1990–92; recipient Zora Ellis Scholarship for doctoral studies; co-author 'Curriculum Development for Classroom Teachers' 1971; 'Locally Initiated School Evaluation' 1973; 'Developing Evaluation Systems in Schools: Organizational Strategies' 1975; 'A Study of Open Area Schools in the Edmonton Public School System' 1978; 'Women and the Canadian Labour Force' 1982; Fellow, Candn. Coll. Teachers; Founding mem., Candn. Assn. Curriculum Studies 1970; Pres.: Winnipeg Teachers' Assn. 1966–67; Acad. Staff Assn. Univ. Alta. 1975; Candn. Soc. Study Edn. 1978–80; Candn. Soc. for the Study of Higher Education 1987–88; Candn. Edn. Assn. 1989–90; mem. Mgmt. Bd., Candn. Tourism Rsch. Inst. 1989–90; Corporate Higher Education Forum 1989–91; Vice Pres., Extve. Ctte., Assoc. of Atlantic Univs. 1988–91; Extve. Comm., Candn. Ctte. for Women in Engrg. 1989–92; Recipient of George Croskery Memorial Award for meritorious service to Canadian Education, 1985; Leadership Award, Atlantic Baptist College 1991; Hon. Life Mem., Candn. Education Assn. 1992; Distinguished Educator, Ont. Institute for Studies in Educ. 1992; Distinguished Service Award, Candn. Assn. for Studies in Educational Admin. 1993; Distinguished Service Award, Candn. Soc. for Studies in Higher Educ. 1993; Grand Dame of Merit, Knights of Malta 1987; mem., Delta Kappa Gamma Soc.; Phi Delta Kappa; recreation: birdwatching; Home: 636 Montreal St., #603, Victoria, B.C. V8V 4Y1.

**HERST, Beth Francine,** B.A., M.A., Ph.D.; playwright; b. Toronto, Ont. 8 Dec. 1962; d. Murray and Roslyn (Ezrin) H.; e. Univ of Toronto B.A. 1985, M.A. 1986; Univ. of London Ph.D. 1989 (Commonwealth Scholar); Governor-General's Gold Medal, Univ. Coll., Univ. of Toronto 1985; First Prize, Questors Theatre Student Playwriting Award (UK) 1988; Playwright-in-Residence, Tarragon Theatre 1990–93; author: 'A Woman's Comedy' (play) 1993, published Playwrights Canada Press, 'The Dickens Hero' (lit. crit.) 1990 and various articles, reviews, etc.; Home: Toronto, Ont.

**HERTZBERG, Peter Alexander,** B.A.Sc., P.Eng.; former consulting engineer; b. Toronto, Ont. 6 Oct. 1921; s. Charles Sumner and Jessie Todd (Alexander) H.; e. Royal Mil. Coll. Kingston Dipl. 1941; Officer's Staff Course Sarafand, Palestine Cert. 1944; Univ. of Toronto B.A.Sc. 1950; m. Marjorie A. d. Archibald and Constance Bruce 22 May 1943; children: Stephen Alexander, Deborah Jane; retired from Proctor & Redfern Ltd.; comnd. Candn. Army, Royal Candn. Engrs. 1941; Active Service 5th Candn. Armoured Div. U.K., Central Mediterranean and N.W. Europe 1941–46; Dept. of Nat. Defence Ottawa 1946–47; joined Proctor & Redfern Ltd. 1950, Assoc. 1958, Dir. 1974–85, Pres. and Gen. Man. 1980–1985; former Trustee and Treas. Candn. Indian Centre Toronto; former Trustee and mem. Extve. Comte. Candn. Jr. Internat. Equestrian Foundation; former Trustee and Vice Pres., Past Chrmn. Bldg. & Housing Comtes. Art Gallery of Ont.; Gov., The Corp. of Massey Hall and Roy Thomson Hall, Co-Chrmn., Property Comte.; Assn. Prof. Engrs. Prov. Ont.; Mil. Engrs. Assn. Can.; Home: 8 Tanager Ave., Toronto, Ont. M4G 3R1.

**HERTZMAN, Lewis,** Ph.D.; university professor; historian; author; b. Toronto, Ont. 7 July 1927; s. Harry and Pauline (Herţanu) H.; e. Univ. of Toronto, B.A. 1949; Harvard Univ., A.M. 1950, Ph.D. 1955; Univ. de Paris, 1950–51; PROF. OF HISTORY, YORK UNIV., since 1968 and Chrmn. of Dept. 1967–70; PROFESSOR EMERITUS 1988; SENIOR SCHOLAR, YORK UNIV. 1988– ; Correspondent on cultural subjects, 'L'Express' (Toronto) and other publs.; Teaching Fellow in Gen. Educ., Harvard Univ., 1953–55; Instr. in Social Science, Drake Univ., 1955–56; Instr. in Hist., Princeton Univ., 1956–59; Asst. Prof. of Hist., Univ. of Alta., 1959–63; Assoc. Prof. 1963–65; joined present Univ. as Assoc. Prof. of Hist., 1965; Mellon post-doctoral fellow, Univ. of Pittsburgh, 1963–64; Visiting Assoc. Prof. of Hist., Univ. of Toronto, 1965–66; Univ. of Guyana, ext. examiner, 1968–73; Dir. Grad. Prog. in Hist., York Univ., 1973–74; author: 'DNVP: Right-Wing Opposition in the Weimar Republic' 1963; co-author; 'Alliances & Illusions: Canada and the NATO-NORAD Question' 1969; other writings incl. articles in various journs. and newspapers; mem. Extve., Comité Internat. des Sciences Hist., membre assesseur du Bureau, 1970–80; mem. Candn. Hist. Assn.; German Studies Assn.; Champlain Soc.; Buddhist Soc. London; del., Can. Comn. for UNESCO, 1972–75; Chrmn., York Univ. Faculty Assn., 1967–68; recreations: dance theatre, photography, swimming, gardening, travel; Home: 102 Mildenhall Rd., Toronto, Ont. M4N 3H5.

**HERVIEUX-PAYETTE, Hon. Céline,** P.C., B.C.L.; b. l'Assomption, Qué. 1941; d. late Lionel and Madeleine (Gariépy) Hervieux; e. Congrégation de Notre-Dame, l'Assomption; Ste-Anne Acad. Montréal; CEGEP Maisonneuve and St-Laurent, D.E.C.; Univ. de Montréal B.C.L. 1973; m.; children: Nathalie, Isabelle, Dominique; VICE-PRES., REGULATORY AND LEGAL AFFAIRS, FONOROLA INC. (specialized firm in telecommunications) 1992– ; Extve. Vice Pres. and Partner, Donancy Ltd. (specializing in Employee Assistance Programs) 1991–93; served as Project Dir. Premier's Office Qué.; Legis. Asst. Office of Min. of Social Affairs Qué.; Special Asst. to Depy. Min. of Labour & Manpower Qué. 1976–78; Dir., Pub. Relations Steinberg Inc. 1978–79; el. to H. of C. for Montréal-Mercier 1979, re-el. 1980, def. 1984; Parlty. Secy. to Solr. Gen. of Can. 1980–82; Min. of State for Fitness and Amateur Sports, Can. 1983–84; first Min. of State for Youth Jan.-June 1984; Chairperson Lib. Party Can. Policy Ctte. and mem. Nat. Exec. 1978–80, 1990– ; mem. Qué. Bar Assn.; Candn. Bar Assn.; recreations: skiing, tennis, golf, cycling, photography, painting, theatre; Address: c/o FONOROLA Inc. 500, René-Lévesque Blvd. W., Ste. 305, Montréal, Qué. H2Z 1W9.

**HERZ, Carl Samuel,** Ph.D.; educator; b. New York City, N.Y. 10 Apr. 1930; s. Michael and Natalie (Hyman) H.; e. Cornell Univ. B.A. 1950; Princeton Univ. Ph.D. 1953; m. Judith d. Philip Scherer 28 Feb. 1960; children: Rachel, Nathaniel; PROF. OF MATH., McGILL UNIV. 1970– ; Peter Redpath Prof. of Pure Mathematics 1993– ; Instr., Cornell Univ. 1953, Asst. Prof. 1956, Assoc. Prof. 1958, Prof. 1963–70; mem. Inst. Advanced Study 1957–58; Visiting Prof. Brandeis Univ. 1969–70; Prof. associé, Univ. de Paris 1964–65, 1968; Alfred P. Sloan Fellow 1962–63; author various publs. harmonic analysis; mem. Candn. Math Soc. (Pres. 1987–89); Am. Math. Soc.; Home: 228 Simcoe, Montreal, Que. H3P 1W9; Office: Burnside Hall, 805 Sherbrooke St. W., Montreal, Que. H3A 2K6.

**HERZBERG, Gerhard,** P.C. (1992), C.C. (1968), D.Sc., LL.D., F.R.S. (1951), F.R.S.C.; scientist; b. Hamburg, Germany 25 Dec. 1904; s. Albin and Ella (Biber) H.; e. Darmstadt Inst. of Tech., Dr. Ing. 1928; Univ of Göttingen, 1928–29, and Univ. of Bristol, 1929–30, post-grad. studies; children: Paul Albin, Agnes Margaret (by late 1st wife); m. 2ndly Monika Tenthoff 1972; DISTINGUISHED RESEARCH SCIENTIST, NATIONAL RESEARCH COUNCIL, since 1969; Chancellor, Carleton Univ. 1973–80; Lecturer and Chief Asst., Physics Dept., Darmstadt Inst. of Technol. 1930–35; Research Prof. of Physics, Univ. of Sask., 1935–45; Prof. of Spectroscopy, Yerkes Observatory, Univ. of Chicago, 1945–48; Princ. Research Officer, Nat. Research Council, Ottawa, Ont., 1948–49 and Dir., Div. of Pure Physics there 1949–69; George Fisher Baker Non-Res. Lectr. in Chem., Cornell Univ. 1968; mem., Am. Chem. Soc.; Am. Astron. Soc.; Faraday Soc.; Am. Phys. Soc.; Optical Soc. Am.; Hon. Fellow, Indian Acad. of Sciences, 1954; author of 'Atomic Spectra and Atomic Structure,' 1936, 2nd ed. 1944; 'Molecular Spectra and Molecular Structure,' Vol. 1, 'Diatomic Molecules,' 1939, 2nd ed. 1950, Vol. 2, 'Infra-red and Raman Spectra of Polyatomic Molecules,' 1945, Vol. 3, 'Electronic Spectra and Electronic Structure of Polyatomic Molecules ' 1966; 'The Spectra and Structures of Simple Free Radicals: An Introduction to Molecular Spectroscopy' 1971; 'Constants of Diatomic Molecules' (with K.P. Huber) 1979; more than 250 original papers on problems of atomic and molecular structure, chem. and astrophys. applications; awarded Henry Marshall Tory Medal by Roy. Soc. Can., 1953; LL.D. Sask. 1953; Toronto 1958; Dalhousie 1960; Alta. 1961; St. Francis Xavier 1972; Simon Fraser 1972; D.Sc. McMaster 1954; Nat. Univ. of Ireland, 1956; Oxford 1960; Brit. Columbia 1964; Queen's 1965; New Brunswick 1966; Chicago 1967; Carleton 1967; Memorial 1968; York 1969; Windsor 1970; Roy. Mil. Coll. 1971; Drexel 1972; Montreal 1972; Sherbrooke 1972; Cambridge 1972; McGill 1972; Manitoba 1973; Bristol 1975; Andhra 1975; Osmania 1976; Delhi 1976; Western Ontario 1976; Laval 1979; Ph.D., Weizmann Inst. of Science 1976; (hon.) Univ. of Toledo 1984; Dr., rer. nat., Göttingen 1968; Hamburg 1974; Dr. phil. nat. Frankfurt, 1983; Fil. Hed. Dr., Stockholm 1966; Pres., Candn. Assn. Physicists, 1956–57; Vice-President, International Union of Pure and Applied Physics, 1957–63; President, Royal Society Canada, 1966; awarded Chair Francqui at University of Liège 1960; Frederic Ives Medal, Optical Soc. Am. 1964; Academician, Pontifical Acad. of Sciences 1964; Willard Gibbs Medal, Am. Chem. Soc. 1969; Gold Medal, Prof Inst. of Public Service of Can. 1969; Faraday Medal, Chem Soc. of London 1970; Linus Pauling Medal, Am. Chem. Soc. 1971; Royal Medal, Roy. Soc. London, 1971; Chem. Inst. Canada Medal 1972; Nobel Prize in Chemistry 1971 for 'his contributions to the knowledge of electronic structure and geometry of molecules, particularly free radicals'; Earle K. Plyler Prize, Am. Physical Soc. 1985; apptd. Mem. of the Queen's Privy Council for Canada 1992; Hon. mem., Optical Society of Am.; Spectroscopy Society of Canada; Japan Acad. 1976; Chem. Soc. of Japan 1978; Honorary Fellow, Chem. Society of London; Chem. Institute of Can.; Hon. mem., Hungarian Acad. Science, 1964; Hon. Foreign mem., Am. Acad. Arts & Sciences, 1965; Foreign mem., Am. Philosophical Soc. 1972; Foreign mem. (Physics), Roy. Swedish Acad. of Sci. 1981; Bakerian Lecture, Royal Soc. London, 1960; named Foreign Assoc., U.S. Nat. Acad. of Sciences, 1968; Office: 100 Sussex Dr., Ottawa, Ont. K1A 0R6.

**HERZOG, John P.,** B.Sc., Ph.D.; educator; b. Canton, Ohio 28 Aug. 1931; s. Phil Charles and Frances Lillian (Norris) H.; e. Univ. of Cal. Berkeley, B.Sc. 1958; Ph.D (Business Adm.) 1962 m. Sharon Lee Prosser, 26 June 1969; one d., Lisa M.; PROF. of BUS. ADM. AND ECON., SIMON FRASER UNIV. since 1969; Acting Chrmn., Dept. of Econ. & Comm. 1969–71; Asst. Prof., Univ. of Wis. Sch. of Comm., 1961; Assoc. Prof., Claremont Grad. Sch., Dept. of Business Econ., 1965; served with U.S. Air Force 1950–54; Russian Translator /Interpreter; rank Staff/Sgt.; author, 'The Dynamics of Large-Scale Housebuilding,' 1963; 'Home Mortgage Delinquency and Foreclosure,' 1970; also articles in various prof. journs.; mem. Am. Finance Assn.; Am. Econ. Assn.; Am. Real Estate and Urban Econ. Assn.; W. Finance Assn. (Pres. 1975); W. Econ. Assn.; Phi Beta Kappa; Beta Gamma Sigma; Protestant; Office: Burnaby, B.C. V5A 1S6.

**HESELTINE, Gilbert F.D.,** B.A., LMCC, D. Psych., FRCP(C), FRC (Psych), FAPA; educator; psychiatrist; b. Winnipeg, Man. 15 Nov. 1929; s. Charles D. and Freda Mary H.; e. Univ. of Man. B.A. (Indust. Psychol.) 1952; West London Med. Sch. LMSA 1958; LMCC 1960; McGill Univ. Dipl. in Psychiatry 1964; m. Ethel d. William J. and Alice McKeag 20 Sept. 1952; children: Geoffrey, Christopher, Pamela; FOUNDING DEAN OF MEDICINE, SULTAN QABOOS UNIV., SULTANATE OF OMAN; Chrmn., Univ. Hosp. Bd., Joint Health Ctte. for Oman; Past Pres., Internat. Health Services Consortium Ltd.; Assoc. Prof. 1969–71 McGill Univ.; Visiting Prof. 1981– ; Assoc. Clin. Dir., Allan Mem. Inst. Montreal 1969–71; Prof. and Chrmn. of Psychiatry, Univ. of Western Ont. 1971–85, Chief of Psychiatry, Univ. Hosp. Health Sciences Centre, London 1971–81; Dir., Northern Health Services and Extended Campus Health Programme, Univ. of Western Ont.; Chrmn. or mem. numerous boards, volunteer, govt. and community agencies; Chrmn., Trustee, U.S. Canada Alcoholic Beverages Med. Rsch. Found.; Extve. Coordinator, Mental Health Policy & Planning, Ont. Prov. Min. of Health 1981–83; recipient various research grants in Biological and Behavioural Psych.; Ed. author or co-author numerous med. publs. incl. research and govt. reports; McLaughlin Travelling Fellow 1962–63; Ont. Min. of Health Travelling Fellowship 1977–78; mem. various national and internat. profl. orgns.; Protestant; recreations: swimming, sailing, golf; Home and Office: College of Medicine, Sultan Qaboos Univ., P.O. Box 32485, Al Khod, Muscat, Sultanate of Oman.

**HESS, Peter C.;** executive; b. Hamilton, Ont. 15 March 1940; s. Charles David and Philis Ada (Gauld) H.; e. Hamilton Inst. of Technol. Electronic Dip. 1962; Ryerson Polytech. Inst. Mktg. Dip. 1967; Univ. of W. Ont. Mgmt. Training 1984; children: Dean, Lori; SR. VICE PRES. COMMUNICATION PRODUCTS GROUP, SONY OF CANADA LTD. 1988– ; Component Sales, Philips Electronic Industries Ltd. 1967; Broadcast Hardware Sales, Ampex of Canada Ltd. 1969; Vice Pres. Mktg. Richmond Hill Laboratores Ltd. 1972; Nat. Sales Mgr. present Co. 1975, Vice Pres. Mktg. & Sales 1983; recreation: sailing; Home: 12 MacPherson Ave., Unit 4,

Toronto, Ont. M5R 1W8; Office: 411 Gordon Baker Rd., Willowdale, Ont. M2H 2S6.

**HESSER, James E.,** M.A., Ph.D.; astronomer; b. Wichita, Kans. 23 June 1941; s. J. Edward and Ina (Lowe) H.; e. Univ. of Kans. B.A. 1963; Princeton Univ. M.A. 1965, Ph.D. 1966; m. Betty d. Max and Violet Hinsdale 24 Aug. 1963; three d. Nadja Lynn, Rebecca Ximena, Diana Gillian; DIR. DOM. ASTROPHYSICAL OBSERV., NATIONAL RESEARCH COUNCIL 1986– and DIR., OPTICAL ASTRONOMY AND SPECTROSCOPY 1993– ; Adjunct Prof. of Physics & Astron. Univ. of Victoria 1988– ; Rsch. Assoc. Princeton Univ. Observ. 1966–68; Jr., Asst., Assoc. Astron. and Assoc. Dir. Cerro Tololo Inter-Am. Observ. La Serena, Chile 1968–77, mem. Time Allocation Ctte. 1989–91; Assoc., Sr. Rsch. Offr. present Observ. 1977, Assoc. Dir. 1984; ed. 'CTIO Facilities Manual' 1973, 1978; 'Star Clusters' 1980; co-ed. 'Late Stages of Stellar Evolution' 1974; author over 175 rsch. publs.; mem. Astron. Soc. of Pacific (Dir. 1980–87, Vice Pres. 1984–86, Pres. 1987–88); Am. Astron. Soc. (Councilor 1984–87, Vice Pres. 1991–94); Candn. Astron. Soc. (Chrmn. Jt. Subctte. Space Astron. 1984–89); Royal Astron. Soc. Can. (Dir. Victoria Centre 1987– ); Internat. Astron. Union; Chrmn., AURA Observatories Visiting Ctte. 1991– , Chair 1992– ; Mem., Astronomy Planning & Priorities Ctte., Can. 1991; Review of Physics in Denmark Ctte. 1991; Chair, Astrom. Review Ctte., Univ. Texas 1993; Mem., York Univ. Natural Science Review Ctte. 1993; Mem., CTIO Dir. Search Ctte. 1993; Mem., GEMINI Telescopes (Dir. Search Ctte.) 1993–94; recreations: hiking, gardening; Home: 1874 Ventura Way, Victoria, B.C. V8N 1R3; Office: 5071 W. Saanich Rd., R.R.5, Victoria, B.C. V8X 4M6.

**HETENYI, Geza Joseph,** M.D., Ph.D.; educator; b. Budapest, Hungary 26 Sept. 1923; s. Geza Joseph and Margaret (Wabrosch) H.; e. Univ. of Budapest M.D. 1947; Univ. of Toronto Ph.D. 1960; F.R.C.P.(C) 1987; m. Caroline E., M.D., F.R.C.P.(C) d. late Geza Scossa; 15 July 1947; PROFESSOR EMERITUS, UNIV. OF OTTAWA 1989– ; joined Dept. of Physiol. Univ. of Toronto 1957, Asst. Prof. 1960, Assoc. Prof. 1964, Prof. 1967; cross appts. Inst. Clin. Science and Inst. Biomed. Engn.; Prof. and Head of Physiol., Univ. of Ottawa 1970–79; Vice Dean, Fac. of Health Sciences, Univ. of Ottawa 1979–86; Prof. of Physiology, Univ. of Ottawa 1987–89; Scientific Advisor to the Pres., Medical Research Council of Canada 1987–91; Dir., Acad. Affairs, Heart Inst., Univ. of Ottawa 1992–94; mem., National Diabetes Adv. Bd. (DHW) 1989–91; Chrmn., Nat. Rsch. Bd., Candn. Diabetes Assoc. 1992– ; recipient, Commemorative Medal for 125th Anniversary of Candn. Confederation 1993; co-author 'The Story of Insulin' 1962, German trans. 1963, Dutch 1964, Japanese 1965; 142 papers in Am. Candn. Brit. German and other scient. journs.; emeritus mem. Candn. Physiol. Soc. (Vice Pres. 1975–76, Pres. 1976–77); Am. Physiol. Soc.; mem., Candn. Diabetes Assn. (Chrmn. Grants Comte. 1975–79); Home: 417 Crestview Rd., Ottawa, Ont. K1H 5G7.

**HETHERINGTON, Charles R.,** B.S., M.S., Sc.D.; company president; b. Norman, Oklahoma, 19 Dec. 1919; s. William Leslie and Helen Rowena (Hudgens) H.; e. Univ. of Oklahoma, B.S. 1940, M.S. 1941; Mass. Inst. of Tech., Sc.D. 1943; m. 1stly Jane Helen, d. Stanton F. Childs, 28 Aug. 1943; children: William Leslie II, Childs Pratt, Helen Jane, Gail Ann; 2ndly, Rose Cosco Scurlock, 17 July 1967; stepchildren: Robert H., Donald S.; President and C.E.O., Panarctic Oils Ltd. 1970; Dir., Panarctic Oils Ltd.; Hetherington Ranches Ltd.; obtained field and other experience during summers while at college; Research Engr. with Research and Devel. Dept. of Standard Oil Co. of Cal. and subsequently California Research Corpn., Richmond, Cal., Sept. 1942–Aug. 1946; Engr. with Ford, Bacon & Davis, Inc., New York City engaged in prof. consulting engn. with particular emphasis on petroleum and natural gas technol., becoming Sr. Engr. of the Co., 1946–52; apptd. Vice-Pres. of Westcoast Transmission Co. Ltd. in charge of all engn. functions 1952; Vice-Pres. for Production and Mfg., Pacific Petroleums Ltd., while maintaining the position with Westcoast Transmission Co. 1956; subsequently Mang., Dir., Pacific Petroleums Ltd.; during 2nd World War, retained as a civilian in the Office of Nat. Defense Research Comte. of the Office of Scient. Research & Devel., U.S.A.; mem., Am. Chem. Soc.; Am. Gas Assn.; Candn. Gas Assn.; Anglican; recreations: polo, fishing, hunting, tennis, amateur radio; Clubs: Calgary Petroleum; Calgary Golf & Country; Mount Pleasant Racquet; Calgary Polo; El Dorado Country; El Dorado Polo; Home: 1001 – 300 Meredith Rd. N.E., Calgary, Alta. T2E 7A8.

**HETHERINGTON, Linda,** F.A.; artist; b. Lunenburg, N.S. 30 April 1945; d. William and Charlotte (Bezanson) Campbell; e. St. Lawrence Coll. F.A.Dip. 1989; m. Brian s. Lloyd and Daphne H. 31 Oct. 1964; children: Terrence, Lisa; professional painter since 1971; exbns incl. O'Keefe Centre 1992, '93; Evergreen Juried Art Exbn. 1991, '92; Rideau Valley Art Fest. 1981–93; Buckhorn Wildlife Art Fest. 1993; Toronto Internat. Art Fest. 1991; Alumni Invitational Exbn., St. Lawrence Coll. 1993; Lambeth Art Fest. 1993; rep. by Agnes Etherington Gall. Kingston; Burdette Gall. Ltd. Orton, Ont.; Libby's of Toronto; Art Mode Gall. Ottawa; The Gallery on the Lake Buckhorn, Ont.; works appear in Dupont Canada Art Collection, Thorne, Ernst & Whinney C.A.s, Beatrice Foods Inc., McCormick & Lock Inc.; Acad. Council Award of Distinction, St. Lawrence Coll. & Gov. Gen. Acad. Medal 1989; subject of TV series Germotte's Studio; Mem., Kingston Regional Arts Council; Kingston Artists Assn.; recreations: quilting, gardening; Address: R.R. 2, 2078 Sunbury Rd., Inverary, Ont. K0H 1X0.

**HETLAND, Forrest M.;** commissioner; b. Naicam, Sask. 17 Aug. 1925; s. Joseph Ingolf and Olena (Brenna) H.; e. Univ. of Saskatchewan, Sch. of Agriculture grad. 1946; m. Doris d. Fred and Mabel Proctor 21 June 1952; children: Bill, Betty-Jane, Barbara; ASSISTANT CHIEF COMMISSIONER, CANADIAN WHEAT BOARD 1990– ; farmed in Naicam, Sask. until 1971; Comnr., Candn. Grain Comn. 1971–76; Candn. Wheat Board 1976–90; Chair, Candn. Internat. Grains Inst. Bd. of Dirs.; 1970 Master Farm Family Award, Prov. of Saskatchewan; Dir., Sask. Branch, Candn. Seed Growers Assn.; Founding Pres., Sask. Rapeseed Assn.; Dir., Rapeseed Assn. of Canada; Mem., United Church; recreations: tennis; clubs: Manitoba Club; Home: 905 – 323 Wellington Cres., Winnipeg, Man. R3M 0A4; Office: 423 Main St., Winnipeg, Man. R3B 1B3.

**HEWAK, Hon. Benjamin,** B.A., LL.B.; chief justice; b. Winnipeg, Man. 12 Nov. 1935; s. Michael and Stephania (Kokowska) H.; e. St. John's High Sch. 1952; Univ. of Man. B.A. 1956, LL.B. 1960; three d. Deborah, Donna, Darcia; CHIEF JUSTICE, COURT OF QUEEN'S BENCH, MAN. 1985– ; Crown Atty. 1960–65; Defence Counsel 1965–71; Partner, Pollock Nurgitz Bromley Myers & Hewak; Judge, Co. Court Winnipeg 1971; Judge, Court of Queen's Bench 1977; former Ald. City of West Kildonan, Man.; Past Pres., Ukrainian Nat. Youth Fedn.; Past Chrmn., Rusalka Ukrainian Dance Ensemble; Seven Oaks Hosp. Foundation; Hon. Bd. mem., Ukrainian Cultural & Ednl. Centre; mem., Policy Counc., Centre for Ukrainian Candn. Studies; mem., Adv. Bd., Holy Family Nursing Home; mem., Osvita Found.; mem., Candn. Bar Assn.; Candn. Inst. Adm. Justice; Candn. Judge's Conf.; Candn. Judicial Counc.; Ukrainian Cath. Ch.; Office: Upper Level, Law Courts Bldg., Winnipeg, Man. R3C 0V8.

**HEWETT, F. Robert;** executive; b. Toronto, Ont. 11 Oct. 1945; s. Frank Victor Charles and Irene T. (Petersen) H.; e. Blythwood Pub. Sch., Upper Can. Coll., Oakwood Coll. Inst. Toronto; Lakefield (Ont.) Coll. Sch.; m. Lynn Ellen, d. Frank A. Hardy, Tucson, Ariz. 29 June 1968; children: Frank Gregory, Jeffrey Robert, Dana Ellen; EXECUTIVE VICE-PRES., TELEMEDIA INC.; Pres., Simpark Ltd.; former Pres. & C.E.O., Commercial Financial Corp. Ltd.; former Chrmn., Wellington Trust; P. Conservative ; Anglican; recreations: golf, hunting, fishing; Clubs: Osler Bluff Ski; King Valley; Nicholson's Island; Goodwood; Y.P.O.; Home: 93 Kennedy St. W., Aurora, Ont. L4G 2L8.

**HEWETT, Frederic G.,** B.Sc., P.Eng.; geologist, engineer, mining executive; b. New Denver, B.C. 30 Aug. 1944; s. Reginald John and Alma May (Watson) H.; e. St. Georges Sch. 1962; Univ. of B.C. B.Sc. 1972; m. Colleen D. d. Edna and Marshall Weaver 5 May 1972; VICE-PRES. & MGR. OF EXPLORATION, INTERNATIONAL NORTHAIR MINES LTD. 1981– ; Mine Geologist, Cassiar Mining Co. 1972–75, Chief Engineer 1975–80; Sr. Explor. Geol., Brinco Mining Ltd. 1980–81; Dir. & Vice-Pres., Newhawk Gold Mines Ltd.; Norcal Resources Ltd.; Tenajon Resources Corp.; Camnor Resources Ltd.; Arauco Resources Corp.; Life Mem., Candn. Inst. of Mining & Metallurgy; Assn. of Profl. Engrs. of B.C.; A.I.M.E.; Fellow, Geol. Assn. of Can.; author of 1 article; recreations: tennis, golf; clubs: Terminal City, Tower Courts Raquet; Home: 2419 Oranda Ave., Coquitlam, B.C. V3K 3A5; Office: 860 – 625 Howe St., Vancouver, B.C. V6C 2T6.

**HEWGILL, Roland William Dowler;** actor; b. Montréal, Qué. 11 Feb. 1929; s. Francis Percy Lovelace and Doris Evelyn (Dowler) H.; e. Kingston Coll. & Vocational Inst. 1948; Webber-Douglas, London, Eng. 1950; mem. Stratford Festival 1954–57, 1970–73; Candn. Players Co.; performed maj. regional theatres, most recently Toronto theatres Tarragon, CentreStage, Theatre Plus; TV performances incl. series 'Airwaves' Atlantis-CBC; recipient Dora Mavor Moore Award 1986; nominated Genie 1987 (film 'John and the Missus'), Dora 1987–88 (Best Actor 'Play Memory'); recreation: gardening; Address: 246 James St., Barriefield, Kingston, Ont. K7K 5P5.

**HEWITT, James D.,** B.Math., M.B.A.; insurance executive; b. Kitchener, Ont. 9 Aug. 1949; s. Donald Stewart and Lois Young (Horncastle) H.; e. Lorne Park Secondary 1967; Univ. of Waterloo B.Math 1970; McMaster Univ. M.B.A. 1972; m. Linda d. John and Mary Bellefleur 23 Dec. 1980; children: Lauren, Harrison; Extve. Vice-Pres., Candn. Gen. Insur. Group 1988; Finan. Analyst / Leasing Rep., IAC Limited 1972–74; Vice-Pres. Finan. & Admin., Scotia-Toronto Dominion Leasing 1974–78; joined The Mortgage Insur. Co. of Can. 1978; Extve. Vice-Pres. & Chief Op. Offr., 1982–88; Anglican; recreations: golf; clubs: Mississauga Golf & Country (Dir.); Home: 590 Shenandoah Dr., Mississauga, Ont. L5H 1V9; Office: 2206 Eglinton Ave. E., Scarborough, Ont. M1L 4S8.

**HEWITT, James J.,** F.C.M.A.; corporate executive; b. Toronto, Ont. 28 Jan. 1933; s. James Henry and Mary (Harrison) H.; e. Humberside Coll.; Fellow, Soc. Mgmt. Accts. (F.C.M.A.); m. Dorothy d. John and Mabel Barber 27 Dec. 1980; children: James Russell, Catherine Lee, Robert Allen, Ronald William; CHAIRMAN AND CHIEF EXECUTIVE OFFICER, FARM CREDIT CORPORATION 1987– ; Fruehauf Trailer of Canada Ltd. 1958–62; Dir. of Field Serv., B.C. Credit Union League 1962–67; Gen. Mgr., Penticton Credit Union 1967–76; Ald. City of Penticton 1971–76; Dir. Regional Dist. Okanagan-Similkameen 1972–74 and Union of B.C. Muns. 1974–76; el. M.L.A. for Boundary-Similkameen prov. g.e. 1975, re-el. 1979, 1983, 1986; Min. of Agric. 1976–78; Min. of Energy, Mines & Petroleum Resources 1978–79; Min. of Agriculture & Food 1979–82; Min. of Consumer and Corporate Affairs, B.C. 1982–86; Min. of Education, B.C. 1986; Fellow, Soc. of Mgmt. Accts. of Can.; Social Credit; United Church; recreations: golf, skiing; Home: 3536 Albert St., Regina, Sask. S4S 3P5; Office: P.O. Box 4320, Regina, Sask. S4P 4L3.

**HEWITT, William Edward,** B.A., M.B.A., C.F.A.; insurance executive; b. Orillia, Ont. 9 Aug. 1940; s. Cecil Medley and Mary Margaret (Moon) H.; e. Victoria Univ., Univ. of Toronto B.A. 1963; Fac. of Management Studies, Univ. of Toronto M.B.A. 1967; m. Diane E. d. Robert Thomas Hayes 12 July 1964; children: Kimberly Anne, George Edward; VICE-PRES., SECURITIES INVESTMENTS, SUN LIFE ASSURANCE CO. OF CANADA 1992– ; Securities Analyst, Bache & Co. Inc. 1967–70; Treas., Allpak Products Limited 1970–73; Vice-Pres. Finance 1974–78; Manager, Financial Operations, Imperial Oil Limited 1978–80; Pension Investment 1981–88; Pension & Employee Funds 1988–91; Treas. & Mem., Extve. Ctte., Victoria Univ., Univ. of Toronto; Trustee, The George R. Gardiner Mus. of Ceramic Art; Mem., Marketing and Publicity Ctte., The Royal Ontario Museum; Financial Extves. Inst. of Canada; St. George's United Church (Mem. of Official Bd., Bd. of Stewards, Chair, Investment Ctte.); recreations: fly fishing, nature appreciation, fine woodworking, genealogy; clubs: Ontario Club, East Hill Skeet Club, London Club, London Hunt & Country Club; Home: 26 Glengrove Ave., Toronto, Ont. M4N 1E7; Office: 225 King St. West, Suite 11, Toronto, Ont. M5V 3C5.

**HEWSON, Edgar Wendell,** M.A., D.I.C., Ph.D., F.R.S.C., F.A.M.S., F.R.Met.S; meteorologist; b. Amherst, N.S. 12 July 1910; s. Edgar Ellis and Helen Clarissa (Bell) H.; e. Cumberland Co. Acad., Amherst, N.S.; Mt. Allison Univ., B.A. 1932; Dalhousie Univ., M.A. 1933; Univ. of Toronto, M.A. 1935; Imperial Coll. of Science and Technol., D.I.C. 1937; (Beit Scient. Research Fellow) Univ. of London, Ph.D.1937; m. Julia Elizabeth, d. Dr. G. W. O'Brien, Amherst, N.S., 17 Aug. 1935; children: David Garnet, Barbara Elizabeth DuCharme; PROF. EMERITUS, DEPT. ATMOSPHERIC SCIENCES, OREGON STATE UNIV. 1981– ; Research Meteorol., Meteorol. Service of Can., 1938–39 and 1946–47; Dir. of Diffusion Project, Mass. Inst. of Tech. 1948–53; Consult Meteorol., Consol. Mining & Smelting Co. of Can. Ltd., 1939–46; U.S. Bur. of Mines, 1939–40 and 1945–46; Asst. Controller for Training and Research Services, Meteorol. Service Of Can., 1947–48; formerly Prof. of Meteorol., Univ. of Mich.; established Dept. of Atmospheric Sci., Oregon State Univ. 1969; Chrmn. 1969–76; Prof. 1969–81; holder of Roy. Soc. of Can. Fellowship, Imperial Coll., London, Eng., 1938; awarded Buchan Prize of the Roy. Meteorol. Soc. 1939;

author (with R. W. Longley), 'Meteorology, Theoretical and Applied,' 1944; contrib. articles to Encycl. Brit., 1946–47; publ. over 70 articles on a wide range of meteorology subjects; held numerous consult. pos'ns; Prof. mem., Comte. on Climatology, Nat. Acad. of Sci., 1957–61; Am. Meteorol. Soc. (Assoc. Ed., 'Journ. of Meteorol,' 1944–54, Councillor, 1945–47 and 1952–54, Publ. Comte. 1946–57; Chrmn., Bd. of Reviewing Eds., 'Meteorol. Monographs,' 1948–58; Chrmn., Air Pollution Abatement Comte., 1951–56, rec'd Award for Outstand. Contrib. to the Advancement of Applied Meteorology 1969; Chrm. Nom. Comte., 1971; mem., Nom. Comte. of Fellows and Hon. Mem., 1972–73); Amer. Wind Energy Assn. (rec'd Award of Excellence for Contributions to the Development of Wind Resource Assessment 1983); mem., Soc. of Friends; Am. Meteorological Soc.; Royal Meteorological Soc.; Int. Soc. of Biometeorol.; recreations: canoeing, hiking; Address: 1770 Avenida del Mundo, #1604, Coronado, CA 92118 USA.

**HEWSON, John,** B.A., M.A., D.del'U.; university professor; b. Tugby, England 19 Dec. 1930; s. George Arthur and Margery (Shaw) H.; e. Univ. College, London B.A. 1952; Inst. of Edn., London P.G.C.E. 1953; Univ. Laval M.A. (French) 1958, (Linguistics) 1960, D.de l'U. 1964; m. Irene d. Raphael and Mary O'Neill 18 April 1954 (divorced 1992); m. 2ndly Janet, d. Angus and Mildred Drover 18 July 1992; children (by previous marriage): Anne, Jean, Paul; (by second marriage) Valerie; UNIVERSITY RESEARCH PROFESSOR, DEPT. OF LINGUISTICS, MEMORIAL UNIVERSITY OF NEWFOUNDLAND 1985– ; Asst. Prof. of French, Memorial Univ. 1960–64; Assoc. Prof. of French 1964–68; Prof. of Linguistics 1968– ; Head, Dept. of Linguistics 1968–84; Vice-Pres., Candn. Linguistics Assn. 1968–70; Pres. 1970–72; Mem., Linguistic Soc. of Am.; Linguistics Assn. of Great Britain; Philological Soc.; Candn. Linguistics Assn.; Soc. de Linguistique Romane; author: 'Oral French Pattern Practice' 1963, 'La Pratique du français' 1965, 'Article and Noun in English' 1972, 'The Beothuk Vocabularies' 1978; 'A Computer-Generated Dictionary of Proto-Algonquian' 1993; co-author: 'Fundamentals for a Science of Language' 1984, 'The Micmac Grammar of Father Pacifique' 1990; recreations: sports, music; Home: 1 Cambridge Ave., St. John's, Nfld. A1A 3N5; Office: St. John's, Nfld. A1B 3X9.

**HEYWOOD, J(ohn) C(arl),** R.C.A., O.S.A.; artist; educator; b. Toronto, Ont. 6 June 1941; s. John William and Margaret Wight (Downs) H.; e. Ont. Coll. of Art Toronto A.O.C.A. 1963; Atelier 17 Paris, France 1967–69; m. Renate Antonie d. Anton Laxgang, West Germany 18 Aug. 1969; PROF. OF ART, QUEEN'S UNIV. 1974– ; (FULL PROFESSOR 1986– ); High Sch. Teacher Ont. 1966–67; Teaching Master of Printmaking and Drawing, Sheridan Coll. 1969–71; Visiting Lectr. at 40 universities and colleges of art in Canada, US, Britain 1976–94; 70 solo exhibitions at public and private galleries 1969–94 incl. Mira Godard Gallery 1975, 76, 78, 81, 85, 87, 89, 92; Art Gallery of Ontario touring exhibitions 1974–76, 77–78; Canadian Cultural Centre, Paris 1973; Univ. of Guelph 1974, 78, 85; etc.; three person exhibition 'Beyond the Repeatable Image' London, Paris, Brussels, Aberdeen, Glasgow; tours Europe 1984–85; Participated in every major international print biennale since 1970, notably Crakow, Ljubljana, Britain, Norway, Switzerland, Germany, etc. (winning 16 Print Awards incl. World Print Edition Purchase Award, San Francisco 1983); prints incl. 48 maj. pub. colls. incl. Metropolitan Museum NY; Victoria & Albert, London; etc.; Can., USA, W. and E. Europe, Gt. Brit.; key prints published: Pages From My Notebook 1974; Beware the Past 1975, Stasis 1976, Stereo Vectographs 1977, Persistence of Memory 1978, Carpe Diem 1979, Vanity Vanity 1980, Triple Entendre 1981, Japan Flowers 1982, Red Niche 1983, Braque Variations 1984, Toccatas and Drypoints 1985; Japan Collé Portfolio 1987; St. Armand Suite 1988; Portraits of the Artist 1989; Peeler Variations 1990; Bagatelles & Recollection 1991; Anxious Objects 1992/93; extensive articles in Print Voice Magazine, Univ. of Alta 1985 and Medicine Hat Print Catalogue 1988; Grants: Can. Council for vectograph 1976; for Colour Prints 1978; Ont. Arts Council Grants to train Apprentice Printmakers 1977, 78, 81, 84, 93; mem. Ont. Soc. Artists; Royal Candn. Acad.; Print & Drawing Council Can.; recreations: travel in Egypt, India, Japan, Turkey, Europe, Pakistan, N. Africa etc., weight lifting, canoeing, hiking in Canada, Peru, Switzerland, Nepal; Office: Queen's Univ., Dept. of Art, Kingston, Ont. K7L 3N6.

**HIBBARD, Arthur G.,** B.Sc.; oilwell drilling executive; b. Peace River, Alta. 29 Jan. 1947; s. Stanley Howard and Justine Marie (Craig) Hibbard; e. London Univ. B.Sc. 1976; children: Tina Marie, Derek Arthur; PARTNER, PHELPS DRILLING INTERNATIONAL LTD. 1983– ; Peter Bawden Drilling Services Ltd. (Canada & Calif.) 1969–73; Reading & Bates Corp. (Texas & London, U.K.) 1973–82; Dir. & Past Pres. (current), Candn. Assn. of Oilwell Drilling Contractors; Dir., Petroleum Industry Training Service; Past Dir., Offshore Petroleum Industry Bd. (U.K.); recreations: golf, skiing; clubs: Petroleum, Pinebrook Golf & Country; Home: 206, 1732 – 9A St. S.W., Calgary, Alta. T2T 3E6; Office: 1450, 101 – 6th Ave. S.W., Calgary, Alta. T2P 3P4.

**HIBBARD, Rear Admiral James Calcutt,** D.S.C. and Bar; Royal Canadian Navy (retired); b. Hemison, Ste-Malachie, Que., 26 Mar. 1908; s. late Rev. Gerald Fitzmaurice and Elfreda H.; e. Hemison (Que.) Pte. Sch.; (summer training) with R.C.N.V.R., 1924–26; Cadet, R.C.N., 1926; Royal Naval Training 1926–31; 1st m. Inez Jessie, d. late David R. Ker, Victoria, British Columbia, 25 March 1933; 2nd m. Helen Davis 5 Nov. 1988; children: Richard James, William Robert; entered R.C.N. in 1926 and in same year went overseas for training in H.M.S. 'Erebus' and R.N. Coll., Greenwich; promoted Midshipman while serving in Battleship 'Emperor of India'; returned to Can. in 1931 and saw service in the destroyers 'Vancouver' and 'Champlain'; returned overseas in 1936 and later became Extve. Offr. of the Brit. destroyer 'Ambuscade'; later held similar post in H.M.S. 'Bulldog' and served on Non-Intervention Patrol off coast of Spain during Spanish Civil War; apptd. to Halifax, 1938 joining training schooner 'Venture'; in 2nd World War was serving on destroyer 'Restigouche,' but joined 'Assiniboine' in Eng., Oct. 1939; Commanded destroyer 'Skeena,' 1940–42 in battle of Atlantic; D.S.C and Bar; apptd. to Staff of Capt. (D) as Training Commdr. for ships engaged in battle of Atlantic; apptd. to Command of H.M.C.S. 'Iroquois,' July 1943; awarded Bar to D.S.C. 1944; Legion d'Honneur (France); Croix de Guerre (avec Palmes); King Haaken Cross of Liberation (Norway); Depy. Chief of Navy Personnel, Ottawa, 1945–47; C.O., H.M.C.S 'Ontario' 1947–49; Nat. War Coll., Wash., D.C., 1949–50; Chief of Naval Personnel and mem. of the Naval Bd., Ottawa, 1950–53; Flag Offr., Pacific Coast, 1953–56; Hon. Citizen, City of Victoria; Life mem., Cancer Foundation of B.C.; Hon. Gov., Corps of Commrs. of Van. Is.; Hon. Trust., Maritime Museum of B.C.; mem. Anglican; Home: 206 - 1211 Beach Drive, Victoria, B.C. V8S 2N4.

**HIBBEN, Alan R.,** B.Comm., C.A., CFA; investment banker; b. Toronto, Ont. 21 Apr. 1953; s. Arthur Roy and Barbara Frances (Dean) H.; e. Upper Canada College 1959–71; Trinity Coll., Univ. of Toronto B.Comm. (Hons.) 1975; Chart. Accountant (Ont.) 1977; m. Elizabeth d. John and Anne Storms 20 Apr. 1990; children: Jennifer, Brandon, Turner; DIRECTOR, RICHARDSON GREENSHIELDS OF CANADA LTD.; Audit Supvr., Peat, Marwick 1975–80; Project Finance, Bank of Montreal 1980–82; Advr., Kaiser Resources 1982–84; Sr. Vice-Pres., Corp. Finan., Bank of Montreal 1984–88; Sr. Vice Pres. & C.F.O., First City Trustco Inc. 1988–91; C.O.O., First City Trust Co. 1989–91; Pres., North American Trust Co. 1991–93; Dir., RealFund; Industrial Funding Corp.; recreations: squash; clubs: Toronto Cricket; Home: 40 Otter Cres., Toronto, Ont. M5N 2W4; Office: 130 Adelaide St. W., Toronto, Ont. M5H 1T8.

**HIBBERT, Kenneth M.,** B.Eng.(Chem.); business executive; b. Valleyfield, Que. 11 Oct. 1932; s. David Dixon and Alice (Middlebrook) H.; e. McGill Univ. B.Eng. 1955, dipl. Bus. Admin. 1968; Harvard Univ., advanced mngt. prog. 1972; m. Jean d. George and Gladys Muir 25 June 1957; children: Keith, Kevin, Glenn, Sheryl; SR. VICE PRES. BUSINESS DEVELOPMENT, LIQUID CARBONIC INTERNATIONAL; Linde Gases Div., Union Carbide Can. Ltd. 1955–62; joined Liquid Carbonic Inc. 1962; Vice-Pres. Sales 1968; Sr. Vice-Pres. Div. 1974; Pres. & Chief Op. Offr. 1987; Pres. & C.E.O. 1990; Bd. of Dir., Can., U.S.A., Venezuela, Brazil; Mem., Candn. Mfrs. Assn.; Office: 810 Jorie Blvd., Oakbrook, IL 60521 USA.

**HIBBITTS, Bernard John,** M.A., LL.M.; lawyer; educator; b. Halifax, N.S. 29 June 1959; s. Rev. Dr. John Bernard and June Marie (Hilchey) H.: e. Queen Elizabeth H.S. (mem., national champ. 'Reach for the Top' team 1975); Univ. of King's Coll. (Gov.-Gen.'s Medal)/Dalhousie Univ. (Gold Medal in Pol. Sci.) B.A. 1980; Carleton Univ. M.A. 1981; Oxford Univ. B.A. 1983 (Rhodes Scholar) M.A. 1989; Dalhousie Univ. LL.B. 1984 (Const. Law Prize); Univ. of Toronto LL.M. 1986 (Duff-Rinfret Scholar); Harvard Law Sch. LL.M. 1988 (Frank Knox Fellow); Most Valuable Player Award, Oxford Univ. Ice Hockey Club 1983; m. Carrie Marie Cottreau 21 Nov. 1992; ASSOCIATE PROFESSOR, SCHOOL OF LAW, UNIVERSITY OF PITTSBURGH 1992– ; apptd. Law Clerk (1984–85) to Chief Justice Bora Laskin (d. 1984), Supreme Court of Can., Sept. 1983; summer law student, McCarthy & McCarthy 1984; Law Clerk to Hon. Gerald Le Dain, Justice, Supreme Court of Canada 1984–85; articled clerk, McInnes, Cooper & Robertson 1986–87; called to N.S. Bar 1987; Visiting Asst. Prof., Sch. of Law, Univ. of Pittsburgh 1988–89, Asst. Prof. 1989–92; recipient, Excellence-in-Teaching Award, School of Law, Univ. of Pittsburgh 1993; Anglican; author and co-author journal articles; recreations: books, international shortwave radio, swimming, travel; Home: 5642 Northumberland St., Pittsburgh, PA 15217, U.S.A.

**HIBON, Georges,** M.B.A.; business executive; b. Roubaix, France 3 Nov. 1937; s. Henri and Yvonne (Sonneville) H.; e. Écoles des Hautes Etudes Commerciales M.B.A. 1961; m. Agnes Duchene 13 Feb. 1965; children: Henri-Frederic, Delphine, Maxime; CHAIRMAN & CHIEF EXECUTIVE OFFICER, CONNAUGHT LABORATORIES LTD. 1990– ; several marketing & management positions with various companies 1963–80; Vice-Pres. Mktg., Merck Sharp & Dohme Internat. (US) 1981–86; Pres., ST Dupont 1986–88; Vice-Pres. & C.E.O., Librairie Larousse 1989; Sr. Vice-Pres., Pasteur Mérieux serums et vaccins, 1990– and Chairman of Virogenetics 1991– ; recreations: cycling; golf; club: Cercle de l'Union Interalliee; Home: 45 East 89th St., Apt. 39D, New York, NY 10128; Office: CLI: Route 611, P.O. Box 187, Swiftwater, PA 18370 USA; CLL: 1755 Steeles Ave. W., Willowdale, Ont. M2R 3T4.

**HICK, John W.W.,** B.A., LL.B.; business executive; b. Toronto, Ont. 16 July 1949; s. John W. and Irene L. H.; e. Univ. of Toronto B.A. 1973; Univ. of Ottawa LL.B. 1976; children: Amy K.L., Jennifer E.S.; PRESIDENT, JOHN W.W. HICK CONSULTANTS INC. 1992– ; Lawyer, Risk Cavan Gardner 1978–80; Fasken & Calvin 1980–81; Vice-Pres., Gen. Couns. & Sec., Dome Mines Group 1981–87; Sr. Vice-Pres. Corp., Placer Dome Inc. 1987–90; Sr. Vice-Pres., Grafton Group Ltd. 1990, Pres. & C.E.O. 1990–92; Dir., Discovery West Corp.; Smoky River Coal Ltd.; Seiferts International Holdings Ltd.; clubs: National, Fitness Inst.; Address: 6 Duggan Ave., Toronto, Ont. M4V 1Y2.

**HICKEN, Hon. Barry,** M.L.C.; politician; b. P.E.I. 8 Aug. 1946; s. Harold and Rita (Irving) H.; e. Pembroke Sch.; Montague Reg. High; m. Louise d. the late Lawrence and the late Cephenia McHerron 25 Nov. 1972; children: Charlene, Jason; MINISTER OF ENVIRONMENTAL RESOURCES 1993– ; Mem., Treas. Bd. & Rural Devel. Bd.; Liberal M.L.A. for 5th Kings; first elected to prov. govt. 1986; served as Depy. Speaker of the Legislative Assembly 1988–89; Min. of Energy & Forestry, also Min. resp. for P.E.I. Energy Corp, P.E.I. 1989–91; Min. of Community and Cultural Affairs and Min. of Fisheries and Aquaculture, P.E.I. 1991–93; served var. legis. & cabinet cttes. incl. Agric., Transp. & Public Works, Energy & Forestry, Fisheries, Indus. Tourism & Labour, Legis. Proposals Intersessional; Chrmn., Special Ctte. on the Meech Lake (Constitutional) Accord; Mem., Special Ctte. on the Constitution of Canada; operated own trucking business; later established a sandblasting & equipment business; Home: Gaspereaux, Montague R.R. 4, P.E.I. C0A 1R0; Office: P.O. Box 2000, Charlottetown, P.E.I. C1A 7N8.

**HICKEY, Brian Edward,** B.A., M.B.A.; publishing executive; b. Toronto, Ont. 20 Feb. 1945; e. Univ. of Toronto B.A. 1967; M.B.A. 1970; m. Wendy; children: Christopher, Joshua; PRES. & CHIEF EXTVE. OFFR., HARLEQUIN ENTERPRISES 1988– ; Product Mgr., General Foods; var. positions incl. Area Dir. for Asia, Mktg. Support Mgr. Asia/Pacific, S.C. Johnson & Son Ltd.; Corp. Vice-Pres. Mktg., present firm 1981; Extve. Vice Pres. N. Am. 1982; Pres. & Chief Op. Offr. 1987; Dir., F.M. Harris Music Co.; University of Toronto Press; recreations: golf; club: Bayview Golf & Country; Home: 96 Woodland Acres Cres., Maple, Ont. L6A 1G1; Office: 225 Duncan Mill Rd., Don Mills, Ont. M3B 3K9.

**HICKEY, Donal A.,** B.Sc., Ph.D.; educator; b. Co. Kerry, Ireland 13 July 1948; s. William and Margaret Mary (Daly) H.; e. Nat. Univ. of Ireland B.Sc. 1970; Harvard Univ. Ph.D. 1977; m. Margaret Moriarty d. Eugene and Hanna M. 1976; children: Hannah, Maeve, Owen; PROF. OF BIOLOGY, UNIV. OF OTTAWA 1988– ; Rsch. Fellow INED Paris 1977–78; Asst. Prof. Brock Univ. 1978–81; Asst. Prof. present Univ. 1981, Assoc. Prof. 1983, Prof. 1988; Dir. Biotechnol. Rsch. Inst. 1986–87; Fellow, Candn. Inst. Advanced Rsch.; Candn. Genetics Soc. Lectr. 1986; mem. Genetics Soc.

Am.; Candn. Genetics Soc.; Home: 36 Burnham Rd., Ottawa, Ont. K1S 0J8; Office: 30 Marie Curie, Ottawa, Ont. K1N 6N5.

**HICKEY, John Leo;** insurance executive; b. Toronto, Ont. 14 Sept. 1935; s. Leo Joseph and Adele Charlotte (Knowlton) H.; e. St. Michael's Coll. Sch. 1953; Assumption Univ., Windsor 1953–54; m. Joan d. Gordon and Rosalind McKnight 9 Mar. 1973; children: John Vincent, Mathew MacDonald; step-children: William Dennis, Sean Hugh Gaherty; PRES., HARGRAFT WOOD FLEMING LIMITED 1960– ; Underwriter, Union Insur. Soc., Toronto 1955–57; London, England 1957–59; Dir./Treas., The Toronto Insur. Conf.; Pres., Blind Leo Investments Limited; Dir., Friends of the HMCS Haida; Roman Cath.; Mem., The Jesters Club (Sec. 1976–79); Ont. Squash Racquets Assn. (Pres. 1969–72); Candn. Squash Racquets Assn. (Sec. 1974–77); recreations: squash, golf, tennis, skiing, sailing; clubs: Royal Candn. Yacht (Vice Commodore 1979–82), The Toronto Hunt (Golf Capt. 1988–89; Dir.), The Caledon Hunt & Riding, The Hamilton Squash, Devil's Pulpit Golf, Bonita Bay (Fla.); Office: 1 Eglinton Ave. E., Toronto, Ont. M4P 3A1.

**HICKINGBOTTOM, Donald George;** company president; b. Toronto, Ont. 1 July 1932; s. George Lane and Williamette (Le Drew) H.; e. Sch. of Comm., Toronto, Ont. 1952; m. Audrey Joyce, d. Clifford Webb, Toronto, Ont. 22 Oct. 1955; children: Stephen Donald, Karen Anne, Wendy Lynn; Dir., G.E. Barbour Co. Ltd.; Corporate Foods Ltd.; Management positions Corporate Foods Ltd., 1951–71; Pres., C.E.O. & Dir., Eastern Bakeries Ltd. 1971; Conservative; United Church; recreations: golf, reading, travelling; Club: Union; Home: 90 Horton Rd., Country Club Heights, East Riverside, Saint John, N.B. E2H 1R1.

**HICKLING, David,** M.A., P.Eng.; b. London, Eng. 8 Feb. 1933; s. Richard Anderson and Betha Joy (Winterbotham) H.; e. Felsted Sch. Essex, Eng. 1951; Cambridge Univ. B.A. 1956, M.A. 1960; m. Elizabeth A. S. Rogers 25 July 1959; children: Richard Anderson, Heather Mary; PRESIDENT, ECODYNE LTD. since 1977; Service Engr. Permutit Co. Ltd. London, Eng. 1956–59; Sales Engr. present co. 1959, Div. Mgr. 1966, Vice Pres. 1972; served with RA, rank Lt.; Dir., Machinery and Equipment Mfrs. Assoc. of Can.; mem. Assn. Prof. Engrs. Prov. Ont.; Am. Water-Works Assn.; Candn. Pulp & Paper Assn.; P. Conservative; United Church; recreations: sailing, squash, tennis; Clubs: Oakville; Port Credit Yacht; Caledon Ski; Home: 55 Howard Ave., Oakville, Ont. L6J 3Y4; Office: 2201 Speers Rd., Oakville, Ont. L6L 2X9.

**HICKMAN, John Roy,** B.Pharm., M.Sc., A.C.T.; public servant; b. Wellington, Shropshire, U.K. 19 April 1934; s. Alfred John and Lilla Irene (Davies) H.; e. George Dixon Grammar Sch.; Birmingham Coll. of Adv. Tech. B.Pharm. 1955; Univ. of Birmingham M.Sc. 1956; m. Christine d. Edith and Leslie Elkington 30 May 1964; children: Sarah Ruth, Christopher James; DIRECTOR GENERAL, ENVIRONMENTAL HEALTH, HEALTH PROTECTION BR., HEALTH CANADA 1988– ; Scientific Officer, U.K. Atomic Energy Rsch. Establishment, Harwell 1956–67; Sci. Advr., Health & Welfare Canada 1967–71; Project Dir., Internat. Food Irradiation Project Germany 1971–74; Dir., Bur. of Chem. Hazards, Health & Welfare Can. 1974–88; Mem., Council of Public Health Consultants; N.S.F. Internat.; Prog. Adv. Ctte., Internat. Program on Chem. Safety; Sci. Adv. Ctte. (Chair), UNEP Internat. Register of Toxic Chem.; Consultant to WHO, FAO, IAEA, PAHO, OECD & UNEP; Chair, IJC Council of Great Lakes Research Managers; Environmental Leadership Award, NSF Internat.; Adv. Bd., Univ. of Toronto/McMaster Inst. of Envir. & Health; Ottawa/Carleton univs. Joint Inst. of Environ. Chem.; Univ. of Windsor Rsch. Council; McGill Sch. of Occupational Safety & Health; Home: R.R. 1, Dunrobin, Ont. K0A 1T0; Office: Ottawa, Ont. K1A 0L2.

**HICKMAN, Philip Douglas,** B.E.S., M.Sc.; environment consultant; b. Whitby, Eng. 25 Nov. 1956; s. John Douglas Young and Juliet Dorothea Chassereau (Williams) H.; e. Leighton Park Sch. Reading, Eng. 1975; Univ. of Waterloo B.E.S. (environmental studies) 1980; Univ. of Toronto M.Sc. 1985; m. Pamela d. Melville and Marguerite Hunter 27 June 1981; three d. Angela Lindsey, Connie Marie, Jennifer Lee; SR. CONS. SNC-LAVALIN INC. 1988– ; Partner, Rowantree Enterprises 1985– ; Cons. Resource Integration Systems Ltd. 1982–86, devel. first mun. blue box recycling prog.; Waste Mgmt. Policy Adv. Dep. Min. of Environment Ont. 1986–88; course instr. Univ. of Toronto 1991; mem. Exec. Ctte. Whitchurch- Stouffville Recycling Group 1983– , Pres. 1986–90, mem. Town Council Waste Mgmt. Ctte.; mem. Recycling Council Ont. 1989– ; Fedn. Ont. Naturalists; author, co-author, ed. various tech. reports since 1982; recreations: canoeing, camping, skiing; Home: Box 1613, 197 Second St., Stouffville, Ont. L4A 8A4; Office: 2235 Sheppard Ave. E., Willowdale, Ont. M2J 5A6.

**HICKMAN, Hon. Chief Justice Thomas Alexander,** Q.C., LL.B., LL.D.; judge; b. Grand Bank, Nfld. 19 Oct. 1925; s. Percival and Myrtle (Foote) H.; e. Un. Ch. Acad. Grand Bank 1942; Memorial Univ. of Nfld. 1944; Dalhousie Univ. LL.B. 1947; Hon. LL.D., Dalhousie Univ. 1986; m. Nancy J. Mews 4 July 1953; children: Alexander, Peter, Harry, and Heather; CHIEF JUSTICE, SUPREME COURT OF NEWFOUNDLAND, TRIAL DIVISION 1979– ; called to Bar of Nova Scotia 1947 & Bar of Nfld. 1948; cr. Q.C. 1964; practiced law in St. John's with Barron, Lewis & Hickman 1948–53; Sr. Partner, Halley, Hickman & Hunt 1953–79; Chrmn., Rent Control Bd. of Nfld. 1952–66; Min. of Health 1968–69; Min. of Justice and Atty. Gen., 1966–69, 1972–79; Min. of Finance and Govt. House Leader 1978–79; Min. of Edn. 1979; Chrmn., Roy. Com. of Inquiry into 'Ocean Ranger' Marine Disaster; Royal Comn. on the Donald Marshall, Jr., Prosecution; Chrmn. Un. Ch. Sch. Bd. for St. John's 1959–66; Mem. Bd. of Govs., Dalhouse Univ.; served as Vice Pres. Candn. Bar Assn.; Bencher and Hon. Secy. Law Assn. Nfld.; mem. Bars of N.S. and Nfld.; United Church; recreations: tennis, curling; Clubs: Kiwanis (Past Pres.); Home: 62 Carpasian Rd., St. John's, Nfld. A1B 2R4; Office: Judges' Chambers, Court House, Duckworth St., St. John's, Nfld. A1C 5M3.

**HICKS, Bruce Maxwell;** journalist & machinery of government expert; b. Stettler, Alta. 18 May 1961; s. Maxwell Fraser and Sidney Agnes (Gidney) H.; e. Ashbury College 1972–79; McGill Univ. 1979–84; PRESIDENT & OTTAWA BUREAU CHIEF, HICKS MEDIA 1992– ; Chrmn., Stemax Holdings Ltd. (Alta.) 1980–82; Gov., 'No-Vote' Committee, Quebec Referendum 1980–81; Volun., Min. of Justice, Attorney Gen. of Can. & Min. of State for Social Devel. 1980–82; Vice Pres., Stud. Soc. of McGill Univ. 1982–83, Pres. 1983–84; Campaign Advr. for John Ciaccia (MLA Mount Royal), Leadership, Liberal Party of Que. 1983; Co-ord., (IYY-PSAs), Dept. of Econ. & Social Information, UN (N.Y.) 1984–85; Pres. Candn. IAU Conference Sec. 1984–85; Co-ord., (Quinquennial Gen. World Conf.), Internat. Assn. of Univs., UNESCO (Paris, France) 1984–85; Spokesperson (IYY), UN (N.Y.) 1985; Pres., Candn. Orgn. for the Promotion of Edn. Inc. 1986–88; Pres., Bruce M. Hicks Cons. Ltd. 1986– ; Vice Pres. & Managing Dir., Stemax Venture Capital Ltd. 1987–88; Managing Dir., Stemax Foreign Investment Assistance 1987–88; Editor-in-Chief, Candn. Parliamentary DataBase 1988– ; Editor-in-Chief, 'The Financial Post' Directory of Government 1988–93; Campaign Manager, Municipal Candidate Richard Cannings (By-Rideau Ward), City of Ottawa 1991; Ottawa Bureau Chief, United Press Internat. (UPI) 1992– ; Ottawa Bureau Chief, NewsEast 1992– ; Pres., Candn. Parliamentary Services 1992– ; Campaign Manager (Tom Van Dusen), Federal PC Nomination (Carleton-Gloucester) 1993; National Campaign Manager, Liberal National 'Blitz' Team (Judy Initiative) 1993; National Co-ordinator (Marked List Collection), Liberal Party of Canada 1993; Hon. Engr., McGill Univ.; Knight of the Round Table (Hon.); Member, Candn. Parliamentary Press Gallery; Pres., Bruce M. Hicks Edn. Found.; Former Sec.-Treas., Arts Foundation; Former Sec.-Treas., Hicks Family Foundation for the Arts; Former Gov., Trustee & Fellow, McGill Univ.; Former Dir., Graduates' Society of McGill Univ.; Former Mem., Royal Institute for the Advancement of Learning; club: Royal N.S. Yacht Squadron; Home: 5, 300 Cooper St., Ottawa, Ont. K2P 0G7; Office: 350–N Centre Block, House of Commons, Ottawa, Ont. K1A 0A6.

**HICKS, Robert V.,** Q.C., B.A., LL.B.; lawyer; b. Windsor, Ont. 16 Jan. 1917; s. Robert and Iva (Haight) H.; e. Univ. of W. Ont. B.A. 1939 (Gov. Gen.'s Medal); Osgoode Hall Law Sch. 1942; m. Mary c. Reginald and Edith Pattinson 24 June 1944; children: Peter Robert, Douglas Reginald, Nancy Kathryn; PARTNER EMERITUS, HICKS MORLEY HAMILTON STEWART STORIE; Dir., Matthews Group Ltd.; Former Dir., Colgate Palmolive Ltd.; CKR Inc.; Gray Coach Lines Ltd.; St. Lawrence Cement Inc.; Wabasso Ltd.; cr. Q.C. 1953; mem. Ont. Govt. Ctte. on Process of Labour Arbitrations 1960; Bennett Comn. on Collective Bargaining in Ont. Pub. Hosps. 1963–64; part-time mem. Fed. Pub. Service Arbitration Tribunal 1968–72; Director, Project on Communications & Information, Ctte. on Govt. Productivity in Ont. 1972; Counsel to Special Study Regarding Med. Prof. 1973; Former Pres. and mem., Bd. Trade Metrop. Toronto; Former Pres. & mem., Stratford Shakespearean Festival Foundation; Former Dir., Ont. Chamber Comm.; Toronto Symphony Orchestra; mem., Candn. Bar Assn.; Clubs: Lambton Golf & Country; Pine Tree Country; Residences: 2000 Islington Ave., PH 7, Weston, Ont. M9P 3S7 and 3009 S. Ocean Blvd., PH 4, Highland Beach, Fla.; Office: 30th Flr., Toronto-Dominion Tower, P.O. Box 371, Toronto-Dominion Centre, Toronto, Ont. M5K 1K8.

**HICKS, Sidney Agnes;** businesswoman, educator; b. Sandy Cove, N.S. 6 June 1936; d. Sydney Lambert and Edna Genevieve (Bruce) Gidney; e. Dalhousie Univ.; N.S. Teachers Coll.; Albright-Knox Mus.; St. Mary's Univ.; Univ. of Ottawa; m. Maxwell Fraser s. Maxwell and Isabel (Bishop) H. 30 July 1960; divorced 1974; one s.: Bruce Maxwell; CHRMN. & OWNER, GIDNEY NEWS & PUBLISHING LIMITED 1993– ; various teaching posts Alta., Ont. & N.S.; Learning Disabilities, Ottawa Bd. of Edn. 1965–74; Dir. & Corp. Sec., M.F. Hicks & Son Ltd. 1971–77; Corp. Sec., Tuff Kote Rustproofing (Atlantic Can.) 1972–74; Work Adjustment Prog., Windsor Reg. Bd. of Edn. 1977–87; Spec. Edn./Work Prog., Windsor Reg. Bd. of Edn. 1987– ; Editor, Candn. Parl. DataBase 1987–90; Editorial Cons., 'The Financial Post' Directory of Government 1988–91, Sr. Editor 1991– ; Chrmn. & Owner, Bruce M. Hicks Cons. Ltd. 1989– ; Chrmn. & Owner, Hicks Media 1992– ; Candidate, Federal Liberal Nomination (Annapolis Valley Hants) 1992; Organizer, Internat. Youth Year (Can.) 1985; Founder, 'Artists for Youth' Auction 1984; Organizer, Internat. Women's Year (N.S.) 1975; Pres. & Gov., Hicks Family Found. for the Arts; Gov., Bruce M. Hicks Edn. Found.; Pres., Arts Found.; Dir., Candn. Orgn. for the Promotion of Edn. (COPE); Gov., Education Inc.; author: 'Planning a Truly National Gallery of Canada for the '90s' 1987, 'The Effect of Legislation on Information Flow' (South Africa, a case in point) 1980; Liberal; Anglican; recreation: lace-work; Home: 949 O'Brien St., Windsor, N.S. B0N 2T0; Office: P.O. Box 362, Stn. A., Ottawa, Ont. K1N 8V3.

**HIDE, Peter Nicholas;** sculptor/university professor; b. Carshalton, Surrey, England 15 Dec. 1944; s. Gordon Walter and Clarice Marna (Ashcroft) H.; e. Croydon Coll. of Art 1961–64; St. Martins Sch. of Art 1964–67 (under Anthony Caro); m. Hilary d. Jack and Hilda Prince 14 July 1967; children: Sarah, Michael; PROF. OF SCULP., UNIV. OF ALTA. 1977– ; selected one-man & group exhibs.: UK: annual shows at Stockwell Depot 1968–79, 'The Condition of Sculpture' Hayward Gallery 1975, Serpentine Gallery 1976, Battersea Park Silver Jubilee Exhib. 1977, Arnolfini Gall. 1979; Can.: Edmonton Art Gallery (1 man shows) 1978, '82, '86, 'Sculpture City' Edmonton Art Gallery 1985, 'Peter Hide in Canada' 1986; Martin Gerard Gall. (1 man shows) 1980, '82, '84; Mira Godard Gall. (1 man show) 1988; U.S.: Clayworks Gall., N.Y. (1 man show) 1984; Andre Emmerich Gall., N.Y. (1 man show) 1990; First Triangle Workshop 1982 & '85 (Sculp. Leader), '86 (Triangle Barcelona); Triangle Workshop 1990 (Invited artist); Emma Lake Artists Workshop 1989 (Sculp. Leader); Hardingham Sculp. Workshop, Norfolk, Eng. 1986, '88 & 90; Philip Berman Sculpture Workship, Allentown, PA (Invited artist); 'Sculpture by Invitation' Law Court Plaza, orgn. by E.A.G. 1986–93; public collections: Tate Gall. (UK); Arts Counc. of Great Brit.; Mus. of Fine Arts – Hines Collection, Boston; Edmonton Art Gall.; Glenbow Inst., Calgary; Can. Counc. Art Bank; cities of Edmonton, Red Deer & Medicine Hat; City of Barcelona; Founder-Mem., Artists Co-op. Studio, Stockwell Depot 1967 (organized & participated in annual painting & sculpture exhibs. 1968–79); Teacher, Norwich Sch. of Art (UK) 1968–74 (devel. sculp. dept. towards successful appl. for Nat. dipl. status); St. Martin's Sch. of Art 1971–78; recreations: travelling, reading; Home: 11620 – 49 Ave., Edmonton, Alta. T6G 0H1; Office: Edmonton, Alta. T6G 2E5.

**HIEATT, A(llen) Kent,** B.A., Ph.D.; professor; b. Indianapolis, Ind. 21 Jan. 1921; s. Allen Andrew and Violet Rose (Kent) H.; e. Univ. of Louisville, B.A. 1943; Columbia Univ., Ph.D. 1954; m. Constance d. Arthur & Eleonora Bartlett 25 Oct. 1958; children: Alice K. Allen, Katherine M.; PROF. EMERITUS, UNIV. OF WEST. ONT. 1986– ; Lectr., Instr., Asst. Prof., Assoc. Prof. of English, Columbia Univ. 1944–68; Prof., Univ. of West. Ont. 1968–86; Wm. Riley Parker Prize (M.L.A.) 1985; recipient of grants from Can. Counc., SSHRCC, Univ. of West. Ont. Found.; F.R.S.C.; Spenser Soc. (Pres. 1982–83); N. Cent. Conf. of Renais. Soc. of Am. (C.E.O. 1973–79); Modern Language Soc. and others; Sr. Founding Ed., 'Spenser Newsletter'; Ed. Bd., 'Duquesne Studies,' 'Renaissance and Reformation,' 'Spenser Studies,' 'Assays'; author: 'Short Time's Endless Monument' 1960, 'Chaucer, Spenser, Milton' 1975; co-author: 'Golden Book of the Canterbury Tales'; co-editor: 'College Anthology of British & American Verse' 1964, 'Edmund Spenser, Selected Poetry' 1970; 'Poetry in English: An Anthology' 1987; co-ed. & co-transl.: 'Canterbury Tales' 1964, 'Lorenzo Valla, On Pleasure'; Ed. Consultant: 'Spenser Encyclopedia' 1991; author num. articles and reviews; Home: 304 River Road, Deep River, CT 06417 U.S.A.

**HIEATT, Constance Bartlett,** A.M., Ph.D., F.R.S.C.; educator; b. Boston, Mass. 11 Feb. 1928; d. Arthur Charles and Eleonora (Very) Bartlett; e. Friends Semy. New York City 1945; Smith Coll. Northampton, Mass.; Hunter Coll. New York City A.B. 1953, A.M. 1957; Yale Univ. Ph.D. 1959; m. Allen Kent s. Allen and Violet Hieatt 25 Oct. 1958; PROFESSOR EMERITUS, UNIV. OF WESTERN ONTARIO 1993– ; Lectr., City Coll. of N.Y. 1959–60; Asst. Prof.-Assoc. Prof. Queensborough Community Coll. C.C.N.Y. 1960–65; Assoc. Prof.-Prof. St. John's Univ. Jamaica, N.Y. 1965–69; Prof. of English, Univ. of W. Ont. 1969–93; mem. Adv. Bd., PMLA 1978–82, Cons. Papers on Lang. & Lit., Chaucer Review and other journs.; author 'The Realism of Dream Visions' 1967; 'Beowulf and Other Old English Poems' transl. 1967, 2nd ed. 1983; 'Essentials of Old English' 1968; 'Karlamagnus Saga' Vols. I and II 1975, III 1980, transl.; 'An Ordinance of Pottage' 1988; co-author 'The Canterbury Tales of Geoffrey Chaucer' 1964, rev. ed. 1981; ed./transl.; 'Pleyn Delit: Medieval Cookery for Modern Cooks' 1976, rev. ed. 1979; 'Curye on Inglysch: English Culinary Manuscripts of the Fourteenth Century' 1985; 'La novele cirurgerie' 1990; contbr. to scholarly journs., author several children's books; rec'd., Yale Univ. Fellowship, Lewis-Farmington Fellowship 1957–59; Can. Council, Social Science & Humanities Research Council Grants; mem., Modern Lang. Assn. Am.; Medieval Acad. Am.; Assn. Candn. Univ. Teachers Eng.; Intnl. Arthurian Assn.; Soc. Advanc. Scandinavian Studies; Anglo-Norman Text Soc.; Early English Text Soc.; Intnl. Saga Soc.; Intnl. Soc. Anglo-Saxonists; Home: 304 River Rd., Deep River, CT 06417, U.S.A.

**HIGGINBOTHAM, John,** B.A., M.A.; foreign service officer; b. Regina, Sask. 8 June 1943; s. Chris and Charlotte (Howe) H.; e. Univ. of Saskatchewan B.A. 1965; McGill Univ. M.A. 1969; m. Michèle d. Wilfred and Connie Allard 20 June 1969; children: Matthew, Ian; COMMISSIONER FOR CANADA, HONG KONG 1989– ; joined External Affairs 1969; Mandarin Language Training Hong Kong 1971–73; served in Candn. Embassy Beijing 1973–75, 1980–83; Dir., International Economic Relations 1983–85; Dir.-Gen., Policy Planning 1985–89; Chair, Festival Canada '91 Board of Directors (Hong Kong 1990–91); Fellow, Centre for Internat. Affairs, Harvard Univ. 1979–80; Home: 6 Goldsmith Rd., Hong Kong; Office: 14th Floor, Tower 1, Exchange Square, Central, Hong Kong.

**HIGGINS, Elizabeth,** B.F.A., M.F.A.; artist; b. Toronto, Ont. 21 Apr. 1960; d. Dr. Hubert Patrick McLoughlin and Julia Agnes (Higgins) H.; e. St. Joseph's Coll. Sch. 1979; Banff Sch. of Fine Art 1982–83; Queen's Univ. B.F.A. 1983 (incl. study of Italian Art Venice 1980); Parson's Sch. of Design N.Y.C. M.F.A. 1985; m. William Pickering s. William and Elizabeth Jones 29 June 1984; solo exhbns. incl. Prince Street Gallery N.Y.C. 1987, 1991, 1994 (group exhbns. 1987, 1988, 1990, 1991, 1993); Nancy Poole's Studio Toronto 1989, 1990; rep. various group exhbns. incl. Ingber Gallery 'Young Masters' N.Y.C. 1988; Addison/Ripley Gallery Washington, D.C. 1988; DeBello Gallery Toronto 1987; A.W.N.Y. Juried Exhn. N.Y.C. 1987; Coll. of William & Mary Williamsburg, Va. 1986; Ward-Nasse Gallery N.Y.C. 1986; U.S. Coll. Art Assn. 2 yr. Travelling Juried Exhn. 1984; Agnes Etherington 'Painters On View' 1983; Ont. Soc. Artists Annual Juried Exhn. 1982; rep. various colls. incl. VIA Rail Coll.; Bryn Mawr Coll., Philadelphia, PA; Univ. of Toronto; cited various mag. articles; mem. Candn. Soc. N.Y.; recreations: music, gardening, sailing; Club: RCYC; Address: 14 Edgehill Dr., Darien, Conn. 06820 USA.

**HIGGINS, Hubert Patrick McLoughlin,** M.D., F.R.C.P.(C), F.A.C.P.; physician; educator; b. Toronto, Ont. 4 May 1924; s. Peter McLoughlin and Irene (Clow) H.; e. St. Michael's Coll. Sch. 1942; St. Michael's Coll. Univ. of Toronto 1942–43; Khaki Univ. of Can., U.K. 1945–46; Univ. of Toronto M.D. 1950; m. Julia Agnes d. James and Julia Higgins 18 Aug. 1951; children: Maureen, Catherine, Peter, Julia, Mary Elizabeth, Brian, Shelagh, Norah, Kevin; Physician-in-Chief, St. Michael's Hospital 1979–89, Dir. 1982–86, Chrmn. Med. Adv. Ctte. 1982–86; Prof. of Med. Univ. of Toronto 1979– ; internship and residency St. Michael's Hosp., Sunnybrook Hosp. Toronto; Rsch. Asst. Brit. Post-Grad. Med. Sch. London, Eng. 1955–56; Clin. teacher in Med. Univ. of Toronto 1956, Assoc. in Med. 1966, Asst. Prof. of Med. 1967, Assoc. Prof. 1969; joined present Hosp. as Dir. Radioactive Isotope Lab. 1956–76, Chief Div. Endocrinol. & Metab., Chief Nuclear Med. 1970–76 (estbd. Dept. Nuclear Med. and Endocrine Clinic), Prog. Dir. Internal Med. 1979–89; Cons. in Med. Scarborough Gen. Hosp. 1956– ; Phys.-in-Chief, St. Joseph's Hosp. and Dir. of Med. Edn. 1976–79, mem. Sr. Staff 1979– ; recipient Helen L. Vandervere Fellowship Banting Inst. Univ. of Toronto 1953–54; Samuel R. McLaughlin Travelling Fellowship 1955–56; William F. Goldie Prize 1959, The Reeve Prize 1960 Univ. of Toronto; served with Candn. Armed Forces World War II; Visiting Prof. Univ. of Ottawa 1977; Session Chrmn. Panasian Oceanic Conf. Endocrinol. Auckland, N.Z. 1971; guest speaker various confs.; Chrmn. Med. Ctte. Pope John Paul II Metrop. Toronto Visit 1984; author or co-author numerous publs., abstracts; Fellow, Royal Soc. Med. London, Eng.; mem., Soc. Nuclear Med. USA; Endocrine Soc. USA; Am. Thyroid Assn.; Candn. Soc. Clin. Investig.; Ont. Med. Assn.; Candn. Med. Assn.; Candn. Soc. Nuclear Med.; Candn. Soc. Endocrinol. & Metabolism; Calcium & Bone Club; recreations: skiing, sailing; Club: Royal Candn. Yacht; Home: 10 Douglas Dr., Toronto, Ont. M4W 2B3; Office: 38 Shuter St., Toronto, Ont. M5B 1A6.

**HIGGINS, Michael W.,** B.A., M.A., B.Ed., Ph.D.; university professor, biographer, documentarist; b. Toronto, Ont. 24 Oct. 1948; s. Joseph Michael and Margaret Mary (Browne) H.; e. Vaughan Rd. C.I. 1966; St. Francis Xavier Univ. B.A. 1970; York Univ. M.A. 1971, Ph.D. 1979; Univ. of Toronto B.Ed. 1974; m. Krystyna d. Boleslaw and Frances Peterson 15 Sept. 1973; children: Rebecca, Andrew, Sarah, Alexa; ASSOC. PROF., ENGLISH & RELIGIOUS STUDIES, ST. JEROME'S COLLEGE, UNIV. OF WATERLOO 1983– ; Teacher, St. Michael's College Sch. 1974–82; Asst. Prof., St. Michael's Coll., Univ. of Toronto 1981–83; Founding Dir., St. Jerome's Ctr. 1982–90; Dir., Inst. for Studies in Theological Renewal 1987– ; Editor of 'Grail: an Ecumenical Journal' 1987; Assoc. Dean, St. Jerome's Coll. 1989– ; Book Review Ed., 'Catholic News Times' 1981–92; Cons. Ed., 'Gamut Internat.' 1985–87; Poetry Ed., 'The New Quarterly' 1983–86; Columnist, 'The Toronto Star' 1986; Roman Catholic; Mem., Candn. Soc. for the Study of Religion; Internat. Thomas Merton Soc.; co-editor & author: 'Thomas Merton' 1983, 'Women and the Church' 1986; co-author: 'Portraits of Canadian Catholicism' 1986, 'My Father's Business: A Biography of Emmett Cardinal Carter' 1990; writer, narrator and editor of 25 scripts for CBC 'Ideas,' 'Testament,' and 'Celebration'; recreations: travel, theatre, walking; Home: 38 Gordon Ave., Kitchener, Ont. N2H 1N8; Office: 200 University W., Waterloo, Ont. N2L 3G3.

**HIGGINS, Paul;** food processing executive; b. Collingwood, Ont.; s. Stafford and Belinda (Byrnes) H.; e. St. Michael's Coll., Toronto; m. Evelyn, d. P.D. Bowlen, Tyler, Texas, 25 Nov. 1939; children: Sandra (Mrs. Donald Campbell), Patty-Anne (Mrs. Latham Burns), Shelagh (Mrs. David Wilson), Paul Jr., Michael; CHRMN. & PRES., MOTHER PARKER'S TEA & COFFEE INC. and CHRMN. & PRES., HIGGINS & BURKE LTD.; Chrmn. & Pres., Sandra Tea & Coffee Ltd.; since leaving school in 1929 has been continuously in the food business; Dir. & Chrmn. Emeritus, St. Bernard's Hospital, Toronto; Chrmn. Emeritus, Food Industry Assoc. of Can., Knight of the Golden Pencil; Dir., Tea Council of Can.; Mem., Grocery Products Mfrs. of Can.; Catholic; recreations: golf, shooting, riding; Clubs: Granite; Briars Golf; Coral Ridge Country, Ft. Lauderdale, Fla.; Coral Ridge Yacht, Ft. Lauderdale, Fla.; Office: 2530 Stanfield Road, Mississauga, Ont., L4Y 1S4.

**HIGGINS, The Hon. Robert James;** justice; b. Saint John, N.B. 13 Jan. 1934; s. John James and Mary Helen (McGuire) H.; e. St. Vincent's H.S. 1952; St. Francis Xavier Univ. B.A. (Hons.) 1956; Univ. of N.B., B.C.L. 1960; m. Rosemary d. James and Catherine Keenan 13 May 1961; children: Helen Ann, Robert Austin, Michael Leonard, James Andrew; JUSTICE, COURT OF QUEEN'S BENCH, N.B. 1979– ; Student Pres., St. Francis Xavier & Univ. of N.B. Law Schs.; Counc., City of Saint John 1964–66; Deputy Mayor 1966; el. M.L.A. for Saint John 1967, 1970, 1974; Min., Econ. Growth 1967–70; Chrmn., Atlantic Prov. Transp. Task Force 1968–69; Min. of Municipal Affairs 1970; Finance Critic for Opposition 1971; Opposition Leader (of Liberal Party) 1971–78; cr. Q.C. 1978; Pres., Candn. Assn. of Mentally Retarded (Saint John Br.) 1969–72; D.C.L. (Hon.), Univ. of N.B. 1990; Home: 5 Bedell Ave., Saint John, N.B. E2K 2C1; Office: 110 Charlotte St., Saint John, N.B. E2L 2J4.

**HIGGS, Lloyd Albert,** B.Sc., D.Phil.; research scientist/astronomer; b. Moncton, N.B. 21 June 1937; s. Maxwell Lemert and Reta Mae (Jollimore) H.; e. Univ. of New Brunswick, B.Sc. 1958; Univ. of Oxford (Rhodes Scholar), D.Phil. 1961; m. Kathleen d. James and Catherine Fletcher 15 Jan. 1966; children: Kevin, Scott, Michelle; Dir., Dominion Radio Astrophysical Observatory, NRC, 1981– ; Rsch. Offr., Nat. Rsch. Council 1961– ; on leave Univ. of Leiden 1964–65; Mem., Candn. Astron. Soc. (Pres. 1992–94); Royal Astron. Soc. of Can. (Pres. 1988–90); Am. Astron. Soc.; Internat. Astron. Union; Boy Scouts Canada (local leader); author of 50 research papers; editor: 'Journal of the Royal Astron. Society of Canada' 1976–80; recreations: tennis, skiing; Home: 126 Brentview Place, Penticton, B.C. V2A 8H2; Office: D.R.A.O., Box 248, Penticton, B.C. V2A 6K3.

**HIGHAM, Kenneth Robert,** B.Comm.; diplomat; b. Edmonton, Alta. 29 July 1942; s. Kenneth Richard and Marguerite Elizabeth (Holland) H., e. Univ. of Alberta 1964 B.Comm.; m. Marie-Louise d. Paul and Charlotte Côté 26 Dec. 1964; children: Marguerite Louise, Lise Suzanne, Anne Catherine; CANADIAN AMBASSADOR TO MOROCCO, DEPT. OF FOREIGN AFFAIRS & INTERNAT. TRADE 1991– ; joined Candn. trade Comnr. Serv. 1964; served in Accra, Liverpool, Boston & Bangkok 1965–74; External Affairs Ottawa 1974–78; Perm. Rep. for Can. to UN Food & Agric. Agencies Rome 1978–82; Counsellor (Agric./Fish.), Candn. Mission to EEC Brussels 1982–86; Dir. Gen. Internat. Trade Pol., Agric. Can. 1986–89; Dir. Gen. Personnel, External Affairs 1989–91; recreations: amateur musician, golf; Office: Canadian Embassy, P.O. Box 709, 13bis. Zankat Jaafar As-Sadik, Rabat-Agdal, Morocco.

**HIGHWAY, Tomson,** C.M.; playwright; artistic director; b. Brochet, Man. 6 Dec. 1951; s. Joe and Pelagie Philomene H.; e. Guy Indian Res. Sch., The Pas., Man. 1967; Churchill H.S. 1970; Univ. of W. Ont. 1975; Artistic Dir., Native Earth Performing Arts Inc. 1986–92; Cultural Worker, Native Peoples' Resource Ctr. 1975–78; Prog. Analyst, Ont. Fed. of Indian Friendship Ctrs. 1978–81; Arts/Cultural Cons., Ont. Min. of Citizenship & Culture 1981–83; freelance theatre artist 1983–85; Artistic Dir., De-ba-jeh-mu-jig Theatre Co. 1985–86; Bd. Mem., The Theatre Centre 1987–89; Mem., Playwrights' Union of Can.; Native Candn. Ctr. of Toronto; Winner, Wang Festival Prize 1989; author: 'The Rez Sisters' 1988 (nom., Gov. Gen. Literary Award 1988; winner of Dora Mavor Moore Awards 1986/87) and 'Dry Lips Oughta Move to Kapuskasing' 1989 (winner of Dora Mavor Moore Awards 1988/89; nom. for Gov. Gen. Literary Award 1989; winner Floyd S. Chalmers Canadian Play Award 1989) and 5 unpublished plays: 'The Sage, The Dancer and the Fool' 1984, 'A Ridiculous Spectacle in One Act' 1985, 'Jukebox Lady' 1985, 'Aria' 1987, 'Annie and the Old One' 1988; Member of the Order of Canada 1994; Hon. D.Litt.: Univ. of Winnipeg 1993; Univ. of Western Ont. 1993; Home & Office: 4 Sackville Pl., Toronto, Ont. M4X 1A4.

**HILBORN, Colonel Robert Harvey,** L.V.O., M.B.E., C.D.; company director; b. Preston, Ont. 20 July 1917; s. Gordon Verne and Sadie Winifred (Devitt) H.; m. Mary Elizabeth, d. Frank Pattinson, Preston, Ont., 16 Oct. 1946; children: David Hedley, Lynn Irving; Dir., Mackenzie Trust Co. 1986– ; Vice Pres. and Gen. Mgr., George Pattinson & Co. Ltd. (Textile Mfrs.), 1948; Vice-Pres. and Gen. Mgr., Farlinger Development Ltd. (Constr. and Land Devel.), 1956; Vice-Pres. and Gen. Mgr., Gibson Brothers Ltd. (Real Estate), 1958; Pres., Harry Price, Hilborn Ins. Ltd., 1963; Sr. Vice Pres. and Dir., Marsh and McLennan Ltd. 1971; Chrmn. of Bd., Exchequer Trust Co., 1977; Sr. Vice Pres. and Dir., Johnson & Higgins Willis Faber Ltd., 1982–87; Chrmn., Canadian Insurance Exchange 1985–87; Lieut., The Highland Light Inf. of Can., 1937; Staff Capt., 9 Candn. Inf. Bgde., 1942; p.s.c. Camberley, 1943; G.S.O. 2, Hdqrs. 1 Candn. Corps (Italy and N.W. Europe) 1944–45; Bgde. Major, 10 Candn. Inf. Bgde., 1945; M.B.E.; Mentioned in Despatches; Lt.-Col. commanding Toronto Scottish Regt. 1960–63; Hon. Lt. Col. 1968–71, Hon. Col. 1971–77, Candn. Equerry to H.M. Queen Elizabeth The Queen Mother, 1965, 74, 79, 81, 85, 87 and 89; Dir. Gen., Royal Visit 1984; Past Chrmn., Empire Club Foundation; Past Pres., Empire Club of Can.; Duke of Edinburgh's Award in Can.; Fort York Br., Royal Candn. Legion; Bd. of Trade, Metrop. Toronto; Nat. Assn. Surety Bond Producers (U.S.); Anglican; Clubs: Empire; Bd. of Trade (Toronto); Royal Can. Mil. Inst.; Home: 157 Cobblestone Place, Rockwood, Ont. N0B 2K0.

**HILDEBRAND, Alan Russell,** B.Sc., Ph.D.; planetary scientist; b. Fredericton, N.B. 10 May 1955; s. John Frederick Thomas and Isabel Ruth (Ewing) H.; e. Univ. of New Brunswick B.Sc. 1977; Univ. of Arizona Ph.D. 1992; PLANETARY SCIENTIST, GEOLOGICAL SURVEY OF CANADA 1991– ; worked in mineral exploration industry 1977–82; discovered that Cretaceous/Tertiary (K/T) boundary impact had occurred between the Americas and led an effort that proved the K/T crater was buried on the Yucatán Peninsula of Mexico; Helen Sawyer Hogg Memorial Lecturer 1992; Mem., Royal Astronomical Soc. of Can.; Meteoritical Soc.; Geol. Soc. of Am.; Geol. Assn. of Can.; Am. Geophysical Union; Nat. Space Inst.; Space Studies Inst.; author/co-author of sci. papers & popular articles; recreations: hiking, scuba diving; Home: 146A Fourth Ave., Ottawa, Ont. K1S 2L4; Office: 1 Observatory Cres., Bldg. 3, Ottawa, Ont. K1A 0Y3.

**HILDEBRAND, Elmer;** broadcast executive; management consultant; b. Altona, Man. 1937; s. Jacob I. and Anne (Friesen) H.; e. Altona High Sch. 1956; children: Robin, Sanford; PRES., C.E.O. AND DIR., GOLDEN WEST BROADCASTING LTD. (operating radio stns. in Altona, Steinbach, Winkler/Morden, Boissevain, Swift Current, Shaunavon, High River, Ajax, Moose Jaw, Calgary, Hamilton); Pres., Elmer Hildebrand Ltd. (Mgmt. Cons.); Altona Mall Developments Ltd.; Red River Valley Echo; Altona Builders Ltd.; Pres., Golden West Media Consultants Ltd.; South Park Village Ltd.; Altona Mall Travel; Copywriter, CFAM Altona 1957, Sales 1958, Sales Mgr. 1960, Gen. Mgr. 1965; named Broadcaster of Yr. W. Assn. Broadcasters 1978 and 1989; Man of the Month 'Trade and Commerce' mag. 1978; recipient Honor Citation Nat. Religious Broadcasters 1983; received Candn. Assn. of Broadcasters Gold Ribbon Award for Broadcast Excellence 1991; Past Chrmn., Candn. Assn. of Broadcasters 1989; Past Pres., Dir. & Secy.-Treas. Western Assn. Broadcasters; Radio Bureau Can.; Dir., BBM; Dir., Candn. Women in Radio & TV; Past Pres., Broadcast Assn. Man.; Dir., Heritage Village Museum; recreation: golf; Home: (P.O. Box 216) Altona, Man. R0G 0B0; Office: (P.O. Box 950) Altona, Man. R0G 0B0.

**HILDEBRAND, Henry Peter,** C.M., M.A., D.D.; educator; b. Steinfeld, S. Russia 16 Nov. 1911; s. Peter and Anna (Froese) H.; came to Can. 1925; e. Winnipeg Bible Coll. Grad. Dipl. 1933, Postgrad. Dipl. 1934; Wheaton Coll., Winona Lake Sch. of Theol. B.A. 1964, M.A. 1966; Winnipeg Theol. Semy. D.D. 1975; m. Inger d. Olaf Soyland, Norway 12 Aug. 1937; children: Marcia (Mrs. P. Leskewich), Evelyn (Mrs. R. Moore), David, Paul, Glen; CHANCELLOR, BRIERCREST BIBLE COLL. since 1977, Founder and Pres. 1935–77; Dir. Candn. Sunday Sch. Mission 1945–86; Pres. Assn. Candn. Bible Colls. 1976–80; Radio Pastor, Briercrest Bible Hour 1937–78; Dir., Africa Inland Mission 1979–87; author: ''In His Loving Service': Memoirs of Dr. H. Hildebrand'; 'Contemporary Leadership Dynamics'; 'The Model of Servant-Leadership'; rec'd Queen's Silver Jubilee Medal 1977; Order of Canada, 1979; Man ofthe Year, Am. Biograph. Inst., Inc. 1991; Interdenominational; recreations: golf, gardening, fishing; Address: Briercrest Biblical Seminary, 337–2451 Gladwin Rd., Clearbrook, B.C. V2T 3N8.

**HILDERLEY, Robert N.,** B.A., M.A.; publisher, editor; b. Woodstock, Ont. 16 June 1952; s. Ray William and Dorothy Lorna Isabel H.; e. Carleton Univ., B.A. (Hons.) 1974; Washington State Univ., M.A. 1978; m. Marjorie Ann d. Norman and Helen Brooks 6 Aug. 1977; children: Erika Rae, Alicia Jayne; PUBLISHER, QUARRY PRESS 1986– ; Teaching Master, Algonguin Coll. & St. Lawrence Coll. 1981–87; Dir., Upper Can. Writers Workshop 1982–87; Dir., Kingston Sch. of Writing (Creative Writing Sch. & Bus. Writing Cons. Div. of Quarry Press); Dir., Kingston Regional Arts Counc.; Chair, Literary Press Group of Can.; Doct. Fellow, SSHRCC; editor: 'Words on Waves: Selected Radio Plays of Earle Birney' 1985; co-editor with Ken Norris: 'Poets 88'; editor: 'Images of Kingston'; Home: P.O. Box 389, Sydenham, Ont. K0H 2T0; Office: P.O. Box 1061, Kingston, Ont. K7L 4Y5.

**HILL, Daniel G.,** Ph.D.; retired officer of the Legislature; b. Independence, Missouri 23 Nov. 1923; s. Daniel Grafton and May Louise (Edwards) H.; e. Howard Univ. (Cum Laude) 1948; Univ. of Oslo 1948; Univ. of Toronto M.A. 1951, Ph.D. 1960; m. Donna d. George Bender 8 June 1953; children: Dan Jr., Lawrence, Karen; Ombudsman, Province of Ontario 1984–89; Instr. Sociology, Morgan State Coll. 1952–53; Res. Dir. Social Planning Counc. of Metrop. Toronto 1955–57; Exec. Sec., North York Area Social Planning Counc. 1957–60; Asst. Dir. Atty.-Gen.'s Proj. on Skid Row Habitué 1960–62; Lectr. Sociology Univ. of Toronto 1961–62; Dir. Ont. Human Rights Comn. 1962–71, Chrmn. 1971–73; Founder Daniel G. Hill & Assoc. Inc. 1973; Adjunct Prof., Fac. of Social Work, Univ. of Toronto 1974–76, Spec. Advr. to Pres. of Univ. (Human Rights and Civil Liberties) 1974–83; Consultant, Candn. Civil Liberties Assn. 1976–83; Sp. Advr. on Cults, Ont. Govt. and Atty. Gen. 1978–80; Sp. Advr. Toronto Mayor's Ctte. on Community and Race Relns. 1980–81; Cons. Bermuda Human Rights Comn. 1982–83; Cons. Federal Sp. Parlty. Cotte. on Participation of Visible Minorities in Candn. Soc. 1983; Chrmn. Certificate Review Adv. Ctte., Ont. Min. of Educ. 1974–83; Cons. Ont. Min. of Correctional Services 1983–83; Cons. Fed. Comn. of Inquiry on Equality in Employment 1983–84; Mem., Candn. Human Rights Tribunal 1989– ; Mem., Public Review Bd., Candn. Auto Workers 1991– ; Founder and Pres. Ont. Black Hist. Soc. (Award Winner 1984); awarded Sidney Hillman Award 1951; Centennial Medal 1967; Jewish Labour Ctte. Award 1970; Award of Merit, City of Tornto 1984; Delos Rogest Davis Soc. Award 1984; Sp. Human Rights Award B'Nai Brith League for Hum. Rights 1984; Human Rights Award, Candn. Labour Congress 1984; LL.D., St. Thomas Univ., N.B. 1986; awarded Order of Ontario 1993; author: 'A Brief Pictorial History of Blacks in Nineteenth-Century Ontario' 1972; 'Human Rights in Canada: A Focus on Racism' 1986; 'Study of Mind Development Groups, Sects and Cults in Ontario' 1980; 'The Freedom Seekers - Blacks in Early Canada' 1981; numerous scholarly articles, papers and booklets; recreations: travel, walking, hiking, reading, jazz.

**HILL, David H.,** Q.C.; lawyer; b. Ottawa, Ont. 27 Nov. 1939; d. Hinson and Gertrude (Bathgate) H.; e. Queen's Univ., B.A. (Hons.) 1962, LL.B. 1965; m. Carolyn E. Smith; children: Michael David, Trevor Carl Beck, Cheryl Louise Beck; SR. PARTNER, MESSRS. PERLEY-ROBERTSON, PANET, HILL & MCDOUGALL 1971– ; Called to Bar of Ontario 1967; Queen's Counsel 1982; articled to Messrs. Gowling, MacTavish, Osborne & Henderson 1965–66; Law Clerk, Chief Justice of Ont. 1967–68; Assoc., Messrs. Gowling, MacTavish, etc. 1968–70; Asst., Bar Admission Course, Toronto, Law Soc. of U.C. 1967–68; Instructor, Bar Admission Course, Ottawa 1975–81; Lectr., Cont. Ed. 1977–86; Guest Lectr., Univ. of Ottawa 1977–84; contrib. author: 'Shopping Centre Leases' 1976; ed.: 'Criminal Reports' 1967–68; mem., Nat. Council Candn. Bar Assn. 1976–80; Candn. Bar Assn. 1967– ; Law Soc. of Upper Canada 1967– ; Carleton County Law Assn. 1967– ; Ottawa-Carleton Home Builders' Assn. 1980– ; Fellow, The Found. for Legal Res. in Canada 1977– ; recipient, Canada Volunteer Award Cert. of Merit 1990; Commemorative Medal for 125th Anniversary of Candn. Confederation 1992; Chrmn., Bd. of Trustees, Ottawa Civic Hosp. 1979–81; Vice-Chrmn. 1978–79; mem. 1976–83; Chrmn., Adv. Ctte., Woodroffe Centre, Ottawa Civic Hosp. 1987–91; Chrmn., Adv. Ctte., Loeb Rsch. Inst., Ottawa Civic Hosp. 1991– ; mem. Ont. Cancer Treatment & Res. Found. 1983–85; Bd. of Dir., Nat. Cancer Inst. of Canada 1984–86 and 1988–89; Hon. Life Mem., Candn. Cancer Soc. 1987; Nat. Vice-Pres. 1987–89; Chrmn., Nat. Public Issues Ctte. 1986–89; Pres., Ont. Div. 1983–85; Pres.-Elect 1982–83; 1st V.P. 1981–82; V.P. 1980–81; Treas. 1971–81; Bd. of Dir. 1975–89; Pres., Carleton Dist. 1975–77; Camp. Chrmn. for Metro. Ottawa 1974; Mem., Nat. Bd. of Dir. & Extve. Ctte., Candn. Cancer Soc. 1983–89; Vice-Chrmn., Ottawa-Carleton Reg. Dist. Health Council 1987–88 (Mem. 1985–88); Mem., Candn. College of Health Service Extves.; Mem., Candn. Assn. of Healthcare Human Resources Mgmnt.; Mem., Council., Queen's Univ. 1970–83; Pres., Queen's Alumni Assn., Ottawa 1977–78; Founder & Pres., Pinecrest Comm. Assn. 1969–74; Dir., Fed. of Citizen Assns. 1972–73; Chrmn., Ottawa Police Services Bd. 1987–92 (mem. 1986–92); Assoc., Candn. Assoc. of Chiefs of Police 1987–92; Assoc., Internat. Assoc. of Chiefs of Police 1989–92; Mem., Ont. Assoc. of Police Bds. 1986–92; Candn. Assoc. of Police Bds. 1990–92; Hon. Life Mem.: Sr. Officers' Mess, Ottawa Police 1990; Ottawa Police Assoc. 1992; Candn. Assoc. of Chiefs of Police 1992; Hon. Mem., Teachers' Federation of Carleton 1993; Club: Rideau; Home: 635 Richmond Rd., Townhouse 44, Ottawa, Ont. K2A 0G6; Office: 99 Bank St., Ottawa, Ont. K1P 6C1.

**HILL, Douglas,** Ph.D.; teacher, writer; b. Fort Wayne, Indiana 15 July 1940; s. Douglas Baldwin and Catharine (Holliday) H.; e. Kenyon Coll., Gambier, OH, A.B. 1962; Columbia Univ., M.A. 1963, Ph.D. 1969; m. Sandy Newton d. H.V. Newton and Barbara Boyd 16 Oct. 1986; children: Douglas III, Samuel, Bridget; ENGLISH DEPT., ERINDALE COLL., UNIV. OF TORONTO 1969– ; book reviewer in Candn. publications 1975– ; 'Paperbacks' column, Globe & Mail 1983–90; author: 'The Second Trap' 1982 (novel); Home: 18 35th St., Toronto, Ont. M8W 3J7; Office: Mississauga, Ont.

**HILL, F. Marguerite,** M.A., M.D., LL.D., F.R.C.P.(C); physician; b. Toronto, Ont. 24 May 1919; d. Frederick Walter James and Gertrude Mary (Spragg) H.: e. Univ. of Toronto B.A. 1940, M.A. 1941, M.D. 1952, F.R.C.P.(C) 1957; Hon. LL.D. Queen's Univ. 1984; HON. STAFF PHYSICIAN, WOMEN'S COLLEGE HOSPITAL 1989– ; Director Emeritus, Canadian Imperial Bank of Commerce; Captain, C.W.A.C., Personnel Section 1942–46; staff physician Women's College Hosp. 1957–68, Physician-in-Chief 1968–84; Prof. of Med. Univ. of Toronto 1968, Prof. Emeritus 1984; Trustee, R. Farquharson Visiting Professorship Ctte.; Jean Davey Trust Fund Ctte.; F.M. Hill Hon. Fund Ctte.; mem., Am. Coll. of Physicians; Bd. of Dirs., Women's Coll. Hosp. 1990– ; Home: 70 Weybourne Cres., Toronto, Ont. M4N 2R7.

**HILL, Frederick Walter,** D.F.C., C.M., B.A., M.B.A.; executive; b. Regina, Sask. 2 Sept. 1920; s. Walter H. A. and Grace E. Hill; e. Lakeview Pub. Sch.; Campion High Sch.; Univ. of Sask. B.A.; Harvard Grad. Sch. of Business Adm. M.B.A.; m. Margaret Shirley d. Patrick J. Mulvihill, 1 Feb. 1944; children: Paul J., Terrence F., Daniel W., Colleen P., Marylyn A.; Chrm. and Dir., McCallum Hill Ltd; Western Surety Co.; Harvard International Resources Ltd.; Harvard Developments Ltd.; Marathon Investments Ltd.; Famhill Investments ltd.; Pres. and Dir., Regina Shoppers Mall Ltd.; Dir., Hudson Inst. Bd. of Trustees; Ohio Gas Co.; Chancellor, The Athol Murray College of Notre Dame, Wilcox, Sask.; Ald. City of Regina 1954–55; served with RCAF 1941 (med. discharge), US Army Air Force 1942–45, pilot heavy bombers 15th Air Force Italy and 8th Air Force Eng.; awarded Air Medal with 3 oak leaf clusters; Distinguished Flying Cross; Home: 27 Trudeau Bay, Regina, Sask. S4S 6V3; Office: 20th Flr., McCallum Hill Centre, 1874 Scarth St., PO Box 527, Regina, Sask. S4P 2G8.

**HILL, Graham Roderick,** M.A., M.L.S.; university librarian; b. Richmond, Surrey, Eng. 4 Apr. 1946; s. Herbert Edgar and Elsie (Davies) H.; e. Univ. of Newcastle-on-Tyne B.A. 1968; Univ. of Lancaster M.A. 1969; Univ. of W. Ont. M.L.S. 1970; m. Penelope Mary d. Maj. John Potts 31 Aug. 1968; one d. Lindsay; UNIV. LIBRARIAN, McMASTER UNIV. 1979– ; Assn. of Research Libraries (Dir. 1983–86); Candn. Assn. of Research Libraries (Pres. 1985–87); Ont. Counc. of University Libraries (Chrmn. 1984–86); Bd. of Govs., Hillfield-Strathallan Coll. (Chrmn. 1989–91); Hamilton Assn. (Councillor 1979–85); joined present lib. 1971 holding various positions incl. Assoc. Univ. Lib. (Collections Dev.); Council on Lib. Resources Acad. Lib. Mang. Intern, Ind. Univ. Lib. 1977–78; Home: 15 Forestview Dr., Dundas, Ont. L9H 6M9; Office: 1280 Main St. W., Hamilton, Ont. L8S 4L6.

**HILL, John Lorne Amos,** M.A., LL.B.; lawyer; b. Cobourg, Ont. 18 Sept. 1946; s. Lorne Clifford and Ann Helen (Fitzmaurice) H.; e. Queen's Univ. B.A. 1969, M.A. 1971, LL.B. 1973; PRISONER RIGHTS LAWYER, JOHN L. HILL, Barrister and Solicitor 1988– ; articled with Siskind, Cromarty, London; called to Bar of Ont. 1975; estbd. own law firm London 1975; Dir., Correctional Law Project, Queen's Univ. 1985–87; Staff Solicitor, Legal Assistance of Windsor and Sessional Lecturer, Univ. of Windsor, 1987–88; accredited child representation lawyer; Liberal cand. for Northumberland fed. g.e. 1984; Past Dir., Ont. Humane Soc.; Lakeshore Summer Festival Cobourg, Ont.; Pres. London Humane Soc. 1984–85; ed. 'O'Connors Prison Law and Administration in Canada' 1985; author 'Correctional Law in Canada' 1986; mem. Am. Correctional Assn.; Vice-Pres., Northumberland Law Assoc. 1993– ; R. Catholic; recreations: scuba, golf; Address: 532 George St., Cobourg, Ont. K9A 3N2.

**HILL, Kathleen L. (Kay);** author; b. Halifax, N.S. 7 Apl. 1917; d. Henry and Margaret Elizabeth (Ross) H.; e. elem., high and bus. schs.; author published plays: 'Midnight Burial' 1955, 'Three to get Married' 1962, 'Cobbler, Stick To Thy Last' 1967; children's books: 'Glooscap and His Magic' 1963 (USA, Can., Eng. & Japan); 'Badger, the Mischief Maker' 1965; 'And Tomorrow the Stars' 1968; 'More Glooscap Stories' 1970; 'Joe Howe, the Man Who Was Nova Scotia' 1980; writer numerous plays, serials, series, documentaries CBC radio and TV; various stories and articles mags. and newspapers, unpublished radio plays adapted and produced on stage; readings in libs. and schs. under Can. Council and Writers Fedn. N.S. progs.; sometime lectr. and guest speaker; recipient N.S. Drama Award 2 yrs.; CLA Book of Yr. for Children 1969; Vicky Metcalf Award 1971; Evelyn Richardson Meml. Lit. Award 1981; mem. Writers Fedn. N.S.; recreation: oil painting; Address: Ketch Harbour, N.S. B0J 1X0.

**HILL, Kenneth Willis John,** B.Sc., P.Eng.; mining executive; b. Sioux Lookout, Ont. 6 Feb. 1939; s. Uno John and Alice Mae (Countryman) H.; e. Haileybury (Ont.) Sch. of Mines Mining Dip. 1958; Mich. Technol. Univ. B.Sc. 1962; m. Mary d. Herbert and Olive Tompson 10 July 1965; children: Martin Gregory, Sally Ann Stephanie; GENERAL MANAGER, IZOK PROJECT, METALL MINING CORP. 1992– ; Vice Pres. Campbell Resources Inc.; Dir. N.W.T. Chamber of Mines; Northwest Gold Corp.; Sonora Gold Corp.; M.S.V. Resources Inc.; Vice Pres. Eng. J.S. Redpath Ltd. North Bay, Ont., Tempe, Ariz. 1974–80; Vice Pres. Mine Devel. Placer Dome Inc. 1980–88; Vice Pres. Operations Northgate Exploration Ltd. 1988–92; mem. Assn. Profl. Engs. Prov. Ont.; Candn. Inst. Mining & Metall.; Bd. Trade Metrop. Toronto; Club: Engineers; Home: 2579 Jarvis St., Mississauga, Ont. L5C 2P9.

**HILL, Paul James,** B.S., B.A., M.B.A.; business executive; b. Cambridge, Mass. 20 Oct. 1945; s. Frederick and Shirley M. (Mulvihill) H.; e. Campion Coll.; Georgetown Univ., B.S., B.A. 1963; Univ. of W. Ont., M.B.A. 1967; m. Carol Rosanne d. Walter and Edna Erb 28 Dec. 1963; children: Rosanne, Shannon, Matthew, Janaury, Kathryn;; PRES., MCCALLUM HILL COMPANIES 1978– ; Investment Analyst, Burns Fry Ltd. 1969–72; Mgr., 1972–76; Vice-Pres. & Gen. Mgr. 1976–78; Dir., Western Surety Co.; Harvard Development Limited; Marathon Investments Limited; North Canadian Oils Limited; Harvard Internat. Resources Ltd.; Saskatchewan Roughriders Football Club; Lakeshore Estates Club; Can. Trust Co.; Asia Pacific Found.; Nat. Employers Support Ctte. for the Armed Services; Dir., Candn. Council for Aboriginal Business; Saskatchewan Chrmn., Candn. Forces Liaison Council; Vice-Chrmn., C.D. Howe Inst.; Sask. Chrmn., Counc. for Candn. Unity; Sask. Chrmn. & Trustee, Olympic Trust of Canada; Bd. of Regents, Athol Murray Coll. of Notre Dame; Sask. Chrmn., Prince Philip Appeal for Commonwealth Veterans (Can.); Trustee, Fraser Inst.; Hon. Col., 16 (Sask.) Service Battalion; Outstanding student award, S.A.M.; awarded Commemorative Medal for 125th Anniversary of Candn. Confederation 1992; Mem., Young Pres. Orgn., Delta Phi Epsion; recreations: jogging, squash, tennis, skiing, golf; Clubs: Assiniboia, Wascana, St. Charles, Lakeshore Estates; Home: 10 McNiven Pl., Regina, Sask. S4S 3X2; Office: P.O. Box 527, Regina, Sask. S4P 2G8.

**HILL, Rev. Peter Allen,** B.A., B.Th.; chaplain; b. Guelph, Ont. 23 Aug. 1940; s. Ven. Fredrick Allen and Margaret Edna (Wallace) H.; e. McMaster Univ. B.A. 1962; Huron Coll. Univ. of W. Ont. B.Th. 1965; m. Nancy d. Frederick and Julia Morrow 2 Feb. 1963; CHAPLAIN, ST. GEORGE'S COLLEGE 1989– ; Asst. Curate St. John's Ch. Thunder Bay, Ont. 1965–68; Rector St. Joseph Island Parish, Richard Landing, Ont., also Teacher Central Algoma Secondary Sch. 1968–76; Chaplain Trinity Coll. Sch. Port Hope, Ont. 1976–85; Headmaster, Queen Margaret's Sch. 1985–89; Anglican; Address: 118 Exeter Rd., Ajax, Ont. L1S 2K5.

**HILL, Peter B.,** D.F.C., B.Eng.; consultant; b. Toronto, Ont. 1 March 1923; s. Clarence Bruce and Charlotte Muriel (Allen) H.; e. Ridley Coll., St. Catharines, Ont. (1932–36); St. Catharines Coll. Inst. (1936–41) m; McGill Univ., B.Eng. 1949; Mang. course, Univ. of W. Ont. (1959); m. Marjorie Gertrude, d. R. A. Hanright, St. Catharines, Ont., 26 Dec. 1944; children: Derek Peter Bruce, Susan Virginia; Vice Pres., Hillmar Glen Enterprises Ltd., Sales, Mktg. & Mfg. Consultants; served in 2nd World War, enlisting with R.C.A.F., May 1941; Grad. as Sgt. Air Observer, Feb. 1942; Overseas, 1942 attached to R.A.F.; Commissioned 1943; repatriated July 1944; discharged with rank of Flight Lt.; D.F.C.; Operations Wing & Bar; mem., Niagara Peninsula Armed Forces Inst.; Royal Candn. Legion; Pres. (1971–72) St. Catharines & Dist. Chamber of Comm.; Conservative; Anglican; recreations: fishing, hunting; Home: 6 Strathmore Rd., St. Catharines, Ont. L2T 2C5; Office: P.O. Box 922, St. Catharines, Ont. L2R 6Z4.

**HILL, Peter C.,** B.A., M.A., Ph.D.; university president; b. Kentville, N.S. 14 July 1944; s. Lloyd Kenneth (dec.) and Irene H.; e. Univ. of N.B. B.A. 1966; Univ. of Toronto M.A. 1967, Ph.D. 1971; children: Susannah, Caitlin, Michael; President, University College of Cape Breton 1989; var. teaching positions 1967–71; Teaching Master, John Abbott College 1971–72; Academic Dean, Lennoxville Campus, Champlain Regional College 1972–73; Principal 1973–78; Acting Campus Principal, St. Lambert Campus 1974–75; Dean, Applied Arts & Hospitality, Sir Sanford Fleming College (SSFC) 1978–82; Principal, Sutherland Campus & Sr. Academic Offr. 1982–88; Chairman & Organizer, Candn. Studies Conf. 1975; of a Nuclear Disarmament Conf. 1976; Founder, Centennial Theatre Cultural Series 1976–78; Governor General's Bronze Medal and several other acad. awards on H.S. grad.; Class of 1969 prize for outstanding achievement; fellowships: 2 declined, 1 hon. mention, Univ. of Toronto Open, Prov. of Ont. 1967–68, Canada Council 1968–69, 1969–70; Mem., Order of Outstanding Young Canadians; extensive community serv. incl. Chair, United Way Campaign, SSFC 1988; Mem., Greater Peterborough C. of C. 1978– ; Candn. Mfrs. Assn. Edn. Branch 1982– ; College-City Liaison Ctte. 1982– ; Data Collection Ctte., Vision 2000 1988– ; Chair, Senior Academic Officers & College Ctte. on Academic Officers 1987–88; author of several papers, presentations & workshops; recreations: minor hockey; clubs: Rotary Internat., Saint George's (Pres. 1976, '77); Home: 455 King's Road, Sydney, N.S. B1S 1B6.

**HILL, Peter C.,** P.Eng.; insurance executive; b. 1 March 1943; m. Evelyn Schindler; one child: Ingo; SENIOR VICE-PRES., INVESTMENTS, STANDARD LIFE ASSURANCE CO.; Pres. & Dir., Standard Life Portfolio Mngt. Limited; Past Pres., Montreal Soc. of Financial Analysts; Past Officer & Dir., The Candn. Council of Financial Analysts; Mem., Assn. of Professional Engrs. of Ont.; Institute of Mining & Metallurgy; Vice-Pres., Austrian Soc.; Home: 392 Corot St., Nun's Island, Que. H3E 1L6; Office: 1245 Sherbrooke St. W., Montreal, Que. H3G 1G3.

**HILL, Robert George,** B. Arch.; architect; editor; b. Toronto, Ont. 28 June 1949; s. Leighton Carlos and Edna Grace (Frise) H.; e. Ryerson Polytech. Inst. Dipl. in Arch. Technol. 1968; Univ. of Toronto Sch. of Arch. B.Arch. 1972; EDITOR AND COMPILER, BIOGRAPHICAL DICTIONARY OF ARCHITECTS IN CANADA 1800–1950, 1977– ; mem. Barton Myers Associates, Architects/Planners 1975–87, Assoc. 1978–84; recipient Toronto Chapter Ont. Assn. Archs. Prize 1969; Canada Mortgage and Housing Corp. Travelling Scholarship 1971 (European Study); Toronto Arch. Guild Medal 1972; George Goulstone Travelling Scholarship 1972; Ont. Heritage Foundation Grant; Samuel and Saidye Bronfman Foundation Grant 1980; Social Sciences & Humanities Research Council Can. Grant (Dictionary project) 1982. 1983, 1985; mem. Ont. Assn. Archs.; Royal Arch. Inst. Can.; Soc. Study Arch. in Can.; Arch. Conservancy Ont.; recreations: photography, reading; Office: P.O. Box 1066, Stn. A, 25 The Esplanade, Toronto, Ont. M5W 1G6.

**HILLIARD, Robert I.,** B.A., M.D., M.Ed., F.R.C.P.(C), F.A.A.P.; pediatrician; b. Fowling, China 29 Nov. 1943; s. Irwin M. and Agnes (Magee) H.; e. Nutana Collegiate Inst., Saskatoon, Sask. 1960; Univ. of Sask. B.A. 1963; Univ. of Toronto M.D. 1967, M.Ed. 1990; m. Jean Marie d. Jack Harper 4 July 1968; children: Michael Robert, Elizabeth Ann; MEM., DIV. OF GEN. PEDIATRICS, HOSP. FOR SICK CHILDREN 1979– ; ASSOC. PROF. DEPT. OF PEDIATRICS, FAC. OF MED., UNIV. OF TORONTO 1982– ; Assoc. Staff., Centre for Studies in Med. Educ., Fac. of Med., Univ. of Toronto; Jr. Rotating Intern Toronto Gen. Hosp. 1967–68; Jr. and Sr. Asst. Resident Hosp. for Sick Chidren Toronto 1970–72; Resident III Montreal Children's Hosp. 1972–73; Asst. Lectr. Univ. of Nairobi, Kenya 1973–74; Chief Pediatric Resident Hosp. for Sick Children Toronto 1974–75; Med. Offr. Maseno Hosp. (Anglican Ch.) Maseno, Kenya 1968–70; Registrar Kenyata National Hosp. Nairobi 1973–74; Pediatre Inst. Med. Evangelique, Kimpese, Zaire and Med. Dir. Inst. Technique Med. de Kimpese, Zaire 1975–78; Mem. Examining Bd. in Pediatrics for the Royal Coll. of Physicians and Surgeons of Can. 1987– ; Chrmn., Examining Bd. in Pediatrics, R.C.P.S. 1991– ; mem. Ed. Bd. Modern Medicine of Can.; former Missionary, United Ch. of Can.; Elder and Sunday Sch. Teacher Bloor St. United Ch.; mem. Candn. Pediatric Soc.; Am. Acad. of Pediatrics; recreations: music (trombone); jogging (completed 5 marathons); triathlons; hockey; Home: 24 Moccasin Trail, Don Mills, Ont. M3C 1Y7; Office: 555 University Ave., Toronto, Ont. M5G 1X8.

**HILLIER, James,** M.A., Ph.D., F.A.P.S.; retired research executive; pioneer in electron microscopy; b. Brantford, Ont. 22 Aug. 1915; s. James and Ethel Anne (Cooke) H.; e. Univ. of Toronto, B.A. 1937 (Math. and Physics), M.A.(Physics) 1938, Ph.D. (Physics) 1941; D.Sc. (Hon.) Univ. of Toronto 1978; D.Sc. (Hon.) New Jersey Inst. of Tech. 1981; m. Florence Marjory, d. William Wynship Bell, 24 Oct. 1936; two s., James Robert, William Wynship; Extve. Vice Pres., Research & Engn., RCA Corp., 1969–76; Research Asst., Banting Inst. of Univ. of Toronto Med. Sch., 1939–40; designer and builder (with Albert Prebus) 1st successful high-resolution electron microscope in W. Hemisphere, 1937–40; Research Physicist and Engr., RCA, 1940–53; Dir. of Research Dept., Melpar, Inc., 1953; Adm. Engr., Research & Engn., RCA 1954; Chief Engr., RCA Comm. Electronics Products 1955–57; Gen. Mgr., RCA Laboratories 1957; Vice-Pres., RCA Laboratories, 1958–68; Vice-Pres., Research & Engn. 1968–69; Extve. Vice Pres., Research and Engn. 1969–76; Extve. Vice Pres. and Sr. Scientist 1976–77 (ret.); mem. of Nat. Acad. of Engineering; Fellow, Am. Assn. Advance. Science; Fellow, Inst. Elect. & Electronic Engrs., Fellow, Am. Phys. Soc.; Eminent mem., Eta Kapp Nu; Past Pres., Electron Microscope Soc. of Am.; Am. Public Health Assn. (Albert Lasker Award, 1960); Pres., Indust. Research Inst. 1963–64; Pres., Indust. Reactor Labs., 1964–65; Comm. Tech. Adv. Bd., U.S. Dept. Comm. 1964–70; Chrmn., Adv. Council to Dept. Elect. Engn., Princeton Univ., 1965; Gov. Bd., Am. Inst. Physics 1964–65; mem., Adv. Council, Coll. of Eng., Cornell Univ. since 1966; mem., N.J. Higher Educ. Study Comte., 1963–64; mem. Joint Consult. Com., U.S. Agency for Internat. Devel/Egyptian Acad. of Sci. Research & Technol. 1978–84; mem. of Bd., National Inventors Hall of Fame Foundation 1992– ; Sigma Xi; Publications: co-author of 'Electron Optics and the Electron Microscope,' 1945; about 150 papers dealing mainly with fields of electron microscopy and research management; holds 41 patents in his name; medalist, Ind. Research Inst. 1975; inducted Nat. Inventors Hall of Fame (U.S.) 1980; Commonwealth Award laureate 1980; Founders Medal Inst., Electric & Electronic Engrs. 1981; Presidential Award, Microprobe Analysis Soc. 1989; Protestant; Home: 22 Arreton Rd., Princeton, N.J., 08540 USA.

**HILLIKER, John Arthur Charles,** B.A.; financial executive; b. Toronto, Ont. 17 Feb. 1928; s. Arthur Ellwood and Kathleen (Keyes) H.; e. Univ. of Toronto B.A. 1951; Univ. of Alta. Banff Sch. Advanced Mgmt.; Harvard Univ. Advanced Mgmt. Program; m. Barbara Doreen d. Russell E. Kenny, Almonte, Ont. 20 Feb. 1954; children: Nancy Lynne, David John; INVESTMENT CONSULTANT; Dir., Continental Insurance Co. of Can.; Thornmark Corporate Management Inc.; St. Lawrence Starch Co. Ltd.; The Sumitomo Bank of Can.; Upper Lakes Group Inc.; Cairn Capital Inc.; Bd. of Govs., Queen Elizabeth Hosp.; joined Canadian Imperial Bank of Commerce 1951, Mgr., Montego Bay, Jamaica 1960, Ottawa 1964; Asst. Gen. Mgr. and Mgr. Main Br. Toronto 1965–70; Vice Pres. H.O. 1971; Sr. Vice Pres. and Regional Gen. Mgr. B.C. 1973; Sr. Vice Pres. Domestic Regions 1976 and Extve. Vice Pres. 1978; Vice Chrmn. & Dir. 1980–82; Chrmn., C.E.O. & Dir., Canada Permanent Trust Co. and Canada Permanent Mortgage Corp. 1982–85; Chrmn. & Dir., Canada Trustco Mortgage Corp./The Canada Trust Co. Jan. 1, 1986; Pres., C.E.O. & Dir., Bimcor Inc. 1986–92; Sr. Partner, J.A.C. Hilliker & Associates 1993; recreations: golf, boating, tennis, bridge; Clubs: Toronto; Granite; Rosedale Golf; Address: 22 McGlashan Court, Toronto, Ont. M5M 4M6.

**HILLIS, Bryan V.,** B.A., M.A. (Oxon.), Ph.D.; b. Regina, Sask. 9 June 1956; s. Samuel Victor and Alma Laura (Maier) H.; e. Univ. of Regina, B.A. (Great Distinction) 1978; Univ. of Man. 1977–79; Oxford Univ. M.A. 1981; Univ. of Chicago Ph.D. 1988; Ford of Can. Scholarship 1974; Gen. Proficiency Awards 1974–77; Gov. Gen. Medal 1978; Univ. of Man. Grad. Fellowship 1978–79; Rhodes Scholar 1979; Ph.D. Student, Univ. of Chicago 1983–88 (Tuition award 1983–84, 85–86, SSHRC Doctoral Fellowship 1986–87); SSHRC Canada Rsch. Fellow 1990–93; m. Dr. Joanne Patricia Kavanagh 14 June 1986; ASST. PROF., RELIGIOUS STUDIES, LUTHER COLL., UNIV. OF REGINA; Corp. Devel. Analyst, Sask. Govt. Ins. 1981–82; Lectr., Univ. of Regina 1984–85; Instr., Memorial Univ. of Nfld. 1988; Instr., Religious Studies Program, York Univ. 1988–89; Asst. Aquatics Supr. 1977–81, 1983; Pool Mgr. 1985; Nat. Lifeguard & Swim Inst. 1974–90; Cert. of Thanks, Royal Life Saving Soc. 1980; Mem., Prov. Water Polo Team 1974–83; Chrmn., Aquarama Ctte., RLSS 1985; Dir., Regina Rowing Club 1983, 1985; Dir. & Vice-Pres., Sask. Water Polo Assn. 1976–81; Mem., Bd. of Dirs., Sask. Sport Hall of Fame and Museum, Regina, Sask.; Chrmn., Sport History Project Ctte.; Editor, Regina Rowing Club Newsletter (Newsweep); Editor, 'For the Record' (a periodical of the Candn. Lutheran Historical Assn.) 1992– ; Secy. of Bd. of Elders, Grace Lutheran Ch. 1990– ; recipient, 'Vital Link Award' awarded for volunteer work; author: 'Can Two Walk Together Unless They Be Agreed? American Religious Schisms in the 1970's' 1991; recreations: sports; Clubs:

Masters Swimming, Rowing; Home: 195 Angus Cres., Regina, Sask. S4T 6N3; Office: Luther Coll., Univ. of Regina, Regina, Sask. S4S 0A2.

**HILLIS, Richard Lyle,** B.Ed., M.F.A.; writer; educator; b. Nipawin, Sask. 3 Feb. 1956; s. Lyle Arthur and Joyce Annie (Morgan) H.; e. Univ. of Sask. B.Ed. 1979; Univ. of Iowa M.F.A. 1985; Stanford Univ. 1988–90, Stegner Fellow; m. Patricia d. Elmer and Mary Appelgren 29 Aug. 1988; children: Cullen Richard, Cassidy Patricia; School teacher Sask. 1980–82; Instr. Saskatoon Community Coll. 1985; Fiction Lectr. Univ. Cal. Hayward 1989; Jones Lectr. in Fiction Writing, Stanford Univ. 1990–93; recipient Commonwealth of Cal. Silver Medal 1991; Fellowships to Yaddo and Chesterfield Film Writers Project; Can. Council, Sask. Arts Bd. grants; author 'Blue Machines of Night' poetry 1988 (finalist, 1988 Lampert Award); 'Limbo River' short stories 1990 (Drue Heinz Lit. Award 1990); co-author 'Canadian Brash' short stories 1990; publs. various lit. mags. and anthols.; mem. Sask. Writers Guild; ACTRA; PEN; Home: 499A Thompson Ave., Mountain View, CA 94043 USA; Office: Stanford, Ca. 94305 USA.

**HILLMAN, Donald Arthur,** O.C., M.D.; b. Montreal, Que. 25 June 1925; s. Daniel and Bertha Jean H.; m. Elizabeth d. Fred Sloman, Clinton, Ont. 29 Dec. 1955; 5 children; PROF. OF PEDIATRICS, MEMORIAL UNIV. OF NFLD.; DIR. CHILD HEALTH PROGRAM, UGANDA 1983–87; served with RCA Overseas 1943–46; Officer, Order of Canada 1994; Anglican; Home: 102 New Cove Rd., St. John's, Nfld.; Office: PO Box 4619, Kampala, Uganda.

**HILLMER, George Norman,** M.A., Ph.D.; historian; teacher; b. Niagara Falls, Ont. 24 Nov. 1942; s. George Powell and Monica Gertrude (Goodrow) H.; e. Blythwood Pub. Sch.; North Toronto Collegiate Inst.; Univ. of Toronto Hons. B.A. Modern Hist. 1966, M.A. Hist. 1967; Cambridge Univ. Ph.D. Hist. 1974; m. Anne Mary d. Frederick W. and Lois (Serson) Trowell 16 Sept. 1978; one s.: Michael; PROF. OF HIST., CARLETON UNIV. 1990– ; Pitman's Publishing Co., London, Engl. 1966; West Humber Collegiate Inst., Rexdale, Ont. 1967–68; Lectr. to Visiting Prof., Dept. of Hist. Carleton Univ. 1972–89; Historian, Directorate of Hist. Dept. of Nat. Defence, Ottawa 1972–90 (Sr. Historian 1980–90); Visiting Prof. of Modern Commonwealth Hist., Leeds Univ., Engl. 1978–79; Cons. 'Canadian Encyclopedia' 1980–87 and 'Junior Encyclopedia of Canada' 1987–90; author, 'Negotiating Freer Trade: The United Kingdom, the United States, Canada, and the Trade Agreements of 1938' 1989; 'For Better or For Worse: Canada and the United States to the 1990s' 1991; numerous articles and reviews; Ed., nine books on Canadian foreign policy, WW II, and the Commonwealth; awarded Queen's Silver Jubilee Medal 1977; I.O.D.E., Univ. of London, Mackenzie King and Canada Counc. Fellowships 1970–72; Commonwealth Scholar 1968–70; St. Michael's Coll. Gold Medal for Modern Hist. 1966; mem. Candn. Hist. Assn. (Eng. Lang. Sec. 1974–81; Distinguished Service Award 1981; Hon. Life Mem. 1982); Pres. Candn. Ctte. for Hist. of the Second World War 1983– ; mem. C.I.I.A.; R. Catholic; recreations: tennis, golf; Clubs: Kappa Alpha Soc.; Cambridge Soc.; Rideau Tennis; Larrimac Golf; Home: 22 Downing St., Ottawa, Ont. K1S 2W1; Office: Dept. of History, Carleton Univ., Ottawa, Ont. K1S 5B6.

**HILSDEN, Laura Jill,** B.Ed., C.A.; insurance executive; b. Regina, Sask. 12 Sept. 1951; d. Harry William and Eileen (Seaker) H.; e. Univ. of Saskatchewan B.Ed. 1972; Mem., Candn. Inst. of C.A.s 1978; Inst. of C.A.s of Sask. 1978; Inst. of C.A.s of Ont. 1990; SR. VICE-PRES. & CHIEF FINANCIAL OFFICER, SIMCOE ERIE GROUP 1989– ; Articling Student, C.A. Program, Peat Marwick Mitchell & Co. 1974–77; C.A. 1977–78; Corporate Controller, Fennell Cochrane Group of Cos. 1978–83; Manager, Crown Investments Corp. of Sask. 1982–83; Asst. Vice-Pres. Finance, Saskatchewan Govt. Insur. 1983–85; Vice-Pres. Finance 1985–89; Bd. of Dir., Simcoe & Erie Gen. Insur. Co.; Elite Insur. Co.; Gan Canada Insur. Co.; Robert Bradford of Canada Limited; Mem., Bus. Devel. Adv. Ctte., City of Burlington; Home: 3050 Swansea Dr., Oakville, Ont. L6L 6H6; Office: 649 North Service Rd. W., Burlington, Ont. L7R 4L5.

**HIMMS-HAGEN, Jean,** B.Sc., D.Phil.; educator; b. Oxford, Eng. 18 Dec. 1933; s. Frederick Hubert and Margaret Mary (Deadman) Himms; e. Milham Ford Sch. Oxford 1949; Univ. London B.Sc. 1955; Oxford Univ. D.Phil. 1958; m. Paul Beo Hagen 29 Sept. 1956; children: Anna Jean, Nina Jean; PROF OF BIOCHEM., UNIV. OF OTTAWA since 1967; Research Fellow, Harvard Univ. 1957–59; Asst. Prof. Univ. of Man. 1959–64; Assoc. Prof. Queen's Univ. 1964–67; Assoc. Prof. present Univ. 1967, Prof. 1971, Acting Chrmn. 1975–77, 1987, Chrmn. 1977–82; rec'd Bond Award Am. Oil Chemists, Soc. 1972; Ayerst Award Candn. Biochem. Soc. 1973; elected to Royal Soc. of Can., 1980; mem. M.R.C.: mem. Metabolism Grants Ctte. 1969–75 (Chrmn. 1972–75), Counc. mem. 1970–75, mem. Extve. 1970–73, mem. Ctte. on Cttes. 1977–78, Scholarship Selection Ctte. 1981–83, Equipment Grant Ctte. 1983–84, Career Investigators Ctte. 1984–87; mem. Candn. Counc. on Animal Care 1970–78; Assoc. Ed. Candn. Jour. Biochem. 1967–71; Assoc. Ed., Candn. Jour. Physiol. and Pharmacol. 1971–75; Assoc. Ed. American Jour. Physiol. 1979–88, 1992– ; mem. Ed. Bd. Proc. Soc. Exp. Biol. Med. (U.S.). 1984–90; Consultant Hoffmann-La Roche Inc. New Jersey U.S. 1984–88; invited speaker at over 80 universities, Rsch. Inst. or Symposia; author of 91 research publications and of 39 scientific review articles or book chapters; Council Mem., Soc. Exp. Biol. Med. (U.S.) 1991– ; mem. Candn. Biochem. Soc.; North Am. Assoc. Study of Obesity; Am. Physiol. Soc.; Biochem. Soc. (UK); Am. Inst. Nutr.; Nutr. Soc. (UK); Soc. Neurosci.; Am. Soc. Pharmacol. & Exper. Therapeutics; recreations: swimming, cross-country skiing; Home: 233 Tudor Pl., Ottawa, Ont. K1L 7Y1; Office: 451 Smyth Rd., Ottawa, Ont. K1H 8M5.

**HINDMARCH, Gladys Maria,** M.A.; writer; educator; b. Ladysmith, B.C. 1 Jan. 1940; d. Robert and Taimi (Aho) H.; e. Ladysmith High Sch. 1957; Univ. of B.C., B.A. 1962, M.A. 1967; div.; one s. Lars Andstein; CO-ORDINATOR OF ENGLISH, CAPILANO COLL.; author: 'A Birth Account' non-fiction 1976; 'The Peter Stories' short stories 1976; 'The Watery Part of the World' novel 1988; Home: 1750 Parker St., Vancouver, B.C. V5L 2K8; Office: 2055 Purcell Way, North Vancouver, B.C. V7J 3H5.

**HINDS, Hon. David Bertram,** B.A., LL.B.; judge; b. Goudhurst, Kent, Eng. 4 May 1927; s. Alfred Bertram and Marjorie Gertrude (Pargiter) H.; e. Univ. of B.C. B.A. 1949, LL.B. 1950; m. A. June d. Roy and Beulah Brett 27 July 1951; children: Diane Beverley, Patricia Lynn; JUDGE, COURT OF APPEAL OF B.C. 1990– ; read law with Frank Wilson, Chilliwack, B.C.; called to Bar of B.C. 1951; cr. Q.C. 1971; law practice Chilliwack 1951–74; Judge, Co. of Westminster, B.C. 1975; Judge, Supreme Court of B.C. 1980; Trustee, Sch. Dist. No. 33 1966–72; Bencher, Law Soc. B.C. 1967–75; Pres., Kinsmen's Club Chilliwack 1959; United Church; recreations: gardening, swimming, golf; Club: Chilliwack Golf & Country; Home: 47455 Mountain Park Dr., Chilliwack, B.C. V2P 7P7; Office: Law Courts, 800 Smithe St., Vancouver, B.C. V6Z 2E1.

**HIND-SMITH, Michael,** B.A.; executive; b. Windsor, Eng. 7 Oct. 1930; s. Norman William and Ann (O'Hagan) H-S.; e. Univ. of B.C. B.A. 1951; Univ. of Toronto Grad. Sch. 1951–52; m. Sandra d. Norman F. and Lauretta McKee 8 May 1970; children (from previous marriage): Stephanie, Jennifer, David; Pres. & C.E.O., Candn. Cable Television Assn. 1975–90; TV Producer and Stn. Mgr. CBC 1952–61; Vice Pres. Prog. and Dir. CTV Television Network Ltd. 1961–66; Vice Pres. Media & Prog. Foster Advertising Ltd. 1967–72; Gen. Mgr. MH Video (div. MacLean Hunter Ltd.) 1972–75; Hon. Vice Pres. Broadcast Execs. Soc.; former Trustee, Internat. Inst. Communications; former Pres. Couchiching Inst. Pub. Affairs; Clubs: Rideau; Toronto Lawn Tennis; Address: P.O. Box 54, Portland, Ont. K0G 1V0.

**HIND-SMITH, Sandra Patricia McKee,** B.Sc.; foundation executive; b. Ottawa, Ont. 6 July 1935; d. Norman Frederic and Loretta Regina (Larivière) McKee; e. Syracuse Univ., B.Sc. 1957; Columbia Univ.; Univ. of San Diego; Univ. of Montreal; m. Michael s. Anne O'Hagen and Norman H. 8 May 1970; Pres., Children's Hosp. of Eastern Ont. Found. 1987–90; Radio, TV & Film Coord., Expo '67 1966–68; Radio, TV & Film Advr., Dept. of Indian Affairs & Northern Devel. 1968–69; Dir., Public Relns., Promotion & Advtg., St Lawrence Ctr. for the Arts 1969–71; Special Relns. Rep., Bell Can. 1971–72; Producer-Hostess-Interviewer, CJOH TV, Ottawa 1976–80, 1961–66; Vice-Pres., CHEO Found. 1983–87; Bd. of Gov., Elmwood Sch., Ottawa; Former Mem., Bd. of Trustees, CHEO; Past Dir., Carleton Unit, Candn. Cancer Soc.; Past Dir., March of Dimes; Heart Found. of Ottawa; Mem., Special Cttes. Civic Hosp. Fund, United Appeal, Muscular Dystrophy Telethon; Former Mem., Adv. Counc., Post Office; Dir., Theatre Ballet of Ottawa; Mem., The Military and Hosp. Order of Saint Lazarus of Jerusalem; clubs: Variety, Press, Couching Inst. on Public Affairs, Good Bears of the World; Home: 100 Rideau Terrace, Unit 11, Ottawa, Ont. K1M 0Z2.

**HINES, William James;** transportation executive; b. Toronto, Ont. 16 Sept. 1911; s. late William Albert and late Annie Francis (Beatty( H.; e. N. Toronto Coll. Inst., 1929; War Staff Coll., Royal Mil. Coll., 1945; Univ. of Toronto; m. Gunda (dec.), d. late Henry Herbert Mason, 17 Feb. 1935; m. 2ndly Audrey Huntingford Taylor 7 Aug. 1987; two s., William Henry Charles, John Anthony; CONSULTANT, LAND TRANSPORT, CANADA STEAMSHIP LINES LTD. since 1976, formerly Sr. Vice-Pres. (1973–76); Past Pres., Kingsway Transports Ltd.; Kingsway Freight Lines Ltd.; Kingsway Dalewood Ltd.; Bennet & Elliott Co. Ltd.; Laurentide Transport Ltd.; Drummond Transit Ltd.; Past Vice Pres. and Dir., Provincial Transport Enterprises Ltd.; Past Dir., John N. Brocklesby Transport Ltd.; Chmr. of Bd., Peelco Mfg. Ltd.; Dir., Floor Trader and Office Mgr., Hambly, Peaker & Trent (now Alfred G. Bunting & Co.) 1934; Acct. and Office Mgr., Atlas Polar Co. Ltd., 1940–42; Acct. and subsequently Secy.-Treas. and Dir., Webster Air Equipment Ltd., London, Ont., 1945; Vice Pres., Gen. Mgr. and Dir., Husband Transport Ltd., 1949; Asst. Gen. Mgr., Kingsway Transports Ltd., 1952; Gen. Mgr. 1961; Vice Pres. and Pres. subsidiary co's 1969; joined present co. as Vice Pres.-Land Transport., 1969; served with R.C.A. Service Corps in Can., Eng. and N.W. Europe 1942–45; rank Maj. on discharge; Former Trustee, Elder, Kingsway Lambton Un. Ch.; Dir. and Past Pres., Ont. Trucking Assn.; Beta Theta Pi; P. Conservative; United Church; recreations: golf, boating; Clubs: St. George's Golf & Country; RCYC; Venice Yacht (Venice, Fla.); Home: 39 Old Mill Rd., Apt. 2103, Toronto Ont. M8X 1G6.

**HINZ, Evelyn J.,** B.A., M.A., Ph.D.; distinguished university professor, editor; b. Humboldt, Sask. 7 Dec. 1938; d. Andrew B. Hinz and Aloysia A. Nenzel; e. Univ. of Saskatchewan B.A. (cum laude) 1961, High Honors 1966, M.A. 1967; Univ. of Massachusetts Ph.D. 1973; single; PROFESSOR OF ENGLISH, UNIVERSITY OF MANITOBA 1972– ; Social Worker, Sask. Govt. 1961–63; Writer-Producer, CFQC-TV (Saskatoon) 1963–65; Instructor, Univ. of Sask. 1966–68; Mem., Delegate Assembly, Modern Language Assn. of Am. 1989–91; Co-Editor, 'The Canadian Review of American Studies' 1977–79; Editor, 'MOSAIC' 1979– ; Mem. Editorial Bd. 'English Studies in Canada' 1991– ; Authorized Biographer of Anais Nin and Second Literary Executor, Anais Nin Estate 1977– ; Governor General's Medal for Academic Proficiency 1957; Killam Post Doctoral Rsch. Fellow 1973–75; Winner, William Riley Parker Prize for an outstanding essay pub. in PMLA 1977; RH Inst. Award for Interdisciplinary Scholarship 1979; Mem., Modern Language Association; Assn. of Candn. Univ. Teachers of English; Humanities Assn. of Canada; Conf. of Editors of Learned Journals (Pres. 1988–90); author: 'The Mirror and the Garden: Realism and Reality in the Writings of Anais Nin' 1971, rpt, enlarged 1973 and over 90 critical articles & reviews in leading scholarly jours. & books; editor: 'A Woman Speaks: The Lectures, Seminars, and Interviews of Anais Nin' 1975, '78, '79 (Am., Brit., German & French eds.); 'The World of Anais Nin: Critical and Cultural Perspectives' 1978; 'Beyond Nationalism: The Canadian Literary Scene in Global Perspective' 1981; 'Death and Dying' 1982; 'For Better or Worse: Attitudes Toward Marriage in Literature' 1985; 'Literature and Altered States of Consciousness' 1986; 'Data and Acta: Aspects of Life-Writing' 1987; 'Troops versus Tropes: War and Literature' 1990; 'Diet and Discourse: Eating, Drinking and Literature' 1991; co-editor: 'The Definitive Edition of Roger Williams' "A Key into the Language of America"' 1973, 'Henry Miller's The World of Lawrence: A Passionate Appreciation' 1980, '85; Home: 136 Wellington Cres., Winnipeg, Man. R3M 0A9; Office: Winnipeg, Man. R3T 2N2.

**HIRSH, Michael;** film producer; b. 8 Feb. 1948; m. Elaine Waisglass; children: Jamie (Waese), Jonathan (Hirsh); CO-FOUNDER & CHAIRMAN., NELVANA LTD.; Prod., 'Cadillacs and Dinosaurs' (13 eps) 1993 (animated tv series); 'Tales of the Cryptkeeper' (13 eps) 1993 (animated tv series); 'Jim Henson's Dog City' (23 eps) 1993 (muppets and animation); 'Savage Steve Holland's Eek the Cat' (26 eps) 1993 (animated tv series); 'Rupert' (39 eps) 1993 (animated tv series); 'The Adventures of Tintin' (39 eps) 1992 (animated tv series); 'Rupert' (26 eps) 1992 (animated tv series); 'Barbar' (65 eps) 1992 (animated tv series); 'Beetlejuice' (65 eps) 1989–91 (animated tv series); 'Little Rosey' (13 eps) 1990 (animated tv series); 'The Droids' (13 eps) 1984 (animated tv series); 'Inspector Gadget' (65 eps) 1983 (animated tv series); 'T and T' (65 eps) 1987–89 (live action tv series); 'The Edison Twins' (65 eps) 1983–86 (live action tv series); 'Twenty Minute Workout' (95 eps) (tv syndication); 'Babar: The Movie' 1989 (animated feature film); 'The Care Bears Adventure in

Wonderland' 1987 (animated feature film); 'The Care Bears Movie' 1984 (animated feature film); 'Rock and Rule' 1983 (animated tv special); 'Take Me Up To The Ballgame' 1980 (animated tv special); 'Easter Fever' 1980 (animated tv special); 'Romie-O and Julie-8' 1979 (animated tv special); 'Intergalactic Thanksgiving' 1979 (animated tv special); 'The Star Wars Special' 1978 (animated tv special); 'The Devil and Daniel Mouse' 1978 (animated tv special); 'Cosmic Christmas' 1977 (animated tv special); num. awards incl. ACE, Day Time Emmy, Gemini, Sept d'Or; Office: 32 Atlantic Ave., Toronto, Ont. M6K 1X8.

**HIRST, Peter C.,** M.A., F.I.A., F.C.I.A., F.C.A., A.S.A., F.Inst.D., C.H.R.P.; actuary; b. Nairobi, Kenya 22 Aug. 1943; e. Oxford Univ. M.A. 1965; m. Audrey 27 July 1968; children: Philippa Anne, Sara Elizabeth; SR. VICE-PRES., BUCK CONSULTANTS LTD. (merged with Actrex Partners Ltd. 1993); Supvr. Group Pension Dept. Imperial Life 1968; Consulting Actuary, Kates Peat Marwick & Co. 1971; Sr. Consulting Actuary, Johnson & Higgins, Willis Faber Ltd. 1974, Asst. Vice Pres. 1975; Founder Hirst Consultants Ltd. 1976, merged with Tillinghast, Nelson & Warren Inc. 1980; Pres., Candn. Operations, Tillinghast; Co-Founder & Pres., Actrex Partners Ltd. (acquired Candn. Subsidiary of Tillinghast, Nelson & Warren Inc. 1986); Past Pres., Candn. Inst. of Actuaries; Past Pres., Candn. Pension Conf.; Personnel Assoc. of Ont. (former Bd. Mem.); Mem., Public Sector Pensions Adv. Bd., Ont.; Conf. of Consulting Actuaries (Bd. Mem.); Assn. Candn. Pension Mang.; Bd. Trade Metrop. Toronto; Inst. of Corporate Dirs. in Canada; Profit Sharing Counc. of Canada; Candn. Compensation Assn.; Internat. Assoc. of Actuaries; Internat. Assoc. of Consulting Actuaries; Clubs: Mississaugua Golf & Country; Canadian; Bd. of Trade of Metro. Toronto; recreations: sports, theatre, reading; Home: 1381 Queen Victoria Ave., Mississauga, Ont. L5H 3H2; Office: Suite 1500, P.O. Box 15, 95 Wellington St. W., Toronto, Ont. M5J 2N7.

**HIRUKI, Chuji,** B.Sc., Ph.D., F.R.S.C.; university professor; b. Fukue, Nagasaki-ken, Japan 16 June 1931; s. Chuichi and Mitsu (Kawamuko) H.; e. Kyushu Univ. B.Sc. 1954, Ph.D. 1963; m. Yasuko d. Tokio and Yoshie Hijikata 26 Dec. 1961; children: Tadaaki, Lisa; UNIV. PROF., PLANT SCI., UNIV. OF ALTA. 1991– ; Plant Pathologist, Hatano Tob. Expt. Sta. 1954–65; Vis. Plant. Pathol., Univ. of Calif., Berkeley 1963–64; Hon. Fellow, Biochem., Univ. of Wisc., Madison 1964–66; Asst. Prof., Plant Sci., Univ. of Alta. 1966–70, Assoc. Prof. 1970–76, Prof. 1976–91; Vis. Prof., State Agric. Univ. Netherlands 1972; Univ. of Queensland 1984–85; Univ. of Tokyo 1984; Hokkaido Univ. 1985, 1991; Kyoto Univ. 1988; Univ. Hohenheim 1990; Vis. Sci., INRA Versailles, France 1972; Inst. for Plant Virus Rsch., Japan 1973; fellowships: Distinguished Hon. Sci., Paulownia Res. Ctr. China 1993; FAO UNDP Internat. Consultant 1993; Brit. Counc. Intervarsity in Biotech. 1987; NSERC travel 1981; NRC travel 1972; The Netherlands Internat. Agric. Ctr. Sr. Rsch. 1972; Fulbright Exchange 1958; Can. Phytopath. Soc. Fellow Award 1993; Am. Phytopath. Soc. Pacific Division Lifetime Achievement Award 1993; J. Gordin Kaplan Rsch. Excell. Award 1993; Japanese Govt. Rsch. Award for Distinguished Foreign Sci. 1991; Phytopath. Soc. Japan Rsch. Excell. Award 1990; Rep. China NSC Lectureship 1989; Am. Phytopath. Soc. Fellow Award 1988; A.G. McCalla Rsch. Professorship 1987; CSFP Australian Govt. Vis. Sr. Prof. 1984; NSERC Internat. Collaborative Rsch. Award 1984; NSERC Internat. Sci. Exch. Award 1982, 1990; Candn. Plains Rsch. Ctrs. Rsch. Travel Award 1981; Japan Soc. for Promo. of Sci. Sr. Rsch. Prof. 1978, 1988; Mem., Candn. Phytopath. Soc. (Vice-Pres. 1988–89; Pres.-Elect 1989–90; Pres. 1990–91); Am. Phytopath. Soc.; Phytopath. Soc. Japan; Indian Phytopath. Soc.; Plant Path. Soc. of Alta.; Soc. for Gen. Microbiol.; Indian Virol. Soc.; African and Middle-East Virol. Soc.; Internat. Orgn. for Mycoplasmol.; Candn. Soc. for Plant Mol. Biol.; Internat. Soc. for Plant Mol. Biol.; New York Acad. Sci.; Chrmn., Internat. Working Group on Plant Viruses with Fungal Vectors; Internat. Working Group on Viroids; Internat. Working Group on Legume Viruses; Internat. Working Group on Ornamental Viruses; Internat. Soc. of Plant Pathol. Subcomte. on Plant Virus Epidemiol.; Internat. Union of Forest. Res. Orgn. Working Party on Virus and Mycoplasma Diseases of Trees; Internat. Union of Forest. Res. Orgn. Project Group on Agroforestry; editor: 'Tree Mycoplasmas and Mycoplasma Diseases' 1988 as well as over 180 sci. rsch. pubs. & 300 rsch. paper presentations & sci. confs.; recreation: swimming, fishing, skiing; Home: 152 Windermere Cres., Edmonton, Alta. T6R 2H6; Office: 4–10D Agric. & Forestry Center, Univ. of Alta., Edmonton, Alta. T6G 2P5.

**HISCOCKS, Richard Duncan,** M.B.E., B.A.Sc., P.Eng.; b. Toronto, Ont. 4 June 1914; s. William Duncan and Elizabeth Gertrude (Barnes) H.; e. Univ. of Toronto, B.A.Sc. 1938; Hon. degrees: Carleton, McGill and McMaster; m. Bettie Eileen, d. Wilfred S. Jacobs; children: Peter, Susan, Patricia, David Christopher; Consultant, Aero Research & Design 1980– ; formerly, Nat. Research Council, Ottawa; Vice Pres. (Ind.): De Havilland Aircraft of Canada Ltd. Vice Pres. (Eng.); Hon. Fellow, Candn. Aerospace Inst.; Engn. Inst.; mem., Candn. Acad. of Engn.; Home: 2095 Beach Ave., Apt. 704, Vancouver, B.C. V6G 1Z3.

**HITCHCOCK, Barry,** B.A.Sc., P.Eng.; executive; b. Sydney, Australia 31 Dec. 1929; s. Heber Stan and Jenny (Duncan) H.; e. Sydney Technical H.S. (Hons.) 1947; Sydney Tech. Coll., dipl. (civil engr.) 1953; Univ. of Toronto B.A.Sc. (Hons.) 1958; m. Elizabeth d. Frederick and Ellen Simpson 25 May 1957; children: David, Kylie, Ruth, Jenny, William; DIRECTOR, CANDN. COUNCIL OF PROFESSIONAL ENGRS.; Engineering Trainee, Water Conservation & Irrigation Comn. of N.S.W. Australia 1948–54; Foundation Supvr., Dept. of Highways, Ont. 1954–56; Structural Designer, Kilborn Engr. 1956–57; Project Engr., Candn. Brit. Engineering Consultants 1958–59; Resident Engr., Super Tanker Berth, Shell Co. of Australia Limited 1959–61; Sr. Vice-Pres., Giffels Associates Limited 1961–92; Pres., Assn. of Profl. Engrs. of Ont. 1991–92; Fellow, Candn. Soc. for Civil Engr.; mem., Institution of Engrs., Australia; Olympic Celebration Award, Govt. of Canada for Oustanding Services to the Community 1988; Gov., Scarborough Gen. Hosp.; Past Pres., Kiwanis Club of the Golden Mile (Scarborough) 1972; recreations: dinghy sailing; clubs: Toronto Sailing and Canoe; Home: 25 Dorcot Ave., Scarborough, Ont. M1P 3K3.

**HITCHCOCK, Roger Bramwell,** M.A., M.Sc.; financial executive; b. Bulawayo, Zimbabwe 31 Aug. 1947; s. Ebenezer Theodore and Edna Elvin (Gavin) H.; e. Hamilton H.S. (Zimbabwe) 1965; Cambridge Univ. (U.K.) B.A. (Hons.) 1969, M.A. (Hons.) 1972; Univ. of Warwick (U.K.) M.Sc. 1973; m. Christine d. Frederick and Beatrice Berry 24 June 1972; children: Stephen, Rachel; CHIEF FINANCIAL OFFICER, ORACLE CORP. CANADA INC. 1991– ; Operations Research Analyst, Alfred Herbert Ltd. (U.K.) 1969–73; var. sr. finance positions, Massey-Ferguson (U.K.) 1974–85; Mgr., Planning & Analysis, Varity Corp. (Toronto) 1985–88; Dir. of Planning & Analysis, Innopac Corp. 1988–90; Vice-Pres. & Controller, Oracle Corp. Canada Inc. 1990–91; Dir., Oakville Christian Sch.; Pentecostal; recreations: squash, tennis, boating; Home: 2171 Cleaver Ave., Burlington, Ont. L7M 3W3; Office: 110 Matheson Blvd. W., Mississauga, Ont. L5R 3P4.

**HITCHMAN, George C.;** b. Toronto, Ont. 10 Aug. 1914; s. Percy R. and Effie (Roger) H.; e. Pub. and High Sch., Tottenham, Ont.; m. Muriel Robinson, New York, 14 June 1942; one d. Barbara Ann; DIRECTOR, ALGOMA CENTRAL CORPORATION; Chrmn. & Dir., Fine Line Circuits Ltd.; Dir., Algoma Central Railway; Magna Intnl. Inc.; Schindler Elevator Corp.; Welded Tube of Canada Ltd.; joined The Bank of Nova Scotia, Woodbridge, Ont. 1931; br. mgr., London, Eng., 1947–51; mgr. Edmonton Br. 1952–53; supvr., Que. Brs., 1954–56; General Office, Toronto, Asst. Gen. Mgr. 1957; Depy. Gen. Mgr. 1963; Joint Gen. Mgr. 1968; Exec. Vice Pres. 1972; Deputy Chrmn. and Dir., 1974; retired 1981; Dir. of Bank, 1981–84; Hon. Dir. 1985; mem. Adv. Bd., Humford Developments Ltd.; served with the 104th U.S. Infantry in France, Belgium, Holland and Germany, 1942–45; rank of Staff Sergeant; Anglican; recreation: golf; Clubs: National; Toronto; Home: 60 Old Mill Rd., Toronto, Ont. M8X 1G7; Office: 289 Bay St., P.O. Box 7000, Sault Ste. Marie, Ont. P6A 5P6.

**HITZIG, Ken,** B.Com., C.A.; financial executive; b. Montreal, Que. 27 Jan. 1932; s. Samuel and Yetta (Fallen) H.; e. McGill Univ., B.Com. 1952, C.A. 1956; m. Glenys d. Joseph and Esther Hargreaves; children: Simon, Jeremy, Rupert; FOUNDER & PRES., ACCORD BUSINESS CREDIT INC. 1978– ; Audit Mgr., Richter, Usher & Vineberg 1952–59; various posts, lastly as Vice-Pres., Ont. & West, Aetna Factors Corp. Ltd. 1960–78; Dir., Accord Business Credit Inc.; M-Corp Inc.; Home: 97 Glengowan Rd., Toronto, Ont. M4N 1G5; Office: 77 Bloor St. W., Suite 1803, Toronto, Ont. M5S 1M2.

**HLECK, Paul,** Q.C., B.A., LL.B.; b. Englefeld, Sask., 7 July 1931; e. Englefeld Pub. and High Schs.; Univ. of Sask. B.A. 1953, LL.B. 1956; m. Mary Lou; children: Mary Ann, Peter; SR. PARTNER, HLECK, KANUKA,

THURINGER; Dir., Cairns Homes Ltd.; Avonlea Mineral Indus. Ltd.; read law with MacPherson, Neuman & Pierce; called to Bar of Sask. 1957; cr. Q.C. 1974; served 5 yrs. on City of Regina Planning Comn.; mem. Community Planning Assn. Can.-Regina Br. (Extve. 1961–69); Housing and Urban Devel. Assn. Regina; active Ukrainian Greek Orthodox Ch. (Extve. Regina Parish 10 yrs.; Nat. Extve. Lay Organ.; Dir. Mohyla Ukrainian Student Residence Saskatoon 10 yrs.) ; mem. Regina and Candn. Bar Assns.; Regina Chamber Comm.; Clubs: Assiniboia; Candn. Men's; Kiwanis (Pres. 1968; Lt. Gov. Div. 4 W. Can. Dist. 1970); Home: 118 Patterson Dr., Regina, Sask., S4S 3W9; Office: 1500, 2500 Victoria Ave., Regina, Sask. S4P 3X2.

**HNATYSHYN, His Excellency the Right Hon. Ramon John,** P.C., C.C., C.M.M., C.D., Q.C.; b. Saskatoon, Sask. 16 Mar. 1934; s. the Hon. John (Senator) and Helen Constance (Pitts) H.; e. Victoria Pub. Sch. and Nutana Coll. Inst. Saskatoon; Univ. of Sask. B.A. 1954, LL.B. 1956; m. Karen Gerda Nygaard d. George Andreasen, Saskatoon, Sask. 9 Jan. 1960; two s. John Georg, Carl Andrew Nygaard; GOVERNOR GENERAL AND COMMANDER-IN-CHIEF OF CANADA 1990– , Chancellor and Principal Companion of the Order of Canada, Chancellor and Commander of the Order of Military Merit 1990– ; called to Bar of Sask. 1957, to Ont. Bar 1986; cr. Q.C. for Sask. 1973; apptd. Q.C. for Canada 1988; law practice Saskatoon 1956–58; Private Secy. and Extve. Asst. to Govt. Leader in Senate 1958–60; rtn'd to law practice 1960 Saskatoon; Lectr. in Law, Univ. of Sask. 1966–74; el. to H. of C. for Saskatoon-Biggar g.e. 1974, re-el. g.e. 1979, 1980 and 1984 for Saskatoon West; apptd. Depy. House Leader of Official Opposition and co-ordinator of Question Period 1976; sworn to the Privy Council 1979; Min. of State for Science & Technol. 1979; Min. of Energy, Mines and Resources 1979–80; House Leader for Official Opposition 1984; Government House Leader 1984–86; Pres. of the Queen's Privy Council for Canada 1985–86; Min. Responsible for Regulatory Affairs 1986; Min. of Justice and Attorney General of Canada 1986–88; Chrmn., Caucus Ctte. on Justice and Legal Affairs 1980–84; Justice Critic 1980–84; Solicitor General Critic 1984; RCAF Reserve Training Plan 1951–56; former mem. RCAF 23 Wing (Auxiliary) Saskatoon 1956–58; Past Pres. UN Assn. Can. (N. Sask. Br.); Bencher, Law Soc. Sask. 1970–74 (Pres. 1973–74, Hon. Life Mem. 1989); Chrmn. Saskatoon Un. Way Campaign 1972; Dir. Un. Community Funds Sask. 1968–74; Vice Pres. Saskatoon YMCA 1973–74; Pres. Saskatoon Gallery and Conserv. Corp. 1974; mem. Saskatoon Bar Assn.; Candn. Bar Assn.; rec'd St. Volodymyr Medal Award, World Congress of Ukrainians 1989; LL.D. (hon. causa): Univ. of Saskatchewan 1990; Open Univ. of B.C. 1991; Royal Military Coll., Kingston 1991; Queen's Univ. 1991; Univ. of Manitoba 1992; McGill Univ.; State Univ. of Chernivtsi in Ukraine; Carleton Univ. 1992; D.Cn.L. (hon. causa), Univ. of Emmanuel College, Saskatoon 1993; Doctorate of Civil Law (honoris causa) Bishop's Univ. in Lennoxville, Que. 1993; Hon. Fellowship, Royal Coll. of Physicians and Surgeons of Can. 1990; Doctorate of the Univ., Univ. of Ottawa 1991; Diploma of the Coll., Loyalist Coll., Belleville, Ont. 1992; Ukrainian Greek Orthodox; Home: 1 Sussex Dr., Ottawa, Ont. K1A 0A1.

**HOAKEN, Paul Clement Spencer,** B.A., M.D., F.R.C.P.(C), F.A.P.A.; psychiatrist; educator; b. Toronto, Ont. 18 Dec. 1930; s. Clement Muller and Kathleen Nora (Bingham) H.; e. Runnymede Pub. Sch. and Humberside Collegiate Inst., Toronto; Univ. of Toronto B.A. 1953, M.D. 1957; m. Ellen d. Bernard and Lucy Moore 4 Nov. 1961; children: Susan (Bergeron), Eric, Nancy (Trivett), Peter; PROFESSOR OF PSYCHIATRY, QUEEN'S UNIVERSITY 1983– ; DEPUTY CHIEF, DEPT. OF PSYCHIATRY, HOTEL DIEU HOSP. KINGSTON; Rsch. Fellow Dept. of Psychiatry, Univ. of N. Carolina 1962–63; Asst. Clinical Dir. Female Service, Kingston Psychiatric Hosp. 1963–64; Geographic Full-Time Teacher Dept. of Psychiatry, from Lectr. 1964 to Prof. 1983; co-author 'Psychopathology in Klinefelfer's Syndrome' 1964; author 'Jealousy as a Symptom of Psychiatric Disorder' 1976; 'Paranoid-Depressive Relationships' 1973; Pres. Ont. Dist. Br., Am. Psychiatric Assn. 1973; Pres. Ont. Psychiatric Assn. 1980; mem. Am. Assn. for Advancement of Sci.; recreations: tennis, reading, creative writing; Home: Box 247, Bath, Ont. K0H 1G0; Office: Hotel Dieu Hospital, 166 Brock St., Kingston, Ont. K7L 5G2.

**HOAR, William Stewart,** O.C., M.A., Ph.D., D.Sc., L.L.D., F.R.S.C. (1955); professor emeritus; b. Moncton, N.B. 31 Aug. 1913; s. George W. and Nina B. (Steeves) H.; e. Univ. of New Brunswick (Beaverbrook Schol.), B.A. 1934; Univ. of W. Ont. M.A. 1936; Boston Univ.,

Ph.D. 1939; D.Sc., Univ. of N.B. 1965, Memorial Univ. 1967; St. Francis Xavier 1976; Univ. West. Ontario 1978; L.L.D. Simon Fraser 1980; Univ. of Tor., 1981; m. Margaret M., d. Angus MacKenzie, Thamesville, Ont., 13 Aug. 1941; children: Stewart, David, Kenzie, Melanie; HON. PROF. OF ZOOLOGY, UNIV. OF BRIT. COLUMBIA, (Head of Dept. 1964–71); mem., Nat. Research Council 1965–70; Fish. Res. Bd. Can. 1965–71; NATO Sci. Affs. Comte. on Research 1972–78; Counc. Mem., Pacific Science Assn. 1966–79; Demonst. in Zool., Univ. of W. Ont., 1934–36; Asst. in Histol. & Embryol., Boston Univ., 1936–39; Asst. Prof. of Biol., Univ. of N.B., 1939–42; Research Assoc. in Physiol., Univ. of Toronto, 1942–43; Prof. of Zool., Univ. of N.B., 1943–45; apptd. Prof. in present Univ. 1945; John Simon Guggenheim Mem. Foundation Fellowship, Oxford Univ., 1958–59; Flavelle Medal, RSC 1965; Fry Medal, CSZ 1974; Shinkishi Hatai Medal, Pacific Sc. Assn. 1991; Hon. Life mem. Pacific Sc. Assn., 1979; United Church; Home: 3561 W. 27th. Ave., Vancouver, B.C. V6S 1P9.

**HOBBS, Clement Francis,** B.Sc., F.I.S., F.S.S.; mathematician; b. London, England 8 Mar. 1927; s. Francis Walter James and Margaret (Pearmine) H.; e. William Ellis Secondary Sch.; Norwood Tech. Coll., 1948–49; Birbeck Coll. (London Univ.), B.Sc. 1955; came to Canada 1955; m. Marie-Marguerite Sonia, d. Roland Rousseau, Nicolet, Que., 9 Dec. 1960; children: Frances Margaret, Clement Francis, Jr.; ASST. PROF., CARLETON UNIV., SCHOOL OF BUSINESS, OTTAWA 1982; with Medical Research Council, England, 1949–53; Fairey Aviation Company Weapons Div., U.K., 1953–55; Sr. Ballistics Offr., Inspection Services, Dept. of Nat. Defence, Ottawa, 1955–59; Chief of Systems Analysis, Army Equip. Engn. Estab., Dept. of Nat. Defence, 1959–65; Supt. Systems Engn., P.O. Dept., 1965; Director of Operational Research 1966; Director General, Post Office Dept. (1966–72); Vice Pres. Finance, Adm. & Personnel, Canadian International Development Agency 1972–74; Dir. Gen., Planning and Systems, Secy. of State Dept. 1974–82; co-author of 'Tables for Inspection by Attributes,' 1962 (first statistical standard publ. by Canadn. Govt.); author or co-author of a number of systems and methods studies; served with British Army 1944–48; mem. Assn. Prof. Engrs. Ont., Anglican; recreations: swimming; sailing, skating, judo; Home: 10 Edenbrook Court, Country Place, Nepean, Ont. K2E 7H4.

**HOBBS, Gerald Henry Danby;** private investor; corporate director; b. Vancouver, B.C. 11 March 1921; s. Charles D. and Victoria M. (Danby) H.; e. Vancouver Coll.; m. Phyllis Rae Nicolson 1 May 1947; children: David, Leslie, Janet, Philip; Dir., The Bank of Nova Scotia; British Columbia Telephone Co.; MacMillan Bloedel Ltd.; North American Life Assurance Co.; Glenayre Electronics Ltd.; Suncor Inc.; Minequest Exploration Assocs. Ltd.; Inter-Pacific Resources Corp., First Mineral Securities Inc.; Valdora Minerals Pty. Ltd.; QPX Minerals Inc.; Sales Mgr. Pacific Bolt Manufacturing Co. 1946–54; Gen. Mgr. Western Canada Steel Ltd. 1955, Pres. 1964, Chrmn. and Chief Extve. Offr. 1968–72; Vice Pres. Vancouver, Cominco Ltd. 1968, Vice Pres. Pacific Region 1969, Extve. Vice Pres. 1972, Pres. 1973, Chrmn. 1978–80; Chrmn. West Kootenay Power and Light 1978–80; Gov. Univ. of B.C.; Dir. St. John Ambulance Assn.; mem. Adv. Bd., KCTS Assn.; mem. Greater Vancouver Adv. Bd. Salvation Army; named Commdr. Order of St. John; served with Royal Candn. Army Service Corps 1940–46; Anglican; Clubs: Vancouver; Faculty Club, Univ. of B.C.; Address: 205 - 7230 Adera, Vancouver, B.C. V6P 5C5.

**HOBBS BIRNIE, Elizabeth (Lisa),** B.A.; writer; b. Melbourne, Australia; d. Robert and Ellen Margaret (Lynch) Allan; e. Univ. of Melbourne; Lone Mountain, Univ. of San Francisco B.A. 1958; Stanford Univ., Ford Found. Fellowship 1967; m. A. Wilfrid Birnie 24 Feb. 1982; children (from 1st marriage to J.E. Hobbs): Crispin and Jonathan Hobbs; started as Reporter, Australian daily newspaper; worked on Fleet Street, England for (now defunct) Melbourne Argus 1951–54; Reporter, then Columnist, San Francisco 'Examiner' 1959–67; Special Correspondent, S.F. 'Chronicle' (Cambodia, Loas, Vietnam) 1968; joined 'Vancouver Sun' 1970; apptd. full-time Mem., Nat. Parole Bd. of Canada 1978 (resigned 1986); Delegate, 1st Am. Newspaper Guild Nat. Conf. on Women's Rights, Chicago 1970 (rep. Vancouver & San Francisco); Founding Mem., Vancouver Status of Women; Winner, United Press Inter./Assoc. Press Award 1967; National Magazine Found. of Can. Award 1992; Dir., Criminal Justice Assn. of B.C.; Mem., John Howard Soc.; Soc. for Children & Youth; Elizabeth Fry Soc.; Contr. Ed., Saturday Night Magazine; author: 'I Saw Red China' (U.S. best seller, a book club selection, & translated into 4 languages: Japanese ed. pub. by Kajima Inst. for Peace) 1966, 'India, India' 1967, 'Running Towards Life' 1970, 'Love and Liberation: Up Front With the Feminists' 1971, 'A Rock and A Hard Place' 1990, 'Such a Good Boy' 1992; plus hundreds of articles in magazines such as 'Saturday Night,' 'Chatelaine,' 'Parents,' 'Readers Digest,' etc.; 'Living on Vancouver Island' 1977 (anthologized in 'Short Essays: Models for Composition' by Gerald Levin); recreations: travelling, hiking, reading, cooking; club: Vancouver Lawn Tennis; Office: c/o Macmillan, 29 Birch Ave., Toronto, Ont. M4V 1E2.

**HOBDAY, John Charles;** foundation administrator; b. Richmond, Surrey, Eng. 7 July 1935; s. Stephen Henry and Kathleen Hawtrey (White) H.; e. Rugby (Eng.) Sch.; m. Helga d. Jürgen and Johanna Stock 22 June 1962; children: Heidi Andrea, Oliver John, Tina Karina; EXEC. DIR. SAMUEL & SAIDYE BRONFMAN FAMILY FOUND. 1983– ; Exec. Dir. Corporate Donations Joseph E. Seagram & Sons Ltd. 1982– ; Special Adv. Philanthropy to Charles R. Bronfman, O.C. 1988– ; Producer/Dir. CBC Radio Drama and Features 1957–65; freelance and contract writer, dir., actor, lectr. London, Eng., radio and TV assignments BBC, CBC, Central Office Info.; Theatre Dir. Confedn. Centre for Arts Charlottetown 1966–68; Adm. Dir. Neptune Theatre, Halifax 1968–71; Nat. Dir. Candn. Conf. Arts Toronto and Ottawa 1971–82; Mem. Extve. Ctte., Inst. Donations & Pub. Affairs Rsch.; Dir. CRB Found. Montreal; CBAC Awards Judge, Council Bus. & Arts Can.; Dir. McCord Museum Candn. Hist. Montreal; Mem. Bd. of Mngmt. Saidye Bronfman Centre Montreal; former mem. Candn. Comn. UNESCO; frequent guest lectr. fundraising, trustee development, sponsorship workshops, cultural seminars; author numerous commentaries, book reviews; recipient Queen's Silver Jubilee Medal 1977; Govt. of Ont. Volunteer Service Award 1986; 2 Ohio State Univ. Awards radio drama prodns.; Fellow, Royal Soc. Arts, Manufactures & Comm. London, Eng.; mem. Cndn. Assn. Arts Adm. Educators; Assn. Cultural Execs. (Mem. Senate Ctte.); Candn. Friends Beth Hatefutsoth; recreations: reading, arts, swimming; Club: M.A.A.A.; Home: Habitat '67, 2600, av. Pierre-Dupuy, Suite 1011, Montréal, Qué. H3C 3R6; Office: 8F, 1170 Peel St., Montreal, Que. H3B 4P2.

**HOBERG, George G. Jr.,** B.S., Ph.D.; university professor; b. Devon, Pennsylvania 29 July 1958; s. George G. and Shirley A. (Keiser) H.; e. Univ. of Calif. at Berkeley, B.S. 1980; Massachusetts Inst. of Technol., Ph.D. 1987; m. Kathryn Harrison d. Anne and Robert Harrison 23 May 1987; ASSOC. PROF., UNIV. OF B.C.; Policy analyst, U.S. Cong. Office of Technol. Assessment periodically over period 1980–85; UBC Killam Faculty Rsch. Fellowship 1992–93; Mem., Candn. & Am. Pol. Sci. Assns.; author of books and a number of scholarly envir. policy articles; recreations: basketball, skiing, softball; Office: 1866 Main Mall, Vancouver, B.C. V6T 1W5.

**HOBKIRK, Alan Arthur,** LL.B.; barrister and solicitor; b. Vancouver, B.C. 7 Nov. 1952; s. Donald Alexander and Helen Louise (Nowlan) H.; e. Univ. of B.C., B.A. 1974; Oxford Univ. B.A. 1976; Univ. of B.C., LL.B. 1979; Rhodes Scholar 1974; Bobby Gaul Mem. Trophy 1979; UBC Big Block Award (5 times); m. Susan d. Ronald and June Grantham 2 June 1979; three s.: Michael Donald, Steven Ronald, Brian Grantham; PARTNER, SWINTON & COMPANY 1981– ; law clerk, Court of Appeal, B.C. 1979–80; articled law student present firm 1980–81; Adjunct Prof. of Law, Univ. of B.C. 1990– ; Bd. of Trustees, St. John Shaughnessy Anglican Ch.; Peoples Warden; Dir. Sport B.C.; Dir., Counselling Group; mem. Olympic Club of Can.; B.C. Field Hockey Assn. (Sec.); Candn. Field Hockey Assn.; Vincents Club; Candn. Assn. of Rhodes Scholars; Lawyers Inn; B.C. Law Soc.; Candn. Bar Assn.; UBC Big Block Club; Candn. National Field Hockey Team 1971–83 (Captain 1975–79); participant in Olympic Games, Pan American Games (4 medals), World Cup, Intercontinental Cup, Esanda World Tournament; 15 Internat. Tours; past team mem. & capt. Oxford Univ.; Br. Univ. All-Stars; Univ. of B.C., B.C. and National Champs.; contrib.: 'Community Participation and the Spatial Order of the City' 1975; recreations: field hockey, golf, classical music; Clubs: Vancouver Hawks Field Hockey; Ladykillers; Kitsilano Yacht; Point Grey Golf and Country; Home: 3450 W. 38th Ave., Vancouver, B.C.; Office: 1000 – 840 Howe St., Vancouver, B.C. V62 2M1.

**HOCHACHKA, Peter William,** Ph.D., FRSC; university professor; b. Therien, Alta. 9 March 1937; s. William and Pearl (Krainek) H.; e. Univ. of Alta. B.Sc. (Hons.) 1959; Dalhousie Univ. M.Sc. 1961; Duke Univ. Ph.D. 1965; m. Brenda d. Henry and Dorothy Clayton 12 Dec. 1970; children: Claire, Gail, Gareth; PROF., DEPT. OF ZOOLOGY & SPORTS MED., UNIV. OF B.C. 1966– ; has travelled worldwide as research/senior scientist and visiting investig./prof. 1967– (over 25 field trips, most recent: Sr. Rsch. Sci., U.S. Antarctic Rsch. Prog., M/V Polar Duke Expedition to the Antarctic; Sr. Sci. and Organizer, 'High Altitude Adaptation in Man' program, La Raya, Peru 1988–89); editor: 'The Mollusca' 2 vols. 1983; lecturer; conf. organizer; Mem., NSERC Animal Biol. Grants Sel. Ctte. 1986– ; Bd. of Trustees, 'Biological Abstracts'; NRC Negotiated Grant 1976; Guggenheim Fellowship 1977–78; Fellow, Am. Assn. for the Adv. of Sci. 1977; Royal Soc. of Can. 1983; Ed. Bd., 'Molecular Physiol.,' 'Am. J. Physiol.,' 'Biochem. Systematics & Ecol.,' 'J. Comp. Physiol. (also Adv. Bd.),' 'Functional Ecol.'; Queen Elizabeth II Sr. Fellowship 1983; Killam Rsch. Prize, U.B.C. 1987–89; B.C. Sci. Counc. Gold Medal 1987; Flavelle Medal, Royal Soc. of Canada 1990; Killam Memorial Prize in Science, Canada Council 1993; Mem., Sigma XI; Candn. & Am. Socs. of Zool.; Am. Physiol. Soc.; N.Y. Acad. of Sci.; Am. Soc. of Biol. Chem.; Soc. of Exper. Biol.; Royal Soc. of Med. (U.K.); author: 'Living without Oxygen' 1980; co-author: 'Metabolic Arrest and the Control of Biological Time' 1987 and 2 others; Home: 4211 Doncaster Way, Vancouver, B.C. V6S 1W1; Office: Vancouver, B.C. V6T 2A9.

**HOCHSTADT, John Webster,** B.A., M.P.A.; university fundraiser; b. New York, N.Y. 13 July 1946; s. Jack and Agnes Gertrude (Houghton) H.; e. City Univ. of New York B.A. 1967; Queen's Univ. M.P.A. 1988; m. Lea d. Paul and Jennye Clearwater 3 March 1972; children: Holly Ann, Toni Beth; DIRECTOR, PLANNED GIFTS & BEQUESTS, UNIV. OF TORONTO 1990– ; Psychiatric Social Worker (US) 1968–72; Contractor (alternate energy) 1973–83; Extve. Dir., P.E.I. Council of the Disabled 1984–87; Acting Asst. Dean, Fac. of Mngt., Univ. of Toronto 1988–89; Graduate Fellowship, Queen's Univ. 1987–88; Founding Bd. Mem. & Vice-Pres., Community Legal Information Assn. of P.E.I.; Founding Bd. Mem., Candn. Assn. of Gift Planners; Chair, 1st Nat. Candn. Conf. on Gift Planning 1994; author: 'Improved Pollination: P.E.I. Honeybees' 1984, 'Eating Miss Daisy' short story in 'Descant' 1991; recreations: wilderness hiking, photography; Home: 92 Walmer Rd., Toronto, Ont. M5R 2X7; Office: 21 King's College Cir., Toronto, Ont. M5S 1A1.

**HOCHSTEIN, Alan Peter,** B.Comm., M.A., Ph.D.; university professor; b. Montreal, Que. 16 July 1945; s. Kermit and Esther (Pittal) H.; e. Sir George Williams Univ., B.Comm. 1966; McGill Univ., M.A. 1969, Ph.D. 1979; m. Debby d. Frances and Melvin Green 1 July 1971; children: Lorin Michael, Eric Glen; ASSOC. PROF. OF FINAN. & FORMER ACAD. DIR. OF MBA PROG., CONCORDIA UNIV.; active in teaching & devel. of extve. MBA prog. and aviation MBA prog.; author: 'An Introduction to Microeconomic Theory: An Advanced Introduction' 1993 (textbook) as well as conf. papers, journal & popular media articles; has presented papers at confs. in Can., U.S. & Eur.; Office: 1455 de Maisonneuve W., Montreal, Que. H3G 1M8.

**HOCKIN, Alan Bond,** M.A.; finance executive; b. Winnipeg, Man. 7 Nov. 1923; s. Harold and Ethel (Bond) M.; e. Univ. of Manitoba, B.A. (Hons.) 1944; Univ. of Toronto, M.A. 1946; Mng. Dir., Sentinel Associates Ltd.; Dir., London Life Insurance Co.; London Insurance Group; Royal LePage Mortgage Corp.; Trilon Financial Corp.; Commemorative Services of Ont.; Candn. Counc. of Christians and Jews; joined Dept. of Finance, Ottawa in 1946; Financial Attaché, Canada House, London, 1951–52; Second Secy. (Finance), Permanent Cdn. Del. to NATO & OEEC, Paris, 1952–53; Vice-Chrmn., Cdn. Del. to GATT session in Geneva 1956; Alternate Extve. Dir., on the Internat. Monetary Fund, Internat. Bank for Reconstr. & Devel., and Internat. Finance Corp., and Financial Counsellor, Cdn. Embassy, Washington, 1957–59; Dir., Financial Affairs & Econ. Analysis Div., Dept. of Finance, Ottawa, 1959–64; Asst. Depy. Min., Dept. of Finance 1964–69; Alternate Governor for Canada of Internat. Bank for Reconstr. and Development, and later of Internat. Monetary Fund; Dpy. to Min. of Finance on the Group of Ten; Alternate mem. of Extve. Comte. of Bank of Canada; Dir., Royal Canadian Mint; Cdn. Chrmn., U.S.-Candn. Balance-of-Payments Comte. 1964–69; with Morgan Stanley & Co. 1970–71; Deputy Chief General Manager Investment Division, Toronto-Dominion Bank 1971–72; Extve. Vice-Pres., Invest. Div., 1972–84; Dean, Faculty of Admin. Studies, York Univ. 1984–88; Clubs: Toronto; Royal Candn. Yacht; Office: 165 University Ave., Suite 200, Toronto, Ont. M5H 3B9.

**HOCKIN, Hon. Tom,** P.C., M.P., Ph.D.; member of Parliament/cabinet minister; b. London, Ont. 5 Mar. 1938; s. Thomas A. and Margaret (McKillop) H.; e. Univ. of West. Ont., B.A. (Hon.) 1961; Harvard Univ., M.Pub.Admin. 1963, Ph.D. 1966; m. Marion V. d. Mario and Elmer Schaefer 9 June 1967; children: Kirsten, Victoria, Thomas; Minister of International Trade, Govt. of Canada 1993; Pres., Markham Imports 1972– ; Prof. 1973– (taught Pol. Sci., York Univ. & Bus. Admin., Univ. of West. Ont. Sch. of Bus.); Headmaster, St. Andrew's Coll. 1974–81; Pres., Sotheby's Can. 1981–83; elected to House of Commons 1984 as P.C. Mem. for London West (P.C. candidate in 1981 by-election); Min. of State, Finance 1986–89; Min. of State, Small Business & Tourism, Govt. of Can. 1989–92; Min. for Science & Min. of State, Small Bus. & Tourism, Govt. of Can. 1993; Fin. Offr., Dept. of Fin. 1963; Part-time mem., Ont. Police Comn. 1980–84; a founding Director of Candn. Ctr. for Creative Technol. and a founding Director of Candn. Ctr. for Arms Control & Disarmament; Past Bd. Mem., Clarke Inst. of Psych., Toronto; Thames Valley Children's Ctr., London; Co-Chrmn., Special Parliamentary Joint Ctte. on Can. Internat. Relns. 1985–86; author: 'Government in Canada' 1976; 'Apex of Power' 1973, 2nd. ed. 1977; 'The Canadian Condominium' 1971; recreations: tennis, golf, canoeing, baseball-watching; Clubs: Albany (Dir. 1980–86); London Hunt & Country; Home: 549 Ridout St. N., PH 4, London, Ont. N6A 2P8; Office: 248 Pall Mall St., Suite 400, London, Ont. N6A 5P6.

**HOCKING, Martin Blake,** B.Sc., Ph.D., F.C.I.C. F.R.S.Chem.; university professor; b. London, England 25 Nov. 1938; s. Brian and Jocelyn May (Hicks) H.; e. Univ. of Alberta B.Sc. 1959; Univ. of Southampton Ph.D. 1963; m. Diana d. Maurice and Dorothy Crane 14 July 1962; children: Jennifer, Philippa, Jeffrey; ASSOC. PROF., DEPT. OF CHEM., UNIV. OF VICTORIA 1975– ; Rsch. Chem. and Group Leader, Dow Chemical of Canada, Ltd. 1963–71; Asst. Prof., present univ. 1971–75; Chair, Environ. Studies 1975–76; Panel Mem., Mercury, Assoc. Ctte. on Sci. Criteria for Environ. Quality, NRC 1977– ; Hibbert Memorial Fellow & Visiting Prof., McGill Univ. & Pulp & Paper Rsch. Inst. of Can. 1978–79; Consultant, MacMillan Bloedel Ltd. 1985–87; Rsch. Fellow, Univ. College London 1987–88; Dist. Visitor, Massey Univ., Palmerston North, New Zealand 1991; Visiting Prof., Univ. of New South Wales, Sydney, Australia 1992; Rsch. interests: organic synthesis, pulp and paper, water-soluble synthetic polymers, environmental chem., life cycle analysis with particular reference to reusable and disposable cups; holder of 8 Candn. & U.S. patents as sole or co-inventor in fields of monomers, process chem., medicine; Fellow: Chem. Inst. of Canada; Royal Soc. of Chem. (U.K.); Mem., Am. Chem. Soc.; Chartered Chemist; author: 'Modern Chemical Technology and Emission Control' 1985 (currently in translation) & num. rsch. papers & book chapters; assoc. ed.: 'Effects of Mercury in the Canadian Environment' 1979; Referee, 'Accounts of Chemical Research,' 'AOSTRA Journal of Research,' 'Biorheology,' 'Canadian Journal of Chemistry,' 'Environment International,' 'Environmental Management,' 'Environmental Pollution,' 'Journal of Luminescence,' 'Spectroscopy: An International Journal,' 'Water, Air & Soil Pollution'; Office: P.O. Box 3055, Victoria, B.C. V8W 3P6.

**HODGE, A. Trevor,** Ph.D.; educator; b. Belfast, N. Ireland; s. Alfred C. and Agnes Edith (Shanks) H.; e. Royal Belfast Acad. Inst.; Gonville & Caius Coll. Cambridge B.A. 1951, M.A. 1955, Ph.D. 1956, Dip. in Classical Arachaeol. 1952; m. Colette d. Flavien and Renée Fabre 16 June 1965; three d. Anne, Christine, Claire; PROF. OF CLASSICS, CARLETON UNIV. 1966– ; Sch. Student Brit. Sch. of Archaeol. Athens 1952; Rome Scholar, Brit. Sch. at Rome 1953–54; Instr. in Classics Stanford Univ. 1957; Asst. Prof. Cornell Univ. 1958, Univ. of Pa. 1959; Asst. Prof. present Univ. 1960, Assoc. Prof. 1963, Chrmn. of Classics 1967–73; commentator CBC radio; writer and interviewer CBC 'Ideas' series; runner-up in Armstrong awards (New York) for most innovative radio programme (for CBC prog. 'Court of Ideas: Pontius Pilate'), 1988; Ottawa ACTRA award best radio documentary writer (for CBC prog. 'Searching for Atlantis') 1986; wrote and appeared in 50 progs. CTV 'University of the Air' classical topics; 'Court of Ideas' (CBC) 10 progs.; Chrmn., Archaeological Inst. of America, international colloquium 'Future Currents in Aqueduct Studies,' New York 1987; author: 'The Woodwork of Greek Roofs' 1960; 'Future Currents in Roman Aqueducts' 1991; 'Roman Aqueducts and Water Supply' 1992 and various articles in learned journals; contributor: 'Globe and Mail,' 'Scientific American'; mem. Hellenic Soc.; Archaeol. Inst. Am.; Am. Philol. Assn.; Classical Assn. Can.; recreations: detective/spy stories, railway operation; Home: 18 Madawaska Dr., Ottawa, Ont. K1S 3G6; Office: Carleton Univ., Ottawa, Ont. K1S 5B6.

**HODGE, Carl Cavanagh,** B.A., M.A., Ph.D.; political scientist; b. London, Ont. 29 Nov. 1950; s. Matthew Cavanagh and Florence Mary (Chavner) H.; e. Carleton Univ. B.A. (Highest Hons.) 1982, M.A. 1983; London Sch. of Econ. Ph.D. 1987; LECTURER IN COMPARATIVE POLITICS, OKANAGAN UNIVERSITY COLL. 1991– ; Civil Servant, Dept. of Energy, Mines & Resources, Nat. Defence 1974–80; doct. cand./teacher, London Sch. of Econ. 1983–87; Lectr. in Comparative Politics, Univ. of Toronto 1987–89; St. Francis Xavier Univ. 1989; Senate Medal of Carleton Univ. 1982; Doctoral fellow, SSHRCC, educated Boyle Scholar (UK); Mem., Candn., Am. & Internat. Pol. Sci. Assns.; author of scholarly articles; recreations: German & French lit., long-distance running; Home: 526 Vintage Terrace Rd., Kelowna, B.C. V1W 2Z8.

**HODGES, Robert S.,** B.Sc, Ph.D., F.R.S.C.; university professor; b. Saskatoon, Sask. 30 Dec. 1943; s. Bertrum and Frances (Cummins) H.; e. Univ. of Saskatchewan B.Sc. (Hons.) 1965 (Hons. Scholarship); Univ. of Alberta Ph.D. 1971 (MRC Studentship); m. Phyllis 23 Aug. 1978; children: Clinton J., Sherylynn J.; PROFESSOR, BIOCHEMISTRY, UNIV. OF ALBERTA 1984– ; Rsch. Scientific Serv. Officer, Dept. of Nat. Defence 1965–67; Postdoctoral Fellow & Rsch. Assoc., Rockefeller Univ. 1971–74 (MRC Fellowship); Asst. Prof., Biochem., Univ. of Alta. 1974–77; Assoc. Prof. 1977–84; Pres., Alberta Peptide Inst. 1985– ; President & C.E.O., Synthetic Peptides Inc. 1986– ; Mem., MRC Group in Protein Structure & Fuction 1974– ; Protein Engr. Network of Centres of Excellence 1990– ; Fellow, Royal Soc. of Can. 1991; contributions to biotechnology, Govt. of Alta. 1986; Sask. Hall of Fame; Candn. Speed Skating Assn. Hall of Fame; Competitor Speed Skating Winter Olympics: Grenoble France 1968, Sapporo Japan 1972; Mgr., Candn. Speed Skating Team Winter Olympics Lake Placid, N.Y. 1980; Vice-Chair, Speed Skating Winter Olympics Calgary 1988; Vice-Pres., Advanced Prog., Candn. Amateur Speed Skating Assn. 1976–83; Mem., Protein Soc.; Am. Peptide Soc.; N.Y. acad. Sci.; Candn. Biochem. Soc.; Am. Chem. Soc.; Sigma Xi; The Sci. Rsch. Soc.; editor: 'Peptide Res.' 1988– ; author/editor: 'High Performance Liquid Chromatography of Peptides & Proteins' 1991; author: 'HPLC of Proteins, Peptides and Polynucleotides' 1991, 'Computer-Assisted Method Development for High Performance Liquid Chromatograpy' 1990, 'The Amphipathic Helix' 1993, 'Chromatography in Biotechnology' 1993, 'Calmodulin Antagonists and Cellular Physiology' 1985 and over 200 journal articles; Home: 9045 Saskatchewan Dr., Edmonton, Alta. T5G 2B2; Office: Edmonton, Alta. T6G 2H7.

**HODGETTS, John Edwin,** O.C., M.A., Ph.D., LL.D., D.Litt., F.R.S.C.; b. Omemee, Ont. 28 May 1917; s. late Alfred Clark and Mary Elsie (Birnie) H.; e. Cobourg (Ont.) Coll. Inst.; Univ. of Toronto, B.A. 1939 (Gold Medallist); M.A. 1940; Univ. of Chicago (Fellowship 1940–43); Ph.D. 1946; Rhodes Scholar, Ont., 1939; LL.D., Mount Allison 1970; Queen's 1973; Carleton Univ. 1982; D.Litt., Memorial Univ. 1971; m. Ella Ruth (dec. 1992), d. late Rev. W. P. Woodger, 26 June 1943; children: Edwin Clark, Peter Geoffrey, Eleanor Anne; PROF. EMERITUS OF POL. SCIENCE, UNIV. OF TORONTO 1982– ; Principal of Victoria College 1967–70 and Pres. 1970–72; Lecturer in Political Science, University of Toronto, 1943–45; successively Lectr., Assistant Prof., Associate Prof. and Professor of Pol. Science, apptd. to the Hardy Chair of Pol. Science (1961–62) all at Queen's Univ., 1945–65; Nuffield Travelling Fellow in Social Sciences, Oxford Univ., 1949–50; Skelton-Clark Research Fellow, Queen's Univ., 1954–55, 1992–93; Editorial Dir., Royal Comn. on Govt. Organization, 1960–62; Can. Council Sr. Research Fellow (sabbatical leave in Oxford Univ., Nuffield Coll. Visiting Fellow) 1962–63; Editor, 'Queen's Quarterly,' 1956–58; mem., Acad. Adv. Panel, Canada Council, 1966–69; Visiting Prof., Northwestern Univ., 1975; Dalhousie, 1975–76, 1982–87; Memorial, 1976–77; Fellow, Royal Soc. of Can. 1963; Publications: 'An Administrative History of the United Canadas,' 1956; (with J. A. Corry) 3rd ed. of 'Democratic Government and Politics'; (with D. C. Corbett) 'Canadian Public Administration: A Book of Readings'; 'Administering the Atom for Peace'; 'The Canadian Public Service, 1867–1970'; (jt. author) 'The Biography of an Institute: The Civil Service Commission of Canada, 1908–1967; (with O.P. Dwivedi) 'Provincial Governments as Employers'; numerous articles in scholarly journs.; mem., Candn. Pol. Science Assn. (Pres. 1971–72); Inst. Public Adm. Can.; Internat. Pol. Science Assn. (mem. Extve. Comte. 1961–64); mem, Royal Comn. on Financial Mang. and Accountability 1976–79; Awarded 1981 Vanier Gold Medal by Inst. of Public Administration of Canada, for a lasting and significant contribution to Canadian Public Administration; apptd. Officer, Order of Canada 1989; Phi Delta Theta; United Church; recreations: sailing, fishing, wood-carving; Home: 48 Earl St., Kingston Ont. K7L 2G6.

**HODGETTS, Ross Birnie,** B.Sc., M.S., Ph.D.; university professor; b. Midland, Ont. 27 May 1941; s. Alfred Birnie and Helen Nicholl (Ross) H.; e. Queen's Univ. B.Sc. 1963; Yale Univ. M.S. 1965, Ph.D. 1967; m. Daralyn d. Guy Francis and Dorothy Simpson 13 June 1964; children: Christopher, Lisa; PROF., DEPT. OF GENETICS, UNIV. OF ALBERTA 1984– ; post-doct. fellow, Yale Univ. 1967–68; Calif. Inst. of Technol. 1968–70; Asst. Prof., present univ. 1970–74; Assoc. Prof. 1974–84; Chrmn., Dept. of Genetics 1993– ; Chrmn., NSERC grant selection panel: Molecular & Devel. Genetics 1990–91; N. Am. Drosophila Bd. 1990–91; Western Dir., Genetics Soc. of Can. 1989–91; Ont. Govt. Scholarship 1959; Union Carbide Scholarship, Queen's 1959–63; Stirling Fellowship, Yale 1966–67; Jane Coffin Childs Fellowship, Yale & Caltech 1967–69; Mngt. Ctte., Clifford E. Lee Nature Sanctuary (Edmonton); Mem., Genetics Soc. of Can.; of Am.; Candn. Nature Fed.; Candn. Parks & Wilderness Soc.; author of more than 30 articles in learned sci. journals incl. 'Nature,' 'Proceedings Nat. Acad. Sci.,' 'Developmental Biol.,' 'Genetics' and 'Embo J.'; recreations: ski mountaineering, wilderness canoeing; club: Centre Club; Home: Site 15, RR 5, Box 49, Edmonton, Alta. T5P 4B7; Office: Edmonton, Alta. T6G 2E9.

**HODGINS, Bruce W.,** M.A., Ph.D.; professor of history; b. Kitchener, Ont. 29 Jan. 1931; s. Stanley Earl and Laura Belle (Turel) H.; e. Univ. of West. Ont., B.A. 1953; Queen's Univ. M.A. 1955; Duke Univ. Ph.D. 1965; m. Carol d. Prescott and Frieda Creelman July 1958; children: Shawn Prescott, Geoff Stanley; PROF. OF HISTORY, TRENT UNIV. 1972– ; Teacher, Prince of Wales Coll. 1955–58, 1961–62; P.E.I. Advr. on Fed.-Prov. Affairs 1957–58; P.E.I. Prov. Archivist 1961–62; Lectr. then Asst. Prof. of Hist., Univ. of West. Ont. 1962–65; Asst. then Assoc. Prof., Trent Univ. 1965–72; Prof. 1972– ; Acting Master, Peter Robinson Coll. 1979; Chrmn., Dept. of Hist. 1980–84; Dir., Frost Ctr. for Candn. Heritage & Devel. Studies 1986–92; Hon. Fellow, Austral. Nat. Univ. 1970; Vis. Prof. of Candn. Studies, Macquarie Univ. 1985; Vis. Fellow, Griffith Univ. 1986; Can. Cent. Medal 1967; Cruikshank Medal for Hist. Writing 1968; Weyerhauser Award, Forest Hist. Soc. 1982; Mem., U.N. Assn. of Can. (Past Chrmn., 2 natl. cttes.); Candn. Inst. of Internat. Affairs (Chrmn., London Br. 1964–65); Candn. Hist. Assn. Counc. 1961–64; Ont. Conserv. Counc. 1975– ; Ont. Recreat. Canoeing Assn. (Pres. 1981–83); N.D.P. (Peterborough Extve. 1965–85, incl. prov. & fed. pres. & 1968 fed. candidate); Asst. Dir., Camp Wanapitei, Temagami 1956–70; Dir. 1971–93; Pres., Camp Wanapitei Coed Camps Ltd. 1971– ; Ont. appointee to Wendaban Stewardship Authority, Temagami 1991– ; author: 'John Sandfield Macdonald: 1812–1872' 1971; 'Paradis of Temagami' 1976; co-editor & contbr. 'Canadian History Since Confederation' 1971, 1979; 'Federalism in Canada and Australia' 1978; 'Nastawgan: The Canadian North by Canoe and Snowshoe' 1985; 'Federalism in Canada and Australia: Historical Perspectives 1920–88' 1989; co-author (with Jamie Benidickson): 'The Temagami Experience: Recreation, Resources, and Aboriginal Rights in the Northern Ontario Wilderness' 1989; co-editor & contbr., 'Using Wilderness: Essays on the Evolution of Youth Camping in Ontario' 1992; 'Co-Existence? Studies in Ontario-First Nations Relations' 1992; recreations: canoe tripping; Home: 7 Engleburn Pl., Peterborough, Ont. K9H 1C4; Office: Peter Robinson Coll., Trent Univ., Peterborough, Ont. K9J 7B8.

**HODGINS, Charles John,** B.A., C.A.; chartered accountant, businessman; b. Toronto, Ont. 1 Aug. 1946; s. Lorne Vincent and Mary Catherine (Leonard) H.; e. Univ. of Western Ont. B.A. 1971; Inst. of C.A.s of Ont. C.A. 1974; children: Paul, Michele, Courtnay; CHAIRMAN, FIRST MERCHANT EQUITIES MANAGEMENT CORP. 1984– ; Ernst & Young (London Ont.) 1971–74; Deloitte & Touche (Prince George B.C.) 1974–78; (Saskatoon) 1978–84; Partner 1976–84; Chairman, Acctg. & Auditing Bd. 1982–84; Co-Founder, First Merchant Equities-Venture Capital Co. 1984– ; Dir. of several Candn. corps.; Special Advisor, Prov. of Saskatchewan; Dir., Saskatoon Airport Econ. Devel. Bd.; Mem., Candn. Inst. of C.A.s Auditing Standards Bd. 1981–84; recreations: golf, hockey, travel; clubs: Riverside Country Club, Saskatoon Club; Home: 529 Mt. Allison Place, Saskatoon, Sask. S7H 4A8.

**HODGINS, Jack Stanley,** B.Ed.; writer; b. Comox, B.C. 3 Oct. 1938; s. Stanley and Reta (Blakely) H.; e. Univ. of B.C. B.Ed.(Sec.) 1961; m. Dianne Child Dec. 1960; children: Shannon, Gavin, Tyler; ASSOCIATE PROFESSOR, UNIV. OF VICTORIA 1985– ; Teacher of High School English, Nanaimo, B.C. 1961–80; Writer-in-Residence, Simon Fraser Univ., 1977; Writer-in-Residence, Univ. of Ottawa, 1979; Visiting Prof., Univ. of Ottawa, 1981–83; Visiting Prof., Univ. of Victoria, 1983–1985; Workshop Instructor, Sask. Summer School of the Arts, 1979, 1980, 1981, 1982; author 'Spit Delaney's Island' 1976; 'The Invention of the World' 1977; 'The Resurrection of Joseph Bourne' 1979; 'The Barclay Family Theatre' 1981; editor 'The Frontier Experience' 1975; 'The West Coast Experience' 1976; mem. Writers' Union of Can.; mem. International P.E.N.; rec'd President's Medal, Univ. of W. Ont., 1973; Eaton's B.C. Book Award, 1977; Gibson's First Novel Award, 1978; Governor General's Award, 1980; Canada-Australia Award 1986; recreations: canoeing, reading; Fine Arts Bldg., P.O. Box 1700, Univ. of Victoria, Victoria, B.C. V8W 2Y2.

**HODGSON, Allan Archibald,** B.A.; executive; b. Montreal, Que. 13 Oct. 1937; s. Jonathan Archibald and Anne Churchill (Hyde) H.; e. McGill Univ. Hons. B.A. 1958; Harvard Univ. Advanced Mgmt. Prog. 1976; m. Victoria d. Stuart and Mary Webster 12 Apr. 1978; children: Lucinda Nora, Jonathan Welbourn, Anne Gregory; Vice-President and Chief Financial Offr., Alcan Aluminium Ltd. 1982–93; Dir., Alcan Aluminium Ltd. 1987–93; Dir. Investment Rsch. C.J. Hodgson & Co. Inc. 1964–67; Asst. Treas. present firm 1969–72; Fin. Dir. Indian Aluminium Co. Ltd., Calcutta 1972–76; Treas. Aluminum Co. of Can. Ltd. 1976–80; Treas. present firm 1980–82; Dir., Spar Aerospace Ltd.; Dir., Allendale Mutual Ins. Co.; recreations: skiing, gardening; Clubs: Bengal, India; University, Montreal; Home: 523 Argyle Ave., Westmount, Que. H3Y 3B8; Office: 1188 Sherbrooke St. W., Montreal, Que. H3A 3G2.

**HODGSON, Barbara L.,** B.A.; book designer; b. Edmonton, Alta. 3 Mar. 1955; d. Stanley and Beatrice Theresa (Connaughton) H.; e. Simon Fraser Univ. B.A. 1977; Capilano Coll. Dip.Graphic Art 1982; PRINC., BARBARA HODGSON DESIGN 1991; Associate, Byzantium Books; Book Designer, Douglas & McIntyre, New Star, Pines & Palms, Viking/Penguin; Book Designer and Art Dir. Douglas & McIntyre 1982–89; lectr. in book design, Simon Fraser Univ. Publ. Prog.; Sessional Instr., Dept. of Comm. S.F.U. 1990; Instr., Graphic Design, Emily Carr Sch. of Art and Design 1990–93; Mem. Graphic Designers of Can. (MGDC); recipient Alcuin Soc. Design Award 1989 (2), 1990 (2); Studio Mag. Award 1986, 1989; GDC Award 1987 (3), 1991 (2); Gilbert Paper Letterhead Award 1988; books designed incl. 'Architecture of Arthur Erickson', 'A Life in the Country', 'Islands on the Edge', 'Asian Dream', 'Cedar', 'Jack Shadbolt', 'Robert Davidson', 'The Egyptian Jukebox'; recreations: painting, photography, travel; Studio: 401 - 28 Powell, Vancouver, B.C. V6A 1E7.

**HODGSON, Gordon Wesley,** B.Sc., M.Sc., Ph.D., F.C.I.C.; educator; b. Islay, Alta., 25 May 1924; s. Wesley White and Olive (Trevithick) H.; e. Univ. of Alta., B.Sc. 1946, M.Sc. 1947; McGill Univ., Ph.D. 1949; m. Jeannette F. Doull, 25 May 1953; children: Patricia, Kathryn, Robin, Lauren, Shannon; SR. RSCH. ASSOCIATE, ARCTIC INST. OF NORTH AMERICA, UNIV. OF CALGARY; Writer/Publisher, Career Seven; Editor, 'Arctic,' Arctic Inst. of North America, Univ. of Calgary until 1989; Professor Emeritus 1985; Prof. Fac. of Engineering, Univ. of Calgary, 1982–1985; Director, Kananaskis Centre for Environmental Research, Univ. of Calgary, 1973–1982; Univ. of Calagary, 1969–1972; with Research Council of Alta., Edmonton, 1949–67; latterly Head, Petroleum Research; Visiting Prof., Tohoku Univ., Sendai, Japan, 1962; NASA Ames Research Center, Moffett Field, Calif., 1967; Stanford Univ. Med. Center, 1968; joined present Univ. 1969; invented capsule pipe lining; author of over 150 articles in various prof. journs.; mem. Chem. Inst. Can.; Am. Chem. Soc.; Geochem. Soc.; Astron. Soc. Am.; Presbyterian; Home: 18 Varbay Pl. N.W., Calgary, Alta. T3A 0C8.

**HODGSON, John Murray,** Q.C., L.S.M., B.A.; b. Toronto, Ont. 21 Sept. 1921; s. Gregory Sanderson and Isabel (Murray) H.; e. Brown Sch. and Upper Can. Coll., Toronto; Trinity Coll., Univ. of Toronto, B.A. 1943; Osgoode Hall Law Sch.; m. Joan Weir, d. late James Walter Morris, 11 Oct. 1952; children: James Sanderson, John Matthew Russell, Barbara Morris; read law with Blake, Cassels & Graydon; called to Bar of Ont. 1949; cr. Q.C. 1968; Law Soc. of Upper Canada Medal 1988; law practice with Blake, Cassels & Graydon; Lectr. on Estate Tax, Osgoode Hall Law Sch., 1958–63; served with Candn. Forces 1943–46 (Italy 1944–45); Hon. Dir., Can. Centre for Philanthropy (founding Pres. 1981–86); Dir., Agora Foundation; Quetico Foundation; mem., Laidlaw Found.(Dir. 1967–84); Candn. Bar Assn. (Ont. Pres. 1971); Am. Coll. of Trust and Estate Counsel, Estate Planning Counc. Toronto (Pres. 1983); Kappa Alpha; Trustee, Deer Park United Church; Club: University; Home: 129 Strathallan Blvd., Toronto, Ont. M5N 1S9; Office: Box 25, Commerce Court W., Toronto, Ont. M5L 1A9.

**HODGSON, Marjorie Jane;** artist; teacher; b. Hamilton, Ont. 30 March 1932; d. George Henry and Florence (Tweddell) Botting; e. Hamilton Tech.; private art lessons; Artists' Workshop; Toronto Ont. Coll. Art; Doon Sch. Fine Arts; m. Joshua s. Joshua and Louise Hodgson 23 Dec. 1950; three s.: Mark Andrew, Joshua Clarke, Duncan Albert; grandchildren: Kimberlea, Ian, Sarah; Ont. Soc. Artists exhns. incl. Image 76 (Molson Purchase Award), Image 77 (Ellerslie Invests. Purchase), Image 80 (Hiram Walker Purchase Award), Image 83 (Union Gas Purchase Award); Candn. Soc. Painters in Water Colour (CSPWC) exhns. incl. open juried exhns. 1967, 1972–84; Japan-Can. Watercolours Exchange Exhn. 1975–76; selected works CSPWC Exhibit Acadia Univ. 1979, Nat. Ballet Exhns. 1978, 1981, 1985, 1990; 'On View' Exhn. Visual Arts Ont. 1976; Nancy Poole's Studio Toronto 1975; Ont. House London, Eng. 1986; opening of new Ontario House, London, Eng. 1988; members shows: O.S.A., C.S.P.W.C.; one man show, Kingsmount Gall. 1991; represented by Kingsmount Gall., Toronto; watercolour teacher; rep. various pub. and private colls. incl. Royal Collection of Drawing and Watercolours, Windsor Castle; mem. Candn. Soc. Painters in Water Colour (Dir. 1974–75, Sec. 1975–79, volunteer coordinator 1986); Ont. Soc. Artists (Dir. 1977–78, 1984, Exhn. Chrmn. 1978–79); recreation: gardening; Home: One East Haven Dr., Scarborough, Ont. M1N 1L8.

**HODGSON, Patrick W.E.,** B.S.; executive; b. Buffalo, N.Y. 6 Sept. 1940; S. Patrick H. and Wilhelmina O. (Schoellkopf) H.; e. Univ. of Pa. B.S. 1962; m. Camille Perrotta 23 Oct. 1963; children: Patrick C., Sayre S.; PRES., CINNAMON INVESTMENTS LTD.; Dir., Old Canada Investment Corp. Ltd.; Fairwater Capital Corp., Toronto; Niagara Share Corp., Buffalo; Manufacturers' and Traders Trust Co., Buffalo; First Empire State Corp, Buffalo; Niagara Blower Co., Buffalo; Scott's Hospitality Inc., Toronto; Todd Shipyards Corp., Seattle, WA (Chrmn.); Exolon Esk Co. Inc., Tonawanda, N.Y.; First Carolina Investors, Charlotte, N.C.; Pres. London Machinery Co. Ltd. 1964–89; mem. Young Pres. Orgn. (Chapter Chrmn. 1988); clubs: London, Washington Athletic; Buffalo Tennis & Squash; Home: 20 Gibbons Pl., London, Ont. N6A 2Y7; Office: 248 Pall Mall St., Ste. 400, London, Ont. N6A 5P6.

**HOEMBERG, (Mrs.) Elisabeth,** M.A.; author; university lecturer; b. Toronto, Ont. 31 Aug. 1909; d. Rev. Robert Arthur and Beatrice (Atkinson) Sims; e. Havergal Coll., Toronto, Ont.; Univ. of Toronto, B.A. 1931 and M.A. 1934; Sorbonne (Paris) 1931–32; Ont. Coll. of Educ., 1932–33; Gertrude Davis Exchange Schol., Univ. of Berlin, 1934–35; Geography Dept., Univ. of Toronto, 1936–38; m. late Dr. Albert Hoemberg, 3 Sept. 1938; children: Philip, Peter, Beata; Reader on the British Dominions, Univ. of Münster 1946–73; Civilian Interpreter, B.A.-O.R., 1945–46; author of 'Thy People, My People' (a diary of the war inside Germany) 1950; Address: c/o 5716 Heather Place, Nanaimo, B.C. V9T 5N7.

**HOENIG, Julius,** M.D.; educator; b. Prague, Czechoslovakia 11 Apr. 1916; s. Josua and Berta (Graz) H.; m. Inge d. late Ernst Greve 31 Jan. 1942; children: Elisabeth, Peter; Prof. and Chrmn. of Psychiatry, Memorial Univ. of Nfld. 1969–1980; co-author 'The Desegregation of the Mentally Ill' 1969; co-translator, 'General Psychopathology' (1963) and 'The Nature of Psychotherapy' (1964) by K. Jaspers; served with RAMC 1943–46; Fellow, Royal Coll. Phys. (UK); Royal Coll. Psychiatrists (UK); Royal Coll. Phys. (C); Office: Clarke Institute of Psychiatry, 250 College St., Toronto, Ont. M5T 1R8.

**HOENIGER, Frederick J. David,** M.A., Ph.D.; educator; b. Goerlitz, Germany 25 Apl. 1921; s. George J. and Elli (Dohne) H.; e. Quaker Sch. Eerde, Ommen, Holland, Oxford Sch. Cert. 1938; Univ. of Toronto, Victoria Coll. B.A. 1946, M.A. 1948; Univ. of London Ph.D. 1954, m. Judith (dec. 1987) F. M. d. Guy Whitaker 13 Sept. 1954; children: Brian, Cathleen; Prof. Emeritus, Victoria Coll., Univ. of Toronto; Lectr. Univ. of Sask. 1946–47; Lectr. present Coll. 1948–51, 1953–55, Asst. Prof. 1955, Assoc. Prof. 1961, Prof. 1963–86, Chrmn. of English 1969–72, Dir. Centre for Reformation & Renaissance Studies 1964–69, 1975–79; Brit. Council Scholar 1951–53; Guggenheim Fellow 1964–65; Gen. Ed. 'The Revels Plays' 1971–85; ed. or co-ed. various publs.; author: 'Medicine and Shakespeare in the English Renaissance' 1992; mem. North-Central Br. Renaissance Soc. Am. (Co-ordinating Secy. 1965–73); Candn. Soc. Renaissance Studies (Pres. 1976–78); Internat. Shakespeare Assn.; Toronto Field Naturalists (Pres. 1960–62); recreations: ornithology, book selling, travel; Home: 133 Roxborough Dr., Toronto, Ont. M4W 1X5; Office: 101 Pratt Library, Victoria Coll., Toronto, Ont. M5S 1K7.

**HOEY, Eamon,** B.A.; telecommunications consultant; b. Argentia, Nfld. 24 Oct. 1941; s. Robert E. and Marie-Paule (Morin) H.; e. Carleton Univ. B.A. 1971; one d. Vanessa; PRES. AND SR. PARTNER HOEY ASSOCIATES 1981– ; joined Bell Canada 1970–76; Sr. Partner The Durham Group 1976–80; Vice Pres. Mktg. & Sales Executone Ltd. 1980–81; regular commentator telecommunications nat. newspapers; recreation: sailing; Club: Mimico Yacht; Home: 379 Belsize Dr., Toronto, Ont. M4S 1N3; Office: 303, 146 Laird Dr., Toronto, Ont. M4G 3V7.

**HOFF, Rita,** B.Comm.; financial executive; b. 10 Feb. 1947; e. Univ. of Bombay B.Comm. 1966; m. Eivind Hoff; children: Alexander, Sean; PRESIDENT & CHIEF EXTVE. OFFR., FIRST CANADA SECURITIES CORP. 1986– ; Bond Trader, Dominion Securities Ltd. 1970–76; Bond Sales, Mead & Co. 1976–80; Vice-Pres., Bond Sales, First Canada Securities Corp. 1980–86; Former Dir., Investment Dealers Assn.; Dir., C.A.A. Toronto; Granite Club; Adelaide Club; recreations: skiing, swimming, gardening, golf, bridge; Home: 22 Old Yonge St., North York, Ont. M2P 1P7; Office: Suite 950, 70 York St., Toronto, Ont. M5J 1S9.

**HOFFER, William Martin,** B.A.; antiquarian bookseller; publisher; b. Winnipeg, Man. 29 May 1944; s. Abram and Rose Beatrice (Miller) H.; e. Univ. of Sask. B.A. 1966; Simon Fraser Univ., Ph.D. studies; PROP., WILLIAM HOFFER BOOKSELLER LTD. 1983– ; commenced second hand bookselling 1969; publisher trade and limited editions lit. and bibliog. 1976– ; mem. Bd. Visitors Hist. Dept. Simon Fraser Univ. 1985; Nat. Archival Appraisal Bd. 1979; mem. Antiquarian Booksellers Assn. Can.; Internat. League Antiquarian Booksellers; Antiquarian Bookseller's Assn. (Internat.); recreation: snooker; Address: 60 Powell St., Vancouver, B.C. V6A 1E7.

**HOFFMAN, Paul Felix,** B.Sc., M.A., Ph.D., F.R.S.C.; geologist; b.Toronto, 21 Mar. 1941; s. Samuel Israel (Hochbaum) and Dorothy Grace (Medhurst); e. Humberside Collegiate, Toronto; McMaster Univ., B.Sc. 1964; John Hopkins Univ., Baltimore, U.S.A., M.A. 1965, Ph.D. 1970; m. Erica, d. Peggy Mackay & Eric Westbrook, Sept. 1984; 1 s.: Guy Samson; PROFESSOR, SCHOOL OF EARTH AND OCEAN SCIENCES, UNIV. OF VICTORIA 1992– ; Field Asst., Geol. Survey of Can. 1962–67, Rsch. Scientist 1969–92; Lectr.: Franklin and Marshall Coll., Lancaster, U.S.A. 1968–69, Univ. of California at Santa Barbara 1971–72; Fairchild Scholar, California Inst. of Technol., Pasadena 1974–75; Vis. Prof., Univ. of Texas at Dallas 1978; Adjunct Prof., Carleton Univ. 1989–92; Visiting Prof., Columbia Univ. 1990; rsch. on geological evolution of continents, Precambrian earth history and environments; rcvd. Link Award, Candn. Soc. Petroleum Geology; Matson Award, Soc. Economic Paleontologists and Mineralogists; Sproule Award, Am. Assn. of Petroleum Geologists; Past Presidents' Medal, Geol. Assn. of Can. 1976; Fellow, Royal Society of Canada; Bownocker Medal, Ohio St. Univ. 1989; Alumni/Alumnae Award, McMaster Univ. 1989; Douglas Medal, Candn. Soc. Petroleum Geology 1992; Logan Medal, Geol. Assn. of Can. 1992; Foreign Assoc., Nat. Acad. of Scis (U.S.A.) 1992; Fellow, Am. Acad. of Arts and Sci. 1993; mem.: Geol. Soc. of Am.; Am. Geophysical Union; Geol. Assn. of Can.; distinguished lecturer for Am. Assn. of Petroleum Geologists, Geol. Assn. of Can., Can. Inst. of Mining and Metallurgy; author in 'Annual Reviews of Earth and Planetary Sciences' 1988; 'The Geology of North America - An Overview' 1989; Home: 3018 Blackwood St., Victoria, B.C. V8T 3X4; Office: Sch. of Earth and Ocean Scis., Univ. of Victoria, P.O. Box 1700, Victoria, B.C. V3W 2Y2.

**HOFFMAN, Randy G.,** B.Eng., M.B.A.; publisher, professor; b. Saint John, N.B. 26 May 1944; s. Peter A. and Rhona G. H.; e. McGill Univ., B.Eng. 1966; York Univ., M.B.A. 1972; m. Wai Wo d. Chu and Kit Kam Lai 3 June 1986; PRES., CAPTUS PRESS INC. 1986– ; Sales Engr., Radionics Ltd. 1966; Regional Sales Mgr.

1969; Vice-Pres., Bus. Devel. in Charge of Planning & Mng., New Strategic Initiatives 1972; Asst. Prof., York Univ. 1977; Assoc. Prof. 1984– ; Contrib. Ed., Sailing Canada 1981–85; 1st degree black belt awarded by All Japan Karate Fed. 1985; author: 'Canadian Management Policy' 1981; co-author: 'Confrontation: A Strategic Management Simulation' 1989; recreations: sailing; clubs: Higashi Sch. of Karate; Home: Vaughan, Ont.; Office: Rm. 251, Atkinson Coll., York Univ., 4700 Keele St., North York, Ont. M3J 1P3.

**HOFFMANN, Ellen,** M.L.S.; librarian; b. Cape Girardeau, Mo. 28 July 1943; d. George E. and Margaret (Riggs) Hafstad; e. Univ. of Wis. B.A. 1965, M.L.S. 1966; m. Richard s. Arthur and Verna Hoffmann 18 June 1966; one d. Kate; UNIVERSITY LIBRARIAN, YORK UNIV. 1984– ; Yale Univ. Lib. 1966–71; York Univ. Lib. 1971– ; mem. Assn. Rsch. Libs. (Bd. 1988–91); Ont. Council Univ. Libs. (Exec. Ctte. 1988– ); Candn. Assn. Rsch. Libs. (Bd. 1985–87); Office: 310 Scott Library, North York, Ont. M3J 1P3.

**HOFFMANN, Geoffrey William,** B.Sc., M.Sc., Ph.D.; university professor; b. Hamilton, Australia 20 Oct. 1944; s. Frederick William and Olga Viola (Menzel) H.; e. Hamilton H.S. 1958–61; Concordia College 1962; Melbourne Univ. B.Sc. (Hons.), M.Sc. 1968; Göttingen Univ. 1968–69; Max Planck Inst. for Biophysical Chem. Ph.D. 1972; m. Monika d. Otto and Emmy Runge 29 May 1971; children: Vivian Eliza, George William; ASSOC. PROFESSOR, DEPT. OF PHYSICS & DEPT. MICROBIOLOGY AND IMMUNOLOGY, UNIV. OF B.C. 1979– ; post-doctoral studies at IBM Research Labs., San Jose 1972–73; Mem., Basel Inst. for Immunology 1974–79; a theoretical biologist interested mainly in 'network theory' of immunology & simple brain models called 'neural networks'; work in immunology led to insights about autoimmunity, developmental work on an AIDS therapeutic and vaccines for autoimmunity; Founder & Pres., Immune Network Research Ltd. (Immunology rsch.); co-editor: 'Paradoxes in Immunology' 1986; recreation: movies; Home: 3311 Quesnel Dr., Vancouver, B.C. V6S 1Z7; Office: 2 - 2095 West 45th Ave., Vancouver, B.C. V6M 2H8.

**HOFFMANN, Peter Conrad Werner,** Ph.D.; educator; b. Dresden, Germany 13 Aug. 1930; s. Wilhelm and Elfriede Frances (Müller) H.; came to Can. 1970; e. Univ. of Stuttgart; Univ. of Tübingen; Univ. of Zürich; Northwestern Univ.; Univ. of Munich Ph.D. 1961; m. Helga Luise, d. August Hobelsberger 22 July 1959; children: Peter F.; Susan J.; PROFESSOR, DEPT. OF HISTORY, MCGILL UNIVERSITY 1970– ; William Kingsford Professor 1988– ; author 'Die diplomatischen Beziehungen zwischen Württemberg und Bayern im Krimkrieg und bis zum Beginn der Italienischen Krise (1853–1858)' 1963; 'Widerstand, Staatsstreich, Attentat' 1969 (4th rev. ed. 1985); 'Die Sicherheit des Diktators' 1975; 'The History of the German Resistance 1933–1945' 1977; 'Hitler's Personal Security' 1979; 'Widerstand gegen Hitler: Probleme des Umsturzes' 1979; 'La résistance allemande contre Hitler' 1984; 'German Resistance to Hitler' 1988; 'Claus Schenk Graf von Stauffenberg und seine Brüder' 1992; numerous articles in profl. journals; mem. Royal Soc. of Can.; Deutsche Schillergesellschaft; Württembergische Bibliotheksgesellschaft; Candn. Comte. for the History of the Second World War; Württembergischer Geschichts- und Altertumsverein; Knightly Order of the Hosp. of St. John of Jerusalem (ER); Home: 4332 Montrose Ave., Montreal, Que. H3Y 2A9; Office: Dept. of History, McGill University, 855 Sherbrooke St. W., Montreal, Que. H3A 2T7.

**HOFFMEISTER, Maj-Gen. Bertram Meryl,** O.C. (1982), C.B. (1945), C.B.E. (1944), D.S.O. (1943), E.D.; b. Vancouver, B.C., 15 May, 1907; s. Louis George and Flora Elizabeth (Rodway) H.; e. Pub. and High Schs., Vancouver, B.C.; m. Donalda Strauss 1935; commissioned in N.P.A.M. 1927 with Seaforth Highlanders Can.; promoted Capt. in 1934, Maj. 1939 and given command of a company; served in 2nd World War with great distinction: Seaforth Highlanders Can. in Eng., 1939–40; returned to Can. and attended Jr. War Staff Course 1942; promoted Lieut.-Col. 1942 and O.C. Seaforth Highlanders Can.; led his regt. in assault on Sicily, July 1943 (D.S.O.); promoted Brig. and in command of 2nd Inf. Brig., Oct. 1943, taking part in Battle of Ortona 1943 (Bar to D.S.O.); promoted to Maj.-Gen., and apptd. to command 5th Armoured Divn. 1943 and took part in Liri Valley operation in 1944, terminating in smashing of Gustav, Hitler, and Gothic Lines (2nd Bar to D.S.O. and C.B.E.); took 5th Armoured Divn. into action in N.W. Europe, March 1945, into the campaigns around Nimegen and Arnheim; assigned to assault on the heavily fortified Frisian Islands when war ended (C.B.); apptd. Commdr. 6th Candn. Divn. (for operations in the Pacific) May 1945; retired from active service in September 1945; apptd. to command 15th Inf. Bgde. (Reserve) 1946; prior to war was Sales Mgr., Candn. White Pine Co. Ltd., Vancouver, B.C.; Commdr., U.S. Legion of Merit 1947; apptd. Vice-Pres. (Production), H. R. MacMillan Export Co. Ltd. (predecessor Co.) 1949; Pres., MacMillan & Bloedel Ltd., 1949, Chrmn., 1956–58; Order of Orange Nassau with Crossed Swords; Military Order of Italy; Agt. Gen. in London (Eng.) for B.C., 1958–61; Pres., Council of Forest Industries of Brit. Columbia 1961–68; Chrmn., The Nature Trust of British Columbia 1971– ; Officer, Order of Canada 1982; recreations: shooting, skiing; Clubs: Vancouver; Capilano Golf & Country; Vancouver Rowing; Canadian; Address: 1501 - 2240 Bellevue, West Vancouver, B.C. V7V 1C6.

**HOFMANN, Theo,** D.Sc.; educator; b. Zurich, Switzerland 20 Feb. 1924; s. Edwin and Hedwig (Moos) H.; e. Evangelische Mittelschule Schiers, Switzerland 1943; Swiss Fed. Inst. of Technol Dipl. Chem. Engn. 1947; D.Sc. 1950; m. Doris Topham d. late John Forbes 15 July 1953; three s. Martin Ian, Tony David, Peter Adrian; PROFESSOR EMERITUS OF BIOCHEM., UNIV. OF TORONTO 1989– , Prof. of Biochem., 1964–89; Post-doctoral Fellow, Univ. of Aberdeen 1950–52; Scient. Offr. Hannah Dairy Research Inst. 1952–56; Lectr. Univ. of Sheffield 1956–64; Visiting Assoc. Prof. Univ. of Wash. 1962–63; Visiting Sr. Scient. C.S.I.R.O., Animal Genetics Div. Sydney, Australia 1972; Visiting Prof. Univ. of Calif. Santa Cruz 1981; Visiting Scientist Univ. of Lund, Sweden 1984 and 1987; mem. Grants Comte. Med. Research Council Can. 1970–74; Assoc. Ed. 'Canadian Journal of Biochemistry' 1970–72; author over 100 articles and reviews structure & function of proteins scient. journs. and books; mem. Candn. Biochem. Soc.; Biochem. Soc. (UK); Am. Soc. Biol. Chems.; Treas. 1977–78, Univ. of Toronto Faculty Assn.; NDP; recreations: ornithology, canoeing, Scottish country dancing, photography, hiking, skiing; Home: 199 Arnold Ave., Thornhill, Ont. L4J 1C1; Office: Toronto, Ont. M5S 1A8.

**HOGAN, James William,** B.A.; librarian; b. London, Eng. 13 Aug. 1938; s. James Anthony and Olive (Stanners) H.; e. Univ. of London, Kings Coll. B.A. 1959, Univ. Coll. Postgrad. Dipl. Librarianship 1964; m. Gillian Collins 29 Sept. 1964; children: Simon, Sarah; UNIV. LIBRARIAN, BROCK UNIV. 1970– ; served with RAF 1959–61 as Chinese Linguist; Westminster City Pub. Libs. London, Eng. 1961–62, 1963–64; Lib., Hong Kong Govt. Office London, Eng. 1964–67; served as Circulation & Science Reference Lib., Serials Lib., Acting Univ. Lib. present Univ. 1967–70; mem. Ont. Council Univ. Libs. (Chrmn. 1986–88); mem. St. Catharines Public Lib. Bd. 1986–91 (Chrmn. 1990–91); mem., Ont. Library Service, Escarpment Bd. 1987–89; mem., Southern Ont. Library Service Bd. 1989–93; mem. Bd. Lib. Coordination 1977–84 (Chrmn. 1977–79); Sch. Lib. Consultant Lincoln Co. Bd. Educ. 1978, 1981; mem. Regional Adv. Comte. Niagara Regional Lib. System 1969–84; Adv. Comte. Lib. Tech. Program Niagara Coll. Applied Arts & Technol. 1968–89 (Chrmn., 1974–78, 1986–88); mem., UNICAT/TELECAT Mgmt. Comte. 1973–80; ; mem. Lib. Assn. (UK); Candn. Lib. Assn.; Candn. Assn. Coll. & Univ. Libs.; mem. Western New York/Ont. Chapt. ACRL; Archaeol. Inst. Am.; Royal Asiatic Soc. (Hong Kong); R. Catholic; recreations: books, racquet sports; Home: 11 Briarfield Cres., St. Catharines, Ont. L2T 3T4; Office: St. Catharines, Ont. L2S 3A1.

**HOGAN, Terrence Patrick,** M.A., Ph.D.; educator; b. Dubuque, Iowa 10 May 1937; s. Clement Joseph and Clarissa Elizabeth (Theis) H.; e. Loras Coll. B.A. 1959; Cath. Univ. of Am. M.A. 1961, Ph.D. 1963; m. the late Elizabeth d. Henry and Joan Gonner 15 June 1963; children: Maureen Anne, Timothy Patrick, Sean Michael; VICE-PRES., (RESEARCH AND EXTERNAL PROGRAMS), UNIV. OF MANITOBA 1991– ; Prof. of Psychol. 1975– ; Prof. of Community Health Services 1991– ; Dir. Psican Behavior Development Systems Ltd.; Chief Psychol. Veterans Adm. Hosp. Clinton, Iowa 1963–65; Asst. Prof. of Psychol. and Business Adm. Bradley Univ. Peoria, Ill. 1965–67; private consulting Marshfield Clinic, Wis. 1967–69; Assoc. Prof. present Univ. 1969, Dir. Clin. Training Psychol. 1970–77, Dir. Psychol. Service Centre 1970–77, Assoc. Head of Psychol. 1975–77, Assoc. Dean of Arts 1977–80, Dean of Grad. Studies 1980–82, Assoc. Vice Pres. (Acad.) 1982–91; indust. consultant; psychol. consultant, Health Sciences Centre Winnipeg; Visiting Prof./Lectr. Univ. of York (U.K.), St. Mary's Univ., Mem. Univ. of Nfld., Dalhousie Univ., York Univ., Univ. of Windsor, Univ. of Victoria, Univ. of Sask., Univ. of Regina, Univ. of Miami, St. Louis Univ., Univ. of Iowa, Wright State Univ. (Ohio), Colls. of William and Mary, Univ. of Wis.; Univ. of the West Indies; Univ. of Zambia; Basselin Scholar Cath. Univ. Am.; mem., Bd. mem. Candn. Plains Research Centre Regina; N. Research Centre Churchill; HVDC Centre; TRLabs; Social Science Fed. Can. Ottawa 1979–83; Social Sci. and Humanities Research Counc. of Can. 1983–86; Internat. Union Psychol. Sciences; mem. Extve. Counc., Candn. Soc. for Studies in Higher Educ. 1988–90 (Pres. 1991–92); ed. 'Business Administration: An Introduction' 1967; 'Family Therapy: An Introduction to Theory and Technique' 1972, Book Club ed. 1975, 2nd ed. 1981; (with Pierre L.J. Ritchie, Timothy V. Hogan) 'Psychology in Canada: The State of the Discipline, 1984' 1988; various papers, articles prof. journs.; Fellow, Foundation for Econ. Educ.; Candn. Psychol. Assn. (Pres. 1982–83); Soc. Personality Assessment; mem. Am. Psychol. Assn.; Internat. Assn. Applied Psychol.; Internat. Council Psychols.; Interam. Soc. Psychols.; Am. Assn. Advanc. Science; Psychol. Assn. Man.; Man. Psychol. Soc.; Psi Chi; Sigma Xi; R. Catholic; recreations: reading, theatre, music; Home: 598A Stradbrook Ave., Winnipeg, Man.; Office: 206 Administration Bldg., Winnipeg, Man. R3T 2N2.

**HOGARTH, Murray E.;** retail gasoline executive; b. Kingston, Ont. 3 Oct. 1930; s. Edgar C. and Gertrude I. (Hunter) H.; e. Queen's Univ. 1950–53; m. Diana Ruth 28 June 1958; children: Gregory, Geoffrey, Timothy, Peter, Christopher; PRES. & CHIEF EXECUTIVE OFFICER, THE PIONEER GROUP INC.; Pioneer was started in 1956 as a retail service station chain in Hamilton and has grown to some 230 stations in Ont. & Manitoba rep. 5% of the Ont. retail gasoline market or 2% of the Candn. market; Pioneer's partnership cos. develop real estate in Florida & Ont., mfg. & sell auto. vehicle washing equipment, ice products and operate Tim Horton Donut Shops, dry cleaning stores, recreational park facilities; Dir of num. Pioneer Group Cos.; Scott's Hospitality Inc.; Atlantis Resources Ltd.; E.D. Smiths & Sons, Limited; awarded 'Canadian Enterpriser of the Year,' by the Candn. Assn. of Family Enterprise 1989; Founder, Napanee & Dist. Found.; Family Enterprise Found.; Adv. Bd. & Founding Dir., The Candn. Assn. of Family Enterprise; Bd. of Gov., Joseph Brant Memorial Hospital; Mem., The Presidents Club & Bus. Adv. Council, McMaster Univ.; Bd. of Dirs., Art Gallery of Hamilton; recreations: tennis; clubs: Roseland Tennis, Burlington, The Racquets Club of Ocean Reef, Holimont Ski Club (Ellicottville, NY); Home: 2320 Lakeshore Rd., Burlington, Ont. L7R 1B2; Office: 5360 South Service Rd., Burlington, Ont. L7L 5L1.

**HOGG, Derek T.,** Q.C., B.A., LL.B.; provincial court judge; b. London, Ont. 29 Aug. 1941; s. William Henry Victor and Blanch M. (Tancock) H.; e. Univ. of West. Ont., B.A. 1964; Osgoode Hall Law Sch., LL.B. 1967; called to Ont. Bar 1969; divorced; children: Colin, Kathleen; PROVINCIAL COURT JUDGE, CRIMINAL DIV., YORK JUDICIAL DIST. 1984– ; litigation practice in criminal & civil law 1969–84; Q.C. 1982; Past Mem., Ont. Legal Aid Extve. in Toronto; Advocates Soc.; Crim. Lawyers Assn.; Pres., Judges Assn.; Chrmn., Judicial Stress Ctte.; presides over mock trials in cont. edn. courses for young lawyers & students; author of numerous judgments on criminal cases & papers; recreations: skiing, hiking, golf; clubs: Advocates Soc.; County of York Law Assn.; Candn. Bar Assoc.; Home: 14 Chestnut Park, Toronto, Ont.; Office: 60 Queen St. W., Toronto, Ont. M5H 2M4.

**HOGG, Peter Wardell,** O.C., Q.C., LL.B., LL.M., Ph.D., F.R.S.C.; university professor; b. Lower Hutt, New Zealand 12 March 1939; s. Eric Thomas Edward and Mary Elizabeth (Wardell) H.; e. Victoria Univ. of Wellington, LL.B. 1962; Harvard Univ., LL.M. 1963; Monash Univ., Ph.D. 1970; m. Frances d. Francis and Miriam Benson; children: Anne, David; PROF. OF LAW, YORK UNIV. 1970– ; called to N.Z. bar 1962; practiced briefly in N.Z.; taught law in N.Z. and Australia; called to Ont. bar 1973; has taught law in Can. since 1970; appears as counsel in constitutional cases; Univ. Prof., York Univ. 1986; Fellow, Royal Soc. of Canada 1988; Officer, Order of Canada 1991; author of books and articles on Candn. constitutional law, incl. 'Liability of the Crown' 1971, 1989; 'Constitutional Law of Canada' 1977, 1985, 1992; Home: 134 Glenrose Ave., Toronto, Ont. M4T 1K8; Office: Osgoode Hall Law School, 4700 Keele St., North York, Ont. M3J 1P3.

**HOGG, Robert Lawrence,** Ph.D.; writer/university professor; b. Edmonton, Alta. 26 Mar. 1942; s. George Harold and Florence (Drebert) Hogg; e. Univ. of B.C., B.A. 1964; S.U.N.Y. at Buffalo, Ph.D. 1982; m. Leslie Joy d. Harry Dudley and Beatrice Flaig; children: Ethan,

Cyrus, Sarada; writing career began as part of TISH poetry movement, Vancouver, early 1960s; influenced by Black Mountain Sch. of Poetics; studied under Charles Olson (Am. poet); author: 'The Connexions' 1966, 'Standing Back' 1972, 'Of Light' 1978, 'Heat Lightning' 1986 (poetry), 'There Is No Falling' 1993; Co-ed., 'TISH' 1964, 'Motion' 1963–64; Prof., Carleton Univ. 1968– specializing in modern & post-modern American and Canadian poetry; Mem., Candn. Organic Growers; Organic Crop Improvement Assn.; maintains organic farm which produces wheat and mills flour; Home: R.R. 3, Mountain, Ont. K0E 1S0; Office: Dept. of English, Carleton Univ., Ottawa, Ont. K1S 5B6.

**HOGG, Roy D.,** C.A.; chartered accountant; b. Winnipeg, Man. 6 March 1937; e. Univ. of Manitoba; m. Hilda; children: Tracy, Trent; CANADIAN TAX PRACTICE DIRECTOR, ARTHUR ANDERSEN & CO.; responsible for seven offices across Canada, Canada-wide tax training and num. tax pubns. of the firm incl. co-author of annual 'Preparing Your Income Tax Returns'; Dir., Candn. Opera Co.; Toronto Chapter, Kidney Found.; Mem., Inst. of C.A.s of Ont.; Inst. of C.A.s of Manitoba; Estate Planning Council; Little Trinity Ch.; Home: 15 Oriole Parkway, Toronto, Ont. M4V 2C9; Office: P.O. Box 29, Toronto-Dominion Centre, Toronto, Ont. M5K 1B9.

**HOHM, Dale Jonathan,** B.Comm., C.A.; energy executive; b. Melville, Sask. 25 March 1958; s. Irvin Harry and Irene Helen H.; e. Univ. of Alberta B.Comm. (with distinction) 1980; m. Charlotte d. Fred and Erma Martin 25 Aug. 1984; children: Ashley, Rebecca, Kelsey; VICE-PRESIDENT, AUDIT, NUMAC ENERGY INC. 1993– ; Manager, Deloitte & Touche 1980–90; Vice-Pres. & Treas., Numac Oil & Gas. Ltd. 1990–93; Vice-Pres., Treas. & Corp. Sec. 1993; Mem., Candn. Inst. of C.A.s; Inst. of C.A.s of Alta.; Financial Extves. Inst.; Home: 16032 McKenzie Lake Way S.E., Calgary, Alta. T2Z 1Y1; Office: 321 – 6th Ave. S.W., Calgary, Alta. T2P 3H3.

**HOILETT, Hon. Keith Alexander,** B.A., LL.B.; judge; b. Jamaica, W.I. 5 Feb. 1933; s. Philip Adolphus and Clara Emily (Davis) H.; e. Univ. of Toronto, B.A. 1960, LL.B. 1964; m. Judith Donna d. Reuben and Edith Yourt Nov. 1968 (separated); children: Philip, Sarinda; JUDGE, ONTARIO COURT OF JUSTICE (GEN. DIV.) 1990– ; called to Ont. Bar 1966; Asst. Crown Attorney, Judicial Dist. of York 1966–75; Spec. Asst. & Legal Offr., then Exec. Dir., Ont. Ombudsman's Office 1975–81; Hearing Offr., N. Pickering Hearings 1976–78; District Ct. Judge, Ont. 1981–90; Assoc., Scarborough Coll., Univ. of Toronto; Chrmn., Dr. Daphne DaCosta Found.; mem. Adv. Ctte., Scarborough Youth Services; Bd. mem., YouthLink (formerly Big Sister Assoc.); Anglican; recreations: bridge, table tennis, cross-country skiing, reading, walking; Home: 65 Scadding Ave., #604, Toronto, Ont. M5A 4L1; Office: Court House, 361 University Ave., Toronto, Ont. M5G 1T3.

**HOLBROOK, Elizabeth Bradford,** R.C.A.; sculptor; b. Hamilton, Ont. 7 Nov. 1913; d. William Ashford and Alma Victoria (Carpenter) Bradford; (great-great-grand-daughter of Hon. John Willson); e. elem. schs. Hamilton; Hamilton Tech. Sch. (Art) and Hamilton Conserv. of Music (Piano) 1929; Ont. Coll. of Art (Sculpture) 1934, postgrad. work with E. Hahn 1937–38 (Lt. Gov.'s Silver Medal for Sculpture 1935); Royal Coll. of Art London, Eng. 1936; Cranbrook Acad. of Art Bloomfield Hills, Mich. (w. Carl Milles) 1948; m. John Grant Holbrook, D.D.S. 3 Aug. 1936; children: John David, M.D., Elizabeth Jane B.A., William Howard (d.); Lectr. and Teacher; World Traveller; Assoc. and Alumnist, O.C.A.; Art Lectr. and Instr. in Sculpture, Dundas Valley Sch. of Art 1964, 1968; 'My Grandfather' John O. Carpenter, plaster 1931 (destroyed in studio fire) 1952; bronze life size head John W. Bradford (coll. of artist) 1932; bronze head and shoulders Dr. W.H. Hewlett, Centenary Ch., Hamilton 1934; Owen Merriman Memorial stone sculpture Royal Bot. Gdns. Hamilton 1937; Geo. Nelson, portrait plaster 1940, destroyed in fire 1952; limestone direct carving 1/2 life size female torso, (coll. of artist) 1942; Jane Holbrook, portrait plaster 1943, destroyed in fire 1952; bronze portrait Dr. J.H. Holbrook Chedoke Gen. Hosp. Hamilton Ont. 1945; bronze life size head William Howard Holbrook (coll. of artist) 1947; garden sculpture for fountain, bronze standing female figure (coll. of artist) 1948; Dancing Bear and Hound, plaster destroyed in fire 1952; Dr. Geo. C. Gilmour, Pres. & Chancellor McMaster Univ. bronze in Divinity Coll., Hamilton Ont. 1948; bronze head & shoulders self portrait (coll. of artist) 1948; Garden Sculpture, standing nude female figure 18" (coll. of Robert Glenny); Garden Sculpture, standing nude female figure on shell, 4' bronze (coll. of artist) 1949; Rev. Norman Rawson bronze United Ch. of Can. 1949; Percé Taçon O.C.E., bronze (coll. of Mrs. Taçon) 1949; bronze on marble life size head John David Holbrook 1949; bronze portrait (coll. of artist) Reginald Godden 1952; bronze life size head Scott Bradford (coll. of J.W. Bradford) 1953; bronze portrait Harry Somers (coll. of artist) 1953; 2 twelve ft. stone panels Hamilton Fed. Bldg. 1955; bronze portrait #1 Emanuel Hahn Nat. Gallery Can. 1957; oil painting life size seated figure Judge G.A.P. Brickenden (coll. of Mrs. Dorinda Fuller) 1959; bronze 18' standing figure St. Brendan coll. of the late Bishop W. Bagnall 1960; bronze portrait Barbara Narusi (coll. of artist) 1964; Wm. Robertson bronze portrait (coll. Dow Chemical Co.) 1964; Meml. bronze plaque Meredith Brockwell Onandaga Camp Minden, Ont. 1965; Centennial Fountain Dunnville Ont. 1967; bronze portrait Ellen M. Fairclough Parlt. Bldgs. 1967, and Fairclough Bldg. Hamilton 1983; Roy G. Cole, bronze 1969, permanent coll., Art Gall. of Hamilton 1992; Rabbi Bernard Baskin, bronze, Anshe Shalom Temple Hamilton, Ont. 1969; Dr. Charles Comfort, bronze, Arts & Letters Club (Toronto); R.C.A. Diploma Collection 1971; Carl Schaefer bronze, A.G.O. 1974; Frank Panabaker bronze, Art Gall. of Hamilton, also Emanuel Hahn #2 1974; E. Hahn #3 bronze, Arts and Letters Club, Toronto 1975; bronze thoro. stallion on marble (edition of 3), E.W. Shaver 1974, Hamilton Club, Ont. 1975, Ralph Cooper 1989; James Babcock bronze, Hamilton Golf & Country Club 1976; designed & executed pendant cast in sterling silver, jewelry for Women's Ctte., Art Gall. of Hamilton, 1977; bronze portrait Francis Deck Pres. Candn. Restaurant Assoc. Toronto 1977; bronze portrait Mrs. Eilleen Peer 1979; E. Hahn #4, plaster, O.C.A. 1979, E. Hahn #5, London Regional Art Gallery & Museum 1992; ; bronze 24' standing figure cadet, Royal Mil. Coll. 1979; bronze family group, Ross & Robinson – Barristers, Hamilton 1979; bronze plaque former Mayor Lloyd Jackson in Lloyd Jackson Square, Hamilton 1979; holy family figures (silver) on altar, St. John's Ang. Ch. Ancaster 1961; oak wood carving liturgical sculpture Altar Frontal there 1978, two angels relief panels added 1991; oak wood carving St. Mark's Ch. Kitsilano Vancouver, B.C. 1980–81; bronze portrait Hon. John Diefenbaker (coll. of artist) 1980; bronze portrait #1 Dr. James Robinson Nat. Portrait Gall., Washington, D.C. 1980; #2 bronze of Dr. J. Robinson, Candn. Crossroads Internat. Office, Toronto 1985; A.R.W. McKay, bronze 1983; struck bronze medal of Ambassador Kenneth D. Taylor 1980; bronze trophy and medal Gartshore Memorial Award Royal Agric. Winter Fair 1982; bronze portrait Mrs. Dorinda Brickenden Fuller of London, Ont. 1984 (acquired by London Regional Art Gall. & Museum for permanent coll. 1992); St. John's Eagle, bronze award medal, St. John's Church, Ancaster 1985; Dr. J.G. Holbrook struck bronze medal, for retirement 1985; bronze portrait Thor Carlsen, Thor Wing of Carlsen Cosmetic Surg., Woodbridge, Ont.; The Brickenden Trophy, Royal Agri. Winter Fair, Horse Show, Toronto 1987; series of life size charcoal drawings Jane, Susan, & Christopher, William Holbrook, Margaret Kelley, Ogilvie children 1985; liturgical drawings and Holy Mother and Child, bronze, collection of Arch Deacon Robert Grigg, Dundas, Ont.; Hamilton Acad. of Med. 1985; bronze plaque of Sir William Osler – 1849–1949; bronze Homage to Henry Moore Medal, A.G.O.; Homage to Albert Einstein Medal (bronze; special centenary ed.); bronze medal James Robinson Award, Crossroads International, Canada 1985; bronze presentation medal Dr. J.H.T. Wade, Ret. Dean of Mech. Engineering, McMaster Univ. 1984; #1 heroic bronze Sir Winston Churchill, Churchill Park, St. John's Nfld. 1986; #2 bronze of Sir Winston Churchill for Ship's Harbour, Nfld. 1991; Maquette for portrait of Lieut. Gov. of Ont. Lincoln Alexander 1987; bronze head & shoulders ex-mayor Victor K. Copps of Hamilton 1986–87 (maquette only); Tree of Knowledge, with three figures, for Scarborough High Sch. of Comm. 1988; Annual Award Medal, Candn. Hunter Improvement Soc. 1970; Annual Team Award Medal, Candn. Equestrian Fed. 1972; Award Medal, Ont. Soc. Artists 1980; designed and executed bronze medal for U.N. 'Child-to-Child' Care Programme (Worldwide Presentation) 1983; solo sculpture exhns. London Art Gall. 1948; Art Gall. of Hamilton 1974; Sisler Gallery Toronto 1976; McMaster Med. Centre Gallery 1978; rep. in Fed. of Internat. Medallists Prague, Cologne, Helsinki, Cracow, Lisbon, Florence, Stockholm, Colorado Springs 1987, Budapest 1994; Women Medallists of Can. Pub. Archives Ottawa 1980; recent exhbns. Hamilton Artists 1910–1950, Art Gall. of Hamilton 1986; Hamilton Now, Old Hamilton Lib. 1986; author, 'Leading Ladies,' Bannister Pub., Ottawa; one man exhbn. Royal Botannical Gardens Gall. 1987; exhbn.: retrospective of all works, McMaster Univ. Gallery 1989; Dr. Chas Comfort, bronze, life size on marble, Arts and Letters Club, Toronto 1989; The Hamilton YWCA Centennial Award Medal (2 sided bronze 4"); The Grand Prix Dressage, bronze 6" medal, presented to equestrian Cindy Ishoy & Dynasty 1989; The Women's Athletic Alumnae of Univ. of Western Ont. 3" bronze medal 1989; The Maurice Saval Plaque (28" x 18" bronze), in City Hall and St. John's Univ., St. John's, Nfld. 1989; St. Paul, The Apostle (18" model) 'In Revelation' 1990; Col. Geo. F. Stanley (Designer of the Candn. Flag) life size portrait head & shoulders bronze for City Hall, Stoney Creek, Ont. 1990 in personal coll. of Col. Stanley; The Catherine Lorillard Wolfe juried Art Exhibit, National Arts Club, New York, N.Y., Best Bronze Portrait Award for Mrs. Dorinda Fuller 1988; portrait life size bronze head & shoulder of A.J. Billes, ret'd Pres. of Candn. Tire Corp., in head office, 1990; bronze equestrian statue, Queen Elizabeth II, 1/4 life size, priv. coll. 1990; Two sided bronze medal for 1992 FIDEM Congress in London, Eng., at British Museum: 'Jacques Cousteau' on obverse 'Calypso diver' on reverse 1992; 3" bronze medal for President's Award, McMaster Univ., Hamilton 1993; large bronze relief plaque: life size portraits of Pres. Franklin D. Roosevelt and Sir Winston Churchill at signing of Atlantic Charter on H.M.S. Prince of Wales 1942, for St. John's Nlfd. 1992; contributor, 'Ontario Collection' by Fern Bayer 1984; 'Climbing the Cold White Peaks' Contemporary Art in Hamiton by Stuart McCuaig 1986; illus. lectures: 'Art & Religion'; 'Henry Moore'; 'Four Candn. Women Sculptors'; 'Relief Sculpture'; 'Carl Milles & Ivan Mestrovic'; rec'd Gold Medal for Portraiture, Nat. Sculpture Soc. New York 1969; estbl'd Elizabeth Bradford Holbrook Sculpture Scholarship O.C.A. 1978; mem. Candn. Hunter Improvement Soc. (Hon. Dir., Past Pres. 1968–69); Candn. Pony Club (Adv. Bd.); mem. and founder Cdn. branch, New Forest Pony Breeding Soc.; Ont. Soc. Artists; Sculptors Soc. Can.; Candn. Equestrian Fed. (retired Sr. Judge Ont. Div.); mem., Royal Candn. Acad. of Arts (elec. 1973), Counc. mem., RCA 1982, 83, 84; Women of the Year in the Arts, Local Counc. of Women, City of Hamilton 1988; Patron Mem., London Regional Art Gall. & Museum, London, Ont. 1992; Life mem., A.G.O.; Benefactor, Art Gallery of Hamilton; mem., U.E.L.; Zonta Club, Hamilton; Eng. Speaking Union, Hamilton Br.; Assoc. of Sisters of St. John the Divine Convent, Willowdale since 1962; Liberal; Anglican; recreation: equestrian; Clubs: Anglican Business & Profl. Women's; Hamilton Hunt; Home: 'Brookford' 1177 Mineral Springs Rd., R.R.3, Dundas, Ont. L9H 5E3.

**HOLBROOK, George W.,** M.Sc., Ph.D.; retired Canadian public servant; b. Asquith, Sask. 16 Dec. 1917; s. Alfred and Florence (Cutler) H.; e. Hastings Private Sch., Eng.; London Univ.; Eng., B.Sc. 1938, Ph.D. 1956; Queen's Univ. 1948–49, M.Sc. Elec. Engn.; D.Sc. (H.C.) Royal Mil. Coll.; D. Eng. (H.C.) Technical Univ. of Nova Scotia; m. Frances Mary (Fletcher) 22 Nov. 1944; children: John Adam Duncan, Mary Jane Louise; CONSULTANT; Transmission and Devel. Lab., Standard Telephone & Cables (London, Eng.); Brit. Terr. Army Feb. 1939; Royal Corps of Signals, armoured and airborne formations until demob. rank of Major, Feb. 1946; Candn. Army as Chief Instr., Royal Candn. Sch. of Signals 1946; Lieut. Col., Dept. of Elect. Engn., Royal Mil. Coll. 1950; Head of Dept. Prof. of Elect. Engn. Jan. 1952; Pres. and Vice-Chrmn., Nova Scotia Tech. Coll. 1961–71; Dir.-Gen. Communications Research Centre, Dept. of Communications to July 1975; Adjunct Prof., Tech. Univ. of N.S., Nov. 1977; mem., Inst. of Elect. Engrs.; Fellow, Engn. Inst. Can.; Assn. Prof. Engrs., N.S.; Anglican; recreation: sailing; Office: Tantallon, Halifax County, N.S. B0J 3J0.

**HOLDCROFT, Steven,** B.Sc., Ph.D.; university professor; b. Manchester, Eng. 8 June 1961; s. Ronald Arthur and Eunice (James) H.; e. Univ. of Salford B.Sc. (Hons.) 1983; Simon Fraser Univ. Ph.D.; m. Amanda d. Bart and Anne Van Dijk 16 Aug. 1986; children: Trevor Arthur, Kevin Andrew; ASST. PROFESSOR, CHEMISTRY, SIMON FRASER UNIV. 1990– ; NSERC Postdoctoral Fellow (with Dr. Guillet, U. of T. studying photoprocesses in polymers) 1988–90; B.C. Advanced Systems Inst. Fellow 1992–93; research focus: electronic & microelectronic properties of plastics; Mem., Chem. Inst. of Canada; Am. Chem. Soc.; author/co-author of 27 sci. rsch. pubs.; recreations: soccer, squash; Home: 307 Highland Way, Unit 6, Port Moody, B.C. V3H 3V6; Office: Burnaby, B.C. V5A 1S6.

**HOLDEN, Derek J.;** business executive; b. Liverpool, England 24 Feb. 1938; s. Joseph and the late Mabel H.; e. A.M.I. Mech. E. (UK), H.N.D. Liverpool College, England 1962; m. Joan; two children; VICE PRESIDENT, GOVERNMENT & INDUSTRY RELATIONS & BUSINESS DEVELOPMENT, OWENS CORNING FIBERGLAS 1993– ; Mechanical Engineer, Fiberglas Canada Inc. 1966; Design Engr. 1967; Sr. Project Engr. 1970;

Mech. Design Supvr. 1973; Mgr., Product & Process Development 1976; Mgr., Research & Devel. 1988; Group Vice-Pres., TR&C 1990 Extve. Vice-Pres. 1990; Pres. & C.E.O., Fiberglas Canada Inc. 1990–93; Mem., Profl. Engrs. of Ont.; recreations: sailing, gardening; Office: 4100 Yonge St., Toronto, Ont. M2P 2B6.

**HOLDEN, Hélène P.;** writer; b. Montréal, Qué. d. Phrixos Basil and Mariette (Vachon) Papachristidis; e. Acad. St-Paul; Coll. Marguerite Bourgeoys, Sir George Williams Univ.; divorced; children: Arthur, Christopher, Caroline; Co-founder & co-owner of The Double Hook, an all-Candn. bookshop in Montréal; author: 'The Chain' 1969; 'La chaine' 1970; 'Goodbye, Muffin Lady' 1974; 'After the Fact' 1986; 'Snow' forthcoming (novels) and several short stories in French & English; Prix de littérature Benson & Hedges 1977 (short story); mem., PEN Internat.; The Writers' Union of Can; Address: c/o Writers' Union of Can., 24 Ryerson Ave., Toronto, Ont. M5T 2P3 and The Double Hook, 1235A Greene Ave., Westmount, Que. H3Z 2A4.

**HOLDEN, Richard B.,** Q.C., B.A., B.C.L.; lawyer; b. Montreal, Que. 7 July 1931; s. John Hastie and Rita (Hutcheson) H.; e. Westmount High Sch. 1948; Univ. de Grenoble, France 1951; McGill Univ. B.A. 1952; Univ. de Montreal 1953; McGill Univ. B.C.L. 1955; Columbia Univ. 1971; div.; children: Arthur, Christopher, Caroline; el. to Nat. Assembly (Que.), Westmount Constituency 1989– ; joined the P.Q. 1992; practised Maritime and Civil law 1956–84; Sec. Montreal Bar 1965; Special Asst. to Que. Ombudsman 1969; cr. Q.C. 1971; Lectr. McGill Law Fac. 1975–78; Vice Chrmn., Restrictive Trade Practices Comn. 1984–87; author: 'The Quebec Crucible' 1970; mem. Candn. Bar Assn.; United Ch. of Can.; past mem. and Dir. Prog. Conservative Party; past mem. and Dir. Candn. Counc. of Christians and Jews; recreations: skiing, swimming, tennis; Office: Hôtel du Parlement, Rm. 303b, Québec, Qué. G1A 1A4 and 5165 Sherbrooke St. W., Room 101, Montréal, Qué. H4A 1T6.

**HOLDSWORTH, David James,** B.A., M.A.; public service executive; b. Toronto, Ont. 14 April 1943; s. James Darrell and Violet Dorothy (Walsh) H.; e. Univ. of Toronto, Victoria College B.A. (Hons.) 1965, M.A. 1966; Univ. of Texas at Austin 1966–70; children: Douglas James, Donald Kenneth; VICE-PRESIDENT (CORPORATE MANAGEMENT) CANADIAN INTERNATIONAL DEVELOPMENT AGENCY 1993– ; Policy and Operational Roles, Ottawa and Consulting to Internat. Red Cross, Geneva, Switz., Candn. Internat. Devel. Agency 1970–77; Counsellor, Candn. High Comn. New Delhi, India 1977–80; Acting Asst. Sec. to Cabinet, Fed.-Prov. Relations Office Ottawa 1981–82; Vice Pres. (Asia) 1986–93; Home: 25 Lindenlea Rd., Ottawa, Ont. K1M 1A9; Office: 200 Promenade du Portage, Hull, Que. K1A 0G4.

**HOLE, Harry,** P.Eng.; professional engineer; b. Edmonton, Alta. 14 Sept. 1921; e. Victoria H.S.; Univ. of Alta. B.Sc.; m. Muriel d. Sam and Nellie Sweetnam 26 Mar. 1949; children: Elaine Louise, Mary Barbara, Janice Lynn, Karen Anne; Pres., Lockerbie and Hole Western Limited; Lieutenant, Royal Candn. Engineers 1944, 1946; Pres., Frobisher Devel. Ltd.; Beaufort Buildings Ltd.; Frobisher Bay Holdings Ltd.; Hole Developments Ltd.; Dir. Emeritus, Candn. Imperial Bank of Commerce; Dir., Westcan Malting Ltd.; Melcor Devel. Ltd.; Northwestern Utilities Ltd.; Marlboro Investments Ltd.; Edmonton Westin Hotel; Hon. Lieutenant-Colonel, 15 (Edmonton) Service Battalion; Past Dir., Candn. Reserve Oil & Gas; Star Oil & Gas; O.P.I. Ltd.; Arteco Mortgage Investment Co.; Western Can. Racing Assn.; Edmonton Broadcasting Co. Ltd.; Alta. Charter Dir., Western Can. Lottery Found.; Past Pres., Edmonton Northlands; Edmonton Klondike Days Assn.; N. Alta. Chap., Am. Soc. Heating & Air Conditioning Engineers; Mem., Edmonton Royal Trust Adv. Bd.; Chrmn., Mayors Spirit of Edmonton Ctte.; Former Dir., Edmonton Tourism; Grant MacEwan Community Coll. Found.; Counc. Alta. Assn. Profl. Engrs., Geol. & Geophys. of Alta.; Mem., Govt. House Found.; Red Shield Ctte.; Concordia College Foundation; clubs: Edmonton Petroleum, Mayfair Golf & Country; Home: PH1, 9929 Saskatchewan Dr., Edmonton, Alta. T6E 5J9; Office: 10835 – 120 St., Box 414, Edmonton, Alta. T5J 2J6.

**HOLETON, David Ralph,** B.A., M.Div., S.T.M., M.Th., D.enS.Th., D.enSc.Rel.; university professor, anglican priest; b. Vancouver, B.C. 9 March 1948; s. William Ralph and Lillian Victoria (Johanson) H.; e. Prince of Wales 1966; Univ. of B.C. B.A. (Hons.) 1970; Nashotah House M.Div. 1973, S.T.M. 1974; Inst. Sup.de Liturgie Paris M.Th. 1979; Inst. Catholique Paris D.enSc.Th. 1983; Univ. of Paris IV Sorbonne D.enSc.Rel. 1983; m. Penelope d. William and Margaret (Lubbock) Rathbone 27 May 1972; one d.: Elena Anne; DEAN OF DIVINITY, TRINITY COLLEGE, UNIV. OF TORONTO 1993– ; Rector, St. Richard's N. Vanc. 1974–77; Asst. Priest, Grace Church on-the-Hill Toronto 1981–83; Asst. Prof. of Liturgy & Early Church History, Vanc. Sch. of Theol. 1983–87; Asst. Prof. of Liturgy, Trinity Coll. 1987; Assoc. Prof. 1989– ; Chair, Internat. Anglican Liturgical Consulation 1987– ; Consultation on Common Texts 1992– ; Sec., Societas Liturgica 1991– ; Anglican Ch. of Canada; author of numerous articles & books; Home: 30 Keewatin Ave., Toronto, Ont. M4P 1Z8; Office: Toronto, Ont. M5S 1H8.

**HOLGERSON, Ronald Charles,** B.A., M.A.; public servant; b. Port Arthur, Ont. 29 April 1949; s Ralph Arthur and Irene Mildred (Avery) H.; e. Forest Hill Collegiate (Hons.) 1968; Glendon College, York Univ. B.A. (Hons.) 1972; Univ. of Alta. M.A. 1974; single; uncle to Leonard Holgerson; MANAGER, ARTS MARKETING, DISTRIBUTION & CONSUMER DEVELOPMENT, GOVT OF CANADA 1992– ; Managing Dir., Choreographer, Dancer, Alberta Contemporary Dance Theatre 1974–77; Actor, Citadel Theatre 1976–77; Copy Editor, Radio & TV Coord., The Bay Edmonton 1977–78; Special Events & Fashion Promotion Manager 1978–80; Reg. Dept. Mgr., The Bay, Montreal 1981–83; Community's Sponsor Devel. Animator, Touring Office, Canada Council 1983–86; Mktg. & Communications Coord., Touring Office, Canada Council 1986–88; Sr. Policy Analyst, Arts Policy, Dept. of Communications Canada 1988–89; National Coordinator, Canadian Arts Consumer Profile, Dept. of Communications, Govt. of Canada 1989–92; Acting Dir., Cultural Initiatives Prog. 1990–91; Guest Prof., University of Ottawa 1988–92; Guest Speaker: London England, Seattle Washington, Portland Oregon & across Canada; Vice-Pres., Bd. of Dir., Alberta Ballet School; Editor-in-Chief, 'Canadian Arts Consumer Profile' 1992; Canada Council 'Touring Office Facilities Directory 1988; recreations: scuba diving, film; Office: 300 Slater St., Room 356, Ottawa, Ont. K1A 0C8.

**HOLGUIN, Hector,** M.S., P.Eng.; executive; b. El Paso, Texas 15 Oct. 1935; s. Hector Trinidad and Antonia (Medina) H.; e. Univ. of Texas, El Paso, B.S. (Civil Eng.) 1958, Austin, M.S. 1959; m. Rosario d. Everardo and Concepcion Gomez 14 Apr. 1964; children: Rosario, Mara Isabel, Lilia Marcela, Annaelisa; CHRMN. AND CHIEF EXECUTIVE OFFR., ACCUGRAPH CORP.; Project Eng. Douglas Space Systems Center Huntington Beach, Cal. 1961–66; Vice Pres. and Chief Operating Offr. Cremans Inc. El Paso 1966–71; Pres. and Chief Exec. Offr. Holguin Corp. El Paso 1971, merged with present co. 1986; Pres. & C.O.O., Accugraph Corp. 1987; Dir. Un. Way 1977–79; El Paso C. of C. 1977–79; Univ. of Texas El Paso Alumni Assn., Dir. Devel. Bd.; named Outstanding Ex-Student 1982; Trustee, Tomas Rivera Center; Chrmn. Bd. Comnrs. El Paso Housing Authority 1979–81; Dir. Fed. Reserve Bd. Dallas El Paso Br. 1985–86; Chrmn., El Paso Chamber of Commerce 1992; author extensive series tech. handbooks eng. design by computers since 1971; named Eng. of Yr. El Paso Chapter Texas Soc. Profl. Engs. 1980, Pres. of Chapter 1975–76; recipient Key to City of El Paso 1981; Outstanding Citizen Award LULACS 1981; Nat. Innovation Award from Pres. Reagan 1985; recreations: tennis, reading, writing; Clubs: El Paso Tennis; Rotary (Pres. El Paso 1981–82); Home: 425 Camino Real, El Paso, Texas 79922; Office: 5822 Cromo, El Paso, Texas 79912.

**HOLLAND, Jane Carolyn,** B.A.; public relations consultant; b. Solihull, Eng. 30 May 1952; d. Stanley Jacques and Nesta Jane (Lewis) Butler; e. Univ. of Bristol B.A. 1973; Sorbonne, Paris 1972; Univ. of Birmingham Dip. in Edn. 1974; Harvard Univ. Dip. in Arts Adm. 1976; m. Clarence L. Poirier; children: Carolyn Jane Butler Poirier, Claire Elizabeth Butler Poirier; FOUNDER AND PRES. LEWIS CARROLL COMMUNICATIONS INC. 1988– ; held publicity positions Univ. of Birmingham Drama Dept. and BBC Radio 1974–75; publicist, fund raiser, adm. various theatre co's 1976–79 Toronto incl. Theatre Plus, Toronto Arts Prodns. (now Canadian Stage Co.), Open Circle Theatre, Comus Music Theatre, David Warrack Prodns.; Promotions Mgr. Village by the Grange residential, comm. & retail complex Toronto 1980; Publ Relations Dir. Ayliffe & Elias Advt. Toronto 1981; Pres., Lewis Carroll Public Relations Inc. 1982–88; First Runner-Up William J. Wylie Award for Arts Admns. Ont. Arts Council 1976; recipient Wintario Grant to attend Harvard 1976; Publicity Co-Chrmn. Juvenile Diabetes Found. 1984–86; recreations: modern dance, tennis; Office: 68 Scollard St., Toronto, Ont. M5R 1G2.

**HOLLAND, Hon. John,** B.A.; judge; b. Toronto, Ont. 4 Oct. 1917; s. late John and late Hannah Clark (Christie) H.; e. Univ. of W. Ont. B.A. 1941; Osgoode Hall Law Sch. 1948; m. Mary Agnes d. Courtney Chick, 24 Feb. 1944; children: Nan Polleys, John C., Melissa Costigan, Mary Agnes, Dan; JUSTICE, SUPREME COURT OF ONT. 1975–92, Supernumerary since 1992; called to Bar of Ont. 1948; cr. Q.C. 1958; Assoc. McTague law firm 1945–58, Partner 1948–75; served with RCNVR 1940–45; mem. Candn. Bar Assn.; Advocates Soc.; Essex Co. Med. Legal Soc.; Essex Law Assn.; Internat. Assn. Ins. Counsel; mem. Royal Candn. Mil. Inst.; Anglican; recreations: swimming, golf; Clubs: Windsor; Windsor Yacht; Lambton Golf & Country; Home: 57 Widdicombe Hill Blvd., Weston, Ont. M9R 1Y4.

**HOLLAND, Ray Geoffrey Lewis,** M.A., B.M., B.Ch. (Oxon), F.R.C.P.(C); psychiatrist; b. Belfast, N. Ireland 30 Oct. 1931; s. John and Mary H.; e. Univ. of London Intermediate B.Sc. 1952; Oxford Univ. (London Country Council Scholarship) B.A. 1959, B.M., B.Ch. 1963, M.A. 1964; Inst. of Aviation Med. Toronto grad. 1965; Fellow, Royal College of Physicians of Canada 1978; Dipl. Am. Bd. of Psychiatry & Neurology 1980; one s. Sean Richard; private practice in Gen. Psychiatry 1978– ; Flight Surg. to RCAF Aerobatic Team, Moose Jaw, Sask. 1964–65, No. 1 Fighter Wing Marville, France 1965–67, Sr. Med. Offr. and Flight Surg. on 'Bonaventure' 1968 and Fleet Air Arm Shearwater 1967–69, rank Lt. Commdr.; Resident in Psychiatry, Buffalo State Hosp. 1969–70, State Univ. of N.Y. 1970–71; gen. practice in med. with emphasis on psychiatry Port Colborne, Ont. 1971–75; Resident in Psychiatry, State Univ. of N.Y. 1976–77; Chief Resident in Psychiatry 1978, Fellowship in Child Psychiatry 1977–78, Asst. Clin. Prof. Dept. Health Sciences 1978–80 and Dept. Psychiatry 1978–82, Buffalo, N.Y.; implemented the inclusion of 'large groups' in OHIP schedule; author 'Consumers' Guide to the Psychotherapies' 1986; 'Personality Categories' 1986; 'Child Development in Turbulent Times' 1988; and numerous articles on social issues 1986– ; Affiliate mem., Royal Soc. Med. (London, Eng.); Cdn. Med. Assn.; Cultural Doctorate in Therapeutic Philosophy for service to community and medicine (in particular social issues and group therapy), World University Roundtable 1985; mem. N.Y. Acad. of Sciences 1986; Hon. Dr. of Sci. in Psych. & Neurology, Min. of Foreign Affairs, Education & Culture, Malta G.C. in conjunction with Univ. of Madrid and the Albert Einstein Internat. Acad. Found. 1987; Life Patron & Holder of World Decoration (1989), Am. Biog. Inst. (Raleigh, N.C.); el. Bd. of Govs., Am. Biograph. Inst. Rsch. Found., Raleigh, N.C. 1987; Depy. Dir. General, Internat. Biographical Assoc., Cambridge, Eng. 1988 (Fellow; Hon. Life Mem. 1989); apptd. Depy. Mem., Assembly, Internat. Parliament for Safety and Peace (assoc. with UN), Palerno, Sicily; 500 Personalities of the World, Internat. Biographical Assoc., Cambridge, Eng. 1989; awarded Alfred Nobel Medal, Albert Einstein Found. 1991; Internat. Man of the Year, Internat. Biographical Assoc., Cambridge, Eng. 1992–93; recreations: skiing, sailing, karate; Address: 80 Fraser St., Port Colborne, Ont. L3K 1E4.

**HOLLAND, Hon. Richard Estcourt,** B.A., LL.B., Q.C.; b. London, Eng., 9 Sept. 1925; s. Percy Estcourt and Nesta (Owen) H.; e. Primary Schs., France and Eng.; Univ. of Toronto, B.A. 1947; Osgoode Hall Law Sch., 1950; m. Nancy Margaret, d. John Milford Wyatt, 28 Aug. 1948; two d., Anne Estcourt Holland-McCowan, Suzanne Estcourt Leggett; COUNSEL, GENEST MURRAY DESBRISAY LAMEK; called to Bar of Ont. 1950; cr. Q.C. 1962; practised with Hughes, Agar, Amys & Steen, Toronto for 4 yrs.; assisted in forming firm of Bassel, Sullivan, Holland & Lawson, continuing practice in partnership until appt. as judge; Judge, Supreme Court of Ont. 1972–90; served with Candn. Army 1943–45; Past Pres., Cdn. Inst. for Administration of Justice; Anglican; recreations: fishing, shooting; Clubs: The York; Caledon Mountain Trout; Canard Gun; Grimersta Estate, Isle of Lewis, Scotland; Home: 103 Crescent Rd., Toronto, Ont. M4W 1T7.

**HOLLANDER, Samuel,** B.Sc.Econ., A.M., Ph.D., F.R.S.C.; b. London, Eng 6 Apl. 1937; s. Jacob and Rachel Lily (Bornstein) H.; e. Letchworth Grammar Sch. Eng. 1951; Hendon Co. Sch. London, Eng. 1953; Gateshead (Eng.) Talmudical Acad. 1954; Hendon Tech. Coll. London 1955; Kilburn Polytech. London 1956; London Sch. of Econ. B.Sc. (Econ.) 1959; Princeton Univ. A.M. 1961, Ph.D. 1963; m. Perlette d. late Elie Kéroub 20 July 1959 in Paris, France; children: Frances, Isaac; UNIVERSITY PROFESSOR AND PROF. OF ECON. UNIV. OF TORONTO, apptd. University Prof. 1984; rec'd Sir Edward Gonner Prize 1959; Fulbright

Award 1959; Guggenheim Fellowship 1968–69; Sr. Canada Counc. Grant 1969–71; Killam Fellowship 1973–75; SSHRCC Research Grant 1981–84, 1988–92, 1993–96; Connaught Sr. Fellowship 1984–85; author 'The Sources of Increased Efficiency' 1965; 'The Economics of Adam Smith' 1973; 'The Economics of David Ricardo' 1979 (SSFC 50th Anniversary Award 1990); 'The Economics of John Stuart Mill' 1985; 'Classical Economics' 1987; various articles prof. journs.; Jewish; Home: 278 Major St., Toronto, Ont. M5S 2L6; Office: 150 St. George St., Toronto, Ont. M5S 1A1.

**HOLLANDS, Kenneth George Terrence,** B.A.Sc., Ph.D., P.Eng.; educator; b. Hamilton, Ont. 3 June 1936; s. George Alfred and Doris Irene (Laugher) H.; e. Univ. of Toronto B.A.Sc. 1959; McGill Univ. Ph.D. 1967; m. Mara d. Norman and Gladys Willoughby 8 July 1961; children: Justin George, Judith Anne; PROF. OF MECH. ENG. UNIV. OF WATERLOO 1978– ; Exper. Offr./Rsch. Sci. Commonwealth Sci. and Ind. Rsch. Orgn. Melbourne, Australia 1961–63, 1967–70; Asst. Prof. present Univ. 1970, Assoc. Prof. 1972; Eng. Cons. to govt. and ind. in renewable energy 1975– ; In-House Cons. Palo Alto Rsch. Labs. Lockheed Aircraft Co. Cal. 1976; Visiting Rsch. Sci. Nat. Rsch. Council Can. Ottawa 1982–83, mem. Adv. Ctte. Solar Energy 1979–85; Dir. Solar Thermal Rsch. Centre Univ. of Waterloo 1987– ; recipient Brace Bequest Fellowship 1963–66; James T. Teetor Award, Soc. Automotive Engs. 1973; Solar Energy Soc. Can. Inc. Award 1985; Christopher Weeks Award (co-winner), Internat. Solar Energy Soc. 1989; author or co-author approx. 150 tech. papers eng. jours. & conf. proceedings; several book chapters; Assoc. Ed. Solar Energy Jour. 1984– ; co-ed. Proceedings INTERSOL '85 1986; Fellow, Candn. Soc. Mech. Engs.; mem. Internat. Solar Energy Soc. (Dir. 1978–85, Editor 1994– ); Am. Soc. Mech. Engs. (Chrmn. Solar Energy Div. 1978); Candn. Soc. Mech. Eng.; Solar Energy Soc. Can. Inc. (Dir. 1975–76, 1980–84); recreations: swimming, walking, reading, jazz; Club: University; Home: 36 Lennox Cres., Kitchener, Ont. N2N 2H4; Office: Waterloo, Ont. N2L 3G1.

**HOLLENBERG, Charles H.,** O.C., M.D., F.R.S.(C), D.Sc., F.R.C.P.(C), M.A.C.P.; educator; physician; b. Winnipeg, Man. 15 Sept. 1930; e. Univ. of Man. B.Sc. 1950, M.D. and B.Sc. (Med.) 1955, D.Sc. (h.c.), Univ. of Man. 1983, McGill Univ. 1985; m. Mimi one s. Anthony; Pres. and C.E.O., Ont. Cancer Treatment and Rsch. Found. 1991– ; Sr. Phys. Toronto Gen. Hosp. 1981– ; Dir. The Great West Life Assurance Co.; Past Pres., The Gairdner Foundation; internship, residency and rsch. training Winnipeg Gen. Hosp., Montreal Gen. Hosp., New Eng. Center Hosp. Boston 1954–60; Lectr. in Med. McGill Univ. 1960, Asst. Prof. 1962, Assoc. Prof. 1964, Prof. 1969–70; Jr. Asst. Phys. Montreal Gen. Hosp. 1960–61, Asst. Phys. 1964, Asst. Dir. McGill Univ. Med. Clinic 1964, Assoc. Phys. 1964, Sr. Phys. 1966–70; Prof. and Chrmn. of Med., Sir John and Lady Eaton Prof. of Med. present Univ. 1970–81, Charles H. Best Prof. of Med. Rsch. 1981–83, Prof. of Medicine, Univ. of Toronto 1981–92; Dir. Banting & Best Diabetes Centre 1981–92, mem. Governing Council of Univ. 1982–83; Phys.-in-Chief Toronto Gen. Hosp. 1970–81; mem., Metrop. Toronto Dist. Health Council; Ont. Council Health; Council, Royal Coll. Phys. & Surgs. (Can.); Univ. of Man. Gold Medal 1955; Markle Scholar in Med. Sci. 1960; Annual Lectr., Royal Coll. Phys. & Surgs. Can. 1975; Queen's Silver Jubilee Medal 1978; Sir Arthur Sims Commonwealth Prof. Australia, N.Z. and Gt. Britain 1980; Mastership, Am. Coll. of Phys. 1983; Fellow, Royal Soc. of Can. 1987; Officer of the Order of Canada 1991; mem., various cttes. Med. Rsch. Council Can.; Arteriosclerosis & Hypertension Adv. Ctte. Nat. Heart & Lung Inst. Nat. Insts. of Health U.S.A.; mem., Council Royal Coll. Phys & Surgs. Can.; author or co-author numerous publs.; Fellow, Montreal Medico-Chirugical Soc.; mem., Am. Assn. Advanc. Sci.; Am. Fed. Clin. Rsch.; Am. Physiol. Soc.; Am. Soc. Clin. Investigation; Assn. Am. Phys.; Assn. Profs. Med. Can. (Past Pres.); Candn. Biochem. Soc.; Candn. Soc. Clin. Investigation (Past Pres.); Candn. Soc. Endocrinol. & Metabolism (Past Pres.); Club de Recherche; Clinique du Qué.; Endocrine Soc.; Peripatetic Club; Office: 3 CCRW 845, Toronto General Hosp., 200 Elizabeth St., Toronto, Ont. M5G 2C4.

**HOLLENBERG, Morley Donald,** M.Sc., D.Phil., M.D.; research physician; educator; calligrapher; b. Winnipeg, Man. 2 July 1942; s. Jacob and Esther (Gorsey) H.; e. Univ. of Man. B.Sc. 1963, M.Sc. 1964; Oxford Univ. (Rhodes Scholar) D.Phil. 1967; The Johns Hopkins Univ. Sch. of Med. M.D. 1972; m. Joan d. Alan and Lucille Omson, Winnipeg, Man. 15 Aug. 1965; children: Elisa Michelle, Daniel Benjamin; PROF., DEPT. OF PHARMACOL. AND THERAPEUTICS AND DEPT. OF MEDICINE, UNIV. OF CALGARY 1979– and Head of Pharmacol. & Therapeutics, Fac. of Med. 1979–89; Asst. Prof. of Pharmacol. & Exper. Therapeutics, The Johns Hopkins Univ. Sch. of Med. 1973–79, Instr. in Med. 1974–75, Asst. Prof. of Med. 1975–79; Investigator, Howard Hughes Med. Inst. 1974–79; recipient Nat. Research Council Can. Scholarship 1963–64; Johns Hopkins Med. Soc. Award for Undergrad. Research 1971, Fellowship in Med. 1971–72, Upjohn Award Clin. Proficiency 1972; Med. Research Council Can. Fellowship 1972–73; author numerous book chapters, articles; mem. Am. Fed. Clin. Research; Pharmacol. Soc. of Can.; Am. Soc. Pharmacol. & Exper. Therapeutics; Am. Soc. Clin. Investigation; Candn. Soc. Clin. Investigation; Alta. Soc. Artists; Meeting Point Artists Soc.; recreations: music, literature; Home: 2004 Urbana Rd. N.W., Calgary, Alta. T2N 4B8; Office: 3330 Hospital Dr., Calgary, Alta. T2N 4N1.

**HOLLINGSWORTH, Margaret,** A.L.A., B.A., M.F.A.; writer/educator; b. London, England; d. George and Nellie (Potts) H.; e. Hornsey H.S.; Sch. of Librarianship, Loughborough A.L.A.; Lakehead Univ. B.A.; Univ. of B.C. M.F.A.; currently teaching creative writing at Univ. of Victoria, BC; playwright and short story writer; best known stage plays are 'Ever Loving' (Chalmers Award) and 'War Babies' (Gov. Gen's Award nomination); Asst. Prof., Univ. of Victoria in Nelson 1981–83; author: 'alli alli oh' 1979; 'Mother Country' 1980; 'Operators/Bushed' 1981; 'Ever Loving' (Chalmers Award) 1982; 'Islands' 1983; 'Willful Acts: 5 plays' (incls. 'War Babies': Gov. Gen's Award nomination) 1985; 'Endangered Species' (4 plays) 1988 and num. short stories in Candn. lit. mags.; 1st collection 'Smiling Under Water' 1989; Address: c/o Lazara Press, P.O. Box 2269, VMPO, Vancouver, B.C. V6B 3W2.

**HOLLINGWORTH, Hon. Allan Henry,** B.A., B.Com., LL.B.; judge; b. Brockville, Ont. 28 Aug. 1918; s. Fred Allan and Ida Jane (Barker) H.; e. Brockville Coll. Inst.; Queen's Univ. B.A. 1942, B.Com. 1942; m. Veronica d. Arthur and Dorilla Delorme 30 June 1945; two d. Michelle, Roxanne; JUDGE, ONTARIO COURT OF JUSTICE (GENERAL DIVISION) 1990, Supernumerary; called to Bar of Ont. 1948; cr. Q.C. 1958; mem. H. of C. 1953–57; Co. Court Judge 1972; Judge, Supreme Court of Ont. 1977–90; recreations: languages, tennis, travel; Home: 3202, 65 Harbour Sq., Toronto, Ont. M5J 2L4.

**HOLLOWS, (Arthur) Jeremy,** B.A., ACMA (UK); financial executive; b. Bramhall, Cheshire, U.K. 16 Dec. 1953; s. Peter Twist and Joan Hurst (Smith) H.; e. Kingswood School Bath 1965–71; Univ. of Newcastle-upon-Tyne B.A. 1975; m. Barbara d. Mr. & Mrs. J.M. Coyne 3 Jan. 1987; children: Jessica, Sophie; VICE-PRES. & CHIEF FINANCIAL OFFR., UNILEVER CANADA LTD. 1990– ; various positions with Unilever Group 1975–83; Sr. Auditor, Unilever Nigeria 1983–85; Commercial Planning Mgr., Unilever Export Ltd. UK 1985–87; Commercial Operations Manager, Unilever Export Group, Europe 1987–88; Asst. to Spec. Ctte. (Chief Extve. Offr.), Unilever London 1988–90; Trustee, Internat. Contact Trust; Mem., Planning Forum; Toronto Bd. of Trade; recreations: walking, sailing, theatre, music; Home: 261 Cortleigh Blvd., Toronto, Ont. M5N 1P8; Office: 160 Bloor St. E., Ste. 1500, Toronto, Ont. M4W 3R2.

**HOLMAN, Donald Morison,** C.D., B.Sc., M.Eng.; teacher (ret.); b. Pittsburgh, Pa. 15 Feb. 1916; s. late Prof. William Ludlow and Mary (Morison) H.; e. Univ. of Toronto Schs.; Royal Mil. Coll., Dipl. (Hons.); Univ. of Toronto, B.Sc. (Aeronautical-Hons.); Royal Mil. Coll., M.Eng.; RCAF Staff Coll.; Nat. Defence Coll.; m. Frances Margaret, d. late Donald Macdonald, 15 June 1940; children: Donald Fraser, Susan Ellen, Robert Alan; during World War II served with Air Force HQ (Aero Engr.); Test and Devel. Estab. (Chief Project Engr.); RCAF Overseas HQ (Aero Engr.); various Candn. bomber bases in U.K.; ended War as Chief Tech. Offr., RCAF Stn. Wombleton; Field Information Agency (Tech.), Germany; mem., Candn. Jt. Staff, Washington, D.C. and RCAF Resident Engn. Offr., Avro (Canada) Ltd., 1946–48; held various staff appts. RCAF Air Material Command, 1950–58; RCAF Air Div. Europe, Planning Team and Staff Offr. Aeronautical Engn., 1952–53; Dir. of Instrument & Elect. Engn. Air Force HQ, 1959–60; Depy. Chief, Logistics Div., Air Material Comd., becoming Chief, 1960–65; Depy. Chief of Staff Logistics, Candn. Forces Material Command, 1965–66; Air Force mem., Dir. Staff, Nat. Defence Coll. 1966–68, Commandant 1968–69; retired from armed forces, rank Air Commodore; Associate Professor Mechanical Engineering, Royal Military College 1970–1980; Fellow, Canadian Aero. and Space Inst.; Alpha Delta Phi; Anglican; recreations: sailing, skiing, music; Clubs: Kingston Yacht; RMC Ex Cadet; Home: 56 Riverside Dr., Milton-on-the-St. Lawrence, R.R. 1, Kingston, Ont. K7L 4V1.

**HOLMES, A. Bruce,** C.L.U.; insurance executive; b. Newton, Ont. 5 Nov. 1928; s. Alexander E. and Mary Stuart (Magwood) H.; e. Listowel High Sch.; m. Grace d. John Harris 1949; children: Linda, Deborah, Pamela, Paul, Mark; VICE PRES. PERSONAL INS., METROPOLITAN LIFE INSURANCE CO. 1980– ; joined H.O. Manufacturers Life Insurance Co. 1946; Agt. present Co. 1951, Asst. Mgr. Scarborough Dist. 1952, Field Training Instr. CHO 1955, Territorial Field Supvr. CHO 1955, Dist. Mgr. London 1959, Regional Sales Mgr. Toronto 1969; mem. Bd. Trade Metrop. Ottawa; Life Underwriters Assn. Can.; Candn. Life & Health Ins. Assn.; Past Chrmn., LIMRA Candn. Comte.; Past Chrmn., Senior Marketing Officers, CLHIA; Corporate Sec. Chrmn., 1984, 1985 Ottawa United Way; Dir., Royal Ottawa Hosp. Found.; recreations: sports, reading, gardening; Club: Rideau; Home: 5509 Island Park Dr., Manotick, Ont. K4M 1J2; Office: 99 Bank St., Ottawa, Ont. K1P 5A3.

**HOLMES, David Bryan;** painter and printmaker; b. Harrow-on-the-Hill, Middlesex, Eng. 8 Aug. 1936; s. Harold P. and Ivy E. (Gregg) H.; e. Twickenham Tech. Coll., Eng.; London Sch. Art & Design, Eng.; Harrow Sch. Art, Eng.; Queen's Univ. (Kingston, Ont.); Art Students' League (New York); typographic and graphic designer, compositor, Saint John, N.B. 1960–64; freelance artist, Kingston, Ont. from 1964; Teaching Master, St. Lawrence Coll. Applied Arts Kingston, Ont. painting, drawing, artistic anatomy, etching, graphic design 1968–74; one-man shows: Galerie Gauvreau, Montreal 1969–70; Wally Findlay Galleries Internat., N.Y. 1974, '76, '78, '80, '82, '83, '85, '87, '89, '92, '94; Chicago 1977, '85, '92, '93; Beverly Hills, Calif. 1979; Palm Beach, Fla. 1981, '84, '86, '90, '91; Agnes Etherington Art Centre (Queen's Univ.) Kingston, Ont. 1967; group shows: Queen's Univ. Spring Exhns., Kingston, Ont. 1964–72; Soc. Candn. Artists Exhns. 1968–71; Tom Thomson Gallery, Owen Sound, Ont. 1971; served with Royal Marines, 42 Cdo 1957–59; mem. Print & Drawing Counc. Can.; Kingston Arts Counc. (Vice-Pres. 1971–73); Soc. Candn. Artists; Art Students' League, N.Y.; Internat. Soc. Artists, N.Y.; Address: R.R. 3, Odessa, Ont. K0H 2H0.

**HOLMES, J. Willard,** B.A.; art gallery director; b. 6 Mar. 1949; s. John and Eveline H.; e. Univ. of B.C., B.A. 1972; m. Laurie Pryce 24 Oct. 1980; children: Wynn Eveline, Pryce Leroy; Dir., Vancouver Art Gallery 1987; Asst. to Dir., Fine Arts Gall., U.B.C. 1972–73; Curator of Exhib., Vancouver Art Gallery 1973–74; Founder & Dir., Pender St. Gall. 1975–78; Head Curator of Contemp. Art, Art Gall. of Gr. Victoria 1978–79; Asst. Cur. of Contemp. Art, Nat. Gall. of Can. 1980–82; Head of Exhib. 1982–85; Acting Coord., New Bldg. Project 1984–85; Chief Curator, present gallery 1985–86; Curator, Organizer, Focus Candn. Art 1960–85, Cologne Internat. Art Fair 1986; Acting Dir., Curatorial Studies Prog., Charles H. Scott Gall., Emily Carr Coll. of Art & Design 1986–87; Cons., Govts. of Can. & B.C.; Simon Fraser Univ.; Dir., Vancouver Cultural Alliance; Home: 639 W. 21st Ave., Vancouver, B.C. V5Z 1Y9.

**HOLMES, Hon. Jack Kenneth,** B.A., LL.B.; judge; b. Ponoka, Alta. 2 Jan. 1928; s. Robert G. and Emily V. (Holben) H.; e. Univ. of Alta. B.A. 1950, LL.B. 1951; m. Jean d. George A. and Mina M. Gourley 28 July 1956; children: John D., Marion L. Moore, Donald G., Gordon B., Douglas K.; JUDGE, COURT OF QUEEN'S BENCH, ALTA. 1979– ; called to Bar of Alta. 1952; cr. Q.C. 1975; law practice Red Deer, Alta. 1952–76; Partner, Holmes, Crowe, Power, Johnston, Ming & Scammell; Judge, Dist. Court of Alta. 1976; Bencher, Law Soc. Alta. 1975; Office: 4909, 48 Ave., Red Deer, Alta. T4N 3T5.

**HOLMES, James,** B.Sc.(Econ.); executive; b. Stacksteads, Lancashire, Eng. 24 Oct. 1919; came to Can. 1949; s. David Thomas and Emily (Hill) H.; e. Univ. of London B Sc.(Econ.), 1949; m. Mildred Alice d. John David Deans 14 July 1943; children: David Caird, Barbara Mary; PRES., HOLMES & CO. 1983–; PRES., CAIRD HOLMES MGMT. LTD. 1984– ; Pres., Bartram Holmes Inc. 1992– ; held various positions with Canadian Pacific incl. Sr. Research Econ., mem. of planning team in the office of Chrmn. and Pres., Treasurer of C.P. Ltd. and C.P. Investments Ltd., 1949–69; Vice Pres., Finance, Falconbridge Nickel Mines Ltd. (Toronto) and Falconbridge Dominicana (Santa Domingo, D.R.), 1970–76; Chrmn. and Chief Extve. Offr., Electrohome Ltd., Kitchener, 1977–80; Chrmn. Central

Ont. Telev. Ltd., Kitchener, 1977–80; served with RAF, 1940–46; Anglican; Club: Oakville; recreations: squash, tennis, skiing; Office: #1005, 2170 Marine Dr., Oakville, Ont. L6L 5V1.

**HOLMES, Jeffrey;** association executive; author; b. Bradford, Yorks., Eng. 16 Aug. 1934; s. the late Frederick and the late Gertrude (Wilkinson) H.; e. Bradford (Eng.) Grammar Sch.; Univ. of Toronto; m. Diane d. Thomas (dec.) and Bradley Matheson 1 June 1963; children: Bryn, Ian, Thane; ASSOCIATE, PARLIAMENTARY CENTRE, seconded to Inst. for Rsch. on Public Policy 1987–91; seconded to Comn. of Inquiry on Candn. Univ. Educ. 1990–91; seconded as Vice-pres., Research and Services, Candn. Bureau for International Educ. 1993– ; seconded as National Dir., Candn. Authors Assoc. 1991–93; joined Brit. Army 1952, comnd. 1953, promoted Lt. 1955, RCAF aircrew training 1957–58; Journalist 1958–67, Fredericton 'Gleaner,' Halifax 'Mail-Star,' 'Sunday Express' London, Eng., UPI Montreal, 'Marketing' Toronto, 'Financial Post' Ottawa; Dir. of Information and Secy. of Bd. 1967–71, Assn. Univs. & Colls. Can.; Extve. Dir. Assn. Atlantic Univs. 1971–78; Dir. Educ., Science & Culture, Statistics Can. 1978–81, Dir.-Gen. Communications (acting) 1981–82; Nat. Dir., Candn. Conference of the Arts 1982–83; Dir. of Information, Social Sciences and Humanities Rsch. Counc. of Can. 1983–87; author abridgement of 'To Know Ourselves' ('The Symons Report') 1978; novels: 'Farewell to Nova Scotia' 1974; 'Shakespeare Was a Computer Programmer' 1975; 'The Hijacking of the P.E.I. Ferry' 1976; co-author 'Systems of Higher Education: Canada' 1978; 'Leisure,' 'Perspectives III' 1980; 'A Little Applebert/Le Petit Applebert' 1983; '20/20 Planning' 1985; Pres.: Candn. Soc. Study Higher Educ. 1980–81; Soc. Coll. & Univ. Planning 1978–80 (recipient of first SCUP 'distinguished service award' 1989); Writers' Fed. N.S. 1977–78; Candn. Authors' Assn. 1981–82, 1993– ; Treas., Writers' Union Can. 1981–82; mem. Bd., Social Science Fed. Can. 1982–83; recreations: reading, walking, squash; Home: 224 Cooper St., Apt. 1, Ottawa, Ont. K2P 0G4; Office: 275 Slater St., 5th Flr., Ottawa, Ont. K1P 5H9.

**HOLMES, John Leonard,** Ph.D., D.Sc., F.C.I.C., F.R.S.(Can.); educator; b. London, Eng. 29 Nov. 1931; s. Leonard Thomas and Jessie Ethel (Doble) H.; e. Haberdashers Askes Hampstead Sch. 1949; Univ. of London B.Sc. 1954, Ph.D. 1957 (Univ. Coll.) D.Sc. 1983; m. Una d. George and Clara Watts 12 Dec. 1958; children: Susan, Jonathan; PROF. OF CHEM., UNIV. OF OTTAWA 1973– ; Postdoctoral Fellowship, Nat. Rsch. Council Can., Ottawa 1958–60; I.C.I. Fellow Edinburgh Univ. 1960–61, Lectr. 1961–62; joined present Univ. 1962; Nuffield Visiting Prof., Univ. of Ghana 1971; Overbeek Visiting Prof., Univ. of Utrecht 1979; Distinguished Visiting Scholar, Univ. of Adelaide 1984; Visiting Rsch. Fellow, Australian National Univ. 1993; Internat. Visiting Fellow, Univ. Bern 1993; recipient Barringer Rsch. Award, Spectroscopy Soc. Can. 1980; Chemical Inst. of Canada Medal 1989; Herzberg Award, Spectroscopy Soc. Can. 1990; author over 200 papers refereed sci. jours.; N. Am. Ed. 'Organic Mass Spectrometry' 1976–93; Internat. Yacht Racing Union; Judge for World, Internat. & Nat. Yachting Championships; mem. Royal Yachting Assn.; Candn. Yachting Assn.; recreations: yachting, reading, music; Club: Britannia Yacht; Home: 58 – 121 Buell St., Ottawa, Ont. K1Z 7E7; Office: Ottawa, Ont. K1N 6N5.

**HOLMES, Mark,** M.A., B.Ed., Ph.D.; professor; b. Yorkshire, England 3 July 1935; s. Maurice and Margaret Ruth (Bland) H.; e. Douglas H.S. for Boys, Isle of Man 1953; Univ. of Cambridge, B.A. 1956, M.A. 1960; Univ. of N.B., B.Ed. 1965; Univ. of Chicago, Ph.D. 1969; m. Leanora d. John and Leanora Forrester 27 July 1960; children: Thomas, Jane, Kristen, Sarah; EDUCATION SPECIALIST; Teacher, Saint John, N.B. 1958–61, 1962–63; Clacton, Engl. 1961–62; Prin., var. schs., Saint John, N.B. 1963–67, 1968–71; Dir. Instr. Serv. N. Isl. Sch. Bd. 1971–73; Dir.-Gen. 1973–75; Sr. Admnr., O.I.S.E. 1975–83; Prof. of Education Admin., Ont. Inst. for Studies in Education 1983–93; Cons., Prov. of Ont. & B.C.; Secondary Prins. of N.B.; Fed. & Ont. Lib. Parties; State of N.J.; Counc. of Ont. Univs.; SSHRC; Orgn. of Educ. Admin. Officials of Ont.; Comn. on Priv. Schs. in Ont.; Ont. Teachers' Fedn.; Anglican; frequent commentator on educ. topics on radio, television and in Toronto based newspapers, magazines; author: 'What Every Teacher and Parent Should Know About Student Evaluation' 1982; 'Models of the Relationship between Students' Achievement in School and Later Success' 1986; co-author: 'Helping Schools Change' 1979; 'Making the School an Effective Community: Belief, Practice and Research in Administration' 1989; co-editor & co-author: 'The House That Ryerson Built' 1984; 'Policy for Effective Schools' 1989; 'Educational Policy for the Pluralist Democracy' 1992; recipient, R.W.B. Jackson Award for journal article 1992; recreations: tennis, cross country skiing, gardening, hiking, film; Home: Darlings Island, R.R. 2, Hampton, N.B. E0G 1Z0.

**HOLMES, Nancy Sandra,** M.A.; writer; b. Edmonton, Alta. 9 Feb. 1959; d. Alexander McDonald and Rosalie (Frinski) H.; e. Univ. of Calgary B.A. 1982, M.A. 1990; children: Douglas, Ian, Alex; author 'Valancy and the New World' poetry 1988; 'Down to the Golden Chersonese: Victorian Lady Travellers' poetry & prose 1991; Instr. in English and Creative Writing, Okanagan Coll.; author poetry and fiction various nat. periodicals; recipient 1st Prize Alta. Culture Short Story Competition 1987; 1st Prize Kalamalka New Writers Soc. Nat. Poetry Competition 1988; Alta. Found. Lit. Arts Grants 1987, 1989; anthologized various lit. publs.; Address: 168 Yorkton Ave., Penticton, B.C. V2A 3V2.

**HOLMES, Philip D. Pemberton,** D.F.C., C.D., K.C.L.J., F.R.I., R.I. (B.C.); retired; b. Victoria, B.C. 2 Feb. 1924; s. Henry Cuthbert and Philippa Despard (Pemberton) H.; e. Brentwood Coll., Victoria, 1935–40; Univ. of Victoria, 1940–41; m. Catherine Anne, d. late Capt. C.J. Webb, R.N., 22 Aug. 1964; children: Diana, Susan, Jennifer; Pres. & Dir., Pemberton, Holmes Ltd. 1965–89, joined firm (4th generation) 1945; Pres. Internat. Real Estate Fed., F.I.A.B.C.I., 1975–77; Pres., Victoria Ins. Agents Assn., 1958; Victoria Real Estate Bd., 1960; B.C. Assn. Real Estate Bds. 1961; mem., Council of Ins. Agents of B.C., 1959; Real Estate Inst. B.C., 1961, (Gov. of Div. 1961–65); Pres., Candn. Assn. Real Estate Bds., 1966; Dir., National Assn. of Real Estate Bds. (U.S.A.) 1966; Chrmn., Candn. Chapter, Internat. Real Estate Fed. 1974–75; mem., Real Estate Council of B.C., 1962–68; apptd. to Canadian Housing Design Council 1967; to Saanich Adv. Planning Comn. 1967; Dir., Victoria Visitors Bureau, 1968; Vice-Pres., MacPherson Playhouse Fdn. 1980–83; Pres., Victoria Downtown Business Assn. 1979–81; Greater Victoria Chamber Comm. 1970; Pres., Assoc. Chamber Comm. of Van. Is. 1973; served with 433 Sqd., # 6 Bomber Grp. RCAF in Europe, 1941–45; retired as Sqdn. Leader; 1st C.O., # 2455 A.C. & W Sqdn. (Auxiliary), 1950; Pres., Air Force Offrs. Assn. of Vancouver Island, 1950; App't Hon. Colonel #11 (Victoria) Service Battalion 1986; Gov., Brentwood Coll. Sch. 1972– ; Extve., Candn. Council of Christians and Jews; Hon. Citizen, City of Victoria; Hon. A. de C. to Lt. Gov. of B.C., 1978– ; Chrmn. Provincial Capital Comn. 1982–84; Vice-Chrmn. Bd. of Gov., Univ. of Victoria 1980–83; Chrmn., Bd. of Gov., Can. Corps of Coms. 1982–84; Chrmn., B.C. Govt. House Found. 1988–93; P. Conservative; Protestant; recreation: photography, hiking, sailing, golf; Clubs: Union; Royal Victoria Yacht; Ardmore Golf; Home: 677 Beach Dr., Victoria, B.C. V8S 2M8.

**HOLMES, Richard Brian,** M.D., M.Sc., LL.D., FRCPS(C); educator; b. London, Ont. 11 Dec. 1919; s. Dr. L. Seale and Haroldine (Goble) H.; e. Univ. W. Ont. M.D. 1943, M.Sc. 1949, LL.D. 1978; m. Barbara Louise, d. Hubert H. Reid, 28 Apl. 1945; children: Richard Seale, Diane Elizabeth, Erin Louise, Katherine Jane; Deputy Vice Chancellor Health Sciences, United Arab Emirates Univ., Al Ain 1989–91; Prof. and Chrmn. Dept. of Radiol., Univ. of Toronto 1965–72; Dean of Medicine there 1973–80; Radiologist-in-Chief, Toronto Gen. Hosp. 1965–1972 and 1984–86, Consultant Radiologist 1986–89; Chrmn., Ont. Council Health 1981–86; Councillor, United Arab Emirates Univ., Fac. of Med. 1987–89; External Auditor, Sultan Qaboos Univ., Coll. of Med., Oman 1987– ; served with RCAMC during World War II; rank Capt.; Fellow, Am. Coll. Radiol. 1956 (Gold Medallist 1980); mem. Candn. Assn. Radiols. (Past Pres.); Bd. of Dirs., Gairdner Fdn. 1975–89; Bd. of Gov., Queen Elizabeth Hosp., Toronto 1981–89 (Chrmn. 1987–89); Radiol. Soc. N. Am. (Pres. 1976, Gold Medallist 1981); Am. Roentgen Ray Soc.; Ont. Med. Assn.; Assn. Candn. Med. Coll. (Pres. 1977); Life Mem. Candn. Med. Assn.; Queen Elizabeth II Silver Jubilee Award; recreations: golf, tennis, philately; Clubs: Toronto Hunt; Aesculapian (Pres. 1986–87); Home: 103 Glen Rd., Toronto, Ont. M4W 2V8.

**HOLMES, Ronald Raymond,** B.Com., LL.B.; judge; b. Newmarket, Ont. 11 Sept. 1939; s. Raymond Lewis and Dorothy May H.; e. Univ. of B.C. B.Com. 1963, LL.B. 1964; m. Naomi Roxy Stewart; JUDGE, SUPREME COURT OF B.C. 1989– ; law practice Guild Yule & Co. 1965–89; Past Pres. Burrard Lions Club; Home: 2788 Wallace St., Vancouver, B.C. V6R 3V7; Office: 800 Smithe St., Vancouver, B.C. V6Z 2E1.

**HOLMES, Thomas Edward;** insurance executive; b. Regina, Sask. 10 Nov. 1932; s. Edward Sloan and Mary Ulah (McFadden) H.; e. Magee High Sch. Vancouver, B.C.; m. Cecilia Theresa d. Henry Karl Linnhoff 4 Sept. 1954; children: Karen Teresa, Paul Karl; CHRMN., ALL WEATHER BOATS INTERNATIONAL LTD. 1993– ; Prop., T.E. Holmes Insurance Agency Ltd. Vancouver 1961–66; Gen. Mgr. B.C. Motorist Insurance Co. and B.C.A.A. Holdings Ltd. 1966–76; Sr. Vice Pres. Autoplan, Insurance Corp. of B.C. 1976–80; Pres., C.E.O. & Dir., Insurance Corp. of B.C. 1980–92; Dir., Canada Safety Council (Mem. Extve. Ctte.); Chrmn., 1984 Campaign, United Way of Lower Mainland; mem. Vancouver Bd. of Trade; Bus. Counc. of B.C.; The Conf. Bd. of Can.; Am. Mgmt. Assn.; Presidents' Assn.; North Vancouver Chamber of Commerce; Candn. Club of Vancouver; The Hon. Order of the Blue Goose Internat.; Anglican; recreations: numismatics, golf, curling, skiing; Clubs: North Shore Winter; Vancouver; Seymour Golf & Country.

**HOLOWNIA, Thaddeus,** B.A.; artist; educator; b. Bury St. Edmunds, Eng. 2 July 1949; s. Jerzy Henryk and Zofia Teresa (Skarzenski) Czerny-Holownia; e. Rothesay High Sch. 1967; Univ. of Windsor B.A. 1972; common-law Gay Hansen 1982; children: Joseph, Inga, Theo, Julian; PROF. OF ART MOUNT ALLISON UNIV. 1977– , devel. and Dir. Photog. Prog.; Founder and Dir. Anchorage Press Jolicure, N.B. 1987– ; Dir. Ships Co. Theatre Parrsboro, N.S. 1985–89; exhbns. incl 'Dykelands' at Art Gallery of Windsor 1985; Art Gallery of Hamilton 1986; Photographers Gallery Saskatoon 1986; Owens Art Gallery, Sackville, N.B. 1989; 'Maritime Landscapes 1977–1987' 1988, 'Headlighting' 1990 Jane Corkin Gallery; 'Avalon Views' James Baird Gallery, St. Johns, Nfld. 1993; 'Sable Island' The Drabinsky Gallery, Toronto, Ont. 1993; co-author 'Dykelands' 1989; recreation: birdwatching; Home: R.R.3 Sackville, N.B. E0A 3C0; Office: Dept. of Fine Art, Mount Allison Univ., Sackville, N.B. E0A 3C0.

**HOLROYD, Margaret Drabble;** see DRABBLE, Margaret (Holroyd).

**HOLST, Rev. Dr. Wayne Alfred,** B.A., M.Div., C.d'E.O., D.Min.; minister of religion, university teacher-researcher; b. Kitchener, Ont. 12 June 1942; s. Alfred Carl and Marieta Lillian (Boyd) H.; e. Wilfrid Laurier Univ. B.A. (Dean's Hon. Roll) 1964; Waterloo Luth. Sem. M.Div. (Grad. Fellowship) 1967; Univ. of Geneva C.d'E.O. 1968; Univ. of Alta., St. Stephen's Coll. D.Min. 1989; m. Gail D. d. Marvin and Winnifred Henker 23 May 1992; children (blended family): Jacqueline Ann, Gina Marieta (Holst) and Bruce William, Kevin Scott, Peter Glen (Copithorne); RSCH. ASSOC., TEACHER & CONS., UNIV. OF CALGARY, ARCTIC INST. OF N. AM. 1989– ; Luth. Ch. in Am.: Missionary Trinidad 1968–70; Ch. Extve. Winnipeg (Asst. to Bishop) 1970–77; New York City (Dir., Mission Office) 1977–80; Parish Pastor Calgary 1980–87; listed in several ref. books; Past Dir., Lutheran Welfare Soc./Bethany Care Ctr. & St. Mary's Cath. Coll.; Dir., L'Arche Calgary 1990– (Pres. 1993– ); Mem., Candn. Soc. for the Study of Religion; Am. Soc. of Missiology; The Alban Institute, Washington, D.C.; The Centre for Catholic and Evangelical Theology; The Church Law Assn. of Can.; author: 'Planning Christian Witness in Canada's North' 1989, new edition (Edwin Mellon Press, Lewiston, NY) 1993 and num. sch. & pop. articles; recreations: travel, music, reading; Home: 3412 Varna Cres. NW, Calgary, Alta. T3A 0E6; Office: 2500 University Dr. N.W., Calgary, Alta. T2N 1N4.

**HOLSTI, Kalevi J.,** M.A., Ph.D., F.R.S.C.; educator; b. Geneva, Switzerland 25 Apl. 1935; s. Eino Rudolf and Liisa Anniki (Franssila) H.; e. Stanford Univ. B.A. 1956, M.A. 1958, Ph.D. 1961; children: Liisa, Matthew, Karina; PROF. OF POL. SCI., UNIV. OF B.C. 1961– ; Head of Pol. Sci. 1980–85; Visiting Prof. McGill Univ. 1972–73; Kyoto Univ. 1977; Hebrew Univ. of Jerusalem 1978; Rsch. Fellow Sch. of Pacific Studies Australian Nat. Univ. 1983; Visiting Prof., International Univ. of Japan Apr.-July 1988, Sept.-Dec. 1992; Bd. mem., Candn. Inst. for Internat. Peace and Security 1987–90; Can. Counc. Killam Award 1987–88; U.B.C. Killam Rsch. Prize 1992; author 'Suomen Ulkopolitiikka Etsimässä (Directions in Finnish Foreign Policy) 1962; 'Why Nations Realign' 1982; 'The Dividing Discipline: Hegemony and Pluralism in International Theory' 1985 (transl. Japanese 1989, Italian 1992); 'International Politics; A Framework for Analysis' 7th ed. 1994 (transl. Japanese 1972, Chinese 1985, Indonesian 1987); 'Peace and War: Armed Conflicts and International Order, 1648–1989' 1991 (transl. Japanese 1993); 'Change in the International System: Essays on the Theory and Practice of International Politics' 1991; ed. Internat. Studies Quarterly 1971–76; co-ed. Candn. Jour. Pol. Sci. 1980–83; various articles nat. and internat. jours.; mem.

Candn. Pol. Sci. Assn. (Pres. 1984–85); Internat. Studies Assn. (Pres. 1986–87); World Assn. Internat. Relations (Vice Pres. 1984– ); recreations: water polo, skiing; Home: 2565 York Ave., Vancouver, B.C. V6K 1E4; Office: Vancouver, B.C. V6T 1Z1.

**HOLT, Linda R.,** B.A.; civil servant; b. Saint John, N.B. 30 Sept. 1951; s. George S. and Madeline F. (Barnett) Dashwood; e. Saint John H.S. 1969; Univ. of N.B. B.A. 1973; m. Douglas s. Malcolm and Elsie H. 1 Dec. 1973; one d.: Jessica Elizabeth; DIRECTOR, CANADA/NEW BRUNSWICK YOUTH STRATEGY 1992– ; Human Resource Officer, City of Saint John; Human Resource Mgr., Northern Telecom Nat. Bargaining Team; Consultant/Owner, Human Resource Management 1982–89; Canada/N.B. Youth Strategy is a pilot program responding to youth unemployment; provides training to young adults on variety of job related topics; Gov., U.N.B. Bd. of Gov. 1992–96 and Chair, Personnel Policy; Nominating Ctt.; Dir., Candn. Cancer Soc. (N.B. Div.) 1986– ; Pres., Assoc. Alumnae 1992–94 (1st V.P. 1990–92; Chair, Scholarship Ctte.); Dir., Co-Op Store; 1st Vice-Pres., Family Serv. Saint John; numerous charitable memberships; active on variety of groups, clubs; author of several articles and one book chapter; recreations: skating (speed), swimming, outdoor pursuits, horseback riding; Home: 65 Hazen Court, Fredericton, N.B. E3B 5K9; Office: 470 York St., Rm. 205, Fredericton, N.B. E3B 5H1.

**HOLT, Lt-Col. Peter James,** CD, rmc, pcsc, B.Eng., P.Eng.; Canadian Forces officer and professional engineer; b. Kingston, Ont. 28 July 1949; s. the late John Samuel and Mary Anita (Tracey) H.; e. Coll. Militaire Royal St-Jean dipl. 1966–69; Royal Military College B.Eng. 1971, M.Eng. 1981; m. Shirley d. Fred and Mabel Atwood 14 July 1973; children: Carol, Norah, Robert; DIRECTOR OF ADMINISTRATION, ROYAL MILITARY COLLEGE OF CANADA 1992– ; commanded maintenance platoons in Petawawa & London, Ont., Churchill, Man. & Lahr, Germany 1971–75; Staff Officer, Candn. Forces Eur. at Lahr, Liaison Offr. with German Army 1975–77; Instructor, CFB Borden 1977–79; Project Mgr. of various small capital projects after post-grad training 1979–84; commanded large Electrical & Mech. Engr. (EME) Workshop Winnipeg, then Sr. Staff Officer EME, Air Command H.Q. Winnipeg 1985–89; Commander, Tech. Serv. Br. in Lahr, Germany 1989 (supported Gulf War & opns. in Yugoslavia from this position); Mem., APEO & CSME 1977– ; Scouts Canada (Beaver Leader 1990– ); DGLEM commendation 1977 for tech. work on intro. of Leopard tank into Candn. Forces; won Commonwealth Armies Essay Competition 1985 for essay on Hitler's strategy in World War II; KNBLO Silver Cross and Crown 1993 for completion of sixth 100 mile military forced march, Nijmegen, Holland; Mem., Anglican Ch. of Can. (lay reader 1979– ); Kingston Choral Soc.; recreations: swimming, hiking, canoeing, nordic skiing; Home: 74 Lundy's Lane, Kingston, Ont. K7K 5G8; Office: Kingston, Ont. K7K 5L0.

**HOLT, Richard C.,** Ph.D.; computer scientist; b. Oklahoma 13 Feb. 1941; s. C.P. and V.Y.H.; e. Cornell Univ., B.E.P. 1964, Ph.D. 1970; m. Marie-France d. Chas. and Barbara Beyer; children: Adam, Sarah; PROF. OF COMP. SCI., UNIV. OF TORONTO 1970– ; Chrmn., Comp. Systems Rsch. Inst., Univ. of Toronto 1982–84; author of 13 books incl.: 'Structured Programming Using PL/1 and SP/k'; 'Fundamentals of Structured Programming Using Fortran with SF/k and WATFIV-S'; 'Concurrent Euclid, Unix and Tunis'; 'Introduction to Computer Science Using the Turing Programming Language'; recipient, ITAC/INSERC Award 1994; Home: 19 Gormley Ave., Toronto, Ont.; Office: Comp. Systems Rsch. Inst., Univ. of Toronto, Toronto, Ont. M5S 1A4.

**HOLT, Steven,** B.Mus.; financial executive, musician; b. Montreal, Que. 9 Apr. 1954; s. David (dec.) and Helen (Margolian) H.; e. Wagar H.S.; McGill Univ. B.Mus. 1981, with distinction; m. Dhiresha d. Robert and Marjorie Gillis 9 Sept. 1989; one d.: Leela Marissa Devi; VICE-PRES. & SR. INVESTMENT ANALYST, WOOD GUNDY INC. 1992– ; Asset Mngt., Stelee Mngt. Corp. 1980–85; Investment Analyst, Candn. Food Merch. 1985–87; Vice-Pres. & Sr. Investment Analyst, Midland Walwyn Capital Inc. 1987–91; Vice-Pres. & Sr. Investment Analyst, Richardson Greenshields of Canada Ltd. 1991–92; music career: one of Canada's premier jazz pianists; self-taught pianist (began at age 4); played in Montreal jazz clubs; McGill's 1st ever B.Mus. majoring in jazz performance; also studied with Kenny Barron in New York; appt. Instr. of Jazz Improvisation, McGill 1981; debut recording 'The Lion's Eyes' 1983 (1 of 5 final JUNO nom. for best jazz album 1983); has since recorded 3 additional albums as leader; has performed with Larry Coryell, James Moody, Archie Shepp; plays live in Toronto & continues to record; Mem., Toronto Soc. of Finan. Analysts; Mem. & Supporter, Light of Truth Universal Shrine (Virginia).

**HOLZMAN, Jacquelin;** politician; b. Ottawa, Ont. MAYOR, CITY OF OTTAWA 1991– ; Councillor, Richmond Ward, City of Ottawa 1982–91; apptd. to numerous boards and committees 1982– ; extensive voluntary work incl. most recent: Mem., Kiwanis Club of Ottawa 1992– ; Bd. Mem., Kidney Found. of Can., Ottawa Valley Chapter 1987– ; Chair, Adv. Ctte. on Rest Homes, Prov. of Ont. 1987–89; Royal Ottawa Hosp. & Reg. Rehab. Ctr. 1977–82; Ottawa Health Sciences Centre 1979–83; City of Ottawa Disabled Citizens Adv. Ctte. 1981; Office: 111 Sussex Dr., Ottawa, Ont. K1N 5A1.

**HOMBURGER, Walter F.,** C.M.; concert manager; b. Karlsruhe, Germany 22 Jan. 1924; s. Victor and Lotte (Fruehberg) H.; came to Canada 1941; e. Schs. in Germany; Eastbourne Coll., Eng. 1939–40; Central Technical School 1941–42. Cantab Coll., Toronto (Sr. Matric.) 1943; m. Emmy Schmid, 23 June 1961; children: Michael, Lisa; MANAGER OF JAMES EHNES; Consultant to Business and the Arts 1987; Founder and Pres. since inception 1946 of International Artists Concert Agency (sold to Toronto Symphony 1981.); Mgr., National Ballet of Can. 1951–55; Mgr., Toronto Symphony 1962–87; over past 40 yrs. has been Mgr. of various artists incl. Glenn Gould, Jan Rubes, Victor Conrad Braun, Donald Bell, Alfred Brendel and Louis Lortie; served in Cdn. Army 1943–45; Appt. a Member of the Order of Canada June 1984; Jewish; Home: 278 Heath St. E., Toronto, Ont. M4T 1T4.

**HOMEL, David,** M.A.; writer; journalist; b. Chicago, Ill. 15 Sept. 1952; s. Irving and Bernice Isaac Brenner H.; e. Ind. Univ.; Univ. de Paris B.A. 1973; Univ. of Toronto M.A. 1976; common-law m. Marie-Louise d. Colette Fontaine and Bernard Gay; two s. Gabriel, Jacob; fiction writer, journalist in arts & politics , transl. some 25 lit. works from French primarily by Que. authors; freelance since 1977; lectr. in transl. program and writing prog., Concordia Univ. Montreal; cons. several Candn. got. agencies cultural matters; Chrmn., Pub. Lending Right Comn. 1990–92; recipient IBBY Award of Merit children's book transl. 1981; for television production 'Visions' series for Television Ont., early 1980s, six awards from different Am. film and TV festivals; Can. Council Writing Grant 1989–90, 1991, 1992–93; Que. Govt. writing grant 1991–92; short-listed Books in Can./W.H. Smith Best First Novel 1989 and Gov. Gen.'s Award for Transl. 1989; for 'Rat Palms' paperback of the year, Found. for the Advancement of Candn. Letters, through the Periodical Marketers of Canada 1993; author 'Electrical Storms' novel 1988; 'Mapping Literature: The Art and Politics of Literary Translation' essay coll. 1988; 'Rat Palms' novel 1992 (foreign lang. editions in Fr. and Greek); Past Pres., Lit. Transls. Assn.; recreation: baseball; Address: 773, avenue Davaar, Outremont, Que. H2V 3B3.

**HOMER, Gordon James,** B.A.Sc., M.B.A.; investment banker; b. Toronto, Ont. 19 Mar. 1947; s. William James and Enid Jean (Kirby) H.; e. Etobicoke Collegiate 1965; Univ. of Toronto B.A.Sc. Ind. Engrg. 1969; Harvard Univ. M.B.A. 1971; m. Carolyn d. Donald and Catherine Silmser 31 Dec. 1980; three s.: Christopher, Michael, Ryan; PRESIDENT, GORDON J. HOMER INC.; joined Wood Gundy Inc. 1971, Vice Pres. 1976, Dir. 1977, Chief Fin. Offr. 1981–82, Dir. of New Issues 1982–87, Extve. Vice Pres. 1987, Vice-Chrmn. 1988–90; mem. Theta Delta Chi; recreations: skiing, golf; Clubs: Granite; Beacon Hall Golf; Caledon Ski; Home: 38 Stratheden Rd., Toronto, Ont. M4N 1E4; Office: Ste. 2550, Toronto Dominion Bank Tower, Toronto, Ont. M5K 1E7.

**HOMER-DIXON, Thomas Fraser,** B.A., Ph.D.; university professor, consultant, writer; b. Victoria, B.C. 22 April 1956; s. Douglas Fraser and Constance Elizabeth (Armstrong) H.; e. Univ. of Victoria 1975–78; Carleton Univ. B.A. (1st Class Hons.) 1980; M.I.T. Ph.D. 1989; m. Jill d. Robert and Carol Lazenby 14 Dec. 1991; ASST. PROF., POLITICAL SCIENCE, UNIV. OF TORONTO 1991– ; Founder & First Nat. Co-ord., Candn. Student Pugwash 1979–82; Computer Software Developer, Project Athena, M.I.T. 1984–85; Dir., Peace & Conflict Studies Program, univ. of Toronto 1989– ; Co-dir. & Lead Researcher, Project on 'Environ. Change & Acute Conflict' 1990–93; Cons., World Resources Int., U.N. Devel. Prog.; Adjunct Rsch. Assoc., Ctr. for Sci. & Internat. Affairs, Harvard Univ. 1986–88; SSRC/MacArthur Dissertation Fellowship 1986–88; SSHRCC postdoct.fellowship 1989–91; large rsch. grants from Donner Candn. Found. & Rockefeller Found.; Mem., Internat. Security Ctte., Am. Assn. for the Advancement of Sci.; author of journal articles; recreations: wilderness hiking and camping, photography; Office: University College, U. of Toronto, Toronto, Ont. M5S 1A1.

**HONDERICH, John Allen,** B.A., LL.B.; journalist/editor; b. Toronto, Ont. 6 July 1946; s. Beland H. and Florence I. (Wilkinson) H.; e. Neuchatel Jr. Coll. 1964; Univ. of Toronto, B.A. (Hons.) 1968, LL.B. 1971; called to Ont. Bar 1973; m. Katherine d. George and Doris Govier 27 Feb. 1981; children: Robin Christian, Emily Rose; EDITOR, 'TORONTO STAR' 1988– ; Reporter, 'Ottawa Citizen' 1973–76; Ottawa Reporter, Toronto Star 1976–79; Ottawa Bureau Chief 1979–80; Washington Bureau Chief 1980–82; Dep. City Ed. 1982–84; Bus. Ed. 1984–86; Editorial Page Editor 1987–88; Dir., Starnews Credit Union 1985–86; author: 'Arctic Imperative' 1987; recreations: music, tennis, skiing; Home: 54 Farnham Ave., Toronto, Ont.; Office: One Yonge St., Toronto, Ont. M5E 1E6.

**HONE, James A.,** B.Comm., B.A.; financial executive; b. Montreal, Que. 28 Oct. 1944; s. George Albert and Isabella Fairbairn (Ritchie) H.; e. McGill Univ. B.Comm. 1966; York Univ. B.A. 1969; m. Barbara d. George and Jeanne Rivard 3 Dec. 1966; children: Christopher, Jason; VICE-PRES. & TREASURER, ABITIBI-PRICE INC. 1993– ; Cost Analyst, Ford of Canada 1966–70; Financial Analyst, Ford U.S. 1970–72; Finan. Mngt., Ford of Canada 1972–76; Treas., Pratt & Whitney Canada 1976–82; Asst. Treas., Internat. Finance, United Technologies Corp. (Hartford, CT) 1982–88; Vice Pres. & Treas., Atibiti-Price Inc. 1988–91; Vice Pres. Financial Services, Commercial Business 1991–93; Mem., Soc. of Internat. Treasurers; Finan. Extve. Inst.; recreations: tennis; Home: 1818 Bayview Ave., #606, Toronto, ON M4G 4G6; Office: 207 Queen's Quay West, Suite 680, Box 102, Toronto, Ont. M5J 2P5.

**HONEY, Terrence Weir;** newspaper publisher/editor; b. Regina, Sask. 8 Aug. 1931; s. Clayton Alexander and Evelyn Jessie (Greig) H.; e. Burford Dist. H.S.; Univ. of W. Ont.; m. Joan d. Andrew and Lenore Foote 20 Oct. 1956; children: Robin, Kimberley, Valerie; EXTVE. DIR., ATLANTIC PRESS COUNCIL 1991– ; Reporter, Elmira Signet 1953–54; Reporter/Photographer 1954–60; Asst. News Ed. 1960–66; Ed., Editorial Page, The London Free Press 1966–74; Asst. Pub., The Cambridge Reporter 1974–76; Publisher & Gen. Mgr., Truro Daily News 1976–91; Dir., The Candn. Daily Newspaper Pub. Assn.; The Candn. Press; Founding Mem., The Atlantic Press Council; Founding Pres., Press Inst. of Canada; Pres., Colchester Family YMCA 1979–80; United Way of Truro and District 1983; Truro Rotary 1990–91; mem., First United Church; editor: 'London Heritage' 1973; recreations: golf, farming, curling; Clubs: Truro Golf, Truro Curling; Home: 7 Muir St., Truro, N.S. B2N 5Z8 and R.R. 1, Londonderry, N.S. B0M 1M0; Office: 577 Prince St., Truro, N.S. B2N 5G6.

**HONISCH, Martin Volker,** B.Ed., M.Ed.; artist; b. Zwittau, Czech. 29 Dec. 1942; s. Franz Karl and Martha Julia (Klima) H.; e. Univ. of Hamburg, Germany, W.U.S. scholarship 1964–65; Univ. of B.C. B.Ed. 1967; Univ. of Western Washington, M.Ed. 1981; m. Usha d. Shamlal and Shanti Devi Sharma 14 July 1979; children: Stefan Sunandan, Erika Supria; first one-man exhib., Vancouver 1972; regular exhibs. in Vanc., Toronto, Victoria, Seattle; solo exhib. at World Bank, Washington 1986; solo exhibits in various public galls. incl. Art Gall. of Greater Victoria, Surrey Art Gall., Richmond Art Gall., etc.; Art Teacher, secondary sch. 1968–69, 1973–82; part-time, Malaspina Coll. 1982–89; since 1975 has followed a spiritual path requiring strict vegetarianism & disciplined way of life, daily meditation; recreations: enjoys quiet way of life, family closeness, daily studio work, nature appreciation, non-involvement politically; Home: 9912 Cedar St., P.O. Box 853, Chemainus, B.C. V0R 1K0.

**HOO, Sing,** A.R.C.A. (1948), R.C.A. (1965); sculptor: b. Canton, China 15 May 1911; s. Kin and Lili (Chow) H.; came to Canada 1922; m. Norah, d. late Dr. W.J. Chambers, 7 Dec. 1937; one d. Catherine: e. Ont. Coll. of Art (Grad. 1933); Slade Sch., London, Eng. (1937); mem., Ont. Soc. of Artists (1938); Sculptors Soc. Can. (1952); Fellow, Internat. Arts & Letters, Geneva, 1959; mentioned in Who's Who in Amer. Art 1965, Who's Who in the Midwest U.S.A Section of Marquis National, Biographee 1963; Men of Achievement, Internat.

Biog. Centre, Cambridge, Eng. 1975; mem., Academia Italia Delle Artie Del Lavoro, Italy, 1980; Conservative; United Church; Address: 139 Livingstone Ave., Toronto, Ont. M6E 2L9.

**HOOD, Hugh,** O.C., M.A., Ph.D.; writer; university professor; b. Toronto, Ont. 30 Apr. 1928; s. Alexander Bridport and Margaret Cecile (Blagdon) H.; e. De La Salle Coll. 'Oaklands,' Toronto, 1945; Univ. of Toronto, B.A. 1950, M.A. 1952, Ph.D. 1955; m. Ruth Noreen, d. Dwight Harcourt Mallory, D.D.S., 22 Apr. 1957; children: Sarah Barbara, Dwight Alexander, John Arthur Mallory. Alexandra Mary; Teaching Fellow, Univ. of Toronto, 1951–55; Asst. and Assoc. Prof., Saint Joseph Coll., Hartford, Conn., 1955–61; Prof. asst., puis agrégé, enfin prof. titulaire, Univ. de Montréal, since 1961; rec'd Pres.'s Medal, Univ. of W. Ont., 1962, 1969; Sr. Artists Award, Can. Council, 1971; author: 'Flying A Red Kite' (stories) 1962; 'White Figure, White Ground' (novel) 1964; 'Around the Mountain: Scenes from Montreal Life' (short stories) 1967; 'The Camera Always Lies' (novel) 1967; 'Strength Down Centre' (sports) 1970; 'A Game of Touch' (novel) 1970; 'The Fruit Man, the Meat Man and the Manager' (stories) 1971; 'You Cant Get There From Here' (novel) 1972; 'The Governor's Bridge Is Closed' (essays) 1973; The New Age/Le nouveau siècle, Vol. I, 'The Swing in the Garden' (novel) 1975; 'Dark Glasses' (short stories) 1976; the New Age/Le nouveau siècle, Vol. II, 'A New Athens' (novel) 1977; 'Selected Stories' (short stories) 1978; 'Scoring: Seymour Segal's Art of Hockey' (art criticism) 1979; The New Age/Le nouveau siècle, Vol. III, 'Reservoir Ravine' (novel) 1979; 'None Genuine Without This Signature' (short stories) 1980; The New Age/Le nouveau siècle, Vol. IV, 'Black and White Keys' (novel) 1982; 'Trusting the Tale' (essays) 1983; The New Age/Le nouveau siècle, Vol. V, 'The Scenic Art' (novel) 1984; 'August Nights' (stories) 1985; The New Age/Le nouveau siècle, Vol. VI, 'The Motor Boys In Ottawa' (novel) 1986; 'Five New Facts About Giorgione' (short novel) 1987; The Collected Stories, Vol. I, 'Flying a Red Kite' (stories) 1987; The New Age/Le nouveau siècle, Vol. VII, 'Tony's Book' (novel) 1988; The Collected Stories, Vol. II, 'A Short Walk in the Rain' (stories) 1989; The New Age/Le nouveau siècle, Vol. VIII 'Property and Value' (novel) 1990; The Collected Stories, Vol. III 'The Isolation Booth' (stories) 1991; 'Unsupported Assertions' (essays) 1991; 'You'll Catch Your Death' (stories) 1992; The New Age/Le nouveau siècle, Vol. IX, 'Be Sure to Close Your Eyes' 1993; The Collected Stories, Vol. IV 'Around the Mountain: Scenes From Montreal Life' (stories) 1994; also many stories and articles in Candn., Am. and European mags. and anthols.; mem., Candn. Assn. Univ. Teachers; Sr. Artists Award, Can. Council, 1974 and 1978; City of Toronto Literary Prize, 1975; Officer, the Order of Canada 1988; recreations: music, sports; Club: Arts and Letters; Home: 4242 Hampton Ave., Montreal, Que. H4A 2K9.

**HOOD, Russell,** B.Eng., F.E.I.C., F.C.S.C.E., F.C.A.E.; planning executive; b. Sydney, Australia 4 Nov. 1932; e. Univ. of N.S.W. B.Eng. 1953; Sydney Tech. Coll. Assoc. 1957; m. Wanda Joy; VICE-PRES., PLANNING & DEVELOPMENT, UMA GROUP 1987– ; assisted in design & construction of civil works assoc. with extension of railways for City of Sydney and later civil work assoc. with major substations devel., N.S.W. Electricity Comn. 1953–58; Resident Engr., UMA Engr. 1958–60; Sr. Project Engr. Manitoba 1961–62; Chief Engr. of Man. & N.W. Ont. Br. 1962–66; Area Mgr., Man. & N.W. Ont. Opns. 1966–86; Mem., Assn. of Profl. Engrs. of Man. (Past Chair, Bd. of Dir.); Engr. Inst. of Can. (Past Pres.; Fellow); Candn. Soc. of Civil Engrs. (Fellow); Fellow, Candn. Acad. of Engineering; Inst. of Engrs., Australia; Roads & Transp. Assn. of Canada; Chrmn., Economic Innovation & Technology Council (Man.); Past Chair, Bd. of Dir., Man. Rsch. Council; Comnr., Nat. Capital Comn. (Extve. Ctte. Mem.); Past Mem., Internat. Peer Review Ctte., Networks of Centres of Excellence Program; Past Chair, Indus. Adv. Ctte., Fac. of Engr., Univ. of Man.; Bd. of Trustees, Victoria Gen. Hosp. Winnipeg; clubs: Niakwa Golf & Country, Fort Garry Rotary; Home: No. 8 – 1800 Wellington Cres., Winnipeg, Man. R3P 2E5; Office: 1479 Buffalo Place, Winnipeg, Man. R3T 1L7.

**HOOD, The Hon. Mr. Justice Sherman Willet,** B.A., LL.B., Q.C.; supreme court judge; b. Sault Ste. Marie, Ont. 11 Aug. 1933; s. Alexander and Lillian Alberta H.; e. Carleton Univ., B.A. 1957; Univ. of B.C. Law Sch., LL.B. 1960; m. Roberta d. Ralph K. and Myrtle Johnson 25 Feb. 1966; children: Shannon, Sherman, Suzanne; SUPREME COURT JUDGE OF BRITISH COLUMBIA 1989– ; articled with Russell & DuMoulin 1960–61; Assoc. 1961–68; Sr. Counsel & Partner 1968–89; recreations: golf, fishing, sports; Club: Capilano Golf & Country; Home: 625 Newdale Rd., West Vancouver, B.C. V7T 1W7; Office: Court House, 800 Smithe St., Vancouver, B.C. V6Z 2E1.

**HOOD, William Clarence,** M.A., Ph.D., LL.D., F.R.S.C.; Canadian public servant; economist; b. Yarmouth, N.S., 13 Sept. 1921; s. Percy Alexander and Vida Barr (Webster) H.; e. Mount Allison Univ., B.A. (Hons. in Econ.) 1941, LL.D. 1970; Univ. of Toronto, M.A. (Econ.) 1943, Ph.D. (Econ.) 1948; Univ. of Chicago Fellow 1949–50; m. Alville Mary Lennox, 4 June 1948; children: Ronald Douglas, Nancy Anne; Economic Counsellor and Dir. of Research, Int. Monetary Fund 1980–86, Economic Consultant 1987– ; Depy. Min. of Finance 1979; Associate Depy. Min. of Finance, 1975–78; (Assistent Deputy Minister 1970–74); taught Econ. at University of Sask., 1944–46; apptd. to Staff of Dept. of Pol. Econ., Univ. of Toronto. 1946; Prof. 1959; Advisor, Bank of Canada 1964–69; Research Assoc. at Cowles Comn. for Research in Econs. Univ. of Chicago, 1949–50; has served on a number of special assignments for Candn. Govt. including as negotiator of financial services portion of Can.-U.S. Free Trade Agreement 1986–87; Publications: 'Studies in Econometric Method,' 1953, 'Output Labour and Capital in the Canadian Economy' (with A. D. Scott), 1958; 'Financing of Economic Activity in Canada,' 1959; many articles on econ. theory and stat.; Fellow, Royal Soc. of Can.; Royal Econ. Soc.; Econometric Soc.; mem., Candn. Econ. Assn.; Am. Econ. Assn.; engaged in special meterol. work during part of war period; Head of special UNESCO 3–mth. mission to Sierra Leone to study educ. and econ. devel. 1961; on partial 2–yr. leave as Econ. Adv. and Dir. of Research for Royal Comn. on Banking & Finance 1961; Named Alternate Gov. for Can. of the I.M.F., 1970; Dir., CMHC, 1977; United Church; Address: 9513 Liberty Tree Lane, Vienna, Virginia, U.S.A. 22182.

**HOOEY, Wayne Leonard,** Q.C., LL.B.; lawyer; b. Barrie, Ont. 13 Feb. 1940; s. Albert Leonard and Verna Mildred (Green) H.; e. Woodville Public & Continuation Sch.; Orono H.S.; Bowmanville H.S.; Univ. of Western Ont.; Osgoode Hall Law Sch. LL.B. 1962; m. Anne d. Horace and Marjorie Best 26 Aug. 1961; children: Jill Anne, Paul Leonard; LAWYER, HOOEY REMUS; read law with Holden Day Wilson 1963; called to Bar of Ontario 1964; Q.C. 1976; Dir., CAA Toronto; CAA Insur. Co. (Ont.); Houghton Mifflin Canada Ltd.; Gananoque Light & Power Ltd.; Westside Cemeteries Ltd.; Vice-Pres. & Dir., Toronto Rehabilitation Centre; Chrmn., Candn. Automobile Assn. Ottawa; Mem., Phi Delta Phi Legal; Candn. Bar Assn.; Internat. Bar Assn.; clubs: The Ontario (Pres. 1978 and 1993); Rosedale Golf Club; Toronto Cricket, Skating & Curling; Home: 136 Highland Cres., Toronto Ont. M2L 1H1 and Hemlock Point, Lake Muskoka, R.R. #2, Gravenhurst, Ont. P1P 1R2; Office: Metropolitan Place, Suite 400, 1 University Ave., Toronto, Ont. M5J 2P1.

**HOOFT, Hendrik G.A.,** LL.D.; lawyer; investment advisor; b. Amsterdam, Netherlands 8 Nov. 1939; s. Hendrik W.C. and Ebba M. (Schumacher) H.; e. Leiden Univ. LL.D. 1963; Oxford Univ. patristic studies; m. Eliane d. Ambassador F.A. Calkoen 3 Feb. 1968; children: Emilie E.E., Wynanda A., Cornelis P., Daniel E.; PRES. AND CHIEF EXTVE. OFFR. WOODMONT HEAD MANAGEMENT LTD. 1980– ; Dir., Stork, Candiac, Qué.; The Ondaatje Corp., Toronto; Sutherland-Schultz, Kitchener; served with Royal Netherlands Army 1964–66; Barrister and Solr. Amsterdam 1966–71; Exec. Vice Pres. Pierson Heldring & Pierson Bank, Amsterdam 1971–75; Pres. and Chief Extve. Offr., Oryx Investments, Dubai, U.A.E. 1975–80; Past Vice Pres. Bd., Chamber Players Toronto; Past Chrmn., Toronto French Sch.; Past Chrmn., Candn. Chem. & Phys. Olympiads; Kt. Sovereign Order St. John Netherlands; author various articles newspapers & periodicals; recreations: farming, skiing, tennis, painting, Greek, travel, music; Clubs: Royal Candn. Mil. Inst.; Address: 9 High Point Rd., Don Mills, Ont. M3B 2A3.

**HOOPER, Cleeve Francis Wilfrid,** B.A., A.M., B.Litt.; diplomat; b. Toronto, Ont. 29 Nov. 1924; s. late Mortimer Cleeve, Q.C. and Irene Mildred (Wood) H.; e. Lawrence Park Coll. Inst. Toronto; Univ. of Toronto B.A. 1947; Harvard Univ. A.M. 1948; Oxford Univ. B.Litt. 1950 (Nuffield Student); m. Katherine Patricia d. late Robert S. Ingram, Orillia, Ont. 18 March 1950; children: Alison Mary, Jonathan Thomas, Jeremy Cleeve; CONSULTANT: SECURITY, INTELLIGENCE AND ACCESS-TO-INFORMATION MATTERS; joined Dept. of External Affairs 1950, Vice Consul Caracas 1952, Third Secy. Buenos Aires 1953, Second Secy. 1955, Ottawa 1956 (Information Div.), Second Secy. New Delhi 1958, Ottawa 1961, First Secy. Dar Es Salaam 1964, London 1966, Counsellor 1967, Ottawa 1970 (Depy. Dir. E. European Div.), Co-ordinator for Candn. participation in Conf. on Security and Co-op. in Europe 1972–76, Dir. E. European Div. 1974–76, High Commr. Jamaica with concurrent accreditation to Bahamas and Belize 1976–78; Dir. Gen. Bureau of Intelligence Analysis and Security, Ottawa 1978–82; Asst. Under-Secy. of State for External Affairs, Ottawa 1982–83; Foreign Service Visitor, Trent Univ. 1983–84; Special Adv., Security Services Bureau, Dept. of External Affairs 1984–87, retired; served with RCNVR 1944–45; Baptist; recreations: shooting, walking; Home: P.O. Box 1, Perth, Ont. K7H 3E2.

**HOOPER, Douglas Graeme,** B.Sc., M.B.A., P.Geo., FGAC; financial executive; b. Port Credit, Ont. 9 Nov. 1960; s. Robert Lawrence and Mary Gwendolyn (Ferguson) H.; e. Univ. of B.C. B.Sc. 1984, M.B.A. 1989; m. Susan d. William and Elizabeth Nicholson 12 Oct. 1985; children: Robyn Nicole, John William; PRESIDENT, TELSOFT MOBILE DATA INC. (formerly Equity Investments Corp.) 1991– ; Consulting Geologist 1984–89; Vice President, Secretary & Portfolio Manager, The Equity Group of Companies 1989–91; Registered Prof. Geoscientist in B.C.; Fellow, The Geol. Assn. of Canada; recreations: squash, hockey, skiing; Home: D68, R.R. #1, Bowen Island, B.C. V0N 1G0; Office: 1010 – 400 Burrard St., Vancouver, B.C. V6C 3A6.

**HOOPER, Frank Clements,** B.A.Sc., D.I.C., F.E.I.C., F.C.S.M.E., P.Eng.; professor emeritus of mechanical engineering; b. Toronto, Ont. 10 Apr. 1924; s. Thomas Henry and Bertha May (Saunders) H.; e. Univ. of Toronto B.A.Sc. 1946; Univ. of London D.I.C. 1953; m. Gladys (Gay) d. Hannah and William Jones Dec. 1952; children: Della Elaine, Jeffrey Thomas; PROF. EMERITUS, MECHANICAL ENGINEERING, UNIV. OF TORONTO 1989– ; Lectr. 1946–55; Asst. Prof. 1955–60; Assoc. Prof. 1960–65; Prof. 1965–89; Chrmn., Div. of Engr. Sci. 1977–82, 1988–89; Pres.: Internat. Assembly for Heat Transfer 1978–82; Royal Candn. Inst. 1981–82; Hooper and Hix 1973–76; Hooper & Angus Assoc. 1976–86; Envirogetics Ltd. 1974–79; Dir., Toronto District Heating Corp. 1984–92; Sr. Cons., Proctor and Redfern Group 1986–93; Chief Engineer, Prime-Drive Inc. 1993– ; Engineering Alumni Medal, U. of T. 1987; Engineering Medal (A.P.E.O.) 1976; Candn. Cong. of Applied Mech. Medal 1978; E.K. Campbell Award of A.S.H.R.A.E. 1980; Candn. Silver Jubilee Medal; Stackiewitz Medal of C.S.M.E. and C.S.Ch.E. 1986; Fellow, Engineering Inst. of Can. 1976; Fellow, Can. Soc. for Mech. Engineering 1991; inducted into the Engineering Alumni Hall of Distinction, Univ. of Toronto 1991; Counc., Royal Candn. Inst. 1980–90 (Past Pres.); Mem., Candn. Soc. for Mech. Engineering (Past Pres.); Candn. Solar Energy Soc.; author of more than 190 tech. papers in confs. & journals; co-author: 'Engineering Dynamics' 1954; recrecreations: sailing, golf; clubs: Royal Candn. Yacht, Univ. of Toronto Faculty; Home: 92 Three Valleys Dr., Don Mills, Ont. M3A 3B9; Office: Mech. Engineering, Univ. of Toronto, Toronto, Ont. M5S 1A4.

**HOOPER, Gerald Allen,** C.A.; financial executive; b. Kitchener, Ont. 1 May 1943; s. Robert Alfred and Jeanette Anne (Toker) H.; e. Univ. of Waterloo C.A. 1970; m. Margaret d. Dr. Robert and Dorothy Gibb 17 Sept. 1966; children: Robert Bryan, Stephen Jeffrey, Susan Janette; VICE-PRES. & CHIEF FINAN. OFFR., SCHNEIDER CORP. 1985– ; Partner, Peat Marwick Thorne 1975; Ont. Dir. of Personnel 1975; of Marketing 1985; Office Mng. Partner Hamilton 1985; Dir., Kitchener-Waterloo Hosp. Found.; Mem., Candn. Inst. of C.A.s; Financial Extves. Inst.; Conservative Bus. Assn.; clubs: Westmount Golf & Country (Dir.), Northfield Racquet; Rotary Club of Waterloo; Home: 296 Hiawatha Dr., Waterloo, Ont.; Office: 321 Courtland Ave. E., Box 130, Kitchener, Ont. N2G 3X8.

**HOOVER, Donald L.,** B.Sc., AACI; agricultural consultant; b. Worsley, Alta. 18 Nov. 1942; s. Lester R. and Mary S. (Childs) H.; e. Univ. of Alta., B.Sc. (Agric.) 1964; Appraisal Inst. of Can., Accredited Appraiser 1970; Certified Mgmt. Consultant 1978; m. Muriel d. Naomi Herbig 28 Nov. 1964; children: Scott, Nicola; SERECON CONSULTANTS 1991– (specializes in agricultural economics, management consulting, environmental assessments, property appraising; Alta. Govt. 1964–65; Farm Mngt. Offr., Farm Credit Corp. Alberta 1965–67; P.E.I. 1967–69; Ottawa 1969–71; Agric. Cons., Sibbald Group 1971–76; Partner, Deloitte & Touche Management Consultants 1976–91; partner and operator of 2,500-acre grain, oilseed farm in Peace River area of Alta.; Past Pres., Alberta Inst. of Agrologists 1981–82, Profl. Recognition Award, Alta. Inst. of Agrologists

1985; Pres., Agricultural Inst. of Can. 1989–90; numerous presentations and reports prepared on land values, expropriation and farm finance in Alta. and Can.; recreations: skiing, hiking, squash; club: Royal Glenora; Home: 361 Hedley Way, Edmonton, Alta. T6R 1T8; Office: 600 First Edmonton Place, 10665 – Jasper Ave., Edmonton, Alta. T5J 3S9.

**HOPKINS, Bernard;** actor/director/teacher; b. Liverpool, U.K. 4 Mar. 1937; s. Bernard and Hilda (Grigg); e. St. Francis of Assisi Jr.; Toxteth Grammar; Royal Acad. of Dramatic Art (all U.K.); BD. MEM., GRAND THEATRE, LONDON 1991– ; MEM., MAIN CO., STRATFORD FESTIVAL 1989– ; early theatre career in U.K.; Candn. debut, Manitoba Theatre Ctr. 1971 season; has directed and acted in all major theatres countrywide; Mem., Stratford Festival Co. 1974–79; Artistic Dir., Theatre London Ont. 1980–84; Head of Drama, Banff Ctr. of Fine Arts 1984–87; Mem., Stratford Festival Co. 1988– ; Dir., Young Co., Stratford 1989–91; teaching: Bishop's Univ.; Nat. Theatre Sch.; George Brown Coll.; Ryerson; Univ. of Alta.; Univ. of Calgary; Univ. of Iowa; Florida State Univ; Carnegie Mellon; recreations: reading, music, cooking; Home: 194 Langarth St., London, Ont. N6C 1Z5; Office: Box 520, Stratford, Ont. N5A 6V2.

**HOPKINS, George W.;** B.A.Sc., P.Eng.; banker; b. Thunder Bay, Ont. 27 Feb. 1938; s. Malcolm M. and Gladys (Paxton); e. Fort William Coll. Inst.; Can. Services Coll, Royal Roads B.C.; Roy. Military Coll. Kingston 1960; Univ. of Toronto B.Sc. 1961; P. Eng. 1961; AMP Harvard Business Sch. 1986; m. Marion Catherine d. Fred Thom 27 Dec. 1960; children: Malcolm Todd, Lisa Catherine; EXECUTIVE VICE PRES., CORPORATE STAFF, BANK OF MONTREAL; RCAF Telecommunications Officer 1960–65; joined IBM Can. as Data Processing Systems Eng. 1966; Marketing Rep. 1969; Marketing Mgr. 1971; Br. Mgr., Montreal 1973; Dir., IBM Computer Centres 1975; Dir. Admin. IBM Can. 1979; joined Bank of Montreal as Sr. Vice Pres., Operations & Systems Div., Toronto 1981; apptd. Extve. Vice Pres., Operations & Systems Group (now Electronic Data Processing Systems Group) 1984; Dir., Trillium Found.; mem. Assoc. of Prof. Engrs. of Ont.; Clubs: Royal Mil. Coll. Club of Can. (Kingston); The Harvard Club of Toronto; Office: 55 Bloor St. W., Toronto, Ont. M4W 3N5.

**HOPKINS, Leonard,** M.P., B.A.; b. Argyle, Ont., 12 June 1930; s. John James and Victoria Maude (Brown) H.; e. Argyle (Ont.) Pub. Sch.; Woodville (Ont.) High Sch.; Ryerson Inst. of Technol.; Queen's Univ., B.A. (Hons.); North Bay (Ont.) Teachers Coll.; Ont. Coll. of Educ., Univ. of Toronto; m. Lois Mary, d. William Albert Gust and Lena (Mohns), Petawawa, Ont., 28 June 1958; children: Sherri Lynne, Douglas Leonard; Opposition Critic Regional Development 1990–93; Elem. Sch. Teacher for 7 yrs. and Princ. for 4 yrs.; High Sch. Teacher for 5½ yrs. and Vice-Princ. 1964–65; mem. Petawawa Twp. Council 1963–65; Charter Pres., Rotary Club of Petawawa, 1961; el. to H. of C. in g.e. 1965; re-el 1968, 1972, 1974, 1979, 1980, 1984, 1988, 1993; Vice Chrmn., H. of C. Standing Comte. on Industry, Energy & Mines 1966–68; Chrmn., H. of C. Standing Comte. on National Resources & Public Works 1968–72; apptd. Parlty. Secy. for Defence 1972, re-apptd. 1973 & 1974; apptd. Parlty. Secy. to Min. of Energy, Mines & Resources, Mar. 1984; apptd. Official Opposition Critic for Nat. Defence, Nov. 1984; apptd. Official Opposition Critic for Supply and Services and Assoc. Critic for Nat. Defence, Jan. 1987; Apptd. Official Opposition Critic for Treasury Bd., and Assoc. Critic for Nat. Defence, Jan. 1988; apptd. Opposition Critic for Financial Mgmt. of the Govt. and Assoc. Opposition Critic for Nat. Defence 1989; apptd. Chrmn. designate and el. Chrmn., H. of C. Public Accounts Ctte. 1988–91; el. Chrmn., East. Ont. Liberal Caucus 1989; el. Vice Chrmn., Ont. Region, Nat. Liberal Caucus 1989; Chrmn. of the Candn. NATO Parlty. Assoc. 1980–84 (led N. Atlantic Assembly Delegations to meetings in Portugal, Federal Republic of Germany, Belgium, Holland, Denmark, Britain, Luxembourg, Italy, etc.); el. Vice-Pres. of North Atlantic Assembly (NATO), The Hague, Holland, Oct. 1983, re-el. 1984; a Keynote Speaker, World Tourism Orgn., The Hague, Holland 1989; Hon. mem., Royal Candn. Legion Branch 72, Pembroke and Branch 517, Petawawa; Hon. Mem., Lanark and Renfrew Scottish Regiment; Liberal; Presbyterian; recreations: skating, fishing, camping, boating; Club: Rotary; Home: 33 Sunset Cres., Petawawa, Ont. K8H 2L8; Office: House of Commons, Ottawa, Ont. K1A 0A6.

**HOPKINS, Robert Harold,** B.Sc.; management consultant; b. Toronto, Ont. 1 Jan. 1947; s. Harold Edgar and Geneva Adelaide (Babcock) H.; e. Weston Collegiate 1964; Univ. of Toronto B.Sc. (Hons.) 1969; m. Barbara d. Arthur and Evelyn Bezzo 31 Aug. 1968; VICE-PRESIDENT, CGI GROUP 1992– ; Systems Analyst, DCF Systems Ltd. 1969–72; Ford Motor Co. 1972–73; DCF Systems Ltd. 1973–74; Gellman-Hayward & Partners Ltd. 1974–92; Partner 1978; President, MTCC 597 (condominium of residence); recreations: travel, photography; Home: 35 Church St., Apt. 716, Toronto, Ont. M5E 1T3; Office: 33 Yonge St., Toronto, Ont. M5E 1G4.

**HOPKINS, Tom,** B.F.A., M.F.A.; artist; b. Summerside, P.E.I. 9 Dec. 1944; s. Archibald Sherard and Frances May (McCulloch) H.; e. Mt. Allison Univ. B.F.A. 1970; Concordia Univ. M.B.A. 1987; m. Rita d. Leslie and Irene Markovits 13 Dec. 1986; children: Jacob, Anna; exhibitions incl.: Equinox Gall., Vanc.; Virginia Miller Gall., Miami 1992; Art Gall. of N.S., The Drabinsky Gall. Toronto, Philippe Daverio Gall. New York 1991; Equinox Gall. Vanc. 1988, '90; Galerie Michel Guimont Qué., Grunwald Gall. Toronto, Art 45 Montréal 1989; Kozen Gall. Montréal, 1988; Gal. Michel Guimont, Qué., Concordia Univ. Art Gall., Anna Leonowens Gall. Halifax 1987; Grunwald Gall. Toronto 1983, '85, '86, '88; Gal. Lacerte & Guimont, Qué. 1983, '85; Gal. Michel Tétreault Art Contemporain Montréal 1984; Anne Doran Gall. 1983; Prof., Painting & Drawing, McGill Univ. 1980–83; Concordia Univ. 1983– ; Dawson Coll. 1982–87; Vice-Pres., Candn. Inst. for Psychosynthesis 1973–78; Can. Counc. Grants 1980, '81, '85; Min. des Affaires culturelles de Québec grants 1988, '90; collections include: Alcan, Allan Schwartz, Art Gall. of Windsor, Art Gall. of Nova Scotia, Dept. of External Affairs, Hart House, Mount Allison Univ., The Cumming-Langford Coll., The Royal Bank of Can., Musée du Qué., The Rideau Ctr., Univ. of N.B., Toronto Dominion Bank Collection; recreations: music, archery, cycling; Home: 489, rue Ste-Madeleine, Montréal, Qué. H3K 2K8; Office: 999, rue du Collège #30, Montréal, Qué. H4C 2S3.

**HOPPENHEIM, Howard Barnett,** B.Comm.; Trustee in Bankruptcy; b. Montreal, Que. 26 June 1944; s. Moe Norman and Rhoda Bessner H.; e. Concordia Univ. B. Comm. 1969; m. Arlene d. Lewis and Millie Lutter 19 Oct. 1980; children: Martine, Jonathan; MANAGING PARTNER, HOPPENHEIM & ASSOC. 1982– ; various managerial positions 1969–73; Principal, Richter, Usher & Vineberg C.A.s 1973–79; Vice-Pres., Ernst & Whinney Inc. & Principal, Ernst & Whinney C.A.s 1979–82; Mem., Candn. Insolvency Practitioners Assn.; Que. Insolvency Assn.; recreations: hockey, squash; club: Montreal Amateur Athletic Assn.; Home: 3228 The Boulevard, Westmount, Que. H3Y 1S3; Office: 625 President Kennedy Ave., Ste. 900, Montreal, Que. H3A 1K2.

**HOPPER, Wilbert Hill,** O.C., B.Sc., M.B.A., LL.D.; petroleum executive; b. Ottawa, Ont. 14 March 1933; s. Wilbert Clayton and Eva (Hill) H. (both deceased); e. Rockcliffe Park Public Sch., Ottawa; Lisgar Coll., Ottawa; Scots Coll., Sydney, Australia; Wellington Coll., Wellington, N.Z.; American Univ., Washington, D.C., B.Sc. (Geol.) 1955; Univ. of Western Ont., M.B.A. 1959; LL.D. (Hon.), Wilfrid Laurier Univ.; m. Patricia Marguerite d. Reginald Gordon Walker 12 Aug. 1957; children: Sean Wilbert, Christopher Mark; Chrmn. C.E.O., & Dir., Petro-Canada 1979–93; Dir., Westcoast Energy Inc.; ICG Propane Inc.; Bd. mem., Bi-Provincial Upgrader Joint Venture; Petroleum Geol., Imperial Oil Ltd. 1955–1957; Petroleum Econ., Foster Associates 1959–1961; Energy Econ., Nat. Energy Bd., Ottawa, 1961–64; Sr. Petroleum Consultant, Arthur D. Little, Inc. Cambridge, Mass. 1964–73; Asst. Depy. Min., Energy Policy, Dept. of Energy, Mines and Resources, Ottawa 1973–75; Pres., C.E.O. and Dir., Petro-Canada 1976–79; Chrmn., C.E.O. & Dir. 1979– ; Bd. of Govs., The Oxford Inst. for Energy Studies; Internat. Adv. Counc., The Centre for Global Energy Studies; Mem., Candn. Economic Assoc.; Am. Economic Assoc.; Candn. Soc. of Petroleum Geologists; Am. Assoc. of Petroleum Geologists; Candn. Inst. for Advanced Rsch., Candn. Inst. of Mining and Metallurgy; Soc. of Petroleum Engrs.; Adv. Ctte., Sch. of Bus. Admin., Univ. of Western Ont.; Officer of the Order of Canada; Address: 500 Eau Claire Ave. S.W., Apt. H302, Calgary, Alta. T2P 3R8.

**HORE, Marlene;** writer; b. Montreal, Que. 7 Aug. 1944; d. Stanley Sam and Mollie (Kushner) Abelson; e. McGill Univ., McDonald Coll., Sir George Williams; m. Ron s. Sid and Dorothy H. 7 July 1968; children: Seanna, Melissa; VICE-CHAIRMAN, J. WALTER THOMPSON CO. LTD. 1986– ; Sr. Writer, CFCF Radio/TV 1966–68; Copywriter, V&B 1968–69; Vice-Pres. & Creative Dir., J. Walter Thompson Co. Ltd. (Montreal) 1978; Vice-Pres. & Nat. Creative Dir., J. Walter Thompson Co. Ltd. Canada 1983; Mem., Canadian Bd. of Dir. 1984; Mem., World Bd. 1986; Extve. Vice-Pres. 1986; Bd. of Dirs., Art Directors Club of Toronto 1990– ; Bd. of Dirs., NABS (Nat. Advertising Benevolent Soc. of Can.) 1991– ; Bd. of Dirs., Candn. Advertising Found. 1991– ; Home: 81 Roxborough St. W.; Office: 160 Bloor St. E., Toronto, Ont. M4W 3P7.

**HORLICK, Louis,** M.Sc., M.D., C.M., F.R.C.P.(C); university professor; b. Montreal, Que. 2 Dec. 1921; s. Philip and Sophie (Katz) H.; e. McGill Univ., B.Sc. 1944, M.D., C.M. 1945, M.Sc. 1952; F.R.C.P.(C) 1952; m. Ruth Lenore, d. late Garfield George Hood 1952; children: Jonathan, Andrew, Allan, Simon; EMERITUS PROF. OF MEDICINE, COLL. OF MEDICINE, UNIV. OF SASK.; Past Pres., and Patron, Sask. Heart and Stroke Foundation; past Chrmn. Candn. Council on Hosp. Accreditation; mem. Am. Coll. of Physicians; Past Pres., Candn. Atherosclerosis Soc. 1988–89; recreation: music; Home: 1215 Elliott St., Saskatoon, Sask. S7N 0V5.

**HORN, Michiel Steven Daniel,** B.A., M.A., Ph.D.; professor of history; b. Baarn, The Netherlands 3 Sept. 1939; s. Daniel and Antje Elisabeth (Reitsma) H.; e. Victoria H.S.; Victoria College, Univ. of B.C. B.A. 1963; Freiburg Univ. West Germany; Univ. of Toronto M.A. 1965, Ph.D. 1969; m. Cornelia (M.A., LL.B.) d. Dr. Otto and Dr. Elfriede Schuh 29 Dec. 1984; children: Daniel André, Patrick Benjamin; PROFESSOR, DEPT. OF HISTORY, YORK UNIV., GLENDON COLLEGE 1982– ; Jr. Officer, Bank of Montreal 1956–58; Lecturer in history, Glendon College, York Univ. 1968; Asst. Prof. 1969; Assoc. Prof. 1973; Co-ord. of Candn. Studies 1972–73, 1986–89; Chair, Dept. of History 1973–78, 1982–93; Assoc. Principal, Finance & Admin. 1978–81; Chair, York Univ. Faculty Assn. 1972–73; Extve. Ctte., Candn. Assn. of Univ. Teachers 1973–75; Chair, Ont. Conf. of Univ. Fac. Assns. 1976–77; Academic Freedom and Tenure Ctte., C.A.U.T. 1984–90; Academic Co-ord., Living and Learning in Retirement 1976– ; Woodrow Wilson Nat. Fellowship 1963; Canada Council Leave Fellowship 1974; SSHRCC Research Grants 1986, 1990; Glendon College Leave Fellowship 1993; North York Historical Bd. & Local Architectural Conservancy Adv. Ctte. 1977–80; Mem., Candn. Historical Assn.; Candn. Inst. of Internat. Affairs; Candn. Assn. for the Advancement of Netherlandic Studies; author: 'The League for Social Reconstruction' 1980, 'Years of Despair' 1986; co-author: 'A Liberation Album' 1980 (translated as 'De Canadezen in Nederland' 1981); 'Canada: A Political and Social History' 1982; editor: 'The Dirty Thirties' 1972, 'Studies in Canadian Social History' 1974, 'A New Endeavour' 1986, 'Academic Freedom' 1987, 'The Depression in Canada' 1988; recreations: reading, opera, squash, baseball; clubs: Massey College Alumni, Glendon Squash & Athletic; Home: 360 Lippincott St., Toronto, Ont. M5S 2P7; Office: 2275 Bayview Ave., Toronto, Ont. M4N 3M6.

**HORN, Steven A.,** B.A., B.L.S., LL.B., Dip.L.D.; lawyer, civil servant; b. Baarn, Netherlands 19 May 1944; s. Daniel and Antje Elizabeth (Reitsma) H.; e. Univ. of Victoria B.A. 1967; Univ. of Toronto B.L.S. 1969; Univ. of Saskatchewan LL.B. 1983; Univ. of Ottawa Dip.L.D. 1989; CHIEF LEGISLATIVE COUNSEL, DEPT. OF JUSTICE, GOVT. OF THE YUKON 1991– ; Cataloguing Librarian, Carleton Univ. 1969–73; Chief Cataloguer, Brampton Public Lib. 1973–74; Justice of the Peace & Court Clerk, Court Serv., Prov. of B.C. 1975–80; Articled Student & Lawyer, Victoria, B.C. 1983–86; Chief Librarian, City of Yellowknife 1986–87; Dep. Registrar of Land Titles, N.W.T. L.R.D. 1987–88; Legislative Counsel, Govt. of the Yukon 1989–91; Mem., Law. Soc. of B.C. 1984– ; Law Soc. of Yukon 1989– ; Candn. Bar Assn.; Candn. Assn. for the Admin. of Justice; author: 'Liquor Offences Under the Indian Act' 1983, 'Courtwatcher's Manual' 1978; Home: 19 Roundel Rd., Apt. 301, Whitehorse, Yukon Y1A 3H3; Office: P.O. Box 2703, Whitehorse, Yukon Y1A 2C6.

**HORNE, Arthur Edward Cleeve,** R.C.A.; painter; sculptor; b. Jamaica, B.W.I. 9 Jan. 1912; s. Arthur Charles Washington and Gladys Lillian (Grant) H.; e. Ont. Coll. of Art (Lieut-Gov's Medal, painting) 1934; sculpture, D. Dick of Eng., 1927–28; painting, J.W. Beatty and John Russell, 1932–34, Europe 1936; m. Jean Mildred, d. William Thomas Harris, 11 Feb. 1939; children: Robert Cleeve, Arthur William, Richard Rowley; served World War, 1943–46, C.I., Cam. Wing, C.E.T.C., retired with rank of Capt.; paintings include portraits of people prominent in industry, law, gov't, banking, educ., etc.; sculpture comns. incl., Alexander Graham Bell, Brantford, Ont., 1948; William Shakespeare, Stratford, Ont., 1950; War Memorial, Law Soc. of Upper Can., Osgoode Hall, Toronto, 1951; Bank of Can., Toronto, 1958; R.S. McLaughlin, R.O.M. Planetarium, Toronto, 1970; artist consultant, Imperial Oil Building, Toronto, 1953–58; St. Lawrence Power Project Adm. Bldg., 1957–59; Canadian Imperial Bank of Commerce H.O., Montreal, 1960–62; Commerce Court, Toronto, 1970–73; Chairman R.C.A. Art Consultant Committee to Ont. Government Queens Park Project, 1968–70; Ont. Hydro H.O., Toronto, 1974–76; R.A.I.C. Allied Art Award, 1963; Centennial Medal; Silver Jubilee Medal; Commemorative Medal for 125th Anniversary of Candn. Confederation 1993; OSA Award, 1982; Fellow, Ont. Coll. of Art 1987; Order of Ont. 1987; mem. Ont. Soc. of Artists (Pres. 1949–51); Sculptors' Soc. of Can.; Anglican; Clubs: Arts and Letters (Pres. 1955–57); York; Studio Home: 181 Balmoral Ave., Toronto, Ont. M4V 1J8.

**HORNE, Edward P.W.,** B.Sc., Ph.D.; scientist; b. Halifax, N.S. 1 Jan. 1952; s. Reginald Allison and Jessie Elizabeth (MacMichael) H.; e. Dalhousie Univ. B.Sc. 1974, Ph.D. 1978; m. Heather d. Walter and H. Aileen Hubley 3 May 1980; children: Ted, Benjamin; RESEARCH SCIENTIST, BEDFORD INST. OF OCEANOGRAPHY 1980– ; Post Doctoral Investigator, Woods Hole Oceanographic Inst. 1978–80; author of journal articles; recreations: gardening, sailing; clubs: Dahha Soc. of N.S.; home: 1665 Walnut St., Halifax, N.S. B3H 3S3; Office: Box 1006, Dartmouth, N.S. B2Y 4A2.

**HORNER, Dr. Hugh M.,** M.D., B.Sc., LL.D; transportation consultant; b. Blaine Lake, Sask. 1 Feb. 1925; s. Ralph Byron and Mae Victoria (MacArthur) H.; e. Univ. of Sask. B.Sc.; Univ. of W. Ont. M.D. 1950; m. Jean Claire d. Dr. Charles Findley 17 Aug. 1947; children: Richard, Bruce, Daniel, Donald, Dougla; TRANSPORTATION CONSULTANT WESTGLEN FARMS LTD.; Vice Chrmn. Via Rail Inc.; Westglen Milling (1989) Ltd.; Dir. Prince Rupert Grain; M.P. Jasper-Edson 1958–67; M.L.A. Lac Ste. Anne 1967–71; M.L.A. Barrhead 1971–79; Dep. Premier and Min. of Agric., Alta. 1971–75; Dep. Premier and Min. of Transp., Alta. 1975–79; Dep. Premier and Min. of Econ. Devel., Alta. 1979–80; Co-ordinator Grain Transp. Authority, Winnipeg 1979–80; Pres. Jamaica Hosp. and Med. Equipment Soc.; Hon. LL.D. Univ. of Alta. 1984; recreation: golf; Club: Barrhead Golf & Country; Home: 4932 47th St., Barrhead, Alta. T7N 1H6.

**HORNER, Hon. Jack H.,** P.C. (1977); rancher; farmer; b. Blaine Lake, Sask. 20 July 1927; s. Senator Ralph Byron and Mae (Macarthur) H.; m. Leola Funnell, 11 April, 1950; children: Blaine, Craig, Brent; Chrmn., Canadian National Railway 1981–84; Administrator, Prairie Grain Agency 1984–88, now retired; first elected to H. of C. 1958; re-elected, 1962, '63, '65, '68, '72, '74; joined Lib. Party 1977; apptd. Min. of Industry Trade & Commerce, 1977; def. g. e. 1979; author: 'My Own Brand' (autobiography) 1980; United Church; Home: Pollockville, Alta. T0J 2L0.

**HORNER, Pamela Mary;** writer, homemaker, retired secretary; b. Davidson, Sask. 25 Sept. 1927; d. Lewis Raymond and Elsie Ann (Cook) Thomas; e. Davidson Elem. & H.S.; Balfour Tech.; Okanagan Coll., Vernon Campus, U.B.C.; m. Ralph s. Marjorie and Ralph H. 14 June 1952; children: James Douglas, Susan Jean, Gordon Hugh; var. secretarial positions in Regina, Whitehorse, Vancouver, Vernon beginning at age 17; writing, always an avocation, became serious pursuit on retirement in 1987; author: 'Osteoporosis, The Long Road Back (One Woman's Story)' 1989; Mem., N.D.P. (P.R. & media work); Unitarian Ch. (var. posts); Armstrong Group Ctte. (Boy Scouts; Sec. in the 1960s); 4H Garden Club Leader 1968–69; Co-Founder & Pres., Vernon Osteporosis Support Group (an affiliate of OSTOP, the Osteoporosis Soc. of B.C.) 1992– ; recreations: reading, contract bridge, hiking, travel, gardening; Home: 1903 – 29 Crescent, Vernon, B.C. V1T 1Y6.

**HORNSTEIN, Reuben Aaron,** C.M. (1991), M.B.E. (1946), M.A. Hon. D.Litt.; retired public servant; meteorologist; radio and television artist: b. London, Ont. 18 Dec. 1912; s. Morris and Sophia (Rosenthal) H.; e. London Central Coll.; Univ. of W. Ont., B.A. 1934 (Gold Medal in Hon. Physics), M.A. 1936; Univ. of Toronto, M.A. 1938; Hon. D.Litt., Saint Mary's, 1982; m. Helen Christina MacDonald, 1956; Demonst. in Physics, Univ. of W. Ont., 1934–37; joined Meteorol. Br., Dept. of Transport and served at St. Hubert and Malton Airports 1938–40; placed in charge of Halifax Office, serving all three Brs. of Armed Forces 1940–46; in charge of Halifax Atlantic Weather Central 1946–72; author of 22 scientific and technical papers, (booklets) 'Weather Facts and Fancies' 1948; 'It's in The Wind' 1950; 'Weather and Why' 1954; 'The Weather Book' 1980; 'Après La Pluie, Le Beau Temps' 1981; vol. in prod. of talking books, tapes for blind and disabled; awarded The Patterson Medal for distinguished Service to Candn. meteorol., 1962; Special Merit Award, Fed. Inst. of Mang., 1977; Volunteer of the Year, Sir Frederick Fraser Sch. 1983; Hon. Big Brother, Big Brothers of Dartmouth-Halifax, 1976–77; awarded Commemorative Medal for 125th Anniversary of Candn. Confederation 1992; Life Mem., N.S. Inst. of Science; Life Mem., Candn. Meteorol. and Oceanographic Soc.; Life Mem., Candn. Assn. Physicists; Life Mem., ACTRA; Emeritus Mem., PIPSC; mem., Federal Superannuates Nat. Assn.; mem., Friends of Halifax Br., Victorian Order of Nurses; John Howard Soc.; The Vanier Inst. of the Family; The Writers Guild of Canada; Roman Catholic; recreations: golf, bridge; Clubs: Ashburn Golf & Country; Saraguay; Home: 1074 Wellington St., Apt. 301, Halifax, N.S. B3H 2Z8.

**HORNUNG, Richard I.,** Q.C., B.A., LL.B., LL.M.; lawyer; b. Grayson, Sask. 15 Apr. 1946; s. I. John and Mary E. (Eckes) H.; e. Univ. of Sask., B.A. 1968, LL.B. 1969; London Sch. of Econ., LL.M. 1971; m. Sharon d. Peder Skotheim 29 Aug. 1970; children: Jonathan, Jennifer, Jeffrey; Q.C. 1985; VICE-CHRMN., CANADA LABOUR RELATIONS BD.; Chrmn., Saskatchewan Labour Relations Board; Chrmn. Candn. Law Information Counc.; Instructor, Harvard Law Sch., P.I.L.; Member: National Academy of Arbitrators; Prof. of Law, Univ. of Alta. 1971–73; Private Practice of Law 1973–88; Mem., Candn. Human Rights Comm.; Bencher, Law Soc. of Sask. 1982–88; Lectr., Bar Admission Course and Candn. Bar Assn.; Lectr., Ctr. for Dispute Settlement Inc.; Chrmn. of vast number of arbitration boards; mediator of labour disputes; Bronze Medal for Bravery 1987; Home: 10 Bayport Private, Ottawa, Ont.; Office: C.L.R.B., 4th Flr. W., 240 Sparks St., Ottawa, Ont. K1A 0X8.

**HORNYKIEWICZ (HORNYKEWYCZ), Oleh,** M.D.; neuroscientist; educator; b. Sychiw, Ukraine 17 Nov. 1926; s. Theophilus and Anna (Yaworsky) H.; came to Can. 1967; e. Univ. of Vienna, Austria M.D. 1951; m. Christina, d. late Sergius Yablonowski, 18 July 1962; children: Maria-Christina; Nikolai; Stephan; Joseph; PROFESSOR AND CHRMN., DEPT. OF BIOCHEMICAL PHARMACOLOGY, UNIV. OF VIENNA, 1977– ; Prof., Dept. of Pharmacology and Dept. of Psychiatry, Univ. of Toronto 1976–91, Professor Emeritus 1992– ; Clinical Asst., Rudolfs-Hosp., Vienna 1952; Asst. Assoc. Prof., Dept. of Pharmacol., Univ. of Vienna 1953–67; Brit. Counc. Scholar, Univ. of Oxford (England) 1956–58; Visiting Prof., Univ. of Toronto 1967–68; Prof., Dept. of Pharmacol. 1968–77; Prof., Dept. of Psychiatry 1973–77; mem., Pharmacological Soc. of Can.; Amer. Soc. of Pharmacology and Therapeutics; German Acad. of Natural Scientists 'Leopoldina'; Austrian Acad. of Sciences; Ševchenko Scientific Society, and many other profl. assns.; awarded Hon. M.D., Univ. of Cagliari, Italy 1976; Research Medal. Amer. Assn. for Research in Nervous and Mental Disease 1969; Internat. Gairdner Found. Award 1972; Wolf Found. Award in Med. 1979 and many others; co-author (with F. Bruecke and E.B. Sigg) 'The Pharmacology of Psychotherapeutic Drugs' 1969; author numerous articles in profl. journals; Ukrainian Catholic; recreations: reading, music; Home: Este Pl. 7/10 A-1030 Vienna, Austria; Offices: Inst. of Biochem. Pharmacol., Univ. of Vienna, Borschkeg 8A, A-1090 Vienna, Austria or c/o Clarke Institute of Psychiatry, 250 College St., Toronto, Ont. M5T 1R8.

**HOROWITZ, Myer,** O.C., B.A., M.Ed., Ed.D., LL.D., D.A.U., F.C.C.T., F.R.C.A.; educator; b. Montreal, Que. 27 Dec. 1932; s. Philip and Fanny (Cotler) H.; e. Comm. High Sch., Montreal, 1949; Sch. for Teachers, Macdonald Coll., Teacher's Cert. 1952; Sir George Williams Coll., (now Concordia Univ.), B.A. 1956; Univ. of Alta., M.Ed. 1959; Stanford Univ., Ed.D. 1965; Hon. LL.D.: McGill Univ. 1979; Concordia Univ. 1982; Univ. of B.C. 1990; Univ. of Alta 1990; Hon. D.A.U., Athabasca Univ. 1989; m. Barbara, d. Samuel and Grace Rosen, Montreal, 3 Oct. 1956; two d.: Carol Anne, Deborah Ellen; PROFESSOR EMERITUS OF EDUCATION, UNIV. OF ALBERTA; Teacher, Elem. and High Schs., Prot. Sch. Bd. of Greater Montreal, 1952–60; joined McGill Univ. as Lectr. in Educ., 1960–63; Asst. Prof. 1963–65, Assoc. Prof. 1965–67, Asst. to the Dir., 1964–65; Prof. of Educ., 1967–69; and Asst. Dean 1965–69; Prof. and Chrmn., Dept. Elementary Educ., Univ. of Alta. 1969–72; Dean of Educ., 1972–75; Vice Pres. (Acad.), 1975–79; Pres., 1979–89; Research and Teaching Asst., Stanford Univ., Chrmn., Candn. Comte. on Early Childhood; Pres., Early Childhood Educ. Council, Alta. Teachers' Assn.; Chrmn. Adv. Comte., Study of Mental Retardation, Univ. of Alta.; Pres., Edmonton Chapter, Candn. Coll. of Teachers; Project Dir., Tanzania Educ. Project; contrib. several articles to prof. and educ. mags. and journs.; Officer, Order of Canada 1990; Fellow, Candn. Coll. of Teachers; Fellow, Royal Soc. of the Arts; Life mem., Prov. Assn. of Prot. Teachers of Que.; Hon. mem. Alta Teachers' Assn.; Jewish; Home: 14319, 60 Ave., Edmonton, Alta. T6H 1J8.

**HORRICK, James Stanley;** insurance executive; b. Montréal, Qué. 14 June 1940; s. Stanley D. and Anne (Lukian) H.; e. Sir George Williams Univ.; PRES. AND CHIEF EXECUTIVE OFFR., ALEXANDER & ALEXANDER / REED STENHOUSE LTD. 1988– ; Pres. & C.E.O., Alexander & Alexander / Reed Stenhouse Companies Ltd. 1989; Dir., Ruben-Winkler Entertainment Insurance Ltd.; Alexander Consulting Group Ltd.; Mem., Global Retail Operations Ctte., Global Retail Bd. and Global Retail Operations Bd., Alexander & Alexander Services Inc.; mem., Ins. Brokers Assn. Prov. Qué. and Ont.; Inst. of Corp. Dirs. in Can.; Bus. Counc. on Nat. Issues; Candn. Institute of Internat. Affairs; recreations: golf, fishing, hunting; Clubs: The Toronto, Mount Royal; Lambton Golf & Country; Royal Candn. Yacht; Griffith Island; Home: 155–B Hudson Dr., Toronto, Ont. M4T 2K4; Office: Reed Stenhouse Tower, Ste. 2200, 20 Bay St., Toronto, Ont. M5J 2N9.

**HORROCKS, Norman,** B.A., M.L.S., Ph.D., F.L.A., A.L.A.A.; librarian; publisher; b. Manchester, Eng. 18 Oct. 1927; s. Edward Henry and Annie (Barnes) H.; e. Burnage High Sch. Manchester 1939–1943; Manchester Coll. of Science & Technol. Sch. of Librarianship 1948–50; Univ. of W. Australia 1957–61; Univ. of Pittsburgh 1963–70; m. Sandra d. Roy and Helen Sheriff, Pittsburgh, Pa.; children: Julie Carol, Carl Scott, Gina Louise, Anne Patricia, Sarah Helen; VICE PRES., EDITORIAL, SCARECROW PRESS, a Grolier Co., Metuchen, N.J. 1986– ; Asst. Librarian, Manchester Pub. Lib. Eng. 1943–45, 1948–53; Librarian, Brit. Council, Cyprus 1954–55; Tech. Librarian, State Lib. of W. Australia 1956–63; Part-time Lectr. in Librarianship, Perth Tech. Coll. 1961–63; Teaching Fellow, Instr., Asst. Prof., Grad. Sch. of Lib. & Information Science, Univ. of Pittsburgh 1963–71; Assoc. Prof. and Asst. Dir. Sch. of Lib. Service, Dalhousie Univ. 1971; Prof. and Dir., Sch. of Lib. Service there 1972–86; Dean, Faculty of Management Studies, Dalhousie Univ. 1983–86; Summer Sch. Faculty, Grad. Sch. of Lib. Studies, Univ. of Hawaii 1969; Adjunct Prof., Dept. of Lib. & Info. Studies, Rutgers Univ. 1987– ; Extension Lectr. Program for Certification of Lib. Assts., State Lib. of Pa. 1966–71; External Examiner, Dept. Lib. Studies, Univ. of W. Indies 1976–81; Bd. of Visitors, Pratt Inst. Sch. of Lib. & Info. Sci., 1981– ; Program Assoc., Dept. of Lib. & Info. Studies, Rutgers Univ. 1986– ; served with Brit. Army Intelligence Corps 1945–48, Egypt, Palestine, Cyprus; rec'd W. H. Brown Prize 1949; Atlantic Provs. Lib. Assn. Merit Award 1979; Univ. of Pittsburgh Distinguished Graduate 1982; Assoc. for Lib. & Info. Sci. Educ. Service Award 1990; Hon. Life Mem., N.S. Lib. Assoc.; Series Ed., 'The Great Bibliographers' 1974– ; regular contrib. to lib. press Can. and U.S.; mem. various journ. adv. bds.; mem. Am. Inst. of Parliamentarians 1988– ; mem. Am. Lib. Assn. (Extve. Bd. 1977–81; Council 1972–81, 1983– ); Am. Soc. for Info. Sci.; Assn. Am. Lib. Schs. (Chair Ed. Bd. 1971–76, Ex-Officio mem. Extve. Bd. 1971–76); Assn. for Lib. & Info. Sci. Ed. (Pres. 1985); Atlantic Provs. Lib. Assn.; Candn. Lib. Assn. (2nd Vice Pres. Council & Bd. Dirs. 1978–80); Intelligence Corps Assoc. (Life Mem.); Lib. Assn. (U.K.); Australian Library and Information Assn.; Adv. Bd., Sci. and Technological Infor., Nat. Research Counc. Can. (Chair 1984–86); Nat. Library Adv. Bd. Comte., Bibliographic & Info. Services, Soc. Sc. and Humanities Counc. of Can. 1982–86; Can. Counc. Writing and Pub. Panel mem. 1982–85; Beta Phi Mu (Nat. Treas. 1968–71; Pres. 1991–93); New Jersey Center for the Book 1990– ; N.S. Lib. Assoc.; United Church; recreations: parliamentary procedures, editing, publishing, spy stories; Home: 3 Dewey Court, Piscataway, N.J. 08854 USA; Office: P.O. Box 4167, Metuchen, NJ 08840 USA.

**HORSEY, (William) Grant,** B.Com.; industrialist; b. Buffalo, N.Y. 17 Oct. 1915; s. late J. William and late Clara (Banford) H.; came to Canada 1920; e. Pub. Schs. of Buffalo, Toronto and Montreal; McGill Univ., B.Com. 1938; m. Eleanor Mae Child, 17 Feb. 1940; one d. Mrs. Susan H. Dees; PRES., WILGRAN INC. 1962– ; The J. William Horsey Foundation; Dir., The J. William Horsey Foundation; Hon. Trustee, The Toronto Hosp.; Mem., The Scott Mission Finance/Investment Ctte.; Vice Pres. Salada Foods Ltd. (formerly Salada-Shirriff-Horsey Inc.) 1946–50 (Pres. 1950–64, Chrmn. 1964–67); Dir., Plant Industries Inc. (formerly Orange Crystals Inc.) 1954–63; Marine Bank & Trust

Co. (now Sun Bank of Tampa Bay) 1955–58; Central Florida Cold Storage Warehouse Inc. circa 1955; Green Giant of Canada Ltd. 1956–60; Hardee Farms Internat. Ltd. 1959–69; DRG Inc. (formerly Globe Envelopes Ltd.) 1960–86 (Vice Pres. 1960–62, Chrmn. 1962–84); Iroquois Glass Ltd. 1960–65; Canadian Food Products Ltd. 1960–67; Versafood Services Limited (now Versa Services Ltd) 1961–67 (Chrmn. 1962–67); Pilot Insur. Co. 1961–83; Dictaphone Canada Ltd. 1962–68; General Mortgage Corporation of Canada Ltd. 1962–67; National Trust Co. 1964–86; National Victoria and Grey Trustco Ltd. 1984–86; Consolidated Graphics Ltd. 1966–69; Crush Internat. Ltd. 1967–70; General Bakeries Ltd. 1969–80; Dir., South Florida Baptist Hosp. 1953–55; Ontario Soc. for Crippled Children circa 1960; Trustee, Toronto Western Hosp. 1964–83 (Hon. Trustee 1983–86); Dir., Gage Research Inst. 1979–87; Dir., Florida Canners Assn. (now Florida Citrus Processors Assn.) 1947–55; National Canners Assn. (now Nat. Food Processors Assn., Washington, D.C.) 1952–54; mem., State of Florida Concentrate Quality Ctte. 1957–58; Founding Dir., Grocery Products Manufacturers of Canada 1960–63; Lieut., Candn. Army Overseas (R.C.A.) 1943–46; Presbyterian; Theta Delta Chi; Clubs: Granite; York; The Toronto; Belleair Country (Clearwater, Fla.); Office: 120 Eglinton Ave. E., Ste. 1000, Toronto, Ont. M4P 1E2.

**HORSMAN, Bryce Eldon,** B.Eng.; transportation executive; b. Moncton, N.B. 4 Jan. 1938; s. Clifford Garfield and Iva (Lutes) H.; e. Mount Royal High Sch. 1955; McGill Univ. B.Eng. (Civil) 1960; m. Anne d. Alexander and Lillian Stuart 15 Sept. 1973; children: Andrew, Chelsea; PRES., CANAC INTERNATIONAL LTD. 1993– ; Asst. Eng. CN Rail, Montréal 1960, Supr. Freight Train Operations 1965, Mkt. Mgr. 1970, Dir. Mktg. Planning 1973, Asst. Chief Transp. 1975; Asst. Vice Pres. Mktg. Conrail, Philadelphia 1977; Vice Pres. Operations VIA Rail 1980; Extve. Vice Pres., VIA Rail 1982; Vice Pres. Planning & Coordination 1987–91; Vice Pres., Strategic Issues, Candn. National Railway Co. 1991; Mem., Adv. Counc., Candn. Inst. of Guided Group Transport (C.I.G.G.T.); mem. Adv. Bd. Concordia Transp. Centre; el. to Chart. Inst. Transport; recreations: hockey, squash, tennis, sailing; Clubs: MAAA; Knowlton Boating; Bruce Trail; Home: 491 Victoria St., Montréal (Westmount), Qué. H3Y 2R3; Office: 1100 University St., 5th Floor, Montréal, Qué. H3B 3A5.

**HORSMAN, Hon. James Deverell,** Q.C., M.L.A., B.Com., LL.B.; politician; b. Camrose, Alta. 29 July 1935; s. George Cornwall and Kathleen (Deverell) H.; e. Meeting Creek, Alta.; Alexandra Pub. Sch. and Central Coll. Inst. Moose Jaw, Sask.; Univ. of B.C., B. Com., LL.B.; m. Elizabeth Marian d. Thompson and Marian Whitney, Medicine Hat, Alta. 4 July 1964; children: Catherine Anne, Diana Lynn, Susan Marian; Depy. Premier, Alta. 1988–93; Min. of Federal and Intergovernmental Affairs, Alta. 1982–93; mem., Finance & Priorities and Treasury Bd.; Vice-Chrmn. of Economic Planning 1986– ; Chrmn., Cabinet Internat. Trade Negotiations Task Force 1985– ; Chrmn., Strategic Planning Ctte. 1988–89; Chrmn., Senate Reform Task Force 1988–90; Chrmn., Spec. Select Ctte. on Const. Reform 1991–92; Chrmn., Const. Reform Task Force 1990–91; Vice-Pres., Pacific Northwest Econ. Region 1991– ; Candn. sponsor of the Canada/U.S.A. Legislative Project 1985–90; Hon. mem. (representing Can.), Bd. of Dir., (U.S.) State Legislative Leaders Found. 1985– ; Co-Chrmn., Alberta/Montana Boundary Advisory Ctte. 1986– ; cr. Q.C. 1980; Cand. prov. g.e. 1967, 1971 def.; el. M.L.A. for Medicine Hat prov. g.e. 1975, re-el. 1979, 1982, 1986, 1989; Min. of Advanced Educ. and Manpower 1979–82; Depy. Govt. House Leader 1979–87; Attorney General 1986–88; Govt. House Leader 1988–92; mem.: Candn. Delegation to Uruguay Round, General Agreement on Trade and Tariffs (GATT) 1986 and 1988; Alta. Delegation to First Ministers Conferences on Constitution 1982–89; Alta. Delegation to Multilateral Negotiations on the Constitution 1992; Chrmn., Prov. Ministers Responsible for Manpower 1982–85; mem. and Chrmn. Bd. Govs. Medicine Hat Coll. 1972–74; Pres. Medicine Hat Chamber Comm. 1971–72; Elder St. John's Ch. Medicine Hat; P. Conservative; Presbyterian; Mem.: Law Soc. of Alberta; Kinsmen (Past Pres., Past Dist. Offr.); Clubs: Cypress; Edmonton.

**HORTE, Vernon L.,** B.Sc.; company president; b. Kingman, Alta. 12 July 1925; s. Thor and Marit (Haugen) H.; e. Univ. of Alta., B.Sc. (Chem. Engn.) 1949; m. Thelma Margaret Boness, 18 Feb. 1950; children: Joan, Robert, Douglas; PRES. V.L. HORTE ASSOC. LTD. 1977– ; Dir., Atcor Resources Ltd.; PanCanadian Petroleum Ltd.; Morgan Hydrocarbons Inc.; Can. Utilities Ltd.; ProGas Ltd.; Engr., Chem. and Geol. Labs., Edmonton, Alta., 1949–50; Gas Engr., The Alta. Petroleum Natural Gas Conserv. Bd., Calgary, 1950–52; Petroleum Engr., DeGolyer & MacNaughton, Consulting Petroleum Engrs., Dallas, Texas, 1952–57; joined TransCanada PipeLines, Chief Gas Supply Engr., 1957; Mgr. of Gas Supply 1959; Vice Pres., Gas Supply 1961; Group Vice Pres., 1966; Pres. 1968; Pres., Candn. Arctic Gas Study Ltd., 1972–77; served as Navig. with RCAF 1943–45; mem., Assn. Prof. Engrs. Alta.; Assn. Prof. Engrs. Texas; recreations: skiing, golf, hunting; Clubs: The Ranchmen's; Calgary Petroleum; Earl Grey Golf; Glencoe; Home: 113 – 5555 Elbow Dr. S.W., Calgary, Alta. T2V 1H7; Office: 4100 – 400 Third Ave. S.W., Calgary, Alta. T2P 4H2.

**HORVATH, Rev. Tibor,** S.J., M.A., S.T.L., S.T.D.; educator; b. Bánhida, Hungary 28 July 1927; s. János and Rozália (Markus) H.; e. Esterházy Gymnasium (Tata, Hungary) Sr. Matric.; Aloysianum (Szeged, Hungary) Philos. Studies 1948; Univ. of Innsbruck 1949; Aloysianum (Chieri, Italy) 1949–51; Coll. Philos. (St. Albert, Louvain) M.A., L.Phil. 1952–54; Facultad Teologica (Granada, Spain) S.T.L. Theol. Studies 1954–58; Univ. Gregoriana (Rome, Italy) S.T.D. 1960–62; Univ. of Chicago post-doctoral studies Info. Sci. and Computer Sci. 1970–71; entered Soc. of Jesus 1946; o. to Priesthood 1956; PROFESSOR OF SYSTEMATIC THEOLOGY, REGIS COLLEGE, FEDERATED COLL. OF UNIV. OF TORONTO 1962– ; Prof. Toronto Sch. of Theology 1968– ; Pastoral experience: Germany 1951–52, 1959–60; Spain 1958–59; Visiting Prof. of Theology St. Paul's Univ. (Ottawa) 1967–69; Founder and Gen. Ed. 'Ultimate Reality and Meaning: Interdisciplinary Studies in the Philosophy of Understanding' 1978– ; Founder and Dir. Inst. for Encyclopedia of Human Ideas on Ultimate Reality and Meaning 1970– ; Pres. Internat. Soc. for the Study of URAM 1985–87; Founder and first Gen. Secy., Internat. Soc. for Encyclopedia of Church History in Hungary 1986– ; Consultor of the Pontifical Counc. for Dialogue with Non-Believers, Vatican City 1990–95; Gen. Editor: 'Essays in Church History in Hungary' 1992–94; first headmaster of the Fényi Gyula Jesuit Gymnasium Miskolc, Hungary 1994–95; author several books and articles on theology, philosophy, and faith; mem. R. Catholic Ch.; Soc. of Jesus; Am. Philosophers; Systematic Theologians; Anthropologists; Internat. Community Service; Am. Candn. Indians; recipient Deutsche Forschungsgemeinschaft 1966; recreations: hiking, mountain climbing, concerts; Home: 2 Dale Ave., Toronto, Ont. M4W 1K4; Office: Regis College, 15 St. Mary St., Toronto, Ont. M4Y 2R5.

**HORWITZ, Clifford Allen,** B.Comm.; entertainment industry executive; b. Durban, S. Africa 10 March 1949; s. Sydney and Tilly (Greenberg) H.; e. Carmell College H.S. 1966; Univ. of Natal B.Comm. 1970; m. Joanne d. Leslie and Marcia Port 27 June 1971; children: Carla, Brett; PRESIDENT & C.E.O., JUMBO VIDEO INC. 1990– ; dabbled with a career in finance 1970–74; Founder, Alida Clothing Mfrs. (Pty.) Ltd. 1974 (sold 1987); emigrated to Canada 1987; Vice-Pres. Finance, Leisure World Inc. 1987; Extve. Vice-Pres. 1988; Extve. Vice-Pres. & Chief Operating Offr., Jumbo Video Inc. 1990; Pres., Jumbo Video Am. Inc.; Chair, Academy of Learning U.S.A.; Vice-Chrmn., Candn. Franchise Assn.; Mem., Bd. of Gov., Video Software Dealers Assn.; recreations: golf; clubs: Emerald Hills Golf & Country; Office: 1075 N. Service Rd. W., Suite 101, Oakville, Ont. L6M 2G2.

**HORWOOD, Harold Andrew,** C.M.; author; b. St. John's, Nfld. 2 Nov. 1923; s. Andrew and Vina (Maidment) H.; m. Cornelia Lindismith 1 July 1973; children: Andrew, Leah; taught creative writing Mem. Univ. of Nfld. and Univ. of W. Ont.; Writer in Residence Univ. W. Ont. 1976–77; Univ. of Waterloo, 1980–82; mem. Arts Adv. Panel Can. Council 1977–80; Lib. mem. for Labrador, House of Assembly Nfld. 1949–51; def. NDP cand. for Trinity-Conception; author 'Tomorrow Will Be Sunday' 1966, rev. ed. 1992 (Beta Sigma Phi Novel for 1966); 'The Foxes of Beachy Cove' 1967 (Best Scient. Book 1967); 'Newfoundland' (travel) 1969, 1977; 'White Eskimo' (novel) 1972; 'Voices Underground' (poetry ed.) 1972; 'Beyond the Road' (travel) 1976; 'Bartlett, the Great Canadian Explorer' (biog.) 1977, 1979; 'The Colonial Dream' (hist.) 1979; 'Only the Gods Speak' (fiction) 1979; 'Tales of the Labrador Indians' (folklore) 1981; 'A History of Canada' 1984; (with E. Butts) 'Pirates and Outlaws of Canada, 1610–1932' (hist.) 1984; 'A History of The Newfoundland Ranger Force' (hist.) 1986; 'Corner Brook, A Social History of a Paper Town' (hist.) 1986; (with John de Visser) 'Historic Newfoundland' (hist.) 1986; 'Remembering Summer' (novel) 1987; 'Dancing on the Shore' (science, nature) 1987; (with E. Butts) 'Bandits and Privateers, Canada in the Age of Gunpowder' (hist.) 1987; 'Joey, the Life and Political Times of Joey Smallwood' (biog.) 1989; numerous articles for mags. and lit. journs.; mem. Writers Union Can. (Vice Chrmn. 3 times, Chrmn. 1980–81); recreations: music, mathematics, boating, ornithology, gardening; Address: P.O. Box 489, Annapolis Royal, N.S. B0S 1A0.

**HOSEIN, H. Roland,** M.Sc., Ph.D.; corporate executive; b. Trinidad 18 Nov. 1945; s. Ibrahim and Jaitoon H.; e. Univ. of London B.Sc. 1971, M.Sc. 1972; Univ. of W. Ont. Ph.D. 1983; m. Shaffina d. Shaheed and Isha Hosein 12 Sept. 1967; two s. Hanson Riad, Ian Riaz; VICE PRES. GE CANADA 1990– ; Rsch. Assoc. Lung Rsch. Center Yale Univ. 1971–75; Occupational Health Head, Alta. Govt. 1975–78; Assoc. Prof. of Occupational Health Faculty of Med. Univ. of Toronto 1978–80, Assoc. Prof. of Environmental Health 1980–90, Assoc. Gage Rsch. Inst. 1988–90; Assoc. St. Michael's Hosp. Occupational Health Clinic 1980–90; Cons. Egypt Project Candn. Pub. Health Assn. 1987–90; Mgr. Health, Safety & Environment GE Canada and Latin Am., Toronto 1980–90; co-author 'Health Hazard in Printmaking' 1976; 'Occupational Hygiene Management Guide' 1989; ed. 'Occupational Health and Safety Series' 1979; 'Solvents: Health Hazards' 1987; author or co-author over 35 sci. jour. articles; Pres. Occupational Hygiene Assn. Ont. 1988; mem. Am. Ind. Hygiene Assn.; Conf. Bd. Can. Adv. Council on Environment; recreation: tennis; Club: Unionville Tennis; Home: 38 Library Lane, Unionville, Ont. L3R 5T8; Office: 2300 Meadowvale Blvd., Mississauga, Ont. L5N 5P9.

**HOŠEK, Chaviva Milada,** B.A., A.M., Ph.D.; educator; b. Chomutov, Czechoslovakia 6 Oct. 1946; d. Emil and Hedy (Weiss) H.; e. Adath Israel Acad. 1963; McGill Univ. B.A. Hons.Eng. 1967; Harvard Univ. A.M. 1968, Ph.D. 1973; m. Alan Thomas Pearson s. Thomas Joseph and Jessie (Wright) P. 1991; DIRECTOR, POLICY AND RESEARCH, OFFICE OF THE PRIME MINISTER 1993– ; Co-Chair, Platform Ctte. of the Liberal Party of Canada which was responsible for producing the 1993 Liberal Electoral Platform 'Creating Opportunity'; Assoc. Prof. of English, Victoria College, Univ. of Toronto 1978–87; mem. Governing Council, Univ. of Toronto 1983–86, Chrmn. Academic Affairs Ctte. 1984–85; Partner, Gordon Capital Corp., Toronto 1985–87; el. M.P.P. for Oakwood 1987; Min. of Housing, Prov. of Ont. 1987–89; Sr. Policy Advisor to the Leader of the Opposition and Dir., National Liberal Caucus Rsch. Bureau 1990–93; author chapters in 'And No One Cheered: Federalism, Democracy & The Constitution Act' 1983; 'Oxford Companion to Canadian Literature' 1983; co-ed. (with Pat Parker) 'Lyric Poetry: Beyond New Criticism' 1985; co-ed. 'Circle & Labyrinth: Essays in Honour of Northrop Frye' 1983; Pres. National Action Ctte. on the Status of Women (1984–86); mem., Economic Counc. of Can. 1986–87; B'nai Brith Woman of the Year 1984; YWCA, Woman of Distinction 1986; Office: House of Commons, Room 129A, Ottawa, Ont. K1A 0A6.

**HOSKING, Ronald G.,** B.Comm., C.A.; biotechnology executive; b. Toronto, Ont. 23 June 1944; s. Edward and Audrey (Lockie) H.; e. Univ. of Toronto B.Comm. 1968, C.A. 1971; m. Joan; children: Scott, Tony; GENERAL MANAGER, ADI DIAGNOSTICS INC. 1992– ; Controller, Peoples Jewellers Ltd. 1971–72; Vice Pres. Finance, Heintzman & Co. Ltd. 1972–75; Daltons (1834) Ltd. 1975–82; Dir. of Mktg. & Finance, Ortho Diagnostic Systems 1982–89; Dir. of Finance, ADI Diagnostics Inc. 1989–91; Past Div. Gov., Toastmasters Internat.; Dir., MEDEC (Medical Devices Can.); Dir., Financial Extves. Inst.; Mem., Bd. of Trade; recreations: sailing, squash; Office: 30 Meridian Rd., Rexdale, Ont. M9W 4Z7.

**HOSKINS, Donat Hamilton,** APR; public relations executive; b. Saskatoon, Sask. 10 Aug. 1932; s. Edmond Hamilton and Margaret Jane (Christie) H.; e. Craven H.S.; Campion Coll. 1951; m. Diane Isabel d. Philip and Isabel Simpson 16 July 1955; children: Christie Dawn, Hunt Hamilton, Donata Diane; VICE-PRES., MKTG., MEDIA TAPES & TRANSCRIPTS LTD. 1992– ; Sports Dir., CFAR Radio 1953–56; CKX Radio and TV 1956–58; News & Sports Dir., CJFB-TV 1958–60; Sr. Reporter, CJAY-TV 1960–61; Publ. Relns. Offr., Candn. Army 1961–63; TransAir Ltd. 1963–67; Supvr., Tourist Promo., Govt. of Man. 1967–68; Supvr., Pub. Affairs, Internat. Nickel 1968–73; Dir. 1973–76; Dir., Communications, Candn. Cable TV Assn. 1976–78; Vice-Pres., Canada NewsWire Ltd. 1978–92; Honorary Aide de Camp to the Lt. Gov. of Manitoba 1970–73; Vice-Pres., Michener Awards Foundation 1990–92; (Dir. 1984– ); Mem., Candn. Pub. Relns. Soc. 1965– ; Accredited 1971 (Pres., Ottawa Chap. 1981–82, 1982–83; Chrmn., Nat. Conf. 1984, 1985; Chrmn., Nat. Fin. Adv. Bd. 1981–82,

1982–83, 1983–84; Nat. Extve. Ctte. 1984–87; Nat. Pres. 1986–87; Presiding Offr., Nat. Conf. Ctte. 1987–90); Ottawa-Carleton Bd. of Trade 1979–92; Internat. Assn. of Bus. Communicators 1970– ; Clubs: Nat. Press Club of Can. 1978 (Fin. Ctte. 1982–87); Home: 1730 Meadowview Cres., Orleans, Ont. K1C 1V1; Office: 600–60 Queen St., Ottawa, Ont. K1P 5Y7.

**HOSPITAL, Clifford George,** B.A., B.D., Ph.D., A.T.C.L.; university professor; b. Rockhampton, Australia 9 March 1937; s. Henry George and Elizabeth Grace (Sharrod) H.; e. Rockhampton H.S. 1954; Queensland Teachers Coll. 1955; Univ. of Queensland B.A. 1961, B.D. 1964 (1st Class Hons.); Harvard Univ. Ph.D. 1973; m. Janette d. Adrian and Elsie Turner 5 Feb. 1965; children: Geoffrey Eliot, Cressida Denise; PROF., COMPARATIVE RELIGION, QUEEN'S UNIV. & QUEEN'S THEOL. COLL. 1983– ; Public sch. teacher, Queensland 1956–58; Sr. Tutor, Kings Coll., Univ. of Queensland 1963; Assoc. Min., West End Meth. Mission, Brisbane 1964–66; Lectr., Queen's Theol. Coll. 1971–73; Asst. Prof. 1973–78; Assoc. Prof. 1978–83; Principal, 1983–92; Head, Dept. of Religion, Queen's Univ. 1983–90; Organist & Choir Dir., Rosemead, Calif. 1967; Winthrop, Mass. 1967–71; First Bapt. Ch., Kingston 1972–82; Bd. of Dir., Shastri Indo-Candn. Inst. 1980–83, 1985–89 (Sr. Fellow 1977–78); Ed. Bd., 'Studies in Religion' 1983–86; Chair, Ctte. on Candn. Affairs of the Assn. of Theol. Schools 1984–89; Hon. Canon, St. George's Cathedral, Kingston 1983– ; ordained Min., Un. Ch. of Can.; Mem., Candn. Soc. for the Study of Religion; Am. Acad. of Religion; Royal Candn. Coll. of Organists; Hum. Assn. of Can.; author: 'The Righteous Demon: A Study of Bali' 1984, 'Breakthrough: Insights of the Great Religious Discoverers' 1985; recreations: music (piano, organ), walking, canoeing; Home: R.R. 1, Kingston, Ont. K7L 4V1; Office: Kingston, Ont. K7L 3N6.

**HOSPITAL, Janette Turner;** writer; b. Melbourne, Australia 12 Nov. 1942; d. Adrian Charles and Elsie Evelyn (Morgan) Turner; e. Univ. of Queensland B.A. 1966; Queen's Univ. M.A. 1973; m. Clifford George s. Henry and Grace H. 5 Feb. 1965; children: Geoffrey, Cressida; H.S. Teacher, Queensland 1963–66; Librarian, Harvard Univ. 1967–71; Lectr. in English 1973–82; Writer, full-time 1982– ; Visiting Writer-in-Residence, M.I.T. 1985–86, winter/spring 1987, spring 1989; Writer-in-Residence, Univ. of Ottawa, fall 1987, Writer-in-Residence, Univ. of Sydney, Australia 1989; Adjunct Professor in English, Univ. of Ottawa 1990– ; also Writer-in-Residence for one semester per year at La Trobe Univ., Australia 1990– ; winner Seal First Novel Award 1982; 'Atlantic First' for Short Story (U.S.A.) 1978; 1st Prize Mag. Fiction, Found. for Adv. of Candn. Letters 1982; CBC Literary Prize for short story 1986; 'Borderline' shortlisted for National Fiction Award (Australia) and Victoria Premier's Literary Award (Australia) 1986; 'Charades' shortlisted for the Miles Franklin Award and the Banjo Award (Australia) 1989; 'The Last Magician' shortlisted for Trillium Award, Canada and Miles Franklin Award, Australia; mem., P.E.N. Internat.; author: (novels) 'The Ivory Swing' 1982; 'The Tiger in the Tiger Pit' 1983; 'Borderline' 1985; 'Charades' 1989; 'The Last Magician' 1992; (short stories) 'Dislocations' 1986 (Fiction Award, Fellowship of Australian Writers 1988; Torgi Talking Book Award, C.N.I.B. 1988); 'Isobars' 1991; books publ. in USA, UK, Australia and in several European translations; short stories publ. in numerous literary mags. internationally; recreations: collecting med. music by early music groups, collecting facsimile eds. of med. 'Books of Hours,' running, hiking; Home: Kingston, Ont. and Australia; Office: c/o McClelland & Stewart, 481 University Ave., Toronto, Ont. M5G 2E9.

**HOSSACK, Duncan John,** M.A., P.G.C.E.; educator, administrator; b. Newcastle-upon-Tyne, England 21 Sept. 1952; s. John Kimber and Anne McHardy (King) H.; e. Eltham Coll. Kent, England 1970; Open Scholarship, Univ. of St. Andrews, Scotland M.A. (Hons.) 1974; Univ. of London, post-grad. cert. of edn. 1975; m. R. Janet d. Dr. Vincent and Mrs. Mary Young 1983; children: Charles Lester, James Vincent; HEADMASTER, SEDBERGH SCHOOL 1990– ; apptd. headmaster following 12-year teaching career at Sedbergh Sch.; Mem., Candn. Educational Standards Inst. Inspection Team 1988; Contbr., 'Report,' Nunavik Educational Task Force 1991; Captain of school rugby 1st XV; recreations: writing, sports, the outdoors; club: Seignory; Home: The Delaney House, Kensington, P.E.I. C0B 1M0; Office: Montebello, Que. J0V 1L0.

**HOSSIE, Ross Douglas,** B.Sc.Phm., M.Sc.Phm., Ph.D.; public servant; b. Sarnia, Ont. 9 Sept. 1940; s. Andrew Douglas and Marie Matilda (Gray) H.; e. St. Marys Dist. C.I.; Univ. of Toronto, B.Sc.Phm. 1965, M.Sc.Phm. 1967; Univ. of London Chelsea Coll., Ph.D. 1970; m. Marion d. Gordon and Lottie Burgin 23 Sept. 1967; children: Ian Douglas, Christopher Gordon, Heather Elizabeth; CHIEF, INTERNAT. CONTROL & LICENCING, DEPT. OF NAT. HEALTH & WELFARE 1980– ; Cons., Ont. Ctte. on the Healing Arts, Priv. Clin. Labs. 1967; Vice-Pres., Rsch. & Devel., Nucro-Technics Ltd. 1972–74; Rsch. Sci., Dept. of Nat. Health & Welfare 1970–72, 1974–80; mem., Ont. Coll. of Pharm.; Chem. Inst. of Can.; Pres., Kanata-Carleton Rotary Club 1982–83; Extve., Kanata Girls Hockey Assoc. 1990–93; author of sci. pubns. on human drug absorption, metabolism & distribution; recreations: coaching youth soccer, sailing, carpentry; Clubs: Home: 29 Milne Cres., Kanata, Ont. K2K 1H7; Office: 122 Bank St., Ottawa, Ont. K1A 1B9.

**HOTCHKISS, Harley Norman,** B.Sc.; geologist; b. Tillsonburg, Ont. 10 July 1927; s. Morley R. and Carrie E. (Todd) H.; e. Mich. State Univ. B.Sc. (Geol.) 1951; m. Norma Rebecca d. Gordon A. Boyd 3 Oct. 1951; children: Paul G., Brenda E., John S., J. Richard, Jeffrey A.; self-employed personal invests. oil and gas, real estate, agriculture and professional sports since 1976; Dir. Nova Corp. of Alberta; Conwest Exploration Co. Ltd.; Telus Corp.; Paragon Petroleum Corp.; Calgary Flames Hockey Club; Michigan State Univ. Found.; Vice Chrmn., Olympic Trust of Canada; Chrmn., Foothills Provincial Gen. Hosp. Bd.; Geol. Canadian Superior Oil Ltd. 1951–53; Geol. and Asst. Mgr. Oil & Gas Dept. Canadian Imperial Bank of Commerce 1953–59; Pres., Alcon Petroleums Ltd. 1959–67 and Sabre Petroleums Ltd. 1967–76; served with Canadian Merchant Marine 1944–45; Fellow, Geol. Assn. Can.; mem. Candn. Soc. Petrol. Geols.; Am. Assn. Petrol. Geols.; Candn. Inst. Mining & Metall.; Soc. Petrol. Engrs. (A.I.M.E.); Phi Kappa Phi; President's Club and Frank S. Kedzie Soc., Mich. State Univ.; recreations: sports, reading, travel, gardening; Clubs: Ranchmen's; Griffith Island; Calgary Petroleum; Home: 40 Eagle Ridge Pl. S.W., Calgary, Alta. T2V 2V8; Office: 1206 Dome Tower, Toronto-Dominion Sq., 333 – 7th Ave. S.W., Calgary, Alta. T2P 2Z1.

**HOUGEN, Rolf B.,** O.C.; executive; b. Can. 17 Dec. 1928; s. Berent and Margrethe (Blackstad) H.; e. Banff Sch. Advanced Mgmt.; m. Margaret Van Dyke 3 May 1955; children: Craig, Kelly, Erik, Greta, Karen, Maureen; PRESIDENT, HOUGEN'S LTD. 1944– ; Dir., Cominco Ltd.; Finning Ltd.; Alberta Power Co. Ltd.; Northwestel (B.C.E. Co.); Founder & Dir., (Cancom) Canadian Satellit Communications Inc.; Pres., Yukon Wholesale Co. Ltd. 1960; Northern Television Systems Ltd. 1965; Klondike Broadcasting Co. Ltd. 1969; Whitehorse Motors Ltd. Ford/Mercury 1969; Dir., Duke of Edinburgh Awards; Consul of France; Chrmn., Yukon Foundation 1981–88; mem. Yukon Order Pioneers; Candn. Parents for French; Vancouver Consular Corps.; Past Chrmn., Canadian Chamber of Commerce; Mem., Stamp Adv. Ctte., Canada Post; Businessman of the Year 1986; Honours List, Candn. Cable Assn. 1986; Yukoner Award – Tourism 1987; Officer of the Order of Canada 1987; Officer National Order of Merit (France); Commemorative Medal, 125th Anniversary of Candn. Confedn.; recreations: fishing, hunting; Home: 210 Rogers St., Whitehorse, Yukon Y1A 1X2; Office: 305 Main St., Whitehorse, Yukon Y1A 2B4.

**HOUGH, Michael,** R.C.A.; landscape architect; b. Nice, France 5 Aug. 1928; s. William and Hortense (Rocher) H.; e. Bradfield Coll. Pub. Sch. Eng. 1947; Edinburgh Coll. of Art Dipl. Arch. 1955; Univ. of Pa. Master of Landscape Arch. 1958; m. Bridget d. Richard Woodhams, Sedbergh, U.K. 24 July 1956; children: Timothy, Adrian, Fiona; FOUNDER & PARTNER, HOUGH STANSBURY & WOODLAND LTD. 1964– ; Prof. of Environment Studies, York Univ. 1970– ; Consultant to Royal Comn. for the Future of the Toronto Waterfront 1988–91; Asst. Arch., Basil Spence & Partners, Edinburgh 1955–56; Landscape Arch.; various U.S. landscape arch. practices 1958–59; Project Planning Associates Ltd. Toronto 1959–62; Planning Office Univ. of Toronto 1962–65; Assoc. Prof. of Landscape Arch. Univ. of Toronto 1963–70, Acting Head Div. Landscape Arch. 1966–67; recipient Am. Soc. Landscape Archs. Honor Award (Inst. Planning – Scarborough Coll.) 1967, Merit Award (Parks & Recreational Planning – Ont. Place) 1975, Honor Award (Design Guidelines for Forest Mang.) 1978, Honor Award (Res - City Form & Natural Process) 1988; Am. Assn. Sch. Adms. Exhns. Sch. Arch. Award (Site Devel. Elem. Schs. K-6) 1970; Am. Soc. Interior Designers Internat. Design Award (Ont. Place) 1975; Ontario Renews Award, Site Renovation Category, Min. for Municipal Affairs & Housing 1984; author 'The Urban Landscape' 1971; 'People & City Landscapes' 1987; 'Out of Place' 1990; recipient ASCA Bradford Williams award for Journalistic Excellence 1990; recipient Toronto Arts Awards for architecture and design 1991; co-author 'Oxford Companion to Gardens' 1986; 'In Celebration of Play' 1980; author 'City Form and Natural Process' 1984; co-author 'Land Conservation and Development' 1984; served with Brit. Army (Dorset Regt.) 1947–49, Malay and Singapore 1948–49; mem. Ont. Assn. Landscape Archs.; Fellow, Candn. Soc. Landscape Archs. (Pres. 1985–86); Anglican; recreations: music, painting, carpentry, gardening; Home: 29 Cornish Rd., Toronto, Ont. M4T 2E3; Office: 916 The East Mall, Suite B, Etobicoke, Ont. M9B 6K1.

**HOUGHTON, Wilfred Anthony,** F.R.I.; real estate executive; b. Toronto, Ont. 2 May 1939; s. Wilfred Tudor and Ena May (Willmot) H.; e. Trafalgar H.S.; Univ. of Toronto Forestry; Banff Sch. of Adv. Mngt. 1981; m. Elizabeth d. Maxine and Gutag Wisniewski 26 Sept. 1964; children: Todd Anthony, Jennifer Elizabeth; SR. VICE PRES. & GEN. MGR., CAPITAL MANAGEMENT SERV., ROYAL LEPAGE CAPITAL MANAGEMENT SERVICES 1992– ; Mortgage Mgr., Investment Div., Canada Life 1963–68; Mgr., Mortgage Banking, Metropolitan Trust 1968–73; Vice Pres., Mortgages, Morguard Trust Co. 1973–75; Sr. Vice Pres., Investments, Morguard Investments Ltd. 1975–92; Association Canadian Pension Management, Real Estate Institute of Canada, Past Director; Rotary Club of Toronto 1991–93 and Past Chair, Rotary Found. 1991–92; Dir. 'YES' Youth Employment Services 1993/94; recreations: sailing, skiing, golf, tennis: clubs: Alpine Ski; Home: 275 King St., Oakville, Ont. L6J 1B8; Office: 33 Yonge St., Suite 900, Toronto, Ont. M5E 1S9.

**HOULD, Claudette,** L.ès L., M.A., Ph.D.; b. Montréal, Qué. 6 Apl. 1942; d. Maurice and Yvonne (Girardeau) H.; e. Univ. de Montréal B.A. 1965, L.ès L. 1969, M.A. 1971; Ecole des Hautes Etudes en Sciences sociales, Paris Ph.D. 1990; DIR., MAISON DES ÉTUDIANT CANADIENS, PARIS 1992– ; PROF. OF ART HIST. UNIV. DU QUÉ. à MONTRÉAL 1976– , Dir. of Dept. 1979–81, 1983–84, 1984–89; Teacher 1960–71; Curator Montreal Museum Fine Arts 1975–76, Acquisition Ctte. since 1982; mem. Bd. Internat. Festival Art Films since inception 1981, initially Vice Chrmn. becoming Chrmn. 1986–89; mem. Bd. Trustees Nat. Gallery Can. 1990–93; Musée d'art contemporain de Montréal 1987–90; Musée du Québec 1984–85, Acquisition Ctte. 1989; Nat. Museums of Can. 1985–90; Trustee UQAM 1988–89; recipient Prix d'excellence, Assn. des Musées canadiens 1989; Remise de la médaille en argent du Bicentenaire de la Révolution française 1989; Prix Publication, Assn. des Musées Québécois 1990; ed. 'Iconographie et image de la Révolution française' 1990; 'L'image de la Révolution française' 1989, Traduction 'Images of the French Revolution'; co-ed. 'Code d'éthique de l'estampe originale' 1982, Traduction 'A Code of Ethics for the Original Print' 1990, Traduit en portugais 'Codigo de Etica da Estampa Original' 1990; 'Répertoire des livres d'artistes au Québec 1900–1980' 1982; 'Répertoire des livres d'artistes au Québec 1981–90' 1993; mem. Soc. d'histoire de l'art français; Am. Soc. Eighteenth Century Studies; Conseil internat. des musées; Assn. d'art des univs. canadiennes; Home: 249 Bloomfield, Outremont, Qué. H2V 3R6; Office: UQAM, C.P. 8888 succ. A, Montréal, Qué. H3C 3P8 and 31 Boul. Jourdan, 75014 Paris, France.

**HOULDEN, Hon. Lloyd William;** judge; b. Toronto, Ont. 16 Sept. 1922; s. Everett Bruce and Mary Jane (Ball) H.; e. Humbercrest Pub. Sch. and Runnymede Coll. Inst., Toronto; Victoria Coll., Univ. of Toronto, B.A. 1944; Osgoode Hall Law Sch., Toronto, 1948; m. Joyce Beryl, d. Marshall Peter Laing Wood, 30 Sept. 1950; children: Pauline Jane, Brent Marshall Wood, Robyn Leslie; JUSTICE, COURT OF APPEAL, ONT. 1974– ; read law with I.E. Houser, Toronto; called to Bar of Ont. 1948; cr. Q.C. 1962; Special Lectr. for Law Soc. of Upper Can., 1954, 1956, 1965; apptd. a Justice, Supreme Court of Ont. 1969; served with R.C.N.V.R. 1944–45; author 'Houlden & Morawetz: Bankruptcy Law of Canada'; mem., Bd. Trade Metrop. Toronto (Bankruptcy Comte.): Phi Delta Phi; Presbyterian (Elder); recreations: gardening, reading, travelling; Home: 48 Anglesey Blvd., Islington, Ont. M9A 3B5; Office: Osgoode Hall, Toronto, Ont. M5H 2N6.

**HOULE, Guy,** B.A., LL.L.; public utilities executive; b. Montreal, Que. 6 Apl. 1935; s. late Lucien and Jeanne (Morin) H.; e. Ste. Marie Coll., B.A. 1955; Univ. of Montreal, LL.L. 1958; McGill Univ. 1959; m. Celine. d. late Herve Bienvenu, Montreal, Que. 24 Dec. 1960; children: Sylvie, Marie-Josee, Christine, Jean; VICE PRES. & CORPORATE SECRETARY, BELL CANADA 1980–,

AND VICE PRES. & CORPORATE SECRETARY, BCE INC. 1983– ; Dir., Bell Canada International Inc.; Tele-Direct (Publications) Inc.; Télébec Ltée; read law with Lacoste, Lacoste, Savoie & Laniel; called to Bar of Que. 1959; private law practice Lacoste, Lacoste, Savoie & Laniel, Montreal, 1959–61; Legal Counsel to Royal Comn. of Inquiry on Educ. (Parent Comn.) 1961–66; Secy. and Legal Counsel to General Investment Corp. of Quebec, 1964–67; joined Bell Canada as Asst. Vice Pres. (Law), 1967–68, General Counsel, 1968–80; Mun. Judge St. Bruno; St. Bruno Chamber Commerce; Dir. Fondation Hôpital Notre-Dame; Opera de Montréal; mem., Can. Bar Assn.; Bar Prov. Que.; Candn. Inst. of Internat. Affairs, Montreal; Assn. Candn. Gen. Counsel; Montreal Bd. Trade; Can. Chamber of Commerce; Intl. Assoc., Am. Bar Assn.; Am. Soc. of Corp. Secretaries, Inc.; The Inst. of Chartered Secretaries and Administrators; Nat. Assoc. of Corp. Directors; Internat. Chamber of Comm. (Internat. Business Law and Practice); R. Catholic; recreations: music, travel, history, golf; Clubs: Richelieu Golf & Country; St.-Denis; Home: 1895 de la Duchesse St., St. Bruno-de-Montarville, Que. J3V 3M1; Office: 1050 Beaver Hall Hill, Rm. 1420, Montreal, Que. H2Z 1S4.

**HOULGATE, Major Brian James,** C.D., B.A.; military officer, pilot, educator; b. St. Andrew's Scotland 31 Jan. 1955; s. Frederick Victor and Stella Maureen (Cook) H.; e. Royal Military College of Canada B.A. 1978; Candn. Land Forces Command and Staff Coll. 1987; m. Catherine E. d. Donald and Ruth Carpenter 29 Dec. 1978; children: Mark Philip, Kevin Michael, Carolyn Elizabeth; STAFF OFFICER CAREERS, ROYAL MILITARY COLLEGE 1990– ; Militia, Ont. Regiment and KO Calgary Regiment, Candn. Forces 1971–74; Royal Military College 1974–78; Pilot Training 1978–79; Helicopter Pilot/Opns Offr. 427 Sqn. Petawawa 1979–83; Standards Officer, Air Ground Opns. School Gagetown 1983–85; Instr. 403 Opn. Training Sqn. Gagetown 1985–87; Flight Commander 444 Sqn. Lahr, Germany 1987–90; career focus: devel. of improved tactics & training & esp. devel. of leadership training; City of Portage la Prairie Flying Award 1979; 403 sqn. Roll of Merit 1987; Canada 125 Medal 1993; Chair, Pittsburgh Township Community Policing Ctte.; Coach/Chair, RMC Varsity Pistol Team; recreations: camping, cycling, hiking, competitive shooting; club: RMC Club of Can.; Home: 15 Bernadette Court, Kingston, Ont. K7K 6L5; Office: Kingston, Ont. K7K 5L0.

**HOUSE, (John) Douglas,** M.A., Ph.D.; educator; public servant; b. Buchans, Nfld. 23 Feb. 1944; s. Edgar George and Margaret (Butt) H.; e. Bishop Feild Coll. 1960; Bishop's Coll. 1961; Meml. Univ. of Nfld. B.A. 1964; Oxford Univ. (Rhodes Scholar) M.A. 1967; McGill Univ. Ph.D. 1972; Univ. of Aberdeen studies offshore oil ind.; m. Jean d. Charles and Marjorie Hunter 22 July 1967; children: Vanessa, Matthew, Adrian; CHRMN., ECONOMIC RECOVERY COMN., GOVT. OF NFLD. AND LABRADOR 1989– ; Chrmn. of the Bd., Enterprise Nfld. and Labrador Corp. 1989– ; Prof. of Sociol., Meml. Univ. of Nfld. 1984– , Rsch. Dir., Inst. of Social & Econ. Rsch., Queen's Coll., present univ. 1984–89, mem. Senate; Prin. Doug House Consultants; Asst. Prof. of Sociol. Univ. of Calgary 1971–75; joined present univ. 1975; Dir. Ocean Ranger Found.; Nfld. Lung Assn.; Chrmn. Nfld. Royal Comn. Employment & Unemployment 1985–86; author 'Contemporary Entrepreneurs: The Sociology of Residential Real Estate Agents' 1977; 'The Last of the Free Enterprisers: The Oilmen of Calgary' 1980; 'The Challenge of Oil: Newfoundland's Quest for Controlled Development' 1985; 'Building on Our Strengths: Report of the Royal Commission on Employment and Unemployment' (principal author) 1986; 'But Who Cares Now? The Tragedy of the Ocean Ranger' 1987; ed. 'Fish Versus Oil: Resources and Rural Development in North Atlantic Societies' 1986; Pres. Atlantic Assn. Sociols. & Anthropols. 1986–87; recreation: tennis; Clubs: Riverdale Tennis; Green Belt Tennis; Home: 31 Roche St., St. John's, Nfld. A1B 1L6; Office: St. John's, Nfld. A1C 5S7.

**HOUSTON, Arthur Hillier,** B.Sc., M.A., Ph.D.; university professor; b. Quebec City, Que. 7 May 1931; s. Ernest Francis and Ida Gladys (Hillier) H.; e. McMaster Univ. B.Sc. (Hon.) 1954; Univ. of Brit. Columbia M.A. 1956, Ph.D. 1958; m. Ida Marietta d. Walter and Anna Graber 9 Nov. 1955; PROFESSOR, BIOLOGICAL SCIENCES, BROCK UNIV. 1971– ; Asst. Prof., Dalhousie Univ. 1958–60; Asst. & Assoc. Prof., Univ. of Man. 1960–64; Assoc. Prof., Univ. of Wisconsin 1964–65; Assoc. & Full Prof., Marquette Univ. 1965–71 (Asst. Chair Biol. 1968–71); Adjunct Assoc. Prof., Marquette Med. Sch. 1968–71; Chair, Biol. Sci., Brock Univ. 1971–74; Acting Dean, Math. & Sci. 1977, '81; Dean 1984–89; Adjunct Prof. of Zool., Univ. of Toronto 1982–87; Univ. of Guelph 1982– ; Canada 125 Medal; Listed in 'American Men and Women of Science'; Mem., Am. Physiol. Assn.; Am. Zool. Soc.; Candn. Soc. of Zool. (Counsellor 1973–76; Edit. Adv. Bd. 1991– ); N.Y. Acad. of Sci.; Sigma Xi Sci. Soc.; Niagara Military Inst.; author: 'Wound Medals and Next-of-Kin Awards fo the Great War' 1993 and over 90 reviews, sci. journal & popular articles; recreations: militaria collecting, lawn bowling; clubs: Orders & Medals Soc. of Am., Orders & Medals Rsch. Soc., Glenridge Lawn Bowling; Home: 35 Adelene Cres., St. Catharines, Ont. L2T 3C6; Office: St. Catharines, Ont. L2S 3A1.

**HOUSTON, James A.,** O.C., D.Litt., D.F.A., D.H.L., LL.D., F.R.S.A.; author; designer; b. Toronto, Ont. 12 June 1921; s. James Donald and Gladys Maud (Barbour) H.; e. John Wanless Pub. Sch. and Northern Vocational High Sch. Toronto; Ont. Coll. of Art 1939 (Hon. Fellow 1981); Ecole Grande Chaumiere, Paris 1947; Unichi Hiratsuka, Tokyo printmaking 1958–59; Atelier 17, Paris, engraving, 1962; D.Litt. Carleton Univ., Ottawa 1972; D.F.A., Rhode Is. School of Design, Providence, R.I. 1979; D.H.L., Rhode Is. College, Providence, R.I. 1975; LL.D., Dalhousie Univ., Halifax 1987; m. Alice d. Prof. William and Elizabeth Watson 9 Dec. 1967; two s. John James, Samuel Douglas; MASTER DESIGNER, STEUBEN GLASS 1988– ; Devel. Inuit Art & Co-ops Candn. Arctic 1948–62; Arctic Adv. Candn. Guild of Crafts 1949–52; Civil Adm., N. Service Offr. Candn. Govt. W. Baffin Island 1953–62; Assoc. Dir. of Design, Steuben Glass 1962–88; served with Toronto Scot. Regt. 1940–45; Past Chrmn., mem. Bd. Candn. Eskimo Arts Council Ottawa 1962–79; Past Chrmn. Am. Indian Art Centre NYC; Art Adv. 'Ksan Art Council B.C.; Bd. Dir.: Alaska Indian Arts, Haines Alaska; Wye Inst. Queenstown, Md. (also art instr.); Inuit Art lectr. various univs., museums Can. and USA; May Hill Arbuthnot Honor Lectr. 1987; Gov. Anthrop. Museum Brown Univ.; mem. N. Arts Ctte. N. Am. Arctic Inst. Calgary; mem. Inuit Art Adv. Ctte., A.G.O., Toronto; Bd. Dir., Arctic Soc. of Canada, Inuit Tapirisat of Canada; past mem., Primitive Art Ctte. Metrop. Museum NYC; recipient Book of Yr. Medal (Children's Lit.) Candn. Lib. Assn. 1966, 1968, 1980; Metcalf Award Candn. Authors Assn. 1977, 1981; Max & Gretta Ebel Award CANSCAIP 1989; Candn. Author's Assn. Literary Award for Fiction 1990; Am. Indian & Eskimo Cultural Found. Award Washington, D.C. 1966; Inuit Kuavati Award Merit 1979; Nominee for Can., Hans Christian Andersen Award 1987, 1991; Citation of Merit Award, Royal Candn. Acad. of Arts; shared 26 documentary film awards; author 'Eskimo Prints' 1967; 'The White Dawn' novel 1971, screenplay (Paramount film) 1973; 'Ojibwa Summer ' 1972; 'Ghost Fox' novel 1977; 'Spirit Wrestler' novel 1980; 'Eagle Song' novel 1983; 'White-out' (novel and screenplay) 1988; 'Running West' (novel) 1989; 15 children's books pub. 1965–92; co-author 'Sculpture Inuit' 1972; ed. 'Lyon's Private Journal' 1974; Profile: 'The Man,' 'The New Yorker,' 1988; mem. Producers Guild Am.; Writers' Union of Can.; Steuben Glass (NYC) Retrospective 1987, 1991; One-Man Show, Century Assn. (NYC) 1991; Anglican; recreations: fishing, sketching; Clubs: Century Assn. (NYC); Explorers (NYC); Home: 24 Main St., Stonington, Conn. 06378 (winter); P.O. Box 43, Tlell, Queen Charlotte Islands, B.C. V0T 1Y0 (summer); Office: 717 Fifth Ave., New York, N.Y. 10022 USA.

**HOUSTON, Paul A.;** business executive; PRESIDENT AND CHIEF EXECUTIVE OFFICER, BLACK'S, BLACK PHOTO CORP.; Office: 371 Gough Rd., Markham, Ont. L3R 4B6.

**HOW, Douglas George,** B.A.; author; b. Winnipeg, Man. 5 Feb. 1919; s. George Herbert and Althea (Dobson) H., e. Dorchester (N.B.) High Sch. (Grad. 1936); Mount Allison Univ., B.A. 1971; children: Patricia, Susan, Dwight; joined Moncton, N.B. 'Daily Times' as a Reporter, 1937; Canadian Press, Halifax Bureau 1940–41; after army service (Lieut., Cape Breton Highlanders) 1941–43 became War Corr., edited CP News, then went to Italy; with Candn. Press in Parlty. Press Gallery, Ottawa, 1945–53; free-lanced in N.S. 1953–55; Extve. Asst. to Hon. Robert Winters, Min. of Public Works, Ottawa, 1955–57; with 'Time' mag. in Ottawa, Toronto and N.Y., 1957–59; Mang. Ed. in Can., The Reader's Digest 1959–69; Dir. of Extension, Mount Allison University, 1973–76; author: 'The 8th Hussars' (a regimental hist.); 'Canada's Mystery Man of High Finance' (biog. of financier Izaak Walton Killam); 'Night of the Caribou' (the story of a wartime sinking); 'Blow Up the Trumpet in the New Moon' 1993; co-author: 'K.C.' (a biography of K.C. Irving) 1993; editor: 'The Canadians at War, 1939–45,' 1969; Anglican; recreations: reading, golf; Address: St. Andrews, N.B. E0G 2X0.

**HOWARD, Brigadier General Barry Allen,** CD, KLJ, B.A.Sc., P.Eng.; business and military executive; b. Toronto, Ont., 25 Oct. 1928; s. Awrey Leslie and Rosamond Bernice (McHenry) H. (both deceased); e. Univ. of Toronto Sch. 1947; Royal Rds. Military Coll., Comn. RCAF pilot 1949; Univ. of Toronto, B.A.Sc. 1952; m. Colleen Diana d. the late George and the late Margaret Henry 1950; children: Barry Jr., Michael, Lynn (Britton), Gregory; CHRMN., WHEEL & RIM CO. OF CANADA LTD. 1967– ; Pilot and undergrad. student, RCAF 1947–52; Commdr., various posts, RCAF Reserve 1952–75; various posts, Sun Oil Co., Canada Foundries & Forgings Ltd., Litton Industries 1952–67; Pres., Heavy Duty Distrib. Counc. 1984–85; Candn. Dir., Nat. Wheel & Rim Assn. 1978–81; Dir., Candn. Paper Box Mfrs. Assn. 1973–75; Mem., Assn. of Profl. Engrs. 1952– ; Hon. Aide de Camp to Gov. Gen. 1967–70; admitted Military and Hospitaller Order of St. Lazarus in grade of Knight 1975; Found. Vice-Pres., Candn. Inst. of Strategic Studies 1975–81; Nat. Pres., RCAF Assn. 1979–81; Chrmn., Conf. of Defence Assns. 1971; Chrmn., Candn. Corps of Commissionaires (Toronto & Region) 1982–84, Life Gov. 1993; Pres., Royal Military Coll. Club of Can. 1984–85; mem., Adv. Bd., Candn. Military Colleges 1990– ; recreations: flying, golf; Clubs: Granite, Royal Candn. Military Inst.; Rosedale Golf; Office: 32 Atomic Ave., Toronto, Ont. M8Z 5L3.

**HOWARD, Charles John,** B.A., C.A.; financial executive; b. Sherbrooke, Que. 22 May 1942; s. Douglas Stevens and Euphemia Morrison (Turner) H.; e. Bishops Coll. Sch. 1955; Trinity Coll. Sch. Port Hope 1960; Univ. of W. Ont. B.A. 1965; C.A. 1968; m. Diana d. Frank and Marion Baillie 13 June 1964; children: Baillie, Susan, Jennifer, Douglas; PRES., CHIEF EXEC. OFFR. AND DIR. AUSNORAM HOLDINGS LTD. 1989– ; Dir., Kingswood Exploration Ltd.; Coolawin Resources Ltd., Australia; former Dir. Airship Industries Ltd., UK; Charterhall Oil Ltd., UK; Trustee, Hugh MacMillan Centre; Past mem. Pension Comn. Ont.; Past Dir. Women's Coll. Hosp. Found.; Past Chrmn.: Invest. Dealers Assn.; Upper Can. Chapter Young Pres. Orgn.; recreations: golf, hunting, fishing, skiing; Clubs: Toronto Golf; Caledon Ski; Caledon Trout; Bray Island Plantation (S.C.); Oakville Golf (Past Pres.); Home: 1122 Lakeshore Hwy. W., Oakville, Ont. L6L 1G1.

**HOWARD, Christopher Eugene,** B.Mus.; composer; b. Ottawa, Ont. 25 Aug. 1967; s. Harold Eugene and Jessie Dianne (Morrell) H.; e. Dartmouth (N.S.) High Sch. 1985; Mount Allison Univ.; McGill Univ. B.Mus. 1989, M.Mus. (Dean's Honour List) 1993; m. Anne d. Joseph and Kathleen Cronin 13 May 1989; children: Devon Christopher, Katalin Grayce; Student-Composer-in-Residence, McGill Univ. 1987– ; DMA, Univ. of B.C. 1992– ; composer numerous works for orch., orch. with choir, choir, chamber ensemble, solo piano, tape/computer, voice with piano since 1985 incl. 'Lakelife Reflections' (broadcast 1985), 'Annapolis Sketches' (1st orch. performance 1985 Chebucto Orch. Halifax); other maj. performances incl. P.E.I. Symphony 1986, 1987, Symphony N.S. 1988 ('Mittenthal Variations'), McGill Chamber Winds 1988, Winnipeg Symphony Orch. 1989, performances S.Am. 1989; 'Places Apart' Juilliard Sch. 1991; 'Mittenthal Variations' Cambridge Univ. 1991; 'Stigmata' McGill Alumni Concert 1993; 'Barnet's Cove' Symphony Nova Scotia 1992; 'Prelude, Chorale and Fantasy' McGill Symphony Orch. 1992; lectr. undergrad. theory classes McGill; lectr. in theory & orchestration at UBC; Asst. Conductor McGill Contemporary Orch. 1989–90; work in film and television since 1990; MIDI consultant for Baldwin Piano and Organ Co., Cincinatti; Pre-concert lectr., Vancouver Symphony Orch. 1994– ; mem. Pro Can.; recipient CFRMTA Nat. First Prize 1985, 1986; 3 orch. comns. 1985, 1986, 1992; Brock Award 1986; BMI Award Student Composers 1989; Cinq Saisons Award 1987; Sir William Peterson Award 1989; SMCQ Award 1989; SOCAN Award 1989, 1991; Hons. in Composition with Distinction McGill 1989; Canada Council Grant 1992; Address: 116 - 5750 E. Hastings St., Burnaby, B.C. V5B 1R6.

**HOWARD, Helen Barbara,** R.C.A.; artist; b. Long Branch, Ont. 10 March 1926; d. Thomas Edmund and Helen Margaret (MacIntosh) H.; e. elem. schs. Toronto, Thunder Bay, Chatham; Chatham Coll. Inst.; W. Tech. & Comm. Sch. Toronto; Ont. Coll. of Art A.O.C.A. 1951 (Silver Medal for Drawing & Painting); m. Richard Daley Outram 13 Apr. 1957; co-founder and proprieter with husband The Gauntlet Press 1960– ; solo exhns. incl. Picture Loan Soc. Toronto 1957, 1958, 1960, 1965; Towne Cinema, Internat. Cinema Toronto 1962; Wells Gallery 1966; Fleet Gallery Winnipeg 1966; Victoria Coll. Toronto 1966; Sisler Gallery Toronto 1974,

1976; Prince Arthur Galleries Toronto 1980; Wells Gallery (Ottawa) 1982; Yaneff Gall. Toronto 1983; Wells Gall. Ottawa 1984; Massey Coll., Toronto 1984; Latcham Gallery Stouffville 1985; O'Keefe Centre, Toronto 1986; National Library of Canada 1986; University Coll., Toronto 1987; Georgetown Cultural Ctr. 1988; The Arts & Letters Club of Toronto 1993; rep. in group exhns. Art Gallery of Ont. 1958, 1960, 1961 (Toronto Collects), 1976 (Drawings & Sculpture); Nat. Gallery of Can. (Candn. Watercolours, Drawings & Prints) 1966 and other exhns.; rep. numerous pub., private and corporate colls. Can., Eng. and USA incl. Nat. Gallery of Can.; Art Gallery of Ont.; Nat. Lib. Can.; Brit. Museum; Bodleian Lib. Oxford; Am. Lib. Cong.; Haughton Library, Harvard Univ.; Univ. of Toronto Rare Books Coll.; books designed and/or illustrated: 'Creatures' 1972; 'Seer' 1973; 'Thresholds'1973; 'Locus' 1974; 'Turns and Other Poems' 1975; 'Arbor' 1976; 'The Promise of Light' 1980; 'Selected Poems' 1984; 'Man In Love' 1985, 'Hiram and Jenny' 1988, all by Richard Outram; 'The Bass Saxophone' by Josef Skvorecky 1977; 'Whale Sound' 1977; 'The Music is in the Sadness' 1988 by James Cameron; rep. in various bibliogs.; mem. Extve. Council Royal Candn. Acad. Arts 1980–82; Hon. Artist Life Mem., Art Gall. of Ont. 1988; recreations: music, gardening, bookbinding; Club: The Arts and Letters; Addresses: c/o Kathryn Minard, Contemporary Fine Arts Services, Toronto, Ont. and 226 Roslin Ave., Toronto, Ont. M4N 1Z6.

**HOWARD, John Arnold,** B.Sc., P.Eng.; executive; b. Calgary, Alta. 21 Jan. 1947; s. Harold J. and Ellen (Miquelon) H.; e. Univ. of Alta. B.Sc. Chem. Engr. 1968; children: David, Nicholas; PRESIDENT AND CHIEF EXEC. OFFR., SEAGULL ENERGY CANADA LTD. 1987– ; Prodn. and Reservoir Engr. Banff Oil Ltd. 1968–70; Reservoir Engr. Ashland Oil Can. Ltd. 1970–73; Engr. Coordr. Brascan Resrouces Ltd. 1973–76; Vice-Pres. Prodn. Marline Oil Corp. 1976–81; Pres. & C.E.O. Aberford Resources Ltd. 1981–87; Past Chrmn. Independent Petroleum Assn. of Can.; mem. Candn. Inst. of Mining and Metallurgy; Assn. of Profl. Engrs., Geologists and Geophysicists of Alta.; Soc. of Petroleum Engrs. of AIME; recreations: golf, skiing, fitness; Clubs: Calgary Petroleum; Calgary Golf and Country; Ranchmen's; Glencoe; Home: 918A Royal Ave. S.W., Calgary, Alta. T2T 0L5; Office: Box 2870, Calgary, Alta. T2P 2M7.

**HOWARD, John Francis,** Q.C., B.Com.; lawyer; b. Colombia, S.A. 8 Dec. 1924; s. Edward Francis and Susan McIntyre (Cowan) H.; e. Forest Hill Village Pub. and High Schs. Toronto 1942; Royal Candn. Naval Coll. 1942–44; Univ. of Toronto B.Com. 1949; Osgoode Hall Law Sch. 1953; m. Nancy Madeline Claire d. late F.H.M. Jones 16 June 1952; children: Gillian L., Peter F.C., Ian C., Margot C.; PARTNER, BLAKE, CASSELS & GRAYDON 1958– ; Vice Chrmn. Hawker Siddely Canada Inc.; called to Bar of Ont. 1953, Sask. 1971, Alta. 1976; cr. Q.C. 1965; served with RCNVR 1944–46, rank Lt.; Trustee, Ont. Jockey Club; mem. Jockey Club of Can.; Advocates' Soc.; Am. Coll. of Trial Lawyers; recreations: riding, fishing; Club: Toronto; Home: 10320 Pine Valley Dr., R.R.2, Woodbridge, Ont. L4L 1A6; Office: P.O. Box 25, Commerce Court West, Toronto, Ont. M5L 1A9.

**HOWARD, Kenneth S.,** Q.C., B.A.; b. Montreal, Que. 24 May 1924; s. Wilbert Harvard, Q.C. and Annie Olive Partridge (Simpson) H.; e. Bishop's Coll. Sch., Lennoxville, Que., 1937–41; McGill Univ., B.A. 1946, Law 1949; m. Marie Elizabeth, d. late Knud Iversen, 25 Oct. 1950; children: Todd, Erika, Brett: COUNSEL, OGILVY RENAULT; Dir., United Corporations Ltd.; Robert Mitchell Inc.; Can. Starch Co. Inc.; Royal Trust Corp. of Canada; read law with Montgomery, McMichael, Common and Howard; called to the Bar of Quebec, 1949; cr. Q.C. 1964; served as Pilot Offr. with RCAF and as Sub-Lt. with R.N. Fleet Air Arm during World War II; Unitarian; recreations: boating, golf, curling; Clubs: Mount Bruno Country; Royal Montreal Curling; University Montl.; Home: 1289 Caledonia Rd., Town of Mount Royal, Que. H3R 2V7; Office: 1981 McGill College Ave., Montreal, Que. H3A 3C1.

**HOWARD, Kenneth William Frank,** M.Sc., Ph.D., P.Hg.; scientist; educator; b. London, Eng. 9 Dec. 1952; s. William Henry and Patricia Ellen (Field) H.; e. Bromley Grammar Sch. UK 1971; Univ. of Exeter B.Sc. 1974; Univ. of Birmingham M.Sc. 1975, Ph.D. 1979; m. Sally d. Arthur and Jean Tucker 8 May 1976 (div. 1987); one d. Helen Patricia; DIR. GROUNDWATER RSCH. GROUP, SCARBOROUGH CAMPUS, UNIV. OF TORONTO 1986– , Assoc. Prof. of Phys. Sci's 1988– (cross appt. Dept. Geol. 1981– , Grad. Sch. 1983– , Inst. Environmental Studies 1986– ), Asst. Prof. 1981–88; Rsch. Assoc. Geol. Sci's Univ. of Birmingham 1975–78 and Civil Eng. 1978–80, Rsch. Fellow Civil Eng. 1980–81; Cons. Robertson Research Internat. UK 1980–81; MacLaren Plansearch, Toronto 1984– ; Dir. and Treas. Utilization Fossil Seas of Sahel 1987– ; author or co-author over 40 rsch. articles sci. jours. and conf. proceedings; Corporate mem. Instn. Geols.; mem. Geol. Soc. Am.; Nat. Well Water Assn.; Candn. Assn. Water Pollution Rsch. & Control; Internat. Assn. Water Pollution Rsch. & Control; Am. Inst. Hydrol. (Sec. Ont. Chapter 1987); Internat. Assn. Hydrogeols.; recipient numerous maj. rsch. awards since 1982; Home: 120 Ling Rd., Scarborough, Ont. M1E 4V9; Office: Dept. of Earth and Environmental Science, Scarborough, Ont. M1C 1A4.

**HOWARD, Lloyd H.,** B.A., M.A., Ph.D.; university professor; b. Los Angeles, Calif. 8 Dec. 1951; s. Jerry and Florence (Glazer) H.; e. Univ. of B.C. B.A. 1973; Johns Hopkins Univ. M.A. 1975, Ph.D. 1976; CHAIR, DEPT. OF HISPANIC AND ITALIAN STUDIES, UNIV. OF VICTORIA 1989– ; Instructor, State Univ. of N.Y., Oswego 1976–77; Asst. Prof. (without tenure) 1977–82; (with tenure) 1982–90; Assoc. Prof. 1990–93; Gilman Fellowship; SSHRCC general grants; discovered some 30 formulas of repetition employed by Dante in 'Divine Comedy'; Edit. Bd. Mem., 'Can. J. of Italian Studies'; Adv. Bd. Mem., Candn. Soc. of Italian Studies; author of numerous refereed articles; recreations: gardening; clubs: Horticultural Soc. of Victoria; Hallmark Soc. of Victoria; Home: 686 Mountjoy Ave., Victoria, B.C. V8S 4K9; Office: P.O. Box 3045, Victoria, B.C. V8W 3P4.

**HOWARD, Thomas Palmer,** Q.C., B.A., B.C.L.; b. Montreal, Que. 19 Aug. 1910; s. Thomas Palmer and E. Daisy (Taylor) H.; e. Selwyn House Sch. and Lower Can. Coll., Montreal, Que.; McGill Univ., B.A. 1931, B.C.L. 1934; m. Katharine, d. Charles Chipman Pineo, 22 Dec. 1934; children: Mrs. Anne Howard Osterholm, Thomas P. (C.A.); read law with Lafleur, MacDougall, Macfarlane & Barclay; called to Bar of Que. 1934; cr. Q.C. 1960; mem. Law Soc. of Alta. 1969; Formerly Sr. Partner, Howard, McDougall, and Graham & its predecessors & latterly counsel to McMaster, Meighen; now retired; served in 2nd World War, R.C.A.F. 1942–46; rank Squadron Leader, Capacity Senior Judicial Officer; Life Governor (Past President Bd. Govs. and Past Chrmn. Bd. Trustees) Martlet Foundation; Life Gov., Montreal Gen. Hosp.; mem. R.C.A.F Benevolent Fund (Past Chrmn. and Hon. Solr. Montreal Br.); Life Gov. and mem. Bd. of Trustees, Pan Canada Foundation; Anglican; Clubs: University; St. James's; Montreal; Montreal Badminton & Squash; Royal Bermuda Yacht; Home: Apt. 804, 4300 de Maisonneuve West, Westmount, Que. H3Z 3C7.

**HOWARD, William Arnold,** C.M.M., C.M., C.D., Q.C.; b. Calgary, Alta. 19 Oct. 1918; s. late Horace Arnold and Elizabeth (Johnson) H.; e. Earl Grey Pub. Sch., King Edward High and W. Can. High Schs. Calgary 1936; Univ. of Alta. B.A., LL.B. 1941; m. Margaret, Elizabeth d. late George A. Hannah 8 Apr. 1950; children: Mary Louise, John Arnold, Barbara Joanne; COUNSEL, HOWARD, MACKIE; Dir., Calgary Military Museum Society; Calgary Police Museum Soc.; read law with W.H. McLaws, Q.C.; called to Bar of Alta. 1942; cr. Q.C. 1955; joined McLaws, Cairns & McLaws, Calgary 1946; Cairns & Howard 1947–51; Mahaffy & Howard 1951–57; present firm since 1957; joined Cdn. Army 1942 as Lt. serving overseas, C.O. King's Own Calgary Regt. rank Lt. Col. 1955–57, Brig. 22nd Militia Group, Militia Advisor (W. Can.) to Depy. Chief (Reserves) CFHQ 1966, Maj. Gen. Reserves, Advisor on Reserves to Chief of Defence Staff 1970–73, Col. Commandant Royal Candn. Army Cadets 1973–78, and Hon. Col. King's Own Calgary Regt. 1973–87; Col. Commandant, Armour Br., Candn. Forces 1987–90; Chrmn. Calgary Police Comm. 1976–82; Gov., Cdn. Corps of Commissionaires (National); mem. Calgary Bar Assn. (Past Pres.); Candn. Bar Assn.; Law Soc. Alta.; United Church; recreation: golf; Clubs: Ranchmen's; Calgary Golf & Country; Glencoe; Royal Cdn. Mil. Inst.; Royal Alta. United Services Inst.; Home: #4, 68 Baycrest Place S.W., Calgary, Alta. T2V 0K6; Office: 1000 Canterra Tower, 400 – 3 Ave. S.W., Calgary, Alta. T2P 4H2.

**HOWARD, William James,** B.A., M.A., Ph.D.; university professor; b. Prince George, B.C. 21 May 1945; s. William James and Dorothy (Bowering) H.; e. Prince George Sr. Secondary 1963; Univ. of B.C. B.A. 1967, M.A. 1969; Univ. of Leeds Ph.D. 1975; m. Heather d. Douglas and Eileen Dewar 20 Dec. 1969; children: William James Sean, Ronald Douglas; PROFESSOR OF ENGLISH, UNIV. OF REGINA 1985– ; Asst. Prof. of English, Univ. of Regina 1975–80; Assoc. Prof. of English 1980–85; Asst. to the Dean of Graduate Studies and Research 1979–82; Head, Dept. of English 1984–87, 1990–91; Editor 'Wascana Review' 1976–82; Assoc. Ed. 'Prairie Forum' 1977–81; Mem., Bd. of Gov., Univ. of Regina 1989– ; Mem., Wordsworth/Coleridge Assn.; The John Clare Soc.; The Byron Soc.; ACUTE; author: 'John Clare' 1981 and articles on William Wordsworth, John Clare and other writers of the Romantic Period; recreations: golf, curling, gardening; clubs: Emerald Park Golf; Home: 115 Quincy Dr., Regina, Sask. S4S 6L9; Office: Regina, Sask. S4S 0A2.

**HOWARD-LOCK, Helen Elaine,** B.Sc., Ph.D., F.C.I.C.; research scientist; educator; b. Hamilton, Ont. 5 Jan. 1938; d. John Wilfred and Leila St. Claire (Cummins) Howard; e. Westdale Secondary Sch. Hamilton; McMaster Univ. B.Sc. 1959, Ph.D. 1968; m. Colin James Lyne s. Lyne and Amy Hilda Irene Lock 21 May 1960; children: Nicola Elaine Simmons, Philippa Edlyne; PROF., SCI. LABORATORIES FOR INORGANIC MEDICINE, McMASTER UNIV. 1981– , McLaughlin Career Sci. in Gerontol. 1987, Assoc. Prof. of Pathol. 1987–88, Asst. Prof. of Eng. Phys. 1970–78; NRC Post-doctorate Fellow Univ. of Toronto 1968–70; Cons. Environment Can. 1973–74; Vice Pres. (Rsch.) and Treas. Howard Concrete & Materials Ltd. 1977–82; Pres., Howard Lock Associates Inc. 1988– ; Pub. Sch. Trustee Halton Bd. Edn. 1973–81; Dir. Burlington Social Planning Council 1974–78; Burlington Family Y, Capital Fundraiser 1979–80; author or co-author over 70 publs. sci. jours.; mem. Royal Bot. Gdns.; Candn. Power & Sail Sqdns.; C.I.C.; recreations: sailing, swimming; Clubs: Royal Hamilton Yacht; University Women's; Home: 138 Northshore Blvd. E., Burlington, Ont. L7T 1W4; Office: Dept. of Chem., McMaster Univ. ABB-266A, Hamilton, Ont. L8S 4M1.

**HOWARTH, Thomas,** Ph.D., FRIBA, FRAIC, Hon. Doc. (Stirling), Hon. F.A.I.A., Hon. OAA, Hon. OALA; university professor (emeritus), architect, author; b. Wesham, England 1 May 1914; s. Lawrence and Agnes (Cornall) H.; e. Kirkham Grammar School; Univ. of Manchester 1934–39; Univ. of Glasgow 1941–46, Ph.D. 1949; m. Edna d. Thomas Rainford and Sarah Marland 6 July 1940; separated 1971; children: John Rainford, Katharine Anne; PROFESSOR EMERITUS, SCHOOL OF ARCHITECTURE AND LANDSCAPE ARCHITECTURE, UNIV. OF TORONTO 1982– ; Organist & Piano Teacher 1928–34; Lectr., Glasgow Sch. of Arch. & night classes Glasgow Sch. of Art 1939–46; Lectr., then Sr. Lectr. in Arch., Univ. of Manchester 1946–58; Dir., Sch. of Arch., Univ. of Toronto 1958–67; Dean, Faculty of Arch., Urban & Reg. Planning & Landscape Arch. 1967–74; Campus Planner, Glendon Coll. & Advr. to Bd., York Univ. 1960–87; Campus Planner, Laurentian Univ. 1961– ; Nat. Capital Comn. 1968–80 (Commissioner two years, Mem. Adv. Ctte. on Design, Chair 2 years); Mem., Toronto Hist. Bd. 1978–86; Candn. Rep. (RAIC), Commonwealth Assn. of Architects 1963–89; Mem., CAA Council & Bd. of Arch. Edn. & latterly Reg. Rep. of the Americas (Can. & the Caribbean); visited many countries of the Commonwealth; prepared proposals for a Sch. of Arch. for Univ. of West Indies 1967 and a Ctr. for Edn. & Tech. Advancement at Singapore 1969; many lectures world wide; designed several exhibitions; Alfred Bossom Rsch. Fellowship of RIBA London 1952; 1st non-Am. to win Annual Book Award, Soc. of Arch. Hist. (U.S.) and the Alice Davis Hitchcock Medal 1953; Killam Sr. Rsch. Scholar, Univ. of Calgary 1978; Civic Award & Medal for Serv. to Community, City of Toronto 1983; Mem., Candn. Soc. of the Decorative Arts (Founder Mem. & Past Pres.); St. George's Soc.; R.O.M.; Art Gall. of Ont.; Twenty-five Year Club, U. of T.; Charles Rennie Mackintosh Soc. Glasgow; author: 'Charles Rennie Mackintosh and the Modern Movement' 1952, '77, '90, 'RAIC College of Fellows' 1962, '77; 'Two Cultures Two Cities' 1976 (proceedings); contributor: 'A History of Architecture on the Comparative System' (by Banister Fletcher) 1961, 'Chambers' Encyclopaedia,' 'Encyclopaedia Britannia,' 'Macmillan's Enc. of Arch.,' 'Who's Who in America 1974–75,' 'Glasgow Girls' 1990 and many other papers & articles; recreations: collecting, music, theatre, visual arts, travel; clubs: Royal Candn. Yacht; Arts & Letters; Home: 131 Bloor St. W., Apt. 1001, Toronto, Ont. M5S 1R1

**HOWE, Bruce Iver;** executive; b. Dryden, Ont. 19 May 1936; s. Norman I. and Laura A. (Locking) H.; e. Queen's Univ. Chem. Engn. 1958; Harvard Univ. Mgmt. Devel. 1961; LL.D. (Hon.) Lakehead Univ. 1983; m. Elsie Evelyn Ann Ferguson 25 Aug. 1962; children: Karen, Norman, Kristina; PRESIDENT & C.E.O., ATOMIC ENERGY OF CANADA LTD. 1993– ; Acting Pres. & C.E.O., Atomic Energy of Canada Ltd.

1992–93; Past Dir., Advanced Systems Inst., Vancouver; Nat. Museum of Science & Technology; Bank of Montreal; B.C. Place; Conference Bd. of Can.; Canada Harbour Place Corp.; Candn. Co-Chrmn., Canada-Korea Bus. Counc.; joined MacMillan Bloedel 1963, Group Vice Pres., Pulp & Paper 1971, Sr. Vice Pres. Operations 1977–79; Pres., C.O.O. and Dir., 1979–80; Chrmn., C.E.O. & Dir., British Columbia Resources Investment Corp. 1980–86; Deputy Min., Energy, Mines & Resources 1988–93; Deputy Min., Western Economic Diversification 1993; Chrmn. & C.E.O., Energy Supplies Allocation Bd. (ESAB) 1989–93; Trustee, Queen's Univ. 1983–91; Adv. Counc., Faculty of Commerce, Univ. of B.C. 1981–86; mem. Internat. Trade Adv. Ctte., Fed. Govt. 1985–86; Comnr. Gen., Canada Pavilion, Expo 1986; Secy. to Min. of State for Science & Technology and Chief Science Advisor to Govt. 1986–88; Secy., Prime Minister's Counc. on Science & Technology 1987–88; Bd. of Dirs., Petro-Canada International 1989–92; Chrmn., Petroleum Monitoring Agency 1992–93; author various articles pulp and paper prof. mags.; mem. City & Guilds; London Inst. (Insignia Award); Assn. Prof. Engrs. Prov. B.C.; recreations: diving; Clubs: Vancouver; Vancouver Lawn Tennis; Past Pres., Canadian Club of Vancouver.; Home: 111 Echo Dr., Townhouse 4, Ottawa, Ont. K1S 5K8; Office: 18th Flr., 344 Slater St., Ottawa, Ont. K1A 0S4.

**HOWE, Gordon,** O.C. (1971); hockey player; b. Saskatoon, Sask. 31 March 1928; s. Albert Clarence and Katherine (Schultz) H.; e. Westmount and King George Schs., Saskatoon, Sask. 1944; m. Colleen Janet, d. Valerian Mark, Joffa, 15 April 1953; children: Marty Gordon, Mark Steven, Cathleen Jill, Murray Albert; Pres., Gordon Howe Enterprises; Breeder Reg'd. Polled Hereford & Simmental cattle, Jackson, Mich.; commenced prof. hockey for Galt (Ont.) 1944–45, and Omaha (Neb.) 1945–46; joined Detroit Hockey Club 1946 and with that Organ. until retirement 1971 when joined World Hockey Assn. (Houston Oilers and later Hartford Whalers); scored 1000 NHL career goal, 1979–80; Awards incl., Hart Memorial Trophy; Art Ross Trophy; Lester Patrick Trophy; mem. 1st All Star Team 12 times and 2nd All Star Team 9 times; named Candn. Athlete of the Yr. 1963; mem. Hockey Hall of Fame; Sports Hall of Fame; co-author of 'Hockey, Here's Howe' 1963; co-author, 'Gordie Howe, No. 9'; also numerous articles for sports publs.; mem. Hockey Hall of Fame; Protestant; recreations: golf, fishing; Club: Plum Hollow Golf.

**HOWE, Robert D.,** LL.B.; labour relations adjudicator; b. Windsor, Ont. 9 May 1948; s. Clarence Bennett and Helen Grace (Rogers) H.; e. Univ. of Windsor LL.B. 1972 (Gold Medallist); m. Lynda G. Hutchison d. Robert W. and Dorothy M. H. 23 June 1973; VICE-CHAIR, ONT. LABOUR RELATIONS BD. 1980– , Acting Chair May-Sept. 1984; Prof. of Law Univ. of Windsor 1972–77, Special Lectr. in Labour Law and Labour Arbitration 1977–80; law practice as Assoc. Gignac, Sutts, Windsor 1977–80; called to Bar of Ont. 1974; mem. Candn. Bar Assn.; Candn. Civil Liberties Assn.; United Church of Can.; Office: 400 University Ave., 4th Floor, Toronto, Ont. M7A 1V4.

**HOWELL, Alfred David,** C.M.A., R.P.A.; trust company executive; b. Berwick, N.S. 10 Sept. 1947; s. Edwin Alfred and Marjorie Joyce (Frederick) H.; e. Herman's Coll. H.S. 1965; Soc. of Mngt. Accts. C.M.A. 1973; Coll. of Registered Public Appraisers R.P.A. 1986; m. Helen d. Marjorie and Henry Prosper 23 Apr. 1966; children: Vincent, Cynthia; EXTVE. VICE-PRES., EVANGELINE SAVINGS & MORTGAGE; C.A. 1965–66; Accountant, John Penny & Son Ltd. 1966–67; joined present firm 1967 and worked in various posts; Dir., Circuit Investment Ltd.; Pres., Hampshire Mngt. Ltd.; Mem., Rotary Club of Windsor (Past Pres.); Windsor Tree Comn. (Past. Chrmn.); recreations: golf, running, fishing; clubs: Avon Valley Golf & Country; Home: R.R. #1, Windsor, N.S. B0N 2T0; Office: P.O. Box 638, Windsor, N.S. B0N 2T0.

**HOWELL, James Mort,** M.B., B.S., D.C.H., D.P.H., F.R.C.P.(C), F.F.P.H.M.; physician; b. Farnworth, England 7 Dec. 1934; s. Norman Lloyd and Marjorie (Mort) H.; e. Manchester Grammar Sch.; St. Mary's Hosp. Med. Sch., Univ. of London, M.B., B.S. 1957; m. Jacqueline d. William and Myra Harrington 4 July 1959; children: David, Andrew, Jill; MEDICAL OFFICER OF HEALTH, EDMONTON BD. OF HEALTH 1975– ; Med. Offr. of Health, Sturgeon Health Unit 1967–75; Clin. Prof., Univ. of Alta.; Assoc. Prof., Univ. of Calgary; editor/co-author: 'Think Prevention' 1987; author of var. papers; Home: 23 Kingswood Dr., St. Albert, Alta. T8N 5M8; Office: Ste. 500, 10216–124 St., Edmonton, Alta. T5N 4A3.

**HOWETT, Jack Reginald;** business executive; b. Wimbledon, England 20 Sept. 1921; s. late Frank and Gertrude Georgina (Wright) H.; e. Marlborough Coll. 1935–39; Cambridge Univ., Spec. Engr. Offrs. Course 1940–41; m. Betty d. late Norman and Gladys Lye 11 Aug. 1951; children: David Michael, Peter Charles; PRES., J.R. HOWETT CONSULTING INC.; Captain, Royal Engrs. 1939–46; Sales Rep., Jack Olding & Co. Ltd., U.K. 1947; S.E. Asia 1952; Overseas Serv. Mgr., Vickers-Armstrongs Tractors Ltd. 1955; Mgr. 1956; Ont. Mgr., Candn. Vickers Ltd. 1962; Div. Sales Mgr. 1967; Gen. Sales Mgr. 1971; Vice-Pres., Indus. Sales 1976; Dir., Vickers Can. Inc. 1978; Vice-Pres., Indus. Sales, Versatile Vickers Inc. 1981; Govt. Affairs 1984; Vice-Pres., Govt. Affairs & Mktg., Versatile Corp. 1986–87; Dir., Orgn. of CANDU Industries; recreations: golf, sailing; Club: Irish Hills Golf and Country; Home and Office: 10 - 889 Bermuda Ave., Ottawa, Ont. K1K 0V8.

**HOWIE, Kenneth Earle,** B.A., LL.B.; lawyer; b. Toronto, Ont. 16 Sept. 1925; s. James Augustus and Lily Rae (Timmins) H.; e. Univ. of Toronto B.A. (Hons.) 1948; Osgoode Hall Law Sch. LL.B. 1951; m. Ruth S. d. Percy and Florence Hurley 16 June 1950; d. Carol Lynne, Heather, James R., Robert; MANAGING PARTNER, THOMSON, ROGERS, BARRISTERS & SOLICITORS; admitted to Law Soc. of U.C. 1951; Past Dean, Internat. Acad. of Trial Lawyers; Past Pres., Co. of York Law Assn.; Medico-Legal Soc. of Toronto; The Advocates' Soc.; Hon. Life Mem., Ont. Insur. Adjusters Assn.; Bencher, Law Soc. of U.C. 1983; Fellow, Am. College of Trial Lawyers 1985; Lectr., Bar Admission Course, Law Soc.of U.C.; Trial Demonstrator, Osgoode Hall Law Sch.; Past Chair, Certification Bd., Law Soc. of U.C.; Co-Chair, Joint Ctte. on Court Reform in Ont.; Chair, Finance & Admin., Law Soc. of U.C.; specialist in civil litigation; practice is largely in area of personal injury litigation, incl. med. malpractice; recreation: golfing; clubs: Mississauga Golf & Country; University Club of Toronto; Home: 1530 Pinetree Cres., Mississauga, Ont. L5G 2S8; Office: 390 Bay St., Ste. 3100, Toronto, Ont. M5H 1W2.

**HOWISON, Alan G.;** executive; b. London, Eng. 9 June 1932; s. James Condie and Molly Beatrice H.; e. Loretto Sch., Musselburgh, Scot. 1950; m. Nancy Louise d. C. Gordon Smith, Winnipeg, Man. 1 Oct. 1955; children: Tricia, Jamie, Bruce; United Canadian Shares Ltd.; joined Oldfield Kirby & Gardner Ltd. 1956–67; Partner Invest. Div. 1961–67; Br. Mgr. Winnipeg Office, Francis I. Du Pont & Co. 1967–70; Richardson Securities of Canada 1970–75, Resident Mgr. Winnipeg Br. 1974–75; Extve. Dir. The Winnipeg Found. 1976–89, Dir. Development 1990–92; served with The Black Watch (R.H.R) 1950–53, attached 1st Bn. Kings African Rifles 1951–52, service in E. Africa and Malaya, Queen's Own Cameron Highlanders (Reserve) 1953–55, rank Lt.; Sinking Fund Trustee, City of Winnipeg; Presbyterian; recreations: golf, gardening; Clubs: St. Charles Country (Dir. 1966–73); Home: 362 Country Club Blvd., Winnipeg, Man. R3K 1X6.

**HOWISON, Jean-Pierre,** B.Com., C.A.; executive, b. Montreal, Que. 25 Jan. 1933; s. Alfred and Cécile (Racette) H.; e. Loyola Coll. B.Com. 1956; McGill Univ. C.A. 1959; m. Dorothy M. Harris 14 Nov. 1959; children: Robert, Nathalie; FINANCIAL CONSULTANT; Asst. Treas. Davie Shipbuilding Ltd. Lauzon, Que. 1959–66; Vice Pres. Finance Admin., Sidbec, Montreal 1966–81; Vice Pres. (Finance & Admin.) & Treasurer, Quebecair 1981–86; mem. Candn. Inst. C.A.'s; R. Catholic; recreation: travel; Home: 4 Hazel Dr., Dollard-des-Ormeaux, Que. H9B 1C5.

**HOWITT, Peter W.,** B.A., M.A., Ph.D., F.R.S.C.; university professor; b. Toronto, Ont. 31 May 1946; s. C. William E. and D. Ruth (Wilkinson) H.; e. McGill Univ. B.A. (Hons.) 1968; Univ. of Western Ont. M.A. 1969; Northwestern Univ. Ph.D. 1973; m. Pat d. Edith and Herbert Zettel 6 Sept. 1969; children: Suzanne Edith, Paul Herbert Eaton, Katherine Elizabeth; BANK OF MONTREAL PROF. OF MONEY & FINANCE, UNIV. OF WESTERN ONT. 1990– ; Assoc. Prof., present univ. 1977–81; Prof. 1981– ; Visiting Prof., Hebrew Univ. Jerusalem 1980; Univ. Laval 1985; M.I.T. 1988; Univ. de Paris I 1989; Pres., Candn. Econ. Assn. 1993–94; Assoc. Ed., 'Can. J. of Econ.' 1978–81; Mem., Bd. of Eds., 'Am. Econ. Review' 1980–83; Mem., Bd. of Eds., 'J. Econ. Literature' 1992– ; Fellow, The Royal Soc. of Canada 1992; author: 'Monetary Policy in Transition: A Study of Bank of Canada Policy 1982–85' 1986, 'The Keynesian Recovery and Other Essays' 1990; Home: 15 Normandy Pl., London, Ont. N6H 4K3; Office: London, Ont. N6A 5C2.

**HOWLAND, Hon. William Goldwin Carrington,** O.C., O.Ont., C.St.J., B.A., LL.B., LL.D., D.Litt.S.; b. Toronto, Ont. 7 Mar. 1915; s. Dr. Goldwin William and Margaret Christian (Carrington) H.; e. Upper Canada Coll., Toronto, 1923–32; University of Toronto, B.A. (Law) 1936, LL.B. 1939; Osgoode Hall Law Sch. (Silver Medallist); m. Margaret Patricia, d. late Kenneth Alfred Greene, 20 Aug. 1966; Chief Justice of Ont. 1977–90; retired 1990; Advisory Council, The Toronto Symphony; read law with Rowell Reid Wright & McMillan; called to Bar of Ont. 1939; cr. Q.C. 1955; has practised law with McMillan, Binch 1939–75; Justice, Court of Appeal, Ont., 1975–77; Lectr. in Mortgages, Osgoode Hall Law School, 1950–67; served with Canadian Army 1942–45; Captain RCASC; appointed Staff Captain, Canadian Army Pacific Force; National Pres., U.N. Assn. in Canada, 1959–60 Pres., Univ. Coll. Alumni Assn., 1958; Churchwarden, Grace Church on-the-Hill, 1959–61; Extve., Council for Social Service, Ang. Ch. of Can. for many yrs. to 1967; mem., Bd. of Govs., Upper Can. Coll. 1968–70, 1977–90; mem. of Senate, York Univ. 1968–69; el. Bencher, Law Soc. Upper Can. 1961 and 1966 (Treas. 1968–70); Life Bencher 1969; Chrmn., Legal Educ. Comte. 1964–68; mem., Candn. Bar Assn. (Council 1959–62); Pres., Fed. of Law Socs. of Can. 1973–74; Gov., Candn. Judicial Centre 1988–90; Trustee, Wycliffe Coll. 1975–90; Chrmn. Adv. Counc., for Order of Ontario 1986–90; Admitted as Commander of the Order of St. John 1984; Hon. LL.D. Queen's Univ. 1972; Univ. of Toronto 1981; York Univ. 1984; Law Soc. of Upper Can. 1985; Hon. D.Litt.S. Wycliffe College 1985; Human Relations Award by Candn. Counc. of Christians and Jews 1990; apptd. to the Order of Ont. 1991; Officer of the Order of Canada 1991; Robinette Medal Award of Excellence, Osgoode Hall Law Sch. Alumni Assn. 1993; Mem., University Coll. Ctte., Univ. of Toronto; Hon. Life Mem., Assoc. of Provincial Criminal Court Judges of Ont.; Hon. Life Mem., The Advocates Soc.; Phi Delta Phi (Hon. mem.); Delta Upsilon (Pres. 1936); Anglican; recreation: travel; Clubs: Toronto; National; Toronto Hunt; Canadian; Empire; Home: 2 Bayview Wood, Toronto, Ont. M4N 1R7.

**HOWSE, Claude Kilborn,** D.Sc.; geologist; b. Burin, Nfld. 7 Nov. 1907; s. Rev. Dr. Charles and Elfrida (Palmer) H.; e. Grand Bank (Nfld.) Acad.; Meth. Coll., St. John's, Nfld.; Dalhousie Univ., Memorial Univ. B.Sc., 1933, one yr. post-grad. studies; Mem. Univ. of Nfld., D.Sc. 1974; m. (Mary) Phyllis, d. William King Mercer, 4 Oct. 1937; two d. Claudia Florence (Temple), Barbara Jean (Shaffer); Nfld. Rep., Iron Ore Co. of Canada 1959–74; Consult., Iron Ore Co. of Can. 1974– ; Dir., Asst. Govt. Geol., Geol. Survey of Nfld. 1934–37; Assoc. Govt. Geol. 1937–42; Govt. Geol. 1943–49; Depy. Min. of Mines, Dept. of Mines, Nfld. 1950–55; St. John's Rep., British Newfoundland Corp. 1955–59; mem. Un. Ch. Bd. of Educ., St. John's 1939–64; Bd. of Regents, Mem. Univ. of Nfld. 1950–69; United Church; recreations: writing, photography; Address: 213 – 1 Heritage Way, Lindsay, Ont. K9V 5P9.

**HOWSE, Robert,** B.A., LL.B., LL.M.; university professor; b. Toronto, Ont. 21 Aug. 1958; s. Herbert Lloyd and Susan Gladys (Winsor) H.; e. Univ. of Toronto B.A. 1980, LL.B. 1989; Harvard Law Sch. LL.M. 1990; m. Denyse d. Leo and Madeleine Goulet 23 June 1984; ASST. PROF., LAW, UNIV. OF TORONTO 1990– ; study and travel in U.S. & Eur. 1980–82; Foreign Serv. Officer, External Affairs Canada 1982–86; Asst. Dir., Internat. Bus. & Trade Law Prog., Fac. of Law, Univ. of Toronto 1990–93; Co-editor-in-Chief, Univ. of Toronto Faculty of Law Review 1988–89; Co-founder: Canada for All Canadians 'No' Ctte. 1992 Constitutional Referendum; author: 'Economic Union, Social Justice and Constitutional Reform' 1992; co-author: 'Trade and Transitions' 1990, 'No Deal' 1992, 'International Trade Regulation' 1994; recreations: swimming, cycling, art history; Home: 294 Ontario St., Apt. 6, Toronto, Ont. M5A 2V7; Office: 84 Queen's Park Cres., Toronto, Ont. M5S 1A1.

**HOY, Claire,** B.A.; journalist; author; b. Brockville, Ont. 21 July 1940; s. James David and Jennie May (Richmire) H.; e. Ryerson Polytech. Inst. B.A. (Jour.) 1964; m. Beverley Sykes (dec. 1976); children: Paul, Katherine; m. lydia huber d. Alois and Maria Pfisterer 15 May 1982; children: Zachary, Clayton, Scarlet; SYNDICATED FREELANCE COLUMNIST/AUTHOR 1988– ; journalist, Belleville Intelligencer 1965–66, Kitchener-Waterloo Record 1967–68, Toronto Telegram 1968–70, Toronto Star 1970–74; Columnist/Journalist, Toronto Sun 1975–88; pol. commentator Global TV 1980; author: 'Bill Davis' (biog.) 1985; 'Friends in High Places' (pol.) 1987; 'Margin of Error' (pol.) 1989; 'Clyde Wells: A Political Biography' 1992; co-author: 'By Way of Deception - A devastating insider's portrait of the

Mossad' (international) 1990; Presbyterian; recreation: golf; Home: 23 Clarendon Ave., Ottawa, Ont. K1Y 0P3; Hffice: Parliamentary Press Gallery, Centre Block, Parliament Hill, Ottawa, Ont. K1A 0A6.

**HOYLES, John Denison Villiers,** B.A., LL.B.; lawyer; b. Val d'Or, Que. 16 Oct. 1950; s. Newman John Sankey and Elizabeth Esther (Delamere) H.; e. Percival Co. H.S. 1968; Univ. of Ottawa B.A. 1972; Osgoode Hall Law School, York Univ. LL.B. 1975; called to Bar of the Prov. of Ont. 1977; m. Sally Ann d. James and Claire Kilgour 13 Aug. 1977; children: Julie, Lesley; EXECUTIVE VICE-PRES. & GENERAL MANAGER, NATIONAL CAPITAL COMN. 1991– ; Partner, Smith & Hoyles 1977–79; Dir. of Tour, Office of the Prime Minister 1979–80; Founding Partner, Byck, Hoyles & Grant 1980–90; Extve. Dir., GST Consumer Information Office 1990–91; Mem., Children's Aid Found.; Mem. Bd. of Govs., Camelot Golf & Country Club; Former Chair, Temiskaming Hosp. Bd.; Former Mem., Criminal Injuries Compensation Bd. (Govt. of Ont.); Former Acting Crown Attorney, Prov. of Ont.; Office: 161 Laurier Ave. W., Ottawa, Ont. K1P 6J6.

**HOYT, Erich;** author; journalist; naturalist; b. Akron, Ohio 28 Sept. 1950; s. Robert Emmett and Betty Jane (Shutrump) H.; e. Campion Jesuit H.S. (Prairie du Chien, Wis.) 1964–67; m. Dr. Sarah Elizabeth Wedden d. Peter Wedden and Janet Moss; one s. Moses Erich; one d. Magdalen Marisa; Freelance Writer 1978– ; Lectr. to Coll., Univ. and conservation groups 1981– ; Field Corr., Defenders of Wildlife (Washington, D.C.) 1985– ; Cons., Whale and Dolphin Conservation Soc. 1991– ; studio, outdoor and nature photography in Victoria, Vancouver and Winlaw B.C. 1969–75; Documentary film sound man and co-producer, Vancouver 1973–74; original music scores for documentaries and feature dramatic films, Vancouver 1973–78; Contributing Editor, Equinox Magazine 1982–87; Ed. Bd., Cetus Magazine 1986–88; Cons., Internat. Bd. for Plant Genetic Resources (UN Food and Agriculture Orgn., Rome, Italy) 1987–88; Knight (formerly Vannevar Bush) Fellow in Science Journalism, Massachusetts Inst. of Technology 1985–86; Visiting Lectr., Mass. Inst. of Technology 1986–87; Lectr., Ohio State Univ. 1992; James Thurber Writer-in-Residence, Columbus, Ohio 1992; Invited participant, IV World Congress on Parks and Protected Areas, Caracas, Venezuela 1992; Consultant, Krent-Paffett Associates Inc., Boston, researching, writing and design for new exhibit halls of the New York Botanical Gardens ('How Plants Become Food'), the Missouri Botanical Gardens (The Tropical Rainforest), the Museum of Arts, Science and Industry (Bridgeport, CT), Networks (Boston, Mass.) and the Bell History Center (Boston, Mass.) 1986–90; Project Offr., World Wide Fund for Nature, Gland, Switzerland, writing and editing five language versions of publication 'Conserving the Wild Relatives of Crops' 1988–91; author 'Orca: The Whale Called Killer' 1981, rev. 1984 and 1990; 'The Whale Watcher's Handbook' 1984, German ed. 1987; 'The Whales of Canada' 1984; 'Seasons of the Whale' 1990, Fr. ed. 1993; 'Extinction A-Z' 1991; 'Meeting the Whales' 1991; 'Riding with the Dolphins' 1992; articles on sci., wildlife, travel, and the environment in National Geographic, Equinox, The New York Times, The Guardian, New Scientist, Reader's Digest, Nature Canada, BBC Wildlife, EnRoute, Owl, Defenders; mem., Writers' Guild; Nat. Assn. of Sci. Writers; Am. Soc. of Journalists & Authors; Outdoor Writers of Can.; Soc. for Marine Mammalogy; Internat. Science Writers Assn.; Orgn. for Tropical Studies; Soc. for Economic Botany; Xerces Soc.; winner Francis H. Kortright Award for article in Equinox 1982; Environment Canada Award for article in Equinox 1985; BBC Wildlife Writing Award, 2nd prize 1988; recreations: composing and playing music; Office: 29 Dirleton Ave., No. 11, North Berwick EH39 4BE Scotland; Contact: c/o Dr. Sarah E. Wedden, Dept. of Anatomy, Univ. of Edinburgh Med. Sch., Teviot Place, Edinburgh EH8 9AG Scotland.

**HOYT, George Calvin,** M.A., Ph.D.; retired educator; b. N.J., 5 Oct. 1924; s. George Stanley and Annie Elizabeth (Wright) H.; e. Stanford Univ., A.B. 1950; Univ. of Chicago, M.A. 1954; Univ. of Cal. Berkeley, Ph.D. 1962; m. the late Eugenia, d. late Peter Zappas, 26 March 1951; children: David, Barbara, Riley, Carl; former: Prof. and Dean, Business Adm., Simon Fraser Univ.; Pres., Vancouver Opera; Gov., B.C. Business Counc.; served with Edwin S. Hewitt Assoc. as Consultant; Bechtel Corp.; Univ. of Cal.; Univ. of Iowa; Mass. Inst. of Technol.; Consultant to various firms in Can. and U.S.; author of numerous articles on community study, organ. leadership and decision making, indust. retirement policy; Dir., Fraser Valley Univ. Soc.; mem. & Dir., Ft. Lang Chamber of Comm. and several municipal comns.; mem., Candn. Assn. Administrative Sciences; Gamma Beta Sigma; Omicron Delta Epsilon; recreations: fishing, hiking, horses; Clubs: Vancouver Bd. of Trade; University Club of Vancouver; Home: 10128 McKinnon Cres., Langley, B.C. V3A 8G6.

**HOYT, Hon. William Lloyd,** M.A.; judge; b. Saint John, N.B. 13 Sept. 1930; s. Lloyd Albert and Dorothy Alice (Fraser) H.; e. Acadia Univ. B.A. 1952; M.A. 1952; Cambridge Univ. B.A. (Law) 1956, M.A. 1979; m. Joan d. William and Isabelle Millier 4 Sept. 1954; three d. Martha, Janet, Susan; CHIEF JUSTICE OF N.B. 1993– ; called to Bar of N.B. 1957; Assoc., Limerick & Limerick, Fredericton 1957–59; Partner, Limerick, Limerick & Hoyt and successor firm Hoyt, Mockler, Allen & Dixon 1959–81; Judge, Court of Queen's Bench N.B. 1981–84; Judge, Court of Appeal N.B. 1984– ; cr. Q.C. 1972; part-time lectr. Univ. of N.B. Law Sch. 1959–61; Gov. Beaverbrook Art Gallery 1979–86, Chrmn. Acquisitions Ctte. 1980–86; author various publs.; United Church; Office: P.O. Box 6000, Fredericton, N.B. E3B 5H1.

**HOZUMI, Nobumichi,** M.D., Ph.D.; physician; b. Japan 25 Feb. 1943; s. Shozo and Miyoko H.; e. Keio Univ., Tokyo, M.D. 1968, Ph.D. (Molecular Biol.) 1972; m. Yuriko d. Kenichi and Toshiko Onuma 1972; children: Tadaaki, Hikaru; SR. SCIENTIST, MT. SINAI HOSP. RSCH. INST. 1985– ; Mem., Basel Inst. for Immunology 1975–78; Sr. Scientist, Ont. Cancer Inst. 1979–85; Assoc. Prof., Fac. of Med., Univ. of Toronto 1984–88, Prof. 1988– ; rec'd David Pressman Meml. Award 1983; Boehringer Mannheim Can. Prize, Candn. Biochem. Soc. 1984; mem. Am. Assn. of Immunologists; Candn. Soc. of Immunologists; recreations: tennis, skiing; Home: 307 Willard Ave., Toronto, Ont. M6S 3R1; Office: 600 University Ave., Toronto, Ont. M5G 1X5.

**HRABOWSKY, Ivan,** D.D.S., F.A.G.D., F.A.D.I., F.P.F.A.; dentist; b. Toronto, Ont. 2 Aug. 1931; s. late Nestor and late Klimentia (Semen) H.; e. King Edward Pub. Sch., Toronto 1944; Harbord Coll. Inst., Toronto 1949; Univ. of Toronto, Faculty of Dent., D.D.S. 1954; m. Vlada, d. late Petras Karvelis and Rose Zukus, 12 Sept. 1953; children: Ivan Mark, Michael Peter, Yvonna Vladislava; Pres. (1970–71), Ont. Dental Assn. Pres., Denpropco Ltd.; Gov., Candn. Dental Assn. (mem. Extve. Council 1967–73); Fellow, Acad. General Dent.; Fellow, Acad. of Dentistry Intnl.; Fellow, Pierre Fauchard Academy, Federation Dentaire Internationale; Founder, Downtown Dental Centre, St. Catharines; Past Pres., St. Catharines Torch Club; Pres., Kurelek Club; Vice-Pres., Niagara Falls Art Gallery & Museum; C.O.T.C. (R.C.D.C.) 1951–54; rank 2/Lt.; Mensa; P. Conservative; recreations: travel, photography, philately; Address: 421 St. Paul St., St. Catharines, Ont. L2R 3N4.

**HRACS, Frank John,** M.A.; economist; b. Welland, Ont. 18 Dec. 1951; s. Frank and Barbara (Lactoczy) H.; e. Welland Eastdale Secondary Sch. 1972; Brock Univ. B.A. 1976; Univ. of Guelph M.A. 1977; m. Avril d. Kenneth and Kathleen Jennings 29 Dec. 1979; two s. Brian, Austin; VICE PRES., CHIEF ECONOMIST, RBC DOMINION SECURITIES 1987– ; Rsch. Asst. Niagara Region Study Review Comn. Thorold, Ont. 1976; Econ. Bank of Nova Scotia 1978–80; Monetary Economist 1980; Vice Pres. McLeod Young Weir 1983–84; Economist, Coopers & Lybrand Consulting Group 1984–87; Office: P.O. Box 21, Commerce Court S., Toronto, Ont. M5L 1A7.

**HRANCHUK, Kenneth Barry,** B.Sc., M.A., Ph.D., C.Psych.; psychologist; b. Regina, Sask. 23 May 1944; s. Daniel and Mary H.; e. Scott Coll. 1963; North Dakota State Univ., B.Sc. 1967; Carleton Univ., M.A. 1969, Ph.D. 1974; wife: Donna Christie d. Don and Theresa Johnson 1978– ; children (prev. marriage): Melinda May, Kenneth Barry, Jr.; (present marriage): Kieva Sofia, Alexis Anna; Psychologist, Rideau Reg. Ctr. 1972–79; Prof., Fac. of Edn., Univ. of Ottawa 1979–80; Dir., Behavior Therapy & Biofeedback Unit, Royal Ottawa Hosp. 1980–84; Vis. Rsch. Sci., Nat. Rsch. Counc. of Can. 1984–87; Cons., Children at Risk, Ottawa, Ont. 1980– ; Hon. Adjunct Prof. of Psychol., Carleton Univ.; Lectr./Undergrad. & Grad. Thesis Ctte. involvement/Clinical Training Supervision 1977–87, 1990–93; Cons., Arnprior & Dist. Assoc. for Community Living; Assoc. for Community Living, Renfrew & Dist.; Children at Risk; Family Builders; Grand River View Homes; K.C. MacLure Habilitation Ctr.; Ottawa Valley Autistic Homes; Renfrew Co. Sep. Sch. Bd.; Sonshine Families; Stormont, Dundas & Glengarry Children's Aid Soc.; Tamir Found.; pioneering psychologist in Canada in the devel. of Applied Behavior Analysis as it pertains to human behavior; Former Mem., Bd. of Dir., Candn. Mothercraft; Fgn. Student Academic Scholar (undergrad.); Ont. Scholar (grad. sch.); Mem., Assn. for Behavior Analysis; Assn. for the Advancement of Behavior Therapy; Candn. Psychol. Assoc.; Candn. Registry of Health Service Providers in Psychol.; author of profl. articles & num. invited addresses to both clinical & experimental groups; recreations: avid antique collector, world traveller; Clubs: Huntley Hist. Soc.; Candn. Wildlife Fed.; Heritage Can. Found.; Address: R.R. 1, Carp, Ont. K0A 1L0.

**HUBBARD, Hon. John Michael,** LL.B.; judge; b. Liverpool, Eng. 19 Jan. 1939; s. Alfred John and Doreen (Newall) H.; e. Liverpool Coll. 1957; Liverpool Univ. LL.B. 1960; m. Barbara d. Walter and Margot Krausz 3 June 1972; two d. Tanya Elizabeth, Kyla Doreen; JUDGE, PROV. COURT OF B.C. 1982– ; Solr. Supreme Court of Eng. 1962; Barrister and Solr. Y.T. 1965, B.C. 1968; recipient Centennial Medal 1967; Capt. Yukon Team Centennial Canoe Pageant Rocky Mt. House to Montréal; Gov. St. Michael's Univ. Sch.; recreations: sailing, mountaineering, kayaking, canoeing; Clubs: Royal Victoria Yacht; Alpine; Union Club of B.C.; Office: 850 Burdett Ave., Victoria, B.C. V8W 1B4.

**HUBBARD, M. Ruth,** B.A., M.S., AMP; public servant; b. Toronto, Ont. 27 June 1942; d. John S. and Winifred (Moreton) Willis; e. Queen's Univ. B.A. 1965; Ohio State Univ. M.S. 1969; Harvard Univ. AMP 1987; m. Martin s. Richard G. and Muriel H. May 1973; one s.: James Nielsen; MASTER OF THE ROYAL CANADIAN MINT; Stats. Can. 1967–77; Dir., Program Br., Treas. Bd. Secretariat 1977–84; Asst. Sec. 1983–84; Assoc. Comnr., FIRA 1984–85; Extve. Vice-Pres., Investment Can. 1985–88; Depy. Min., National Revenue, Customs & Excise 1988–92; Deputy Min./Chairperson, Employment and Immigration Canada 1992; Home: 440 Emerson Ave., Apt. 503, Ottawa, Ont. K1Y 2L8; Office: 320 Sussex Dr., Ottawa, Ont. K1A 0G8.

**HUBEL, Vello,** R.C.A.; industrial designer; artist; educator; b. Tallinn, Estonia 6 July 1927; s. Gustav and Hilda (Kunkmann) H.; came to Can. 1947; e. Ont. Coll. of Art Indust. Design A.O.C.A. 1955; Mass. Inst. of Technol. summer 1962, 1971, 1973 (Nat. Design Council Scholarships); m. Nelly d. Anton Gustavson, Toronto, Ont. 10 Apr. 1965; two d. Kalli Ann, Tiina Katrin; PROP., VELL HUBEL DESIGNS 1958– ; indust. design consultant to Candn. mfrs.; designer many wood, plastic and metal products, comm. interiors, yacht interiors, and exhibits; consultant to fed. and various prov. govts. on design; initiated and directed no. of design based symposiums and events; served on various design and art juries; teacher Ont. Coll. of Art since 1965 (Chrmn., Industrial Design Dept., Retired 1993); OCA A.J. Casson Award 1989; co-author 'Focus on Designing' (textbook) 1983; prepared over 300 colour drawings of old Toronto houses 1970–76; recipient numerous design awards; City of Toronto Medal of Service; exmem. Art Adv. Comte. Toronto City Hall; Hon. Treas. Royal Candn. Acad. Arts 1978–81; mem. Assn. Candn. Indust. Designers (Vice Pres. 1965–67, Ont. Chapter Pres. 1970–72, Pres. 1988– ); Candn. Power Sqdn.; Estonian Fed. in Can. (Pres. 1979– ; Community Citation); Protestant; recreations: walking, sailing, drawing, painting; Address: 531 Soudan Ave., Toronto, Ont. M4S 1X1.

**HUBERT, His Excellency Jean-Paul,** B.A., B.C.L., M.I.A., Ph.D.; diplomat; b. Grand-Mère, Qué. 16 Dec. 1941; s. Jean-Paul and Cécile (Laperrière) H.; e. Laval Univ. B.A. 1963; McGill Univ. B.C.L. 1966; admitted to Bar of Que. 1967; Columbia Univ. M.I.A. 1969; Univ. de Paris Ph.D. 1971; m. Mireya d. Roberto Melgar 28 July 1967 (div. 1985); children: Jean-Philippe, Jean-Charles, Alexandra; SENIOR ADVISOR FOR THE COMMONWEALTH, 'la FRANCOPHONIE AND HEMISPHERIC AFFAIRS 1994– ; joined Cdn. diplomatic serv. (External Affairs) 1971; Vice-consul, Spain & Morocco 1972–74; Legal Adv. Div. 1974–76; Personnel Div. 1976–78; 1st Sec. & Consul, Cuba 1978–81; Pol. Counsellor, France & Canada's Perm. Rep. to Agency for Cult. & Tech. Coop., Paris 1981–85; Dir., Econ. & Treaty Law Div. 1985–86; Fed. Coord. for 'La Francophonie' 1986–88; Personal Rep. of Canada's Prime Minister, Francophone Summits 1988–90; Pres., Internat. Follow-up Ctte., Que. Summit 1988–89; Ambassador to Senegal, Mauritania, Guinea, Guinea-Bissau & Cape Verde & High Comnr. to Gambia 1988–90; Ambassador (1st), Permanent Rep. of Canada to the Orgn. of American States 1990–93; Federal Coordinator, 1993 Francophonie and Commonwealth Summits 1993; Ordre de la Pléiade, Internat. Assn. of French-speaking Parlementarians 1989; Home: 48, Rouen, Gatineau, Que. J8T 1G9.

**HUBICKI, John Michael,** B.A.Sc., O.A.A., M.RAIC, P.Eng.; consulting engineer, architect, planner; b. Toronto, Ont. 5 Sept. 1931; s. Leo and Rose Helen (Krasicki) H.; e. Western Tech. H.S. 1951; Univ. of Toronto B.A.Sc. 1956; m. Dorothy Amy d. George and Dorothy Burfield 14 Sept. 1956; children: Wendy Lee, Michael John, Lisa Rose, Laura Dawn; PRINCIPAL, TOTTEN SIMS HUBICKI ASSOC. LIMITED 1963– ; Mem., Siting Task Force for Low Level Radioactive Waste in Canada; Asst. County Engr., Co. of Peel, Ont. 1956–59; County Engr., Co. of Peterborough 1960–62; Totten Sims Hubicki has a staff of 300 engineers, architects, planners, etc. involved in public & private work; recognized Expert in Land Use Planning, Ont. Municipal Bd.; Ontario Renews Award in Planning 1983; Mem., Ont. Assn. of Architects; Royal Architectural Inst. of Canada; Am. Soc. of Civil Engrs.; Ont. Assn. of Profl. Engrs.; recreations: canoeing, sailing, theatre, Northumberland Players; Home: 403 Lake Shore Dr., Cobourg, Ont. K9A 1S2; Office: P.O. Box 398, 1A King St. E., Cobourg, Ont. K9A 4L1.

**HUCK, Herb,** B.B.A., C.A., C.M.A.; insurance executive; b. Toronto, On. 11 Jan. 1957; s. Hermann and Else (Kunzelmann) H.; e. Northview Hiehgts; York Univ. B.B.A. 1980; m. Wendy d. Fred and Jane Ann Quance 2 Aug. 1982; children: Heather Allison, Colleeen Michelle; VICE-PRESIDENT, TAXATION, THE NATIONAL LIFE ASSURANCE CO. OF CANADA 1988– ; Senior Accountant, Arthur Andersen 1980–84; Comptroller, National Life Assur. Co. of Canad 1984–88; York Univ.: Entrance Scholarship, In Course Scholarship, Gordon G. Shaw Award, Undergrad. Business Award; Mem., Newtonbrook West Community Assn.; Candn. & Ont. Inst. of C.A.s; Soc. of Management Accountants; Candn. Life & Health Insur. Assn.; recreations: woodworking, baseball, volleyball, camping; Home: 53 Charlton Blvd., Willowdale, Ont. M2M 1C1; Office: 522 University Ave., Toronto, Ont. M5G 1Y7.

**HUCKER, Stephen John,** M.B., B.S., F.R.C.Psych., F.R.C.P.(C); forensic psychiatrist; educator; b. Emsworth, England 23 March 1947; s. John Charles and Elsie (Williams) H.; e. Univ. of Newcastle-Upon-Tyne, England M.B., B.S. 1975; m. Mary Ann d. Richard Hall and Gladys McCoy 31 July 1978; three s. John, Andrew, William; PROFESSOR & CHAIRMAN, DIVISION OF FORENSIC & CORRECTIONAL PSYCHIATRY, QUEEN'S UNIVERSITY; Assoc. Prof., Univ. of Toronto; Staff Psychiatrist Clarke Inst. of Psychiatry 1976–81; Head, Forensic Div., Clarke Inst. of Psychiatry and Dir. Metrop. Toronto Forensic Service 1981–93; Cons. in Forensic Psychiatry, Correctional Service Can., Min. Health Ont., Atty. Gen. State of Mich., RCMP; Sec. Kenneth G. Gray Found.; co-ed. 'Mental Disorder and Criminal Responsibility' 1981; 'Clinical Criminology' 1985; 'Dangerousness: Probability and Prediction, Psychiatry and Public Policy' 1985; recreations: music, art appreciation; Office: Kingston, Ont. K7L 3N6.

**HUDDART, Hon. Carol Mahood,** B.A., LL.B.; judge; b. Peterborough, Ont. 25 May 1938; d. Samuel Kenneth and Reta Mae (Wilson) Mahood; e. R.H. King Secondary Sch. Scarborough 1955; Univ. of Toronto, B.A. 1959; Osgoode Hall Law Sch., LL.B. 1963; m. J. Larry s. Jack and Evelyn Huddart 12 Feb. 1970 (dec.); children: Stephen, Bob, Susan; JUDGE, SUPREME COURT OF B.C. 1987– ; Judge, Co. Court of Vancouver 1981–87; Office: 800 Smithe St., Vancouver, B.C. V6Z 2E1.

**HUDON, Jean-Guy,** B.A.; member of parliament; b. La Pocatiere, Que. 24 Apr. 1941; s. Leo and Marguerite (Bilodeau) H.; e. Univ. de Sherbrooke, degree of teacher edn. 1959; Univ. of Montreal, A.A. 1967, B.A. 1968; m. Colombe d. Georges Dagenais 3 Aug. 1963; children: Stephane, Isabelle; former Parliamentary Secretary for the President of the Privy Council and Min. resp. for Constitutional Affairs; Teacher, 1959–72, Chief of Staff 1972–78; Superintendant, Moissons Sch. Bd. 1978–84; Town Counsellor & Mayor, Beauharnois 1974–78, 1982–84; M.P. for Riding of Beauharnois-Salaberry 1984– ; Parliamentary Sec. for Employment & Immigration 1984–85; Parlty. Sec. for External Affairs 1985–88; Parlty. Sec. for National Defense 1989–91; C.R. 1 Couns. in Indus. Relns.; Home: 142, Trudeau, Beauharnois, Que. J6N 2L4.

**HUDSON, Alan Roy,** M.B., Ch.B., F.R.C.S.Ed., F.R.C.S.(C); neurosurgeon; educator; b. Cape Town, S. Africa 16 March 1938; s. John George H.; e. Rondebosch Boys' High Sch.; Univ. of Cape Town; Univ. of Toronto; Oxford Univ.; M.B.Ch.B. 1960; F.R.C.S. Ed. 1964; L.M.C.C. 1965; F.R.C.S.(C.) 1968; came to Can.; m. Susan Elizabeth d. Roy Hurd 1962; children: Jean, Katherine, Erin, Roy; PRESIDENT & C.E.O., THE TORONTO HOSPITAL; former James Wallace McCutcheon Chair, Surgeon-in-Chief, The Toronto Hosp.; former Depy. Chrmn., Dept. of Surgery and Prof. of Neurosurgery, Univ. of Toronto; author numerous papers and chapters on peripheral nerve injuries; Hon. Pres., Congress, World Fed. Neurosurgical Soc.; recreation: yachting; Office: Toronto General Hosp., 585 University Ave., BW 1–658, Toronto, Ont. M5G 2C4.

**HUDSON, Arthur J.,** M.D., B.Sc., F.R.C.P.(C); educator; b. Toronto, Ont. 3 Aug. 1924; s. Arthur Willie and Dorothy (McGookin) H.; e. Maurice Cody Pub. Sch. and N. Toronto Coll. Inst.; Univ. of Toronto, M.D. 1950, B.Sc. (Neuroanat.) 1952; m. Jean d. Alcwyn and Aeronwen Glanville 22 Dec. 1956; children: Nicholas James, Robert Glanville, Anna Victoria; RSCH. DIR., UNIV. HOSP. 1988– , Dir., Neurochemistry Lab., Univ. Hosp. 1974–88; Prof. of Med., Univ. of W. Ont. 1974– , Prof. of Clin. Neurol. Sci. 1974– , Professor Emeritus 1990– , Hon. Lectr. in Biochem. 1964–90; Mem., Bd. of Govs., Univ. of W. Ont.; Neurol. Cons. Univ. Hosp. London; internship and residency Toronto Gen. Hosp. 1950–51, Med. Rsch. Council Fellow in Neurol. 1953–54, 1956–57; J.H. Richardson Rsch. Fellow Univ. of Toronto 1951–52; Royal Victoria Hosp. Montréal 1952–53; Montréal Neurol. Inst. 1954–55; Clk. Nat. Hosp. London, Eng. 1955–56; Rsch. Fellow in Neurochem. Montréal Gen. Hosp. Rsch. Inst. 1957–58; Instr. in Med. present Univ. 1958, Asst. Prof. 1967, Assoc. Prof. 1969, mem. Senate 1980–82 & Senate Ctte. Univ. Planning & Ctte. Budget Finance 1982–85; Sr. Mem., Candn. Med. Assoc. 1990; served with RCAF 1943–45; recipient Muscular Dystrophy Assn. Can. Rsch. Award 1960–74; Med. Rsch. Council Can. Rsch. Award 1960–74, 1989–92; Candn. Diabetic Assn. Rsch. Award 1982–84; Ont. Mental Health Rsch. Award 1980–82; Ont. Mental Health Found. Rsch. Award 1984–86; Phys. Services Inc. Rsch. Award 1985–87; author or co-author over 100 publs.; Co-Founder & Past Chrmn. Sci. Adv. Ctte. Amyotrophic Lateral Sclerosis Soc. Can. (ALS); mem. Sci. Adv. Ctte. ALS Assn. USA; Co-Founder Biennial Rossiter Rsch. Conf.; mem. Am. Acad. Neurol.; Am. Assn. Advanc. Sci.; Candn. Biochem. Soc.; Candn. Med. Assn.; Candn. Neurol. Soc. (Pres. 1975); Candn. Cong. Neurol. Sci's (Pres. 1975, Chrmn. ALS Symposium 1987); Multiple Sclerosis Soc. Can. (Pres. Ont. Div. 1975); Internat. Brain Rsch. Orgn.; Ont. Med. Assn.; Soc. for Neurosci. USA; Alpha Omega Alpha; Home: 8 Doncaster Ave., London, Ont. N6G 5A5; Office: 339 Windermere Rd., London, Ont. N6A 5A5.

**HUDSON, Donald J.,** B.A.; investment executive; b. Vancouver, B.C. 26 Sept. 1930; e. Univ. of B.C. B.A. 1952; LL.D. honoris causa, Simon Fraser Univ. 1993; PRESIDENT, VANCOUVER STOCK EXCHANGE 1982– ; joined The Shell Oil Co. of Canada Ltd. 1952; Canadian Pacific Airlines Ltd. 1953–64 (last position held Dir. of Sales Devel.); The T. Eaton Co. Ltd. 1964–81 (last position held Sr. Vice Pres., Pacific Div.); Chrmn., Internat. Financial Centre; Found. Bd. Chrmn., Simon Fraser Univ.; Mem. Adv. Counc., The Niagara Inst.; Mem., B.C. & Yukon Counc. of the Duke of Edinburgh's Award in Canada; Mem., Sr. Adv. Bd., YMCA of Gter. Vancouver; Mem., Bd. of Govs., Vancouver Stock Exchange; Mem. Bd. of Dirs., Pacific Corridor Enterprise Council; Dir.: British Pacific Properties Limited; Norwich Union Life Insurance Soc., Candn. Board; Clubs: Vancouver Club; Vancouver Lawn Tennis; Office: (P.O. Box 10333) 609 Granville St., Vancouver, B.C. V7Y 1H1.

**HUDSON, James, F.,** B.A., M.B.A.; bank executive; b. Vancouver, B.C. 9 Oct. 1942; s. George Frederick Victor and Katherine Maude Josephene (Wright) H.; e. Univ. of Brit. Columbia B.A. 1965; Univ. of Western Ont. M.B.A. 1967; m. Anita Y. d. Herman and Anne Beeftink 26 Sept. 1970; children: Amber G., Michael E.J.; SENIOR VICE-PRES., PACIFIC DIVISION, TORONTO-DOMINION BANK; joined Toronto-Dominion Bank 1967; various domestic & internat. assignments: Toronto, London (UK), Hong Kong, N.Y.; Office: P.O. Box 10001, Pacific Centre, Vancouver, B.C. V7Y 1A2.

**HUDSON, Susanne;** magazine publisher; b. Toronto, Ont. 13 Oct. 1944; d. Morgan and Claire (Watson) Hudson; children: Julie and Stephanie Beattie; PUBLISHER, CANADIAN GEOGRAPHIC MAGAZINE 1988– ; Registered Nurse, Wellesley Hospital Toronto 1966–78; Fashion Buyer, T. Eaton Co. Ltd. 1978–81; Harrowsmith Magazine 1981; Advtg. & Mktg. Dir., Toronto Life Magazine 1981–85; Publisher, Your Money Magazine 1985–88; Extve., Magazines Canada; Writer's Development Trust Ottawa; Bd. of Trustees, Candn. Mus. of Nature 1990– ; Home: Ottawa, Ont.; Office: 39 McArthur Ave., Vanier, Ont. K1L 8L7.

**HUEGLIN, Thomas O.,** Ph.D., Dr.habil.; professor of political science; b. Munich, W. Germany 24 May 1946; s. Hans O. and Renate (Wachendorff) H.; e. Univ. of St. Gall, Switz. Ph.D.; Konstanz Univ., W. Germany Dr.habil.; partner: Julia Roberts; children: Hannah (from 1st m.), Christian (Julia's d.); PROFESSOR OF POLITICAL SCIENCE, WILFRID LAURIER UNIVERSITY; fellowships: Italy (European Univ. Inst. Florence) and Queen's Univ. (Skelton & Clark Fellow); Bd. Mem., Ctte. on Socio-Pol. Pluralism; Internat. Pol. Science Assn.; author: 'Tyrannei der Mehrheit' 1977, 'Sozietaler Foederalismus' 1991, 'Politics in Federal States' forthcoming; publications & research focus on comparative federalism, regionalism, pol. econ. & history of pol. thought (Althusius, Machiavelli); referreed schol. articles have appeared worldwide; recreations: tennis; clubs: Waterloo Tennis; Home: 184 Front St., New Dundee, Ont. N0B 2E0; Office: Waterloo, Ont. N2L 3C5.

**HUESTIS, Douglas William,** M.D.; physician/university professor; b. London, Ont. 21 Mar. 1925; s. Richard Douglas and Marie Marguerite (Hinde) H.; e. Trinity Coll. Sch. 1942; Univ. of Toronto, Fac. of Med. 1942–44; McGill Univ., M.D. 1948; m. Rosemary Lucille d. John and Lucy Colford 11 June 1955; children: Lucy, Marilyn, Andrew, Karen, Peter; EMERITUS PROF. OF PATHOLOGY, UNIV. OF ARIZONA 1993– ; Postgrad. work in Can., Sweden, Eng., U.S.A. 1949–55; Pathologist, W. Pennsylvania Hosp. 1955–60; Blood Transfusion Spec., Mt. Sinai Hosp. (Chicago) 1960–69; Prof. of Pathology, Univ. of Arizon 1969–93; current work incl. spec. blood component therapy, transplantation immunology; Med. Dir., S. Ariz. Red Cross Blood Ctr. 1970–77; Chief, Transfusion Medicine, Univ. Med. Ctr., Tucson 1969– ; Cons., U.S. Public Health Serv. Food & Drug Admin.; Exchange Sci., USSR; John Elliott Award, Am. Assn. of Blood Banks 1975; Dir., Am. Assn. of Blood Banks 1964–68; Vice-Pres. 1968; Counc., Internat. Soc. Blood Transfusion 1978–86; Mem., Am. Soc. Hematology, Am. Soc. Clinical Pathologists; Sr. author: 'Practical Blood Transfusion' 4th ed. 1988; editor: 'Technical Manual, Am. Assn. of Blood Banks' 4th & 5th eds.; Mem., Ed. Bd., 'Transfusion' 1964– ; 'Revue Francaise de Transfusion' 1968– ; 'Journal of Clinical Apheresis' 1981– ; author & co-author of approx. 90 sci. articles; recreations: walking, cycling, gardening, amateur linguist (five languages); Home: 6750 w. Camino del Cerro, Tucson AZ 85745.

**HUESTON, Frank Harris,** B.A.Sc., P.Eng.; association executive; b. Toronto, Ont. 30 July 1930; s. Alexander William and Marjorie Irene (Harris) H.; e. Etobicoke Coll. Inst.; Univ. of Toronto B.A.Sc. 1954; Chalk River Reactor Sch. Cert. 1960; Am. Mgmt. Assn. Cert. Gen. Mgmt. 1977; m. Lois d. John and Evelyn Wilson 5 Nov. 1960; children: Sandra Jane, James J.A., R.C. Scott; Chrmn. Municipal Electric Assn. 1990–91; Chrmn. Hydro Electric Comn. Town of Port Hope 1986– , Vice Chrmn. 1980–85; mem. Bd. Saft Batteries (Canada) Ltd. 1988–91; Assoc., R.J. McClure & Associates 1989– ; Plant Eng. Ind. Chem. Div. Canada Packers 1954–56; Eldorado Resources Ltd. 1956–88, various tech. and mgmt. positions, latterly Mgr. Eng. Maintenance & Utilities and Asst. Gen. Mgr.; 1st Vice Chrmn. present Assn. 1989, mem. Bd. since 1987; Chrmn. Planning Bd. Town of Port Hope 1978–79; Pres. Port Hope & Dist. Boy Scout Council 1973; author various articles, presentations; Freemason; Anglican; recreations: duplicate bridge, curling; Club: Dalewood Golf & Curling; Home: 1 Silver Cres., Port Hope, Ont. L1A 2C4.

**HUFF, Thomas Allan;** herpetoculturist & conservationist; b. San Francisco, Ca. 17 May 1947; s. Lotus Austin and Dorothy Jane (Gullette) H.; e. Lowell H.S. 1965; Univ. of Cal. at Davis 1965; San Francisco City Coll. 1966–68; m. Caren d. Calvert T. and Helen Bird 22 July 1967; children: Jeremy Carter, Leah Alexandra, Jessica Lynn; MANAGER, LITTLE CATARAQUI CREEK CONSERVATION AREA; Consulting Herpetoculturist and Lecturer; Pres., Forked-Tongue Farms; Reptile Educ. and Conservation Trust; The Exotarium, and Herpetoculture Information Search Service; Assoc. Dir. & Co-Founder, Inst. for Herpetol. Rsch., Stanford, Ca. 1972– ; Natural Sci. Staff mem., Josephine D. Randall Jr. Museum, San Francisco 1966–68; Animal Keeper, San Fran. Zool. Gdns. 1968–72; Dir. of Conservation and Education, Reptile Breeding Found. 1973–91; Rsch. Assoc., Royal Ont. Mus. 1988– ; Field Assoc., Nat. Mus. of Natural Sci. 1988– ; Chrmn. Ann Farwell Pub. Lib. Milford, Ont. 1978–90; Dir., Quinte Summer Music 1982–84; Volunteer Cons., Candn. Exec. Serv. Orgn.; recipient Award of Merit as Citizen of Yr. Prince Edward C. of C.; author over 50 papers herpetoculture; ed. 'The Herpetoculturist'; keynote speaker Conf. Breeding Reptiles in Captivity, Cartagena, Colombia;

cons. Granby Zoo opening new reptile house 1984; Fellow, Candn. Assn. Zool. Parks & Aquariums; Assoc., Am. Assn. Zool. Parks & Aquariums; mem., Am. Soc. Ichtyols. & Herpetols.; Dir., Prince Edward C. of C. 1979–82; recreations: hiking, swimming, antiques; club: Rotary (Dir. & Past Pres., Picton, Ont.); Home: R.R. 3, Picton, Ont. K0K 2T0; Office: 1641 Perth Rd., Glenburnie, Ont. K0H 1S0.

**HUFFMAN, Alvin Donald,** B.A.Sc., P.Eng.; business consultant; b. Windsor, Ont. 2 May 1924; s. Donald Alfonso and Dora Katherine (Bailey) H.; e. Univ. of Toronto, B.A.Sc. 1949; m. L. Joyce d. Herbert and Georgina Smale 1 Aug. 1949; children: Robert, Janet, Catherine; Flying Offr./Pilot, RCAF 1942–45; Plant Engr. then Prodn. Supr., Sifto Salt Div., Domtar Ltd. 1949–53; Supt. then Plant Mgr. 1953–57; Tech. Dir. then Indus. Sales Mgr. 1957–63; Gen. Sales Mgr., Lime Div. 1963–67; Mktg. Mgr. then Asst. Gen. Mgr., Sifto Salt Div. 1967–71; Gen. Mgr., Converted Papers Div. 1971–77; Pres., Prairie Malt Ltd. 1978–85, Dir. 1981–85; C.E.O., CSP Foods Ltd. 1985–90; mem., Assn. of Profl. Engrs. of Sask.; of Ont.; of Manitoba; Chem. Inst. of Can.; Engr. Inst. of Can.; recreations: skiing, gardening; Home: 8615 Kingcome Cres., Sidney, B.C. V8L 5C8.

**HUFFMAN, Edward Drew,** B.Sc., M.B.A., P.Eng., C.M.C.; management consultant; b. Hamilton, Ont. 23 Nov. 1949; s. Keith Cameron and Dorothy Jean (Scott) H.; e. Queen's Univ. B.Sc. 1972; Univ. of Ottawa M.B.A. 1979; m. Martha d. George and Helen Krick 28 Apl. 1979; two s. Brenton, Peter; PARTNER, THE BAY CONSULTING GROUP 1989– ; Eng. Bell Canada 1972–74; Mgr. Arthur Andersen & Co. mgmt. cons. 1974–80; Mgr. Corporate Performance Improvement Currie, Coopers & Lybrand 1981–86; Prin., The Coopers & Lybrand Consulting Group 1986–89; Lectr. in Mgmt. Methods, Computing and Finance: Univ. of Ottawa, Candn. Inst. C.A.'s, Soc. Mgmt. Accts., Retail Council Can.; Hosp. Financial Mgmt. Assoc.; Am. Coll. of Hosp. Admin.; Conf. Chrmn./Moderator Financial Post Confs. Health Care in Can. 1987, Inst. Internat. Rsch. Effective Hosp. Mgmt. 1989; Dir. QUESSI 1971–72; Dir., mem. Exec. Ctte. and Treas. Toronto Free Theatre 1984–87, The Candn. Stage Co. 1987–90; Chrmn. Ottawa Mayoralty Debates 1979; mem'ship Sec. Kiwanis Ottawa 1975–79; Entrance Ctte. Inst. Mgmt. Cons. 1983–84; author 'Introspective Profiteering' 1981; 'Cash Management' 1981; 'To the Rescue: Winning the Productivity Battle' 1986; recreations: skiing, sailing; Club: Cedar Highlands Ski; Home: 82 Willowbank Blvd., Toronto, Ont. M5N 1G6; Office: 1033 Bay St., Suite 304, Toronto, Ont. M5S 3A5.

**HUGESSEN, Hon. James K.,** M.A., B.C.L., judge; b. Montreal, Que. 26 July 1933; s. Adrian Knatchbull and Margaret Cecelia Ross (Duggan) H.; e. Bishop's Coll. Sch., Lennoxville, Que.; Oxford Univ., B.A. 1954, M.A. 1958; McGill Univ., B.C.L. 1957; m. Mary Rosamond, d. R. E. Stavert, Montreal, Que., 12 Sept. 1958; children: Jaime William, Kathleen Jill, Alicia Mary, Alexander Ewart, Ross Adrian; JUSTICE, FEDERAL COURT APPEAL 1983– ; Justice, Superior Court of Que., 1972–83; Associate Chief Justice there 1973–83; Anglican; recreations: skiing, sailing, curling; Clubs: Royal St. Lawrence Yacht; Rideau; Red Birds Ski; Home: 81 Queen St., Almonte, Ont. K0A 1A0; Office: Federal Court of Canada, Ottawa, Ont. K1A 0H9.

**HUGGAN, (Jean) Isabel,** B.A.; writer; b. Kitchener, Ont. 21 Sept. 1943; d. (Cecil) Ronald and Catherine Innes (MacLennan) Howey; e. Elmira Dis. H.S. 1961; Univ. of West. Ont., B.A. 1965; m. Bob s. Robert and Mary H. 31 Dec. 1970; one d.: Abbey Clare; Ed. Asst., Macmillan Pub. Co. 1965–66; Teacher, Ont. secondary schs. 1968–72; Reporter, Photographer, Columnist, The Belleville Intelligencer 1973–76; Teacher, Creative Writing, Univ. of Ottawa 1985–87; Author: 'The Elizabeth Stories' 1984, 1987 (fiction); Anthol. contbr.: 'First Impressions' 1980 (short stories); 'Best Canadian Stories' 1983; 'Stories by Canadian Women' (Vol. II) 1987; 'New American Short Stories' 1988; 'Cradle and All' 1989 (anthology); 'Soho Square' 1990 (anthology); 'The Time of Your Life' 1992 (anthology); 'You Never Know' 1993; 'Unbecoming Daughters of The Empire' 1993 (anthology); 'Serpent à Plumes' 1994 (anthology); First prize, film script, NFB contest for women writers 1977; Quality Paperback Book Club's annual Joe Savago Award – New Voice of 1987; annual Alan Swallow Literary Award for 1987; recreations: walking, reading, music; Home: Ottawa, Ont. (Los Banos, Philippines, until 1997).

**HUGGARD, Richard James,** M.Sc., P.Ag., F.A.I.C.; public servant; b. Norton, N.B. 18 June 1935; s. Russell Clyde and Lillian Erna (Gillies) H.; e. Belleisle Regional H.S. 1953; N.S. Agric. College diploma 1956; MacDonald Coll., McGill Univ. B.Sc. 1958; Univ. of Illinois M.Sc. 1965; m. Marjorie d. John and Dorothy MacRae 16 April 1960; children: Richard James, Lesley Anne; DEPUTY MINISTER, N.S. DEPT. OF AGRICULTURE AND MARKETING 1991– ; Beef Fieldman, Livestock Br., N.S. Dept. of Agric. & Mktg. 1958; Livestock Supt. 1965; Dir., Livestock Br. 1973–75; Dir., Extension Serv. 1975–86; Chief Dir., Operations 1986–90; Extve. Dir., Admin. Serv. 1990; Lectr., Animal Science, N.S.A.C. 10 years; Pres., N.S. Inst. of Agrologists 1972–73; Past Council Mem.; Dir., Candn. Soc. of Animal Sci. (Eastern Br.) & Nat. Body (Past Pres. of both orgns.); Past Chair, Adv. Council on Sci. Affairs, Agric. Inst. of Can. (has served on Nat. Council & Nat. Extve.; Pres. 1978–79); Mem., Mngt. Bd., N.S. Animal Breeders Coop.; Mngt. Bd., N.S. Prov. Exbn.; Past Dir., Atlantic Winter Fair; Dir., Royal Agric. Winter Fair; Vice-Pres., Candn. Agric. Hall of Fame Assn.; Past Mem., N.S. Min. of Environ. Task Force on Clear Water; Award of Merit, Candn. Soc. of Animal Sci.; Erland Lee Award, Fed. Women's Inst. of Canada; Fellowship, Agric. Inst. of Can.; Warden, St. John's Anglican Ch. 1985–87; St. John's Laymens Assn. 1987– ; Hon. Life Mem., Candn. Soc. of Extension; recreations: fishing; clubs: Cobequid Salmon Assn. (Dir.), N.S. Salmon Assn., Atlantic Salmon Fed., Gamma Sigma Delta; Home: 59 Shannon Dr., Truro, N.S. B2N 3V7; Office: Box 190, Halifax, N.S. B3J 2M4.

**HUGGINS, Charles B.,** B.A., M.Sc., M.D., D.Sc., LL.D., F.R.C.S.(Edin. & Eng.) F.A.C.S., Hon. F.R.S. (Edin.); surgeon; cancer researcher; b. Halifax, N.S., 22 Sept. 1901; s. Charles Edward and Bessie (Spencer) H.; e. Acadia Univ., B.A. 1920, D.Sc. 1946; Harvard Univ., M.D. 1924; Yale Univ., M.Sc. 1947; D.Sc.: Washington Univ. 1950, Leeds Univ. 1953, Turin Univ. 1957, Trinity Coll. 1965, Wales 1967, Univ. of Cal. 1968, Univ. of Mich. 1968; Gustavus Adolphus Coll. 1975; Med. Coll. of Ohio (Toledo) 1973; Univ. of Louisville 1980; Wilmington Coll. (Ohio) 1980; LL.D.: Univ. of Aberdeen 1966, York Univ. 1968; D.P.S.: George Washington Univ. 1967; Sigillum Magnum, Bologna Univ. 1964; Hon. Prof., Madrid Univ. 1956; m. Margaret Wellman, 29 July 1927; children; Charles Edward, Emily Fine; Prof. of Surg., Univ. of Chicago, since 1936; Dir., The Ben May Lab. for Cancer Research, 1951–69; William B. Ogden Distinguished Service Prof., 1962; Intern in Surg., Univ. of Mich., 1924–26; Instr. in Surg. 1926–27; joined Univ. of Chicago as Instr. in Surg., 1927–29; Asst. Prof. 1929–33; Assoc. Prof. 1933–36; Prof. surgery, 1936– ; rec'd. Nobel Prize for Med. and Physiol. 1966; other honors incl.: Am. Med. Assn. for Scient. Exhibits Gold Medal, 1936 and 1940; Katherine Berkan Judd Award for Cancer Research 1942; Charles L. Mayer Award 1944; Gold Medal (Prix Fenwick) 1947; Francis Amory Prize 1948; Am. Urology Assn. Award 1948; Meyer Bodansky Lecture, Univ. of Texas, 1952; Ramon Guiteras Lecture, Am. Urology Assn. 1952 and Medal and Award 1966; Judd Lecture, Univ. of Minn., 1953; Bertner Lecture, M. D. Anderson Hosp., Houston, Texas, 1953; Am. Pharm. Mfrs. Assn. Research Award 1953; Wolbach Mem. Lecture, Harvard Univ. 1955; Am. Assn. Genito-Urinary Surgs. Gold Medal 1955; Assn. Am. Med. Colls., Borden Award and Gold Medal 1955: Order 'Pour le Merite' by German Fed. Republic 1958; Comfort Crookshank Prize for Cancer Research 1958; Charles Mickle Fellowship 1958; Cameron Prize in Practical Therapeutics 1958; City of Hope Award 1958; MacEwen Mem. Lecture, Univ. of Glasgow 1958; Centennial Lecture, Gesellschaft deutscher Naturforscher u. Aerzte, Wiesbaden, 1958; Marnoch Lecture, Univ. of Aberdeen, 1959; Orden 'El Sol del Peru,' Class Grand Offr., 1961; Walker Prize for 1955–60 awarded by Royal Coll. of Surgs. of Eng., 1961 and Moynihan Lecture there, 1963; Oscar B. Hunter Award 1962; First Ferdinand Valentine Award 1962: Albert Lasker Award for Clin. Research 1963; Rudolf Virchow Med. Soc. Gold Medal 1964; Markle Lecture 1965; Passano Foundation Award 1965; The Worshipful Soc. Apothecaries London Gold Medal in Therapeutics 1966; Gairdner Award, Toronto, 1966; Chicago Med. Soc. Award 1967: Acadia Univ. Centennial Medal 1967; Hamilton Award 1967; Bigelow Medal 1967; Univ. of Mich. Sesquicentennial Award 1967: Lincoln Acad. Medal 1967: St. Louis Univ. Silver Medal 1968; Chancellor Acadia Univ., 1972–79; I. S. Ravdin Lect. (Am. Coll. Surgs.) 1974; Tracy O. Powell Lect. (Los Angeles Urol. Soc.) 1975; Lucy Wortham James Lect. of the James Ewing Soc. 1975; Robt. V. Day Lect. (Am. Urol. Assn., Portland) 1975; Franklin Medal, Am. Philosophical Soc. 1985; Sesquicentennial Commemorative Award, The National Library of Medicine 1986; author of over 200 articles in sc. & med.; Hon. Fellowship Inst. of Med. of Chicago, 1968; mem., Royal Soc. Med. (Hon.): Candn. Med. Assn. (Hon.); Nat. Acad. Sciences: Am. Philos. Soc.; Am. Assn. Cancer Research (Hon.): La Academia Nacional de Medicina, Mexico (hon.); Alpha Omega Alpha; Home: 5807 Dorchester Ave., Chicago, IL 60637; Office: 5841 S. Maryland, Chicago, IL 60637.

**HUGGINS, Robert John,** B.A.; publisher, editor-in-chief; b. North York, Ont. 4 June 1958; s. James and Annie Calder (McPherson) H.; e. Univ. of Waterloo B.A. 1981; m. Brenda Anne d. William Russell and Doris Joan (Elliott) Bunker 24 Aug. 1984; PUBLISHER & EDITOR-IN-CHIEF, THIS COUNTRY CANADA PUBLISHING INC. 1992– ; Candn. Depository for Securities Toronto 1981–83; Regional Mgr., The Globe and Mail, InfoGlobe Ottawa 1983–90; Publishing Con., Woodcuts Magazine 1991–92; Sponsor, ABC Canada, The Found. to Promote Literacy in Can.; Candn. Found. for Ileitis & Colitis; Dir., Torbolton Historical Soc., W. Carleton 1990–92; recreations: squash, wood carving, nordic skiing; clubs: National Press Club of Can.; Home: R.R. 3, Woodlawn, Ont. K0A 3M0; Office: P.O. Box 220, Dunrobin, Ont. K0A 1T0.

**HUGHES, Andrew,** M.A., D.Phil.; university professor; b. London, England 3 Aug. 1937; s. Horace and Nora (Lake) H.; e. Merchant Taylors' Sch. 1950–55; Worcester Coll. (Oxford) 1957–64; m. Diane d. Robert and Leonora Rycroft 19 Sept. 1959; one d. Penelope Anne; PROF., UNIV. OF TORONTO 1969– ; UNIVERSITY PROFESSOR 1992; Lectr., Queen's Univ. (Belfast) 1962–64; Asst. Prof., Univ. of Illinois 1964–67; Assoc. Prof., Univ. of N. Carolina 1967–69; Bd. of Dir., Am. Musicological Soc. 1972–74; Counc., Mediaeval Acad. of Am. 1985–88; 'Majestas' 1985– ; Henry Hadow Scholarship (Oxford) 1955; John Lowell Osgood Mem. Prize (Oxford) 1958; Fellow, Guggenheim Found. 1973–74; Trinity coll., Toronto 1980; Mediaeval Acad. of Am. 1987; author: 'Manuscript Accidentals: Ficta in Focus' 1972, 'A Bibliography of Medieval Music' 1974, 2nd ed. 1980, 'Medieval Manuscripts for Mass and Office' 1981, 1986, 'Style and Symbol: Medieval Music 800–1453' 1989 and num. articles in learned jours.; editor: 'Fifteenth Century Liturgical Music' 1968; co-editor: 'The Old Hall Manuscript' 1969, 1973; dir./ed., videotapes: 'Liturgical Manuscripts of the Middle Ages' (2 parts) 1982, 'The Coronation of Henry V of England' 1973, 1985, 'Easter Matins for 14th-Century French Nuns' 1987; prod. of several other medieval reconstructions such as Easter dramas; extensive travel & lectures; recreations: travel, wine-making, computers, tournament croquet; Home: 47 Larkfield Dr., Don Mills, Ont. M3B 2H3; Office: Univ. of Toronto, Fac. of Music, Centre for Medieval Studies, Toronto, Ont. M5S 1A1.

**HUGHES, Barbara Dorothy,** Q.C.; barrister/banking executive; b. Bournemouth, England 22 Jan. 1928; d. William James Pope and Dorothy Margaret (Carter) P.; e. Bournemouth Sch. for Girls 1946; Univ. of London, LL.B. 1949; called to bar, Gray's Inn, London, Eng. 1950, N.S. 1951; m. Gordon F. s. John and Anne H.; one s.: Trevor Ian; PRES., EVANGELINE FINANCIAL SERVICES CORP., EVANGELINE SAVINGS & MORTGAGE CO. & EVANGELINE TRUST CO.; legal practice, Windsor, N.S. 1951– ; appointed Q.C. 1971; Dir., Circuit Investment Ltd.; Maritime Telegraph & Telephone Co.; Ocean Co. Ltd.; Town of Windsor Civic Award 1978; Dir., Participaction 1972–85; Chrmn. 1977–82; Gov. 1985– ; Gov., Kings-Edgehill; Hon. Corresponding Secy., Royal Over-Seas League; Mem., Candn. Bar Assn.; N.S. Barristers Soc.; N.S. Bar Counc. 1956–58; Pres., Hants Co. Barristers Soc. 1979; Home: 1049 King St., Windsor, N.S.; Office: P.O. Box 10, 535 Albert St., Windsor, N.S. B0N 2T0.

**HUGHES, Charles David,** B.A., B.C.L.; lawyer; b. St. Stephen, N.B. 15 June 1942; s. Charles J.A. and Edith B. (Atwater) H.; e. Univ. of New Brunswick B.A. 1964; B.C.L. 1966; m. Pamela d. Roland and Myrna Waddingham 20 Nov. 1971; children: Peter, Lindsay; LAWYER, HUGHES CAMPBELL AND ASSOCIATES; cr. Q.C. 1984; Home: 311 St. John St., Fredericton, N.B. E3B 4B5; Office: 551 Charlotte St., Fredericton, N.B. E3B 1M1.

**HUGHES, David John Llewellyn,** B.A.; business executive; b. Surrey, England 30 Jan. 1934; s. Arthur Llewellyn and Florence Alberta (Sims) H.; e. Marlborough Coll.; Cambridge Univ., B.A. (Hons.) 1957; m. Mary d. Benjamin and Betsy Ball 29 Oct. 1960; children: Christopher, David, Jeremy, Robyn; VICE-PRES., BUSINESS DEVELOPMENT, SIERRA SYSTEMS CONSULTANTS INC. 1988– ; Computer Prog./Analyst, ICL England 1958–61; Mktg. Mgr., ICL Rhodesia 1961–63; Overseas Mktg. Mgr., ICL England 1963–66; Mgr., Computer Hardware & Info. Serv., Candn. Gen. Electric 1966–73; Dir. of Mngt. Info. Serv. & Gen. Mgr., Computer Commun. Group & Gen. Sales, B.C. Tel. Co.

1973–82; C.E.O., Cue Datawest Ltd. 1982–88; var. advs. cttes. to edn. insts. incl. Langara Coll. & B.C. Inst. of Tech.; MART ctee., Sci. Counc. of B.C.; Univ. Computer Science Accreditation Council; Past Chrmn., Candn. Assn. of Data & Profl. Serv. Orgns.; Past Pres., Candn. Info. Processing Soc. (Vancouver Section); Chrmn., B.C. Software Productivity Ctr. 1992– ; Chrmn., BC Technology Industries Assn.; recreation: sailing; Clubs: Vancouver; Home: 3557 W. 8th Ave., Vancouver, B.C. V6R 1Y8; Office: 1400 – 1177 W. Hastings, Vancouver, B.C. V6E 2K3.

**HUGHES, Edward John,** R.C.A.; artist-painter; b. N. Vancouver, B.C. 17 Feb. 1913; e. Vancouver Sch. of Art (teachers incl. F.H. Varley and J.W.G. MacDonald) 1929–35; m. the late Rosabell Smith 1940; free-lance comm. artist in Vancouver 1935–39; collab. on murals for First Un. Ch. and W. K. Oriental Gardens, Vancouver; Malaspina Hotel, Nanaimo and B.C. display in W. States Bldg., Golden Gate Expn., San Francisco, 1939; el. mem., Candn. Group of Painters, 1948 (later resigned); comnd. by Standard Oil Co. to travel on tanker to paint series of B.C. coast, 1954; cross-country trip to paint Candn. cities, 1956; rec'd Can. Council grants to travel and sketch on coast and in interior of B.C., 1958, 1963; painted covers for B.C. telephone directory, 1958–61; mural for Royal York hotel, 'View from Qualicum Beach,' 1958; Canada Post stamp for 125th Anniversary 1992; one-man exhn., Vancouver Art Gallery and York Univ., Toronto, 1967; retrospective exhn.: Surrey Art Gallery 1983; Victoria Art Gallery; Edmonton Art Gallery; Glenbow Museum, Calgary; National Gallery; Beaverbrook Gallery, Fredericton 1984; Heffel Gall., Vancouver 1990; Dominion Gall., Montreal 1991; Madrona Gall., Malaspina Coll., Nanaimo, B.C. 1993; group exhn., Stratford Art Gallery, Stratford, Ont., 1978; Work in permanent colls. of Nat. Gallery Can., Montreal Museum of Fine Art, Art Gallery of Ont., Vancouver and Victoria Art Galleries, Hart House, Toronto, Beaverbrook coll. and other pub. and pte. colls.; enlisted R.C.A. as Gunner 1939; became Army artist (Sgt.) 1940; official Army War Artist (Capt.) in Can., Gt. Brit. and Aleutians, 1942–46; awarded Emily Carr Scholarship 1947; Can. Council Award 1967 and 1970; Mem., Royal Candn. Acad. 1967; Home: Duncan, B.C.; Address: c/o Dominion Gallery, 1438 Sherbrooke St. W. Montreal, Que. H3G 1K4.

**HUGHES, Francis Norman,** B.S., Phm.B., M.A., LL.D., D.Sc.; dean emeritus; b. Dresden, Ont. 23 Jan. 1908; s. Charles Harvey Norman and Ella May (McKim) H.; e. Sarnia (Ont.) Coll. Inst.; Ont. Coll. of Pharmacy (Univ. of Toronto), Phm.B. 1929; Purdue Univ., B.S. (Pharm.), 1940, and Hon. LL.D., 1954; Univ. of Toronto, M.A. 1944, LL.D. (hon. causa) 1980; m. 1st Helen Laird Hamilton (died 11 Apl. 1953), 2 Sept. 1935; 2ndly, Lorna Felice Roberts Hunt, 25 June 1954; children: Judith, Mary, Margaret, Elizabeth, David, Donald, Linda; DEAN EMERITUS, FACULTY OF PHARMACY, UNIV. OF TORONTO since 1973; Dean upon estab. of the Faculty 1953–73; Apprentice in Ingersoll Bros. Pharmacy, Sarnia, Ont., 1924–27 and Partner there 1930–37; mem., Bd. of Examiners, Ont. Coll. of Pharm., Toronto 1930–37; apptd. Asst. Prof. of Materia Medica, Ont. Coll. of Pharm. 1938, Prof. 1946, Asst. Dean 1948 and Dean 1952; mem. of Diocesan Bd. of Religious Educ., Toronto Diocese 1948–56; Publications: 'New Products Index' Vols. 1 to 13, 1951–58; 'Compendium of Pharmaceutical Specialties' 1960, 1963, 1967–79; Pres. 1956–57 Candn. Found. for Adv. Pharm. and Chrmn. of Comte. on Pharm. Educ. and Research; mem., Council, Ont. Coll. of Pharmacy 1953–73; Pres., Can. Conference Ph. Fac. 1952–53; Pres., Assoc. Fac. Ph. of Can. 1970; Assoc. Deans Ph. of Can. 1966–69; Pharm. Examining Bd. Can. 1964–66; mem. Ed. Bd., Applied Therapeutics (1959–65); Contrib. Ed., 'Canadian Pharmaceutical Journal' to 1979; Registrar-Treas., Pharmacy Examining Bd. Can., 1973–81; Hon. Life mem., Candn. Pharm. Assn.; Candn. Soc. Hosp. Pharm.; Ont. Pharm. Assn.; Assn. of Fac. of Pharm. of Can.; Assn. of Deans of Pharm. of Can.; Ont. Coll. of Pharmacists; Hon. LL.D., Purdue 1954; Dalhousie 1973; Toronto 1980; Hon. D.Sc., Memorial Univ. 1990; Kappa Psi; Rho Pi Phi (Rokeah Chapter, Hon. Chancellor); Conservative; Anglican; Home: 74 Batson Dr., Aurora, Ont. L4G 3P8.

**HUGHES, Gerald Francis George,** B.Sc.; diplomat; b. Sayabec, Que. 10 Mar. 1919; s. Samuel George and Catherine May (Bellenger) H.; e. Campbellton (N.B.) High Sch.; Univ. of N.B. B.Sc. (Elect. Engn.) 1940; m. Mary d. William and Helena Wade 28 Feb. 1942; three s. Michael, Christopher, Timothy; Engr., Canadian General Electric Co. Toronto 1940–41; R.C.N.V.R. 1941–45; rank Lieut. Cdr. (Electrical); joined Candn. Govt. Trade Commr. Service 1945; Trade Commr. Glasgow 1946–48, Comm. Secy. Ankara and Istanbul 1948–52, opened Govt. Trade Office Beirut 1952, Asst. Dir. Trade Commr. Service Ottawa 1957, Comm. Counsellor Stockholm 1961–62, Dir. Indust. Promotion Br. 1962–64, Dir. Internat. Trade Centre Expo '67 Montreal 1964–67, Min.-Counsellor Rome 1968–71, Ambassador to Turkey 1971–74, Dir. in F.I.R.A. Ottawa 1974–76, Min. (Comm.) London 1976–80; High Commr. to Malaysia 1981–83; 'Freedom of City of London' Apr. 2 1980; retired 1984 from Dept. of External Affairs; Anglican: recreations: golf, fishing; Clubs: White Pine Fishing (Ottawa); Country Club, Aylmer; Home: 402 Island Park Dr., Ottawa, Ont. K1Y 0A9.

**HUGHES, Gordon Frederick;** O.C.; executive; b. Windsor, N.S. 30 March 1924; s. John Frederick and Annie Margaret H.; e. Windsor (N.S.) Acad.; m. Barbara Dorothy Pope; one s. Trevor Ian; CHRMN., OCEAN CO. LTD.; Chrmn., Evangeline Financial Services Corp.; Dir., Circuit Investment Ltd.; John Labatt Ltd.; Part-time mem. Candn. Radio TV Comn. 1968–74; Officer, Order of Canada (1979); served with RCAF as Wireless Airgunner 1943–46; Home: Hampshire Court, 1049 King St., Windsor, N.S. B0N 2T0; Office: Box 10, King St., Windsor, N.S.

**HUGHES, Graeme Clive,** M.A.T.S., M.A., LL.B., N.D.C.; association executive; business consultant; b. Sydney, Australia 28 Oct. 1938; s. Lance Clive and Edna Martha (Saville) H.; e. Univ. of Sydney (Australia) LL.B. 1960; post-grad. studies in law, London Univ. 1962; Nat. Def. Coll. (Kingston, Ont.) N.D.C. 1980; York Univ. M.A. 1982; Inst. of Transpersonal Psychology, M.A.C.T.S. 1993; practised law as Barrister, Sydney, Australia 1962–68; joined Candn. Mfrs.' Assn. 1968–85; involved in public policy issues affecting mfrs.; Sr. Extve. Vice-Pres. and Sec., Candn. Mfrs.' Assn. 1980–85; Pres. & Sec., Candn. Business Equipment Manufacturers' Assn. 1985–87; Pres. & Sec., Information Technology Assoc. of Can. 1987–90; Adjunct Prof. of Mgmt. Studies, Univ. of Waterloo 1990–91; Consultant 1991–93; author: 'The Foreign Investment Review Act' 1975; 'Foreign Investment Law in Canada' 1983; numerous articles on bus.-govt. relations, information technology and transpersonal studies; recreations: travel, reading, music, athletics; Address: #103, 2061 Beach Ave., Vancouver, B.C. V6G 1Z3.

**HUGHES, John Noel;** investment dealer; b. Jamaica, W. Indies 5 Jan. 1930; s. Noel W. and Mary (Crosse) H.; e. De Carteret Prep. Sch. and Munro Coll., Jamaica; Trinity Coll. Sch., Port Hope, Ont.; m. Janice, d. Lawrence Jackson, 12 Sept. 1958; children: Peter, Sarah; Vice-President, Levesque Beaubien Geoffrion Inc. 1989– ; Chrmn. & Dir., J.L. Graham & Co. Ltd. 1951–70; Chrmn. & Dir., Burgess Graham Securities Ltd. 1970–87; Vice-Chrmn. & Dir., Geoffrion Leclerc & Co. Ltd. 1987–89; mem. Toronto Stock Exchange; Invest. Dealers' Assn. of Can.; Anglican; recreations: golf, tennis, fishing, hunting; Clubs: Badminton & Racquet; Toronto Hunt; Home: 37 Elderwood Dr., Toronto, Ont. M5P 1W8.

**HUGHES, Linda J.,** B.A.; newspaper publisher; b. Princeton, B.C. 27 Sept. 1950; d. Edward Rees and Madge Preston (Bryan) H.; e. Univ. of Victoria, B.A. 1972; m. George Ward 16 Dec. 1978; children: Sean Edward, Katherine Ruth; PUBLISHER, THE EDMONTON JOURNAL 1992– ; joined Victoria Times 1972–76, Reporter, Legis. Bureau Chief; present newspaper 1976, Reporter, Ed. Writer, City Ed., News Ed., Asst. Mng. Ed., Editor 1987–92; recipient Southam Fellowship, Univ. of Toronto 1977–78; Office: P.O. Box 2421, Edmonton, Alta. T5J 2S6.

**HUGHES, Margaret Eileen,** B.A., M.S.W., LL.M.; educator; b. Saskatoon, Sask. 22 Jan. 1943; d. E. Duncan and Eileen (Shaver) Farmer; e. Univ. of Sask. B.A. 1965, LL.B. 1966 (Brown Prize as top graduate 1966); Univ. of Mich. M.S.W. 1968, LL.M. 1968 (William Cooke Fellowship 1966–68); m. James Roscoe s. Roscoe and Irene Hughes 21 May 1966; two d. Shannon Margaret, Krista Lynn; PROF. OF LAW, UNIVERSITY OF CALGARY, Dean of Law 1984–89 (1st woman dean of a Candn. Law Sch.); mem. Fac. of Law, Univ. of Windsor 1968–75; Exec. Interchange Prog., Dept. of Justice, Can. 1975–77, Counsel Dept. Justice 1977–78; Prof. of Law, Univ. of Sask. 1978–84; Fac. mem., Senior Univ. Administrators Course Banff 1990– ; ed. 'National Trends in Family Law' 1988 and numerous law casebooks Univs. of Windsor, Sask. and Calgary; author various book chapters, briefs; presented invited papers lawyer's confs.; cons. family law projects Dept. Justice, Ottawa; Chair, Council of Candn. Law Deans 1987–88; mem. Law Soc. Alta.; Law Soc. Upper Can.; Law Soc. Sask.; mem., Exec. Ctte. & Bd. of Dirs.: Industrial Relations Research Group 1990– ; Candn. Inst. of Resources Law 1984–89; Candn. Rsch. Inst. for Law and The Family 1984–89; Candn. Assn. Children & Adults Learning Disabilities (National Legal Resources Ctte.) 1982–86; recreations: swimming, skiing; Office: Univ. of Calgary, Calgary, Alta. T2N 1N4.

**HUGHES, Monica Mary;** writer; b. Liverpool, Eng. 3 Nov. 1925; d. Edward Lindsay and Phyllis (Fry) Ince; e. Eng. & Scot.; m. Glen s. Edward and Leta Hughes 22 Apr. 1957; children: Elizabeth, Adrienne, Russell, Thomas; author (juvenile fiction) 'Gold-Fever Trail' 1974; 'Crisis on Conshelf Ten' 1975; 'Earthdark' 1977; 'The Tomorrow City' 1978; 'Ghost Dance Caper' 1978; 'Beyond the Dark River' 1979; 'The Keeper of the Isis Light' 1980; 'The Guardian of Isis' 1981; 'The Isis Pedlar' 1982; 'The Beckoning Lights' 1982; 'The Treasure of the Long Sault' 1982; 'Hunter in the Dark' 1982; 'Ring-Rise, Ring-Set' 1982; 'Space Trap' 1983; 'My Name is Paula Popowich!' 1983; 'Devil on My Back' 1984; 'Sandwriter' 1985; 'The Dream Catcher' 1986; 'Blaine's Way' 1986; 'Log Jam' 1987; 'The Refuge' 1989; 'Little Fingerling' 1989; 'The Promise' 1989; 'Invitation to the Game' 1990; 'The Crystal Drop' 1992; 'A Handful of Seeds' 1993; recipient Beaver Award 1980; Vicky Metcalf Award 1981; Alta. Culture Juvenile Novel Award 1981; Can. Council Prize Children's Lit. 1981, 1982; IBBY Cert. of Honour 1982; Lib. Assn. Young Adult Novel Award 1983; Guardian Award runner-up 1983; Writers Guild Alta. R. Ross Annett Award 1983, 1984, 1987, 1992; Silver Feather Award (Germany) 1986; Bookenleeuw (Netherlands) 1987–88; Writer-in-Residence Univ. of Alta. 1984–85, Edmonton Public Lib. 1988–89, Henry Kreisel Lectr. 1987; short residencies incl. Boys & Girls House Toronto, Jasper, Windsor, Medicine Hat; served with WRNS 1943–46; came to Can. 1952; Lab. Tech. Nat. Rsch. Council 1952–57; mem. Internat. P.E.N.; Writers Union Can.; Writers Guild Alta.; Candn. Soc. Children's Authors, Illustrators & Performers; Speculative Writers' Assoc. of Can.; recreations: swimming, walking, reading, beachcombing; Home: 13816 – 110A Avenue, Edmonton, Alta. T5M 2M9.

**HUGHES, Pamela Susan,** B.A., LL.B., LL.M.; securities lawyer, executive; b. Winnipeg, Man. 27 Nov. 1951; d. Edgar Murray and Selma Margaret (Miller) McClarty; e. Vincent Massey Collegiate; McGill Univ. B.A. (Hons.) 1974, LL.B. 1977; Univ. of Toronto, Fraser & Beatty Fellowship LL.M.; m. David Philip s. Charles and Joan H. 3 June 1972; children: Peter David, Andrew Hunter, Christopher Blake; DIRECTOR, INTERNATIONAL MARKETS / CAPITAL MARKETS, ONTARIO SECURITIES COMMISSION 1991– ; Part-time Journalist, 'Canadian Business' 1971–81; Lawyer, Tory Tory DesLauriers & Binnington 1980–87; Corp. Finance Solicitor, Ont. Securities Comn. 1987–88; Dep. Dir., Corp. Finance 1988–89; Dir., Internat. Markets 1989–91; primary negotiator for Canada of multi-jurisdictional disclosure system between Canada & U.S.; Mem., Internat. Orgn. of Securities Comns. (IOSCO) 1987– ; Working Party on Internat. Equity Offers & Working Party on Secondary Markets 1992– ; Chair, Internat. Markets Ctte., Candn. Securities Administrators; Mem., Capital Markets Ctte.; Consultative Ctte. between EC and IOSCO; author of journal articles; recreations: cycling, swimming, walking, gardening; Home: 217 Riverside Dr., Toronto, Ont. M6S 4A8; Office: 20 Queen St. W., Suite 800, Box 55, Toronto, Ont. M5H 3S8.

**HUGHES, Samuel Frederick;** executive; b. Toronto, Ont. 25 Aug. 1929; s. Samuel Ashfield and Alice Lambson (Mann) H.; e. Upper Can. Coll.; Univ. of W. Ont. Sch. of Bus. Adm.; m. Joan L. d. Frederick and Stella Sasse 12 Apl. 1958; children: Stephen S., Heather A., Cynthia F.; CHRMN. CORPORATION HOUSE LTD.; Pres. Candn. C. of C. Ottawa; Chrmn., Bd. Carleton Univ.; Dir., Royal Candn. Geog. Soc.; Clubs: Toronto, Rockcliffe Park Tennis, Jonathan's Landing Golf & Country; Home: 186 Acacia Ave., Rockcliffe Park, Ont. K1M 0L5; Office: 1400, 60 Queen St., Ottawa, Ont. K1P 5Y7.

**HUGHES, Hon. Samuel Harvey Shirecliffe,** Q.C., M.A.; retired judge; b. Victoria, B.C. 24 Oct. 1913; s. Maj.-Gen. Garnet Burk, C.B., C.M.G., D.S.O., and Elizabeth Irene Bayliss (Newling) H.; e. Stowe Sch., (England); Upper Canada Coll., Toronto, Ont.; Univ. of Toronto, (Trinity Coll.) B.A. 1934; Oxford Univ., (Balliol Coll.) B.A. 1936, M.A. 1951; Osgoode Hall, Toronto, Ont.; m. Helen Beatrice, d. late L. B. Spencer, Q.C., 27 July 1940; children: Lynn Spencer (Mrs. John H. Clappison), Samuel Garnet Spencer; Justice, Supreme Court of Ont. 1958–59 and 1962–88; read law with L. B. Spencer, Q.C., Welland, Ont.; called to the Bar of Ont. 1947; cr. Q.C. 1955; History Master, Ridley

Coll., St. Catharines, Ont., 1936–39; practised law with Raymond Spencer Law & MacInnes, Welland, Ont. 1947–55; Chrmn., Ont. Highway Transport Bd. 1955–58; Chrmn. Civil Service Comn. Can. 1959–62; apptd. to conduct Roy. Comn. on Atlantic Acceptance Corp. 1965 (reported to Ont. Govt. 1969); apptd. to conduct Roy. Comn. on Waste Mang. Inc. 1977 (reported to Ont. Govt. 1978); apptd. Chrmn., Ont. Electoral Boundaries Comn. 1983; Chrmn., Federal Electoral Boundaries Comn. for Ont. 1986; apptd. to conduct Royal Comn. of Inquiry into the Response of the Nfld. Criminal Justice System to Complaints 1989 (reported to Nfld. Govt. 1991); Alderman, City of Welland, 1953, 1954, 1955; served in 2nd World War; Overseas with Gov. Gen. Horse Guards as Lieut. 1941; trans. to Candn. Intelligence Corps 1942; Italy (1st Candn. Inf. Div.) 1943–44; Historical Sec., Gen. Staff; Lieut.-Col. on retirement, Apr. 1946; Zeta Psi; Protestant; Clubs: University; Leander (Henley-on-Thames, England); Home: 260 Forest Hill Rd., Toronto, Ont. M5P 2N5.

**HUGHES, Stanley John,** D.Sc., F.M.L.S., F.R.S.C.; mycologist; b. Llanelli, Dyfed, Wales 17 Sept. 1918; s. John Thomas and Gertrude (Roberts) H.; e. Llanelli Grammar Sch. 1938; Univ. Coll. of Wales B.Sc. 1941, M.Sc. 1943, D.Sc. 1954; m. Lyndell Anne d. late Wilfred Conway Rutherford 11 Oct. 1958; children: Robert Conway, Glenys Anne, David Stanley; HON. RESEARCH ASSOC., CENTRE FOR LAND AND BIOLOGICAL RESOURCES RESEARCH, CENTRAL EXPER. FARM 1983– ; Asst. to Adv. Mycologist, Nat. Agric. Adv. Service, Univ. Colls. of Wales, Aberystwyth and Cardiff 1941–45; Asst. Mycologist, Commonwealth Mycological Inst., Kew, Eng. 1945–52; Mycologist, Central Exper. Farm, Agric. Can. Ottawa 1952–58, Sr. Mycologist 1958–62; Princ. Mycologist 1962–83; invited scient. Univ. of Ghana 1949; tour of Herbaria univs. and museums of Europe 1955; Sr. Research Fellow, DSIR, Auckland, N.Z. 1963; Nat. Research Councils of Can. and Brazil Exchange Scient. Univ. of Pernambuco, Recife 1974; rec'd Jakob Eriksson Gold Medal 1969; George Lawson Medal, Candn. Bot. Assn. 1981; Distinguished Mycologist Award, Mycol. Soc. Am. 1985; elected Foreign Member, Linnean Soc. of London 1986; author over 120 publs.; Assoc. Ed. 'Canadian Journal of Botany' 1968–79; Ed. 'Fungi Canadenses' 1973–83; Foreign Vice Pres. and Hon. Mem., Brit. Mycol. Soc. 1987; mem., Mycol. Soc. Am. (Pres. 1975); Internat. Mycol. Assn. (Vice Pres. 1977–83); United Church; Home: 360 Hamilton Ave., Ottawa, Ont. K1Y 1C5; Office: Mycology Unit, Centre for Land and Biological Resources Research, Saunders Bldg., Central Experimental Farm, Ottawa, Ont. K1A 0C6.

**HUGHES ANTHONY, Nancy,** B.A.; public servant; g. Montreal 3 July 1949; d. Maurice E. and Ruth E. (McDiarmid) Hughes; e. McGill Univ. B.A. 1970; m. Brian s. Frederick and Gladys Anthony 1979; children: Elizabeth, David; DEPUTY MINISTER OF VETERANS AFFAIRS CANADA 1993– ; var. positions, Dept. of Sec. of State, The Canada Council, Treasury Bd. Secretariat, External Affairs & Energy Mines & Resources 1970–86; Special Asst. & Advisor, Dept. of Energy & Forestry then Secretary for Intergov. Affairs, Govt. of P.E.I. 1987–89; Deputy Minister, Office of Privatization & Regulatory Affairs 1990; Deputy Min., Consumer and Corporate Affairs, Govt. of Canada 1991; Bd. Mem., Inst. of Public Admin. of Canada; Federal Business Devel. Bank; Trustee, Public Service Management Insur. Plan and Trustee, Ottawa Gen. Hosp.; Home: 109 Powell Avenue, Ottawa, Ont.; Office: Lord Elgin Plaza, 66 Slater St., Ottawa, Ont. K1A 0P4.

**HUGO, John Robert Yeomans,** B.P.H.E., B.A., LL.B.; barrister and solicitor; b. Newmarket, Ont. 18 Dec. 1932; s. Howard Victor and Georgia (Hewitt) H.; e. Pub. and High Sch., Newmarket; Univ. of Toronto, B.P.H.E. 1955, B.A. 1956; Osgoode Hall Law Sch., LL.B. 1960; m. Gloria Dianne, d. Charles Noakes, 26 May 1978; children: Michael John, Tracy; SOLE PRACTITIONER; read law with Fraser, Beatty, Tucker, McIntosh & Stewart, 1958–62, McDonald, Davies & Ward, 1962, Partner, 1963; Partner, McDonald & Zimmerman, 1966; mem., Candn. Bar Assn.; Candn. Tax Foundation; United Church; recreations: golf, squash, tennis, swimming; skiing; Clubs: Cambridge; Lambton Golf & Country; Oxford; Office: Suite 1200, 8 King St. E., Toronto, Ont. M5C 1B5.

**HULBERT, Richard Elliot,** M.A.I.B.C., F.R.A.I.C., R.A.I.A., M.Arch., A.I.A., R.C.A.; architect; b. St. Louis, Mo. 25 Dec. 1945; s. Sidney and Lillian (Waisman) H.; e. Univ. of Ariz. B.Arch. 1969 (Silver Medal Am. Inst. Archs.); Univ. of Calif. Berkeley M.Arch. 1970; PRINCIPAL ARCHITECT, THE HULBERT GROUP 1974– ; joined GRV Design Group 1970, Pres. Los Angeles Div. 1972–74; Fellow, Royal Arch. Inst. of Can.; Former Past Chrmn., Candn. Housing Design Council; has won a design award every year for the past 19 yrs., including Governor General's Awards for Architecture; jury mem. various award programs; rep. Can. 1981, 1987 Can./Japan Housing Meetings Tokyo; frequent guest speaker innovative design and planning and computer applications to architecture nat. and internat. meetings; author over 50 articles; Mem., Coll. of Fellows, Royal Architectural Inst. of Can.; Academician, Royal Candn. Acad. of the Arts; Past Pres., Architectural Inst. of B.C.; Former Dir., Candn. Wood Counc.; Past Chrmn., Candn. Housing Design Counc.; Past Dir., Urban Development Inst., Pacific Region; Founding Chrmn., Arts Umbrella Found. School for Visual and Performing Arts; Founding Mem., Ed. Adv. Bd., Building Renovation Magazine; Mem., The Am. Resort and Residential Development Assoc.; The Royal Australian Inst. of Architects; Queensland, Australia Bd. of Architects; New South Wales Bd. of Architects; California Bd. of Architects; Florida Bd. of Architects; Office: 2429 Marine Dr., West Vancouver, B.C. V7V 1L3.

**HULCHANSKI, John David,** B.A., M.Sc.(Pl.), Ph.D.; educator; b. Syracuse, NY 23 May 1949; s. John and Dorothy (Koczan) H.; e. Siena Coll. (Loudonville, NY) B.A. Pol. Sci. and Hist. 1971; Univ. of Toronto M.Sc. (Pl.) Urban & Regional Planning 1974, Ph.D. Urban & Regional Planning 1981; m. Elizabeth Rea Devakos d. Thomas and Mary D. 28 Apr. 1984; one d. Anna Mary Devakos; PROFESSOR, HOUSING POLICY, FACULTY OF SOCIAL WORK, UNIV. OF TORONTO 1991– ; Dir., Centre for Human Settlements, Univ. of B.C. 1988–91 and Prof., Sch. of Community and Regional Planning, Univ. of B.C. 1983–91; Rsch. Assoc. Univ. of Toronto Centre for Urban and Community Studies 1978–83; part-time Instr. Univ. of Toronto Urban Studies Prog. 1975–83; Cons. Urban Planning and Residential Devel. 1973–76, 1980– ; Visiting Prof., Kyoto Univ., Japan 1986; author: scholarly articles, rsch. monographs, govt. studies on housing policy, community planning and hist. of Candn. planning and housing; North Am. Editor, 'Housing Studies' (journal) 1993– ; Ed. U.B.C. Planning Papers 1985–91; Ed. Papers on Planning and Design, Univ. of Toronto 1977–81; Housing Rsch. Cons.: Ont. Human Rights Commission 1992–93; Ont. Fair Tax Commission 1990; Yukon Housing Corp. 1986; Ont. Comn. of Inquiry into Residential Tenancies 1984; Canada Mortgage and Housing Corp. 1982–86; Soc. Planning Counc. of Metrop. Toronto 1982–83; Ont. Min. of Municipal Affairs and Housing 1982; Co-operative Housing Found. of Can. 1981–83; mem. Candn. Housing and Renewal Assn.; Candn. Inst. of Planners; Am. Planning Assn.; Office: 246 Bloor St. W., Rm. 602, Toronto, Ont. M5S 1A1.

**HULL, Brian Allan Rodger,** M.A.; economist; b. Ottawa, Ont. 9 May 1942; s. Lt. Gen. (R) Allan Chester, CMM, DFC, CD and Katherine Jane (Currier) H.; e. Lakefield Coll. Sch. Ont. 1960; Univ. of Toronto, B.A. 1964; Cambridge Univ. B.A. 1966, M.A. 1969; Yale Univ. grad. studies econ. 1966–69; m. (2ndly) Theresa Lynn d. Lt. Cdr. (R) Thomas V. and Patricia Stephens 15 Apr. 1989; PRINCIPAL, BRIAN HULL & ASSOCIATES 1981–89, 1993– ; joined Ont. Min. of Treasury & Econ. 1970, Sr. Budget Adv. Personal Taxes, Income Security & Pensions 1974 and Fiscal Policy 1975–80; Exec. Dir. Candn. Found. for Econ. Edn. 1980–81; Special Adv. Fed. Sales Tax Reform consultations Dept. Finance Ottawa 1984–87; Staff Mem., Global Secretariat, The Hunger Project, N.Y.C. 1988; Principal Rsch. Assoc., The Conference Bd. of Can. (Business and Environment Program) 1990–93; Lectr. in Internat. Econ. Atkinson Coll. York Univ. 1973–77; Candn. Spokesperson Live Aid for Africa 1985; Bd. Mem., Hunger Project, Canada 1992– (Chrmn. 1993– ; volunteer 1978– ); recipient Hon. Woodrow Wilson and Commonwealth Fellowships; Can. Council, Yale Fellowships; author 'International Development: Challenge to Christians' 1970; 'The Post Transition Economy' 1986; co-author (with Barry Sadler) 'In Business for Tomorrow: The Transition to Sustainable Development' highlights of Globe '90, 1990; author or co-author various papers, articles, submissions; mem. Parish Council and Churchwarden, Ch. of Holy Trinity Toronto 1972–76; recreations: jogging, swimming, skiing; Home: 766 St. Andre Dr., Ottawa, Ont. K1P 5P7; Office: P.O. Box 632, Station B, Ottawa, Ont. K1P 5P7.

**HULL, Robert (Bobby) Marvin,** O.C.; hockey player (retired) farmer; b. Pointe Anne, Ont. 3 Jan. 1939; s. Robert Edward and Lena (Cook) H.; m. Joanne McKay, 1960 (div.); children: Bobby Jr., Blake, Brett, Bart; Commentator, Hockey Night in Canada 1982– ; turned pro with Chicago Black Hawks 1957–58 season playing left wing in NHL through 1971–72 campaign before shifting to Winnipeg Jets of WHA 1972–79; briefly player-coach before returning to playing only; second to Gordie Howe in goals, points scored; in 15 NHL seasons played in 1,036 regular schedule games scoring 604 goals, 67 assists for 129 points and 102 penalty minutes; in four WHA seasons played in 330 games, scored 255 goals, 261 assists, 516 points 160 penalty minutes; five 50–plus goal seasons with Chicago; first team all-star NHL 10 times, WHA four times; second team NHL twice; Lady Byng Trophy (most gentlemanly NHL) 1964–65; Lester Patrick Award (service to hockey in US) 1969; Gary Davidson Trophy (WHA MVP) 1973, 1975; nickname Golden Jet; fastest left-handed slap shot 118.3 mph, fastest skater 29.7 mph; author 'Hockey is My Game'; Pres., Bobby Hull Enterprises.

**HULL, Russell D.,** M.B.B.S., M.Sc., F.R.C.P.(C), F.A.C.P., F.C.C.P.; b. Hobart, Tasmania, Australia 24 Aug. 1945; s. Leslie Norman and Nancy Mansfield (Russell) H.; e. Univ. of Sydney M.B.B.S. 1968; McMaster Univ. M.Sc. 1981; m. Lillian d. John and Alice O'Leary 4 Sept. 1973; children: Janet, Alexandra, Kathryn, James, Elizabeth, Margaret, Jonathan; DIRECTOR, CLINICAL TRIALS UNIT and PROF. OF MED. UNIV. OF CALGARY 1988– ; Ont. Heart Fellow Chedoke-McMaster Hosps. Hamilton 1974–78, Lectr. in Med. 1976–78, Asst. Prof. of Med. 1978–82, Dir. Non-Invasive Venous Vascular Lab. 1980–88, Chief of Med. Chedoke Hosp. Div. 1981–88, Assoc. Prof. of Med. McMaster Univ. 1982–88, Prof. 1988, Assoc. Appt. Dept. Clin Epidemiol. & Biostats. 1982–88; Dir. Clin. Trials Unit present Univ. 1988– ; Head Div. Gen. Internal Med. Foothills Hosp. 1988–93; recipient Commonwealth Scholarship 1963–68; Rotary Postgrad. Fellowship 1970–71; CIBA Fellowship 1972; Candn. Heart Fellow 1976–78; Candn. Heart Scholar 1978–84; Distinguished Scientist Award, Candn. Soc. for Clinical Investigation 1993; College Medallist Lectr., Am. College of Chest Physicians 1993; author or co-author numerous articles, abstracts, book chapters; over 400 sci. presentations nat. and internat. meetings & symposia; mem. Am. Heart Assn. (Exec. Ctte. Council Thrombosis); Central Soc. Clin. Rsch.; Heart & Stroke Found. Ont. (Med. Rsch. Ctte.); Alta. Heart & Stroke Found. (Sci. Review Ctte.) and numerous other profl. socs.; mem. Westwind Chorus Calgary; recreation: vocal arts (counter-tenor); Home: 339 Edelweiss Pl., Calgary, Alta. T3A 3R2; Office: 3330 Hosp. Dr. N.W., Calgary, Alta. T2N 4N1.

**HULLAH, William Arthur,** B.Sc.Agr., M.Sc., C.F.E.; food industry executive; b. Toronto, Ont. 2 June 1943; s. Arthur Havelock and Ida Brenda (Sheridan) H.; e. Univ. of Guelph, B.Sc.Agr. 1967; Univ. of B.C., M.Sc. 1969; m. Evelyn d. John Russell and Doris Camelon 27 June 1970; children: Joanne, Karen, Gary; FOUNDER, PRES., CHIEF EXTVE. OFFR. & DIR., FTI FOODTECH INTERNATIONAL INC. 1985– ; Prof. of Microbiol., Ryerson Polytech. Inst. 1969–83; Founder/Op., Industrial Bacteriol. Serv. 1969–76; Food Microbiol. Cons., 1976 Summer Olympics, Montreal; Founder & Pres., Cardinal Biologicals Ltd. (incl. Cardinal Labs., Cardinal Kitchens) 1976– ; author of several food rsch. papers & patents; C.F.E.; Past Warden, Anglican Ch. of the Ascension; Pres., Toronto Br., Candn. Food Serv. Extve. Assn. 1984–85; Vice-Pres., Nat. 1985; Mem., Candn. Inst. of Food Sci. & Technol.; recreations: badminton, tennis, hiking; Office: 43 Railside Rd., Don Mills, Ont. M3A 3L9.

**HUMBER, Charles Joseph,** B.A., M.A.; publisher; b. St. Lambert, Que. 14 July 1936; s. Charles Maitland and Evelyn Audrey (Jarvis) H.; e. Temple Univ. B.A. 1962; Univ. of Wisconsin M.A. 1970; m. Gayle d. Raymond and Beatrice Jenkins 22 Nov. 1961; children: Kristan Laura, Karyn Anna, Charles William, Scott Nicholas; PUBLISHER, HEIRLOOM PUBLISHING INC. 1985– ; Mktg. & Sales, Toronto Telegram 1956–59; Teacher, Thomas L. Kennedy S.S. 1962–66; Streetsville S.S. 1967–68; Lawrence Park C.I. 1969–77; Oakwood C.I. 1977–83; freelance editor & writer 1983–85; Night School Instr. in Antiques (Etobicoke Bd. of Edn.) 1973–75; Hon. Mem., The Hereditary Order of Descendents of The Loyalists & Patriots of the Am. Revolution; Chevron, Hosp. Order of Saint John of Jerusalem; Companion, Most Hon. Order of Meritorious Heritage; Ont. Bicentennial Serv. Award 1984; Protestant (Baptist); Pres., The John W. Fisher Soc. 1985– 93; The United Empire Loyalists' Asn. of Can. 1982–84; Gov. Simcoe Branch 1980–82; Dir., John Graves Simcoe Assn. 1981–93; Mem., Monarchist League of Can.; Toronto Toronto Postcard Club; Co-editor: 'Loyal She Remains' 1984; author: 'Foreword' to 'Loyalist Mosaic: A Multi-cultural Heritage' 1984; Publisher-editor: 'Canada: From Sea Unto Sea' 1986, rev. 1988, 'Canada's Native Peoples' 1988, rev. 1989, 'Allegiance: The Ontario Story'

1991, Pathfinders: Canadian Tributes' 1994; collaborated with several authors incl. most recent: Patricia Fleming in 'Traditions in Wood' 1987; participant, 'Georgian Canada,' Bicentennial Exbn., Royal Ont. Museum 1984; recreation: collector, Canadiana; Home: 1821 Deer's Wold, Mississauga, Ont. L5K 2H1; Office: 6509B Mississauga Rd., Mississauga, Ont. L5N 1A6.

**HUMBER, William Arthur,** B.A., M.E.S.; college executive; b. Toronto, Ont. 9 Sept. 1949; s. Alfred and Betty Louise (Westlake) H.; e. Univ. of Toronto, B.A. 1972; York Univ. M.E.S. (Environmental Studies) 1975; m. Catherine Ellen d. John and Ruth McConkey 10 Aug. 1974; children: Bradley Arthur, Darryl Arthur, Karen Ellen; CHRMN. CONTINUING EDN. SENECA COLL. OF APPLIED ARTS & TECHNOL. 1983– ; Pub. Participation Offr. N. Pickering Project 1974–76; Community & Continuing Edn. Co-ordinator Seneca Coll. 1977–83; Mem. Bd. of Govs., Candn. Baseball Hall of Fame and Museum 1993– ; Founding Vice-Pres., Soc. for Internat. Hockey Rsch. (SIHR), Kingston, Ont. 1991; mem. Newcastle Community Services Planning Bd. 1983–86; Pres. Visual Arts Centre Newcastle 1975–76; Sec. Soc. Am. Baseball Rsch. 1982–83; author 'The Soccer Book' 1994; 'The Baseball Book' first release of the Sports Trophy Series 1990; 'Let's Play Ball' 1989; 'Freewheeling: The Story of Bicycling in Canada' 1986; 'Cheering for the Home Team: The Story of Baseball in Canada' 1983; co-author (with Doris Falls) 'The Story of Central Public School, Bowmanville: 1889–1989' 1989; subject specialist to the Royal Ont. Museum for its major exhibit on baseball in 1989; recipient Central Mortgage & Housing Corp. Fellowship 1973; Anglican; Home: 15 Beech Ave., Bowmanville, Ont. L1C 3A1; Office: 1750 Finch Ave. E., Willowdale, Ont. M2J 2X5.

**HUME, Catherine Douglas,** B.Comm.; investor relations consultant; b. Moose Jaw, Sask. 3 May 1951; d. H. Douglas and Idelhia Louise (Ironside) Hume; e. Univ. of Guelph B.Comm. (Hons.) 1974; VICE-PRES., KIERAN & CO. INC. 1993– ; Claims Adjuster & Supervisor, Candn. General & Liberty Mutual 1976–80; Registered Rep., Richardson Greenshields of Canada 1980–86; Vice Pres., Registered Rep., Deacon Barclays de Zoete Wedd Limited 1986–91; Co-owner/Operator of Group of Moneysworth & Best Quality Shoe Repair franchises (downtown Toronto) and built a N. Am. mktg. & distbn. network of 70 distributors of personal & health care products 1989–present; private pilot licence 1978; Candn. Investment Finances parts I & II for designation F.C.S.I. 1984; Dir. & Offrs. Exams for Brokers & Securities Dealers 1988; Centre for Resource Studies, Queen's Univ. 1-week intensive mining course; French Studies, Alliance française Paris 1974–75; Dir., Bd. of Gov., Univ. of Guelph; Extve. Ctte. of the Bd. & Chair, External Relns. Ctte.; club: Wellington; Home: 117 Cowan Ave., Toronto, Ont. M6K 2N1; Office: 224 Parliament St., Toronto, Ont. M5A 3A4.

**HUME, (John) Christopher (William),** B.A.; newspaper critic; b. Farnborough, UK 23 Apl. 1951; s. Michael Patrick and Jacqueline (Boy) H.; e. N. Toronto Coll. Inst. 1969; Univ. of Toronto Faculty of Music 1969–70; Glendon Coll. York Univ. B.A. 1975; m. Eileen d. Vern and Lucille Fawcett 7 Aug. 1980; two d. Jessica, Alexandra; ART AND ARCH. CRITIC THE TORONTO STAR 1981– ; contbr. maj. mags and newspapers Can. and U.S.; frequent appearances Candn. Radio and TV; served numerous art and arch. juries; frequent lectr.; Nat. Newspaper Award nominee Critical Writing 1988, 1992; Citation, Ont. Assn. of Architects; ed. 'From the Wild' non-fiction art 1986; Home: 28 Riverdale Ave., Toronto, Ont. M4K 1C3; Office: One Yonge St., Toronto, Ont. M5E 1E6.

**HUME, James Nairn Patterson,** M.A., Ph.D., F.R.S.C.; educator; b. Brooklyn, N.Y. 17 March 1923; s. James Smith and Jean Frances (Nairn) H. (both Candn.); e. Goderich, Ont. pub. and high schs.; Univ. of Toronto B.A. (Math. & Physics) 1945, M.A. (Physics) 1946, Ph.D. (Theoretical Atomic Spectroscopy) 1949; m. Patricia d. H.A.S. Molyneux, Toronto, Ont. 8 Aug. 1953; children: Stephen, Philip, Harriet, Mark; Prof. Emeritus, Univ. of Toronto 1988– ; Master Emeritus, Massey Coll., Univ. of Toronto 1988– ; Demonst. in Physics present Univ. 1945, Instr. in Math. (Ajax) 1946–49, Asst. Prof. of Physics 1950, Assoc. Prof. 1957, Assoc. Dean (Physical Sciences) Sch. of Grad. Studies 1968–72, Chrmn. of Computer Science 1975–80; Prof. of Physics and of Computer Science Univ. of Toronto 1963–88; Master, Massey Coll., Univ. of Toronto 1981–88; Instr. in Physics Rutgers Univ. 1949–50; CBC TV programs incl.: 'Focus on Physics' 1958; 'Two for Physics' 1959; 15 short programs on Physics for children Can. and U.S. 1960; 'The Nature of Things' 1960–65; 'The Ideas of Physics' 1962; 'The Nature of Physics' 1963; 'The Constants of Physics' 1966; co-writer 4 films produced by Phys. Science Study Comte. U.S.A.; audio tape with slides lectures 'Fortran'; recipient Special Citation Edison Foundation for best science educ. film 1962 ('Frames of Reference'); Scient. Inst. Rome Silver Medal 'Random Events'; Ohio State Award for 'Count on Me' from 1962 'Nature of Things' and for 'Order or Chaos?' from 1962 'Ideas of Physics' series; Centennial Medal 1967; Silver Core Award Internat. Fed. for Information Processing, Stockholm 1974; Sesquicentennial Long Service Honour Award Univ. of Toronto 1977; Distinguished Service Citation Amer. Assn. Physics Teachers, N.Y. 1979; Civic Award of Merit, City of Toronto 1987; author 'Programmers' Guide' 1963; 'Programmers' Guide (Fortran IV)' 1966; 'Relativity, Electromagnetism and Quantum Physics' Vol. II of 'Physics in Two Volumes' 1974; co-author 'Trancode Manual' 1955; 'High-speed Data Processing' 1958; 'Structured Programming Using PL/1 and SP/k' 1975; Fundamentals of Structured Programming Using Fortran with SF/k and Watfiv-S' 1977; 'Programming Fortran 77' 1979; 'Programming Standard Pascal' 1980; 'UCSD Pascal: A Beginner's Guide to Programming Microcomputers' 1982; 'Pascal under Unix' 1983; 'Better Basic for the Apple' 1983; 'Better Basic for the IBM Personal Computer' 1983; 'Vax Pascal' 1984; 'Introduction to Computer Science using the Turing Programming Language' 1984; 'Fortran 77 for Scientists and Engineers' 1985; 'Structured MS Basic for the Macintosh' 1986; 'A Guide to the PC-Turing Interpreter' 1986; 'Turing Tutorial Guide' 1988; author or co-author numerous articles; mem. Assn. Computing Machinery; Sigma Xi; recreations: theatre, painting; Club: Arts & Letters; Home: 51 Matson Dr., RR #2, Bolton, Ont. L7E 5R8; Office: Massey College, 4 Devonshire Pl., Toronto, Ont. M5S 2E1.

**HUME, Stephen,** B.A.; editor; writer; journalist; b. Blackpool, U.K. 1 Jan. 1947; s. James and Joyce (Potter) H.; e. Mount Douglas S.S. 1966; Univ. of Victoria, B.A. 1971; m. Susan Winifred d. Arthur William and Winifred Mayse 29 July 1970; COLUMNIST-AT-LARGE, THE VANCOUVER SUN 1989– ; Copyboy and Proofreader, Edmonton Journal 1966; entered summer intern prog. for reporters 1967; Copy Ed., Victoria Daily Times 1968; Ed., Univ. of Victoria Newspaper 'The Martlet' 1968; Reporter, Victoria Daily Times 1969–71; Edmonton Journal 1971; Arctic Corr. 1971–73; Energy Reporter 1974; Ed. Writer 1975; City Ed. 1975–77; Weekend Ed. 1978; News Ed. 1979–81; Editor 1981–87; General Mgr., The Journal 1987–89; Univ. of Victoria English Dept. Essay Prize 1967; Alma Mater Soc. Prizes for Journalism (1968), Spec. Pubns. (1969); Alta. Writer's Guild Literary Award, best book of non-fiction 1989 ('Ghost Camps'); Southam President's Award for Commentary 1990; National Newspaper Awards citation for column writing 1990; very active in sports 1966–74 (some records set); author: 'Signs Against an Empty Sky' (poetry) 1981; 'And the House Sank like a Ship in the Long Prairie Grass' (poetry) 1987; 'Ghost Camps' (essays) 1989; recreations: fly-fishing, writing, various outdoor sports; Office: Editorial Dept., Vancouver Sun, 2250 Granville St., Vancouver B.C. V6H 3G2.

**HUME, Valerie Elizabeth,** Ph.D.; federal civil servant; b. Auckland, N.Z. 24 Apr. 1934; d. Frank Seddon and Edna (Russell) H.; e. Epsom Girls' Grammar Sch. Auckland 1951; Auckland Teachers' Coll. 1952–53; Auckland Univ. Coll. Univ. of N.Z. B.A. 1957, Dip. Ed. 1960; Univ. of Edinburgh Ph.D. 1970; Nat. Defence Coll. Can. 1975–76; POLICY CO-ORDINATOR OF SUSTAINABLE DEVELOPMENT, DEPT. OF INDIAN AFFAIRS AND NORTHERN DEVELOPMENT 1989– ; Teacher: Meadowbank Sch. Auckland 1954; Otara Intermed. Sch. Auckland 1955; Epsom Girls' Grammar Sch. 1956–60; Waverly Sch. Stettler, Atla. 1960–61 (exchange); Roedean Sch. Eng. 1961–62; Châtelard Sch. Switzerland 1962–66; Tutor Edinburgh Univ. 1967–69; Asst. Prof., Tutor and Don, York Univ. Toronto 1969–76 (Fellow McLaughlin Coll.); Head, Policy & Planning N. Transp. Infrastructure, Dept. of Indian Affairs & N. Devel. Can. 1976–87; Head, Land Programs, Dept. of Indian Affairs & N. Devel., Can. 1987–88; Canada Interchange assignment: Dir., Physical and Mathematical Sciences, Natural Sciences and Engineering Rsch. Counc. 1988–89; Founding Pres., Candn. Ctte. for UNIFEM 1993– ; mem. Candn. Assn. Geogs.; Assn. Am. Geogs.; Candn. Inst. Internat. Affairs (Chrmn. Nat. Capital Br. 1984–86); Zonta Club of Ottawa (Pres. 1992– ); Ottawa-Carleton Br., Candn. Red Cross Soc. (Council 1991– , Sec. 1992– ); Candn. Assn. for the Club of Rome; Ottawa Field Naturalists' Club; Candn. Power Squadron; Club: Britannia Yacht; Home: Unit 14, 655 Richmond Rd., Ottawa, Ont. K2A 3Y3; Office: Ottawa, Ont. K1A 0H4.

**HUMMEL, Solon Lamont (Monte),** M.A., M.Sc.F.; conservationist; b. Toronto, Ont. 4 Dec. 1946; s. Solon George and Laura Matilda (Platte) H.; e. Univ. of Toronto B.A. 1969, M.A. 1970, M.Sc.F. 1979; m. Sherry d. R.K. Pettigrew and A.L. Masterman 10 Nov. 1990; children (by previous marriage): Robin Louise, Guy Douglas; PRES. WORLD WILDLIFE FUND CANADA 1985– ; Co-founder Pollution Probe 1969; Co-ordinator Environmental Studies Prog., Univ. of Toronto 1973–80; Assoc., Inst. for Environmental Studies, Univ. of Toronto; Exec. Dir. present orgn. 1978; Exec. Co-ordinator Wildlife Toxicol. Fund; Founding Dir. and mem. Exec. Ctte., Candn. Coalition on Acid Rain and Candn. Council on Ecological Areas; Dir.: Arctic Internat. Wildlife Range Soc.; Mem., WWF Internat. Adv. Counc., Gland, Switzerland; Mem. Adv. Counc.: Coll. of Biological Sciences, Univ. of Guelph; Hon. Fellow Innis Coll. Univ. of Toronto; Mem. Adv. Counc., Univ. of Toronto, Faculty of Forestry; Mem. Bd. of Dir., Midlands Project, Tuscon, Ariz. USA; recipient E. J. Sanford Gold Medal in Philos. 1969; Past Pres. Labrador Retriever Club Ont.; co-author 'Pollution Probe' 1972; author 'Arctic Wildlife' 1984; 'Endangered Spaces' 1989; 'Wild Hunters' 1991; author over 100 jour. and mag. articles; recreations: wilderness canoe tripping, astronomy, running; Home: R.R. 3, Cookstown, Ont. L0L 1L0; Office: 504, 90 Eglinton Ave. E., Toronto, Ont. M4P 2Z7.

**HUMPHREY, John Peters,** O.C. (1974), O.Q. (1985), K.St.J., B.C.L., Ph.D., D.Sc.Soc., LL.D., D.C.L., D.Litt.; b. Hampton, N.B. 30 Apr. 1905; s. Frank M. & Nellie (Peters) H.; e. Rothesay Coll.; Mt. Allison Univ.; McGill Univ., B.Comm. 1925, B.A. 1927, B.C.L. 1929, Ph.D. 1945; Dr. of Univ. of Algiers (hon. causa 1944); Dr. of Soc. Sciences, Ottawa 1966; LL.D.: Carleton 1968, St. Thomas 1971, Dalhousie 1975, McGill 1976, McMaster 1992; D.C.L., Mt. Allison 1977; D.Litt., Acadia 1980; Saint Mary's 1984; Award of Highest Honour, Soka Univ., Japan 1992; Hon. doctorate, Soka Univ. 1993; Macdonald Travelling Schol. in Law, University of Paris, France 1929–30; m. 1stly Jeanne Marie Louise Godreau (dec.) 3 September 1929; 2ndly Dr. Margaret Kunstler, 21 June 1981; called to the Quebec Bar 1929; practised law with Wainwright, Elder and McDougall, Montreal, 1930–36; appointed Lectr. in Roman Law, McGill University, 1936; awarded Fellowship by Carnegie Foundation for Internat. Peace to pursue studies in internat. law at Univ. of Paris, 1936–37; Secy., Faculty of Law, McGill Univ., 1937–46; apptd. Gale Prof. of Roman Law and Dean of Law Faculty, McGill Univ., 1946; Prof. Law and Political Science, 1966–71; Dir., Div. of Human Rights, U.N. Secretariat, 1946–66; author of 'The Inter-American System: A Canadian View' 1942; 'Human Rights and the United Nations: A Great Adventure' 1984; ('La grande aventure, Les Nations unies et les droits de l'homme' 1989); 'No Distant Millenium: The World Law of Human Rights' 1989; many articles on internat. pol. and legal subjects; mem., Candn. Inst. Internat. Affairs (Vice-Chrmn. Montreal Br. 1943–44; Chrmn. N.Y. Br., 1961–66); U.N. Assn. in Can. (Nat. Pres. 1968–70; Pres. Montreal Br. 1945–46); Pres., Candn. Comn. Internat. Year for Human Rights 1968; mem., U.N. Sub-Comn. on Prevention of Discrimination and Protection of Minorities (Chrmn. 1970); mem., Royal Comn. on Status of Women in Can.; Extve. Secy., U.N. Conf. on Freedom of Information, Geneva 1948; U.N. Conf. on Refugees and Stateless Persons, Geneva 1951; U.N. Conf. on Status of Stateless Persons 1954; Principal Secy. to U.N. Mission to Viet Nam 1963; Rapporteur, Internat. Law Assn. Comte. on Human Rights; Rapporteur, U.N. Seminar on Human Rights (Jamaica) 1967; Vice-Chrmn., U.N. Seminar on Racial Discrimination (New Delhi) 1968; Mem., Internat. Comn. of Inquiry into the 1932–33 Famine in the Ukraine 1988–90; Rapporteur, Conf. on Human Rights and the Protection of Refugees (Montreal) 1987; Hon. Mem., War Amputations of Canada; Hon. Mem., Union of Bulgarian Lawyers; Mem., Order of Kliment Ohridské; Hon. mem., Assoc. des Avocats pour les Droits de l'Auteur (Paris); Hon. Citizen, City of Edmonton 1964; Internat. Cooperation Year Citation (Can. 1965); World Jewish Cong. Citation 1966; 'World Legal Scholar' award, World Peace through Law Centre (1973); John Reid Medal (Canadian Council of Internat. Law, 1973); Officer, Order of Canada 1974; World Federalists of Can. Peace Award 1981; Nova Scotia Human Rights Comn. Award 1982; Saul Hayes Human Rights Award (Cdn. Jewish Cong.) 1983; Order of Quebec 1985; Order of St. John of Jerusalem 1986; Citation, Govt. of Nova Scotia 1988; Citation, Amnesty Internat. (Can.) 1988; apptd. Great Montrealer 1992; Inaugural Lecturer, John Humphrey Lecturship on Human Rights, McGill Univ. 1988; United Nations Award for outstanding achievements in the field of human rights 1988; Quebec Bar medal for advancement of justice 1991; Personnalité de la Semaine, La Presse, Montréal 1991; Visiting Prof., Univ. of Toronto, 1971–72; Univ. of

Western Ont. 1981–82; Past Pres., Amnesty Internat. (Canada) (mem. Council 1981); Pres. Emeritus, Candn. Human Rights Foundn. (Pres. 1978–85, Chrmn. 1985–86, resigned 1991); Vice Pres., Internat. Comn. of Jurists; International Law Assn. (Rapporteur on Human Rights); Vice-Pres., UNESCO Conf. on Teaching of Human Rights, Malta. 1987; Life Hon. Mem., Candn. Council of International Law; Hon. Mem., Phi Delta Phi; Conseil d'Administration, Société Quebecoise de Droit International; Adv. Bd., World Federalists of Canada; Bd. mem., Internat. Trustees, Atwater Inst.; Pres., Candn. Br., World Conf. on Religion and Peace; Clubs: University (Montreal); McGill Fac.; Montreal Amateur Athletic Assn.; Home (summer): Brackley Beach, P.E.I. C0A 2H0; Permanent Address: 30 Thurlow Rd., Hampstead, Montreal, Que. H3X 3G6.

**HUMPHREY, Robert J.,** B.Comm.; business executive; b. Windsor, Ont. 25 June 1947; s. Hugh A. and Dorilla (Gore) H.; e. Univ. of Windsor B.Comm. (Hons.) 1970; divorced; children: Christian Steven, Andrew David; PRESIDENT AND CHIEF OPERATING OFFICER, HARRY ROSEN INC.; Branch Accountant, Royal Bank of Can. 1970–72; Credit Officer, Federal Bus. Devel. Bank 1972–73; C.F.O., Tip Top Tailors 1973–75; C.F.O., Opns. Mgr, Gen. Mgr., Pres. & C.E.O., Harry Rosen Inc. 1975– ; Dir., Ont. C. of C.; Pres., Harry Rosen Inc. USA; Dir., Univ. of Windsor Alumni Assn. (Pres. Toronto Chapter); recreations: alpine skiing, powerboating; Office: 11 Adelaide St. W., Toronto, Ont. M5H 1N1.

**HUMPHREY, William A.,** B.S.; mining engineer; b. Potrerillos, Chile 12 Jan. 1927; s. Thomas Zenas and Ethel Katherine (Kolbe) H.; e. Rutgers Univ. 1946–47; Univ. of Ariz. B.S. 1950; m. Edna Lillian Joule 20 Dec. 1947; children: Patricia, Nancy, Katherine, William; Bd. Vice Chrmn., Homestake Mining Co. 1992, Pres. and C.O.O. 1991–92; Dir. and mem. Extve. Comte. Homestake Mining Co.; Homestake Gold Australia Ltd.; Homestake Copper Co.; Homestake Forest Products Co.; Homestake Gold Ltd.; Homestake Internat. Sales Corp.; Homestake Lead Co. of Missouri; Homestake Mineral Devel. Co.; Homestake New Zealand Exploration Ltd.; Homestake Smelting Co.; Uranium Holdings Co.; Geol. Cananea Consolidated Copper Co. Sonora, Mexico 1950–55, Foreman Underground Div. 1955, Planning Engr. 1959, Asst. to Mgr. 1965, Gen. Supt. 1968, Vice Pres. and Asst. Gen. Mgr. 1968, Extve. Vice Pres. Gen. Mgr. and Dir. 1971–75; Vice Pres. Planning Mont. Div. Anaconda Co. Butte 1975; Vice Pres.-Operations, Newmont Mining Corp. 1975–81; Extve. Vice Pres.-Operations, Homestake Mining Co. 1981–91; served with USNR 1945–46; mem. Am. Inst. Mining Engrs.; The Mining and Metallurgical Soc. of Am.; Tau Beta Phi; Protestant; Home: 2469 Biltmore Dr., Alamo, CA 94507 USA.

**HUMPHREYS, Helen Caroline;** writer; b. Kingston, England 29 March 1961; d. Anthony Cecil and Frances (Brett) H.; writer: 'Gods and Other Mortals' 1986, 'Nuns Looking Anxious, Listening to Radios' 1990 (both poetry), 'Ethel on Fire' 1991 (novel); 'What Wants to be Spoken, What Remains to be Said' (film script) 1992; (under the pseudonym Catherine Brett) 'Things Just Aren't the Same' 1987; 'S.P. Likes A.D.' 1989 (both novels for young adults); Mailing address: P.O. Box 256, Stn. P, Toronto, Ont. M5S 2S8.

**HUMPHRIES, George Edward,** M.B.E., P.Eng.; b. Wolverhampton, England 31 Dec. 1907; s. Walter William and Clara Louise (Whitcomb) H.; e. Elem. Schs. and Tech. Coll., Eng., and at various Colls. (Extension courses); m. Margaret Merle, d. John Stewart, 25 May 1940; two s., David George, Walter John; came to Can. 1928 after having worked on steam power plant design in Eng. (1926); with Hamilton Bridge Co. Ltd., Hamilton, Ont., as Structural Draftsman, 1928; with Hydro-Elect. Power Comn. of Ont., 1929–30; McClintic Marshall Corp., Pittsburgh, 1930–31; engaged as Engr. in N. Ont. gold fields 1932–40; with M. Murray Dillon estbd. firm of M.M. Dillon; served as Chief Engr., President, Chrmn., retired 1989; served in 2nd World War with R.C.E., U.K. and N.W. Europe, 1940–45; awarded M.B.E.; Mentioned in Despatches; Offr., Candn. Army (R) 1946–56; retired with rank of Lieut.-Col.; Hon. mem. Assn. Consulting Engrs. Can. (Pres. 1963); Fellow, Engn. Inst. Can. (Pres. 1964–65; Julian C. Smith Medal 1974); Fellow, Inst. of Civil Engrs.; Fellow, Cdn. Acad. of Engr.; mem., Royal Canadian Legion (Vimy Branch); Assn. Prof. Engrs., Ont.; Chartered Engr., U.K.; Anglican; recreations: gardening; Club: The London.

**HUMPHRIES, John Thomas,** B.Comm., C.L.U.; financial executive; b. Halifax, N.S. 19 Dec. 1943; s. James Gordon and Hilda Bernice (Ireland) H.; e. West Van H.S. 1961; Univ. of B.C., B.Comm. 1967; m. Anne d. Garth and June Griffiths 22 July 1967; Children: Sara Anne, James John Garth; FOUNDING PARTNER, GRANVILLE WEST GROUP LTD. 1982– ; joined Mutual Life of Can. 1967; obtained Chartered Life Underwriter designation 1973; Bd. of Dir., Life Underwriters Assn. of Can. 1977; Chrmn. of Bd. 1982–84; Dir. & Shareholder, Granville West Securities Ltd. 1986; Granville West Agencies Ltd. 1987; Dir., Export Devel. Corp. 1986; Alderman, Dist. of West Van. 1978–82; Founding Dir., Collingwood Sch.; Dir., Lions Gate Hosp. 1978–80; Trustee, Crofton House Sch. Edn. Found.; St. George's Sch. Edn. Found.; Chrmn., Community Serv. Adv. Comn.; Group Ctte., West Van. United Ch. 1970–71; mem., Ch. Bd. 1972–74; recreations: tennis, skiing, jogging, boating; Clubs: West Vancouver Tennis; Vancouver; West Vancouver Yacht; Home: 3024 Proctor Ave., West Vancouver, B.C. V7V 1G1; Office: 1425 - 1075 W. Georgia St., Vancouver, B.C.

**HUMPHRYS, Richard,** B.A., F.S.A., F.C.I.A.; financial consultant; b. Jasmin, Sask. 27 March 1917; s. William and Olive Mary (Maher) H.; e. Public and High Sch., Kelliher, Sask.; Univ. of Manitoba, B.A. 1937; F.S.A. 1944; m. Wilma Kay Grant, 3 Oct. 1942; joined Great-West Life as Actuarial Clerk 1939; apptd. to Fed. Dept. of Ins. as Actuarial Asst. 1940; Assoc. Actuary 1944; joined Teachers Ins. & Annuity Assn. in New York as Asst. Actuary 1947 and promoted Assoc. Actuary in 1948; rejoined Fed. Dept. of Ins. as Chief Actuary 1948 and promoted Asst. Supt. of Ins. 1956; Supt. of Ins. 1964–82; Fellow, Soc. of Actuaries (Vice-Pres. 1979–81); Fellow, Candn. Inst. of Actuaries (Pres. 1965–66); recreations: golf, skiing, music, reading; Club: Ottawa Hunt & Golf; Address: 50 Rothwell Dr., Ottawa, Ont. K1J 7G6.

**HUNDAL, Nancy Lynn,** B.A.; teacher, librarian; b. Vancouver, B.C. 31 Jan. 1957; d. John Alexander and Doris Anna Mae (Erickson) Ferguson; e. Sir Winston Churchill S.S.; Univ. of B.C. B.A., teaching cert.; m. Derek S. s. Bakhshis (Buck) and Ranjit (Jeto) H. 6 Aug. 1983; children: Joshua, Bianca; B.C. Book Prize 1991 (Sheila A. Egoff Children's Prize) for 'I Heard My Mother Call My Name'; author: 'Mallory's Rainy Day' (in 1987 Canadian Children's Annual) 1987, 'I Heard My Mother Call My Name' (children's picture book) 1990, 'November Boots' 1993 and various other stories & poems in magazines for children; Mem., Vancouver Children's Literature Roundtable; recreations: singing in madrigal group, craftwork, painting, reading; Home: 1517 W. 58th Ave., Vancouver, B.C. V6P 1W6.

**HUNEAULT, Louis R.,** B.A., M.A.; public servant; b. Chelmsford, Ont. 16 May 1942; s. Léo Paul and Fernande (Bélanger) H.; e. Laurentian Univ., B.A. 1964; Ottawa Univ., B.Sc. Hons. 1965, M.A. 1967; m. Rachel Patricia d. Roger and Alma Groulx 19 Aug. 1967; children: Alain, Sylvie; DEPUTY MIN., CUSTOMS & EXCISE, NAT. REVENUE 1986– ; Publ Serv. Comn., Govt. of Can. 1967–68; Regl. Econ. Expansion 1968–73; Dir., Opns., Health & Amateur Sports 1973–76; Mem., Decentral. Team, Sec. of State 1976–77; Dir. Gen., Personnel, Indian and North. Affairs 1977–80; Asst. Dep. Min., Personnel, Transp. Can. 1980–83; Asst. Dep. Min., Excise Branch, Customs & Excise, Nat. Revenue 1983–86; Home: 2388 Wyndale Cres., Ottawa, Ont. K1H 7A5.

**HUNG, Chung;** see CHUNG, Hung.

**HUNGERFORD, George William,** O.C., Q.C., B.A., LL.B.; solicitor; b. Vancouver, B.C. 2 Jan. 1944; s. Roderick M. and Florence Mary (Farrell) H.; e. Univ. of B.C., B.A. 1965, LL.B. 1968; m. Jane d. Nairn and Jane Knott 17 June 1967; four children; SR. PARTNER, HUNGERFORD SIMON 1972– ; called to Bar of B.C. 1969; Dir. Mutual Life Assurance Co. of Canada; recipient Olympic Gold Medal Rowing, Tokyo 1964; Bd. Govs. Simon Fraser Univ. 1978–84; Chrmn., Greater Vancouver Adv. Bd. Salvation Army; Gov. Olympic Trust of Can.; Past Presidents' Adv. Ctte., B.C. Sports Hall of Fame & Museum; Past Chrmn., St. George's Sch.; Chrmn., Pacific Salmon Found.; recreations: swimming, boating, fishing, skiing; Clubs: Vancouver (Past Pres.); Shaughnessy Golf & Country; Arbutus; Office: 1725, 555 Burrard St., Vancouver, B.C. V7X 1J8.

**HUNGERFORD, John G.,** C.M., LL.B., Q.C.; retired; b. London, Ont. 15 Nov. 1905; s. Walter Francis and Maude Margaret (MacLaren) H.; e. Univ. of Western Ont., B.A. (Hon. Pol. Econ.) 1926; Osgoode Hall, Toronto, Ont. 1929; called to Bar of Ont. 1929; m. Persis Stephanie, d. Norman Seagram of Toronto, Ont.; Past Chrmn., National Trust Co. Ltd.; Past Chrmn. & Hon. Dir., Canada Life Assnce. Co.; Hon. Trustee, Hosp. for Sick Children, Toronto; Chrmn., The R. Samuel McLaughlin Foundation; Zeta Psi; Anglican; Clubs; Toronto; York; Toronto Golf; Home: 252 Forest Hill Rd., Toronto, Ont. M5P 2N5.

**HUNKIN, John Stewart,** B.A., M.B.A.; investment executive; b. Toronto, Ont. 14 Apr. 1945; s. Peter and Ethel (Valor) H.; e. Univ. of Man., B.A. 1967; York Univ., M.B.A. 1969; m. Barbara d. Robert and Janet Becker 27 Sept. 1969; children: Dawn, Tara, Lauren; PRESIDENT, INVESTMENT & CORPORATE BANK, CIBC 1992– ; Gen. Mgr., Internat. Money Market Opns., Candn. Imperial Bank of Commerce 1979; Gen. Mgr., U.S.A. 1980; Vice-Pres., Eastern Reg., U.S.A. 1982; Sr. Vice-Pres., U.S.A. 1984; Extve. Vice-Pres., The Americas, Investment Bank (CIBC) 1986; Pres. & C.O.O., Wood Gundy Inc. 1988, Depy. Chrmn. & C.E.O. 1990; Dir., John P. Robarts Rsch. Inc.; The Wellesley Hosp. Found.; Mem., Adv. Counc., Faculty of Admin. Studies, York Univ.; Gov., York Univ. Bd. of Govs.; Dir. and Pres., Candn. Psychiatric Rsch. Found.; recreations: skiing, tennis, reading, horseback riding; Home: R.R. #3, Schomberg, Ont. L0G 1T0; Office: Commerce Court, Toronto, Ont. M5L 1A2.

**HUNLEY, Hon. Helen,** O.C.; b. Acme, Alta. 6 Sept. 1920; e. high sch. Rocky Mountain House, Alta.; Lt.-Gov. of Alta. 1985–91; served with Candn. Women's Army Corp. (CWAC) 1941–46, Overseas 1943–45, rank Lt.; served 9 yrs. with implement and truck dealership also ins. agency, purchased business 1957 and held International Harvester franchise Rocky Mountain House until 1968; holds Journeyman's Cert. as 'Partsman'; owned and managed Helen Hunley Agencies Ltd. (ins. agency) 1968–71; served as Town Councillor 6 yrs., mayor of Rocky Mountain House 5 yrs.; el. M.L.A. for Rocky Mountain House prov. g.e. 1971, re-el. 1975; Min. without Portfolio 1971, Solr. Gen. 1973, Min. of Social Services & Community Health 1975–79; LL.D. (Hon.), Univ. of Alberta; Officer of the Order of Canada 1992; served various voluntary orgns. and adv. cttes. incl. Alta. Girls Parlt. and Prov. Mental Health Adv. Council.

**HUNSLEY, Terrance Michael,** B.A., M.A., M.Ed.; research and consulting executive; b. Amherst, N.S. 28 Feb. 1947; s. Ernest William and Jesse Fillmore (Knowlton) H.; e. Univ. of N.B., B.A., M.A.; St. Francis Xavier Univ., M.Ed.; Fed. Training Ctr., Cert. in Public Admin.; m. Patricia, d. Harold and Edith Nutter 21 June 1969; children: Timothy, Christopher; PRINCIPAL, TM HUNSLEY SERVICES INC. (Research & Consulting); RESEARCH FELLOW, QUEEN'S UNIV. 1990– ; Social Development Co-ordinator, Grand Lake Development Corp. 1968–69; Instr., Sociology, Univ. of N.B. 1970; Consultant, N.B. Social Services Dept. 1970–73; Dir., Social Develop. and Rehabilitation, Prov. of N.B. 1973–76; Partner, SEAS Assoc. 1973–76; Dir., Educ. Consulting, Public Service Commn. of Can. 1976–77; Sr. Policy Consultant, Internat. Relations, Labour Can. 1977–78; Dir., Social Services Div., Health and Welfare Can. 1978–80; Extve. Dir., Candn. Council on Social Development 1980–90; Partner, Allied Infosearch 1982–90; Visiting Prof., Queen's Univ. 1990–91; awarded Candn. Physical Fitness Scholarship and Paul William Alexander Scholarship 1964; mem. Extve. Comte., Coalition of National Voluntary Organizations; Adv. Comte., Burns Memorial Chair of Child Welfare, Univ. of Calgary; editor, 'The Social Contract in Canada's Future' 1991; 'Social Policy in the Global Economy' 1992; author, several articles in CCSD publications; 'Perception' and 'Overview'; in major newspapers and magazines, incl. The Globe and Mail, Toronto Star, Financial Post, Montreal Gazette, Ottawa Citizen, Winnipeg Free Press. Calgary Herald, The Sunday Star, Policy Options, Canadian Housing, The Spectator, Canadian Home Economics Journal; policy briefs to Royal Comns. and Parlty. Comtes.; Home: 235 Bradford St., Ottawa, Ont. K2B 5Z5; Office: 55 Parkdale Ave., Ottawa, Ont. K1Y 4G1.

**HUNT, Brian A.,** B.Com., C.A.; executive; b. 13 May 1951; e. Univ. of Windsor B.Com. 1974; C.A. 1976; PRES. PHH CANADA INC. 1989– ; Office: 350 Burnhamthorpe Rd. W., Mississauga, Ont. L5B 2C2.

**HUNT, D. Earl,** M.D.; physician; surgeon; b. Honeywood, Ont. 16 Mar. 1915; s. John and Myrtle (Lockhart) H.; e. Univ. of Toronto, M.D. 1946; m. Jean M., d. Charles Blundell, St. Catharines, Ont., 26 July 1944; children: Margaret, Elizabeth, John, Douglas; Pres. (1966) Coll. of General Practice of Can.; post-grad. work, St. Michael's Hosp., Toronto; while at univ. was on staff of Dept. of Anatomy and assisted with research for R.C.A.F. for 3 yrs; Lectr., St. John's Ambulance for several yrs.; ACTIVE STAFF, ST. CATHARINES GEN. AND HOTEL DIEU HOSPITALS, St. Catharines; former Chief, Sec. of Gen. Practice, St. Catharines Gen. Hosp., Past Dir., Out Patient Dept., there; former Lectr. in Hematology, Mack Training Sch.; Past Chief Family Physicians Hotel Dieu Hosp., St. Catharines; taught sch., Melancthon, Simcoe, Muskoka for 4 yrs.; during 2nd World War served with C.O.T.C., Univ. of Toronto; on Active Service 1 1/2 yrs.; Med. Dir., Diabetic Assn., Niagara Chapt. for 26 years; Fellow, Coll. of Family Physicians of Can.; mem. Candn. Med. Assn. (Past Secy., Sec. Gen. Practice); Ont. Med. Assn. (Past Chrmn., Educ. Comte., Sec. Gen. Practice; mem., Tariff Comte.; awarded Glenn Sawyer Award 1989); Coll. of Family Physicians (Past Pres., Ont. Chapter; Past Chrmn., Bd. Dirs.); Lincoln Acad. Med.; received 50 yr. pin & certificate, Scottish Rite Lodge, Barrie, Ont. 1992; 32 Freemason; United Church; recreations: hunting, fishing, flytying, coin and gun collecting, bonsai, calligraphy, Chinese cooking; Clubs: Niagara Arms Collectors; St. Catharines Game & Fish Assn.; St. Catharines Coin (Hon. mem.); Address: R.R. 3, 352 Martindale Rd., St. Catharines, Ont. L2R 6P9.

**HUNT, David Owen;** publishing executive; b. Bistroff, France 3 Mar. 1964; s. Owen and Doreen (Goring) H.; e. John Abbott Coll.; Concordia Univ.; Banff Ctr. Sch. of Fine Arts; Stanford Univ.; m. Carolyn d. Sheila and Earl Whitzman 10 Aug. 1985, 23 Aug. 1987; National Dir., Canadian Book Information Centre (the marketing arm of the Assoc. of Candn. Publishers) 1990; Dir. & Treas., Candn. Give the Gift of Literacy Found. 1990– ; Policy & Admin. Dir., Assn. of Candn. Publishers 1989–90; Mem., Ed. Bd. 'This Magazine'; Guest Lectr. in English, John Abbott Coll.; Home: 52 Cornwall St., Toronto, Ont. M5A 4K5.

**HUNT, Gary William,** B.A., M.Ed., Ed.D.; educator; b. Toronto, Ont. 18 May 1944; s. Glyndwr and Edna May (Cunneyworth) H.; e. Lakeshore Teachers' Coll. Ont. Teaching Cert. 1963; York Univ. B.A. 1972; Ont. Inst. Studies in Edn. M.Ed. 1976; US Internat. Univ. Ed.D. 1980; two s. Jason James, Timothy Hamilton; CHAIRMAN, ELEMENTARY EDUCATION & STUDENT SERVICES, FACULTY OF EDN. UNIV. OF TORONTO 1989– ; Teacher, Fern Ave. Pub. Sch. Toronto 1964–67; Sci. Cons. Toronto 1967–71; Prin. High Park Sch. Toronto 1969–71; Lectr. in Sci. Edn. Faculty of Edn. present Univ. 1971–73, Chrmn. of Elem. Edn. 1973–85; Chrmn., Continuing Education & Student Services 1985–89; field-based teacher education coordinator; partnerships in teacher education; Active Learning program consultant; family and adolescent counselling; recipient City of Toronto Volunteer Award 1986, 1989; Toronto Bd. of Edn. Trustee 1972–74; Chair, Community Adv. Bd.; co-author 'Primary Encounters in Science' 1972; 'Ages 9 Through 12' 1986; Chair, Swansea Community Adv. Board 1991– ; Mem. Bd. of Dirs., Adventure Place 1992– ; mem. Candn. Soc. Studies Edn.; Candn. Assn. for Young Children; Phi Delta Kappa; Home: 62 Armadale Ave., Toronto, Ont. M6S 3X2; Office: 371 Bloor St. W., Toronto, Ont. M5S 2R7.

**HUNT, R.H. (Ray),** B.Ap.Sc., P.Eng.; professional engineer; b. Cranbrook, B.C. 11 Feb. 1937; s. Horace Edwin and Gwynneth Isobel (Backs) H.; e. Mission H.S. 1955; Univ. of B.C. B.Ap.Sc. 1961; m. Jacque d. Fred and Eileen Johnstone 12 Sept. 1959; children: Kelly Orene, Tracy Ann; PRESIDENT & CHIEF OPERATING OFFICER, B.C. HYDRO 1991– ; Graduate Engineer in Training, B.C. Hydro 1961–65 (4-year program of 8 6-mo. rotations); Project Control Engr. 1965; Electrical Stations Constructon Engr. 1967; Construction Mgr., GMS Generating Station 1972; Asst. Mgr., Construction Div. 1974; Mgr., Corp. Services 1977; Chief Engineer 1979; Senior Vice-Pres., Engineering 1984; Executive Vice-Pres. & Chief Op. Offr. 1980; Dir., Powertech; recreations: racquetball, hunting, fishing, golf; clubs: YMCA, Carnoustie Racquets, Pitt Meadows Golf; Office: 6911 Southpoint Dr., Burnaby, B.C. V3N 4X8.

**HUNT, Tony;** hereditary chief; native indian artist; gallery director; b. Alert Bay, B.C.; s. Henry and Helen (Nelson) H.; e. elem. and secondary schs.; indian carving and dancing instrn. from grandfather Mungo Martin; children: Tony Jr., Steven, Debbie; FOUNDER AND DIR. ARTS OF THE RAVEN GALLERY 1969– ; Hereditary Chief of Fort Rupert Kwa-Gulth; Asst. Carver Thunderbird Park Victoria, B.C. 1962–72; completed many museum projects with father during above period; numerous maj. private comns. since 1967 incl. native indian totem poles, masks, jewellry exhns. incl. Royal Ont. Museum 1975, Lahr, Germany 1976, Nat. Museum of Man Osaka, Japan 1977, 1978, Bonn, W. Germany 1979, Hamburg 1979, Candn. Embassy Mexico City 1979, Field Museum Chicago 1980–81, Souchow, China 1981, New York 1984; Chief Designer and Artist Fort Rupert (B.C.) Long House 1985; solo exhns. incl. Eaton's Contemporary Victoria 1964; Bon Marche Gallery Seattle 1965; Gallery Libre Montréal 1967; Vancouver Art Gallery 1967; Lowie Museum Berkeley, Cal. 1970; Field Museum Chicago 1972; group exhns. incl. Candn. Indian Art Royal Ont. Museum 1974, Am. Indian Arts & Crafts Show Oakland, Cal., Seattle, Scottsdale, Ariz. 1975; De Young Museum San Francisco 1978; Gallery Hennimann Bonn, W. Germany 1980; Hunt Family Heritage (4 museums) Nat. Museum Man Ottawa 1981; Internat. Trade Show Frankfurt 1981, Tokyo 1982; 'Robes of Power' Australia 1985; Via Rail comm. painting 'Spirits of Deer Island' Montreal, Que. 1989; numerous dance performances since 1966 incl. Queen Elizabeth II 1983, Premier of China 1984; subject of many books, articles, interviews, film, video, radio; First Instr. Kitamax Sch. of Northwest Coast Indian Art Hazelton, B.C. 1967; Vice Pres. B.C. Indian Arts & Crafts Soc. 1974–82, Bd. mem.; Candn. Craft Council Del. to World Craft Council Conf. Kyoto, Japan 1978; guest reception for Queen Elizabeth II 1978, presentation Killerwhale painting 1983; Exec. Sec.-Treas. Nat. Indian Arts & Crafts Corp. Ottawa 1981–82; Hon. Life Mem., Univ. of B.C. Alumni Assn. 1982; accompanied 'People of Cedar' to Caracas, lectr. N.W. Coast art Rio de Janeiro and Sao Paulo 1984; Hon. Gov. 'Islands '86' (Expo '86 Ctte.) Victoria 1985; Royal Candn. Acad. of Arts, Certificate of Merit 1985.

**HUNTER, Bryce McClelland,** B.A., C.A., A.I.I.C.; insurance broker; b. Toronto, Ont. 21 Oct. 1945; s. Bryce Pepall and Elizabeth Jane (McClelland) H.; e. Upper Can. Coll. 1964; Univ. of W. Ont. B.A. 1967; Clarkson Gordon C.A. 1970; Ins. Inst. of Can. A.I.I.C. 1975; m. Corneila Doelman 4 Apr. 1980; children: Stephanie Brooke, Scott Bryce, Thomas Nicholas Todd, Carrie Elizabeth; PRESIDENT, HUNTER ROWELL & CO. LTD. 1978– ; Acct., Clarkson Gordon 1967–71; Hunter Rowell & Co. Ltd. 1971– ; Dir., Orthopaedic and Arthritic Hosp.; Candn. Assoc. of Family Enterprises; Intersure Ltd.; Presbyterian Ch.; Liberal Party; recreations: family activities, golf, squash; Clubs: Toronto Golf, Royal & Ancient Golf (St. Andrews, Scot.); The Toronto; Badminton & Racquet; University (Past Pres.); Devil's Glen Ski; Eastbourne Golf; Mad River Golf; Roon The Ben Soc.; Home: 40 Oriole Gardens, Toronto, Ont. M4V 1V7; Office: 595 Bay St., Ste. 1002, Toronto, Ont. M5C 2E3.

**HUNTER, David Ian;** publisher & author; b. Brighton, Sussex, England 3 June 1941; s. Francis Reginald and Olive Joan (Breem) H.; e. Hove Co. Grammar Sch. (UK); Univ. of London (UK); m. Kathaline Mary Steers 16 Mar. 1963; OWNER & PUBLISHER, MILE OAK PUBLISHING INC. 1992– ; var. capacities, Royal Insur. 1959–62; Systems Analyst, General Accident Assur. 1962–69; Sr. Mgr., MIS, KPMG Peat Marwick 1969–88; Pres., Kathda Consulting 1988–89; Mng. Dir., Cabledata Canada 1989–92; Occasional writer, broadcaster, CFRB 1010, Toronto; Past Pres. & 5-yr. Bd. Mem., Peel Condominium Corp. #154; Dir. & Past Sec., Toronto Brigantine Inc.; 25-yr. Mem., Data Processing Mngt. Assn.; Vice Pres., 'Shellback Club' (founded RCYC in 1934) 15 yrs.; Mem., Mary Rose Soc., UK (King Henry VIII sunken warship, 1545 AD); Hamilton & Scourçe Soc. (2 1812 sunken warships); Mississauga Hist. Soc.; author: 'Along the Interstate - 75' (Candn. Best Seller) 1992; recreations: sailing, historical writings; club: Port Credit Yacht (Sec. & Dir. 1972–74, 1983–86; Historian-archivist 1973– ); Address: Ste. 81, 20 Mineola Rd. E., Mississauga, Ont. L5G 4N9.

**HUNTER, Donald W.,** B.E.Sc., M.B.A., C.A., C.I.S.A.; accounting executive; b. Kirkland Lake, Ont. 9 Nov. 1946; s. George Andrew Addie and Ruth Elizabeth (Large) H.; e. Univ. of Western Ont. B.E.Sc. 1970; York Univ. M.B.A. 1974; m. Joan d. Grant and Lyla MacLennan 15 Aug. 1970; children: Sarah, Andrea, Katie; PARTNER, ENTREPRENEURIAL BUSINESS SERV., PRICE WATERHOUSE; experience in acquisitions & mergers, computers & audit; Lectr., Univ. of Toronto 1974–77; Candn. Inst. of C.A.s; seminars & presentations for Am. Mngt. Assn., Candn. Assn. of Business Valuators & others in Canada, Mexico, S. America & Hong Kong; Trustee, Islington Un. Ch. 1987– ; Pres., Islington Residents & Ratepayers Assn. 1977–78; Vice-Pres., Red Cross Soc., Toronto Central 1982–86; author of articles on computers, acquisitions and accounting; recreations: golf, skiing, bridge; clubs: Albany, St. Georges Golf & Country, Sturgeon Point Golf, Toronto Athletic, Bd. of Trade; Home: 12 Holloway Rd., Etobicoke, Ont. M9A 1E8; Office: 20 Queen St. W., Suite 200, Box 75, Toronto, Ont. M5H 3V7.

**HUNTER, Ian A.,** B.A., LL.B.; educator; b. Toronto, Ont. 18 May 1945; s. James Hogg and Margaret Elizabeth (Diggins); e. Univ. of Toronto B.A 1966 (Victoria Coll.), LL.B. 1969; one d. Alison, one s. Colin; PROF. OF LAW, UNIV. OF WESTERN ONT. 1978– ; Asst. Prof. of Law Carleton Univ. Ottawa 1970–74; Assoc. Prof. present Univ. 1974–78; Visiting Scholar, Wolfson Coll. Cambridge 1985–86; Part-time Asst. Crown Atty. 1980– ; Mediator and Labour Arbitrator 1976– ; mem. Lt. Gov.'s Adv. Review Bd. 1986– ; mem. Free Trade Panel, North Am. Free Trade Agreement 1994– ; mem. Adv. Council, Candn. Human Rights Found. 1978–88; Counsel: Ont. Human Rights Comn. 1970–78; Comn. of Inquiry on Equal Opportunity in Athletics 1982–83; Gen. Counsel, Internat. Comn. of Jurists Inquiry into the Famine in the Ukraine 1988–89; recipient Univ. of W. Ont. Gold Medal for Teaching Excellence 1983; author 'The Immigration Appeal Board of Canada' 1976; 'Malcolm Muggeridge: A Life' 1980; 'Nothing to Repent: The Life of Hesketh Pearson' 1986; ed. 'Things Past: Malcolm Muggeridge' 1978; 'A Lover's Quarrel With the World' 1985; recreation: walking; Home: Unit 4, 810 Maitland St., London, Ont. N5Y 2W5; Office: Faculty of Law, Univ. of Western Ont., London, Ont. N6A 3K7.

**HUNTER, James,** M.A., C.A., F.C.A.; chartered accountant; b. Ayr, Scotland 19 Nov. 1951; s. William James and Mary Dalrymple Seymour (Wright) H.; e. Marr Coll.; Edinburgh Univ. M.A. 1973; m. Jane d. Norman Stuart and Shirley Wood 29 Sept. 1979; one d.: Emma Jane; PARTNER, PEAT MARWICK THORNE 1987– ; trained as an accountant with Dixon Wilson & Co., London, Engl. (articled to Sir Charles Hardie C.B.E.); A.C.A. (Eng. & Wales) 1976; C.A. (Ont.) 1980; F.C.A. (Eng. & Wales) 1982; Senior Vice-Pres. Peat Marwick Thorne Inc. 1987; Past Mem. of Council, Candn. Insolvency Practitioners Assn.; Past Pres. Ont. Insolvency Assn.; Trustee in Bankruptcy; Mem., Assoc. of Certified Fraud Examiners; Dir., Candn. Centre for Ethics and Corporate Policy; Club: University Club of Toronto; Home: 40 Kingsway Cres., Toronto, Ont. M8X 2R4; Office: 3300 Commerce Court W., Toronto, Ont. M5L 1B2.

**HUNTER, Jane Proud;** artist; b. Sarnia, Ont. 12 Jan. 1939; d. John Paul and Frances Madeline (Grace) James; e. Doon Sch. of Fine Arts 1956; Ont. Coll. of Art Toronto, Art Edn. Certificate 1959; Toronto Teachers Coll. 1960; Schneider Sch. of Fine Arts 1974; m. John Donald s. John and Laura Hunter 5 Aug. 1961; children: Christopher Mark, Jonathon Scott, Jennifer Anne; taught elem. sch. Sarnia, Ont. and Ohio, Usa; began painting in water-colour 1974; solo exhns. Sarnia and London, Ont.; rep. group exhns. Sarnia, London, St. Thomas, Bayfield, Bright's Grove and Toronto; exhibits regularly with Candn. Soc. Painters in Water Colour (CSPWC); chosen to rep. Sarnia in 'Suncor Crossroads Series'; painting selected for CSPWC Diamond Jubilee Coll. Windsor Castle; painting selected for 'International Waters' a joint exhbn. and tour by the C.S.P.W.C., the Am. Watercolor Soc. and the Royal Watercolour Soc.; rep. pub., private and corporate colls. Can., USA, UK, S.Africa, Australia, Hong Kong; winner several juried awards pub. galleries and Purchase Award CSPWC Annual Exhn. Toronto 1979; recipient Ont. Arts Council Grant 1975 and Grants for 'Creative Artists in Schools' 1977, 1980, 1983; Cons. Gallery in the Grove, Bright's Grove, Ont.; mem. CSPWC; Candn. Cancer Soc.; Anglican; recreations: walking, swimming, cross-country skiing, church choir; Home: 440 Charlesworth Lane, Sarnia, Ont. N7V 2R2.

**HUNTER, Lawson A.W.,** Q.C., B.Sc., LL.B., LL.M.; lawyer; b. Florenceville, N.B. 11 Jan. 1945; s. Donald McKenzie and Hildred Eleanor (Welch) H.; e. Univ. of N.B., B.Sc. 1967, LL.B. 1970; Harvard Law Sch. LL.M. 1971; m. Camrose d. T.H. and Janet Burdon 26 Oct. 1974; children: Jared Edwin, Rosalind Dorothy; PARTNER, STIKEMAN, ELLIOTT 1993– ; Legal Advr. Legal Rsch. and Policy Sect., Dept. of Justice 1972–73; Exec. Asst. to Depy. Min., Dept. of Consumer & Corporate Affairs 1973–74; Policy Devel. Coordr., Bur. of Competition Policy 1974–77; Special Asst. to Depy. Min. of Justice 1977–78; Gen. Counsel and Dir. Legal Services, Dept. of Consumer & Corp. Affairs 1978–81; Asst. Depy. Min. Bureau of Competition Policy and Dir. of Investig. & Rsch. Combines Investig. Act, Dept. of Consumer & Corp. Affairs 1981–85; Editor-in-Chief, Canadian Competition Policy Record 1986–92; Vice Chrmn. Fraser & Beatty 1992, Partner 1986–92; Adv. Bd., Antitrust & Trade Regulation Report; Candn. Corporate Counsel; Dynatek Automation Systems Inc.; author numerous articles; mem. Law Soc. of New Brunswick; Law Soc. of Upper Canada; Candn. Bar Assn. (Vice Chrmn., National Competition Law Section 1992– ); Internat.

Bar Assn.; recreations: squash, philately, piano, cooking; Club: Rideau; Home: 88 Waverley St., Ottawa, Ont. K2P 0V2; Office: Suite 914, 50 O'Connor St., Ottawa, Ont. K1P 6L2.

**HUNTER, Maureen Elizabeth,** B.A.; playwright; b. Indian Head, Sask. 28 Sept. 1947; d. Victor Edward and Stella May Margarita (Henry) Horsman; e. Squirrel Hills Sch. 1961; Indian Head H.S. 1965; Univ. of Sask. B.A. 1970; m. Gary Michael s. Ken and Margaret H. 26 May 1973; Journalist, Saskatoon Star-Phoenix and Winnipeg Tribune 5 years; Information Writer, Candn. Wheat Board until 1977; Extve. Asst. to the Bd., then Sec. to the Bd., then Extve. Dir., Admin. (all 1st woman to be apptd.) 1977–82; work has been produced in theatres across country; Playwright-in-Residence, Manitoba Theatre Centre 1993–94; Mem., Manitoba Assn. of Playwrights; Candn. Union of Playwrights; Manitoba Writers Guild; Candn. Authors Assn.; author: 'Transit of Venus' published by Blizzard Publishing 1992 (premiere prodn., Manitoba Theatre Ctr. Nov. 1992 becoming 1st play by a Manitoba writer to be prod. on M.T.C.'s main stage in 25 years), 'Beautiful Lake Winnipeg' published by Blizzard Publishing 1990 (premiere, M.T.C. at The Warehouse 1990), 'The Queen of Queen Street' 1989 (premiere, Agassiz Theatre 1989), 'Footprints on the Moon' published by Blizzard Publishing 1988 (nominated for Gov. General's Award for Drama 1988; premiere, Agassiz Theatre 1988); 'Poor Uncle Ernie in His Covered Cage' (Agassiz 1986) (plays); co-author: 'I Met a Bully on the Hill' 1986 (play); Monologue from 'The Queen of Queen Street' in 'The Perfect Piece' 1991, Monologue from 'Footprints on the Moon' in '"And do you have anything else?": Audition pieces from Canadian Plays' 1992; Address: 6 Riverside Dr. E., Winnipeg, Man. R3T 0E8.

**HUNTER, Payson Young,** B.A., B.Comm., M.B.A., C.A.; chartered accountant; b. New York, N.Y. 7 Apr. 1950; s. Payson and Alma Odette (Young) H.; e. Kent State Univ. B.A. 1972; Dalhousie Univ. B.Comm. 1974, M.B.A. 1975; m. Shauna Jane d. Vernon and Isabel Krause 12 Sept. 1975; VICE-PRES., CORP. DEVEL., EMPIRE COMPANY LTD. 1990– ; Accountant (CPA), Peat, Marwick Mitchell & Co. 1979; Treas., Imp Fishing Gear (U.S.) 1981; Mgr., Corp. Admin., IMP Group 1981; Dir., Centennial Hotels 1986; Treas., Centennial Group of Companies 1987; Vice-Pres., Finance, Centennial Hotels 1988; Dir., N.W. Drug Co. Limited 1990– ; Pres., Morningside Farm Limited; Chrmn., P.Y. Hunter & Assoc. Limited; Lectr., Acadia Univ. 1982–83; C.P.A. (Maine); Mem., C.I.C.A., A.I.C.P.A., M.S.C.P.A., I.C.A.N.S.; recreations: sailing, skiing; clubs: Royal N.S. Yacht Squadron (past V.C. sailing); Home: P.O. Box 854, Cedar Dr., Stellarton, N.S. B0K 1S0; Office: 115 King St., Stellarton, N.S. B0K 1S0.

**HUNTER, Peter David,** LL.M.; lawyer; b. Toronto, Ont. 8 May 1943; s. Peter and Basya H.; e. Univ. of Toronto B.A. 1966; Osgoode Hall Law Sch. LL.B. 1976, LL.M. 1983; m. Janet d. Cyril and Catharine Saddington 20 March 1970; one s. Ari Parnell; PARTNER, AIRD & BERLIS 1990– ; Chrmn. Fed. Ctte. on Youth 1971; Exec. Co-ord. Prov. Offences Act Min. Atty.-Gen. Ont.; Counsel Niagara Escarpment Comn.; author various publs.; Club: Ontario; Home: 34 Alcina Ave., Toronto, Ont. M6G 2E8; Office: BCE Place, Suite 1800, Box 754, Toronto, Ont. M5J 2T9.

**HUNTINGTON, Hon. (Arthur) Ronald,** P.C., B.S.A.; b. Vancouver, B.C. 13 Feb. 1921; s. Sam Clegg and Winifred Ethel (Macintyre) H.; e. Univ. of B.C., B.S.A.; m. the late (Sydney) Jean d. late John R. Christie 13 Apl. 1943; children: Victoria Jean, Ronald Miles; m. Miriam Haig 1990; Chrmn., Service Packing Co. Ltd.; el. to H. of C. 1974, re-el. 1979 & 1980, Chrmn. Standing Comte. on Pub. Accts. 1977–79; Min. of State for Small Business and Industry 1979–80; served on Standing Cttes., H. of C. for Transport & Comm., Finance Trade & Econ. Affairs, Miscellaneous Estimates, and Special Ctte. on Standing Orders & Procedure; el. Chrmn., Nat. Progressive Conservative Caucus 1982–83; Vice Chrmn., Commonwealth Parlty. Assn., Candn. Group 1983–84; Chrmn., Ridley Terminals Inc. 1985–90, appt. Pres. and C.E.O. 1990– ; Chrmn., Canada Ports Corp. 1985–91; former mem. B.C. Inst. Agrols.; served with RCN 1941–45, rank Lt. Commdr. (retired); rec'd Queen's Silver Jubilee Medal; Commemorative Medal, 125th Anniversary; Naval Offrs. Assn. Can.; author: 'Closing the Loop' 1982; various articles; Anglican; recreations: yachting, fishing; Clubs: Kiwanis (Pres. 1971–72); West Vancouver Yacht (Commodore 1967); Vancouver Club; Office: 14834 Prospect Ave., White Rock, B.C. V4B 2B1.

**HUOT, Guy E.;** music administrator; b. Ottawa, Ont. 21 Mar. 1943; s. Eugène J. and Monique M. (Duchesne) H.; SECRETARY GENERAL, INTERNATIONAL MUSIC COUNCIL (UNESCO) 1987– ; Head, Music Section, Can. Counc. 1966–73; Music Adm., National Arts Centre Ottawa 1973–75; Ed.-in-Chief 'MUSICANADA' 1976–87; Secy. Gen., Canadian Music Counc. 1976–87; author various articles nat. and internat. publs., music reviews, prog. notes; mem. numerous music competition juries; frequent guest speaker various assns.; Candn. del. to internat. confs.; past Pres. Espace Musique Concert Soc.; past 1st Vice Pres. Inter Am. Music Counc. (O.A.S. Washington); past mem. Adv. Ctte. to Bd. Assn. Candn. Orchestras; past mem. Bd. Ottawa Choral Soc.; past Bd. mem., Ontario Choral Fedn. 1986–87; recreations: writing, travel, reading, organ & harpsichord playing, art; Home: 44, rue de Moscou, 75008 Paris, France; Office: 1, rue Miollis, 75732 Paris, Cedex 15, France.

**HURET, Jérôme,** M.A., Ph.D., M.B.A.; executive; b. Mende, France 29 May 1941; s. Jacques E. and Monique Marie (Mahoudeau) H.; e. Ecole Supérieure d'Electricité (Paris) Master's in Engrg. 1962; Univ. de Paris Ph.D. sciences 1964; Inst. d'admin. des entreprises, Paris M.B.A. 1966; m. Sophie d. René and Hermance Audet 15 July 1966; one s. Grégoire; CHRMN., NORTHERN TELECOM-FRANCE; joined CIT-Alcatel (France) 1966, Project Mgr. 1967, Gen. Mgr. Automatism Div. 1971, Vice-Pres. Internat. Product and Strategic Mktg. Office Equip. Group 1976; Exec. Vice-Pres., AES Data Inc. 1983–85; Chrmn. Sperry-France 1986; Chrmn., Olivetti-France 1989; mem. French C. of C. in Can.; mem. U.S. C. of C. in Paris; recreations: ski, tennis; Home: 58 Av. Theophile Gautier, Paris, France 75016.

**HURKA, Thomas Michael,** D.Phil.; educator; b. Toronto, Ont. 10 Aug. 1952; s. Anthony Emmanuel and Edith Dita (Heller) H.; e. Univ. of Toronto Schs. 1971; Univ. of Toronto Trinity Coll. B.A. 1975; Corpus Christi Coll. Oxford B.Phil 1977 (John Locke Prize in Mental Philos. 1976), D.Phil. 1980; PROF. OF PHILOS., UNIV. OF CALGARY 1992– , Sessional Lectr. 1978, Asst. Prof. 1979, Assoc. Prof. 1984; Annual Fellow, Calgary Inst. for Humanities 1989–90; author: 'Principles' The Globe and Mail (weekly column) 1989–92; 'Perfectionism' 1993; 'Principles: Short Essays on Ethics' 1993; co-editor: (with Harold Coward) 'Ethics and Climate Change: The Greenhouse Effect' 1993; over 20 articles, reviews philos. jours.; mem. Candn. Philos. Assn.; Am. Philos. Assn.; Sidgwick Soc.; recreations: golf, theatre, oldtimers hockey; Home: 2603 – 23 Ave. S.W., Calgary, Alta. T3E 0H9; Office: Univ. of Calgary, Calgary, Alta. T2N 1N4.

**HURLBUT, Robert St. Clair,** B.Com., LL.B.; company chairman; b. Toronto, Ont. 10 June 1924; s. St. Clair and Maude I. (Burleigh) H.; e. Earl Haig Collegiate, Toronto, Ont., (Sr. Matric.); Univ. of Toronto, B.Com. 1948; Osgoode Hall Law Sch., LL.B. 1951; m. Anne Marilyn, d. Walter T. Moffat, 2 May 1953; two s. David, Andrew; CHAIRMAN & PRESIDENT, GENSTAR CAPITAL CORP. 1989– ; Dir.: North Amer. Life Assurance Co.; Consumers' Gas; Rio Algom Ltd.; Northern Telecom Ltd.; North American Trust Co.; North American Mortgage Co.; read law with Robert Pringle, Q.C.; called to the Bar of Ontario 1951; practised law with Daly, Thistle, Judson and McTaggart, Toronto 1951–52; joined Colgate-Palmolive, Toronto, as Salesman 1952; Brand Mgr. 1953–54; Group Mgr. 1954–55; Product Mgr., General Foods Inc. 1956–59; Product Group Mgr. 1959–62; Mgr. Sales Operations Mar.-Nov. 1962; Devel. Mgr. 1962–63; Adv. and Merch. Mgr. 1963–65; Nat. Sales Mgr. 1965–66; Mktg. Mgr. May-Nov. 1966; Vice-Pres. Mktg. 1966–67; Pres. 1967–84; Chrmn. 1984–89; Ordinary Seaman Apr. 1943–Dec. 1943 when commissioned; discharged Sept. 1945 as Lieut. R.C.N.(R.); past Chrmn. Grocery Prod. Mfrs. of Can.; Assn. of Candn. Advertisers 1964–68; Founding Mem., Business Counc. on Nat. Issues; Gov.: Olympic Trust of Can.; North York General Hosp. 1984–93; Guelph Univ. 1970–76; Sigma Nu; Conservative; Anglican; Clubs: Granite; Rosedale Golf; National; recreations: sailing, photography, golf; Home: 3 – 3100 Bayview Ave., Willowdale, Ont. M2N 5L3; Office: Scotia Plaza, Ste. 4900, Toronto, Ont. M5H 4A2.

**HURLEY, (Marie)-Adèle Margaret,** B.A., M.E.S.; conservationist; b. St. Catharines, Ont. 15 Nov. 1952; d. Cecil Vincent and Eleanor Melanie (Peckham) H.; e. York Univ., Glendon Coll. B.A. 1974, Faculty Environmental Studies M.E.S. 1976; FOUNDER, CANDN. COALITION ON ACID RAIN 1981– ; Dir., Ontario Hydro; Pres., Hurley and Assoc. Inc. 1992; Assoc., Inst. Environmental Studies Univ. of Toronto; Researcher, Environment Portfolio, Ont. Lib. Party 1978–80; recipient: Lt. Gov.'s Conservation Award 1989; 'White Hat Award' 1985 Pennsylvania Fish Comn.; Acid Rain Citizen's Award 1984 New Hampshire Citizens Task Force; Conserv. Achievement Cert. Fedn. Ont. Naturalists 1984; Inaugural lectr., Walter Gordon Series in Public Policy, Massey Coll., Univ. of Toronto 1990; recreation: canoeing, equestrian riding; Office: 401, 112 St. Clair Ave. W., Toronto, Ont. M4V 2Y3.

**HURLEY, Brian A.;** insurance executive; b. Liverpool, England 3 May 1934; s. Edmund A. and Catherine (Reid) H.; e. English public school; m. Nan d. Hannah and John Stevenson 29 Nov. 1958; VICE-PRES., CREDIT, LAURENTIAN FINANCIAL INC. 1989– ; Inspector, Mortgages, Credit Foncier Franco Canadien 1956–68; Asst. Supt., Mortgages, Manufacturers Life INsur. Co. 1968–72; Asst. Vice-Pres., Mortgages, City Savings & Trust Co. 1972–78; Extve. Dir., Mortgage Investments, The Imperial LIfe Assur. Co. of Canada 1978–89; Past Pres., Soc. of Real Estate Appraisers (Ont.); Mem., Appraisal Inst. of Canada; Appraisal Institute (U.S.); Pres., The Toronto Consort; recreations: golf, tennis, squash, music; clubs: Bd. of Trade Country; Home: #1909 – 820 Burnhamthorpe Rd., Etobicoke, Ont. M9C 4W2; Office: 95 St. Clair Ave. W., Toronto, Ont. M4V 1N7.

**HURLEY, Daniel M.,** Q.C., C.D., B.A., B.C.L., LL.M., Ph.D., LL.D.; educator; b. Barnaby River, N.B. 4 May 1929; s. Daniel Michael and Clara (Mahar) H.; e. St. Thomas Acad. 1946; St. Thomas Univ. B.A. 1950, LL.D. 1982; Univ. of N.B. B.C.L. 1958; Univ. of London LL.M. 1960, Ph.D. 1970; m. Hanora Kathleen (Kate) d. Patrick Joseph and Julia Anne Murphy 27 June 1960; children: Daniel Joseph Colman, Clarissa Hanora (Claire); PROF. OF LAW, UNIV. OF N.B. 1970– , Assoc. Dean of Law 1982–88; served with Candn. Army (Korean campaign) 1950–55; summer session The Hague Internat. Law Acad. 1959; Asst. Prof. of Law present univ. 1960, Assoc. Prof. 1965; sabbatical leave Va. Law Sch. 1966–67; recipient Beaverbrook Scholarships (Can.) 1955–58, (overseas) 1958–60; Excellence in Teaching Award Univ. of N.B. 1982; apptd. Q.C. (N.B.) 1989; Gov. St. Thomas Univ.; Chrmn. Bd. of Sch. Trustees 1971–89; Chrmn. N.B. Parole Bd. 1964– ; Mem., Nat. Parole Bd. 1980–84; N.B. Prov. candidate 1967, 1974; Fed. candidate 1980; author various publs.; N.B. ed. Halsbury's Laws of England 1961–62; mem. John Howard Soc.; Charter and continuing mem. Atlantic Provs. Corrections Assn. (now Criminology & Corrections); mem., Internat. Assoc. of Penal Law 1980– , Sec./Treas. Cdn. Sec. 1990– ; Alternate Chrmn. N.B. Labour Rlns. Bd. 1965–66; mem. Candn. Bar Assn.; Law Soc. N.B.; Fredericton Law Soc.; N.B. Liberal Assn. (mem. Extve. 1974–84); York-Sunbury Lib. Assn. (Pres. 2 yrs); Fredericton S. Lib. Assn.; R. Catholic; Liberal; recreations: gardening, skating, walking; Home: 216 Turnbull Court, Fredericton, N.B. E3B 4L1; Office: Fredericton, N.B. E3B 5A3.

**HUROWITZ, Bonnie,** B.A.; magazine editor; b. Toronto, Ont. 8 Sept. 1956; d. Stanley G. and Tanya F. (Rubinoff) H.; e. Jarvis Coll. Inst. 1974 (Ont. Scholar); Univ. of Toronto, B.A. (Hons.) 1977; Osgoode Hall Law Sch. 1977–78; m. Michael Fuller 26 June 1983; EDITOR-IN-CHIEF, YM; Reporter, The Markham Econ. and Sun, summer 1977; The Toronto Star, part-time 1977–78; City News & Lifestyle, The Ottawa Citizen, summer 1978; Fashion Reporter, The Toronto Star 1978–80; Sportswear Ed., Women's Wear Daily 1980–83; Columnist, Flare Mag. and Contrib. Fashion Writer 'All the Rage,' Maclean's Mag. 1981–83; Editor, Flare Magazine 1983–89; recreations: reading, cooking, eating fine cuisine, swimming, skiing, camping; Office: Gruner-Jahr Publishing, 685 Third Ave, 28th Flr., New York, NY 10017 USA.

**HURST, D.G.,** M.Sc., Ph.D., F.R.S.C.; physicist; b. St. Austell, England 19 Mar. 1911; s. George Leopold and Sarah Ellen (Inns) H.; e. McGill Univ., B.Sc. 1933, M.Sc. 1934, Ph.D. 1936; Univ. of Cal. 1936–37; Cavendish Lab., Cambridge Univ. (1851 Exhn. Scholar.) 1937–39; m. Margaret Christina, d. D. A. McCuaig, 23 Dec. 1939; children: Dorothy June, David Alan; with Division of Physics, National Research Council, Ottawa, 1939–44; Montreal Lab., N.R.C., 1944–45; joined Chalk River Lab., 1945; Dir., Div. of Reactor Research & Devel. 1961–65; 1965–67 on leave as Dir., Nuclear Power and Reactors Div., I.A.E.A., Vienna, Austria; Dir., Applied Research and Develop., Chalk River Nuclear Labs. 1967–70; Pres., Atomic Energy Control Bd. 1970–74; Fellow, Royal Soc. of Can.; Fellow, Am. Nuclear Soc.; Outstanding Contribution Award, Candn. Nuclear Assn. 1990; 'Tommy Thompson' Award (the highest ANS award for outstanding contributions in the field of nuclear reactor safety), Am. Nuclear Soc. 1994; mem.,

Candn. Assn. of Physicists; United Church; Address: 7 Frontenac Cresc., P.O. Box 274, Deep River, Ont. K0J 1P0.

**HURST, F(rederick) Warren,** B. Com., M.B.A., F.C.A.; retired executive; b. Toronto, Ont. 4 May 1926; s. Frederick Clarence, F.C.A. and Alice (Moody) H.; e. Univ. of Toronto Schs. Matric. 1943; Univ. of Toronto, Trinity Coll., B.Com. 1947; Harvard Grad. Sch. of Business Adm., M.B.A. 1949; Inst. of Chart Accts. of Ont. C.A. 1953, Fellow 1965; m. Cynthia Masson d. Cyril M. Smith, Q.C. 24 Jan. 1953; children: David Warren, Wendy Ann, Graham John Britton; Dir., Mackenzie Financial Corp.; Midland Walwyn Inc.; Padinox Inc.; Fairbank Lumber Co. Ltd.; Financial Adv. Board, Ganonoque Steel Forgings Inc.; with Mang. Adv. Services Sec. of Price Waterhouse & Co. 1949–55; joined The Consumers' Gas Co. in 1955 as Comptroller and was chief financial offr. till 1971 when apptd. Extve. V.P., Commercial Operations (Dir. of the Co. 1971–73); Dir., Extve. Comte., Home Oil 1972–73; Pres., F.H. Deacon & Co. Ltd. 1975–76; Pres., F.H. Deacon, Hodgson Inc. 1977; Vice-Chrmn. and Dir. 1978–84; Sr. Policy Advisor, Investment Dealer's Assoc. of Can. 1984–86; Co-Chrmn., Ctte. for Equal Treatment of Asbestos Minority Shareholders 1986– ; Dir., Extve. Comte., Northstar Res. Ltd. 1978–84; Dir., Lake Louise Lifts Ltd. 1972–81; GLN Investments Ltd. 1982–84; White Rose Nurseries Ltd. 1971–84; Extve. Dir., The Ontario Comte. on Taxation, 1963–67; Treas., Candn. Inst. of Chart. Accts. 1965–68; Pres., Bureau of Mun. Research of Metro Toronto 1965–70; Vice Chrmn., Metrop. Toronto Planning Bd. 1970–76; Treas., Ont. Boy Scout Assn. 1976; Treas., Nat. Boy Scout Assn. 1989–91 (Finance Ctte. 1993– ); Delta Kappa Epsilon; Anglican; Clubs: Donalda; National; Osler Bluff Ski; Home: Oakhurst Point, R.R. #2 Days Rd., Gananoque, Ont. K7G 2V4.

**HURST, William Donald,** C.M. (1972), M.S.C.E., F.C.A.E., P.Eng., P.E.; b. Winnipeg. Man. 15 Mar. 1908; s. William and Magdalene (Unger) H.; e. Winnipeg Public and High Sch., Matric. 1925; Univ. of Manitoba, B.Sc. (in C.E.) 1930; Virginia Polytechnic. Inst., and State Univ. M.S.C.E. 1931; m. Gytha Johnson, Winnipeg, Man., 2 June 1934; children: Marilyn Ragna, William Helgi Donald; CANDN. REPRESENTATIVE, AM. PUBLIC WORKS ASSOC. 1976– ; Consulting Civil Engr. since 1972; City Engr. and Commr. of Bldgs., Winnipeg (retired) 1944–72; Chairman, Winnipeg Building Comn. 1944–60; Chrmn. of Commrs., Greater Winnipeg Water Dist. & Greater Winnipeg Sanitary Dist. 1949–60; Chrmn., River & Streams Protection Authority 1951–72; Comnr. of Works and Operations, Winnipeg 1972–73; Sr. Research Assoc., Am. Public Works Assn., Kansas City, Mo. 1972 to present; Candn. Rep. Amer., Can. Public Works Assoc. 1986– ; Pres., Winnipeg Symphony Orchestra, 1955–56; Teaching Fellow, Civil Engn., Virginia Polytechnic. Inst., Blacksburg, Va., 1930–31; rejoined Engn. Dept., Winnipeg, rising to Engr. of Water Works, 1934–44; Asst. City Engr., 1944; served as Secy.-Engr., Bd. of Engrs., Greater Winnipeg Sanitary Dist., 1935–39; apptd. Commr., Winnipeg-St. Boniface Harbour Comn., 1946; Commr., Nat. Capital Comn., Ottawa, 1971–76; mem. Exec. Comte., Chrmn., Land Comte.; mem., Assoc. Comn. on Geotech. Research, NRC, Ottawa, 1967–71; served in 2nd World War, 10th Dist. Engrs., R.C.E., Capt. O/C 1st Workshop and Park Co.; mem., The Royal Candn. Legion, Fort Rouge Br., #97, Winnipeg; mem., Assn. of Prof. Engrs., Man. (Pres. 1950 and 1951); Engn. Inst. of Can. (Chrmn., Winnipeg Br., 1938 and 1951); Am. Water Works Assn. (Chrmn., Minnesota Sec., 1947–48; Chrmn. Candn. Sec., 1952–53; Dir., 1952–55; Nat. Vice Pres. 1961–62; Nat. Pres., 1962–63); Am. Pub. Works Assn. (Dir. 1954–57, Vice Pres. 1957–58, Pres. 1959–60); Hon. Fellow, Inst. of Water and Environmental Management (U.K.); Life mem., Fellow, American Society of Civil Engineers; Vice-Chrmn., Rsch. Foundn., Am. Public Works Assn.; Trustee Eme., Pres., Inst. for Municipal Engineering 1966–67; Diplomate Am. Acad. of Environmental Engrs.; Brit. N. Am. Philatelic Soc.; Reg'd. Prof. Engr., Man. and Minn.; Hon. Reg'd. Architect, Manitoba; Hon. Mem.: Assn. of Prof. Engrs., Man. 1977; Am. Waterworks Assn. 1966; Candn. Public Works Counc. 1983; Am. Public Works Assn. 1985; Public Works Historical Soc. (U.S.A.) 1988; Member, Order of Canada 1972; awarded Queen's 25th Anniversary Medal; Commemorative Medal, 125th Anniversary, Candn. Confedn. 1992; Candn. Council of Professional Engrs. Gold Medal 1993; Fellow, Candn. Acad. of Engr. 1989; George Warren Fuller Award, Am. Water Works Assn.; Pub. Works Man of the Year, Kiwanis Internat. and Am. Pub. Works Assn. 1962; Hon. Mem., Pub. Works Historical Soc., Chicago. Ill., Career Oral Interview publ'd. 1984 – 1st Cdn. recipient; Samuel Greeley Service Award; author of many technical papers; Chrmn. Nat. Ed. Ctte., Building Canada, History of Public Works in Canada 1986–88; Phi Delta Theta; Golden Legion; Freemason (Scottish Rite 33$); A.A.O.N.M.S. (Khartum Temple); Royal Order of Jesters; United Church; recreations: golf; philately; Clubs: Manitoba (Life Mem.); Carleton; Collectors, New York; Home: 67 Kingsway, Winnipeg, Man. R3M 0G2.

**HURSTFIELD-MEYER, Jonathan Robert,** B.Com., C.A.; executive; b. Lusaka, Zambia 12 Feb. 1945; s. Johannes and Joan M. (Chaplan) Meyer; e. Madrid Univ.; McGill Univ. B.Com. 1969, LIA 1971, C.A. 1971; m. Lynn d. Guy and Pauline René de Cotret 18 July 1980; children: Julie, Richard, David; PRES., C.E.O. & DIR., CLEYN AND TINKER (1989) INC. 1991– ; Dir., Cleyn and Tinker International; Keltico; Kent Manufacturing Co.; Auditor, Peat Marwick, Mitchell 1969–76, Partner Income Tax 1979–84; Treas. S.N.C. Inc. 1976–79; Vice Pres., Innocan Inc. 1984–91; recreations: tennis, scuba diving, golf; Club: Mount Royal Country; Home: 244 Kindersley Ave., Montréal, Qué. H3R 1R7; Office: 2350 Cohen, Saint-Laurent (Montréal), Qué. H4R 2N6.

**HURTEAU, Gilles D.,** B.A., M.D., C.M., F.R.C.S.(C), F.A.C.O.G.; educator; b. Cornwall, Ont. 28 Nov. 1928; s. Joseph A. and Antoinette (St-Laurent) H.; e. Univ. of Ottawa B.A. 1951; McGill Univ. M.D., C.M. 1955; m. Janine Anita d. Percy and Anita Carrière 16 June 1956; children: Michèle, Jean, Louise, Pierre, Gilles-André; EXECUTIVE DIRECTOR, ROYAL COLLEGE OF PHYSICIANS AND SURGEONS OF CANADA 1990– ; post grad. training in Surg. Case Western Reserve Univ. 1956–58 and in Obstetrics & Gynecol. Yale Univ. 1958–61; Instr. and Clin. Asst. Yale Univ. Med. Sch. 1961–62; Asst. Prof. Univ. of Ottawa Med. Sch. 1962, Assoc. Prof. 1966, Prof. and Chrmn. of Obstetrics & Gynecol. 1967–76; Dean of Health Sciences and Sch. of Medicine, Univ. of Ottawa 1976–89; Trustee Children's Hosp. of E. Ont. 1977–89; Chrmn., Jt. Rsch. Review Task Force Ont. Council of Health 1977–81; author of many publs. and book chapters; mem., various ed. bds.; Pres., Assn. Candn. Med. Colls. 1981–83; Fellow, Royal Coll. Physicians and Surgeons of Canada (Counc. 1970–78, Vice Pres., Surg. 1976–78); mem. of Council, Ontario Cancer Treatment & Rsch. Foundation 1983–92; mem., Ont. Min. of Health Advisory Ctte. on High Technology, 1984; mem. of Council, Ottawa-Carleton District Health Council 1978–84; grants' ctte., Physician's Services Inc. (P.S.I.) Foundation 1984–86; mem. Candn. Delegation to Moscow Peace Conf., Comn. of Physicians and Biomedical Scientists, Moscow 1987; mem., Cercle Universitaire d'Ottawa; Soc. of Obstetricians & Gynecologists of Can.; Am. Coll of Obstetrics & Gynecology; Royal Coll. of Physicians & Surgeons of Can.; Alpha Omega Alpha Honor Med. Soc. (Fac. Mem.); recreations: skiing, swimming, boating; Office: 774 Echo Dr., Ottawa, Ont. K1S 5N8.

**HURTIG, Mel,** O.C.; L.L.D.; book publisher and author; b. Edmonton, Alta. 24 June 1932; m. Kay Eleanor Studer, 18 Nov. 1981; children: Barbara, Gillian, Jane Anne, Leslie; PRESIDENT, HURTIG COMMUNICATIONS LTD.; formerly Pres., New Canadian Encyclopedia Publishing Ltd. and Hurtig Publishers Ltd.; estbd. bookstore Edmonton 1956 subsequently expanding to three; sold retail book operations 1972 to concentrate on publishing Cdn. books; named Cdn. Book Publisher of the Yr. 1974 and 1981; former Pres. Edmonton Art Gallery; former mem. Univ. of Alta. Senate; City of Edmonton's Grants Comte.; served in adv. capacity Can. Council, Pollution Probe, Can. Council on Social Devel.; founding Chrmn., The Council of Cdns. 1985–87; founding mem. Comte. for an Independent Can. (Past Nat. Chrmn.); Past Chrmn. Bd. Cdn. Booksellers' Assn.; Order of Can. 1980; LL.D.: York Univ. 1980; Wilfrid Laurier Univ. 1985; Univ. of Lethbridge 1986; Univ. of Alberta 1986; Concordia Univ. 1990; Univ. of British Columbia 1992; Eve Orpen Award for Publishing and Literary Excellence 1985; Silver Ribbon Award, City of Edmonton 1985; Centenary Medal, Royal Soc. of Can. 1986; Alberta Achievement Award 1986; Toastmasters Internat. Communications and Leadership Award 1986; President's Award, Candn. Booksellers Assn. 1986; Quill Award, Windsor Press Club 1986; Speaker of the Year Award, Candn. Speech Communicators Assoc. 1986; Corporate Citizen of the Year Award, Community of Bus. and Profl. Associates of Can. 1988; Lester B. Pearson Man of the Year Peace Award 1988; author: 'The Betrayal of Canada' (non-fiction) 1991; 'A New and Better Canada' 1992; el. Leader, The National Party of Canada 1992; Home: 9905 – 115 St., Edmonton, Alta. T5K 1S4.

**HURTUBISE, Jacques-Claude,** B.A., D.Phil.; educator; b. Montréal, Qué. 12 Mar. 1957; s. Jacques Edouard and Margaret (Ching) H.; e. Coll. Jean-de-Brébeuf D.E.C. 1975; Univ. de Montréal B.A. 1978; Oxford Univ. D.Phil. 1982 (Rhodes Scholar); m. Odile Marcotte 1986; ASSOC. PROFESSOR, McGILL UNIV. 1988– ; Prof. de Mathématiques, Univ. du Québec à Montréal 1982–88; Membre-Associé, C.R.M. Univ. de Montréal; Dir., Candn. Math. Soc. 1985–87; Mem., Inst. Adv. Study, Princeton 1987–88; Centennial Fellowship, Am. Math. Soc. 1993; Office: 805 Sherbrooke St. W., Montreal, Que. H3A 2K6.

**HURTUBISE, Pierre J.,** O.M.I., M.A.Phil. L.Th., L.Hist.Eccl., Ph.D.; university professor; b. Ottawa, Ont. 15 Feb. 1933; s. Samuel J. and Marguerite M. (Daoust) H.; e. Univ. of Ottawa M.A.Phil. 1961; L.Th. 1961; Gregorian Univ., Rome, L.Hist. Eccl. 1965; Sorbonne, Paris. Ph.D. 1969; RECTOR, SAINT PAUL UNIV. 1985– ; Academic Vice-Rector there 1980–83; Lectr. in Phil., Univ. of Ottawa 1961–63, Visiting Prof. of History 1969– ; Assoc. Prof. of Theology, Saint Paul Univ. 1968–76, Prof. 1976– ; Dir., Rsch. Centre 1976–79, 1984– ; author 'Correspondance du nonce en France, Antonio Maria Salviati (1572–1578)' 1975; ed. 'Le laic dans l'Eglise canadienne-française de 1830 à nos jours' 1972; 'Une famille-témoin: les Salviati' 1985; mem., Royal Soc. Can. (Hon. Secy. 1992– ); Dir., Soc. canadienne d'études de la Renaissance 1984–86; mem. Programme Comte., Candn. Academic Centre in Italy 1980– ; Vice Pres., Candn. Mediterranean Inst. 1987–90; Bd. mem., Internat. Fedn. of Catholic Univs. 1988– ; Gov., Univ. of Ottawa 1984–85; recreations: music, cross-country skiing; Club: Cercle Universitaire d'Ottawa; Home: 175 Main St., Ottawa, Ont. K1S 1C3; Office: 223 Main St., Ottawa, Ont. K1S 1C4.

**HURTUBISE, René,** B. ès A., LL.L., M.A.; juge et éducateur; né Montréal, Qué. 1 avril 1933; fils Louis-Vincent et Bernadette (Brunet) H.; é. Univ. de Montréal, B. ès A., 1954; LL.L., 1957; Univ. d'Oxford, M.A. (Jurisprudence), 1960; Univ. de Montréal, M.A. (Droit), 1961; ép Jeannine, f. Fortunat Carrier, 10 août 1957; enfants: Patrice, Martin, Frederic; JUGE À LA COUR SUPÉRIEURE DU QUÉBEC; a contribué des articles à plusieurs revues; co-auteur de (Les mécanismes de législation d'administration et d'interprétation de la fiscalité fédérale) 'Legislation, Administration and Interpretation Processes in Federal Taxation'; L'Université-La Société et Le Gouvernement' 1970, 'L'Université Québécoise du Proche Avenir' 1973; ex membre du Conseil, des Universités du Qué.; ex Prés., du Comité sur les Objectifs de l'Enseignement Supérieur du Conseil des Univs.; Conseiller auprès du représentant permanent du Can. lors de la 33ème Sess. de la Comm. des droits de l'homme des Nations-Unies (1977); Prés. de l'Assoc. Can. des organismes statutaires pour la protection des droits de l'homme (1977–78); invité à titre d'expert par l'UNESCO au colloque 'L'Homme et la Paix,' à Paris, Oct. 1977, et à Montréal, comme expert et rapporteur, en juillet 1978, 'Le Racisme et l'Histoire'; invité à titre d'expert et de conférencier par le Centre des droits de l'homme de l'Office des Nations Unies (Genève) au colloque auprès des juges de la Cour suprême de Justice à Bucarest (Roumanie) en septembre 1991; Prés. de la Comm. des Droits de la personne du Quebec 1975 a 1980; ant. Dir. gén. de la Conférence des recteurs et des principaux des univ. du Québ. Catholique; Administrateur de l'Institut Canadien d'Administration de la Justice, 30 novembre 1993; résidence: 3546, ave Marcil, Montréal, Qué. H4A 2Z3; Bureau: Palais de Justice, 1 Notre-Dame est, bureau 15.65 Montreal, Qué. H2Y 1B6.

**HUSBAND, Harold;** company president; b. Troy, N.Y. 1905; became a naturalized Candn. 1929; s. late John Husband; e. New York and Montreal Schs.; m. Margaret Kay Lindsay, 1937; three d.; PRES., HUSWEST ENTERPRISES CORP.; Director, Victoria Chamber Comm.; worked for C.P.R., particularly in connection to constr. of hotels at Banff and Lake Louise; worked with the late J.S.H. Matson, organ. and buying bus lines on Vancouver Island; later became Gen. Mgr. of Vancouver Island Transportation Co. and Vancouver Island Coach Lines Ltd., subsequently buying these co's from C.P. Rly. Co.; for many yrs. was active in publishing business and was Mang. Dir. of 'Victoria Colonist,' a Dir. of Candn. Daily Newspapers Assn. and a mem. of The Candn. Press; owned and op. Victoria Machinery Depot Co. Ltd. 1947–81; Pres., Candn. Ship Building and Ship Repairing Assn. 1957–60, B.C.; mem., Victoria Chamber of Comm. (Past Pres.); Victoria and Island Publicity Bureau (Past Pres.); recreation: golf; Clubs: Victoria Golf; Union; Vancouver; Home: 3150 Rutland Rd., Uplands, Victoria, B.C. V8R 3R8; Office: (Box 1117) 343 Bay St., Victoria, B.C. V8W 2S6.

**HUSER, Glen Anton,** B.Ed., M.A.; writer, artist, teacher; b. Elk Point, Alta. 1 Feb. 1943; s. Harry Oliver and Beatrice (Daily) H.; e. Ashmont P.A.; Eastglen H.S. 1960; Univ. of Alta. 1960–62; Vanc. Sch. of Art 1965–66; Univ. of Alta. B.Ed. (with distinction) 1970, M.A. 1988; one s.: Casey Lawrence Huser; Teacher (Edmonton) 1963– ; studied creative writing under Rudy Wiebe, Margaret Atwood and W.O. Mitchell; short stories 'Dance' pub. in 'Prism International' Fall 1977, 'The Recital' in 'Dandelion' 1982, 'Nudities' in 'Boundless Alberta' 1993; in 1978 he developed 'Magpie' a mag. of student writing & graphics for Edmonton Public Schools and continues as Managing Ed.; began a long career working as a teacher-librarian 1970; co-editor, Nelson mini-anthologies series for Junior High students 1992, 1993; Consultant in Learning Resources, Edmonton Pub. Schs.; M.A. thesis 'The Flowers of Alberta' was chosen by NeWest Press as 2nd in Nunatak Fiction Series and an expanded and retitled ('Grace Lake') version was nom. for W.H. Smith–Books in Canada first novel award 1990 & the Writers' Guild of Alta. for Novel Award 1990; 1st Prize, Edmonton Jour. Lit. Awards for Short Fiction 1974, Poetry 1979, One-Act Play 1980; Alta. Heritage Wilfrid R. May Scholarship for Career Devel. 1986; Greater Edmonton Reg. Learning Resources Council Award of Merit 1991; Extve. Mem., Children's Literature Roundtable (Edmonton); Bd. of Dir., Young Alta. Book Festival Soc.; recreations: as an artist has an interest in figure-drawing, the Alta. landscape, & children's book illustration; keen interest in film history & film aesthetics; Office: c/o NeWest Publishers, 310 – 10359 Whyte Ave., Edmonton, Alta. T6E 1Z9.

**HUSHLAK, Gerald,** B.Ed., M.F.A., R.C.A.; educator; artist; b. 1944; e. Royal Coll. of Art London, Eng. M.A.R.C.A. 1973; PROF. OF ART, UNIV. OF CALGARY 1992– ; Assoc. Prof. 1975–92; 20 solo exhns. nat. and internat. museums and art galls.; 9 solo exhns. nat. comm. galls.; rep. 24 museum and pub. art colls.; 12 distinguished lectures on computer art various Candn. art galls. and univs.; subject of TV documentary on vector drawings; juried into 70 exhns.; incl. in SIGGRAPH computer art exhns. past 3 yrs; rep. Can. in Museum of Modern Art Paris (Electra Exhn.); Can. Counc. Computer Rsch. Grant and 3 project grants, 3 Alta. Culture visual arts grants, 3 Univ. of Calgary rsch. grants; incl. in 43 publs.; subject various publs.; Home: Box 14, Site 24, R.R. 12, Calgary Alta. T3E 6W3; Office: Art Bldg. (722), 2500 University Dr. N.W., Calgary, Alta. T2N 1N4.

**HUSSEY, Valerie,** B.A.; publisher; b. New York, N.Y. 18 Nov. 1950; d. Edward Baker and Paula (Handler) H.; e. SUNY Buffalo B.A. 1972; m. J. Ian s. Dr. Christopher and Dorothy Graham 22 Sept. 1978; one s.: Andrew; PUBLISHER-PRESIDENT, KIDS CAN PRESS LTD. 1979– ; Writer, Westinghous Learning Corp. 1972–73; Editor, Macmillan 1973–74; General Publishing 1975–76; Harcourt, Brace, Jovanovish 1977–79; Faculty, Banff Publishing Workshop; Vice-Pres., Council, Assoc. of Cdn. Publishers; Chair, Candn. Children's Book Centre, 4 yrs.; Ctte. Chair, Childrens Ctte., Profl. Devel. Ctte.; Bd. of Dir., Planned Parenthood of Toronto; Book Reviewer, 'Globe & Mail' 1979–80; author of sundry articles in periodicals, incl. piece in collection 'Writers on Writing' ed. D. Booth; Mentor in Step-Up program for Women in Business; Office: 29 Birch Ave., Toronto, Ont. M4V 1E2.

**HUSTON, M.J.,** M.Sc., Ph.D.; retired university dean; b. Ashcroft, B.C. 4 Sept. 1912; s. William Mervyn and Irene Mary (Gray) H.; e. Univ. of Alta. B.Sc. (Pharm.) 1934, M.Sc. (Biochem.) 1938; Univ. of Wash., Ph.D. (Pharmacol.) 1941; Hon. LL.D., Dalhousie Univ. 1982; Hon. D.Sc., Univ. of Alta. 1988; m. Helen Margaret McBryan, 18 Dec. 1939; children: Bryan Mervyn, Dorna Helen; joined staff of Univ. as Lect. 1939, Asst. Prof. 1943, Acting Dir. Sch. of Pharm., 1946, Dir., 1948; Dean, Faculty of Pharmacy and Pharmaceutical Sciences, Univ. of Alberta, 1955–78; Pres. (1970), Candn. Foundation for Advanc. of Pharm.; Candn. Pharm. Assn. (President 1968–69); mem., Alta. Pharm. Assn.; Am. Pharm. Assn.; Candn. Conf. of Pharm. Faculties (Chrmn. 1948–49); author of 'The Great Canadian Lover' 1964; 'Toast to the Bride' 1969; 'Canada Eh to Zed' 1973; 'Great Golf Humour' 1977; 'Golf and Murphy's Law' 1981; 'Gophers Don't Pay Taxes' 1981; Ed.-in-Chief, Candn. Journ. of Pharm. Science 1965–78; has publ. two textbooks and written many papers for tech. journs.; rec'd. Dr. E.R. Squibb Award 1971; Alta. Achievement Award Medal 1971; Hon. Life Mem.: Cdn. Pharmaceutical Assn. 1977; Alta. Pharmaceutical Assn. 1978; Man. Pharmaceutical Assn. 1978; B.C. Pharm. Assn. 1978; Sask Pharm. Assn. 1978; Stephen Leacock Memorial Medal for Humour 1982; Sigma Xi; Phi Sigma; Phi Delta Theta (Adv. 1948–50); Rho Chi; Freemason (32$); Conservative; United Church; recreations: music, sports; Home: 11562–80 Ave., Edmonton, Alta. T6G 0R9.

**HUTCHEON, Hon. Henry Ernest,** B.A., LL.B.; b. Brantford, Ont. 26 July 1920; s. James and Florence (Carey) H.; e. Univ. of Toronto, B.A. 1948; Univ. of B.C., LL.B. 1950; m. Valerie Marie, d. Albert John McCullagh, 9 March 1955; children: Bruce, Craig, Kerry; JUSTICE, COURT OF APPEAL FOR B.C., 1980– ; read law with R. N. Shakespeare; called to the Bar of B.C. 1951; cr. Q.C. 1967; Partner, Shakespeare & Hutcheon, 1958–68; Guild, Yule, Schmitt, Lane, Hutcheon & Collier 1968–73; apptd. Judge Co. Court 1973; Justice, Supreme Court of B.C. 1974–80; served with the Royal Canadian Corps of Signals 1939–45; Protestant; recreation: golf; Club: Point Grey Golf & Country; Home: 2327 W. 35th St., Vancouver, B.C. V6M 1J7; Office: Court House, 800 Smithe St., Vancouver, B.C. V6Z 2E1.

**HUTCHEON, Linda,** Ph.D., F.R.S.C.; educator; b. Toronto, Ont. 24 Aug. 1947; d. Vincent Roy and Elisa Euphemia (Rossi) Bortolotti; e. Univ. of Toronto B.A. 1969, Ph.D. 1975; Cornell Univ. M.A. 1971; F.R.S.C. 1990; m. Michael s. Alexander and Kathleen Hutcheon 30 May 1970; PROF. OF ENG. & COMPARATIVE LIT., UNIV. OF TORONTO 1988– ; John P. Robarts Prof. of Candn. Studies York Univ. 1988–89; Asst., Assoc. and Full Prof. of Eng. McMaster Univ. Hamilton 1976–88; other teaching incls. Internat. Summer Inst. Semiotic & Structural Studies 1984 and 1990; Italian Assn. Candn. Studies 1986; recipient Woodrow Wilson Fellowship 1969; Killam Jr. Fellowship 1978–80, Sr. Rsch. Fellowship 1986–88; Connaught Sr. Fellowship 1991–92; Guggenheim Fellowship 1992–93; author: 'Narcissistic Narrative' 1980, 1984, 'Formalism and the Freudian Aesthetic' 1984, 'A Theory of Parody' 1985, 'The Canadian Postmodern' 1988, 'A Poetics of Postmodernism' 1988, 'The Politics of Postmodernism' 1989; 'Splitting Images: Canadian Ironies' 1991; transl. 'Allegro' by Felix Leclerc 1974; co-ed. 'Other Solitudes: Multicultural Fiction and Interviews' 1990; 'Likely Stories' 1993; 'A Postmodern Reader' 1993; ed. 'Double-Talking' 1992; mem. numerous ed. bds.; mem. various profl. assns. incl. Toronto Semiotic Circle (Pres. 1981–83); ACCUTE (Exec. 1979–81); CCLA (Sec. 1981–82); Modern Lang. Assn. (Extve. Council 1993–96; Del. Assembly 1985–87, Elections Ctte. 1987–89, ed. bd. PMLA 1990–92); recreations: piano, cycling; Home: 8 High Park Gardens, Toronto, Ont. M6R 1S9; Office: 7 King's College Circle, Univ. of Toronto, Toronto, Ont. M5S 1A1.

**HUTCHINGS, John Barrie,** B.Sc., M.Sc., Ph.D., FRSC; research scientist; b. Johannesburg, S. Africa 18 July 1941; s. John P. and Margaret A. (Niven) H.; e. Diocesan Coll., Cape Town 1957; Witwatersrand Univ., B.Sc. 1962, M.Sc. 1963; Cambridge Univ., Ph.D. 1967; m. Patricia Masters Oct. 1967; children: Claire, Jessica; RESEARCH SCIENTIST, DOMINION ASTROPHYSICAL OBSERVATORY, NRC OF CAN. 1969– ; PDF, Dom. Astrophys. Observ. 1967–69; rsch. on hot stars, binary stars, x-ray sources, quasars & active galaxies; involvement in space hardware & experiments (U.S., U.S.S.R., Eur., Can.); Principal Rsch. Offr., N.R.C. 1988– ; Fellow, Royal Soc. of Can. 1987; Mem., Am. & Candn. Astronomical societies; Internat. Astron. Union; author of over 300 rsch. papers; editor of various sci. books & pubns.; Home: 1615 McTavish Rd., Sidney, B.C. V8L 3S1; Office: 5071 W. Saanich Rd., Victoria, B.C. V8X 4M6.

**HUTCHINGS, Murray R.;** university professor; b. Regina, Sask. 22 Sept. 1940; s. Donald Eldridge and Aileen (McKillop) H.; e. McMaster Univ., M.B.A. 1969; Univ. Western Ont., B.A. 1965; m. Janet, d. Herbert and Olive Lindsay, 23 Oct. 1965; children: Greg; Heather; Cameron; EXTVE. DIR., UNIVERSITY DEVELOPMENT, UNIV. OF REGINA; Tech. Sales Rep. (Sask.), Alchem Ltd. 1965–67; Lectr. and subsequently Asst. Prof., Faculty Admin. Studies, Dept. Acctg. and Finance, Univ. of Man. 1969–75; joined present univ. in Faculty of Admin. 1975; Assoc. Prof. 1977; Asst. Dean 1976–81; Acting Dean 1981–82; Dean 1982; Instructor in professional programs of Insts. of Chartered Accts., Sask. and Man. and Soc. Mgmt. Accts.; Mem., Candn. Federation of Deans of Mgmt. and Admin. Studies; Dir., Regina Chamber of Comm.; Admin. Sciences Assn. Can.; recreation: golf; Home: 4520 Pasqua St., Regina, Sask. S4S 6L5; Office: Administration Humanities, Room 435, Univ. of Regina, Regina, Sask. S4S 0A2.

**HUTCHINSON, Allan Charles,** LL.B., LL.M.; educator; b. Manchester, Eng. 16 Oct. 1951; s. Charles Paylor and Marie (Beaumont) H.; e. Hulme Grammar Sch. Oldham, Eng.; Univ. of London LL.B. (Hons.) 1974; Manchester Univ. LL.M. 1978; Barrister Grays Inn 1975; three d. Katie, Emily, Rachel; ASSOC. DEAN 1994– and PROF. OF LAW, OSGOODE HALL LAW SCH. YORK UNIV. 1982– , Ed.-in-Chief 1983–85, Chrmn. Senate Rsch. Ctte. 1985–87; Lectr., Univ. of Newcastle-Upon-Tyne, Eng. 1980–82; Barrister and Solicitor, Law Soc. of Upper Canada; author various publs. legal and scholarly jours.; 'The Rule of Law: Ideal or Ideology' 1987; 'Dwelling on the Threshold: Critical Essays in Modern Legal Thought' 1988; 'Critical Legal Studies' 1988; 'Law and Community' 1990; 'Access to Justice' 1991; 'Canadian Civil Litigation' 1992; recreations: soccer, squash, music, Van Morrison, colourful ties; Office: 4700 Keele St., Downsview, Ont. M3J 2R5.

**HUTCHINSON, Bruce George,** B.E., M.Sc., Ph.D., P.Eng.; university professor and department chair; editor; b. Sydney, Australia 29 Oct. 1934; s. George Thomas and Winifred Emily (White) H.; e. Univ. of Sydney, B.E. 1956; Queen's Univ., M.Sc. 1959; Univ. of Waterloo, Ph.D. 1965; m. Douglas Mary d. Thomas and Helen McCollum Sept. 1959; children: Douglas Jean, Thomas, Susan; CHAIR, DEPT. OF CIVIL ENGINEERING 1992– and PROF. OF CIV. ENGR., UNIV. OF WATERLOO 1962– ; civ. engr. on a major Australian hydro-elec. dam 1956–57; Alta. Rsch. Counc. 1960–62; joined Univ. of Waterloo 1962; Vis. Prof., Swiss Fed. Inst. of Technol. 1975–76; Kuwait Univ. 1982 and 1988–89; Univ. of New South Wales 1975–76, 1984–85; cons. to World Bk. and var. Candn. and Australian orgns.; C.D. Howe Meml. Fellowship 1968; mem. Assn. of Profl. Engrs. of Ont.; Fellow, Candn. Soc. of Civ. Engrs.; Am. Soc. of Civ. Engrs.; author 'Principles of Urban Transport Systems Planning' 1974; co-ed. 'Systems Analysis in Urban Policy-Making and Planning' 1983; 'Optimization and Discrete Choice in Urban Systems' 1985; 'Advances in Urban Systems Modelling' 1986; author of about 120 tech. papers in the areas of transp. planning & engr.; Ed., Candn. Journ. of Civil Engr.; Home: 105 William St. W., Waterloo, Ont. N2L 1J8; Office: Waterloo, Ont. N2L 3G1.

**HUTCHINSON, Hon. Ralph Maurice James,** M.A.; judge; b. Iringa, Tanzania 25 Apl. 1930; s. Geoffrey George Steele and Ina Bryony (Joseph) H.; e. Pembroke House Kenya; Hilton Coll. Natal; Rugby Sch. Eng. 1948; Magdalene Coll. Cambridge B.A. 1952, M.A. 1964; m. Dorothy d. Alexander and Anne Johnstone 27 Apl. 1957; children: Bryony, John; JUDGE, SUPREME COURT OF B.C. 1990– ; Cadet, Colonial Service Kenya 1948–49; called to Bar of B.C. 1956; Barrister & Solr. Vancouver 1956–60; Partner Heath, Hutchinson, Nanaimo 1960–80; Co. Court Judge Prince Rupert 1980–84, Vancouver 1984–86, Nanaimo 1986–90; Chrmn. Un. Appeal Nanaimo 1972; Pres. John Howard Soc. Vancouver Island 1975–77; Bencher, Law Soc. B.C. 1978–80; Dir. Continuing Legal Edn. Soc. B.C. 1976–80; recreations: mountaineering, squash, skiing; Clubs: Alpine Club Can. (Vice Pres. 1980–82); B.C.M.C.; Home: 3358 Stephenson Pt. Rd., Nanaimo, B.C. V9T 1K2; Office: Court House, 35 Front St., Nanaimo, B.C. V9R 5J1.

**HUTCHINSON, Thomas Cuthbert,** B.Sc., Ph.D.; educator; b. Sunderland, U.K. 18 Feb. 1939; s. Walter and Margaret Amelia (Bell) H.; e. Bede Grammar Sch., Sunderland, Engl.; Manchester Univ., Hons.B.Sc. 1960; Sheffield, Ph.D. 1966; div.; one d., Sally Louise; PROFESSOR OF BIOLOGY AND CHAIR, ENVIRONMENTAL RESOURCE STUDIES, TRENT UNIV. 1991– ; Asst. Prof. Dept. of Botany Univ. of Toronto 1967, Assoc. Prof. 1971, Prof. 1974–91 (and Chrmn. Dept. of Botany 1976–82); Acting Dir. Inst. of Environ. Studies, Univ. of Toronto 1973–74; author 125 sci. publ. incl. 5 books; Chrmn. Assoc. Ctte. on Sci. Criteria for Environ. Quality, National Rsch. Counc. 1984–86; mem. and Chrmn. Population Biology Grant Selection Ctte. (1978–82), NSERC; mem. Am. Ecological Soc.; Am. Agron. Soc.; Arctic Inst. N. Am.; Candn. Botanical Assn.; British Ecological Soc.; recipient George Lawson Medal, Candn. Botanical Assn. 1983; Fac. Alumni Award, Univ. of Toronto 1984; Fellow, Royal Soc. of Can. 1985; Home: RR #2, Indian River, Ont. K0L 2B0; Office: Dept. of Environment and Resource Studies, Trent Univ., Peterborough, Ont. K9J 7B8.

**HUTCHISON, The Rt. Rev. Andrew S.,** L.Th., D.D.; anglican bishop; b. Toronto, Ont. 19 Sept. 1938; s. Ralph Burton and Kathleen Marion (Van Nostrand) H.; e. Lakefield College Sch.; Upper Canada Coll.; York Univ.; Trinity Coll.; m. Lois d. Florence Mary (Bedford) and Thomas H. Knight 7 May 1960; one s.: David Andrew Thomas; BISHOP OF MONTREAL, THE ANGLICAN CHURCH OF CANADA 4 NOV. 1990– ; Ordained Deacon, St. James' Cathedral 1969; Ordained

Priest, Christ Church, Deer Park Toronto 1970; Rector, Parish of Mindon Toronto 1970–74; St. Francis of Assisi Toronto 1974–81; St. Luke's East York Toronto 1981–84; Dean of Montreal, Rector of Christ Ch. Cathedral 1984–90 (steered Cathedral through massive redevel. of its ministry & bldgs. which are now housed in a 35-storey bldg. behind the Cathedral & beneath it is a shopping mall of 140 stores opening onto a metro station); Consecration, Christ Ch. Cathedral Montreal 1990; an activist in ecumenical and cross cultural affairs; Officer of the Order of St. John of Jerusalem and its Quebec Chaplain; Ecclesiastical Grand Cross, Order of St. Lazarus; Chaplain, 6087–22 C.A.R. Overseas Assn.; Last Post Fund Que.; Hon. Chaplain, Candn. Grenadier Guards; Pres., Montral Diocesan Theol. Coll.; Visitor, Bishop's Univ. Lennoxville; Home: 3630 de la Montagne, Montreal, Que. H3G 2A8; Office: 1444 Union Ave., Montreal, Que. H3A 2B8.

**HUTCHISON, Hamish Rodney,** B.Com.; investment management executive; b. England, 1931; e. McGill Univ. B.Com. 1956; PRES., MONEYWARE INC. 1984– ; Dir., The International Trust Co.; FRI Corp.; Partner and Mgr. Bond Dept. Greenshields Inc. 1957–63; Vice Pres. and Dir. Rsch., Loomis, Sayles & Co. (Canada) Ltd. 1964–72; Vice Pres. and Dir. AGF Management Ltd. 1964–72; Pres., AGF Toronto Investment Management 1973–76; Chrmn., Toronto Investment Management Inc. 1976–85; Mng. Dir., Rogers, Casey & Barksdale (Canada) Inc. 1985–87; Home: 52 High Park Ave., Toronto, Ont. M6P 2R9; Office: Box 76, North Tower, Royal Bank Plaza, Toronto, Ont. M5J 2J2.

**HUTCHISON, Patricia Anne,** M.D., C.M., F.R.C.P.(C); physician; b. Regina, Sask. 27 Dec. 1930; d. Leslie James and Marguerite Honora (McGahey) H.; e. Queen's Univ. M.D., C.M. 1954; Univ. of W. Ont. Dip. in Adm. (Urban/Regional) 1982; Med. Health Offr. City of Regina 1983–92, retired; Coroner 1993– ; Clin. Asst. Prof. of Paediatrics Univ. of Sask. Regina 1982–92, retired; mem. Exec. Mackenzie Infant Care Centre 1985– ; residency paediatrics Hosp. for Sick Children Toronto, Univ. Hosp. Saskatoon and Children's Hosp. Winnipeg 1955–59; paediatric practice St. Boniface (Man.) Clinic 1960–62; Paediatrician City of Regina Health Dept. 1962–72, Asst. Med. Health Offr. 1972–83; recipient Women of Distinction Award (Health) Soroptimist Internat. 1988; Courtesy Staff, Regina General Hosp. 1962–92, Pasqua Hosp. 1962–92 and Wascana Rehabilitation Centre 1965–92; mem. of first board, SCEP Centre 1968; mem. Regina Health Edn. & Welfare Ctte. 1972–76; Regina Area Mun. Rd. Ambulance Bd. 1979–81; Home Care Adv. Bd. 1969–82; co-author various profl. publs.; mem. Sask. Coll. Phys. & Surgs.; Sask. Med. Assn.; Candn. Med. Assn.; Candn. Paediatric Soc.; Candn. Pub. Health Assn. 1963–92; Sask. Pub. Health Assn. (Exec. 1981–91, Pres. 1986–87); Sask. Paediatric Soc.; Cath. Family Services Soc. Exec. 1981; Treas. Wascana Toastmasters 1986–87; Bd. & Extve. of Wascana Home Care Bd. 1989–92; Bd. Regina Assessment and Placement Service 1989–92; Bd. Mackenzie Infant Care Centre 1985– ; Bd. SCEP Centre 1993– ; R. Catholic; recreations: bridge, music, travel; Club: Federation of University Women; Seniors' Univ. Group; Home: 2714 Aster Cres. E., Regina, Sask. S4V 1Z6.

**HUTCHISON, Thomas Sherret,** B.Sc., Ph.D., Hon.D.Sc.(Queen's 1985), F.Inst.P., F.A.P.S., F.R.S.E.; educator; b. Arbroath, Angus, Scot. 12 Aug. 1921; s. Thomas and Elizabeth Sherret (Smith) H.; e. Arbroath H.S. 1939; Univ. of St. Andrews B.Sc. 1942, Ph.D. 1948 (Physics Medallist, Colours in Golf); m. Anne Margaret d. Patrick and Grace MacDonald 19 Sept. 1946; children: Janet Elizabeth Murray, Gavin Patrick Sherret; PROFESSOR EMERITUS, ROYAL MILITARY COLL. OF CAN. 1986; served with Brit. Admiralty 1942–45 part of team producing CCR torpedo pistol; SSO Harwell 1948–50, rsch. exper. physicist solid state physics & structure analysis; chief contributions in internal friction; lectr. Can., USA, UK, Italy, Germany; Prof. of Physics, Royal Military Coll. of Can. 1950–86; headed dept. present Coll. and contrib. to devel. of crygenic lab., Dean of Sci. 1959–62, 1972–80, introduced Grad. Sch. and served as Dean 1962–72; Acad. Adv. to Candn. Offr. Devel. Bd. and Candn. Defence Ednl. Estabs. 1968–71 HQ Ottawa; Hon. mem. of Senate present Coll., Distinguished Prof.; co-recipient Merit Award of Civil Service for work in acoustic in-flight monitoring of mil. aircraft 1980; Candn. Metal Physics Conf. Medal 1978; co-author 'Physics of Engineering Solids' 1963, rev. 2nd ed. 1968; author over 60 reviewed publs. to ind. jours.; recreations: Brit. mil. hist., golf; Clubs: Royal Mil. Coll. (Hon. Life mem.); Glen Lawrence Golf & Country; Home: Sibbit Rd., RR 1, Kingston, Ont. K7L 4V1; Office: RMC, Kingston, Ont. K7K 5L0.

**HUTCHISON, William George,** B.Eng., P.Eng., CMC; business executive; b. New Liskeard, Ont. 10 Jan. 1938; s. William Leslie and Ellen Milne (Weeks) H.; e. McGill Univ. B.Eng. (Elec.) 1962; m. Sandra Lee d. Gori and Rena Cioci June 1989; children: Laurie, Lynn, Sue, Cathy, Stephanie, Shannon; MANAGING PARTNER & NATIONAL DIRECTOR, INFORMATION TECHNOLOGY, ERNST & YOUNG 1989– ; var. positions ending as Regional Dir., Central Canada, Honeywell Ltd. 1962–69; Internat. Vice-Pres., then Pres. & Chief Extve. Offr., Consolidated Computer 1969–76; Chair, Telnor Holdings Ltd. & Pres., William G. Hutchison & Co. Ltd. 1976–89; Dir., Precarn Assoc. Ltd.; Vision 2000; Chair, Extve. Ctte., CANARIE (Candn. Network for Adv. Rsch., Industry and Edn.); Chair, Sci. & Industry Adv. Ctte., Ont. Laser Lightwave Rsch. Int.; Past Dir., Torstar Corp., OLLRC, Candn. Adv. Technol. Assn.; Award of Distinction for Private Sector Leadership, CATA; Scarlet Key, McGill; Past Vice Chair & Mem., Nat. Adv. Bd. for Sci. & Technol.; Past Gov., West Park Hosp.; Past Dir., West Park Hosp. Found.; Mem., Candn. Information Processing Soc.; Assn. of Profl. Engrs. of Ont.; Engineering Inst. of Can.; recreations: skier, golfer, tennis player; Clubs: Rotary of Toronto (Past Dir.); World Trade; St. George's Golf; Home: 11 Cobble Hills, Etobicoke, Ont. M9A 3H6; Office: P.O. Box 251, T.D. Centre, Toronto, Ont. M5K 1J7.

**HUTNER, Paul;** artist; b. Toronto, Ont. 29 Feb. 1948; s. Arthur Matthew and Dorothy (Heller) H.; e. New Sch. of Art Toronto 1969; m. Martha d. James and Margaret Black 23 Aug. 1974; solo exhbns. Toronto incl. Dunkelman Gallery 1972; Jared Sable Gallery 1975, 1976; Sable-Castelli Gallery 1976–80 inclusive, 1983, 1985, 1988, 1989; numerous group exhbns. incl. Edmonton Art Gallery 1972, 1974; Winnipeg Art Gallery 1975, 1977, 1981; Montreal XXI Olympiad 1976; Art Gallery of Ont. 1984, 1989; rep. numerous pub. colls. incl. Nat. Gallery Can., Art Gallery of Ont., Can. Council Art Bank; maj. comns. incl. Dept. Pub. Works, Cineplex Odeon Tampa, Fla.; rep. many private colls.; recipient Sr. Can. Council Grant 1989; recreation: sailing; Club: Toronto Hydroplane & Sailing; Home: 1081 Bathurst St., Toronto, Ont.; Office: c/o The Sable-Castelli Gallery, 33 Hazelton Ave., Toronto, Ont. M5R 2E3.

**HUTT, William,** C.C. (1969), O.O., M.M., D.F.A., D.Litt., LL.D.; actor-director; b. Toronto, Ont. 2 May 1920; s. Edward DeWitt and Caroline Frances Havergal (Wood) H.; e. Vaughan Road Coll. Inst., Toronto, Ont.; N. Toronto Coll. Inst. (1941); Trinity Coll., Univ. of Toronto, B.A. 1949; Hon. D.F.A., Univ. of Ottawa 1969; Hon. D.Litt., Univ. of Guelph 1973; Hon. LL.D., Univ. of W. Ont. 1981; began prof. field in 1947 with summer stock co. in Bracebridge, Ont.; one season as Asst. Mgr. & leading man with Candn. Repertory Theatre, Ottawa; also dir. Little Theatre groups throughout Ont. and adjudicated for W. Ont. Drama League; 1948–52, played with various summer stock theatres; joined Stratford Shakespearen Festival Co. its first year (1953) playing Sir Robert Brackenbury and Capt. Blunt in 'Richard III' and Min. of State in 'All's Well That Ends Well'; in 1954 acted Froth in 'Measure for Measure,' Hortensio in 'The Taming of the Shrew,' and Leader of the Chorus in 'Oedipus Rex' (1st recipient, Tyrone Guthrie Award); in 1955 acted Ligarius and Cinna the Poet in 'Julius Caesar,' Old Gobbo in 'The Merchant of Venice,' Chorus Leader in 'Oedipus Rex'; in 1956 Leader of the Chorus in film version of 'Oedipus Rex,' Canterbury in 'Henry V' and Ford in 'The Merry Wives of Windsor'; 1957 Polonius in 'Hamlet'; 1958 Worcester in 'Henry IV Part I' and Don Pedro in 'Much Ado About Nothing'; 1959 Lodovico in 'Othello' and Jaques in 'As You Like It'; appeared in several Candn. Players tours in various Shakespearean parts and lead in Noel Coward's 'Private Lives' 1963–64; has often appeared on CBC-TV and ABC-TV in Britain; in Eng. starred at Bristol Old Vic as James Tyrone in 'Long Day's Journey Into Night'; Noel Coward's 'Waiting in the Wings' and in several films on TV for BBC; toured US in Coward's 'Sail Away'; toured with Canadian Players as Lear in 'King Lear' and Thomas Mendip in 'The Lady's Not For Burning'; returned to Stratford Festival for 10th Season to play Prospero in 'The Tempest,' Banquo in 'Macbeth' and Carson de Castel-Jaloux in 'Cyrano de Bergerac'; has appeared in 3 Broadway prod.; originated role of Tsar Nicholas II in world premiere of 'Nicholas Romanov,' Man. Theatre Ctr.; at Stratford (Ont.) Festival played Pandarus in 'Troilus and Cressida' 1963; title role in 'Richard II' and Sparkish in 'The Country Wife' 1964; Brutus in 'Julius Caesar,' Justice Shallow in 'Henry IV Pt. II' and Gaev in 'The Cherry Orchard' 1965; Chorus in 'Henry V,' Warwick in 'Henry VI,' Grand Duke Michael in world premiere of 'Last of the Tsars' 1966; Khlestakov in 'The Government Inspector' (repeated at Expo 1967), Clarence in 'Richard III,' Enobarbus in 'Antony and Cleopatra,' (repeated at Expo 1967); played title role in 'Tartuffe' (later recorded for Caedmon Records), Trigorin in 'Seagull,' and dir. 'Waiting for Godot' 1968; with Nat. Theatre, Chichester, Eng., played Don Adriano de Armado in 'Love's Labour Lost' and Alcibiades in 'Timon of Athens' 1964; on Broadway played Lawyer in Edward Albee's 'Tiny Alice' opposite John Gielgud and Irene Worth 1964; played Tsar Nicholas in MGM film 'The Fixer' 1967; played Warwick in Shaw's 'St. Joan,' Lincoln Centre, N.Y. 1968; title role in Moliére's 'Tartuffe' 1968–69; played Epicure Mammon in 'The Alchemist' 1968–69, and again at Chichester Festival, Eng. 1970; apptd. Assoc.-Dir., Stratford Nat. Theatre 1970–71, directing 'Much Ado About Nothing' and playing title role in 'Volpone'; dir. 'As You Like It,' title role in 'King Lear' 1971–72; led Stratford Nat. Theatre as 'King Lear' on tour of European capitals incl. Moscow, Leningrad, Warsaw 1973; led Stratford Nat. Theatre in title role 'The Imaginary Invalid' on tour of Australia, repeated role in Stratford 1974; as Dir., Festival Stage under artistic dir. Robin Phillips, played Duke of Vienna in 'Measure for Measure,' in 'Captain Brazen,' 'Trumpets and Drums,' and Lady Bracknell in 'The Importance of Being Earnest'; also dir. 'St. Joan' for Festival Stage and 'Oscar Remembered' for The Third Stage, Stratford 1975; apptd. Artistic Dir., Theatre London (Ont.) and Dir., Festival Stage, Stratford 1976; with Theatre London directed Shaw's 'Candida' and played James Tyrone opposite Jessica Tandy in 'Long Day's Journey into Night' (dir. by Robin Phillips); played Pastor Manders in 'Ghosts,' King of France in 'All's Well that Ends Well' and David in 'Hay Fever' at Stratford 1977; title role in 'Uncle Vanya,' title role in 'Titus Andronicus' and Falstaff in 'Merry Wives of Windsor' at Stratford 1978; title Role in 'Titus Andronicus' (revived) Stratford 1980; Feste in 'Twelfth Night,' Dorn in 'Seagull' (with Maggie Smith), Fool in 'Lear' (with Peter Ustinov); James Tyrone in 'Long Day's Journey into Night' (with Jessica Tandy); Schill in 'The Visit' (with Alexis Smith); starred in 'The Wars' (film of Timothy Findley's novel, dir. by Robin Phillips) and in 'Models' (film dir. by Jean Claude Lord) both in 1981; Sir in Ronald Harwood's 'The Dresser,' Vancouver Playhouse 1982; starred in Bill Davis' 'Mass Appeal,' Vancouver Playhouse 1983; inaugural season of The Grand Theatre Co., London, Ont. 1983–84 (dir. Robin Phillips) title role in Shakespeare's 'Timon of Athens,' Sir Ralph Bloomfield Bonnington in Shaw's 'Doctor's Dilemma,' and Abby Brewster in 'Arsenic and Old Lace'; in 1984–85 season with Vancouver Playhouse, played Thomas More in 'A Man For All Seasons' and Clarence Darrow in one-man show 'Darrow' (both under dir. of Walter Learning); Nat. Arts Ctr., Ottawa, and CentreStage, Toronto, starred as Bob in world premiere of John Murrel's play 'New World' (dir. Robin Phillips); starred as George in Edward Albee's 'Who's Afraid of Virginia Woolfe' for Vancouver Playhouse (Dir. Walter Learning); returned to Stratford Festival 1986 to play Thomas More in 'A Man for All Seasons' (dir. Walter Learning) and Cardinal Wolsey in Shakespeare's 'Henry VIII'; Sir Peter Teazle in 'School for Scandal' and Leonato in 'Much Ado About Nothing' Stratford Festival 1987; 1988: title role in 'King Lear' with Stratford Festival's Young Co. (Dir. Robin Phillips); Sheridan Whiteside in 'The Man Who Came to Dinner' (Dir. Peter Moss) Grand Theatre, London, Ont.; 1989: Shaw Festival, Roebuck Ramsden in 'Man and Superman' and Sir William Gower in 'Trelawny of the 'Welles''; 1990: Shaw Festival, General St. Pé in 'Waltz of the Toreadors' (by Jean Anouilh; Dir. David Giles); Grand Theatre, London, Marius in 'Road to Mecca' (by Fugard; Dir. Diana Lablanc); Bradley in 'The Cocktail Hour' (by A.R. Gurney; Dir. Peter Moss); 1991: Citadel Theatre, Edmonton, Bradley in 'The Cocktail Hour' (as above); 1992: Citadel Theatre and Manitoba Theatre Centre, Saunders in 'Lend Me A Tenor' (Dir. Robin Phillips); Banff Sch. of Fine Arts, Dir. 'Twelfth Night'; 1992–93: Grand Theatre, London, Ont.: Actor #1, in 'Dining Room' (by A.R. Gurney: Dir., Martha Henry); Scrooge in 'A Christmas Carol' (musical version by Mavor Moore; Dir. Miles Potter); Harry Raymond in 'The Stillborn Lover' (by Timothy Findley; world premiere); 1993: Stratford Festival, Argan in 'Imaginary Invalid' (by Moliere; Dir. Albert Millaire); subj. of bio. 'William Hutt – A Theatre Portrait' (by Keith Garebian); given key to city of Ottawa, offic. recog. by Speaker of H. of C. 1984; served in 2nd World War, 1941–46 with 7th Cdn. Light Field Ambulance (front-line service in Italy, France, Belgium, Holland); awarded Military Medal; Earl Grey ACTRA for best performance on TV as Sir John A. MacDonald in 'The National Dream' 1975; (won ETROG – Best Actor in Can. films); Prix Anik for performance of Bernard Shaw in CBC TV prod. 'First Night of Pygmalion' 1975; Toronto Drama Bench Award for contribution to Canadian Theatre 1988; Order of Ontario 1992; Governor General's Lifetime Achievement Award in Performing Arts 1992; mem. Actor's Equity Assn.; Assn. Candn. TV and Radio Artists; Liberal; Anglican; recreations: fishing, golf, swimming, playing piano; Address: 4 Waterloo St. N., Stratford, Ont. N5A 5H4.

**HUXLEY, Herbert H.,** M.A.; emeritus professor; b. Brooklands, Cheshire, Eng., 29 July 1916; s. Henry and Amy (Bland) H.; e. Sale High Sch., Cheshire, Eng., 1927–29; Manchester (Eng.) Grammar Sch., 1929–35; St. John's Coll., Cambridge Univ., B.A. 1939, M.A. 1942; Trinity Coll., Dublin, M.A. 1961; m. Joan Mary, d. late Rev. Thomas Peers, 30 Aug. 1941; two s., Martin Neil, Ph.D., Andrew David, M.A., B.C.L.; Joan Mary d., Oct. 22 1974; 2ndly m. Margaret Elizabeth, d. late Rev. G. E. P. Cox; Supervisor in Classics, St. John's College, Cambridge, 1979–85; Lectr. in Classics, Leeds Univ., Eng., 1944–51; Sr. Lectr. in Latin, Univ. of Manchester, Eng., 1951–62; Reader in Latin 1962–68; Prof. of Classics, Univ. of Victoria, 1968–82; Emeritus Prof. 1982– ; Visiting Lectr. in Classics, Dublin Univ., 1961; Visiting Assoc. Prof. of Classics, Brown Univ., 1966–67; Visiting Fellow of Univ. Coll., Cambridge Univ., 1970–71; Visiting Fellow of St. Cross Coll., Oxford 1978–79; Visiting Fellow of St. Edmund's Coll. Cambridge 1980; el. mem. of Classical Fac., Univ. of Cambridge, 1980– ; Co-author, (with F.J. Lelièvre) 'Across Bin Brook' 1992; Ed., 'Claudian: The Rape of Proserpine' (transl. Leonard Digges; an ed. of a book publ. 1617) 1959; 'Virgil, Georgics I & IV' 1963, 1965 and 1979; 'Carmina MCMLXIII' 1963; 'Corolla Camenae' 1969; 'What Proper Person?' 1984; 'Proceedings of the Virgil Soc.' Vol. XIX, 1988; other writings incl. over 400 Latin poems publ. in over 40 different metres; contrib. to 'Horace 2000: A Celebration' (ed. N. Rudd 1993) and numerous journals; Fellow, 'Latinitas' Fdn. (Vatican) 1977; Fdn. Life Mem., The Cambridge Society 1977; mem., Classical Assn. Can.; The Oxford Society; Classical Assn. (GB); Virgil Soc. (Pres. 1992–93); Cambridge Philol. Soc.; Cambridge Theol. Soc. (Counc. Mem. 1988–90); Oxford Philol. Soc.; Leeds Lit. & Philol. Soc.; Hon. mem., Manchester Microscopical Soc. (estbl.1880) 1986; Life Fellow, Royal Soc. for the Protection of Birds; Anglican; recreations: natural history, microscopy, music; Home: 12 Derwent Close, Cambridge, CB1 4DZ England.

**HUYCKE, F.A.M.,** Q.C.; b. Toronto, Ont. Oct. 1924; s. George Meredith and Ottilie (Avery) H.; e. Toronto Public Schs.; Trinity Coll. Sch. 1943; Trinity Coll., Toronto, 1948; Osgoode Hall, Toronto, 1951; m. Catherine, d. John LeBel 1952; children: Catherine, Mary, Margot, Graeme, Jennifer; Bd. Chrmn., Dir. & Extve. Ctte., Bow Valley Energy Inc.; Dir., The Consumers Gas Co. Ltd.; served in R.C.A. 1943–45; called to the Bar of Ont. 1951; mem. Can. Bar Assn.; County of York Law Soc.; Anglican; recreations: skiing, tennis, golf; Clubs: The Toronto; Toronto Golf; Badminton and Racquet; Osler Bluff Ski; Home: 39 Rosedale Hts. Dr., Toronto, Ont. M4T 1C2.

**HYDE, Christopher;** writer; b. Ottawa, Ont. 26 May 1949; s. Laurence and Bettye Marguerite (Bambridge) H.; e. Crichton St. P.S.; York St. P.S.; Lisgar C.I. (expelled 1965 after compl. gr. 9 and part gr. 10); m. Mariea d. Rod and Krystyna Sparks 23 July 1975; children: Noah Stevenson Sparks, Chelsea Orianna Sparks; freelance broadcaster, CBC Ottawa 1966–68; CBC Vancouver 1969, 1973–75; CJOH TV Ottawa 1970–71; CBC, CTV, OECA 1971–72; full-time writer 1977– ; Pres., Ripping Yarns Inc.; Partner, Nicholas Chase Prodns.; Owner, Plain Brown Wrapper Puzzles; author: 'The Wave' 1978 (publ. 6 countries); 'The Karus Seal' 1979; 'Styx' 1980; 'The 10th Crusade' 1981; 'Maxwell's Train' 1984; film options on 'Styx' and 'Maxwell's Train'; co-author (as Nicholas Chase): 'Locksley' 1983; forthcoming: 'Whisperland' 1986; 'Jericho Falls' 1986; 'Holy Ghost' 1987; 'Echo Drive' (co-author) 1983; recreations: travel, reading; Clubs: YMCA; Briane Nasimok Sunday Brunch; Address: c/o Lucinda Vardey Agency, 297 Seaton St., Toronto, Ont. M5A 2T6.

**HYDE, Michael Arthur,** P.Eng.; environmental executive; b. Kingston, Ont. 17 Apl. 1942; s. Arthur Edwin and Mary Isabelle (Moran) H.; e. Queen's Univ. P.Eng. (Eng.Chem.); m. Yoko d. Kazua Igaya 19 May 1981; children: David Michael, Andrew Tyler (by previous marriage), Keri Kazumi, Amanda Izumi; DIR. ENVIRONMENTAL AFFAIRS PLASTICS DEPT. DOW CHEMICAL CANADA INC. 1988– ; Tech. Mgr. Constrn. Rsch. Dow Chemical 1971, Dir. Rsch. Dow Chemical Japan 1976, Dist. Sales Mgr. Constrn. 1980, Nat. Sales Mgr. Constrn. Dow Chemical 1983, Bus. Devel. Mgr. Constrn. 1984, Mgr. Mergers & Acquisitions Dow Chemical Canada Inc. 1986; holds various patents; Dir. Mod-Lok Wall Systems Ltd. 1986–88; Pres. Harmony Bay, Kirk, Kove Coalition 1984–86; mem. Fire Test Bd. Nat. Bldg. Code Ottawa 1974–76; Dir. Recycling Council Ont. 1990 (Mem. Personnel and Membership Cttes.; Mem. Extve. Ctte. 1993– ; Chair, Policy Ctte.); mem. Environment & Plastics Inst. Can. (mem. Recycling Ctte., Anti-litter Ctte., Degradable Ctte. and Mgmnt. Ctte; Chrmn., Energy from Waste Ctte.); Dir. Ont. Ind. Roofing Assn. 1981–84; mem. Packaging Assn. Can.; Candn. Polystyrene Recycling Assn. (Chrmn. 1989–91); Mem., Markets & Technical Development Ctte., Ont. Multi-Materials Recycling Inc. (OMMRI); Mem., Waste Reduction Office, Strategic Team for Plastics (Mem. Steering Ctte.; Regulatory and Municipal, Industrial, Commercial, Institutional Task Forces), Ont. Min. of the Environment; Mem., Candn. Standards Assn., Tech. Ctte. for Waste Mngmt. Planning 1993– ; P. Conservative; recreations: boating, cross-country skiing; Home: 61 Greengrove Cres., Don Mills, Ont. M3A 1H8; Office: 20 Carlson Court, Etobicoke, Ont. M9W 6V4.

**HYDE, Paul N.,** B.Comm.; professional manager; b. Deep River, Ont. 1 Jan. 1953; s. Arthur S.C. and Elsa M. H.; e. Univ. of Ottawa B.Comm. (Hons.) 1980; Queen's Univ. Extve. Program; m. Catherine d. Andrew and Anne McMahon; one s.: Jordan Andrew; PRESIDENT & CHIEF EXECUTIVE OFFICER, KASTEN CHASE APPLIED RESEARCH 1990– ; General Motors of Canada 1980–82; CMHC 1982–84; Northern Telecom (Canada & Europe) 1984–90; Bd. of Dir., Temple Ridge Ltd.; Bd. of Dir., Disys Corp.; Chrmn., A.M. McMahon Scholarship Ctte., Queen's Univ.; club: Toronto Bd. of Trade; Young Presidents Organization; Office: Orbitor Place, 5100 Orbitor Dr., Toronto, Ont. L4W 4Z4.

**HYDE, Peter J.;** translator, editor, reviser; b. London, England 21 Nov. 1924; s. Cyril and Lena (Hutchings) H.; e. Maidenhead College and Royal Agric. College, Eng.; m. Anne Veronica (dec.) d. late Harry and Sally Hereford 5 Nov. 1949; children: David Julian, May Elizabeth; Sub-Lt. (Air) Royal Naval Volunteer Reserve 1943–46 (maintenance test pilot, Admiralty Islands, S.W. Pacific); Technical Offr., Defence Rsch. Northern Lab., Defence Rsch. Bd., Fort Churchill, Man. 1949–51; Communications Offr., Commun. Security Establishment Ottawa 1951–67; assisted in first 'Miles for Millions' fundraising 40-mile walks (Oxfam Canada) 1968; freelance translator of Russian and French literature 1967–93; revisor/ed. 2nd Internat. Conf. on Permafrost, USSR contbn. at request of U.S. Nat. Acad. Sc. 1978; 1st Sec. Gen., Internat. League for Animal Rights 1976; organized humane edn. award-giving ceremony for Anahareo, widow of 'Grey Owl,' Vancouver 1978; accredited observer at Internat. Whaling Comn. meeting on behav., commun. & intelligence of cetacean animals Washington, D.C. 1980; Press Summary Offr., External Affairs & Internat. Trade Canada 1988–91; recreations: walking, skiing, swimming, reading, music; Home: 1107 – 2625 Regina St., Ottawa, Ont. K2B 5W8.

**HYDE, Ralph Ernest,** B.A., LL.B.; judge (ret'd); b. Edmonton, Alta. 27 June 1922; s. Ernest Elmer and Mildred Mary (Jolliffe) H.; e. Highlands Pub. and Eastwood High Schs. Edmonton; Royal Mil. Coll.-Kingston 1940–42; Univ. of Alta. B.A. 1949, LL.B. 1950; m. Marion Webster d. late William Alexander and Lillian (Webster) Milroy, 9 Aug. 1945; children: Jill, Pamela, Marion, John; JUDGE OF THE PROVINCIAL COURT since 1978; read law with Nelles Victor Buchanan; called to Bar of Alta. 1951, Bar of N.W.T. 1964; cr. Q.C. 1968; articled Wood Buchanan Campbell 1950–51, assoc. 1951; Partner Wood Haddad Moir Hyde & Ross 1953; senior partner, Newson Hyde, 1973–77; served with Royal Candn. Armoured Corps 1942–46 UK, Sicily, Italy, N.W. Europe; Reserve Army 1946–57, A.D.C. Lt. Gov. of Alta.; Law Soc. Alta.; Loyal Order Blue Goose Internat.; P. Conservative; Anglican; recreations: golf, skiing, hunting, fishing; Clubs: Kiwanis Internat.; Crestwood Curling; RMC; Pender Golf and Country; Home: 3707 Port Rd., Pender Island, B.C. V0N 2M0.

**HYLAND, Barbara A.,** B.A., B.L.S.; publisher; b. Sherbrooke, Que. 7 Nov. 1942; d. Gordon Hamilton and Ruth Marter (Tilley) Moffat; e. Bishop Strachan Sch. 1960; Bishop's Univ. B.A. 1963; Univ. of Toronto B.L.S. 1965; two s. Mark Stephen Tait, Patrick Colin; PUBLISHER, INVESTMENT EXECUTIVE 1992– ; Gen. Mgr. Info Globe 1980, Dir. of Electronic Pub. 1985, Dir. of Info. and Mktg. 1988–89, mem. Mgmt. Ctte. The Globe and Mail 1985–92; Publisher, Financial Times of Canada 1989–92; mem. Sectoral Adv. Ctte. Internat. Trade; Gov. Bishop Strachan Sch.; former Bd. mem. Young People's Theatre, Assn. Women Execs.; Adv. Council Grad. Sch. Journalism Univ. of W. Ont.; Club: Toronto Lawn Tennis; Home: Toronto, Ont.; Office: 362 Sackville St., Toronto, Ont. M4X 1S4.

**HYLAND, Frances,** O.C.; actress, educator; b. Regina, Sask.; e. Royal Acad. Dramatic Art (Eng.) under Sir Kenneth Barnes; m. George McCowan (divorced); one s., Evan McCowan; first prof. performance Stella in 'A Streetcar Named Desire' London, Eng.; others incl. 'The Winter's Tale' with Sir John Gielgud, directed by Peter Brooks; 'Crime and Punishment'; 'The Idiot'; 'A Woman of No Importance'; 'The Dark Is Light Enough'; invited to Stratford Festival (Can.) by Tyrone Guthrie, 1954; played Isabella in 'Measure for Measure' opposite James Mason, Portia opposite Frederick Valk; Ophelia opposite Christopher Plummer etc.; toured with winter co., The Canadian Players; appeared in 'Look Homeward Angel' New York; 'A Time to Laugh' London, Eng. under the direction of Tyrone Guthrie; helped pioneer regional theatres in Can. such as Man. Theatre Centre, Vancouver Playhouse; Dir., Canadian Theatre; Shaw Festival Theatre; apptd. mem. Can. Council 1974; Winner of the Drainie Award for Distinguished Contribution to Broadcasting, 1981; Officer of the Order of Canada; LL.D. (Hon.): Univ. of B.C.; Univ. of Sask.; Univ. of Windsor; Address: c/o Candn. Actors' Equity Assn., 260 Richmond St. E., 2nd Flr., Toronto, Ont. M5A 1P4.

**HYNDMAN, Douglas McCrae,** B.A., M.B.A.; b. Edmonton, Alta. 29 Sept. 1950; s. William Alexander and Mary Alice (McCrae) H.; e. Univ. of B.C., B.A. 1972; Univ. of W. Ont., M.B.A. 1975; m. Jean d. Stephen and Marie Booy 17 May 1975; 1 s. Matthew; CHRMN., B.C. SECURITIES COMN. 1987– ; var. positions in B.C. Min. of Fin. 1975–82; Dir., Econ. & Fiscal Policy, Min. of Fin. 1982–84; Asst. Dep. Min. of Fin. & Dep. Sec. to Treasury Bd. 1984–87; Office: 1100 – 865 Hornby St., Vancouver, B.C. V6Z 2H4.

**HYNDMAN, Frederick Eardley;** insurance executive; b. Charlottetown, P.E.I. 5 Feb. 1939; s. Hon. Frederick Walter and N. Cecile (Shannon) H.; e. Charlottetown elem. schs.; Kings Coll. Sch. Windsor, N.S.; Dalhousie Univ.; m. Shirley Lillian d. Guy Gamester, Charlottetown, P.E.I. 9 July 1966; two d. Helen Elizabeth, Norah Joanne; MANG. DIR., HYNDMAN & CO. LTD.; Dir. Bank of Canada; Northumberland Ferries Ltd.; Padinox Canada Ltd.; comnd. Candn. Army (Reserve) 1960; active supporter P. Cons. Party; Fellow, Ins. Inst. Can.; mem. Ins. Agts. Assn. P.E.I. (Past Pres.); P. Conservative; Anglican; recreation: sailing; Clubs: Charlottetown; Halifax; Home: 98 Brighton Rd., Charlottetown, P.E.I. C1A 1V1; Office: 57 Queen St., Charlottetown, P.E.I. C1A 7L9.

**HYNDMAN, Roy David,** M.A.Sc., Ph.D., F.R.S.C.; research scientist; b. Vancouver, B.C. 20 Feb. 1940; s. Andrew William and Joan (McDonald) H.; e. Univ. of B.C. B.A.Sc. 1962, M.A.Sc. 1964; Australian Nat. Univ. Canberra Ph.D. 1967; m. Jennifer G. d. John F. and Marjorie Close 1969; children: Arn C., Kyle C.; RSCH. SCI. V PACIFIC GEOSCIENCE CENTRE, NATURAL RESOURCES CAN., Victoria, B.C. 1987– ; Adjunct Prof. Univ. of Victoria 1987– ; Asst. Prof. Dalhousie Univ. 1967–71, Assoc. Prof. 1972–74; Assoc. Prof. Univ. of B.C. 1971–72; Visiting Prof. Univ. Paris 1974–75; Rsch. Sci. present Dept. 1975–82; Dir. Pacific Geoscience Centre Victoria 1983–86; Visiting Prof. Cambridge Univ. 1987–89; Rsch. Sci. Geol. Surv. Can., Ottawa 1993–94; author over 150 sci. publs. various jours. and volumes; mem. CGU; GAC; AGU; Fellow, Royal Soc. of Canada; Office: P.O. Box 6000, Sidney, B.C. V8L 4B2.

**HYNE, James Bissett,** B.Sc., Ph.D.; educator; industrial scientist; b. Dundee, Scot. 23 Nov. 1929; s. William Simpson and Winnifred Moore (Bissett) H.; e. St. Andrew's Univ. B.Sc. 1951, Ph.D. 1954; m. Ada Leah d. Nathan and Fannie Jacobson 3 Sept. 1958; EMERITUS PROF. OF CHEM., UNIV. OF CALGARY 1990– , Dean of Grad. Studies 1966–89; Rsch. Dir., Alberta Sulphur Research Ltd. 1964– ; Internat. Scient. Consultant oil, gas, and sulphur industries; recipient Candn. Centennial Medal 1967; CNGPA Award of Merit for contribs. to Candn. Nat. Gas Industry in Sulphur Production 1974; R.S. Jane Mem. Lecture Award 1977; Queen's Silver Jubilee Medal 1977; Alta. Achievement Excellence Award 1980; Higher Education Forum Award for Research, Bell Canada 1990; Arthur B. Purvis Memorial Lectr., Soc. of Chemical Industry 1991; author over 275 papers nat. and internat. journs.; mem. Candn. Soc. Chem. Engn.; Candn. Gas Processors Assn.; Am. Chem. Soc.; Chem. Soc.; Chem. Inst. Can.; Home: 312 Superior Ave. S.W., Calgary, Alta. T3C 2J2; Office: Dept. of Chemistry, Univ. of Calgary, 2500 University Dr. N.W., Calgary, Alta. T2N 1N4.

**HYNES, Hugh Bernard Noel,** Ph.D., D.Sc., F.R.S.C.; educator; b. Devizes, Eng. 20 Dec. 1917; s. Harry

George Claude and Anna Minnie Lucy (Meyer) H.; e. Prices Sch. Fareham, Eng. 1934; Royal Coll. of Science, Univ. of London, ARCS 1938, B.Sc. 1938, Ph.D. 1941, D.Sc. 1958; Hon. D.Sc., Univ. of Waterloo 1987; (External Research Student Fresh. Biol. Assn. Windermere 1938–40); Imp. Coll. of Tropical Agric. Trinidad, Colonial Service Cadet 1941–42; m. Mary Elizabeth d. late Edward Hinks 24 Oct. 1942; children: Richard Olding, Elisabeth Anne Grant, Andrew John, Julian David; PROF. OF BIOL. UNIV. OF WATERLOO since 1964, Emeritus Prof. since 1984; Chrmn. of Biol. 1964–71; Colonial Agric. Service special Anti-Locust work Ethiopia, Kenya and Somalia 1942–46; Faculty mem. Dept. Zool. Univ. of Liverpool 1946–64; Visiting Prof. of Zool. Ind. Univ. 1960, Monash Univ. Melbourne 1971–72; Visiting Research Assoc. in Bot. Univ. of Tasmania 1978; Distinguished Visiting Scholar in Zool., Univ. of Adelaide, 1979; Visiting Prof., Addis Ababa Univ. 1984; Wallace Prof., Univ. of Louisville 1985; served Fisheries and Oceans Rsch. Adv. Council, Govt. of Can., various Nat. Research Council comtes.; Internat. Biol. Program; mem. and Candn. Chrmn. (2 yrs.) Bd. Govs. group of schs. Educ. Dept. Liverpool 1960–64; awarded Centennial Medal 1967; Kentucky Colonel 1985; author 'The Biology of Polluted Waters' 1960; 'The Ecology of Running Waters' 1970; over 150 articles scient. journs.; mem., Freshwater Biol. Assn.; Internat. Assn. Limnology; N. Am. Benthol. Soc.; Candn. Soc. Zool.; Australian Soc. Limnol.; recreations: camping, canoeing, nordic skiing; Home: 127 Iroquois Pl., Waterloo, Ont. N2L 2S6; Office: Waterloo, Ont. N2L 3G1.

**HYNES, Lawrence,** Q.C.; b. Toronto, Ont. 8 Sept. 1915; s. James P. and Anna L. (O'Brien) H.; e. St. Michael's Coll.; Univ. of Toronto B.A. 1938; Osgoode Hall Law Sch. 1941; m. Barbara Ann d. Frederic J. and Veronica Boland 23 Sept. 1944; one s. John L.; Lawyer, Fraser & Beatty 1959–93, retired; Dir. Cara Operations Ltd.; Lt., R.C.N.V.R. 1941–45 (Combined Operations, Mediterranean Theatre 1942–44); practiced law in Toronto since 1945; cr. Q.C. 1961; R. Catholic; Clubs: The National; Royal Candn. Yacht; Home: 161 Glenrose Ave., Toronto, Ont. M4T 1K7.

**HYNES, William Anthony,** B.A.; writer; educator; b. New York City, N.Y. 20 Aug. 1943; s. William Thomas and Linga (Caravano) H.; e. Far Rockaway High Sch. NYC 1961; Harpur Coll. State Univ. of New York, B.A. 1966; m. Mary d. Michael and Tess Trapani 19 June 1965; one s. Douglas Allen Beamish; author (juvenile fiction) 'Aventure à Ottawa' 1984; 'Mystère en Suisse' 1986; 'Secrets Dangereux' 1987; to be published: 'Aventure en Afrique,' 'Mystère en Belgique,' 'Erik's Daughter' (adult fiction); various articles edn., mil., pol. & tech. fields in newspapers and mags.; Court Interpreter and Legal/Tech. Translator Toronto Area 1977– ; Teacher, NYC 1966–71, Toronto Area 1972–82, 1983– ; Acting Prin. and Teacher Cadotte Lake and Little Buffalo, Alta. 1982–83; Chief Educ. Offr., Mattagami Band, Ojibway First Nation 1988; founded Canadians for Real Education (Éducation Réaliste) and co-founded Alliance for Educational Renewal to defend learner-centered (progressive) educ. 1993; Vice Pres. Hynesco; mem. Dragon Soc.; Art Gallery Ont.; Royal Ont. Museum; Metrop. Toronto Zool. Soc.; Writers' Odyssey; Bruce Trail Assn.; Ont. Teachers Fedn.; Ont. Modern Lang. Teachers Assn.; NDP; R. Catholic; recreations: hiking, camping, reading, old movies; Home: 214, 25 Sunny Glenway, Don Mills, Ont. M3C 2Z5.

**HYNNA, Y.A. George,** B.A., LL.B.; lawyer; b. Thunder Bay, Ont. 13 Oct. 1937; s. Ilmari and Selma (Lamppu) H.; e. Port Arthur Coll. Inst.; Univ. of Toronto Univ. Coll. B.A. 1961 (Gertrud Davis Exchange Fellow, German Acad. Exchange Service Scholar); Univ. of Freiburg and Free Univ. of West Berlin 1961–62; Osgoode Hall Law Sch. LL.B. 1965; m. Martha d. Andrew and Peggy Brewin 24 June 1967; children: Ann, Aleksander, Mark; PARTNER, GOWLING, STRATHY & HENDERSON 1975– ; articled with Herridge, Tolmie, Gray, Coyne and Blair 1965–66; called to Bar of Ont. 1967; joined Gowling, MacTavish, Osborne and Henderson (now present firm) 1967; Life mem. Candn. Suomi Found.; mem. Candn. Nordic Soc. (Pres. 1987–89); Candn. Friends of Finland; Shoppers Co-op. Inc. (Pres. 1983–85); Kappa Alpha; Candn. Inst. of Internat. Affairs; mem. Law Soc. Upper Can. (Instr. Bar Admission Course Ottawa 1983–86); Patent & Trademark Inst. Can. and Candn. Bar Assn. (Jt. Copyright Legis. Ctte.); Copyright Soc. USA; recreations: reading, skiing, windsurfing, squash, golf; Clubs: Le Cercle Universitaire d'Ottawa; Larrimac Golf; Gatineau Fish & Game (Dir. 1978–86); Home: 696 Echo Dr., Ottawa, Ont. K1S 1P3; Office: 2600, 160 Elgin St., Ottawa, Ont. K1N 8S3.

**HYSOP, D. Gary,** B.Sc., E.E.; business executive; b. Deloraine, Man. 28 Nov. 1944; s. D.F. Frank and N. Vivien (Collins) H. e. Killarney Collegiate 1962; Univ. of Man. B.Sc.E.E. 1966; m. Vicky d. Reginald and Winnifred Bridges 1 Oct. 1966; children: Lara, Brent; VICE-PRES., TORONTO OPERATIONS, KNOLL NORTH AMERICA 1992– ; joined Westinghouse Canada Inc. as engineer 1966; advanced to mngt. Indus. Serv. Div.; Vice-Pres. Electronics, Control & Distribution Products Div. 1983; Vice-Pres., Quality & Strategic Resources 1987; Vice-Pres. Human and Strategic Resources 1990–92; Mem., Conf. Bd. of Canada, Council. on Mngt. of Total Quality; Dir., United Way of Burlington, Hamilton-Wentworth (1988 Campaign Chrmn.); recreations: hunting, fishing, curling, skiing, canoeing; clubs: Burlington Curling (Past Pres.); Home: 1264 Tyandaga Park Dr., Burlington, Ont. L7P 1M8; Office: 1000 Arrow Rd., Weston (Toronto), Ont. M9M 2Y7.

# I

**IACOBUCCI, The Honourable Frank,** B.Com., LL.B., LL.M., Dip. Intl. Law, LL.D., L.S.M.; supreme court judge; educator; jurist; b. Vancouver, B.C. 29 June 1937; s. Gabriel and Rosina (Pirillo) I.; e. Britannia High Sch. Vancouver 1955; Univ. of B.C. B.Com. 1961, LL.B. 1962; Cambridge Univ. LL.M. 1964, Dipl. in Internat. Law 1966; LL.D. (Hon.) U.B.C. 1989, LL.D. (Hon.) Univ. of Toronto 1989; m. Nancy Elizabeth d. late James S. Eastham 31 Oct. 1964; children: Andrew Eastham, Edward Michael, Catherine Elizabeth; JUDGE, SUPREME COURT OF CANADA 1991– ; Assoc., Dewey, Ballantine, Bushby, Palmer & Wood, New York 1964–67; Univ. of Toronto, Assoc. Prof. of Law 1967–71, Prof. of Law 1971–85, Assoc. Dean, Fac. of Law 1973–75, Vice Pres. Inter. Affairs 1975–78, Dean of Law 1979–83, Vice Pres. & Provost of Univ. 1983–85; Depy. Min. of Justice and Depy. Attorney General, Dept of Justice, Govt. of Can. 1985–88; Chief Justice, Federal Court of Canada 1988–91; Member, Court Martial Appeal Court 1989–91; Visiting Fellow, Wolfson Coll. Cambridge Univ. 1978–79; Consultant, Select Comte. on Co. Law, Ont. Legis. 1968–70; Dept. Consumer & Corporate Affairs, Govt. of Can. 1974–78; Dept. Consumer Affairs, Alta. 1974–75; called to Bar of Ont. 1970; created Q.C. 1986; mem., Ont. Securities Comn. 1982–85; Islington Residents & Ratepayers Assn. 1971–85; Dir., Multicultural Hist. Soc. Ont. 1976–88; Vice-Pres. and mem., Bd. of Govs., Candn. Inst. for Advanced Legal Studies 1981–85, 1991– ; Chrmn., Ont. Law Deans 1983; Gov. Candn. Judicial Ctr. 1989–91; Gov., National Judicial Inst. 1992– ; mem. Bd. of Dirs., Cambridge Candn. Trust 1984–91; Mem., Adv. Council, Internat. Ctr. for Criminal Law Reform and Criminal Justice Policy 1991– ; Dir., Toronto District, Nat. Congress of Italian Canadians 1979–83; Vice Pres., Nat. Congress of Italian Canadians 1980–83; former Elder, Islington Un. Ch.; recipient, Man of the Year Award, Canadian-Italian Bus. and Profl. Assoc. of Toronto 1985; Italo Canadian of the Year Award, Confratellanza Italo Canadese (Vancouver) 1985; Law Soc. Medal, Law Soc. of Upper Canada 1987; Distinguished Fiji Award, Fraternity of Phi Gamma Delta 1987; Ordine al Merito Award, Nat. Congress of Italian Canadians (Toronto District) 1989; Commemorative Medal, 125th Anniversary, Candn. Confedn. 1992; Commendatore dell'Ordine Al Merito della Repubblica Italiana 1993; co-author 'Canadian Business Corporations' 1977; 'Business Associations Casebook' 1979; 'Cases and Materials on Partnerships and Canadian Business Corporations' 1983; co-ed. 'Materials on Canadian Income Tax' 1973, 1974, 1976, 1980, 1983, 1985; author various book chapters, articles, reports and papers; former mem., Law Soc. Upper Can; Candn. Assn. Univ. Teachers; Candn. Assn. Law Teachers; Candn. Judicial Counc. (mem. Educ. Ctte. 1988–91, Extve. Ctte. 1990–91); mem., Candn. Bar Assn.; Supreme Court Hist. Soc.; Phi Gamma Delta; Sigma Tau Chi; United Church; recreations: sports, music, reading; Clubs: Rideau (Ottawa); West Ottawa Tennis; Sporthèque (Hull, P.Q.); Office: Supreme Court of Canada, Supreme Court Bldg., Kent & Wellington Streets, Ottawa, Ont. K1A 0J1.

**IACOVETTA, Franca,** B.A., M.A., Ph.D.; university professor; b. Toronto, Ont. 14 Sept. 1957; d. Giovanni and Dalinda (Carmosino) Lombardi-Iacovetta; e. York Univ. B.A. (Hons.) 1980, M.A. 1981, Ph.D. 1988; m. Ian s. Sydney and Margaret Radforth 6 Nov. 1982; PROFESSOR, CANADIAN HISTORY, UNIV. OF TORONTO 1990– ; Postdoctoral Fellow, Univ. of Guelph 1988–89; Canada Research Fellow, SSHRCC 1989–90; accepted tenure track appt., Univ. of Toronto 1990; Floyd Chalmers Award in Ontario History 1992; Toronto Historical Bd. Award of Merit 1992; Candn. Historical Review Best Article 1992; Hilda Neatby Prize (CHA) for Best Article Pub. in Canada in Women's History 1986; Mem., Candn. Hist. Assn. (Extve. Mem., Ctte. on Women's Hist. 1990–93); Series Co-ed., 'Social History of Canada' series 1992– ; author: 'Such Hardworking People' 1992; co-editor: 'Gender Conficts' 1992; recreation: gardening; Home: 64 Livingstone Ave., Toronto, Ont. M6E 2L8; Office: Toronto, Ont. M5S 1A1.

**IANNI, Ronald William,** C.M., Q.C., B.A., B.Com., LL.B., Ph.D.; educator; b. Sault Ste. Marie, Ont. 27 Aug. 1935; s. Giuseppe and Mary Anne (Mantello) I.; e. Sault Ste. Marie Coll. Inst.; Univ. of Windsor B.A. 1957, B.Com. 1958; Osgoode Hall Law Sch. LL.B. 1961; Univ. of Paris C.U.E.C.E. Dipls. in Common Market & Internat. Law 1967, 1968; Univ. of London Ph.D. (Law) 1971; m. Mina d. Dave and Sonia Grossman 25 July 1968; PRESIDENT AND VICE-CHANCELLOR, UNIV. OF WINDSOR 1984– ;read law with I.A. Vannini, Q.C.; called to Bar of Ont. 1963; cr. Q.C. 1976; Asst. Prof. of Law Univ. of Windsor 1971, Assoc. Prof. 1972, Dir. Community Law Program 1973, Assoc. Dean of Law 1973–1975; Dean and Prof. of Law 1975–84; Arbitrator, Ont. Labour Mgmt. Bd.; Ont. Civil Service Dispute Settlement Bd.; Chair, Industry Labour Adjustment Program Comte. Windsor 1981–83; Premier's Council on Economic Renewal 1991; Chair, Ont. Comm. on Interuniversity Athletics 1990–93; Vice-Chair, Council of Ont. Universities 1993– ; Chair, Govt. Task Force on Paralegals in Ont. 1988–89; Chair, Govt. Task Force on Mandatory Retirement 1986–88; Chrmn. CAW/Chrysler Legal Services Plan Ctte. 1986– ; Chair, CAW/Ford and General Motors Cdn. Legal Services Plan Comte. 1985– ; Pres., Art Gall. of Windsor 1993– ; former Pres. Un. Way of Windsor and Essex Co.; Windsor-Essex Mediation Centre; named Offr., Order of Merit Repub. of Italy 1982; mem. Candn. Mission to U.N. (6th Comte.) 1982; mem., Order of Canada 1987; Negev Tribute 1989; Nat. Leadership Award, National Fed. of Cdn.-Italian Bus. & Profl. Assoc. Inc. 1991; Law Soc. Upper Can.; Candn. Bar Assn.; Candn. Council Internat. Law; Am. Soc. Internat. Law; Candn. Assn. Law Teachers; Chair, Ctte. of Ont. Law Deans 1977–78; Chair, Counc. of Can. Law Deans 1977–78; Phi Delta Phi; Home: 197 Sunset Ave., Windsor, Ont. N9B 3A6; Office; Windsor, Ont. N9B 3P4.

**IBBITSON, John Perrie,** B.A., M.A.; writer/journalist; b. Gravenhurst, Ont. 9 June 1955; s. Joseph Henry and Phyllis Alberta (Boyd) I.; e. Trinity Coll., Univ. of Toronto, B.A. (Hons.) 1979; Univ. of West. Ont., M.A. 1988; COLUMNIST, OTTAWA CITIZEN 1990– ; Editor, Collier Macmillan Can., Inc. 1986–87; Reporter, Ottawa Citizen 1988–90; formerly writer of plays & teleplays incl. CBC adaptation of 'Mayonnaise' 1980, 1983 and 'Country Matters' 1982; both plays 1st presented by Phoenix Theatre, Toronto (Graham Harley, dir.); writer of young-adult fiction for Maxwell Macmillan incl. novel '1812' 1991 (nominated for 1992 Governor-General's Award) and novellas 'The Big Story' 1990, 'Starcrosser' 1990, 'The Wimp and Easy Money' 1987, 'The Wimp and the Jock' 1986, and 'The Wimp' 1985; author: 'Mayonnaise' (Simon & Pierre) 1982; 'Catalyst' (Simon & Pierre) 1976; mem., Candn. Assoc. of Journalists; recreations: music; Home: 80 Patterson Ave., Apt. 1, Ottawa, Ont. K1S 1Y3; Office: The Ottawa Citizen, 1101 Baxter Rd., Ottawa, Ont. K2C 3M4.

**ICHINO, Yoko;** ballet dancer; b. Los Angeles, Cal.; trained intensively with Mia Slavenska; m. David Nixon June 1985; Principal Dancer, Nat. Ballet of Canada 1984; joined Joffrey II, New York City and promoted to main co.; repetoire incl. 'Viva Vivaldi,' 'Remembrances' and 'Deuce Coupe'; joined Stuttgart Ballet leaving to teach 1976; became first Am. to win medal Third Internat. Ballet Competition Moscow 1977; Soloist, Am. Ballet Theatre 4 seasons, leaving to pursue guest engagements; joined Nat. Ballet Can. 1982; extensive repetoire incls. 'Theme and Variations,' 'Undertow,' 'The River,' 'Sleeping Beauty,' (Aurora), 'Swan Lake' (Odette/Odile), 'Don Quixote' (Kitri), 'The Nutcracker' (Snow Queen/Sugar Plum Fairy), 'The Dream' (Titania), 'La Fille Mal Gardee' (Lise), 'Etudes,' La Bayadere' (Nikiya), 'Components' and many other ballets; danced at 2nd World Ballet Festival, Tokyo 1979 and with Tokyo Ballet 1982; toured USA with 'Alexander Godunov and Stars' 1982 later dancing 'Coppelia' with Sydney Ballet Australia; danced with New Zealand Ballet and in Australia 1984; filmed 'Le Corsaire' with Godunov 1984; 'Chat Botte' created by Roland Petit for her (premiered in Paris) 1985; guest dancer with Deutsche Opera Ballet, W. Berlin 1985 ('Giselle'), 1986 ('Romeo and Juliet,' 'Cinderella'); other guest appearances incl. Los Angeles Hollywood Bowl with 'Bujones and

Friends,' Fla., Chicago (Ruth Page's prodn. 'The Nutcracker'); guest appearances during 1987–89 incl. Ballet National de Marseilles (Roland Petit) 1987, Deutsche Oper Ballett (W. Berlin), Bayerische Staatsoper Ballett (Munich, W. Germany), Australian Ballet and the filming of 'The Merry Widow' with the National Ballet of Canada; dancing partners incl. Rudolf Nureyev, Fernand Bujones, Helgi Tomasson, Danilo Radojevic and David Nixon; has taught many workships, summer sessions, nat. and internat. ballet co's incl. Tokyo Ballet, Australian Ballet, Devische Oper Berlin Ballet, Joffrey Sch.; danced 2 premieres 'Duetto' and 'Lamento' 4th World Ballet Festival Tokyo 1986; Address: Schillerstr, 35, 1000 Berlin 12, Germany.

**IDE, (Thomas) Ranald,** C.M., B.A., L.L.D.; b. Ottawa, Ont. 20 Feb. 1919; s. Richard and Lola (Scharfe) I.; e. elem. sch. Ottawa; high sch. Saint John, N.B.; Mount Allison Univ. B.A. 1940; L.L.D., Queen's Univ., Kingston Ont., 1978; L.L.D., Univ. of Waterloo, Waterloo, Ont., 1978; m. 1st. Eleanor (d. 1965) d. late Dr. F. A. Aylesworth, 18 June 1942; m. 2nd. Arlene d. late Maj. Hugh G. Miles, 14 Apl. 1967; three s. Richard, John, Douglas; PRES., T.R. IDE CONSULTANTS INC.; Spec. Adv. on Planning, C.B.C. 1983–86; Chrmn.: Comte. on Computers & Inf. Soc., Sci. Counc. of Can. 1978–82; Communications Rsch. Adv. Bd. 1980–83; The Donwood Inst. 1980–82; Teacher, Vice-Prin. and Prin. Port Arthur (Ont.) Coll. Inst. 1947–62; Dist. Inspr. of Secondary Schs. N.W. Ont., 1963–65; Supt. of Secondary Schs. Port Arthur 1965–66; Dir. Educ. Television Br. Ont. Dept. Educ. 1966–70; served with RCAF as Navig. in Can. and UK during World War II, rank Flying Offr.; Gov. Ont. Teachers' Fed. 1959–61 (Chrmn. Audio-Visual Comte. 1961–62) Vice Chrmn. Ont. Educ. Television Assn. 1959–62; Dir. of Courses on Educ. Television Ryerson Polytech. Inst. 1960–62; mem. Planning Comte. on Scope and Organ. Ont. Curriculum Inst. 1964–66; mem. Curriculum Comte. to revise courses of study for Student Occupations; Candn. Rep. Third E.B.U. Internat. Conf. on Educ. Radio and TV, Paris 1967; Chrmn. E.T.V. sub-comte. Educ. Media Comte. Council Mins. Educ. 1969; mem. Media & Communications Standing Comte. Ont. Inst. for Studies in Educ. 1973; Mem. Steering Comte. for a Nat. (U.S.) Conf. on the new Literacy 1977; Chrmn. and CEO, Ont. Educ. Commun. Authority, 1970–79; Dir. Agency for Instructional Television (U.S.A) 1973–79; Dir. Ont. Educ. Research Council 1976–78; author various articles in prof. journs.; Fellow: Ont. Inst. for Studies in Educ.; Ont. Teachers' Fedn.; mem. Candn. Assn. for the Club of Rome; World Future Studies Fed.; Club of Rome; Queen's Silver Jubilee Medal, 1967; Col. Watson Award, 1979; Anglican; recreations: tennis, music; Address: 307 Chartland Blvd. South, Scarborough, Ont. M1S 3P4.

**IDLER, David Richard,** D.F.C., Ph.D., D.Sc., F.R.S.C.; scientist; educator; b. Winnipeg, Man. 13 Mar. 1923; s. Ernest and Alice (Lydon) I.; e. Univ. of B.C. B.A. 1949, M.A. 1950; Univ. of Wis. Ph.D. 1953 (Babcock Fellowship 1952–53); m. Myrtle Mary Betteridge 12 Dec. 1956; children: Louise, Mark; PATON RESEARCH PROF., OCEAN SCIENCES CENTRE, MARINE SCIENCES RESEARCH LAB. and Prof. of Biochem. Memorial Univ. of Nfld; Mem. & past Chrmn., NSERC Grants Selection Comte. for Animal Biol. and for Univ. Rsch. Fellowships; served with RCAF 1942–45, rank Flying Offr.; Ed. 'Steroids in Nonmammalian Vertebrates' 1972; author over 250 publs.; mem. ed. bds. various scient. journs.; Steroids and Pituitary Hormones; Founding mem. European Soc. Comparative Endocrinol.; mem. Candn. Biochem. Soc.; Candn. Zoological Soc. (Vice-Pres. 1986–87, Pres. 1987–88); Am. Assn. Advanc. Science; Am. Zool. Soc.; Endocrine Soc.; N.Y. Acad. Sciences; Anglican; interest: philately; Home: 44 Slattery Rd., St. John's, Nfld. A1A 1Z8; Office: St. John's, Nfld. A1C 5S7.

**IGLAUER, Edith Theresa,** B.A., M.S.; writer; b. Cleveland, Ohio; d. Jay and Bertha (Good) Iglauer; e. Wellesley Coll. B.A. 1938; Columbia Univ. M.S. 1939; Zimmern Sch. Internat. Studies Geneva, 1937; m. Philip Hamburger 24 Dec. 1942 (div.); two s. Jay Philip, Richard Shaw; m. John Heywood Daly 1 March 1976 (dec. 1978); STAFF WRITER, THE NEW YORKER MAG. 1961– ; freelance writing MacLean's, Saturday Night, Candn. Weekly and other publs.; landed immigrant Can.; recipient various writing awards incl. short list Gov. Gen.'s Award non-fiction 1988; author 'The New People: The Eskimo's Journey into Our Time' 1966; 'Denison's Ice Road' 1975, reprinted 1982, 2nd reprint 1991; 'Inuit Journey' 1979; 'Seven Stones: A Portrait of Arthur Erickson, Architect' 1981; 'Fishing with John' 1988, reprinted 1991; 'The Strangers Next Door' 1991; mem. Writers Union Can.; B.C. Civil Liberties Assn.; Amnesty Internat.; Candn. Arctic Resources Ctte.; B.C. Arts in Edn. Council; Sunshine Coast Arts Council and other orgns.; recreations: swimming, travel, walking; Clubs: Cosmopolitan (N.Y.); Cleveland Play House; Home: Box 116, Garden Bay, B.C. V0N 1S0; Office: 20 West 43rd St., New York, N.Y. 10036.

**IGLOLIORTE, James Jonathan,** B.Sc., B.Ed., LL.B.; provincial court judge; b. Hopedale, Labrador 16 July 1949; s. Matthew and Susan (Mitsuk) I.; e. Memorial Univ. of Nfld., B.Sc., B.Ed. 1973; Dalhousie Law Sch., LL.B. 1985; m. Linda d. Llewlyn and Alma Carter 12 Aug. 1972; children: Gareth, Mark, Heather, Justin; JUDGE, PROV. COURT OF NEWFOUNDLAND 1980– (circuit covers 9 communites along Labrador coast serving white, Inuit & native peoples); Vice-Principal & Teacher, St. James All-Grade Sch., Lark Harbour Bay of Islands, Nfld. 1973–80; apptd. Magistrate, Nfld. Prov. Court 1980; Internat. Grenfell Assn.; recreations: hunting, gardening; Home: Box 633, Stn. C., Happy Valley, Goose Bay, Labrador A0P 1C0; Office: Box 3026, Stn. B., Happy Valley, Goose Bay, Labrador A0P 1C0.

**IGNATIEFF, Michael,** Ph.D.; writer; historian; b. Toronto, Ont. 12 May 1947; s. George and Alison (Grant) I.; e. Upper Can. Coll. 1965; Univ. of Toronto Trinity Coll. B.A. 1969; Harvard Univ. Ph.D. 1975; Cambridge Univ. M.A. 1978; m. Susan d. Clifford and Barbara Barrowclough 30 Dec. 1977; children: Theo, Sophie; editorial columnist 'The Observer' (London) 1990–93; Reporter, The Globe and Mail 1966–67; mem. Campaign Staff Lib. Party Can. 1968 el.; Teaching Fellow in Social Studies Harvard Univ. 1971–74; Asst. Prof. of Hist. Univ. of B.C. 1976–78; Sr. Rsch. Fellow King's Coll. Cambridge 1978–84; writer and broadcaster London 1984– ; Host, BBC TV 'Thinking Aloud' 1986– , Channel Four's 'Voices' 1986; host 'The Late Show' BBC-2, 1989– ; Visiting Prof. Ecole des Hautes Etudes Paris 1985; author 'A Just Measure of Pain: The Penitentiary in the Industrial Revolution' 1978; 'The Needs of Strangers' 1984; 'The Russian Album' 1987; Governor General's Award 1988; 'Asya' 1990; 'Scar Tissue' 1993; 'Blood and Belonging: Nationalism in the Nineties' 1993; co-author 'Wealth and Virtue: The Shaping of Classical Political Economy in the Scottish Enlightenment' 1983; '1919' (screenplay) 1985; recreations: tennis, swimming, wine; Club: The Groucho (London); Address: 37 Baalbec Rd., London N5 1QN, England.

**ILLIDGE, John James,** B.A., B.B.A.; investment banker; b. Toronto, Ont. 4 Jan. 1953; s. Jack and Beverly (Shea) I.; e. Malvern Coll. Inst.; Ryerson Polytech. Inst. B.A. 1974, B.B.A. 1975; m. Ellen d. Edward Fox 27 June 1975; three d. Rebecca, Emma, Sara; PRES. & C.O.O., CREDIFINANCE SECURITIES LIMITED 1991– ; Chrmn., Conquest Capital Ltd.; Dir., Emcor, New York, Toronto; Vice-Pres., Bache Securities Canada 1980–83; Vice-Pres., Citicorp N.A. 1983–86; Pres. & C.E.O. Royal Cougar Financial 1983–86; Sr. Vice-Pres., Mgr., Dir. Prudential Bache Capital Markets 1986–90; Dir., Multibanc Financial Corp. 1986–1990; recreations: squash, tennis; Clubs: Granite; Cambridge; Albany; Home: 69 Devere Gdns., Toronto, Ont. M5M 3E8; Country address: R.R. #1, Glenmount, Ont.

**ILLMANN, Margaret Louise;** classical ballet dancer; b. Adelaide, South Australia 1965; d. Kevin Murray and Jennifer Coralie Manser I.; e. Annesley College 1982 (Sch. Capt.; Capt., State Debating Team; Dux of Arts Subjects); dance training: Dorothy Noye F.I.S.T.D., Australian Ballet School coached by Maina Geilgud, Peggy Van Pragh, Madame Vaussard, Serge Golovine, Yvette Chauvré, Reid Anderson, Natalia Makarova, Sergiu Stefanschi, Magdalena Popa; PRINCIPAL DANCER, NATIONAL BALLET OF CANADA 1991– ; Corps de Ballet, Australian Ballet Co. 1985–89 (promoted to 1st Soloist 1987; toured Japan, China, Russia, England and Greece; recipient, Louise Pommery Ballet Grant 1987); roles included: Eurydice in Glen Tetley's 'Orpheus' (in opening night at Covent Garden with David Ashmole); Junior Girl in Lichine's 'Graduation Ball'; Queen of France in Prokovsky's 'The Three Musketeers'; Carlotta Grisi, Pas de Quatre, Inner Self, in Jiri Kylian's 'Transfigured Night'; Corps de Ballet, Nat. Ballet of Can. 1989– ; roles include: Sweet Young Thing in Tetley's 'La Ronde'; Principal role in 'Gloria'; 1st Movement in Macmillan's Concerto; Kitri in 'Don Quixote'; Olga in Cranko's 'Onegin'; The Snow Queen/Sugar Plum Fairy in 'The Nutcracker'; Aurora in Nureyev's 'The Sleeping Beauty'; Principal role in 'Paquita'; Swan Queen in 'Swan Lake'; Bianca in 'The Taming of the Shrew'; Red Couple in Kylian's 'Forgotten Land'; Juliet in 'Romeo and Juliet'; Title role in 'Giselle'; premiere as Swanilda in 'Coppélia' 1994; Broadway debut Dec. 2 1993, Victoria Page in 'The Red Shoes' based on the 1949 movie; Guested with Raeffaelle Paganini (Rome Opera Theatre 'Nutcracker') partners have included: Stephen Heathcote, David McAllister, Kelvin Coe, Jeremy Ransom, Gregory Osborne, Rex Harrington, Kevin Pugh, Fernando Bujones and Raeffaello Paganini; Office: 157 King St. E., Toronto, Ont. M5C 1G9.

**IMBEAULT, Bernard,** B.Sc.Comm., M.Sc.Comm., M.B.A.; food industry executive; b. Matane, Que. 16 April 1945; e. Univ. of Moncton B.Sc.Comm. 1967, M.Sc.Comm. 1968, M.B.A. 1969; Ecole Nat. d'Admin., Paris, post-grad. studies 1970; CHAIRMAN & PRES., PIZZA DELIGHT CORP. LTD.; Pres. & Chief Extve. Offr., General Finan. Corp. Ltd.; Dir., Tekmin Inc.; Assumption Mutual Life Insur. Co.; San Andreas Resources Corp.; Adv. Mngt. Prog. for Hospitality Indus., Sch. of Hotel & Food Mngt., Univ. of Guelph; Assomption Mngt. Found., Univ. of Moncton; Home: 21 Main St., Sackville, N.B. E0A 3C0; Office: P.O. Box 2070, Station A, Moncton, N.B. E1C 8H7.

**IMBERT, Patrick Louis,** M.A., Ph.D.; educator; b. Paris, France 4 Feb. 1948; s. Gerald Louis and Odette Cécile (Linsart) I.; e. Institut catholique de Paris, Licence 1969; Univ. of Ottawa M.A. 1970, Ph.D. 1974; m. Nicole d. Marcel and Gisèle Baril 7 June 1980; children: Sacha, Maxime; PROF. OF LETTRES FRANCAISES, UNIV. OF OTTAWA 1984– ; Part-time Prof. Univ. of Ottawa 1969–74, Asst. Prof. 1975–80; Asst. Prof. McMaster Univ. 1974–75; Mem. Bd. of Dirs., Candn. Fed. for Humanities 1989–92; author Sémiotique et description balzacienne' 1978; 'Roman québécois contemporain et clichés' 1983; 'L'Objectivité de la Presse' 1989; mem., Société de Philosophie de l'Outaouais (Pres. 1992–94); Internat. Assn. Semiotic; Candn. Semiotic Assn. (Pres. 1979–80); P.E.N.; Candn. Comparative Lit. Assn.; Assoc. for Candn. and Que. Lit. (Pres. 1988–90); recreation: sailing; Club: Georgian Bay Sailing Center; Home: 774 Lonsdale Rd., Ottawa, Ont. K1K 0K1.

**IMBODEN, Roberta Ann,** B.A., M.A.; university professor; b. Buffalo, N.Y. 11 July 1934; d. Robert Henry and Margaret Doris (Morford) I.; e. Mercyhurst Coll., B.A. 1956; Canisius Coll., M.A. 1961; Univ. of Toronto, M.A. 1977; m. David s. Josephine and James Grimshaw 4 June 1977; PROF. OF LITERATURE, RYERSON POLYTECHNICAL INST. 1965– ; Lit. Teacher, Loyola Coll. 1964–65; mem., Delta Epsilon Sigma; Catholic Univ. Liberal Arts Hon. Soc. (U.S.A.); author: 'From the Cross to the Kingdom: Sartrean Dialectics and Liberation Theology' 1987; 'The Huperbolical Project of Cristina: A Derridean Analysis of Ricci's *Lives of the Saints*' in Dalhousie Review, Spring 1992, Vol. 72, No. 1; recreation: swimming; Home: 190 St. George St., #302, Toronto, Ont. M5R 2N4; Office: 350 Victoria St., Toronto, Ont. M5B 2K3.

**INFELD, Eric (Eryk),** B.A., M.A., Ph.D., D.Sc.; professor of theoretical physics; b. Toronto, Ont. 8 Jan. 1940; s. Leopold (FRSC) and Mary Helen (Schlauch) I.; e. Cambridge Univ. B.A. 1962, M.A. 1968; Warsaw Univ. Ph.D. 1966; Soltan Inst. D.Sc. 1972; one d.: Ewa Joanna Infeld; dual citizenship: Canadian and Polish; PROFESSOR AND HEAD OF PLASMA PHYSICS GROUP, THEORY DEPT., SOLTAN INSTITUTE (WARSAW); Bursar, Trinity College, Cambridge Univ. 1959–62; Scientist, Soltan Inst. Warsaw 1963; Culham Rsch. Assoc. UK 1964–65; Assoc. Prof., Soltan Inst. 1973; Prof. 1990– ; Principal Rsch. Fellow, Warwick Univ. 1978; Sr. Visitor, Mathematics, Cambridge Univ. (7 visits) 1973–90; Visiting Prof., Centre de Rech. Math., Univ. of Montreal 1990–91; Rsch. Fellow, Univ. College, London 1992–93; Vice-Pres., Plasma Physics Section, Polish Academy of Sciences 1983–87 and 1992– ; Pres., Polish Electromagnetic Soc. 1990–91; Mem., Am. Physical Soc.; Am. Math. Soc.; Candn. Applied Math. Soc.; Polish Physical Soc. (Extve. 1982–85); Soc. for the Interaction between Math. and Mechanics; Polish Soc. for Science; Gold Cross, Poland 1989; Polish Academy of Sciences Award 1990; Mem., Solidarity (Poland) 1980–83; co-author: 'Nonlinear Waves, Solitons and Chaos' 1990, '92 (Book of the Month, Macmillan-Newbridge Book Club 1990); author: 'Leopold Infeld' 1978; Assoc. Ed., 'J. of Plasma Physics' 1989; Journal of Tech. Physics 1993; mem., Scientific Council, Cosmic Rsch. Institute, Warsaw; recreations: horses; clubs: Oxford and Cambridge Soc. of Montreal; Home: Boya 2 m 8 Warsaw 00621, Poland; Soltan Institute, Hoza 69, Warsaw 00681, Poland.

**ING, John R.;** executive; b. Montréal, Qué. 1 Jan. 1947; s. Fred and Blossom I.; e. McGill Univ.; m. Tracey 30 Dec 1971; PRES. AND CHIEF EXEC. OFFR. MAISON PLACEMENTS CANADA INC. 1984– ; former portfolio mgr. Jones Heward & Co. Montréal; joined Mead &

Co. 1971 becoming Sr. Vice Pres. and Dir.; Vice Pres., Mgr. Investor Services Pitfield Mackay Ross 1980 and becoming Vice Pres. and mem. Invest. Strategy Ctte. Dominion Securities Pitfield; long-time gold analyst; mem. Toronto Soc. Financial Analysts; Toronto Mining Analyst; Chinese Candn. Investment Professional Assoc.; Candn. Inst. Mining & Metall.; Fellow, Candn. Securities Inst.; Phi Kappa Pi; Club: Cambridge; Office: 906, 130 Adelaide St. W., Toronto, Ont. M5H 3P5.

**INGHAM, David Keith,** M.A., Ph.D.; educator; actor; b. London, Ont. 30 Sept. 1950; s. George Kenneth and Louise Adele (Cox) I.; e. St. Jerome's Coll. Waterloo B.A. 1973; Univ. of Waterloo M.A. 1976; Univ. of B.C. Ph.D. 1985; m. Kathleen Elizabeth Barnett 1991; PROF. OF ENG. UNIV. OF LETHBRIDGE 1990– ; computer cons., tech. writer 1985–87; Prof. of Eng., Univ. of Sask. 1987–90; profl. actor since 1971; cons., regional co-ordinator Horizon Pacific Ventures Ltd. Vancouver; served with Candn. Armed Forces 1976–79, rank Lt.; nominee Master Teacher Award 1989; author numerous articles and reviews Candn. lit. and tech. manuals computers & word processing; mem. Candn. Univ. Teachers Eng.; Assn. Candn. & Que. Lit.; Amnesty Internat.; Sierra Club; Greenpeace; World Wildlife Fedn.; Wilderness Canoe Assn.; Am. Contract Bridge League; Life Master bridge 1979; recreations: whitewater canoeing, duplicate bridge; Home: 591 Columbia Blvd. W., Lethbridge, Alta. T1K 5N4; Office: Lethbridge, Alta. T1K 3M4.

**INGLE, Lorne Edward,** Q.C., B.A., LL.B.; lawyer; b. Rainbow, B.C. 16 Oct. 1915; s. Albert Edward and Mary Etta (Ingle) Pattison; e. elem. and high schs. Jasper and Edmonton, Alta., McBride, B.C.; Univ. of Alta. B.A. 1939 (Econ.), LL.B. 1940; m. Alice Laird d. Kenneth and Mabel Reikie 8 Nov. 1940; children: Barbara, Margot, Roger; m. Nita Marguerite d. Louis and Mabel Guilbault 19 May 1973; DIR. DOUGLAS-COLDWELL FOUND. 1985– ; articled with S.Bruce Smith 1940 and A.L. Marks 1946, Edmonton; called to Bar of Alta. 1946, Sask. 1958, Ont. 1962; served with Candn. Army 1940–45, Adjt. Inf. Bn., GSO HQ Pac. Com'd., DAAG NDHQ, rank Major; Nat. Rsch. Dir. CCF 1946–50, Nat. Sec. 1950–57; Solr. Atty.-Gen.'s Dept. and Govt. Finance Office Regina 1957–61; Solr. Jolliffe, Lewis & Osler Toronto 1962–65; Candn. Gen. Counsel Un. Steelworkers of Am. 1966–79; Counsel, Metrop. Toronto Police Assn. 1979–83; Columnist People's Weekly, Edmonton 1937–40; Prov. Sec. CCF Alta. 1938, Prov. Treas. 1945–46 and NDP Ont. 1965–67; Fed. Treas. NDP 1972–74; compiled and ed. 'Meech Lake Reconsidered' 1989; mem. Lawyers for Social Responsibility; Candn. Econ. Assn.; recreations: music, medieval history; Address: 805, 45 Huntingdale Blvd., Scarborough, Ont. M1W 2N8.

**INGLIS, Stephen Robert,** Ph.D.; research executive; b. Vancouver, B.C. 21 Sept. 1949; s. Robert and Joy Gloria (Carter) I.; e. Univ. of B.C., B.A. 1973, Ph.D. 1984; Calcutta Univ. M.A. 1977; m. Erica d. Gertrude and Eric Claus Nov. 1986; children: Jasmine, Maya; DIRECTOR, RESEARCH, CANDN. MUSEUM OF CIVILIZATION 1992– ; Chief, Candn. Centre for Folk Culture Studies, Candn. Mus. of Civilization 1991–92; Curator, South & W. Asia, Candn. Mus. of Civilization 1984–91; Visiting Lectr. in Anthropology, Carleton Univ.; Acting Chief, Candn. Ctr. for Folk Culture Studies, Candn. Mus. of Civilization; Chairperson, Cultural Prog., Shastri Indo-Candn. Inst.; Ed. Bd. mem., 'Culture' (Candn. Ethnol. Soc.); Home: 106 Hopewell, Ottawa, Ont. K1S 2Z1; Office: P.O. Box 3100, Station B, Hull, Que. J8X 4H2.

**INGOLD, Keith U.,** B.Sc., D.Phil., F.R.S.C. (1969), F.R.S. (1979), F.C.I.C.; research chemist; b. Leeds, Eng. 31 May 1929; s. Sir Christopher Kelk and Lady Edith Hilda (Usherwood) Ingold; e. Univ. Coll., Univ. of London, B.Sc. (Hon. Chem.) 1949; Oxford Univ., D.Phil. 1951; m. Carmen Cairine, d. Frank G. Hodgkin, Ottawa, Ont. 7 Apr. 1956; children: Christopher Frank (dec.), John Hilary, Diana Hilda; DISTINGUISHED RESEARCH SCIENTIST, STEACIE INST. FOR MOLECULAR SCIS., N.R.C. 1991– ; Adjunct Prof., Dept. of Biochemistry, Brunel Univ., U.K. 1983– ; Adjunct Rsch. Prof., Dept. of Chemistry, Carleton Univ., Ottawa 1991– ; post-doctoral fellow, Div. of Pure Chem., N.R.C. 1951–53; Defense Rsch. Bd. post-doctoral Fellow, Chem. Dept., Univ. of B.C. 1953–55; Rsch. Offr., Div. of Applied Chem., N.R.C. 1955; Visiting Prof., Chevron Research Co., Richmond, Cal. 1966; Univ. Coll., London 1969 and 1972; Carnegie Fellow of Univ. of St. Andrews, Scotland 1977; Assoc. Dir., Div. of Chem., National Research Council 1977–90; Adjunct Prof., Dept. of Chemistry & Biochemistry, Univ. of Guelph, Guelph, Ont. 1985–87; numerous lectures including: Frank Burnett Dains Memorial Lecture, Univ. of Kansas 1969; The J.A. McRae Memorial Lectures in Chemistry, Queen's Univ., Kingston, Ont. 1980; Douglas Hill Memorial Lecture, Duke Univ., N. Carolina 1987; Rayson Huang Lecture, Univ. of Hong Kong 1988; Peter de la Mare Memorial Lecture, Univ. of Auckland, New Zealand 1993; Gilman Lecture Series, Iowa State Univ. 1993; rec'd Am. Chem. Soc. Petroleum Chem. Award 1968; Queen's Jubilee Medal 1977; Award in Kinetics and Mechanism, Chem. Soc. (London) 1978; Chem. Inst. of Can. Medal 1981; Centennial Medal, Roy. Soc. of Can. 1982; Syntex Award, Chem. Inst. of Can. 1983; Hon. D.Sc., Univ. of Guelph 1985; Henry Marshall Tory Medal, Roy. Soc. of Can. 1985; LL.D. (hon. causa) Mount Allison Univ. Sackville, N.B. 1987; Pauling Award, Am. Chem. Soc. 1988; Alfred Bader Award in Organic Chem., Candn. Soc. for Chem. 1989; Hon. D.Sc., Univ. of St. Andrews, Scotland 1989; Sir Christopher Ingold Lectureship Award, Royal Soc. of Ch. (U.K.) 1991; Humboldt Rsch. Award, Alexander von Humboldt Found., West Germany 1989; VERIS Award, Vitamin E Rsch. Information Services (U.S.) 1989; Davy Medal, Royal Soc. (London) 1990; Mangini Prize in Chem., Univ. of Bologna, Italy 1990; Lansdowne Visitor Award, Univ. of Victoria, Canada 1990; Arthur C. Cope Scholar Award, Am. Chem. Soc. 1992; Izaak Walton Killam Memorial Prize, The Canada Counc. 1992; Hon. D.Sc., Carleton Univ., Ottawa, Ont.; Nat. Sci. Counc. Letureship, Republic of China 1992; Van Arkel Visiting Prof., Leiden Univ. (Holland) 1992; James Flack Norris Award in Physical Organic Chem., Am. Chem. Soc. 1993; el. Fellow, University Coll., London 1987; Vice Pres., Candn. Soc. for Chem. 1985–87; Pres., Candn. Soc. for Chem. 1987–88; Fellow, Chem. Inst. of Can.; mem. Am. Chem. Soc.; Royal Soc. Chem. (London); recreations: skiing, windsurfing; Home: 72 Ryeburn Dr., Gloucester, Ont.; Office: National Research Council, Sussex Dr., Ottawa, Ont. K1A 0R6.

**INGRAM, Donald C.,** B.A.Sc., M.B.A., P.Eng.; engineering executive; b. Toronto, Ont. 3 Aug. 1937; e. East York Coll. Inst. Sr. Matric. 1956; Univ. of Toronto B.A.Sc. Mech. Engr. 1960; McMaster Univ. M.B.A. 1975; m. Kathleen d. Hazel Baker 2 Sept. 1960; children: Paul, Kristen, Peter; Pres., International Pipeline Engineering Ltd. 1984; Pres., Pipetronix Inc. (Houston, U.S.A.) 1988– ; Design Engr. Clark Bros. Co. (Olean, N.Y.) 1960–64; Sr. Design Engr. James Howden & Parsons of Can. Ltd. 1964–68; Mgr. Eastern Region Union Gas Ltd. 1976, Vice-Pres. Engrg. and Gas Supply 1976–84; Dir. Ont. Natural Gas Assn. 1981–84; Chrmn. Approvals Managing Ctte., Candn. Gas Assn. 1983–84; mem. Assn. Profl. Engrs. of Ont.; Vice-Chrmn. and Chrmn. Fund Raising Ctte., United Way of Chatham-Kent; Gold Medallist, McMaster M.B.A. Class as part-time student 1975; recreations: skiing, golf, squash; Club: Holimont Ski; Home: 1355 Lorne Park Rd., Mississauga, Ont. L5H 3B2.

**INGRAM, James Allan,** B.A., LL.B.; lawyer; b. Toronto, Ont. 21 Nov. 1949; s. G. Allan and Mary L. I.; e. Univ. of Toronto 1971; Univ. of Ottawa B.A. 1976; Osgoode Hall LL.B. 1978; m. Karen d. Wilbert and Maria Voll 13 Aug. 1977; children: Matthew, Andrew; LAWYER, KMART CANADA LIMITED 1980– ; Lawyer, National Trust 1978–79; Lawyer, Royal Bank 1979–80; Mem., Inst. of Chartered Secretaries & Administrators; Law Soc. of U.C.; Candn. Secondary Schools Rowing Assn.; Home: 65 Leeward Dr., Brampton, Ont. L6S 5V9; Office: 8925 Torbram Rd., Brampton, Ont. L6T 4G1.

**INGSTRUP, Ole Michaelsen,** Ph.D.; correctional services executive; b. Aarhus, Denmark 4 May 1941; s. Alf and Edith (Sorensen) I.; e. Aarhus Univ., B.A. 1961, M.A. 1966, Ph.D. (law) 1970; Internat. & Social Law, Training in Mngmt., and Media Relns. & Commun. dipls.; m. Marie-ève d. Jean and Georgette Marchand 26 Feb. 1983; children: Benedicte, Anne, Emmanuel, Mélissa; PRINCIPAL, CANADIAN CENTRE FOR MANAGEMENT DEVELOPMENT; Assoc. Prof. of Law, Aarhus Univ. 1966–69; Dep. Warden; Warden 1972; Visiting Professor, U.N. Training Inst., Tokyo, Japan 1972; Chrmn., Planning Ctte., Danish Min. of Justice 1973; Danish Govt. Rep., Eur. Ctte. on Crime Problems & Chrmn., Select Ctte. on Prison Regimes & Prison Leave for Counc. of Eur. 1977; Spec. Adv. to Comnr. of Correctional Serv. of Can. 1983; Chrmn., Nat. Parole Bd., Govt. of Can. 1986–88; Comn., Correctional Service of Canada 1988–92; Chrmn. & Mem., num. cttes. & task forces in Denmark Council of Europe & Can.; Examiner, Law Fac., Aarhus Univ.; assigned to UN Soc. Def. Rsch. Inst. (Rome); decorated by Her Majesty the Queen of Denmark with the Order of Knights; Mem., Candn. Inst. for Admin. of Justice; Candn. Crim. Justice Assn.; Am. Correctional Assn.; author of numerous articles & book reviews; co-author: 'Prisoner's Legal Rights,' 'Structural Change in Prison Management,' 'Use and Abuse of Prison Leave,' 'Criminal Responsibility,' 'Essays in Criminal Law,' 'Crime Control in Denmark' 1980; Office: 373 Sussex Dr., Ottawa, Ont. K1N 8V4.

**INKPEN, Linda L.,** B.Sc., B.Ed., B.Med.Sc., M.D., L.M.C.C.; physician; educational administrator; b. Toronto, Ont. 15 Jan. 1948; d. Roland and Beulah (Case) I.; e. Prince of Wales Coll. 1954–65; Memorial Univ. of Nfld. B.Sc. 1969, B.Ed. 1970, B.Med.Sc. 1972, M.D. 1974; L.M.C.C. 1974; rotating internship, affil. hosps. of Memorial Univ. Med. Sch. 1974–75; m. Dr. Nizar B. Ladha 21 June 1974; children: Justin, Michael, Jonathan; various summer positions; Hostess, CBC-TV Youth Current Affairs Prog. 1966; CBC-TV Current Affairs & Musical Prog. 1969; Asst. in Stats. Lab., Dept. of Math., Memorial Univ. of Nfld. 1968–70; High School Subs. Teacher 1970–71; estab. med. practice in St. John's, Nfld. (manager of 3-doctor office & supportive staff) 1975–87; Staff Health Physician, St. Clare's Mercy Hosp. 1976–87; Staff Physician, Queen St. Mental Health Ctr. Toronto 1979–80; Comn., Royal Comn. on Employment & Unemployment 1985–86; Pres. & Chief Extve. Offr., Cabot College of Applied Arts, Technology and Continuing Education 1987–93; numerous scholarships & awards 1954–74 incl. highest prov. school-leaving aggregate mark, Dux Medal, Governor Gen.'s Medal 1965; Active Med. Staff, St. Clare's Mercy Hosp.; Courtesy Staff, Grace Gen. Hosp. & Wterford Hosp.; Mem., Candn. & Nfld. Med. assns.; Coll. of Family Phys. of Can.; St. John's Gen. Practitioners Assn.; Women Interested in Sci. & Engr. 1988– ; Adv. Bd., Brother T.I. Murphy Learning Resource Ctr. 1988–93; Hon. Chair, Big Brothers, Big Sisters 1989 Annual Campaign; Terry Fox 1989 Campaign; Mem., Nfld. & Lab. Sci. & Technol. Adv. Counc. 1990–93 (Vice-Chair 1988–90); Vice-Chair, Atlantic Prov. Econ. Counc. 1990– (Gov. 1988–90); Vice-Chair, Nat. Innovations Adv. Counc. 1990– (Mem. 1989–90); Mem., Environ. Partnership Fund for Nfld. 1990– ; St. John's Hosp. Counc. 1987–93; Extve. Devel. Ctte. (prov. govt.) 1988–93; Seabright Corp. Bd. of Dir. 1988–93; Adjustment Steering Ctte., Nat. Priv. Sector Project on Women in Engr. 1990–92; Adjunct Prof. of Med., Meml. Univ. 1990– ; Mem., Nfld. Power Bd. of Dir. 1990– ; NRC Indus. Rsch. Assistance Prog. Adv. Bd. 1991; Nat. Adv. Bd. of Sci. & Technol. 1991– ; and other past extve. positions; Chairperson, Nfld. & Labrador Business Hall of Fame 1992; Chairperson, Fortis Educ. Found. 1992– ; Chairperson, Industrial Inquiry 1993; Home: Box 432, R.R. #1, St. Phillips, Nfld. A1L 1C1.

**INKSTER, Commissioner Norman David,** B.A. (Hons. Socio.); b. Winnipeg, Man. 19 Aug. 1938; s. Harold McFarlane and Martha Mae (Brown) I.; e. Univ. of N.B., B.A. Hons. Socio. 1971; full-time French lang. training 1976–78; m. Mary Anne d. Everett and Christine Morrison 17 Nov. 1961; children: Leslie Anne, Scott, Dana; apptd. COMMISSIONER, ROYAL CANDN. MOUNTED POLICE and Chairperson, Sr. Exec. Ctte. 1987– ; joined RCMP 1957 performing mun. and prov. policing duties Settler, Three Hills and Red Deer, Alta.; adm. duties Ottawa, Fredericton and Montréal 1962–78; Offr.-in-Charge Montréal Sub-Div. 1978, Exec. Offr. to Commr. 1979; Offr.-in-Charge Staffing & Personnel Br. for Offrs. 1980–82; C.O. RCMP 'A' Div. Ottawa 1982; Dir. Orgn. & Personnel Hdqrs. 1984; Depy. Commr., Operations (Criminal) and mem. Sr. Exec. Ctte. 1985–87; Pres., ICPO - Interpol 1992; recipient Queen's Silver Jubilee Medal 1977; RCMP Long Service Medal; Officer Brother, Order of St. John of Jerusalem 1988; awarded Commemorative Medal for 125th Anniversary of Candn. Confederation 1992; mem. Candn. Assn. Chiefs of Police; Internat. Assn. Chiefs of Police; Home: 1265 Royal Maple Dr., Cumberland, Ont. K4C 1B5; Office: 1200 Vanier Parkway, Ottawa, Ont. K1A 0R2.

**INKSTER, Timothy John,** B.A., G.D.C.; publisher, printer, book designer; b. Toronto, Ont. 26 Sept. 1949; s. Walter James and Rita Marie (Walters) I.; e. University College, Univ. of Toronto B.A. 1971; m. Elke d. Alma and Johannes Koehler Aug. 1970; CO-FOUNDER/PUBLISHER (WITH ELKE INKSTER), PORCUPINE'S QUILL 1974– ; Porcupine's Quill has pub. over 100 titles under its own imprint primarily in the area of contemporary Candn. Lit. & Art; all titles are produced on the premises in a turn-of-the-century storefront in the village of Erin; many have won awards for design & production excellence notably from the Alcuin Soc., The Malahat Review, Design Canada and The Look of Books; Bronze Medal, Leipzig Book Fair 1984; Silver Medal 1980; N.Y. Art Directors' Club Citations 1980, '83; Profl. Mem., Graphic Designers of Canada; Treas., Assn. of Candn. Publishers 1986–90; Mem., Leage of

Candn. Poets 1973–83; author: 'For Elke/No Parking' 1970 (poetry chapbook); 'The Topolobampo Poems' 1972, 'Mrs. Grundy' 1973, 'The Crown Prince Waits for a Train' 1976, 'Blue Angel' 1981 (poetry); 'An Honest Trade' 1983 (memoir); subject of a 15-min. film 'The Colours of a Poet' 1976; anthologized in 'The Penguin Book of Canadian Verse' 1975, 'The Poets of Canada' 1978; subject of special issue of 'Amphora' Spring 1991; recreations: gardening; Home & Office: 68 Main St., Erin, Ont. N0B 1T0.

**INLOW, Edgar Burke,** A.B., M.A., Ph.D.; educator; b. Forest Grove, Oregon 14 Dec. 1914; s. Harvey Edgar and Eva Lou (Skaggs) I.; came to Can. Aug. 1961; e. Washington State Univ., A.B. 1937; Univ. of Calif. M.A. 1939; Johns Hopkins Univ. Ph.D. 1949; General Theological Seminary 1950; m. Louise Maurer 21 Oct. 1971; children: Rush; Morgan; Gerd; Brand; Shane; PROFESSOR EMERITUS, DEPT. OF POL. SCI., UNIV. OF CALGARY 1981– ; served in Infantry, U.S. Army, 1941–45; Instr., Princeton Univ. 1947–49; ordained Priest, Episcopal Church 1950; Parish Priest in California and Pennsylvania 1950–57; U.S. Dept. of Defense (M.A.I.) 1957–61; Prof., Univ. of Calgary 1961–81 (Head of Dept. of Political Sci. 1961–71); Visiting Prof., Vanderbilt Univ., Nashville 1964–65; Univ. of Teheran 1970; Project Dir., Royal Comm. on Health Services, Canada 1962–64; mem. Candn. Comte. for the Universal Commemoration of the 2500th Anniversary of the Founding of the Persian Empire 1971–72; Hon. Asst., St. Stephen's Anglican Church, Calgary until retired 1981; author 'The Patent Grant' 1949; 'Studies in Canon Law' 1957; 'Shahanshah, The Monarchy of Iran' 1979; numerous articles on comparative legal theory; mem. Royal Soc. Asian Affairs (Hon. Sec. for Can. 1971–81); Brit. Inst. of Persian Studies; Fellow, Can. Council; Social Science Research Council (U.S.A.); mem. Union Club of B.C.; Phi Beta Kappa; Home: 2340 Magnolia Blvd. W., Seattle, WA 98199 USA; Office: 2500 University Dr. N.W., Calgary, Alta. T2N 1N4.

**INMAN, Robert Davies,** B.A., M.D., FRCP(C), FACP; university professor, physician; b. Toronto, Ont. 6 March 1949; s. Robert Eric and Elizabeth Jean (Davies) I.; e. Yale College B.A. 1971; McMaster Univ. M.D. 1974; Vanderbilt Univ. 1977 Internal Med. Cert.; Cornell Univ. 1979 Rheum. Cert.; Research, Hammersmith Hosp. London England; m. Straughn d. Stan and Emily Eastman 31 Jan. 1971; children: Susan Davies, David Stanley, Kathryn Abbott; PROFESSOR OF MEDICINE & IMMUNOLOGY, UNIV. OF TORONTO 1990– ; joined Faculty, Univ. of Toronto 1983; Dir., Univ. of Toronto Rheumatic Disease Unit 1991; Toronto Hosp. Arthritis Ctr. 1991; Mem., Bd. of Dir., Am. College of Rheumatology; Pres., House of Compassion of Toronto; The Arthritis Soc. Ont. Div.; Mem., Yorkminster Park Baptist Ch. (Bd. of Deacons); Candn. Rhem. Assn.; Am. Coll. of Rheum. (Reg. Pres. 1988–90); Christian Med. Soc.; Candn. Soc. Clin. Investigation; Am. Assn. of Immunology; Assoc. Ed., 'The J. of Rheum.'; Home: 118 Hillsdale Ave. W., Toronto, Ont. M5P 1G6; Office: Toronto Western Hosp., 399 Bathurst St., Toronto, Ont. M5T 2S8.

**INNES, Christopher David,** B.A., M.A., B.Phil., D.Phil., FRSA, FRSC; university professor; b. Liverpool, Eng. 6 Oct. 1941; s. Alexander and Mary Margaret I.; e. Oxford Univ. B.A. 1965, M.A. 1967 B.Phil. 1968, D.Phil. 1969; Munich Univ. 1965–66 (King Edward VII Found. Scholarship); Freie Universität 1968–69 (DAAD Scholarship); m. Eva d. George and Gudrun Felso-Eör Nagy; one s.: Alexander Carlyon; PROFESSOR, ENGLISH, YORK UNIV. 1981– ; English Dept., York Univ. 1969– ; Initiator & Dir., Interdisciplinary Grad. Prog.; Rsch. Fellow, Corpus Christi Coll. 1983–84; Benian's Fellow, St. John's Coll. 1989–90; Visiting Eminent Scholar, Univ. of Newcastle 1992; Cons., Chinese Univ. of Hong Kong 1992; Fellow, Royal Soc. of Can. 1992; Royal Soc. of Arts 1983; Bd. of Dir., Candn. Stage Co. 1992– ; Mem., Internat. Assn. of Univ. Prof. of English; Internat. Theatre Inst.; Candn. Assn. for Irish Studies (Treas. 1973–75); Liveryman of Salters Co., City of London; Founding Ed., 'Director in Perspective' series & 'Canadian Playwrights' series; Co-editor: 'Lives of the Theatre' series, 'Drama East and West' & 'Modern Drama'; has designed and directed plays; author: 'Pisator's Political Theatre' 1972, '77, 'Modern German Drama' 1979, '80, 'Holy Theatre' 1981, '84, 'Edward Gordon Craig' 1983, 'Politics and the Playwright: George Ryga' 1986, 'Twentieth-Century British Drama' 1992, '94, 'Avant Garde Theatre' 1993, '94, and over 40 articles; Contbg. Co-ed., 'The Cambridge Guide to World Drama' 1988; recreations: painting, sailing, skiing; Home: 124 Glen Rd., Toronto, Ont. M4W 2W2; Office: 249 Winters College, 4700 Keele St., North York, Ont. M3J 1P3.

**INNES, Frank Cecil,** M.A., B.Sc., Ph.D.; university professor; b. Edinburgh, Scotland; s. James Alexander Lindsey and Kathleen Grace (Thurston) I.; e. Dollar Acad. 1953; Univ. of Glasgow, B.Sc. (Hons.) 1957; McGill Univ., M.A. 1960, Ph.D. 1967; m. Willa d. Myrtle and William Banfill 1961; children: Dawn, Joy, Jon; PROF., HIST. & MED. GEOGRAPHY, UNIV. OF WINDSOR 1972– ; Glasgow/McGill Exchange Scholar 1958; Sess. Asst., Assoc. Prof., Geog., McGill Univ. 1959–72; Prof. & Head, Dept. of Geog., Univ. of Windsor 1972–78; Dir., Sermons from Sci., Expo '67, Man and His World 1965–67; Sandwich Comm. Health Ctr. 1985– ; Bd. Chrmn., Sandwich Community Health Center 1990–92; Guest Lecturer, Cunard Cruise Lines 1990 and 1993; Royal Viking Lines 1993; Cons., S.W. Ont. Perinatal Adv. Ctte.; Mem., Regional Children's Centre Ctte., Windsor Western Hosp.; Chrmn., Iona Coll. 1978–80; Elder, St. Andrews Presbyn. Ch. 1986– ; Treas., Candn. Assn. of Geog. 1963–70; Chrmn., OCPLACS 1980–82, 1987–88; co-editor: 'Health Welfare and Development in Latin America and the Caribbean' 1981; co-author: 'Atlas of Montreal' Royal Comn. on Bilingualism & Biculturalism 1967; author of over 20 articles, book chapters, etc.; recreations: gardening, stamp collecting; Home: 1467 Guildwood Cres., Windsor, Ont. N9H 2B3; Office: Windsor, Ont. N9B 3P4.

**INNES, Richard D.;** business executive; b. Woodstock, Ont. 10 May 1939; s. James Durno and Frances Georgina (Dent) I.; e. Univ. of West. Ont., (Hons.) B.A. 1961; m. Roberta d. Howard and Eileen Rogers 18 Aug. 1962; children: Stephanie, Sarah; PRES., INDUSTRIAL DIVISION, AULT FOODS LTD. 1989– ; Mktg. Mngt., Procter & Gamble 1961–70; Vice-Pres. & Dir., Candn. Mktg. Assoc. 1970–72; Dir. of Mktg. then Vice-Pres., Mktg. & Mfg. then Pres., Playtex Ltd. 1973–82; Vice-Pres., Planning, Nabisco Brands Ltd. 1982–83; Pres., Grocery Div., 1983–87; Pres., Catelli Inc. 1987–89; Past Pres., Body Fashion Mfr. Assn.; Dir. & Exec. Ctte., National Dairy Counc.; recreations: tennis, skiing; Clubs: Toronto Cricket Curling & Skating; Home: 4 Binscarth Rd., Toronto, Ont. M4W 1Y1; Office: 405 The West Mall, Etobicoke, Ont. M9C 5J1.

**INOUE, Masayasu,** B.Econ.; forest industry executive; b. Kyoto, Japan 6 Dec. 1935; s. Masao and Miyo (Urakami) I.; e. Kyoto Univ. B.Econ. 1958; m. Masako d. Iwao and Michiko Otabe 8 March 1963; children: Yasuko, Satoshi, Utako, Keiko; CHAIRMAN AND CHIEF EXECUTIVE OFFICER, CRESTBROOK FOREST INDUSTRIES LTD.; joined Mitsubishi Corp. 1958; served var. assignments worldwide: Tehran (Iran), Vancouver & Cranbrook, Atlanta, and Bahrain; Vice-Pres. & Gen. Mgr., Mitsubishi Internat. Corp. Atlanta; Sr. Asst. to Mng. Dir., Mitsubishi Corp. Tokyo; Chair & Mng. Dir. Mitsubishi Corp. (Middle East) Bahrain; recreation: golf; clubs: Kasumigasaki Country, Richmond Country; Home: 4492 Haggart St., Vancouver, B.C. V6L 2H5; Office: 1200 - 1055 W. Hastings St., Vancouver, B.C. V6E 2E9.

**INUKPUK, Johnny,** R.C.A.; artist; b. 1911; medium: sculpture, prints; 45 group exbns. incl.: Hudson's Bay Co. Collection of Inuit Art, Winnipeg Art Gall. 1992; Arctic Artistry, Hastings-on-Hudson, N.Y. 1991, 1992; Granville Island Candn. Inuit Sculpture, Vancouver Inuit Art Soc. (two exhibs.) 1991; 'Mother and Child: Sculpture & Prints' Albers Gall., San Francisco, Ca. 1991; 'Espaces Inuit' Maison Hamel-Bruneau, Ste-Foy, Qué. 1990–91; Images of the North, San Francisco, Ca. 1990; 'Arctic Mirror' Candn. Mus. of Civilization, Hull, Qué. 1990; 'In the Shadow of the Sun: Contemporary Indian & Inuit Art in Canada' Candn. Mus. of Civilization, Hull, Qué. 1989; 'Stories in Stone: Soapstone Sculptures From Northern Québec and Kenya' La Fed. des Co-op du Nouveau-Qué. 1988–90; 'The Spirit of the Land' The Koffler Gall. 1986; Masterwork Sculpture 1985, Inuit Gall. of Vancouver; 'The Arctic/L'Artique' UNESCO, Paris, France 1983; 'Inuit Sculpture 1982' The Raven Gall., Minneapolis, USA; 'Eskimo Sculpture and Art Exhibit' Yerkes Internat. Gall., N.Y. 1980; 'Eskimo Art' Embankment Gall., London, Eng. 1978; 'The Art of the Eskimo' Simon Fraser Univ., B.C. 1971; 'The Eskimo Art Collection of the Toronto-Dominion Bank' Toronto 1967; 'Eskimo Carvings: Coronation Exhibition' Gimpel Fils, London, Eng. 1953; solo exbns.: Galerie Le Chariot, Montreal 1987; Arctic Artistry, Hartsdale, N.Y. 1984; Cottage Craft Gifts and Fine Arts Ltd., Calgary, Alta. 1980; works in 19 collections incl.: Agnes Etherington Art Centre, Queen's Univ., Kingston, Ont.; Art Gall. of Greater Victoria; Art Gall. of York Univ.; Bessie Bulman Collection, Winnipeg Art Gall.; Glenbow Museum, Calgary; Klamer Family Coll., Art Gall. of Ont.; Metro. Museum of Art N.Y.; Musée de la civilisation Québec City; Rothmans Permanent Coll. of Eskimo Sculpture, Toronto; Musée des beaux-arts de Montréal; elected Mem., Royal Candn. Academy of Arts 1978; carving 'Mother Nursing Child' appeared on cover of 'Inuit Art Quarterly' Summer 1990; subject of numerous selected references; Home: Inukjuak, Qué.; Office: La Federation des Co-op. du Nouveau-Qué., 19950 Clark Graham, Baie D'Urfe, Qué. H9X 3R8.

**INWOOD, Martin J.,** B.Sc., M.D., F.R.C.P.(C); physician/university professor; b. United Kingdom 11 Apr. 1935; s. Harold and Nora (Curran) I.; e. Univ. of London, F.I.M.L.S. 1959; Laurentian Univ. B.Sc. 1964; Univ. of West. Ont. M.D. 1969; m. Elizabeth d. William and Rheta Shannon 21 Dec. 1983; children: Karen, Hilary, Nicola, Jacqueline, Taylor, Ryan; PROF. OF MED., UNIV. OF WEST. ONT. & CHIEF, DIV. CLIN. HEMATOL./ONCOL., DEPT. OF MED., ST. JOSEPH'S HEALTH CTR. 1981– ; other current positions: Prof., Oncol., UWO; Chief Div. of Lab. Hematol. & Blood Transfusion, St. Joseph's Health Ctr.; Med. Dir., S.W. Ont. Reg. Hemophilia Prog.; Cons. Physician, Children's Psych. Rsch. Inst.; Cons. privileges, Univ. Hosp., Victoria Hosp., Cons., O.C.F., London and Reg. Cancer Ctr.; Royal Army Med. Corps 1953–55; Intern, St. Joseph's Hosp. 1969–70; Clin. Rsch. Fellow 1970–72; Sr. Res. & Rsch. Fellow, McMaster Univ. 1972–73; Sr. Res., UWO 1973–74; Lectr., Asst. & Assoc. Prof., UWO & var. posts, St. Joseph's Hosp. 1974–80; num. degrees, diplomas, rsch. grants & awards; mem. of 28 local prov., nat. & internat. soc.; num. current & past extve. ctte. posts (soc., univ. & hosp.) 1974– ; extensive lectr.; author of 21 book chapters, 114 articles, and num. abstracts; recreations: antique autos; antiques; Address: 1358 Brookline Rd., London, Ont. N5X 2R6; Office: 268 Grosvenor St., London, Ont. N6A 4V2.

**IONIDES, Rudolf John,** B.Sc., M.Eng.; executive; b. Nicosia, Cyprus 14 Jan. 1937; s. John and Edith I.; e. Glasgow Univ. B.Sc. 1960; McGill Univ. M.Eng. 1964; m. Jean d. Mike and Helen Charal 29 May 1969; children: Rudolf Jr., Eleni; PRES. & DIR., BECHTEL CANADA INC. 1987– ; Sr. Vice Pres., Bechtel Corp. 1989; Dir., Bantrel Inc.; Pres., Bechtel Quebec Ltée; Bechtel Found. of Canada; Chief Elec. Eng. Cyprus Mines, Cyprus 1960–62; Project Eng. MECO Montreal 1964–65; Chief Elec. Supr. GECO Toronto 1965–69; Sr. Elec. Supr., Asst. Project Eng. and Chief Elec. Eng. Canadian Bechtel Ltd. Montreal 1969–74; Exec. Vice Pres. Devel. & Constrn. International Plaza Ltd. Vancouver 1974–76; Project Mgr. present Co. 1976 becoming Eng. Mgr. and Mgr. Projects & Eng., Pres. and Dir.; mem. Assn. Prof. Engs. Provs. Que., Ont., B.C. and Alta.; Eng. Inst. Can.; Candn. Inst. Mining, Metallurgy and Petroleum; Bus. Couns. on Nat. Issues; Greek Orthodox; Home: 139 Abbeywood Trail, North York, Ont. M3B 3B6; Office: 12 Concorde Place, Suite 200, North York, Ont. M3C 3T1.

**IP, Irene Kellow,** B.A., M.A.; economist; b. London, England 21 May 1934; d. the late Thomas Edwin and Emily May (Crooke) Kellow; e. Notre Dame H.S. (U.K.) 1950; Toronto Teachers' Coll. Cert. 1958; Trent Univ. B.A. (Hons.) 1975; Univ. of Toronto M.A. 1976; m. Anthony s. Philip and Maria Ip 30 April 1960; children: Michael, David, Gregory, Claire; RESEARCH ADVISER, BANK OF CANADA 1993– ; Elementary Sch. Teacher 1958–64; Rsch. Asst., Econ. Dept., Trent Univ. 1973–74; Economist, Wood Gundy Inc. 1976–88 (Chief Forecaster 1979–88; Asst. Vice-Pres. 1980; Vice-Pres. 1984); Sr. Policy Analyst, C.D. Howe Inst. 1988–93; Mem., Edit. Bd., Candn. Business Econ. 1992– ; Mem., Bd. of Dir., Toronto Assn. of Bus. Econ. 1990–93; Sessional Lectr., Dept. of Econ., Univ. of Toronto 1987; Occasional Guest Lectr., Brock Univ.; Canada Council Spec. M.A. Scholarship 1975–76; Symons Medal, Trent Univ. 1975; Gov., Trent Univ. 1973–75; Roman Catholic; Mem., Catholic Conf. on Devel. & Peace; author: 'Big Spenders: Provincial Government Finances in Canada' 1991, 'Strong Medicine: Budgeting for Recession and Recovery' 1991; co-author: 'Dividing the Spoils: The Federal-Provincial Allocation of Taxing Powers' 1992; 'A Partnership in Trouble: Renegotiating Fiscal Federalism' 1993; editor: 'Roundup' 1982–88; author/co-author of num. articles, book chapters, commentaries, reports; recreations: theology, hiking, classical music; Home: 111 Wurtemburg St., Apt. 1005, Ottawa, Ont. K1N 8M1.

**IPEELEE, Osuitok,** R.C.A.; artist; b. 23 Oct. 1923; m. Nipisha; medium: sculpture, prints; 80 group exhbns. incl. most recent: Winnipeg Art Gall. 1992, The McMichael Candn. Art Collection Kleinburg, Ont. 1991–92, Inuit Gall. of Vancouver 1990, 1991, Vancouver Inuit Art Soc. 1991, Arctic Inuit Art Richmond, Va. 1991, Virginia Mus. of Fine Arts Richmond, Va. 1990–91, Feheley Fine Arts Toronto 1990, Candn. Mus. of Civilization Hull, Que. 1990; solo exhbns.: Eskimo Art

Gall. Toronto 1987, Feheley Fine Arts 1987, Inuit Galerie Mannheim, Germany 1983, Theo Waddington, N.Y. 1979, 1980, Pucker/Safrai Gall., Boston, Mass. 1978, Waddington Galleries Toronto 1978, Candn. Guild of Crafts Que. Montreal 1973; works in 29 collections incl. art galleries of Nova Scotia, Ontario (Klamer Family & Sarick colls.), Winnipeg (Hudson's Bay Co. & Twomey colls.), Canada Council Art Bank Ottawa, Candn. Mus. of Civilization Hull, Que., National Gallery of Can. Ottawa, Inuit Cultural Inst. Rankin Inlet, N.W.T., Metro. Mus. of Art N.Y., Nunatta Sunaqutangit Mus. Iqaluit, N.W.T.; comnd. to carve figures on mace of N.W.T. 1955; created carving of H.R.H. Queen Elizabeth (presented to her on the occasion of her visit to Can.) 1959; comnd. by Public Works Canada to create inukshuk at External Affairs H.Q. 1970; attended openings at 'Sculpture / Inuit' Leningrad 1972, solo exhbn. Candn. Guild of Crafts Que. 1973, inuit exhbn. Sydney, Australia 1973, Klamer exhbn. of Inuit art, Art Gall. of Ont. (awarded travel grant) 1983, Nat. Gall of Canada (gala opening) 1988; R.C.A. 1973; subject of several articles and catalogues; Home: Cape Dorset, N.W.T.; Office: c/o Dorset Fine Arts, 33 Belmont St., Toronto, Ont. M5R 1P9.

**IPPERSIEL, Fernand,** B.A.; writer; b. Cheneville, Qué. 6 Apl. 1921; s. Victor and Alice (Blais) I.; e. Univ. of Ottawa B.A. 1944; m. Alma d. André Provencher 6 July 1944; children: Roger, Gérard, Andrée, Jean-Luc, Roch; served newspaper 'Frontière' Rouyn, Qué. 1945; radio stns. CKRN Rouyn 1946–47, CHFA Edmonton 1949–51, CFNS Saskatoon 1952–56, Radio-Can. (TV) Montréal 1956–84; author 'Les Cousins ennemis' 1990; 'G.E. Cartier' forthcoming; mem. Soc. St-Jean Baptiste; Retraités de Radio-Can.; Parti Québécois; recreations: cinema, reading; Address: 1025 Sherbrooke St. E., Montréal, Qué. H2L 1L4.

**IQULIQ, Tuna;** sculptor; b. near Baker Lake, N.W.T. 1935; children: Johnny, Louie, Camille; 53 group exbns. incl.: 'The Art of Keewatin' Arctic Artistry, N.Y. 1993; 'Drawings and Sculpture from Baker Lake' Winnipeg Art Gall. 1992/1993; 'Art Inuit' Galerie Maite Aubert 1991; 'Animals of the Arctic' Richmond, VA 1991; Beeldhouwkunst van de Inuit (Canada) by l'Iglou Art Esquimau, Douai, France at Amphora Finippon pvba, Sint Andries, Brugge, Belgium 1990; 'Baffin Images' Orca Aart, Chicago IL 1989; 'Art of the Eskimo: Contemporary Sculpture & Drawings from the Canadian Arctic' Gallery 100 Hudson, N.Y. 1988; 'Tundra & Ice: Stone Images of Animals and Man' Adventurers' Club, Chicago, IL 1988; 'Sixty Diminutive Eskimo Carvings' Images of the North, San Francisco, CA 1986; 'Arctic Vision: Art of the Canadian Inuit' Dept. of Indian Affairs and Northern Development and Candn. Arctic Producers, Ottawa, Ont. 1984–86; 'Baker Lake - Sculpture and Wallhangings' Candn. Guild of Crafts Québec 1981; 'Sculpture of the Inuit: Masterwork Exhibitors of the Canadian Arctic' Inuit Gall. of Vancouver 1979; 'Sheokju of Cape Dorset & Eleven Sculptors of Baker Lake' Victor Waddington Gall., London, Eng. 1977; 'INUA: 50 Works from the Cappadocia Collection of Inuit Art' McMaster Art Gall., Hamilton, Ont. 1972; 'Sculpture/Inuit: Masterworks of the Canadian Arctic' Candn. Eskimo Arts Council, Ottawa, Ont. 1971–73; 'Arctic Values '65' New Brunswick Museum; 'Eskimo Carvers of Keewatin, N.W.T.' Winnipeg Art Gall. 1964; solo exbns.: Inuit Galerie, Mannheim, Germany 1981; The Guild Shop, Toronto 1979; The Innuit Gall. of Eskimo Art, Toronto 1977; collections: art galleries of Ontario (Sarick & Williamson colls.) and Winnipeg (Millard, Swinton & Twomey colls.); Candn. Mus. of Civilization; Dennos Mus. Ctr., N.W. Michigan Coll., Traverse City, Mich.; Eskimo Mus., Churchill, Man.; Inuit Cultural Inst. Rankin Inlet, N.W.T.; Nat. Gallery of Can.; Winnipeg Art Gall.; subject of numerous selected references; Home: Baker Lake, N.W.T.; Office: c/o Candn. Arctic Producers, 1645 Inkster Blvd., Winnipeg, Man. R2X 2W7.

**IRANI, Ray R.,** B.S., Ph.D.; energy executive; b. Beirut, Lebanon 15 Jan. 1935; s. Rida and Naz I.; e. American Univ. B.S. (summa cum laude) 1953; Univ. of Southern Cal. Ph.D. 1957; m. Ghada; children: Glenn R., Lillian M., Martin R.; CHAIR, PRES. & CHIEF EXECUTIVE OFFICER, OCCIDENTAL PETROLEUM CORP. 1990– ; various executive positions, Olin Copr. Chemicals Group 1973–80; C.O.O., Olin Corp. 1981–83; Pres. & Dir. 1980–83; Extve. Vice-Pres., Occidental Petroleum 1983–84 ; C.E.O., Occidental Chem. Corp. (now OxyChem) 1980–91 (Chair 1980– ); Dir., Occidental Petroleum Corp. 1984– ; Pres. & C.O.O. 1984–90; Chair, Candn. Occidental Petroleum Ltd. 1987– ; Dir., Nat. Asn. of Mfrs.; Am. Petroleum Inst.; Kaufman & Broad Inc.; Mem., Nat. Petroleum Council; Am. Inst. of Chemists; Am. Chem. Soc.; Sci. Rsch. Soc. of Am.; Industrial Rsch. Inst.; Conf. Bd.; Calif. Business Roundtable; Am. Inst. of Chem. Hon. Fellow Award 1983; Polytechnic Univ. Creative Tech. Award 1988; Chem. Mktg. Rsch. Assn. Man of the Year Award 1990; Trustee, Univ. of S. Calif. & Mem., C.E.O. Bd. of Advisers, USC Sch. of Bus. Admin.; Trustee, Am. Univ. of Beirut; Nat. Hist. Museum of L.A.; St. John's Hosp. & Med. Ctr. of Santa Monica; Mem., Bd. of Gov., Los Angeles Town Hall; World Affairs Council; author: 'Particle Size' 1963 and over 50 tech. papers; Office: 10889 Wilshire Blvd., Los Angeles, CA 90024.

**IRELAND, Denise;** artist; b. Manchester, England 1949; e. Ont. Coll. of Art; solo exhibitions incl.: Annual Solo Show, Nancy Poole's Studio 1979–89, Exhib. of Drawings 1986; Algoma Pub. Lib. 1984; Rodman Hall Pub. Gall. 1983; MacKenzie Gall., Trent Univ. 1982; Upper Level Gall. North Bay 1981; St. Lawrence Coll. Gall. Kingston 1980; Durham Pub. Lib. & Art Gall. 1980; ten others in the 1970s; collections: Robert McLaughlin Pub. Gall.; The Queen's Silver Jubilee Art Coll.; Canada Council Art Bank; MacKenzie Gall. & Peter Robinson Coll., Trent Univ.; St. Lawrence Coll. Gall.; Winnipeg Art Gall.; Norcen Corp. Coll.; Vanguard Trust Corp.; Canadore Coll. North Bay; Burnaby Art Gall.; Crown Life Corp.; Univ. of Guelph Art Gall.; McCarthy & McCarthy Corp. Coll.; Westinghouse Can.; Halifax Insur. Co. Toronto; E. York Bd. of Edn. Pub. Coll.; General Electric Canada; awards: Canada Council Jury 1984; Ontario Arts Council Grant 1980; Canada Council Arts Bursary 1975–76; Office: c/o Nancy Poole's Studio, 16 Hazelton Ave., Toronto, Ont. M5R 2E2.

**IRELAND, James Arthur;** art director; b. York, Yorks., Eng. 1 July 1945; s. Arthur and Margaret (Early) I.; e. St. George's Sch. York; York Sch. of Art; Brighton Coll. of Art Nat. Dip. of Design 1965; m. Patricia d. James and Phyllis Towers 14 July 1972; children: Elizabeth, Christopher; FOUNDER, JAMES IRELAND DESIGN INC. 1989– ; Art Dir., Imperial Oil Review, Chatelaine, Edn. Forum, Physician's Guide, FirstBank News, U of T Magazine; served as Art Dir. various mags. and newspapers incl. Maclean's, Toronto Life, Canadian Art, Globe and Mail and affiliated mags.; taught mag. design Ryerson Sch. of Journalism, Banff Pub. Workshop, Candn. Periodical Pub. Assn.; recipient numerous Art Dirs. Club Toronto Awards, Nat. Mag. Awards; recreations: fishing, painting; Home: 35 Petman Ave., Toronto, Ont. M4S 2S9; Office: Suite 400, 145 Berkeley St., Toronto, Ont. M5A 2X1.

**IRELAND, William Edmund,** Q.C., B.A., LL.B.; lawyer; b. Winnipeg, Manitoba 23 Mar. 1934; s. Brian Warren and Emma Georgina (MacNachtan) I.; e. Univ. of Man. B.A. 1955; Manitoba Law Sch. LL.B. 1959; m. Heather Alda d. Johannes and Bergljot Sigurdson 10 Aug. 1962; children: William David, Signy Margaret, Erik Brian; PARTNER, OWEN, BIRD 1970– ; Assoc. & Partner, Pitblado & Hoskin Winnipeg 1959–70; Chrmn., Empire Stevedoring Co. Ltd.; Empire Internat. Stevedores Ltd.; Dir., Greyhound Lines of Canada Ltd.; Motor Coach Industries Ltd.; Fletcher Challenge Investments II Inc.; Q.C. (B.C.) 1984; Past Chrmn./Trustee, B.C. Cancer Agency; Counc. of University Teaching Hospitals; Mem., Finance Ctte., Science World; Anglican, Lambda Alpha International, Phi Delta Theta Fraternity; recreations: reading, skiing, cycling, boating, windsurfing; club: Burrard Yacht; Home: 940 Younette Dr., W. Vancouver, B.C. V7T 1S9; Office: P.O. Box 49130, 595 Burrard St., Vancouver, B.C. V7X 1J5.

**IRISH, Maureen Frances,** B.A., LL.B., LL.M., D.C.L.; educator; b. Simcoe, Ont. 28 Oct. 1949; d. Raymond Francis and Bernice Norma (Stevens) I.; e. Univ. of Toronto, Victoria Coll. B.A. 1970, LL.B. 1974; McGill Univ. LL.M. 1982, D.C.L. 1992; ASSOC. PROF. OF LAW, UNIV. OF WINDSOR 1984– ; called to Bar of Ont. 1976; private practice Ottawa 1976–78; Teaching Asst. in Law McGill Univ. 1979–80; Asst. Prof. present Univ. 1980–84; author 'Customs Valuation in Canada' 1985; co-ed. 'The Legal Framework for Canada-United States Trade' 1987; Office: Windsor, Ont. N9B 3P4.

**IRVINE, Rev. Donald Fredrick,** Ph.D.; educator; b. Vancouver, B.C. 31 July 1934; s. Arthur Donald and Beatrice Margaret (Brown) I.; e. Univ. of W. Ont. B.A. 1960; Huron Coll. B.Th. 1962; Univ. of Waterloo M.A. 1966, Ph.D. 1978; m. the late Joyce Reid d. Elizabeth Spanier 20 Sept. 1958; children: Karl Frederick, Kathryn Elizabeth, Peter Andrew; Prof. of Philos., of Religion and Ethics and mem. Corp. Huron Coll. 1976–90; former Acad. Dean of Theology, Huron Coll.; o. Deacon 1962; Priest (Ang.) 1963; Assoc. Priest, St. Aidan's Ch. Windsor, Ont. 1962–65 and Ch. of the Holy Saviour Waterloo, Ont. 1965–68; Lectr. present Coll. 1968; Associate, The Institute of Public Administration of Canada; mem., The Candn. Centre for Ethics and Corporate Policy; mem. Bd. and Corp. London Pastoral Inst. 1982–90; Candn. Philos. Assn.; Dir. and Fellow, Assn. Case Teaching; Soc. Christian Philosophers; recreation: calligraphy; Home: 856 Berkshire Dr., London, Ont. N6J 3S7; Office: London, Ont. N6G 1H3.

**IRVINE, Donald Grant,** M.A., Ph.D.; research scientist; b. Victoria, B.C. 28 Oct. 1930; s. Roy Milne and Helen Georgina (Grant) I.; e. Gordon Head and Mt. Douglas High Schs. Victoria; Victoria Coll.; Univ. of B.C. B.A. 1952, M.A. 1954; Univ. of Sask. Ph.D. 1981; m. Isabelle d. Clive and Fannie Davis 4 Sept. 1954; children: Ian Douglas, Rosalee Anne, Kenneth Duncan; SR. RSCH. SCI., TOXICOLOGY RSCH. CENTRE, UNIV. OF SASK. 1990– , Rsch. Sci., Toxicology Rsch. Centre, Univ. of Sask. 1983–90, Adjunct Prof. of Toxicology Faculty of Grad. Studies & Rsch. 1985– ; Rsch. Asst. in Zoology Univ. of B.C. 1952–54; Rsch. Asst. in Physiol. Univ. of Sask. 1954–58, Rsch. Assoc. in Psychiatry, Univ. of Sask. 1969–72; Rsch. Sci. Psychiatric Rsch. Div. Sask. Health 1958–83; cons. various univs., govts. and ind. toxicology; recipient various undergrad. and grad. awards; mem. Saskatoon Opera Assn. (Dir. 1983–87); Trustee, Gustin/Trounce Heritage Trust (Inaugural 1989); discovered and documented oldest remaining bldg. in Saskatoon and initiated preservation as heritage property; co-author 'You and Toxicology' 1986; author or co-author numerous papers, tech. reports, book chapters; ed. proceedings 5 sci. meetings; Life mem. World Assn. Theoretical Organic Chemists; Soc. Env. Geochem. & Health; mem., Sask. Soc. Clin. Chems. (Sec.-Treas. 1981–82); Soc. Toxicol. Can.; Candn. Biochem. Soc.; Air & Waste Mgmt. Assn.; Saskatoon Heritage Soc.; Soc. of Env. Toxicology and Chemistry - Europe (SETAC); Internat. Soc. Reg. Tox. & Pharm.; ASTM; recreations: historical archaeology, gardening, travel; Club: Rotary; Home: 144 Salisbury Dr., Saskatoon, Sask. S7H 3J7; Office: Saskatoon, Sask. S7N 0W0.

**IRVINE, Marie A.,** LL.B.; lawyer; b. Walrous, Sask. 20 Feb. 1948; d. Thomas and Mary Grant (MacDonald) I.; e. Osgoode Hall Law Sch. LL.B. 1980; married; one d.: Tracy; SOUTHERN ALBERTA DIR., CHILDREN'S ADVOCATE OFFICE 1991– ; Extve. Dir., Canadian Foundation for Children, Youth & The Law 1983–91; Mem., Law Soc. of U.C.; Candn. Bar Assn.; Nat. Assn. of Counsel for Children; Calgary Assn. of Women and the Law; editor: 'Justice for Children & Youth' newsletter; contbr.: 'In Trouble With the Law,' 'Canadian Women's Legal Guide'; author of numerous briefs on youth legal issues; Home: 1026 Centre Ave. N.E., Calgary, Alta.; Office: 406 - 301 14th St. N.W., Calgary, Alta. T2N 2A1.

**IRVING, Edward,** M.A., Sc.D., F.R.A.S., F.R.S.C., F.R.S.; Emeritus research scientist; b. Colne, Eng. 27 May 1927; s. George Edward and Nellie (Petty) I.; e. Colne Grammar Sch. 1945; Univ. of Cambridge B.A. 1950, M.A. 1957, Sc.D. 1965; Carleton Univ. D.Sc. 1979; Memorial Univ., Nfld., D.Sc. 1986; m. Sheila Ann d. William Arthur Irwin, Victoria, B.C. 23 Sept. 1957; children: Kathryn Jean, Susan Patricia, Martin Edward, George Andrew; EMERITUS RESEARCH SCIENTIST, PACIFIC GEOSCIENCE CENTRE, SIDNEY, B.C. 1992– ; Adjunct Prof. and Part-time Lectr., Carleton Univ. 1967–81; Rsch. Scientist, Pacific Geoscience Centre, Sidney, B.C. 1981–92; Adjunct Prof., Univ. of Victoria 1985– ; Rsch. Fellow, Fellow and Sr. Fellow Dept. of Geophysics Australian National University 1954–64; Research Offr. Mines and Tech. Surveys, Ottawa 1964–66; Prof. of Geophysics, Univ. of Leeds 1966–67; Research Scientist, Earth Physics Br., Dept. Energy, Mines and Resources, Ottawa, 1967–81; served with Brit. Army 1945–48, 2 yrs. Middle E.; awarded: Christien Mica Gondwanaland Medal, Mining Geol. & Metall. Inst. of India 1960–62; Logan Medal Geol. Assn. Can. 1975; Walter H. Bucher Medal, Am. Geophysical Union 1979; Wilson Medal, Candn. Geophysical Union 1984; author 'Paleomagnetism and Its Application to Geological and Geophysical Problems' 1964; author numerous articles scient. journs.; Hon. Fellow, Geol. Soc. London; Fellow, Am. Geophys. Union; mem. Geol. Assn. Can.; Candn. Geophys. Union; United Church; recreations: gardening, singing, carpentry; Home: 9363 Carnoustie Cres., R.R.2, Sidney, B.C. V8L 5G7; Office: Pacific Geoscience Centre, 9860 West Saanich Rd., P.O. Box 6000, Sidney, B.C. V8L 4B2.

**IRVING, Harold Alexander,** B.A., M.A.; executive; b. Calgary, Alta. 4 Mar. 1927; s. Frederick Lorne and Elizabeth (MacBeth) I.; e. West. Canada H.S.; Univ. of Alta.; McGill Univ. B.A.; Univ. of Calgary M.A.; m. Sheila d. Jack and June Copeland 11 Jan. 1973; children: Harold Alexander, Frederick Lorne (dec.), Jill, Polly,

Sally, Julie; PRESIDENT, IRVING HOLDINGS LTD. 1954– ; IRVING INDUSTRIES (IRVING WIRE PRODUCTS DIV.) LTD.; Pres. and Dir., H.A.I Resources Inc.; Dir., Irvco Resources, Irvco Industries Inc.; Munich Reinsurance Co.; Munich Canada Mgmnt. Corp. Ltd.; Great Lakes Reins. Co. of Can.; Great Lakes Reinsurance Holdings Ltd.; Past Chrmn. & Dir., Can-Al Pipeline System, PA U.S.A; Past Dir., Lake Louise Lifts; Nova Corp.; Alberta Gas Ethylene; Roughneck, Pacific Petroleums 1952; Landman, Shell Oil Co. 1952–53; Past Vice-Pres. & Dir. Calgary C. of C.; Past Gov. Univ. of Calgary; mem. The Associates, Univ. of Calgary; Past Regional VP, McGill Grad. Soc.; Past Chrmn., Calgary McGill Advancement; founding mem. and past Chrmn. Alta. Chapter, Young Pres's Orgn.; Past Chrmn. and Dir. Woods Christian Homes for Children; Past Chrmn. (Corporate) Calgary United Appeal; Sidesman, St. Peters Anglican Church; played profl. and college football: quarterback and co-captain McGill (League Winners) Allstar 1951; captain and quarterback, Univ. of Alta. Golden Bears (undef.); captain and quarterback, Calgary West-End Tornadoes Jr. Football Team (undef. 1945 & 1946); Team Mem. (quarterback and defensive half back) 1948 Calgary Stampeders (undef.); played hockey Univ. of Alta. Golden Bears, Halpenny Trophy winners 1949, and McGill Redmen 1950–51; played horse polo 1954–74 (Team Member, Calgary Polo Club, winners Pacific N.W. Tournament, Portland, Oregon 1956); mem. Delta Upsilon; recreations: golfing, hiking, skiing, swimming, skating; Clubs: Glencoe, Ranchmen's, Calgary Golf and Country, Calgary Petroleum, Calgary Polo; Home: 1002 - 32 Ave. S.W., Calgary, Alta. T2T 1V3; Banff Residence: 123 Grizzly St., Banff, Alta.; Ranch: Priddis, Alta.; Office: 709 - 7015 Macleod Trail S.W., Calgary, Alta. T2H 2K6.

**IRVING, Howard H.,** B.S., M.S.W., Ph.D.; b. Providence, R.I. 4 July 1936; s. Samuel and Sylvia (Rosensweet) I.; e. Univ. of Rhode Isl., B.S. 1960; Univ. of Connecticut, M.S.W. 1962; Univ. of Toronto, Ph.D. 1970; m. Fahla d. Phil and Shirley Granovsky 26 July 1981; children: Jonathan, Jennifer, Adam, Jay; PROF., FAC. OF SOCIAL WORK, UNIV. OF TORONTO 1970– , Lectr. Fac. of Law, Univ. of Toronto: Pres., Family Mediation Can.; Dir., Ctr. for Dispute Resolution; Former Rsch. Dir., Shared Parenting Project; Ed. Bd. Mem., 'Canadian Family Law Quarterly' 'Canadian Journal of Family Law'; Director, Family Mediation cert. Prog., Univ. of Toronto; Laidlaw Fellowship; Health & Welfare Fellowship; Past Bd. Mem., Big Brothers Assn.; Couns. Mem., Am. Assn. of Marriage and Family; Coll. of Profl. Social Serv.; author: 'The Family Myth' 1972, 'Divorce Mediation' 1980, 'Family Law: An Interdisciplinary Approach' 1981; co-author: 'Family Mediation: Theory and Practice' 1986; Home: 285 Glengrove Ave. W., Toronto, Ont. M5N 1W3; Office: 304 St. Clair Ave. W., Toronto, Ont. M4V 1S3.

**IRVING, Janet Turnbull,** B.A., M.A.; literary agent; b. Toronto, Ont. 16 Apr. 1954; d. Donald Gibson and Joan Heloise (Kitchen) T.; e. Bishop Strachan Sch. 1973; Univ. of Toronto B.A. 1978, M.A. 1979; m. John Irving 1987; PRES., THE TURNBULL AGENCY 1987– ; Pres., Curtis Brown Canada Ltd. 1989– ; Editor, Bantam Canada Inc.; Founding Pres., The Candn. Business Task Force on Literacy; Editor, Authors' Marketing Services Ltd. 1979; Editor, Doubleday Canada Ltd. 1980, Mng. Editor 1981; Vice-Pres., Publisher & Dir., Seal Books 1984–87; Office: 200 First Ave., Toronto, Ont. M4M 1X1.

**IRWIN, Colin John, M.A., Ph.D.;** research fellow; explorer; b. Eastbourne, Eng. 22 May 1946; s. Gerald and Lillian (Fautly) I.; e. St. Peters Sch. Bournemouth, Eng.; Univ. of Man. M.A. 1981; Syracuse Univ. Ph.D. 1985; m. Theresa d. Kako and Aupudluck 1 May 1974; children: Ookpik, Mellisa, Christina; designed and lived in first underwater house with self contained artificial atmosphere for one week at depth of 30 feet in Plymouth Sound 1965; salvaged 4000 yr. old dugout canoe Poole Harbour and served as diving instr. Red Sea 1966–67; built yacht to sail through N.W. Passage 1970 and began voyage from central Alaska 1971; after wintering in Cambridge Bay, N.W.T. crossed Arctic N. Am. from Hudson Bay to Alaska by dog team and canoe 1973; sailed to Belliot Straits 1975 est. record furthest single-handed sailing of yacht without auxiliary power through N.W. Passage; Special Adv. to Keewatin Inuit Assn. 1977; Killam Fellow Dalhousie Univ. 1985; completed study social and econ. conditions Candn. Inuit for Min. of Health & Welfare 1988 and apptd. Hon. Rsch. Fellow Queen's Univ. Belfast; recipient Brit. Sub-Aqua Club Duke of Edinburgh Sci. Award 1966; Royal Cruising Club Medal 1978; SSHRC awards 1980–81, 1981–85, 1987–89; Killam Fellowship 1985–87; recreations: sailing, diving, arctic travel, hunting; Home: Chesterfield Inlet, N.W.T. X0C 0B0; Office: Dept. of Social Anthropology, The Queen's Univ. of Belfast, Belfast BT7 1NN Northern Ireland.

**IRWIN, (Marjorie) Eleanor Gray ,** M.A., Ph.D.; educator; b. Toronto, Ont. 29 Apl. 1937; d. Joseph Everard and Gladys (Malcolm) Gray; e. Jarvis Coll. Inst.; Univ. of Toronto, Univ. Coll. B.A. 1959, M.A. 1960, Ph.D. 1967; m. John W. s. John C.W. and Annie Elizabeth Irwin 16 Dec. 1961; children: John Joseph, Marjorie Elizabeth, Peter David Gordon, Andrew James Gray; ASSOC. PROFESSOR OF CLASSICS, SCARBOROUGH COLL., UNIV. OF TORONTO 1973– ; Asst. Prof. Div. of Humanities present Coll. 1968, Assoc. Chair of Humanities 1980–82, Chair Coll. Council 1984–85, Assoc. Dean (Acad.) 1985–88; Vice Prin. and Assoc. Dean Scarborough Coll., Univ. of Toronto 1989–93, Assmem. Council Ont. Univs. 1986–88; Chair, Internat. Service Fellowship 1984–92; Candn. Bapt. Fedn. Council 1985– ; Chs. Council Theol. Edn. 1986–92; author 'Colour Terms in Greek Poetry' 1974; mem. Classical Assn. Can.; Candn. Soc. Patristic Studies; recreation: botany; Home: 81 Bayview Ridge, Willowdale, Ont. M2L 1E3; Office: 1265 Military Trail, Scarborough, Ont. M1C 1A4.

**IRWIN, George MacDonald,** B.A.; executive; b. Toronto, Ont. 3 May 1950; s. Samuel MacDonald and Elinor Jane (Somerville) I.; e. Ridley Coll. St. Catharines, Ont.; Univ. of W. Ont. B.A. 1972; m. Susan d. Donald and Marjorie McQuigge 6 Oct. 1975; two s. George Douglas, Peter Andrew; PRES., IRWIN TOY LTD. 1991– ; Dir., Irwin Toy Ltd.; Salesman present Co. 1972, Product Mgr. 1975, Group Product Mgr. 1977; Vice Pres. 1983–91; Dir. Ridley Coll.; Clubs: Toronto Golf; Osler Bluff Ski; Badminton & Racquet; Home: 230 Inglewood Dr., Toronto, Ont. M4T 1J1; Office: 43 Hanna Ave., Toronto, Ont. M6K 1X6.

**IRWIN, Grace Lillian,** M.A., D.Litt.S. (Hon.); speaker, writer; b. Toronto, Ont. 14 July 1907; d. John and Martha (Fortune) Irwin; e. Parkdale Coll. Inst., Toronto, Ont.; Victoria Coll., Univ. of Toronto, B.A. 1929 and M.A. 1932; Teacher of Latin, English, Hist. at Humberside Coll. Inst., Toronto, Ont., 1931–42 and Head of Latin and Greek Dept. there 1942–69; Co-pastor, Emmanuel Congregational Christian Ch. 1974– ; Pastor, o. 1980–87; author: 'Least of All Saints' (novel) 1952; 'Andrew Connington' (novel) 1954; 'In Little Place' (novel) 1959; 'Servant of Slaves' (biog. novel) 1961; 'Contend With Horses' (novel) 1968; 'The Seventh Earl' (biog. novel) 1976; 'Three Lives in Mine' (biography) 1986; contrib. of poems in 'Little Songs for Little People' and of occasional poems and articles to mags.; Past Pres., Toronto Classical Club; mem. Extve. Comte., Ont. Classical Assn.; Candn. Classical Assn.; Senate, Univ. of Toronto 1952–56; Mem. Bd. Cons. Cong. Christian Churches of Am. 1987–89; awarded Centennial Medal 1968; D.Litt.S., Victoria College (honoris causa) 1991; Christian; Home: 33 Glenwood Ave., Toronto, Ont. M6P 3C7.

**IRWIN, Janet Elizabeth,** B.A., B.Ed.; theatre director; educator; writer; b. Cornwall, Ont. 10 Oct. 1947; d. Ernest George and Helen Elizabeth (MacLachlan) I.; e. Queen's Univ. B.A. 1969; Univ. of Toronto B.Ed. 1970; m. Gordon Victor s. John and Ella Cullingham 13 Jan. 1988; Teacher, Lawrence Park Coll. Inst. Toronto 1970–71; Cornwall 1972–76; Glebe Coll., Ottawa 1987; Ottawa Sch. of Speech and Drama; freelance dir.: Great Canadian Theatre Co., Nat. Arts Centre; J-B Theatre Co-op., Univ. of Ottawa, Easy Street Prodns.; Upper Can. Playhouse Morrisburg; Man. Popular Theatre Alliance Winnipeg; mem. arts award juries Can. Council (Explorations), Ont. Arts Council; Co-founder, Another Shakespeare Project; Co-Prod., Ottawa Shakespeare Festival (1992 inaugural season); Co-founder, Rideau Watch (cassette heritage tours 'Talking up the Rideau,' 'Talking up the Ottawa,' 'Talking up the St. Lawrence'); author: 'Side Effects' play 1985; co-author: 'Easy Avenue' (play) 1990; 'A Seaway Story' (play) 1993; mem. Candn. Actors Equity Assn.; Theatre Ont. 'Talent Bank'; recreations: boating, touring; Address: 6, 325 Clemow Ave., Ottawa, Ont. K1S 2B7.

**IRWIN, John Wesley,** B.A.; book publisher; b. Toronto, Ont. 11 July 1937; s. John Coverdale Watson and Annie Elizabeth (Hiltz) I.; e. Whitney Pub. Sch. Toronto 1949; Pickering (Ont.) High Sch. 1955; Univ. Coll. Univ. of Toronto B.A. 1959; m. Marjorie Eleanor, Ph.D. d. Joseph Everard Gray 16 Dec. 1961; children: John Joseph, Marjorie Elizabeth (Robertson), Peter David Gordon, Andrew James Gray; PUBLISHING CONSULTANT 1988– ; Dir., Frederick Harris Music Co. Ltd.; teacher 1959–60; joined Irwin Publishing Inc. 1960, Gen. Mgr. 1967–71, Pres., 1971–88; Chrmn. Candn. Copyright Inst. 1982, 1984–90; Treas. Assn. Candn. Publishers 1977, Dir. 1973–86; Trustee and Senate Mem., (and Vice Chrmn., Bd. of Trustees 1987, Chrmn. 1988– ) McMaster Divinity Coll., Hamilton 1985– ; Inter-Varsity Christian Fellowship, Dir. 1973, Chrmn. 1979–91; mem. Finance Comte., Internat. Fellowship of Evangelical Students 1981– ; Chair, Bd. of Dirs., Candn. Feed the Children 1992– ; awarded Centennial Medal 1967; Baptist; recreation: sailing; Clubs: Peiromai; Empire; Address: 81 Bayview Ridge, Willowdale, Ont. M2L 1E3.

**IRWIN, Neal Alexander,** B.A.Sc., P.Eng.; consulting engineer; b. Toronto, Ont. 2 Jan. 1932; s. William Arthur and Jean Olivia (Smith) I.; e. N. Toronto Coll. Inst. 1950; Univ. of Toronto, B.A.Sc. (Engn.-Physics) 1955; m. Carol Anne, d. Dr. J. H. Howson; children: Christine Alice, Anne Olivia, Arthur Campion, Alexander James Howard; MANAGING DIR., IBI GROUP; Chrmn. InterBase Inc.; Pres. N.A. Irwin Consulting Ltd.; Nuclear Power Stn. Designer, English Electric Co., U.K. 1955–57; Nuclear Power Design Engr. Atomic Energy of Can. Ltd. and several other Candn. cos. 1957–60; Sr. Project Engr., Traffic Research Corp.; Vice-Pres. i.c. U.S. operations Traffic Research Corp. (subsidiary co.) 1961–66; Extve. Vice-Pres. KCS Ltd. 1966; Sr. Partner, Kates, Peat, Marwick & Co. (merger) 1967–74; formed own firm of Neal A. Irwin Ltd. and apptd. Sr. Partner, IBI Group 1974– ; Partner, Beinhaker/Irwin Associates, Architects, Engineers and Planners 1974– ; with Univ. Naval Training Div. 1950–53, Acting Sub-Lt. RCN(R); Fellow, Inst. Traffic Engrs.; past Chrmn., Technical Counc., Roads and Transportation Assoc. of Can.; mem., Urban Transportation Council, Transportation Assn. of Canada; Past Treas., Counsulting Engrs. of Ont.; Past Pres., Candn. Transp. Research Forum; Chrmn., Transportation Policy Ctte., Assn. of Consulting Engineers of Canada; mem. Assn. Prof. Engrs. Ont.; Candn. Soc. of Civil Engrs.; Phi Gamma Delta (Pres. 1955); recreations: music, athletics, building; Home: 18 Lawrence Cres., Toronto, Ont. M4N 1N1; Office: 230 Richmond St. W., Toronto, Ont. M5V 1V6.

**IRWIN, Patrick Hamilton,** F.C.M.C., C.A.; management consultant; b. Montreal, Que. 6 Feb. 1923; s. W. Eric C. and Caroline (Guthrie) I.; e. Westmount (Que.) High Sch. 1941; C.A. 1947; Harvard Advanced Mang. Program 1964; PRES., PATRICK H. IRWIN CONSULTING SERVICES INC. 1983– ; joined McDonald, Currie & Co. 1941, Partner 1951; trans. to Urwick, Currie Ltd. on its formation 1955 (now Coopers & Lybrand Consulting Group), Partner 1962, Dir. of Strategic Mgmt. Services 1970–83, Chrmn. 1982–83; author 'How To Make A Profit Plan' 1961; 'Business Planning: Key To Profit Growth' 1969; author/lectr. numerous strategic mang. articles and seminars; Lt., R.C.N.V.R. 1943–45; writer/composer numerous skits and songs Fossils Club of Montreal revues 1947–69; Fellow, Inst. Mang. Consultant Que. (Pres. 1970–71); Inst. Mang. Consultant Can. (Pres. 1972–74); Order C.A.'s Que.; Pres., Montreal Diet Dispensary 1988–91; Dir., Candn. Ski Museum; recreations: tennis, skiing, squash, music; Clubs: Montreal Badminton & Squash (Hon. Treas. 1956–60); Mount Royal Tennis (Pres. 1986–88); J.B. Ski (Pres. 1956–57, 1970–72); Address: Apt. 1104, 4900 Cote St. Luc Rd., Montreal, Que. H3W 2H3.

**IRWIN, Peter John,** B.E., P.Eng.; industrial executive; b. Montréal, Qué. 3 Jan. 1934; s. Selwyn and Gertrude Florence (Sharp) I.; e. Lower Can. Coll. Montreal 1950; McGill Univ. B.E. (Chem.) 1955; Univ. of W. Ont. Mktg. Mgmt. Course 1977; m. Mary Koerner d. Fred and Jane Reid 10 Sept. 1955; children: Peter J., James R., Wendy K. Parker; PRES., C.E.O. AND DIR., THE CANADA METAL CO. LTD. 1985– ; joined Canadian Industries Ltd. 1955–59; McArthur Irwin Ltd. 1959–67; present co. 1967; mem. Assn. Prof. Engs. Prov. Ont.; recreation: tennis; Club: Granite; Home: 130 Stratford Cres., Toronto, Ont. M4N 1C8; Office: 721 Eastern Ave., Toronto, Ont. M4M 1E6.

**IRWIN, The Honourable Ronald A.,** C.M., LL.B., Q.C., P.C., M.P.; politician; e. Osgoode Hall Law School LL.B. 1962; m. Margaret Frech; three children; MINISTER OF INDIAN AFFAIRS AND NORTHERN DEVELOPMENT, CANADA 1993– ; Mayor of Sault Ste. Marie 1972–74 (Dir., Ont. Municipal Assn. & Fed. of Candn. Municipalities); Comnr., Candn. Radio-TV & Telecommunications Comn. 1977–80; Lawyer actively involved in Native issues rep. First Nations & Métis interests in N. Ont.; Lecturer, Lake Superior State Univ. 1988–91; 1st elected as Member for Sault Ste. Marie to House of Commons 1980; Parly. Sec. to Min. of Justice (served on Parly Ctte. on the Constitution) and Attorney Gen., to the Min. of State for Social Development, to the Sec. of State for External Affairs; Chair, Sub-

Ctte. on Acid Rain; re-elected 1993 g.e.; Order of Canada 1975; Sault Jaycee Outstanding Canadian and Sault Ste. Marie Conservation Man of the Year Awards; Queen's Jubilee Medal 1977; Canada 125 Medal 1992; former appointments: Trustee, Sault Ste. Marie Bd. of Edn.; Alderman; Mem., Community Services Bd.; Historical Sites Bd.; Public Utilities Comn.; former Dir., Sault Ste. Marie Mus.; C. of C.; Former Pres., Sault Ste. Marie Law Assn.; Office: Room 583, Confederation Bldg., House of Commons, Ottawa, Ont. K1A 0A6.

**IRWIN, Samuel Macdonald (Mac),** B.A.; toy manufacturer; b. Toronto, Ont. 11 June 1927; s. Samuel Beatty and Beatrice Isobel (Whiteside) I.; e. Ridley Coll. St. Catherines, Ont.; Univ. of Toronto B.A. 1949; m. Elinor Jane d. George A. Somerville 4 June 1949; children: George Macdonald, David Samuel, Peter Matthews, Patti-Ann; CHRMN. OF THE BOARD, IRWIN TOY LTD. 1991– ; Dir. Kenner Products (Canada) Ltd.; Ideal Toy Co. of Canada; Salesman present Co. 1949, Exec. Vice Pres. 1954, Pres. & Dir. 1983–91; Past Chrmn., Ridley Coll.; Children's Broadcast Inst.; Ont. Assn. Governing Bodies Independent Schs.; Chrmn. Candn. Toy Mfrs. Assn.; Anglican; P. Conservative; recreations: golf, tennis, squash; Clubs: Lambton Golf & Country; Badminton & Racquet; St. Andrews (Delray, Fla.); Country C. of Fla. (Delray, Fla.); Toronto Golf; Peterboro Golf; Home: 92 Maclennan Ave., Toronto, Ont. M4T 2H5; Office: 43 Hanna Ave., Toronto, Ont. M6K 1X6.

**IRWIN, Scott;** toy industry executive; SENIOR VICE-PRESIDENT & DIRECTOR, IRWIN TOY LTD.; Office: 43 Hanna Ave., Toronto, Ont. M6K 1X6.

**IRWIN, William Arthur,** O.C., LL.D., B.A.; b. Ayr, Ont. 27 May 1898; s. Rev. Alexander J., B.A., B.D., D.D., and Amelia J. (Hassard) I.; e. Univ. of Manitoba; Univ. of Toronto, B.A. (Pol. Science) 1921; Univ. of Victoria, LL.D. (Hon.) 1977; m. 1stly, Jean Olive (dec. Oct. 1948), d. Rev. W.E. Smith, M.D., Toronto, Ont. 1922; children: Neal A., Sheila A. Irving, Patricia J. Morley; 2ndly, Patricia K., d. late Maj.-Gen. L.F. Page, Dec. 1950; sometime Rodman, Candn. Northern Rly. construction; later Reporter, Toronto 'Mail & Empire' and subsequently Reporter, Corr. (Parlty. Press Gallery, Ottawa) and Ed. Writer, Toronto 'Globe'; Assoc. Ed., Maclean's Mag., 1925–42, Mang. Ed. 1943–45 and Editor 1945–50; Commr. and Chrmn., Nat. Film Bd. Can. 1950–53; High Commr. for Can. in Australia, 1953–56; Ambassador to Brazil, 1956–59; Ambassador to Mexico, 1960–64; Ambassador to Guatemala, 1961–64; Publisher, Victoria Daily Times, and Vice-Pres., Victoria Press Ltd. 1964–71; served in 1st World War with C.E.F., 10th Batty., Candn. Garrison Arty., France; former Pres., Toronto Writers' Club; former mem., Nat. Extve. and Research Comte., Candn. Inst. of Internat. Affairs; 'Candn. Writers' Market Survey,' 1931; author of 'The Wheat Pool,' brochure reprinted from 'Maclean's Mag.,' 1929; author, Motor Vehicle Transportation Briefs: Royal Comn. on Railways & Transportation 1932, Royal Comn. on Transp. in Ont. 1937; Candn. Del. to Brit. Commonwealth Relations Conf., London, Eng., 1945; mem., Candn. del. to U.N. Conf. on Freedom of Information, Geneva, 1948; Candn. Alternate Del. to XIV and XV Gen. Assemblies of U.N., 1959 and 1960; co-author 'The Machine' (ice ballet) 1939; Address: 3260 Exeter Road, Victoria, B.C. V8R 6H6.

**ISAACS, Avrom,** C.M., B.A., LL.D.; art dealer; b. Winnipeg, Man. 19 Mar. 1926; s. Isaac and Manya Isaacovitch; e. Univ. of Toronto, B.A. (Hon.) 1950; one d. Renann Miriam; OWNER, THE ISAACS/INNUIT GALLERY 1970– ; exhibits early North American Indian Art, specializing in the Northern Tribes (from Haida on the west coast to Mic-Mac on the east coast) and Inuit Art (both contemporary and prehistoric); book & record publisher; sponsor of poetry readings, underground film screenings, mixed media concerts; served on Govt. Adv. Bds., Municipal, Provincial & Federal; Chrmn., Candn. Film Distribution Co-operative 1981–82; recipient, 1991 RCAIC silver medal; Assoc. Fellow, Calumet Coll., York Univ., Hon. Fellow, Ont. Coll. of Art; Member of the Order of Canada 1992; LL.D. York Univ. 1992; Silver Medal 125 Years Canada 1992; Metro Toronto Arts Award for Lifetime Contribution to the Arts 1992; Bd. Mem., The Textile Museum, Toronto; recreation: cycling; Office: 9 Prince Arthur Ave., Toronto, Ont. M5R 1B2.

**ISAACS, Colin Francis Weeber,** B.Sc., A.R.C.S., C.Chem.; environmentalist; b. New Malden, Surrey, England 16 Sept. 1948; s. Denis and Mary (Weeber) I.; e. Bancroft's Sch.; Univ. of London B.Sc. (Hons.); Imperial College A.R.C.S. 1969; Univ. of Western Ont. C.Chem.; m. Heide d. Edward and Adele Cieply 29 June 1973; CONSULTANT; Researcher, univ. admin., Counc. of Ont. Univ. 1973–79; Mem. of Counc., Town of Stoney Creek 1976–79; M.P.P. for Wentworth (NDP, critic for mun. affairs & the environment) 1979–81; Cons. in univ. admin. 1982; Extve. Dir., The Pollution Probe Found. 1982–92; Financial Post environment columnist; director OMMRI: Corporations in support; mem. Adv. Bd., Clean Environment Mutual Funds; sr. consulting assoc., Niagara Inst.; Past Mem., Ont. Recycling Adv. Ctte.; Mem., Ont. Round Table on Envir. & Econ.; Mem., Environmental Advisory Panel to Ontario Hydro; Adv. Council to the Institute for Environ. Policy & Stewardship, Univ. of Guelph; Dir., Knowledge of the Environment for Youth Foundation; Sec., Univ. of London Flying Club 1967–69; Officer Cadet, Univ. of London Air Squadron, Royal Air Force Volunteer Reserve 1967–69; Pres., Soc. of Grad. Students, U.W.O. 1971–73; recreations: canoeing, cross-country skiing; Home: 2 Lakeview Dr., Stoney Creek, Ont. L8E 5A5.

**ISAAK, Nancy Jane;** writer; b. New Westminster, B.C. 13 Oct.; d. Bruno and Constance Ada (Vowles) I.; e. John Oliver H.S. 1976; Corporal, 744 (Vanc.) Communications Squadron 1976–78; writer of plays, screenplays & articles; 'Number Four Mine at Kemptanooga Bay' Am. Radio Theatre 1987; 'Not By Choice' NFB Montreal 1988; 'RoboKid' (Beachcombers) CBC 1989; 'Oh, Those Baby Blues' NFB 1989; 'Northwood' CBC 1990; 'Nancy Drew' USA 1991; 'Under African Skies' Family Channel 1992; 'Liar, Liar...' CBC/CBS 1993; 'Bad Boy' CBC 1993; 'Deep Deception: The Killing of Clementine' CBC 1994; participant, Drama Lab, Nat. Screen Inst. of Can. 1987; awards incl. Am. Radio Theatre 1985; Writers' of the Future 1985; Mem., ACTRA; BCMPA; Agents: (Canada) Great North, 350 Dupont St., Toronto, ON M5R 1V9; (USA) ICM, 8942 Wilshire Blvd., Beverly Hills, CA 90211 USA.

**ISBISTER, Claude Malcolm,** B.A., Ph.D.; economist; consultant; b. Winnipeg, Man. 15 Jan. 1914; s. Claude and Margaret Ethel (McKechnie) I.; e. Univ. of Man. B.A. 1934; Univ. of Toronto 1938–39; Harvard Univ. Ph.D. (Econ.) 1946; m. Ruth d. late William Cunningham 18 June 1938; children: John William, Alex James, Kathryn Ruth; CONSULTANT since 1978; joined Publ. Service of Can. 1945, served successively as Asst. Dom. Stat., Asst. Depy. Min. Trade & Comm. and of Finance, Depy. Min. Citizenship and Immigration, Mines and Tech. Surveys and Energy Mines & Resources, Chrmn. Dominion Coal Bd., Dir. Canadian National (West Indies) Steamships Ltd.; Extve. Dir. World Bank Group Washington and Chrmn. Jt. Audit Comte. 1970–75; Royal Commr. on Petroleum Products Pricing Prov. Ont. 1975–76; Consulting Partner, Currie, Coopers & Lybrand, 1976–77; in recent years consultant to World Bank, I.M.F., Caribbean Develop. Bank and African Develop. Bank; Govt. of Can.; recreations: public affairs, swimming; Clubs: Canadian; Canadian Inst. of Internat. Affairs; Address: 260 Heath St. W., Suite 1703, Toronto, Ont. M5P 3L6.

**ISELER, Elmer Walter,** O.C., B.Mus., LL.D.; choir conductor; choral editor; b. Port Colborne, Ont. 14 Oct. 1927; e. Waterloo Lutheran Univ. (now Wilfrid Laurier) organ and church music with Ulrich Leupold; Univ. of Toronto B.Mus. 1950; Ont. Coll. of Educ. 1951; Dalhousie Univ. LL.D. 1971; Brock Univ. LL.D. 1972; Waterloo Lutheran Univ. LL.D.; CONDUCTOR, ELMER ISELER SINGERS 1978– ; conducted Univ. of Toronto Symphony Orchestra and All-Varsity Mixed Chorus 1950–51; Asst. Rehearsal Conductor, Toronto Mendelssohn Choir 1951–52 becoming Conductor 1964; taught orchestral and choral music Toronto high schs. 1952–64; helped found Toronto Festival Singers 1954 serving as Conductor 24 yrs.; taught choral music Univ. of Toronto 1965–68; began editing 'Festival Singers of Canada Choral Series' 1968; awarded Gold Civic Award of Merit, City of Toronto 1973; Silver Medal, Soc. d'Encouragement de Paris 1973; Candn. Music Council Medal 1975; Officer of the Order of Canada 1975; first Hon. Life Mem., Assoc. of Candn. Choral Conductors 1984; Elmer Iseler Day proclaimed, Toronto 3 Nov. 1984; Address: c/o Toronto Mendelssohn Choir, 60 Simcoe St., Toronto, Ont. M5J 2H5.

**ISENBAUM, Hy,** F.C.A.; chartered accountant; b. Toronto, Ont. 26 Nov. 1926; s. Isaac and Esther (Weinberg) I.; e. Central H.S. of Comm. (Gold Medalist 1945); Inst. of C.A.s, C.A. 1949; Fellow, Inst. of C.A.s 1988; m. Myrna d. Herman and Beatrice Teitelbaum 19 May 1958; one d. Lori; FOUNDER AND SR. PARTNER SOBERMAN, ISENBAUM & COLOMBY CHARTERED ACCTS. 1958– ; Dir., Bioniche Inc.; Bd. Chrmn. Reliacare Inc.; articled with David Vise & Co. C.A.s 1945–49, Supvr. 1949–52, Partner 1952–58, when estbd. firm in partnership with Max Soberman; Trustee and Chrmn. Emeritus, Mount Sinai Hosp.; Gov. Baycrest Centre for Geriatric Care; Weizmann Inst. of Sci., Israel; recreations: golf, tennis, running, reading, concerts; Clubs: Primrose; Maple Downs Golf and Country; Home: 1703–63 St. Clair Ave. W., Toronto, Ont. M4V 2Y9; Office: 2 St. Clair Ave. E., Toronto, Ont. M4T 2T5.

**ISGUR, Nathan,** Ph.D., F.R.S.C.; physicist; educator; b. Houston, Texas 25 May 1947; s. Moses Abraham and Betty (Winograd) I.; e. Cal. Inst. Technol. B.S. 1968; Univ. of Toronto Ph.D. 1974; m. Karin d. Daniel and Joyce Bergsagel 1 Sept. 1984; children: Abraham (Bram) Daniel Bergsagel, Benjamin Isaac Bergsagel; THEORY GROUP LEADER at CEBAF (Continuous Electron Beam Accelerator Facility) 1990– ; NSERC Postdoctoral Fellow, Univ. of Toronto 1974, Asst. Prof. 1976, Assoc. Prof. 1980, Prof. of Physics 1983–92; recipient Herzberg Medal Candn. Assn. Phys. 1984, Rutherford Medal 1989; Steacie Fellowship NSERC 1986–87 and Prize 1986; Fellow, Am. Physical Soc. 1990; author over 100 sci. articles; Home: 216 Richard Burbydge, Williamsburg, VA 23185; Office: CEBAF, 12000 Jefferson Ave., Newport News, VA 23606.

**ISH, Daniel Russell,** B.A., LL.B., LL.M.; educator; b. Loon Lake, Sask. 28 Aug. 1946; s. Leme Jay and Obeline Delia (Sicotte) I.; e. St. Thomas Coll. North Battleford, Sask. 1964; Univ. of Sask. B.A. 1970, LL.B. 1970; Osgoode Hall Law Sch. York Univ. LL.M. 1974; m. Bonnie d. Clarence and Jean Bolger 22 Dec. 1970; children: Jason, Rachel; PROF. OF LAW, UNIV. OF SASK. 1975– , Dir., Centre for the Study of Co-operatives, Dean of Law 1982–88; called to Bar of Alta. 1971, Sask. 1979; Queen's Counsel 1991; articled and practised law with H. Lloyd MacKay, Banff, Alta. 1970–71; mem. faculty McGill Univ. Law Sch. 1972–75; joined faculty present Univ. 1975, Asst. Dean of Law 1977–79; Visiting Prof. of Law Univ. of Auckland 1980–81, 1989; inducted into U.S. National Acad. of Arbitrators 1989; Dir. Botron Film Productions and Tormont Film Productions 1978–80; Chrmn. of Bd. Univ. Credit Union 1979–80; author 'The Law of Canadian Co-operatives' 1981; 'The Taxation of Canadian Co-operatives' 1975; numerous articles learned journs.; Bencher, Law Soc. Sask. 1982–88; Trustee, Sask. Law Foundation 1982–88; recreations: hiking, running; Home: 1421 – 13th St. E., Saskatoon, Sask. S7H 0C7; Office: Saskatoon, Sask. S7N 0W0.

**ISHWARAN, Karigoudar,** Ph.D., D. Litt.; university professor; b. India 1 Nov. 1922; s. Channappa and Basamma Patil; e. Univ. of Bombay, M.A. 1947; Univ. of Karnatak, Ph.D. 1954; Oxford Univ., B. Litt. 1956; Univ. of The Hague, M.S.S. 1957; Univ. of Leiden, D.Litt. 1959; m. Wobine, May 1960; children: Arundhati, Hemant, Shivakumar; PROF. OF SOCIOL., YORK UNIV.; Lectr., J. G. Coll. of Comm. and S. K. Art Coll., Hubli, India, 1947–52; Princ., Sangameshvar Coll., Sholapur, India, 1953–54; Research Fellow of the Netherlands' Univs. Foundation for Internat. Cooperation, The Hague, 1956–59; Reader and Chrmn., Dept. of Grad. Studies in Social Anthrop., Karnatak Univ., Dharwar, India, 1959–62; Univ. Prof. and Chrmn. of Dept., 1962–64; Visiting Prof., Memorial Univ. of Nfld., 1964–65; author of 'Family Life in the Netherlands' 1959; 'Tradition and Economy in Village India' 1966; 'Politics and Change' 1967; 'Shivapur: A South Indian Village' 1968; 'Change and Continuity in India's Villages' 1969; 'The Canadian Family' 1971, rev. 1976; co-author of 'Urban Sociology' 1965; 'Family, Kinship and Community: A Study of Dutch-Canadians' 1977; 'A Populistic Community and Modernization in India' 1977; 'Childhood and Adolescence in Canada' 1979; 'Canadian Families: Ethnic Variations' 1980; 'Canadian Family' 1983; 'Marriage and Divorce in Canada' 1983; 'Religion and Society among the Lingayats of South India' 1983; 'Basava and the Lingayat Religion' 1987; 'Family and Marriage - cross-cultural perspectives' 1989; 'Speaking of Basava - Lingayat Religion and Culture in South Asia' 1992; ed. no. of bks. and written papers for internat. journs.; Ed. 'International Journal of Comparative Sociology'; 'Journal of Asian and African Studies'; 'Journal of Developing Societies' (formerly 'Contributions to Asian Studies'); 'International Journal of Comparative Religion and Philosophy'; 'International Journal of Comparative Family and Marriage'; 'International Journal of Comparatice Race and Ethnic Studies'; Kannada Literary Award, Karnatak State, India 1983; Publisher, de Sitter Publications Inc. 1993– ; recreations: reading, writing, travelling; Home: 374 Woodsworth Rd., Toronto, Ont. M2L 2T6.

**ISLEY, Hon. Ernest Douglas,** B.Ed., M.L.A.; politician, farmer; b. Vermillion, Alta. 29 June 1937; s. Wesley Herbert and Mary Helen (Ross) I.; e. Univ. of Alta. B.E. (with distinction) 1969; m. Sheila Anne d. Lorne Franklin 18 Aug. 1958; children: Floyd Ernest,

Lori Anne, Thea Roxanne, Tracy Lynn; ten grandchildren; MINISTER OF AGRICULTURE & RURAL DEVELOPMENT, PROV. OF ALBERTA 1992– ; 1st elected to Alta. Legis. g.e. 1979; re-elected g.e. 1982, 1986, 1989; apptd. Min. of Manpower 1982–86; Min. of Public Works, Supply & Services 1986; Min. of Agric. 1989, re-appted. 1992; mem., Agenda & Priorites Ctte.; Vice Chrmn., Standing Policy Ctte. on Agric. & Rural Develop. and the S.P.C. on Financial Planning; operates a mixed farm in Bonnyville & has acted as an agent for a large insur. co.; Principal, Altario Sch. 1961–71; Bonnyville Centralized High School 1971–78; Dir., Bonnyville Agric. Soc. 1973–78; Dir. & Vice-Pres., Bonnyville P.C. Assn. 1974–78; Pres., Lakeland Tourist Assn. 1975; Mem., Bonnyville C. of C.; Party: P.C.; United; recreations: coaching sports teams; Riding Office: Box 7580, Bonnyville, Alta. T9N 2H9.

**ISON, Terence George,** LL.D.; professor; b. Hitchen, Eng. 26 Sept. 1934; s. George Henry and Edith Elsie (Cook) I.; e. Univ. of London LL.B. 1957, LL.D. 1981; Harvard Law Sch. LL.M. 1959; PROF. OF LAW, OSGOODE HALL LAW SCH. YORK UNIV. 1980– ; legal practice B.C. 1960–62; mem. Faculty of Law Univ. of B.C. 1962–68, Queen's Univ. 1968–80; Chrmn. Workers' Compensation Bd. B.C. 1973–76; cons. various govt. depts. and agencies workers' compensation; author: 'The Forensic Lottery' 1968; 'Credit Marketing and Consumer Protection' 1979; 'Accident Compensation' 1980; 'Workers' Compensation in Canada' 1983, 2nd ed. 1989; recreations: sailing; Home: 42 Roselawn Ave., Toronto, Ont. M4R 1E4; Office: 4700 Keele St., North York, Ont. M3J 1P3.

**ISRAEL, Charles Edward,** B.A. B.H.L.; writer; b. Evansville, Ind. 15 Nov. 1920; s. Edward Leopold and Amelia (Dryer) I.; e. Baltimore City Coll. 1937; Univ. of N.C.; Univ. of Cincinnati B.A. 1942; Hebrew Union Coll. B.H.L. 1943; m. Gloria Isabel Varley; staff mem. UN Relief & Rehabilitation Adm. and successor Internat. Refugee Organ. 1946–50, European program; fulltime prof. writer since 1950; Program Head, Screenwriters' Workshop, Banff Sch. of Fine Arts 1987–91; accumulated over 550 credits Candn. and U.S. radio, TV and film work; author 'How Many Angels' 1956; 'The Mark' 1958; 'Rizpah' 1961; 'Who Was Then the Gentleman?' 1963; 'Shadows on a Wall' 1965; 'The Hostages' 1966; 'Five Ships West' 1966; co-author 'The True North' 1957; Gen. Ed. and contrib. author 'The Newcomers' 1979; monthly column and numerous features on wines and spirits 'Toronto Calendar Magazine,' 'Toronto Life,' 'Toronto' (Globe and Mail) and others; recipient Prix Italia City of Genoa Award for TV Drama 1964 (nominated 1965, 1969); Best Scenario Prague TV Film Festival 1965; Best Screenplay Yorkton Internat. Film Festival 1973; rec'd Margaret Collier Award, Gemini Awards, Acad. of Candn. Cinema and Television 1986; served with U.S. Merchant Marine 1943–45; mem. Acad. TV Arts & Sciences (US); Acad. Candn. Cinema and Television; Wine Writers' Circle; ACTRA; Writers Guild Am. (US); Writers' Guild of Can.; Writers' Union Can.; Internat. P.E.N.; Jewish; recreations; wine-tasting, cooking, hiking; Address: 21 Dale Ave., Apt. 647, Toronto, Ont. M4W 1K3.

**ISRAEL, Milton,** M.A., Ph.D.; educator; b. Hartford, Conn. 27 July 1936; s. Archie and Jean (Tulin) I.; e. Bristol (Conn.) High Sch., 1954; Trinity Coll., Hartford, B.A. 1958; Univ. of Mich., M.A. 1959, Ph.D. 1965; Fulbright Fellow in India 1963–64; Internat. Studies Fellow (Univ. of Toronto) in India 1970–71; m. Beverly, d. Arthur Stein, Springfield, Mass., 22 Aug. 1959; children: Lauren Beth, Andrew Shale; PROF. OF HISTORY, UNIVERSITY OF TORONTO 1990– ; joined present Univ. as Lectr. 1964, Assoc. Prof. of Hist. 1972, Asst. to Dean, Sch. of Grad. Studies 1967–70, Assoc. Chrmn. Dept. of Hist. 1972–74, Vice Provost, 1974–79, Dir., Centre for South Asian Studies 1981–91, Prof. of Hist. 1990; Pres., Shastri Indo-Canadian Inst. 1976–79, Resident Dir. in India 1980–81; Editor: 'Pax Britannica' 1968; 'Islamic Society and Culture: Essays in Honour of Professor Aziz Ahmad' 1983; 'National Unity: The South Asian Experience' 1983; 'Nehru and the Twentieth Century' 1991; Co-Editor: (with N.K. Wagle) 'Religion and Society in Maharashtra' 1987; (with D.W. Attwood and N.K. Wagle) 'City, Countryside and Society in Maharashtra' 1988; (with J.T. O'Connell, W.G. Oxtoby and with W.H. McLeod and J.S. Grewal) 'Sikh History and Religion in the Twentieth Century' 1988; Author: 'Communications and Power, Propaganda and the Press in the Indian Nationalist Struggle, 1920-1947' 1994; author of articles and reviews for various journs.; Chrmn. of Bd. of Dirs., Multicultural History Soc. of Ont.; mem. Assn. Asian Studies; Candn. Soc. Asian Studies; Pi Kappa Alpha (Past Pres.); Jewish; recreation: reading, travel, antiques; Address: Rm. 2045, Sidney Smith Hall, Univ. of Toronto, Toronto, Ont. M5S 1A1.

**ISRAEL, Werner,** O.C., M.Sc., Ph.D.; educator; b. Berlin, Germany 4 Oct. 1931; s. Arthur Israel; e. Cape Town High Sch. 1948; Univ. of Cape Town B.Sc. 1951, M.Sc. 1954; Dublin Inst. for Advanced Studies 1956–58; Trinity Coll. Dublin Ph.D. 1960; m. Inge d. late Leo V. Margulies 26 Jan. 1958; children: Pia Lee, Mark; came to Can. 1958; UNIVERSITY PROFESSOR OF THEORETICAL PHYSICS, UNIV. OF ALTA. 1985– ; Prof. of Theoretical Physics there since 1971; Visiting Prof. Dublin Inst. for Advanced Studies 1966–68; Sherman Fairchild Distinguished Scholar, Cal. Inst. of Technol. 1974–75; Sr. Visitor, Dept. Applied Math. and Theoretical Physics Univ. Cambridge 1975–76; Maitré de Recherche Associé, Institut Henri Poincaré, Paris 1976–77; Visiting Prof., Univ. of Berne 1980; Visiting Fellow, Gonville and Caius Coll., Cambridge 1985; Visiting Prof., Kyoto Univ. 1986; Fellow, Candn. Inst. for Advanced Research since 1986; Ed. 'Relativity, Astrophysics and Cosmology' 1973; co-ed. 'General Relativity: An Einstein Centenary Survey' 1979; '300 Years of Gravitation' 1987; various papers black hole physics, relativistic stat. mechanics and gen. relativity; Fellow, Royal Soc. of London 1986; mem. Royal Soc. Can.; Internat. Astron. Union; Candn. Assn. Physicists (Chrmn. Theoretical Physics Div. 1971–72; Medal foent in Physics 1981); Candn. Astron. Soc.; awarded Univ. of Alta. Rsch. Prize 1983; Izaak Walton Killam Memorial Prize 1984; Alta. Achievement Award for Excellence 1984; D.Sc. (hon. causa) Queen's Univ., Kingston 1987; Docteur Honoris Causa, Université de Tours, France June 1994; Officer, Order of Canada 1994; Jewish; recreation: music; Home: #1403, 11027 87th Ave., Edmonton, Alta. T6G 2P9; Office: Edmonton, Alta. T6G 2J1.

**ISRAELSON, David Birrel,** B.A., LL.B.; journalist; b. Toronto, Ont. 18 March 1954; s. Shmarya Reuven (Reeve) and Barbara May I.; e. Univ. of Toronto 1972–74, B.A. 1988; Hebrew Univ. Jerusalem 1974–75; Osgoode Hall Law Sch. LL.B. 1978; Carleton Univ. Sch. of Journalism 1980–81; m. Susan d. Clifford and Maxine Elliott 21 May 1982; children: Jacob Michael Elliott Israelson, Tessa D'Arcy Elliott Israelson; called to Ontario Bar 1980; pursued writing career after qualifying as a lawyer: Sportswriter / Reporter / part-time Editorial Writer, 'Kitchener-Waterloo Record' 1981–83; Ed. Bd. Mem., Toronto Star 1983–85; Environment Reporter 1985–87, 1989–90; Housing Reporter 1987–89; European Bureau Chief, Toronto Star (London, Eng.) 1990–93; particular areas of expertise are environmental issues & internat. politics; Western Ont. Newspaper Awards 1981, '82; Mem., Foreign Press Assn. (London); Royal Inst. of Internat. Affairs; author: 'Silent Earth: The Politics of Our Survival' 1990, paperback 1991; recreations: music (guitar, saxophone, piano, clarinet), sports (riding, cycling, canoeing, sailing, running); Office: c/o Toronto Star, One Yonge St., Toronto, Ont. M5E 1E6.

**ITUKALLA, Juanisi Jakusi (Joanassie Jack);** artist; b. south of Povungnituk, Que. 2 Dec. 1949; s. Aisa Avialiajuk I.; medium: sculpture, prints; began carving at age twelve; central theme of work is struggle for survival, which pits man against animal, animal against animal and man against his environment; 35 group exbns. incl.: 'Recent Stone Sculpture from Arctic Quebec' Arctic Artistry, Hastings-on-Hudson, N.Y. 1992; Granville Island Canadian Inuit Sculpture Exhib. (second exhib.), Vancouver Inuit Art Soc. 1991; 'Masters of the Arctic: An Exhibition of Contemporary Inuit Masterworks' presented by Amway Corp. at the United Nations Gen. Assembly, N.Y. 1989; 'Stories in Stone: Soapstone Sculptures From Northern Québec' La Fed. des Co-op. du Nouveau-Qué., Montreal 1988–90; l'Iglou Art Esquimau, Douai (toured 6 cities) France 1987–90; 'The Art of the Eskimo' Newman Galleries, Bryn Mawr, PA 1986; 'Visions of Rare Spirit' Museum of Indian Archaeology, London, Ont. 1984/1985; 'Miniature Show' The Guild Shop, Toronto 1983; 'The Year of the Bear' The Arctic Circle, Los Angeles, CA 1981; 'A Taste of Arctic Québec' Marion Scott Gall., Vancouver 1980; 'Arctic Québec Sculpture' Vita Inuit, Pavia, Italy 1978; 'Art/Inuit/Art: The Rothmans Permanent Collection of Eskimo Sculpture' Toronto, Ont. 1975; solo exbns.: Juliane Galleries, Toronto 1976, 1980; Man and His World, Montreal 1969; collections: Art Gall. of Windsor; Avataq Cultural Inst. Montreal; Musée de la civilisation, Québec City; Musée du Qué. Québec City; Rothmans Perm. Coll. of Eskimo Sculpture, Toronto; Saputik Mus., Povungnituk, Qué.; Toronto-Dominion Bank Coll., Toronto; demonstrated art of carving in Ottawa, Toronto and at 'Man and His World' Montreal 1969; submitted maquette for stone decoration, Parliament Bldgs. Ottawa 1982; subject of documentary film 'Inukshuk' 1985; Co-winner (with Peter Itukulla and Paulusie Novalinga), 1st prize for Québec Sculpture, Internat. Sculpture Competition, Quebec's Winter Carnival 1988; demonstrated carving in Leningrad in conjunction with the opening of exhib. 'Tundra Taiga' (a joint venture between USSR and le musée de la civilisation de Qué. 1989; Popular Prize, Nat. Snow Sculpture Comp., Carneval de Qué. 1990; participant, Inuit Art Conf., McMichael Candn. Art Coll. 1991; subject of numerous articles and catalogues; Home: Povungnituk, Que.; Office: La Federation des Co-op. du Nouveau-Qué., 19950 Clark Graham, Baie D'Urfe, Qué. H9X 3R8.

**IVANIER, Isin;** O.C., D.Sci.(h.c.); industrialist; b. Vijnita, Romania 9 Apr. 1906; s. Jacob and Perl (Weintraub) I.; m. the late Fancia d. David and Amalia Herling; children: Paul, Sydney; came to Can. 1949; CHAIRMAN, IVACO INC.; Dir., Ivaco Inc.; Canron Inc.; Wrights Can. Ropes Ltd.; Docap (1985) Corp.; Bakermet Inc.; Club: Montefiore; Office: 770 Sherbrooke St. W., Montreal, Que. H3A 1G1.

**IVANIER, Paul,** Ph.D., F.R.S.A., C.A.; executive; b. Cernauti, Romania 12 Oct. 1932; s. Isin and the late Fancia I.; e. Baron Byng High Sch. Montréal; McGill Univ.; C.A. 1957; Ben-Gurion Univ., Ph.D.; m. Lily d. Regina and Isac Neilinger 13 June 1954; children: Shirley Retter, Janet Neuman, Philip; PRESIDENT, CHIEF EXEC. OFFR. AND DIR., IVACO INC. 1976– ; Dir. Canron Inc.; Wrights Canadian Ropes Ltd.; Docap (1985) Corp.; Bakermet Inc.; served pub. acctg. practice one yr. after grad.; joined family business Sivaco Wire and Nail Co. (now present Co.); held various positions incl. Vice Pres. Operations and Exec. Vice Pres. (1969); was guiding force in taking firm public in 1970 (at $11 million in sales), and guided through growth stage to current position in top 100 companies in Can. (1992 sales were $1.1 billion); Dir. & Past Vice Chrmn., Candn. Steel Producers Assoc.; Mem. Bd. of Dir., Candn. Steel Trade and Employment Congress (Founding Mem.); Laureate, Club des Entrepreneurs, Conseil du Patronat du Québec, 1989; Grand Patron Montréal Museum of Fine Arts (mem. acquisition ctte. for Candn. Art); Mem. Bd. of Gov., Univ. de Montréal and Co-Chrmn., Capital Fund Raising Campaign; Mem. Bd. of Govs., Concordia Univ. of Montréal and Chrmn., Real Estate Devel. Ctte.; Mem., Bd. of Gov., Royal Victoria Hosp. Corp of Montréal; mem. Internat. Bd. of Govs. of Ben-Gurion Univ.; mem. Bd. of Dir., Weizmann Inst. of Sciences; mem. Bd. of Dir., Med. Rsch. Found., Jewish Gen. Hosp. of Montréal; Past Pres. B'Nai Brith (Mount Scopus Lodge) Montréal; a founder, Mount Sinai Hosp., Miami, Fla.; Clubs: Elmridge Golf & Country; St. James's; Turnberry Isle Golf, Miami, Fla.; Office: 770 Sherbrooke St. W., Montréal, Que. H3A 1G1.

**IVANY, J.W. George,** B.Sc., M.A., Ph.D., LL.D.; educator; b. Grand Falls, Nfld. 26 May 1938; s. Gordon and Stella (Skinner) I.; e. Meml. Univ. of Nfld. B.Sc 1960; Columbia Univ. M.A. 1962; Univ. of Alta. Ph.D. 1965; m. Marsha d. Norman and Betty Gregory 24 March 1983; children: Leslie, George, Jessica, Sarah; PRESIDENT, UNIVERSITY OF SASKATCHEWAN 1989– ; Asst. Prof. Univ. of Alta. 1965–66; Columbia Univ. 1966–68, Assoc. Prof. 1968, Dept. Head 1973; Prof. and Dean of Edn. Meml. Univ. of Nfld. 1974–77; Prof. and Dean of Education, Simon Fraser Univ. 1977–84, Acting Pres. 1983, Vice Pres., Academic 1984–89; author, 'Today's Science' 1973; 'Environment: Readings for Teachers' 1968; co-author 'Federal-Provincial Relations: Education Canada' 1981; 'Teaching Elementary Science: Who's Afraid of Spiders' 1988; Assoc. Ed. 'Journal Research in Science Teaching' 1966–68; Past Dir. Nat. Assn. Rsch. in Sci. Teaching; Bd. of Mgmt., TRIUMF, 1984–89; Bd. Mem., National Institute of Nutrition 1991– ; Office: Univ. of Sask., Saskatoon, Sask. S7N 0W0.

**IVERS, Irving N.;** entertainment executive; b. Montreal, Que. 23 Feb. 1939; s. Jack and Annie (Dizgun) Itzkovitch; e. Baron Byng H.S. 1955; Sir George Williams Univ. 1957; m. Dorothy Siddall 26 Sept. 1963; children: Adam Jason, David Jacob; PRESIDENT, ASTRAL DISTRIBUTION 1992– ; various radio & TV positions 1962–80; Extve. Vice-Pres., Worldlwide Mktg., 20th Century Fox (LA) 1980–83; Pres., Worldwide Mktg., MGM 1983–86; Vice-Pres., Mktg., Warner Bros. Internat. 1986–91; lecturer; Mem., Acad. of Motion Pictures Art & Sciences; Bd. Mem., Motion Picture Found. of Can.; Candn. Motion Picture Pioneers; 1st recipient, Marketing Achievement Awrd, Nat. Assn. of Theatre Owners; Hon. Citizen of Toronto 1980; recreations: reading, tennis, piano, music, travelling; Home: 13 Berryman St., Toronto, Ont. M5R 1M7; Office: 181 Bay St., Ste. 100, Toronto, Ont. M5J 2T2.

**IVES, Glenn Antony,** B.Math.(Hons.), C.A.; chartered accountant; b. Gravesend, Eng. 19 June 1960; s. Kenneth Martin and Daphne Anne (Goodger) I.; e. Univ. of Waterloo B.Math. (Hons.) 1984 (Dean's Honour Roll); m. Katherine A. d. Sam and Sybil Horton 29 Aug. 1981; children: Geoffrey, William, Anna Jane; VICE-PRES. FINANCE & CHIEF FINANCIAL OFFICER, VENEZUELA-GOLDFIELDS INC. 1993– ; acctg. student, Clarke, Henning & Co. 1980–85 (U.F.E. Gold Medalist, Ont. C.A. exams 1984); Manager, Coopers & Lybrand 1985–88; Dir. of Finance, Consolidated TXV Mining Corp. 1988–91; Vice-Pres. Finance, TVX Gold Inc. 1991–93; Dir., Venezuelan Goldfields; Dir., Boliver Goldfields Ltd.; United Church; recreations: soccer, tennis; Office: 200 Burrard St., Ste. 1788, Vancouver, B.C. V6C 3L6.

**IVEY, Beryl Marcia,** B.A.; foundation executive; b. Chatham, Ont. 28 Dec. 1924; d. Col. W. I. and Beatrice Alice (Heaton) Nurse; e. Univ. of W. Ont. B.A. 1947; Ont. Coll. of Ed. 1948; m. Richard M. s. Richard G. and Jean Ivey 6 August 1949; children: Richard, Jennifer, Rosamond, Suzanne; VICE PRES. AND DIR. THE RICHARD IVEY FOUNDATION 1972– ; Pres., Beehive Investments Ltd., London 1973– ; Dir., Ivest Corp. 1974– ; World Wildlife Fund (Can.) 1975– ; University Hosp. Found., London 1988– (Pres. 1990–92); Foundation Western 1993– ; Mem., Hon. Adv. Bd., Candn. Assoc. for Community Living 1992– ; Mem., Visual Arts Adv. Counc., Univ. of Western Ont. 1992– ; Teacher Phys. Ed. and Engl., Sec. Sch., London, Ont. 1948–49; Dir. Canada Trustco Mortgage Co. 1982–89; CT Financial Services Inc. 1987–89; Theatre London 1965–67; Nat. Theatre Sch., Montreal 1971–72; The Trillium Found. of Ont., Toronto 1982–88; Shaw Festival Theatre, Niagara-on-the-Lake 1969–75 (Dir. and Vice-Pres. 1977–82); National Ballet Sch., Toronto 1975–80, 1983–84; London Art Gall. Assn. 1969–80; Candn. Centre for Philanthropy, Toronto 1982–83; Adv. Bd., Parkwood Hosp., London 1982–89; Trustee, Alternate Mem., Art Gall. of Ont. 1974–77; Mem., Inuit Art Ctte., Art Gallery of Ont. 1989–93; Dir., Eskimo Arts Counc., Ottawa 1975–78; University Hosp., London 1982–92; Pres., Arboretum Adv. Counc., Univ. of Guelph 1987–93; Home: 990 Wellington St., London, Ont. N6A 3T2; Office: 618 Richmond St., London, Ont. N6A 5J9.

**IVEY, Donald Glenn,** M.A., Ph.D.; physicist and educator; b. Clanwilliam, Man. 6 Feb. 1922; s. Carle R. and Bessie Luella (Reid) I.; e. Univ. of British Columbia, B.A. 1944, M.A. 1946; Univ. of Notre Dame, Ph.D. 1949; m. Marjorie Eileen Frisby, 1944; children: Donna Marleen, Sharon Eileen, David Donald Glenn; PROF. OF PHYSICS (EMERITUS), UNIVERSITY OF TORONTO; Principal of New Coll., Univ. of Toronto, 1963–74; Assoc. Chrmn., Dept. of Physics, 1978–80; Vice Pres. Inst. Rel., 1980–84; engaged also in preparation and presentation of educ. television programmes for C.B.C.; has prepared award-winning physics teaching films used internationally; Publications: 'Physics' 1954; 'Classical Mechanics and Introductory Statistical Mechanics' 1974; tech. articles to journals; mem., Canadian Assn. Physicists; Canadian Association University Teachers; Am. Phys. Soc.; Am. Assn. of Physics Teachers; Anglican; recreation: tennis; Clubs: Queens; Toronto Cricket, Skating & Curling; Home: 34 Yewfield Crescent, Don Mills, Ont. M3B 2Y6.

**IVEY, Richard Macaulay,** C.M., LL.D., Q.C.; b. London, Ont. 26 Oct. 1925; s. Richard Green and Jean (Macaulay) I.; e. Ridley Coll., St. Catharines, 1943; Univ. of W. Ont., B.A., 1947; Osgoode Hall, Toronto, Ont., LL.B. 1950; Univ. of W. Ont., Hon. LL.D., 1979; m. Beryl Marcia, d. Col. W. I. Nurse, Chatham, Ont., 6 Aug. 1949; children: Richard William, Jennifer Louise, Rosamond Ann, Suzanne Elizabeth; CHRMN., IVEST CORPORATION; Dir., Livingston Group Inc.; Eaton Yale Ltd.; Hon. Dir., Bank of Montreal; Pres., The Richard Ivey Foundn.; Dir., John P. Robarts Research Inst.; World Wildlife Fund (Canada); mem. Adv. Bd., The Grand Theatre Co., London, Ont.; Hon. Trustee, Royal Ont. Museum; Hon. Adv. Bd., St. Joseph's Hosp., London, Ont.; Clubs: London; London Hunt & Country; Toronto; Home: 990 Wellington St., London, Ont. N6A 3T2; Office: 618 Richmond St. London, Ont. N6A 5J9.

**IVEY, Richard William,** B.A., LL.B.; lawyer; b. London, Ont. 15 Aug. 1950; s. Richard Macaulay and Beryl Marcia (Nurse) I.; e. Ridley Coll. St. Catharines, Ont. 1968; Univ. of W. Ont. Sch. of Business Adm. B.A. 1972; Univ. of Toronto Law Sch. LL.B. 1975; m. Donna Lois, d. J.A. Smith, Thunder Bay, Ont. 6 Sept. 1980; CHRMN., LIVINGSTON GROUP INC. and PRES. & C.E.O., IVEST CORPORATION; Assoc., Tory, Tory, Deslauriers & Binnington 1977–81; read law with above firm; called to Bar of Ont. 1977; Dir., CT Financial Services Inc.; The Canada Trust Co.; Canada Trustco Mortgage Co.; The Richard Ivey Foundn.; Vice-Chrmn., Bd. of Trustees, Lester B. Pearson Coll. of the Pacific; Mem., Western Business Sch. Adv. Ctte.; recreations: skiing, tennis, golf; Clubs: London; London Hunt & Country; Badminton and Racquet; Toronto; Osler Bluff; Home: 430 St. George St., London, Ont. N6A 3B4; Office: 618 Richmond St., London, Ont. N6A 5J9.

**IYAITUK, Matiusie;** sculptor; b. near Cape Smith, N.W.T. 20 Nov. 1950; s. Markusi I. (a carver); 34 group exbns. incl. most recent: 'Le Nouveau Monde Nouveau Territoires ...' Montreal 1992, Min. de la santé et des services sociaux Que, Que. 1992, Surrey Art Gallery Surrey, B.C. 1992, York Quay Gall. & Leo Kamen Gall. Toronto 1991, The Guild Shop Toronto 1990–91, Maison Hamel-Bruneau Ste-Foy, Que. 1990–92, Winnipeg Art Gall. 1990–92, l'Iglou Art Esquimau, Douai (toured 6 cities) France 1989–90; 8 solo exbns.: Aux Multiples, Quebec City 1992; Images of the North, San Francisco 1991; The Guild Shop 1986, '90; Inuit Galerie Mannheim, Germany 1990; Gallery Phillip Don Mills, Ont. 1983; Images of the North San Francisco, Calif. 1981; The Beckett Gallery Hamilton, Ont. 1980; works in 6 collections incl. art galleries of Winnipeg (Millard Coll.) and Ontario (Sarick Coll.), Candn. Mus. of Civilization Hull, Que., Musée du Québec Qué., Qué., Nat. Gallery of Canada Ottawa; attended openings: 'Images of the North' 1981, Guild Shop 1986, 'Arctic Quebec' exbn. Galerie le Chariot Montreal 1988; submitted maquette for stone decoration to Parl. Bldgs. Ottawa 1982; demonstrated carving Gallery Phillip exbn. 1982; Guest Speaker, 'Canada's Peoples – Cultural Contributions' conf. 1983; Explorations Grant, Canada Council 1984; attended workshop Ottawa Sch. of Art 1991; invited to teach in Labrador workshop by Inuit Artists' College 1991; Artist-in-Residence, The McMichael Candn. Art Collection Kleinburg, Ont. (one week 1992); invited to lead cross-cultural workshop, Ottawa Sch. of Art 1994; subject of articles and catalogues; Home: Ivujivik, N.W.T.; Office: c/o La Fédération des Coopératives du Nouveau-Québec, 19950 Clark Graham, Baie d'Urfé, Qué. H9X 3R8.

**IZUMI, Kiyoshi,** B. Arch., M.C.P., R.C.A., F.R.A.I.C.; educator; environmental design consultant; b. Vancouver, B.C. 24 March 1921; s. Tojiro and Kin (Fujii) I.; e. Vancouver Tech. Sch. 1939; Regina (Sask.) Coll. 1943; Univ. of Man. B.Arch. 1948; AA Sch. of London, Eng. 1949; London Sch. of Econ. 1949; Mass. Inst. of Technol. M.C.P. 1952; Harvard Univ. 1952; m. Amy Nomura 11 Apl. 1950; children: James Kiyoharu, Gordon Satoshi, Mary Kiyoko; Environmental Design & Planning Consultant 1968– ; private arch. practice Izumi, Arnott & Sugiyama, Regina, Sask. 1953–68; Chrmn. Human Information and Ecology Program Univ. of Sask. Regina 1968–71; Resident Consultant Ministry of State for Urban Affairs Ottawa 1971–72; Prof. of Urban & Regional Planning, Univ. of Waterloo 1972–86 (Retired); former Dir., Domain Bio-dynamics Research Found., Breslau, Ont. (Retired); Trustee, Nat. Museums Can. 1968–74; Chrmn. Visiting Comte. Nat. Gallery Can. 1970–74; mem. various comtes. devel. and review Nat. Bldg. Code Govt. Can. 1954–74; Chrmn. Comn. Prof. Status Teachers Sask. 1962; mem. Health & Environment Research Comte. Nat. Health & Welfare Can.; Mental Health Survey Comte. State of Colo., Nat. Inst. Mental Health Govt. U.S.A. 1962; rec'd Can. Council Killam Fellowship 1968–71; author 'Psychiatric Hospital Design and Planning Standards' 1965; various articles, papers; recreation: golf; Home: 289 Hiawatha Dr., Waterloo, Ont. N2L 2V9.

# J

**JABES, Jak,** B.A., M.A., Ph.D.; university professor; b. Istanbul, Turkey 8 Oct. 1945; s. Leon and Ester (Abeni) J.; e. Robert Coll., B.A. 1968; Univ. of Kansas M.A. 1970, Ph.D. 1973; m. Vicky d. Sami and Perla Akohen 28 Dec. 1974; children: Jascha Leon, Boris Samuel; PRINCIPAL ADMINISTRATOR, SIGMA PROGRAMME, O.E.C.D. (PARIS, FRANCE) 1993– ; Asst. Prof. 1973–80, Assoc. Prof. 1980–89, Prof., Organizational Behaviour, Ottawa Univ. 1989–93; Invited Prof., ESCP, Paris 1979–81, and ESC Reims 1987–88; cons., public & private sector worldwide; Mem., Inst. of Public Admin. of Can.; author: 'Individual Processes in Organizational Behavior' 1978, 'Gestion Stratégique Internationale' 1988 and journal articles; co-author: 'Traité des Organisations' 1982 (spec. mention, Harvard L'Expansion); 'Vertical Solitude: Managing in the Public Sector' 1989; 'Management: Aspects Humains et Organisationnels' 1991; Editor-in-Chief: 'Optimum: The Journal of Public Management'; Associate Editor: 'International Review of Administrative Sciences'; Home: 23 rue de Laos, Paris, France; Office: 38 Boulevard Suchet, 75016 Paris, France.

**JACEK, Henry J.,** B.S.S., M.A., Ph.D.; educator; b. Derby, Conn. 31 Oct. 1941; s. Henry John and Elizabeth Mary (Sapach) J.; e. Fairfield (Conn.) Univ. B.S.S. 1963; Georgetown Univ. M.A. 1967, Ph.D. 1969; m. Catherine d. Leo and Mary Fields 13 May 1967; children: Anne Elizabeth, Michael Fields, Annice Marie; PROF. OF POL. SCI., MCMASTER UNIV. 1991– ; Rsch. Asst., Center for Population Rsch., Georgetown Univ. 1966–67; Lectr. present univ. 1967–69; Asst. Prof. 1969–75; Assoc. Prof. 1975–91; Assoc. Chrmn., Dept. of Pol. Sci. 1982–83; Chrmn. 1983–86; co-author 'An Essay Guide for Political Science' 1980; 'Regionalism, Business Interests and Public Policy' 1989; author of various articles on pol. sci.; analyst for Candn. television & radio stations on elections, urban problems, Am. pol., and other subjects; Coach Dundas Girls Soccer League; Pres. & Chrmn., McMaster Savings and Credit Union 1981–94; Past Pres. Dundas Heritage Assn.; mem. Candn. Pol. Sci. Assn. (Dir.); Inst. Pub. Adm. Can.; Am. Pol. Sci. Assn.; Conf. Group on Italian Pol. & Soc.; Conf. Group on German Pol. & Soc.; Counc. for Eur. Studies; Pi Sigma Alpha; R. Catholic; recreations: fitness, running, soccer; Clubs: McMaster Univ. Faculty (Dir.); Hamilton Automobile; Home: 49 Hillside Ave. S., Dundas, Ont. L9H 4H7; Office: Hamilton, Ont. L8S 4M4.

**JACK, Donald Lamont;** author; b. Radcliffe, Manchester, Eng. 6 Dec. 1924; s. Robert Paterson and Sarah (Lamont) J.; e. Bury (Lancs.) Grammar Sch.; Marr Coll. Troon, Ayrshire; m. Nancy (dec. 1990) d. Frederick Tolhurst 1952; two d. Maren Jean, Mary-Louise Victoria; served with RAF 1943–47; joined export packing firm Manchester 1948–51, Transport Mgr.; came to Can. 1951; Candn. citizen 1964; held various positions Can. incl. script writer Crawley Films Ltd. Ottawa 1955–57; free-lance full-time writer since 1957; 39 TV plays produced, 22 radio plays, numerous documentary films and 4 stage plays incl. 'The Canvas Barricade' (only original Candn. play to be produced Stratford Festival main stage, 1961); author 'Where Did Rafe Madison Go' novelette 1959; 'Exit Muttering' play 1972; 'Sinc, Betty and the Morning Man' hist. 1977; 'Rogues, Rebels & Geniuses: The Story of Canadian Medicine' hist. 1981; 'The Bandy Papers' (series 7 vols. comic novels, 3 rec'd Leacock Awards, one Author's Award Periodical Distributors Can.): 'Three Cheers For Me 1962, 1973, 'That's Me in the Middle' 1973, 'It's Me Again' 1975, 'Me Bandy, You Cissie' 1979, 'Me, Too' 1982, 'This One's On Me' 1987; 'Me So Far' 1989; private papers with Univ. of Calgary; author numerous mag. articles; Address: c/o Doubleday Publishers, 105 Bond St., Toronto, Ont. M5B 1Y3.

**JACKMAN, Barbara Louise,** B.A., LL.B.; lawyer; b. Toronto Ont. 23 Oct. 1950; d. William Stephen and Agnes Veda (Tully) J.; e. White Oaks S.S. 1969; Univ. of Windsor B.A. (Hons.) 1972; Univ. of Toronto LL.B. 1976; unmarried; one d.: Sara Teresa Ahmadian Jackman; called to Bar, Law Soc. of U.C. 1978; specialist in immigration & refugee law with Knazan, Jackman & Goodman; then Chiasson, Jackman to 1988; then P. Zambelli & M. Silcoff to 1990; then to Jackman, Joseph and Associates to 1991; presently priv. practice with Hoppe Jackman; Instr., Bar Admis. Prof., Law Soc. of U.C. 1983–86; Lectr., 1984–85, 1987–90; Fac. of Law, Queen's Univ. 1988–90, 1991–93; Osgoode Hall Law Sch., York Univ. 1988–89; Chair, Immigration Law, Candn. Bar Assn. (Ont.) 1987–89 (Extve. Mem. 1984–90); Dir., Candn. Civil Liberties Assoc. 1989–93; Extve. Mem., Immigration Law, Candn. Bar Assn. 1989–93; Former Dir., Working Women Comm. Ctr.; Intercede; Mem., Law Union of Ont.; Candn. Bar Assn. (Ont.); Candn. Counc. for Refugees; author of various papers & articles & contbr. to 3 books; del., Trans-Atlantic Legal Exchange on Refugee Law 1986–87; Office: Ste. 300, 196 Adelaide St. W., Toronto, Ont. M5H 1W7.

**JACKMAN, Frederic (Eric)** Langford Rowell, O.St.J., Ph.D., C. Psych.; executive; psychologist; b. Toronto, Ont. 17 May 1934; s. late Henry Rutherford, O.C., K.St.J., Q.C. and Mary Coyne (Rowell) J., LL.D., D.S.L., G.D.C.L.J.; e. Rosedale Pub. Sch., Toronto; Trinity Coll. Sch., Port Hope 1952; Univ. of B.C. 1952–53; Trinity Coll., Univ. of Toronto B.A. (Econ.) 1957, M.A. (Psychol.) 1962; Univ. of Chicago Ph.D. (Human Devel.) 1980; m. Sara Ellyn 4 Nov. 1978; children: Tara Griffith, Thomas Frederic Rowell, Robert Wesley Graydon; CHRMN. JACKMAN FOUND., PRES. AND DIR. INVICTA INVESTMENTS INC. 1978– ; Officer of the

Order of St. John and member of national investment ctte.; recipient Commemorative Medal for 125th Anniversary of Candn. Confederation; Career: Invest. Dealer, Burns Bros. and Denton Ltd. Toronto 1958–60; Psychology Intern, Ontario Hosp. (999 Queen), Toronto 1962; Clin. Psychol. Univ. of Chicago Service, Ill. Mental Health Insts. 1966–70; extensive consulting service with various psychiatric hospitals, juvenile courts, agencies for the blind and disabled, restaurants and public utilities in the United States and Canada 1965–78; P. Cons. Cand. for H. of C., Fed. Riding of Spadina g.e. 1980; Professional Registrations: Ont. Bd. of Examiners in Psychology 1965– ; Nat. Register of Health Service Providers in Psychol. (U.S.A.); Candn. Register of Health Service Providers in Psychol. 1987– ; mem., Ill. Group Psychotherapy Soc. (Past Pres.); Ill. Psychol. Assn. (Past Chrmn. Clinical Sec.); Founding mem., Candn. Group Psychotherapy Assoc. (Chrmn., Budget and Finance Comte. 1979–89); Pres., Candn. Group Psychotherapy Fdn. 1992– ; Ont. Psychol. Found. (Chrmn. 1986–90; Pres. 1991– ); recipient, C.M. Hincks National Award for Mental Health, C.M.H.A. 1991; Hon. Consulting Psychol., Distress Centre 1992– ; Gov., Univ. of Windsor 1989– ; Trustee & Vice Pres., Art Gall. of Ont. 1983– ; Founding Gov., Candn. Journalism Fdn. 1990– ; Rosedale P.C. Assn. (Vice-Pres.); Chrmn., Hon. Bd. of Dirs., Multiple Sclerosis Soc. of Can., Toronto Chapter (Pres. 1986–87); Chrmn., Hon. Adv. Comm., Boundless Adventures 1991– ; Cdn. Student Debating Fed. 1989– ; Gov., N. Amer. Model United Nations 1989– ; Metro Internat. Caravan; Dir., Empire Club of Canada 1987– (Pres. 1993–94); Candn. Fed. of Friends of Museums 1991– ; Candn. Hearing Soc. Fdn. 1992– ; Adv. Bd., Bereaved Families of Ontario; Youth Challenge International 1991– ; Bond Street Nursery Sch. 1988– ; Prime Mentors 1989– ; Hon. Patron, Cabbagetown Community Art Centre; Hon. Trustee, Ont. Coll. Art; C.N.I.B.; Mem., Candn. Inst. of Internat. Affairs; Bd. of Trade of Metro. Toronto; Founding Pres., Univ. of Chicago Alumni Club of Canada 1982–84; Founding Chrmn., Leaders of the Way Div., United Way of Greater Toronto 1982–85; formerly Dir., Stratford Festival 1985–88; Trinity Coll. Sch. 1988–90; Couchiching Inst. on Public Affairs 1983–88; Tarragon Theatre 1980–83; Victorian Order of Nurses; Group Psychotherapy Foundn., U.S.A. 1982–84; Steward, Metrop. United Church 1983–86; P. Conservative; Zeta Psi; United Church; recreations: photography, skiing, boating; Clubs: Albany; Empire; University; Badminton and Racquet; Toronto Golf; Osler Bluff Ski; Canadian; Home: 9 Drumsnab Rd., Toronto, Ont. M4W 3A4; Office: Ste. 1300, 44 Victoria St., Toronto, Ont. M5C 1Y2.

**JACKMAN, Colonel The Hon. Henry Newton Rowell,** C.M., K.St.J., LL.D.; executive; b. Toronto, Ont. 10 June 1932; s. Henry Rutherford, O.C., K.St.J., Q.C. and Mary (Rowell) J.; e. Upper Can. Coll. Toronto; Univ. of Toronto Schs.; Univ. of Toronto B.A. 1953, LL.B. 1956; London Sch. of Econ.; m. Maruja Trinidad d. James Stuart Duncan, C.M.G., LL.D. 14 Aug. 1964; children: Henry, Duncan, Maria Victoria, Consuelo, Trinity; apptd. LIEUTENANT GOVERNOR OF ONTARIO 19 Nov. 1991, sworn in 11 Dec. 1991 (Ontario's 25th Lieutenant Gov. since John Graves Simcoe arrived in Upper Canada as the 1st, 200 years ago. Prior to his apptd. as Lieutenant Gov., resigned from the following business positions: Chrmn. of the Bd. of Dirs., National Trust Co.; The Empire Life Insurance Co.; Economic Investment Trust Ltd.; The National Trustco Ltd.; E-L Financial Corp. Ltd.; E-L Financial Services Ltd.; Fulcrum Investment Co.; Algoma Central Corp.; United Corporations Ltd.; Vice Chrmn., The Dominion of Canada General Insurance Co.; Pres., Canadian and Foreign Securities Co. Ltd.; Canadian Northern Prairie Lands Co. Ltd.; The Debenture and Securities Corp. of Canada Ltd.; Dominion and Anglo Investment Corp. Ltd.; Dir., Mercantile & General Reinsurance Co. of Canada Ltd.; Peoples Jewellers Ltd.; Premier Trust Co.; Hollinger Inc.; Doubleday Canada Ltd.; Refuge Group PLC; Connecticut Nat. Life Insur. Co.; Hon. Trustee, Toronto Western Hosp.; Stratford Shakespearean Festival; also the following Charitable Bds.: Pres., Cdn. Opera Company 1984–86; Ballet Opera House Corp. 1986–89; Chrmn., Atlantic Council of Can.; Chrmn. Adv. Bd. Toronto Old Aged Men's and Women's Homes; Chrmn. Bd. of Trustees, Candn. Red Cross Pension Fund; Founding Chrmn., Regent Park Community Health Centre; Vice Chrmn., Candn. Opera Co. Found.; 1991 Glory of Mozart Competition; 1993 Internat. Choral Festival; Empire Club Found.; Vice Pres. & Mem. Nat. Ctte., Candn. Institute of Internat. Affairs; Vice Pres., Candn. Foundation for AIDS Rsch.; Hon. Treas. & Dir., Stratford Shakespearean Festival Found. of Can.; Dir., Institute for Rsch. on Public Policy; Candn. Institute for Strategic Studies; Ont. Heritage Found.; Univ. of Toronto Settlement House; Trustee, Stratford Found. Festival Fund; Toronto Western Hosp.; Art Gall. of Ont.; Mem. Bd. of Govs., York Univ.; Shaw Festival; St. Andrew's Coll.; Upper Canada Coll.; Mem. of the Council, Bureau of Municipal Rsch.; mem. Metro. Toronto Adv. Bd., The Salvation Army; mem. Ont. Finance and Investment Cttes., Order of St. John; mem. Candn. Affairs Adv. Bd., Americas Soc., New York City; mem. Bd. of Stewards, Metro. United Church; Chrmn., The Cardinal's Dinner 1989; Tribute Dinner 1990, Candn. Friends of the Hebrew Univ. (Co-Chrmn.); Hon. Chrmn., 'The Great Valentine Gala' Candn. Found. for Physically Disabled Persons 1989–90; Extve. Asst. to Min. of Pub. Works Can. and Min. in Charge of Central Mortgage & Housing Corp. Ottawa 1959–61; Pres., Rosedale Riding P. Cons. Assn. 1963–65 and P. Cons. Businessmen's Club Metrop. Toronto 1968–70; former cand. for H. of C., Rosedale Riding; currently Chrmn. of the Bd., J.P. Bickell Foundation; Canada's representative, Council of the Internat. Institute for Strategic Studies; Honours & Distinctions: LL.D. (honoris causa), Univ. of Windsor 1991 and Univ. of Toronto 1993; LL.D. (jure dignitatis) Univ. of Western Ont. 1993; apptd. Hon. Colonel, Governor General's Horse Guards 1992 (Hon. Lieutenant Col. 1989–92; Mem., Order of Canada 1991; Hon. Commander, Fort Henry Guard, Kingston 1992; invested into Pickering College 'Class of 1842' distinguished Alumni Award 1992; apptd. Paul Harris Fellow, Rotary Found. 1992; Knight of Justice in the Most Venerable Order of the Hospital of St. John of Jerusalem, and Vice-Prior, Ont. Council of the Order 1992; Knight Commander, Military and Hospitaller Order of St. Lazarus of Jerusalem 1975; Commander of Merit 1990; recipient, Univ. of Toronto Faculty of Mngmt. Distinguished Business Alumni (DBA) Award 1992; apptd. Hon. Colonel of 429 (Tactical Transp.) Squadron, CFB Trenton (first Hon. Colonel in the Bison Squadron's history); Phi Gamma Delta; P. Conservative; United Church; Clubs: York; Toronto; Albany (Pres. 1982–84); R.C.Y.C.; Royal Candn. Military Institute; Canadian; Empire Club of Canada (Pres. 1971–72); Mount Royal (Montreal); as Lieutenant Gov. has become Hon. Patron of more than 150 organizations in the arts and sciences, sports, and charitable communities throughout the province of Ontario; Office: Office of the Lieutenant Governor, Queen's Park, Toronto, Ont. M7A 1A1.

**JACKMAN, Nancy Rowell,** B.A., M.A., D.H.L.; feminist activist & philanthropist; b. 6 Jan. 1942; e. London School of Economics 1962; Covenant College theol. dipl. 1967; York Univ. B.A. 1969; Hebrew Univ. 1969; Whitworth, Spokane M.A. 1977; Univ. of Toronto, Theol. 1972–73, 1986–87 (grad. studies in Christian theology); PRESIDENT, 443472 ONT. LTD. 1980– (investment company), 983963 ONT. LTD. (land development company) and NANCY'S VERY OWN FOUNDATION 1985– ; extensive experience with religious, profl. & edn. orgns. in Canada, Britain & U.S. 1972–80; Interim Minister, Metro. Un. Church 1986; Co-Founder & Mgr. The Charter of Rights Coalition 1982– ; Leader, Women's Charter of Rights issues, Ad Hoc Ctte., Women on the Constitution (Ontario) 1987– ; Candn. Women on the Constitution 1981– ; the Meech Lake Accord; Equality Eve; The Women's Agenda & 1992 constitutional negotiations 1981– through public speaking, edn. & devel. of audio visuals; Staff Assoc., Naramata Centre for Cont. Edn. (B.C.) 1973–76; Mngt. Consultant to Archbishops of Canterbury & York, Comn. on Evangelism, England 1977; Dir., Saratech Inc. (incontinence products); Internat. Inst. of Concern for Public Health; Candn. Women's Found. (Co-founder); former Dir., Economic Council of Canada; Fulbright Found. Canada/USA; Gov., Mount St. Vincent Univ.; The Candn. Centre for Global Security; Pres. & Co-founder, LEAF Found.; Co-founder & Dir., LEAF 1984–86; Sky Works Charitable Found. (Adv. Ctte.); Womanly Way Prodns.; Hon. Dir. Massey Centre; John Black Aird Gallery (Adv. Ctte.); Friends of Shopping Bag Ladies; Candn. Soc. of Painters in Watercolour; Scarborough Women's Centre; Theatre Direct Canada; Several past political positions, P.C. party; P.C. candidate, 1993 Ont. by-election St. George-St. David; 1990 Ont. prov. election, St. Andrew-St. Patrick; federal P.C. nominee, Rosedale Riding 1988; Bd. of Dir., St. Andrew-St. Patrick P.C. Assn. 1991–93; St. George-St. David P.C. Assn. 1989–93; Rosedale P.C. Assn. 1989– ; extensive public speaker; applies profl. orgn. & devel. skills to the management of philanthropic activites; D.H.L. (honoris causa), Mount St. Vincent Univ. 1989; Woman of Distinction Special Award, Metro Toronto YWCA 1988; Tribute Dinner announcing the LEAF Nancy Rowell Jackman Award 1988; Trustee, The Jackman Found. 1979–88; founded, endowed and served on selection ctte. for doctoral scholarship for a feminist scholar, Toronto Sch. of Theol. 1979– ; Nancy Rowell Jackman Chair in Women's Studies, Mt. St. Vincent Univ. 1988, Nancy R. Jackman Jubilee Scholarship 1986– ; Nancy Rowell Jackman Child Care Centre, Internat. Feminist Univ. (Norway) 1988; has given major support to economic devel., cultural, educational & community, health & environ., internat., peace and disarmament, and women's organizations & institutions; Home: 184 Roxborough Dr., Toronto, Ont. M4W 1X8.

**JACKMAN, Neal,** C.A.; airline executive; b. Grand Falls, Nfld. 18 June 1950; s. Arthur R. and Ruby P. (Parsons) J.; e. Dianne d. Cecil and Madeline Byrne 8 July 1971; children: Arthur, Agnela; PRESIDENT, AIR ATLANTIC LTD. 1986– ; Lee & Martin C.A.s 1968–71; Eastern Provincial Airways Ltd. 1971–85; Sealand Helicopters Ltd. 1985; Home: St. John's, Nfld. A1A 4E9; Office: P.O. Box 9040, St. John's, Nfld. A1A 2X3.

**JACKMAN, Peter J.;** broadcasting executive; b. Toronto, Ont. 18 Aug. 1941; e. Ryerson Polytech. Inst. Bus. Adm. & Mktg.; m.; 6 children; Pres. & Chief Gen. Mgr., CKO Radio Inc. 1988; joined Wright Line of Canada Ltd. Ottawa 1965–66; Paul Mulvihill Ltd. Toronto 1966–69; Stephens & Towndrow Co. Ltd. Toronto, Acct. Exec. TV 1969–73, Asst. Gen. Mgr. and Sales Mgr. TV Div. 1973–75, Vice Pres., Gen. Mgr. 1975–80; Stanford Prize Merchandising Toronto, Vice Pres. and Gen. Mgr. 1980–82; C.A.P. Communications Toronto, Kitchener, Sales Mgr. 1982–83; CKO Radio Inc., Gen. Mgr. CKO Vancouver 1983, Vice Pres. W. Region 1985, Exec. Vice Pres. Toronto 1986.

**JACKMAN, Sydney W.,** B.S., M.A., Ph.D., D.Litt. (Hon.), F.S.A., F.R.Hist.S.; historian; educator; b. U.S.A. 25 Mar. 1925; s. Ensleigh Ellsworth and Dorothy (Anfield) J.; e. Victoria (B.C.) High Sch.; Univ. of Wash., B.S. 1946, M.A. 1947; Harvard Univ., M.A. 1948, Ph.D. 1953; Univ. of Lethbridge D.Litt. (Hon.) 1989; Univ. of Victoria D.Litt. (Hon.) 1991; Prof. of History, Univ. of Victoria, B.C. 1964–90; Fellow of St. Edmund's Coll., Cambridge, 1990; Instr., Phillips Exeter 1952–56; Asst. and Assoc. Prof., Bates Coll. 1956–64; Mem. Bd. of Dir., Art Gallery of Greater Victoria 1965–70; Humanities Rsch. Counc. 1976–81; Candn. Fedn. for the Humanities 1981; mem. Adv. Comte., Maltwood Museum; Prov. Jt. Bd. of Teacher Educ. 1972–73; Gov., Univ. of Victoria 1982–87; corresp. mem., Council Soc. for Army Hist. Res.; Woodbury-Lowry Mem. Scholar; Rockefeller Fellow; Penrose Fellow; Visiting Fellow, Aust. Nat. Univ.; Visiting Prof., Univ. of Tasmania; Univ. of Mich.; Univ. of Papua, New Guinea; Visiting Scholar, Trinity Hall, Cambridge 1978–79; Fellow, Yale Center for British Art 1986; author: 'Galloping Head' 1958; 'Man. of Mercury' 1965; 'Portraits of the Premiers' 1969; 'Men at Cary Castle' 1972; 'Vancouver Island' 1972; 'Tasmania' 1974; 'Nicholas Cardinal Wiseman' 1977; 'A Slave to Duty' 1979; 'The People's Princess' 1984; Ed., F. Marryat 'Diary in America' 1962; 'With Burgoyne From Quebec' 1963; 'English Reform Tradition' 1963; 'American Voyageur' 1969; 'Romanov Relations' 1969; 'The Journal of William Sturgis' 1978; Ed., 'Acton in America' 1979; 'A Curious Cage' 1981; 'At Sea & By Land' 1984; 'Een Vreemdelinghe in den Haag' 1984; 'Romanov Relaties' 1987; 'Chère Annette' 1990; mem. Ed. Adv. Bd., 'American Neptune'; other writings incl. articles in various scholarly journs.; Fellow, Roy. Irish Soc. Antiquaries; Scottish Antiquaries; Roy. Soc. Arts; Society of Antiquaries (London); Royal Hist. Soc.; mem. Colonial Soc. Mass.; Mass. Hist. Soc.; Am. Antiquarian Soc.; Soc. Army Hist. Research; Royal Soc. Tasmania; Royal Commonwealth Soc.; Hasty Pudding Inst. 1770; recreations: travel, collecting pictures; Clubs: Union (Victoria); Atheneum (London); Authors (London); St. Stephen's Green (Dublin); military service W.W. II; Home: 1065 Deal St., Victoria, B.C. V8S 5G6.

**JACKS, Allan Milton;** executive; b. Hamilton, Ont. 29 Jan. 1953; s. Donald Grant and Dorothy Elaine (Macleay) J.; e. Burlington Cent. H.S.; Kelvin H.S.; Univ. of Man.; m. Evelyn d. Harry and Elfrieda Schimke 10 May 1975; children: Cordell, Donald; Chief Extve. Offr., U & R Tax Services 1980; Mgr., White Cap Boat Serv. 1973–85; Tax Preparer, U & R Tax Serv. 1975; Brandon Dist. Mgr. 1976; Franchise Dir. 1978; Winnipeg Dist. Mgr. 1979; regd. trade sch. instr.; Man. Dept. of Edn. Prog. Review Ctte. Mem.; Past Pres., Candn. Assn. of Income Tax Practitioners; Past Pres., Wasagaming C. of C.; Past Comdr., Clear Lake Yacht Club; Mem., Phi Delta Theta frat.; Man. Assn. of Career Coll.; Man. Assn. of Tax Discounters; Nat. Assn. of Tax Practitioners (U.S.); Candn. Tax Found.; Editorial Adv. Bd. Mem., Manitoba Business Magazine; co-prod./host 'Jacks on Tax' TV show; frequent public appearances: radio, TV, print, seminars; recreations: fishing, windsurfing, coaching soccer, travel, kids' hockey; clubs:

Winnipeg Winter (Gov.), Lake George Fishing (Dir.), Internat. Game Fish Assn., Ducks Unlimited.

**JACKSON, Andrew Carlisle;** corporate executive; b. Horsforth, England 2 June 1948; s. Charles William and Margaret Hawley (Carlisle) J.; e. Froebelian P.S. 1956; Bradford Sch. 1966, Oxford & Cambridge Bd.; m. Charlene d. Basil and Gwen Norman 1980; one s.: William Andrew; Mgr., U.K. Dealer Network, Volkswagen (G.B.) 1966; Gen. Mgr. (group of V.W. franchises) 1970; joined Caterpillar orgn. in UK & moved to Alta. as divisional Gen. Mgr. of a Caterpillar dealership 1980; Pres. & C.E.O., Willcock Industries 1986–91; Chief Operating Offr., Griffith Oil Tool (a div. of Dreco Energy Services) 1991–93; Pres., Westank-Willock; Willock Truck Internat.; Willock Truck & Equip.; Past Pres., Candn. Truck Trailer Mfrs. Assn.; Bd. of Dirs., Dreco Group of Companies; Mem., British Shooting Team for 10 yrs. rep. Britain in European Championships, Commonwealth Games & World Championships: ranked 1 in UK and 5th in the World; author: 'The Edmonton Soaring Club: The First Twenty-Five Years'; recreations: soaring, golf; clubs: Edmonton Soaring (Pres.); Home: 78 Fairway Dr., Edmonton, Alta. T6J 2C4; Office: 3660 – 93 St., Edmonton, Alta.

**JACKSON, Andrew Nussey,** B.Sc., M.Sc.; economist; b. Hereford, U.K. 28 Aug. 1952; s. John Nicholas and Kathleen Mary J. e. London Sch. of Econ., B.Sc. 1973, M.Sc. 1975; m. Karen Marilyn d. Charles and Margory Ort 12 Aug. 1979; one d.: Caitlin; SENIOR ECONOMIST, CANADIAN LABOUR CONGRESS 1989– ; Instr., Capilano College 1978–80; Policy Researcher-Economist, New Democratic Party 1980–87; Prog. Offr., Canadian Labour Market & Productivity Ctr. 1988–89; Dir., Candn. Ctr. for Policy Alternatives; Candn. Counc. on Social Devel.; Social Planning Counc. of Ottawa-Carleton; Contbr.: 'Federalism in Canada' 1989, 'The Free Trade Deal' 1988; Home: 23 Kinnear St., Ottawa, Ont. K1Y 3R7; Office: 2841 Riverside Dr., Ottawa, Ont. K1V 8X7.

**JACKSON, Andrew Sander,** F.C.A.; retired executive; b. Winnipeg, Man. 15 June 1925; s. Esther Secelia (Lindgren) and late Alfred Sander J.; e. Daniel McIntyre Coll.; Univ. of Manitoba, C.A. 1948; F.C.A. 1970; m. Elsie Mary, d. late William Edmund Collicutt, 12 June 1948; children: Brian, Barbara, Sandra; retired Extve. Vice Pres., Investors Group; Dir., Investors Group Trust Co. Ltd.; Investors Syndicate Ltd.; Winpak Ltd.; Apprentice, Glendinning, Gray & Roberts 1942; Income Tax Dept. 1948–50; with Peat, Marwick, Mitchell & Co. 1950; Comptroller, Investors Syndicate of Canada Ltd. 1955, Asst. Gen. Mgr. and Treas. 1963, Vice-Pres. and Treas. 1964, Exec. Vice-Pres. 1970; President, Investors Syndicate Ltd. 1974; served in R.C.N.V.R. 1943–45; Dir., Children's Hosp. of Winnipeg Research Found. Inc.; mem. Inst. Chart. Accts. of Man.; Anglican; recreations: golf, curling, painting; Clubs: The Manitoba; Winnipeg Winter; Granite Curling; St. Charles Country; Home: 476 South Drive, Winnipeg, Man. R3T 0B1.

**JACKSON, (William) Bruce,** M.D., FRCSC; ophthalmologist, university professor and administrator; b. Peterborough, Ont. 2 May 1943; s. William Herbert and Marjorie Powell (Robinson) J.; e. Univ. of Western Ont. M.D. 1967; FRCSC Ophth. McGill Univ. 1972; Diplomat of Am. Bd. of Ophth. 1973; m. Mary Lou d. Dorothy and John Sparrow 13 May 1967; children: David Bruce, Julie Alicia; CHIEF OF OPHTHALMOLOGY, OTTAWA GENERAL HOSPITAL 1991– and DIRECTOR GENERAL, EYE INSTITUTE, UNIVERSITY OF OTTAWA 1991– ; Prof. and Chrmn., Dept. of Ophthalmology, Univ. of Ottawa 1991– ; Assoc. Prof., McGill Univ. 1978–87; Prof. of Ophth. 1987–91; Ophthalmologist-in-Chief, Royal Victoria Hosp. 1986–91; Chair, Ophth., McGill Univ. 1987–91; Francis I Proctor Fellow; Mem., Candn. Ophth. Soc.; author/co-author of 43 research articles; recreations: skiing, tennis; Home: 1693 Amberdale Cres., Ottawa, Ont. K1H 7B2; Office: Ottawa Gen. Hosp., 501 Smyth St., Ottawa, Ont. K1H 8L6.

**JACKSON, Bruce Leslie,** B.A., C.A.; publishing executive; b. Toronto, Ont. 21 Apr. 1946; s. Les and Hazel (Workman) J.; e. McMaster Univ. B.A. 1968; Ernst & Young C.A. 1971; m. Sally d. Marion Smith 15 July 1972; children: Lesley, Scott; CHIEF FINANCIAL OFFICER, TORONTO SUN PUBLISHING CORP.; Partner, Ernst & Young Chartered Accountants; Chrmn., Bowes Publishers Limited; Dir., The Financial Post Co.; T.S. Pubns. (Florida) Inc.; Comprint Inc. (Washington); One: 1362 Birchwood Heights Dr., Mississauga, Ont. L5G 2Y2; Office: 333 King St. E., Toronto, Ont. M5A 3X5.

**JACKSON, David Phillip,** B.Sc., M.A., M.A.Sc., Ph.D.; physicist; b. Toronto, Ont. 2 Oct. 1940; s. Peter Morris and Bertha Belle (Morris) J.; e. Riverdale C.I.; Univ. of Toronto, B.Sc. 1962, M.A. 1964, M.A.Sc. 1966, Ph.D. 1968; Univ. of Ottawa, dipl. Eng. Mngt. 1985; Univ. of Ottawa M.Eng.Mngt. 1991; m. Susan Jane d. Peter and Shirley Bell 30 May 1975; children: Scott Peter, Timothy David; DIR., NATIONAL FUSION PROGRAM, CHALK RIVER LABS., ATOMIC ENERGY OF CAN. LTD. 1986– ; IBM 1962–63; Rsch. Asst., Inst. for Aerospace Studies, Univ. of Toronto 1965–68; Vis. Sci., Max Planck Inst. for Plasmaphysics, Garching Germany 1975–76; joined present firm 1968; Rsch. Offr., Solid State Sci. Br. 1968–80; Sr. Rsch. Offr. 1981–84; Mgr., Fusion Breeder Blanket Prog. 1982–85; Mgr., Fusion 1985–86; Assoc. Prof. (part-time), Dept. of Engr. Physics, McMaster Univ. 1978–81; Prof. (part-time) 1981– ; Inst. for Materials Rsch., McMaster 1979– ; Inst. for Energy Studies 1980– ; Cons. Vis. Prof., AT&T Bell Labs. 1982–87; Adv. Ctte., Internat. Conf. on Fusion Reactor Materials 1984– ; Fusion Power Coord. Ctte., Internat. Energy Agency 1985– ; Internat. Fusion Rsch. Counc., Internat. Atomic Energy Agency 1988– (Chrmn. 1993– ); Cons. d'admin., Ctr. candn. de fusion magnétique 1988– ; mem., federal interdepartmental Panel on Energy Rsch. and Devel. 1992– ; Royal Candn. Navy Reserve 1958–75; mem., Chem. Inst. of Can.; author of 75 sci. papers, abstracts & reports; recreations: sailing; clubs: Deep River Golf; Naval Officers Assn. of Can.; Home: 117 Frontenac Cres., Deep River, Ont. K0J 1P0; Office: Chalk River, Ont. K0J 1J0.

**JACKSON, Donald K.,** B.A., M.B.A.; executive; b. Castor, Alta. 6 Apr. 1944; e. Univ. of Alta. B.A. 1965; Univ. of W. Ont. M.B.A. 1967; children: Andrea, Sara; PRES. & C.E.O., LAIDLAW INC.; Dir., Derlan Industries, ADT Limited; Attwoods plc; Public Policy Forum, Conf. Bd. of Can.; Pres., Tricil Ltd. 1973–76; Chrmn., Tricil Ltd. 1976–87; Group Vice Pres., Trimac Ltd. 1976–77; Dir. Trimac Ltd. 1981–87; Pres., Nat. Tank Truck Carriers, Inc. 1984; Chrmn., Young Pres.' Cdn. Council 1984–86; mem. YPO; Dir., Derlan Industries; Clubs: Glencoe Golf & Country; York; Founders.

**JACKSON, Douglas,** B.A.; film director; b. Montréal, Qué. 26 Jan. 1940; s. Frederick and Joyce J.; e. Sir George Williams Univ. B.A. 1960; m. Tanya; son: Misha; wrote or co-wrote screenplays for over 30 films directed for Nat. Film Bd., CBC and U.S. television; most recently directed feature films, 'Stalked' (starring Jay Underwood, Maryam D'Abo and Lisa Blount) and 'The Paperbox' (starring Alexandra Paul, Mark Marut, William Katt for producer Tom Berry and The Image Organization, L.A.); also directed 'Deadbolt' (feature film for CBS telecast), starring Justine Bateman and Adam Baldwin, 'Whispers' (feature film) starring Victoria Tennant, Jean Leclerc and Chris Sarandon, two episodes of 'Street Legal', 'Counterstrike' (filmed in Paris), 'Friday The 13th,' 'Wise Guy' and two episodes of 'Twilight Zone' for CBS and 'Banshee' starring Peter O'Toole for HBO (winner of Best Directing Ace Award, U.S. Cable TV); co-wrote, produced and directed 'The Heatwave Lasted Four Days' (first Candn. feature film to receive U.S. Network telecast) ABC 1975; directed half the episodes of CBC mini-series 'Empire, Inc.' (sold to TV in 38 countries incl. U.S. 1985); directed 3 TV dramas for Atlantis Films 1985 incl. Mordecai Richler's 'Bambinger' and Brian Moore's 'Uncle T' starring Gordon Pinsent; films won over 30 internat. awards incl. Oscar Nomination 1969, Am. Film Festival Award, N.Y. 1986; recreations: tennis, skiing; Clubs: Montreal Indoor Tennis; Mount Royal Tennis; Home: 408, 225 Olivier Ave., Montréal, Qué. H3Z 2C7.

**JACKSON, Douglas Northrop,** M.Sc., Ph.D.; psychologist; educator; b. Merrick, N.Y. 14 Aug. 1929; s. Douglas N. and Caya (Cramer) J.; e. Cornell Univ. B.Sc. 1951; Purdue Univ. M.Sc. 1952, Ph.D. 1955; Menninger Foundation Topeka, Kans. postdoctoral fellow 1955–56; m. Lorraine J. d. late Jacob Morlock 28 June 1962; children: Douglas III, Lori, Charles Theodore; SR. PROF. OF PSYCHOL., UNIV. OF W. ONT. 1964– ; Pres., Research Psychologists Press Inc.; Chrmn., Can. Council Fellowship Comte. (Psychol.) 1976–78; Special Rsch. Review Comte. U.S. Pub. Health Service 1971– ; Scient. Adv. Comte. Psych. Systems Inc. 1981– ; Mgmt. Adv. Comte. Applied Psychological Measurement 1980– ; Psychol., U.S. Veterans Adm. 1951–52, 1953–55; Rsch. Psychol. Menninger Foundn. 1952–53, U.S. Pub. Health Service postdoctoral Fellow 1955–56; Asst. and Assoc. Prof. Pa. State Univ. 1956–63, Visiting Prof. 1978–79; Consultant, Educ. Testing Service 1958–64, Visiting Scholar 1971–72; Distinguished Visiting Prof., Univ. of Iowa 1983; Rsch. Consultant Family Services London (Ont.); Consultant London Police Dept.; Dir. London (Ont.) French Sch. 1970–71; co-ed. 'Problems in Human Assessment' 1967, 1977; over 150 scient. articles; author 'Jackson Vocational Interest Survey' and other psychol. tests; mem. bd. eds. various journs,; Fellow, Candn. Psychol. Assn.; Am. Psychol. Assn.; mem. Psychometric Soc.; Soc. Multivariate Exper. Psychol. (Pres. 1975–76); recreations: fishing, boating, music; Home: 29 Maldon Rd., London, Ont. N6G 1W2; Office: London, Ont. N6A 5C2.

**JACKSON, Edwin Sydney,** B. Comm., F.S.A.,F.C.I.A.; financial services executive; b. Regina, Sask. 17 May 1922; s. late Dorothy Hazel (Bell) and late Edwin J.; e. Univ. of Man., B.Comm. 1947; m. Nancy Joyce, d. late Gordon Stovel, Winnipeg, 19 May 1948; three d., Patricia, Barbara, Catherine; VICE-CHAIRMAN, THE MANUFACTURERS LIFE INSURANCE COMPANY 1990– ; joined Acturial Dept. of present co. in 1948; Pres. and C.E.O. 1972; Chrmn. & C.E.O. 1985–87; Chrmn. 1987–90; Dir., The Manufacturers Life Capital Corp. Inc.; Chrmn., Arthritis Soc.; Business Fund for Candn. Studies in the U.S.; mem.: Bus. Council on National Issues; Cdn. Inst. Actuaries (Pres. 1966–67); Soc. of Actuaries; recreations: skiing, golf, curling; Clubs: Toronto; Granite; Rosedale; Home: 101 Stratford Cres., Toronto, Ont. M4N 1C7; Office: 200 Bloor St. E., Toronto, Ont. M4W 1E5.

**JACKSON, G. Ernest;** insurance executive; b. Toronto, Ont. 2 Feb. 1921; s. George Ernest and Jean Tinsely (McNeill) J.; e. London (Ont.) S. Coll. Inst.; m. Wilma (Reid) Mossman; Dir., Reed Stenhouse Ltd. (Sr. Vice Pres. 1973–86); Br. Mgr. Canadian Pittsburgh Industries 1946; Partner Cronyn Pocock & Robinson 1948; Dir. Reed Shaw Osler 1968; served with Royal Candn. Regt. Eng. Sicily and Italy 1939–45, rank Capt.; el. M.P.P. for London S. 1955–59; Campaign Mgr. for Ont. Progressive Conservatives in gen. elects. 1963–67; Hon. J.P. Robarts Leadership Campaign; Shriner; P. Conservative; Anglican; recreations: golfing, fishing, hunting; Clubs: Griffith Island; Albany; Rosedale Golf; Toronto Hunt; Home: 78 Cluny Drive, Toronto, Ont. M4W 2R3; Office: Reed Stenhouse Tower, 20 Bay St., Toronto, Ont. M5J 2N9.

**JACKSON, J.T. Blair,** B.A., FRI, RI (B.C.), CAE; corporat; executive; b. Vernon, B.C. 9 Aug. 1931; s. George T. and Kathleen (Galbraith) J.; e. Public and High Schs., Ottawa, Ont.; Carleton Univ.; Univ. of Brit. Columbia, F.R.I. 1961; m. . 1954; children: Suzanne, Todd, Mark; PRES. REALTY WORLD INTERNATIONAL and PRES. & DIR., JACKSON, DORAN & ASSOC. LTD.; Pres. & Dir., RW Internat. Marketing Corp.; RW Asia Pacific Marketing Corp.; RW Americas Marketing Corp.; RW European Marketing Corp.; RW Mid-East Marketing Corp.; RW Eastern Europe Marketing Corp.; RW China Marketing Corp.; Innova Concepts Ltd.; Verndale Develop. Ltd.; Dir., Realty World Corp. (U.S.); Exec. Comm. & Bd. Mem., Internat. Real Estate Fedn. (Paris); with Household Finance Corp., Br. Mgr. Ottawa 1951–54; Credit Mgr., Galbraith & Sons Ltd., Vernon, B.C. 1954, Gen. Mgr. 1956–58; Pres., Verndale Devel. Ltd., Vancouver, B.C. 1959– ; Pres. and Gen. Mgr., Verndale Const. Ltd. 1959–65; Reg. Mgr., Capitol Holdings Ltd., Vancouver 1963; Mortgage Appraisal Mgr., Wolstencroft Corp., New Westminster, B.C. 1965, Vice-Pres. and Asst. Gen. Mgr. 1968; Dir. Rsch. and Public Relations, Candn. Assn. Real Estate Bds., Toronto, Ont. 1968–70; Extve. Vice-Pres. & Gen., Mgr., Candn. Real Estate Assn. 1971–79; Sr. Vice Pres., Century 21 Real Estate Can. Ltd. 1980, Exec. Vice-Pres. 1981–91; Pres. Neighbourhood Financial Corp. 1982–90; Pres., Goldshield Services Ltd. 1983–91; Pres., Century 21 Real Estate Services Ltd. 1983–91; served with R.C.A.F. as Flying Offr. 1950–51; mem. Soc. Real Estate Appraisers; Internat. Council Shopping Centres; Urban Devel. Inst.; Housing and Urban Devel. Assn. Can.; Real Estate Inst. Can.; Real Estate Inst. B.C.; Candn. Real Estate Assn.; Internat. Real Estate Fed.; Canada Chamber of Commerce; Un. Church; recreations: tennis, riding, skiing, boating, photography; Address: 1736 West 59 Ave., Vancouver, B.C. V6P 1Z4.

**JACKSON, James Robert de Jager,** M.A., A.M., Ph.D., F.R.S.C.; professor; b. St. Andrew's, Scotland 14 July 1935; s. Reginald and Clara (Farrell) J.; e. Trinity Coll. Sch.; Queen's Univ., B.A. (Hons.) 1957, M.A. 1958; Princeton Univ., A.M. 1960, Ph.D. 1961; Univ. of London, Ph.D. 1963; m. Heather d. Colman and Margaret Murphy 5 Sept. 1969; children: Katherine, Elizabeth; PROF., VICTORIA COLL., UNIV. OF TORONTO 1973– ; Vis. Rsch. Fellow, Birkbeck Coll., Univ. of London 1962–63; Asst. Prof., McMaster Univ. 1963–64; Victoria Coll., Univ. of Toronto 1964–67; Assoc. Prof. 1967–73; Guggenheim Fellowship 1972–73; Killam Sr. Scholarship 1975–76; Killam Rsch. Fellowship 1982–84; Connaught Sr. Fellowship 1985–86; author: 'Romantic Poetry by Women: A Bibliography, 1770-1835' 1993; 'Historical Criticism and the Meaning of Texts' 1989, 'Annals of English Verse 1770–1835' 1985, 'Poetry of the Romantic Period' 1980, 'Method and Imagination in Coleridge's Criticism' 1969; editor: 'Coleridge: The Critical Heritage Volume 2: 1834–1900' 1991; S.T. Coleridge, 'Logic' 1981, 'Coleridge: The Critical Heritage' 1970; Home: 55 Boswell Ave., Toronto, Ont. M5R 1M5; Office: Dept. of English, Victoria Coll., Toronto, Ont. M5S 1K7.

**JACKSON, John David Allan,** B.Comm., LL.B.; lawyer; b. Chatham, Ont. 29 Jan. 1947; s. Allan Sutherland and Valerie Evelyn (Frosdick) J.; e. University of Windsor B.Comm. 1969; Osgoode Hall Law School LL.B. 1972; m. Ann Maureen d. Achille E. and Catherine P. Caza 5 June 1971; PARTNER, BLAKE, CASSELS & GRAYDON 1980– ; joined Blake, Cassels & Graydon on graduation from Osgoode Hall Law Sch. 1972; called to Bar in Ont. 1974; Co-Chair, Securities Law Practice Group; Dir., Investors Group Inc.; Dayton Mining Corp.; Federal White Cement Ltd.; Cominco Fertilizers Ltd.; Pilkington Sales (North America) Limited; M.I.M. (Canada) Inc.; Granges Inc. & several Candn. subs. of internat. corps. & other private Candn. companies; University of Windsor Gold Medal in Business Admin.; has lectured & written on securities & corp. law topics incl. chairing or participating in panels sponsored by Candn. Fed. of Law Socs., Law Soc. of U.C. & private orgns.; recreations: golf, reading; clubs: Albany Club of Toronto, Donalda Club; Home: 17 Daleberry Place, North York, Ont. M3B 2A5; Office: Box 25, Commerce Court W., Toronto, Ont. M5L 1A9.

**JACKSON, John James,** M.Sc., Ph.D.; educator; b. Silsden, Eng. 5 Oct. 1935; s. Albert and May (Atkinson) J.; e. Keighley Boys' Grammar Sch. 1954; Borough Rd. Coll. Inst. of Educ. Univ. of London Teacher's Cert. 1958; Carnegie Coll. Leeds D.P.E. 1959; Univ. of Ottawa M.Sc. 1970; Univ. of Alta. Ph.D. 1975; m. Enid d. Frank and Muriel Foster 12 Aug. 1959; children: Deborah Louise (Hungerford), Richard John; PROFESSOR OF PUBLIC ADMINISTRATION, UNIV. OF VICTORIA 1993– ; served with RN 1954–56; Asst. Master Teignmouth Grammar Sch. Devon 1959–65; Exchange Teacher Cy-Fair High Sch. Houston, Texas 1963–64; Asst., Univ. of Aberdeen 1965–66; Asst. Master Hele's Sch. Exeter 1966–70; Research Asst., Univ. of Ottawa 1968–69; Tech. Rep./Regional Offr. (SW), CCPR/The Sports Council (Eng.) 1970–73; Instr., Univ. of Alta. 1973–75; Dir. of Recreation City of Edmonton 1975–76; Asst. Prof. of Educ. and Phys. Educ. present Univ. 1976, Assoc. Prof. 1978, Prof. 1982–93 and of Public Admin. 1985–92 (part-time), Dir. Sch. of Phys. Educ. 1980–82, Dean, Faculty of Educ. 1982–87; Assoc. Vice-Pres., Rsch. 1987–93, Dir., Business and Industry Development Centre 1987–92; Visiting Fellow, East-West Center, Honolulu 1985; Sr. Rsch. Scholar, Corpus Christi Coll., Cambridge 1986; Visiting Sr. Mem., Linacre Coll., Oxford 1993; Visiting Fellow, ANU, Canberra 1993; Dir.: B.C. & Yukon Council Duke of Edinburgh Award in Can. 1981– (Vice Pres. 1988–93; Pres. 1993– ); Victoria Heart Inst. Foundation 1988– ; numerous publs.; Home: 4404 Meadowood Place, Victoria, B.C. V8X 4V7; Office: Victoria, B.C. V8W 2Y2.

**JACKSON, John Nicholas,** B.A., Ph.D.; professor emeritus; b. Nottingham, England 15 Dec. 1925; s. Alexander (Alec) and Phyllis Elizabeth (Oldfield) J.; e. King Edwards Sch., Birmingham; Univ. of Birmingham, B.A. 1949; Univ. of Manchester, Ph.D. 1960; m. Kathleen d. Sam and Nellie Nussey 10 May 1951; children: Andrew, Susan, Paul; PROF. EMERITUS, BROCK UNIV. 1991– ; Rsch. Offr., Co. Planning Dept., Herefordshire Co. Counc. 1950–53; Sr. Rsch. Offr., Hull C.B. 1954–56; Lectr., Town & Country Planning, Univ. of Manchester 1956–65; Prof. of Applied Geog., Brock Univ. 1965–91; Vis. Assoc. Prof., Community & Regl. Planning, Univ. of B.C. 1962–63; Mem., Town Planning Inst. 1960; Dir., Bruce Trail Assn. 1977–82; Dir., Welland Canals Found. 1981– (Pres. 1986–90); author: 'Surveys for Town and Country Planning' 1963; 'Recreational Development and the Lake Erie Shore' 1968; 'The Industrial Structure of the Niagara Region' 1971; 'The Urban Future' 1973; 'The Canadian City' 1972; 'Welland and the Welland Canal' 1975; 'A Planning Appraisal for the Welland Urban Community' 1975; 'St. Catharines, Ontario' 1976; 'Values in Conflict' 1976; 'The Welland Canals: A Comprehensive Guide' 1982; 'The Four Welland Canals: A Journey of Discovery in St. Catharines and Thorold' 1988; 'Names Across Niagara' 1989; co-author: 'Railways in the Niagara Peninsula' 1978; 'The Welland Canals: The Growth of Mr. Merritt's Ditch' 1988; 'St. Catharines: Canada's Canal City' 1992; co-editor: 'Practical Geography' 1972; recreations: travel, gardening, bridge; Home and Office: 80 Marsdale Dr., St. Catharines, Ont. L2T 3S3.

**JACKSON, Kenneth Ronald,** M.Sc., Ph.D.; educator; b. Montréal, Qué. 3 March 1951; s. Reginald Ronald and Evelyn Mary (Skelton) J.; e. Silverthorne Coll. Inst. Etobicoke 1969; Univ. of Toronto B.Sc. 1973, M.Sc. 1974, Ph.D. 1978; Yale Univ. Postdoctoral Rsch. 1981; m. Ivana d. Stanislava and Miodrag Zivič 14 July 1983; PROF. OF COMPUTER SCI., UNIV. OF TORONTO 1992– , Asst. Prof. 1981, Assoc. Prof. 1986, Assoc. Chrmn. of Dept. 1987–89; Univ. Rsch. Fellow (NSERC) 1981–91; author or co-author various papers internat. sci. jours.; Chrmn., SIAM Ctte. on Human Rights of Mathematical Scientists; Home: 18 Brûlé Gdns., Toronto, Ont. M6S 4J2; Office: Computer Science Dept., Univ. of Toronto, Toronto, Ont. M5S 1A4.

**JACKSON, Lawrence James,** B.Sc., M.B.A.; international business executive; b. Canada 27 Sept. 1946; s. Irwin George and Annie Muriel (Miller) J.; e. Univ. of Guelph B.Sc. 1968; York Univ. M.B.A. 1970; m. Susan d. Robert and Catherine Storey 13 Sept. 1969; children: Michael, Matthew; PRESIDENT, GLOBAL GROWTH PARTNERS LIMITED 1990– ; Product Mngt., S.C. Johnson, T.J. Lipton, Bristol-Myers 1970–76; New Products Devel. Mgr., S.C. Johnson Inc. USA 1976–81; Mng. Dir., S. Africa 1981–85; Area Dir., Europe 1985–86; Pres. S.C. Johnson & Son Ltd., Canada 1986–90; Pres. & C.E.O., Brewers Retail Inc. 1990–92; recreations: golf, skiing, travel; clubs: Osler Bluff Ski; Blue Mountain Golf; Address: P.O. Box 4399, R.R. 4, Collingwood, Ont. L9Y 4T9.

**JACKSON, Margaret;** retired accountant; b. Toronto, Ont. 15 July 1922; d. Hugh Allen and Lucy C. (Bailie) J.; e. Runnymede Pub. Sch. 1934; Western Comml. Sch. 1937; Dominion Bus. Coll. 1938; PAST PRESIDENT, CANADIAN FEDERATION OF BUSINESS AND PROFESSIONAL WOMEN'S CLUBS; Treas., Sr. Talent Bank Assoc. of Ont.; Bookkeeping, switchboard, secretarial Dental Company of Canada 1938–48; Credit Mgr. and Office Mgr. Leyland Motors (Canada) Ltd. 1948–54; Acctg. Supvr., Chief Acct., Computer Operator, Credit Asst. United Dominions Corp. (Canada) Ltd. 1955–82; Acct. United Dominions Investments Ltd. until retired 1982; Pres. Young Women's Candn. Club 1950–52; Toronto Bus. and Profl. Women's Club 1970–71; Bus. and Profl. Women's Clubs of Ont. 1974–76; Treas. and Trustee, Elsie Gregory MacGill Meml. Found.; mem. Women's Coll. Hosp. Volunteer Auxiliary; Volunteer Red Cross Nurse; Volunteer Runnymede Hosp.; Life mem. in CFBPWC conferred by Toronto BPWC 1978; recreations: theatre, music, baseball, travel, volunteer work; Home: 205–45 Oakmount Rd., Toronto, Ont. M6P 2M4.

**JACKSON, Paul Conrad;** journalist; b. Halifax, England 8 Feb. 1944; s. William Craven and Dorothy (Saunders) J.; e. Southcoates H.S.; Hull College of Commerce; EDITOR, CALGARY SUN 1989– ; Reporter, Saskatoon Star-Phoenix 1964–67; Business Writer, Edmonton Journal 1967–69; City Editor, Calgary Albertan 1969–71; Mem., Parliamentary Press Gallery 1971–82 writing for papers incl. Vancouver Sun, Edmonton Journal, Calgary Herald, & Ottawa Journal; Extve. Asst. to Premier Grant Devine of Sask. 1982–86; Columnist, Saskatoon Star-Phoenix 1986–89; major achievement in journalism was exposé in 1978 of Soviet spy ring in Canada, followed by four years of writing about East Block espionage in Canada; also, only Western journalist to cover a war crimes trial in Titograd, Yugoslavia (coverage won the release of an accused Edmonton, Alta. man who was charged with being commander of a Nazi-style death squad) 1979; frequent guest & talk show host on radio & TV; Mem., Calgary C. of C.; Roman Catholic; co-author: 'Battleground: The Socialist Assault on Grant Devine's Canadian Dream' 1991; recreations: classical music, history; club: Commerce; Home: Suite 502, 354 – 3rd Ave. N.E., Calgary, Alta. T2E 0H4; Office 2615 – 12th St. N.E., Calgary, Alta. T2E 7W9.

**JACKSON, Richard Lee,** B.A., M.B.A.; educator; b. Ottawa, Ont. 7 June 1943; s. Richard Crompton and Margaret Elizabeth (Lee) J.; e. Royal Mil. Coll. Kingston B.A. 1966; Queen's Univ. M.B.A. 1971; m. Lalage Moira d. Sinclair and Lalage (Graves) Pritchard 29 Oct. 1966; children: Sarah, Gregory; ASSOC. PROF. OF LABOUR RELATIONS, SCHOOL OF BUSINESS, QUEEN'S UNIV. 1992– ; Offr. RCN 1966; Personnel Offr. Carleton Univ. 1971; Lectr. and Adm. Sch. of Bus. present Univ. 1974, Asst. Prof. of Labour Relations 1979, Chrmn., Undergraduate Program, School of Business 1980–84, 1990–91, 1992– ; Assoc. Dean of Bus. 1989–90, 1992–93; Assoc. Prof. of Labour Relns. 1992– ; arbitrator and fact finder pub. and private sector labour disputes; mem. Ont. Pub. Service Grievance Bd. 1981–87; Cons. Candn. Police Coll. Ottawa 1978–86; Cons. and Investig. Royal Comn. Inquiry Niagara Regional Police Force 1989; Hon. Pres. Queen's Comm. Soc. 1987–88, Queen's Alma Mater Soc. 1988–89; recipient Queen's Comm. Soc. Teaching Excellence Award 1987, Queen's Comm. Soc. Student-Life Award 1990, 1991 & 1992; author: 'Fact Finding Under The Teachers' and School Boards Collective Negotiations Act' 1989; co-ed. 'Conflict and Cooperation in Police Labour Relations' 1980; various jour. articles, textbook chapters, case studies; mem. Candn. Ind. Relations Assn.; recreations: sailing, Am. Civil War hist.; Clubs: R.M.C.; Kingston Yacht; Home: 152 College St., Kingston, Ont. K7L 4L8; Office: School of Business, Queen's Univ., Kingston, Ont. K7L 3N6.

**JACKSON, Richard Wayne;** labour executive; b. St. Thomas, Ont. 17 Oct. 1947; s. Charles Edward and Lillian Grace (Clark) J.; e. Arthur Voden Secondary Sch. St. Thomas 1964; Ryerson Polytech. Inst. Toronto Communications 1974; Labour College Can. 1977; m. Elizabeth d. Etienne and Helen Gluckstal 27 Dec. 1985; children: Angela, Erin, Christopher, (by previous marriage); DIR. INTERNAT. AFFAIRS DEPT. CANDN. LABOUR CONG. 1987– ; served with Candn. Armed Forces (Navy) 1964–72; Communications Specialist Dept. External Affairs Ottawa 1973–77; Nat. Edn. Offr. Pub. Service Alliance Can. 1977–81, Exec. Asst. to Pres. 1981–82; Project Co-ord. Inter-Am. Regional Workers Orgn. Mexico City 1982–83; Nat. Rep. Internat. Affairs Dept. present Cong. 1983–87; Dir.: Gateway Recovery Home Ottawa 1983– ; Council on Addictions Progs. Ottawa 1980–82; mem. Internat. Affairs Ctte. NDP 1986– , Nat. Policy Review Ctte. 1979–81; Office: 2841 Riverside Dr., Ottawa, Ont. K1V 8X7.

**JACKSON, Robert John Donald,** M.A., D.Phil.; educator; b. Gosfield Twp. N., Ont. 29 May 1936; s. Donald and Dorothy (Wilkinson) J.; e. Leamington (Ont.) Dist. High Sch. 1956; Univ. of W. Ont., B.A. 1960, M.A. 1962; Oxford Univ. D.Phil. 1965; m. Doreen d. Kenneth and Velma Sholdice 4 July 1959; one d. Nicole Janine; PROF. OF POL. SCI., CARLETON UNIV. 1965– , Chrmn. 1976–83; Sr. Policy Adv. to the Leader of the Opposition, H. of C. 1987–89; Dir. Parlty. Internship Prog. H. of C. 1980–85; Guest Prof. Freie Universitat Berlin 1979; Fellow, Atlantic Inst. Internat. Affairs Paris; Visiting Fellow, Australian Nat. Univ. Canberra 1984 and 1989; Visiting Prof. McGill Univ. 1968, 1986; Legis. Adv. and Dir. Rsch. Office Pres. Privy Council 1972–73; Prin. Investig. Crisis Study Group Prime Min. 1977; syndicated columnist Toronto Star 1982–84; commentator Candn. & Foreign Politics CBC and Global TV; Exec. Sec. Ctte. Atlantic Studies; Exec. Sec. Internat. Rsch. Ctte. Politics & Bus.; author: 'Rebels and Whips: Dissension, Discipline and Cohesion in British Parties' 1968; author and ed. 'Continuity of Discord: Crises and Responses in the Atlantic Community' 1985; author and co-ed. 'Contemporary Canadian Politics' 1987; 'The Politicization of Business in Western Europe' 1987; 'Europe in Transition'; co-author and ed. 'Issues in Comparative Politics' 1971; co-author 'The Canadian Legislative System: Politicians and Policy Making' 1980; 'Politics in Canada: Culture, Institutions, Behaviour and Public Policy' 2nd ed. 1990; 'Stand Up for Canada: Leadership and the Canadian Crisis'; 'Contemporary Government and Politics: Democracy & Authoritarianism'; Home: 339 Mountbatten Ave., Ottawa, Ont. K1H 5W2; Office: Colonel By Dr., Ottawa, Ont. K1S 5B6.

**JACKSON, Sarah Jeanette,** M.A.; artist; b. Detroit, Mich. 13 Nov. 1924; e. Wayne State Univ. B.A. 1946, M.A. 1948; m. Anthony Jackson 1949; children: Timothy, Melanie; Artist-in-Residence, Technical Univ. of N.S. 1978–89; Dir., Art & Tech. Program and accompanying annual Festivals; solo exhns. sculpture, drawings, copier art and bookworks (electrographics) incl.; Apollinaire Gallery London 1951; New Vision Gallery London 1956; Arts Club Montreal 1956; Montreal Museum Gallery Twelve 1957; Robertson Galleries Ottawa 1959; Here & Now Gallery Toronto 1960; Roberts Gallery Toronto 1961; Jerrold Morris Internat. Gallery Toronto 1963; Galerie Libre Montreal 1964, 1966, 1968; Dalhousie Univ. 1965; Mt. St. Vincent Univ. 1967, 1968, 1981; Zwicker's Gallery Halifax 1971; St. Mary's Univ. 1973; Gallery Danielli Toronto 1975, 1976; Tech. Univ. N.S. 1976, 1979, 1985; Gallerie Scollard Toronto 1976; Pa. State Univ. 1978; Gadatsy Gallery Toronto 1979; Sandor Teszler Library, Wofford Coll., S.C. 1983; Pictura Museum, Sweden 1984; Bass Museum & Continuum Gallery, Miami Fla. 1985; Lytesome Gall., Antigonish, N.S. 1986; Manuge Gallery, Halifax, N.S. 1988–89; Micro Hall Art Ctr., West Germany 1989; Exhib. of Copier Art Murals, sponsored by Federal & Provincial Governments for Japanese Trade Mission, Nova Scotian Hilton Hotel, Halifax, N.S. 1989; Westchester Community Coll., Valhalla, N.Y. 1990; Copier Art Bookworks, WCBA, Minneapolis, MN 1990; Valentine's Day Copier Art Festival, Halifax (Artistic Dir.) 1991; Guest Artist & Artistic Adv., Internat. Mail/Copier Art Festival, Museum of Civilization, Ottawa 1992; One person Exhib. & Copier Art Show, Ace Art 1993; Sarah Jackson Electrographic Art, Winnipeg 1993; Art Treasure Hunt in Halifax Sept. 1993 and lectures on 'The Pixel and I' 1993; 'My Bosnia Murals' at Conference, Conn. College, New London, Conn. 1994– ; Murals for 'Bruckner Fantasy' Conn. College, Internat. Music Conference on Bruckner; Dir., Summer Arts Festivals & Copier Art Festivals 1981–86; Internat. Copier Art Bookworks Exhbn. & triptych catalogue 86 'Books Build Bridges' Tech. Univ. of N.S., Halifax; Initiator & co-Curator, Internat. Mail/Copier Art Exhbn. (with bookworks), London, Eng. 1987; 'Sarah Jackson Mail-Copier Art Collection' acquired by Nat. Postal Museum of Can. for their archives to be housed in the Candn. Mus. of Civilization 1988; numerous group exhns. Can., Europe, U.S.A. incl. Womens' Bookworks, Powerhouse Gallery, Montreal 1982; Mirrorings, Womens' Art, originated by Mt. St. Vincent Art Gall. 1983; Internat. Soc. of Copier Artists, N.Y. 1984, 1988–89; exhbn. of Copier Art, London Olympia, London, England 1989; Dreams Come True Exhbn., Eye Level Gall., Halifax, N.S. 1989; A Space Exhbn. 'Artware: Artists' Books' Toronto, Ont. and travelling exhbn. 1989; Copier Art Festival, Tech. Univ. of N.S., Halifax, N.S. 1989; 'Artitudes' Internat. Art Competition, Green Street Gall., N.Y.C. 1989; 'Groupe A-Z' Xántus János Múzeum and Vasarely Múzeum, Budapest 1992; rep. perm. colls, incl. Hirshorn Museum & Sculpture Garden; Nat. Coll. Fine Arts (Smithsonian Inst.); Nat. Gallery Can.; Art Gallery Ont.; musée des Beaux-arts de Montréal; Musée d'Art Contemporain Montréal; subject of film 'Sarah Jackson Halifax 1980' (sponsored by Nat. Film Bd.) 1980; participated with Ramuna Macdonald for film 'Spirit Journey' 1981; commissioned multi-discipline work based on her bookwork 'Spirit Journey/Voyage de l'Esprit' and Margaret Harry's poetry 1983–85; dance choreographed by Pat Richards based on her copier art bookwork 'Finding Herself' 1984; lectr. many colls. and galleries incl. Mexico City Coll. 1948; Tate Gallery, London, Eng. 1954–55; Nat. Gallery, Ottawa 1957; Nova Scotia Coll. of Art & Design 1970; Univ. of B.C. 1979; Univ. of Quebec at Montreal 1980–81; guest artist: Works Arts Festival, City of Edmonton 1990; artist bookworks: Tate Gallery Library Coll., Nat. Library of Can., Bruce Peel Coll. (U. of Alberta), Princeton U. Library, Hirshorn Mus. Library; Victoria & Albert Museum, London, Eng.; National Museum of Women in the Arts, Washington, D.C.; Boymans Van Beuningen Museum, Rotterdam, Holland; Award of Excellence, Art Museum Assn. of America for catalogue to International Mail/Copier Art Exhibition 85, (Tech. Univ. of N.S. & London, Eng.) 1985, 1988–89; Address: 1411 Edward St., Halifax, N.S. B3H 3H5.

**JACKSON, Terry Allan,** B.Comm., M.B.A.; investment dealer executive; b. Montreal, Que. 16 Mar. 1948; e. McGill Univ. B.Comm. 1969; Univ. of Western Ont. M.B.A. 1973; m. Bonnie Lanthier; children: Joanna, Heidi, Holly; VICE-CHAIRMAN, NESBITT THOMSON INC.; Trustee, Securities Indus. Inst.; Mem., Sales & Mktg. Ctte., Securities Indus. Assn.; Treas. and Bd. Mem., Juvenile Diabetes Foundation International; Bd. of Govs., Oakville Family Y; Former Gov., St. Mildreds Lightbourne School; Past Chrmn., Juvenile Diabetes Foundation Canada; Past Pres., Diabetes Canada; clubs: Toronto Golf, Oakville; Home: 1161 Colborne Court, Oakville, Ont. L6J 6B9; Office: Suite 2200, 150 King St. W., Toronto, Ont. M5H 3W2.

**JACKSON, William Robert;** member/commissioner; b. Stonewall, Man. 15 June 1945; s. William Jackson; e. Univ. of Winnipeg; Ryerson Polytech. Inst. Cert. in Pub. Health Inspection 1966; Red River Community Coll. Winnipeg; Univ. of Ottawa; m. Betty Helen d. Henry Haak, Clearbrook, B.C. 25 March 1973; children: Heidi Karen, William David John; MEMBER, IMMIGRATION AND REFUGE BOARD OF CANADA 1989– ; Dir. of Admin., Candn. Organization for Development Through Education 1985–89; Extve. Dir., Hopital Albert Schweitzer, Deschapelles, Haiti 1981–85; Pres. and CEO, Nat. Union of Prov. Govt. Employees 1979–81; Vice Pres. 1976–79; Pres., Man. Govt. Employees' Assn. 1976–79; Vice Pres., Man. Fed. of Labour 1976–78; Treas. & Dir., Internat. Child Care 1989– ; Mennonite; recreations: curling, golf; Home: 33 MacIntosh Cr., St. Catharines, Ont. L2N 7M5; Office: 70 University Ave., Toronto, Ont. M5J 2M5.

**JACOB, Ellis,** B.Comm., M.B.A., C.A., C.M.A.; accountant; b. Calcutta, India 5 Oct. 1953; s. Raymond and Tryphosa J.; e. McGill Univ. B.Comm. 1974; York Univ. M.B.A. 1976; C.A. (Que. & Ont.); C.M.A.; m. Sharyn 2 July 1978; children: Lauren, Resa; CHIEF FINANCIAL OFFICER, CINEPLEX ODEON CORP. 1987– ; Chartered Accountant, Peat Marwick Thorne 1974–76; var. financial positions, Ford Motor Co. 1977–80; Mfg. Controller, Motorola Canada 1981–87; Office: 1303 Yonge St., Toronto, Ont. M4T 2Y9.

**JACOBS, Eugene E.,** B.Com.; b. Buffalo, N.Y. 16 June 1930; s. Eugene Edwin and Margaret May (O'Shea) J.; e. St. Michael's Choir Sch. 1945; De La Salle 'Oaklands' Toronto 1948; Univ. of Toronto B.Com. 1952; m. Ann d. Frank and Edna Foy 27 Dec. 1958; children: Eugene III, Elizabeth, Joseph, Michael, Thomas; Chrmn., Jacobs & Thompson Inc. 1955–86; Dir. Angene Investments Inc.; Amalcon Corp. Ltd.; past Chrmn. Bd. Govs. Ont. Inst. Studies in Edn.; mem. Bd. Trade Metrop. Toronto; mem., Etobicoke General Hosp. Found. Bd.; Past Pres. Serra Club Toronto N.; mem. Archdiocesan Bldg. Ctte.; recreations: golf, tennis; Home: 72 Golf Ave., Woodbridge, Ont. L4L 3A5.

**JACOBS, Jane;** writer; b. Scranton, PA. 4 May 1916; d. Dr. John Decker and Bess Mary (Robison) Butzner; e. Columbia Univ.; m. Robert Hyde s. Robert Sr. and Leila J. 27 May 1944; children: James Kedzie, Edward Decker, Mary Hyde; contbr.: 'The Exploding Metropolis' 1958; author: 'The Death and Life of Great American Cities' 1961; 'The Economy of Cities' 1969; 'The Question of Separatism' 1980; 'Cities and the Wealth of Nations' 1984; 'The Girl on the Hat' 1989 (children's fiction); 'Systems of Survival: A Dialogue' 1993; Address: c/o Random House of Canada, 33 Yonge St., Toronto, Ont. M5E 1G4.

**JACOBS, John Arthur,** M.A., Ph.D., D.Sc., D.Sc. (h.c.), F.R.S.C., F.R.A.S.; b. London, England 13 Apr. 1916; s. Arthur George and Elfrida Malvine (Boeck) J.; e. Dorking High Sch., Surrey, Eng. (1927–34); Univ. of London, B.A. 1937, M.A. 1939, Ph.D. 1949, D.Sc. 1961; m. 1stly Daisy Sarah Ann Montgomerie 7 Nov. 1941 (d. 1974); two d. Coral Elizabeth, Margaret Ann.; m. 2ndly Margaret Jones 4 Oct. 1974 (div. 1980); m. 3rdly Ann Grace Wintle 24 June 1982; EMERITUS PROF., UNIV. OF CAMBRIDGE; Hon. Prof., Univ. Coll., Aberystwyth, Wales 1988– ; Sr. Lectr. in Applied Maths., Royal Naval Engn. Coll., Devonport, Eng. (also Depy. Training Commdr.) 1944–46; Lectr. in Applied Maths., Univ. of London 1946–51; Assoc Prof., Applied Maths., Univ. of Toronto 1951–54 and Assoc. Prof. of Geophysics there 1954–57; Prof. of Geophysics, Univ. of B.C. 1957–61, Dir. Inst. of Earth Sciences there 1961–67; Killam Mem. Prof. of Sciences, Univ. of Alta. 1967–74, Dir. Inst. of Earth & Planetary Physics there 1970–74; Prof. of Geophysics, Univ. of Cambridge 1974–83; Lieut.-Commdr., R.N.V.R. 1941–46; author: 7 books; more than 150 scient. papers in tech. journs.; recipient Cent. Medal of Can. 1967; Gold Medal, Cdn. Assn. of Physicists 1975; J. Tuzo Wilson Medal, Cdn. Geophysical Union 1982; D.Sc. (hon. causa) Univ. of B.C. 1987; recreations: walking, music; Home: 4, Castell Brychan, Aberystwyth, Dyfed SY23 2JD, U.K.

**JACOBS, Peter Daniel Alexander,** B.A., M.Arch.,M.L.Arch.; university professor; b. Montreal, Que. 3 Dec. 1939; s. Joseph Jacob and Francis (Alexander) J.; e. Antioch College B.A. 1961; Harvard Grad. School of Design M.Arch. 1964, M.L.Arch. 1968; m. Ellen-Gail d. Alex and Flo Vinebreg 17 Aug. 1967; children: Merav Beth, David Avrum; PROFESSOR OF LANDSCAPE ARCHITECTURE, ECOLE D'ARCH. DE PAYSAGE, UNIV. DE MONTREAL; Fellow & Past Pres., Candn. Soc. of Landscape Architects; Canada's Sr. Delegate, Internat. Fed. of Landscape Architects; Fellow, Am. Soc. of Landscape Architexts; Chair, Edit. Advisory Ctte., 'Landscape Architecture'; Past Chair, Environ. Planning Comn.; Internat. Union for Conservation of Nature & Natural Resources (12 yrs.); Kativik Environ. Quality Comn. for northern territories, Prov. of Que.; Chair, Public Adv. Ctte., Canada's State of Envir. Reporting; has served on num. Candn. cttes., comns. & public hearings; Mem., Que. Round Table on the Environ. & the Econ.; Mem., Bd. of Dir., Environmental Choice Prog.; Consultant, City of Montreal; has worked on restoration of Mount-Royal Park, orig. designed by F.L. Olmsted; re-design of St. Helen's and Notre Dame Islands (former site of Expo '67); design of a new urban square in downtown Montreal, Place Berri; author & editor of num. pubs. incl. 'Sustainable Development and Environmental Assessment' 1990; mem. of num. sci. & profl. edit. adv. cttes. incl. 'Eco-Decision'; recreations: sports, photography; clubs: Mount Royal Tennis, Montreal Badminton and Squash; Home: 644 Belmont Ave., Westmount, Que. H3Y 2W2; Office: 5620 Darlington Ave., Box 6128, Station A, Montreal, Que. H3C 3J7.

**JACOBSEN, Carl G.,** B.A., M.Phil., Ph.D.; university professor and consultant; b. London, England 13 May 1944 (Norwegian-British descent); s. Frithjof H. (former Norwegian Sec. of State for Foreign Affairs & former Ambassador to Canada 1959–61, the USSR 1960–65, 1970–75, & the U.K. 1975–81) and Elsa (Tidemand-Andersen) J.; e. Carleton Univ. B.A. 1966; Glasgow Univ. M.Phil. 1968, Ph.D. 1971; m. Trudy d. Felix and Irene Brand 1971; children: Leah, Meghan, Kai; DIRECTOR, EURASIAN SECURITY STUDIES ORU, CARLETON UNIV. 1992– ; Dir. of Soviet & Strategic Studies Programs, Univ. of Miami Grad. Sch. of Internat. Studies 1980–85; Dir. of Soviet Studies, Stockholm Internat. Peace Research Inst. 1985–87; Dir., Inst. of Soviet & East Eur. Studies 1990–92; other acad. appointments at Acadia, Columbia, and Harvard univs.; Consultant, Soviet, Russian, Eurasian & Strategic Issues; recipient of British & U.S. honours incl. Choice 'Outstanding Academic Book ... 1989'; Mem., Bd. of Dir., Canadian Pugwash; Edit. Bd. Mem., 'European Security'; Mem., Am. Assn. for the Advancement of Slavic Studies, Brit. Assn. for Slavic & East Eur. Studies and others; author: 'The Nuclear Era' 1982, 'Sino-Soviet Relations since Mao' 1981, 'Soviet Strategic Initiatives' 1979, 'Soviet Strategy – Soviet Foreign Policy' 1974 and others; editor & co-author: 'Strategic Power: USA/USSR' 1990, 'Soviet Foreign Policy' 1989, 'The Uncertain Course' 1987, 'The Soviet Defense Enigma' 1987 and others; recreations: sailing, skiing, tennis; Home: 206 James St., Ottawa, Ont. K1R 5M7; Office: Ottawa, Ont. K1S 5B6.

**JACOBSEN, Pat,** B.A.; financial services executive; b. St. Thomas, Ont. 5 June 1946; d. Walter D. and Charlotte R. (Hamilton) Crozier; e. Silver Heights Collegiate 1964; Univ. of Man. B.A. 1967; m. Peter s. Mary and John Jackman 4 Sept. 1981; one d.: Kathleen; SR. VICE PRES., HUMAN RESOURCES & CORP. SERV., MANULIFE FINANCIAL 1992– ; Advtg., Eaton's 1967–69; Dir. of Communications, var. Ministries, Ont. Govt. 1969–81; Extve. Dir., Ind. Mktg., Industry & Trade 1981–83; Extve. Dir., Real Estate, Gov. Serv. 1983–86; Asst. Dep. Min., Management Bd. 1986–87; Dep. Min., Executive Resources 1987–90; Dep. Min., Transportation 1990–92; Lecturer, Queen's Univ. Bus. Sch.; Mem., Public Policy Forum; Conf. Bd. of Canada; Founding Mem., Ontario Council on Customer Serv.; Bd. of Trails Youth Initiatives; Univ. of Toronto Adv. Bd. on Human Resources; Home: 20 Nanton Ave., Toronto, Ont.; Office: 200 Bloor St. E., Toronto, Ont. M4W 1E5.

**JACOBSON, Ernie W.,** B.A., M.A.; financial executive, educator; b. Radway, Alta. 16 May 1948; s. Tony W. and Tyyne A. (Pasanen) J.; e. Univ. of Alta. B.A. (Hons.) 1970, M.A. 1971; m. Barbara d. John and Florence Scollon 24 May 1969; children: Shelley, Lisa; CHRMN. & DIR., CAPITAL CITY SAVINGS & CREDIT UNION 1991– ; Researcher, Govt. of Sask. 1971–73; Teaching Admin., N. Alta. Inst. of Technol. 1973– ; Athabasca Univ. 1980– ; Dir. & Bd. Sec., Edmonton Savings & Credit Union 1983–87; tutor; teaches seminar and teleconf. courses; D.A. MacGibbon Gold Medal in Econ.; recreations: golf, squash; clubs: Windermere Golf & Country, Centre; Home: 10520 – 35 Ave., Edmonton, Alta. T6J 2L9; Office: 300 – 8723 – 82 Ave., Edmonton, Alta. T6C 0Y9.

**JACOX, Gordon G.,** B.Sc., M.B.A.; steel industry executive; b. Seattle, Washington 26 June 1931; s. Clarence David and Mary Olive (Ritter) J.; e. Univ. of Alberta B.Sc. 1955; Univ. of Western Ont. M.B.A. 1957; Erie County Tech. (N.Y.), dipl. Metallurgy 1960; m. Nancy Jane d. Charles and Hazel Garnett 5 May 1954; children: Susan, Jill, Grahame, Jeffrey; PRES. & DIR., KUBOTA METAL CORP., FAHRAMET DIV. 1990– ; Supt., Stainless Steel Prodn., Atlas Steels 1957–67; Vice-Pres., Norcast Foundry Div., Corp. Planning Mfg. Div., Noranda Inc. 1967–84; Vice-Pres., Fahramet Div., Falconbridge 1984–90; Dir., Orillia Economic Devel. Comn.; Kubota Metal Corp.; Mem., Duke of Edinburgh Commonwealth Study Conf. 1962; Bd. of Govs. (Chair 1992), Georgian Coll. (Barrie) 1991–93; Anglican; Mem., St. Paul's (Washago); P.C. Canada; Simcoe East P.C. Assn.; Simcoe North P.C. Assn.; Royal Soc. of Arts (U.K.); Candn. Inst. of Mining & Metallurgy; Am. Foundry Soc.; Candn. Foundry Assn. (Past Pres. 1984); Am. Inst. of Mining Engineers; Engineering Inst. of Can. (Past Chrmn., Niagara Branch); clubs: Albany; Home: Quarry Point Rd., Longford Mills, Ont. L0K 1L0; Office 25 Commerce Rd., Orillia, Ont. L3V 6L6.

**JACQUES, Hector J.,** M.Eng., P.Eng.; engineering and environmental science executive; e. Univ. of Cambridge, gen. cert. of edn. 1960; Indian Inst. of Technol. B.Eng. 1966; N.S. Tech. Coll. M.Eng. 1968; PRESIDENT, CHIEF EXTVE. OFFR. & PRINCIPAL GEOTECHNICAL ENGINEER, JACQUES WHITFORD GROUP OF COMPANIES 1972– ; Geotch. Engr., Warnock Hersey Internat. Ltd. 1967–68; Div. Mgr. & Sr. Geotech. Engr. 1968–72; recipient, Engineering Award, Ass. of Profl. Engrs. of N.S.; Beaubien Award, Assn. of Cons. Engrs. of Canada; awarded Canada 125 Anniversary Medal; Mem., Assn. of Profl. Engrs. of N.S., P.E.I., Nfld. & N.B.; Internat. Soc. of Soil Mech. & Found. Engr.; Engr. Inst. of Canada; candn. Geotech. Soc.; Am. Soc. for Testing Materials; N.S. Cons. Engrs. Assn. (Pres. 1976–77, 1989–90); Assn. of Cons. Engrs. (Past Dir.); Candn. Inst. of Mining; N.S. Mining Soc.; N.S. Council of Applied Sci. & Technol.; N.S. Voluntary Planning Bd. (Bd. Mem. & Past Chair, Profl. Serv. Indus. Sector); Tech. Univ. of N.S. (Mem., Bd. of Gov., Extve. Ctte. & Policy & Planning Ctte.); Bd. Mem. & Past Chair, N.S. Bus. Capital Corp.; Victoria Gen. Hosp.; expert witness; chair for several seminars & confs. & presenter of num. papers; involved in variety of community based orgns.; Home: 60 French Masts Lane, Bedford, N.S. B4A 3W7; Office: 3 Spectacle Lake Dr., Dartmouth, N.S. B3B 1W8.

**JADD, Bernard R.,** M.C.I., C.M.A.; financial executive; b. Buffalo, N.Y. 21 Aug. 1938; s. William and Ruth A. J.; e. Candn. Credit Inst. M.C.I. 1965; Soc. of Mngt. Accts. C.M.A. 1977; m. Esther d. Aaron and Bella Keller 7 Sept. 1958; children: Jerome L., Mark I., Suzanne; VICE-PRES., FINANCE & ADMIN., ATLANTIC PKG. PROD. LTD. 1992– ; Corp. Credit Mgr., Cole Steeel Internat. Ltd. 1960–65; Controller, Kent Steel Prod. Ltd. 1965–69; Corp. Credit Mgr., Castrol Oil Can. Ltd. 1969–70; Office Manager, Atlantic Pkg. Prod. Ltd. 1970–74; Controller 1974–92; Chair, Financial Serv. Ctte., Candn. Corrugated Cartons Assn.; Home: 147 Simonston Blvd., Thornhill, Ont.; Office: 111 Progress Ave., Scarborough, Ont. M1P 2Y9.

**JAEGER, Leslie Gordon,** M.A., Ph.D., D.Sc.(Eng.), D.Eng., F.R.S.E., P. Eng.; educator; b. Southport, Eng. 28 Jan. 1926; s. late Henry and late Beatrice Alice (Highton) J.; e. King George V Sch. Southport, Eng. 1943; Gonville & Caius Coll. Cambridge Univ. B.A. 1946, M.A. 1950 (State Scholar 1943–45, Scholar of Coll. and Prizeman 1944–45); Univ. of London Ph.D. 1955; D.Sc.(Eng.) 1986; Carleton Univ. D.Eng. (honoris causa) 1991; Memorial Univ. of Nfld. D.Eng. (honoris causa) 1994; m. 1stly Annie Sylvia d. late William Arthur Dyson 3 Apr. 1948; two d. Valerie Ann, Hilary Frances; m. 2ndly Kathleen Grant d. late Hugo Allen 24 July 1981; RESEARCH PROFESSOR, TECHNICAL UNIV. OF NOVA SCOTIA 1987– ; Fellow, Magdalene Coll. Cambridge 1959–62; Fellow, The Royal Soc. of Edinburgh 1966; Prof. of Civil Engn. and Applied Mech. McGill Univ. 1962–64 and 1966–70; Regius Prof. of Engn. and Head of Dept. Edinburgh Univ. 1964–66; Dean of Engn. Univ. of N.B. 1970–75; Vice Pres. (Acad.) Acadia Univ. 1975–80; Special Asst. to the Pres., and Vice Pres. (Rsch.)., T.U.N.S. 1980–87; Pres., Candn. Soc. for Civil Engr. 1992–93; Consultant to various firms incl. Rolls Royce Ltd.; United Aircraft of Canada Ltd.; co-leader team structural design theme bldgs. Expo 67; Consultant design hwy. bridges Ont. Govt. and Karachi Development Authority; N.B. Electric Power Comn.; Chrmn. 1975 Candn. Congress Applied Mech.; mem. Candn. Nat. Comte. on Earthquake Engn. 1973–76; served with RN 1945–48, rank Lt.; Dir. N.B. Prot. Orphans Home 1973–75; mem. Maritime Provs. Higher Educ. Comn. 1974–78; author 'The Analysis of Grid Frameworks and Related Structures' 1958; 'Elementary Theory of Elastic Plates' 1962; 'Cartesian Tensors in Engineering Science' 1964; 'Bridge Analysis Simplified' 1985; 'Bridge Analysis by Microcomputer' 1989; 'Soil-Steel Bridges' 1993; also over 140 papers mainly in field of structural engn. with emphasis on behaviour of bridges, tall bldgs. and nuclear power stns. in earthquakes; Fellow, Engn. Inst. Can.; Fellow, Candn. Soc. for Civil Engrg.; Past Fellow, Inst. Civil Engrs. (London); Past Fellow, Inst. Structural Engrs. (London); Freemason; Liberal; Anglican; recreations: golf, curling, contract bridge; Clubs: Saraguay; Home: P.O. Box 1000, Halifax, N.S. B3J 2X4.

**JAEGGIN, Ronald Paul,** B.Eng., M.B.A.; business executive; b. Montreal, Que. 24 Dec. 1933; s. Paul G. and Doris M. (Johnstone) J.; e. McGill Univ. B.Eng. 1957; Univ. of West. Ont. M.B.A. 1960; m. Lola d. Edward and Marie-Belle Viney 25 June 1960; children: Lisa, Peter; VICE-PRES., CORP. DEVEL., ITT CANADA LTD. 1981– ; Mngt. Cons., Currie, Coopers & Lybrand 1960–64; Factory Mgr., Sklar-Peppler Furniture Inc. 1964–69; Vice-Pres., Sales & Mktg., Hydraulics Div., Houdaille Indus. 1969–77; Gen. Mgr., Kysor Indus. of Canada 1977–78; Gen. Mgr., ITT Milrod Div., ITT Can. Ltd. 1979–81; Dir., Candn. Mfrs. Assn. (Chrmn., Internat. Trade Ctte.); Dir., Formtech Inc.; Mem., Econ. Devel. Ctte., Metro Toronto Bd. of Trade; Mem., Defence Indus. Preparedness Adv. Ctte., Dept. of Nat. Defence; served on Royal Comn. on Govt. Orgn. 1960–61; Mem., Profl. Engrs. Ont.; Inst. of Indus. Engr.; Soc. of Autom. Engrs.; Assn. for Corp. Growth; The Planning Forum; recreations: jogging, skiing, tennis: Office: Box 138, Toronto-Dominion Ctr., Toronto, Ont. M5K 1H1.

**JAENEN, Cornelius John,** M.A., B.Ed., Ph.D., LL.D., F.R.S.C.; educator; b. Cannington Manor, Sask. 21 Feb. 1927; s. John (Jan) and Rosa Adolphine (Minet) J.; e. Univ. of Man. B.A. 1947, M.A. 1950, B.Ed. 1958; Univ. de Bordeaux Diplôme de Fin d'Etudes 1948; Univ. of Ottawa Ph.D. 1963; Univ. of Winnipeg LL.D. 1981; F.R.S.C. 1992; m. Ina May d. William and May Turner 20 July 1949; children: Elizabeth, Anne, Margaret Rose, Jeannette, John, Suzanne, Mark, Michelle, Daniel; PROF. OF HIST. UNIV. OF OTTAWA 1967– ; Richardson Housemaster, St. John's-Ravenscourt Sch. 1948–52; Ministry of Edn. Imp. Ethiopian Govt. 1952–55; high sch. teacher Winnipeg schs. 1955–58; Asst. Prof. of Hist. Meml. Univ. of Nfld. 1958–59; Asst. and Assoc. Prof. of Hist., United Coll. Winnipeg 1959–67; Assoc. Prof. present Univ. 1967; Full Prof. 1970; mem. Man. Adv. Ctte. Bilingualism & Biculturalism 1963–64; Etats-Généraux du Can. Français (Man.) 1965–66; Cons. Fortress of Louisbourg project 1968–72; Candn. Comn. UNESCO 1970–72; Cons. Ethnic Studies Dept. Sec. of State Can. 1971–87; Chrmn. Ethnic Hists. Adv. Panel 1971–86; Appraisals Ctte. Ont. Council Grad. Studies 1973–76; Cons. Native Awareness Progs. Dept. External Affairs 1982–84; recipient Ronsard Medal French Govt. 1947; Gold Medal in Edn. Univ. Man. 1958; Sainte-Marie Prize in Candn. Hist. 1974; author 'Friend and Foe' 1976; 'The Role of the Church in New France' 1976; 'The French Relationship with the Native Peoples of New France' 1985; co-author 'Emerging Identities' 1986; 'Canada, A North American Nation' 1988; 'A History of the Canadian Peoples' Vol. I 1993; 'Les Franco-Ontariens' 1993; 8 booklets, 28 book chapters and over 50 articles refereed sci. jours. & proceedings acad. confs.; Founding Pres. Candn. Ethnic Studies Assn. 1971–73; Vice Pres. CESA/SCEE 1985–87; Pres. French Colonial Historical Soc. 1986–89; Pres., Candn. Hist. Assn. 1988–89; Soc. French Hist. Studies; Institut d'Histoire de l'Amérique française; Internat. Assn. Candn. Studies; Champlain Soc.; recreations: gardening, camping; Home: 9 Elma St., Kempark, Gloucester, Ont. K1G 3N2; Office: 155 Séraphin Marion Priv., Univ. of Ottawa, Ottawa, Ont. K1N 6N5.

**JAGO, Charles Joseph,** B.A., Ph.D.; college administrator/professor; b. St. Catharines, Ont. 21 March 1943; s. Charles Alfred and Margaret Edith (Heyes) J.; e. Univ. of West. Ont. B.A. (Hons.) 1965; Cambridge Univ. Ph.D. 1969; m. Mary-Louise d. Elizabeth and Harold McDonagh 27 Aug. 1967; children: Charles 'David,' Jonathan 'Noel,' Christopher 'Paul'; PRINCIPAL, HURON COLLEGE 1987– ; Asst., Assoc. & Prof. of Hist., McMaster Univ. 1970–87; Bd. Chrmn., Senate Ctte. on Long-Range Planning 1978–81; Chrmn., Dept. of Hist. 1983–87; Woodrow Wilson Scholar (Hon. mention); Commonwealth Scholar; Mem., Anglican Ch. of Can.; Soc. for the Study of Spanish & Portuguese Hist.; Internat. Comn. for the Study of Parl. & Representative Insts.; author of several scholarly articles; Home: 35 Pine Ridge Dr., London, Ont. N5X 3G7; Office: London, Ont. N6G 1H3.

**JAIN, Arvind K.,** B.Tech., D.I.I.Sc., M.S.I.A., Ph.D.; university professor; b. Delhi, India 1 March 1945; s. Anand P. and Kiran J.; e. I.I.T., Bombay B.Tech. (Hons.) 1966; I.I.Sc., Bangalore, D.I.I.Sc. 1968; Carnegie-Mellon Univ., M.S.I.A. 1970; Univ. of Michigan Ph.D. 1979; married; one child: Gitanjali Jain; ASSOC. PROF., CONCORDIA UNIV. 1990– ; Prod. Engr., K.M.C. Pvt. Ltd. (Bombay) 1966–67; Sr. Fin. Analyst, Getty Oil Co. (US) 1970; Lectr., Univ. of Dar-es-Salaam (Tanzania) 1974–76; Advr., Min. of Econ. Devel. 1975–76; Mexican Coffee Inst. (Mexico) 1976–77; Assoc. Prof., McGill Univ. 1979–89; Visiting Assoc. Prof., Indiana Univ. 1989–90; Cons. to banks & other firms; Mem., Bd. of Dir., Que. Drama Federation, Montreal; Mem., Acad. of Internat. Bus.; Am. Fin. Assn.; Am. Econ. Assn.; Ed. Bd., 'Journal of International Business Studies'; author: 'Commodity Futures Markets and Law of One Price' 1980, 'International Financial Markets' 1994, and numerous articles & book chapters; recreations: sailing, hiking, swimming, theatre, diving; Home: 538 Grosvenor Ave., Westmount, Que. H3Y 2S4; Office: Dept. of Finance, Concordia Univ., 1455 de Maisonneuve W., Montreal, Que. H3G 1M8

**JAIN, Harish Chand,** M.B.A., Ph.D.; educator; b. India 1 Dec. 1936; s. Data Ram and Padam Sri J.; e. Ind. Univ. M.B.A. 1962; Univ. of Wis. Ph.D. 1970; m. Constance d. Anne and Arthur Turski Dec. 1969; children: Raja, Ravi, Deena; PROF. OF HUMAN RESOURCES & LABOUR RELATIONS, McMASTER UNV. 1970– ; Instr. St. Bonaventure Univ. 1962–64; Dir. of Rsch. N.S. Dept. Labour 1964–67; Panel mem. Candn. Human Rights Tribunal 1986–92; Cons. Special Parlty. Ctte. Visible Minorities Candn. Soc. 1983–84; Past Pres., Candn. Ind. Relations Assn. 1987–88; mem. Fed. Task Force Micro-electronic Technol. & Employment 1982; Dir.: Internat. Exec. Devel. Prog. Bata Ltd. 1973–75; Slater Steel Sr. Exec. Devel. Prog. 1975; Recipient, Ont. Psychological Foundation's Community Service Award 1990; Recipient, Award for 'Excellence in Race Relations' Federal Dept. of Multiculturalism & Citizenship 1992; Visiting Fellowship Award, SHASTRI Indo-Candn. Inst. 1990–91 and 1992; Candn. External Affairs Dept. Grant 1990–91; author: 'Racial Minorities and Affirmative Action/Employment Equity Legislation in Canada' in 'Relations Industrielles' vol. 44, 1989; 'Employment Equity and Visible Minorities: Have the Federal Policies Worked?' (Candn. Labour Law Journal) 1993; co-author: 'Equal Employment Issues' 1981; 'Measuring Effectiveness of Employment Equity Programs in Canada: Public Policy and a Survey' in 'Canadian Public Policy' vol. XV, 1989; 'Human Resource Management Practices of Japanese and Other Foreign Companies in Developing Countries' (proceedings of the IRRA) 1992; editor: 'Contemporary Issues in Canadian Personnel Administration' 1974; 'Emerging Trends in Canadian Industrial Relations' 1988; co-editor: 'Behavioural Issues in Management' 1977; 'National Conference on Racial Equality in the Workplace: Retrospect & Prospect' 1991; Pres. Internat. Mahavira Jain Mission (Can.); mem., Bd. of Dirs., Human Resource Professional Assn. of Ont. 1990–92; Home: 67 Flatt Ave., Hamilton, Ont. L8P 4N2; Office: MGD 404, 1280 Main St. W., Hamilton, Ont. L8S 4M4.

**JAKHU, Ram S.,** B.A., LL.B., LL.M.(Pb.), LL.M., D.C.L.; executive; b. India 10 Feb. 1946; s. Amar Chand and Chanan Kaur (Bangar) J.; e. Panjab Univ., B.A. 1967, LL.B. 1970, LL.M. 1972; McGill Univ., LL.M. 1978, D.C.L. 1983 (Dean's Hon. list); m. Brij Bala Sood d. Agya Ram and Shankari Devi 16 Feb. 1975; children: Virat, Vikas; ASST. DIR., INSTITUTE OF AIR & SPACE LAW, FACULTY OF LAW, MCGILL UNIV. 1990– ; Mem., Candn. Human Rights Tribunal Panel; Pres., Consultants Northam, Montreal; Dir., var. companies & individuals; Mem., Internat. Bar Assn.; Internat. Inst. of Space Law; Internat. Inst. of Commun.; Candn. Counc. on Internat. Law; Life mem., Nat. Indo-Canadian Counc.; author/co-author num. articles; Bd. of Ed.: 'The Utrecht Studies in Air and Space Law' (The Netherlands) and 'Annals of Air and Space Law' (Montreal); recreations: badminton, camping, yoga; Home: 9057, Rimouski, Brossard, Que. J4X 2S3; Office: 3661 Peel St., Montreal, Que. H3A 1X1.

**JALBERT, Maj. Rene Marc,** CV, C.D.; b. Québec City, Qué. 20 Feb. 1921; s. Paul Gabriel and Marie Yvonne (Gagnon) J.; e. Commercial Acad. Qué. 1942; Laval Univ.; m. Phyllis Nanette d. Ray and Florence Studor 3 July 1948; children: Richard Marc, Linda Anne; Gentleman Usher of the Black Rod, The Senate of Canada 1985–90; served with Royal 22nd Regt. 1942–69 Eng., France, Korea, Indochina, Cyprus; Extve. Asst. to Agt. Gen. Qué. House, N.Y. 1969–71; Asst. Chief of Protocol Qué. Govt. 1971–74; Sgt.-at-Arms Qué. Nat. Assembly 1974–85; recipient Cross of Valour 1984; Kt. Mil. Order St. Lazarus of Jerusalem, Cross of Merit; Carnegie Gold Medal; Order St. John's of Jerusalem Gold Medal; recreations: horseback riding, sailing, golf, fishing; Clubs: Qué. Garrison; Qué. Mil. Inst.; Home: 1503, 9 Jardins Mericy, Québec City, Qué. G1S 4S8.

**JAMES, Brian Robert,** B.A., M.A., D.Phil., C.Chem, F.R.S.Chem, F.C.I.C., F.R.S.C.; university professor; b. Birmingham, England 21 Apr. 1936; s. Herbert Arthur and Frances Vera (Stride) J.; e. Oxford Univ., B.A. 1957, M.A. 1960, D.Phil. 1960; m. Mary Jane d. Howard Edward and Lillian Beatrice Thompson 6 Oct. 1962; children: Jennifer Ann, Peter Edward, Sarah Elizabeth, Andrew Francis; PROF., DEPT. OF CHEM., UNIV. OF B.C. 1974– ; postdoct. fellow, U.B.C. 1960–62; Sr. Sci. Offr., U.K. Atomic Energy Authority, Harwell 1962–64; Asst. Prof., present univ. 1964; Assoc. Prof. 1969; Vis. Lectr., Univ. of Sussex 1970–71; Vis. Prof., Univ. of Waterloo 1970–71; Univ. of West. Ont. 1984; Univ. of Veszprem, Hungary 1984; Univ. of Venice 1984; Vis. Nato Prof., Univ. of Pisa 1979; Univ. of Amsterdam 1990; Visiting Fellow, Australian National Univ., Canberra 1991; Visiting Prof., Enichem Company, Novara,

Italy 1991; several past extve. positions incl. Chem. Inst. of Can., NSERC & Royal Soc. of Can.; Editor, 'Can. J. Chem.' 1978–88; Ed. Bd. Mem., 'Inorg. Chem.' 1993– , 'J.Chem. Soc. Dalton' 1992– , 'J. Mol. Catal.' 1989– , 'React. Kin. & Cat. Letters' 1988– , and 4 others; Noranda Award 1975; FRSC 1982; Guggenheim Fellowship 1983; Jacob Biely Award 1986; Dow Lectureship in Catalysis 1987; Killam Rsch. Prize 1988; UBC Sr. Killam Fellowship 1990; Candn. Catalysis Award 1990; Canada Council Killam Fellowship 1993; Mem., Wadham Coll. Soc.; N.Y. Acad. of Sci.; Am. Chem. Soc.; N.A. Catal. Soc.; author: 'Homogeneous Hydrogenation' 1973 (U.S.S.R. ed. 1976); co-author: 'Biological Aspects of Inorganic Chem.' 1977, 'The Porphyrins' 1978, 'Adv. in Organometal. Chem.' 1979, 'Comprehensive Organometallic Chem.' 1982; editor: 'Catalysis by Metal Complexes' 14 vols. 1976–93; author/co-author of 250 papers & 3 patents; recreations: squash, cricket, bridge, music; Home: 4010 Blenheim St., Vancouver, B.C. V6L 2Y9; Office: Vancouver, B.C. V6T 1Z1.

**JAMES, Christopher Robert,** M.A.Sc., Ph.D.; university professor; b. Vancouver, B.C. 15 Nov. 1935; s. Christopher Robert and Lillian Bernice (Shaw) J.; e. Univ. of Brit. Columbia, B.A.Sc. 1960, M.A.Sc. 1961, Ph.D. 1964; rec'd Assn. Prof. Engrs. Gold Medal for Engn. in B.C. 1960; Oxford Univ., Post Doctoral Fellow 1964–65; m. Arline Sigrid, d. Alwyn Fox, 21 April 1956; children: Alison Elaine, Margo Arline, Heather Gail, Cheryl Kirstin, Maureen Beth; PROFESSOR OF ELECTRICAL ENGINEERING, UNIV. OF ALBERTA since 1971, Chairman of Dept. 1974–87; joined the University as Asst. Prof. 1965, Assoc. Prof. 1967, Vice Pres. (Rsch.) 1987–92; Bd. of Dirs., Alberta Laser Inst.; Alberta Rsch. Coun.; Natural Science and Engineering Rsch. Council; Candn. Microelectronics Corp.; mem., Assn. Prof. Engrs., Geols. and Geophysicists of Alta.; Candn. Assn. Physicists; Eng. Inst. of Can. Am. Physical Soc.; Am. Assn. Advanc. Science; recreations: hunting, gardening, skiing; Clubs: Alberta Fish & Game; Edmonton Sporting Dog Club; Home: 4836 - 122 A St., Edmonton, Alta. T6H 3S7.

**JAMES, David B.,** B.A.; financial services executive; b. Moncton, N.B. 1 June 1953; s. Willard Murray and Marian (Chapman) J.; e. Queen's Univ. B.A. 1976; VICE PRES. TRANS CANADA CREDIT CORP., A Norwest Financial Company 1992– ; Dir., CGT Insurance Co.; joined Traders Group 1977–80; Central Guaranty Trust 1980–88; Trans Canada Credit Corp. Limited 1988–92; Exec. Vice Pres., Newphos Ltd. (sub of TCC) 1991–92; present Co. 1992; recreation: golf; Home: 1729 Riverbend Court, Mississauga, Ont. L5M 5J1; Office: 402, 703 Evans Ave., Etobicoke, Ont. M9C 5E9.

**JAMES, David Fielding,** B.Sc., M.Sc., M.A., Ph.D., P.Eng.; university professor; b. Belleville, Ont. 9 July 1939; s. Hedley Gordon and Lilian May (Parsons) J.; e. Queen's Univ. B.Sc. 1962; Calif. Inst. of Technol. M.Sc. 1963, Ph.D. 1967; Univ. of Cambridge M.A. 1974; one d.: Joan Susan James-Tanner; CHRMN., DIV. OF ENGINEERING SCIENCE, UNIVERSITY OF TORONTO 1991– ; Asst. Prof., present univ. 1967–71; Assoc. Prof. 1971–79; Prof. 1979– ; Commonwealth Fellow, St. John's Coll., Cambridge, England 1974–75; Chevron Visiting Prof., Calif. Inst. of Technol. 1987–88; Sr. Fellow, Massey Coll., Univ. of Toronto 1987– ; University Visiting Prof., Monash Univ., Australia 1993; Pres., S+J Engineering Inc.; Office: Toronto, Ont.

**JAMES, Donald Wesley,** C.M., M.Mus., B.A., A.R.C.T.; conductor, teacher; b. Enderby, B.C. 6 Aug. 1946; s. Joseph Harold and Ruth Viola (Fletcher) J.; e. Toronto Conservatory A.R.C.T. Piano Perf. 1965; Seattle Pacific Univ. B.A. (magna cum laude) Music Theory & Lit. 1970; Univ. of Washington M.Mus. Orch. Conducting 1972; m. Terry-Lyne Sabine d. Joyce and Harold Danbrook 1990; children: Brent Wesley, Michael Andrew, Jeffrey Jaun, Marnie Melyne; FOUNDER & MUSIC DIRECTOR, POWELL RIVER ACADEMY OF MUSIC 1981– ; Teacher of Music, School Dist. #47 (Powell River) 1973– ; Founder Conductor, Powell River Boys, Girls, & Youth choirs 1974–90; Powell River Academy Singers 1979– ; Co-Founder & Music Dir., Internat. Choral Kathaumixw 1982– ; sessional instr. music history, theory & choral music, Malaspina College; guest lectr., Univ. of Victoria, Chorus Am., Sask. Choral Fed. & others; adjudicator; guest conductor; 10 internat. concert tours with the Powell River Acad. Singers 1980– and 5 recordings conducting P.R.A.S.; TV & radio broadcasts: Mexico, Hungary, Poland, Canada, Finland, England; choral prizes: Canada, Engl., Poland, USA; Willan Award for outstanding serv. to B.C. Choral Fed. 1988; Order of Canada for outstanding contbn. to choral music in Canaa 1990; Bd. of Dir., B.C. Choral Fed. 1980– ; Assn. of Candn. Choral Conductors 1982–84 (Pres. 1984–88; Past Pres. 1988–92); Internat. Fed. for Choral Music 1985– ; Mem., Extve. Ctte. planning 1993 World Symposium on Choral Music (Vanc. 1933) 1990–93; mem., Am. Choral Dirs. Assoc. (ACDA); Assoc. of Candn. Choral Conductors (ACCC); Internat. Fedn. for Choral Music (IFCM); B.C. Choral Fedn. (BCCF); author of several articles; recreations: canoeing, hiking, interior design, woodwork; Home: 3297 Windsor Ave., Powell River, B.C. V8A 1B2; Office: Box 334, Powell River, B.C. V8A 5C2.

**JAMES, Geoffrey,** M.A.; photographer, writer; b. St. Asaph, Wales 9 Jan. 1942; s. Capt. Arthur Sedgwick and Beryl (Williams) J.; e. Wellington Coll., Crowthorne, Berk, U.K. 1960; Wadham Coll., Oxford B.A. 1964, M.A. 1967; m. Jessica d. Harvard and Amy Bradley 5 Sept. 1981; children: David, Charles, Matthew; Contbg. & Assoc. Ed., Time Canada 1967–75; Head, Visual Arts Section, Canada Council 1975–82; Visiting Prof., Visual Arts, Univ. of Ottawa 1982–84; Fellowship, Graham Found. for Advanced Studies in the Fine Arts Chicago 1984; Can. Counc. 'A' Grant 1987; Fellowship, Guggenheim Found. 1989; Victor Lynch Staunton Prize, Canada Counc. 1992; major photographic exhibs.: Royal Inst. of Brit. Architects London 1986; Palazzo Braschi Rome 1986; Documenta IX, Kassel, Germany; The Power Plant, Toronto 1993; author: 'Genius Loci' 1986, 'Morbid Symptoms, Arcadia & the French Revolution' 1987, 'The Italian Garden' 1991, 'La Campagna Romana' 1991; editor: 'An Inquiry into the Aesthetics of Photography' 1975; '13 Essays on Photography' 1990; Home: 4579 ave. Coloniale, Montreal, Que. H2T 1W1.

**JAMES, Norman Graham;** executive; b. Cottesloe, W. Australia 19 Oct. 1923; s. Alfred Edward and Millicent Marie (Bradshaw) J.; e. Eng. and France; m. Noel M. Simpson 1 Apr. 1977; children: Deborah, Colin, Valerie; CHRMN. & C.E.O., CANDN. NAT. SPORTSMEN'S SHOWS 1969– ; Chrmn. & C.E.O., Outdoor Canada Publishing Ltd.; Chrmn.: Western Sportsman Magazine, Regina; Boating Business; Dir. Financial Life Assurance Co. of Canada; a founding Dir. Hamilton Trust & Saving Corp.; former Dir. Laurier Life Insurance Co. of Canada; Vice-Pres., External Affairs, Univ. of Toronto 1974–76; Chrmn. & Pres. ITT-Abbey Life Insurance Co. of Canada, Hamilton, Ont. 1964–74; Exec. Vice Pres. and a Founding Dir. Income Life Insurance Co. of Canada, Hamilton 1964–66; Vice Pres. Mktg. Global Life Insurance Co. of Canada, Toronto 1962–64; various sales positions and Br. Mgr. Canada Life Assurance Co. Toronto 1951–62; Journalist and Ed. 'Hamilton Spectator' and CJSH-FM Hamilton 1946–51; served with Royal Air Force and Royal Indian Air Force as pilot, Squadron Comdr., Air Staff Offr., in U.K., Canada, India, Burma and Malaya, W.W. II; pilot and Flight Comdr., 424 Squadron, Royal Candn. Air Force Reserve 1947–56; recipient Inst. Chart. Life Underwriters Gold Medal 1955; mem., Ad Personam Counc. of HRH The Duke of Edinburgh, World Wildlife Fund Internat., Gland, Switzerland; Trustee, mem. Exec. Ctte., Chrmn. Finance Ctte., N. Am. Wildlife Found. Washington, D.C. (operating Delta (Man.) Waterfowl & Wetlands Rsch. Stn.); Trustee, Nature Conservancy of Can.; Vice Chrmn. and founding Dir. 'True North' Can.'s Challenge for America's Cup, Perth, Australia 1986–87; Dir.: World Wildlife Fund Canada; Operation Raleigh Canada; Patron, Arctic Quest; mem., Adv. Council, The Inst. for Environ. Policy and Stewardship; P. Conservative; Anglican; recreations: downhill skiing, hunting, fishing, travel, languages, aviation, music, historical lit.; Clubs: Royal Air Force Club, London, U.K.; Holimont Ski; Goodwood; Home: 142 Edgecliffe Pl., Burlington, Ont. L7L 3Z3.

**JAMES, Paul Clive,** B.Sc., D.Phil.; ornithologist, ecologist, conservation biologist; b. Taplow, U.K. 23 Jan. 1953; s. Kenneth Cyril and Eileen (Roberts) J.; e. Simon Fraser Univ. B.Sc. 1980; Oxford Univ. D.Phil. 1984; m. Marilyn; children: Nicholas, Matthew, Neil, Keating, Mauray; CURATOR OF ORNITHOLOGY, ROYAL SASK. MUSEUM 1987– and ADJUNCT PROF., BIOLOGY DEPT., UNIV. OF REGINA 1989– ; Rsch. Asst., Queen's Univ. Rsch. Station Churchill Man. 1978; Mitlenatch Isl., B.C. 1979–80; Doctoral Stud., Boreal & Subtropical Atlantic Islands 1980–84; Post-doct. Fellow, Univ. of Sask. 1984–86 (NSERC); Univ. of Calgary 1986–87; Teacher, ecol. & bird anat., Univ. of Sask. 1984–86, ornithology, Univ. of Regina 1989– , grad. students 1992– ; Reg. Rep., Pacific Seabird Group 1985–89; Candn. Dir., Raptor Rsch. Found. 1989– ; Dir. and Mem., Sask. Nat. Hist. Soc. 1988– ; Regina Nat. Hist. Soc. 1988–91; Leader, Boy Scouts of Can. 1987–89; Big Brother 1975–80; Mem., Am. & Brit. Ornithol. Unions; Candn. Soc. of Ornithol.; Soc. Cons. Biologists; Int. Soc. Ecol. Economics; Raptor Rsch. Found.; Candn. Nature Fed.; author/co-author of over 60 sci. & pop. articles about birds; recreations: music, squash, skiing, reading; Home: Box 193, Pilot Butte, Sask. S0G 3Z0; Office: 2340 Albert St., Regina, Sask. S4P 3V7.

**JAMES, R. Scott,** B.A.; executive; b. Oxford, Engl. 1 Nov. 1943; s. Eric William and Peggy (Lidgett) J.; e. Univ. of Wales B.A. Hons. Hist. 1965; London Univ. post-grad. cert. in Edn. 1966; children: Louise, Spenser; MANAGING DIRECTOR, TORONTO HISTORICAL BOARD 1984– ; joined City of Toronto Archives 1967, Dir. of Records and City Archivist 1975; Chrmn. Albert Franck Ctte. (responsible for ann. exch. of artists with Amsterdam, Toronto's twin city) 1975–84; Chrmn., Toronto Sesquicentennial Pub. Ctte. 1980–84; founded Toronto Area Archivists Group 1973; Dir., T.A.A.G. Educ. Found. 1987–89; mem. Assn. of Candn. Archivists; Candn. Urban Hist. Assn.; Candn. Mus. Assn.; Ont. Mus. Assn.; Heritage Canada; City of Toronto's Records and Archives Prog. rec'd. Distinguished Service Award, Soc. of Am. Archivists' 1981 (first Candn. Inst. and first municipality to do so); awarded scholarship to attend M.A. (Hist. Prog.), Dalhousie Univ. 1966–67; Vice Pres., Mariposa Folk Foundation 1993– ; recreations: visual arts, music, squash; Club: Toronto Athletic; Office: 205 Yonge St., Toronto, Ont. M5B 1N2.

**JAMES, William,** B.Sc., Dip.HE, D.Sc., Ph.D., FCSCE, FASCE, P.Eng.; university professor; b. Johannesberg, S. Africa 15 Aug. 1937; s. William and Helena Cornelia (Fowlds) J.; e. Univ. of Natal B.Sc. 1958; Delft Tech. Univ. Dip.HE 1962; Univ. of Aberdeen Ph.D. 1965; Univ. of Natal D.Sc. 1985; m. Evelyn Mary d. Robert and Vera Stephen 1965; children: Robert, Iain; DIRECTOR, SCH. OF ENGINEERING, UNIV. OF GUELPH 1988– ; Natal Prov. Water Engineer 1958–59; M.S. Zakrzewshi & Partners 1960–61; grad. studies 1962–64; Sr. Lectr., Univ. of Natal 1965–70; Prof., McMaster Univ. 1971–85; Cudworth Chair of Computational Hydrology, Univ. of Alabama 1986–87; Chair of Civil Eng., Wayne State Univ. 1987–88; Visiting Prof., Univ. of Lund, Univ. of Lulea, Queen's Univ., Univ. of Witwatersrand, Univ. of Michigan; C.E.O., Computational Hydraulics Internat.; consults widely to govt. & indus., Canada, U.S., etc.; Fellow, Candn. Soc. of Civil Eng.; Am. Soc. of Civil Eng.; Mem., Am. Soc. of Civil Eng.; Am. Geophysical Union; Internat. Assn. for Hydro. Sci.; Eng. Inst. of Can.; Am. Water Resources Assn.; Assn. of Profl. Eng. of Ont.; Cand. Soc. of Civil Eng.; Candn. Water Resources Assn.; Internat. Great Lakes Rsch. Assn.; author of 160 sci. papers, 175 reports, 12 edited conf. proceedings; editor: 'Current Practices in Modelling the Management of Stormwater Impacts' 1992, 'New Techniques for Modelling the Management of Storm-Water Quality of Pollution Control Planning' 1991, 'Pollution Control Planning' 1987; co-author: 'A Sufficient Quantity of Pure and Wholesome Water' 1978; recreations: sailing, tennis, canoeing; club: Cutten; Address: 36 Stuart St., Guelph, Ont. N1E 4S5.

**JAMES, William,** M.A., Ph.D.; mining executive; b. Ottawa, Ont. 5 Feb. 1929; s. William Fleming and Lenore (McEvoy) J.; e. pub. and high schs. Toronto; Univ. of Toronto B.A. 1951, M.A. 1954, McGill Univ. Ph.D. 1957; m. Joanna d. Fred T. Watson, 15 Sept. 1954; children: Paul, William, Anne, Mary, George, John; Dir., Air Canada; Cameco; Canadian Imperial Bank of Commerce; Convest Exploration Co. Ltd.; CGC Inc.; Export Develop. Corp.; Falconbridge Ltd.; Falconbridge Dominicana, C. por A.; Fishery Products Internat. Ltd.; Morrison Petroleums Ltd.; The Mutual Life of Canada; The Mutual Group (U.S.); James & Buffam 1961–67, Partner 1967–73; Noranda Mines Ltd. 1973–82; Falconbridge Ltd. 1982–89; Former Chrmn., Pres. & C.E.O. Falconbridge Ltd. 1989– ; Dir., Olympic Trust of Can.; Cambrian Coll. Found.; St. Michael's Hosp.; Mem., Ont. Round Table on Environment & Economy; mem., Assn. Prof. Engrs. Ont.; Cdn. Inst. of Mining & Metallurgy; Am. Inst. of Mining, Metallurgical and Petroleum Engineers; R. Catholic; Clubs: Engineers; York; Toronto; Office: P.O. Box 39, Commerce Court North, Toronto, Ont. M5L 1A1.

**JAMES, William (Bill);** artistic director; choreographer; b. Cleveland, Ohio 25 Nov. 1951; s. Dr. William H. and Rosalie (Hume) J.; e. Univ. of N.D. 1969–70; Univ. of Portland 1970–71; Royal Winnipeg Ballet Sch. 1972–73; Banff Sch. of Fine Arts 1974; Artistic Dir., Dancemakers 1988; Actor, Persephone Theatre Saskatoon 1974–75; Dancer/Choreog. Le Groupe de la Place Royale Montreal and Ottawa 1975–85; Guest Lectr. York Univ. Toronto 1986, Univ. of Quebec, Montreal 1988; freelance choreog./teacher 1985–88; mem. Adv. Bd. Dancers Transition Centre Toronto; Dance Assessor The Can. Council Ottawa; mem. Candn. Assn. Profl. Dance Orgns. Ottawa; Address: 298 Logan Ave., Toronto, Ont. M4M 2N7.

**JAMES-FRENCH, Dayv,** B.A.; writer; b. Summerside, P.E.I. 18 Aug. 1953; e. Carleton Univ. B.A. 1979; Univ. of Victoria; invited participant at Kingston Conference (New Writers/New Critics) 1986; author: 'Victims of Gravity' 1990 (short stories); stories anthologized in 'Journey Prize Anthology V', '92: Best Canadian Stories' 1992, 'The New Story Writers' 1992, 'The Macmillan Anthology' 1990, '88: Best Canadian Stories' 1988, 'Coming Attractions' 1986; Home: 2592 Hobson Rd., Ottawa, Ont. K1V 8M7.

**JAMESON, Albert George,** FCGA; association executive; b. Sudbury, Ont. 4 May 1936; s. Albert and Elizabeth Maria (Gardiner) J.; e. Eastern H.S. of Commerce 1953; Cert. Gen. Acct. 1962; Fellow, Inst. Cert. Gen. Acct. 1980; m. Helen d. Jack and Margaret Beattie 18 Nov. 1961; children: Philip Alan, Catherine Ann, Sharon Lynn, Sandra Marie; PRES., FINANCIAL EXECUTIVES INST. CANADA 1987– ; joined IBM 1953; controller 1968; Vice-Pres. & Treas. 1972; Vice-Pres., Fin. 1979; Vice-Pres., Mngt. Serv. (resp. for real estate, comm., corp. prog., personnel, quality) 1985; Chrmn., Centenary Hosp. Bd., Couns. of Fin. Extves.; recreations: tennis, squash; club: Granite; Home: 46 Creekwood Dr., West Hill, Ont. M1E 4L7; Office: 1701 – 141 Adelaide St. W., Toronto, Ont. M5H 3L5.

**JAMIESON, Christopher Warren,** B.Sc., M.B.A.; energy company executive; b. Toronto, Ont. 5 July 1954; s. Warren J. and Ann T. J.; e. Queen's Univ. B.Sc. (Hons.) 1976, M.B.A. 1978; m. Harriet d. Robert and Mary Hipwell 1 May 1976; children: John, Rob; SENIOR VICE-PRESIDENT & CHIEF FINANCIAL OFFICER, UNION ENERGY INC. 1986– ; Asst. Mgr., Credit (King/Bay Branch), Toronto Dominion Bank 1978–80; Vice-Pres. & Asst. Treas., Cadillac Fairview Corp. 1980–85; Home: 8 St. Andrew Gardens, Toronto, Ont. M4W 2E1; Office: 21 St. Clair Ave. E., Toronto, Ont. M4T 2T7.

**JAMIESON, John Kenneth;** company director; b. Medicine Hat, Alta. 28 Aug. 1910; s. John Locke and Kate (Herron) J.; e. Univ. of Alta.; Mass. Inst. of Tech., Grad.; m. Ethel May Burns, 23 Dec. 1937; children: John Burns, Anne Frances; DIR., RAYCHEM. CORP. 1977– ; has been engaged in the oil industry since 1931; el. a Dir. of Imperial Oil Co., Ltd., Toronto, Ont., 1952; Vice Pres. 1953; Pres., International Petroleum Co., Ltd., 1959–61; Vice President and Dir., Exxon Co. (U.S.) 1961–62; Extve. Vice Pres. 1962–63; Pres. 1963; Extve. Vice Pres. and Dir. Exxon Corp. 1964–80; Pres. 1965–69; Chrmn. and Chief Extve. Offr. 1969–75; mem., Association of Prof. Engrs. Ont.; Lambda Chi Alpha; Episcopalian; Clubs: Houston (Texas) Country; Augusta National Golf; Office: 1100 Milam Bldg., Suite 4601, Houston, Texas 77002.

**JAMIESON, Walter,** Ph.D., ACP, MCIP; university professor; b. Montreal, Que. 11 Apr. 1945; s. Joseph Walter and Angel Therese (Plano) J.; e. York Univ. B.A. 1970, M.E.S. 1973; Edinburgh Coll. of Art/Heriot-Watt Univ. M.Sc. 1974; Univ. of Birmingham Ph.D. 1978; m. Delphine 14 Sept. 1973; children: Christopher, Michelle; PROF. OF PLANNING, DIR., HIST. RESOURCES INTERN PROGRAMME & DIR., CENTRE FOR LIVABLE COMMUNITES, UNIV. OF CALGARY 1986– ; var. acad. posts 1975–78; Assoc. Prof., present univ. 1978–86; Chrmn., Prog. Ctte., Candn. Inst. of Planners Annual Conf. 1990; Profl. Exam. Bd. in Community Planning 1989– ; Vice Pres., Urban & Reg. Info. Systems (Alta.) 1989– ; Mem., Assn. for Preserv. Technol. (APT) (Past Pres. 1987–89; Pres. 1983–87; Vice-Pres. 1980–83; Sec.-Treas. 1978–80; Chrmn., Annual Conf. 1982); Professional Advisor, CMHC Scholarship Program 1992; Vice-Chair., World Tourism Education Rsch. Centre 1992; various extve. positions ICOMOS Can. & Internat. and Candn. Inst. of Planners (Alta.); Teaching Excellence Award, Univ. of Calgary Student's Union 1988–89; APT Award for outstanding serv. 1987; Edmonton River Valley comp., 4 awards; Calgary City Counc. Award for hist. preserv. work 1984; Heritage Canada's Lt. Gov. Award 1984; editor of several symposium & conf. proceedings and reports; co-editor: 'Plan Canada' 1991–94; mem./past mem. of numerous community & hist. assns.; Home: 4028 Chatham Place N.W., Calgary, Alta. T2L 0Z6; Office: Calgary, Alta. T2N 1N4.

**JANCI, William A.,** B.A., M.B.A.; business consultant; b. Detroit, Mich. 8 May 1946; s. Anthony J. and Josephine B. J.; e. Univ. of Windsor, B.A. 1967, M.B.A. 1969; m. Anne M. d. Tina and Bill Cherrie 1972; children: Bill Jr., Nicole, Bevin; PRES., BJ BUSINESS CONSULTANTS 1992– ; Pres. & Chief Extve. Offr., Agnew Group Inc. 1987; var. posts, Chrysler Can. 1969–76; Corp. Controller, Chrysler S. Africa 1976; Dir. of Pricing Chrysler U.S.A. 1978, Dir. of Fin. 1979, Uniroyal Tire U.S.A. 1980; Corp. Controller, Electrohome Ltd. 1982, Vice-Pres., Fin. & Chief Fin. Offr. 1984; Mem., Fin. Extve. Inst.; recreations: golf, curling, tennis; clubs: Westmount Golf & Country (Bd. of Dirs.); Northfield Racquet; Home: 587 Manorwood Court, Waterloo, Ont. N2K 3L7.

**JANES, Robert R.,** B.A., Ph.D.; museum executive; b. Rochester, Minn. 23 April 1948; s. Joseph Mowat and Helen Viola (Johnson) J.; e. Univ. of the Americas; Univ. of Calif. at Berkeley; Lawrence Univ. B.A. (cum laude) 1970; Univ. of Calgary Ph.D. 1976; m. Priscilla d. William Harold and Annette Ray Bickel 28 Aug. 1971; children: Erica Helen Janes, Peter Bickel Janes; EXECUTIVE DIRECTOR & CHIEF EXECUTIVE OFFICER, GLENBOW-ALBERTA INSTITUTE 1989– ; arch. field asst., supervisor, crew chief, principal investigator, consultant in U.S.A., Africa, Yukon & N.W.T. 1970–86; Founding Dir., Prince of Wales Northern Heritage Centre 1976–86; Postdoctoral Fellow, Arctic Inst. of N. Am. 1981–82; Founding Extve. Dir., Sci. Inst. of the N.W.T. & Sci. Advisor, Govt. of the N.W.T. 1986–9; Adjunct Prof. of Arch., Univ. of Calgary 1990– ; Assoc. Ed. 'Arctic' 1987– ; Mem., Bd. of Dir., Museums West 1990– ; Candn. Art Museum Directors' Orgn. 1992– ; Alberta 2005 Centennial History Soc. 1991– ; several past executive positions various orgns.; Canada Council Doctoral Fellow 1973–76; Foreign Fellow, Am. Anthropological Assn. 1977; Cert. of Accreditation, Candn. Museums Assn. 1982; Fellow, Arctic Inst. of N. Am. 1984; First Hon. Life Mem., Candn. Museums Assn. 1986; Distinguished Alumni Award, Univ. of Calgary 1989; Lucia R. Briggs Distinguished Achievement Award, Lawrence Univ. 1991; Outstanding Achievement Award for Museum Mngt., Candn. Museums Assn. 1992; Award of Merit for O/S Achievement, Alta. Museums Assn. 1992; Who's Who in America 1991–94; Sigma Xi Sci. Rsch. Soc. 1993; Candn. Studies Writing Award, Assn. for Candn. Studies 1989; Mem., Candn. Arch. Assn. (Vice-Pres. 1980–82; Pres Elect 1982–84; Pres. 1984–86); Arctic Inst. of N. Am. (Vice-Chair of Bd. 1985–89); Soc. of Am. Arch.; Current Anthropology (Assoc.); Candn. Museums Assn.; Am. Anthropological Assn.; Am. Assn. of Museums; Alta. Museums Assn.; Internat. Council of Museums; author: 'Archaeological Ethnography among Mackenzie Basin Dene' 1983, 'Preserving Diversity' 1991 and approx. 50 articles, chapters, notes, comments & reviews in journals & mags.; recreations: hiking, nordic skiing, camping, gardening, reading; clubs: Ranchmen's Club; Home: Box 32, Site 32, R.R. 12, Calgary, Alta. T3E 6W3; Office: 130 – 9 Ave. S.E., Calgary, Alta. T2G 0P3.

**JANISCH, Andrew,** B.Sc.; petroleum executive; b. Wallern, Austria 7 Nov. 1931; s. Joseph and Anna (Summer) J.; came to Can. 1935; e. Univ. of Man. B.Sc. (Civil Engn.) 1953; m. Jessie Patterson d. Thomas Dickson 26 Aug. 1953; children: Stephen Alexander, Gregory Joseph, Mark Richard, Matthew Lawrence; Pres., Jandess Ltd.; Dir. & Chrmn., Mark Resources Inc.; Dir., Westrock Energy Corp.; Pointer Exploration; joined Gulf Oil Canada Ltd. 1953; Vice Pres. and Gen. Mgr., Gulf Minerals Canada Ltd., Pres. 1975; Sr. Vice Pres. Petro-Canada 1977; Pres. 1979; Pres. Cdn. Superior Oil Ltd. 1982–86; mem. APEGGA; R. Catholic; recreations: golf, curling; Clubs: Calgary Petroleum; Home: 118 Pumpridge Place S.W., Calgary, Alta. T2V 5E7.

**JANISCH, Hudson Noel,** B.A., M.A., LL.B., M.C.L., LL.M., J.S.D.; educator; b. Cape Town, S. Africa 12 Nov. 1938; s. John Ralph and Margaret (Paterson) J.; e. Diocesan Coll. 1956; Rhodes Univ. B.A. 1959; Cambridge Univ. M.A. 1961, LL.B. 1962; Univ. of Chicago M.C.L. 1963, LL.M. 1965, J.S.D. 1971; m. Alice d. Charles and Dorothy Arthur 13 July 1968; one d. Ellen Barbara; PROF. OF LAW, UNIV. OF TORONTO 1978– ; called to Bar of Ont. 1971; Asst. Prof. of Law, Univ. of W. Ont. 1968, Assoc. Prof. 1970–72; Assoc. Prof. of Law, Dalhousie Univ. 1972, Prof. 1975–78; mem. Adv. Ctte. Regulatory Reference, Econ. Council Can. 1980–81; Ont. Pub. Comm. Vehicle Act Review Ctte. 1982–83; Adv. Ctte. Centre for Study Regulated Inds. McGill Univ.; Chrmn. Regulated Inds. Prog. Consumer's Assn. Can. 1979–82; Founding mem. and mem. Steering Ctte. Univ. of Toronto-Waterloo Univ. Coop. on Info. Technol. 1981–85; Invited Guest Hokkaido Univ. and Nippon Telephone and Telegraph Co. Japan 1987; cons. telecommunications ind. and govt. regulatory agencies and depts.; author 'The Regulatory Process of the Canadian Transport Commission' 1978; co-author 'Administrative Law, Cases Text and Materials' 3rd ed. 1989; 'Canadian Telecommunications Regulation Bibliography' 1987; numerous articles and chapters adm. law, regulation & telecommunications; Assoc. Ed. 'Administrative Law Reports'; mem. Old Diocesan Union; Candn. Assn. Law Teachers; Law Soc. Upper Can.; recreation: fishing; Home: 84 Summerhill Ave., Toronto, Ont. M4T 1A8; Office: 78 Queen's Park, Toronto, Ont. M5S 2C5.

**JANISCHEWSKYJ, Wasyl,** B.A.Sc., M.A.Sc., FIEEE; university professor; b. Prague, Czechoslovakia 21 Jan. 1925; s. Ivan and Hanna (Rawych); e. Univ. of Toronto B.A.Sc. 1952, M.A.Sc. 1954; m. Emilia d. Mykhailo and Maria Miszczuk 7 Jan. 1951; children: Roxolana, Marko; PROF. EMERITUS, DEPT OF ELECTRICAL ENGR., UNIV. OF TORONTO 1990– , Prof. 1970–90; Elect. Engr., Aluminium Labs. Ltd., Kingston, Ont. 1955–59; Lectr., Dept. of Electr. Engr., Univ. of Toronto 1959–62; Asst. Prof. 1962–65; Assoc. Prof. 1965–70; Asst. Head of Dept. 1964–70; Assoc. Dean, Fac. of Applied Sci. & Engr. 1978–82; Vis. Prof., Univ. of Liverpool 1970; Tech. Univ. of Munich 1970; Fed. Univ. of Rio de Janeiro 1982; Univ. of Rome 'La Sapienza' 1989; Vis. Sci., Elect. de France, Rsch. Labs. at Clamart 1982; NSERC Sr. Indus. Fellow, Trench Electric 1983; Cons., Elect. Engr. Consociates 1968– ; Fellow (& mem.) Inst. of Elect. and Electronics Engr.; mem. Assn. of Profl. Engrs. of Prov. of Ont.; Candn. Electr. Assn.; 'CAGE CLUB' (founding); Internat. Electrotech. Comn.; Internat. Spec. Ctte. on Radio Interference; Internat. Conf. on Large High-Voltage Electric Systems; Candn. Nat. Ctte. COPIMERA; Internat. Comm. on Rules for Approval of Elect. Equipment; Candn. Standards Assn. (extensive current & prev. extve. & ctte. positions in all above assns.); Ukrainian Free Acad. of Scis.; Extve., Candn. Taras Shevchenko Scientific Soc.; Dir., Ukrainian Chair Found.; author of over 140 scholarly papers & over 50 scholarly lectrs. presented on 5 continents; Ukrainian Greek Orthodox; recreations: swimming, volleyball, chess, tennis; Home: 65 Humbercrest Blvd., Toronto, Ont. M6S 4K6; Office: Toronto, Ont. M5S 1A4.

**JANNETEAU, Gérald M.,** B.A.; television executive; b. Notre-Dame du Nord, Qué. 6 April 1942; s. Marcel J. and Eglantine (Pleau) J.; e. Coll. Sacré-Coeur Sudbury; Univ. Laurentienne B.A. 1963; McMaster Univ. C.M.A. 1971; m. Pauline C. d. Eugène and Isabelle Bourgeault 26 December 1963; children: Marcel G., Jean E., Josée A.; PRES. AND GEN. MGR. LE RÉSEAU DES SPORTS 1989– ; Cost Acct. Spruce Falls Pulp & Paper Co. Ltd. Kapuskasing 1964–68; Acctg. Mgr. Borg Textiles Elmira, Ont. 1968, Asst. to Dir. Mfg. Delavan, Wis. 1970–71; Financial Analyste Siège Social Radio Can. Ottawa 1972, Adjoint au Dir. Régional CBC Qué. Montréal 1974, Producer CBC TV News Montréal 1976, Asst. Mng. Ed. Nat. TV News Toronto 1980, Dir. of Television CBC Ottawa 1984, Dir. Régional CBC/Radio Can. Ottawa 1989; recreations: squash, golf, reading, cinema; Home: 2130 Pelletier, Varennes, Qué. J3X 1E6; Office: 300, 1755 boul. René-Lévesque est, Montréal, Qué. H2K 4P6.

**JANSA, Lubomir F.,** M.Sc., Ph.D.; senior research scientist; b. Czechoslovakia 15 Nov. 1933; s. Frantisek and Marie (Kralova) J.; e. Masaryk Univ., Brno M.Sc. 1956; Charles Univ., Prague Ph.D. 1966; m. Hana Marie Sebestova d. Eduard Sebesta 20 June 1957; children: Hana, Michal; GEOLOGICAL SURVEY OF CANADA 1971– ; Geologist: Coal Expl. Co., Czech. 1956–58; Geol. Survey of Czech. 1958–60; Minerals Prospecting Co., Ostrava, Czech. 1960–65; Head, Coal Lab., Coal Research Inst., Radvanice, Czech. 1966–68; Research Assoc., Illinois Geol. Surv. & Univ. of Illinois 1968–69; NRC postdoct. fellow, Inst. of Sedimentary & Petroleum Geol., Calgary 1970–71; Adjunct Prof., Dalhousie Univ. 1984– ; NRC postdoct. fellowship; recipient, Prof. Purkyne medal for contributions to sedimentary and marine geology, awarded by Czechoslovak Geological Societies and Geological Survey 1992; discoverer of the first meteorite impact crater in the ocean; Chairman of Symposia at Internat. Sedim. Congresses, Hamilton 1982; Canberra, Aust. 1986; 28th Internat. Geol. Congress (Washington) 1989; Mem., Geol. Soc. of Am.; Internat. Sedimentol. Soc.; Candn. Soc. of Petro. Geol.; Soc. of Econ. Paleontol. & Mineralog.; author of over 150 scientific papers published in international journals; assoc.-editor: Sedimentary Geology Journal; recreations: skiing, mountaineering, classical music; Home: 32 Birchwood Terrace, Dartmouth, N.S. B3A 3W3; Office: Atlantic Geosci. Center, Bedford Inst. of Oceanography, P.O. Box 1006, Dartmouth, N.S. B2Y 4A2.

**JANSON, Peter S.,** B.Sc., P.Eng.; engineer; b. Vasteras, Sweden 28 May 1947; s. the late Helge A. and Dorothy W. (Burgers) J.; e. Queen's Univ., B.Sc. (Elect. Engr.) 1969; m. Margaret d. Archibald and Marion Ross 18 Sept. 1971; children: Jennifer, Elizabeth, Allison; PRES. & C.E.O., ASEA BROWN BOVERI INC. 1988– ; Chrmn., CITEQ (Centre d'innovation sur le transport d'énergie du Qué.); Dir., Energy Council of

Canada; Laurentian Bank of Canada; Laurentian Trust of Canada Inc.; Power Serv Pacific Inc.; Training Engr., ASEA Inc. 1969–70; Sales Application Engr. 1971–73; Prod. Mgr. 1973–77; Dist. Sales Mgr., Indus. Div. 1977–79; Dept. Mgr. 1979–82; Gen. Mgr. & Extve. Dir., ASEA Electric (S. Africa) 1982–86; Pres., ASEA Inc. 1986–88; Mem., Business Council on National Issues; National Advisory Bd. on Science and Technology; Assn. of Professional Engineers of Ont.; Clubs: Forest & Stream; West Island Tennis; Home: 111 Elm Cres., Baie d'Urfé, Qué. H9X 2P5; Office: 3000 Halpern, St. Laurent, Qué. H4S 1R2.

**JANSSON, Harri Elis,** B.A.; banker; b. Helsinki, Finland 23 Dec. 1945 (Cdn. Citizen); s. Kurt Gunnar and Eeva J.; e. New York State Univ. at Buffalo B.A. 1967; m. Judith d. Norm Bowen 26 Oct. 1974; children: Linnea, Anna-Liisa, Kirsti; SR. VICE-PRES., BC DIV., PERSONAL & COMMERCIAL BANKING, BANK OF MONTREAL 1990– ; var. Br. Mgr. postings, IAC Limited 1969–78; Vice-Pres. Mktg., Scotia Leasing Limited 1978–80; Vice-Pres., Grindlays Bank Can. Ltd. 1980; joined present bank 1980; Vice-Pres. East. & N. Ont. 1985, Vice-Pres. Manitoba 1986; Sr. Vice-Pres., Commercial Banking, Prairies 1987–90; Mem., B.C. Ctte., Cdn. Bankers' Assn.; 1992 Chrmn., Leadership Vancouver; External Adv. Bd. Mem., Simon Fraser Univ. Faculty of Business Admin.; Financial Regulation Internship Adv. Ctte., Univ. of B.C. Faculty of Commerce & Business Admin.; Chrmn., Vancouver General Hospital Found.; Corp. Fundraising Ctte., Vancouver Symphony Orchestra; Mem., Finnish Candn. Chamber of Commerce; British Candn. Trade Assn.; Canada/Japan Soc.; recreations: golf; clubs: Shaughnessy Golf & Country; The Vancouver Club; The Canadian Club; Vancouver Bd. of Trade; Office: 595 Burrard St., Box 49500, Vancouver, B.C. V7X 1L7.

**JANTHUR, Heinz Joachim (Joe),** Ec.D., FICB; financial executive; b. Glogau, Germany 19 July 1934; s. Adolf J. Karl and Elly Hildegard (Jantz) J.; e. Waterloo C.I.; Queen's Univ.; Ryerson; York Univ.; m. Theresa d. Dominic and Mary McCaffrey 12 April 1958; children: Marlene, Charles; PRESIDENT, DEPAG DEPOSIT AGENCY OF CANADA INC. 1983– ; progressed through all phases of banking within Candn. Imperial Bank of Commerce & Bank of America Canada in Canada, Switz. & Germany; reorganizes & strategically positions client corps. for growth; Chair, Fed. of Export Clubs Can.; Central Ont. Export Club; Canada-Romania Bus. Council; Canada-Moldova Bus. Council; Waechtersbach Canada Limited; Waterloo N. Condominium Corp. No. 185; Ronneburg Plazas Inc.; Vice Chair, Share Life Charities of Archdiocese of Toronto; Candn. Exporters Assn. (Ont.); Vice-Pres., Insur. & Banking Phila. Soc. of G.B.; recreations: reading, curling; club: Albany of Toronto; Home: 22 Danville Dr., Willowdale, Ont. M2P 1J1; Office: 67 Yonge St., Suite 1402, Toronto, Ont. M5E 1J8.

**JANVIER, Alex,** R.C.A.; artist; b. Le Goff, Alta. 28 Feb. 1935; s. Harry and Mary J.; e. Alta. Coll. of Art Calgary grad. 1960; m. Jacqueline d. Jacob Wolowski 20 Apl. 1968; children: Dean, Tricia, Duane, Kyle, Jill, Brett; teacher Univ. of Alta. Dept. Extension 1960–62; Co-Owner Triple Jay Cattle Co. 1962–65; Dept. Indian Affairs 1965–67; Alta. Newstart Lac La Biche 1968–71; mem. Candn. Cultural Exchange Tour China 1985; full-time artist since 1971; first N.Am. Indian painter creating modern art; exhbns.: 'Land Spirit Power' Nat. Art Gall. 1992; 'Alex Janvier, First Thirty Years' retrospective, Thunderbay Art Gall., Thunder Bay, Ont. 1993; mem. CARFAC; Candn. Artist Representation; Alta. Indian Arts & Crafts; Southwestern Assn. Indian Affairs Inc.; recreation: hockey; Club: Cold Lake Old Timers; Address: P.O. Box 8130, Cold Lake, Alta. T0A 0Y0.

**JANZEN, Henry Frank,** B.Sc., M.A., Ed.D.; university dean; b. Winnipeg, Man. 7 June 1940; s. Jake and Sadie J.; e. Univ. North Dakota, B.Sc. 1964; Univ. Northern Colorado, M.A. 1966; Ed.D. 1970; m. Judy, d. Leslie Munro; children: Dean; Joanne; DIR./DEAN FACULTY PHYS. ED. & RECREATION STUDIES, UNIV. MAN. since 1978; joined Winnipeg Blue Bombers 1959; chosen Rookie of the Year 1959; chosen Outstanding Candn. with Blue Bombers 1962–65; chosen All-Star Candn. 1965; Teacher, Jr. High and High Sch. (Winnipeg) 1964–65; Coach, Univ. Man. Bisons 1966–70; Bisons Candn. Coll. Bowl Champions 1969, 1970; Athletic Dir., Sch. Phys. Ed., Univ. Man. 1965–78; named Candn. Coll. Football Coach of the Year 1979; author several articles published in athletic education journals; Hon. Citizen Winnipeg; Dean's List, Univ. North Dakota and Univ. Northern Colorado; Course Conductor, Level 1, 2 and 3, Nat. Coaching Certificate Programs; mem., Winnipeg Blue Bomber - Hall of Fame; Nat. Advisory Counc., Fitness and Amateur Sport; Bd. Dirs., Man. Sports Fed.; Bd. Dirs., 1290 Fox & 9.94 Radio Stations; mem. Fort Garry Sch. Div.; Home: 569 Parkwood Pl., Winnipeg, Man. R3T 3A3; Office: Fac. of Phys. Ed. and Recreation Studies, Univ. of Man., Room 102, Frank Kennedy Centre, Winnipeg, Man. R3T 2N2.

**JAQUES, Louis B.,** M.A., Ph.D., D.Sc., F.R.S.C.; professor; b. Toronto, Ont. 10 July 1911; s. late Robert Herbert and Ann Bella (Shepherd) J.; e. Univ. of Toronto (Trinity Coll.), B.A. 1933, M.A. 1935, Ph.D. 1941; Univ. of Sask. D.Sc. 1974; m. Helen Evelyn, d. late Thomas J. Delane, Huntsville, Ont., 15 May 1937 (dec. 22 May 1987); one d. Catherine Mary Ann (Hall); m. the late Georgina Merrick Powell, Toronto, Ont. 16 Nov. 1991; EMERITUS PROF. PHYSIOLOGY AND RESEARCH ASSC. OF DENTISTRY, UNIV. OF SASK., 1979; Fellow, Royal Soc. Can. 1952; Fellow, New York Academy of Sciences 1955; Hon. Lay Canon, Ang. Dioc. of Saskatoon, 1981; Surgery (under a grant from Banting Foundation) Univ. of Toronto, 1934–35; Fellow, Dept. of Physiology 1936–38 and Research Asst., 1938–42; Research Asst., Dept. of Physiol. Hygiene, 1939–42; Lectr and Research Assoc., Dept. of Physiol., 1943–44; Asst. Prof., 1944–46; Prof. and Head Dept. of Physiol. Pharmacol., Univ. of Sask., 1946–71; Prof. of Physiology, Univ. of Sask, and Head of Haemostasis-Thrombosis Unit, 1971–79; Lindsay Prof., 1972–79; author of 'The Prayer Book Companion' 1963; 'Anticoagulant Therapy' 1965; numerous articles in scient. journ.; mem., New York Acad. Sciences; Med. Research Council, 1960–61; Gen. Synod, Ang. Ch. Can., 1952–59; Gen. Comn. on Union, Ang.-Un. Ch. of Can. 1967–73; Adv. Comte., Med. Div., Nat. Research Council, 1952–55, 1958–60; Internat. Comte. for Standardization of Nomenclature of the Blood Clotting Factors 1954–66; mem., Candn. Physiol. Soc.; Pharmacol. Soc. Can.; Am. Soc. of Hematol.; Anglican; Home: 682 University Drive, Saskatoon, Sask. S7N 0J2.

**JARDINE, Andrew Kennedy Skilling,** B.Sc., M.Sc., Ph.D., C.Eng., P.Eng.; university professor; b. Edinburgh, Scotland 25 Jan. 1941; s. Andrew and Catherine Kennedy (Skilling) J.; e. Univ. of Strathclyde, B.Sc. 1964, M.Sc. 1965; Univ. of Birmingham, Ph.D. 1973; m. Kathleen d. George and Davina Robertson 30 May 1964; children: Niall, Alison, Bruce; PROF. & CHRMN., DEPT. OF INDUS. ENGINEERING, UNIV. OF TORONTO 1986– ; Engr. appren., Nairn-Williamson 1956–60; Lectr., Strathclyde Univ. 1966–71; Birmingham Univ. 1971–77; Assoc. Prof., Univ. of Windsor 1977–79; Assoc. Prof. & Prof.-in-Charge, Engr. & Mngt. Prog., Royal Military Coll. of Can. 1979–81; Prof. & Head, Dept. of Engr. Mngt. 1981–86; editor: 'Operational Research in Maintenance' 1970; author: 'Maintenance, Replacement and Reliability' 1973; co-author: 'Essentials of Statistics in Marketing' 1974, 'Statistical Methods in Quality Control' 1975; Home: 90 Willingdon Blvd., Etobicoke, Ont. M8X 2H7; Office: Toronto, Ont. M5S 1A4.

**JARISLOWSKY, Stephen A.,** O.C., B.Sc., M.A., M.B.A., LL.D. (Hon.); investment counsel; b. Berlin, Germany 9 Sept. 1925; s. Alfred and Kaethe (Gassmann) J.; e. Ecole du Moncel, Jouy-en-Josas, France; Asheville Sch., NCUSA 1942; Cornell Univ., B.Sc. 1944; Univ. of Chicago, M.A. 1947 (Phi Beta Kappa); Harvard Univ., M.B.A. 1949; m. Margaret Gail, d. late Harold Merilees, 11 Apl. 1968; children: Stephen Alfred, Michael Andrew, Alexandra Cecile, Marika Ann; CHAIRMAN, JARISLOWSKY, FRASER & COMPANY LTD. (Canada's largest pension fund manager); Dir. and mem. Extve. Comte. SNC Lavalin Inc.; Fraser Bros.; past Dir.: Prefac Concrete; OE Inc.; Abitibi-Price Diversified Group; past Chrmn. Finance-Admin. Comte., Montreal Mus. of Fine Arts (Past Dir. Extve. Comte.); Pres. & Dir. Didier Refractories Canada Ltd.; Chrmn., Montreal Learning Associates; Chrmn., Montreal Learning Centre; Vice-Chrmn. & Dir., Régie des Rentes du Qué.; Dir., Southam Inc., The Daily Telegraph (U.K.); Growth Oil & Gas Investment Fund; Goodfellow Lumber Co.; J.J. Barker Co. Ltd.; North American Refractories Inc.; Swiss Bank Corp. (Canada); Unimedia Lteé.; Candn. Marconi; Dir., Musée d'Art Contemporain; Extve. Comte., Comité Qué., C.D. Howe Research Inst.; Dir., C.D. Howe Inst.; Past Dir., Chambre de Comm. de Montréal; SPCA Montreal; Past Chrmn. Qué. MBA Assn.; Past Extve. Council, Candn. Chamber of Comm.; Past Pres., Japan-Canada Soc.; served with Alcan Aluminum Ltd. as Plant Engr., Sales Adm., Finance Adm. and Area Supvr., Asia, Africa and Australia, 1949–52; The Twin Editions, Art Publishing, New York, 1952–55; estbd. Growth Oil & Gas Investment Fund, 1952; General Impact Extrusions Ltd. 1953; estbd. present firm 1955; has reorganized various other firms and served as extve. incl. Vice Pres. and Dir., Phénix Mills (1966); taught invest. analysis, Dept. of Comm., McGill Univ., 1956–60; consultant to various banks and corps.; frequent contrib. to newspapers, radio, television on econ. topics; served with US Army 1944–46, Japan; Counter Intelligence Corps; rec'd Order of Chrysanthemum (4th Class) Japan; Officer, Order of Canada 1994; Unit Citation Medal; Hon. LL.D., Queen's Univ.; Univ. of Alta.; Chrmn., Montreal Learning Centre; Trustee, Asheville Sch. (N.C.); mem., Chamber Comm. Finance Comte.; Candn. Econ. Policy Comte.; Financial Analyst Soc.; Trustee, Children's Hosp., Montreal; Protestant; recreations: hiking, tennis, swimming, music, gardening; Clubs: Mt. Royal; Hillside Tennis; Laurentian Ski; Home: 9 Murray Ave., Westmount, Que. H3Y 2X9; Office: 1110 Sherbrooke St. W., Montreal, Que. H3A 1G8.

**JARMAIN, William Edwin Charles,** M.Sc., P.Eng.; company president; b. London, Ont. 25 May 1938; s. Edwin Roper and Ruth Winifred (Second) J.; e. Mass. Inst. of Technol., B.Sc. (Elect. Engn.) 1961, M.Sc. (Elect. Engn.) 1964, M.Sc. (Indust. Mang.) 1964; m. Anna Stahmer 31 Dec. 1990; three d. Catherine Carroll, Anne Beatrice, Ellen Ruth; PRESIDENT, JARMAIN GROUP INC. (Toronto) and CHAIRMAN, FCA INTERNATIONAL LTD. (Montreal); Dir., The Equitable Companies Inc. 1992– ; The Equitable Life Assurance Soc. of the United States 1992– ; Donaldson, Lufkin & Jenrette, Inc. 1993– ; AXA Insurance (Canada) 1989– ; Anglo Gibralter Insurance Group 1987– ; Counc. Candn. Unity 1987– ; formerly Pres., London Biochemistry Reference Laboratory; Pres., Canadian Cablesystems Ltd.; Staff mem., Sch. of Indust. Mang., Mass. Inst. of Technol., 1961–64; Assoc., McKinsey & Co., Inc. (mang. consultants), New York, 1964–66; Visiting Lectr. in Business Adm., Univ. of W. Ont., 1967; mem., Assn. Prof. Engrs. Prov. Ont.; Candn. Cable TV Assn. (Dir. 1968–73; Chairman 1970–72); Dir., Ont. Development Corp. 1972–80; Dir., Ont. Energy Corp., 1980–86, Chrmn. 1982–86; Dir., Suncor Inc. 1982–86; Dir., American Cablesystems Corp. 1981–88; Dir., Ont. Assn. Medical Laboratories 1986–88, Pres. 1987–88; Clubs: Toronto; University (N.Y.); Royal Canadian Yacht; Craigleith Ski; recreations: skiing, sailing; Address: 56 Castle Frank Rd., Toronto, Ont. M4W 2Z8.

**JARRELL, Richard Adrian,** A.B., M.A., Ph.D.; university professor; b. Connersville, Indiana 29 Aug. 1946; s. Maurice Adrian and Eileen (Atterbury) J.; e. Indiana Univ., A.B. 1967; Univ. of Toronto, M.A. 1969, Ph.D. 1972; ; m. Martha d. Delmont and Mildred Mafit 7 Sept. 1968; children: D'Arcy R.G., Courtney M.G.; PROF., ATKINSON COLL., YORK UNIV. 1970– ; Vis. Lectr., Univ. of Toronto 1976–78; Mem., Grad. Hist. prog., present univ. 1984– ; Co-founder, Candn. Sci. & Tech. Hist. Assn. 1980 (Sec. Treas. 1980–91); Founding Editor, 'Scientia Canadensis' 1976–88; organizer of 6 nat. 'Kingston Conferences' on hist. of Candn. sci., tech. & med. 1981–91; Dir., The Scientia Press Ltd.; Ed. Advr., 'Social Studies of Science'; Cons. to several acad. & scholarly orgns. & pubs.; Atkinson Coll. Rsch. Fellow 1984–85; Mem., History of Sci. Soc.; Candn. Hist. Assn.; Royal Astron. Soc. of Can.; Candn. Soc. for Hist. & Phil. of Sci. (Vice-Pres. 1979–84; author: 'Building Canadian Science' 1992; 'Science, Technology and Medicine in Canada's Past' 1991, 'The Cold Light of Dawn' 1988, 'Critical Issues in the History of Canadian Science, Technology & Medicine' 1983, 'Science, Technology and Canadian History, '1980, 'A Curious Fieldbook' 1974; recreations: hiking, cycling, cooking; Home: 29 Nicholson Way, Thornhill, Ont. L3T 5B4; Office: 4700 Keele St., North York, Ont. M3J 1P3.

**JARRETT, Peter Malcolm,** ndc, B.Sc., M.Sc., Ph.D., P.Eng.; university professor and engineer; b. Blackpool, England 10 Oct. 1941; s. Norman Randall and Alice (Croft) J.; e. Leamington College for Boys; Univ. of Nottingham B.Sc. 1963; Queen's Univ. M.Sc. 1965; Univ. of Glasgow Ph.D. 1971; Nat. Defence College ndc 1989; m. Lesley d. Wilfred and Muriel Burkitt 1 April 1961; one d.: Carol Lorraine; HEAD, DEPT. OF CIVIL ENGINEERING, ROYAL MILITARY COLLEGE OF CANADA 1984– ; Research Officer, National Research Council of Canada 1964–67; Lecturer, Univ. of Glasgow 1967–73; Prof., Royal Military College of Canada 1973– ; Pres., Bathurst Jarrett and Assoc.; Mem., Am. Soc. for Testing and Materials (Former Vice-Chair of Committee D18 on Soil and Rocks); Bd. of Gov., St. Lawrence Coll. St. Laurent 1986–88, 1990– (Chair 1992–93); Mem., College Standards and Accreditation Council Bd.; Salvation Army Adv. Bd. Kingston; Profl. Engrs. of Ont. (Mem., Academic Requirements Ctte. 1983– ; Chair 1992– ); editor: 'Testing of Peats and Organic Soils'; co-editor: 'The Application of Polymeric Reinforcement in Soil Retaining Structures'; recreations: squash, sailing, curling; clubs: RMCYC, Cataraqui

Golf & Country; Home: PH4, 50 Market St., Gananoque, Ont. K7G 2M3; Office: Kingston, Ont. K7K 5L0.

**JARRY, Gilles,** B.Comm.; banking executive; b. Montreal, Que. 14 Sept. 1941; s. Aphtère and Irene J. (Maynard) J.; e. Grand Falls N.B. H.S.; Waterloo Que. H.S. 1958; McGill Univ., B.Comm. 1969 (Bank of Montreal scholarship); m. Helen d. Thomas and Julienne Johnson 27 Jan. 1962; children: Pierre (Peter), Michel, Brigitte; SR. VICE-PRES., QUEBEC DIVISION, BANK OF MONTREAL 1990– ; joined Bank of Montreal 1958; various managerial positions, 1965–75; Mgr. for Computer Oper. for E. Canada 1975–77; Vice-Pres., Que. Div. 1977–83; Vice-Pres. & District Extve., Montreal Dist., E. Region, Domestic Banking 1983–86; Sr. Vice-Pres., E. Region, Personal Banking 1986–90; Pres., Fond. Hosp. Maisonneuve Rosemont; Dir., Extve. Ctte., Univ. of Quebec in Montreal Foundation; Bd. Mem., Les Jeunes Entreprises du Québec Inc.; Montreal Symphonic Orch.; I Musici of Montreal Chamber Orchestra; CIREM; Mem., Bd. of Trade; Chambre de Commerce de Montréal; Chambre de Commerce Française; recreations: reading, fishing, skiing, golf; Clubs: Saint Denis; Laval sur le Lac Golf; Home: 7300 Milan boul., Brossard, Que. J4Y 1S7; Office: 105 St. Jacques, Montreal, Que. H2Y 3S8.

**JARVIE, Ian Charles,** B.Sc., Ph.D., F.R.S.C.; university professor; b. South Shields, England 8 July 1937; s. Charles Purves and Eleanor Marshall (Carver) J.; e. Dover Co. Grammar Sch. 1955; London Sch. of Econ., B.Sc.Econ. 1958, Ph.D. 1961; m. May d. David and Hélène Friedman 1962; divorced 1984; children: Suzanne Karen, Alexander Max; DISTINGUISHED RSCH. PROF. OF PHILOSOPHY, YORK UNIV. 1993– ; Lectr. in Phil., Univ. of Hong Kong 1962–66; Assoc. Prof., present univ. 1967–69, Prof. 1969–93; FRSC 1988; author: 'The Revolution in Anthropology' 1964, 'Concepts and Society' 1972, 'Rationality and Relativism' 1984, 'Thinking about Society: Theory and Practice' 1985, 'Philosophy of Film' 1987, 'Hollywood's Overseas Campaign' 1992 and many others; Home: 924 Manning Ave., Toronto, Ont. M6G 2X4; Office: 4700 Keele St., North York, Ont. M3J 1P3.

**JARVIS, Daniel Owen,** B.A., M.B.A.; resort executive; b. Toronto, Ont. 26 Apr. 1950; s. Thomas and Mary-Louise J.; e. Queen's Univ. B.A. (Hons.) 1972; Harvard Univ. M.B.A. 1975; m. Wendy Harris 25 Aug. 1979; children: Ian, Cameron, Bronwyn, Colin, Elizabeth; EXECUTIVE VICE PRESIDENT AND CHIEF FINANCIAL OFFICER, INTRAWEST CORP. 1989– ; Dir. Intrawest Corp.; Asst. Vice-Pres. Wood Gundy Ltd. 1976–79; Dir. Fin. Analysis Bell Canada 1980–81, Asst. Vice-Pres. 1981–83; Vice-Pres. & Treas., BCE Inc. 1983–86; Extve. Vice Pres., Finance & C.F.O., BCE Development Corp. 1986–89; recreation: skiing, tennis; Clubs: Vancouver Club; Vancouver Lawn Tennis; University (Montreal); Home: 6090 Blenheim St., Vancouver, B.C.; Office: Intrawest Corp., 8th Flr., 200 Burrard St., Vancouver, B.C. V6C 3L6.

**JARVIS, Kenneth Phillips,** Q.C., RCA; sculptor; lawyer; b. Toronto, Ont. 25 Dec. 1926; s. Guy Meredith and Dorothy Aunger (Phillips) J.; e. University Coll. Univ. of Toronto B.A. 1952; Osgoode Hall Law Sch. 1956; cr. Q.C. 1967; art education: Univ. of Toronto, Central Tech. Sch., private studies with Elizabeth Wynn Wood and Emanuel Hahn; m. Ellen Marie d. Richard Lankaster and Estrid Lea (Holme) Hearn 24 Sept. 1956; one s. Brian Hearn; served in World War II with R.C.N.V.R.; practised law with Wright & McTaggart 1956–58; Lectr. and Head of Sect., Bar Admission Course, Osgoode Hall; Depy. Secy., Law Society of Upper Can. 1958–66, Secy. 1966–87, Under Treasurer 1987–88, Hon. Bencher; mem. Advy. Review Bd. and Central Review Bd., Mental Hospitals Act 1971–78 (Chrmn. Central Review Bd. 1978); Rep. Fedn. of Law Societies of Can. 1966–80; Hon. Counsel; Chrmn., Jt. Ctte. on Accreditation; (Pres. Interprofessional Liaison Ctte. 1973–74, 1981–82); mem. Counc., Candn. Bar Assn. 1984–86; Secy., Law Found. of Ont. 1974–81; Trustee, Law Soc. Found.; Dir., Osgoode Soc.; Mem., Candn. Inst. for Advanced Legal Studies; 1st prize for sculpture, Hart House, Univ. of Toronto 1948; exhbd. with Ont. Soc. of Artists, Art Gall. of Ont. 1950; el. to RCA 1984; Council, Royal Candn. Acad. of Arts 1987–91 (Pres. 1991); Fund Raising Ctte., St. John Ambulance 1991– ; portraits in bronze of many prominent Canadians; works displayed in Parliament Bldgs., Supreme Court of Canada Bldg. (Ottawa); Ont. Legislative Bldg., Osgoode Hall, Univ. of Toronto, York Univ., Ont. Medical Assn. Bldg., Guild Inn, Ont. Coll. of Art, Campbell House (Toronto); Royal Mil. Coll. (Kingston); Windsor Art Gall.; Roy Thomson Hall; du Maurier Theatre (Toronto); Royal Acad. of Music (England); The Univ. of Sask.; Univ. of Alta.; and in private collections in Canada and abroad; sculptures include portraits, bas reliefs, medals, equestrian statue; recreations: trap and skeetshooting, fishing; Clubs: Arts and Letters (Pres. 1984–86); Caledon Mountain Trout (Dir. 1984–87); Albany Club; Home: 94 Alexandra Blvd., Toronto, Ont. M4R 1L9; Studios: Toronto and New York.

**JARVIS, Richard Colborne,** P.Eng.; consultant; b. Nelson, B.C. 17 July 1937; s. Reginald Colborne Botsford and Madeline Anne (MacDonald) J.; e. Gonzaga Univ., B.S.E.E. 1961; m. Dolores d. Edward and Elizabeth Hamilton 10 Feb. 1961; children: Kevin C., John H., Marcia Ann; OFFR. & DIR., JARVIS ENGINEERING LIMITED 1967– ; Project Engr., Joseph M. Doyle & Assoc. 1961–63; Skidmore Owings & Merrill 1963–67; Pres./Dir., Jarvis Consultants Ltd.; Dir., Rotary Club of Edmonton 1985–87; Alberta Art Found. 1982–85 (Chairman 1985–91); Chrmn., Alberta Foundation for the Arts 1991– ; Mem., Assoc. of Profl. Engrs., Geologists & Geophysicists of Alta.; Mem., Pres. Counc., Univ. of Alta.; Illuminating Engr. Soc.; P.C. Assn. of Edmonton Glenor (Dir. 1978–82; Pres. 1982–84); recreation: golf; Clubs: Centre, Faculty, Edmonton Country, Tucson Nat. Golf; Home: 14116 – 95 Ave., Edmonton, Alta. T5N 0A2; Office: 17406 – 106A Ave., Edmonton, Alta. T5S 1E6.

**JARVIS, Robert E.,** Q.C., B.A., LL.B.; lawyer; b. Ottawa, Ont. 15 Nov. 1935; s. Earl Roland and Marjorie Marie (Goodhouse) J.; e. Univ. of Alta. B.A. 1960, LL.B. 1963; Osgoode Hall Law Sch. LL.B. 1964; m. Joan E. d. John and Kay Bales 15 Dec. 1956; three s. R. David, Donald B., Douglas E.; SR. PARTNER, GOODMAN AND CARR 1983– ; SR. PARTNER, GOODMAN LAPOINTE FERGUSON 1988; Chrmn., Skylight Theatre Inc. 1988– ; Dir., Dora Mavor Moor Awards 1992– ; served with RCAF 1956–62, Pilot; called to Bar of Ont. 1966; law practice Thomson Rogers, Toronto 1966–73, Partner 1970–73; estbd. own firm Jarvis Blott Fejer Pepino, Toronto 1973–82; Past Chrmn., Canada Mortgage & Housing Corp. 1985–90; el. to H. of C. for Willowdale 1979–80; Parliamentary Sec. Energy Mines & Resources; Office: Suite 2300, 200 King St. W., Toronto, Ont. M5H 3W5.

**JARVIS, William Esmond,** M.Sc.A.; agrologist; b. Gladstone, Man. 10 Dec. 1931; s. Frederick Roberts and Dorothy Welles (Tuckwell) J.; e. Univ. of Man. B.Sc.A. 1955; Mich. State Univ. M.Sc.A. 1960; m. Leona; children: Cheryl, Darrell, Dennis, Morgan; CANDN. HIGH COMMR. 1990– ; joined Dept. Agric. Man. 1955, Depy. Min. of Agric. 1962–67; Asst. Depy. Min. of Agric. Can. and Assoc. Depy. Min. 1967–77; Chief Commissioner, Candn. Wheat Board 1977–90; rec'd Nuffield Foundation Travelling Research Fellowship, Univ. of Man. Alumni Assn. Jubilee Award 1981; mem. Agric. Inst. Can.; Man. Inst. Agrols.; United Church; recreations: sporting and outdoor activities; Club: Gyro; Home: 11 Dillon St., Lowry Bay, Eastbourne, N.Z.; Office: Canadian High Commission, P.O. Box 12–049, Thorndon, Wellington, New Zealand.

**JARVIS, Hon. William Herbert,** P.C., Q.C. (1979) B.A., LL.B.; lawyer; b. Hamilton, Ont. 15 Aug. 1930; s. Garfield and Nina (McBean) J.; e. Univ. of W. Ont. B.A. 1953, LL.B. 1962; children: Elizabeth, Richard; Assoc. with McCarthy Tétrault, Barristers and Solicitors (formerly Clarkson Tétrault); el. to H. of C. g.e. 1972, re-el. 1974, 1979, 1980; Min. of State for Fed.-Prov. Relations 1979; el. Pres., Progressive Conservative Party of Canada 1986; Office: 1000 - 275 Sparks St., Ottawa, Ont. K1R 7X9.

**JARVLEPP, Jan Eric,** B.Mus., M.Mus., Ph.D.; musician; b. Ottawa, Ont. 3 Jan. 1953; s. Eric and Leena (Hirvonen) J.; e. Univ. of Ottawa B.Mus. 1976; McGill Univ. M.Mus. 1978; Univ. of Calif., San Diego Ph.D. 1981; a catalogue of over 25 original compositions most of which have been performed & broadcast in var. countries; several comns. from Canada Council & Ont. Arts Council; recordings: 'Soundtracks of the Imagination' 1989, 'Chronogrammes' 1986 (available from Candn. Music Ctr.); Cellist, Ottawa Symphony Orch. & var. chamber ensembles since 1981; Part-time Instr., Ottawa Bd. of Education & Ottawa Univ.; part-time location recording business; produces computerized music notation, digital recordings & electronic music in home MIDI studio; composes in postmodern style; frequent guest artist with Open Score ensemble; participant on CBC chamber music broadcasts; lecturer; Artistic Dir., Espace Musique Concert Soc. 1993– ; Adjudicator of original compositions for Kiwanis Music Festival; Winner, Nat. PRO Canada Composers Competitions 1980, '81, '82; Julius Schloss Award, McGill Univ. 1978; Mem., SOCAN; Candn. League of Composers; Candn. Electroacoustic Community; Candn. Music Ctr.; Am. Fed. of Musicians; author of 3 journal articles; recreations: wine, women and song; Home: 2 – 424 Lisgar St., Ottawa, Ont. K1R 5H1; Office: Jarvlepp Productions, Box 2684, Station D, Ottawa, Ont. K1P 5W7.

**JASMIN, Gaëtan,** B.A., M.D., Ph.D. F.R.C.P.(C); educator; b. Montreal, Que. 24 Nov. 1924; s. Horace and Antoinette (Piquette) J.; e. Coll. St-Laurent B.A. 1945; Univ. de Montréal M.D. 1951, Ph.D. 1956; C.S.P.Q. 1968; F.R.C.P.(C), 1978; m. Suzanne Dupont 18 Oct. 1952; children: Eve, Luc, Pierre; PROF. OF PATHOLOGY, UNIV. DE MONTREAL; affiliated Hôpital Ste-Justine; Ed. 'Mechanism of Inflammation' 1953; 'Endocrine Aspects of Disease Processes' 1968; 'Methods and Achievements in Experimental Pathology' Vols. 1–13, 1966–86; author numerous publs.; mem. Assn. Pathols. Qué.; Fed. Médecins Spécialistes Qué.; Internat. Acad. Pathol.; Soc. Exper. Biol. & Med.; Fed. Am. Biol. Socs.; Candn. Fed. Biol. Socs.; Histochem. Soc.; Soc. Française de Microscopie électronique; The Joseph F. Morgan Rsch. Found.; Goups for Research in pathology Educ.; Assn. Can. française pour l'avancement des sciences; Soc. de physiologie de Montreal; N.Y. Academy of Sc.; Internat. Soc. for Heart Research; Am. Physiolog. Soc.; Cercle Français Pathologie ultrastructurale; Can. Soc. for Clinical Investigation; Muscular Dystrophy Assn. of Can.; Soc. Can. de physiologie; Am. Assn. for Advancement of Sc.; R. Catholic; Home: 6150 du Boisé, Montreal, Qué. H3S 2V2.

**JASMIN, The Hon. Pierre,** B.A., LL.B.; judge; b. Montreal, Que. 5 May 1946; s. Yvon and Claire (Trudeau) J.; e. College André Grasset B.A. 1965; Univ. of Montreal LL.B. 1968; McGill Inst. of Air and Space Law diploma 1975; divorced; children: Olivier, Maude; JUDGE, SUPERIOR COURT OF QUEBEC 1991– ; practising lawyer 1969–91 specializing in insurance law and arbitration in labour field; Chair, Montreal Young Bar Assn. 1975–76; Home: 44 Robert St., Outremont, Que. H3S 2P2; Office: 1 est Notre Dame, Montreal, Que. H2Y 1B6.

**JASMIN, Yves,** O.C., A.P.R.; public relations consultant; b. Lachine, Que. 27 Feb. 1922; s. Aquila and Rachel (Valois) J.; e. Cath. High Sch.; Univ. de Montréal; m. Micheline d. Jean and Marguerite Vermet 19 July 1973; children: Claude-Guy, Pierre, Elisabeth; Reporter 'Le Canada' Montreal 1945–52; Pub. Relations Air Canada 1952–56, 1970–73; Molson Brewery 1956–60; Ford of Canada 1961–64; Expo '67 1964–68; Asst. Sec. Gen., Nat. Museums Can. 1975–77; self-employed Public Relations firms 1968–70, 1973–75, 1977– ; accredited mem., Candn. Pub. Relations Soc. (APR), (Nat. Pres. 1962–63; Attainment Award 1967); Pub. Relations Soc. America (Golden Anvil 1967); Officer, Order of Canada 1967; recreations: golf, sailing; Club: Royal St. Lawrence Yacht; Home: 519 Querbes Ave., Outremont, Que. H2V 3W4.

**JASPER, Herbert H.,** O.C. (1972); M.D., Ph.D., D. ès.Sc., F.R.S.C.; neurophysiologist; b. La Grande, Oregon, 27 July 1906; s. Franklin M. and Lina (Dupertuis) J.; e. Reed College, Portland (Oregon) B.A. 1927; University of Oregon (Eugene), M.A. 1929; University of Iowa, Ph.D. 1931; Laureat of Acad. Sciences, Paris, 1933; University of Paris, D.ès.Sc. 1935; McGill University, M.D.C.M. 1943; Doctorat, honoris causa, Univ. de Bordeaux 1949; Univ. d'Aix Marseille 1960; McGill Univ. 1971; Univ. of W. Ont. 1977; Queen's Univ. 1979; Memorial Univ. of Nfld. 1983; m. Margaret E. d. Hon. Lincoln Goldie Aug. 1940 (died 26 Dec. 1982); children: Stephen, Joan; m. 2ndly Mary Louisa McDougall 28 Dec. 1983; PROF. EMERITUS, Centre de Recherche en Sciences Neurologiques, DEPT. DE PHYSIOL., UNIV. DE MONTREAL since 1976; Prof. Neurophysiology, 1965–76; Acting Dir., Dept. of Physiol., 1971–72; Nat. Research Council Fellow, Paris, 1931–33; Asst. Prof., Brown Univ., 1933–38; joined McGill Univ. as Asst. Prof. in 1938; Prof. Exper. Neurol., 1946–64; Dir., Labs of Neurophysiology and Electroencephalography of the Montreal Neurol. Inst.; 1st Extve. Secy., Internat. Brain Research Organization (IBRO); author, 'Epilepsy and the Functional Anatomy of the Human Brain,' with Dr. W. Penfield; 'Nobel Laureates in Neuroscience,' with T. Sourkes; published numerous papers in scient. and med. journs.; rec'd Karl Lashley prize of Am. Philosphical Soc. 1982; Ralph Gerard Prize of the Soc. for Neuroscience; William Lennox Prize for research in epilepsy; The McLaughlin Medal and Prize, Royal Soc. of Can.; Fanny Embden Prize, French Acad. of Sci., Paris; Prix de l'Association des Medecins de Langue Française; Officer of the Order of Canada 1972; Distinguished Scholar Award, Med. Coll. of Virginia, Virginia Commonwealth Univ. (Outstanding Contrib. in Electrophysiology and Neuroscience)

1990; Besta Medal and Award for outstanding rsch. in epilepsy, Milano; Am. Epilepsy Soc. & Milken Family Medical Found. Senior Prize for rsch. in epilepsy 1993; Hon. Fellow, Am. Assn. for the Advancement of Science; Hon. Mem.: Am. Neurol. Assn.; Polish Soc. for EEG and Clin. Neurophysio.; Belgian Academy of Medicine; Royal Soc. Medicine (London); Italian Academy of Science; Mem.: Am. Med. Assn.; Am. Physiol. Soc.; Candn. Neurol. Soc.; Hon. mem. & First Pres., Am EEG Soc.; First Pres., Internat. Fed. of Soc. for EEG & Clin. Neurophysiol.; founding ed., EEG Journal; served in 2nd World War with R.C.A.M.C. 1943–45; Liberal; Presbyterian Church; recreations: skiing, sailing; Home: 4501 Sherbrooke St. West, Apt. 1F, Westmount, Que. H3Z 1E7.

**JAVED, Naseem,** B.A.; marketing executive; b. Delhi, India 17 May 1944; s. Mohamed and Amtul (Haseen) Omar; e. Marie Colaco & St. Patrick H.S.; Univ. of Karachi B.A. 1964; m. Lucie E. d. Anna and Peter Pomarico 6 Nov. 1980; one s.: Tashi; PRES. & DIR., ABC NAMEBANK INT'L. INC. 1979– ; Corporate and Product Name Consultant to IBM, BellSouth, Peat Marwick, General Motors, Johnson & Johnson, Ford, Honeywell, Radio Shack, Petro-Canada, Bell Canada, Sasktel, Telus, Molson, BBDO Worlwide; Minnova, Genexxa, Cara; Consultant Mktg. & Promotions 1976 Montreal Summer Olympic Games 1970–76; Dir. & Mngt. Cons. Candn. Direct Mktg. Cons. Group Ltd. 1976–79; Mng. Dir. Inst. of Electro Ergonomics; Dir. Tradewriters Ltd. 1984– ; CDMMA Award, Best in Category for Graphics, Design and Marketing in Canada 1976; author 'How to Name a Business or New Product' 1985; 'Brand Name Considerations' 1986; 'Corporate and Business Name Trends' 1987; 'Dangers of Elementary Naming' 1991; recreations: squash, painting, chess; Club: Rotary; Home: One St. John's Rd., Brampton, Ont.; Offices: (U.S.) 90 Park Ave., Suite 1600, New York, N.Y. 10016; (Canada) P.O. Box 2360, Brampton, Ont. L6T 3Y9.

**JAWORSKA, Tamara,** M.F.A., R.C.A.; painter; tapestry maker; b. Archangielsk, Russia; d. Antoni Jankowski; came to Can. 1969; e. State Acad. Fine Arts, Lodz, B.F.A. (Hons.) 1950, M.F.A. (art weaving) 1952; m. Tadeusz, s. Zygmunt J. 1957; children: Eva, Pyotr; Asst. Prof., Sr. Asst. Prof. and Lect., State Acad. Fine Arts, Poland 1952–58; exhns. incl. Warsaw and Lodz Art Galleries 1965; Pushkin Museum, European Art Gallery, Moscow 1966; Richard Demarco Gallery, Edinburgh and Scot. Woolen Art Gallery, Galashields, Scot. 1968; Fine Art Museum, Plymouth, Eng. 1968; Merton Gallery, Toronto 1970; Hermitage Leningrad, USSR 1968; Nat. Art Gallery, Teheran, Iran 1968; Museum Modern Art, Mexico City 1969; Art Gallery of Ont. 1971 and 73; major commercial solo exhbn., Leo Kamen Gallery, Toronto 1987; one-woman exhns. in Art Galleries of London & Windsor Ont. 1971; Glendon Art Gall., Toronto 1972; major solo exh. Art Gall. of Hamilton 1980; Academician, Academia Italia delle Arti e del Lavoro 1980; solo exhib. France, West Germany, Belgium, Switzerland, Luxemburg 1982; major exhib. of tapestries, new coll., Galerie Inard, Centre National de la Tapisserie D'Abusson, Paris 1984; exh. later travelled to major Museums & Galleries in Madrid, Barcelona, Valencia, San Sebastian, Tarragona, Malaga 1980–81 & Paris 1981; Munchen, West Germany, Paris, Grand Palaise, 1981–82; West Berlin, Zurich, Suisse, Paris & Toulousse, France, 1983; Centre National De la Tapisserie D'Abusson, Paris, France (major exhib.-retros. 'Tapestries for Corporate and Private Collectors' 1991; Royal Acad. of Arts, John B. Aird Gallery, Toronto 1992; rep. by Centre National de la Tapisserie D'Abusson Galerie Inard, Paris, Boulevard St. Germain, France; tapestries owned by museums, galleries, public and private collectors in U.S., USSR, Poland, U.K., Switzerland, Sweden, France and Can.; Won Competition for tapestry, Hart House Great Hall, U of T, Toronto; Bank of Montreal, Calgary, Alberta; comns. incl. 'Unity' (32x22 ft.), Place Bell Canada, Ottawa 1972; IDS-Finch-1000, Metropolitan Life H.O., tapestry (18x9 ft.) 1974–75; 'Quartet Modern' (4 tapestries, ea. 15x9 ft.), Bank of Montreal, First Canadian Place, Toronto; Govt. of Canada, Ext. Affairs Dept., Candn. Embassy in Riyad, Saudi Arabia (main lobby, 10x17 ft.); Gold Medallist, Internat. Exhn. Interior Design and Arch., Triennale de Milano 1957; Award for Excellence 'Wool Gathering 73' Montreal 1973; Master of Painting Honoris Causa by the Accademia Italia, Italy, 1982; Golden Centaur, for the achievements in the international art field by Academia Italia, Italy, 1982; Gold Medal and First Prize, Internat. Juried Art Competition, N.Y.C., U.S.A. 1985; awarded Commemorative Medal for 125th Anniversary of Candn. Confederation 1993; Num. articles in mag. and art books in N. America and Europe; Num. films, radio and TV programmes and interviews about artist and her work; Fellow, R.C.A.; mem., Royal Acad. of Arts; Home: 49 Don River Blvd., Willowdale, Ont. M2N 2M8.

**JAWORSKI, Tad,** M.F.A., R.C.A. film and TV producer-director; b. Poland 20 Feb. 1926; s. Zygmunt and Teofila (Wroblewska) J.; came to Canada 1969; e. Gymnasium and Lyceum, Lodz, Poland 1945; Univ. of Lodz 1947; Leon Schiller Acad. of Film & Theatre, Lodz, B.F.A. 1950, M.F.A. and Film Producer-Director Diploma 1952; m. Tamara, d. Antoni Jankowski, Warsaw, Poland 1957; children: Eva, Pyotr; Film Prod., Dir., Scriptwriter, Polish National Film Board 1952–68; TV Drama Producer, Polish National TV 1967–68; Documentary Film Producer and Dir., U.N., WHO Geneva, Switzerland 1964–68; Feature Film Producer-Director 'Kamera' Group, Polish National Film Board 1967–68; writer, producer and dir. of numerous documentaries, features films, radio and TV dramas incl. 'Africa '60' (best radio documentary award, ZAIKS) 1960; 'The Source 1962 (Warsaw Mermaid Critics Prize; Min. Culture & Art Great Prize; Bronze Dove, Leipzig Film Festival; Grand Prix & Golden Dragon Prize, Cracow Film Festival); 'The Secretary' 1966 (Silver Laikon Award, Cracow Film Festival); 'I was Capo' (Special Prize, Oberhausen Internat. Film Festival) 1963; 'The Boys' 1966 (numerous awards incl. Golden Screen Independent Prize); 'A Cry in the Emptiness of the World' 1967 (Best Stage Production and Most Outstanding TV Drama Award, Polish Min. Broadcasting & TV); recent Candn. works incl. 'Miniatures' CBC 1970; 'Selling Out' (feature documentary, Golden Etrog. Best Candn. Film 1972 & Academy Award 'Oscar' Nomination 1973) 1972; 'Canadian Artists' CBC 1972; also several documentary feature films in assoc. with CBC and private Candn. film cos.; Prod., dir. and co-author of 6 hour documentary drama series, 'The Jesus Trial' 1977–78; Writer, Prod. & Dir., 6 half-hour mini series: 'The Challenge of Karl Marx' (with Host Irving Layton); 'A Modern Country' a mini series (with Host Leon Whiteson); Writer, Prod. Dir., Docu-drama 'The Island'; Pres. & C.E.O., Co-Producers Fund of Canada Ltd. (Film/TV Productions), Toronto; Councillor, Royal Candn. Acad. of Arts 1992– ; Tutorial Film Leader, Stong Coll. York Univ.; Master of Cinematog. and Resident Film Producer, Humber Coll.; Elected Mem., Royal Canadian Academy of Arts, 1978; Curator & Dir., RCA Examination '92, Toronto; RCA Examination '93, Toronto; awards incl. Laureate of State Prize, Min. Culture and Art, Poland 1967; Cavalier Order Cross 'Polonia Restituta' 1967; awarded Commemorative Medal for 125th Anniversary of Candn. Confederation 1993; mem. Internat. Film Makers Assn.; Internat. Authors Assn.; author of numerous articles on aesthetic problems in film and TV; Lecturer in film and TV subjects at Canadian univs. and colls. since 1970; Home: 49 Don River Blvd., Willowdale, Ont. M2N 2M8.

**JAY, Charles Douglas,** C.M., M.Div., M.A., Ph.D., D.D. (United Church); educator; b. Monticello, Ont. 10 Oct. 1925; s. Rev. Charles Arthur and Luella Gertrude (McPherson) J.; e. Humberside Coll. Inst., Toronto, 1942; Univ. of Toronto, B.A. (Victoria Coll.) 1946, M.A. 1948, B.D. (Emmanuel Coll.) 1950; Univ. of Edinburgh, Ph.D. 1952; Queen's Univ., D.D. 1971; Wycliffe Coll., D.D. 1976; Regis Coll. D.D. 1980; Univ. of St. Michael's Coll., D.D. 1983; Member, Order of Canada 1988; m. Ruth Helen, d. late Mervyn Arthur Crooker, 30 Jan. 1948; three s. David, Ian, Garth; Principal, Emmanuel Coll., Univ. of Toronto (1981–90); PROF., PHILOS. OF RELIGION & ETHICS, EMMANUEL COLL., UNIV. OF TORONTO 1963–91; Dept. of Philos., Queens Univ. 1946–47; o. 1950; Min., Elk Lake-Matachewan, 1952–54 and Trafalgar-Sheridan, 1954–55; joined Emmanuel Coll. as Asst. Prof., Philos. of Religion & Christian Ethics, 1955; Registrar 1958–64; AATS Fellow 1963; founding Dir., Toronto School of Theology, 1969–80; served on Comn. on Accreditation, Am. Assn. Theol. Schs., 1962–68; Vice-Pres., Assoc. of Theol. Schs. in U.S. and Can., 1976–78, Pres., 1984–86; R. P. McKay Mem. Lectr. various univs. and colls. across Can., 1966–67; Special Lectr. at Hankuk Theological Seminary, Seoul, Korea, 1978; Federal Theological Seminary, Pietermaritzburg, South Africa 1981; Union Theological Seminary, Manila, The Philippines; Nanjing Theological Seminary, Nanjing, P.R.C. 1991; mem. Working Group, Dialogue with People of Living Faiths and Ideologies, World Council of Churches 1970–83; Chrm., Division of World Outreach, United Church of Canada, 1975–82; writings incl. various book chapters; served with COTC 1943–45; Chaplain, RCN (R), 1956–59; mem., Am. Soc. Christian Ethics; Candn. Theol. Soc.; recreations: skiing, gardening; Home: 1606 Watersedge Rd., Mississauga, Ont. L5J 1A4; Office: Emmanuel Coll., 75 Queen's Park Cres., Toronto, Ont. M5S 1K7.

**JAY, R(aymond) Harry,** B.A., B.C.L.; diplomat; b. Lachine, Que. 13 Aug. 1919; s. Lincoln P. and Mary Higginson (Dilworth) J.; e. St. Albans Sch., Brockville, Ont.; Northwestern High Sch., Detroit, Mich.; Wayne Univ.; McGill Univ., B.A. 1941, B.C.L. 1948; m. Dorothy V., d. Rev. (Maj.) Harry Andrews, M.B.E., E.D., 7 Sept. 1945; three s: Lincoln A., Michael H., Stephen D.; joined Dept. of External Affairs 1948; served in Ottawa, India (1950–53), Indochina (1955), Geneva (1956–59); Depy. Perm. Rep., Candn. Del. to NATO, Paris, 1963–65; High Commr. in Jamaica, 1965–68; External Affairs Rep., Candn. Nat. Defence Coll., 1968–70; Dir. Gen., Bureau of U.N. Affairs 1970–73; Ambas. to Sweden 1973–76; Ambas. & Permanent Rep. to U.N., Disarmament & GATT in Geneva 1976–79; Chief Air Negotiator, 1979–81; has attended numerous internat. confs.; negotiated and signed for Can. U.N. Anti-Slavery Convention; Chrmn. Exec. Cmte., U.N. Comm. for Refugees 1978–79; ret. from Dept. External Affairs, 1981; Exec. Sec., Xth World Congress on Prevention of Occupational Accidents and Diseases, 1981–83; Head of Delegation, CSCE Human Rights Experts Meeting 1984–85; served with RCAF 1941–45; P.O.W. Germany 1943–45; Sigma Chi; Anglican; recreations: golf, swimming, tennis, boating, flying, travel, music, theatre; Clubs: Royal Ottawa Golf; Address: Home: 806 - 20 Driveway, Ottawa, Ont. K2P 1C8.

**JAYE, Elisabeth Anne;** market research executive; b. London, England 3 Nov. 1945; d. Harry Joseph and Rene Vivienne (Hill) Mornington (both dec.); e. Burlington Grammar Sch. (U.K.); Univ. of Toronto; m. Ivan s. Leah and Louis (dec.) Jaye 29 Dec. 1968; children: Paul Daniel, Naomi Ruth; VICE-PRESIDENT & DIRECTOR OF SPECIAL SERVICES, CREATIVE RESEARCH INTERNATIONAL INC. 1985– ; Acct. Executive in an advtg. agency (U.K.); Advtg. Mgr., Canadian Opera Co. 2 years; Sales & Sales Management, Xerox Canada 1980–85; Past Pres. (Toronto Chapter) & Mem., Professional Market Research Soc.; Chair, AIDS Ctte., Holy Blossom Temple 1988–90; Bd. Mem. & Chair, Dept. of Jewish Living, Social & Outreach Prog., Holy Blossom Temple 1990–92; recreations: aspring cyclist, movie buff, concert goer and avid reader; Home: Toronto, Ont.; Office: 100 Sheppard Ave. E., Suite 700, North York, Ont. M2N 6N5.

**JEAN, Hon. Bernard A.,** M.A.; judge; b. Lameque, N.B. 2 March 1925; s. Azade and Esther (Duguay) J.; e. Couvent Jesus Marie, Lameque, N.B.; Univ. St. Joseph B.A. 1946; Laval Univ. M.A. 1949; m. Corinne d. late Majorique Lanteigne, Caraquet, N.B. 3 Sept. 1955; children: Suzanne, Rodrigue, Maurice, Monique, Françoise, Isabelle; JUDGE, COURT OF QUEEN'S BENCH N.B.; el. M.L.A. N.B. 1960–72, Speaker of Legislature 1963–66, Min. of Justice 1966–70; mem. Candn. Centennial Comn. 1963–67; Bd. Govs. Univ. of N.B. 1965–71; called to Bar of N.B. 1951; cr. Q.C. 1966; R. Catholic; Home: (P.O. Box 267) Caraquet, N.B. E0B 1K0; Office: Queen's Bench Chambers, P.O. Box 5001, Court House, Bathurst, N.B. E2A 3Z9.

**JEAN, Michèle S.,** B.A., M.Ed., M.A.; public servant; b. Quebec, Que. 24 Jan. 1937; d. Roger Henry and Françoise (Gamache) Stanton; e. Laval Univ. B.A. 1957; Univ. of Montreal M.Ed. 1974, M.A. 1975; m. Pierre s. Hélène and Phidelem J. 27 June 1959; now separated; children: Dominique, Nathalie, Madeleine, Philippe; DEPUTY MINISTER, HEALTH CANADA 1993– ; Journalist, 'Le Soleil' 1957–59; Adult Edn. Counsellor, Coll. Bois-de-Boulogne 1975–84; Chair, Comn. of Inquiry on Vocation & Socio-Cult. Training for Adults in Que. 1980–82; Consultant, Internat. Inst. for Edn. Planning (IIEP) (Paris) 1982; Asst. Dep. Min. & Dir. Gen., Profl. Training Div., Que. Dept. of Manpower & Income Security 1984–88; Extve. Dir., Employment, Employment and Immigration Canada 1988–91; Assoc. Deputy Min., Employment & Immigration 1991–92; Under-Secy. of State, Sec. of State Dept. 1992–93; Past Dir., Univ. of Montreal; Conseil québécois de statut de la femme; Comité nat. sur les innovations; Comn. de la construction du Qué.; currently Cons., IIEP; Bd. Mem., Elder Hostel Canada; National Film Bd. Canada; participant in several internat. meetings; One of 10 women of the year at 'Salon de la Femme' (Montreal 1979; 'Career Woman of the Year,' Coll. O'Sullivan (Montreal) 1981; 'Special Recognition Award,' Candn. Assn. for Univ. Cont. Edn. 1991; author of several books & pubns. incl. 'Québécoises du XX ème siècle' 1974, 'L'Histoire des femmes au Québec de la Nouvelle-France à nos jours' 1982 (2nd ed. 1992), 'Learning, a voluntary and responsible action' 1982; recreations: skiing, tennis, swimming; Home: 460 Champagneur, Outremont, Que. H2V 3P5; Office: Jeanne Mance Bldg., Tunney's Pasture, Ottawa, Ont. K1A 0K9.

**JEAN, Paul E.;** communications executive; b. Quebec City 27 May 1937; s. Emile and Noella (Villeneuve) J.; children: Claude, Helene; PRES., CANTEL QUEBEC, ROGERS CANTEL MOBILE INC., 1990– ; var. positions incl., Sales Rep., Sales Mgr., Product Mgr., Nat. Acct. Extve., Xerox Canada Inc. 1966–80; Nat. Mktg. & Sales Mgr., All Steel Canada 1980–84; Reg. (East) Sales Mgr., present firm 1984–86; Vice Pres. Eastern Reg. 1986–90; Mem., Bd. of Dirs., D-Trois-Pierres; Mem., Prov. of Que. C. de C.; mem. National Assn. for Photographic Art; Former Président National of 'La Fédération des Jeunes Chambres de Commerce du Canada français' 1971–72; recreations: photography; club: Montreal Camera; Home: 23 Place Andelot, Lorraine, Que. J6Z 3N9; Office: 6315 Cote de Liesse, Ville St. Laurent, Que. H4T 1E5.

**JEANNIOT, Pierre Jean,** O.C.; transportation executive; b. Montpellier, France 9 Apr. 1933; s. Gaston and Renee (Rameau) J.; e. Sir George Williams Univ., Montreal B.Sc. (Science-Physics and Mathematics) 1957; McGill Univ. and Univ. de Montréal, Masters degree courses 1966–69; came to Canada 1947; m. Marcia David 28 Apr. 1979; children: Pierre Jean, Michel, Lynn; DIRECTOR GENERAL, INTERNATIONAL AIR TRANSPORT ASSN. (IATA) 1993– ; Dir., Bank of Nova Scotia; M3i; career: designer of aircraft and marine instrumentation, Sperry Gyroscope of Canada 1952–55; joined Air Canada and held various positions in rsch., development and management of technical operations, contributing to the development of the first comprehensive flight data recorder (or 'black box') 1955–68; Vice Pres. Computers & Communications, Univ. du Québec 1969; Vice Pres., Computer and Systems Services, Air Canada 1970–76; subsequently held senior extve. positions in the airline including sales, marketing and planning and subsidiary companies; Extve. Vice Pres. & C.O.O. 1983; Pres. and C.E.O. 1984–90; Pres. & C.E.O., JINMAG Inc. 1990–92; Pres., Candn. Operational Rsch. Soc. 1966; Chrmn., Air Transport Assn. of Canada 1984; Mem. Extve. Ctte., Chair Ctte. and Chrmn., Strategic Planning Sub-Ctte., IATA 1988–90; Chrmn. of Bd., Univ. du Qué. à Montreal 1972–78; Prés., Fondation Univ. du Québec à Montréal 1978–92; Chrmn. of Bd. & C.E.O., La Revue Commerce magazine 1977–82; Past Hon. Chrmn., fund raising campaign, Candn. Cancer Soc.; Jerry Lewis Telethon for Muscular Dystrophy; CBC Telethon for the Quebec Soc. for Disabled Children; President of fund raising campaign for Youth and Music Canada Foundation 1990; Participant and section leader in the various conferences on the Candn. Constitutional Renewal 1992; author of numerous technical papers, notably in the area of applied rsch.; Chrmn., The Council for Canadian Unity 1991–94; Honours: Honorary Doctorate, Univ. du Québec 1988; Mgmt. Achievement Award, McGill Univ. Faculty of Management; apptd., Officer of the Order of Canada 1989; Prix Roger Demers 1991; apptd., Chevalier dans l'Ordre de la Légion d'Honneur 1991; Transportation Man of the Year (Canada) 1992; Addresses: 2000 Peel St., Montreal, Que. H3A 2R4 and Route de l'Aéroport 33, P.O. Box 672, 1215 Geneva 15 - Airport, Switzerland.

**JEFFERIS, Jeffrey Douglas,** M.A., Ph.D., D.C.L.; emeritus professor; b. London, Eng. 10 Feb. 1906; s. Percy William and Lillian (Douglas) J.; e. Christ's Hosp., Horsham, Eng.; Bishop's Univ., B.A. 1927; McGill Univ., M.A. 1929; Univ. of Toronto, Ph.D. 1934; Bishop's Univ., D.C.L. 1968; Fellow, Candn. Coll. of Teachers; m. Elizabeth (d. 1974), d. Frank Spooner, Cobourg, Ont. 1936; Asst. Master, Mount Royal High Sch. 1927–30; Crescent Sch., Toronto 1930–31, 1936–38; Lectr. in Classics, Queen's Univ. 1932–33; Sr. Classical Master, Trinity Coll. Sch., Port Hope, Ont. 1934–36; Prof. of Classics, Waterloo Coll., Univ. of W. Ont. 1938–44; Prof. of Educ., Bishop's Univ. 1944–68; Reserve Army, 1940–45; with Univ. C.O.T.C.; author: 'An Introduction to Educational Psychology' 1958; Anglican; Address: Central Park Lodge, 33 Argyle Ave., St. Lambert, Que. J4P 3P5.

**JEFFERS, Stanley,** B.Sc., A.R.C.S., D.I.C., Ph.D.; university professor; b. Northern Ireland 1 Nov. 1941; s. Samuel and Charlotte (Crawford) J.; e. Imperial College, Univ. of London B.Sc. (special hons.), A.R.C.S. 1963, D.I.C., Ph.D. 1968; ASSOCIATE PROFESSOR OF PHYSICS AND ASTRONOMY, YORK UNIV.; postdoctoral fellow, Dept. of Astronomy, Univ. of Toronto 1968–69; Asst. Prof., Physics and Astronomy, York Univ. 1969–74; Visiting Assoc. Prof., Dept. of Astrogeophysics, Univ. of Colorado 1979–80; Mem., Science for Peace (Treas. 1987–88); Internat. Astronomical Union; Native Canadian Centre; recreations: martial arts, motorcycling; Home: 316 Kennedy Ave., Toronto, Ont. M6P 3C3; Office: 4700 Keele St., North York, Ont. M3J 1P3.

**JEFFERSON, Anne Lily,** B.Ed., M.Ed., Ph.D.; university professor; b. Saskatoon, Sask. 29 Aug. 1953; d. Norman Gordon and Lillian Veronica (Riley) J.; e. Univ. of Alta. B.Ed. (with distinction) 1975, M.Ed. 1979, Ph.D. 1982; ASSOCIATE PROF., UNIV. OF OTTAWA 1990– ; Teacher, various Alta. schools 1975–78; Rsch. & Admin. Asst., Alta. Dept. of Edn. 1979–80; Rsch. Asst., Univ. of Alta. 1980–81; Writer, Candn. Sch. Extve. 1981–84; Sessional Lectr., Univ. of Alta. 1981–82; Asst. Prof., Univ. of Man. 1982–88; Assoc. Prof., Univ. of Windsor 1988–90; Visiting Prof., Univ. of Victoria summer 1982; Univ. of Newcastle Australia summer 1990; Australian Nat. Univ. summer 1990; Brandon Univ. summer 1992; Mem., Nat. Ctr. for Edn. Statistics Tech. Planning Panel, U.S. Dept. of Edn. 1993– ; Extve. Dir., Nat. Consortium of Sci. & Edn. Soc. 1992– ; Dir., Bd. of Dir., Am. Edn. Finance Assn. 1990–93; Financial Advisor, Candn. Union of Edn. Workers 1985–86; Consultant, DIAND 1983; Consultant, CEA Short Course 1983; Consultant, Alta. Dept. of Edn. 1982; Publicity Chair, Phi Delta Kappa, Winnipeg Chapter 1986–87; Distinguished Serv. Award, Am. Edn. Finance Assn. 1993; Merit Award, Univ. of Windsor 1989; Phi Delta Kappa Award of Excellence in Rsch. 1982; Mem., Am. Edn. Finance Assn.; Assn. for the Study of Higher Edn.; Eur. Assn. for Institutional Rsch.; Commonwealth Council for Edn. Admin.; Candn. Soc. for the Study of Higher Edn.; Candn. Soc. for the Study of Edn.; editor: 'J. of Educational Administration & Foundations' 1985–91; co-author of 1 book chapter; sole author of 1 book chapter; author of over 70 articles, several technical reports & invited presentations; recreations: horse-back riding, skiing (alpine & nordic), flying, canoeing, hiking, adventurous travel; Office: Faculty of Edn., Univ. of Ottawa, Ottawa, Ont. K1N 6N5.

**JEFFERY, Frederick Lawrence,** B.F.A.; playwright; b. Vancouver, B.C. 28 Sept. 1953; s. Frederick Emmitt McGill and Margaret Elaine (Twilley) J.; e. York Univ. B.F.A. 1976; author (plays) 'Clay' 1982 (produced by Factory Theatre Toronto 1982, Touchstone Theatre Vancouver 1983; short-listed Gov. Gen's Award Drama 1982, nominated Dora Mavor Moore Award 1982; 'Tower' 1983 (produced by Tarragon Theatre Toronto 1983; nominated Dora Mavor Moore Award 1983); 'Precipice' 1988 (produced by Factory Theatre Toronto 1987); 'Chinese Canadians, Voices from a Community' Evelyn Huang with Lawrence Jeffery, pub. 1992; 'Four Plays' pub. 1992; 'Who Look In Stove' pub. 1993; mem. Playwrights Union Can.; ACTRA; International P.E.N.; Writers Guild of Can.; Home: 23I, 20 Prince Arthur Ave., Toronto, Ont. M5R 1B1.

**JEFFERY, Joseph,** O.B.E. (1946), C.D. (1976), Q.C. (1955), LL.B. (1991), LL.D. (1975); retired insurance executive; b. London, Ont. 1 Sept. 1907; s. late James Edgar and Gertrude (Dumaresq) J.; e. London Pub. and Secondary Schs.; Osgoode Hall Law School, Toronto; Hon. LL.D., Univ. of W. Ont. 1975; m. Nora Alicia, d. late Rev. John Morris, St. Williams, Ont. 19 Oct. 1949; d. Elizabeth (by former m.); two s., Joseph and John Gordon; three d., Alicia, Jennifer, Deborah; PARTNER, JEFFERY & JEFFERY; Counsel, Jeffery Associates; Chrmn., Advisory Ctte., Covent Garden Building Inc.; Past Pres. & Dir., Covent Garden Building Inc.; London Hunt Kennels Ltd.; Pres. & Dir., London Winery Ltd.; Vice-President and Dir., Forest City Investments Ltd; Past Secy.-Treas. & Past Dir. London Broadcasters Ltd.; Secy. and Dir. Lonwin Holdings Ltd.; Treasr. and Dir., Dunwell Holdings Ltd.; mem. Extve. Comte. and Dir., Trilon Financial Corp.; Past Dir., Toronto-Dominion Bank; Two Hundred Queens Ave. Ltd.; Boug Realty Ltd.; London Health Assn.; Hiram Walker Resources Ltd.; read law with Phelan and Richardson and with Jeffery and Jeffery; called to the Bar of Ont. 1930; cr. Q.C. 1955; served with R.C.N. 1940–46, retiring with rank of Captain; also acted as Secretary and mem., Naval Board of Canada; Past Hon. Col., London Service Bn.; Hon. Past Pres., Ont. Business & Comm. Teachers' Assn.; Hon. Vice-Pres., London United Services Inst. (Past Pres.); Trustee, Y.M.C.A.-Y.W.C.A.; Dir. Candn. Council of Christians & Jews; Candn. Extve. Service Overseas; Can.-Israel Chamber Comm. and Indust.; Canada Comte.; Hon. Life mem. (Past Pres.), Victorian Order of Nurses for Canada; Candn. Bar Assn. (Past Vice Pres.; Past Ont. Vice-Pres.); Inst. of Electrical & Electronics Engrs.; Hon. mem. (and former mem.) Extve. Comte. of Adv. Comte. of Sch. Business Adm., Univ. of W. Ont. (Past Chrmn., Bd. of Govs. there); Dir. and former Vice-Chrmn., Candn. Council, Intl. Chamber of Comm.; mem. Adv. Bd., London Little Theatre; Candn. Arthritis & Rheumatism Soc. (Hon. Vice Pres.); Inst. Radio Engrs.; life mem., Law Soc. of Upper Can.; Adv. Comte, Royal Candn. Naval Benev. Fund; Candn. Bus. & Indust. Adv. Comte., Organ. for Econ. Co-op. and Devel.; London Chamber of Comm. (Past Pres.); Candn. Council, Internat. Cham. of Comm. (past Vice-Chrmn.); Ont. Chamber of Comm. (Past Pres.); Candn. Chamber Comm. (mem. Adv. Comte., past Pres.); Candn. Inst. of Internat. Affairs; Candn. Inst. of Public Affairs; Inst. of Radio Engrs.; St. John Ambulance Assn.; Ont. Council, London Historical Museums Adv. Comte.; U.N. Assn., London Br. (Past Pres.); Ont. Bus. and Comm. Teachers' Assn. (Hon. Past Pres.); Hon. mem., Middlesex Law Assn.; London Amateur Radio Club; rec'd. Human Relations Award, Candn. Council of Christians & Jews 1956; Freemason; A.F. & A.M. (Tuscan Lodge); Liberal; Anglican; recreations: riding, fishing, yachting, amateur radio; Clubs: Canadian Legion (Past Pres., Vimy Br.); London Hunt & Country; Sarnia Yacht; Great Lakes Cruising; London Baconian; London City Press; The London; The Toronto; Royal Canadian Naval Sailing Assn.; Home: Black Acre Place, 458 Kains Rd., R.R. 3, London, Ont. N6A 4B7; Office: 174 King St., London, Ont. N6A 1C6.

**JEFFERY, Michael I.,** Q.C., B.A., LL.B., LL.M.; lawyer; b. Toronto, Ont. 15 Feb. 1942; s. Harold and Laura Louise (Donnenfield) J.; e. Univ. of Toronto LL.B. 1965, B.A. 1966; Osgoode Hall Law Sch. LL.M. 1984; m. Josine Alix d. Dorothy and David Cowan 16 Dec. 1965; children: Alison Laurel, David Scott, Lindsey Andra, Adam Cowan; PARTNER, FRASER & BEATTY & HEAD, ENVIRONMENTAL LAW GROUP 1990– ; Visiting Prof. (part-time), Fac. of Environmental Studies, York Univ. 1992– ; called to Bar of Ont. 1967; Q.C. 1978; Partner, Rubin & Jeffery 1968–76; Sr. Partner, Jeffery, Grierson & Traves 1976–81; Vice Chair, Environmental Assessment Bd. of Ont. 1981–86; Chrmn. 1986–90; Chair Emeritus, Internat. Bar Assn.'s Internat. Environ. Law Ctte.; Founding Mem. & Past Chair, Counc. of Candn. Admin. Tribunals; Past Chair, Am. Bar Assn. Internat. Ctte. (Urban, State & Local Govt. Law); Special Advisor to Council on Internat. Issues, Am. Bar Assn. (Urban State & Local Govt. Law) 1993–94; Past Member-at-Large, Candn. Bar Assn. (Ont.), Section on Environ. Law; Past Mem., Adv. Ctte. on Admin. Law, Law Reform Comn. of Can.; part-time faculty, Banff Ctr. Sch. of Mngt.; Chair, Policy & Legisl. Steering Ctte., Globe '90 Environ. Trade Fair & Conf. 1990; Co-Chair 1992; Chair, Candn. Young Citizens' Edn. Found. 1983–93; Invited speaker, Oxford Law Colloquium, Univ. of Oxford 1993; Mem., Law Soc. of U.C. 1967– ; Internat. Bar Assn. 1978– ; Am. Bar Assn. 1990– ; Environ. Law Assn. of N.S.W. 1983– ; Elected mem., Conservation Council of Ont. 1993– ; author: 'Environmental Approvals in Canada' 1989 and numerous articles in refereed law jours.; Founder & Editor-in-Chief: 'Candn. J. of Admin. Law & Practice' 1986– ; Candn. Section Ed., 'Environ. & Planning Law J.' 1986– ; extensive experience as presentor, chair & lecturer at seminars & confs. worldwide; recreations: tennis, motorcycling, skiing, hiking, flying; clubs: Valley Tennis, Caledon Ski; Home: 40 Plymbridge Cres., Willowdale, Ont. M2P 1P5; Office: Box 100, 1 First Candn. Pl., Toronto, Ont. M5X 1B2.

**JEFFREY, Brian,** F.I.I.C.; insurance executive; b. Belfast, N. Ireland 27 Apr. 1945; s. George and Elizabeth (Dunseath) J.; e. Lisnasharragh Primary; Annadale Grammar Sch., adv. sr. level 1964; m. Marion d. John and Elizabeth Harvey 27 July 1966; children: Elizabeth Ann, Christine; PRES., KNOX VICARS MCLEAN 1988– ; var. positions ending as Branch Property Casualty Supt., Comml. Union Group 1964–73; var. ending as Underwriting Projects Mgr. for Can., Head Office, Firemans Fund 1973–76; Acct. Rep. & Asst. Vice-Pres., Marsh & McLennan 1976–79; Extve. Vice-Pres. & Chief Extve. Offr., Knox Vicars McLean (Ont.) Ltd. 1979–85; Dir., KVM International Holdings Inc.; Knox Vicars McLean Inc.; Knox Vicars McLean (Ont.) Ltd.; KVM (Bermuda) Ltd.; Dir., Toronto Ins. Conf., Ins. Inst. of Ont.; Soc. of Fellows; F.I.I.C.; Reg. Ins. Broker; Life Ins. Agent; Presbyterian; Pres., Ont. Greyhound Assn. 1984; Mem., Nat. Greyhound Assn.; recreations: reading, sports and greyhound racing; Clubs: Markland Wood Country; World Trade; Home: 19 Laver Rd., Etobicoke, Ont. M9C 3K4; Office Ste. 210, 214 King St. W., Toronto, Ont. M5H 3S6.

**JEFFREY, Clarence,** B.A., M.Ed., Ph.D.; educator; b. Halifax, N.S. 24 May 1940; s. Alfred Joseph and Ida Marie (Bourque) J.; e. Coll. Ste-Anne B.A. 1960; Univ. de Moncton B.Ed. 1962, M.Ed. 1967; Univ. of Ottawa Ph.D. 1969; McGill Univ. Exper. Psychol. 1964–65; m. Simonne d. Marie and Albéo Allain Melanson 4 July 1964; children: Michel, Gilberte, Claude; PROFESSOR, UNIV. DE MONCTON 1986– , Prof. of Psychol. there 1963– , Research Consultant N.B. Newstart Inc. 1969–

71; Dir. of Psychol. present univ. 1970–73; Acad. Vice Pres. Univ. Sainte-Anne 1978–79; Dean of Grad. Studies and Rsch., Univ. de Moncton 1980–85; author over 15 articles exper. and applied psychol.; mem. N.B. Psychol. Assn. (Extve. 1970–71, Vice Pres. 1971–72, Pres. 1972–73); Candn. Psychol. Assn.; Assn. Advanc. Behavioral Therapy; Candn. Mental Health Assn.; recreations: golf, hunting, fishing; Home: 57 Liberty Cres., Moncton, N.B. E1A 6H4; Office: Moncton, N.B. E1A 3E9.

**JEFFREY, Paul Goforth;** executive; b. Toronto, Ont. 12 Feb. 1926; s. David Ivory (missionary) and Ruth (Goforth, d. of Dr. Jonathan Goforth, a pioneer Presb. missionary in China from 1888–1938) J.; e. Chefoo, N. China; French Indo-China; Kimball Union Acad., Meriden, N.H.; Queen's Univ., B.A. (Econ.) 1949; m. Jane, d. J. Worden Edwards, 17 June 1950; children: Mary Elisabeth, Jennifer Susan, John Stephen David; CHRMN. & DIR., CANAUSTRA CAPITAL CORP.; Pres. & Dir., P.G. Jeffrey & Co. Ltd.; Dir., United Tristar Resources Ltd.; Cliff Resources Ltd.; SCC Resources Inc.; mem. Adv. Bd., Bloorview Children's Hosp.; served in 2nd World War with 1st Candn. Parachute Bn., 6th (U.K.) Airborne Div.; Anglican; Clubs: University; Toronto Golf; Goodwood; Home: Ste. 603, 25 George St., Toronto, Ont. M5A 4L8.

**JELINEK, Otto John;** businessman; b. Prague, Czechoslovakia 20 May 1940; s. Henry and Jarmila (Zizka) J.; e. Appleby Coll., Oakville, Ont.; Oakville Trafalgar H.S. and Thomas A. Blakelock H.S.; Swiss Alpine Business Coll. Davos, Switzerland 1958–59; m. Leata Bennett 17 Aug. 1974; two sons; PRESIDENT, JELINEK INTERNATIONAL 1993– ; former competitive skater; with his sister Maria won the Pairs title for Canada, World Figure Skating Championships, Prague 1962; elected to H. of C. 1972, re-el. 1974, '79, '80, '84, '88; Min. of State (Fitness and Amateur Sport) 1984–88; Min. of State (Multiculturalism) 1985–86; Min. of Supply and Services and Receiver General for Canada 1988–89; Min. of National Revenue 1989–93; P. Conservative; Protestant; Home: Oakville, Ont.; Office: 182 Brookfield Cres., Oakville, Ont. L6K 1A9.

**JELLINEK, Gabor,** B.Sc., M.B.A.; distillery executive; b. Budapest, Hungary 19 July 1934; e. Tech. Univ. Budapest (Chem. Engn.) 1956; McGill Univ. M.B.A. 1974; m. Eva Rosenfeld 17 Dec. 1967; children: Michael, Dana; CHRMN., JOSEPH E. SEAGRAM & SONS, LIMITED 1991– ; Extve. Vice-Pres., Manufacturing, The Seagram Spirits & Wine Group 1991– ; Chem., Distillers Corp. Ltd. LaSalle 1957, Special Assignment Venezuela 1960, Engn. Dept. Head, Waterloo, Ont. 1961, Plant Mgr. LaSalle 1964, Opns. Mgr. 1966, Dir. of Production 1970; Vice Pres. Production, The House of Seagram Ltd. 1974; Extve. Vice Pres. Mfg. present Co. 1978, Extve. Vice Pres. and Chief Oper. Offr. 1980; Pres. & Dir., 1982–91; Vice-Pres., Production & Offr., The Seagram Co. Ltd. 1987; Adv. Bd., Juvenile Diabetes Found.; Dir., Joseph E. Seagram & Sons, Ltd.; BioTechnica Internat. Inc.; Candn. Extve. Service Overseas; Orchestre symphonique de Montréal; recreations: skiing, swimming, tennis; Clubs: M.A.A.A.; Nuns' Island Indoor Tennis; Office: 1430 Peel St., Montreal, Que. H3A 1S9.

**JENKIN, Michael Richard Maclean,** M.Sc., Ph.D.; educator; b. Toronto, Ont. 24 Oct. 1959; s. Richard Derek and Norma Lilian (Maclean) J.; e. Univ. of Toronto B.Sc. (Trinity Coll.) 1982, M.Sc. 1984, Ph.D. 1988; m. Heather d. Ronald and Margaret Maclay 23 June 1984; two d. Emma Siobhan, Sarah Eleanor; Assoc. Prof. of Computer Sci. York Univ. 1987– ; co-editor: (with L. Harris) 'Spatial Vision in Humans and Robots'; author or co-author over 50 publs. sci. jours., confs., book chapters; mem. A.C.M.; I.E.E.E.; recreations: sailing, squash; Club: RCYC; Office: 4700 Keele St., North York, Ont. M3J 1P3.

**JENKINS, David John Anthony,** M.D., Ph.D., D.Sc., FRCP(C); university professor; b. London, England 20 July 1942; s. John Robert Frances Esmond and Betty Olive (Dudrenac) J.; e. Christ Ch. Sch. 1960; Merton Coll., Oxford Univ. & Middlesex Hosp. Med. Sch., London, M.A., Ph.D. 1970, M.D., D.Sc. 1986, FRCP(C); m. Alexandra Louisa d. Elbert and Willy E. (Henning) Waller 28 July 1979; two d.: Amy Elizabeth Julia Ann, Wendy Margarita Nina; PROF., DEPT. OF MED. & DEPT. NUTRITIONAL SCIENCES, UNIV. OF TORONTO 1984– ; Sci. Staff (Clin.), Med. Rsch. Counc., Gastroentenol. Unit, London 1972–77; Rsch. Assoc. & Prof. of Med., Radcliffe Infirmary & Mem., Fac. of Biol. Sci., Oxford Univ. 1977–80; Assoc. Prof., present univ. 1980–84; Dir., Clin. Nutrition & Risk Factor Modification Ctr., St. Michael's Hosp. 1988– ; Borden Award 1983; Can. Goldsmiths Award in Clin. Nutrition, AMCN 1985; Theist with a respect for world's trad. religions; a politically conservative conservationist; vegetarian; numerous memberships in med. & sci. societies; author of sci. papers on nutritional issues; recreations: Roman Archeology; Home: 52 Playter Cres., Toronto, Ont. M4K 1S5; Office: Toronto, Ont. M5S 1A8.

**JENKINS, Hon. John Howard,** B.A., Q.C.; justice; b. Galt, Ont. 15 July 1933; s. Howard Arthur and Lavelle (Culham) J.; e. Univ. of W. Ont. B.A. 1955; Osgoode Hall Law Sch. 1959; m. Edythe d. Albert and Grace Crossman 5 Aug. 1960; children: John, Carole, Elizabeth; JUSTICE, ONT. COURT OF JUSTICE GEN. DIV. 1990– ; Sr. Partner Simmers, Harper, Jenkins & Gowling Henderson until 1986; Sr. Dist. Court Judge Regional Dist. of Durham 1986–90; apptd. Queen's Counsel 1971; Office: 605 Rossland Rd. E., Whitby, Ont. L1N 9G7.

**JENKINS, Kenneth J.W.,** C.M., B.Sc., M.Sc., Ph.D.; research scientist; b. Montreal, Que. 1 Oct. 1929; s. James William and Emily (Vickers) J.; e. McGill Univ. B.Sc. 1951; Univ. of Sask. M.Sc. 1953; Univ. of Wis. Ph.D. 1958; m. Betty Anne Harris 1969; one d. Victoria; PRIN. RSCH. SCI. ANIMAL RSCH. CENTRE AGRIC. CAN. 1965– ; Head, Animal Products Rsch. & Devel. Defence Rsch. Med. Labs. 1953; Teaching Asst. Univ. of Wis. 1954; Asst. Prof. Univ. of Guelph 1958; recipient Nat. Rsch. Council Fellowship 1952–53; Univ. of Wis. Alumnus Fellowship 1957–58; Borden Award 1974; Canada Packers Medal for Excellence in Nutrition 1984; Profl. Inst. Gold Medal 1985; Pub. Service Can. Merit Award 1986; Candn. Soc. Animal Sci. Cert. Merit 1987; C.M. 1989; author over 102 sci. publs.; co-author 'Selenium in Nutrition' 1983; mem. US NRC Subctte. on Selenium; Ctte. on Animal Nutrition; Candn. Biochem. Soc.; Candn. Soc. Nutrition Sci.; Candn. Soc. Animal Sci.; Am. Dairy Sci. Assn.; Sigma Xi; recreations: tennis, travel, horticulture; Club: Barrhaven Tennis; Home: 63 Larkin Dr., Nepean, Ont. K2J 1B3; Office: Ottawa, Ont. K1A 0C6.

**JENKINS, Philip Robert,** B.A.; writer; b. London, England 15 June 1951; s. Eric Edward and Josephine Anne (Weir) J.; e. Merchant Taylors' Liverpool; Lancaster Univ. B.A. 1973; BOOK COLUMNIST, OTTAWA CITIZEN 1991– ; Slaughterman, nylon spinner 1973; College Teacher 1975; Arts Administrator 1976–78; emigrated to Canada 1978; Bartender / Roadie / Film Critic / Magazine Journalist / Folk Musician 1978–89; Coordinator of adult literacy orgn. in Ottawa & singer/songwriter & writer 1989– ; author: 'Fields of Vision: A Journey to Canada's Family Farms' (non-fiction) 1991; recreations: Tae-Kwan-Do (red belt), scuba diving; allergic to clubs of all denominations; Home: R.R. 3, Wakefield, Que. J0X 3G0.

**JENKINS, Rebecca;** singer, songwriter, film star; b. Innisfail, Alberta 1960; e. Dalhousie Univ.; Univ. of Waterloo; Vancouver Playhouse Acting School 1984; back-up singer, The Parachute Club, Jane Siberry, Micah Barnes, Holly Coles, and others; films include: 'Bye Bye Blues', 'Bob Roberts,' 'South of Wawa,' 'Till Death Do Us Part,' 'Split Images,' 'Family Reunion' (nom. Genie Award), 'Cowboys Don't Cry'; plays incl. 'How to Succeed in Business Without Really Trying,' 'Shadows and Light'; brief stint with Second City Auxiliary Touring Co.

**JENKINS, William,** M.Sc., Dr. P.A.; association executive; b. New York City, 17 Oct. 1916; s. Hugh Alexander and Florence Ann (MacInnis) J.; e. N.S. Agric. Coll. (1938); Macdonald Coll., McGill Univ., B.Sc. (Agric.) 1942; M.Sc. 1947, Cornell Univ.; Harvard Univ. (1952–53) M.P.A.; Dr. P.A. 1961; m. Rebecca Jean, d. William Retson, 1 July 1943; two d. Catherine Faye, Heather Jo; ATLANTIC PROVS. ECON. COUNCIL, ret. as Extve. Vice-Pres. 1977; formerly Princ. N.S. Agric. Coll.; Chrmn. Maritime Provinces Higher Educ. Comm; Assoc. Dir., Extension N.S. Dept. of Agric., 1951–61; Chrmn., N.S. Land Settlement Bd., 1961–64; served in 2nd World War, Offr., 1st Candn. Parachute Bn.; mem., N.S. Inst. Agrols.; Freemason; Baptist; Clubs: Golden K, Truro; Home: #7 Retson Court, 143 Ryland Ave., Truro, N.S. B2N 6L4.

**JENKINS, William Alexander,** Q.C.; judge; b. London, Ont. 9 Nov. 1936; s. Frederick Lionel and Norah J.; e. Trinity Coll. Sch.; Univ. of W. Ont. B.A. 1959, LL.B. 1962, LL.D. (Hon.) 1986; m. Ann d. Murray Boulton 6 July 1962; children: Alexandra Ann, William Andrew; JUSTICE OF THE ONTARIO COURT OF JUSTICE (GENERAL DIV.) 1990– ; Partner, Shepherd, McKenzie, Plaxton, Little and Jenkins 1967–88; called to Bar 1964; awarded Q.C. 1976; mem., Middlesex Law Assn. 1964–88; Trustee, Middlesex Law Assn. 1970–78 (Pres. 1978); Advocates' Soc. of Ont. 1972– (Dir. 1981–84); Candn. Bar Assn. 1964–92; Superior Court Judge Assn. of Ontario 1992– (Dir. 1993– ); Sessional Lectr., Univ. of W. Ont. Law Sch. 1966–69; Ont. Bar Admission Course Instructor 1976–82, 1986; Gov., Fanshawe Coll. 1972–73; Univ. of W. Ont. 1976–85 (Chrmn. Bd. of Govs. 1983–85); mem., Ont. Counc. of Regents of Applied Arts & Tech. 1970–71; Bd., London Regional Art Gall. 1974–77 (Chrmn. 1977); Dir., Matthews Group Ltd. 1979–88; Found. Western 1982–87, 1988–92 (Chrmn. 1989–91); Dir., Robarts Research Inst. 1986–93; Dir., Victoria Hosp. Corp. 1986–92; apptd. District Court Judge 1988; Anglican; Conservative; recreations: tennis, squash; Clubs: London; London Hunt & Country (Dir. 1979–81, 1990–94, Vice-Pres. 1991–92, Pres. 1992–93); London Squash Racquets (Dir. 1971–77; Pres. 1977); Home: 67 Hampton Cres., London, Ont. N6H 2P1; Office: 80 Dundas St., London, Ont. N6B 1T6.

**JENNEKENS, Jon Hubert Felix,** O.C., B.Sc., P.Eng.; b. Toronto, Ont. 21 Oct. 1932; s. Hubert Joseph and Laura Sessla (Thorvaldson) J.; e. Royal Mil. Coll. Can. 1954 (Ridout-Van der Smissen Award 1954); Queen's Univ. B.Sc. (Hon.) 1956; m. Norah Margaret Aylesworth Magee 5 June 1954; children: Sandra Ellen, Jon Darren, Jennifer Norah; Depy. Dir. Gen., Safeguards, Internat. Atomic Energy Agency 1987; Past Pres., Atomic Energy Control Bd. 1978–87; served with Royal Can. Elect. & Mech. Engrs. 1954–58, U.N. Forces S. Korea 1954–55, rank Lt.; mem. Chalk River Nuclear Labs. 1958–62; Atomic Energy Control Bd. 1962–87; apptd. Officer of the Order of Canada 1987; mem. Assn. Prof. Engrs. Prov. Ont.; Fellow, Candn. Acad. of Engineering; United Church; recreations: skiing, boating, swimming; Home: 1815 Dorset Dr., Ottawa, Ont. K1H 5T7.

**JENNINGS, I.H. (Tony),** R.P.F.; association executive; b. Toronto, Ont. 12 Aug. 1940; s. Ian Leslie and Sarah Elizabeth (Pepler) J.; e. Upper Canada College 1958; Univ. of Toronto B.Sc.F. 1963; further studies in biol., hydrology, planning & mngmnt.2 yr. masters prog. in biol.; m. Maria A. d. Col. Harry and Dorothy Gow 8 Aug. 1964; children: Timothy S.W., Katherine H.; CHIEF EXEC. OFFR. MUNICIPAL ELECTRIC ASSN. 1989– ; served Ont. Govt. 23 yrs.; prior Extve. Dir., Gov. General's Candn. Study Conference; Conserv. Authority Br. Energy & Resources Mgmt., Mins. of Environment and of Natural Resources; held exec. positions Civil Service Comn. and Min. of Energy; served Ont. Profl. Foresters Assn., Inst. Pub. Adm. Can., Univ. of Toronto Alumni, Boy Scouts, Un. Way, Federated Health, Interfaith; recipient Award of Merit IPAC 1986; Office: P.O. Box 2004, 20 Eglinton Ave. W., Toronto, Ont. M4R 1K8.

**JENNINGS, Honourable Mr. Justice John R.R.,** B.A., LL.B., Q.C.; Ontario Court Judge; b. Toronto, Ont. 10 July 1937; s. Robert Douglas and Mary Adelaide (Rogers) J.; e. Upper Canada College 1955; Trinity College, Univ. of Toronto B.A. (Hons.) 1959; Osgoode Hall Law Sch. LL.B. 1962; m. Eyton d. Alan and Jean Embury 4 April 1964; children: Evan, Simon; JUDGE, ONTARIO COURT, GENERAL DIVISION 1991– ; called to Bar of Ont. 1964; Partner, Kingsmill Jennings 1969–91; Q.C. 1976; Pres., Candn. Bar Assn. 1989–90; The Advocates Soc. 1987–88; Co. of York Law Assn. 1976–77; Hon. Mem., Law Soc. of England & Wales; Law Soc. of Sask.; Fellow, Am. College of Trial Lawyers; Mem., Royal Candn. Military Institute; recreations: golf, tennis, squash; clubs: Toronto Golf; Badminton and Racquet; Toronto Racquet; Rideau; Home: 181 Glenrose Ave., Toronto, Ont. M4T 1K7; Office: Court House, 361 University Ave., Toronto, Ont. M5G 1X9.

**JENNINGS, Peter Charles,** LL.D.; television anchorman; b. Toronto, Ont. 29 July 1938; s. Charles and Elizabeth (Osborne) J.; e. Trinity Coll. Sch. (Port Hope, Ont.); m. Kati Marton; children: Elizabeth, Christopher; CORRESPONDENT/ANCHOR, ABC NEWS; CBC Montreal; CJOH-TV Ottawa; Parliamentary Corr., Network Anchorman, CBC TV, Ottawa; Network Anchorman, Nat. Correspondent, ABC News from 1964; Anchor, Chief Foreign Correspondent and Foreign Desk, London, World News Tonight 1978–1983; Anchor & Sr. Editor, ABC News 1983; also involved in production of numerous documentaries; Mem., Internat. Radio & TV Soc. Club; Overases Press; Office: c/o ABC Press Relations, 47 West 66th Street, New York, N.Y. 10023.

**JENNINGS, Robert G.,** B.A., C.F.A.; investment banker; b. Toronto, Ont. 28 March 1946; s. Col. R.D. and M.A. (Rogers) J.; e. Upper Canada College 1965;

Brock Univ. B.A. 1968; Univ. of Virginia C.F.A. 1973; divorced; PRESIDENT, JENNINGS CAPITAL INC.; Dir., McLeod Young Weir 1968–78; Founder & Partner, Carson Jennings & Assoc. 1979–88; former Sr. Vice-Pres. & Dir., Midland Walwyn Capital Inc.; Dir., Summit Resources; Encal Energy; Former Chair, Mayors Office Calgary Winter Olympics 1988; Former Gov., Alberta Stock Exchange; Office: Suite 2600, 520 – 5 Ave. S.W., Calgary, Alta. T2P 3R7.

**JENSEN, Ben;** artist; b. Skive, Denmark 25 March 1932; s. Jorgen Christian and Anne (Mehlsen) J.; e. Ryerson Inst. Arch. Drafting 1961; Univ. of Toronto; Univ. of Western Ont.; m. June d. Fred and Velma Baxter 29 Dec. 1956; children: David, Cindy; began oil paining in 1962 as a hobby while working for Zurich Insur. Co. (24 years); full-time profl. artist 1987– ; notable recipients of his work: Premier David Peterson, Paul Martin Jr., Premier Bob Rae, City of Toronto archives, Mayor Warsaw Poland presented by Mayor of Toronto and several large Candn. institutions; 1st Prize for Best Oil Painting, Huronia Festival of the Arts 1986; People's Choice Award 1st Prize, McLaughlin Gall. Oshawa 1991; Pres., Cottam Rotary Club 1975–76; recreations: hiking, fishing, travelling, reading; Address: 86 Mill Creek Cres., Kingsville, Ont. N9Y 3P9.

**JENSEN, Elsabeth,** R.N., B.A., B.Sc.N.; association executive; b. Copenhagen, Denmark 26 Apl. 1950; d. Aage and Anna Margrethe J.; e. Hamilton (Ont.) Civic Hosps. Sch. of Nursing R.N. 1972; Univ. of W. Ont. B.A. 1981, B.Sc.N. 1989 (M. Josephine Flaherty Award l989); m. Leonard D. s. Joseph and Beatrice Kushnier 27 Sept. 1980; children: Emerald Suzanne, Bradley Jensen; NURSE MANAGER, CHILD AND ADOLESCENT PSYCHIATRY UNIT, VICTORIA HOSP., LONDON 1990– ; nursing staff London (Ont.) Psychiatric Hosp. 1972–81; Lectr. in Community and Continuing Edn. Fanshawe Coll. London, Ont. 1982–87; R.N. Outpatient Psychiatry Univ. Hosp. London 1982–90; Pres., Reg'd. Nurses Assn. Ont. 1989–90, Pres. Elect 1987–89, Dir. 1982–87; Co-chair White Oaks Community Centre Ctte. 1984–87; mem. Candn. Nurses Assn. (Dir. 1989–90); Mem. Bd. of Dirs., Project Turnabout 1990–91; mem. London-Middlesex Child Abuse Council 1990–93; Dir., Co-ordinating Council for Children and Youth for London and Middlesex 1992–93; Anglican; recreations: reading, camping, hiking, cross-country skiing; Address: 80 Archer Cres., London, Ont. N6E 2A5.

**JENSEN, Susan E.,** B.Sc., Ph.D.; educator; scientist; b. Edmonton, Alta. 30 Jan. 1950; d. Ernest Gustav and Margaret Anne (McKim) Stoby; e. Univ. of Alta. B.Sc. 1970, Ph.D. 1975; m. Chris L. s. Christian R. Jensen 3 Dec. 1971; ASSOC. PROF. OF MICROBIOL. UNIV. OF ALTA. 1984– ; Postdoctoral Fellow, Univ. of B.C. 1974–76; Rsch. Assoc. and Sessional Lectr. present univ. 1977, Asst. Prof. 1981; Alta. Heritage Found. for Med. Rsch. Scholar 1981– ; mem. Candn. Soc. Microbiol.; Am. Soc. Microbiol.; Home: 8808 - 187 St., Edmonton, Alta. T5T 1R9; Office: Edmonton, Alta. T6G 2E9.

**JENSEN-STEVENSON, Monika,** B.F.A.; journalist, author; b. Germany 14 April 1944; d. Gerhard Fritz and Erika (Wohlfahrt) Rasch; e. Univ. of Wisconsin B.F.A. 1967; m. William Henri s. William S.; 12 Nov. 1984; one d.: Alexandra Stevenson; Mng. & Assoc. Ed., 'Arts in Society' 1967–73; Faculty, Univ. of Wisconsin; Reporter / Producer, CTV National News, 'W5,' 'CTV Reports,' 'Canada AM' 1975–81; Staff Producer, '60 Minutes,' CBS 1981–86; freelance journalist for a variety of broadcast outlets, newspapers & magazines incl. PBS, NBC, The Toronto Star, Washington Post and Town & Country Magazine; author; Consultant, Public TV, Thailand, Population Devel. Assn.; Emmy for 'Sixty Minutes' prodn. 'In the Belly of the Beast'; Gold medal for CTV prodn. 'The Miracle Seekers'; recipient, Vietnam Veterans National Medal; co-author: 'Kiss the Boys Goodbye: How the United States Betrayed its own POWs in Vietnam' (Best Selling pub. in cloth & paper in Canada, U.S. & England); recreations: tennis, equestrian, swimming; Home: currently residing in Thailand while working on book & film project; Mailing address: c/o McClelland and Stewart, 481 University Ave., Toronto, Ont. M5G 2E9.

**JEPHCOTT, Samuel Charles;** film & television production and marketing executive; b. Southampton, UK 23 July 1944; s. Ronald Dickson and Joan (Clapson) J.; e. Arts Educational Trust London; m. Katherine d. Verne and Muriel Martin 19 Nov. 1975; one s. Jonathan Charles; one d. Emily Kate; PRES., CYCLOPS COMMUNICATIONS CORP. 1978– ; Dir. Mktg., 'The Adventures of Dudley the Dragon' TV Series for Breakthrough Films/TV Ontario; Publisher 'Home Video for the Inquisitive' mail order catalogue; joined BBC TV as child actor 1956; TV Comm. Prodn. 1960–67; came to Can. 1968; freelance feature film and TV prodn. mgmt. exec. incl. Supr. of Prodn. for Torstar's Nielsen-Ferns Div. 1977–81; Distribution & Foreign Sales Exec. incl. Mgr. of Distribution CBC Enterprises 1982–84; Pres., Candn. Film & Television Assn. 1984–90; Producer 'The Last Frontier' TV series for Mako Films/CTV Television Network Ltd. Inc. 1985–87; Dir., Gen. Mgr., Candn. Film & Television Production Assn. 1990–92; Exec. Sec., Dir. and Offr. Directors Guild of Can. 1969–75; Mem., YMCA; Address: 44 Gibson Ave., Toronto, Ont. M5R 1T5.

**JEROME, Hon. Mr. Justice James,** P.C.; Judge b. Kingston, Ont. 4 March 1933; s. Joseph Leonard and Phyllis (Devlin) J.; e. St. Michael's Coll. High Sch., Toronto Univ. of Toronto, B.A. 1954; Osgoode Hall Law Sch., grad. 1958; m. Barry Karen Hodgins, 7 June 1958; children: Mary Lou, Paul, Jim Jr., Joey (dec.), Megan Phyllis; ASSOC. CHIEF JUSTICE, FEDERAL COURT OF CANADA 1980– ; Privy Councillor 1981– ; Elected to Sudbury City Council, 1965; el. to H. of C. for Sudbury in g.e. 1968; re-el., 72, 74 & 79; Vice Chrmn., Standing Comte. on Privileges and Els.; Chrmn., Special Committee on El. Expenses, 1970; Parlty. Secy. to Pres. of Privy Council and Govt. House Leader, 1970; mem. Can. delegation to NATO, 1972; Chrmn., Standing Comte on Justice and Legal Affairs, 1972–74; elected Speaker of the House of Commons, 1974, and in 1979 became the first Speaker to be re-elected after a change of government; el. Pres. of the Commonwealth Parliamentry Assn., 1976; Liberal; R. Catholic; recreations: golf; music; Home: 1051 Cahill Dr. W., Ottawa, Ont.; Office: Supreme Court of Canada Building, Ottawa, Ont. K1A 0H9.

**JÉRÔME-FORGET, Monique,** Ph.D.; executive; b. Montréal, Qué. 8 Aug. 1940; d. Frederick G. and Cécile (Labelle) Jérôme; e. Coll. Basile-Moreau 1960; McGill Univ. Ph.D. 1976; m. Claude E. s. Lucien and Isola Forget 25 March 1960; children: Nicolas, Elise; successively First Vice Pres. Candn. Adv. Council Status of Women, Asst. Dep. Min. Health & Welfare Can., Vice Rector Concordia Univ. 1982–86; Pres. & C.E.O., Comn. de la Santé et de la Sécurité du Travail Que. 1986–90; Pres. & C.E.O., Institute for Rsch. on Public Policy 1991– ; previously served prog. devel. and mgmt. and practicing psychol. health and social service instns.; recent activities incl. Chair, OECD Task Force Social Policy; Internat. Union Family Orgns. Family Health Ctte.; Vice Pres. XII World Cong. Internat. Social Security Assn.; mem. several dels. to confs. and meetings World Health Orgn. and UNESCO; Bd. Dirs. many orgns. incl. Candn. Council Social Devel., Fédération des femmes du Qué., Corp. profl. psychols. Qué.; Founding and Affiliated Faculty mem. Kellogg Center 1977– ; co-author 'The Family a Part of Larger Systems; the Community; Working with the Family in Primary Care' 1984; recreations: sailing, skiing, travel; Clubs: M.A.A.A.; University; Home: 82, 1227 rue Sherbrooke Ouest, Montréal, Qué. H3G 1G1; Office: 1470 Peel St., Suite 200, Montréal, Qué. H3A 1T1.

**JERRETT ENNS, Victor,** B.A.; writer; association executive; b. Winnipeg, Man. 3 Apr. 1955; s. Frank F. and Susann (Klassen) E.; e. Mennonite Coll. Inst. 1972; Univ. of Man., B.A. 1979; m. Sheila d. Gerald and Evelyn Jerrett 14 Aug 1982; children: Jay Alden, Theodore John, Bronwyn Evelyn; EXECUTIVE DIRECTOR, MANITOBA ARTS COUNCIL 1993– ; Univ. of Man. Students Union 1973–79; Editor, 'The Manitoban' 1974–75; Communications Dir. 1977–78; Student, Writer, Journalist & Broadcaster 1973–81; Extve. Dir., Sask. Writers Guild 1982–88; Administrator/General Manager, Globe Theatre 1988–91; Gen. Mgr., Rainbow Stage 1991; Theatre and Dance Officer, Manitoba Arts Council 1992; Acting Executive Dir., Manitoba Arts Council Dec. 1992–June 1993; Extve. Mem., Sask. Arts Alliance 1986–90; Founding Mem. & Vice-Pres., Man. Writers Guild 1980 & 1981; Mem., Assn. of Cultural Extves.; author: 'Jimmy Bang Poems' 1979, 'Correct in this Culture' 1985; Gen. Ed. (in-house) & Prodn. Supvr.: 'Saskatchewan Literary Arts Handbook' 1985, 'On Saskatchewan Writing' 1986; recreations: reading, writing, swimming, children; Home: 200 Lenore St., Winnipeg, Man. R3G 2C5.

**JERVIS, Robert E.,** M.A., Ph.D., F.C.I.C., F.R.S.C., P.Eng.; educator; b. Toronto, Ont. 21 May 1927; s. Bertram Chas. W. and Mary Elizabeth (Gibbings) J.; e. E. York Coll. Inst.; Univ. of Toronto B.A. 1949, M.A. 1950, Ph.D. 1952; m. Jean d. John B. and Edith McCourt 30 Dec. 1950; children: Ann Kathleen, Peter R.; PROF. OF CHEM. ENG. UNIV. OF TORONTO 1958– ; Assoc. Rsch. Offr. Atomic Energy Canada Ltd. Chalk River 1952–58; Asst. Prof. present Univ. 1958, Assoc. Prof. 1960, Prof. 1966; Dir. SLOWPOKE Nuclear Reactor 1970–82, 1986–92, Assoc. Dean of Eng. (Rsch. & Advanced Studies) 1974–77, Chrmn. Rsch. Bd. 1981–85, mem. Centre for Nuclear Eng. 1983– , Assoc. Inst. Environmental Studies 1975– ; Dir. Chemical Engineering Research Consultants Ltd. Toronto 1963– ; Cons., Internat. Atomic Energy Agency 1967– ; Cons., Atomic Energy Control Bd. Can. (Chair, Adv. Ctte. Nuclear Safety) 1980– ; Visiting Prof. of Radiochem. Univ. of Tokyo 1965–66; Visiting Prof., Cambridge Univ. 1978; Visiting Prof., Nat. Univ. Malaysia 1979; author or co-author over 210 sci. publs. in books, internat. jours. and conf. proceedings on applied nuclear chem., environment, trace analysis, biomed. studies; Fellow, Candn. Christian Scient. Affiliation; Fellow, Royal Soc. of Canada; Fellow, Chemical Inst. of Canada; Hon. Fellow Indian Acad. Forensic Sci's; Honors: Hevesy Medal (internat. radioanal. chem.) 1978; W.B. Lewis Medal, Can. Nuclear Soc. 1991; T. Ressosky Medal, Russia Acad. of Sci. 1992; Dir.: Inter-Varsity Christian Fellowship 1960–87; Candn. Soc. for Chem. 1986–89; Home: 30 Chestergrove Cres., Agincourt, Ont. M1W 1L4; Office: Toronto, Ont. M5S 1A4.

**JESSIMAN, The Hon. Duncan J.,** B.A., LL.B., LL.M.; senator, barrister; b. 5 June 1923; e. Univ. of Man. B.A., LL.B., LL.M.; Hon. LL.D. Univ. of Winnipeg 1976; Q.C. 1959; spouse: Alix; children: Duncan, Robert, Sally; SENATOR, GOVERNMENT OF CANADA 1993– ; Barrister, Johnston, Jessiman & Gardner 1948–71; Pitblado & Hoskin 1971– ; Bd. Mem. (16 years) and Past Chair, Univ. of Winnipeg; Bd. Mem. (15 years) and Past Chair, Victoria Gen. Hosp.; Mem., Candn. & Man. Bar assns.; appointed to the Senate 26 May 1993; Past Pres. & Mem., Rotary Club of Winnipeg; Past Bd. Mem., Rainbow Stage, Candn. Arthritis Soc.; Past Mem. of Cabinet, United Way in Winnipeg; Office: Room 623, 140 Wellington, Ottawa, Ont. K1A 0A4.

**JESTIN, Richard W.,** B.Sc.; telecommunications executive; b. Calgary, Alta. 24 June 1947; s. Warren James and Isobel Dorothy Elizabeth (Rowden) J.; e. Univ. of Calgary B.Sc.(EE) 1969; m. Marjorie d. Richard and Mollie Chapman 16 Aug. 1969; one s. Wayne Douglas; EXEC. VICE PRES. TELESAT ENTERPRISES INC. 1988– , Dir. Telecommunication Services; Chief Operating Offr. Mediasat Advertising Services; Dir. Digital Video Services; served 18 yrs. telecommunications ind. incl. 9 yrs. with Bell Canada, 2 yrs. as cons.; joined Telesat Canada as Mgr. Voice/Data Services 1982; Advanced Amateur Radio Operator; mem. Assn. Profl. Engs. Prov. Ont.; Home: 69 Heritage Rd., Russell, Ont. K4R 1W3.

**JESTIN, Warren,** Ph.D.; economist; b. 28 Feb. 1949; e. Univ. of Guelph B.A. (Hon.) 1971, M.A. 1971; Univ. of Toronto Ph.D. 1977; m. Deborah 15 Dec. 1987; children: Andrew, Daniel, Victoria; SR. VICE-PRES. & CHIEF ECONOMIST, THE BANK OF N.S. 1990– ; Prof. of Econ., Simon Fraser Univ. 1973–74; Brock Univ. 1974–75; Economist, The Bank of Canada 1975–77; Sr. Econ., The Bank of N.S. 1978–86; Dep. Chief Econ. 1986–88; Vice-Pres. & Chief Econ. 1988–90; Bd. of Trustees, The Fraser Inst.; Mem., Econ. Policy Ctte., Candn. C. of C.; Home: 9 James Speight Rd., Markham, Ont. L3P 3G3; Office: 44 King St. W., Toronto, Ont. M5H 1H1.

**JESTLEY, William Garth,** B.Sc., M.B.A.; executive; b. Vancouver, B.C. 9 Sept. 1946; s. Hilliard Lyle and Gwendolyn (Newton) J.; e. Univ. of B.C., B.Sc. 1968; Univ. of W. Ont., M.B.A. 1971; m. Mary d. Richard and Norah Fladgate 5 July 1969; children: Skye, Mark, Erin, Kathleen; PRES., CHIEF EXTVE. OFFR. & DIR., MIDDLEFIELD VENTURES LTD. 1986– ; Sr. Investment Analyst, Prudential Insur. Co. of Am. 1971–74; various pos. ending as Vice Pres., Citibank 1974–80; Vice Pres., Project Fin., Bank of Montreal 1981–84; Vice Pres., Mktg. 1985; Dir., H.E.R.O. Industries Ltd.; Gravure International Corp.; R-Tek Corp.; Sequel Industries Inc.; several univ. scholarships; Christian; Mem., Evangel Temple, North York; recreations: running, swimming, tennis; Home: 69 St. Leonard's Ave., Toronto, Ont. M4N 1K4; Office: 58th Floor, Box 192, First Canadian Place, Toronto, Ont. M5X 1A6.

**JEWERS, Hon. Gerald Oliver,** LL.M.; judge; b. Winnipeg, Man. 19 May 1932; s. Ernest John and Kathleen Victoria (Green) J.; e. Kelvin H.S. Winnipeg 1949; Univ. of Man. Ll.B. 1955, LL.M. 1957; m. Claire d. Norman and Beulah Woodcock 21 Aug. 1954; children: Judith, Robin, Leslie; JUDGE, COURT OF QUEEN'S BENCH, MAN. 1984– ; cr. Q.C. 1975; law practice Newman, McLean and Associates, Winnipeg 1956–61; Partner, Fillmore & Riley, Winnipeg 1961–77; Judge, Co. Court of Winnipeg 1977–84; mem. Manitoba Law Reform Comn. 1985; Chrmn. Comn. Enquiry Private Operators

Lotteries man.; Pres. Man. Bar Assn. 1975; recreations: golf, skiing; Home: 1120 Rue Des Trappistes, Winnipeg, Man. R3V 1B8; Office: Law Courts, Broadway & Kennedy, Winnipeg, Man.

**JEWETT, Marcus L.,** Q.C.; b. Montreal, Que. 28 May 1945; s. Dr. Beverly L. and Dr. Marie Anne (Copeman) J.; e. Univ. of N.B., B.A. 1966, LL.B. 1969; Trinity Coll., Cambridge, LL.B. 1972, Dipl. Internat. Law 1973; ASST. DEPY. MIN. & COUNSEL, DEPT. OF FINANCE, CANADA 1990– ; called to N.B. Bar 1969; with Hoyt, Mockler, Allen & Dixon (Fredericton, N.B.) 1969–70; Counsel, Const. Admin. and Internat. Law Section, Dept. of Justice 1972–74; Dir. Legal Servs., Min. of State for Urban Affairs 1975; Gen. Counsel Anti-Inflation Bd. 1976–78; Gen. Counsel, Dept. of Nat. Revenue, Taxation 1977–80; Gen. Counsel, Constitutional & Internat. Law, Dept. of Justice 1980–86; cr. Q.C. 1982; with Debevoise & Plimpton, New York, N.Y. 1986–87; Tax Counsel and Gen. Dir., Tax Policy & Legislation Br., Dept. of Finance, Canada 1987–90; mem. Exec. Bd. Candn. Counc. on Internat. Law; Vice-Pres., Internat. Law Assoc. (Canada); mem. Candn. Bar Assn. (Vice-Chrmn. Internat. Law Sect.); N.B. Barristers Soc.; Am. Soc. of Internat. Law; Internat. Fiscal Assoc.; author articles in Internat. Legal Materials, Candn. Yearbook of Internat. Law, Candn. Bar Review; Office: 140 O'Connor St., 21st Flr., East Tower, Ottawa, Ont. K1A 0G5.

**JEWISON, Norman Frederick,** C.C., B.A., LL.D.; film producer and director; b. Toronto, Ont. 21 July 1926; s. Percy Joseph and Irene (Weaver) J.; e. Malvern Coll. Inst., Toronto, Ont. (Matric.); Victoria Coll., B.A. 1940–44; Univ. of Toronto, 1950; LL.D. Western Ont. 1974; m. Margaret Ann, d. James Nelson Dixon, 11 July 1953; children: Kevin Jefferie, Michael Philip, Jennifer Ann; joined CBC, 1952–58; CBS, 1958–61; Universal Studios, 1961–64, where he directed the motion pictures '40 Pounds of Trouble,' 'The Thrill of It All,' 1963; 'Send Me No Flowers' 1964; as a Free Lance, 1964–68; directed 'Art of Love,' 'The Cincinnati Kid' 1965; prod. and dir. 'The Russians Are Coming' 1966; dir. 'In The Heat of The Night,' prod./dir. 'The Thomas Crown Affair' 1967; dir. 'Gaily, Gaily' 1968; prod. 'The Landlord' 1969; prod./dir. 'Fiddler on The Roof' 1970; 'Jesus Christ Superstar' 1972; prod. 'Billy Two Hats' 1972; 'Rollerball' 1974; prod./dir. 'F.I.S.T.' 1977; 'And Justice for All' 1979; Extve. Prod. 'Dogs of War' 1980; prod./dir. 'Best Friends' 1982; Extve. Prod. 'Iceman' 1983; Extve. Prod./Dir. 'A Soldier's Story' 1984; 'Agnes of God' 1985; 'Moonstruck' 1987; Extve. Prod. 'The January Man' 1988; 'In Country' 1989; Extve. Prod./Dir. 'Other People's Money' 1991; 'Just In Time' 1994; honoured by American Civil Liberties Union in California 1984; mem. Bd., Festival of Festivals, Toronto 1981; named Officer, Order of Canada, 1982; Mem., Order of Ontario 1989; Companion, Order of Canada 1993; presenter of C.N.E. student film award, 1980 and 1981; mem. Senate, Stratford Festival; dir. Belafonte, Jackie Gleason, Andy Williams, Judy Garland, Danny Kaye TV shows; produced 1981 Academy Awards; nomimated by D.G.A. for 'outstanding directorial achievement' in 1984; rec'd. Academy Award Nominations 1966–67, 72, 74, 84, 88 (Best Dir.); Directors Guild Nominations 1966–67; Golden Globe Award (Foreign Press) 1966; Emmy Award 1960; Emmy Nominations, 1961 and 1962; TV Directors Award, 1961; Candn. Liberty Award, 1958; Judge of Monte Carlo Internat. TV Festival, 1966; served as Pres. of Jury, Avoriaz Film Festival (France) 1981; Best Dir., Berlin Film Festival 1988; Hon. degrees: Trent Univ. 1985; Victoria College (U. of T.) 1985; Ryerson Institute 1986; Founder and Co-Chrmn., Candn. Centre for Advanced Film Studies 1986; Faculty mem., Inst. for America Studies 1969, Salzburg, Austria; Goals and Purposes Comte., Directors Guild of America, 1982; el. Bd. of Govs., Acad. Motion Picture Arts and Sciences 1988; served with R.C.N., 1945–46; Liberal; Protestant; recreations: skiing, yachting, tennis; Office: Yorktown Productions Ltd., 18 Gloucester St., 5th Floor, Toronto, Ont. M4Y 1L5.

**JILES, Paulette,** B.A.; writer; b. Salem, Missouri; d. Robert Leonard and Ruby Lee (Racy) J.; e. Univ. of Missouri, B.A. 1968; came to Canada 1969; freelance radio reporter for CBC; travelled in Eur. & N. Africa 1970–72; worked in Arctic & subarctic for Native Communications groups 1973–83; Teacher, David Thompson Univ., Nelson, B.C. 1984–85; writer-in-res., Phillips Acad., Andover, MA 1987–; Mem., Writers Union of Can.; Gov. Gen. Award, Pat Lowther Award, and Gerald Lampert 1984: all for 'Celestial Navigation,' 1st and only time one book of poetry has won all 3; ACTRA award for 'best writer, original drama' 1989; author: 'Waterloo Express' 1973, 'Celestial Navigation' 1983, 'The Jesse James Poems' 1987 (poetry); 'Golden Hawks' 1976 (juvenile); 'Sitting in the Club Car Drinking Rum & Karma-Kola' 1986, 'The Late Great Human Roadshow' 1986 (fiction); 'Blackwater' 1988 (collection); 'Song to the Rising Sun' 1989.

**JIM, Harvey,** C.A.; financial executive; b. Lillooet, B.C. 10 June 1932; s. San and Jane (Wong) J.; e. Univ. of B.C. B.Sc. 1957; McGill Univ. C.A. 1965; m. Christine Hori Aug. 1962; one s.: Calvin; Sr. Vice-Pres., Finance, Saskpower 1989–93; Engr., Candn. Chemical Co. Ltd., Celanese Can. Ltd. 1957–62; Chief Acct., Churchill Falls Power Project, Candn. Bechtel 1965–68; Mgr. Budget & Finan. Analysis, Allied Chem. Co. of Can. 1968–70; Finan. Cons./Asst. V.P. & Cont. Acres Ltd., Trader's Group Ltd., Guaranty Trust Co. of Can. 1970–74; CFO/VP Finan., Assoc. Engineering Ltd./Assoc. Kellogg Ltd. 1974–81; V.P. Finance, Techman Engr. Ltd. 1981–83; V.P. Finan. present firm 1984–88; Dir., Finan. Extves. Inst. (Past Pres. Regina Ch.); Mem., Candn. Inst. of C.A.s; Assoc. of Profl. Engrs., Geol. & Geophy. of Alta.; Insts. of C.A.s of Sask. & Que.; Assiniboia Club; Former Extve., Boy Scouts of Canada; United Way; recreations: golf, tennis, bridge; clubs: Wascana Golf & Country, Silver Springs Golf & Country; Home: 343 Avon Dr., Regina, Sask. S4V 1L8; Office: 2025 Victoria Ave., Regina, Sask. S4P 0S1.

**JIMBOW, Kowichi,** M.D., Ph.D., FRCP(C); university professor and director; b. Nagoya Aichi-ken, Japan 4 June 1941; e. Sapporo Medical College Japan 1960–66; Intern, Sapporo Med. College Hosp. 1966–67 (M.D. 1966), Ph.D. studies 1968–70 (Ph.D. 1974); Fellow, Dept. of Dermatology, Massachusetts Gen. Hosp., Harvard Med. Sch. 1970–74; m. Mihoko; children: Takatoshi, Mie, Eri, Atsuko; PROF. & DIR., DIV. OF DERMATOLOGY & CUTANEOUS SCIENCES, UNIV. OF ALBERTA 1987– ; Instr., Harvard Med. Sch. 1974–75; Asst. Prof., Sapporo Med. Coll. 1975–76; Assoc. Prof. 1976–87; Prof., Dept. of Pathology, Univ. of Alta. 1988– ; Assoc. Visiting Prof., Univ. of Arkansas 1975–78; 'Am. J. of Derm.' 1979– ; Pres., Western Candn. Soc. for Clin. & Investigative Dermatology 1990– ; Ed. Bd., 'Pigment Cell Research' 1987– ; Fellow, Am. Acad. of Derm. 1987– ; W.H.O. Mem. for Evaluation of Methods of Diagnosis & Treatment of Melanoma 1983– ; past mem. of several cttes.; Mem., Am. Soc. of Cancer Rsch.; Am. Soc. of Photobiology; Candn. Derm. Assn.; Alta. Med. Assn.; Am. Acad. of Derm.; Finnish Derm. Assn. (Hon. Mem.); Internat. Soc. of Pigment Cell Rsch. (Councillor); Japan Soc. of the Reticuloendothelial System; Eur. Soc. of Derm. Rsch.; and several others; FRCP(C); Heritage Medical Scientist 1988; Seiji Memorial Prize, Japanese Soc. of Derm. 1984; Alfred-Marchionini Prize, Internat. Assn. of Derm. 1982; recipient of several research grants; author: 'Malignant Melanoma: Basic and Clinical Features' 1987 & num. articles, reviews, book chapters & abstracts; editor: 'Structure and Function of Melanin' 4 vols. 1984–87; has presented num. lectures & symposiums; participant in over 200 workshops & major nat. & internat. meetings; Office: Edmonton, Alta. T6G 2S2.

**JOAKIM, Chris,** B.A., C.A.; chartered accountant, financial executive; b. Cyprus 20 Oct. 1954; s. Charley Savva and Pauline (Stephanou) J.; e. Univ. of Toronto B.A. 1980; m. Mary d. George and Georgia Nicholas 11 Sept. 1976; children: Christopher, Paul, Melissa; PARTNER, ORENSTEIN & PARTNERS 1991– ; Student-in-accounts, Spencer, Pal and Gould C.A.s 1980–84; C.A. 1983; Sr. Accountant, Orenstein & Partners 1985–87; Mgr. 1988–91; areas of expertise: real estate, health care, syndications, financing, business acquisitions & business consulting; Candn. Securities Course 1988; Past Banking Chrmn. & Treas., Juvenile Diabetes Found.; recreations: cycling, photography, gardening, woodworking, stained glass; clubs: Bayview Country; Markham Health; Home: 78 Wrenwood Court, Unionville, Ont.; Office: 595 Bay St., Suite 300, Toronto, Ont. M5G 2C2.

**JOBIN, Pierre,** C.M., M.D., F.R.C.S.(C); retired university professor; b. Que. 8 Sept. 1907; s. Albert and Julie-Anna (Delage) J.; e. Que. Semy.; Laval Univ., B.A. 1927, M.D. 1932; post-grad. studies in France and Eng., 1934–37; m. Blanche C. de Léry, Quebec, 6 Feb. 1970; one s., Pierre; Prof. of Anatomy, Laval Univ., 1944–75; Asst. étranger en Chir. de Lyon, France, 1935; Asst. Surg., Hôtel-Dieu Hosp., Que., 1937; Lectr. in Anat., Laval Univ., 1938, Assoc. Prof. 1940, Prof. 1941, Head of Dept. of Anat. 1940, Dir. Continuing Med. Educ. 1963; apptd. Med. Consultant to Royal Comm. on Health Services, July 1961; Assn. des Méd. de Langue Française du Can.; Am. Assn. Anat.; Assn. French-speaking Doctors (Pres. 1960); Médaille du Centenaire de la Confédération Canadienne 1967; Membre de L'Ordre du Canada 1986; Liberal; Roman Catholic; recreations: fishing, golf, singing; Clubs: Richelieu; Home: 610 Chemin St-Louis, Quebec, Que. G1S 1B8.

**JODREY, John J.;** industrialist; Chrmn., Maritime Paper Products Ltd.; Minas Basin Holdings Ltd.; Scotia Investments Ltd.; Dir., Avon Valley Greenhouse Ltd.; CKF Inc.; Cobi Foods Inc.; The Montserrat Company Ltd.; Chancellor Emeritus, Technical Univ. of Nova Scotia; Freemason (Scot. Rite); Baptist; recreations: golf, boating; Clubs: Halifax (N.S.); Montserrat Golf (Montserrat, West Indies); Office: Prince St., Hantsport, N.S. B0P 1P0.

**JOE, Rita Ann,** O.C.; writer; b. Whycocomagh, N.S. 15 March 1932; d. Joseph and Annie (Googoo) Bernard; e. Millbrook Day Sch.; Indian Residential Sch. Shubenacadie, N.S. 1948; Eskasoni C.B. N.S. Grade XII 1989; Eskasoni Bus. Ed. 1981; m. Frank s. Stephen and Isobel Joe 16 Jan. 1954; children; Phyllis, Evelyn, Bernadette, Frances, Caroline, Ann, Bernard,, Basil; writer Micmac News since 1969; Owner craftshop Minvitagn; resource person schs. Can. and USA; recipient Lit. Award (Hon. Mention) N.S. Writers Fedn. 1974; author 'Poems of Rita Joe' 1979; 'Song of Eskasoni' 1989; mem. Eskasoni Women's Auxiliary; recreation: bingo; Address: c/o Ragweed Press Inc., P.O. Box 2023, Charlottetown, P.E.I. C1A 7N7.

**JOFFE, David Herschel,** B.A.; industrial relations executive, labour negotiator; b. Montreal, Que. 20 Aug. 1947; s. Alec and Sahra (Fine) J.; e. Univ. of Windsor B.A. 1972; m. Marie Louise Sutton 5 Aug. 1992; children (from previous marriage): Aaron Philip, Dana Ann; VICE-PRES., INDUSTRIAL RELATIONS, THE OSHAWA GROUP 1990– ; Mfg., Chrysler Canada Ltd. 1964–72; Labour Relns. & Human Resources Specialist 1972–76; Mgr., Peronnel & Indus. Relns., Assembly Div. 1976–79; Dir., Personnel & Indus. Relns., Kaiser Aluminum Canada Ltd. 1979–84; Dir., Labour Relns., The Oshawa Group Limited 1984; Home: 599 Dovercourt Rd., Toronto, Ont. M6H 2W5; Office: 302 The East Mall, Etobicoke, Ont. M9B 6B8.

**JOHNS, Harold Elford,** O.C., Ph.D., LL.D., F.R.S.C. (1951); university professor; b. Chengtu, West China 4 July 1915; s. Alfred Edward and Myrtle Madge J.; e. McMaster Univ., B.A. 1936; Univ. of Toronto, M.A. 1937, Ph.D. 1939; Univ. of Sask., LL.D. 1959; McMaster 1970; D. Sc. Carleton Univ., 1976; D.Sc. Univ. of Western Ont., 1978; m. Alice Sybil, d. late Stonewall Jackson Hawkins, 15 June 1940; children: Gwyneth, Claire, Marilyn; PROF. OF MED. BIOPHYSICS, UNIV. OF TORONTO, since 1962; Head, Physics Div., Ont. Cancer Inst. 1956–80; Prof., Dept. of Physics, Univ. of Toronto, since 1956; Lectr. in Physics, Univ. of Alberta, 1939–45; during 2nd World War, Lectr. in radar to Air Force and Navy Personnel, Univ. of Alberta, 1939–45; Official Radiographer of aircraft casting for W. Can., 1942–45; Asst., Assoc. Prof. of Physics, Univ. of Sask., 1945–56 (also Physicist, Sask. Cancer Comn.); named Saskatoon's (Sask.) Citizen of the Year, 1952; Roentgen Award, Brit. Inst. of Radiology, 1953; Henry Marshall Tory Medal, Royal Royal Soc. Can.; Gairdner International Award 1973; Offr. Order of Can. 1977; Gold Medalist, Am. Coll. of Radiology, 1980; Hon. mem., Ont. Med. Assn., 1981; R.M. Taylor award, Cdn. Cancer Soc., 1982; Candn. Med. Assn. 1983; Medal, Amer. Nuclear Industry 1983; W.B. Lewis Award Candn. Nuclear Soc. 1985; author of: 'The Physics of Radiation Therapy' 1953; 'The Physics of Radiology' 1961 (4th ed. 1983); also over 200 papers in scientific journals; holds a number of patents on the design of Cobalt 60 units for treatment of cancer; Chrmn., Healing Arts Radiation Protection Cmte., 1981–82; mem., British Institute of Radiol.; Candn. Assn. Radiol.; Candn. Assn. Physicists; Candn. Assn. Med. Physicists (Pres. 1962); Am. Phys. Soc.; Am. Radium Soc.; Am. Assn. of Physicists in Med.; Soc. of Photographic Scientists & Engrs.; Radiation Research Soc.; United Church; Home: Suite 220, Briargate, 4567 Bath Rd., Amherstview, Ont. K7N 1A8.

**JOHNS, Martin Wesley,** M.A., Ph.D., F.R.S.C. (1958); physicist; retired university professor; b. Chengtu, Szechuan, W. China 23 March 1913; s. Rev. Alfred Edward and Myrtle Madge J.; e. Canadian Sch., W. China; High Schs. in Tacoma, Wash., Vancouver, Brandon and Exeter, Ont.; Brandon Coll. (1928–31); McMaster Univ., B.A. 1932, M.A. 1934; Univ. of Toronto, Ph.D. 1938; m. late Margaret Mary, d. Edwin Hilborn, Hamilton, Ont., 15 July 1939; children: Robert, Elizabeth, Kenneth and Kathryn (twins); re-married, Elsie North, 1981; Prof. of Physics, McMaster Univ., 1953–81; Co-ordin., Part-time Degree Studies in Adult Educ., 1977–81; Part-time Research Assistant Nuclear Data Project McMaster 1982– Chrmn. of Dept. of Physics, 1961–67 and 1970–76; Lectr. in Physics; Brandon Coll., 1937–38;

Prof. of Physics there, 1938–46; Assoc. Research Physicist, Nat. Research Council, Chalk River, Ont., 1946–47; Asst. Prof., McMaster Univ., 1947–48, Assoc. Prof., 1948–53; Visiting Prof., Oxford Univ., 1959–60; Colombo Plan 'expert' sent to Pakistan, 1960; Visiting Scientist Chalk River Nuclear Labs., 1967–68; served in C.O.T.C., 1940–41; research concerned with neutron physics (Chalk River), nuclear spectroscopy (McMaster); Publications: 100 papers in these fields; actively interested in Un. Ch. as Layman, and has served on many Ch. Comtes. at Local and Nat. level; Co-Chrmn., Family Life Comte. of Un. Ch. 1954–67; Pres. of Bd., Family Services of Hamilton-Wentworth 1976–77; Pres. Hamilton United Way 1977–79; Pres. Ont. Assn. of Family Service Agencies 1979–81; Pres. Family Services Canada 1984–86; recreations: swimming, hiking, gardening; Home: 115 Dalewood Cres., Hamilton, Ont. L8S 4B8.

**JOHNSON, Albert Wesley,** O.C., M.A., M.P.A., Ph.D., LL.D.; educator; b. Insinger, Sask. 18 Oct. 1923; s. Rev. Thomas William and Louise Lillian (Croft) J.; e. Wilcox (Sask.) Secondary Sch.; Univ. of Sask. B.A.; Univ. of Toronto M.A.; Harvard Univ. M.P.A., Ph.D.; LL.D. (H.C.) Univ. of Regina 1977; LL.D. Univ. of Sask. 1978; LL.D. Mount Allison Univ. 1982; Queen's Univ. LL.D. 1992; m. Ruth Elinor, d. Rev. R.W. Hardy 27 June 1946; children: Andrew, Frances, Jane, Geoffrey; PROFESSOR EMERITUS, UNIV. OF TORONTO and ADVISOR ON PUBLIC POLICY AND ADMINISTRATION 1991– ; served with Candn. Army 1942; Depy. Prov. Treas. & Secy. to the Treas. Bd., Govt. of Sask. 1952–64; Asst. Depy. Min. Finance 1964–68; Econ. Advisor to P.M. on Constitution 1968–70; Secy. Treasury Bd. 1970–73; Depy. Min. of National Welfare 1973–75; Pres., C.B.C. 1975–82; Skelton-Clark Fellow, Queen's Univ. 1982–83; Prof. of Political Science, Univ. of Toronto 1983–89; Sr. Fellow, Candn. Centre for Management Development 1989–91; Internat. Consultant on public administration, Indonesia (1988 and 1991) and South Africa (1992–93); rec'd. Order of Canada; Gold Medal, Prof. Inst. of Pub. Service of Can.; Vanier Medal; Mem., Candn. Broadcasting League; mem., Candn. Pol. Science Assn. (Extve. Council 1963–64); Inst. of Pub. Adm. Can. (Pres. 1962–63); Dir. Nat. Film Bd. 1970–82; Nat. Arts Centre 1975–82; author: Task Force Report 'Federal Financing of Post-Secondary Education and Research in Canada' 1985; 'Social Policy in Canada: the Past as it Conditions the Present' 1987; 'Reflections on Administrative Reform in the Government of Canada 1962–1991' 1992; Task Force Report 'Saskatchewan Universities: Programs, Governance, and Goals' 1993; 'What is Public Management? An Autobiographical View' 1993; has contrib. articles to prof. publs.; United Church; Home: 1042 Castle Hill Cres., Ottawa, Ont. K2C 2A7.

**JOHNSON, Arthur Joseph Fynney,** M.B.E., C.D., Q.C., M.A., B.C.L.; b. Vancouver, B.C. 15 Feb. 1915; s. Joseph Fynney and Alice Gertrude (Jones) J.; e. Sir William Van Horne Pub. Sch. and John Oliver Secondary Sch., Vancouver, 1931; Univ. of B.C., B.A. 1935, M.A. 1936; Oxford Univ. (Rhodes Scholar for B.C. 1936), B.A. 1938, B.C.L. 1939, M.A. 1942; m. Catharina, d. late H. W. van der Ploeg, Holland, 10 Jan. 1946; children: Harold M. G., Nelie Catharina, Philip D. A.; COUNSEL RETIRED, DAVIS & COMPANY; read law with E. Slade, St. John's Coll., Oxford; called to Bar of B.C. 1939; cr. Q.C. 1969; Asst. to Supvr. for B.C. Foreign Exchange Control Bd., 1939–41; Second Secy., Dept. of External Affairs, Ottawa, 1946–47; served with Candn. Army Overseas 1941–46; Lt. Col. Commdg. B.C. Regt., Candn. Militia, 1951–54; mem. Vancouver Sch. Bd. 1964–68 (Chrmn. 1968); mem. Vancouver Police Commission 1970–74; Governor, St. George's Sch., Vancouver; mem., Candn. and Vancouver Bar Assns.; Un. Services Inst. Vancouver (Past Pres.); Psi Upsilon; Anglican; recreations: golf, hiking, gardening; Club: Shaughnessy Golf & Country; Home: #244–658 Leg-in-Boot Square, Vancouver, B.C. V5Z 4B3.

**JOHNSON, Bob R.,** M.Sc.; curator; b. Grimsby Beach, Ont. 25 Jan. 1948; s. David Ross and Anne (Reid) J.; e. Univ. of Toronto B.Sc. 1971; York Univ. M.Sc. 1985; m. Dianne d. Charles and Dorothy Devison 1952; one d. Cassia Danielle Devison; CURATOR OF AMPHIBIANS AND REPTILES METROPOLITAN TORONTO ZOO 1980– ; Keeper present Zoo 1973–77; Sr. Keeper Regent's Park Zoo London, Eng. 1977–79; author 'Amphibians and Reptiles in Metropolitan Toronto: Inventory and Guide' 1983; 'Familiar Amphibians and Reptiles of Ontario' 1989; Chair, IUCN Species Survival Comn. Declining Amphibian Populations Task Force; Chair, Am. Assn. Zool. Parks & Aquariums Amphibian Adv. Group; Co-ord. Puerto Rican Crested Toad Species Survival Plan; Co-chair, Eastern Massasauga Rattlesnake Recovery Team; IUCN Captive Breeding Specialist Group, Herpetol. Group; Ont. Herpetol. Soc. (Dir.); Soc. Study Amphibians & Reptiles; Toronto Field Naturalists; Fedn. Ont. Naturalists; recreation: natural hist.; Office: P.O. Box 280, West Hill, Ont. M1E 4R5.

**JOHNSON, Bradley R.,** B.F.A., M.L.A., R.C.A.; landscape architect; b. Toronto, Ont. 9 Oct. 1936; s. Robert Theodore and Ethel Isabel (Lisk) J.; e. Univ. of Ill. B.F.A. 1958 (Edward L. Ryerson Fellow); Harvard Univ. Grad. Sch. of Design, Master of Landscape Arch. 1963 (Charles Elliot Fellow); m. Mary d. Wallace Irl Johnston 28 Feb. 1959; two d. Lisa, Brooke; PRES., BRAD JOHNSON & ASSOC. LTD: 1982– ; joined Project Planning Associates Ltd. Toronto 1958–66, Chief Landscape Arch. 1965–66; Partner and Dir., Johnson Sustronk Weinstein and Assoc. 1966–82; planning and design of land devel., new communities, waterfront devel.; consultant to municipal, prov. and fed. agencies for numerous park and recreation studies and designs incl. the master plan for the Metro Toronto Zoo, urban design for various priv. and pub. proj.; numerous community and prof. activities incl. various arts and design award juries; mem. Adv. Bd., Univ. of Toronto Sch. of Arch. & Land. Arch.; Adjunct Prof. of Landscape Arch. Univ. of Toronto; Univ. of Guelph; Conway Sch.; Fellow and Pres. (1987–88) Candn. Soc. Landscape Archs.; mem. Ont. Assn. Landscape Archs.; Am. Soc. Landscape Archs.; Academician, Royal Candn. Academy of Arts; Office: Box 54, R.R. #1, Elgin, Ont. K0G 1E0.

**JOHNSON, Brian Arthur,** B.Comm., M.B.A., F.L.M.I.; insurance executive; b. Manitoba 20 Mar. 1944; s. Frank Halvor and Winnifred May (Pepper) J.; e. Univ. of Man., B.Comm. (Gold Medalist) 1965; Univ. of Penn., M.B.A. 1968; m. Sherril d. Miller and Marjorie Stewart 10 July 1965; children: Shannon, Chris, Cameron; PRES. & CHIEF EXTVE. OFFR., CROWN LIFE INSURANCE COMPANY 1993– ; Chrmn. & Pres., C.A.L. Investment Services, Inc.; CLICO Properties Ltd.; Crown America Holding Co.; Chrmn., Crown America Investment Management, Inc.; Crown America Financial Corp.; Crown Financial Management Ltd., U.K.; Dir., CILC Corp. (U.S.); Crown Life Investment Management, Inc.; Crown Life Insurance Co.; Western Surety Co.; Investment Analyst, Great-West Life Assurance (Winnipeg) 1965; worked in senior finance, investment and administration positions in both the service and manufacturing industries as well as a financial management consultant with Booz Allen & Hamilton; Sr. Vice-Pres., Finance, Investments and Internat. Banking, Continental Bank of Canada 1980–87; Sr. Vice-Pres. & Chief Financial Offr., Crown Life Insurance Co. 1987–91; Sr. Vice-Pres. & Chief Investment Offr. 1991–93; Clubs: Boulevard; Lambton Golf & Country; Kingsway Platform Tennis; Assiniboia Club; Wascana Golf and Country; Home: 3726 Currie Bay, Regina, Sask. S4S 7C7; Office: 1901 Scarth St., P.O. Box 827, Regina, Sask. S4P 3B1.

**JOHNSON, Brian Derek,** B.A.; writer; b. Cheadle Hume, Cheshire, England 24 June 1949; s. Theodore Neville and Lola Christine (Rosenvinge) J.; e. Norseman P.S.; Upper Canada Coll. 1966; Univ. of Toronto B.A. 1969; common law spouse: Marni d. Clyde and Olive Jackson; children: Casey Johnson; SENIOR WRITER, MACLEAN'S 1985– ; Editor, 'The Varsity' Univ. of Toronto 1969–70; Staff Writer, 'Toronto Telegram' 1971; 'The Gazette' Montreal 1971–74; freelance prod. & writer of CBC Radio documentaries 1975; On-Air Reporter, CBC 'Day Break' Montreal 1976; freelance weekly columnist, 'The Globe & Mail' Toronto 1977–78; performed & recorded as profl. musician (toured with bands in Canada & the U.S.) and composed & recorded soundtracks for film & theatre 1977–81; freelance magazine writing with feature articles pub. in 'Saturday Night,' 'Rolling Stone,' 'Maclean's,' 'Chatelaine,' 'Equinox,' 'Harrowsmith,' 'Quest,' 'City Woman,' 'Toronto Life,' 'The Globe & Mail'; Film Critic, Maclean's 1987– ; Co-host, CBC Newsworld's 'On the Arts' TV 1991– ; 2 nat. mag. awards for pol. & for travel 1983; 1 sci. jour. award from Candn. Sci. Writers Assn. 1986; author: 'Marzipan Lies' 1975 (poetry), 'Railway Country: Across Canada by Train' 1985; co-author: 'The XV Olympic Winter Games: The Official Commemorative Book' 1988; recreations: music, swimming, hockey, skiing; Home: 53 Seymour Ave., Toronto, Ont. M4J 2T3; Office: 777 Bay St., 7th Floor, Toronto, Ont. M5W 1A7.

**JOHNSON, Christopher David;** actor; b. Montréal, Qué. 29 Nov. 1955; s. David Merrill and Sheila Anne (Edgar) J.; e. Westmount High Sch. Montréal; Stanstead Coll. 1973; Univ. of N.B. 1974–77; Vancouver Playhouse Acting Sch. grad. 1981; m. Diane d. Frank P. and Marjorie D'Aquila 12 July 1987; children: Alexandra, Samuel; mem. acting co. Theatre New Brunswick 1978–79, Vancouver Playhouse 1979–81, Nat. Arts Centre 1981–83, Stratford Festival 1984; also performed Man. Theatre Centre, Theatre Calgary and others; played Charlie Marsh 'Red Serge' 1985 and Chuck Tchobanian 'Street Legal' 1986–91 CBC TV; mem. ACTRA; Candn. Actors' Equity Assn.; Acad. Candn. Cinema & TV; Performing Artists Nuclear Disarmament; recreations: fishing, baseball; Office: 208, 501 Yonge St., Toronto, Ont. M4Y 1Y4.

**JOHNSON, Conrad F.,** B.A.Sc., M.B.A., P.Eng.; tire company executive; b. Iroquois Falls, Ont. 24 Aug. 1935; s. Alexander and Irene (Larivière) J.; e. Ecole Polytechnique Univ. de Montréal B.A.Sc. Eng. 1962; Univ. of W. Ont. M.B.A. 1968; m. Marie d. Alphee Arsenault 7 Oct. 1932; children: Martin, Christine, Dominique; PRES., SERVICE DE PNEUS CTR. LTEE. 1987– ; VICE PRES. Sales Eastern Region GAZ MÉTROPOLITAIN INC. 1985– ; Vice-Pres., Gaz Inter-Cité (Québec) 1982– ; Dir., Bridgestone/Firestone Canada Inc.; La St. Maurice, Casualty & Liability Insur.; various engn. positions 1962–66; Assoc. Dir. Gen. Dept. Edn. Que. 1968–69; Extve. Vice Pres. Laiterie Laval Ltée; Pres. C.F. Johnson & Associates 1974–75; Pres. and Gen. Mgr. Montel Inc. 1975–82, Chrmn. 1982–83; Div. Chrmn. Fund Raising Campaign Centraide Qué.; Pres. C. of C. and Ind. Que.-Metro 1980–81; Chrmn. Marketing Mgmt. Ctte., Candn. Gas Assn. 1984–85; Chrmn., MBA Assn. Prov. Que. 1982–83; mem. Engn. Inst. Can.; Que. Order Engrs. 1985; Chrmn. Eye Sickness Found. (Formoeil); Club: Quebec Garnison; Home: 1652 Place De Bruyère, Sainte-Foy Qué.; Office: 128, av. St-Sacrement, Québec, Qué. G1N 3X6.

**JOHNSON, Daniel,** B.A., LL.M., Ph.D., M.B.A.; financial executive; politician; b. Montreal, Que. 24 Dec. 1944; s. Daniel and Reine (Gagne) J.; e. Univ. of Montréal B.A. 1963, LL.L. 1966; Univ. of London (UK) LL.M. 1968, Ph.D. 1971; Harvard Bus. Sch. M.B.A. 1973; children: Philippe, Stephanie; PRIME MINISTER OF QUÉBEC 1994– ; Corp. Sec., Power Corp. of Can. 1973–78; Vice-Pres. & Sec. 1978–81; Mem., Nat. Assembly of Que. for Vaudreuil 1981– ; Min. of Industry & Comm. 1985–88; Chrmn., Treasury Bd. of Qué. 1988–94; Office: Bldg. J, 3rd Floor, 885 Grande-Allée East, Quebec, Qué. G1A 1A2.

**JOHNSON, David Alan,** B.Sc.; information security officer; b. Newcastle, England 22 July 1946; s. Douglas and Eleanor Margaret (Spawls) J.; e. McMaster Univ. B.Sc. 1967; m. Eleanor d. Arthur and Marion Norrie 21 June 1969; children: Pamela, Gregory; SUPERVISOR, SECURITY & ACCESS SERVICES, STELCO INC.; 26 years active & continuous involvement in Information Systems field; recognized authority on computer security issues & practices; leading proponent of the need for Candn. orgns. to develop plans for the continuity of critical bus. functions in the event of disaster; public engagements incl. Chair, Contingency Planning Expo '93; Co-Chair, 3rd & 4th Annual N. Am. Information System Security Symp.; Guest Speaker, 5th Annual Candn. Computer Security Symp.; System Software Conf. '93 and others; Mem., Planning Ctte., 4th World Conf. on Disaster Mngt.; Pres., Toronto Chapter, Disaster Recovery Information Exchange 1991– ; Toronto Top Secret Users 1992– ; interviews pub. Globe and Mail & Datapro Internat. Candn. Newsletter; recreations: reading, travel; Home: 192 Mohawk Rd., Ancaster, Ont. L9G 2W9; Office: Stelco Tower, P.O. Box 2030, Hamilton, Ont. L8N 3T1.

**JOHNSON, F. Ross,** O.C., B.Com., M.B.A.; industrial executive; b. Winnipeg, Man. 13 Dec. 1931; s. Frederick Hamilton and Caroline (Green) J.; e. Univ. of Man., B.Com. 1952; Univ. of Toronto, M.Com. 1956, M.B.A.; LL.D. (Hon.) Univ. St. Francis Xavier (Antigonish N.S.) 1978; LL.D. (Hon.) Memorial Univ. of Nfld. 1980; LL.D. (Hon.) Barry Univ. (Miami Shores, Fla.) 1987; two s. Bruce, Neil; m. 2ndly Laurie Ann; CHRMN. & C.E.O., RJM GROUP, INC. (Atlanta, Georgia) a private internat. mgmt. & advisory orgn. 1989– ; Pres., C.E.O. & Dir., RJR Nabisco, Inc. (Atlanta, GA) 1985–89, Chrmn., Extve. Ctte. 1987–89; Dir., National Service Industries (Georgia); American Express (New York); Power Corp. of Canada (Montreal); Archer Daniels Midland (Decatur, IL); Black & McDonald (Toronto); U.S. Golf Assn. Found.; began at Canadian General Electric; joined T. Eaton Co. as Vice Pres., Merchandising 1964; Extve. Vice Pres. & C.O.O., GSW Ltd.; Pres. & C.E.O., Standard Brands Ltd., Can. 1971; Chrmn. & C.E.O., Standard Brands Inc. 1976; Pres. & C.O.O. & Chrmn., Extve. Ctte., Nabisco Brands (upon the merger of Standard Brands and Nabisco, Inc.) 1981; Vice Chrmn. & C.E.O. 1984; Chrmn., The Economic Club of New York 1983–86; N.Y. Chapter, Multiple Sclerosis Soc. 1978–86; Vice

Chrmn., Extve. Counc., Found. of the Commemoration for the Constitution (Bicentennial); Clubs: Atlanta Country (GA), The Brook, The Links, Blind Brook, Deepdale (N.Y.); Jupiter Hills (Fla.), Country Club of the Rockies (CO); recreations: golf, skiing, tennis; Home: 4385 Whitewater Creek Rd., Atlanta, GA 30327; Offices: RJM Group, 200 Galleria Pkwy., Ste. 970, Atlanta, GA 30339.

**JOHNSON, Frank,** B.Sc., M.A.Sc., Ph.D., C.Eng., P.Eng., F.I.E.E.; medical engineer, educator, industrialist; b. Nuneaton, U.K. 7 Aug. 1947; s. Albert Edward and Irene Winifred (Tweed) J.; e. King Edward VI Grammar Sch.; Univ. of Salford B.Sc. 1968; Univ. of Toronto M.A.Sc. 1970, Ph.D. 1973; m. Sharon Dawn d. Ray and Gladys Ostrander 24 Sept. 1971; children: Gregory, Kara-Lee; DIRECTOR, INSTITUTE OF MEDICAL ENGINEERING, UNIV. OF OTTAWA 1991– ; Medical Physicist Liverpool 1973–75; Sr. Medical Physicist 1975; Sr. Physicist, Queens Med. Ctr. 1975–79; Lectr. in Bioengineering, Med. Sch., Nottingham 1979–82; Rsch. Mgr., Oxford Medical Systems 1983–84; Technical Mgr. 1984–85; R&D Mgr., Richard Brancker Rsch. Ltd. Ottawa 1986–89; Elect. Eng. Coord., Univ. of Ottawa Heart Inst., EVAD Project 1989–91; Pres., Ottawa Instrumentation Ltd. 1991– ; Dir., RBR Ltd. 1988–89; Founding Dir., Biological Engr. Soc. U.K. (Hon. Treas. 1981–84); Fellow, Inst. of Electrical Engrs.; Mem., A.P.E.O.; C.M.B.E.S.; People's Warden, Anglican Ch. of the Ascension (Ottawa); author: 'Principles of Cooking' 2nd ed. 1992; co-editor: 'Theoretical and Applied Aspects of Eye Movement Research' 1984; author/co-author of num. sci. papers & book chapters; recreations: music, kayaking, photography; Address: 169 Fifth Ave., Ottawa, Ont. K1S 2M8.

**JOHNSON, Hon. Frederick William,** O.C., S.O.M., Q.C., B.A., LL.B.; b. Sedgley, Staffordshire, Eng. 13 Feb. 1917; s. Edwin Priestley and Laura (Caddick) J.; e. Univ. of Sask., B.A. 1947, LL.B. 1949; m. Joyce Marilyn d. William Laing, Stockholm, Sask. 30 July 1949; children: William Frederick, Dr. Royce Laing Caddick, Sheila Frederika; Lieut. Gov. of Sask. 1983–88; called to Bar of Sask. 1950; cr. Q.C. 1963; law practice Johnson, Bayda, Trudelle & Beke; apptd. Justice, Court of Queen's Bench Sask. 1965; apptd. Chief Justice there 1977; served with RCA 1941–46 UK and W. Europe; Hon. Colonel 10th Field Reg't. R.C.A.; apptd. Officer of Order of Canada 1990; recipient, Sask. Order of Merit 1991; Trustee Regina Pub. Sch. Bd. 1956–60; Chrmn. Royal Comn. on Govt. Adm. (Sask.) 1964–65; Bencher, Law Soc. Sask. 1960–65; United Church; Clubs: Assiniboia; Royal United Services Inst.; Home: 121 Leopold Cres., Regina, Sask. S4T 6N5.

**JOHNSON, The Hon. George,** B.Sc., M.D., LL.D.; b. Winnipeg, Man. 18 Nov. 1920; s. Jonas George and Laufey J.; e. Univ. of Man. B.Sc. 1947, M.D. 1950; m. Doris d. August and Gudrun Blondal 31 Dec. 1943; children: Janis, Jennifer, Daniel, Jon, Joann, Gillian; LT. GOV. OF MAN. 1986– ; med. practice Gimli, Man. 1950–58, Winnipeg 1970–78; el. M.L.A. Man. 1958–69, Min. of Health & Pub. Welfare 1958–61, Min. of Health 1961–63, Min. of Edn. 1963–68, Min. of Health & Social Devel. 1968–69; Chief Med. Cons. Dept. Health & Community Services Man. 1979; Acting Dep. Min. of Health and Vice Chrmn. Man. Health Services Comn. 1979–81; Med. Cons. to Min. of Health, Chrmn. Standing Ctte. Med. Manpower 1981–86; served with Candn. Armed Forces 1941–45, rank Lt.(N) RCNVR; Honorary Captain (N) HMCS Chippawa (88); Past Pres. 'Betel' (Icelandic) Home Found.; Chrmn. Med. Adv. Ctte. Selkirk and Gimli Betel Homes; Past mem. Adv. Bd. St. Benedict's Priory Middlechurch, Man.; Past Pres. Gimli C. of C.; Hon. Life mem. Man. Med. Assn.; Winnipeg Med. Soc.; Man. Teachers Soc.; Gimli Kinsmen; Life mem. Candn. Med. Protective Assn.; Fellow, Coll. Family Phys. Can.; mem. Council Coll. Phys. & Surgs. Man. 1974–78; Lutheran; recreations: jogging, golf, fishing, reading; Address: Unit 9C, 2366 Portage Ave., Winnipeg, Man. R3J 0N4.

**JOHNSON, Gordon Edward,** B.Sc.Phm., M.A., Ph.D.; educator; b. Welland, Ont. 21 Sept. 1934; s. Edward and Dorothy (Williams) J.; e. Univ. of Toronto B.Sc.Phm. 1957, M.A. 1959, Ph.D. 1961; m. Mary-Jane Graham d. Graham Bowles, Toronto, Ont. 20 Sept. 1958; children: Dorothy, Ian, Warren, Louise, Edward, Rebecca; PROF. DEPT. OF PHARMACOLOGY UNIV. OF SASK. 1986– ; Dir., Compliance, Patented Medicine Prices Review Bd., Govt. of Canada 1990–91; Dir., Bureau of Human Prescription Drugs, Health and Welfare, Canada 1988–90; Asst. Prof. Univ. of Toronto 1963, Assoc. Prof. 1966, Prof. 1971–73; Prof. and Head of Pharmacol. Univ. of Sask. 1973–86; Visiting Prof. Med. Research Council Can., Drug Metabolism Labs. CIBA Ltd. Basel, Switzerland 1968–69; author: 'Essentials of Drug Therapy' 1991; 'PDQ Pharmacology' 1988, 'Pharmacology and the Nursing Process' 1983, 1987 and 1992, 'Blue Book of Pharmacologic Therapeutics' 1985, 'Manual de Terapeutic Farmacolgica' as well as over 50 scient. articles; mem. Pharmacol. Soc. Can.; Am. Soc. Pharmacol. & Exper. Therapeutics; Am. Soc. Clin. Pharmacol. Therapeutics; Candn. Soc. Clin. Pharmacol.; Candn. Hypertension Soc.; Lambda Chi Alpha; Protestant; recreations: music; farming; Home: R.R. 5, Box 166, Saskatoon, Sask. S7K 3J8; Office: Univ. of Sask., Saskatoon, Sask. S7N 0W0.

**JOHNSON, Irene,** M.A.; Canadian public service; b. Winnipeg, Man. 5 March 1925; d. Charles and Irène Alyea (LaBerge) Flint; e. Univ. of Toronto, B.A. (Law) 1947, M.A. (Econ.) 1949; London Sch. of Econ., postgrad studies in Econ. 1949–51; m. Geoffrey Phipps Johnson, Dec. 1953, div. 1973; one s., Blaine; Consultant, Economics, Public Administration & Human Resource Development; Lectr., Sch. of Business Adm., Univ. of W. Ont., 1952–54; Econ., N.S. Dept. Trade & Indust., Halifax, 1956–62; Econ. & Research Br., Dept. of Labour, Ottawa, 1962–64; Econ., Area Devel. Agency, Dept. of Indust., 1964–67; Finance Officer, Econ. Devel. Div., Dept. of Finance, 1967–69; Chief, Analysis & Devel. Sec., Dom. Bureau of Stat., 1969–71; Group Chief, Manpower Group, Social & Cultural Div., Treas. Bd., 1971; Commn., Pub. Service Comn. of Can., 1971–76; Ex: Dir., Employment Training, Can. Employment & Immig. Comn., 1976–78; Cdn. High Commissioner, Wellington, N.Z., Dept. External Affairs with Accreditation to Fiji, Western Samoa, Tonga, Kiribati and Tuvalu 1978–81; Asst. Dep. Min., Personnel & Mmgt. Practices, Energy, Mines and Resources Can. 1981–83; Consul Gen. of Canada at Philadelphia, U.S.A., Dept. of External Affairs 1983–86; Nat. Women's Director, Liberal Party of Can. 1986–87; Economic Cons., own account 1988– ; N.V.R. since 1952, rank Sub-Lt.; former Dir., Civil Service Recreational Assn.; mem. Candn. Inst. Internat. Affairs (Chrmn. 1967–68); Candn. Econ. Assn.; Inst. of Pub. Adm. of Canada; Internat. Personnel Mang. Assn.; Am. Economic Assn; Civil Service Co-op. Credit Soc. (Mem. of Exec. 1978–); Board of Gov. Carleton Univ. (1976–78, 1982–83); Mem. Bd. of Dirs., Candn. Extve. Services Orgn. 1988–94; recreations: theatre, opera, music, reading, skiing, cycling, trekking, wilderness canoeing; Home: 205 Irving Pl., Ottawa, Ont. K1Y 1Z7.

**JOHNSON, John Edward (Ted);** business executive; lawyer; b. London, Ont. 1 Feb. 1946; s. George Herbert and Mary Ewing (Code) J.; e. Univ. of W. Ont., B.A. (Hons.) 1968; Inst. d'études pol. de Paris, C.d'E.P. 1971; Queen's Univ., LL.B. 1976; m. Sharon d. William E. and Evelyn Vance, 20 Sept. 1985; VICE PRES., GEN. COUNSEL & SECY., POWER CORPORATION OF CANADA 1985– ; Sp. Asst., Federal Min. of Justice 1976–78; called to Bar 1978; Sp. Asst., Fed. Min. of Finance 1978–79; Tax Counsel, Dept. of Justice 1979–80; Extve. Asst. to Prime Minister of Canada 1980–84; Lawyer, Lang, Michener, Cranston, Farquharson and Wright 1984–85; Vice Pres., Gen. Counsel & Secy., Power Financial Corp. 1985– ; Mem. Bd. of Dirs., Montreal Symphony Orchestra; National Theatre Sch. of Can.; Anglican; Liberal; recreations: canoeing, skiing; Clubs: University; Montreal Racket; Five Lakes; Home: 621 Murray Hill, Westmount, Que. H3Y 2W7; Office: 751 Square Victoria, Montreal, Que. H2Y 2J3.

**JOHNSON, Maj.-Gen. Leonard Verne,** C.D.; freelance writer and lecturer; b. Ridgedale, Sask. 12 Aug. 1929; s. Joseph and Vera (Frazer) J.; e. Luther Coll. Regina 1944–45; The Pas Coll. Inst. 1945–46; U.S. Armed Forces Staff Coll. Norfolk, Va. 1966; Nat. Defence Coll. Can. 1972–73; Univ. of Man. 2 yrs. B.A. course; m. Shirley d. Reginald and Anna Hutcherson 11 Sept. 1954; children: Julianne, Ross, Raymond, Paula; joined RCAF pilot training 1950–51; Transport Pilot - Instr. Pilot Edmonton, Trenton, Ottawa 1951–62; Staff Offr., Sqdn. Commdr., Base Commdr. Trenton, Ottawa & Edmonton 1962–74; Commdr. Training Command Winnipeg and Candn. Forces Training System Trenton 1974–78; Assoc. Asst. Depy. Min. (Policy) and Chief of Evaluation 1978–80; Commandant, Nat. Defence Coll. Kingston 1980–84; Dir. Energy Probe Rsch. Found.; mem. Veterans Against Nuclear Arms; Gens. for Peace & Disarmament; Chair, Candn. Pugwash Group; author: 'A General for Peace' 1987; Chair, Project Ploughshares; Address: R.R. 2, Westport, Ont. K0G 1X0.

**JOHNSON, Neil Alexander,** B.Comm., Ph.D.; investment executive; b. London, Ont. 17 July 1948; s. Leonard Naismith and Josephine (DeVries) J.; e. McGill Univ. B.Comm. (Hons.) 1970; Johns Hopkins Univ. Ph.D. 1978; m. Gail M. d. Preston R. and Marie Cook 9 June 1975; children: Alexander J.C., L. Gregory C.; CHIEF ECONOMIST & PORTFOLIO STRATEGIST, NESBITT THOMSON 1980– ; Asst. Prof., Tehran, Iran 1975–76; Senior Economist, DRI 1976–80; Dir., Nesbitt Thomson Inc.; club: Granite; Home: 116 Lascelles Blvd., Toronto, Ont. M5P 2E4; Office: 150 King St. W., Toronto, Ont. M5H 3W2.

**JOHNSON, Norm K.,** B.Comm.; business executive; b. Winnipeg, Man. 1 May 1950; s. Norman O. and Margaret J. (Fogg) J.; e. Univ. of Calgary B.Comm. 1973; m. Linda C. d. Lois and Charlie Roberts 17 Jan. 1970; children: Shauna Rae, Trevor Alon; VICE-CHRMN. & C.E.O., JOSS ENERGY LTD.; Pres. & Chief Executive Officer, Devstar Properties Ltd.; Home: 12823 Canso Place S.W., Calgary, Alta. T2W 3A7; Office: #2350, 444 – 5th Ave. S.W., Calgary, Alta. T2P 2T8.

**JOHNSON, Patrick Trench,** M.A.; retired investment executive; b. Assam, India 4 Apr. 1926; s. Francis Richard, D.F.C., and Phyllis Mary (Wilkinson) J.; e. Oxford Univ. B.A. 1951, M.A. 1956; m. Eleanor Jean d. Andrew D. and Laura McCain 21 Aug. 1954; children: Patrick Trench Jr., Derek Wallace McCain; Pres., Candn. Securities Inst. 1981–90; Dean of Boys, Graham Eckes Sch. 1951–53; Master, Rossall Sch. 1953–58; Principal, Upper Canada Coll. 1965–75; Asst. Gen. Mgr., The Bank of Nova Scotia 1975–81; served as Capt. and Adjutant, 9th Gurkha Rifles, Indian Army 1944–48; Sec.-Treas. Candn. Headmasters' Assn. 1967–75; Gen. Mgr. Spencer Hall Found. 1976–81; Bd. Chrmn. The Terry Fox Humanitarian Award Prog.; Bd., National Ballet Sch.; Mem. Bd., Variety Village; recreations: theatre, tennis, walking, bridge; Home: 116 Dunvegan Rd., Toronto, Ont. M4V 2R1.

**JOHNSON, Peter E.,** B.A., LL.B., Q.C.; lawyer; b. Vancouver, B.C. 20 Aug. 1937; s. Robert A.C. and Josephine (Henigman) J.; e. Univ. of Sask. B.A. 1959, LL.B. 1962; m. Vicky d. Victor and Audrey Thomas 1965; children: David, Patricia, Jennifer; CHIEF LEGISLATIVE COUNSEL, JUSTICE (CANADA) 1987– ; law articles & private practice, Walker, Agnew 1962–65; Municipal Solicitor, Dept. of Municipal Affairs, Govt. of Sask. 1965–67; Asst. Legis. Counsel 1967–72; Legal Advisor, Privy Council Office Section, Justice Canada 1972–76; Dir. 1976–78; Legislative Drafter 1978–86; Home: 68 Amberwood Cr., Nepean, Ont.; Office: 222 Queen St., Ottawa, Ont. K1A 0H8.

**JOHNSON, Hon. Pierre Marc,** B.A., LL.L., M.D.; former provincial premier; b. Montreal, Qué. 5 July 1946; s. late Daniel (Prime Min. of Qué. 1966–68) and Reine (Gagné) J.; e. Coll. Jean-Brébeuf Montréal B.A. 1967; Univ. de Montréal LL.L. 1970; Univ. de Sherbrooke M.D. 1975; m. Marie-Louise d. Douglas Parent 30 June 1973; children: Marc Olivier, Marie-Claude; called to Bar of Qué. 1971; admitted Qué. Coll. of Phys. & Surgs. 1976; mem. Bd. and various comtes. Oxfam Can. and Oxfam Qué. 1969–76; el. M.N.A. for Anjou 1976–87; mem. Nat. Extve. Council Parti québécois 1977–79; Min. of Labour and Manpower 1977–80; Min. of Consumer Affairs, Cooperatives and Financial Institutions 1980–81; Min. of Social Affairs, Qué. 1981–84; Min. of Justice, Attorney General and Min. Resp. for Canadian Intergovernemental Affairs 1984–85; Pres., Parti québécois 1985–87; Premier of Québec, Oct. 1985–Dec. 1985; Leader of Official Opposition, Qué. National Assembly 1985–87; Prof. of Law, McGill Univ.; Lectr., various univs.; Practice of law with Guy & Gilbert Law Offices; Dir. of Environment's Program, McGill Center for Medicine, Ethics and Law; Vice-Chair, National Round Table on Environment and Energy; Mem. of Bd., Internat. Inst. on Sustainable Development (Winnipeg); mem. Bd. of Dirs., UNIMEDIA (Hollinger, Québec); mem. Bd. S.N.C.; Special Advisor to U.N. Sec. Gen. of Conf. on Environment and Development (Rio '92); R. Catholic; recreations: swimming, ski, music; Home: Outremont, Qué.; Office: 770 Sherbrooke St. W., Suite 2300, Montréal, Qué. H3A 1G1.

**JOHNSON, (James) Richard,** B.B.A.; advanced financial planner; b. Saint John, N.B. 1 Apr. 1956; s. late Terence Joseph and Mary Eileen (Stanton) J.; e. St. Malachy's Meml. High Sch. Saint John 1974; St. Francis Xavier Univ. Antigonish B.B.A. 1977; m. Ginette d. Laurier and Carmen Levesque 25 Oct. 1980; two s.: Denis Richard, Philip Andre; INVESTORS GROUP; joined J.K. Associates Ltd. 1973–81, Mgr. Service; Lantic Sugar 1981–85, Personnel Supr. present co. 1985; Pres. P. Cons. Party N.B. 1988–89, Vice Pres. Finance Saint John P. Cons. Assn. (Federal); Pres. Saint John Chapter St. Francis Xavier Alumni Assn. 1987–91; Dir., St. Francis Xavier Alumni Bd. 1992– ; mem. Saint John

Bd. Trade; Volunteer Saint John Un. Way; R. Catholic; recreation: downhill skiing; Home: 24 Clarwood Dr., Rothesay, N.B. E2E 4K2; Office: 50 Crown St., Saint John, N.B. E2L 2X6.

**JOHNSON, Richard Golding,** B.A., LL.B.; retired consultant; b. Calgary, Alta. 3 Mar. 1913; s. Percy Wilfrid and Lottie May (Golding) J.; e. Pub. Schs., Calgary, Alta.; Strathcona High Sch., Edmonton, Alta., Univ. of Alberta, B.A. 1933; LL.B. 1935; m. Emily Irene, d. C. W. Loney, Owen Sound, Ont., 1940; has one s., Robert Golding; admitted to the Bar of Alta., 1936; articled at law and practised with Milner, Steer & Co., Edmonton, Alta., 1935–37; Estates Offr., London & Western Trusts Co. Ltd., Toronto, and Trusts Offr. at the Co's. H.O., London, Ont., 1937–40; Solr., Legal Br., Dept. of Mun. & Supply, 1940–41; Contracts Offr., Asst. Dir. and Dir., Defence Projects Br., Dept. of Mun. & Supply, 1941–44; Secty. Dept of Reconstruction and Supply, 1944–45; Gen. Mgr., Candn. Construction Assn., 1945–55; loaned to Candn. Govt. as Constr. Consultant, Candn. Commercial Corpn., Oct. 1950; Pres. and Gen. Mgr., Defence Construction (1951) Ltd. (Crown Co.) 1950–63 (on loan from Candn. Construction Assn., 1950–55); Extve. Vice-pres., Canadn Inst. of Steel Construction, 1963–66; Pres. of C.I.S.C., 1966–78; Hon. Life Mem., Candn. Construction Assn.; Hon Mem., Engrg. Inst. of Can.; recreations: golf, swimming; Home: R.R. 3, Wiarton, Ont. N0H 2T0.

**JOHNSON, S. Ross,** B.Com., CLU.; insurance executive; b. Calgary, Alta., 18 Apl. 1929; s. Stanley and Margaret (Fisher) J.; e. Univ. of B.C. B.Com. 1952; Chartered Life Underwriter designation (CLU) 1959; m. Muriel (Fairley) 15 July 1953; children: Susan Kim, Judy Lynn, Grant Ross, Warren Scott; PRESIDENT, THE PRUDENTIAL INSURANCE COMPANY OF AMERICA, CANADIAN OPERATIONS; Pres. & Dir., Industrial Trust Co.; Pres. & Dir., Prudential Growth Fund of Can. Ltd.; Prudential Income Fund of Can.; Prudential Dividend Fund of Can.; Prudential Money Market Fund of Can.; Prudential Precious Metals Fund of Can.; Prudential Natural Resource Fund of Can.; Prudential Diversified Investment Fund of Can.; Chrmn. & Dir., Prudential of Am. General Insur. Co. (Canada); HSG Health Systems Group Ltd.; PIC Realty Can. Ltd.; Dir., Prudential Fund Management Ltd. (PFM); New York Life 1952–69, joined as agent in Vancouver, B.C. and held various positions of increasing responsibility; Resident Vice Pres. of Canada, New York Life 1969–79; Extve. Vice Pres., National Life of Canada 1979–85; Pres. & C.E.O., National Life of Can. 1985–89; Pres. & Founder, People Count management consulting firm, 1989–90; Dir., Addiction Prevention Fund; Depy. Chrmn., 1990 Metro Toronto United Way Campaign; mem. Bd. of Adv., Stokes Seeds 1989; Honours: Univ. of B.C. Alumnus of the Year 1974; Canada Award of Business Excellence 1988; motivational speaker across Canada and the U.S.; recreations: boating; model building; Clubs: Univ. Club of Toronto; Home: Oakville, Ont.; Office: 200 Consilium Place, Scarborough, Ont. M1H 3E6.

**JOHNSON, Steven F.;** oil and gas executive; b. Winnipeg, Man. 27 April 1956; s. Norman Olafur and Margaret Joyce (Fogg) J.; e. Stratchcona Tweedsmuir H.S.; Univ. of Calgary 2.5 yrs.; m. Gail d. Jack and Barb Campbell 14 Aug. 1982; children: Ryan, Ashley; PRES. & CHIEF OPERATING OFFICER, JOSS ENERGY LTD. 1983– ; Sales Rep., Atco Structures 1979–80; Industrial Sales Rep. 1981–82; Calgary Dist. Mgr. 1982; Contracts Mgr., Candn. Operations, Spartan Drilling 1982–83; Dir., Devstar Properties Ltd. (21% owner); recreations: bird hunting, skiing; clubs: Silver Springs Golf, Spruce Creek Uplands; Home: 12716 Canso Place S.W., Calgary, Alta. T2W 3A8; Office: 2350, 444 – 5 Ave. S.W., Calgary, Alta. T2P 2T8.

**JOHNSON, Susan Maureen,** M.A., Ed.D.; educator; psychologist; b. Chatham, Eng. 19 Dec. 1947; d. Arthur and Winifred (Wright) Driver; e. Univ. of Hull B.A. 1968; Univ. of B.C., M.A. 1980, Ed.D. 1984; m. John s. Harry and Elma Douglas 1 Oct. 1988; children: Timothy Douglas, Emma Douglas; ASSOC. PROF. OF PSYCHOL. AND PSYCHIATRY UNIV. OF OTTAWA 1989– ; reg'd psychol. 1985; Ednl. Co-ordinator The Maples Centre for Emotionally Disturbed Adolscents, B.C. 1975–80; Asst. Prof. of Psychol. present Univ. 1984–88, Co-ordinator of Training, Centre Psychol. Services; Dir., Marital & Family Clinic Civic Hosp. Ottawa; co-author 'Emotionally Focused Therapy for Couples' 1988; numerous articles; superviser, Am. Assn. Marital & Family Therapy; Home: 33 Mary Dr., Gloucester, Ont. K1G 3N3; Office: 11 Marie Curie, Ottawa, Ont. K1N 9A4.

**JOHNSON, Terence L.,** BFA, MFA;; artist; educator; b. Baltimore, Md. 27 Feb. 1940; s. Ernest A. and Barbara (Kanouse) J.; e. Rhode Isl. Sch. of Design, BFA 1962; Ohio Univ., post-grad. study; Univ. of Washington, MFA 1964; m. Joyce d. Willis and Josephine Leonard 1960; children: Gregory Scot, Ahna Sarah; INSTR., EMILY CARR COLL. OF ART & DESIGN 1990– ; Dir. of Fine Art 1984–88, & Co-Princ. 1985–86; num. solo exhibits incl.: S. Alta. Art Gall., Confederation Art Gall., Univ. of Lethbridge Gall., Dalhousie Univ. Art Gall., Memorial Univ. Art Gall. 1982; Mendel Art Gall., Mercer Union 1983; Art Gall. of W. Australia, Peter Whyte Gall. 1985; Equinox Gall., Vancouver 1988, '89, '92; Mira Godard Gall., Toronto 1990; Vancouver Art Gall. 1992; Pub. Collections incl.: Nat. Gall. of Can., Can. Counc. Art Bank, Glenbow Mus., Univ. of Lethbridge, Dalhousie Univ., Vancouver Art Gall.; Instr., Univ. of Penn. 1962–64; Asst. Prof., Moore Coll. of Art 1964–65; Assoc. Prof., Univ. of Kentucky 1965–71; Head, Sculpture Dept. 1971–80 & Chair, Studio Div., 1977–80 N.S. Coll. of Art & Design 1971–80; Head, Art Studio, Banff Sch. of Fine Arts 1980–84; Assoc. Dean, Studio Div., Emily Carr Coll. of Art & Design 1988–90, Faculty E.C.C.A.D. 1991– ; Can. Counc. 'A' Grant 1991; recreation: sailing; Home: 1015 Ironwork Psq., Vancouver, B.C. V6H 3R4; Office: 1399 Johnston St., Vancouver, B.C. V6H 3R9.

**JOHNSON, William Denis Hertel,** C.M., L.Ph., M.A.; journalist; b. Kapuskasing, Ont. 23 Apr. 1931; s. William Martin and Eglantine (Levert) J.; e. Coll. Jean de Brébeuf 1947; Loyola Coll. B.A. 1949; Regis Coll. L.Ph. 1956; Univ. de Montréal M.A. 1958; entered the Soc. of Jesus 1949, withdrew 1959; Univ. of Toronto; Univ. of Cal. Berkeley; m. Joan Carol d. Earl and Orlu Sergeant 21 Mar. 1964 (div. 1981); children: Marc Laurier, Susanna Kate; m. Carol Jane Dutcher Bream d. Russell and Helen Dutcher 28th Sept. 1991; OTTAWA COLUMNIST, THE GAZETTE 1987– ; Reporter, The Globe and Mail 1967–87, Washington Bureau Chief 1984–87; Lectr. in Sociol. Univ. of Man. 1961–62, Univ. of Toronto 1964–67; Correspondent, The Globe and Mail, Montreal 1971–72, Parlty. Corr. Ottawa 1973–76, Corr. Nat. Assembly Que. 1977–81; Nat. Columnist, The Globe and Mail 1978–84; elected Financial Secy. National Press Club, Washington, D.C. Dec. 1985; author: 'Anglophobie Made in Quebec' (book:essay) 1991; co-author 'Toute ma vérité: Les confessions de l'agent SAT 945–171' memoirs 1981; co-author and translator 'The Informer: Confessions of an Ex-Terrorist' 1982; awarded Order of Canada 1982; awarded National Newspaper Award for Columns 1987; Certificate of Merit, National Newspaper Awards 1988, 1990; Home: 257 Jacques-Cartier St., Gatineau, Que. J8T 2W3; Office: Rm. 505, 151 Sparks St., Ottawa, Ont. K1P 5E3.

**JOHNSON, William McAllister,** M.A., M.F.A., Ph.D., F.R.S.C.; educator; art historian; b. Columbia, Mo. 24 Oct. 1939; s. Durfee McAllister and Fern Dolores (Hammer) J.; e. Univ. of Mo. B.A. 1960, M.A. 1962; Princeton Univ. M.F.A. 1964, Ph.D. 1965; PROF. OF FINE ART GRAD. DEPT. HIST. OF ART, UNIV. OF TORONTO 1977– , Lectr. 1965, Asst. Prof. 1967, Assoc. Prof. 1969; mem. Prints & Drawings Comte. Art Gallery of Ont. 1977– ; Adv. Comte. to Dir. McMichael Candn. Collection 1982–86; Fulbright Fellow 1960–61; Guggenheim Fellow 1978–79; Prix Bernier Académie des Beaux-Arts, Institut de France 1982; author 'French Lithography: The Restoration Salons 1817–1824' 1977; 'French Royal Academy of Painting and Sculpture: Engraved Reception Pieces 1673–1789' 1982; 'Art History: Its Use and Abuse' 1988; 'Hugues-Adrien Joly. Lettres à Karl-Heinrich von Heinecken 1772–1789' 1988; co-author 'Estienne Jodelle. Le Recueil des Inscriptions 1558' 1972; 'The Paris Entries of Charles IX and Elisabeth of Austria 1571' 1974; 'The Royal Tour of Charles IX and Catherine de' Medici 1564–1566' 1979; ed. 'Ontario Association of Art Galleries Art Gallery Handbook' 1982; 'RACAR (Revue d'art canadienne/Canadian Art Review)' 1977–85; Société 'Le Vieux Papier'; mem. Am. Soc. for Eighteenth Century Studies; Renaissance Soc. Am.; Société de l'Histoire de l'Art français; Phi Beta Kappa; Office: Toronto, Ont. M5S 1A1.

**JOHNSTON, Alexandra Ferguson,** M.A., Ph.D., LL.D., D.D.; educator; b. Indianapolis, Ind. 19 July 1939; d. Geoffrey Deane and Alexandra Ferguson (Sherwood) J.; e. Brantford (Ont.) Coll. Inst. & Vocational Sch. 1957; Univ. of Toronto B.A. 1961 (Victoria Coll.), M.A. 1962, Ph.D. 1964; PROF. OF ENGLISH, VICTORIA COLL., UNIV. OF TORONTO 1978– ; Asst. Prof. of Eng. Queen's Univ. 1964–67; Asst. Prof. present Coll. 1967, Assoc. Prof. 1970, Principal 1981–91; mem. Adv. Bd., Eng. Drama, Art & Music; Adv. Comte., Index of Middle Eng. Prose; Pres., Internat. Soc. for Medieval Theatre 1989–92 (Secy. 1986–89); Pres., Medieval and Renaissance Drama Soc., Modern Language Assoc. of Am. 1989– ; Dir., Records of Early Eng. Drama 1976– ; author 'The York Records, Records of Early English Drama' 2 vols. 1979; Mem. Unit II 'Life Education and Mission' World Council of Churches 1992– ; Chrmn. Bd. of Ministry Presb. Ch. in Can. 1981–84; Elder, Rosedale Presb. Ch. 1973; LL.D. Queen's Univ. 1984; D.D. The Presbyterian Coll., Montreal 1990; Home: 39 Elgin Ave., Toronto, Ont. M5R 1G5; Office: 150 Charles St. W., Toronto, Ont. M5S 1K9.

**JOHNSTON, Archibald Frederick,** B.Com.; executive; b. Peter's Rd., P.E.I. 9 March 1919; s. Frederick William and Christy Annie (MacLeod) J.; e. elem. and high schs. Murray River and Charlottetown, P.E.I. 1937; Prince of Wales Coll. Charlottetown 1945–46; Queen's Univ. B.Com. 1949; m. 1stly Frances Ann d. James Haunts, Kingston, Ont. 20 Feb. 1945 (d.); children: James Archibald Frederick, Heather Ann Ellen, Alexandra Frances, Margaret Ellen MacLeod; m. 2ndly Elizabeth d. Ferdinand Van Siclen Parr and Helene (Ham) P., Morristown, N.J. 6 March 1982; FINANCIAL AND PLANNING CONSULTANT 1983– ; Vice Pres. and Western Rep., Inst. of Donations and Public Affairs Rsch. 1988–91; Returning Officer, Federal Electoral Dist. of Calgary Southwest 1987–91; joined Candn. Gen. Electric Co. Ltd. as Consultant to Appliance Dealers 1949, Mgr. Operations W. Ont. Dist. 1953 and W. Dist. (B.C. & Alta.) 1955, Mgr. Finance Wholesale Dept. 1957, Mgr. Que. Dist. Wholesale Dept. 1960, Mgr. Corporate Planning and Services 1966, Mgr. Corporate Relations 1968, Vice Pres. & Gen. Mgr. Supply Sales & Distribution Dept. 1970 and Gescan Business Dept. 1974–79; Vice Pres. Pub. Affairs and Govt. Relations 1979–82; named Elect. Man. of Yr., Elect. News & Engn. 1970; served with Royal Candn. Corps Signals 1939–45 Can. & Overseas, rank Capt., Reserve Army 1945–52; Dir., Inst. Pol. Involvement; Jr. Achievement Metrop. Toronto 1979–83; Queen's Univ. Alumni 1981–83, Pres., Oakville-Mississauga Br. 1981–82, Pres., Calgary Br. 1986–88; Dir., Calgary Queen's Business Club 1988–91; Dir., Candn. Electrical Distributors Assn. (CEDA) 1972–78; Vice Pres. CEDA 1977–78; Dir., Electrical and Electronic Mfrs. Assn. (EEMAC) 1979–82; Dir., Atlantic Winter Fair 1992– ; Mem. Advisory Bd., Nova Scotia Centre on Aging; P. Conservative; Anglican; recreations: sailing, golf, photography, cross-country and Alpine skiing, reading; Clubs: Royal Candn. Mil. Inst.; Ashburn Golf Club (Halifax); Chester Golf Club (Chester, N.S.); Halifax Club; Address: The Meadows, 166 Bedford Hwy., Halifax, N.S. B3M 2J6.

**JOHNSTON, Brian Kenneth,** B.Comm., C.A.; real estate executive; b. Huntsville, Ont. 28 Sept. 1958; s. Kenneth D. and Lecily C. (White) J.; e. Huntsville H.S. 1977; Univ. of Toronto B.Comm. 1981; C.A. 1983; m. Colleen d. Christene and Earl Duffy 19 Oct. 1985; children: Emily Elizabeth, Katherine Grace; DIRECTOR, MONARCH DEVELOPMENT CORP. 1992– ; Price Waterhouse 1981–84; Asst. Controller, Monarch Development Corp. 1984; Controller 1987; Treas. 1988; Vice-Pres. 1990; recreations: jogging, reading; Home: 117 Cassandra Blvd., North York, Ont.; Office: 2025 Sheppard Ave. E., Willowdale, Ont. M2J 1V7.

**JOHNSTON, Rear-Admiral Bruce,** C.M.M., C.D., B.A.; Canadian Forces; b. Vancouver, B.C. 14 March 1942; s. George Herbert and Evelyn Dorain (Boyes) J.; e. Univ. of B.C. B.A. 1964; Royal Naval Staff Coll. 1974–75; m. Lynne d. Cecil and Beverly Watson 20 Aug. 1965; two s. Christopher, Keith; DEPY. CHIEF OF STAFF OPERATIONS, SUPREME ALLIED COMMANDER ATLANTIC; joined RCN 1959 (ROTP); initial sea appt. HMCS MacKenzie 1964; Operations Offr. HMCS Terra Nova Halifax 1969–70; shore appts. incl. RN 1972–74 specialized Electronic Warfare & Communications; served staff Maritime Warfare Sch. Halifax; Exec. Offr. HMCS Margaree; promoted Cdr. 1976 and Sr. Staff Offr. Communications to Comd. Maritime Command; command HMCS Kootenay 1978; Comd. Sea Training Pacific 1980; promoted Capt. (N) 1982, Dir. Curriculum Devel. and Maritime Studies Candn. Forces Command and Staff Coll. Toronto; C.O. HMCS Protecteur 1984; Commandant Cdn. Forces Fleet Sch. Halifax 1986; promoted Commodore 1987, Dir. Gen. Maritime Doctrine & Operations NDHQ; Dir. Gen. Mil. Plans and Operations, NDHQ 1989; Home: 1423 Trouville Ave., Norfolk, Va USA 23505; Office: SACLANT HQ, Norfolk, Va USA 23511–6696.

**JOHNSTON, Charles Bernie Jr.,** B.A., M.B.A., educator; b. Sudbury, Ont. 3 June 1931; s. Charles Bernie and Beatrice Eileen (Gilpin) J.; e. Sch. of Business Adm. Univ. of W. Ont. B.A. 1954, M.B.A. 1957; m. Carol Jean

d. Ernest T. Querney, Sudbury, Ont. 22 Aug. 1953; children: Charles David, Jeffrey Philip, Craig Matthew, Laura Isobel Myerling, Nancy Anne Beatrice; PROF. OF BUSINESS ADM., UNIV. OF W. ONT.; Mem. Adv. Counc., Candn. Ctr. for Management Development 1988–90; Dir., Canada Publishing Corp.; Promotion Co-ordinator, Procter and Gamble Inc. 1954; Gen. Mgr. C. B. Johnston Ltd. 1955; joined Univ. W. Ont. 1957, Assoc. Dean of Business Adm. 1975–78, Dean 1978–89; Visiting Prof. IMEDE Mang. Devel. Inst. Lausanne, Switzerland 1967–68; Keio Business School, Hiyoshi, Japan 1991; Visiting Scholar, Nat. Univ. of Singapore 1991; Dir. Mang. Training Course 1972–88; co-author 'How Industry Buys' 1959; Contrib. 2nd Ed. 1965 and co-author 3rd Ed. 1972 'Canadian Problems in Marketing'; author numerous cases in Marketing; Delta Upsilon; Protestant; Home: 165 Hunt Club Dr., London, Ont. N6H 3Y8; Office: London, Ont. N6A 3K7.

**JOHNSTON, Charles Murray,** B.A., M.A., Ph.D.; university professor emeritus; consultant; b. Hamilton, Ont. 1 Apr. 1926; s. Lawrence Druce and Kathleen Mary (Hunt) J.; e. McMaster Univ., B.A. 1949; Univ. of Penn., M.A. 1950, Ph.D. 1954; m. Lorna d. Leslie and Eva Chaffey; children: Brock, Kathleen, Kent, Patricia; Prof. of History, McMaster Univ. 1966–88; joined McMaster Univ. 1953; Exchange Prof., West Va. Univ. 1957; Duke Univ. Commonwealth Studies Fellowship 1957; Can. Counc. Leave Fellowship 1963; SSHRC Leave Fellowships 1975, 1982; mem. Archeol. & Hist. Sites Bd. of Ont. 1965–70; mem. Candn. Hist. Assn.; Ont. Hist. Soc.; author: 'The Head of the Lake: Wentworth County' 1958, 1967; 'Brant County: A History' 1967; 'McMaster University' 1976 (vol. 1), 1981 (vol. 2); 'E.C. Drury: Agrarian Idealist' 1986 (rec'd Floyd S. Chalmers Award in Ont. History); co-author 'Student Days: An Illustrated History of Student Life at McMaster Univ.' 1986; ed. 'The Valley of the Six Nations: A Collection of Documents on the Indian Lands of the Grand River' 1964, 1971; author of numerous articles on Candn. hist.; currently researching Br. Imp. hist.; rec'd Distinguished Alumni Scholar Award in Arts, McMaster Univ. 1989; Home: 7 Ravina Cres., Ancaster, Ont. L9G 2E5.

**JOHNSTON, David L.,** B.A.Sc., M.A.Sc.; mining executive; b. Terrace, B.C. 6 Sept. 1939; s. Albert and Marie (Desjardins) J.; e. Univ. of B.C., B.A.Sc. (Mining Engr.) 1963, M.A.Sc. 1969; m. Dolly d. Guglielmo and Maria DePaoli 24 July 1965; children: Anita, Brock, Bruce; VICE PRES., MINE OPNS., COMINCO METALS 1989– ; Rsch. & Devel. Dept., Kennecott Copper Corp. 1963–64; joined Cominco as Rsch. Asst. 1964–69; Devel. Engr./Op. Supt., Pine Pt. Operations 1969–73; Op. Supt., Fording Operations 1973–75; Gen. Mgr. 1975–80; Gen. Mgr., Valley Copper Mines 1980–81; Vice-Pres. 1981; Gen. Mgr., Northern Group 1981–83; Vice-Pres., Northern Operations, Cominco Metals 1983–89; Pres. & C.E.O., Pine Point Mines Ltd. 1985– 90; Dir., Cominco Engr. Services; mem. Candn. Inst. of Mining & Metallurgy; Profl. Engrs. of B.C.; MITEC Adv. Counc. for Mineral Processing; Vancouver Bd. of Trade; Office: 500 Waterfront Centre, 200 Burrard St., Vancouver, B.C. V6C 2R2.

**JOHNSTON, David Lloyd,** A.B., LL.B., LL.D., D.D.; university administrator; lawyer; b. Sudbury, Ont. 28 June 1941; s. Lloyd Allen and Dorothy (Stonehouse) J.; e. Sault Coll. Inst.; Harvard Univ. A.B. 1963; Cambridge Univ. LL.B. 1965; Queen's Univ. LL.B. 1966; Law Soc. Upper Can. LL.D. 1979; m. Sharon d. Reid Downey 29 Aug. 1964; children: Deborah, Alexandra, Sharon, Jennifer, Catherine; PRINCIPAL AND VICE CHANCELLOR, McGILL UNIVERSITY and Prof. of Law there 1979– ; Asst. Prof. of Law Queen's Univ. 1966–68; Asst. Prof. of Law Univ. of Toronto 1968, Assoc. Prof. 1969, Prof. 1972; Dean and Prof. of Law, Univ. of W. Ont. 1974–79; Barrister and Solr. Supreme Court of Ont. 1969– ; Comnr. Ont. Securities Comn. 1972–79; Pres. Assn. of Univ. and Coll. of Canada 1985–87; Chrmn., National Round Table on the Environment and the Economy 1988–91; mem. Harvard Univ. Bd. 1992– ; rec'd Honorary Doctorates from 9 insts.; author 'Canadian Securities Regulation' 1977; co-author Supplement 1982; 'Business Associations' 1979, 3rd ed. 1989; 'Canadian Companies and the Stock Exchange' 1980; Anglican; recreations: jogging, skiing; Home: 18 Sunnyside, Westmount, Que.; Office: 845 Sherbrooke St. W., Montreal, Que. H3A 2T5.

**JOHNSTON, Hon. Dick,** B.A., M.B.A., F.C.A.; politician; b. Lethbridge, Alta. 5 Mar. 1940; s. Archibald Stewart and Jeanetta E.; e. Lethbridge sch. system; Univ. of Calgary (B.A.); Univ. of Alta. (M.B.A.); m. Janice Lynn d. Douglas T. and Hazel Phillips, Lethbridge, Alta. 16 May 1964; children: Carolyn, Suzanne, Barbara, David;

Provincial Treasurer, Govt. of Alta. 1986; el. M.L.A. for Lethbridge E. 1975; re-el. 1979, 1982, 1986, 1989; apptd. Minister of Municipal Affairs, Govt. of Alta. 1975; Min. of Federal & Intergovernmental Affairs 1979; Min. of Advanced Education, 1982; Min. Responsible for the Status of Women 1983; C.A. practice D. Johnston & Associates, Lethbridge, Alta. 1969–75; Mgmt. Consultant, D. Johnston Management Consultants, Lethbridge, Alta. 1969–75; past Dir. Lethbridge Community Coll.; past Dir., Lethbridge Br., Victorian Order Nurses; Fellow, Inst. of C.A.'s of Alta.; P. Conservative; United Church; recreations: reading, skiing.

**JOHNSTON, Hon. Donald James,** P.C., Q.C., B.A., B.C.L.; politician; legal counsel; b. Ottawa, Ont. 26 June 1936; s. Wilbur Austin and Florence Jean Moffat (Tucker) J.; e. Montreal High Sch.; McGill Univ. B.A., B.C.L.; Grenoble Univ.; m. Heather Bell d. James Maclaren and Dorothy Bell, Halifax, N.S. 11 Dec. 1965; children: Kristina, Allison, Rachel, Sara; COUNSEL, HEENAN BLAIKIE; joined Stikeman, Elliott 1961; Lectr., Fiscal Law, Faculty of Law, McGill Univ. 1964– 77; el. House of Commons, St-Henri-Westmount riding in by-el. 1978; re-el., general elections 1979, 1980, 1984; Pres. of Treasury Bd. 1980–82; Min. of State for Economic and Regional Development, Science and Min. of State for Science and Technology 1982–84; Min. of Justice and Attorney General of Canada June 1984– Sept. 1984; re-el. 1984; Finance & External Affairs critic posts in Opposition; did not seek re-election in 1988; el. Pres., Liberal Party of Canada 1990– ; Mem. of the Bd., BCE Inc.; Unimédia (1988) Inc.; Québec Hospital Assn. (retired); Centre de Santé St-Henri; author: 'How to Survive Canada's Tax Chaos' 1974; 'Up the Hill' 1986; 'With a Bang Not a Whimper' 1988; Ed.: 'Lac Meech, Trudeau parle' 1989; Honours: numerous prizes incl. Gold Medal of the Faculty of Law; studied on scholarship, Univ. of Grenoble; mem. Que. & Ont. Bar Assns.; Club: Montreal Indoor Tennis; Mount Royal Club; Liberal; Protestant; recreations: writing, tennis, piano; Home: 4080 Highland Ave., Montreal, Que. H3Y 1R3; Office: 1250 René-Lévesque Blvd. W., Suite 2500, Montréal, Qué. H3B 4Y1.

**JOHNSTON, Donald William Cooper,** M.D., F.R.C.S.(C); orthopaedic surgeon; b. 6 Oct. 1950; s. Donald Cooper J.; e. Univ. of Alberta M.D. 1975, F.R.C.S. 1982; m. Mary Inez Johnston; children: Susan, Ronald, Laureen, Elizabeth; ORTHOPAEDIC SURGEON-IN-CHIEF, UNIVERSITY OF ALBERTA HOSPITALS 1986– ; Provisional Staff, Univ. of Alta. Hospitals 1983–84; Active Staff 1984– ; Pres., Medical Staff 1992–94; Assoc. Clin. Prof. 1986–96; Clin. Prof. 1992– ; Mem., Alta. Orthopaedic Soc.; Alta. Med. Assn. Red Sweater Club; Edmonton Ortho. Soc.; Candn. Med. Assn.; Candn. Orth. Assn. (Chair, Trauma Ctte. 1988–91; Edn. Ctte. 1991– ); Dewar Ortho. Soc.; Trauma Assn. of Can. (Chair, Edn. Ctte.); Ortho. Trauma Assn.; Am. Assn. for the Surgery of Trauma; S.I.C.O.T.; author of med. rsch. pubs.; Office: Edmonton, Alta. T6G 2E8.

**JOHNSTON, George,** M.A., Ph.D., D.D., LL.D.; educator; Minister, United Church of Can.; b. Clydebank, Scotland, 9 June 1913; s. William George and Jennie (McKeown) J.; e. Glasgow Univ., M.A. (Hons.), 1935 and B.D. (with Distinction) 1938, D.D. 1960; Marburg Univ., 1938; Cambridge Univ., Ph.D. 1941; United Theological Coll., D.D. 1974; Montreal Diocesan Theological Coll., D.D. 1975; Mt. Allison Univ., LL.D. 1974; Brown Downie Fellow in New Testament, 1937; Black Theol. Fellow, Glasgow Univ., 1938; Maxwell Forsyth Fellow, Trinity Coll., Glasgow, 1938; Cleland & Rae Wilson Gold Medals in New Test. & Ch. Hist. & Divinity; A.A.T.S. Faculty Fellowship, 1967; Canada Council Leave Fellowship, 1975–76; m. Alexandra, d. late John Gardner, M.D., 6 Aug. 1941; children: Christine, Ronald, Janet; EMERITUS PROFESSOR OF RELIGIOUS STUDIES, McGILL UNIV. 1982– ; Prof., New Testament there 1959–81 and Dean, Faculty of Religious Studies 1970–75; Fac. Lectr. 1981– ; Gov., McGill Univ. 1971–75; Bruce Lectr., Trinity Coll., Glasgow, 1940–43; Min. of Martyrs' Ch., St. Andrews, Fife, Scot., 1940–47; Pres., Ch. of Scot. Young Men's Guild, 1942– 45; Assoc. Prof. of Ch. Hist. & New Testament, Hartford (Conn.) Semy. Foundation, 1947–52; Kellner Mem. Lectr. in New Testament, Episcopal Theol. Sch., Cambridge, Mass., 1951; Prof. of New Testament Lit. and Exegesis, Emmanuel Coll., Victoria Univ., Toronto, Ont., 1952–59; Principal, United Theol. Coll., Montreal, 1959–70, Prof. 1976–90; R.T. Orr Visitor, Huron Coll., London, Ont., 1971; Visiting Prof., St. Mary's Coll., Univ. of St. Andrews, Scotland 1976; served in 2nd World War; Acting Chaplain, 7th Black Watch, 51st Highland Div., 1945; author of: 'The Doctrine of the Church in the New Testament' 1943; 'The Secrets of the

Kingdom' 1954; 'Ephesians-Philippians-Colossians-Philemon' (The New Century Bible) 1967; 'The Spirit-Paraclete in the Gospel of John' 1970; 'Discovering Discipleship' 1983; 'Opening the Scriptures' 1992; Ed. 'The Church in the Modern World' (with W. Roth) 1967; contrib. 'Peake's Commentary' 1962; 'Interpreter's Dict. of the Bible' 1962; 'Hastings' Dict. of the Bible' 1963; several composite vols. and Festschriften, and various religious journs.; Commr. Un. Ch. Gen. Council, 1958, 1966, 1968; mem., Soc. of Biblical Lit.; recreations: music, early Christian art & Celtic archaeology; Address: 399 Clarke Ave., Apt. 1C, Montreal, Que. H3Z 2E7.

**JOHNSTON, George Benson,** M.A., LL.D., D.Litt.; retired professor, poet, translator; b. Hamilton, Ont. 7 Oct. 1913; s. Benson Edward and Margaret Ellen (Black) J.; e. Univ. of Toronto B.A. 1936, M.A. 1945; m. Jeanne d. Duncan and Susan McRae 3 July 1944; children: Robert, Margaret, Andrew, Cathleen, Nora, Mark; Asst. Prof. of English, Mount Allison Univ. 1947–49; Carleton Univ. 1950–62; Prof. 1962–79; served with Royal Candn. Air Force 1940–45: General Reconnaissance pilot in Africa; instructor in N. Ireland & Canada; Anglican; Mem., Lit. Translators' Assn. of Canada; League of Candn. Poets (Life Mem.); Candn. Assn. of Univ. Teachers; Assn. of Candn. Univ. Teachers of English; author: 'The Cruising Auk,' 'Home Free,' 'Happy Enough,' 'Taking a Grip,' 'Ask Again,' 'Auk Redivivus' (poetry); 'Endeared by Dark' (collected poems); translations: 'The Saga of Gisli,' 'The Greenlanders' Saga,' 'The Faroe Islanders' Saga' (from Old Icelandic); 'Rocky Shores' (from Faroese); 'Wind over Romsdal,' 'Bee-Buzz, Salmon-Leap' (from Norwegian); 'Pastor Bodvar's Letter' (from Modern Icelandic); 'BARBARA' (from Danish); 'Carl, Portrait of a Painter' (letters from Carl Schaefer); 'George Whalley: Collected Poems'; Home: 27 Henderson, P.O. Box 788, Huntington, Que. J0S 1H0.

**JOHNSTON, H. Douglas,** B.Sc., P.Eng.; consultant; government administrator, retired; b. Montague, P.E.I. 25 Oct. 1933; s. Louis A. and Annie (McGowan) J.; e. Univ. of New Brunswick B.Sc. (Civil Eng.) 1958; m. Beverley Ann d. Beverly & Velma Wheaton, 24 May 1958; children: A. Catherine, H.B. William, D. Alexander; Consultant Engr., Fisheries' Sector, Private Enterprise & Government 1990– ; Engr. & Prod., Pulp & Paper Indus. 1958–66; var. positions to Asst. Dep. Min., Pacific & Freshwater Fishes, Fisheries & Oceans, Can. 1966–82; Fed. Econ. Devel. Co-ordinator, P.E.I., Dept. of Reg. Indus. Expansion 1982–86; Dep. Min., P.E.I. Dept. of Fisheries 1986–90; Trustee, Kings County Mem. Hosp.; Mem., Profl. Engr. Assn. of P.E.I.; Session Mem. United Ch. of Can.; recreation: recreational hockey, golf, gardening, sailing; Club: Brudenell Golf; Home: Robertson Rd., Brudenell, P.E.I. C0A 1R0.

**JOHNSTON, Heather Erika,** D.D.; ecumenist; b. Cölbe, Germany 22 Aug. 1930; d. Bernhard and Ruth (Bartels) Heppe; e. Fröbelseminary, Germany; Interpreter, Eng. Inst. Heidelberg 1953–55; Oxford Univ. 1955; Knox Coll. Toronto D.D. 1984; m. John Alexander s. Joseph and Halley Johnston 20 Feb. 1957; children: Andrew, Ian, Mary; adv. to women's group Lagos, Nigeria 1964–66; mem. Family Life Ctte. Presb. Ch. in Can. 1967–74; mem. Ecumenical Relations Ctte. 1973– 91; Chair of Ctte. 1976–84; Co-founder and mem. Multicultural Soc. Hamilton, Ont. 1972–80; mem. Central Ctte. World Council Chs. Geneva 1975–83; Pres. Candn. Council Chs. 1979–82; Dir. Ecumenical Devel. Co-op. Soc. Holland 1984–90; Founder and Chair Candn. Support Assn. 1983– ; Chair Candn. Christian Jewish Consultation 1986–92; Co-Chair, Candn. Christian Festival IV 1992–94; nat. and internat. guest speaker; mem. internat. team to observe els. Guyana 1981; invited by China Christian Council Shanghai as Leader Candn. Ch. Leaders 1981; Internat. Meeting World Council Chs. Dresden 1982; recreations: swimming, reading, friends, family; Address: 183 Chedoke Ave., Hamilton, Ont. L8P 4P2.

**JOHNSTON, James Clifton,** B.A., M.A.; environmental planner; b. Brockville, Ont. 25 Mar. 1951; s. Robert Harold and Bessye Josephine (Sheffield) J.; e. Brockville C.I.; Waterloo Lutheran Univ., B.A. 1973; Univ. of Waterloo/Wilfrid Laurier Univ. M.A. 1976; CHIEF, NEW PARK PROPOSALS - NORTH, NATIONAL PARKS SYSTEMS BRANCH, CANADIAN PARKS SERVICE 1991– ; Resource Planner, Govt. of Man. 1976; Nat. Park Planner, Prairie Reg., Candn. Parks Serv. 1977–80; Head, Nat. Parks Planning Section, Prairie & North Region, National Parks Service 1980–91; Acting Supt., Wood Buffalo Nat. Park 1982; Riding Mountain Nat. Park 1983; Cons. to Internat. Union for Conserv. of Nature & Nat. Resources & Peoples Rep. of China 1986 (summer); Cons., Internat. Union for Conserv. of Nature & Nat. Resources; Mem., Soc. for Study of Archit. in Can.; author of park management plans, num. newsletters & tech. reports; recreations: skiing, boating, woodworking; Club: Candn. Power & Sail Squadrons; Office: Jules Leger Bldg., 25 Eddy St., 4th Floor, Hull, Qué. K1A 0M5.

**JOHNSTON, Lawrence Hugh,** B.Com., F.C.A.; retired manufacturer; b. Hamilton, Ont. 4 May 1918; s. Lawrence Bastedo and Aleda Pearl (Neil) J.; e. Queen's Univ., B.Com. 1940; m. Mildred Kathleen, d. John C. Wright, 9 Apl. 1949; three children; joined Price Waterhouse & Co., Toronto, 1940–51; trans. to Hamilton, Ont., 1951–58; joined Canadian Canners Ltd. 1958; Pres. & C.E.O. 1965–83; served with R.C.N.V.R. 1941–45; Chrmn., Hamilton & Dist. C.A.'s Assn., 1958–59; Pres., Hamilton Chapter, Financial Extves. Inst., 1965–66; Pres. Cndn. Food Processors Assn., 1972–73; C.E.O., Canadian Canners Ltd. 1965–83; Bd. of Gov., McMaster Univ. 1975–83; Dir. Wellington Ins. Co. 1975–93; Bd. of Trustees, McMaster University Medical Centre, 1970–79, Chrmn. 1978–79; Bd. of Trustees Chedoke-McMaster Hospitals 1980–93, Chrmn. 1982–83; United Church; recreations: golf, curling, fishing; Clubs: Hamilton; Hamilton Golf & Country; Home: 202 – 150 Wilson St. W., Ancaster, Ont. L9G 4E7.

**JOHNSTON, Malcolm Carlyle;** banker; b. Glasgow, Scotland 10 July 1934; s. Malcolm and Margaret B. (MacPherson) J.; e. Kelvinside Acad., Glasgow; Fellow, Inst. of Canadian Bankers, Gold Medal 1983; m. Anna Maria d. Henri and Josefina Bindels of the Netherlands 7 Sept. 1963; children: Margareta, Malcolm; EXTVE. VICE-PRES., INTERNAT. BANKING, THE BANK OF N.S.; joined The Clydesdale & N. Scotland Bank 1951; The Bank of W. Africa 1955; joined Bank of N.S. 1969; Asst. Agent, N.Y.; Spec. Rep., Hong Kong; Mgr., Kuala Lumpur, Malaysia; Mgr., The Bank of N.S. Jamaica Ltd.; Asst. Gen. Mgr., Internat. Corp. Credit; Asst. Gen. Mgr., later Gen. Mgr., Caribbean Reg. Office; Sr. Vice-Pres. & Deputy Gen. Mgr., Candn. Commercial Credit; Dir., BNS Internat. (U.K.) Ltd.; The Bank of N.S. Asia Ltd.; The Bank of N.S. Jamaica Ltd.; The Bank of N.S. Trinidad & Tobago Ltd.; The Bank of N.S. Trust Co. of Trinidad & Tobago Ltd.; Boracay Ltd.; Brit. Caribbean Insur. Co. Ltd.; Caribbean Mercantile Bank N.V.; Export Finan. Corp. of Can. Ltd.; Indus. Finan. Corp.; Indus. Finan. Holdings Ltd.; Maduro & Curiel's Bank N.V.; Scotiabank Jamaica Trust & Merchant Bank; Scotia Realty Antilles N.V.; West India Co. of Merchant Bankers; Chrmn., Scotia Export Finan. Corp.; Mem., Ch. Inst. of Bankers; Asean-Can. Bus. Counc.; Rep., Canada-China Trade Counc.; Canada-Korea Trade Counc.; Pacific Basin Econ. Counc.; Military Serv., The Royal Highland Regiment, The Black Watch; recreations: reading, scuba diving: clubs: The National, The Hong Kong; Office: 44 King St. W., Toronto, Ont. M5H 1H1.

**JOHNSTON, Norman George,** B.A., C.A.; business executive; b. Montreal, Que. 12 Feb. 1934; s. Archibald Downie and Isabella Rattray (Webster) J.; e. Concordia Univ. B.A. 1970; McGill Univ. C.A. studies 1956; m. Eugenia d. Nicholas and Mary Butrey 3 June 1961; children: Hamish, Stewart, Colin; DIRECTOR OF FINANCE & TREASURER, UNILEVER CANADA LIMITED; articles with Coopers & Lybrand (McDonald Currie) Montreal; held senior management positions in the electronics, constructon and health care industries; Audit Ctte., Fleming Canada Investment Trusts; Mem. Editorial Bd., Canadian Treasury Management Handbook; Mem., Inst. of C.A.s (Que. and Ont.); Financial Executives Inst.; Toronto Board of Trade; recreations: golf, reading; clubs: Board of Trade; Office: 160 Bloor St. E., Ste. 1500, Toronto, Ont. M4W 3R2.

**JOHNSTON, Patrick;** B.A., B.Ed., M.S.W.; executive; b. Kitchener, Ont. 26 July 1949; s. Lloyd Robert Theodore and Jeanne Margaret (Thrush) J.; e. York Univ., B.A. 1973; Queen's Univ., B.Ed. 1975; Univ. of Toronto, M.S.W. 1980; EXECUTIVE DIR., CANADIAN COUNCIL ON SOCIAL DEVELOPMENT; Prog. Dir., Social Serv. & Health, Candn. Counc. on Social Devel. 1980–82; Extve. Dir., Nat. Anti-Poverty Orgn. 1982–86; Co-chair, federal Liberals' election platform ctte. 1986–88; Sr. Advisor, Ont. Social Assistance Review 1986–88; Sr. Policy Advisor to the Premier of Ontario 1989–90; Home: 103 James St., Ottawa, Ont. K1R 5M2.

**JOHNSTON, Peter,** B.F.A.; sculptor; b. England 25 Sept. 1949; s. Noel Peter and Nancy J.; e. Queen's Univ. B.F.A. 1973; frequent solo exhibitions; Instr. in Sculpture, Queen's Univ., 15 years; works in many public & private collections; rep. by Klonaridis Inc. Toronto & Robertson Gallery Ottawa; Address: Univ. of Guelph, Dept. of Fine Arts, Guelph, Ont. N1G 2W1.

**JOHNSTON, Peter Arthur Edward,** B.A.; retired diplomat; b. Toronto, Ont. 18 Sept. 1921; s. George Arthur, Q.C. and Gladys Madeleine (Baker) J.; e. Univ. of Toronto, B.A. 1948; m. the late Valerie, d. Dr. Francis Farewell, Whitby Ont. June 1947; children: Mrs. Celia Hunter, Stuart, Geoffrey and Mrs. Sarah Lalumière; m. 2ndly Rosanne d. Rupert Hughes, 15 Sept. 1973; joined Nat. Research Council Ottawa 1948–57; Dept. of External Affairs 1957, First Secy. London 1962, Counsellor Dar-Es-Salaam 1966, Dir. Security and Intelligence Liaison Div. Ottawa 1968, Min. Tokyo 1972, Ambassador to Indonesia 1974–77; Amb. to Czechoslovakia 1977–81; Ambassador to Venezuela and Dominican Republic 1981–83; Foreign Service Visitor, Univ. of Victoria 1983–84; active interest in encouraging democratic institutions in Third World countries, having monitored elections in El Salvador (1990), Nicaragua (1991) and Angola (1992); served with Candn. Army UK, Sicily, Italy, France, Holland 1940–45, Mentioned in Despatches; recreations: reading, music, foreign languages, golf; Clubs: Union Club of BC; Uplands Golf; Address: 1908 Beach Drive, Victoria, B.C. V8R 6J5.

**JOHNSTON, Richard William,** B.Sc., B.S.W., M.A.; management consultant; b. Shenyang, China 21 Oct. 1928; s. Harry Kay and Jean Christina (Cross) J.; e. Univ. of Man., B.Sc. 1950, B.S.W. 1953; Univ. of Sask., M.A. 1955; m. Carolyn d. Robert and Ruth Hall 12 Sept. 1953; children: Brock, Laurie; PARTNER, JOHNSTON SMITH FROMKIN MCCULLOCH INC. 1990– ; probation offr., Sask. Govt. 1952–55; Personnel Asst., C-I-L Inc. 1955–57; Sr. Interviewer, Westinghouse Can. 1957–59; Placement Supr., H.V. Chapman & Assocs. 1959–63; Functional Dir., P.S. Ross & Partners 1963–65; Founding Partner, Hickling-Johnston Ltd. 1965–78; Chrmn., SpencerStuart & Assoc. Can. Ltd. 1989–90, Pres. 1978–89; Past-Pres., Candn. Assoc. of Mgmt. Cons.; Fellow, Inst. of Certified Mgmt. Cons.; Mem., Adv. Counc., Fac. of Mgmt. Studies, Univ. of Toronto; Reg'd. Psychologist (Ont.); recreations: sailing, scuba diving, skiing; Home: 334 North Shore Blvd. E., Burlington, Ont. L7T 1W9; Office: Suite 1002, 145 King St. W., Toronto, Ont. M5H 3X6.

**JOHNSTON, Rita Margaret;** politician; b. Melville, Sask. 22 April 1935; d. John R. and Annie (Chyzzy) Leichert; m. George J. 28 April 1951; children: Darlene, Colleen, Rock; Premier, B.C. Govt. Apr. 1991–Nov. 1991 (first Candn. female Premier in history); Depy. Premier, B.C. Govt. 1990–91; Min. of Transportation and Highways, B.C. Govt. 1989–91; Steno, Household Finance & Bank of Montreal; Mgr., Bell Fin. Ltd.; Alderman, Dist. of Surrey for 9 yrs. during period 1970–1983; Social Credit M.L.A. 1983– ; Min. of Munic. Affairs, Recreation & Culture, B.C. Govt. 1986–89; mem. Surrey C. of C.; Surrey B.P.W.; Home: 6595 King George Hwy., Surrey, B.C. V3W 4Z4.

**JOHNSTON, Robert Stanley,** LL.B., Q.C.; historian; of U.E.L. descent; b. Hamilton, Ont. 13 Sept. 1905; s. Robert Lawrence and Emma Matilda (Martindale) J. e. Osgoode Hall, Toronto, Ont.; m. Marjorie Lloyd, d. H. A. Webber, 26 Sept. 1936; has one s., Robert Douglas, and one d., Roseanne M.; Partner, Johnston and Peart; read law with Mortimer Clark & Co., Toronto, Ont.; called to Bar of Ont. 1930; cr. Q.C. 1958; Hon. Life mem., V.O.N. Canada (Past Pres., Prov. Ont. Br. and Hamilton-Wentworth Br. 1957); Past Chrmn. and Hon. Solr., Royal Candn. Humane Assn.; Mem., Law and the Community; mem., Estate Planners Council, Hamilton; Pres., Dom. Council, U.E.L. Assn. Can., 1939–45; mem., Hamilton Art Gallery; Candn. Bar Assn.; Chamber of Comm., Hamilton; Freemason 33$ (mem. of all Scot. Rite bodies); Acacia Lodge #61; Past Chrmn., Scottish Rite Club (Hamilton); Chrmn. Bd. of Trustees, St. Giles United Church; past mem., Exec. Gen. Council, United Church of Can.; Bd. mem., Candn. Bible Soc., Hamilton; Dir., Hamilton-Wentworth Branch, Victorian Order of Nurses Found.; Clubs: Lawyer's; Canadian; Scottish Rite; Home: 1202 - 136 Bay St. S., Hamilton, Ont. L8P 3H5; Office: 403 - 20 Hughson St. S., Hamilton, Ont. L8N 3C8.

**JOHNSTON, Wayne Gerard,** B.A., M.A.; writer; b. Goulds, Nfld. 22 May 1958; s. Arthur Reginald and Genevieve (Everard) J.; e. Memorial Univ. of Nfld., B.A. 1978; Univ. of N.B., M.A. 1984; m. Rosemarie d. Jan and Mary Langhout 1981; Reporter, St. John's Daily News 1978–80; Poetry Ed., 'The Fiddlehead Magazine' 1984–86; 1st prize The Nfld. Arts & Letters Competition 1982; author 'The Story of Bobby O'Malley' 1985 (W.H. Smith Books in Canada First Novel Award); 'The Time of Their Lives' 1987 (Air Canada Award for Best Young Writer) 'The Divine Ryans' 199 (The Atlantic Fiction Prize for Best Atlantic Novel); Home: 811-B Duplex Ave., Toronto, Ont. M4W 1W6; Office: c/o HarperCollins Publishers Ltd., Ste. 2900, Hazelton Lanes, 55 Avenue Rd., Toronto, Ont. M5R 3L2.

**JOHNSTON, William A.,** B.A.; management consultant; b. Toronto, Ont. 9 Dec. 1943; s. William A. and Marianne E. (Fitch) J.; e. Oakland Univ., B.A. 1967; Wayne State, M.I.R.; children: William, Brent; PRES., WORKFORCE ASSOCS. 1991– ; Labour Relns., Ford Motor Co. Can. Ltd. 1967–75; Employment & Placement Mgr. 1975–79; Labour Relns. Mgr., Windsor Opns. 1979–84; Dir., Human Resources & Public Affairs, Uniroyal Can. Ltd. 1984–85; Vice-Pres., Human Resources, & Public Affairs, Speedy Muffler King 1985–87; Pres. & Prin. Partner, Verity Internat. Limited 1987–89; Partner, Peat Marwick Stevenson & Kellogg 1989–91; Dir., Ontario Arts Counc.; Mem., Bd. of Trade; Personnel Assns. of Ont.; recreations: golf, tennis, squash, photography; club: Mayfair; Home: 42 Hillside Dr., Toronto, Ont. M4K 2M2.

**JOHNSTON, William E. Jr.,** B.A., M.B.A.; manufacturing executive; b. Gary, Indiana 3 Sept. 1940; s. William E. and Helen Rachel (Street) J.; e. St. Joseph's Coll., B.A. 1963; Univ. of Chicago, M.B.A. 1973; divorced; children: Allen, William, Jennifer; VICE-PRES., FINANCE & OPERATIONS, MORTON SALT DIVISION, MORTON INTERNATIONAL INC./DIV. PRES., MORTON SALT/PRES., SALT GROUP 1977– ; U.S. Steel 1959–69; Group Controller, Allis-Chalmers 1969–77; Pres & Dir., The Candn. Salt Co. Ltd., Morton Bahamas Limited; Dir., Ecuatoriana de Sal Y Productos C.A.; Mem., Salt Inst. (C.E.O. Council); Grocery Mfrs. of Am. Inc.; Bd. of Trustees, Food Industry Crusade Against Hunger (FICAH); Bd. of Trustees, Saint Joseph's Coll.; mem. Canadian Club of Chicago; recreations: sailing, skiing, tennis; Clubs: Chicago Yacht: East Bank; Tower; Home: 155 N. Harbor Dr., Apt. 3412, Chicago, Ill. 60601; Office: 755 Boul. St. Jean, Pointe Claire, Que. H9R 5M9.

**JOHNSTONE, (Kenneth) Alvin,** B.Com., C.A.; dairy processor executive; b. Moose Jaw, Sask. 24 Apl. 1930; s. Ellis Alvin and Emma Lucinda (Davies) J.; e. Red Deer High Sch. 1948; Univ. of Alta. B.Com. 1952; C.A. 1961; m. Joan d. Fred and Daisy Harvey 5 Apl. 1958; children: Jeffrey, Nancy; EXTVE. VICE PRES., AGRIFOODS INTERNATIONAL COOPERATIVE LTD. 1992– ; joined Royal Bank of Canada 1952–58; Staff Acct. Deloitte, Haskins & Sells 1958–62; Comptroller, Central Alta. Dairy Pool 1962, Mktg. Mgr. 1972, Asst. Gen. Mgr. 1974–75, Gen. Mgr. 1975–92; Steno. Alta. Dairy Control Bd. Policy Adv. Ctte.; Dir. and Past Chrmn. Nat. Dairy Council; Past Dir. Red Deer Coll. Found.; Past Pres. and Life Dir. Westerner Expn. Assn.; Dir., Internat. Ice Cream Assn.; mem. Red Deer C. of C.; Calgary Chamber of Commerce; Past Pres. and Life mem. Alta. Dairymen's Assn.; Past Treas. Gaetz Meml. Un. Ch. Red Deer; recreations: golf, fishing; Clubs: Red Deer Golf & Country; Rotary; Kinsmen (Past Pres. and Life mem. Red Deer); Home: 32 Aikman Close, Red Deer, Alta. T4R 1G2; Office: P.O. Bag 550, Red Deer, Alta. T4N 5G4.

**JOHNSTONE, John,** F.I.I.C.; insurance executive; b. Glasgow, Scot. 20 March 1946; s. John and Mary McKenzie (Hill) J.; e. Hyndland Sr. Secondary Sch. Scot.; York Univ.; m. Jackie Arnold; children: Mark, Paul, David, Rebecca; EXEC. VICE PRES. AND DIR. MARSH & McLENNAN LTD. 1989– ; underwriter Norwich Union UK prior to immigrating to Can. 1967; Acct. Exec. present Co. 1972, Asst. Vice Pres. 1975, Vice Pres. 1978, Sr. Vice Pres. 1981; Mng. Dir. Marsh & McLennan Inc. 1983; mem. Internat. Affairs Ctte. Candn. C. of C.; Bd. Trade Metrop. Toronto; Presbyterian; P. Conservative; recreations: golf, shooting, reading; Clubs: Donalda; Adelaide; National; Home: 68 George Henry Blvd., Toronto, Ont. M2K 1E6; Office: Canada Trust Tower, BCE Place, 161 Bay St., P.O. Box 502, Toronto, Ont. M5J 2S4.

**JOHNSTONE, Robert,** B.A., M.Sc.; b. New York, N.Y. 30 Dec. 1932; s. Edmund and Eleanor (Warden) J.; e. Univ. of Toronto B.A. 1954; Univ. Laval M.Sc. 1957; m. Louise d. George and Micheline Craig 7 Dec. 1957; children: Lesley, Ian, Christopher, Nicholas; CONSULTANT, SENIOR POLICY ADVISOR, GOVT. OF ONT.; Dir., Eurocopter Canada Ltd.; London Insurance Group; London Life Insur. Co.; Promis Systems Corp.; Quorum Funding Corp.; Asst. Dir. Research Royal Comn. on Banking & Finance 1961–64; Asst. Chief Research Dept. Bank of Canada 1964, Depy. Chief 1966; Adviser Research & Stat. Dept. Internat. Monetary Fund Washington 1967, Extve. Dir. for Can., Ireland,

Jamaica and Guyana 1968; Advisor to Gov. Bank of Can. 1971; Extve. Dir., Anti-Inflation Bd. Govt. of Can. 1975; Depy. Under-Secy. (Econ.) Dept. of External Affairs 1977; Personal Rep. of the Prime Minister for Economic Summits; Depy. Min. of Industry, Trade & Comm. 1980; Depy. Min. Internat. Trade and Coordr. Internat. Econ. Relations Dept. of External Affairs 1982; Consul General of Canada in New York and Commissioner to Bermuda 1984; Extve. Dir., Ont. Centre for Internat. Business 1988; Address: 167 Major St., Toronto, Ont. M5S 2K9.

**JOHNSTONE, Rose M.,** Ph.D.; university professor; administrator; b. Lodz, Poland 14 May 1928; d. Jacob Shea and Esther (Rotholz) J.; e. McGill Univ., B.Sc. 1950, Ph.D. 1953; m. Douglas Frederick J. 9 Aug. 1953; children: Michael Trevor, Eric Stephen; Chair, Dept. of Biochem., McGill Univ. 1980–90; Gilman-Cheney Chair 1985; Asst. Prof. 1960–66; Assoc. Prof. 1966–78; Prof. 1978– ; Mem., Candn. Biochem. Soc. (Pres. 1985–86); Am. Soc. of Biol. Chem.; Internat. Assn. of Women Biosci. (Sec.-Treas. 1984–88); Queen's Jubilee Silver Medal 1978; Fellow, Royal Soc. Can. 1987 (Treas. 1990– ); author of sci. articles; recreations: tennis, folk dancing; Home: 4064 Oxford Ave., N.D.G., Que. H4A 2Y4; Office: 3655 Drummond St., Montreal, Que. H3G 1Y6.

**JOLI-COEUR, Henri,** A.S.A., B.A., B.Comm.; insurance executive; b. 27 May 1936; s. Achille and Marie-Paul (Langelier) J.; e. Laval Univ. B.A., B.Comm. 1961; widowed; two children; PRESIDENT AND CHIEF OPERATING OFFICER, OPTIMUM GROUP INC. 1969– ; Mercantile & Gen. Reinsurance 1961–67; Mutuelle des Fonctionnaires 1967–69; Pres. & Dir., Nat.Insur. Group Inc.; Dir., Nat. Frontier Insur.; B.C. Insur. Co.; Nat. Insur. Co. Inc.; Optimum Foncier Inc.; Vie Optimum (France); St. Lawrence Reassur. Co.; Optimum Insur. Co. (Texas); Optimum Consulting; Underwriters Adjustment Burea; Dir. Fond. des Grands Brûlés; Mem., Soc. of Actuaries; Corp. des Admin. Agréés; recreation: travel; club: Garrison; Home: 264, ave McDougall, Outremont, Que. H2V 3P2; Office: 425, de Maisonneuve Blvd. W., Ste. 1700, Montreal, Que. H3A 3G5.

**JOLICOEUR, Louise,** LL.B.; lawyer; b. Montreal, Que. 1953; e. Univ. of Montreal LL.B.; m. Jean Proulx; SECRETAIRE GENERALE ET DIRECTRICE DESSERV. JURIDIQUES, SOC. QUEECOISE DE DEVELOPPEMENT DE LA MAIN-D'OEUVRE 1993– ; Vice-Pres., Legal Affairs & Corp. Sec., General Trust of Canada until 1993; Mem., Candn. Bar Assn.; Montreal C. of C. (Bus. Women's Ctte.); Candn. Corp. Counsel Assn.; Trust Cos. Assn. of Can. (Que. Section); Administrator, Soc. Immobiliere Trans-Que. Inc.; Office: 1100 University St., Montreal, Que. H3B 2G7.

**JOLICOEUR, Paul,** M.D., Ph.D.; university professor, researcher; b. Beauceville, Que. 4 Jan. 1945; s. Philippe and Eva (Rodrigue) J.; e. Laval Univ., B.A. 1964, M.D. 1968, Ph.D. 1973; m. Claudine Tremblay 10 Apr. 1976; DIR., LAB. OF MOL. BIOL., CLINICAL RSCH. INST. OF MONTREAL 1976– ; Med. Dir., LAMA-KARA Hospital (SUCO), Togo (Africa) 1968–69; general practice, Gaspésie, Qué. 1970; postdoctoral fellow, M.I.T. 1973–76; Prof., Dept. of Microbiol. & Immun., Univ. of Montreal; Dept. of Experimental Med., McGill Univ.; Centennial Fellowship, Med. Rsch. Counc. of Can. 1975–76; Mem., Royal Soc. of Can. 1989; author of more than 80 sci. papers; recreatings: skiing, swimming; Home: 5296 Durocher, Outremont, Que. H2V 3Y1; Office: 110 Pine Ave. W., Montreal, Que. H2W 1R7.

**JOLIN, The Hon. Paul,** B.A., L.L.L., J.C.S.; superior court judge; b. Giffard, P.Q. 2 May 1933; s. Henri and Madeleine (La Rochelle) J.; e. Jesuit's Coll., Que. B.A.; Laval Univ., L.L.L.; London Sch. of Econ. (U.K.); m. Celine d. Armand Poulin July 1961; children: Bernard, Marie, Catherine, David; SUPERIOR COURT JUDGE, SUPERIOR COURT OF QUE. 1988– ; Partner, Lachapelle & Jolin 1960–65; Legal Couns. & Sec., Sid-BEC 1965–67; Partner, Blain-Piché 1967–80; Sr. Partner, Heenan-Blaikie 1980–88; Sec., Marine Industries, Forano Inc., Volcano Inc. 1967–70; mem., Candn. Bar Assn.; former Reserve Offr., Candn. Forces (Captain R.C.A.); recreations: golf, tennis, R-Ball; club: Beloeil Golf; Home: 2055 Melba St., St-Bruno, Que. J3V 3R9; Office 1 est Notre Dame, Montreal, Que. H2Y 1B6.

**JOLLEY, David Richard,** M.B.A.; executive; b. Toronto, Ont. 19 Feb. 1942; s. Malcolm Porter and Grace Ethyl (Middleton) J.; e. Univ. of Toronto, Engineering Degree 1964; Stanford Univ. M.B.A. 1967; child: Malcolm Mckinnon; OFFICE OF THE C.E.O., TORSTAR; PUBLISHER & PRES., TORONTO STAR NEWSPAPERS LTD.; Management Consultant, Currie Coopers & Lybrand Ltd. 1967–70; Part., Can. Consulting Group Inc. 1970–80; Home: 84 Woodlawn Ave. W., Toronto, Ont. M4V 1G7; Office: One Yonge St., Toronto, Ont. M5E 1E6.

**JOLLIFFE, Edward Bigelow,** Q.C., M.A.; arbitrator; b. Luchow, China 2 March 1909; s. Rev. Charles and Gertrude (Bigelow) J.; e. Rockwood Pub. Sch. 1922; Candn. Sch., Chengtu, 1924; W. China Union Univ. 1925; Guelph Coll. Inst., Ont. 1927; Victoria Coll., Toronto, (Rhodes Schol. 1931); Christ Ch., Oxford, 1934; Gray's Inn, London (Arden Schol.); called to the English Bar 1934; Ontario. 1936; K.C. 1944; m. Ruth Conger, d. Charles Herbert Moore, Dundas, Ont., 26 October 1935; children: Naomi, John, Nancy, Thomas; from time to time with The Candn. Press as Reporter, Cable Ed. and Counsel, Toronto, Montreal, N.Y., 1930–43; def. cand. to H. of C. for Toronto St. Paul's g.e. 1935, and York E., g.e. 1940; Ont. C.C.F. Leader 1942–53; Leader of the Official Opposition in the Leg. 1943–45 and 1948–51; practised law with Lang and Michener, Toronto, 1936–43; Jolliffe, Lewis, and Osler, 1945–69 Candn. gen. counsel for United Steelworkers and other internat. and nat. unions and prof. organizations; apptd. Chief Adjudicator under Canada Public Service Staff Relations Act, 1969, also Depy. Chrmn. P.S.S.R. Bd. 1975–79; Vice Chrmn., Ont. Public Service Grievance Settlement Bd. 1980–88; contributed to Candn. Bar Review, American Administrative Law Review, McGill Law Journ., MacLean's and other U.S. and Candn. periodicals; co-author 'Witness to a Generation' (history) 1966; author 'The First Hundred' (novel) 1972; mem., Candn. Bar Assn.; Nat. Acad. Arbitrators; Life mem., Alliance of Canadian Cinema, Television and Radio Artists; Hon. mem. Candn. Veterinary Med. Assn.; Vice-Chrmn. of Bd., Central Hosp., Toronto 1967–69; Chrmn. Atai Arctic Creative Devel. Foundation 1975; Pres., Empire Club of Canada, 1968–69; recipient, Gov.-Gen. commendation for distinguished public service 1940; Clubs: University; Rideau; Home: 806 Sunset Dr., Saltspring Island, B.C. V0S 1E0.

**JOLLIFFE, N. Lynn,** B.A., M.B.A.; retail executive; b. Kitchener, Ont. 16 March 1952; d. Robert E. and Jean G. J.; e. Queen's Univ. B.A. 1973; Univ. of Toronto M.B.A. 1979; m. Howard s. George and Doris Hutchison 28 Dec. 1984; children: Gregory Howard, Kevin Norman; SENIOR VICE-PRES. & CHIEF FINANCIAL OFFICER, HOLT RENFREW & CO., LIMITED 1992– ; Sales & Mktg., Bell Canada 1973–79; Human Resources (2 yrs), Commercial & Corp. Lendin (4 yrs), Bank of Montreal 1979–85; Vice-Pres. Controller & MIS, Holt Renfrew & Co., Limited 1985–87; Vice-Pres. Human Resources 1987–91; Vice-Pres. & Gen. Mgr., Bloor St. Store (also resp. for Human Resources) 1991–92; Mem., Selection Ctte., Beth Park Memorial Scholarship Fund; recreations: tennis, skiing, camping: Office: 50 Bloor St. W., Toronto, Ont. M4W 1A1.

**JOLY, Jean-Marie,** M.A., Ph.D.; éducateur et administrateur; né Cap St-Ignace, Qué. 28 déc. 1925; f. François R.J. (décédé) et Wilhelmine (Leclerc) J. (déc.); é. Univ. Laval, B.A. 1946; Univ. d'Ottawa, M.A. 1949; Syracuse Univ., Ph.D. 1957; ép. Mariette, f. J.E. Bélanger (décédé) 13 juin 1953; enfants: Mathieu, Dominique, Elisabeth, Martine, Michèle; Professeur Titulaire, Faculté d'Education, Univ. d'Ottawa 1977–90; retiré; enseignement: univ. d'Ottawa 1949, Syracuse Univ. 1953, Univ. Miami 1955, Univ. Laval 1956; Dir. gen. des Programmes et des Examens, Min. de l'Educ. Qué. 1964; Dir. Inst. de Recherche pédagogique, Min. de l'Educ. Qué. 1967; Vice-recteur adjoint, Univ. of Ottawa, 1971–77; mem. Soc. candn. pour l'étude de l'éduc. (Vice-Prés. 1974–75); Assn. candn. des chercheurs en éduc.; auteur de plusieurs articles; reçu Whitworth Award, Conseil candn. de la recherche en éduc. 1971; Catholique r.; loisirs: musique, lecture, ski, jardinage; résidence: 44 Rideau River Lane, Ottawa, Ont. K1S 0X1.

**JOLY, Jean R.,** M.D., F.R.C.P.(C.), M.S.P.H., M.B.A.; university professor; b. Montreal, Que. 6 Jan. 1950; s. Maurice and Marcelle (Gaboury) J.; e. Univ. de Montréal M.D. 1975, F.R.C.P.(C.) 1979; Univ. of Washington M.S.P.H. 1981; Univ. of Concordia M.B.A. 1993; m. Johanne d. J.P. and C. (Laperrière) Hubert 26 May 1973; children: Jean-Sébastien, Marie-Soleil; DIRECTOR OF RESEARCH CENTRE, HOPITAL DU SAINT-SACREMENT 1991– ; rsch. training in epidemiology, Univ. of Washington; Rsch. Scholar, Fonds de la Rech. en Santé du Qué. 1981–87; Nat. Health Scholar 1987–92; main areas of research: Legionnaire's disease, epid. of HIV infection & sexually transmitted diseases; has been mem. of num. peer review cttes for NHRDP, FRSQ & other rsch. funding agencies in Can.; Vice-Pres., Candn. Soc. for Epid. & Biostatistics 1991–93; Pres. 1993–95; author/co-author of over 50 sci. journal articles; Office: 1050 chemin Ste-Foy, Quebec, Que. G1S 4L8.

**JONAS, George;** writer; b. Budapest, Hungary 15 June 1935; s. Dr. George M. Hubsch and Magda (Klug) J.; e. Lutheran Gymnasium, Budapest; studied theatre and film arts under F. Hont, Budapest; one s., Alexander; came to Can. 1956; author 'The Absolute Smile' (poems) 1967; 'The Happy Hungry Man' (poems) 1970; 'Cities' (poems) 1973; co-author 'By Persons Unknown' (non-fiction) 1977; 'Pushkin' (stage play commissioned by Theatre Plus) 1978; 'Final Decree' (novel) 1981; 'The Scales of Justice' (anthology of radio plays) 1983; 'Vengeance' (non-fiction) 1984; 'Crocodiles in the Bathtub' (journalism) 1987; 'Greenspan: The Case for the Defence' (biography with E.L. Greenspan) 1987; 'A Passion Observed' (non-fiction) 1989; 'Politically Incorrect' (journalism) 1991; other writings incl. numerous radio & TV plays; librettos for operas by Tibor Polgar, 'The European Lover' (toured Canada 1966) and 'The Glove' (commissioned by Canadian Opera Company 1973); contributed poems, articles and reviews to various journals; regular columnist, Toronto Sun, Toronto Life Magazine, Canadian Lawyer, The Idler; winner, Edgar Allan Poe Award for Best Fact Crime Book, 1977; ACTRA 'Nelly' Award for Best Radio Program 1982, 1986; Gold Medal, Internat. Radio Festival of New York 1986; mem., Assn. TV Producers & Dirs.; Composers, Authors & Publishers Assn. Can.; Poets & Writers, N.Y. State Council on Arts; recreation: motorcycle riding; Address: c/o M.G.A., 10 St. Mary St., Suite 510, Toronto, Ont. M4Y 1P9.

**JONCAS, Hon. Judge Claude,** B.A., LL.B.; judge; b. Montreal, Que. 15 May 1930; s. Louis E. and Lea (Bissonnette) J.; e. Stanislas Coll. B.A. 1949; Univ. of Montreal LL.B. 1954; McGill Univ. 4th yr. Law 1955; m. Hon. Claire d. Cecile and Jean Barrette 21 Dec. 1963; children: Louis, Lucie; JUDGE, COURT OF QUEBEC 1973– ; practiced Law, Montreal 1955–73; Alderman for City of Outremont 1966–73; Partner Lacoste, Savoie, Joncas, Smith, Leger; Pres. Jr. Bar of Montreal 1961; mem. Counc., Bar of Montreal; Bar of Prov. of Que.; Candn. Bar Assn.; Pres. Que. Conf. of Judges 1982; Que. Rep., Candn. Assn. of Provl. Court Judges 1982; Dir. Candn. Inst. for Admin. of Justice; cr. Q.C. 1972; recreations: golf, curling; Clubs: Rosemere Golf; Outremont Curling; Home: 261 Cote Ste Catherine, Outremont, Que.; Office: 1 Notre Dame E., S. 541, Montreal, Que. H2Y 1B6.

**JONES, Barbara Ellen,** B.A., M.A., Ph.D.; university professor; b. Philadelphia, Pa. 19 Dec. 1944; d. Charles Leslie and Ella (Yeager) J.; e. Univ. of Delaware B.A. 1966, M.A. 1969; master's thesis, Fac. de Méd., Lyon, France; Univ. of Delaware, Ph.D. 1971; m. John Gordon s. Gordon and Elizabeth Galaty 12 Aug. 1972; one s.: James Gordon Jones Galaty; PROF., MCGILL UNIV. 1989– ; predoct. fellow, Fac. de Méd., Lyon France 1968–69; postdoct. fellow, Coll. de France, Paris France 1970–73; Rsch. Assoc., Univ. of Chicago 1973–77; Asst. Prof., McGill Univ. 1977–82; Assoc. Prof. 1982–89; Killam Fellow, Montreal Neurol. Inst. 1977; MRC Scholar 1978–83; Fonds de la Rech. en Santé du Qué. Chercheur-Bouriser 1984–89; Visiting Scientist, Oxford Univ., England 1984–85; Invited Prof., Univ. de Genève, Switzerland 1991–92; Mem., Am. Assn. for the Adv. of Sci.; Am. Assn. of Anatomists; Sleep Rsch. Soc. (USA & Canada); Soc. for Neuroscience (USA); author of multiple rsch. reports & reviews in sci. journals & chapters in books; recreations: horseback riding; Home: 97 Arlington Ave., Westmount, Que. H3Y 2W5; Office: Montreal Neurological Inst., 3801 University St., Montreal, Que. H3A 2B4.

**JONES, Barry Douglas Walter,** B.Sc., M.D.C.M., F.R.C.P.(C); educator; psychiatrist; b. Montréal, Qué. 4 May 1951; s. Douglas Wyman and Florence Muriel (Witts) J.; e. McGill Univ. B.Sc. 1972, M.D.C.M. 1976; Harvard Med. Sch. Psychopharmacol. 1980 (Med. Rsch. Council Can. Fellow); m. Sylvia d. Ivars and Zenta Garnis 17 Aug. 1974; children: Brendon, Inara; CHIEF, SCHIZOPHRENIA BRANCH, INSTITUTE OF MENTAL HEALTH RSCH., ROYAL OTTAWA HOSP. and Assoc. Prof. of Psychiatry Univ. of Ottawa 1987– ; Residency in Psychiatry McGill Univ. 1976–80; mem. staff Allan Meml. Inst. Montréal 1981–84; joined Univ. of B.C. 1984 becoming Dir. Schizophrenia Service, Health Sci's Centre Hosp. and Asst. Prof.; Chrmn., Candn. Alliance for Research on Schizophrenia; Chrmn. Rsch. Review Ctte. present Hosp.; recipient Edgar G. Wilson Bursary McGill Univ. 1968–74; Sutherland Gold Medal in Biochem. McGill 1973; First Prize Resident Rsch. Day, Allan Meml. Inst. 1979; MRC Fellow 1980; author or co-author numerous profl. publs.; Fellow, Candn. Coll. Neuropsychopharmacol. (Councillor

1987); mem. Candn. Soc. Clin. Pharmacol.; Corp. Phys. & Surgs. Qué.; B.C. Med. Assn.; Candn. Med. Assn.; N.Y. Acad. Sci's; Candn. Psychiatric Assn.; Ont. Med. Assn.; Harvard Alumni Assn.; Home: 36 Fardon Way, Ottawa, Ont. K1G 4N3; Office: 1145 Carling Ave., Ottawa, Ont. K1G 7K4.

**JONES, Brian Rendel;** artist; b. Chatham, Ont. 1 June 1950; e. H.B. Beal S.S., spec. art course 1969–71; m. Susanne Tausig 14 May 1983; solo exhibitions incl.: Nancy Poole's Studio 1975–78, '80, '82, '84, 1987–90, '92, '93; Kitchener / Waterloo Art Gall., Chatham Cultural Ctr. 1987; Concourse Gall., Wilfrid Laurier Univ. 1985; London Reg. Art Gall. 1978; group exhibitions incl.: 'Toronto Harbour' Market Gallery 1988, 'Paintings of People' Memorial Univ. 1987, Ont. Soc. of Artists Annual Juried Exhib. Toronto 1985, McIntosh Gall., Univ. of W. Ont. 1984, '11 London Artists' The Gallery/Stratford 1979 & several others; collections incl.: Confed. Art Gall. P.E.I., Queen's Silver Jubilee Collection, Canada Council Art Bank, London Reg. Art Gall., McIntosh Gall. Univ. of W. Ont., Via Rail Corp. Coll., Wilfrid Laurier Univ., Prov. of Ont., Crown Life, T. Eaton Co., London Free Press, City of Toronto Corp. Coll.; Glaxo Canada Inc.; awards and grants incl.: Ont. Arts Council 1974–76, 1978; A.L. Hanna Mem. Award, Thames Theatre & Arts; 'Young Achiever' 1982 (ceremony attended by Queen & P.M.); Best Oil in Show Award, Ont. Soc. of Artists 1985; McDonald's of Can. Fine Arts Comp. 1985 & several others; subject of numerous magazine & newspaper articles and catalogues; Office: c/o Nancy Poole's Studio, 16 Hazelton Ave., Toronto, Ont. M5R 2E2.

**JONES, Brian William,** M.B.A.; insurance executive; b. Toronto, Ont. 18 July 1951; s. Kenneth Frederick and Marion Katherine (Sebert) J.; e. Upper Can. Coll. Toronto 1970; Univ. of W. Ont. H.B.A. 1974; Univ. of B.C. M.B.A. 1975; m. Jill Sloski 7 July 1983; children: Kim, Marc; SR. VICE PRES. AND BRANCH MGR., JOHNSON & HIGGINS LTD. 1985– ; Dir., Go Vacations Ltd.; Smed Manufacturing Ltd.; Safedesign Apparel Ltd.; Bluewing Environmental Services Inc.; joined present firm 1976; Dir., Toronto Symphony; Special Adv. Easter Seal Soc.; Ducks Unlimited (Can.); Univ. of Western Ont. Business Sch. Club of Toronto; Chrmn., Univ. of Western Ont. Development & Fund Raising Ctte.; recreations: squash, skiing, fishing, hunting; Clubs: Cambridge; Home: 495 Arrowhead Rd., Mississauga, Ont. L5H 1V5; Office: Scotia Plaza, P.O. Box 1010, 40 King St. W., Toronto, Ont. M5H 3Y2.

**JONES, Brian William,** H.B.A., M.B.A.; business executive; b. Toronto, Ont. 11 Sept. 1948; s. William L. and Muriel M. (Meaden) J.; e. Ridley Coll. 1968; Univ. of West. Ont. H.B.A. 1972, M.B.A. 1974; m. Diana d. Michael and Natalie Carroll 23 Dec. 1971; children: Andrew Michael William, Matthew Hadyn Mitchell; PRES. & CHIEF EXTVE. OFFR., RADIO MARKETING BUREAU INC. 1990– ; Dir., Goldcorp Inc.; CAB; BBM; BES; Emerson Summers Ltd.; Chrmn., Vision 2000 Mngt. Group Inc.; Fac. Mem., U.W.O. Sch. of Bus. Admin. 1972–73; Product Mgr., General Foods Ltd. 1974–78; Mktg. Mgr., Laura Secord Ltd. 1978–81; Vice-Pres. Mktg. & Sales, E.D. Smith & Sons Ltd. 1981–86; Pres., Candn. Nat. Sportsmen's Shows Ltd. 1986–90; Mem., Young Pres. Orgn.; Forum K; Past Pres. & Dir., Western Bus. Sch. Club of Toronto; Past Pres., Am. Mktg. Assn. of Toronto; Past Pres., Alumnae Assn. Ridley Coll.; recreations: tennis, golf, squash; club: Oakville; Home: 149 Balsam Dr., Oakville, Ont. L6J 3X4; Office: 146 Yorkville Ave., Toronto, Ont. M5R 1C2.

**JONES, Christopher Prestige,** M.A., Ph.D., F.R.S.C.; educator; b. Chislehurst, Eng. 21 Aug. 1940; s. William Prestige and Irene May (McCreddie) J.; e. Rugby Sch. Eng. 1958; Oxford Univ. B.A. 1962, M.A. 1967; Harvard Univ. Ph.D. 1965; PROF. OF CLASSICS AND HISTORY, HARVARD UNIV. 1992– ; Lectr. Univ. of Toronto 1965, Asst. Prof. 1966, Assoc. Prof. 1968, Prof. of Classics 1975–92, Assoc. Chrmn. of Classics 1983–85, Chrmn. 1986–90, Acting Vice Dean of Arts & Sci. 1985–86; Visiting Lectr. Harvard Univ. 1968; mem. Inst. Advanced Study Princeton 1971–72, 1982–83, Visitor 1987, 1990–91; Prof. Associé, École Normale Supérieure de Jeunes Filles Paris 1979; Professeur associé, École Normale Supérieure, Paris 1992; author 'Plutarch and Rome' 1971, 2nd ed. 1972; 'The Roman World of Dio Chrysostom' 1978; 'Culture and Society in Lucian' 1986; transl. 'Philostratus: Life of Apollonius' 1971; mem. Am. Philol. Assn. (ed. bd. 1974–76; Chrmn. 1975–76); Fellow, Am. Numismatic Soc.; Corresponding mem., German Archaeological Institute; Sr. Fellow, Byzantine Studies, Dumbarton Oaks 1993– ; recreations: music, travel; Home: Apt. 107, 130 Mount Auburn St., Cambridge, Mass. 02138 U.S.A.

**JONES, David Charles,** Ed.D.; educator; b. Edmonton, Alta. 7 Oct. 1943; s. Harry and Dagmar Maria J.; e. Univ. of Victoria B.Ed. 1966; Univ. of B.C., M.Ed. 1968, Ed.D. 1978; m. Anita E. d. Ann and Bob Busenius 8 May 1976; children: Wesley T., Abbie L., Kyle L.; PROF. OF EDN., UNIV. OF CALGARY 1987– ; High Sch. Teacher Revelstoke, B.C. 1966–74; apptd. present Univ. 1977; author: 'Midways Judges and Smooth Tongued Fakirs' 1983, 'Empire of Dust' 1987 (Special Merit Award Alta. Culture); co-author: 'The Weather Factory: A Pictorial History of Medicine Hat' 1988; editor: 'We'll All Be Buried Down Here' 1986; co-editor: 'Shaping the Schools of the Canadian West' 1979, 'Schooling and Society in 20th Century B.C.' (Candn. Hist. Assn. Regional Hist. Award) 1980, 'Approaches to Educational History' 1981, 'Building Beyond the Homestead' 1985, 'Schools in the West' (Candn. Hist. of Educ. Assoc. Award) 1986; editor 'Wake Up, Canada' by C.W. Peterson 1989; 'A Funny Bone That Was: Humor Between The Wars' 1992; general co-editor: 'Aberhart: Outpourings and Replies' 1991; Reynolds-Alberta Museum Transportation and Agriculture History Series 1992; 'Pioneer Policing in Southern Alberta: Deane of the Mounties' 1993; author or co-author over 40 articles; recipient Student Union Teaching Excellence Award 1988; Distinguished Lectr., Education Faculty 1990; Chinook Arch Author's Award 1992; recreations: curling, basketball, swimming; Home: 125 Sandpiper Place N.W., Calgary, Alta. T3K 3T9; Office: Calgary, Alta. T2N 1N4.

**JONES, David Haney,** Q.C.; retired transportation executive; b. Winnipeg, Man. 13 Mar. 1925; s. late Stanley Neville Kennedy and Miriam Margaret (Haney) J.; e. Pub. Schs. and St. John's-Ravenscourt Sch., Winnipeg; Univ. of Man., Law Sch., LL.B. 1948; Univ. of Cambridge, Dipl. in Comparative Legal Studies 1950; m. 1stly, late Kathleen Elizabeth Barry 2 Sept. 1950; children: Sarah Kennedy, Andrew Robert O'Neill; 2ndly, Evelyn Constance Hyndman 16 Sept. 1989; Commr., Candn. Transport Comn. 1967–87; called to Bar of Man. 1949; cr. Q.C. (Fed.) 1972; served in Office of Econ. Adv. to Premier, Govt. of Man., 1949–50; Solr., Dilts, Baker, Laidlaw & Shepard, Winnipeg, 1951–53; Partner of law firm Thompson, Dilts and Co., Winnipeg, 1953–67; Lectr., Man. Law Sch., Univ. of Man., 1952–66; Chrmn., Rly. Transport Comte., 1967–79; Chrmn., Water Transport Comte. 1979–82; Chrmn., Commodity Pipeline Transport Comte. 1982–87; Sub-Lt., R.C.N.V.R. 1943–45; Lt. R.C.N. (Reserve) 1950–56; mem., Law Soc. of Man.; Life Mem., Adv. Bd. of Ottawa, Salvation Army; Zeta Psi; Anglican; recreations: reading, railway history, travel; Home: 97 Park Rd., Ottawa, Ont. K1M 0C1.

**JONES, David Robert,** B.Sc., Ph.D., F.R.S.C.; educator; b. Bristol, Eng. 28 Jan. 1941; s. William Arnold (dec.) and Gladys Margery (Parker) J.; e. Southampton Univ. B.Sc. 1962; Univ. of E. Anglia, Ph.D. 1965; m. Valerie d. Gordon and Agnes Gibson 15 Sept. 1962; two d. Melanie Ann, Vivienne Samantha; PROF. OF ZOOL. UNIV. OF B.C. 1969– ; Lectr. Univ. of Bristol 1965–69; Killam Found. Fellow 1973, 1989; Fry Medal, Candn. Zool. Soc. 1992; Killam Rsch. Prize (UBC) 1993; author or co-author over 150 sci. papers diving & exercise physiol.; mem. Soc. Exper. Biol.; Am. Physiol. Soc.; Am. Zool. Soc.; Candn. Zool. Soc.; Candn. Physiol. Soc.; Home: 3545 W. King Edward Ave., Vancouver, B.C. V6S 1M4; Office: 6270 University Blvd., Vancouver, B.C. V6T 2A9.

**JONES, David William,** B.Sc., M.D.; physician; b. Vancouver, B.C. 14 March 1946; s. William Ivor and Vera Olive (Allin) J.; e. Sir Winston Churchill and Magee Secondary Schs. Vancouver; Univ. of B.C., B.Sc. 1967, M.D. 1970; m. M. Patricia d. Stephen and Trudy Herbrik; children: Russell, Keith, Michael, Ashley; commenced family practice Vancouver 1971, Burnaby, B.C. 1975; Active Staff, Burnaby Hosp. 1976– , Visiting Staff, Vancouver Gen. Hosp. and Grace Hosp., Vancouver 1971– ; mem. Candn. Acad. Sports Med. 1974– ; Team Phys. Vancouver Candn. Baseball Club 1978–90, also amateur lacrosse, baseball and ice hockey teams; Mem. Bd. of Dirs., MD Advisory Bd. 1989– (Chrmn. 1993– ); mem. Candn. Med. Assn.; B.C. Med. Assn.; mem. ed. bd. B.C. Med. Jour. 1972–85; Dir. B.C. Med. Assn. 1980–91 (mem. Finance Ctte. 1980–88, Chrmn. Communications Ctte. 1983–87, Exec. Ctte. 1984–89, Pres. 1987–88); Dir. Candn. Med. Assn. 1989–91 (mem. Finance Ctte. 1983–89); mem. Christian Med. Dental Soc. Can. (Treas. 1972–81); Home: 6507 Crestview Dr., Delta, B.C. V4E 2Z6; Office: 204, 6440 Royal Oak, Burnaby, B.C. V5H 3P2.

**JONES, Rt. Rev. Derwyn Dixon,** B.A., L.Th., D.D.; retired bishop; b. Chatham, Ont. 5 Aug. 1925; s. Rev. Walter and Mary Rosalie (Dixon) J.; e. Sir Adam Beck Coll. Inst. London, Ont. 1942; Huron Coll. London L.Th. 1946, D.D. 1983; Univ. of W. Ont. B.A. 1946; m. A. Carole d. Carl and Audrey Dilamarter 18 Apl. 1960; children: Paula Mary, Evan Frederick Peter; o. Deacon 1946; o. Priest (Ang.) 1947; Curate Holy Trinity Ch. Winnipeg 1946–48, All Saints' Ch. Windsor 1948–49; Rector St. Andrew Meml. Ch. Kitchener and St. George's Ch. New Hamburg 1949–52; Asst. Rector St. Paul's Cath. London 1952–55; Rector Canon Davis Meml. Ch. Sarnia 1955–58; Rector St. Barnabas' Ch. Windsor 1958–66; Bishop's Examining Chaplain for Deacons 1962–66; Rector St. Peter's Ch. Brockville and Canon of St. George's Cath. Chapter Kingston 1966–69; Rector St. James' (Westminster) London 1969–82; Canon Precentor 1970; Archdeacon of Middlesex 1978–82; el. Bishop Suffragan of Huron 1982; Coadjutor Bishop of Huron 1983; Ninth Bishop of Huron Diocese 1984–90 (retired); Hon. Sr. Fellow Renison Coll. Waterloo 1982; recreations: music, journalism; Club: London; Home: Suite 301, 7 Picton St., London, Ont. N6B 3N7.

**JONES, Douglas Gordon,** F.R.S.C.; retired educator; b. Bancroft, Ont. 1 Jan. 1929; s. Gordon W. and Arlene M. (Ford) J.; e. The Grove Sch. Lakefield, Ont.; McGill Univ. B.A. 1952; Queen's Univ. M.A. 1954; D.Litt. (Hon. causa) Univ. of Guelph, 1982; m. Monique Baril 1 Dec. 1976; children: (by previous marriage) Stephen, Skyler, Tory Joanne, North; Prof. of English, Univ. de Sherbrooke 1963–94, retired; lectr. Royal Mil. Coll. 1954–55; Guelph Agric. Coll. 1955–61; Bishop's Univ. 1961–63; recipient Univ. of W. Ont. Pres.'s Medal for Poetry 1976; Gov. Gen.'s Award for Poetry 1977; Mich. State Univ. A.J.M. Smith Prize for Poetry 1977–78; QSPELL Award for Poetry 1989; Gov. General's Award for Translation; author (criticism) 'Butterfly on Rock' 1970; (poetry) 'Frost on the Sun' 1957; 'The Sun is Axeman' 1961; 'Phrases from Orpheus' 1967; 'Under the Thunder the Flowers Light Up the Earth' 1977; translator 'The Terror of the Snows' 1976 (selected poems of Paul-Marie Lapointe); enlarged Candn. edition, 'The Fifth Season' 1985; 'Categorics' (Normand de Bellefeuille) 1992; ed. ''The March to Love': selected Poems of Gaston Miron' 1986; 'A Throw of Particles: Selected and New Poems' 1983; 'Balthazar and Other Poems' 1988; 'A Thousand Hooded Eyes' (8 colour engravings by Lucie Lambert and 9 poems by D.G. Jones) 1991; Fellow, Royal Soc. of Can.; Home: P.O. Box 356, North Hatley, Que. J0B 2C0; Office: Sherbrooke, Que. J1K 2R1.

**JONES, Frank Edward;** university professor; b. Montreal, P.Q. 28 Oct. 1917; s. Richard James and Victoria Lemire (Hughes) J.; e. McGill Univ., B.A. 1949; M.A. 1950; Harvard Univ., Ph.D. 1954; m. Jean, d. D.S. McEachran, 14 Sept. 1946; children: David M.; Dilys L.; PROF. EMERITUS, DEPT. SOCIOLOGY, MCMASTER UNIV.; Chief, Research Div., Candn. Citizenship Branch 1953; Asst. Prof. Soc., McMaster Univ. 1955–59; Chrmn., Dept. Soc. 1958–65; Assoc. Prof. Soc. 1959; Prof. Soc. 1964; Chrmn. 1982–86; Dir., Labour Studies 1981–87; author 'An Introduction to Sociology,' 1961; co-author (with B.R. Blishen, K.D. Naegele and John Porter) 'Canadian Society: Sociological Perspectives,' 1961, 1964, 1968, 1971; co-author (with M. Boyd, J. Goyder, H. McRoberts, P. Pineo and J. Porter) 'Ascription and Achievement: Studies in Mobility and Status Attainment in Canada' 1985; author various articles in professional journals on occupations, organizations, immigrants and immigration; rec'd. visiting appointments Univ. B.C.; Australian Nat. Univ.; McGill Univ.; served Royal Candn. Navy 1940–45; mem. Candn. Sociology and Anthropology Assn.; Am. Sociological Assn.; recreations: tennis; music; reading; Home: 19 Brentwood Dr., Dundas, Ont. L9H 3N2; Office: Dept. Sociology, McMaster Univ., 1280 Main St. W., Hamilton, Ont. L8S 4M4.

**JONES, Geoffrey Melvill,** M.A., M.B., B.Ch., F.R.S., F.R.S.C., F.C.A.S.I., F.R.Ae.S.; university professor; b. Cambridge, Eng. 14 Jan. 1923; came to Can. 1961; s. Benett Melvill and Dorothy Laxton (Jotham) MJ.; e. King's Choir Sch., Cambridge, 1930–35; Dauntsey's Sch., Wiltshire, 1935–40; Cambridge Univ. B.A. 1944, MA. 1947, M.B., B.Ch. 1949; Middlesex Hosp., London 1945–49; Addenbrooke's Hosp., Cambridge 1949–51; m. Jenny Marigold Burnaby (dec.) 21 June 1953; children: Katharine F., Francis H., Andrew J., Dorothy H.; PROF. (ADJUNCT) OF CLINICAL NEUROSCIENCES, UNIV. OF CALGARY and PROF. (EMERITUS) OF PHYSIOLOGY, MCGILL UNIV.; first incumbent of the Hosmer Research Professorship in applied physiology, McGill Univ.; Visiting Prof.: Stanford Univ. 1971–72; Collège de France, Paris 1979; Green visiting scholar Univ. of

Texas Galveston 1982; Heritage Visiting Prof. Univ. of Calgary 1983; Consultant in Neurosciences to NASA Skylab and Spacelab programs; served with RAF (Inst. of Av. Med.), 1951–55, rank sqdn. leader, Flying Personnel Med. Offr.; Offr. (External Staff) Med. Rsch. Council Gt. Brit. 1955–61; rec'd. Harry G. Armstrong Lectureship Award, Aerospace Medical Assn. 1968; Arnold D. Tuttle Award for outstanding rsch. in aerospace medicine 1971; Skylab Achievement Award, 1974; Quinquennial Gold Medal award, Internat. Bárány Soc.; 1st recipient, Dohlman Medal, Dohlman Soc., Univ. of Toronto; Wilbur Franks award, Candn. Soc. for Aerospace Med.; Stewart Memorial Lectureship Award, Royal Aeronautical Soc., London 1989; Buchanan Barbour Award, Royal Aeronautical Soc., London 1990; McLaughlin Medal Award, Royal Society of Canada, for Medical Scientific Rsch. 1991; author 'Mammalian Vestibular Physiology' 1979; ed., 'Adaptive Mechanisms in Gaze Control' 1985; articles in over 150 scientific publs.; el. Fellow, Royal Soc. of London 1979; el. Fellow, Royal Soc. of Can. 1979; Fellow, Candn. Aeronautics and Space Inst.; Fellow, Aerospace Med. Assn.; Fellow, Royal Aeronautical Soc.; mem., UK Physiol. Soc.; Candn. Physiol. Soc.; Candn. Soc. of Aerospace Med.; Mtl. Physiol. Soc.; Society for Neuroscience; Intl. Collegium of Otolaryngology; Bárány Soc.; Anglican Protestant; recreations: outdoor activities, tennis, sailing, music, reading; Office: Dept. of Clinical Neurosciences, Faculty of Medicine, Univ. of Calgary, 3330 Hospital Drive N.W., Calgary, Alta. T2N 4N1.

**JONES, Llewellyn Edward,** B.Sc.(C.E.), M.A.Sc., Ph.D., F.I.Mech.E., F.E.I.C., P.Eng., C.Eng.; university professor, professional engineer; b. Montreal, Que. 25 Mar. 1910; s. William and Lilian (Varley) J.; e. Univ. of Man. B.Sc.(C.E.) 1931 (magna cum laude, 2 gold medals); Univ. of Toronto M.A.Sc. 1933, Ph.D. 1941; m. Dorothy d. James and Florence (Davies) Mudge 30 July 1938; children: James Llewellyn, William Ruell; PROF. EMERITUS OF MECHANICAL ENGINEERING, UNIV. OF TORONTO 1975– ; Jr. Engr., C.P.R. 1929–30; Man. Prov. Govt. 1931–33; Emergency Lectr., Univ. of Man. 1932; Dem., Instr., Lectr., Rsch. Asst., (Appl. Physics), Univ. of Toronto 1936–44; Asst. Prof. to Prof. (Mech. Engg.) 1944–75; Engineering Archivist 1970– ; Assoc., Inst. for Environ. Studies 1971– ; Hydraulic Engr., Ont. Hydro 1941–57; General Cons. 1957– ; certificate designer, calligrapher; extensive public service to students; many years of voluntary instruction; F.I.Mech.E. 1964; Sons of Martha Medal 1965; F.E.I.C. 1974; Queen's Silver Jubilee Medal 1977; several awards from students, alumni, staff, Univ. of Toronto incl. Sesquicentennial Long Serv. Award 1977; Life Mem., Royal Candn. Inst. 1990– ; Boy Scouts Canada Medal of Merit 1992; awarded Commemorative Medal for 125th Anniversary of Candn. Confederation 1993; Anglican; Conservative; Mem., Ont. Assn. of Profl. Engrs.; Am. Soc. of Civil Engrs.; Am. Soc. of Mech. Engrs.; Brit. Inst. of Mech. Engrs.; Royal Candn. Inst. (Hon. Sec. 1982–86); Boy Scouts Assn. of Can.; Camp 1, The Ritual of the Calling of an Engineer; editor: 'The Next Hundred Years' (for Centennial of Fac. of Appl. Sci. and Engg., Univ. of Toronto 1973); author of some 200 discussions, reviews, reports, biographies, hist. summaries, articles & papers in tech. journals; recreations: choral singing, photography, woodworking, writing, composing humorous verse, calligraphy; clubs: Faculty, Hart House; Home: 29 Prince George Dr., Islington, Ont. M9A 2X9; Office: 35 St. George St., Toronto, Ont. M5S 1A4.

**JONES, Hon. Malachi C.,** B.A., LL.B.; judge; b. Rockingham, N.S. 2 Sept. 1929; s. late Alexander William, K.C. and Lillian Agatha (Lyons) J.; e. Rockingham (N.S.) Pub. Sch. and St. Patrick's High Sch., 1946; St. Mary's Univ., 1946–48, B.A. 1970; Dalhousie Univ., LL.B. 1951; m. Catherine Ann Marie, d. late Dugald MacDonald, 2 Aug. 1952; children: Roseanne, Barbara, Maureen, Sheila, Colleen, Monica, Jennifer, Stephanie, Stephen; JUSTICE, SUPREME COURT OF N.S., since 1970; appointed to the Appeal Division, 1979; read law with Walter Barss, K.C. and John A. Y. MacDonald, K.C., Depy. Atty. Gen. N.S.; called to Bar of N.S. 1952; cr. Q.C. 1967; cont. to practice with Dept. of Atty. Gen. N.S. after receiving law degree; Leg. Counsel for N.S. 1966–67; apptd. Asst. Depy. Atty. Gen. 1967, Assoc. 1969; has appeared on numerous occasions before Supreme Courts of N.S. and Can. and various prov. adm. bds.; rep. of N.S. on Conf. of Commrs. on Uniformity of Leg. in Can.; has lectered at St. Mary's and Dalhousie Univs.; Past Vice Chrmn., Halifax Housing Authority; mem. Bd. of Govs., St. Mary's Univ., 1966–70 (Pres. Alumni Assn. 1963–65); past mem. Bd., Home of the Good Shepherd, Halifax; mem. N.S. Barristers' Soc.; Candn. Bar Assn.; R. Catholic; recreations: sailing, swimming, walking; Home: 14 Turnmill Dr., Halifax, N.S. B3M 4H2; Office: The Law Courts, 1815 Upper Water St., Halifax, N.S. B3J 3C8.

**JONES, Marsha Susan,** CMP; management executive; b. Brampton, Ont. 13 Sept. 1951; d. Charles Wesley and Ena Jean (Alderson) J.; e. Georgetown Dist. H.S.; m. Clive s. C. Richter 22 Oct. 1988; one d.: Alexis Richter; PRESIDENT/OWNER, MCC PLANNERS INC. 1988– ; various management positions until 1988; Pres., Meeting Planners Internat. Toronto Chapter 1993–94; occasional speaker, Ryerson Tourism/Meeting Mngt. Course; Guest Speaker, ACE Convention; Volunteer work for St. Louise Outreach, Rett Syndrom, Alzheimer Assn.; Mem., Meeting Planners Internat.; Candn. Hotel & Mktg. Sales Extves.; Metro Toronto Convention & Visitors Assn.; Home: 90 Moregate Cres., Brampton, Ont. L6S 3K9; Office: 33 Niagara St., Toronto, Ont. M5V 1C2.

**JONES, Paul Charles,** B.A.; publisher; b. Swanage, Dorset, UK 20 May 1949; s. Patrick Charles and Mona Elizabeth (Park) J.; e. Saltfleet High Sch. Stoney Creek, Ont. 1966; Univ. of Toronto B.A. 1972 (Beatty Admission Scholarship, Wintercorbyn Award for Eng., Univ. Coll. Honour Award); m. Rona d. Max and Fredelle Maynard 20 Oct. 1970; one s. Benjamin; EXEC. VICE PRES. AND DIR. CB MEDIA LTD. 1990– ; Publisher 'Canadian Business' and 'Profit' mags. 1990– ; joined 'The Financial Post' 1974–78; Rsch. Dir., Sales Devel. Mgr. 'Maclean's' mag. 1978–81, Dir. of Mktg. 1982, Gen. Mgr. 1984, Assoc. Pub. 1987–90; Exec. Dir. Canadian University Press Media Services Ltd. 1981–82, Dir. and Treas. 1983–85; Chrmn., Print Measurement Bureau 1992– (Treas. 1985–90); Chrmn. Postal Options Ctte. Candn. Mag. Publishers Assn. 1990–93; Periodical Dist. Task Force 1991–92; Dir. Candn. Bus. Press 1990–92; Candn. Mag. Publishers Assn. 1991–93; Nat. Mag. Awards Found. 1989–93 (Treas. 1989–91); ABC Canada 1990–92; Junior Achievement of Canada 1992– ; Candn. Congress of Advertising 1992–93; Pres. Bus. Task Force on Literacy 1987–90; Comnr. The Baseball Pool 1983– ; ed. 'A Survey of Managerial and Professional Canadians' 1978; 'Measuring the Costs of Illiteracy in Canada' 1988; frequent speaker literacy issues confs., conventions, media; recreations: wine-tasting, golf, health spas; Clubs: Cambridge; Greystone Golf; Office: 5F, 777 Bay St., Toronto, Ont. M5W 1A7.

**JONES, Peter,** Ph.L., S.T.L., Ph.D.; b. Warwickshire, Eng. 10 Dec. 1938; s. William Edward and Doris Ellen (Simpson) J.; e. St. Philips Grammar Sch. Eng.; Gregorian Univ. Rome Ph.L. 1960, S.T.L. 1964; Oxford Univ. 1972–73; McGill Univ. Ph.D. 1973; m. Elizabeth Margaret d. G.D. Meredith, San Francisco, Cal. 27 Dec. 1968; children: Martin David, Marc Andrew, Simon Francis; PRESIDENT, UNIVERSITY COLLEGE OF THE FRASER VALLEY 1987– ; Chrmn., North Fraser Investment Corporation 1991– ; Lectr. Marianopolis Coll. (Univ. de Montréal) 1964–65; Asst. Prof. and Dir. Dept. Interdisciplinary Studies, mem. Senate Loyola Coll. Montreal 1965–74; Pacific Region Dir. Candn. Council of Christians & Jews Vancouver 1974–75, Asst. to Pres. 1975–76; mem. Acad. Council Sch. of Continuing Studies Univ. of Toronto 1977–79; Pres., Candn. Council of Christians and Jews 1976–79; Exec. Dir., Univ. of B.C. Alumni Assoc., 1979–84; Dean, B.C. Inst. of Technology, 1984–85; Vice Pres, Student Services and Educational Support, B.C. Inst. of Technology, 1985–87; Vice-Pres., Advanced Education Council of B.C. 1990–91; R. Catholic; recreations: gardening, camping; Club: Canadian; Home: 1345 McKenzie Rd., Abbotsford, B.C. V2S 4N2; Office: 45600 Airport Rd., Chilliwack, B.C. V2P 6T4.

**JONES, Philip H.,** B.A.Sc., M.S., Ph.D.; educator; b. Tredegar, Gwent, U.K. 30 Jan. 1931; s. Reginald Salisbury and Evelyn Ann (Harrhy) J.; e. Univ. of Toronto B.A.Sc. Hon. 1958; Northwestern Univ., Evanston, Ill. M.S. 1963, Ph.D. 1965; m. Eileen d. Steve and May Ryan 11 Dec. 1954; children: Denise, Lisa, Glyn, Ian; PROFESSOR EMERITUS, CIVIL ENGINEERING AND ENVIRONMENTAL STUDIES 1990– ; PRES., PHILIP H. JONES LTD., CONSULTING ENVIRONMENTAL ENGRS. 1990– ; particled pupil to Borough Engr., Slough, U.K. 1946–50; Asst. Engr. Borough of Surbiton, U.K. 1950–51; Asst. Engr. Volta River Project, Ghana, W. Africa 1951–54; Project Engr. Town Planning Cons., Toronto 1954–58; Gen. Mgr. Contracting Co., Toronto 1958–59; Partner Franklin McArthur Assoc. Cons. Engr., Toronto 1959–62; Grad. Sch. 1962–65; Prof. of Civil Engineering, Univ. of Toronto 1965–90; Foundation Prof. of Environmental Engineering, Griffith Univ., Brisbane, Australia; Founding Dir., Inst. of Environmental Studies, Univ. of Toronto 1971–90; started grad. prog. in Environ. Engrg.; Cons. to World Health Orgn. 1969– ; Cons. to OECD, IBRD, various govt. and ind. in Can. and U.S.A.; Founding Pres. Candn. Assn. on Water Pollution Rsrch. and Control; Pres. Conf. of Internat. Assoc. on Water Pollution Rsch.; Past Nat. Chrmn. Environ. Engr. Div., Candn. Soc. for Civil Engrg.; Past Chrmn. Sport Ont.; Past Exec. Vice-Pres. Sports Fedn. of Can.; past Warden Trinity Ch., Aurora (Anglican Ch. of Can.); recreations: swimming, photography, video movie making.

**JONES, Phillip Clarence,** C.A.; financial executive; b. Saint John, N.B. 10 July 1942; s. Willard Clarence and Grace Vivian (Waddell) J.; e. Saint John H.S. 1960; C.A. Prov. of N.B. 1965; VICE-PRESIDENT, FINANCE, T.S. SIMMS & CO. LTD. 1986– ; Coopers, Lybrand 1960–67; joined T.S. Simms & Co. Limited 1967; Past Dir., Mosley Stone Ltd. U.K.; Life Mem., Kinsmen Club of Saint John (Past Pres.); Past Sec., Maritime Chess Assn.; Sec., Woolastook Investments Club IV; Home: P.O. Box 3395, Stn. B., Saint John, N.B.; Office: P.O. Box 820, Saint John, N.B. E2L 4C5.

**JONES, Phyllis Edith,** B.Sc.N., M.Sc., R.N., F.A.P.H.A., DNSc. (Hon.); nursing administrator; b. Barrie, Ont. 16 Sept. 1924; d. Colston Graham and E. (Shand) J.; e. Barrie Coll. Inst. 1943; Univ. of Toronto B.Sc.N. 1950; M.Sc. 1969; PROF. EMERITUS, UNIV. OF TORONTO 1990– ; Prof., Univ. of Toronto 1972–89; Dean, Faculty of Nursing, Univ. of Toronto 1979–88; Co-Chairperson Candn. Public Health Assn. Comte. to develop 'A Statement of Functions and Qualifications for the Practice of Public Health Nursing in Canada,' 1964–66; Mem. Bd. Dir. Victorian Order of Nurses, 1971–79, 1985–87; Ont. Council Health Task Force on Evaluation of Primary Health Care Settings, 1975; Task Force, Coll. of Nurses of Ont., 1978–80; Adv. Comte., Toronto Gen. Hosp. Patient Classification Study, 1978–80; Adv. Comte. to George Brown Coll. Diploma Nursing programme, 1981–86; Metro. Toronto Dist. Health Council, 1981–82; WHO cons. 1985, 1986; author of various articles with reference to the primary health care sector and nursing diagnoses; mem., Candn. Public Health Assn.; Ont. Public Health Assn.; Candn. Assn. of Univ. Schs. of Nursing (Council member); Candn. Council of Social Development; Candn. Nurses Assn.; R.N. Assn. of Ont.; Charter Mem., N. Amer. Nursing Diagnosis Assn.; Honorary Mem., The Finnish Soc. of Pro Nursing; Hon. DNSc., Univ. of Turku, Finland; Protestant; recreations; skiing, reading, walking, cooking; Home: R.R. 2, Owen Sound, Ont. N4K 5N4.

**JONES, R. Michael,** B.Sc., P.Eng.; geological engineer; b. Kingston, Ont. 23 Nov. 1963; s. Richard Edward and Mary (Milsap) J.; e. Univ. of Toronto B.Sc. 1985; PRESIDENT AND CHIEF EXECUTIVE OFFICER, CATHEDRAL GOLD CORP. 1991– ; Founder, Utex Gold Syndicate 1984; Glimmer Resources Inc. 1987; Vice-Pres., Cathedral Gold Corp. 1990–91; recreations: skiing, hiking, sailing; Office: 601 W. Hastings St., 8th fl., Vancouver, B.C. V6B 5A6.

**JONES, Richard Allan,** M.A., Ph.D.; educator; b. Kearny, N.J. 7 July 1943; s. Richard Ditzel and Evelyn Antoinette (Allen) J.; Candn. citizen 1958; e. Princeton Univ. B.A. 1965; Univ. Laval M.A. 1966, Ph.D. 1972; m. Lilianne d. Victor-Edouard and Georgette Plamondon 8 June 1974; children: Marie-Noëlle, Stéphanie, Serge-André, Charles-Denis; PROF. OF HIST., LAVAL UNIV. 1970– , Dir. of Advanced Studies 1988–90; Visiting Prof. of Candn. Hist.: The Johns Hopkins Sch. of Advanced Internat. Studies 1977; Center for Candn. Studies, Duke Univ. 1983–84; Univ. of York, England 1990–91; author 'Community in Crisis: French-Canadian Nationalism in Perspective' 1967, 1972; 'L'Idéologie de l'Action catholique' 1974; 'Vers une hégémonie libérale' 1980; 'Duplessis et le gouvernement de l'Union nationale' 1983; 'L'Association des universités partiellement ou entièrement de langue française; une idée en marche' 1987; co-author 'Histoire du Québec' 1976; 'Origins: Canadian History Before Confederation' 1988, 1992; 'Destinies: Canadian History Since Confederation' 1988, 1992; ed. 'Revue d'histoire de l'Amérique française' 1985–88; mem. Institut d'histoire de l'Amérique française; Candn. Hist. Assn.; recreation: gardening; Home: St-Cyrille-de-L'Islet, Qué. G0R 2W0; Office: Québec, Qué. G1K 7P4.

**JONES, Rev. Richard Ditzel,** O.C. (1972), M.A., B.S.T., LL.D.; b. Elizabeth, N.J. 17 Sept. 1906; s. John Richard and Hannah M. (Ditzel) J.; e. Elizabeth, N.J.; Wesleyan Univ., B.A. 1928; Boston Univ., Sch. of Theol., M.A. 1932 and B.S.T. 1933; Windsor Univ., LL.D. 1968; York Univ. 1975; m. Evelyn A., d. John M. Allen of Gladstone, N.J., 26 June, 1937 (dec'd. 1986); children: Richard, Nancy; PRES., CANADIAN COUNCIL OF CHRISTIANS AND JEWS, 1967–76; Pres. Emeritus, 1976; mem. Newark, N.J., Conf. of the Meth.

Ch.; taught Latin and English at Athens Coll., Athens, Greece, 1928–31; Pastor, Gladstone (N.J.) Meth. Ch., 1934–37; Grace Meth. Ch., Kearny, N.J., 1937–47; Extve. Dir., Candn. Counc. of Christians and Jews 1947–67; attended World Brotherhood Conf. at UNESCO House, Paris, June 1950, and 2nd Conf. in Brussels, 1955; Past Chrmn., West Hudson Am. Cancer Soc.; has travelled and lectured in many countries; toured Iraq and Iran with Richard Haliburton; served in 2nd World War with U.S. Merchant Marine; author 'A Life Long Pursuit of Brotherhood' (autobiography) 1988; contributed various articles on human relations to numerous journs.; recipient of Beth Sholom Brotherhood Award; Award of Merit, Corp. of City of Toronto 1972; Canadian Citizen October 1957; apptd. Chaplain, Metrop. Toronto Police Assn., 1968; Chaplain Emeritus 1987; apptd. Officer, Order of Canada 1972; rec'd award of John Diefenbaker Memorial Foundation 1984; Commemorative Medal, 125th Anniversary, Candn. Confedn. 1992; Extve Comte., St. Albans Boys and Girls Club; Finance Chrmn., John G. Diefenbaker Memorial Fdn.; Bd. Delta Tau Delta; recreations: fishing, travelling; Clubs: Rotary (Hon.); Kiwanis; Home: 2466 Shepard Ave., Mississauga, Ont. L5A 2H6.

**JONES, Richard Norman,** Ph.D., D.Sc., F.R.S.C.; research scientist; b. Manchester, Eng., 20 March 1913; s. late Richard Leonard and Blanche (Mason) J.; e. Manchester Univ., B.Sc., M.Sc., Ph.D., D.Sc.; D.Sc. (Hon.) Univ. of Poznan, Tokyo Inst. of Technology; m. Magda, d. late Eugene Kemeny, 11 July 1939; two s.; Richard Kemeny, David Leonard; Guest Researcher, Dept. of Chem., Tokyo Inst. Technology 1985–86; Adjunct Prof., Queen's Univ. 1984; Distinguished Visitor, Dept. of Chem, Univ. of Alta. 1983; Guest Prof., Dept. of Chemistry, Tokyo Inst. of Technology, 1979–82; Commonwealth Fund Fellow, Harvard Univ., 1937–42; Lectr. and Asst. Prof., Dept. of Chem., Queen's Univ. 1942–46; Principal Research Offr., Div. of Chem., Nat. Research Council Can., 1946–78; Guest Worker 1978–92; Guest Scientist, Dept. of Chem., Univ. of Alta. 1992– ; author of three books and over 250 tech. papers in chem. and spectroscopic journs.; Fellow, Royal Society of Canada; Chem. Inst. Can.; mem., Am. Chem. Soc.; Royal Soc. Chem. (London); Internat. Union Pure & Applied Chem. (Past Pres., Phys. Chem. Div.); I.C.S.U. Comm. on Data for Science and Tech., Spec. Soc. Can.; recreations: travel, photography, history of science; Home: Claridge House, Apt. 1003, 11027 87th Ave., Edmonton, Alta. T6G 2P9.

**JONES, Robert Howell,** B.Comm.; executive; b. Toronto, Ont. 31 Jan. 1925; s. late Daniel Howell and late Nellie Jones; e. Univ. of Manitoba B.Comm. 1948; m. Thelma d. John and late Martha Laubenstein 23 June 1950; children: Diane, Barbara, Lorraine; DIR. INVESTORS GROUP INC. 1981– ; Chrmn. & Dir., United Candn. Shares Ltd.; Dir.: Investors Syndicate Ltd.; Investors Mutual of Canada Ltd.; Investors International Mutual Fund Ltd.; Investors Growth Fund of Canada Ltd.; Investors Japanese Growth Fund Ltd.; Provident Stock Fund Ltd.; Investors Dividend Fund Ltd.; Investors Group Trust Co. Ltd.; Power Corp. of Can.; The Great-West Life Assurance Co.; TransCanada Pipelines; joined Investors Syndicate of Can. Ltd. as Security Analyst 1948, Mgr. of Securities Investment Div. 1958, Vice-Pres. 1963; name of firm changed to Investors Group 1964; Vice-Pres. 1964, Exec. Vice-Pres. 1970, Pres. and C.E.O. 1971, Chrmn. & C.E.O. 1981, Chrmn. 1985–91; United Ch.; recreation: golf; Clubs: Manitoba; St. Charles Country; Home: 200 Tuxedo Blvd., Winnipeg, Man.; Office: One Canada Centre, 447 Portage Ave., Winnipeg, Man. R3C 3B6.

**JONES, Roger M. (Rod) Jr.,** B.A., M.B.A.; shipping executive; b. Cleveland, Ohio 4 Feb. 1954; s. Roger M. and Frances (Taylor) J.; e. Colby College B.A. 1975; Amos Tuck Sch. of Business, Dartmouth Univ. M.B.A. 1984; m. Joanne d. Robert and Shirley Muther 7 June 1980; children: Kimberly, Emma, Trevor; PRESIDENT, CSL INTERNATIONAL 1992– ; Lieutenant Jr. Grade U.S. Navy 1976–80; Supervisor, Navios Corp. 1980–82; Dir., New Business Van Ommeren 1984–85; Dir. of Mktg., Canada Steamship Lines 1985–90; Sr. Cons., Jones, Bardelmeier & Co. 1990–92; Home: 44 William Fairfield Dr., Wenham, Ma. 01984; Office: 55 Tozer Rd., Beverly, Ma. 01915.

**JONES, Ronald Webster,** B.Sc., P.Eng.; association executive; b. Bittern Lake, Alta. 26 Jan. 1929; s. Johnney David and Rhoda (Watkin) J.; e. Univ. of Alta. B.Sc. (C.E.) 1949; m. Sharon d. Ed and Greta Paugh 30 Aug. 1986; children: Melanie Dawn, Holly-Anne; PRES. ALTA. CONSTRN. ASSN. 1986– , Chrmn. 1975; Pres. RMH Industries Ltd.; Project Eng. PFRA (Agric. Can.) St. Mary River Irrigation Project Lethbridge 1949–56;

Project Constrn. Mgr., Vice Pres. Oland Construction Co. Ltd. Lethbridge 1956–65; Calgary 1965–86; Pres. Calgary Constrn. Assn. 1972; mem. Eng. Inst. Can. (Chrmn. Lethbridge Br. 1963); APEGGA; Univ. of Alta. Alumni Assn. (Vice-Chrmn.); Pres. Lethbridge Y's Men's Club 1965; Calgary W. Rotary 1978–79; Chrmn. Lethbridge YMCA 1965; Anglican; P. Conservative; recreations: hiking, camping, cross-country skiing, curling; Clubs: Glencoe (Calgary); Edmonton; Address: 52 Shawmeadows Rise S.W., Calgary, Alta. T2Y 1C6.

**JONES, Trevor Glyndwr,** B.A.; consultant; b. UK 5 May 1939; s. Owain Peter and Esther Abigail (Fairchild) J.; e. Latymer Upper Sch. London, Eng. 1955; Univ. of Toronto Cert. in Bus. 1969; York Univ. B.A. 1972; m. Eurwen d. Glyn and Enid Williams 28 Dec. 1964; children Siân Myfanwy, Iola Gwenllian; CONSULTANT & DIR., NEWBRIDGE NETWORKS CORP.; Dir. Montreal Trust Securities Inc.; joined maj. Candn. chart. bank London, Eng. 1955; emigrated to Can. 1957; held various positions Candn. banking and trust ind.; Regional Vice Pres. Ont. Montreal Trust Co. 1984, Vice Pres. Br. Operations H.O. Montreal 1986; Sr. Vice Pres. 1990; Gold Medallist Rugby Ont. Summer Games 1974; mem. Retail Merchants Assn. Can. (Ont.) Inc. (Dir.); Brit. Candn. Trade Assn.; recreations: rugby, squash, skiing; Clubs: Ontario; Scarborough Golf & Country; MAAA; Westmount Rugby; Office: 806, 175 Bloor St. E., Toronto, Ont. M4W 3R8.

**JONES, William David,** B.A., Ph.D.; university professor; b. Liverpool, Engl. 3 Feb. 1945; s. Walter Dodgson and Lilian (Jennings) J.; e. Univ. of Sheffield B.A. 1967, Ph.D. 1970; m. 1stly Jacqueline Morton (div.); 2ndly Diane Birley 1 Nov. 1975; children: Benjamin, Siân; CHAIR, PSYCHOLOGY DEPT., CARLETON UNIVERSITY, Prof. 1978– ; Lectr. Birkbeck Coll., Univ. of London 1969–70; Univ. of Queensland, Brisbane, Australia 1970–74; Visiting Prof. Univs. of Waterloo, W. Ont. 1972–73; Pres., Ont. Confederation of University Faculty Associations 1982; author numerous publs. in learned journs; recreations: polo, horse-racing; Office: Dept. of Psychology, Loeb Bldg., Rm 552, 1125 Colonel By Drive, Ottawa, Ont. K1S 5B6.

**JONES, William John;** historian, university professor; b. London, U.K., 4 July 1932; s. Gwilym Lemuel and Grace Bronwen J.; e. Univ. Coll. London, B.A.(1st class hons. Hist.) 1954, Ph.D. 1958; D.Lit. 1984; m. Leila, d. Abdelghani and Huda el Karmy, 30 Dec. 1958; children: Riyad, Riel, Hasna Rhuanedd; PROFESSOR EMERITUS OF HISTORY, UNIV. OF ALBERTA, 1992– ; Hist. of Parliament Trust, Westminster: Asst. 1957–59, Sr. Asst. 1959–61; with Univ. of Alta. since 1961, Prof. of Hist. 1969–91; Vis. Assoc. Prof., Univ. of California (Davis) 1965–66, (Berkeley) 1967; Chrmn., History Dept. Univ. of Alta. 1975–77; McCalla Rsch. Prof., Univ. of Alta. 1981–82; Ed. Bd., Am. Jour. of Legal History 1963–; Counc. of the List and Index Soc. 1969–80; mem. of Grants Ctte., Legal Hist. Prog., Am. Bar Found. 1968–79; mem. of Doctoral Grants Ctte. (Hist.), Can. Counc. 1971; Canadian Rep., Cttee. for the Anglo-Am. Conf. of Historians, London 1977, '79, '81, '82; mem.: Econ. Hist. Soc., Selden Soc., Past and Present Soc., N. Am. Conf. of Brit. Studies, Lancashire and Cheshire Record Soc., The Historical Assoc., Am. Soc. for Legal Hist., Friends of the Huntington Library, Société Jean Bodin; Friends of the Provincial Museum Edmonton, and of the Glenbow Museum Calgary; received numerous grants and fellowships, incl. Guggenheim Fellowship 1968; Fellow of the Royal Historical Soc. 1973, Fellow of the Royal Soc. of Can. 1982; author of 'The Elizabethan Court of Chancery' 1967, 'Politics and the Bench' 1971, 'The Foundations of English Bankruptcy' 1979; contbr. (188 items) in 'History of Parliament 1559–1601' (London 1982–83) 3 vols.; scholarly essays, articles and reviews; Panellist, 'International Review of Periodical Literature: British History' 1988, (pub. 1989); recreations: cricket, chess; Club: Nat. Liberal Club, London, U.K.; Office: Dept. of History, Univ. of Alta., Edmonton, Alta. T6G 2H4.

**JOÓS, Béla,** Bacc., B.Sc., Ph.D.; university professor; b. Montreal, Que. 7 Aug. 1953; d. Ernest and Irma (Kemnitz) J.; e. Coll. Stanislas de Montréal Bacc. 1971; Loyola of Montreal B.Sc. 1974; McGill Univ. Ph.D. 1979; ASSOCIATE PROFESSOR, DEPT. OF PHYSICS, UNIV. OF OTTAWA 1987– ; NSERC Postdoctoral Fellow, Univ. of Calif. at Berkeley 1979–81; Research Assoc., Simon Fraser Univ. & Univ. of B.C. 1981–82; Asst. Prof., Simon Fraser Univ. 1982–83; Univ. of Ottawa 1984–87; Edit. Bd., 'Can. J. of Physics' and 'Physics in Canada'; Sec.-Treas., Div. of Condensed Matter Physics, Candn. Assn. of Physicists; NSERC 1967 Science Scholar 1974–78; NSERC Postdoctoral Fellowship 1979–81; NSERC Univ. Rsch. Fellowship 1982–83;

Mem., Candn. Assn. of Physicists; Am. Physical Soc.; Materials Rsch. Soc.; Assn. can.-française pour l'avancement des sciences; recreations: nordic skiing, outdoor activities in general; Home: 636 Brierwood Ave., Ottawa, Ont. K2A 2H9; Office: 150 Louis Pasteur, Ottawa, Ont. K1N 6N5.

**JOPLIN, Albert Frederick,** B.Ap.Sc., P.Eng.; executive; b. Victoria, B.C. 22 Feb. 1919; s. Albert Edward and Emily Eliza (Norford) J.; e. Univ. of B.C., B.Ap.Sc. (Civil Engn.) 1948); m. the late Margaret McMorragh-Kavanaugh, 26 May 1947; one d. Mary Lynn Barbara; 2nd. m. Dorothy Anne Cook, 29 July 1977; PRESIDENT AND C.E.O., CENTRAL OCEAN INDUSTRIES LTD. 1987– ; Chrmn. & Dir., Leaders Equity Corp.; Advanced Smelters Technology Inc.; Dir., Shaw Industries Ltd.; joined Canadian Pacific as Transitman, Roadmaster, Div. Engr., B.C. 1947–62, Special Engineer, Calgary 1962–65, Development Engineer Vancouver 1965; Manager, Special Projects, Canadian Pacific Investments Ltd. and Gen Mgr., Marathon Realty, Vancouver, 1966; initiated Project 200 devel. scheme for Downtown Vancouver; System Mgr. Planning & Devel., Canadian Pacific Ltd., Montreal 1968, Dir. Devel. Planning 1969; Vice Pres., Marketing & Sales, CP Rail 1971; Vice-Pres, Operation and Maintenance, CP Rail 1974; Pres. & C.E.O., Canadian Pacific (Bermuda) Ltd. 1976–84; Commissioner and Dir. Gen., Candn. Pacific Pavilion, EXPO 86 1984–87; served with RCAF 1941–45; rank Flight Lt.; Life mem. Assn. Prof. Engrs. and Geoscientists of Prov. B.C.; Life mem. Candn. Soc. for Civil Engineering; Life mem. Engn. Inst. Can.; Vancouver Maritime Arbitrators Assn.; Candn. Maritime Law Assn.; The Indian Ocean Flying Boat Assn.; Inst. of Corporate Dirs. in Can.; The Internat. Soc. For Planning and Strategic Mgmt.; Rly. Assn. Can.; Assn. Boy Scouts of Canada; Vancouver Maritime Museum; Life mem. Bermuda Maritime Museum Assn.; Bermuda National Trust; Paul Harris Fellow; Clubs: Mount Stephen; Western Canada Railway; Canadian Railway; Royal Montreal Golf; Traffic; Vancouver Rotary; Airforce Officers' Assoc.; Canadian Forces Vancouver Officers' Mess; Terminal City; Order of St John; Beta Theta Pi; Home: 4317 Staulo Cres., Vancouver, B.C. V6N 3S1.

**JOPLING, Samuel Haigh,** B.E., M.Sc., D.Phil.; educator; b. Kingston, N.Y. 6 Sept. 1928; s. late Samuel Haigh and Nellie (Bennett) J.; e. Georgia Inst. Technol. B.E. (Mech. Engn.) 1950; Pa. State Univ. M.Sc. 1965, D.Phil. 1975; m. Anneliese d. late Frederick F. and Elise (Nagel) Schmitz, Germany 1 Aug. 1959; children: Mary Louise, Frederick Haigh; PROF. OF ACCOUNTING, 1982– and MEMBER, BOARD OF GOVERNORS, SAINT MARY'S UNIV. 1990– ; joined Cal. State Univ. Los Angeles 1972, Assoc. Dean (1973–76) and Accounting faculty mem. Sch. of Business & Econ.; joined Saint Mary's Univ., Dean of Comm. 1976–82; Founder (1975) and first Mang. Ed. 'Los Angeles Business and Economics' mag.; co-author (with F. Dougherty, A. Francia, M. Porter and R. Strawser) 'Managerial Accounting In Canada' 1983; Financial Executives Inst. (Past Pres. Maritime Provs. Chapter); Candn. Acad. Accts. Assn. (Past National Pres.); Club: Halifax; Home: 1038 Robie St., Halifax, N.S. B3H 3C5; Office: Halifax, N.S. B3H 3C3.

**JORGENSEN, Erik,** M.F.; educator; consultant; b. Haderslev, Denmark 28 Oct. 1921; s. Johannes and Eva Bromberg (Hansen) J.; e. Akad. Aarhus (Denmark), 1940; Royal Veterinary and Agric. Coll., M.F. 1946; m. Grete, d. Osvald Moller, Fredericia, Denmark, 13 June 1946; children: Marianne, Birthe; Adjunct Prof., Faculty of Forestry, Univ. of Toronto 1987–89; former Dir., Univ. of Guelph Arboretum and Prof., Environmental Biol., 1978–87; Research Offr., Danish Forest Exper. Stn., Springforbi, Denmark, 1946; Forest Pathol., Royal Veterinary and Agric. Coll., 1949; Research Offr., Forest Pathol. Lab., Science Service, Can. Dept. of Agric., Maple, Ont., 1955; Asst. Prof., Faculty of Forestry, Univ. of Toronto, 1959–63; mem. Grad. Dept. of Bot., 1959–73; i.c. Shade Tree Research Lab. 1962–72, Assoc. Prof. 1963, Prof. 1967; Assoc., Inst. of Environmental Sciences & Engn., 1971–73; Chief, Urban Forestry Program, Forest Mang. Inst. Candn. Forestry Service, Dept. of the Environment, 1973–78; served with Danish Army 1946–48; rank 2nd Lt.; consultant govt. agencies, private individuals and firms 1959–73; participated in devel. of urban forestry concept in Can. and in devel. of techniques for study and control of Dutch Elm Disease and other tree diseases; Founding mem. Dutch Elm. Disease Control Comte. for Metrop. Toronto & Region (forerunner Ont. Shade Tree Council), 1961; rep. for S. Ont. Sec., Candn. Inst. Forestry on Conserv. Council of Ont., 1966–69; mem. Bd. of Examiners, Ont. Inst. Parks Extves., 1967–70; mem., Ont. Ornamentals Research Comte.; author of over 60 articles and scient. papers on urban forestry and tree diseases; rec'd 'Author's Citation,' Internat. Shade Tree Conf., Inc., 1970; Life Mem., Ont. Prof. Foresters Assn.; Fellow, Candn. Institute of Forestry 1991 (Dir. 1967, Chrmn. Bd. Examiners 1970) Chrmn. S. Ont. Sec. 1966); Internat. Shade Tree Conf., Inc. (Gov. 1966–72, Pres. Candn. Chapter 1967–68); Ont. Shade Tree Council (Pres. 1970–71); recipient, 'Trees for Tomorrow Award' Candn. Forestry Assn. 1993; Sigma Xi; Danish Lutheran; Home: 507 - 172 Metcalfe St., Guelph, Ont. N1E 6T5.

**JOSEFOWITZ, Nina,** Ph.D., C.Psych.; psychologist; b. Los Angeles, U.S.A. 27 Aug. 1950; d. Sam and Natasha (Chapro) J.; e. Swiss Maturité Féd. 1968; Brandeis Univ., B.A. (Hons. Psych. Magna Cum Laude) 1972; London Sch. of Econ., M.Sc. 1973; Univ. of Toronto, Ph.D. 1981; one d.: Laura Hava Josefowitz Shell; two s.: Aaron Frazer Josefowitz Myran, Daniel Thomas Josefowitz Myran; CONSULTANT TO COUNSELLING CTR., ATKINSON COLL., and to SEXUAL HARASSMENT EDUCATION AND COMPLAINT CTR., YORK UNIV., and LECTR., UNIV. OF TORONTO 1989– ; Vis. Lectr., Univ. Gadjah Mada (Indonesia) 1974–75; Co-ordinator, Student Couns. Serv. & Asst. Prof., Candn. Memorial Chiropractic Coll. 1979–83; Dir., Counselling & Career Ctr., Glendon Coll., York Univ. 1984–88; Lectr., York Univ. 1989–90; author of articles in profl. jours.; Office: Counselling Centre, Atkinson Coll., York Univ., 4700 Keele St., Toronto, Ont. M3J 1P3.

**JOSEPHSON, Joseph Edward,** M.D., C.M., B.Sc. (Med.), F.R.C.P.(C); F.A.C.P.; D.Sc.(Hon.); pathologist; educator; b. Hamilton, Ont. 29 Nov. 1911; s. Samuel Ellis and Katherine (Wolkin) J.; e. Hamilton (Ont.) Central Coll. Inst.; Queen's Univ., M.D., C.M. 1934; Univ. of Toronto, B.Sc. (Medicine) 1936; D.Sc. (Hon.) Memorial Univ. of Nfld.; m. Vivian Mary, d. Sir John Charles and Lady Puddester, 22 Mar. 1948; two s., Clayton Glenn, Dr. Bruce; CLINICAL PROF. OF PATHOL., FACULTY OF MED., MEMORIAL UNIV. OF NFLD.; Recipient of Queen's Jubilee Medal; Hon. Consultant, St. John's Gen. Hospital in Health Sciences Complex; Consultant Pathol., Waterford Hosp., St. Clares Hosp., Grace Hosp., Janeway Children's Hosp.; Consultant, Red Cross Blood Transfusion Service, and former Medical Director, St. John's, Nfld. Centre; In 1942 organized and started the first voluntary Blood Bank Services in Newfoundland and had stored 1,000 units of frozen fresh Blood Plasma for use in the event of a War emergency locally; Candn. Red Cross took over the service in 1958; served as M.O. (Capt.) to Nfld. Militia 1942–45; Major, R.C.A.M.C. (R); holds Specialist Cert., R.C.P. & S. (Can.) in Path., Bacteriol. and Internal Med.; Past Pres., Nfld. Med. Assn. (1957); Past Pres. Med. Council of Can. (Pres. 1965–66); Past President, Candn. Assn. of Pathols.; Past Pres., Nfld. Assn. of Pathols.; Ret. Chrmn., Dep't of Lab. Med. and Chief Pathologist, St. John's Gen. Hosp.; Ret. Dir. Nfld. Pub. Health Labs and Prov. Pathologist, Nfld.; Past Pres. Med. Staff, mem. of Adv. Council, St. John's General Hospital; former mem. Bd. of Mang., Nfld. Div., C.N.I.B.; former Extve. mem. Nfld. Div., Candn. Cancer Soc.; Freemason, Scottish rite; recreations: fishing, hunting; Clubs: St. John's Curling; Bally Haly Golf; Murray's Pond Fishing (former director); Royal Newfoundland Yacht (former Fleet Surgeon); Home: 25 Tiffany Lane, Apt. 311, St. John's, Nfld. A1A 5B4.

**JOSEPHSON, Joshua Ellis,** B.S., O.D., F.A.A.O., F.A.C.L.P.(UK); optometrist; business executive; b. Toronto, Ont. 22 Feb. 1944; s. David Ralph and Merryl (Lewis) J.; e. Forest Hill Coll. Inst. 1963; Ohio State Univ. B.S. 1966, O.D. (Optometry) 1968; m. Barbara Caffery d. Duncan and Janet MacPhail 9 Feb. 1984; children: Lisa, Kate; 1st Candn. Clin. Investig. Soft Contact Lenses 1969; Sci. Cons.: Griffin Labs. Inc. 1969–74; Bausch & Lomb Inc. 1976–78, 1987; Barnes-Hind Inc. 1983–84; 3M Inc. 1987–89; University Optics Inc. 1987–88; American Hydron Inc. 1984; Sr. Partner Drs. Josephson, Caffery, Tepperman Associates 1987–89; Dir. Josephson Opticians Ltd. 1989– ; Co-prop. The Cookbook Store, Toronto; Chrmn. Ophthalmic Devices Sect. Standards Council Can. 1982– ; Chrmn. Contact Lens Ctte. Candn. Gen. Standards Bd. 1987– ; Chrmn. Position Papers Ctte., Am. Optometric Assn. 1988–90; clin. investig. over 40 internat. mfrs. contact lenses, materials, solutions 1969–89; frequent guest lectr. ocular field; invited researcher The Morton Sarver Inst. Cornea & Contact Lens Rsch. Univ. of Cal. Berkeley; cons. US Triservice Aerospace Rsch. Council mil. use contact lenses; author or co-author over 90 papers profl. jours., book chapters; contbg. ed. various ocular jours.; mem., Internat. Editorial Bd., The Journal of the British Contact Lens Assn.; Charter mem. Internat. Soc. Contact Lens Rsch. 1980, mem. Council 1988– ; Founder, Pres. Candn. Contact Lens Soc. 1982; mem. Internat. Soc. Contact Lens Specialists; mem. Adv. Bd. Candn. Sjögrens Found. 1989– ; mem. Assn. Rsch. & Vision in Ophthalmol.; Internat. Soc. Dakryology; Am. Optometric Assn.; Brit. Contact Lens Assn.; Soc. Ophthalmic Photogs.; Ont. Assn. Optometrists (Merit Award 1978, Recognition Award 1979); York Co. Optometric Soc.; Candn. Assn. Optometrists; recreations: scuba diving, wine tasting, travel; Clubs: Chevalier de la Confrerie de la Chaine des Rotisseurs; Confrerie des Chevaliers du Tastevin; Maître de l'Ordre International des Anysetiers; Home: 616 Avenue Rd., Toronto, Ont. M4V 2K8; Office: 705, 60 Bloor St. W., Toronto, Ont. M4W 3B8.

**JOSHI, Sadhna,** Ph.D., D.Sc.; university associate professor; b. Udaipur, India 22 Feb. 1956; d. Vraj Raj and Saraswati J.; e. Univ. of Paris VII B.Sc. 1974, Licence 1975, M.Sc. 1976, Attestation d'Etudes Approfinies 1977, Dip. d'Etudes Approfondies 1977, Ph.D. 1979, D.Sc. 1983; m. Ram N. s. Bhagwan Lal Sukhwal 28 June 1979; ASSOC. PROF. & DIR., HIV RESEARCH LAB., MICROBIOLOGY, FAC. OF MEDICINE, UNIV. OF TORONTO 1988– ; Rsch. Fellow, Inst. Jacque Monod Paris 1976–83; Postdoct. Fellow, Univ. of Leiden 1980–82; Rsch. Scientist, Allelix Inc. 1983–87; Principal Investigator, AIDS & Immune Regulation (Allelix) 1987–88; Sr. Rsch. Sci. & Prin. Investigator 1988; Mem., Sch. of Grad. Studies, Univ. of Toronto 1989– ; Reviewer, Ont. Min. of Health; Nat. Health Rsch. Devel. Prog.; Med. Rsch. Council's AIDS rsch. projects; Mem., Internat. & Candn. societies for AIDS Rsch.; Am. Soc. for Virology; Univ. of Toronto Fac. Assn.; Am. & Candn. societies for Microbiologists; recreations: writing poems, singing, music, dancing; Home: 74 Faywood Blvd., Toronto, Ont. M3H 2X3; Office: 150 College St., #212, Toronto, Ont. M5S 1A8.

**JOSLIN, A. Barry,** B.A., M.B.A.; executive; b. Montréal, Qué. 25 Aug. 1944; s. Clarence Ettric and Margaret Elizabeth (Grubert) J.; e. Loyola Coll. Montréal B.A. 1964; Univ. of W. Ont. M.B.A. 1970; m. Catherine d. Henry and Lorvinia George 29 Dec. 1983; one d. Martha; SR. VICE PRES., CORPORATE AND PUBLIC AFFAIRS, THE MOLSON COMPANIES 1992– ; Sr. Cons. Bureau of Mgmt. Consulting Ottawa 1970–73; Chief of Evaluation Treasury Bd. Ottawa 1973–76; Special Policy Asst. to Chrmn. Anti Inflation Bd. Ottawa 1976–78; Dir. of Progs. Bus. Council on Nat. Issues 1978–80; Dir. Pub. Affairs The Molson Companies 1980–83; Vice Pres. Pub. Affairs Molson Breweries 1983–87; Sr. Vice Pres., Molson Breweries 1987–92; Dir. Candn. Found. Econ. Edn.; Tourism Ind. Assn. Can.; Canada-U.S. Bus. Assoc; Ont. C. of C.; recreations: travel, theatre; Home: 298 Berkeley St., Toronto, Ont. M5A 2X5; Office: 40 King St. W., Ste. 3600, Toronto, Ont. M5H 3Z5.

**JOSLING, Brian T.,** B.Comm., M.B.A.; communications executive; b. Toronto, Ont. 19 Dec. 1942; s. Cecil F. and Catherine I. (Hart) J.; e. Univ. of Toronto B.Comm., M.B.A.; m. Margaret J. d. Murdo and Peggy MacKenzie 1966; children: Tracy, Kelly, Bradley; Vice Pres., Retail Div., Capitol Records E.M.I. Ltd. 1974–78; Sr. Vice Pres., CBS Records Canada Ltd. 1978–82; Pres., Sydney Devel. Corp. 1983–84; Pres., Cantel West, Rogers Cantel Mobile Inc. 1985–93; Home: 960 Sherwood Lane, W. Vancouver, B.C. V7V 3X9.

**JOUBIN, Franc R.;** retired mining geologist and technical mine consultant; b. San Francisco, Calif. 15 Nov. 1911; s. Auguste and Marthe Jeanne (Renault) J.; e. Pub. and High Sch., Victoria, B.C. (Matric. 1929); Victoria Coll. 1931–32; Univ. of Brit. Columbia B.A. (Chemistry) 1936; M.A. (Geol.) 1942; P.Eng. B.C. 1947; P.Eng. Ont. 1948; m. Mary Toine Torvinen 21 Dec. 1938; one d., Marion Frances; Mining Expl. Geol., Pioneer Gold Mines of B.C., Western Can. 1936–43; in charge of E. Can. Exploration, 1948–52; self-employed Geol. Cons. for Candn. and Am. clients (travelled extensively throughout Can. and Central. Am.) 1948–52; publicly regarded as one of Canada's specialists in uranium exploration through discoveries in the Blind River Dist. of Ont., the Beaverlodge Dist. of Sask. and in B.C.; Consultant to U.N. Tech. Assistance Programs 1962–79; author 'Not for Gold Alone' (autobiography) 1989; author of many tech. papers on mining exploration topics for tech. journs. in Can., U.S.A. and U.K.; mem., Geol. Assn. of Can.; CIIM; P & D Assn.; Assn. Geoscientists for Int. Dev. & B.C. & Yukon Chamber of Mines; awarded Leonard Medal, Engn. Inst. of Can. 1956; Blaylock Medal, Candn. Inst. Mining & Metall. 1957; P & D Assn. Dist. Service Award 1982; Mem., Order of Canada 1983; W.B. Lewis Award, Can. Nuclear Assn. 1984; Great Trekker Award, Alumni B.C. 1985; Mem., Order of Ont. 1987; Candn. Mining Hall of Fame 1989; D.Sc.: U.B.C. 1958; Dalhousie Univ. 1985; Hon. LL.D.: St. Francis Xavier 1972; York Univ. 1979; Protestant; recreations; reading, writing, painting; Club: Toronto Geological Disc.; Home: 581 Avenue Rd., Toronto, Ont. M4V 2K4.

**JOUDRIE, H. Earl;** executive; b. 27 Mar. 1934; e. Univ. Alta., B.A. 1957; children: Neale, Carolyn, Colin, Guy; CHAIRMAN OF THE BOARD, GULF CANADA RESOURCES LTD. and ALGOMA STEEL INC.; Dir. & Pres., A&G Resources Corp.; Dir., Abitibi-Price Inc.; Candn. Insurance Group Ltd.; Canadian Tire Corporation, Limited; Canadian Utilities Ltd.; Consolidate Carma Corp.; Dorset Exploration Ltd.; Rayrock Yellowknife Resources Inc.; United Financial Management Ltd.; Chrmn. Emeritus, Public Policy Forum, Ottawa; Mem., Prime Minister's Advisory Ctte. on Govt. Restructuring; Chief Landman & Office Mgr., United Producing Company (merged with Ashland) 1961–63; Candn. Div. Mgr., Ashland Oil and Refining Co. 1963–65; Pres. & C.E.O., Ashland Oil Canada Ltd. 1965–68, Chrmn. & C.E.O. 1968–76; Sr. Vice Pres. & Group Operating Offr., Ashland Oil, Inc. (Kentucky) 1976–78; Chrmn. of the Bd., Ashland Oil Canada Ltd. 1976–78; Pres. & C.E.O., Nu-West Group Ltd. and Voyager Petroleums Ltd. 1979–85; Pres. & C.E.O., Dome Canada Ltd. and Encor Energy Corp. Inc. 1985–88; Personal Business Investments in Oil and Gas, Real Estate, Securities 1988–89; Chrmn. & C.E.O., American Eagle Petroleums Ltd. 1990–91; Chrmn., Rayrock Yellowknife Resources Inc. 1990–92; Clubs: Calgary Petroleum; Ranchmen's; Canyon Meadows Golf & C.C.; Bearspaw Golf & C.C.; Home: Site 16, P.O. Box 46, SS #1, Calgary, Alta. T2M 4N3.

**JOUDRY, Patricia;** playwright; b. Spirit River, Alta. 18 Oct. 1921; m. 1st, Delmar Dinsdale (divorced 1952); two d.; 2ndly, John Steele, Toronto (divorced 1975); three d.; author of plays, radio & TV scripts 'Teach Me How To Cry' (play; Dom. Drama Festival Best-play Award, 1956) produced off-broadway theatre; script writing incl. the 'Henry Aldrich Show' for four years, and 'Penny's Diary' both radio serials; other works: 'The Sand Castle' (comedy); 'Three Rings for Michele' (play); 'The Song of Louise in the Morning' (one act drama); 'Stranger in My House' (play); 'Walk Alone Together' (comedy; prize winner, Stratford-Globe playwriting competition and London West End 1959); 'Semi-Detached' (drama, Broadway theatre 1960); 'Valerie' (comedy); 'Don The Dinted Armour' (comedy; 1st Prize Winner, Nat. Playwriting Seminar, London, Ont.); 'God Goes Heathen' (drama); 'Think Again' (comedy) 1969; 'Now' (science-fiction, multi-media drama) 1970; 'I Ching' (drama) 1971; 'The Dweller on the Threshold' (novel) 1973; 'And the Children Played' (non-fiction) 1975; 'Spirit River to Angels' Roost' (Non-fiction) 1977; 'The Selena Tree' (novel) 1980; 'A Very Modest Orgy' (play) 1981; 'Sound Therapy for the Walk Man' (non-fiction) 1984; co-author (with Maurie D. Pressman, M.D.): 'Twin Souls' (non-fiction) 1993; Address: Box 616, Dalmeny, Sask. S0K 1E0.

**JOVANOVIC, Miodrag Stevana,** M.D., F.R.C.P. & S. (C), F.A.C.S.; surgeon; educator; b. Tabanovic, Yugoslavia 3 May 1936; e. Coll. of Sabac B.A. 1954; Univ. of Belgrade M.D. 1963; m.; 3 children; SURGEON, JEFFREY HALE'S HOSPITAL 1972– ; Surg. Hôpital Notre-Dame de l'Espérance 1972– ; Prof. of Human Anat. Fac. of Med. Laval Univ. 1972– ; internship France, Europe 1963–65; internship and residency in surgery Quebec City, Montreal and Sherbrooke 1965–70; Asst. Chief Resident Univ. of Sherbrooke 1970–71, Chief Resident 1971–73; Fellow, Am. Coll. Chest Phys.; Internat. Coll. Surgs.; Am. Coll. of Surgeons; Royal Coll. of Phys. & Surgs. Can. (Surgery); Address: 2219 Bourbonnière St., Sillery, Que. G1T 1A9.

**JOY, Nancy Jean Hannah Grahame;** medical illustrator; educator; b. Toronto, Ont. 15 Jan. 1920; d. Ernst Grahame and Dorothy Ewart (Primrose) J.; e. St. Clement's Private Sch. for Girls, Toronto 1938; Ont. Coll. Art Dept. Drawing & Painting 1942 (Hughes Owens Prize), night courses Life Drawing & Water Colour 1963–65; Univ. of Toronto Special Student Anat., Histol., Pathol. Embryol., Neuroanat. 1942–44; Univ. of Ill. Pupil Apprentice Med. Illustration 1944–47; Ryerson Polytech. Inst. TV Studio Production Cert. 1971; Illustrator, Dept. Anat. Univ. of Toronto 1947–52, 1954–56 (also Dept. Radiol.); freelance med. illustrator Eng. and Scot. 1952–54; Med. Illustrator Dept. Surg. Univ. of Man. 1956–59, Asst. Prof. of Med. Illustration 1959–62; Assoc. Prof. and Chrmn. of Art as applied to Med. Program, Univ. of Toronto 1962–73, Prof. and Chrmn. 1973–85; Prof. & Dir., B.Sc. AAM Prog. 1985–86; on admin. leave 1986–87; Dir. of AAM Services 1962–69; author or co-author numerous articles, reviews, bibliogs., reports, monographs-vocational guidance; scholarly addresses and seminar panels; illustrations contrib. to numerous med. books, films, projection slides; co-inventor Constudium Carrel 1969; production co-ordinator and/or designer med. exhibits, film 'Dizziness' 1969 (Med. Educ. Award and one other Biocommunications '70 Houston 1970, Internat. Med. Videotape & Film Festival Williamsburg 2nd place 1970); Hon. Fellow, Ont. Coll. of Art 1984; mem. Ont. Coll. Art Alummi Assn.; Assoc. mem. Acad. Med.; mem. Assn. Med. Illustrators; Candn. Science Film Assn.; Anglican; Club: Heliconian; Home: 8 Oaklawn Gardens, Toronto, Ont. M4V 2C6.

**JOYAL, Hon. Justice L. Marcel,** B.A., B.C.L.; judge; b. Haileybury, Ont. 19 July 1924; s. Dr. & Mrs. J. Hector J.; e. Univ. of Ottawa B.A. Magna Cum Laude 1943; R.C.N.V.R. 1944–45; McGill Univ. B.C.L. 1948; m. Pauline Elizabeth d. Dr. and Mrs. Stuart Ramsey 29 June 1957; children: Diane, Lorraine, Richard; called to Bar of Que. 1948, Bar of Ont. 1949; Law Practice Ottawa, Ont. 1949–63; Exec. Asst. to Min. of Transport 1963; Special Asst. to Secy. of State 1964–65; Sr. Partner Honeywell, Wotherspoon Barristers 1966–84; apptd. 29 June 1984 Judge of Federal Court of Can., Trial Div. and mem. ex officio Federal Court of Appeal; apptd. 23 Aug. 1984 mem. Court Martial Appeal Court; past Sr. Instr. Bar Admission Course, Law Soc. of Upper Can.; past Chrmn. Ctte. on Natural Resources, Candn. Bar Assn.; mem. Bench and Bar Counc. 1984; Pres. Assn. des juristes d'expression française de l'Ont. 1983–84; past Hon. Couns. Royal Candn. Geog. Soc.; past Hon. Couns. Candn. Counc. on Social Devel.; R. Catholic; mem. Atty-Gen.'s Adv. Ctte. on French Lang. Services 1983–84; recreations: skiing, tennis; Clubs: Rideau; Cercle Universitaire d'Ottawa; Rockliffe Lawn Tennis; Office: Federal Court of Canada, Ottawa, Ont. K1A 0H9.

**JOYAL, Serge,** P.C., B.A., LL.L., LL.M., M.Phil.; lawyer; b. Montreal, Que. 1 Feb. 1945; s. Fernand and Rachel (Desrosiers) J.; e. Univ. de Montréal B.A., LL.L.; Sheffield Univ. LL.M.; London Sch. of Econ. & Pol. Sci. M.Phil.; Secretary of State, Can. 1982–84; Pol. Asst. to Hon. Jean Marchand 1972–73; el. M.P. for Maisonneuve-Rosemont g.e. 1974; Founding Mem. Mun. Action Group Montreal 1978; Cand. Montreal Mayoralty 1978; re-el. M.P. for Hochelaga-Maisonneuve 1979, 1980, def. 1984; Parlty. Secy. to Pres. of Treasury Bd. 1980; Founding mem. Special Jt. Comte. Senate and H. of C. on Official Langs. 1980; Co-Chrmn. Special Jt. Comte. on Constitution 1980; Min. of State 1981; Vice Pres. Lib. Party of Can. (Que.) 1974–75; Pres. Classical Coll. Students Assn. Que. 1963–64; Pres. by interim Que. Student Union 1946; Candn. del. World Assembly of Youth 1964; recipient Lomer Gouin Prize for Distinction in Law 1966; Lord Reading Soc. Prize Distinction in Civil Procedure 1966; Internat. Law Faculty Bursary 1969–70; Rotary Internat. Bursary 1970–71; Vice Chrmn. Musée d'Arts de Joliette, Qué.; Dir. Candn. Museum Assn. 1974–75; Heritage Montréal 1977–78; Pres. Que. Museum Assn. 1974–75; Collaborateur Vie des Arts (Revue); Dir. 'La Collection Beaux-Arts des Cahiers du Québec'; mem. Que. Bar Assn.

**JOYCE, Douglas Alick,** B.A., A.M., Ph.D.; university professor; b. Carbonear, Nfld. 20 July 1922; s. Joseph Gilbert and Susan Mellett (Carlton) J.; e. McGill Univ. B.A. 1943; Harvard Univ. A.M. 1944, Ph.D. 1952; Univ. of Göttingen/Marburg 1952–53; Univ. of Tübingen 1953, 1956; m. Dorothy Mary d. Albert and Florence Johnson 16 Apr. 1960; children: David, Andrea; PROFESSOR EMERITUS, UNIV. OF TORONTO 1988– ; Teaching Fellow, Harvard Univ. 1945–49; Lectr. of German, Univ. of Toronto 1950–55; Asst. Prof. 1955–63; Assoc. Prof. 1963–67; Prof. 1967–88; Guest Lectr., Volkshochschule, Kassel 1952–53; Harvard Univ. 1961; Univ. of Buffalo 1965; Instr., Goethe Inst., Toronto 1963–65; External Appraiser, Brock Univ. Dept. of Germanic & Slavic Studies 1985; Founding mem. Candn. Assn. of Univ. Teachers of German 1961– ; Founding mem., 'Seminar: A Journal of Germanic Studies' 1965; author 'Hugo von Hofmannsthal's 'Der Schwierige.' A Fifty-Year Theatre History' 1993, and of var. papers, articles, and lectures on German lit.; Modern Langs. Assn. of Am.; Hofmannsthal Soc. (Frankfurt/Vienna); Wagner Soc. of Toronto; Toronto Camera Club; Elder & Mem. of Session, Bloor St. United Ch. 1957– ; Co-Founder, Toronto Chap., Ont. Assn. for Children with Learning Disabilities 1973; Adv. Counc. to Spl. Edn., Toronto Bd. of Edn. 1974–76; recreations: music, photography; Home: 58 Colin Ave., Toronto, Ont. M5P 2B9; Office: Trinity Coll., Univ. of Toronto, Toronto, Ont. M5S 1H8.

**JOYCE, Hugh Kirkpatrick,** B.B.A.; paper company executive; b. Toronto, Ont. 19 March 1921; s. Thomas Wolsey and Lail Kirkpatrick (Hyslop) J.; e. Upper Canada Coll., grad. 1938; Univ. of W. Ont., B.B.A. (Univ. Gold Medalist; Hons.) 1949; m. Nancy Jane, d. B.J. Waters, Fort Point, Liverpool, N.S. 6 Jan. 1943; children: Richard Kirkpatrick, John Waters; Past Dir., Bowater Corp., London; Bowater China Ltd., London; Past Chrmn. and Dir., Bowater Canadian Ltd.; Dir., Kay Corp.; Conn. Bank and Trust Corp.; Chrmn., Bd. of Trustees, Holderness Sch., Plymouth, N.H.; joined Mersey Paper Co. Ltd., Liverpool, N.S. 1949, Personnel Mgr. 1950, Asst. to Gen. Mgr. 1955, Asst. Gen. Mgr. 1960–62; Vice Pres. Bowaters Newfoundland Ltd., Corner Brook, Nfld., 1962–65, Pres. and Gen. Mgr. 1965–68, Dir. 1966–80; Pres. & Dir., Bowater Sales Co. 1970–72; Pres., CEO and Dir., Bowater North Amer. Corp. 1972–82; retired as Chrmn. 1984; served with R.C.N.V.R. 1939–45, discharged with rank of Lieutenant Commdr.; mem., Bd. of Visitors, Univ. of Conn. Sch. of Bus. Admin.; Dir., Greenwich (Conn.) Hosp.; Greenwich Emergency Med. Service; Naval Officers Assn. of Can.; Anglican; recreations: sailing, golf, skiing, reading, photography; Clubs: Blomidon Country, Corner Brook, Nfld. (Past Pres.); Greenwich Country; Canadian Soc. of New York; Metropolitan (N.Y.C.); Montserrat Yacht (W.I.); Home: Birch Lane, Greenwich, Conn. 06830.

**JOYNT, Carman Millar,** B.Comm., C.A.; chartered accountant; b. Ottawa, Ont. 12 Nov. 1943; s. George A. and Reta E. (Pettapiece) J.; e. Fisher Park H.S. 1964; Carleton Univ. B.Comm. 1966; m. Gail Catherine Ryan; children: David Andrew, Peter Michael; PARTNER, DELOITTE & TOUCHE 1975– ; C.A., Riddell Stead 1967–69; Touche Ross & Co. 1969–71; P.S. Ross & Son 1971–72; Touche Ross & Co. 1972–90; Deloitte & Touche 1990– ; Extve. Interchange, Fed. Govt., Anti-Inflation Bd. 1975–76; Teacher, Algonquin Coll. (2 yrs. in 1970s); served on transition team of the P.C. Party in 1984; Past Pres., Le Cercle Univ. d'Ottawa; Ottawa C.A.'s Assn.; Past Chrmn., Ottawa Civic Hosp. Found.; Past Dir., Jr. Achievement of Ottawa; Christie Lake Boys Camp; Past Gov., Ottawa Sch. of Art.; Past Adv., Youth Enterprise Ctr., YM/YWCA; Past Mem., Edn. Ctte., Ottawa Bd. of Trade; Fees Mediation Panel Ont., Inst. of C.A.'s; Mem., Elections Ctte., Gen. meeting, P.C. Party of Can.; co-author: 'Touche Ross & Co. Business Valuations 1985'; recreations: skiing, bicycling, gardening, wine; Clubs: Le Cercle Univ. d'Ottawa; Club Champêtre; Home: 497 Mayfair Ave., Ottawa, Ont. K1Y 0L1; Office: 90 Sparks St., Ottawa, Ont. K1P 5B4.

**JUBINVILLE, Alain,** M.Soc.Sci.; retired banker; b. Somerset, Man. 23 Aug. 1928; s. Laurent and Eliane (Landry) J.; e. Coll. de Saint-Boniface, Univ. of Man.: Latin & Philos.; Laval Univ.: M.Soc.Sci. (economics); m. Marguerite d. Adrien Taillefer 23 Jan. 1960; children: Yves, Louise, Denis, François; Depy. Governor, Bank of Canada 1974–88; Alternate Dir., Federal Business Development Bank 1984–88 and Export Development Corp. 1984–87; Research Econ. Bank of Canada 1953, Research Offr. 1963, Chief Foreign Exchange 1963, Chief Internat. 1971; Principal Dir., Banque du Zaïre 1981–83; sch. bds. La Commission scolaire Outaouais-Hull and La Commission scolaire régionale de l'Outaouais 1972–81; recreation: golf, photography, cross-country skiing; Club: Outaouais Golf (Founding mem. & mem. Bd. of Dirs. & Treas. 1992–93); Home: 555 place Foxview, Ottawa, Ont. K1K 4E1.

**JULIEN, Gilles,** D.Sc.; private consultant; b. Sillery, Que. 23 Apr. 1935; s. Louis Georges and Yvonne (Huot) J.; e. Séminaire de Québec B.A. 1954; Univ. Laval B.Sc. 1959, D.Sc. (Pharm.) 1966; m. Françoise d. Maurice and Fernande Delisle 26 May 1962; children: François, Nathalie, Louis, Nicolas; Extve. Vice Pres., Natural Sciences & Engineering Rsch. Council (NSERC) 1988–92, Extve. Dir. 1978–88; Assoc. Prof. of Biol. Faculty of Sciences Univ. Laval 1962–65, Prof. of Pharmacol. Faculty of Med. 1965–71; Awards Offr. Office of Grants & Scholarships Nat. Research Council 1971–76, Dir. of Office 1976–78; Dir. général Assn. canadienne-française pour l'avancement des sciences 1970; Conductor, Choir Les Chansonniers Ottawa; Founding Pres. Choeur V'la l'Bon Vent Québec 1958; Chrmn. OECD Group on Univ. and Scientific Rsch. 1987–1991; Administrator, NATO Science Fellowships; mem. Candn. Assn. Univ. Research Adms.; Assn. Scient., Engn. & Technol. Community Can.; Soc. Research Adms. U.S.A. and Can.; Home: 44 Valewood Cres., Gloucester, Ont. K1B 4E8.

**JULIEN, Pierre,** M.Sc., Ph.D.; educator; b. Sherbrooke, Qué. 12 Nov. 1947; s. Majella and Raymonde (Montminy) J.; e. Laval Univ. B.Sc. 1971, M.Sc. 1974, Ph.D. 1977; m. Louise d. Marcel and Françoise Bourassa 6 June 1971; children: Héryk, Eve; ASSOCIATE PROF. OF MED., LAVAL UNIV. 1993– ; Career Scientist, Fonds de la Recherche en Santé du Qué 1987–93, Rsch. Fellow 1977–79; Rsch. Fellow Ont. Heart Found. 1979–81, K.M. Hunter Fellow 1980; Scholar, Candn. Heart Found. 1981–87; Lectr. in Med. Univ. of Toronto 1982–84, Asst. Prof. 1984–87; Asst. Prof., present univ. 1987–93; recipient Yves Morin Prize Qué. Heart Inst. 1975; author or co-author numerous publs.; mem. Internat. Soc. Heart Rsch.; Candn. Biochem. Soc.; Am. Heart Assn. (Council on Arteriosclerosis); Candn. Atherosclerosis Soc. (Treas. 1990– ); N.Am. Assn. Study Obesity; Club de Recherches Cliniques du Qué.; Club Lipidologie du Qué.; Candn. Soc. Clin. Investig.; R.Catholic; Home: 795 Le Cavelier, Ste-Foy, Qué. G1X 3J2; Office: Lipid Research Centre, 2705 blvd. Laurier, Ste-Foy, Qué. G1V 4G2.

**JULIEN, Yves,** B.Sc., S.M., Ph.D.; business executive; b. Montreal, Que. 15 June 1946; s. Lucien and Rachel (Lacasse) J.; e. École Polytechnique B.Sc. 1969; M.I.T. S.M. 1970; Rensselaer Polytechnic Inst. Ph.D. 1972; m. Suzanne Lussier; children: Antoine, Benoit, Etienne; SENIOR VICE-PRESIDENT & DIRECTOR, MERRILL LYNCH CANADA INC. 1984– ; Financial Advisor, Que. Fed. Caisses Populaires 1972–73; Treas. & Chief Financial Offr., School Council, Island of Montreal 1973–81; Vice-Pres., Merrill Lynch Canada Inc. 1981–84; Dir., Coll. de Montréal Found.; Mem., Investment Dealers Assn. Que. Div. (Chair 1992–93); recreations: squash, tennis, skiing, windsurfing; club: Mount Royal Tennis; Home: 27, ave Rosemount, Westmount, Que. H3Y 3G6; Office: 1800 McGill College Ave., Ste. 2500, Montreal, Que. H3A 3J6.

**JUNEAU, Denis,** R.C.A.; artiste; né Montréal, Qué. 30 Sept. 1925; f. Laurent Edmond et Marguerite (Angrignon) J.; é. Institution des Sourds de Montréal, diplômé 1942; Ecole des Beaux-Arts de Montréal 1943–50 (prix du Ministre, peinture); Stage chez Georges Delrue, orfèvre de Montréal 1951–52; Chez Gilles Beaugrand, orfèvre d'église de Montréal 1952–53; Centro Studi Arte Industria de Novara (Italie), études sur l'esthétique industrielle, diplômé 1956; L'Atelier Jean Ouellet, architecte de Montréal 1963–65; expositions solo: Galerie Denise Delrue Montréal 1958, 1963; Musée des Beaux-Arts Montréal 1962 (Galerie Norton), 1970; Galerie Nova et Vetera Montréal (rétrospective, peintures, sculptures et dessins) 1962; Galerie du Siècle Montréal 1967; Galeria Carmen Lamanna Toronto 1968, 1973; Galerie le Gobelet Montréal 1969; Musée Provincial de Québec 1970; Centre Culturel de Trois-Rivières 1971; Centre audio-Visuel de l'Université de Montréal 1971; Symposium des Arts Plastiques, Centre Culturel de Drummondville 1971; Galerie de Montréal 1973; Galerie Bourguignon Montréal (58 dessins de 1954–66) 1974; Galerie Optica Montréal (perspective des oeuvres de 1969–78) 1979; Galerie le Groupe de Somerville Montréal 1981; Galerie Treize Montréal 1981; expositions itinerante: Consulat Général du Can. New York, Centre Culturel Canadien à Paris, Centre Culturel de l'Ambassada du Can. à Bruxelles, Can. House à Londres, 1975–76; expositions nombreaux groupe, collections publiques et privées (comprenant Musée d'Art Contemporain et Musée des Beaux-Arts Montréal, Conseil des Arts du Can. et Galerie Nationale du Can. Ottawa); prix: Boursier du Conseil des Arts du Can. 1961–62, 1962–63, 1968–69, 1969–70, 1972–73, 1974–75; Mention honorable, Concours Nat. de l'arch. du Can., Alcan 1957; Grand prix du concours du trophée pour le grand prix de l'urbanisme de la prov. de Qué. 1965; Mention, concours artistiques du Qué. 1967, 1971; Mention, Show Winnipeg 1968; Subvention du service de l'aide à la recherche et à la création du ministère des affaires culturelles du Qué. 1970; Address: c/o Royal Canadian Academy of Arts.

**JUNEAU, Jean-Pierre,** B.A., M.A.; diplomat; b. Quebec, Que. 24 April 1945; s. Paul-Henri and Madeleine (Bouchard) J.; e. Coll. des Jésuites B.A. 1965; Laval Univ. B.A. (Hons.) 1968, M.A. (Political Science) 1969; Banff Sch. of Adv. Mngt. grad. of 55th session 1984; m. Emitza d. Francisco and Lucila Escobar 4 Sept. 1979; children: Jean-Philippe, Marie-Caroline; AMBASSADOR TO SPAIN 1991– ; joined Dept. of External Affairs 1969; folowing postings in N.Y., Havana & Paris was assigned as Counsellor, Candn. Embassy in Washington 1981–85; Minister-Counsellor, Paris 1985–88; Dir. Gen., Western Europe Bur. at H.Q. 1988–91; Address: P.O. Box 500 (Madrid), Ottawa, Ont. K1N 8T7.

**JUNEAU, Pierre,** O.C. (1975), LL.D.; public servant; b. Verdun, P.Q. 17 Oct. 1922; s. Laurent Edmond & Marguerite (Angrignon) J.; e. Coll. Ste-Marie, Montréal, B.A.; Inst. Cathol., Paris, L.Ph.; m. Fernande, d. Hector Martin, 17 March 1947; children: André, Martin, Isabelle; Visiting Prof., Univ. of Montreal; Pres., Canadian Broadcasting Corp. 1982–89; joined Nat. Film Bd. in 1949 as Montreal Dist. Rep.; apptd. Asst. Regional Supervisor, Que. 1950; Chief, Internat. Distribution 1951; Asst. Head of European Office 1952; Secretary 1954; Sr. Asst. to Commr. and Dir. of French Lang. Prod. 1964; Vice Chrmn. Bd. of Broadcast Govs. 1966; Chrmn. Candn. Radio-TV Comn. 1968; Co-founder and Pres. Montreal International Film Festival 1959–68; Min. of Communications 1975; joined Prime Minister's staff as special policy advisor 1975; def. in by-el. to H. of C. Oct. 1975; apptd. mem. and Chrmn. of Nat. Capital Comn. 1976; Under Secretary of State, Feb. 1978; Depy. Min. of Communication 1980; Officer, Order of Canada; mem. Roy. Soc. of Canada; Club of Rome; Hon. LL.D., York Univ., Toronto 1973; Trent Univ., Peterborough 1987; Univ. of Moncton 1988; Roman Catholic; recreations: tennis, music, reading; Address: 165 Chemin Ste Catherine, Apt. 1003, Outremont, Que. H2V 2A7.

**JURIST, Paul Michael,** B.B.A., M.B.A.; bank executive; b. New York, N.Y. 5 July 1951; s. Dr. Irving and Judith (Caplan) J.; e. Baruch College, City Univ. of N.Y. B.B.A. 1972; York Univ. M.B.A. 1974; m. Vesna d. Lola Leman 30 Nov. 1984; one s.: Michael; SR. VICE-PRES., UNION BANK OF SWITZERLAND (CANADA) 1988– ; Union Carbide Canada 1974–75; Vice-Pres., Morgan Bank 1975–82; Sr. Vice-Pres., Bank of Montreal 1982–88; Bd. of Dir., National Ballet of Canada; clubs: Royal Candn. Yacht, Boulevard, Caledon; Home: 93 Lonsdale Rd., Toronto, Ont. M4V 1W4; Office: 154 University Ave., Toronto, Ont. M5H 3Z4.

**JUROCK, Oswald Erich,** F.R.I., C.M.R.; real estate executive; b. Cologne, Germany 5 Jan. 1944; s. Erich and Erna (Schwarz) J.; e. Severins H.S. 1962; m. Josefina d. Pilar and Victor Gochuico 7 July 1967; children: Marc Oswald, Liesl Robyn; CHRMN., PRES. & C.E.O., NATIONAL REAL ESTATE SERVICES LTD. (NRS) 1990– ; Pres., Prophase Systems Inc. 1990– ; Pres., National Real Estate Service (US) 1990– ; Pres., Royal LePage Asia Ltd. 1988–90; Pres., Datum Real Estate Management Co. Taipei 1989–90; Pres., Royal LePage Residential Real Estate Serv. 1986–88; Vice-Pres. & Gen. Mgr., Royal LePage (B.C.) (also Dir., Nat. Res. Bd.) 1984–86; Vice-Pres. & Gen. Mgr., A.E. Lepage (B.C.) 1979–84; Br. Mgr., Melton/A.E. LePage 1974–79; Sales Rep., A.E. Austin/Melton 1969–74; Hotel Extve., Devonshire Hotel (BC) 1966–69; Past Pres., Real Estate Bd. of New Westminster, Burnaby Coquitlam, BC 1978–79; Dir. & Chrmn., Arbitration Ctte., Vanc. Real Estate Bd. 1981–84, 1986; Mem., Adv. Bd., B.C. Inst. of Technol. 1984–86; Dir., Real Estate Council of B.C. 1992; Quality Council of B.C.; Pres., Canada/Taiwan Assoc.; Mem., Real Inst. of Can.; Candn. Real Estate Advisory Bd., U.B.C.; Mgmnt. Bd., Real Estate Institute of Canada, Vancouver Chapter; The President's Club, Simon Fraser Univ.; extensive public speaker; 1st prize 1981 and 1992, article, Real Estate Inst. of Can.; Winner, Morguard Literary Awards Competition (practising industry lay writers category) 1992; recreations: skiing, sailing, swimming; Club: The Vancouver; Address: 1311 Howe St., Vancouver, B.C. V6Z 1R7.

**JUYAL, Shreesh,** B.A., M.A., Drs.Cum laude, D.Sc.(Kandidat), C.I.I.A.; university professor; b. Dehra Dun, India 22 Nov. 1941; s. Ravi Datt and Kushleswari Devi J.; e. Agra Univ. B.A. 1953, M.A. 1961; Nijmegen Univ. Drs.Cum laude 1972; Univ. of Amsterdam D.Sc.(Kandidat) 1975; m. Zillah Amelia d. F.X. and M. Muttoo 14 Aug. 1971; children: Anshumala, Malini; ASSOC. PROF. OF POL. SCI., UNIV. OF REGINA 1983– ; Extve. Sec., Nat. Council of Univ. Students of India, New Delhi 1962–66; Special Lecturer, Univ. of Regina 1971–74; Asst. Prof. 1974–83; Pres., Montessori College of W. Canada 1981– ; Visiting Prof., Univ. of Bombay 1988–89; M.S. Univ. of Baroda 1992; Univ.of Lucknow 1992; Summer Studies Instructor Univ. of Victoria 1991, '92; Inst. Fellow, Candn. Inst. of Internat. Affairs 1993– ; Extve. Dir., Office of Internat. Model U.N., Univ. of Regina 1986–88; Dir., U.S. Fed. of Sci. & Schoalrs 1988– ; Mem., Comn. of the World Fed. of Sci. Workers 1989– ; Pres., Internat. Assn. on U.N. & Peace Affairs 1990– ; several past positions involving U.N. & Disarmament 1988– ; Pres., Sask. Assn. on Human Rights 1973–75, 1983–84; Candn. Inst. of Internat. Affairs, S. Sask. Br. 1976–79, 1992– ; editor: 'International Issues and Model United Natons' 1988, 'Equality Rights' 1986; co-editor: 'The United Nations and World Peace' 1990; recreations: reading, travelling; clubs: Faculty, Univ. of Regina; Home: 2639 McCallum Ave., Regina, Sask. S4S 0P6; Office: Regina, Sask. S4S 0A2.

# K

**KADECHUK, Barry James,** B.A., M.B.A.; general management executive; b. Yorkton, Sask. 15 Dec. 1942; s. John and Dorothy (Windjack) K.; e. Brock Univ. B.A. 1977; Southern Methodist Univ., Texas M.B.A. 1989; m. Linda d. Lennox and Mary Hunter 17 June 1967; children: Kerri-Lynn, Scott; PRES., FIRESTONE AGRICULTURAL TIRE DIV. 1991– ; Ind. Engr., Textile Plant, Dunnville, Ont. 1963–65; joined Firestone Canada Inc. 1965: Ind. Engr. 11 yrs., Prodn. Mgr. Hamilton Ont. 2 yrs., Plant Mgr. Whitby Ont. 1979, Plant Mgr. Hamilton 1981; Plant Mgr. Oklahoma City; Plant Mgr. Des Moines, Iowa; Plant Mgr., Firestone Tire & Rubber Co. Ltd. 1980–91; participant Gov.-Gen.'s Study Conf. 1983; Home: 1065 Bradford Place, West Des Moines, Iowa 50266; Office: 730 East Second St., Des Moines, Iowa 50309.

**KADLEC, Robert Edward,** B.A.Sc., P.Eng.; b. Calgary, Alta. 24 June 1933; e. Univ. of Toronto B.A.Sc. 1958; m. Roberta Hazel Johnston 17 June 1960; 2 children; PRES., CHIEF EXEC. OFFR. AND DIR., BC GAS INC. (formerly Inland Natural Gas Co. Ltd.) 1972– ; Dir., Trans Mountain Pipe Line Co. Ltd.; Questar Corp.; Mountain Fuel Supply Co.; Bank of Montreal; British Pacific Properties Ltd. & Affliated Companies; joined the Consumers' Gas Co. Toronto 1958–64; joined present Co. 1964, Pres. 1972; Extve. Mem., Bd. of Govs., B.C. Bus. Council; Gov., Vancouver Bd. of Trade (Past Chrmn. 1987–88); Dir., Conference Bd. of Can.; Pacific Coast Gas Assn. (Past Chrmn. 1985–86); Candn. Gas Assn. (Past Chrmn. 1980–81); Trustee, Simon Fraser Univ. Foundation; Hon. Chrmn., Vancouver Bd. of Trade Found.; Adv. Ctte. to Bd. of Dirs., Lions Gate Hosp. Found.; Sr. Adv. Bd., YMCA of Greater Vancouver; Clubs: Vancouver; Hollyburn Country; Canadian; Office: 24F, 1111 W. Georgia, Vancouver, B.C. V6E 4M4.

**KAHL, Alfred Louis,** B.A., M.B.A., Ph.D.; university professor; b. Michigan City, Indiana 4 Oct. 1932; s. Alfred Louis and Marion Carr (Wheeler) K.; e. Univ. of Maryland B.A. 1960; Univ. of Pittsburgh M.B.A. 1962; Univ. of Florida Ph.D. 1969; m. Lola Latini 3 Dec. 1955; children: Karen, Kevin; PROFESSOR, FACULTY OF ADMIN., UNIV. OF OTTAWA 1974– ; Prof., Univ. of Georgia 1965–70; Univ. de Tunis 1970–72; Dept. Chairman, Mankato State Univ. 1972–74; listed in num. Who's Whos; author: 'Introduction aux affaires' 1993, 'Morin Spreadsheet Applications in Engineering Economics' 1992, 'West Canadian Financial Management' 3rd ed. 1991; Home: 183 Craig Henry Dr., Ottawa, Ont. K2G 3Z8; Office: Ottawa, Ont. K1N 6N5.

**KAIHLA, Paul,** B.A.; journalist; b. Sault Ste. Marie, Ont. 19 Oct. 1959; s. Mauno Olavi and Terttu Helmi Elizabeth Kaihla (Tähtinen) K. (father served as hon. consul for Finland 1963–84 and was awarded White Rose of Finland, Knight, 1st class); e. Univ. of Toronto B.A. (with high distinction) 1986; ONTARIO BUREAU CHIEF, MACLEAN'S 1992– ; freelance writer 1986–88; Assoc. Nat. Ed., Maclean's 1988–92; Faculty Scholar, Univ. of Toronto 1986; Southam Fellowship 1993–94; Vice-Pres., Candn. Friends of Finland; Dir., Candn. Friends of Finland Educational Found.; Lutheran; coauthor: 'Savage Messiah' 1993 (non-fiction); recreations: nordic skiing, baseball; Home: Box 622, Stn. P, Toronto, Ont. M5S 2Y4; Office: 777 Bay St., 7th fl., Toronto, Ont. M5W 1A7.

**KAIN, Gary David,** B.A., M.B.A., C.A., C.B.V.; business executive; b. Hamilton, Ont. 13 March 1946; s. Lyle H.K.; e. McMaster Univ. B.A. 1969, M.B.A. 1973; Ont. Inst. of C.A.s C.A. 1975; Candn. Assn. of Ch. Bus. Valuators C.B.V. 1980; m. Elizabeth d. Leslie McKinnell 10 July 1971; children: Brandon, Aimee; CHAIRMAN, REGIONAL CABLESYSTEMS INC. 1992– ; Senior Vice-Pres. & C.F.O., Candn. Satellite Communications Inc. 1984–87; Extve. Vice-Pres. & C.O.O. 1987–88; Pres. & C.E.O., Regional Cablesystems Inc. 1988–92; Dir., Cable 2000 Inc.; Regional Cable TV (Atlantic, Central, Western & USA) Inc.; Regional Cablesystems Inc.; M.B.A. Grad. Sch. Rsch. Fellowship; Mem., Local Network Convergence Ctte.; Ont. & Candn. Insts. of C.A.s; Candn. Assn. of Ch. Bus. Valuators; author of 2 journal articles; club: Oakville Golf; Home: 268 Rambler Ct., Oakville, Ont. L6H 3A6; Office: 710 Dorval Dr., Ste. 300, Oakville, Ont. L6K 3V7.

**KAIN, Karen;** ballerina; b. Hamilton, Ont.; 28 March 1951; d. Charles A. and Winifred Mary (Kelly) K.; e. Fessenden Pub. Sch., Ancaster, Ont.; Springfield Pub. Sch., Erindale, Ont.; Nat. Ballet Sch., Toronto, Ont.; joined Corps de Ballet, Nat. Ballet Co. of Can. 1969; became princ. dancer 1970; rec'd Ont. Arts Foundation, Can. Council and Ford Motor Co. Scholarships 1964–69; Hon. Awards, Prov. of Ont., Cities of Mississauga and Toronto 1973; Silver Medalist, Internat. Competition Moscow 1973; Companion, Order of Can. June 1976; Hon. Degress: U.B.C.; Trent Univ.; York Univ.; Protestant; recreations: reading, swimming, theatre, music; Address: c/o The National Ballet of Canada, 157 King St. E., Toronto, Ont. M5C 1G9.

**KAISER, Colin Frederick;** business executive; b. Ayr, Queensland 3 Dec. 1933; e. Univ. of Queensland diploma in Metallurgy; m. Eugene; two sons; DIRECTOR, GRANGES INC. 1989– ; Chrmn. & Pres., Hycroft Resources & Devel. Corp. (Winnemucca, Nevada) 1989– ; Dir., International Curator 1989– ; Dir., M.I.M. Expl. Pty. Ltd. 1989– ; Dir., Hycroft Resources; Gen. Mgr., B.H.P. Minerals Co. Ltd., Australia 1975–80; Chief Gen. Mgr. & Dir., Houston Oil & Minerals, Australia 1980; Gen. Mgr. & Dir., Oaky Creek Coal Pty. Ltd., Australia 1981–84; Dir., Dalrymple Bay Coal Terminal & Dir., Abbot Point Coal Terminal 1981–84; Gen. Mgr. & Dir., Carpentaria Exploration Co. Pty. Ltd. (subsidiary of M.I.M. Holdings Ltd.), Australia 1984–87; Dir., Australia Diamond Exploration 1984–87; Extve. Gen. Mgr. Exploration & Gold Operations, Carpentaria Exploration Co. (subsiary of M.I.M. Holdings Ltd.), Chrmn. Bds. of Mngmnt., Carpentaria Gold, Carpentaria Exploration in Australia and Carpentaria Exploration Corp., New Zealand 1987–89; Dir., Teck Corp. (Vancouver) 1987–89; Pres. & C.E.O. Granges Inc. 1989–93; Mem., A.I.M.E.; C.I.M.; M.A.C.; P.D.A.C.; Office: 23rd floor, 885 W. Georgia St., Vancouver, B.C. V6C 3E8.

**KAISER, Jr., Edgar Fosburgh,** B.A., M.B.A.; executive; industrialist; b. Portland, Ore. 5 July 1942; s. Edgar Fosburgh and late Sue (Mead) K.; e. Stanford Univ. B.A. 1965; Harvard Univ. M.B.A. 1967; married; 2 children; CHRMN. OF THE BD., PRES. & C.E.O., KAISER RESOURCES LTD. 1970– ; Special assignments in Vietnam, U.S. Agency for Internat. Devel. 1967–68; White House Fellow (Asst. to Pres. Johnson) 1968; Special Asst. to Secy. of the Interior, U.S. Dept. of Interior 1969; Chrmn. & C.E.O., Kaiser Steel Corp. 1970–81; Chrmn. of the Bd., Pres. & C.E.O. Bank of British Columbia 1984–86; Chrmn. & Founder, Kaiser Youth Found.; Chrmn., Extve. Ctte., Harvard Capital Corp.; Dir., Boys' and Girls' Club, Vancouver (Hon. Dir.); Vancouver Gen. Hosp. Found.; Principal, Council for Excellence in Govt.; Chrmn. Emeritus, Henry J. Kaiser Family Found.; Trustee, The Salk Inst.; Woods Hole Oceanographic Institution; Mem., Business Council on National Issues; Denver Broncos Youth Found. (Adv. Ctte.); Friends of Alta. (Adv. Ctte.); Governor Dummer Acad. (Internat. Adv. Counc.); The Trilateral Commn.; Advisory Council, Faculty of Commerce and Business Admin., U.B.C.; White House Fellows Assn.; Woods Hole Oceanographic Inst. (Corp. Mem.); World Presidents' Orgn.; Young Presidents' Orgn.; Hon. Vice-Counsel, The Republic of Colombia in Vancouver, B.C.; Patron, Vancouver Public Aquarium Assn. (former Gov.); past Chrmn., Amer. Acad. of Achievement; past Chrmn. & C.E.O., Denver Broncos Football Club; past Chrmn. & Founder, Denver Broncos Youth Found.; past Chrmn., Special External Advisory Ctte. on Education Reform, Min. of Education, Govt. of B.C.; past Co-Chrmn., Amer. Cancer Soc.; past Pres., The Coal Assn. of Canada; past Dir., Amer. Iron & Steel Inst.; Bell Canada Enterprises Development Corp.; B.C. Place Ltd.; Canadair Ltd.; Candn. Arthritis & Rheumatism Soc.; Earth Day 1990; Internat. Iron & Steel Inst.; John G. Diefenbaker Memorial Found. Inc.; Man in Motion World Tour Inc.; Sadat Peace Found.; Stanford Univ. Alumni Assn.; Toronto-Dominion Bank; Univ. of Colorado Found.; Vancouver Symphony Soc.; past Advr./Dir., Private Investment Co. for Asia (PICA) S.A.; Vancouver General Hosp. Found.; Past Hon. Patron, Candn. Diabetes Assn. (B.C. Div.); former Gov., The Arts and Science Centre (Vancouver); Business Council of B.C.; Candn. Atherosclerosis Soc.; Downtown Vancouver Assn.; Honorary Captain, Canadian Navy, Second Canadian Destroyer Squadron; former Trustee, California Inst. of Technology; Nat. Choral Arts Soc., Washington, D.C.; Vancouver Gen. Hosp.; past Mem., Extve. Ctte., Asian Centre, Vancouver, B.C.; Business Council of B.C.; Canada-Japan Bus. Co-op. Comte.; Canada-Korea Business Counc.; Candn.-American Comte.; Counc. on Foreign Relations; School of Education Graduate Sch. Visiting Ctte., Harvard Univ.; HRH, The Duke of Edinburgh's Fifth Commonwealth Study Conference Canada 1980; Adv. Ctte., Internat. Financial Centre (Vancouver); Junior Achievement (Chrmn., Candn. Business Leadership Conference) 1986; National Adv. Comte. on Mining Industry (NACOMI); Pacific Basin Economic Council,

Candn. Ctte. Salk Institute; S.R.I. Internat. Counc.; Bus. Adv. Counc., Fac. of Bus., Univ. of Alta.; Awards: Golden Plate Award, Amer. Acad. of Achievement 1978; B.C. Businessman of the Year 1979; Edgar A. Scholz Award, B.C. and Yukon Chamber of Mines 1984; Marketing Executive of the Year 1986, Sales and Marketing Extves. of Vancouver; Round-the-World Speed Record Holder and eight speed-over-distance records in a BAe twin-engined jet aircraft, February 1988; Office: 20th Flr., 1500 West Georgia St., Vancouver, B.C. V6G 2Z8.

**KAISER, Karl J.,** B.Sc.; enologist (winemaker); b. St. Veit of Goelsen, Lower Austria 22 Sept. s. Karl and Katharina (Renz) K.; e. Brock Univ. B.Sc. (Hons.) 1974; m. Silvia (Regina) d. Hilde and Silvio Petritsch; children: Magdalena, Andrea, Maximillian; WINEMAKER & VICE-PRESIDENT, INNISKILLIN WINES INC.; Guest Teacher (speaker), George Brown College; Mem., Deans Council, Brock Univ., Fac.of Math. & Science; Mem., Candn. Chem. Soc.; Am. Soc. of Enology & Viticulture (Profl. Mem.); Candn. Soc. of Enol. & Viriculture; Am. Wine Soc.; Soc. of Wine Educators; recreations: skiing, fishing; Address: RR 1, Niagara-on-the-Lake, Ont. L0S 1J0.

**KAISER, Nicholas,** B.Sc., Ph.D.; university professor; b. England 15 Sept. 1954; s. Thomas Reeve and Pamela (Pound) K.; e. Leeds Univ. B.Sc. 1978; Cambridge Univ. Part III Maths Tripos 1979, Ph.D. 1982; m. Penelope d. Thomas and Evelyn Corbett 17 Dec. 1983; children: Alexander Nicholas, Louis Thomas; PROFESSOR, CANADIAN INST. FOR THEORETICAL ASTROPHYSICS, UNIV. OF TORONTO 1988– ; Lindemann postdoctoral fellowship, Univ. of Calif. at Berkeley 1983; postdoctoral positions, Univ. of Calif. at Berkeley and Santa Barbara 1984; NSERC Advanced Fellow, Inst. for Astronomy, ambridge 1985–87; Fellow, Candn. Inst. for Adv. Rsch. 1988; Helen Warner Prize, Am. Astron. Soc. 1989; NSERC Steacie Fellow 1991–92; Hertzberg Medal, Candn. Assn. of Physicists 1993; Home: 53 Templeton Ct., Scarborough, Ont. M1E 2C3; Office: 60 St. George St., Toronto, Ont. M5S 1A7.

**KALANT, Harold,** M.D., Ph.D., F.R.S.C.; educator and researcher; b. Toronto, Ont. 15 Nov. 1923; s. Max Isaac and Sophie (Shankman) K.; e. Kent Pub. Sch. and Bloor Coll. Inst. Toronto; Univ. of Toronto M.D. 1945 (Cody Silver Medal Med.), B.Sc. (Med.) 1948, Ph.D. 1955 (Starr Medal for Research); m. Oriana d. Pablo and Maria Josseau 22 July 1948; PROF. EMERITUS, UNIV. OF TORONTO and DIR. EMERITUS OF BIOBEHAV. RESEARCH (ARF) 1989– ; residencies in Internal Med. Saskatoon Veterans' Hosp., Toronto Gen. Hosp., Hosp. del Salvador (Santiago, Chile) 1947–50; Post-Doctoral Fellow Cambridge Univ. 1955–56; Biochem. Sect. Head Defence Rsch. Med. Labs. Downsview, Ont. 1956–59; Assoc. Prof., Univ. of Toronto 1959–64, Prof. of Pharmacol. 1964–89; Asst. Rsch. Dir., Addiction Research Foundation Ont. 1959–64, Assoc. Research Dir. 1964–89; Expert Panel on Drugs of Dependence World Health Orgn. 1978–83; Sci. Adv. Bd. Addiction Rsch. Foundation Palo Alto, Cal. 1974–82; Banting Rsch. Foundation 1976–80; Comte. Problems Drug Dependence U.S.A. 1978– ; Comité des Centres de Recherche FCAC Qué. 1983–84; Chrmn. Bd. Sci. Counsellors Nat. Inst. Alcoholism & Alcohol Abuse U.S.A. 1983–87; Bd. mem., Candn. Centre on Substance Abuse 1989–93; Pres., Int. Soc. Biomed. Rsch. Alcoholism 1990–94; recipient Jellinek Meml. Award, Amsterdam 1972; Raleigh Hills Foundation Gold Medal, Irvine, Cal. 1981; Rsch. Soc. Alcoholism Award 1983; Upjohn Award, Pharmacol. Soc. Canada 1985; Nathan B. Eddy Memorial Medal, Comte. Problems Drug Dependence U.S.A. 1986; co-author 'Experimental Approaches to the Study of Drug Dependence' 1969; 'Drugs, Society and Personal Choice' 1971, French transl. 1973, Norwegian transl. 1974; 'Amphetamines and Related Drugs: Clinical Toxicity and Dependence' 1974; co-ed. 'Alcoholic Liver Pathology' 1975; 'Cannabis and Health Hazards' 1983; series co-ed. 'Research Advances in Alcohol and Drug Problems' Vols. 1–9; Assoc. Ed. Candn. Jour. Physiol. & Pharmacol. 1975–81; Field Ed. Jour. Studies on Alcohol 1983–92; mem. various ed. bds.; Home: 2701, 965 Bay St., Toronto, Ont. M5S 2A3; Office: Toronto, Ont. M5S 1A8.

**KALISKI, Stephan Felix,** M.A., Ph.D.; educator; b. Warsaw, Poland 4 Nov. 1928; s. late Jacob and late Ludwika (Romanus) K.; e. Univ. of B.C. B.A. 1952; Univ. of Toronto M.A. 1953 (Alexander Mackenzie Research Fellow 1953–54); Cambridge Univ. Ph.D. 1959 (Research Fellow Social Science Research Council 1956–57, Fellow Candn. Social Science Research Council 1957–58); m. Marian Ieleen d. late Abel J. Nelson and late Hilda N. 6 Oct. 1960; one d. Susan Maria; PROF. OF ECON. QUEEN'S UNIV. since 1969; Stat. Dom. Bureau of Stat. 1951–52; Lectr. Queen's Univ. 1954–56; Jr. Research Officer, Dept. Applied Econ., Cambridge Univ. 1957–58; Research Fellow in Econ. Stat. Manchester Univ. 1958–59; Asst. Prof. Carleton Univ. 1959, Assoc. Prof. 1962, Prof. 1965–69, Chrmn. Econ. Dept. 1962–63, 1964–66; Research Supvr. Royal Comn. on Taxation 1963–64; Research Assoc. Univ. of Cal. Berkeley 1966–67 (Can. Council Sr. Fellowship, Dept. of Labour Univs. Research Comte. Grant); Hon. Research Assoc. in Econ. Harvard 1973–74 (Can. Council Leave Fellowship); Mang. Ed. 'Canadian Journal of Economics' 1976–79; Director, McGill-Queen's Univ. Press, 1978–80; Dir. Nat. Bureau Econ. Research, (U.S.A.), 1979–84; author or co-author numerous publs. on applied econ., internat. econ., unemployment, inflation; mem. Candn. Econ. Assn. (Vice-Pres. 1984–85; Pres.-Elect 1985–86; Pres. 1986–87; Past Pres. 1987–88); Am. Econ. Assn.; Royal Soc. Can.; Home: 649 Fernmoor Dr., Kingston, Ont. K7M 8K5; Office: Kingston, Ont. K7L 3N6.

**KALLEN, Evelyn,** Ph.D., F.R.S.C.; educator; b. Toronto, Ont. 30 Sept. 1929; d. Martin and Bess (Karry) K.; e. Univ. of Toronto B.A. 1950, Dip. CS 1953, Ph.D. 1969; m. David Rees s. Thomas Richard and Elizabeth Hughes 14 March 1975; EMERITUS PROF. OF SOCIAL SCI. AND ANTHROP. YORK UNIV. 1991– ; Asst. Prof. of Social Sci. present Univ. 1970, Assoc. Prof. of Social Sci. & Anthrop. 1974; Prof. of Social Sci. & Anthrop. 1984; Holder Hon. Chair of Human Rights, Human Rights Rsch. & Edn. Centre Faculty of Law Univ. of Ottawa 1989–90; author 'Spanning the Generations: A Study in Jewish Identity' 1977; 'The Western Samoan Kinship Bridge' 1982; 'Ethnicity and Human Rights in Canada' 1982; 'Label Me Human: Minority Rights of Stigmatized Canadians' 1989; co-author 'The Anatomy of Racism: Canadian Dimensions' 1974 (Candn. Human Rights Found. Annual Prize); mem. Candn. Human Rights Found. (Nat. Council 1982–91); Candn. Ethnic Studies Assn. (Dir. 1982–84); Candn. Sociol. & Anthrop. Assn. (Exec. Ctte. 1979–82); recreations: swimming, walking; Home: 11 Davy Pt. Circle, Keswick, Ont. L4P 3H2; Office: 362 NBC, 4700 Keele St., North York, Ont. M3J 1P3.

**KALLER, Cecil Louis,** B.A., B.Ed., M.A., Ph.D.; educator; b. Humboldt, Sask. 26 March 1930; s. Frank Joseph and Cecilia Johanna (Hinz) K.; e. Elem. and High Schs. Sask.; Sask. Normal Sch., Saskatoon; Univ. of Sask., B.A. 1954, B.Ed. 1954, M.A. 1956; Purdue Univ., Ph.D. (Math. Stat.) 1960; m. Theresa Ann, d. Clarence Fricke, Ohio, 26 May 1962; four s. Kevin Paul, Damon Michael, Brian Francis, Alan Matthew; Teacher, Elem. and High Schs. 1948–52; Asst. Research Stat. Educ. Div., Dom. Bureau of Stat., Ottawa 1955; Research Stat., Upjohn Co., Kalamazoo, summers 1958–60; Asst. Prof. of math., Univ. of Sask. 1960, Assoc. Prof. 1964, trans. Regina campus as Assoc. Prof. and Chrmn. Dept. of Math. 1965, Prof. and Chrmn. of Math. 1967–70; President, Notre Dame Univ. of Nelson, also Prof. of Math. and mem. Bd. of Govs. 1970–76; Instructor of Mathematics, Okanagan Coll., Kelowna, B.C. 1976–92; author articles in various prof. and scholarly journs.; Vice Pres. Computer Science Assn. 1963–70; Assn. Computing Machinery 1967–70; Biometric Soc. 1959–70; Inst. Math. Stat. 1959–68; Trustee St. Joseph's Sch. Nelson 1973–75; Dir., Kelowna Minor Hockey Assoc. 1976–78; Vice-Pres., Catholic School Trustees Assoc. of B.C. 1977–80; Vice Pres., Faculty Assn. of Okanagan College, 1979–81; Trustee St. Joseph's & Immaculata School 1978–80; B.C. Dir. on Cdn. Catholic School Trustees Assn., 1980–84; Chrmn., 4th Kelowna Boy Scout Assn., 1978–81; St. Thomas More Coll. Corp., Univ. of Sask. 1982– ; Dir., Kelowna Right-To-Life Soc.; mem. Am. Math. Soc.; Math. Assn. Am.; Candn. Math. Soc.; Am. Stat. Assn.; Sigma Xi; Humanities Assn. Can.; R. Catholic; Home: #103, 539 Sutherland Ave., Kelowna, B.C. V1Y 5X3.

**KALLMANN, Helmut,** C.M., B.Mus., LL.D.; retired music librarian and historian; b. Berlin, Germany 7 Aug. 1922; s. late Dr. Arthur and late Fanny (Paradies) K.; e. Elem. and High Schs., Berlin, 1928–39; Sr. Matric., Toronto, 1946; Royal Conserv. of Music, Grade X Piano 1948; Univ. of Toronto, B.Mus. 1949, LL.D. 1971; m. late Ruth, d. late Israel Singer, Toronto, 31 Dec. 1955; one step-d., Lynn Proctor (Mrs. R. Salter); Chief of Music Div., Nat. Library Can. 1970–87; CBC Toronto Music Lib. 1950–70; Music Clk. 1950–51, Music Lib. 1951–61, Sr. Music Lib. 1961–62, Supvr. of Music Lib. 1962–70; author 'Catalogue of Canadian Composers' (rev. ed. only) 1952; 'A History of Music in Canada 1534–1914,' 1960 (reprint and paperback 1969, 1987); co-ed., 'Encyclopedia of Music in Canada' 1981 (2nd ed. 1992); 'Encyclopédie de la Musique au Canada' 1983 (2nd ed. 1993); Ed., 'The Canadian Musical Heritage, vol. 8: Music for Orchestra 1' 1990; other writings including book chapters, dict. and music journ. articles; collab. in various bibliog. publs.; Candn. Music Council Medal for 'outstanding service to Candn. musical life,' 1977; apptd. Member, Order of Canada 1986; mem., Candn. Music Council (Vice Pres. 1971–76); Candn. Assn. Music. Libs.; Internat. Assn. Music Libs.; Bibliog. Soc. Can.; Assoc. pour l'avancement de la recherche en musique du Québec; Chrmn., Can. Musical Heritage Soc. 1982– ; recreations: music, travel; Home: 38 Foothills Dr., Nepean, Ont. K2H 6K3.

**KALMAN, James Alexander,** B.A.Sc., M.Sc., M.B.A.; oil and gas industry executive; b. Budapest, Hungary 26 Dec. 1946; e. Univ. of Toronto B.A.Sc. 1970, M.Sc. 1972; Univ. of Western Ont. M.B.A. 1974; m. Marilynn; two children; EXTVE. VICE-PRES., OIL & GAS DIV., CONWEST EXPLORATION CO. LIMITED 1978; Asst. Mgr., Metals & Mining, Toronto Dominion Bank 1974–78; joined Conwest Exploration as Vice-Pres. 1978; Dir., Cogas Energy; Paragon Petroleum Ltd.; recreations: tennis, squash; clubs: Bow Valley, Glencoe, Glencoe Golf & Country; Home: 102 Eagle Ridge Drive S.W., Calgary, Alta. T2V 2V4; Office: 800, 407 – 8th Ave. S.W., Calgary, Alta. T2P 1E5.

**KALOW, Werner,** M.D., F.R.S.C.; educator; b. Cottbus, Germany 15 Feb. 1917; s. Johannes Bernhard and Maria Elisabeth (Heyde) K.; e. high sch. Cottbus; med. studies Univs. of Greifswald, Graz, Gottingen; Univ. of Konigsberg M.D. 1941; m. Brigitte D. d. Wilhelm and Hertha von Gaza 21 Dec. 1946; children: Peter Bernard, Barbara Irene; m. Patricia M. d. Frederick and Mary E. Arnold 3 May 1991; PROF. OF PHARMACOL., UNIV. OF TORONTO 1962– ; Rsch. Asst. Berlin Univ. 1947–49; Rsch. Fellow and Instr. Univ. of Pa. 1949–51; Lectr. present Univ. 1951, Asst. Prof. 1953, Assoc. Prof. 1955, Chrmn. of Pharmacol. 1966–77; Dir. of Biol. Rsch. C.H. Boehringer Sohn, Ingelheim, W. Germany 1965–66 (on leave-of-absence); Samuel Hahnemann Lectr. Univ. of Cal. San Francisco 1977; Upjohn Award Pharmacol. Soc. Can. 1981; mem. Drug Rsch. Bd. Nat. Acad. Sci's Washington, D.C. 1972–76; Oscar B. Hunter Award, Am. Soc. for Clinical Pharmacol. and Therapeutics 1993; Rsch. Recognition Award, Candn. Anaesthetists Soc. 1993; Steering Comte. Toronto/Guelph Centre for Toxicology; Assoc. Inst. of Environmental Studies 1971– ; Cons., Nat. Insts. Gen. Med. Sci's Pharmacol.-Toxicol. Prog. Bethesda, Md. 1972–76 and 1986– ; author 'Pharmacogenetics, Heredity and the Response to Drugs' 1962; co-ed. 'Pharmacogenetics' 1968; 'International Symposium on Malignant Hyperthermia' 1973; 'Ethnic Differences in Reactions to Drugs and Xenobiotics' 1986; ed. 'Pharmacogenetics of Drug Metabolism' 1992; Hon. mem. Candn. Anaesthetists Soc.; mem. Pharmacol. Soc. Can. (Pres. 1963–64); Am. Soc. Pharmacol. & Exper. Therapy; Deutsche Pharmakologische Gesellschaft; Soc. Toxicol. Can.; Candn. Physiol. Soc.; Fellow, Roy. Soc. of Canada; Genetics Soc. Can.; Toronto Biochem. & Biophys. Soc. (Pres. 1963–64); Candn. Soc. Clin. Pharmacol. & Chemotherapy (Pres. 1975–77); Home: 130 McGill St., Toronto, Ont. M5B 1H6; Office: Toronto, Ont. M5S 1A8.

**KALYMON, Basil A.,** B.Sc., Ph.D.; university professor; b. Horlyci, Ukraine 4 April 1944; s. Ananij and Maria (Drimalyk) K.; e. De La Salle Collegiate 1962; Univ. of Toronto B.Sc. 1966; Yale Univ. Ph.D. 1970; m. Olia d. Dmytro and Anna Romanenchuk 1965; children: Taras, Natalie; PROFESSOR, UNIV. OF TORONTO, FACULTY OF MANAGEMENT 1975– ; Prof., Univ. of Calif. 1969–71; Univ. of Toronto, Fac. of Mngt. 1971–73; Harvard Univ. Business Sch. 1973–75; Assoc., Cooper & Lybrand Consulting Group 1982– ; Visiting Scholar, Nat. Centre for Management Research Devel. 1987; Dir., Community Trust Co.; Newport Devel.; Economic Policy Ctte., Candn. C. of C.; Visiting Lectr., Internat. Mngt. Inst. Kiev; Bd. of Gov., Univ. of Toronto 1989– ; Business Bd., Univ. of Toronto 1989– ; Ukrainian Catholic; Mem., Inst. of Mngt. Sciences; Admin. Sci. Assn. of Can. (Past Dir.); Financial Extves. Inst.; author: 'The Management of Canadian Resources' 1981, 'Global Innovation: The Impact on Canada's Financial Markets' 1989; recreations: tennis, skiing; clubs: Cranberry Village, Boulevard; Home: 56 Ridgevalley Cres., Islington, Ont. M9A 3J6; Office: 246 Bloor St. W., Toronto, Ont. M5S 1V4.

**KAMAL, Musa Rasim,** B.S., M.Eng., Ph.D.; educator; b. Tulkarm, Jordan 8 Dec. 1934; s. Rasim Kamal Ismail and Aminah Adu Hadbah; e. Univ. of Ill. B.S. 1958; Carnegie-Mellon Univ., Pittsburgh, Pa. M.Eng. 1959, Ph.D. (Chem. Eng.) 1961; Columbia Univ., N.Y. Grad. studies in Economics; m. Nancy Joan d. Arthur Edgar 23 Dec. 1961; children: Rammie, Basim; DIR., BRACE RESEARCH INST. 1987– and PROF. CHEM. ENG. DEPT., McGILL UNIV. 1973– ; Pres., Tulkarm Enterprises Ltd. (Consultants & Planners); Research Chem. Eng., Central Research Lab, Amer. Cyanamid Co., Stamford, Conn. 1961–65; Research Group Leader, Plastics & Resins Divn., Amer. Cyanamid, Wallinford, Conn. 1965–67; joined present Univ. as Assoc. Prof. of Chem. Eng. in 1967; Head Micro-Economics & Sectoral Studies Grp., Morocco 5–Year Ind. Devt. Plan, Rabat, Morocco 1977; Chrmn., Chem. Eng. Dept., McGill Univ., 1983–93; author 'Weatherability of Plastics Materials' 1967; over 170 publications in fields of Chem. Eng. and Polymer Technology; 6 U.S. patents; mem. Advisory Bd., 'Polymer Engineering and Sci. Journal'; Ed. Bd., 'Advances in Polymer Tech. Journal,' 'Polymer Eng.,' 'International Polymer Processing,' 'Polymer Contents'; mem., Que. Order of Engineers; Can. Soc. of Chem. Engrs. (past Treas.); Inst. of Chem. Sci. and Tech. (Mngmt. Ctte. 1992– ); Fellow, Chem. Inst. of Can. (Bd. of Dirs., Dir., Econ. & Bus. Mgmt. Div., past mem. Finance Comte.); Soc. of Plastics Engrs. (past Dir., Plastics Analysis & Engineering Structure & Properties Divns.); Candn. Advanced Industrial Materials Forum (Adv. Bd. 1988– ); Plastics Inst. of Amer. (past Dir.); Amer. Chem. Soc.; Amer. Inst. of Chem. Eng.; Amer. Inst. of Physics; Candn. Plastics Institute (Bd. of Govs. 1986– ); Amer. Assn. for Advancement of Sci.; Amer. Acad. of Mechanics; Soc. of Rheology; Candn. Inst. of Internat. Affairs; U.N. Assn. of Can; McGill Assn. of Univ. Tchrs.; various academic & admin. comtes., McGill Univ.; Progm. Chrmn., 2nd World Congress of Chem. Engrs. 1981; Annual Technical Conf., Soc. of Plastics Engrs. 1973; IUPAC POlymers 1990; Internat. Polymer Processing Group (Chrmn. 1981– ); Polymer Processing Soc. (Founding Offr. 1985–89); Kuwait Prize for Applied Sciences 1983; Soc. of Plastics Engrs., Internat. Education Award 1984; SPI Canada, Canplast Award 1986; Tau Beta Pi; Phi Lamda Epsilon; Pi Mu Epsilon; Sigma Xi; Clubs: Montreal Amateur Athletics Assn.; McGill Univ. Faculty; recreations: reading, travel; Home: 338 Roslyn Ave., Westmount, Que. H3Z 2L6; Office: 3480 University St., Montreal, Que. H3A 2A7.

**KANAREK, Alexander David,** B.Sc., Ph.D., A.R.C.S., M.C.I.M.; biotechnology consultant; b. London, Eng., 19 April 1930; s. Jacob R. and Lily P. (Packer) K.; e. Imperial Coll. B.Sc. 1950; Univ. of Cambridge Ph.D. 1954; Inst. of Marketing M.C.I.M. 1974; m. Tina d. Anchel and Sylvia Newman 9 Nov. 1958; children: Melanie Ruth, Julian Victor; Sr. Scientist, Wellcome Rsch. Labs., Wellcome Found. Ltd. U.K. 1954–71; Product Group Mgr., Biologicals 1971–75; Connaught Labs. Ltd. 1975–79; emigrated to Canada 1979; European Regional Mgr. 1981–84; directed vaccine technology transfer to Pakistan Nat. Inst. of Health; Dir., Viral Vaccines & Vaccine Devel. 1984–90; Dir., Business Devel. 1990–93; founded consultancy April 1993; Mem., Sci. Adv. Bd., Stressgen Inc.; recreations: tai chi, dressage riding: Address: 38 Col. Sharpe Crescent, Uxbridge, Ont. L9P 1T7.

**KANE, Hon. Joseph C.;** judge; b. Stratford, Ont. 19 Oct. 1928; s. Frederick H. and Lillian May (Jones) K.; e. Oakwood Coll. Inst. Toronto 1948; Univ. of Toronto Victoria Coll. B.A. 1951; Ont. Coll. of Educ. 1952; Osgoode Hall Law Sch. 1957; m. Janet Wylie d. Ernest Henry Perkins 30 June 1956; children: Terrance, Wendy, Timothy, Steven, Christopher; JUDGE, DISTRICT COURT OF ONTARIO; called to Bar of Ont. 1957; cr. Q.C. 1974; Protestant; Home: 169 Munro Blvd., Willowdale, Ont. M2P 1C9; Office: Court House, 361 University Ave., Toronto, Ont. M5G 1T3.

**KANE, Robert G.,** B.Sc., B.Eng.; business executive; b. St. John, N.B. 17 Nov. 1953; s. George C. and Doris G. (Watson) K.; e. Dalhousie Univ. B.Sc. (Psych.); Technical Univ. of N.S. B.Eng. (Chem.Eng.) 1979; m. Sharon d. Benson and Alice Auld 10 May 1979; PRESIDENT AND GENERAL MANAGER, CAE FIBERGLASS LTD. 1991– ; various positions in engineering, manufacturing, sales, marketing and R&D, Dow Chemical 1979–86; responsible for marketing & technical functions, Celfortec 1986–91; Home: 106 Three Valleys Dr., Don Mills, Ont. M3A 3B9; Office: 219 Jamieson Bone Rd., Belleville, Ont. K8N 5B2.

**KANE, T. Gregory,** Q.C., LL.B.; lawyer; b. Kingston, Ont. 24 Aug. 1942; s. James Baxter and Mary Graham (Sewell) K.; e. Queen's Univ.; Univ. of Ottawa LL.B. 1969; m. Adrian Ilene d. George and Dorothy Solomon 1 Dec. 1990; children: Graeme, Adam, Oliver; step-children: Dean, Matthew, Blake, Christina; MANAGING PARTNER, OTTAWA OFFICE, STIKEMAN, ELLIOTT 1981– ; General Legal Council, Accra, Ghana 1969–71, 1973–75; General Counsel, Consumers Assn. of Canada 1975–78; Assoc. General Counsel, Candn. Radio-TV and Telecommunications Comn. 1978–80; sole practioner 1980–81; Adjunct Prof. of Law, Fac. of Common Law, Univ. of Ottawa 1981–87 and Sch. of Grad. Studies 1988– ; Bd. Chair, Ottawa Ballet 1989– ; Past Chair, Media & Telecommunications Nat. Section, Candn. Bar Assn.; Founding Ed., 'The Regulatory Reporter' 1980; author: 'Consumers and the Regulators: Consumer Intervention in the Federal Regulatory Process' 1980, 'Regulation of Specific Businesses' in 'Doing Business in Canada'; numerous articles for journals and conference proceedings; recreations: skiing, tennis; clubs: Rideau, Country; Home: 470 Acacia Ave., Ottawa, Ont. K1M 0M2; Office: Suite 914, 50 O'Connor St., Ottawa, Ont. K1P 6L2.

**KANE, Thomas Douglas,** B.A., M.B.A., C.A.E.; association executive; b. Toronto, Ont. 15 Jan. 1951; s. Robert James and Dorothy Mary (Ames) K.; e. Lawrence Park Collegiate Inst. Toronto 1969; York Univ. B.A. 1972, M.B.A. 1978; Cert. Assn. Exec. (C.A.E.) 1984; m. Ann d. Grant and Elizabeth Gillespie 9 Sept. 1972; children: Brandon Thomas, Lesley Ann; PRESIDENT, ONT. DAIRY COUNCIL 1980– ; Office Mgr. Donlands Dairy Co. Ltd. Toronto 1972–79; Adm. Mgr. present Counc. 1979–80; Dir. Royal Agric. Winter Fair Assn.; Industrial Accident Prevention Assoc.; recreations: philately, curling; Home: 1421 Bridgestone Lane, Mississauga, Ont. L5J 4E1; Office: 6533 Mississauga Rd., Unit D, Mississauga, Ont. L5N 1A6.

**KANEE, Sol,** O.C., B.A., LL.B., LL.D.; executive; b. Melville, Sask. 1 June 1909; s. Sam and Rose (Lercher) K.; e. Univ. of Man., B.A. 1929, LL.D. 1974; Univ. of Sask., LL.B. 1932; m. Florence Barish, 10 Apl. 1935; one s., Stephen Charles; Chrmn., Kanee Grain Canada Ltd.; Chrmn., GIII Ltd.; Dir., Grant Park Plaza Ltd.; Hon. Dir., Canadian Airlines International Ltd.; read law with J.W. Estey, K.C., Saskatoon; called to Bar of Sask. 1933; with law firm Kanee & Deroche, Melville, Sask., 1933–40; Shinbane, Dorfman & Kanee, Winnipeg, 1945–65; served with RCA in Europe and S. Pacific 1940–45; rank Maj.; Past Pres., Candn. Jewish Cong.; Un. Way of Greater Winnipeg; Community Welfare Planning Council; Royal Winnipeg Ballet; Services for Handicapped (Man.) Inc.; Mem. of Executive World Jewish Cong.; Past Chrmn.: Federal Business Development Bank; Bd. Govs., Univ. of Man.; Candn. Nat. Millers Assn.; Officer, Order of Can. 1977; Liberal; Jewish; recreation: fishing; Club: Glendale Golf & Country; Office: 274 Jarvis Ave., Winnipeg, Man. R2W 3A5.

**KANFER, Julian Norman,** M.Sc., Ph.D.; biochemist; educator; b. Brooklyn, N.Y. 23 May 1930; s. Benjamin N. and Clara (Lichtenberger) K.; e. Brooklyn Coll. B.Sc. 1954; George Washington Univ. M.Sc. 1958, Ph.D. 1961; m. Beverly; children: Brian, Rachel; Prof. and Head of Biochem., Univ. of Man. 1975–86; Consultant, Health Sciences Center Winnipeg 1976–86; mem. Med. Adv. Bd. Nat. Tay-Sachs Foundation New York 1970– ; mem. Study Sec. on Pathobiol. Chem. Nat. Insts. Health 1974–78; mem. Panel on Clinical Postdoctoral Fellowships, Med. Rsch. Counc. 1983–86; recipient Travel Award, Am. Soc. Biol. Chems. 1967; Visiting Scientist Award, Med. Rsch. Counc. 1980, 1982, 1986; Tokyo Soc. Med. Sciences and Faculty of Med. Univ. of Tokyo Award; Visiting Prof., Univ. of Pittsburgh Sch. of Medicine 1993–94; INSERM Fellow 1983–86; author 'Sphingolipid Biochemistry' 1982; Fellow, I.N.S.E.R.M., France 1983, 1986; mem. Am. Soc. Biol. Chem.; Am. Neurochem. Soc.; Internat. Neurochem. Soc.; Am. Chem. Soc.; Am. Assn. Advanc. Science; Fed. Am. Socs. Exper. Biol. (Nat. Corr.); Candn. Fed. Biol. Socs.; Multiple Sclerosis Soc. Can. (Winnipeg Chapter); Office: 770 Bannatyne Ave., Winnipeg, Man. R3E 0W3.

**KANG, Chil-Yong,** F.R.S.C., D.Sc., Ph.D., Dipl. V.Sc.; university professor; b. Republic of Korea 28 Nov. 1940; s. Whashik and Ungee (Song) K.; e. Malling Agric. coll. (Denmark), Dip.V.Sc. 1963; Kon-Kuk Univ. (Korea), B.S.A. 1965; McMaster Univ., Ph.D. 1971; Carleton Univ. D.Sc. 1991; m. Myung Ja (Oh) d. Daewon and Unsook Oh 17 Dec. 1966; children: Julie, Rosanne, Matthew; PROF. & DEAN, FACULTY OF SCIENCE, THE UNIV. OF WESTERN ONT. 1992– ; Rsch. Asst., Connaught Med. Rsch. Labs. 1966–68; Nat. Cancer Inst. of Can. pre-doct. fellow, McMaster Univ. 1970–71; Nat. Cancer Inst. of Can. Post-doct. fellow, Lab. of Dr Howard M. Temin, Univ. of Wisconsin 1971–74; Asst. Prof., Univ. of Texas SW Med. Sch. 1974–77; Assoc. Prof. 1978–82; Prof. & Chrmn., Dept. of Microbiol. & Immunol., Univ. of Ottawa 1982–92; Co-Dir., Univ. of Ottawa Biotechnol. Rsch. Inst. 1985–87; Dir. 1987–92; Sci. Cons., Virus Rsch. Institute, Cambridge, MA; Korean Green Cross Corp.; Hon. Prof., Chinese Acad. of Prev. Med. 1987– ; Vis. Sci., Lab. of Molecular Genetics, Dr Lazzarini's Lab. NINCDS, NIH, Bethesda, USA (sabb.) 1981; Visiting Sci., NERC Institute of Virology, Oxford, United Kingdom 1986; Mem., Am. Soc. for Virology; Am. Soc. for Microbiol.; Am. Assn. for Adv. of Sci.; Candn. Soc. of Microbiol.; Genetics Soc. of Can.; NY Acad. of Sci.; Korean Soc. of Virology; Assn. of Korean-Candn. Sci. & Engr.; Fellow, The Royal Soc. of Canada 1993; recreations: golf, music; Clubs: Sunningdale Golf, London; Camelot Country, Ottawa; Home: 111 Glenridge Cres., London, Ont. N6G 4X9; Office: Western Science Centre, Faculty of Science, The Univ. of Western Ont., London, Ont. N6A 5B7.

**KANGAS, Martti,** B.A., M.B.A.; editor, publisher, public relations consulant; b. London, Ont. 22 July 1958; s. Lauri Hendrick and Joan Isabel (McNamara) K.; e. Univ. of Toronto B.A. 1980, M.B.A. 1982; Ryerson Polytechnical Inst. 1988; m. Jennifer d. Earle and Jacqueline Scahffenburg 29 June 1985; one s.: Mikael; CANADIAN EDITOR/PUBLISHER, T.V. BUSINESS MAGAZINE (MACLEAN HUNTER GERMANY) 1991– ; Account Extve. & Proprietor, Jack Roberts Mktg. Services Ltd. 1983–89; Editor-in-Chief, Canadian Printer Magazine (Maclean Hunter Ltd.) 1989–92; Assoc., National Public Relations 1993– ; Maclean Hunter Award of Excellence 1990; Three Top 5 Awards, K.R. Wilson Bus. Publishing Awards 1992; Kappa Alpha Alumni Assn.; recreations: skiing, swimming, photography, tennis; Home: 269 Beresford Ave., Toronto, Ont. M6S 3B4.

**KANN, Isabel,** RCA, OSA, B.A.; artist; b. Bangalore, India 1921 (of English parents); e. Bournemouth Art Sch. 1942; Edinburch Coll. of Art (Sir Wm. Gillies 1942–43) & 1946–48 (1 yr. post-grad. scholarship); Univ. of Toronto B.A. 1974; solo exhibitions: Nancy Poole's Studio 1975, 76, 77, 80, 82, 83, 84, 86, 88, 90; Silverstone Gall., Montreal 1989; group exhibitions: RCA House, Opening Show for Members 1987, 'Personal Vision' Cambridge Pub. Gall. 1987, OSA-ASA 'Expression East-West' 1984, Lynwood Arts Ctr. Simcoe 1983, OSA 'Women on the Move' Toronto 1981; OSA juried exhib. Toronto 1977–81, 'Image 75' Toronto 1975, New English Art Club London, Eng. 1942; collections: Canada Council Art Bank; Dupont Can. Inc.; Imperial Oil; Mary Kay Cosmetics; Shell Canada; Union Gas; Claridge; Royal Bank; Vanguard Trust; General Electric, Canada Inc.; Glaxo Canada Inc.; catalogue: 'Personal Vision in Landscape' 1988; subject of article Globe & Mail 2 Mar. 1982; 'Isabel Kann' by Harry Thurston in City & Country Home 1991; represented in Ontario: Nancy Poole's Studio, 16 Hazelton Ave., Toronto, Ont. M5K 2E2; Quebec: Westmount Gallery, 4912 Sherbrook St. W., Westmount, Montreal, Que. H3Z 1H3.

**KANTAROFF, Maryon;** sculptor; fine arts foundry founder; feminist-artist; lecturer; writer; b. Toronto, Ont. 20 Nov 1933; d. Christopher and Irene (Somlev) K.; e. ARCT, piano, Royal Cons. of Music 1953; Univ. of Toronto, Hon. Art & Archaeology 1957; Postgrad. study, Brit. Mus. 1958–59; Postgrad. sculp., Birkshire Coll. of Art 1958–59; Postgrad. study, painting, Sir John Cass Coll. of Art 1959–60; sculp., Chelsea Coll. of Art, Univ. of London 1959–62; Asst. Curator, Art Gallery of Toronto 1957–58; Art Teacher, England 1958–59; Art Critic, Brit. Broadcasting Corp., E. Europe Broadcasting 1959–62; freelance sculp., Brit. Broadcasting Corp.; Independant TV; Art Teacher, Secondary Sch., London 1962; 1st profl. exhbn. 1962; Spearhead Postgrad. course in Metallergy, Brunel Univ. 1968–69; 1st Resident Sculp., Seneca Coll. 1970; Art Lectr. & feminist 1970– ; creations incl. 20 environ. sculps., ltd. jewellery eds., numerous solo and group exhbns.; founded The Art Foundry Inc. 1974 (closed 1988); Organizer, New Feminists in Toronto 1969; 1st Retrospective Exhbn., Los Angeles, Calif. 1987 (25 yrs. since 1st show, Milan 1962); recent comn.: sculpture for Candn. Embassy in Tokyo (installation 1991); memorial sculpture, Beth Sholom Synagogue (installation 1992); mem., Sculp. Soc. of Can.; Candn. Art Assn.; Toronto Profl. & Bus. Women's Assn.; Nat. Action Ctte.; Artists for Peace; Amnesty Internat.; Scholarship, Can. Counc. for the Arts 1958; Zonta Adventure Award 1975; Woman of Distinction Award, YWCA 1982; President's Award for best sculpture, Sculptor's Soc. of Canada 1992; art & feminist mag. contrbr.; recreations: reading, music, swimming; Club; Heliconian; Home: 148 Lyndhurst Ave., Toronto, Ont. M5R 2Z9.

**KANUNGO, Rabindra Nath,** B.A., M.A., Ph.D.; university professor, author, consultant; b. Cuttack, India 11 July 1935; s. Kshirode Chandra and Mahindramani (Mohanty) K.; e. Utkal Univ. B.A. (Hons.) 1953; Patna Univ. M.A. 1955; McGill Univ. Ph.D. 1962; m. Minati d. Laxmiaarayan and Indubala Das 25 Nov. 1957; children: Siddhartha, Nachiketa; PROFESSOR, FACULTY OF MANAGEMENT, MCGILL UNIV. 1973– ; Lecturer, Ravenshaw College India 1955–60; Asst. Prof.,

Indian Inst. of Mngt. Calcutta 1962–64; Head, Social Science Div., Indian Inst. of Tech. Bombay 1964–65; Assoc. Prof., Dalhousie Univ. 1965–69; McGill Univ. 1969–73; Chair, Fac. of Mngt. 1988– ; consultant to num. orgns. such as CBC and Xerox Canada; research & consultant in N. Am., Eur. & Asian countries; Fellow, Candn. Psych. Assn.; Visiting Scholar, Univ. of Calif. at Berkeley; Distinguished Indo-Candn. Award, NACOI Montreal 1991; served on several boards incl. Shastri Indo-Candn. Inst., Internat. Sociological Assn., 'Can. J. of Behavior Sci.' (Edit. Bd.), etc.; mem. of several profl. orgns. in both psych. & mngt. fields; Past Pres., India-Can. Assn. Halifax & Montreal; Past Vice-Pres., NACOI Ottawa; author: 'Biculturalism and Management' 1980, 'Work Alienation' 1982 and over 100 refereed journal articles; co-author: 'Affect and Memory' 1975, 'Compensation' 1992; editor: 'South Asians in the Canadian Mosaic' 1984; co-editor: 'Behavioral Issues in Management' 1977, 'Management of Work and Personal Life' 1984, 'Charismatic Leadership' 1988, 'Management in Developing Countries' 1990, 'South Asian Canadians' 1992; Office: 1001 Sherbrooke St. W., Montreal, Que. H3A 1G5.

**KAO, Kuo Nan,** B.Sc., M.S.A., Ph.D., F.R.S.C.; researcher; b. Jen Yee, Kiangsu, China 5 Apl. 1934; s. Pang Tsing and Jin Wu (Hwu) Kao; e. Chung-Hsing Univ. Taiwan B.Sc. 1956; Univ. of Guelph M.S.A. 1964; Univ. of Sask., Ph.D. 1968; m. Wen-jou d. Pei-chi and Chin-ling Wang 20 Sept. 1962; two d. Anna Ching-Chi, Valeria Ching Mei; SR. RSCH. OFFR. PLANT BIOTECHNOL. INST. NRC 1980– ; Adjunct Prof. Univ. of Sask. 1984– ; Rsch. Asst. Taiwan Provl. Agric. Rsch. Inst. 1958; Teaching Asst. Chung-Hsing Univ. Taiwan 1958–62; Postdoctoral Fellow, Univ. of Guelph 1968–69 and Prairie Regional Lab. 1969–70; Asst. Rsch. Offr. present Inst. 1970–74, Assoc. Rsch. Offr. 1974–80; recipient Distinguished Grad. in Agric. Award 1986; author or co-author over 60 sci. rsch. papers; mem. Genetic Soc. Can.; Tissue Culture Assn.; New York Acad. Sci's; Internat. Assn. Plant Tissue Culture; recreation: outdoor activity; Home: 385 Birch Cres., Saskatoon, Sask. S7N 2M6; Office: 110 Cymnasium Rd., Saskatoon, Sask. S7N 0W9.

**KAO, Raymond Wen-Yuan,** B.Sc., M.B.A., M.A.; professor of entrepreneurship; b. Nanking, China 11 Oct. 1924; s. Wing-Sun and Han-Shih (Han) K.; e. Univ. of Toronto, M.B.A. 1961; Univ. of Manchester, M.A. 1976; m. Flora Maria d. Isidro and Rosalina Con 6 Oct. 1956; children: Yolanda, Belinda, Kenneth, Rowland, Christine; PROF. OF ENTREPRENEURSHIP, CENTRE FOR ENTREPRENEURSHIP FAC. OF MGMT., UNIV. OF TORONTO; Visiting Prof., School of Accountancy and Business, Nanyang Technological University, Singapore 1992–94; Chrmn., National Entrepreneurship Development Inst. Onatio Network 1989–93, Exec. Dir., 1989–90; Distinguished Prof. of Entrepreneurial Studies, Ryerson Polytech. Univ. 1986–89; Pres., Internat. Counc. for Small Business – Canada 1982–86; Internat. Counc. for Small Business 1987–89; mem., Small Bus. Cons. Ctte. to the Min. of State for Small Bus., Govt. of Can. 1983, 1986; Entrepreneurship Curriculum Development Cons., Ngee Ann Polytechnic, Singapore 1988; Mem., Founding Counc. for the National Entrepreneurship Development Inst. 1988; Visiting Prof., Brock Univ. 1989; Founder, Pub. & Extve. Ed., 'Journal of Small Business & Entrepreneurship' 1982– ; Editorial Advisor, 'Journal of Enterprising Culture', Singapore 1993– ; mem., Ed. Bd. 'internat. gewerbearchiv,' St. Gall Grad. Sch. of Econ., Switzerland 1986– ; mem. Adv. Bd., 'American Journal of Small Business' 1979–84; Reviewer, 'Front Runner' TVO; 'Entrepreneurship' Cdn. Found. for Econ. Edn.; First Tasman Fellow, Univ. of Canterbury, New Zealand 1982; Wilford L. White Fellow, Internat. Counc. for Small Bus. 1984; Ryersonian 1975; mem., Meech Lake Round Table on Entrepreneurship 1987; author: 'Small Business Management, A Strategic Emphasis' 1982, 1984; 'Big GAAP versus Little GAAP' 1986; 'Entrepreneurship and Enterprise Development' 1989; co-author: 'Entrepreneurship and New Venture Management, Readings and Cases' 1987; recreations: gardening, dining out, walking, tropical fish; Home: 76 Hilton Ave., Toronto, Ont. M5R 3E7; Office: 246 Bloor St. W., Toronto, Ont. M5S 1V4.

**KAPLAN, Allan Saul,** A.A., B.A., M.Sc., M.D., F.R.C.P.(C), Dipl. Psychiatry; physician; b. Providence, R.I. 7 Feb. 1952; s. Philip and Esther (Koffler) K.; e. Yeshiva Univ. A.B., B.A. 1974; Univ. of Toronto M.D. 1978, dipl. Psychiat. 1983; F.R.C.P.(C) 1983; Univ. of Toronto, M.Sc. 1988; m. Rochelle d. Bill and Judy Rubinstein 30 June 1974; children: Jess, Zekiel, Alisha; SR. STAFF PSYCHIATRIST, THE TORONTO HOSP. 1983– & ASSOC. PROF., DEPT. OF PSYCHIATRY, UNIV. OF TORONTO 1985– ; Ont. Mental Health Rsch. Fellow, Toronto Gen. Hosp. 1983–85; Dir. Eating Disorder Ctr. 1985– ; Dir., Postgrad. Edn., Dept. of Psychiatry 1985– ; Dir., Fellowship Training Program 1993– ; House Staff Liaison Ctte. 1985– ; Human Review Ethics Ctte., Dept. of Psychiatry, Univ. of Toronto; Pfizer Prize, best rsch. paper, annual dept. rsch. day, Univ. of Toronto 1982; Candn. Psychiatric Research Foundation Award, Best Poster, Annual Research Day, Univ. of Toronto 1987; Mem. Ont. and Candn. Med. Assns.; Candn. Psychiatric Assn.; Am. Psychosomatic Soc.; Am. Psychiatric Assoc.; author of 23 jour. articles, 20 book chaps. & edited 2 books; Home: 110 Old Forest Hill Rd., Toronto, Ont. M5P 2R9; Office: Eating Disorder Ctr., Toronto Gen. Hosp., 200 Elizabeth St., Toronto, Ont. M5G 2C4.

**KAPLAN, Robert Phillip,** P.C., Q.C., B.A., LL.B.; b. Toronto, Ont. 27 Dec. 1936; s. Solomon Charles and Pearl (Grafstein) K.; e. Univ. of Toronto B.A. (Univ. Coll.) 1958, LL.B. 1961; m. Estherelke, d. Joseph & Faye Tanenbaum, Toronto, Ont., 10 Oct. 1961; children: Jennifer Mia, John David, Raquel Katherine; called to Bar of Ont. 1963; practised law Toronto; el. to H. of C. for Don Valley g.e. 1968, def. g.e. 1972, el. M.P. for York Centre 1974, 1979, 1980, 1984, 1988; Solicitor General of Canada 1980–84; Past Chrmn. Joint Standing Cttee. on Scrutiny of Regulations; Past Chrmn. H. of C. Standing Cttee. on Finance, Trade & Econ. Affairs; Past Candn. Del. to UN Gen. Assembly; mem. Can.-US Parlty. Group; served as Consultant on Candn. Affairs Hudson Inst. of N.Y. lecturing on this subject at Inst. confs. in N. Am. and abroad; mem. National Liberal Club (London, England); Beth Tzedec Synagogue (Toronto); Candn. Bar Assn.; The Law Society of Upper Canada; Candn. Civil Liberties Assn.; Rideau Club (Ottawa); Liberal; Jewish; Home: Toronto, Ont.; Office: House of Commons, Ottawa, Ont. K1A 0A6.

**KAPLAN, William Edward,** LL.B., M.A., J.S.D.; educator; lawyer; arbitrator; b. Toronto, Ont. 24 May 1957; s. late Igor and Cara Ruth (Feldman) K.; e. Univ. of Toronto, Victoria Coll. B.A. 1980, M.A. 1985; York Univ. LL.B. 1983; Stanford Law Sch. J.S.D. 1988; m. Susan d. Horace and Elizabeth Krever 8 June 1985; children: Maxwell Bernard, Simon Avery, Hannah Beth; ASSOC. PROF. OF LAW, UNIV. OF OTTAWA 1991– and Faculty Ed. 'Ottawa Law Review' 1987–89; Asst. Prof. of Law 1986–91; apptd. General Counsel and Dir. of Rsch., CBA Task Force 1990 on the Independence of Federal Administrative Tribunals and Agencies in Canada 1990; apptd. Mem., Public Service Staff Relations Bd. 1988–93; apptd. Vice-Chairperson, Ont. Crown Employees Grievance Settlement Bd. 1990– ; apptd. to Ont. Min. of Labour List of Approved Arbitrators 1992; apptd. Deployment Recourse Investigator, Public Service Commission of Can. 1993; articled with Cavalluzzo, Hayes & Lennon 1983–84; author: 'Everything that Floats: Pat Sullivan, Hal Banks and the Seamen's Unions of Canada' 1987; 'State and Salvation: The Jehovah's Witnesses and their Fight for Civil Rights' 1989; ed., contr. 'Belonging: Essays on the Meaning & Future of Canadian Citizenship' 1993; co-ed, contr.: 'Law Policy and International Justice: Essays in Honour of Maxwell Cohen' 1993; co-ed.: 'Moscow Despatches: Inside Cold War Russia' 1987; 'Labour Arbitration Yearbook' (first published) 1991– ; 'The Canadian Labour Law Journal' 1992; awarded Fellowship in Legal Hist., Osgoode Soc. 1989–90; mem., Law Soc. Upper Can.; Osgoode Soc.; Am. Soc. for Legal Hist.; Candn. Civil Liberties Assn.; Candn. Assoc. of Law Teachers; Candn. Historical Assoc.; Lawyers Against Apartheid; The Selden Society; Jewish; Offices: University of Ottawa, Ottawa, Ont. K1N 6N5 and Suite 200, 70 Bond St., Toronto, Ont. M5B 1X3.

**KAPLANSKY, Kalmen,** C.M., D.U.; labour consultant; b. Bialystok, Poland 5 Jan. 1912; s. late Abraham and Masha (Wisotsky) K.; e. High Sch., Poland (Matric. 1929); D.U. (Hon.), Univ. of Otawa 1983; m. Esther, d. late Nathan Kositsky, 21 June 1945; children: Marsha Anne, Frances F.; DIR. OF CAN. BR. OFFICE AND SPECIAL ADV. TO DIR.-GEN., INTERNAT. LABOUR OFFICE, 1967–80; mem., Econ. Counc. of Can. 1978–88, Refugee Status Adv. Comte., Employment and Immigration Comn. 1978–88; Dir., Candn. Civil Liberties Assn.; Gov., Carleton Univ. 1971–82; Gov. Body, ILO 1960–66; Typesetter and Linotype Operator, 1932–43; Nat. Dir., Jewish Labour Comte. of Can., 1946–57; Secy. Publications Comte., Candn. Labour Reports, 1946–57; Dir., Dept. of Internat. Affairs, Candn. Labour Congress, and Secy. Nat. Comte. for Human Rights, 1957–66; served in 2nd World War with Candn. Army (Active) 1943–46; def. cand. to Quebec Leg. (C.C.F.) 1944, and Fed. by-el. for Cartier, 1950; Chrmn., Montreal Organ. of Workmen's Circle (1940–43); mem., Internat. Typographical Union since 1932; substitute mem., Extve. Bd., ICFTU, 1957–66; Alternate mem., Candn. Nat. Comn. on UNESCO, 1957–66; mem. Candn. del. to 10th Session of Gen. Conf. of UNESCO, Paris, 1958 and to 18th General Assembly of the United Nations (1963); Advr. to Worker's Del. of Can. to 40th, 42nd, 43rd, 44th, 45th, 46th, 47th, 48th, 49th and 50th sessions, I.L.O., Geneva (1957–66); Sr. Fellow, Human Rights Center, Univ. of Ottawa; Pres., Douglas-Coldwell Foundation; Chrmn. Special Staff Group on Employment and Econ. Opportunities for Native Northerners, Dept. Indian & N. Affairs 1970–74; Hebrew; recreation: reading; Home: 771 Eastbourne Ave., Manor Park, Ottawa, Ont. K1K 0H8.

**KAPTAINIS, Arthur David,** B.A.; music critic; b. Toronto, Ont. 3 Nov. 1955; s. Arthur Stanley and Muriel Joyce (Bews) K.; e. Oakwood C.I.; Univ. of Toronto, B.A. 1980; m. The Rev. Roberta d. James and Barbara Clare 6 Sept. 1980; one s. Anton; MUSIC CRITIC, MONTREAL GAZETTE 1986– ; Entertainment Ed., Varsity 1978–79; Freelance music critic, Globe and Mail, Musical America, Canadian Composer 1981–86; Staff Writer, Univ. of Toronto Bulletin 1984–86; recreations: cycling, travel; Office: 250 St-Antoine W., Montreal, Que. H2Y 3R7.

**KAPTEIN, Tim,** C.A.; provincial public servant; b. The Hague, Holland 9 Feb. 1921; s. Dirk and Abeltje Jantina (Westerdiep) K.; e. high sch. The Hague 1938; Ryksbelasting Acad. Rotterdam, Master at Law 1946; Inst. C.A.'s Ont., C.A. 1962; m. Ursula d. Paul and Olga Prabucki 17 Sept. 1954; children: Michael Andrew; Sylvia Karen; Tax Assessor Dept. of Finance Holland 1946–51; private practice as Tax Consultant 1951–53; came to Can. 1953, Candn. Citizen 1958; Chief Acct. MacLaren Advertising 1958–66; Comptroller, Fine Papers Ltd. 1966–70; Auditor General of P.E.I. 1970–86 (retired); Past Pres. Inst. C.A.'s P.E.I.; Charter mem. and Past mem. Bd. Govs. Candn. Comprehensive Auditing Foundation; mem. various comtes. Prov. and Candn. Insts. C.A.'s; United Church; recreations: tennis, sailing; Home: 61 York Lane, Charlottetown, P.E.I. C1A 2A5; Office: PO Box 2000, Charlottetown, P.E.I. C1A 7N8.

**KAPYRKA, Peter J.;** publisher; b. Quaregnon, Belgium 13 Feb. 1950; s. Leo and Olga (Mitchenko) K.; e. Glebe C.I., Ottawa; m. Cheryl d. Charlie and Faith LaRocque; children: Julie, Amy; PUBLISHER, 'CAPE BRETON POST' 1990– ; Proofboy, Copy Desk Clerk, Salesman, 'Ottawa Journal' 1968–77; Asst. Sales Mgr., 'Ottawa Today' 1977–78; Salesman, 'Niagara Falls Review' 1978; Advtg. Mgr., 'Peterborough Examiner' 1978–84; Advtg. Cons., Thomson Newspapers 1984–87; Publisher, 'The Barrie Examiner' 1987–90; Office: 255 George St., Sydney, N.S. B1P 6K6.

**KARAFILLY, Irena Friedman,** B.A., M.A., M.F.A.; fiction writer / university lecturer; b. Orenburg, Russia 31 Aug. 1944; d. Jacob and Eugenia (Ivanova) F.; e. Sir George Williams Univ. B.A. 1971; McGill Univ. M.A. 1973; Univ. of B.C. M.F.A. 1975; divorced; children: Ranya; fiction writer & poet; work widely published in Canada & abroad in both literary & consumer magazines; occasionally anthologized & broadcast over the CBC; 1990 winner of the CBC literary competition (fiction) & author of 'Night Cries,' a collection of stories set in Greece & published by Oberon Press 1990; Office: c/o Emilie Jacobson, Curtis Brown Literary Agency, Ten Astor Place, New York, NY 10003.

**KARDISH, Laurence ('Larry'),** M.F.A.; curator; author; film maker; b. Ottawa, Ont., 5 Jan. 1945; s. Samuel and Tillie (Steinberg) K.; e. Lisgar Coll. Inst., Ottawa, 1962; Carleton Univ., B.A. 1966; Columbia Univ., M.F.A. 1968; (divorced); one d., Naomi Frances; ASSOC. CURATOR, EXHIBITIONS, DEPARTMENT OF FILM, MUSEUM OF MODERN ART, N.Y.; founded Carleton Univ. Cine Club 1964; New Am. Cinema Group; Film-makers' Distribution Center; one of maj. retrospectives mounted at present museum 'New Cinema From Quebec' 1972; 'Senegal: Fifteen Years of an African Cinema, 1962–1977' 1978; 'Cinema Quebecois, 1972–78'; Nat. Film Board of Canada; rec'd Art Gallery of Ont. award 'Best Narrative – Canadian Film' 1969; author 'Reel Plastic Magic' 1972; other writings incl. 'Brussels Sprouts' (play) 1969; 'Bronx Lullaby'; 'Slow Run' (film), 1968; 'Soft Passions' (screenplay) 1973; 'Egg Cream' (play) 1975; 'Of Light and Texture' (monograph) 1981; 'Michael Balcon and the Idea of a National Cinema' (essay in book) 1983; mem. Nat. Film Theatre (Ottawa); Candn. Film Inst.; Candn. Fed. Film Socs.; Comité d'honneur of the festival Internat. du film de la critique quebecoise Montreal Home: 165 Christopher St., New York, N.Y. 10014; Office: 21 W. 53rd St., New York, N.Y.

**KAREDA, Urjo,** M.A.; artistic director; critic; b. Tallinn, Estonia 9 Feb. 1944; s. Endel and Helmi Johanna (Urm) K.; e. Bathurst Heights Secondary Sch. 1962; Univ. Coll. Univ. of Toronto B.A. 1966, M.A. 1967; King's Coll. Cambridge 1967–70; m. Shelagh d. Alison and A.W.B. Hewitt 4 Oct. 1969; one child: Maia; ARTISTIC DIR., TARRAGON THEATRE 1982– ; directed 'L'Amante Anglaise' 1985; 'The Island' 1986; 'Undersea' 1988; 'April Fish' 1989; 'Wing's Chips' 1990; co-directed 'Aunt Dan and Lemon' 1987; 'The Crackwalker' 1990; 'A Woman's Comedy' 1992; Film Critic, The Toronto Star, 1970–71, Drama Critic 1971–75; Lectr. in Eng. Erindale Coll. Univ. of Toronto 1970–75; instructor in playwriting, York Univ. 1983–88; Lit. Mgr. Stratford Festival 1975–80; Dir. of Script Devel. Radio Drama CBC 1981–82; Film Critic, Maclean's 1975–76; freelance writer/critic The Globe and Mail, The New York Times, Maclean's, Opera News, Dance in Canada, Canadian Forum, Saturday Night; broadcaster/critic CBC radio and TV; Consultant to Can. Council (served on Periodicals Comte.), Ont. Arts Council; mem. jury Gov. Gen's Award; co-dir. Stratford Festival's Uncle Vanya 1977, The Woman 1978, Love's Labour's Lost 1979, The Seagull 1980; mem. Actors Equity; ACTRA; Prof. Assn. Candn. Theatres; Office: 30 Bridgman Ave., Toronto, Ont. M5R 1X3.

**KARL, Gabriel,** Ph.D., F.R.S.C.; professor; b. Cluj, Romania 30 April 1937; s. Alexander and Frida (Izsak) K.; e. Univ. of Cluj, dipl. 1958; Univ. of Toronto, Ph.D. 1964; m. Dorothy d. Frederick and Ethel Searle 11 Apr. 1965; one d.: Alexandra; PROF. OF PHYSICS, UNIV. OF GUELPH, 1975– ; post-doct. fellow, Univ. of Toronto 1964–66; NRC (Oxford Univ.) 1966–69; Asst. Prof., Univ. of Guelph 1969–71; Assoc. Prof. 1971–75; F.R.S.C. 1984; Trustee, Aspen Ctr. for Physics 1983; recipient, Humboldt Award 1993; Mem., Candn. Assn. of Physicists; Am. Physical Soc.; author of spec. articles in theoretical physics; recreations: hiking; Home: 11 Borden St., Guelph, Ont.; Office: Dept. of Physics, Univ. of Guelph, Guelph, Ont. N1G 2W1.

**KARMALI, Mohamed Abdulhamid,** M.B., Ch.B., FRCP (Glasg.), FRCP(C); medical microbiologist / university professor; b. Pretoria, S. Africa 21 Sept. 1947; s. Abdulhamid and Kulsum (Virjee) K.; e. Univ. of Glasgow, M.B., Ch.B. 1972; m. Patricia d. Robert and Sarah Forsyth 20 Oct. 1978; children: Jena Kulsum-Noor, Tazmin Patricia; MICROBIOLOGIST-IN-CHIEF, THE HOSP. FOR SICK CHILDREN & PROF., DEPT. OF MICROBIOL., UNIV. OF TORONTO 1991– ; FRCP (Glasg.) 1988; FRCP(C) 1977; Career Scientist, Ont. Min. of Health 1982–86; Staff Bacteriol., The Hosp. for Sick Children 1980–88; Sec., Internat. Ctte. of Systematic Bacteriol.; Subctte., Taxonomy of Campylobacter; Vice-Pres., Candn. Assn. for Clinical Microbiology and Infectious Diseases (CACMID), Editor, CACMID Newsletter; Mem. Rsch. Council, Lois Joy Galler Found. for Hemolytic Uremic Syndrome; Mem., Candn. Med. Assn.; Candn. Assn. of Med. Microbiol.; Candn. Assn. of Clin. Microbiol. & Infect. Diseases; Am. Soc. of Microbiol.; author of over 70 sci. papers; recreations: swimming, squash; club: North York YMCA; Home: 388 Princess Ave., North York, Ont. M2N 3S9; Office: 555 University Ave., Toronto, Ont. M5G 1X8.

**KARMAN, Robert;** retired commercial artist; b. Montréal, Qué. 17 Feb. 1933; s. Frank and Paula (Reinholz) K.; e. St. Louis de France Montréal; Earl Haig Coll. Inst. and Northern Vocational Toronto; m. Beverly d. Charles and Joan Seymour 29 Sept. 1988; two s. Gregory, Derek; Prin. Robert Karman & Associates 1970; painting exhns. Toronto, Montréal and Hamilton Galleries; began photo retouching 1950; served Brigden Engravers 8 yrs., Pacesetters Art Studio, Wheeler & Scott Studio, Haughton Studios, Art & Design Studios; freelance past 20 yrs.; recipient several awards for re-touching and Best Retoucher Award 1967; recreations: sailing (crossed N.Atlantic, N.Sea & Baltic Ocean in 35 ft. Ketch), welding; Club: Queen City Yacht; Home: R.R. 1, Orangeville, Ont. L9W 2Y8.

**KARON, Ralph R.,** C.A., M.B.A.; insurance executive and financial consultant; b. 9 Feb. 1938; s. Kurt S. and Irene (Tillich) K.; e. C.A. 1960; Concordia Univ. B.A. 1962; Columbia Univ. M.B.A. 1963; m. Irene d. R.W. Sims 4 March 1961; children: Kim, Ann, Ted; Price Waterhouse & Co. 1959–62; Internal Auditor, Exxon Corp. 1963–65; Financial Mgr., Imperial Oil Limited 1965–74; var. positions as Asst. Gen. Mgr. in Comptroller's, International, Domestic Regions & Systems, Canadian Imperial Bank of Commerce 1974–82; Vice-Pres. & Comptroller, N. Am. Life Assur. Co. 1983–89; Senior Vice-Pres. & Comptroller, The Prudential Insur. Co. of America, Candn. Operations 1989–92; Awarded, Beta Gamma Sigma; Vice-Chrmn. & Treas., United Way of Greater Toronto 1983–86; Board of Trustees 1978–86; Mem., C.A. Inst. of Ont.; Finan. Exec. Inst. (Past Dir., Toronto Chap.); Inst. of Directors; Candn. Red Cross Soc. (Past Vice-Pres., Ont. Div. & Toronto Central Br. Treas.); Financial Assoc., The Toronto Symphony; recreations: tennis, badminton, jogging, skiing; club: Granite; Home: 58 Highland Cr., North York, Ont. M2L 1G6.

**KARP, Allen,** LL.M., Q.C.; company president; b. Toronto, Ont. 18 Sept. 1940; s. David and Mollie (Newman) K.; e. Bathurst Heights Coll. Inst.; Univ. of Toronto LL.B. 1964; Osgoode Hall Law Sch. York Univ. LL.M. 1975; m. Sharon d. Mollie and Nathan Silver 23 May 1961; children: Debra Anne, Amy Lynn, Melanie Claire; PRES. & C.E.O., CINEPLEX ODEON CORP. 1990– ; Sr. Partner, Goodman and Carr 1970–86; Dir. and/or Offr., Cineplex Odeon Corp.; Plitt Theatres, Inc.; RKO Century Warner Theatres, Inc.; called to Bar of Ont. 1966; joined Goodman and Carr 1966; joined Cineplex Odeon Corp. 1986; former Head of Corporate and Comm. Law Sec. Bar Admission Course Ont.; Chrmn. and Lectr. various legal educ. programs field of business law; Past Dist. Pres. and mem. Nat. Extve. B'Nai Brith Youth Organ.; former Campaign Capt. Lawyers' Div. Un. Way Metrop. Toronto; Co-Chrmn. Endowment Laskin Chair Hebrew Univ. of Jerusalem; Chrmn. Frederick G. Gans Mem. Fund; Dir. Can. Coll. Jerusalem; Dir. Toronto Chapter Weizman Inst. for Sci.; author numerous articles, papers, publs. franchising and other corporate matters; recreation: sailing; Home: 6 Strathearn Rd., Toronto, Ont. M6C 1R3; Office: 1303 Yonge St., Toronto, Ont. M4T 2Y9.

**KARPATI, George,** M.D., FRCP(C); university professor; e. Dalhousie Univ. M.D. 1960; m. Shira Tannor; children: Adam, Joshua; I.W. KILLAM CHAIR OF NEUROLOGY, MONTREAL NEUROLOGICAL INST., MCGILL UNIV. 1985– ; training in neurol. & neurosci., Montreal Neurol. Inst.; in internal med., Henry Ford Hosp.; in rsch., Nat. Inst. of Health, Bethesda, MD; engaged for 25 yrs. in practice & teaching of neurol. with spec. clin. & rsch. interest in neuromuscular diseases; Montreal Neurol. Inst.; Dir., Neuromuscular Rsch.; Chrmn., Sci. Med. Bd., Muscular Dystrophy Assn. of Can.; Assoc. Ed., 'Muscle & Nerve'; 'J. Neurol. Sci.'; 'Can. J. Neurol. Sci.'; Ed. Bd., 'Neuromuscular Disorders,' 'Clinical and Investigative Medicine,' 'Cell Transplantation'; co-author: 'Pathology of Skeletal Muscles'; co-editor of 2 books; author of 165 sci. articles; recipient, Gov. General's Anniv. Medal 1993; Office: 3801 University St., Montreal, Que. H3A 2B4.

**KARSH, Yousuf,** C.C. (1990), O.C. (1967), D.C.L., LL.D., D.H.L., F.R.P.S., R.C.A.; portraitist; photographer; b. Armenia 23 Dec. 1908; s. Amsih and Bahia (Nakash) K.; came to Canada 1924; naturalized 1947; e. LL.D., Carleton Univ., Queen's Univ., Emerson Coll., Boston; D.H.L., Dartmouth Coll.; Mt. Allison and Ohio Univs. 1968; D.C.L. Bishop's 1969; D.H.L., Univ. of Detroit 1978; D.F.A. Amherst College, 1979; D.H.L. Univ. of Hartford, 1980; D.F.A. Tufts Univ., 1981; Silver Shingle Award, Boston Univ. Law School 1983; D.F.A., Syracuse Univ. 1986; D.F.A., Yeshiva Univ. 1989; D.F.A., Columbia Coll., Chicago 1990; D.F.A., Univ. of B.C. 1991; m. 1st Solange Gautier, (d. 1961), 1939; 2nd., Estrellita, d. late Philip Nachbar, Chicago, Ill., 28 Aug. 1962; studied photography under his uncle George Nakash in Sherbrooke, Que., and in Boston with John Garo; settled in Ottawa in 1932, and shortly after estbd. his studio there; has since established an internat. reputation for his portraits of famous men and women, notably Sir Winston Churchill (1941), and many others throughout the world; Fellow, Royal Photographic Soc. (Eng.); Photo. Soc. of Am.; mem., Candn. Photo. Soc. (Hon. Life); Publications: 'Faces of Destiny' 1947; 'This is the Mass' 1958; 'This is Rome' 1959; 'Portraits of Greatness' 1959; 'This is the Holy Land' 1960; 'These are the Sacraments' 1963; 'The Warren Court' (Frank and Karsh) 1964; 'Karsh Portfolio' 1967; 'Faces of Our Time' 1971; 'Karsh Portraits' 1975; 'Karsh Canadians' 1978; 'Karsh: A 50–Year Retrospective' 1983; 'Karsh: American Legends' 1992; one-man exhibitions: Canadian Pavilion, Expo '67; Montreal Museum Fine Arts; Boston Museum Fine Arts; Corning Museum, 1968; Corcoran Gallery; Detroit Art Museum; Seattle Art Museum 1969–70; Kalamazoo Inst. of Arts; Philadelphia Civic Centre; Grand Rapids Art Museum; Hackley Art Gallery 1971; Nelson Gallery of Art; Sedona Arts Centre; Reading Museum; St. Petersburg Museum of Arts 1972; Palm Springs Desert Museum; Albright-Knox Art Gallery; Santa Barbara Art Museum; Toledo Museum of Art 1973; Flint Inst. of Arts; State Univ. of N.Y.; Ulbrich Art Gallery (Wichita) 1974; Loch Haven Art Center (Orlando); Honolulu Contemporary Arts Center 1975; Kenosha Pub. Museum (Wis.) 1976; Ulbrich Art Gallery (Wichita) 1977; Museum of Science and Indust. (Chicago) 1978; Albrecht Museum, (St. Joseph, Missouri); Evansville Art Gallery, (Evansville, Ind.) 1979; Palm Springs Desert Museum, 1981; opening exhibition 'Museum of Photography and Film,' Bradford, Eng. 1983; Internat. Center of Photography, N.Y. City 1983; touring U.S. throughout 1986; Nat. Portrait Gall., London 1983; Nat. Gall., Edinburgh, Scotland 1983; Helsinki, Finland; National Museum, Beijing, China 1985; Muscarelle Museum of Art, Coll. of Wm. & Mary 1986 and 1987; Muscarelle Museum Show (touring U.S. museums) 1988–94; 'Karsh: A Birthday Celebration' Barbican Centre, London, England 1988, touring Europe 1988–89; 'Karsh: The Art of the Portrait' National Gallery, Can. 1989; Huntington Museum, Calif. 1989; Vancouver Art Gallery 1990; Karsh Tribute Exhibition, National Portrait Gallery, London 1991; Glenbow Museum, Calgary 1991; Halifax Art Gallery 1991; Montreal Museum of Fine Arts 1992; Montreal Museum 1992; 'Karsh: American Legends' Exhibition, International Center of Photography 1992; Corcoran Gallery, Washington 1993; Mint Museum, Charlotte, N. Carolina 1993; 10th Anniv. Inaugural Exhib., Museum of Photography, Film & Television, Bradford, Eng. 1993; 'Karsh: Selected Portraits' from Nat. Archives of Canada Collection, Candn. Embassy, Washington, D.C. 1994; one-man exhn.: 'Men Who Make Our World' acquired by Nat. Gallery Australia, Museum Contemporary Arts, Tokyo and Prov. of Alta.; awarded Can. Council Medal, 1965; Centennial Medal; Guest of Hon., Arles, (France) Arts Festival & Exhn. 1975; Visiting Prof. of Photog. Art. Ohio Univ. 1967–68; Emerson Coll. 1970–72; el. R.C.A. 1975; Achievement in Life Award, Encyclopaedia Brittanica, 1980; Gold Medal (for promoting Candn.-Am. understanding), Americas Soc. 1989; Lotos Medal of Merit, Lotos Club, New York 1989; first recipient, Creative Edge Award, New York Univ. and Time, Inc., N.Y. 1989; Infinity Award, Master Photography, Internat. Center of Photography, N.Y. 1990; Companion of the Order of Canada 1990; Gold Medal, National Soc. Arts and Letters 1991; CBC documentary film, 'Karsh: The Searching Eye' prod. by Harry Rasky, shown on CBC network and distributed worldwide, 1986; rec'd Gold Medal for contributing to Candn. and U.S. relations, The Americas Soc.; Office: Chateau Laurier Hotel, Ottawa, Ont. K1N 8S7.

**KARTHA, Kutty Krishnan,** M.Sc., Ph.D.; scientist; b. Shertallai, India 9 Aug. 1941; s. Deven Raman and Ammu Kutty (Kunjamma) K.; e. Jawaharlal Nehru Agric. Univ. M.Sc. 1965; Indian Agric. Rsch. Inst. Ph.D. 1969; m. Françoise d. Jean and Anne Quemeneur 23 Sept. 1972; children: Ravi, Cyril; HEAD, CELL TECHNOL. LAB., PLANT BIOTECHNOL. INST., NAT. RSCH. COUNC. OF CAN. (SASK.) 1983– ; post-grad. rsch., Inst. Nat. de la Rech. Agron. (France) 1969–72; Vis. Sci., Plant Biotechnol. Inst. 1973–74; Asst. Rsch. Offr. 1974; Assoc. Rsch. Offr. 1976; Sr. Rsch. Offr. 1981; Adjunct Prof., Univ. of Sask.; supvr., 2 Ph.D. students; Mem., Grad. Adv. Ctte.; Cons., U.N. Internat. Atomic Energy Agency prog. on plant biotechnol.; keynote speaker, Rockefeller Found., etc.; George M. Darrow Award for excel. in rsch., Am. Soc. for Horticultural Sci. 1981; Mem., Internat. Assn. for Plant Tissue Culture; Candn. Soc. of Plant Physiol.; Candn. Phytophathol. Soc.; author/co-author of over 100 rsch. pubs.; editor: 'Cryopreservation of Plant Cells and Organs' 1985, 'J. of Plant Physiol.' (2 issues) 1987; recreations: reading, badminton, table tennis; Home: 214 Auld Cres., Saskatoon, Sask. S7H 4W9; Office: 110 Gymnasium Rd., Saskatoon, Sask. S7N 0W9.

**KASHA, Kenneth John,** O.C., M.Sc., Ph.D., LL.D., F.R.S.C.; educator; b. Lacombe, Alta. 6 May 1933; s. John Clarence and Mary Jeannette (Proudfoot) K.; e. Lacombe High Sch. 1951; Univ. of Alta. B.Sc. 1957, M.Sc. 1958; Univ. of Minn. Ph.D. 1962; Univ. of Calgary LL.D. (Honorary) 1986; m. Marion Eileen d. Karl and Bertha Lenz 14 Aug. 1958; children: Lorelei Marion, David John; PROF. OF CROP SCI. UNIV. OF GUELPH 1974– ; Rsch. Asst. Univ. of Minn. 1958, Rsch. Fellow in Agronomy & Plant Genetics 1961–62; Rsch. Sci. Forage Sect. Ottawa Stn. Agric. Can. 1962–66; Asst. Prof. present Univ. 1966, Assoc. Prof. 1969; Cons. Haploid Rsch. Lab. Ciba-Geigy Seeds Ailsa Craig, Ont. 1974–81; Internat. Rice Rsch. Inst. Philippines 1984; Dir. Plant Biotechnol. Centre of Guelph-Waterloo Biotech 1984–87, Exec. 1985–87; Prog. Chrmn. XVI Internat. Cong. Genetics Toronto 1988; orgn. 1st Internat. Symposium 'Haploids in Plants' 1974, ed. proceedings; Nilsson-Ehle Lectr. Sweden 1987; recipient Sigma Xi Distinguished Rsch. Award 1974; E.C. Manning Award of Excellence 1983; Grindley Medal Agric. Inst. Can. 1977; OAC Distinguished Rsch. Award 1984; Fellow,

Royal Soc. of Canada 1990; Officer, Order of Canada 1994; author or co-author over 280 rsch. publs.; mem. various ed. bds.; mem. Genetics Soc. Can. (Sec. 1966–69, Dir. 1970–72, Pres. 1976–77); Genetics Soc. Am.; Am. Soc. Agronomy; Candn. Soc. Plant Molecular Biol.; Internat. Assn. Plant Cell & Tissue Culture (Candn. Corresp. 1990–94); Sigma Xi; Home: 28 Halesmanor Ct., Guelph, Ont. N1G 4E2; Office: Guelph, Ont. N1G 2W1.

**KASS, Heidi,** B.Ed., B.Sc., Ed.M., Ph.D.; professor of science education and research design; b. Tallinn, Estonia 17 June 1939; d. Julius and Lydia (Anton) K.; e. Univ. of Alta. B.Ed. 1961, B.Sc. 1963; Harvard Univ. Ed.M. 1965; Univ. of Alta. Ph.D. 1969; children: Tracy Lynne and Tanya Jane Kass; CO-DIR., CENTRE FOR MATHEMATICS, SCIENCE AND TECHNOLOGY EDUCATION (1991– ) and PROF. OF SCIENCE EDN. & RESEARCH DESIGN, DEPT. OF SECONDARY EDN., UNIV. OF ALTA. 1976– ; H.S. Teacher, Queen Elizabeth H.S. 1961–64, 1965–66; Asst. Prof., Univ. of Alta. 1969–72; Assoc. Prof. 1972–76; Co-Principal Investigator, 2nd Internat. Science Study, Internat. Assn. for the Evaluation of Edn. Achievement 1981–88; Visiting Prof., Memorial Univ. 1972; Univ. of Sask. 1974; Univ. of B.C. 1979; Monash Univ. (Australia) 1983–84; Univ. of Victoria 1990; Curtin Univ. (Australia) 1993; Co-Editor, Int. Sci. Edn. Section, 'Science Education' 1988– ; Evaluation Team, Internat. Council of Sci. Unions; Testing Prog. Mem., Nat. Sci. Found. 1990– ; Ed. Bd., 'J. of Res. in Sci. Teaching' 1986–89; Chair, Strategic Grants Div., SSHRCC 1987–89; Doct. & Post Doc. Fellowship Div. 1987; McCalla Rsch. Prof., Univ. of Alta. 1985; Presidential Citation, Assn. for Edn. of Teachers of Sci. (AETS) 1988; Nat. Sci. Teachers Assn. Medal 1978; NRC Fellowship 1969; Dir., AETS 1978–81; Task Force Chair 1985–88; Finan. Adv. Ctte. 1988; Policy Adv. Ctte., Nat. Assn. for Rsch. in Sci. Teaching 1990– ; num. profl. affiliations incl. The Chem. Inst. of Can.; Internat. Union of Pure & Applied Chem.; Candn. Soc. for the Study of Edn.; Am. Edn. Rsch. Assn.; Science Council, Alta. Teachers Assn. (Pres. 1978–79); co-author: 'Elements of Chemistry' 1966, 'Science Education in Canada' 2 vols. 1985, 1989 and num. rsch. papers 1969– ; over 40 conf. presentations; chaired & served on orgn. cttes. of several internat. confs. in sci. edn.; recreations: piano, gardening, travel, reading; club: Orchid Soc. of Alta.; Home: 38 Valleyview Cres., Edmonton, AB T5R 5S6; Office: Dept. of Secondary Education, The Univ. of Alberta, Edmonton, Alta. T6G 2G5.

**KASSIRER, Mark D.,** B.Sc., M.B.A., C.F.A.; financial executive; b. Welland, Ont. 2 Oct. 1946; s. A.L. Kassirer; e. Univ. of Toronto B.Sc. (Hons.) 1968; York Univ. M.B.A. 1973; C.F.A. 1975; m. Hanna; children: Matthew, Emma, Laura; EXECUTIVE VICE-PRES. & DIR., BURNS FRY LIMITED, BURNS FRY FINANCE CORP. & BURNS FRY HOLDINGS CORP. 1990– ; joined Fry Mills Spence 1969 and has held various positions in Burns Fry incl. Bank Analyst & Money Market Trader; set up Futures Trading group 1981; assumed resp. for Money market opns. 1983; Capital Markets 1985; Bond Dept. 1989; Inst. Equity Trading 1990; Chair, Chief Extve. Offr. & Dir., Burns Fry Managed Futures Inc.; Vice-Chair & Dir., Burns Fry International Inc.; Dir., Burns Fry Analytics Inc.; Burns Fry Fund Management Inc.; Burns Fry Shareholders Holdings Corp.; Burns Fry Inc.; Office: P.O. Box 150, First Canadian Place, Toronto, Ont. M5X 1H3.

**KATER, Michael H.,** B.A., M.A., Ph.D., F.R.S.C.; Distinguished Research Professor; b. Zittau, Germany 4 July 1937; s. Heinz and Annemarie Agnes (Gensichen) K.; e. Humanistisches Gym. Krefeld; St. Michael's Coll. H.S.; Univ. of Toronto, B.A. (Hons.) 1959; M.A. 1961; Univ. München; Univ. Heidelberg, Ph.D. 1966; m. Barbara d. Berthold and Katharina Streit July 1965; children: Eva Dorothea, Anya; DISTINGUISHED RSCH. PROF. OF HISTORY, ATKINSON COLL., YORK UNIV. 1991– ; Lectr., Univ. of Maryland 1965–66; Asst. Prof., Atkinson Coll., York Univ. 1967; Assoc. Prof. with tenure 1970; Prof. 1973; Jason A. Hannah Vis. Prof. of Hist. of Med., Fac. of Health Sci., McMaster Univ. 1985–86; Fellowships: Can. Counc. (leave) 1973–74, Guggenheim 1976–77, Can. Counc. Sr. Killam 1978–79, 1979–80, 1993–94, SSHRCC (leave) 1982–83, Atkinson Rsch. 1984–85, York Walter L. Gordon 1990–91; Am. Hist. Assn. First Prize for Best Article in Central Eur. Hist. 1972; Candn. Hist. Assn., W.K. Ferguson Prize, Hon. Mention, Best Book in non-Candn. Hist. in Last Two Years 1986; Konrad Adenauer Research Award, 1990–91; Jason A. Hannah Medal 1991; Can. Council Sr. Killam 1993–94; author: 'Das "Ahnenerbe" der SS 1935–1945' 1974, 'Studentenschaft und Rechtsradikalismus in Deutschland 1918–1933' 1975, 'The Nazi Party: A Social Profile of Members and Leaders, 1919–1945' 1983, 2nd printing 1985, 'Doctors Under Hitler' 1989, 'Different Drummers: Jazz in the Culture of Nazi Germany' 1992 and 70 scholarly articles pub. worldwide; Home: 134 Chartwell Rd., Oakville, Ont. L6J 3Z6; Office: 4700 Keele St., North York, Ont. M3J 1P3.

**KATES, Josef,** B.A., M.A., Ph.D., LL.D., P.Eng., F.E.I.C., FICM; executive; b. Vienna, Austria 5 May 1921; s. Baruch and Anna (Entenberg) Katz; e. Goethe Real Schule, Vienna 1938; Internat. Corr. Schs. Radio Engn. Course 1942; Licensed by Assn. of Profl. Engrs. of Ont. (Electronics) 1946; Univ. of Toronto B.A. 1948, M.A. 1949, Ph.D. (Physics) 1951; m. the late Lillian S. d. late Louis Kroch 24 Dec. 1944; children: Louis, Naomi, Celina, Philip; PRES., JOSEF KATES ASSOCIATES, INC. 1974– ; Pres. SETAK Computer Services Corp. Ltd. (formerly KCS Ltd.) 1954– ; Chrmn. Teleride/Sage Ltd. 1977– ; joined Imperial Optical Co. Toronto 1942 in charge of precision optics for naval equipment; Special Projects Engr. Rogers Electronics Tubes (now Philips Electronics Ltd.) 1944–48; joined Computation Centre, Univ. of Toronto 1948; designed and built first pilot model (UTEC) of Electronic Computer in Can.; also designed first electronic game playing machine (Bertie the Brain), exhibited Candn. Nat. Exhn. 1950; served as computer consultant to numerous Candn. and Am. firms and organs.; estbd. KCS Ltd. Toronto 1954 subsidiary Traffic Research Corp., subsequently expanded to other Candn., Am. and UK centres; designed world's first computer controlled signal system in Metrop. Toronto, capacity improvement of Welland Canal, computer models for urban and regional transport. and land use planning utilized by numerous cities and regions in N. Am. and Europe; consulting operations KCS Ltd. in 1967 merged with consulting div. Peat, Marwick, Mitchell & Co. in Can. to form Kates, Peat, Marwick & Co. (Can.), Peat, Marwick, Kates & Co. (Eng.) and Peat, Marwick & Livingstone & Co. (US), remained Depy. Mang. Partner of Candn. firm until 1968; computer operations of KCS Ltd. continued by SETAK Computer Services Corp. Ltd. from 1967; formed Teleride Corporation in 1979 to specialize in development and installation of transportation information, communications and control systems; mem. Science Council Can. 1968–74; Chrmn. Science Council Can. 1975–78; mem. Bd. New Mount Sinai Hosp.; past mem. Bd., Candn. Weitzmann Inst. of Science; Candn. Technion Soc.; Hospital Computing Services of Ont. Inc.; Past Pres. Operations Research Soc.; Past Chrmn. Operations Research Comte. Candn. Indust. Traffic League; former mem. Nat. Research Council Adv. Comte. on Computers; Past. Vice Pres. Candn. Assn. Data Processing Service Organs.; Ont. Inst. Mang. Consultants; Fellow, Engn. Inst. Can. (Past Chrmn. Mang. Sec. Toronto Region); Fellow, Inst. of Certified Mgmt. Consultants; elected Chancellor, Univ. of Waterloo, 1979–82; re-elected 1982–85; elected Chancellor Emeritus 1993; recreations: tennis, skiing; Club: Donalda; Home: 265 Upper Highland Cres., Willowdale, Ont. M2P 1V4.

**KATES, Morris,** M.A., Ph.D.; educator and researcher; b. Galati, Romania 30 Sept. 1923, s. Samuel and Tobe (Cohen) K.; e. Parkdale Coll. Inst. Toronto 1941; Univ. of Toronto B.A. 1945, M.A. 1946, Ph.D. 1948; m. Pirkko Helena Sofia d. Urho Makinen, Korso, Finland, 14 June 1957; children: Anna-Lisa, Marja Helena, Ilona Sylvia; PROF. OF BIOCHEM., UNIV. OF OTTAWA 1968–89; PROF. EMERITUS 1989– (and Chrmn. of Biochem. there 1982–85; Vice-Dean (Research) 1978–82); Nat. Research Council Postdoctoral Fellow 1949–51, Research Offr. Ottawa 1951–68; Visiting Scient. Nat. Inst. for Med. Research, London, Eng. 1959–60; Visiting Prof. Univ. of Helsinki 1975, Japanese Soc. for Promotion of Science 1975, 1985; recipient: Prize for Scient. Achievement, Ottawa Biol. and Biochem. Soc. 1977; Staff Rsch. Lectureship, Univ. of Ottawa 1981; Supelco Award for Lipid Rsch., Am. Oil Chemists' Soc. 1984; author 'Techniques of Lipidology' 1972, 2nd ed. 1986; co-ed. 'Metabolic Inhibitors' Vol. III 1972, Vol. IV 1973; 'Membrane Fluidity' 1980; 'Biomembranes' Vol. XII, 1984; 'Handbook of Lipid Research' Vol. 6, 1990; 'The Biochemistry of Archaea (Archaebacteria)' 1993; 'Canadian Journal of Biochemistry' 1974–84; over 200 scient. articles original research lipid biochem. and metabolism; Fellow, Chem. Inst. Can. (Councillor 1966–69); Candn. Biochem. Soc. (Councillor 1971–74, Pres. 1987–88); Fellow, Royal Soc. Can. 1973; Am. Chem. Soc.; Am. Oil Chemists' Soc.; Am. Soc. Biol. Chems.; Biochem. Soc. (London); Ottawa Biol. & Biochem. Soc. (Pres. 1974–75); recreations: music composition, chamber music playing (violin, viola), swimming, skiing; Home: 1723 Rhodes Cres., Ottawa, Ont. K1H 5T1; Office: 40 Marie Curie, Ottawa, Ont. K1N 6N5.

**KATES, Paul Allan;** insurance executive; b. Toronto, Ont. 3 Feb. 1926; e. Toronto Schs.; m. Claire Gelfond 15 Aug. 1955; children: Kathryn, Valerie; Pres., Coronet Insurance Agencies Ltd. 1954–61; Pres., Kates-Duncan and Assocs. Ltd. 1961–88; Sr. Partner, Creative Planning Insurance Agencies Ltd. 1972–85; former Pres., BRB Life Insurance Agency Ltd.; mem., Pension Comn. Ont. 1968–83; served in Candn. Intelligence Corps (R) 1948–49; Life Mem., Million Dollar Round Table; Campaign Chrmn. Metro Toronto Federal P.C.s 1972–74; Past Pres., Temple Emmanuel; recreations: callisthenics, history, classical music, walking; Home: 812, 3900 Yonge St., Toronto, Ont. M4N 3N6.

**KATO, Hiroshi,** L.èsA.L.S.; bank executive; b. Akita, Japan 2 Oct. 1953; s. Kinero and Ritsuko (Hasegawa) K.; e. Uinv. of Tokyo Lic. ès arts-liberaux-supérieurs 1976; Ancien élève de Todai-Kyoyogakka 1976; m. Kakuko d. Dr. Hiroshi and Izumi Kondo 8 Dec. 1980; children: Shu, Mari, Yuri, Yu; Vice-Pres. & Gen. Mgr. Montreal, The Bank of Tokyo Canada 1989; joined Bank of Tokyo, Ltd. Tokyo April 1976; Mngt. Trainee, Univ. de Dijon 1979; Paris Br. 1980; Asst. Mgr., Corp. Banking Div. Tokyo 1982; seconded as Asst. Dir., Japan Nat. Oil Corp. Tokyo 1985; ret. to bank as Asst. Gen. Mgr., Money Market Planning Div. Tokyo 1987; Principal, Japanese Lang. Sch. of Montreal for Japanese Children; Dir., Que.-Japan Business Forum; Dir., Montreal Japanese Assn. of Commerce & Industry; Home: 200 Lansdowne, Apt. 107, Westmount, Que. H3Z 3E1.

**KATO, Laszlo,** M.D.; microbiologist; educator; b. Medgyes, Hungary 5 July 1914; s. Denes and Gizella (Panczel) K.; e. Univ. Pazmany Peter, Budapest, M.D. 1939; Research Training Courses in Biochem., Bacteriol. and Serol. 1940, in Clin. Pathol. 1944; m. Vilma Dombos, 29 June 1940; children: Laszlo, Gabor; DIR. RESEARCH, THE SALVATION ARMY, CATHERINE BOOTH HOSPITAL CENTRE, MONTREAL 1979– ; Prof., Hansen Chair of Rsch., Inst. Armand Frappier, Univ. Que. (in collab. with W.H.O.); Asst. Prof., Exper. Pathol., Univ. Pazmany Peter, Budapest 1942; Med. Offr., UNRRA Operations, Germany 1944–48; came to Can. 1951 as Head, Lab. of Exper. Pathol., Univ. of Montreal; Assoc., Candn. Extve. Service Overseas for Brazil 1969, for Brazil, Senegal and Cameroon 1972; Head, Hansen Lab. 1970; served in 2nd World War, Lieutenant Medical Corps; service with combatting troops, Royal Hungarian Army, Eastern Front 1942–43; awarded Fire Cross 1st Class with Swords; Order for Heroism; Expert, W.H.O. Communicable Diseases, Leprosy Sec., H.Q. Geneva; Hon. mem. Argentinian Soc. Biochems.; Brazilian Soc. of Leprol.; mem. Am. Pavlovian Soc.; Am. Coll. Neuropsychopharmacol.; Coll. Phys. and Surgs. P.Q.; Internat. Leprosy Assn.; Candn. Assn. Microbiols.; Assn. Internat. Léprologues de langue française; Adv. Comte., Candn. Leprosy Council; Kt., Mil. and Hosp. Order St. Lazarus of Jerusalem; Cross of Merit, Sovereign Order of Malta; Publications: 'Horn, Clapper and Bell' 1972; 'Studies on phagocytic stimulation' 1957 and 'Acute Inflammation' 1970 (both with B. Gözsy); Ed. Monography Series, Inst. Microbiol. and Hygiene; author of over 404 original publs. in field of exper. pathol. and leprosy and the iconography and hist. of leprosy; Presbyterian; recreations: cabinetmaking; mosaics; Home: 6 Kilburn Cres., Hampstead, Que. H3X 3B9; Office: Dept. of Research, The Salvation Army, Catherine Booth Hospital Centre, 4375 Montclair Ave., Montreal, Que. H4B 2J5.

**KATTAN, Naim,** O.C.; author; public institution executive; b. Bagdad, Iraq 26 Aug. 1928; s. late Nessim and Hela (Saleh) K.; e. Alliance Israélite Universelle Bagdad 1943; Tafayoudh (Coll.) Bagdad 1943–45; Univ. de Bagdad Faculté de Droit 1945–47, Sorbonne 1947–51; m. Gaétane d. late Avila Laniel July 1961; one s. Emmanuel; ASSOCIATE PROFESSOR, UNIV. DU QUÉBEC 1994– ; Head, Writing & Publishing Section, Canada Council 1967–90, Assoc. Dir. 1990–91; Writer-in-Residence, Univ. du Québec 1992–94; author: Essai critique, 'Le réel et le théâtral' 1970 (Prix France-Can. 1971); 'La mémoire et la promesse' 1978; 'Ecrivains des Amériques' Tome I Les Etats-Unis, Tome II Le Canada Anglais, Tome III L'Amérique latine 1980; théâtre, 'La discrétion et autres pièces' 1974; Roman, nouvelles, 'Dans le désert' 1975; 'La Traversée' 1977; 'Le Rivage' 1979; 'Adieu Babylone' 1976; 'Les Fruits Arrachés' 1978; 'Le Sable de l'île' 1981; 'The Neighbour 1982; 'La mémoire et la promesse' 1983; 'La fiancée promise' 1983; 'La reprise' 1985; 'Le Repos et L'Oubli' 1987; 'La Fortune du Passager' 1989; 'Le Père' 1990; 'Farida' 1992; 'La Réconciliation' 1992; 'Portraits du Pays' 1994; numerous articles various publs.; Vice Pres. & Pres. of Academy I; mem. Royal Soc. Can. 1987–89; Société des Cent Associés; Acad. Canadienne Française des Lettres du Qué.; Officer, Order of Canada; Officer, Order of

Arts & Letters of France; National Order of Québec; Jewish; Home: 3463 rue Ste Famille, Apt. 2114, Montreal, Que. H2X 2K7.

**KATZ, John Stuart,** B.A., M.A., Ed.D.; educator; b. Cincinnati, Ohio 21 June 1938; s. Maurice G. and Helen (Klein) K.; e. Miami Univ. Ohio B.A. 1960; Columbia Univ. M.A. 1961; Harvard Univ. Ed.D. 1967; div.; one child: Jesse; PROF. OF FILM YORK UNIV. 1972– ; Dir., Donald Brittain Documentary Study Centre, York Univ., Faculty of Fine Arts; frequent lectr.; former Prog. Dir. Flaherty Film Seminar N.Y. 1980; author 'Perspectives on the Study of Film' 1971; 'A Curriculum in Film' 1972; 'Autobiography' 1978; co-author 'Image Ethics' 1989; co-screenwriter 'Isaac Littlefeathers' feature film 1985; produced and dir. several documentary films incl. 'Rubin' (premiered Museum of Modern Art New York 1972); prog. documentaries and independent features Toronto Festival of Festivals 3 yrs.; reviews films for Classical 96 Toronto FM radio stn.; Programme Consultant, Toronto Jewish Film Festival; mem. UFVA; SCS; Acad. Candn. Film & TV; recreation: running; Home: 59 Bowden St., Toronto, Ont. M4K 2X3; Office: 218 Fine Arts Centre III, 4700 Keele St., North York, Ont. M3J 1P3.

**KATZ, Leon,** O.C. (1974), M.Sc., Ph.D., Dr.Sc., F.R.S.C.; emeritus professor; b. Russia, 9 Aug. 1909; s. Jacob and Malka K.; came to Can. 1920; e. Queen's Univ., B.Sc., M.Sc. 1936; Calif. Inst. of Tech., Ph.D. 1942; m. Georgina May Caverly, 4 Jan. 1941; children: Sylvan, Zender, David, Malka Faye; consultant; formerly Dir. Science Policy Secretariat, Govt. of Sask. formerly Head, Physics Dept., Univ of Sask and Dir., Accelerator Lab.; has written over 60 scient. papers on thermodynamics and nuclear physics; Univ. of Sask. Rep., Candn. Research Mang. Assn.; mem. (Founding) Candn. Assn. for Club of Rome; Counc. Trustees, Inst. for Rsch. Public Policy 1974–89; mem., Sci. Counc. of Can. 1966–72; mem. Canadian Assn. Physicists (Past Pres.); Fellow, Am. Phys. Soc.; Hebrew; Home: 203 Ball Cresc., Saskatoon, Sask. S7K 6E1.

**KATZ, Myer,** B.A., M.S.W., Ph.D.; educator; b. Montreal, Que. 19 March 1928; s. Joseph and Rachel K.; e. Sir George Williams Univ. B.A. 1949; McGill Univ. B.S.W. 1950, M.S.W. 1951; Columbia Univ. Ph.D. 1959; m. Rose d. Hyman and Shayna Goldstein 26 Dec. 1949; children: Hester Ruth, Joel David, Michael Isa; PROF. OF SOCIAL WORK, MCGILL UNIV. 1959– , Instr. 1953–56, Assoc. Prof. 1959–69, Prof. 1969; Visiting Prof. The Chinese Univ. of Hong Kong 1966–67; External Examiner in Social Work, University of Hong Kong 1977–80; Chargé de Cours, Univ. de Montréal 1972–76, Univ. Laval 1971–75; Consultant, Centre de Consultation Matrimoniale Montréal and Service de Therapie Conjugale Qué. 1971; mem. Corp. des Travailleurs Sociaux de Qué.; Am. Psychol. Assn.; Am. Assn. Marriage & Family Therapy (Fellow, Approved Supvr.); Candn. Assn. Schs. Social Work (Past Pres.); Assn. des Therapeutes Conjugeaux et Familiaux du Qué. (Fellow, Approved Supvr.); Home: 656 Grosvenor Ave., Westmount, Que. H3Y 2S8; Office: 3506 University St., Montreal, Que. H3A 2A9.

**KATZ, Stanley Martin,** B.E., M.B.A., CMC; management consultant; b. Brooklyn, N.Y. 10 Sept. 1945; s. Harry and Gertrude (Wolveck) K.; e. Brooklyn Tech. High Sch. 1963; N.Y. Univ. Bronx, N.Y., B.E. (E.E.) 1967; York Univ. M.B.A. 1976; m. Debra d. Abe and Tobi Kaufman 27 Nov. 1971; children: Naomi Leah, Aaron Shane; Pres., SMK Associates Inc., Management Consultants 1989– ; joined RCA Computer Systems Div. 1967–68; U.S. Army Signal Corps 1968–70, rank 1st Lt.; RCA Ltd. 1970–71; Canadian Permanent Trust Co. 1971–72; Versa Management Services Ltd. 1972–73; Woods Gordon 1973–75; S.M. Katz & Associates 1975–76; Inter Bake Foods Ltd. 1976–79, Dir. Info. Systems; Peat Marwick Stevenson Kellogg 1979–89 (Principal); Vice Pres., Sales, MicroTurbo Canada Inc. 1987–88; Dir., Paradigm Consulting Ltd. 1992–93; Prof. Candn. Sch. of Mgmt. 1985– ; Founding Pres. MSA Accts. Payable Users Group, Dir. Candn. Payroll Users Group; mem. Cdn. Info. Processing Soc.; Inst. Cert. Mgmt. Cons. Ont.; Pres. Cummer Park Fitness Club 1980–81; recreations: photography, science fiction, model building; Club: American of Toronto (Pres.); Home: 138 Rodeo Dr., Thornhill, Ont. L4J 4Y5.

**KATZ, Welwyn Leigh Wilton,** B.Sc.; writer; b. London, Ont. 7 June 1948; d. Robert and Marion Annabelle (Taylor) Wilton; e. Univ. of W. Ont. B.Sc. 1969; Althouse Coll. of Edn. Dip. Edn. 1970; m. Albert s. Bernard and Mollie Katz 8 Sept. 1972 (div.); one d. Meredith Allison; m. Douglas s. Wilfred and Thelma Bale 10 Aug. 1991; author (novels) 'The Prophecy of Tau Ridoo' 1982; 'Witchery Hill' 1984; 'Sun God, Moon Witch' 1986; 'False Face' 1987; 'The Third Magic' 1988; 'Whalesinger' 1990; 'Come Like Shadows' 1993; (short stories) 'Cat Mundy's Magic' 1988; 'Their Joyous Strain' 1988; 'Unicorn' 1992; 'You Can Take Them Back' 1993; Writer-in-the-Lib. Stratford (Ont.) Pub. Lib. 1989–90, Windsor (Ont.) Pub. Lib. 1992–93; Cons. Grants Can. Council, Ont. Arts Council; three times runner-up Candn. Lib. Assn. Book of Yr.; winner Internat. Children's Fiction Contest 1987; Ebel Award 1987; twice nominated Ruth Schwartz Award; three times nominated, Gov. Gen.'s Award; winner Gov. Gen.'s Award 1988; Sch. Lib. Jour. 'Best Book' author 1988; winner, 'Short Grain' Contest 1992; mem. Writers union Can.; Candn. Soc. Chldren's Authors, Illus. & Performers; Candn. Authors' Assn.; recreations: flute playing, reading; Address: 346 Blackacres Blvd., London, Ont. N6G 3C9.

**KATZENBERG, M. Anne,** B.A., M.A., Ph.D.; university professor; b. Pittsburgh, Pennsylvania 13 Nov. 1952; d. Frank and Connie (Bowen) K.; e. Univ. of Cincinnati B.A. (Hons.) 1974, M.A. 1976; Univ. of Toronto Ph.D. 1983; ASSOC. PROF., DEPT. OF ARCHAEOLOGY, UNIV. OF CALGARY 1989– ; Asst. Prof., Anthropology, Univ. of Toronto 1983–85; Univ. of Calgary 1985–89; Asst. Dean, Fac. of Social Sciences 1988–91; Cons. to Chief Med. Examiner's Office of Alta.; 'Forensic Anthropology'; Fulbright Scholarship 1992; 2 rsch. grants from SSHRC to study bone chem. & prehistoric diet; Mem., Sigma Xi; The Scientific Rsch. Soc. (Univ. of Calgary Chap. Pres. 1990–91); Am. Assn. of Physical Anthropol.; Candn. Assn. for Physical Anthropol. (Prog. Chair 1990; Pres. 1993– ); Am. Anthropol. Assn.; Am. Acad. of Forensic Sciences (Provisional Mem.); author: 'Chemical Analysis of Prehistoric Human Bone from Five Temporally Distinct Populations in Southern Ontario' 1984 and author/co-author of 15 journal articles, 6 book chapters, 2 conf. proceedings, 6 book reviews & num. conf. presentations; co-editor: 'The Skeletal Biology of Past People' 1992; recreations: hiking, skiing, piano; Office: Calgary, Alta. T2N 1N4.

**KAUFMAN, C. Marty;** artist; instructor; b. Regina, Sask. 15 Sept. 1954; s. Nicholas Andrew and June Elizabeth (Gardiner) K.; e. The Alta. Coll. of Art Dip. in Visual Arts 1981; Head of Glass Dept., Alta. Coll. of Art 1991–92; Chair of Negotiations Ctte. 1991–92; constructed Drakemunn Glass Studio Calgary 1981 producing sculptures and glass pieces; entered partnership and expanded operations as Double Struggle Studio 1985, sold partnership 1990; instr. in Glass Dept. present Coll. 1986, perm. faculty status 1988, Pres. Faculty Assn. 1990, Treas. 1988–90; taught Red Deer Series Prog. 4 summers, Red Deer Coll. Alta., cons. constrn. glass studio; lectr. Palomar Coll. San Diego, Cal. 1989; exhns. incl. Kesik Gallery Regina 1979; Art Objects Calgary 1982; Koffler Gallery Toronto 1982; Muttart Conserv. Edmonton 1982–84; Edmonton Convention Centre 1983; Candn. Glass Assn. Exhn. Montreal 1983; Candn. Nat. Exhn. Toronto 1983; Harbourfront Gallery Toronto 1984; Wells Gallery Ottawa 1984; Alta. Coll. Art 1985; Nickle Arts Museum Calgary 1985; Alta. Crafts Council Touring Exhn. 1985–86; Thomas Gallery Winnipeg 1987; Neo-Faber Gallery Toronto 1989; Glass Art Gallery Toronto 1984–90; O.C.C. Museum Toronto 1991; Faculty Exhib., Alta. College of Art 1992; 'The Works Exhibition,' Cream of the Crop, Glasswork Alta. Craft Council Gallery Edmonton, Alta. 1992; 'Red Series Exhibition,' Red Deer College 1992; selected by jury to participate in Alta. crafts exhn. Morristown, N.J.; selected to exhibit in Candn. Craftsmen '83 tour Pacific Rim; curated Art of Glass Candn. Survey Show '85 Nickle Arts Museum Calgary; rep. various pub., corporate and private colls. incl. Alta. Art Found., Alta. Trade Comn. N.Y.C., Nickle Arts Museum; rep. various Candn. publs.; mem. Alta. Coll.-Inst. Faculties Assn. Pres's Council 1989– ; recreation: cycling; Home: 918 – 16 Ave. S.W., Calgary, Alta. T2R 0T3; Office: 1407 – 14 Ave. N.W., Calgary, Alta. T2N 4R3.

**KAUFMAN, Donna Soble,** B.C.L., LL.M.; lawyer; b. Toronto, Ont. 23 Nov. 1943; d. Kenneth David and Frances Reeve (Leibel) Soble; e. McGill Univ. B.C.L. 1984; Univ. de Montréal LL.M. 1986; m. The Hon. Fred Kaufman, C.M., Q.C. s. Richard and Alice K. 9 Apr. 1967 children: Leslie Ann, David Richard; PARTNER, STIKEMAN, ELLIOTT; joined CHCH-TV 1961; Extve. Dir., Public Affairs Prog. 1965–68; Candn. Assn. of Broadcasters Award 1967 for 'The Mood of Quebec'; Dir., Selkirk Communications Limited 1987–89 (Chrmn. & C.E.O. 1988–89); Chrmn. & Dir., Niagara Television Limited 1988–89; Dir., TransAlta Corp. 1988– ; The CRB Found. 1988– ; Southam Inc. 1990–93; Sir Mortimer B. Davis - Jewish General Hosp. Foundation; Candn. Bar Assn.; Que. Bar Assn.; Am. Bar Assn. (Antitrust section); author: 'Broadcasting Law in Canada: Fairness in the Adminstrative Process' 1987 and num. jour. articles; Clubs: University (Montreal), York (Toronto), Knowlton Golf; Home: Apt. 1405, 1 Wood Ave., Westmount, Que. H3Z 3C5; Office: Suite 3900, 1155 René-Lévesque Blvd. W., Montreal, Que. H3B 3V2.

**KAUFMAN, Hon. Fred,** C.M., Q.C., B.Sc., B.A., B.C.L., M.B.A., D.C.L.; lawyer and arbitrator; b. Vienna, Austria 7 May 1924; s. late Richard and Alice (Singer) K.; e. Bishop's Univ., B.Sc. 1946; Univ. de Montréal, B.A. 1953; McGill Univ., B.C.L. 1954; Bishop's Univ., D.C.L. (Hon.) 1976; Concordia Univ. M.B.A. 1991; m. Donna Joy d. late Kenneth D. Soble and Frances Reeve (Leibel), Hamilton, Ont. 9 Apr. 1967; children: Leslie Ann, David Richard; COUNSEL, YAROSKY, DAVIAULT, LA HAYE, STOBER & ISAACS, barristers and solicitors; formerly Justice Que. Court of Appeal 1973–91 (acting Chief Justice of Quebec Jan.–June 1988); former Sr. Partner, Kaufman, Yarosky & Fish; read law with Joseph Cohen, Q.C.; called to Bars of Que. 1955, N.W.T. 1961, Alta. 1968; cr. Q.C. 1971; Lectr. in Criminal Law, McGill Univ. 1962–68, Asst. Prof., Med. Jurisprudence, Faculty of Medicine, McGill Univ. 1968–73; Adjunct Prof., Ethics in Business, Faculty of Management, McGill Univ. 1991–94; Visiting Lectr., Extve. M.B.A. Program, Faculty of Commerce and Admin., Concordia Univ. 1991–93; mem. of Corp. (1970–82) and Chrmn., Extve. Comte. (1973–76) Bishop's Univ.; author 'The Admissibility of Confessions in Criminal Matters' 1960, 3rd ed. 1979, and numerous journal articles on law and related topics; mem. and Que. Chrmn. Criminal Justice Sec. (1969–71), Candn. Bar Assn.; Que. Chrmn. Rhodes Scholarship Selection Ctte. (1984–89); Part-time mem., Que. Securities Comn. 1992–94; Member of the Order of Canada 1992; Clubs: University, Montefiore, Knowlton Golf; Home: Apt. 1405, 1 Wood Ave., Westmount, Que. H3Z 3C5; Office: Suite 2536, 800 René-Lévesque Blvd. West, Montreal, Que. H3B 1X9.

**KAUFMAN, Martin,** C.A.; investment analyst; b. Montreal, Que. 28 June 1935; s. Samuel and Molly (Schwartz) K.; e. McGill Univ. C.A. 1960; m. Marsha d. Max and Becky Karpman 24 March 1963; children: Reesa, Mitchell Alan; VICE-PRESIDENT, NESBITT THOMSON INC. 1970– ; Greenberg Stores Limited 1964–70; Trustee, Baron de Hirsch Soc.; Home: 82 Place Dephoure, Dollard-des-Ormeaux, Que. H9B 1C2; Office: 355 St. Jacques St. W., Montreal, Que. H2Y 1P1.

**KAUFMAN, Miriam Elizabeth,** B.Sc. (N), M.D., F.R.C.P.(C); paediatrician; b. Cleveland, Ohio 2 Jan. 1954; d. Nathan and Rita (Friendly) K.; e. Duke Univ. B.Sc.(N) 1976; Queen's Univ. Kingston M.D. 1980; common-law spouse: E. Roberta Benson; s. Robert Ormand and Queenie; children: Jacob, Aviva Rose; STAFF PHYS. HOSP. FOR SICK CHILDREN 1985– , Acting Dir. Div. Adolescent Med. 1987; Asst. Prof., Paediatrics, Univ. of Toronto; paediatric residency training McMaster Univ. 1980–82; present Hosp. 1982–83, Adolescent Med. Fellowship 1983–84; Fellow of the Royal College of Physicians & Surgeons 1984; Chair, Candn. Paediatric Soc. Adolescent Medicine Ctte.; frequent TV appearances and speaker adolescent med. (eating disorders, teen mothers, adolescent sexuality & reproductive technology); Active in environmental, peace and lesbian-feminist movements; Dir. Hassle-Free Clinic; Bd. of Advs., Toronto Birth Centre; Past Pres. Bd. Dirs. McMurrich-Sprouts Daycare; Founding mem. Best Babysitting Co-op.; mem. Karma Food Co-op.; author: 'Menstrual Dysfunction' Paediatric Medicine Quarterly (Winter 1988); 'Talking With Teens About Sexuality' Paediatric Medicine Quarterly (Spring 1991); 'STD's and Youth' Mediscan (Fall 1990); 'Answering Parents' Questions About Homosexuality' Candn. Family Physician (vol. 37, May 1991); 'Counselling Pregnant Adolescents' Can. J. of OB/GYN and Women's Health (Vol. 4 #2); 'Discussing Sexuality with the Adolescent' Can. J. OB/GYN & Women's Health (Vol. 4 #3); 'More to Love: Parenting Your Overweight Child' 1994; Charles T. Fried Lectr., Edmonton Alta.; Community Adv. Bd., Women's College Sexual Assualt Care Team; mem. Canadian Paediatric Soc.; Ctte. on Adolescence; Soc. for Adolescent Med.; N.Am. Soc. Paediatric & Adolescent Gynecol.; Soc. for Rsch. in Adolescence; recreation: goldsmith, children's writer (unpublished), reading; Home: 28 Atlas Ave., Toronto, Ont. M6C 3N7; Office: 555 University Ave., Toronto, Ont. M5G 1X8.

**KAUFMAN, Nathan,** M.B.E., M.D., C.M.; pathologist; professor; b. Lachine, Que. 3 Aug. 1915; s. Solomon and Anna (Sabesinsky) K.; e. McGill Univ., B.Sc. 1937, M.D., C.M. 1941; Intern., Royal Victoria Hosp., Montreal, 1941–42; Jewish Gen. Hosp., Montreal, Res.

in Path., 1946–47; Cleveland City Hosp., Asst. Res. in Path., 1947–48; m. Rita, d. Jack Friendly, 1946; children: Naomi Friendly, Michael David, Miriam Elizabeth, Hannah Esther, Judith Anne; Secy. Treasurer & Extve. Dir., United States and Candn. Academy of Pathology 1986–91; Secy. Treas. (U.S.) Candn. Div., Internat. Acad. of Pathology 1979–86; Prof. and Head, Dept. of Path., Queen's Univ., 1967–79; Attending Staff, Kingston Gen. Hosp., 1967–81; Honourary Staff 1981– ; Prof. Emeritus, Queen's Univ. 1981– ; Pathologist-in-Chief, Kingston (Ont.) Gen. Hosp., 1967–79; Consultant, Hotel Dieu Hospital; Chrmn., Med. Research Council Grants Comte. for Pathol. and Morphol., 1971–74; mem., Med. Research Council and Extve., 1971–77; Clinical Prof. of Humanities, Medical Coll. of Georgia, 1980–85; began teaching at Western Reserve Univ. Med. Sch.; Instr. in Path., 1948, Sr. Instr. 1951, Asst. Prof. 1952, Assoc. Prof. 1954; Prof., Duke Univ. Sch. of Med., 1960–67; Dir., Grad. Studies, Dept. of Path., there 1965–67; at Cleveland City Hosp. (later Cleveland Metrop. Gen. Hosp.); Asst. Pathol., 1948–52, Pathol., i/c, 1952–60, Dir., Sch. of Cytol., 1955–60; Consulting Pathol., Marymount Hosp., Cleveland; Assoc. Ed., Lab. Investig., 1952–66 and Ed. 1972–75, Edit. Bd. 1975– ; mem. Edit. Bd. Am. Journ. Path., 1967–71; Editor, Modern Pathology 1988; served as Capt., R.C.A.M.C., 1942–46; M.B.E., Mentioned in Despatches; mem., Amer. Medical Assn.; Internat. Acad. of Path. (Pres. 1976–78, Pres. U.S.-Candn. Division 1973–74); Publications: numerous scient. articles on iron metabolism and nutrition in major scient. and med. journs.; mem., Am. Soc. Clin. Pathols.; Am. Assn. Pathols.; Candn. Med. Assn.; Am. Med. Assn.; Cleveland Soc. Pathols. (Pres., 1958–59); Internat. Acad. Path. (mem., Council 1967–70); Am. Assn. Advanc. Science; Soc. Exper. Biol. and Med.; Am. Assn. Cancer Research; N.Y. Acad. Sciences; Medical Assn. of Georgia; Candn. Assn. Pathols.; Candn. and Am. Socs. Cytology; Coll. Am. Path.; Ont. Assn. Pathols.; recipient Duke Univ. Distinguished Alumnus Award; Sigma Xi; Jewish; Address: 2211 Dartmouth Rd., Augusta, GA 30904.

**KAVANAGH, Els;** board member; b. Amsterdam, The Netherlands 16 Aug. 1938; d. William B. and Elisabeth M.B. De Ryk Mesman; e. Lyceum 'Fons Vitae'; m. Kevin P. s. Martin and Katherine (Powers) K.; children: Sean Kevin, Jennifer Thea; Vice-Chair, St. Boniface Gen. Hosp.; Dir., Candn. Mus. of Nature; Vice Chair, Care Canada; Past Chair, Candn. Club of Winnipeg; Manitoba Arts Council; Manitoba Historical Soc.; Past Mem. of Bd., Royal Winnipeg Ballet; Roman Catholic; recreations: tennis, golf, biking; clubs: Winnipeg Winter; Bear's Paw Country Club (Naples, Fla.); Home: 131 Grenfell Blvd., Winnipeg, Man. R3P 0B6.

**KAVANAGH, Kevin Patrick,** B.Comm.; b. Brandon, Man. 27 Sept. 1932; s. Martin and Katherine (Power) K.; e. Brandon Coll.; Univ. of Man. B.Comm. 1953; Hon. LL.D., Univ. of Manitoba 1990; m. Elisabeth M. Mesman July 1963; children: Sean K., Jennifer T.; Insurance executive, Great-West Life Assurance Company 1953–79; Pres. & C.E.O. 1979–90; Pres. & C.E.O., Great-West Lifeco Inc. 1986–92; Bd. of Dirs., Great-West Lifeco Inc.; The Great-West Life Assurance Co.; National Advisory Board for Science & Technology; Council for Cdn. Unity; Chrmn., Crown Corporations Council (Manitoba); Univ. of Manitoba, Assocs. of the Fac. of Mgmt.; Immed. Past Chrmn., Cdn. Life and Health Ins. Assn.; Conference Bd. of Canada; Mem., Manitoba Commission of Inquiry into Univ. Education; recreations: tennis, boating, skiing; Clubs: Manitoba; Toronto; Home: 131 Grenfell Blvd., Winnipeg, Man. R3P 0B6; Office: 100 Osborne St. N., Winnipeg, Man. R3C 3A5.

**KAVANAGH, Sarah B.,** B.A., M.B.A.; financial executive; b. Boston, Ma.; e. Williams College B.A. 1978; Harvard Business School M.B.A. 1983; VICE-PRES., CORPORATE FINANCE, PEOPLES JEWELLERS LIMITED 1991–93; Lehman Brothers (N.Y.) 1983–90.

**KAY, Cyril Max,** Ph.D., F.R.S.C.; educator; b. Calgary, Alta. 3 Oct. 1931; s. Louis and Fanny (Pearlmutter) K.; e. Central Coll. Inst. Calgary 1949; McGill Univ. B.Sc. 1952; Harvard Univ. Ph.D. 1956; m.Faye d. Alter Bloomenthal, Calgary, Alta. 30 Dec. 1953; children: Lewis Edward, Lisa Franci; PROF. OF BIOCHEM. UNIV. OF ALTA. since 1958; Co-Dir., Med. Research Council Group in Protein Structure and Function 1974– ; Mem., Protein Engineering Network Centres of Excellence 1990– ; Postdoctoral Fellow in Biochem. Cambridge Univ. 1956–57; Rsch. Physical Biochem., Eli Lilly & Co., Indianapolis 1957–58; Med. Rsch. Counc. of Can. Visiting Scient. Weizmann Inst. of Science, Israel 1969–70; Visiting Prof., Weizmann Ins. of Science, Rehovot, Israel, Summers of 1973, 1975, 1977, 1980; rec'd Ayerst Award in Biochem., Candn. Biochem. Soc. 1970; Distinguished Scientist Award, Fac. of Med., Univ. of Alta. 1988; co-author 'Muscle' 1964; over 200 research publs. phys. biochem., protein chem. and muscle biochem.; Ed.-in-Chief, Pan American Assn. Biochem. Socs. Review; Assoc. Ed., Candn. Journ. Biochem.; Fellow, N.Y. Acad. Sciences; mem. Candn. Biochem. Soc. (Pres. 1977–78); Am. Soc. Biol. Chems.; Biophys. Soc.; Med. Adv. Bd., Gairdner Foundation 1980–89; Med. Rsch. Counc. of Can. 1982–88; Dir., Candn. Soc. for Weizmann Inst. of Sci.; Bd. of Dirs., Protein Engineering Network Centres of Excellence 1991– ; Sigma Xi; Jewish; Home: 9408–143 St., Edmonton, Alta. T5R 0P7; Office: Edmonton, Alta. T6G 2H7.

**KAY, Guy Gavriel,** B.A., LL.B.; author; producer; b. Weyburn, Sask. 7 Nov. 1954; s. Samuel Kopple and Sybil (Birstein) K.; e. Sir William Osler Elem. Sch. and Grant Park High Sch., Winnipeg; Univ. of Man. B.A. 1975; Univ. of Toronto, LL.B. 1978; m. Laura d. Leonard and Alice Cohen 15 July 1984; Assoc. Producer & Prin. Writer, CBC Radio 'The Scales of Justice' 1981–89; retained by estate of J.R.R. Tolkien to assist in ed. constrn. of posthumously published 'The Silmarillion' 1974–75; called to Bar of Ont. 1981; recipient Candn. Bar Assn. and Candn. Law Reform Comn. Award Best Media Treatment of a Legal Issue 1986; Casper and Aurora Awards, Best Candn. Speculative Fiction Work 1986, 1990; author: 'The Fionavar Tapestry' comprising 3 novels: 'The Summer Tree' 1984, 'The Wandering Fire' 1986, 'The Darkest Road' 1986; 'Tigana' (novel) 1990; 'A Song For Arbonne' (novel) 1992; Address: c/o MGA Agency, 10 St. Mary St., Ste. 510, Toronto, Ont. M4Y 1P9.

**KAY, Jack M.;** association executive; b. Winnipeg, Man. 14 Nov. 1940; s. Zachariah and Rae (Lev) K.; e. Univ. of Sask., R.P.N. 1963; m. Patricia Ann d. Myles and Shirley McCormick 18 March 1987; children: Katherine Lynn, Patricia Joan, Shawn David, Joshua Myles, Zachary Aaron; Chrmn., Candn. Drug Manufacturers Assn. 1991–93; Pres., Sabra Pharmaceuticals Ltd. 1970–72; Vice Pres. and Co-Gen. Mgr., ICN Can. Ltd. 1972–82; Exec. Vice Pres., Apotex Inc. 1982; Dir., AFI Inc.; Star Plex Scientific; Apo-Scientific Inc.; NCS Diagnostics; Candn. Schizophrenia Found.; recreations: racquetball, squash, tennis; Home: 23 Bryson Dr., Richmond Hill, Ont. L4C 6E2; Office: 4120 Yonge St., Suite 606, North York, Ont. M2P 2B8.

**KAZMER, Allan Joseph;** retired advertising executive; b. Detroit, Mich. 7 June 1941; s. Joseph Francis and Katherine Ruth (Shaffer) K.; e. Univ. of Detroit; Wayne State Univ.; m. Karen d. Jerome and Edna Goodman 26 Apl. 1968; one s. Aaron Joseph; Internat. Creative Dir., DDB Needham Worldwide, retired; began advt. career Detroit 1960; joined Goodis Goldberg Soren Toronto 1968; Assoc. Creative Dir. Spitzer, Mills & Bates; McCann Erickson Advertising 1972, Sr. Vice Pres. and Dir. 1977; Creative Dir. and Sr. Vice Pres. Doyle Dane Bernbach 1981; Extve. Vice Pres. & Creative Dir., Carder Gray DDB Needham 1986; recipient numerous awards incl. 12 Clios, Gold and Silver Medals N.Y. Art Dirs. Club One Show, Toronto Art Dirs. Show, Mktg. Award, Candn. TV Commercials Festival; finalist Cannes TV Comm. Festival; cited various Candn., Am. and Eur. publs.; Les Usherwood Award creative excellence Toronto Art Dirs. Club 1989.

**KEALEY, Gregory Sean,** B.A., M.A., Ph.D., F.R.Hist.S.; university professor, writer; b. Hamilton, Ont. 7 Oct. 1948; s. Michael Francis and Doris Marguerite (Wilson) K.; e. St. Michael's College Sch.; Univ. of Toronto B.A. (Hons.) 1970; Univ. of Rochester M.A. 1971, Ph.D. 1977; m. Linda d. Raymond and Virginia Bailey 8 June 1968; one d.: Caitlin Elizabeth; UNIVERSITY RESEARCH PROFESSOR, MEMORIAL UNIV. OF NEWFOUNDLAND 1992– ; Asst. Prof. of History, Dalhousie Univ. 1974–79; Assoc. Prof. of History 1979–81; Memorial Univ. of Nfld. 1981–83; Professor of History 1983– ; Mem., Univ. Senate 1989– ; Chair, Senate Research Ctte. 1989–93; Chief Negotiator, Memorial Univ. of Nfld. Faculty Assn. 1985–89; Sec. 1990–92; Visiting Distinguished Prof., Univ. of Alta. 1984; Visiting Prof., Univ. of Guelph 1985, Univ. of Sydney, Univ. of New England & Griffith Univ. 1993; Program for the Exchange of Cultural Personalities, Assn. for Candn. Studies in Australia & N.Z.; Fellow, Royal Historical Soc. 1983– ; Short List, Toronto Book Award 1981; Sir John A. Macdonald Prize, CHA 1980; A.B. Corey Prize 1984; Pres. Award for Outstanding Rsch. MUN 1985; Maurice Cody Memorial Prize, Univ. of Toronto 1970; fellowships: Woodrow Wilson 1970–71, CMHC 1971–72, Canada Council Doctoral 1972–74, SSHRCC leave 1980–81, 1984–85; recipient of several research grants; Mem., Candn. Hist. Assn. (Nom. Ctte. 1981–83; Council 1983–86; Candn. Ctte. on Labour Hist. (Treas. 1974– ); Assn. for Candn. Studies (Vice-Pres. 1988–92; Acting Pres. 1991–92); Sec.-Treas., Candn. Assn. for Learned Journals 1990–94; Mem., Gen. Assembly, Social Sci. Fed. of Can. 1985–87, 1989– ; Bd. of Dir. 1990–91; Vice-Pres., Rsch. Communications 1991–92, 1992–94; Chair, Joint Mngt. Bd., Aid to Scholarly Pub. Prog. 1992–93; Mem. 1991–94; author: 'Toronto Workers Respond to Industrial Capitalism, 1867–1892' 1980, 'Workers and Canadian History' forthcoming; co-author: 'Dreaming of What Might Be' 1982, 'Labour and Hibernia' 1993; editor of 18 scholarly monographs, 'Labour/Le Travail' 1976– and the McClelland & Stewart Social History series 1980– ; Labour Columnist, 'Evening Telegram' 1989– ; Home: 96 Freshwater Rd., St. John's, Nfld. A1C 2N7; Office: St. John's, Nfld. A1C 5S7.

**KEAN, John E.,** B.Sc., B.Eng., P.Eng.; association executive; b. St. John's, Nfld. 31 May 1934; s. Michael and Victoria Arabella (Gardener) K.; e. Prince of Wales Coll.; Memorial Univ. of Nfld. B.Sc.; Technical Univ. of N.S. B.Eng. (Hons.); m. Jane Campbell 27 July 1960; children: Jonathan, Jocelyn, Jennipher; PRESIDENT & CHIEF EXTVE. OFFR., CANADIAN STANDARDS ASSN. 1987– ; joined Candn. Standards Assn. 1958 and has served in var. engineering, inspection & managerial functions; successively Mgr., Pacific Reg. Br. Office; Mgr., Inspection Serv.; Dir., Certification Div.; Mng. Dir. 1974; Pres. 1981; Mem., Assn. of Profl. Engrs. of Ont.; Engineering Inst. of Can.; Toronto Bd. of Trade; Ontario Club; Candn. Soc. of Assn. Extves. (Chrmn., Industry Assn. Extves. Council); Standards Council of Can. (Extve. Ctte.; Vice-Pres. Technical); Chrmn. Technical Mngmt. Bd., Internat. Organization for Standardization (ISO - Geneva); Winston Gordon Award Ctte., Candn. Nat. Inst. for the Blind; Dir., Am. Soc. for Testing and Materials (ASTM Philadelphia); Candn. Welding Bureau and the Quality Management Institute; Councillor, McMichael Candn. Art Collection; Home: Box 175, Kleinburg, Ont. L0J 1C0; Office: 178 Rexdale Blvd., Rexdale (Toronto), Ont. M9W 1R3.

**KEANE, David Roger,** B.Sc., B.M., M.M.; educator; composer; author; b. Akron, Ohio 15 Nov. 1943; s. David Francis and Pauline Morin (Price) K.; E. Ohio State Univ. B.Sc. 1965, B.M. 1965, M.M. 1967; m. Melba Cuddy d. William Alexander and Melba (Smith) Cuddy 14 Aug. 1982; PROF. OF MUSIC, QUEEN'S UNIV. 1985– , Dir. Electroacoustic Music Studios; Grad. Teaching Asst. Ohio State Univ. 1965–67; Music Specialist, Worthington (Ohio) Sch. System 1966–67, B.C. Sch. Dist. #46 (Surrey) 1967–69; Instr. Simon Fraser Univ. 1969–70; Lectr. present Univ. 1970, Asst. Prof. 1972, Assoc. Prof. 1976, Prof. 1985; Double Bassist, Columbus Symphony Orch. 1964–67; Vancouver Symphony Orch. 1969–70; Kingston Symphony Orch. (Prin.) 1970–75; Freelance Music Producer CKWS-TV Kingston 1974–79; Dir. Kingston Camerata 1975–77; Dir. Kingston Chamber Orch. 1973–76; recordings: 'David Keane: Lyra' 1980; 'David Keane: Aurora' 1985; 'Electroacoustic Music' 1990; '20th Century Canadian Chamber Music' 1991; 'Dialogics' 1993; author 'Polyphony' 1972; 'Twentieth-Century Composition' 1972; 'Tape Music Composition' 1980; various articles music jours. and mags.; comns. incl.: Ont. Arts Council 1977, 1979, 1981, 1985 (2), 1986, 1987 (3), 1990, 1992, 1993 (2); Can. Council for Arts 1978, 1982, 1985, 1986 (2), 1987 (2), 1992, 1993; CBC 1977; also various orgns. UK, Can., Cuba, France, Hungary & USA; recipient grants Can. Council, Candn. Dept. External Affairs, Ont. Arts Council, Ont. Min. Citizenship & Culture, Social Sci.'s & Humanities Rsch. Council; mem., Candn. Electroacoustic Community (Bd. of Dir. 1987–93); Candn. League Composers (Nat. Council 1983–93); Am. Soc. Univ. Composers (Internat. Coordinator 1986–90); Confed. Internat. de Musique Electroacoustique (founding mem.); recreations: cooking, hiking; Home: 38 Meadowcliffe Dr., Scarborough, Ont. M1M 2X9; Office: School of Music, Queen's Univ., Kingston, Ont. K7L 3N6.

**KEARNEY, John F.,** B.C.L., LL.M., B.A., D.Eur.L., M.B.A.; mining executive; b. Dublin, Ireland 3 March 1951; s. Donal T. and Kathleen (Tuite) K.; e. St. Finians Coll. Mullingar, Ireland; Univ. Coll. Dublin B.C.L. 1971, LL.M. 1973, B.A. 1976, D.Eur.L. 1979; Univ. of Dublin Trinity Coll. M.B.A. 1974; Law Soc. Ireland Law Sch. Solr. 1972; m. Katherina Margaret d. Martin and Marie O'Doherty 3 July 1976; children: James, Elisa, Joanne; CHAIRMAN AND DIR., NORTHGATE EXPLORATION LTD. 1992– ; Chrmn. and Dir., Campbell Resources Inc.; North West Gold Corp.; Sonora Gold Corp.; Dir., Ennex International plc; Legal Counsel and Asst. Sec. Tara Mines Ltd. Dublin 1973–79; Sec.-Treas. present Co. Toronto 1979, Exec. Vice Pres., Sec.

and Dir. 1981, Pres. and Dir. 1987, Chrmn. & Dir. 1992; mem. The Ireland Fund of Can.; Law Soc. Ireland; Inst. Chart. Secs. & Adms. London, Eng.; Assn. Bus. Adm. Grads. Ireland; Prospectors & Developers Assn.; Candn. Inst. Mining & Metall.; Bd. Trade Metrop. Toronto; recreations: running, squash; Clubs: University (Toronto); Univ. Coll. Dublin Athletic; Home: 86 Bessborough Dr., Toronto, Ont. M4G 3J1; Office: 2701, 1 First Canadian Place, P.O. Box 143, Toronto, Ont. M5X 1C7.

**KEARNS, James H.,** B.Com., F.C.A.; retired transportation executive; b. Toronto, Ont. 21 Feb. 1920; s. Frederic Carey and Emily (Halliwell) K.; e. Univ. of Toronto B.Com. 1942; m. Mary d. J. Gilbert and Ethel Shoebridge 15 Jan. 1946; children: Carolyn, Susan, Mark; joined Price Waterhouse 1946–53; Toronto Transit Comn. 1953–77, Treas., Gen. Mgr. of Operations; Pres. & C.E.O., Gray Coach Lines Ltd. 1977–85 (retired); Past Pres. Candn. Motor Coach Assn.; Candn. Transit Assn.; Electric Club Toronto; recreations: golf, curling; Club: Thornhill Country; Home: 39 Kirk Dr., Thornhill, Ont. L3T 3K8.

**KEAST, Ronald Gordon,** B.A., M.A., Ph.D.; television executive; b. Toronto, Ont. 8 Dec. 1933; s. Gordon Marshall and Muriel (Hughes) Keast; e. McMaster Univ. B.A. 1963, M.A. 1969, Ph.D. 1974; m. Elizabeth d. Wilfred and Margaret Shoemaker 14 June 1958; children: Randall, Mark, Tabitha; PRES. & CHIEF EXTVE. OFFR., VISION TV 1987– ; began at CKVR-TV, Barrie; CHCH-TV 1956–63; produced first edn. credit course on TV in Can.; estab. closed circuit TV system/audio visual dept. as well as grad. work at McMaster Univ. 1963; Dir., Adult Prog., TV Ont. 1973; Gen. Mgr., Eng. Prog. 1976–80; Chrmn., Sch. of Radio & TV Arts, Ryerson 1980–88 (instrumental in planning Ryerson's Ctr. for Communications & Computer Sci.); communications consultant; author: 'Technology and Education' 1983 and several govt. studies & journal articles; Home: 345 Aurora Cres., Burlington, Ont.; Office: 315 Queen St. E., Toronto, Ont. M5A 1S7.

**KEATING, Charles V.;** communications executive; b. Dartmouth, N.S. 17 Sept. 1933; s. Charles C. and Beatrice L. (Redmond) K.; e. St. Peters Sch. and Dartmouth High Sch. N.S.; St. Francis Xavier Univ. Dip. in Eng. 1958; children: Anne Marie, Gregory, Catherine, Susan; OWNER AND CHRMN., ACCESS CABLE TELEVISION LTD.; Owner & Pres.: Kings Kable Ltd.; Kings County Cable; Lakeview Shopping Centre Ltd.; Downeaster Beverage Room; Lakeview Hardware and Building Supplies; Bluewater Rentals Ltd.; Old Favourite Beverage Room; Digby Cable TV Ltd.; Delmar Stores Ltd.; Dir. Nova Scotia Crime Stoppers Assoc.; Halifax Cablevision Ltd.; Shaw Cablesystems Ltd.; Shaw Cablesystems (N.S.) Ltd.; Past Chrmn., Atlantic Canada Plus; Past Dir., Atlantic Child Guidance Centre; Better Business Bureau; mem. Royal Commonwealth Soc.; mem. N.S. Lib. Party; Honours List Candn. Cable TV Assn. (Past Chrmn.); former Chrmn. Loto Canada Inc.; former Pres. Dartmouth C. of C.; Past Dir.: Canadian Home Shopping Network; Dartmouth Gen. Hosp.; N.S. Voyageurs Hockey Club; Atlantic Provs. Econ. Council; Dartmouth Regional Vocational Sch.; N.S. Volunteer Bureau/Help Line; Atlantic Provs. C. of C.; Dir. Youth Alternative Soc.; Past Pres. Dartmouth Boys' and Girls' Club; Liberal; R. Catholic; recreations: singing, swimming, baseball, hockey, boxing; Clubs: Brightwood Golf & Country; World Trade Centre; The Halifax; Home: 37 Woodland Ave., Dartmouth, N.S. B3A 3J6; Office: 190 Victoria Rd., Dartmouth, N.S. B3A 1W2.

**KEATING, Diane Margaret,** B.A.; writer; b. Winnipeg, Man. 20 July 1943; d. Ernest Sidney and Muriel Beatirce (Dudley) Heys; e. Univ. of Manitoba B.A. 1963; m. Christopher s. Martha and William K. 1967; children: Stephanie, Justin; Vice-Pres., Keating Educational Tours; nom., Governor General's Award for Poetry 1982; nom., Journey Prize 1991; Mem., League of Canadian Poets 1980–88; author: 'In Dark Places' 1978, 'No Birds or Flowers' 1982, 'The Optic Heart' 1984 (poetry); Home: 55 Heath St. W., Toronto, Ont. M4V 1T2.

**KEATING, Michael Irvine,** B.A.; environment writer and consultant; b. Toronto, Ont. 27 Feb. 1943; s. Michael James and Doretta (Gage) K.; e. Saugeen Dist. H.S.; Ryerson Polytech Inst., Dipl. Journalism 1965, B.A. 1973; m. Nicole d. Georges and Marcelle Préhu 17 Dec. 1971; Assoc., Inst. for Environmental Studies, Univ. of Toronto; Reporter, The Owen Sound Sun-Times 1965–67; The Windsor Star 1977–81 (former mem. Queen's Park and Ottawa Bureaux); The Globe & Mail (former Environment, Educ., Mun. Affairs, and Court Reporter) 1971–88; Hon. Mention, Candn. Sci. Writers' Assn. 1983; Citation Candn. Meteorological and Oceanographic Soc. 1984; UN Envir. Prog. Award 1984; Environment Canada Writing Award 1986; ROSE Award, World Media Inst. 1987; Harry E. Schlenz Medal, Water Pollution Control Fedn. 1987; Fellow, Fac. of Environmental Studies, York Univ.; Founder & Co.-Dir., Environmental Issues for Journalists Course; Mem. Bd. of Dirs., Candn. Global Change Program, Royal Soc. of Canada; mem. Inst. for Risk Research; mem. Editorial Board, Ecodecision; author: 'Cross-Country Canada' 1977; 'Cross-Country Ontario' 1979; 'To The Last Drop: Canada and the World's Water Crisis' 1986; 'The Earth Summit's Agenda for Change' 1993; 'Covering the Environment' 1993; recreations: canoeing, skiing; Home: 10 Astor Ave., Toronto, Ont. M4G 3M2.

**KEATING, Michael James,** M.A., Ph.D., AIL; university professor; b. Hartlepool, England 2 Feb. 1950; s. Michael Joseph and Margaret Watson (Lamb) K.; e. St Aidan's Grammar Sch.; Univ. of Oxford, B.A. 1971, M.A. 1975; Glasgow Coll. of Tech., Ph.D. 1975; m. Patricia Ann d. Patrick and Margaret McCusker 22 Feb. 1975; one s.: Patrick David; PROF., DEPT. OF POL. SCI., UNIV. OF WESTERN ONT. 1988– ; Sr. Rsch. Offr., Univ. of Essex 1975–76; Lectr., North Staffs. Polytechnic 1976–79; Lectr./Sr. Lectr., Univ. of Strathclyde 1979–88; Vis. Prof., Virginia Polytechnic Inst. & State Univ. 1987–88; Univ of Strathclyde 1989– ; author: 'Glasgow: The Politics of Urban Regeneration' 1988, 'State and Regional Nationalism' 1988; 'Comparative Urban Politics' 1991; 'The Politics of Modern Europe' 1993; co-author: 'Labour and Scottish Nationalism' 1979, 'The Government of Scotland' 1983, 'Labour and the British State' 1985, 'Decentralisation and Change in Contemporary France' 1986, 'Remaking Urban Scotland' 1986, 'Scottish Government & Politics' 1990; editor: 'Regional Government in England' 1982, 'Regions in the European Community' 1985; recreations: sailing, music, hiking; Home: R.R. 3, Komoka, Ont. N0L 1R0; Office: London, Ont. N6A 5C2.

**KEBARLE, Paul,** Ph.D., F.C.I.C., F.R.S.C.; educator; b. Sofia, Bulgaria 21 Sept. 1926; s. Paul and Kathryn (Mihailov) K.; e. Gymnasium Sofia, Bulgaria 1944; ETH, Zurich, Switzerland Dipl. Chem. 1952; Univ. of B.C. Ph.D. 1956; m. Beverly Jean d. Walter Harris, North Vancouver, B.C. 14 Jan. 1955; children: Kathy, Karen, Paula; PROF. OF CHEM. UNIV. OF ALTA. 1966– ; Postdoctoral Fellow Nat. Research Council, Ottawa 1956–58; Asst. Prof. Univ. of Alta. 1958, Assoc. Prof. 1962; Prof. 1966; developed method of ion equilibria studies in gases; author over 220 research articles Candn. and internat. science journs.; elected mem., N.Y. Acad. of Sci. 1968; Fellow: Chemical Soc. of Can. 1965; Royal Soc. of Can. 1978; recipient Alta. Achievement Award 1980; rec'd medal Chem. Inst. of Can. 1986; recipient, Am. Chem. Soc. Award for Outstanding Achievement in Mass Spectrometry 1994; mem., Am. Chem. Soc.; Am. Soc. for Mass Spectrometry (Dir. 1976–77); recreations: sailing, canoeing, scuba diving, backpacking, skiing; Home: 7816 - 119 St., Edmonton, Alta. T6G 2L4; Office: Edmonton, Alta. T6G 2G2.

**KEDDY, Paul A.,** Ph.D.; university professor; b. London, Ont. 29 May 1953; s. Norman Cyril and Dorothy Jean (Urch) K.; e. York Univ., B.Sc. 1974; Dalhousie Univ., Ph.D. 1978; m. Catherine d. Phillip and Margaret Pointing 1986; children: Martin Philip, Ian Cyril; PROF., DEPT. OF BIOLOGY, UNIV. OF OTTAWA 1989– ; Asst. Prof., Univ. of Guelph 1978–82; Asst. Prof., present univ. 1982–85; Assoc. Prof. 1985–89; Hon. Rsch. Fellow, Univ. Coll., London 1985; Vis. Lectr., Univ. of Sheffield 1986; Mem., Subctte. for Plants, Ctte. on the Status of Endangered Wildlife in Can. 1984– ; Co-ord., Sci. Ctte., Candn. Counc. on Ecol. Areas 1986–90; Population Biol. Grant Selection Ctte., NSERC 1986–89; Sci. Adv. Ctte., World Wildlife Fund 1986–90; Endangered Species Recovery Fund 1989–91; rsch. & fund-raising for N.S.'s first Ecological Reserve; two Ont. Wetlands designated 'Areas of Natural and Sci. Interest' based on his rsch.; NRC 1967 Sci. scholarship 1974–78; Royal Soc. Vis. Fellowship 1986; Gleason Prize 1991; Lawson Medal 1992; Buddhist; Founding Pres., Halifax Field Naturalists 1975–78; author: 'Competition' 1989 and over 50 sci. papers; recreations: hiking, canoeing; Office: Ottawa, Ont. K1N 6N5.

**KEDWELL, William Robert;** retired petroleum executive; b. Petrolia, Ont. 26 July 1909; s. Horace McGregor and Lucy (Hallam) K.; e. Humberside Coll. Inst. Toronto; Harvard Bus. Sch. 39th A.M.P. 1961; m. Jean d. Frank and Evelyn Houghton 20 Nov. 1937; two s. Barry Houghton, Roger Hallam; served in Mktg. Imperial Oil Ltd. 42 yrs. becoming Mgr. Retail Sales Ont. 1950–52, Dist. Mgr. Hamilton and Toronto 1953–54, Ont. Sales Mgr. and Asst. Region Mgr. Ont. 1954–61, Mgr. Retail Sales Can. 1961–72; cons. Indian Affairs, Ottawa; Founding mem. and Vice Pres. York Central Hosp. Found., Trustee (1976–88) and Chrmn. of Bd. York Central Hosp. Assn. (1986–88); el. Vice Pres., Co-ord. Counc., Mental Health Region of York 1988; Chrmn. Richmond Hill Chapter Candn. Cancer Soc.; Warden St. Mary's Ang. Ch.; mem. Metro. Toronto Bd. of Trade; Home: 2960 – 16th Ave., Markham, Ont. L3R 0K8.

**KEEFE, Francis Paul,** C.A.; trust company executive; b. Ottawa, Ont. 18 Aug. 1943; s. Joseph Leslie and Helen (Carragher) K.; e. C.A. 1966; m. Birgitte Scheel 28 July 1990; EXTVE. VICE-PRES., FINANCE, MONTREAL TRUST; Deloitte & Touche incl. predecessor firms & Coopers & Lybrand 1961–67; var. positions ending as Vice-Pres. & Chief Finan. Offr., Traders Group Limited 1967–79; Vice-Pres., Treas. Opns. then Vice-Pres., Mortgages, Bank of Montreal 1979–82; joined Montreal Trust as Chief Finan. Offr. 1983; Chrmn. of the Bd., CANDEV Financial Services Ltd.; Montreal Trustco Leasing Inc.; Dir., Helix Investment Limited; Roynat Inc.; clubs: Royal Montreal Golf, University Club of Montreal, Montreal Amateur Athletic Assn., Forest & Stream Club, Donalda Club, Toronto; Home: 3445 Ave. du Musée, Montreal, Que. H3G 2C8; Office: 1800 McGill College, Montreal, Que. H3A 3K9.

**KEEFE, Peter Huntley,** M.D., F.R.C.P.(C); psychoanalyst; internist; b. Toronto, Ont. 29 Sept. 1952; s. Thomas Joseph and Norma Frances (Peppin) K.; e. Univ. of Toronto Schs. 1970; Univ. of Toronto St. Michael's Coll. 1970–72 (Henry Carr Scholarship), M.D. 1976; Am. Bd. Internal Med. Cert. 1980; Cert. Candn. Internal Medicine 1981; Am. Bd. Psychiatry & Neurol. Cert. 1984; Cert. Can. Psychiatry 1983; Toronto Inst. Psychoanalysis 1983–89; m. Kathleen d. James and Pauline Saunders 7 Nov. 1982; children: Anna Louise, Dennis, Stephen; ASST. PROF. OF PSYCHIATRY, UNIV. OF TORONTO 1986– ; Staff Psychiatrist Mount Sinai Hosp. 1983– ; internship Toronto Gen. Hosp. 1976–77; Residency Internal Med. Univ. of Toronto 1978–80, Stanford (Cal.) Univ. Psychiatry 1980–83 (Rsch. Fellowship Candn. Heart Found. 1982–83); Rsch. Grant Candn. Psychiatric Rsch. Found. 1984–85; author or co-author various papers; mem. Toronto Psychoanalytic Soc.; Candn. & Internat. Psychoanalytic Assns.; Ont. Med. Assn.; Candn. Assn. Irish Studies; recreations: tennis, windsurfing, skiing; Home: 14 Wendigo Way, Toronto, Ont. M6S 2T9; Office: 600 University Ave., Suite 936, Toronto, Ont. M5X 1G5.

**KEELER, R. Bryan,** B.Com., C.A.; mining executive; b. Winnipeg, Man. 28 Dec. 1945; s. Ronald H. and Margaret (Hives) K.; e. Univ. of Toronto B.Com. 1970; C.A. 1974; m. Susan M. d. Norman and Beatrice Geick 14 May 1976; one s. Richard Craig; Vice Pres., Denison Mines Ltd. 1987; Staff Acct. Clarkson Gordon & Co. 1970–76; various financial positions Canadian Cellulose Co. Ltd., Westar Timber (Div. Controller, Corporate Controller, Dir. Pulp Mktg. Adm.) 1976–85; Noranda Forest Inc. 1985–86; joined present Co. 1987; recreations: squash, bridge; Club: Adelaide; Address: 402 - 160 Frederick St., Toronto, Ont. M5A 4H9.

**KEELING, Nora,** M.A.; writer; b. Owen Sound, Ont. 25 Dec. 1933; d. James Henry and Kathleen Coralie (Walker) K.; e. Owen Sound Coll. & Vocational Inst.; Royal Acad. Dramatic Art London, Eng. 1954; Univ. of W. Ont. B.A. 1963, M.A. 1964; m. Graham Ward s. Allan and Lena Hall 28 Jan. 1967; one s. James Graham (Barney); RADA studies, painting exhn. Piccadilly Circus Gallery London, Eng. 1956; various acting roles Paris, France 1956–61; Lectr. in French Univ. of W. Ont., Head Oral and Spoken French 1966–71; Instr. in French and Eng. Fanshawe Coll. 1975–80; recipient Dom. Drama Festival Best Actress Award (Medea) Montreal 1962; Can. Council and Ont. Arts Council grants; Bd. Govs.' Gold Medal French Lang. & Lit. Univ. W. Ont. 1963; recipient, Chautauqua Scholarship (summer 1950) NY; C.N.E. Girls' Public Speaking Championship 1951; Best Actress Award (The Heiress) O.S.C.V.I., Owen Sound 1951; author: 'The Driver' short stories, one novella 1982; 'chasing her own tail' short story coll. 1985; 'A Fine and Quiet Place' short stories 1987; 'A Fine & Quiet Place' short stories 1991; short fiction various anthols.; recreations: non-fiction reading, legal procedure & the justice system in Canada, medical technology & administration, police recruitment and procedure, architecture, photography, collecting fine art, antique furniture; Address: 894 Notre Dame Dr., London, Ont. N6J 3C4.

**KEENAN, Hon. Mr. Justice Harry Joseph,** Q.C., B.Comm., LL.B.; judge; b. Toronto, Ont. 15 Sept. 1932; s. John Stephen and Margaret Ellen (Fitzgerald) K.; e.

St. Francis Xavier Univ. B.Comm. 1955; Osgoode Hall Law Sch. LL.B. 1959; m. Barbara d. George and Eileen Bull 21 June 1973; children: Anne Louise, Jacqueline (previous marriage), Harrison, Ashley; ONTARIO COURT OF JUSTICE 1990– ; articled law student G. Arthur Martin Q.C., Arthur Maloney Q.C. 1957–59; private law practice 1959–61; Corp. Mngmt., Toronto and Nassau, Bahamas 1961–69; Founding Pres. & Dir., Orangeroof Canada Limited (Candn. Franchisee – Howard Johnson's) 1969–71; Resort Ctte., American Hotel & Motel Assn.; return to private law practice 1972; Apptd., Queen's Counsel 1978; Judge, District Court of Ontario 1980–90; Mem., Advocates Soc.; Candn. Bar Assn.; Candn. Inst. for Admin. of Justice; Dir., Ont. Superior Court Judges Assn.; Lectr. & Panelist, seminars by National Judicial Institute; recreations: golf, ski, tennis; clubs: Rosedale Golf, Granite; Home: 11 Forest Glen Cres., Toronto, Ont. M4N 2E7; Office: 361 University Ave., Toronto, Ont. M5G 1T3.

**KEENAN, Patrick John,** F.C.A., B.Comm., A.C.I.S.; b. Montreal, Que. 7 Jan. 1932; s. Thomas Philip and Kathleen (Collins) K.; e. D'Arcy McGee High Sch. Montreal; McGill Univ. B.Comm. 1954 (Laddie Millen Mem. Scholarship 1952); C.A., Chart. Secy. 1956; m. Barbara Gwendolyn d. Charles Douglas Fraser, Oakville, Ont. 14 Feb. 1959; children: Dr. Sean Patrick, Gwendolyn Mary, Katharine Ann, Christina Fraser; PRESIDENT & CHIEF EXTVE. OFFR., THE ONTARIO JOCKEY CLUB; Chrmn. & C.E.O., Keewhit Investments Limited 1975– ; Chrmn. & Dir., Canada Development Investment Corp.; Chrmn. & Dir., St. Michael's Hosp.; Past Chrmn., ShareLife; Dir., Brascan Limited; Canada Eldor Inc.; Cartierville Financial Corp. Inc.; Fairwater Capital Corp.; The Hume Group Ltd.; The Ireland Fund of Canada; Keywhit Inc.; London Insurance Group Inc.; London Life Insurance Co.; Petro-Canada; Scott's Hospitality Inc.; Westmin Resources Limited; Dir., The National Ballet Foundation; Trustee, Ontario Jockey Club; Patron, Grenville Christian Coll.; Asst. Treasr. and Controller Patino Mining Corp. 1964; Treasr. 1965–66; Vice Pres. Fin. and Treas. 1967–70; Treas. and Dir., Patino N.V., The Hague 1971; Vice Pres., Treas. and Dir. 1972–74; Pres., CEO and Dir. Patino, N.V. 1975–81; C.E.O. and Dir., Consolidated Tin Smelters Ltd., London, Eng. 1971–74; Vice Chrmn. 1975; C.E.O., Amalgamated Metal Corp. Ltd. 1971–75; Chrmn. & Dir., Barnes Wines, Ltd. 1981–88; Vice Chrmn. & Dir., Polysar Energy & Chemical Corp. (formerly Canada Development Corp.) 1985–88; Chrmn. & Dir., Henge Properties Inc. 1988–90; rec'd Gold Medal, Inst. Chart. Secy's 1962; Fellow, Inst. of C.A.'s Ont. 1988; mem.: Inst. C.A.'s Ont.; Order C.A.'s Que.; Inst. Chart. Secy's; Delta Sigma Phi; R. Catholic; recreations: skiing, golf; Clubs: Founders Club, Skydome (Dir.); Toronto Golf; National; Caledon Ski; Devil's Pulpit Golf Assoc.; Caledon Mtn. Trout; Coral Beach & Tennis Club (Bermuda); Belmont Golf & Country Club (Bermuda); Mid Ocean (Bermuda); Valderrama Golf (Sotogrande, Spain); Home: 16 Whitney Ave., Toronto, Ont. M4W 2A8; Office: Crown Life Place – North Tower, Ste. 750, P.O. Box 6, 175 Bloor St. E., Toronto, Ont. M4W 3R8.

**KEENBERG, Ronald Douglas,** B.F.A., M.Arch., R.C.A., M.A.A.; architect; educator; b. Winnipeg, Man. 30 Dec. 1941; s. Abraham Alexander and Mary (Burtnick) K.; e. Pratt Inst. New York B.F.A. 1965; Univ. of Man. M.Arch. 1989; m. Holly d. Rob and Ilene Robinson 19 Sept. 1971; children: Breen Robby, Sean Michael, Megan Paige; CO-FOUNDER, PARTNER AND CHIEF DESIGNER, IKOY ARCHITECTS 1968– ; Mng. Dir. IKOY Ventures 1973– ; Adv. Sch. of Arch. Univ. of Waterloo 1982, Prof. of Arch. 1983–89; Prof. of Arch. Univ. of Man. 1986–87; recipient numerous awards incl. Gov. Gen.'s Medal 1982, 1986 and Award 1986, 1990; Man. Design Inst. Award of Merit 1971; Candn. Housing Design Council Award 1971, 1981; Sask. Assn. Archs. Annual Design Awards 1978, 1980 (2), 1988; Premier's Award Design of Merit 1982, Award of Excellence 1988; MAA Award of Excellence and Citation 1989; winning competitions incl. Harbour View Park Winnipeg 1981, Wm. G. Davis Computer Centre Univ. of Waterloo 1984, Aquatic Centre London, Ont. 1988; finalist Winnipeg Art Gallery 1968, Museum of Civilization Ottawa 1983, MacKenzie Art Gallery Regina 1988; exhns. incl. Akademie der Kunste Berlin 1983, Nanjing Inst. of Technol. Peoples' Repub. of China 1987; co-author: 'Architecture - Fundamental Issues' 1990; author numerous arch. publs.; frequent nat. and internat. lectr.; recreations: fishing, hunting; Club: Manitoba Club; Office: 396 Assiniboine, Winnipeg, Man. R3C 0Y1.

**KEENE, Susan Warner,** B.A., A.O.C.A.; artist; b. Toronto, Ont. 28 Jan. 1949; d. Norman Reeve and Elizabeth Carthew (Eakins) K.; e. Lisgar C.I. 1965; Mackinac College B.A. 1970; Ont. College of Art A.O.C.A. (Hons.) 1979; textile artist exhibiting wall reliefs in Canada & abroad since 1980; principal exbns.: 7th Internat. Triennial of Tapestry Lodz Poland 1992; Candn. Mus. of Civilization (4 recently acquired works) 1991; 'Directions: From Historical Sources' Museum for Textiles Toronto 1989; 'Restless Legacies: Contemporary Craft Practice in Canada' Olympics Cultural Festival Calgary Alta. 1988; 'Feltmaking: Four Major Installations' Burlington Cultural Ctr. 1986; 'Canada Mikrokosma: Contemporary Canadian Tapestry' London England, Madrid Spain, Krefeld Germany, Copenhagen Denmark 1982–85; public collections: Candn. Mus. of Civilization, Canada Council Art Bank, Ont. Crafts Council, U.B.C. Mus. of Anthropology, Cartwright Gallery Coll. Vancouver, The Gallery Cambridge, Ont.; served on juries for Canada Council, Ont. Arts Council, Metro. Toronto Cultural Affairs Div., Candn. Bookbinders & Book Artists Guild & many other orgns.; has taught num. workshops & courses across Canada; Saidye Bronfman Award for Excellence in the Crafts 1991; comnd. by Ont. Municipal Employees Retirement Systems to produce a large work for Constitution Sq., Ottawa 1987; Pres., Surfacing: The Textile Dyers and Printers Assn. of Ont. 1992–93; Advisor, The Textile Studio, Harbourfront Toronto 1987–92; Mem., Candn. Bookbinders and Book Artists Guild; Mem., Public Art Policy Advisory Ctte., Metropolitan Toronto 1992– ; curator: 'Pictorial Space: New Textile Images' exhbn. & catalogue for Mus. for Textiles 1990; Assoc.-Ed.: 'Ontario Craft' mag. 1979–88; Studio: 26 Noble St., Unit 11, Toronto, Ont. M6K 2C9.

**KEENLEYSIDE, Donald William,** B.A., M.D., C.M.; b. Port Colborne, Ont. 7 Sept. 1930; s. late James Ord and late Ida Pearl (La Fortune) K.; e. Queen's Univ., B.A. 1954, M.D., C.M. 1956; m. Linda Jane Seguin 24 Oct. 1992; children (from previous marriage): Laura, David, Timothy; P. Conservative; Anglican; recreations: golf, curling; Club: Cataraqui Golf & Curling; Home: 20 Gore St., Apt. 403, Kingston, Ont. K7L 2L1; Office: 800 Princess St., Kingston, Ont. K7L 5E4.

**KEENS-DOUGLAS, Richardo;** actor/writer/storyteller; b. Grenada, W.I. 17 May 1953; s. Templeman and Muriel K.; e. Presentation Bros. Coll. 1969; Dawson Coll. 1977; single; wrote & starred in 'The Obeah Man' (Dora Mavor Moore Award nominee for best actor) 1985; 'Once Upon An Island' (Sterling Award Nominee for Best Touring Production) 1991; Mem., Stratford Shakespearean Fest. 1978; Stage credits include: roles incl. Peter in 'Souvenirs,' Fermin in 'Two Brothers,' 'Ain't Misbehavin',' title role in 'Pinocchio,' Macheath in 'Threepenny Opera'; Playboy in 'Playboy of the West Indies,' 'The Boyfriend,' 'Dames at Sea,' 'Twelfth Night,' 'The Unseen Hand,' 'Once Upon an Island'; film & TV performances incl.: 'Zero Patience,' 'Adderly,' 'Inside Stories - Dance to Remember,' 'Fields of Endless Days,'; noted storyteller - 'Once Upon An Island' (cassette), 'To Ski or Not to Ski' (cassette) and 'The Nutmeg Princess' (cassette); aired on CBC Radio Morningside Drama; Host, 'Cloud 9' CBC National Radio; author: 'Freedom Child of the Sea' (children's novel) 1994; 'The Nutmeg Princess' (children's novel) Annick Press 1992; 'Caribbean Cindy' (play) 1992; 'Take Five' 1991– ; Movement Teacher, Children's Theatre 1974–77; recreation: fitness enthusiast; Home: 10 Beaconsfield Ave., Apt. 4, Toronto, Ont. M6J 3H9.

**KEEP, John Leslie Howard,** Ph.D.; educator; b. Orpington, UK 21 Jan. 1926; s. Norman Marion Howard and Phyllis Mary Rolls (Austin) K.; e. Univ. of London B.A. 1950, Ph.D. 1954; m. Ann Elizabeth 17 Dec. 1948; Prof. of Russian History, Univ. of Toronto 1970–88 (retired); Lectr., Reader in Russian Hist. Sch. of Slavonic & E. European Studies Univ. of London 1954–70; John S. Guggenheim Fellow 1978–79; Connaught Fellow 1981; author 'The Rise of Social Democracy in Russia' 1963; 'The Russian Revolution: A Study in Mass Mobilization' 1976; 'Soldiers of the Tsar: Army and Society in Russia, 1462–1874' 1985; ed. and trans. 'The Debate on Soviet Power' 1979; various articles Russian hist., politics; served with Brit. Army 1943–47, rank Capt.; mem. Candn. Assn. Slavists; Am. Assn. Advanc. Slavic Studies; Address: 'Les Planettes', Chemin de Chaloie, CH-3973 Venthone VS, Switzerland.

**KEEPING, Max;** broadcast journalist; b. Grand Bank, Nfld. 1 Apl. 1942; s. Heber and Polly (Pike) K.; e. Bishop Feild Coll. St. John's 1957; VICE PRES.-NEWS NATION'S CAPITAL TV 1972– ; Sports Ed. Evening Telegram St. John's 1956–61; VOCM Radio St. John's 1961–63; CJCH Radio-TV Halifax 1963–65; Parlty. Corr. CFRA Radio Ottawa 1965–66, CTV Nat. News 1966–72; Hon. Chrmn. Heart & Stroke Found., Children's Wish Found., Juvenile Diabetes Found., Children's Aid Soc. Centennial Campaign; Patron, Alzheimer Soc. & Elizabeth Bruyere Health Centre; recipient Ont. Good Citizenship Medal 1983; Howard Caine Meml. Award Central Candn. Broadcasters Assn. 1987; Order of Canada 1991; awarded Commemorative Medal for 125th Anniversary of Candn. Confederation 1992; Home: 1606, 1140 Fisher Ave., Ottawa, Ont. K1Z 8M5; Office: 1500 Merivale Rd., Ottawa, Ont. K2E 6Z5.

**KEESAL, Norman J.,** B.A., M.B.A.; management educator and consultant; b. Chicago, Ill. 5 Oct. 1927; s. late Harry Edward and Celia (Gordon) K.; e. Harvard Univ., B.A. (Econ.) 1950; Harvard Grad. Sch. of Business Adm., M.B.A., 1952; m. Miriam, d. late Samuel Shapiro, 15 Feb. 1959; children: Sheldon Ian, Brenda Joy, Nancy Beth; ASSOC. PROF. OF MGMT., FACULTY OF MGMT., MCGILL UNIV. 1984– ; Dir., Mgmt. Inst. 1984–92; Pres., Norman Keesal & Assocs. Management Consultants 1984– ; Invest. Counsellor and Analyst, Stein, Roe & Farnham, Chicago 1952–54; Vice-Pres., Red Comet (Canada) Ltd. of Montreal 1954–60; Lectr., McGill Univ. since 1957; Extve. Devel. Inst. since 1958; Queen's Univ. 1964–66; Vice-Pres. & Gen. Mgr., Cartier Chemicals Ltd. 1960–84; served with U.S. Air Force during 2nd World War; Chief Air Inspr. 103 Weather Group; author of numerous articles for prof. journs.; Chrmn., Econ. Development Ctte., Project Renewal Beersheva; past Pres., Reconstructionist Synagogue of Montreal; Bd. of Golden Age Assn. of Montreal; past mem. Extve. Comte. and Bd. Trustees, Allied Jewish Community Services of Greater Montreal; Past Vice-Pres. YM-YWHA; Dir, Extve. Devel. Inst.; Jewish Peoples and Peretz Schs.; mem., Harvard Business Sch. Club of Montreal; Montreal Bd. Trade; K. of P.; Hebrew; recreations: public speaking, teaching; Home: 5611 Hartwell, Cote St. Luc, Que. H4W 1T5; Office: 1001 Sherbrooke W., Montreal, Que. H3A 1G5.

**KEEVIL, Norman B.,** B.A.Sc., Ph.D., P.Eng.; b. Mass. 28 Feb. 1938 (came to Can. 1939); s. Norman Bell and Verna Ruth (Bond) K.; e. Univ. of Toronto B.A.Sc. (Applied Geol.) 1959; Univ. of Cal. Berkeley Ph.D. 1964; m. Joan Ellen Macdonald Dec. 1990; children: Scott, Laura, Jill, Norman III; CHRMN., PRES. AND C.E.O., TECK CORPORATION; Chrmn., Cominco Ltd.; Past Chrmn., Mining Assn. of Can.; mem., Soc. Exploration Geophysics; Candn. Inst. Mining & Metall.; recipient Honorary LL.D., Univ. of B.C. 1993; Protestant; recreations: golf, tennis, fishing, photography; Clubs: Vancouver; Shaughnessy Golf & Country; Office: 700, 200 Burrard St., Vancouver, B.C. V6C 3L9.

**KEFFER, James Fennell,** M.A.Sc., Ph.D.; educator; b. Toronto, Ont. 15 Dec. 1933; s. James Wellington and Helen McKim (Fennell) K.; e. Univ. of Toronto B.A.Sc. (Mech. Engn.) 1956, M.A.Sc. 1958, Ph.D. 1962; Cavendish Lab. Cambridge Univ. Post Doctoral Fellow 1962–64; m. Anne Rosemary d. John Floyd Hooper, Cambridge, Ont. 24 Sept. 1955; two s. James David, John Wellington; PROF. OF MECH. ENGN., UNIV. OF TORONTO; consulting engr. for industry and govt.; Visiting Prof. Institut de Mécanique Statistique de la Turbulence, Marseille, France; Univ. of Barcelona, Tarragona, Spain; Assoc. Dean, Sch. of Grad. Studies, Univ. of Toronto 1980–84; Vice-Provost, Univ. of Toronto 1985–88; Vice-Pres., Rsch. and Internat. Relations, Univ. of Toronto 1988–93; author over 100 papers on fluid mechanics and turbulent flows; mem., Sigmi Xi; Assn. Prof. Engrs. Prov. Ont.; recreations: sailing, skiing, squash; Home: 76 Amelia St., Toronto, Ont. M4X 1E1; Office: King's College Rd., Toronto, Ont. M5S 1A4.

**KEILTY, G.C.,** B.P.E., B.A., M.S., Ed.D.; civil servant; b. Canterbury, N.B. 12 March 1940; s. Allan J. and Bernice B. (McInnis) K.; e. Univ. of N.B. B.P.E. 1964, B.A. 1967; Springfield College Mass. M.S. 1966; Boston Univ. Ed.D. 1975; m. Patricia J. d. Bernard and Geraldine McCarthy 9 July 1966; children: Krista, Peter, Jill; DEPUTY MINISTER OF EDUCATION, PROVINCE OF N.B. 1992– ; Public School Teacher Oromocto & Saint John schools 1959–62, 1964–65; Univ. Teacher & Administrator, Univ. of N.B. 1966–76; Concordia Univ. 1976–77; joined Prov. of N.B. Civil Service 1977; Dir. of Profl. Development; Extve. Dir. of Instruction; Asst. Dep. Min.; Rsch. Assoc. & Mem., Bd. of Gov., Univ. of N.B.; Home: 7 Burnham Court, Fredericton, N.B. E3B 5T6; Office: P.O. Box 6000, Fredericton, N.B. E3B 5H1.

**KEIRSTEAD, James Lorimer;** artist; b. Saint John, N.B. 18 Dec. 1932; s. George Lorimer and Greta Margaret (Clayton) K.; m. Elizabeth Ann Hibbard 20 July 1957; two d. Brenda Jane, Janice Dawn; m. Robere d. Thomas Kenneth and Dorothy Mae Robertson 14 May 1988; served in Korea 1952–53; Const. Ont. Prov. Police Kingston 1954–65; full-time artist oils & watercolours

Candn. heritage subjects since 1965; over 100 solo exhns.; over 180 reproductions and 17 collector plates; named Artist of Yr. Plate Collector Clubs Can. 1984; author 'Keirstead's Canada' 1991; co-author 'Keirstead: My Art and Thoughts' 1979; apptd. 22 June 1993 Honorary Inspector & Art Advisor, Ont. Provincial Police by Commnr. Thomas B. O'Grady replacing Dr. A.J. Casson - Group of Seven; major collector, Dennis R. Roy; Keirstead's Address: 4 Aragon Rd., R.R.1, Glenburnie, Ont. K0H 1S0.

**KEIRSTEAD, Walter Mitchell (Mitch),** B.Sc.; artist; b. Whitby, Ont. 6 Feb. 1948; s. George Lorimer and Greta Margaret (Clayton) K.; e. Burnhamthorpe Collegiate 1966; Univ. of Toronto B.Sc. 1970; children: David Christopher, Darryl James, Christopher James; first one-man show Etobicoke Nov. 1969; became full-time artist June 1973 over 50 one-man exbns to date; primary affiliation: The Menger Gallery Gormley Ont.; oils, watercolours; over 50 limited edition reproductions (many sold out); teaches twice yearly at Buckhorn Sch. of Fine Art; best known work 'The Autumn Ritual'; known as life painter; works incl. studies of people & horses, at work and at play, street scenes, landscapes, portraits; paintings signed only with stylized 'Mitch'; member of Canada's first family of art; recreation: baseball (Coaching Devel. Mgr., Waterloo Minor Baseball Assn.); Home: 659-B Pinerow Cres., Waterloo, Ont. N2T 2K5.

**KEITH, Patrick L.,** CMA; paper industry executive; b. Kingston, Ont. 9 Nov. 1954; s. Fred Lawrence and Barbara Edith (Smith) K.; Cert. Mngt. Accountant 1978; m. Gail d. Frank and Margaret Archibald 10 Dec. 1977; children: Tricia, Justin, Holly; VICE-PRES., CORPORATE DEVEL., QUNO CORP. 1992– ; Imperial Oil Ltd. 1974; Spruce Falls Pulp & Paper 1976; Kimberly-Clark 1977; QUNO Corp. 1978; Mill Cost Accountant, Supvr., Gen. Acctg. 1980; Mktg. Controller 1981; Mgr., Treas. Operations 1983; Dir., Corp. Planning 1985; Office: 80 King St., St. Catharines, Ont. L2R 7G2.

**KEITH, William John,** M.A., Ph.D., F.R.S.C.; educator; literary critic; b. London, Eng. 9 May 1934; s. late William Henry and late Elna Mary (Harpham) K.; e. Brentwood Sch. Essex, Eng. 1952; Jesus Coll. Cambridge B.A. 1958; Univ. of Toronto M.A. 1959, Ph.D. 1961; m. Hiroko Teresa d. late Norio Sato 26 Dec. 1965; PROF. OF ENG., UNIV. COLL. UNIV. OF TORONTO 1971– ; Lectr. in Eng. McMaster Univ. 1961–62, Asst. Prof. 1962–66; Assoc. Prof. Univ. of Toronto 1966–71; served with Royal Army Educ. Corps 1953–55; author 'Richard Jefferies: A Critical Study' 1965; 'Charles G.D. Roberts' 1969; 'The Rural Tradition' 1974; 'The Poetry of Nature' 1980; 'Epic Fiction: The Art of Rudy Wiebe' 1981; 'Canadian Literature in English' 1985; 'Regions of the Imagination' 1988; 'Introducing 'The Edible Woman'' 1989; 'A Sense of Style: Studies in the Art of Fiction in English-Speaking Canada' 1989; 'An Independent Stance: Essays on English-Canadian Criticism and Fiction' 1991; 'Echoes in Silence' (poems) 1992; 'Literary Images of Ontario' 1992; Ed. 'Charles G.D. Roberts: Selected Poetry and Critical Prose' 1974; 'A Voice in the Land: Essays by and about Rudy Wiebe' 1981; co-ed. 'The Arts in Canada: The Last Fifty Years' 1980; author numerous articles Eng. and Candn. lit.; Fellow, Royal Soc. of Can.; Hon. Pres. Richard Jefferies Soc. (Swindon, Eng.) 1974–91; Ed. 'University of Toronto Quarterly' 1976–85; recreations: walking, ornithology; Home: 142 Hilton Ave., Toronto, Ont. M5R 3E9; Office: Toronto, Ont. M5S 1A1.

**KELAHER, John Terrence,** B.Comm., F.I.I.C.; insurance executive; b. Montreal, Que. 24 Mar. 1943; s. Walter Francis and Glenna Margaret (Shaw) K.; e. Resurrection of Our Lord H.S.; Sir George Williams Univ., B.Comm. 1963; m. Linda d. Wib and Lois Hastings 29 Dec. 1979; children: Tracy, Derek; PRESIDENT AND DIR., THE ALLSTATE INSURANCE COMPANIES OF CAN.; Dir., Allstate Insurance Co. of Canada; Allstate Life Insurance Co. of Canada; Chrmn., Allstate Investment Management Co. of Canada; Dir. & Chrmn., Insurance Bureau of Canada; Dir., Insurance Crime Prevention Bureau; Vehicle Information Centre of Canada; Dir., Policy Management Systems Corp. of Canada; Dir., Equifax Canada Ltd.; var. positions, Royal Ins. Co. 1963–68; Phoenix Ins. Co. 1968–74; The Personal Ins. Co. 1974–83; Home Ins. Co. 1983–85; The Personal Ins. Co. 1985–88; Clubs: Mississauga Golf & Country; Bayview Country Club; Office: 10 Allstate Parkway, Markham, Ont. L3R 5P8.

**KELEHER, Donald Peter,** B.Sc., B.E., P.Eng.; university executive; b. Halifax, N.S. 6 Nov. 1947; s. the late Thomas Joseph and Beryl Veronica (Lean) K.; e. Saint Mary's Univ. Dip. Eng. 1969, B.Sc. 1970; Tech. Univ. of N.S. B.E. 1972; one d. Tara Constance; DIR. OF UNIV. ADVANCEMENT, SAINT MARY'S UNIV. 1982– ; joined ABCO Ltd. 1972–75, 1976–79; AMF Waterbury, Conn. 1975–76; Cons. NATCO Halifax 1979–82; Past Nat. Pres., Candn. Assoc. of Education Develop. Officers; Past Nat. Pres., Candn. Council for the Advancement of Education; Past Nat. Pres.-Elect Candn. Progress Club, Past Pres. Halifax Br.; Past Pres. Saint Mary's Univ. Alumni Assn.; Past Vice Commodore RNSYS; mem. World Trade Club Halifax; R.Catholic; Clubs: R.N.S.Y.S.; Halifax; Waegwoltic; World Trade Centre; Home: 5456 Inglis St., Halifax, N.S. B3H 1J7; Office: Halifax, N.S. B3H 3C3.

**KELLER, Arnold,** B.A., M.A., M.A., Ph.D.; university professor; b. Montreal, Que. 26 July 1943; s. Albert and Anne (Caplan) K.; e. Sir George Williams Univ. B.A. (Hons.) 1966; Claremont Grad. School M.A. 1967; Concordia Univ. M.A. 1979, Ph.D. 1982; m. Polly d. John and Betty Horvath 8 June 1978; children: Jonathan, Emily, Rebecca; DIRECTOR OF WRITING, UNIV. OF VICTORIA; professional interest lies in computer applications to education; Winner, Governor-General's Medal for Studies in Literature; Woodrow Wilson Fellowship; taught at var. institutions in Canada & U.S.; author: 'When Machines Teach' 1987 and a number of studies in computer applications to edn.; co-author: var. U.S. & Candn. eds. of 'English Simplified' 1991; Home: 4430 Chartwell Dr., Victoria, B.C. V8N 2R3; Office: Dept. of English, Univ. of Victoria, Victoria, B.C. V8W 3P4.

**KELLER, Betty Carol,** B.A.; writer, festival producer; b. Vancouver, B.C. 4 Nov. 1930; d. Harry Burritt and Anne (White) Devine; e. Langley H.S. 1948; Univ. of B.C., teaching cert. 1963, B.A. 1967; divorced; children: Christopher Philip and Perry Neil Keller; PRODUCER & FOUNDER, SUNSHINE COAST FESTIVAL OF THE WRITTEN ARTS 1983– ; Teacher of English & Drama, B.C. secondary schools 1963–75; Fac. Assoc., Simon Fraser Univ. (Edn.) 1975–76, 1978–79; Instr., Creative Writing, Univ. of B.C. 1980–81, 1986; Teacher, Nigeria 1977–78; author: 'Trick Doors' (collection of 14 short plays) 1974, 'Opening Trick Doors' 1975, 'Taking Off' 1975, 'Pauline: A Biography of Pauline Johnson' 1982, 'Black Wolf: A Life of Ernest Thompson Seton' 1984, 'On the Shady Side: Vancouver 1886–1914' 1986, 'Improvisations in Creative Drama' 1988; co-author: 'Legends of the River People' 1976; recipient, 1991 Lescarbot Award in recognition of outstanding contributions to regional cultural activities; Home: R.R. 1 Sandy Hook, Sechelt, B.C. V0N 3A0; Office: Box 2299, Sechelt, B.C. V0N 3A0.

**KELLER, Terrence John;** artist, painter, sculptor; b. Edmonton, Alta. 29 Jan. 1947; s. John Joseph and Elsie May (Richards) K.; e. Alberta Coll. of Art, dipl. – fine art 1973; m. Patricia d. Walter and Clara Hagerty 7 July 1990; Instructor of Art, Dept. of Extension, Univ. of Alta. 1979–80; Lectr., Dept. of Art & Design 1981–83; var. workshops incl. The Triangle Workshop (N.Y., Spain); solo exhibns.: Edmonton, Calgary, Montreal, N.Y.; group shows: Edmonton, Calgary, Saskatoon, Toronto, N.Y. & Barcelona; galleries: Vanderleelie Gallery, Edmonton; Paul Kuhn Fine Arts, Calgary; Douglas Udell Gallery, Vancouver; represented in several private & public collections incl. The Edmonton Art Gallery, The Glenbow Museum Calgary, The Canada Council Art Bank Ottawa, City of Barcelona, Spain, & The Boston Museum Collection; recreations: T'ai Chi Chuan, fishing, gardening; Home: 11703 – 39 Ave., Edmonton, Alta. T6J 0M8.

**KELLEY, David H.,** Ph.D.; archaeologist; b. Albany, N.Y. 1 Apl. 1924; s. Gilbert David and Helen Ensworth (Humiston) K.; e. Harvard Coll. B.A. 1949; Harvard Univ. Ph.D. 1957; m. N. Jane d. William C. and Olive Holden 11 June 1958; children: Rebecca Ann, Thomas Michael, Dennis Walter Curry, Nancy Megan; Fulbright Scholar Peru 1957–58 and Teaching Fellow Uruguay 1963; taught anthrop. Texas Technol. Coll. 1958–63, Univ. of Neb. 1964–68; joined Dept. of Archaeol. Univ. of Calgary 1968, Prof. 1970, Prof. Emeritus 1989– ; author 'Deciphering the Maya Script' 1976; co-author 'The Alphabet and the Ancient Calendar Signs' 1969; numerous jour. articles; Fellow, Am. Soc. Genealogists; Address: 2432 Sovereign Cr. S.W., Calgary, Alta. T3C 2M2.

**KELLS, Virginia Constance;** public relations consultant; b. Toronto, Ont.; d. Frank Ernest and Sarah (Hudson) Adlam; FOUNDER AND PRES. VIPR COMMUNICATIONS 1976– ; Dir., Toronto Press Club 1991– ; former Maclean-Hunter Bus. Paper Ed.; former Mktg. Dir. and Ed. Toronto Real Estate Bd.; Exec. Gov. Toronto Chapter, Who's Who Internat. 1986–89; Pres., Candn. Pub. Relations Soc. (Toronto) Inc. 1983–84; Nat. Chrmn. 1982–83 and mem. Cons.' Inst.; Candn. Pub. Relations Soc. (Nat. Award of Excellence 1981); recipient Kenneth R. Wilson Award 1964; recreations: sailing, theatre, music; Office: 40 Orchard View Blvd., (Courtyard Level), Toronto, Ont. M4R 1B9.

**KELLY, Alan,** B.Sc., F.C.A.; business executive; b. England 20 July 1948; s. the late Arthur K.; e. Univ. of Hull B.Sc. 1970; C.A. 1973; m. Vivian Whitley 20 Sept. 1992; SENIOR VICE-PRESIDENT, FINANCE & DEVELOPMENT (CHIEF FINANCIAL OFFICER), BATA LIMITED 1988– ; Auditor, Arthur Andersen 1970–73; var. finance positions, Westinghouse Electric, Eur. 1974–76; Div. Controller, Northern Telecom Ltd. 1976–81; Vice-pres., Corp. Development, Jannock Ltd. 1981–87; Mem., The Inst. of C.A.s in England & Wales; recreation: tennis; Office: 59 Wynford Dr., Don Mills, Ont. M3C 1K3.

**KELLY, Burton Vincent,** B.Com.; retired banker; b. Woodstock, N.B. 16 June 1932; s. late Burton Murrant K.; e. Woodstock (N.B.) High Sch.; Sir George Williams Univ. B.Com.; m. Mary Pamela Ludford d. late John B.L. Taylor, St. Andrew, Jamaica 31 Aug. 1957; one s. John B.V.; RETIRED SR. EXTVE. VICE-PRES., ROYAL BANK OF CANADA 1992; Chrmn. & Dir., The Sunnybrook Foundation; Dir., Am. Management Assn.; Atlantic Salmon Federation; Chrysler Canada Ltd.; Pacific Basin Economic Council; Royal Life Insur. Co. of Canada; Salmon Waters Holdings Ltd.; Mem. Bd. of Trustees, Sunnybrook Health Science Centre; Assoc., Inst. Cdn. Bankers; Clubs: Toronto; The Goodwood; Rosedale Golf; Toronto Golf; Royal Montreal Golf; Address: R.R. 5, Colborne, Ont. K0K 1S0.

**KELLY, The Hon. Francis Bernard 'William,'** B.A., LL.B.; justice; b. Charlottetown, P.E.I. 9 Jan. 1937; s. Lucius Owen and Ethel Anna (Murphy) K.; e. St. Dunstans Univ., B.A. 1960, Dalhousie Law Sch., LL.B. 1967; m. Helena d. A.J. (Gus) and Mary Dowling 28 Dec. 1963; children: Lawrence Owen, Heidi Mary Catherine, Shannon Liam; Justice, Supreme Court of N.S., Trial Div. 1985– ; Royal Candn. Navy; law prac., Kelly, Evans, MacIsaac & MacIsaac 1967–84; Judge, Family Court of N.S. 1984; Q.C.; Regional Vice-Pres., Internat. Commission of Jurists, Candn. Sector; Hon. Life Mem., Benevolent Irish Soc. of P.E.I.; Past Pres., Charitable Irish Soc. of Halifax; c/o Supreme Court of Nova Scotia, 1815 Upper Water St., Halifax, N.S. B3J 1S7.

**KELLY, (Howard) Garfield,** M.D., C.M., LL.D., F.R.C.P.(C), F.A.C.P.; retired medical consultant, teacher, administrator; b. Kingston, Ont. 16 Aug. 1917; s. Howard and Hazel Dell (Lewis) K.; e. Queen's Univ. M.D., C.M. 1940, distinguished service award 1981, LL.D. 1984; postgrad. studies Queen's Univ. Kingston Gen. Hosp., McGill Univ. Royal Victoria Hosp. Montreal Neurol. Inst., Univ. of Toronto Banting Inst. Toronto Gen. Hosp., Post-grad. Med. Sch. London, Eng.; m. Grace Ellen d. David Southall, Kingston, Ont. 17 Oct. 1941; two d. Diane Grace Burkom, Joan Champ; served with RCAF 1941–46, rank Sqdn. Leader, Med. Services; Past Chrmn. Health Rsch. & Development Counc. of Ont.; past Chrmn., Physicians Services Inc. Found.; Past Chrmn., Ont. Council of University Health Sciences; retired Vice Principal Health Sciences, Queen's Univ. and Emeritus Prof. of Med. there; Hon. Life Mem., Can. Arthritis Soc.; Past Pres., Kingston Branch of Can. Arthritis Soc.; Sr. mem. Candn. Med. Assn.; Life mem. Ont. Med. Assn.; Life mem. Bd. of Gov., Kingston Gen. Hosp.; Grant Hall Soc., Queen's Univ.; Le Royer Patron, Corp. of the Religious Hospitallers of St. Joseph of the Hotel Dieu of Kingston; mem. hon. cons. staff, Kingston Gen. & Hotel Dieu Hosps.; Past Pres. Candn. Rheumatism Soc.; recreation: swimming, photography; Home: 77 Alwington Ave., Kingston, Ont. K7L 4R4.

**KELLY, Gary Donald,** B.A., M.A., D.Phil., FRSC; university professor, broadcaster; b. Toronto, Ont. 18 Sept. 1943; s. Donald Gorden and Lillian June (Bray) K.; e. Univ. of Toronto B.A. 1965; Oxford Univ. M.A. 1972, D.Phil. 1972; m. Jennifer d. Thomas and Irene Stanley 1 May 1984; children: Rory, Alice, Christabel; PROF., ENGLISH, UNIV. OF ALBERTA 1976– ; Lectr., Univ. of N.B. 1972–73; postdoctoral fellow 1973–74; Canada Council Killam Found. postdoctoral scholar 1974–76; McCalla Rsch. Prof., Univ. of Alta. 1988–89; Canada Council Killam Found. Sr. Rsch. Fellow 1990–92; freelance broadcaster CBC radio (language & culture) 1987– ; Fellow, Royal Soc. of Canada 1992; Mem., N.D.P.; Modern Language Assn. of Am.; Assn. of Candn. College & Univ. Teachers; Candn. Soc. for Eighteenth-Century Studies; N. Am. Soc. for Studies in Romanticism; Brit. Assn. for Romantic Studies; author:

'The English Jacobin Novel 1780–1805' 1976, 'English Fiction of the Romantic Period' 1989, 'Revolutionary Feminism' 1992, 'Women, Writing, and Revolution 1790–1827' 1993; editor: 'Mary Wollstonecraft, 'Mary' and 'The Wrongs of Woman' 1976; recreations: music, walking, book collecting; Home: 11009 – 85 Ave., Edmonton, Alta. T6G 0W5; Office: Edmonton, Alta. T6G 2E5.

**KELLY, Gemey June,** B.A., B.F.A.; curator; b. Toronto, Ont. 26 July 1948; d. Donald and Lillian June K.; e. Univ. of Toronto B.A. 1972; N.S. Coll. Art & Design B.F.A. 1979; m. John s. Donald and Edith Murchie 30 July 1988; CURATOR AND DIR. OWENS ART GALLERY MOUNT ALLISON UNIV. 1989– , Lectr. in Art Hist. 1990–91, 1991–92; Curator Dalhousie Art Gallery 1979–89; art critic and art reviewer CBC Radio 'Artsnational' 1980, 1981, also 'ArtsAtlantic' and 'Vanguard' mags.; mem. Can. Council Adv. Ctte. 1986–89, Jury mem. 1984, 1986, 1991; Pres. Atlantic Provs. Art Galleries Assn. 1990–91; Dir. Eye Level Gallery 1981–85; Atlantic Centre for Contemporary Photog. 1981–82; Exhn. Ctte. Visual Arts N.S. 1984–86; author (exhn. catalogues) 'Arthur Lismer: Nova Scotia, 1916–1919' 1983; 'Rockwell Kent: The Newfoundland Work' 1987; 'J.E.H. MacDonald, Lewis Smith and Edith Smith in Nova Scotia' 1990; 'Alex Colville: Selected Drawings' 1993; Home: 60 Pondshore Rd., R.R.2 Sackville, N.B. E0A 3C0; Office: Sackville, N.B. E0A 3C0.

**KELLY, M.T. (Milton Terrence),** B.A., B.Ed.; writer; poet; playwright; novelist; b. Toronto, Ont. 30 Nov. 1946; s. Milton Thomas and Sybil Lucy (Preston-Vores) K.; e. York Univ. B.A. 1970; Univ. of Toronto B.Ed. 1976; freelance writer, Edinburgh, 1973–74; City Hall reporter, Moose Jaw Times Herald, 1974–75; Teacher of Eng., Sudbury Bd. of Ed., 1976–77; Columnist, 'Between the Sexes,' The Globe and Mail, 1979–80; book reviewer 1979–86; Teacher, Creative Writing, York Univ. 1987–92; Contrib. Interviewer, TVO's literary show 'IMPRINT' 1989– ; Writer-in-Residence, North York Public Library 1992; Metropolitan Toronto Reference Library 1993; Publications: 'I Do Remember the Fall' (novel) 1978, repr. 1988 (a finalist in the Books In Can. Best 1st Novel competition, 1978); 'Country You Can't Walk In' (poetry) 1979, repr. 1984; 'The More Loving One' (a novel and 3 stories) 1980; 'The Ruined Season' (novel) 1982; 'The Green Dolphin' (play) 1982; 'Wildfire, The Legend of Tom Longboat' (screenplay) CBC 1983; 'Country You Can't Walk In and Other Poems' 1984; 'A Dream Like Mine' (novel) 1987 (winner Governor General's Award for Fiction 1987) released as movie 'Clearcut' 1991 (transl. into Japanese, Polish, Dutch, French, Danish & Italian); 'Breath Dances Between Them' (short stories) 1990; 'Arctic Argonauts' by Walter Kenyon (edited & introduced by M.T. Kelly) 1991; rep. in numerous nat. and internat. anthols.; has also published in several Candn., Mexican and American journals, reviews and quarterlies; Ont. Arts Council grants; Can. Council grants; finalist, best first novel, Books in Can. 1978; nominated for best short story (fiction) Nat. Mag. Awards 1983; Toronto Arts Counc. Award for Poetry 1986; Winner, Governor General's Award for Literature 1987; mem., Writers' Union of Can.; Champlain Soc.; Internat. PEN; recreation: canoeing; Home: 60 Kendal Ave., Toronto, Ont. M5R 1L9; Office: c/o Stoddart Publishing Co. Ltd., 34 Lesmill Rd., Don Mills, Ont. M3B 2T6.

**KELLY, Nora Hickson;** author; b. Burton-on-Trent, Staffordshire, Eng., 8 Mar. 1910; d. Samuel Charles and Kate Elizabeth (Bagnall) Hickson; e. Pub. and High Sch., North Battleford, Sask.; Saskatoon Normal Sch., 1st Class Teacher's Diploma, 1929; m. William Henry, R.C.M.P., s. William George Kelly, 10 July 1940; taught pub. sch. in rural and urban Sask., for about nine yrs.; author 'Highroads to Singing' (children's songs); 'The Men of the Mounted' 1949; co-author: 'The Royal Canadian Mounted Police: A Century of History' 1973; 'Policing in Canada' 1976; 'The Horses of the Royal Canadian Mounted Police: A Pictorial History' 1984; contrib. 'The Americana Annual' (American Encyclopedia Yearbook) 1974; 'The Academia American Encyclopedia' 1980; 'Canadian Geographical Journal'; 'Canadian Red Cross Junior'; has publ. children's plays and songs; sch.-help work books in health, citizenship; operettas; Talks for C.B.C.; shadow plays; stories, articles and plays in school readers; pre-school 'Look and Learn'; teacher's manuals in lit.; Life mem., Nat. Assn. for Advancement of Coloured People; Voluntary Euthanasia Society (Gr. Brit.); Rationalist Press Assn. (Gr. Brit.); recreation: music; Home: 2079 Woodcrest Rd., Ottawa, Ont. K1H 6H9.

**KELLY, Robert P.,** B.Comm., C.A., M.B.A.; banking executive; b. Halifax, N.S. 1954; e. St. Mary's Univ. B.Comm. 1975; C.A. 1978; The City Univ., London, U.K. M.B.A. 1986; EXTVE. VICE-PRESIDENT FINANCE, THE TORONTO DOMINION BANK 1993– ; Senior Inspector, Toronto 1981; Manager, Finance, London, U.K. 1984; Manager, Capital Markets 1986; Asst. Gen. Mgr., Capital Mkts., Corp. & Investment Banking Group Toronto 1987; Gen. Mgr., Capital Markets 1988; Gen. Mgr., Capital Markets & Fixed Income 1989; Sr. Vice-Pres. Atlantic Div. 1990; Sr. Vice-Pres., Finance & Control Div., The Toronto Dominion Bank 1992; Office: Head Office, T.D. Centre, Toronto, Ont. M5K 1A2.

**KELLY, Terence Vincent,** B.A., B.C.L., Q.C.; lawyer; b. Toronto, Ont. 28 May 1931; s. John Joseph and Beatrice Edna (Nicholson) K.; e. St. Malachy's Coll., Belfast, N. Ireland H.S.; Univ. of N.B., B.A. 1951, B.C.L. 1953; children: Timothy John, Jane Elizabeth; LAWYER, KELLY, ZULY, GREENWAY, BRUCE 1956– ; Dir., Toronto Maple Leafs Hockey Club and Maple Leaf Gardens Ltd.; called to Bar of N.B. 1953; Bar of Ont. 1953; cr. Q.C. 1964; Vice-Pres. Advocates Soc. Ont. 1969; mem. Candn. Bar Assn.; Pres. Ont. Soccer Assn. 1961–67; Pres. National Lacrosse Assn. 1968; Exec. Mem., Bd. of Govs., Canada's Sports Hall of Fame (Chairman, Selection Ctte.); Founding Chrmn., Oshawa Sports Hall of Fame; Founding Chrmn., Durham Recycling; Founding Dir., Oshawa Green Gaels Lacrosse Club; Hon. Mem., Oshawa Kinsmen Club; Former Pres., Oshawa Vikings Rugby Football Club; Dir., Oshawa Generals Hockey Club; Oshawa Legionnaires Hockey Club; Dir., Multicultural Council of Oshawa Durham; Dir., William Hayball Found.; R. Catholic; Liberal; Centennial Medal 1967; Queen's Silver Jubilee Medal 1977; Ont. Bicentennial Medal 1984; one of three Young Men of the Year, Jr. C. of C., Ont. 1967; Celebration 88, Certificate of Merit 1988; named Paul Harris Fellow, Rotary Internat. 1989; Commemorative Medal, 125th Anniversary of Candn. Confedn. 1992; Volunteer Service Award, Ont. Min. of Citizenship; recreation: watching sporting events; Clubs: Deer Creek Golf; Oshawa Curling; Royal Candn. Mil. Inst.; Toronto Press; Office: 114 King St. E., Oshawa, Ont. L1H 7N1.

**KELLY, Hon. William McDonough,** B.A.Sc., F.E.I.C.; senator; executive; civil engineer; b. Georgetown, Ont. 21 July 1925; s. John Doyle and Margaret Shirley (Carpenter) K.; e. Georgetown H.S.; Univ. of Toronto, B.A.Sc. (Hons.) 1950; Univ. of Illinois; Harvard Bus. Sch.; m. Elizabeth Anne d. Reginald Paul 1944; children: Ann (Walsh), Patricia (Parr); Lieut., Candn. Army, 1944–46; Cadet Engr., Consumers' Gas Co. 1951; retired as Sr. Vice Pres. 1971; Pres., Can-Arctic Construction Ltd. 1972–80; Summoned to Senate 23 Dec. 1982; Chrmn., Sen. Ctte. on Terrorism & Public Safety; Mem., Senate Ctte. on Banking, Trade & Commerce, Nat. Finance (Vice Chrmn.); Nat. Defense; Chrmn., Rothman's Inc. 1985– ; Pres., Kelco Mgmt. Ltd.; Severn Boat Haven Ltd.; Dir., Contrans Inc.; Rothmans Internat. PLC (United Kingdom); Rothmans Internat. NV (The Netherlands); Comdr., Order of St. Lazarus of Jerusalem; Life Mem., World Wildlife Fund Canada; Fellow, Eng. Inst. of Canada; Mem., Inst. of Gas Engrs. U.K.; Gov., Canada's Sports Hall of Fame; Past Chrmn., Ryerson Polytech. Inst.; Church of England; Progressive Conservative; Masonic Lodge (Credit 219); recreations: sailing, hunting, tennis; Clubs: Toronto; Albany; Rideau; Home: 1300 Bloor St. #2406, Mississauga, Ont.; Office: P.O. Box 370, Toronto-Dominion Ctr., Toronto, Ont. M5K 1K8.

**KELLY, William Patrick;** industrial relations consultant; b. Toronto, Ont. 24 Mar. 1924; s. Patrick Joseph and Alice Lavina (Dennison) K.; e. Western Commerce, Toronto, Ont. grad. 1941; m. Jean Eloise d. Isaac Earl and Mary Ada Hooper 23 June 1956; one s. Michael Patrick; BD. OF DIRS. & SPECIAL COUNSEL, GOVERNMENT CONSULTANTS INTERNAT. 1989– ; Visiting Prof., Univ. of Ottawa 1989–92; elected mem., Ontario Press Council 1989– ; apptd. Mem., Royal Commission on a National Transportation System for the 21st Century 1989–92; RCAF Pilot 1942–45; Trainman CP Rail 1945–58; Vice-Pres., Brotherhood of Railroad Trainmen (now United Transp. Union) 1960–66; Labour Can.: Dir. Conciliation & Arbitration Br. 1966–71; Asst. Depy. Min. Ind. Relns. 1972–80; Sr. Asst. Depy. Min., Federal Mediation and Conciliation Service 1980–84; Assoc. Depy. Min., Labour Canada 1985–89; Charter Mem., Soc. of Profls. in Dispute Resolution; Gov., Canadian Inst. for Conflict Resolution; recipient Merit Award, Incentive Bd. of Publ. Service of Can. 1971; Order of Can. 1984; Outstanding Achievement Award of the Public Service of Canada 1987; Commemorative Medal, 125th Anniversary, Candn. Confedn. 1992; Home: 60 Sullivan Ave., Nepean, Ont. K2G 1V2.

**KELMAN, Steven G.,** B.Sc., M.B.A., C.F.A.; investment counsellor, writer; b. Toronto, Ont. 21 Dec. 1945; s. David and Molly (Bernholtz) K.; e. McMaster Univ. B.Sc. 1967; York Univ. M.B.A. 1969; Inst. of C.F.A.s C.F.A. 1976; VICE-PRES., CORP. & PUBLIC RELATIONS, DYNAMIC FUND MANAGEMENT 1985– ; Portfolio Mgr., The Excelsior Life Insur. Co. 1970–74; Sr. Analyst, May Mikkila & Co. 1975; Investment Editor, Financial Times of Canada 1975–85; Part-time Lectr., Admin. Studies, York Univ. 1981–85; Advisory Ed., Mutual Fund Sourcebook and Advisor, Mutual Fund Sourcedisk for Southam Bus. Communications Inc.; author: 'RRSPs 1994,' 'Understanding Mutual Funds'; co-author: 'Investment Strategies,' 'Investing in Gold'; Office: 40 King St. W., 55th Floor, Toronto, Ont. M5H 4A9.

**KEMENY, John;** film producer; b. Budapest, Hungary; e. Acad. of Comm., Budapest; PROD., INTERNAT. CINEMEDIA CENTER CORP. II; Asst. Ed., Ed., Dir., Prod., Extve. Prod., Nat. Film Bd. of Can. 1957–69; Pres., Internat. Cinemedia Ctr., Ltd.; Internat. Cinema Corp.; Principal, Alliance Entertainment Corp.; ed., dir., prod., over 100 theatrical shorts, documentaries & TV programs incl.: 'Ladies & Gentlemen, Mr. Leonard Cohen,' 'Memorandum,' 'The Best Damn Fiddler from Calaboogie to Kaladar'; 'Bethune'; feature film prod.: 'Don't Let the Angels Fall,' 'Un Enfant Comme les Autres,' 'The Apprenticeship of Duddy Kravitz' (1st prize, Berlin Film Festival), 'White Line Fever,' 'Ice Castles,' 'Atlantic City' (1st prize, Venice Film Festival & the Golden Globes, 5 Academy Award nominations incl. Best Picture), 'Quest for Fire,' (one Academy Award and 2 Cesars of French Film Acad.) 'The Bay Boy' (won 6 Genie Awards incl. Best Picture), The Boy in Blue,' 'The Wraith,' 'The Gate,' 'Nowhere to Hide,' 'Iron Eagle II'; mini-series incl.: 'Louisiana,' 'Blood of Others'; 'The Murderers Among Us: The Simon Wiesenthal Story' (4 ACE Awards incl. Best Picture of the Year); 'Red King, White Knight'; 'The Josephine Baker Story' (5 Emmy Awards); Lifetime Achievement Award, Academy of Candn. Cinema & Television; recipient of over 40 internat. awards for various films produced; Candn. Centennial Medal in recognition of valuable serivice to the nation; Mem., Acad. of Motion Picture Arts & Sci.; Acad. of Candn. Cinema and Television.

**KEMP, Anthony Leslie,** B.Arch., MRAIC, ARIBA, RCA; architect; b. Kingston-On-Thames, Eng. 9 July 1936; s. Leslie Hagger and Louise (Winter) K.; e. Sherborne Sch. Dorset; Ridley Coll. St. Catharines, Ont.; Univ. of Toronto B.Arch.; came to Can. 1947; m. Patricia Ann Fraser July 1968; one d. Katharine Nicole; PRESIDENT, KEMP ARCHITECTS INC. 1969– ; Pres., Anthony Kemp Associates Ltd.; Pres., Fairwinter Developments Ltd.; Extve. Asst. to John C. Parkin, Parkin Architects and Engineers 1964–69; Adv. Counc., Ridley Coll.; Trustee, The Riverdale Hosp., Toronto; Gov., Branksome Hall Sch.; Past Pres. Associates of Toronto Symphony; recipient various design awards incl. Candn. Housing Design Council, Ont. Masonry Council, Candn. Arch. Yearbook; mem. Royal Can. Acad. of Arts; Ont. Assn. Archs.; Royal Arch. Inst. Can.; Toronto Soc. Archs.; Royal Soc. Arts UK; Hon. Co. Freeman City of London in N. Am. (Past Master); Worshipful Co. of Gardners London, Eng.; Delta Upsilon; Anglican; recreation: sailing; Club: RCYC; Home: 104 Balmoral Ave., Toronto, Ont. M4V 1J4; Office: 517 Wellington St. W., Toronto, Ont. M5V 1G1.

**KEMP, Linda Patricia Frayne,** CSPWC, OSA, SCA; artist; b. St. Catharines, Ont. 26 Jan. 1956; d. Ralph Haskings and Alice Beverly (Gibson) Frayne; e. Fanshawe Coll.; m. Barry James s. Robert and Elma K. 21 May 1977; children: Jamie Linn and Eric William Frayne Kemp; exhibited in major juried & invitational shows incl. Rodman Hall, Hamilton Art Gallery, John B. Aird, Burlington Cultural Centre, O'Keefe Ctr., Mississauga Civic Ctr., Homer Watson, etc. 1979– ; solo shows: Lindsay Gall. 1994, Grimsby Art Gall. 1982, '88, '95 (planned), Anthony Gall. 1988, '90, Royal Botanical Gardens 1989, Hennipen Gall. 1989, Harbour Gall. 1991 and others; work incl. in corp., govt. & private collections in Can., U.S., U.K., Eur. & Russia; teacher & guest lectr. in Canada and U.S. for orgns., art schools & societies; recipient of many awards & honours for competitions; Ont. Arts Council Visual Arts grants 1989, '90, '91, '93; Mem., Candn. Soc. of Painters in Watercolour; Ont. Soc. of Artists; Soc. of Candn. Artists; Pres., Central Ont. Art Assn. 1990–92; recreations: hiking, music, theatre, ballet; Home: 3797 Main St., Jordan, Ont. L0R 1S0.

**KEMP-GEE, Alan Keith;** chartered accountant; b. Tunbridge-Wells, England 23 Apr. 1940; s. Peter Murray and Valerie (Oswald-Smith) K.; e. Gordonstoun; m. Stephanie d. James and Winnifred Green 1983; children: Michelle, Mark, Scott, Meghan, Jonathan; PRES., PAN FINANCIAL INC.; Dir., Firan Corp.; Partner, Peat Marwick Mitchell & Co. 1971–87; C.A. 1962; Dunwoody & Co. 1957–60; Clarkson Gordon & Co. 1960–71; Dir. & Pres., Peat Marwick Limited 1972–84; Dir. & Chrmn. 1984–87; Sr. Vice Pres., Merchant Banking, Central Capital Corp. 1989–91; mem., Inst. of C.A.s of Ont. and B.C.; author: 'Insolvency in Practice: A Receiver's View' 1982; recreations: squash, tennis, golf, skiing; Clubs: Capilano Golf; Vancouver; Lambton Golf & Country, Toronto Lawn; Oxford; Office: 353 Iroquois Shore Road, Oakville, Ont. L6H 1M3.

**KENDALL, David John Winston,** M.Sc., Ph.D.; space scientist; b. Teddington, Middlesex, Eng. 8 Feb. 1948; s. John Henry and Evelyn Agnes Daisy (Lewis) K.; e. Thames Valley Grammar Sch. Twickenham, Eng. 1966; Univ. Coll. Swansea, Univ. of Wales B.Sc. 1969; Univ. of Calgary M.Sc. 1972, Ph.D. 1979; children: Christopher, Susannah, Katie; PROG. SCIENTIST, SPACE SCI. PROG., CANDN. SPACE AGENCY 1989– ; FACULTY, INTERNAT. SPACE UNIV. 1990– ; Co-Chrmn., Phys. Sci. Dept., Internat. Space Univ. 1994; Rsch. Assoc. Physics, Univ. of Calgary 1972–75; Rsch. & Devel. Sci. Bomem Inc. Quebec 1978–82; Prog. Scientist, Candn. Centre Space Sci. 1982–84, Space Div. 1984–89 Nat. Rsch. Council; Prin. Investig. OGLOW experiment shuttle mission STS-41G 1984; Co-investig. CANOPUS experiment 1985– ; Co-investig. OGLOW-2 experiment 1992; Chrmn., Solar Terrestrial Relations Advisory Ctte., Candn. Space Agency 1989–92; National Representative, Scientific Ctte. on Solar Terrestrial Physics (SCOSTEP) 1992– ; Mem., Space and Astronomy Grant Selection Ctte., NSERC 1992–95; Earth Observation Internal. Coordination Working Group 1988– ; Science Advisory Ctte., Candn. Network for Space Research 1990– ; author of approx. 90 papers published or given at conferences; mem. Am. Geophys. Union; Candn. Aeronautics and Space Inst.; recreations: soccer, squash, cross-country skiing, gardening, organizing & judging sch. sci. fairs/olympics; Home: 208 - 225 Alvin Rd., Ottawa, Ont. K1K 4H6; Office: 100 Sussex Dr., Ottawa, Ont. K1A 0R6.

**KENDALL, Gerald Robert,** B.Sc.; development-construction executive; b. Winnipeg, Man. 10 July 1935; s. Henry Charles and Beatrice Alice (Wynn) K.; e. Univ. of Manitoba B.Sc. 1957; m. Joan d. Edwin and Dorothy Canfield 1 June 1957; children: Clayton, Janice, Kathryn, Nancy; Branch Mgr., Regional Vice-Pres. & Sr. Vice-Pres., Dominion Construction & Devel. Inc. (Winnipeg) 1972–93, retired; Application Engr., Carrier Air Conditioning Corp. (N.Y.) 1957–59; Design Engr., Leo A. Daly Co., Architexts & Engrs. (Nebraska) 1959–63; Chief Engr., GBR & Assoc., Arch. & Engr. (Winnipeg) 1963–70; Mgr., Reid Crowther & Partners 1970–72; recreations: golf, gardening; clubs: Niakwa Golf & Country, Carleton; Home: 155 Victoria Cres., Winnipeg, Man. R2M 1X6.

**KENDALL, Perry Robert William,** M.B.B.S., M.Sc., F.R.C.P.C.; public health official; b. London, England 2 Feb. 1943; s. Ronald and Violet Edith (Newland) K.; e. Univ. Coll. Hosp. Med. Sch., London, England, M.B.B.S. 1968; Univ. of B.C., M.Sc. 1983; F.R.C.P.C., Community Med. 1984; m. Rena d. Rita and David Herbert S. 23 June 1982; children: Maximilian Zulu, Sahara Katrina Chava; MED. OFFICER OF HEALTH, CITY OF TORONTO DEPT. OF PUBLIC HEALTH 1989– ; Sr. House Offr., Univ. of the W. Indies 1971–72; Gen. practice & Hassle Free Clinic, Toronto 1972–74; Asst. Med. Dir., North Health Unit & Med. Offr., Youth Health Serv., Vanc. Health Dept. 1974–78; Unit Med. Offr. & Unit Dir. E. & S. Units 1978–84; Area Med. Offr., Public Health Br., Min. of Health, Ont. 1985; Physician Mgr., Disease Control & Epidem. Serv. 1985–87; Med. Health Offr., Capital Reg. Dist., Community Health Serv., Victoria, B.C. 1987–89; Special Advr., to the Depy. Min. of Health (Ont.) on Long Term Care Reform & Population Health Issues 1992–93; Mem., Candn. & Am. Public Health Assns.; Royal Coll. of Phys. & Surg. of Can.; Coll. of Phys. & Surg. of Ont. and B.C.; Internat. Phys. for the Prevention of Nuclear War; author of several med. articles; Home: 34 Fenwick Ave., Toronto, Ont. M4K 3H3; Office: 7th Floor, East Tower, 100 Queen St. W., Toronto, Ont. M5H 2N2.

**KENDLE, John Edward,** B.A., Ph.D., F.R.Hist.S.; educator; b. London, Eng. 14 Apr. 1937; s. Arthur and Sybil Violet Mary (Jordan) K.; e. Lord Roberts Jr. High and Gordon Bell High Schs. Winnipeg 1955; Univ. of Man., Un. Col. B.A. 1958, M.A. work 1959–61; King's Coll. Univ. of London Ph.D. 1965; m. Judith Ann d. late Charles Halsey 3 Aug. 1963; children: John Stephen, Andrew Bruce, Nancy Elizabeth; PROF. OF HIST. ST. JOHN'S COLL. UNIV. OF MAN. 1965– ; IODE Doctoral Fellow 1961–63; Can. Council Doctoral Fellowship 1964–65, Leave Fellowship 1971–72, 1978–79, 1985–86; Post-doctoral Fellowship 1967–68; Tutorial Studentship in Imp. Hist. Univ. London 1964–65; Margaret McWilliams Medal, Man. Hist. Soc. 1980; Visiting Rsch. Fellow, Australian Nat. Univ. and Auckland Univ. 1967–68; Commonwealth Fellow, St. John's College, Cambridge 1985–86; mem. Ed. Bd., Candn. Hist. Assn. Papers 1973–78; mem. Adv. Bd., Jr. of Imp. & C.W. Hist. 1988– ; Chrmn. Dept. of History. Univ. of Man. 1982–85, 1990– ; Chairperson., Historic Sites Adv. Bd. of Man. 1982–84; author 'The Colonial and Imperial Conferences 1887–1911' 1967; 'The British Empire-Commonwealth 1897–1931' 1972; 'The Round Table Movement and Imperial Union' 1975; 'John Bracken: A Political Biography' 1979; 'Ireland and the Federal Solution: The Debate over the United Kingdom Constitution 1870–1921' 1989; 'Walter Long, Ireland, and the Union, 1905–1920' 1992; various articles imp. fed., fed. and devolution in UK; mem. Candn. Hist. Assn. (Vice Pres. 1980–81, Pres. 1981–82); Am. Comte. Irish Studies; Am. Hist. Assn.; recreations: curling, cycling, reading; Home: 149 The Glen, Winnipeg, Man. R2M 0B5; Office: Winnipeg, Man. R3T 2M5.

**KENDRICK, Bryce,** Ph.D., D.Sc., F.R.S.C; educator; b. Liverpool, Eng. 3 Dec. 1933; s. William and Lillian Maud (Latham) K.; e. Univ. of Liverpool B.Sc. 1955, Ph.D. 1958, D.Sc. 1980; m. Laureen d. Fraser and Willa Carscadden 14 Dec. 1977; children: Clinton, Kelly; PROF. OF BIOL., UNIV. OF WATERLOO 1971– ; Nat. Research Council Postdoctoral Fellow 1958–59; Research Offr. Agric. Can. 1959–65; Asst. Prof. of Biol. present Univ. 1965, Assoc. Prof. 1966; Guggenheim Fellow 1979–80; Convenor, Plant Biol. Subj. Div., Acad. of Sci., Roy. Soc. of Can. 1984–85; Hon. Secy., Acad. of Sci., R.S.C. 1985–91; Assoc. Dean of Science for Graduate Affairs 1985–93; author: 'Fungi, Algae and Bryophytes' 1978; 'The Fifth Kingdom' 1985 (2nd rev. ed. 1991); 'A Young Person's Guide to the Fungi' 1986; co-author: 'Genera of Hyphomycetes' 1980; 'A Survey of Plants' 1981; 'An Evolutionary Survey of Fungi, Algae and Plants' 1992; editor: 'Taxonomy of Fungi Imperfecti' 1971; 'The Whole Fungus' 2 vols. 1979; 'Biology of Conidial Fungi' 2 vols. 1981; mem. Candn. Bot. Assn.; Mycological Soc. Am.; recreations: reading, writing and publishing (proprietor, Mycologue Publications), scuba, photography, family, travel, music; Home: 331 Daleview Pl., Waterloo, Ont. N2L 5M5; Office: Waterloo, Ont. N2L 3G1.

**KENDRICK, Mary;** artist; b. Woodslee, Ont. 3 May 1928; d. Russell John and Gertrude Agnes Mitchell; e. studied with Edwin Matthews & Mitch Keirstead, Buckhorn Sch. of Fine Art; m. James G. Kendrick 18 Sept. 1948; children: Linda, Danny, Brad; started painting 1965; paintings are in homes & galleries all over the world; uses unique palette knife style (canvases come alive with colour); teacher, Buckhorn Sch. of Fine Art 1989–94; exbns: Buckhorn Wildlife Festival, Cobourg Canada Day Festival, Art in the Park (Windsor); originals, prints, hasti-notes, & coffee mugs are displayed at Gallery on the Lake (also for sale), Burdette Gall. Orton, Ont., Anneka's Bay Galleries in Belleville & Kingston; Address: c/o The Gallery on the Lake, Box 10, Buckhorn, Ont. K0L 1J0.

**KENINS, Talivaldis,** B.Litt.; professor emeritus; b. Liepaja, Latvia 23 April 1919; s. Atis and Anna (Rumanis) K.; e. Acad. de Grenoble France B.Litt.; State Conservatory of Latvia with Joseph Wihtol 1940–44; Conserv. Nat. Sup. de Musique de Paris with Simone Plé-Caussade, Tony-Aubin & Olivier Messiaen, Grand Prix Laureate 1945–50; UNESCO Fellowship Award in Music (Paris) 1950; m. Valda d. Karlis and Alma Dreimanis 2 Dec. 1950; children: George, Andrew; PROFESSOR EMERITUS, FACULTY OF MUSIC, UNIV. OF TORONTO 1984– ; Music Dir., Latvian St. Andrews Ch. (Toronto) 1951; Lectr., Asst. Prof., Assoc. Prof. & Full Prof., Fac. of Music, Univ. of Toronto 1952–84; Candn. citizen since 1956; composer of 8 symphonies, 12 concertos, major chamber music & choral works, performed internationally; Publishers: Boosey and Hawkes (England and Canada); Société d'Editions Musicales Internationales, Paris, France; Leeds Music (Canada) Ltd.; Berandol Music Ltd.; The Frederick Harris Music Co. Ltd.; Gordon V. Thompson Ltd.; Jaymar Music Ltd.; Waterloo Music Co. Ltd., Canada; Dir., Candn. League of Composers 1958–76 (Pres. 1973, '74); Lectr., Schola Cantorum Toronto 1958–66; Commentator, Radio-Canada music programs; Guest Lectr. on contemp. music topics & Canadiana worldwide; Festival Adjudicator & Jury Mem., Conservatoires of Paris & Que.; Composer-in-Res., Kalamazoo College; Guest Composer, Darmstadt Festival of New Music Germany; Hon. Prof., Music Acad. of Latvia; Champollion Silver Medal, Grenoble, France; Prix Perilhou; Prix Halphen; Prix Gouy d'Arcy music prizes France; Grand Prix Music Award; Am.-Latvian Cong.; Sr. Music Awards, Canada Council; honoured with 'Kenins Crescent' in Kanata, Ont.; Mem., Candn. League of Composers, Society of Composers, Authors and Music Publishers of Canada (SOCAN); Société des Auteurs et Compositeurs Dramatiques, Paris, France; Internat. Soc. for Contemp. Music; Assoc. Mem., Candn. Music Centre; compositions published & recorded worldwide; listed in several biographical reference books incl.: 'Encyclopedia of Music in Canada' or the 'CMC Directory'; recreations: international railway history, systems & schedules, extensive travelling, old & contemporary sacred monuments, cathedrals & churches of the world, internat. tennis; Home: 73 Parkview Ave., Willowdale, Ont. M2N 3Y3.

**KENNEDY, Alan,** B.A., M.A., Ph.D.; university professor; b. Vancouver, B.C. 23 March 1942; s. Albert Edgar and Effie Grace (Nahirney) K.; e. Univ. of B.C., B.A. 1964, M.A. 1966; Univ. of Edinburgh, Ph.D. 1973; m. Oopalee Operajita; d. B. and P.N. Das; 1 child: Ayus Aditya; PROF. OF ENGLISH AND HEAD OF DEPT. OF ENGLISH, CARNEGIE MELLON UNIV., Pittsburg, PA; joined Dalhousie Univ. 1974; Prof. of Eng. 1982; Chrmn., Dept. of English 1986–89; Ed., The Dalhousie Review 1980–86; Dir., Shastri Indo-Candn. Inst. 1987– ; Hon. Fellow, Pearson Inst. for Internat. Devel.; mem. Modern Lang. Assn.; Candn. Assn. for Commonwealth Lang. & Literary Studies; author: 'The Protean Self: Dramatic Action in Contemporary Fiction' 1974; 'Meaning and Signs in Fiction' 1981; 'Reading as Resistance and Value' 1988; recreation: hunting; Home: 5418 Beacon St., Pittsburgh, PA; Office: Dept. of English, Carnegie Mellon Univ., Pittsburg, PA 15213.

**KENNEDY, Arlene Marie,** B.A.(Hons.), Dip.Ed., M.A.; museum director; b. Toronto, Ont. 6 May 1948; d. Vernon Drew and Eilleen Mary Rose (Latham) K.; e. Univ. of Western Ont. B.A. (Hons.) 1971; Memorial Univ. Dip.Ed. 1972; N.S. Coll. of Art & Design M.A. 1978; DIRECTOR, MCINTOSH GALLERY, UNIV. OF WESTERN ONTARIO 1989– ; Art Educator 1971–79; Exhbn. Co-ord., McIntosh Gallery 1979–82; Dir., Oakville Galleries 1982–89; Pres., Ont. Assn. of Art Galleries 1986–87 (Bd. Mem. 1984–88); Pres., Profl. Managerial Assn., Univ. of W. Ont. 1993– ; University Community Centre Gov. Council 1993; Mem., Candn. Art Museum Directors Assn.; author of articles, catalogues and reports; recreations: growing orchids and bonsai, swimming; Office: London, Ont. N6A 3K7.

**KENNEDY, Betty (Mrs. G. Allan Burton),** O.C. (1982), LL.D.; b. Ottawa, Ont. 4 Jan. 1926; d. late Walter Herbert and Janet Kincaid (McPhee) Styran; e. Lisgar Coll. Inst.; LL.D. (Hon.), York Univ. 1982; LL.D., Univ. of Western Ont. 1987; D.Hum.Litt., Mount Saint Vincent Univ. 1989; m. 1stly Gerhard William Thomas Kennedy (d. 1975); children: Mark, Shawn, D'Arcy, Tracy; m. 2ndly G. Allan Burton 1976; Broadcast Journalist and Pub. Affairs Ed. Radio Stn. CFRB 1959–1986; retired from daily public affairs show but continues in special broadcast capacity; Panelist CBC-TV 'Front Page Challenge' since 1962; Extve. Producer and Host of two 20 episode series 'Insight' for TV Ontario 1971–72; Dir. Simpsons Ltd. 1974–79; Bank of Montreal since 1975; Akzona Inc. 1976–82; Ex-Cal Resources Ltd. 1982–92; Northern Telecom Ltd. 1987; mem. Metrop. Toronto Hosp. Planning Council 1965–70; Gov. Council Univ. of Toronto and mem. various comtes. incl. Extve. Comte. and Chrmn. External Affairs Comte. 1972–77; first non med. mem. Coll. Phys. & Surgs. Ont. Complaints Comte. 1970–75; Adv. Comte. on Communications, Comte. on Govt. Planning Ont., Adv. Comte. Special Study regarding med. prof. in Ont. comnd. by Ont. Med. Assn. (Pickering Report 1972–73), mem. Citizens Adv. Comte. of Assn. 1973–76; served on Special Program Review Comte. to recommend efficiencies in Prov. spendings 1975; first woman Chrmn. Nat. Brotherhood Week, Candn. Council Christians & Jews 1975; mem. of Bd., Toronto Western Hospital 1976–85; mem. Selection Comte. for Outstanding Achievement Award in Pub. Service of Can. 1972 (Chrmn. 1973); mem. Adv. Comtes. for Ont. Educ. Communications Authority, Ryerson Polytech. Inst. (Radio, TV Arts), Univ. of W. Ont. (Sch. of Journalism); mem. Conference Council, Gov. Gen.'s Candn. Study Conf. 1983; mem. Adv. Comte. on Financial Institutions for Min. of State for Finance 1984; Hon. Nat. Chrmn., Canadian Cancer Society 1983–84; Bd. mem., Conference Bd. of Canada

1985–88; Mem., Coll. of Physicians & Surgeons of Ontario's Task Force on the Relationship between Physicians and the Pharmaceutical Industry 1990; Mem., Princess Margaret Hospital Council 1990; author 'Gerhard' 1976; 'Hurricane Hazel' 1979; Officer, Order of Canada 1982; el. to News Hall of Fame 1983; inducted into the Broadcasting Hall of Fame 1991; Address: 68 Old Mill Rd., Toronto, Ont. M8X 1G8.

**KENNEDY, Desmond Francis,** B.A.; writer; b. Liverpool, Eng. 6 Sept. 1945; s. Thomas and Eileen Mary (Shevlin) K.; e. Passionist Monastic Sem. B.A. 1968; m. Sandra d. William and Gladys Lesyk 22 Oct. 1970; High School Teacher, Vancouver 1968–69; Social Worker 1969–71; Native Land Claims Cons., Nazko & Kluskus Indian Bands 1974–76; writer and performer (incl. freelance writing for mags. & newspapers in US & Can.; speaker & humorist; TV & radio broadcast journalism) 1976– ; environmental activist living a self-sufficient, conservative lifestyle incl. land stewardship; arrested for civil disobedience at Clayoquot Sound 1993; Commemorative Medal, 125th Anniversary of Confed. of Canada 1992; Nat. Journalism Awards 1990; Dir., Denman Conservancy Assn. 1991–94; Pres., Denman Is. Ratepayers & Residents Assn. 1990–91; Vice-Pres., Friends of Strathcona Park 1988–89; author: 'Living Things We Love to Hate' 1992, 'Crazy About Gardening' 1994; recreations: camping, hiking, nature study, gardening; Home: Box 3, Pickles Rd., Denman Island, B.C. V0R 1T0.

**KENNEDY, James Cecil,** B.A., M.D., Ph.D.; educator; physician; scientist; b. Toronto, Ont. 14 March 1935; s. Cecil Hobson and Jessie Nicol (Donaldson) K.; e. Weston (Ont.) Coll. Inst. 1953; Univ. of Toronto, B.A. 1957, M.D. 1961, Ph.D. 1966; m. Ruth d. Felix and Euphemia Hermosa 23 July 1966; children: David, Andrew, Marta, Peter, Sara, Samuel, Joseph; PROF. OF ONCOLOGY, QUEEN'S UNIV. 1991– ; Assoc. Prof. of Pathol. 1974– ; Adjunct Prof., Dept. of Chem. & Chem. Engr., Royal Military Coll. of Can. 1991– ; Career Sci. Ont. Cancer Treatment & Rsch. Found. 1983– ; mem. Attending Staff in Oncology, Kingston Gen. Hosp. 1977– ; Cons. in Med. Trenton Meml. Hosp. 1983– ; Cons. in Med., Ongwanada Hosp. 1990– ; Asst. Prof. of Pathol. present Univ. 1969–74; Assoc. Prof. of Oncology 1977–91; Adjunct-Assoc. Prof., Dept. of Chem. & Chem. Engr., Royal Military Coll. of Can. 1989–91; Rsch. Scholar, Nat. Cancer Inst. Can. 1969–72, Rsch. Assoc. 1972–77; Rsch. Assoc. present Found. 1977–83; mem. Attending Staff in Pathol. present Hosp. 1969–77; mem. Am. Soc. Photobiol.; European Soc. Photobiol.; recreations: canoeing, wilderness travel; Home: 299 Glen Cairn Terr., Kingston, Ont. K7M 4A6; Office: Ontario Regional Cancer Centre, 25 King St. W., Kingston, Ont. K7L 5P9.

**KENNEDY, James Macoun,** B.A., M.A., Ph.D.; retired; b. Ottawa, Ont. 25 Apr. 1928; s. Howard and Mary (Macoun) K.; e. Univ. of Toronto B.A. 1949, M.A. 1950; Princeton Univ. Ph.D. 1953; m. Norah Hilda d. Harold Arthur Leake 9 Sept. 1950; Professor, Dept. of Computer Science, Univ. of B.C. 1968–93, Retired; Vice-Pres., Univ. Services 1980–84; Research Offr., Atomic Energy of Can. Ltd. 1952; joined Univ. of B.C. 1966 as Dir. of Computing Ctr., Acting Head of Dept. 1968–69 and 1973–74); author of many articles and addresses on technical & social aspects of computers; Bd. Mem., Vancouver Community Coll. 1976–80 (Chrmn. 1976–78); mem. Candn. Information Processing Soc. (Pres. 1971–72; Hon. Mem. 1987); Candn. Assn. of Physicists; Candn Mathematics Assn.; Can. Applied Math. Assn.; Anglican; Club: U.B.C. Faculty; recreation: music; Home: 1891 Acadia Rd., Vancouver, B.C. V6T 1R2.

**KENNEDY, Hon. James T.,** B.A., B.C.L.; judge; b. Montréal, Qué. 29 Apr. 1929; s. Frederick William and Elizabeth (McKay) K.; e. St. Francis Xavier Univ. B.A. 1951; McGill Univ. B.C.L. 1955; m.(1) Louyse Drouin (dec.) 19 Sept. 1961; children: Andrew, Suzanne; m.(2) Karlene Miller Curran 21 May 1983; children: William, Kevin, Sean; JUDGE, SUPERIOR COURT OF QUE. 1983– ; law practice with W.J. McQuillan and George V. Broderick; c.r. Q.C. 1976; Past Pres. St. Patrick's Soc. Montréal; Trustee, Montréal St. Patrick's Foundation; Dir. St. Patrick's Devel. Found.; Sacred Heart Sch. Montréal; Father Dowd Found.; St. Mary's Hosp. Found.; mem. Candn. Bar Assn.; Club: Royal Montréal Golf; Home: 20247 Lakeshore Rd., Baie d'Urfé, Qué. H9X 1P9; Office: 12.30 Palais de Justice, 1 est, Notre Dame, Montréal, Qué. H2Y 1B6.

**KENNEDY, John R. (Ted);** distribution executive; b. Toronto, Ont. 1 Aug. 1933; s. John James and Elaine (Hodgetts) K.; e. Univ. of Toronto, P.&H.E. 1953–54; m. Marie d. Dr. Galbraith Williams; children: Terry, Steve, Keith, Rick; PRES., EMCO DISTRIBUTION GROUP 1990– ; Vice-Pres. & Gen. Mgr., Price Wilson 1954–71; Vice-Pres. Mktg., Rubbermaid Can. Inc. 1971–78; Vice-Pres. & Gen. Mgr., Lee Canada Inc. 1978–81; Vice-Pres., Can. Corp. Mgmt. Co. Ltd. 1981–86; Pres. & Chief Extve. Offr., Federal Indus. Consumer Group Inc. 1986–89; Dir., Canada Starch Co. Inc.; Cardinal Meat Specialists; Walters Consulting Group; Westroc Indus. Limited; The Business Depot Ltd.; Pres., Candn. Hardware & Housewares Assn. 1976; Dir., Junior Achievement Canada; recreations: fishing, hunting, squash; clubs: Ontario, Board of Trade, Mississaugua Golf & Country, Caledon Ski, Nut Island Shooting; The Caledon Mountain Trout; Home: 1138 Tecumseh Park Dr., Mississauga, Ont. L5H 2W1; Office: 2000 Argentia Rd., Plaza Three, Ste. 102, Mississauga, Ont. L5N 1V9.

**KENNEDY, Joseph Frederick;** trade union executive, retired; b. London, Ont. 29 Sept. 1926; s. George Cornelius and Agnes (Ida) McFarland K.; e. Beaver Creek P.S.; George Harvey S.S.; courses at York Univ., Univ. of Toronto; children: George Richard, Robert Wayne; Business Mgr., Internat. Union of Operating Engrs. 1974–92; Mem., Internat. Union of Operating Engrs., 42 yrs.; Pres., 2 terms; Treasurer, 23 yrs.; Trustee, Local 793 Benefit Plan; Past Chrmn., Candn. Bd., Internat. Found. of Employee Benefit Plans; Mem., Constr. Indus. Adv. Bd., Prov. of Ont.; Vice Pres., Prov. Bldg. Trades Counc. of Ont.; part-time mem., Ont. Labour Relns. Bd. 1983– ; Dir., Constr. Safety Assn. of Ont.; Roy A. Phinnemore Award 1976; Candn. Infantry Corps. 1944–45; Club: Royal Cdn. Legion, Br. 57, Silverthorn; Masonic Lodge No. 22; Home: 60 Sylvan Valleyway, Toronto, Ont. M5M 4M3.

**KENNEDY, Richard J.,** M.D., F.R.C.P.(C), F.C.C.P.; physician; university professor; b. Montréal, Qué. 21 May 1936; s. John Martin and Bertha (Hamelin) K.; e. Cardinal Newman H.S. 1953; McGill Univ., B.Sc. 1958; Queen's Univ., M.D. 1963; m. Helen Ann d. Helena and Joseph Karpowicz 20 May 1963; children: Stephen Richard, Cheryl Ann, Laura Lynn, Deborah Aileen; Active staff, Montreal Chest Hosp. 1969–77; St. Mary's Hosp. 1971–77; Calgary Gen. Hosp. 1977– (Dir., Respiratory Diseases Div. 1979–84); Peter Lougheed Hosp. 1988– ; Assoc. Staff, Montreal Gen. Hosp. 1969–77; Lectr., Med., McGill Univ. 1972–77 Clin. Asst. Prof., Med., Univ. of Calgary 1979– ; Cons. (pulmonary diseases & allergies), Alta. Children's 1978–87, Col. Belcher, Holy Cross, Rockyview Hosps. 1978– ; Mem., Acute Care Funding Steering Ctte., Dept. of Health, Alta. 1989–92; Mem., CMA Political Action Ctte. 1989–92; Chrmn., AMA Convention Ctte. 1987–89; Mem., AMA Govt. Affairs Ctte. 1989– ; Chrmn., AMA Ad Hoc Ctte., 'Future of Health Care' 1988; Bd. Mem., Alta. Med. Assn. 1982–89; Pres. 1986–87; Pres. Elect, Candn. Med. Assn. 1992 (Bd. Mem. 1987–89); Mem., Min. Adv. Liaison Ctte., Alta. Hosp. & Med. Care 1987–89; FRCP(C) 1972; FCCP 1978; Assoc. Fellow, Am. Coll. of Allergy & Immunology 1982; Bd. Mem., Spirit of Rockies Color Guard 1979; Pro Musica Calgary 1985–89; Calgary Minor Soccer Assn. 1983–85; S.W. Chinooks Soccer Assn. (& Vice-Pres.) 1985–88; Mem., Alta. Assn. of Internists 1977– (Chrmn., Fees Comm. 1990–92); Alta. Thoracic Soc. 1977– ; Mem., AMA Ad Hoc Ctte., 'Ambulatory Care' 1992; Pres., Mission Lung Function Laboratory 1990– ; recreations: skiing, model railroading, jazz; Clubs: Calgary Flying; Glencoe; Calgary Med. Curling; Home: 1316 – 70th Ave. S.W., Calgary, Alta. T2V 0R3; Office: 900 – 2303 4th St. S.W., Calgary, Alta. T2S 2S7.

**KENNEDY, Russell Jordan,** M.C., M.S., D.Sc.; educator; b. Dunrobin, Ont. 23 Nov. 1917; s. James Abbott and Mabel Lois (Sweeney) K.; e. Carp (Ont.) Cont. Sch.; Nepean (Ont.) High. Sch.; Queen's Univ. B.Sc. (Civil Engn. Medal) 1941; Iowa State Univ. M.S. (Hydraulics) 1949; Queen's Univ. D.Sc. (Hon.) 1993; m. 1stly Shirley C. Workman (d. 1966); m. 2ndly Marjorie M. d. Frederick W. and Gertrude Rice 12 Oct. 1968; children: Ian Charles, Robert James, Nancy Patricia, Barbara Jean; EMERITUS PROF. OF CIVIL ENGN., QUEEN'S UNIV. 1984– ; joined present Univ. 1946, Prof. 1959, Assoc. Dean of Grad. Studies & Rsch. 1968–69, Vice. Princ. Admin. 1970–76; served with RCE 1941–46; recipient Angus Medal Engn. Inst. Can. 1958; Queen's Univ. Council Distinguished Service Award 1978; United Church; recreations: skiing, building log house on tree farm; Home: 2 Grenville Rd., Kingston, Ont. K7M 2C5; Office: Queen's Univ., Kingston, Ont. K7L 3N6.

**KENNEDY, Thomas Charles,** B.A.A.; journalist; b. St. John's, Nfld. 12 April 1952; s. Bernard Joseph and Margaret Jean (Bickerton) K.; e. Brother Rice H.S. 1969; Portobello College (Edinburgh) 1969–70; Memorial Univ. of Nfld. (Chem.) 1970–73; Ryerson Polytechnical Inst. B.A.A. (Journalism) 1976; m. Sylvie d. Gerard and Fleur-Ange Goulet 1 Nov. 1980; children: Mathieu, Julie; JOURNALIST, CBC-TV, QUEBEC CITY (coverage of evolving political situation) 1991– ; part-time, 'Globe & Mail' 1975–76; Reporter, Montreal, CBC-TV 1976–80; Quebec City (coverage of R. Levesque's govt.) 1980–83; Network Reporter, covering Prov. of Que. 1983–86; Asia Correspondent 1986–89 (rec. Gemini Award for coverage of Tienanmen massacre); also worked for Radio Canada (Asia) 1986–89; Toronto 1989–90; Occasional Performer for St. John's Symphony Orch., Edinburgh Symph., Savoy Opera Co. (Edinburgh) 1968–73; Mem., Bd. of Dir., St. John's Symph. 1971–72; recreations: chess, golf; club: Scarborough Chess; Office: 1055 rue Conroy, Quebec, Que. G1R 5J4.

**KENNEDY, Thomas Mann;** insurance underwriter; b. Glasgow, Scotland 12 Aug. 1945; s. David and Catherine McGee (Mann) K.; e. St. Aloysius Coll., Langside Coll.; m. Susan G. d. George and Olive Heron 28 Aug. 1971; children: Michelle Suzette, Theresa Denise, Richard Thomas, Joanne Evelyn; SENIOR UNDERWRITER, COMMERCIAL PROPERTY & BOILER AND MACHINERY UNDERWRITER, ZURICH CANADA 1973– ; Commercial Underwriter, Commercial Union Insur. 1964–67; Comm. Property Underwriter, Royal Insur. 1967–70; Property & Liability Underwriter, Central Mutual Insur. 1970–73; Mem., Candn. Boiler & Machinery Underwriters Assn.; Property Casualty Underwriters Club; Mariners Club; Grad., Christopher Leadership Course, Lumen Inst.; Am. Mutual Assn. Mngt. Course; Coach, Ajax Spartan Minor Baseball Assn.; Oshawa Minor Soccer; Treas., Legion of Mary; recreations: fishing, baseball, reading; Home: 889 Finley Ave., Ajax, Ont.; Office: 375 University Ave., Toronto, Ont. M5G 2S7.

**KENNETT, William A.,** B.A., M.Sc.; retired Canadian public servant; b. Toronto, Ont. 4 Sept. 1932; s. late Horace and Lena (Thorburn) K.; e. Univ. of Toronto, B.A. 1955; London Sch. of Econ. M.Sc. 1957; m. Valerie Cosby d. late Frank S. Spence Jan. 1958; children: Steven, Brenda; Consultant; Inspr. Gen. of Banks 1977–86; Harshman Fellowships Soc.; Rideau Valley Field Naturalists; Ottawa YM/YWCA; Chancellor's Council, Victoria Univ.; Madawaska Highlands Adv. Ctte.; Home & Office: RR #3, Maberly, Ont. K0H 2B0.

**KENNEY, John Herbert,** B.A., LL.B.; association executive; b. Vancouver, B.C. 19 May 1935; s. H. Martin K.; e. Appleby Coll. 1954; Trinity Coll. Univ. of Toronto B.A. 1957; Osgoode Hall Law Sch. LL.B. 1960; called to Bar of Ont. 1962; PRES. & CHIEF EXTVE. OFFR., THE ONTARIO JOCKEY CLUB 1987– ; articled Fraser & Beatty; practiced law Fraser & Beatty 1962–64; joined Ont. Jockey Club 1964; Pres. 1975; Dir., Thoroughbred Racing Assn. of Am.; Harness Tracks of America; Race Tracks Can.; el. to Candn. Horse Racing Hall of Fame 1990; Bd. of Gov., Appleby Coll.; Dir., St. Michael's Hosp. Found.; Kappa Alpha Soc.; club: Toronto; Office: 555 Rexdale Blvd., P.O. Box 156, Rexdale, Ont. M9W 5L2.

**KENNIFF, Patrick,** B.Sc., B.A., LL.L., Ph.D.; university administrator; b. St. Paul, Minn. 15 June 1943; s. Thomas Joseph and Georgina (Guilbault) K.; e. Loyola Coll. Montréal B.Sc. 1964, B.A. 1965; Univ. Laval LL.L. 1969; Univ. of London Ph.D. (Laws) 1973; RECTOR AND VICE CHANCELLOR, CONCORDIA UNIV. 1984– ; Assoc. Prof. of Law Univ. Laval 1973–78; Asst. Dep. Min. of Municipal Affairs, Québec 1978–79, Dep. Min. 1979–84; Pres. World Univ. Service Can., Ottawa 1985–89; Dir. Les Grands Ballets Canadiens, Montréal 1985–89; Dir., Chambre de Commerce de Montréal 1985–89; Dir., Montréal Stock Exchange 1988–92; Pres., 'Celebrations du 350e anniversaire de Montréal,' 1988–93; Pres., CREPUQ, Conf des recteurs et principaux des univs. du Qué. 1989–91; author 'Quebec Municipal Commission' 1978; co-author 'Government Control of Administrative Tribunals' 1978; mem. Govt. Comn. Waste Water Treatment Montréal 1984–87; Pres. Candn. Assn. Law Teachers 1976–77; mem. Québec Bar; Candn. Bar Assn.; Candn. Inst. Pub. Adm.; R. Catholic; recreations: reading, tennis, squash, skiing, sailing; Clubs: M.A.A.A.; University; Office: 1455 de Maisonneuve Blvd. W., Montréal, Qué. H3G 1M8.

**KENNING, Brian G.,** B.A., M.B.A.; financial executive; b. 1949; e. Univ. of Victoria, B.A. 1971; Queen's Univ., M.B.A. 1973; CHRMN. & MNG. PARTNER, B.C. PACIFIC CAPITAL CORP. 1988– ; Project Mgr., Marathon Realty 1973; Br. Mgr., Coronation Credit Corp. Ltd. 1975; Vice-Pres. 1976; Mgr., Corp. Planning, Versatile Corp. 1980; Asst. Vice-Pres., Corp. Planning 1984; Pres. & Mng. Partner, B.C. Pacific Capital Corp.

1987–90; Pres. & Dir., BRL Enterprises Inc.; Varitech Investors Corp.; Dir., F.T. Capital; Westfield Minerals Ltd.; Candn. Northstar Corp.; Chrmn. Bd. of Gov., Brentwood Coll. Sch.; Trustee, Vancouver Museum; recreations: skiing, tennis; Home: 3865 West 36th Ave., Vancouver, B.C. V6N 2S5; Office: Ste. 1632 – 1055 W. Georgia St., P.O. Box 11179, Royal Centre, Vancouver, B.C. V6E 3R5.

**KENNY, David Joseph,** B.Sc., D.D.S., Ph.D.; paediatric dentist; b. Stratford, Ont. 25 Feb. 1942; s. H. James and Anne M. (Chapman) K.; e. Univ. of Waterloo B.Sc. 1966; Univ. of W. Ont. D.D.S. (cum laude) 1970; Univ. of Toronto Dip. Paedodontics 1973, Ph.D. 1976; m. Judith d. Frederick J. and Molly O. Beale Sept. 1965; two d. Sarah Ruth, Megan Jane; DENTIST-IN-CHIEF, HOSP. FOR SICK CHILDREN 1981– ; Prof. of Dentistry Univ. of Toronto; Cons. Depts. of Dentistry & of Rsch. The Hugh MacMillan Rehab. Centre Toronto; joined staff present hosp. 1973; estbd. private practice Toronto 1976; estbd. Div. of Dentistry Children's Hosp. of E. Ont. Ottawa 1977; former teaching appts. Faculties of Med. Univ. of W. Ont. and Univ. of Ottawa; recipient Ont. Min. of Health Fellowships 1971–72; Med. Rsch. Council Fellowships 1973–74; Candn. Dental Rsch. Found. Award 1974; Ed. 'Ontario Dentist' 1981–87; Fellow, Acad. Dentistry for Handicapped; Am. Acad. Cerebral Palsy & Developmental Med.; recreations: sailing, antique cameras; Club: RCYC; Home: 53 Lascelles Blvd., Toronto, Ont. M5P 2C9; Office: 555 University Ave., Toronto, Ont. M5G 1X8.

**KENNY, Douglas T.,** B.A., M.A., Ph.D., LL.D.; professor and educator; b. Victoria, B.C. 1923; s. late John Ernest and late Margaret (Collins) J.; e. Victoria Coll., Victoria, B.C.; Univ. of B.C. B.A. 1945, M.A. 1947, Univ. of Wash. Ph.D. 1952; LL.D. (hon. causa) Univ. of B.C. 1983; m. Margaret Lindsay, d. late William Howieson; children: John Douglas, Kathleen Margaret; PRESIDENT EMERITUS AND PROF. OF PSYCHOL., UNIV. OF BRITISH COLUMBIA 1989; faculty mem. of present Univ. 1950–89; Head of Dept. of Psychol. 1965–69; Acting Dean, Faculty of Arts 1969–70; Dean, Fac. of Arts 1970–75, Pres. & Vice Chancellor of Univ. of B.C. 1975–83; has taught psychol. Univ. of Wash. 1947–50, Wash. State Univ. 1953 and Harvard Univ. 1963–65; Past Pres. Brit. Col. Psychol. Assn. 1951–52; Past Pres. Faculty Assn. Univ. of Brit. Col. 1961–62; Past Pres. Vancouver Inst. 1973–74 (Past Hon. Pres. 1975–83); Past Honorary Pres. Alumni Assn., U.B.C. 1975–83; mem. Bd. Trustees: Vancouver Gen. Hosp. 1976–78; Can. Council 1975–1978; Soc. Sciences & Humanities Research Council 1978–83; Monterey Inst. of Internat. Studies, Monterey Calif. 1980–83; The Discovery Found. (B.C.) 1979–83; Founding mem., Bd. of Gov., Arts, Sciences & Technology Centre, Vancouver (1980); Past mem.: Commonwealth Assn. of Universities; Internat. Assn. of Univ. Pres.; Hon. Patron, The Internat. Found. of Learning since 1983; mem. Amer. Psychol. Assn. 1950– ; mem., Amer. Psychol. Soc. 1990– ; author numerous articles and chapters on psychol. and educ. in Candn., US and Japanese learned journs. and books; Recipient Queen's Silver Jubilee Medal 1977; Park O. Davidson Memorial Award for Outstanding Contribution to the Development of Psychology 1984; Speaker, The Pacific Circle Consortium, Hiroshima, Japan 1982; Special Guest Speaker, 10th Anniversary of the Univ. of Tsukuba, Japan 1983; new psychol. building at Univ. of B.C. named 'The Douglas T. Kenny Bldg.' 1984; recreations: collecting Chinese and Japanese art, painting; Clubs: Vancouver; Fac. Club, Univ. of B.C.; Vancouver; Home: 4180 Crown Cres., Vancouver, B.C. V6R 2A9.

**KENNY, Hon. James Colin Ramsey,** B.Sc.; senator; petroleum executive; b. Montreal, Que. 10 Dec. 1943; s. Robert Allen and Evelyn Constance Salmon (Carroll) K.; e. Bishop's Coll. Sch. Lennoxville, Que.; Norwich Univ., Northfield, Vermont B.Sc. 1966; Amos Tuck Sch. of Bus. Admin., Dartmouth Coll. Hanover, New Hampshire (Publ. Service Fellowship 1967); m. Petra d. Patricia and Harold Horne 26 July 1969; children: Robert Allen, Thomas Frederick, James Armstrong; SENATOR 1984– ; mem. Standing Senate Ctte. on Internal Economy, Budgets & Admin., Standing Senate Ctte. on Energy & Natural Resources; Mem. Special Ctte. of the Senate on Terrorism & Public Safety; various positions on staff of Prime Min. of Can. 1970–79; Petroleum Executive; Extve., Dome Petroleum 1980–84; Exec. Dir. Liberal Party of Ont. 1968; mem. Canada-Europe Parlty. Group; Can.-U.S. Inter-Parlty. Group; Candn. Br. Commonwealth Parlty. Group; Candn. Br. Commonwealth Parlty. Assn.; Candn. NATO Parlty. Assn.; Candn. Group, Inter-Parlty. Union; Anglican; Liberal; Gov. of Ashbury Coll., Ottawa; Clubs: Ranchmen's (Calgary); Rideau (Ottawa); Office: Senate of Canada, Ottawa, Ont. K1A 0A4.

**KENT, Donald Martin,** B.Sc., M.Sc., Ph.D., P.Eng.; university professor; b. Medicine Hat, Alberta 25 Jan. 1933; s. George Wyman and Alice Marie (Choiniere) K.; e. Campion College; Univ. of Saskatchewan B.Sc. 1957, M.Sc. 1959; Univ. of Alberta Ph.D. 1968; 1st. m. Alvina Dolores d. Roy and Katherine Deverou 8 March 1962; deceased 1984; childen: Mark J., Christopher D., Paul E., Teresa M., Carmel J.; 2nd m.: Joyce Margurite d. Edward and Teresa Barton 10 Oct. 1987; stepchildren: Crystal T., Terri E., Douglas J. (Abrahamson); PROFESSOR, DEPT. OF GEOLOGY, UNIV. OF REGINA 1991– ; Jr. Rsch. Geologist, Sask. Dept. of Mineral Resources 1958–60; Sr. Rsch. Geologist 1960–71; Sessional Lectr., Univ. of Regina 1968–70; Assoc. Prof. 1971–77; Prof. 1977– ; Head, Dept. of Geology 1982–88, 1991– ; Pres., D.M. Kent Consulting 1981– ; Dir., Colray Resources 1983–89; Pan-American Petroleum Corp. Research Fellowship 1960–61; Mem., Assn. of Profl. Engrs. of Sask.; Am. Assn. Petrol. Geol.; Candn. Soc. Petrol. Geol.; Internat. Assn. of Sedimentologists; Soc. for Sedimentary Geol.; Sask. Geol. Soc. (Prs. 1965, '70, '75); Holy Cross Ch. Pastoral Council; co-editor & contbr.: 'Anatomy of a Cratonic Oil Province' 1987; Assoc. Ed. & contbr.: 'Geological Atlas of the Western Canada Sedimentary Basin' forthcoming; contbr.: 'Occurrence and Petrophysical Properties of Carbonate Reservoirs in the Rocky Mountain Region' 1988; author of more than 30 tech. papers; recreations: training & evaluation of football officials, 27 years of onfield officiating, incl. 2 yrs. in CFL; clubs: Football Sask. (Dir. 1980–91); Sask. Amateur Football Official Assn. (Pres. 1975– ); Candn. Football Official Assn.; Home: 86 Metcalfe Rd., Regina, Sask. S4V 0H8; Office: Regina, Sask. S4S 0A2.

**KENT, Hon. Mr. Justice James C.,** B.A., LL.B., LL.M.; judge; b. Peterborough, Ont. 22 July 1941; s. Fred Barton and Lacuta Crystelle (Munday) K.; e. Waterloo Lutheran Univ. B.A. 1963; Univ. of W. Ont. LL.B. 1967 (Dean's Honour List, Ivan C. Rand Honour Award); Osgoode Hall, York Univ. LL.M. 1986; m. Carol Johnston d. Burton and Jeanna J. 23 July 1966; children: Alyson Elizabeth, Johnston James; JUDGE, ONTARIO COURT OF JUSTICE (GENERAL DIV.) 1982– ; Partner, Waterous, Holden, Kellock & Kent and Waterous, Holden Kent & Amey 1969–82; Ald. City of Brantford 1973–74; Chrmn. Boston-Brantford Classic Run 1983–86; Dir. Brantford Regional C. of C. 1980–82; Pres. and Dir. St. Leonard's Soc. 1968–82; author 'When is a Director Not a Director' Vol. 6, Univ. of W. Ont. Law Review; United Church; recreations: running, skiing; Home: 335 Mount Pleasant Rd., Brantford, Ont. N3T 1V3; Office: Court House, 70 Wellington St., Brantford, Ont. N3T 2L9.

**KENT, Lionel Pelham,** F.C.A.; b. N. Vancouver, B.C. 13 Oct. 1914; s. Gerald Aldwyn and Ethel Mary (Felton) K.; e. Lynn Valley Pub. Sch. 1920–26; Churchers Coll., Hants., Eng. 1927–31 (grad. with Hons. Sr. Cambridge Sch. Cert.; London Matric.); m. Josephine Hope, d. late Henry Brealey (dec.) 2 March 1939; children: Judith Hope (Mrs. Robert J. Cowling), Michael Pelham, Brian Brealey (dec.), Lionel Richard, David Pelham, Patrick Henry; Dir., Alcan Aluminum Ltd. 1979–88; Chrmn. Bd of Mgmt., McLintock Main Lafrentz & Co. 1977–79; Chrmn. Thorne Riddell Assocs. Ltd. 1974–77; articled Clerk with Riddell, Stead, Graham & Hutchison, Vancouver, 1931–38; C.A. 1938; Partner 1945, Partner i.c. Vancouver Office 1955; Extve. Partner Riddell Stead & Co. Montreal 1959–74 (Chrmn. Mang. Comte. 1963–67); Chrmn. Riddell Stead & Assocs. Ltd. 1973–74; Extve. Partner, Thorne Riddell & Co. 1974–77 Financial Advr. to Counsel for B.C. in series of freight rate cases 1946–50; Financial Advr. to Board of Transport Commissioners for Can. 1950–57; served in 2nd World War with R.C.A.F. 1940–45 (Dir. of Accts. & Finance, Overseas); discharged with rank of Group Capt.; mem., Inst. of Chart. Accts. of B.C. (mem. Council 1946–47), Que., Ont.; Gov., Crofton House School 1947–59 (Chrmn. 1957–59); St. George's School 1957–59 (Dir. 1958–59); Trinity College School (Dir. 1965; Life Gov. 1966); Trustee, Bishops Univ. 1980–89; mem., Air Force Offrs. Assn. (Dir. 1956–57); Candn. Chamber Comm. (Chrmn. Extve Council 1968–69; Nat. Dir.); Pacific Basin Economic Council (Chrmn. Candn. Comte. 1971–72); Can. Japan Business Co-op. Comte.; Anglican; recreations: shooting, fishing, golf, bridge, horses; Clubs: Vancouver; Capilano Golf & Country; Mount Royal; Mount Bruno Country; Forest & Stream; Toronto Golf; Home: R.R. #3, Ayer's Cliff, Que. J0B 1C0.

**KENT, Peter J.,** B.A., LL.B.; lawyer, corporate executive; b. Kisvarda, Hungary 16 July 1946; s. Paul and Judith (Roth) K.; e. Univ. of Toronto B.A. (Hons.) 1969, LL.B. 1972; Law Soc. of U.C., admitted to Bar 1974; divorced; children: Jonathan, Robyn; Vice-Pres., Gen. Counsel & Sec., TecSYN Internat. Inc. 1984; Partner, Laird, Laird & Kent 1974–76; Olch, Torgov, Cohen & Kent 1976–83; Dir., TecSyn Internat. Inc.; TecSyn Inc.; TecSyn (PMP) Inc.; Playfield Indus. Inc.; Connoisseur Prod. Inc.; Poli-Twine Southern Inc.; Polytech Netting Indus. Inc.; PNI, Inc.; Mem., Candn. Bar Assn.; Law Soc. of U.C.; Taddle Creek Soc.; Patron, Bora Laskin Library; recreations: travel, photography; Home: 1129 Windrush Dr., Oakville, Ont. L6M 1S9.

**KENT, Thomas Worrall,** O.C., M.A., LL.D.; writer; retired executive; b. Stafford, Eng., 3 Apr. 1922; s. John Thomas and Frances (Worrall) K.; e. Wolstanton (Eng.) Grammar Sch.; Corpus Christi Coll., Oxford, B.A. 1941 (1st Class Hons. in Modern Greats); Univ. of Oxford, M.A. 1950; Hon. LL.D., Dalhousie Univ. 1989; m. Phyllida Anne, d. M.R. Cross, Aston Tirrold, Eng., 3 June 1944; children: Duncan M.S., Oliver R.T., Andrew J.F.; ADJUNCT PROF. OF PUBLIC ADMIN., DALHOUSIE UNIV. 1983– ; VISITOR, SCHOOL OF POLICY STUDIES, QUEEN'S UNIV. 1992– ; engaged in intelligence service for U.K. War Office and Foreign Office, 1942–45; Edit. Writer for the 'Manchester Guardian,' 1946–50; Asst. Editor, 'London Economist,' 1950–54; Editor, 'Winnipeg Free Press,' 1954–59; Vice-Pres., Chemcell Ltd., Montreal, Que., 1959–61; Special Consultant to late Rt. Hon. Lester B. Pearson, P.C. 1961–63; def. cand. to H. of C. for Burnaby-Coquitlam in g.e. 1963; Co-ordinator of Programming & Policy Secy. to Prime Min., 1963–65; Dir. of Special Planning Secretariat, P. Council Office, 1965; Deputy Min., Dept. of Manpower and Immigration, 1966–68; Deputy Min., Dept. of Regional Econ. Expansion, 1968–71; Pres. & Chief Exec. Offcr., Cape Breton Devel. Corp., 1971–77; Pres. and C.E.O., Sydney Steel Corp., 1977–79; Dean, Fac. of Administrative Studies, Dalhousie Univ. 1980–83; Chrmn., Royal Comm. on Newspapers, 1980–81; Visiting Prof., Univ. of King's Coll. 1989; Hon. Fellow, Inst. for Research on Public Policy 1985–91; author of 'Social Policy for Canada' 1962; 'Management for Development' (with I. McAllister) 1985; 'A Public Purpose' 1988; 'Getting Ready for 1999: Ideas for Canada's Politics and Government' 1989; Editor, 'Policy Options' 1980–88; contrib. to various books and periodicals on pol. and econ. subjects; Invested as Officer of the Order of Canada, 1979; Home: Box 29, R.R. 1, Inverary, Ont. K0H 1X0.

**KENYON, Andrew G.,** B.Com., C.A.; banker; b. Vancouver, B.C. 6 Jan. 1947; s. Arthur G. and Ruth A. (Graham) K.; e. McGill Univ. B.Com. 1969; C.A. 1972; m. Joanne d. James and Thelma Stevenson Dec. 1981; children: Naomi F., Tyler S., SR. VICE PRES. TAXATION, CANADIAN IMPERIAL BANK OF COMMERCE 1986– ; Auditor, Ernst & Ernst, Montréal 1969–72; Auditor Taxation, Revenue Can. Ottawa 1972, seconded to Independent Ctte. Review Office of Auditor Gen. Can. 1974, Appeals Offr. 1975; joined present Bank 1975; Pres. Toronto Chapter (1986–87), Tax Execs. Inst.; Chrmn., Taxation Ctte. Candn. Bankers Assn. 1987–89; Vice-Pres., Region I, Tax Execs. Inst. 1991–92; Bd. Trade Metrop. Toronto; Office: Commerce Court, Toronto, Ont. M5L 1A2.

**KENYON, Peter A.;** retail executive; b. Senlac, Sask. 14 March 1950; e. John Taylor Collegiate 1967; Pennsylvania State Univ. Logistics Prog. for Extves. 1992; misc. courses; m. Mona McCoy Aug. 1972; children: Lisa, Steve; VICE-PRES., LOGISTICS & INVENTORY MNGT., KMART CANADA LIMITED 1991– ; joined S.S. Kresge Co. 1971; Operational Store Asst. 1971–72; Asst. Store Mgr. 1972–74; Kresge Store Mgr. 1974–76; Dist. Mgr. 1976–82; Store Mgr. 1982–84; Distbn. Mgr., Central Merch. System 1984–85; Dir. 1985–87; Sr. Dir., Inventory Mngt. 1987–91; recreations: ice hockey, racquet ball, camping; Office: 8925 Torbram Rd., Brampton, Ont. L6T 4G1.

**KEON, Wilbert Joseph,** M.D., M.Sc., F.R.C.S.(C), F.A.C.S.; surgeon; b. Sheenboro, Que. 17 May 1935; e. St. Paul's High Sch. Sheenboro, Que. and St. Patrick's Coll. High Sch. Ottawa; Univ. of Ottawa, St. Patrick's Coll. B.Sc. 1957, M.D. 1961; McGill Univ. M.Sc. (Exper. Surg.) 1963; children: Claudia, Ryan, Neil; Prof. & Chrmn. of Surgery, Univ. of Ottawa 1976–91, Chrmn. Div. Cardiothoracic Surg. 1974– , Dir. Heart Inst. 1969– ; Co-Chrmn., Med. Adv. Comte., Candn. Heart Foundation; Ottawa Civic Hospital, Chief, Div. of Cardiothoracic Surg. 1969– ; Surgical Traveler, James IV Assn. of Surgeons Inc. 1979; post-grad. training Ottawa Civic Hosp., Montreal Gen. Hosp., Toronto Gen. Hosp., Toronto Hosp. for Sick Children, Peter Bent Brigham Hosp. and Harvard Med. Centre 1961–

69; Dir. Ont. Heart Foundation; rec'd Peter Ballantine Ewing Gold Medal-Surgery; McLaughlin Fellowship; Ont. Heart Foundation Sr. Fellowship; Man of the Yr. Award, Ottawa Knockers Club; Univ. of Ottawa Staff Research Award 1975; Carleton Univ. Outstanding Alumnus Award 1977; B'Nai Brith Man of the Year Award 1984; Officer, Order of Canada 1985; Booster Award 86 Ottawa Visitors & Convention Bureau; Knight of the Order of St Gregory the Great 1987; CAMMD Medical Achievement Award 1987; Order of Ontario 1988; Apptd., Senate of Canada 1990; author or co-author numerous publs.; frequent speaker; Fellow, Am. Heart Assn. Council on Clin. Cardiol.; Am. Coll. Cardiol.; Affiliate, Royal Soc. Med.; mem. Ont. Med. Assn.; Candn. Med. Assn.; Acad. Med. Ottawa; Candn. Cardiovascular Soc. (1st Vice Pres. 1986–87; Pres. 1988–90); Candn. Heart Foundation (Past Chrmn. Scient. Sub-comte.; Chrmn. Medical Adv. Comte. 1980–83; Vice-Pres. Medical 1983–84); Med. Research Council (Grants Comte. for Heart & Lung); Vice Pres., Med. Rsch. Counc. 1988–90; Internat. Cardiovascular Soc.; Am. Assn. Thoracic Surg.; Soc. Thoracic Surgs.; Ont. Cancer Treatment & Research Foundation (Adv. Med. Bd.); Candn. Assn. Clin. Surgs.; Candn. Soc. Clin. Investigation; Soc. Vascular Surg.; Exec. Ctte., Med. Research Counc. 1986–88; Counc. mem., Royal Coll. of Physicians & Surgeons 1988– (Mem. of Extve. 1989– ); Alpha Omega Alpha (Hon. mem.); Home: 11 Barlow Cres., Dunrobin, Ont. K0A 1T0.

**KEOUGH, Kevin Michael William,** B.Sc., M.Sc., Ph.D.; university administrator and professor; b. St. George's, Nfld. 2 Aug. 1943; s. William Joseph and Gertrude Clara (O'Brien) K.; e. Univ. of Toronto B.Sc. (Hons.) 1965, M.Sc. 1967, Ph.D. 1971; m. Joan d. Agnes and Burgess Murphy 14 Aug. 1967; children: Shanna, Valerie; VICE-PRESIDENT (RESEARCH), MEMORIAL UNIVERSITY OF NEWFOUNDLAND 1992– ; Postdoctoral Fellow of the Muscular Dystrophy Assn. of Can., Chemistry, Univ. of Sheffield 1971–72; Asst. Prof., Dept. of Biochem., Memorial Univ. of Nfld. 1972–76; Assoc. Prof. 1976–82; Prof. 1982– ; Head (pro tem) 1977; Head 1986–92; Assoc. Prof., Discipline of Pediatrics 1981–82; Prof. 1982– ; Visiting Prof., Joint Program in Neonatology, Dept. of Ped., Harvard Med. Sch. summer 1981; Dir., Seabright Corp.; Candn. Centre for Fisheries Innovation; Candn. Centre for Marine Communications 1993– ; Bd. of Dir., Nfld. Symphony Orchestra 1981–82; Mem., Medical Research Council of Canada 1993– ; Assoc. Ed., 'Biochemistry and Cell Biology' 1982– ; Vice-Pres., Candn. Biochem. Soc. 1987–88; Pres. 1988–89; Past-Pres. 1989–90; Pres.-Elect, Candn. Fed. of Biological Societies 1989–90; Pres. 1990–91; Past-Pres. 1991–92; Home: 35 Carpasian Rd., St. John's, Nfld. A1B 2P9; Office: Memorial Univ. of Nfld., St. John's, Nfld. A1C 5S7.

**KEPPEL-JONES, Arthur Mervyn,** M.A., B.A., Ph.D., D.Litt.; educator; b. Cape Town, S. Africa 20 Jan. 1909; s. Harold and Evelyn Frances (Bickley) K.; e. S.A. Coll. Sch.; Univ. of Cape Town B.A. 1928, Ph.D. 1943; Oxford Univ. B.A. (Hons.) 1931, M.A. 1940; Rhodes Scholar 1929; Hon. D. Litt. (Natal) 1988; m. late Eileen Bate 16 Dec. 1935; children: David, Michael, Diana (Margaret); PROFESSOR EMERITUS OF HISTORY, QUEEN'S UNIVERSITY 1976– ; temporary Lectr., Hist. Dept., Univ. of Witwatersrand 1933–34; Lectr. Hist. Dept. Natal Univ. Coll. 1935; Lectr. Univ. of Witwatersrand 1936–44, Sr. Lectr. 1945–53; Visiting Lectr., Dept. of Hist., Queen's Univ. 1953–54; Prof. of Hist., Univ. of Natal 1954–59; Queen's Univ. 1959–76 (and Chrmn. 1964–68); Visiting Prof. of Hist., Duke Univ. 1963; teacher, summer schools: Johns Hopkins Univ. 1954, Univ. of Alta. 1961, Univ. of B.C. 1964; Pres. Transvaal Workers' Educ. Assn. 1937–53; Chrmn. Johannesburg Counc. of Adult Educ. 1950–53; Gov. Michaelhouse Sch., Natal 1955–59; Anglican Ch. (licensed sub-deacon by Bishop of Natal); mem., S.A. Hist. Soc.; Candn. Hist. Assn.; Candn. Inst. of Internat. Affairs; author: 'When Smuts Goes' 1947; 'South Africa: A Short History' 1949; 'Friends or Foes?: A Point of View and a Programme for Racial Harmony in South Africa' 1950; 'Rhodes and Rhodesia' 1983; also many articles, papers, chapters and sections of books; editor: 'Philipps, 1820 Settler' 1960; Home: 1 College St., Kingston, Ont. K7L 4L5; Office: Dept. of History, Queen's Univ., Kingston, Ont. K7L 3N6.

**KEPROS, Peter G.,** B.S., M.S., Ph.D.; educator; b. Salt Lake City, Utah 25 Mar. 1936; s. George N. and Maria P. (Deliezas) K.; e. Univ. of Utah B.S. 1960, M.S. 1963, Ph.D. 1965; m. Anne, d. Louis and Edna D'Amour 15 Aug. 1980; one d. Stephanie; PROF. OF PSYCHOL., UNIV. OF N.B. 1976– , Asst. Prof. of Psychol. present Univ. 1965, Assoc. Prof. 1970, Assoc. Dean (Soc. Sci's.) Fac. of Arts 1972, Acting Dean of Arts July-Dec. 1977, Dean of Arts Jan. 1978 – Jun. 1988; Mem.-at-Large Social Sci. Rsch. Council Can. 1975–78; Vice Pres. Social Sci. Fed. Can. 1977–78; Mem. Sigma Xi; mem. Candn. Psychol. Assn.; Am. Psychol. Assn.; Mid-Western Psychol. Assn.; Rocky Mountain Psychol. Assn.; Psychonomic Soc.; New York Acad. of Scis.; Home: 652 Valleyview Court, Fredericton, N.B. E3B 2B2; Office: Dept. of Psychology, Univ. of N.B., Fredericton, N.B. E3B 5A3.

**KER, John William,** B.A.Sc., M.F., D.For., D.Sc.; forester; retired university dean; b. Chilliwack, B.C., 27 Aug. 1915; s. John and Ellen (Fitz-Gibbon) K.; e. Univ. of British Columbia, B.A.Sc. (Forestry) 1941, D.Sc. 1971; Yale Sch. of Forestry, M.F. 1951, D.For. 1957; m. Marguerite Frances, d. late Seth Witton, 26 April 1943; children: John Gerald, Kerry Ann, Wendy Rena; Prof., Faculty of Forestry, Univ. of British Columbia; Dean, Faculty of Forestry, Univ. of N.B. 1961–82; mem., Science Council of Can. 1966–68; Candn. Inst. of Forestry (Pres. 1971–72); Candn. Forestry Advisory Council 1970–81; B.C. Natural Resources Conf. (Forestry), 1955–57; Pacific Science Cong. (Del. to Tenth Cong., Honolulu 1961); Assn. of B.C. Foresters (Chrmn. Bd. of Examiners 1955; mem. Counc. 1956); Assn. of Reg'd. Prof. Foresters of N.B.; Forest Engr. (P.Eng.) admitted into Assn. Prof. Engrs. of N.B. 1971; mem. Candn. Council Rural Devel. 1972–73; Natural Sciences and Engineering Rsch. Council of Can. 1980–83; C.I.D.A. expert, Agric. University Malaysia 1973–74; I.D.R.C. consultant, People's Republic of China 1987; publications: co-author of a number of books related to forestry; many articles in prof. journs.; Anglican; recreations: gardening, family-tree research; Home: 760 Golf Club Road, Fredericton, N.B. E3B 4X4.

**KERANS, Marion Douglas,** B.A., B.S.W., M.S.W.; community and peace activist, writer, retired social worker; b. Grand Rapids, Mich. 20 Dec. 1927; d. James John and Agnes Mary (Douglas) Roche; e. Marianapolis (Montreal) B.A. 1948; McGill Univ. B.S.W. 1949; Univ. of Toronto M.S.W. 1967; 1st. m. William M. Kellerman 1952 (dec. 1965); 2nd m. Patrick s. Philip and Julia Kerans 31 July 1973; children: Karen, Maureen, Joanne, Patrick, Robert (Kellerman), Evelyn (Kerans); practised & taught social work 1950s–70s in Montreal, Vancouver, Toronto & Ottawa; primary care giver to six children 1953–65; organized public participation in mun. & prov. planning 1975–78; The People's Food Comn. 1978–79; peace coalitions incl. the Halifax-Dartmouth Coalition against Nuclear War 1983, the Coalition of Candn. Women's Groups (initiated by Voice of Women) which sponsored Internat. Women's Peace Conf. (Halifax) 1985 & the Atlantic Peace Coalition 1986; currently researching biography of Muriel Duckworth (peace activist); rep. Voice of Women, Women's Internat. Peace confs. Brussels 1979, Geneva 1982, '84; visited NATO & OECD as invitee of Dept. of External Affairs 1980; rep. Candn. Peace Coalition, Internat. Conf. on Disarmament Moscow 1987; Mem., Voice of Women Can.; Group of 78; Ploughshares; Extve. Mem., Ont. Assn. of Social Workers 1970–73; N.S. Assn. of Social Workers 1974–76; Chair, Community Planning Assn. of N.S. 1982; Mem., Consultative Group on Disarmament to the Ambassador for Disarmament 1980–85; author of 3 book chapters, 'Report' of People's Food Comn. 1979 and several articles; recreations: walking, gardening; Home: 6236 Willow St., Halifax, N.S. B3L 1N9.

**KERANS, Hon. Roger Philip,** B.A., LL.B.; judge; b. Lashburn, Sask. 6 Jan. 1934; s. Philip Francis and Julia Ella (Loran) K.; e. Univ. of Alta. B.A. LL.B.; m. Marilynn d. Ethel and Wyman Murphy 20 Aug. 1957; children: Christopher, Patrick, Katherine; JUDGE, COURT OF APPEAL, ALTA. and COURT OF APPEAL, N.W.T. 1980– ; law practice Edmonton 1957–70; apptd. to Dist. Court of N. Alta. and Local Judge of Supreme Court of Alta., Edmonton 1970–75, Assoc. Chief Judge Dist. Court, Alta. Calgary 1975–79, Depy. Judge Supreme Court of Y.T. 1976– , Puisne Judge Court of Queen's Bench, Alta. 1979–80; Office: 611 – 4th St. S.W., Calgary, Alta. T2P 1T5.

**KERBEL, Robert S.,** B.Sc., Ph.D.; research scientist, university professor; b. Toronto, Ont. 5 April 1945; s. Phillip and Anne Gertrude (Feldman) K.; e. Vaughan Rd. C.I. 1964; Univ. of Toronto B.Sc. 1968; Queen's Univ. Ph.D. 1972; Inst. for Cancer Research, London, England, postdoctoral training 1972–74; m. Diane d. Wilf and Evelyn Smith Nov. 1970; one d.: Alyssa Jane; DIRECTOR OF CANCER RESEARCH, SUNNYBROOKE HEALTH SCIENCE CENTRE 1991– ; Asst. Prof. Pathology & Research Scholar, National Cancer Inst., Queen's Univ. 1975–80; Assoc. Prof. & Rsch. Assoc. 1980–85; Terry Fox Research Scientist 1986– ; Prof. of Medical Biophysics & Medical Genetics, Univ. of Toronto 1986– ; Dir., Div. of Cancer Biology, Mt. Sinai Hospital 1985–90; Mem., Ed. Bd. 'Cancer Research,' 'Clinical & Experimental Metastasis,' 'Molecular and Cellular Biology'; Editor-in-Chief, 'Cancer & Metastasis Reviews' 1990– ; Adjunct Prof. of Cell Biology, M.D. Anderson Cancer Ctr., Texas; Mem., Nat. Reviewers Registry, Nat. Insts. of Health, USA 1990– ; King George VI Silver Jubilee Cancer Rsch. Fellow, Nat. Inst. of Canada 1973; Chrmn., Gordon Research Conf. on Cancer 1991; Home: 48 Bennington Heights Dr., Toronto, Ont. M4G 1A9; Office: Reichmann Research Bldg., 2075 Bayview Ave., Toronto, Ont. M4N 3M5.

**KERMALLI, Jaffer Mohomed,** F.C.A., C.A.; executive; b. Zanzibar, Tanzania 24 Feb. 1947; s. Mohomed Kermalli and Nargis Gulamhussein (Dharsi); e. King George VI School 1964; Inst. of C.A.s in England & Wales A.C.A., F.C.A. 1970–79; British Inst. of Management A.M.B.I.M. 1974; Inst. of C.A.s in Ont. C.A. 1976; Univ. of Western Ont. MACFEE 1979; Tax Executives Inst. T.E.I. 1982; m. Sabira d. Mohamedalli and Zainab Esmail 30 Jan. 1972; children: Shelyna, Shehnaz, Fatema; VICE-PRESIDENT & GENERAL MANAGER, BRAZILIAN CANADIAN COFFEE CO. LTD. 1991– ; articled clerk, Carter Chaloner & Kearns 1965–70; Senior Auditor, Coopers & Lybrand 1970–71; Chief Accountant, Kilimanjaro Textiles Corpn. Ltd. 1971–72; Advisor to Financial Dir., Somaltex S.p.A. 1972–74; various posts ending as Asst. Treasurer, Nestle Enterprises Limited 1974–84; Chief Financial Officer, Goodhost Foods (1983) Limited (Nestle subs.) 1984–86; Vice-Pres. & Treas., Nestle Capital Corp. Limited 1987; Dir. of Finance & Treas., Nestle Enterprises Limited 1987; Vice-Pres. & Gen. Mgr., Club Group of Companies (div. of Nestle Foodservice) 1988–89; Chief Operating officer, S & O Copiers Inc. 1990; Pres. & Dir., Biashara Investments Inc.; Caledon East Co-Tennancies Inc.; Unguja Investments Inc.; Sikera Ltd.; JG International Inc.; Mem., Islamic Shia Ithna-Asheria Jamaat of Toronto (Chair, Strategic Planning and Adult/Youth Liaison cttes.; Past External Auditor); Jaffery Bus. & Profl. Assoc. (Chrmn., Ont. Chapt.); JIBA Internat. C. of C. (Vice Chrmn.-Americas); Sajjadiyya Trust (Treasurer); recreations: golf, bridge; Home: 37 Trafford Cres., Unionville, Ont. L3R 7H9; Office: 1260 Martingrove Rd., Rexdale, Ont. M9W 4X3.

**KERMOYAN, Mireille;** film board executive; b. Nice, France; d. Felix and Marie Germaine (Hamon) Sacco; e. France; m. Ara Kermoyan 11 May 1968; children: Delphine, Mathieu; SEC. TO BD. OF TRUSTEES NAT. FILM BD. OF CAN. 1991– ; Sec.-Treas. Art Global Inc. Montréal; former Dir. of Communications and Dir. Internat. Devel. present Bd.; recreations: books, films; Club: Gastronomique; Office: Box 6100, Stn. A, Montréal, Qué. H3C 3H5.

**KERN, Rolf Robert,** Dr. rer. pol.; insurance executive; b. Freiburg, Germany 5 Aug. 1927; s. Friedrich Albert and Lina (Mattmueller) K.; e. Elem. and High Schs., Freiburg, Germany; Univ. of Freiburg, Dipl. rer. pol. 1953, Dr. rer. pol. 1955; post grad. work univs. France and U.S.; m. Inge Elizabeth, d. Emil Schmidt, 26 Aug. 1958; children: Rona Elizabeth Lina, Barbara Diana, Petra Ruth; PRES. AND DIR., GERLING GLOBAL REINSURANCE CO. since 1980; Pres. and Dir., Gerling Global General Insurance Co. since 1980; Dir., Gerling Global Offices, Inc., New York 1984; commenced in market research Badische Anilin & Sodafabrik A.G., Ludwigshafen, Germany 1955; Jr. Extve., Gerling-Konzern, Cologne 1957; joined present Co. as Mgr. and Secy.-Treas. 1958, Vice-Pres. 1968, Sr. Vice-Pres. and Secy.-Treas. 1971; Adm. Mgr., Gerling Global General Insurance Co. 1964, Sr. Vice-Pres. and Secy.-Treas. 1971; Vice-Pres. and Secy., Gerling Service Corp. Ltd. 1969; Extve. Vice-Pres. and Secy. Treas., Gerling Global Reinsurance 1976–80; Extve. Vice-Pres. and Secy., Gerling Global General Ins. Co., 1976–80; mem. Ins. Accounting and Stat. Assn.; Reinsurance Research Council (Past Pres. and Dir.); Protestant; recreations: swimming, yoga, tennis; Clubs: Bayview Country; Granite; Office: 480 University Ave., Toronto, Ont. M5G 1V6.

**KERNAGHAN, Edward J.,** B.A.; investment executive; b. Toronto, Ont. 7 Jan. 1941; s. the late Edward Benson and Gertrude Jean (McNeill) K.; e. Upper Canada Coll.; Univ. of West. Ontario B.A. (Hons.) 1965; m. Alice Gould Vanstone June 1968; children: Edward Hume, Elizabeth Anne; CHAIRMAN & CHIEF EXECUTIVE OFFICER, THOMSON KERNAGHAN & CO. LIMITED 1982– ; Pres., Kernaghan & Co. Ltd. 1968–82; Dir., General Leaseholds Limited; Mem., Toronto Stock Exchange; Investment Dealers Assn.; recreations: shooting, fishing, golf, tennis, skiing; clubs: Toronto, Granite, Rosedale Golf, Cambridge, Goodwood, Ojibway, Osler Bluff Ski, Ticker, Sigma Chi; Home: 11 Glengown Road, Toronto, Ont. M4N 1E9; Office: 200 – 365 Bay St., Toronto, Ont. M5H 2V2.

**KERNAGHAN, (William David) Kenneth,** M.A., Ph.D.; educator; b. Hamilton, Ont. 18 Dec. 1940; s. William Robert and Margaret Jane (King) K.; e. McMaster Univ. B.A. 1962; Duke Univ. M.A. 1964, Ph.D. 1966; m. Helgi d. Richard and Marianne Kond 7 Sept. 1963; children: Kevin, Scott, Kris; PROF. OF POL. SCI. AND MGMT. BROCK UNIV. 1968– ; joined Univ. of Waterloo 1965–67, Carleton Univ. 1967–68; Chrmn. of Politics present Univ. 1970–73, Founding Dir. Sch. of Adm. Studies 1974–78; Dir. Ednl. Rsch. Bureau Exec. Edn. Pub. Service Comn. Can. 1974–75; Founding Dir. Case Prog. Candn. Pub. Adm. 1975–79; Pres. Inst. Pub. Adm. Can. 1987–88; Vice Pres. Internat. Assn. Schs. & Insts. Adm. 1986–89; Mem., Acad. Adv. Ctte. Ont. Council Univ. Affairs 1981–90 (Chrmn. 1988–90); author 'Ethical Conduct: Guidelines for Government Employees' 1975; 'Canadian Cases in Public Administration' 1977; co-author 'Coordination in Canadian Governments: A Case Study of Aging Policy' 1983; 'Ethics in the Public Service: Comparative Perspectives' 1985; 'Public Administration in Canada: A Text' 1987, 2nd ed. 1991; 'The Responsible Public Servant' 1990; ed. 'Do Unto Other: Ethics in Government and Business' 1991; 'Canadian Public Administration: Discipline and Profession' 1983; 'Bureaucracy in Canadian Government' 2nd ed. 1973; 'Public Administration in Canada: Selected Readings' 5th ed. 1985; Ed., Candn. Pub. Adm. Jour. 1979–87; Ed., Internat. Review of Admin. Sciences 1989– ; recreations: tennis, farming; Home: 586 Foss Rd., Fenwick, Ont. L0S 1C0; Office: St. Catharines, Ont. L2S 3A1.

**KERNALEGUEN, Anne Paule M.,** B.Sc., B.Ed., M.A., Ph.D.; university professor emeritus; b. St. Brieux, Sask. 15 Feb. 1926; d. Pierre Paul and Marguerite (Sainte Alexia) K.; e. Univ. of Sask., B.Sc. 1948; Univ. of Alta., B.Ed. 1957; Michigan State Univ., M.A. 1963; Utah State Univ., Ph.D. 1968; Specialist in Aging cert. 1987; PROF. EMERITUS, UNIV. OF ALBERTA; Prof., Univ. of Alta. 1970–87; Dist. Home Econ., Ont. Agric. 1948–51; Teacher, Schs. of Agric., Alta. Agric. 1951–54; Red Deer Comp. H.S. 1954–60; Candn. Edn. Bilingual Rep., McCalls Corp (NY) 1960–62; Asst. Prof., Michigan State Univ. 1963–64; Univ. of Sask. 1964–66; Assoc. & Dept. Chrmn., Utah State Univ. 1968–70; Dept. Chrmn., Univ. of Alta. 1970–80; Extve. Dir., Claridge House Condominium 1986– (Mem., Bd. of Dir. 1979– ); Designer, MacPhee Workshop; Church Banners; Govt. Alta. Achievement Award 1983; Fellow, Alta. Home Econ. Assn. 1984; Fellow, Assoc. of College Professors of Textiles and Clothing 1989; nom. for E.C. Manning Award for creative contrib.; Treas., Alta. Rhythmic Sportive Gymnastics Federation; U of Agers, Seniors Gymnastics Team; Handicraft co-ord., Alta. Senior Games; Past Pres., Assn. of Textiles & Clothing Profs.; Past Bd. Mem., Am. Home Econ. Assn.; author 'Clothing Designs for the Handicapped' 1978 (transl. into German & Japanese; 5 printings); author of var. articles; display designer; speaker, var. confs.; Clubs: U of Agers; Seniors Gymnastics Team; Home: 605, 11027 – 87 Ave., Edmonton, Alta. T6G 2P9.

**KERNER, Fred,** B.A., F.A.C.W.; publisher; b. Montreal, Que. 15 Feb. 1921; s. Sam and Vera (Goldman) K.; e. Baron Byng High Sch., Montreal; Sir George Williams Univ., B.A. 1942; m. Sally Dee, d. Fred Stouten, Valley Stream, N.Y., 18 May 1959; children: David, Diane, Jon; PRESIDENT, PUBLISHING PROJECTS INC. 1967– ; Vice-Pres. & Ed.-in-Chief, Harlequin Enterprises Ltd. 1975–83, Ed. Emeritus and Senior Consulting Editor 1983– ; Dir., Communications Unltd.; Colophon Publishing Inc.; Centaur House, Inc.; National Mint Inc.; Publitex International Corp.; Veritas International Publishers; Personalized Services, Inc.; Paramount Securities Corp.; Peter Kent, Inc.; Ed. Writer, Saskatoon Star-Phoenix 1942; Asst. Sports Ed. and Fine Arts writer, Montreal Gazette 1942–44; News-Ed. and roving correspondent, The Candn. Press, Montreal, Toronto & N.Y. 1944–50; Night City Ed. and roving corr., The Associated Press, N.Y. 1951–56; Sr. Ed., Hawthorn Books 1957–58; Extve. Ed., Fawcett World Lib., N.Y. 1959–62, Ed.-in-Chief 1962–64; Pres. and Ed.-in-Chief, Hawthorn Books, Inc., N.Y. 1964–67; Pres., Centaur House, Inc., N.Y. 1964–79; Pres., Paramount Securities Corp. 1965–68; Vice-Pres., Publitex International Corp., King of Prussia, PA 1967–78; Publishing Dir., Books and Educ. Divisions, Reader's Digest Assn. (Canada) Ltd. 1969–75; Pres., Athabaska House 1975–77; author 'Love Is a Man's Affair' 1958; 'Stress and Your Heart' 1961; 'Watch Your Weight Go Down' (pseudonym: Frederick Kerr) 1962; 'A Treasury of Lincoln Quotations' 1965; 'It's Fun to Fondue' (pseudonym: M.N. Thaler) 1968; 'Careers in Writing' 1986; 'Mad About Fondue' 1987; 'Home Emergency Handbook and First Aid Guide' 1990; co-author: 'Eat, Think and Be Slender' 1954; 'The Magic Power of Your Mind' 1956; 'Ten Days to a Successful Memory' 1957; 'Secrets of Your Supraconscious' 1965; 'Buy High, Sell Higher' 1966; 'What's Best for Your Child – and You' 1966; 'Nadia' 1976; 'Prospering Through the Coming Depression' 1988; 'The Writer's Essential Desk Reference' 1991; 'Lifetime' 1992; editor: 'The Canadian Writer's Guide' 9th ed. 1985, 10th ed. 1988, 11th ed. 1992; 'Short Fiction: Guidelines to Canadian Magazines' 1993; books transl. into French, German, Japanese, Portuguese, Spanish, Italian; contributed to 'Chambers's Encyclopedia'; 'Words on Paper'; 'The Overseas Press Club Cookbook'; 'Successful Writers and How They Work'; 'The Canadian Writer's Guide'; 'The Seniors' Guide to Life in the Slow Lane'; 'Lifetime: A Treasury of Uncommon Wisdoms' and various mags.; T.V. and radio script writer; recipient Montreal Y.M.C.A. Literary Awards 1937, 1938, 1939; Crusade for Freedom Award, Am. Heritage Found. 1954; Journalism Award, P.T.A. 1967; Distinguished Service Award, Overseas Press Club 1967; Literary Award, Air Canada 1978; Queen's Silver Jubilee Medal 1979; Allan Sangster Award 1982; Second Prize, Short Story Competition, Toronto Star 1988; Mercury Award 1990; N.A.A.N. Award 1990; Drama festival adjudicator, 1940–48; Playscript consultant ('play doctor') Broadway 1948–57; Gov. Concordia Univ. 1975–77; Trustee, Benson & Hedges Lit. Awards, Gibson Lit. Awards, Candn. Authors Association Lit. Awards, Rothman Literary Award of Merit; Judge, William Henry Drummond National Poetry Contest 1975; Mem., National Comte., American Newspaper Guild 1949–54, Wire Service Guild 1954–57 (Chair, National Negotiating Ctte.; Chair, Grievance Ctte.); mem. Local Sch. Bd., Dist. 4, N.Y. 1968; Pres., Sir George Williams Univ. Alumni Assn. 1971–74 (Pres., N.Y. Branch 1960–62); Chrmn. (1973) Sch. Comte. (ombudsman) Westmount (Que.) High Sch.; mem. Sch. Comte. Roslyn School, Westmount, Que.; Hon. Life mem., Candn. Authors Assoc.; Hon. Life mem., Candn. Book Publishers Council (Chrmn. Copyright Comte.; Dir. 1977–78); Hon. Life mem., Am. Assoc. of Publishers; Gov., Vice Chrmn., and Fellow, Canadian Copyright Inst., 1977– ; Gov. Candn. Writer's Foundation 1982– ; Vice Pres., Fellow & Dir. Academy of Candn. Writers 1986– ; Mem., European Acad. of Arts, Sciences and Humanities; Bd. mem., Book and Periodical Council; Founding Dir. and Bd. mem., Toronto Book and Magazine Fair; Avodah Honour Soc., Montreal; Founding Dir., Toronto Men's Press Club 1944–46; Founding Dir. Organization of Candn. Authors and Publishers 1977–81; Pres., Candn. Assn. for the Restoration of Lost Positives 1969–94; Chrmn. (1965) Internat. Affairs Conf. for Coll. Editors; Chrmn. Book Publishers Comte., Edward R. Murrow Meml. Fund; mem., Mystery Writers Am. (Ed. 'Third Degree' bulletin; Co-chrmn., Awards Comte.); Candn. Authors Assn. (Nat. Pres. 1982–83; Regional Vice-Pres. 1972–78; Pres. Montreal Br. 1974–75; Chrmn. Awards Comte. 1972–81; Chrmn. Special Projects Comte. 1983–87; Chrmn., Publications Comte. 1986–92; Chrmn., Grievance Comte. 1983–93; Chrmn. Fiction/Romance Writers Workshop 1984–88; Founder Chrmn. Toronto Literary Luncheon program; Founder Chrmn. The CAA Fund to Develop Candn. Writers 1983–92); Founding Extve. Ctte. mem., Vice-Chair, Public Lending Rights Comn. 1986–89; Vice-Chrmn. and Fellow, Candn. Copyright Institute; Am. Mgmt. Assn.; Author's League; Author's Guild; Soc. of Prof. Journalist's Presidents' Club; The Writers' Union of Can. (Chair, Grievance Comte., Contracts Comte.); Periodical Writers Assoc. of Can. (Chair, Mediation Comte.); Internat. Platform Assn.; National Speakers Assn.; Am. Acad. of Political and Social Sciences; Adjunct Lectr., Long Island Univ.; Univ. of W. Ont.; Panelist at confs. of Am. Book Publishers Counc.; Candn. Authors Assn.; Mystery Writers Assn.; Overseas Press Club of Am., International P.E.N. Ed.-in-residence: Southwestern Writers Conf.; Breadloaf Writers Conf.; Cape Cod Writers Conf.; Oakland Coll. Writers Conf.; Am. River Univ. Writers Conf.; Sun Coast Writers Conf.; recreations: music, skating, walking; Clubs: Author's (London); Advertising (N.Y.); Dutch Treat (N.Y.); Authors League (N.Y.); Authors Guild (N.Y.); Overseas Press, (N.Y.) (Chrmn., Election Comte., Lib. Comte., Book Night Comte., Awards Comte.); Town Hall (N.Y.); Toronto Men's Press; Candn. Soc. N.Y.; Deadline (N.Y.); Sigma Delta Chi; Home: 25 Farmview Cres., Willowdale, Ont. M2J 1G5; Office: 55014 Fairview Mall, Toronto, Ont. M2J 5B9.

**KERNICK, John O.;** electronics executive; b. London, England 29 May 1939; s. Sidney and Lily N. (Maybourne) K.; e. Henley Gr. Sch.; Columbia Univ. 1980; EPBA Grad. Bus. Sch.; m. Pauline May d. Edgar and Doris Stansbury 31 Aug. 1964; children: Simon J., Nicholas P.; PRES. & CHIEF EXTVE. OFFR., OLIVETTI CAN. LIMITED 1985– ; var. mngt. pos. in Europe incl. Br. Mgr., British Olivetti 1976; Gen. Mgr., Sharp Electronics (UK) Ltd. 1978; Div. Mgr., British Olivetti 1984; Sr. Vice-Pres. Sales, Olivetti Can. Limited 1985: Dir., Info. Technol. Assn. of Can.; Mem., Bd. of Trade; recreations: golf; Home: 16 Seinecliffe Rd., Thornhill, Ont. L3T 1K4.

**KERR, Andrew Brent,** B.Sc., LL.B.; lawyer; b. Saskatoon, Sask. 6 Aug. 1956; s. Andrew Wayne and Irene May (Parchman) K.; e. Univ. of Saskatchewan B.Sc., LL.B. 1979; C.I.C.A. In-Depth Tax Course 1980–81; m. Rowena d. Len Kong Lim 1 Sept. 1978; children: Julia Mckenzie, Andrew Chartwell; RESIDENT PARTNER, HONG KONG OFFICE, MCCARTHY TÉTRAULT 1990– ; Partner, McCarthy Tétrault 1979–90; Dir., PMS Information Systems Ltd.; Mem., Tax Adv. Bd., Continuing Legal Edn. Soc. of B.C.; Candn. C. of C. in Hong Kong; Hong Kong Trustees' Assn.; Inter-Pacific Bar Assn., Tax Law Ctte.; extensive lecturer and presentor at seminars; co-author: 'Deductibility of Legal Fees'; Office: 3703 Edinburgh Tower, 15 Queen's Road Central, Hong Kong.

**KERR, David Wylie,** B.Sc., C.A.; business executive; b. Montréal, Qué. 14 Dec. 1943; s. Dudley Holden and Cecilia (Maguire) K.; e. Town of Mount-Royal High Sch.; McGill Univ. B.Sc. 1965; C.A. 1969; m. Sheryl d. Alpin and Margaret Drysdale 1 Nov. 1969; children: Ross, Tamara; PRES. & C.E.O., NORANDA INC. 1990– ; Dir.: Brascan Ltd.; Brunswick Mining & Smelting Corp. Ltd.; Carena Developments Ltd.; Falconbridge Ltd.; Hees International Bancorp Inc.; Hemlo Gold Mines Inc.; Noranda Inc.; MacMillan Bloedel Ltd.; Noranda Forest Inc.; Norcen Energy Resources Ltd.; Ontario Hydro; joined Touche Ross & Co. 1965–72; Vice Pres. and Chief Financial Offr. Edper Investments Ltd. 1972–78; C.O.O., Hees International Corp. 1978–85; Extve. Vice Pres., Brascan Ltd. 1985–87; Pres., Noranda Inc. 1987–90; recreations: squash, hockey, golf; Clubs: Toronto Racquet; Granite; Rosedale; Office: P.O. Box 755, Suite 4100, BCE Place, 181 Bay St., Toronto, Ont. M5J 2T3.

**KERR, James W.,** B.Sc.; company executive; b. Hamilton, Ont. 11 Mar. 1914; s. George Robert and Helen Robertson (Bews) K.; e. Pub. Sch. and Delta Coll. Inst., Hamilton, Ont.; Univ. of Toronto, B.Sc. (Applied Sc. & Engn.) 1937; m. Ruth Eleanor, d. Charles H. Marrs, Hamilton, Ont., 5 Oct. 1940; children: David, Barbara; CONSULTANT, TRANS-CANADA PIPELINES 1984– ; Dir., Internat. Minerals & Chem. Corp. (Can.) Ltd.; Dir. Emeritus, Canadian Imperial Bank of Commerce; Great Lakes Gas Transmission Co.; former Dir., Bell Canada; Bell Canada Enterprises Inc.; Northern Telecom Ltd.; Maple Leaf Mills Ltd.; The Manufacturers Life Insurance Co.; Algoma Steel Corp. Ltd.; commenced work with Canadian Westinghouse Company Limited, Hamilton, Ont. 1937; served in various positions, becoming Vice-Pres. and Gen. Mgr., Apparatus Products Group 1956; joined present Co. as Pres. and Chief Extve. Offr. 1958, Chrmn. and Pres. 1961, Chrmn. and C.E.O. 1968, Consultant & Dir. 1979; served in 2nd World War, R.C.A.F.; rank Sqdn. Ldr.; Hon. mem., Bd. Govs., Queen Elizabeth Hosp.; Past Chrmn., Territorial Adv. Bd. Extve., The Salvation Army; Past Pres., Candn. Gas Assn.; Bd. Trade Metrop. Toronto; Hon. Pres. Internat. Gas Union; Assn. Prof. Engrs. Ont.; Fellow, Candn. Acad. of Engr.; Engn. Inst. Can.; Theta Delta Chi; recreations: golf, gardening; Clubs: The Toronto; York; Rosedale Golf; Home: 503 – 33 Jackes Ave., Toronto, Ont. M4T 1E2; Office: TransCanada PipiLines, 8th Flr., 55 Yonge St., Toronto, Ont. M5E 1J4.

**KERR, John Custance,** B.A., M.B.A.; executive; b. Vancouver, B.C. 21 Sept. 1944; s. Leslie John and Barbara (Custance) K.; e. St. George's Sch. Vancouver; Univ. of B.C., B.A. 1965; Univ. of Cal. Berkeley M.B.A. 1967; m. Judith (Bell); children: Timothy, Sarah, Susannah, Kate, Molly; CHRMN. LIGNUM LTD.; Past Chrmn. Council Forest Inds., mem. Exec. Ctte.; Mem., Internat. Chapter, Young Presidents' Orgn.; mem., B.C. Chapter, Young Pres.' Orgn.; recreations: tennis, fishing, golf; Clubs: Bohemian (San Franciso, Ca.); Shaughnessy Golf & Country; Vancouver Lawn Tennis & Badminton; Vancouver; Meadowood Country (Cal.); Home: 3479 Point Grey Rd., Vancouver, B.C.; Office 1200, 1090 West Georgia St., Vancouver, B.C. V6E 3V7.

**KERR, John Gregory,** B.A., B.Ed.; politician; b. Annapolis Royal, N.S. 8 Oct. 1947; s. John Roland K.; e. Annapolis Royal Regional Acad. 1966; Mount Allison

Univ. B.A. 1970, B.Ed. 1971; m. Marcia Lee d. Bernard Longmire, Hillsburn, N.S. 22 Aug. 1970; children: Gillian Loring, Megan Bernice; el. M.L.A. for Annapolis West prov. g.e. 1978; Caucus Chrmn. P. Cons. Party 1979–80; Min. of Culture, Recreation and Fitness 1980–81, 1986–87; Min. of Environment 1981–83; Min. of Finance, N.S. 1983–92; Min. of Tourism & Culture and Chair of Policy Bd. 1992; Chrmn. of Bd. of Resource Development, Policy Bd. 1983; Minister in charge of the Lottery Act 1986–92; Min. of Housing, N.S. 1988–89; Chrmn. of Management Bd. & Min. responsible for the Civil Service Act 1991–92; Historic Restoration Soc. Annapolis Co.; Gov. Heritage Foundation Annapolis Royal; P. Conservative; Anglican; recreations: squash, racketball, farming, watersports; Home: R.R. 1, Granville Ferry, Annapolis Co., N.S. BOS 1K0.

**KERR, John Williamson, Jr.;** publishing executive; b. Toronto, Ont. 9 Aug. 1951; s. John Williamson and Wendy Marjorie (Lamb) K.; e. Upper Can. Coll. 1960–70; Univ. of West. Ont., B.A. 1973; m. Diana Elizabeth d. David Cape 12 Oct. 1984; children: John, Julia; PRES. & C.O.O., KERRWIL PUBLICATIONS 1987– ; Dir., Kerrwil Publications Ltd.; Periodical Publishers Exchange; Chrmn., Canadian Business Press; Dir., Les Publications Industrielles Ltée; Candn. Yachting Assn.; Olympic Bronze Medallist 1984 Olympics (Los Angeles); World Cup, Soling Class 1978, '82, '83; European Soling Class Champion 1978, '82, '83; Candn. Soling Class Champion 1973, '75, '78, '80, '83, '84; U.S. Champion 1978, '80; Gold Duke of Edinburgh Award 1970; Mem., Kappa Alpha Soc.; recreations: sailing, squash, skiing, running; Clubs: Royal Candn. Yacht; Madawaska; Skyloft; Home: 23 Cornish Rd., Toronto, Ont. M4J 2E3; Office: 395 Matheson Blvd. E., Mississauga, Ont. L4Z 2H2.

**KERR, Margaret G.,** M.D., DIH, C.B.O.M.; telecommunications executive; b. Ont. 5 Mar. 1945; d. James William and Mary Jane (Stone) K.; e. Univ. of Toronto M.D. 1970, DIH 1978, C.B.O.M. 1980; children: Davis, Megan, Caitlin; SENIOR VICE-PRES., ENVIRONMENT & ETHICS, NORTHERN TELECOM LTD. 1987– ; Med. Dir., Shell Can. 1978–82; Vice-Pres., Environ., Occupational Health & Safety, Alcan Aluminium Ltd. 1982–87; Dir. & Vice Chrmn., World Environ. Ctr.; Dir., Arthur D. Little, Inc.; John Labatt Ltd.; Home: 143 Glenrose Ave., Toronto, Ont. M4T 1K7; Office: 3 Robert Speck Parkway, Mississauga, Ont. L4Z 3C8.

**KERR, Robert Bews,** O.B.E., M.A., M.D., F.R.C.P., FRCPC, M.A.C.P.; professor emeritus; b. Hamilton, Ont. 20 Aug. 1908; s. George Robert and Helen Robertson (Bews) K.; e. Hamilton C.I.; Univ. of Toronto B.A. 1930, M.D. 1933, M.A. 1936; m. Lois d. Robert E. Reynolds 21 Sept. 1937; children: John Reynolds, James Bews, Charles Robert; PROFESSOR EMERITUS, UNIVERSITY OF B.C. 1974– ; Demonstrator, Dept. of Med., Univ. of Toronto 1939; Assoc. Prof. and Head, Dept. of Therapeutics 1947–50; Eric W. Hamber Prof. of Med. and Head Dept. of Med., Univ. of B.C. 1950–74; Head Dept. of Med. Vancouver Gen. Hosp. 1950–74; Lt. Col., R.C.A.M.C. 1940–45 (Engl. and N.W. Europe Candn. Hosps.); O.B.E. 1945; mem. United Ch.; Royal Coll. of Physicians & Surgeons of Canada (Pres. 1966–67); Med. Counc. of Can. (Pres. 1968); author: 'History of Medical Council of Canada' 1979; co-author: (with Douglas Waugh) 'Duncan Graham - Medical Reformer and Educator' 1989; Home: 311 – 3755 West 8th Ave., Vancouver, B.C. V6R 1Z2.

**KERR, Robert John;** motion picture systems executive; b. Galt, Ont. 28 Aug. 1929; s. John Robert and Jessie Christena (MacKay) K.; e. G.C.I. & V.S. Cambridge (Galt) Ont., Sr. Matric. 1947; m. Margaret d. Edwin and Margaret Vaughn 2 Feb. 1984; children: Barbara, Nancy Jean; CONSULTANT, IMAX SYSTEMS CORP. 1994– ; Pres., John Kerr & Son Ltd. 1950–67; Co-Ord., 'Polar Life' for Expo 67, 1965–67; Founder & Chrmn., Imax Systems Corp. 1967–94; Alderman, City of Galt 1957–63; Mayor 1964–67; Prov. Candidate, Waterloo S. CCF 1955, 1959; NDP 1967; Chrmn., Grand River Disaster Relief Fund 1974; Mayor, City of Cambridge 1975–76; Centennial Medal, Jubilee Medal, Pilot of the Year Award, W-W Flying Club 1969; recreations: restoration of classic wooden boats, woodworking; Home: 55A Avenue Rd., Apt. 412, Toronto, Ont. M5R 2G3; Office: 38 Isabella St., Toronto, Ont. M4Y 1N1.

**KERR, Robert William,** B.A., LL.B., LL.M.; university professor, association president; b. Fredericton, N.B. 7 Aug. 1943; s. James Milton Fowler and Sarah Jane (Warrell) K.; e. Univ. of N.B. B.A. 1964; Dalhousie Univ. LL.B. 1967; Harvard Univ. LL.M. 1968; Univ. of Calif. at Berkeley, post-grad.; PROFESSOR, FACULTY OF LAW, UNIV. OF WINDSOR 1976– ; Law Teacher, Univ. of N.B. 1968–76; Consulant, N.B. Dept. of Justice on Legislation 1970–76 and on Constitutional Matters 1976–78; Mem., Human Rights Bd. of Inquiry or Tribunal for N.B. 1971–76, for Ont. 1978– , for Canada 1979– ; Public Intervenor, Telephone Rate Review for N.B. 1975–76; Mem., Task Force on Position of Official Languages in N.B. 1980–84; Consultant on Official Lang. to N.B. Govt. 1974–78 and to N.W.T. Govt. 1988; Frank Knox Fellowship, Harvard Univ. 1967–68; Sir James Dunn Scholarship, Dalhousie Univ. 1964–67; author: 'Labour Board Remedies in Canada' 1993; Mem., Law Soc. of N.B. 1967– ; Law Soc. of U.C. 1978– ; Candn. Bar Assn. 1967– ; Candn. Assn. of Law Teachers 1967– (Sec.-Treas. 1989–90; Vice-Pres. 1990–91; Pres. 1991–92); Candn. Assn. of Univ. Teachers 1976– (Vice-Pres. 1985–87, 1989–90; Pres. 1990–91); P.C. Party of Canada 1960– (Pres., Young P.C.s 1969–70; Vice-Pres., P.C. Youth 1970–72; P.C. Party of N.B. 1960–76; of Ont. 1976–82); Office: Windsor, Ont. N9B 3P4.

**KERR, Shelagh Duncan,** B.Sc.; dietitian; b. Fredericton, N.B. 15 Aug. 1955; d. James Cowie and Margaret Campbell (Cownie) K.; e. Ridgemont High Sch. Ottawa 1973; Univ. of Ottawa B.Sc. 1977; Calgary Gen. Hosp. Postgrad. Dietetic Internship 1978; VICE PRES. CORP. AND ENVIRONMENTAL AFFAIRS, COCA-COLA LTD. CANADA 1991– ; Edn. Dietitian Calgary Gen. Hosp. 1978–79; Product Devel. Mgr.: Controlled Foods Internat. Vancouver 1979–80; White Spot Restaurants (General Foods) 1980–81; Nutrition/Food Ed. Fair Lady Mag. Cape Town, R.S.A. 1981–83; Pub. Health Nutritionist Brantford, Ont. 1984; Dir. Sci. Affairs, Grocery Products Manufacturers of Can. 1985–89, Vice Pres. 1989–91; mem. Nat. Packaging Task Force, Candn. Council Mins. Environment 1989–91; Mem. Advisory Bd., Environment Can.'s Environmental Choice Program 1992– ; mem., Communications Implementation Ctte., Nutrition Recommendations for Candns. 1987–89; mem. Candn. Dietetic Assn.; Ont. Dietetic Assn.; Chair, Ontario Multi Material Recycling Inc. 1992– ; Bd. Mem., Candn. Found. for Dietetic Rsch. 1992– ; Mem., Public Affairs Ctte., Toronto Home Care Program 1991– ; recreations: hiking, tennis, travel; Home: Toronto, Ont.; Office: 42 Overlea Blvd., Don Mills, Ont. M4H 1B8.

**KERSELL, John Edgar,** B.A., M.A, Ph.D.; university professor; b. Simcoe, Ont. 29 Jan. 1930; s. Ivan and Olive Alverda (Cook) K.; e. Queen's Univ. B.A. 1953, M.A. 1954; London Sch. of Econ. Ph.D. 1958; m. Marjorie (Mardi) d. Arthur and Dora Eastbury; children: Monty, Heather, John; PROF., UNIV. OF WATERLOO 1967– , Founding Dir. of Candn. Studies 1969–72; Prof., Univ. of West. Ont. 1954–59; McMaster Univ. 1959–67; (Adjunct) Internat. Coll. of the Cayman Islands 1978– ; Bermuda Coll. 1979–82; Pres., Luminaire Consulting Serv. 1986– ; specialist in devel. admin. of small dependencies and in team work; Commonwealth of Australia Sr. Fellow 1965; First in Ont., Fraser Inst. 'Economy in Government' Competition 1992; Mem., Inst. of Pub. Admin. (Gen. Chrmn., Centennial Year Conf. 1967); Candn. Pol. Sci. Assn.; author: 'Parliamentary Supervision of Delegated Legislation' 1960; co-editor: 'Comparative Political Problems' 1968; various articles on public admin. and Candn. public policy; consultant to govts. in Can. and the West Indies; served with the RCAF and the RCR; recreations: scuba diving, tennis, golf, sailing; club: Westmount Golf & Country; Office: Waterloo, Ont. N2L 3G1.

**KERSHAW, Kenneth Andrew,** Ph.D., D.Sc., F.R.S.C.; educator; b. Morcambe, Eng. 5 Sept. 1930; s. Andrew and Margaret (Carr) K.; e. Ashbourne (Eng.) Grammar Sch. 1949; Manchester Univ. B.Sc. 1952; Univ. of N. Wales Ph.D. 1957; Univ. of Wales D.Sc. 1968; m. Ellen d. Alexander and Ismay Bruce 1 Apr. 1967; three s. Daniel Kenneth, Andrew Duncan, Matthew Alexander; Prof. of Biology, McMaster Univ. 1969–88; Dir. Kershaw Old Maps & Prints, 355710 Ontario Ltd.; Lectr. Imperial Coll. London 1957–62, 1964–69; Sr. Lectr. (seconded) Ahmadu Bellow Univ. Zaria, Nigeria 1962–64; author 'Quantitative and Dynamic Plant Ecology' 1962, 2nd ed. 1973, 3rd ed. 1985; 'Physiological Ecology of Lichens' 1985; 'Early Printed Maps of Canada, 1540–1703' 1993; Home: 601 Old Dundas Rd., Ancaster, Ont. L9G 3J3.

**KERSLAKE, Susan M.;** writer; b. Chicago, Ill. 20 Apr. 1943; d. Youart Herbert and Martha Elizabeth (Muckley) K.; e. Roycemore Sch. Evanston, Ill. 1960; Univ. of Mont.; Beloit Coll. Wis.; served Kroch's & Brentano's Bookstore, Chicago 1962–66; Dalhousie Univ. Libs. 1966–73; St. Joseph's Children's Centre 1973–80; Izaak Walton Killam Hosp. for Children 1980–85; short listed 1984 Gov. Gen's Award; listed '45 Below' CBIC; author 'Middlewatch' 1976; 'The Book of Fears' 1984; 'Penumbra' 1984; 'Blind Date' 1989; mem. Writers Union Can.; Writers Fedn. N.S.; Address: 304, 5713 Victoria Rd., Halifax, N.S. B3H 2Y3.

**KERT, Norman L.;** advertising executive; b. Ottawa, Ont. 2 Sept. 1933; s. Charles and Minnie (Gencher) K.; e. Lisgar Coll. Inst. Ottawa; Carleton Univ.; m. Ellin d. Jules and Faye Goldberg 9 Apr. 1957; children: Karen, Charles, Eric; CHRMN. & C.E.O., KERT ADVERTISING LTD. 1966– ; Pres. and Dir.: Muller Jordan Weiss Ltd.; Owner, Huron Yonge Investments Ltd.; Announcer, Radio Stns. CHRO Pembroke, CHOK Sarnia and CFRA Ottawa; apptd. Promotion Dir. and Sales Rep. CFRA; estbd. Mayer Kert Advertising Co. Ltd. Ottawa 1963; estbd. present co. Toronto 1966; Dir.: Inst. Candn. Advertising; Candn. Soc. for Weizmann Inst. Sci.; Koffler Gallery; Gov.: Mount Sinai Hosp., Toronto; recreations: golf, tennis, sailing, skiing; Clubs: Oakdale Golf and Country; YMCA; Boca Point (Fla.) Country; Home: 405 Glenayr Rd., Toronto, Ont. M5P 3C8; Office: 600, 2200 Yonge St., Toronto, Ont. M4S 1S5.

**KERWIN, Claire,** R.C.A.; artist; b. Chatelet, Belgium; d. Emile and Elisabeth (Fremersdorf) Roland; e. Belgium; came to Can. 1947; m. George s. Patrick and Georgina (Mace) Kerwin 1 Feb. 1947; children: Michael, Shawn; rec'd Medal of Merit City of Toronto; mem. Print & Drawing Council Can.; Royal Canadian Academy (Council Mem. 1982–83); former mem. Soc. of Candn. Artists; Ont. Soc. of Artists; several one-man shows in Canada and abroad: Merton Gall.; Pascal Gall.; Alice Peck Gall., Burlington; Art Dialogue Gall.; 80 Spadina; St. Jean de Luz, France; group shows: Candn. Embassy, Paris; Ontario House, London (Eng.); Royal Candn. Acad. of Art; Univ. of Waterloo; Ont. Soc. of Artists; John Aird Gall. (Counc. mem. 1990–93); Shaw-Remington Gall.; volunteer artist, Royal Ont. Museum; commissioned to design and create set, The Toronto Dance Theatre 1991; recreations: tennis, squash, farming; Club: Toronto Lawn Tennis; Address: 20 Monteith St., Toronto, Ont. M4Y 1K7.

**KERWIN, Edward Philip,** B.Sc., LL.B.; barrister and solicitor; b. St. Catharines, Ont. 22 Oct. 1946; s. Patrick Kilroy and Mary Gertrude (Doyle) K.; e. St. Michael's Coll., Univ. of Toronto, B.Sc. 1968; Osgoode Hall Law Sch., York Univ., LL.B. 1971; called to Bar of Ont. 1973; Alta. 1981; m. Ann d. Robert C. and Naomi C. Scrivener 5 Aug. 1972; children: Caitlin Sarah, Stephanie A.; PARTNER, McCARTHY TÉTRAULT, BARRISTERS & SOLICITORS 1979– ; Assoc. 1973–79; Mng. Partner, Calgary Office 1985–87; Mng. Partner, London, U.K. & Eur. Office 1987–90; Instr., Corp. & Comm. Law, Bar Admission Course, Law Soc. of U.C. 1974–79; Sec., Woodbridge Foam Corp. 1978–84; Pres., Univ. of Toronto Alumni Assn. 1982–83; Pres., St. Michael's Coll. Alumni Assn. 1976–78; Mem. of Board, Candn. Stage Company; Roman Catholic; P.C.; Sigma Chi; contrib. ed., 'Securities Law & Practice' 1984; co-editor, 'Osgoode Hall Law Journal' 1970–71; recreations: running, hiking, skiing, tennis, squash, golf, music, theatre; clubs: The Royal Automobile (London); Toronto Golf; The Badminton & Racquet; Glencoe and Glencoe Golf & Country (Calgary); Home: 45 Elm Ave., Toronto, Ont. M4W 1N6; Office: Suite 4900, Toronto-Dominion Bank Tower, Toronto-Dominion Centre, Toronto, Ont. M5K 1E6.

**KERWIN, Larkin,** C.C., O.Q., M.Sc., D.Sc., LL.D., F.R.S.C., D.C.L., F.R.S.A., F.C.A.E. Eng., O.L.H.; K.G.C.H.S., D.H.C.; physicist; b. Quebec, Que., 22 June 1924; s. Timothy John and Catherine (Lonergan) K.; e. St. Patrick's High Sch., Quebec, 1941; St. Francis Xavier Univ., B.Sc. 1944; Univ. of Toronto, 1944–45; Mass. Inst. of Technol., M.Sc. 1946; Univ. Laval, D.Sc. 1949; LL.D.: St. Francis Xavier 1970; Concordia Univ. 1976; Univ. of Alta. 1983; Dalhousie Univ. 1983; D.Sc.: Univ. of B.C. 1973, Univ. of Toronto 1973, McGill Univ. 1974; Memorial Univ. 1978; Univ. of Ottawa 1981; Roy. Mil. Coll., Kingston 1982; Univ. of Winnipeg 1983; Univ. of Windsor 1984; Univ. of Moncton 1985; D.C.L.: Bishop's 1978; D.H.C. univ. de Montréal 1991; m. Maria Guadalupe, d. André Turcot, Sillery, Que., 10 June 1950; children: Lupita, Alan, Larkin, Terence, Rosa-Maria, Gregory, Timothy, Guillermina; President, Canadian Space Agency 1989–92; Pres., National Rsch. Counc. of Can. 1980–89; Rector, Univ. Laval, 1972–77, and Prof. of Physics; Professor Emeritus 1991– ; joined present University as Assistant Professor 1946; Chairman, Physics Dept., 1961–67; Vice Dean, Faculty of Science, 1967–68; mem. various scholarship and grants committees of Prov. of Que., Nat. Research Council and Defence Research Bd.; Internat. Union Pure and Applied Physics, Secy. Gen. 1972–84, First Vice-Pres. 1984–87,

Pres., 1987–90; Pres. du Conseil, Univ. Laval; Vice Pres., Que. Br., U.N. Assn. Can., 1958–59; Vice-Pres., Natural Sciences & Eng. Research Council, Canada 1978–80; Pres. Assn. Univs. and Colls. of Can. 1974; Vice-Pres. Royal Soc. of Can. 1974, Pres. 1976; Pres. Acad. of Sc., Royal Soc. of Can. 1973; Mem., National Advisory Bd. on Science & Technology 1986–90; Pres., Cdn. Acad. of Engr. 1989–90; awarded Prix David 1951; Médaille Pariseau 1965; Centenary Medal 1967; Medal of Canadian Assn. Physicists 1969; Kt., Order of Holy Sepulchre 1970; Queen's Jubilee Medal 1977; Officer, Order of Canada 1978, Companion 1981; Commemorative Medal, 125th Anniversary, Candn. Confedn. 1992; Medal 'Gloire del'Escolle,' the Anciens de Laval 1978; Michener Visitor, Queen's Univ. 1982; Gold Medal, Candn. Council of Profl. Eng. 1982; Pariseau Medal, l'ACFAS 1964; Rousseau Medal, l'ACFAS 1983; Ordre National du Québec 1988; Award for distinguished Public Service Canada 1987; Officier de la Légion d'Honneur de France 1989; contrib. to prof. new devices for focusing ion and electron beams, the discovery of phosphorous-8 molecule, of various excited states of atmospheric gases; author: 'Atomic Physics: an Introduction' 1963; 'Introduction à la physique atomique' 1964; 'Introduction a la Fisica Atomica' 1968; other writings incl. chapters for prof. books and over 50 scient. papers on atomic physics; mem., Assn. Canadienne Française pour l'Avance. des Sciences; Candn. Assn. Phys. (Pres. 1955); Am. Phys. Soc.; Mexican Phys. Soc.; Royal Astron. Soc. Can.; Order des ingénieurs du Québec; R. Catholic; recreations: skiing, sailing, canoeing, history; Home: 2166 Bourbonnière Park, Sillery, Quebec, Que. G1T 1B4.

**KESSELMAN, Jonathan Rhys,** B.A., Ph.D.; university professor; b. Columbus, Ohio 17 March 1946; s. Louis Coleridge and Jennie (Stregevsky) K.; e. Oberlin College B.A. (Hons.) 1968; Massachusetts Inst. of Technology Ph.D. 1972; m. Sheila d. Sue and Nathan Kaplan 12 March 1973; one d.: Maresa; PROF. OF ECONOMICS, UNIV. OF B.C. 1981– ; Dir., Centre for Rsch. on Economic and Social Policy, U.B.C. 1992– ; Systems Analyst & Econ., Systems Research Group Toronto 1970; Econ., Office of Econ. Opportunity Washington 1972; Rsch. Assoc., Inst. for Rsch. on Poverty, Univ. of Wisconsin-Madison 1974–75; Visiting Scholar, Delhi Sch. of Econ. India 1978–79; Visiting Fellow, Australian Nat. Univ. 1985; Asst. & Assoc. Prof. of Econ., Univ. of B.C. 1972–81; Cons., Canada Dept. of Finance; Treas. of N.Z.; B.C. Min. of Finance; Employment & Immigration Canada; Dept. of Nat. Health & Welfare; B.C. Workers' Comp. Bd.; Ont. Min. of Treas. & Econ. and private industry; Professorial Fellowship in Econ. Policy, Reserve Bank of Australia 1985; Dir., Tibetan Refugee Aid Soc. 1980–82; Trustee, Univ. of B.C. Pension Plan 1988–90; Edit. Bd., 'Canadian Taxation' 1979–82; Chrmn. & Representative, Musqueam Indian Band Taxation Advisory Council 1992– ; Mem., Am. Econ. Assn.; Candn. Tax Found.; author: 'Financing Canadian Unemployment Insurance' 1983, 'Rate Structure and Personal Taxation' 1990 and numerous journal articles, contbns. to conf. volumes & edited volumes; recreations: investment, carpentry; club: U.B.C. Faculty; Home: 4273 Musqueam Dr., Vancouver, B.C. V6N 3R8; Office: Vancouver, B.C. V6T 1Z1.

**KEVAN, Peter Graham,** B.Sc., Ph.D., F.R.E.S.; university professor; b. Edinburgh, Scotland 17 June 1944; s. Douglas Kieth McEwan and Kathleen Edith (Luckin) K. e. McGill Univ. B.Sc. (Hons.) 1965; Univ. of Alta. Ph.D. 1970; m. Sherrene d. Betty and Carl Kent; children: Colin Douglas, Kathleen Hannah; PROF., UNIV. OF GUELPH 1982– ; Nat. Co-ord., Internat. Biolog. Prog. (CT) 1969–70; Contract Biolog., Candn. Wildlife Serv. (Inuvik/Edmonton) 1970–71; Post-Doct. Fellow, Can. Agric. (Ottawa) 1971–72; Project Mgr., Mem. Univ. 1972–75; Town Counc., Pouch Cove, Nfld. 1974–75; Asst. Prof., Univ. of Colorado 1975–82; Cons., Food & Agric. Orgn. (Rome) 1983, 1984; CIDA, IDRC in Can. & Far East; Palm Oil Rsch. Inst. of Malaysia 1983 and others; F.R.E.S.; several NRC scholar/fellowships; Mem., Entomol. Socs. of Can. & Ont.; Botanical Soc. of Am.; Brit. Ecolog. Soc.; Internat. Assn. for Ecol.; Internat. Bee Rsch. Assn.; Royal Entomol. Soc.; author of over 100 sci. articles & several book chapters; co-editor of one book; recreations: natural history, gardening, woodwork; Home: 352 River Rd., Cambridge, Ont. N3C 2B7; Office: Guelph, Ont. N1G 2W1.

**KEYES, Ken,** B.A., M.Ed., N.D.C.; politician; b. Wolfe Island, Ont. 16 Sept. 1930; s. John and Elsie (Allum) K.; e. Toronto Teachers Coll. 1950; Queen's Univ. B.A. 1965; Univ. of Ottawa M.Ed. 1972; Nat. Defence Coll. 1981; m. Carrie d. Thomas and Sarah Richmond 25 Aug. 1951; 4 d., 2 s.; Parliamentary Asst. to the Min. of Education 1989; served as Ald. City of Kingston 12 yrs., Dep. Mayor 5 yrs., Mayor 4 years; el. M.P.P. for Kingston and the Islands 1985; Solr. Gen. and Min. of Correctional Services 1985–87; Parlty Asst. to the Min. of Health 1987–89; mem. Ont. Pub. Sch. Teachers' Fedn.; recreations: boating, amateur theatre; Home: 339 Norman Rogers Dr., Kingston, Ont. K7M 2R9.

**KEYFITZ, Nathan,** Ph.D., LL.D., F.R.S.C.; professor; b. Westmount, P.Q. 29 June 1913; s. Arthur and Anna (Gerstein) K.; e. McGill University, B.Sc. 1934; University of Chicago, Ph.D. 1952; Univ. of N. Carolina, 1946; m. Beatrice, d. Henry Orkin, Oct. 1939; children: Barbara, Robert; HEAD, POPULATION PROGRAM, INTERNATIONAL INST. FOR APPLIED SYSTEMS ANALYSIS, VIENNA 1984– ; engaged in Census, Soc. Analysis, External Trade Dept. 1936–46; Math Advisor, Central Rsch. and Development Staff, Dominion Bureau of Statistics 1946–50; Sr. Research Stat., Dom. Bureau of Statistics 1950–59; Dir., Colombo Plan Bureau. 1956–57; recipient Gold Medal, Profl. Inst. of the Civil Service of Canada 1957; Technical Asst. missions Burma 1951; Indonesia 1952–3, 1985–90; Argentina 1960; Chile 1963; Beijing 1981; Senegal 1982; Indonesia 1985–88 and others; Prof., Dept. Pol. Econ., Univ. of Toronto 1959–63; Univ. of Montreal 1962–63; Prof., Dept. of Sociol., Univ. of Chicago 1963–68 (Chrmn. of Dept. 1965–67); Prof. of Demography, Univ. of Cal., Berkeley 1968–72; Prof., Harvard Univ. 1972–83 (Chrmn. of Dept. 1978–80), Emeritus 1983; Lectr. in Demography, Univ. of Moscow 1978; Lazarus Prof., Ohio State Univ. 1981–83, Emeritus 1983; Rosenstadt Prof., Univ. of Toronto 1983–84; apptd. Acad. Adv., Royal Comn. on Biling. & Bicult., Feb. 1964; Dir., Social Sci. Rsch. Counc. 1959–64; LL.D.: Univ. of Western Ont. 1972; Univ. de Montréal 1984; McGill Univ. 1984; Univ. of Alta. 1984; Univ. of Siena 1991; Carleton Univ. 1993; Univ. de Québec 1993; recipient, Commonwealth Award 1991; Austrian Cross of Honour for Science, First Class 1993; publications: 'An Introduction to the Mathematics of Population' 1968; 'World Population Growth and Aging (with Wilhelm Flieger) 1991; 'Applied Mathematical Demography' 1977; 'Population Change and Social Policy' 1982; papers in scient. journs.; Fellow, Am. Stat. Assn.; el. to Roy. Soc. of Can. 1959; Nat. Acad. of Sciences (U.S.) 1977; mem., Internat. Stat. Inst.; Population Assn. of Am. (Pres. 1970–71); Candn. Pol. Science Assn. (Vice-Pres. 1962); Am. Acad. of Arts and Sciences, Phi Beta Kappa; Address: 1580 Massachusetts Ave., Apt. 7C, Cambridge, MA 02138 U.S.A.

**KEYS, John David,** M.Sc., Ph.D., P.Eng.; Consultant; b. Toronto, Ont. 30 Sept. 1922; s. David Arnold and May Irene (Freeze) K.; e. Montreal West (Que.) and Lower Can. Coll. Montreal, 1939; McGill Univ., B.Sc. 1947, M.Sc. 1948, Ph.D. (Nuclear Physics) 1951; m. Ruth Olivet, d. George Henry Harris, 23 Oct. 1945; children: Susan Irene, David George; CONSULTANT 1981– ; Prof. of Physics and subsequently Head of Dept., Candn. Services Coll., Royal Roads, 1951–58; joined Dept. of Mines and Tech. Surveys, Mines Br., Mineral Sciences Div. as Research Scientist, 1958; apptd. Head, Mineral Physics Sec., 1963; Chief, Hydrologic Sciences Div., Inland Waters Br., Dept. of Energy, Mines and Resources, 1967–70; Science Adv., Treasury Bd. Secretariart 1970–71; Asst. Vice Pres. (Labs.) Nat. Research Council 1971–74, Vice Pres. (Program) 1974–76; Asst. Depy. Min. (Science & Technol.) Dept. of Energy, Mines & Resources 1976–81; served with RCNVR attached to RN (Combined Operations), 1941–45; rank Lt.(n) on discharge; spent 5 months at Semiconductor Inst., Leningrad and research estabs. in Moscow, Baku and Tashkent under auspices of Nat. Research Council – Soviet Acad. of Sciences Exchange Program, 1963; mem., Am. Assn. Advanc. Science; Am. Phys. Soc.; Candn. Assn. Physicists; Royal Astron. Soc.; Sigma Xi; Psi Upsilon (Pres., McGill Chapter, 1945); Protestant; recreations: tennis, scuba diving; Home: 39 Rideau Terrace, Ottawa, Ont. K1M 2A2.

**KEYSER, J. James,** B.A.; management consultant; b. Toronto, Ont. 1 Sept. 1936; s. James M. and Laura; e. Univ. of Toronto B.A. 1960, post-grad. work 1961; m. Mary H., d. Dr. W.D. Harding, 1 July 1962; children: Murray, Ellen, Nancy; PRESIDENT, KEYSER CONSULTING INC. and HUMAN RESOURCES CONSULTING PARTNER – THE COOPERS AND LYBRAND CONSULTING GROUP; Personnel Mgr. Traders Group Ltd. 1966, Dir. of Personnel 1971, Vice Pres. Personnel and Organ. 1973; Personnel Supvr. Bank of Nova Scotia 1969; Dir. and Vice Pres. Personnel Assn. Toronto; Dir. and Vice Pres., Personnel Assn. of Ont.; Extve. Mem. Ont. Soc. Training & Devel. (Bd.); Phi Kappa Sigma (Vice Pres.); Club: Mayfair; Home and Office: 66 Silverbirch Ave., Toronto, Ont. M4E 3K9.

**KEYSER, Walter Alan,** B.A.; real estate finance and consulting; b. London, Ont. 1 Aug. 1936; e. Univ. of W. Ont., B.A. (Hons. Business Adm.) 1958; PRES. W.A. KEYSER & ASSOCIATES LIMITED since 1978; with Bank of Canada, special assignment, Can. Conversion Loan 1958; joined Gairdner & Co. Ltd., Toronto, Invest. Dealers to estab. Money Market Dept. 1959; retired from Co. as Sr. Vice-Pres. March 1973; to assist in forming Heitman Canadian Realty Investors, a public real estate investment trust; Chrmn. & C.E.O. Heitman Financial Services Ltd. 1973–78; Vice Pres.-Investments & Treas., The Dominion Life Assurance Co. 1983–85; W.A. Keyser & Associates Ltd. originates and administers NHA-insured and conventional mtge. loans and acquires commercial real estate on behalf of domestic and non-resident financial institutions; served in RCASC rank Lt.; Dir., AGF Management Ltd., Dir., Hardit Corp. Ltd.; Tor.; Dir., AGF Trust Co.; Dir., Transmetro Properties Ltd.; Dir., Cathedral Square Partnership and various other real estate joint ventures of City of Toronto with private developers; Beta Theta Pi; P. Conservative (Past Pres. UWO Young P. Cons. Assn.); Un. Church; recreations: golf, skiing; Home: R.R. 1, Terra Cotta, Ont.; Office: R.R. #1, Terra Cotta, Ont. L0P 1N0.

**KEYSERLINGK, Michaela;** textile conservator; b. Breslau, Germany 1 Aug. 1939; d. Dr. Adalbert Graf and Dr. Gisela Graefin (Baronin von Schaumberg) von Keyserlingk; e. Kempfhausen, Germany, teacher's diploma; Munich Univ. child psychology 1961; Algonquin College Museology diploma 1978; m. Robert s. Robert and Sigrid Keyserlingk 11 May 1963; children: Andrea, Thomas, Alexander, Martin; SR. TEXTILE CONSERVATOR, CANADIAN CONSERVATION INST., GOVT. OF CANADA, MIN. OF CANADIAN HERITAGE 1978– ; taught private school Tübingen, Germany 1961–62; Custodian, Chalice Well Trust, Glastonbury, England 1962–63; Extve. Mem., Candn. Assn. of Profl. Conservators; Asst. Coord., Textile Group, Internat. Ctte. of Musuems; Mem., Internat. Inst. of Conservation, Candn. Group (Treas. 1983); author of numerous articles; co-author: 'CCI Notes'; recreations: interior design, gardening; Home: 675 Gilmour St., Ottawa, Ont. K1R 5L9; Office: 1030 Innes Rd., Ottawa, Ont. K1A 0C8.

**KEYSERLINGK, Robert Henry,** B.A., M.A., Ph.D.; retired university professor; b. Berlin, Germany 16 May 1933; s. Robert Wendlin and Sigrid (von der Recke) K.; e. Lower Can. Coll.; Loyola H.S.; Loyola Coll., B.A. 1949; Fribourg Univ.; Göttingen Univ.; Univ. of Toronto, M.A. 1958; Univ. of London (England), Ph.D. 1964; m. Michaela d. Graf Adalbert von Keyserlingk 11 May 1963; children: Andrea, Thomas, Alexander, Martin; Prof., History Dept., Univ. of Ottawa 1963–93, retired; Corresponding Sec., Pax Romana, Fribourg, Switz. 1950–51; Fgn. Serv. Offr., Govt. of Can. 1958–61; Vis. Prof., Univ. of P.E.I. 1972, 1973; Dir., Candn. Military Hist. Assn.; Candn. Immigration Hist. Soc.; Ed. Bd., 'Canadian Review of Studies in Nationalism'; German & Austrian Acad. Insts. scholarships; Can. Counc. & SSHRCC scholarships; Roman Catholic; Mem., Knights of Malta; Candn. Inst. of Internat. Affairs; Candn. Ethnic Studies Assn.; Candn. Hist. Assn.; author: 'Canada: The Role of Middle Powers in World Politics' 1969, 'Survival for Charity: History of the Sovereign Order of Malta' 1974, 'Media Manipulation: The Press and Bismarck in Imperial Germany' 1977, 'Austria in World War II: An Anglo-American Dilemma' 1988, 1990 and 30 articles; recreations: politics, gardening, running; Home: 675 Gilmour St., Ottawa, Ont. K1R 5L9; Office: Ottawa, Ont. K1N 5N6.

**KHAN, Abrahim Habibulla,** B.S., B.D., M.A., Ph.D.; philosopher of religion; b. British Guiana 13 Apr. 1943; s. Habibulla and Delasia (Chatrupaul) K.; e. Howard Univ. Washington, D.C. B.S. 1965; Yale Univ. B.D. 1968; McGill Univ. M.A. 1971, Ph.D. 1973; m. Pamela d. Peter and Sadie O'Neill 11 Oct. 1969; children: Tariq K., Roshan S., Laith T.; LECTR. IN DEPT. FOR THE STUDY OF RELIGION, RSCH. ASSOC. IN ARTS, TRINITY COLL. AND ASSOC. MEM. OF CENTRE FOR BIOETHICS, UNIV. OF TORONTO; Concurrent, Assoc. Prof. (Visiting), Dept. of Religion, Concordia Univ. 1991–92; Convenor, Kierkegaard Circle present univ. 1987– , Lectr. in Religious Studies and Rsch. Assoc. in Arts at Trinity Coll., Univ. of Toronto 1986– ; Lectr. in Religious Studies McGill Univ. 1973, Rsch. Assoc. in Philos. 1974–75, Asst. Prof. 1979–81; Lectr. in Religious Studies Concordia Univ. and Champlain Coll. 1974–75; Asst. Prof. of Religious Studies Univ. of Man. 1975–76, Univ. of Toronto 1976–79; Lectr. in Philos. Trent Univ. 1982, Asst. Prof. 1983–84; Assoc. Prof. of Religious Studies, McMaster Univ. summer 1984–85; Rsch. Assoc. Trinity Coll. Univ. of Toronto 1984–85, Hon. Fellow and Rsch. Reader Centre for Religious

Studies 1985–86; Bd. mem., Candn. Federation for the Humanities 1993– ; Bd. mem., Dialogue Centre Montréal 1969–75; Mem., Ethics Ctte., Clarke Inst. of Psychiatry 1990– ; Extve. Mem., North Am. Assn. for the Study of Religion 1990– ; Co-organizer, Søren Kierkegaard Soc. (USA); recipient McConnell Summer Fellowship 1971, Univ. Summer Fellowship 1973, Rsch. Grant, McGill Univ. 1980–81; Qué. Rsch. Grant participant, 1972–73; SSHRCC Rsch. Grant 1979–80, 1985, 1986, 1988, 1989, 1990; Int'l. Travel Grant 1985, 1987; author: ''Salighed' As Happiness? Kierkegaard on the Concept Salighed' 1985; 'Rethinking Philosophy of Religion in a Theological Context' TJT 1989; 'The Academic Study of Religion with reference to Islam' in Scottish Journal of Religious Studies, 1990; 'The Idea of Person with Reference to Islam' 1990; 'Playing With Fire: On Prometheus Rebound' TJT 1991; 'Kierkegaard's Acknowledged Works: Introduction to Four Essays' TJT 1992; 'Melancholy: An Elusive Dimension of Depression?' Journal of Medical Humanities 1994; num. articles, reviews and other publs.; mem. Candn. Soc. Study Religion; Candn. Theol. Soc. (Pres. 1985–86; Ed. Newsletter 1984–87); Assn. Advanc. Scandinavian Studies Can.; Am. Acad. Religion (Chair, Kierkegaard Seminar 1985–89); Candn. Philos. Soc.; Søren Kierkegaard Soc.; recreation: volleyball; Home: 1045 Escott Court, Pickering, Ont. L1X 1P2; Office: Trinity College, Univ. of Toronto, 6 Hoskin Ave., Toronto, Ont. M5S 1H8.

**KHANER, Julie;** actor; b. Montreal, Que. 5 Dec. 1957; d. Lyon and Valentina (Shpilman) K.; e. Westmount H.S.; Dawson College/Dome Theatre 1974–78; PRINCIPAL ACTOR (ALANA NEWMAN), 'STREET LEGAL', CBC; roles in 'Videodrome' (David Cronenberg), 'Escape from Iran' (Lamont Johnson), 'For Those I Loved' (Robert Enrico); various roles at Stratford Festival 1985–86; guest roles: 'Adderly,' 'Night Heat,' 'The Twilight Zone,' 'Forgiving Harry,' 'My Secret Identity' and 'E.N.G.'; Mem., ACTRA, EQUITY, Academy of Canadian Cinema & TV; Office: c/o ACI, 205 Ontario St., Toronto, Ont. M5A 2V6.

**KHARAS, Firdaus James,** B.A., M.A.; political scientist; b. Calcutta 18 Nov. 1955; s. Jimmy P. and Coomi J.K.; e. Univ. of Cambridge, Indian Sch. Cert. 1972; Comm. of Penn., Hon. Dipl. 1974; Thiel Coll., B.A. (magna cum laude) 1978; Carleton Univ., M.A. 1979; Program for Senior Managers in Govt., John F. Kennedy School of Government, Harvard Univ. 1992; m. Elizabeth Service 6 Aug. 1988; children: Nicholas, Kaitlin; ASST. DEP. CHRMN. (OTTAWA/ATLANTIC REGION), IMMIGRATION AND REFUGEE BD. OF CAN. 1989– ; Intern, U.N. Info. Ctr., Wash. D.C.; Rsch. analyst, Commonwealth of Penn.; Pres., Global Outlook 1980–82; Extve. Dir., United Nations Assn. in Can. 1982–87; Consultant – Policy Advisor (Immigration) to the Min. of Employment & Immigration of Can. 1988–89; Mem., several Candn. U.N. & U.N.A. dels., worldwide incl. 40th UN General Assembly; Extve. Ctte., World Fed. of U.N. Assns.; recipient, UN Peace Medal; Medal of the World Fed. of U.N. Assns.; several scholarships & acad. awards; former Rotary exchange student; rel.: Parsee; author of several articles; recreations: travelling, music; Office: 240 Bank St., Ottawa, Ont. K1A 0K1.

**KHATRI, Aslam;** business executive; VICE-PRESIDENT, FINANCE & TREASURER, KAUFEL GROUP LIMITED; Office: 1811 Hymus Blvd., Dorval, Que. H9P 1J5.

**KIDD, Bruce,** B.A., A.M., M.A., Ph.D.; university professor; b. Ottawa, Ont. 26 July 1943; s. James Robbins and Margaret Edith (Easto) K.; e. Univ. of Toronto B.A. (Hons.) 1965; Univ. of Chicago A.M. 1968; York Univ. M.A. 1980, Ph.D. 1990; m. Phyllis Berck 7 May 1988; PROFESSOR, SCHOOL OF PHYSICAL AND HEALTH EDUCATION, UNIV. OF TORONTO 1991– ; Lectr., Maharajah's College & Information Officer, Colombo Plan Project, Univ. of Rajasthan 1965–66; Community Prog. Offr., Ont. Dept. of Edn. 1966–67; Extve. Asst. & Rsch. Offr., Sec. of the Treasury Bd., Govt. of Ont. 1968–70; Lectr., Univ. of Toronto 1970–73; Asst. Prof. 1973–79; Assoc. Prof. 1979–91; Co-ord., Candn. Studies, Univ. College 1986–90; Dir., School of Physical and Health Edn. 1991– ; Chair, Olympic Academy of Can. 1983–93; Lou Marsh Trophy 1961; Candn. Press, Athlete of the Year 1961, '62; T.A. Loudon Trophy, Univ. of Toronto 1964; Prov. of Ont. Achievement Award 1965; Queen's Message Relay, Buckingham Palace 1966; Amateur Athletic Union of Canada Hall of Fame 1966; Canada's Sports Hall of Fame 1968; City of Toronto Merit Award 1971; Prov. of Ont. Merit Award 1975; U.N. Special Ctte. against Apartheid special citation 1985; Univ. of Toronto Hall of Fame 1988; Canada 125 Medal 1993; several past community & sports executive appointments incl. Dir., Toronto Ont. Olympic Council 1990; Mem., Candn. Olympic Assn. 1981– ; Dir., Stadium Corp. of Ont. 1990– ; author: 'The Political Economy of Sport' 1979, 'Tom Longboat' 1980, 'Hockey Showdown' 1980, 'Who's a Soccer Player' 1980; co-author: 'The Death of Hockey' 1972, 'Athletes' Rights in Canada' 1982; recreations: reading, cycling, hiking; Home: 72 Greensides Ave., Toronto, Ont. M6G 3P7; Office: 320 Huron St., Toronto, Ont. M5S 1A1.

**KIDD, George Pirkis,** M.A.; retired diplomat; b. Glasgow, Scotland 6 June 1917; s. George Watson and Mary Hood (McIntyre) K.; came to Canada, 1922; e. St. Michaels Sch. (1928–32) and Brentwood Coll., Victoria, B.C. (1932–36); Univ. of British Columbia, B.A. 1939; Univ. of Illinois, (Fellowship) M.A. 1941; m. Lola M., d. R. H. Calverley, Loveland, Colo., 1949; joined Dept. of External Affairs, 1946; Candn. Legation, Warsaw, 1947–49; Candn. Embassy, Paris, 1949–51; student at Nat. Defence Coll., 1951–52; with the Dept. at Ottawa, 1952–54; Charge d'Affaires, Candn. Embassy, Tel Aviv, 1954–57; returned to the Dept. at Ottawa, 1957–59; mem. of Directing Staff, Nat. Defence Coll., 1959–61; Ambassador to Cuba & Haiti, 1961–64; Minister Candn. Embassy, Washington, 1964–67; Vice-Pres., Canadian Inter. Development Agency, 1967–71; Asst. Secretary-General, Commonwealth Secretariat, London, 1971–74; High Commr. Nigeria and concurrently Sierra Leone, 1974–77; served in 2nd World War with Candn. Army, 1941–46; served overseas with Queens Own Cameron Highlanders of Can. in U.K. and France; wounded in action; Past Chrmn., Bd. of Gov., Univ. of Victoria; Past Pres., Bd. of Trustees, Art Gallery of Greater Victoria; Hon. Doctor of Laws, Univ. of Victoria 1992; Pres., Art Gallery of Greater Victoria Found.; Anglican; Address: 1033 Belmont Ave., Suite 704, Victoria, B.C. V8S 3T4.

**KIDD, Kenneth E.,** M.A.; university professor; b. Barrie, Ont. 21 July 1906; s. D. Ferguson and Florence May (Jebb) K.; e. Univ. of Toronto (Victoria Coll.) B.A. 1931, M.A. 1937; Univ. of Chicago, 1939–40; m. Martha Ann, d. late O.V. Maurer, Oct. 1943; PROF. EMERITUS OF ANTHROPOL., TRENT UNIV. 1973– (Prof. 1968–73; Chrmn. of Dept. 1967–70; 1st Chrmn., Indian-Eskimo Studies 1969–70); joined staff of Royal Ont. Museum 1935; Asst., Dept. of Ethnol. 1942, Jt. Curator 1956, Hon. Curator (Ethnology) 1981; in charge of numerous archaeol, excavations, incl. Ste. Marie I (site of Jesuit mission of 1639–49); Huron Indian ossuary, Ossossané 1947–48; publications: 'The Excavation of Ste. Marie I' 1949; 'Canadians of Long Ago' 1951; 'Indian Rock Paintings of the Great Lakes' (with S. Dewdney) 1961; 'A classification for glass beads for the use of field archaeologists' (with M.A. Kidd) 1977; 'Glass bead-making from the middle ages to the early 19th century' 1979; 'Excavations at Cartier-Brébeuf Park, Quebec City, 1959' 1980; 'The Dating of Cutlery Objects for the Use of Archaeologists' (microfiche) 1983; 'Blackfoot Ethnography' 1986; awarded Guggenheim Mem. Fellowship 1951–52; Cornplanter Medal 1970; Award for Eminent Service, Trent Univ. 1983; J.C. Harrington Medal, Soc. for Historical Archaeology 1985; Award 'for Outstanding Contributions to Amer. Archaeol.,' Soc. for Amer. Archaeol. Denver, Colorado 1985; Fellow, Am. Anthropol. Assn.; Royal Anthrop. Inst. of Gt. Britain & Ireland; Trent Univ. LL.D. (honoris causa) 1990; awarded Commemorative Medal for 125th Anniversary of Candn. Confederation 1992; mem., Soc. Am. Archaeol. (Past Vice-Pres.); Am. Indian Ethnohist. Conf. (Extve. Comte.); Internat. Cong. of Americanists; Am. Ethol. Soc.; Am. Soc. for Ethnohist.; Soc. for Hist. Arch.; British Museum Soc.; Candn. Rock Art Rsch. Assocs.; Candn. Sociol. & Anthrop. Soc.; Indian-Eskimo Assn. Can.; Ont. Archeol. Soc.; Ont. Hist. Soc.; Candn. Archaeological Assn.; Hon. Life mem. R.O.M. since 1964, nominated Hon. Curator; mem. Scient. Adv. Comte. of Quetico Foundn.; el. mem., Explorers' Club of N.Y., 1979; Protestant; recreation: travel; Office: Trent University, Peterborough, Ont. K9J 7B8.

**KIDD, Robert Hugh,** B.Com., M.B.A., F.C.A.; executive; b. Toronto, Ont. 1 June 1944; s. Donald Alexander K.; e. Univ. of Toronto Schs. 1962; Univ. of Toronto B.Com. 1966; C.A. 1969; York Univ. M.B.A. 1973; m. Elizabeth Maria; children: Donald, Scott, Susanne; SR. VICE PRES. AND CHIEF FINANCIAL OFFR. & DIR., GEORGE WESTON LTD. 1981– ; Dir. Loblaw Companies Ltd.; E.B. Eddy Forest Products Ltd.; B.C. Packers Ltd.; Credit Suisse Canada; Partner, Thorne Riddell & Co. Toronto 1973–81; Lectr. Sch. of Business Univ. of Toronto 1969–81; recipient various undergrad. scholarships, awards; Gov. Gen.'s Gold Medal, Candn. Inst. C.A.'s 1968; Silver Medal 1967, Gold Medal 1968 Ont. Inst. C.A.'s; Edmund Gunn Prize 1968; Fred Page Higgins' Award 1967; author various publs.; Chrmn., Appleby College Found.; mem. Candn. Inst. C.A.'s; Candn. Tax Foundation; Council Financial Extves.; Conf. Bd. Can.; Candn. Cancer Soc. Investment Ctte.; United Church; recreations: skiing, boating, tennis; Club: Caledon Ski; Office: 2001, 22 St. Clair Ave. E., Toronto, Ont. M4T 2S7.

**KIDDER, Margot;** actress; b. Yellowknife, N.W.T. 17 Oct. 1948; e. Univ. of B.C.; m. 1stly Tom McGuane (divorced); one d. Maggie; m. 2ndly John Heard (divorced); began career Candn. theatre and TV; film debut 'Gaily, Gaily' 1969; other films incl. 'Quackser Fortune Has a Cousin in the Bronx' 1970; 'Sisters' 1972; 'Gravy Train' 1974; 'The Great Waldo Pepper' 1975; 'The Reincarnation of Peter Proud' 1975; '92 in the Shade' 1977; 'Superman' 1978; 'The Amityville Horror' 1979; 'Superman II' 1981; 'Some Kind of Hero' 1981; 'Heartaches' 1981; 'Trenchcoat' 1983; starred TV series 'Nichols' 1972; other TV appearances incl. 'Switch,' 'Baretta,' 'Barnaby Jones,' 'Hawaii Five-O, Mod Squad'; TV movie 'Honky Tonk' 1974.

**KIEFL, Barry,** B.A., M.Sc.; communications executive; b. Ottawa, Ont. 26 Apl. 1949; s. Richard Francis and Theresa Mary (Quinn) K.; e. Carleton Univ. B.A. 1970; Boston Univ. M.Sc. 1973; m. Mary d. Floyd and Kathleen Lemon 7 Jan. 1989; children: Mika, Sarah; DIR. OF RSCH. CBC/RADIO-CANADA 1983– ; radio announcer/producer CBC 1970–71; policy analyst and writer/ed. Dept. Communications and Candn. Radio-Television & Telecommunications Comn. 1972–76; Sr. Rsch. CBC 1976–83; Visiting Prof. Univ. of Ottawa; frequent lectr. univs., guest speaker confs.; Dir. Candn. Advt. Rsch. Found.; Bureau Broadcast Measurement; author numerous reports and studies broadcasting & communications; mem. Profl. Mkt. Rsch. Soc.; Candn. Communications Assn.; Broadcast Rsch. Council; recreation: tennis; Home: 17 Castlethorpe Cres., Nepean, Ont. K2G 5P6; Office: Box 8478, Ottawa, Ont. K1G 3J5.

**KIERAN, Michael Eric Robert;** author, business executive; b. St. Catharines, Ont. 23 Sept. 1953; s. Jon William and Sheila Harriet (Ginzler) K.; e. Jarvis C.I. 1972; m. Jane Elizabeth d. Goldwyn and Lula Faint 21 June 1981; children: Christopher, Andrew; PRESIDENT, DESKTOP PUBLISHING ASSOCIATES 1985– ; Science researcher/writer, TVOntario 1973–80; Reporter, The Globe & Mail 1980–83; Sales Manager, Compuserve 1983–85; senior executive & principle of a Toronto-based training & consulting co. specializing in electronic publishing 1985– ; Ed. Bd. Mem., 'Electronic Composition & Imaging' magazine 1990–92; Guest Speaker, MacWorld Expo, the Seybold Pub. Conf., Color Connections, Aldus Colour Forum, the Electronic Design Show, the Electronic Desktop Pub. Assn., the Assn. for Systems Management, the Candn. Computer Show, ComGraph, Graphic Trade, Vicom and others; awarded special citation from U.S. Air Force for excellence in mathematics 1972 and for excellence in life sciences 1973 for science fair projects; Mem., Bd. of Dir., Toronto Waldorf School 1990– ; author: 'Desktop Publishing in Color' 1991 and more than 200 newspaper & magazine articles; colour editor & columnist: 'Electronic Composition & Imaging' magazine 1989–92; editor: 'Computer Products Update' 1985–86; recreations: woodworking, birdwatching; Home: 35 Edgar Ave, Richmond Hill, Ont. L4C 6K2; Office: 1992 Yonge St., Suite 301, Toronto, Ont. M4S 1Z7.

**KIERAN, Sheila Harriet;** b. Toronto, Ont. 4 May 1930; d. Seymour Robert and Ida (Schulman) Ginzler; e. elem. and high schs. Toronto and New York City; Columbia Univ. Sch. of Extension; Univ. of Toronto Dept. of Extension; m. 1951; divorced 1968; children: Susan (dec. 1991), Michael, Patricia, Mark, Jon, Frances, Andrew; SR. EDITORIAL ADVISOR AND MEMBER OF THE HOUSEHOLD, the Rt. Hon. Ramon Hnatyshyn, Governor General of Canada; Editor, all published documents of Royal Comm. on the Future of the Toronto Waterfront and other govt. reports and documents; Sr. Policy Advr., Min. of the Environment 1985–87; speechwriter, various Cabinet ministers 1987–90; author, Canada's submission to the World Comm. on Environment and Development (the Brundtland Comm.); Dir. of Public Participation of the Royal Comm. on Violence in the Communications Industry (the 'LaMarsh Commission') 1975–77; author 'The Family Matters: Two Centuries of Family Law and Life in Ontario' 1986; 'The Non-Deductible Woman: A Handbook for Working Wives and Mothers' 1970; contrib. 'The Chatelaine Guide to Marriage' 1974; author numerous articles, radio and TV commentaries, speeches, brochures; Bd. mem. of various Comm. and voluntary groups and agencies; Office: Rideau Hall, 1 Sussex Dr., Ottawa, Ont. K1A 0A1.

**KIERANS, Hon. Eric William,** P.C., B.A., LL.D. (Hon.), D.C.L. (Hon.); economist; executive; b. Montreal, P.Q. 2 February 1914; s. Hugh and Lena (Schmidt) K.; e. Loyola Coll., B.A. 1935; McGill Univ. (1947–51) Grad. Research in Econ.; St. Thomas Univ., LL.D. (Hon.), 1979; McGill Univ., LL.D. (Hon.) 1981; Bishops Univ., D.C.L. (Hon.) 1983; King's Coll. (Halifax) D.C.L.; McMaster Univ. LL.D.; Concordia Univ. LL.D. 1987; Dalhousie Univ. LL.D. 1991; m. Teresa Catherine, d. late Edw. P. Whelan, 12 Nov. 1938; children: Thomas Edward, Catherine Anne; Dir., Sch. of Comm., McGill Univ., and Prof. of Comm. and Finance there 1953–60; Pres., Montreal and Canadian Stock Exchanges 1960–63; el. to Que. Leg. for Notre Dame de Grace, by-el. Sept. 1963, re-el. June 1966; Minister of Revenue, Que. 1963–65; Min. of Health, Que. 1965–66; Pres., Que. Lib. Fed. 1966–68; cand. for Fed. Liberal leadership 1968; el. to H. of C. June 1968; apptd. Postmaster General (also Min. responsible for Dept. of Communications) July 1968; Min. of Communications May 1969; resigned from Cabinet 29 Apr. 1971; Prof. of Econ., McGill Univ. 1972–80; Prof. of Economics, Dalhousie Univ. 1983–84; Dir.: Sidbec-Dosco Ltée. 1978; Caisse de Dépot et Placement du Qué. 1979; Chrmn., Canadian Adhesives Ltd. 1980; Pres., Kara Investments Limited 1982; engaged by Manitoba Govt. as a Consultant on Resources Policy, Apr. 1972; Lt., 2nd Battation (Res.), Victoria Rifles of Can. 1942–46; author: 'Challenge of Confidence: Kierans on Canada' 1967; 'Report on Natural Resources Policy in Manitoba' 1973; (with Walter Stewart) 'Wrong End of the Rainbow'; 1983 Massey Lectr. (5 Lectures on Globalism and the Nation State); Dal Grauer Memorial Lectr., Univ. of B.C. 1984; David Alexander Meml. Lect., Memorial Univ. 1985; Fellow in Residence, Inst. for Rsch. on Public Policy 1985; Dir., Lester Pearson Inst. for Internat. Development; The Dalhousie Medical Rsch. Found.; Mem. of Counc., N.S. Barristers' Soc. 1990– ; Chrmn., N.S. Working Ctte. on the Constitution; Liberal; Roman Catholic; recreation: sports; Clubs: M.A.A.A. (Past Pres.); Seigniory, Montebello, Que.; Faculty (McGill); University (Montreal); Coral Beach and Tennis (Bermuda); The Saraguay; Faculty (Dalhousie Univ.); Home: 1000 Winwick Rd., Halifax, N.S. B3H 4L5.

**KIERANS, P. Emmet,** Q.C., B.A., B.C.L.; lawyer; b. Montreal, Que. 23 March 1915; s. late Thomas and Margaret (McAran) K.; e. St. Patrick's and D'Arcy McGee High Sch., Montreal; Univ. of Montreal; Sir George Williams Univ.; Queen's Univ., B.A. 1945; McGill Univ., B.C.L. 1948; m. Doris May, d. Joseph Daigle, Edmundston, N.B., 7 May 1949; children: Patrick, David, Mark, Elaine, Louise, Renée; SR. PARTNER, KIERANS & GUAY, since 1973; Quebec Agent: Ludlow Canada Inc.; G C Services Corp.; Consolidated Rail Corp.; read law with Dixon, Claxton, Senécal, Turnbull & Mitchell; called to Bar of Que. 1948; cr. Q.C. 1963; Partner, Dixon, Senécal, Turnbull, Mitchell, Stairs, Culver & Kierans, 1956; Senécal, Kierans & Stairs, 1963; Kierans & Guay, 1964; Kierans, Kisilenko & Guay, 1967–73; Lectr. in Civil Law, McGill Univ., 1957–63; served as Civil Math. Instr., RCAF, St. Hubert during World War II; Vice-Pres., Que. Lib. Fed. 1956–58; Westmount Lib. Assn. 1967–69; N.D.G. Lib Assn. 1952–58; Rental Commr. of Que., 1960–66; mem. Council of Montreal Bd. Trade, 1976–81; Secy. and Charter mem., Fed. Eng. Speaking Cath. Teachers Inc. 1939–41; Secy., Jr. Bar Assn. Montreal, 1951–53; Life mem., St. Patrick's Soc. Montreal; mem., Montreal, Que. and Candn. Bar Assns; Liberal; R. Catholic; recreations: Canadian history, art, antiques; Club: St. James's (Montreal); Mount Royal Tennis; Home: 3548 Ave. de Vendôme, Montreal Que. H4A 3M7; Office: Suite 440, Canada Cement Bldg. 606 Cathcart St., Montreal, Que. H3B 1K9.

**KIERANS, Thomas Edward,** B.A., M.B.A.; b. Halifax, N.S. 2 Dec. 1940; s. the Hon. Eric William and Teresa Catherine (Whelan) K.; e. McGill Univ., B.A. (Honours Econ. & Pol. Sci.) 1961; Univ. of Chicago, M.B.A. 1963 (Dean's Honours List); m. Mary Louise, d. Daniel and Anne Janigan 3 Dec. 1988; children: Renata Anne, Julia Alexandra; PRES. & C.E.O., C.D. HOWE INST. 1989– ; Chrmn., Ipsco Inc.; First Marathon Inc.; Adjunct Prof., Sch. of Policy Studies, Queen's Univ.; Dir., The Manufacturers Life Insurance Co.; Southam Inc.; TransCanada PipeLines Ltd.; Fishery Products Internat.; Old Canada Investment Corp.; Petro-Canada; Mem. Investment Ctte., Ont. Hosp. Assn. 1991–93; Chrmn., The Royal Ontario Museum 1989–92; Dir., The Writers' Development Trust 1986–92; Vice Pres., Dir. and Princ., Nesbitt, Thomson & Co. Ltd. 1963–74; Sr. Vice Pres. and Dir., Pitfield Mackay Ross Ltd. 1974–80; Pres., McLeod Young Weir Ltd. 1980–88 and ScotiaMcLeod Inc. (its successor) 1988–89; Chrmn., Energy Options Adv. Ctte. (to Fed. Govt.) 1987–88; past Chrmn., Ont. Econ. Council; former Dir., Inst. for Rsch. on Public Policy; former Special Policy Adv., Govt. of Ont.; Mem. Adv. Counc., Fac. of Admin. Studies, York University 1988–92; former Adv., Internat. Finance Corp.; former mem., Business Counc. on Nat. Issues; Chrmn., United Way of Gter. Toronto 1987–89; columnist 'Report on Business Magazine', The Globe and Mail; frequent contributor to Candn. public policy journals; mem. Ed. Bd. 'Options'; recreations: literature, history, scuba diving, bicycling, shooting, back-packing, trekking; Clubs: Albany (Dir.); Griffith Island; Fitness Inst. (all of Toronto); University (Montreal); Coral Beach and Tennis (Bermuda); Home: 4 Woodland Heights, Toronto, Ont.; Office: 125 Adelaide St. E., Toronto, Ont. M5C 1L7.

**KIERNAN, Allan F.,** B.Sc., P.Eng.; energy industry executive; b. Lloydminster, Sask. 30 July 1940; s. Byron F. and M. Irma (Miller) K.; e. Univ. of Alberta B.Sc. 1962; Banff School of Advanced Management 1977; m. Carolyn d. Zupito and Metha D'Amico 1 Aug. 1964; children: Patrick J., Cindy M.; SENIOR VICE-PRESIDENT, ALBERTA ENERGY COMPANY 1988– ; Shell Canada Limited 1962–69; Milar Engineering Limited 1969–70; Hudson's Bay Oil and Gas Co. 1970–82; Dome Petroleum Limited 1982–85; Chieftain Development Co. Ltd. 1985–88; Lectr., Petroleum Industry Training Serv.; Dir., Palliser-Bayview Community Assn. 3 years; Pres. 1975; Mem., Assn. of Profl. Engrs., Geologists & Geophysicists of Alta. (Council Mem. 1991– ); Canadian Gas Processors Assn. (Pres. 1981); Canadian Heavy Oil Assn.; clubs: Priddis Greens Golf & Country, Calgary Petroleum; Home: 224 Pumphill Rise S.W., Calgary, Alta. T2V 4C8; Office: 3900, 421 – 7 Ave. S.W., Calgary, Alta. T2P 4K9.

**KIERNAN, James Thomas, Jr.,** M.B.A.; investment executive; e. Harvard, M.B.A.; Brown, A.B.; PRES., GOLDMAN SACHS CANADA 1988– ; joined Goldman Sachs & Co. 1976; London 1978; Vice-Pres. 1982; Internat. Product Mgr. 1984; Sales Mgr., Goldman Sachs Can. 1987; Office: 150 King St. W., Toronto, Ont. M5H 1J9.

**KIKANO, Khalil Naoum,** C.P.A.; banker; b. Tahwita, Lebanon 20 Aug. 1938; s. Naoum and Margo (Baddour) K.; m. Nellie Farah 22 Nov. 1959; children: Naoum, Maya, Lara; VICE-PRESIDENT, LENDING, ROYAL BANK OF CANDA 1988– ; var. banking positions, Beirut, Middle East, Montreal, Africa, London with Banque Sabbag SAL, Whinney Murray & Co. and Royal Bank of Canada 1956–84; Vice-Pres., International Banking, Royal Bank 1988– ; club: RAC; Home: 6 Cornwall Mansions, 33 Kensington Ct., London W8 5BG; Office: 71 Queen Victoria St., London EC4V 4DE, England.

**KILBOURN, William Morley,** C.M., B.A., A.M., Ph.D., F.R.S.C.; writer; university professor; b. Toronto, Ont. 18 Dec. 1926; s. late Kenneth Morley and Mary Rae (Fawcett) K.; e. Upper Can. Coll., Toronto, Ont. (1937–44); Trinity Coll., Univ. of Toronto, B.A. 1948; Harvard Univ. A.M. 1949, Ph.D. 1957; Oxford Univ. (1949–51), B.A. 1952, M.A. 1956; m. Mary Elizabeth, d. late Rev. Philip Sawyer, Hespeler, Ont. 10 Sept. 1949; children: Philippa, Hilary, Nicholas, Timothy, Michael; WRITER and PROF. OF HISTORY AND HUMANITIES, YORK UNIV.; (Chrmn. of Humanities Div., 1962–67); mem., Dept. of Hist., McMaster Univ., 1951–62; Teaching Fellow, Harvard Univ., 1953–55; Publications: 'The Firebrand: William Lyon Mackenzie and the Rebellion in Upper Canada' 1956 (2nd ed. 1960; London, 1958; winner of Univ. of B.C. President's Medal for Biog. 1956); 'The Elements Combined: A History of the Steel Company of Canada' 1960; 'The Writing of Canadian History' in 'The Literary History of Canada' 1965, rev. ed. 1976; 'The Restless Church' 1966; 'The Making of the Nation' 1966, rev. ed. 1973; 'Religion in Canada' 1968; 'Pipeline: TransCanada, and the Great Debate' 1970; 'Canada: A Guide to the Peaceable Kingdom' 1970; 'Inside City Hall: The Years of the Opposition' 1972 (co-auth. D. Crombie, K. Jaffary, J. Sewell); 'The Toronto Book' (an anthology) 1976; 'Toronto' (essays and photography) 1977, rev. ed. 1983; (with Robert Bothwell) 'C.D. Howe: A Biography' 1979 (winner of Corey Prize awarded jointly by the Canadian and the American Historical Assns.); 'Canada in the 1880's' 1980; 'Toronto Remembered: Celebration of the City' 1984 (winner of Gutenberg Medal of Printing Trades of North America); (with William Dendy) 'Toronto Observed: its Architecture, Patrons and History' (City of Toronto Book Award 1986); 'The Peaceable Kingdom Still' (in 'In Search of Canada') 1989; 'Intimate Grandeur: One Hundred Years at Massey Hall' 1993; and articles and reviews in various books, newspapers, encycs., and journs.; Past Pres., Toronto Book and Magazine Fair; former mem., Canada Council; former Trustee, Art Gallery of Ont.; mem.-at-large, Can. Nat. Comm. for UNESCO; Adv. Bd., CJRT-FM; Conservation Counc. of Ont.; past Chrmn., Toronto Arts Council; Bd. mem., New Music Concerts; Toronto Internat. Festival; Candn. Opera Co. Archives Ctte.; mem., Candn. Hist. Assn.; Isaacs Gallery Ensemble for performance of mixed media compositions; Alderman, City of Toronto 1970–76; mem. Metrop. Council and City of Toronto Extve. Comte. 1973–76; awarded Civic Medal of Service, City of Toronto 1982; Award of Merit, Toronto Historical Bd. 1985; residency at Rockefeller Center in Italy, Spring 1992; Member, Order of Canada 1993; Liberal; Anglican; recreations: piano, art, tennis; Home: 66 Collier St., #12C, Toronto, Ont. M4W 1L9.

**KILGOUR, David Errett,** B.A.; editor; b. Toronto, Ont. 3 Apr. 1955; s. David Goldie and Elizabeth Dewar (Anderson) K.; e. Jarvis C.I. 1973; Univ. of Toronto, B.A. 1977; CHILDREN'S BOOK EDITOR, PENGUIN BOOKS CANADA LIMITED 1988– ; Editor, Dorset Publishing Inc. 1977–78; Trade Ed., Scholastic-TAB Pubs. 1978–83; Sr. Ed., Penguin Books Can. Limited 1983–88; freelance editor of adult non-fiction 1988– ; editor of more than 50 books; awards given to books edited incl. the first Nat. Business Book Award (Best & Shortell: A Matter of Trust), the Candn. Libr. Assn. Book of the Year for Children (Pearson: A Handful of Time) and the Boston Globe/Horn Book Honor Book (Little: Little by Little); James S. Harris Award for Gen. Proficiency incl. Latin & Greek (U. of T.); Ont. Scholar; Home: 150 Crawford St., Toronto, Ont. M6J 2V4; Office: 10 Alcorn Ave., Toronto, Ont. M4V 3A9.

**KILIAN, Andre,** B.A., LL.B.; diplomat; b. S. Africa 4 Oct. 1946; e. Univ. Pretoria B.A. 1967; Univ. of the Witwatersrand LL.B. 1970; m. Karen Sunde 22 Jan. 1972; children: Nicole, Marc, Michelle; AMBASSADOR OF THE REPUBLIC OF SOUTH AFRICA TO CANADA 1992– ; Office: 15 Sussex Dr., Ottawa, Ont. K1M 1M8.

**KILIAN, Crawford,** M.A.; educator; writer; b. New York, N.Y. 7 Feb. 1941; s. Victor William Cosgrove and Verne (Debney) K.; e. Columbia Univ. B.A. 1962; Simon Fraser Univ. M.A. 1972; m. Alice d. Virgil and Louise Fairfax 8 Apr. 1966; two d. Anna Catherine, Margaret Cathleen; INSTR. IN ENGLISH & COMMUNICATIONS, CAPILANO COLL. 1968– , Co-ordinator, Communications Dept. 1974–83, 1987– ; Columnist, Vancouver Province 1982– ; author (juvenile) 'Wonders, Inc.' 1968; 'The Last Vikings' 1974 (nonfiction) 'Go Do Some Great Thing: The Black Pioneers of British Columbia' 1978; 'School Wars: The Assault on B.C. Education' 1985; (novel) 'The Empire of Time' 1978; 'Icequake' 1979; 'Eyas' 1982; 'Tsunami' 1983; 'Brother Jonathan' 1985; 'Lifter' 1986; 'The Fall of the Republic' 1987; 'Rogue Emperor' 1988; 'Gryphon' 1989; 'Greenmagic' 1992; (textbook) 'Exploring British Columbia's Past' 1983; frequent contbr. mags. and newspapers; author 6 radio plays CBC 1972–75; frequent speaker edn. confs.; Host 'Profiles' TV interview prog. 1984–86; Instr. in Eng. Guangzhou (China) Inst. Foreign Langs. 1983–84; Instr. in Eng. Vancouver Community Coll. 1967–68; Tech. writer-ed. Lawrence Berkeley Lab. Calif. 1966–67; served with US Army 1963–65; Dir. Verbotronic Productions 1985– ; Sch. Trustee N. Vancouver 1980–82; recipient Black Cultural & Hist. Soc. B.C. Achievement Award 1983; Chair, Summer Pops Youth Orchestra 1989–91; Bd. mem., Candn. Inst. of Arts for Young Audiences 1990–91; recreations: hiking, reading; Home: 4635 Cove Cliff Rd., North Vancouver, B.C. V7G 1H7; Office: 2055 Purcell Way, North Vancouver, B.C. V7J 3H5.

**KILIMNIK, Robert F.,** B.A., M.B.A., C.F.A.; insurance investment executive; b. Kitchener, Ont. 1 Apl. 1947; s. Joseph and Antoinette (Hintz) K.; e. Univ. of Waterloo B.A. 1970; McMaster Univ. M.B.A. 1971; m. Janice d. Len and Alice Cronkwright 9 Oct. 1976; children: Jennifer, Ian; VICE PRES. INVESTMENTS, MUTUAL LIFE OF CANADA 1991– ; Dir., Newcourt Credit Group Inc.; Tuckahoe Leasing Inc.; Princeton Developments Ltd.; Candn. Environmental Energy Corp.; Pinnacle II Capital Corp.; joined present Co. 1971 becoming Dir. Invest. Rsch. before trans. to private placement operation 1981; Adjunct Asst. Prof. of Econ. Univ. of Waterloo 1972–86; Woodrow Wilson Fellow 1970–71; co-author "Raising Capital: Perspectives and Approaches' 1989; R.Catholic; recreation: golf; Clubs: Westmount Golf (Kitchener; Dir.); Albany (Toronto); Home: 408 Clairbrook Cres., Waterloo, Ont. N2L 5V7; Office: 227 King St. S., Waterloo, Ont. N2J 4C5.

**KILLAM, G. Douglas,** B.A., Ph.D.; educator; b. New Westminster, B.C. 26 Aug. 1930; s. Harry and Margaret

Marion (Currie) K.; e. Univ. of B.C. B.A. 1954; Univ. of London Ph.D. 1964; m. Helen Shelagh d. H.C. Anderson, Creston, B.C. 22 Aug. 1959; children: Christopher, Sarah; Prof. of Eng. Univ. of Guelph since 1977; taught in Sierra Leone 1963–65, Nigeria 1967–68, Tanzania 1970–72, Edmonton (Alta), York Univ. Toronto 1968–73, Acadia Univ. 1974–77 (Head Dept. Eng. 1974–76, Dean of Arts 1976–77); held Prof'ship and Chair of Lit. Dar Es Salaam, Tanzania; Visiting Candn. Fellow, Macquarie Univ., Sydney, Australia 1984; Brooks Fellow, Univ. of Queensland, Brisbane, Australia 1988; author 'Africa in English Fiction' 1968; 'Novels of Chinua Achebe' 1968 (republished as 'The Writings of Chinua Achebe' 1977); 'African Writers on African Writing' 1972; 'An Introduction to the Writings of Ngugi' 1980; 'Contexts of African Criticism'; also articles on Can. literature and new lits. in Eng.; 'Critical Perspectives on Ngugi' 1985; Ed.: 'East and Central African Literatures in English' 1985; Ed. 'World Literature Written in English' 1979–89; Co-Ed., 'Canadian Journal of African Studies' 1979–81; Pres., Assn. of Commonwealth Literature and Language Studies (ACLALS) 1980–83; mem. Assn. Candn. Univ. Teachers Eng. (Extve.); Candn. Assn. African Studies (Past Pres.); Internat. Assn. of Univ. Professors of English; Asst. Secy., FILLM 1984–87, Vice-Pres. 1993– ; Chrmn., Candn. Assn. of Chrmn. of English 1985–86; Chrmn., Div. 33, MLA 1983–88; Protestant; recreations: gardening, dogs, cooking; Home: 112 Glasgow St., Guelph, Ont. N1H 4W3.

**KILLEEN, Karen L.,** B.Comm., C.A.; financial executive; e. University of Manitoba B.Comm. (Hons.) 1978; C.A. 1981; CHIEF FINANCIAL OFFICER AND TREASURER, THE GOLDFARB CORPORATION; Office: 17th floor, 4950 Yonge St., North York, Ont. M2N 6K1.

**KILLINGER, Barbara Elizabeth,** B.A., M.A., Ph.D.; psychologist, writer; b. London, Ont. 6 June 1934; d. Wesley 'Cuyler' Stewart and Eva Lillian (Hobbs) Henderson; e. Univ. of Western Ont. B.A. 1955; York Univ. B.A. (Hons.) 1972; York Univ. M.A. 1974, Ph.D. 1977; children: Katherine, Michael, Suzanne; Interne at Psych. Services, York Univ. 1972–73; North York Gen. Hosp. 1973–74; Toronto East Gen. Hosp. 1974–75; Research Asst., York Univ. 1975–76; research project at C.M. Hincks Treatment Centre 1978; Clinical Psych., North York Gen. Hosp. 1978–80; Clinical Psych., Private Practice, Toronto 1980– ; Pres., Henderson Publications Inc.; consultant; speaker at workshops, seminars, meetings; Student, Ont. College of Art; Mem., Ont. Psych. Assn.; C.G. Jung Found. of Ont.; Bd. Mem., Extension Gallery; author: 'Workaholics: The Respectable Addicts' 1991, '92 (New York, Australia, Britain), (French translation 1992, German & Spanish 1993, Estonian & Hungarian editions forthcoming) and two book chapters; recreations: skiing, tennis, swimming, bicycling, sculpture; clubs: Toronto Cricket, Skating & Curling; Home: 5 Finchgate Court, Willowdale, Ont. M2K 2C8; Office: 60 Pleasant Blvd., Suite B, Toronto, Ont. M4T 1K1.

**KILNER, Douglas L.,** B.A.Sc., P.Eng.; construction executive; b. Toronto, Ont. 28 July 1938; s. David James and Gertrude Creek (Rason) K.; e. Univ. of Waterloo B.A.Sc. (Civil) 1964; m. Dorothy d. Norman and Ethel Howard 21 July 1962; children: Brent, Barbara, Christine; PRES. ORLANDO CORP. 1973– ; joined R.E. Winter & Associates Consulting Engs. 1955–58, 1969–73; teacher 1964–69; Lectr. Ont. Mun. Engs. Assn.; Judge Mississauga City Hall Design Competition; Chrmn. Mississauga Planning Ctte.; mem. Steering Ctte. Regulatory Reform Ont.; Gov. Credit Valley Hosp. Mississauga; author 'Perimeter, Area, Volume' high sch. math. text 1965; mem. Assn. Prof. Engs. Prov. Ont.; recreations: skiing, hockey, antique automobiles; Clubs: Antique Classic Car Can.; Hidden Valley Highlands Ski; Home: 962 Streamway Cres., Mississauga, Ont. L4Y 2P4; Office: 6205 Airport Rd., Mississauga, Ont. L4V 1E3.

**KILODNEY, Crad,** B.Sc.; writer; b. Queens (Borough) N.Y.C. 13 Feb. 1948; e. Univ. of Michigan B.Sc. 1968; self-publishing author selling own books on streets of Toronto 1978– ; claims to be only author in the world so engaged as sole occupation; founded private imprint Charnel House 1979; numerous mag. pubns. in Canada, U.S. & Great Britain; author: 'Girl on the Subway' 1990, 'Malignant Humors' 1988, 'Pork College' 1984, 'Lightning Struck My Dick' 1980 plus 28 private editions 1978–92; intends to disappear without warning before the year 2000; Business: Charnel House, 1712 Avenue Rd., P.O. Box 54541, North York, Ont. M5M 4N5.

**KIMBER, Stephen Edward;** educator; writer; b. Halifax, N.S. 25 Aug. 1949; s. Edward Grey and Marion Eva (Roome) K.; e. Queen Elizabeth High Sch. Halifax 1967; Dalhousie Univ. 1967–70; m. Jean d. Max and Mildred Steinbock 27 June 1976; children: Matthew, Emily, Michael; ASST. PROF. OF JOURNALISM UNIV. OF KING'S COLL. 1982– ; Field Producer CTV Reports Ottawa 1977–78; Mng. Ed. Atlantic Insight Mag. 1979–81; Ed. Commercial News 1982–84; Ed. and Publisher Cities Mag. 1987–89; N.S. Corr. Maclean's mag. 1979–80; Atlantic Corr. Today Mag. 1980–81; Pres. MariMedia Associates Ltd. 1983–89; recipient Dan MacArthur Award Radio Documentary 1970; Atlantic Journalism Award 1982; Centre Investigative Journalism Author's Award 1987; Candn. Food Writer's Award 1987; author: 'Net Profits: The Story of National Sea Products' 1989; Co-author: 'The Spirit of Africville' 1992; Gen. Ed., Report Royal Comn. on Donald Marshall Jr. Prosecution 1990; Gen. Ed., 'Creating Our Own Future: A Nova Scotia Economic Strategy' 1991; Host, Maritime Magazine, CBC Radio 1992; Reporter, The Leading Edge, MITV 1992– ; Home: 2533 Beech St., Halifax, N.S. B3L 2X9; Office: Coburg Rd., Halifax, N.S. B3H 2A1.

**KIMMERLY, The Hon. Roger Stephen,** B.A., LL.B.; retired; b. Ottawa, Ont. 27 Jan. 1948; e. Carleton Univ. B.A. 1968; Queen's Univ. LL.B. 1972; Min. of Justice & Govt. Serv., Yukon Govt. 1985–89; Crown Attorney, N.W.T. 1977–78; Judge, Territorial Court, Yukon 1978–81; priv. law practice 1981–85; elected NDP mem., Whitehorse South Centre, Yukon Legis. Assembly 1981; Home: 9842 Fir St., Chemainus, B.C. V0R 1K0.

**KIMURA, Doreen,** Ph.D., C.Psych., F.R.S.C.; professor, researcher, consultant; b. Winnipeg, Man.; e. McGill Univ., B.A. 1956, M.A. 1957, Ph.D. 1961; one d.: Charlotte Vanderwolf; PROF., DEPT. OF PSYCHOLOGY, UNIV. OF WESTERN ONTARIO 1974– ; Fellow, Montreal Neurol. Inst. 1960–62; Lectr., Sir George Williams Coll. 1960–61; Rsch. Assoc., U.C.L.A. Med. Ctr. 1962–63; Geigy Fellow, Kantonsspital, Zürich, Switz. 1963–64; Rsch. Assoc., McMaster Univ. 1964–67; Assoc. Prof., present univ. 1967–74; Hon. Lectr., Clin. Neurol. Sci., U.W.O. 1982– ; Supvr., Clin. Neuropsych., Univ. Hosp. 1975–83; Co-ord., Clin. Neuropsych. Prog., U.W.O. 1983– ; CPA award for Disting. Contrib. to Candn. Psych. as a Science 1985; Candn. Assn. for Women in Sci. award for Outstanding Sci. Achievement 1986; F.R.S.C. 1989; John Dewan Award for outstanding research, Ont. Mental Health Foundation 1992; Hon. LL.D., Simon Fraser Univ. 1993; Fellow, Candn. & Am. Psych. Assns.; Am. Psych. Soc.; Mem., Internat. Neuropsych. Symp.; Acad. of Aphasia; Soc. for Neurosci.; author 'Neuromotor Mechanisms in Human Communication' 1993 and over 70 sci. papers; Founding Pres., Society for Acad. Freedom and Scholarship; Office: London, Ont. N6A 5C2.

**KINCAID, Keith William,** B.A.; news agency executive; b. Toronto, Ont. 4 Jan. 1935; s. Frank S. and Vera I. (Lubbock) K.; e. Univ. of W. Ont. B.A. Hon. Journalism 1958; m. Noreen A. d. Vera E. and James A. Lumsden 27 Dec. 1958; children: Kerry, Peter, Andrew; PRES. & C.E.O., THE CANADIAN PRESS 1982– ; Reporter and Ed. The Candn. Press in Calgary, Halifax and Toronto 1958–64; Picture Ed. 1964; Exec. Asst. 1969; Gen. Exec. 1973; Gen. Mgr. 1978; Chief Exec. Broadcast News Ltd. and Press News Ltd.; mem. Selection Ctte. Southam Fellowships, Univ. of Toronto; Candn. Selection Ctte. Nieman Fellows, Harvard Univ.; Commonwealth Press Union; Internat. Press Inst.; Chrmn., Internat. Press Telecommunications Counc.; Merit Award, Univ. of W. Ont.; 1969 Media Award, N. Am. Assn. of Alcoholism Prog.; Clubs: Metrop. Bd. of Trade; The University Club; Home: 95 Airdrie Rd., Toronto, Ont. M4G 1M4; Office: 36 King St. E., Toronto, Ont. M5C 2L9.

**KINCAIDE, Barbara Louise,** B.Sc.; convention management consultant; professional speaker; b. Halifax, N.S. 17 Sept. 1922; d. Thaddeus Mark and Elizabeth Hazlett (Dobson) Sieniewicz; e. Halifax Ladies Coll. 1939; Dalhousie Univ. 1944; m. Cyril M. s. Flora and George K. 16 Feb. 1946; children: Robert J., David M., John W.; OWNER; CONVENTION CONSULTANTS OF CAN. LIMITED 1973– and SPEAKERS BUREAU INTERNAT. 1978– ; Dept. of Biol., Univ. of N.B. 1944–46; Dept. of Path., New England Deaconess Hosp. 1947–49; Dir., Bur. of Rsch. Volunteers, Ont. Heart Found. 1965–66; Presenter, Convention Planning & Mngt., Cont. Edn., Univ. of N.B.; Founder, Meeting Planners Internat., 1st Internat. Chapter, Toronto 1978 (Faculty, Internat. Meetings, Hong Kong 1984; Internat. Bd. of Dir. 1978–81); Faculty, 1st Internat. Conv. of Meeting Planners & Travel Agents, Beijing P.R.C. 1981; Founding Mem. & Past Pres., Internat. Group of Agencies & Bur. 1989–90 (Candn. Rep., Internat. Bd. of Dir.); Bd. Mem., St. Lawrence Ctr. for the Arts 1969–71; Pres., Guild of St. Lawrence Ctr. for the Arts; Bd., Toronto Workshops Prodns. 1986–88; Trustee, Candn. Student Debating Fedn.; Adv. Bd. to 1993 Couchiching Inst. on Pub. Affairs; Mem., Jr. League of Halifax, Boston & Toronto (past extve. positions); editor: 'Speakers Directory' 1985– ; recreations: travel, reading, theatre, and the arts; club: Toronto Lawn Tennis; Home: 6 Glen Edyth Dr., Toronto, Ont. M4V 2V7; Office: 961 Eglinton Ave. E., Ste. 200, Toronto, Ont. M4G 4B5.

**KINDRED, Herbert George,** C.D., B.E., B.Ed., M.Ed., P.Eng.; b. Moose Jaw, Sask. 23 Apl. 1933; s. Henry George and Gladys Rachael (Harrison) K.; e. Univ. of Sask. B.E.(Chem.) 1956 (Chem. Inst. Can. Prize 1956), B.Ed. 1964, M.Ed. 1972; m. Frances d. William and Charlotte McCullough 6 Aug. 1955; five s.: Gregory, Clinton (dec.), Norman, Thomas, David; PROF. AND DEAN OF UNIV. EXTENSION UNIV. OF REGINA 1980– , mem. Senate; Pres. Kindred Enterprises; Refinery Eng. Husky Oil & Refining 1956–60; Gas Eng. British American Oil 1960–62; Teacher, Evening & Summer Sch. Prin., Dir. Cont. Edn. & Special Services Moose Jaw Pub. Sch. Bd. 1963–71 (honoured by Bd. for service to edn. 1984); Assoc. Prof. and Head Bus. & Profl. Div. Extension Dept. Univ. of Sask. Regina 1971–73; Assoc. Prof. and Dir. of Extension present Univ. 1973–80; mem. Assn. Profl. Engs. Sask.; Eng. Inst. Can.; Sask. Assn. Lifelong Learning; Nat. Univ. Cont. Edn. Assn.; Candn. Assn. Univ. Cont. Edn. (Pres. 1981–82); Candn. Assn. Adult Edn.; Candn. Assn. Distance Edn.; Regina Lions Band Assn. (Pres. 1977–79); Elks; Kiwanis; recreations: bandsman, water & downhill skiing, woodworking; Home: 10 Coral Place, Emerald Park, Sask. S4L 1A7; Office: Regina, Sask. S4S 0A2.

**KING, A. Douglas,** B.A., M.B.A.; banker; b. Toronto, Ont. 13 Feb. 1941; e. Univ. of Toronto B.A. 1963, M.B.A. 1965; SR. VICE-PRES. & DEPUTY CHIEF INSPECTOR, TORONTO-DOMINION BANK 1991– ; joined Toronto-Dominion Bank 1965; New York 1967–69; Hong Kong/Singapore 1972–75; Sr. Vice-Pres., Europe, Mid-East & Africa, London England 1980–88; Pres. & Dir., Toronto-Dominion Securities Inc. 1988–91; recreations: golf, skiing; clubs: Scarboro Golf, Fitness Inst.; Office: Aetna Tower, 21st Floor, Toronto, Ont. M5K 1A2.

**KING, Allan,** B.A.; film producer and director; b. Vancouver, B.C. 6 Feb. 1930; s. John Owen and Kathleen Mary (Keegan) Winton; e. Univ. of B.C. B.A. (Philos.) 1954; m. Phyllis April, d. Douglas M. Leiterman, Pickering, Ont. 10 May 1952; one d. Anna Augusta; 2ndly Patricia Watson 30 June 1970; one d. Maggie Amanita, one s. Robert Alexander; 3rdly Colleen Murphy 15 Apr. 1987; one s. August Lucian Murphy; formed Allan King Associates Ltd. 1961 and later Allan King Associates England Ltd.; films incl. 'Skidrow' (documentary) 1956 (won 3 awards in Can. and U.S.); 'The Yukoners' 1956; 'Pemberton Valley' 1957; 'Rickshaw' 1960 (won awards at Leipzig and Vancouver Festivals, 1961); 'Dreams' 1961; 'Warrendale' (won 2 awards at 1967 Cannes Festival, top Candn. film of 1967, shared Brit. critics' Best Foreign Film award 1967, won 2 prizes in Austrialia and was named Best Documentary of 1968 by U.S. film critics); has directed and produced works ranging from TV commercials to documentary features; credits incl.: 'Lynn Seymour' (ballerina) 1964; 'Bjorn's Inferno' 1964 (shown by invitation at 9th Annual San Francisco Film Festival); 'Running Away Backwards' 1964 (won awards at 1966 San Francisco and Sydney Film Festivals and was screened by invitation at Venice, Montreal, Vancouver and Mannheim Festivals); recent films (1974–84) incl.: TV dramas 'A Bird in the House' (four Candn. Film Awards), 'Baptising' (Best Drama Yorkton Festival), 'Red Emma,' and 'Six War Years,' 'Ready for Slaughter' (awarded Best Non-Continuing Drama, Banff TV Fest) 1983, 'Who's in Charge?' (shown by invitation at London Film Festival and at INPUT Internat. TV Fest), 'The Last Season' CBC 1986; and feature films 'Who Has Seen the Wind' (Grand Prix Paris Film Festival), 'One Night Stand' (four Candn. film awards), 'Silence of the North'; 'Termini Station' Astral Films 1989; four retrospectives of his work have been shown by Cinematheque Canadienne, Montreal; Commonwealth Film Festival, London; Mea Roma el. R.C.A. 1975; Canada House, London, 1985; Pres., Dirs. Guild Can., Chrmn., Ont. Dist. Council; mem.: Assn. Cinematograph & TV Techs. (U.K.); C.T.F.A.; recreations: music, reading; Address: c/o Ralph Zimmerman, Great North Artists Mgmt., 350 Dupont St., Toronto, Ont. M5R 1V9.

**KING, Brian Maxwell,** B.Chem.E.; executive; b. Adelaide, Australia 10 Jan. 1933; s. Stanley Roger and Kathleen Lavaria (Beckman) K.; e. Adelaide High Sch. 1950; Univ. of Adelaide B.Chem.E. 1955; m. Madelyn d. Douglas and Alice Wetmore 4 Apr. 1959; three s. David,

Donald, Geoffrey; DIR., ONEX CORP.; Bioresearch Laboratories; Vengrowth Capital Funds; The Healthcare and Biotechnology Venture Fund; Sales Engr. Cominco Ltd. Vancouver 1956–61; Fisons Ltd. London, Eng. 1961–70, Dir. of Marketing to Mang. Dir. Internat. Div.; Pres. and Dir. Fisons Corp. and Fisons Inc. Boston, Mass., Fisons Corp. Ltd. Toronto 1970–78; Sr. Vice Pres., Canada Development Corp. 1978–87; Chrmn., Pres. & C.E.O., Connaught Biosciences Inc. 1978–90; mem. Candn. Soc. Chem. Engrs.; Chem. Inst. Can.; recreations: tennis, golf, jogging; Home: 69 Sherwood Ave., Scarborough, Ont. M1R 1N6.

**KING, Charles;** communications consultant; b. Vancouver, B.C. 27 Nov. 1926; s. late Eileen Edith (Arnoldi) and Harold George K.; e. Pub. and High Schs., Vancouver, B.C.; Univ. of Brit. Columbia; m. Pauline Ida, d. late J.J. Trueb, Campbell River, B.C., 1 June 1948; children: John C.P., Terry E.; PRES., CHARLES KING CONSULTING LTD., Ottawa; joined Circulation Dept., 'Vancouver Sun' 1941; Reporter, 'Vancouver Daily Province' 1944, and after several positions became Asst. News Ed. 1956; apptd. to Ottawa Bureau, Southam News Services, March 1957–62 and became Chief of Ottawa Bureau, July 1960; Nat. Newspaper Award 1961; Dir., Candn. Parlty. Press Gallery, 1960–62; Broadcaster and Commentator, Stn. CFCF and CFCF-TV Montreal, 1958–62; Chief of London Bur., Southam News Services, 1962–67; Assoc. Editor, 'Ottawa Citizen' 1967–77; Vice Pres. and Ed., 'Ottawa Today' 1977–78; formed own company 1978; freelance commentator CBC and BBC; has covered news assign. in Candn. Arctic, Japan, Africa, Britain and W. Europe, U.S. and Can. from coast to coast; served in 2nd World War with Candn. Army 1945; Home and Office: 128 Lisgar Rd., Rockcliffe Pk., Ottawa, Ont. K1M 0E6.

**KING, David Thomas;** executive; b. Perth, Ont. 22 June 1946; s. Rev. Dr. Albert Edward and Ethel (Dickson) K.; e. Univ. of Victoria 1964–65; Univ. of Alta. 1965–67, 1969–70, B.A. (Pol. Sci.); m. Clare Elaine Ann d. late Oliver Piven 19 Oct. 1968; three s. Troy Oliver Albert, Jason Darren Todd, Cory Michael; PRES., EFFECTIVE STRATEGIES INC.; el. to Leg. Assembly Alta. 1971, re-el. 1975, 1979, 1982; Min. of Educ. 1979–86; Min. of Technology, Research and Telecommunications, Alta. 1986; Extve. Dir., Public Sch. Boards' Assn. of Alta.; P. Conservative; United Church; Home: 11248 - 63rd St., Edmonton, Alta. T5W 4E6.

**KING, Egerton Warren,** B.Sc., D.Sc. (Hon.), P.Eng., F.C.A.E.; corporate director; b. Calgary, Alta. 19 May 1919; s. Arthur Blake and Grace Donald (Riddell) K.; e. Univ. of Alta., B.Sc.; m. Olive Mary d. Charles and Jessie Phillips 5 Nov. 1943; children: Donald, Peter, Helen, Michael, David; test engr., Candn. Gen. Elec. 1942–43; Elec. Lieut., Royal Candn. Navy 1943–45; elec. engr., East Kootenay Power Co. 1945; Mgr., McGregor Telephone & Power Constrn. Co. 1955; joined Candn. Utilities Ltd. as Transmission & Distbn. Supt. 1956; Gen. Mgr., Yukon Elec. Co. and Yukon Hydro Co. (acquired by Candn. Utilities) 1958; Vice-Pres., Northland Utilities 1961; Gen. Mgr., Candn. Utilities 1966; Pres. & Dir. of both cos. 1968; also Pres. & Dir., Northwestern Utilities Ltd. and Candn. Western Natural Gas Co. 1969; Pres., Alta. Power Ltd. 1972; Pres. & C.E.O., Canadian Utilities operating cos. 1972; C.E.O., Candn. Utilities Ltd. & subs. cos. 1981–84; Chrmn., Echo Bay Mines 1973–80; former Dir., Candn. Utilities Ltd.; C.I.L.; Canadian Airlines International; Royal Trustco; Echo Bay Mines; ATCO Ltd.; Rolls-Royce Inds. Can. Inc.; Ducks Unlimited Can.; Past Chrmn., Candn. Gas Assn.; Past Pres., Candn. Elec. Assn.; Edmonton C. of C.; Chrmn., Univ. of Alta. Hosps. Bd. 1984–90; Delta Upsilon Frat.; life mem. Alta. & B.C. Assns. of Profl. Engrs.; recreations: shooting, fishing; Clubs: Edmonton; Edmonton Flying; Derrick Golf & Winter; Mayfair Golf & Country; Edmonton; Home: 46 Marlboro Rd., Edmonton, Alta. T6J 2C6.

**KING, Eldred;** politician, farmer; b. Scarborough, Ont. 1 July 1927; s. Albert William and Mary Pearl (Shadlock) K.; e. Stouffville H.S. 1945; m. Beulah d. Argyle and Blanche Rutledge 27 Sept. 1958; children: Jeffrey, Rodney, Jan; CHAIR OF COUNCIL & CHIEF EXECUTIVE OFFICER, THE REGIONAL MUNICIPALITY OF YORK 1984– ; elected School Trustee 1965–68; elected Councillor, Markham Twp. Council 1969–70; Town of Whitchurch-Stouffville 1972–78; Mayor 1978–84; Mem., Reg. Mun. of York Police Serv. Bd. 1984– ; Bd. Mem., GO Transit (Vice-Chair 1993); Bd. Mem., Region of York Housing Corp. 1989– ; Metro Toronto & Region Conservation Authority 1978– ; Mem., Markham-Stouffville Hosp. Bd. 1989–90; Active Mem., 4H Agric. Clubs; Mem., Ont. Jr. Farmers Assn. (local & co. offices 1946–54); established Holstein Dairy Herd (Internat. Recognition 1954–67); Mem. & Dir., York Co. Holstein Assn.; York County Milk Bd.; York Co. Crop & Field Assn.; Markham & East York Agric. Soc.; Mem., Stouffville Un. Ch.; club: Unionville Curling; Home: 15 Bayberry St., Stouffville, Ont. L4A 7Z1; Office: Box 147, 17250 Yonge St., Newmarket, Ont. L3Y 6Z1.

**KING, Frank Walter,** O.C., LL.D., B.Sc., P.Eng.; business executive; b. Redcliff, Alta. 22 Aug. 1936; s. Walter and Mildred Laura K.; e. Central H.S. (Hons.) 1954; Univ. of Alta. B.Sc. 1958; individual courses in engineering, business, finance, mktg. & public relns.; m. Jeanette Elizabeth 4 Oct. 1958; children: Diane Elizabeth, Linda Gail, David William, Stephen Walter; PRES., C.E.O. & DIR., CAMBRIDGE ENVIRO. SYSTEMS INC. 1993– ; Pres. & Dir., Metropolitan Investment Corp. 1978– ; Chem. Engr., CIL, Polymer Corp. & CAE Industries 1958–63; Gen. Mgr., Durethane Indus. Ltd. (later N.W. Indus. Ltd.) 1963–69; Gen. Mgr., Ralph M. Parsons Canada Ltd. 1969–74; Sr. Vice-Pres., Mfg., Turbo Resources Limited 1974–82; Pres., C.E.O. & Dir., Candn. Turbo Inc. 1991–92; Co-Pres. & Dir., Canada 125 Corporation 1991–92; Chrmn. & Chief Extve. Offr., XV Olympic Winter Games 1981– ; Dir., Toronto Sun Publishing Co.; Sherritt-Gordon Inc.; Air BC Ltd.; honours (1988): Officer of the Order of Canada; Hon. LL.D., Univ. of Calgary; Olympic Order in Gold; Gold Medal, Champion D'Afrique; MacLean's Top 12 Canadians of the Year; Person of the Year, Tourism Indus. Assn.; Person of the Year, Calgary Herald; Alberta Achievement Award; Calgary Sports Media Club Award; City of Edmonton Special Citation; Calgary Booster Club Award (also 1982); num. other awards prior to 1988; Mem., Assn. of Profl. Engrs., Geol. & Geophys. of Alta. 1961– ; Nat. Speakers Bureau 1988– ; Mem. Alta. Chap., World Business Council 1988– ; Extve.-in-Residence, Fac. of Mngt., Univ. of Calgary 1988–90; extensive involvement in community activities and organizations; author: 'It's How You Play the Game' 1991 (the inside story of the Calgary Olympic Games); recreations: active in sports; Clubs: Calgary South Rotary; Glencoe; Home: 3931 Edison Cres. S.W., Calgary, Alta. T2S 0X1; Office: 4600 - 400 3rd Ave. S.W., Calgary, Alta. T2P 4H2.

**KING, G. Edmund,** B.A. (Econ.); financial executive; b. Toronto, Ont. 4 Aug. 1933; s. Frances Glenny and Ella Alexandria K.; e. Univ. of Toronto B.A. (Econ.); m. Beverley Joyce d. Bill and Margaret Warwick 19 Apr. 1959; children: Jeffrey, Julia, Diana, Meghan; CHRMN. & C.E.O., THE CIBC WOOD GUNDY CORP. 1992– ; joined Wood Gundy 1957; Mgr. Montreal Money Market Div. 1959–62; Toronto 1962–70; Pres., Wood Gundy Corp. N.Y. 1971–74; Corp. Finan. Div. 1974–86; Vice-Chrmn. 1986; Chrmn. & Chief Extve. Offr. 1988; Chrmn., Wood Gundy Inc. 1990–92; Chrmn., Investment Dealers Assn.; Chrmn., Ont. Cancer Institute / Princess Margaret Hosp.; Dir. & Corp. Canvass Chrmn., Shaw Festival; recreations: golf, skiing, tennis; clubs: Granite, National, Toronto, York, Beacon Hall, Muskoka Lakes, Greenwich Connecticut, Founders; Home: 122 Dawlish Ave., Toronto, Ont. M4N 1H3; Office: P.O. Box 500, BCE Place, Toronto, Ont. M5J 2S8.

**KING, Gerald Wilfrid,** Ph.D., D.Sc., F.R.S.C., F.C.I.C., C.Chem., F.R.S.C. (U.K.); educator; b. West Hartlepool, Eng. 22 Jan. 1928; s. Wilfrid James and Doris Amelia (Jackson) K.; e. Highgate Sch. London 1943–45; Univ. Coll. London B.Sc. 1949, Ph.D. 1952; Univ. of London D.Sc. 1970; m. Gwyneth d. David Emrys Jones, Gwynedd, Wales 27 March 1954; children: Richard James, Juliette Mary, Jennifer Wyn, Gillian Clare; EMERITUS PROF. OF CHEM., McMASTER UNIV.; Vice-Pres., Summit Halfway House Inc. 1990– ; Scient. Offr. Atomic Weapons Research Estab. Aldermaston, Eng. 1952–54; Lectr. Univ. Coll. London 1954–57; Asst. Prof. McMaster Univ. 1957, Assoc. Prof. 1959–64, Prof. 1964–89; rec'd Sir William Ramsay Medal 1952; author 'Spectroscopy and Molecular Structure' 1964; numerous papers and articles phys. chem. especially spectroscopy, molecular structure and laser applications; Chrmn. Phys. Chem. Div. Chem. Inst. Can. 1963–64, Vice Chrmn. 1962–63; Pres. McMaster Faculty Assn. 1973–74, 1986–87; Chrmn., Chemistry Dept., McMaster Univ. 1979–82; Bd. of Gov., McMaster Univ. 1985–88; mem. Optical Soc. Am.; Ed. 'Canadian Journal of Chemistry' 1974–79; mem. several ed. bds. prof. journs.; rec'd Gerhard Hertzberg Award of the Spectroscopy Soc. of Can. 1981; Anglican; Home: 674 Northland Ave., Burlington, Ont. L7T 3J7; Office: Hamilton, Ont. L8S 4M1.

**KING, Jack Avery,** B.A., LL.B., Q.C.; lawyer/health executive; b. Peterborough, Ont. 4 July 1934; s. John Frederick and Olive Mary (Avery) K.; e. Peterborough Coll. V.S.; Queen's Univ. B.A. 1957, B.L. 1960; m. Noreen Joan d. Major Norman and Kathleen Hancock 1 June 1960; one d.: Dr. Alison Jane; PRES., CHRMN., BD. OF DIR., ADMIN. & CORP. GEN. COUNS., FOREST GROVE CARE CTR. LTD. 1972– ; called to Alta. Bar 1961; Pres., Admin. & Chrmn., Bd. of Dirs., Meadowbrook Management Ltd. 1961–72; Mktg. Lawyer, Royalite Oil Co. Ltd. 1964–67; Pres. & Chrmn., Bd. of Dirs., Persona Care Ltd. 1969–70; Mem., Am. Health Care Assn.; Coll. of Am. Health Care Admins.; Fac. Mem. & Grad., Candn. Hosp. Assn. Extended Care Mgmt. Course 1974– ; Cons., Nat. Long Term Care Forum; Extve. Mem., Candn. Coll. of Health Serv. Extves. 1985; Cert. Cons. 1986; Vice-Chrmn. & Dir., Candn. Task Force on Energy Mgmt. in Health Care Facilities 1988–89; Q.C. 1986; Dir., Alta. Long Term Care Assn. 1983– ; Candn. Long Term Care Assn. 1984–85 1st Vice Pres. 1985–86; Pres. 1986–87; Past Pres. 1987–88; Founding Mem., 1st Pres. & 1st Hon. Dir., Candn. Long Term Care Found. 1989 & apptd. Chrmn. 1991; Mem., Un. Ch. of Can.; Calgary Bar Assn.; Law Soc. of Alta.; Candn. Bar Assn.; co-founder, vice pres. & cons. ed., 'Geriontion Journal': A Canadian Review of Elder Care 1986–87; Mem., Ed. Ad. Bd., 'Health Care Magazine' 1991; recreations: tennis, skiing, swimming, scuba diving; Clubs: The Ranchmen's; 400; Silver Springs Golf & Country,;P.P.C.L.I. Officers Mess; Home: 32 Varsity Place N.W., Calgary, Alta. T3B 2Z3; Office: 10 Forest Grove Place S.E., Calgary, Alta. T2A 7G6.

**KING, Jen Genia;** transportation executive; b. Edmonton, Alta. 16 Aug. 1922; d. Joseph and Marie (Stadnyk) Pawlyshyn; e. McDougall Comm. Edmonton 1941; m. Harry Joseph (dec.) s. August and Theresia King 21 June 1947; three s. David Joseph Paul, Michael Robert, Brian Christopher; PRES. WHITE SADDLE AIR SERVICES LTD. (a helicopter charter co.) 1977– ; served 50 yrs. in bus. adm. primarily self-employed; mem. Candn. Owners & Pilots Assn.; B.C. Aviation Council; Candn. Wildlife Fedn.; Candn. Nature Fedn.; Life mem., BC Mountaineering Club; Alpine Club of Canada; awarded Commemorative Medal for 125th Anniversary of Candn. Confederation 1993; recreations: gardening, skiing, photography; Club: Tatla Lake Community; Address: P.O. Box 22, Tatla Lake, B.C. V0L 1V0.

**KING, Leslie John,** M.A., Ph.D., F.R.S.C.; educator; b. Christchurch, N.Z. 10 Nov. 1934; s. Lawrence Charles and Phyllis Ivy (Walter) K.; e. Christchurch Boys High Sch.; Univ. of Canterbury N.Z. B.A. 1955, M.A. 1957; Univ. of Iowa Ph.D. 1960; m. Doreen M. d. Kenneth and Mercia Brown 22 Oct. 1960; children: Loren Antony, Andrew Brett; PROF. OF GEOG., McMASTER UNIV. 1970– ; Lectr. Univ. of Canterbury N.Z. 1960–62; Asst. Prof. McGill Univ. 1962–64; Assoc. Prof./Prof. Ohio State Univ. 1964–70; Chrmn. of Geog. present Univ. 1970–73, Dean of Grad. Studies 1973–79, Vice Pres. Acad. 1979–89; Visiting Prof. E.T.H. Zurich, Switzerland 1972; recipient Fulbright Award 1957; Distinguished Service Award Assn. Am. Geogs. 1976; Queen's Silver Jubilee Medal 1977; Can. Council Leave Fellowship 1978; award for scholarly distinction, Candn. Assn. Geographers 1984; Commonwealth Prestige Fellow in New Zealand 1986; author 'Statistical Analysis in Geography' 1969; 'Central Place Theory' 1984; co-author 'Readings in Economic Geography' 1968; 'Cities, Space and Behavior' 1978; numerous book chapters, articles urban and econ. geog. prof. journs.; Founding Ed. 'Geographical Analysis: An International Journal of Theoretical Geography' 1969–74; Pres. Candn. Assn. Geographers 1986–87: mem. Candn. Assn. Geogs.; Assn. Am. Geogs.; recreations: reading, squash, golf; Club: Hamilton Golf & Country; Home: R.R. #3, Dundas, Ont. L9H 5E3; Office: Hamilton, Ont. L8S 4K8.

**KING, The Hon. Lynn,** M.A., LL.B.; provincial court judge; b. Sudbury, Ont. 19 Apr. 1944; d. Harry and Madelin (Tarshis) Waisberg; e. Univ. of Toronto, B.A. 1967; Fletcher Sch. of Law & Diplomacy, M.A. 1968; Univ. of Toronto Law Sch., LL.B. 1971; m. M.T. Kelly s. Sybil and Milton Kelly 1981; two s.: Jonah Preston Kelly, Max Milton Kelly; JUDGE, ONT. PROV. COURT, FAMILY DIV. 1985– ; Partner, Copeland, King 1973–75; Lectr., Osgoode Hall Law Sch. 1975–76; Partner, King & Sachs 1976–86; Instr., Bar Admission Course 1979–85; author: 'What Every Woman Should Know About Marriage, Separation and Divorce' 1980; co-author; 'Women Against Censorship' 1986, 'Law, Law, Law' 1975; recreations: cycling, canoeing, swimming, skiing; Home: Toronto, Ont.; Office: 311 Jarvis St., Toronto, Ont. M5B 2C4.

**KING, Robert H.,** B.A., LL.B.; deputy judge; b. Regina, Sask. 19 June 1915; s. Arthur Joseph and Grace Mary (Galloway) K.; e. Univ. of Saskatchewan B.A.

1940, LL.B. 1947; m. Dorothy Ledford 6 Dec. 1947; children: Laureen Susan, Douglas Robert; Deputy Judge, Tax Court of Canada 1988–93; General Motors Products of Canada 1951–61; Provincial Court Judge 1961–85; retired 1985; Chair, Labour Relations Bd., Saskatchewan for 7 years in 1970s; Office: 200 Kent St., Ottawa, Ont. K1A 0M1.

**KING, Robin Geoffrey,** M.A.; college administrator; b. Bradford-on-Avon 24 Nov. 1943; s. Percy and Eileen Murial (Brooks) K.; e. Headlands Grammar School; Oxford College of Technology; York Univ. M.A. 1979; CHAIRMAN, COMMUNICATION, MEDIA AND PERFORMANCE, FACULTY OF THE ARTS, SHERIDAN COLLEGE; Royal Military College of Science (England); emigrated to Canada 1965; Physics Research Technologist, Univ. of Waterloo 1965; joined Sheridan College 1971; grad. rsch. at York Univ. involved application of gen. systems theory to creative behav. in the Visual Arts 1976–79; estab. Canada's first post-diploma prog. in Computer Graphics for the Arts 1981; has lectured extensively throughout N. Am., Japan, Australia & Europe incl. U.C.L.A., Minneapolis College of Art & Design, Univ. of Toronto, Calif. Inst .for the Arts, Art Centre School of Design; has held var. of positions in internat. computer graphics orgns.; Pres., Imagina Computer Graphics Corp. 1985– ; Visual Arts Cons., The Mississauga Living Arts Ctr.; Computer Graphics Cons., S. Illinois Univ.; Mem., Nat. Computer Graphics Assn.; SIGGRAPH; author of several articles; Office: Oakville, Ont. L6H 2L1.

**KING, Roger S.,** B.A., M.B.A.; banker; b. Philadelphia, PA 29 June 1948; s. Samuel McConnell and Carolyn Joan (Stewart) K.; e. West Georgia Coll. B.A. 1970; East Carolina Univ. M.B.A. 1976; m. Judith Berk d. Arnold and Violet Straussman 9 Sept. 1984; SENIOR VICE-PRES., LLOYDS BANK (seconded to HONG KONG BANK OF CANADA) 1990– ; various jobs in insurance 1970–75; Asst. Vice-Pres., Lloyds Bank Plc (Atlanta, Ga.) 1982–84; Vice-Pres., N. Am. Head Office (N.Y.) 1984–86; Vice-Pres. & Mgr., N. Am. Loans (London, Eng.) 1986–87; Sr. Vice-Pres., Credit, Lloyds Bank Canada 1987–90; recreations: sailing, camping, art, history; club: Bruce Trail Assn.; Home: 159 Lyndhurst Ave., Toronto, Ont. M5R 3A1; Office: 70 York St., 3rd fl., Toronto, Ont. M5J 1S9.

**KING, Thomas Brown;** Canadian glass researcher (retired); executive; b. Hamilton, Ont. 6 June 1913; s. James Watt and Hannah Brewster (Brown) K.; e. Hillcrest; Selwyn House; McGill Univ.; m. Helen d. Gerald and Ethel Campbell 9 Sept. 1939; children: Diana Brown, Cynthia Helen; joined Dominion Glass Co. Ltd. 1932; served w. Kent. Regt. in Canada and 4 Dorsets overseas 1939–45; Asst. Sec., Domglas 1945–56; Corp. Sec. 1956–78; Dir. 1966; retired 1978 with 46 years serv.; Counc. Mem., Montreal Bd. of Trade 1971–73; Founder & Coordinator, GLASFAX 1967–78 (Chrmn. 1978– ); Gov., Montreal Gen. Hosp.; Sr. Elder, Ch. of St. Andrew & St. Paul (Presbyn.); FCIS; FCCS; author: 'Glass in Canada' 1987; Club: Royal Montreal Curling; Home: 499 Elm Ave., Westmount, Que. H3Y 3H9.

**KING, Thomas H.;** transportation executive; b. Golden, B.C. 10 Sept. 1940; s. Howard and Agnes V. (Gable) K.; e. Golden H.S.; B.C. Tech. Inst.; m. Patricia d. Joseph and Lulu Spitzig 2 May 1970; Pres. & C.E.O., Federal Industries Transport Group Inc.; Career summary: Previously 20 years with Canadian Freightways, 11 positions in 20 yrs., left as Dir. of Terminals in 1978; joined The White Pass & Yukon Corp. Ltd. 1979 as Extve. Vice-Pres. & G.M.; named Pres. 1980 and apptd. to Bd. of Dirs. & Pres. of Federal Industries Transport Group in 1984; currently Pres. & C.E.O., Federal Industries Transport Group Inc.; Pres. & C.E.O., The White Pass and Yukon Corp. Ltd.; Chrmn.: Thunder Bay Terminals Ltd., Motorways (1980) Limited, Kingsway Transports Ltd., Consolidated Fastfrate Transport, Cougar Freight Systems, Servall Transport Ltd.; Chrmn., Pres. & C.E.O. Tri-Line Expressways Ltd.; Dir. & Chrmn., White Pass Systems Ltd.; Dir., Junior Achievement of Canada; Dir., Canadian Trucking Assn.; Mem., Winnipeg C. of C. Transp. Counc.; Mem., Indus./Gov. Adv. Forum; Mem., Univ. of Man. Transport Inst.; Fellow, Chartered Inst. of Transport (FCIT); recreations: boating, fishing: clubs: The Manitoba, The Canadian; Home: 63 Park Royal Bay, Winnipeg, Man. R3P 1P2.

**KINGAN, Ted,** N.D.D., A.T.D. (MANC.), R.C.A.; retired; b. Lytham-St-Annes, Lancs., Eng. 12 Oct. 1927; s. James Edward and Elsie (Charnley) K.; e. Bluecoat Sch. for Boys Stamford, Eng. 1938; St. John's Sch. Lytham-St-Annes, Eng. 1941; Blackpool (Eng.) Sch. of Art Nat. Dipl. in Design 1952; Regional Coll. of Art Manchester, Eng. Art Teacher's Dipl. 1953; Victoria Univ. Manchester Art Teacher's Cert. 1953; m. 1stly: Nelly (dec.) d. late John Snow 11 July 1948; one s. Randolph Paul; m. 2ndly: Marny Carla d. late Christian F. Bertelsen, Oct. 1987; step-daughter: Erin Lee Tupper; Lectr. in Painting, Studio Art Program, Capilano Coll. 1973; conducts painting and design workshops through Emily Carr Coll. of Art Outreach Program; art teacher secondary schs. Eng. and Can. 1953–73; solo exhn. Bau-Xi Gallery Vancouver 1970; group exhns. incl.: Surrealist Group Show Swindon 1948; B.C. Soc. Artists and several juried annual shows Vancouver Art Gallery 1960–70; Galerie Allen Vancouver 1971–75; Alma Mater Gallery Univ. of B.C. 1975; Gallery Move Vancouver 1975–80; Internat. Surrealist Exhn. Camden Arts Centre London, Eng. 1978; Agnes Etherington Art Centre Queen's Univ., Can. House London and Centre Culturel Canadien Paris 1979; West Coast Surrealists Grp. Exhbn., Gallery Move, Vancouver 1980; 'Collaborations' Robson Sq. Media Centre, Vancouver 1981; R.C.A. Grp. Exhbn., Kenneth Heffel Gallery, Vancouver 1981; Bau-XI Gallery, Vancouver 1984; Exposição Internacional Surrealismo e Pintura Fantástica, Lisbon 1984; Pitt Internat. Gall., Vancouver 1986; PHASES French Surrealists, Le Havre, Montlucon, St. Etienne, France 1987; PHASES French Surrealists, Internat. Group exhbn., Musée des Beaux-Arts André Malraux, Le Havre, France 1988; West Coast Surrealists, Threshold Gallery, Vancouver 1989; 'ARTROPOLIS-90' Vancouver 1990; 'Eros at Alpha' Alpha Gallery, W. Vancouver; 'Rainforests of the Mind' and 'Fantastic Visions,' Alpha Gallery, W. Vancouver 1991; 'Jeu Overt' surrealist group show, 'Actuel' Gallery, Paris, France 1992; rec'd Can. Council Project Grant 1978, Travel Grant 1978; rep. in B.C. Govt. Perm. Coll. and various private colls. Eng., Can. and USA; served with Royal Signals Eng. and Germany 1946–48; mem. Prison Arts Foundation (B.C.); recreations: magic (especially card manipulation), reading, underwater photography, travel; Club: Vancouver Magic Circle; Home: #202, 2020 Fullerton Ave., North Vancouver, B.C. V7P 3G3.

**KING-FARLOW, John,** M.A., Ph.D., F.R.S.C.; educator; b. London, Eng. 9 July 1932; s. Hugh St. Denys Nettleton K-F, M.B.E. and (Barbara) Hazel (Guggenheim) K-F; e. Westminster Sch. London 1951; Christ Ch. Oxford B.A., M.A. 1955; Duke Univ. A.M. 1958; Stanford Univ. Ph.D. 1960; m. Elizabeth A. d. Kenneth E. and Doreen Slater 16 May 1992; PROF. OF PHILOS. UNIV. OF ALTA. 1968– ; Flying Offr. RAF 1955–57; Lectr. in Philos. San José State Coll. Cal. 1959–60; A.W. Mellon Post-Doctoral Fellow Univ. of Pittsburgh 1960–61; Lectr. Amherst Coll. Mass. 1961–62; Asst. Prof. of Philos. Univ. of Cal. Santa Barbara 1962–65; Leverhulme Found. Post-Doctoral Fellow Univ. of Liverpool 1966–68; Visiting Prof. present Univ. 1968, Assoc. Prof. 1969; Visiting Prof.: Univs. of Guelph 1971–72, Ottawa 1972–73, P.E.I. 1976, Lethbridge 1977; Visiting Prof.'s privileges for rsch. McGill Univ. 1974; Trustee, Philos.' Info. Service Ohio; mem. various cttes. SSHRCC; author 'Reason and Religion' 1959; 'Self-Knowledge and Social Relations' 1978; 'The Dead Ship' poetry 1968; co-author 'Faith and the Life of Reason' 1972; 'Self-Deception and Self-Healing' 1988; co-ed. 'Contemporary Canadian Philosophy Series' 4 vols. Eng. Candn. Essays 1977; 'L'universe la philosophie' 4 vols. French Candn. essays 1973; poetry pub. various lit. jours. and mags.; frequent guest speaker various univs. and assns.; Founding ed. Candn. Jour. of Philos. 1970; Ed. Bd., Apeiron; mem. Candn. Philos. Assn. (Dir., Sec., Vice Pres. and Pres. 1970–78); Am. Philos. Assn.; Oxford Union Soc. (former Sec. and Lib.); Anglican; NDP; recreations: poetry, opera, politics, history, fiction; Club: Athenaeum (London, Eng.); Home: 2201, 8210 – 111 St., Edmonton, Alta. T6G 2C7; Office: Rm. 4–105 Humanities Centre, Edmonton, Alta. T6G 2E1.

**KINGHAM, Douglas James (Jim),** B.A., Ph.D.; provincial public servant; b. Kitchener, Ont. 1 Sept 1941; s. Ernest William and Pearl Marguerite (Shoemaker) K.; e. McMaster Univ. B.A. 1964; Univ. of Waterloo Ph.D. (Inorganic Chem.) 1968; m. Dr. Anastasia d. Dr. Michael and Maria Shkilnyk 1984; children (by previous marriage): Sharon, Scott, Brian; VICE-CHRMN., ONTARIO ENVIRONMENTAL ASSESSMENT BD. 1987– ; joined federal pub. service as rsch. sci. (chem.) 1968; developed Candn. Ocean Dumping Control Bill and negotiated Candn. positions marine sci. rsch. and transfer of technol. for Law of the Sea Convention 1973–77; Dir. Environmental Emergency Programme 1977–82; Dir. Policy and Expenditure Mgmt. Br. Environmental Protection Service 1982–83; Reg. Dir. Gen. Environment Can., Ont. Region 1984–86; Candn. Chrmn. Internat. Jt. Comn.'s Great Lakes Water Quality Bd. 1984–87; Fed. Chrmn. Review Bd. Can.-Ont. Agreement Respecting Great Lakes Water Quality 1984–87; Office: P.O. Box 2382, 2300 Yonge St., Suite 1201, Toronto, Ont. M4P 1E4.

**KINGHORN, Niall Bindon;** theatre manager; artistic director; b. Esher, Surrey England 26 Apr. 1946; s. James Agnew and Audrey Constance (Blood) K.; e. Prior Park Coll. Bath, England; Wimbledon Sch. of Art, Eng.; London Acad. of Music & Dramatic Arts, Eng.; m. Christine d. William and Alice Maude (Spencer) Bennett 30 May 1980; two d. Nyree Christine, Lucinda May; THEATRE MGR., UNIV. OF VICTORIA 1980– ; Adjudicator, Theatre B.C.; Artistic Dir. Shakespeare Plus 1987–88; Asst. Stage Mgr. Bristol Old Vic Co. 1968, Stage Mgr. 1969–71; Co. Mgr. Liverpool Playhouse 1971–73; Tech. Dir. Theatre Dept. present Univ. 1973–80; mem. Royal Scottish Country Dance Soc.; Asian Arts Soc.; Home: 941 Meares St., Victoria, B.C. V8V 3J5; Office: P.O. Box 1700, Victoria, B.C. V8W 2Y2.

**KINGSLEY, Jean-Pierre,** B.Comm., M.H.A.; public servant; b. Ottawa, Ont. 12 July 1943; s. Oscar and Françoise (Charette-Bertrand) K.; e. Univ. of Ottawa, B.Comm. 1965, M.H.A. (Hosp. Admin.) 1969; m. Suzanne d. Georges and Meldréa Potvin 19 Aug. 1967; children: Marie-France, Justin, Michèle; CHIEF ELECTORAL OFFICER OF CANADA 1990– ; Programmer, IBM 1965–66; Field Supvr., Travelers Insur. 1966–67; Chief, Hospitals, Veterans Affairs 1969–71; Prof. Offr., CMHC 1971; Extve. Dir., Charles Camsell Hosp. 1971–73; Sr. Extve. Offr. to the Depy. Min. of Welfare 1973–74; Group Chief, Treas. Bd. 1974–76; Dir. Gen. Audit, Pub. Serv. Comn. 1976–77; Pres. & Chief Extve. Offr., Ottawa Gen. Hosp. 1977–81; Dep. Sec., Prog. Delivery Br., Min. of State for Social Devel. 1981–84; Dep. Sec., Treasury Bd., Personnel Policy Branch 1984–87; Asst. Depy. Registrar General, Govt. of Canada 1987–90; Bd. Chrmn., Montfort Hosp., Ottawa 1982–90; Home: 274 Bruyère, Ottawa, Ont. K1N 5E6; Office: 1595 Telesat Court, Ottawa, Ont. K1A 0M6.

**KINGSMILL, Ardagh Sidney,** Q.C.; b. Cambridge, Mass. 17 June 1927; e. Univ. of W. Ont., Business Adm. grad. 1950; Osgoode Hall Law Sch., 1954; m. Alva Marjorie Coles, 7 July 1956; two s., Andrew Winnett, David Ardagh; PARTNER, McCARTHY TÉTRAULT; Dir., Canadian Pacific Limited; Laidlaw Inc.; Ampex Canada Inc.; FBM Distillery Co. Ltd.; Suncor Inc.; Cummins Diesel of Can. Ltd.; The Tapecoat Co. of Canada, Ltd.; Sandoz Agro Canada Inc.; Unitel Communications Inc.; The Corp. of Massey Hall and Roy Thomson Hall; called to Bar of Ont. 1954; cr. Q.C. 1968; mem., Candn. Bar Assn. (Past Chrmn. Ont. Taxation Subsec.); Candn. Tax Foundation; Internat. Fiscal Assoc.; Internat. Bar Assn.; Bd. of Trade; Phi Delta Phi; recreations: sailing, badminton, swimming; Clubs: Toronto; Granite; Home: 322 Lytton Blvd., Toronto, Ont. M5N 1R8; Office: Toronto Dominion Bank Tower, Toronto-Dominion Centre, Toronto, Ont. M5K 1E6.

**KINGSTON, Robert Arnold,** Q.C., B.A.; b. Prescott, Ont. 17 Sept. 1915; s. Paul and Elizabeth Theresa (Coughlin) K.; e. Trinity Coll., Univ. of Toronto, B.A. 1936; Osgoode Hall, Toronto, LL.B. (Gold Medallist); m. Jeanne Elizabeth, McFarlane, Toronto, Ont., 8 Sept. 1944; children: Susan, Barbara, John, Judith; PARTNER, BLAKE, CASSELS & GRAYDON; Adv. Ctte., Sotheby's (Canada) Inc.; mem. of Senate, Univ. of Toronto, 1952–56; Chrmn. of Convocation, Trinity Coll., 1950–52; read law with Fennell, Porter & Davis, Toronto, Ont.; called to Bar of Ont., 1940; cr. Q.C. 1955; author, 'Ontario Corporation Manual,' 1949; 'Canada Corporation Manual,' 1950; mem. Candn. Bar Assn; Delta Chi; Freemason; Anglican; recreations: curling, golf; Clubs: Toronto; Granite; Ticker; Home: 33 Elmhurst Ave., Apt. 2310, Willowdale, Ont. M2N 6G8; Office: Box 25, Commerce Court W., Toronto, Ont. M5L 1A9.

**KINKAIDE, Perry Studley,** B.A., M.Sc., Ph.D., C.M.C.; management consultant; b. New York, N.Y. 7 April 1942; s. Edwin Lincoln and Patricia Lenore (Ibbotson) K.; e. Colgate Univ. B.A. 1964; Univ. of Alberta M.Sc. 1967, Ph.D. 1972; m. Alexandra d. George and Milka Chruma 23 Sept. 1972; children: Paul Francis, Peter Alexander; PARTNER, KPMG MANAGEMENT COMSULTING 1990– ; Teaching Fellow, Univ. of Alberta 1969–72; Rsch. Assoc., Centre for Study of Mental Retardation 1972–73; Regional Coord., Serv. for Handicapped, Alta. Govt. 1973–81; Regional Dir., Alta. Social Services & Community Health 1981–82; Asst. Deputy Min. 1982–84; Dir., Corp. Devel. 1985; Pres., Perry S. Kinkaide Mngt. Serv. Ltd. 1985–87; Principal, KPMG Management Consulting 1987–89; Teacher, Univ. of Alta. 1964–72; Instr., Grant MacEwan Community College 1972–74; Board Mem., Inst. of Cert.

Mngt. Consultants of Alta. 1991– ; Univ. of Alberta Teaching Fellow 1966; Queen's Jubilee Award 1977; Nat. Research Fellow 1970; Outstanding Leadership in Student Govt. 1960; All Eastern U.S. Chorus 1959, '60; Bd. Mem., Goodwill Rehab. Services 1982–86; Vice-Pres., St. Albert Assn. for the Handicapped 1983–87; Alberta Psychologists Assn.; Edmonton C. of C.; Author: 'Kenny – Will I Ever Grow Up' 1985, 'The Quest – In Search of Kinkaide' 1991 (unpub.) and numerous journal articles & newsletters; Founding editor, 'The Mental Retardation Bulletin; KPMG's 'The Executive's Digest'; 'Alberta Social Service's: The News'; Founder, Alberta's Futures Network; recreations: tennis, genealogy, sailing, gardening; club: Royal Glenora; Home: 45 Windermere Crescent, St. Albert, Alta. T8N 3P1; Office: 2610, 10104 - 103 Ave., Edmonton, Alta. T5J 0H8.

**KINNEAR, Michael Stewart Read,** B.A., M.A., D.Phil., F.R.Hist.S., F.R.G.S.; university professor; b. Saskatoon, Sask. 13 Aug. 1937; s. William and Agnes K.; e. Univ. of Sask. B.A. (Chem.) 1958, B.A. (Hist.) 1960; Univ. of Oregon, M.A. 1961; Oxford Univ. D.Phil. (Politics) 1965; m. Mary d. Harry and Alice Preston 4 July 1964; children: David, Andrew, Sara, Lucy; PROF. OF HIST., UNIV. OF MAN. 1965– ; joined Hist. Dept., Univ. of Man. 1965; Chrmn., Man. Mosaic Congress; Sr. Rsch. Assoc., St. Antony's Coll., Oxford Univ.; Bye Fellow, Robinson Coll., Cambridge Univ.; Visiting Fellow, Australian National Univ. 1993; awarded Can. Counc. M.A. and Ph.D. Scholarships; Woodrow Wilson Fellowship; IODE Overseas Scholarships; SSHRCC & Canada Council Leave Fellowships; Judge, 1993 CABIRA award (Canada-Australia Bicentennial Institutional Rsch. Award, Dept. of External Affairs); Anglican; author: 'The British Voter' 1968, 1981; 'The Fall of Lloyd George' 1973, 1974; 'Gleanings and Memoranda, 1893–1968' 1975; var. articles and reviews; Manitoba mem., Historic Sites & Monuments Bd. of Canada 1990– ; recreation: collecting political ephemera; club: Nat. Lib. (U.K.); Home: 754 Cloutier Dr., Winnipeg, Man. R3V 1L2; Office: Winnipeg, Man. R3T 2M8.

**KINOSHITA, Gene,** B.Arch., M.Arch., O.A.A., F.R.A.I.C., R.C.A.; architect; b. Vancouver, B.C. 18 Jan. 1935; s. Zenichi and Yoshi (Maikawa) K.; e. Univ. of B.C. B.Arch. (Hons.) 1959; Yale Univ. M.Arch. 1962; m. Dorothy d. Yaichi and Chiyoko Fukui 1 Sept. 1962; children: Mark, Michelle, Eric; PRES., MOFFAT KINOSHITA ASSOC. INC. estab. 1965; Pres., Royal Candn. Acad. of Arts 1984–88, Counc. Mem. 1979–81, Chrmn., Bldg. Ctte. 1976–87, 1st Vice-Pres. 1981–84; Dir., Visual Arts Ont. 1990–94; Hon. Trustee, Ont. Coll. of Art Found.; Bd. Mem., Arts Found. of Greater Toronto 1988–92; Pres., Arts Found. of Greater Toronto 1993–95; Arch. Design Critic, Univ. of Toronto 1969–71, 1980–84; Awards Jury Mem., Ont. Masonry Awards Prog. 1975; OAA Awards Program 1979; MAA Awards Program 1989; firm recipient of over 35 architectural design awards/distinctions; seven scholarships at UBC 1956–59; National Design Award of Pilkington travel. fellowship 1959; Yale Univ. scholarships 1961, 1962; Fellow, Royal Arch. Inst. of Can.; Academician, R.C.A.; Dir./Extve. Mem., Oolagen Community Serv. 1977–81; Life Mem., R.O.M.; architect for R.O.M. 1974–94; CHCH TV 11 1986; Univ. of Toronto, Fac. of Law Lib. & Fac. of Mus. Lib. 1986–91; Univ. of Western Ont., Sciences Complex Additions 1988–91; Whitby Psychiatric Hospital Redevelopment 1990–96; Cobourg Cultural Centre 1990–93; recreations: art collection & appreciation, fishing, tennis, skiing, gardening; Clubs: Empire, Georgian Peaks; Home: 278 Sheldrake Blvd., Toronto, Ont. M4P 2B6; Office: 124 Merton St., Toronto, Ont. M4S 2Z2.

**KINSELLA, Noël A.,** Hon. B.A., B.D., L.Ph., S.T.L., Ph.D., S.T.D.; b. Saint John, N.B. 28 Nov. 1939; s. John A. and Anna M. (Monahan) K.; e. elem. and high schs. Saint John; Univ. Coll. Dublin B.A. 1960; Pontifical Lateran Univ. Rome B.D. 1962, S.T.L. 1964, S.T.D. 1966; St. Thomas Univ. (Angelicum) Rome L.Ph. 1964, Ph.D. 1965; Licenced mem. Coll. Psychols. N.B.; SENATE OPPOSITION WHIP; Chrmn., Standing Senate Ctte. on Social Affairs, Science and Technology; Mem., Finance Ctte.; Mem., Foreign Affairs Ctte.; Assoc. Under Secy. of State for Canada 1989–90; Chrmn. N.B. Human Rights Comn. 1967–88; Chrmn. Ind. Training & Certification Bd. N.B. Dept. of Labour 1969–71; Chrmn. of Psychol. St. Thomas Univ. Fredericton 1967–78, Vice Pres. (Acad.) 1980–81; Comnr. Ind. Inquiry Comn. Ind. Relations Act N.B. 1975; Pres. Candn. Human Rights Found. 1988; Pres. Candn. Assn. Statutory Human Rights Agencies 1974, 1980; Pres. N.B. Region Inst. Pub. Adm. Can. 1977–78; arbitrator numerous labour disputes pub. and private sector; mem. Min. of Finance Ctte. Equal Pension Benefits Can. 1984; mem. N.B. Dels. to First Mins.' Conf. Candn. Constn. 1981–83; Visiting Scholar UN Inst. Training & Rsch. 1972; mem. numerous Candn. dels. to UN Human Rights Comn., UN Econ. & Social Council, UNESCO Conf. Human Rights Edn.; recipient Queen's Silver Jubilee Medal 1977; Kt. Sovereign & Mil. Order St. John Jerusalem, Rhodes & Malta; author 'Toward a Theory of Personality Development' 1966; 'Moral Orientation of the Mentally Retarded' 1967; 'Ego-Idenity and Indian Education' 1971; 'Tomorrow's Rights in the Mirror of History'; 'Civil Liberties in Canada' 1982; 'Some Psychological Considerations of the Trusting Attitude' 1973; mem. Candn. Psychol. Assn.; Pres. N.B. Psychol. Assn. 1969–70; U.S. Trotting Assn.; Candn. Trotting Assn.; R. Catholic; recreation: standard bred horses; Home: 151 Wetmore Rd., Fredericton, NB E3B 6M4; Office: Rm. 900, Victoria Bldg., 140 Wellington St., Ottawa, Ont. K1N 5V4.

**KINSELLA, T. Douglas,** B.A., M.D.,C.M., F.A.C.P., F.R.C.P.(C); physician; educator; b. Montreal, Que. 15 Feb. 1932; s. James Gerald and Mary Alice (Nelson) K.; e. Loyola Coll. Montreal B.A. 1953; McGill Univ. M.D.,C.M. 1957; m. Lorna d. Earl and Irene Cleary 18 June 1955; children: Warren, Kevin, Lorne; PROF. OF MED. UNIV. OF CALGARY 1975– and DIRECTOR, OFFICE OF MED. BIOETHICS 1993– , Asst. Dean (Med. Bioethics) 1984–92; Asst. and Assoc. Prof. of Med. Queen's Univ. 1968–73; Assoc. Prof. of Med. McGill Univ. 1973–75; Visiting Scholar Center Med. Ethics Univ. of Chicago 1988–89; Chrmn. & Pres., Nat. Council Bioethics Human Rsch.; mem. Nat. Council Bioethics Human Rsch.; recipient Queen's Silver Jubilee Medal 1977; Pew Found. Trust Ethics Scholar 1988; author or co-author over 60 jour. articles and book chapters med., arthritis, immunol. & med. bioethics; Adv. Bd. Ed. Internat. Jour. Rheumatol.; mem. Candn. Arthritis Soc.; Candn. Rheumatism Assn.; Candn. Bioethics Soc.; Liberal; R. Catholic; Office: Health Sciences Center, 3330 Hospital Dr. N.W., Calgary, Alta. T2N 4N1.

**KINSELLA, William Patrick,** B.A., M.F.A.; author; b. Edmonton, Alta. 25 May 1935; s. John Matthew and Olive Mary (Elliott) K.; e. Eastwood H.S. Edmonton 1953; Univ. of Victoria B.A. 1974; Univ. of Iowa M.F.A. 1978; m. 1stly Myrna Salls Dec. 1957; m. 2ndly Mildred Clay-Heming Sept. 1965; m. 3rdly Ann Ilene Knight Dec. 1978; children: Shannon, Lyndsey, Erin; author 'Dance Me Outside' (17 stories) 1977; 'Scars' (16 stories) 1978; 'Shoeless Joe Jackson Comes to Iowa' (10 stories) 1980; 'Born Indian' (14 stories) 1981; 'Shoeless Joe' (novel) 1982; 'The Moccasin Telegraph' (16 stories) 1983; 'The Ballad of the Public Trustee' 1982; 'The Thrill of the Grass' (10 stories) 1984; 'The Alligator Report' (26 stories) 1985; 'The Iowa Baseball Confederacy' (novel) 1986; 'The Fencepost Chronicles' (13 stories) 1986; 'Five Stories' (5 stories) 1987; 'Red Wolf, Red Wolf' (13 stories) 1987; 'The Further Adventures of Slugger McBatt' (10 stories) 1988; 'The Miss Hobbema Pageant' (14 stories) 1989; 'The Rainbow Warehouse' (poetry, with Ann Knight) 1989; 'Two Spirits Soar: The Art of Allen Sapp' (non-fiction) 1990; 'Box Socials' (novel) 1991; 'The Dixon Cornbelt League' (9 stories) 1993; recipient Houghton Mifflin Lit. Fellowship 1982; Books in Canada First Novel Award 1982; Candn. Authors' Assn. Award for Fiction 1982; Writers Guild Alta. Award for Fiction 1982, 1983; Vancouver Award for Writing 1987; Stephen Leacock Medal for Humor 1987; Canadian Booksellers Assoc. Author of the Year 1987; mem. Am. Atheists; Enoch Emery Soc.; Am. Amateur Press Assn.; Soc. Am. Baseball Researchers; Mailing Address: P.O. Box 2162, Blaine, WA 98230.

**KINSEY, Bernard Bruno,** B.A., Ph.D., F.R.S.C.; retired university professor; b. London, England 15 June 1910; s. Rudolf Julius and Marie Angeline Josephine (Voss) K.; e. Cambridge Univ., B.A. 1932, Ph.D. 1937; Univ. of Calif. at Berkeley, grad. student; m. Marian Hall 26 Jan. 1968; children (from previous marriage): Jennifer, Nicholas, Peter; Lectr., Liverpool Univ. 1936–39; Telecommun. Rsch. Estab. 1939–42; Atomic Energy, England 1942–44; Can. 1944–54; Guest, Radiation Lab., Univ. of Calif. at Berkeley 1954–55; Rsch. Sci., AERE, Harwell, England 1955–58; Prof. of Physics, Univ. of Texas 1958–76; Founder, Scientific Services 1979; Founder, Topline Publishers 1988; FRSC 1954– ; Fellow, Am. Physical Soc.; author: 'Slow to Learn' 1989 and sundry physics pubs.; recreations: swimming; Home: 102 Skyline Dr., Austin, TX 78746.

**KINSLOW, Valerie Elaine,** B.A.; singer (soprano); b. Glace Bay, N.S. 10 Dec. 1949; d. George Ernest and Margaret Rose (Bagnell) K.; e. McGill Univ. B.A. 1980; performs regularly through N. Am. & Europe; recognized as one of Canada's leading interpreters of Baroque music; has performed as soloist with Tafelmusik & Studio de Musique Ancienne as well as num. chamber orchs., symphonies & ensembles; Guest Artist, Symphony N.S. 1991; formed Duo Seraphim with countertenor Allan Fast which has performed to critical acclaim across Canada 1981; featured in many recitals of 20th century music; heard frequently on CBC & Radio-Canada; has recorded for Radio Spain & Radio France Internat.; has given num. master-classes at var. univs., workshops & art centres; Teacher, Concordia Univ. 1978– ; Univ. of Montreal (voice) 1991– ; Past Bd. Mem., Musique Royale; Scholar, N.S. Talent Trust 1974, '75 (studied Early Music in London England); recreations: golf, nordic skiing; Address: Faculty of Music, Univ. de Montréal, CP 6128, Succ A, Montréal, Qué. H3C 3J7.

**KINSMAN, Jeremy K.B.;** civil servant; b. Montreal, Que. 28 Jan. 1942; s. Ronald D.L. and Katharine Nixon (Bell) K.; e. Lower Can. Coll. 1959; Princeton Univ. 1963; Inst. d'Etudes Pol., Paris 1965; m. Hana Gregor; one d.: Juliet Bibby; AMBASSADOR OF CANADA IN MOSCOW 1993– ; Aluminum Co. of Can. 1965–66; Dept. of External Affairs 1966; served in several capacities with External Affairs 1966–74; Candn. Embassy & Mission to EEC, Brussels, Candn. Embassy, Algiers, Permanent Mission of Can. to U.N., N.Y. 1975–80; Min. & Depy. Permanent Rep., Candn. Deleg. to the U.N., N.Y. 1979–80; Chrmn., Policy Planning Secretariat, Ottawa 1980–81; Min., Political Affairs, Candn. Embassy, Washington 1981–85; Asst. Depy. Min., Cultural Affairs & Broadcasting, Dept. of Communications, Govt. of Can. 1985–89; Asst. Depy. Min., Political and International Security Affairs, Dept. of External Affairs, Govt. of Can. 1990–92; Club; Rideau Tennis, Princeton Club of N.Y.; Office: Canadian Embassy, 23 Starokonyushenny Pereulok, Moscow, Russia.

**KIPPEN, Walter Bruce,** B.Comm.; oil executive; b. Montreal, Que. 30 Jan. 1926; s. Col. Eric Douglas Bruce, O.B.E. and Marguerite Beresford (Stethem) K.; e. Lower Canada College, Westmount H.S.; McGill Univ. B.Comm. 1949; m. Claire Elfride Audley 1 May 1958; children: Alexander Bruce, Julia Francesca, Winston David Bruce; PRES., PETROKIPP CAPITAL CORP. INC.; Pres., Westcan Corp. Inc. & Jiffy Auto Ltd. 1949–56; Dir., Kippen & Co. Inc. 1958–64; Chair & C.E.O. 1964–74; Sr. Vice-Pres. & Dir., Bongard, Leslie & Co. Ltd. 1974–75; Dir., Jetoils Ltd.; Pathfinder Petroleums Ltd.; Canadian Diamond Coring Ltd.; organized Medaillon Petroleums Ltd. (later absorbed into Norcen Energy Resources); served RCAF, 2nd World War; discharged as Pilot Offr.; Queen Elizabeth II Jubilee Medal for efforts in devel. Council for Candn. Unity; Mem., Am. Metal Miniing Assn.; Independent Petroleum Assn. of Can.; Montreal, Toronto, Can. & Midwest (Chicago) Stock Exchanges; Investment Dealers Assn. of Can.; Gov., Can. Stock Exchange 1962–63; Montreal YMCA 1965–69; Vice-Pres., Council for Candn. Unity 1965–73; Alpha Delta Phi; Anglican; co-author & sponsor: 'Option Canada: The Economic Consequences of Separatism' 1966; recreations: shooting, skiing, golf, tennis, writing; clubs: University, Knickerbocker (N.Y.), M.A.A.A., Hillside Tennis; Home: 478 Mount Pleasant Ave., Westmount, Montreal, Que. H3Y 3H3.

**KIRBY, Charles William, Jr.;** dancer/choreographer; b. Little Rock, Ark. 28 April 1926; s. Charles William and Eva Rose (Horton) K.; e. Little Rock Jr. Coll. 1945; PRINCIPAL CHARACTER ARTIST, NAT. BALLET OF CAN. 1985– ; prin. soloist, Ballet Soc. Ark. 1947; Assoc. Dir., Acad. Ballet Arts, Little Rock 1948–50; Co-dir., Acad. Dance Arts, Memphis, Tenn. 1950–65; prin. dancer, choreographer, etc., several U.S. theatres 1950– ; Mem., Nat. Ballet Can. 1965–72; Soloist 1972–76; Principal Dancer 1976–85; Co. Mgr., Dance Repertory Co., N.Y.C. 1972; TV appearances incl.: 'Swan Lake' 1967, 'Cinderella' 1968 (Emmy), 'Sleeping Beauty' 1972 (Emmy), 'Giselle' 1975, 'La Fille Mal Gardee' 1979, 'Onegin' 1985, 'The Merry Widow' 1987; choreographer, 'La Rondine' 1971, 'Maurice Ravel Cent. Concert' 1975 (TV specials); summer opera fests.; Nat. Arts. Ctr.; Candn. Opera Co.; author, dir., choreographer, narrator, 'Spectrum: A Retrospective Look at Dance' 1973; served AUS 1944; Key to City of Little Rock 1965; Co-founder/owner (with Jacques Wensvoort) Abundance Restaurant, Inc. 1980– ; Adv. Bd., George Brown Coll.; Extve. Ctte., Candn. Actors Equity Assn.; Mem., ACTRA; Episcopalian; Office: c/o Nat. Ballet of Can., 157 King St. E., Toronto, Ont. M5C 1G9 and 35 Church St., #614, Toronto, Ont. M5E 1T3.

**KIRBY, M. Robert,** B.Arch., M.Arch.; professor of architecture; b. Nokomis, Sask. 28 May 1940; s. Howard Herbert and Irene Elizabeth (Gasser) K.; e. Univ. of

Manitoba B.ARch. 1967; M.I.T. M.Arch. 1970; m. Elaine d. Fred and Mia Heck June 1987; children: Tyler, Ian; PROF. OF ARCHITECTURE, FAC. OF ENVIRONMENTAL DESIGN, UNIV. OF CALGARY 1970–74, 1978– ; Architect, #10 Arch. Group Winnipeg 1967–70, 1974–78; Part-time Prof., Univ. of Manitoba 1968–70; Partner, Nokomis Consultants Community Design & Development; Mem., Sustainable, Affordable Housing Soc.; Home: 6939 Bow Cres., Calgary, Alta.; Office: 2500 University Dr. N.W., Calgary, Alta. T2N 1N4.

**KIRBY, The Hon. Michael J.L.,** B.Sc., M.A., Ph.D.; senator; b. Montreal, Que. 5 Aug. 1941; s. John Charles and Monica Mary (Cooper) K.; e. Dalhousie Univ. B.Sc. 1961, M.A. 1962; Northwestern Univ. Ph.D. 1965; m. Dianne Glenna Laham 1 March 1986; children: Coleen, Bruce, Sean; step-children: Shane, Lee Ann; MEMBER OF THE SENATE OF CANADA 1984– ; Mem. Bd. of Dirs.: Quaker Oats; Crownx; RJR Macdonald; Westbury Canadian Life; joined Research Analysis Corp. 1964; various teaching positions Univs. Chicago, Dalhousie and Kent (Canterbury, Eng.) 1965–70; Asst. Dean of Arts & Science Dalhousie Univ. 1969–70, Prof. of Comm. & Business Adm. and Dir. Govt. Studies Program 1973–74, Prof. of Pub. Adm. and Business Adm. 1976–80; Princ. Asst. to Premier of N.S. 1970–73; Asst. Princ. Secy. to Prime Min. of Can. 1974–76; mem. N.S. Bd. Commrs. Pub. Utilities 1976–77; Pres. Inst. for Research on Pub. Policy 1977–80; Secy. to Cabinet for Fed.-Prov. Relations Govt. Can. 1980–82; Depy. Clk. of Privy Council 1981–82; Chrmn. Task Force on Atlantic Fisheries 1982–83; Sr. Corp. Vice Pres., Canadian National Railways 1982–84; Chrmn. of the Leader's Strategy Ctte., Liberal Party of Canada (1988 Fed. elec. campaign); Liberal mem., 'Political Pundits Panel' CTV; author over 40 papers prof. journs.; recreations: squash, jogging, golf; Home: 2538 River Rd., Manotick, Ont. K4M 1B4; Office: The Senate, Ottawa, Ont. K1A 0A4.

**KIRBY, Hon. William John Cameron,** C.D., Q.C.; retired judge; b. Calgary, Alta. 12 Jan. 1909; s. William John and Catherine Georgina (Gray) K.; e. Rocky Mountain House (Alta.) Pub. Sch.; Hanna (Alta.) High Sch.; Univ. of B.C., B.A. 1930; Univ. of Alta., Grad. Sch. of Educ., 1931–32; Vancouver Law Sch. 1938–41; m. Marion Jean, d. Stanley Floyd and Ethel Torrance, Calgary, Alta., 10 Apl. 1954; children: William John Torrance, Catherine Elaine; JUSTICE, COURT OF QUEEN'S BENCH OF ALBERTA until retirement 1984; read law with Dugald Donaghy, K.C., Vancouver, B.C.; called to Bar of B.C. 1943, Alta. 1945; High Sch. Teacher, Hussar, Alta., 1932–35; Princ., Okotoks (Alta.) Schs., 1935–38; practised law in Red Deer, Alta., 1945–60 (Partner, McClure & Kirby, 1945–47; Kirby, Murphy, Armstrong, Beames & Chapmen, 1947–60); Chrmn., Bd. of Review of the Admin. of Justice in the Prov. Courts of Alta. 1973–78; Chrmn., Federal Electoral Boundaries Comn., Alta. 1983; served with Candn. Army Active Service 1941–45; Inst., Offrs. Training Centre, Victoria, B.C., 1941–43; Troop Commdr., 25th and 24th Field Regts. RCA 1943–44; Legal Offr., Pacific Command HQ, 1944–45; M.L.A. Alta. 1954–59; Prov. Leader, P. Cons. Party of Alta., 1958–59; Pres., Red Deer Br., Royal Candn. Legion, 1950–53; Freemason; Anglican; recreations: golf, gardening, bridge; Clubs: Ranchmen's; Union; Home: 1774 Orcas Park Terrace, Sidney, B.C. V8L 4A7.

**KIRK, K. Lloyd,** C.L.U.; insurance executive; b. Thunder Bay Ont. 12 Jan. 1933; s. A. Raymond W. and Enid M. (Faulkner) K.; e. Fort William Coll. Inst. 1953; Univ. of W. Ont. 1956; C.L.U. 1965; m. Carole Visseau 24 Jan. 1957; children: Jeffrey Lloyd, Robert John, Kendall Elizabeth; Exec. Vice Pres. & Chief Operating Offr., North American Life Assurance Co. 1985; Dir., First North American Insurance Co.; Chateau Insur. Co.; Jedal Resources Inc.; Nalafund Investors Ltd.; Agt., Supr. Great-West Life Assurance Co. 1958–62; Mgr., Supt. of Agencies, Commercial Union Assurance Co. Toronto and Montréal 1962–72, Exec. Asst. to Gen. Mgr. London, Eng. 1972–74, Dep. Dir. of Agencies, Toronto 1974–75; Agency Vice Pres. present co. 1975–80, Sr. Vice Pres. 1980–85; recreations: skiing, swimming; Club: National; Home: 14 Wellesbourne Cres., Willowdale Ont. M2H 1Y7.

**KIRKCONNELL, Paul Andrew,** B.A., M.B.A.; pharmaceutical executive; b. Ottawa, Ont. 10 Mar. 1958; s. Russell Stewart and Edna Irene (Gilmour) K.; e. Univ. of Toronto, B.A. 1980; Univ. of West. Ont., M.B.A. 1983; EXTVE. DIR., BUSINESS PLANNING AND DEVELOPMENT, CONNAUGHT LABORATORIES INC. 1990– ; Analyst, Finan. Planning, Northern Telecom Internat. Limited 1983; Mgr., Mktg. Support 1984; Bus. Devel. 1985; Auditor, Opns. Control & Review Group, Northern Telecom Limited 1986; Sr. Cons., Strategic Mngt. Serv., Coopers & Lybrand Cons. Group 1986; Manager, Strategic Mngt. Serv., The Coopers & Lybrand Cons. Group 1988–90; Lectr., Univ. of Toronto 1988; published in Globe & Mail, Univ. of W. Ont. Business Quarterly; Internat. Business Scholarship, U.W.O.; Dir., The Toronto Chap. of the Planning Forum 1986–89; Phi Delta Theta of Toronto Limited 1979–81, 1983–89; Address: Route 611, P.O. Box 187, Swiftwater, PA 18370.

**KIRKHAM, Peter Gilbert,** B.A.Sc., M.B.A., M.A., Ph.D., r.m.c.; economist; Canadian public servant; banker; b. Red Deer, Alta. 24 Oct. 1934; s. Norman Kennedy K.; e. Royal Mil. Coll., Kingston, Ont. 1957; Univ. of Brit. Columbia, B.A.Sc. 1958; Univ. of Western Ont. M.B.A. 1963, M.A. (Econ.) 1964; Princeton Univ. Ph.D. (Econ.) 1970; m.; SR. VICE-PRES., HUMAN RESOURCES, BANK OF MONTREAL 1982– ; Prof. of Econ., Univ. of Western Ont. 1964–65, 1969–73; Asst. Chief Statistician, Statistics Can. 1973–75; Chief Statistician 1975–80; Sr. Vice Pres. and Chief Economist, Bank of Montreal 1980–82; served in Royal Candn. Engrs. 1953–60; rank on retirement Capt.; mem. Candn. Econ. Assn.; Am. Econ. Assn.; Office: First Canadian Place, Toronto, Ont. M5X 1A1.

**KIRKLAND, Douglas;** photographer; b. Toronto, Ont. 16 Aug. 1934; s. Morley David and Evelyn (Reid) K.; m. Françoise 1967; children: Mark, Karen, Lisa Foley; freelance photog. USA and Eur. since 1960; former photog. 'Look' and 'Life' mags.; author/photog. 'Light Years' autobiog. 1989; 'Icons' computer imaged book 1993; Address: 9060 Wonderland Park Ave., Los Angeles, Cal. 90046.

**KIRKLAND, Ellis Galea,** OAA, MRAIC, B.Arch., MAUD; architect, urban designer, association executive; b. Rabat, Malta 30 Sept. 1955; d. Paul Carmel and Mary Helen (Micallef) Galea; e. Univ. of Toronto B.Arch. 1981; Harvard Univ. MAUD 1984; OAA; MRAIC; m. J. Michael s. Joseph Walton and Gleannis (Howell) K. 10 June 1989; children: Cleo, Gilly; PRINCIPAL, THE KIRKLAND PARTNERSHIP 1989– ; Mgr., Core Area W. Ottawa, Nat. Capital Comn. 1985; Chair, Ctte. of Candn. Architectural Councils 1994; has worked in urban design, planning & arch. fields 1976– ; projects incl. Nat. Film Bd. Offices: Theatre, Film & Video Lib., North York Civic Sq.; Lecturer, Univ. of Toronto, Univ. of Waterloo; Teaching Asst., Harvard Univ.; firm has won num. awards incl. Prix Jean A. Laurent 1991, 1st Place of 403 submissions for internat. comp. in Japan 'Style for the Year 2001' 1985; Delegate, Commonwealth Conf. for Young Leaders 1987; CMHC Full Schoalrship to Harvard Univ. 1982; Royal Arch. Inst. of Canada Medal 1981; Jules Wegman Travelling Fellowship 1981, Alpha Rho Chi Medal 1981, Frederick Coates Fellowship 1978; Treas. & Dir., Mariposa Folk Found. 1990–93; elected 1st President, Ont. Assn. of Architects (1st woman in 104 year history) 1993; re-elected President 1994; Sr. Vice-Pres. & Treas. 1992; Vice-Pres. 1991; author: 'Trade Centres' 1993; recreations: artist, writer, cultural voyeur; club: still seeking a club resplendent with the zeitgeist of the Austrian & French 'Discourse Parlours' of the Art Nouveau Period; Home: 120 Rosedale Valley Rd., Suite 105, Toronto, Ont.; Office: 225 Richmond St. W., Ste. 500, Toronto, Ont. M5V 1W2.

**KIRKLAND, James Leslie,** M.D., M.Sc., Ph.D., F.R.C.P.(C); physician; b. Montréal, Qué. 22 March 1952; s. Norman George and Audrey Louise K.; e. Univ. of Toronto, M.D. 1977; Univ. of Manchester, M.Sc. 1982; Univ. of Toronto, Ph.D. 1990; CHIEF, GERIATRICS SERVICE, THE QUEEN ELIZABETH HOSP. 1985– ; Med. Dir., Central Service, Univ. of Toronto Regional Geriatrics Program; Dir. of Geriatrics Services, Toronto Hosp. 1985– ; Asst. Prof. of Med., Univ. of Toronto 1990– ; Resident in Med. Toronto Gen. Hosp. 1977–80; Rsch. Assoc. in Geriatric Med. Univ. of Manchester 1980–82; Guest Worker, Nat. Inst. on Aging, Nat. Insts. of Health 1982–84; Instr. in Med. Johns Hopkins Univ. 1983–84; mem. Endocrine Soc.; Am. Geriatrics Soc.; Brit. Geriatrics Soc.; Brit. Soc. Rsch. Aging; Alpha Omega Alpha; Office: 1104, 550 University Ave., Toronto, Ont. M5G 2A2.

**KIRKLAND, John Michael,** B.Arch., M.Arch., M.Urban Design; architect; educator; b. Miami, Fla. 31 March 1943; s. Joseph W. (d.) and Gleannis L. (Howell) K.; e. Harvard Univ. M.Arch. 1968, M.Urban Design 1970; American Acad. in Rome, Dip. 1971; PRINCIPAL, THE KIRKLAND PARTNERSHIP ARCHITECTS 1988– ; Adjunct Prof. of Architecture, Univ. of Toronto 1990– ; Assoc. Chief Arch. and Dir. of Rsch. New York Urban Development Corp. 1970–73; Dir. of Urban Design and Princ. Urban Designer Manhattan, New York 1973–75; New York City 1973–75; Lectr., Inst. for Arch. and Urb. Studies, N.Y. 1973–74; Asst. Prof. Columbia Univ. 1971–73; Visiting Prof. Harvard Univ. 1974 & 1987, Univ. of Pa. 1975, Univ. of Mich. 1984, New York St. Univ. 1986–88, Univ. of Waterloo 1987–88, Nanjing Inst. 1987; Assoc. Prof. of Arch. Univ. of Toronto 1976–90; Distinguished Internat. Prof., Univ. of Wisconsin 1989; Assoc. Barton Myers 1976–78; J. Michael Kirkland Arch. 1974–82; Jones & Kirkland Architects 1982–88; Fulbright Fellow 1970; Prix de Rome 1969–70; Frederick Sheldon Fellow Harvard 1970; Loeb Fellow, Harvard 1974; Prog. Arch. Awards 1975, 1977, 1983; Arch. Design Awards 1983, 1984, 1988; Awards of Excellence O.A.A. 1987–88; Award of Excellence, North York Civic Square 1989; Gov. Gen. Award for Architecture 1990; Jean-Alaurent Grand Prix Award of Distinction 1991; Bringing Back the Don Award for Planning Excellence 1992; Fellow, Am. Acad. in Rome; R.A.I.C.; N.C.A.R.B.; mem., Candn. Rome Prize Ctte.; Reg. Arch., Mass., Ont., N.Y., N.B., Fla.; Competition Awards, Fountainbleu 1965, Roosevelt Island N.Y. 1976, Edmonton City Hall 1980, Mississauga City Hall 1982, West Hollywood Civic Centre 1987; St. Clair Terraces 1988; Kitchener City Hall 1989; author (bldgs. & projects) 'Low Rise, High Density Prototype' 1974; North York Civic Pool, Square, Gardens 1981–88; Mississauga City Hall 1982–87; King West Centre 1986–89; Nat. Film Bd. of Can. 1988–90; Ataratiri Plan 1990; The Railways Lands Urban Design 1992; Shanghai Culinary Centre 1993; Lower Don Plan 1993; Office: 225 Richmond St. W., Suite 500, Toronto, Ont. M5V 2C7.

**KIRKLAND, Hon. Marie Claire,** C.M., Q.C., B.A., B.C.L., LL.D. (Hon.); b. Palmer, Mass., U.S.A., 8 Sept.; d. late Rose A. (Demers) and late Dr. Charles Aimé Kirkland (former M.L.A. for Jacques-Cartier, 1939–61 for whom the city of Kirkland, P.Q. was named); e. Villa-Maria Convent; McGill Univ., B.A. 1947; McGill Univ. Faculty of Law, B.C.L. 1950; LL.D. (Hon.), Moncton Univ. 1965; York Univ. 1975; m. P. Casgrain (divorced); children: Lynne-Marie, Kirkland, Marc; m. 2ndly Wyndham A. Strover; Judge, Prov. Court of Que.; retired 1990; with law firm of Cerini, Jamieson 1952; cr. Q.C. 1969; first el. to Que. Leg. in by-el. for Jacques-Cartier, Dec. 1961 (1st woman to sit in Que. Leg.); at the 1962 gen. el., rec'd one of the largest majorities ever recorded in the province (50,000 vote majority); Quebec promoter and sponsor of the first important bill to amend the Civil Code (1964) giving married women equal rights; First Woman Cabinet Min. in Que.; Min. Transport & Communications 1964; re-el for Marguerite-Bourgeoys g.e. April 1970; Min. of Tourism, Fish and Game 1970; Min. of Cultural Affairs 1972 until retired 1973; Judge (1st woman), Prov. Court of Que. 1973–90; seconded the address in reply to speech from the Throne at 1st session of Leg. 1962; first woman to plead before the private bills comte. in Que. 1953; sponsor of a bill (in the Que. Legis.) that estbld. the advisory council of the Status of Women (for the Prov.).; Founder and Pres. Candn. Chapter, Internat. Alliance of Women; mem. Kappa Alpha Theta; honorary member of the Quebec Safety League; life member of the Douglas Hospital in Montreal; life member of the Phi Alpha Delta Legal Fraternity of America; Chevalier de L'Ordre National du Québec; Grande Dame de L'Ordre Souverain Militaire de Saint-Jean de Jérusalem (Chevaliers de Malte); apptd. Mem., Order of Canada 1992; Gov.-Gen's. Prize Commemorating the 1929 Case which declared a woman to be a 'person' 1993; recreations: golf, fishing, travels; Home: 2879 Rothesay Rd., P.O. Box 700, Rothesay, N.B. E0G 2W0.

**KIRKLEY, Richard David,** C.D., B.A.; retired provincial public service; b. St. Boniface, Man. 2 Nov. 1931; s. Edwin Wheeler and Isabella Stuart (Berry) K.; e. Queen's Univ. B.A. 1969; m. Olive Annette d. Crawford Mason 12 Oct. 1952; children: Paul, Bruce, Terry, Stuart, David, John; former Asst. Depy. Min., Bd. of Management, Govt. of N.B. 1984–88; Chrmn. Information Systems Steering Ctte.; Central Vehicle Mgmt. Ctte.; joined RCAF 1950, Air. Navig. 405, 407 CEPE 436 Sqdn.; Instr. 2(M) OTU, RAF exchange 1958–60; Staff Offr. Mgmt. Services, Candn. Forces Europe 1972–74; retired 1974 with rank Maj.; Mgmt. Cons. N.B. Dept. of Treasury Bd. 1974–77; Exec. Dir., Adm. Div., Dept. of Health N.B. 1977–84; Chrmn., Productivity Program for N.B. Civil Services 1983–84, 1984–85; recipient C.D. and Bar; Home: P.O. Box 83, Cherry Valley, Ont. K0K 1P0.

**KIRKPATRICK, Douglas Allen,** B.A.; government advisor; b. Toronto, Ont. 8 Sept. 1955; s. Roger M. and D. Isobel (Cody) K.; e. Trinity Coll. Sch. Port Hope, Ont. 1974; Trinity Coll. Glenalmond, Perth, Scot. 1972–73; Univ. of W. Ont. B.A. 1978; Sr. Adv. to Premier of Ont. 1989; Adv. to Min. of State (Mines) 1980–81; Sr.

Adv. to Pres. Treasury Bd. Can. and Sec. Cabinet Ctte. Ont. Mins. 1982–84; Dir. of Operations Office Premier of Ont. 1985–87; Dep. Prin. Sec. Office Leader of Opposition, Ottawa 1987–88; Anglican; Liberal; recreations: skiing, squash, cooking, cycling, reading, travel; Home: 155 Spadina Rd., Toronto, Ont. M5R 2T9.

**KIRKPATRICK, James Balfour,** Ed.D.; retired university dean; b. Saskatoon, Sask. 20 Apr. 1909; s. Wilbur Allan and Elizabeth (Balfour) K.; e. Univ. of Sask., B.A. 1929, B.Ed. 1930, M. Ed. 1935; Teachers' Coll., Columbia Univ., Ed.D. (Physical Educ.) 1944; Hon. LL.D., Univ. of Saskatchewan 1990; m. Mary d. late John Convey, 30 Oct. 1943; eight children; served as High Sch. Instr., Melfort, Sask., 1930–33; Instr., Bedford Rd. Coll., Saskatoon, 1934–39; Physical Educ. Instr., Edmonton (Alta.) Normal Sch., 1939–42; Dir. of Physical Fitness and Recreation, Dept. of Educ., Regina, Sask., 1944–48; Dir., McGill Sch. of Physical Educ., Montreal, P.Q., 1948–56; Dean of Education, Univ. of Sask., 1956–76; rep. Candn. Conf. on Educ., 1956, 1962; Pres., W. Can. Regional Conf. on Teacher Educ., 1960–61; inducted to Sask. Sports Hall of Fame 1991; served in 2nd World War 1942–44; P.T. and Drill Offr., R.C.A.F.; co-author, 'Physical Fitness,' 1944; Catholic; Address: Apt. 108, 1421 Egbert Ave., Saskatoon, Sask. S7N 2L8.

**KIRKPATRICK, John Gildersleeve,** Q.C., B.Sc., B.C.L.; lawyer; b. Toronto, Ont. 28 Jan. 1917; s. Herbert Rutherfoord and Edna Margaret (Nelles) K.; e. Westmount (P.Q.) Public Schs.; Trinity Coll. Sch., Port Hope, Ont.; McGill Univ., B.Sc. 1939, B.C.L. 1942; m. Irena, d. William Groten, 24 June 1944; children: Xenia, Kathleen, Patricia; COUNSEL, OGILVY, RENAULT; called to Bar of Que. 1943; cr. Q.C. 1961; practised with present firm and its predecessors since 1943; Anglican; Club: St. James's, Mount Royal; Home: Apt. 507, 4444 Sherbrooke St. W., Montreal, Que. H3Z 1E4; Office: Suite 1100, 1981 McGill College Ave., Montreal, Que. H3A 3C1.

**KIRKPATRICK, Lesmere Forrest,** D.S.O., F.C.A.E., D.Eng., F.E.I.C.; retired public utility executive; b. Parrsboro, N.S. 19 Oct. 1916; s. Rupert Edwin and Vera Lavina (Ward) K.; e. Parrsboro High Sch.; Mount Allison Univ. (Engn. Cert. 1936); N.S. Tech. Coll., B.Eng., 1938; Atlantic Sch. of Business Adm., June-July, 1957; m. Eva Katherine, d. Augustus P. Gavin, 25 Sept. 1948; children: Kathie Jane, Mary Leslie; Former Vice-Pres. and Dir., Nova Scotia Tidal Power Corp.; Former Chrmn. & Dir. Halifax Water Comn.; Former Chrmn. & Dir., Blue Cross Atlantic Canada; Former Dir., 644 Main Inc.; mem. and former Dir., Candn. Acad. of Engr.; former Dir. and Past Pres., Can. Electrical Assn.; former Dir., Candn. Nuclear Assn. and N.S. Energy Council; Supt., Parrsboro Mun. Elect. Light System, 1938–40; Constr. Engr., Canada Electric, March-Dec. 1946, and Res. Engr., 1947–49, Steam Plant Supt., Amherst, N.S., 1949–55; Comm. Supt., N.S. Power Comn., 1955; Asst. Mgr., 1959; Gen. Mgr., N.S. Power Comn., Dec. 1959; Pres. and Gen. Mgr. N.S. Power Corp. 1973–78; Pres., CEO and Dir., N.S. Power Corp. 1978–82 (ret.); served in 2nd World War, 1940–42; with 2nd R.C.A., Halifax, Lieut.; promoted Capt. 1942 and trans. to 106th Coast Batty., Nfld.; Overseas, Oct. 1943; posted to 12th Candn. Field Regt., France, June 1944; promoted to Major i/c 16th Field Batty., 1945; awarded D.S.O.; mem. and Past Dir., Halifax YMCA; Past Pres., Candn. Council of Prof. Engrs.; Fellow, Candn. Acad. of Engr.; Eng. Inst. of Can.; mem., Assn. of Prof. Engrs. of N.S.; Halifax Bd. Trade (past dir.); Bd. mem. Technical Univ. of N.S.; past Dir. and Chrmn., Atlantic Industrial Research Inst.; past Dir., Halifax Children's Hospital; Dir., Grace Maternity Hospital Foundation; Freemason; United Church; recreations: curling, golfing, fishing, tennis; Clubs: Halifax (past Pres.); Halifax Curling; Parrsboro Golf; Ashburn Golf & Country; Burnside Tennis; Waegwoltic; Home: 2259 Macdonald St., Halifax, N.S. B3L 3G2.

**KIRKWOOD, David Herbert Waddington,** M.A.; executive; b. Toronto, Ont., 8 Aug. 1924; s. late Dr. William Alexander and Dr. Mossie May (Waddington) K.; e. Univ. of Toronto Schs., 1941; Univ. of Toronto, B.A. (Physics & Chem.) 1945, M.A. (Pol. Science) 1950; m. Diana Thistle, d. late Henry R. T. Gill, Ottawa, Ont., 6 June 1953; children: Peter Henry Alexander, Gill David William, Melissa Macdonald Thistle, John Robert Waddington; CHRMN., ENVIRONMENTAL ASSESSMENT PANEL ON AIR TRANSPORTATION PROPOSALS FOR THE TORONTO AREA 1991– and CHRMN., ENVIRONMENTAL ASSESSMENT PANEL ON DECOMMISSIONING OF URANIUM MINES AT ELLIOT LAKE 1993– ; Research Physicist, Canadian atomic energy program 1945–48; Asst., Dept. of Pol. Econ., Univ. of Toronto, 1949–50; Foreign Service Offr., Dept. of External Affairs, 1950–69; serving in Ottawa, Paris, Athens, Bonn; Asst. Secy. to the Cabinet 1969–72; Asst. Depy. Min., Dept. Nat. Defence, 1972–75; Sr. Asst. Depy. Min. Transport Canada, 1975–78; Chrmn. Anti-Dumping Tribunal 1978–80; Depy. Min. (Services), Dept. of Supply and Services, and Depy. Receiver Gen. for Can. 1980–83; Depy. Min., Health and Welfare Canada 1983–86; Pres., Candn. Mediterranean Inst. (CMI) (a non-profit orgn. which assists Candn. univs' scholarly and artistic work in Med. countries) 1986–90; Dir., Candn. Med. Inst. 1986– ; Royal Candn. Geographic Soc. 1987– ; Hospice of All Saints 1987– ; Anglican; recreations: skiing, fishing, tennis, sailing; Home: 260 Metcalfe St., Apt. 1B, Ottawa, Ont. K2P 1R6.

**KIRSCHBAUM, Stanislav J.,** B.Sc.Soc., M.A., Dipl.R.E.E.S., Dipl.s.r.e.p., D.Rech., N.D.C.; university professor; b. Bratislava, Slovakia 6 Aug. 1942; s. Joseph M. and Maria Magdalena (Danihel) K.; e. Univ. of Ottawa B.Sc.Soc. 1964; Univ. of Toronto M.A. 1966; Dipl. in Russian & East Eur. Studies 1968; Univ. de Paris Dipl. supérieur de rech. d'études pol. 1970; Doctorate de Rech., mention 'Etudes pol.' 1970; Nat. Defence College of Canada 1982; m. Agnes d. John Stanley and Alta Whitfield 8 June 1974; children: Olga, Sophia, Alexandra; PROFESSOR, YORK UNIVERSITY, GLENDON COLLEGE 1989– ; Asst. Prof., Queen's Univ. 1969–70; York Univ., Glendon College 1970–75; Assoc. Prof. 1975–89; Visiting Prof., Univ. de Montréal 1970; Exchange Prof., Univ. Laval 1974–75; Visiting Prof., Univ. Laval 1977; Jr. Fellow, Massey College, Univ. of Toronto 1965–66; Internat. Fellow, Internat. Fellowship Prog. for Soviet & East Eur. Studies, Volkswagenwekr Stiftung, Germany 1986–87; Sec., Internat. Council for Soviet & East European Studies 1980– ; Officer Cadet, Royal Canadian Air Force 1962–64; commissioned Flying Offr. 1964; Mem., Candn. Assn. of Slavists; Candn. Inst. of Internat. Affairs; Candn. Inst. of Strategic Studies; Can. Pol. Sci. Assn.; Centre québécois des relns. internat.; Am. Assn. for the Advancement of Slavic Studies; Internat. Inst. for Strategic Studies; Slovak Studies Assn.; author: 'Slovaques et Tchèques' 1987; editor: 'Slovak Politics' 1983; 'East European History' 1988, 'La coopération France-Canada et la sécurité maritime' 1991; co-editor: 'Reflections on Slovak History' 1987; recreations: squash, tennis, hockey, opera, theatre; Home: 104 Braeside Rd., Toronto, Ont. M4N 1Y1; Office: 2275 Bayview Ave., Toronto, Ont. M4N 3M6.

**KIRTON, John James,** M.A., Ph.D.; educator; b. Welland, Ont 30 Apr. 1948; s. James Samuel and Margaret Isabel (Bulman) K.; e. Univ. of Toronto B.A. 1971; Carleton Univ. M.A. 1973; Johns Hopkins Univ. Ph.D. 1977; m. Mary d. Deane and Hope Harris 12 July 1975; children: Michael John, Joanna Elizabeth; ASSOC. PROF. OF POL. SCI., UNIV. OF TORONTO 1982– , Co-ordinator Internat. Relations Prog. 1978–89, Co-director of Research, Centre for Internat. Studies 1986–90, Fellow Trinity Coll. 1978– ; Vice-Pres., Kirton Associates; Rsch. Fellow Inst. Internat. Relations Univ. of B.C. 1977; Asst. Prof. present univ. 1977–82; Woodrow Wilson Fellow 1971; co-author 'Canada as a Principal Power' 1983; co-ed. 'Canadian Foreign Policy: Selected Cases' 1992; 'Canada and The New Internationalism' 1988; ed.: 'Canada, the United States and Space' 1986; co-ed.: 'The International Joint Commission Seventy Years On' 1981; Dir., Couchiching Inst. of Public Affairs 1985– ; mem. Candn Inst. Internat. Affairs (Assoc. Dir. Rsch. 1983–85); Candn. Profs. Peace in Middle E. (Vice Chrmn. 1983–87); Mem., Foreign Policy Ctte., Nat. Roundtable on the Economy and the Environment 1990– ; Dir., Canada-Japan Soc. of Toronto 1990–91; Anglican; P. Conservative; recreation: squash; Home: 91 Roe Ave., Toronto, Ont. M5M 2H6; Office: 100 St. George St., Toronto, Ont. M5S 1A1.

**KIRZNER, Eric,** B.A., M.B.A.; educator; b. Toronto, Ont. 17 Jan. 1945; s. Paul Marvin and Sarah (Meyer) K.; Univ. of Toronto B.A. 1967, M.B.A. 1970; m. Helen d. Stanley and Ida Rakowsky 7 July 1968; two d. Jennifer, Diana; ADJUNCT ASSOC. PROF., FACULTY OF MANAGEMENT, UNIV. OF TORONTO 1989– ; Dir. AME Ltd. 1988– ; Dir., Equitable Trust 1992– ; Lectr. McMaster Univ. 1974–77; Asst. Prof. of Pol. Econ. and Prog. Co-ordinator Sch. of Continuing Studies, Univ. of Toronto 1977–80; Asst. Prof. Accounting Group, Univ. of Waterloo 1980–89; Chrmn., Investors and Issuers Advisory Ctte., Toronto Stock Exchange 1990– ; mem. Adv. Bd., 'Canadian Investment Review'; W. Finance Assn.; S.W. Mktg. Assn.; Acad. Mktg. Sci's; co-author 'CCH Canadian Guide to International Investing' 1984; 'Global Investing, The Templeton Way' 1988; 'Investments, Analysis and Management' 1988; various jour. articles; contbg. ed. 'The Moneyletter' 1984– ; recreations: gardening, sports, bridge; Home: 302 Green Lane, Thornhill, Ont. L3T 7A6; Office: 246 Bloor St. W., Toronto, Ont. M5S 1V4.

**KISSICK, (William) Norman,** B.A.Sc.; executive; b. Toronto, Ont. 3 Oct. 1930; s. late William John and late Evelyn Elizabeth (Hayes) K.; e. Bloor Coll. Inst. Toronto 1948; Univ. of Toronto B.A.Sc. 1952; m. Lois Elizabeth d. late John Joseph Caddell 2 June 1956; three s. James Stephen, John David, William Peter; Chrmn. & C.E.O., Union Carbide Canada Ltd. 1983–91 (retired); Dir. Toronto-Dominion Bank; Nova Corp. of Alberta; Canadian Pacific Forest Products Ltd.; Union Carbide Canada Ltd., Montreal E. 1955–65, Asst. Plant Mgr. 1965–69, Business Mgr. Chemicals 1969–73; Gen. Mgr. Businesses 1974–75 Plastics & Chemicals Toronto, Vice Pres. 1975–81, Dir. 1975– ; Pres. & C.E.O. 1981–83; mem. Soc. Chem. Industry (Can.) (Chrmn. 1978–79; Dir. 1977–80); Candn. Soc. Chem. Engrs.; Order of Engineers of Québec; Protestant; Home: 40 Wakefield Cres., Agincourt, Ont. M1W 2C2.

**KITCHEN, David Neild,** B.E.; financial executive; b. Toronto, Ont. 6 Nov. 1936; s. Irving Dixon and Lilian Audrey (Neild) K.; e. Univ. of Toronto B.E. (Hons.) 1961; Columbia Univ. Executive Program 1974; m. Margot Lynne d. Della and Bernard Taylor 5 May 1962; children: Taylor Timothy, Kelly Anne, David Bernard; SENIOR VICE-PRES. & GENERAL MANAGER, ALBERTA, ROYAL BANK OF CANADA 1986– ; Trainee, Royal Bank 1962; worked at Yonge & Richmond Br. as well as in the Toronto Dist. Gen. Mgr.'s Dept. & Head Office (Montreal) prior to taking up post of Credit Officer, Vanc. Dist. Gen. Mgr.'s Dept. 1964; Asst. Mgr. 1966; Sr. Asst. Mgr., Main Br. Winnipeg 1969; Inspector, Loans, Head Office 1971; Loans, Canadian 1973; Mgr., Calgary 1975; Vice-Pres. & Mgr., Toronto Main Br. 1978; Vice-Pres., Commercial Banking Alberta 1982; Sr. Vice-Pres., Global Energy Group 1984; Chair, United Way of Calgary 1988; Bd. Mem., Calgary C. of C. 1989; Bd. of Gov., The Univ. of Calgary 1990; The Calgary Found. 1991; recreations: nordic skiing, hiking, jogging; clubs: Calgary Petroleum, Ranchmen's, Calgary Golf & Country; Home: 4607 Coronation Dr. S.W., Calgary, Alta. T2S 1M5; Office: 24th floor, 335 – 8th Ave. S.W., Calgary, Alta. T2P 2N5.

**KITCHEN, Martin,** B.A., Ph.D., F.R.Hist.S., F.R.S.C.; educator; b. Nottingham, Eng. 21 Dec. 1936; s. John Sutherland and Margaret Helen (Pearson) K.; e. Sherborne Sch.; Magdalen Coll. Oxford; Sch. of Slavonic & E. Eur. Studies Univ. of London B.A. 1963, Ph.D. 1966; PROF. OF HISTORY, SIMON FRASER UNIV. 1976– ; mem. Cambridge Group for Population and Social Studies, Cambridge Univ. 1965–66; joined present Univ. 1966; author 'The German Officer Corps 1890–1914' 1968; 'A Military History of Germany' 1975; 'The Silent Dictatorship: The Politics of the German High Command Under Hindenburg and Ludendorff' 1976; 'Fascism' 1976; 'The Political Economy of Germany 1815–1914' 1978; 'The Coming of Austrian Fascism' 1980; 'Germany in the Age of Total War' 1981; 'British Policy Towards the Soviet Union During the Second World War' 1986; 'Europe Between the Wars' 1988; 'The Origins of the Cold War in Comparative Perspective: American, British and Canadian Relations with the Soviet Union, 1941–48' 1988; 'A World in Flames' 1990; recreations: music, sailing, skiing; Club: The Vancouver; Home: 24B - 6128 Paterson Ave., Burnaby, B.C. V5H 4P3; Office: Dept. of History, Simon Fraser Univ., Burnaby, B.C. V5A 1S6.

**KITCHEN, Michael B.;** insurance executive; b. Ontario 3 July 1945; e. Ryerson Polytech. Inst. Bus. (Hons.) 1968; LIMRA Field Officers Sch. 1976; Aetna Life & Casualty Advanced Mngt. Prog. 1983; m. Mary-Jane; children: Carolyn, Steven; PRESIDENT, CHIEF EXECUTIVE OFFICER & DIR., THE CUMIS GROUP LIMITED 1992– ; The CUIS Program Venture Manager 1992– ; Group Insur. Underwriter, Confederation Life Insur. Co. 1968; Sr. Group Rep. 1969–76; Supt. of Agencies, S.E. U.S. Region 1976–78; Sr. Acct. Extve. 1978–80; Mgr., Toronto Group Office, Aetna Canada 1980–84; Vice-Pres., Life & Health Mktg., Group Div. 1984–89; Sr. Vice-Pres., Group Div. 1989–91; Cons., Candn. Imperial Bank of Commerce 1991–92; President, Chief Extve. Offr. & Dir., The CUMIS Group Limited; CUMIS Life Insur. Co.; CUMIS Gen. Insur. Co.; Candn. Northern Shield Insur. Co. 1992– ; Dir., Credit Union Central of Canada; Co-op. Trust Co. of Canada; CUNA Mutual Insurance Group; Office: P.O. Box 5065, Burlington, Ont. L7R 4C2.

**KITCHEN, Paul Howard,** B.A., B.L.S.; government relations consultant; b. Toronto, Ont. 14 Nov. 1937; s.

Percy Floyd and Mary Henrietta (Price) K.; e. Hopewell Pub. Sch. Ottawa; Glebe Coll. Inst. Ottawa; Carleton Univ. B.A. 1963; Univ. of B.C., B.L.S. 1964; m. Anne d. Frank and Mona Heaney 23 Aug. 1963; two s. Kevin, Peter; PRES. PAUL KITCHEN AND ASSOC. 1986– ; joined Nat. Lib. of Can. 1964, Chief Bibliog. Div. 1966–70, Special Asst. to Nat. Lib. 1970–72, Govt. Libs. Liaison Offr. 1972–75; Extve. Dir., Candn. Library Assn. 1975–85; mem. Bd. Book & Periodical Devel. Council 1975–85; Dir. Inst. Assn. Extves. 1982–86, Pres. Ottawa Chapter 1982–83; apptd. Cert. Assn. Extve. (C.A.E.) by Inst. Assn. Extve. 1982; annual contrib. to Am. Lib. Assn. Yearbook 1975–85; Chrmn. Lib. Science Group Prof. Inst. Pub. Service Can. 1967–69; mem. Candn. Soc. of Assoc. Extves.; Inst. of Public Admin. of Can.; recreations: cycling, hockey, hockey history rsch.; Club: National Press; Home: 502 Penhill Ave., Ottawa, Ont. K1G 0V6.

**KITCHING, Maj.-Gen. George,** C.B.E. (1945), D.S.O. (1943); Canadian Army retired; Lord of the Manor of Bluntisham-Alias-Stockings of Cambridgeshire, Eng.; b. Canton, China 19 Sept. 1910; s. George Charlesworth and Florence Dagmar (Rowe) K.; e. Cranleigh Sch., Eng.; Roy. Mil. Coll., Sandhurst; commissioned in Gloucestershire Regt. 1930–38 serving in Singapore, Malaya and India; m. Audrey Katherine Calhoun, Oct. 1946; children: George, Katherine (deceased); served in 2nd World War 1939–45; Royal Candn. Regt. 1939–40; G.S.O. III, H.Q. 1st Candn. Divn. 1941; Staff Coll., 1941–42; G.S.O. II, H.Q. 1st Candn. Corps 1942; Lieut.-Col. commdg. Loyal Edmonton Regt. 1942; G.S.O. I, 1st Candn. Divn., 1943; Brig. Commdg. 11th Candn. Inf. Bgde. 1943–44; G.O.C., 4th Candn. Armoured Divn. (Acting Maj.-Gen.) 1944; mentioned in Despatches 1944; B.G.S. and C. of S., 1st Candn. Corps 1944–45; on return from overseas Aug. 1945 apptd. Vice-Q.M.G., at N.D.H.Q.; in Washington D.C., Nat. War College, 1947–48; Brig. Gen. Staff (Plans) Army Hdqrs. 1948–51; subsequently Commandant, Candn. Staff Coll. and Commdr., B.C. Area; apptd. Vice-Chief of the Gen. Staff, Ottawa, 1956 and later Chrmn., Candn. Jt. Staff, London; G.O.C. Central Command 1962–65; Commissioner, Ont. Pavilion, Expo 70, Osaka, Japan; Chrmn., L.C.B.O. 1970–76; Colonel Commandant, Royal Canadian Infantry Corps, 1974–78; Pres., Nat. Council, Duke of Edinburgh's Award in Can. 1967–70; Legion of Merit (U.S.); Commander, Order Orange Nassau (Netherlands); Commander, Military Order of Italy; author 'Mud and Green Fields' 1986; mem., Inst. Internat. Affairs; Chrmn. Gurkha Welfare Appeal (Can.) 1974–77; Patron, Old Fort York 1975; Sir Edmund Hillary foundation; Patron Pearson College; Hon. Pres., Pro-Patria Branch No. 31, Royal Candn. Legion 1985–88; Anglican; recreations: gardening, stamps; Home: 3434 Bonair Place, Victoria, B.C. V8P 4V4.

**KITSIKIS, Dimitri,** B.A., M.A., Ph.D.; university professor; b. Athens, Greece 2 June 1935; s. Nikos and Beata (Petychakis) K.; e. Lycée Lakanal & Lycée Carnot Paris 1952; Univ. of Paris (Sorbonne) B.A., M.A. 1958, Ph.D. 1962; m. Ada d. Yannis and Pota Nikolaros 26 Jan. 1975; children: Tatiana, Nicolas, Agis, Kranay; PROF. OF INTERNATIONAL RELATIONS, DEPT. OF HISTORY, UNIV. OF OTTAWA 1983– ; Research Attaché, Grad. Inst. of Internat. Studies, Geneva 1960–62; Ctr. of Internat. Relns., Nat. Found. of Political Science Paris 1962–65; Nat. Ctr. of Scientific Research Paris 1965–70; Assoc. Prof., Univ. of Ottawa 1970–83; Visiting Prof., Laval Univ. 1972–73; Senior Rsch. Scholar, Nat. Ctr. of Social Research Athens 1972–74; Visiting Prof., Deree College Athens 1976–78; Bogaziçi Univ. Istanbul 1981–82; Bilkent Univ. Ankara 1991–92; Vice-Pres., Assn. des auteurs de l'Ont. 1990–91; several other past extve. & consulting positions; First Prize in Poetry, Abdi Ipekçi Peace and Friendship Prize, U.N., Greece & Turkey 1991; nom., Univ. of Ottawa Award for Excellence in Research 1991; Citation for valuable achievements, Bogaziçi Univ. 1981; Personal Guest, Chinese leader Deng Xiao-ping, China 1974; Pres., Rep. of Turkey, Turgut Ozal 1990; Special Guest, Iranian Govt. to Tehran 1990; Adviser to Greek leader Konstantinos Karamanlis 1967–70; Adviser to Turkish President Turgut Ozal 1990–92; Unofficial Rep. of the Greek Government to Turkish part of Cyprus and Turkey 1975, and of Mayor of Greek Sparta to Isparta, Turkey 1988; Co-organizer, 1st and 2nd Internat. Symposium on Orthodoxy & Islam Athens 1990 and 1992; part of 8-mem. official Greek Del. headed by late vice-prime min. of Greece to P.R. of China 1958; extensive, varied scholarly contbns. have made him a highly controversial scholar; author of 16 books, most recent incl.: 'The Third Ideology and Orthodoxy' 1990, 'L'Empire ottoman' 1985, '91, 'A Comparative History of Greece and Turkey' 1978, '90 and 56 scholarly articles; poetry books incl. 'Omphalos. Poème' 1977, 'L'Orroc dans l'âge de Kali' 1985; 'Le paradis perdu sur les barricades' 1993; co-author of 17 books incl. 'Turquie, Moyen Orient, Communauté européenne' 1989, 'Communist Parties in Western Europe,' 'La Moyenne Puissance au XXe siècle' 1988; recreations: science-fiction, art; Office: Dept. of Hist., Univ. of Ottawa, Ottawa, Ont. K1N 6N5.

**KITTS, Dean Carson,** Q.C., B.A.Sc., LL.B.; lawyer; executive; b. Matheson, Ont. 9 Dec. 1934; s. James and Evelyn K.; e. Univ. of Toronto B.A.Sc. (Chem. Engn.) 1958; Osgoode Hall Law Sch. LL.B. 1963; m. Elizabeth Ann d. James and Claire Brawley, St. Thomas, Ont. 24 May 1958; children: Dean, Robert, Mary; called to Bar of Ont. 1963; cr. Q.C. 1979; joined John Labatt Ltd. as Patent Agent 1964; Corporate Counsel 1966, Vice Pres. and Secy. 1971; Vice Pres. & Gen. Counsel 1981–90, retired; mem. Ont. Securities Commn.; mem. Assn. Prof. Engrs. Prov. Ont.; Candn. Bar Assn.; Patent & Trade Mark Inst. Can.; Delta Chi; Clubs: St. Thomas Golf & Country; Home: 8 Drake St., St. Thomas, Ont. N5R 2H5.

**KITZ, Leonard Arthur,** Q.C., LL.B., D.C.L.; b. Halifax, N.S. 9 Apr. 1916; s. Harry and Yetta (Lesser) K.; e. Dalhousie Univ., LL.B.; Univ. of King's College, Halifax D.C.L. 1980; m. 1stly Dr. Alice Duff d. Robert Findlay, 17 Oct. 1945 (dec'd 1969); children: Hilary Ann, John Findlay, Alan Lawrence; m. 2ndly Janet Brownlee, 18 Dec. 1971; COUNSEL, PATTERSON KITZ; Pres., The Provincial Realty Co. Ltd.; read law with Pearson, Rutledge and Donald; called to Bar of N.S. 1939; cr. Q.C., 1959; served with Princess Louise Fusiliers as Capt.; 12th Candn. Light Brigade as Staff Offr.; Founding mem., Halifax Grammar Sch.; mem., Bd. Technical Univ. of N.S. 1973–81; mem. Bd., Univ. of King's College 1983–87; Trustee, Candn. Mediterranean Inst. 1985– ; former Chrmn. Atlantic Industrial Research Inst.; Mayor of Halifax, 1955–57; Past Pres., The John Howard Soc. of N.S.; Chrmn., N.S., Candn., Inst. of Internat. Affairs; Trustee, National Arts Centre, 1967–73; Pres., N.S. Barristers Soc., 1968–69; Prov. Vice-Pres., Candn. Bar Assn. 1969–71; Founding Dir., Atlantic Trust Co.; Honourary Dir., Halifax Developments Ltd.; Dir., Internat. Churchill Societies; Chrmn., Churchill Ctte. Statue erected Halifax; Chrmn., Sir John S.D. Thompson Ctte. Statue Study (Halifax); Chrmn., Fountain Trust-fountain erected Law Courts (Halifax); Hon. Chrmn., Chinese Students' and Scholars' Assn. of Nova Scotia; Vice-Chrmn., N.S. Provincial Court Task Force 1989–90; Liberal; Jewish; recreations: greenhouse, fishing, bridge, gardening; Clubs: Halifax; R.N.S.Y.S.; Saraguay; Home: 1110 Rockcliffe Street, Halifax, N.S. B3H 3Y6; Office: Suite 1600, 5151 George St., Halifax, N.S. B3J 1M5.

**KIVENKO, Jack,** B.Comm., M.B.A.; apparel industry executive; b. Montreal, Que. 18 Feb. 1940; s. Saul I. and Esther (Steinberg) K.; e. McGill Univ., B.Comm. (Hon.) 1961; Stanford Univ.; M.B.A. 1963; m. Linda Nudelman; children: Gary Allan, Daniel Lawrence, Joshua Adam, Sharon Freda; Vice Pres., JACK SPRATT MFG. INC. 1978; joined Jack Spratt Mfg. 1963; Chrmn., Apparel and Shoe Sectoral Adv. Group on Internat. Trade; Pres., Candn. Apparel Federation; mem., Internat. Trade Adv. Ctte.; Home: 321 Dufferin Rd., Hampstead, Que. H3X 2Y6; Office: 9880 Esplanade, Montreal, Que. H3L 2X5.

**KIVENKO, Ken,** B.S.; aerospace industry executive; b. Toronto, Ont. 25 July 1942; s. Louis and Lily (Stein) K.; e. McGill Univ. B.S. 1964; m. Marilyn d. Nathan and Esther 21 June 1964; children: Leigh, Bram; CHAIRMAN, ALLIEDSIGNAL CANADA INC. & PRES., ALLIEDSIGNAL AEROSPACE CANADA 1989– ; var. mngt. positions, Dept. of Nat. Defence 1964–66 and Canadian Marconi Co. 1966–84 leaving as Vice-Pres., Components Div.; Chair & Pres., Bendix Avelex Inc. 1984–89; Mem., Metro. Toronto Bd. of Trade 1990; Chair, Aerospace Indus. Assn. of Can. 1991–92; Council Mem., Montreal Bd. of Trade 1989–92; QPMA 1992–93; Pres., Canada Quality Council; Bd. Mem., Nat. Quality Inst.; author: 'Managing Work in Process Inventory' 1981, 'Quality Control for Management'; noted lecturer on Total Quality; Home: 35 Aldershot Cres., North York, Ont. M2P 1L7; Office: 240 Attwell Dr., Etobicoke, Ont. M9W 6L7.

**KLAASSEN, David Jerome,** B.A., M.D., F.R.C.P.(C), F.A.C.P.; medical oncologist; b. Rosthern, Sask. 8 Dec. 1936; s. John William and Mary (Kinzel) K.; e. Univ. of Sask. B.A. 1958, M.D. 1961; m. Louise d. Kornelius and Helen Toews 2 Sept. 1961; children: Timothy, Robert, Carolyn, Adam; DIR., VANCOUVER CLINIC 1987– ; Clin. Prof. of Med. Univ. of B.C. 1987– ; internship and residency Saskatoon City Hosp., Victoria Hosp. and Univ. of W. Ont., Montreal Gen. Hosp. and McGill Univ.; Sr. Cancer Clinic Assoc. Saskatoon Cancer Clinic and Lectr. in Med. Univ. of Sask. 1966–67; Sr. Med. Oncologist Ottawa Cancer Clinic, Ottawa Civic Hosp., Head of Med. Oncology of Hosp., Lectr. and Asst. Prof. of Med. Univ. of Ottawa 1967–80; Dir. Saskatoon Cancer Clinic, Med. Dir. Sask. Cancer Found., Prof. and Head of Oncol. Univ. of Sask. 1980–87; Chief Extve. Offr. & Dir., B.C. Cancer Agency 1987–93; mem. Nat. Cancer Inst. Can., Chrmn. Clin. Epidemiol. Rsch. Adv. Group, mem. Cancer Rsch. Coordinating Ctte. Can., mem. Bd., Chrmn. Clin Trials Ctte.; mem. World Health Orgn. working party on colorectal cancer; author or co-author numerous sci. publs.; Pres., Christian Med. Dental Soc. Can. 1990–92 (Pres. Sask. Chapter 1981–84); Pres. Saskatoon Palliative Care Assn. 1983–85; mem. Council (1986–87) and Chrmn. Med. Oncology Specialty Ctte. (1982–88) Royal Coll. Phys. & Surgs. Can.; mem. B.C. Med. Assn.; Vancouver Med. Soc.; Candn. Med. Assn.; Candn. Oncology Soc. (Pres. & mem. Bd. 1982–83); Candn. Assn. Med. Edn.; Am. Soc. Clin. Oncology; Am. Soc. Preventive Oncology; Am. Assn. Cancer Edn.; Am. Assn. Med. Dirs.; Candn. Assn. Med. Oncology; recreations: sailing, hiking, swimming, skiing; Home: 3833 West 11th Ave., Vancouver, B.C. V6R 2K8; Office: 600 West 10th Ave., Vancouver, B.C. V5Z 4E6.

**KLASSEN, Gerald Arthur,** M.D., F.R.C.P.(C), F.A.C.C., F.A.C.P.; physician and university professor; b. Kerrobert, Sask. 12 Jan. 1933; s. William Peter and Agnes Margaret (Hamm) K.; e. Univ. B.C., M.D. 1957; m. Andree, d. A.E.F. Dauphinee 29 Sept. 1961; children: Timothy William; Sonja Elizabeth; PROF., MEDICINE, PHYSIOLOGY AND BIOPHYSICS, DALHOUSIE UNIV.; Pres., Pathfinder Med. Inc.; Internship, Royal Victoria Hosp. (Montreal); Brit. Counc. Scholar, Inst. Cardiology (London, Eng.) 1958–59; Residency Internal Med. & Cardiology, Vancouver Gen. & Royal Victoria Hosp.; Postgrad. training, Johns Hopkins Univ. 1963–65; Sr. Physician, Royal Victoria Hosp.; Dir., Cardiovascular Div. 1974–77; Prof. Visiteur, Univ. Laval 1971–72; Carnegie and Rockefeller Prof. Physiology and Biophysics & Dept. Head, present univ. 1977–81; Vice Pres., Academic & Research 1981–83; Vice Pres., Research 1983–84; Prof. a contratto, Univ. di Pisa (Italy) 1986–87; Consultant, Camp Hill Hosp.; Assoc. Physician, Victoria Gen. Hosp.; author approx. 134 articles published in med. journals; co-author (with Masari and Lesch) 'Primary and Secondary Angina Pectoris,' 1978; (with Kajiya, Spaan and Hoffman) 'Coronary Circulation' 1990; mem., Candn. Med. Assn.; N.S. Medical Soc.; Nova Scotia Soc. Internists; Candn. Cardiovascular Soc.; Candn. Soc. for Clinical Investigation; Candn. Physiological Soc.; Am. Fed. for Clinical Research; Alpha Omega Alpha; Cardiovascular Systems Dynamics Soc.; Counc. on Circulation, Am. Heart Assn.; Am. Physiological Soc. (Fellow, Circulation Group); Candn. Hypertension Soc.; Rsch. Ctte., Royal Coll. Phys. & Surg. of Can.; Nat. Counc. on Bioethics in Human Rsch.; United Church; Home: 6955 Armview Ave., Halifax, NS B3H 2M5; Office: Maritime Heart Centre, Victoria General Hospital, Halifax, N.S. B3H 2Y9.

**KLASSEN, Sarah,** B.A., B.Ed.; teacher, poet; b. Winnipeg, Man. 6 Oct. 1932; d. Gerhard and Helen K.; e. Univ. of Manitoba, B.A. 1963, B.Ed. 1971; Teacher, North Kildonan 1952–57; Fort Garry Sch. Div. 1957–59; Brandon Sch. Div. 1963–65; Teacher, River East Sch. Div. 1965–90; Gerald Lampert Memorial Award for 'Journey to Yalta' 1988; mem. Man. Writers' Guild; League of Candn. Poets; River East Mennonite Brethren Ch.; author: 'Journey to Yalta' 1988; 'Violence & Mercy' 1991; 'Borderwatch' 1993; recreations: nordic skiing, travel, walking, cycling; Home: 19 Del Rio Place, Winnipeg, Man. R2G 1K9.

**KLASSEN, William John,** M.F.; business executive; b. Franklin Mun., Man. 23 June 1944; s. Peter J. and Annie (Guenther) K.; e. Ross L. Gray High Sch. Sprague, Man.; Univ. of Alaska, B.Sc. 1976; Yale Sch. of Forestry M.F. 1981; m. Rayanne d. Raymond and Marianne Squires 5 Dec. 1969; children: Delwyn Michael, Katrina Marie, Roxanne Sherry, Carolyn Gail; PARTNER, TRANSARCTIC TOURS LTD. and PARTNER, TRANSNORTHERN CONSULTING 1990– ; Constable, RCMP in B.C., Y.T. and N.W.T. 1964–70; Game Guardian Yukon Territorial Govt. (YTG) Game Br. Watson Lake, Y.T. 1970–72; Environmental Protection Biol. YTG Wildlife Br. 1976–78; Dir. Project Devel. YTG Intergovernmental Relations 1978–80, 1981–82; Depy. Min. of Health & Human Resources, Y.T. 1982–85; Depy. Min. of Renewable Resources, Y.T. 1985–90; mem. Elders Bd. Riverdale Bapt. Ch. Whitehorse 1977–80, 1982–86, 1988–90; Chrmn., Yukon Workers Compensation, Health and Safety Bd. 1992– ; recreations: canoeing, skiing, hunting, fishing, reading; Home: P.O.

Box 4896, Whitehorse, Y.T. Y1A 4N6; Office: P.O. Box 5383, Whitehorse, Y.T. Y1A 2Z1.

**KLAWE, Maria M.,** B.Sc., Ph.D.; university professor; b. Toronto, Ont. 5 July 1951; d. Janusz Jozef and Kathleen Wreath (McCaughan) K.; e. Strathcona Composite H.S. 1968; Univ. of Alta., B.Sc. (Hon.) 1973, Ph.D. 1977; Univ. of Toronto, grad study computer science 1978–79; m. Nicholas J. s. Mary and Robert Pippenger 12 May 1980; children: Janek Klawe, Sasha Pippenger; HEAD & PROF. OF COMPUTER SCIENCE, UNIV. OF B.C. 1988– ; Asst. Prof., Dept. of Math Sci., Oakland Univ. 1977–78; Dept. of Computer Sci., Univ. of Toronto 1979–80; Mgr., Discrete Mathematics Group, IBM Rsch. 1984–88; Mgr., Dept. of Math & Related Comp. Sci., IBM Rsch. 1985–87; Rsch. Staff Mem., IBM Almaden Rsch. Ctr. 1980–89; Univ. Adv. Ctte., IBM Toronto Lab.; Weiss Cup, S.C.H.S. 1968; I.N.C.O. Scholarship 1968–72; NRC postgrad. fellowship 1973–77; IBM Outstanding Innovation Award 1989; mem., Premier's Advisory Council on Science and Technology 1992– ; mem., Bd. of Govs., Science World BC 1990– ; mem., Bd. of Trustees Am. Math. Soc. 1992– ; mem., Computer Rsch. Bd. 1990– ; Bd. of Dir., Candn. Math Soc. 1985–89; Sci. Adv. Bd., Ctr. for Discrete Math. & Theoretical Comp. Sci. 1989– ; Mem. of Counc., Soc. Indust. Applied Math. 1989–91; Chair, SIAM Disc. Math. Act. Group 1985–88; Ed. Bd. Mem., 'Combinatorica,' 'SIAM Journal on Computing,' and 'SIAM Journal on Discrete Mathematics'; recreations: running, painting; Home: 3708 W. 34 Ave., Vancouver, B.C. V6N 2L1; Office: Vancouver, B.C. V6T 1Z2.

**KLEIN, Bonnie Sherr,** M.A.; film director and producer; writer, broadcaster, disability rights activist; b. Philadelphia, Pa. 1 Apr. 1941; e. Barnard Coll. New York City B.A. 1961; Stanford Univ. M.A. 1966; m. Dr. Michael Klein 19 Aug. 1967; children: Seth, Naomi, Misha; film dir. and producer Nat. Film Bd. Challenge for Change 1967–70, Studio D 1975–87; on disability leave since 1988; film credits incl.: 'Mile Zero: The Sage Tour'; 'Speaking Our Peace Series'; 'Not A Love Story: A Film About Pornography'; 'Patricia's Moving Picture'; 'Harmonie'; 'Citizen's Medicine'; 'The Alinsky Series'; 'VTR-St-Jacques'; radio credits: 'Finding My Place' CBC Centrepoint; Address: 210 - 1450 Pennyfarthing Dr., Vancouver, B.C. V6J 4X8.

**KLEIN, Kurt Kenneth,** B.S.A., M.Sc., Ph.D.; university professor; b. Canwood, Sask. 29 Oct. 1943; s. Oliver and Ruth K.; e. Canwood H.S. 1961; Univ. of Sask., Dip. 1963, B.S.A. 1970, M.Sc. 1972; Purdue Univ., Ph.D. 1976; PROF., ECON. DEPT., UNIV. OF LETHBRIDGE 1981– ; Owner/operator, mixed beef-grain farm 1961–71; Rsch. Econ., Agric. Can. Rsch. Station (Lethbridge) 1971–81; Acting Chrmn., Econ. Dept., Univ. of Lethbridge 1985–86; Vis. Prof., Dept. of Agric. Econ., Univ. of B.C. 1986–87; Vis. Prof., Hokkaigakuen, Sapporo, Japan Sept.-Dec. 1988; Visiting Prof., Otaru Univ. of Commerce, Japan 1992–93; Cons., var. fed. & prov. govt. depts.; Most outstanding journal article, Candn. Jour. of Agric. Econ. 1974, 1981; Most outstanding Masters Thesis, Candn. Agric. Econ. Soc. 1972; Univ. of Sask. Scott Prize Most Distinguished Grad. 1963, Silver Medal High Standing in Grad. Class 1963; Co-Chrmn. Fed. Div., Lethbridge Un. Way 1977–78; Councillor, Western Agric. Econ. Assn. 1990–93; Counc. & Awards Ctte. Chrmn., Candn. Agric. Econ. & Farm Mgmt. Soc. 1983–85; Extve. Mem., Alta. Agric. Econ. Adv. Ctte. 1979–87; editor: 'Economics of Agricultural Research in Canada' 1985; 'Canadian Agricultural Trade' 1990; co-author: 'Farm Finances in Western Canada' 1985; 'Western Canadian Beef in the Japanese Market' 1989; author or co-author of over 180 research papers; Home: 2815 – 22 Ave. S., Lethbridge, Alta. T1K 1K1; Office: 4401 University Dr., Lethbridge, Alta. T1K 3M4.

**KLEIN, Lothar,** M.A., Ph.D.; composer; educator; b. Germany 27 Jan. 1932; s. Vigdor Michael and Mary Sophie (Haynitszch) K.; e. Washburn Sr. H.S. 1950; Free Univ. of Berlin, Hochschule für Musik 1959; Univ. of Minn,. M.A. 1960, Ph.D. 1962; m. Marjorie d. Elmer and Alice Johnson 27 Sept. 1957; children: Eric Victor, David Gabriel; compositional catalogue contains all genres with emphasis on symphonic orchestral music incl. a series of poly-hist. concerti 1965– , a jazz study 'Musique a Go-Go' 1965 and the ballet 'Canadiana' 1980; high points have been assn. with Igor Stravinsky 1965 and programming of his work by major internat. orchs. & conds. incl. Ancerl, Barbirolli, Andrew Davis, Dutoit, Previn, Szell; Music Ed., Schmitt, Hall & McCreary 1960–62; Music Advr., CBS TV, Stravinsky documentary 1965; Fulbright Examiner, West Berlin 1958–60; Chrmn., Dept. of Music, Univ. of Toronto; Rockefeller New Music Prize 1964, 1968; Fellow, MacDowell Colony, N.Y.; Edna St. Vincent Millay Fellow in Music; Chalmers Creative Arts Award; Mem., Perf. Rights Orgn. Can.; Coll. Music Soc.; Minn. Composers Forum; Candn. League of Composers; Candn. Music Ctr.; author: 'Tale of a Father and Son' opera in collab. with W. Gunther Plaut; recreations: athletics, rabelaisiana, Peter De Vries; Home: 44 Wallingford Rd., Don Mills, Ont. M3A 2T9; Office: Faculty of Music, Univ. of Toronto, 80 Queens Park Cres., Toronto, Ont. M5S 1A1.

**KLEIN, Michael L.,** B.Sc., Ph.D., F.R.S.C., F.C.I.C.; research scientist; educator; b. London, Eng. 13 March 1940; s. Jack and Bessie (Bloomberg) K.; e. Univ. of Bristol B.Sc., 1961, Ph.D. 1964; m. Brenda d. George and Marion Woodman 3 June 1962; two d. Paula Denise, Rachel Anne; HEPBURN PROFESSOR OF PHYSICAL SCIENCES AND DIR., NATIONAL SCIENCE FOUND. MATERIALS RESEARCH LABORATORY, UNIV. OF PENNSYLVANIA 1987– ; part-time Prof. of Chem. McMaster 1979–89; CIBA-Giegy Fellow Genoa, Italy 1964–65; ICI Fellow (Chem.) Univ. of Bristol 1965–67; Rsch. Assoc. (Physics) Rutgers Univ. 1967–68; Assoc. Rsch. Offr. 1968, Sr. Rsch. Offr. 1974; Prin. Rsch. Offr. Nat. Rsch. Council 1985–87; Prof. Associé Univ. de Paris 1975–76; JSPS Fellow Kyoto, Japan 1982; Fellow Commoner Trinity Coll. Cambridge 1985–86; Louis Née Visiting Prof., École Normale Superieure, Lyon, France 1988; Guggenheim Fellow 1989–90; mem. Ed. Bd. of the journs.: 'Physics Reports'; 'Chemical Physics'; 'Computational Materials Science'; 'Molecular Physics'; 'Journal of Physical Chemistry'; ed. 'Rare Gas Solids' Vol. 1 1976, Vol. II 1977; 'Inert Gases' 1985; author or co-author over 300 sci. articles; mem. Internat. Relations Ctte. NSERC 1982–84, Chem. Grant Ctte. 1985–86; mem. EEC Ctte. TRIUMF 1987–93; Home: 133 West Atlantic Blvd., Ocean City, New Jersey 08226; Office: Dept. of Chemistry, Univ. of Pennsylvania, Philadelphia PA 19104–6323.

**KLEIN, Hon. Ralph Phillip;** provincial premier; b. Calgary, Alta. 1 Nov. 1942; e. Calgary Business Coll.; m. Colleen; PREMIER OF ALBERTA 1992– ; Dir. of Public Relns., Alta. Div., Candn. Red Cross 1963–66; Calgary and District United Way 1966–69; Sr. Civic Affairs reporter, CFCN Radio and TV 1969–70; el. Mayor of Calgary 1980, re-el. 1983, '86; el. MLA Calgary Elbow 1989; Min. of the Environment 1989; el. leader, P.C. Party of Alta. 1992; former Principal, Calgary Business Coll.; former mem. Candn. Public Relns. Soc.; Calgary Press Club; Alta. Motion Pictures Assoc.; awarded Order of St. John 1986; Olympic Order 1988; Office: 307 Legislature Bldg., Edmonton, Alta. T5K 2B6.

**KLEIN, Robert,** D.L.C.; railroad executive; b. Paris, France 1 Aug. 1932; e. Loughborough Univ. D.L.C. (Hons.) 1954; m. Felicia Kastner 24 June 1956; children: Laura, Mark; SENIOR VICE-PRES., ADMIN., CP RAIL SYSTEM 1993– ; Systems Engr., Northern Electric 1954–56; Eng. & Program Mgr., CAE Electronics 1966–71; Dir., Tech. R&D, Candn. Pacific Limited 1971–75; Mgr. Research 1975–81; Gen. Mgr. Rsch. Dept. 1981–83; Asst. Vice-Pres. Planning & Rsch. 1983–85; Vice-Pres., Admin., CP Rail 1985–92; Dir., Railroad Assn. Insur. Ltd.; Transp. & Railroad Assur. Co.; Past Pres. & Bd. Mem., Jewish Rehab. Hosp.; recreations: golf, tennis, fishing, reading; club: Summerlea Golf & Country; Home: 3455 Drummond, Apt. 703, Montreal, Que. H3G 2R6; Office: P.O. Box 6042, Stn. A, Montreal, Que. H3C 3E4.

**KLEIN, Stuart Walter,** M.D., F.R.C.P.(C); F.A.C.P., F.A.C.C.; cardiologist; b. Windsor, Ont. 27 June 1938; S. Joseph and Rose (Stern) K.; e. Forster C.I.; Univ. of West. Ont., M.D.; m. Francie d. Samuel and Hortense Norris 25 Jan. 1975; children: Sherri Elise, Justin Norris; CARDIOLOGIST, NORTH YORK GEN. HOSP. 1969– ; Rotating Intern, Toronto Gen. Hosp. 1962–63; Asst. Res., Ann Arbor University Hosp. 1963–64; Mount Sina Hosp. (N.Y.) 1964–65; Res. in Cardiol., N.Y. Hosp.-Cornell Med. Ctr. 1965–66; Fellow in Cardiol., Toronto Gen. Hosp. 1966–68; Fellow in Clin. Pharmacol., Harvard Med. Sch., Mass. Gen. Hosp. 1968–69; Cons., Wellesley Hosp. 1969– ; Asst. Prof. of Med., Dept. of Med., Univ. of Toronto 1969– ; F.R.C.P. 1968; Am. Bd. of Internal Med., dipl. 1969, dipl., Subspec. of Cardio. Disease 1975; F.A.C.P. 1973; F.A.C.C. 1976; Fellow, Counc. of Clin. Cardiol. (Am. Heart Assn.) 1976; Mem., Ont. Med. Assn. (Chrmn., Dist 11 1978–86; Pres., Oriole Br. 1976–78); Candn. Med Assn.; N.Y. Acad. of Sci.; Candn. Cardio. Soc.; Alpha Omega Alpha Hon. Soc.; recreations: squash, tennis, golf; Home: 59 Magpie Cres., Willowdale, Ont. M2L 2E6; Office: 1333 Sheppard Ave. E., Ste. 220, Willowdale, Ont. M2J 1V1.

**KLEIN-LATAUD, Christine;** professor; translator; b. Courbevoie, France 30 Aug. 1940; d. André and Simone (Magnen) Lataud; e. Agrégation de lettres classiques 1963; m. Michel s. Roger and Marcelle Klein 28 May 1964; children: Mélusine, Alexis; DIR. SCH. OF TRANSLATION, GLENDON COLL. YORK UNIV. 1984–88, 1990–92; Prof. au lycée de Sèvres, Conseillère au Centre Internat. d'études pédagogiques 1965–78; recipient Palmes académiques; lit. critic Radio-Can. 1982– and 'Spirale'; author 'Le Rouge et le Noir' 1971; 'Précis des Figures de Style' 1991; 'Paroles Rebelles' 1992; French transl. 'A Bird in the House' by Margaret Laurence 1989; Editorial Bd., 'Canadian Women Studies/Les Cahiers de la femme' 1986–92; cert. mem. Assn. Translators & Interpreters Ont.; Pres. Candn. Assn. Schs. Transl. 1986–88; mem. Bd. APFUCC 1985–89; mem. Assn. Candn. Studies in U.S.; Referee for Meta, Ed. Bd. TTR; mem. Literary Translator's Assn. of Can. (LTAC); recreations: theatre, opera, hiking; Home: 16 Munro Blvd., Willowdale, Ont. M2P 1B9; Office: 2275 Bayview Ave., Toronto, Ont. M2P 1B9.

**KLEMP, John Peter Christian,** O.St.J., C.D., K.C.L.J., G.C.M.L.J., B.B.A., C.L.A., F.I.I.C.; business executive; b. Oslo, Norway 4 Nov. 1928; s. Ragnar J. and Ingrid (Huseby) K.; e. Ullern Sr. High Sch. Oslo 1947; Royal Norwegian Mil. Coll. 1947–49; OTH Sch. of Bus. Oslo B.B.A. 1951; Sir George Williams Univ. Bus. Adm. 1952–53; Univ. of Toronto grad. Ins. Mgmt. Course; McQuaig Inst. Exec. Devel.; Chart. Loss Adjuster; Fellow, Insurance Inst. of Canada; m. Esther d. John Hulland 25 July 1959; children: Karen Ingrid, Christine Andrea; CHRMN. & C.E.O., NOREG INVESTMENTS 1982– ; Chrmn. & C.E.O., The Wine Shop Ltd. 1985– ; Chrmn. & Dir., Canmark Internat. Resources Inc. 1993– ; Underwriting Mem., Lloyd's of London 1983– ; joined Guardian Group of Insurance Co.'s Montreal 1952, Toronto 1954, Calgary 1956, Mgr. Adm. Toronto 1966–67; Brouwer Group Calgary 1968–81; Vice Pres., Dir., W. Regional Mgr., Head Nat. & Internat. Special Risks Divs.; Morden & Helwig 1981–82; Chrmn., Alberta Petroleum Inv. Corp. 1983–89; Dir. Moneta Porcupine Resources Ltd., Albany Oil and Gas 1985–87; Chrmn. and Dir. Trans Dominion Energy Corp. 1985–92; Chrmn., Albany Corp. 1985–92; mem., Mngmt. Advisory Council, Univ. of Calgary 1989– ; served with Resistance Forces Norway 1944–45; Royal Norwegian Air Force 1949–51, Capt.; RCAF(R) Toronto and Calgary 1954–64, Flight Lt.; Maj. Calgary Highlanders 1964–66, 1968–70, Toronto Scot. Regt. 1966–67, Sen. Staff Offr., Southern Alta. Militia Dist. 1974–75, Candn. Armed Forces (R) 1970– ; recipient numerous awards & decorations incl. Order of St John; Commemorative Medal for 125th Anniversary of Candn. Confederation; Canadian Forces Decoration (CD); Resistance Medal (Norway); Croix du combattant de l'Europe (France); Chevalier du L'Ordre du Mérite Agricole (France); Cross of Freedom (Poland); Sphinx Cross (Interallied Resistance Decoration); Soc. of Fellows Ins. Inst. Can., Past Pres., Past Nat. Dir.; Candn. Ins. Man of Yr. 1973; Alta. Achievement Award 1988; Citations Lt. Gov. Alta. 1982 and HRH Prince Philip, Duke of Edinburgh 1983; Compagnon de Bordeaux; Commandeur d'Honneur, l'Ordre Commanderie du Boutemps de Medoc et des Graves 1993; Ctte. mem., Museum of the Regiments (Calgary Military Museum Soc.); Past mem. Alta. Aviation Council; Past Chrmn., St. John Ambulance (Calgary); Calgary C. of C.; Past Chrmn. Alta. Historic Sites Bd.; Hon. Life Mem. and Past Assoc. Dir., Calgary Exhn. & Stampede Ltd.; Past Vice Pres. Nat. Council Duke of Edinburgh's Award in Can., Founding & Past Pres. Alta. Div., mem. Past Pres.'s Ctte.; Ctte. mem. OCO 88; Vice Chrmn. Norwegian Olympic Support Ctte.; Ctte. mem. W. Can. Summer Games, Alta. 75 Celebrations; mem. Adv. Council N.Am. Ctte. Internat. Wine & Food Soc., Past Pres. Calgary Br.; mem. Alta. Hist. Resources Found.; Sir Winston Churchill Soc.; Hon. Life mem. Candn. Ins. Claims Mgrs. Assn., Past Nat. Pres.; Past Sec./Treas. and Dir. Alta. Assn. Ins. Adjusters; mem. Royal Alta. Un. Services Inst.; Clubs: Glencoe; Commerce; recreations: skiing, hiking, badminton, sailing, reading, oenology, politics, mil. hist.; Home: 7240 Kananaskis Dr. S.W., Calgary, Alta. T2V 2N2; Office: 202, 815 – 17th Avenue S.W., Calgary, Alta. T2T 0A1.

**KLENMAN, Norman Albert,** B.A.; film and television writer; broadcaster; b. Brandon, Man. 2 Aug. 1923; e. Univ. of B.C., B.A. 1948, Postgrad. studies in Anglo Saxon; m. Daphne D.J. d. Alwyn and Mai Timmins 2 Feb. 1951; children: Alexander C.J., Anna Abigail; CO-FOUNDER CKVU TV 1976; writer, co-prod., TV and feature prodns.; Reporter, Vancouver Sun 1946–49; PA Reuter Newsagency London, Eng. 1949–52; Playwright BBC TV 1951–52; Filmmaker, Film Bd. Can. Ottawa 1952–55; Founder, Klenman Davidson Productions Ltd.

Toronto 1957–60; CBC Toronto 1955–64; Dramatist first Jack Kerouac and Henry Miller stories for TV; writer and producer Morley Callaghan feature film 'Now That April's Here' and 'Ivy League Killers'; writer Steve Allen Show Los Angeles and Les Crane Show ABC New York 1964–65; writer TV and film 20th Fox, Columbia, Warner Brothers & Universal Studios; original screenplay 'The Swiss Conspiracy'; 'Flint: Dead on Target'; commuted to Toronto 1969–74 writing CBC TV Drama and co-founded Galanty Films Ltd. CITY-TV; served RCAF 1943–45, Flying Offr. Observor; Co-founder Internat. Writers Guild, London 1965; mem. Writers Guild Am. (W.); WGC; Address: RR2, 130 Bittancourt Rd. C-11, Salt Spring Island, B.C. V0S 1E0.

**KLEWIN, Thomas W.,** B.A., B.D., B.Sc., M.A.; public servant; b. Sheboygen, Wisconsin 31 January 1921; s. Emil Herman and Wilhelmina (Gottoske) K.; e. Concordia Coll. A.A. 1941; Concordia Seminary B.A. 1945, B.D. 1945; Washington Univ. M.A. 1946; m. Jean S. d. Tranie and Natalie McDaniel; children: Diana, Michael, Leslie, Matthew, Shelley; Extve. Dir., P.E.I. Human Rights Comn. 1979–88; Chaplain (Lt.-Col.), U.S. Air Force 1951–73; Health Edn. Dir., Southshore Health Maintenance Orgn. (US) 1975–77; Instr., Ricker Coll. 1963–66; B.Sc. in Anthropol., Stockton State Coll.; 'St. Martin of Tours' Medal, Lutheran Ch.; Korean War Medal; Valley Forge Freedom Found. Medal 1963, 1968; Vietnam Medal; Vice-Pres., P.E.I. Civil Liberties Assn. 1977–79; Youth Bd. Mem., Lutheran Ch. 1947–51; author/co-author (with Jean Klewin): 'Love Thy Teenager' 1970, 'Preparing for Retirement' 1972, 'Thinking of Drinking' 1977, 'Abortion, A View of' 1978, 'When the Man you Marry is an Alcoholic' 1980 and ca. 2000 periodical articles; Contrib. Ed.: 'Pastoral Life,' 'This Day'; Home: Box 58, Crapaud, P.E.I. C0A 1J0.

**KLIBANSKY, Raymond,** M.A., D.Phil., F.R.H.S., F.R.S.C. (1970); university professor; b. Paris, France 15 Oct. 1905; s. the late Hermann and Rose (Scheidt) K.; e. Univs. Heidelberg, Kiel, Hamburg; D.Phil., Heidelberg 1928; Oxford Univ., M.A. (by decree) 1935; D.Phil. (h.c.) Ottawa; D.Phil. (h.c.) Marburg; EMERITUS PROF., MCGILL UNIVERSITY; Frothingham Prof. of Logic and Metaphysics there 1946–75; FELLOW OF WOLFSON COLLEGE OXFORD 1981– ; Asst. Heidelberg Acad. of Science & Letters 1927–33; Lect. in Philos., Heidelberg Univ. 1931–33; King's Coll., Univ. of London 1934–36; Oriel Coll., Oxford 1936–48; Forwood Lectr. in Phil. of Religion, Univ. of Liverpool 1938–39; Dir. of Studies, The Warburg Inst., Univ. of London 1947–48; Vis. Prof. of History of Phil., Univ. de Montréal 1947–68; Malon Powell Prof. of Philos., Univ. of Indiana 1949–50; served as Chief Intelligence Officer, P.W.E., Foreign Office, London 1941–46; Cardinal Mercier Prof. of Philos., Univ. of Louvain 1956; Foundation Lectr., Univ. of Rome 1957; Visiting Prof.: Faculty of Philos., Univ. of Rome 1961; Univ. of Genoa 1964; Sorbonne, Paris 1967; Univ. of Tokyo; Keio University, Tokyo 1971; Ecole Pratique des Hautes Etudes, Sorbonne, Paris 1972; Teheran Univ. and Aryamehr Univ., Teheran 1974; Medallist, Univs. of Louvain and Liège, Belgium; Gauss Medal, Brunswick 1990; Prof. Emeritus, Heidelberg Univ. 1975– , Hon. Senator 1986– ; Guggenheim Foundation Fellow 1954, 1965; Vis. Fellow, Wolfson Coll., Oxford 1976–78; Jt. Chrmn., Internat. Ctte. for Comparative Philosophy, Louvain-la-Neuve; Pres.: Inst. Internat. de Philosophie, Paris 1966–69 (Hon. Pres. 1969– ); Société Internationale pour l'étude de la Philos. Médiévale, Louvain 1968–72 (Hon. Pres. 1972– ); (Medal 1992) Candn. Soc. for Hist. and Phil. of Science 1959–72 (Pres. Emeritus 1972– ); Internat. Ctte. for Anselm Studies 1970– ; Centro di Studi Medievali e Rinascimentali, Parma 1990– ; Fellow: Royal Soc. of Canada, Ottawa; Royal Historical Soc., London; Accademia Nazionale dei Lincei, Rome; Acad. of Athens; Acad. Internat. d'Histoire des Sciences, Paris; Iranian Acad. of Philosophy, Teheran; Accad. Mediterranea delle Scienze, Catania; Accad. delle Belle Arti, Scienze e Lettere, Acireale; Corresponding Fellow: Mediaeval Acad. of America, Cambridge, Mass.; Heidelberg Acad. of Scis.; Wissenschafte Gesellschaft, Blaunschweig; Hon. Foreign Mem.: Am. Acad. of Arts and Sciences; Hon. Mem.: Assoc. des Scientifiques de Roumanie, Bucarest; Hon. Fellow: Oriel Coll., Oxford; Warburg Inst., Univ. of London; Accad. Ligure delle Scienze (Ligurian Acad. of Sciences), Genoa; Allgemeine Gesellschaft für Philosophie in Deutschland; Candn. Mediterranean Inst., Athens, Rome, Cairo; Winner, Killam Award (Sr. Rsch. Fellowship), Canada Counc., Ottawa 1976; recipient of the distinction 'Reconnaissance de mérite scientifique', Univ. de Qué. à Montréal 1991; Dir., Candn. Academic Centre in Italy 1980; mem. Exec. Counc., Union Académique Internationale 1978–80; Comité Directeur, Fedn Internat. des Socs de Philosophie 1958–83; mem. of Dir. Council, Internat. Centre of Humanist Studies, Rome; Nat. Research Council, mem. Candn. Nat. Comte. for Hist. and Philos. of Science and (1969–81) Candn. Nat. Comte. for Internat. Council of Scient. Unions; Candn. Secy., Union Internat. Philos. and Hist. of Sciences 1969–81; former mem., Extve. Comte., Am. Philos. Assn.; Gen. Ed., Corpus Platonicum Medii Aevi (Plato Latinus and Plato Arabus), Union Académique Internat. & Brit. Acad. 1937– ; Joint Ed., 'Magistri Eckardi Opera Latina' 1934–36; 'Philosophy and History' (ed. with H.J. Paton) 1936; 'Philosophical Texts' 1951–62; 'Mediaeval and Renaissance Studies' 1941–68; Ed. 'Mussolini's Memoirs 1942–43'; Philosophy and World Community 1957–91; 'Philosophy in the Mid-Century' vols. I-IV 1958–59; 'Contemporary Philosophy' vols. I-IV 1968–71; Dir. 'Bibliographie de la Philosophie' 39 vols., 1954–92; 'Philosophical foundations of human rights' Unesco 1986; author: 'Ein Proklos-Fund und seine Bedeutung' 1929; Heidelberg Acad. edn. 'Opera Nicolai de Cusa' 5 vols 1929–82; 'The Continuity of the Platonic Tradition' 1939 (enlarged 3rd edn. incl. 'Plato's Parmenides in the Middle Ages and the Renaissance' 1981, 1982); 'Leibniz' Unknown Corr. with Eng. Scholars and Men of Letters' 1941; (with E. Panofsky and F. Saxl) 'Saturn and Melancholy' 1964 (Italian ed. 1983, Japanese 1991); enlarged French, German, Spanish edns. 1989–91; articles in Jahresberichte d. Heidelberger Akademie, Proceedings of British Acad., Enciclopedia Italiana, and elsewhere; Jewish; recreation: music; Home: 3660 Peel St., Apt. 29, Montreal, Que. H3A 1W9; Office: Wolfson College, Oxford 0X2 6UD; Leacock Building, McGill Univ., Montreal, Que. H3A 2T7.

**KLIGER, Allan Stephen,** LL.B.; business executive; b. Toronto, Ont. 11 Apr. 1958; s. Bernard and Ethel (Weinbrom) K.; e. Univ. of West. Ont., LL.B. 1982; PRES. & FOUNDER, VICTORY'S KITCHEN 1985– , a leading processor and supplier of soups, sauces, and prepared food entrees to the North Am. foodservice and healthcare trade, incl. hospitals & prominent restaurant chains; called to Bar of Ont. 1984; articled with Holden, Murdoch & Finlay; Sr. Consultant, Mergers & Acqusition Group, Ernst & Whinney (also responsible for foreign investment services) 1985; Univ. of West. Ont., highest standing in corp. taxation; recreations: mountaineering, cycling, water and snow skiing; Home: 1675 Bathurst St., Upper, Toronto, Ont. M5P 3J8; Office: 30 Gunns Rd., Toronto, Ont. M6N 3S5.

**KLINCK, James William,** B.Math.; insurance executive; b. Kitchener, Ont. 12 Dec. 1951; s. Armand A. and Imogene (Sim) K.; e. Univ. of Waterloo B.Math (Hon.) 1974; m. Viola d. Foster and Florence Wright 17 Sept. 1977; children: David James, Bonnie Anne; VICE-PRESIDENT, METROPOLITAN LIFE INSURANCE COMPANY; joined present firm 1974 and held var. positions of increasing responsibility within Information Systems, Corp. Services & Human Resources; ISP (Information Systems Professional of Canada) designation from CIPS (Candn. Information Processing Soc.) May 1989; Mem., CIPS; Home: 34 Richlin Cres., Ottawa, Ont. K2B 8K4; Office: 99 Bank St., Ottawa, Ont. K1P 5A3.

**KLINE, Donald W.,** B.A., M.A., Ph.D.; university professor and administrator; b. London, England 22 Jan. 1944; s. Winard and Maria J. (Huber) K.; e. Univ. of Calgary B.A. 1967; Univ. of S. Calif. M.A. 1971, Ph.D. 1972; m. Theresa Jean d. Lon and Francis Babbitt 3 June 1989; PROFESSOR & HEAD, DEPT. OF PSYCHOLOGY & DIR., VISION & AGING LAB., UNIV. OF CALGARY 1986– ; Visiting Asst. Prof., Univ. of S. Calif. 1972–73; Asst. Prof., Univ. of Notre Dame 1973–79; Assoc. Prof. 1979–86; Prof. 1986–87; Dir. Grad. Studies 1981–82, 1985–86; Asst. Chair & Dir. of Undergrad. Studies 1976–79; Visiting Scholar, Northwestern Univ. 1984–86; Sr. Scientist, Ard Corp. (Columbia, MD); expert witness re effect of aging on task performance incl. Flight Engr. role; consultant re design of visual displays (highway signs, etc.) for use by older persons; Prof. Thomas P. Madden Award for Excellence in Teaching, U. of Notre Dame 1977; Rsch. Career Devel. Award, Nat. Inst. on Aging, NIH 1984–89; Fellow, Gerontological Soc. of Am.; Mem., Assn. for Rsch. in Vision & Ophthalmology; Candn. Assn. of Gerontology; Candn. Psych. Assn.; co-editor, 'Aging & Human Visual Function' 1982; author of numerous research jour. articles & book chaps. and several questionnaire instruments assessing knowledge of aging & effects of sensory aging on perf. of daily tasks; recreations: sailing, skiing, woodworking; Home: 16 Artist View Way W., Box 16, Site 23, RR 12, Calgary, Alta. T3E 6W3; Office: 2500 University Dr. N.W., Calgary, Alta. T2N 1N4.

**KLINKHAMMER, Frederic Thomas,** C.M.A.; communications executive; b. Brantford, Ont. 30 March 1945; s. Albert Francis and Mary (Vinal) K.; e. Ryerson Polytech. Inst. Bus. Adm., Computer Systems 1968; C.M.A. 1970; Candn. Inst. Mgmt. P.Mgr. 1978; m. Victoria d. William and Tina Froehlich 26 Aug. 1967; Pres. & C.E.O., Imax Systems Corp. 1990; Mgr. Acctg. Maclean-Hunter Cable TV Ltd. H.O. 1970–73, Gen. Mgr. St. Catharines and Thorold Systems 1971–73; Vice Pres. and Treas. CityTV Toronto 1974, Vice Pres. Finance & Operations 1975, Vice Pres. Finance & Stn. Mgr. 1977, Vice Pres./Gen. Mgr. and Dir. 1978–83; Pres. and Chief Exec. Offr. & Dir. Cablenet Ltd. Canada; U.S. Cablenet Inc.; Cablenet Inc.; Cablenet Development Corp. Toronto and Chicago 1983–84; Pres. & C.E.O., First Choice Candn. Communications Corp. 1984–90; Past Comndr., Toronto Power & Sail Squadron; mem., Broadcast Extve. Soc.; Soc. of Mgmt. Accts.; Candn. Inst. of Mgmt.; Acad. of Candn. Cinema; recreations: sailing, squash; Home: 50 Roxborough Dr., Toronto, Ont. M4W 1X1.

**KLODAWSKY, Helene,** B.F.A.; film-maker; b. Toronto, Ont. 28 March 1956; d. Anszel and Bluma (Rotenberg) K.; e. N.S. Coll. Art & Design B.F.A. 1977; Queen's Univ.; York Univ.; m. John s. Robert and Ida Lucas 4 May 1986; children: Simone, Yasmine; documentary film researcher, writer, producer and dir. since 1979; co-producer film 'All of our Lives' (winner First Prizes 1984 Candn. Film & TV Awards and Am. Film Festival); producer and dir. 'Painted Landscapes of the Times: The Art of Sue Coe' (winner Gold Prizes 1987 Nat. Film & Video Festival Oakland, Ca., Golden Sheaf Awards Yorkton, Sask., Gold Ducat Award and Jury Prize Outstanding Ednl. Film 1987 Mannheim Internat. Film Festival, Special Jury Award (Second Prize) Visual Arts/Performing Arts Category 1988 San Francisco Internat. Film Festival); conceived and directed 'Love's Labour' TV Ont. 1986 (winner First Prize Health & Sci. 1987 Columbus Internat. Film Festival, 1987 Media Award Coalition Sr. Citizens Ont., Bronze Prize for Community Programming 1987 N.Y. Internat. Film & Video Awards); Dir. 'Shoot and Cry' 1988 Nat. Film Bd. (premiered Channel 4 TV UK); 'No Time To Stop' Nat. Film Bd. 1990 (rec'd Honourable Mention, Best Documentary Film 'La Mondiale de Films et Vidéos Quebec' 1991; Certificate of Honourable Mention, Social Studies Category, Columbus Internat. Film and Video Festival, Ohio 1991); 'Motherland: Tales of Wonder' (feature documentary), National Film Bd. of Canada 1994; mem. Assn. des réalisateurs et réalisatrices de films du Québec; Candn. Ind. Film Caucus (Montreal Chapter); Home: 5385 Durocher, Outremont, Que. H2V 3X9; Office: National Film Board, CP 6100 Succ. A, Montreal, Que. H3C 3H5.

**KLOEPFER, Clarence Victor,** B.Sc.; professional engineer; b. Calgary, Alta. 24 May 1933; s. Arthur Thomas and Philomena Agnes (Gilker) K.; e. Univ. of Oklahoma B.Sc. 1954; m. Olive Mary d. Walter and Harriet Sultan 27 April 1957; children: Susan, Jay, Anthony; PRESIDENT, PERMEZ PETROLEUMS LTD. 1982– ; Engr., Husky Oil Ltd. 1954–59; Engineering Group Supvr., Pan American Petroleum Corp. 1959–65; Chief Engr., Banff Oil Ltd. 1965–70; Mgr., Engineering, Aquitaine Co. of Canada 1971–72; Principal Engineer, Kloepfer and Associates Ltd. (now Coles Gilbert Assocs. Ltd.) 1972–82; Bd. Chair, Computalog Ltd.; Dir., Enertech Geophysical Services Ltd.; Hoko Investments Ltd.; CIM Distinguished Serv. Award 1981; Mem., Candn. Inst. of Mining Metallurgy & Petroleum; Petroleum Soc. of CIM; Assn. of Profl. Engrs., Geologists & Geophysicists of Alta; Rotary Club of Vancouver; past mem. of 12 boards of public companies; author of technical papers; recreations: genealogy, politics, golf, cycling; Home: 2328 Mathers Ave., West Vancouver, B.C. V7V 2H6; Office: 505, 520 5th Ave. S.W., Calgary, Alta. T2P 3R7.

**KLOPFER, Alex E.,** B.E., M.Eng.Sc.; executive; b. Budapest, Hungary 23 July 1940; s. Eugene and Gertrude K.; e. Univ. of Sydney, B.E. 1962; Univ. of New South Wales, M.Eng.Sc. 1965; m. Sherrill d. Tom and Grace Arnott 10 March 1970; children: Ronald Gregory, Jennifer Joan; PRES. & C.E.O., EPIC DATA INC. 1989– ; joined IBM 1965, Mktg. Mgr. Ottawa 1969, Mgr. Corporate Plans 1974, Br. Mgr. Calgary 1976, Mgr. Systems Mgmt. 1977, Mktg. Operations Mgr. 1981, Vice Pres. W. Region 1984; Exec. Vice Pres. and Chief Operating Offr., MacDonald Dettwiler and Assocs. 1986–89; Past Chrmn. Devel. Council B.C. Inst. of Technol.; Gov. Science World; Past Vice Pres., Vancouver Symphony Soc.; Dir., BC Infohealth Ltd.; Modatech Inc.; recreations: skiing, sailing, running; Clubs: Hollyburn Country; Vancouver; Home: 244 Stevens Dr., W. Vancouver, B.C.; Office: 7280 River Rd., Richmond, B.C.

**KLOPPENBURG, Henry Ronald,** B.A., LL.B., B.C.L., Q.C.; lawyer; b. Humboldt, Sask. 21 June 1945; s. Henry Joseph and Lena Marie (Kobelsky) K.; e. St. Augustine Sch. and Humboldt Coll. Inst. 1963; St. Thomas More Coll. Univ. of Sask. B.A. 1965, Coll. Law LL.B. 1968; Exeter Coll. Oxford (Rhodes Scholar) B.C.L. 1970; m. Cheryl L. d. Harold and Hazel V. Roycroft 19 May 1973; PARTNER, KLOPPENBURG & KLOPPENBURG 1991– ; called to Bars of Sask. 1971, N.W.T. 1977, Alta. 1980, Manitoba 1986; Queens Counsel for Sask. 1993; Clk. to Hon. Mr. Justice Emmet M. Hall, Supreme Ct. of Can. 1971–72; law practice Goldenberg, Taylor & Tallis, Saskatoon 1972–77; private practice Saskatoon 1977–78; Partner, Kloppenburg & Kloppenburg 1978–89; Partner, Kloppenburg Kloppenburg & Kobrynsky 1989–91; Lectr. in Law Univ. of Sask. 1972–73, Lectr. in Comm. 1973–81; Chairperson, Mendel Art Gallery; Lectr., Bar Admission Course 1989– ; mem. Adv. Ctte. Child Protection Sask., Min. of Social Services; Ctte. Ethics Human Exper. Univ. Hosp. Saskatoon; Dir. Kidney Found. Sask. 1982– ; Kt. of Malta 1983; western region Vice Pres., Order of Malta 1989–92; Q.C. 1993; mem. Law Soc. Sask.; Law Soc. N.W.T.; Law Soc. Alta.; Candn. Bar Assn.; Am. Bar Assn.; Am. Soc. Law & Med. 1984; Candn. Inst. Adm. Justice; Bldg. Fund Appeal Comte., Exeter College, Oxford 1984–89; Sask. Dir., Campaign for Oxford 1989; Bd. of Trustees, Saskatoon Gallery and Conservatory Corp. 1986 (Secy. 1987, Chairperson 1991– ); recreations: walking, collecting Inuit and 20th-century Candn. art, personal computing; Club: Saskatoon; Univ. of Sask. Faculty; Home: 814 Saskatchewan Cres. E., Saskatoon, Sask. S7N 0L3; Office: 333 – 728 Spadina Cres. E., Saskatoon, Sask. S7K 4H7.

**KLOSLER, George,** B.Sc., M.S.A., P.Ag.; educator; b. Roumania 10 Aug. 1938; s. Martin and Maria K.; e. Univ. of Guelph B.Sc. 1962, M.S.A. 1965; m. Gerhilde d. Peter and Mathilde Menning 14 June 1962; three s. George Peter, Paul Edward, David Philip; PROF., FANSHAWE COLLEGE, LONDON, Ont.; Pres. Klosler Brothers Ltd.; Triple 'K' Hog Enterprises Ltd.; Klosler-Rooke Custom Farming Ltd.; J & G Developments Ltd.; Pres. Ingersoll Elevators Ltd. 1979–81; Travel Trust Inc. 1981–83; Bus. Partner Elmhurst, Ingersoll 1980–83; Trustee Oxford Co. Bd. of Edn. 1983– , Chrmn. 1987; Dir. Farm Credit Corp. Ottawa 1985– , Chairperson Audit Ctte. 1987– ; Dir. Ont. Pub. Sch. Bds. Assn. 1988– ; mem. Tribunal Discipline Ctte. Inst. C.A.'s Ont. 1988– ; Special Cons. Office of Auditor Gen. Ottawa 1988– ; private farm cons. 1965–68; Asst. Prof. O.A.C. Univ. of Guelph 1968–72; Co-ordinator Farm Bus. Mgmnt. Prog., Fanshawe Coll. Woodstock 1972–91; Dir. Woodstock & Dist. C. of C. 1982–85; Ont. Found. Rural Living 1984–86; recipient Co. Council Award 1978; Bicentennial Cert. of Merit Min. of Agric. & Food 1984; initiated prodn. film 'A Question of Balance' 1978–79 (Award of Merit Soil Conserv. Soc. Am. 1984); author various publs. farm related matters; frequent guest speaker; expert witness courts agric. issues; mem. Candn. Inst. Profl. Agrols.; Ont. Inst. Profl. Agrols.; Soil Conserv. Soc. Am.; Nat. Assn. Regulatory Utility Comnrs. USA; Candn. Agric. Hall of Fame Assn.; Address: R.R. 2, Mount Elgin, Ont. N0J 1N0.

**KLOWAK, The Honourable Madam Justice G.R.,** B.A., LL.B., Q.C.; judge; b. Grimsby, Ont. 7 June 1942; d. Harry and Sophia (Haluk) K.; e. Grimsby H.S. 1960; McMaster Univ. B.A. 1963; Osgoode Hall Law School LL.B. 1966; called to Bar 1968; m. The Hon. Judge Michael s. Phil and Janet Caney 30 Aug. 1968; children: Christina, Colleen, Stacey; JUDGE, ONTARIO COURT OF JUSTICE (GENERAL DIV.) 1991– ; articled & juniored Haffey, Sherwood 1967–71; Partner, Caney & Klowak 1971–80 (initiated & participated in legal rep. of children in adoption & child welfare proceedings) 1971–80; Counsel, Baker, Blakely, Freeman, Reim 1980–83; Personal Rights Panel Lawyer, Office of Official Guardian & Panel Lawyer, Support & Custody Orders Enforcement 1983–90; Judge, High Court of Justice, Supreme Court of Ont. 1990; 1980s: Lectr., Bar Admissions Course; Orgn. & 1st Chair, Bench & Bar Ctte.; Family Court Toronto; Extve. C.B.A.O.; Dep. Judge, Prov. Court, Civil Div. (Jud. dists. of York & Durham); Q.C. 1980; Dir., Candn. Opera Womens' Ctte. 1980–83; Vice-Pres. 1986–87; Dir. & Vice-Pres., North Toronto Gyros Athletics Inc. 1983–84; Dir., North York Aquatic Club 1983–84; Co-chair, Univ. of Toronto Discipline Tribunal 1980–90; To 1990: Mem., C.B.A.O.; Ukrainian Candn. Advocates Soc.; Lawyers Club; recreations: swimming, skiing; clubs: Toronto Granite, Skyloft Ski.

**KLUCKNER, Michael John;** artist; writer; b. Vancouver, B.C. 4 Apr. 1951; s. Albert Ralph and Lois Theodora (Findlay) K.; e. Univ. of B.C. B.Sc. 1972; m. Christine d. Jeffery and Nancy Allen 17 Feb. 1984; one d. Sarah Jane; writer and illus. newspapers Vancouver and San Francisco (1974); comm. artist Vancouver 1976–80; rep. various public and private colls.; author and illus. 'Vancouver the Way It Was' 1984; 'Victoria the Way It Was' 1986; 'Toronto the Way It Was' 1988; 'Vanishing Vancouver' 1990; 'Paving Paradise' 1991; 'British Columbia in Watercolour' 1993; active as an advocate for the preservation of buildings and heritage landscaping, through shows of watercolour paintings and lectures; recreations: gardening, music, sheep raising; Home: 'Killara,' Langley, B.C.; Office: 21733 - 8th Ave., Langley, B.C. V3A 7R2.

**KLUGE, Holger,** B.Comm., M.B.A.; banker; b. Hamburg, West Germany 11 Mar. 1942; e. Sir. George Williams Univ. (now Concordia), Montreal. B.Comm. (with honors) 1971; Sophia Univ., Tokyo, M.B.A. 1977; m.; 2 children; PRESIDENT, PERSONAL AND COMMERCIAL BANK, CIBC 1990– and Bd. of Dirs. 1992– ; joined CIBC (Montreal) in 1959 working in branch operations; over the years he held progressively more responsible positions in branch mgmnt. in Canada and in corporate and internat. banking in Singapore, Japan and Hong Kong; Vice Pres., Asia Pacific Opns., Hong Kong 1981; Sr. Vice Pres., Internat. Operations 1984; Extve. Vice Pres., Support Services, Corporate Bank 1986; Extve. Vice Pres., Eastern Canada, Europe, Middle East, Africa and Latin Am., Corporate Bank 1988–90; Extve. Vice Pres., International, CIBC, 1990; Chrmn. & Dir., CIBC Securities Inc.; CIBC Mortgage Corporation; CIBC Insurance Mngmt. Co. Ltd.; Dir., CIBC Trust and Merchant Bank (Barbados) Limited; CIBC Jamaica Ltd.; CIBC Trust and Merchant Bank (Jamaica) Limited; CIBC Holdings (Cayman) Limited; CIBC Caribbean Limited; CIBC West Indies Holdings Limited; Canadian Imperial Private Currencies Fund Limited; CEF Holdings Ltd.; CEF Capital Ltd.; Husky Oil Holdings Ltd.; Husky Oil Ltd.; Vice-Chrmn. Bd., Covenant House, Toronto; Mem. Extve. Ctte., Candn. Bankers Assn.; Office: Commerce Court W., Toronto, Ont. M5L 1A2.

**KLUGE, J. Hans,** executive; b. Czechoslovakia 14 May 1928; s. Johann and Elizabeth (Czeike-Zentzitsky) K.; e. Prague, Salzburg, Vienna, B.A. 1951; Ryerson Polytech. Inst. Toronto Engn. Technol. 1955; m. Maria de Györössy-Czepreghy 4 Apr. 1956; children: Florian, Clara; PRES. & C.E.O., AUTOMATIC SWITCH CO., FLORHAM PARK, N.J., U.S.A.; Labourer, Neilson's Chocolates, Toronto 1951–52; Labourer, Assemblyman, D. M. Fraser Ltd. 1952–58; Inspr., Wireman, Draftsman, Estimator, Engn. Mgr. 1958–67; Vice Pres., Gen. Mgr. and Pres., Ward Leonard of Canada 1967–71; Pres. & C.E.O., Ascolectric Ltd. 1971–87; Member of the Board: New Jersey Chamber of Commerce; ANSI, Am. Nat. Standards Inst.; New Jersey Export Counc.; Past Chrmn., Candn. Mfrs. Assoc.; Candn. Standards Assn.; Internat. Standards Adv. Comte.; Elect. & Electronic Mfrs. Assn. Can.; Elect. Mfrs. Sector Metric Comn.; Chrmn. Candn. Mfrs. Assn. Ont. Div.; Pacific Area Standards Cong.; mem. Illuminating Engn. Soc.; Ont. Assn. Cert. Techs. & Technols.; author various business papers metric conversion, elect. energy use and conserv.; recreations: model air craft, trap shooting, fly fishing, fly tying; Clubs: Brantford; Brantford Golf & Country; Rotary (Past Pres.); Home: 35 Elmhurst Ave., Apt. 307, Toronto, Ont. M2N 6G8 and 35 Woodcrest Dr., Convent Station, N.J. 07961, U.S.A.; Office: 50 Hanover Rd., Florham Park, New Jersey 07932.

**KNAPPER, Christopher Kay,** B.A., Ph.D.; educator; b. Crewe, Eng. 4 March 1940; s. Harold Alfred Kay and Hilda (Nevitt) K.; e. Crewe Co. Grammar Sch. 1958; Univ. of Sheffield B.A. 1961; Univ. of Sask. Ph.D. 1969; m. Laurel Jeanne d. Arthur and Beatrice Thom 1976; DIR., INSTRUCTIONAL DEVELOPMENT CENTRE, and PROF. OF PSYCHOLOGY, QUEEN'S UNIV. 1992– ; Prof. of Environmental Studies and of Psychol., Univ. of Waterloo 1977–93, Dir. of Teaching Resources & Continuing Edn. 1985–93; Liaison & Info. Offr. Cutlery Rsch. Council Sheffield, Eng. 1961–62; Ind. Rsch. (Nuffield Found. & Dept. Sci. & Ind. Rsch. sponsorship) Psychol. Dept. Univ. of Sheffield 1962–66; Asst., Assoc. and Full Prof. of Psychol. Univ. of Sask. Regina (now Univ. of Regina) 1966–76; Chrmn. and Head of Psychol. Univ. of Regina 1969–76, Adjunct Prof. 1978–80, Chrmn. Faculty Assn. 1970–71; Rsch. Fellow in Psychol. Waikato Univ. N.Z. 1974; Visiting Fellow, W. Australian Inst. of Technol. Perth 1982; Visiting Sci. Internat. Assn. Traffic Safety Sci's Univ. of Osaka, Japan 1982; Adjunct Prof. of Rural Extension Studies Univ. of Guelph 1986– ; Internat. Visitor, Trenton State Coll., New Jersey 1988; Distinguished visitor, Monash Univ. (Australia) 1989; author: 'Evaluating Instructional Technology' 1980; co-author: 'The Perception of People and Events' 1968; 'Lifelong Learning and Higher Education' 1985 (2nd ed. 1991); ed. 'If Teaching is Important: The Evaluation of Instruction in Higher Education' 1977; 'Expanding Learning Through New Communications Technologies' 1982; mem. various ed. bds.; Chrmn. Doctoral Fellowship Selection Ctte. Can. Council 1976–77; mem. Social Sci's & Humanities Rsch. Council Can. Leave & Postdoctoral Fellowships Jury 1984–85; Fellow, Brit. Psychol. Soc.; Registered Psychol., Ontario; Chartered Psychol. (U.K.); mem. Candn. Assn. Univ. Teachers (Exec. various cttes.); Co-founder and first Coordinator Soc. Teaching & Learning in Higher Edn.; recreations: walking, cooking, gardening, travel; Club: National Liberal (Eng.); Home: 200 Piper St., Ayr, Ont. N0B 1E0; Office: Kingston, Ont. K7L 3N6.

**KNEEBONE, Thomas Selwyn Oscar;** actor; writer; b. Auckland, N.Z. 13 May 1935; s. Thomas Keith and Nancy Bergit (Matheson) K.; e. Mt. Albert Grammar, N.Z.; The Bristol Old Vic Theatre Sch.; ARTISTIC DIR., SMILE THEATRE CO.; appearances with London Old Vic, Candn. Opera Co., Shaw Festival, Stratford Festival (The Dauphin in 'St Joan'; Feste in 'Twelfth Night'), Charlottetown Festival, Nat. Tap Dance Co.; cabaret appearances incl.: 'Oh Coward!'; 'The Apple Tree'; 'Gilbert & Sullivan Tonight!'; 'Hey Porter!'; 'Noel and Gertie' (wrote and devised latter three shows); one-man show 'T.K.'s Kabaret'; CBC radio appearances 'Noel Coward' and 'Kurt Weill in America'; appearing as Bennett, Christopher Plummer's butler in 'Counterstrike' T.V. series; Address: 7 Jackes Ave., Suite 107, Toronto, Ont. M4T 1E3.

**KNEEN, Brewster Beattie,** B.A., M.Div.; writer; b. Cleveland, Ohio 21 July 1933; s. Harold Fitch and Carol Dora (Beattie) K.; e. Cornell Univ. B.A. 1955; New Coll. Edinburgh; Union Theol. Semy. N.Y. M.Div. 1961; m. Cathleen d. Horace and Anna Rosenberg 20 May 1964; children: Rebecca, Jamie; freelance broadcaster, cons. in econ. and theol., Exec. Dir. Centre Study Instns. & Theol. Toronto 1965–71; farmer N.S., Dir. N.S. Fedn. Agric., Dir. and Exec. Sec. Sheep Producers Assn. N.S., Founding Dir. and Mktg. Organizer Northumberland Lamb Mktg. Co-operative, Founding Dir. Brookside Abattoir Co-operative 1971–86; writer, food system analyst since 1986; served with US Navy 1955–57; recipient Social Sci's & Humanities Rsch. Council Grants 1987, 1989; researcher Award CBC TV Centennial Special 'Therefore Choose Life' 1967; 'Shepherd of the Year' Award N.S. Sheep Producers Assn. 1985; author 'The Economy of Sugar' 1971; 'From Land to Mouth: Understanding the Food System' 1989, 2nd ed. 1993; 'Trading Up: How Cargill, the World's Largest Grain Company, is Changing Canadian Agriculture' 1990; 'The Rape of Canola' 1992; co-ed. 'The Ram's Horn' monthly newsletter 1980– ; Anglican; recreations: swimming, cycling; Address: 125 Highfield Rd., Toronto, Ont. M4L 2T9.

**KNELMAN, Fred Harold,** B.A.Sc., M.Eng., D.I.C., Ph.D.; adjunct professor, writer, consultant; b. Winnipeg, Man. 9 Oct. 1919; s. Morris Jacob and Bessie Deborah K.; e. Univ. of Toronto B.A.Sc. 1943; McGill Univ. M.Eng. 1950; Imperial Coll. of Science (U.K.) D.I.C. 1953; Univ. of London (U.K.) Ph.D. 1953; m. Anna Suzy d. John and Mary Gordon Dec. 1985; children: Kevin Mark, Linda; VICE-PRES., HEALTH GUARD PRODUCTS (Vancouver); Chief Engr., Monarch Battery 1946–50; Dir., Rsch. & Devel., Stuart/Givaudan 1953–62; Assoc. Prof., Gen. Edn., York Univ. 1962–67; Prof., Interdisciplinary Studies, Concordia Univ. 1967–85; Visiting Prof., Univ. of Calif. at Santa Barbara 1973–74, 1978–79; at Santa Cruz 1984–85; Pres., Knelman Consulting Serv. 1985– ; Vice-Pres., Health First Products 1989–92; Policy Advr., Sci. Council of Canada & Environment Canada 1977–78; State Govt. of Calif. 1981–82; Dir. & Vice-Pres., Whistler Found. for a Sustainable Environ.; recipient, World Wildlife Canada Prize 1967; World Federalists Peace Essay Prize 1970; White Owl Conservation Award 1972; Ben Gurion Univ. Medal of Merit 1985; U.N.A. Special Achievement Award Montreal 1983; Meritorious Serv. Award, Candn. Peace Edn. & Rsch. Assoc. 1987; Commemorative Medal for 125th Anniversary of Candn. Confederation 1992; World Peace Prize (World Federalists) 1994; Office: Victoria, B.C. V8W 2Y2.

**KNELMAN, Judith,** B.Ped., B.A., M.A., Ph.D.; university professor; b. Winnipeg, Man. 30 April 1939; s. John M. and Marion (Medovy) K.; e. Univ. of Manitoba B.Ped. 1959; Univ. of Toronto B.A. 1968, M.A. 1972, Ph.D. 1978; divorced; children: Tom Gelmon, John Gelmon; PROFESSOR OF JOURNALISM, UNIV. OF WESTERN ONT. 1988– ; public School Teacher, Winnipeg & Toronto 1959–66; Writing Workshop Instructor, York & Univ. of Toronto 1968–73; Freelance Writer (Maclean-Hunter, Globe and Mail, etc.) 1960– ; Prof.

of English, Bishop's Univ. 1979–80; Writer & Ed., Univ. of Toronto Dept. of Communications 1981–88; Mem., Ont. Council on Univ. Affairs 1992–95; Univ. of Western Ont. Senate 1990–92; Faculty Assn. Extve. 1991–93; author of scholarly articles on Victorian social history esp. women & crime in 19th-century England; clubs: Victoria League; Home: 143 Wolfrey Ave., Toronto, Ont. M4K 1L4; Office: Univ. of Western Ontario, London, Ont. N6A 5B7.

**KNELMAN, Martin,** M.A.; writer; b. Winnipeg, Man. 17 June 1943; s. John and Marion (Medovy) K.; e. Luxton Sch. Winnipeg 1958; St. John's High Sch. 1960; Univ. of Man. B.A. (gen.) 1964, B.A. (hons.) 1967; Univ. of Toronto M.A. 1971; m. Bernadette Sulgit 12 June 1975; children: Joshua, Sara; Reporter, Copy Desk, The Globe and Mail 1964–66, Movie Critic 1969–76; Movie Critic Toronto Star 1967–69; Lectr. York Univ. 1970–73; Can. Council Sr. Arts Fellow 1973–74; Critic and Contrib. Ed., Saturday Night; Arts & Entertainment columnist, Toronto Life; recipient Nathan Cohen Award for Drama Criticism 1982, 1989; Imperial Oil Award for Arts Journalism 1992; The White Award for criticism 1993, City and Regional Magazine competition (William Allen White Sch. of Journalism, Univ. of Kansas); author 'This is Where We Came In' 1977; 'A Stratford Tempest' 1982; 'Home Movies' 1987; various mag. articles; Address: 62 Bernard Ave., Toronto, Ont. M5R 1R5.

**KNIEWASSER, Andrew Graham,** O.C. (1967), B.A., F.C.S.I.; executive; b. Ottawa, Ont., 9 Sept. 1926; s. Andrew Vernon and Helen Graham (Cooch) K.; e. Lisgar Coll., Ottawa, Ont.; Queens Univ., B.A. (Hon. Econ.) 1949; m. Jacqueline Marie, d. late Wilfred Delaney and Marguerite Rousseau, 3 Aug. 1951; children: Andrew Peter, James David, John Hugh, Andréa Hélène; PRES., ROCKCHAPEL ENTERPRISES 1991– ; Econ., Economics Rsch. and Devel. Br. Dept. of Trade and Comm., Ottawa, 1949; Econ., Dept. of Defence Prod., Ottawa, 1950; Trade Commr. service 1951; Asst. Trade Commr., Candn. Embassy, Athens, 1952; Acting Trade Commr. a.i., Beirut, 1953, Cairo 1954; Asst. Comm. Secy., Candn. Embassy, Caracas, 1955, Comm. Secy., Caracas 1957; Area Trade Offr. for Latin Am., Dept. Trade and Comm., Ottawa, 1957; Extve. Asst. to the Depy. Min. of Trade and Comm., 1958; Comm. Counsellor, Candn. Embassy, Paris, Candn. Del. to Bureau of Internat. Exhns., and Candn. Del. to Co-ordinating Comte. (NATO) 1960; Gen. Mgr., Expo '67, 1963–67; Asst. Dep. Min. (Trade Promotion), Dept. Trade and Comm.; Dir. Can. Corp. for 1967 World Exhibition; Dir., Export Credits Ins. Corp., 1968; Sr. Asst. Depy. Min. (Indust. & Trade Devel.), Dept. Indust., Trade and Comm., Can. 1970; Pres., Investment Dealers Assn. of Can. 1972–91; former Dir., Export Development Corp.; Candn. Standards Assoc.; Standards Counc. of Can.; 'Cours Claudel,' Ottawa; Dir., The Candn. Securities Inst.; Atlantic Counc. of Can.; Atlantic Inst.; The Donwood Inst.; Queen Elizabeth Hosp.; National Club; Goodwood Farms; Trustee, Children's Hosp. of Eastern Ont.; former mem., Extve. & Devel. Comte., Atlantic Salmon Fedn.; The Canadian Club (Pres. 1980–81); Le Cercle Canadien (Founding Dir. 1986–87); former Trustee, Children's Hosp. of Eastern Ont.; served with Candn. Inf. Corps 1945; Commandeur de l'Ordre du Merite agricole 1966; Officer of the Order of Canada 1967; Fellow, Candn. Securities Inst. 1986; recreations: hunting, fishing; Clubs: National (Dir.); Rideau; Goodwood (Dir.); United Church; Home: R.R. 2, Pontypool, Ont. L0A 1K0.

**KNIGHT, Arthur Robert,** F.C.I.C., B.Sc., M.Sc., Ph.D.; educational administrator; b. St. John's, Nfld. 24 Feb. 1938; s. Herbert Arthur and Dorothy (Byrne) K.; e. Memorial Univ. B.Sc. 1958, M.Sc. 1960; Univ. of Alberta Ph.D. 1962; m. Phyllis (dec. 1986) d. Harry and Dulcie Oake 18 May 1959; m. Ineke d. Sophia and Aage Postma 22 Nov. 1986; children: Katherine (Mrs. D.H. Ervin), David, Barbara (Mrs. K. Fredrickson), Susan, Jennifer (Mrs. R. Harder), Robert, Mark, Marieke; PRES., SASKATCHEWAN INSTITUTE OF APPLIED SCIENCE AND TECHNOLOGY 1993– ; Postdoctoral Fellow, Univ. of Alta. 1962–64; Assist. Prof., Dept. of Chem. and Chemical Engineering, Univ. of Sask. 1964–68, Assoc. Prof. 1968–72, Prof. 1972–93, Prof. and Dept. Head 1976–81; Dean of Arts & Sci. 1981–90; Acting Assoc. Vice-Pres. (Academic) 1990–92; Assoc. Vice Pres. (Academic), Univ. of Sask. 1992–93; author: 'Introductory Physical Chemistry,' 1970; author or co-author of 51 refereed scientific articles on Photochemical Research; Saskatoon Catholic Bd. of Ed., Trustee 1970–73, Chrmn. 1973–76; Saskatchewan School Trustees Assn. Pres., Urban Section 1972–73; recreation: carpentry; Home: 3523 Balfour St., Saskatoon, Sask. S7H 3Z5; Office: 1401 - 606 Spadina Cres. E., Saskatoon, Sask. S7K 2H6.

**KNIGHT, Douglas Walker,** B.A., M.Sc.; publishing executive; b. Toronto, Ont. 14 Feb. 1952; s. Eliot Douglas and Patricia Edith (Gilverson) K.; e. Univ. of Toronto B.A. (Hons.) 1976; London Sch. of Econ. M.Sc. 1977; m. Colleen Flood 27 June 1981; children: Molly Jane, Emma Leigh; PUBLISHER, THE FINANCIAL POST CO. 1988– ; Chrmn., Securities Valuation Co.; joined present newspaper 1978; Hon. Chrmn., Opera Atelier; Pres., Theatre Beyond Words; Dir., Toronto Symphony; Junior Achievement; Print Measurement Bureau; Home: 74 Hilton Ave., Toronto, Ont. M5R 3E7; Office: 333 King St. E., Toronto, Ont. M5A 4N2.

**KNIGHT, Eric E.;** business executive; b. Montreal, Que. 10 Aug. 1954; s. a. Gordon and Jean Urquart (Chatfield) K.; e. Carlton Univ. 1975; m. Barbara d. Alexander and Sylvia Szita 1 Oct. 1977; children: Ryan, Vanessa; PRES., EXECUCOR FINANCIAL LIMITED 1983– ; Sales Mgr., Equip Div., Misener Financial Corp. 1980–83; piloted an antique aircraft across Canada; recreations: hockey, boating, coaching hockey and baseball; clubs: York Mills Hockey Assn.; Home: 93 Lynnhaven Dr., Toronto, Ont. M6A 2L1; Office: 119 Denison St., Markham, Ont. L3R 1B5.

**KNOWLES, Arthur Francis,** C.A.; executive; b. Montreal, Que. 17 Aug. 1922; s. William Francis and Beatrice (Anyon) K.; e. McGill Univ. Extension Courses leading to C.A. 1946; m. Audrey d. John and Kathleen McGruther 7 Sept. 1946; children: David, Brian, Audrey, Ross; DIRECTOR EMERITUS, POWER CORP. OF CANADA 1991– ; Dir., Great-West Lifeco Inc.; joined McDonald Currie & Co. Pub. Acctg. 1940–52; Gen. Auditor Shawinigan Water & Power Co. 1952–62; Treas. Shawinigan Engineering Co. Ltd. 1962–64; Pres., C.O.O. & Dir., present company 1964–91; mem. Candn. Inst. C.A.'s; Que. Order C.A.'s; Ont. Inst. C.A.'s; recreation: golf; Clubs: St. James; Summerlea Golf & Country; The Country Club of Florida; Home: Apt. 801, 230 Hymus Blvd., Pointe Claire, Que. H9R 5P5; Office: 751 Victoria Square, Montreal, Que. H2Y 2J3.

**KNOWLES, Arthur Neville;** executive; b. London, Ont. 31 July 1927; e. Appleby Coll. Oakville, Ont.; m. Verna June 1954; children: Peter Allen, Arthur Neville, James Laurie, Elizabeth June; EXTVE. V.P. & DIR., LONDON WINERY LTD.; Dir. & Pres., Knowlwin Holdings Ltd.; Dir., Elizabeth's of London Gifts Limited; Dir. & Gen. Manager, Westminster Transport Ltd.; Home: R.R. 2, PT Lot 19, Conc. 12, West Lorne, Ont. N0L 2P0; Office: 560 Wharncliffe Rd. South, London, Ont. N6J 2N5.

**KNOWLES, Henry Joseph,** Q.C., B.A., LL.B., LL.M., M.B.A.; business lawyer and financial consultant; b. London, Ont. 22 Jan. 1932; e. London S. Coll. Inst. 1952; Univ. of W. Ont. Sch. Business Adm. Honors B.A. 1956; Osgoode Hall Law Sch. 1960; Yale Univ. Law Sch. LL.M. 1961; Univ. of Toronto Sch. of Business M.B.A. 1962; m. Marilyn Anne Radcliffe 1960; 2 children; BUSINESS LAWYER AND FINANCIAL CONSULTANT; Counsel, Bastedo, Sheldon, McGivney & Peck, Barristers & Solicitors; Dir., Samuel Manu-Tech Inc.; Durkin Hayes Publishing Ltd.; The Gore Mutual Insurance Co.; Algonquin Mercantile Corp.; The Inst. of Corporate Directors in Can.; Lectr., Univ. of Toronto, Faculty of Engineering 1991– ; Chrmn. of Bd., Algonquin Mercantile Corp. 1989–91; Pres. & C.E.O., United Financial Management Ltd. 1987–89; legal and financial practice 1984–87; Visiting Kimber Fellow, Faculty of Administrative Studies, York Univ. 1983; Chrmn., Ont. Securities Comn. 1980–83; called to Bar of Ont. 1960; cr. Q.C. 1978; law practice Borden & Elliot 1961–64; Smith, Lyons, 1965–68, Partner 1969–80; Seminar Instr. in Corporate Law 1966–69 and in Income Tax Law 1974, 1976, 1977, Osgoode Hall Bar Admission Course; author 'Partnership' (statutory annotation) 1978; 'International Securities Regulation' 1985 (Candn. author and ed.); 'Competing with the Financial Conglomerate and Financial Supermarket' 1986; 'Concentration of Power in the Financial Services Industry' 1988; 'Individual Involvement in the Take-Over Process' 1988; 'Corporate Governance and Canadian Capital Markets' 1989; 'Directors and Officers' 1989; 'Business Self Government and Accountability in a Global Market' 1989; co-author 'So You Want A Fight-Shareholder Rights and Remedies in Canada' 1986; mem. Candn. Bar Assn.; Candn. Tax Foundation; Co. York Law Assn.; Inst. Law Clks. Ont. (Hon. mem. 1978); Candn. Ski Instructors' Alliance; Delta Upsilon; Phi Delta Phi; recreations: skiing, jogging; Clubs: Granite; Cambridge; Alpine; Address: 1800 Dundas St. W., Suite 1800, Toronto, Ont. M5G 1Z8.

**KNOWLES, Hon. Stanley Howard,** P.C., O.C., B.A., B.D., LL.D.; b. Los Angeles, Calif. 18 June 1908; s. Stanley Ernest and Margaret Blanche (Murdock) K. (both born in Canada); e. Elem. and High Sch., Los Angeles; Brandon Coll., Man., B.A. 1930 (Gen. Prof. Medal); Univ. of Man. (Theol. and post grad. studies in Philos. and Econ. 1930–34); B.D. 1934 (Gen. Prof. Medal); Hon. LL.D.: Brandon Univ. 1967; McMaster Univ. 1973; Queen's Univ. 1976; Univ. of Toronto 1976; Trent Univ. 1978; York Univ. 1979; m. Vida Claire, d. Chas. Gordon Cruikshank, Winnipeg, Man., 9 Nov. 1936 (dec. 20 Apr. 1978); one son (m.) and one d. (m.); Ald., City of Winnipeg 1941–42; 1st el. to H. of C. for Winnipeg N. Centre, 1942, in by-el. to succeed late J. S. Woodsworth; re-el. g.e. 1945, 1949, 1953, 1957; def. g.e. 1958; re-elected, g.e. 1962, 1963, 1965, 1968, 1972, 1974, 1979 and 1980; Chief C.C.F. Whip 1944–57; C.C.F. Depy. Leader, 1957–58; Extve. Vice-Pres., The Candn. Labour Cong., 1958–62; Chrmn., C.C.F. Nat. Convention, 1948, '50, '52, '54, '56, '58, active in formation of N.D.P.; Chrmn., Nat. Comte. for New Party, 1958–61; House Leader, N.D.P. Caucus in H. of C.; Candn. Del. to U.N. Gen. Assembly (1st session) 1945–46; Workers' Del. for Canada at I.L.O. Conf., Geneva, 1959, '60 and '61; mem. of 1st Bd. of Dirs. of Red River Co-operative Supply Ltd., Winnipeg; mem., Winnipeg Local No. 191 of Internat. Typographical Union; Candn. Inst. of Internat. Affairs (Winnipeg Br.); Nat. Council and Nat. Extve. of C.C.F. (Man. Prov. Chrmn. 1935–36 and 1939–41; el. Nat. Vice-Chrmn. 1954); mem., Fed. Council, N.D.P.; apptd. Chancellor of Brandon Univ., Manitoba, 1970–90, Chancellor Emeritus 1990– ; in recognition of 38 years of service in the House, apptd. Honorary Officer, House of Commons 1984 for his future years; author of: 'The New Party' ('Le Nouveau Parti') 1961; sworn in as Mem. of Queen's Privy Council for Canada 1979; Officer, Order of Canada 1985; named in his honour: Stanley Knowles Sch., Winnipeg, 1988; Stanley Knowles Housing Co-operative, Toronto; Stanley Knowles Park, Winnipeg; Knowles-Douglas Students' Bldg., Brandon Univ.; Stanley Knowles Endowed Chair in Public Policy, Brandon Univ.; N.D.P.; United Church; Club: Canadian; Home: Apt. 513, Rideau Place, 550 Wilbrod St., Ottawa, Ont. K1N 6N2; Office: House of Commons, Ottawa, Ont. K1A 0A6.

**KNOWLES, Valerie Jean,** M.A., B.J.; writer; b. Montreal, Que. 2 Aug. 1934; d. Trevor Durnford and Margaret Jean (Mackay) Ross; e. Smith Coll. Northampton, Mass. B.A. 1956; McGill Univ. M.A. 1957; Carleton Univ. B.J. 1964; m. David Clifford s. Rev. Dr. E. Clifford and Dorothy Knowles 11 March 1961; Instr. in Hist. Prince of Wales Coll. P.E.I. 1958–59; Hist. Teacher Elmwood Sch. Rockcliffe Park, Ont. 1959–60; Instr. in Hist. Carleton Univ. Ottawa summer 1961, discussion group leader and bibliog. Hist. Dept. 1964–1972; Archivist, Pub. Archives Can. 1961–63; freelance writer since 1964; author 'Leaving With A Red Rose' 1981; 'First Person' 1988; 'Strangers At Our Gates' 1992; various articles newspapers, mags. and fed. govt. publs.; mem. Media Club of Ottawa (Exec. 1977–83); Zonta Club of Ottawa (Exec. 1989–91); Writers' Union Can.; Anglican; recreations: reading, walking, tennis, photography; Club: University Women's (Montreal); Address: 554 Piccadilly Ave., Ottawa, Ont. K1Y 0J1.

**KNOWLTON, Thomas A.,** B.A., M.B.A.; executive; b. Toronto, Ont. 16 June 1946; s. Dr. William George and Grace K.; e. Univ. of Windsor B.A. 1968, M.B.A. 1970; m. Janice 8 June 1968; children: Kimberly, Tricia, Jeffrey, Andrea; CHRMN., KELLOGG CO. OF GREAT BRITAIN 1990– ; EXECUTIVE VICE PRES., KELLOGG COMPANY, BATTLE CREEK; AREA DIR., KELLOGG EUROPE 1992– ; Brand Mgmt. Colgate Palmolive, Toronto 1970–73; Product Mgr. General Foods, Toronto 1973–75; Vice Pres. and Dir. Client Services, Leo Burnett, Toronto 1975–79; Vice Pres. Kellogg Co., Battle Creek, Mich.; Pres. & C.E.O., Kellogg Canada Inc. 1979–88; Mng. Dir., Kellogg Co. of Gt. Britain 1989–90; mem. Upper Canada Chapt., Young Pres.' Orgn.; Univ. of Windsor Alumni; recreations: squash, golf; Club: York Downs Golf & Country; Home: 32 Congleton Rd., Adlerley Edge, Cheshire, England SK9 7AB; Office: Stretford, Manchester M32 8RA.

**KNOWLTON, W. Leo.,** Q.C.; executive; b. Toronto, Ont. 1905; e. St. Michael's Coll. Sch.; Univ. of Toronto, B.A. (Gold Medal in Philos.): Osgoode Hall Law Sch., Toronto, Ont.; m. the late Mary Teaffe, Ottawa, Ont., 1931; two d., Mary, Adele; m. 2ndly Margaret MacKenzie (Webber) 7 May 1982; Director, Lake Erie Tobacco Co. Ltd.; called to the Bar of Ontario, 1930; cr. Q.C.

1948; joined Can. Permanent Trust Company as a Trust Offr. 1930; Mgr. of Toronto Br. of the Co., 1940–54; apptd. Asst. Gen. Mgr., 1955, Gen. Mgr. 1956 and Vice Pres. 1961, Extve. Vice Pres. 1965; Pres., Trust Co.'s Assn. Can., 1962–63; mem., Toronto Bd. Trade; Clubs: National; Lawyers; Granite; Toronto Hunt; Home: 53 Widdicombe Hill Blvd., Weston, Ont. M9R 1Y3.

**KNOX, George,** B.A., M.A., Ph.D.; art historian; b. London, England 1 Jan. 1922; s. Inman and Hilda (Ball) K.; e. Westminster Sch., England; London Univ., Courtauld Inst. of Art, B.A. 1950, M.A. 1954, Ph.D. 1969; 1st m. Ursula d. David Leacock 1945; 2nd m. Patricia d. Alan Isaacs 1964; children: Benedict, Sarah, Matthew, Martha, Erasmus, Emma; PROFESSOR EMERITUS, UNIV. OF B.C. 1987– ; Lectr., Slade Sch. of Fine Art, Univ. Coll., London 1950–52; Univ. of Durham 1952–58; Sr. Lectr., Portsmouth Coll. of Art 1963–69; Asst. Prof., Queen's Univ. 1969–70; Prof., Dept. of Fine Arts, U.B.C. 1970–87; Mem., Inst. of Advanced Studies, Princeton 1980–81; Candn. Ctte. for the History of Art 1980–92 (Pres. 1985–92); Comité internat. d'hist. de l'art 1985– ; Vice-Pres., Candn. Soc. for 18th Century Studies 1985–86; Pres. 1986–87; Socio, Ateneo Veneto 1986– ; author/co-author of numerous exhibition catalogues, monographs, articles & reviews incl. most recently 'Giambattista Piazzetta, 1682–1754' 1992; '18th Century Venetian Art in Canadian Collections' 1989; 'Master Drawings from the National Gallery of Canada' 1988–89; 'The Robert Lehman Collection, VI: Italian Eighteenth-Century Drawings' 1987; 'G.B. Piazzetta' 1983; 'Giambattista and Domenico Tiepolo' 1980; Home: 3495 West 11th Ave., Vancouver, B.C. V6R 2K1.

**KNOX, James Wilson,** M.B.E., E.D.; Registered Insurance Broker (Ont.); b. Westmount, P.Q. 17 Apr. 1915; s. Frank John and Mary Luceneth (Jones) K.; e. Lower Canada Coll., Montreal, P.Q.; m. Georgina W., d. George W. Grier, Montreal, Que., 17 Feb. 1945; children: Victoria W., Frances J., Georgina M., Alexandra J.; DIR., KVM CANADIAN HOLDINGS INC. (estbd. 1908); began with the Royal-Liverpool Group of Ins. Co's. at Candn. H.O., Montreal 1933; joined present Interests 1938; joined N.P.A.M., The Black Watch (RHR) of Can., 1934 with rank of Lieut.; served in 2nd World War with 1st Bn. of this Unit, 1939–45 in U.K., and on General Staff, N.W. Europe; Dir., Staff, Staff Coll., Camberley; awarded M.B.E.; 1946–53, The Black Watch (Militia) retired Lieut.-Col. Commanding; 1963–68 Col. of the Regt.; Candn. Red Cross Soc., Que Div. (Hon. Vice-Pres., and Past Pres.); St. Andrews Soc. of Montreal (Past Pres.); Fellow, Royal Commonwealth Soc.; Gov., Douglas Hosp.; Montreal Gen. Hosp.; Royal Victoria Hospital; Presbyterian (Elder and Former Trustee); recreations: yachting; music; amateur radio (VE3AAP and J37XP); Clubs: St. James's; Royal St. Lawrence Yacht; Candn. Yachting Assn.; Great Lakes Cruising; Canadian Power Squadrons; St. Lawrence Cruising; Canadian Legion; The Pistol of Montreal; The Highland Brigade (Scotland); Kingston and Granada (W.I.) Amateur Radio; Home: 1005, 165 Ontario St., Kingston, Ont. K7L 2Y6.

**KNOX, John Keith,** Q.C., B.A., LL.B.; executive; b. Winnipeg, Man. 12 June 1933; s. John James and Lillian Mary (Bennett) K.; e. Univ. of Man. B.A. 1955, LL.B. 1959; m. Sally Marie d. Frederick A. and Elizabeth R. Wansbrough 21 June 1958; children: Allison E., J. David, James M.; VICE PRES. AND GEN. COUNSEL, SECY., JAMES RICHARDSON & SONS LTD. 1979– ; Dir. Richardson Greenshields of Canada Ltd.; read law with Pitblado & Hoskin, Winnipeg; called to Bar of Man. 1959; cr. Q.C. 1978; private law practice 1959–72; part-time Crown Prosecutor 1967; part-time Prov. Judge 1968–72; lectr. various aspects litigation Man. Bar Admission Course 1964–72; Regional Counsel, W. Region, Canadian Pacific Law Dept. 1972–79; Anglican; mem. Winnipeg Chamber Comm.; Candn. Tax Foundation; Candn. Bar Assn.; Law Soc's Man. and Sask.; recreations: golf, skiing, tennis, reading; Clubs: Manitoba; St. Charles Country; Unicity Racquet; Home: 300 Cordova St., Winnipeg, Man. R3N 1A4; Office: 30th Floor, One Lombard Place, Winnipeg, Man. R3B 0Y1.

**KNOX, Marilyn H.,** B.Sc.; food manufacturing executive; b. Montreal, Que. 1950; e. Mount Allison Univ. B.Sc. 1971; Vancouver Gen. Hosp. dietetic internship 1972; Univ. of Toronto grad. dipl. 1975; SR. VICE-PRES., NESTLE CANADA INC. 1992– ; Therapeutic Dietitian, Grace Gen. Hosp. St. John's Nfld. 1972–74; Public Health Nutritionist, Ottawa-Carleton Reg. Health Unit 1975–78; Cons., Health Protection Br., Health & Welfare Can. 1979–80; Vice-Pres., Grocery Products Mfrs. of Can. 1980–88; Extve. Dir., Premier's Council on Health Strategy 1988–90; Asst. Dep. Min., Ont. Min. of Agric. & Food 1990–91; Dep. Min., Ont. Tourism & Recreation 1991–92; Fellow, Candn. Dietetic Assn.; Women on the Move Award, Toronto Sun; Award of Honour, Ont. Dietetic Assn.; Elizabeth Chant Robertson Award; Dir., Participaction; Co-Chair, Children's Ctte., Premier's Council on Health Well-being & Soc. Justice; Dir., Workers' Compensation Rsch. Institute; Dir., Candn. Council for Drug-Free Sport; Dir., Candn. Dietetic Assn. 1984; Pres., Ont. Dietetic Assn. 1984; Pres., Nfld. Diet. Assn. 1972; recreations: rowing, outdoor sports; Office: 1185 Eglinton Ave. E., Toronto, Ont. M3C 3C7.

**KNUDSEN, Conrad Calvert,** B.A., LL.B.; executive; b. Tacoma, Wash. 3 Oct. 1923; s. Conrad and Annabelle (Callison) K.; e. Univ. of Wash. B.A. 1948, LL.B. 1950; Columbia Univ. Fellow in Law 1951; m. Julia Lee (dec'd) d. David Morgan Roderick 22 Nov. 1950; children: Calvert Jr., Elizabeth Page, Colin Roderick, David Callison; DIR., MacMILLAN BLOEDEL LTD.; Dir., Cascade Corp.; Portland General Corp.; Safeco Corp.; Seafirst Corp.; Seattle First National Bank; Penwest Ltd.; West Fraser Timber Co. Ltd.; Dir. Emeritus, Candn. Imperial Bank of Commerce, Toronto; called to Bar of Wash. 1950; Assoc. and Partner, Bogle, Bogle & Gates, Seattle 1951–61; Extve. Vice Pres. and Dir., Aberdeen Plywood & Veneer Inc., Aberdeen, Ore. 1961–63; Pres. and Chief Adm. Offr., Vice Chrmn., Evans Products Co., Portland, Ore. 1963–68; Sr. Vice Pres. Corporate Growth, Weyerhaeuser Co., Tacoma, Wash. 1969–76; Chrmn., C.E.O. & Dir., MacMillan Bloedel Ltd. 1976–83; Vice Chrmn. & Dir. 1983–90; served with U.S. Army 1942–46; mem. Am. and Wash. State Bar Assns.; recreations: tennis, jogging, vineyards, skiing; Clubs: Vancouver; Rainier (Seattle); Seattle Tennis; University (Seattle); Arlington (Portland); Multnomah Athletic (Portland); Racquet (Portland); Home: 602 - 36th Ave. E., Seattle, WA 98112; Office: 925 West Georgia St., Vancouver, B.C. V6C 3L2.

**KNUDSEN, Helge,** M.Sc.; computer scientist; b. Rejsby, Denmark 6 Nov. 1944; s. Jens Jorgensen and Anna Kathrine (Andersen) K.; e. Ribe Kathedralskole, Ribe 1963; Technical Univ. of Denmark M.Sc. 1968; m. Inger d. Anna and Niels Rasmussen 28 Sept. 1970; children: Else Marie, Anders; VICE-PRES., SOFTWARE DEVEL. CTR. (MEADOWVALE), AMDAHL CANADA LTD. 1981– ; Technical Univ. of Denmark 1968–75; postdoctoral fellow, IBM Corp. (Los Angeles & Palo Alto) 1975–77; joined Amdahl Canada Ltd. as Computer Architect (Sunnyvale, USA) 1977–78; Mktg. (Scandinavia) 1978–81; Home: 46 8th Concession East, R.R. 1, Freelton, Ont. L0R 1K0; Office: 2000 Argentia Road, Plaza 2, Suite 200, Mississauga, Ont. L5N 1V8.

**KNUTSON, Harry L.;** financial executive; b. Prince Rupert, B.C. 18 Jan. 1946; e. Simon Fraser Univ. (Econ. & Commerc.); children: Harry Louis III, Todd Murray James, Kristiana Gudrun, Kai Harry; Chrmn., Nova Bancorp Financial Services (Canada) Ltd.; Nova Bancorp Group (Canada) Ltd.; Nova Bancorp Investments Ltd.; Nova Bancorp Capital Management Ltd.; Nova Bancorp Developments Ltd.; Nova International Limited; Dir., Envirocon Pacific Ltd.; CanOcean Engineering Ltd.; joined Aetna Life & Casualty, Hartford Conn. 1969; Dir. of Pensions & Financial Services, Excelsior Life Insurance Co. 1971; Vice Pres. and Dir., AGF Toronto Investment Mgmt. Inc. 1972; Pres. & Trustee, Candn. Realty Investors 1975; Pres. & Dir. Pocklington Financial Corp. 1979; recreation: hunting; Office: Suite 650, 999 West Hastings, Vancouver, B.C. V6C 2W2.

**KOBIE, Franklin Lewis,** M.B.A., F.C.M.A.; energy executive; b. Edmonton, Alta. 1 Oct. 1933; s. Lewis and Mary Margaret (Tesch) K.; e. Univ. of Manitoba B.Comm. (Hons.) 1971; Univ. of Alta. M.B.A. 1978; Soc. of Mngt. Accountants Manitoba F.C.M.A. 1972; m. Elizabeth Relkoff 7 April 1956; children: Allan, Karen, Keith; Pres. & Chief Extve. Offr., Dreco Energy Services 1990–92; Inspector, Royal Candn. Mounted Police 1952–78; Partner, Deloitte & Touche 1978–90; Dir., Edmonton Northlands; Good Samaritan Soc. Edmonton; Candn. Corps. of Commissionaires Northern Alberta; Edmonton Power; Concordia College; Concordia Foundation; clubs: Mayfair Golf & Country, Edmonton Petroleum; Home: 417 Butchart Dr., Edmonton, Alta. T6R 1Z5; Office: 3716 – 93 St., Edmonton, Alta. T6E 5N3.

**KOCH, Eric Alfred,** B.A., LL.B.; writer; part-time professor; b. Frankfurt/Main Germany 31 Aug. 1919; s. Otto and Ida (Kahn) K.; e. Goethe Gymnasium 1929–35; Cranbrook Sch. 1935–37; Cambridge Univ. 1937–40; Univ. of Toronto 1942–43; m. Sonia d. Philip and Dora Mecklenburg 11 May 1948; children: Tony, Monica, Madeline; COURSE DIR., YORK UNIV.; German Section, Internat. Serv., CBC 1944–53; Prod., Extve. Prod. & Area Head 1953–71; Reg. Dir. (Montreal) 1971–77; author: 'The French Kiss' 1969, 'The Leisure Riots' 1973, 'The Last Thing You'd Want to Know' 1976, 'Good Night Little Spy' 1979, 'Deemed Suspect' 1980, 'Inside Seven Days – The Show That Shook The Nation' 1986, 'Kassandrus' (in German) 1988, 'Xananta' (in German) 1992, and two documentary films; 20 half-hour tv plays incl. 'The Ninety-Ninth Day' and co-authored (with Vincent Tovell) '1999'; recreations: violin and viola in amateur string quartets; Office: 4700 Keele St., Downsview, Ont. M3J 1P3.

**KOCZAPSKI, Andrzej Bohdan,** B.Sc., M.D., C.C.F.P. ,F.R.C.P.(C); psychiatrist; b. Torquay, England 3 Sept. 1949; s. Adam Wtadystaw and Pamela Mary (Hutt) K.; e. Chilliwack S.S. 1962; Univ. of B.C. B.Sc. 1970, M.D. 1976; Univ. of Ottawa C.C.F.P. 1978; Univ. of B.C. F.R.C.P.(C) 1992; m. Debra d. Jim and Alice Gilman 15 Sept. 1984; one d.: Karina Marie; STAFF PSYCHIATRIST, UNIVERSITY HOSP., UNIV. OF B.C. 1989– ; Musician 1970–72; Resident in Family Med., Univ. of Ottawa & Ottawa Gen. Hosp. 1976–78; medical doctor (family practice) 1978–89; active staff, Riverview Hosp. 1978–89; Chrmn., Riverview Hosp. Med. Staff Orgn. 1984–87; devel. specialized ward for assessment & treatment of severe self-induced water intoxication in patients with schizophrenia 1983–85; continued rsch. in water balance, temperature regulation & biol. rhythms in schizophrenia 1984– ; pilot project for helping severely ill hosp. schizophrenics return to community living 1987–89; clinical trials of new antipsychotic medications 1988–89; rsch. project to prevent rehosp. of persons with mood & anxiety disorders 1991–92; Resident in Psychiatry, Univ. of B.C. 1989–92; Clin. Instr., UBC, Fac. of Med.; Mem., UBC Med. Student Mentorship Prog.; awarded 1992 Laughlin Fellowship (Am. Coll. of Psychiatrists); Pres., UBC, Psychiatric Residents Assn. 1991–92; Mem., Candn. Psychiatric Assn.; Am. Psychiatric Assn.; N.W. Pacific Soc. of Neurology & Psychiatry; West Coast Coll. of Biological Psychiatry; author/co-author of several rsch. papers; recreations: music, reading, computers, outdoors; Office: Dept. of Psychiatry, Univ. of B.C., 2255 Wesbrook Mall, Vancouver, B.C. V6T 2A1.

**KOENDERMAN, Paul P.,** B.A.Sc.; business executive; b. Dordrecht, Netherlands 17 Nov. 1946; s. Paul Philip and Wilhelmina (Poppeliers) K.; e. Univ. of Waterloo, B.A.Sc. 1971; m. Suzanne d. Frank and Pearl Gillard 23 Aug. 1969; children: Aaron, Julianne; SENIOR VICE PRES., POWER GENERATION GROUP 1993– ; joined Babcock & Wilcox as student engr. 1969; Design Engr., Package Boiler Dept. 1971; Proj. Engr. 1973; Sr. Proj. Mgr. 1976; Mgr., Commercial Applications Dept. 1978; Mgr., Fossil Equipment Dept. 1980; Mgr., Mktg. & Sales 1982; Vice Pres. Mktg. & Sales 1986; Vice Pres. & Gen. Mgr., Babcock & Wilcox Internat. 1987; Vice Pres. & Gen. Mgr., Fossil Power Division 1991; Past Chrmn., Candn. Exporters Assn.; Past Chrmn., Candn. Nuclear Assn.; Dir.: USA/ROC Bus. Counc.; recreations: skiing, jogging, carpentry; Office: 20 South Van Buren, Barberton, Ohio.

**KOERNER, Michael Milan,** C.M., S.B., M.B.A.; executive; b. Prague, Czechoslovakia 26 Aug. 1928; s. Walter Charles and Marianne (Hikl) K.; e. Cheltenham (Eng.) Jr. Sch.; St. George's Sch. Vancouver; King Edward High Sch. 1945; Mass. Inst. of Technol. S.B. 1949; Harvard Grad. Sch. of Business Adm. M.B.A. 1952; m. Sonja d. Enrique Novak, Lima, Peru 18 Dec. 1951; children: Alexandra Maria, Jacqueline Laura, Michelle Diane; PRES., CANADA OVERSEAS INVESTMENTS LTD.; Sylva Investments Ltd., Vancouver; Dir., CAE Industries Ltd.; CUC Ltd.; Commercial Union of Canada Holdings Ltd.; Co-Steel Inc.; Finning Ltd.; GEAC Computer Corp. Ltd.; Helix Investments Ltd.; Huron Technologies Inc.; Morgan Bank of Canada; Pratt & Whitney Canada Inc.; Suncor Inc.; Taurus Fund Ltd.; Trustee, Canada Trust Income Investments; Asst. Mgr. of New Developments, Abitibi Power and Paper Co. Ltd. 1952–56; Investment Mgr., United North Atlantic Securities Ltd. (UNAS Investments Ltd.) 1956–59; Associate Trustee, Art Gallery of Ont. (Past Pres. 1982–84); Mem. of Corp., Mass. Inst. of Tech.; Member of the Order of Canada; Anglican; recreations: music, tennis, squash; Clubs: Badminton & Racquet; National; York; Granite; Home: 14 Ridgefield Rd., Toronto, Ont. M4N 3H8; Office: P.O. Box 130, Ste. 5010, Scotia Plaza, 40 King St. W., Toronto, Ont. M5H 3Y2.

**KOERNER, Roy Martindale,** B.A., M.A., Ph.D., P.M. & bar; research scientist; b. Portsmouth, U.K. 3 July 1932; s. Bernard William and Minnie (Martindale) K.; e. Portsmouth Southern Grammar (U.K.); Univ. of Sheffield B.A. (Hons.) 1954, M.A. 1961; London Sch. of Economics Ph.D. 1966; m. Anna d. Anna and Roman

Kowalczyk 28 Sept. 1964; children: Eva, Justin, Davina, Kristina; RESEARCH SCIENTIST, DEPT. OF ENERGY MINES & RESOURCES, GOVT. OF CANADA 1969– ; Sr. Meteorologist, Hope Bay, Antarctica with Falkland Is. Dependencies Survey 1957–60; Glaciologist, Arctic Inst. of N. Am. on Devon Is., N.W.T. 1961–62 & summers 1963, '65, '66; Rsch. Assoc., Ohio State Univ. (Antarctica) 1963–63, (E. Antarctica) 1966–67; Glaciologist, British TransArctic Expedition 1968–69 (crossed from Point Barrow, Alaska to the island near Spitsbergen via the North Pole; wintered on the Arctic Ocean); one of few people who have been to both North & South Pole; Head, Ice Core Lab.; Adjunct Prof., Geography, Carleton Univ.; Polar Medal for work in Antarctica with FIDS; bar to Polar Medal for 1st crossing of Arctic Ocean; U.S. Antarctic Serv. medal; author of over 50 sci. papers; recreations: running, nordic skiing; clubs: National Capital Runners Assn.; Home: 3369 Daoust Ave., Gloucester, Ont. K1T 1P5; Office: 601 Booth St., Ottawa, Ont. K1A 0E8.

**KOFFLER, Adam Harrison,** B.A.; hotelier; developer; b. Toronto, Ont. 20 Feb. 1959; s. Murray Bernard and Marvelle (Seligman) K.; e. Upper Can. Coll. and A.Y. Jackson Secondary Sch.; Univ. of W. Ont.; Univ. of Toronto B.A. 1980; m. Shayla Dee d. Mort and Gwen Ison 6 June 1982; children: Zachary, Logan, Quade; PRES., KING RANCH HEALTH SPA & FITNESS RESORT 1985– ; Dir. Koffler Gallery; The Koffler Centre for the Arts; Mem. Editorial Adv. Bd., Canadian Hotel & Restaurant Magazine; Founding Mem., I/SPA (International Spa Assn.); recreations: Tae Kwon Do (3rd Degree Black Belt), skiing, scuba, equestrian; Clubs: Park Jong Soo Tae Kwon Do; Craigleith; Office: R.R.2, King, Ont. L0G 1K0.

**KOFFLER, Murray Bernard;** C.M., O.Ont., Phm.B., Ph.C., Ph.D. (Hon.), LL.D. (Hon.); executive; b. Toronto, Ont. 22 Jan. 1924; s. late Leon and Tiana K.; e. Oakwood Coll.; Faculty of Pharm., Univ. of Toronto, Phm.B. 1946; m. Marvelle, d. Irving Seligman; children: Leon, Tom, Adam, Theo, Tiana; Dir., Four Seasons Hotels Ltd.; Imasco 1978; Bank Leumi 1981; Manufacturers Life Insurance Co. 1983; Pharmacist, Koffler Drug Stores (estbd. 1921), Toronto, 1946, later Prop.; Pres., Koffler Stores Ltd., 1968–71; Chrmn., Shoppers Drug Mart Ltd. 1971–86; Hon. Chrmn. 1986; Dir., Toronto Symphony until 1978; Univ. of Toronto until 1979; Co-Chrmn., Candn. Council of Christians and Jews; Dir., Mt. Sinai Hosp.; Candn. Jewish News; Un. Jewish Welfare Fund; World Wildlife Fund; Jerusalem Found.; Olympic Trust of Can.; Candn. Found. for Refugees; Hon. Chrm., Toronto Outdoor Art Show; Gov., Massey Hall; Olympic Trust; Chrmn., Weizmann Inst. of Science; Chrmn. Emeritus, Candn. Soc. for Weizmann Inst. of Science; Hon. Chrmn. and Dir., Council on Drug Abuse; Pres., Jokers Hill Horse Trials; Patron, Lester B. Pearson Coll. of Pacific; Hon. Chrmn., Candn. Council for Native Business; mem., Bd. of Trade of Metrop. Toronto; Candn., Ont. and Rokeah Pharm. Assns.; Candn. Found. for Advancement of Pharm.; Candn. Hotel Assn.; Candn. Equestrian Team; mem. Order of Can. 1977; rec. B'nai B'rith Dist. Cit. Award 1969; Ont. Soc. for Crippled Children Dist. Serv. Citation 1972; Can. Council of Christians and Jews Humanitarian Award 1974; A.H. Robins 'Bowl of Hygeia' 1976; Award of Merit, City of Toronto 1986; Candn. Retailer of the Year (Candn. Retail Counc.) 1986; Centennial Award, Ont. Med. Assoc. 1988; Candn. Business Hall of Fame 1991; Order of Ontario 1992; Pi Lambda Phi; Rho Pi Phi; recreations: skiing; sailing; golf; tennis; Clubs: Canadian; Empire; Toronto & North York Hunt; Craigleith Ski; York Tennis; Oakdale Golf & Country; Homes: 23 Beechwood Ave., Willowdale, Ont. M2L 1J2; Jokers Hill, R.R. No. 3, King, Ont. L0G 1K0.

**KOFFMAN, Moe (Morris);** musician; b. Toronto, Ont. 28 Dec. 1928; e. began studying violin at 9 and alto saxophone at 13; Toronto Conserv. of Music clarinet, theory; studied with Gordon Delamont during 1940's and during 1950's in New York with Harold Bennett (flute) and Leon Russianoff (clarinet); winner CBC 'Jazz Unlimited' poll as best alto saxophonist 1948; made first recording in Buffalo 1948; moved to USA 1950 playing in big bands of Sonny Dunham, Jimmy Dorsey and others; returned to Toronto 1955 dividing career between his jazz group and studio work; first Toronto appearance at House of Hambourg; became booking agent George's Spaghetti House 1956, and still remains in this capacity; recording of own composition 'Swinging Shepherd Blues', recently awarded BMI award for over 1 million performances logged, brought international recognition as flutist (1958); appearances in mid 1960's incl. 6 times as soloist on NBC TV 'Tonight Show'; became lead alto and featured soloist Boss Brass in 1972 and has played in Candn. orchestras led by Benny Goodman, Woody Herman and Quincy Jones at Candn. Nat. Exhn; recordings include arrangements of music by various classical composers, also 'Solar Explorations,' 'Live at George's' 1975, 'Museum Pieces' 1977, 'One Moe Time' 1986, 'Moe-Mentum' 1987, 'Oop Pop A Da' (with featured guest Dizzy Gillespie) 1988; 'Moe Koffman Plays...' 1990; 'Music For The Night' (symphonic, chamber & jazz interpretations of the music of Andrew Lloyd Webber) 1991; tours Canada and U.S.A. regularly; performed at many festivals including Expo 67, Shaw, Stratford, CBC Festival series in W. Can., Ontario Place Jazz Festival, Monterey Jazz Festival, Bracknell Festival (London, Eng.) and Montreal and Toronto Jazz Festivals; gave special performances for Her Majesty Queen Elizabeth II, for the Chancellor of West Germany, for Canadian Consul General Ken Taylor in N.Y. City and for Princess Margaret; various appearances with symphony orchestras including Toronto, Hamilton, Sudbury, London and Kitchener/Waterloo; major performances in Lewiston, N.Y. (Artpark), UCLA, Australia and S. America; performed chamber music with the Orford String Quartet; soloist with many pop recordings and has played in various jazz-oriented TV orchestras; winner of the 1981 Harold H. Moon award for outstanding contribution to Canadian music; affiliate PRO Canada; performs often with Dizzy Gillespie in both Can. & U.S. and most recently at Budapest Spring Festival 1989; toured W. Germany spring 1990; performer and contractor for many feature films; contractor for 'Phantom of the Opera' and 'Showboat' Toronto and all live Entertainment Corporation of Canada musicals; Juno Award nominee 'Instrumental Artist of the Year' 1991; recipient, Toronto Arts Award 1991; Apptd. Officer, Order of Canada 1994; recipient, 1993 Annual SOCAN awards for Songwriters in the Jazz Category; Address: c/o Swinging Shepherd Enterprises, 60 Duncannon Dr., Toronto, Ont. M5P 2M2.

**KOFSKY, Harvey,** B.Sc.Eng.; engineer, business executive; b. Montreal, Que. 14 Dec. 1942; s. Jack and Ruth (Martin) K.; e. Univ. of Toronto B.Sc.Eng. 1966; m. Sandra d. David and Doris Sonin 31 Jan. 1971; one s.: Tev Lorne Ronald; CHAIR, PRES. & CHIEF EXECUTIVE OFFICER, PROMATEK INDUSTRIES LTD. 1969– ; developed radar & assoc. devices, Candn. Marconi 1966–69; present firm designs & manufactures ergonomic video analysis & legal charge back acctg. systems; holder of 15 patents; presenter of various profl. papers; recreation: amateur radio operator; club: Manuscript Soc.; Home: 394 Dufferin Rd., Hampstead, Que. H3X 2Y7; Office: 8390 Mayrand St., Montreal, Que. H4P 2C9.

**KOGAWA, Joy Nozomi,** C.M., LL.D., D.Litt.; author; b. Vancouver, B.C. 6 June 1935; d. Gordon Goichi and Lois Masui (Yao) Nakayama; e. R. I. Baker Sch. Coaldale, Alta. 1953; Univ. of Alta. 1954; LL.D. (hon. causa) Univ. of Lethbridge 1991; Univ. of Guelph D.Litt. (hon. causa) 1992; Simon Fraser Univ. LL.D. (hon. causa) 1993; children: Gordon Kyosei, Deidre Jan; writer, Prime Min.'s Office 1974–76; Writer-in-Residence, Univ. of Ottawa 1978; author poetry: 'The Splintered Moon' 1967; 'A Choice of Dreams' 1974; 'Jericho Road' 1977; 'Woman in the Woods' 1985; novel: 'Obasan' 1981 (rec'd Books in Can. First Novel Award 1981; Candn. Authors' Assn. Book of the Yr. Award (fiction) 1982; Amer. Book Award, Before Columbus Foundation 1983; Notable Book, Amer. Library Assn. 1982; Periodical Distributors of Canada and Foundation for the Advancement of Canadian Letters award for paperback fiction 1983; publ. in U.S. and Germany; French translation 1989; instrumental in influencing the Candn. Govt.'s 1988 settlement with Japanese-Canadians for their loss of liberty and property in Canada during World War II); 'Itsuka' (a sequel to 'Obasan') 1992, U.S. 1994; children's book: 'Naomi's Road' 1986 (publ. in Canada); 'Naomi No Michi' (publ. in Japan) 1988; Member of the Order of Canada; Address: c/o Writers' Union of Canada, 24 Ryerson Ave., Toronto, Ont. M5T 2P3.

**KOKEN, Bernd Krafft;** executive; b. Munich, Germany 25 March 1926; e. Ont. Coll. of Arts 1942; ICS (Mech. Eng.) 1954; m. Marguerite Thomson; children: Kristine, Peter, Robert, Bruce, Kenneth; CHRMN., ABITIBI-PRICE INC. 1991– ; Dir.: Brunswick Corp.; David R. Webb Co. Inc.; Vice Pres. Bldg. Materials & Packaging Group Abitibi Paper Co. Ltd. 1969; Vice Pres. Lumber & Kraft Products Group 1975; Pres. Groundwood Papers & Kraft Products Div. Abitibi-Price Sales Corp. 1977, Chrmn. & C.E.O. 1978; Group Vice Pres. present Co. 1980; Exec. Vice Pres. and Chief Oper. Offr. 1982; Pres., Chief Oper. Offr. and Dir. 1983; Pres. & C.E.O. 1985; Chrmn. & C.E.O. 1987; recreations: golf, travel, art, music; Clubs: Longboat Key (Fla.); Tournament Players (Jacksonville, Fla.) The Oaks (Osprey, Fla.); Home: 916 MacEwen Dr., Osprey, Fla. 34229; Office: 207 Queen's Quay W., PO Box 102, Toronto, Ont. M5J 2P5.

**KOLACZ, Jerzy,** R.C.A.; painter, illustrator; b. Czeladz, Poland 6 Sept. 1938; s. Edward and Stanislawa (Wozniczko) K.; e. Fine Art Academy Warsaw Poland grad. 1962; m. Ewa d. Stanislaw and Anna Brudek 20 March 1990; children: Peter Kolacz, Patrycia Barszczewski (stepdaughter); OWNER, J.K. ART & DESIGN; Instructor, Art Dept., Pedagogical Inst. Szczecin 1962–67; Head Art Dir., WAG Szczecin-Wydawnictwo Artystyczno Graficzne 1967–75; spent 1 year in Sweden; emigrated to Toronto 1978; Display Designer 1978–81; pursued career in commerical illustration since 1981; works have been shown in Poland, W. Germany, Austria, Czech., Hungary, Holland, England, Denmark, Belgium, Sweden, the U.S. & Can. 1963– ; Instructor, Ont. College of Art; agent: Reactor Art & Design; recipient of num. awards & honours incl. Toronto Art Directors' Club gold & silver awards and awards of merit 1981–91, Communications Arts Award of Excellence 1984–85, Nat. Magazine Award 1979; Polish Contemporary Painting Festivals (7 awards) 1963–76; Mem., Royal Candn. Academy of the Arts; author: 'Duet' 1987, 'Paranoid Guide to Them' 1983–84; internat. pub. in all major mags. since 1981; recreations: travel; Home: 7 Valleywoods Rd., Unit 140, Don Mills, Ont. M3A 2R4; Office: 51 Camden St., Toronto, Ont. M5V 1V2.

**KOLBER, Hon. Ernest Leo,** B.A., B.C.L.; senator; b. Montreal, Que., 18 Jan. 1929; s. late Moses and Luba (Kahan) K.; (now Mrs. P. Lassar); e. Westhill (Que.) High Sch.; McGill Univ., B.A. 1949, B.C.L. 1952; m. Sandra, d. Haim Maizel, Montreal, Que., 8 Sept. 1957; children: Marna Lynne, Jonathan; CHRMN. & DIR., CINEPLEX ODEON CORPORATION; Dir., The Seagram Company Ltd.; E.I. duPont de Nemours & Co.; The Toronto-Dominion Bank; read law with Mendelsohn, Rosentzveig, Shacter & Taviss; called to Bar of Que. 1952; summoned to the Senate 1983; Gov., YM/YWHA of Montreal; United Talmud Torahs; Jewish Hosp. of Hope; Hebrew Free Loan Association; Jewish General Hospital; mem., Shaar Hashomayim Synagogue; Hebrew; recreation: golf; Clubs: Montefiore; Elm Ridge Golf & Country; Mount Royal; Mount Royal Tennis; Palm Beach Country; Home: Summit Circle, Westmount, Que.; Office: 1170 Peel St., 8th Floor, Montreal, Que. H3B 4P2.

**KOLBER, Sandra,** C.M., B.A.; writer, film consultant; b. White Plains, N.Y.; d. Haim and Stella (Kornbluth) Maizel; e. McGill Univ. B.A. 1955; m. E. Leo, now Senator Kolber 1957; children: Lynne Halliday, Jonathan; DIR., CANADIAN BROADCASTING CORP. 1990– (apptd. by Candn. Govt. Order-in-Council); Writer, Anglo-Jewish Press 1968–74; Head, Story Dept., Sagittarius Prodns. Inc. 1970–73; Cons., Candn. Film Devel. Corp. (now Telefilm Canada) 1972–79; Dir., Creative Devel., Astral Film Prodns. Ltd. 1979–83; Vice-Pres., Candn. Internat. Studios Inc. 1983–86; Dir., Cineplex Odeon Corp. 1984–90; award from Tel Aviv Univ. for Israel/Can. Co-prodn. of feature film 'Tell Me That You Love Me' 1983; Vice-Pres., Orch. symphonique de Montréal; Mem., PEN Internat.; Composers, Authors, Publishers Assn. of Can.; Acad. of Candn. Cinema & TV; author: 'Bitter Sweet Lemons and Love' 1967, 'All There Is of Love' 1968 (poetry); Apptd. Mem., Order of Canada 1993; club: Mount Royal Tennis; Home: 100 Summit Circle, Westmount, Que. H3Y 1N8; Office: 1170 Peel St., 8th floor, Montreal, Que. H3B 4P2.

**KOLHATKAR, Frank,** M.B.A., LL.B., C.A.; chartered accountant; b. Pen, India 19 May 1942; s. G.M. and S.G. K.; e. Bombay Univ. B.Comm. 1961, LL.B. 1963; Univ. of Wisconsin M.B.A. 1966; m. Rowena d. Thomas and Susanne Moore 22 Nov. 1969; children: Sheelah, Amanda; SENIOR PARTNER, DELOITTE & TOUCHE 1990– ; joined Deloitte & Touche 1969; admitted to partnership 1980; currently National Partner for Financial Institutions and Dir. of Audit, Toronto; co-author: 'Leases – Financial Analysis'; editor: 'Deloitte & Touche Financial News' (quarterly); co-editor: 'Deloitte & Touche, Computing for Executives'; recreations: tennis, cycling, travel; clubs: University, Bd. of Trade; Home: 401 Queen's Quay W., Apt. 206, Toronto, Ont.; Office: BCE Place, 181 Bay St., Toronto, Ont. M5J 2V1.

**KOLISNYK, Peter,** R.C.A.; artist; b. Toronto, Ont. 30 Nov. 1934; s. Fred and Mary (Koszlok) K.; e. Western Tech. and Comm. Sch.; m. Anne Bernadette, d. T.B. Buckley, Mimico, Ont. 20 June 1960; children: Peter, Beth; Lecturer and Dir., Art Prog., Dept. of Multi-disciplinary Studies, Glendon Hall, York Univ. 1975– ; Visiting Artist, Emily Carr Coll. of Art, Outreach Programme 1982; Artist in the Schools Programme, Ont. Arts Council 1982, 1983; Curator, Cobourg Art Gallery, 1964–69; teaching assignments: Koffler Gallery; Elliott Lake Centre for Continuing Educ.; McMaster Univ.; Rothman Art Gallery, Stratford, Ont.; Brock Univ.; Trent Univ.; Ont. Dept. Educ. Community Programmes; Glendon Coll., York Univ.; Whitby Art Gallery; exhns. incl.: Montreal Museum of Fine Art's Spring Shows; Royal Candn. Acad.; Ont. Soc. Artists; Candn. Soc. Painters Watercolour; Nat. Gallery IV Candn. Biennial; 1st Winnipeg Biennial; St. Catharines Spring Shows, Rodman Hall; Art Inst., Centennial Travelling Exhn.; Jerrold Morris Gallery, 1967; Hart House, Univ. of Toronto. 1961; Albright Knox Museum, 1968; 'A Plastic Presence,' Jewish Museum, N.Y., Milwaukee Art Centre, San Francisco Museum of Art, 1969; '3D into the 70's,' Art Gallery Ont.; 'Transparent and Translucent Art,' St. Petersburg Museum Fine Arts and Jacksonville Art Museum, Fla. 1971; '49th Parallels – New Canadian Art,' Museum Contemp. Art, Chicago, Ill. 1971; Jeunesses Musicales du Canada, Orford Arts Centre 1971; Ont. Soc. Artists – 100 Years 1872–1972; '5 Candn. Artists' Ukrainian Inst. of Mod. Art 1972; 'Plastic Fantastic' London Art Gallery 1972; Kitchener-Waterloo Art Gallery, Hamilton Art Gallery, Art Gallery Ont., 1975–76; Harbourfront Gallery, Toronto, The Gallery, Stratford, Cobourg Art Gallery, Whitby Art Gallery, Quinte Arts Council, Belleville, Queen's Silver Jubilee Exhn., Toronto, 1977; 50 years – The Canadian Society of Painters in Watercolour; 'Ontario Now – A Survey of Contemporary Art' Art Gallery of Hamilton; 'Limits, Lines, Prosections' The Gallery, Stratford; 'Rehearsal: An Exhibition of Sculpture,' Harbourfront Gallery, 1977; 'The Winnipeg Perspective,' Winnipeg Art Gallery; '4 Sculptors' The Ukrainian Inst. of Mod. Art.; 'Performance: An Exhibition of Sculpture' Harbourfront Art Gallery; Monmumental Sculpture, Toronto-Dominion Centre; Sculpture Out of Doors, Agnes Etherington Art Centre, 1978; 'Sails by Artists' Harbourfront Gallery 1979; Art Toronto '80 – Outdoor Sculpture on the Waterfront, 1980; Group Exhibitions: 'Down Under' Harbourfront Gallery 1981; First Purchase Art Gallery at Harbourfront, 1981; 'The Constructivist Heritage' Harbourfront Gallery 1981; 'White Art' Harbourfront Gallery 1981; Contemporary Outdoor Sculpture, Guildwood Hall, Toronto 1982; 'Rational Alternatives' Harbourfront Gallery 1983; 'Works on Paper' Ukrainian Inst. of Mod. Art 1983; Proposals for the Art Gallery of Peterborough National Outdoor Sculpture Competition, Peterborough, Ont. 1986; one-man exhns. incl.: Pollock Gallery, Toronto, 1965, 1968, 1969, 1970; York Univ. Glendon Coll. 1970; 'Inventory' Robert McLaughlin Gallery, Oshawa; Art Gallery of Brantford 1973; Ukrainian Inst. of Mod. Art, Chicago 1975; 'Artist with his Work' Art Gallery of Ont., Univ. of Toronto 1975; 'Peter Kolisnyk' Art Gall. of Ont., Art Gallery of Windsor, Sir George Williams Galleries, Dalhousie Art Gallery, 1977; Alta. Coll. Art Gallery, 'Artists with their works' circ. by Art Gallery of Ont., Art Gallery of Lindsay, 1980; 'Peter Kolisnyk Drawings' The Gallery, Stratford; Glendon Gallery, York Univ.; MacIntosh Gallery, Univ. of Western Ont.; The Nickle Arts Museum, Univ. of Calgary 1981–82; Kolisnyk, Extensions – Mercer Union, Toronto, Ont. 1983; Peter Kolisnyk – Art Gallery of Lindsay, Ont. 1983; The Manning Gall., Toronto 1986; Ukrainian Inst. of Modern Art, Chicago, Ill. 1987; Geraldine Davis Gall., Toronto 1992; Galerie Lallouz-Watterson-Mont. 1993; Whitby Art Gall. 1993; Blackwood Gall., Erindale Coll., Univ. of Toronto 1994; incl. in perm. colls. of Art Gallery Ont., Cobourg Art Gallery; Robert McLaughlin Gallery; Can. Council Art Bank; Ont. Council for the Arts Centennial Collection; Queen's Silver Jubilee Art Collection; Ukrainian Inst. Modern Art, Chicago; awarded comn. for 'Three Part Ground Screen' Art Gallery of Peterborough – Nat. Outdoor Sculpture Competition 1985–86; invited by the pre-selection jury, XV Olympic Winter Games, to submit medal designs for the Olympic Sport Medal and the Olympic Demonstration Sport Medal; rep. in private collections in Canada, U.S.A. and Eng., The Winnipeg Art Gallery and The Gallery Stratford; Agnes Etherington Gallery, Queen's Univ.; Art Gall. of Ont.; Art Bank Canada Council; The Robert McLaughlin Art Gall.; Ukrainian Institute of Modern Art, Chicago; Queen's Silver Jubilee Art Collection; theatre design for: 'Fortune and Men's Eyes' (Kingston); 'Creeps' (Toronto); 'The Odd Couple' (Cobourg); 'Branch Plant' (Toronto); rec'd C.S.P.W. Watercolour Award 1962; Candn. Artists '68 Sculpture Award; Ont. Soc. Artists Sculpture Award; Canada Council Senior Arts Grant, 1975–76; Province of Ont. Council for the Arts Grant. 1975–77, 1978–79, 1981–82, 1983–87; apptd. to Acquisition Comte. for the Purchase of International Contemporary Art, Art Gallery of Ont. 1980–85; Art Advisor to the Prison Arts Fdn. 1979–80; Trustee, Art Gallery of Ont. 1982; mem. Ont. Arts Counc., Ctte. for Re-evaluation of Alternate Art Schools 1984–85; Jury mem., Canada Counc. Art Bank 1984; apptd. to Jury, Art Gallery of Ont. Phase III Architectural Competition, Reconstruction Programme 1986–87; mem., Ont. Soc. Artists; Royal Candn. Acad. Arts; C.A.R.O.; Candn. Soc. Painters Watercolour.

**KOLKO, Gabriel,** B.A., M.S., Ph.D., F.R.S.C.; educator; b. Paterson, N.J. 17 Aug. 1932; s. Philip and Lillian (Zadikow) K.; e. Kent State Univ. B.A. 1954; Univ. of Wis. M.S. 1955; Harvard Univ. Ph.D. 1962; m. Joyce d. Wray and Mary Manning 11 June 1955; EMERITUS DISTINGUISHED RSCH. PROF. OF HIST. YORK UNIV. 1986– ; Prof. of Hist. 1970– ; Assoc. Prof. Univ. of Pa. 1964–68; Prof. State Univ. of N.Y. Buffalo 1968–70; recipient Transp. Hist. Prize Orgn. Am. Historians 1963; Guggenheim Found. Fellow 1966–67; Am. Council Learned Soc's Fellow 1971–72; Killam Rsch. Fellow Can. Council 1974–75, 1982–84; author 'Wealth and Power in America' 1962; ' The Triumph of Conservatism' 1963; 'Railroads and Regulation, 1877–1916' 1965; 'The Politics of War' 1969; 'The Roots of American Foreign Policy' 1969; 'Main Currents in Modern American History' 1976; 'Anatomy of a War' 1986; 'Confronting the Third World' 1988; 'War and the Shaping of the 20th Century' 1994; co-author 'The Limits of Power' 1972; recreations: hunting mushrooms, travel; Home: 305, 330 Spadina Rd., Toronto, Ont. M5R 2V9.

**KOLOSHUK, Victor,** B.Sc., M.B.A., C.F.A.; investment executive; b. Germany 27 Oct. 1945; e. McGill Univ., B.Sc. 1966, M.B.A. 1968; Univ. of Va., C.F.A. 1974; m. Dr. Shelley Rae Saunders; CHRMN., KOLOSHUK FARRUGIA CORP. 1988– ; Dir., Chateau Stores of Can. Ltd.; The Poplar Corp.; Office: P.O. Box 54, 95 Wellington St. W., Toronto, Ont. M5J 2N7.

**KOMAR, Luba,** M.D., F.R.C.P.(C), F.A.A.P.; pediatric emergency physician; b. Toronto, Ont. 5 Oct. 1958; d. Markian and Anna (Pidlashecky) K.; e. Victoria Coll., Univ. of Toronto 1977–79, Fac. of Med., Univ. of Toronto MD 1979–83; ASSISTANT PROF., DEPT. OF PEDIATRICS, DIV. OF EMERGENCY MEDICINE, HOSP. FOR SICK CHILDREN 1992– ; Rotating Internship, St. Joseph's Health Centre 1983–84; Pediatric Residency, Hosp. for Sick Children 1984–87; Pediatric Cardiology Subspecialty 1987–89; Clin. Asst., Dept. of Pediatrics 1989–92; Mem., Candn. Med. Assn.; Candn. Pediatric Soc. (CPS); Candn. Pediatric Soc., Emergency Section; Ont. Med. Assn.; Ukrainian Med. Assn.; Univ. of Toronto Fac. of Med. Chornobyl Project; Dir., Univ. of Toronto Fac. of Med. Chornobyl Project Bursary Program; Fellow, CPS; Royal College of Physicians & Surgeons; Am. Acad. of Pediatrics; Collaborator, Ukraine Environ. Health Project; Collaborator, Children's Chernobyl Project; recreations: reading, photography, hiking, canoeing, golf; Office: Emergency Dept., Hosp. for Sick Children, 555 University Ave., Toronto, Ont. M5G 1X8.

**KOME, Penney Jeffries;** writer; b. Chicago, Ill. 2 Nov. 1948; d. Hal and Jane Elizabeth (McCahan) K.; m. Robert S. (Bob) s. Marion and Sanford Pond 25 July 1987; two s.: Sanford & Graham Kome-Pond; RSCH. ASSOC., CANDN. RSCH. INST. FOR THE ADVANCEMENT OF WOMEN (CRIAW); professional writer since 1971; author: 'Somebody Has To Do It: Whose Work is Housework?' 1982, 'The Taking of Twenty-Eight' 1983, 'Women of Influence: Canadian Women & Politics' 1985, 'Every Voice Counts' 1989; co-editor: 'Peace: A Dream Unfolding' 1986; wrote 'Woman's Place' column for Homemaker's mag. 1976–88; currently Columnist, Calgary Herald and Calgary Contrib. Ed., NeWest Review; mem., Ombudsboard, Mt. Royal College newspaper 'The Reflector'; articles have appeared in journals such as Maclean's, Saturday Night, The Globe & Mail, Toronto Star, Calgary Herald, Homemaker's, Quest, Chatelaine, Financial Post Magazine, Now Magazine, This Magazine; Robertine Barry Prize 1984, CRIAW; Metro Toronto YWCA Woman of Distinction 1987 (communications); Pres. (1983–84) & Dir. (1984–85), Bain Apt. Co-op. Inc.; Charter mem., CRIAW; Periodical Writers Assn. of Can.; Ctr. for Investigative Journalism; mem., The Writers' Union of Canada; PEN Internat.; Candn. Assn. of Journalists; recreations: cycling, reading, letters-to-the-editor; Home: 2319 Uxbridge Dr. NW, Calgary, Alta. T2N 3Z7.

**KON, Jeremy O'Neill,** M.A., P.Eng.; engineering / construction executive; b. Reading, England 3 March 1940; s. Stanislaus Kazimierz and Phyllis May (Edmunds) K.; e. Bradfield College 1958; Cambridge Univ. B.A. 1962, M.A. 1965; m. Edith d. August and Olga Funk 10 July 1965; children: Janina, Martin; EXECUTIVE VICE PRESIDENT, UMA GROUP 1991– ; Designer / Project Engr. / Project Mgr. / Chief Estimator / V.P., George Wimpey & Co. 1963–69, 1972–74; Management Consultant, Urwick Currie 1970–71; Regional Mgr., UMA Spantec (div. of UMA Group) 1974, Gen. Mgr. 1977; Pres., UMA Spantec & Spantec Constructors 1980– ; Dir., UMA Group 1980– ; SoilTech Inc. 1991– ; Mem., Assn. of Profl. Engrs. (Ont.); Inst. of Civil Engineers (U.K.); recreations: skiing, tennis, swimming; club: Oakville; Home: 2090 Glenforest Cres., Oakville, Ont. L6J 2G4; Office: 5080 Commerce Blvd., Mississauga, Ont. L4W 4P2.

**KONDO, Norman H.,** B.A., LL.B.; association executive; b. Montreal, Que. 28 Sept. 1946; e. York Univ. B.A. (Hons.) 1968; Univ. of Windsor LL.B. 1976; called to Bar of Ont. 1978; EXECUTIVE DIRECTOR, CANADIAN INSOLVENCY PRACTITIONERS ASSN./ASSN. CANADIENNE DES PROFESSIONNELS DE L'INSOLVABILITÉ 1983– ; Lawyer, James, Geisler-James, Kondo (Cambridge, Ont.) 1978–79; various positions with Candn. Inst. of C.A.s 1979–83; Mem., Candn. Bar Assn.; Insol Internat.; author and editor of 'The Review' CIPA; club: Wellington; Office: 277 Wellington St. W., Toronto, Ont. M5V 3H2

**KONG, Shiu Loon,** C.M., B.A., M.Ed., Ph.D., LL.D., F.I.I.P.; psychologist; educator; b. Hong Kong 1 May 1934; s. Shiu-Ying and (Chueng) Yuk Kong; e. Wah Yan Coll. Hong Kong Dipl. 1953; Hua Kiu Univ. B.A. 1958; Univ. of Ottawa M.Ed. 1959, Ph.D. 1961; children: Lana Ann, Raymond Tao, Norman Holt; PROFESSOR EMERITUS, UNIV. OF TORONTO 1990– ; Assoc. Prof. Nanyang Univ. Singapore 1961; Tutor, Queen's Univ. 1961–62; Asst. Prof. Brandon Univ. 1962–64; Dir. Research Dept. North York Bd. Educ. 1964–67; Assoc. Prof., Univ. of Toronto 1967–72; Prof. of Educational Psych., Univ. of Toronto 1967–89; Dean and Chair Prof. Sch. of Educ., The Chinese Univ. of Hong Kong 1972–75; Pres., Ont. Adv. Counc. on Multiculturalism and Citizenship 1987–90; Pres., Multiheritage Community Alliance of Toronto; author 'Learning from Teaching' 1957; 'Summer Sixteen' 1958; 'Humanistic Psychology and Personalized Teaching' 1970; 'Cognitive Processes Applied to Education' 1973; 'An English-Chinese Glossary of Social Sciences and Education' 1975; 'The Foundation of Modern Mathematics' 1975, 2nd ed. 1979; 'Psychological Considerations in Personalized Teaching' 1979; co-ed. 'Unity Within Diversity' 1978; 'The Development of American Secondary and Higher Education' 1980; 'Psychology for Teaching and Caring' 1982; 'Fables and Legends From Ancient China' 1985; 'Korean Folk Tales' 1986; 'The Magic Pears' 1986; 'Multicultural Education, Programmes and Method' 1986; 'Chinese Culture and Lore' 1989; recreations: painting, swimming, music appreciation; Home: 52 Granby St., Toronto, Ont. M5B 2J5.

**KONKEL, Kazimierz Gerard Edward,** B.A., M.A.; novelist; police officer; b. Rotterdam, Netherlands 27 Aug. 1950; s. Edward and Anna (Van Zelst) K.; e. Univ. of Waterloo, B.A. (Hons.) 1972, M.A. (Internat. Relns.) 1973; m. Robin d. Roy and Margaret Devine 17 Feb. 1979; one d.: Laura Grace; STAFF SGT., METROPOLITAN TORONTO POLICE FORCE 1976– ; Insp. of Police, Royal Hong Kong Police Force 1974–76; Internat. Expert (Oriental Crime); Lectr., Candn. Police Coll., Ont. Police Coll.; regular panelist, 'Life-Time' (CTV talk show); has rec'd several awards for police bravery; author 'The Glorious East Wind' (novel) 1987 and numerous profl. papers and reviews; Fellow, Royal Soc. of Arts and Letters 1989; Hon. Life Mem., The Hamilton Club 1989; mem. Imperial Offrs. Assn. of Can.; Internat. Police Assn.; Candn. Comprehensive Auditing Found.; Empire Club of Can.; R. Catholic.

**KOOLURIS DOBBS, Linda Kia,** A.A., B.F.A.; artist; b. Orange, NJ 28 Jan. 1949; e. Pine Manor Coll. A.A. 1968; Sorbonne and Academic Year Abroad Program 1968–69 (private studies with Nicolas Manev); Sch. of Visual Arts B.F.A. (Hons.) 1972 (studied with William T. Williams, Marshall Arisman, Paul Spina, Gerry Moriarty, Gilbert Stone); m. Kildare Dobbs 7 May 1981; several college teaching positions 1975–93; 40 exhibitions incl. most recent: Gallery Sheila Roth Toronto, Newbury Fine Arts, Boston & Edgartown, Mass., Prior Editions, Vancouver, London Regional Art Gallery 1992, '93, Art Gallery of Hamilton, Toronto Watercolour Soc. Vancouver Maritime Museum 1992; works included in over 79 collections in Canada and over 33 in other countries; Annual Art Purchase Prize, Pine Manor Coll. 1968; 2nd Prize (Paintings), Financial Post Annual Reports Awards 1981; Mem., Heliconian Club 1984– ;

selected for Ont. Living Magazine 'Gallery' 1985; chosen for two covers featuring living painters in Can., Can. Med. Assn. Journal 1985; 'Creative Decade' Merit Award 1986; Perm. Mem., Toronto Watercolour Soc. and Hon. Mention, Annual Fall Show 1991; featured in 'Applied Arts Magazine' Feb./March 1993 issue; most recent portrait commissions: Mr. Gerald Turner, Retiring Pres. of Mt. Sinai Hosp. Toronto; Mr. Eddie Goodman, Founder of Goodman & Goodman Law Firm; Dr. William Callahan, Founder of the Eye Research Inst. of Can.; Mrs. A. Tanenbaum, Mother of Joseph Tanenbaum; Address: 330 Spadina Rd., Ste. 1005, Toronto, Ont. M5R 2V9.

**KOPELCHUK, Honourable Lorne Allan,** M.L.A.; politician; b. Canora, Sask. 4 Aug. 1938; s. Steve Phillip and Susie (Procyshen) K.; e. Coll. of Commerce, Univ. of Sask.; m. Doris d. George and Marguerite Samuel 9 Aug. 1961; children: Karen, Kathryn, Karolyn, Kristen; M.L.A., Canora, Min. of Parks & Renewable Resources, Govt. of Sask. 1986; Alderman, Town of Canora 1964–68; Mayor 1980–85; Mem., Canora C. of C.; Canora Kiwanis Club; Canora Masonic Lodge; St. Andrew's Un. Ch.; Canora Agric. Soc.; Home: Box 927, Canora, Sask. S0A 0L0.

**KOPSTEIN, His Hon. Robert Lionel,** B.A., LL.B.; judge; b. Winnipeg, Man. 5 Aug. 1932; s. Maxwell Eul and Sylvia (Danzker) K.; e. B.A., 1955, LL.B. 1958; m. Jean d. Leo and Freda Robin 23 June 1954; children: Ivy Faye, Ruth Leanne, Alan Neil; JUDGE, PROV. COURT OF MAN. 1971– ; called to Bar 1958; law prac., Kopstein, Kimelman & Kopstein 1958–71; employed by Man. Govt. to draft legisl. & reguls. for auto. insur. plan 1971; apptd. Commissioner to review auto insurance plan (report publ.) 1988; apptd. Chair Man. Workers' Compensation Bd. 1989–92; Past Mem., City of Winnipeg, Charities Endorsement Bureau; Past Bd. Mem., Winnipeg Hebrew Sch.; I.L. Peretz Folk Sch. (Chrmn., Bd. of Edn.); Jewish Hist. Soc.; Shaarey Zedek Synagogue; Past Pres., Redboine Lions Club; Past Pres., Man. Prov. Judges Assn.; author of several pub. judgments; recreations: reading, photography; Home: 38 Lancaster Blvd., Winnipeg, Man.; Office: Judges Chambers, 408 York Ave., Winnipeg, Man. R3C 0P9.

**KORBA, Larry W.,** M.A.Sc., P.Eng.; senior research officer; b. Winnipeg, Man. 7 June 1950; s. Alphons and Jean (Luby) K.; e. Univ. of Man., B.A.Sc. EE 1973; Univ. of Toronto, M.A.Sc. EE 1977; m. Anne Marie d. Shaun and Merna Mayne 27 May 1978; one d.: Sarah Louise; RSCH. OFFR., NAT. RESEARCH COUNCIL, MED. ENGR. SECTION 1980– ; Telecommun. Engr., CP Telecommunications 1973; Test Engr., IBM Canada 1973–75; FBM Can. 1977–78; Design Engr., IBM Can. Laboratory 1978–80; thesis advr. for 4th yr. Carleton Univ. electr. engr. students; Mentor, Coop. Edn. Prog., Carleton Bd. of Edn.; mem., Inst. for Electrical & Electronic Engrs.; mem., Assn. of Profl. Engrs. of Ont.; Rehab. Engr. Soc. of N. Am. (Chair, Robotics Group 1990–91); editor: 'International Inventory of Robotics Projects in the Healthcare Field' 1989; author/co-author over 80 sci. & tech. papers; Home: 11 Lakeside Ave., Ottawa, Ont. K1S 3H1; Office: National Research Council of Canada, Inst. for Inform. Tech., Room 318a, Bldg. M-50, Montreal Rd., Ottawa, Ont. K1A 0R6.

**KORDAN, Bohdan Stephan,** B.A., M.A., Ph.D.; university professor; b. Toronto, Ont. 8 Apr. 1955; s. Andrij and Fenna (Kapeluch) K.; e. Univ. of Toronto, B.A. (Hons.) 1977; Carleton Univ., M.A. 1981; Arizona State Univ., Ph.D. 1988; SR. LECTURER, GRANT MACEWAN COLL. 1988– ; Rsch. Assoc. & Visiting Asst. Prof., Univ. of Alta. 1982–85; Neporany post-doct. fellow 1987–88; Fellow, Chair of Ukrainian Studies 1985– ; Research Fellow, Univ. of Alta. 1989– ; Visiting Prof., Erindale College, Univ. of Toronto 1991–92; Fellow, Institute of Internat. Relations and World Economy, Kiev, Ukraine 1992– ; Ed. Bd., 'Journal of Contemporary Political Thought' 1992– ; 'Journal of Ukrainian Studies' 1985–89; author: 'Ukrainians in Canada and the 1981 Census' 1985, 'XVII and XVIII Century Maps of Ukraine' 1985; 'A Delicate and Difficult Question' 1986, 'Land of the Cossacks' 1987, 'Anglo-American Perspectives on the Ukrainian Question' 1987, 'The Famine and the Foreign Office' 1988, 'On Guard for Thee' 1988, 'Creating a Landscape' 1989; 'In the Shadow of the Rockies' 1991.

**KORDYBACK, Michael R.,** B.A., C.A.; business executive; b. Edmonton, Alta. 23 July 1948; s. Albert and Franchea (Maguire) K.; e. York Univ. B.A. 1970; C.A. 1975; m. Frances d. Francis and Ann Young 21 July 1988; children: Eve Kathleen, Clare Maguire; EXECUTIVE VICE-PRES., STRATEGY, FINANCE & DEVELOPMENT, JANNOCK LIMITED 1994– ; joined Thorne, Ernst & Whinney 1972–78; Price Waterhouse 1977–78; Asst. Treas. becoming Treas. Crownx 1978–80; Treas. 1980, Vice Pres. Finance 1983, Sr. Vice Pres. and Chief Financial Offr. 1987; Exec. Vice Pres. and Dir., Unicorp Canada Corp. 1988–90; Sr. Vice Pres., Scotts Hospitality Inc. 1990–93; Club: Cambridge; Home: 310 Inglewood Dr., Toronto, Ont. M4T 1J5.

**KOREY-KRZECZOWSKI, George,** D.Sc.Econ., LL.M., LL.D., C.M.C., F.R.E.S.; college administrator; b. Kielce, Poland 13 July 1921; s. Antoni-Marian Kniaz, Judge of the Castle Court and Zofia Emilia Wanda (Chmielewska) Korczak-Krzeczowski; e. State High Sch. and State Coll., Kielce, Poland; Dept. of Law and Adm., Jagellonian Univ., Cracow, Poland, LL.M. 1945; Post Grad. studies at Acad. of Pol. and Social Science, Warsaw, Poland; Dept. of Internat. Law, Univ. of Bucharest, Rumania; Inst. of Internat. Law, and Dept. of Law and Pol. Science, Univ. of Fribourg, W. Germany, LL.D. 1949; Dept. of Econ. Science, Univ. of Tuebingen, W. Germany, D.Sc. (Econ.) 1950; grad. Inst. of Educat. Mgmt., Harvard Univ. 1975; 6 hon. doctorates; m. Irene Marie, d. Wladyslaw Latacz, 15 July 1944; one s. Andrew George; PRES., CANDN. SCH. OF MANAGEMENT AND HONORARY CHANCELLOR, NORTHLAND OPEN UNIVERSITY; Grand Master, Sovereign Order of the St. John of Jerusalem; Distinguished International Prof. of Strategic Mgmt., International Mgmt. Centre, Buckingham, Eng.; Distinguished Visiting Prof. of Business Admin., Florida Atlantic Univ.; Prof., Polish Univ. (London, Eng.); Adj. Prof. and Trustee, Union Grad. Sch. (Cincinnati, Ohio); Pres., Univ. Without Walls Internat. Council; formerly Actg. Pres., Exec. Vice Pres. and Dean of Business, Ryerson Polytechnical Inst., 1971–77; former Chrmn., Ont. Adv. Council on Multiculturalism; Vice-Pres. and Dir. York-Ryerson Computing Centre; Pres., Ryerson Applied Rsch. Ltd.; Pres., Korey International Ltd., Toronto; Dir., Candn. Operations, Canadian Textile Consultants Ltd.; Dir., Werner Management Consultants (Canada) Ltd.; Dir. of Dept. Min. of Culture and Arts, Poland 1945; Vice-Pres., Council of Arts and Sciences, Kielce, Poland 1945; Press Attaché, Polish Embassy, Bucharest, Rumania; Vice-Consul of Poland; Cultural Counsellor of Embassy 1946; Dir. and Prof. of Polish Inst., Bucharest; Consul of Poland in Bucharest, Rumania; Econ. Adv. of Embassy; Counsellor, Min. of Foreign Affairs, Warsaw, Poland 1947; Consul of Poland in Berlin, Germany; Consul of Poland in Baden-Baden, W. Germany 1948–50; Head of Econ. and Restitution Mission 1949–50; in these capacities often took part in internat. negotiations; resigned diplomatic career for pol. reasons and came to Can. 1951; Assistant Supervisor, Indust. Engn. Dept and Contract Estimating Dept. Canadair Ltd.; Asst. Mang. Dir. and Controller, Damar Products of Canada Ltd. and Around-the-World Shoppers Club (Canada) Ltd.; Vice-Pres. and Mang. Dir., Schlemm Assoc. Ltd., Mgmt. Consultant on own account; Pres., Pan-American Mgmt. Ltd.; apptd. Dean of Business and Vice-Pres., Ryerson Polytech. Inst. 1971, Extve. Vice-Pres. and Dean, External Programmes 1973–77; Acting Pres. 1974; publications: 'Siedemnasta Wiosna' 1938; 'Rytm Serca' 1938; 'Goloborze' 1939; 'Pamietnik Poetycki' 1939; 'Internationale Rechtsverhaeltnisse Polens Im Gebiete des Strafrechts' 1949; 'Plannung in der Polnischen Landwirtschaft' 1950; 'Liryki Nostalgiczne' 1974; 'Lunch w Sodomie' 1976; 'Korey's Stubborn Thoughts' 1980; 'New Role for the Canadian Economy in the Age of World Food Shortage' 1975; 'Attitudes in the Business and Health Care sectors towards Nontraditional Management Education' 1980; 'University Without Walls' 1981; 'Tree of Life' 1982; 'Alternative Tourism' 1984; 'Managerial Futuristics' 1985; 'Wszedzie i Nigdzie' poems, Eds. Dembinski Paris 1990; numerous articles on mang., econ. planning, internat. affairs, foreign markets, and marketing; publ. a series on European Common Market and Canada's Econ. Policies in 'Industrial Canada' and 'Canadian Textile Journal'; a market mgmt. series in 'Marketing'; mgmt. consulting series in 'Canadian Textile Journal'; Guest Lectr. on radio and T.V. talks and interviews; has had mgmt. consulting experience in over 50 countries in many types of industries; Fellow, Royal Econ. Soc.; Candn. Inst. of Certified Admin. Mgrs. (F.C.A.M.); Acad. Marketing Sc. (U.S.A.); Bailie, Grand Cross of Justice, Sovereign Order of St. John of Jerusalem; Knight, Military Constantinian Order of St. George; Knight-Commander, Sovereign Order of Cyprus; Kt. Grand Cross, Military Order of St. Agatha di Paterno; Kt. Commander, Order of St. Ladislas (Free Hungarian); decorated with the Cross of Polish Home Army (1939–45), awarded Polish Military Medal for W.W.II; Polish Gold Cross of Merit; Queen's Jubilee Medal; Interallied Distinguished Service Cross; Royal Yugoslav Croix de Guerre; Croix de la Victoire; Allied Cross; Knight, Guard of Honour, Apostolic Throne (Patriarch of Alexandria); European Combattants Cross; Gold Medal, Candn. Polish Congress; mem. Inst. Mang. Consultants Que. and Ont.; Fellow N.Y. Acad. Sc.; Fellow, Royal Society of Arts; Companion, British Inst. of Mgmt.; Pres. & Fellow, Can. Inter. Acad. of Humanities and Social Sc.; Am. Mgmt. Assn.; Acad. of Mang. U.S.A.; Inter-Am. Rsch. Inst.; Acad. Internat. Business; Candn. Council for Internat. Co-op (Dir.); Candn. Inst. Public Affairs; European Foundation Mgmt. Devel.; Internat. Inventors Assn.; Polish Inst. (U.K.); mem. several other assns. and comtes.; Pres. (1966) Nat. Council, Candn. Polish Cong.; mem., Nat. Counc. of Poland (in exile); Companion, Internat. Soc. of Hereditary Nobility; Mem., Soc. of Descendants of the Latin Kingdom of Jerusalem; World Council of Poles (1978–81); Hon. Citizen, City of Winnipeg and Miami Beach; Roman Catholic; Home: 55 Tanbark Cres., Don Mills, Ont. M3B 1N7.

**KORHONEN, Edwin John,** B.Sc.; food industry executive; b. Sudbury, Ont. 23 May 1935; s. Aku and Irja (Pulkinnen) K.; e. Queen's Univ. B.Sc. (E.E.) 1957; m. Gail d. Thomas and Isobel Buchanan 3 June 1961; children: Bruce, Kristen; Pres., Maple Leaf Mills 1989; joined Allen-Bradley Canada Ltd. 1957–63; Campbell Soup Co. Ltd. 1963–73, various assignments U.S. and Can., Pres. Candn. Operations 1973–77; Nabisco Brands Ltd. 1977–89, Pres. Confectionery, Ind. Products & Grocery Divs.; Gov. Queensway Gen. Hosp.; Candn. Nat. Millers Assn. (Dir.); recreations: golf, skiing, jogging; Clubs: Mississauga Golf; Craigleith Ski; Cambridge; Home: 2206 Pineneedle Row, Mississauga, Ont. L5C 1V3.

**KORMAN, Gordon Richard,** B.F.A.; writer; b. Montreal, Que. 23 Oct. 1963; s. Charles Isaac and Bernice (Silverman) K.; e. Thornlea S.S. 1981; New York Univ., B.F.A. 1985; began writing at age 12 as grade 7 English project; 30-year-old author of 19 best selling novels aimed at juvenile & young adults; worldwide sales over 4½ million in several languages & eds.; public speaker at numerous schs., libraries, confs., etc., Can. & U.S.; Air Canada Literature Award 1981; Ont. Youth Medal 1985; Town of Markham Civic Award for Cultural Achievement 1987; Internat. Reading Assoc. Children's Choice Award ('I Want To Go Home') 1986; Am. Lib. Assoc. Best Book List ('Son of Interflux') 1987; Internat. Reading Assoc. Children's Choice Award ('Our Man Weston') 1987; ALA Best Book List ('A Semester in the Life of a Garbage Bag') 1988, ('Losing Joe's Place') 1990; Junior Library Guild selection - 'The Twinkie Squad'; Mem., The Writers Union of Can.; Candn. Authors' Assn.; CANSCAIP; The Soc. of Childrens Book Writers; ACTRA; author: 'This Can't Be Happening at Macdonald Hall' 1978, 'Go Jump in the Pool' 1979, 'Beware the Fish' 1980, 'Who is Bugs Potter?' 1980, 'I Want To Go Home' 1981, 'Our Man Weston' 1982, 'The War With Mr. Wizzle,' 1982, 'Bugs Potter LIVE at Nickaninny' 1983, 'No Coins Please' 1984, 'Don't Care High' 1985, 'Son of Interflux' 1986, 'A Semester in the Life of a Garbage Bag' 1987; 'The Zucchini Warriors' 1988; 'Radio Fifth Grade' 1989; 'Losing Joe's Place' 1990; 'Macdonald Hall Goes Hollywood' 1991; 'The Twinkie Squad' 1992; (with Bernice Korman) 'The D-Minus Poems of Jeremy Bloom' 1992; 'The Toilet Paper Tigers' 1993; contbr. to num. mags. & newspapers; recreations: travel, music, sports; Home: 20 Dersingham Cres., Thornhill, Ont. L3T 4E7.

**KORN, David Ashley,** M.D.; public health physician; b. Toronto, Ont. 26 1942; s. Stanley Philip and Betty (Goodman) K.; e. Univ. of W. Ont. M.D. 1967; London (Eng.) Sch. of Hygiene & Tropical Med. D.T.M.&H. 1971, D.T.P.H. (Distinction) 1975; Amer. Acad. of Health Care Providers in Addictive Disorders, Certified Addiction Specialist (C.A.S.) 1990; m. Laura d. Ralph and Barbara Palmer 24 Oct. 1981; one d. Ashley Rebecca; one s. Zachary Morgan; PRES. & C.E.O., THE DONWOOD INST. 1987– ; Asst. Prof. in Preventive Med. & Biostats. Univ. of Toronto 1983– ; Family Phys. Toronto 1968–69; Govt. Med. Offr. (Clin.) Repub. of Zambia 1971–74; Cons. Epidemiol. Smallpox Eradication Prog. World Health Orgn. Ethiopia 1975–76; Asst. Prof. of Preventive Med. Dept. Environmental Health Univ. of Cincinnati Coll. of Med. 1976–77; Med. Offr. of Health and Exec. Offr. Simcoe Co. Dist. Health Unit, Midhurst, Ont. 1978–83; Chief Med. Offr. of Health, Ont. 1983–87; mem. Ont. Interministerial Ctte. Pollutants & Health (Chrmn. 1984–85); mem. Fed./Prov. Adv. Ctte. on Occupational & Environmental Health 1985–87; mem. Metro Toronto YMCA, Health Adv. Ctte. 1985– ; Mem., Admin. Ctte., Doctors on Chemicals Program, Coll. of Physicians and Surgeons of Ont. 1986–93; mem., Min. of Health's Panel on Health Goals for Ont. (Spasoff Report) 1987; mem., Candn. Bar Assoc's Working Group on Mandatory Drug Testing 1987; Mem., Bd. of Govs., Metro Toronto YMCA 1985–92;

Candn. Cancer Soc., Ont. Div., Public Issues Ctte. 1988–91; Co-founder, OPTIMA, a Candn. group dedicated to personal and community well-being 1987; The Toronto Mayor's Task Force on Drugs 1991–93; Adv. Council, Addictions & Rehab. Dept., The Salvation Army Harbour Light, Toronto 1989– ; Mem. Internat. Adv. Bd., Am. Acad. of Health Care Providers in the Addictive Disorders 1991– ; Editorial Adv. Bd. 'Wellness MD' 1992– ; recipient Recognition Award Twp. of Medonte for role in CPR Derailment & fire 1982; Order of Bifurcated Needle, World Health Orgn. for work Global Smallpox Eradication Prog. 1976; Fellow, Royal Society of Tropical Medicine & Hygiene 1975; author or co-author numerous articles, reports, papers; mem. Ont., Candn. & Am. Pub. Health Assns.; Candn. Soc. for Internat. Health; Nat. Assn. Pub. Health Policy; Am. Coll. of Preventive Med.; Candn. Medical Soc. on Alcohol and Other Drugs; Am. Soc. of Addiction Medicine; Amnesty Internat.; Candn. Physicians for the Prevention of Nuclear War; Ont. Track & Field Assn.; Scarborough YMCA; recreations: long distance running, jazz, travel, canoeing; Home: 290 Forman Ave., Toronto, Ont. M4S 2S7; Office: The Donwood Inst., 175 Brentcliffe Rd., Toronto, Ont. M4G 3Z1.

**KORNBLUM, Warren F.;** communications executive; b. Toronto, Ont. 27 Aug. 1952; s. Philip and Shirley (Pollock) K.; m. Tricia d. Grant and Evelyn Barron 15 Feb. 1987; CHRMN., C.E.O. & EXTVE. CREATIVE DIR., KORNBLUM INTERNAT. 1986– ; Partner, KWT Worldwide, Coconut Grove, Florida; began as Acct. Exec. 1973, then became Exec. Asst. to Chrmn. of an American advert. agency; Pres. & C.E.O., Gray O'Rourke Sussman Internat. 1981–86; has spoken extensively throughout world on both retail mktg. and advertising creativity; voted Toronto Man of Style 1987; Mem. Nat. Retail Merchants Assoc.; Retail Counc. of Can.; Dir., Sportsnacks Holdings; WFK Racing Stables; Westwood Pictures Inc.; Nat. Co-Chrmn., Starlight Foundation (also Internat. Bd. Mem.; Internat. Extve. Cttee. Mem.); Screenwriter; Awards incl. Internat. Clio Finalist; Marketing Awards; Bessie Awards; recreations: yachting, photography, creative writing, travel; Office: Kornblum Internat. Bldg., 64 Merton St., Toronto, Ont. M4S 1A1.

**KORNELSEN, Ernest Victor,** B.Sc., M.Sc., Ph.D.; physicist; b. Swift Current, Sask. 2 Oct. 1930; s. Henry H. and Minna (Ewert) K.; e. Univ. of Sask. B.Sc. 1952, M.Sc. 1953; McGill Univ. Ph.D. 1957; m. June Y. Girvan 18 May 1987; PHYSICIST, INSTITUTE FOR MICROSTRUCTURAL SCIENCES, NATIONAL RESEARCH COUNCIL 1957– ; early work on vacuum technology & surface science; since 1985 semiconductor materials, fabrication & electronic devices; co-author: 'The Physical Basis of Ultrahigh Vacuum' 1968; Home: 333 Besserer St., Ottawa, Ont. K1N 6B4; Office: Bldg. M-50, Montreal Rd., Ottawa, Ont. K1A 0R6.

**KORNELUK, Robert George,** B.Sc., M.Sc., Ph.D., F.C.C.M.G.; university professor, biomedical researcher; b. Sault Ste. Marie, Ont. 3 Nov. 1950; s. Ihor and Katherine (Katynsky) K.; e. Bawating H.S. 1969; Univ. of Toronto B.Sc. (Hons.) 1973, M.Sc. 1976, Ph.D. 1982; m. Margo d. Gerald and Ruby Clowes 27 Dec. 1969; children: Yolanda, Paul; DIRECTOR OF MOLECULAR GENETICS, RESEARCH INST. CHILDREN'S HOSP. OF EASTERN ONT. 1985– ; MRC Post-doct. Fellow, Genetics, Research Inst., Hospital for Sick Children 1982–85; Asst. Prof., Paediatrics and Microbiology & Immunology depts., Univ. of Ottawa 1986–90; Assoc. Prof. 1990– ; Ottawa Lab. Chief, Ikeda Genosphere Project, Japan Research & Devel. Corp./Univ. of Ottawa; Fellow, Candn. Coll. of Med. Geneticists (F.C.C.M.G.); scientific achievements: identificaiton of genetic defect causing myotonic dystrophy 6 Feb. 1992; ident. of myotonic dystrophy gene 6 Mar. 1992; signing of collaborative agreement between Dr. Korneluk & Dr. Ikeda (Univ. of Ottawa & Japan Rsch. & Devel. Corp.) 24 Mar. 1992; recipient of several research grants; member of several cttes.; author of 55 sci. papers & 63 sci. abstracts; recreations: hockey, baseball, guitar playing; Home: 1901 Tweed Ave., Ottawa, Ont. K1G 2L8; Office: 401 Smyth Rd., Box 8010, Ottawa, Ont. K1H 8L1.

**KORTHALS, Robert W.,** B.Sc., M.B.A.; banker; b. 7 June 1933; e. Univ. of Toronto B.Sc. (Chem. Engn.) 1955; Harvard Business Sch. M.B.A. 1961; PRES., TORONTO DOMINION BANK 1981– ; Chrmn., TD Trust Company; Dir., TD Mortgage Corp.; Toronto Dominion Bank; Hayes-Dana Inc.; Co-Steel Inc.; Jannock Ltd.; Supt., Gen. Mgr. of Nat. Accts. Div. 1972, Vice Pres. Adm. 1972, Extve. Vice Pres. and Chief Gen. Mgr. 1978; Gov., Central Hosp. Toronto; mem., Ontario Business Advisory Council; Office: P.O. Box 1, Toronto Dominion Centre, Toronto, Ont. M5K 1A2.

**KOSHAL, Arvind,** M.B.B.S., M.S., FRCSC(Gen. Surg.), FRCSC(CVT); b. London, England 13 May 1948; s. Krishan Dev and Surya Kanta (Sondhi) K.; e. Christ Ch. Boys H.S. 1964; Ravishankar Univ. M.B.B.S. 1971 (Five gold medals 1970 and Pfizer post-grad. Med. Award & Gold Med. in Med. 1970); All India Inst. of Med. Sci., M.S. 1975 (gold medallist); Univ. of Ottawa, FRCSC(Gen. Surg.) 1978, (Cardiac Surg.) 1979; m. Arti d. Tejbhan and Indira Malhotra 25 Nov. 1974; children: Arjun, Anurag, Amit; Director and Surgeon-in-chief, Division of Cardiovascular and Thoracic Surgery; Clinical Prof., Univ. of Alberta Hospitals, Edmonton 1991– ; Surgical Co-ordinator, Univ. of Ottawa Heart Inst. Cardiac Transplant Prog. 1984–91; Chief Admin. Res. in Surg., Univ. of Ottawa 1976–77; Sr. Res., Cardiovascular & Thoracic Surg. 1977–79; Candn. Heart Found. Rsch. Fellow, Harvard Med. Ctr. 1979–80; Lectr., Univ. of Ottawa 1980–82; Asst. Prof. 1982–86; Assoc. Prof. Cardiothoracic Surg. 1986–91; Prog. Dir., Cardio. & Thor. Surg. 1986–91; Courtesy Staff, Childrens Hosp. of E. Ont. 1986–91; Fellow, Royal Coll. of Phys. & Surg. of Can.; Am. Coll. of Cardiol.; Am. Coll. of Chest Phys.; Mem., Candn. Cardio. Soc.; author of num. med. articles; recreations: tennis, chess; Home: 85 Westbrook Dr., Edmonton, Alta. T6J 2C8; Office: Walter MacKenzie Centre, 8440 – 112 Street, Edmonton, Alta. T6G 2B7.

**KOSIANCIC, John M.,** B.Sc., C.L.U.; insurance executive; b. Nelson, B.C. 27 Dec. 1937; s. Joseph and Josephine (Schiavon) K; e. Michigan Tech. Univ. B.Sc. 1960; m. Elizabeth M. d. James and Margaret Byrne 9 Feb. 1963; children: Michael, Paul, Elizabeth Ann; PRES., C.E.O. & DIR., COLONIA LIFE INS. CO., TORONTO 1984– ; Pres. and Dir. Colonia Life Holdings Ltd. 1984– ; profl. hockey player 1960–63; Mgmt. Trainee Manufacturers Life Ins. Co. 1963, Br. Mgr. Calgary 1967, Br. Mgr. Hamilton 1971, Dir. of Agy. 1973, Agy. Vice-Pres. 1973, Vice-Pres. Candn. and Internat. Mktg. 1977, Vice-Pres. Candn. and Caribbean Div. 1982; Past Dir., Life Ins. Mktg. and Rsch. Assoc.; Past Dir., Candn. Life and Health Insurance Assoc. Inc.; past Chrmn. various Life Ins. Ind. Cttes.; recreations: tennis, skiing, hockey; Home: 4010 Lantern Lane, Burlington, Ont. L7L 5Z2; Office: 2 St. Clair Ave. E., Toronto, Ont. M4T 2V6.

**KOSICH, George John,** B.Comm.; business executive; b. Vancouver, B.C. 3 Aug. 1934; s. John and Mary (Tomasevich) K.; e. Univ. of B.C., B.Comm.; m. Joan d. William and Barbara Gray Dec. 1957; children: William, Georgina Ann, John, Barbara Ann, Robert; PRES. AND CHIEF EXEC. OFFR., HUDSON'S BAY CO. 1990– ; Trainee present Co. Vancouver 1960, Divisional Merchandise Mgr., Victoria Store; Store Mgr., Victoria Store; Gen. Merchandise Mgr., Calgary Store; Gen. Mgr., Calgary Region; Gen. Mgr., Toronto Region; joined Simpsons Ltd. as Vice-Pres. Store Opns., subsequently apptd. Pres.; Exec. Vice Pres. and Dir. present co. 1985; Pres. & C.O.O. 1987–90; Pres. & C.E.O. 1990– ; recreations: skiing, golf, hunting; Office: 401 Bay St., Toronto, Ont. M5H 2Y4.

**KOSISKI, Leszek Antoni,** M.A., Ph.D.; university professor; b. Warszawa, Poland 13 June 1929; s. Jakub and Emilia (Opacka) K.; e. Univ. of Warsaw M.A. 1954; Polish Acad. of Sciences Ph.D. 1958; m. Marytka d. Antoni and Wanda Bodakiewicz 1951; PROF., GEOGRAPHY, UNIV. OF ALBERTA 1969– ; Researcher, Inst. of Town Planning and Arch. (Warsaw) 1951–54; Inst. of Geog., Polish Acad. of Sciences 1954–68; Visiting Prof., Queen's Univ. 1968; Univ. of Warsaw 1956–68; Univ. of Calif. at Berkeley 1962; Indiana Univ. 1962; Univ. of Minnesota 1967; Northwestern Univ. 1968; Pennsylvania State Univ. 1968; Univ. of Washington 1971; Univ. of Liverpool 1981; Autonomous Univ. of Mexico 1981; Univ. of Guadalajara 1985; Cons., Inst. for Rsch. on Public Policy; Statistics Canada; Internat. Fed. of Documentation (the Hague); U.N. Fund for Population Activities (N.Y.); Attorney Gen. Alta.; Employment & Immigration Can.; Internat. Orgn. for Migration (Geneva); Ctte. for Internat. Coop. in Nat. Rsch. in Demography (Paris); Alta. Advanced Edn. and Manpower; Price Waterhouse (Ottawa); Inst. für Wissenschaften von Menschen (Vienna); External Examinor/Assessor, univs. of Malaya, Karachi, Bar Illam, Yaoundé, Jahangirnagar, Manitoba, Lethbridge, New Univ. of Ulster, Australia Nat. Univ., Memorial Univ. of Nfld., Tirupati, India, Makarere, Uganda; Hon. Mem., Soc. de Géog. (France) 1989; Polish Geog. Soc. 1990; Corresp. Mem., Akad. für Raumforschung und Landesplanung 1982; Soc. Geog. Italiana 1989; Medal, S. African Geog. Soc. 1987; Fellow, Royal Soc. of Can. 1991; Bd. Mem., Candn. Global Change Prog. 1991–94; Extve. Ctte., Internat. Human Dimensions of the Global Envir. Change Prog. 1991– ; Sec.-Gen. & Treas., Internat. Geog. Union 1984–92; Extve. Mem., Int. Soc. Sci. Council 1986–90; Mem., Union for Sci. Study of Population 1967– ; Eur. Assn. for Population Studies 1984– ; Assn. internat. des démographes de langue française 1998– ; Assn. Am. Geog. 1967– ; Population Assn. of Am. 1967– ; Candn. Assn. of Geog. 1968– ; Candn. Assn. of Slavists 1967– (Bd. Mem. 1976–78); Candn. Population Soc. 1974– (Vice-Pres. 1982–84; Pres. 1984–86); Cand. Fed. of Demographers (Bd. Mem. 1986–90); author of over 20 books and over 100 reports & articles pub. in 21 countries in 12 languages; recreations: skiing, photography, reading; Home: 7419 Saskatchewan Dr., Edmonton, Alta. T6G 2A5; Office: Edmonton, Alta. T6G 2H4.

**KOSSUTH, Selwyn Barnett,** M.A., B.Comm.; executive; b. Johannesburg, S. Africa 16 Aug. 1937; s. (late) Barnett Reginald and Lyrice Beryl K.; e. Univ. of Stellenbosch, S.A., B.Comm.; Oxford Univ., M.A.; Inner Temple, Engl. Barrister; Rhodes Scholar (Transvaal) 1958; Oxford Field Hockey blue; m. Philippa d. Neil and Gwen Holford 4 July 1964; children: Guy Barnett, Donald Graham, Robert Stephen; PRES. & C.E.O., INVESTMENT FUNDS INSTITUTE OF CANADA 1991– ; Extve. Dir., Ont. Securities Commission 1989–91; Marketing and Regional Co-ordination, Shell Internat. Petroleum Co. Ltd. 1961–66; Sec. to Exec. Ctte., Anglo Am./De Beers Group 1967–76; Dir. of Admin., Brascan Brazil 1977; Hochschild Group 1978–81; Vice-Pres. & Dir., Corp. Finance, Nesbitt Thomson Deacon Inc. 1981–90; recreations: curling, golf; Clubs: The National; Mississaugua Golf and Country; Deerfield Golf; Blue Mountain Golf and Country; Vincents (U.K.); Home: 1160 Cloverbrae Cres., Mississauga, Ont. L5H 2Z8; Office: 80 Bond St., Toronto, Ont. M5B 1X8.

**KOSTER, Emlyn Howard,** B.Sc., Ph.D.; geologist and science centre / museum administrator; b. Suez Canal Zone, Egypt 18 March 1950; s. the late Douglas Albert and Dorothy Muriel (Roberts) K.; e. Christchurch Grammar Sch. UK Advanced Certs. 1968; Univ. of Sheffield UK B.Sc. (Geol.) 1971; Univ. of Ottawa Ph.D. (Geol.) 1977; m. Maryse d. André and the late Madeleine Rémillard 22 June 1974; children: Véronique Justina, Simon Emlyn; DIR. GENERAL, ONTARIO SCIENCE CENTRE (AGENCY OF ONTARIO MINISTRY OF CULTURE, TOURISM & RECREATION), TORONTO 1991– ; Dir. and Chair, Education Ctte., Challenger Ctr. for Space Sci. Educ., Washington, D.C.; Dir., Marc Garneau Collegiate Inst. 1991– ; Mem., Candn. Ctte., Global Sedimentary Geology Program 1988–92; Assoc. Cons. GeoAnalysis Ltd. Ottawa 1975–76; Asst. Prof. of Geol. Concordia Univ. Montréal 1976–77; Asst. Prof. of Geol. Sci's Univ. of Sask. 1977–80; Project Mgr. and Rsch. Offr. Alta. Geol. Survey, Alta. Rsch. Council Edmonton 1980–86; Dir., Royal Tyrrell Museum of Palaeontol. and Field Stn., Alta. Culture and Multiculturalism 1986–91; Adjunct Prof. of Geol. & Geophys. Univ. of Calgary 1987–91; Visiting Prof. Univ. of Buenos Aires 1988; Dir., Drumheller Regional Econ. Devel. Authority 1987–90; Dir., Drumheller Valley Tourism Devel. Bureau 1987–91; mem., Candn. dinosaur-hunting expedition to China's Gobi Desert 1987; Host of Space Link '92 between Prime Minister Brian Mulroney and Astronaut Dr. Roberta Bondar 1992; Guest of the Government of France, Paris 1993; Invited speaker, Internat. Conference on 'Quality Management of Urban Tourism' Victoria, B.C. 1994; Internat. Symposium on 'When Science Becomes Culture' Montreal, April 1994; Candn. Museums Assn., Regina 1993; Royal Astronomical Soc., Toronto 1993; Royal Candn. Institute, Toronto 1992; World Conf. on Tourism Develop. and the Environment, Canary Islands, Spain 1989; Sr. Editor, Candn. Soc. Petrol. Geols. 'Memoir 10' 1984; author or co-author over 40 jour. papers, conf. abstracts, book reviews, and over 150 invited speeches; recipient Tracks Award Candn. Soc. Petrol. Geols. 1985; Fellow, Geol. Assn. Can. (Prog. Ctte. Chrmn. & mem. Exec. Council 1988–91); recreations: cultural tourism, fishing; Office: 770 Don Mills Rd., Ont. M3T 1C3.

**KOSTUCH, Mitchell J.,** M.B.A.; business executive; b. Toronto, Ont. 11 Feb. 1931; s. Antoni and Karolina (Nowak) K.; e. Ryerson Inst. of Technology 1953; York Univ. M.B.A. 1973; m. June Lulchak 18 June 1957; children: James George, Lynn Michelle; PRESIDENT, CO-FOUNDER & DIRECTOR, SB CAPITAL CORPORATION LTD. 1973– ; Vice-Pres. & Dir., Southam Business Communications 1951–70; Dir., Hemosol Inc.; Kostuch Communications Ltd.; Kostuch Engineering Ltd.; North American Ventures Mngt. Ltd.; SB Capital Internat. Inc. (UK); Mem., Candn. Environ. Indus. Assn.; Candn.-Czech C. of C.; Bd. of Trade; Assn. of Candn. Venture Capital Companies; Nat. Assn. of

Small Business Investment Companies; Candn. Advanced Technology Assn.; Home: 3 Alvarado Pl., Don Mills, Ont. M3A 3E8; Office: 2 Bloor St. E., Ste. 3304, Toronto, Ont. M4W 1A7.

**KOSTUIK, (Stephen) Paul,** B.Sc., M.Sc.; business and mining executive; b. Malarctic, Que. 3 Nov. 1939; s. John and Mable Anne (Beadman) K.; e. Queen's Univ. B.Sc. 1961, M.Sc. 1964; m. Donna Jean d. Donald and Olive Martin 11 Nov. 1961; children: Jennifer Anne, Stephen Peter, Martin Leslie, Paula Nicole; PRES., PK ASSOCIATES 1992– ; underground miner/miner's helper, four summers 1957–60; Underground Shift Boss, Kerr Addison Mines Limited 1961–62; Chief Mine Engr., Underground Supt., Internat. Minerals and Chem. Corp. 1964–67; Tech. Asst. to Pres., Kerr Addison Mines Limited 1967–69; Vice-Pres. & Gen. Mgr., Mining & Explor., Molycorp Inc. 1970–74; Pres., S.E. Div., Vulcan Materials Co. 1974–77; Extve. Vice-Pres., Constr. Materials & Dir. 1977–84; Pres., Quintette Coal Limited 1985–91; Past Chrmn., Coal Assn. of Can.; Past Chrmn., Queen's Univ. Engr. Adv. Counc.; Mem., Assn. of Profl. Engrs. (Ont.); Candn. Inst. of Mining & Metallurgy; Am. Inst. of Mining Engrs.; Mining & Metallurgical Soc. of Am.; recreations: golf, curling, skiing; Clubs: Shaughnessy Golf & Country, Hollyburn Country, Sandestin Country; Home: 5325 Montiverdi Place, West Vancouver, B.C. V7W 2W8; Office: Ste. 1500 – 701, W. Georgia St., Vancouver, B.C. V7Y 1A1.

**KOSTYNIUK, Ronald P.,** M.S., M.F.A., R.C.A.; artist; educator; b. Wakaw, Sask. 8 July 1941; s. George and Ann (Shutter) K.; e. Univ. of Sask. B.A. (Biol.) 1963, B.Ed. 1963; Univ. of Alta. B.F.A. 1969; Univ. of Wis. (Fellowship) M.S. 1970, M.F.A. 1971; m. Jeanette d. Jack Pellizzari 1963; one s. Christopher; PROFESSOR OF ART, UNIV. OF CALGARY 1984– , Chrmn. of Div. of Design 1971–76, 1982–84; Co-ordr., Grad. Studies, Dept. of Art 1976–82; Teacher of Biol. Brandon, Man. and Edmonton High Schs. 1963–68; joined Univ. of Calgary Art Dept. 1971; Assoc. Prof. 1978–84; apptd. Prof. 1984; solo exhns, incl. Brandon Allied Arts Centre 1965 and Univ. 1966; Edmonton Art Gallery 1969; Bradley Gallery Milwaukee 1970; Univ. of Man. 1971, 1979; Univ. Alta. 1971; Mendel Art Gallery Saskatoon 1971; Univ. of Calgary 1972, 1978; Glenbow Art Foundation Calgary 1972; York Univ. Toronto 1973; Beaverbrook Art Gallery Fredericton 1973; Dalhousie Univ. 1973; Meml. Univ. of Nfld. 1973; Inst. Modern Art Chicago 1973; Gallery Oseredok Winnipeg 1974; Sarnia Art Gallery 1974; Univ. of Moncton 1974; Mt. St. Vincent Univ. 1975 Gallery III, Univ. of Man. 1979– ; Brian Melnychenko Art Gallery, Winnipeg, 1981; Nickle Museum, Calgary, Alta., 1983; South. Alta. Art Gallery, Lethbridge, 1983; Medicine Hat Art Gallery and Museum, 1983; rep. numerous group exhns. incl. 7th Biennial of Candn. Painting Nat. Gallery Can. 1968; Museum of Contemporary Art Chicago and Herron Museum Indianapolis 1969; 5 Candn. Artists Inst. Modern Art Chicago 1972 and Evanston Art Centre (Ill.); Alta. Art Japan tour 1979; Evolution of Constructed Relief 1913–1979 W. Can. tour 1979–80; Harbourfront Art Gallery, Toronto 1981; rep. various pub., corporate and private colls. incl. Alta. Govt. Art Foundation, Can. Council Art Bank; participant various radio and TV programs; Visiting Artist, Univ. of Man. 1970, 1979; Visiting Speaker, Mendel Art Gallery Saskatoon 1980; Univ. of Alta. 1980; recipient numerous awards incl. Alta. Govt. Visual Arts Grant 1968, Culture Project Grant 1978, 1979; Winnipeg Biannual Prize 1968; Can. Council Art Bursary 1969, Grants 1975, 1976, 1978, 1979, 1980; Univ. of Calgary Research Grant 1976–77, 1983, 1986; External Affairs Foreign Exchange Scholar Can.-USSR 1978; Killam Resident Fellowship Univ. Calgary 1979; Lipschultz Foundation for the Arts Grant 1979; Univ. of Calgary Special Projects Grant 1979, 1981; British Council Grant; subject numerous bibliogs.; author various publs. including 'The Evolution of the Constructed Relief 1913–1979,' 1979; 'Ron Kostyniuk: Art and Sources' 1983; 'Constructive Art in Poland 1919–1991' 1991; 'Neo-Constructions' 1992; mem. Candn. Assn. Univ. Teachers; Univ. Art Assn. Can.; Coll. Art Assn. Am.; Alta. Soc. Artists; Royal Canadian Academy; Public Commissions; Home: 4907 Viceroy Dr., Calgary, Alta. T3A 0V2; Office: Univ. of Calgary, Calgary, Alta. T2N 1N4.

**KOTAITE, Assad,** Docteur en Droit (Paris); barrister; b. Hasbaya, Lebanon 6 Nov. 1924; s. Adib and Kamlé AbouSamra K.; e. French Univ. of Beirut, law grad. 1948; Univ. of Paris, Docteur en Droit 1952, Inst. des hautes études internat.; Acad. of Internat. Law, The Hague; m. Monique Ayoub; PRES. OF COUNCIL, INTERNAT. CIVIL AVIATION ORGAN. 1976– ; Secy. Gen. 1970–76; barrister at law Beirut 1948–49; Chief, Legal Services, Ministry of Pub. Works, Lebanon, 1953–56; Rep. of Lebanon on Council of present organ. 1956–70; Home: 5955 Wilderton Ave., Apt. 04A, Montreal, Que. H3S 2V1; Office: 1000 Sherbrooke St. W., Montreal, Que. H3A 2R2.

**KOTCHEFF, William Theodore (Ted);** director; b. Toronto, Ont. 1931; joined CBC 1952–57; ABC TV London 1957; dir. plays incl.: 'Of Mice and Men'; 'Desparate Hours'; 'Progress in the Park'; 'Luv'; 'Maggie May'; dir. films incl.: 'Life at the Top' 1965; 'Two Gentleman Sharing' 1970; 'Outback' 1971; 'Billy Two Hats' 1973; 'The Apprenticeship of Duddy Kravits' 1974; 'Fun with Dick and Jane' 1977; 'Who is Killing the Great Chefs of Europe?' 1978; 'Joshua Then and Now' 1985; dir., writer film 'North Dallas Forty' 1979.

**KOULACK, David,** B.A., M.S., Ph.D.; university professor, writer; b. New York, N.Y. 21 Dec. 1938; s. Isadore and Annette K.; e. Brandeis Univ. B.A. 1960; Yeshiva Univ. M.S. 1961, Ph.D. 1967; m. Jane Cahill; children: Joshua, Daniel, Leah Cahill, Anna Cahill, Samuel; PROF., DEPT. OF PSYCHOLOGY, UNIV. OF MANITOBA 1977– ; Lectr., Psychology, Brooklyn College 1964–66; Asst. Prof., Washington State Univ. 1966–68; Univ. of Manitoba 1968–70; Assoc. Prof. 1970–77; author: 'To Catch a Dream: Explorations of Dreaming' 1991; co-author: 'Single Father's Handbook: A Guide for Separated and Divorced Fathers' 1979; co-editor: 'Readings in Social Psychology, Focus on Canada' 1973; Home: 323 Kingsway, Winnipeg, Man. R3M 0G6; Office: Winnipeg, Man. R3T 2N2.

**KOUWENHOVEN, Simon;** banker; b. Delft, The Netherlands 24 Oct. 1932; e. School of Commerce, The Netherlands; m. Martha 6 Sept. 1955; children: Wendy, Stephen John, Joanne D., Franciska A.; SR. VICE PRES., ATLANTIC PROVINCE DIV., BANK OF MONTREAL; Fellow, Institute of Candn. Bankers; Dir., Edmonton Economic Development Authority; Edmonton Symphony; recreations: jogging, hiking, skiing; Clubs: The National; Centre; Office: P.O. Box 2207, Halifax, N.S. B3J 3C4.

**KOVAL, Patricia Anne,** B.A., LL.B., M.B.A.; lawyer; b. London, Ont. 3 Sept. 1955; d. Lloyd Douglas and Marian (Hodgson) Temple; e. York Univ. B.A. (Hons.; summa cum laude) 1977; Osgoode Hall Law Sch., York Univ. LL.B., M.B.A. 1981; m. Alan s. Michael and Nina K. 9 May 1980; PARTNER, TORY TORY DESLAURIERS & BINNINGTON 1988– ; joined present firm as Assoc. 1982; practice primarily in corp. finan., mergers & acquisitions & securities law; frequent speaker at legal & bus. edn. confs.; Gov. Gen.'s Gold Medal for Acad. Achievement 1977; Dir. & Pres., African Wildlife Conserv. Fund; Dir., Candn. Assn. for the U.N. Environment Prog.; Mem., Candn. Bar Assn.; author of several articles; recreations: travel, reading, nordic skiing; Home: 358 Conley St., Thornhill, Ont. L4J 6S4; Office: Ste. 3000, IBM Tower, Box 270, Toronto-Dominion Centre, Toronto, Ont. M5K 1N2.

**KOVALIK, Tibor F.;** artist; b. Poprad, Czecho-Slovakia 21 Sept. 1935; s. Vladimir and Maria Irma (Hatrikova) K.; e. elem. and high schs. Czecho-Slovakia; m. Julia Ambrusova 9 June 1955 (div.); two s. Peter Paul, Igor Daniel; m. 2ndly Roseline Boucher, 1984, d. Sofia Marie; author 'From Tale to Tale' 1979; 'Raise and Fall of Byzantine Art' 1984; co-author 'Slovak Culture Through the Centuries' 1976; 'Say Nothing' 1981; 'Silence, You Left Behind' 1988; recipient 1st Prize Bombay, India 1968; Ont. Arts Council Grants 1974, 1978, 1981, 1989; mem. Soc. Candn. Artists (Vice Pres. 1972–73, Pres. 1973–74); Candn. Conf. Arts; Slovak World Cong.; R. Catholic; Office: C.P. 244, 75 Chemin des Cretes, Lac Beauport, Que. G0A 2C0.

**KOVALSKI, Maryann;** children's author; illustrator; b. New York, N.Y. 4 June 1951; d. Samuel and Alice Dorothy (Caputo) K.; e. St. Barnabas Grammar & High Schs. New York; Sch. of Visual Art New York; m. Gregory s. John and Bernadette Sheppard 31 Aug. 1975; two d. Genevieve, Joanna; author/illustrator: 'Brenda and Edward' 1983; 'The Wheels on the Bus' 1987; 'Jingle Bells' 1988; illustrator: 'Molly and Mr. Maloney' 1982; 'Sharon, Lois & Bram's Mother Goose' 1986; 'I'll Make You Small' 1986; 'My King Has Donkey Ears' 1986; 'The Cake That Mack Ate' 1986; co-estbd. The Dinsmore Gallery (original children's books) 1982–83; mem. Children's Book Centre; C.A.N.S.C.I.P. (Vice Pres.); recreations: swimming, antiquarian etiquette books; Club: McGill; Home: 138 Balmoral Ave., Toronto, Ont. M4V 1J4.

**KOVITZ, Muriel,** C.M. (1977); LL.D.; b. Calgary, Alta. 20 Feb. 1926; d. Norman and Ethel Rose (Shapiro) Libin; e. Calgary pub. and high schs.; Univ. of Toronto 1944–45; London Royal Schs. of Music LRSM 1944; m. David M. Kovitz 2 Aug. 1945; children: Jeffrey Wayne, Ronald Stephen, Ethel Rose; Chancellor (Emeritus), Univ. of Calgary, 1978– ; Chancellor, Univ. of Calgary 1974–78; Chrmn. Senate Extve. Comte. and Senate, mem. Extve. Comte. Bd. of Govs. there; Dir. Centennial Packers of Canada Ltd.; Imperial Oil Ltd.; Alberta Investments Ltd.; The Reader's Digest Ass. (Can.) Ltd.; Inst. of Donations and Publics Affairs Research; mem. Extve. Bd. Dirs. Candn. Council Christians and Jews (W. Region); Co-Chrmn. 3rd Internat. Banff Conf. on Man and His Environment 1978; mem. Fed. Govt. Task Force on Candn. Unity; Pres. Calgary Sec. Nat. Council Jewish Women of Can. 1959–61 (Nat. Extve. Comte. 1961–73, Nat. Program Chrmn. 1963–67, Nat. Chrmn. Sch. for Citizen Participation 1967–73); mem. City Calgary Recreation Bd. 1966–69; Pres. Calgary Social Planning Council 1967–69; mem. Bd. Vocational & Rehabilitation Research Inst. Calgary 1968–69; Calgary Housing Authority 1968–72; participant various nat. confs. and seminars 1959–73; el. to Senate Univ. of Calgary 1970, apptd. to Bd. of Govs. 1972, served on various univ. comtes.; Dir. Calgary and Dist. Foundation; mem. Alta. Rhodes Scholarship Selection Comte. 1976; received Alberta Achievement Award Oct. 1977; Clubs: Canyon Meadows Golf & Country; Glenmore Racquet; Home: 4708 Britannia Dr. S.W., Calgary, Alta. T2S 1J7.

**KOVRIG, Bennett,** M.A., Ph.D.; educator; b. Budapest, Hungary 8 Sept. 1940; s. John and Clara Radoczi Mattyok K.; e. Jarvis Coll. Inst. Toronto 1958; Univ. Coll. London 1959–60; Univ. of Toronto B.A. 1962, M.A. 1963; London Sch. of Econ. & Pol. Science Ph.D. (Internat. Relations) 1967; m. Patricia Anne Cooper; children: Michael John, Ariana Julia, Alexander Nicholas; PROF. OF POL. SCIENCE, UNIV. OF TORONTO 1974– ; Group Relations, Candn. Corp. 1967 World Exposition, Montreal 1966–67; Asst. Prof. Queen's Univ. 1967–68; Asst. Prof. of Pol. Science present Univ. 1968, Assoc. Prof. 1970–74, mem. Governing Council 1975–78, cross-appt. Trinity Coll. 1975; Chrmn. Dept. of Pol. Econ. 1979–82; Dir., Candn. Scene 1981–87; Centre Stage Co. 1981–84; Exec. Dir., Hungarian Rsch. Inst. of Can. 1985– ; Pres., Am. Assn. for the Study of Hungarian History 1986–87; Chrmn. of Pol. Sci. , Univ. of Toronto 1982–87; Rsch. Dir., Radio Free Europe, Munich 1987–88; author 'The Hungarian People's Republic' 1970; 'The Myth of Liberation: East-Central Europe in U.S. Diplomacy and Politics Since 1941' 1973; 'Communism in Hungary from Kun to Kadar' 1979; 'Of Walls and Bridges: The United States and Eastern Europe' 1991; numerous articles East-West relations, E. European politics and hist.; mem. Amer. Assn. for the Advancement of Slavic Studies; recipient, Order of Merit of the Republic of Hungary; Office: Toronto, Ont. M5S 1A1.

**KOWALCHUK, Reginald William,** B.Sc., C.A.; banker; b. Winnipeg, Man. 30 Apl. 1942; s. William and Mary (Buyar) K.; e. Univ. of Man. B.Sc. 1963; Inst. C.A.'s Man. C.A. 1968 (Outstanding Grad.), Que. 1971, Ont. 1984; m. Doreen d. Karl and Ruby Doern 9 Nov. 1963; children: Kimberly, Karla, Roderick, Kyle; SR. VICE PRES. TAXATION THE BANK OF NOVA SCOTIA 1989– ; Commissioned Offr., Royal Candn. Naval Reserves 1962; joined Coopers & Lybrand Winnipeg and Montreal 1963–73; Royal Bank of Canada Montreal 1973–76; Bank of Montreal, Montreal 1976–78; Bank of Nova Scotia Toronto 1978– ; Lectr. McGill Univ. Centre for Continuing Edn. 1971–76; Dir., Past Internat. Pres., Past Pres. Toronto Chapter, Tax Execs. Inst. Inc.; mem., Toronto Br. Naval Offrs. Assn. Can.; Founding Dir. and mem. UNTD Assn. Upper Can.; Trustee, Candn. Naval Meml. Trust; mem., Minister's Adv. Counc. on Tax Admin. 1986–91 and IRS Commissioner's Adv. Group 1993; Gov., Candn. Tax Found.; mem. Bd. Trade Metrop. Toronto; Candn. C. of C. (Tax Ctte.); recreations: fitness, golf; Club: Fitness Inst.; Home: 1594 Calverton Court, Mississauga, Ont. L5G 2W3; Office: 44 King St. W., Toronto, Ont. M5H 1H1.

**KOWALICZKO, Béatrice,** M.A., CAPES; executive; b. Paris, France 25 July 1947; d. Roman B. and Zofia (Kowalczykowska) K.; e. Paris Lycée, Baccalauréats lettres 1965; Paris-Censier, Duel lettres 1971; Paris-Sorbonne, Licence lettres modernes 1972; Capes lettres 1975; McGill Univ., M.A. 1981; m. Brian Young 24 July 1982; one s.: Julien Leloup; EXTVE. DIR., THE ROYAL SOCIETY OF CANADA 1993– ; Prof., French Lit., Sec. & Post-Sec. levels; Que. Office Dir., Assn. for Candn. Studies 1983–85; Assoc. Dir. 1985–86; Extve. Dir., Assn. for Candn. Studies 1986–93; Bd. of Dir., Assn. Can.-Fran. pour l'Adv. des Sci. 1986–88; Candn. Fed. for the Humanities 1987–89; Candn. Fed. Soc. Sciences 1988–92; Vice-Prés., Québec dans le monde 1990–93; Prés., Conseil Inter. d'études francophones 1993–

(Vice-Prés. 1989–93); Office: C.P. 9734, Ottawa, Ont. K1G 5J4.

**KOYL, Donald H.;** retired realtor; appraiser; b. Saskatoon, Sask. 27 Dec. 1918; s. late Arthur Leon and Josephine Elizabeth (Eckstein) K.; m. Doris, d. late A. P. Moodycliffe; children: Donald Gavin, Mary Lee Morrow; PRES. & DIR., HOME PROPERTIES LTD.; joined present Co. in 1937, rejoining in present position 1945; served in 2nd World War, R.C.A.F. as Pilot in 1940; discharged 1945 with rank of Sqdn. Leader; Founding Treas., Saskatoon Auditorium Foundation; Founding Pres. Saskatoon Gallery Corporation (Mendel Gallery); served 20 years as member and Chrmn., Assessment Bd., City of Saskatoon; Alderman, City of Saskatoon, 1962–64, 1967–73; Past Pres. and Life Mem., Candn. Real Estate Assn. (1959); Past Pres. (1950–51) and Life Mem., Saskatoon Real Estate Bd.; Past Pres., Fellow and Life Mem., Real Estate Inst. Can. 1962; Exchange Dir., Nat. Assn. of Real Estate Bds. (U.S.A.) 1959; United Church; Clubs: The Saskatoon; Riverside Country; Home: 1333 Temperance St., Saskatoon, Sask. S7N 0P4.

**KOZIAK, James V.,** B.A.Sc., M.B.A.; executive; b. Alta. 29 June 1941; s. Max and Olga K.; e. Univ. of B.C., B.A.Sc. 1964; Univ. of W. Ont. M.B.A. 1968 (Dean's List); m. Linda Jean d. Fred and Olga Bartholomew 3 Oct. 1964; two d. Lynn, Jill; SPECIAL ASST. TO CHIEF EXTVE. OFFR., DEVTEK CORP.; Dir., Fleck Manufacturing Ltd.; Asst. to Pres. and Mgr. Dealer & Br. Operations, Canadian Kenworth Co., Vancouver, B.C. 1968–71; Asst. to Pres. and Br. Manager, Cummins Diesel Sales of B.C., Vancouver, B.C. 1971–72; Mktg. Mgr., Regional Sales Mgr., Operations Mgr., Canadian Kenworth Co., Ste-Thérèse, Qué. 1972–79; Pres., C.E.O. & Dir., King Truck Engineering Ltd., Woodstock, Ont. 1979–81; Pres., C.E.O. & Dir., Western Star Trucks Inc., Toronto, Ont. 1981–86; Consultant, Mergers & Acquisitions, Derlan Industries, Toronto, Ont. 1986–87; Pres., C.E.O. & Dir., Gormont Ltd., Markham, Ont. 1987–88; former Executive Vice-Pres., Fairwater Capital Corp.; mem. Young Pres., Orgn.; Soc. Automotive Engs.; Candn. Inst. Mgmt.; Home: 16 Princess Anne Cres., Islington, Ont. M9A 2P1; Office: 100 Allstate Parkway, Suite 500, Markham, Ont. L3R 6H3.

**KOZIAK, Julian G.J.,** Q.C., M.L.A., LLB.; innkeeper; b. Edmonton, Alta. 16 Sept. 1940; s. John H. and Marie (Woytkiw) K.; e. Univ. of Alta. B.A. 1962; LL.B. 1963; m. Barbara Lee d. late Joseph Melnychuk 19 Aug. 1961; children: Leanne, Donald, Deborah, Susan, Julian; called to Bar of Alta. 1964; Partner, Kosowan & Wachowich 1964–75; el. M.L.A. for Edmonton Strathcona 1971, re-el. until 1986; Min. of Educ. 1975–79; Min. of Consumer & Corporate Affairs 1979–82; Min. of Municipal Affairs 1982–86; Pres., Chateau Louis Hotel & Conference Centre 1987– ; P. Conservative; Ukrainian Catholic; Home: 4715 Malmo Rd., Edmonton, Alta. T6H 4L7.

**KRAAG, Gunnar R.,** M.D.,C.M., F.R.C.P.(C); physician; educator; b. Constance, W. Germany 4 March 1944; s. Arnold Eric and Nady (Booth) K.; e. Queen's Univ. M.D.,C.M. 1969; postgrad. studies Univ. of Toronto, McMaster Univ.; m. Marilyn d. David and Bessie Boak 8 July 1967; children: Scott, Sheila; CHIEF OF RHEUMATOL. AND CHIEF OF STAFF, OTTAWA CIVIC HOSP. and Prof. of Med. Univ. of Ottawa 1991– ; Cons. Ottawa Gen. Hosp., St. Vincent's Hosp.; Mem. of Bd. of Trustees, Ottawa Civic Hosp.; recipient Arthritis Soc. Award of Merit 1981; author or co-author over 50 publs. med. jours.; mem. Am. College of Rheumatology; Candn. Rheumatism Assn.; Candn. Med. Assn.; Ont. Med. Assn.; recreations: golf, tennis; Home: 2374 Rembrandt Rd., Ottawa, Ont. K2B 7P5; Office: 1053 Carling Ave., Ottawa, Ont. K1Y 4E9.

**KRAINTZ, Leon,** M.A., Ph.D.; educator; b. Johnstown, Pa. 3 Oct. 1924; s. late Franz and late Marie (Peterlin) K.; e. Harvard Univ. A.B. 1950; Rice Inst. M.A. 1952, Ph.D. 1954; Oak Ridge Inst. for Nuclear Studies, Radioisotope techniques in Biochem. Cert. 1952; m. Frances Draper d. late Warren Draper Whitcomb, Waltham, Mass. 29 Aug. 1949; children: Dona Sturmanis, Erika Schmidt, Franz Peterlin; PROF. EMERITUS, UNIV. OF B.C. 1987– ; Lecturer, Nutrition 1990–93; Prof. of Oral Biol. 1964–87; Head of Oral Biol. 1970–82; Hon. Prof. of Physiol. 1966–90; Rsch. Asst. in Psychiatry, Boston Psychopathic Hosp. 1947–48; Rsch. Asst. in Clin. Investigation, Sloan-Kettering Inst. for Cancer Rsch. and Cornell Univ. 1948–50; Rsch. Scientist in Exper. Med., Univ. of Texas M.D. Anderson Hosp. for Cancer Rsch. Houston 1950–51; Instr. in Radiobiol., Endocrinology, Physiol. and Micro-biol. Rice Inst. Houston 1950–54, Research Assoc. in Biol. (U.S. Atomic Energy Comn. Grant) 1951–52; Nat. Sci. Found. Fellow, Biomedical Scis.; Visiting Lectr. and Instr. in Physiol. Baylor Univ. 1956–64; Visiting Prof. of Biol. Univ. of St. Thomas, Houston 1958–64; Prof. of Biol. and Assoc. Dir., Nat. Inst. Dental Research Training Grant, Rice Univ. 1962–64; Visiting Assoc. Clin. Prof. of Physiol. & Curriculum Consultant, Univ. of Texas Dental Br. 1962–64, Visiting Prof. Dental Science Inst. 1981–82; Visiting Prof. of Physiol. Emory Univ. Sch. of Med. 1964–68; Visiting Scient. Physiol. Dept. Univ. of Melbourne 1969–70; Sr. Research Fellow, Nat. Insts. of Health U.S. 1969–70; mem. Independent Assessors Panel, Nat. Health & Med. Rsch. Counc., Australia 1972– ; served with U.S. Navy 1942–45, Reserve 1945–48, N. Atlantic, N. Africa, Mediterranean, Sicily, Italy invasions; rec'd Unit Commendations N. Africa, Sicily; author over 80 publs. scient. journs., book chapters physiol., endocrinol, and mineral metabolism; Fellow, Am. Assn. Advanc. Science; mem. Soc. Exper. Biol. & Med. (Councilor 1975–77); Internat. Assn. Dental Research (Councilor 1975–78, Pres. B.C. Sec. 1966–69, 1980); Endocrine Soc.; Am. Physiol. Soc.; Candn. Physiol. Soc.; Soc. Neurosciences; U.B.C. Sigma Xi (Pres. 1976, 1990–94, Sec. 1978–80, 1982–87); Nat. Del. 1975, 1978–80, 1984–94, Dir. 1974– ; Pres., Texas Med. Center Research Soc. 1960–62; Quaker; recreations: music, carving, cross-country skiing, camping, enology; Club: Harvard; Home: 6478 Dunbar St., Vancouver, B.C. V6N 1X6; Office: 2199 Wesbrook Mall, Vancouver, B.C. V6T 1W5.

**KRAJDEN, Sigmund,** B.Sc., M.D., C.M., F.R.C.P.(C); physician; b. Germany 9 Apr. 1946; s. Jacob and Halina K.; e. Baron Byng High Sch. Montréal; McGill Univ. B.Sc. 1967, M.D.,C.M. 1971; m. Jeanie Cohen d. Mildred and Saul Cohen 30 March 1974; children: Selig Micah, Ari Zev, Miriam Rachel, Dov Azer; DIR. OF MICROBIOL., ST. JOSEPH'S HEALTH CENTRE 1980– and Chief of Infectious Diseases; Univ. Prof., Microbiol. & Med. Univ. of Toronto; cons. in infectious diseases, St. Michael's Hosp., Queen Elizabeth, Branson and Queensway General Hosp.; internship and residency Montréal, McGill Hosp. 1971–73; Fellow in Infectious Diseases Univ. of Cal. 1974; Resident in Microbiol. Univ. of Toronto 1977–80 and in Med. 1976; various TV and newspaper interviews and lectures; co-author 'Occupational Mycoses' 1983; 'Dermatologic Immunology and Allergy' 1985; author or co-author over 60 publs. Candn. and other med. jours.; reviewer & editorial bd. of Candn. and Am. med. jours.; mem. Candn. Med. Assn.; Ont. Med. Assn.; Candn. Pub. Health Assn.; Soc. for Tropical Med.; Am. Soc. Microbiol.; Cons. to Microprobe (Seattle), Epitope (Oregon), STD Branch of Centres for Disease Control (Atlanta); and Federal Govt. (Health & Welfare); listed in 'The International Who's Who' Cambridge, England; International Biographical Centre's 'Dictionary of International Biography'; fungus named in his honour for contbns. in infectious diseases in Canada: 'Trichophyton krajdenii'; recreations; swimming, jogging, piano; Home: 80 Shelborne Ave., Toronto, Ont. M5N 1Z3; Office: St. Joseph's Health Centre, 30 Queensway, Toronto, Ont. M6R 1B5.

**KRAMER, Burton,** M.F.A., B.Sc., R.C.A., A.G.I., F.G.D.C.; graphic designer; educator; b. New York City, N.Y. 25 June 1932; s. Sam and Ida (Moore) K.; e. Bronx High Sch. of Science Dipl. 1949; State Univ. of N.Y. 1949–51; Inst. of Design of IIT Chicago B.Sc. in Graphic Design 1954; Royal Coll. of Art London, Eng. Fullbright Scholar Design 1955–56; Yale Univ. Sch. of Art & Arch. M.F.A. (Graphic Design) 1957; m. Irène Margarite Thérèse d. late Johann Jacob Mayer 24 Feb. 1960; children: Gabrielle Kimberly, Jeremy Jacques; PRES. AND CREATIVE DIR., KRAMER DESIGN ASSOCIATES LTD. 1967– ; Instr. in Design Ont. Coll. of Art 1978– ; Designer, Geigy Chemical Corp. New York 1959–61; Chief Designer, Halpern Advertising Zurich 1961–65; Dir. Corporate Graphics, Clairtone Sound Corp. Toronto 1967; Speaker at VICOM '87, '88, '89, Toronto; Guest Lectr. in Graphic Design Rochester Inst. of Technol. 1976 and Lectr. 'Designer-in-Residence' 1981; Visiting Lectr. Cincinnatti Univ. 1980; Guest Speaker ICOGRADA Edmonton 1975; maj. works incl. Symbol and Visual Identity Programs for Canadian Broadcasting Corp., Reed Paper; North American Life Assurance, Onex Packaging Inc.; Decoustics; St. Lawrence Centre for the Arts, Copps Coliseum, Teknion Furniture Systems,Ont. Educ. Communications Authority, Candn. Crafts Council, Ont. Guild of Crafts; Design of Exterior Graphics Candn. Discovery Train; Signage Systems for Eaton Centre Toronto, CBC Broadcast Centre Toronto, Centenary Hosp., Hosp. for Sick Children Toronto, Metro Central YMCA, Toronto Union Station, Erin Mills New Town Mississauga; Logo and signing system for St. Lawrence Centre for the Arts; signing system for the O'Keefe Centre for the Performing Arts; Graphic Design Program for Royal Ont. Museum; Map-Directory System & Graphics Expo 67 Montreal; work in permanent coll.: Smithsonian Inst.; Library of Congress; rep. many nat. and internat. design exhns.; rec'd Gold Medal Internat. Typographic Composition Assn. 1971, Art Dirs. Club Toronto 1973; numerous awards for Design Excellence; Bronze medal, Leipzig, for design of Candn. art book 'The Art of Norval Morrisseau' 1979; 'Passionate Spirits' (hist of Royal Candn. Acad. Arts) 1980; author Candn. sec. 'Trademarks and Symbols of the World'; co-author 'Report on Canadian Road Sign Graphics' Transport Can.; author various articles and editor of special issue on Canadian graphic design 'Idea' mag. Tokyo; work published by numerous nat. and internat. annuals, books and journals.; Fellow, Soc. Graphic Designers Can. (Past Pres.); mem. Alliance Graphique Internationale (AGI); R.C.A.; Royal Candn. Academy of Arts; AIGA; Can. Post Postage Stamp Design, Adv. Comte. 1982–85; Toronto Folk Festival 1978 (Bd.mem.); recreations: music, sailing, painting, sculpture, photography, books, art; Home: 101 Roxborough St. W., Toronto, Ont. M5R 1T9; Office: 103 Dupont St., Toronto, Ont. M5R 1V4.

**KRASNOW, Stephen M.,** B.Comm., M.B.A.; investment manager; b. Montreal, Que. 7 May 1947; s. Morris A. and Goldie (Warsaw) K.; e. McGill Univ. B.Comm. 1968; Harvard Univ. M.B.A. 1970; m. Esther Holtzman June 1970; children: Lisa, Stefanie; PRESIDENT, CANFUND ENERGY CAPITAL LTD. 1990– ; Investment Analyst, Greenshields Inc. 1970–73; Vice-Pres. Finance & Dir., The Resource Service Group Ltd. 1973–87; Pres., Krasnow Financial Ltd. 1988– ; Dir., Camberly Energy Ltd.; Vice-Pres. & Dir., Calgary Jewish Community Council; Dir. & Past Chair, Calgary Jewish Centre; Home: 925 Prospect Ave. SW, Calgary, Alta. T2T 0W6; Office: 400 – 3rd Ave. SW, Ste. 1550, Calgary, Alta. T2P 4H2.

**KRATOCHVIL, Byron George,** M.Sc., Ph.D., F.C.I.C., F.A.A.A.S.; educator; b. Osmond, Neb. 15 Sept. 1932; s. Frank James and Mabel Louise (Schneider) K.; e. Iowa State Univ. B.Sc. 1957, M.Sc. 1959, Ph.D. 1961; m. Marianne d. James and Margaret Spain Nov. 1961; children: Susan Joan, Daniel James, Jean Marie, John David; PROF. OF CHEM. UNIV. OF ALTA. 1971– , Chrmn. 1989– ; served with US Army 1953–55; Instr. in Chem. Univ. of Wis. 1961, Asst. Prof. 1962–67; Assoc. Prof. of Chem. present Univ. 1967–71; Prof. 1971– ; recipient Fisher Lecture Award Analytical Chem. Candn. Soc. Chem. 1990; co-author 'Chemical Analysis' 1969, 'Chemical Separations and Measurements' 1974; 'Introduction to Chemical Analysis' 1981; over 100 papers sci. jours.; Sr. Ed. Candn. Jour. Chem. 1988–93; Fellow, Am. Assoc. Adv. Sci.; Chem. Inst. Can.; mem. Am. Chem. Soc.; Candn. Soc. Chem. (Dir. 1977–80); Home: 11240 – 58 Ave., Edmonton, Alta. T6H 1C4; Office: Edmonton, Alta. T6G 2G2.

**KRAUSE, Jerome Clark,** M.F.A.; educator; artist; b. Columbus, Ohio 4 May 1943; s. Jack Cletus and Beatrice Anne (Hamerla) K.; e. Layton Sch. of Art Milwaukee B.F.A. 1965; Cranbrook Acad. of Art Bloomfield Hills, Mich. M.F.A. 1967; Instituto Allende San Miguel de Allende, GTO Mexico 1964; PROF. OF PAINTING AND DRAWING, CONCORDIA UNIV.; univ. teacher since 1967; Assoc. Prof. present Univ. (then Sir George Williams Univ.) 1973; former Faculty mem. Penn State Univ.; over 50 art exhns. museums, univs. and galleries; rep. various pub., corporate and private colls. incl. Art Inst. Chicago, Santa Barbara Museum of Art, Nat. Pub. Archives Can., Art Bank Can.; Past Chair and mem. Gov. Council Lacolle Centre for Ednl. Innovation; recipient rsch. grants U.S. Nat. Endowment for Arts, Can. Council, Social Sci. & Humanities Rsch. Council; author various articles innovations in teaching & learning; recreations: flying, aircraft design & constrn., solar energy systems, wilderness canoeing; Home: 561 Ch. Guay, Ayer's Cliff, Que. J0B 1C0; Office: VA-318, 1455 De Maisonneuve Blvd. W., Montreal, Que. H3G 1M8.

**KRAUSE, Judith Ann,** B.A., B.Ed.; writer / teacher / editor; b. Regina, Sask. 11 Jan. 1952; d. Frank Ernest and Mary Patricia (Blair) K.; e. Univ. de Caen, cert. du français 1971; Univ. of Sask. B.A. (mention bilingue) with great distinction 1974; Univ. of Regina, B.Ed. (with great distinction) 1991; one d.: Alexis Claire Fruman; Pres., Sask. Writers Guild 1977–79; Mem., Coteau Books Pub. Coop 1979–80; Lit. Arts Cons., Sask. Arts Bd. 1980–81; Co-ord., Creative Writing Prog., Sask. Sch. of the Arts 1980, 1981, 1982; Instr., Univ. of Regina, Extension Div., Creative Writing 1983–84; Sask. Sch. of the Arts 1988, 1989; Sage Hill Writing Experience 1991, 1992, 1993; GRAIN poetry editor 1993–94; Ed., 'Windscript' 1982–83, 1986–87, 1987–88; Ed. Asst., 'Salt Magazine' 1978–79; Sask. Writers Guild Lit. Awards Poetry 1982, Hon. Mention 1987; Hon. Mention Creative non-Fiction 1992; Robert Kroetsch Scholarship 1979; Sask. Arts Bd. Individual Assistance Award 1984, 1989, 1994; City of Regina Writing Award 1988; Mem., Sask. Writers Guild; League of Cdn. Poets; local writing group, Poets' Combine; author: 'What We Bring Home' 1986, 'Half the Sky' 1994 (poetry); 'No. 1 Northern' 1977, 'Going for Coffee' 1981, 'Other Channels' 1984, 'Heading Out' 1986, 'Labour of Love' 1989, '200% Cracked Wheat' 1992, 'Vintage '92' 1993, 'Lodestone' 1993 (anthologies), 'Knowing Women' forthcoming; co-editor: 'Out of Place' 1991.

**KRAUSE, William Edward,** B.A.; association executive; e. Rutgers Univ. B.A. 1967, postgrad. studies 1967–69; married with four children; PRESIDENT, THE ECONOMISTS', SOCIOLOGISTS' AND STATISTICIANS' ASSN. (ESSA) 1991– ; Asst. Dir., Statistics Canada, Senior Investment Analyst, Investment Canada; Chief, Corp. Planning, Sec. of State; Chief, Economic Analysis, Operations Research, Canada Post; Mem., ESSA Negotiating Team & Finance Ctte.; Investment Canada Steward & Occupational Health & Safety Ctte.; Am. Statistical Assn.; Office: Suite 700, 220 Laurier Ave. W., Ottawa, Ont. K1P 5Z9.

**KRAUSZ, Peter Thomas;** artist; gallery director; educator; b. Brasov, Romania 19 Aug. 1946; s. Tibor Thomas and Judith Noemi (Mozes) K.; e. Fine Arts Acad. Bucharest, Romania 1964–69; m. Irina d. Theodor and Riva Kozak 14 Sept. 1971; one d. Anne-Nathalie; PROF., DEP. HISTOIRE DE L'ART, UNIV. DE MONTRÉAL 1991– ; Exhbn. Dir., The Saidye Bronfman Centre 1980–91; Lectr. Concordia Univ. Montréal 1980–91; exhns. incl. Marlborough/Godard Gallery Montréal 1976; Forum/76, Montreal Museum Fine Arts; Mira Godard Gallery Toronto 1979; Waddington Gallery Montréal 1979, Toronto 1980; L'Eau et le Vent Québec City 1984; Montréal Tout-Terrain, Clinique Laurier Montréal 1984; Optica Gallery Montréal 1985; Montréal-Geneve Exchange, Centre d'art visuel Geneva 1986; Galerie Articule Montréal 1986; Martina Hamilton Gallery New York 1986; 'Stations' C.I.A.C., Montreal 1987; Galerie J. Yahouda Meir, Montreal 1988, 1989; Galerie Dresdnere, Toronto 1988, 1989, 1990; Robert McLaughlin Gallery, Oshawa 1989; Musee du Québec 1990; 49th Parallel, N.Y. 1991; Dél. Québec, Paris 1991; De Natura (Humana), Centre d'Art contemporain, Montpellier, Centre Saidye Bronfman and Galerie Lallouz, Montreal 1992 and Galerie Dresdnere, Toronto 1993; organized and curated numerous exhns.; recipient Can. Council Grants 1975, 1977, 1979, 1984, 1986, 1992; Ministère des Affaires Culturelles Grant 1983, 1988, 1989, 1992, 1993; author: 'Drawing-A Canadian Survey 1977–1982' 1983; '10 Aspects-Recent Concerns in Canadian Drawing' 1984; Office: P.O. Box 6128, Station A, Montreal, Que. H3C 3J7.

**KRAVIS, Janis,** B.Arch.; architect; interior and industrial designer; b. Riga, Latvia 20 Oct. 1935; s. Arvids Ludvigs and Laima (Mednis) K.; e. Sweden 1944–50; Bloor and Earl Haig Coll. Insts.; Univ. of Toronto Sch. of Arch. B.Arch 1959; m. Helga Milda d. late Herbert Braslis, 23 Apl. 1960; children: Leif, Nils, Guntar; PRESIDENT, JANIS KRAVIS ARCHITECT 1963– ; Pres. Janis Kravis Consultants Ltd. (estbd. 1969); estbd. Karelia Studio Ltd. 1959; architectural, interior, graphic and indust. designs incl.: Three Small Rooms (awarded Ont. Tourism Award 1967 and Ont. Assn. of Architects 25 year Award 1991) and Number Twenty-two Lounge Windsor Arms Hotel, Credit Valley and York Regional Schs. of Nursing, Richview Lib., Etobicoke Hydro H.O. Bldg., Inn on the Park Athletic Club, Univ. Centre Carleton Univ., Four Seasons Hotel (Belleville, Ont.), Aurora Highlands Golf Club, Young & Rubicam Ltd., Constellation Hotel, North Albion Lib., Tax Court of Canada (Toronto), Good Shepherd Community Church (Toronto), Historic Tom Taylor Bldg., BGM Image Centre, and other indust. pub. and residential bldgs.; founded Karelia International 1969; opened Karelia store Vancouver 1973; rec'd Eedee Award in Lounge Seating category furniture design 1967; mem. Ctte. on the Environment, Ont. Assn. Archs.; mem., Royal Arch. Inst. Can.; Latvian Architect's Assn.; Assn. Candn. Indust. Designers – Ont.; Royal Candn. Acad.; mem. Art Gallery of Ont.; mem., Ontario Crafts Council; Swiss Candn. Chamber of Commerce; Heritage Canada; Chrmn., Interiors Ctte., RAIC (Royal Arch. Inst. of Can.); Interiors Ctte., A.I.A. (Am. Inst. of Arch.); AIA Ctte. on the Environment; Steering Group, Ctte. on the Environment, Ont. Assn. of Architects; recreations: farming, sailing, tennis; Home: 38 Cedarbank Cres., Don Mills, Ont. M3B 3A4.

**KRAVITZ, Henry,** B.A., M.D.,C.M., F.R.C.P.(C), F.A.C.P.; psychiatrist; educator; b. Poland 18 Oct. 1918; s. Julius and Erna (Hops) K.; e. McGill Univ. B.A. 1940, M.D.,C.M. 1949; m. Mona Brenda d. Peter and Shirley Samuels 1 July 1971; one d. Susan Rachel; EMERITUS CHIEF OF PSYCHIATRY, JEWISH GEN. HOSP. 1988– , Chief of Psychiatry 1967–88; Chrmn. Med. Exec. Comte. 1970–85, Prof. of Psychiatry, McGill Univ. 1970– , Chrmn. Dept. of Psychiatry there 1985–86; Dir., Candn. Psychoanalytic Inst., National 1989–91 (Q.E. 1977–83); mem. Comité de la Santé du Qué. 1983–84; Chief Examiner Psychiatry Royal Coll. Phys. & Surgs. (C) 1978–82, Chrmn. Psychiatry 1982–86; cons. film on Freud; author over 30 articles prof. journs.; 2 training films; Life Fellow, Am. Psychiatric Assn.; Roy. Coll. of Phys. & Surgs. (Can.); Fellow, Am. Acad. Psychoanalysis; Am. Coll. Psychiatry; Am. Coll. Psychoanalysts; Life mem., Candn. Psychiatric Assn.; Life mem., Candn. Psychoanalytic Soc. (Pres. 1967–71); Jewish; recreations: music, art; Home: 4994 Circle Rd., Montreal, Que. H3W 1Z7; Office: 4333 Cote Ste-Catherine Rd., Montreal, Que. H3T 1E2.

**KRAWETZ, Stephen Andrew,** B.Sc., Ph.D.; molecular biologist; assistant professor; b. Fort Frances, Ont. 17 Sept. 1955; s. Stephen and Michaelene (Medynski) K.; e. Victoria Park S.S.; Univ. of Toronto B.Sc. 1977, Ph.D. 1983; m. Lorraine d. Harold and Ruth St. John 19 Aug. 1977; children: Rhochelle, Tairaesa; ASST. PROF., DEPTS. OF OBSTETRICS AND GYNECOLOGY AND MOLECULAR BIOLOGY AND GENETICS, C.S. MOTT CENTER FOR HUMAN GROWTH AND DEVELOPMENT AND CENTER FOR MOLECULAR MEDICINE, WAYNE STATE UNIV. 1992– ; freelance biotechnol. cons. to several major biotech. firms 1985– ; occasional teacher, Scarborough Bd. of Edn. 1976–77; Doctoral student, Univ. of Toronto 1977–83; Postdoctoral Fellow, Dept. of Med. Biochem., Fac. of Med., Univ. of Calgary 1983–89; Asst. Prof., Dept. of Molecular Biology and Genetics, Wayne State Univ. 1989–92; Asst. Prof. (Rsch.) Dept. Molecular Biol. & Genetics and Ctr. for Molecular Biol. 1989; Dir., Molecular Biology Computer Facility, Wayne State Univ. 1990–92; Co-founder, Genetic Imaging Inc. 1988; fellowships: B.C. Children's Hosp. Rsch. 1984; Alta. Heritage Found. for Med. Rsch. 1985, 1986, 1987, 1988; recipient, IntelliGenetics Computer Application Award 1988; Mem., Candn. Biochem. Soc. 1980– ; Am. Assn. for the Advancement of Sci. 1981– ; Am. Men and Women of Sci. 1988– ; New York Acad. of Scis. 1989– ; Comprehensive Cancer of Metro. Detroit 1989; Am. Assn. for Human Genetics 1990– ; Founding Mem., Int. Soc. for Matrix Biology 1993– ; author of num. sci. papers pub. in learned jours. 1978– ; Ed. Bd. Mem. and reviewer for learned journals and govt. agencies; Bd. Mem., Hutzel Hospital Fetal Therapy Bd.; rsch. interests: gene therapy, control of eucaryotic gene expression during devel., the evolution of struc. & functional domains of proteins & the 'Human Genome Initiative', molecular diagnostic probes for human and animal disease, expression of elastic-tissue genes; recreations: skiing, Porsche car racing, jogging, 4-channel quadraphonic music systems; clubs: Porsche Club of Am. (PCA); Southeastern Michigan Region PCA; Home: 805 Canterbury Rd., Grosse Pointe Woods, MI 48236 U.S.A.; Office: Dept. of Obstetrics & Gynecology and Molecular Biol. & Genetics, Wayne State Univ., 253 C.S. Mott Ctr., 275 E. Hancock, Detroit, Michigan 48201.

**KRESGE, Alexander Jerry,** B.A., Ph.D., F.R.S.C.; educator; b. Wilkes-Barre, Pa. 17 July 1926; s. Alexander Marion and Helen Clementine (Ertner) K.; e. pub. and high schs. Kingston, Pa. 1944; Cornell Univ. B.A. 1949; Univ. of Ill. Ph.D. 1953; m. Yvonne Chiang 6 Dec. 1963; children: Nell, Peter, Nicole; PROF. OF CHEM. UNIV. OF TORONTO 1974– , Chrmn. Chem. Group Scarborough Coll. 1974–78, Visiting Prof. 1970–71; Fulbright Scholar Univ. Coll. London 1953–54; Rsch. Assoc. Purdue Univ. 1954–55, M.I.T. 1955–57; Assoc. Chem. Brookhaven Nat. Lab. 1957–60; Asst. Prof. I.I.T. 1960, Assoc. Prof. 1964, Prof. 1968–74; Visiting Lectr. Bedford Coll. London 1964; Visiting Prof. Oxford Univ. 1965; Univ. of Mich. 1979; Univ. of Lausanne 1981; Tech. Univ. of Denmark 1982; Univ. of Sao Paulo 1984; Fed. Univ. of Santa Catarina 1984; Visiting Sci. M.I.T. 1965; Fritz Haber Inst. 1981; Univ. of Goteborg 1983; N.S.F. Sr. Fellow 1964; Guggenheim Fellow 1965; Mardi Gras Lectr. 1981; Mobay Lectr. 1982; Killam Fellow 1984–86; Yamada Fellow 1985; Nelson J. Leonard Lectr. 1986; Morley Medal 1988; Syntex Award 1988; Richard and Doris Arnold Lectr. 1989; Ingold Lectr. 1994; Chrmn. Gordon Rsch. Conf. Chem. & Physics of Isotopes 1968; Chrmn. Organizing Ctte. Internat. Symposium Physical Organic Chem. 1979; author over 200 publs. phys. organic chem. various jours.; Office: Dept. of Chem., Univ. of Toronto, Toronto, Ont. M5S 1A1.

**KRESS, Edward Charles,** B.Comm., C.A.; financial executive; b. Toronto, Ont. 9 June 1944; s. Albert Edward and Augusta K.; e. Etobicoke C.I.; Univ. of Toronto B.Comm. 1967; m. Patricia d. Elizabeth and Herbert Brangam 15 Oct. 1977; one child: Morgan; EXTVE. VICE-PRES. AND CHIEF FINANCIAL OFFR., BRASCAN LIMITED 1974– ; Pres. & Dir., Great Lakes Power Inc. 1991– ; Dir., Westmin Resources Limited 1991– ; Great Lakes Power Limited 1983– ; Student to Mgr., Clarkson Gordon 1967–74; Dir. & Past Chrmn., Central Marketing Serv. 1982; Mem., Financial Extves. Inst.; recreations: golf, sailing, cycling; Home: 8 Reigate Rd., Islington, Ont.; Office: BCE Place, 181 Bay St., Toronto, Ont. M5J 2T3.

**KREVER, Hon. Horace,** B.A., LL.B.; judge; b. Montreal, Que. 17 Feb. 1929; s. Morris and Leah (Levy) K.; e. Harbord and N. Toronto Coll. Insts.; Univ. of Toronto, Univ. Coll. B.A. 1951, LL.B. 1954; Osgoode Hall Law Sch. 1956; m. Elizabeth Mardane, d. late Herbert Wiggin, 15 Oct. 1954; children: Catherine, Susan, Barbara, Bruce; JUSTICE, COURT OF APPEAL FOR ONTARIO 1986– ; Justice, Supreme Court of Ont., High Court of Justice, 1975–86; read law with Goodman & Goodman, Toronto; called to Bar of Ont. 1956; cr. Q.C. 1970; law practice Kimber & Dubin 1956–64; part-time Lectr. in Law Univ. of Toronto 1962–64, Prof. 1964–68; Prof. of Law and Special Lectr. Faculty of Med., Univ. of W. Ont. 1969–74; Prof. of Law and Prof. of Community Med., Univ. of Toronto 1974–75; mem. Senate, Univ. of Toronto 1960–64; Comte. on Healing Arts (Ont.) 1966–70; Fed. Community Health Centre Project (Hastings Comte.) 1971–72; Bencher Law Soc. of Upper Can. 1970–75 (Chrmn. Legal Educ. Comte 1974–75); mem. Rules Comte. under Judicature Act and Courts of Justice Act (Ont.) 1972–75 and since 1977; Ont. Council of Health (Extve. Comte. and Chrmn. Comte. on Human Resources) 1971–75; Commr., Royal Comn. on The Confidentiality of Health Records in Ont. 1977–80; Adv. Council, Medal for Good Citizenship Prov. of Ont. 1972–76; Alternate Chrmn., Ont. Adv. Review Bd. 1976–86; mem., Comte. on Accreditation Canadian Medical Schools 1979–85; Comte. on Human Exper. Rsch. Inst., Hosp. for Sick Children Toronto 1966–75; Arbitrator, Ont. Labour-Mgmt. Arbitration Comn. 1973–75; rec'd Faculty Award, Univ. of Toronto Alumni Assn. 1975; Ed.-in-Chief Dominion Law Reports, Ontario Reports, Canadian Criminal Cases 1967–75 (Ed. 1965–67); mem. Candn. Bar Assn.; Co. York Law Assn.; Medico-Legal Soc. Toronto (Pres. 1976–77; Chrmn. Special Comte. Human Tissue Gift Act 1971–75); Gov., Univ. of Toronto 1982–84; Candn. Pol. Science Assn.; Am. Judicature Soc.; Pres., Candn. Inst. for the Admin. of Justice 1987–89; Co-Chrmn., Royal Soc. of Can. Study of AIDS in Canada 1987–88; Commissioner, Royal Commission of Inquiry on the Blood System in Canada 1993– ; Home: 134 Roxborough Dr., Toronto, Ont. M4W 1X4; Office: Osgoode Hall, Toronto, Ont.

**KREYSZIG, Erwin,** Ph.D.; university professor; m. Herta K., Ph.D.; DISTINGUISHED RESEARCH PROFESSOR OF MATHEMATICS AND PROFESSOR, DEPT. OF MATHEMATICS, CARLETON UNIV. 1991– ; Mathematics Advisor, John Wiley & Sons, Inc., New York; author: 'Statistische Methoden und ihre Anwendungen' 1987 7th ed., 'Advanced Engineering Mathematics' 1993 7th ed., 'Introductory Functional Analysis with Applications' 1989; co-author (with M. Kracht): 'Methods of Complex Analysis in Partial Differential Equations' 1988; 'Differential Geometry' 1991; (with E.J. Normintour) 'Maple Computer Manual for Advanced Engineering Mathematics' 7th ed. 1994; Office: Ottawa, Ont. K1S 5B6.

**KREYSZIG, Walter Kurt,** Ph.D.; associate professor of music; b. Jugenheim a.d. Bergstrasse, Germany 3 Sept. 1955; s. Prof. Dr. Erwin O. and Dr. Herta K. K.; e. Univ. of Windsor B.Mus. 1977; Univ. of West. Ont. M.A. 1980; Yale Univ. M.Phil. 1983, Ph.D. 1989; Akademie für Musik und Darstellende Kunst, Graz, 1966–67; Robert-Schumann-Konservatorium, Düsseldorf 1967–71; trained as flutist under Prof. Hans Florey (Graz) 1966–67; Kammermusiker Prof. Richard Vogel (Düsseldorf) 1967–71; Prof. Klaus Tippach (Karlsruhe) 1971–72; Prof. Wilm Coolen (Karlsruhe) 1972–73; Prof. Shaul Ben-Meir (Detroit) 1973–77; Prof. Nicholas Fiore (London, Ont.) 1977–79; Prof. Per Oien (London, Ont.) 1979–80; Prof. Julius Baker (N.Y.) 1980–85; ASSOC. PROF. OF MUSIC, UNIV. OF SASKATCHEWAN 1990– ; Asst. Prof. of Music 1985–90; Dir., Collegium Musicum Saskatchewanense 1985–91; Visiting Prof. of Musicology, Univ. of Vienna 1991– ; Mem., Ed. Adv. Ctte., Thesaurus Musicarum Latinarum (Indiana Univ.) 1990– ; Mem., Bd. of Dirs., Institutum Musices Feldkirchense (Feldkirch, Austria) 1991– ; Third Vice-Pres., Mons Serenus (Halle a.d. Saale, Germany) 1992– ;

Corresponding Mem., Institute of Advanced Musical Studies, King's Coll. (London, Eng.) 1993– ; Founding Mem., Int. Leopold Mozart Gesellschaft 1993– ; Mem., Candn. Univ. Music Soc.; Am. & Internat. Music. socs. (Life Mem.); Soc. for Music Theory; Coll. Music Soc. (Life Mem.); Am. Mus. Instrument Soc.; Am. Bach Soc.; Early Music America; Internat. Heinrich Schütz Soc.; Internat. Handel Soc.; Internat. Fasch Soc.; Internat. Stiftung Mozarteum; Renaissance Soc. of Am. (by invitation); and musicological socs. of Austria, Germany, Netherlands, and Switzerland; author: 'Anonymous Compositions from the Late-Fourteenth and Early-Fifteenth Centuries' (Vienna 1984); 'The Life and Works of Hugues de Berzé: Commentary and Critical Edition of His Chansons' with Lane M. Heller (Ottawa 1994); Franchino Gaffurio's 'Theorica musice' trans. with intro. & notes (New Haven 1993); 'Franchino Gaffurio's Theorica musice: A Study of the Sources' (Vienna 1994); and articles on Mozart, Scheidt, Webern, 15th century secular music, and editorial practices of Medieval and Renaissance Music Theory in Mozart-Jahrbuch; Dietrich Buxtehude and Samuel Scheidt: An Anniversary Tribute (Sask. 1988); Studien zur Musikwissenschaft; Musiktheorie; Festschrift Luther Ditttmer (Ottawa 1990); Office: Dept. of Music, Univ. of Saskatchewan, Saskatoon, Sask. S7N 0W0.

**KRIEGLER, Elisabeth Caroline,** B.A.; crown corporation executive; b. Pecs, Hungary 12 Feb. 1939; d. Elemer Anthony and Judith (Milkovitch-Scholz) De Gosztonyi; e. Acad. of Sacred Heart, Montréal 1956; Univ. of Toronto B.A. 1961; two s. Andrew Joseph, Paul Gregory; SR. VICE PRES. ADMINISTRATION, CANADA POST CORP. 1983– ; Econ. T. Eaton Co. Ltd. 1961–66; Combines Investigation, Consumer & Corporate Affairs 1966–69; Econ.: Candn. Transport Comn. 1969–71; Regional Econ. Expansion 1971–73; Policy Adv. Indian & N. Affairs 1973–77; Sr. Policy Adv. Treasury Bd. Can. 1979–80; Dir. Gen.: Communications Econ., Dept. Communications 1980–82, Broadcasting & Social Policy 1982–83; mem. Bd. Ottawa Women's Credit Union 1982; Tradex Invest. Fund Ltd. 1985; Mem. Bd., Ottawa YM/YWCA 1990–93; mem. Bd. Ottawa-Carleton Economic Development Corp.; Mem., President's Adv. Counc., Carleton Univ.; mem. Candn. Assn. Bus. Econs.; Clubs: Cercle Universitaire; The Hunt Club; Canadian; Home: 517 Bay St., Ottawa, Ont. K1R 6B2; Office: Canada Post Place, 2707 Riverside Dr., Ottawa, Ont. K1A 0B1.

**KRIESER, Thomas P.;** pulp and paper machinery executive; b. Banska Bystrica, Slovakia 17 May 1938; s. Oscar and Edith (Filo) K.; e. St. Francis Xavier. Eng. Cert. 1959; Concordia Univ. B.A. Theol. Studies; two s. Paul, Mark; PRES. AND CHIEF EXEC. OFFR. KVAERNER HYMAC INC. 1985– ; Chrmn. and C.E.O., Kvaerner Hymac Corp., Atlanta, Ga.; Dir., Mechanical and Chemi-Mechanical Wood-Pulps Network - Paprican 1990– ; Dir. & Chrmn., Machinery & Equip. Manufacturers' Assn. of Can. 1990– ; Dir., Canada-USSR Business Council 1990– ; Kanco Ltd. 1990– ; You Are Church Inc. 1993– ; Forest Sector Adv. Council 1990– ; joined Frigistors Ltd. 1961–66, Sales Mgr.; present co. 1967, Export Sales Mgr., Gen. Sales Mgr. 1969, Vice Pres. Mktg. and Dir. 1973, Exec. Vice Pres. 1984; author various tech. articles; Chrmn. of Forest Sector Adv. Council, Machinery Sub-Ctte. 1990– ; R. Catholic; Home: 2466 Blvd. des Oiseaux, Ste-Rose, Laval, Que. H7L 3M3; Office: 1867 Berlier St., Laval, Que. H7L 3S4.

**KRISHNA, Vern,** Q.C., F.R.S.C., F.C.G.A., B.Comm., LL.B., M.B.A., LL.M., Dip.Law; professor of law; executive; b. India 18 Sept. 1943; s. Radha and Savitri K.; e. Univ. of Manchester, B.Comm. 1963; Univ. of Alta., LL.B. 1974, M.B.A. 1969; Harvard Univ., LL.M. 1975; Dip.Law 1987; m. Linda d. John and Vivian Fleming 30 Dec. 1975; children: Nicola, Alexander; PROF. OF LAW, UNIVERSITY OF OTTAWA 1981– ; Exec. Dir., Tax Rsch. Centre, Univ. of Ottawa; professional accountant UK & Canada 1963–68; Prof. of Acctg., Univ. of Alta. 1969–74; Prof. of Law, Dalhousie Univ. 1975–78; Chief of Tax Policy, Govt. of Can. 1979–80; Tax Counsel in private practice 1981– ; Tax Couns., Koskie & Minsky (Toronto); Elected Bencher, Law Soc. of Upper Canada 1991– ; Bd. of Gov., Cert. Gen. Accountants Assn. of Ont. 1985– ; Secy.-Treas. 1990–91; Vice Pres. 1991– ; Q.C. 1989; F.R.S.C. 1992; F.C.G.A. 1989; Extve. Dir., Joint Ctte. on Accreditation, Fed. of Law Soc. of Can. 1983– ; Dir., Shastri Indo-Candn. Institute 1990; Mem., Candn. Tax Found.; Candn. Bar Assn. of Can.; Am. Bar Assn.; Internat. Fiscal Assn.; author: 'Fundamentals of Canadian Income Tax' 1985, 1986, 1989, 1993, 'Taxation of Capital Gains' 1981, 'Canadian Taxation' 1980, 'Tax Avoidance' 1990; Mng. Ed., 'Canadian Current Tax'; Editorial Bd. 'Ontario Law Reports' 1991– ; recreations: swimming, photography, tennis; club: Rideau; Home: 78 John St., Ottawa, Ont. K1M 1N4; Office: Common Law Section, 57 Louis Pasteur, Ottawa, Ont. K1N 6N5.

**KRISTIANSON, Gerald Lawrence,** B.A., Ph.D.; management consultant; b. Shaunavon, Sask. 11 Nov. 1940; s. Edwin Leonard and Annie Mae (Small) K.; e. Univ. of Brit. Columbia B.A. (Hons.) 1962; Australian Natl. Univ. Ph.D. 1966; m. Diana d. Jakko and Martha Taipalus 19 Aug. 1961; children: Eric James, Leif Roland (dec.); PRESIDENT, PACIFIC PUBLIC AFFAIRS 1976– ; Asst. Prof., Univ. of Sask. 1965–67; Fgn. Serv. Officer, Dept. of External Affairs (Ottawa, Tokyo, Seoul, Georgetown) 1967–73; Extve. Asst., Liberal Caucus, B.C. Legis. 1973–76; Sessional Lectr. in Pol. Sci., U.B.C. 1974– ; Univ. of Victoria 1975–85; School Trustee, Saanich 1974–84; Pres., Pacific Public Affairs 1976– ; Pres., Western Brewers Assn.; Dir., Cerebral Palsy Assn. of Vancouver Is.; Pres., Victoria Crime Stoppers; Gr. Pearkes Found. for Children; Trustee, Piers Is. Improvement Dist.; Chair, Nat. Parks Citizens Centennial Ctte. 1983–86; Mem., SSHRC 1982–85; Liberal Candidate, Esquimalt-Saanich 1980, '84; Policy Chair, B.C. Liberal Party 1981–85; Mem., Liberal Platform Ctte. 1983–84; United Ch.; author: 'Politics of Patriotism' 1966 and numerous journal articles; political analyst: CBC-TV, CTV, CBC Radio, CJVI Radio, CFAX Radio; recreations: squash, sportfishing; club: Union; Home: 67 McKenzie Cr., Sidney, B.C. V8L 3X9; Office: 2-1441 Store St., Victoria, B.C. V8W 3J6.

**KRISTJANSON, Kristjan,** C.M., M.Sc., Ph.D.; insurance executive; b. Gimli, Man. 4 Jan. 1921; s. late Hannes and Elin Thordis (Magnusdottir) K.; e. Univ. of Man. 1939–42; Univ. of Alta. B.Sc. 1943; Univ. of Toronto M.Sc. 1946; Univ. of Chicago summer 1946; Univ. of Wis. Ph.D. 1954; m. Lois d. late Hugh Hill 24 Dec. 1952; children: Ruth, Helga, Ingrid, Stefan; retired CONSULTANT, GREAT-WEST LIFE ASSURANCE CO.; Research Econ. Dominion Econ. Div. Saskatoon 1943–44; Lectr. in Econ. Univ. of Guelph 1945–46; Research Econ. and Teaching Asst. U.S. Forest Service & Univ. of Wis. 1946–48; Research Econ. U.S. Dept. Agric. Brookings, S.D. 1949–53; Assoc. Prof. Univ. of Neb. 1953–56; Sr. Administrator Govt. Can. Ottawa 1956–61; Dir. Econ. Div. Man. Hydro Electric Bd. Winnipeg 1961–66, Asst. Gen. Mgr. Adm. Man. Hydro 1966–71; Chrmn., Manitoba Hydro Electric Bd. 1980–82; Vice Pres. Corporate Planning & Personnel, Great-West Life Assurance Co. 1971–82; Dir. Museum of Man & Nature; Winnipeg Chamber Comm.; Chrmn., Nat. Research Council Med. Biohazards Comte.; Pres. Can. Iceland Foundation; mem. Inst. Pub. Adm. Can. (Pres. 1967–68); Dir., Victoria Hosp.; P. Conservative; recreations: swimming, tennis, golf, billiards; Home: 283 Queenston St., Winnipeg, Man. R3N 0W9.

**KRISTJANSON, Leo Friman,** C.M., M.A., Ph.D.; educator; economist; b. Gimli, Man. 28 Feb. 1932; s. Hannes and Elin Thordis (Magnusdottir) K.; e. Un. Coll. Winnipeg B.A. 1954; Univ. of Man. M.A. 1959; Univ. of Wis. Ph.D. 1963; Univ. of Winnipeg, LL.D. 1980; m. Jean Evelyn d. Hector M. Cameron, Moorepark, Man. 29 June 1957; children: Terri Elin, Darryl Cameron, Brenda Jean, Johanne Alda; former Pres., Univ. of Saskatchewan, retired 1989; has served on several adv. comtes. to govt.; Awarded, Member of the Order of Canada 1990; author various articles in fields of co-operatives, demography and agric. policy; mem. Candn. Econ. Assn.; Candn. Agric. Econ. Assn.; Home: Box 5, Gimli, Man. R0C 1B0.

**KRNJEVIC, Kresimir Ivan,** O.C., M.B., Ch.B., B.Sc., Ph.D., F.R.S.C.; neurophysiologist; b. Zagreb, Croatia, Yugoslavia 7 Sept. 1927; s. Juraj and Nada (Hirsl) K.; e. Primary Sch. Geneva, Switzerland 1935–39; High Sch. Realna Gimnazija, Zagreb 1939–41; Wynberg Boys' High Sch. Capetown, S. Africa 1941–43; Edinburgh Univ. M.B., Ch.B. 1949, B.Sc. (Physiol.) 1951, Ph.D. 1953; m. Jeanne W. d. late John Herbert Bowyer 27 Sept. 1954; two s. Peter Juraj, Nicholas John; DIR. OF ANAESTHESIA RESEARCH DEPT. McGILL UNIV. since 1965; JOSEPH MORLEY DRAKE PROF. OF PHYSIOL. since 1978; Chrmn. of Physiol. Dept. 1978–87; Goodsir Mem. Fellow 1950–52; Beit Mem. Fellow 1952–54; Demonst. in Physiol. Edinburgh Univ. 1950–54; Research Assoc. and Asst. Prof. of Physiol. & Biophysics, Univ. of Wash. 1954–56; Visiting Fellow, John Curtin Sch. of Med. Research, Australian Nat. Univ., Canberra 1956–58; Princ. becoming Sr. Princ. Scient. Research Offr., A.R.C. Inst. Animal Physiol., Babraham, Cambs., Eng. 1959–65; Visiting Prof. of Physiol. McGill Univ. 1964–65; Forbes Lectr. Woods Hole 1978; mem. Conseil de la Recherche en Santé du Qué. 1974–79; Ed. 'Canadian Journal of Physiology and Pharmacology' 1972–78; author numerous articles in physiol. and neuroscient. journs.; Hon. mem. Soc. royale de medecine mentale de Belgique 1969; Fellow, Royal Soc. of Canada 1975; Mem., Croatian Acad. of Science 1992; mem. Physiol. Soc. (U.K.); Internat. Brain Research Organ.; Peripatetic Club; Internat. Soc. Neurochem.; Soc. for Neuroscience (Pres. E. Candn. Chapter 1973–74); Candn. Physiol. Soc. (Pres. 1979–80); Montreal Physiol. Soc. (Pres. 1977–78); Intl. Union of Physiological Societies (mem. Council 1983–93; Chrmn., Admissions Ctte. 1983–93; Chrmn. Comn. on Neurotransmission 1978–86); Hon. mem. Croatian Pharmacological Assn.; Sarrazin Award, Canadian Physiological Soc. 1984; Gairdner International Award 1984; Officer, Order of Canada 1987; Zagreb Union Alumni Assn., Hon. Pres., Québec Chapter 1990– ; recreations: mountaineering, skiing, swimming, reading, music; Home: 653 Belmont Ave., Westmount, Que. H3Y 2W3; Office: 3655 Drummond St., Montreal, Que. H3G 1Y6.

**KROEGER, Arthur,** O.C., M.A.,; Canadian public servant, retired; b. Naco, Alta. 7 Sept. 1932; s. Heinrich and Helena (Rempel) K.; e. Consort (Alta.) High Sch. 1950; Univ. of Alta. B.A. 1955; Pembroke Coll. Oxford Univ. (Rhodes Scholar) M.A. 1958; m. late Gabrielle Jane Sellers, Toronto, Ont. 7 May 1966; two d., Nina Alexandra, Kate Megan Jane; VISITING PROF., UNIV. OF TORONTO 1993–94; Chrmn., Public Policy Forum 1992; Chancellor, Carleton Univ., Ottawa; former Dir., Petro Canada; Northern Transportation Company Ltd.; Sessional Instr. Univ. of Alta. 1954–55; Master, St. Johns-Ravenscourt Sch., Winnipeg 1955–56; joined Dept. External Affairs 1958 becoming Secy. GATT Del. Geneva 1960, Second Secy. New Delhi 1961, Ottawa 1964 (seconded to Dept. Nat. Defence 1967–68), Counsellor Washington 1968; Treasury Bd. Secretariat, Program Br., Dir. External Affairs and Defence 1971, Asst. Secy. 1972, Depy. Secy. 1972; Depy. Min. of Indian Affairs & Northern Development 1975; Depy. Min. of Transport 1979; Secy., Min. of State for Economic & Regional Development 1983; Special Advr. to Clerk of the Privy Counc. 1984–85; Deputy Min. of Regional Industrial Expansion 1985–86; Depy. Min. of Energy, Mines & Resources 1986–88; Depy. Min./Chrmn., Employment & Immigration 1988–92; Officer of the Order of Canada; Outstanding Achievement Award 1989; Honorary Doctorate of Laws 1991; Club: Five Lakes; Home: 245 Springfield Rd., Ottawa, Ont. K1M 0L1.

**KROEKER, Hans-Rudi,** B.A.Sc., P.Eng.; corporate president and director; b. Winnipeg, Man. 24 Nov. 1953; s. Dr. George and Johanna Irene (Dick) K.; e. Clarke Rd. S.S. (London, Ont.); Univ. of Waterloo B.A.Sc. (Elec. Engr.) 1978; m. Yvette d. Romuald and Dorothy Charlebois 1 July 1978; children: Adam Oliver, Erik Ian, Martha Helena; PRES., CHIEF EXTVE. OFFR. & DIR., WHITING EQUIPMENT CANADA INC. 1993– and CHRMN., CHIEF EXTVE. OFFR. & DIR., WHITING EQUIPMENT SERVICES CO. LTD. 1994– ; Plant Electrical Engr., General Motors – Diesel Div. 1976–79; Sr. Design Engr., Ford Essex Engine Plant 1979–84; Mgr., Mfg. Engr., NAVISTAR Internat. Corp. 1984–86; Mgr., Tech. Serv., AMCAN Castings Limited 1986–88; Sr. Vice-Pres., Opns., GSW Water Products Co. 1988–90; Pres. & Dir., Hamilton Gear & Machine Co. 1990–92; Vice-Pres. & Dir., Compro Ltd. 1991–92; Sr. Mem., Soc. of Mfg. Engrs.; Mem., Assn. of Profl. Engrs. of Ont.; Soc. of Auto. Engrs.; I.E.E.E.; Candn. Soc. for Elec. Engr.; Engr. Inst. of Can.; Dir., Inst. for Improvement in Quality & Productivity 1988–90; Mem., Candn. Manufacturers' Assn.; Mem., Welland Club; Protestant; recreations: hunting, fishing, canoeing; Home: 90 Hands Dr., Guelph, Ont. N1G 3H3; Office: Box 217, Alexander St., Welland, Ont. L3B 5P4.

**KROETSCH, Robert,** M.A., Ph.D.; writer; university professor; b. Alta. 26 June 1927; Paul and Hilda (Weller); e. Heisler (Alta.) Pub. Sch.; Red Deer (Alta.) High Sch., 1945; University of Alta., B.A. 1948; McGill Univ. 1954–55; Middlebury Coll., M.A. 1956; Univ. of Iowa, Ph.D. 1961; m. first Mary Jane, d. George Clinton Lewis, Wilmington, N.C., 13 January 1956; two d., Laura Caroline, Margaret Ann; remarried Smaro Kamboureli 1982; PROF. OF ENGLISH, UNIV. OF MANITOBA 1978– (Distinguished Prof. 1985); Purser on Mackenzie River riverboats 1948–50; Dir. of Information and Educ., U.S. Air Force, Goose Bay, Labrador 1951–54; joined State Univ. of N.Y. as Asst. Prof. of Eng. 1961; Assoc. Prof. 1965–68; Prof. 1968–78; Fellow, Univ. of Iowa 1960–61; Fellow, Bread Loaf Writers Conf. 1966; rec'd. Gov. Gen.'s Lit. Award (for novel 'The Studhorse Man') 1969; Fellow, Royal Soc. of Can. 1986; Killam Award 1986–88; author of the following novels: 'But We Are Exiles' 1965; 'The Words of My Roaring' 1966; 'The Studhorse Man' 1969; 'Gone Indian' 1973; 'Badlands' 1975; 'What the Crown Said' 1978; 'Alibi' 1983;

'The Puppeteer' 1992; poetry: 'The Stone Hammer Poems' 1975; 'Seed Catalogue' 1977; 'The Sad Phoenician' 1979; 'Field Notes' 1981; 'Advice to My Friends' 1985; 'Excerpts from the Real World' 1986; 'Completed Field Notes' 1989; 'The Lovely Treachery of Words: Essays Selected and New' 1989; travel: 'Alberta' 1968; journal: 'The Crow Journals' 1980; other writings incl. short stories, poems and book chapters in various mags. and journs.; Office: Winnipeg, Man. R3T 2N2.

**KROFT, Hon. Guy Joseph,** LL.B.; judge; b. St. Boniface, Man. 27 May 1934; s. Charles and Heloise (Cohn) K.; e. Univ. of Man. B.A. 1955, LL.B. 1959; m. Hester Lee d. late A. Montague Israels, Q.C. 10 June 1956; children: Jonathan Barry, Deborah Faith, David Joseph, Sarah Lynn; JUDGE, COURT OF APPEAL, MAN.; called to Bar of Man. 1959; cr. Q.C. 1978; Court of Queen's Bench, Manitoba 1979; former Partner, Thompson, Dorfman, Sweatman; Dir., Can. Judges Conf.; Extve., Jewish Found. of Manitoba; The Winnipeg Found.; Past Pres.: Man. Div. Red Cross Soc.; Candn. Club Winnipeg; Winnipeg Jewish Community Council; former mem.: Nat. Bd. Can. Israel Comte.; Nat. Extve. Candn. Jewish Cong.; Nat. Extve., Canada Council of Jewish Federations; Nat. Council, Candn. Bar Assn. (Past Vice Pres. Man. Sec.); former Bencher, Law Soc. Man.; Sigma Alpha Mu; recreation: tennis; Home: 352 Oxford St., Winnipeg, Man. R3M 3J7; Office: Judges Chambers, Law Courts Bldg., Winnipeg, Man. R3C 0V8.

**KROFT, Richard Henry,** B.A., LL.B.; executive; b. Winnipeg, Man. 22 May 1938; s. Charles and Heloise (Cohn) K.; e. Kelvin H.S., Univ. of Man., B.A. 1959, LL.B. 1963; m. Hillaine d. Nathan and Anryette Jacob 22 Dec. 1960; children: Elizabeth Sarah, Steven Harold Jacob, Gordon Nathan Jacob; PRES., TRYTON INVESTMENT CO. LTD. 1969– ; called to Man. Bar 1963; articled law, Pitblado, Hoskin & Co.; Brown Shipley & Co. and Schwartz & Co. (U.K.) 1963–64; Asst. Sec. & Treas., McCabe Grain Co. Ltd. 1964–67; Spec. Asst. to Min. of Fin., & Extve. Asst. to Sec. of State for External Affairs, Govt. of Can. 1967–69; Chrmn. & C.E.O., Controlled Environments Ltd.; Vice-Pres. & Dir., John A. Flanders Ltd.; Vice-Chrmn. & Dir., Precision Metalcraft Inc.; Mem., Winnipeg 2000 Leaders Ctte.; Chrmn., Investment Ctte., Jewish Found. of Man.; Past Dir. & Chrmn., Venture Capital Ctte., Fed. Bus. Devel. Bank; Past Dir., Bird Constr. Co. Ltd.; Past Dir., Royal Winnipeg Ballet (Past Chrmn., Bldg. Ctte. & Past Pres.); Past Bd. Mem., Assoc. of Fac. of Mngt., Univ. of Man.; Past Dir. & Extve. Ctte. Mem., num. orgns.; Jewish; Liberal; Mem., Law Soc. of Man.; recreations: golf, tennis, windsurfing, snooker; Clubs: Glendale Golf & Country; Manitoba; Home: 85 Ash St., Winnipeg, Man. R3N 0P4; Office: 720 – 305 Broadway, Winnipeg, Man. R3C 3J7.

**KROGH, Thomas Edvard,** M.Sc., Ph.D.; curator; b. Peterborough, Ont. 12 Jan. 1936; s. Johan Edvard and Marjorie Ruth (Byers) K.; e. Queen's Univ. B.Sc. 1959, M.Sc. 1961; Mass. Inst. Technol. Ph.D. 1964; m. Kathleen d. Roger and Helen Myers 9 Sept. 1961; children: Erik, Kari, Sara, Jason; CURATOR, ROYAL ONT. MUSEUM 1975– ; Staff Sci. Carnegie Instn. of Washington 1964–75; devel. techniques used worldwide for precise dating geol. materials now essential in studies of earth hist.; Prof. of Geol. Univ. of Toronto 1976– ; recipient Logan Medal Geol. Assn. Can. 1989; named Fellow, Am. Geophysical Union 1990; recipient, J.T. Wilson Medal Candn. Geophysical Union 1991; Hon. Doctor of Science, Queen's Univ. 1991; recreations: gardening, cooking; Home: 73 Kennedy St. W., Aurora, Ont. L4G 2L6; Office: 100 Queen's Park, Toronto, Ont. M5S 2C6.

**KROLL, Robert Melvyn,** B.Sc, M.Sc., Ph.D.; speech pathologist; educator; b. Montréal, Qué. 15 June 1947; s. Max and Esther (Emerson) K.; e. West Hill High Sch. Montréal 1964; Sir George Williams Univ. B.Sc. 1969; McGill Univ. M.Sc. 1971; Bowling Green (Ohio) Univ. Ph.D. 1974; m. Karen d. Iain and Bernice (Tedd) Henderson 16 Sept. 1979; two s.: Aaron, Noam; HEAD OF SPEECH PATHOL. CLARKE INST. 1974– ; Clin. Educator Div. Speech Pathol. Univ. of Toronto 1975– , Asst. Prof. of Speech Pathol. Psychiatry 1983– , Assoc. mem. Grad. Dept. Speech Pathol. 1986– ; Speech Pathol. Intern Royal Victoria and Jewish Gen. Hosps. Montréal 1971; Project Evaluator Toledo (Ohio) Pub. Schs. 1972–74; Sr. Speech Pathol. Hadassah Univ. Hosp. Jerusalem 1984–85; Cons. Inst. for Stuttering Treatment & Rsch. 1987– ; mem. Profl. Adv. Bd. She'arim Hebrew Day Sch. 1982–84; recipient Ont. Speech & Hearing Assn. Honours 1982; author: 'Manual of Fluency Maintenance: A Guide for Ongoing Practice' 1986; mem. various ed. bds. sci. jours.; mem. Ont. Assn. Speech-Lang. Pathols. (Exec. Council 1975–77); Candn. Assn. Speech-Lang. Pathols.; Am. Speech-Lang. Hearing Assn.; YM-YWHA; recreations: squash, travel, hiking, birdwatching; Home: 23 Ravengloss Dr., Thornhill, Ont. L3T 4C8; Office: 250 College St., Toronto, Ont. M5T 1R8.

**KRONICK, Doreen,** M.A.; psychoeducational consultant; b. Winnipeg, Man. 9 Nov. 1931; d. Leon and Elsie (Weinstein) Pape; e. Skidmore Univ. Saratoga Springs B.A. 1974; York Univ. M.A. 1976; m. Joseph s. Samuel and Gertrude Kronick 7 Sept. 1950; children: Noah, Sarah, Adam; Private Psychoeducational Consultant; retired Assoc. Prof. of Education, York Univ. 1983–87; Dir. Intgra Found. 1970–84; Teacher Trainer Ont. Min. of Edn., Trillium Sch. 1979– , Cons. Support Services Learning Disabled Post-secondary Students 1984–87; mem. Review Ctte., Ont. Min. of Education and Community & Social Services 1985–86; Lectr. York Univ. 1977, Asst. Prof. 1981; Special Lectr. Univ. of Toronto 1977–79, 1982–83, 1987–89; Lectr. Nipissing Univ. 1982; lectured widely U.S.A., Can., Australia, New Zealand and Central Am.; Cons. TV Ont. 1977–79, 1984–85, mem. Bd. Pine Ridge Sch. 1971–84; Profl. Adv. Bd. Can. & Ont. Learning Disabilities Assn. 1970– and Perceptions Inc. 1975–84; recipient Lowen, Ondatje, McCutcheon Award 1980; Therese Casgrain Award 1983; author: 'Social Development of Learning Disabled Persons' 1981; 'New Approaches to Learning Disablilties: A Cognitive, Metacognitive Holistic Approach' 1988; 'All Children Are Exceptional' 1993; co-author 'Toward Productive Living' 1983; author or contrib. author numerous publs. disabled persons; Founder, Learning Disabilities Assoc. of Ont. 1964, Sec. 1964–66, Pres. 1967–89, Adv. Bd. 1989– ; Founder, Learning Disablities Assoc. of Can. 1967 (Pres. 1967–68, 1971–72; Adv. Bd. 1972– ); Contrib. Ed., Academic Therapy 1967–89; Journal of Learning Disabilities 1970– ; recreations: music, travel, cooking, reading, art; Home: 221 Broadway Ave., Toronto, Ont. M4P 1W1.

**KRÓTKI, Karol Józef,** M.A., Ph.D., F.R.S.C.; educator; b. Cieszyn, Poland 15 May 1922; s. Karol Stanislaw and Anna Elzbieta (Skrzywanek) K.; e. Fabiani High Sch. Radomsko, Poland 1939; Cambridge Univ. 1946–48 B.A., M.A.; Princeton Univ. 1958–60 M.A., Ph.D; m. Joanna d. Maria and Józef Patkowski 12 July 1947; children: Karol Peter, Jan Józef, Filip Karol; UNIV. PROF. EMERITUS, UNIV. OF ALTA. 1991– ; Univ. Prof. 1983–91; Prof. of Demography 1968–83; Rsch worker Ministry of Town & Country Planning, Eng. 1948–49; Depy. Dir. (Tech.) of Stats. Sudan Govt. and Census Controller 1st Population Census of Sudan 1949–58; Visiting Fellow Princeton Univ. 1958–60; Rsch. Adv. Pakistan Inst. of Devel. Econ. 1960–64; Asst. Dir. (Census Rsch.) Dom. Bureau of Stats. Can. 1964–68; Visiting Lectr. in Econ. Univ. of Cal. Berkeley 1967; Visiting and Adjunct Prof. of Biostats. Univ. of N.C. 1970–73; Visiting Prof. of Sociol. Univ. of Mich. 1976; recipient Achievement Award Govt. Alta. 1970; awarded Commemorative Medal for 125th Anniversary of Candn. Confederation; served in French campaign 1940, Libyan campaign 1941–42 and subsequently with RAF (pilot); co-author 'The People of Karachi' 1964; 'Population Growth Estimation: A Handbook of Vital Statistics Measurement' 1974; 'Family and Childbearing in Canada: A Demographic Analysis' 1993; ed. 'Developments in Dual System Estimation of Population Size and Growth' 1978; also 8 other books, over 120 articles learned jours. and some 90 reviews; various ed. bds.; Fellow, Am. Stat. Assn.; Council mem. Internat. Stat. Inst. 1979–83; Pres. Fed. Candn. Demographers 1981–84; Vice Pres., Academy of Humanities & Social Sciences, Royal Society of Canada 1984–86 (Pres. 1986–88); Vice Pres., Central and East Eur. Study Soc. of Alta. 1984–86, and Pres. 1986–88; Founder & First Pres., Soc. of Edmonton Demographers; Extve. Dir., Candn. Futures Rsch. Institute, Univ. of Alberta 1993– ; mem. 18 nat. and internat. learned soc's; recreations: cross-country skiing, opera appreciation, reading; Home: 10137 Clifton Pl., Edmonton, Alta. T5N 3H9; Office: Edmonton, Alta. T6G 2H4.

**KROUSE, Howard Roy,** B.Sc., Ph.D., F.Inst.P., F.C.I.C.; professor of physics; b. Simcoe, Ont. 8 Jan. 1935; s. Howard and Mary Watson (Davidson) K.; e. Hagersville H.S. 1952; McMaster Univ. B.Sc. (Hons.) 1956, Ph.D. 1960; m. Irene Mary 25 Oct. 1958; children: Donald Roy, Ian Howard; PROF., DEPT. OF PHYSICS, UNIV. OF CALGARY 1971– ; appts. in profl. ranks, Dept. of Physics, Univ. of Alta. 1960–71; Head, Dept. of Physics, Univ. of Calgary 1971–74; Visiting Short Term Appts. in insts. in U.S., Australia, Japan, Malagasy Rep., Czech., Poland, Germany, N.Z. & former USSR; estab. Stable Isotope Labs at univs. of Alta. & Calgary; Fellow, Inst. of Physics (London) 1972; Geochm. Soc., 'Best Paper in Organic Geochem.' 1973; Prov. of Alta. 'Achievement Award' in Excellence Category 1988; Fellow, Chem. Inst. of Canada 1990; Mem., Candn. Assn. of Physicists; Chem. Inst. of Canada; Am. Geophysical Union; Geochem. Soc. of Am.; Mass Spectrometry Soc. of Japan; Inst. of Physics; Sigma Xi; Candn. Geophysical Union; extensive ctte. work for various insts. incl. UN and NRC; co-editor: 'Stable Isotopies: Natural and Anthropogenic Sulphur in the Environment' 1991; author/co-author of over 200 refereed papers on applications of stable isotope rsch. in many disciplines; clubs: National Model Railroad Assn. (Life Mem.; Master Builder, Cars); Prairie Mountain Fiddlers (Calgary); Home: 2043 Ungava Rd. N.W., Calgary, Alta. T2N 4B3; Office: Dept. of Physics, Rm. SB135, 2500 University Dr. N.W., Calgary, Alta. T2N 1N4.

**KRUEGER, Peter J.,** M.Sc. D.Phil., F.C.I.C., F.R.S.Chem.; educator; university administrator; consultant in university affairs; b. Altona, Man. 11 Nov. 1934; s. Jacob J. and Elisabeth (Friesen) K.; e. Mennonite Coll. Inst. Gretna, Man. 1951; Univ. of Man. B.Sc. 1955, M.Sc. 1956 (Nat. Research Council Can. Bursary); St. John's Coll. Oxford Univ. D.Phil 1958 (Univ. of Man. Travelling Fellowship, Shell Commonwealth Scholarship); m. Dorothy Isabel d. late Lawrence Lashley, Lanark, Ont. 18 July 1959; children: Kathryn, Vivian, Jonathan; PROF. EMERITUS, UNIV. OF CALGARY 1991– ; Post-doctoral Research Fellow Nat. Research Council of Can. Ottawa 1958–59; Asst. Prof. of Chem. Univ. of Alberta, Calgary 1959, Assoc. Prof. Univ. of Alta, Calgary 1964–66; Prof., Univ. of Calgary 1966–91, Head, Dept. of Chem. 1966–70, Vice Dean (Budget and Phys. Planning) Faculty of Arts and Science 1970–72, mem. Bd. of Govs. 1970–73, Senate (ex officio) 1976–90, Vice Chrmn. Gen. Faculties Council (ex officio) 1976–90, Vice-Pres. (Acad.) and Provost, 1976–90; Visiting Scient. Nat. Research Council Can. Ottawa 1966–67; Brit. Council Visitorship 1974; NRC/CNRS Scient. Exchange Programme (France) 1974; rec'd Coblentz Soc. Award in Spectroscopy 1967 (1st Candn.); Gerhard Herzberg Award in Spectroscopy 1973; Alta. Achievement Award 1974; past and present mem. educ./scient. comtes. univ., prov. and nat. levels; author over 70 research publs. in scient. journs.; Fellow, Chem. Inst. of Can.; Chartered Chemist and Fellow, Royal Soc. of Chem.; mem. Spectroscopy Soc. Can.; Coblentz Soc.; Sigma Xi; Baptist; recreation: squash; Home: 88 Brown Cres. N.W., Calgary, Alta. T2L 1N5; Office: 2500 University Dr. N.W., Calgary, Alta. T2N 1N4.

**KRUEGER, Ralph R.,** M.A., Ph.D.; educator; b. Huron Co., Ont. 10 March 1927; s. late Elmer G. and Myrtle M. (Horner) K.; e. London (Ont.) Normal Sch.; Univ. of W. Ont. B.A. 1952, M.A. 1955; Ind. Univ. Ph.D. 1959; m. B. June d. late J. Everet Hambly 30 June 1949; two d. Karen, Colleen; PROFESSOR EMERITUS, UNIV. OF WATERLOO 1993– , Prof. of Geography 1962–93; mem. Faculty Wayne State Univ. 1957–59; Waterloo Lutheran Univ. 1959–62; Founding Chrmn. of Geog. and Planning, Univ. of Waterloo 1962–70; mem. Kitchener Planning Bd. 1960–72; Waterloo Co. Area Planning Bd. 1966–72; author 'Canada: A New Geography' 1969; 'Urban Problems' 1970; 'Managing Canada's Renewable Resources' 1977; 'This Land of Ours' 1992; 'Low-Temperature Injury to Quebec Orchard Industry' 1992; numerous articles and book chapters Can.'s agric. land base particularly orchard lands; mem. Candn. Assn. Geographers (Pres. 1978–79); recreation: skiing, tree farming; Home: R.R. #2, Clarksburg, Ont. N0H 1J0.

**KRUGER, Arthur M.,** Ph.D.; educator; b. Toronto, Ont. 4 Nov. 1932; s. Joseph and Anna Martha (Barron) K.; e. Univ. of Toronto B.A. 1955; Mass. Inst. of Technol. Ph.D. 1959; m. Betty Mina d. Francis and Levy Jacober 19 Aug. 1958; children: Sarah Anne, Helen Nina, Gerald Zev, Naomi Vered; DIRECTOR, ONTARIO INSTITUTE FOR STUDIES IN EDUCATIONS (OISE) 1992– ; Asst. Prof. Wharton Sch. Univ. of Pa. 1959–61; joined Univ. of Toronto 1961, Chrmn. Div. of Social Sciences Scarborough Coll. 1969–70, Assoc. Chrmn. of Pol. Econ. 1970–74, Princ. Woodsworth Coll. 1974–77; Dean of Arts & Science, Univ. of Toronto 1977–82; Prof. of Econ., Univ. of Toronto; Principal of Woodsworth Coll. 1984–91; Dir., Ontario Institute For Studies in Education (OISE) 1992– ; arbitrator and mediator in labour disputes; author: 'Public Services Under Stress' 1993; various articles related to labour; mem. Am. Econ. Assn.; Indust. & Labour Relations Assn.; Candn. Econ. Assn.; Jewish; Home: 34 Shallmar Blvd., Toronto, Ont. M6C 2J9; Office: Toronto, Ont. M5S 1A1.

**KRUGER, Joseph, II,** B.Sc., D.Sc.; business executive; b. Montreal, Que. 1945; e. Clarkson College B.Sc. 1967; m. Susan; 2 children; CHAIRMAN & CHIEF EXECU-

TIVE OFFICER, KRUGER INC.; Clarkson Univ. Honorary Doctor of Science 1987; Dir., Bank of Canada; clubs: Mount Royal, Club St-Denis, St. James's, Lyford Cay (Nassau, Bahamas); Office: 3285 Bedford Rd., Montreal, Que. H3S 1G5.

**KRULL, Ulrich Jörg,** B.Sc., M.Sc., Ph.D.; educator; b. Berlin, W. Germany 28 Oct. 1956; s. Horst Wilhelm and Anneliese Martha Elisabeth (Schaefer) K.; e. Univ. of Toronto B.Sc. Chem. 1979, M.Sc. Analytical Chem. 1980, Ph.D. Analytical Chem. 1983; m. Carol Bernice d. Dorothy and Stanley Walters 31 May 1980; two s., Jeffrey Michael, Justin Ulrich; ASSOC. PROF. OF CHEMISTRY, UNIVERSITY OF TORONTO 1990– ; Head-Dept. Chem., Erindale Campus, Univ. of Toronto 1990–92; devel. selective biochemical transducers based on lipid membrane tech. leading to patents; Visiting Asst. Prof./Rsch. Assoc., Dept. of Chem., Univ. of Toronto 1983–85, Asst. Prof. 1985–90, appt. to Grad. Sch. 1987; co-founder Univ. of Toronto Chem. Sensors Group 1983, cross appointment to Univ. of Toronto Inst. for Environmental Studies 1989; Assoc. of the Univ. of Toronto Centre for Plant Biotechnology 1992; devel. of first surface stabilized lipid-based electrochemical transducer 1984; co-author 'Lipid Membrane Dipole Perturbation and Chemoreception as Models for Selective Chemical Sensing'; 'The Primary Events in Chemical Sensory Perception: Olfaction as a Model for Selective Chemical Sensing'; 'Towards a Fluorescent Chemoreceptive Lipid Membrane-Based Optrode'; 'Fiber-Optic Chemical Sensors'; over 100 original sci. rsch. publ. and reviews; joint Rsch. Dir. Univ. of Toronto Chem. Sensors Group; recipient, 'CNC/IUPAC Travel Award' Chem. Inst. of Can.; Erindale Campus Community Award; Faculty Teaching Award, Erindale Campus; McBryde Medal for Analytical Chem., Chem. Inst. of Can.; Fellow, Chem. Inst. of Can. (Chair of Analytical Div. Exec. 1992–94); Councillor, Royal Candn. Inst. (2nd Vice-Pres. 1993–94); mem., Royal Astronomical Soc. of Can.; recreations: studies in astronomy, mineralogy; Home: 1920 Sandown Rd., Mississauga, Ont. L5M 2Z8; Office: Dept. of Chem., Erindale College, Mississauga, Ont. L5L 1C6.

**KRUPSKI, Zbigniew Henry,** B.Sc.; retired executive; b. Pressbaum, Austria 1 Sept. 1910; s. Henry and Sophy (Schramm) K.; e. Vienna Tech. Univ. Dipl. Engn. (B.Sc.) Elect. Engn. 1935; m. Barbara Jean, d. late Dr. Wesley Bourne, 29 Sept. 1951; one d. Anne; joined Bell Can. as Asst. Engr., Montreal, 1948; served in various engn. mang. positions, Montreal, 1948–54 and 1956–60; Radio Systems Engr. 1954; Area Chief Engr., Toll Area, Montreal, 1961; Vice-Pres. Bell Canada and Chrm. Trans-Canada Telephone System 1964–71; 1964; Extve. Vice-Pres., Bell Can 1971–75; served with RAF (Polish Unit) in N.W. Europe and UK 1940–48; rank Flight Lt. (A/Sqdn. Leader); mem., Engn. Inst. Can.; Royal Ottawa Golf; Home: 1500 Riverside Dr., Apt. 1007, Ottawa, Ont. K1G 4J4.

**KUBÁLEK, Antonín;** concert pianist; educator; b. Libkovice, Czech Republic 8 Nov. 1935; s. Antonin and Helena (Kubálek-Kříbala) Špička; e. Prague Conserv. of Music 1952–57; Charles Univ. Acad. of Music 1957–59; m. Patricia d. David and Jewel Wotherspoon 31 July 1993; children: Ildiko, Helen, Darius; PROF. OF MUSIC, ROYAL CONSERVATORY OF MUSIC, UNIV. OF TORONTO 1980– ; came to Can. 1968; concert appearances N.Am. with various prominent conductors; concert tours incl. E. and W. Germany, Hungary, Rumania, Bulgaria, Belgium, Switzerland, USA and most recently the Czech Republic (after 23 yrs. of absence); over 46 comm. recordings of 26 Candn. composers; 11 CD's (Dorian) since 1988; Juno Award Nominations for Smetana Czech. Dances 1991 (Dorian) and Brahms Vol. II 1992 (Dorian); recipient Hon. Dip. 1958 George Enesco Internat. Festival Bucharest; Nat. Award Best Performance Bach's Concerto in D and 1st Prize Best Performance Liszt's Sonata in B 1957; recreations: reading, poetry, art; Address: 20 Rogate Pl., Scarborough, Ont. M1M 3C3; Office: 273 Bloor St. W., Toronto, Ont. M5S 1W2; Agent: Andrew Kwan Artists Mgmt., 385 Yonge St., Ste. 300, Toronto, Ont. M5B 1S1.

**KUBAS, Christopher Patrick,** B.B.A., M.B.A.,; marketing consultant; b. Trenton, Ont. 9 Dec. 1962; s. John Leonard and Kathleen (Lonergan) Kubas; e. York Univ. B.B.A. 1985, M.B.A. 1986; DIRECTOR, MARKETING, KUBAS CONSULTANTS 1989– ; Project Dir. & Research Executive, Kubas Consultants 1986–88; Retail Copywriter, Saffer Advtg. 1988–89; special competence in retail marketing research, consulting, retail sales modelling & forecasting; widely quoted by media on retailing issues; Mem., Profl. Marketing Research Soc.; editor: 'How to Improve Profitability Through Managing Advertising Rate Structures' 1990, 'Re-Building Advertising Revenues with New Concepts in Rate Cards' 1994; recreations: punk, ska; club: No Trump; Office: 2300 Yonge St., Ste. 2002, Toronto, Ont. M4P 1E4.

**KUBAS, Leonard,** C.D., M.A.; marketing executive; b. Winnipeg, Man. 15 May 1937; s. John F. and Jean M. (Ziola) K.; e. Royal Mil. Coll. Can. B.A. 1960; Univ. of Wisc. 1966; Syracuse Univ. M.A. 1969; m. Kathleen Mary d. Ed and Leona Lonergan 1 July 1961; one s. Christopher Patrick; PRES. KUBAS CONSULTANTS 1977– ; served with RCAF as Navig., Pub. Relations Offr.; former Mktg. Mgr. Toronto Star; Corporate Planning Mgr. Torstar Corp.; Mktg. Services Dir. Toronto Star; cons./mktg. rsch. Communications Rsch. Center, Retail Mktg. Communications; author 'How to Improve Profitability by Managing Newspaper Advertising Rate Structures' 1978, rev. 1990; 'Profitable Customer Service Techniques' 1986; Royal Comn. on Newspapers Vol. 1 1981; mem., Bd. of Dirs., Canex (Cdn. Armed Forces Exchange System); mem. Am. Mktg. Assn.; Prof. Mktg. Rsch. Assn.; Retail Council Can.; YMCA; recreations: racquetball, jogging; Home: 171 Stibbard Ave., Toronto, Ont. M4P 2C4; Office: 2300 Yonge St., Suite 2002, Toronto, Ont. M4P 1E4.

**KUCHARCZYK, Walter,** M.D., F.R.C.P.; university professor, physician; b. Toronto, Ont. 22 April 1955; s. Michael and Aleksandra (Sak) K.; e. Univ. of Toronto M.D. 1979; m. Dale d. John and Mary Babij 19 May 1979; children: Michael Jonathan, Peter Alexander, Jennifer Marie; PROFESSOR & CHAIR, RADIOLOGY, UNIV. OF TORONTO 1991– ; Internship & Residency, Diagnostic Radiology, Univ. of Toronto 1979–83; Specialty Training UCSF 1984, Toronto Hospital 1985; Visiting Faculty, UCSF 1986; joined Faculty, Univ. of Toronto and Toronto Hosp. 1986; Dir., Tri-Hosp. Magnetic Resonance Centre 1987; cross-apptd. to Hosp. for Sick Children & Mt. Sinai Hosp.; Cons. to Metro Toronto Dist. Health Council for Magnetic Resonance Imaging and Govt. of Canada for Magnetic Resonance Imaging Guidelines; Silver Medal, Fac. of Med., Univ. of Toronto 1979; McLaughlin Fellow 1984; Mem., Candn. Assn. of Radiologists; Am. Soc. of Neuroradiol.; Soc. of Magnetic Resonance in Med.; Soc. of Magnetic Resonance Imaging; author: 'Magnetic Resonance Imaging of the Central Nervous System' 1990; recreations: basketball, tennis; club: Univ. of Toronto Faculty; Office: Rm. 127, FitzGerald Bldg., Toronto, Ont. M5S 1A8.

**KUDO, Akira,** B.Sc., M.Sc., Ph.D., Dr.Eng.; senior research officer and visiting professor; b. Nobeoka, Japan 6 April 1939; s. Masao and Misao (Morizumi) K.; e. Kyoto Univ. B.Sc. 1963, M.Sc. 1965; Univ. of Texas Ph.D. 1969; Kyoto Univ. Dr.Eng. 1979; m. Yumiko d. Shoji Morimoto 16 June 1974; children: Hiroki, Satoshi; SENIOR RESEARCH OFFICER, NATIONAL RESEARCH COUNCIL OF CANDA 1973– & VISITING PROF., UNIV. OF OTTAWA 1975– ; Research Engr., Kyoto Univ. Atomic Reactor Inst. 1965; Univ. of Texas at Austin 1965–68; Acting Dir., AEC Project 1968–69; Kyoto Univ. Atomic Energy Inst. 1969–74; Postdoctoral Fellow, NRC 1971–73; Assoc. Ed., 'J. of Envir. Conserv. Engr.' 1981– ; Mem., Canada-Japan Sci. Exchange 1976, 1991, 1992; Japan Soc. for Promotion of Science 1985; Canada-France Scientific Exchange 1981, '84, '85, '91; Chair, Task Ctte., Am. Soc. of Civil Engrs.; Fellow, Am. Soc. of Civil Engrs. 1992; Organizing Ctte., IAWPRC Kyoto Conf.; co-editor: 'Toxic Materials: Methods for Control' 1983; recreations: swimming; clubs: Rotary Club of Ottawa 1979– ; Home: 1838 Beattie Ave., Ottawa, Ont. K1H 5R8; Office: Room 236 (M-12), NRC, Montreal Rd., Ottawa, Ont. K1A 0R6.

**KUEPPER, Karl J.,** M.A., M. Ed., Dr.phil.; university professor b. Cologne, Germany 8 Aug. 1935; s. Josef and Elisabeth (Kurschildgen) K.; e. Hansagymnasium Cologne, Univ. of Cologne M.A. 1961, M.Ed. 1963; Amherst Coll. Mass.; Univ. of Muenster Dr. phil 1970; m. Gisela d. Fritz and Aenne Herrmann 10 June 1963; children; Mark, Sabina; Prof. of German and Dean of the Faculty, Bishop's Univ. 1979–87; Asst. Prof., Univ. of N.B. 1965, Assoc. Prof. 1972, Assoc. Dean 1975–76, 1977–78, Prof. 1978; mem., Candn. Assn. of Univ. Teachers of German; Candn. Assn. for the Advancement of Netherlandic Studies; Candn. Assn. of Applied Linguistics; author 'Studien zur Verbstellung' 1971; contrib., 'Brockhaus Enzyklopädie' 1975–76; 'Der grosse Brockhaus' 1977–81; articles in applied linguistics; Dir., World Univ. Serv. of Can 1967–69, 1978–80; Home: 46 Speid St., Lennoxville, Que. J1M 1S4; Office: Bishop's University, Lennoxville, Que. J1M 1Z7.

**KUERTI, Anton,** B.M., D.M., D.L.; pianist/composer; b. Vienna, Austria 21 July 1938; s. Gustav and Rosi (Jahoda) K.; e. Cleveland Inst. of Music, B.M. 1956; Curtis Inst. of Music, Diploma 1958; m. Kristine d. Lajos and Anna Bogyo 13 Sept. 1974; children: Julian, Rafael; Nat. Music League Award, Philadephia Orchestra Youth Prize, Leventritt Award 1957; debut N.Y. Philharmonic, Carnegie Hall 1957; performed with leading conductors & orchs. in 30 countries; incl. 45 records and CD's complete Beethoven Piano Sonatas & Concertos and Schubert Piano Sonatas; compositions incl. works for piano, string quartet, violin, cello, a symphony and a piano concerto; Founder, Festival of Sound, Parry Sound, Ont.; Juno Award; Candn. Grand Prix du Disque; Hon. doctorate York Univ.; Laurentian Univ.; Bd. Mem., Pollution Probe; Mem., Amnesty Internat.; Candn. Ctte. of Sci. & Scholars; NDP candidate for Parliament in 1988 Fed. Election; recreations: mountaineering, sailing; Home: 20 Linden St., Toronto, Ont. M4Y 1V6.

**KUFFEL, Edmund,** D.Sc., Ph.D.; educator; b. Poland 28 Oct. 1924; s. Franciszek and Marta (Glodowska) K.; e. Univ. Coll. Dublin B.Sc. 1953, M.Sc. 1954, Ph.D. 1959; Univ. of Manchester D.Sc. 1967; m. Alicja d. Peter and Amalia Gromnicka 4 Oct. 1952; children: Anna, John, Richard, Peter; PROF. AND DEAN EMERITUS, DEPT. OF ELEC. ENG., UNIV. OF MAN. 1989– ; Prof. of Elec. Eng. 1968–70, 1978–79, Head of Elec. Eng. 1978–79, Dean of Eng., Univ. of Man. 1979–89; Head of Elec. Eng. Univ. of Windsor 1970–78; Rsch. Eng. Metropolitan Vickers Electric Co. Manchester, Engl. 1954–60; mem. Faculty Elec. Eng. U.M.I.S.T. 1960–68; cons. to various mfrs. high voltage cables; Dir. Man. Hydro Elec. Bd. 1979– ; Consulting Prof. Xi'an Jiaotong Univ., China 1986– ; co-author 'High Voltage Engineering' 1970; 'Fundamentals of High Voltage Engineering' 1984; 'Introductory Electromagnetics' 1984; author or co-author over 150 tech. papers high voltage eng.; Fellow, Inst. Elec. & Electronic Engs.; Fellow, Can. Acad. Eng.; Home: 2661 Knowles Ave., Winnipeg, Man. R2G 2K7; Office: Rm. 563, Engineering Bldg., Winnipeg, Man. R3T 5V6.

**KUHN, John Henry,** B.S., M.S.; manufacturing executive; b. New York, N.Y. 1 Aug. 1930; s. Franz A. and S. Elfriede (Engler) K.; e. St. John Cath. H.S. 1948; Rutgers Univ. B.S. 1952; State Univ. of N.Y., M.S. 1957; Syracues Univ., M.S. 1957; m. Theresa d. Duilio and Elvira Meola 29 Nov. 1958; children: Eric Joseph, Elaine; PRES., JOHN H. KUHN CONSULTING INC. 1990– ; Rsch. Asst., Lowe Paper Co. 1954–55; Supvr., Supt., Plant Mgr., Rsch. Mgr., Container Corp. of Am. 1956–73; Corp. Mfg. Mgr., Chicago HQ 1973–85; Vice Pres., Paper Mills, Belkin Inc. 1985–87; Vice-Pres., Gen. Mgr. & Dir., Cincinnati Paperboard Corp. 1987–90; Trustee, Paper Indus. Mgmt. Assn. (Bd. of Dirs.); Tech. Assn. of the Pulp & Paper Indus.; CPPA; Guest Lectr., Univ. of Maine; Georgie Inst. of Technol.; Dir., Syracuse Pulp & Paper Found.; Boxboard Rsch. & Devel. Assn.; Survivors Club of Finland; Albert Award, TAPPI; PIMA Glen T. Renegar Award, International Conference, Toronto; Dir., Delvor Hosp. Found.; Roman Catholic; Past Vice Pres., Whitpain Twp. Bd. of Sch. Dirs.; Mem., Republican Nat. Ctte.; Past Mem., Bd. of Dirs., Optimist Club; Nat. Defence Ctte.; author: 'Vapor Phase Corrosion Inhibitors in Paper Packaging' 1956 and other articles & papers; recreations: travel, photography, cross-country ski touring; Address: 5340 Aspenknoll Court, Cincinnati, OH 45230, USA.

**KÜHNLEIN, Urs,** B.Sc., Ph.D.; professor; b. Zürich, Switz. 17 Sept. 1940; s. Victor and Hedwig (Göhner) K.; e. Fed. Inst. of Technol. (Switz.), B.Sc. 1965; Univ. of Geneva, Ph.D. 1970; Stanford Med. Sch., post-doct. fellow, 1970–72; m. Harriet d. William and Mildred Kling 29 July 1972; children: Letitia, Matthew, Peter; PROF., DEPT. OF ANIMAL SCI., MCGILL UNIV. 1985– ; Rsch. Biochem., Univ. of Calif. 1972–76; Rsch. Scholar, Nat. Cancer Inst. of Can. & Sr. Sci., B.C. Cancer Rsch. Ctr. 1984–85; recreations: skiing, mountaineering; Home: 20790 Lakeshore Rd., Baie d'Urfé, Qué. H9X 1R9; Office: Macdonald Coll., St. Anne de Bellevue, Qué. H9X 3V9.

**KUJAWA, Serge,** Q.C., B.A., LL.B.; lawyer; civil servant; b. Radin, Poland 25 Nov. 1924; s. Jacob and Vera (Makarevich) K.; e. Univ. of Sask. B.A. 1958, LL.B. 1957; m. Betty d. Orlan and Rita Brydges 1954; children: Ivy, Judy, Kim, Mandi, Melodi, Melissa; Assoc. Dep. Min. of Justice and Gen. Counsel, SASK. 1980–88; served over 25 yrs. prosecution maj. criminal cases Sask. becoming Dir. Pub. Prosecutions; served over 26 yrs. as Vice Chrmn. Securities and mem. Mental Patients Bd. of Review; mem. and past Nat. Pres. Uniform Law Comn. Can.; Bencher, Law Soc. Sask.; Home: 3002 Assiniboine Ave., Regina, Sask. S4S 1E1.

**KUKAL, Olga,** B.Sc., M.Sc., Ph.D.; university professor; b. Prague, Czech. Rep. 17 Oct. 1956; d. Stewart and Jarmila Kukalová-Peck (Daková) Peck; e. Carleton Univ. B.Sc. (Hons.) 1979; Univ. of Guelph M.Sc. 1984; Univ. of Notre Dame Ph.D. 1988; m. Thomas Allen s. Allene and Furman K. 6 March 1990; ASST. PROF., ACADIA UNIV. 1993– ; Visiting Rsch. Sci., Leningrad State Univ. 1979–80; self-employed, insect collections from Asia, Africa, Indonesia, Australia 1980–82; Rsch. Assoc., Michigan State Univ. 1988–89; Ohio State Univ. 1989–90; Univ. of Victoria 1990–91; Adjunct Prof. 1991–93; recipient of several grants and awards; Mem., Entomol. Soc. of Am.; Am. Soc. of Zool.; Arctic Inst. of N. Am.; Am. Assn. for the Advancement of Sci.; Northern Heritage Soc.; Soc. for Cryobiol.; Sigma Xi; Entomol. Soc. of Can.; author of journal articles and book chapters; frequently interviewed; extensive public speaker & lecturer; Office: Acadia Univ., Wolfville, N.S. B0P 1X0.

**KUKALOVÁ-PECK, Jarmila,** B.A., M.S., Ph.D., F.R.S.C.; paleoentomologist; b. Prague, Czech Rep. 28 July 1930; d. Karel Daněk and Jindřiška Vomáčková; e. Drtina Gymnasium B.A. (Hons.) 1947; Charles Univ. M.S. (magna cum laude) 1956, Ph.D. 1962; m. Stewart B. s. William E. and Ellen Louise (Stewart) Peck 30 July 1976; children: Olga, Hana; RESEARCH ADJUNCT PROF., EARTH SCIENCES, CARLETON UNIV. 1988– ; Teaching Asst., Paleontology, Charles Univ. Prague 1952–55; Asst. Prof. 1955–68; NSF Fellow, Pal., Harvard Univ. 1964–65; Alex. Agassiz Lectr., Biol. 1968–69; Assoc. Prof., Pal., Charles Univ. 1968–70; Rsch. Assoc., Geol., Carleton Univ. 1974–75; Adjunct Prof. 1975–88; invited lectr., var. univs.; Fellow, Royal Soc. of Canada 1992; Mem., Candn. Entomol. Soc.; Internat. Orthopterists Soc.; author: 'A Phylogenetic Tree of the Animal Kingdom,' 'Fossil History and Evolution of Hexapod Structures and 57 sci. jour. articles; recreation: collecting insects; club: Ottawa Entomology; Home: 993 Normandy Cres., Ottawa, Ont. K2C 0L3; Office: Ottawa, Ont. K1S 5B6.

**KUKIEL, Edward Alexander,** B.Sc., B.Comm., C.F.A.; financial executive; b. Toronto, Ont. 4 Oct. 1954; s. Aleksander and Genowefa (Kulaga) K.; e. Univ. of Toronto B.Sc. 1977; Univ. of Windsor B.Comm. 1979; C.F.A. 1982; m. Lesley M. d. Olive and Leslie Nelson 16 March 1990; PRESIDENT, GARBELL HOLDINGS LIMITED & GARDINER GROUP CAPITAL LIMITED 1990– ; Investment Analyst, Sonor Investments Ltd. 1979–83; Vice-Pres., Sales, Gardiner Group Stockbrokers Inc. 1983–88; Vice-Pres., Trading & Client Services, Chief Trading Offr., Portfolio Mgr., Green Line Investor Services Inc. 1988–90; Dir., Garbell Holdings Limited; Gardiner Group Capital Limited; Green Line Investor Services Inc.; GSW Inc.; Gardiner Farms Limited; George R. Gardiner Foundation; TD Trust Company; Mem., Toronto Soc. of Financial Analysts; Asst. Dir., Study Seminar for Financial Analysts, Univ. of Windsor; recreations: fishing; Home: 2285 Lakeshore Blvd. W., #913, Etobicoke, Ont. M8V 3X9; Office: P.O. Box 53, Toronto-Dominion Centre, Toronto, Ont. M5K 1E7.

**KUKSIS, Arnis,** B.Sc., M.Sc., Ph.D., F.R.S.C.; professor; b. Trikata, Valka, Latvia 3 Dec. 1927; s. Eduards and Emma (Sene) K.; e. Iowa State Univ., B.Sc. 1951, M.Sc. 1953; Queen's Univ., Ph.D. 1956; m. Inese d. Bernhards and Anna Jekabsons 12 Sept. 1953; children: Anda, Davis, Lauris, Inga; CAREER INVESTIGATOR, MEDICAL RESEARCH COUNCIL OF CANADA 1960– ; Dir., MRC Regional Mass Spectrometry Facility, Banting & Best Dept. of Med. Rsch., Univ. of Toronto 1972– ; Rsch. Asst. & Demonstrator, Queen's Univ. 1953–56; postdoctoral fellow, Royal Military Coll. 1956–58; Rsch. Assoc., Queen's Univ. 1958–60; Asst. Prof. Queen's Univ. 1960–65; Asst. Prof., Banting & Best Dept. of Med. Rsch. & Dept. of Biochem., Univ. of Toronto 1965–67; Assoc. Prof. 1967–74; Prof. 1974– ; F.R.S.C. 1988; Mem., Candn. Soc. of Biochem. & Mol. Biol.; Candn. Atherosclerosis Soc.; Am. Soc. of Biochem. & Mol. Biol.; Am. Oil Chem. Soc.; Am. Heart Assn. Counc. on Arteriosclerosis; Am. Inst. of Nutrition; author: 'Fatty Acids and Glycerides, Handbook of Lipid Research' vol. 1 1978; 'Membrane Fluidity' 1980, 'Fat Absorption' vols. 1 & 2 1986; 'Chromatography of Lipids in Biomedical Research and Clinical Diagnosis' 1987; Home: 129 Underhill Dr., Don Mills, Ont. M3A 2K3; Office: 112 College St., Toronto, Ont. M5G 1L6.

**KULA, Sam,** B.A.; archivist; b. Montreal, Que. 11 Oct. 1932; s. Nathan and Bella (Winkler) K.; e. Concordia Univ. B.A. 1953; Univ. of London, Dip. in Librarianship 1962; m. Eleanor d. Cyril and Constance Phillips 25 Nov. 1964; children: Helen, Jocelyn; ASST. DIRECTOR GENERAL, ARCHIVES AND GOVERNMENT RECORDS BRANCH, NAT. ARCHIVES OF CAN. 1991– ; Archivist, Nat. Archives of Can. 1954–57; Dep. Curator, National Film Archives, Brit. Film Inst. 1959–62; Librarian, Rschr., Lectr., Univ. of S. Calif. 1962–68; Archivist & Asst. Dir., Am. Film Inst. 1968–73; Dir., Moving Image & Sound Archives Div., National Archives of Can. 1973–87 & 1988–89; Dir., West Memorial Bldg. Project, Archives Headquarters Accommodation Project, Nat. Archives of Can. 1989–91; Exec. Dir., Candn. Centre for Advanced Film Studies 1987–88; has consulted and taught seminars for UNESCO on mgmt. of archives in var. countries; has lectured on Candn. and world cinema at Concordia Univ. and Carleton Univ.; author: 'The Archival Appraisal of Moving Images' Paris: Unesco, 1983; Home: 448 Mansfield Ave., Ottawa, Ont. K2A 2S7; Office: 395 Wellington St., Ottawa, Ont. K1A 0N3.

**KULESHA, Gary Alan,** ARCT, ARCT, LMusTCL, FTCL; musician (composer/conductor/pianist); b. Toronto, Ont. 22 Aug. 1954; s. Protazy 'Peter' Grigorievich and Emilia 'Millie' (Gryszkiewicz) K.; e. Royal Conservatory of Music, Toronto, ARCT (Piano) 1973, ARCT (Comp.) 1978; Trinity Coll. of Music (UK), Licentiate in Theory 1976; Fellowship in Comp. 1978; m. Larysa d. Mychajlo 'Mike' and Paraskeia Kuzmenko 30 Dec. 1983; Prod., CBC Radio, Winnipeg 1977; Organist & Choir Dir. 1976–83; Mus. Dir., Toronto Doctors' Orch. 1973–76; Scarborough Concert Band 1976–78; Principal Conductor, Festival Theatre, Stratford Fest. 1983–85; Art. Dir., Composers' Orch. 1987– ; broadcasts as conductor, pianist, reviewer 1978– ; guest conducting 1980– ; comp. & performer, Stratford Festival 1982– ; freelance composer; music performed throughout N. Am., Eur., Iceland, Australia; performers include: Maureen Forrester, Toronto Symph., Kitchener-Waterloo S.O., Regina S.O., Edmonton S.O., Candn. Brass, Chamber Players of Toronto, Manitoba Chamber Orch., CBC Orch. (Vanc.), The Netherlands Clarinet Quartet, Arraymusic, etc.; apptd. Composer-in-Residence, Kitchener-Waterloo S.O. 1989–92; apptd. Composer-In-Residence, Candn. Opera Co. 1992; teaching appointments, Wilfrid Laurier Univ. 1990–92; Univ. of Toronto 1991– ; Performing Rights Orgn. of Can. (Pro Can.) Concert Music Award 1985; Candn. Rep., Internat. Rostrum of Composers, Paris 1986; Mem., Assoc. Composers, Candn. Mus. Ctr.; Candn. League of Comp.; author on 2 articles; sound recordings: 'Angels' Centrediscs CMC 2786, 'Third Chamber Concerto' Centrediscs CMC CD 3488; 'Toccata' CMC CD 4592; 'Mysterium Coniunctionis' CMC CD 4392; recreations: automobiles; Home: 54 Springbrook Gardens, Toronto, Ont. M8Z 3C1.

**KULYK, Karen Gay,** B.F.A.; visual artist; b. Toronto, Ont. 19 July 1950; d. Joseph and Natalie Melanie (Solowski) K.; e. York Univ. B.F.A. (Hons.) 1973; Founder & Curator, Seedlings Gall. Toronto 1973–75; established studios worldwide 1975– ; solo exhbns.: Nat. Gall. of Thailand, The Rotunda Exchange Square & Gov. of Ont. Offices Hong Kong, Marianne Friedland Gall. Florida 1991; Marianne Friedland Gall. Toronto 1975, '77–78, '80, '81, '83, '87, '85, '89–90; Los Angeles Art Exposition, N.Y. City Art Exposition 1986; Chicago Internat. Art Exposition (1st Candn. represented) 1984; Seedlings Gall. 1973; group exhbns.: Touchstone Gall. Hong Kong 1991; Marianne Friedland Gall. Florida 1990; Important Candn. Artists, Sotheby Toronto 1989; Chicago International Art Expositon 1986–89; The Gallery, Elmwood Club Toronto 1984, '86–88; priv. exhbn. Ottawa 1978; Marianne Friedland Gall. Toronto 1977, '78–91; Seedlings Gall. 1973–75; York Univ. 1973; museum exhbns.: National Gall. of Thailand 1991; The Station Gall. Whitby, W.B. Lewis Library Deep River, New College (Univ. of Toronto) Toronto 1982; Blyth Centre for the Arts, Manitouwadge Rec. Ctr., Cedar Ridge Studio Gall. Scarborough 1981; touring exhbns.: Thai paintings, Nat. Gall. of Thailand 1991; French paintings, Art Gall. of Ont., 'Karen Kulyk: Colourscapes on Paper' 1981; forthcoming exhbns.: Marianne Friedland Gall. 1993; Kitchener-Waterloo Art Gall., Touchstone Gall. Hong Kong 1992; selected collections: Citibank Canada, Canada Trust, Dominion Trust, Toronto Dominion Bank, The Permanent, Manufacturers Life Insur., Halifax Insur. Co., Shell Canada, Huskey Oil, Texaco, Trimor Serv., Hotel Victoria Toronto, Martin Atkins Realty, McCauley-Chusid Toronto, MacDonalds Canada, Paul Duval Toronto, IBM Ltd., Financial Concepts Mass., Felton Empire Winery Calif., Pierre Hautot Paris, Othon Hotels Brazil, Personality Inc. Japan, Thai Airways Internat., Candn. Airlines Internat., Elmwood Club Toronto, Govt. of Ont.; private collections in Canada, France, U.K., Hong Kong, Japan, U.S.; 6 catalogues; 6 reproductions; 4 hand pulled studio print edns.; has taught in several institutions Canada & Thailand; Treviso Internat. Art Competition Italy, Grollo d'Oro 1983; subject of several newspaper articles; illustrator: 'Orff, 27 Dragons, and a Snarkel'; Home: 110 Balmoral Ave S., Hamilton, Ont. L8M 3J9; Office: c/o Marianne Frieldand Gallery, 122 Scollard St., Toronto, Ont. M5R 1G2.

**KUMAR, Pradeep,** B.A., M.A., Ph.D.; university professor; b. Deeg, India 2 Feb. 1940; e. Rajasthan Univ. India B.A. 1958, M.A. 1961; Queen's Univ. M.A. 1969, Ph.D. 1973; m. Sudha Mathur 10 June 1966; one child: Rahul; PROFESSOR, SCHOOL OF INDUSTRIAL RELATIONS, QUEEN'S UNIV. 1992– ; Assoc. Prof., Queen's Univ. 1983–92; Asst. Dir., Sch. of Industrial Relations/Indus. Rel. Ctr. 1975–82; Assoc. Dir. 1983–92; Acting Dir. 1990–91; Visiting Prof., Univ. of Tasmania 1990; Research consultant, various govt. agencies; Mem., Adv. Ctte. on Labour Stats., Statistics Canada 1988– ; Adv. Group on Labour Market Rsch., McDonald Comn. 1983–85; Candn. Industrial Relns. Assn. (Rsch. Ctte. Mem.); Industrial Relns. Rsch. Assn.; Internat. Industrial Relns. Assn.; author: 'Industrial Relations in Canada and the United States: From Uniformity to Diversity' 1993; 'Relative Wage Differentials in Canadian Industry' 1976; co-author: 'Canadian Labour Relations: An Information Manual' 1991; 'Industrial Relations in Canada: Trends and Emerging Issues' 1989, 1991; 'The Canadian Union Movement in the 1980s' 1988; author/co-author of numerous articles, books and book chapters in the area of unionism, collective bargaining, and on the North American automobile industry; Home: 241 Phillips St., Kingston, Ont. K7M 3A3; Office: Kingston, Ont. K7L 3N6.

**KUMAR, Shrawan,** B.Sc., M.Sc., Ph.D.; university professor; b. Allahabad, India 1 July 1939; s. Tribeni and Dhairyavati (Devi) S.; e. Univ. of Allahabad B.Sc. 1959, M.Sc. 1962; Univ. of Surrey Ph.D. 1971; m. Rita d. R.C. Srivastava 7 July 1965; children: Rajesh, Sheela; PROFESSOR, UNIV. OF ALBERTA 1982– ; Lecturer in Zool., CMP Degree Coll., Allahabad 1962–66; Demonstrator, Univ. of Surrey 1968–70; PDF, Trinity College Dublin 1971–73; Pool Offr. in Orth. Surgery, All India Inst. of Med. Sciences 1973–74; Rsch. Assoc. in Rehab. Med., Univ. of Toronto 1974–77; Asst. Prof., Univ. of Alta. 1977–79; Assoc. Prof. 1979–82; McCalla Rsch. Prof. 1984–85; Visiting Prof., Univ. of Michigan 1983–84; Chair, Grad. Program 9 years & Dir. of Rsch. 5 years; currently directs Ergonomics Rsch. Lab. with rsch. funded by MRC, NSERC & other sources; consultant; teaches undergrad. & grad. courses in ergonomics, kinesiology & electromyography; nom. three times for Gordon Kaplan Prize for Excellence in Rsch.; Chair, Internat. Ergonomics Assn.'s Cttes. on 'Rehab.' and 'Ethics in Ergonomics'; Sec., Internat. Found. for Internat. Ergo. & Safety Rsch.; Pres., Indo-Candn. Soc. of Alta. 1987–91; Council of India Soc. of Edmonton 1989–90; author: 'Functional Evalution of Human Back' 1991; editor: 'Advances in Industrial Ergonomics and Society' IV 1992; recreations: travelling, camping, sports; Home: 2807 – 118 St., Edmonton, Alta. T6J 3R1; Office: 3 – 75 Corbett Hall, Univ. of Alta., Edmonton, Alta. T6G 2G4.

**KUNII, Toshio,** B.A.; automobile industry executive; b. Japan 29 Dec. 1935; e. Tokyo Univ. of Foreign Study, B.A.; m. Hiroko; children: Akihiro, Nobuko; PRES. & DIR., TOYOTA CANADA INC. 1989– ; joined Toyota Motor Corp., Japan 1958 & held various positions in Japan, Mexico, and Peru; prior to present appt. he was Gen. Mgr., Export Latin Am. Dept., Toyota Motor Corp., Japan; clubs: Bayview Country, Cherry Downs Golf & Country; Office: One Toyota Place, Scarborough, Ont. M1H 1H9.

**KUNOV, Hans,** Ph.D., P.Eng.; university professor; b. Copenhagen, Denmark 14 Mar. 1938; s. Jens Christian and Ruth (Valeur) K.; e. Roskilde Katedralskole (high sch.) 1957; Technical Univ. of Denmark, M.A.Sc. 1963, Ph.D. 1966; m. Diana Clare d. Tom and Jean Lamb 1 Aug. 1977; children: Mads (Mark) Jacob, Niels Peter; PROF., INST. OF BIOMEDICAL ENGINEERING, UNIV. OF TORONTO 1982– ; Asst. Prof. 1967–73; Assoc. Prof. 1973–82; Assoc. Dir. 1984–86; Dir. 1989–94; Assoc. Chrmn., Div. of Engr. & Sci. 1987–88; Asst. Prof., Dept. of Elec. Engr. 1967–73; Assoc. Prof. 1973–82; Prof. 1982– ; Assoc. Prof., Dept. of Otolaryngology 1980–82; Prof. 1982– ; Pres., Artel Engr.; Dir. of Rsch., Poul Madsen Medical Devices Ltd.; Big Brother of the Year (Toronto) 1985, (Etobicoke) 1986, (Metro Toronto) 1986; Dir., Bd. of Big Brothers of Metro. Toronto 1988–91; mem., IEEE, Danish Engr. Soc., Candn. Med. Biol. Engr. Soc.; APEO, ISA, AAAS, Acoust. Soc. Am., Can. Acoust. Assn., AAEE, Sigma Xi; author/co-author of numerous research papers; Assoc. Ed., IEEE Transactions on Biomedical Engineering 1991–93; Mem., Natural Sciences and Engineering Rsch. Council, Grant Selection Ctte. 1990–93; recreations: sailing, big brothering; Home: 4 Princeton Rd., Etobicoke, Ont. M8X 2E2; Office: Toronto, Ont. M5S 1A4.

**KUNTZ, Sr. Dolores,** M.A., Ph.D., educator; b. London, Ont. 4 Dec. 1925; d. Edward John and Margaret Helen (Ward) K.; e. Brescia Coll. Univ. of W. Ont. B.A. 1946; Detroit Univ. M.A. 1962; Queen's Univ. Ph.D. 1968; PRINCIPAL AND DEAN, BRESCIA COLL. 1977– ; High Sch. Teacher, Grimsby, Ont. 1947–48; The Pines, Chatham, Ont. 1948–58; St. Mary's High Sch. Edmonton 1958–59; Univ. teacher present Coll. 1959– , Dean of Residence 1960–63; Psychol. Brockville Psychiatric Hosp. summers 1968–74; mem. Ursuline Community of Chatham Union; Address: 1285 Western Rd., London, Ont. N6G 1H2.

**KUNUK, Zacharias;** artist, film producer; b. Kapuivik, N.W.T. 27 Nov. 1957; medium: sculpture, photography; 10 group exbns. incl. most recent: Surrey Art Gallery Surrey, B.C. 1992, Bunkamurra Art Gallery Tokyo, Japan 1991, National Gallery of Canada Ottawa 1990; collections: Candn. Mus. of Civilization Hull, Que., National Gallery of Canada; Producer, Inuit Broadcasting Corp.; Artist-in-residence, Winnipeg Art Gallery 1991; invited to attend conf. 'Fragmented Power' at Queen's Univ. 1991; subject of articles and catalogues; Home: Igloolik, N.W.T.; Office: c/o Ingo Hessel, Indian and Northern Affairs Canada, Les Terrasses de la Chaudière, Ottawa, Ont. K1A 0H4.

**KUPCIS, O. Allan,** B.A.Sc., M.A.Sc., Ph.D., P.Eng.; utility executive; b. Latvia 15 Jan. 1944; s. Janis and Valija (Kanepe) K.; e. Univ. of Toronto B.A.Sc. 1966, M.A.Sc. 1968, Ph.D. 1970; m. Baiba d. Boris and Lucija Glebovs 20 May 1967; children: Laura, Jennifer; PRESIDENT, ONTARIO HYDRO 1993– ; Research Assoc., Univ. of Toronto 1972–73; Research Div., Ont. Hydro 1973–88; Dir., Corp. Programming Div. 1988–91; Vice-Pres., Procurement & Power System Planning 1992; Acting Pres. 1992; Bd. of Dir., Energy Council of Canada; Gov. Bd., World Assn. of Nuclear Operators, Atlanta Centre; Mem., Candn. Electrical Assn.; Home: 118 Thompson Ave., Etobicoke, Ont. M8Z 3V2; Office: 700 University Ave., Toronto, Ont. M5G 1X6.

**KUPIN, Russell S.,** B.Sc., M.B.A.; gas industry executive; b. LLoydminster, Sask. 23 Sept. 1945; e. Univ. of Alberta B.Sc. Civil Eng. 1970, M.B.A. 1977; m. Merna; PRESIDENT, K-FIVE ENERGY CONSULTING INC.; Office: 1200, 250 – 5th Avenue S.W., Calgary, Alta. T2P 3H7.

**KUPSCH, Walter Oscar,** M.Sc., Ph.D., F.R.S.C., F.A.I.N.A., F.R.C.G.S., F.G.A.C., F.G.S.A.; b. Amsterdam, Netherlands, 2 March 1919; s. Richard Leopold and Elizabeth (Heuser) K.; e. Univ. of Amsterdam, B.Sc. 1946; Univ. of Michigan, M.Sc. 1948; Ph.D. 1950; m. Emmy Hélène d. C. B. de Jong, Amsterdam, 2 Oct. 1945; children: Helen Elizabeth, Yvonne Irene, Richard Christopher; PROFESSOR EMERITUS OF GEOL., UNIV. OF SASK.; Dir., Inst. for Northern Studies 1965–73; University of Michigan 1948–49; joined teaching staff, Univ. of Saskatchewan 1950; Consultant, Sask. Dept. Mineral Resources and Gulf Oil Corp. 1950–58; with J.C. Sproule, Consulting Engr. 1959–65; Extv. Dir., Adv. Comm. on Devel. of Govt. in N.W.T. 1965–66; Dir., Churchill River Study 1973–76; served in Netherlands Army 1939; principal or co-author of over 70 scient. papers on geol.; Vice-Chrmn., Science Adv. Bd. N.W.T. 1976–84; Chrmn., Commissioner's Award Comte., N.W.T. 1967–91; recipient, N.W.T. Commissioner's Award for Public Service at the Highest Level 1992; Mem., Science Council Can. 1976–82; Northern Development Adv. Counc. (Sask.) 1985–88; Mining Sect. Sask. Round Table Environ. 1989–91; Am. Assn. Petroleum Geols.; Home: 319 Bate Cr., Saskatoon, Sask. S7H 3A6.

**KURIAN, George,** B.A., M.S.Sc., D.Litt.&Phil.; university professor; b. Manganam Kottayam, Kerala 24 Oct. 1928; s. Kalarickal Kurian and Accamma Chackalayil (Mani) K.; e. Univ. of Madras B.A. 1950; Inst. of Social Studies, The Hague, Netherlands M.A. 1955, M.Sc. 1956; State Univ. of Utrecht, Netherlands D.Litt.&Phil. 1961; m. Dr. Susannah d. Prof. M.O. Varkey 6 Feb. 1964; PROFESSOR OF SOCIOLOGY, UNIV. OF CALGARY 1976– ; Reader, Rural Sociology, Osmania Univ. India 1962–63; Lectr. & Acting Head, Dept. of Asian Studies, Victoria Univ. of Wellington N.Z. 1963–64; Asst. Prof. of Sociology, Univ. of Calgary 1966–69; Assoc. Prof. 1969–75; Fellow, Royal Asiatic Society, London, U.K.; Founder-Editor, 'Journal of Comparative Family Studies' 1970– (the world's leading pubn. on cross-cultural family studies); author: 'The Indian Family in Transition' 1961, 'The Family in India: A Regional View' 1974, 'Cross-Cultural Perspectives in Mate-Selection and Marriage' 1979, 'Women in the Family and the Economy: An International Comparative Survey' 1981, 'Overseas Indians: A Study in Adaptation' 1983; 'Parent-Child Interaction in Transition' 1986; editor: 'Journal of Comparative Family Studies' 1970– ; 'Family and Religion' special issue 1974, Editor Chakralata, India-Candn. Assn. monthly newsletter 1984– ; Outstanding Service Award, India-Canada Assn. 1993; Sr. Rsch. Fellowship, Shastri-Indo-Canadian Institute 1987 and 1992; recreations: golf; Home: 40 Varsity Place N.W., Calgary, Alta. T3B 2Z3; Office: 2500 University Dr. N.W., Calgary, Alta. T2N 1N4.

**KUSHNER, Donn J.,** S.B., M.Sc., Ph.D.; educator; writer; b. Lake Charles, La. 29 March 1927; s. Sam and Lily (Donn) K.; e. Lake Charles, La.; Harvard S.B. 1948; McGill Univ. M.Sc. 1950, Ph.D. 1952; m. Eva d. Josef Dubsky and Anna Dubska 15 Sept. 1949; three s.: Daniel, Roland, Paul; PROF. OF MICROBIOL. & BOTANY, UNIV. OF TORONTO 1988– ; Postdoctoral Fellow McGill-MGH Rsch. Inst. 1952–54; Rsch. Sci. Forest Insect Lab. Sault Ste. Marie, Ont. 1954–61; Nat. Rsch. Council Can. Ottawa 1961–65; Assoc. Prof., Univ. of Ottawa 1965–67, Prof. of Biol. 1967–89, Professor Emeritus 1989; Visiting Sci./Prof. Nat. Inst. Med. Rsch. London, UK 1958–59; Institut Pasteur (Paris) 1972; Macdonald Coll. 1979; Cornell Univ. 1980; Institut Jacques Monod Paris 1986–87; Assoc., Candn. Inst. Advanced Rsch. 1987–93; recipient Ottawa Biol. & Biochem. Soc. Award 1986; Candn. Lib. Assn. Award 1981; IODE Can. Chapter Award 1988; Candn. Soc. Microbiols. Award 1992; author (short stories) 'The Witnesses and Other Stories' 1980; (children's novels) 'The Violin-Maker's Gift' 1980; 'Uncle Jacob's Ghost Story' 1984; 'A Book Dragon' 1987; 'The House of the Good Spirits' 1990; 'The Dinosaur Duster' 1992; 'A Thief Among Statues' 1993; ed. and contbr. 'Microbial Life in Extreme Environments' 1978, Russian transl. 1981; ed. Candn. Jour. Microbiol. 1978–83; Archives of Microbiol. 1983– ; mem. Candn. Soc. Microbiols. (Pres. 1980–81); Am. Soc. Microbiol.; Am. Soc. Biochem. Mol. Biol.; Writers Union Can.; Candn. Soc. Children's Authors, Illustrators & Performers; Jewish; recreation: playing violin & viola amateur chamber music groups & orch.; Home: 63 Albany Ave., Toronto, Ont. M5R 3C2; Office: Toronto, Ont. M5S 1A8.

**KUSHNER, Eva,** M.A., Ph.D., F.R.S.C.; educator; author; b. Prague, Czechoslovakia 18 June 1929; d. Josef and Anna (Kafkova) Dubsky; e. elem. sch. Prague 1935–39; Coll. classique de jeunes filles, Cognac, Charente, France 1939–45; Coll. Marie de France, Montreal B.Ph. 1946; McGill Univ. B.A. 1948, M.A. (Philos.) 1950, Ph.D. (French Lit.) 1956; m. Donn Jean Kushner, Lake Charles, La. 15 Sept. 1949; children: Daniel Peter, Roland Joseph, Paul Joel; PROF. OF FRENCH AND COMPARATIVE LITERATURE and PRESIDENT, VICTORIA UNIVERSITY IN THE UNIVERSITY OF TORONTO 1987–94; Sessional Lectr. in Philos. Sir George Williams Univ. 1952–53; Sessional Lectr. in French, McGill Univ. 1952–55; Instr. McGill French Summer Sch. 1956, 1958, 1961, 1962, 1967, 1968, 1969; Lectr. Univ. Coll. London, Eng. 1958–59; Lectr. Carleton Univ. 1961, Asst. Prof. 1963, Assoc. Prof. 1965, Prof. of French & Comparative Lit. 1969–76, Chrmn. of Comparative Lit. 1965–69, 1970–72, 1975–76; Hon. Adjunct Prof. of Comparative Lit., Carleton Univ. 1976–79; Prof. of French and Comparative Lit., McGill Univ. 1976–87; elected to Académie Européenne des lettres, des sciences et des arts (1980); Royal Society of Can. (1971); Pres. of Acad. des lettres et sciences humaines and Vice-Pres., Roy. Soc. of Can. 1980–82; mem. (and mem. Extve. Comte.) Can. Council 1975–81; mem., Comité-Conseil F.C.A.C., Dept. of Education Québec; Conseil d'administration, Fond de soutien et aide à la recherche 1980–84; Mem. (1983–86), Vice-Pres. (1984–86), Social Sciences and Humanities Rsch. Council of Can.; Adv. Bd. Nat. Lib. of Can. 1977–81; Pres. Humanities Rsch. Council Can. 1970–72; mem. Rsch. Counc., Candn. Inst. for Advanced Rsch. 1983–87 (and mem. Extve. Comte.); Observer, Archives Counc. of Can. 1985–86; mem. Bd. of Dirs., McGill Queen's Press (1986–87), Univ. of Toronto Press Bd. (1989–90); mem., Candn. Ctte. for women in engineering 1989–91; Vice-Chrmn., Gardiner Museum for Ceramic Arts; author 'Patrice de La Tour du Pin' 1961; 'Le mythe d'Orphée dans la littérature française contemporaine' 1961; 'Chants de Bohême' 1963; 'Rina Lasnier' coll. 'Ecrivains canadiens d'aujourd'hui' 1964; 'Rina Lasnier' coll. 'Poètes d'aujourd'hui' 1969; 'Saint-Denys Garneau' 1967; 'François Mauriac' 1972, Japanese transl. 1976; author of an anthology of Quebec poetry, translated into Hungarian 1978 and Polish 1985; co-editor 'Proceedings of the VIIth Congress of the Internat. Comparative Lit. Assn.'; Vol IV (Evolution of the Novel) of the IX ICLA Congress Proceedings; ed. of the XIth ICLA Congress Proceedings; ed. 'Renewals in the Theory of Literary History' 1984; numerous articles and papers on 16th Century French Lit., 20th Century poets of France and Québec, comparative lit. and comparative lit. theory; co-editor and co-author Renaissance vols. 'Histoire comparée des littératures de langues européennes' (vol. I 'L'avènement de l'esprit nouveau [1400–1480]' 1988); co-editor and co-author 'Théorie littéraire: problèmes et perspectives' Paris 1989; mem. ed. comte. 'Canadian Comparative Literature Review'; 'Dalhousie French Review'; 'Synthesis'; Etudes Montaignistes; Chair, Internat. Adv. Bd., 'Recherches littéraires' (ICLA); mem. Am. Comparative Lit. Assn. Adv. Bd. 1980–83; Internat. Comparative Lit. Assn. (Vice Pres. 1973–78; Pres. 1979–82; Chair. Publication Policy Comte. 1983–88); Modern Lang. Assn. Am. (mem. Del. Assembly, twice Chrmn. 16th century French Lit. Div., mem. Extve. Council 1983–86, mem. Nominating Ctte. 1986–88); Vice-Pres., Internat. Fedn. for Modern Languages and Literatures 1987–93; Assn. internat. des études françaises; Assn. des profs. de français des univs. canadiennes; Assn. canadienne de littérature comparée (Vice Pres. 1969–71); Internat'l Assoc. for Neo-Latin Studies; Soc. canadienne d'études de la Renaissance; Assn. des littératures canadienne et québecoise; Candn. Soc. Semiotic Research; Office: Victoria Univ., 73 Queen's Park Cres., Toronto, Ont. M5S 1K7.

**KUSHNIR, Victor Michael,** B.Sc., M.Sc., P.Eng.; university professor; b. Montreal, Que. 2 Dec. 1941; s. Steve and Julia Lily (Zakrzewski) K.; e. Oakwood C.I. 1960; Univ. of Western Ont. B.S. 1964, M.Sc. 1966; APEO Ont. P.Eng. 1980; m. Hildegard d. Conrad and Katherine Felder 5 Nov. 1966; children: Christopher Michael, Geoffrey Steven, Brian Conrad; PROFESSOR, DEPT. OF MATHEMATICS, PHYSICS & COMPUTER SCIENCES, RYERSON POLYTECHNIC UNIVERSITY 1985– ; DeHavilland Aircraft, Spar Aerospace ISISA Satellite 1966–68; Instructor, Ryerson 1968–71; Instructor Supervisor, Physics 1971–78; Dir., Physics Technology 1975–77; Continuing Education Coordinator 1981–88; Asst. Chair, Math., Physics & Computer Science 1983–85; Chair 1985– ; Gold Medal, Radio Physics, Univ. of W. Ont. 1964; Mem., ASEE, APEO; recreations: amateur radio: VE3GGG; clubs: Logic; Home: 2640 Barnstone Cres., Mississauga, Ont. L5K 2C1; Office: 350 Victoria St., Toronto, Ont. M5B 2K3.

**KUTCHER, Stan P.,** M.A., M.D., F.R.C.P.(C); b. Toronto, Ont. 16 Dec. 1951; s. Walter Victor and Ria (Osypowich) K.; e. McMaster Univ. B.A. 1973, M.A. 1974, M.D. 1979; Univ. of Toronto Dip. Child Psychiatry 1984; m. Jane d. Robert and Norah Sheppard 22 Dec. 1974; children: Daniel, Matthew, Leah; HEAD, DIV. OF ADOLESCENT PSYCHIATRY SUNNYBROOK HEALTH SCIENCES CENTRE 1989– ; Assoc. Prof. of Psych. Univ. of Toronto 1990– , Asst. Prof. 1986; Med. Rsch. Council Gt. Brit. Univ. of Edinburgh Brain Metabolism Unit 1985; McLaughlin Fellow in Med. 1984; numerous rsch. awards; author numerous med. articles; recreation: ice hockey; Office: 2075 Bayview Ave., Toronto, Ont. M4N 3M5.

**KUTNEY, Peter Ray,** B.Sc.; executive; b. Lethbridge, Alta. 12 July 1931; s. Harry and Helen K.; e. Lethbridge Secondary Schs.; Univ. of Alta., B.Sc. (Chem. Engn.); m. Laura Mae Stillings, 14 Aug. 1959 (divorced); one s. Peter Douglas; m. Irene Ruth Brooks, 3 Dec. 1972; Dir., Pegasus Gold Inc.; past Chrmn., Pres. & Dir., Coseka Resources Ltd.; past Vice-Pres., Westcoast Transmission Co. Ltd.; Comnd. as Flying Offr., R.C.A.F. (R); Clubs: Calgary Petroleum; The Vintage Club; The Vancouver; Vancouver Lawn Tennis; Home: 802 - 300 Meredith Rd. N.E., Calgary, Alta. T2E 7A8.

**KUWABARA, Bruce Bunji,** B.Arch., O.A.A., M.R.A.I.C.; architect; b. Hamilton, Ont. 18 March 1949; s. Masao and Esther (Ennyu) K.; e. Univ. of Toronto, B.Arch. 1972; PARTNER, KUWABARA PAYNE McKENNA BLUMBERG ARCHITECTS 1987– ; Asst. Archit., George Baird Archit. 1972–75; Asst. Archit., Barton Myers Assoc. 1975–77; Associate, Barton Myers Assoc. 1977–87; Vis. Tutor, Univ. of Toronto 1978–82; Vis. Lectr., U.C.L.A. 1979–81; Coord., 2nd Year Design Studio, Univ. of Toronto 1983–84; Vis. Prof., Univ. of Toronto 1985; Adjunct Assoc. Prof. 1986–88, 1990–93; Visiting Design Critic, Harvard Univ. 1990–91; Mem., Adv. Ctte. on Design, Nat. Cap. Comn. 1986–92; King James Place 1992; Nicolas 1991; Marc Laurent 1986–91; Tudhope Studios 1989; Dome Productions 1989; Kitchener City Hall 1989–93; Oasis 1992; mem. Ont. Assn. of Archit.; Home: 61 Robert St., Toronto, Ont. M5S 2K4; Office: 322 King St. W., Toronto, Ont. M5V 1J2.

**KUZIAK, Myron A.,** B.A., LL.B.; public servant; b. Canora, Sask. 15 Aug. 1938; s. Gerald David and Betty Ann (Thompson) K.; e. Univ. of Saskatchewan B.A. and LL.B. 1964; 1st m.: Sheila M. Smith 1962; 2nd m.: Barbara Nymark 1985; children: Natalya, Sara; CHIEF ELECTORAL OFFICER, PROVINCE OF SASKATCHEWAN 1992– ; Lawyer (private practise) Regina 1964–69, 1972–92; Lawyer, Dept. of Attorney-General Manitoba 1969–72; Lecturer, Sch. of Human Justice, Univ. of Regina 1989–92; Office: Ste. 301, 2222 13th Ave., Regina, Sask. S4P 3M7.

**KUZMICKI, André R.,** B.A., M.B.A.; real estate executive; b. Brussels, Belgium 19 June 1951; s. Kazimierz Jan and Tamara-Hélène (Poorten) K.; e. McGill Univ. B.A. 1972, M.B.A. 1976; m. Nadine d. Vivian and Sam Rabinovitch 1990; one d.: Fanny; SENIOR VICE-PRES., PROPERTY INVESTMENTS, THE PRUDENTIAL INSURANCE CO. OF AMERICA 1990– ; Underwriter, Mortgage Insur. Co. of Canada 1973–74; Real Estate Appraiser Montreal, The Prudential Insur. Co. of Am. 1976–78; Investment Mgr. 1978–81; Gen. Mgr. 1981–82; Dir., Property Devel. Toronto 1982–85; Vice-Pres. 1985–90; Dir., Bentall Corp.; Vice-Pres., Institute of Candn. Real Estate Investment Managers; Past Pres., Scarborough C. of C.; Office: 200 Consilium Place, Scarborough, Ont. M1H 3E6.

**KWAN, Alan H.L.,** M.D., C.M., M.Sc., F.R.C.S.(C)., F.A.C.S.; university professor, surgeon; b. Canton, China 2 May 1943; s. Wai-Hung and Ying-Woon (Tso) K.; e. McGill Univ., B.Sc. 1964, M.D., C.M. 1968; M.Sc. 1972; m. Sylvia d. David and Cornelia Lam 6 Sept. 1969; children: Andrea, Vanessa; DIR., NFLD. CANCER CLINIC & MED. DIR., NFLD. CANCER TREATMENT & RESEARCH FOUND. 1985– ; interned at Royal Victoria Hospital and completed Surgical Residency in Gen. Surg. at Montreal Gen. Hosp.; completed Surg. Oncol. Fellowship, Sloan Kettering Cancer Ctr. (New York) 1975; Asst. Prof. of Surgery, Memorial Univ. of Nfld. 1975; promoted through ranks & apptd. Prof. of Surg. 1988; Mem., Exam. Bd. in General Surg., Royal Coll. of Phys. & Surg. of Can.; Roman Cath.; Mem., Candn. & Nfld. Med. assns.; Candn. Assn. of Surg. Oncol.; of Gen. Surg. (Adv. Bd. Mem. 1984–88); Candn. Oncol. Soc.; recreations: fishing, gardening, reading; Home: 55 Fagan Dr., St. John's, Nfld. A1A 3N2; Office: Health Sci. Ctr., Prince Phillip Dr., St. John's, Nfld. A1B 3V6.

**KWAN, Chiu-Yin,** M.Sc., Ph.D.; educator; b. Canton, China 19 Aug. 1947; s. Richard T.A. and Lily L.W. (Lian) K.; e. Chu-Hai Coll. Hong Kong B.Sc. 1969; Wilkes Coll. Pa. M.Sc. 1971; Univ. of Pa. Ph.D. 1976; m. Kanly Hsiao 10 Jan. 1975; children: Tony, William, Emily; PROF. & HEAD, PHYSIOLOGY, UNIV. HONG KONG 1992– and PROF. OF BIOMED. SCIENCES, McMASTER UNIV. 1988– ; Rsch. Fellow Candn. Heart Found. 1978– ; Asst. Prof. present Univ. 1980, Assoc. Prof. 1984; Visiting Sci.: Nat. Inst. for Physiol. Sci. Okazaki, Japan 1985; NIEHS, NIH, N.C. 1989; Visiting Prof.: Peking Union Med. Univ. Beijing, China 1989–91; Shanghai Med. Univ. China 1992–93; Sun Yat-Sen Univ. of Med. Sci's Guangzhou, China 1989–94; mem. Grants Review Ctte. Med. Rsch. Council Can. 1987–90; Dir. Candn. Ginseng Rsch. Found.; Chair Bd. Trustees Hamilton Chinese Sch.; recipient Young Investigator Award Candn. Hypertension Soc.; Career Investigator Award Heart & Stroke Found. Ont.; mem. Chinese Candn. Soc. (Pres. 1988–89); Chinese Culture Assn.; Hamilton Mundialization Ctte.; Fedn. Can.-China Friendship Assns.; ed. 'Membrane Abnormalities in Hypertension' 2 vols. 1989; author or co-author over 300 sci. publs. since 1975, over 20 book chapters; Home: 228 Crestwood St., Ancaster, Ont. L9G 1X6; Office: 1200 Main St. W., Hamilton, Ont. L8N 3Z5.

**KWAN, Mackenzie M.L.,** B.Sc., M.B.A., Ph.D.; energy executive; b. China 21 Aug. 1947; e. McGill Univ. B.Sc. 1968; Case Western Reserve Univ. Ph.D. 1973; Queen's Univ. M.B.A. 1979; m. Miranda B.H. Wu 19 May 1973; children: Michael, Mark; VICE-PRESIDENT, FINANCE & CORP. DEVELOPMENT, PAN-CANADIAN PETROLEUM 1992– ; Lectr. & Rsch. Assoc., Physics Dept., Queen's Univ. 1973–77; Treas. Corp. Planning & Production Depts., Imperial Oil 1979–84; Treas. Dept., Exxon Co. U.S.A. 1984–87; Asst. Treas. & Corp. Finance Mgr., Imperial Oil 1987–90; Vice-Pres. Business Serv., Imperial Oil Resources 1990–92; Dir., Candn. Children's Found., Calgary Chapter; Office: P.O. Box 2850, Calgary, Alta. T2P 2S5.

**KWINTER, Monte;** politician; b. Toronto, Ont. 22 March 1931; s. Aaron and Mildred Kwinter; e. Ont. Coll. of Art 1954; Nat. Ind. Design Post-Grad Scholarship (NIDPGS) to Syracuse Univ. 1955; NIDPGS to Mass. Inst. of Tech. 1956; NIDPGS to Inst. of Contemporary Art 1957, 1958; Univ. of Montreal (Hons.) 1959; m. Wilma Frankel 1956; children: Richard David, Robert Eric, Lisa, Kathryn; MEMBER OF PROVINCIAL PARLIAMENT 1985– ; Indus. Des./Sales Dev., Dunlop Canada 1955–56; Ed. Dir., Wallace Pub. Co. 1957–61; Sec.-Treas., Canada Compound Co. 1962–64; Owner/Dir., Camp Kawagama 1965–71; Vice Pres., Ont. Coll. of Art 1970–72; Murray Goldman Real Estate Ltd. 1972–78; Pres., Monte Kwinter Real Estate Ltd. 1978–85; Min. of Consumer and Commercial Relations, and Min. of Financial Institutions, Prov. of 1985–87; Min. of Industry, Trade and Tech. 1987–90; Lectr., Ryerson Inst. 1956; Consultant 1969; Teacher, N. York Bd. of Educ. 1969–71; Toronto Bd. of Educ. 1969–71; Mem., Gov. Coun., Ont. Coll. of Art 1969–71; Faculty Mem. & Vice Pres. 1970–72; Cons., Ont. Dept. Educ. 1971–72; Course Conductor, Scar. Bd. of Educ. 1977– ; Accredited Instr., Cert. Prog., Ont. Real Estate Assn. 1985; Extve. Mem., League for Human Rights; Bd. of Dir., Mem., Extve. Ctte. & Chrmn. Finance Ctte., Upper Canada Zoological Soc.; Founding Pres., Toronto Reg. Coun. of B'nai B'rith; Chrmn., Toronto Harbour Commissioner; Interim Mgmt. Ctte., Toronto Humane Soc.; Port Captain, 1984 Toronto Sesqui. Tall Ships Visit; Mem., Metro Toronto & Region Conservation Authority/Found.; Sec.-Treas., Toronto Area Indus. Devel. Bd.; Dir., Candn. Nat. Exhibiton; Mem. Bd. Trustees, Molson Indy; el. to 'Who's Who in Engineering' 1959; Ed. Dir. & Contrib. author of numerous pubns.; Home: 311 Richview Ave., Toronto, Ont. M5P 3G4; Office: Rm. 340, Parliament Bldgs., Queen's Park, Toronto, Ont. M7A 1A2.

**KWITKO, Marvin L.,** O.St.J., B.A., M.D., F.A.C.S., F.I.C.S., F.R.C.S., F.R.C.Ophth.; author; lecturer; ophthalmic surgeon; b. New York 3 March 1931; s. Louis and Rose (Gomberg) K.; e. Univ. of West. Ont., B.A. 1955, M.D. 1956; m. Alicja; children: Geoffrey, Jacqueline, Lara, Adam; ASST. PROF. OF OPHTHALMOLOGY, MCGILL UNIV.; Chief of Ophthalmology, St. Mary's Hosp., Montreal; invited to lecture & operate in Asia, India, the Middle East, Europe, S. America, Northern Finland (Lapland); began 1st successful lens implant operation series for cataract patients in Canada in 1966; joined group of 8 internat. eye surgeons performing this type of surgery in 1966; has personally instructed over 300 ophthalmic surgeons on the technique which is now practiced worldwide; performed 1st radial keretotomy surg. procedure in Can. 1979 & remains one of the leaders in this field; Founder & Pres., Candn. Implant Assn. 1975; Co-founder, Am. Intraocular Implant Soc. 1975; Founding Mem., Internat. Intraocular Implant Club 1972; Sec., Internat. Soc. of Geog. Ophthal. (orgn. symposiums in Yellowknife, Cadiz, Tunis, Sardinia & Rio de Janiero); Prof. Ignacio Barraquer Meml. Award 1970; Am. Acad. of Ophthal., Hon. Award 1975, Sr. Hon. Award 1989; Univ. of West. Ont., Hon. Award 1956; Medale d'Honneur, Assoc. Française des Imp. Intraoc.; Officer of the Order of St. John; Apptd. Chrmn. Advisory Ctte. on the Excimer Laser for Health and Welfare Canada 1990, reapptd. 1991; Mem., Pan Am. Assn. of Ophthal.; Am. Acad. of Ophthal.; Am. Coll. of Surg.; Candn. Ophthal. Soc.; Assn. for Rsch. in Ophthal.; Ophthal. Soc. of the U.K.; Internat. Coll. of Surg.; Royal Coll. of Surgeons of Can.; Hellenic Ophthal. Soc. (Hon. Mem.); Royal Coll. of Ophthalmol. (Engl.); Ophthalmological Soc. of the Barraquer Inst. (Spain); Hon. Surgeon Ophthalmatrion Eye Hosp. (Athens); Variety Club Internat.; author (medical text books): 'Glaucoma in Infants and Children' 1973, 'Surgery of the Infant Eye' 1979; 'Pseudophakia, Current Trends and Concepts' 1980, 'Geriatric Ophthalmology' 1985, 'A Comprehensive Review of Eye Diseases' 1993, 'Keratorefractive Surgery' forthcoming; and over 100 scientific medical articles; Ed. Bd. ophthalmic journals: 'Glaucoma,' 'Metabolic Ophthalmology,' 'Annals of Ophthalmology,' 'Journal of Cataract Surgery,' 'Afro-Asian Journal of Ophthalmology,' 'Ocular Surgery News Journal'; Bd. of Dirs., Nat. Assoc. for Visually Handicapped; Sci. Adv. Bd., The Kerato-Refractive Society; Bd. of Govs., Internat. Glaucoma Congress 1980; recreations: editorial writing, Dixieland jazz, Klezmer music, Cajun music, travel (has crossed the Arctic circle), ballroom dancing, golf, collects antique cars; Clubs: Elmridge Golf & Country; Home: 3800 Ave. de Ramezay, Westmount, Que. H3Y 3K1; Office: 5591 Cote des Neiges, Montreal, Que. H3T 1Y8.

**KWO, Chin Charles,** M.Sc., M.D.; physician, surgeon; b. Loyang, Honan, China 28 Oct. 1926; s. Foo Show and Mary Man (Han) K.; e. Nat. Defence Med. Coll. Taipei, Taiwan M.B., M.D. 1952; McGill Univ. M.Sc., M.D. 1969; m. Toa-Tzu Dorothy d. Huan Tsai Chen 8 July 1961; children: Jean, Jennie, John; DIR., CANDN. INST. OF CHINESE MED. SCIENCE AND ACUPUNCTURE; Pres. & Principal, Inst. of Chinese Languages and Culture, Montreal; mem. Med. Staff, Consultant, Montreal Chinese Hosp. 1969– , Reddy Mem. Hosp. 1970– , Montreal Pain Clinic 1972– ; Assoc. Research in Anesthesia, Royal Victoria Hosp. 1973– ; a pioneer, Candn. use of acupuncture analgesia for surgery and dental surgery; Intern, Nat. Defence Med. Coll. Hosp. Taipei 1951–52, Resident in Surg. 1952–56, Chief Resident in Surg. and in Orthopaedic Surg. 1957–60, Surg., Orthopaedic Instr. and Specialist in Tumor Surgery 1961–62; Intern, Reddy Mem. and Montreal Children's Hosps. 1964–65; Resident in Surg. Lake Shore Gen. Hosp. Que., St. John Gen. Hosp. N.B., Hosp. du Sacré Coeur Montreal, Hosp. Ste-Justine; Orthopaedic Research Fellow in Exper. Surgery Hosp. Ste-Justine, Verdun Gen. Hosp. Montreal 1966–70; mem. Candn. Med. Assn.; Gen. Med. Council London; Vt. Med. Bd.; Prof. Corp. Physicians Qué.; recreations: photography, paintings, Chinese calligraphy; Office: 1414 Drummond St., Suite 517, Montreal, Que. H3G 1W1.

**KWOK, Sun,** M.S., Ph.D.; educator; astronomer; b. Hong Kong 15 Sept. 1949; s. Chuen-Poon and Pui Ling (Chan) K.; e. McMaster Univ. B.Sc. 1970; Univ. of Minn. M.S. 1972, Ph.D. 1974; m. Emily Shiu-Tseng d. Chun-Ming Yu 16 June 1973; two d. Roberta Wing-Yue, Kelly Wing-Hang; PROF. OF ASTRONOMY, UNIV. OF CALGARY 1988– ; Postdoctoral Fellow Univ. of B.C. 1974–76; Asst. Prof. Univ. of Minn. 1976–77; Rsch. Assoc. Centre for Rsch. in Exper. Space Sci. York Univ. Toronto 1977–78; Rsch. Assoc. Herzberg Inst. of Astrophysics, Nat. Rsch. Council Can. Ottawa 1978–83; Asst. Prof. present Univ. 1983, Assoc. Prof. 1985, Prof. 1988– ; Visiting Fellow, Joint Inst. for Lab. Astrophysics, Univ. of Colorado 1989–90; Project Specialist Internat. Adv. Panel Chinese Univ. Devel. Project of World Bank 1984; mem. Grant Selection Ctte. Space & Astronomy, Natural Sci.'s & Eng. Rsch. Council 1985–88; mem. Assoc. Ctte. Astronomy, Nat. Rsch. Council 1986–88; Mem., Nat. Facilities Bd., Nat. Rsch. Counc. 1988–90; mem., Joint Sub-Ctte. on Space Astronomy 1989–92; mem., Advisory Panel, Institute for Astronomy and Astrophysics, Academia, Taiwan 1993– ; co-editor: 'The Late Stages of Stellar Evolution' 1987; editor: 'Astronomical Infrared Spectroscopy' 1993; author over 130 articles profl. sci. jours.; mem. Internat. Astron. Union; Candn. Astron. Soc.; Am. Astron. Soc.; rsch. field: stellar evolution and interstellar medium; Home: 139 Edgeland Rd. N.W., Calgary, Alta. T3A 2Y3; Office: Dept. of Physics & Astronomy, The Univ. of Calgary, Calgary, Alta. T2N 1N4.

**KYBETT, Brian David,** Ph.D., FCIC; university professor; b. Oxford, England 10 May 1938; s. Henry and Gwenllian (Williams) K.; e. Univ. of Wales, B.Sc. 1960, Ph.D. 1963; m. Gaynor d. Tudor and Gainor Davies 31 Aug. 1963; one s.: Gareth; DIR., ENERGY RSCH. UNIT (1987– ) and PROF. OF CHEM., UNIV. OF REGINA 1981– ; Rsch. Assoc., Rice Univ., Houston 1963–65; Asst. Prof., Univ. of Regina 1965; Mem., CIC; ACS; RSC; CIMM; MAC; CSS; SIGMA XI; SSYO (Pres. 1981–83); CAYO (Pres. 1986–87); author of numerous tech. articles & reports on Energy & Coal Chem.; Home: 9 Estey Place, Regina, Sask. S4S 4J7; Office: Energy Rsch. Unit, Univ. of Regina, Regina, Sask. S4S 0A2.

# L

**LABARGE, Margaret Wade,** CM, F.R.S.C., B.Litt., D.Litt., LL.D.; historian/writer; b. New York, N.Y. 18 July 1916; d. Alfred Byers and Helena (Mein) Wade; e. Convent of the Sacred Heart 1933; Harvard Univ., B.A. (Hon.) 1937; Oxford Univ., B.Litt. 1939; m. Raymond s. Charles and Martha Labarge 20 June 1940; children: Claire, Suzanne, Charles, Paul; ADJUNCT PROF. OF HIST., CARLETON UNIV. 1983– ; part-time lectr., Carleton Univ. and/or Univ. of Ottawa 1950–62; full-time writer 1962– ; Order of Canada; Fellow, Royal Soc. of Can.; D.Litt., honoris causa, Carleton Univ.; LL.D., honoris causa, Univ. of Waterloo; Phi Beta Kappa; J.H. Newman Honor Key; Bene Merenti Medal; Radcliffe Coll. Alumnae Recognition Award; Bd. of Gov., Carleton Univ. 1984– ; Bd., Saint Vincent Hosp. 1969–81 (Chrmn. 1977–79); Vice-Chrmn. & Chrmn., Vanier Reg. Nursing Sch. Bd. 1967–74; Dir., Candn. Nurses Assn. 1980–83; Rehab. Inst. of Ottawa 1973–81 (Chrmn. 1979–81); Counc. on Aging 1986–93 (Pres. 1989–91); Soc. of Candn. Medievalists (Pres. 1993–94); Roman Catholic; Mem., Med. Acad. of Am.; Catholic Health Assn. of Ont. (Pres., 1987–88, Dir. 1985–90); Ottawa-Carleton Reg. Dist. Health Counc., Cont. Care Bd. 1975–79, Chrmn., Hosp. Adv. Bd. 1981–83; author:

'Simon de Montfort' 1962, 'A Baronial Household of the Thirteenth Century' 1965, 'Saint Louis' 1968, 'The Cultural Tradition of Canadian Women, the Historical Background' (Royal Comn. on Status of Women) 1971, 'Court, Church and Castle/Cour, Eglise et Chateau' 1972, 'Henry V, the Cautious Conqueror' 1975, 'Gascony, England's First Colony' 1980, 'Medieval Travellers, the Rich and the Restless' 1982, 'Women in Medieval Life' (U.S. title: 'A Small Sound of the Trumpet') 1986 and acad. articles; recreations: travel, reading, walking; Address: 402 - 555 Wilbrod St., Ottawa, Ont. K1N 5R4.

**LABARGE, Suzanne,** B.A., M.B.A.; public servant; b. Ottawa, Ont. 19 Sept. 1946; d. Raymond Clement and Margaret Mein (Wade) L.; e. McMaster Univ. B.A. 1967; Harvard Univ. Sch. of Bus. Admin, M.B.A. 1971; DEPUTY SUPERINTENDENT, OFFICE OF THE SUPERINTENDENT OF FINANCIAL INSTITUTIONS 1987– ; Asst. Mgr., Main Br., Ottawa, The Royal Bank of Canada 1972–73; Sr. Asst. Mgr. Vancouver 1973–75; Winnipeg 1975–77; District Inspector, Montreal & Que. East Districts 1977–79; Asst. Gen. Mgr., Loans, Internat. Div. 1979–81; Commercial Banking, Internat. Div. 1981–82; Gen. Mgr., The Royal Bank (Suisse) 1982–84; Vice-Pres., World Corp. Banking, Que. & Atlantic 1984–85; Asst. Auditor General, Office of the Auditor Gen. of Canada 1985–87; Home: 126 Lewis St., Ottawa, Ont. K2P 0S7; Office: 13th floor, 255 Albert St., Ottawa, Ont. K1A 0H2.

**LABBÉ, Paul,** B.A., B.C.L.; export corporation executive; b. Buckingham, Que., Can. 11 March 1939; s. Arthur and Dorothy Frances (Gorman) L.; e. Univ. of Ottawa B.A. 1961; McGill Univ. B.C.L. 1964; Bar: Que. 1965; student, École Nationale d'Administration Paris 1969; Hvd. Grad. School of Business 1990; m. Kathryn Grace Cameron 10 July 1965; children: Marie-Paule, Marc, Philippe, David, Robert; PRES. & CHIEF EXECUTIVE OFFICER, EXPORT DEVELOPMENT CORP. 1991– ; Commercial Sec., Candn. Embassy Paris 1966–69; Exec. Asst. to Min. of Industry, Trade & Comm. 1969–73; Assoc., Intermico Inc. 1973–75; Pres. 1975–81; Pres., Candn. Indus. Renewal Bd. 1981–85; Commr., Fgn. Investment Review Agency 1985; Pres., Investment Can. 1985–91; Pres. & C.E.O. Export Devel. Corp. 1991– ; club: Rideau, Hunt; Home: 216 Clemow Ave., Ottawa, Ont. K1S 2B6; Office: Export Development Corp., 151 O'Connor St., Ottawa, Ont. K1A 1K3.

**LABEAUME, Régis,** B.S.; mining executive; b. Roberval, Que. 2 May 1956; s. Maurice and Thérèse (Bolduc) L.; Univ Laval B.S. 1981; m. Louise d. Christian Vien 14 July 1985; children: Catherine, Laurent; FOUNDER, PRESIDENT & CHIEF EXECUTIVE OFFICER, SOC. MINIERE MAZARIN INC. 1985– ; Political Advisor, Govt. of Que. 1980–85; Chair, Asbestos Corp. Ltd., Bell Asbestos Ltd. & Atlas Turner Inc. 1992– ; Pres., Pétro Gaspé Inc. 1989– ; administrator of var. mining companies; Pres., Que. Prospector Assn. 1986–88; Administrator, Prospector & Developer Assn. of Can. (PDAC) 1986–88; Life Mem., PDAC; co-author: 'Les innovations dans le monde minier québécois' 1990; Home: 963, Chemin Royal, Saint-Laurent, Ile d'Orléans, Que. G0A 3Z0.

**LABELLA, Frank S.,** Ph.D.; MRC career investigator; university professor; b. Middletown, Conn. 23 Sept. 1931; s. Angelo S. and Felicetta (Salafia) L.; e. Wesleyan Univ., B.A. 1952, M.A. 1954; Emory Univ., Ph.D. 1957; m. Arlyne d. Charles and Katherine McDowell 26 July 1952; children: Jennifer, Michael, Lisa; PROF. PHARMACOL. & THERAPEUT., FAC. MED., UNIV. MANITOBA 1967– ; Asst. Biol., Wesleyan Univ. 1952–54; Asst. Physiol., Emory Univ. 1954–58; Asst. Histol. 1955–57; Instr. Physio. 1957–58; Lectr. Pharmacol. 1958–60; from Asst. Prof. to Prof. 1960–67; Career Investr., Med. Res. Counc. Can. 1966– ; Am. Heart Assn. Fellow, Emory Univ. 1957–58; Candn. Rheumatism & Arthritis Soc. Res. Fellow, Univ. Man. 1958–61; Estab. Investr., Am. Heart Assn. 1961–66; Mem., Counc. on Arteriosclerosis; Man. Environ. Rsch. Ctte.; rsch. areas: narcotic drugs & endorphins; mechanisms of general anesthesia; neuroendocrin.; neurochem.; neurotoxicol.; digitalis drugs; Receptor Pharm.; aging; John J. Abel Award 1967; E.W.R. Steacie Prize 1969; Upjohn Award 1982; Sigma XI Award for Rsch. 1982; Internat. Award St. Boniface Gen. Hosp. Rsch. Found. 1983; Mem., Candn. Biochem. Soc.; Endocrine Soc.; AAAS; Candn. Assn. Gerontol.; Candn. & Amer. Pharmacol. socs.; and numerous others; Home: Box 4059, R.R. 1, Oakbank, Man. R0E 1J3; Office: Winnipeg, Man. R3E 0W3.

**LABELLE, Huguette,** O.C., Ph.D., LL.D.; public servant; b. Rockland, Ont.; e. Univ. of Ottawa Ph.D. 1980; LL.D. (Hon. causa): Brock Univ. 1982; Univ. of Saskatchewan 1984; Carleton Univ. 1986; Univ. of Ottawa 1986; York Univ. 1990; Univ. of Windsor 1990; Manitoba Univ. 1992; Officer of the Order of Canada 1990; PRESIDENT, CANDN. INTERNATIONAL DEVELOPMENT AGENCY 1993– ; has held positions in the fields of health science and education, nursing education and health care planning; Consultant, Governments of Haiti and Cuba 1974–76; Director Gen. of Policy, Research and Evaluation, Indian and Inuit Affairs Prog. 1976–78; Asst. Depy. Minister, Corporate Policy, Dept. of Indian and Northern Affairs 1979–80; Under Sec. of State for Can. 1980–85; Assoc. Secty. to the Cabinet & Depy. Clerk of the Privy Counc., Govt. of Can. 1985; Chrmn., Public Service Comn. of Can. 1985–90; Deputy Min. of Transport Canada 1990–93; past positions: Pres. Candn. Red Cross Soc.; Chrmn. Bd. of Trustees, Ottawa General Hosp.; Chrmn. of the Bd., Ottawa Health Sciences Centre Inc.; Pres., Transportation Assn. of Canada; Chrmn. of the Bd., Algonquin Coll.; Chrmn. of the Bd., Ottawa-Carleton United Way; Pres., Management Consulting Inst.; Pres., Candn. Nurses Assn.; Vice-Pres., Candn. Safety Council; mem. Bd. of Govs., Carleton Univ.; mem., Internat. Aviation Management Training Institute; mem. of Bd. of Govs., Candn. Comprehensive Auditing Found.; mem. Council of Govs., Candn. Centre for Occupational Health and Safety; mem. Bd. of Dirs., Collaboration Santé Internationale; mem. Extve. Ctte., Inst. of Public Admin. of Canada; mem. Master of Public Management Adv. Council, Faculty of Business, Univ. of Alta.; mem. Adv. Bd., School of Public Admin., Dalhousie Univ.; currently: mem., Bd. of Govs., McGill Univ.; mem. Bd. of Dirs., Public Policy Forum; mem. Faculty of Admin. Adv. Bd., Univ. of Ottawa; Internat. Development Rsch. Centre; Export Development Corp.; Internat. Centre for Human Rights and Democractic Development; Internat. Institute for Sustainable Development; Office: 12th Floor, Place du Centre, 200 promenade du Portage, Hull, Que. K1A 0G4.

**LABERGE-COLAS, Hon. Rejane,** B.A., LL.L., D.C.L. (h.c.); judge; b. Montreal, Que. 23 Oct. 1923; d. Dr. Louis Xiste and Isabelle (Lefebvre) Laberge; e. Villa-Maria Convent, Montreal, 1940; Coll. Marguerite-Bourgeois, Westmount, B.A. 1943 (cum laude); Univ of Montreal, LL.L. 1951 (cum laude), D.C.L. (Hon. causa) Bishop's 1971; m. Emile Jules Colas, Q.C., D.C.L., C.Eng. 25 Oct. 1958; children: Bernard, Hubert, Francois; Justice, Superior Court, Que., 1969; called to Bar of Que. 1952; cr. Q.C. 1968; legal Dept., The Aluminum Co. of Canada Ltd., Montreal, 1952–57; mem. of firm Geoffrion & Prud-homme, Montreal, 1957–69; former mem., Jr. Bar Council, 1955–56; Vice Chrmn. Candn. Consumers Council 1968–70; specialized in corp. law; Founding Pres. Féd. des Femmes du Québec; mem. Montreal Pub. Safety Comn. 1960–64; toured Europe with Montreal Bach Choir (contralto) singing at Edinburgh Festival, Brussels, Basel, London and Paris, 1958; Dame of Magistral Grace, Order of Malta; Roman Catholic; recreations: music, golf, skiing, tennis, swimming; Club: Hermitage Country; Home: 1 Summerhill Terrace, Montreal, Que. H3H 1B8.

**LABOSSIÈRE, Robert L.J.,** M.F.A., LL.B.; lawyer, association executive; b. Russell, Manitoba 15 April 1952; s. Léo Raymond (dec.) and Mary (Struss) L. (dec.); e. Nova Scotia College of Art & Design M.F.A. 1985; Osgoode Hall Law School LL.B. 1989; m. Dr. Laurie A. Gillies d. Ronald Kenneth (dec.) and June Cole Gillies 3 July 1983; LAWYER, private practice 1991– ; Trustee, McMichael Canadian Art Collection 1991– ; Home: 314 - 48 Abell St., Toronto, Ont. M6J 3H2; Office: 489 College St., Suite 303, Toronto, Ont. M6G 1A5.

**LABOW, Rosalind S.,** B.Sc., M.S., Ph.D.; scientist, university professor; b. Montreal, Que. 8 Jan. 1942; d. Reuben and Helen (Greenfield) Fisher; e. McGill Univ., B.Sc. 1962; Univ. of Michigan, M.S. 1964, Ph.D. 1966; m. Stanley s. Pearl and Isaac Labow 11 June 1961; children: Brian, Daniel; DIR., TAICHMAN LAB., UNIV. OF OTTAWA HEART INST., OTTAWA CIVIC HOSP. 1988– ; post-doct. fellow, N.Y. State Dept. of Health 1966–68; Rsch. Asst., Dept. of Biochem., Univ. of Ottawa 1969–81; Rsch. Assoc., Biol. Sci., Nat. Rsch. Counc. 1981–84; Scientist, Candn. Red Cross 1984–88; Asst. Prof. of Surgery, cross-appt. in Biochem., Univ. of Ottawa 1988– ; Sixma Xi 1966– ; co-author of 130 pubns.; Home: 1642 Featherston Dr., Ottawa, Ont. K1H 6P2; Office: 1053 Carling Ave., Ottawa, Ont. K1Y 4E9.

**LABRECQUE, Jacques,** B.A., F.S.A., F.I.C.A.; insurance executive; b. Quebec City, Que. 19 Feb. 1946; s. Marcel and Irène Giroux L.; e. Petit Séminaire de Qué. B.A. 1966; Laval Univ. actuarial sciences; m. Louise d. Maurice and Dolores Gignac 19 Sept. 1970; children: Annie, Jean-Francois, Sylvain, Martin; PRESIDENT AND CHIEF OPERATING OFFICER, GROUPE MFQ INC. 1991– ; Actuarial Mgr., Laurentienne-Vie 1969–75; Sr. Mgr., Individual Life Opns., MFQ Vie 1975–83; Pres. & C.E.O., La Capitale, cie ass. gén. 1983–89; C.E.O., The Personal Insur. Co. of Can. 1988–89; Pres. & C.O.O., MFQ Vie 1989– ; Bd. of Dir., Groupe MFQ Inc.; Compcorp; Les Nordiques de Qué.; Club de Golf Lorette Inc.; Office: 625, rue St-Amable, Quebec City, Que. G1R 2G5.

**LABRIE, Fernand,** O.C., O.Q., M.D., Ph.D., F.R.C.P. (C), F.R.S.C.; physician; educator; scientist; b. Quebec, Que. 28 June 1937; s. François-Xavier and Rose-Alma (Dubois) L.; e. Séminaire de Québec, B.A. 1957; Laval Univ. M.D. 1962, Ph.D. 1966; Univs. of Cambridge and Sussex, Eng., postdoctoral studies 1966–69; m. Nicole d. Henri and Françoise Cantin; children: Claude, Pierre, Danielle, Anne, Isabelle; HEAD OF MOLECULAR ENDOCRINOL. 1972– and DIR. OF RESEARCH, LE CENTRE HOSPITALIER DE L'UNIVERSITE LAVAL 1982– , Phys. in Endocrinol. 1972– ; internship and residency in Internal Med. l'Enfant-Jesus Hosp. and L'Hôtel-Dieu de Québec 1961–63; Asst. Prof. 1966–69, Assoc. Prof. 1969–74, Full Prof. 1974– (Head, Dept. Physiology 1990– ), Dir. Molecular Endocrinol. Lab. 1969– , Laval Univ.; Tutor in Biochem. Cambridge Univ. 1966–67, Sussex Univ. 1967–68; Fellow, Med. Res. Council Can. 1962–68, MRC Centennial Fellow 1968–69, Scholar 1969–73, Dir. Medical Research Counc. Group, Molecular Endocrinology Group 1973– , MRC Assoc. 1973– ; Dir. Found. du CHUL; Found. Prostate Cancer; Mem., Foundation Eye Res.; recipient Prince of Wales Award 1957; Gov. Gen.'s Medal 1957; Jobin Award 1958; Morin Award 1958, 1959; Coll. Phys. & Surgs. Que. Award 1959; Grant Medal 1960; Frank W. Horner Medal 1961; Order Student Merit Laval Univ. 1962; Fondamental Res. Award Assn. des Médecins de Langue Française du Can. 1972; Vincent Medal Assn. Canadienne Française pour l'Avancement des Sciences 1976; City of Nice Medal 1977; Fellow, Royal Soc. of Canada; Acad. of Sciences of Can. 1979; Res. Award, Soc. for the Study of Reproduction 1980; O.C. 1981; Fondation de Recherche en Hormonologie Award 1981; MDS Health Group Award 1981; Medal of Coll. of France 1984; Fideides Award, Chamber of Commerce, Ste-Foy. 1984, 1985; Chevalier, Order of Malta 1985; Excel Award 1985; Scientifique Canadien Francophone 1989, Radio-Canada; Michel Sarrazin Award, Can. Phys. Soc. 1990; Michel Sarrazin Award, Club Rech. Québec 1990; most cited Canadian Scientist 1973–88, Inst. for Sci. Information; Ordre National du Québec 1991; Grand Québecois 1991; Gloire de L'Escolle 1991; mem. Fellowships Comte. MRC 1972–73; Med. Adv. Bd. Gairdner Found. Toronto 1979–85; Adv. Bd. Fond. de Recherche en Hormonologie, Paris 1979–83; Trustee, Fonds de Recherche en Santé du Qué. 1981–88; mem., Science Counc. 1983–87; Pres., Fonds de Recherche en Santé du Qué. 1992– ; frequent guest speaker; author or co-author over 750 publs. and 1200 communications; Assoc. Ed. 'Canadian Journal of Biochemistry' 1973–78; 'Journal of Molecular and Cellular Endocrinology' 1973–81; co-ed. various publs., mem. various ed. bds.; Assoc., Royal Coll. Phys. & Surgs. Can. 1973– ; Affiliate, Royal Soc. Med. (Eng.); mem. Council Royal Soc. Can. 1983–84; mem. Coll. des Médecins et Chirurgiens de la Prov. de Qué.; Assn. des Médecins de Langue Française du Can. (Gen. Council 1970–75, 1985–89); Am. Assn. Advanc. Sci.; Assn. Canadienne-Française pour l'Avancement des Sciences; Biochem. Soc. (Gt. Brit.); Endocrine Soc. (U.S.); Candn. Biochem. Soc. (Extve. 1974–78); Candn. Physiol. Soc.; Club de Recherches Cliniques du Qué. (Sci. Sec. 1974; Extve. 1974–77); Candn. Soc. Clin. Investig. (Pres. 1981–82); Am. Soc. Cell. Biol.; Candn. Soc. Endocrinol. & Metabolism (Extve. 1974–80, Pres. 1978–79); Am. Soc. Andrology (Council 1982–85); Internat. Soc. Endocrinol. (Extve. 1980–88, Central Comte. 1976–84); Chrmn., Org. Comte., 7th Internat. Congress of Endocrinology 1984; Internat. Soc. Neuroendocrinology (Sec.-Treas. 1984–92); Candn. Acad. Sciences and other prof. assns.; Alpine Chrmn. Skibec Zone 1980–85; Vice Pres. Skibec 1980–82; Pres. Que. Ski Show 1980, 1981; Pres., Quebec Ski Fed. 1982–87; Pres. Quebec Water Ski Assn. 1987–89; Trustee, Fondation Skibec Alpin 1981– ; recreations: alpine skiing, water skiing, swimming, scuba diving, music; Clubs: Mt. Ste-Anne Ski (Alpine Chrmn. 1977–79, Pres. 1979–82); Home: 2989, de la Promenade, Ste-Foy, Qué. G1W 2J5; Office: 2705 Boulevard Laurier, Ste-Foy, Qué. G1V 4G2.

**LABROSSE, Hon. Jean-Marc,** B.A., LL.B.; judge; b. Masson, Que. 2 June 1935; s. Olida and Gracia (Pilon) L.; e. Ecole St. Charles Ottawa 1949; Univ. of Ottawa High Sch. 1953; Univ. of Ottawa B.A. 1957, LL.B. 1960; m. Louise d. Armand Dumas, Malartic, Que. 1 Dec. 1962; children: Danielle, Michèle, Marc; JUDGE,

COURT OF APPEAL OF ONTARIO 1990– ; called to Bar of Ont. 1962; law practice Sudbury, Ont. 1962–75; Judge, Supreme Court of Ont. 1975–90; served with U.N.T.D. 1957–60, retired as Sub-Lt. 1961; while in Sudbury actively engaged in Jr. Hockey and served as Dir. of Sudbury Wolves Jr. Hockey Club; Dir. Sudbury Dist. Boys Home; mem. Candn. Bar Assn.; Advocates' Soc.; R. Catholic; recreations: golf, skiing, fishing, hunting; Office: 130 Queen St. W., Toronto, Ont. M5H 2N5.

**LABROSSE, Leo E.,** B.Com.; retired company executive; b. Montreal, Que. 22 Nov. 1925; s. Eddy Joseph and Hortense (Crevier) L.; e. Sir George Williams Coll., B. Com. 1956; m. Claire, d. late Georges Lesage, 24 June 1950; children: Pierre, Johanne; Dir., B.C. Sugar Refinery Ltd.; Roman Catholic; recreations: skiing, golf, swimming, tennis, reading; Clubs: St.-Denis; Islesmere Golf and Country; Home: 6111 du Boisé ave., Apt. PH-E, Montreal, Que. H3S 2V8.

**LACAILLE, Philippe G.,** B.A.C.; pharmaceutical executive; b. Neuilly/Seine, France 26 Sept. 1954; s. Alexis and Denise (Quinquet) L.; e. Paris Academy B.A.C. 1972; Sch. of Med. Paris 1973–74; Fac. of Sci. Paris 1975–76; Sr. Extve. prog., Univ. of Western Ontario cert. 1990; m. Veronique d. Henry and Simone Mory 19 May 1979; children: Audrey, Julien, Emilie, Kevin; EXECUTIVE VICE-PRES. & CHIEF OPERATING OFFICER, BIOCHEM PHARMA INC. 1991– ; various sales positions in pharm. industry 1979–85 in Europe and Canada; Div. Mgr., Ophthalmics Group, Pharmacia Can. Inc. 1986; Gen. Mgr. 1987; Vice-Pres. Ophthalmics Group 1988–90; Vice-Pres. Health Care Group 1990–91; Interim Pres. & C.E.O., IAF BioVac Inc. 1993– ; Mem., Long-Range Strategic Planning Group, Pharmacia Ophthalmics AB Sweden 1989–91; Bd. of Dir., BioChem Therapeutic Inc.; BioChem ImmunoSystems Inc.; IAF BioVac Inc.; Alumni, Univ. of W. Ont.; Mem., Presidents Assn., Am. Mngt. Assn.; Bd. of Trade of Montreal and Laval; recreations: music, tennis, skiing; Home: 45 Alouette, Dollard des Ormeaux, Que. H9A 3H3; Office: 2550 Daniel-Johnson Blvd., Ste. 600, Laval, Que. H7T 2L1 and 3100 Le Carrefour Blvd., Suite 770, Laval, Que. H7T 2L1.

**LACE, Francis Dwyer,** D.S.O., O.B.E., E.D.; investment dealer; b. Qu'Appelle, Sask. 20 Nov. 1911; s. Algernon Francis Doyne and Marion Edith (Leonard) L.; e. Upper Can. Coll., Toronto, Ont., 1922–28 (Sr. Matric.); Royal Mil. Coll., Kingston, Ont. Grad. 1932; m. Barbara Lynne, d. W. Boyd Caldwell, Toronto, Ont., 12 Sept. 1939; children: Roger Dwyer, Catherine Anne; Hon. Dir., RBC Dominion Securities Inc.; Hon. Trustee, Toronto Hospital; Jr. with A.E. Ames & Co. Ltd., Invest. Dealers, Toronto, Ont. 1932–37; joined Matthews and Co. Ltd. in 1937 as Salesman; Partner 1946, Vice-Pres. 1952, Pres. 1960, Chrmn. 1972–75; served with Candn. Militia 1932–39; Candn. Army Active, Overseas 1939–45; promoted to rank of Brig. on active service Oct. 1944, C.R.A. 2 Candn. Div.; awarded D.S.O., O.B.E.; Chrmn., Ont. Dist., Invest. Dealers Assn. Can. 1958–59; Anglican; recreations: golf, tennis; Clubs: Toronto Golf; Toronto; Badminton & Racquet; Address: 15 Hillholm Road, Toronto, Ont. M5P 1M1.

**LACEY, Veronica Suzanne,** B.A., M.A., M.Ed.; educational executive; b. Hungary; e. York Mills C.I.; Univ. of Toronto B.A. (Hons.) 1967, M.A. 1970, M.Ed. 1981; DIRECTOR OF EDUCATION AND SECRETARY TREASURER, NORTH YORK BOARD OF EDUCATION 1989– ; Teacher, Principal, Superintendent & Dir. of Edn. 26 years; promotes greater parental influence in the school system through var. programs; fluent in English, French, Spanish, Hungarian; one of the Canadian school system's most innovative leaders in building new partnerships among schools, business, industry, labour & govt.; Bd. of Dir., Conf. Bd. of Canada Nat. Council on Edn.; Univ. of Toronto Bd. of Gov.; Bd. of Dir. for Candn. Network for the Advancement of Research, Industry and Edn. CANARIE Inc.; Bd. of Dir., Nat. Quality Inst.; Prosperity Steering Group, Govt. of Canada (contbr. to report: 'Inventing Canada's Future'); Distinguished Educator Award, OISE 1993; Gov. Gen. Medal for Community Commitment 1993; YMCA's Woman of Distinction Award 1991; Phi Delta Kappa's Educator of the Year Award 1991; O.S.S.T.F. 'Woman of Year' Award 1988, '89; Ont. Sec. School Teachers' Fed. Woman of the Year Award 1988; Selection Ctte., Marshall McLuhan Distinguished Award for Outstanding Teachers; Principal, Leadership Courses for Principals, Ont. Govt.; Bd. of Dir., Metro Action Ctte. on Public Violence Against Women & Children; Chair, U.N. 50th Year Edn. Ctte.; recreation: tennis; Office: 5050 Yonge St., North York, Ont. M2N 5N8.

**LACHANCE, Denis,** B.Sc., Ph.D.; research program manager; b. Quebec City, Que. 2 Feb. 1939; s. Alcide and Clementine (Bernier) L.; e. Laval Univ. B.Sc. 1962; Univ. of Wisconsin Ph.D. 1966; m. Ruth Gagnon; children: Simon, Vincent, Renée; RESEARCH MANAGER, CAN. FOREST SERVICE, NAT. RESOURCES CAN., QUEBEC REGION 1989– ; Research on conifer root rots, 1966; on stem cankers of deciduous trees from 1970; Tree Disease Specialist, Forest Insect & Dis. Survey Unit, Que. Region 1976– ; Head 1978– ; leader of a large rsch. project on effects of environ. stress on the forest 1988– ; Candn. Sci. Coord. joint U.S./Canada Rsch. Project, The N. Am. Maple Project; Nat. Coord., Green Plan Bio-Monitoring Activity, Can. Forest Service; Mem., Candn. Phytopath. Soc. (Sec.-Treas. 1971–73); Ordre des Ingénieurs forèstiers du Qué.; Candn. Inst. of Forestry; Que. Soc. for Plant Protection (Vice-Pres. 1984, Pres. 1985); author: 'Sugarbush Management: A Guide to Maintaining Tree Health' 1989; co-editor: 'Foret Decline Concepts' 1992; Home: 3374 Beauchamps, Sainte-Foy, Que. G1X 2C6; Office: P.O. Box 3800, Sainte-Foy, Que. G1V 4C7.

**LACHANCE, Gustave,** C.M., B. ès L., B.D.S., D.D.S.; retired educator; b. Quebec City, Que. 20 Dec. 1912; s. late Joseph Michel Eusebe and late Edith Pritchard (Guité); e. Hist. Guide of Que. Cert. 1928; Que. Little Semy. B. ès L. 1930; Univ. Montreal, Certificate of P.C.B. 1933; Univ. Montreal B.D.S. 1935, D.D.S. 1937; m. Jeanne d. late Pierre Poirier, New Richmond, Bonaventure Cty., Que. 16 Oct. 1937; children: Jacques (m. Rita Dorion), Odette (m. François Labrousse), Louis de Gaspé, André (dec'd 1988); Editor-in-chief, Univ. Montreal's Newspaper: 'Le Quartier Latin'; Assoc. Ed., Univ. Montreal's Grad. magazine: 'L'Action Universitaire'; dental practice New Richmond, Que. 1937–50, Quebec City 1950–72; Asst. Prof. of Dental Med., Laval Univ. 1972, Assoc. Prof. 1978, Dir. of Clinics 1972–80, Archivist & Historian 1974– , Life mem. Laval Univ. Foundation 1975; Special Counsellor, Laval Univ. Service of Expansion Bd. 1980; Past Pres. Inst. Canadien de Que. 1966–69; La Croix Rouge Canadienne, New Richmond Dist. 1946–49; La Caisse Populaire Desjardins New Richmond 1948–50; La Soc. Dentaire de Qué. 1954–55; Le Congrès Internat. Richelieu, Que. 1961–62; Poly-Glot (1963) Inc. Que. 1963–68; Bibliothèque Municipale de Qué. 1966–69; Jeunesses Musicales du Can. Que. Sec. 1967–68; Consulting Dentist, Qué. Workmen's Compens. Bd., 1969–72; Gov., Qué. Symphonic Orchestra, 1979–; Past Dir. Assn. des Medecins et Dentistes de la Gaspésie 1939–50; Corp. du Theatre du Vieux-Que. 1967–68; Corp. du Theatre Le Trident Inc. Que. 1970–71; Gov., Ordre des Dentistes du Que. 1968–72; Assn. Dentaire Canadienne (Exécutif des Congrès Nat. Toronto) 1968–69; Corp. de l'Opéra du Qué. 1971–75; Gov., Que. Symphonic Orchestra since 1980; Corp. du Pavillon des Jeunes Inc. St. Damien since 1975; Adm., Laval Hospital Inst. of Cardiology 1981; Adm., La Fond. de l'Opera de Qué. 1983– ; rec'd Order of Merit, Univ. of Montreal 1936; Centennial Medal 1967; 125th Anniversary of the Confederation of Canada Medal, 1992; Order of Canada 1978; mem. emeritus 1977 Inst. Canadien de Que. (Pres. 1966–69); Hon. Citizenship of City of Lafayette, Louisiana, U.S.A. 1987; mem. Canadian Opera Guild 1974– ; Heritage Canada 1975– ; Can. Dental Assn.; Order Dentists Que. (Gov. 1968–72); Am. Assn. Dental Faculties; Que. City Dental Club (Past Pres.); Candn. Soc. for the History of Med. (Que. City Sect.; Offr. of Extve. 1983); Adv. Bd., Les Presses de l'Université Laval 1979– ; mem. Hollywood (Fla.) Art & Culture Centre; mem., La Soc. Historique de la Gaspésie; La Soc. Historique de Sillery; La Soc. des Amis de l'orgue de Québec; Liberal; R. Catholic; recreations: music, reading, writing, travel; Home: 1695 Parc des Sources, Sillery, Que. G1S 4B6.

**LACHAPELLE, Diane,** B.Sc., RDH, M.Sc.; university professor and administrator; b. Montreal, Que. 29 Jan. 1952; d. Paul and Georgette (Giard) L.; e. Ahuntsic Coll. Dipl. 1971; Univ. of Montreal B.Sc. 1974; Laval Univ. M.Sc. 1980; m. Dr Yves s. Isidore and Aurore Harvey 5 May 1973; children: Simon-Pierre, Jean-Daniel; PROF. & ASSISTANT DEAN, FAC. OF DENTAL MEDICINE, LAVAL UNIV. 1992– ; began teaching Laval Univ. 1975; main researcher and/or collaborator in many rsch. projects fin. by Med. Rsch. Council, Nat. Health Rsch. & Devel. Prog. & Fonds de rech. en santé du Qué.; Consulting Practicing Dental Hygienist, Faculty Prof. Dental Clinic 1975– (one day per week); extensive lecturer; Founding Mem., Corp. prof. des hygiénistes dentaires du Qué. 1975–79; Mem., Internat. Assn. for Dental Rsch. 1985– ; Assn. can. de rech. dent. 1985– ; Mem. in good standing, Corp. prof. des hygiénistes dent. du Qué. 1975; author/co-author of over 50 sci. pubns. & num. sci. communications; recreations: winter skiing, golf,; clubs: Quebec Garrison; Home: 1799 chemin Gomin, Sillery, Que. G1S 1P2; Office: Quebec, Que. G1K 7P4.

**LACHAPELLE, Guy F.,** B.A., M.Sc., M.A., Ph.D.; university professor; b. Montreal, Que. 14 Jan. 1955; s. Bernard and Gilberte (Choinière) L.; e. Concordia Univ., grad. dipl. in commun. 1979; Univ. of Montreal, B.A. 1977, M.Sc. 1981; Northwestern Univ., M.A. 1982, Ph.D. 1986; m. Lyne d. Robert and Denise Lalonde; children: Marc-Olivier, Camille; PROF., DEPT. OF POL. SCI., CONCORDIA UNIV. 1984– ; Dir., M.A. Prog. in Pub. Policy/Pub. Admin., present univ. 1990–91; Asst. Dir., Parlty. Internship Prog. (Ottawa) 1988–92; Mem., Bd. of Dir., Candn. Pol. Sci. Assn. 1988; review editor: 'Revue Politique' [québécoise de science] 1990–92; (with Gérald Bernier, Daniel Salée and Luc Bernier) 'The Quebec Democracy: Structure, Processes & Policies' McGraw-Hill Ryerson 1993; 'Polls and the Media in Canadian Elections: Taking the Pulse' (Royal Commission on Electoral Reform and Party Financing, Dundurn Press) 1991; co-author: 'Québec: Un Pays incertain – réflexion sur le Québec post-referendaire' 1980; recreations: nordic skiing, swimming; Office: 7141 Sherbrooke St. W., Montreal, Que. H4B 1R6.

**LACHAPELLE, Roger;** b. Montreal, Que. 5 Apr. 1925; e. Lachine (Que.) High Sch.; Sir George Williams Coll.; McGill Univ.; m. Jeanne Carey; Dir., Corby Distilleries Ltd.; BNP (Canada); Industrial Alliance Life Insur. Co.; Rolland Inc.; National Life of Canada; Bouverie Investments Ltd.; F.C.A. Internat. Ltd.; joined Transparent Paper Products Ltd. as Secy. Treas. 1949–60, Extve. Vice-Pres. 1960–66, Pres. 1966; Pres. & C.E.O., Meaghers Distillery Ltd. 1967–78; Extve. Vice Pres., Corby Distilleries Ltd. 1978; Pres. and C.E.O. 1979–90; Chrmn., 1990–92; Retired; served in 2nd World War with RCAF 1943–45; recreations: boating, fishing, hunting, skiing; Clubs: St. Denis (former Pres.); Home: 11807 de Meulles, Cartierville, Que. H4J 2E4.

**LACK, Kelvin;** broadcasting executive; b. London, Eng. 26 Oct. 1938; e. UK; m. Morag McDonald 1982; children (by previous marriage): Simon, Robert, Yolanda; MANAGER, CBC RADIO WORKFORCE STRATEGY 1993– ; served 32 yrs. with CBC in TV, Radio and Radio Can. Internat. (RCI); various journalistic and mgmt. roles CBC TV Montreal, RCI and Nat. TV & Radio News Toronto; Dep. Mng. Ed. Nat. Radio News 1979–82; Dir. of Radio for Ont. 1982–88; Manager, Radio Production Centre, CBC Toronto 1988–93; career counsellor Univ. of Toronto; author various articles cooking, travel, current affairs for mags. and newspapers; recreations: golf, sailing; Office: Broadcast Centre, 250 Front St. W., Rm. 2G207, Toronto, Ont. M5V 3G5.

**LACK, Stephen H.,** B.A., M.F.A.; painter; filmmaker; b. Montréal, Qué. 27 Aug. 1946; s. David Melvin and Sybil (Glickman) L.; e. McGill Univ., B.A. 1967; Instituto Allende, Univ. of Guanajuato, Mexico M.F.A. 1968; m. Lilly d. Lindsay and Josephine Glidden 6 Aug. 1982; two s. Jasper Nile, David Asher; solo painting exhns. incl. Vehicle Art Montréal 1974, 1977; internat. exhns. since 1982; rep. various corporate and pub. colls. incl. Nat. Gallery Australia and New York Pub. Lib. Prints & Books; films incl. 'Montreal Main' (co-author) 1974; 'Rubber Gun Show' (co-author & co-producer) 1977; nominated 1979 Genie Best Script; 'Dead Ringers' 1989; 'All the Vermeers in New York' 1990; author 'Just Get Me Out of Here' (18 miniature etchings) 1987; film lead 'Head On' 1979 retitled 'Fatal Attraction' with Sally Kellerman and John Huston and 'Scanners' by David Cronenberg 1979; recipient 'Print' Magazine's Regional Designers Award N.Y. 1985; Nat. Endowment Arts Award USA 1987; Nat. Endowment Award (N.E.A.) Painting 1993; Canada Council Award 1991; Home: 9 Willow Ave., Rockleigh, NJ 07647 USA and P.O. Box 83, East Greenwich, NY 12826 USA.

**LACOMBE, Trefflé,** B.Com., B.A., M.A.; public servant; b. Montréal, Qué. 3 May 1940; s. Gérard and Béatrice (Doyle) L.; e. Sir George Williams Univ. B.Com. Bus. Admin. 1963, B.A. Econ. 1966; Carleton Univ. M.A. Pub. Admin. 1968; m. Yolande d. Lucie and Maurice Vaillancourt 14 Mar. 1964; children: Francis, Gabriel, Nathalie; CHIEF EXTVE. OFFICER, STCUM, MONTRÉAL; Office Mgr., Bell Canada 1963; Asst. to the Princ., Sir George Williams Univ. 1963; Dir. Student Services, Univ. of Montréal 1968; Asst. Vice-Rector, Univ. of Ottawa 1970; teacher at M.B.A. level Personnel Mgmt. and Ind. Relns., Univ. of Ottawa 1976–83; Commissioner, Public Service Comn. of Canada 1983–88; Executive Director, Québec Region, Employment and Immigration Canada 1988; recreation: tennis; Home: 8055 Neuchatel, Brossard, Qué. J4Y 2G8;

Office: 800, de la Gauchetière St. W., Room F-2100, P.B. 2000, Place Bonaventure, Montréal, Qué. H5A 1J6.

**LACOSTE, Gérald Alexandre,** Q.C., B.A., LL.L., LL.M., b. Lac Lacoste, Labelle Co., Que. 18 July 1943; s. the late Judge Marc and late Jacqueline (Barsalou) L.; e. Coll. St-Viateur d'Outremont B.A. 1963; Univ. of Montreal LL.L. 1966; Univ. of London LL.M. 1968; L.S.E. (Pub. Adm.) 1969; m. Fernande d. W. Boutin, 2 Sept. 1967 (dec'd.); children: Marie Catherine, Alexandra, Hugo; PRESIDENT AND CHIEF EXTVE. OFFR., MONTREAL STOCK EXCHANGE 1994– ; Partner, Martineau Walker and Fasken Martineau, Montreal 1982–93 (business law with emphasis on securities and financial institutions); called to Bar of Que. 1967; mem. Extve. Comte. and Gen. Council Bar Prov. Que. 1975–76; Counsellor Bar of Montréal 1975–77 (Secy. Jr. Bar 1972–73); Chrmn, Que. Securities Comn., 1976–81; Pres., Advisory Ctte., Quebec Financial Institutions 1987; Legal Advisor to Senate Ctte. for the reports on the reform of financial institutions 1986 and 1990; Mem., Binational Panel Review, Canada-U.S. Free Trade Agreement 1989–93; R. Catholic; recreations: fishing, hunting, skiing, windsurfing; Home: 35 ave. Springrove, Outremont, Qué. H2V 3J1.

**LACOSTE, Paul,** O.C., LL.L., Ph.D.; lawyer, professor; b. Montreal, P.Q. 24 Apr. 1923; s. Juliette (Boucher) and the late Wing Commdr. Emile L., C.G.A.; e. Univ. of Montreal, B.A. 1943, M.A. 1944, L. Ph. 1946, LL.L. 1960; Univ. of Chicago, 1946–47; Univ. of Paris, Ph.D. 1948; LL.D. (Hon.) McGill Univ. 1975; Univ. of Toronto 1978; D.d'Univ. (Hon.) Univ. Laval 1986; m. Louise Marcil, 31 Aug. 1973; two d., Helene, Anne-Marie; one s., Paul-André; RECTOR, UNIV. OF MONTREAL 1975–85; Prof. of Philos. (1946–86), and Law (1962–70, 1985–87), Professor Emeritus (1987), Univ. of Montreal; Practicing Lawyer, 1964–66; Commentator and Moderator on C.B.C. Radio and Television, 1948–63; mem. Royal Comn. on Biling. & Biculturalism (1963–71); mem. Superior Council of Educ., Qué. 1964–68; Que. Univs. Council (1969–77); Council of City of Montreal and of Montreal Urban Community (1970–74); Chrmn. & Pres., I Musici Orchestra of Montreal 1991–93, Mem. 1983– ; Ecole polytechnique de Montréal 1975–85; Ecole des hautes études commerciales de Montréal 1982–85; Inst. de recherches cliniques de Montréal 1975–87; Assn. des universités partiellement ou entiérement de langue française 1975–81 (Pres. 1978–81); Fonds international de coopération universitaire (1975–81); Association of Commonwealth Universities (1977–80); Candn. Scholarship Trust Plan 1988– ; Quebec Bar Found. 1991–92; Vice-Pres., Canada Studies Foundation (1972–79); Chrmn., Commission and Cttees. of the Federal Environmental Assessment Review to the Great Whale Hydro-electric Project 1991– ; Officer of the Order of Canada (1977); Chevalier de la Légion d'Honneur, France, 1984; Human Relations Award, Candn. Council of Christians and Jews 1981; Pres., Soc. de Philosophie de Montréal 1951–57; Vice Rector, Univ. of Montreal 1966; Extve. Vice Rector 1968–75; Pres., Conf. of Rectors & Principals of Que. Univs. 1977–79; Pres., Assn. of Universities & Colleges of Canada 1978–79; mem. Bd. C.S.T. Foundation (Candn. Scholarship Trust); mem., Nat. Counc., Candn. Human Rights Found.; Amnesty Internat. (Can.); Montreal Museum of Fine Arts; Publications (with others): 'Justice et paix scolaire' 1962; 'A Place of Liberty' 1964; 'Principes de gestion universitaire' 1970; 'Education permanente et potentiel universitaire' 1977; Home: 356 Woodlea Ave., Montréal, Qué. H3P 1R5; Office: Univ. de Montréal, C.P. 6128, Succ. Am Pavillon 2910, Suite 6, Montréal, Qué. H3C 3J7.

**LACOURCIERE, Hon. Maurice-Norbert;** judge; b. Montmartre, Sask. 8 Oct. 1920; s. Joseph-Emile, Q.C. and Atala (Fortin) L.; e. Coll. Mathieu, Gravelbourg, Sask., Univ. of Ottawa, B.A. 1940; (Gold Medal, Phil.; Gold-Silver Medal, French Lit.) Osgoode Hall Law Sch.; m. Marguerite Gauthier 7 April 1956; children: Luc, Marc, Brigitte, François, Chantal, Michel; JUSTICE, COURT OF APPEAL, ONT., since 1974; read law with Phelan, O'Brien & Phelan, Toronto, and J. E. Lacourcière, Q.C., Sudbury; called to Bar of Ont. 1949; served 1 yr. with H.O. Crown Life Ins. Co., Toronto after call to Bar; thereafter in partnership with father, J. E. Lacourcière, Q.C., in Sudbury; apptd. Judge of Co. Court, Nipissing District, 1964; Justice, Supreme Court of Ontario 1967; served with the R.C.A.F. 1941–45, rank Flying Offr.; (mem., Bd. of Govs., Laurentian Univ. 1962–69); Past Gen. Chrmn., Sudbury & Dist. Un. Welfare Fund; Pres., Sudbury Law Assn., 1955; Past Dist. Gov. (1956), N. Ont. Richelieu Soc.; Past Pres., Société Historique du Nouvel Ont.; Past Chrmn., Editorial Advisory Bd., Cdn. Bar Review; mem. (1968–72) Bd. of Govs., Univ. of Toronto; Inst. of Judicial Admin.; Internat. Law Assn.; Centennial Medal; Queen's Jubilee Medal; 125th Anniversary of the Confederation of Canada Medal, 1992; Hon. doctorate (D.U.), Univ. of Ottawa 1989; R. Catholic; recreations: golf, swimming; Club: York Downs Golf & Country; Office: Osgoode Hall, Toronto, Ont. M5H 2N5.

**LA COUTURE, Jean,** F.C.A.; financial executive; b. Montreal, Que. 1946; e. C.A. 1967; PRES. AND CHIEF EXTVE. OFFR. THE GUARANTEE CO. OF NORTH AMERICA 1989– ; Partner Le Groupe Mallette 1967–72, Pres. and Chief Extve. Offr. 1980–89, Pres. Calculus, Cie d'Informatique Ltée 1972–80 (subsidiary); Chrmn., Assn. of Candn. Insurers; Dir., C.D.M. Laminates Inc.; Home: 625 St-Germain, Outremont, Qué. H2V 2V7; Office: 1560 Place du Canada, Montreal, Qué. H3B 2R4.

**LACROIX, Benoît;** éducateur; né à St-Michel-de-Bellechasse, Qué., 8 septembre 1915; f. Caius et Rose-Anna (Blais) L.; é. Lectorat en théologie, Ottawa 1941; Maîtrise ès sciences médiévales, Toronto 1946, Doctorat ès sciences médiévales, Toronto 1951; Harvard Univ. 1959–60 (Bourse Guggenheim); PROFESSEUR, INSTITUT d'ETUDES MEDIEVALES, UNIV. DE MONTREAL 1945–85; Directeur-fondateur de 'Vie des Lettres Canadiennes' 1956–75; Professeur invité aux universités de Kyoto, Butare et Caen; Directeur, Institut d'Etudes Médiévales, Univ. de Montréal 1963–69; Centre d'études des religions populaires (Montréal) depuis 1970; Prof. invité au Dép. d'histoire (CELAT), Univ. Laval 1978–82; Dir. de l'édition critique Lionel Groulx, Montréal, 1979; Chercheur à l'Inst. québ. de recherche sur la culture, Qué., 1980; Prix du Qué., 1981; auteur: 'Pourquoi aimer le moyen âge?' 1950; 'Les débuts de l'historiographie chrétienne...' 1950; 'L'histoire dans l'antiquité...' 1951; 'Vie des lettres et histoire canadienne' 1954; 'Compagnon de Dieu' 1961; 'Le P'tit Train' 1964; 'Orose et ses idées' 1965; 'Le Japon entrevu' 1965; 'Le Rwanda: mille heures au pays des mille collines' 1966; 'L'historien au moyen âge' 1971; 'Les cloches' 1974; en collaboration 'The Development of Historiography' 1954; 'Classiques canadiens' ('Saint Denys Garneau' 1956, 'Lionel Groulx' 1967); 'Edition critique des Oeuvres de Saint Denys Garneau' 1971; 'Folklore de la mer et religion' 1980; 'Les Pèlerinages au Québec' 1981; 'Célébration des saisons' 1981; 'Quelque part en Bellechasse' 1981; 'Religion populaire, religion de clercs?' (sous la dir. de Benoît Lacroix et Jean Simard) 1984; 'Religion populaire au Québec...' (sous la dir. de Benoît Lacroix et Madeleine Grammond) 1985; 'La religion de mon père' 1986; 'Trilogie en Bellechasse' 1986; 'Marie de Saint-Michel' 1986; 'Le choix de Benoît Lacroix dans l'oeuvre de Benoît Lacroix' 1987; 'Silence' 1989; 'La piété populaire: le Québec, répertoire bibliographique, Canada, tome 1' 1989; 'Jeunes et croyants' 1989; 'Célébration des âges et des saisons' 1993; articles nombreux; mem. Société Royale du Can.; Académie des Sciences Morales et Politiques; Officier de l'Ordre du Canada 1985; Doctorat honoris causa, Univ. de Sherbrooke 1990; Ordre National du Québec 1990; Catholique; Adresse: 2715, Côte-Sainte-Catherine, Montréal, Qué. H3T 1B6.

**LACROIX, Georgette;** auteur et journaliste; née Québec, Que. 6 avril 1921; f. Jean Baptiste et Alice (Mercier) L.; é. Congrégation Notre Dame St. Malo; Inst. Jean Thomas; cours privés pour l'espagnol et l'italien; une f. Hélène; 24 années de radio CHRC et 2 années de journ. à 'L'Action Québec'; collaboration à 'Echos-Vedettes,' 'Québec en Bref' et 'Audace' (revue belge); Dir. de la revue 'Poésie' de la Soc. des Poètes Candn.-Français; série de 17 émissions à CFCM-4, Télévision de Qué., 'D'Hier à Aujourd'hui' (petite histoire des lieux et des gens); de 1972 à 1985 à l'emploi du Gouv. du Que., Min. des Affaires culturelles; d'abord comme attaché de presse du min., puis agent d'information au Service des Lettres, agent culturel au Service de la Recherche; rédactrice du bulletin d'information 'Archives en tête,' des Archives nationales du Qué. 1978–81; archiviste au Centre de la Capitale 1981–84; auteur de 'Mortes Saisons' 1967; 'Entre Nous ... Ce Pays' 1970 (Prix France Que. 1971); 'Le Creux de la Vague' 1972; 'Aussi Loin que Demain' 1973; 'Dans L'Instant de ton Age' 1974; 'Au large d'Eros' 1975; 'Vivre l'automne' 1976; 'Québec 1608–1978' (1978); 'Québec, Capitale de la Neige' 1979; 'Québec' 1979; 'Faire un enfant' 1980; 'Hommage au Québec, Eugène Kedl Photographe' 1980; 'Artistes du Quebec' 1980; 'Germain Larochelle, L'homme et le Peintre' 1981; 'Astrorama' 1982; 'Tatoushak' 1982; 'Sports en fête' 1983; 'Le carnaval de Québec 1894–1954–1984' 1984; 'L'Acadie...avec les yeux du coeur' 1984; 'Les Fermières d'Armagh pour la terre et pour le foyer' 1984; 'De Tadoussac à Mistassini' 1984; 'Le Carnaval aux Souvenirs' 1985; 'Tableaux-poèmes sur le Temps d'Autrefois' 1985; 'Charlevoix Mes Amours' 1985; 'Le Salon se raconte' 1986; 'Histoires de mots et d'animaux' 1986; 'Adieux du Québec à M. Yourcenar' 1988 (Collectif); 'La Sinfonia, 25 Ans de Musique' 1988; 'La Petite Scène des Grandes Vedettes' 1988 (Collaboration); 'Grands Peintres du Québec' 1990; 'Adieux du Québec à Alice Parizeau' 1991 (collectif); auteur des textes de 21 chansons sur disques, interprétées par André Lejeune, Rui Mascarenas et Guy Lepage; a mérité 2 prix de poésie de la Soc. du Bon Parler Francais, Montréal 1963, 1969; prix France-Québec 1971; prix des Arts et Poésie de Touraine (France) 1972; Mention d'Honneur de la Société des Écrivains Canadiens de Langue Française pour 'Le Carnaval de Québec 1894–1954–1984'; Certificat d'honneur de la Ville de Qué. pour 'Le Carnaval de Québec 1894–1954–1984'; 1er prix de Poésie du Concours la Voie des mots, de Via Rail 1990: Hommage de la Ville de Mistassini à l'Occasion de son Centenaire 1892–92; Présidente Générale, la Soc. des Ecrivains Can. 1982–83; mem. du Salon internat. du livre de Qué. 1977–89; mem. de Québec-Acadie; mem. du comité de la collection Civilisation du Qué du min. des Aff. culturelles; 1981–82 et 1982–83; mem. hon. à vie du club Lions de Baie St-Paul Inc. pour 'Charlevoix, Mes Amours'; mem. hon. à vie de la Société de géographie de Québec; catholique r.; récréations: lecture, natation, cinéma, voyages; residence: 694 rue St-Jean, Québec, Que. G1R 1P8.

**LACROIX, Guy R.;** textile executive; b. Ottawa, Ont. 4 Aug. 1948; s. Lucien and Cécile (Bélisle) L.; e. Algonquin Coll.; m. Louise d. Rolland and Yvette Roussy 14 June 1969; children: Guy, Renée; Pres., Dominion Fabrics Co., subs. Dominion Textile Inc. 1987–91; var. pos. with Royal Bank of Can. 1969–80; Noranda Mines 1980–83; joined Dominion Textile Inc. 1983; Club: Univ. Club of Montreal.

**LACROIX, Marcel,** P.Eng.; company president; b. Ste. Marie, Beauce Co., Que., 13 March 1930; s. Charles and Marie (Giroux) L.; e. Laval Univ., Civil Engn., 1953; m. Louise, d. Fernand Boutin, Quebec City, Que., 9 Oct. 1954; children: Monique, Charles, Camille; PRES., MARCEL LACROIX INVESTMENTS LTD.; Dir., The Canam Manac Group; Restaurants Sportscene Inc.; mem., Corp. Prof. Engrs. Que.; K. of C.; Roman Catholic; recreations: golfing, skiing; Home: 16 Jardins Mérici, Apt. 742, Québec, Qué. G1S 4V9; Office: 2125 boul. Charest ouest, St.-Foy, Qué. G1N 2G2.

**LACROIX, Richard;** painter-engraver-sculptor; b. Montreal, Que. 14 July 1939; s. Simon and Reine (Despres) L.; e. Inst. of Graphic Arts of Prov. of Que., Montreal, Dipl. 1960; Montreal Sch. of Fine Arts, Cert. of Pedagogy and Methodology 1960; Inst. of Applied Arts, Montreal, Cert. of Aesthetics and Art Hist. 1960; rec'd Can. Council Award to study engraving in various European studios 1961–64; with help of Que. Ministry of Cultural Affairs founded Atelier Libre De Recherches Graphiques for graphic research; co-founder of Fusion Des Arts, Inc. 1964; with aid of Min. of Cultural Affairs, Que., and Can. Council founded The Graphic Guild, dedicated to publishing original Candn. prints 1966; further scholarships (1968, 1971, and 1978) from Qué. Min. of Cultural Affairs; scholarship for free work from Prov. Bank of Can. 1978; directed environment design for 7th Montreal Film Festival 1966; designed plastic program and poster for 'Festival du Quebec' 1967; directed kinetic sculpture 'Fusion des Arts' Expo; 'Frappez la Cocotte' Mus. Contemp. Art, Montreal 1967; kinetic sculptures for Montreal Internat. Airport, Radio-Quebec 1968; Invited Teacher, Dept. of Art History, Univ. Que., Montreal 1969–70; designed cloth banner for Confederation Museum, Charlottetown, P.E.I. 1970 murals Pie-X School, Montreal, Cath. Sch. Bd. 1971; supv. organ. Graphic Guild 1972; mem. of Jury, 10th Salon Internat. de la Caricature 1973; one man shows: Gallerie l'Art Francais, Montreal 1961; Maison du Can., Paris 1962–63; Dorothy Cameron Gallery, Toronto 1963; Gallerie Agnes Lefort, Montreal 1963; Gallery XIII, Montreal Mus. of Fine Arts 1964; Art Centre of Jeunesse Musicules, Mont-Orford 1966; Fleet Gallery, Winnipeg 1966; Triangle Gallery, San Francisco 1968; Dunkelman Gallery, Toronto 1968; Univ. of Sask. 1969; Boutique Soleil, Montreal 1969; Open House, 4677 St. Denis, Montreal 1970; Mont-Orford, Que. 1978; Place des Arts, Montreal 1978; Galerie 'A,' Montreal 1980; Retrospective Exhibition of engravings and paintings (1959–84), La Guilde Graphique, Montreal 1984; Retrospective Exhibition of engravings and paintings Québec 1985; Galerie Nurihiko Tokyo 1985; Galerie Calligramme Ottawa 1986, 1990; Galerie Estampe Plus Québec 1987, 1990; has exhibited in group shows in Can., Europe, S. Am., U.S. and Asia including Internat. Biennal of Engraving; Internat. Triennal of Engravings; Bienal Americanna de grabado/Am. Biennal of Engraving; Québec Pavillion, Osaka, Japan 1970; Place des Arts

Montréal 1988; Via Rail Murale 1990; Salon de la "SAGA" Paris 1990; author of deluxe portfolios 'Sept Eaux-Fortes' 1959; 'Pierres du Soleil' (poems and lithos) 1960; 'Bestiaire' (etchings) 1961; 'Metamorphose de la Pitoune' 1969; 'Poems d'Alain Grandbois' (illus.) 1970; 'Mutations' 1970; 'Cristaux' 1971; 'Danses Carrées' 1973; 'Keys' 1975; 'Kamis,' 1977; films & documentaries, 'Le Graveur,' C.B.C. TV; 'La Fougere et La Rouille,' N.F.B. Can.; 'Il Ne Faut Pas se Couper l'Oreille pour Ça,' N.F.B. Can; 'Il Faut Que l'Hippopotame Poursuive sa Démarche,' Que. Film Bd.; 'L'Univers de Richard Lacroix' T.V. documentary 60 mn Radio Québec 1987; received First Prize, Fête des Fleurs, 1960 and Purchase Award, Spring Show, 1962, Montreal Museum of Fine Arts; Prize, Second Burnaby Nat. Print Show, 1963; Candn. Graphic Assn., 1964; Internat. Biennale of Graphic Art, Lugano, Switzerland, 1964; First Prize, Painting Sec., Hadassah Exhn., Montreal, 1965, 2nd Prize, 1966; Purchase Award 10th Annual Print Exhn., Calgary 1970; 1st choise, Montreal Catholic Sch. Bd. contest for murals, 1971; 1st Prize, Graphics, Hadassah Auction, Montreal 1974; Prize, Que. Engraving concourse, Cult. Centre, Sherbrooke Univ., 1977; lectures & seminars on engraving & sculpling, Montreal Mus. F.A.; Univ. of Qué.; U.B.C., Vancouver; Studio of Graphic Guild, Montreal; rep. in collections in Can. & abroad, incl. Montreal Mus. Fine Arts, Nat. Gallery of Can., Art Gallery of Ont., Victoria & Albert Museum (London, Eng.), Museum of Modern Art (N.Y.), Cabinet des Estampes, Bibliothèque Nationale de Paris; Canada Council; Radio-Canada, Montreal; mem., Cinématheque canadienne; Soc. des Artistes prof. du Que.; Candn. Soc. of Graphic Art; Home: 4273 Fabre, Montreal, Que. H2J 3T5; Studio & Office: La Guilde Graphique, 9 St. Paul Ouest, Old Montreal, Que. H2Y 1Y6.

**LACROIX, Robert L.,** B.A.; industrial relations / human resources executive; b. Quebec City, Que. 27 Apr. 1944; s. Lucien A. and Agnes M. (Walton) L.; e. Loyola of Montreal, Concordia Univ., B.A. 1965; m. Marie d. Francoise and Ernest Livernois 13 Aug. 1966; now divorced; children: Christine, Kevin; personnel & labour relns. positions, Allied Chemical Canada Ltd. 1966–72; Mgr., Atlantic Reg., Dir., Labour Relations, Vice-Pres.; Maritime Employers Association 1972– ; Certified Instr., Effective Communications & Public Speaking; Home: 10 Harris Court, Bedford, N.S.; Office: One Sackville Place, 5121 Sackville St., Suite 200, Halifax, N.S. B3J 1K1.

**LADANYI, Branko,** Ph.D., F.R.S.C., F.E.I.C., F.C.A.E., P.Eng.; educator; b. Zagreb, Croatia 14 Dec. 1922; s. Adalbert and Zora (Kniewald) L.; e. elem. and secondary ed. Zagreb 1929–41; Univ. of Zagreb B.E. Dip. (Civil Eng.) 1947; Univ. of Louvain Ph.D. (Soil Mechanics) 1959; m. Nevenka d. Franjo and Stanka Zilic 14 Dec. 1946; children: Branka, Thomas, Marc; PROF. OF CIVIL ENGINEERING, ECOLE POLYTECHNIQUE 1977– , Dir. Northern Engineering Centre 1972– ; Design Eng. Dept. Transport Zagreb 1947–52; Teaching Asst. Soil Mechanics Inst. Univ. of Zagreb 1952–58; Research Eng. Belgian Geotech. Inst. Ghent, Belgium 1958–62; Assoc. Prof.-Prof. of Civil Eng. Laval Univ. 1962–67; Prof. of Mining Eng. Ecole Polytechnique 1967–77; recipient Que. Sci. Award 1974; R.F. Legget Award Candn. Geotech. Soc. 1981; E.E. De Beer Award, Belgian Geotechnical Soc. 1986; Elbert F. Rice Memorial Award, Am. Soc. of Civil Engrs. 1991; Roger J.E. Brown Memorial Award, Candn. Geotechnical Soc. 1993; co-author 'Geotechnical Engineering for Cold Regions' 1978; 'Permafrost Engineering, Design and Construction' 1981; author over 160 sci. and tech. papers on mechanics of soils, rocks and permafrost; Fellow, Royal Society of Canada; Candn. Soc. Civil Engs.; Am. Soc. Civil Engs.; Candn. Acad. of Engr.; mem. Tunnelling Assn. Can. (Pres. 1983–85); Order Engs. Que.; Candn. Geotech. Soc.; Candn. Inst. Mining & Metall.; Internat. Soc. Rock Mechanics; Am. Soc. Testing & Materials; Home: 321, 3355 Queen Mary Rd., Montreal, Que. H3V 1A5; Office: C.P. 6079, Succ. A., Montreal, Que. H3C 3A7.

**LADHANI, Nazeer Aziz,** M.B.A.; foundation executive; b. Morogoro, Tanzania 20 Aug. 1947; s. Abdulaziz and Shireen (Dhallaly) L.; e. Inst. Europeen d'Admin. des Affaires, Fountainbleau, France M.B.A. (with distinction); cert. mngt. accountant; dipl. in agric.; m. Gulabi d. Sultanali Ladhani 14 Aug. 1974; children: Noor, Aliya; CHIEF EXTVE. OFFR., AGA KHAN FOUNDATION CANADA 1985– ; conducted corp. evaluations in 25 countries incl. Eur., Africa & Middle East 1971–77 for Exxon Corp.; Alberta Gas Ethylene Co. (Nova Corp. subsidiary) 1978; Lectr., Univ. of Alta. & N. Alta. Inst. of Technol. (finance, small bus. mngt. & entrepreneurship) 1979–80; Admin., Aga Khan Found. Can. 1981; Bd. Mem., Candn. Ctr. for Philanthropy; Pres., Internat. Development Extves. Assn. (IDEA Group); has undertaken several missions overseas & served on var. task forces & cttes. on behalf of CIDA, South Asia Partnership & Candn. Counc. for Internat. Coop.; Office: Constitution Sq., 350 Albert St., Suite 1820, Ottawa, Ont. K1R 1A4.

**LADLY, Frederick Bernard,** B.A.; health care & financial services executive; b. Toronto, Ont. 14 July 1930; s. John Bernard and Olivia Montgomery (Fennimore) L.; e. Univ. of Toronto B.A. 1951; m. Sharon Mary Davidson children: Martha Jane, Patricia Anne, Lois Elizabeth, Katharine Olivia, Sarah Jane, Mary Meghan; PRES. & C.E.O., CROWNX INC. and PRES. & C.E.O., EXTENDICARE HEALTH SERVICES INC.; Chrmn. & C.E.O., United Health Inc.; Chrmn., International Care Services (U.K.); Dir., Crownx Inc.; Crown Life Insurance Co.; Cobi Foods Inc.; Home: R.R. 1, Fallbrook, Ont. K0G 1A0; Office: 3000 Steeles Ave. E., Suite 700, Markham, Ont. L3R 9W2.

**LADNER, Thomas Ellis,** D.S.C., Q.C., B.A., LL.B.; solicitor; b. Vancouver, B.C. 8 Dec. 1916; s. Leon Johnson and Jeanne (Lantzius) L.; e. Shawnigan Lake (B.C.) Sch.; The Leys Sch. Cambridge, Eng.; Univ. of B.C., B.A. 1937; Osgoode Hall Law Sch. Toronto LL.B. 1940; m. Janet Susan d. Bryce W. Fleck 1945; children: Nancy Edmonds, Peter, Stephen, Janet, Wendy Beaudry, Christopher; Partner, Ladner Downs 1945–93; called to Bar of B.C. 1940; cr. Q.C. 1964; served with RCNVR, RCN 1940–45, on loan to RN, rank Lt.-Cdr.; awarded D.S.C. and Bar; mem. Bd. Police Commrs. Vancouver 1960–64; Leon and Thea Koerner Foundation; The Hamber Found.; Public Mem. of Counc., Inst. of Chartered Accountants of B.C. 1989–93; Anglican; recreations: boating, fishing, squash, skiing; Clubs: Vancouver; Royal Vancouver Yacht; West Vancouver Yacht; Men's Canadian (Pres. 1958–Vancouver); Vancouver Lawn Tennis; Vancouver; Home: 4610 Connaught Dr., Vancouver, B.C. V6J 4E2; Office: 900 Waterfront Centre, 200 Burrard St., P.O. Box 48600, Vancouver, B.C. V7X 1T2.

**LADOUCEUR, Roland J.,** M. Com.; b. Trois-Rivières, Qué. 2 March 1929; s. Elzéar and Yvonne (Landry) L.; e. Laval Univ. Sch. of Adm. B.Com. 1951, M.Com. 1952; Univ. of Ottawa Sch. of Pol. Sciences Dipl. 1953; Candn. Soc. of Mgment. Accountants, R.I.A, 1953; m. Henriette d. late Paul Martel, Q.C. 19 June 1954; CONSULTANT IN COMMUNICATIONS AND CULTURAL AFFAIRS 1990– ; joined Nat. Film Bd. Can. 1953 serving as Assoc. Dir. of Distribution 1961–66; Asst. Govt. Film Commr. Montreal 1966–68; Dir. for Europe, Middle East and Africa, Paris 1968–74, U.S. Gen. Mgr. N.Y. 1974–78, Dir. of Pub. Relations Montreal 1978–80; Extve. Dir., Film Canada Center, Los Angeles 1980–84; joined Telefilm Canada as Dir., Paris Office 1984–89; Sr. Advr., Planning and Policies, Montreal 1989–90; Pub., 'MOMENTUM' (newsletter) 1980–84; articles on cinema and television in Variety, On Location, La Presse, Le Devoir, Toronto Trade Forum, Candn. Cable Magazine, Cinema Canada, EBU Review (European Broadcasting Union); recipient Queen's Silver Jubilee Medal 1977; Accredited mem. Candn. Pub. Relation Soc.; mem. Candn. Cultural Extves.; Conf. on Candn. Information; Acad. Candn. Cinema; Am. Film Inst.; Nat. Assn. of Television Program Extves. (U.S.A.); Internat. Inst. of Communication (London); Assn. des Conseils et Experts du Cinéma et de la Communication Audiovisuelle (Paris); Internat. Soc. of Strategic Mngmnt. and Planning; Guest speaker: Am. Film Inst. (Los Angeles), Banff Television Film Festival, Festival des films du monde (Montréal), Rencontre du Film (Bruxelles), Film Sch. of the Univ. of Calif. at Los Angeles, Unifrance Film; R. Catholic; recreations: cultural activities, travel, golf, skiing; Home: 30 rue Berlioz, Apt. 910, Ile des Soeurs, Verdun, Qué. H3E 1L3.

**LAFLAMME, Guy;** executive; b. Levis, Qué. 6 May 1937; s. Eugene and Blandine (Dionne) L.; e. St-Louis de Gonzague, Québec; Sacred Heart Univ. Bathurst, N.B.; Univ. Laval; m. Marthe Paul Vaillancourt 23 May 1959; children: Jean, Jacques, Marc, Richard, Marie-Josee; CHRMN. & C.E.O., SOUTH SHORE INDUSTRIES LTD.; SOUTH SHORE INDUSTRIES INC., Blackstone, Va.; PRES., 118280 CANADA INC.; Pres., Club St. Vincent Inc.; Pres. Bd. of Govs. & Dir., Noël Du Bonheur; Gov., Faculte Adm. Univ. Sherbrooke; Jeunes Entrepreneurs Que. Metro; Finance Ctte. Québec 2002; Fondation J.M. Brochu; Fondation Hotel Dieu Levis; Chrmn. of Bd., Conseil du Patronat du Qué.; Mem., Internat. Trade Advisory Ctte. (ITAC); Mayor, Mun. Ste-Croix 1973–75, 1979–81; mem. UN Indust. Devel. Organ.; Corp. C.M.A.; H.E.C.; recreations: hunting, fishing, travel; Clubs: Optimist; Garnison; St. Vincent; Office: C.P. 190, Ste-Croix, Lotbinière, Qué. G0S 2H0.

**LAFLEUR, Guy Damien;** hockey player; b. Thurso, Que. 20 Sept. 1951; s. Rejean and Pierrette L.; m. Lise (Barre) 16 June 1973; children: Martin, Mark; RETURNED TO NHL, 1988–89 SEASON WITH NEW YORK RANGERS; spotted by scouts while leading Thurso team to class C title in 1962 Quebec international peewee tournament; at 14 joined Quebec City junior B team; following year played eight junior A games scoring first of 315 junior A goals with Quebec Ramparts; in first full junior campaign scored 30 goals, added 50 next year, 103 third season; scored 130 goals, 79 assists for 209 points in final junior season; Montreal's first choice and first overall in 1971 amateur draft; scored 29 goals as rookie and in six years three times has cleared 50 goals; through 1971–77 in 445 games scoring 243 goals, 312 assists for 555 points, 221 penalty minutes, plus 67 playoff games scoring 32 goals, 44 assists for 76 points, 38 penalty minutes; three times first team all-star right winger; Art Ross Trophy 1976, 1977; Lester B. Pearson Trophy 1976, 1977; Hart Trophy 1977; Conn Smythe Trophy 1977; Sport Magazine playoff MVP award 1977; mem., Team Canada 1976, 1981; Address: 7400 Anne Barbel, Quebec, Que. G2K 2C4.

**LAFLEUR, Jean H.,** Q.C., B.A., B.C.L., D.E.S.Econ.; lawyer; b. Montreal, Que. 6 May 1938; s. Robert and Gabrielle (Ste-Marie) L.; e. Brébeuf & Loyola Colleges; McGill Univ. B.A. 1956, B.C.L. 1959; Univ. Sorbonne, D.E.S.Econ. 1961; m. Louise d. Leopold Limoges 27 Aug. 1960; children: Jean Jr., Diane; PARTNER, MARTINEAU WALKER, MONTREAL 1981– ; called to Bar of Quebec 1960; Q.C. 1976; Lawyer, Lafleur & Gagnon 1961–62; Riel-Ledain 1962–64; Partner, Gagnon Lafleur 1965–81; Dir., Peerless Carpet Corp.; United Distillers Canada Inc.; Birks Gold Medal for Leadership & Admin. 1954; Elizabeth Torrance Gold Medal, McGill Univ. 1959; recreations: tennis, golf; clubs: St-Denis, Mount Royal, Nun's Island Tennis; Home: 1455 Sherbrooke St. W., Apt. 2306, Montreal, Que.; Office: 3400 The Stock Exchange Tower, P.O. Box 242, Victoria Sq., Montral, Que. H4Z 1E9.

**LAFLEUR, Robert S.,** LL.B.; federal civil servant; b. Ottawa, Ont. 29 Feb. 1940; s. Lorenzo and Yvonne (Lavoice) L.; e. B.P.Sc. 1963; Univ. of Ottawa, LL.B. 1966; Osgoode Hall Law Sch.; m. Louise d. Georges and Cecile Fleury 10 Sept. 1966; children: Marie Josée, Eric; DEPY. SECY., HUMAN RESOURCES DEVELOPMENT BRANCH, TREASURY BOARD SECRETARIAT 1990– ; called to Bar of Ont. 1968; joined Federal Govt. as legal adv. 1968, Dir. General Appeals Branch Public Service Commission 1974–78, Dir. Aeronautical Standards & Legis. and Dir. Review & Aviation Safety Implementation, Transport Can. 1979–84, Dir. Gen. Aviation Regulation 1984; Candn. rep. various internat. forums civil aviation; Asst. Dep. Min., Realty Services PWC 1987–90; Dep. Secretary, Treasury Bd. of Canada 1990– ; recipient Award of Excellence Transport Inds. Can.; Legal Adv. Assn. France-Can.; recreations: theatre, ballet; Club: Ottawa Athletic; Home: 12 Carlyle Ave., Ottawa, Ont. K1S 4Y3; Office: L'Esplanade Laurier, Ottawa, Ont. K1A 0R5.

**LAFOND, Georges,** B.A., M.Com., F.C.A.; educator; b. Montréal, Qué. 1931; e. Coll. St-Laurent B.A. 1951; École des Hautes Études Commerciales M.Com. 1957, C.A. 1958; m.; 4 children; EXTVE.-IN-RESIDENCE ÉCOLE DES HAUTES ÉTUDES COMMERCIALES DE MONTRÉAL 1990– ; Chrmn., CTI Capital Inc.; Auditor Touche Ross, Bailey & Smart 1957–60; Credit Offr. Federal Business Development Bank 1960–62; Asst. Treas. Crédit Saint-Laurent Inc. 1962–65; Asst. Treas. becoming Treas. Hydro-Québec 1965, Vice Pres. Finance 1981, Extve. Vice Pres. Mktg. 1982, Extve. Vice Pres. External Mkts. 1984–86; Sr. Vice Pres. Finance La Conféderation des caisses populaires et d'économie Desjardins du Québec 1986–87; Pres. and Chief Extve. Offr. Caisse Centrale Desjardins 1987–90; Chaire des sciences comptables present École 1986; author various publs.; Club: St-Denis; Home: 425 Brookfield, Town of Mount-Royal, Qué. H3P 2A9; Office: 5255 ave. Decelles, M210, Montréal, Qué. H3T 1V6.

**LAFONTAINE, Raymond,** B.A., B.A.Sc., M.Phil.; business executive; b. Montreal, Que. 30 July 1941; s. Gerard and Pauline L.; e. Univ. of Montreal, B.A. 1960, B.A.Sc. 1964; Univ. of London, M.Sc. 1966; Dip. in Applied Econ., l'Ecole des Hautes Etudes Comm., Montreal 1968; m. Estelle d. Cyprien and Angeline Pelletier 5 Sept. 1964; children: Marie-Anik, Sylvie-Ninon; PRES., LGS GROUP INC. 1984– ; var. mktg. & mgmt. positions, IBM Canada 1966–79; co-founder, LGS (an information systems consulting firm with 15 branch offices across Canada and in France) 1979; mem. Order of Engrs. of Que.; Inst. of Mgmt. Consultants of Que.;

Montreal C. of C.; Montreal World Trade Center; Mem. Bd. of Gov., Conseil du Patronat du Qué.; Mem. Bd. of Dirs., EDI (electronic data interchange) Institute; Bd. Chrmn., Fond. des Grands Brûlés du Qué.; Mem. Bd. of Dirs., Société Nationale d'Assurances; Past Pres., Candn. Info. Processing Soc.; CIEQ (Software Industry's Permanent Comn. at the Conseil de l'Industrie Electronique du Qué.); Dir., Esso Scholarship, Univ. of Montreal; Commonwealth Scholarship, Univ. of London; recreations: sailing, skiing; Club: St-Denis; Home: 1645 Croissant Salzbourg, Brossard, Que. J4X 1V8; Office: Suite 1070, 1253 McGill College Ave., Montreal, Que. H3B 2Y5.

**LA FOREST, Gerard V.,** B.C.L., M.A., LL.M., J.S.D., LL.D., D.U., D.C.L., F.R.S.C. (1975); Judge; b. Grand Falls, N.B. 1 Apr. 1926; s. J. Alfred and Philomene (Lajoie) La F.; e. Grand Falls (N.B.) Pub. and High Schs.; St. Francis Xavier Univ., 1944–46; Univ. of N.B., B.C.L. 1949; Rhodes Scholar 1949; St. John's Coll., Oxford Univ. B.A. Juris. 1951, M.A. 1956; Yale Univ. (Yale Grad. Fellow), LL.M. 1965, J.S.D. 1966; LL.D., Univ. of Basel 1981; D.U., Univ. of Ottawa 1985; D.C.L., Univ. of N.B. 1985; LL.D., St. Francis Xavier Univ. 1988; LL.D. St. Thomas Univ. 1988; LL.D. Univ. of Alberta 1988; LL.D. Univ. of Moncton 1988; LL.D. Bates College 1990; Fellow, Royal Society of Canada 1975; Fellow, World Academy of Art and Science 1975; m. D. Marie Warner, 27 Dec. 1952; children: Marie, Kathleen, Anne, Elizabeth, Sarah; JUSTICE, SUPREME COURT OF CANADA 1985– ; called to the Bar of N.B. 1949; cr. Q.C. 1968; law practice Grand Falls, N.B. 1951–52; Adv. Counsel, Legal Br., Dept. of Justice, Ottawa, 1952–55; Legal Advisor, Irving Oil, Saint John, N.B., 1955–56; Assoc. Prof. Univ. of N.B. 1956–63; Prof. 1963–68; Dean of Law, Univ. of Alberta, 1968–70; Visiting Prof., Fac. of Law, Univ. of Montreal 1962–63; Lectr., Univ. of Ottawa, Fac. of Law (Civil Law Section) 1971–78; Lectr., Fac. of Law, McGill Univ. 1971, 1979; Asst. Depy. Atty. Gen. of Can. (Research & Planning) 1970–74; Commissioner, Law Reform Com. of Canada, 1974–79; Prof. Law and Dir. Legislative Drafting Prog., Faculty of Law (Common Law Section) Univ. of Ottawa 1979–81; Justice, New Brunswick Court of Appeal 1981–85; frequent consultant to federal and provincial governments; served on Glassco Royal Commission 1959 and Royal Comn. on Pilotage 1965; Adviser to Special Counsel on Constitution to Min. of Justice and Prime Min. 1967–70; mem. Extve. Ctte. Task Force on Computers and Privacy 1971–72; Extve. Vice Chrmn., Candn. Bar Assn. Ctte. on the Constitution 1977–78; Chrmn., Fed.-Prov. Inquiry on Kouchibouguac Nat. Park, 1980–81; publs. incl. 'Disallowance and Reservation of Provincial Legislation'; 'Extradition To and From Canada'; 'Natural Resources and Public Property Under the Canadian Constitution'; 'The Allocation of Taxing Power Under the Canadian Constitution'; co-author 'Water Law in Canada - The Atlantic Provinces'; 'Le Territoire Québecois'; also numerous articles; R. Catholic; Home: 170 Minto Pl., Rockcliffe Park, Ottawa, Ont. K1M 0B7; Office: Supreme Court Bldg., Wellington St., Ottawa, Ont. K1A 0J1.

**LAFORGE, Réjean,** C.M.A., C.S.A.; financial executive; b. Montreal, Que. 1 Aug. 1946; s. Roger and Jeannine (Collin) L.; e. Hautes Etudes Commerciales de Montréal C.M.A. 1972, C.S.A. 1973; m. Andréa d. Eugène and Phoebe McIntyre 24 May 1969; children: Geneviève, Dominic; CONTROLLER & TREASURER, TQM PIPELINE 1981– ; Material Control & Cost Acctg. Dept., United Aircraft 5 years 1966–71; Internal Auditor for a Maritime agency company 1971–73; Regional Controller, Eastern & Atlantic Provinces, Consumer Glass 1973–76; Manager, Planning & Cost Accounting, Chromasco 1976–81; Secretary, Fond. Centre Hospitalier Côte-des-Neiges 1991– , 2nd Vice-Pres. 1993; Pres., Assn. Pipeline Longitude 75$ 1992–93, Pres. ex-officio 1993–94; recreations: alpine skiing, golf, softball, theatre, music; Office: 1 Place Ville Marie, Suite 2220, Montreal, Que. H3B 3M4.

**LAFORTE, Conrad,** D.ès L.; professeur titulaire; né à Kénogami, Qué. 10 nov. 1921; f. Philippe et Marie-Mathilda (Dallaire) L.; é. Univ. de Montréal Bacc. en bibliothéconomie et bibliographie 1949; Univ. Laval B.A. 1946, L.ès L. 1968, diplôme d'études supérieures 1970, D.ès L. 1977; ép. Hélène f. Emile et Alice (Duval) Gauthier 24 août 1957; enfant: Esther; Professeur Titulaire au Departement d'Histoire et Celat, Fac. des Lettres, Univ. Laval 1981–88; Chercheur émérite au CELAT, Univ. Laval 1984; Chargé de cours 1965–67, Prof. Asst. 1967–73, ajoint 1973–77, agrégé 1977–81; Bibliothécaire-archiviste aux Archives de folklore Univ. Laval 1951–75, Secrétaire 1973–75; Dir. des études de premier cycle en arts et civilisation 1981–83; Enquêtes ethnographiques au Qué. dans les comtés de Chicoutimi, Lac-St-Jean et Bagot 1954–67,; 1,132 enregistrements sonores sur 67 rubans magnétiques de deux heures chacun (comprenant contes, chansons, légendes et airs de danse) classés et conservés aux Archives de folklore Univ. Laval; Recherches subventionnées par le Conseil des Arts du Can. et le Conseil de recherches en sciences humaines du Can. pour rédaction du 'Catalogue de la chanson folklorique française' 1971–83; auteur 'Le chanson folklorique et les écrivains du XIXe siècle (en France et au Québec)' 1973; 'Poétiques de la chanson traditionnelle française' 1976, 2$^{e}$ éd. 1993; 'Catalogue de la chanson folklorique française' 6 vols. 1977–87; 'Menteries drôles et merveilleuses' 1978; 'Survivances médiévales dans la chanson folklorique' 1981; deuxième prix littéraire de Radio-Canada 1946; Prix Raymond-Casgrain 1959; Médaille Luc-Lacourcière 1981; Distinguished Candn. Folklorist, Folklore Studies Assn. of Can. 1984; membre de la Société Royale du Can.; retraité; Adresse: 949 rue Gatineau, Ste-Foy, Qué. G1V 3A2.

**LAFRAMBOISE, G. Guy,** M.D., F.R.C.S.(C); otolaryngologist; educator; b. Ottawa, Ont. 24 Aug. 1927; s. George Etienne and Marie Antoinette (Smith) L.; e. Loyola Coll. Montreal B.A. 1948; Univ. of Ottawa L.B., L.M.C.C. 1954; Johns Hopkin's Hosp. Postgrad. Residency Training Otolaryngol. 1954–59; m. Mary Anne d. John Darcy Coulson 6 Oct. 1951; children: Lise Anne, Lorraine, Julie, Estelle, Moira, Guy Jr., Deirde, Nicole; ASSOC. PROF. OF OTOLARYNGOLOGY, UNIV. OF OTTAWA 1983– (Chrmn. of Otol. there 1964–82, 1986–87); Former Chrmn. of Otolaryngol. Ottawa Gen. Hosp. 1963–92; Reg. Chrmn., Nat. Annual Meeting of CSO H&N 1987; Consultant Otolaryngol. Riverside Hosp., Ottawa Civic Hosp., St. Louis Marie de Monfort Hosp., Hôpital Sacré Coeur of Hull, Centre Hospitalier de Buckingham, Centre Hospitalier de Maniwaki, Nat. Defence Med. Centre; Pembroke General Hosp.; Renfrew Victoria Hosp.; has contributed and organized Rhinoseptoplasty courses Univ. of Toronto, Univ. of Montreal; service with Hull Regt. Armoured Corps (Reserve); has presented papers on Rhinoseptoplasty in Children; mem. Ottawa Acad. Med.; Candn. and Ont. Med. Assns.; R. Catholic; recreations: fly fishing, upland bird shooting, farming; Home: Luskville, Que.; Office: Ottawa General Hospital, 501 Smyth Rd., Ottawa, Ont. K1H 8L6.

**LAFRAMBOISE, James G.,** B.Sc., B.A.Sc., M.A., Ph.D.; researcher; educator; b. Windsor, Ont. 26 July 1938; s. Percy Emmanuel and Annabel (St-Pierre) L.; e. Univ. of Windsor B.Sc. 1957; Univ. of Toronto B.A. Sc. 1959, M.A. 1960, Ph.D. 1966; m. Mary Catherine d. Austin F. and Gertrude Newton Hall 29 Sept. 1962; children: Robert James, Claire Eileen; PROF. OF PHYSICS, YORK UNIV. 1977– ; Asst. Prof. of Math. Univ. of Windsor 1965–67; Rsch. Assoc. Space Physics Lab. Univ. of Mich. summers 1966, 1967; Asst. Prof. present univ. 1967, assoc. Prof. 1971–77; sabbatical leave Groupe de Recherches Ionosphériques, Orléans-La Source, France 1973–74; rsch. contracts U.S. Air Force Office of Sci. Rsch. on high altitude spacecraft elec. charging 1976–81 and Geophysics Lab. on auroral zone spacecraft elec. charging 1983–86; on a review of theory for electrostatic probes in plasmas 1985–86, on high-voltage space power systems 1987–89, on spacecraft-environment interactions 1988–92, on particle sensor simulation development for Candn. Space Agency 1991– ; mem. project team WISP Shuttle experiment 1980– , OEDIPUS rocket experiment 1983– , theory group for SPEAR rocket experiment 1987–89, peer-review panel for NASA 'ACTIVE' Space Plasma Physics Program 1989, on science team for TPA experiment on Planet-B (Mars) spacecraft 1991– ; author over 60 sci. papers; assoc. Ed. Jour. of Geophysical rsch., Space Physics 1983–85; mem. Candn Assn. Physicists; Am. Geophys. Union; Planetary Soc.; Home: 182 Baythorn Dr., Thornhill, Ont. L3T 3V5; Office: North York, Ont. M3J 1P3.

**LAFRANCE, Carole M.;** advertising executive; b. North Bay, Ont. 16 Oct. 1944; d. Adélard and Laurette (Dignard) L.; e. Univ. of Toronto; Laurentian Univ.; Owner/Pres. Mgmt. Course, Harvard Bus. Sch. 1985–87; PRESIDENT, CALA H.R.C. LTD. 1978– founded in Montreal 1978, opened Calgary, affiliated with JPW Recruitment Advertising, London, Eng. 1979, opened Ottawa and Toronto 1981, Edmonton 1986; affiliated with Deutsch, Shea and Evans Recruitment Advertising, New York, Los Angeles, San Francisco, Mountain View, Denver, Salt Lake City, Boston and Chicago, U.S.A. 1988, opened Vancouver 1989; Toronto 1990; Reg. Dir., public relations firm W.W. Inc. 1971–72; opened and operated Am. advtg. agency NAS Inc. 1972–78; Clubs: EPOC Montreal (Extve. Bd. Dir. 1981–86, Chair 1987–89); Les Valentines 1985–91; les Amies d'Affaires du Ritz, L'Assoc. des femmes d'affaires du Québec 1991–93; Montreal Chamber of Commerce; A.P.R.H.Q. Que.; Harvard Alumni; The Committee of 200 – USA (first Cdn. mem.) 1987– ; YPO 1988– ; The Public Policy Forum (Bd. Dir. 1988, Extve. Bd. 1989– ); Cdn. Commercial Corp. (Bd. Dir. 1989–92); Lester B. Pearson Coll. of the Pacific-United World Colleges (Bd. Dir. 1989–93); Cdn. Chamber of Commerce (Bd. Dir. 1990, Officer 1994– ); Offices: 63, de Brésoles St., Montréal, Qué. H2Y 1V7; 294 Albert St., Suite 404, Ottawa, Ont. K1P 6E6; 146 Front Street W., Suite 750, Toronto, Ont. M5J 1G2 and 550 - 11th Ave. S.W., Suite 503, Calgary, Alta. T2R 1M7.

**LAFRANCE, Yvon,** D.Ph., Doct.Etat; educator; b. Montreal, Que. 1 Dec. 1930; s. Lorenzo and Anna (Ouellette) L.; e. Univ. de Montréal B.A. 1951; Univ. of Sao Paulo D.Ph. 1964; Univ. of Louvain D.Ph. 1967; Univ. of Paris Doct.Etat 1982; m. Gracia d. Avila Malo 14 Dec. 1970; PROFESSOR OF PHILOSOPHY, UNIVERSITY OF OTTAWA 1971– ; Prof. of Philos. Univ. of Sao Paulo, Brazil 1962–64, Univ. of Sherbrooke 1967–69, Univ. of Que. (Montreal) 1969–71; Founder, Laboratoire de recherches en pensée antique et médiévale 1979; author 'La théorie platonicienne de la doxa' 1981; 'Méthode et exégèse en histoire de la Philosophie' 1983; 'Pour interpréter Platon' Vol. I 1987, Vol. II 1993; 'Les Présocratiques. Bibliographie analytique (1879–1980)' Vol. I, 1988; Vol. II, 1989; ed. 'L'Univers de la Philosophie' 1973; 'Noêsis' 1979; Founder 'Philosophiques' review 1974; Comité scientifique 'Encyclopédie Philosophique Universelle' (Paris); mem. Assn. Guillaume Budé (Paris); Assn. canadienne de Philosophie; Assn. brésilienne de Philosophie (1962–64); Soc. Promotion Hellenic Studies (London); Société de Philosophie du Qué. (conseil d'adm. 1982–84); Fellow, Royal Soc. of Can. 1987; Killam Scholarship du Conseil des Arts du Canada 1989–91; Home: 1417 Cheverny, Orléans, Ont. K4A 3C8; Office: Ottawa, Ont. K1N 6N5.

**LAFRENIERE, Rene,** D.E.C., M.D., C.M., F.R.C.S.(C), F.A.C.S.; surgeon; educator; b. Shawinigan, Qué. 13 July 1953; s. Jean-Paul and Olivette (Lambert) L.; e. Coll. St-Jean sur Richelieu, Qué. D.E.C. 1972; McGill Univ. M.D., C.M. 1977; m. Zam Zam Saad 18 Sept. 1961; children: Annie, Richard, Safi; Surg. Foothills Hosp., Tom Baker Cancer Centre; Dir. Flow Cytometry Facility; Prof. and Head, Dept. of Surg. Univ. of Calgary 1992– ; mem. Melanoma, Biol. Therapeutics, Oncology and Immunol. Sci's Rsch. Groups; Resident Gen. Surg. Miami, Fla. 1977–82, Fellow Surg. Oncology 1982–84, Instr. in Surg. Div. Surg. Oncology 1982–86; Fellow, Tumor Immunol. Nat. Cancer Inst. Bethesda, Md. 1984–86; recipient Alta. Heritage Found. Med. Rsch. Scholarship 1986–91; mem. Am. Assn. Cancer Rsch.; Am. Assn. Immunols.; Candn. Oncology Soc.; Candn. Assn. Immunols.; Office: 3330 Hospital Dr. N.W., Calgary, Alta. T2N 4N1.

**LAGACE, Hon. Maurice E.,** B.A., LL.L.; judge; b. Montreal, Que. 29 Oct. 1931; s. Omer and Blanche (Legault) L.; e. Coll. Ste.-Marie Montréal B.A. 1952; Univ. of Montreal LL.L. 1956; m. Louise, Dt. (well-known author of 6 books on nutrition, including 'Feeding Your Child') d. Lt. Col. Paul Lambert, Montreal, Que. 5 Aug. 1961; children: Pascale, Janique, Marie-Claire; JUDGE, SUPERIOR COURT MONTREAL; called to Bar of Que. 1956; cr. Q.C. 1972; former Sr. Assoc. Martineau, Walker, Allison, Beaulieu & Associates; R. Catholic; Home: 4150 Trafalgar Rd., Montreal, Que. H3Y 1R2.

**LAGASSE, Jacques;** notary & title attorney; b. St-Hyacinthe, Que. 24 Aug. 1916; s. Joseph Arsene and Yvonne (Cadorette) L.; e. Acad. of Sacred Heart, Windsor, Que.; St. Charles Semy., Sherbrooke, Que.; Univ. of Montreal; Notary 1939; L.L.D. (hon.c.) Univ. of Sherbrooke; m. Suzanne, d. Dr. Jean Marcoux, Sherbrooke, Que., 22 Feb. 1941; children: Françoise L. (Mrs. Pierre Boily), Jacques, Pierre, Louis; Mem., Lagasse, Lagasse (est. 1939); Dir. and Mem. of Extve. Counc. of Banque Canadienne Nationale 1972–80; Past Pres., Bd. of Notaries Que.; Memb. Admin. Counc. Univ. of Sherbrooke; Liberal; Roman Catholic; recreations: golf, skiing; Clubs: Social; Golf Longchamp Inc.; Sherbrooke Golf; Reform; Mount Royal; Home: 245 Heneker St., Sherbrooke, Que. J1J 3G5.

**LAHEY, Kathleen A.,** B.A., J.D., LL.M.; educator; b. Urbana, Ill. 18 July 1946; d. Edward Andrew and Ruth Evelyn (Wilson) L.; e. Univ. of Ill. B.A. 1969; DePaul Univ. J.D. 1974; York Univ. LL.M. 1977; children: Kate, Michèle; PROF. OF LAW, QUEEN'S UNIV. 1987– ; former Prof. of Law, Windsor Univ., Lectr. in Law Osgoode Hall Law Sch.; active women's issues especially taxation, pub. policy and constl. law; mem. Ont. Adv. Council Women's Issues 1988–90; previously affiliated with Harvard Univ. and Monash Univ. as scholar and lectr.; author 'Corporate Taxation' 1984; Founding Ed. Candn. Jour. Women and the Law 1984–89; Atty. and Counselor Supreme Court of Ill.; mem. Law Soc. Upper Can.; Home: 86 Beverley St., Kingston, Ont. K7L 3Y6; Office: Fac. of Law, Queen's Univ., Kingston, Ont. K7L 3N6.

**LAHEY, Most Rev. Raymond John,** M.Th., Ph.D.; bishop; b. St. John's, Nfld. 29 May 1940; s. Raymond John and Marguerite Mary (Murphy) L.; e. St. Bonaventure's Coll. St. John's Nfld.; Univ. of Ottawa B.Th. 1961, M.Th. 1963, Ph.D. 1966; Gregorian Univ. Rome and Cambridge Univ. post-doctoral studies; BISHOP OF ST. GEORGE'S, NFLD. 1986– ; Principal, St. John's Coll. Mem. Univ. of Nfld. 1968–81, Asst. Prof. of Religious Studies 1968, Assoc. Prof. 1972, Acting Head of Dept. 1974–75, Prof. 1980–81, Head of Religious Studies 1977–81; Vicar-Gen., Archdiocese of St. John's, Nfld. 1981–86; Pastor, St. Peter's Parish, Mount Pearl, Nfld. 1982–86; named Prelate of Honor to his Holiness 1985; mem., Pontifical Counc. for Promoting Christian Unity 1989– ; mem., Governing Bd. Candn. Council of Churches; Pres., Episcopal Commn. for Liturgy for Canada; author 'James Louis O'Donel in Newfoundland 1784–1807: The Establishment of the Roman Catholic Church' 1984; co-author 'Bishops and Writers: Aspects of the Evolution of Modern English Catholicism' 1977; 'Early European Exploration and Settlement in Atlantic Canada' 1984; 'Creed and Culture: The Place of English-Speaking Catholics in Canadian Society' 1993; various articles religious hist.; contrib. to 'Dictionary of Canadian Biography'; R. Catholic; Home and Office: Bishop's Residence, 16 Hammond Dr., Corner Brook, Nfld. A2H 2W2.

**LAHN, Mervyn Lloyd,** B.A.; trust company executive; b. Hanover, Ont. 24 June 1933; s. Charles Henry and Emma Wilhelmine Frederika (Leifso) L.; e. Hanover (Ont.) Pub. and High Schs., 1951; Waterloo Coll., Univ. of W. Ont., B.A. 1954, Grad. Mang. Training Course 1964; LL.D., Wilfred Laurier Univ. 1978; m. Myra Ann Helen, d. late J. Herbert Smith, 17 Sept. 1960; two s.: John Geoffrey, Pearce Alexander, one d. Margaret Ann; DIR., CT FINANCIAL SERVICES INC., THE CANADA TRUST CO. & Can. Trustco Mortgage Co.; Dir., Ault Foods Ltd.; CAMECO; Dana Corp.; Hayes-Dana Inc.; John Labatt Ltd.; Cadillac Fairview Inc.; Laidlaw Inc.; Sifton Properties Ltd.; Ellis-Don Inc.; Truscan Realty Ltd.; ADT Limited; Bauer Industries Ltd.; Livingston Group Inc.; MacLean Hunter Ltd.; joined Waterloo Trust and Savings Co. 1955; apptd. Asst. Treas. 1958, Treas. 1960, Asst. Gen. Mgr. and Treas. 1967; Asst. Gen. Mgr., Canada Trust 1968, Depy. Gen. Mgr. 1972, Sr. Vice Pres. & Gen. Mgr. 1973; Extve. Vice Pres. 1974; Pres. and Chief Operating Officer, 1978; Pres. & C.E.O. Dec. 1979; Chrmn. & C.E.O. Mar. 1987–90; P. Conservative; Lutheran; recreations: curling, golf; Clubs: London Hunt; The London; Home: 1597 Ryersie Rd., London, Ont. N6G 2S2; Office: Canada Trust Tower, City Centre, 275 Dundas St., London, Ont. N6B 3L1.

**LAI, David Chuenyan,** C.M., Ph.D.; educator; b. Canton, China 16 Sept. 1937; s. Yiu Sang and Mee Yuk (Sau) Lai; e. Univ. of Hong Kong (Hong Kong Government Scholarship) B.A. 1960, M.A. 1964; London Sch. of Econ. & Pol. Sci. (Brit. Commonwealth Scholar 1964–67) Ph.D. 1967; m. Roberta d. Siu Ping Cheung 18 May 1968; children: Jim Yuan, Joan Man; PROF. OF GEOGRAPHY, UNIV. OF VICTORIA 1989– ; Tutor in Geog. Univ. of Hong Kong 1960–64, Lectr. 1967–68; Asst. Prof. of Geog. present Univ. 1968, Assoc. Prof. 1973; Cons. Portland Devel. Comn. 1984, 1986; Found. Group Ltd. Vancouver 1988; Min. Mun. Affairs B.C. 1988–89; Chrmn. Chinatown Redevel. Ctte. Chinese Consolidated Benevolent Assn. 1980– , Acad. Adv.; Vice Chrmn. Sister City Adv. & Liaison Ctte. City of Victoria 1989 and 1990; Chrmn. Heritage & Archival Adv. Ctte. Dist. of Saanich 1983, 1989; Chrmn., Twinned City Advisory Ctte., City of Victoria 1993; named Hon. Citizen City of Victoria 1980; recipient Citation Award Applied Geog. Assn. Am. Geog. 1982; Award of Merit Am. Assn. State & Local Hist. 1983; B.C. and Yukon Regional Community Service Award Heritage Can. Found. 1982; Member of the Order of Canada 1983; Suzanna Seto Meml. Service Award 1987; Cert. of Merit B.C. Hist. Fedn. 1989; Sch. Bd. Dir. Chinese Pub. Sch. Victoria 1977–92; Archives Assn. of B.C. 1993; Hon. Adv. Guangdong Soc. Overseas Chinese Studies 1988– , Guangdong Soc. Hist. Overseas Chinese 1988– ; Dir. Candn. Asian Studies Assn. 1988–90; Dir., Candn. Ethnic Studies Assn. 1989– ; author 'Arches in British Columbia' 1981; 'Chinatowns: Towns Within Cities in Canada' 1988; 'The Forbidden City Within Victoria: Myth Symbol, and Streetscape of Canada's Earliest Chinatown' 1991; co-author 'The Small Industrial Unit in Hong Kong: Patterns and Policies' 1967; Home: 4302, 2829 Arbutus Rd., Victoria, B.C. V8N 5X5; Office: P.O. Box 3050, Victoria, B.C. V8W 3P5.

**LAIDLAW, Robert William Alexander,** B.Sc., M.P.E.; petroleum executive; b. Nanton, Alta. 23 March 1929; e. Mount Royal Coll. Calgary 1949; Univ. of Okla. B.Sc. 1953, M.P.E. 1955; m. Esther Barfield 1956; children: Robert W., Beverlee J. Chasse, Margaret A.; DEPUTY CHAIRMAN OF BOARD, GIBSON PETROLEUM CO. LTD. 1992– ; Dir.: Gibson Group of Co's; Canadian Utilities Ltd.; Reservoir & Drilling Eng. Husky Oil Ltd. 1955–58, Mgr. Crude Oil Mktg. 1958–60; Mgr. Crude Oil Purchasing present Co. 1960–69, Pres. 1969; Chrmn., Calgary Centre Performing Arts. Dir. Petrol. Ind. Training Services; Dir. Jr. Achievement Can.; Chrmn., UPITFOS (Upstream Safety Canadian Assn. of Petroleum Producers C.A.P.P.); Calgary Exhn. & Stampede, Past Pres.; Past Chrmn. Un. Way Calgary; Past Pres.: Wascana Pipe Line Ltd.; Past Dir.: Encor Energy Corp. Inc.; Past Gov., Candn. Petrol Assn.; OCO '88 (Winter Olympics); Calgary C. of C.; Past Chrmn.: Am. Inst. Mining, Metall. & Petrol. Engs.; Candn. Inst. Mining & Metall. Calgary Sect.; Candn. Inst. Mining; Soc. Petrol. Engs.; recreations: golf, hunting, fishing; Clubs: Calgary Petroleum (Past Pres.); Calgary Glencoe; Calgary Golf & Country; Home: 903 Lansdowne Ave. S.W., Calgary, Alta. T2S 1A4; Office: 900, 727 7 Ave. S.W., Calgary, Alta. T2P 0Z5.

**LAIDLAW, Sheila Margaret,** M.A., M.L.S.; university librarian; b. Edinburgh, Scot. 2 Dec. 1931; d. Robert Brownlee and Jessie Barrie (MacKay) L.; e. Musselburgh Grammar Sch. 1950; Edinburgh Univ. M.A. 1953; Univ. of Toronto B.L.S. 1960, M.L.S. 1973, Wycliffe Coll. Lay Cert. of Theol. 1968; Dir. of Libraries, Univ. of N.B. 1982–90; Lib. Adv. and Consultant Bermuda Coll. 1978– ; Asst. Lib. Univ. of Edinburgh 1953–57; Lib. Asst. Univ. of Toronto 1957–60, Circulation Lib. Undergrad. Services 1960–66, 1968–73, Sigmund Samuel Lib. (i/c Undergrad. Lib.) 1973–82; Lib. and Secy. to Dir. Ch. Army in Can. (Ang.) 1966–68; Girl Guides of Can. Div. Commr. N.B. 1983–85, Prov. Training Commr. (N.B.) 1985–89, Prov. Training Commr. (Ont.) 1979–82; mem. Candn. Assn. Research Libs. (Bd. mem. 1983–89); Candn. Lib. Assn. (Council mem. 1979–82); Am. Lib. Assn. (Assn. Coll. & Research Libs., Bd. mem. 1978–79; Chrmn. Western NY/Ont. Chapter 1979–80); Assoc. of Atlantic Univs. Librarians' Counc. (Secy. 1985–89); Atlantic Provs. Lib. Assn.; Counc. of Head Librarians of N.B. Libs. (Chair 1986–88); Federation of Christian Librarians and Information Specialists (Vice-Pres. 1990–92; Pres., 1992–94); Third Thursday Network (Fredericton Women's Network); Beta Phi Mu; Anglican: recreations: travel, crafts, cooking, wood-turning, golf; Home: 15 Chelsea Court, Fredericton, N.B. E3B 4N1.

**LAIDLER, David Ernest William,** B.Sc.Econ., M.A., Ph.D., F.R.S.C.; educator; b. Tynemouth, Eng. 12 Aug. 1938; s. John Alphonse and Leonora (Gosman) L.; e. Tynemouth Sch. Eng. 1956; London Sch. of Econ. B.Sc.Econ. 1959; Univ. of Syracuse M.A. 1960; Univ. of Chicago Ph.D. 1964; m. Antje d. Richard and Irmgard Breitwisch 27 Jan. 1965; one d. Nicole Joanna; PROF. OF ECON., UNIV. OF W. ONT. 1975– , Chrmn. of Econ. 1981–84; Scholar-in-Residence, C.D. Howe Inst. 1990–91, Adjunct Scholar 1991– ; Dir. Philip Allan Publishers Ltd.; Temporary Asst. Lectr. London Sch. of Econ. 1961–62; Asst. Prof. Univ. of Cal. Berkeley 1963–66; Lectr. in Econ. Univ. of Essex, Eng. 1966–69; Prof. of Econ. Univ. of Manchester 1969–75; various Visiting Appts. Stanford Univ., Brown Univ., Stockholm Sch. of Econ., Univ. of Konstanz, Monash Univ., Flinders Univ.; Reserve Bank of Australia; Brit. Assn. Advanc. Science Lister Lectr. 1972; mem. Econ. Adv. Panel to Min. of Finance (Hon. Marc Lalonde) 1982–84; co-ord. Research Adv. Group on 'Economic Ideas and Social Issues' Royal Comm. on Econ. Union and Devel. Prospects for Canada (The Macdonald Commission) 1984–85; author 'The Demand for Money' 1969; 'Introduction to Microeconomics' 1974; 'Essays on Money and Inflation' 1975; 'Monetarist Perspectives' 1982; 'Taking Money Seriously' 1990; 'The Golden Age of the Quantity Theory' 1991; numerous articles learned jours.; mem. Am. Econ. Assn.; Candn. Econ. Assn. (Extve. Comte. 1980–83, Pres. 1987–88); recreations: theatre, opera, concerts; Home: 345 Grangeover Ave., London, Ont. N6G 4K8; Office: London, Ont. N6A 5C2.

**LAIDLER, Keith James,** M.A., Ph.D., D.Sc., F.C.I.C., F.R.S.C.; university professor; b. Liverpool, England 3 Jan. 1916; s. George James and Hilda (Findon) L.; e. Liverpool Coll., 1929–34; Trinity Coll., Oxford (1934–38), B.A., M.A., D.Sc.; Commonwealth Fellow, Princeton Univ. (1938–40), Ph.D. 1940; m. Mary Cabell, d. late John Auchincloss, 22 June 1943; children: late Margaret Cabell (Mrs. Paul McGaw), late Audrey Auchincloss (Mrs. Peter Bunting), James Reid; PROF. EMERITUS OF CHEMISTRY, UNIV. OF OTTAWA, since 1981; Prof. of Chem. 1955–81; Chairman of Dept., 1961–66; Vice-Dean, Faculty of Pure and Applied Science, 1963–66; Research Scientist, N.R.C. (Ottawa), 1940–42; Scient. Offr., Inspection Bd. of U.K., 1942–44; Chief Scient. Offr. Candn. Armaments Research & Devel. Estab., 1944–46; Assoc. Prof., Cath. Univ. of Am., 1946–55; Commonwealth Visiting Prof., Univ. of Sussex, 1966–67; Chrmn., Comte. on Symposia, Royal Soc'y of Can., 1971–87; Chairman, Comn. on Chemical Kinetics, Intl. Union of Pure and Applied Chemistry, 1977–89; Publications: 'Theory of Rate Processes' (with S. Glasstone & H. Eyring) 1941; 'Chemical Kinetics' 1950; 'Chemistry of Enzymes' 1954; 'Chemical Kinetics of Excited States' 1955; 'Chemical Kinetics of Enzyme Action' 1958, 2nd ed. (with P.S. Bunting) 1973; 'Principles of Chemistry' 1966; 'Reaction Kinetics' Vols. I and II 1963; 'Theories of Chemical Reaction Rates' 1969; 'The Chemical Elements' 1970; ' Physical Chem. with Biological Applications' 1978; 'Physical Chemistry' (with J.H. Meiser) 1982; 'Chemical Kinetics' (3rd ed.) 1987; 'The World of Physical Chemistry' 1993; over 250 articles in scient. journs.; Chem. Inst. of Canada Medallist, 1971; Chem. Educ. Award, Chem. Inst. of Canada, 1974; Chem. Teacher Award, Mfg. Chem. Assn. 1975; Queen's Jubilee Medal, 1977; Boomer Lectr., Univ. of Alberta, 1978; Robert A. Welch Lectr., 1982; Centenary Medal, Royal Society of Canada, 1982; Henry Marshall Tory Medal, Royal Soc. of Canada, 1987; recreations: gardening, acting; Home: 734 Eastbourne Ave., Ottawa, Ont. K1K 0H7.

**LAIDLEY, David Howard,** B.Comm.; chartered accountant; b. Montreal, Que. 31 Dec. 1946; s. Wendell Howard and Margaret Mary (Monsarrat) L.; e. Lower Can. Coll. 1963; McGill Univ., B.Comm. 1967; C.A. 1970; m. Valerie d. Stanley and Bette Thomas 19 Feb. 1972; PARTNER, DELOITTE & TOUCHE 1975– ; joined Touche Ross 1967; specialized in income tax consulting 1970–86 returning to auditing in 1986; Chrmn., Royal Victoria Hosp. Corp.; Chrmn., Royal Victoria Hosp. Found.; Councillor, City of Westmount; Past-Pres., Grad. Soc. of McGill Univ.; Past-Pres., Estate Planning Counc. of Montreal; Past Pres., Univ. Club of Montreal; Trustee, The John Dobson Found.; recreations: tennis, squash, rowing, skiing, antique automobiles; clubs: The Mount Royal, The University Club of Montreal, The Hillside Tennis; Montreal Indoor Tennis; Home: 654 Murray Hill, Westmount, Que. H3Y 2W6; Office: Suite 3000, 1 Place Ville Marie, Montreal, Que. H3B 4T9.

**LAING, Crawford E.,** F.C.I.A., F.F.A., A.I.A., A.S.A., F.C.A.; consulting actuary; b. Glasgow, Scotland 21 Dec. 1924; s. James Crawford and Helen Govan (Simpson) L.; e. Hyndland S.S. (Scotland); Balfron H.S., higher leaving cert. 1940; Faculty of Actuaries in Scotland F.F.A. 1952; Assoc., Inst. of Actuaries A.I.A. 1954; Candn. Inst. of Actuaries F.C.I.A. 1966; Soc. of Actuaries A.S.A. 1966; Fellow, Conf. of Consulting Actuaries F.C.A. 1982; m. Sheila Helen Stuart d. John R. and Isabella (Maxwell) Linacre 12 Dec. 1949; children: Alison Helen, Roger Ewing, Kirsteen Stuart; emigrated to Canada Nov. 1965; PRES. & ACTUARY, CRAWFORD E. LAING LTD. CONSULTING ACTUARIES 1970– ; Consulting Actuary to Workers Compensation Boards of Alta., NWT, Yukon; Institutions, Employers & Unions; Pres., Dynamic Pensions Mngt. Ltd.; C.E.D.A.R. Investment Serv. Ltd. 1986– ; Advisor, Trustees of Stabilization Fund for Co-op Housing & Coop. Housing Fed. of Can.; Pioneering Paper on 'Maintained Value Pensions,' 17th Internat. Cong. of Actuaries 1964; IACA paper on 'Index-Linked Leases' 1992; 'Friend of Guiding' Award 1980; Mem., Rotary Club of W. Vanc. (Sec. 1982–83; Pres. 1984–85); Paul Harris Fellow, Rotary Internat.; recreations: travel, photography, computers, home renovations (do-it-yourself); clubs: Vancouver, Canada, Vancouver Bd. of Trade; Home: 3830 Southridge Ave., W. Vancouver, B.C. V7V 3J1; Office: #102, 2221 Folkestone Way, W. Vancouver, B.C. V7S 2Y6.

**LAING, Gertrude M.,** O.C. (1972); b. Tunbridge Wells, Kent, Eng., 13 Feb. 1905; d. Arthur George and Mary Elizabeth (Williams) Amies; e. Univ. of Man., B.A. 1925; Sorbonne, post-grad. studies 1927; m. 16 June 1930; two s.: Colin D. B., Alan R. B.; Teacher, Riverbend Sch. for Girls, Winnipeg, 1928–32; Lectr. in French, Univ. of Man., 1945–50; served as Extve. Secy., War Services Bd. and Central Volunteer Bureau, Winnipeg, 1942–45; apptd. Commr., Royal Comn. on Bilingualism & Biculturalism, 1963; appt. part-time mem.,

Candn. Radio-Television Comn., 1968; W. Regional Vice-Pres., Candn. Welfare Council, 1964–70; Pres., YWCA, Winnipeg, 1941–43; Central Volunteer Bureau, Winnipeg, 1951–52; Social Planning Council, Calgary, 1957–59; mem. Canada Council; named Chrmn. of Canada Council, 1975–78; extve. mem. Candn. Comn. for UNESCO, 1974–75; mem. Candn. Del. UNESCO Gen. Assembly 1974; Lecturer, Univ. of Calgary 1977; Hon. D. Univ., Calgary 1973; U.B.C. 1977; Univ. of Ottawa 1978; Univ. of Man., 1980; Officer of the Order of Canada, 1972; Liberal; recreation: music; Clubs: Calgary Golf & Country; Address: 405, 220, 26 Ave. S.W., Calgary, Alta. T2S 0M4.

**LAJEUNESSE, Claude,** M.A.Sc., Ph.D., P.Eng.; executive; b. Quebec City, Que. 20 June 1941; s. Paul-Henri and Marie-Ange (Rousseau) L.; e. Ecole Polytechnique Montreal B.Sc.A. 1965; Rensselaer Polytechnic Inst. Troy, N.Y. M.Sc.A. 1967, Ph.D. (Nuclear Engn.) 1969; m. Nicole d. Emile Morin, Quebec City, Que. 23 Dec. 1961; children: Christine, France, Marc, Nathalie, Pascale, François; PRESIDENT & CHIEF EXECUTIVE OFFICER, ASSOCIATION OF UNIVERSITIES AND COLLEGES OF CANADA (AUCC) 1988– ; Pres. & C.E.O., Centre for Rsch. on Information Technologies in Montreal (CRIM) 1987–88; Dir., Targeted Rsch., Natural Sciences and Engineering Rsch. Council (NSERC) 1984–88; General Mgr., Candn. Council of Professional Engineers 1978–84; Syndic and Head of Legal Affairs Dept., Ordre des ingénieurs du Qué. 1974–78; Head of Engn. Faculty Université du Québec à Trois-Rivières 1972–74; Head of Engn. Physics Dept. 1971–72; mem., Bd. of Dirs. & Extve. Ctte., Fonds pour la Formation des Chercheurs et l'Aide à la recherche (FCAR) 1987– ; Mem. (1990–91), Chair (1991–92) Bd. of Dirs., Network of Centres of Excellence on High-Performance Concrete; Mem., Bd. of Dirs., 1989 Candn. Engineering Memorial Foundation 1992– ; Mem., Joint Advisory Ctte. on Consultation, The Privy Council Office, Govt. of Canada 1991– ; Assoc. Mem., Corporate-Higher Education Forum 1990– ; Mem., Extve. Ctte, World Fedn. of Engineering Organizations, Paris, France 1983–87; Mem., Bd. of Dirs., Candn. Microelectronics Corp. 1984–87; Mem., Ctte. on Internat. Sci. and Tech. Affairs, Nat. Rsch. Council of Canada 1981–84; Co-Chrmn., Ctte. on Evaluation of Programs, Canada Quebec Subsidiary Agreement on Science and Technology 1986–88; author of numerous publications including the Engineering section 'The Canadian Encyclopedia' Hurtig Publishers Ltd. 1985; Ordre des ingénieurs du Qué.; recreations: tennis, squash; Office: 600 - 350 Albert, Ottawa, Ont. K1R 1B1.

**LAKE, Philip,** C.G.A.; business executive; b. Toronto, Ont. 18 July 1950; s. Arthur R. and Grace L. (Patten) L.; e. Certified General Accountant C.G.A.; m. Janet d. Bruce and Betty Fairgrieve 14 Aug. 1971; children: Jennifer, Bradley; VICE PRESIDENT, CHUBB SECURITY 1989– ; various management positions; Regional Manager, Protection Serv. Div. / Branch Mgr., Southern Alberta / Atlantic Region / Manager, Business Planning & Systems, Honeywell Limited 1975–89; Home: 1151 Cynthia Lane, Oakville, Ont.; Office: 42 Shaft Rd., Rexdale, Ont. M9W 4M2.

**LAKING, Janice R.,** B.A.; mayor; b. Barrie, Ont. 23 Dec. 1929; d. Duncan Fletcher and Laura Isabel (Wilson) McCuaig; e. Univ. of West. Ont., B.A. 1951; Univ. of Toronto 1953; m. John C. s. Wilbur and Alma L. 27 Dec. 1952; children: Wendy, Susan, Jane, Sandra, Paul, John, Ruth; MAYOR, CITY OF BARRIE 1988– ; Liberal Candidate Fed. Election, Simcoe Centre 25 Oct. 1993; Secondary Sch. Teacher, Petrolia, West Lorne, St Thomas; Head of Girls' Phys. & Health Ed. & Guidance, Barrie N. Coll. & Central Coll.; early retirement Jan. 1988; elected Barrie City Alderman Nov. 1972, Mayor Dec. 1988; Dir., Barrie Public Utilities Comn., Barrie Police Comn.; Royal Victoria Hosp. Bd.; Mem., United Ch.; Liberal cand. for Simcoe North in Fed. election 1974; Past Pres., Univ. Women's Club; Past Chrmn., Barrie Dist. United Way; Dir., Simcoe Co. Children's Aid; Kinark Children's Serv.; Barrie Horticulture Assn.; recreations: gardening, woodworking, sewing; Home: 23 Letitia St., Barrie, Ont. L4N 1N7; Office 70 Collier St., Box 400, Barrie, Ont. L4M 4T5.

**LALA, Peeyush Kanti,** M.B., B.S., M.D., Ph.D.; university professor; administrator; b. Chittagong, Bengal, Brit. India 1 Nov. 1934; s. Sudhangshu Bimal and Nanibala (Chaudhuri) L.; e. Calcultta Univ., M.B., B.S. 1957, Ph.D. 1961, M.D. (thesis) 1962; ECFMG (USA) 1962; 1stly m. Arati (dec'd.) d. Kartick and Sarbajoya Roy-Burman 7 July 1962; children: Probal, Prasun; 2ndly m. Shipra Bhattachareya 6 Nov. 1992; PROF. & CHRMN., DEPT. OF ANATOMY, UNIV. OF WEST. ONT. 1983– ; Rsch. Fellow, Saha Inst. of Nuclear Physics 1958–62; Res. in Med., Calcutta Med. Coll. 1958–59; Demonstrator of Pathol. & Hematol. 1959–60; NRS Med. Coll., Calcutta 1961–62; Res. Rsch. Assoc., Div. Biol. & Med. Rsch., Argonne Nat. Lab., Ill. 1963–64; Rsch. Scient. and Asst. Prof. Lab. of Radiobiol., Univ. of Calif. Med. Center, San Francisco 1964–66; Rsch. Sci., Biol. & Health Physics Div., Chalk River Nuclear Labs. 1967–68; Asst. Prof. of Anat., McGill Univ. 1968–72, Assoc. Prof. 1972–77, Prof. 1977–83; Vis. Prof., Walter and Eliza Hall Inst. Med. Res., Univ. of Melbourne 1977–78; discovery of a new mode of cancer therapy (a new mode of immuno-therapy of cancer metastasis); Mem., Grants Panel, Med. Rsch. Counc. of Can.; Nat. Cancer Inst. of Can.; Cancer Rsch. Soc. Inc. (Montréal); Nat. Inst. of Health (U.S.A.); Connaught Ctte. (Toronto); Ed. Bd., 'Leukemia Research,' 'American Journal of Reproductive Immunology,' 'Experimental Hematology,' 'American Journal of Anatomy' (Assoc. Ed.); T. Ahmed Medal in Ophthalmology, Calcutta Univ. 1957; Fulbright Scholar 1962; Univ. of Melbourne Scholar 1977–78; JCB Grant Award, Candn. Assn. of Anat. 1990; Chrmn., Cultural Ctr., Cult. Assn. of India, Montreal 1973–83; Mem., Internat. Soc. for Exper. Hematol.; Internat. Soc. for Immunology of Reproduction (Counc. 1986–89); Soc. for Leukocyte Biol.; Candn. (Chrmn., awards ctte. 1986–89; Vice Pres. 1989–90, Pres.-elect 1990–91, Pres. 1991–93) & Am. Assns. of Anat.; Candn. & Am. Socs. of Immunol.; Am. Assn. for Cancer Rsch.; Am. Soc. of Reproductive Immunol. (Vice-Pres. 1985–86); author of more than 130 rsch. pubns. & 13 book chapters on hematology, immunology, cancer and reproduction; editor: 'Stem Cells in Various Tissues' 1975; Guest Ed., 'American J. Anatomy' (spec. issue on Immune System) 1984; recreations: swimming, music, public speaking on sci.; Home: 1095 Prince George Rd., London, Ont. N6H 4E2; Office: London, Ont. N6A 5C1.

**LALANDE, Richard H.,** B.A.; design contractor; b. Nanaimo, B.C. 10 April 1943; s. Henri Joseph and Rollande (Hurtubise) L.; e. Carleton Univ., B.A. (Geog.) 1969; m. Marilyn Margaret d. Orville O'Byrne 23 July 1966; children: Guy, Chantal; PRES., PRI-TEC CONSTRN. LTD. 1972– ; Area Mgr., Butler Mfg. Co. 1969–72; founded Pri-Tec in 1972; Pres., Pri-Tec Ltd.; Pri-Tec Internat. Inc.; O.S. Outaouais Systems Ltd.; P.C.W. Investments; Kirkland Lake Ind. Plaza Ltd.; Cardevco Ind. Park; West Carleton Bus. Assoc.; Adv. Counc., Algonquin Coll.; recreations: hunting, fishing, squash; Club: Thunderbird Tennis; Home: 12 Buttonwood Trail, SS 2, Stittsville, Ont. K2S 1C9; Office: Box 13090, Kanata, Ont. K2K 1X3.

**LALL, Santosh P.,** B.Sc., M.Sc., Ph.D.; research scientist; b. Motihari, India 8 Sept. 1944; s. Victor C. and Ummedi L.; e. Allahabad Univ B.Sc. 1964; Univ. of Guelph M.Sc. 1969, Ph.D. 1973; m. Barbara d. Robert C. Smith; children: Julie Shirin, Carolyn A.; RESEARCH SCIENTIST, DEPARTMENT OF FISH & OCEANS, BIOL. SCI. BRANCH 1974– ; Research Asst., Agriculture Inst., Allahabad, India 1964–65; Adjunct Prof., Univ. of P.E.I.; N.S. Agriculture College; Dalhousie Univ.; Technical Univ. of Nova Scotia; Mem., Nat. Academy of Science (Subctte. on Fish Nutrition) Washington; Candn. Soc. of Nutritional Sciences; Aquaculture Assn. of Canada; N.Y. Academy of Sciences; author of 40 scientific pubns. incl. chapters in books; Home: 35 Flamingo Dr., Halifax, N.S. B3M 1S6; Office: P.O. Box 550, 1707 Lower Water St., Halifax, N.S. B3J 2S7.

**LALONDE, Fernand,** B.A., LL.L.; lawyer; b. Mont-Laurier, Que. 27 Aug. 1932; e. Collège St-Jean; Collège Ste-Marie B.A. 1951; Univ. of Montreal & McGill Univ. LL.L. 1957; m. Marie Elie 23 Nov. 1957; children: Marie-Claire, Elaine, Benoit; LAWYER, AHERN, LALONDE, NUSS, DRYMER 1986– ; called to Bar 1957; Q.C. 1973; Lawyer, Geoffrion & Prud'homme 1957–71; successively Special Adviser, Qué. Solicitor Gen., Acting Chair, Que. Securities Comn. & Dep. Min., Financial Institutions, Que. 1971–73; Mem., Nat. Assembly of Que. for Marguerite-Bourgeoys 1973–84; Min. of State, Executive Council of Que. 1973–75; Que. Solicitor General 1975–76; Parly. Leader, Official Opposition 1982–84; Chief, successful electoral campaign, Que. Liberal Party 1985; Dir., Air Canada; Culinar Inc.; Socanav Inc.; La Soc. d'énergie Foster Wheeler Ltée (Bd. Chair); Montreal Mus. of Fine Arts (Chair, Bd. of Trustees); Théâtre du Nouveau monde; Montreal Heart Inst. (Past Bd. Chair); Mem., Candn. Bar Assn.; club: University; Office: 1, Pl. Ville Marie, Ste. 3333, Montreal, Que. H3B 3N2.

**LALONDE, Francine Champagne,** B.A.; professeur; b. St-Hyacinthe, Que. 24 Aug. 1940; d. Grégoire and Jeannette Savard (Champagne) L.; e. St-Hyacinthe bacc en psycho-pédagogie, école normale Cardinal-Leger 1960; Univ. de Montréal Licence Hist. 1964; m. Bernard s. Jean-Marie L. 16 Mai 1964 (séparée); children: Dominique, Philippe, Julien; professeur des relations du travail à l'UQAM, aux HEC et de l'histoire du Québec, de l'évolution du mouvement ouvrier, et de l'histoire de la santé & securité au travail à l'UQAC et à l'Univ. de Montreal comme chargée de cours 1985– ; Teacher: (Français) CECM 1960–62; (Latin) Couvent Hochelaga 1962–64; (Hist.) Coll. Basile-Moreau 1964–68; (Hist.) CEGEP St-Laurent 1968–70, 1978–79; Prés. Secteur CEGEP 1970; Prés. FNEQ-CSN 1970–76, 1979–81; Vice-Prés. CSN 1976–78; co-ordonnatrice des fédérations dans le secteur privé, CSN 1981–84; Sec. SCOPEM 1984–85; Ministre Deleguée à la Condition Feminine (Min. Responsible for the Status of Women) gouvernement du Québec: de janv. 1985 à juin 1985; candidate à la présidence du Parti Québécois: de août 1985 à sept. 1985; candidate aux élections provinciales dans le comté de St-Henri en 1985 et 1989; élue conseillier au programme du Parti Québecois en 1991; Home: 127 Clermont, Laval-des-Rapides, Que. H7N 2Z6.

**LALONDE, Jean-Louis,** B.A., R.C.A.; architect; b. Coteau Station, Que. 17 June 1923; s. Charles and Marie-Ann (LeFebvre) L.; e. Coll. St. Marie (Montreal); Univ. of Montreal, B.A. 1944; Beaux Art 1950; Architectural Assn. Sch. of Arch. (London, Eng.), Dipl. in Arch. 1951; m. Gisele, d. Trancrede Bissonnette, 8 July 1950; children: Pier, Marc; Partner, Hebert and Lalonde 1968; with Fry and Drew, Architects, London, Eng. 1951–52; then Breuer-Nervi-Zehrfuss, Paris, France 1952–56; joined Rother-Bland & Trudeau, Architects, Montreal 1957, prior to commencement in private practice, 1960; Chrmn., Adv. Comte. on Design, Nat. Capital Comn.; mem. Prov. Que. Assn. of Arch. (Past Pres.); R.A.I.C. (Pres. 1971); Arch. and Planning Comn., City of Westmount; Extve. Bd. Internat. Union of Archs.; Jacques Viger Comn. (Hist. Monuments), Montreal; Roman Catholic; recreations: tennis, Clubs: Mount-Royal Tennis, Montreal Badminton & Squash; Home: 4328 Montrose Ave., Westmount, Que. H3Y 2A9.

**LALONDE, The Hon. Marc,** P.C. (Can.), O.C., Q.C., LL.L., M.A.; lawyer; b. Ile Perrot, Quebec, 26 July 1929; s. J. Albert and Nora (St. Aubin) L.; e. St. Laurent College, Montreal, B.A. 1950; University of Montreal, LL.L 1954, M.A. (Law) 1955; Oxford University (Econ. & Political Science), M.A. (Oxon) 1957; Ottawa Univ., Dipl. of Superior Studies in Law, 1960; m. Claire, d. J. Georges Tétreau, Montreal, Que., 8 Sept. 1955; children: Marie, Luc, Paul, Catherine; called to Bar of Que. 1955; Prof. of Comm. Law and Econ., Univ. of Montreal, 1957–59; Special Asst. to Min. of Justice, Ottawa, 1959–60; Partner, Gelinas, Bourque, Lalonde & Benoit, Montreal, 1960–68; Lectr. in Adm. Law for Doctorate Students, Univ. of Ottawa and Univ. of Montreal, 1961–62; Policy Adviser to Prime Min. 1967; Princ. Secy. to Prime Min. 1968–72; el. to H. of C. for Montreal-Outremont g.e. 1972, re-el. until 1984; Min. Nat. Health and Welfare 1972–77; Min. of State for Fed.-Prov. Relations 1977–78 and Min. Resp. for Status of Women, 1975–78; Min. of Justice 1978–79; Minister of Energy, Mines & Resources 1980–82; Minister of Finance 1982–84; Partner, Stikeman, Elliott, Montreal; Bd. Chrmn., Hôtel-Dieu of Montreal 1985– ; mem. Bd. of Dir., Citibank Can. 1986– ; Lakewood Energy Inc. 1993– ; CamDev Corporation 1993– ; mem. Internat. Adv. Bd. Air France; Am. Arbitration Assn. 1987– ; Officer of the Order of Canada; mem. Que. Bar Assn.; Upper Canada Law Soc.; Am. Bar Assn.; Internat. Bar Assn.; Liberal; R. Catholic; recreations: jogging, tennis, skiing, swimming, sailing, reading; Home: 5440 Légaré, Montreal, Que. H3T 1Z4; Office: Ste. 3900, 1155 René-Levesque Blvd. W., Montreal, Que. H3B 3V2.

**LAMARRE, Bernard,** Eng., M.Sc., D.I.C., F.E.I.C., LL.D., O.C., O.Q.; b. Chicoutimi, Que. 6 Aug. 1931; s. Emile (dec.) and Blanche (Gagnon) L. (dec.); e. Mont St.-Louis Coll., Sr. Matric. and Dipl. of Sci. 1944–48; Ecole Polytechnique de Montréal B.A.Sc. Civil Engrg. 1952; Univ. of London, England, Imp. Coll. of Sci. and Tech. M.Sc. Engrg. 1953; m. Louise; d. Jean-Paul Lalonde 30 Aug. 1952; children: Jean, Christine, Lucie, Monique, Michele, Philippe, Mireille; SR. ADVISOR, SNC-LAVALIN INC.; Soil Mechanics Engr., Structural Design Engr., Project Engr. in Pub. Works, Lalonde & Valois Cons. Engrs. 1955–60; Chief Engr. 1960–62; Partner, Gen. Mgr. and Pres., Lalonde, Valois, Lamarre, Valois & Associes 1962–72; Pres. & C.E.O., Lavalin Ltd. 1972–91; Past Pres. Mont St-Louis Alumni Assn. 1962; Dir. Coll. Marie de France, Montreal 1975–91; Coll. Stanislas, Montreal 1976– ; Chrmn. Montreal Mus. of Fine Arts 1982–91; Pres. Centennial Bd. 1987; Corp. de l'Ecole Polytechnique 1987–92; Past Chrmn., CDIC 1984–87; Chrmn., Candn. Cultural Property Export Review Board 1992; Mem. of the Bd., Telesystème Inc. 1992; Chrmn. of the Bd., Belledrasse Santé Inc. 1991; Pres., Ordre des Ingénieurs du Québec 1993; Pres., Institut de Design Montreal 1993; Athlone Fellowship 1952; Fellow Engr. Inst. of Can. 1975; LL.D. (h.c.) St. Francis Xavier Univ. 1980; Hon. Fellow Royal Archit. Inst. of Can. 1983; Fellow Candn. Soc. for Civil Engr. 1983; D.Eng. (h.c.), Univ. of Waterloo 1984; D.Eng. (h.c.), Univ. of Montreal 1985; LL.D. (h.c.) Concordia Univ. 1985; Officer, Ordre National du Québec 1985; Officer, Order of Canada 1985; Doctor of Applied Sciences (h.c.), Univ. of Sherbrooke, Que. 1986; D.B.A. (h.c.), Univ. of Quebec, Chicoutimi, Que. 1987; D.Sc. (h.c.), Queen's Univ., Kingston, Ont. 1987; D.Eng. (h.c.) Univ. of Ottawa, Ont. 1988; D.Eng. (h.c.) Technical Univ. of Nova Scotia 1989; D.Eng. (h.c.) Royal Military Coll., Kingston, Ont. 1990; Clubs: Mount Royal; St.-Denis; Laval-sur-le-Lac; Home: 4850 Cedar Cres., Montreal, Que. H3W 2H9; Office: 2 Place Felix-Martin, Montreal, Que. H2Z 1Z3.

**LAMB, James Barrett;** author; b. Toronto, Ont. 30 Nov. 1919; s. Thomas Barrett and Elsie Margaret (Blair) L.; e. Whitney P.S.; Oakwood C.I.; Royal Candn. Mil. Coll.; m. Ruby Edith d. Edward and Edith Evans 23 June 1948; children: Roderick Barrett, James Edward; served six years, Royal Candn. Naval Volunteer Res. in WWII; Comdr., Minesweeper HMCS 'Minas' and Corvette HMCS 'Camrose'; mentioned in despatches at Normandy 6 June 1944; retired as Lt-Comdr.; Journalist (Ont. & Sask.) 1945–50; Ed. & Pub., 'Orillia Daily Packet & Times' 1950–71; Columnist, Toronto Star & var. mags.; retired to Cape Breton 1971 to write; Anglican; Rotarian; Mem., Red Cross; Cancer Soc.; Boy Scouts; Past Chrmn., Orillia Publ. Library; Leacock Award Bd.; and others; author: 'The Other Canada' 1972, 'Clap Hands, Here Comes Charlie' 1973, 'Temple-Tombs and Hillforts' 1975, 'The Hidden Heritage' 1975, 'The Corvette Navy' 1977, 'The Man From the Sea' 1984, 'Gunshield Graffiti' 1984, 'Press Gang' 1979, 'On The Triangle Run' 1986; 'Love and War' 1988; 'A Place Apart' 1989; 'The Gentle Genius' 1990; 'The Celtic Crusader' 1992; 'Jingo' 1992; recreations: sailing, walking, golf, travel; Club: Royal Candn. Mil. Inst.; Home: Big Harbour, RR #2, Baddeck, N.S. B0E 1B0.

**LAMB, John Maxwell,** M.A.; director; b. Montréal, Qué. 23 Nov. 1951; s. John Douglas and Alice Maxwell L.; e. Univ. of Toronto B.A. 1977, doctoral rsch. internat. relations 1978–83; Columbia Univ. M.A. 1978; m. Alison H. d. Kenneth and Hope Lee 16 Aug. 1980; one d. Rosalind Isabella (Bella) Hope; PRINCIPAL, STRATEGIC PLANNING ASSOCIATES 1993– ; Researcher, Operations Rsch. & Analysis Est. Dept. Nat. Defence 1977–78; Teaching Asst. in Pol. Sci. Univ. of Toronto 1979–81; Founder and Extve. Dir., The Canadian Centre for Global Security (formerly The Candn. Centre for Arms Control and Disarmament) 1983–93; author numerous newspaper, mag. and jour. articles arms control; mem. Bd. of Dirs., Candn. Centre for Global Security; recreations: fly fishing, reading, skating; Home & Office: 102 Lorne Ave., Ottawa, Ont. K1R 7G9.

**LAMB, William Kaye,** O.C. (1969), Ph.D., LL.D., D.S. Litt., F.R.S.C.; librarian and archivist (retired); b. New Westminster, B.C., 11 May 1904; s. Alexander and Barbara S. (McDougall) L.; e. Univ. of Brit. Columbia, B.A. 1927, M.A. 1930; Univ. of Paris (Sorbonne), sessions 1928–29, 1930–32; Univ. of London, Eng., Ph.D. 1933; LL.D., Univ. of B.C. 1948; Manitoba 1953; Toronto 1954; Sask. 1956; Assumption 1958; McMaster 1966; Univ. of Victoria 1966; New Brunswick 1967; York 1968; D.S.Litt., Victoria (Toronto), 1961; m. Wessie M. Tipping, 15 May 1939; one d. Barbara Elizabeth; Prov. Librarian and Archivist of B.C. 1934–40; Supt., B.C. Pub. Lib. Comn., 1936–40; Librarian, Univ. of B.C. 1940–48; Dom. Archivist, 1948–69; Nat. Librarian 1953–68; mem., B.C. Pub. Library Comn. 1943–48; The Champlain Soc. (Past Pres.); B.C. Library Association (Past Pres.); Candn. Hist. Assn. (Past Pres.); B.C. Hist. Assn. (Past Pres.); Candn. Library Assn. (Pres. 1947–48); Steamship Hist. Soc. of Am.; Soc. of Archivists (Past Pres.); Soc. of Am. Archivists (Past Pres.); Fellow, Roy. Soc. Can. (Past Pres.); mem. Mass. Hist. Soc.; Am. Antiq. Soc.; Ed., 'B.C. Hist. Quarterly,' 1937–46; contrib. hist. introductions to 'Letters of John McLoughlin' (three series) 1942–45; edited 'Journal of Daniel Williams Harmon' 1957; 'The Letters and Journals of Simon Fraser, 1806–1808' 1960; 'Journal of Gabriel Franchère' 1969; 'Journals and Letters of Sir Alexander Mackenzie' 1970; 'George Vancouver, 'A Voyage of Discovery 1791–1795',' (4 vols.) 1984; author of 'Canada's Five Centuries: From Discovery to Present Day' 1971; (with N. R. Hacking) 'The 'Princess' Story' 1974; 'History of the CPR' 1977; numerous articles in hist., library, and marine journs.; Awarded Tyrrell Medal (Royal Soc. of Can.) 1965; Address: #2105–2055 Pendrell St., Vancouver, B.C. V6G 1T9.

**LAMBART, Evelyn Mary;** film maker; b. Ottawa, Ont. 23 July 1914; d. Frederick Howard John and Helen Marianne (Wallbridge) L.; e. Ottawa Model Sch.; Lisgar Coll. Inst. Ottawa; Ont. Coll. of Art grad. 1937; retired film maker Nat. Film Bd. Can.; recreation: rock gardening; Address: 431 Mudgett Rd., Sutton, Que. J0E 2K0.

**LAMBERMONT, Jeannette Monique,** B.F.A.; theatre director; b. The Netherlands 31 Dec. 1956; d. John Peter and Ingrid Gerlinde (Dewald) L.; e. York Univ. B.F.A. 1978; Co-Artistic Dir. The Next Stage Inc. Toronto 1984–87; Cons. and Casting Dir. Soma Film Producers 1986–87; Mem. of Play Reading Cttee., Candn. Stage Co. 1991 and 1992; Guest Dir., Juilliard Sch., New York 1993; Guest Teacher and Dir. Ryerson Theatre Sch. 1985–87, 1990 and 1992; Guest Dir., George Brown Coll. 1990, 1992 and 1993; Univ. of Alberta 1991; Humber College 1991 and 1992; Univ. of Victoria 1992; Dartmouth College, New Hampshire 1991; Instructor, Maggie Bassett Studio 1990; Instr., Theatre Ontario 1992 and 1993; private monologue and audition coach since 1984; Dir. in Word Festival, Candn. Stage Co. 1991 and 1992; and 'Twelfth Night' 1993 and 1994; Dir., 'On the Verge' Virginia Stage Co., Virginia 1994; Dir., 'Barefoot in the Park,' Huron Country Playhouse 1993; Dir., 'The Trojan Women,' Alumnae Theatre 1993; Dir., 'The Grand Inquisitor' and 'Swan Song,' Stratford Festival 1990; Dir. 'The Miracle Worker' Citadel Theatre 1989, 'Titus Andronicus' Stratford Festival 1989, 'The Great Lover' and '24 Dunsinane Hill' workshops Stratford Festival 1988, 'Easter' Equity Showcase 1987, 'Changes in a Unicorn' Next Stage Inc. 1986; Contbr. Dir., 'The Comedy of Errors' and 'The Relapse,' Stratford Festival, 1989; Asst. Dir. 'Taming of the Shrew' 1988, 'Othello'1987 Stratford Festival, 'Dracula' Young People's Theatre 1988, 'Observe the Sons of Ulster' CentreStage 1988, 'Skin Deep' Theatre Plus 1987; recipient Tyrone Guthrie and Jean Chalmers Awards 1988; Dir. Observer's Award, Candn. Acad. of Cinema and Television 1991; 1st Director's Award Alumnae Theatre; mem. Candn. Actors Equity Assn.; Anthroposophical Soc. Can.; Address: c/o Christopher Banks & Assocs., 219 Dufferin St., Suite 305, Toronto, Ont. M6K 1Y9.

**LAMBERT, Allen Thomas,** O.C.; retired banker; b. Regina, Sask. 28 Dec. 1911; s. Willison Andrew and Sarah (Barber) L.; e. Victoria (B.C.) Pub. and High Schs.; m. Marion Grace, d. William G. Kotchapaw, Winnipeg, Man., 20 May 1950; children: William A., Anne B.; Group Chrmn., Edper-Brascan Financial Services; Dir., Cdn. Satellite Communications Inc.; Trilon Financial Corp.; London Insurance Group; Brascan Ltd.; Great Lakes Group Inc.; Hees International Corp.; Western Internat. Communications Ltd.; Past Pres. Internat. Monetary Conf.; Hon. Trust., Upper Can. Coll. Fdn.; apptd. Head, Roy. Comm. on Financial Mang. and Accountability, 1976; entered service of the Toronto-Dominion Bank at Victoria, B.C., 1927 and subsequently served in Vancouver, Brockville and Montreal; became Mgr. at Yellowknife, N.W.T., 1946; Insp., Winnipeg, Man., 1947; Supv., H.O., Toronto, 1949; Asst. Mgr., Main Office, Montreal 1950; Supt. H.O., Toronto 1953; Asst. Gen. Mgr., 1953; apptd. General Manager, 1956; Vice-President and Director, 1956; President 1960; Chairman of Board 1961 until retirement 1978; served during the 2nd World War with R.C.N., 1943–45; discharged with the rank of Lieutenant; United Church; recreations: golf, fishing, curling; Clubs: Toronto; Toronto Hunt; Toronto Golf; Granite; York; Home: 483 Russell Hill Road, Toronto, Ont. M5P 2S8; Office: P.O. Box 1, Toronto-Dominion Centre, Toronto, Ont. M5K 1A2.

**LAMBERT, Garrett,** B.A.; public servant; b. Toronto, Ont. 20 June 1941; s. Christopher and Muriel L.; e. Univ. of Toronto B.A. 1963; m. Helen 28 Aug. 1965; children: Jason, Alexander; ASSISTANT DEPUTY MINISTER, CORP. MANAGEMENT BRANCH, DEPARTMENT OF FOREIGN AFFAIRS & INTERNATIONAL TRADE 1990– ; Special Asst., Min. of Defence 1966–68; Commercial Counsellor, Iran, W. Germany, E. Germany, Poland 1969–78; Dir. Gen. for Industrial Coop. 1978–82; High Comnr. to Nigeria 1982–85; Dir. Gen. for USA Trade 1985–88; High Comnr. to Malaysia 1988–90; Adv. Bd. Mem., Candn. Passport Office; U. of T. New College Honour Award 1963; Office: 125 Sussex Dr., Ottawa, Ont. K1A 0G2.

**LAMBERT, Geoffrey,** Ph.D.; university professor; b. Scunthorpe, England 26 June 1945; s. Albert and Florence May (Paddison) L.; e. Scunthorpe Grammar Sch.; Manchester Univ. B.A. (Econ.) 1966; Univ. of Minnesota M.A. 1969, Ph.D. 1976; Summer Institutes at Univ. of Michigan and Harvard; Extension courses at Univs. of Toronto and Winnipeg; Prairie Theatre Exchange Sch., Winnipeg; ASSOC. PROF. OF POLITICAL STUDIES, UNIV. OF MANITOBA 1983– ; Lectr., Univ. of Minn. 1968–70; Univ. of N.B. 1970–71; Univ. of Man. 1971–73; Asst. Prof., Univ. of Man. 1973–83; Visiting Scholar, Cntr. of Asian Studies, Univ. of Hong Kong 1978; Rsch. Leave, Univ. of Toronto 1983–85; occasional broadcaster, commentator and consultant on public affairs; Bd. Mem., SSHRCC 1987–94 (Extve. 1989–94); Chair, SSHRC Cttee. to Review Canada Rsch. Fellowships Prog. 1988; Sec. & Rsch. Dir., Min. Adv. Cttee. on Liquor Control Matters, Man. 1980–81; Mem., Univ. Grants Comn., Man. 1980–82; Chair, Ministerial Cttee. to Review Greater Winnipeg Gas Franchise (Man.) 1981–82; Mem., Selection Cttee., Man. Legislative Internship Prog. 1988–91; Mem., Law Enforcement Review Agency, Man. 1991–93; Head, Pol. Studies, Univ. of Man. 1978–83; Provost, Univ. College, Univ. of Man. 1990–91; has chaired several major univ. cttes.; recipient, Stanton Award for Excellence in Teaching, Univ. of Man. 1987; Service Award (U. Service) Univ. of Man. 1989; Outreach Award (Community Service), Univ. of Man. 1991; Commemorative Medal for 125th Anniversary of Candn. Confederation 1992; Cert. of Excellence in Teaching, Univ. of Man. 1993; Anglican; Tory; Mem., pol. sci. assns. of Can., U.S.A. & U.K.; P.C. Party; Assoc. Manitoba Arts Festivals; Zoological Soc. of Man.; Parkinson Foundation; Plan Internat.; Royal Candn. Geographical Soc.; fundraiser for several orgns.; active in minor hockey and amateur theatre; initiator, Manchester Univ. Graduates Assn. in Can.; author, approx. fifty articles and reviews on Can. and comparative politics; regular contbr., 'Canadian Annual Review'; author, over two hundred technical (primarily opinion survey) reports; recreations: all performing arts, genealogy, hockey, squash, walking, collecting books; Home: 189 Elm St., Winnipeg, Man. R3M 3N5; Office: Winnipeg, Man. R3T 2N2.

**LAMBERT, Jean R.;** investment dealer; b. St-Georges of Beauce 12 June 1938; s. Gérard and Juliette (Larochelle) L.; e. Univ. Laval, admin. 1961; Candian Investment Dealer Inst., finances 1968; m. Andrée d. Oliva Coulombe 28 July 1962; children: Renée, Joann, Carol; VICE-PRES. & DIR., LEVESQUE BEAUBIEN GEOFFRION INC.; Pres., Caisse Populaire Desjardins Chauveau; Maison des Régions du Québec; Soc. Immobilière du Canada Inc. 1982; Chair, Harvey Bearings Inc.; Fishery Products Belle Marée Inc.; Dir., Aetna Canada; Caisse de Retraite de l'Université Laval; Québec 2002; Sales Mgr., Bank of Canada CSB Payroll Savings P.Q.; Pres., Groupe Demeter Inc.; Pres. & Dir., Candn. Investment Securities Inst. 1977–85; Endowment Dir., Laval Univ.; Dir. Enfant Jésus Hospital (1st Vice-Pres., Endowment); recreations: skiing, hockey, racquetball; clubs: Garrison; Home: 190 Père Giroux, Beauport, Qué. G1E 2Z8; Office: 2785, boul. Hamel Ouest, Québec, Qué. G1P 2H9.

**LAMBERT, Hon. John Douglas,** B.A., LL.B.; judge; b. Ardrossan, Scot. 30 June 1930; s. James Edward and Jane Grierson (Todd) L.; e. Ardrossan (Scot.) Acad. 1944; Trinity Coll. Glenalmond, Scot. 1948; St. Andrews Univ. 1948–52; Queen's Univ. B.A. 1955; Univ. of B.C. LL.B. 1958; m. Barbara-Rose d. late Adolf George Schwenk 31 Dec. 1956; children: James Matthew, Sheena Louise, John Andrew Bowman; JUDGE, B.C. COURT OF APPEAL AND YUKON TERRITORY COURT OF APPEAL since 1978; Lectr. in Law Univ. of Victoria 1977–81 and Univ. of B.C. 1979–81; called to Bar of B.C. 1959, Ont. 1963; Counsel, Dept. of Justice 1959–64; Solr. B.C. Hydro & Power Authority 1964–67, 1968–69; Advisor, External Aid Program, Barbados 1967–68; Assoc. Davis and Co. Vancouver 1969–71, Partner 1971–78; mem. Law Reform Comn. Vancouver 1976–78, Chrmn. 1978; Presbyterian; recreation: walking; Club: Vancouver; Home: 6435 Wellington Ave., West Vancouver, B.C. V7W 2H7; Office: 800 Smithe St., Vancouver, B.C. V6Z 2E1.

**LAMBERT, Kenneth Henry,** B.Sc., LL.B.; corporate executive; b. Edmonton, Alta. 26 Sept. 1944; s. Leonard Thomas and Margaret Eileen (Lewis) L.; e. Univ. of Alta. B.Sc. 1965, LL.B. 1968; m. Glenna d. Gordon and Dorothy Macdonald 21 Aug. 1971; one d. Sheena Maureen; PRES., CHIEF EXTVE. OFFR. & DIR., NU-GOLD TECHNOLOGY LIMITED 1993– ; Pres., Edmonton International Industries Ltd. 1976– ; Lambert Management Ltd. 1969– ; Chrmn., Downhole Tools Inc. 1987– ; Dir., Coho Energy Inc. 1993– ; Three Sisters Golf Resorts Inc. 1989– ; Chrmn. SDS Drilling Ltd. 1977–88; Chrmn., Coho Resources Limited 1992–93; law practice Bishop & McKenzie Edmonton 1968–69; Corporate Sec. Banister Pipelines Ltd. 1969–73; Vice

Pres. Adm. & Corporate Sec. Banister Continental Ltd. Toronto 1973–76; Extve. Vice Pres. Mined Storage Ltd. 1974–76; law practice Bell Felesky Iverach Calgary 1978–82; Pres. & C.E.O., Coho Resources Ltd. 1980–92; Dir. Calgary French Sch. 1983–84; Lycée Louis Pasteur Soc. 1984–87, Chrmn. 1986–87; Founding Dir. and Chrmn. Small Explorers & Producers Assn. Can. 1986– ; mem. Young Pres. Orgn.; Office: 2010, 255 – 5th Ave. S.W., Calgary, Alta. T2P 3G6.

**LAMBERT, Michael R.,** B.Comm., C.A.; corporate executive; b. Windsor, Ont. 11 Aug. 1955; s. Eugene and Evelyn (Orlando) L.; e. Univ. of Windsor B.Comm. 1978; C.A. 1981; m. Mary d. Robert and Marilyn Dupuis 1 Sept. 1979; children: Andrew, Stephen, Angela; VICE-PRES., FINANCIAL REPORTING, GEORGE WESTON LTD. 1993– ; Coopers & Lybrand 1979–82; Senior Financial Analyst, Candn. Imperial Bank of Commerce 1982–83; Dir. of Internal Audit then Asst. Controller, Loblaw Companies 1983–86; Controller, George Weston Limited 1986–91; Vice-Pres. Finance, Southam Business Communication Inc. 1991; Vice-Pres. Finance, Southam Newspaper Group 1992–93; C.A. 1981 admitted to Ont. Inst. of C.A.s; Office: 1450 Don Mills Rd., Don Mills, Ont. M3B 2X7.

**LAMBERT, Peter John B.,** B.Sc.(Hons.), M.A.; archaeological consultant; b. Toronto, Ont. 5 Apr. 1952; s. John Hugh and Edith May (Bance) L.; e. Upper Can. Coll. 1971; Trent Univ. B.Sc. (Hons.) 1975; Univ. of Man. M.A. 1980; est. Peter J. Lambert, Archaeol. Cons. 1982– ; Archaeol. Rsch. Offr. Parks Br. N.W. Region Ont. Min. of Natural Resources, survey 7 Prov. Parks 1983; Project Dir. N.W. Ont. rock art inventory and recording 1982–83, 1984–86; Curatorial Asst. Faunal Div. Archaeol. Survey of Alta. 1982; Archaeol. Cons. assisting in recording Lake of the Woods petroglyph sites 1981; Archaeol. Reserch N.W. Region Ont. Min. Culture & Recreation 1982, Project Dir. W. Patricia Land Use Plan 1981–82; Archaeol. Researcher Dept. Cultural Affairs & Hist. Resources Man., Garden Site St. Norbert, Man. 1980, Field Excavator and Analyst Aschkibokahn Site 1977; Teaching Asst. in Anthrop. Univ. of Man. 1977, Rsch. Asst. 1978; author or co-author various publs., papers; awarded Archaeological Licences over six years under Ont. Heritage Act.; awarded Doctoral Scholarship in Archael. & Hist. Univ. of Tehran 1978 (declined); mem. Candn. Archaeol. Assn.; Candn. Rock Art Researchers Assn.; Ont. Archaeol. Soc.; Office: 483 Spadina Rd., Toronto, Ont. M5P 2W6.

**LAMBERT, Phyllis,** O.C., CQ, O.A.L., FRAIC, OAQ, RCA, B.A., M.S.Arch., Dr.h.c. Eng., Dr.h.c., D.Litt., LL.D.; architect; b. Montreal, Que. 24 Jan. 1927; d. Samuel and Saidye (Rosner) Bronfman; e. The Study, Montréal 1944; Vassar Coll., N.Y. B.A. 1948; Illinois Inst. of Technol., Chicago, M.S. (Arch.) 1963; Doctorates honoris causa: Technical Univ. of Nova Scotia, 1982; Univ. de Montréal, 1985; McGill Univ., 1986; Concordia Univ. 1986; Bishop's Univ. 1987; Univ. of Windsor 1989; Queen's Univ. 1990; Pratt Institute, New York 1990; Istituto Universitario di Architettura, Venice 1991; Illinois Institute of Technology, Chicago 1991; Univ. of Toronto 1991; Univ. de Laval, Que. 1991; Mount Saint Vincent Univ., Halifax, N.S. 1992; Acadia Univ., N.S. 1992; UBC 1992; Univ. of Victoria 1993; DIRECTOR, CENTRE CANADIEN D'ARCHITECTURE/CANADIAN CENTRE FOR ARCHITECTURE; projects incl. Dir. of Planning, Seagram Bldg., N.Y. 1954–58; Consultant to Fairview and Toronto-Dominion Bank, Toronto-Dominion Centre 1962; Architect, Saidye Bronfman Centre YM-YWHA Montréal 1963–68; Planning studies for Douglas Community Orgn., Chicago 1968–69; Communications Arts Center Study for Vassar Coll., N.Y. 1970; Fogg Museum Space Study 1972; Consultant to Cadillac-Fairview for design architecture, Eaton Centre 1972; Founder and Dir., Curator's Office, Joseph E. Seagram & Sons Inc., N.Y. 1972; consulting architect CCA 1984–89; Bd. Chrmn. & Principal, Ridgway Ltd., Architects/Developers, Los Angeles, 1972–84; Dir., Groupe de recherche sur les bâtiments en pierre grise de Montréal 1973; Consultant to Cadillac-Fairview for design architecture, Les Promenades St-Bruno (Qué.) Shopping Centre 1974; Architect, Jane Tate House renovation, Montréal 1974–76; Dir., Seagram Bicentennial Project 'Court House: A Photographic Document' 1974–79; Architect, cinema in private home, Montréal 1976; Architect-Developer, Biltmore Hotel renovation, Los Angeles 1976; Developer, renovation of housing units, St-Hubert St., Montréal 1979; Founder/Dir., Centre Canadien d'Architecture/Canadian Centre for Architecture, Montréal 1979; Pres., Société d'Amélioration Milton Parc, 700 unit non-profit cooperative housing renovation, Montréal 1979–85; Project Dir., renovation of Ben Ezra Synagogue, Cairo, Egypt 1987– ; Jury member on several cttes. incl. Mississauga City Hall Competition, Ont. 1982; competition for Carnegie Lib., Univ. of Toronto, 1985; Brooklyn Museum Competition 1986; Competition for the renovation and enlargement of the Gallery, Art Gallery of Ont., Toronto 1987; Ballet Opera House, Toronto 1987; House & Garden 1987; Consultative cttes. for the Vieux-Port de Montréal, McGill College Avenue (Montréal) and Downtown Library project of Concordia Univ. (Montréal); Auxiliary Prof., Sch. of Arch., McGill Univ., Montreal; Université de Montréal; exhns. incl.: McCord Museum 1975, 1980; Fourth Floor Gallery, Seagram Bldg., N.Y., 1977; Kunsthaus Lempertz, Cologne, Germany 1982; Art Inst. of Chicago, Chicago 1983; Cooper-Hewitt Museum, N.Y. 1983; Montreal Museum of Fine Arts 1983, 1984; Centre Georges Pompidou, Paris 1984; National Gallery of Can., Ottawa 1984; Candn. Centre for Architecture 1989, 1992; Awards incl.: Massey Medal, Royal Arch. Inst. of Can. 1970; Robinson's Design Award (Biltmore Hotel) 1977; Western Art Directors Club Award of Merit 1977; el. Academician, Royal Candn. Acad. Arts (RCA) 1977; American Inst. of Architects S. Cal. Chapter Award of Honor 1978; Am. Jewish Cong. National Women's Division N.Y. Award 1978; Printing Industries of America Cert. of Award, Graphic Arts Award Competition 1978; Am. Inst. of Architects Design Award 1979; Am. Inst. Graphic Arts Cert. of Excellence 1979; Am. Soc. Interior Designers Internat. Design Award 1980; co-recipient Am. Inst. Architects Nat. Honor Award 1980; Médaille de Mérite Ordre des Architectes du Qué. 1981; Nat. Preservation Honor Award 1981; Fellow, Royal Architecture Inst. of Can. 1983; Am. Inst. of Archs. Twenty-Five Year Award of Excellence 1984; Great Montrealer Award 1984; Member, Order of Canada 1985; Chevalier, l'Ordre national du Qué. 1985; AIA Governor's Award, Indiana Soc. of Architects, Chicago 1987; IIT Alumni Medal, Illinois Inst. of Technology, Chicago 1988; Médaille de l'Académie d'Architecture, Paris (France) 1988; Gabrielle Léger Medal for a lifetime dedicated to national heritage preservation, Heritage Canada Found., Charlottetown 1988; 'Domus' Award as Personality of the Year, APCHQ 1988; New York Landmarks Conservancy Award 1989; 'Grand Ulysse' presented by Greater Montreal Convention & Tourist Bureau; 'Prix d'Excellence' as Personality of the Year, La Presse 1989; 'Grand Prix 1989' Conseil des Arts commauté urbaine de Montréal 1990; Medal of Honour, La Soc. Historique de Montreal 1990; Officer of The Order of Canada 1990; 1991 Phoenix Award, Soc. of Am. Travel Writers; '1991 Award of Merit,' New York Chapter of the Am. Institute of Architects; 1991 Gold Medal Award, Royal Architectural Inst. of Canada; Mem., Royal Soc. of Canada 1991; Prix 'Chomedey de Maisonneuve,' Soc. St-Jean Baptiste, Montreal 1991; 1992 Honor Award, Am. Inst. of Architects; Officer, Ordre des Arts et Lettres, Govt. of France 1992; 1992 Lescarbot Award, Gov. of Canada; frequent guest lectr.; author or co-author various publs. incl. 'Court House: A Photographic Document,' 'Photography and Architecture: 1839–1939,' 'Planned Assaults' 1987, 'The First Five Years' 1988; 'Canadian Centre for Architecture: Building and Gardens' 1989; 'Ernest Cormier and the Université de Montréal' 1990; 'Opening the Gates of Eighteenth Century Montreal' 1992; 'Fortifications and the Synagogue: The Fortress of Babylon and the Ben Ezra Synogogue, Cairo' (working title) in press; work cited numerous articles; Affil: Internat. Confederation of Architectural Museums (ICAM); Temple Hoyne Buell Center for the Study of Am. Arch., Columbia Univ., N.Y. (Bd. Chrmn. 1984–89); Inst. of Fine Arts, N.Y. Univ. (Trustee 1973); mem., Visiting Ctte., Mass. Inst. of Technolgy 1983–89; Soc. of Architectural Historians (Dir. 1985–88); Nat. Gallery Can. (Adv. Bd.); Candn. Conf. of the Arts, (Pres., Qué. Section 1984–90); Candn. Mediterranean Inst., Ottawa (Trustee) 1986; Vieux-Port de Montréal (Dir. 1984); Soc. du Patrimoine Urbain de Montréal (Pres. 1979); Heritage Montreal (Founding Pres.); Mies van der Rohe Archive Museum of Modern Art N.Y. (Adv. Bd.; Chrmn. 1975–80); Adv. Ctte. on Architectural and Urban Hist., Harvard Univ., Grad. Sch. of Design 1988; Bd. of Overseers, Illinois Inst. of Technology, Coll. of Arch., Planning and Design 1988; Mem., Visiting Comm., School of Arch., Princeton Univ.; Mem. Adv. Bd., School of Arch. & Landscape Arch., Univ. of Toronto; Mem. Bd., Learning for a Sustainable Future; Mem. Bd., Société d'Habitation et de Developpement de Montréal; Bd. mem.: journals 'Forces' 1982 and 'Vie des Arts' 1983; Office: 1920, Baile St., Montréal, Qué. H3H 2S6.

**LAMBERT, Ronald Dick,** M.A., Ph.D.; sociologist; educator; b. Sophiasburgh Twp., Prince Edward Co., Ont. 6 Apr. 1936; s. Wilfred Morley and Edith Marjorie (Dick) L.; e. Sudbury (Ont.) High Sch. 1954; McMaster Univ., B.A. 1959, M.A. 1961; Univ. of Mich., Ann Arbor, Ph.D. 1966; m. Marilyn Ruth, d. Emmett Gordon Black, 14 June 1964; three d.; CHAIR, DEPT. OF SOCIOL., UNIV. OF WATERLOO 1990– and PROF. OF SOCIOL. 1987– ; adjunct appt., Grad. Faculty in Pol. Sci., Wilfrid Laurier Univ. 1984–89; joined the Univ. as Asst. Prof. of Sociol. (with cross-appt. in Dept. of Psychol.) 1966; Principal Investigator, 1984 Candn. Nat. Election Study; mem. Candn. Sociol. & Anthropol. Assn.; Candn. Pol. Sci. Assoc.; Assn. Candn. des sociologues et anthropologues de lanque francaise (ACSALF); Candn. Ethnic Studies Assn.; Ont. Genealogical Society; Publications: 'Sex Role Imagery in Children: Social Origins of Mind' 1971; 'Social Process and Institution; The Canadian Case' (text-reader with J. E. Gallagher) 1971; 'The Sociology of Contemporary Quebec Nationalism: An Annotated Bibliography and Review,' 1981; articles in 'Candn. Journ. of Pol. Science'; 'Candn. Review of Sociology and Anthropology' and elsewhere; Home: 11 Ellen St. W., Kitchener, Ont. N2H 4K1.

**LAMBERT-LAGACE, Louise,** B.Sc.; consulting dietitian, author; b. Montreal, Que. 20 Aug. 1941; d. Paul and Lucille (Blais) Lambert; e. Univ. of Montreal B.Sc. 1961; m. Maurice L. 5 Aug. 1961; children: Pascale, Janique, Marie-Claire; OWNER, THE NUTRITION CLINIC, LOUISE LAMBERT-LAGACE & ASSOC. 1975– ; nutrition counselling & edn. through the media: 7 TV series 1974–91 & 10 books published; Pres., Montreal Diet Dispensary; Past Bd. Mem., Professional Corp. of Dietitians of Que.; Bd. Mem., Univ. of Montreal; Adv. Bd., Nestlé; author: 'Feeding Your Baby'; 'The Nutrition Challenge for Women'; 'Feeding Your Preschooler'; recreations: tennis, travelling; Home: 4150 Trafalgar Rd., Montreal, Que. H3Y 1R2; Office: 1259 Guy St., Montreal, Que. H3H 2K5.

**LAMBIE, D. Elizabeth,** B.Sc., P.Dt., M.P.H., F.C.D.A.; university professor; b. Berwick, N.S. 22 July 1930; d. Hugh and Alice Margaret (Blood) MacKinnon; e. Acadia Univ. B.Sc. 1953; St. Luke's Hosp. P.Dt. 1954; Univ. of Michigan M.P.H. 1960; m. Vincent F. s. Richard and Laura (Halsted) L. 6 July 1963; children: Laura Jane, Christopher MacKinnon; ASSOC. PROF., SCHOOL OF NURSING, NUTRITION, DALHOUSIE UNIV. 1972– ; various positions in field of nutrition 1956–65; Lectr., Dalhousie Univ. 1970–72; Asst. Prof. 1972–76; Assoc. Prof. 1976–present; greatest professional joy is promoting Canada's Food Guide; Charter Fellow, Candn. Dietetic Assn. 1989; Halifax Y.W.C.A. Recognition for Women Award; N.S. Dietetic Assn. Merit Award 1984 and several other awards; numerous community appointments, Jr. League of Halifax, Y.W.C.A., Red Cross, Halifax Landmarks Comn., Dartmouth Academy, Acadia Univ., etc.; Mem., N.S. Dietetic Assn., Candn. Dietetic Assn. (Fellow), Nutrition & Food Security Network, Profl. Group on Eating Disorders, Oncology Dietitians Network, N.S. Home Econ. Assn., Candn. Home Econ. Assn., Fed. Internat. pour l'econ. familiale, Candn. Public Health Assn., Candn. Assn. of Univ. Sch. of Nursing, Orgn. for Nutrition Edn., N.S. Nutrition Council, N.S. World Day Ctte., Scotia Festival of Music and others (active in executive positions); author/co-author of several journal articles and papers; recreations: alpine skiing, sailing, family; clubs: Waegwoltic, Royal Nova Scotia Yacht Squadron, Wentworth Valley Ski; Home: 6049 Cherry St., Halifax, N.S. B3H 2K4; Office: Halifax, N.S. B3H 3J5.

**LAMER, Rt. Hon. Antonio,** P.C., LL.D., LL.L., D.U.; judge; b. Montreal, Que., 8 July 1933; s. Antonio and Florence (Storey) L.; e. Coll. St-Laurent, Montreal 1952; Univ. de Montréal, LL.L 1956, LL.D. 1991; Univ. of Moncton LL.D., 1981; Univ. of Ottawa D.U. 1987; Univ. of Toronto LL.D. 1992; m. Danièle Tremblay 10 July 1987; children: Stéphane, Mélanie, Jean-Frédéric; CHIEF JUSTICE, SUPREME COURT OF CANADA 1990– ; Mem., Privy Council of Canada; Deputy Governor General; Chrmn., Candn. Judicial Council; Chrmn., Adv. Council, Order of Canada; Chrmn., National Judicial Institute; Hon. Bencher, Lincoln's Inn; Order of Merit, Univ. of Montréal 1991; Knight, Order of St. John 1993; Hon. Lt. Col. 62nd Field Regt.; Justice Superior Court Que., 1969–78; Justice, Que. Court of Appeal, 1978–80; Justice, Supreme Court of Canada 1980–90; Vice-Chrmn. Nat. Law Reform Comn., 1971–75, Chrmn. 1975–78; Prof. agrégé, Univ. de Montréal since 1967; read law with Cutler, Lamer, Bellemare & Assoc.; called to Bar of Que. 1957; Lectr. for many years, Faculty of Law and Sch. of Criminol., Univ. de Montréal; Lectr., Candn. Judicial Conf.; formerly a Sr. Partner, Cutler, Lamer, Bellemare & Assoc.; Que. Bar Rep. on Govt. Inter-disciplinary Comte. on Structures to be given the new Univ. du Québec; served in R.C.A. (R) 1952; Past Pres. (1960) Montreal Dist. Young Libs.; Secy. (1961–66) Montreal Men's Reform Club; Founder

Defence Attorneys' Association Quebec; Past Nat. Chrmn., Criminal Justice Sec., Candn. Bar Assn.; Pres., Quebec Criminology Soc., 1978; R. Catholic; Clubs: Le Cercle Universitaire (Ottawa); Maganassippi Fish and Game; Office: Supreme Court of Canada, Ottawa, Ont. K1A 0J1.

**LAMON, Jeanne,** B.A; music director; violinist; b. New York, N.Y. 14 Aug. 1949; e. Brandeis Univ. B.A. 1970; studied with Hermann Krebbers, Concertmaster, Concertgebouw Orch. 1970–72; Sigiswald Kuijken (baroque violin) 1972–73; MUSIC DIR., TAFELMUSIK 1981– ; freelance soloist, concertmaster, chamber musician 1973–81; Faculty mem., Royal Conserv. of Mus.; Univ. of Toronto; Office: 427 Bloor St. W., Toronto, Ont. M5S 1X7.

**LAMOND, Robert W.,** B.Sc., geologist; b. Kirkcaldy, Scotland 6 July 1944; s. late Robert and late Jessie (Ward) L.; e. Edinburgh Univ., Scotland B.Sc. 1965; m. Mary, d. late Adolphe Hallaert 30 Mar. 1970; children: Robert Edward; Emeline Jane; Victoria Anne; CHRMN., PRES. & C.E.O., CZAR RESOURCES LTD. since 1980; Chrmn. & Dir., Orbit Oil & Gas Ltd.; Humboldt Energy Corp.; Pres., Frobisher Resources Ltd.; Dir., Goldmark Minerals Ltd.; geologist, Imperial Oil 1965; Geologist, Mesa Petroleum Ltd. 1969; Co-Founder and Chief Geologist, Skye Resources Ltd. 1969; Founder & Pres., current firm 1974; mem. A.A.P.G.; R.M.A.G.; Wyoming Geological Soc.; recreations: tennis, travelling; Clubs: Calgary Petroleum; Ranchmen's; Address: 2100, 144 - 4 Ave. S.W., Calgary, Alta. T2P 3N4.

**LAMONT, Francis B.,** M.A. (Oxon), LL.B.; financier; b. Winnipeg, Man. 23 March 1933; s. John Salmon and May (Bastin) L.; e. Univ. of Man. B.A. 1953; Man. Law Sch. 1953–56; (Isbister Scholar) 1954–56; Oxford Univ. Jesus Coll. 1956–59 (Rhodes Scholar) B.A. (Hons) 1958, M.A. 1972; Univ. of Man. LL.B. 1960; m. Judith d. Robert Barrett, 27 July 1963; children: John R. T., Alexandra M., Dougald F., Laura J.; LEGAL AND ECONOMIC CONSULTANT 1990– ; Gov., Toronto Futures Exhange 1984; read law with Thorvaldson, Eggertson, Bastin & Stringer; called to Bar of Man. 1960; Barrister and Solr. Thorvaldson, Eggertson, Bastin, Saunders & Mauro, Winnipeg, 1960–63; joined Legal Dept. Richardson Securities of Can. 1963, Secy. and Gen. Counsel 1966–76, Partner 1972, Managing Partner 1976–82; Pres. & C.E.O. 1982–84; Vice Chrmn. & Dir. 1984–87; Dir., Investment Dealer's Assn. of Canada 1978–79, 1984–87, Chrmn. 1986–87; Pres. & C.E.O., Investment Corp. of Saskatchewan 1988–90; Lt., Winnipeg Grenadiers (Militia) 1960–65; Past Pres., Better Business Bureau of Greater Winnipeg; Y.M.C.A. of Winnipeg; Canadian Club of Winnipeg; Pres., Candn. Assn. of Rhodes Scholars 1981–83; active at constituency and provincial levels, Liberal Party of Manitoba; Liberal; recreations: rowing, cross-country skiing; Clubs: Vincents; Leander; Isis; Manitoba; Winnipeg Rowing; Address: 47 Harvard Ave., Winnipeg, Man. R3M 0J6.

**LAMONTAGNE, Hon. J.-Gilles,** O.C., P.C., C.D., B.A.; b. Montreal, Que. 17 Apr. 1919; s. Trefflé and Anna (Kieffer) L.; e. Jean-de-Brébeuf Coll. Montreal B.A.; m. Mary Katherine d. Joseph Schaefer, Dayton, Ohio 23 Apl. 1949; children: Michel, André, Pierre, Marie; SENIOR CONSULTANT, CONSILIUM (government & internat. affairs) 1992– ; Bd. Mem., The Candn. Centre on Substance Abuse 1991– ; mem. Que. City Council 1962–65, Mayor 1965–77; mem. Econ. Council of Can. 1974–77; former mem. Planning Council Prov. of Que.; Pres., Union of Muns. of Que. 1974–77; Past Extve. mem. and Vice Pres., Fed. of Muns.; Founding mem. 'Le Progrès civique de Québec' mun. party; el. to H. of C. for Langelier by-el. 1977, re-el. 1979, 1980; Sworn of Privy Council and apptd. Min. without Portfolio 1978; Postmaster Gen. 1978; Min. of Nat. Defence 1980–83; Acting Min. for Veterans Affairs, 1980–81; sworn in as Lieut. Gov. of Québec 28 March 1984–90; served with RCAF 1941–45, rank Capt.; Knight, Order of St. John of Jerusalem; Hon. LL.D., Royal Military Coll., Kingston 1986; Hon. D.B.A., Collège Militaire Royal St.-Jean 1989; Hon. Colonel, #1 Tactical Aviation Wing (Montreal) 1987; Officer of the Order of Canada 1991; elected Grand President, Royal Candn. Legion 1991; R. Catholic; Clubs: Royal Golf; Cercle de la Garnison; Address: 8, Jardins Mérici, app. 1405, Québec, Qué. G1S 4N9.

**LAMONTAGNE, Lieut.-Col. Leopold,** C.D., B.A., Ph.D., D.èsL., F.R.S.C.; writer; b. Mont-Joli, Quebec, 8 July 1910; s. Alphonse and Marie (Joncas) L.; e. Laval Univ., B.A. 1931, L.èsL. 1934; Ottawa Univ. Ph.D. (Lettres) 1944; D.èL., Paris, 1955; m. Cécile d. late Auguste Lepage, 31 Aug. 1940; children: Denis, Marie, André, Marc; Prof., Séminaire de Rimouski, Que., 1934–40; Capt.-Adj., Mil. Instr. Centre, Rimouski, Que., 1940–42; Bureau of Translation, Candn. Army, Ottawa, 1942–48; Assoc. Prof. of French, R.M.C., Kingston, Ont., 1948–52; Dir., Dept. of French, C.M.R., St-Jean, Que., 1952–54; became Prof. and Head Dept. of Modern Lang., Royal Mil. Coll., 1955, Dean, Faculty of Letters, Laval Univ., Quebec, 1963–67; Executive Director, Service for Admission to College and University; President, TRIC Translating Service; awarded Royal Society Candn. Overseas Fellowship (Sorbonne) 1954–55; Publications: 'La Gaspésie,' 1936; 'Les Archives régimentaires des Fusiliers du St-Laurent' 1943; 'Arthur Buies, homme de lettres,' 1957; 'Royal Fort Frontenac' (co-ed. Dr. R. A. Preston), 1958; 'Histoire du 22e Regiment,' 1964; 'Visages de la civilisation au Canada français,' ed. RSC, 1970; 'Le Canada francais d'aujourd'hui,' ed. RSC, 1970; many hist. and other articles in journs. and bulls. incl. 'Queen's Quarterly,' 'London Illustrated,' 'Revue d'histoire d'Amerique française,' etc.; awarded P.Q. Literary Prize, 1958; Royal Society Medal (Belgium) 1974; Cdn Centennial Medal, 1982; mem., Candn. Hist. Assn. (Ed. annual report 1950); Humanities Assn. Can. (Council 1954–55); Humanities Assn. St-Jean (Qué.) Br. Pres. 1953–54); Humanities Assn. Kingston, Ont., Br. (Pres. 1956–57); Alliance Francaise, Kingston, Ont., Br. (Vice-Pres. 1958); Modern Lang. Assn. Am., Sec. VIII (Secy. 1954–56, Pres. 1956–57); R. Catholic; Address: 2238 Lilac Lane, Ottawa, Ont. K1H 6H7.

**LAMONTAGNE, Mary S.,** C.M. (1976), B.Sc.A., B.Ph., M.A.; b. Dayton, Ohio 1 Nov. 1926; d. Joseph J. and Mary (Kette) Schaefer; e. Ravenhill Acad. Philadelphia 1943; Coll. de Bellevue, Que. 1944; Univ. Laval B.Sc.A. (Chem.) 1948, B.A. 1974, M.A. (Phil.) 1982; m. Joseph Gilles Lamontagne 23 Apl. 1949; children: Michel, André, Pierre, Marie; Dir.: CFCF Inc.; Lépine, Cloutier, Bourgie Ltée.; National Bank of Canada; North American Life Assurance Co.; Quaker Oats Co. Canada Ltd; Québecor Inc.; Mem., National Ctte. on Education, Candn. University Women 1962; Founding mem. Que. Sec. UN Assn; Treas. Symphonic Matinees for Children 1960–65; Mem. Bd. of Govs., Laval Univ. 1970–74; Pres. Alumni Assn. Laval Univ. 1971–72; Pres. Comte. 125th Anniversary, Candn. Institute of Quebec; Pres. Candn. Addictions Foundation 1974–75; Bd. mem., Vanier Inst. of the Family 1973–79; Founding Pres., S.O.S. Grossesse (information service for maternity-related problems) 1974; mem., Med. Research Council, Can. 1975–80; mem., MRC Task Force on Human Experimentation 1976–77; Chrmn. Centennial Scholarship Comte. MRC 1977–80; Pres. United Way Fund-raising Drive (Qué. region) 1979; mem. National Biotechnology Advisory Ctte. 1983–88; mem. MRC Standing Comte. on Ethics in Experimentation 1984–91; mem. Bd., Société d'investissement Jeunesse 1986–91; mem. Candn. Inst. for Advanced Rsch.; mem. Orientation Ctte., Science & Engineering Dept., Laval Univ.; mem. Ethics Review Comte., Faculty of Medicine, Laval Univ.; Mem. Bd., Museum of Que. Seminary; Past Pres., Laval Univ. Hosp.; Member of the Order of Canada; Officer, Order of St. John; R. Catholic; Address: 8 Jardin Merici, app. 1405, Quebec, Qu. G1S 4N9.

**LAMONTAGNE, Paul;** executive; b. Québec City, Qué. 17 July 1932; s. Emile and Imelda (Belanger) L.; e. CIST Dip. in Industrial Eng. 1964; m. Monik d. Cyrille and Aimé Lockquell 27 Dec. 1954; children: Sylvie, Pierre, Martin; CHIEF ADMIN. OFFR., OGILVY RENAULT 1989– ; joined Goodyear Tire & Rubber Co. 1952–67, Tech. Services Mgmt., Rsch. & Devel. Dir.; Vachon Inc. 1967–81, Rsch. & Devel. Dir., Mfg. Dir., Pres.; Bombardier Inc. 1981–83, Pres.; Can. Post Ottawa 1983–85, Vice Pres. Tech. Services; Extve. Vice Pres. & C.O.O., Cumberland Drugs 1985–90; Sr. mem. Am. Inst. Ind. Engs.; mem. Candn. Mktg. Assn.; Assn. of Legal Administrators; Montréal C. of C.; recreations: golf, bridge, tennis, swimming; Club: Tennis Val-des-Arbres; Home: 1680 De La Mauricie Duvernay, Laval, Qué.; Office: Suite 1100, 1981 McGill College Ave., Montréal, Qué. H3A 3C1.

**LAMOUREUX, Hon. Lucien,** P.C., Q.C., M.A., L.Ph., LL.D.; diplomat; b. Ottawa, Ont. 3 Aug. 1920; s. Prime and Graziella (Madore) L.; e. Univ. Ottawa, B.A., L.Ph., M.A., LL.D. (Osgood Hall Law Sch.); m. Dr. Jr. Elisabeth Hoffmann; DIPLOMAT; Senior Partner in law firm Lamoureux, Rouleau and Forget, 1954–74; after grad. apptd. Extve. Asst. to Min. of Transport (Hon. Lionel Chevrier); first el. to H. of C. as Lib. mem. for Stormont g.e. 1962; re-el. 1963, 1965; el. as an Independent for Stormont-Dundas in g.e. 1968; re-el. 1972; apptd. Depy. Speaker of H. of C. and Chrmn. of Comtes. of the Whole for 26th Parlt.; Speaker, H. of C. 1965–74; Candn. Ambas. to Belgium & Luxembourg, 1974–80 and to Portugal 1980–85; Past Pres., Bd. of Trustees, Ottawa General Hosp.; Visiting Prof. of Parlty. Law (Grad. Studies), Faculty of Law, Univ. of Ottawa; Past Hon. Pres., Alumnae Assn., Univ. of Ottawa; Past Chrmn., Candn. Council of Commonwealth Parlty. Assn.; Past Pres., Can.-France Inter-parlty. Group; apptd. Chancellor, Univ. of Windsor 1971–78; apptd. Q.C. 1963; mem. Queen's Privy Council for Canada 1974; mem., Brussels Bar (foreign solicitor); Resident Counsel, Fasken Martineau Davis; R. Catholic; Club: Richelieu (Past Pres.); Cercle Royal Gaulois, Brussels; Sept Fontaines Golf, Waterloo; Office: 96A Ave. F. Roosevelt, 1050 Brussels, Belgium.

**LAMPARD, Keith,** B.A.; public servant; b. Hastings, England 26 March 1940; s. Ernest Joseph and Eileen (Walden) L.; e. St. Dunstan's Coll. 1958; Newlands Park Teacher Training Coll., teaching dipl. 1964; Univ. of Sask. B.A. 1971; 1st m.: Eileen C. Egerton 1964; 2nd m.: M. Lorraine (Lorri) d. Eli and Celia Fleece 1985; children: Duff, Tobi, Kristyn, Alexandra; Chief Electoral Offr., Prov. of Sask. 1982–92; Teacher, Richard Albion Sch. (UK) 1964–65; Vice-Prin., Assiniboia P.S. 1965–67; Prin., Sturgeon Landing Sch. 1967–69; Teacher, Humboldt P.S. 1971–72; Clavet Comp. H.S. 1972–77; Caucus Sec./Rsch. Dir./Press Sec., Office of the Leader of the Official Opposition, Sask. 1977–79; Prin., Marcelin Comp. H.S. 1980–82.

**LAMPMAN, Mary;** artist; b. Port Colborne, Ont. 22 Dec. 1926; d. Arthur Norman Charles and May Lily (Kettle) Mathew; e. Welland H.S. 1945; m. Douglas s. Orin and Gertrude Lampman 17 Feb. 1945; children: Dale, Linda, Debra; has been painting for 20–25 years, professionally for 15 years; Home: 594 Stanley St., Port Colborne, Ont. L3K 5W8.

**LAMY, André;** né à Montréal, Que. 19 juillet 1932; f. Adélard et Marie-Antoinette (Crépeau) L.; e. Ecole de technol. méd., Univ. de Montréal 1952–55; Intern dans quatre hôpitaux 1955–56; Faculté des Scs., McGill 1956–57; Cours d'adm. Ecole des Hautes Études comm., Montréal 1969–71; ép. Françoise, f. J. Hector Martin, Outremont, Que. 1958; enfants: Mathieu, Marc, Philippe; Producteur de Film, Galafilm Inc. 1990; Rep. méd., The Upjohn Co. of Canada 1957–62; Dir. des ventes, Producteur, Niagara Films, Montreal 1962–64; Vice-prés. fondateur, Producteur réalisateur, Dir. de la Production et Adm., Onyx Films, 1964–70; Commissaire-Adjoint Office Nat. du Film 1970–75; Commissaire du Gouvernement à la cinematographie canadienne et Pres., Office Nat. du Film/National Film Board 1975–79; Vice Pres., Relations avec l'auditoire Radio Canada 1979; Dir. General, Telefilm Canada 1980–85; Producteur exécutif, Ciné Groupe inc., Montréal, Qué. 1987–90; Adm., Soc. des Amis de l'Enfance Ecole Nouvelle Querbes, Outremont 1965–75; mem. du Conseil d'admin. Radio-Canada/CBC 1975–79; Centre national des Arts/Nat'l Arts Centre 1975–79; Institut Canadien du film (Canadian Film Inst.) 1979– ; Telefilm Canada; New Western Film and Television Foundation 1979– ; Participaction 1979– ; Prés., de l'Association des Producteurs de Film et de Télévision du Qué. (A.P.F.T.Q.) 1990–91; catholique romain; résidence: 245 rue Outremont, Outremont, Qué. H2V 3L9.

**LANAWAY, John Beresford,** B.A., C.A.; business executive; b. London, England 13 Apr. 1950; s. Kenneth Charles and Cecelia Edith Muriel (Browne) L.; e. Univ. of Toronto B.A. 1971; Inst. of C.A.s of Ont. C.A. 1974; m. Janet Susan d. Warren and Mary-Eleanor Morris 13 June 1986; children: Scott, Samantha, Ian, Andrew; SENIOR VICE-PRES., NORTH AMERICA, LAWSON MARDON GROUP LIMITED 1993– ; joined Deloitte Haskins & Sells Toronto 1971; Partner 1980; Dir., Acctg. & Auditing (Toronto) 1985; Vice-Pres., Finan. Reporting & Control, present firm 1985–87; Gen. Mgr. Lawson Mardon Graphics 1988–89; Group Vice-Pres. & Chief Finan. Offr., Lawson Mardon Group Limited 1989–92; Former Bd. Mem. & Treas., York Co. Hosp. Found.; Former Pres. & Bd. Mem., UTS Alumni Assn.; Mem., MENSA Canada Soc.; club: Granite; Home: 32 Mossgrove Trail, Willowdale, Ont. M2L 2W3; Office: 700, 6733 Mississauga Rd., Mississauga, Ont. L5N 6P6.

**LANCASHIRE, Anne Charlotte,** B.A., A.M., Ph.D.; university professor; b. Montreal, Que. 23 Nov. 1941; d. Fay Broughton and Katherine Anne (Savage) Begor; e. Montreal West H.S.; Trafalgar Sch. for Girls 1958; McGill Univ. B.A. (Hons.) 1962; Harvard Univ. A.M. 1963, Ph.D. 1965; m. Ian s. Elizabeth and Ernest L. 25 May 1968; children: Susannah Cannie, David Begor, Ruth Matilda; PROF. OF ENGLISH, UNIV. OF TORONTO 1976– ; cross apptd. to Univ. College 1965– ; to Graduate Drama Ctr. 1975– ; to Cinema Studies Program 1988– ; Assoc. Fellow, Massey Coll. 1986– ; Lectr., 1965–67; Asst. Prof. 1967–71; Assoc.

Prof. 1971–76; Vice-Principal & Program Dir., Univ. Coll. 1990–93; Vice-Provost (Arts & Sci.) & Vice-Provost (Staff Functions) 1987–88; Acting Chair, English Dept. 1983–84; Asst. to Dean, Sch. of Grad. Studies 1974–76; Vice-Pres., Women's Athletic Assn. Directorate 1972–77; Acad. Sec., Dept. of Mod. Languages & Lit. 1969–70; Chair 1970–71; Can. Counc. Leave Fellow 1971–72; SSHRCC Leave Fellow 1986–87; Ed. Bd. 'Medieval & Renaissance Drama in England' 1990– , 'Essays in Theatre' 1991– ; Bd. of Gov., OISE, 1988–91; Joint Counc. on Edn., Univ. of Toronto/OISE 1981–84; Chair, Conf. on Editorial Problems 1975–76; Treas. 1976–78; Lectr., Celebrity Lectr. Series, Stratford Fest. 1983; Chair, Group Ctte., 1st Etobicoke Central Scouts 1985–89; Anglican; Mem., Shakespeare Assn. of Am. (Pres. 1988–89, Trustee 1984–87, 1989–91); Malone Soc. (Candn. Sec.-Treas. 1977–90); Modern Language Assn. of Am. (Inspector, Ctr. for Scholarly Edns. 1986–89); Film Studies Assn. of Can.; ACCUTE; Medieval & Renaissance Drama Soc.; editor: Clifford Leech, 'Christopher Marlowe: Poet for the Stage' 1986; author/editor: 'The Second Maiden's Tragedy' 1978, 'Gallathea' and 'Midas' 1969; editor: 'Editing Renaissance Dramatic Texts: English, Italian, and Spanish' 1976; also num. scholarly articles, papers at scholarly meetings, invited lectrs.; recreations: gardening, karate; Home: 78 Strath Ave., Etobicoke, Ont. M8X 1R5; Office: University College, University of Toronto, Toronto, Ont. M8X 1R5.

**LANCASHIRE, Ian,** M.A., Ph.D.; educator; author; b. Winnipeg, Man. 27 Nov. 1942; s. Ernest Smethurst and Elizabeth (Lawton)L.; e. Winston Churchill H.S. 1960; Univ. of Man., B.A. (Hons.) 1964; Univ. of Toronto, M.A. 1965, Ph.D. 1969; m. Anne Charlotte d. Katherine and Fay Begor 25 May 1968; children: Susannah Cannie, David Begor, Ruth Matilda; PROF. OF ENGLISH, UNIVERSITY OF TORONTO 1981– ; Instr., Univ. of Man. Summer Sch. 1965, 1967; Lectr., Erindale Coll., Univ. of Toronto 1968–69; Asst. Prof. 1969–74; Assoc. Prof. 1974–81; Editorial Bd., Records of Early English Drama 1976– ; Chrmn., Toronto Renaissance & Reform. Colloquium 1977–78; Discipline Rep., Dept. of English, Erindale Coll. 1981–84; Co-ord. for English Studies in Profl. Facs., 1984–86; Founding Dir., Ctr. for Computing in the Humanities 1985– ; Univ. Rep., IBM Can. Ltd. and Univ. of Toronto Co-op. in Humanities Computing 1986–89; Toronto-Waterloo Co-op. in Info. Technol. 1986–89; Pres., Toronto Semiotic Circle 1987–88; Mem., Computing and Emerging Technologies Ctte., Modern Language Assn. 1990– ; Pres., Consortium for Computing in the Humanities / Consortium pour ordinateurs en sciences humanines 1992– ; Assn. for Computing in Humanities; Assn. of Computat. Linguistics; Assn. for Lit. & Ling. Computing; Med. Acad. of Am.; Shakespeare Soc. of Am.; Anglican Ch. (rector's warden); author: 'Computer Applications in Literary Studies' 1983, 'Dramatic Texts and Records of Britain' 1984, 'The Humanities Computing Yearbook' 1988, 1991; num. scholarly articles; verse pub. in Candn. poetry jours.; editor: 'Two Tudor Interludes' 1980, 'Computers and the Humanities' 1986, 'The Dynamic Text' 1989, 'Research in Humanities Computing 1' 1991; 'Computer-based Chaucer Studies' 1993; co-editor: 'The Centre and its Compass: Studies in Medieval Literature in Honor of Professor John Leyerle' 1993; software developer: 'Micro Text-analysis System' 1985, 'TACT' (Text-Analysis Computing Tools) 1992; recreations: film, books, golf; Home: 78 Strath Ave., Toronto, Ont. M8X 1R5; Office: Wetmore Hall, New College, Univ. of Toronto, Toronto, Ont. M5S 1A1.

**LANCASTER, Francis John;** association executive; b. Belleville, Ont. 30 Jan. 1920; s. William and Marguerite Jane (Richardson) L.; e. Belleville Coll. Inst. & Vocational Sch.; Univ. of Ottawa courses in Psychol., Social Psychol. & Pub. Adm.; m. Eva d. Dieudonne and Amanda Leroux 10 June 1978; children: Marilyn Farley, Mark F., John R. Bolger, Julie A. Bolger, Brenda L. Shaw; Past Nat. Pres., Fed. Superannuates Nat. Assn.; Audit Supr. Nat. Revenue Taxation 1946–65, Dir. of Personnel 1969–79; Nat. Sec.-Treas. present Assn. 1980–86; Lectr. in Mgmt. Devel. Pub. Service Comn. and Am. Mgmt. Assn.; co-founder credit union Belleville; Pres. Dist. Council Scouting Belleville; Life mem. Pub. Service Alliance Can.; awarded Commemorative Medal for 125th Anniversary of Candn. Confederation; mem. Regina Symphony Orchestra; People's and Rector's Warden, Ch. of the Resurrection (Ang.) Ottawa 1967–70; recreations: classical music, art, golf, philately; Home: 354 Fulton Dr., Regina, Sask. S4X 1W4.

**LANCASTER, Peter,** B.Sc., M.Sc., Ph.D., D.Sc., F.R.S.C.; mathematician; b. Appleby, Eng. 14 Nov. 1929; came to Can. 1962; s. John Thomas and Emily (Kellett) L.; e. elem. sch. and Sir John Deane's Grammar Sch., Northwich, Eng. 1933–46; Liverpool Coll. Sch. 1946–48; Univ. of Liverpool B.Sc. 1952, M.Sc. 1956, D.Sc. 1987; Univ. of Singapore Ph.D. 1964; m. Edna Lavinia d. Robert J. Hutchinson 3 Sept. 1951; children: Jane, Jill, Joy; PROF. OF MATH, UNIV. OF CALGARY 1967– ; author of 'Lambda-Matrices and Vibrating Systems' 1966; 'Theory of Matrices' 1969 and 1985 (2nd ed.); 'Mathematics: Models of the Real World' 1973; co-author 'Matrix Polynomials' 1982; 'Matrices and Indefinite Scalar Products' 1983; 'Invariant Subspaces of Matrices' and 'Curve and Surface Fitting' 1986; many published articles in scholarly jnls. on math. and its application; Comte. work for Nat. Science and Engn. Research Council, 1976– ; Pres., Can. Math. Society, 1979–81; elected to the Royal Society of Canada 1984; recreations: music, squash, hiking, skiing; Home: 3052 Conrad Dr.,Calgary, Alta. T2L 1B4; Office: Dept. of Math., Univ. of Calgary, Calgary, Alta. T2N 1N4.

**LANCTOT, J.L. Herve,** C.L.U., F.L.M.I.; retired insurance executive; b. Montreal, Que. 11 Jan. 1925; s. late J. Rosario and Christine L.; e. St. Dominic's Acad., Mont.; children: Gloria, Allan, Kathryn, Anne; Pres. & C.E.O., The CUMIS Group Limited 1983–89; Pres. & C.E.O., CUMIS Life Insurance Co., 1976–89; Pres. & C.E.O., CUMIS General Insurance Co. 1980–89; Pres. & C.E.O., CUMIS Services Ltd. 1974–89; Dir. of all four companies; Pres. & C.E.O., Candn. Northern Shield Insur. Co. 1985–89; Dir., Candn. Co-operative Credit Soc.; Dir., Candn. Co-operative Assoc.; Co-operative Trust Co. of Can.; mem., Life Underwriters Assn. of Can.; Accounting Dept., C.P.R., Mont. 1941–53; Managing Dir., Quebec Credit Union League 1955–66; Representative, CUNA Mutual Ins. Soc. 1956, Vice-Pres. & Gen. Mgr., CUNA Mutual Ins. Soc. and CUMIS Ins. Soc. Inc. 1968; Extve. Vice-Pres., C.M.I.S. & CUMIS 1972–89; past positions incl.: Pres., United Way of Can.; Vice-Pres., Sales & Marketing Extve. Club of Hamilton; Dir., Hamilton Cham. of Comm.; Gov., Joseph Brant Memorial Hospital Foundation; Jr. Achievement of Burlington; Chrmn., Hamilton-Wentworth District Health Council; Head Office: P.O. Box 5065, Burlington, Ont. L7R 4C2.

**LANCTÔT, Jean-G.,** CBV, F.C.M.A., F.C.A.; b. Montreal, Que. 7 Nov. 1929; s. Jean-Roméo and Gabrielle (Cadieux) L.; e. École des Hautes Études Commerciales, lic. in comm. science & accountancy 1951; C.A. 1952; m. Denise d. Rosario Fontaine 3 Oct. 1953; children: Jean-Marc, Louise, Michel, Yves, Philippe, Marie-Josée; CONSULTANT, LALIBERTÉ LANCTÔT COOPERS & LYBRAND 1993– ; Extve.-in-Residence, École des Hautes Études Commerciales 1993– ; Mem. Bd. and of Extve. Ctte., The Council on Candn. Unity; Mem. Adv. Ctte., Financial Reporting of the Qué. Securities Commission; Former: Assoc. Prof., Fac. of Admin., Univ. of Sherbrooke 1956–63; Guest Lectr., École des Hautes Études Commerciales 1963–74; Partner, Coopers & Lybrand (formerly McDonald, Currie & Co.) 1965–76; Laliberté Lanctôt Coopers & Lybrand 1976–89; Mem., Mgt. Cttee., Coopers & Lybrand & Extve. Cttee. of Partnership Bd. of the Cdn. firm to 1993; Former Pres., Corp. des comptables en admin. indus. du Qué. for several years; Sec., Cdn. Inst. of C.A.s & Mem., Bd. of Gov., Coord. & Extve. cttees. 1979–82; Former Special Investigator, Que. Securities Comm., Justice Dept.; Vice-Pres., Caisse Populaire de Sherbrooke 1962, '63; expert witness in various court cases; Fellow, Soc. of Mgt. of Canada and of the Ordre des comptables agréés du Québec; Mem., Cdn. Tax Found.; Cdn. Business Valuators Assn.; dir. of several public & private corps. 1986–89; Dir., Théâtre de Quat'Sous de Montréal 1976– ; Bd. Mem., Council on Candn. Unity; Mem. Adv. Ctte., Quebec Securities Commn.; author/editor of several articles; recreations: skiing, sailing, travel, photography, reading, etc.; clubs: Club St-Denis; Office: 1170 Peel St., Montreal, Que. H3B 4T2.

**LANCTOT, Laurent-Léopold,** B.A., Ph.L., Th.L., C.L.L.; priest; publisher (retired); b. Montreal, Que. 30 May 1911; s. Roland-Laurent and Marie-Louise (Perreault) L.; e. Ecole supérieure St-Louis Montreal 1927; Univ. of Ottawa B.A., Ph.L. 1932, Th.L. 1936, C.L.L. 1939; Dir. Univ. of Ottawa Press 1946–82; entered Order of Missy. Oblates of Mary Immaculate 1930; o. Priest 1935; Asst. Dir. Univ. of Ottawa Press 1936–46; Chaplain, French Speaking Girl Guides; author: 'L'Acadie des Origines' 1989; 'Familles acadiennes' 1992; co-author: 'Sors de ta Ouache-Carnet Nature' 1975; many articles on nat. hist.; former mem. (and Treasr.) Assn. Candn. Univ. Presses; Admin., Missionary Guild 1984– ; Assist Treas., Assumption House 1982–85; Treas. Assumption House 1985– ; R. Catholic; recreations: canoeing, ornithology, botany, entomology; Home: 305 Nelson St., Ottawa, Ont. K1N 7S5.

**LANCTÔT, Micheline,** B.A.; actress; writer; film maker; b. Montréal, Qué. 12 May 1947; d. Bernard and Simone (Cadieux) L.; e. Coll. Jesus-Marie d'Outremont, B.A. 1966; Ecole Vincent d'Indy Laureate of Music 1966; m. Hubert Yves s. Henri and Yvette Rose 1981; children: Simone, Francis; PRIN. STOPFILM INC. 1981– ; prize winning actress 'The True Nature of Bernadette' 1972, 'The Apprenticeship of Duddy Kravitz' 1974; writer/dir. 'L'Homme à Tout Faire' 1980 (winner 5 Genie nominations and silver medal San Sebastian Film Festival; second feature film 'Sonatine' winner 1984 Silver Lion Venice Film Festival, also honoured in France and Portugal; author (fiction) 'Armand Dorion, Homme à Toute Faire' 1980; 'Garage Meo Mina' 1982; part-time instr. Concordia Univ. 1980– ; recipient Special Achievement Award 1981 Candn. Film Awards; mem. Bd. Candn. Film Inst.; Candn. Centre Advanced Film Studies; mem. Assn. des réalisateurs/réalisatrices de film du Qué. (Présidence 1981–82); Union des artistes; SARDEC; Cinémathèque Québécoise; Home: 350 rue Birch, St-Lambert, Qué. J4P 2M6.

**LAND, Reginald Brian,** M.A., M.L.S.; Library administrator and library educator; b. Niagara Falls, Ont., 29 July 1927; s. Allan Reginald and Beatrice Beryl (Boyle) L.; e. Oakwood Coll. Inst. (Toronto, Ont.) 1945; Univ. of Toronto (Univ. Coll.), B.A. (Pol. Science & Econ.) 1949, B.L.S. 1953, M.L.S. 1956, M.A. (Pol. Science) 1963; m. Edith Wyndham Eddis, 29 Aug. 1953; Children: Mary, John; PROFESSOR EMERITUS, UNIVERSITY OF TORONTO 1993– ; Extve. Dir., Ont. Legis. Lib. 1978–93; with T. Eaton Co. Ltd. as Copy Editor, Mail Order Advertising, 1949–50; became Reference Librarian, Toronto Public Library, 1953–55; joined University of Toronto Library as Cataloguer, 1955–56 becoming Assistant Chief Librarian 1959–63 and Assoc. Lib. 1963; apptd. Head, Business & Indust. Div., Windsor Pub. Lib. 1956–57; joined 'Canadian Business' magazine, Montreal, as Asst. Ed. 1957–59 (Assoc. Ed. 1958); apptd. Extve. Asst. to Min. of Finance, Ottawa, 1963–64; Prof., Faculty of Library and Information Science, University of Toronto, 1964–93; Prof. Emeritus 1993– ; Dean, Fac. of Libr. & Info. Sci., 1964–72; Commr., Candn. Radio-Television and Telecommunications Comn. 1973–78; rec'd. Kenneth R. Wilson Mem. Award, Bus. Newspapers Assn. of Can., 1959; Distinguished Achievement Award, Ont. Lib. Trustees' Assn. for contribs. to advance. of lib. services in Ont., 1968; Queen Elizabeth II's Silver Jubilee Medal, 1977; Mem. of the Year Award, Toronto Chapt. Special Libraries Assn. 1986; CASLIS Award for Special Librarianship in Canada, Candn. Assn. of Libraries & Information Services 1991; OCULA Merit Award, Ont. College and Univ. Library Assn. 1992; 125th Anniversary of the Confederation of Canada Medal, 1992; author of: 'Directory of Business, Trade and Professional Associations in Canada,' 2nd ed. 1962; 'Eglinton: The Election Study of a Federal Constituency' 1955; 'Directory of Associations in Canada,' 14th ed. 1993; 'Sources of Info. for Candn. Business,' 4th ed. 1985; has contrib. articles and researches to business and library journs.; mem., Assn. of Parliamentary Libns in Canada (Pres. 1982–84); Candn. Council of Lib. Schs. (Chrmn. 1971–72); Am. Lib. Assn. Comte. on Accreditation (Chrmn. 1973–74); Ont. Comte. Deans & Dirs. of Lib. Schs. (Chrmn. 1967–71); Inst. Prof. Lib. Ont. (Pres. 1961–62); Candn. Lib. Assn. (Pres. 1975–76); Am. Lib. Assn.; Ont. Lib. Assn. (Vice President 1962–63); Special Libs. Assn. (Toronto); Assn. for Lib. & Info. Sci. Educ. (Pres. 1973–74); Candn. Assn. for Grad. Educ. in Lib., Archival & Info. Studies (Pres. 1966–67); Candn. Lib. Research and Devel. Council (Vice-Pres. 1965–67); Ont. Prov. Lib. Council (1967–70); Ont. Govt. Lib. Council (Chrmn. 1984–85); Bibliog. Soc. Can.; Ont. Genealog. Soc.; U.E.L. Assn.; Beta Phi Mu; Knight, Hospitaller Order of St. John of Jerusalem; Anglican; Home: 18 Kirkton Rd., Downsview, Ont. M3H 1K7.

**LANDE, Earl,** B.Sc., M.B.A.; financial and investment executive; b. Montreal, Que. 26 Feb. 1950; s. Perry David and Yetta (Gans) L.; e. Mount Royal H.S. 1967; McGill Univ. B.Sc. 1971; Univ. of Western Ont. M.B.A. 1973; m. Diane Roy; SENIOR VICE-PRES., ROYNAT INC. 1973– ; responsible for marketing & operations, merchant banking & equity operations; Dir., Assn. of Candn. Venture Capital Cos.; Candn. Turnaround Mgt. Assn.; Bd. Mem., Internat. Wallcoverings Ltd.; Western Bus. School Club of Toronto; Office: 1 First Canadian Place, Suite 1040, Toronto, Ont. M5X 1B1.

**LANDE, Lawrence M.,** O.C. (1967), LL.B., D.Litt., F.R.S.A.; notary; writer; b. Ottawa, Ont. 11 Nov. 1906; s. Nathan and Rachel Ray (Freiman) L.; e. Westmount (Que.) High Sch., grad. 1924; McGill Univ., B.A. 1928; Univ. of Montreal, LL.B. 1931; Univ. of Grenoble, Dipl. in Philos. 1928; m. late Helen Vera, d. Meyer Leon

Prentis, 14 June 1939; children: Denise (Mrs. Morris Brown), Dr. Nelson Lande; remarried, to Helen Ackerman Rogal, 6 Dec. 1975; served with Civil Protection Comte. during 2nd World War; Hon. Past Chrmn. Herzl Health Centre; Dir., Candn. Writer's Foundation Inc.; author of 'Psalms Intimate and Familiar' 1945; 'Toward the Quiet Mind' 1954; 'The 3rd Duke of Richmond' (hist.) 1956; 'Old Lamps Aglow' (an appreciation of early Candn. poetry) 1957; 'Experience' (poetry written jointly with Prof. T. Greenwood) 1963; 'The Lawrence Lande Collection of Canadiana' (McGill Univ.) 1965; 'L'Accent' 1970; 'Rare & Unusual Canadiana, 1st Supplement to Lande Bibliography' (McGill Univ.) 1971; 'Adventures in Collecting' 1977; 'Canadian Historical Documents and Manuscripts' 1977–83 (6 vols.); 'The Rise and Fall of John Law 1716–1720' (McGill Univ.) 1982; 'The Political Economy of New France as Developed by John Law' and 'Compagnie des Indes and the French-Canadian Traders: A Bibliography' 1983; 'The Founder of our Monetary System – John Law – Companie des Indes and the Early Economy of North America – A Second Bibliography' (McGill Univ.) 1984; 'John Law – The French Régime and the Beginnings of Exploration Trade and Paper Money in North America – A Third Bibliography' (McGill Univ.) 1985; 'John Law – The Influence of His System on the American and French Revolutions and Its Lasting Effect on World Economics – A Fourth Bibliography' (McGill Univ.) 1986; 'John Law – The Creditability of Land and the Development of Paper Money and Trade in North America – A Fifth Bibliography' 1987; 'John Law - Early Trade Rivalries Among Nations and The Beginnings of Banking in North America – A Sixth Bibliography' 1988; 'What Evolved form John Law's System? – A Seventh Bibliography' 1989; 'John Law – His System and Its Influence on Trade & Industry in North America – An Eighth Bibliography' (McGill Univ.) bound together with 'The French Royal Navy' an unpublished manuscript by Louis-Antoine de Bougainville, translated (McGill Univ.) 1990; 'The Development of the Voyageur Contract (1686–1821) A Monograph' 1989; 'A Catalogue of the Lawrence Lande William Blake Collection in the department of rare books and special collections of the McGill Univ. Libraries' (McGill Univ.) 1983; 'A Man called Job' (publ. by Jewish Ed. Counc. of Gter. Montreal 1984); has made 36 long-playing records; composes for piano; Past Pres., Montreal Centre of Canadian Friends of Hebrew Univ.; Past Pres., Candn. Centre P.E.N. Internat.; Hon. Corr. mem. for Que. Royal Soc. of Arts (1968); Order of the Knights of Malta; Sir Thomas More Medal 'for private book collecting for public benefit,' Gleason Library Associates of the Univ. of San Fransisco (first Candn. recipient); Clubs: Grolier (N.Y.); University; Beaver; Montefiore; Palm Beach Country; St. James Lit. Soc.; Homes: 4870 Cedar Cr., Montreal Que. H3W 2H9; (winter): 147 Dunbar Rd., Palm Beach Fla. 33480; Office: Lande Room, 4th Fl., McLennan Library, McGill Univ., 845 Sherbrooke St. W., Montreal, Que. H3A 2T5.

**LANDE, Mildred Queene,** C.M., B.A., LL.D. (h.c.); volunteer; b. Port Arthur, Ont. 5 Nov. 1913; d. Abe and Sophie (Rasminsky) Bronfman; e. McGill Univ. B.A. 1936; m. Bernard s. Nathan and Ray Lande 14 June 1936; children: Neil, Eric, Ruth, Margot; Pres. (first woman) Jewish Community found. Greater Montreal; Pres. (first woman in 140 yrs.) Shaar Hashomayim Synagogue; Chair 1978 (first woman) Montreal Combined Jewish Appeal and Israel Emergency Fund Campaign; Hon. Vice Pres. Jewish Gen. Hosp., Trustee of Corp., Hon. Pres. Women's Aux. (Past Pres.); mem. Extve. Israel Bond Orgn.; Youth Aliyah-Hadassah-Wizo Orgn. (Chrmn. Benefactors & Mothers in Israel); Assoc. Chrmn. Montreal Israel Bond Orgn.; Gov. YM-YWHA; mem. Message Biblique Marc Chagall, France; Adv. Bd. Vt. Studio Sch. Johnson, Vt.; Past Vice Chrmn. Extve. Ctte. Concordia Univ & mem. Emeritus Bd. Govs.; Past Vice Pres. Women's Ctte. Montreal Museum of Fine Arts; Past Chrmn. Women's Div. Combined Jewish Appeal; Past Pres. Women's Fed. Allied Jewish Community Services; Past Chrmn. Women's Div. Combined Health Appeal (Centraide); Que. Heart Campaign; Past Co-Chrmn. Red Cross Campaign; Montreal Sect. Candn. Nat. Ballet; Past Vice Pres. Les Grands Ballets Canadiens; recipient C.M. 1980; Samuel Bronfman Medal Meritorious Service; Jewish Theol. Semy. Am. Medal; Citation Woman of Achievement Shaar Hashomayim Sisterhood and Women's League Conserv. Judaism 1978; Plaque Tribute Bldg. & Strengthening Econ. Israel 1977; Eleanor Roosevelt Centennial Award 1984; 125th Anniversary of the Confederation of Canada Medal, 1992; Hon. LL.D. Concordia Univ.; recreations: tennis, golf; Clubs: Elmridge Golf & Country; Home: 4333 Westmount Ave., Montreal, Que. H3Y 1W2.

**LANDER, Jack Robert,** M.A., M.Litt., F.R.H.S., F.R.S.C.; historian; educator; b. Hinckley, Eng. 15 Feb. 1921; s. Robert Arthur and Hilda Mary (Goodman) L.; e. Alderman Newton's Sch. Leicester, Eng. 1940; Pembroke Coll. Cambridge B.A. 1942, M.A. 1945, M.Litt. 1950; Professor Emeritus, Univ. of W. Ont.; Lectr. and Sr. Lectr. Univ. of Ghana 1950–63; Assoc. Prof. Dalhousie Univ. 1963–65; Prof. present Univ. 1965–70; J.B. Smallman Prof. Univ. of W. Ont. 1970–85; author 'The Wars of the Roses' 1965; 'Conflict and Stability in Fifteenth Century England' 1969; 'Crown and Nobility 1450–1509' 1976; 'Crown and Community: England 1450–1509,' 1980; 'The Limitations of English Monarchy in the Later Middle Ages' 1989; 'English Justices of the Peace, 1461–1509' 1989; articles on fifteenth and early sixteenth century Eng. in various learned journs.; Conservative; recreations: travel, swimming; Club: Reform (London, Eng.); Home: 5 Witherington Road, London N5 1PN England.

**LANDRY, Hon. Alfred R.,** M.A., B.Com., D.C.L.; judge; b. Robichaud, N.B. 21 Apr. 1936; s. Albert and Agnes (Thibodeau) L.; e. Notre-Dame des Victoires High Sch., Barachois, N.B. 1953; Coll. l'Assomption, Moncton, 1955; St-Joseph Univ., B.A. 1957; Univ. of Ottawa, B.Com. 1958; Univ. of N.B. Law Sch., 1958–60; Rhodes Scholar, Oxford Univ., M.A. (Juris.) 1962; St. Thomas Univ., (Hon.) D.C.L. 1973; Univ. de Moncton, (Hon.) D.C.L. 1977; apptd. Q.C. 1978; m. Alfreda d. Albenie J. Leger, Shediac, N.B., 4 July 1964; children: Christian and Chantal; JUDGE, COURT OF QUEEN'S BENCH OF N.B.; former Sr. Partner, Landry, & McIntyre; former Dir.: Mother's Own Bakery Ltd.; (and former mem. Extve. Comte.) N.B. Telephone Co. Ltd.; Natgas Ltd.; Dir. Candn. Council of Christians and Jews; N.B. Heart Foundation; Past Chrmn., Bd. of Trustees, N.B. Extra-Mural Hospital; Past Vice President, N.B. Young P. Cons. Assn.; Past President (Past Treas), N.B. P. Cons. Party; P.C. candidate at 1982 provincial election; Chrmn., N.B. Bicentennial Comn.; Mayor of Shediac 1966–71; Past Secy., N.B. Union of Towns; Founding Co-Pres., N.B. Assn. Nursing Homes; Past Vice Pres., S.E. Tourist Bureau; Past Chrmn., Bd. of Govs. and Extve. Comte. Univ of Moncton; Past Chrmn., N.B. Liquor Corp.; N.B. Rep., Uniform Law Comn.; Past mem., N.B. Rhodes Scholarship Selection Comte; past mem., Candn. Council on Admin. of Justice; Candn. Institute for the Admin. of Justice; Candn. Judges Conference; Assn. des Juristes d'expression francaise du N.-B.; Internat. Commn. of Jurists; Past mem. Bd. Dirs., Georges-L. Dumont Hosp. (Pres. Constr. Comte.); read law with Judge C.I.L. Leger; called to Bar of N.B. 1964; mem., Candn. Bar Assn.; past mem., N.B. Barristers' Soc.; Moncton Barristers' Soc. (Past Secy.); Shediac Lions Club; Moncton Rotary Club; Moncton Bd. Trade; Shediac Chamber Comm.; R. Catholic; mem., Order of Saint Lazarus of Jerusalem; Paul Harris Fellow; recreations: fishing, hunting, raquetball, golf; Home: 85 Sackville St., Shediac, N.B. E0A 3G0; Office: 2nd Floor, Assumption Pl., 770 Main St., P.O. Box 5001, Moncton, N.B. E1C 1E7.

**LANDRY, Edmond E.,** C.M., D.Hum.Sc.; businessman; b. Caraquet, N.B. 12 July 1931; s. Edmond J. and Winnifred Gabriel (Asselin) L.; e. Ecole Petite-Rivière; Univ. du Sacré-Coeur Bathurst, N.B.; St. Thomas Coll. D.Hum.Sc. 1981; MGR. AND OWNER, GRANDE-ANSE SERVICE LTEE; Ins. Agt. Edmond Landry Assurance Ltée 25 yrs.; Mgr. and Owner Grande-Anse Beverages Ltd. 10 yrs.; Owner Le Propane de la Baie des Chaleurs 10 yrs.; Le Salon du Pecheur Ltée 10 yrs.; Pres. Comn. Industrielle de la Péninsule Acadienne 1979, 1980; Dir. N.B. Electric Power Comn. 1970–73; Pres., Village Assn. Prov. N.B. 1980–82; Pres. N.B. Licence Suspension Appeal Bd.; Pres. of Appeal Bd., U.I.C.; Pres. St. John Ambulance N.B.; Comdr. Order St. John Jerusalem; Member, Order of Canada 1983; Chevalier de l'Assn. Internationale des Parlementaires de Langues Françaises 1983; Knight Comdr. of the Order Equestre, of the Holy Sepulchre of Jerusalem; Hon. Citizen Mun. of Paspebiac 1977; Mun. of Bas-Caraquet 1977; La République du Madawaska 1978; mem. Acad. Genium Propache (Rome); Mayor of Grande-Anse 1968–88; Dir., National Art Centre, Ottawa; R. Catholic; recreations: boating, reading; Office: Grande-Anse, N.B. E0B 1R0.

**LANDRY, Fernand;** university professor and administrator; DEAN, SCHOOL OF LAW, UNIVERSITE DE MONCTON; Office: Moncton, N.B. E1A 3E9.

**LANDRY, G.Y. (Yves),** B.Comm., M.Comm.; auto industry executive; b. Thetford Mines, Que. 15 Feb. 1938; e. Laval Univ. B.Comm. 1957, M.Comm. 1958; extve. programs: Queen's Univ. 1967 & Columbia Univ. 1984; m. Henrielle Laplante Aug. 1959; children: Danielle, Jean, Philippe; PRES. & CHIEF EXTVE. OFFR., CHRYSLER CANADA LTD. 1990– and CHRMN., CHRYSLER TAIWAN; sales mngt. & mktg. positions with 2 major oil companies to 1969; Que. Reg. Sales Mgr., present firm 1969; Atlantic Reg. Mgr. 1970; Que. Reg. Mgr. 1972; Mgr., Merch., Head Office 1977; Vehicle Sales 1978; General Sales Mgr. 1979; Vice-Pres. 1980; Vice-Pres., Sales & Mktg. 1985; Gen. Mgr., Import Opns., Chrysler Corp. Detroit 1986; Internat. Sales & Mktg. 1988; played key role in Chrysler's successful re-entry into world markets; Extve. Vice-Pres., Chrysler Canada Ltd. 1989; Dir., Acustar Canada; Chrysler Credit Canada Ltd.; Indus. Alliance Insur. Co.; Immed. Past Chrmn., Motor Vehicle Manufacturers Assn. of Can.; Mem. USA - Canada Select Ctte. on Free Trade; Mem. Adv. Ctte. on Extve. Compensation of the Privy Council of Can.; Mem., Adv. Counc., Fac. of Admin. Sci., Laval Univ.; Windsor & Prov. of Que. C. of C.; Bd. of Dirs., Windsor & Essex Co. United Way; Govt. of Canada Automotive Select Panel on Free Trade (Canada-US); Bd. of Govs., Univ. of Windsor; recipient Hermes Award, Faculty of Business Admin., Laval Univ. 1986; McGill Univ. Mngmt. Award 1993; Hon. Doctorate Degree, Univ. of Ottawa 1993; clubs: Beach Grove Golf & Country (Windsor), Renaissance Club (Detroit); Office: 2450 Chrysler Ctr., P.O. Box 1621, Windsor, Ont. N9A 4H6.

**LANDRY, Hon. J(oseph) Conrad,** M.L.A., B.Sc.Adm.; politician; b. Memramcook, N.B. 14 Nov. 1938; s. Raymond and Aline (LeBlanc) L.; e. Univ. of Moncton B.Sc.Adm. 1964; m. Blanche d. Henri and Lorette Richard 20 Aug. 1964; two s. André, Jacques; Solicitor General, N.B. 1987–91 and mem. Extve. Council; teaching and adm. high sch. 1964–78; automobile dealer 1978–82; el. M.L.A. for Kent-North 1982, re-el. 1987, 1991; Past Chrmn. Cartier Co-op.; Past Pres. Kent Ind. Comn.; Kent-North Lib. Assn.; Clubs: La Marina du Suroit; Richelieu; Home: P.O. Box 429, Richibucto, N.B. E0A 2M0.

**LANDRY, Louis E.;** businessman; b. Cap Pelé, N.B. 7 Nov. 1927; s. Edvard E. and Edith (Leblanc) L.; e. N.B.; m. Rita d. Domenique Cormier 1 Sept. 1951; children: Guy, Joanne, Janice, Yvette, Jacqueline; PRES., MALL CENTRE-VILLE LTD. 1973– ; Vice Chrmn. N.B. Power 1970–87; Pres., L.E. Landry Ltd.; Past Pres., Shediac Downtown Development Corp.; Villa Providence Inc.; Past Dir., Cité d'age d'or Inc.; Villa Heritage Inc.; Shediac Medical Centre Ltd.; farm implement dealer 1949–55; furniture retailer 1953–80; Pres., Atlantic Ski-doo Ltd. 1965–73; real estate 1960– ; jewellry store 1975– and restaurant 1976–91 owner; P. Cons. cand. 3 prov. els.; Co-Chrmn. 2 N.B. prov. els.; served as Vice Pres., Treas. local and prov. P. Cons. organs.; Co-Chrmn. organ. Fed. P. Cons. for N.B.; Ald. Shediac Town Council; P. Conservative; R. Catholic; recreations: hunting, fishing, snowmobiling; Club: Richelieu (Past Pres.); Past Pres. Shediac Lobster Festival Inc.; Home: Marina Beach, N.B. E0A 3G0; Office: P.O. Box 250, Shediac, N.B. E0A 3G0.

**LANDRY, Hon. Louis-Philippe,** B.A., B.Ph., LL.L.; judge; b. Hull, Que. 29 Apl. 1935; s. Ulysse and Marie-Rose (Duval) L.; e. Ottawa, Ont. Semy. 1953; Univ. of Ottawa Inst. of Philos. B.A., B.Ph. 1955, LL.L. 1958; m. Lise d. Antoine Deveault, Hull, Que. 31 May 1958; children: Marc, Suzanne, Hélène, Sylvain; JUDGE, SUPERIOR COURT PROV. OF QUE. since 1979; Lectr. in Law, Univ. Ottawa since 1971; called to Bar of Que. 1959; cr. Q.C. 1969; Legal Offr., Combines Br., Dept. Justice 1959–61 and Criminal Law Sec. 1961–63; Prov. Crown Atty. Montreal 1963–65; Dir. Regional Office, Fed. Dept. Justice Montreal 1965–75; Asst. Dept. Atty. Gen. (Criminal Law) Dept. Justice Ottawa 1975–79; lectr. in Criminal Law, Bar Admission Course Prov. Que. and sometime lectr. Univs. Sherbrooke, Montreal, McGill and Laval; recreations: tennis, fishing, music; R. Catholic; Home: 103 des Capucines, Hull, Que. J9A 1S8; Office: Courthouse, 17 Laurier St., Hull, Que. J8X 4C1.

**LANDRY, The Hon. Monique,** P.C.; politician; b. Verdun, Qué. 25 Dec. 1937; d. Auguste and Antoinette (Miquelon) Bourbeau; e. Univ. de Montréal, Physiotherapy & Occupational Therapy 1957; m. Jean-Guy L. 13 Oct. 1958; children: Jacques, Robert, Michel, Dominique; Secretary of State of Canada, Min. of Communications and Min.-Designate of Canadian Heritage 1993; Physiotherapist, Montreal Children Hosp. 1957–58; priv. Physiotherapist 1958–63; Publicist 1963–80; Owner & Vice Pres. Cordevin Int. 1980–84; el. M.P. for Blainville-Deux-Montagnes 1984, re-el. 1988; Parl. Sec. of Sec. of State 1984; Parl. Sec. of Min. for Internat. Trade 1985; Min. for External Relations and International Development 1986–92; Min. responsible for CIDA 1986–92; Min. of State (Indian and Northern Affairs) 1991–92; Min. responsible for relations with la Francophonie 1991–92; Sec. of State of Canada and Min. resp. for the Status of Disabled Persons 1993; Mem. Cabinet Cttes: Treasury Bd. Ctte., Special Ctte. of Council; Pres., public awareness campaign, Que. Arthritis Soc. 1988; named Woman of the Year, Salon de la Femme of Montreal 1988; recreations: golf, tennis.

**LANDRY, Patrick B.,** B.S., M.S.; actuary; b. New Iberia, Louisiana 19 Mar. 1951; s. Wilbert and Mazie (Boudreux) L.; e. Univ. of S.W. Louisiana B.S. 1973, M.S. 1975; m. Lucy Gorny 20 June 1981; PRINCIPAL, WILLIAM M. MERCER LTD. 1985– ; Sun Life of Am. 1975–78; Sun Life of Canada 1978–83; Bulger Group of Cos. 1983–85; Teacher, Univ. of Toronto 1988–90; Ryerson Polytech. Inst. 1990; Home: 1549 Henry St., Halifax, N.S.; Office: 1770 Market St., Halifax, N.S. B3J 3M3.

**LANDRY, Raymond A.,** C.M., B.A., LL.L., D.E.S.D.; éducateur; né Buckingham, Qué. 6 Aug. 1936; Univ. Laval B.A. 1957; Ecole des Hautes Etudes Commerciales Montréal H.E.C. 1958; Univ. d'Ottawa LL.L. 1961, D.E.S.D. 1964; ép. Francine Lefebvre-Landry (déc.); enfant: Claire; COMMISSAIRE AUX ÉLECTIONS FÉDÉRALES 1992– ; PROFESSEUR TITULAIRE, FACULTÉ DE DROIT, UNIVERSITÉ D'OTTAWA 1991– ; Doyen de la Section de Droit Civil., Univ. d'Ottawa 1979–91; Doyen intérimaire 1967–68; Surintendant des faillites, Ministère Consommation et Corporations Can. 1968–79; Secrétaire, Comité sur la législation en matière de faillite et d'insolvabilité, 1966–70; Prés., Comité sur l'indemnisation du salarié en matière de faillite et d'insolvabilité, 1981; Prés. du Conseil d'adm. Lycée Claudel 1978; Club: Cercle Universitaire (Conseil d'Adm. 1982); Président, Comité des Doyens du Canada 1985–86; Membre du Barreau du Québec; Membre de l'Ordre du Canada 1991; récipiendaire de la médaille commémorative du 125ième anniversaire de la confédération du Canada, 1992; Résidence: 6 – 65 Whitemarl Dr., Rockcliffe Park, Ont. K1L 8J9; Bureau: Fauteux Hall, 57 Louis Pasteur, Ottawa, Ont. K1N 6N5.

**LANDRY, Robert E.,** C.M., B.Eng.; executive; b. Arvida, P.Q. 9 April 1929; s. Reginald and Violet (Thibodeau) L.; e. St. Francis Xavier Univ.; McGill Univ., B.Eng. (Elec.) 1950; married; children: Michael, Peter, Robert, Anthony, Liane, Joanne, Stephanie; PRESIDENT, STRATEGEX CONSULTANTS INC.; Retired Vice-Pres., Imperial Oil Ltd.; Chrmn., Public Affairs Counc., Conf. Bd., Ottawa 1977–79; Vice Pres., Bd. Dirs., Edmonton Symphony Orch. 1970–71, Toronto Symphony Orch. 1972–82; mem. Fed. Cultural Policy Rev. Comn., Ottawa 1980–82; Chrmn., Nat. Theatre Sch. of Can., Montreal 1986–88 (Bd. 1981–92); Chrmn., Ottawa Arts Centre Found. 1987–88; Chrmn., Nat. Arts Centre, Ottawa 1988– ; Chrmn., Bd. of Gov., Univ. of Ottawa 1989– (Bd. 1987– ); Council Mem., World Arts Forum, Geneva 1991– ; Mem. Advisory Bd., Ottawa Heart Institute 1993– ; apptd., Member of the Order of Canada 1991; recreation: tennis, squash, skiing; Clubs: Rideau; Granite (Toronto); Home: 106 – 111 Echo Dr., Ottawa, Ont. K1S 5K8; Office: 541 Sussex Dr., Ottawa, Ont. K1N 6Z6.

**LANDRY, Roger D.,** O.C.; publisher; b. Montréal, Qué. 26 Jan. 1934; s. Charle and Mabel (Desgroseillers) L.; e. Sir George Williams Univ. 1953; Institut des Sciences Politiques Paris postgrad. studies, 1956; m. Suzanne Shepherd; children: Charle, Johane, Geneviève; PRES. & PUBLISHER, LA PRESSE LTEE 1980– ; Mgr. of Marketing Services Bell Canada 1957–63; Inspr. Que. Prov. Police Force 1963–65; Depy. Dir. 1967 World Exhn. 1965–68; Depy. Dir. Air Canada 1968–70; Pres., Beauregard, Landry, Nantel & Associates 1970–75; Sr. Vice Pres. and Chief Adm. Offr. ITT Canada 1975–77; Vice Pres. Marketing and Pub. Affairs, Montreal Baseball Club Ltd. 1977–80; apptd. Pres. (1984) Publications J.T.C., a co. which owns a no. of dailies such as Le Nouvelliste of Trois-Rivieres, La Tribune of Sherbrooke, La Voix de l'Est of Granby, also a no. of weeklies, radio station CHEF in Granby and a commercial printing plant in Trois-Rivières; Past Chrmn. of the Bd., Candn. Daily Newspaper Assn.; Dir., Assn. des Quotidiens du Qué.; Chrmn of the Bd., Canadian Press; named Mktg. Man of Year, Major League Baseball 1980; Candn. Pub. Relations Soc. (Médaille du Président 1980); Médaille Edouard-Montpetit 1984; Member, Order of Canada 1986, Officer 1991; Member, Advisory Council 1991; Officer, Order of Quebec 1992; Member, Order of the Golden Lion, Sons of Italy 1987; Grande Médaille de Vermeil de la Ville de Paris 1989; Doctorate (h.c.): Sherbrooke Univ. 1990; Collège militaire royal de Saint-Jean 1993; Chrmn. of the Bd., Société de la Place des Arts; Office: 7 rue St-Jacques, Montréal, Qué. H2Y 1K9.

**LANDSBERG, Michele,** B.A.; journalist; b. Toronto, Ont. 12 July 1939; d. John Abraham and Naomi Leah (Glassman) L.; e. Univ. of Toronto, B.A. (Hons.) 1962; m. Stephen s. David and Sophie Lewis 30 May 1963; children: Ilana Naomi, Avram David, Jenny Leah; COLUMNIST, TORONTO STAR 1989– ; Reporter, Globe & Mail 1962–65; Freelancer 1965–71; Ed. & Feature Writer, Chatelaine 1971–78; Columnist, Toronto Star 1978–84; Columnist, The Globe and Mail 1985–89; National Newspaper Award (columns) 1980, (feature writing) 1981; author: 'Women & Children First' 1982, 1983; 'Michele Landsberg's Guide to Children's Books' 1986; 'This is New York, Honey! A Homage to Manhattan in Love & Rage' 1989; Office: One Yonge St., Toronto, Ont. M5E 1E6.

**LANE, Elizabeth A. (Mrs. William T.),** C.M. (1979), B.A., LL.D. (S.F.U. 1977); (Elizabeth Ann Greer); b. Vancouver, B.C. 30 Jan. 1928; d. Thomas Hyland and Bettie Maud (Beattie) Greer; e. Prince of Wales Sch., Vancouver; Univ. of B.C., B.A. (Chem.) 1949; m. William Tierney Lane, 1 Dec. 1956; one d. Naomi Elizabeth; one s. Thomas Wallace; served as research chem. with: Nat. Research Council Atomic Energy Project, Chalk River, 1949–50; B.C. Research Council, Vancouver, 1951–52, 1954–56; Royal Sch. of Mines, London, Eng., 1952–53; el. mem. Can. Council 1970–73; Dir., Community Arts Council of Vancouver 1959–81 (Pres. 1964–65); Chrmn., Vancouver Br. Extve., Community Planning Assn. Can., 1963–64; President Vancouver Museums Association, 1968–70; President, Jr. League of Vancouver, 1965–67; also served as Dir., Playhouse Theatre Co.; Vancouver Festival Soc.; Vancouver Housing Assn., Vancouver Art Gallery; mem. Fed. Cultural Policy Review Comte., 1979–82; Convocation mem. of Senate, Univ. of B.C. 1969–78; Pres. Candn. Conf. of the Arts 1976–78; Chrmn. B.C. Arts Bd. 1974–78; Extve. Comte., Candn. Comn. for UNESCO, 1978–81; mem., B.C. Regional Counc., Candn. Music Centre 1985–94; Extve. Mem., B.C. Arts in Educ. Counc. 1986–94; Chrmn., Leon and Thea Koerner Foundation 1982–86; Delta Gamma; Home: 4438 Marguerite St., Vancouver, B.C. V6J 4G6.

**LANE, Hon. Mr. Justice G. Dennis,** B.A., LL.B.; provincial supreme court justice; b. Toronto, Ont. 27 Dec. 1932; s. Clifton H. and Marjorie C. (Neish) L.; e. Victoria Coll. Univ. of Toronto B.A. 1954; Osgoode Hall Law Sch.; called to the bar, 1958 (C.B. Martin Prize); m. Sandra d. Allen and Irene Brown 7 Sept. 1957; three s. Allan, David, Andrew; JUSTICE, ONTARIO COURT (GENERAL DIVISION) 1990– ; called to Bar of Ont. 1958; cr. Q.C. 1973; law practice Robertson, Lane & Co. 1958–60; Ferguson Montgomery & Co. 1960–62; Osler Hoskin & Harcourt 1962, Partner 1968–89; Justice, Supreme Court of Ontario (High Court of Justice) 1989–90; part-time teacher Bar Admission Course 1963–70; mem. Bd. Regents, Victoria Univ. 1966–87 (Hon. Life Mem.), Chrmn. 1978–82, Trustee Pension Plan 1975–88; Dir. Candn. Opera Co. 1980–90, Hon. Secy. 1982–89; Dir., Ballet Opera Hall Corp. 1988–91; Dir., Candn. Opera Foundation 1991– ; Trustee, (Chrmn. Extve. Ctte. 1986) G. R. Gardiner Museum of Ceramic Art 1982–90; Dir. and Vice Chrmn. Presb. Ch. Bldg. Corp. 1966–72; Dir. Ont. Rugby Union 1970–72; Dir. Advocates' Society 1985–88; Dir., Candn. Lawyers Liability Assurance Soc. 1987–89, Chrmn. 1989; mem.: Canadian Bar Assoc.; Lawyers Club of Toronto; Armour Heights Presbyterian Ch. (Chrmn., Trustees 1989– ); recreations: tennis, playing 'old-timers' hockey; Home: 27 Belgrave Ave., Toronto, Ont. M5M 3S9; Office: Osgoode Hall, 130 Queen St. W., Toronto, Ont. M5H 2N5.

**LANE, George Stewart,** B.Com., M.A., Ph.D.; management consultant; educator; b. Nanton, Alta. 21 May 1937; s. George Birtle Irving and Gwendolyn Rachael (Stewart) L.; e. Parkland and Lindsay Thurber Composite High Schs. Alta.; Univ. of Alta. B.Com. 1960; Univ. of Wash. M.A. 1965, Ph.D. 1969; Soc. Mang. Accts. Can. C.M.A. 1965; m. Marcia d. Milton Eliasoph 15 May 1970; two s. Michael, David; PROF. FAC. OF MANAGEMENT, UNIV. OF CALGARY 1976– ; (Dean, 1976–81); Instr. Sask. Tech. Inst. 1960–64, Chrmn. 1962–64; Lectr. Univ. of Alta. 1964–66, Acting Faculty Secy. 1965–66; Predoctoral Lectr. Univ. of Wash. 1966–69; Assoc. Prof. and Consultant Sir George Williams 1972–73; Assoc. Prof. and Acting Dean Univ. of Calgary 1974–76, 1975–76; author 'Ralph Nader is a Marketing Man' 1969; 'Festival of Waste Revisted' 1971; 'Being Made Aware of Your Rights' 1971; 'Marketing in the Canadian Environment' 1973; 'A Canadian Replication of Mason Haire's Shopping List Study' 1975; 'Environmental Forecasting: A New Dimension of Marketing Planning' 1975; recipient Queen Elizabeth Scholarship 1959–60; Can. Council Doctoral Fellowship 1967–69; Edna Benson Dissertation Fellowship 1969; Prov. of Que. Scholarship 1973; Brit. Council Visitorship 1973; mem. Acad. Mang.; Strategic Mgmt. Soc.; Internat. Communication Assn.; Soc. Mgmt. Accts.; Acad. Marketing Sciences; Candn. Assn. Adm. Sciences; Clubs: Canadian Men's; Glencoe; Office: Scurfield Hall, Rm. 432, 2500 University Dr. N.W., Calgary, Alta. T2N 1N4.

**LANE, Hon. J. Gary,** M.L.A., Q.C., B.A., LL.B.; judge; b. Saskatoon, Sask. 2 May 1942; s. Richard Louis and Kathleen May (Flanagan) L.; e. St. Paul's High Sch. Saskatoon; Univ. of Sask. B.A. 1963, LL.B. 1966; m. Elizabeth (Liz) d. Dr. John and Doreen McLaughlin 21 July 1979; four children; JUDGE, SASKATCHEWAN COURT OF APPEAL (Sept.) 1991– ; Formerly (1991): Min. of Justice and Attorney General, Govt. of Sask.; Provincial Secretary; Min. resp. for: Saskatchewan Telecommunications, Sask. Energy Corp. and Sask. Communications Network; Chrmn., Investment Corp. of Sask.; Vice-Chrmn., Sask. Energy Corp. & Sask. Telecommunications; articled Cuelenaere & Beaubier, Saskatoon; called to Bar of Sask. 1966; cr. Q.C. 1982; served as Crown Solr. Dept. Atty. Gen. Sask.; Extve. Asst. to Atty. Gen. Sask.; law practice Regina 1971–76; Sr. Partner Lane & Whitmore, Regina 1976–82; el. M.L.A. Sask. 1971, re-el. since; Provincial Secretary 1982–84; Min. of Intergovernmental Affairs 1982–84; Min. of Justice and Attorney General 1982–85; Min. resp. for Sask. Comp, 1982–88; Min. resp. for Employment Develop. Agency 1984–86; Min. of Finance 1985–89; Min. of Revenue and Financial Services 1986–87; Min. resp. for Potash Corp. of Sask. 1986–89; Min. of Telephones 1982–83, 1986–91; mem. Regina Bar Assn.; Law Soc. Sask.; Candn. Bar Assn.; recreations: reading, golf, skiing; Home: 3055 Angus St., Regina, Sask. S4S 1P2.

**LANE, John Scott,** B.A., M.A.; insurance executive; b. Woodley, England 1 Mar. 1935; s. Norman Esgate and Evelyn (Scott) L.; e. Univ. Coll., Oxford B.A. 1957, M.A. 1959; m. Maria Luisa d. Jose and Luisa Ferrer 26 Sept. 1964; children: Michael, Richard, Alexander; SR. VICE-PRES. INVESTMENTS, SUN LIFE ASSURANCE CO. OF CANADA 1991– ; Chrmn. & Dir.: Spectrum Bullock Funds Inc.; Sun Life Dealer Services Corp.; Dir.: Sun Life Assur. Co. of Canada (U.S.); Sun Life of Canada Investment Management Ltd.; Sun Life Insur. and Annuity Co. of New York; Bullock Growth Fund Ltd.; Century 21 Real Estate Canada Ltd.; Glengarry and Stormont Railway Co.; Spectrum Bullock Services Inc.; Spectrum Bullock Holdings Corp.; Stormont Electric Light and Power Co.; Sun Capital Advisers Inc.; Sun Investment Services Co.; Sun Life Financial Holdings Inc.; Sun Life Savings and Mortgage Corp.; Sun Life Trust Co.; Candn. Investment Fund Ltd. (Bullock/CIF); TransAlta Utilities; TransAlta Corp.; TransAlta Energy; Trustee, The Calvin Bullock Funds; The Spectrum Mutual Funds; Investment Analyst Sun Life of Canada 1957, Asst. Treas. 1965, Fin. Vice-Pres. 1974, Sr. Vice-Pres. & Gen. Mgr. for Canada 1985; Pres. & Dir., Candn. Psychiatric Rsch. Found.; Dir., Candn. Opera Co.; Chartered Fin. Analyst; Clubs: United Oxford and Cambridge University (London, Engl.); Brome Lake Boating (Qué.); Office: 150 King St. W., Toronto, Ont. M5H 1J9.

**LANE, Lauriat, Jr.,** M.A., Ph.D., F.R.S.C.; educator; b. Boston, Mass. 12 Feb. 1925; s. Lauriat and Marguerite (Pierce) L.; e. Browne & Nichols Sch. 1941; Harvard Univ. A.B. 1947, M.A. 1948, Ph.D. 1953; m. Millicent d. William and Elsie Travis 26 Aug. 1957; children: Hannah Marguerite, Lauriat III; PROFESSOR EMERITUS 1990– ; Prof. of English, Univ. of N.B. 1966–90; Tutor and Teaching Fellow Harvard Univ. 1949–53; Instr. and Asst. Prof. Cornell Univ. 1953–60; Asst. Prof. present Univ. 1960, Assoc. Prof. 1962, Assoc. Dean of Grad. Studies 1970–75, Chrmn. of Eng. 1975–77; Can. Council Leave Fellowship 1966–67; ed. 'English Studies in Canada' 1973–84; 'Approaches to Walden' 1961; co-ed. 'The Dickens Critics' 1961; sr. ed. 'The Stature of Dickens' 1971; author over 80 essays and reviews Eng. and Am. lit.; contbr. 'Literary History of Canada' 1976; mem. Royal Soc. of Can.; Modern Lang. Assn.; Assn. Candn. Univ. Teachers Eng.; Candn. Assn. Am. Studies; Melville Soc.; Thoreau Soc.; recreations: swimming, cycling, singing; Home: 807 Windsor St., Fredericton, N.B. E3B 4G7; Office: Fredericton, N.B. E3B 6E5.

**LANE, Patricia Ann,** M.A., Ph.D.; executive; educator; b. Waterloo, N.Y. 26 Jan. 1945; d. Bernard and Dorothy (Jones) Faulstick; e. Hartwick Coll. Oneonta, N.Y. B.A. 1964; State Univ. of N.Y. Binghamton M.A. 1966, Albany Ph.D. 1971; div.; children: Kathryn, David, Suzanne, Jessica; PRES. AND DIR., LANE ENVIRONMENT LIMITED 1993– ; Prof. of Biol. Dalhousie Univ.

1984– , Asst. Prof. 1973–78, Assoc. Prof. 1978–84, Chair Univ. Senate 1989–92; mem. Bd. Govs. 1989–95; Visiting Assoc. Prof. Harvard Sch. Pub. Health 1980–82; Visiting Lectr., Harvard School of Public Health 1982– ; Nova Scotia Roundtable on the Environment and Economy 1990–95; Dir., Resource Futures Internat. Inc. (Ottawa) 1990–92; named Distinguished Woman of the Year – Entrepreneur – Innovator, Halifax Cornwallis Progress Club; named Top Ten Outstanding Campus Achievers, Campus Can. 1985; Fellow, Rawson Acad. Aquatic Sci. (Dir. 1988–92); author or co-author over 80 publs. and tech. reports; mem. Am. Naturalists Soc.; Am. Soc. Limnol. & Oceanography; Ecol. Soc. Am. (Sr. Ecol. Cert. 1985– ); Internat. Assn. Theoretical & Applied Limnol.; N.S. Inst. Sci.; Soc. Candn. Limnols.; Soc. Candn. Zools.; Office: 1663 Oxford St., Halifax, N.S. B3H 3Z5.

**LANE, Patrick;** writer; b. Nelson, B.C. 26 March 1939; s. Albert Stanley and Eileen Mary (Titsworth) L.; e. Vernon Sr. High Sch.; children: Mark Hayden, Christopher Patrick, Kathryn Mary, Michael John, Richard Patrick; writer for past 25 yrs.; author: 'Selected Poems' 1987; rec'd Gov. Gen.'s Award for Poetry 1978; CAA Award for Poetry 1988; mem. League of Candn. Poets; The Writer's Union; ACTRA; Home: R.R. 2, 1886 Cultra Ave., Saanichton, B.C. V0S 1M0.

**LANE, Peter Louis,** M.D., F.R.C.P.(C); emergency physician; b. Ottawa, Ont. 4 July 1952; e. Queen's Univ. M.D. 1976; two s. Dylan Shaw, Max Alexander George; MEDICAL DIR., TRAUMA SERVICES 1991– and EMERGENCY PHYS., VICTORIA HOSP., London 1989– ; Assoc. Prof. of Med., Univ. of Western Ont.; Asst. Prof. of Surg. Univ. of Toronto 1980–88; Residency Training Emergency Med. Queen's Univ. 1976–79; Emergency Phys., Ottawa Gen. Hosp. 1979–80; Sunnybrook Med. Ctr. 1980–88; author or co-author various publs. trauma resuscitation, migraine headache; Founding mem. and Past Pres. Candn. Assn. Emergency Phys.; Founding mem. and Past Pres., Trauma Assn. Can.; Fellow and Mem. Bd. of Dirs., Assn. for the Advancement of Automotive Medicine (AAAM); Hon. mem. British Assn. of Accident and Emergency Medicine; mem. New York Acad. Sci's; Pres. Profl. Assn. Interns & Residents Ont. 1978–79; awarded Commemorative Medal for 125th Anniversary of Candn. Confederation 1993; Office: Victoria Hosp., Suite E301, 375 South St., London, Ont. N6A 4G5.

**LANE, Hon. William Burley,** B.A., LL.B.; judge; b. Picton, Ont. 19 Nov. 1934; s. Wilfrid Slater and Dorothy Irene (Burley) L.; e. Prince Edward Coll. Inst. Picton; Victoria Coll. Univ. of Toronto B.A. 1957; Queen's Univ. LL.B. 1960; m. Doris d. Arthur and Grace Carman 27 June 1959; one s. Bryan Carman; JUSTICE, ONTARIO COURT GENERAL DIVISION (and of predecessor court) 1980– ; private law practice Picton, Ont. 1962–80; Councillor, Town of Picton 1965–70; mem. Prince Edward Co. Bd. Educ. 1970–80, Chrmn. 1977; mem. Co. and Dist. Judges Assn.; Candn. Bar Assn.; Candn. Judge's Conference; United Church; recreations: boating, gardening; Home: 680 Bessborough Dr., Oshawa, Ont. L1G 4H2; Office: The Court House, 605 Rosalind Rd. E., Whitby, Ont. L1N 9G6.

**LANFRANCO, Samuel Louis,** B.A., M.A., Ph.D.; university professor; b. Fresno, Calif. 4 Mar. 1939; s. Edward B. and Catherine E. (Bocchini) L.; e. Fresno State Coll. B.A. 1962; Univ. of Calif. at Berkeley M.A. 1965, Ph.D. 1975; m. Johanna Leichsenring 23 Aug. 1969; children: Carlos, Katerina, Andrea; PROF., DEPT. OF ECONOMICS, ATKINSON COLL., YORK UNIV. 1985– ; Prof., McMaster Univ. 1967–79; Cons. Econ., U.N. conf. on Trade & Devel. 1978–81; Prof., Boston Univ. 1980–81; Univ. of Toronto 1982–85; Fellow, Ctr. for Rsch. on Latin Am. & the Caribbean; Associate, York Centre for Health Studies, York Univ.; Dir., Toronto FreeNet 1993– ; Doctors Hosp. 1989–92 (Chairperson, Community Adv. Ctte. 1989–92); Habitat for Humanity Canada 1988–92; Mem., Candn. Econ. Assn.; Candn. Assn. of Latin Am. & Caribbean Scholars; Candn. Assn. for Studies in Internat. Devel.; Am. Econ. Assn.; Co-ordinator, Distributed Knowledge Project on Computers, Knowledge and Social Process; Home: 43 Ulster St., Toronto, Ont. M5S 1E4; Office: 4700 Keele St., North York, Ont. M3J 1P3.

**LANG, Christopher,** H.B.A.; marketing executive; b. Montréal, Qué. 7 March 1941; s. Howard and Helen (Grant) L.; e. Univ. of W. Ont. H.B.A. 1964; m. Joanne d. Gus Millar 7 Oct. 1971; children: Brian, Susan, Debbie, Shauna; CHRMN. AND FOUNDER, LANG & ASSOCIATES LTD. 1968– ; joined Mercantile Bank of Canada 1964–67; First National City Bank of New York 1967–68; mem. Task Force Sports for Candns. 1968; co-founder Hockey Can. (Sec.-Treas. 1968–94); Coaching Assn. Can.; Clubs: Rosedale Golf; Badminton & Racquet; Devils Glen Ski; Timberlane Tennis & Country; Home: R.R. 2, 15th Sideroad, King City, Ont. L0G 1K0; Office: 100, 4100 Yonge St., Toronto, Ont. M2P 2B5.

**LANG, Hon. Daniel Aiken,** Q.C.; senator; barrister and solicitor; b. Toronto, Ont. 13 June 1919; s. the late Daniel W., Q.C., and Edna (Aiken) L.; e. Upper Canada Coll.; Trinity Coll., Univ. of Toronto; Osgoode Hall Law Sch., 1941 and 1945–47; m. Frances, d. late Dr. H.J. Shields and Cecil (Oatman) S., 24 Sept. 1948; children: Daniel, David, Nancy (Martin), Janet (Young); COUNSEL, LANG MICHENER; read law with Lang & Michener; called to Bar of Ontario 1947; joined firm of Lang, Michener & Cranston; with same firm to date; summoned to the Sen. of Can. 1964; former mem., Bd. of Govs., Univ. of Toronto; former Dep. Chrmn., Bd. of Trustees, Sunnybrook Hosp.; served in 2nd World War with R.C.N.V.R., 1941–45; Home: 43 Hillholm Rd., Toronto, Ont. M5P 1M4; Office: BCE Place, P.O. Box 747, Suite 2500, 181 Bay St., Toronto, Ont. M5J 2T7.

**LANG, Daniel Wallace,** B.A., M.A., Ph.D.; university administrator; educator; b. Gulfport, Mississippi 24 Jan. 1944; s. Daniel Maxwell and Helen Muriel (Young) L.; e. Wesleyan Univ. B.A. 1966, M.A. 1968; Univ. of Toronto Ph.D. 1976; m. Diane d. Donald and Doris Cannan; children: Katherine Elspeth, Timothy Fraser; ASST. VICE-PRES. PLANNING AND UNIV. REGISTRAR, UNIV. OF TORONTO 1983– ; Asst. Dean, Wesleyan Univ. 1967–69; Assoc. Dean and Coordr. of Twelve Coll. Exchange 1969–73; Admin. Offr. for Acad. Prog. Planning, Univ. of Toronto 1975–77, Dir. of Planning 1977–79, Asst. Vice-Pres. and Dir. of Planning 1979–83; Assoc. Prof. Sch. of Grad. Studies (Educational Theory, Ont. Inst. for Studies in Educ.), Univ. of Toronto; author of several published papers on higher educ.; Ed. 'Canadian Journal of Higher Education' 1976–80; Chrmn. Ctte. of Judges Bernard H. McCusker Meml. Trust Fund 1968–73; Ont. Del. Sweden/Ont. Bilateral Exchange 1982, 1983; mem. Extve. Counc. Candn. Soc. for the Study of Higher Educ. 1977–81; Pres. Operations Planning and Analysis Group 1980–84; mem. Soc. for Coll. and Univ. Planning; Chrmn. Evaluation Ctte. Assn. for Instl. Rsch. 1983; Vice-Chair, COU Council on University Planning and Analysis; Chair, Committee on Accountability; mem., Minister's Task Force on Accountability; Gen. Motors Scholar 1962–66; Phillips-Exeter Teaching Fellowship 1965; Root-Tilden Scholar 1966–67; Assoc. Commonwealth Univ./Commonwealth Found. Fellowship 1978; recreations: tennis, gardening, woodworking, theatre; Home: 16 Catalina Dr., Scarborough, Ont. M1M 1K6; Office: Simcoe Hall, Univ. of Toronto, Toronto, Ont. M5S 1A1.

**LANG, Edward J.;** business executive; b. Perth, Scotland 27 Jan. 1937; m. Margaret Jean Whalley; children: Kirstie, Tamaryn, Angus; CHAIRMAN AND CHIEF EXECUTIVE OFFICER, RJR-MACDONALD INC.; Pres., Americas Tobacco Internat., Winston Salem N.C.; Mem., Canadian Tobacco Manufacturers' Assn.; Office: One, First Canadian Place, Suite 6000, Toronto, Ont. M5X 1E8.

**LANG, Frederick Andrew,** F.C.A., LL.D.; Chartered Accountant retired insurance executive; b. Dunrea, Man. 8 June 1910; s. George Frederick and Margaret Elizabeth (Bissett) L.; e. John M. King Sch., Winnipeg, 1918–25; Daniel McIntyre Coll. Inst., 1926–28; Univ. of Man. (Extension), C.A. 1934; Hon. LL.D., Univ. of Manitoba 1978; m. Ruth Hay, d. Alexander and Ruth H. Noble, 6 June 1936; children: Mrs. R. J. Gooding (Charon Ruth), Frederick Stuart, Douglas Andrew; Pres., Candn. Funding Services Ltd., 1975; Student in Acct., William Gray & Co., 1928–34; C.A. 1934; Assessor, Income Tax Dept., Govt. of Man., 1935–38; Corpn. Assessor, Income Tax Dept., Gov. of Can., 1938–41; Secy.-Treas., Systems Equipment Ltd., 1941–55; Pres. & Mang. Dir., Citadel Life Assurance Co. 1955–75; Fellow of Chartered Accts. (Man. Inst.), 1975; mem., B.C. Inst. Chart Accts. 1975; Hon. mem., Bd. of Govs., Regent Coll. Van.; Bd. of Dir., The Citadel Assurance; Man. Inst. of Management Inc.; Protestant; recreations: golf, music; Clubs: Vancouver; Home: 5345 Aspen Dr., West Vancouver, B.C. V7W 3E4.

**LANG, Gordon Saunders,** B.A.Sc., P.Eng.; business executive; b. Toronto, Ont. 5 Mar. 1925; s. late Stuart George and late Vera Noreen (Saunders) L.; e. Humber Crest Sch.; Univ. of Toronto Schs.; Univ. of Toronto BA.Sc. (Elec. Engrg.); children: Stuart William, Donald Gordon, Sherry Maureen, Barbara Joan; CHAIRMAN, CCL INDUSTRIES INC.; Plant Mgr., Samson United (Canada) Ltd. 1949–50; estbd. present co. 1950; served with RCA and Royal Candn. Inf. 1943–45; mem. Candn. Mfrs. Assn.; Assn. Prof. Engs. Prov. Ont.; Candn. Paint Mfrs. Assn.; Candn. Mfrs. Chem. Specialties Assn.; Candn. Cosmetic, Toiletry & Fragrance Assn.; Graphic Arts Inds. Assn.; Packaging Assn.; Proprietary Assn. Can.; Soap & Detergent Assn. Can.; Ont. Paint Assn.; Toronto Soc. Paint Technol.; Am. Prodn. & Inventory Control Soc. Inc.; Chem. Specialties Mfrs. Assn. USA; Clubs: Rosedale Golf; Granite; Muskoka Lakes Golf & Country; Dorado Beach & Tennis (Puerto Rico); United Ch.; Home: 17 Valleyanna Dr., Toronto, Ont. M4N 1J7; Office: 105 Gordon Baker Rd., Willowdale, Ont. M2H 3P8.

**LANG, Howard Jerome,** B. Eng.; industrialist; b. Galt, Ont. 15 June 1912; s. Louis LaCourse and Gertrude O. (Dietrich) L.; e. Galt Coll. Inst., Galt, Ontario; McGill Univ., B.Eng.; (Chem.) 1935; m. Helen Mary, d. George S. Grant, Vancouver, B.C., 29 Oct. 1938; children: David L., Christopher H., Michael J., Martha H., Jennifer M.; remarried: Margaret Barrett Eldridge 1 Dec. 1990; mem., Govs. Appleby Coll., Oakville, Ont.; el. Dir. Pres. and C.E.O. of Canada Iron Foundries Ltd. (now Canron Inc.) July 1960; retired as Chrmn. & Dir. Canron Inc. April 1983; retired as Dir. 1983 Canadian Pacific Ltd., Canadian Imperial Bank of Commerce, Canadian Marconi Inc.; retired as Dir. 1985 Sun Life Assurance Co., Texaco Canada Inc.; retired as Dir., Dofasco Inc. and Canadian Investment Fund Ltd. 1988; mem., Assn. Prof. Engrs. of Ont.; Delta Kappa Epsilon; Catholic; recreations: fishing, shooting, golf; Clubs: York; Toronto Golf; St. Andrews (Fla.); Home: 13 Rosedale Heights Dr., Toronto, Ont. M4T 1C2.

**LANG, K.D. (Katherine Dawn);** singer, composer; b. Consort, Alta. 1961; d. Adam and Audrey L. L.; Mem., Texas Swing Fiddle Band 1982– ; formed band: The Reclines; albums include: 'A Truly Western Experience' 1984, 'Angel with a Lariat' 1986, 'Shadowland' 1988, 'Absolute Torch and Twang' 1990 (Candn. Country Music Awards Album of the Year), 'Ingenue' 1992; actress (film): Salmonberries 1991; recipient Candn. Country Music Awards incl. Entertainer of the Year 1989; Grammy Award 1990; Office: Sire Records, 75 Rockefeller Plaza, New York, N.Y. 10019.

**LANG, Hon. Otto E.,** P.C., Q.C., B.A., LL.B., B.C.L., LL.D.; b. Handel, Sask. 14 May 1932; s. Otto T. and Marie (Wurm) L.; e. Humboldt (Sask.) Coll. Inst.; Univ. of Sask., B.A. 1951, LL.B. 1953; Oxford Univ. (Rhodes Scholar) 1953, B.C.L. 1955; Univ. of Man., LL.D. 1987; m. Adrian Ann Merchant 1963; divorced 1988; m. Deborah J. McCawley, Q.C. 1989; children: (by previous marriage) Maria (dec'd), Timothy, Gregory, Andrew, Elisabeth, Amanda, Adrian; step-children: Andrew, Rebecca; PRESIDENT & CHIEF EXTVE. OFFR., CENTRA GAS MANITOBA INC. 1993– ; read law with W. B. Francis, Q.C.; called to the Bars of Sask. 1956, Ont. 1972, Manitoba 1988; Secy., Rhodes Scholar. Selection Comte. for Sask. 1962–68; prior to political engagement was Dean and Prof. of Law, Univ. of Sask.; el. to H. of C. for Saskatoon-Humboldt g.e. June 1968; apptd. Min. without Portfolio July 1968; Acting Minister Energy, Mines and Resources 1969; Min. of Manpower and Immigration 1970–72; Min. of Justice 1972–75; cr. Q.C. 1972; Min. of Transport 1975–79; Min. responsible for Candn. Wheat Bd. 1969–79; Extve. Vice-Pres., Pioneer Grain Co. Ltd. and Asst. Gen. Mgr., Grain Merchandising, James Richardson and Sons Ltd. 1979–88; Chrmn., Transport Inst., Univ. of Manitoba 1988–93; Board member, Investors Group Trust Co. Ltd. 1978– ; Winnipeg Airport Authority Inc. 1993– ; publications: 'Contemporary Problems of Public Law in Canada' 1967 and numerous articles on labour law, torts, & no-fault auto. ins.; Pres., Assn. of Candn. Law Teachers, 1962; Campaign Chrmn., Un. Way of Winnipeg 1983; Liberal; Roman Catholic; Knight of Malta; Home: 680 Wellington Cres., Winnipeg, Man. R3M 0C2; Office: 560, 444 St. Mary Ave., Winnipeg, Man. R3C 3T7.

**LANG, Reginald Stephen Eduard,** B.E., M.Sc., MCIP, OPPI; professor in environmental studies; b. Assiniboia, Sask. 17 Dec. 1936; s. the late Jacob Stephen and Leontine Marie (Lolacher) L.; e. Univ. of Sask., B.Sc. 1957; Univ. of Man., M.Sc. 1963; Doctoral cand., Ont. Inst. for Studies in Educ.; divorced; children: Michelle Anne, Mary-Ellen Elizabeth; PROF. IN ENVIRONMENTAL STUDIES, YORK UNIV. 1977– , Assoc. Prof. 1971–77; Engr., City of Regina 1957–62; Planner, Can. Mortgage & Housing Corp. 1963–65; Dir., Community Planning, N.S. Dept. of Mun. Affairs 1965–71; Assoc. Prof., York Univ. 1971–77; Prin., Lang Armour Assoc. 1977–86; Reg Lang & Assoc. 1986– ; Intern Couns., Toronto Inst. of Human Relns. 1986–88; Guest lectr., Canada & abroad; Rsch. Assoc., Univ. of Calif., Davis 1979; Cons., Candn. fed./prov./mun. govts.

& private sector; Mem., 3 fed. environ. assessment panels 1977–80; course coordinator, Banff Ctr. Sch. of Mngt.; Cert. of Distinction, Town Planning Inst. of Can. 1963; Queen's Silver Jubilee Medal 1977; Nuffield Travelling Fellowship 1969; Mem., Candn. Inst. of Planners 1964– ; Assn. of Profl. Engrs. of Ont. 1971–90; Ont. Profl. Planners Inst. 1986– ; author: 'Residential Density and Energy Conservation' 1986; co-author: 'Environmental Planning Resourcebook' 1980, 'The Assessment and Review of Social Impacts' 1980, 'Planning Land to Conserve Energy' 1982, 'New Directions in Municipal Energy Conservation' 1980; editor: 'Integrated Approaches to Resource Planning and Management' 1986; recreations: hiking, skiing, gardening, design; Home: 16 Knowles Cres., Aurora, Ont. L4G 1Z7; Office: 4700 Keele St., North York, Ont. M3J 1P3.

**LANG, Stuart William,** B.Sc.; printer; b. Toronto, Ont. 26 Jan. 1951; s. Gordon Saunders and Joan Darlie (Moxon) L.; e. Upper Canada College 1970; Queen's Univ. B.Sc. 1974; m. Kim d. Donald and Dorothy Burnett 6 May 1978; PRESIDENT, CCL LABEL, CANADA, CCL INDUSTRIES, INC. 1990– ; Edmonton Eskimo Football Club 1974–81; Bd. of Dir., CCL Industries, Inc.; Christian; recreations: hockey, golf, tennis, jogging; clubs: Rosedale Golf, Granite; Home: R.R. #22, Cambridge, Ont. N3C 2V4; Office: 3077 Mainway, Burlington, Ont. L7R 4C5.

**LANG, T.E.,** B.Sc.; retired food executive; b. Osage, Iowa 16 May 1919; s. Elmer P. and Martha (Hartnell) L.; e. State Univ. of Iowa, B.Sc. 1941; Harvard Business Sch., 1958; m. Hanne; children: Dr. R. T., Jori, Janelle; Chrmn. & C.E.O., Carnation Inc., July 1985; now retired; joined present co. 1941; held various positions from Plant Supt. to Gen. Supt. of all Plants, 1950; apptd. Asst. Vice Pres., Sales 1953, Vice Pres. 1965, Pres. 1972; served during 2nd World War as Lt. with U.S.N.; Pres., Ont. Processing Council, 1959; Pres., Frozen French Fry Assn.; Chrmn., Nat. Dairy Council; Chrmn., Grocery Products Mfrs. Can.; United Church; recreations: fishing, hunting, gardening, skiing; Clubs: Hunt; Islington Sportsmen (Pres.); Home: R.R. 3, Georgetown, Ont. L7G 4S6.

**LANGDON, Frank Corriston,** Ph.D.; educator; consultant; researcher; b. La Grange, Ill. 3 June 1919; s. Ernest Warren and Julia Ida (Mondeng) L.; e. Harvard B.A. 1941, M.A. 1949; Univ. of Cal. Berkeley Ph.D. 1953; m. Virginia d. Edward and Edith Osborne 25 May 1956; two s. Peter John, Marc Christopher; INST. OF INTERNAT. RELATIONS, UNIV. OF B.C. 1984– , Prof. Emeritus 1984– ; Communications Offr. Naval Japanese Lang. Sch. Stillwater, Okla. 1945–46; Econ. Analyst Foreign Trade, HQ Supreme Commdr. Allied Powers Tokyo 1946–47; Instr. in Pol. Sci. Far E. Prog. Extension Div. Univ. of Cal. 1953–55; Sr. Lectr. in Japanese Australian Nat. Univ. Canberra 1955–58; Prof. of Pol. Sci. present Univ. 1958–84; author 'Politics in Japan' 1967; 'Japan's Foreign Policy' 1973 (Jap. transl. 1976); 'The Politics of Canadian-Japanese Economic Relations 1952–83' 1983; co-author and co-editor 'Superpower Maritime Strategy in the Pacific' 1990; co-editor and contbr. 'Japan in the Posthegemonic World' 1993; mem. Vancouver Mokuyokai Soc.; Candn. Pol. Sci. Assn.; Candn. Asian Studies Assn.; Presbyterian; recreations: hiking, skiing; Home: 4736 W. 4th Ave., Vancouver, B.C. V6T 1C2; Office: Inst. of Internat. Relns., Univ. of B.C., Buchanan C456, 1866 Main Mall, Vancouver, B.C. V6T 1W5.

**LANGDON, The Hon. Mr. Justice Kenneth A.,** LL.B.; judge; b. Brampton, Ont. 9 June 1938; s. Kenneth M. and Patricia (Aylsworth) L.; e. Upper Can. Coll. 1950–56 (Moderns Prize); Univ. of Toronto (Trinity) 1956–58; Osgoode Hall Law Sch., LL.B. 1961 (Rubinoff Prize Legal Hist. 1959); m. Lynda Frances (née Cook); children (by previous marriage): Sharon E., Heather D., Kenneth R.; JUSTICE, ONT. COURT (GEN. DIV.) 1990– ; called to Ont. Bar 1963; law Practice, MacMillan Rooke & Coy 1963–66; Helson & Langdon 1966–69; Helson, Baines & Langdon 1969–74; Solicitor, Georgetown & Dist. Mem. Hosp. 1970–74, Bd. of Dir. 1974–86 (Chrmn. 1981–85); Judge, Ont. Prov. Court (Crim. Div.) 1974–90; Judge, Ont. District Court Apr. 1990–Sept. 1990; Office: P.O. Box 8000, Brampton, Ont. L6V 2M7.

**LANGDON, Steven W.,** M.P., B.A., M.A., Ph.D.; economist; b. Stratford, Ont. 15 July 1946; e. Univ. of Toronto; Carleton Univ.; Univ. of Sussex (Commonwealth Scholar); VISITING SCHOLAR, SCHOOL OF PUBLIC ADMINISTRATION, CARLETON UNIV.; journalist and professor; Assoc. Dir., IDRC; Pres., Student Union, Univ. of Toronto 1968–69; Founder, Candn. Ctr. for Policy Alternatives 1980; taught econ. to trade unionists, Candn. Labour Congress's Labour Coll. 1980–81; el. to H. of C. for Essex-Windsor g.e. 1984; re-el. g.e. 1988; Party Spokesman on Trade Indus. & Econ. Devel.; then on Finance; N.D.P.; Home: Ottawa, Ont.

**LANGE, Gordon Lloyd,** B.Sc., Ph.D.; educator; b. Edmonton, Alta. 1 Mar. 1937; s. Carl John and Margaret Ellen (Losie) L.; e. Univ. of Alta. B.Sc. 1959; Univ. of Cal. Berkeley, Ph.D. 1963; m. Gail d. John and Laura Stephen 4 Apr. 1964; children: Stephen, Margot; PROF. OF CHEM. & BIOCHEM., UNIV. OF GUELPH 1984– ; Rsch. Chem. Procter & Gamble Co. Cincinnati 1962–65; Post-Doctoral Fellow, Univ. of W. Ont. 1965–67; joined present Univ. 1967; recipient Ont. Confedn. Univ. Faculty Assns. Teaching Award 1984; Union Carbide Award Chem. Edn. 1986; 3M Teaching Fellowship 1991; author over 60 publs. chem. jours.; mem. Chem. Inst. Can.; Am. Chem. Soc.; recreations: sports, travel; Home: 8 Crawford St., Guelph, Ont. N1G 1Z1; Office: Guelph, Ont. N1G 2W1.

**LANGELIER, Jean Guy;** financial executive; b. Montreal, Que. 28 Jan. 1950; e. Colgate Univ. international finance 1976; Univ. of Western Ont. international management 1978; McGill Univ. international operations 1979; m. Monique; two children; SENIOR VICE-PRES. & GENERAL MANAGER, CAISSE CENTRALE DESJARDINS 1994– ; Manager, Internat. Banking, Banque Nat. du Canada 1979; Dir., Card Serv. Div. 1981; Dir., Operations, Caisse centrale Desjardins 1981; Vice-Pres., Opns. 1984; Sr. Vice-Pres., Admin. & Banking Serv. 1986; Sr. Vice-Pres., Finance & Admin. 1992–94; Bd. Mem., Candn. Payments Assn.; YMCA; Montreal Country Club; Desjardins FSB Holding Ltd.; Vice Chrmn., Desjardins FSB; recreations: reading: finance and business, golf, hockey; Office: 1, Compl. Desjardins, Ste. 2822, Montreal, Que. H5B 1B3.

**LANGER, H. Peter;** real estate consultant; b. Vienna, Austria 25 Mar. 1916; s. Viktor and Margarete (Wachsmann); e. High Sch., Vienna, Austria (Sr. Matric. 1934); Vienna Agric. Coll.; Reading Univ. Eng. (Intermediate Science) 1939; m. Lillian, d. late Henry Patterson, Toronto, Ont. 3 Sept. 1941; children: Ann, Peter, Paul; former Chrmn. & Dir., Markborough Properties Ltd. (previously Extve. Vice Pres., then Pres.); emigrated to Canada after discharge from U.K. forces in Sept. 1946; joined real estate firm of A.W. Farlinger, Toronto, Ont. 1947; apptd. Mgr. of East End Office 1949, Gen. Mgr. 1951, Extve. Vice-Pres. 1953 (firm name changed to Farlinger and Langer Ltd. 1954); joined A.E. LePage Ltd. as Vice-Pres. and Dir. 1960; served in 2nd World War joining U.K. forces in Feb. 1940; served in France, Eng., N. Africa, Italy; final appt. Depy. Asst. Dir. of Labour, N. Italy with rank of Staff Major; discharged with Hon. rank of Major, Sept. 1946; Fellow of the Real Estate Inst. of Can., C.L.P. (Certified in Land Planning and Devel.); retired mem., Soc. of Indust. and Office Realtors; Past Pres., Urban Devel. Inst. Ont.; Past Pres. and Hon. Life mem., Toronto Real Estate Bd.; mem. Assn. Ont. Land Econs.; has written articles and lect. on real estate matters; appeared as speaker, moderator and panel mem. on real estate and allied subjects on many occasions; Past Pres. and Life Mem. Downtown Club, Candn. Legion; Life mem., Royal Candn. Mil. Inst.; Lambda Alpha; Anglican; Clubs: Donalda; Empire; Home: 225 The Donway West, Suite 204, Don Mills, Ont. M3B 2V7.

**LANGFORD, Arthur Nicol,** M.A., Ph.D., D.C.L. (h.c.); botanist; b. Ingersoll, Ont. 30 July 1910; s. Thomas Eli and Bertha Alexandra (Nicol) L.; e. Queen's Univ., B.A. (Hons. Biol. and Chem.) 1931; Univ. of Toronto; M.A. (Bot.) 1933, Ph.D. (Plant Path.), 1936; m. Anne B. d. George Brodie, July 1938; m. 2ndly Marjorie A. d. William Gilbert, 12 June 1976; children: Mrs. Roberta L. Cone, Peter Arthur, John Stephen; EMERITUS PROF. OF BIOLOGY, BISHOP'S UNIV.; now involved in environmental issues; Secy., Long Point Biosphere Reserve; began at Bishop's Univ. as Lectr., 1937; Visiting Prof. of Biology, Univ. of Botswana and Swaziland, Kwaluseni, Sd. 1976–80; Extve. Dir., Long Point Bird Observatory, Port Rowan, Ont., 1983–84; D.C.L. (h.c.) Bishop's Univ. 1985; United Church; recreations: nature study, philately, photography, squash; Address: P.O. Box 220, Port Rowan, Ont. N0E 1M0.

**LANGFORD, J. Alex,** Q.C.; b. Toronto, Ont. 7 Dec. 1931; s. Henry E., Q.C. and Helen Elizabeth (Uren) L.; e. Univ. of Toronto Schs. 1950; Univ. of Toronto, B.A. (Hon. Mod. Hist.) 1954; Osgoode Hall Law Sch., 1958; m. Marion Grace, d. late Elzwood and Helen E.A. (Reid) Barker, 20 Apl. 1957; children: Mary (Mrs. J. Michael Rolland), Sarah (Mrs. David Kyle), Anne (Mrs. Peter Dotsikas), John, Jane: Dir., E-L Financial Corp.; National Trust Co.; Dominion of Canada General Insurance Co.; Empire Life Insurance Co.; called to Bar of Ont. 1958; cr. Q.C. 1971; comnd.; Hon. Solr., Candn. Inst. Internat. Affairs; mem. Candn. Bar Assn.; Phi Gamma Delta; P. Conservative; United Church; recreations: reading, tennis, skiing, hiking, sailing; Clubs: National; Albany; Granite; Caledon Ski; Home: 129 Coldstream Ave., Toronto, Ont. M5N 1X7; Office: 625 Cochrane Dr., Suite 800, Markham, Ont. L3R 9R9.

**LANGFORD, Martha,** B.E.A., M.A.; museum director; b. Ottawa, Ont. 18 Dec. 1953; d. James Warren and Lucille (Coupal) L.; e. Lisgar C.I. 1971; N.S. College of Art & Design B.F.A. 1975; McGill Univ. M.A. 1991; Dir., Canadian Museum of Contemporary Photography (affiliate mus. of Nat. Gall. of Canada) 1985; Extve. Prod., Still Photography Div., Nat. Film Bd. of Canada 1981–84; Edn. Leave to complete residence requirements for Ph.D. in Art Hist. from McGill Univ. 1992–93; Part-time Lectr., Univ. of Ottawa 1984–85; Govt. of Canada Merit Award 1989; Max Stern Fellowship in Art History 1991–92, 1992–93; Bd. Mem., Soc. for Photographic Edn. 1990–92; author of eight exbn. catalogues; recreations: dogwalking, baking, swimming; Home: 2191 Souvenir St., Montreal, Que. H3H 1R9.

**LANGFORD, Michael John,** M.A., Ph.D.; university professor; b. London, U.K. 29 June 1931; s. Dr. John Charles Cobden and Margaret Alice Jeanette (Higham) L.; e. St. Paul's Sch. 1944–50; New College, Oxford Univ. B.A.(P.P.E.) 1954, M.A. 1958; Westcott House, Cambridge Univ. 1955–56; King's College, London Ph.D. 1966; m. Sally d. James and Kathryn Church 10 Aug. 1985; children: Jeanette Marguerite, Kathryn Marie; PROF. OF MEDICAL ETHICS, FAC. OF MEDICINE, MEMORIAL UNIV. OF NEWFOUNDLAND 1987– ; Anglican Curate, Bristol U.K. 1956–59; Chaplain, Queens' College, Cambridge Univ. 1959–63; Rsch. Student, King's College, London 1963–66; joined Philosophy Dept., Memorial Univ. of Nfld. 1967; Full Prof. 1982– ; Wine Consultant, Nfld. Liquor Corp.; Black Belt Judo (Shodan) and Aikido (Nidan); Anglican Priest (working as Hon. Curate); author: 'Providence' 1982, 'Unblind Faith' 1982, 'The Good & The True' 1985 and several articles on philosophy & med. ethics in refereed jours.; recreations: violin, aikido, fly fishing, wine tasting, Scottish country dancing; Home: 8 Dartmouth Pl., St. John's, Nfld. A1B 2W2; Office: Health Sci. Ctr., St. John's, Nfld. A1B 3V6.

**LANGILL, George F.;** health administrator; b. Ottawa, Ont. 31 Dec. 1946; s. Roy Joseph and Margaret Graham (O'Hara) L.; e. Univ. of Ottawa, B.Sc. (Hons.) 1971, M.H.A. 1973; m. Lorraine d. Norman and Lorraine Brazeau 28 Dec. 1968; children: Norman, Barbara Anne, Kendra; CHIEF EXTVE. OFFR., ROYAL OTTAWA HEALTH CARE GROUP 1982– ; Assoc. Extve. Dir., Royal Ottawa Regn. Rehab. Ctr. 1980–82; Asst. Extve. Dir., Royal Ottawa Hosp. 1974–80; Admin. Co-ord., N.S. Min. of Health 1973–74; Extve. Ctte. Chrmn., Vice Chrmn., Bd. of Govs., Ottawa-Carleton Regn. Hosp. Food Serv. Inc. 1979–82; Chrmn., Ottawa Health Sci. Ctr. Extve. Ctte. 1983–86, 1992– ; Chrmn., Nat. Capital Chapter, Candn. Coll. of Health Serv. Extves. 1985–87; Chrmn., Nat. Profl. Assns. Ctte., Candn. Rehab. Counc. for the Disabled 1985–88; Can. Liquid Air Award 1973; Fellow, C.C.H.S.E. 1991; Fellow, ACHE 1993; Top Acad. Achievement, MHA Prog., Univ. of Ottawa; Young Admin. Essay Forum 1979 Winner (Am. Soc. of Hosp. Admins.); Agnew Peckham Award 1990; Sec. Treas., Royal Ottawa Hosp. Found.; Candn. Del., World Comn., Rehab. Internat., Orgn. & Mgmt. Session; Part-time Lectr. & Adjunct Prof., Univ. of Ottawa; Sch. of Health Admin. & Faculty of Medicine; Algonquin Coll. Health Sci. Cont. Edn. 1976–82; author of numerous pubns. & presentations; recreations: golf, skiing, reading, hockey; Clubs: Kanata Lakes Golf & Country; Home: 17 Windeyer Cres., Kanata, Ont. K2K 2N1; Office: 1145 Carling Ave., Ottawa, Ont. K1Z 7K4.

**LANGLANDS, Robert P.,** B.A., M.A., Ph.D., D.Sc.; professor, mathematician; b. New Westminster, B.C., 6 Oct. 1936; s. Robert and Kathleen Johanna (Phelan) L.; e. Univ. of B.C., B.A. 1957, M.A. 1958; Yale Univ., Ph.D.(math) 1960; D.Sc. (hon. causa) Univ. of B.C. 1985; McMaster Univ. 1985; CUNY, Graduate Centre 1985; D.Math. (hon. causa) Univ. of Waterloo 1988; D.Sc. (hon. causa) Univ. de Paris VII 1989; McGill 1991; Univ. of Toronto 1993; m. Charlotte, d. Lawrence and Helen Cheverie, 13 Aug. 1956; children: William, Sarah, Robert, Thomasin; PROFESSOR OF MATHEMATICS, INSTITUTE FOR ADVANCED STUDY, PRINCETON, 1972– ; Princeton Univ.: instructor 1960–61, lectr. 1961–62, asst./assoc. prof. 1962–67; prof., Yale Univ. 1967–72; mem., Inst. for Advanced

Study 1962–63; Univ. of California, Berkeley: Miller Fellow 1964–65, Sloan Fellow 1964–66; Middle East Tech. Univ. 1967–68; Bonn Univ. 1970–71, 1980–81; chercheur titulaire, Centre de recherches mathématiques, Montréal 1990–93; awards: F.R.S.C. 1972, Wilbur L. Cross Medal, Yale 1975, Fellow, Royal Soc. of London 1981, Cole Prize, Am. Math. Soc. 1982; Common Wealth Award 1984; Nat. Acad. of Sciences Award in Mathematics 1988; mem.: Nat. Acad. of Sci. 1993; Am. Math. Soc.; Can. Math. Soc.; author: 'Euler Products' 1971, 'On the Functional Equations satisfied by Eisenstein Series' 1974; 'Base Change for GL(2)' 1980; 'Les débuts d'une formule des traces stable' 1983; co-author: 'Automorphic Forms on GL(2)' 1970; Home: 60 Battle Rd., Princeton, N.J. 08540; Office: School of Mathematics, Institute for Advanced Study, Princeton, N.J. 08540.

**LANGLEY, George Ross,** B.A., M.D., C.M., F.R.C.P.(C), F.A.C.P., F.R.C.P. (Edin); Physician and University professor; b. Sydney, N.S. 6 Oct. 1931; s. John George Elmer Langley; e. Port Hawkesbury Elem. and New Glasgow High Schs. N.S. 1948; Mt. Allison Univ. B.A. 1952; Dalhousie Univ. M.D., C.M. 1957 F.R.C.P. (C), 1961; m. Jean Marie d. Ernest Pitblado Ballantyne, Ballantyne's Cove, N.S. 22 June 1957; children: Joanne Marie, Mark Ross, Richard Graham; PROF. OF MEDICINE, DALHOUSIE UNIVERSITY and Senior Physician Victoria General Hospital; Lectr. in Med. Dalhousie Univ. 1962, Asst. Prof. 1964, Assoc. Prof. 1966, Prof. 1968; Chief of Service Med. Camp Hill Hosp. 1969–74; Prof. & Head, Dept. of Medicine, Dalhousie Univ. 1974–82; Head, Dept. of Medicine, Victoria General Hosp. 1974–82; Vice Pres. (Medicine), Royal Coll. of Physicians and Surgeons of Can. 1980–82; mem. Bd. of Dirs., Nat. Cancer Inst. Can. (mem. Profl. Awards Panel 1981–85; Comte. on Priorities, Chrmn. 1981–84; Clin. Adv. Comte. 1973–76; Clin. & Epid. Research Adv. Comte. 1978, Chrmn. 1981–84; Clinical and Epid. Research Grants Panel mem. 1973–78, Chrmn. 1978–83); mem. Adv. Comte. to Candn. Blood Comte.; John and Mary Markle Scholar in Acad. Med. 1963–68; recipient Queen's Silver Jubilee Medal; Medal of the Nat. Cancer Inst.; Wightman Visiting Professor, Royal Coll. Physicians and Surgeons of Can. 1990; author over 65 scient. articles red cell metabolism, leukemia, med. educ.; Fellow, Royal Coll. Physic. & Surg. Can.; Fellow, Am. Coll. Physic., Royal Coll. of Physic. of Edinburgh; Candn. Assn. Profl. Med. (Vice Pres. 1980–82; Sec.-Treas. 1978–80); Internat. Soc. Hematology; mem. Am. Soc. Hematology; Am. Soc. Clin. Onco.; Candn. Soc. Onco.; mem. Counc., Royal Coll. Phys. & Surgs. 1978–86 (Chrmn. Hematology Specialty Comte. 1974–80; Chrmn. Examinations Comte. 1980–82; Chrmn. Credentials Comte. 1984–86); Gov. Am. Coll. Phys. 1974–78; mem. Candn. Soc. Clin. Investigation (Council 1966–69, Chrmn. Awards Comte. 1968–69); Med. Research Counc. Can. (Grants Comte. Clin. Investigation 1974–78, Chrmn. 1976–78; Clinical Trials 1990–91); Candn. Hematology Soc. (Pres. 1976–78, Vice Pres. 1974–76); Med. Soc. N.S. (Chrmn. Sec. Internal Med. 1971); N.S. Soc. Internal Med. (Vice Pres. 1970, Pres. 1971); Dalhousie Med. Alumni (Pres. 1973–75, Vice Pres. 1971–73, Secy. Treas. 1967–71); Alpha Omega Alpha; Phi Rho Sigma; United Church; recreations: gardening, reading, skiing; Home: 6025 Oakland Rd., Halifax, N.S. B3H 1N9; Office: Victoria Gen. Hosp., Halifax, N.S. B3H 2Y9.

**LANGLEY, J. Thomas,** B.Comm., M.S., C.G.A.; university administrator; b. Point Tupper, N.S. 6 March 1940; s. Thomas Rhodes and Rose Christina (Malcolm) L.; e. St. Francis Xavier Univ. B.Comm. 1961; Univ. of Nebraska M.S. 1971; Harvard Univ. 6-wk. dipl. in Univ. Admin.; m. Marius E. d. Duncan and Catherine MacIsaac 6 July 1963; children: Jennifer L., Stephanie A., Wendy J., Jeffrey T.; VICE-PRESIDENT, ADM. & SECRETARY-TREASURER, ST. FRANCIS XAVIER UNIV. 1978– ; Accountant, N.S. Pulp Ltd. 1961–63; Business Mgr. & Accountant, St. Francis Xavier Univ. 1963–72; Comptroller & Sec.-Treas. 1972–78; Pres., Candn. Assn. of Univ. Business Officers 1981–82 and Chair, Atlantic Assn. of Univ. Bus. Offrs. 1977–80 (served on Bd. & several cttes. of these assns.); Cert. Gen. Accountants Dipl. 1970; Commonwealth Admin. Travelling Fellowship 1986; Vice-Chair, Bd. of Dir., St. Martha's Hosp. 1982–84; recreations: jogging, swimming, skiing, reading, family activities; Home: 71 St. Ninian St., Antigonish, N.S. B2G 1Y7; Office: Antigonish, N.S. B2G 1C0.

**LANGLOIS, Bernard P.,** F.C.A.; chartered accountant; b. Coniston, Ont. 1 April 1934; s. Alfred J. and Simone (Robineau) L.; m. Mary Argentin 19 July 1958; children: Shelley, David; PRESIDENT, RIDGE RUN RESORTS 1989– ; Revenue Canada Taxation 1960; Partner, Ross & Langlois 1962; Thorne Riddell 1968; Office Managing Partner 1978; Regional Council, Thorne Riddell 1982; Nat. Serv. Expansion Partner 1985–89 (retired); Pres., Daley Mngt. Inc. 1989; FCA 1979; various extve. positions Bd. of Edn., Laurentian Hosp., Univ. of Sudbury, Laurentian Hosp. Found.; Mem., St. Paul Parish Council (Chair 1974–76); author: 'Running Your Own Business' 1971, 'Death of a Taxpayer' 1973 and various articles; Lectr., Sch. of Accountancy; recreations: golf, squash, boating; club: Idylwylde Golf; Address: 427 Kirkwood Dr., Sudbury, Ont. P3E 1X1.

**LANK, David Morris,** B.A., F.R.S.A.; executive; writer; b. Buenos Aires, Argentina 25 Nov. 1937; s. Herbert Hayman and Oriana (Bailey) L.; e. Lower Can. Coll. Montreal; Princeton Univ. B.A. 1960; Univ. de Grenoble, France 1960; children: Cynthia, Gordon, Sarah, David; DORCHESTER INVESTMENT MANAGEMENT 1992– ; Dir. Helix Investments; Isomedix Inc. (Whippany, N.J.); Mirabaud Canada; joined DuPont International Geneva 1960–67; Dep. Head Operations Control Expo '67 1967–68; Partner, Dorchester Investment Mgmnt. 1968–93; Chrmn. McCord Museum of Candn. Hist.; Adjunct Curator Cleveland Museum Natural Hist.; Trustee Bishop's Univ. Lennoxville; Past Gov. Lower Can. Coll., St. George's Sch., The Study Sch.; Dir., Wilderness Preservation Trust; Dir. Atlantic Salmon Fedn. (Pres. 9 yrs.); Chrmn., Shawbridge Found.; Dir., Candn. Found. for Dietetic Rsch.; Pres. Château Montlabert; Vice Pres. Soc. Wilderness Art for Nation Gloucester, UK; guest lectr. numerous Candn. & USA univs., natural hist socs., high schs.; author 'A Gourmet's Geneva' 1964–67; 'The Squirrel Place' (children's lit.) 1966; 'Chateau Montlabert' history 1968; 'The Beckoning Land' adventure 1975; 'Surely the Gods Live Here' adventure 1984; 'Nature Classics' rare books hist. 1985; 'Images From The Wild' wild life art 1986; 'A Dissimulation of Birds' natural hist. 1988; 'The Sketches of Joseph Wolf' art hist. 1988; 'The Gospels According to St. Salmo' humour 1988; 'The Psalms According to St. Psalmo' humour 1989; author and frequently illus. over 400 articles, catalogues, columns various mags. and jours.; Fellow, Am. Antiquarian Soc.; past mem. Can.-UK Ctte. Candn. C. of C., Past mem. Can.-US Ctte.; Clubs; University; Angler's (New York); Grolier (New York); Explorers' (New York, Fellow); Home: Westmount, Que.; Office: 1005, 500 René Lévesque Blvd. W., Montreal, Que. H2Z 1W7.

**LANSDOWNE, James Fenwick,** O.C., R.C.A., LL.D.; artist; b. Hong Kong 8 Aug. 1937; s. Ernest Lansdowne; e. St. Michael's Sch. and Victoria High Sch., B.C.; Elec. mem. Royal Canadian Academy of Arts, 1974; Officer, Order of Canada 1977; Univ. of Victoria LL.D. 1980 (Hon.); co-author: 'Birds of the Northern Forest' 1966; 'Birds of the Eastern Forest' vol. I 1968, vol. II 1970; author-artist 'Birds of the West Coast' Part I 1976, Part II 1980; Fellow, Explorers Club; Anglican; recreations: antiques, book collecting, ornithology; Home: 681 Transit Rd., Victoria, B.C.; Office: 941 Victoria Ave., Victoria, B.C. V8S 4N6.

**LANTHIER, Claude,** B.A.Sc., P.Eng.; consulting engineer; b. Montreal, Que. 24 Jan. 1933; s. Ulric and Berthe (Sauvé) L.; e. Univ. of Montreal B.A.Sc.; Ecole Polytech. de Montréal P.Eng.; several other certificates & diplomas; m. Violet d. Rafaëlo Pietroniro 8 Sept. 1956; children: Marc, Anne-Marie; CHRMN., CANDN. SECTION, INTERNATIONAL JOINT COMMISSION; Arbitrator Engr. Examiner, Order of Architects of Que. 1962– ; Senior Partner, Claude Lanthier, Jean Saia & Assoc. 1959–84; 1st elected M.P., House of Commons, Sept. 1984; Parl. Sec. to Min. of Finan. 1984–85; to Min. for Sci. & Technol. 1986; to Min. of Public Works 1987; Pres., Perm. Ctte., House of Commons on Employment, Work & Immigration 1987; several past extve. positions; as consulting engr. & expert arbitrator in civil engr. supervised as many as 1,500 individual contacts annually for past 20 yrs ranging in value from $1 to $36 million; advisor to priv. indus. incl. Bell, Laurentian Bank, National Bank & several others; Mem., Ordre des Ingén. du Qué.; Engineering Inst. of Can.; Certified Arbitrator, Arbitrators Inst. of Can.; Am. Arbitration Institute; Certified Environmental Inspector, Environmental Assessment Assn.; Singapore Internat. Arbitration Centre; Vancouver Arbitration Centre; Centre d'Arbitrage National et International du Qué.; Gov., Found. of LaSalle Gen. Hosp.; Dir., Fond. Hosp. de Verdun; School Comnr., Sault-Saint-Louis Sch. Bd.; recreations: gastronomy & oenology (Mem. or Pres. of internat. juries for fine wines & spirit tasting contests), gymnastics & fast-walking, cycling, opera, theatre; Home: 382 de Cabano St., LaSalle, Que. H8R 2M1; Office: 100 Metcalfe St., 18th Floor, Ottawa, Ont. K1P 5M1.

**LANTHIER, J. Spencer,** F.C.A.; chartered accountant; b. Montreal, Que. 17 Dec. 1940; s. Edgar J. and Sarah M. (Boyd) L.; e. McGill Univ.; C.A. 1965; m. Diane d. Garrett and Muriel Safford 16 Sept. 1961;; children: Sherrill, Suzanne, John, Sara; CHRMN. & CHIEF EXTVE. OFFR., KPMG PEAT MARWICK THORNE 1993– ; joined Peat, Marwick, Mitchell & Co. 1960; Partner, Montreal 1972; Mng. Partner, London 1977; Mng. Ottawa 1982; Extve. Ctte. 1983; Mng. Partner, Toronto 1984; Vice Chrmn., Toronto Region 1989; awarded F.C.A. by Ont. Inst. of C.A.s 1982; Gov. Counc., Univ. of Toronto; Past Chrmn., Goodwill Industries of Toronto; recreations: golf, platform tennis, reading; Clubs: London Hunt & Country; Royal Montreal Golf; Lambton Golf & Country; London; Kingsway Platform Tennis; Fitness Inst.; Toronto Golf; Home: 12 Kingsway Cres., Toronto, Ont. M8X 2R1; Office: Suite 1200, One Toronto St., Toronto, Ont. M5C 2V1.

**LANTOS, Robert,** B.A., M.A.; film and tv producer; b. Hungary 3 Apr. 1949; s. Laszlo and Agnes (Bodor) L.; e. Northmount High Sch.; McGill Univ. B.A. 1970, M.A. 1972; children: Ari, Sabrina; CHRMN. & C.E.O., ALLIANCE COMMUNICATIONS CORPORATION 1989– (Co-Chrmn. 1985–89); Pres. RSL Entertainment Corp. 1975–85; productions incl. feature films: 'Black Robe' (6 Genies, including Best Picture); official Cannes Competition entry 'Joshua Then and Now' (winner of 5 Genies) and 'In Praise of Older Women' (winner of 4 Genies); television: 'North of 60'; 'E.N.G.' (3 time winner of Gemini Award for Best Dramatic Series); 'Counterstrike'; 'Bordertown'; 'Night Heat' (winner of TV Guide Most Popular Series Award and Gemini Award for Best Dramatic Series); 'A Family of Strangers'; 'Woman On The Run: The Lawrencia Bembenek Story'; 'Sword of Gideon' (winner of 3 Gemini Awards and an ACE Award); Winner of 1991 Air Canada Award for contribution to filmmaking in Canada; winner of CFTPA Chetwyn Award for Entrepreneurial Excellence; mem. Bd. of Dirs., Festival of Festivals, and Candn. Film Centre; mem. of Academy of Canadian Cinema and Television (past Chrmn.); Bd. of Govs., Mt. Sinai Hospital; mem. Academy of Motion Picture Arts and Sciences of Am.; mem. Candn. Champion Water Polo Team 1967–69; Office: 920 Yonge St., Suite 400, Toronto, Ont. M4W 3C7.

**LAOUN, Antoine,** B.Eng., M.B.A.; business executive; b. 15 Dec. 1946; s. Joseph and Marie (Hechema) L.; Canadian citizen; e. McGill Univ. B.Eng. 1968, M.B.A. 1970; m. Violet d. Joseph and Minnie Lynn 29 June 1974; children: Mark Andrew, Brent Philip; PRES. & DIR., DUKE SEABRIDGE LIMITED; Financial Analyst, Air Canada Montreal 1970–71; Incentive Offr., Dept. of Reg. Econ. Expansion 1972–73; Sr. Planning Analyst, Power Corp. of Canada Ltd. 1973–75; Mgr., Corp. Planning, James Bay Devel. Corp. 1975–78; Sr. Staff Advr., B.C. Ctte. on Crown Corps. Vancouver 1978–80; fulfilled var. positions as officer & dir. of Duke Seabridge (A Guinness Family Co.) since 1981; currently: Bd. Chrmn. & Dir., Broadmead Farms Ltd.; Capitol Tractors & Equipment Ltd.; Coast Tractor & Equipment Ltd.; Ince Holdings Ltd.; Vice-Pres. & Dir., Elgistan Mngt. Limited; Offr., Montreal Chap., Planning Extves. Inst. 1973–78; Offr. & Past Pres., Vancouver Chap., N. Am. Soc. for Corp. Planning 1978–82; recreations: fitness, skiing, squash, tennis; clubs: Vancouver, Hollyburn Country; Home: 2316 Nelson Ave., West Vancouver, B.C.; Office: #505, 100 Park Royal, West Vancouver, B.C. V7T 1A2.

**LaPALME, Robert,** O.C., R.C.A.; caricaturist; b. Montreal, Que. 14 Apl. 1908; s. Tancrede and Elodie (Beauchamp) L.; e. autodidact; m. Annette (d. 1978) d. Alphonse Demers, Montreal, Que. 14 Jan. 1935; one s. Pierre; pol. cartoonist Montreal and New York since 1933; FOUNDER AND DIR., INTERNAT. CENTER OF UNIVERSAL HUMOUR 1987; Founder and Dir. Internat. Salon of Cartoons 1963–87; Founder Qué. Mun. Art Gallery; exhns. incl. New York, Montréal (4), Toronto, Rio de Janeiro (2), Sao Paolo, Rome, Paris, Nat. Gallery Can.; painted 3 murals Expo '67 (now in Montreal metro); large tapestry Place des Arts; mural Place Crémazie; Prof. Faculty of Sciences Laval Univ. 3 years.; cited in many books; R. Catholic; recreation: reading; Club: Montreal Press (Hon. Life mem.); Invited Mem., Academie des Grands Montréalais Nov. 1992; Home: 1081 St.-Urbain, S/605, Montréal, Qué. H2Z 1K8.

**LAPERRIERE, Normand J.,** M.D. FRCPC; radiation oncologist; b. Niagara Falls, Ont. 19 Apr. 1953; s. Gaston and Viola (Ouimet) L.; e. Univ. of Toronto Med. Sch., M.D. 1978, Res. in Radiation Oncol. 1984; m. Catherine d. Ken and Doreen Cumming 17 July 1982; children: Michelle, Victoria; RADIATION ONCOLO-

GIST, PRINCESS MARGARET HOSP. 1985– ; training, Princess Margaret Hosp. 1980–84; Staff, Dept. of Radiation Oncol., McGill Univ. 1984–85; Rsch.: clinical investigations of experimental treatments for patients with brain tumors; Home: 121 Aitken Circle, Unionville, Ont. L3R 7L8; Office: 500 Sherbourne St., Toronto, Ont. M4X 1K9.

**LAPIERRE, Hon. Jean C.,** P.C., M.P., LL.L.; politician; b. Basin, Iles de la Madeleine, Qué. 7 May 1956; s. Raymond and Lucie (Cormier) L.; e. Elem. and High Schs. Iles de la Madeleine; CEGEP (legal specialty) Granby, Qué.; Univ. of Ottawa LL.L. 1979; children: Marie-Anne, Jean-Michel; Parliamentary Leader, Bloc Québécois 1990; Special Asst. to Min. for Consumer & Corporate Affairs 1974–76; Extve. Asst. to Min. of State for Urban Affairs 1976–78; el. to H. of C. for Shefford g.e. 1979, re-el. since; mem. Special Jt. Ctte. H. of C. and Senate on Canadian Constitution 1980–81; Parlty. Sec. to Sec. of State and Min. of State for Fitness & Amateur Sports 1981; Parlty. Sec. to Dep. Prime Min. and Sec. of State for External Affairs 1982; Min. of State for Youth and Min. of State for Fitness & Amateur Sports 1984; Official Opposition Critic for Internat. Trade 1984; Official Opposition Critic for Youth and Assoc. Critic for Employment & Immigration 1985; Official Opposition Critic for Rural & Community Development 1985–88; Official Opposition Critic for Federal-Provincial Relations 1988–90; Resigned from Liberal Party to become independent, then joined Bloc Québécois and became its Parliamentary Leader and Justice Critic 1990– ; Pres. Youth Ctte. Qué. Lib. Party and Lib. Party of Can. (Shefford) 1973; Sec. Lib. Caucus of Qué. H. of C. 1980–81; mem. Policy Steering Ctte. 1985; mem. Assn. 'Granby et ses villes jumelées'; Granby C. of C.; Granby Office of Tourism; R. Catholic; recreations: skiing, tennis; Club; Aramis; Home: Granby, Qué.; Office: 117 East Block, House of Commons, Ottawa, Ont. K1A 0A6.

**La PIERRE, Laurier L.,** M.A., Ph.D., LL.D.; university professor; b. Lac Mégantic, Que., 21 Nov. 1929; s. Lionel and Aldora (Bilodeau) L.; e. Univ. of Toronto, B.A. 1955, M.A. 1957, Ph.D. 1962: LL.D., Prince Edward Island 1970; m. Paula, d. late C.H.A. Armstrong, Toronto, 28 May 1960; children: Dominic, Thomas; MAX BELL PROFESSOR, SCHOOL OF JOURNALISM, UNIV. OF REGINA; Assoc. Prof. of Hist., McGill Univ., 1965; Dir., French Can. Studies Programme, McGill; Pres., Comn. of Inquiry into Educ. of Young Children in Ont.; Dir. of the collection. 'La Saberdache Québécoise'; Lectr., Univ. of Western Ont., 1960–62; Asst. Prof., Loyola Coll., 1962–63; McGill Univ., 1963–64; T.V. and Radio Commentator; served as Co-Host, 'This Hour Has Seven Days'; Host, C.B.C. television show 'La Pierre'; Moderator, Radio-Québec television series 'En se racontant l'histoire d'ici'; Commentator and Programmer for C.K.V.U., Vancouver; has written numerous articles for mags. & learned journs.; mem., Candn. Hist. Assn.; Candn. Assn. Univ. Teachers; Office: Regina, Sask. S4S 0A2.

**LA PIERRE, Tom,** A.O.C.A.; R.C.A.; artist; educator; b. Toronto, Ont. 28 Dec. 1930; s. Romeo Paul and Catherine (White) La P.; e. Ont. Coll. of Art 1955; Ecole des Beaux-Arts Paris; La Grande Chaumierr Paris; Atelier 17 Paris; m. Patricia Clemes 27 Sept. 1958; children: Armand, David; Art Instr. Ont. Coll. of Art; rep. nat. and internat. exhns. incl. USA, France, Italy, Japan, S. Am., China; recipient various arts awards, scholarships, Can. Council grants; mem. Candn. Soc. Painters in Watercolour; Royal Candn. Academy; recreations: music, film, literature, theatre, nature; Address: 2067 Proverbs Dr., Mississauga, Ont. L4X 1G3.

**LAPIERRE, Yvon D.,** B.A., M.D., M.Sc., F.R.C.P.(C), F.A.P.A., F.A.C.P.; psychiatrist; educator; b. Bonnyville, Alta. 19 Oct. 1936; s. Existe Roval and Cecile Anne (Bellemare) L.; e. Fort Kent Sch., Coll. St. Jean, Edmonton; Univ. of Ottawa, B.A. 1957, M.D. 1961; Univ. of Montréal, M.Sc. 1970, Dip. in Psychiatry 1970; m. Nicole d. Roland and Jeanne Beauregard 27 Aug. 1960; children: Michel, Denis, Stephan; CHRMN. OF PSYCHIATRY, UNIV. OF OTTAWA & PSYCHIATRIST-IN-CHIEF, ROYAL OTTAWA HOSP. 1986– ; Dir. Gen., Inst. of Mental Health Rsch. 1990– ; Dir. of Rsch., present Hosp. 1978–87, Dir. Outpatient Services, 1980–85; Prof. of Psychiatry & Pharmacol. Univ. of Ottawa 1981– , Chrmn. of Psychiatry 1986; Psych.-in-Chief, Royal Ottawa Hosp. 1986– ; gen. med. practice 1962–65; Sci. Dir. Pierre Janet Hosp. Hull, Qué. 1970–76; Dir. Psychopharmacol. Ottawa Gen. Hosp. 1976–79; Lectr. Univ. of Ottawa 1970, Asst. Prof. 1973, Assoc. Prof. 1976; cons. to Ottawa Civic, St. Vincent's and Ottawa Gen. Hosps., Nat. Defence Med. Centre, Children's Hosp. E. Ont., Elizabeth Bruyere Health Centre, Ottawa; Pierre Janet Hosp. Hull; Brockville Psychiatric Hosp.; Conseil Scientifique Assn. pour la methodologie de la recherche en psychiatrie, Marseilles; Ind. on Psychiatric Rsch.; recipient Tait MacKenzie Medal 1980; Medal of Honour, Candn. Call. of Neuropsychopharmacology 1988; service Candn. Army, rank Maj.; author and co-author 19 Continuing Med. Edn. audio-visual tapes, sci. reviews & editorials, over 200 papers & presentations incl. book chapters & monographs; mem. various ed. bds.; mem. Candn. Med. Assn.; Ont. Med. Assn.; Candn. Psychiatric Assn.; Assn. des Medicins de Langue Française de Can.; Soc. Biol. Psychiatry; Coll. Internationale Neuropsychopharmacologicum; Assn. Methodol. & Documentation in Psychiatry (Sec. Eng. Speaking Sect.); Candn. Coll. Neuropsychopharmacology; Ottawa Neurosci. Soc.; Soc. Clin. Pharmacol. & Therapeutics; recreations: skiing, golf, Candn. hist.; Clubs: Cercle Universitaire Ottawa; Home: 2298 Bowman Rd., Ottawa, Ont. K1H 6V6; Office: 1145 Carling Ave., Ottawa, Ont. K1Z 7K4.

**LAPIERRE-ADAMCYK, Evelyne,** B.Sc., M.A.; professeur; née. St-Pie, Qué. 15 fév. 1940; f. Ovélis and Marguerite (Plouffe) L.; é. Univ. de Montréal B.Sc. 1966, M.A. 1969; ép. Ronald John f. John and Stella Adamcyk 10 juillet 1971; enfants: Martin-Blaise, David-Jan; PROF., DEP. DE DEMOGRAPHIE, UNIVERSITE DE MONTREAL 1985– ; Research, Population Council (N.Y.) 1969–71; Statistics Canada 1971–73; Univ. de Montréal 1973– ; Dir., Groupe de rech. sur la démographie québécoise 1982–89; Chair, Dep. de démographie 1989–93; mem., Nat. Statistics Council 1991– ; Conseil de la langue française 1991– ; mem., Assn. des démographes du Qué.; Population Assn. of Am.; Union for Scientific Study of Population; co-auteur: 'La fin de la revanche des burceaux' 1973, 'Les Enfants qu'on n'a plus au Québec' 1981, 'Family and Childbearing in Canada' 1993; rés.: 928 ave Antonine-Maillet, Outremont, Qué. H2V 2Y9; bureau: C.P. 6128, Montréal, Qué. H3C 3J7.

**LAPLANTE, André;** concert pianist; b. Rimouski, Que. 12 Nov. 1949; s. Roger and Anne-Marie (Demers) L.; e. Coll. Ste-Marie and Coll. Notre-Dame, Montreal 1969; Vincent D'Indy Ecole de Musique, Montreal 1969; Juilliard Sch. of Music, N.Y. 1976–79; m. France d. Henri de Guise, Montreal, Que. 21 Aug. 1976; has toured North America, Europe, Orient, Australia, Russia as concert pianist in recital & with major symphony orchestras; performed Carnegie Hall 1978, 1980; rec'd Silver Medal Tchaikowsky Internat. Competition 1978 (1st Candn. to win prize) Moscow; CBC Record of Grieg Piano Concerto with Vancouver Symphony Orchestra; named Candn. Interpreter of Yr., Candn. Music Council 1978; Distinguished Visiting Prof., Ohio State Univ. 1987–88; Judge, Internat. Piano Competitions; R. Catholic; recreations: swimming, photography, cinema; Home: 155 W. 68th St., #1017, New York City, N.Y. 10023.

**LaPOINTE, Kirk Bradley;** journalist; b. Toronto, Ont. 12 Dec. 1957; s. Lydia L.; e. Ryerson Polytech. Inst., journalism 1981; m. Denise d. Walter and Simone Rudnicki 26 Nov. 1983; children: Vanessa, Michael; OTTAWA BUREAU CHIEF, THE CANADIAN PRESS 1991– ; 'Toronto Star' 1979–80; 'The Globe and Mail' 1981; Gen. Assignment Reporter (Toronto), Canadian Press 1981; Reporter, spec. in communications (Ottawa) 1982; Reporter on broadcasting (Toronto) 1984; Lifestyles Editor 1986; Ottawa News Editor 1987; Host, 'Canada Connection,' CBC Newsworld 1989; 'Meech Lake Review'; 'Week's End' 1990– ; recreations: running, hockey; Home: 21 Harmer Ave. N., Ottawa, Ont. K1Y 0T8; Office: Box 595, Stn. B, 1 O'Connor St., Ottawa, Ont. K1P 5P7.

**LAPOINTE, Marc C.,** Q.C., M.C.L.; labour relations lawyer; b. Montreal, Que. 18 Apr. 1923; s. Edouard Charles and Antoinette (Trudeau) L.; e. St. Vincent Ferrier Pub. Sch. and Coll. André-Grasset; Univ. of Montréal B.A.; McGill Univ. B.C.L., M.C.L. (Labour Relations); Inst. of world Affairs, Cert. in Internat. Law; children: Luc, Judith, Marc Jr., Anne; Chrmn., Canada Labour Relations Bd. 1973–89; called to Bar of Qué. 1947; cr. Q.C. 1964; mem. firm Desaulniers, Lapointe, Lussier 1948; Sr. of law firm Lapointe, O'Brien & Associates 1948–51 and of Lapointe and Levesque & Associates 1951–73; specialist, lectr. (McGill Law Faculty 12 yrs.) and speaker on labour law, leg. and relations; author numerous articles various law reviews; mem. Internat. Bar Assn.; Candn. Bar Assn.; R. Catholic; recreations: boating, tennis, golfing, painting; Address: 1030 Chemin Rauin, St. Lazare, Que. J0P 1V0.

**LAPONCE, Jean Antoine,** Ph.D.; educator; b. Decize, France 4 Nov. 1925; s. Fernand and Fernande (Ramond) L.; e. Institut d'Etudes Politiques Paris, Dipl. 1947; Univ. of Cal. Los Angeles Ph.D. 1956; m. Iza d. Stanislaw Fiszhaut 7 Apl. 1971; children: Jean-Antoine, Marc, Patrice (from 1st marriage), Danielle (from 2nd marriage); PROF. OF POL. SCIENCE, UNIV. OF B.C. and UNIV. OF OTTAWA; author 'The Protection of Minorities' 1961; 'The Government of France Under the Fifth Republic' 1962; 'People vs Politics' 1970; 'Left and Right' 1981; 'Langue et Territoire' 1984 (English edition: 'Languages and their Territories' 1987); and articles on comparative politics, ethnic relations; mem. Candn. Pol. Science Assn. (Pres. 1972–73); Internat. Pol. Science Assn. (Pres. 1973–76); Royal Soc. Can.; Acad. of Humanities and Soc. Sciences (Pres. 1988–91); Office: Dept. of Pol. Sci., U.B.C., Vancouver, B.C. V6T 1W5 and Inst. of Interethnic Relations, Dept. of Pol. Sci., Univ. of Ottawa, Ottawa, Ont. K1N 6N5.

**LAPORTE, Jean-Marc S.J.,** B.A., M.A., D.esSc.Rel.; university professor; b. Edmundston, N.B. 5 July 1937; s. J. Murillo and Laurente (Levesque) L.; e. Loyola Coll. B.A. 1957; Regis Coll. M.A. 1958; Univ. de Strasbourg D.esSc.Rel. 1971; DIRECTOR, TORONTO SCHOOL OF THEOLOGY 1992– ; Professor of Theology, Regis College Toronto 1971– ; Pres. 1975–82; author: 'Patience and Power: Grace for the First World' 1988; Home: 94 Isabella, Toronto, Ont. M4Y 1N4; Office: 47 Queen's Park Cres. E., Toronto, Ont. M5S 2C3.

**LAPP, Philip Alexander,** Sc.D., LL.D., P.Eng. F.R.S.C.; consulting engineer; b. Toronto, Ont. 12 May 1928; s. John Stanley and Victoria (Cotton) L.; e. Malvern Coll. Inst.; Univ. of Toronto B.A.Sc. 1950; Mass. Inst. of Technol. S.M. 1951, Sc.D. 1955; McMaster Univ. LL.D. 1987; m. Caulyne Moiree d. Dr. Rowland and Marjorie Byers 6 Sept. 1952; children: David John, Douglas Foster, Aimee Moiree; PRESIDENT, PHILIP A. LAPP LTD. 1970– ; Chrmn., York Univ. Development Corp. 1985– ; Inst. for Space & Terrestrial Sciences, York Univ. 1988– ; Dir., Spar Aerospace Ltd.; Crowborough Investments Ltd.; MacDonald Dettwiler Associates; General Technology Systems (UK); Gov., York Univ.; Dir., Frontiers Found.; Ortech International; Kenneth Molson Found.; Rsch. Asst. Mass. Inst. Technol. 1950, Instr. 1952, Rsch. Assoc. 1954; Systems Eng. De Havilland Aircraft of Canada Ltd. 1954, Project Eng. 1956, Chief Eng. 1960, Dir. Tech. Operations 1965; Sr. Vice Pres. and Dir. Spar Aerospace Products Ltd. 1967–69; Cons. to Comte. of Pres. Univs. Ont., Dir. Study Eng. Edn. Ont. 1969–70; mem. Sci. Secretariat Studies Upper Atmosphere & Space Rsch. Can.; Candn. Accreditation Bd. 1971–75; Chrmn. NRC Adv. Bd. Sci. & Technol. Info. 1972–77; Task Force on Surveillance Satellites 1976; Task Force on Nat. Surveying and Mapping 1978; Fed. Interdept'al Study Group Ocean Info. Systems 1978–79; Chrmn., Minister's Ocean Group, Dept. of Fisheries and Oceans 1986–87; Mem., Nat. Marine Counc. 1988– ; recipient Harvey Aggett Meml. Scholarship 1948; Goodyear Fellowship M.I.T. 1951; Centennial Medal 1967; Univ. of Toronto Engn. Alumni Medal 1984; Companion of the Order of Sons of Martha 1984; Toronto Beach's Honour Roll 1989; Fellow, Ryerson Polytech. Inst. 1985; CASI C.D. Howe Award 1987; author various papers, reports, studies; Pres., Candn. Counc. of Prof. Engrs. 1987–88; Candn. Acad. of Engr. 1988–89; Hon. mem. Engn. Inst. Can.; mem. Assn. Prof. Engrs. Prov. Ont. (Past Pres., Councillor 1972–84; Pres. 1982–83); Fellow, Royal Soc. of Can. 1982; Fellow, Candn. Acad. of Engr. 1987; Fellow, Candn. Aeronautics & Space Inst. (Pres. 1967–68); Am. Inst. Aeronautics & Astronautics; Inst. Elec. & Electronics Engs.; Candn. Rsch. Mgmt. Assn.; Gamma Alpha Rho; Sigma Xi; recreations: scuba diving, skiing; Home: 128 Elgin St., Thornhill, Ont. L3T 1W6.

**LARAMÉE, Gilles,** B.Comm.; chartered accountant; b. Verdun, Que. 17 Jan. 1961; s. Roland and Jeanne (Senécal) L.; e. Ecole des Hautes Etudes Commercials B.Comm. 1983; m. Julie d. André Rouisse 10 Dec. 1988; children: Marie, Mathieu; TREASURER, SNC-LAVALIN GROUP INC. 1991– ; Senior Auditor, Clarkson Gordon 1984–86; Senior Accountant, The SNC Group Inc. 1986; Asst. Controller 1987; Asst. Treas. 1988; Mem., Candn. Inst. of C.A.s; Treasury Management Assn. of Montreal; Bd. of Honour for the 1983 C.A. exam; Home: 268 d'Angouleme, Boucherville, Que. J4B 7V3; Office: 2 Place Felix-Martin, Montreal, Que. H2Z 1Z3.

**LARGE, Earl Wilbert,** C.A.; chartered accountant; b. Toronto, Ont. 20 June 1936; s. Gerald Leigh and Marion (Pickering) L.; e. Univ. of Victoria Sr. Matric. 1957; m. Alice E. James; children: Christine, Philip, Kimberly; CHAIRMAN AND FOUNDER, DATATECH SYSTEMS LTD. 1963– a computer field engineering firm, listed TSE; Dir., Equi-Ventures Ltd., listed TSE; Dir., various private companies of diverse nature; articled with Bailey, Monteith and Holmes 1958–62; formed Large & Co. Chartered Accts. 1962; Christian; accepted at Sch. of Fine Arts, Univ. of Victoria 1983; recreations: golf, bridge, fitness, fishing; Home: 4060 Granville Ave., Victoria, B.C.; Office: P.O. Box 30036, Saanich Centre, Postal Outlet, Victoria, B.C. V8X 5E1.

**LARGE, Hon. Frederic Alfred;** retired judge; b. Bradalbane, P.E.I. 7 Dec. 1913; s. Ernest Alfred and Georgie Eliza (Leard) L.; e. Mount Allison Acad.; Prince of Wales Coll.; m. Mildred Grace d. late Chester Morgan Cox 7 Nov. 1939; children: David Frederic Holland, M.D., Susan Ruth (Mrs. W.J. Gregory), Donald Philip, Q.C.; retired Judge, Supreme Court of P.E.I., Court Martial Appeal Court; called to Bar of P.E.I. 1937; cr. K.C. 1944; practiced law Charlottetown 1937–39 and 1944–75; Crown Prosecutor 1937–39; Partner, Large & Large 1973–75; Atty. Gen. of P.E.I. 1944–49; Min. of Educ. P.E.I. 1949–53; served with RCNVR 1937–39, rank Lt., R.C.N. 1939–44 overseas and at sea in H.M.C.S. Niagara, also bases Saint John, Halifax and Gaspé, rank Lt. Commdr.; Scoutmaster 1954–60, Prov. Comnr. 1960–63, Boy Scouts Assoc.; Past Pres. Island Hospice Assn.; Past Pres., Law Soc. P.E.I.; P.E.I. Lib. Assn.; Past Prov. Vice Pres. Candn. Bar Assn.; mem. Royal Commonwealth Soc.; United Church; mem., Bd. of Trustees, Queen Elizabeth Hosp. Found. 1986–92; Patron, Confederation Centre of the Arts; recreation: travel; Home: 205 North River Rd., Charlottetown, P.E.I. C1A 3L4.

**LARIVIERE, Louis;** business executive; b. La Sarre, Que. 16 June 1935; s. Joseph and Eva (Gagnon) L.; e. St. Alexandre College; m. Rose-Marie d. Roy Egide 3 Aug. 1961; children: Lucie, Brigitte, Serge; CHAIRMAN, GROUP SANI MOBILE INC.; 27 years with Sani Mobile Inc. and Groupe Sani Mobile Inc.; recreations: golf; clubs: Levis; Office: 350, 6500 blvd. Rive-Sud, Lévis, Que. G6V 7M5.

**LARKIN, David J.,** B.A.; business executive; b. Boston, Mass. 11 Dec. 1939; e. Harvard Univ. B.A. 1961; m. Robin; CHAIRMAN, PRESIDENT & CHIEF EXTVE. OFFR., HONEYWELL LIMITED 1992– ; served four years in U.S. Navy as Naval Aviation Offr.; Sales Rep., Commercial Div., Honeywell Inc. 1965; Br. Serv. Mgr. 1971; Br. Commercial Mgr. 1975; Eastern Regional Dir., Elmsford, N.Y. 1976; Field Dir. Minneapolis 1981; Vice-Pres. of Sales & Mktg. 1984; Vice-Pres. & Gen. Mgr., Commercial Div. 1985; Vice-Pres. & Group Extve., Commercial Bldgs. Group 1986; Bd. of Gov., Nat. Electrical Mfrs. Assn. (NEMA); Mem., Bd. of Trade of Metro. Toronto; Business Council on Nat. Issues; Office: 155 Gordon Baker Rd., North York, Ont. M2H 3N7.

**LARKIN, Leo Paul, Jr.,** A.B., LL.B.; attorney; b. Ithaca, N.Y. 19 June 1925; s. Leo Paul and Juanita (Wade) L.; e. Cornell Univ. A.B. 1948, LL.B. 1950; ASSOC. ATTY., PARTNER & SR. COUNSEL, ROGERS & WELLS and predecessor firms 1950– ; Dir., Indal Ltd. 1979–88; served with U.S. Army Europe 1943–45; mem. Bd. Eds. 'Cornell Law Quarterly'; mem. Am. and N.Y. State Bar Assns.; Assn. Bar City N.Y.; Fed. Bar Council; Delta Phi (Trustee Educ. Fund); Phi Beta Kappa; Phi Kappa Phi; Theta Delta Phi; R. Catholic; recreations: theatre, music, magic; Clubs: University, Sky (N.Y.); Home: 200 E. 66th St., New York, N.Y. 10021; Office: 200 Park Ave., Suite 5200, New York, N.Y. 10166.

**LARKIN, Peter Anthony,** M.A., D.Phil., LL.D., D.Sc., F.R.S.C.; biologist; university professor; b. Auckland, N.Z., 11 Dec. 1924; s. Frank Wilfrid and Caroline Jane (Knapp) L.; e. Balfour Tech. Sch., Regina, Sask.; Regina Coll., 1941–42; Univ. of Sask., B.A., M.A. 1946 (Gov. Gen.'s Gold Medal); Oxford Univ., Exeter Coll. (Rhodes Scholar), D.Phil. 1948; m. Lois Boughton, d. late John G. Rayner, Saskatoon, Sask., 21 Aug. 1948; five d. Barbara, Kathleen, Patricia, Margaret, Gillian; UNIVERSITY PROFESSOR, UNIV. OF B.C. 1988–89; Professor Emeritus 1990– ; Dir., B.C. Packers Ltd.; N.W. Fisheries Investigation, Fisheries Research Bd. of Can., 1944–46; Chief Fisheries Biol., B.C. Game Comn., 1948–55; joined present Univ. as Asst. Prof. 1948–55; Prof. 1959–63 and since 1966; Dean, Fac. of Grad. Studies, 1975–83 and Prof., since 1966; Assoc. Vice Pres. Research, Univ. of B.C. 1980–86, Vice Pres., Research 1986–88; Dir., Inst. of Fisheries at Univ., 1955–63 and 1966–69; Dir., Biol. Stn., Fisheries Research Bd., Nanaimo, 1963–66; el. mem. of Bd. of Dir., B.C. Packers Ltd, 1980; Head Dept. of Zool., U.B.C., 1972–75 Hon. Life Gov., Vancouver Pub. Aquarium; mem. Science Council of Can. 1971–77; Senate UBC 1966–84; mem. Can. Com. Int. Biological Program, (B.C. co-chrmn 1967–73 Subcomte CT, 1967–73; Chrmn P.M. Subcomte 1968–73); Fish. Res. Bd. Can. 1972–79; Extve. Bd. 1972–79; Nat'l Chrmn. Candn. Comte. for Man & the Biosphere 1972–74; int. Centre for Living Aquatic Resource Mgmt. 1977–93; Candn. Comte. for Freshwater Fisheries Research; Pres. Candn. Assn. Univ. Research Administrators 1979–80; mem. Nat'l. Research Council of Can. 1980–84; Gov., Internat. Development Research Centre 1984–92; mem. Natural Sci. & Eng. Research Counc. of Can. 1987–93; Pres., Rawson Acad. of Aquatic Sciences 1988–91; Pres., B.C. Conservation Found. 1988–90; mem. Bd. of Trustees, Internat. Centre for Living, Aquatic Resource Mgmt. 1989–90, Chrmn. 1990–93; mem. Interim Governing Council, Univ. of Northern B.C.; rec'd Candn. Centennial Medal 1967; Master Teacher Award UBC 1970; Nuffield Foundation Fellow 1961–62; Queen's Jubilee Medal, 1977; Fry Medal, Can. Soc. of Zoo. 1978; Can. Sports Fishing Inst. Award 1979; Award of Excellence, Am. Fisheries Soc. 1983; Award for Excellence, Rawson Academy of Aquatic Sciences 1985; Distinguished Canadian Biologist Award, Canadian Council of University Biology (Chrmn. 1991); Carl R. Sullivan Conservation Award, Am. Fisheries Soc. 1993; author, co-author and ed. of numerous publs.; mem., Internat. Limnol. Assn.; Am. Fisheries Soc.; Candn. Assn. Rhodes Scholars.; Pacific Fish Biol. Assn.; Royal Soc. Can. 1965; Candn. Soc. Wildlife & Fisheries Biols. (Vice. Pres. 1961); Candn. Soc. Zools. (Pres. 1972); Home: 4166 Crown Cres., Vancouver, B.C. V6R 2A9.

**LAROCHE, Gilles,** B.A.Sc.; communications executive; b. Coaticook, Que. 17 Aug. 1937; s. Hervé and Edouardina (Cayer) L.; e. Collège Saint-André; Montréal Polytech. Sch. B.A.Sc. 1963; m. Marie Claire Pettigrew 11 April 1966; children: Claude, Caroline, Frédéric, Valérie; PRESIDENT & CHIEF EXECUTIVE OFFICER, QUEBEC TELEPHONE 1992– ; var. engineering & mngt. positions, Québec-Télephone 1963–80; Vice-Pres., Business Devel. 1981; Network Eng. & Construction 1986; Customer Serv. 1987; Pres. & C.O.O. 1991; Pres. & C.E.O. 1992; Mem., Eng. Inst. of Can. 1963; Ordre des ingén. du Qué. 1963; Adv. Ctte., CFLP-CIKI; Dir. & Mem., Extve. Ctte., Nat. Optics Inst.; Dir. & Mem., Audit Ctte., Assem. des Gouv. de l'Univ. du Qué.; Dir., CIREM; Fond. Univ. du Qué. in Rimouski; recreations: golf, skiing, reading, music; Home: 476, Pl. Mgr-Courchesne, Rimouski, Que. G5L 5P1; Office: 6, rue Jules-A-Brillant, Rimouski, Que. G5L 7E4.

**LA ROCHELLE, Pierre Louis,** Ph.D., F.E.I.C., F.R.S.C.; university professor; b. Saint-Michel, Qué. 20 Aug. 1928; s. Emile Joseph and Juliette Marie (Coulombe) L.; e. Sém. de Qué., B.A. 1950; Univ. Laval, B.Sc. 1954, M.Sc. 1956; Univ. of London, Ph.D. 1960; m. Rachel d. Armand Bédard 11 July 1959; children: Judith, Sophie, Anne; PROF., CIVIL ENGR. DEPT., LAVAL UNIV. 1968– ; Asst. then Assoc. Prof., Civil Engr. Dept., Laval Univ. 1960–68; Dept. Head 1963–67; Dir., Graduate Studies, Civil Engr. 1992– ; Pres., Ctte. on Landslides, Internat. Soc. for Soil Mechanics & Found. Engr. 1981–89; Co-founder, 'Canadian Geotechnical Journal'; Assn. Qué. pour le Transp. et les Routes; Cons., geotech. engr. & dam design & constrn.; stabilization of major slides; Past Mem., Cons. Bd., La Grande Project, Bay James; investigation of Saint-Jean Vianney flowslide; landslide specialist; Legget Award 1977; Candn. Geotech. Jour. Prize 1975; Queen Elizabeth's Jubilee Medal 1970; Hogentogler Award 1985; author and co-author of num. articles; recreations: sailing, skying, music; club: Qué. Yacht (Commodore 1982); Home: 2528 des Hospitalières, Sillery, Qué. G1T 1V7; Office: Dépt. Génie civil, Fac. des Sci. & Gén., Université Laval, Québec, Qué. G1K 7P4.

**LaROCQUE, Emma D.,** M.A.; educator; b. Big Bay, Alta. 2 Jan. 1949; e. Goshen Coll. Ind. B.A. 1973; Elkhart, Ind. M.A. (Religion/Peace Studies) 1976; Univ. of Man. M.A. (Candn. Hist.) 1980, Ph.D. (Aboriginal Hist./Literature) in progress; PROF. OF NATIVE STUDIES UNIV. OF MAN. 1976– ; Extve. Mem. Native Hist. Rsch. Project; Univ. of Man. researcher on Aboriginal women, Self-Govt. for Centre for Constitutional Studies, U of A 1993–94; Adv. Ctte. Mem., Justice Research Project on Indigenous Women, Aboriginal Justice Inquiry, Man. 1989; guest-teacher: Social Justice Inst., Newman Coll. Edmonton 1985; cons./lect. Keyano Coll. Fort McMurray, Alta. 1988; guest-teacher: Grant McEwan Community Coll. Edmonton 1989; presenter to Can. Human Rights Comm. Hearing on 'Women and Racial Discrimination,' Winnipeg 1989; recipient Rockefeller Scholarship 1974; Univ. of Man. Grad. Fellowship 1977 and Acad. Award for Rsch. 1983, Faculty of Arts Conference Grant 1986, Rsch./Study Leave Grant 1989; frequent guest lectr.: Native issues, human rights, educ., women and peace, etc.; author: 'Defeathering the Indian' 1975; 'Native Studies: A Selected Bibliography' 1975; 'Three Conventional Approaches to Native People in Society and Literature' 1984 (booklet); numerous articles, both popular and scholarly, on Native people (i.e. racism, identity, history, literature); poetry pub. in the following anthologies: 'Writing The Circle' eds. Jeanne Perreault and Sylvia Vance, with a preface by Emma LaRocque (Edmonton: NeWest Press 1990); 'Native Writers & Canadian Literature' ed. W.H. New (Canadian Literature No. 124-125, Spring/Summer 1990 - UBC Press); 'Our Bit of Truth' ed. Agnes Grant (Winnipeg: Pemmican Publ. 1990); an autobiographical essay 'Tides, Towns and Trains' in Living the Changes ed. Joan Turner (U. of Man. Press 1990); 'Racism/Sexism and its Effects on Native Women' in the Can. Human Rights Commission Report on Women and Racial Discrimination 1990; poetry in various periodicals; other works forthcoming 1990–91; Misc.: Plains Cree-Metis; recreations: reading, photography, music, speaking, walking; Office: Winnipeg, Man. R3T 2N2.

**LaROCQUE, Judith Anne,** CVO, B.A., M.A.; federal civil servant; b. Hawkesbury, Ont. 27 Sept. 1956; d. Olier and Elizabeth (Murray) L.; e. Carleton Univ. B.A. 1979, M.A. 1992; Notary public 1991– ; m. André Roland Lavoie 15 Mar. 1991; SEC. TO THE GOV. GEN. 1990– , Sec. Gen. Order of Can. and Order of Mil. Merit, Herald Chancellor of Can.; Adm. Asst. Internal Audit Directorate Pub. Service Comn. 1979; Writer/Researcher Prime Min.'s Office 1979; Special Asst. Office of Leader of Opposition 1980–82; Ctte. Clk. Cttes. and Private Legis. Br. H. of C. 1982–84; Legis. Asst. to Govt. House Leader 1984–85; Head of House Bus. Office of Govt. House Leader, Pres. Queen's Privy Council for Can. and Min. Responsible for Regulatory Affairs 1985–86; Extve. Asst. to Min. of Justice and Atty. Gen. of Can. 1986–89; Chief of Staff to Govt. Leader in Senate and Min. of State for Fed.-Prov. Relations 1989–90; Office: 1 Sussex Dr., Ottawa, Ont. K1A 0A1.

**LAROSE, Roger,** O.C. (1973), B.A., B.Pharm.; industrialist; b. Montreal, P.Q. 28 July 1910; s. Alfred Fervac & Anna (Contant) L.; e. Coll. Ste. Marie, Montreal; Univ. of Montreal, B.A., B.Pharm. and a degree in Social Pol. & Econ. Sciences; m. Julienne Bégin, 3 Aug. 1961; one d. (by prior m.) Louise; Vice Chrmn. and mem. Extve. Comte., Banque Canadienne Nationale 1969–80; Pres. of the OSM 1978; Pres. and Managing Dir., 1979–81; apptd. (first) Vice Rector (Adm.) Univ. de Montréal (1969–79); Pres., Candn. Pharm. Mfrs. Assn., 1961–62; joined Ciba Co. Ltd., 1936 where he successively held positions of Med. Rep., Production Mgr., Asst. Mgr., Mgr. of Pharm. Div.; el. a Vice-Pres., 1958; el. a Dir. 1967, Pres. 1968–73; Chrmn., Ciba-Geigy Canada Ltd. 1978–82; Dean, Faculty of Pharm., Univ. of Montreal, 1960–65; Governor, Canadian Bankers Institute 1973–80; appointed officer of Ord. of Can. 1973; Roman Catholic; Clubs: St. Denis; Home: Le Tournesol, Apt. 404, 205 Chemin de la Cote Ste. Catherine, Montreal, Que. H2V 2A9.

**LAROUCHE, Gérard-Ludger,** B.A., M.D., L.M.C.C., F.R.C.P.(C); physician; b. Cacouna, Que. 24 Jan. 1918; s. Ernest and Eva (Lamoureux) L.; e. Coll. Ste-Anne de la Pocatière (1932–40); Laval Univ., M.D., L.M.C.C. 1944; Certified Specialist in Internal Medicine and Cardiology; Asst. étranger des Hôpitaux de Paris (1947); F.R.C.P.(C) 1956; m. Luce (déc.), d. Euchariste Michel, 3 June 1950; retired Prof., Faculty of Med. Sherbrooke Univ. (Founder and Dean of the Faculty of Med. 1961–64); Hon. M.D., Univ. of Sherbrooke 1988; mem., Candn. Med. Assn.; L'Assn. des Méd. de Lang. Française du Can. (Councillor 1960–68); Nat. Geog. Soc.; Roman Catholic; Home: 430, rue Denonville, Sherbrooke, Que. J1J 2K2.

**LAROUCHE, Laurent,** B.A., L.Ph., M.Sc., Dr.rer.nat.; educator; b. Bagotville, Que. 7 Oct. 1924; s. Edmond and Marie (Bouchard) L.; e. Laval Univ. B.A. 1946; Jesuit Faculty of Philos. Montreal L.Ph. 1951; Univ. of Montreal B.Sc. 1954, M.Sc. 1955; Woodstock Coll. Md. (USA) L.Th. 1959; Univ. of Muenster (Germany) Dr.rer.nat. 1964; DIR. CENTRE FOR ADULT FAITH DEVELOPMENT AND SPIRITUALITY 1993– ; Prof. of Math. and Modern Logic 1964–69, Vice Pres. Acad. 1974–75 Laurentian Univ.; Vice Pres. Acad., mem. Bd. Govs. and Acad. Senate 1969–72 Univ. of Que. Chicoutimi; Pres., Univ. of Sudbury 1972–75, 1982–92; Pres. Brebeuf Coll. Montreal 1975–81; Consultant Xavier Bd. Educ. India 1981–82; mem. Adv. Council Franco-Ontarian Affairs, Min. of Colls. & Univs., Ont. 1975–76; mem. Bd. of Dirs. Que. Assn. Colls. 1975–81, Pres. 1977–81; mem. Coordinating Comte. Colls. and Univs. Prov. Que. 1978–81; mem. Bd. of Dirs. CADRE 1977–81; mem. Counc. for Franco-Ontarian Educ., Min. of Colls. & Univs., Ont. 1987–88; mem. Bd. of Dirs., Hebdo Le Voyageur, Sudbury, Ont. 1992– ; Asst. to the Pres., Univ. of Sudbury 1992–93; author various articles; Address: Univ. of Sudbury, 935 Ramsey Lake Rd., Sudbury, Ont. P3E 2C6.

**LARSEN, Clemm Erik Dahm,** C.D.; retired commission executive; b. Plaster Rock, N.B. 21 Dec. 1931; s. Karl Madvig and Mary Alice (Field) Dahm-Larsen; e. Sr. Matric. N.S.; Dip. Modern Landscaping; m. Susan d. Dr. Seton and Jean Richardson 10 Oct. 1987; children: Kristofer, Kathryn Warren, Diane Olivotto; Chrmn. N.S. Health Services & Insurance Commn. 1981–89, retired; served with RCAF/CAF 1949–76, Air Traffic Controller; Mgr. Annapolis Co. Exhn. 1977–80; Dir., N.S. Health Services & Insurance Commn. 1980–84; Dir. Lawrencetown Youth Arena 1973–83; Sec.-Coordinator Lawrencetown & Dist. Improvement Ctte. 1976–81; Comnr. Lawrencetown Village Comn. 1979–82 (Chrmn. 1980–81); Vice Chrmn. Lawrencetown Recreation Comn. 1981–83; Sec.-Treas. Annapolis Co. Woodlot Owners Assn. 1974–83; Volunteer Probation Offr. 1979–80; Commissioner, Supreme Court of Nova Scotia 1987– ; Freemason; P. Conservative; recreations: gardening, fishing, silviculture; Home: Wards Brook, R.R. 3, Parrsboro, N.S. B0M 1S0.

**LARSEN, Jenniece Beryl,** R.N., Ph.D.; university professor and administrator; b. Bassano, Alta. 9 Aug. 1942; d. Hans Aldstein and Mary Eliza (Grue) Sagstuen; e. Alta. Hosps., R.P.N. 1964; R.N. 1969; Univ. of Alta. B.Sc.N. 1970, M.Ed. 1976, Ph.D. 1984; divorced; children: Mawney Joan, Christopher; PROF. & DIR., SCH. OF NURSING, UNIV. OF MAN. 1985– ; Staff nurse in psych., med. & intensive care 1969–71; Nursing Instr., Sch. of Nursing, Edmonton Gen. Hosp. 1970–72; Instr., Dept. of Nurs., Grant McEwan Coll. 1973; Chairperson, Allied Health Dept. 1973–76; Asst. Prof., Fac. of Nurs., Univ. of Alta. 1978–82; Assoc. Prof. 1982–85; external reviewer, acad. prof. in nurs.; invited speaker, nat. workshops & confs. concerning women's leadership & mngt. issues; Bd. Mem., Man. Assn. of Reg. Nurses; Women's Health Rsch. Found., Inc.; Past Pres., Candn. Assn. of Univ. Sch. of Nurs.; Ctte. Mem., Univ. of Victoria; Health Sci. Ctr.; Misericordia Gen. Hosp.; St. Boniface Gen. Hosp.; Hon. Pres., Univ. of Man. Alumni Assn.; Cert. of Merit for distinguished serv. to Med., Internat. Who's Who in Med., 1st ed., UK 1986; Diss. of the Year Award, Univ. of Alta.; author of two book chapters and 28 publ. papers; co-editor: 'Canadian Nursing Faces the Future: Development and Change' 1988, 1992; Home: 749 Somerset Ave., Winnipeg, Man. R3C 3E1.

**LARSEN, Lars;** wildlife artist; b. Copenhagen, Denmark 19 April 1938; s. Henry Emile and Inger (Raben) L.; Candn. citizen 1962; e. Royal Danish Acad. of Fine Arts; Acad. for Free and Mercantile Arts; m. Michelle d. Jules and Juliette Harvey 1986; World Wildlife Art Auction Toronto 1985; S.E. Wildlife Art Expo Charleston S. Carolina 1986–93; Buckhorn Wildlife Art Fest.1990–93; Artwork on Browning Firearms 1990–93; comnd. artwork for Ducks Unlimited & Molson; Waterfowl Award Ducks Unlimited 1988; Feature Artist, Atlantic Waterfowl Celebration 1990; N.B. Wildlife Fed., First Conservation Print 1993; Retrospective Exbn. Moncton City Hall Gall.1994; Dir., Arts Prog., Ducks Unlimited Can.; Atlantic Salmon Fed.; Ont. Fed. of Anglers & Hunters; N.B. Arts Fair; Moncton Art Soc.; Subject, CBC Nat. Artist Profile, ATV 1992, The Conservator 1988 (artist profile), Wildlife Art News 1988; Mem., N.B. Wildlife FEd.; Fed. qué. du saumon Atlantique; Candn. Retriever Club; paintings reproduced as limited editions: The Natives 1986, Shediac Island 1987, Absent 1988, At Dusk 1988, Summer Deer 1989, Tantramar Marsh Magic 1990, Springtime Rendez-Vous 1991, Miramichi Prize1992, Moonlight Swim 1993, New Brunswick Legend 1993; recreations: outdoor activities; Home: R.R. 2, Harvey Bank, Albert, N.B. E0A 1A0.

**LARSEN, Col. Layne Raymond,** C.D., B.Eng., M.Eng.; Canadian Armed Forces; b. Asquith, Sask. 7 Sept. 1940; s. George Raymond and Marion Berniece (Turner) L.; e. Moose Jaw (Sask.) Central Coll. Inst.; Royal Roads Mil. Coll. 2 yr. dipl.; Royal Mil. Coll. B.Eng. (Elec.) 1962, M.Eng. 1967; Candn. Forces Coll. Toronto 1976–77; m. Patricia d. Roland and Doris Moore 2 June 1962; two d. Victoria, Catherine; DIR., MILITARY MANPOWER DISTRIBUTION, NDHQ 1991– ; comnd. RCAF 1962; 405 Sqdn. Greenwood, N.S. 1962–64, Instr./Engr. Maritime Radar Training Unit 1964–66; Guided Weapon Systems Analyst Nat. Defence HQ 1967–71; 404 Sqdn. Greenwood 1971–75; Staff Offr. Maritime Command HQ 1975–76; Dir. Defence Services Program Information System and Candn. mem. NATO Force Planning Data Base Comte. 1977–81; Dir. of Cadets, Royal Mil. Coll. of Canada 1981–83; Dir., Technical Intelligence Section, National Defense Headquarters 1983–88; Sr. Action Offr., Automated Command and Control Requirements, SHAPE 1988–91; author 'Improvement of Machine/Operator Interface on Operational Radars' 1967; 'The NATO Force Planning Data Base' 1980; several tech. articles and critiques in mil. tech. and tactical journs. as well as regular column in Candn. Stamp News; Past Vice Pres. Candn. Forces Philatelic Soc.; mem. Inst. Elect. & Electronics Engrs. Inc.; recreations: fishing, gunsmithing, philately; Address: 47 Elvaston Ave., Nepean, Ont. K2G 3X6.

**LARSON, Douglas William,** B.Sc., Ph.D.; university professor; b. Montreal, Que. 19 Mar. 1949; s. Eric Gordon and Joan Truman (Purdy) L.; e. Oakville Trafalgar H.S. 1968; McMaster Univ., B.Sc. 1972, Ph.D. 1975; m. Dawn d. Frances and Arthur Ewings 28 June 1975; children: Virginia Frances Chapman, Nathaniel Douglas Flanders, Nicholas William Kniffen; PROF., DEPT. OF BOTANY, UNIV. OF GUELPH 1990– ; worked on ecology of coastal tundra in extreme northern Ont. 1972–75; Asst. Prof., Univ. of Guelph 1981–; major rsch.: ecology of cliffs and ecology of coastal tundra in extreme northern Ont.; Discoverer of oldest trees and most virgin forest ecosystem in Eastern North America; Con., Johnson and Johnson; Tridel; Ont. Hydro; Min. of the Environment; Environment Canada Parks Service; Min. of Natural Resources; mem., Am. Assn. for Bryology & Lichenology; Candn. Botanical Assn.; British Ecological Soc.; Sigma Xi; Assoc. Ed. 'Canadian Journal of Botany' 1989– ; author/co-author numerous sci. papers and book chapters; Ralph Sherwood Award for Conservation; Province of Ont. Award as a 'Friend of the Niagara Escarpment'; recreations: woodworking; Home: 20 Floral Dr., Guelph, Ont. N1G 1R1; Office: Guelph, Ont. N1G 2W1.

**LARSON, Lorne H.,** B.A., P.Geol.; petroleum executive; b. Saskatoon, Sask. 25 Oct. 1935; e. Univ. of Sask., B.A. 1958, Bus. Adm. Dip. 1958; m. Patricia A. Todd 1958; children: Ronald K., Karen D.; PRES. AND CHIEF EXTVE. OFFR. ProGas Limited 1986– ; Geol. Shell Canada 1958–63; Asst. Mgr. Reserves, TransCanada PipeLines 1963–76; Mgr. Reservoir Geol. Canadian Hunter Exploration Ltd. 1976–78; Sr. Vice Pres. Pan-Alberta Gas Ltd. 1978–86; Dir., Rigec Energy Corp.; Dir., Calgary YMCA; Club: Rotary; Home: 3132 Conrad Dr. N.W., Calgary, Alta. T2L 1B4; Office: 4100 - 400 Third Ave. S.W., Calgary, Alta. T2P 4H2.

**LARUE, Monique,** P.H.D. (doctorat de 3ème cycle); college professor, writer; b. Montreal, Que. 3 April 1948; d. Jean-Paul and Thérèse (Cloutier) L.; e. Univ. of Montreal B.Ph. 1970; Univ. of Sorbonne, maîtrise en philosophie 1971; Univ. of Sorbonne, doctorat de 3ème cycle 1976; m. Norbert Robitaille; 3 children; Mem., U.N.E.Q.; author: 'La Cohorte fictive' 1979, 'Les Faux fuyants' 1982, 'Copies conformes' 1989 (Grand Prix du Livre de Montréal 1990), 'Promenades littéraires dans Montréal' 1989; Home: 764 Stuart, Outremont, Que. H2V 3H5.

**LARY, Nikita Michael,** M.A., D.Phil.; educator; b. Washington, D.C. 6 July 1940; s. Hal Buckner and Natalia Mikhailovna (Boborykina) L.; e. Internat. Sch. Geneva 1956; Haverford Coll. Pa., B.A. 1960; King's Coll. Cambridge, B.A. 1963; Univ. of Sussex, D.Phil 1969; m. Diana d. Arthur and Marie Lainson 1 Sept. 1965 (div. 1989); two d. Tatiana Marie, Anna Nathalie; ASSOC. PROF. OF HUMANITIES, YORK UNIV. 1969– ; author 'Dostoevsky and Dickens: A Study of Literary Influence' 1973; 'Dostoevsky and Soviet Film: Visions of Demonic Realism' 1986; transl. 'The Art of Conjecture' by Bertrand de Jouvenel 1967; recreations: canoeing, skiing; Home: 41 Geneva Ave., Toronto, Ont. M5A 2J9; Office: Rm. 208, Vanier College, York Univ., 4700 Keele St., North York, Ont. M3J 1P3.

**LaSALLE, Gérald,** B.A., M.D., D.H.A.; retired university officer; b. Que. 15 Dec. 1915; s. J. Pierre and Mabel (Ryan) L.; e. Univ. of Montreal, B.A.; Laval Univ., M.D.; Univ. of Toronto, D.H.A.; m. Jeanne, M.A. LL.L, d. J. P. Ménard, Oct. 1941; nine children; Retired Vice-Pres.-in-Charge of Med. Affairs, Univ. of Sherbrooke and Founder and Dir. Inst. Superieur d'Adm. Hop. de l'Univ. de Montréal; Dean, Sch. of Med., Univ. of Sherbrooke; Founder and first Extve. Dir., Que. Hosp. Assn.; Dir., Sandoz (Canada) Ltd.; mem. of Royal Commission on Hospital Problems (Favreau Commission); mem. of Hospital Committee of Ministry of Health, Que., 1956–60; Past Pres., Assn. of Univ. Programs in Hosp. Assn. and Candn. Council on Hosp. Accreditation; Past Registrar of Coll. of Phys. & Surgs. of Que.; Pres., Fourth Internat. Oceanography, St-Malo (France); Roman Catholic; Address: 10 Driveway, Ottawa, Ont. K2P 1C7.

**LASCHINGER, John Gordon,** B.Sc., M.B.A.; consultant; b. Montreal, Que. 1 Sept. 1942; s. Alan Gordon and Elsa Helen Clare (Young) L.; e. McGill Univ. B.Sc. 1964; Univ. of W. Ont. M.B.A. 1966; m. Carol d. Clayton and Katherine Weber 29 July 1967; children: Brett, Jan.; CONSULTANT, associated with GOLDFARB CONSULTANTS, NORTH YORK; with IBM Canada Ltd. 1966–73; Nat. Dir. Prog. Cons. Party of Can. 1973–78; Asst. Depy. Min./Acting Depy. Min. Govt. of Ont. 1981–83; Pres., Dale & Co. Ltd. 1984–86; mem. United Ch. of Can.; Prog. Conservative; recreations: tennis, cross-country skiing, politics; Clubs: Granite; Albany; Home: 50 Donwoods Dr., Toronto, Ont. M4N 2G4.

**LASH, Anthony Baldwin;** computer communications executive; b. Toronto, Ont. 1 Apr. 1939; s. Peter J.B. and Hazel Eileen (Clarkson) L.; e. Trinity Coll. Sch. 1957; m. Marion d. Charles and Joyce Marshall 26 Dec. 1960; children: Peter C.B., John E.A., David M.C.; PRESIDENT, LASH INTERNATIONAL INC. 1993– ; Programmer, IBM 1960–64; Lash Partnership (designed & marketed extve. gifts to Neiman, Marcus, Saks etc.) 1964–68; Founder & Chrmn., TIL Systems 1968–92; recreations: swimming, skiing; clubs: Craigleith Ski, Badminton & Racquet of Toronto; Address: 105 College View Ave., Toronto, Ont. M5P 1K2.

**LASHMAR, Reginald Alexander,** B.A.; real estate finance executive; b. London, England 15 Jan. 1935; s. William Alexander and Lilian Maud (Bray) L.; e. York Univ. B.A. 1976; m. Meredith d. Nelson and Edna Ross 11 Sept. 1959; children: William, John, Elizabeth; SENIOR VICE-PRESIDENT, ROYNAT INC. 1991– ; Real Estate Appraiser, Montreal Trust 1958; Manufacturer's Life 1961; General Mgr., Ont. Property Enterprises (Finan. Agents) 1963; Asst. Vice-Pres., Heller-Natofin 1971; Vice-Pres., Walter & Heller Finan. Corp. 1976; Vice-Pres., Bank of America Canada 1982; Vice-Pres., RoyNat Inc. 1987; recreations: skiing, sailing; clubs: Fitness Inst., Toronto Bd. of Trade; Home: 15 Apple Orchard Path, Thornhill, Ont. L3T 3B5; Office: P.O. Box 51, Suite 1040, 1 First Canadian Place, Toronto, Ont. M5X 1B1.

**LASSERRE, Jean-Paul,** M.B.A.; executive; b. Mirande, France 2 Feb. 1942; s. Henry and Renée (Bertin) L.; e. Ecole Centrale Paris, France P. Eng. 1965; Insead Fontainebleau, France M.B.A. 1977; Pres., Scor Reinsurance Co. 1987; Design Eng. S.O.M. Chicago 1965; Project Eng. Eurochemic Mol, Belgium 1966; Area Mgr. Middle E. OTH International Paris 1972; Internat. Contracts Mgr. CMP-EI Paris 1977; joined Scor Group 1981; Dir. & Vice Pres., Reinsurance Rsch. Council; Dir., Cercle Canadien; Dir., French Candn. C. of C.; Home: 1506, 130 Carlton St., Toronto, Ont. M5A 2K2.

**LASSONDE, Pierre,** B.A., B.Sc., P.Eng., M.B.A., C.F.A.; mining executive; b. St-Hyacinthe, Que. 17 April 1947; s. Raoul and Juliette (Lafond) L.; e. Univ. of Montreal B.A. 1967; Ecole Polytechnique Montreal B.Sc. 1971; Univ. of Utah M.B.A. 1973; Univ. of Virginia C.F.A. 1983; m. Claudette d. Raymond and Therese MacKay 1 Aug. 1970; children: Julie-Alexandra, Christian-Pierre; PRES., FRANCO-NEVADA MINING CORP. 1983– ; Chief Cost Engineer, Bechtel Corp. (San Francisco, CA) 1973–75; Senior Planning Analyst, Rio Algom Ltd. (Toronto) 1975–80; Sr. Vice-Pres., Beutel, Goodman & Co. 1980–91; Pres., Euro-Nevada Mining Corp. 1987– ; Chrmn., Redstone Resources 1988– ; Dir., Tiomin Resources Inc. 1992– ; Mem., Prospectors & Developers Assn.; Candn. Inst. of Mining & Metallurgy; Bd. Trustee, St. Clements School 1987–90; author: 'The Gold Book: The Complete Investment Guide to Precious Metals' 1990; recreations: skiing, travelling; Office: 2000, 20 Eglinton Ave. W., Toronto, Ont. M4T 1K8.

**LAST, John Murray,** M.D., D.P.H., FRCPC; educator; b. Tailem Bend, Australia 22 Sept. 1926; s. Raymond Jack and Vera Estelle (Judell) L.; e. St. Peter's Coll.; Univ. of Adelaide, M.B., B.S. 1949, M.D. 1967; Univ. of Sydney, D.P.H. 1960; m. Janet Margaret d. Walter and Elsie Wendelken 14 Feb. 1957; children: Rebecca, David, Jonathan; EMERITUS PROF. OF EPIDEMIOLOGY, UNIV. OF OTTAWA 1992– ; hosp. residencies and ship's doctor 1950–54; gen. med. practice Australia 1954–59; Visiting Fellow Med. Rsch. Council London, Eng. 1961–62; Lectr. Univ. of Sydney 1962–63; Asst. Prof. Univ. of Vt. 1964–65; Sr. Lectr. Univ. of Edinburgh 1965–69; Dept. Chrmn. present Univ. 1970–78, Sec. Sch. of Med. 1980–82; Visiting Prof. Mt. Sinai Sch. Med. New York 1978–79; Nat. Univ. of Singapore and Chinese Acad. Med. Sci's Beijing 1982; past and present mem. various adv. cttes. Fed., Ont. and US Govt. agencies; cons. and temporary adv. World Health Orgn. and other internat. agencies; recipient Tasmania Prize Royal

Aust. Coll. Gen. Pract. 1967; Distinguished Service Award, Am. Coll. Preventive Med., 1984; Sch. of Med. Award for Teaching Excellence 1988; Univ. of Ottawa Award of Excellence 1990; Special Recognition Award, Am. Coll. Preventive Med. 1991; M.D. (honoris causa) Uppsala, Sweden 1993; el. to Faculty of community Med., Royal Coll. Phys. (UK) as distinguished sci. 1984; author 'Public Health and Human Ecology' 1987; ed.-in-chief 'Maxcy-Rosenau Public Health and Preventive Medicine' 11th edn. 1980, 12th edn. 1985, 13th edn. 1991; ed. 'A Dictionary of Epidemiology' 1983, 2nd edn. 1988; assoc. ed. 'American Journal of Preventive Medicine' 1984–93; sci. ed. 'Canadian Journal of Public Health' 1981–91; Ed. Annals RCPSC 1990– ; approx. 200 sci. & review articles, chapters in 28 books; Found. Fellow, Am. Coll. Epidemiol.; Fellow, Am. Coll. Preventive Med. (Pres. 1987–89); FRACP; FFCM; Pres. Candn. Assn. Teachers Soc. Preventive Med. 1973–74; Pres. Assn. Teachers Preventive Med. (USA) 1983–84; Dir. Candn. Pub. Health Assn. 1981–91; Mem. Council, Internat. Epidemiological Assoc. 1987–1990; Candn. Vice-Pres., Am. Public Health Assn. 1988–89; Fellow or mem. numerous other profl. assns.; recreations: book collecting, travel, cycling, photography; Home: 685 Echo Dr., Ottawa, Ont. K1S 1P2; Office: 451 Smyth Rd., Ottawa, Ont. K1H 8M5.

**LASTMAN, His Worship Mayor Mel;** city mayor; b. Toronto, Ont. 9 Mar. 1933; m. Marilyn 15 Nov. 1953; children: Dale, Blayne; MAYOR, CITY OF NORTH YORK 1972– ; Hon. Chrmn. Children's Wish Found. of Ont.; Patron, Kidney Found. of Cand.; Toronto Rehabilitation Centre 1985–86; Candn. Acad. of Riding for the Disabled; The Puppet Centre; North York Philharmonic Choir; Sculptor's Soc. of Canada; Bd. of Dir., Candn. Soc. for Yad Vashem; mem. Candn. Red Cross, North York Br.; Assn. for Children with Learning Disabilities; Children's Services Ctte., North York Arts Counc., North York Inter-Agency Coun.; North York Symphony; North York Mental Health Counc.; North York Hydro Comn.; Asthma Soc. of Can.; Columbus Centre; Freedom From Fear Found.; Ont. Men's ORT, Candn. ORT Orgn.; Peanut Neighbourhood Youth Centre; Candn. Authors Assoc., North York Br.; Bob Rumball Cantre for the Deaf; African-Canadian Centre; Hungarian Helicon Ball; The Arthritis Soc. Campaign 1988; Run for Research; Stopnitzer Young Men's Benevolent Assn.; Alcohol and Drug Service Network of North York; Metro Metis and Aboriginal Assn.; Na'amat Can.; Hugh MacMillan Med. Centre; Leukemia Rsch. Fund; North York Chamber of Commerce; Solar Stage; Older Adult Centres' Assn.; St. John Ambulance; Kiwanis Club of North York; Joint Community Relations Ctte., Ont. Div., Candn. Jewish Congress; St. John's Rehabilitation Hosp.; Toronto Consolata Missionaries; Youth Assisting Youth; Ont. Div., Toronto Chapter of Dysautonomia Found.; Community Adv. Council, Central Region, League for Human Rights of B'nai Brith Can.; Juvenile Diabetes Found. Can., Toronto Chapter 1990 Raffle & Gala; Candn. Cancer Society (Willowdale Unit); Caritas Project; Arthritis Soc. (Hon. Campaign Chrmn.); Bd. Mem., The Bernard Betel Centre for Creative Living; Hon. Patron, Parents Against Drugs; York-Finch Gen. Hosp. Found.; North York YMCA; North York Arts Counc.; Volunteer Centre of Metro. Toronto; Skylight Theatre Fundraising Campaign; Boy Scouts of Can., Greater Toronto Reg.; North York Seniors Centre - Fund Raising Ctte.; Sunnybrook Med. Centre; North York Gen. Hosp.; Nat. Chamber Orch. of Can.; Renascent Fellowship/Renascent Found. Inc.; Italian Chamb. of Comm. Toronto; The Grotto Cerebral Palsy Found. Inc.; Stadium Corp. of Ont. Ltd., The Stadium Corp.; Variety Club of Ont. Tent 28; Pride of Israel Synagogue; Wilson Heights Lodge B'nai Brith; Clubs: Kinsmen; Rotary; Don Mills Jaycees; North York Civitan; Home: North York, Ont.; Office; 5100 Yonge St. North York, Ont. M2N 5V7.

**LATHAM, Leonard George,** F.I.I.C.; insurance executive; b. Hamilton, Ont. 13 Nov. 1931; s. George Harold and Vera (Hope) L.; e. Central and Westdale Coll. Inst. Hamilton; Ins. Inst. Can. grad.; m. Catherine d. Thomas McDonald 26 Feb. 1954; one d. Diane Louise; PRES., C.E.O. AND DIR., THE GENERAL ACCIDENT ASSURANCE CO. OF CANADA 1981– ; Pres., C.E.O. & Dir.: General Accident Holdings (Canada) Ltd.; General Accident Indemnity Co.; Prudasco Assurance Co.; joined Candn. Underwriters Assn. 1955; present Co. 1959, Property Mgr. Can. 1969, Mid-West Mgr. Calgary 1971, Asst. Gen. Mgr. 1973, Vice Pres. 1976, Sr. Vice Pres. 1977, Extve. Vice Pres. 1979; recreation: golf; Clubs: National; Bd. Trade Metrop. Toronto; Scarborough Golf & Country; Home: 208 Guildwood Parkway, Scarborough, Ont. M1E 1P7; Office: PO Box 410, 2600–2 First Canadian Pl., Toronto, Ont. M5X 1J1.

**LATIMER, E. John,** B.A., B.Ed.; real estate developer; b. Toronto, Ont. 12 July 1946; s. Edward Knox and Helen Louise (Drew) L.; e. Waterloo Lutheran Univ. B.A. 1968; Univ. of Toronto B.Ed. 1970; m. Donna d. Harry and Beverley Johnston 27 Aug. 1976; children: Alison, Kathryn; PRESIDENT, MONARCH DEVELOPMENT CORPORATION 1980– ; Land Rep., Marathon Realty Co. 1971–72; Gen. Mgr. Residential Devel., McNamara Corp. 1972–79; Dir., Urban Devel. Inst.; Chair, Ctte. of Stewards, Westminster United Church; recreations: skiing, golf, curling; clubs: Weston Golf & Country, Millcroft Golf; Home: 140 Church St., Weston, Ont. M9N 1N5; Office: 1201, 2025 Sheppard Ave. E., Willowdale, Ont. M2J 1V7.

**LATIMER, Elizabeth Joan,** B.Sc.N., M.D., CCFP, FCFP; palliative care physician, university professor and administrator; b. Hamilton, Ont. 26 Jan. 1945; d. Cecil Elsworth and Isabelle Myrtle (Magee) L.; e. Delta S.S.; McMaster Univ. B.Sc.N. 1967, M.D. 1979; College of Family Physicians Canada, Cert. 1981; m. Willem s. W. Kamphorst and S. Kamphorst v.d. Vis 10 May 1986; DIRECTOR, PALLIATIVE CARE PROGRAM, HAMILTON CIVIC HOSPTIALS; nurse, hospital & community centres 1967–76; residency in Family Medicine & a Clin. Scholars Appointment 1979–82; joined McMaster Univ. 1982; present rank: Assoc. Prof.; has studied & practiced in field of Palliative Care for 12 yrs and is one of Canada's pioneers in this field of care; activities incl. nat. leadership, health sciences edn., public awareness of needs of dying patients & direct patient care to patients & families; elected Fellow, Coll. of Family Physicians of Canada 1991; author/co-author of 47 medical articles, reports, newsletters & handbooks; Home: 162 Queen St. S., Hamilton, Ont. L8P 3S4; Office: c/o Henderson General Hospital, 711 Concession St., Hamilton, Ont. L8V 1C3.

**LATIMER, John Robert;** children's camp owner; headmaster; b. Toronto, Ont. 13 Oct. 1930; s. Robert Clarke and Zetta Louise (Greenwood) L.; e. Lawrence Park Coll. 1948; Victoria Coll. 1948–50; Acad. of Dramatic Arts 1950–52 (acting scholarship); m. Margaret E. d. Ina M. and John K. Macdonald 29 Apr. 1961; children: David, Jeffrey, Michael; OWNER, KILCOO CAMP 1956– ; HEADMASTER, ROYAL ST. GEORGE'S COLLEGE, Toronto 1988– ; News & Spec. Events Ed./Announcer, CJCS Stratford & CJOY Guleph 1953–54; Extve. Asst., Min. of Econ. & Devel., Govt. of Ont. 1961–62; Cons. on Agency Relns., Min. of Tourism & Recn. & Min. of Citizenship & Culture 1981–84; Ont. Depy. Chief of Protocol 1984–87; Acting Chief of Protocol 1987–88; Pres., Latimer, Macdonald & Assoc.; Dir., Kilcoo Camp 1956–81; Chrmn., St. George's Coll.; Candn. Camping Assn. 'Award of Honour'; Pres., Ont. Camping Assn. 1970–71 (Life Mem.); Candn. Camping Assn. 1971–75; Chrmn., Camp Awakening; Dir., Duke of Edinburgh Awards; Hon. Mem., Am. Camping Assn.; Chrmn., 1st Internat. Children's Camping Congress 1983; Dir. Operation Raleigh; Bd. of Dirs., Candn. Educational Standards Inst.; Comus Music Theatre; Hincks Treatment Centre; Conference of Independent Schools; Founding Chrmn., Ont. Rec. Canoeing Assn.; Pres., Soc. of Camp Directors; Past Offr. of many other orgns.; Public speaker; Anglican Ch. of Can.; author of several articles; co-author: 'Camp Counsellors Handbook' 1980, rev. ed. 1984; recipient, 125th Anniversary of the Confederation of Canada Medal, 1992; recreations: squash, tennis; Clubs: Toronto Cricket; Albany; Home: 24 York Valley Cres., Willowdale, Ont. M2P 1A7; Office: 120 Howland Ave., Toronto, Ont. M5R 3B5.

**LATNER, Steven David,** M.A.Oxon; real estate executive; b. Toronto, Ont. 28 June 1950; s. Albert J. and Florence Thelma (Weinstock) L.; e. Ridley Coll. 1969; Univ. of Pennsylvania B.A. 1973; Oxford Univ., St. Peter's Coll. M.A. 1976; m. Lynda d. Sydney C. Cooper 18 Sept. 1973; children: Lily, Jack, Yael, Phoebe; EXTVE. VICE PRES., GREENWIN DEVELOPMENTS 1977– ; Dir., Dynacare Health Group Inc.; Dir., University of Toronto Press; Office: 20 Eglinton Ave. W., Suite 1600, Toronto, Ont. M4R 2H1.

**LATOWSKY, Lawrence (Larry) Neal,** B.A.; retail executive; b. Toronto, Ont. 20 Aug. 1959; s. Norman and Marcia (Ruskin) L.; e. York Mills C.I. 1977; York Univ. B.A. 1981; m. Karen d. Roy and Jan Gale 13 Oct. 1991; one d.: Tova; SENIOR VICE-PRESIDENT, MERCHANDISING, BIWAY STORES 1992– ; var. retail positions ending as Asst. to Pres., Collegiate Sportsworld (Div. of Imasco Retail) 1981–83; Pres. & C.E.O., Drug World Limited 1983–90; Vice-Pres., Mktg., Biway Stores 1990–92; Mem., Internat. Mass Retail Assn.; Retail Advtg. Club; recreations: golf, tennis, theatre; clubs: Maple Downs Golf & Country, Mayfair Tennis; Home: 6 Shellaray Dr., Thornhill, Ont. L3T 4J6; Office: 115 Commander Blvd., Scarborough, Ont. M1S 3M7.

**LaTRAVERSE, Pierre V.,** D.E.C., B.C.L., LL.B.; attorney; b. Montreal, Que. 27 April 1961; s. Pierre P. and Monique (Jeanneau) L.; e. Coll. Jean-de-Brébeuf D.E.C. 1980; McGill Univ. B.C.L. 1983, LL.B. 1984; admitted to Quebec Bar 1985; to New York Bar 1991; PARTNER, CLARK AND PARTNERS 1981– ; Lectr., Civil Procedure and Evidence, McGill Univ. Law Sch. 1988, '89, '90, '91; Mem., Candn. Bar Assn.; L'Assn. du Jeune Barreau de Montréal; Bar of the Prov. of Que.; Defense Research & Trial Lawyers Assn. (U.S.A.); recreations: squash, swimming, tennis; clubs: MAAA; Hillside Tennis; Home: 3421 Drummond, #125, Montreal, Que. H3G 1X7; Office: 1245 Sherbrooke W., #2000, Montreal, Que. H3G 1G2.

**LATT, Richard Harry,** D.V.M; veterinarian; b. Montreal, Que. 29 March 1944; s. Bernard and Bernice (Solomon) L.; e. Ont. Veterinary Coll. Univ. of Guelph D.V.M. 1969; Johns Hopkins Univ. Sch. of Med. Postdoctoral Fellow Div. Lab. Animal Med. 1969–72, Dept. Pathol. 1972; Diplomate Am. Coll. Lab. Animal Med.; DIR., ANIMAL RESOURCES CENTRE, McGILL UNIV. since 1977, Prof. of Pathol. and Univ. Animal Care Offr.; Cons., Council on Accreditation, Am. Assn. for Accreditation of Lab. Animal Care, Rockville, MD; author 'Drug Dosages For Laboratory Animals' in 'Handbook of Laboratory Animal Science' 1976; mem. Candn. Assn. for Lab. Animal Science (Past Pres.); Candn. Assoc. for Lab. Animal Med. (Past Pres.); Am. Vet. Med. Assn.; Am. Assn. for Lab. Animal Science; Office: 3655 Drummond St., Montreal, Que. H3G 1Y6.

**LATULIPPE, Andréa,** B.Comm., F.C.A., adm.a.; b. Vallée-Jonction 17 March 1939; s. J.-Hector and Gabrielle (Diament) L.; e. Victoriaville Coll., Univ. of Sherbrooke 1954–57; B.Comm. 1961, Master in Acctng. 1962, C.A. 1962, F.C.A. 1991; m. Fleurette Doyon-Latulippe 20 May 1967; children: André, Anne, Alain; PRES. & GEN. MGR., LA SOLIDARITE 1987– ; C.A., Ruel, Roy, Moreau & Assoc. 1962–73; Latulippe, Renaud & Assoc. 1973–86; Raymond, Chabot, Martin, Paré 1986–87; Pres., L'Unique 1987– ; Unicour Inc. 1988– ; Dir., La Solidarité 1977– ; Bd. Mem., Hôp. St-Joseph de Beauceville; Mayor, Munic. du Lac Poulin 1975–79; Ville St-Joseph – Beauce 1976–80; recreations: walking, swimming, hunting; Home: 542, av. Robert-Cliche, St-Joseph de Beauce, Qué. G0S 2V0; Office: 925, chemin St-Louis, Québec, Qué. G1S 1C1.

**LAU, Catherine Yuk Ying,** B.Sc., M.Sc., Ph.D.; scientist / executive; b. Hong Kong 11 Feb. 1951; d. Tsong Yao and Su Wo (Yang) Lieu; e. Indiana Univ., B.Sc. 1972; Yale Univ., M.Phil. 1974, Ph.D. 1976; m. Sek Lun Yuen s. Cheong Ching and Shook Fong Y. 16 July 1977; children: Harold, Heidi Yuen; DIR., BIOL. RSCH. THE R.W. JOHNSON PHARM. RSCH. INST. 1989– ; studied early differentiation of B lymphocytes, Univ. of Toronto 1976–77; Supvr., Immunopharm., Ortho Pharm. (Can.) Ltd. 1977 (major rsch. immunoregulatory functions of thymic peptides in autoimmunity, cancer & aging; solved structure of a novel immunosuppressive molecule 1987); Project Mgr. 1984; Mgr., Biotechnol. Rsch. 1987; Asst. Prof., Univ. of Toronto; Phi Beta Kappa; Ortho High Tech. Achievement Award; PRI Discovery Award; Pinnacle Award for Excellence; author of sci. papers; Mem., Am. Assn. of Immunologists; Am. Assn. of Pharm.; club: The Yale Club of Toronto; Home: 1 Decourcy Court, Unionville, Ont. L6C 1B6; Office: 19 Green Belt Dr., Don Mills, Ont. M3C 1L9.

**LAU, Hang-Tong,** B.Sc., M.Sc., Ph.D.; scientist, educator; b. Hong Kong 7 Sept. 1952; s. Kwan-Wah and Oy-Mui (Wong) L.; e. The Chinese Univ. of Hong Kong B.Sc. 1976; McGill Univ. M.Sc. 1978, Ph.D. 1980; m. Helen Ying-Kit d. Chung-Mo and Pui-Ming Law 6 May 1984; children: Matthew, Lawrence, Tabia; RESEARCH SCIENTIST, BELL-NORTHERN RESEARCH & ADJUNCT PROF., COMPUTER SCI. DEPT., CONCORDIA UNIV. 1982– ; Asst. Prof., Comp. Sci. Dept., Vanderbilt Univ. 1980–82; Award of Excellence, Bell-Northern Research; Reviewer, 'Mathematical Reviews' & 'Zentralblatt für Mathematik'; author: 'Chinese Chess' 1985, 'Algorithms on Graphs' 1989; Home: 750 Abbott St., St. Laurent, Que. H4M 1X1; Office: BNR, 16 Place du Commerce, Verdun, Que. H3E 1H6.

**LAUBITZ, Christopher John,** B.B.A.; consultant; b. Toronto, Ont. 1 Feb. 1953; s. Matthew J. and Leone E. Deboer (Turney) L.; e. Univ. of Western Ont. B.B.A. (Hons.) 1976; m. Carol d. Frank and Carmen Hallett 29 June 1974; children: Carissa, Cayley; CONSULTING PARTNER, THE CALDWELL PARTNERS 1986– ;

Sales, Olivetti Canada 1976–77; Sun Life Canada 1977–78; Sales & Mngt., Xerox Learning Systems 1978–86; frequent speaker to var. groups on leadership & career mngt.; Judge for Woman of the Year and Employer of the Year, Canadian Women in Radio & TV 1993; Mem., Internat. Assn. of Corp. & Profl. Recruiters; recreations: girls soccer (fan, coach), golf, squash; clubs: Univ. of Western Ont. Bus. Sch. Club of Toronto), Markham Golf and Country, Bally Matrix Fitness; Home: 34 Silver Spruce Dr., Scarborough, Ont. M1W 1V5; Office: 64 Prince Arthur Ave., Toronto, Ont. M5R 1B4.

**LAUDENBACH, Joseph Adam,** B.Sc.; business executive; b. Seaforth, Ont. 11 Dec. 1930; s. Louis and Susan (Schaffer) L.; e. Royal Mil. Coll. B.Sc. 1952; Queen's Univ. B.Sc. 1953; m. Margaret d. Edgar and Bertha Bauer 13 Sept. 1958; children: David, Andrew, Ann, Sarah; PRES. AND CHIEF OPERATING OFFR. QUAKER STATE INC. 1988– ; joined Shell Canada London, Ont. 1956, Mgr. Consumer Sales Montréal 1963, Mgr. Lubricants & Asphalt Sales H.O. Toronto 1969, Operations Mgr. Ont. 1976, Mgr. Mktg. Operations H.O. 1980–84; Cons. Celanese Canada 1984–86; Vice Pres. Mktg. present Co. 1986; Founding mem. Croquet Can.; recreations: tennis, croquet; Clubs: Burlington Racquet; Bayfield Croquet; Home: 1208 Havendale Blvd., Burlington, Ont. L7P 4E7; Office: 1101 Blair Rd., Burlington, Ont. L7M 1T3.
LAUGHREN, Hon. Floyd G., M.P.P., B.A.; politician; b. Shawville, Que. 3 Oct. 1935; s. Irvin and Erma (Burton) L.; e. Ryerson Polytechnical Inst., business dipl. 1957; York Univ. B.A. 1969; m. Jeannette d. Burt and Grace Gossen 12 May 1962; MIN. OF FINANCE and DEPUTY PREMIER, GOVERNMENT OF ONTARIO 1993– ; Economics Instr., Cambrian Coll. of Applied Arts & Technol. 1969; 1st elected M.P.P. for Nickel Belt 1971; re-elected 1975, '77, '81, '85, '87, '90; as a senior member of his party while in opposition he served as party critic for a number of portfolios incl. 4 years as party critic for treas. & revenue ministries; Chair, Ont. Cabinet & Policy & Priorities Ctte. of Cabinet; Chair, Treasury Board; Mem., Cabinet Ctte. on Econ. Development; Mem., Premier's Council on the Econ. & Quality of Life; N.D.P.; Protestant; Constituency Office: 125 Errington St., Rear, Chelmsford, Ont. P0M 1L0; Minister's Office: 7th Floor, Frost Bldg. South, 7 Queen's Park Cres., Toronto, Ont. M7A 1Y7.

**LAUGHTON, Robert Joseph,** Q.C., B.A., LL.B.; lawyer; b. Ottawa, Ont. 11 Feb. 1938; s. Robert Charles David and Doris Editha (McCulloch) L.; e. Glebe Coll.; Carleton Univ., B.A. 1959; Queen's Univ., LL.B. 1962; m. Judith-Anne d. Douglas & Isobel Coleman 26 Aug. 1961; children: Robert, Douglas, Michael, Peter; PARTNER, GOWLING, STRATHY & HENDERSON 1971– ; apptd. Queen's Counsel 1983; Past Chrmn., Royal Ottawa Hosp.; mem. Bd. of Govs., Carleton Univ.; National Hon. Counsel, Boy Scouts of Can.; Hon. Counsel, Ottawa Y.M./Y.W.C.A.; United Ch. of Can.; Club: Rideau; Home: 5 Colville Court, Kanata, Ont. K2K 1A9; Office: 160 Elgin St., Ste. 2600, Ottawa, Ont. K1N 8S3.

**LAUMANN, Silken;** rower; e. Lorne Park Secondary Sch.; Univ. of Western Ont. B.A. (English); FEMALE ATHLETE OF THE YEAR, Canadian Press 1992; rower with Canadian National Team; Bronze medal (with sister Danielle), doubles, Summer Olympics, Los Angeles, CA 1984; Gold medal, single sculls, Pan-American Games, Indianapolis 1987; World Cup, single sculls, Lucerne, Switzerland 1991; World Champion, Vienna, Austria 1991; Bronze medal (after leg seriously injured in regatta 10 weeks earlier), single sculls, Summer Olympics, Barcelona 1992; named Ont. Female Athlete of the Year 1991; Canadian Athlete of the Year (Lou Marsh Award) 1991; Address: The Landmark Group, 277 Richmond St. W., Toronto, Ont. M5V 1X1.

**LAUMET, Henri,** Ph.D.; banker; b. Sidi Bel Abbes, Algeria 11 Dec. 1943; e. Political Studies Inst. Ph.D. (Law) 1966; m. Françoise Giovannoli; PRESIDENT, CREDIT LYONNAIS CANADA 1992– ; seconded from Credit Lyonnais to various positions with Union de Banques Arabes et Françaises 1972–79; Mgr., Credit Lyonnais Cairo 1980–82; Area Mgr. for E. Eur. (Internat. Div.) 1983–84; seconded from Credit Lyonnais as General Manager, Gulf Riyad Bank E.C. 1984–87; Asia Pacific Area Mgr. 1987–92; Dir., Crédit Saint-Pierrais; club: University; Home: 637 Sydenham Ave., Westmount, Que. H3Y 2Z3; Office: 2000 Mansfield St., Montreal, Que. H3A 3A6.

**LAUNAY, Viviane Françoise,** M.A.; association executive; b. Montreal, Que. 30 July 1947; d. Jean E.L. and Simone (Salmon) Launay; e. Coll. Marie de France, Montreal; Acad. de Caen, France Baccalauréat en philosophie 1966; McGill Univ.; Carleton Univ. B.A. 1969, M.A. 1970; Univ. d'Ottawa; Univ. de Paris X-Nanterre; Centre de recherche en néologie lexicale, C.N.R.S., Paris; children: Michaël, Arielle; SECY.-GEN., CANDN. COMMN. FOR UNESCO 1991– ; Instr. French Summer Sch. McGill Univ. 1966, 1967; Teaching Asst. Univ. d'Ottawa 1970–71; Offr., Aid to Scholarly Publs. Program, Humanities Research Council Can. and Social Science Research Council Can. 1974–75, Dir. 1975–79; Extve. Dir. Candn. Fed. for the Humanities 1979–90; rec'd Carleton Univ. Fellowship 1969–70; Ont. Grad. Fellowships 1969–70, 1970–71; France-Qué. Fellowship 1971–72; Can. Council Doctoral Fellowships 1972–73, 1973–74; Vice-Pres., Candn. Comn. for UNESCO 1988–90; mem. Assn. Candn. & Que. Lits.; Assn. Candn. Studies; Candn. Soc. for the Study of Higher Educ.; Match Internat.; Amnesty Internat.; Greenpeace; Home: The Mayfair Apartments, 4D-260 Metcalfe St., Ottawa, Ont. K2P 1R6; Office: 350 Albert St., P.O. Box 1047, Ottawa, Ont. K1R 1A4.

**LAUNDY, David Arthur,** B.A.; stock exchange executive; b. Victoria, B.C. 16 Jan. 1942; s. Arthur James Tylden and Dorothy (Kennedy) L.; e. Ryerson Polytech. Inst. Dip. in Jour. 1963, B.A. 1975; m. Janet Lee d. Douglas and Jean Hadden 9 Apl. 1966; two s. Robert Kent, David Christopher; VICE PRES., PUBLIC AFFAIRS, VANCOUVER STOCK EXCHANGE 1990– ; Reporter Edmonton Journal and Vancouver Sun 1963–67; Pub. Relations Cons. James Lovick Ltd. Edmonton and Vancouver 1967–73; Pub. Affairs Mgr. Royal Bank of Canada 1973–84; Dep. Min. Govt. Info. Services & Communications Counsel to Premier of B.C. and Cabinet 1984–87; Pres. Comcore Public Affairs Inc. 1987–90; accredited mem. Candn. Pub. Relations Soc.; mem. Vancouver Bd. Trade; Terminal City Club; United Church; recreation: music (piano); Home: 1361 McBride St., N. Vancouver, B.C. V7P 1G4; Office: 609 Granville St., Vancouver, B.C. V7Y 1H1.

**LAURENT, Brigitte;** artist; b. Montreal, Que. 1961; self-taught; all works have been produced in collaboration with Patrick Amiot; selected exhibitions: Nancy Poole's Studio 1988, 89, 90; Galerie Franklin Silverstone Montreal 1988, 89, 90; Doheny Gall. Vancouver 1990; Grace Gall. Vanc. 1984–86; group exhibitions: New Art Forms Exhib. Chicago 1989; 'Abreath of Canadian Life,' Sunlife of Canada Calgary 1989; collections: Burlington Cultural Ctr.; McDonald's Restaurants; Claridge Investments Limited Montreal; Coca Cola Limited; Hees Internat. Toronto; Bombardier Found. Montreal; Power Corp.; Lignum Indus.; Washington State Art Bank; General Foods Corp. N.Y.; Apple Computers; numerous priv. collections in Can., U.S., Japan, Hong Kong; commissions & awards: winner Business and the Arts Found. award 1986; Washington State Arts Comn. (incl. 2 murals & 3 standing figures) 1986; The Land Plaza Comp. Expo '86 1985; Comn., B.C. Pavillion, Expo '86, ceramic mural 120 sq. ft. 1985; Comn., Govt. of Can. (Can. Harbour Place Pavillion Expo '86) 5 murals, 50 sq. ft. & 5 large portrait sculptures of Candn. Inventors; Office: 4452 De Bullion, Montreal, Que. H2W 2G1.

**LAURENT, Jacques,** LL.L., Q.C.; attorney-at-law; b. Montreal, Que. 7 May 1941; s. Gaston and Yvette (Villeneuve) L.; e. Univ. of Montreal LL.L. 1963; m. Mimi d. Marguerite and Roland Cusson 28 Dec. 1963; children: Anouk, Etienne; PARTNER, GUY & GILBERT, ATTORNEYS-AT-LAW 1970– ; Assoc., Ogilvy, Renault 1965–68; Extve. Asst., Min. of Edn., Govt. of Que. 1968–70; Dir., Export Development Corp.; Autostock Inc.; Sereq; Montreal Neurological Hosp.; Fond. des grands brûlés; Lt., Royal Canadian Navy (Reserve); recreations: tennis, skiing; clubs: University Club of Ottawa, Winchester Fishing Club; Home: 191 Maplewood Ave., Outremont, Que. H2V 2M6; Office: Suite 2200, 770 Sherbrooke St. W., Montreal, Que. H3A 1G1.

**LAURENZO, Vincent D.,** B.A., M.B.A.; industrial management company executive; b. Des Moines, Iowa 31 May 1939; e. Notre Dame B.A. (Finance) 1961; Univ. of Mich. M.B.A. 1964; m.; 3 d., 2 s.; VICE CHRMN. AND PRES., VARITY CORP. 1988– ; joined Ford Motor Co. 1961–66 becoming Supvr. Costs & Reports; Cost Analysis Supvr. Massey-Ferguson N. Am. Operations, Des Moines 1966, Gen. Financial Analysis Mgr. 1970, Gen. Plans and Controls Mgr. H.O. Toronto 1971–72, Comptroller, Dir. Finance, Sr. Dir. Finance N.Am. Operations 1972–78, Comptroller H.O. 1978, Vice Pres. and Comptroller 1978, Sr. Vice Pres. Planning and Adm. 1980, Pres. 1981; Home: 768 Le Brun, Amherst NY 14226 USA; Office: 672 Delaware Ave., Buffalo NY 14209 USA.

**LAURIN, Camille;** psychiatrist, university professor; b. Charlemagne 5 June 1922; s. Eloi and Mary (Morin) L.; e. Univ. of Montreal M.D. 1950; m. Francine d. Luc and Geraldine Castonguay 7 Sept. 1983; children: Pascale, Maryse, Catherine, Dominique; CHIEF PSYCHIATRIST, HOPITAL SACRE-COEUR 1984– ; Head, Dept. of Psych., Univ. of Montreal 1959–63; Chief Psych., Albert Prevost Inst. 1958–66; Parliamentary Leader, Parti Québécois 1970–73; Minister of Cultural & Scientific Development, of Education, of Social Affairs 1976–84; Mem., Assn. Psychanalytique de France; Soc. Psychanalytique de Montréal; author: 'Ma Traversée du Québec' 1970, 'Le Français, Langue du Québec' 1978; recreations: music, reading; Home: 205 ave du Club, Dorion, Que. J7V 2E6; Office: 6555 boul. Gouin West, Montreal, Que. H4K 1B3.

**LAURIN, Cyrille Joseph,** O.B.E., G.C.St.J., C.D., B.A.; b. Montreal, Que. 25 March 1912; s. Joseph Antoine and Lillian Beatrice (Sheppard) L.; e. St. Andrews Coll., Aurora, Ont.; St. Clements Sch., Toronto; Univ. of Toronto, B.A. 1934; m. Elaine Roche, d. Fuller Claflin, Detroit, Mich., 2 Oct. 1946; joined Maclean-Hunter Ltd., Montreal 1934; returning from war service was publisher of each of Maclean-Hunter Consumer mags.; apptd. a Dir. 1958, Vice-Pres. and Dir., 1960; Head Mag. Div. 1958–64, Financial Post Div. 1964–68; retired 1968; served in 2nd World War returning to Canada as Deputy Adj. Gen. with rank of Brig., 1945; awarded O.B.E.; Mentioned in Despatches; Past Pres., Periodical Press Assn.; Mag. Publishing Assn.; Chrmn. Metro Toronto Planning Bd. 1965–67; Dir., Audit Bur. of Circulations 1965–68; Pres., Candn. Club Toronto 1968; Consult. to Organ. Comte., 1976 Olympics; Commr. Metric Comn.; past Chancellor, St. John Ambulance; Boy Scout Medal of Merit; Centennial Medal 1967; Jubilee Medal 1977; Candn. Lifestyle Award 1978; Awarded Knight Grand Cross St. John, 1980; awarded Commemorative Medal for 125th Anniversary of Candn. Confederation 1993; recreation: golf; Clubs: Bayview and Canadian (Toronto); Tequesta Country (Florida); Residence: Apt. 3502, 95 Thorncliffe Park Dr., Toronto, Ont. M4H 1L7; Winter Home: 375 Beach Rd., Penthouse A, Tequesta, Fla. 33469-2804.

**LAURIN, Jean F.,** B.Adm., B.Com., C.A.; insurance executive; b. Buckingham, Que. 28 Nov. 1958; s. Philippe and Valerie Ann (Trukan) L.; e. Hawkesbury Dist. High Sch. 1977 (Meritas Award); Univ. of Ottawa B.Adm. 1980, B.Com. 1981; C.A. 1984; m. Diane R. d. Léo and Claudette St-Denis 8 Aug. 1981; two d. Adèle, Evelyne; SR. VICE PRES. ENCON INSURANCE MANAGERS INC. 1990– ; joined Thorne Riddell C.A.'s 1981–85; Asst. Researcher present Co. 1985, Mgr. Special Risks Div. 1986, Asst. Vice Pres. 1987, Vice Pres. 1988; guest speaker Ont. Ins. Inst.; mem. Ont. Inst. C.A.'s; Candn. Inst. C.A.'s; Property Casualty Underwriters Club; Club: Cercle Universitaire; Home: 1735 Autumn Ridge Dr., Orleans, Ont. K1C 6Z1; Office: 1200, 99 Metcalfe St., Ottawa, Ont. K1P 6L7.

**LAURIN, Pierre,** O.C., B.A., L.Sc.Com., D.B.A.; b. Charlemagne, Que. 11 Aug. 1939; s. Eloi and Mary (Morin) L.; e. Séminaire de Philosophie B.A. 1960; Ecole des Hautes Etudes Commerciales L.Sc.Com. 1963; Harvard Business Sch. D.B.A. 1970; m. Louise Baribeau; children: Pierre-Eloi, Philippe, Anne-Marie; VICE CHRMN. & DIR. GEN., QUEBEC, MERRILL LYNCH CANADA INC.; Co-Founder C.E.G.I.R. (Mgmt. Consultants); author: 'Facteurs Humains de la Croissance des P.M.E.' 1976; co-author 'Orientation and Conflict in Career' 1970; 'Le Management, Textes et Cas' 1973; author various articles; Founder & Editor of 'Gestion' (Business review); Dir. of various private and public corporations, notably: Fondation Hôtel-Dieu de Montréal; IST; Quebecor Inc.; Chrmn. Sidbec-Dosco; Officer of the Order of Canada; recreations: tennis, golf, skiing; Clubs: Saint-Denis; Joyce; Montreal Indoor Tennis; Hillside Tennis; Home: 200 Hall St., Apt. 705, Ile-Des-Soeurs, Que. H3E 1P3; Office: 1800 McGill College Ave., Suite 2500, Montreal, Que. H3A 3J6.

**LAURSEN, Ronald Eric,** B.Comm.; trust company executive; b. Toronto, Ont. 11 June 1957; s. Knud and Maureen (O'Neil) L.; e. McGill Univ. B.Comm. 1980; Concordia Univ. M.B.A. 1992; m. Deborah van Blankers 10 July 1982; children: Melissa, Erik, Jessica; VICE-PRESIDENT, RETAIL PLANNING AND PRODUCT MGMNT., MONTREAL TRUST 1990– ; Manager, Deposits & Fund Admin., Montreal Trust 1984; Asst. to the Chairman & Chief Extve. Offr. 1987; clubs: Summerlea Golf; Montreal Amateur Athletic Assn.; Home: 2912 Coachman's Row, St. Lazare, Que.; Office: 1800 McGill College Ave., 12th floor, Montreal, Que. H3A 3K9.

**LAUTENSCHLAEGER, Gerhardt,** Dr. Econ.; investment and finance (insurance) executive; b. Gefell, Germany 3 May 1927; s. Friedrich and Martha (Hofmann) L.; e. Univ. of Heidelberg, Sr. Matriculation 1947; Univ. of Mannheim, Dr. Econ., 1953; Univ. of Wisconsin (Fulbright Scholarship) 1954; m. Ursula Erna, d. Erich Walther, 11 July 1955; children: Frank, Christine, Gabriele; DIRECTOR, GLOBAL INVESTMENT CORPORATION LIMITED; Dir. and Mem. Extve. Cttes., Gerling Global General Insurance Co., Gerling Global Reinsur. Co.; after employ. with Dresdner Bank, Frankfurt, Mannheim & Heidelberg, Germany, joined Internat. Dept. of Gerling Global Group, Cologne, 1954; emigrated to Canada April 1956 to become assoc. with Gerling Global Group, Toronto, Ont. since its inception, with multiple executive functions and capacities; mem., Swiss Cdn. Chamber of Commerce (Toronto) Inc.; Lutheran; recreation: tennis; Clubs: National; Canadian; Granite; Home: 114 Donwoods Drive, Toronto, Ont. M4N 2G8; Office: 480 University Ave., Toronto, Ont. M5G 1V6.

**LAUZON, Jean-Claude,** M.Ps., F.C.M.C.; management consultant; b. Montréal, Qué. 3 May 1949; s. Jean-Paul and Gisèle (Brouillet) L.; e. Univ. de Montréal, M.Ps. Psychol. 1973; m. Johanne d. Philippe and Jeannette Daoust 1974; children: Maude, Benoit, David; PARTNER, ERNST & YOUNG and CARON BÉLANGER ERNST & YOUNG INC. 1980– ; joined Nabisco Brands 1972–74, Asst. Vice Pres. Personnel, Mgr. Manpower Devel.; Rourke Bourbonnais 1974–80; Cons., Sr. Cons., Prin.; Pres., World Confedn. Productivity Sci.; Pres., Candn. Counc. for Productivity; Dir., Forum National de l'emploi; Club: St. James's (Dir.); Office: 1 Place Ville Marie, Montréal, Qué. H3B 3M9 or 222 Bay St., 25th Floor, Ernst & Young Tower, Toronto-Dominion Centre, Toronto, Ont. M5K 1J7.

**LAUZON, Linda Louise,** CMM; civil servant; b. Potsdam, N.Y. 2 Jan. 1957; d. Paul Ross and Helen Elizabeth (Spencer) Santimaw; e. St. Lawrence College, Behavioral Science Technician; children: Lindsay Catherine Sandelin, Charles Garvie Cruickshank, Adam John Lauzon, Benjamin Robert Cruickshank; SAFETY AND TRAINING OFFR., THE CORP. OF THE CITY OF CORNWALL 1988– ; Library Technician 1976–79; Group Home Manager 1984–86; Teaching Master 1986–88; Pres., Local Chapter of Human Resources Profls. Assn. of Ont.; Mem., Bd. of Dir., Industrial Training Council; recreation: aerobics, power boating; clubs: Long Sault Marina Boaters Assn.; Home: 11 Wellington St. E., Cornwall, Ont. K6H 6W8; Office: Box 877, Cornwall, Ont. K6H 5T9.

**LAVASSANI, His Excellency Mohammad Hossein,** B.Sc., M.Sc.; diplomat; b. Qom 14 July 1937; s. Ahmad and Sadigheh L.; e. Tehran Univ. B.Sc. 1963; Univ. of Colorado M.Sc. 1974; m. Pari Sadat d. Hossein and Batol Araghchi April 1971; children: Ahmad, Omid Ehsan, Hossein; AMBASSADOR OF ISLAMIC REP. OF IRAN TO CANADA 1990– ; General Dir. for Asia & Africa, Min. of Foreign Affairs 1980–88; Dep. Min. for International Affairs 1988–90; visited over 50 capital cities as Head of Delegation or accompanying Min. of Fgn. Affairs & highest ranking officials incl. official visits paid by Prs. Hashemi Rafsanjani; met virtually every country's Fgn. Min. & many Heads of State; much attention devoted to Persian Gulf Affairs incl. peace talks with Iraq; attended all summit meetings of non-aligned countries in Havana, New Delhi, Harare & Belgrade; languages: fluent in Persian, English, and Arabic; Home: 524 Acacia Ave., Rockcliffe Park, Ottawa, Ont. K1M 0M4; Office: 245 Metcalfe St., Ottawa, Ont. K2P 2K2.

**LAVELLE, Patrick J.;** strategic business consultant / association chairman; b. Toronto, Ont. 21 Feb. 1939; s. John Joseph and Wylo Elizabeth (Couzens) L.; e. St. Michael's College Sch.; Univ. of Western Ont.; m. Linda P. d. Hon. H.J. Robichaud P.C. 14 Oct. 1967; children: Mark Andre, Susan Elizabeth; PRES., PATRICK J. LAVELLE & ASSOC. & CHAIRMAN & CHIEF EXTVE. OFFR., CANDN. COUNCIL FOR ABORIGINAL BUSINESS 1991– ; Reporter, Kingston Whig Standard 1959; United Press Internat. 1960; Acct. Extve., McLaren Advtg. 1961–63; Dir., Public Affairs, Liberal Party of Canada 1963; Extve. Asst., Fed. Ministers of Labour, Nat. Health & Welfare 1963–68; Sr. Acct. Extve., Public & Indus. Relations 1968–71; Dir., Mktg. & Sales, Consumers Glass Co. 1971–74; Pres., Automotive Parts Mfrs. Assn. of Canada 1974–85; Agent General, Govt. of Ontario (Paris, France) 1980–81; Deputy Min., Industry, Trade & Technol. 1985–88; Vice-Pres., Corp. Devel., Magna Internat. 1988–91; Dir., Butler Metal Products; Centre for Internat. Business; Meridien Technol. Ltd.; Pallet Pallet Inc.; Slater Industries Inc.; Special Advr. on Internat. Trade & Commerce to the 38th General Assembly, U.N.; Co-Chair, 2 Fed. Task Forces on Future of the Automotive Indus. 1983–84; Mem., Bd. of Gov. & Treas., Central Hosp.; Mem., Liberal Party of Canada; Ont. Chair 1984–88 Leadership Campaigns of Hon. Jean Chretien; Economic Advr. to Leader of the opposition; extensive speaking experience across Canada on econ. & pol. issues; served as 1st Sec. of Premiers Council of Ont. which produced econ. agenda for the province 1986–87; recreations: tennis; Home: 55 Welland Ave., Toronto, Ont. M4T 2H9.

**LAVELLE, Paul Michael,** B.A., M.B.A., C.A.; executive; b. Toronto, Ont. 26 Jan. 1949; s. Herbert Michael and Mollie Ailsa (Lancey) L.; e. York Univ. B.A. 1972; York Univ. M.B.A. 1984; C.A. Ontario 1975; m. Gillian d. Kenneth and Helen Stoker 23 June 1979; children: Geoffrey, Elizabeth; PRESIDENT & CHIEF EXECUTIVE OFFICER, THORNMARK CAPITAL CORPORATION 1986– ; various positions ending as Senior Tax Manager, Clarkson, Gordon 1972–82; Vice-Pres., Thornmark Capital Corp. and predecessors 1982–84; Extve. Vice-Pres. 1984–86; Dir., Upper Lakes Group Inc.; Standard Chartered Bank of Canada; Simmons Canada Inc.; Adjunct Prof., Atkinson College, York Univ. 1980–82; recreations: squash, tennis, golf, photography; clubs: Granite, University Club of Toronto; Home: 94 Yonge Blvd., Toronto, Ont. Office: 22 St. Clair Ave. E., Ste. 1200, Toronto, Ont. M4T 2S3.

**LAVER, Kenneth G.,** B.Sc., M.B.A.; aviation executive; b. Kingston, Ont. 23 May 1951; s. Ernest and Jeanne (Smits) L.; e. Queen's Univ. B.Sc. (Eng. Chem.) 1973, M.B.A. 1976; m. Marilyn d. Robert and Ida Wheeler 31 Dec. 1977; PRESIDENT, DE HAVILLAND INC. 1992– ; Team Mgr., Procter and Gamble Specialties Ltd. 1976–78; Science Procurement Offr., Dept. of Supply and Services 1978–81; Dir. Bus., Vice-Pres. and Gen. Mgr., Boeing Canada (Arnprior Div.) 1981–87; Vice-Pres. Mfg., Vice-Pres. Admin., Boeing Canada (de Havilland Div.) 1987–92; Mem., Bd. of Dirs., de Havilland Holdings Inc. 1992– ; Ont. Aerospace Council 1992– ; recreation: canoeing, hunting, fishing, Opimian Soc.; Office: Garratt Blvd., Downsview, Ont. M3K 1Y5.

**LAVERDURE, Robert R.,** B.A.; financial executive; b. Ottawa, Ont. 14 Oct. 1946; e. Notre Dame Univ. B.A. 1969; Harvard Business School, PMD Course 1981; m. Garrie; SR. VICE-PRES., QUE. DIV., TORONTO-DOMINION BANK 1988– ; joined Toronto-Dominion Bank 1969; Asst. Gen. Mgr. & Mgr., Montreal Main Branch, Toronto-Dominion Bank 1982; Gen. Mgr., Corp. Banking Montreal 1984; Vice-Pres., Corp. Banking 1986; Dir., YMCA; Dir., Candn. Council of Christians and Jews; Mem. Bd. of Examiners, Montreal Office of Port Warden; Office: 500 St. Jacques, Montreal, Que. H2Y 1S1.

**LAVERTU, Gaétan,** M.Pol.Sci., M.B.A., M.P.A.; diplomat; b. St-Hyacinthe, Que. 25 Jan. 1944; s. Paul and Eglantine (Bruneau) L.; e. Laval Univ., M.Pol.Sci. 1967; Univ. of Western Ont., M.B.A. 1968; M.P.A. (Ecole nationale d'administration publique) 1975; m. Donate d. Jean-Marie and Lina Michaud 1 Sept. 1968; children: Francoise, Genevieve; ASST. DEPUTY MIN., POLITICAL AND INTERNATIONAL SECURITY AFFAIRS 1992– ; Offr., Royal Candn. Navy (R) 1962–69; joined fgn. service 1969; NORAD/NATO Div. 1969–70; Personnel Div. 1970–71; Third Sec., Candn. Embassy, Madrid, Spain 1971–73; Second Sec., Rabat, Morocco 1973–74; Fed.-Prov. Coordination Div. 1975–76; First Sec., Caracas, Venezuela 1976–79; Couns., Mission to the EEC, Brussels 1979–82; Sr. Extve. Asst., Dep. Min. (Fgn. Policy) 1982–83; Dir., Intelligence Analysis Div. 1983–85; Dir. Gen., Fgn. Intelligence Bur. 1985–87; Ambassador to Colombia and Ecuador 1987–89; Deputy High Comnr. to United Kingdom 1989–92; Address: Canadian High Commission, Macdonald House, 1 Grosvenor Sq., London W1X 0AB, England.

**LAVERY, John Robert,** C.A.; manufacturer; b. Toronto, Ont. 13 May 1942; s. John Frederick and Margaret Mary (Myles) L.; e. London (Ont.) Central Coll. Ins. 1961; C.A. 1966; m. Elaine Joyce d. Thomas and Lydia Shawlinski 9 Aug. 1969; two d. Shaunna Lyn, Cara Joyce; PRES., CHIEF EXTVE. OFFR., DIR. AND CO-FOUNDER, WINPAK LTD. 1977– ; Dir. LGM Graphics Inc.; Foundations for Health, Winnipeg; with Thorne Ernst & Whinney, London, Toronto & Winnipeg 1961–77, Partner 1973, in charge Winnipeg office; Dir., Health Sciences Centre Rsch. Foundation; Mem. External Adv. Ctte., Univ. of Manitoba Transport Institute; Past Sector Chrmn. Un. Way Winnipeg; recreation: golf; Clubs: St. Charles Country Club; Manitoba Club; Home: 78 Pinevalley Dr., Winnipeg, Man. R3K 1Y1; Office: 100 Saulteaux Cres., Winnipeg, Man. R3J 3T3.

**LAVERY, Kenneth R.,** B.A., C.M.A., C.M.C., F.C.A., C.A.E.; management consultant; b. London, Ont. 29 Jan. 1930; s. Ernest Anderson and Norma Loretta (Reid) L.; e. Westdale Coll. Inst., Hamilton, Ont.; Univ. of Toronto, B.A.; m. Joan Elizabeth, d. Wilfred Charles Langford, Hamilton, Ont., 28 June 1958; children: Shawn, Stephen, Joanne, Kathryn; CHRMN., LAVERY & ASSOCIATES INC., OAKVILLE 1985– ; Riddell Stead, Graham & Hutchison, Toronto, 1954–55; J.T. Symons, C.A., Toronto, 1956–58; Consultant, P.S. Ross & Partners, Toronto, 1958–64; Partner, Montreal, 1964–71; Dir. Internat. Consulting Services and Mang. Partner; Partner, Touche Ross & Co., Montreal and Toronto, 1964–71; Pres. & C.E.O., Brewers Assn. of Canada 1971–85; Project Offr. Glassco Commission; Founding Vice-Chrmn., Alcoholic Beverage Medical Research Foundation; Founding Chrmn., Forum for Young Canadians; served with 79th Field Arty. Regt. and 27 Candn. Inf. Bgde. 1950–53; author 'Selective Inventory Management'; 'Effective Inventory Management'; also articles for various journs.; mem., Inst. C.A.'s Ont.; Inst. Mang. Consultants Ont.; Soc. Mgmt. Accts.; Can. Inst. Assn. Extves.; Anglican; recreations: golf, fishing, tennis; Clubs: Royal Ottawa Golf; Oakville Club; Rockcliffe Lawn & Tennis; National (Toronto); Mississauga Golf & Country (Toronto); Caledon Mountain Trout; Hardy Bay Fishing (North Bay); Home: 224 Robinson St., Oakville, Ont. L6J 1G4.

**LAVIGNE, David Martin,** M.Sc., Ph.D., Dr. philos.; educator; b. Watford, Herts. Eng. 18 March 1946; s. Joseph Martin and Pauline Russell (Martin) L.; e. Univ. of W. Ont. B.Sc. 1968; Univ. of Guelph, M.Sc. 1972, Ph.D. 1974; Univ. of Oslo (Norway), Dr. philos. 1988; m. Susan d. William and Marie Black 24 Aug. 1968; children: Sara Jane, Jodi Anne, Tracy Elizabeth; PROF. OF ZOOL. UNIV. OF GUELPH 1987– ; Extve. Dir., Internat. Marine Mammal Assn. Inc.; Pres. La Vie Wildlife Research Associates Ltd. Rockwood, Ont.; High Sch. Teacher London Bd. Edn. 1968–69; Asst. Prof. of Zool. present Univ. 1973–79, Assoc. Prof. 1979–87; Visiting Sci. Life Sci's Div. Brit. Antarctic Survey, Cambridge, UK 1980–81; mem. Seal Specialist Group, Species Survival Comn. Internat. Union for Conserv. Nature & Natural Resources, Gland, Switzerland; Mem. Ed. Adv. Bd., Candn. Journal of Zoology 1988–92; Cert. Wildlife Biol. Wildlife Soc. Washington, D.C.; co-author 'Seals, Fur Seals, Sea Lions, and Walrus' Status Survey and Conservation Action Plan 1993; 'Harps and Hoods: Ice-breeding Seals of the Northwest Atlantic' 1988; co-ed. 'Marine Mammals and Fisheries' 1985; author over 70 tech. publs.; Chrmn., Wildlife Biols. Sect., Candn. Soc. Zools. 1986; Home: R.R. 1, Rockwood, Ont. N0B 2K0; Office: Guelph, Ont. N1G 2W1.

**LAVIGNE, Marion Judith;** publisher; b. Midland, Ont. 31 July 1942; d. Elmer Arthur and Veronica Martha (Desrochers) L.; e. Ryerson, Journalism 1964; PUB., 'UPHERE MAGAZINE' & PRES., OUTCROP LTD. 1976– ; P.R. Asst., TransCanada Pipeline 1964–67; Ed., Ont. Min. of Transp. 1967–69; Co-ord., Internal Commun., Ont. Civil Serv. Comm. 1969–71; P.R. Mgr., Libby's 1971–72; Commun. Mgr., Clarkson Gordon & Co. 1972–75; Head, Tourism Promo., Govt. of N.W.T. 1975–76; Mem., N.W.T. Bus. Counc. 1984–88; Dir., Travel Indus. Assn. of the N.W.T. 1984–87; Northern Frontier Visitors Assn. 1986–87; Past Pres., Internat. Assn. of Bus. Commrs. (Toronto & Yellowknife chapters); Past Vice-Pres., IABC Can. & Dist. 1; Home: P.O. Box 1114, Yellowknife, N.W.T. X1A 2N8; Office: P.O. Box 1350, Yellowknife, N.W.T. X1A 2N9.

**LAVIGUEUR, Guy A.,** M.B.A., F.C.A.; b. Montreal, Que. 4 March 1937; s. Paul-Emile and Alice (Sicotte) L.; e. Mont St-Louis Coll. Montreal B.A. 1955; Laval Univ. B.Com., L.Sc.Comp., M.Sc.C. 1960; Conserv. of Que. Dipl. Music 1960; C.A. 1961; Columbia Univ. M.B.A. 1962; EXTVE. DIR., CANADA - INTER-AMERICAN DEVELOPMENT BANK 1993– ; Sr. Assoc. Lavigueur & Associés (chartered accountants) 1963; Prof. Montreal Univ. Ecole des Hautes Etudes Commerciales 1963; Mem., Lavigueur & Lavigueur Inc. (Management Consultants) 1965; Advisor Pro Gestuib 1967; Mem., Review Commission on Mirabel Airport and Lemay Comn. on Fusion of Municipalities 1970; joined Candn. Pub. Service 1972, Extve. Dir. Policy & Planning Unemployment Ins. Comn. 1972; Asst. Depy. Min. (Finance) Dept. of Transport 1973; Sr. Assistant Deputy Min. of Ind., Trade & Comm., 1975; Dir. Canada Dev. Corp., 1975; Pres. Fed. Inst. of Mgmt., 1976; Dir., Canadair Ltd., 1976; Extve. Vice-Pres., Fed. Bus. Development Bank, 1977; Dir., Export Development Corp., 1979; Pres., Federal Business Development Bank 1978; Advisor to the Mngmt. Ctte. of ADFIAP (Assn.of Development Financing Institutions in Asia and the Pacific) 1986– ; mem. Public Relations Comte., Order of C.A.'s,

Que., 1967; Montreal Chamber Comm.; Pres., Candn. Music Competition, 1980; Life Gov. & Dir., Douglas Hosp. 1981; mem., Bd. of Dir., Concordia Centre for Management Studies, 1981; Dir., Candn. Ind. Renewal Bd., 1982; Fellow, Order of Chartered Accountants, Quebec 1984; Mem. Bd. of Govs. (Associates), Univ. of Montreal; Governing Body of Wasme (World Assembly of Small and Medium Enterprises) 1984–91; Assoc. Mem. of Alide (Latin Am. Assn. of Development Finance Institutions) 1988; Mem., Inst. of Corp. Dirs. 1986; Clubs: St-Denis; Mount-Royal; Ottawa Athletic; Club des Ambassadeurs; Address: 800 Victoria Sq., 11th Floor, Montreal, Qué. H4Z 1L4.

**LAVIGUEUR, J. Bernard,** F.E.I.C., B.A.Sc., P.Eng.; executive; b. Montreal, P.Q. 1 Mar. 1918; s. Marie H. (Charron) and late Joseph R. L.; e. Mont Saint-Louis Coll.; Univ. of Montreal, Ecole Polytechnique, B.A.Sc., Civil Eng.; m. Moira L., d. late J. P. McKeown, Montreal, two s., Marc, Philippe; Dir., Canadian Centre for Industrial Innovation, Montreal; Fondation de Polytechnique; Pres., Fondation de La Salle; Mem., The Candn. Academy of Engineering; Corp. Ste-Justine Hospital; Roads and Transportation Ass'n. of Canada; Engineering Inst. of Canada; Order of Engineers of Que.; Society of Automotive Engineers; Association des Diplômés de Polytechnique; Les Diplômés de l'Univ. de Montréal; joined Sicard Inc. as Production Engr. 1945, Asst. Gen. Mgr. and Chief Engr. 1949, Gen. Mgr. and Chief Engr. 1952, Extve. Vice-Pres. and Gen. Mgr. 1959., Pres. and Gen. Mgr. 1962, Chairman of the Board 1968–76; Pres. & Principal, La Corp. de l'Ecole Polytechnique de Montréal 1969–84; R. Catholic; Grand Cross of Magistral Grace of the Sovereign and Military Order of Malta; recreations: golf, fishing, music; Clubs: Saint-Denis; Home: 5955 Wilderton Ave., Apt. G-8, Montreal, Que. H3S 2V1.

**LAVIN, David Frances;** executive; b. London, England 8 May 1958; s. Michael and Marise (Owen) L.; e. York Univ.; m. Dianne d. Edna and Albert Bartley; children: Dylan, Carter; PRES., DAVID LAVIN AGENCY LTD. lecture and seminar agency; Chess Master, Internat. Arbiter, World Chess Fed. (F.I.D.E.); Office: 77 Mowat Ave., Ste. 406, Toronto, Ont. M6K 3E3.

**LAVINE, Herbert Alan,** B.S.A.; property management executive; b. Toronto, Ont. 7 Apr. 1927; s. Julius Judah and Belle (Sher) L.; e. Harbord Coll. Inst.; Univ. of Toronto; Ont. Agric. Coll., B.S.A. 1950; m. Ettie; d. Helen and James Green 7 June 1949; children: David Eric, Larry Ian, Barbara Ellen; Pres., Park Property Management Inc. 1979–92; Retired; employed on dairy farm late 1940s; Territory Mgr., John Deere Plow Co., Hamilton 1951–52; Sales Promo. Mgr., Deere & Co., Winnipeg 1952–54; own dealerships, Deere & Co., Dauphin 1954–69; Property Mgr., Cadillac (Fairview) Corp. 1970–79; Extve., Apt. Group of Urban Devel. Inst.; Charter Mem. & Dir., Fair Rental Policy Orgn. of Ont.; Mem., Century Club; OAC alumnus; recreations: sailing (25 yrs), squash; Clubs: Bronte Harbour Yacht; Mayfair Racquet; Home: 143 Gypsy Roseway, Willowdale, Ont. M2N 5Z1.

**LAVOIE, Gilbert,** B.A.; newspaper editor; b. Rimouski, Que. 3 May 1948; s. Rolland and Jeanne Darc (Roy) L.; e. Univ. of Toronto B.A. (Hons.) 1971; m. Joanne d. Fernand and Mariette Mailloux 1 Dec. 1974; children: Dominic, Mathieu; EDITOR-IN-CHIEF, LE DROIT 1992– ; Newscaster, CKAC, Telemedia Montreal 1971; Reporter, TVA Montreal 1973; La Presse 1975; Ottawa Bureau Chief 1983; Asst. Ed. Montreal 1985; Press Secretary, Office of the Prime Minister Ottawa 1989; Office: 47 Clarence St., Ottawa, Ont. K1G 3J9.

**LAVOIE, Lionel A.,** B.A., M.D., CCFP(C); physician; b. St. Brievx, Sask. 24 Aug. 1937; s. Athanase T. and Ella Marie (Mevel) L.; e. Collège Mathieu 1956; Univ. of Ottawa B.A. 1958, M.D. 1964; Royal Univ. Hosp. Saskatoon CCFP(C) 1971; m. Mary d. John and Tekla Luchenski 12 Oct. 1964; children: Robert, Michelle, Nicole, Andrea; ASSOCIATE CLINICAL PROFESSOR, FAMILY MEDICINE, UNIV. OF SASKATCHEWAN 1974– ; Chief Medical Staff Melfort Union Hosp. 1986–91; Prov. Sec., College of Family Physicians 1967–70; Bd. of Dir., Sask. Med. Assn. 1971–76; Vice-Pres. 1974; Pres. 1975; Sask. Acad. Sports Medicine 1986–88; Bd. of Dir., Candn. Medical Assn. 1978–83 (Past Pres. 1992); Chrmn., Med. Edn. Council, 1985–89; Pres. 1991– ; Adv. Ctte., Candn. Cancer Soc. 1986– ; Chrmn., Sask. Summer Games 1988; Award of Merit, Sask. Med. Assn. 1976; Jaycee Outstanding Ward 1975; Dedication Award, Sask. Parks & Rec. 1988; Community Recognition Award Melfort & Dist. C. of C. 1989; awarded Commemorative Medal for 125th Anniversary of Candn. Confederation; Bd. of Dir., Candn. Scholarship Trust Fund.; Sask. Paraplegic Assn. 1978– ; Comnr., M.C.I.C. Sask. 1984–88; Chrmn., Parks & Rec., City of Melfort 1983–86; Melfort & Dist. Minor Sports 1978–80; Mem., Melfort Rotary (Pres. 1987–88); Melfort Knights of Columbus; recreations: curling, golf; Home: 402 Stovel E., Melfort, Sask. S0E 1A0; Office: Associate Medical Clinic, Box 1690, Melfort, Sask.

**LAVOIE, Marc,** B.A., D.E.A., Ph.D.; university professor; b. Ottawa, Ont. 29 Apr. 1954; s. Wilfrid and Reine (D'Anjou) L.; e. Carleton Univ. B.A. (Hons.) 1976; Univ. of Paris I (Econ.) D.E.A. 1977, (Macroecon.) Ph.D. 1979; spouse: Camille d. Jean-Paul and Auriette Lafortune; children: Jérôme, Adrien, Christophe; FULL PROF., DEPT. OF ECON., UNIV. OF OTTAWA 1993– ; Asst. Prof. 1979–86; Assoc. Prof. 1986–93; specializations: money, macroeconomics, economics of sport; Mem., Internat. Adv. Ctte., 'Economie appliquée'; Mem. Editorial Bd. 'Review of Political Economy'; Mem., Candn. Olympic Fencing Team 1976, 1984; Pan-American Games 1975, 1979 (4th), 1983 (3rd in team event); Commonwealth Championships 1974 (4th), 1978 (2nd), 1982 (1st in team); 7 time Canadian Sr. Sabre Champion 1975–79, 1985, 1986; author: 'Macroéconomie: Théorie et controverses post-keynésiennes' 1987, 'Foundations of Post-Keynesian Economic Analysis' 1992 and 46 jour. articles & 14 book chapters; co-editor: 'Milton Friedman et son oeuvre' 1993; recreations: tennis; club: Sporthèque de Hull; Home: 61 rue du Muguet, Hull, Que. J9A 2L6; Office: Ottawa, Ont. K1N 6N5.

**LAVOIE, Roger;** retired banker; b. Montreal, Que. 26 Sept. 1928; s. late Hector and late Cécile (Théoret) L.; e. Coll. Supérieur St-Stanislas Montreal; Ecole des Hautes Etudes Commerciales Montreal 1970; Post University courses; m. Huguette d. late Maurice Mousseau and Cécile Decelles, 3 Oct. 1953; children: Michel, Daniel; Pres., The Laurentian Bank of Canada 1981–90; joined City and Dist. Savings Bank 1946, Asst. Chief Inspr. 1960, Founding Mgr. Methods and Procedures Dept. 1961–67, Founding Mgr. Marketing Dept. 1967–73, Asst. Gen. Mgr. 1973; Gen. Mgr. The Montreal City and District Trustees 1973–76, Extve. Comte. and Dir. 1974; mem. Mang. Comte. present Bank 1973, Gen. Mgr. and Chief Operating Offr. and mem. Extve. Comte. 1976, Vice Pres., Gen. Mgr. and Chief Operating Offr. 1976, Extve. Vice Pres. 1978; Vice-Pres., The Montreal City and District Trustees Ltd., 1978; Pres. and Chief Operating Off'r., The Montreal City and District Savings Bank, 1979; Dir., Credit Foncier Franco-Canadian, 1979; lectr. in Mang., Le Coll. du Gésu 1964; Founder, Mun. of Repentigny Lib. 1963; Dir. Le Gardeur Regional Sch. Bd. 1963 (Pres. Planning Comte. 1964); Pres. Repentigny Sch. Bd. 1966; Dir., Lake Raymond Country & Boating Club, 1966; rec'd Merit Award Internat. System Meeting St. Louis 1968; Hon. Pres., Multiple Sclerosis Soc. 1979; Decorated Hon. mem. Order Sons of Italy in Can. 1979; Annual Fellow, Intl. Biographical Assn. 1980; Del. for Can., 12th World Congress of Intl. Inst. of Savings Banks (Dakar, Senegal) 1980; Del. for Can., 13th World Congress, Intl. Inst. of Savings Banks (Berlin) 1981; awarded Lion d'Or Trophy by Gov. Gen. Mr. Edward Schreyer (for services rendered to Candn. financial community) 1981; Pres. Assn. of Counsels in Methods & Procedures, 1966; nominated Gov., La Jeune Chambre de Montréal 1977; author various articles; recipient of Award for outstanding service as Pres., Ville Marie Chapt., Systems & Procedures Assn., 1966/67; R. Catholic; recreations: skiing, tennis, travel; Clubs: St-James's; St-Denis; Valmorin Golf; Addresses: 2108 – 3ème Ave., C.P. 458, Val Morin, Que. J0T 2R0.

**LAW, Brian John,** F.R.C.O. (chm), L.R.A.M., A.R.S.C.M.; musician; b. London, Eng. 14 Apr. 1943; s. John William and Ethel (Taylor) L.; e. Royal School of Church Music, Croydon, Eng. F.R.C.O., L.R.A.M. 1963; Assoc. Royal School of Church Music (Hon.) 1974; MUSIC DIRECTOR, CHRISTCHURCH CITY CHOIR 1991– ; immigrated to Can. 1965; Organist & Choirmaster, St. Matthews Church (Ottawa) 1965–80; Mus. Dir., Cantata Singers of Ottawa 1965–87; Music Director, Ottawa Choral Society 1967–91; Asst. Cond. & Chorus Master, Festival Ottawa 1970–83, 1988– ; Music Director, Ottawa Symphony Orchestra 1974–91; Founding Cond., Ontario Youth Choir 1971, Cond., 1987; Thirteen Strings (Baroque Ensemble) 1976–91; Conducting Debuts: National Arts Centre Orch. 1970, Victoria Symphony 1976, Calgary Philharmonic 1978, C.B.C. Orchestras (Vancouver, Winnipeg, Atlantic) 1980, Manitoba Chamber Orch. 1981, Toronto Symph. 1982, Festival L'Aquila (Italy) with Ottawa Choral Soc. 1982, Barcelona Symphony Orch. 1989; Assist. Conductor & Chorus Master L'Opéra de Montréal 1986–89 and 1990–91; Edmonton Symphony, Les Grands Ballets Canadiens 1990; Hamilton Philharmonic 1991; emigrated to New Zealand 1991; Music Dir., Christchurch City Choir 1991– ; conducting debuts 1992: New Zealand Symphony Orch., Auckland Philharmonia Orch., Christchurch Symphony Orch., Dunedin Sinfonia, Canterbury Opera; Address (New Zealand): Box 1652, Christchurch, New Zealand; (Canada): c/o Benson St., Nepean, Ont. K2E 5J5.

**LAW, Maureen Margaret,** M.D., D.P.H., M.Sc., F.R.C.P.(C); public servant; b. Calgary, Alta. 3 Jan. 1940; d. William Allen Hay and Norah Mary (Welch) L.; e. Queen's Univ., M.D. 1964; Univ. of Toronto, D.P.H. 1967, M.Sc. 1970; m. Richard s. Wilbur and Laureen Weiler 17 May 1975; children: Robert, David, Lisa; Sr. Advisor, External Affairs, Govt. of Canada 1990; Asst. Med. Offr. of Health, Carleton Co. 1965–66; Dep. Med. Offr. of Health, York Co. 1967–68; Asst. Prof., Queen's Univ. 1968–72; Dir., Community Health, Dept. of Nat. Health & Welfare 1973–76; Dir. Gen. Health Consultants, Dept. of N.H. & W. 1976–78; Asst. Depy. Min., Health Services, Dept. of Nat. Health & Welfare 1978–83; Assoc. Dep. Min., Dept. of Nat. Health & Welfare 1983–86; Depy. Min., Dept. of Nat. Health & Welfare 1986–89; Bd. of Trustees, Queen's Univ.; Extve. Bd. Mem., World Health Orgn.; Roman Catholic; Fellow of Royal Coll. of Physicians & Surgeons of Can.; Ont. Coll. of Physicians & Surgeons; Ont. and Candn. Med. Assns.; Candn. Public Health Assn.; Home: 61 Okanagan Dr., Nepean, Ont. K2H 7G3.

**LAW, R. Warren,** LL.B., LL.M.; lawyer; b. Chatham, Ont. 23 Sept. 1952; s. Herbert Henry and Helen Kathleen (Tucker) L.; e. Univ. of Toronto, University College 1973; Osgoode Hall Law School LL.B. 1976; called to Ont. Bar 1978; Osgoode Hall Law Sch. LL.M. 1986; m. Zinta d. John and Ruth Komarovskis 9 June 1979; children: Jonathan, Tory, Kelsey; VICE-PRES. & GENERAL COUNSEL, LAURENTIAN FINANCIAL SERVICES INC. & LAURENTIAN FUNDS MANAGEMENT INC. 1989– ; private practice Toronto 1978–80; General Solicitor, Coca-Cola Ltd. 1980–83; Legal Counsel, Guaranty Trustco 1983–87; General Counsel, Eaton Financial Services / Eaton Trust / Eaton Life / Eaton Funds Management (Eaton Financial Group) 1987; assumed resp. for legal activities of parts of Imperial Life 1991– ; clubs: St. George's Golf & Country; Home: Etobicoke, Ont. M8X 1K3; Office: 310 Front St. W., 3rd floor, Toronto, Ont. M5V 3B8.

**LAWER, John Vincent,** SBStJ., Q.C., B.A., LL.B., LL.M., F.R.S.A.; barrister and solicitor; b. Toronto, Ont. 31 March 1929; s. Cyril John Edward and Mary Kathleen Humphrys (Robinson) L.; e. Univ. of Toronto, Trinity Coll. B.A. (Hons.) 1951, LL.M. 1975; grad. Osgoode Hall Law Sch. 1955; called to Bar 1955; m. Audrey S. d. Ralph and Stella Robbins 15 Aug. 1986; daughter: Lorraine (Cane); read law with Thomas N. Phelan, Q.C. and Brendan O'Brien, Q.C.; practised with Phelan O'Brien & Co. 1955–86; sole practitioner 1986– ; Q.C. 1966; Sovereign Grand Commander, The Supreme Council 33$ Ancient and Accepted Scottish Rite of Freemasonry of Canada 1991– ; Sec., Scottish Rite Charitable Found. of Canada 1977–91 (Dir. 1977– ); Anglican-Lay Sec., Diocese of Toronto 1981–83; Pres., The English-Speaking Union of Can. 1985–88; Chairman, 1988–92; admitted to the Freedom of the City of London 1988; admitted to the Freedom and Clothed with the Livery of the Worshipful Company of Upholders 1991; Hon. Co. of Freemen of the City of London of N. Am.; Master 1992; serving Brother, The Order of St. John of Jerusalem 1992; Commander, The Military and Hospitaller Order of St. Lazarus of Jerusalem (CLJ) 1992; Knight, Ordo Constantini Magni (KCM) 1989; Fellow, Royal Soc. of Arts; Clubs: Albany, Granite, Royal Candn. Yacht, Metro. Toronto, Bd. of Trade (Chrmn., Insur. Ctte. 1978–85); City Livery, London, Eng.; Home: 604 – 625 Avenue Rd., Toronto, Ont. M4V 2K7; Office: 306 – 40 St. Clair Ave. E., Toronto, Ont. M4T 1M9.

**LAWFORD, Hugh John,** B.A., LL.B., B.C.L.; educator; b. Edmonton, Alta. 8 Sept. 1933; s. John Radomsky and Ruth Havergal L; e. King Edward Sch. and Strathcona H.S. Edmonton; Univ. of Alta. B.A. 1954, LL.B. 1955; Wadham Coll. Oxford (Rhodes Scholar) B.C.L. 1957; m. Corilla Diane d. John and Jessie Mason 23 Aug. 1958; children: Michele, John, Mark; PROFESSOR OF LAW, QUEEN'S UNIVERSITY 1965– ; Pres. QL Systems Ltd. 1973– ; called to Bars of Alta. 1958, Ont. 1962; Asst. Prof. of Law present Univ. 1958, Assoc. Prof. 1962, Dir. QUIC/LAW Project 1968–73; Special Asst. to Govt. House Leader 1964–65; Special Advr. to Prime Min. 1965–66; recreation: running; Home: 65 Earl St.,

Kingston, Ont. K7L 4V1; Office: Kingston, Ont. K7L 2G5.

**LAWFORD, Ross,** B.Sc., Ph.D.; research executive; b. Toronto, Ont. 27 Feb. 1941; s. F. Hugh and Edith M. (Gibson) L.; e. Lawrence Park C.I. 1959; Univ. of Toronto B.Sc. 1963, Ph.D. 1966; m. Beatrice d. Clark and Doris Bradshaw 24 Sept. 1966; children: Janine Alexandra, Grant Alexander; Pres., Ortech Internat. 1990; MRCC post-doct. fellow in U.K. 1966–68; Asst. Prof., Biochem., McMaster Univ. 1968–74; Rsch. Dir., Diversified Research Labs. Limited (div. of George Weston Limited) 1974–77; Tech. Dir. & Gen. Mgr. 1977–89; Mem., Mng. Bd., Candn. Rsch. Mngt. Assn. 1985– ; Vice-Chair, APRO - The Cdn Technology Network; Home: 23 Rumsey Rd., Toronto, Ont. M4G 1N7.

**LAWLESS, Ronald Edward;** transportation executive; b. Toronto, Ont. 28 Apr. 1924; e. elem. and high schs. Toronto; extension courses Univ. of Toronto, McGill Univ. and Concordia Univ.; PRES. & C.E.O., VIA RAIL CANADA INC. 1989– ; Chrmn., Pres., C.E.O. & Dir., Central Vermont Railway, Inc.; Chrmn., Pres. & C.E.O., Duluth, Wpg. & Pacific Railway Co.; Grand Trunk Corp.; Grand Trunk Western Railroad Co.; Chrmn., Railway Assoc. of Canada; Dir., Canadian National Railways; VIA Rail Canada Inc.; Assoc. of American Railroads; Dome Consortium Investments Inc.; Old Brewery Mission; The Montreal Bd. of Trade Heritage Found.; Bishop's Univ.; joined CN Express Dept. Toronto 1941, Employee Relations Offr. HQ 1961, Gen. Supt. Express, Great Lakes Region, Toronto 1962, System Mgr., Container Development, Montreal 1969, Gen. Mgr., Express and Intermodal Systems 1970, Vice Pres., Freight Sales 1972, Vice Pres., Marketing 1974, Pres., CN Rail 1979, Pres. & C.O.O., CN Rail 1982; Pres. & C.O.O., Candn. National Railways 1985; Pres. & C.E.O., Candn. National Railways 1987; Dir., Bd. of Govs., Concordia Univ.; served with RCAF 1943–46; Dir.: Cdn. Transportation Educ. Found. Bursary Bd.; Univ. of Manitoba Adv. Ctte.; mem.: The Corporate Adv. Ctte., Wanuskewin Heritage Park; New York Traffic Club; National Freight Transportation Assoc.; Toronto Railway Club; Transportation Club of Toronto; Montreal Bd. of Trade; Canadian Railway Club; Traffic Club of Montreal; Canadian Club of N.Y.; Canadian Club of Montreal; the McGill Assocs.; awards: Hon. Mem., Cdn. Inst. of Traffic & Transportation; Canada's Transportation Man of The Year 1986; Knight, Order of St. John; Fellow, The Chartered Inst. of Transport; recreations: golf, reading; Clubs: Beaconsfield Golf; Mount Royal; St. James; Vancouver; Home: 337 Penn Rd., Beaconsfield, Que. H9W 1B5; Office: 2 Place Ville-Marie, Montreal, Que. H3B 2C9.

**LAWLOR, Stan D.,** B.A., M.A.; university professor / mayor; b. St. John's, Nfld. 4 Aug. 1943; s. Thomas Joseph and Mary Jane (Dobbin) L.; e. Memorial Univ., B.A. (Hons.) 1964; Univ. of Alta., M.A. 1967; m. Geraldine d. Ernest and Margaret Harvey 3 May 1969; children: Stan M., Sean D.; MAYOR, CITY OF NORTH BAY 1984– and ASSOC. PROF. OF SOCIOLOGY, NIPISSING UNIV. 1967– ; elected to City Council, City of North Bay 1973; has served on numerous local, prov. & fed. bds. & directorates including many charitable orgns.; presented papers at academic & municipal meetings; Dir., Fed. of Candn. Municipalities; Paul Harris Fellow; Chrmn., North Bay Police Comn.; Chrmn., North Bay, Safe Community Project; Host, Easter Seal Telethon 1983–93; Host & Prod., Mid-North Focus (weekly TV interview prog.) 1987–90; Pres., Nipissing Univ. Coll. Fac. Assn.; author of several articles, papers, & workshops; Home: 1951D Peninsula Rd., North Bay, Ont. P1B 8G4; Office: P.O. Box 360, City of North Bay, Ont. P1B 8H8.

**LAWRENCE, Hon. Allan Frederick,** P.C., Q.C., LL.B.; b. Toronto, Ont., 8 Nov. 1925; s. Frederick Charles and Elizabeth Anne L.; e. Jarvis Coll. Inst., Toronto; Victoria Coll., Univ. of Toronto, B.A. 1949; Osgoode Hall Law Sch.; called to the Bar of Ont. 1954; LL.B., York Univ. 1991; m. Moira Patricia McGuffin, 1 Sept. 1949; children: Sean, Alison; SENIOR ARBITRATOR, ARBITRATION ASSOCIATES OF TORONTO; Bd. of Dirs., Hughes-Leitz Optical Technologies Ltd.; Lifetime Bencher, Law Society of Upper Canada; Mem., Her Majesty's Privy Council of Canada; Practised law in Toronto for fifteen years with McLaughlin, Macaulay, May and Soward; cr. Q.C. 1963; el. M.P.P. for Toronto-St. George in Prov. by-el. 1958; re-el. 1959, 1963, 1967 and 1971; Apptd. Min. of Mines for Ontario, Feb. 1968, Min. of Mines and Northern Affairs, 1970; Atty.-General for Ont. and Sr. Min. responsible for policing, law enforcement, justice, court & criminal law admin., correctional institutions, consumer legislation, & corporate affairs March 1971; First Prov. Secy. for Justice Jan. 1972, resigning Sept. 1972 (retired from provincial politics); el. to H. of C. Oct. 1972; re-el. until retirement 1988; Party Spokesman on Consumer and Corporate Affairs, Energy, Justice, Solicitor-General, and Federal-Provincial Relations and Chrmn. of House of Commons Standing Ctte. on Public Accounts (in opposition) 1972–79; Solicitor Gen. of Can. and Min. of Consumer and Corporate Affairs 1979–80; In Opposition, chaired Caucus Ctte. on Justice (Shadow Cabinet) 1980–84; Candn. Delegate, United Nations Assembly 1984–85; U.N. Delegation advisor on justice, illicit drug abuse and trafficking, and defence-related subjects 1986–88; Candn. Chrmn., Canada-U.S. Permanent Joint Board on Defence 1984–89; Candn. Delegate, North Atlantic Assemblies (Paris, Quebec City & Hamburg) 1984–89; Candn. Parliamentary Delegate & Internat. Council Mem., Inter-Parliamentary Union 1972–88; Charter mem. & Treasurer, Internat. Democrat Union 1983–87; served with RCNVR as Seaman 1944–45; Chrmn., Labour Arbitration Bd.: Corporation of City of Toronto and Toronto Firefighters' Assn.; mem., Bd. of Govs., Central Hosp., Toronto; mem., The Chancellor's Council of Victoria Univ., Univ. of Toronto; Adv. Bd., Candn. Student Debating Federation; Commonwealth Parliamentary Assn.; Bd. Mem., Assn. of Former Parliamentarians of Canada; Arbitration and Mediation Inst. of Canada (Ont.); Candn. Bar Assn.; P. Conservative; Anglican; Clubs: Albany; University; Home: 'Fleetwood', R.R. 1, Janetville, Ont. L0B 1K0; Office: 33 Harbour Square, Suite 2611, Toronto, Ont. M5J 2G2.

**LAWRENCE, André H.,** M.Sc., Ph.D.; analytical chemist; b. Cairo, Egypt 1 July 1943; s. Hanna B. and Bertha H. (Méo) L.; e. Jesuite Coll. Cairo 1961; Ain Shams Univ. Cairo, B.Sc. 1966, M.Sc. 1969; Univ. of W. Ont. Ph.D. 1974; m. Marie-Reine d. Naguib and Antoinette Goubran 24 Sept. 1967; children: Dominique, Bernard; DIRECTOR RSCH. AND DEVELOPMENT, CUSTOMS LAB. 1992– ; Rsch. Chem. Celanese 1974–76; Rsch. Sci. Dow-Badische 1976–77; Patent Examiner, Patent Office 1977–78; Rsch. Chem. Customs Lab. 1978–82; Rsch. Sci. Nat. Rsch. Council Can. 1982–92; Part-time Lectr. in Chem. Eng. McGill Univ. 1977–79 and in Chem. Algonquin Coll. 1981–82, 1987 (mem. Adv. Ctte. Chem. & Biochem. Tech. Prog. 1984–86); holds patents trace vapour detection; author or co-author over 75 sci. papers, tech. reports organic & analytical chem.; co-author: 'On-site Sampling and Detection of Drug Particulates' in 'The Analysis of Drugs of Abuse' 1991; 'New Applications for Ion Mobility Spectrometry Detection Techniques' in 'Instrumentation for Trace Organic Monitoring' 1992; Ron Cockcroft Award 1990; mem. Spectroscopy Soc. Can.; Home: 13 Crownhill St., Ottawa, Ont. K1J 7K1; Office: Bldg. M-10, Montreal Rd., Ottawa, Ont. K1A 0R6.

**LAWRENCE, John Edward McCrea,** Q.C., B.A., B.C.L.; communications and public law lawyer; b. Kingston, Ont. 18 Jan. 1932; s. late Edward Gilbert and Edwina Claire (McCrea) L.; e. Bishop's Coll. Sch.; Bishop's Univ. B.A. 1952; McGill Univ. B.C.L. 1956; m. Anne d. Arthur Denys and late Cary (Baker) Cadman, Austin, Texas 14 Sept. 1957; children: Edward Burke, John Cadman, Denys McCrea, Cary Edwina; COUNSEL, BLAKE, CASSELS & GRAYDON, Barristers and Solicitors 1990– ; Teacher, Upper Can. Coll. Toronto 1952–53; called to Bar of Que. 1957; cr. Q.C. 1974; Assoc. and subsequently Partner, Mackenzie Gervais, Barristers and Solicitors, Montreal 1957–71; Gen. Counsel Candn. Radio-Television Comn. 1971–75; mem. Temporary Assignment Pool Treasury Bd. Can. 1975–76; Asst. Sec. to Cabinet, Legis. & House Planning, Privy Council Office 1976–77; Counsel to Privy Council Office 1977–80; Vice-Chrmn., Canadian Radio-television and Telecommunications Comn. 1980–87; Counsel, Lang Michener Lawrence Shaw 1987–90; Chrmn., Private Sector Adv. Ctte. on the Implementation of ISDN in Can. 1988–89; Dir. Tektronix Canada Ltd., Lab-Volt Ltd. and other private co's 1967–71; recipient Candn. Red Cross Soc. Badge of Service; Founding Chrmn. Disaster Relief Services Comte., Candn. Red Cross Soc. Montreal Br. 1961–65, Vice Chrmn. 1968–71; Dir. Federated Appeal Greater Montreal 1969–71; mem. Corp. Bishop's Univ. 1972–75; Ed.-in-Chief 'McGill Law Journal' 1955–56; mem. Bar Prov. Que.; Candn. Bar Assn. (Chrmn. Adm. Law Sect. 1976–78); Inst. Pub. Adm. Can.; Anglican; recreations: cross-country skiing, fishing, bicycling; Home: 98 Ruskin St., Ottawa, Ont. K1Y 4B2; Office: World Exchange Plaza, 20th Floor, 45 O'Connor St., Ottawa, Ont. K1P 1A4.

**LAWRENCE, Karen Ann,** B.A., M.A.; writer; b. Windsor, Ont. 5 Feb.1951; d. Kenneth William and Wanda Mary (Klapowich) L.; e. Univ. of Windsor B.A. (Hons.) 1973; Univ. of Alta. M.A. 1977; m. Robert s. Robert and Lucille Gabhart 18 Dec. 1982; one s.: Devin Lawrence Gabhart; Fiction Editor, 'Branching Out' (Candn. Mag. for Women) 1974–77; Mem., ACTRA; Writers' Union of Canada; author: 'Nekuia: The Inanna Poems' 1980 (poetry); 'The Life of Helen Alone' 1986 (W.H. Smith/Books in Canada First Novel Award; PEN Los Angeles Center Best First Novel Award 1987), 'Springs of Living Water' 1990 (novels); 'The Life of Helen Alone' 1987 (screenplay); Home: 2153 Pine St., San Diego, Calif. 92103–1522.

**LAWRENCE, Lionel H.,** M.A.; international arts training specialist; university sr. administrator; arts consultant; b. Scot. 1936; e. Loretto Sch. Scot. 1954; Queen's Univ. Hon. B.A. (Philos.) 1962; Univ. of Ill. M.A. (theatre - dir.) 1963; Harvard Univ., Inst. for Educational Mgmt. 1988; 3 daughters; INTERNAT. ARTS CONSULTANT (quality and cost analysis) 1990– ; Dir. Victorian College of the Arts, Melbourne, Australia 1985–90; Trustee, Victorian Arts Centre Trust 1986–90; Internat. Counc. of Fine Arts Deans 1980–90, Extve. Ctte. 1983–85; National (Australia) Education and Arts Advisory Ctte. (Federal Min. of Educ.) 1985–87; Dir., Western Australia Acad. of Performing Arts, Perth, S.A. Feb.-June 1985; Dean, Faculty of Fine Arts, and Prof. of Theatre, York Univ., Toronto, Ont. 1980–85, Dir., Grad. Programs in Fine Arts there; Bd. 'World Encyclopedia of Contemporary Theatre' (WECT), York Univ. 1983– ; Chrmn. Nat. Comte. of Arts Administrators (Canada Council-Banff Centre) 1980–84; Chrmn., Candn. Theatre Review Publications 1980–83; Gov., Candn. Conference on the Arts (CCA) 1981–85 (Extve. of CCA 1983–85); Chrmn. 'The Arts: Study and Training in Canada' 1983–84; Chrmn. and Assoc. Prof., Theatre Dept., Dalhousie Univ. 1972–80; Editorial Adv. Bd., 'Canadian Theatre Review' 1972–75; Candn. Del. Intl. Theatre Research Inst., Prague Conf., Prague 1973; Chrmn., Symposium on Education and the Arts, CCA, Ottawa 1982; Co-Chrmn. CCA Prov. Task Force Arts & Education 1977; mem. N.S. Drama Task Force Curriculum Dept. Educ. 1975; mem. Nat. Comte., Candn. Theatre History 1976; Dir. (theatre and opera), producer, actor in numerous plays; adjudicator, media theatre critic, commentator; Andrina McCullough award 1958; CIVDL Best Actor award 1972; Editor 'Quarry 11' 1962; John Golden Travelling Fellowship 1963; Canada Counc. award 1969; Midshipman RNVR 1954–56, Lieut. RCNVR 1959–62; Home: 45 Rideau Terrace, Ottawa, Ont. K1M 2A2.

**LAWRENCE, Minnie,** B.A., C.A.; chartered accountant; b. Yaas, Roumania 7 April 1955; d. Sydney and Rachel Posner; e. Univ. of Toronto B.A. 1976; Candn. Inst. of C.A.s C.A. 1981; m. Arthur Lawrence, C.A.; two children; SOLE PRACTIONER specializing in taxation 1993– ; C.A., Rubinovich, Newton & Back 1976–80; Tax Partner, Orenstein & Partners 1980–93; Lectr., Ryerson Polytech. Inst. for the Candn. Inst. of Bankers; Mem., Candn. Tax Found.; Profl. Adv. Ctte., United Jewish Welfare Fund; Women's Endowment Ctte., UJWF/Toronto Jewish Congress; Endowment Fund, Candn. Weizman Inst.; Candn. Inst. of C.A.s; Inst. of C.A.s of Ont.; Contbg. Ed., 'Retiring Right,' 'Insure Sensibly,' text on U.S. Developments (specialized texts); author of num. articles for Inst. of C.A.s of Ont. & Candn. Inst. of C.A.s; frequent speaker to various business groups; interviewed on TV & radio & quoted by several newspapers; recreations: astrology, psychology, reading, baseball, issues on women in the workforce and travel; Office: 60 Renfrew Dr., Suite 210, Box 620, Markham, Ont. L3R 0E1.

**LAWRENCE, Richard John (Jack),** B.A.; investment dealer; b. Orangeville, Ont. 23 Apr. 1934; s. late Albert and late Reta (Fenton) L.; e. Etobicoke High Sch. Toronto 1952; Univ. of W. Ont. B.A. 1956; m. Janice Letitia d. late John and Helen Boyd; children: Brian, Judy, Wendy, Debbie, Carolyn, Richard Jr.; CHRMN., BURNS FRY LTD. and CHRMN. & C.E.O., BURNS FRY HOLDINGS CORP. 1990– ; Money Market Specialist, Equitable Securities 1956; joined Fry Mills Spence Ltd. 1961, Dir. and Mgr. Money Market & Bond Dept. 1964, Vice Pres. 1967; Pres. & C.E.O., Burns Fry Ltd. 1978–84; Chrmn. & C.E.O., Burns Fry Ltd. 1984–90; mem. Young Pres.'s Organization; C.E.O. Organization; Zeta Psi; United Church; Business Counc. on Nat. Issues; recreations: golf, squash, skiing, flying; Clubs: Lost Tree, Lokahatchee Club; Lambton Golf; Rosedale Golf; Cambridge; Home: 2 Cluny Dr., Toronto, Ont. M4W 2P7; Office: P.O. Box 150, One First Canadian Place, Toronto, Ont. M5X 1H3.

**LAWRENCE, Terence Murray,** B.Sc., P.Eng.; oil industry executive; b. Edmonton, Alta. 12 July 1949; s. Earl Desmond and Patricia Jean (Murray) L.; e. Univ. of Calgary B.Sc. 1971; m. Maxine d. Bert and Anne Critchley 27 Mar. 1975; children: Byron, Candace,

Cory; VICE-PRES., PRODUCTION, PANCANADIAN PETROLEUM LIMITED 1990– ; Petroleum Engr., present firm 1971–80; Mgr., Reservoir Engineering 1980–88; Mgr., Oil Sands 1988–90; recreations: golf, curling, sailing; Office: Box 2850, Station M, Calgary, Alta. T2P 2S5.

**LAWRIE, Robert,** B.Sc.; advertising executive; b. Edinburgh Scotland 12 Apr. 1947; s. Robert and Elizabeth (McDonald) L.; e. Leith Acad. 1965; Univ. of Edinburgh, B.Sc. 1969; m. Frances d. Frederick and Lilian Barnes 18 Apr. 1975; children: Kyle, Ross; PRES., SMW ADVERTISING LTD. 1986– ; Dir., ALLARD/SMW et Associes Inc.; SMW Direct; SMW Research; Inst. of Candn. Advertising; Brand Mngt., Beecham Group London U.K. 1970–76; Warner Lambert 1976–78; General Foods Toronto 1978–80; Acct. Dir., Vice-Pres. Mngt. Suprvr., then Sr. Vice-Pres. Dir. of Client Serv., Saatchi & Saatchi Compton Hayhurst (formerly Hayhurst Advtg.) 1980–86; recreations: reading, the arts, walking; Club: Granite; Founders; Bd. of Trade; Home: 20 Pembury Ave., Toronto, Ont. M4N 3K4; Office: 365 Bloor St. E., Toronto, Ont. M4W 3S3.

**LAWSON, David,** B.S.S., M.A., Ed.D.; writer; educator; b. London, Eng. 11 Oct. 1927; s. Albert and Marjorie (Turner) L.; e. Univ. of City of New York B.S.S.Sc. 1950; Columbia Univ. M.A. 1952; Ed.D. 1959; Asst. to Dir. of Admissions, Foreign Student Desk, Columbia Univ. 1951–54; Teacher, The Harvey Sch. Hawthorne, N.Y. 1954–55; Asst. Leader, Brooklyn Soc. for Ethical Culture, Brooklyn, N.Y. 1955–57; Chief, Stat. Services Div., Dept. of Information, Inst. of Internat. Education, N.Y. 1957–58; Teacher, Midtown Ethical Culture School N.Y. 1958–60; Asst. Prof. of Educ. Univ. of B.C. 1960–63; Asst. Prof. of Educ. Hunter Coll. New York 1963–66; Assoc. Prof. of Educ. Western Wash. State Univ. 1966–68; Assoc. Prof. of Educ. McGill Univ. 1968–70; Visiting Prof. Boston Univ. 1971–72; 'Foreign Expert', Shanghai International Studies Univ., China 1989–90; 'Foreign Expert' Xi'an Inst., Peoples Republic of China 1990–91; Visiting Prof. of English, Xi'an Teachers Univ., Xi'an, Shaanxi, China 1991–92; Visiting Prof. of English, Central China Teachers Univ., Wuhan, Hubei, People's Republic of China 1992–93; summer sessions Univ. of Toronto, Univ. of Vt.; Curator, Montreal Quaker House 1976–78; Mental Health Comte. Beacon Hill Civic Assn. Boston 1972–73; John Reed Centennial Ctte.; speaker, centenary celebration, Harvard Univ., Oct. 1987; Discussion Leader, World Politics, Am. Foundation for Political Educ.; Freedom Agenda Program, League of Women Voters, N.Y. 1955–57; author 'Alcestis: A Narrative Poem' 1967; 'Peregrines: Poems' 1970; 'The Teaching of Values' 1970; 'Patches: A Montage' (novel) 1975; 'Zhongguo' (China - poems) 1993; numerous articles prof. and scholarly journs.; numerous poems, short stories, articles, book reviews various mags., newspapers, tabloids, collections; Mexican writing for publications in Canada, U.S. and U.K., 1985– ; 'Midsummer' an exhibition of art and poetry, Westmount Public Library 1986; Art exhibit, Channing Hall, Montreal 1988; recipient Cert. of Merit 'Men of Achievement' 1979–80 and Dictionary Internat. Biog. 1968; prizewinning poem, Westmount Arts Festival 'Christmas Parmelee' 1985; recreations: walking, chess, music; Home: 551 Argyle Ave., Montreal, Que. H3Y 3B8.

**LAWSON, Donald G.;** stock broker; b. Toronto, Ont. 11 Oct. 1928; s. Frank Gordon and Janet Waters (Ross) L.; e. Blythwood Pub. Sch., Toronto, Ont.; Univ. of Toronto Schs. (Matric. 1947); Univ. of Toronto (Comm. and Finance) 1948–50; m. Lorraine Marilyn Forbes, 10 May 1957; children: Douglas Forbes, Elizabeth Anne, David Andrew, Bruce Gordon; CHRMN. & DIR., MOSS LAWSON & CO. LTD.; Dir., Cabre Exploration Ltd.; Ivaco Inc.; Candn. Anaethetists Mutual Accumulating Fund; Millenium Growth Fund; Chrmn. (1971–72), Bd. of Govs., Toronto Stock Ex.; joined predecessor Co., Moss, Lawson & Co. in June 1950 becoming a Partner in Nov. 1950; Past Pres. and Dir. , Metrop. Toronto YMCA; United Church; recreation: golf; Clubs: National; Granite; Rosedale Golf; Briars Golf; Home: 36 Daneswood Rd., Toronto, Ont. M4N 3J8; Office: One Toronto St., Ste. 410, Toronto, Ont. M5C 2W3.

**LAWSON, Donald Stuart,** B.Sc.; engineer; executive; b. Liverpool, Eng. 18 Jan. 1935; s. Allan Stuart and Jane (Horridge) L.; e. Univ. of Bristol B.Sc. (Hons.) Aeronautical Eng. 1956; m. Rosanne d. Walter Morton 10 Aug. 1957; children: David, Nicholas, Hugh; PRES. AECL CANDU 1984– ; Pres., AECL Technologies, Rockville, Maryland; various positions, nuclear design, testing, assembly, construction & commissioning, English Electric Co. (GEC), 1958–76; VP (responsible for power & desalination projects Saudi Arabia), Sanderson & Porter Inc., N.Y. 1977–78; joined AECL 1978; recipient, James Clayton Prize 1969; Assn. of Professional Engineers of Ont. Engineering Medal - Management Category 1992; Dir., Nuclear Project Mgs., Montréal; mem. Assn. Prof. Engs. Prov. Ont.; Cdn. Nuclear Soc.; Office: AECL CANDU, Sheridan Park Research Community, Mississauga, Ont. L5K 1B2.

**LAWSON, Douglas I.F.,** B.A.; advertising executive; b. Toronto, Ont. 25 Apr. 1931; s. James Irving and Florence Evelyn (Eastmure) L.; e. Trinity Coll. Sch.; Trinity Coll., B.A.; m. Wendy L. d. Harry and Constance Wilson 5 June 1936; children: Brian, Margaret, Richard; PRES., LAWSON MURRAY LIMITED 1971– ; Lever Bros. Limited 1956–65; Foote Cone & Belding Limited 1965–67; Vice Pres., MacLaren Adv. Limited 1967–69; Dir., Sales & Mktg., United Biscuits Canada Limited 1969–71; Adv. Bd., Candn. Paraplegic Assn. (Ont.); Gov., Trinity Coll. Sch.; Anglican; Kappa Alpha Soc.; recreations: golf, tennis, skiing; Clubs: Rideau; Toronto Golf; Badminton & Racquet Club of Toronto; Beaver Valley Ski; Home: 132 Clifton Rd., Toronto, Ont. M4T 2G6; Office: 95 King St. E., Ste. 501, Toronto, Ont. M5C 1G4.

**LAWSON, John Barker,** Q.C.; b. Toronto, Ont. 18 June 1926; s. Hugh Hutchinson and Muriel Maud (Rogers) L.; e. Upper Can. Coll., Toronto, 1944; Trinity Coll., Univ. of Toronto, B.A. 1948; Osgoode Hall Law Sch., 1951; York Univ. LL.B. 1991; PARTNER, McCARTHY TÉTRAULT; Past Chrmn. of the Bd., The Corporation of Massey Hall and Roy Thomson Hall; Pres. The Sir Ernest MacMillan Memorial Found.; Pres., The Glenn Gould Found.; Dir., The Aldeburgh Connection Concert Soc.; Dir., Univ. of Toronto Alumni Assn.; read law with McCarthy & McCarthy (now McCarthy Tétrault); called to the Bar of Ontario 1951; cr. Q.C. 1965; mem., Candn. Bar Assn.; Delta Kappa Epsilon; Anglican; recreation: music; Clubs: University; Toronto; Arts & Letters; Home: 28 Elgin Ave., Toronto, Ont. M5R 1G6; Office: Toronto Dominion Bank Tower, Toronto-Dominion Centre, Toronto, Ont. M5K 1E6.

**LAWSON, John Herries,** B.Comm.; executive; b. Toronto, Ont. 22 Apr. 1942; s. William Joseph and Elizabeth Beatrix (Morse) L.; e. Sir George Williams Univ., B.Comm. 1969; m. F. Juliette d. Ross and Jessie MacKay 21 Aug. 1965; children Michael, Brian, Susan; PRES., JHL MANAGEMENT 1992– ; Asst. to Vice-Pres. Marketing, Computing Devices Co. (Div. of Control Data Corp.) 1969–74; Sen. Cons., DPA Consulting Ltd. 1974–81; Extve. Dir. & C.E.O., Tourism Indus. Assn. of Can. 1981–92; recreations: tennis, badminton, skiing; Clubs: Aylmer Country; Home: 8 Frontenac Dr., Aylmer, Que. J9J 1C4.

**LAWSON, R(uston) William,** O.C., M.A., LL.D.; economist; retired banker; b. Glenboro, Man. 19 Oct. 1917; s. Rev. Dr. Clarke B. and Florence Martha (Ruston) L.; e. United Coll.; Univ. of Manitoba, B.A. 1938; Oxford Univ., B.A. 1940, M.A. 1945; LL.D. Winnipeg 1975; m. Katharine, d. Hon. J.M. Macdonnell, 1 Aug. 1964; one d. Anne; mem. of Statistics and Research Section, Foreign Exchange Control Board, 1940–42 and 1947–50; Economist, Royal Comn. on Coal, 1945–47; joined Research Dept., Bank of Can., 1950, and Chief of Dept., 1956–62; Extve. Asst. to Gov. 1962–64; Depy. Gov. 1964–73; Sr. Deputy Gov., Bank of Canada 1973–84; retired; served in 2nd World War with Candn. Army 1942–45; served in Can., U.K., Belgium, Germany, Holland; Lieut., 2nd Candn. Arty. Survey Regt.; Officer of the Order of Canada 1984; Home: 158 Carleton St., Rockcliffe, Ont. K1M 0G7.

**LAWSON, Walter Reynolds,** B.Sc.; retired company executive; b. Amherst, N.S., 11 Feb. 1918; s. Gerald and Rose (Smith) L.; e. Saint John (N.B.) High Sch.; Dalhousie Univ., B.Sc. 1940; m. Harriet Jane, d. late Harry Senior, 22 June 1946; children: Cecily, Walter Geoff, Tim, Heather; Plant Engineer, Toronto Works, Dominion Tar and Chemical Limited, 1945; Plant Manager, Sifto Salt Co., Sarnia, Ontario, 1947; Works Manager, Domtar Ltd., Toronto, 1950; Plant Manager, Manistee (Mich.) Salt Works, 1951–52; Project Engr., Domtar Engineering Department 1953–54; General Sales Mgr. and Asst. Gen. Mgr., Sifto Salt Div. of Dom. Tar & Chemical Co. Ltd., 1955–56; Vice-Pres. and Gen. Mgr., Sifto Salt 1957–62; Vice-Pres. and Gen. Mgr., Bell Kilgour Div. of Domtar Packaging, 1963–65; Corp. Vice-Pres. Purchasing and Transport., 1966–70; Vice-Pres. and Gen. Mgr. Domtar Packaging 1970–77; Pres., Domtar Packaging 1977–79; Extve. Vice-Pres., Domtar Inc. 1979–82; served in 2nd World War with Candn. Army, 1940–45; discharged with rank of Maj.; served in Eng., N.W. Europe, Philippines, Okinawa; p.s.c.; Gov., Montreal Gen. Hosp.; Candn. Mfrs. Assn. (Nat. Pres., 1974–75, Chrmn., Que. Div. 1964–65); Inst. of App. Econ. Research (Bd. of Govs. 1975–79); Dir., St. James's Club, 1976–79, Chrmn., 1979; Roman Catholic; recreations: golf, shooting, skiing; Clubs: St. James's; Royal Montreal Golf (Dir., 1964–67); Montreal Indoor Tennis; Home: 224 Senneville Rd., Senneville, Que. H9X 3L2.

**LAWTON, Stephen Burrell,** M.A., Ph.D.; educator; b. Indianapolis, Ind. 17 July 1942; s. Burrell C. and Emma Loretta (McCord) L.; e. Univ. of Cal. Santa Barbara B.A. 1964, Berkeley M.A. (Edn.) 1969, M.A. (Stats.) 1970, Ph.D. 1971; m. Ann d. Kam Yuen and Tam Lun Yeung 9 Aug. 1980; children: Jefferay Wing Chung, Sarah Wing Yun; PROF. OF EDNL. ADM. ONT. INST. FOR STUDIES IN EDN. 1987– ; former secondary sch. math. teacher; Lectr. present Inst. 1970, Asst. Prof. 1971, Assoc. Prof. 1973, Acting Chair 1981–82, Chair Ednl. Adm. 1992– ; cons. to Sask. Sch. Finance Review 1990; Nfld. Task Force Sch. Finance 1988–89; McDonald Comn. Sch. Finance Ont. 1984; Shapiro Comn. Private Schs. 1984; recipient Rsch. Grants Social Sci's & Humanities Rsch. Council, Ont. Min. of Edn., OISE; Visiting Scholar Univ. of Mich. 1979; Stanford Univ. 1982; Univ. of Hong Kong 1990; Monash Univ. 1990; author various edn. publs.; mem. Am. Edn. Rsch. Assn.; Am. Edn. Finance Assn. (Dir. 1985–88, 1991–94); Candn. Assn. Study Ednl. Adm. (Vice Pres.); CSSE; ASBO; recreations: tennis, canoeing; Home: 63 Agincourt Dr., Agincourt, Ont. M1S 1M7; Office: 252 Bloor St. W., Toronto, Ont. M5S lV6.

**LAY, David W.,** F.C.A.; b. Winnipeg, Man. 23 Jan. 1933; s. Austin W. and Sybil L. (Bodé) L.; e. Queen's Coll. Nassau, Bahamas; Central Secondary Sch. Hamilton, Ont.; C.A. 1957; m. Elizabeth d. William and Myrtle Bergin 5 July 1958; children: Michael, Christine, Karen, Kathy; Former Deputy Chrmn., Ernst & Young (formerly Clarkson Gordon), Partner 1963, Extve. Partner 1979; Office: Ernst & Young Tower, 222 Bay St., Toronto, Ont. M5J 1P1.

**LAYDEN, Maurice J.,** B.Comm.; financial executive; b. 1935; e. Sir George Williams Univ. (now Concordia) B.Comm. 1962; m. Pauline Jasmin; 3 children; VICE-PRESIDENT, FINANCE & ADMINISTRATION, ROSE & LAFLAMME CO. LTD. 1992– ; Accountant, Pepsi-Cola 1951–60; Office Mgr., Schweppes 1960–63; General Brewing Corp., Calif. 1963–65; Armstrong Beverley Inc. 1965–81; Controller, Rose & Laflamme Co. Ltd. 1982–92; Office: 300 rue St-Jacques, La Prairie, Que. J5R 1G6.

**LAYNE, Donald S.,** M.Sc., Ph.D., F.R.S.C.; scientist administrator; b. Marbleton, Que. 5 Apr. 1931; s. John Graham L.; e. Harrison Coll. Barbados, High Sch.; McGill Univ. B.Sc. 1953, M.Sc. 1955, Ph.D. 1957; Univ. of Edinburgh Postdoctoral 1957–58; m. Alice Edith Common d. Dr. Robert H. Common, Ste. Anne de Bellevue, Que. 25 Apr. 1959; children: Donald Graham, Kathleen Renate, Geoffrey Haddon; RESEARCH CONSULTANT, TORONTO HOSPITAL 1993– ; Research Assoc. Queen's Univ. 1958–59; Scient. Worcester Foundation, Mass. 1959–64; Assoc. Prof. of Biol. Clark Univ., Worcester, Mass. 1964–66; Chief, Pharmacol. Div. Food & Drug Labs Nat. Health & Welfare Ottawa 1966–68; Chrmn. of Biochem. Univ. of Ottawa 1969–75; Vice-Dean, Health Sciences, Univ. of Ottawa 1975–79; Vice-Pres., Research and Technology, Connaught Laboratories 1979–82; Vice-Pres. Research, Toronto Hospital 1982–93; author, 'Metabolic Conjugation and Metabolic Hydrolysis' 1970; 'Advances in Sex Hormone Research' 1974; over 80 scient. articles various journs.; mem. Candn. Bioch. Soc. (Pres. 1976–77); Am. Soc. Biochem. Mol. Biol.; Am. Assn. Advanc. Science; recreations: squash, tennis, sailing; Home: 85 Glenforest Rd., Toronto, Ont. M4N 2A1; Office: 200 Elizabeth St., Toronto, Ont. M5G 2C4.

**LAYTON, Anthony Shakespear;** financial consultant; b. Montreal, Que. 7 Aug. 1951; s. Michael Shakespear and Mia Doris (Fogt) L.; e. Trinity Coll. Sch. 1969; Queen's Univ., B.A. (Hons.) 1974; McGill Univ., M.B.A. 1985; m. Nathalie d. Georges and Céline Cartier 29 Aug. 1981; three d.: Geneviève, Mimi, Anne; PARTNER, EXTVE. VICE PRES., T.E. FINANCIAL CONS. 1983– ; Mktg. Rep., IBM 1977–80; T.E. Fin. Cons. 1980– ; Pres., Candn. Assn. of Fin. Planners; Home: 4121 Marlowe Ave., Montreal, Que. H4A 3M3; Office; Ste. 2510, 600 de Maissonneuve Blvd. W., Montreal, Que. H3A 3J2.

**LAYTON, Irving,** O.C., M.A., D.C.L., D.Litt.; poet; teacher; b. Neamtz, Rumania 12 Mar. 1912; s. Moses Lazarovitch and Klara (Moscovitch) L.; came to Canada Apr. 1913; e. Alexandra Public Sch. and Baron Byng High Sch., Montreal, P.Q.; Macdonald Coll., B.Sc.

(Agric.) 1939; McGill Univ., M.A. 1946; D.C.L. Bishop's Univ., Lennoxville, Que. 1970; D. Litt., Concordia Univ., Montreal 1976; D. Litt., York Univ., Toronto 1979; m. Faye Lynch 13 Sept. 1938, div. 1946; m. 2ndly Betty Frances Sutherland; children: Max Rubin, Naomi Parker; m. 3rdly Aviva Cantor; one s. David Herschel; m. 4thly, Harriet Bernstein, div. 1983; one d., Samantha Clara; m. 5thly, Anna Pottier; Teacher, York Univ., formerly lecturer, Sir Geo. Williams Univ., Montreal; Lieut. in R.C.A., 2nd World War; discharged in 1943; Publications: 'Here and Now' 1945; 'Now Is the Place' 1948; 'The Black Huntsmen' 1951; (with others) 'Cerberus' 1952; 'Love the Conqueror Worm' 1953; 'In the Midst of My Fever' 1954; 'The Long Pea-Shooter' 1954; 'The Cold Green Element' 1955; 'The Blue Propeller' 1955; 'The Bull Calf and Other Poems' 1956; 'The Improved Binoculars' 1956 (repr. 1991); 'Music On a Kazoo' 1956; 'A Laughter in the Mind' 1958; 'A Red Carpet for the Sun' 1959 (Gov.-Gen. Award for English Poetry 1960); 'The Swinging Flesh' 1961; 'Balls for a One-Armed Juggler' 1963; 'The Laughing Rooster' 1964; 'Collected Poems' 1965; ed. 'Love Where The Nights Are Long' (Candn. love lyrics) 1963 (Prix Littéraire de Québec, First Prize, 1963); 'Periods of the Moon' 1967; 'The Shattered Plinths' 1968; 'The Whole Bloody Bird' (prose and poetry) 1969; 'Selected Poems' 1969; 'Nail Polish' 1971; 'Collected Poems' 1971; 'Engagements' (Selected Prose) 1972; 'Lovers and Lesser Men' 1973; 'The Pole Vaulter' 1974; 'Seventy-Five Greek Poems' 1974; 'Il Freddo Verde Elemento' (ed. Giulio Einaudi) 1974; 'The Darkening Fire: Selected Poems 1945–68' 1975; 'The Unwavering Eye: Selected Poems 1969–75,' 1975; 'For My Brother Jesus' 1976; 'The Covenant' 1977; 'Taking Sides' (prose) 1977; 'Selected Poems' 1977; 'The Uncollected Poems of Irvng Layton' 1977; 'The Tightrope Dancer' 1978; 'The Love Poems of Irving Layton' (deluxe edition) 1978; Irving Layton, Carlo Mattioli (Ed. Trentadue, Milan) 1978; Irving Layton/Aligi Sassu Portfolio, 1978; 'Droppings from Heaven' 1979; 'An Unlikely Affair: Layton-Rath Correspondence' 1980; 'For My Neighbours in Hell' 1980; 'The Love Poems of Irving Layton' 1980; 'in un'eta di ghiaccio' ('In An Ice Age'; bilingual Selected Poems) 1981; 'Europe and Other Bad News' 1981; 'A Wild Peculiar Joy' 1982; 'Shadows On The Ground' (portfolio) 1982; 'The Gucci Bag' 1983; 'Le Poesie d'Amore' (bilingual Italian/Eng. ed.) 1983, expanded edition 1993; 'Poemas de Amor' (bilingual Spanish/Eng. ed.) 1983; 'A Spider Danced A Cosy Jig' (ed. E. Cameron) 1984; 'Waiting for the Messiah' (autobiography) 1985; 'Selected Poems' (bilingual Korean/Eng. ed.) 1985; 'Where Burning Sappho Loved' (bilingual Greek/Eng. ed.) 1985; 'Dance With Desire' (love poems) 1986 (repr. 1992); 'A Tall Man Executes a Jig' (portfolio) with Salvatore Fiume (Milan) 1985; 'Final Reckoning: Poems 1982–86' 1987; 'Fortunate Exile' 1987; 'Wild Gooseberries: Selected Letters 1939–89' (ed. by Francis Mansbridge) 1989; 'A Wild Peculiar Joy: Selected Poems 1945–1989' 1989; 'Irving Layton/Robert Creeley Correspondence' 1990; 'A Wild Peculiar Joy' (cassette of 44 poems) 1990; 'Tutto Sommato: Poesie 1945–1988' (a selected bilingual Italian-English ed.) 1989; 'Fornalutx: Selected Poems 1928–1990' 1992; 'The Baffled Hunter' (a selected bilingual Italian/English ed.) trans. by Francesca Valente 1993; 'Danza di Desiderio' (a selected bilingual Italian/English ed.) 1993; co-ed. with L. Dudek of 'Canadian Poems 1850–1952,' 1953; his poems have appeared in translation in Roumanian, Polish, Russian, Korean and in Spanish, Italian in Argentine lit. papers and journs.; in 1956 an American ed. of his selected poems under title 'The Improved Binoculars' with foreword by William Carlos Williams, appeared under the imprint of Jargon Press; 'Italian Critics on Irving Layton' ed. by Alfredo Rizzardi 1988; 'A Catalogue of the Manuscripts in the Irving Layton Collection, Concordia Univ.' compiled by Joy Bennett 1988; 'Irving Layton Bibliography' compiled by Francis Mansbridge, forthcoming; awarded a Canada Foundation Fellowship, 1957; rec'd Can. Council Sr. Arts Fellowship; Candn. Found. Fellowship; Gov. General's Literary Award for Poetry, 1959; Canada Counc. Award 1960; President's Medal, Univ. of Western Ont. 1961; Prix Littéraire de Québec, 1st prize 1963; Canada Counc. Special Arts Award 1963; Can. Counc. Award; Centennial Medal 1967; Can. Counc. Special Arts Award 1968; Can. Counc. Sr. Arts Fellowship and Travel Grant 1973; Order of Canada 1976; Encyclopedia Britannica, Life Achievement Award 1978; Can. Counc. Sr. Arts Fellowship and Travel Grant 1979; Canada Council Arts Award (Long Term) 1979–1981; Poet-in-Residence, Univ. of Guelph, 1969; Univ. of Ottawa, 1978; Visiting Professor, Concordia University, 1978; Writer-in-Residence, Univ. of Toronto 1981; Adjunct Prof., Concordia Univ., fall 1988; Adjunct Prof. and Writer-in-Residence, Concordia Univ., fall 1989; Readings given at the Smithsonian Inst. and in Pittsburgh's Carnegie Hall; N.D.P.; nominated for Nobel Prize by Italy and S. Korea 1982, and again by Italy 1983; 1st non-Italian to be awarded Italy's Petrarch Award for Poetry for 'Danza di Desiderio' 1993; Freethinker; recreations: polemicizing, travelling, chess; Address: c/o McClelland & Stewart, 481 University Ave., Toronto, Ont. M5G 2E9.

**LAYZELL, David Bruce,** B.Sc., M.Sc., Ph.D.; researcher and educator; b. Newmarket, Ont. 20 Dec. 1952; s. George Hubert and Louise Marjorie (Rutledge) L.; e. Univ. of Waterloo B.Sc. 1975; Univ. of Guelph M.Sc. 1976; Univ. of Western Australia Ph.D. 1980; m. Katherine Elizabeth Wynne-Edwards d. Hugh Robert Wynne-Edwards and Stella Julia Gartland (nee Scott) 28 Dec. 1992; PROFESSOR OF BIOLOGY, QUEEN'S UNIV. 1991– ; Postdoct. Fellow, Boyce Thompson Inst. for Plant Sci. Rsch., Cornell Univ. 1980–81; NSERC Univ. Rsch. Fellow (URF) / Asst. Prof., Biology Dept., Queen's Univ. 1981–86; NSERC URF / Assoc. Prof. 1986–91; Visiting Rsch. Fellow, Nat. Inst. of Agrobiology Resources, Tsukuba, Japan 1987; E.W.R. Steacie Mem. Fellow, NSERC 1992–94; Monitoring Ed., 'Plant Physiology' 1993– ; Edit. Bd. Mem., 'Plant Physiology' 1990–92, 'Physiologia Plantarium' 1992–94; Mem., Candn. Soc. of Plant Physiologists (Sec. 1989–91); NSERC Plant Biol. Grant Selection Ctte. 1989–92 (Chair 1991–92); Sci. Adv. Ctte., Inst. du rech. en biol. végétale Montreal 1991–92; Consultant, P.K. Morgan Instruments Inc. (USA) 1992–94; U.S. Dept. Energy, Advisory Panal Mem. 1993; Univ. Rsch. Fellow, NSERC 1981–91; C.D. Nelson Award, Candn. Soc. Plant Physiologists 1990; author/co-author of over 60 sci. rsch. articles or reviews; inventor/co-inventor of instrumentation used in plant sci. rsch. (two patents held, two applied for); recreations: canoeing, bicycling; Home: 134 Lower Albert St., Kingston, Ont. K7L 3V2; Office: Kingston, Ont. K7L 3N6.

**LAZAROVITS, Andrew Ivan,** B.Sc., M.D., F.R.C.P.(C); physician; b. Budapest, Hungary 23 Feb. 1954; s. Dr. Stephen I. and Susan L. (Angyal) L.; e. Upper Can. Coll. Toronto 1972; Univ. of Toronto Trinity Coll. B.Sc. 1975; McMaster Univ. M.D. 1978; Diplomate Am. Bd. Internal Med. 1981; m. Carolyn Jane d. Dr. Premysl and Hana Dobias 21 July 1984; children: Adrian John, James Alexander, Chloe Susan; DIR. OF RENAL TRANSPLANTATION, UNIVERSITY HOSP., London 1988– ; Assoc. Prof. of Med., Univ. of Western Ont. 1988– ; Scientist, John P. Robarts Rsch. Inst., London 1988– ; Fellow, Assn. of Commonwealth Universities, Imperial Cancer Rsch. Fund Laboratories, London U.K. 1992; Asst. Prof. of Med. Univ. of Ottawa 1984–88; Cons. in Nephrol. Children's Hosp. of E. Ont. 1985–88; Nat. Defence Med. Centre 1986–88; Dir. of Renal Transplantation, Ottawa Gen. Hosp. 1984–88; Fellow, Med. Rsch. Council Can. 1982–84; Rsch. Fellow, Harvard Med. Sch. 1982–84; recipient rsch. grants, Med. Rsch. Counc. of Can. and Kidney Found. of Can.; author or co-author numerous publs., abstracts; Fellow, Royal Coll of Phys. & Surg. of Can. 1982; mem. Candn. Med. Assn.; Candn. Transplant Soc.; Transplantation Soc.; Am. Soc. of Nephrology; Am. Soc. of Transplant Physicians; Candn. Soc. of Nephrology; Candn. Soc. of Clinical Investigation; Internat. Soc. Nephrology; Am. Assn. Advanc. Sci.; Am. Assn. of Immunologists; recreations: skiing, travel; Home: 63 Grasmere Cres., London, Ont. N6G 4N7; Office: University Hosp., 339 Windermere Rd., London, Ont. N6A 5A5.

**LAZIER, Colin Gillies,** LL.B.; lawyer; b. Hamilton, Ont. 8 Aug. 1949; s. Colin Simpson and Martha (Gillies) L.; e. Univ. of Western Ont. LL.B. 1972; m. Barbara d. Laird and Jean Jennings 12 Aug. 1971; children: Amy Victoria, Catherine Barbara, Colin Laird, William Robert; recreations: tennis, computers, genealogy; PARTNER, LAZIER, HICKEY, LANGS, O'NEAL 1974– ; firm has been in practice since 1863; Past Chair, Chedoke-McMaster Hospitals; Trustee, Centenary Un. Ch. (Past Chair, Ctte. of Stewards); Dir., Chedoke Health Corp.; Sec.-Treas., The Malloch Found.; Dir., Chedoke-McMaster Hosp. Found.; Former Dir., Hamilton Thistle Club; Mem., Candn. Bar Assn.; Candn. Soc. for the Advancement of Legal Technology; Hamilton Law Assn.; Ont. Genealogical Soc.; The Bergen Co. Hist. Soc. (N.J.); Holland Soc. of N.Y.; clubs: Hamilton, Tamahaac, Hamilton Lawyers; Home: 407 Queen St. S., Hamilton, Ont. L8P 3T8; Office: 25 Main St. W., 17th fl., Hamilton, Ont. L8P 1H1.

**LAZIER, F. Stuart,** B.Sc.Soc., M.B.A.; real estate executive; b. Charlottetown, P.E.I. 14 Sept. 1950; s. Thomas A. and Julia I. (Steacy) L.; e. Univ. of W. Ont. B.Sc.Soc. 1973, M.B.A. 1975; m. Victoria d. Norris and Mollie Mackenzie 23 May 1975; three s. Adam, Michael, Sanders; PRESIDENT, ENTERPRISE PROPERTY GROUP LTD. 1989– ; Chrmn. & Founder, Environmental Planning Inst. of Can.; Mktg. Mgr. Atco Industries Ltd. 1975–80; Pres. Indacom Real Estate Corp. 1980–84; Gen. Mgr. present Co. 1985, Vice Pres. & Partner 1986; mem. BOMA; ICSC; Club: University; Home: 9 Ridge Dr., Toronto, Ont. M4T 1B6; Office: 200, 480 University Ave., Toronto, Ont. M5G 1V2.

**LAZURE, Hon. Denis,** M.D.; né Napierville, Qué. 12 oct. 1925; f. Thomas et Berthe (Durivage) L.; é. Coll. Jean-de-Brébeuf Montréal B.A. 1946; Univ. de Montréal M.D. 1952; Adm. hospitalière certificat 1965; Univ. of Pa. Dipl. in Child Psychiatry 1957; ép. Anne Marie f. Paul Lalande 22 avril 1977; enfants: Gabrielle, Michel, Catherine, Eric-René; DÉPUTÉ DE LA PRAIRIE À L'ASSEMBLÉ NATIONALE DU QUÉBEC et CRITIQUE DE L'OPPOSITION POUR LES PERSONNES HANDICAPÉS ET POUR LA MAIN D'OEUVRE ET LA SÉCURITÉ DU REVENU et VICE-PRÉS. DE LA COMMISSION PARLEMENTAIRE BUDGET ET ADMIN. 1989– ; Psychiatre clinicien, Hôp. Charles le Moyne, Greenfield Park, Que.; Fondateur et dir. Dépt. de Psychiatrie Infantile, Hôpital Ste-Justine Montréal 1957–69; Dir. général Hôpital Rivière-des-Prairies Montréal 1969–74 et Hôpital Louis-H. Lafontaine Montréal 1974–76; Ministre des Affaires sociales, 1976–81; Deputé de Bertrand, Assmeblée National du Québec 1981–84; Min. d'État au Développment Social 1981–82; Ministre délégué aux relations avec les citoyens, 1982–84; député de Chambly 1976 Assemblée Nationale Qué.; auteur 'One Million Children' 1970; Parti Québecois; récreations: tennis, skiing, natation; Adresse: 2068, Bellevue, St-Bruno, Qué. J3V 4A8.

**LEADER, Arthur,** B.A., M.D., FRCSC; gynecologic reproductive endocrinologist; b. Munich, Germany 26 Dec. 1946; s. Henry and Alfreda (Zwilling) L.; e. Univ. of Toronto B.A. 1969; McMaster Univ. M.D. 1972; m. Ellen d. Irving and Pauline Gottheil 18 June 1989; PROF., FAC. OF MEDICINE, UNIV. OF OTTAWA 1986– ; Chief, Div. of Reproductive Endocrinology, Univ. of Ottawa; Cons., Human Reproduction Unit, World Health Orgn., Switz. 1973; MRC Fellow, Karolinska Inst., Sweden 1974–75; Obstetrical/Gyn. resident, U.K. 1975–77; Rsch. Fellow, Sahlgrenska Hosp., Sweden 1977; FRCSC 1980; Asst. Prof., Univ. of Calgary 1982–86; Dir., Program for Assisted Reproductive Technologies, Univ. of Ottawa; Chrmn., Task Force on Obs./Gyn., Coll. of Phys. & Surg. of Ont.; Past Chrmn., Reproductive Biol., Ont. Med. Assn.; ad hoc reviewer for profl. jours. & granting agencies; Bd. Chrmn., Infertility Awareness of Canada 1989–90; primary medical interests: clinical treatment & rsch. into male infertility & quality assurance of med. care to meet profl. goals & public expectations; active in undergrad. and fellowship education; author of over 40 medical articles & several book chapters; recreations: skiing, cycling; Office: Suite 570, 1053 Carling Ave., Ottawa, Ont. K1Y 4E9.

**LEAHEY, Dennice M.,** B.A.; banker; b. Edmonton, Alta. 27 Oct. 1941; e. Mount St. Vincent Univ. B.A. 1964; m. Stephen G. Leahey; children: Douglas, Adrienne; SR. VICE PRES. AND GEN. MGR. (MANITOBA) ROYAL BANK OF CANADA 1992– ; joined present Bank 1971 serving in Personnel, Br. Mgmt. and Corporate Banking; Dir., Royal Winnipeg Ballet; Heart and Stroke Manitoba Branch; St. Boniface Hospital Rsch. Found.; Office: 16th Floor, 220 Portage Ave., Winnipeg, Man. R3C 2T5.

**LEAL, Herbert Allan Borden,** O.C., Q.C., L.S.M., B.A., LL.B., LL.M., LL.D., D.C.L.; b. Beloeil, P.Q. 15 June 1917; s. Frederick William and Marie Ange (Ranger) L.; e. Tweed (Ont.) High Sch.; McMaster Univ., B.A. (Hons. Hist.) 1940 (O.H.A. Scholar 1936, Gov. Gen. Medal 1939, A.G. Alexander Scholar 1939, Rhodes Scholar for Ont. 1940); Osgoode Hall Law Sch. 1945–48; Harvard Law Sch., LL.M. 1957; m. Muriel Isobel, d. Rothsay Eugene Clemens, Hamilton, Ont. 21 March 1942; children: Kathleen Mary (Mrs. Malcolm A. Clark), Allan Ross, James Frederick; Vice-Chrmn., Ont. Law Reform Commission 1981–89; Special Advisor to Premier of Ont. Constitutional Law 1981–82; Chancellor, McMaster Univ., 1977–86; read law with Frank Erichsen-Brown, Q.C., Toronto; called to the Bar of Ontario 1948; practised with Erichsen-Brown and Leal, Toronto 1948–50; Lecturer, Osgoode Hall Law School 1950; Vice-Dean and Professor 1956, Dean and Prof. 1958–66; Chrmn., Ont. Law Reform Comm. 1966–77 (mem. 1964–66); Depy. Atty.-Gen. Ont. 1977–81; Chrmn., Profl. Organizations Comte., Prov. of Ont. 1977–80; Special Lectr., Law Soc. of Upper Can. 1951, 1957, 1960, 1966 and 1977; Special Lectr., Property Law, Faculty of Law, Univ. of Toronto 1972–77; Prov. of Ont. Atty.-Gen.'s Adv. Comte. on Adm. of Justice

1958–64; mem. Council, Medico-Legal Soc. of Toronto (1st Vice-Pres. 1968; Pres. 1969); mem. Extve. Comte., Toronto Br., Candn. Red Cross Soc. 1959–64; Co-Chrmn. Special Comte., Assn. Am. Law Schs. and Assn. Candn. Law Teachers on Candn.-Am. Co-operation 1962–66; Commr. for Ont., Uniform Law Conf. of Can. since 1963, Pres. 1977–78; mem. Adv. Comte., Candn. Civil Liberties Assn. Ont. 1965–66; mem. Faculty, Candn. Judicial Conf. 1969–73 (Dir. 1969–70); Adv. Group on Private Internat. Law and Unification of Law, Gov't. of Can. 1968–86; mem. Candn. delegation to The Hague Conference on Private International Law 1968, 1972, 1976, 1980; Chief of Can. Del. and Vice Pres., Hague Conf. on Private Internat. Law 1980; mem. Can. Del., Special Commission on the Civil Aspects of Internat. Child Abduction 1979; Chief of Can. Del, Int. Diplomatic Conf. on Wills, Washington 1973; Chrmn., Special Comte., Uniform Law Conf. on Intl. Conventions of Private Intl. Law 1971–82; served in 2nd World War, R.C.A. 1943–45 in Can., England and U.S.; grad. War Staff Gunnery Coll., Royal Sch. Arty., Larkhill, England and Royal Coll. Science; retired with rank of Capt.; Publications incl. articles or chapters in several legal books and prof. journs.; mem. Law Soc. Upper Can.; Toronto Arty. Offrs. Assn.; Past Pres., Assn. Candn. Law Teachers; Past Chrmn. Nat. Scholar. Comte. and former Dir., African Students Foundation; created Queen's Counsel 1959; LL.D. (Hon.) McMaster Univ. 1963; LL.D. York Univ. 1978; D.C.L. Univ. of W. Ont. 1982; LL.D. Dalhousie Univ. 1983; Offr. Order of Can. 1983; Law Soc. Medal (L.S.M.) 1987; elected Reeve, Municipality of Village of Tweed 1991– ; Freemason; recreations: sailing, fishing, golf; Home: Box 538, Tweed, Ont. K0K 3J0.

**LEAMY, Cameron J.D.;** insurance executive; b. Montreal, Que. 26 Sept. 1932; s. Andrew (dec.) and Gladys (Cameron) L. (dec.); e. Sir George Williams High Sch.; m. Joan Ghent 19 Apr. 1958; children: Andrew, Sharon; SR. VICE PRES. MARKETING, SUN LIFE ASSURANCE CO. OF CANADA 1981– ; joined present Co. as Agt. 1953, Unit Mgr. 1956, Inspr. of Agencies E. Candn. Div. 1963, Inspr. of Agencies Central U.S. Div. 1964, Asst. Supt. Agencies 1965 and Supt. Agencies Central U.S. Div. 1968, Supt. Agencies E. U.S. Div. 1971, Br. Mgr. Houston 1973–81; mem., Conference Bd. of Canada; Council of Marketing Extves.; Office: Sun Life Cntre, 150 King St. W., Toronto, Ont. M5H 1J9.

**LEAN, Ralph Edward,** B.A., LL.B.; lawyer; b. Toronto, Ont. 16 Oct. 1945; s. Saul Stanley and Lillian (Davidson) L.; e. Univ. of W. Ont., B.A. 1968; Osgoode Hall Law Sch., LL.B. 1971; m. Marcelle d. Jacques and Julie Abergel 4 May 1975; children: Stephen, Joanna, Alexandra; PARTNER, CASSELS, BROCK & BLACKWELL; Dir., Atomic Energy of Canada Ltd.; Canbra Foods Ltd.; Past Gov. and Past Chrmn., Exhn. Pl.; Past Bd. Govs. Canada Sports Hall of Fame; Trustee, Molson Indy Bd. of Trustees; recreation: golf; Clubs: Bayview Golf & Country; Richmond Hill Country; Albany; Home: 26 Dunvegan Dr., Richmond Hill, Ont. L4C 6K1; Office: Scotia Plaza, 2100, 40 King St. W., Toronto, Ont. M5H 3C2.

**LEARNING, Walter J.,** B.A., M.A., D. Litt.; theatre and drama director; b. Quidi Vidi, Nfld. 16 Nov. 1938; s. Edwin James and Maud (Maheal) L.; e. Bishop Feild Coll., St. John's, Nfld. 1957; Univ. of N.B., B.A. 1961, M.A. 1963; Australian Nat. Univ., 1963–66; D.Litt. (Hon) U.N.B. 1968; m. Lea, d. James A. Mersereau, Fredericton, N.B., 14 Feb. 1962; one s., James Warwick Christopher; Artistic Dir., The Confederation Centre of the Arts & Charlottetown Festival 1987; Teaching Fellow, Univ. of N.B., 1961–63; Dir. of Drama, summer seasons 1966–67; Sessional Lectr., Mem. Univ., 1966–67; Lectr. 1967–68; Founder, Theatre New Brunswick 1968; Artistic Dir. and Gen. Mgr., The Beaverbrook Playhouse, 1968–78; Head, Theatre Section, Canada Council 1978–82; Artistic Dir., The Vancouver Playhouse 1982–87; theatrical experience in N.B. 1957–63 incl. Miller in 'Journey's End' (Dom. Drama Festival final), Marco in 'A View from the Bridge' (Dom. Drama Festival Hon. mention) and Roo, 'Summer of the Seventeenth Doll' (Dom. Drama Festival Hon. mention); during this period also involved in design, direction and production; other theatrical experience incls. Toronto summer 1961 and Canberra, Aust., 1963–66 (leading stage roles and Dir. no. of plays); also TV and drama critic, book reviewer during latter period; formed production group Prompt Theatre, Fredericton, 1966; Production Mgr., Playhouse, Fredericton, summer 1967; Asst. Dir. and Dir. several plays and stage roles St. John's, Nfld., 1966–67; Pres. N.B. Drama Soc.; Extve. Offr. N.B. Drama League for 5 yrs., Secy. 2 yrs.; Extve. Offr., Canberra Repertory Theatre, 3 yrs.; Moderator, 1967 Dom. Drama Festival theatre conf. (Nat. Vice Pres. of Festival; has served also as Gov. and Extve. Offr.); Gov., Nat. Theatre School, 1973; Founder, Theatre New Brunswick Young Company, 1974; Pres. and Gen. Mgr., Learning Productions Ltd.; co-author (with Alden Nowlan) 'Frankenstein: The Man Who Became God' 1974; 'The Dollar Woman' 1977; 'The Incredible Murder of Cardinal Tosca' 1978; writer, dir., Story editor, TV series 'Up at Ours' 1978–79; 'Svengali' 1982; 'A Gift to Last' 1982; received Graduate Fellowship 1961–63; Commonwealth Scholarship 1963–66; awarded D.Litt. from Univ. of N.B., 1978; Recipients of Queen's Jubilee Medal, 1978; Dir., Candn. Conf. of the Arts; Candn. Theatre Centre; Address: R.R. 1, Crossroads, P.E.I. C1A 7J6.

**LEATHER, Sir Edwin H.C.,** K.C.M.G., K.C.V.O., K.St.J., LL.D., B.Mil.Sc.; b. Toronto, Ontario, 22 May 1919; s. Harold H., M.B.E. and Grace C. (Holmes) L.; e. Hillfield School, Hamilton, Ontario; Trinity Coll. School, Port Hope, Ontario; RMC of Canada Grad 1939; m. Sheila A.A. d. Major & Mrs. A.H. Greenlees, Hamilton, Ont., 9 March 1940; two d., Hope A., Sarah A. G.; Dir., N.M. Rothschild (Bermuda) and other companies 1977– ; mem. Extve. Comte. and Bd. of Finance, Conservative Party Nat. Extve. Comte. 1965–71, Chrmn. 1970–71; Gov. Yehudi Menuhin Sch.; served in 2nd World War 1939–45; commd. to R.C.H.A.; served Overseas, 1940–45; cand. for S. Bristol, 1945; el. to H. of C. for N. Somerest in g.e. 1950; re-el. to H. of C. g.e. 1951, '55, '59; sometime Depy. Chrmn. Commonwealth Affairs Comte.; mem. Extve. Comte., Brit. Commonwealth Ex-Services League, 1952–63; Chrmn. Bath Festival Soc. 1960–65; Pres. Inst. of Marketing, U.K. 1963–67; Gov. & Commdr.-in-chief, Bermuda, 1973–77 (ret.); Founder and Hon. Patron, Bermuda Festival 1975– ; Trustee, Menuhin Foundation of Bermuda 1975– ; Chrmn., Bermuda Ctte. United World Colleges 1975–91; mem., Extve. Comte., Brit. Commonwealth Producers Organ.; regular Broadcaster; National Governor Shaw Festival, Niagara-on-the-Lake 1990– ; Hon. Ctte. Mem., Candn. Memorial Foundation 1991; Trustee Gurkha Welfare Appeal (Canada) 1991; rec'd. Meritorious Service Medal of Royal Candn. Legion; cr. Kt. Bachelor, 1962; Hon. F.R.S.A. 1970; K.C.M.G. 1974; K.St.J. 1974; K.C.V.O. 1975; Hon LL.D., Bath Univ. 1975; B.Mil.Sc., RMC of Canada 1994; mem. Council, Imp. Soc. of Kts. Bachelor; Gold Medal, Nat. Inst. of Social Sciences, New York, 1976; Hon. Citizen, Kansas City, Mo.; Grand Senechal, Confrerie des Chevaliers du Tastevin 1989– ; Author, 'The Vienna Elephant' 1977; 'The Mozart Score' 1978; 'The Duveen Letter' 1980; Anglican (Lay Reader since 1951); Clubs: York (Toronto); Royal Bermuda Yacht; Hamilton (Hamilton, Ont.); Address: Chelsea, 1 Inwood Close, Paget, Bermuda.

**LEATHERDALE, Marcus Andrew;** photographer; b. Montréal, Qué. 18 Sept. 1952; s. John Bruce and Grace (Andersen) L.; e. Ecole des Beaux Arts Montréal 1971–73; Los Angeles Art Center 1975; San Francisco Art Inst. 1976–77; Sch. of Visual Arts New York City 1978; m. Claudia d. Callie Summers 18 May 1979; solo exhns. incl. Clock Tower-Inst. Art & Urban Resources NYC, S44 Natoma Gallery San Francisco 1982; London (Ont.) Regional Art Gallery, Galerie in der GGK Vienna, Form & Function Gallery Atlanta 1983; Rheinisches Landesmuseum Bonn, Grey Art Gallery NYC 1984; Greathouse Gallery NYC 1984, 1985, 1986, 1987; Paul Cava Gallery Philadelphia, Gallery 291 Atlanta, Artinizer Munich 1985; Michael Todd Gallery NYC, Il Centro Culturale Canadese Wessel O'Conner Gallery Rome 1986; Collier Gallery Scottsdale, Ariz. 1987; Claus Runkel Gallery (London, Eng.) Apr. 1988; Madison Art Center (Wisconsin) Dec. 1988; Wessel O'Connor Gallery (NYC) Mar. 1989; Fay gold Gall. Sept. 1990; Brent Sikkema Gall. (NYC) Oct. 1990; Fahey Klein Gall. (Los Angeles) Nov. 1990; Arthur Rogers Gall. (New Orleans) Feb. 1991; Micheal Neumann Gall. (Dusseldorf) 1991; Runkel Hue-Williams Gall. (London) 1991; Arthur Rogers Gall., N.Y.C. 1992; Lehmann-Sitcoske, N.Y.C. 1992; Gallery Bardamu NYC 1993; group exhns., 49th Parallel Gallery-Center Contemporary Candn. Art NYC 1983; Nat. Museum of Am. Art, Smithsonian (Washington, D.C.) Apr. 1989; Philadelphia Art Alliance, Mar. 1990; Bayly Museum, (Virginia) Mar. 1990; Walker Art Museum (Minneapolis) June 1990; Contemporary Museum of Art (Chicago) Nov. 1989; recipient Nat. Endowment for Arts Grant 1984; recreations: canoeing, travel, curio collector; Address: 281 Grand St., New York City, N.Y. 10002.

**LEATHERS, Winston Lyle,** R.C.A.; artist; educator; b. Miami, Man. 29 Dec. 1932; s. Almer Leathers; e. Miami Coll. Inst. 1952; Univ. of Man. Fine Arts grad. 1956, Art Educ. 1960–61; post-grad. art educ. Mexico 1957; Man. Teachers Coll. maj. in Art Educ. 1959; Univ. of B.C. Festival of the Arts Scholarship student 1962; m. Kathleen Dawn Wilson 30 Jan. 1978; one s. Paul William; PROF. OF ENVIRONMENTAL STUDIES, UNIV. OF MAN.; mem. numerous comtes. on art educ.; solo exhns. incl. Mexico City 1957; Alty Gallery Winnipeg 1960, Toronto 1962; Univ. of B.C. 1961; Point Gallery Victoria 1963; Grant Gallery Winnipeg 1964; W. Candn. Art Circuit 1966–67; Yellow Door Gallery 1967; London, Eng. 1968; Brandon Univ. 1969; Grant Gallery Winnipeg 1969; Upstairs Gallery 1969; Mem. Art Gallery St. John's, Nfld. 1972; Beau-xi Gallery Vancouver 1973; Univ. of Man. Faculty of Arch. 1973; Winnipeg Art Gallery 1974; Albert Whyte Gallery 1975; Brian Melnychenko Gallery Winnipeg 1982; University of Man., Faculty of Architecture 1981; Cardigan-Milne Gallery 1984; rep. in numerous maj. group exhns. incl. 69th Internat. Exhn. Prints, Inst. of Contemporary Arts, Washington, D.C.; Xylon V Internat. Graphics Zurich 1971; Paris Internat. Print Exhn. 1972; Monaco and Bermuda Biennial Internat. Print Exhns. 1972; Brit. Fed. Internat. Argentina 1972; Graphics Can. Art Gallery Ont. and Nat. Travel Show 1973–74; Internat. Print Exhns. Zurich, Lucerne, London, Paris, Japan 1974; 'Manitoba Flashback,' Peterbourough Art Gallery 1981; Gallery III, School of Art, Univ. of Man. 1982; 'The Grand Western Canadian Screen Shop: A Print Legend 1968–1983,' Ukrainian Cultural Centre and Gallery III, Univ. of Man. 1983; Gail Nep, Art Consultant Services 1984; rep. in various pub., corporate and private colls. Can. USA, Europe, Mexico, S.Am.; maj. awards incl. Winnipeg Show 2nd Prize in Oils 1960; Calgary Graphics Purchase Prize 1964; Winnipeg Biennial Purchase Price 1964; Sr. Can. Council Fellowship 1967–68, Grant 1970; Soc. Painter, Etchers & Engravers 1973; Internat. Print Exhn. Zurich 1974; Finalist, Bronfman Award, Candn. Crafts Council 1983; Man. Soc. Arts; Brit. Fed. Arts; Print & Drawing Council Can.; Teacher Indust. Design Dept. Winnipeg Tech. Vocational High Sch. 1958–68; Liberal; recreations: sailing, skiing; Home: 55 Rosyln Cres., Winnipeg, Man., R3L 0H6; Office: Univ. of Man., Faculty of Arch., Winnipeg, Man.

**LEBEL, J. Louis,** Q.C. B.A., LL.B., LL.D.; b. Longueil, Que. 17 Oct. 1918; s. Alfred U. and Margaret Jean (Ivany) L.; e. Laval Univ. B.A. 1940; Univ. of Alta. LL.B. 1943; Harvard Sch. of Business Adm. 1947–48; Stanford Univ. Extve. Devel. Program 1963; m. Therese Marguerite d. Charles Edmond Barry, Edmonton, Alta. 18 Nov. 1950; children: Robert, Pierre, Charles, Marguerite, Louise, Simone; Counsel with Parlee McLaws (Calgary); Retired Pres., Dome Canada Ltd. (Calgary) April, 1985; Retired Vice Pres. and Dir. Chevron Canada Resources Ltd. Oct. 1980; Dir., Amptech Corp.; Scrim Lebel & Assoc. Ltd.; Mountain Minerals Co. Ltd.; called to Bar of Alta. 1947; appointed Queen's Council, 1979; LL.D., Univ. of Calgary 1985; served with Candn. Inf. Corps 1943–46, rank Lt.; Univ. of Calgary Chancellor 1978–82; Past Pres. Calgary Un. Appeal and Alta. Heart Foundation; Past Treas. Candn. Petroleum Law Foundation; former Chrmn. Candn. Petrol. Assn.; mem. Law Soc. Alta.; R. Catholic; recreations: golf, skiing; Clubs: Calgary Petroleum; Calgary Golf & Country; Glencoe; Home: 102, 5555 Elbow Dr. S.W., Calgary, Alta. T2V 1H7; Office: 3400, 707 – 8th Ave. S.W., Calgary, Alta. T2P 1H5.

**LEBEL, M. Maurice,** O.C. (1967), M.A., L. LèsL., Ph.D., D.Litt., D.C.L., F.R.S.C. (1947); educator; b. St. Lin, Can., 23 Dec. 1909; s. André and Eugénie (Robichaud) L.; e. Univ. of Montreal, B.A. 1928; Laval Univ., M.A. 1930; Sorbonne, Dipl. d'études Supérieures en lang. et. lit. classiques 1931; Univ. of London, B.A. (Hons.); Ph.D. (Educ.) 1952; D.Litt., Athens 1957, Hon degrees from the following Universities; Birmingham, Moncton, Memorial, Dalhousie, McMaster, Saskatchewan, Rennes,; m. Eva Sophia, d. Reginald Batt, Camberley, Eng., 7 July 1938; children: Andrew, Mark, Michael; PROF. OF ANCIENT STUDIES, LAVAL UNIV., Faculty of Letters; attended numerous educ. and scient. cong. 1936–39 and 1947; travelled throughout Europe and Russia, touring univs., 1930–39; studied Classical Antiquity for two summers in Greece, 1932–33; Prof. of Greek Lit., Laval Univ. 1937–75; Dean Faculty of Letters, 1957–63 (Secy. 1938–52); winner of Prix David 1945 and Prix Théodore Reinach (France) 1947; Pres., Classical Assn. of Can., 1955–56; mem., Candn. Authors Assn.; Classical Assn. of U.S.A.; l'assn. des Etudes Grecques de France; author of 'L'étude et l'enseignement de l'Anglais,' 1942; 'Suggestions pratiques pour notre Enseignement,' 1939; 'Les Humanités classiques dans la Société Contemporaine,'1944; 'L'Enseignement et l'étude du grec,' 1944; 'Life et le Canada Francais,' 1944; 'Natural Law in Greece'; 'Pourquoi apprend-on le grec,' 1952; 'Explications de Textes français et anglais,' 1953; 'Le Conseil Canadien de recherches sur les Humanités,' 1954; 'Lettres de Grèce,' 1955; 'L'Explication des Textes Littéraires,' 1957; 'Recheres sur les Images dans la Poésie de Sophocle,' 1957; 'Images de la Turquie,' 1957; 'Considérations sur le rôle de l'Université au XXe Siècle,' 1958; 'Humanisme et Technique,' 1959; 'La Langue parlée,' 1959; 3rd ed. 1960; 'Trois Cultures et Sagesse,' 1960; 'Le mirage des États-Unis et de la Russie dans l'enseignement supérieur au Canada,' 1961; 'La Tradition du nouveau,' 1962; 'Propos inédits et interdits sur l'Education,' 1963; 'd'Octave Cremazie à Alain Grandbois,' 1963; 'De Saint François de Sales à Alphonse Daudet,' 1964; 'De René Bazin à Saint-Exupéry,' 1964; 'Sir Philip Sidney Un Plaidoyer pour la Poésie,' 1965; 'Éducation et Humanisme,' 1966; 'Les Humanités classiques au Québec' 1967; Pages choisies d'Eugenio Maria de Hostos' 1969; La Grèce et Nous' 1969; 'Histoire Littéraire du Canada 1970; 'Mgr. Jean Calvet De la Faculté des Lettres au Pro-Rectorat 1939–45' 1970 (Bibliographie); 'Images de Chypre' 1972; 'Académie des Sciences morales et politiques Montréal' 1973; 'De transitu hellenismi ad christianismum de Guillaume Budé' 1974; 'État présent des travaux sur Platon '1975; 'Iacurto Souvenirs' 1976; 'Regards sur la Grèce d'hier et d'aujourd'hui' 1977; 'Mythes anciens et drame moderne,' 1977; 'Mutation de la culture, de l'éducation et de l'enseignement' 1978; 'La Composition Stylistique' de Denys d'Halicarnasse, 1981; 'Souvenirs historiques' 1984; Introduction, Notes et Index pour: Emile Pacault 'La fin du chômage par le partage du travail' 1985; Préfaces, Traduction, Introduction, Notes et Index pour 'Josse Bade (1462–1535)' 1988; Guillaume Budé 'De Philologia' (1532), Traduction, avec introduction, notes et index 1989; D'un livre à l'autre L'esprit des livres 1993; 'L'Ordre Equestre du Saint Sépulcre de Jérusalem Lieutenance du Canada-Québec' 1987; awarded P.J.O. Chauveau Medal 1962; Prix Venizelos, 1962; Prix de l'Académie française 1964; Order of Canada 1967; Commander of the Order of the Phoenix (Greece); Commandeur de l'Ordre du Saint Sépulcre de Jérusalem; Prof. Emeritus, Mem. Emeritus, L'ACFAS; Past Pres., Royal Soc. of Can.; Roman Catholic; Home: 2007, rue Bourbonnière, Québec, Que. G1T 1A9.

**LEBEL, Most Rev. Robert,** B.A., D.Th.; bishop; b. Trois-Pistoles, Que. 8 Nov. 1924; s. Wilfrid and Alexina Bélanger L.; e. Seminaire de Rimouski B.A. 1946; Univ. of Ottawa Faculty of Theol.; Angelicum Univ. Rome D.Th. 1951; BISHOP OF VALLEYFIELD 1976– ; Teacher of Theol. and Patristic Seminaire de Rimouski 1951–65, Rector 1963–65; Rector Coll. of Rimouski 1965–68; Prof. of Religious Sciences Univ. of Rimouski 1970–74; Auxiliary Bishop of St. Jean-de-Québec; mem. Cath. Conf. Candn. Bishops (Pres. 1989–91); mem. l'Assemblee des Eveques du Qué.; mem. Synod of Cath. Bishops, Rome 1980; author various articles religion and pastorals; mem. La Société Canadienne de Théologie; Address: 11 de l'Eglise, Valleyfield, Que. J6T 1J5.

**LEBERG, John Raoul,** C.M.; opera manager; b. Winnipeg, Man. 9 Jan. 1938; s. Felix Harold and Ruth Beatrice (Robinson) L.; e. Univ. of Toronto 1958, Opera Dept. 1968; m. Margaret d. John and Ann Harper 15 Nov. 1957; one s. John Colm; INDEPENDENT PRODUCER 1991– and MANAGING DIR., MICHIGAN OPERA THEATER 1992– ; Opera Instr. Banff Sch. of Fine Arts, Univ. of Toronto; Stage Dir. C.O.C., N.A.C., Calgary, Portland, Kitchener 1969–88; Stage Mgr. Candn. Opera Co. 1967, Prodn. Mgr. 1973, Dir. of Operations 1977, Dep. Gen. Dir. 1988–90; Depy. Gen. Dir., San Francisco Opera 1990–91; Address: 157 Maiden Lane, Box 2528, St. Marys, Ont. N4X 1A3.

**LEBLANC, Alfred Joseph,** B.A., M.A.; seminarian; b. Cheticamp, N.S. 21 July 1957; s. William Thomas and Theresa (Levert) L.; e. Margaree Forks Dist. H.S. 1975; St. Francis Xavier Univ., B.A. (Hons.) 1979; Rhodes Scholar, Oxford, B.A. 1981; Queen's Univ., M.A. 1982; Deputy Editorial Page Editor, Financial Post; Spec. Asst., Min. of External Affairs 1983–84; travelled in Asia & Europe 1984–85; enrolled Le Grand Séminaire 1985, transferred to St. Basil's Coll. and Toronto Sch. of Theology 1986–88; Home: Margaree Forks, Inv. Co., N.S. B0E 2A0.

**LEBLANC, Claude L.,** M.D., L.M.C.C.; medical doctor and administrator; b. Sydney, N.S. 16 Apr. 1932; s. James Armand A. and Kathleen (Meyers) L.; e. St. Anne's Coll, B.A. 1954; Ottawa Univ., B.Sc. 1956, M.D. 1960; m. Sandra d. Norman and Grace Lacey 25 Nov. 1961; children: Mark, Paul, John Douglas; Chief of Staff, Holy Cross Hosp. 1984; Pres., Rockyview Hosp. Staff 1970; Holy Cross Hosp. Staff 1974; Chief of Gen. Prac. 1974–80; Chrmn., Utilization Ctte. 1971–74; Preceptor; Chief of Gen. Prac., Alta. Children's Hosp. 1981–82; Clinical Asst. Prof., Univ. of Calgary Med. Sch.; Med. Dir., Drummond Petroleums Ltd.; Ocelot Industries Ltd.; Tricentrol Oil Ltd.; Mem., Alta. Coll. of Physicians & Surgeons 1961– ; Past Mem., Alta. Med. Assn., Ctte. on Hosps.; AARN Liaison Ctte.; Past vol., Calgary Exhbn. & Stampede Bd.; Bd. Mem., Banff Ctr. 1980–86 (Extve. mem. 1984– ); Dir., Calgary Elbow P.C. Constituency (Extve. Mem.); Bd. Mem., Calgary Mini Bus. Assn. 1980–84; recreation: downhill skiing; Club: Calgary Golf & Country; Home: #23, 3201 Rideau Pl. S.W., Calgary, Alta. T2S 1Z3; Office: 5116 Elbow Dr. S.W., Calgary, Alta. T2V 1H1.

**LE BLANC, Huguette;** redactrice en chef; née Dugal 18 déc. 1943; f. Oscar et Bernadette (Loubert) L.; é. Univ. de Montréal dipl. 1969; Univ. Laval cert. 1982, 1993; enfants: Caroline, David; RÉDACTRICE EN CHEF, REVUE UNIVERS; Lauréate du Salon internat. du livre de Qué. 1979, '80; Finaliste au prix France-Canada 1981 et prix de la C.U.M. 1981; auteure: 'Bernadette Dupuis ou la mort apprivoisée' 1980, 'La nuit des immensités' 1983 (romans), 'Alberto Kurapel, poésie et chant d'exil' 1983 (essai); 'Samina' 1985, 'Le Bouchra' 1985 (nouvelles); résidence: 4710 du Golf, Québec, Qué. G2A 1G7; bureau: 2269, chemin St-Louis, Québec, Qué. G1T 1R5.

**LEBLANC, Michel,** B.A.; transportation executive; b. Trois Rivières, Qué. 18 Sept. 1946; s. Roger and Pierrette (Blais) L.; e. Univ. de Montréal, B.A. 1966; State Univ. of N.Y. Buffalo, M.B.A. 1969; one d. Julie; PRESIDENT AND CHIEF EXTVE. OFFR., ROYAL AVIATION INC. 1991– ; Aviation Roger Leblanc Ltée 1970–77, Vice Pres. Sales; Pres. and Chief Extve. Offr. Conifair Aviation 1978–86; Pres. & C.E.O., Inter-Canadien 1986–91; Pres. Assn. Québécoise des Transporteurs Aériens 1984–86; Home: 4351 Montrose Ave., Westmount, Qué. H3Y 2B2.

**LeBLANC, Raymond,** B.A., B.Ed., L.ès. L., Doctorat; educator; b. St-Wenceslas, Qué. 16 Feb. 1936; s. Henri and Berthe (Lafrenière) LeB.; e. Univ. de Montréal B.A. 1960, B.Ed. 1962, L.ès. L. 1965; Univ. de Grenoble D.E.A. 1969; Univ. d'Aix-Marseilles Doctorat 1970; m. Gisèle d. Bruno and Alice Painchaud 5 Dec. 1959; one s. Michel; PROF. OF SECOND LANGUAGE CURRICULUM AND INSTRUCTION AND OF FRENCH, UNIV. OF OTTAWA 1970– ; Dir. Nat. Core French Study 1984–90, Head of Second Lang. Progs. Univ. de Montréal 1965–67; Head of French Rsch. Sector Pub. Service Comn. Ottawa 1967–68; Chrmn., Second Lang. Inst. present Univ. 1970–80, 1990– , Assoc. Prof. 1980; Prof. 1987; mem. Bibeau Comn. on Second Lang. Progs. Pub. Service Comn. 1975–76; Cons. in Lang. Evaluation Stats. Can., Min. Edn. Qué., Min. Immigration Qué., Comn. des écoles catholiques de Montréal; Guest Lectr. Univ. Laval, Univ. de Montréal; recipient Prix Ghislaine Coutu-Vaillancourt Assn. québécoise des enseignants de français langue seconde 1988; Gold Medal (Foreign Langs. Sect.) Internat. Film & TV Festival New York 1988; Robert Roy Award, Candn. Assn. of Second Language Teachers 1989; numerous rsch. grants various areas second lang. curriculum & instrn.; Keynote and Guest Speaker Candn. and Internat. Confs.; author, co-author or ed. various publs.; mem. Candn. Assn. Applied Linguistics (Treas. 1972–76); Home: 49 Blackburn Ave., Ottawa Ont. K1N 8A4; Office: 600 King Edward St., Ottawa, Ont. K1N 6N5.

**LeBLANC, Hon. Roméo A.,** P.C., M.P., B.A., B.Ed.; senator; b. L'Anse-aux-Cormier, Memramcook, N.B. 18 Dec. 1927; s. Philias and Lucie L.; e. St-Joseph Univ.; Univ. of Paris; m. Joslyn Carter, Montreal, Que. 17 Dec. 1966; children: Dominic, Geneviève; SPEAKER OF THE SENATE 1993– ; former prof. and journalist; Press Secy. to Prime Min. of Can. 1967–71; el. to H. of C. for Westmorland-Kent g.e. 1972, re-el. 74, 79, and 80; not a cand. g.e. 1984; Sworn of Privy Council and apptd. Min. of State for Fisheries 1974; Min. of Fisheries and Environment 1976; Min. of Fisheries and Oceans, Can. 1980–82; Minister of Public Works, 1982–84; summoned to The Senate June 1984; Liberal; R. Catholic; Home: (P.O. Box 93) Grand Digue, N.B.; Office: The Senate of Canada, Ottawa, Ont. K1A 0A4.

**LEBLOND, Charles Philippe,** M.D., Ph.D., D.Sc., F.R.S. (1965), F.R.S.C. (1951), O.C. (1977); university professor; b. Lille, France 5 Feb. 1910; s. Oscar and Jeanne (Desmarchelier) L.; e. Free Univ. of Lille, Lic.-ès-Sciences 1932; Univ. of Paris, M.D. 1934, D.Sc. Sorbonne, 1945; Univ. of Montreal, Ph.D. 1942; m. Gertrude, d. L. W. Sternschuss, New Haven, Conn., 22 Oct. 1936; children: Philippe, Paul, Pierre, Marie Pascale; PROF. OF ANATOMY, McGILL UNIV., since 1948; Lectr. in Anat. and Histol., Univs. of Lille and Paris, 1934–35; Rockefeller Fellow, Yale Univ., Dept. of Anat., 1935–37; Dir. of the Biol. Divn., Lab. de Synthèse Atomique, Paris, 1937–40; Research Fellow in Anat., Rochester Univ., 1940–41; Lectr. in Histol., McGill Univ., 1941–42; apptd. Asst. Prof., 1943; Assoc. Prof. of Anat., 1946; Prof. of Anatomy 1948–; Chrmn. of Dept. McGill U., 1957–74; organ. 'Selection of Personnel' in Free French Army, 1944–45; Pres., The Histochem. Soc. (1955–56); Pres., Am. Assn. Anats. 1962–63; Pres., Candn. Assn. Anats, 1966; mem., Soc. of Exper. Biol. & Med.; Biol. Stain Comn.; Amer. Soc. for Cell Biology; Fellow, Royal Soc., London and Royal Soc. of Canada; Research Adv. Group, Nat. Cancer Inst. of Can. 1953–63; author, 'L'Acide Ascorbique dans les Tissus et sa Detection,' 1936; 'Iodine Metabolism,' in 'Advances in Biological and Medical Physics,' 1948; about three hundred articles of original research work in biol. and med.; rec'd. the following Special Honours; Prix Saintour, French Academy 1935, Iodine Education Bureau Award 1951, NATO Professor, University of Louvain, Belgium 1959, Flavelle Medal, Royal Society of Canada 1961, Medal Leo Pariseau, Assoc, Canadienne-Française pour l'Avancement des Sciences 1962, Gairdner Fdn. Award 1965, Am. Coll. Phys. Award for distinguished contrib. in med. science 1966, Province of Quebec Biology Prize 1968, Honorary Member of the American Academy of Arts and Sciences 1970, Honorary Degree of Doctor of Science: Acadia University, Wolfville, Nova Scotia 1972; McGill University 1982; Université de Montréal 1985; York Univ. 1986; Université de Sherbrooke 1988; Isaac Schour Award of the International Association for Dental Research 1974, Fogarty Scholar of the National Institutes of Health (January to July) 1975, Prix Scientifique de l'Association Canadienne des Médecins de Langue Française 1976, Officer of the Order of Canada 1977, Henry Gray Award of the American Association of Anatomists 1978, J.C.B. Grant Award of the Cdn. Assoc. of Anatomists 1979; McLaughlin Medal of the Royal Society of Canada 1983; Gomori Prize of the Histochemical Soc. 1988; Prix Marie-Victorin de la Province de Québec, 1992; Club: Faculty; Home: 68 Chesterfield Ave., Westmount, Que. H3Y 2M5.

**LEBLOND, Jean-Claude,** M.Sc.; editor; b. Montréal, Qué. 30 June 1947; e. Univ. de Montréal, M.Sc. 1981; children: Nicolas, Alexis; Ed. Banque Canadienne Nationale, Montréal 1977–78; Visual Arts Co-Ordinator Nat. Capital Comn. Ottawa 1983–85; Gen. Mgr. Société des Musées Québécois, Montréal 1985–86; Dir. and Ed., Vie des Arts 1987–92; cons. McCord Museum of Candn. Hist. Montréal; Dept. Cultural Affairs Govt. Qué.; Internat. Council Museum; Assn. Internationale de la Critique d'Art; Office: 200 rue St-Jacques, bureau 600, Montréal, Qué. H2Y 1M1.

**LeBLOND, Paul Henri,** B.A., B.Sc., Ph.D., D.Sc. (h.c.), F.R.S.C.; educator; b. Quebec, Que. 30 Dec. 1938; s. Sylvio and Jeanne (Lacerte) LeB.; e. Petit Séminaire de Chicoutimi B.A. 1957; McGill Univ. B.Sc. 1961; Univ. of B.C. Ph.D. (Phys. Oceanography) 1964; m. Josée d. Gerard and Trina Michaud 18 May 1963 (now div.); children: Michel, Philippe, Anne; DIR., PROGRAM IN EARTH & OCEAN SCIENCES and PROF. OF OCEANOGRAPHY AND PHYSICS, UNIV. OF B.C.; NATO Postdoctoral Fellow, Univ. Kiel, W. Germany 1964–65; Visiting Prof./Research Sci., Bedford Inst. Dartmouth, N.S. 1968; Univ. Havana 1972; Simon Fraser Univ. 1970; Inst. Oceanology USSR Acad. Sci., Moscow 1973; Laval Univ. 1979; State Univ. of N.Y. Stony Brook, L.I., N.Y. 1983; Univ. Marseille 1985; Assoc. Dean, Faculty of Science, U.B.C. 1983–85; co-recipient Pres.'s Prize Candn. Meteorol. & Oceanographic Soc. 1981; Tully Medal, Candn. Meteorol. & Oceanographic Soc. 1991; Foreign mem., Russian Academy of Natural Science; co-author 'Waves in the Ocean' 1978; author or co-author over 70 tech. jour. articles oceanic waves, coastal circulation, beach evolution, Arctic oceanography; mem. various ed. bds.; mem., Fisheries Resource Conservation Council; Bd. mem., Candn. Centre for Fisheries Innovation; Founding Bd. mem. Internat. Soc. Cryptozool. 1982; Bd. Chrmn., B.C. Cryptozoology Club; mem. Candn. Meterol. & Oceanographic Soc.; Am. Geophys. Union; Am. Meterol. Soc.; The Oceanography Soc.; recreations: cycling, hiking, travel, science-fiction; Home: 3773 West 18th Ave., Vancouver, B.C. V6S 1B3; Office: Vancouver, B.C. V6T 1W5.

**LEBRUN, Hon. Guy,** B.A., LL.L.; judge; b. St-Tite, Qué. 30 Jan. 1931; s. Jean-Baptiste and Jeanne (Trottier) L.; e. Juniorat du Sacré-Coeur Ottawa; Seminaire St-Joseph Trois-Rivières; Univ. St-Joseph, Memramcook, N.B., B.A. 1952; Univ. Laval, LL.L. 1957; m. Françoise d. Benoit and Therese Dionne Martin 31 Oct. 1960; children: Christine, Michel, Genevieve; JUDGE, SUPERIOR COURT OF QUE. 1972– ; called to Bar of Qué. 1958; law practice Cap-de-la-Madeleine, Qué. 1959–63; Lebrun & Lamothe 1963–68; Lebrun & Moreau 1968–72; Coroner, Comté Trois-Rivières & Champlain, Qué. 1960–64; Crown Prosecutor Qué. 1964–66; Adm. Caisse

Populaire St-Madeleine, Qué. 1963–72; Law Cons. Town of Cap-de-la-Madeleine 1960–72; First Councillor Local Bar 1972; Dir. Société Charles N. Deblois 1967– ; recreations: golf, skiing; Home: 208 Pie XII, Cap-de-la-Madeleine, Qué. G8T 1R1; Office: #1.05, 250 Laviolette, Trois-Rivières, Qué. G9A 1T9.

**LECERF, Olivier Maurice Marie,** B.A., LL.M.; industrialist; b. Merville-Franceville (Calvados), France 2 Aug. 1929; s. late Maurice and Colette (Lainé) L.; e. Coll. St. Louis de Gonzague, Paris B.A. (Philos.) 1946; Ecole des Sciences Politiques, Paris Dipl. 1950; Univ. of Paris LL.M. 1950; Univ. of Geneva Centre d'Etudes Industrielles grad. 1960; m. Aline Marie-Anne (Annie) d. R. Bazin de Jessey, Paris, France 11 Jan. 1958; children: Christophe, Véronique, Nicolas, Patricia; HON. CHRMN. LAFARGE COPPÉE 1989, Chrmn. & C.E.O. 1974– , Chrmn. of Financiere Lafarge Coppée; Dir., Lafarge Coppée; Orsan, L'Oreal - SEB S.A. Cementia; Compagnie de St. Gobain; mem., Internat. Adv. Ctte. of Morgan Stanley; Asst. Mgr. Omnium for Importation and Exportation, Paris 1951–56; joined Ciments Lafarge, Paris 1956, Asst. Mgr. 1956–60 (serving in Can. 1956–57, Brazil 1958–59); Asst. Mgr. Foreign Dept. 1961, Asst. Comm. Mgr. Paris 1962–64; Gen. Mgr. and Pres. Lafarge Cement of North America, Vancouver 1965; Pres. Ciments Lafarge Quebec, Montreal 1968 becoming Lafarge Canada Ltd. 1969; Gen. Mgr. Canada Cement Lafarge 1970; Extve. Gen. Mgr. Ciments Lafarge Paris 1971–73; Chrmn. & C.E.O., Ciments Lafarge 1974 (company became Lafarge, June 1974; and Lafarge Coppée 1980); Chrmn. & C.E.O. 1984; named Officier, Legion of Honour; Commandeur, Order National du Merite; R. Catholic; recreations: golf, tennis, skiing, swimming; Clubs: Automobile C. de France; Polo C. de Paris; Home: 8, rue Guy de Maupassant, 75116 Paris, France; Office: 61, rue des Belles Feuilles, 75116 Paris, France.

**LECKER, Robert,** B.A., M.A., Ph.D.; university professor/publisher; b. Montreal, Que. 9 Dec. 1951; s. Nathan and Dorothy (Campbell) L.; e. York Univ., B.A. 1974, M.A. 1976, Ph.D. 1980; one d.: Emily; PROF., MCGILL UNIV. 1988– ; McGill Institute for the Study of Can. 1994– ; Asst. Prof., Univ. of Maine at Orono 1978–82; Assoc. Prof. present univ. 1982–88; Dir., M.A. Graduate Program in English 1989–93; Publisher, ECW Press; Dir., Candn. Literary Rsch. Found.; H. Noel Fieldhouse Award for distinguished teaching, McGill Univ. 1985 and recipient of several rsch. grants; Social Sciences and Humanities Rsch. Council of Can. rsch. grant 1992, 1993, 1994; Can. Counc. doct. fellowships 1979, 1978, 1977, 1976, 1975 and several scholarships; Mem., Assn. for Candn. & Que. Literatures (Vice-Pres. 1984–86); ACS; ACQL; ACCUTE; ACSUS; MLA; author: 'On the Line' 1982; 'Robert Kroetsch' 1986; 'An Other I' 1988; editor: 'Twayne's World Authors Series-Canada,' 'Twayne's Masterwork Studies,' 'Critical Essays on World Literature'; editor: 'The Borderlands Anthology: Essays on Canadian-American Relations' 1991; 'Canadian Canons: Essays in Literary Value' 1991; co-editor: 'Essays on Canadian Writing' 1975– ; 'The Annotated Bibliography of Canada's Major Authors' 1979, 1980, 1981, 1983, 1984, 1987, 1988, 1990 (8 vols.); 'Introduction to Poetry' 1981; 'Canadian Poetry' 1982 (2 vols.); 'An Anthology of Maine Literature' 1982; 'Introduction to Fiction' 1983; 'Canadian Writers and Their Works' 1983, 1984, 1986, 1987, 1988, 1989, 1990, 1992 (20 vols.); 'Introduction to Literature: British, American, Canadian' 1987; 'The New Canadian Anthology: English-Canadian Poetry and Short Fiction' 1988; Advisory Bd., Borderlands Rsch. Project on Candn.-Am. Relations 1989– ; author of num. articles, papers & reviews; Home: 4055 Melrose Ave., Montreal, Que. H4A 2S5; Office: 853 Sherbrooke St. W., Montreal, Que. H3A 2T6.

**LECKIE, Keith Ross;** writer; b. Toronto, Ont. 26 Apl. 1952; s. John Myles and Jessie Margarette (Ross) L.; e. Ryerson Polytech. Inst. Photo Arts Degree 1975; Nat. Film Bd. Actor/Writers/Dirs. Workshop 1977–79; m. Mary d. Roy and Connie Young 6 June 1981; children: Toban, Katelyn; feature TV scripts incl. 'Crossbar' CBC 1979 (novelized 1979); 'Special Delivery' 1985 (Columbus Internat. Festival 2nd Prize 1986); 'Where the Spirit Lives' CBC, BBC 1988 (Gemini Award, Best Film 1990); 'Lost in the Barrens' Atlantis films 1989; 'Journey into Darkness: The Bruce Curtis Story' 1989 (Gemini Award 1992); 'The Avro Arrow Story' 1990, 1994; 'The Price of Vengeance' NBC 1993; 'Fortitude Bay' CBC 1994; co-writer 'African Journey' 1989; writer/dir. numerous episodes 'The Beachcombers', 'Spirit Bay', 'Danger Bay' since 1984; author 'The Seventh Gate' novel 1989; recipient San Francisco Internat. Festival Special Jury Award 1987, Columbus Film Festival Chris Award 1987, N.Y. Film Festival Blue Ribbon 1988 for 'Spirit Bay' episode 'Words on a Page' 1986; recreations: flying, sailing, scuba diving; Address: 590 Indian Rd., Toronto, Ont. M6P 2C2.

**LECKY, John MacMillan Stirling,** M.A., LL.B., C.F.A.; holding and operating company executive; b. Vancouver, B.C. 29 Aug. 1940; s. late John and Edna Marion L.; e. Shawnigan Lake Sch.; Neuchatel Jr. Coll.; Univ. of B.C., B.A. 1961; Cambridge Univ. M.A. 1963, LL.B. 1964; m. Frances Ferguson, Montréal, Qué. 1974; children: Caroline, Jonathan, Christopher, Edward, Anton; FOUNDER, CHRMN. AND PRES. THE RESOURCE SERVICE GROUP LTD. 1972– and CO-FOUNDER AND CHRMN., CANADA 3000 AIRLINES LTD. 1988– ; Dir., Lone Star Grinding Co. Inc. Houston, Texas; read law Middle Temple, Inn of Court, London, Eng. 1961–64; Invest. Analyst, Greenshields, Montréal 1965, Asst. to Chrmn. 1968, Mgr. Invest. Mgmt. & Rsch. Dept. 1970; Gov.: Shawnigan Lake Sch.; The Olympic Trust; mem. Extve. Bd. Candn. Olympic Assn.; N. Am. Extve. Ctte. mem. Fedn. Internationale des Societs d'Aviron; Organizing Ctte. 1975 F.I.S.A. World Jr. Rowing Championships Montréal; mem. Calgary C. of C.; Head, Candn. Summer Games Team Los Angeles 1984 Summer Olympics; mem. Extve. Ctte. Calgary 1988 Winter Olmpics, mem. Nominating Ctte., Sponsorship & Licencing Ctte., Chrmn. Finance & Budget Ctte.; honours incl. Silver Medal eight-oared rowing Olympics Rome 1960; Capt. Vancouver Rowing Club 1961; Oxford Cambridge Boat Race Winning Crews 1962–64; Candn. Rugby Team UK Tour 1963; Pres. The Hawks Club Cambridge 1963; MacKenzie King Scholarship Internat. Law 1964; Silver Goblet and Nickalls Challenge Cup Royal Henley Regatta Course Record 1964; Protestant; recreations: running, shooting; Clubs: Mount Royal (Montréal); Vancouver; Vancouver Rowing; Glencoe; Bow Valley; Home: 717 Royal Ave. S.W., Calgary, Alta. T2S 0G3; Office: Suite 2540, Sunlife Plaza, 144 – 4th Ave. S.W., Calgary, Alta. T2P 3N4.

**LeCLAIR, J. Maurice,** C.C., B.Sc., M.D.,C.M., M.Sc. (Medicine), L.L.D., D.Sc.(Hon.c.) F.R.C.P.(C), F.A.C.P.; corporate executive; b. Sayabec, Que. 19 June 1927; s. François and Rose-Anna (Chassé) LeC.; e. McGill Univ., B.Sc. 1947, M.D., C.M. 1951; Univ. of Minn., M.Sc. (Medicine) 1958; m. Pauline, d. Eugène Héroux, Shawinigan, Que., 22 Nov. 1952; children: Suzanne, Marie, François, Manon, Nathalie, Guy; Vice-Chrmn., CIBC 1987–92; Chrmn. & C.E.O., Canadian National, 1985–86; Pres. & C.E.O., 1982–85; Sr. Corp. Vice Pres. 1981; Corp. Vice Pres. 1979; Secy. of Treasury Board 1976; Secy. Min. of Science and Technol. 1974; Depy. Min. of Health and Welfare 1970; Dean, Faculty of Med., Univ. of Sherbrooke, 1968; Head, Dept. of Med., 1965; Vice Dean, Fac. of Med., Univ. of Montréal, 1962; Consulting Internist, Notre Dame Hospital, Montreal, 1958; Fellow, Mayo Clinic, Minn., 1955; G.P., Shawinigan, 1953; Vice Pres., Med. Research Council of Can. 1968–70; Dir., Can. Imp. Bank of Commerce; John Labatt Ltd.; Sceptre Resources Ltd. (Chrmn.); Connaught Laboratories Ltd.; Pasteur Mérieux s.v. (France); Mem. Royal Comn., Intercity Passenger Transportation 1989; author of over 30 publications in Med. & Admin.; Offr. Order of Canada 1980; Commander, Order of St. John 1983; Knight, Order of Malta 1984; Companion, Order of Canada 1986; Roman Catholic; Home: 500 Laird Blvd., Town of Mount Royal, Que. H3R 1Y4.

**LECLERC, Guy,** B.Com.; b. Quebec City, Que. 1933; e. Univ. Laval B.Com. 1953, grad. studies Bus. & Econ. 1954 and later Carleton Univ.; m. one s.; RESEARCH ASSOC., CANADIAN COMPREHENSIVE AUDITING FOUNDATION; served 3 yrs. private financial field; joined Stats. Can. 1957 becoming Asst. Chief Statistician Can.; Trustee & First Vice-Chrmn., Children's Hosp. E. Ont.; del. numerous internat. confs.; served 3 yrs. as mem. exec. U.S. Income & Wealth Conf. Nat. Bureau Econ. Rsch.; Dep. Comptroller Gen. Prog. Evaluation Br., Office of Comptroller Gen. of Canada 1983–91; author numerous papers nat. & internat. levels; Office: The Carriageway, 55 Murray, Suite 210, Ottawa, Ont. K1N 5M3.

**LECLERC, Jean;** editor; director; producer; b. Tracy, Que. 27 Oct. 1948; m. Martine Hudon 14 June 1980; 1 s. Jerome; wrote, edited and directed: 'Les inquietudes d'Elisa' (short film) 1972; 'Les feux de la rampe' (short film) 1974; 'Jalousie' (short film) 1979; 'Jeunesse ad lib' (long feature documentary) 1985; 'Franc parler' (TV special) 1987; 'Borduas' (TV Special) 1988; 'Les Fils du Soleil' (TV Special) 1989; Mad For Ads (TV Series) 1990, 1991, 1992; writer and dir. of many commercials, promotional and ind. films, and videos; Information Services Institute Award 1986; Silver Hugho, Television Sect., Chicago Film & Video Festival 1986; Silver Plaque, Chicago Film & Video Festival 1987; Finalist Award, New York Film Festival 1986; Yorktown Film Festival 1990; Nominations at the Prix Gemeaux, l'Academie du Cinema et de la Television Canadienne 1986, 1987, 1990, 1991, 1992; winner of Prix Gemeaux for Best Editing for 'Les Fils du Soleil'; author of 'Quand on ne voit tout ca!' (biography) 1980; 'Playback' (TV series); Address: 11, 075 Marie-Victorin, Tracy, Que. J3P 5N4.

**LECLERC, Yves,** B.A., M.D., FRCS, FACS; surgeon; b. Quebec, Que. 14 June 1948; s. Maurice and Marie-Jeanne (Paquette) L.; e. Coll. Jesuit B.A. 1965; Laval Univ. M.D. 1973; m. Daniele d. Paul and Pauline Boulet 9 May 1976; HEAD OF CARDIOVASCULAR SURGERY, MONTREAL HEART INSTITUTE 1986– ; Cardiovascular Surgeon, Montreal Heart Inst. 1985; Consultant, Cardiovascular Surgery, Ste-Justine, St-Luc, Maisonneuve Rosemont Hospital 1985– ; recreations: skiing, sailing, photography; Office: 5000, rue Bélanger est, Montreal, Que. H1T 1C8.

**LE CLÈRE, René;** internat. civil servant; writer; b. Oise, France 5 June 1940; s. Édouard Charles and Lucie Charlotte (Battellier) le C.; e. Univ. du Québec à Montréal, Dip. Éducation 1973; Order Profl. Technols. in Applied Sci's of Qué., Eng. Dip. 1983; HUMAN RIGHTS OBSERVER, ORGANISATION OF AMERICAN STATES (O.A.S.), RÉPUBLIQUE D'HAÏTI 1993– ; private sec. Hon. François Leduc 1964, Marquise de Ruzé d'Effiat 1970–74, Don Umberto, The Duke Pini di San Miniato 1984–86; Air Can. Lit. Award Sec. 1976–80, Pres. 1984; terminologist Canatom, VIA Rail Can., Candn. Red Cross 1976–87; Sec. Gen. Fedn. French Alliances Can. 1980–84, Soc. French-speaking Candn. Writers 1975–80, 1983–88; Sec. Gen. Internat. P.E.N. Qué. Center 1988–93; recipient Air Can. Lit. Award 1977; author numerous articles, studies, tech. lexicons, one tech. book; contbr. various newspapers, acad. jours.; Fellow, Augustan Soc. (USA); Hon. mem. Soc. French-speaking Candn. Writers; Dubbed "Knight" by HMSH the Prince Ernest August of Lippe 1977; mem. Alliance française de Montréal; Cercle généalogique de Picardie; Assoc. canadienne pour les Nations unies; Société généalogique canadienne-française; Musée du Château Ramezay, etc.; recreations: genealogy, music, reading; Club: Mount Royal Tennis Club; Home: 418 Claremont Ave., Apt. 32, Montréal, Qué. H3Y 2N2; Office: P.O. Box 329 Victoria Station, Montréal, Qué. H3Z 2V8.

**L'ECUYER, Jacques,** B.Sc., Ph.D.; civil servant; b. St-Jean sur Richelieu, Qué. 6 March 1937; s. Paul and Lucienne (Frenette) L'E.; e. Séminaire de St-Jean B.A. 1956; Univ. de Montréal B.Sc. 1959 (General Motors Scholarship 1956–59), Ph.D. 1965 (NRC Scholarship 1959–61); m. Aline d. Edgar and Alice (Bélanger) Payette 15 Aug. 1959; children: Jacques D., Nicolas, Geneviève; PRESIDENT, COMMISSION D'EVALUATION DE L'ENSEIGNEMENT COLLEGIAL DU QUEBEC 1993– ; Lectr. Univ. de Sherbrooke 1963–64; Prof. Univ. Laval 1964–67; NRC Post-doctoral Fellow, Oxford Univ. 1967–69; Prof. Univ. de Montréal 1969–79, Prés. Syndicat général des professeurs 1973–75, mem. Assemblée universitaire 1973–77, mem. Bd. Govs. 1976–79; Prés. Comm. de la recherche universitaire du Québec 1979–81; Prés. Conseil des universités du Québec 1981–88; Vice-Prés (Academic Affairs) Univ. du Québec 1988–93; author over 40 publs. various sci. jours.; mem. Assn. canadienne pour l'Avancement des Sciences; Hong Kong Council for Acad. Accreditation; Organization of American States Inter-American Ctte. on Education (Washington); Home: 10, 890 rue Berri, Montréal, Qué. H3L 2H5; Office: 905, Aut Dufferin-Montmorency, 3e etage, Quebec, Qué. G1R 5M6.

**LE DAIN, Bruce,** RCA; artist; b. Montreal, Que. 26 April 1928; s. Eric George Bryant and Antoinette Louise (Whithard); e. West Hill H.S. 1945; Sir George Williams College Fine Arts 1947; m. Gertrud d. Gabrielle and Rudolf Zenker 9 May 1959; children: Derek, Timon, Trevor; Art Dir., Odhams Press (U.K.) 1953–54; Mather & Crowther 1954–57; Art Dir./Creative Dir., McKim (Montreal) 1957–77; established studio in Montreal 1977; group exbns.: Montreal Museum Annual Spring 1949/52/53; Royal Candn. Acad. of Arts 87th Annual 1966; Memorial Univ. Art Gallery 1979; Thomas Moore Inst. 1969/90; First Prize, Price Fine Arts Award '67/'69; solo exbns.: Walter Klinkhoff Gall. Montreal (6); Manuge Gall. Halifax (1); rep. in private collections in Canada, U.S., England, France, Germany, Holland, Israel & Japan & over 50 corp. collections; graphic design awards: Art Dir. Club of Montreal 1959/61; Graphica '65, '66, '68, '71; Art Dir. Club of N.Y. 1964/66; Socrates Award USA 1959/62; Chair, Beautification & Devel. Grounds Ctte., Douglas Hospital 1982–88 (area named Bruce Le Dain Park in his honour); elected Royal Canadian Acad. of Arts 1984; Interim Pres. 1991–92; Pres. 1992–93; awarded Commemorative Medal for 125th Anniversary of Candn. Confederation 1993; Invitee and Medalist 1993 Biennale, Société Nationale des Beaux-Arts, Paris; Anglican; recreations: writing, family and friends; clubs: Hon. Life Mem., The Arts Club of Montral; Home/Studio: 21 Stratford Rd., Hampstead, Que. H3X 3C3; Summer Studio: Schooner Cove, N.S.

**LE DAIN, Hon. Gerald Eric,** C.C., Q.C., B.C.L., D. de l'Univ., D.C.L., LL.D.; retired judge; b. Montreal, Que., 27 Nov. 1924; s. Eric George Bryant and Antoinette Louise (Whithard) Le D.; e. West Hill High Sch., 1942; William A. Birks and Sir William Macdonald Schols. to McGill Univ., (Arts), 1942–43; Candn. Army Univ. Course ('With Distinction'), McGill Univ., 1943–44; Khaki University, Eng., 1946; McGill University, B.C.L., 1949; Univ. Scholar; Elizabeth Torrance Gold Medal; Macdonald Travelling Scholarship; Université de Lyon, Docteur de l'Université ('Mention Très Bien'), 1950; Hon. LL.D.'s, York Univ. 1976; Concordia Univ. 1976; McGill University 1985; Hon. D.C.L., Acadia Univ. 1978; m. Cynthia Moira Emily, d. late Colin Ian Roy, 13 Sept. 1947; children: Jacqueline, Catherine, Barbara, Caroline, Eric, Jennifer; Justice, Supreme Court of Canada May 1984 to Nov. 1988; now retired; called to the Bar of Quebec, 1949; cr. Q.C., 1961; practised law with Walker, Martineau, Chauvin, Walker & Allison, 1950–53; Associate Professor and Secy., Faculty of Law, McGill Univ., 1953–59; Legal Dept., Canadian International Paper Co., 1959–61; Partner, Riel, Le Dain, Bissonnette Vermette & Ryan, 1961–66; a counsel to the Attorney General for Quebec in constitutional cases, 1963–67; Prof., Constitutional and Adm. Law, McGill Univ., 1966–67; Prof. of Law, Osgoode Hall Law Sch. York Univ. 1967–75 and Dean of Law there 1967–72; called to the Bar of Ont. 1968; appt'd to Federal Court of Appeal 1975; served with Canadian Army, 1943–46; Gunner, N.W. Theatre, with 7th Medium Regt., R.C.A., 1944–45; Army of Occupation, 1945–46; published several articles on constitutional adm. comm. and civil law and legal educ.; Consultant to Royal Comn. on Bilingualism and Biculturalism; Adv. to Special Counsel on the Constitution to the Min. of Justice 1967; Chrmn., Comn. of Inquiry into Non-Medical Use of Drugs 1969–73; Companion of the Order of Canada 1989; The Justice Gerald Le Dain Award for Achievement in the Field of Law of the Drug Policy Foundation, Washington 1990; Anglican; Club: Rideau; Home: 263 Island Park Drive, Ottawa, Ont. K1Y 0A5.

**LEDDY, (John) Francis,** O.C. (1972), M.A., M.Litt., D.Phil., D.Litt., D.ès L., D.C.L., LL.D., K.C.S.G. (1964), F.R.S.A. (1971); F.R.Hist.S. (1972); former university president; b. Ottawa, Ont. 16 Apr. 1911; s. late John Joseph and Teresa Frances (Dwyer) L.; e. Univ. of Sask., B.A. (Hons. in Latin and French) 1930, M.A. (Latin) 1931, LL.D. 1965; Univ. of Chicago (Grad. Sch.) 1932–33; Oxford Univ., 1933–36; (Sask. Rhodes Schol. at Exeter Coll.), B. Litt. 1935, D.Phil. (for research in Ancient Hist.) 1938 and M. Litt. 1980; D. Litt., St. Francis Xavier 1953; Ottawa 1957; Windsor 1988; D.ès L., Laval 1956; LL.D., Assumption, 1956; D.C.L., St. Mary's 1960; LL.D. Toronto 1966; Hanyang (Korea) 1971; Notre Dame (Nelson, B.C.) 1971; Waterloo Lutheran 1972; West. Ontario 1975; Hon. Fellow, Exeter Coll. 1983; m. Kathleen Beatrice, B.A., d. late W.T. White, 7 May 1938; Instr. in Classics. Univ. of Sask., 1936–39, Asst. Prof. 1939–45 and Assoc. Prof. 1945–46; Prof. and Head of Dept., 1946–64; Dean Coll. of Arts and Science, 1949–64; Vice-Pres. (Academic), 1961–64; Dir., Univ. of Sask. Summer Sch., 1942–49; Chrmn., Educ. Council, Prov. of Sask., 1945–63; mem. of Senate, Univ. of Sask., 1945–64; Pres. & Vice-Chancellor, Univ. of Windsor 1964–78; Extve. mem., Nat. Conf. of Candn. Univs., 1948–50, 1956–57 (Secy. Treas. 1953–56); Hon. Life mem., Sask. Alumni Assn. (Pres., 1940–43); mem. Humanities Research Council of Can. 1943–64 (Chrmn., 1949, 1955); Humanities Assn. of Can. (first Chrmn. 1950–52); Classical Assn. of Can. (Pres., 1956–58); Candn. Inst. Internat. Affairs (Pres. Saskatoon Br. 1943; mem. of Nat. Council 1944 and 1951–55); Pres., Candn. Assn. Rhodes Scholars, 1957–59; President, Candn. Nat. Comn. for UNESCO, 1960–62; mem., Candn. Cath. Hist. Assn. (President General 1960–61); Adv. Bd., CARE of Canada; Candn. Del., Internat. Union of Acads., Brussels, 1953, 1955, 1958, Rome 1956, Stockholm, 1961, Vienna, 1963; Candn. mem., Extve. Council, Assn. of Univs. of Brit. Commonwealth, Melbourne, Aust., Aug. 1955; Hon. Pres., Nat. Fed. of Candn. Univ. Students, 1961–62; Candn. Del., East-West UNESCO Conf., Calcutta, 1961; mem., Bd of Dirs., Assn. Univ. Coll. of Can.1966–69; mem., Prov. Comte. on Aims and Objectives of Educ. in Schs. of Ont., 1965–68; Pres., Candn. Service for Overseas Students and Trainees, 1967–70; Pres. Gen., Eng. Cath. Educ. Assn. of Ont., 1967–69; Vice-Pres., Internat. Extve., World Univ. Service, 1964–68; Hon. Pres., Candn. Univ. Service Overseas (Chrmn. 1962–65); Vice Chrmn. The Can. Council, 1964–69, mem., 1957–60; mem., Nat. Conf. on Centennial1963–67; Chrmn., Organizing Comte., Co. of Young Candns.1965; mem., Council, Candn. Soc. for Asian Studies 1970–72; Hon. Pres., Candn. Assn., The Order of Malta 1981, Pres 1978–81; Hon. Pres. World Federalists of Canada, 1981; Pres. 1979–81; Chrmn., Council, World Assn. of World Federalists, 1983–87; Pres., World Assn. of World Federalists 1987–1991; Human Relations Award, Candn. Council Christians and Jews, 1953; Univ. of Sask., Alumni Assn. Award for Achievement, 1980; University of Windsor Alumni Award 1984; Gov't of Saskatchewan, Special Presentation, 1984; Papal Medal, 'Pro Ecclesia et Pontifice,' 1956; Knight of Malta, 1956; Knight of the Holy Sepulchre, 1959; Knight of St. Gregory 1964; Cardinal Newman Award, Candn. Fed. Newman Clubs, 1958; Lateran Cross, 1963; Gentleman of His Holiness, Pope Paul VI, 1969; and of Pope John Paul I, 1978; and of Pope John Paul II, since 1978; Roman Catholic; Address: The Leddy Library, University of Windsor, Windsor, Ont. N9B 3P4.

**LEDDY, Sister Mary Jo,** Ph.D.; journalist; b. Toronto, Ont. 1 Feb. 1946; d. John Edward and Rita Therese (Wilkinson) L.; e. Univ. Sask., B.A. 1968; B. Ed., 1970; Univ. Toronto, M.A. 1972; Ph.D. 1980; mem. relig. community Sisters of Sion; High Sch. Teacher 1968–70; Campus Minister, Newman Ctr. (Toronto) 1976–77; founder & ed. Catholic New Times 1976; Editor, Catholic New Times 1976–84; Editorial Team, CNT 1985–88; part-time univ. Lectr., Univ. Coll. (Toronto); Maryknoll Seminary (Higham, Mass.); Regis Coll. (Toronto); regular columnist, Toronto Star Religion Page 1979–86; author numerous articles Catholic New Times, Toronto Star, Catalyst, Grail, Compass, National Catholic Reporter; Mandate, the Reporter, Prairie Messenger, etc. 1976–88; Introduction to 'Quiet Heroes' by Andre Stein; 'The Faith That Transforms: Essays in Honor of Gregory Baum' 1987; rec'd. Gov. Gen. Bronze Medal 1963; Govt. Entrance Scholarship 1965; Univ. Undergrad. Scholarship 1966; Govt. Education Scholarship 1967; Ont. Grad. Fellowship 1971; Can. Counc. Doctoral Fellowship 1972; Candn. Univ. Presidents' Award: One of Outstanding Young Women 1978; Candn. Church Press Award: Best Editorial 1978; Candn. Church Press Award: Best Editorial: Best Feature Article 1979, 1988; Catholic Press Assn. Award for Best Nat. Catholic Newspaper in North America 1982; College Theology Soc. Award for best book ('Faith that Transforms') 1988; Ida Nudel Humanitarian Award 1984; Newman Ctr. Bd. Dirs. (Toronto) 1980–81; Sisters of Sion Prov. Counc. 1973–79; Provl. Co-ordinator, N. Amer. Province, Sisters of Sion 1983–88; Moderator, Niagara Inst. 1982; Commentator, Papal Visit CBC TV 1984 and 1987; awarded Candn. Jewish Congress Humanitarian Award 1987; mem. Holocaust Remembrance Comte. Toronto; Catholic Press Assn.; Candn. Church Press; Extve. Council, Candn. Religious Conf. – Ont.; Interfaith Ctte. on Soviet Jewry; Ed. Bd., Grail; Ed. Bd., Frye Publishing; Hon. Dir., Shalom Inst., Vancouver; Address: 48 Wanda Rd., Toronto, Ont. M6P 1C6.

**LEDERIS, Karolis (Karl) Paul,** B.Sc., Ph.D., D.Sc., F.R.S.C.; university professor (emeritus); b. Noreikoniai, Lithuania 1 Aug. 1920; s. Paul Augustus and Franciska Veronika (Danisevicius) L.; e. Linkuva State Gym. 1937; Siauliai Teacher's Coll. (Lith.) 1939; Univ. of Giessen & Muenster 1947; Univ. of Bristol, B.Sc. 1958, Ph.D. 1961, D.Sc. 1968; m. Hildegard d. Hugo and Anna Gallistl 28 Feb. 1952; children: Aldona Franciska, Edmund Paul; EMERITUS PROF. OF PHARMACOL., UNIV. OF CALGARY 1989– ; 'UPJOHN' award in Pharmacology 1990; Rsch. Asst. to Reader in Pharm., Univ. of Bristol 1958–69; postdoct. fellow, Univ. of Kiel 1961–62; Vis. Sci., Univ. of Calif. at Berkeley 1967–68; Prof. of Pharm., Univ. of Calgary 1969–89; Vis. Prof., universities of Lille, Paris, Giessen, Hamburg, Muenchen, Mendoza, Santiago & Valdivia, Vilnius, Kyoto, Bristol 1963–89; Visiting Sci., Institute for Cell Biochem. and Clin. Neurobiology, Univ. of Hamburg 1989– ; Mem./Chair, MRC grants cttees. for endocrin. & prog. grants 1972–92; Mem., MRC: Member of Council 1983–90; Extve. Ctte. 1984–90; Mem., Internat. Peer Review Ctte., Networks of Centres of Excellence; FRSC 1987; Ed.-in-Chief, Pharm. 'Internat. J. for Exper. & Clin. Pharm.' 1977–86; Mem., Candn. Pharm., Physiol., Biochem. societies; U.K. Pharm., Physiol., Endocrin. societies; U.S. N.Y. Acad. of Sci., Endocrine Soc.; Internat. Brain Rsch. Orgn.; editor: 'Subcellular Organization and Function in Endocrine Tissues' Mem. Soc. Ender. Memoirs, Vol. 19, 1970; 'Recent Studies of Hypothalamic Function' 1974; 'Current Studies of Hypothalamic Function' parts I & II 1978; 'Neurosecretion' 1981; author of over 350 original articles, book chapters & reviews; recreations: golfing, fishing, hunting; clubs: Men's Candn., Cabot Cruising Bristol (UK) & Lithuanian Club of London (U.K.); Home: 147 Carthew St., Comox, B.C. V9M 1T4.

**LEDERMAN, Sidney N.,** B.A., LL.B., Q.C.; lawyer; b. Toronto, Ont. 11 Jan. 1943; e. Univ. of Toronto, B.A. 1963, LL.B. 1966; PARTNER, STIKEMAN, ELLIOTT 1979– ; called to Bar 1968; Prof. of Law, Osgoode Hall Law Sch. 1971–77; Q.C. 1982; Pres., Human Rights Tribunal Panel 1985–92; Mem., Civil Rules Ctte. for Ont. Courts; Fellow, Am. College of Trial Lawyers; mem. Corp. Couns. Ctte. of Am. Arbitration Assn.; mem. Police Services Act Board of Inquiry; mem. The Private Court; co-author: 'Law of Evidence in Civil Cases' 1974; 'Law of Evidence in Canada' 1992; Home: 18 Oriole Gardens, Toronto, Ont. M4V 1V7; Office: Suite 5300, P.O. Box 85, Commerce Court W., Toronto, Ont. M5L 1B9.

**LEDOUX, Paul Martin;** writer; b. Halifax, N.S. 4 Nov. 1949; s. Gerrard and Geraldine (Carlin) L.; e. Dalhousie Univ. B.A. (Hist.) 1972; N.S. Coll. of Art & Design 1972–74; m. Ferne d. Don Downey; Co-Founder, Power House Performance Space, Montreal 1976–77; Artistic Dir., Stages Cabaret 1979–80; Dramaturge, Factory Theatre, Toronto 1983–85; Chrmn., Playwrights Union of Can. 1985–87; Lit. Mgr., Theatre Passe Muraille 1988–90; author plays: 'Electrical Man,' 'Dada,' 'Rag Doll,' 'Judy,' 'Broadway Flo,' 'North Mountain Breakdown,' 'The Clockmaker,' 'Children of the Night,' 'The Secret Garden' (adapted from the novel); co-author (with David Young): 'Fire' (winner of Chalmers Award 1989 and Dora Mavor Moore Award 1989), 'Love is Strange,' 'As Time Goes By'; (with Ferne Downey) 'Honky Tonk Angels'; author var. television & film scripts, incl.: 'Johann's Gift to Xmas,' 'Trick of Treasure'; Series: 'The Campbells,' 'Street Legal'; script ed., reader for var. stage cos.; mem. Playwrights Union of Can.; ACTRA; Dramatists Guild of Am.; SOCAN; recreation: music; Home: 41 Cowan Ave., Toronto, Ont. M6K 2N1.

**LEDSOME, John Russell,** M.D.; university professor; b. Cheshire, England 18 June 1932; s. Joseph Williams and Clare Elizabeth (Ashurst) L.; e. Univ. of Edinburgh, M.B., ChB. 1955, M.D. 1962, D.Sc. 1989; m. Joan Allsop 5 July 1957; children: Henry John, Mark, Sarah Elizabeth; PROF., DEPT. OF PHYSIOLOGY, UNIV. OF B.C. 1968– ; House Physician/Surgeon, Leicester Royal Infirmary 1955–56; Surg. Lt., Royal Navy 1956–59; Asst. Lectr., Physiol., Univ. of Leeds 1959–64; Postdoct. fellow, Cardiovascular Rsch. Inst., San Francisco 1964–65; Lectr., Physiol., Univ. of Leeds 1965–68; Head of Dept., Dept. of Physiol., U.B.C. 1980–91; Pres., B.C. Heart Found. 1987–89; Mem., Physiol. Soc.; Candn. Physiol. Soc.; Am. Physiol. Soc.; recreation: sailing; Club: Eagle Harbour Yacht; Home: 5651 Westhaven Rd., W. Vancouver, B.C. V7W 1T5; Office: Vancouver, B.C. V6T 1W5.

**LEDUC, Gilles Germain,** B.A., M.D., F.A.C.C., F.A.H.A.; cardiologist; educator; b. Montreal, Que. 14 Oct. 1923; s. Joseph Octave and Elise Marie (Lussier) L.; e. Univ. of Ottawa B.A. 1944; Univ. of Montreal M.D. 1950; m. Francine d. Oscar Mercier 12 Sept. 1959; children: Bertrand, Martin; CARDIOLOGIST, INSTITUT DE RECHERCHES CLINIQUES; Intern, Hôtel-Dieu de Montreal 1950; Resident 1951–52; Resident (Cardiology) St. Luke's Hosp., N.Y.C. 1952–54; Hôpital Boucicaut, Paris 1954–55; Attending Physician, Hôtel-Dieu Hosp. 1955; private practice specializing in internal medicine and cardiology, Montreal, 1955– ; Consulting Physician, St. Justine Hosp. 1956– ; Prof. of Medicine, Univ. of Montreal 1956– ; Sen. Mem., Inst. Research, Montreal; Fellow, Amer. Heart Assn.; Amer. Coll. of Cardiology; mem. Montreal Cardiac Soc. (past Pres.); Acad. Religion and Mental Health (mem. Adv. Council); Candn. Cardiovascular Soc.; author several scientific papers; Home: 82 Lockhart St., Town of Mont Royal, Que. H3P 1X8; Office: 110 Pine Ave. W., Montreal, Que. H2W 1R7.

**LEDWELL, Frank Joseph,** M.A.; educator; b. St. Peter's Bay, P.E.I. 14 Apr. 1930; s. Thomas Alexander and Anna Faustina (Gillis) L.; e. St. Dunstan's Univ. B.A. 1951; St. Augustine's Semy. Theol. 1955; studies Boston Univ., Boston Coll.; Notre Dame Univ. M.A. 1965; m. Carolyn d. Earl and Annie Duffy 26 Dec. 1970; children: Jane, Patrick, Emily, Thomas, Daniel, Christian; PROF. OF ENGLISH, UNIV. OF P.E.I. 1965– , Chrmn. of Eng. Dept. 1971–74, Dean of Arts 1979–84, mem. Bd Govs. 1976–78, mem. Senate 1972–75 and 1978–83; High Sch. Princ. 1957–61; Univ. Hockey 1961–64 and

Football Coach 1958–64; Univ. Teacher of Engn. Graphics, Descriptive Geom. & Math. 1961–64; pioneered univ. acad. courses by radio P.E.I.; co-author 'Portraits and Gastroscopes' 1972; 'The Dust is Earth' 1979; author numerous poems, short stories and articles various mags. and journs.; 'The North Shore of Home' 1986; 'Crowbush' collected poems 1990; Founder, Ed., Contrib. 'Katharsis, Eastern Canadian Writing' 1967–71; mem. Candn. and Atlantic Assns. Vice Pres. Acad., 1979–83; Candn. and Atlantic Assns. Deans Arts & Science, 1979–83; mem. Nat. Counc. SSHRC 1986–89 and 1989–92 (Extve. 1987–89); Pres., Malpeque PC Assn. 1990– ; Vice-Pres., National Milton Acorn Festival 1988– ; Nat. Dir. Candn. Conf. Teachers Eng. 1972–75; Author Award, P.E.I. Heritage Found. 1986; Outstanding Contribution Award, P.E.I. Counc. of the Arts 1988; Office: 550 University Ave., Charlottetown, P.E.I. C1A 4P3.

**LEE, Alvin A.,** B.A., M.Div., M.A., Ph.D.; educator; b. Woodville, Ont. 30 Sept. 1930; s. Norman Osborne and Susanna Elizabeth (Found) L.; e. Lindsay Coll. Inst., Lindsay, Ont.; Victoria Coll., Univ. of Toronto, B.A. 1953; Emmanuel Coll. M.Div. 1957; Univ. of Toronto M.A. (Eng.) 1958, Ph.D. 1961; m. Annie Hope, d. George Arnott 21 Dec. 1957 children: Joanna, Monika, Fiona, Alison, Margaret; PROF. OF ENGLISH, McMASTER UNIV. 1960– ; Teaching Fellow, Univ. Coll. Univ. of Toronto 1957–59; Asst. Prof. of English, Assoc. and Full Prof., McMaster Univ. 1960 to present, Asst. Dean, Grad. Studies 1968–71, Dean, Grad Studies 1971–73; Vice Pres. (Academic) 1974–79; Pres. & Vice Chancellor 1980–90; author: 'James Reaney' 1968; 'The Guest-Hall of Eden' 1972; co-author (with Hope Lee): 'Wish and Nightmare' 1972; 'Circle of Stories One' 1972; 'Circle of Stories Two' 1972; 'The Garden and the Wilderness' 1973; 'The Temple and the Ruin' 1973; 'The Peaceable Kingdom' 1974; contrib. articles in scholarly journals on Old English poetry, Candn. lit. and literary theory's, awarded Sanford Gold Medal in Divinity, Victoria Univ.; Canada Council Pre-doctoral Fellowship, Sr. Fellowship, Leave Fellowship (twice); Hon. Prof. of English, Univ. of Science and Tech., Beijing 1981; Hon. Prof. Heilongjiang Univ. 1986; Hon. D.Litt.S., Victoria Univ. 1986; Hon. D.Litt. McMaster Univ. 1993; Northrop Frye Prof. of Literary Theory, Univ. of Toronto 1992; Northrop Frye Medal, Bd. of Regents, Victoria Univ.; mem. Assn. Candn. Univ. Teachers of Eng.; Chancellor's Council, Victoria Univ. 1983– ; Ed. Bd., English Studies in Canada 1982–88; Gen. Ed., McMaster Old English Studies and Texts; mem. Adv. Bd., Studies in Medieval Renaissance History 1991– ; Trustee and Vice-Chrmn., Candn. Merit Scholarship Found. 1990–93; mem. of Council, Assn. of Commonwealth Univs. 1984–86, 1987–90; Mediaeval Acad. Am.; Modern Lang. Assn.; Assn. of Univ. & Coll. Can. (mem., Council of Univ. Pres. 1980–90; Bd. of Dir. 1983–85, 1986–88); mem., Candn. Inst. for Advanced Rsch. 1986– ; Community Educ. Coordinating Comte. 1981–90; Chrmn. and Dir., Computer Integrated Mfg. 1980–87; Trustee and mem. Extve. Comte., Chedoke-McMaster Hospital, 1980–90; Chrmn., Chedoke-McMaster Hospitals Foundation/McMaster Univ. Fund-raising Liaison Comte. 1983–90; mem. Conf. Bd. of Can. 1983–86; mem. Corporate-Higher Educ. Forum 1983–90; Council of Ont. Univ. (Chrmn. 1983–85; Vice Chrmn. 1981–83, Chrmn. Extve. Comte. 1983–85; mem. Council 1980–90); Dir., Council of Ont. Universities Holdings Assn. 1981–85; Chrmn., Ont. Commn. on Interuniversity Athletics 1988–90; Education Fond. of the Fedn. of Chinese Candn. Professionals (Ont.), Hon. Patron 1984– ; mem. Hamilton Region Conservation Authority Foundation 1990–93; Hon. Pres., Hamilton Assoc. for the Advancem. of Lit., Sc., and Art 1980–87; Hon. Mem. of the Bd., Operation Lifeline, 1980–90; Hon. Pres., McMaster Univ. Alumni Council, 1980–90; Hon. Mem., McMaster Univ. Lettermen's Assn. 1983– ; McMaster Univ. Eng. Soc., Pres. 1981–90; Chrmn., Health Sci. Liasion Comte. 1988–90 (mem. 1980–90); Dir., Nuclear Activation Services, 1980–87; Dir., Royal Botanical Gardens, 1980–90 (mem. Extve. Comte. 1981–90; Vice Chrmn.; Hamilton and District Chamber of Comm. (mem. 1982–90; mem. Bd. of Dir. 1982–87); Vice-Chrmn., Hamilton-Wentworth Economic Advisory Conference 1983–86; Hon. Patron, Opera Hamilton 1982–90; mem. Adv. Ctte., Bach-Elgar Choir 1987–90; United Church; recreations: gardening, swimming, windsurfing, hiking, canoeing, running, theatre, music, reading; Home: Stormont, West Flamborough, Ont.; Office: Dept. of English, McMaster Univ., 1280 Main St. W., Hamilton, Ont. L8S 4L9.

**LEE, Betty;** journalist; b. Sydney, Australia 18 Dec. 1921; d. Albert George and Violet (Haffenden) L.; e. Sydney (Aust.) High Sch.; Univ. of Sydney; Columbia Univ.; began career in Sydney, Australia as Script Writer, Radio 2UE, 1944–46; Feature Writer and Ed., K. G. Murray Publ. Co., Sydney; Argus (morning newspaper), Melbourne, 1949–51; Reporter, Daily Mirror in London, Eng., 1951–52; Press Offr., Wembley (Eng.) Stadium, 1952–53; came to Can., Oct. 1953 as Sr. Reporter, Ed. Writer, Globe & Mail, Toronto, 1953; in 1954 became freelance writer for various U.S. publs. and later Staff Writer with Street and Smith Publs., N.Y.; returned to Globe & Mail, Toronto, as Reporter and Feature Writer, 1957–75; Sr. Editor of Chatelaine, 1978–80; Freelance contributor to various Candn. publs. and editorial & communications consultant, 1980– ; consulting ed., Your Money magazine 1984–88; Sr. Editor, Canadian Business 1981–83; Personal Finance Editor 1983–92; Contributing Editor 1992– ; author of 'The Stock Market Story,' 'The Borrowers,' 'Insurance: The Magic of Averages,' in Globe & Mail; 'Love and Whisky: The Story of the Dominion Drama Festival' (1973); 'Lutiapik' (1975); rec'd. Candn. Women's Press Club Nat. Award for Spot News Reporting (1965); Nat. Newspaper Award for Feature Writing (1966); Southam Fellow, Univ. of Toronto 1972–73; Home: Toronto, Ont.; Mailing address: c/o Writers' Union of Canada, 24 Ryerson Ave., Toronto, Ont. M5T 2P3.

**LEE, Christopher Alan,** B.Sc.F., R.P.F.; forester; b. Shilo, Man. 27 Aug. 1955; s. George Bernard and Helene Catherine (Guay) L.; e. Vincent Massey Collegiate; Univ. of Toronto B.Sc.F. 1979; Univ. of Saskatchewan Dip.B.A. 1986; m. Bonnie C. d. John and Katherine Braithwaite 31 Aug. 1984; one s.: Scott W.B.; EXECUTIVE DIRECTOR, CANADIAN INSTITUTE OF FORESTRY 1990– ; Operations Planner, Prince Albert Pulpwood (now Weyerhaeuser Can.) 1979–84; Forestry Officer, Candn. Forest Service 1984–87; Program Analyst 1987–88; Policy Advisor, Min. of Forestry 1988–89; Industry, Trade & Technology, Candn. Forest Serv. 1989–90; Adv. Bd., Univ. of Toronto Fac. of Forestry; Bd. of Dir., Candn. Wildlife Fed.; Mem., City of Kanata Envir. Adv. Ctte.; Mem., Ont. Profl. Foresters Assn.; Soc. of Am. Foresters; Candn. Inst. of Forestry; Office: 1005 - 151 Slater St., Ottawa, Ont. K1P 5H3.

**LEE, Dennis Beynon,** O.C., M.A.; author; song-lyricist; editor; b. Toronto, Ont. 31 Aug. 1939, s. Walter Edgar Lorne and Jetret Emma Louise (Garbutt) L.; e. University of Toronto, B.A. 1962, M.A. 1965; m. Donna Alberta, d. Albert Youngblut, 20 May 1961; children: Kevyn, Hilary, Julian; div. 1972; m. Susan Ruth, d. Allan and Belle Perly, 12 Oct. 1985; former Pres. House of Anansi Press; poetry consultant, McClelland & Stewart 1981–84; author: 'Kingdom of Absence' 1967; 'Civil Elegies' 1968, rev. ed. 1972; 'Wiggle to the Laundromat' 1970; 'Alligator Pie' 1974; 'Nicholas Knock and Other People' 1974; 'The Death of Harold Ladoo' 1976; 'Garbage Delight' 1977; 'Savage Fields: An Essay in Literature and Cosmology' 1977; 'The Gods' 1979; 'The Ordinary Bath' 1979; 'Jelly Belly' 1983; 'Lizzy's Lion' 1984; 'The Difficulty of Living on Other Planets' 1987; 'The Ice Cream Store' 1991; 'Riffs' 1993; 'Ping and Pong' 1993; song-lyricist for 'Fraggle Rock' (children's series, co-prod. CBC-TV and Henson Associates) 1982–86; Ed. 'T.O. Now' 1968; 'The New Canadian Poets: 1970–1985' 1985; co-ed. 'An Anthology of Verse' 1965, rev. ed. 1989; 'Second Century Anthology of Verse' 1967; 'The University Game' 1968; Officer, Order of Canada 1994; Address: c/o Sterling Lord Assoc., 10 St. Mary St., Ste. 510, Toronto, Ont. M4Y 1P9.

**LEE, Edward G.,** Q.C., B.A., LL.B., LL.M.; diplomat; b. Vancouver, B.C. 21 Nov. 1931; s. William C. and Dorothy F. (Graham) L.; e. Univ. of B.C., B.A. 1954, LL.B. 1955; Harvard Univ. LL.M. 1956; m. Beverly d. Edwin and Audrey Saul 19 Aug. 1955; children: Kerry, Barbara, Nancy; AMBASSADOR OF CANADA TO AUSTRIA & PERMANENT REPRESENTATIVE TO THE UNITED NATIONS ORGANIZATIONS IN VIENNA & GOV. ON BD. OF THE INTERNAT. ATOMIC ENERGY AGENCY 1990– ; elected mem., Permanent Internat. Court of Arbitration 1987; joined present Dept. 1956, Second Sec. Djakarta 1959–61, Counsellor London, Eng. 1965–69, Dir. of Personnel Ottawa 1970–72, Legal Adv. 1973–75, Ambassador to Israel and High Commn. to Cyprus 1975–79, Asst. Under Sec. for USA Affairs 1980–82, Ambassador to S. Africa and High Comn. to Lesotho and Swaziland 1983–86; Legal Adv. & Asst. Depy. Min. for Legal, Consular & Immigration Affairs, Dept. of External Affairs 1986–90; served with RCAF, Flying Offr.; author numerous articles Candn. law jours.; Extve. mem., Internat. Law Section, Candn. Bar Assn.; Candn. Council Internat. Law; mem., Law Soc. B.C.; Am. Soc. Internat. Law; recreations: swimming, walking, ornithology; Home: 27 Lannerstrasse, 1190 Vienna, Austria; Office: Dr. Karl Lueger-Ring 10, A1010 Vienna, Austria.

**LEE, Ian,** B.A., M.A., Ph.D.; university professor; b. Winnipeg, Man. 13 Jan. 1953; s. Arthur Richard and Ruth Margaret (Whitehead) L.; e. Carleton Univ. B.A. 1981, M.A. 1983, Ph.D. 1989; m. Lyne d. Robert and Danielle Dufault 6 June 1986; children: Kyle Lee, Dominique Dufault; PROF., SCHOOL OF BUSINESS, CARLETON UNIV. 1987– ; Manager, Avco Corp. 1974–78; Manager, Bank of Montreal 1978–81; Policy Analyst, Canada Post Corp. H.Q. 1983–84; Facilitator & Instr., Candn. Management Training & Education Program for Poland; Dir., Centre for Business-Govt.-NGO Relns., Carleton Univ.; mem., Steering Ctte., Greenprint; mem., Ottawa-Carleton Bd. of Trade; mem., Ottawa Carleton Economic Development Corp.; mem., Steering Ctte., Carleton Univ. Academic Staff Assn.; mem., Bd. of Dirs., Ottawa-Carleton Regional Housing Authority; Chair, Conference 'Lobbying in the 90s' Carleton Univ.; Past Candidate PC Party, Ottawa Centre, 1993 Federal Election; research: Business-Govt.-NGO Relns.; Business strategy & competitiveness; Fed. Govt. Labour Relns.; Secretary-Treasurer, Candn. Pol. Sci. Assn.; Inst. of Public Admin. of Canada; Am. Acad. of Mngt.; author: 'The Canadian Post Office: From Nation Builder to Public Utility, 1765–1981' (under review for possible publication) and 7 scholarly articles; Home: 34 Melgund Ave., Ottawa, Ont. K1S 2S2; Office: Room 901, Dunton Tower, Colonel By Dr., Ottawa, Ont. K1S 5B6.

**LEE, Hon. James M.,** P.C.; b. Charlottetown, P.E.I. 26 March 1937; s. late James Matthew and Catherine (Blanchard) L.; e. Queens Square Sch.; St. Dunstan's Univ.; m. Patricia d. late Ivan Laurie 2 July 1960; 3 children; Member, Canadian Pension Commission, D.V.A., P.E.I. 1986– ; ; el. M.L.A. by-el. 1975, re-el. 1978, 1979, 1982; defeated 1986; Min. of Social Services, 1979–80; Min. of Tourism, Parks and Conservation, 1979–80, Min. of Health and Social Services, 1980–81, Leader, P.E.I. Progressive Party, 1981; Premier of P.E.I., 1981–86; sworn into Privy Council of Can. by Her Majesty Queen Elizabeth II, Ottawa 17 Apr. 1982; Intl. Jacyee Senator 1983; P. Conservative; R. Catholic; Home: Stanhope, Little York P.O. (R.R. 1), P.E.I.; Office; P.O. Box 9900, Charlottetown, P.E.I. C1A 8K6.

**LEE, Leonard G.,** B.A.; economist; association executive; company president; b. Wadena, Sask., 17 July 1938; s. William Henry Edwin Morley and Winnifred Marcella (O'Farrel) L.; e. Archerwill High Sch., Sask., 1956; Royal Roads Mil. Coll., Dipl. Civil Engn. 1960; Royal Mil. Coll., 1961 (apptd. Cadet Wing Commdr.); Queen's Univ., B.A. (Econ.) 1963; m. Lillian Lorraine, d. Frank King, Ottawa, Ont., 9 March 1961; two s., Robin, James; PRES. LEE VALLEY TOOLS LTD. since 1978; Dir., The Public Policy Forum; Consul and Asst. Trade Commr., Chicago, 1964–67; First Secy. and Head of Comm. Div., Lima, Peru, 1967–68; Extve. Asst. to Asst. Depy. Min., Dept. Indust. Trade & Comm., 1968–69; Extve. Asst. to Depy. Min., Dept. of Consumer & Corporate Affairs, 1969–70; Dir. Candn. Consumer Council, 1970–71; nominated for Agrarian Medal of Peru 1968; Alcuin Soc.; United Church; recreations: duplicate bridge, golf, sailing; Home: 517 Westminster Ave., Ottawa, Ont. K2A 1T4; Office: 1080 Morrison Dr., Ottawa, Ont. K2H 8K7.

**LEE, Melvin,** M.A., Ph.D.; educator; b. New York City, N.Y. 5 Jan. 1926; s. Herman Israel and Rebecca (Panish) L.; e. Univ. of Cal. (Los Angeles) B.A. 1947, (Berkeley) M.A. 1951, Ph.D. 1957; m. Beverly Mae Low d. late Art Low 4 Feb. 1950; children: David M., Janice Naomi, Jeffrey Wayne, Ronald Alan; came to Can. 1967; PROF. HIROSHIMA JOGAKUIN UNIV., HIROSHIMA, JAPAN and EMERITUS PROF. OF HUMAN NUTRITION, SCH. OF FAMILY AND NUTRITIONAL SCIENCES, UNIV. OF B.C.; Visiting Prof., Gunma Univ., Maebashi, Japan 1986; author over 60 tech. papers research journs., book chapter; mem. Am. Inst. Nutrition; Nutrition Soc. Can.; Sociedad de Nutricion Latinoamericano; Jewish; recreations: swimming, skiing; Home: Residence Shirai, Apt. 303, Ushita Waseda 4 chome, 1-44 Higashi-ku, Hiroshima 732, Japan.

**LEE, Richard Borshay,** M.A., Ph.D., D.Litt.; university professor; b. Brooklyn, N.Y. 20 Sept. 1937; s. Charles and Anne (Borshay) L.; e. Univ. of Toronto B.A. 1959, M.A. 1961; Univ. of Calif., Berkeley Ph.D. 1965; Univ. of Alaska D.Litt. 1990; life companion, Harriet d. Louis and Molly Rosenberg; children: David Haldane, Miriam Judith, Louise Anne; PROF., DEPT. OF ANTHROPOL., UNIV. OF TORONTO 1972– ; Lecturer, Harvard Univ. 1965–70; Assoc. Prof., Rutgers Univ. 1970–72; Field Rsch. in N. Canada 1960, 1984, 1986; E. Africa 1963; S. Africa 1963–65, 1967–69, 1973, 1980, 1983, 1986–87; Cons., BBC TV 1980–81; CBC TV 1983–85; PBS TV 1985; FRSC 1983; Mem., Toronto

Ctte. for Liberation of S. Africa; Pres., Candn. Ethnol. Soc. 1983–84; author: 'The !Kung San' 1979, 'The Dobe !Kung' 1984; co-editor: 'Man the Hunter' 1968, 'The New Native Resistance' 1974, 'Kalahari Hunter-gatherers' 1976, 'Politics and History in Band Societies' 1982 and over 60 articles & book chapters; recreations: canoeing, camping, photography; Home: 147 Delaware Ave., Toronto, Ont. M6H 2T2; Office: Sidney Smith Bldg., 100 St. George St., Toronto, Ont. M5S 1A1.

**LEE, Robert William Mason,** B.Sc.; journalist; b. Bassano, Alta. 8 Nov. 1956; s. William Alexander and Mabel Hettie (Smith) L.; e. United World Coll. of the Atlantic, Internat. Baccalaureate 1974; London Sch. of Econ., B.Sc. (Econ.) 1978; one d. Jacqueline Jean; WRITER AND COLUMNIST, VANCOUVER SUN 1992– ; Reporter, Red Deer Advocate 1979–83; Staff Writer, Alta. Report Mag. 1983; Edmonton Bur. Chief, United Press Can. 1983–85; Parliamentary Bur. Chief, Calgary & Edmonton Sun 1985–86; Nat. Political Writer, Ottawa Citizen 1986–92; Contbr., Saturday Night Mag. 1985– ; Contbr., CBC 'Morningside'; Contbr., CBC Newsworld; author: 'One Hundred Monkeys: The Triumph of Popular Wisdom in Canadian Politics' (pols), 1989; 'Death and Deliverance: The Haunting True Story of the Hercules Crash at the North Pole' 1992; script consultant: 'Ordeal in the Arctic' ABC Network; rec'd Nat. Mag. Award Gold Medal (Religion) and Pres.'s Medal 1986; Asia-Pacific Found. of Can. Journalism Fellowship 1987; Nat. Mag. Award Gold Medal (Pol.) 1987; Southam Newspaper Group Pres.'s Medal 1987, 1990; Nat. Newspaper Award for enterprise reporting 1988; Nat. Newspaper Award for Spot News reporting 1990; Protestant; Mem., Parliamentary Press Gallery; Vancouver Press Club; recreations: swimming, skiing, mountain hiking; Office: 2250 Granville St., Vancouver, B.C. V6H 3G2.

**LEE, Sang Chul,** B.D., Th.M., S.T.M., D.D., LL.D.; minister; b. Siberia, U.S.S.R. 29 Feb. 1924; s. Do-Ill and Do-Soon (Kim) L.; e. H.S., China 1943; Normal Sch., China 1945; Hankak Theol. Sem., B.D. 1951, Th.M. 1956; Union Coll. (B.C.), S.T.M. 1964; Ecumenical Grad. Sch., (Switz.) 1963; Emmanual Coll., Victoria Univ., D.D. 1974; m. Shin d. Chai Choon and Boon Ye Jang 8 Apr. 1953; children: Irene, Grace, Joy; Apptd. CHANCELLOR, THE VICTORIA UNIV., UNIV. OF TORONTO May 1992– ; Past Moderator, United Church of Can. 1988–90; School teacher, China & S. Korea; Min., Presbyn. Ch., Korea 1949–61; Min., United Ch. of Can. (min. related to Japanese-, Korean-, and English-speaking congregations) 1963–88; Korean newspaper columnist; active mem., human rights orgns.; author of three books in Korean and English languages; Hon. LL.D., Mount Allison Univ. 1990; Home: 558 Priddle Rd., Newmarket, Ont. L3X 1X8.

**LEE, William Mark,** B.J.; broadcast journalist; b. Calgary, Alta. 7 Aug. 1956; s. William Anthony Forbes and Doreen Eileen (Croswell) L.; e. Earl of March Secondary Sch. Kanata, Ont.; Carleton Univ. B.J. 1979; National Reporter, CBC Network Radio Sports 1989– ; News Anchor CFCF Radio Montréal 1979; Writer/Reporter nat. newsroom CBC Radio Toronto 1980, Nat. Anchor/Reporter Network Radio Sports 1982; Host/Reporter 'The Inside Track' CBC 1985–89; recipient Foster Hewitt Award (ACTRA Awards) Best Sports Broadcaster 1986 and 1988; recipient of Gabriel Award 1987 for documentary on Jackie Robinson (first black to break colour barrier in major league baseball) 'Jackie Robinson: The Legend and the Legacy'; Finalist, New York International Radio Awards for three-part series on NCAA Football; quarterback Carleton Ravens during univ. yrs.; mem. YMCA-Toronto; recreations: football, hockey, tennis, softball, cycling; Home: 45 Galt Ave., Toronto, Ont. M4M 2Z2.

**LEE, Yoo Il,** LL.B.; automotive executive; b. Seoul, Korea 3 July 1943; e. Yonsei Univ. LL.B. 1966; m. Ock Young Lee; children: Jae Yoon, Jae Shin (daughters); EXECUTIVE DIRECTOR, HYUNDAI MOTOR COMPANY 1990– ; joined Corp. Affairs Dept., Hyundai Motor Co. (Seoul, Korea) 1969; Mgr., Corp. Affairs Dept. 1971–77; Gen. Mgr. 1978–83; Dir., in charge of Export Div. 1983–87; Mng. Dir., Overseeing All Export Operations 1988–89; Pres. & Chief Extve. Officer, Hyundai Auto Canada 1989– ; Home: 31 Cobblestone Dr., Willowdale, Ont.; Office: 75 Frontenac Dr., Markham, Ont. L3R 6H2.

**LEECH, Geoffrey Bosdin,** B.A.Sc., M.Sc., Ph.D., F.R.S.C.; geologist; b. Montreal, Que. 28 Aug. 1918; s. Daniel Herbert and Olive Roberta (Shepherd) L.; e. Univ. of B.C., B.A.Sc. (Geol. Engn.) 1942; Queen's Univ., M.Sc., 1943; Princeton Univ., Ph.D. (Petrol., Econ. Geol.) 1949; m. Mary Jean, d. Roy Winters, Pembroke, Ont., 1 Oct. 1946; one d. Joan Elizabeth (Mrs. B.R. Edwards); Geol., Intl. Nickel Co. of Can. Ltd., 1943–46; B.C. Dept. of Mines, 1947–48; Geol. and Dir., Geol. Survey of Canada 1949–82; Comn. for Metallogenic Map of North Am., 1967–82; Assoc. Sec. Gen. International Assoc. on Genesis of Ore Deposits, 1978–86; investigations concerned with the geology of Rocky Mts., genesis of mineral deposits and evaluation of mineral resources; author of over 30 articles in scient. journs.; Fellow, Royal Soc. Canada (Nom. Comte. 1974); Geol. Soc. Am. (Comtes. Comte. 1967, 1968, Nom. Comte. 1982); Geol. Assn. Can.; Soc. Econ. Geol. (Publications Comte. 1973–76, Chrmn. 1976); Life Mem., Candn. Inst. of Mining, Metall. & Petrol. (Councillor Geology Div. 1974–75); Sigma Xi; Unitarian; Home: 1113 Greenlawn Cres., Ottawa, Ont. K2C 1Z4.

**LEECH, James William,** B.Sc., M.B.A.; executive; b. St. Boniface, Man. 12 June 1947; s. the late BGen. George C. and late Mary E. (Gibson) L.; e. Royal Mil. Coll. Can. B.Sc. (Hon.) 1968; Queen's Univ. M.B.A. 1973; m. Jacqueline Roberts d. Dr. James H.B. and Marjorie Hilton 20 Sept. 1969; children: Jennifer Hilton, Joanna Marjorie, James Andrew Douglas; PRESIDENT & CHIEF EXTVE. OFFR., DISYS CORPORATION; Dir., Harris Steel Group Inc.; 20/20 Financial Corp.; Commissioned Officer, Candn. Armed Forces, Kingston and Germany 1968–71; Extve. Asst. to Pres. Commerce Capital Corp. Ltd. Montreal 1973–74, Vice Pres. 1974–75; Extve. Vice Pres. and Dir. Commerce Capital Trust Co. Calgary 1976–78; Sr. Vice Pres. Commerce Capital Corp. Ltd. Toronto 1978–79; Sr. Vice Pres. Eaton/Bay Financial Services Ltd. Toronto 1979; Dir. & Pres., Unicorp Energy Corp. 1980–88; Pres., C.E.O. and Dir., Union Energy Inc. 1988–93; Vice Chrmn. and Dir., Union Gas Ltd. 1988–93; Chrmn. & Dir., Mark Resources Inc. and Unigas Corp. 1988–93; recipient D.I. McLeod Scholarship 1971–73 and Rsch. Fellowship 1972; Samuel Bronfman Foundation Fellowship (Seagram) 1972; Transp. Devel. Agency Fellowship 1972; Chrmn. and Pres. (1989–93) and Dir. (1984– ), The Canadian Stage Company; Trustee, Queen's Univ. 1984– ; mem. Invest. Ctte., Bd. of Trustees, 1980– ; former Vice Chrmn. Adv. Counc. Sch. of Business 1979–83; mem. Gen. Counc. 1979–85; Queen's Fund Counc. 1988– ; Fellow, Trust Co's Inst.; Clubs: The National; Granite; Ranchmen's (Calgary); Glencoe (Calgary); Roy. Mil. Coll. of Can.; Home: 70 Garfield Ave., Toronto, Ont. M4T 1E9; Office: 719 Clayson Rd., Toronto, Ont. M9M 2H4.

**LEEFE, John Gordon,** M.L.A., B.A., B.Ed., M.A.; politician; teacher; author; b. Saint John, N.B. 21 Mar. 1942; s. James Gurney and Helen Gordon (Sancton) L.; e. Saint John H.S. 1960; Univ. of King's Coll., B.A. 1966; Univ. of N.B., B.Ed. 1968; Dalhousie Univ., M.A. 1970; m. Nancy d. George and Helen Morrison 17 Dec. 1964; children: James Philip, Sarah Elizabeth; Teacher, Saint John schs. 1965–68; Halifax Schs. 1968–70; Head, Soc. Studies Dept., Liverpool Regl. H.S. 1970–79; Asst. to Curriculum Supr., Queen's Dist. Sch. Bd. 1981–83; el. M.L.A. (Queen's) 1978; re-el. 1981, 1984, 1988; apptd. Dep. Speaker 1981; re-apptd. 1982; Min. of Fisheries 1983–89; Min. of the Environment 1989–92; Apptd. House Leader 1991; Min. of Natural Resources 1992–93; Bd. of Gov., Univ. of King's Coll. 1970–72; Mem., Queen's Co. Hist. Soc. (Pres. 1975–78); Pres., Candn. Council of Minister's of the Environment (CCME) 1990–91; Member, National Round Table on Environment & the Economy 1991–92; Member, Nova Scotia Round Table on Environment & the Economy; Chrmn., Legislature Public Accounts Ctte.; author of several publ profl. & hist. articles and 'Atlantic Privateers' 1978; co-author: 'Kejimkujik National Park' 1981, 'A History of Early Nova Scotia' 1983; recreation: canoeing; Clubs: Zetland Lodge #9 A.F.A.M.; Honourary Kinsman; Queen's County Hist. Soc.; Home: 38 Barss St., Liverpool, N.S. B0T 1K0; Office: P.O. Box 1755, Liverpool, N.S. B0T 1K0.

**LEEMING, David John,** B.Sc., M.A., Ph.D.; university professor; b. Victoria, B.C. 8 June 1939; s. Kenneth L. and Mary A. (Costen) L.; e. Univ. of B.C. B.Sc. 1961; Univ. of Oregon M.A. 1963; Univ. of Alberta Ph.D. 1969; m. Yvonne d. James and Yvonne Muir 18 June 1966; children: Heather, Graeme, Robert; PROFESSOR, MATHEMATICS AND STATISTICS, UNIV. OF VICTORIA 1986– ; Instructor, Dept. of Math, Univ. of Victoria 1963–66; Asst. prof. 1969–74; Assoc. Prof. 1974–86; Chair of Dept. 1989–94; Academic Council, Open Learning Agency, Open Univ. 1988– ; Mem., Candn. Math. Soc.; recreations: gourmet cooking; Home: 2796 Tudor Ave., Victoria, B.C. V8N 1L7; Office: Victoria, B.C. V8W 3P4.

**LEENEN, Frans H.H.,** M.D., Ph.D., FRCP(C); academic cardiologist, scientist; b. Linne, The Netherlands 16 Sept. 1943; s. the late Jan H.H. and the late Anna Maria (Hulsbosch) L.; e. Univ. of Utrecht Ph.D. in pharm. 1971, M.D. 1973; Royal Netherlands Med. Assn., board-qual. cardiologist 1978; m. Mindy d. Mitchel and Sylvia Fein 13 April 1986; children: Arjan, Bob-Willem, Sarah C., David A., Peter M.; DIR., HYPERTENSION UNIT, UNIV. OF OTTAWA HEART INST. 1989– ; Rudolf Magnus Inst. Pharm., Univ. of Utrecht, Ph.D. grad. studies 1968–71; Rsch. Fellow, Univ. of Pittsburgh 1972–73; Univ. of Utrecht 1973–74; Resident 1975–78; Asst. Prof. of Med. & Pharm., Univ. of Toronto 1979–85; Assoc. Prof. 1985–88; Prof. 1989– ; Co-ord., Clin. Pharm. Prog. 1985–88; Staff Mem., Dept. of Medicine, Toronto Western Hosp. 1979–88; Vice-Chrmn., Sci. Review Sub-Ctte., Heart & Stroke Found. of Can. 1988–90; Chrmn. 1991–93; Chrmn., Scientific Review Ctte., Heart and Stroke Found. of Can. 1994– ; Ed. Bd. Mem., 'Cardiovascular Pharm.' 1990– , 'Clin. & Investigative Med.' (Assoc. Ed. 1986–90), 'J. of Hyptertension' 1988–90; Pres., Gen. Practice Rsch. Group 1990–; Scientific Advr., pharm. cos.; Merck Sharp & Dohme Internat. Fellowship 1972; Young Investigator's Award, Candn. Hypertension Soc. 1982; FRCPC 1986; Excellence in Clin. Invest. Award (Calif.) 1987; Candn. Heart Found. Rsch. Scholarship 1982–88; Career Investigator, Heart & Stroke Found. of Ont. 1989– ; Mem., Am. Soc. for Clin. Pharm. & Therapeutics (Section Chrmn. 1988–91); Am. Soc. of Hypertension; Candn. Hypertension Soc. (Sec.-Treas. 1984–85; Pres. 1985–86; Chrmn., Ont. Chap. 1989–93; Chrmn., Sci. Review Ctte. 1989–92); Can. Soc. for Clin. Investigation; Fellow, Council for High Blood Pressure Rsch., Am. Heart Assn.; Royal Coll. of Phys. & Surg. of Can.; senior author of over 100 sci. pubns.; co-editor: 'How to control your BP and get more out of life' 1986, 'Down with High Blood Pressure' 1990, 'A Bas L'Hypertension' 1990; Home: 198 Lisgar Rd., Rockcliffe Park, Ont. K1M 0E6; Office: H360, Ottawa Civic Hosp., 1053 Carling Ave., Ottawa, Ont. K1Y 4E9.

**LEEPER, Cyril G.F.,** P.O.I.P., A.B.A.R., P.I.N.Y.; portrait artist, violinist; b. Toronto, Ont. 5 Oct. 1949; s. Robert Patrick and Muriel Margaret (Reuben) L.; formal art studies: Art School at the Grange 1958–61; with H.D. Sheppard 1961–68; Accademia di Belle Arte di Roma 1968–72; Escuela Sup. de Bellas Artes de San Fernando 1972–73; with Kenneth Forbes 1973–79; m. Anne Cameron 16 April 1977; children: Jean Paul, Celeste, Marian; portraits include Queen Elizabeth II (forthcoming), HRH Prince Andrew, The Duke of York, Malcolm Muggeridge, Lady Colin Campbell, Hamilton Southam, Peter Lougheed, Grant Devine, Lincoln Alexander Emmett Hall, Hon. Frank Iacobucci, 8 Lieutenant-Governors, Premiers, Chief Justices of Provincial and Federal Courts, Chancellors and Presidents of Universities, The Military and Corporate elite; Past Pres., Ont. Inst. of Painters; Mem., Accademia di Belle Arte di Roma; Portrait Inst. of N.Y.; Grad., Sup. Sch. of Fine Arts, Madrid, Spain; Former Concermaster, Huronia Symphony (performed under baton of Walter Susskind, Victor Feldbrill, Leopold Stokowski, Boyd Neal); recreations: music, skiing; clubs: Toronto Arts and Letters; Home: 93 Huron St., Clinton, Ont. N0M 1L0.

**LEESON, Thomas Sydney,** M.A., M.D., Ph.D., F.R.S.H.; b. Halifax, Eng. 26 Jan. 1926; s. Charles Ernest and Gladys (Stott) L.; e. Cambridgeshire High Sch., Higher Sch. Cert.; St. Catharines Coll., Cambridge, B.A., 1946, M.A. 1947, Ph.D. 1971; King's Coll. Hosp. Med. Sch., London, M.B.B. Chir. 1950; Cambridge, M.D. (by thesis) 1959; m. Catherine Mary, d. Thomas Witcomb, Newent, Glos., U.K., 6 Sept. 1952; children: Roland Paul, Susan Gillian, Helen Clare; Prof. of Anatomy, Univ. of Alberta (and Chrmn. of the Dept. 1963–83); Demonst. in Anat., Cambridge Univ. 1950; Lectr. in Anat., Univ. of Wales, 1955–57; Asst. Prof. in Anat., Univ. of Toronto 1957–60, Assoc. Prof. 1960; served in R.A.F.-V.R. G/D Pilot, 1945–50; R.A.F. Med. Br., 1951–55; Sqdn. Ldr., 1955–57; Med. Offr. 1957–59; co-author: 'Histology' (with C.R. Leeson and A.A. Paparo) 5th ed. 1985; 'Atlas of Histology' (with C.R. Leeson and A.A. Paparo) 2nd ed., 1985; 'Text Atlas of Histology' (with C.R. Leeson and A.A. Paparo) 1988; 'Human Structure' (with C.R. Leeson) 1989; has written some 130 articles in med. and scient. journs. mainly in respect of electron microscopy; Part Inventor of Sims-Leeson Ultramicrotome 1956; Anglican; recreations: hunting, angling; Address: 45–903 109 St., Edmonton, Alta. T6J 6R1.

**LEESTI, Mart,** B.Eng., P.Eng.,; public servant; b. Tallinn, Estonia 28 May 1941; s. Georg and Lonni Luise (Vaus) L.; e. Royal Roads Military College 1963; Royal Military College of Can. B.Eng. 1965; m. Steffanie d.

William and Tracey Christie 8 May 1965; children: Martin, Tracey; COMMISSIONER OF PATENTS, REGISTRAR OF TRADE MARKS & CHIEF EXTVE. OFFR., CANADIAN INTELLECTUAL PROPERTY OFFICE, INDUSTRY CANADA 1992– ; Officer & Pilot, HS-50 Sqn., RCN 1965–68; Patent Examiner, Patent Office 1968–71; Tec. Adv. Services, Bur. of Corp. Affairs 1971–75; Dir., Elect. & Phys. Sciences, Patent Office 1980–83; Mngt. Serv., Bur. of Corp. Affairs 1983–84; Policy & Prog. Planning, Intellectual Property 1984–87; Extve. Dir., Intellectual Prop. 1987–92; Mem., Assn. of Profl. Engrs., Prov. of Ont.; recreations: fishing, sailing, travel, computers; Home: 14 Aberfeldy St., Nepean, Ont. K2H 6H5; Office: 50 Victoria St., Hull, Que. K1A 0C9.

**LEEW, Edward Alexander,** B.A., LL.B.; lawyer; b. Calgary, Alta. 19 March 1953; s. Alex and Eva Victoria (Morris) L.; e. Univ. of Alberta B.A. 1974, LL.B. 1975; m. Jeanie d. John and Peggy Hutton 16 Aug. 1975; children: Blake John Alexander, Ian Edward, John Hutton; VICE-PRESIDENT, LEGAL, NORCEN ENERGY RESOURCES LIMITED 1992– ; articled with Macleod Dixon 1976–77; Assoc. Lawyer 1977–81; Partner 1981–92; Gen. Counsel, Norcen Energy Resources Limited 1992; Office: 715 – 5th Ave. S.W., Calgary, Alta. T2P 2X7.

**LEFAIVRE, W. Paul;** retired banker/company director; b. Edmonton, Alta. 20 Oct. 1923; s. William McCormick and Eugenie Ann (Pineau) L.; e. St. Angelas; St. Mary's Boys; West. Can. Coll., Calgary; Banff Sch. of Adv. Mngt.; m. Marlyn d. John and Mary Horne 15 Sept. 1948; children: Maryann, Paula, Michelle; Royal Candn. Navy, N. Atlantic & Normandy 1942–45; var. positions (Alta.) Royal Bank of Can. 1940–73; Supvr., Loans, Atlantic Provs. 1973–75; Regl. Mgr., Edmonton 1975–76; Asst. Gen. Mgr., Alta. N. 1976–81; Vice-Pres. Alta. N. 1981–82; retired 1982; Dir., P.T.I. Group Inc.; Edmonton Telephones Corp.; Chrmn. Bd. of Govs., Alberta Real Estate Foundation; Pres., Bd. of Trustees, Franciscan Fathers of W. Can.; Roman Catholic; Mem., Royal Candn. Legion; recreation: golf; Clubs: Edmonton Country; Edmonton; Home: 32 St. Georges Cres., Edmonton, Alta. T5N 3M7; Office: 1524 – 10117 Jasper Ave., Edmonton, Alta. T5J 1W8.

**LEFEBER, Louis,** Ph.D.; educator; b. Budapest, Hungary 5 July 1924; e. Trefort Sch. of the Pazmany Peter Univ. Budapest 1942; Jozsef Nador Tech. Univ. Budapest 1942–44; Mass. Inst. of Technol. 1953–57, Ph.D. 1957; m. Rosalind Rudy 1958; PROF. OF ECON. YORK UNIV. 1972– , Founding Dir. Centre for Rsch. Latin Am. & Caribbean 1978–84; Instr. and Asst. Prof. Harvard Univ. 1956–60; Assoc. Prof. Mass. Inst. Technol. 1961–65; Visiting Prof. Stanford Univ. 1965–66; F.C. Hecht Prof. Brandeis Univ. Waltham, Mass. 1966–76; Cons. various UN orgns., foreign govts., Ford Found., Panamerican Union (Alliance for Progress) 1962, World Bank 1976, Bank of Greece 1981–89, Econ. Council Can. 1977–78; mem. Rsch. Adv. Ctte. The Brookings Instn. 1962–64; Dir. Sociedad Interamericana de Planificacion 1984–87; Dir., Black Creek Found. Toronto 1985–87; Ford Faculty Rsch. Fellow 1964–65; Ford Found. Prof. Inst. Econ. Growth Delhi Univ. 1969–70, V.K. Ramaswami Meml. Lectr., Delhi School of Economics 1975; author: 'Allocation in Space' 1958, 'Location and Regional Planning' 1971; co-author: 'Capital Formation and Economic Development' 1964, 'Regional Development: South and Southeast Asia' 1969; co-ed. and co-author: 'Democracy and Development in Latin America' 1980; ed. and co-author: 'La Economia Politica del Ecuador' 1985; contbr. various profl. jours. and books; mem., Organizing Ctte., IXth World Congress of the International Economic Assn. 1989; Contbr., Pugwash Conferences 1993; mem. Am. Econ. Assn.; Can. Econ. Assn.; CALACS; Home: 99 Clifton Rd., Toronto, Ont. M4T 2G3; Office: 4700 Keele St., North York, Ont. M3J 1P3.

**LEFEBVRE, Gilles,** O.C., C.Q.; cultural agency executive; b. Montréal, Qué. 30 June 1922; s. Hubert and Germaine Handfield (Gravel) L.; e. Univ. of Ottawa 1942; music studies Paris 1946–50; Univ. de Montréal, Hon. Dr. (Arts) 1978; Univ. de Sherbrooke, Hon. Dr. (Arts) 1986; Assoc. Dir. The Canada Council 1983–87; Founder 1949, Pres. 1950–51 and Dir. Gen. 1951–72, Jeunesses Musicales du Canada; Founder 1950, Dir. 1950–72, Centre d'Arts d'Orford JMC; Assoc. Artistic Dir. World Festival for Expo 1967, 1964–67; Dir. Candn. Cultural Centre Paris 1972–78; Dir. Gen. Bureau of Internat. Cultural Relations, Dept. of External Affairs 1979–83; Assoc. Dir., Canada Council 1983–87; Officer of the Order of Canada 1967; Chevalier de l'Ordre National du Québec 1985; Officier des Arts et Lettres, France 1988; Calixa-Lavallée Medal Société St-Jean-Baptiste de Montréal 1963, de Sherbrooke 1971; Diplôme d'honneur Candn. Conf. of Arts 1978; Medal and plaque Kodaly Inst. in Kecskemet 1982; Candn. Music Council Medal 1982; Pres., Conseil des arts de la Communauté urbaine de Montréal 1991; Hon. mem. Internat. Music Council; Home: 2160 Goyer, Montréal, Qué. H3S 1G9.

**LEFEBVRE, Guy,** C.M.A., C.A.; city auditor; b. Montreal, Que. 9 July 1939; s. Adrien and Cécile (Pagé) L.; e. Coll. André-Grasset, B.A. 1960; Univ. of Montreal, Hautes Etudes Comm., C.M.A., C.A. 1963; m. Françoise d. Francois Caillée 16 Oct. 1965; children: François, Julie, Marc; CITY AUDITOR, CITY OF MONTREAL 1987– ; Auditor, hospitals & colleges 1963–67; municipalities (launching of a data ctr.) 1964–68; Cons., General Computer Corp. 1969; Head of P.P.B.S. Study Group, City of Montreal 1970–73; implementation of finan. systems 1974–78; Depy. City Auditor 1979–80; Dir. of Revenue 1981–86; Mem., Inst. of Mngt. Cons.; author of an annual report; Home: 11920 Guertin, Montreal, Que. H4J 1V6; Office: 276 ouest St-Jacques, Ste. 605, Montreal, Que. H2Y 1N3.

**LEFEBVRE, Robert,** B.èsA., M.Ed.; éxécutif des ressources humaines; né. Hammond, Qué. 31 janvier 1944; f. Charles Edouard et Marie Rose (Lavigne) L.; é. Coll. privé de Bourget 1962; Univ. d'Ottawa, B.èsA. 1966, M.Ed. 1974, cert. gén. en droit 1988; ép. Solange Godin 28 mai 1966; enfant: Yves; SURINTENDANT DES RESSOURCES HUMAINES À LA SECTION CATHOLIQUE DU CONSEIL SCOLAIRE DE LANGUE FRANÇAISE D'OTTAWA-CARLETON 1992– ; Enseignant à l'École sec. d'Eastview 1966–68; Enseignant et chef, de la section Histoire à l'École sec. de Plantagenet 1968–72; Dir. adjoint 1972–79; Dir. par intérim de l'École l'Escale de Rockland 1979–80; Dir. adjoint de l'École sec. de Plantagenet 1981–82; Agent de supérvision au bur. rég. du min. de l'Édn. à Toronto 1981–82; Dir. de l'École sec. l'Escale de Rockland 1982–83; Sur. de l'édn. au Conseil scolaire de Prescott-Russell 1984–89; Conseil des écoles cath. de Prescott-Russell 1989; Sur. des ressources humaines au Conseil plénier du Conseil scolaire de langue française d'Ottawa-Carleton 1989–92; Prix commémoratif Luc M. Sauvé 1976; Méd. du 25e anniversaire de sa Majesté la Reine Élizabeth II 1977; mem., Bur. des Gouv. de l'Univ. d'Ottawa; Conseil d'admin. du Centre culturel Ste-Famille-de-Rockland; Adresse: 6237, rue Beauséjour, Orléans, Ont. K1C 6X9.

**LEFEBVRE, Wilfrid,** B.A., LL.B.; lawyer; b. Montreal, Que. 11 Jan. 1947; s. Wilfrid and Renee (Bastien) L.; e. Coll. St-Laurent B.A. 1966; Univ. of Montreal LL.B. 1969; called to Bar of Que. 1970; m. Lise d. Jacques and Mariette Dussault 11 Aug. 1972; one s. Julien; SENIOR PARTNER with OGILVY, RENAULT, Montreal; Legal Offr., Dept. of Supply and Services 1970–72; Counsel, Tax Litigation Section 1972–76; Dir., Taxation Serv., Revenue Canada 1976–78; Gen. Counsel, Tax Litigation Services, Dept. of Justice, Can. 1978–86; part-time teacher, Ottawa Univ. 1974–86; Lectr. Sherbrooke Univ. and Bar Admission Courses (Que. and Ont.); recreation: golf; Home: 1965 La Corne, St-Bruno, Que. J3V 5A1; Office: 1981 McGill College, Montreal, Que. H3A 3C1.

**LEFFEK, Kenneth Thomas,** B.Sc., Ph.D., F.R.S.Chem., F.C.I.C., F.R.S.A.; educator; b. Nottingham, Eng. 15 Oct. 1934; s. Thomas and Ivy Louise (Pye) L.; e. Clacton Co. High Sch. 1951; Univ. Coll. London Univ. B.Sc. (Chem.) 1956, Ph.D. 1959; m. Janet Marilyn d. J. C. M. Wallace, Grimsby, Ont. 26 Sept. 1958; children: Katharine, Geoffrey; Dean of Grad. Studies, Dalhousie Univ. 1972–90 and Prof. of Chem. 1972; Postdoctoral Research Fellow Nat. Research Council Ottawa 1959–61; Asst. Prof. of Chem. present Univ. 1961, Assoc. Prof. 1967; Leverhulme Visiting Research Fellow Univ. of Kent, Canterbury, Eng. 1967–68; author over 70 research papers in phys.-organic chem.; Fellow, Chem. Inst. Can. (Vice Pres. 1985–86, Pres. 1986–87); Royal Soc. of Arts (Chair, Atlantic Chapter 1987–91); Home: 1155 Belmont-on-the-Arm, Halifax, N.S. B3H 1J2.

**LEFSRUD, Erik Sigurd,** Q.C., B.A., LL.B.; b. Viking, Alta. 25 Aug. 1933; s. late Sigurd, Q.C. and Jennie (Ness) L.; e. Univ. of Alta. B.A. 1955, LL.B. 1956; m. Helen Hazel d. the late Melvin Carlson 2 June 1956; children: Erik Gregory, Kristin Lee, Karin Marie; JUSTICE, COURT OF QUEEN'S BENCH OF ALBERTA 1991– ; Sr. Partner, Lefsrud, Coulter & Kerby till 1991; Lutheran; recreations: curling, golf; Club: Derrick Golf & Winter; Home: 68 Westbrook Dr., Edmonton, Alta. T6J 2E1; Office: The Law Courts, Edmonton, Alta. T5J 0R2.

**LEGARE, Most Rev. Henri Francis,** O.M.I., LL.D., B.A., M.A., D.Sc.Soc. (R.C.) bishop; b. Willow Bunch, Sask. 20 Feb. 1918; s. Philippe and Amanda (Douville) Légaré; e. Coll. Cath. de Gravelbourg, Sask.; Sacred Heart Scholasticate (Philos. and Theol.) Lebret, Sask.; Social, Econ. and Pol. Sciences at: Laval, Cath. Univ. of America, St. Francis Xavier Univ., Catholic Univ. of Lille, France, Fribourg Univ., Switzerland; LL.D. Carleton 1959, Assumption 1960, Queen's 1961, Sask. 1963, Waterloo Lutheran 1965; D.U., Ottawa 1984; ARCHBISHOP OF GROUARD-McLENNAN since 1972; Bishop of Labrador-Schefferville 1967–72; Nat. Chaplain and Executive Director, Catholic Hospital Assn. of Can. 1952–57; o. Priest, June 1943; Prof. of Sociology, Laval Univ., Quebec, 1946; Treas, and Prof. at Grand Semy., St. Norbert, Manitoba, 1947–48; Prof. of Sociology, Grand Semy., St. Boniface, Man., 1950–52; Prof. of Sociology (fall term 1951), Univ. of Ottawa; Prof. of Med. Ethics, Faculty of Med., Univ. of Ottawa, 1955–58; Dean of the Faculty of Social, Econ. & Pol. Science, 1954–58, second Vice-Rector, 1955–58; Rector, 1958–64; Dir. of Studies, Oblate Prov. of Manitoba, 1966 and Prov. Superior there same year; consecrated 9 Sept. 1967; Asst. Editor of French Weekly 'La Liberte et le Patriote,' Winnipeg, Man., 1950–52; Editor, 'L'Ami du Foyer' (mag.), 1950–52; Dir., Sch. of Social Action, St. Boniface, Man., 1951–52; mem., Internat. Acad. of Pol. Science; Candn. Welfare Council (French Comn.); mem., Ont. Cancer Treatment & Research Foundation; Pres. (1960–62), Nat. Conf. of Candn. Univs. & Colls.; Chrmn. (1960–62), Candn. Univs. Foundation; Pres., Western Catholic Conference of Bishops, 1974–80; Pres., Candn. Catholic Conference of Bishops, 1981–83; Vice-Pres., World Univ. Service of Can.; Hon. mem., 'Le conseil de la vie française en Am.'; Hon. Prof. of Ottawa, 1967; Address: Box 388, McLennan, Alta. T0H 2L0.

**LEGARE, Jacques;** éducateur; né Montréal, Qué. 11 mai 1938; f. Arthur et Louisa (Laporte) L.; é. Univ. de Montréal B.Sc. 1960; Univ. de Paris Diplôme d'expert démographe 1963, Doctorat-Démographie 1969; ép. Gisèle Graton 12 décembre 1970; PROFESSEUR AU DEPARTEMENT DE DEMOGRAPHIE, UNIV. DE MONTREAL; Professeur à l'Université de Montréal depuis 1965, Directeur du Département de démographie 1973–89, Professeur titulaire depuis 1976; auteur 'Démométrie et planification des ressources humaines' 1972; en collaboration 'Evolution démographique du Québec et de ses régions 1966–86' 1969; En collaboration 'Répertoire des actes de baptême, mariage, sépulture et des recensements du Québec ancien,' 1980–1991 (47 vol.); en collaboration, 'Evolution de la mortalité au Canada et au Québec 1831–1931: Essai de mesure par génération' 1982; en collaboration, 'Naissance d'une population: Les Français établis au Canada au XVIIe siècle' 1987 (in English: 'The First French-Canadians: Pioneers in the St. Lawrence Valley' 1993); en collaboration 'The Family in Crisis: a Population Crisis? Crise de la famille, crise démographique?' 1989; mem. Société royale du Can.; Union internationale pour l'étude scientifique de la population; Population Assn. Am.; Candn. Population Soc.; Assn. des démographes du Qué.; Adresse: 5637 Plantagenet, Montréal, Qué. H3T 1S3; Bureau: CP 6128, Succ. 'A,' Montréal, Qué. H3C 3J7.

**LEGAULT, Albert,** M.A., (Hon.) Dr. de l'U. (Paris); educator; b. Montreal, Que. 7 June 1938; s. Fortunat and Félécilda (Geoffrion) L.; e. Coll. St-Laurent B.A. 1959; Univ. of Chicago M.A. 1961; Grad. Inst. Internat. Studies Geneva, Docteur ès sciences politiques 1964; Univ. de Paris-Sud, Dr. de l'U. (Paris) 1976; m. Cosima d. Max Dittus 27 July 1964; one d. Cornelia; PROF. OF POL. SCIENCE, LAVAL UNIV. since 1969; Lectr., Grad. Inst. Internat. Affairs, Geneva 1964–66; Asst. Dir. Internat. Information Centre on Peace-Keeping Operations, Paris 1966–68; Visiting Prof. Chair of Strategic Studies, Queen's Univ. 1968–69; Dir. Gen., Centre québécois de relations internationales 1973–80; co-author 'The Dynamics of Nuclear Balance' 1974, French and German tranls.; 'Quarante-trois ans d'espoir, Le Canada et le désarmement, 1945–88' 1989, English ed.: 'A Diplomacy of HOPE, Canada and Disarmament, 1945–88' 1992: over 60 articles scient. journs. and newspapers; mem. Internat. Inst. Strategic Studies; Internat. Studies Assn; Internat. Peace Acad.; Atlantic Inst.; Candn. Inst. Internat. Affairs (Assoc. Extve. Dir. 1975–80); Task Force to Review Unification of the Armed Forces, 1979; Can. Expert, U.N. Study Group on Nuclear Weapons, 1979; Special Adv., Dept. of Nat. Defence, Ottawa, Sept 1980–82; Dir., Candn. Inst. of Internat. Peace and Security 1984–87; Special Advisor, Candn. Del. to UNSSOD III, 1988; R. Catholic; Home: 2038 blvd. Laurier, Sillery, Qué. G1T 1B6; Office: Pavillon de Koninck, Laval Univ., Québec, Qué. G1K 7P4.

**LEGAULT, François,** B.A.A., C.A.; financial executive; b. Montreal, Que. 25 April 1956; s. Guy R. and Anne-Marie (Painchaud) L.; Hautes Études Comm. B.A.A. 1978, C.A. 1980; m. Sylvia d. Reginald and Pauline Johnson 2 June 1984; children: Laura, Frederic; SENIOR VICE-PRES. FINANCE & TREAS. BIOCHEM PHARMA INC. 1987– ; Auditing, Coopers & Lybrand 1978–80; Insolvency Dept. 1980–84; Dir. of Finance, SQT (Holding) 1984–87; Dir., BioChem ImmunoSystems Inc.; IAF BioVac Inc.; BioChem Therapeutic Inc.; IFCI CloneSystems S.p.A.; Chemila S.p.A.; Soc. Québécoise du Développement de la Main-d'Oeuvre; Pharmaceutical Mfrs. Assn. of Canada (Financial Sector); Home: 1088 Waterloo, Town of Mount-Royal, Que. H3B 2L2; Office: 2550 Daniel-Johnson Blvd., Ste. 600, Laval, Que. H7T 2L1.

**LEGAULT, Josée,** B.A.; political scientist; b. Montreal, Que. 1 Oct. 1960; d. Gaston and Micheline (Trottier) L.; e. Univ. of Que. at Montreal B.A.; Ph.D. in progress; TEACHER, POLITICAL SCIENCE & HISTORY, UNIV. OF QUEBEC AT MONTREAL 1990– ; fields of interest: Anglo-Quebecers, English Canada, Charter of Rights, Language, Minority-Majority Relations, The Constitutions; frequent public speaker across Canada; Mem., Adv. Bd., Theatre 1776 (only bilingual theatre in Montreal); Candn. & Que. Political Science assns.; Fellowship, SSHRCC; author: 'L'Invention d'une minorité: Les Anglo-Québécois' (1992) and several articles; contbr.: 'Répliques aux détracteurs de la souveraineté' 1992, 'Les Objections de 20 spécialistes aux offres fédérales' 1992, 'René Lévesque: L'homme, la nation, la démocratie' 1992, 'Counter Revolution in Canada' forthcoming; recreations: long walks, theatre, swimming; Home: 8005 St-Denis, Montreal, Que. H2R 2G2.

**LEGENDRE, Louis,** B.A., B.Sc., Ph.D., M.S.R.C.; professeur; né Montréal, Qué. l6 février 1945; f. Vianney et Marguerite (Venne) L.; é. Univ. de Montréal B.A. 1964, B.Sc. 1967; Dalhousie Univ. Ph.D. 1971; Univ. de Paris VI, Station marine de Villefranche-sur-Mer, France Stagiaire post-doctoral OTAN; PROF., DEP. BIOLOGIE, UNIV. LAVAL 1981– , Prof. adjoint 1973, Prof. agrégé 1977; mem. Groupe interuniv. rech. océanogr. Québec 1973– , Sec. gén. 1977–79, Coord. Rech. 1980–86, Vice-prés. 1989– ; Cons. Rech. sci. nat. génie Can. Com. Biol. Populations 1980–83, Com. Océans 1985–89, Prés. groupe sci. vie 1989–92; Fonds FCAR Com. Centres 1988–89; Prés. Com. sci. Actions structurantes 1990; Sci. Com. Oceanic Res. (ICSU) Working Groups 73 1983–87 and 86 1988– ; Inst. océanogr. Paris Com. Perfectionnement 1981– ; Univ. française Pacifique Com. Sci. Cultur 1990– ; Arctic Ocean Sci. Bd. Chrmn. Sci. Coord. Group, Internat. Arctic Polynya Programme 1989– ; NATO Adv. Res. Workshop Numerical Ecol. co-dir. 1985–86; Réseau de Centres Excell. OPEN mem. Bd. 1989–90; Cons. Hydro-Québec et SEBJ 1975–77, UNESCO 1980; Prof. invité Univ. Paris VI 1978, 1980; Vrije Univ. Brussels 1980; Univ. Corse 1987; Univ. Malaga 1989; Univ. Barcelona 1991; Chev. Malte; Acfas: Prix Léo-Pariseau 1985; Prix Michel-Jurdant 1986; auteur ou co-auteur de plus de 15 livres et chapitres, 100 publications en océanographie biol. et écol. numérique dans des périodiques scientifiques et compte-rendus de conf.; co-ed. 'Developments in Numerical Ecology' 1987; mem. divers conseils rédac.; Bureau: Québec, Qué. G1K 7P4.

**LEGENDRE, Pierre,** B.A., M.Sc., Ph.D., F.R.S.C.; university professor; b. Montréal, Qué. 5 Oct. 1946; s. Vianney and Marguerite (Venne) L.; e. Coll. Saint-Viateur, Univ. de Montréal B.A. 1965; McGill Univ. M.Sc. 1969; Univ. of Colorado Ph.D. 1971; m. Ghislaine d. Fernand and Carmen Ouellette 12 June 1969; children: Eric, Marie-Pierre; PROFESSOR, BIOLOGY, UNIV. DE MONTREAL 1984– ; postdoctoral fellow, Genetiska Inst., Lunds Univ. Sweden 1971–72; Rsch. Assoc. then Rsch. Dir., Ctr. de rech. en sci. de l'envir., and lastly Prof., Dép. de physique, Univ. de Qué. at Montréal 1972–80; Assoc. Prof., Biol., Univ. de Montréal 1980–84; Killam Rsch. Fellowship 1989–91; Visiting Prof., Univ. des Sci. et Tech. du Languedoc France 1985; Fac. des Sci., Univ. cath. de Louvain Belgium 1987, '88, '89; has held several executive academic and assn. positions; Bd. of Dir., Soc. francophone de Classification 1984– ; Mem., Benthos Ecol. Working Group, Internat. Council for the Exploration of the Sea 1989– ; Com. d'experts en santé envir., Hydro-Québec 1989– ; Killam Selection Ctte. 1990–93 (Chair, subctte. on nat. sci. 1992–93); Sec.-Treas., Internat. Fed. of Classification Societies (IFCS) 1988–92; Chair, Nom. Ctte., Classification Soc. of N. AM. 1992–93; Sec., Sci. Awards Ctte., Internat. Fed. of Classification Soc. 1992–93; Edit. Bd. Mem., 'Le Naturaliste canadien' 1981– , 'Can. J. of Zool.' 1987– , 'Annals of the Royal Belgian Zool. Soc.' 1989–93; Assoc. Ed., 'J. of Environmental Statistics' 1993; Michel-Jurdant Prize for Envir. Sci., ACFAS 1986; Fellow, Royal Soc. of Canada 1992– ; Life Sci. Fellowship Rev. Ctte., Acad. of Sci. 1992–95; co-author of 6 books incl. most recent: 'Ecologie numérique, deuxième édition revue et augmentée' 2 vols. 1984; co-editor: 'Developments in Numerial Ecology' 1987; Home: 559, ave. Champagneur, Outremont, Qué. H2V 3P4; Office: C.P. 6128, Succ. A, Montréal, Qué. H3C 3J7.

**LEGER, Franklin Oswald,** B.A., B.C.L., LL.D. (hon.); Q.C.; barrister and solicitor; b. St. John, N.B. 4 June 1930; s. Leo Oswald and Muriel Florilla (Whelpley) L.; e. St. Francis Xavier Univ. B.A. 1951; Univ. of N.B., B.C.L. 1954; London Sch. of Econ., Univ. of London 1955; m. Priscilla d. Arthur and Barbara Doyle 23 Apr. 1966; children: Jennifer, Mark, Alexandra, Rebecca; PARTNER PALMER, O'CONNELL, LEGER, RODERICK, GLENNIE 1985; read law with Teed, Palmer & O'Connell 1952–53; called to Bar of N.B. 1954; Assoc. Teed, Palmer & O'Connell 1955–59; Assoc. and Partner Teed, Palmer, O'Connell & Leger 1959–64; Partner Palmer, O'Connell, Leger & Turnbull 1964–68; Partner Palmer, O'Connell, Leger, Turnbull & Turnbull 1968–83; Palmer, O'Connell, Leger, Guerette 1983–85; cr. Q.C. 1973; author: 'One Hundred Years in the Practice of Law: 1888–1988'; mem. Bd. of Dir., Candn. Lawyers Insur. Assoc. 1988– ; Sec. and mem. Bd. of Gov. St. Thomas Univ. 1972– ; former Chrmn. and mem. Bd. of Dir. St. Joseph's Hosp. Found. Inc.; Pres. N.B. Div., Candn. Red Cross Soc. 1978–80; mem. Law Soc. of N.B.; Candn. Bar Assn.; R. Catholic; Clubs: Union; Riverside Country; Home: 15 Almon Lane, P.O. Box 265, Rothesay, N.B. E0G 2W0; Office: One Brunswick Sq., Suite 1600, Saint John, N.B. E2L 4H8.

**LEGER, Rev. Hector,** B.A., S.Th.L., Ph.D. (R.C.); retired; b. St. Anthony, N.B., 18 Jan. 1911; s. Ferdinand and Marie-Blanche (Allain) L.; e. St. Joseph's Univ., B.A. 1930, Ph.D. 1949; entered Congregation of Holy Cross 1930; Grand Semy., Montreal, 1931–35; S.Th.L. 1935; Prov. Superior of Congregation of Holy Cross, Acadian Province 1945–68; Prof. of Philos., St. Laurent Coll., Montreal, 1935–36; St. Joseph's Univ. 1936–41; Prof. of Theol., Holy Cross Semy., St. Genevieve, Que., 1941–44; Dir. there 1942–44; Pres., St. Joseph's Univ., 1944–48; Extve. Secy. of CRC-A (Atlantic Provs.) 1970–72; Chaplain, N.D.S.C. Motherhouse, Moncton 1969–78; retired with part time ministry as chaplain since 1978; Address: 24 Kendra St., Apt. 3, Moncton, N.B. E1C 4J8.

**LEGER, Jacques A.,** Q.C., LL.B.; lawyer; b. Montréal, Qué. 1 Feb. 1945; s. Jacques and Jacqueline (Lanctot) L.; e. Univ. de Montréal m. Hélène Lapierre 4 Oct. 1968; children: Martin, Isabelle, Vincent; SR. PARTNER, LEGER ROBIC RICHARD / ROBIC 1971– ; called to Bar of Qué. 1968; law practice Bohemier Chenard & Leger 1968–71; Chrmn. of Bd. Canadian Patents & Development Ltd.; Lectr. Candn. Inst., P.T.I.C., Internat. League Competition Law; Pres. René Richard Found.; Co-Ed. 'Canadian Trade Marks Annotated' 1984; Co-editor, 'Canadian Copyright Act' annotated 1993; Gen. Ed. 'Civil Remedies in Copyright Law' 1983; apptd. Queen's Counsel 1992; Office: 55 St.-Jacques St., Montréal, Qué. H2Y 3X2.

**LEGER, Hon. Jean-Louis,** B.A., B.Ph., B.L.L.; juge; né Montréal, Qué. 24 Sept. 1927; f. Damase et Elizabeth (Lefebvre) L.; é. Coll. Sainte-Croix, Univ. de Montréal, Univ. McGill; é. Gisèle f. Maurice Viger et Blanche Laurin 11 Juin 1951; enfants: Stéphane, Nathalie; JUGE, COUR SUPÉRIEURE DU QUÉBEC 1987– ; Prés. Commission scolaire Chomedey-Laval 1968–71; membre exécutif C.E.G.E.P. Montmorency-Laval 1969–75; échevin Ville de Laval, Prés. Assoc. de bienfaisance des avocats de Montréal; C.R. en 1976; Catholique; Résidence: 690, ave. Bernard, Laval, Qué. H7V 1T3; bureau: 1 est, rue Notre-Dame, 6.56, Montréal, Qué. H2Y 1B6.

**LEGER, Joseph Claudius Ignace de Loyola,** Q.C., B.C.L.; b. Saint John, N.B. 9 Sept. 1920; s. Jean Edmond and Léona Béatrice Marie (Johnson) L.; e. Moncton High Sch. 1940; St-Joseph Univ.; St-Thomas Univ.; Univ. of N.B. B.C.L. 1946; m. Julia C. Bowser; called to Bar of N.B. 1946; cr. Q.C. 1962; M.L.A. 1948–52; apptd. County Court Judge for Counties of Kent and Westmorland 1963; Chief Judge, County Court of N.B. 1972, elevated to Supreme Court of N.B., Queen's Bench Div. 1972; Judge, Court of Queen's Bench, N.B. and ex officio Judge, Court of Appeal, N.B. 1979; mem. Candn. Bar Assn.; R. Catholic; recreation: golf; Club: Moncton City; Home: 224 MacBeath Ave., Moncton, N.B. E1C 7A3.

**LÉGER, Viola,** O.C., M.F.A., D.ès L.; actress; teacher; director; b. Fitchburg, Mass. 29 June 1930; d. André É. and Nathalie M. (LeBlanc) L.; e. Univ. de Moncton B.A. 1964, B.Ed. 1971, D.ès L. 1976; Boston Univ. M.F.A. 1970; Univ. St-Anne, N.S. D.ès L. 1981; Saint Thomas Univ., N.B. D.ès L. 1986; ARTISTIC DIR. LA COMPAGNIE VIOLA LÉGER INC. (theatre co.) 1985– ; appeared over 1000 performances in French and Eng.'La Sagouine' by Antonine Maillet 1971, Candn. and New Eng. tours, Eur. tour 1976; performed 16 episodes Radio-Can. (TV); Théâtre d'Orsay de Jean-Louis Barrault et Madeleine Renaud, Paris 16 performances; Festival d'Avignon, France 1978; other roles performed Théâtre du Rideau Vert, Montréal; Nat. Arts Centre Ottawa; CentreStage Toronto; Théâtre de l'Ile, Hull; served as Drama Teacher N.B. high schs.; Artist-in-Residence; Visiting Prof.; Guest, John Grinder Workshop, Neuro-Linguistic Prog. Monterey, Cal.; Seminar Communications Technol. Higher Edn. Univ. de Moncton; recipient Prix Littéraire de La Presse 1976; named Chevalier de l'Ordre de la Pléiade 1978; Dora Mavor Moore Award Outstanding Performance 1978; nominated Earle Grey Award best acting performance TV; Médaille du Conseil de la Vie Française en Amérique 1987; O.C. 1989; Chevalier de l'Ordre français des Arts et des Lettres 1991; Home: 297, rue Highfield, Moncton, N.B. E1C 5R4; Office: C.P. 39, Moncton, N.B. E1C 8R9.

**LEGERE, Martin J.,** O.C. (1974), M.Sc.Com., D.Sc.Soc., D.Sc.Adm., LL.D.; retired banker; b. Caraquet, N.B., 17 November 1916; s. Jean B. and Beatrice (Godin) L.; e. Caraquet (N.B.) Sch.; St.-Francis-Xavier Univ.; Laval Univ.; Hon. M.Sc.Com., St. Joseph 1950; D.Sc.Soc., Sacred Heart Univ. 1953; D.Sc.Adm., Moncton 1971; LL.D. St. Francis Xavier 1974; m. Anita Godin, 5 June 1950; children: Louise, Louis, René, Jean-Claude; General Manager, La Federation Des Caisses Populaires Acadienne Ltee from 1946–81; Pres., newspaper L'Evangeline, 1980–81; General Manager, La Société d'Assurance des Caisses Populaires Acadienne 1947–81; L'Institut de Coopération Acadien (1978–81); Secretary, L'Union Coopérative Acadienne 1945–81; Director, La Caisse Populaire de Caraquet, 1938–72; Co-Operative Fire and Casualty Insurance, 1964–77; Co-operative Life Insurance, 1964–77; Co-operative Insurance Services, 1964–77; La Compagnie de Gestion Atlantique Ltée 1975–82; started career as Fieldman, Co-op. Movement, St-Francis-Xavier Univ., Antigonish, N.S. 1938; Auditor of Credit Unions, Prov. of N.B. 1940–46; Pres., Le Conseil Candn. de la Co-op 1952–82; La Co-op. de Caraquet 1947–78; N.B. Industrial Finance Bd., 1960–76; Secy., Chambre de Comm. de Caraquet; Treas., La Ville Beauséjour of Caraquet; Dir., La Société des Artisans 1950–81; Chancelier, Le Conseil de Vie Française; Les Coopérants 1981–90; General Manager, La Fondation Culturelle Acadienne 1982–89; Caraquet Hosp., 1960–75; Patrimoine Caraquet Inc. 1983; Prés., Les Oeuvres de Presse Acadienne, 1977–81; mem. Adv. Bd., Bathurst Coll., 1970–73; mem. Central Comte., Internat. Co-op. Alliance 1970–81; Mun. Councillor 1950–55; Treas., Children's Aid Soc., Gloucester Co. 1948–66; Pres., Catholic Youth Assn. 1940–50; Dir., Atlantic Provs. Econ. Council 1956–62; mem. Community Devel. Corp. (N.B.) 1965–66; mem. Extve. Cttee., Le Centre de Bénévolat de la Péninsule Acadienne Inc. 1981–86; awarded 'Bene Merentis' medal by His Holiness Pope Pius XII, 1950; mem. Order of La Pleiade, 1980; Knight of Order of St. Lazarus of Jerusalem 1981; Chosen 'Personality of the Year' by Richelieu International 1990; mem. Club des Cent Associes, 1980; Club: Richelieu; Home: 312 W., Blvd. St. Pierre, Caraquet, N.B. E0B 1K0; Office: Caraquet, N.B. E0B 1K0.

**LEGGE, Bruce Jarvis,** C.M.M., CM, K.St.J., E.D., C.D., Q.C.; lawyer; b. Toronto, Ont. 20 Jan. 1919; s. late W.R. and Mina Loretta (Jarvis) L.; e. Univ. of Toronto 1941; Osgoode Hall Law Sch.; m. Laura Louise d. late James and Lucy Down 21 July 1950; children: Elizabeth (Mrs. George Meanwell), John, Bruce; PARTNER, LEGGE & LEGGE since 1955; Dir., Candn. Inst. of Strategic Studies 1990– ; Vice Pres., Atlantic Council of Canada 1990– ; called to Bar of Ont. 1949; cr. Q.C. 1960; Dist. Solr. and Pensions Advocate Dept. Veterans' Affairs 1950–64; Chrmn. Ont. Workmen's Compensation Bd. 1965–73; Pres., Assn. of Workmen's Compensation Bds. of Canada 1970–71; Chrmn. of Comns. Inquiry into Workmen's Compensation Y.T. and N.W.T. 1966–67, N.W.T. 1973–74; mem. Gov.'s Comn. to Study Workmen's Compensation Laws State of N.J. 1972–73; Hon. Life Gov., Corps of Commissionaires since 1985; served continuously in the Cdn. Forces, active and reserve since 1938; Cmdg. Offr., 5 Armoured Divisional Column, RCASC 1958–62; Pres., Royal Cdn. Army Service Corps, Assoc. of Can. (RCASC) 1963; Vice-Chrmn., Comn. on the Reorgn. of the Candn. Army (Militia), Govt. of Can. 1964; Cmdg. Offr., 1st Toronto Service Battalion 1965–66; Chrmn. Conf. Defence Assns. Can. 1965; Candn. delegate to CIOR 1965–

78; Col. and apptd. Militia Adv., Toronto District 1966–70; Brig. Gen. and Commdr. Central Militia Area 1970–73; apptd. Militia Adv. to Comdr. of Mobile Command 1973; promoted Maj.-Gen. and apptd. Maj.-Gen. Reserves for Can. 1975–78; Secy. Gen. Interallied Confed. Reserve Offrs. (NATO) 1978–80, Past Secy. Gen. 1980–82; Hon. Life Mem., Extve. Ctte., CIOR since 1982; Col. Commandant Logistics 1982–87; Hon. Col. 25 (Toronto) Service Battalion since 1987; One of five Candn. lawyers to tour China as guests of the Chinese Govt. 1958; In charge of transport, Anglican World Congress, Toronto 1963; Chrmn., Internat. Seminar on rehabilitation programmes in workers' compensation and related fields 1969; Patron, 2nd Pan-Pacific Congress Games 1973; Mem., Ctte. of Honour, 6th Internat. Conf. on alcohol, drug and traffic safety 1974; Chrmn. of Bd., Can. Safety Council 1974–75, Pres. 1972–74; Participant on the Candn. Nat. Ctte. for Habitat '76, The U.N. Conf. on Human Settlements; Trustee, Sunnybrook Med. Centre 1981–87; Trustee, First Sunnybrook Fund 1986–90; Trustee Emeritus, Sunnybrook Health Science Centre 1991– ; Chrmn. for Programme, Confed. of church and business people 1985–87; Pres. Empire Club Can. 1958–59 and Foundation 1977–86; Chrmn., Inst. Pub. Adm. Toronto 1964–65; Royal Candn. Legion Fort York Br. 1965; Royal Candn. Mil. Inst. 1966–68, Hon. Pres. 1971–75, elected Hon. Life Mem. 1991– ; Internat. Assn. Indust. Accident Bds. & Comns. 1971–72 (Adm. of Yr. Award 1973); Good Neighbours' Club Aged Men (Un. Appeal) 1971–74; Medico-Legal Soc. 1973–74; Chrmn., Royal Commonwealth Soc. Toronto 1978–81, Hon. Life Chrmn. (Toronto) since 1981, Nat. Chrmn. 1982–87, Hon. Pres. 1987, Hon. Life Vice-Pres. (London) 1988; Life mem. Reserve Offrs. Assn. U.S.A. 1980 (Bronze Eagle Award 1987); Dir. Ch. of Good Samaritan since 1965; Chrmn., Metro Internat. Caravan since 1981; mem. Governing Counc.: Candn. Bar Assoc. 1972–75; Rehabilitation International 1973–74; Candn. mem., Bd. of Regents, IAI-ABC 1973–77; Candn. Inst. of Mgmt. 1974–78; Duke of Edinburgh's Award in Can., Nat. Counc. 1979–89; Trustee, Wycliffe Coll. since 1981; Vice-Pres., Canada-Korea Soc. 1982–91, Pres. 1991–92; Vice-Pres., Atlantic Counc. of Can. 1991– ; mem., Bd. of Trade, Metro. Toronto (Chrmn., Military Affairs Ctte. since 1984); Candn. Inst. Internat. Affairs; Candn. Inst. of Strategic Studies; John Howard Soc.; Art Gall. of Ont.; U.N. Assoc.; English-Speaking Union; Royal Candn. Mil. Inst. Curling Club; Bishop's Co. (Anglican); Honorary Counsel, Prayer Book Soc.; Chrmn., The Council of Honorary Colonels, Candn. Forces 1994– ; recipient Efficiency Decoration (ED) 1956; Centennial Medal 1967; Cdn. Forces Decoration (CD) 1968; Award of Merit, City of Toronto 1972; Knight Ordre Souverain et Militaire du Temple de Jerusalem, Norway 1974; Queen's Silver Jubilee Medal 1977; Comdr. of the Order of Military Merit (CMM) 1978; Cert. of Achievement, R.O.A. 1978; Knight of Grace, The Military and Hospitaller Order of St. Lazarus of Jerusalem (KLJ) 1979; Golden Salute Award for Outstanding Service to the Reserves of Germany and NATO, Armed Forces of the Fed. Republic of Germany 1980; Knight of Grace of The Order of St. John of Jerusalem (KStJ) 1981; Knight of Merit, Ordo Constantini Magni 1984; Royal Danish Decoration of Hon., by Denmark at Rome 1984; Member of the Order of Canada 1987; Medal of Merit, Baltic Veterans' League in Canada 1989; Freedom of the City of London (at Guildhall) U.K. 1989; Jerusalem Medal, Jewish War Veterans 1989; Phi Delta Phi; Anglican; Clubs: Empire; Canadian; Arts & Letters; Home: 301 Lonsdale Rd., Toronto, Ont. M4V 1X3; Office: 60 St. Clair Ave. E., Toronto, Ont. M4T 1N5.

**LEGGE, Elizabeth,** Ph.D.; curator; b. Toronto, Ont. 25 March 1952; d. Bruce Jarvis and Laura Louise L.; e. Bishop Strachan Sch.; Univ. of Toronto B.A. 1973; Cambridge Univ. B.A. 1976; Courtauld Inst. Univ. of London Ph.D. 1986; m. George Dewar s. Robert W. and Joyce Meanwell 14 Dec. 1979; one s. Max; CURATOR UNIV. OF TORONTO ART COLL. 1988– ; Assoc. Curator Winnipeg Art Gallery 1979–81; Asst. Prof. Univ. of Winnipeg 1985–88; Asst. Prof., Fine Art Dept., Univ. of Toronto 1992– ; Roland Penrose Meml. Lectr. Tate Gallery London 1991; mem. Man. Adv. Council Status Women 1980–81; Bd. Visual Arts Man. 1985–87; Bd. Toronto Mendelssohn Choir 1989; Curatorial Bd. Extension Gallery Print & Drawing Council Can. 1990; author 'Faded Allusions: Later Nineteenth Century Academic Art' 1981; 'Max Ernst, The Psychoanalytic Sources' 1989; co-author 'Kurelek' catalogue 1980; mem. ed. adv. bd. Univ. of Toronto Quarterly 1990; recreation: soft sculpture (caricatures); Home: 43 Appleton Ave., Toronto, Ont. M6E 3A4; Office: 15 King's College Circle, Toronto, Ont. M5S 1A1.

**LEGGE, Laura Louise,** Q.C., B.A., LL.D. (h.c.); lawyer; b. Delhi, Ont. 27 Jan. 1923; d. James and Lucy (Pratt) Down; e. Univ. of W. Ont. B.A. 1944; Toronto Gen. Hosp. Sch. of Nursing R.N. 1945; Osgoode Hall Law Sch. 1948; m. Bruce Jarvis Legge 21 July 1950; children: Elizabeth (Mrs. George Meanwell), John Bruce Jarvis, Bruce Richard Warren; PARTNER, LEGGE & LEGGE since 1955; called to Bar of Ont. 1948; cr. Q.C. 1966; Solr. Ont. Dept. of Health 1948–54; Dir. Home Care Program Metro Toronto 1975–83; Bd. Chrmn., Ont. Safety League 1986–88; mem. Council Ont. Coll. of Art 1980–83; Bd. Govs. Women's Coll. Hosp. 1983–93; Bencher, Law Soc. Upper Can. since 1975, el. Treas. 1983, 1984 and 1988; Pres., Fedn. of Law Societies of Can. 1988; Women's Law Assn. Ont. (Pres. 1964–66); Dir., Bd. of Trade for Metrop. Toronto 1983–87; Canada Life Assurance Co.; Commissioner, Toronto Parking Authority 1985–92; mem., Toronto Economic Development Corp.; awarded LL.D. (hon. causa), Law Soc. of Upper Canada 1988; Internat. Legal Fraternity, Phi Delta Phi; Anglican; Club: Soroptimist Internat. of Toronto (Pres. 1974–76); Home: 301 Lonsdale Rd., Toronto, Ont. M4V 1X3; Office: 60 St. Clair Ave. E., Toronto, Ont. M4T 1N5.

**LEGGE, Russel Donald,** B.A., S.T.B., Ph.D.; educator; b. Milton, N.S. 31 Jan. 1935; s. James Farish and Shirley Evelyn (MacNutt) L.; e. Queen Elizabeth High Sch. Halifax, N.S. 1952; HMC Dockyard apprenticeship Ship's Fitter 1956; Transylvania Univ. Lexington, Ky. B.A. 1962; Harvard Univ. S.T.B. 1965; McMaster Univ. Ph.D. 1972; m. Elma d. Earl and Doris Dingwell 20 Aug. 1960; children: Cheryl Lee, Scott Douglas, Suzanne Rae, James Earl; ASSOC. PROF. OF RELIGIOUS STUDIES, UNIV. OF WATERLOO 1982– ; Lectr. in Religious Studies present Univ. 1970, Asst. Prof. 1972–82; Dean, St. Paul's United Coll., Univ. of Waterloo 1978– ; Dir. of Centre for Society, Technology and Values, Univ. of Waterloo 1986–89; Ship's Fitter, HMC Dockyard 1956–57; Br. Service Mgr. Neptune Meters Ltd. Halifax 1957–58; Student Asst. Min. Harvard Cong. Ch. 1963–65; Min.: Guelph Christian Ch. (Disciples of Christ) 1965–67; Winger Christian Ch. 1967–70; Moderator, Christian Ch. (Disciples of Christ) in Can. 1980–82; Pres. Candn. Council Chs. 1982–85; Chairperson, Nat. Tripartite Liaison Ctte. 1983–86; Home: 259 Lourdes St., Waterloo, Ont. N2L 1P2; Office: St. Paul's United College, Univ. of Waterloo, Waterloo, Ont. N2L 3G5.

**LEGGET, Robert Ferguson,** C.C. (1989), M.E., D.Eng., D.G.Sc., LL.D., D.Sc., F.R.S.C. (1956),; b. Liverpool, Eng., 29 Sept. 1904; s. Donald and Mercy (Thomson) L.; e. Merchant Taylor's Sch., Great Crosby, Eng.; Univ. of Liverpool, B.E. (Hons.) 1925, M.E. 1927; LL.D. McMaster, 1961, Queen's 1966, New Brunswick 1969, Toronto 1969, Glasgow 1971; D.Sc. Waterloo, 1963, Western 1969; D.G.Sc., Charles (Prague) 1969; D.Eng. Liverpool 1971; Nova Scotia Tech. Coll., 1972; D.Sc. Clarkson Coll. of Technol. 1972; Sir George Williams Univ. 1972; D.Eng. Carleton 1974; m. the late Lillian S., d. S.A. Free, Stratford, England, 28 February 1931; has one s., David; Assistant Engineer, C.S. Meik and Buchanan, Westminster, England, 1925–29; Resident Engr., Power Corporation of Canada Ltd., engaged on water power projects 1929–32; Engr., Candn. Sheet Piling Co. Ltd., Montreal, 1932–36; Lectr. in Civil Engn., Queen's Univ., 1936–38; Asst. Prof. of Civil Engn., Univ. of Toronto, 1938–43; Assoc. Prof. 1943–47; Dir., Div. Building Research, Nat. Research Council 1947–69; Officer of the Order of Canada 1967; Companion of the Order of Canada 1989; 1st recipient, Medaille d'or, Candn. Council Prof. Engrs. 1972; Julian C. Smith Medal 1971, Sir John Kennedy Medal 1978, Engn. Inst. Can.; Logan Gold Medal, Geol. Assn. Can. 1972; Leo B. Moore Gold Medal, Standards Engrs. Soc. 1974; Dumont Gold Medal, Geol. Soc. of Belgium 1976; 1st recipient, Wm. Smith Medal, Geol. Soc. of London 1977; Royal Bank Award 1989; Hon. Fellow, Inst. of Civil Engineers (London) 1980; Hon. M.A.S.C.E. (Am. Soc. of Civil Engrs) 1977; Hon. Fellow, Royal Arch. Inst. Can., Geol. Soc. (London), Roy. Soc. of Edinburgh 1983; Gold Medal Assn. Profl. Engrs. of Ont. 1970; Pres., Am. Soc. for Testing and Materials, 1965–66; Pres., Geol. Soc. Am. 1966; Pres., Internat. Council on Building Research 1966–69; Pres. (founding), Candn. Acad. of Engr. 1987; author of 'Geology and Engineering' 1939 (2nd ed. 1962, 3rd ed. (with A.W. Hatheway) 1988); 'Rideau Waterway' 1955 (2nd ed. 1986); 'Standards in Canada' 1970; 'Railways of Canada' 1973 (2nd ed. 1987); 'Cities and Geology' 1973; 'Ottawa Waterway' 1975; 'Canals of Canada' 1976; 'Candn. Railways in Pictures' 1977; 'The Seaway' 1979; 'Ottawa River Canals' 1987; co-author (with C.P. Disney) 'Modern Railroad Structure' 1949; (with P.F. Karrow) 'Handbook of Geology in Civil Engineering' 1983; Editor, 'Soils in Canada' 1961 and 'Reviews in Engineering Geology' Vol. 1 (with T.W. Fluhr), 1962 and Vol. 5 'Geology under Cities' 1982; ed., 'Glacial Till,' 1976; has contributed numerous papers on engn. and research in field of soil mechanics; Home: 531 Echo Dr., Ottawa, Ont. K1S 1N7.

**LEGGETT, Stephen George,** B.A., LL.B., Q.C.; lawyer; b. Toronto, Ont. 12 July 1936; s. William Cecil and Izet Isabella (Ashenhurst) L.; e. Upper Canada College 1954; Trinity College, Univ. of Toronto B.A. 1957; Osgoode Hall Law School LL.B. 1962; m. Suzanne Estcourt d. The Hon. Richard and Nancy Holland 25 May 1991; CROWN ATTORNEY, NORTH YORK, ONT. 1989– ; called to Bar of Ont. 1962; Lawyer, Holden, Murdoch, Walton 1962–64; Asst. Crown Attorney, Judicial Dist. of York 1964; Dep. Crown Attorney 1974; North York 1977; Q.C. 1975; Anglican; Mem., Royal Regt. of Canada Officers Assn.; Law Soc. of U.C.; Crown Attorneys Assn.; recreations: travel, fly fishing; clubs: Royal Canadian Yacht; Home: 18 Wimpole Dr., Toronto, Ont. M2L 2K9; Office: 1000 Finch Ave. W., Downsview, Ont. M3J 2V5.

**LEGGETT, Wiliam C.,** B.A., M.Sc., Ph.D., D.Sc., F.R.S.C.; educator; b. Orangeville, Ont. 25 June 1939; s. Frank Gay and Edna Irene (Wheeler) L.; e. Orangeville Dist. High Sch. 1959; Waterloo Univ. College B.A. 1962; Univ. of Waterloo M.Sc. 1965, D.Sc. 1992; McGill Univ. Ph.D. 1969; m. Claire d. Britton and Marjorie Holman 9 May 1964; two s. David Scott, John William; VICE-PRINCIPAL ACADEMIC, McGILL UNIV. 1991– , Prof. of Biol. 1979– ; Rsch. Sci. Essex Marine Lab. 1965–70; Asst., Assoc. Prof. present Univ. 1970–79, Chrmn. of Biol. 1981–85, Gov. 1988, Dean of Sci. 1986–91; mem. Candn. Ctte. Fishery Rsch. 1979– ; mem. and Chrmn. Grant Selection Ctte. Population Biol. Natural Sci's & Eng. Rsch. Council Can. 1978–82, Strategic Grants Selection Ctte. Oceans 1984–86; mem. Sci. Adv. Bd. World Wildlife Fund Can. 1986–89; Pres. Groupe Interuniversitaire de Recherche Oceanographiques du Que. 1986–91; mem. Conseil Scientifique Institut Nat. de Recherche Scientifique 1986–89; Nat. Marine Council 1988–91; Pres. and Chrmn. Huntsman Marine Sci. Centre 1980–83, Vice Pres. Rsch. 1986–87, Chrmn. 1987–89 and 1990–92, Vice Chrmn. Rsch. 1989–90; recipient D.W. Webster Award of Excellence Am. Fisheries Soc. 1989; Fry Medal, Candn. Soc. Zoologists 1989; Award of Excellence in Fisheries Education, Am. Fisheries Soc. 1990; Fellow, Rawson Acad. 1987; Fellow, Royal Soc. of Canada 1989; author or co-author over 90 sci. publs.; mem. various ed. bds; Home: 161 Sommerhill Ave., Dollard des Ormeaux, Que. H9A 1W9; Office: 853 Sherbrooke St. W., Montreal, Que. H3A 2T6.

**LE GOFF, T.J.A.,** B.A., Ph.D.; historian; b. Vancouver, B.C. 12 Dec. 1942; s. Antoine Jacques and Kathleen (Skinner) L.; e. Vancouver Coll. 1961; Univ. of B.C., B.A. 1965; Univ. Coll. London, Ph.D. 1969; m. Judith d. Harry and Emily (Knowles) Stafford 27 Dec. 1970; children: Henry Jacques Louis, Pauline Elisabeth; ASSOC. PROF. OF HIST. YORK UNIV. 1973– ; Lectr. present Univ. 1969, Asst. Prof. 1970; Lectr. Univ. of Reading, UK 1979–80; Visiting Prof. Univ. Laval 1983; Visiting Fellow, Balliol Coll. Oxford 1983–84; mem. Extve. Council Internat. Comn. Maritime Hist. 1986–90; mem. Extve. Comm., Soc. for French Historical Studies 1989– ; author 'Vannes and its Region: A Study of Town and Country in Eighteenth-Century France' 1981, French transl. 1989; author or co-author numerous articles early Candn. hist., French hist. & popular counter-revolutionary movement during French Revolution; ed. bd. French Hist. Studies 1981–83; French Hist. 1986– ; Histoire sociale/Social History 1987– ; recipient Garneau Medal Candn. Hist. Assn., Hon. Mention 1983; Koren Prize French Hist. Soc. 1975, Hon. Mention 1984; W.K. Ferguson Prize Candn. Hist. Assn. 1984; Keith Matthews Prize, Candn. Nautical Rsch. Soc. 1987; mem., Soc. for French Historical Studies; Société d'Histoire moderne et contemporaine; Candn. Hist. Assn. (Extve. Council 1991– ); Comn. française d'histoire maritime; recreations: squash, music; Home: 580 Palmerston Ave., Toronto, Ont. M6G 2P7; Office: 4700 Keele St., Downsview, Ont. M3J 1P3.

**LEHMAN, Hugh Stephen,** A.M., Ph.D.; educator; b. New York City, N.Y. 8 Dec. 1936; s. Philip and Marion (Horwich) L.; e. Union Coll. A.B. 1958; Harvard Univ. A.M. 1960, Ph.D. 1963; m. Barbara d. David and Helen Stewart 6 Sept. 1958; children: Stephanie, Keith, Bram, Lance, David; PROF. OF PHILOS. UNIV. OF GUELPH 1983– ; joined Smith Coll. Northampton, Mass. 1962–63; Western Wash. Univ. Bellingham 1963–66; Iowa State Univ. Ames 1966–69; present Univ. 1969; author 'Introduction to the Philosophy of Mathematics' 1979; various scholarly articles; co-ed. Jour. of Agric. and Env. Ethics; co-editor 'The Pesticide Question: Environment, Economics and Ethics'; mem. Am. Philos. Assn.; Candn.

Philos. Assn.; Home: 11 Heather Ave., Guelph, Ont. N1G 1P2; Office: Guelph, Ont. N1G 2W1.

**LEHMANN, Arlene Mary,** B.A.A.; video executive; b. Toronto, Ont. 6 Nov. 1950; d. Arthur William and Kathleen Anne (Amsbury) Bradley; e. Ryerson Polytech. Inst., B.A.A. 1974 (radio & TV arts); m. Eric s. Paula and Ewald L. 13 Mar. 1982; Vice-Pres., Marketing, Magnetic North 1983–90; Prod. Asst. to Prod., Corp. Videos, M.R. Communication Cons. 1974–77; Assoc. Prof. 'Nashville Swing,' 'Peter Appleyard Presents,' 'Pete's Place,' Wm. F. Cooke Television 1977–82; Co-owner with husband of Cherry Hill Arabians breeding straight Egyptian Arabian horses, which has included importing bloodstock directly from Egypt; Mem., Candn. & Am. Arabian Horse registries; Candn. Equestrian Fed.; Internat. Arabian Horse Assn.; The Pyramid Soc.; author of numerous articles about personal travels & the horses of Egypt; Home: R.R. #3, Stouffville, Ont. L4A 7X4.

**LEHMANN, Heinz E.,** O.C., M.D., F.R.S.C.; psychiatrist; b. Berlin, Germany 17 July 1911; s. Richard R. and Emmy (Grönke) L.; e. Mommsen Gymnasium, Berlin 1920–1929; Univ. of Freiburg 1929, 1930–31; Univ. of Marburg 1929–30; Univ. of Vienna 1932–33; Univ. of Berlin 1934 M.D. 1935; m. Annette d. late Urbain Joyal 28 July 1940; one s. François; EMERITUS PROF. OF PSYCHIATRY, McGILL UNIV. 1981; Prof. of Psychiatry 1965–81; Visiting Prof. Univ. of Cincinnati; Consultant Royal Victoria Hosp.; Douglas Hosp. (Verdun); Lakeshore Gen. Hosp. (Pointe Claire); Montreal Gen. Hosp.; Reddy Mem. Hosp. (Montreal); St. Mary's Hosp. (Montreal); Psychiatrist, Verdun Prot. Hosp. 1937–47; Clin. Dir. Douglas Hosp. Verdun 1947, Dir. of Research 1966–76; Chrmn. Dept. Psychiatry McGill Univ. 1971–74; Deputy Commissioner of Research, Office of Mental Health, State of New York, U.S.A., 1981– ; rec'd Albert Lasker Award 1957; Fellow, The Royal Society of Canada (1970); Officer of the Order of Canada, (1976); The Taylor Manor Hospital Psychiatric Award, 1978; The Psychiatric Outpatient Centres of America Award, 1980; LL.D.(honoris causa) Univ. of Calgary, 1980; 'Heinz Lehmann Annual Award' est. by Candn. Coll. of Neuro Psycho-pharmocology, May 1982; Award for Excellence in Psychiatry, Que. Psychiatric Assoc. 1986; Medal for Excellence, Candn. Coll. of Neuro Psychopharmacology 1987; Silv. Arieti Award, Am. Acad. of Psychoanalysis 1988; 'Heinz Lehmann Rsch. Award' est. by New York State Office of Mental Health 1990; Van Gieson Award, Columbia Univ. 1991; co-author 'Handbook of Psychiatric Treatment in Medical Practice' 1962; 'Pharmacotherapy of Tension and Anxiety' 1970; 'Experimental Approaches to Psychiatric Diagnosis' 1971; 'Diagnosis and Treatment of Old Age Dementias' 1989; author book chapters and over 300 prof. publs. on psychiatry and psychopharmacol.; mem. Am. Coll. Neuropsychopharmacol. (Past Pres.); Collegium Internat. Neuro-Psychopharmacologium (Past Pres.); Candn. Psych. Assn.; Am. Psych. Assn.; Liberal; recreations: skiing, scuba diving, astronomy, gem collecting, lapidary; Home: 1212 Pine Ave. W., Apt. 908, Montreal, Que. H3G 1A9; Office: 1033 Pine Ave. W., Montreal, Que. H3A 1A1.

**LEHMANN, Kenneth Edward,** B.S., B.A.; newspaper executive; b. Louisville, Ky. 13 Jan. 1942; s. Otto Wilhelm and Cecilia Charles (Blincoe) L.; e. Xavier Univ. Cincinnati, B.S., B.A. 1964; m. Bonnie d. Joseph and Agnes Roos 28 May 1966; children: Eric, Heidi, Bridgit; EXTVE. VICE PRES. THE OTTAWA SUN 1988– ; Pres. Property Management Group; played football with Ottawa Rough Riders 1964–72, Schenley Lineman of Yr. 1968, runner-up 1966, 6 times EFC All-Star, five times All-Candn.; played 3 Grey Cups winning 2; Radio Advt. Salesman; Co-Founder and Owner The Ottawa Sunday Herald newspaper 1983 (bought by Toronto Sun Publishing and named The Ottawa Sun); Office: P.O. Box 9729 Station T, Ottawa, Ont. K1G 5H7.

**LEIGHTON, David Struan Robertson,** B.A., M.B.A., D.B.A., LL.D.; writer; educator; director; b. Regina, Sask. 20 Feb. 1928; s. Gordon Ernest and Mary Haskins (Robertson) L.; e. Glebe Coll. Inst., Ottawa, Ont., 1941–46; Queen's Univ., B.A. 1950 (Tricolour Soc.); Univ. of Toronto, 1950–51; Harvard Univ. (George F. Baker Scholar), M.B.A. 1953, D.B.A. 1956; Windsor Univ. LL.D. 1972; Queen's Univ. LL.D. 1993; m. Margaret Helen, d. John Albert House, St. Catharines, Ont., 25 Aug. 1951; children: Douglas, Bruce, Katharine, Jennifer, Andrew; Nabisco Brands Professor, Univ. of Western Ontario; formerly Dir., Nat. Centre for Management Research & Development; formerly Chrmn., Nabisco Brands Ltd., Toronto; formerly Pres., XV Olympic Winter Games Org. Comte., Calgary; Formerly Pres., Dir., Banff Sch. of Fine Arts and Centre for Continuing Educ.; formerly Prof., Harvard Univ.; Dir., Camco Inc.; Gulf Canada Ltd.; GSW Inc.; Rio Algom Ltd.; Cambridge Shopping Centres; Montreal Trust Co.; Telemedia, Inc.; The Blackburn Group Inc.; Dir. and Past Chrmn. (1st) Candn. Consumer Council; past Gov., Can. Conference of the Arts; Centre Stage; Telefilm Canada; Council on Bus. & the Arts; Candn. Centre for Philanthropy; Resources for the Future Inc.; Glenbow-Alberta Institute; Marketing Science Institute; Better Business Bureau of Can.; Muttart Foundation; Toronto Symphony; Banff Television Festival; Conference Bd. of Can.; Gov., Queen's Univ.; Social Science & Humanities Rsch. Council; Ont. Selection Ctte., Rhodes Scholarship Trust; co-author: 'Problems in Marketing' (2nd ed.) 1957; 'Canadian Problems in Marketing' 1959 (rev. eds. 1965, 1972); 'How Industry Buys' 1959 (won Media-Scope Award 1960); 'The Distribution of Packaged Consumer Goods: An Annotated Bibliography' 1963; 'International Marketing' 1965; 'Canadian Marketing: Problems and Prospects' 1973; 'Case Problems in Marketing' 1973; 'Artists Builders and Dreamers: 50 Years at The Banff School' 1983; co-ed. 'Marketing in Canada' 1958; mem., Am. Marketing Assn. (Founding Pres., London Chapter, 1958–61; Nat. Dir. 1964–66; Vice-Pres. 1969–70; Nat. Pres. 1971–72; Internat. Marketing Fed. Pres. 1972–73); Alberta Order of Excellence 1985; Distinguished Service Award, Queen's Univ.; recreations: tennis, skiing, music,; Home: Old River Rd., R.R. 3, Komoka, Ont. N0L 1R0.

**LEIPCIGER, Nathan Leon,** B.A.Sc., P.Eng.; consulting engineer; b. Poland 28 Feb. 1930; s. Jacob and Faygel Leah (Percik) L.; e. Univ. of Toronto, B.A.Sc. (Elect.) 1955; m. Bernice d. Saul and Molly Collis 7 Sept. 1954; children: Lisa (Mrs. Stephen Pinkus), Ronda (Mrs. Cary Green), Arla (Mrs. Zvi Litwin); 8 grandchildren; MNG. DIR. AND PRES., LEIPCIGER, KAMINKER, MITELMAN & PARTNERS INC.; Design Eng. H.H. Angus, Consulting Engs. 1955–58; Vice Pres. Eng., Plan Electrical Contractors 1958–62; Hon. mem. Technion Israeli Inst. of Technol.; Dir. Doctors Hosp. Toronto 1980–83; Community Hebrew Acad. Toronto 1975–85; Vice Pres./Treas. Friends of Candn. Technion 1980–82; mem. Extve. Toronto Jewish Cong., Chrmn. Holocaust Remembrance Ctte. 1981–88; Co-Chrmn. Candn. Gathering of Holocaust Survivors and their children (Ottawa) 1985; Founder, Holocaust Education & Memorial Centre, Toronto; Candn. Jewish Cong. Ont. Region 1981– ; Pres. Civitan Parkwoods Club Don Mills 1965–67; Dir. Civitan Candn. Dist. 1967–69; co-author 'Guide for Electrical Systems in Patient Care Areas in Hospitals' 1983; 'Illumination Systems in Hospitals' 1979; mem. Assn. Profl. Engs. Prov. Ont.; Assn. Profl. Engs. B.C.; Assn. Profl. Engs. Manitoba; Candn. Standards Assn.; Environment Conditions Health Care Facilities (Standing Ctte. mem. 1975– ); Pres. Temple Emanu-El Toronto 1973–75; Chrmn., National Holocaust Remembrance Ctte., Candn. Jewish Congress 1989; recreations: skiing, sailing; Clubs: Beaver Valley Ski; Home: 102 Banstock Dr., Willowdale, Ont. M2K 2H6; Office: 235 Lesmill Rd., Don Mills, Ont. M3B 2V1.

**LEISS, William,** M.A., Ph.D.; educator; b. New York City, N.Y. 28 Dec. 1939; s. William and Ethel (Walter) L.; e. Fairleigh Dickinson Univ. B.A. 1960; Brandeis Univ. M.A. 1963; Univ. of Cal. San Diego Ph.D. 1969; m. Marilyn Lawrence 20 Sept. 1973; PROF. OF COMMUNICATION, SIMON FRASER UNIV. 1980– (Chrmn. of Communication 1980–85), Vice Pres. Rsch. 1990– , Dir., Ctr. for Policy Rsch. on Science and Technology 1989– ; Asst. and Assoc. Prof. of Pol. Science Univ. of Regina 1968–73; Assoc. Prof. of Environmental Studies York Univ. 1973–75, Prof. of Pol. Science & Environmental Studies 1976–79; Assoc. Prof. of Sociol. Univ. of Toronto 1975–76; Fellow, Royal Soc. of Can.; author 'The Domination of Nature' 1972; 'The Limits to Satisfaction' 1976, Revised ed. 1979, republished 1988; 'Social Communication in Advertising' 1986, 1990; 'C.B. Macpherson' 1988; 'Under Technology's Thumb' 1990; Ed. 'Ecology Versus Politics in Canada' 1979; 'Prospects and Problems in Risk Communication' 1989; various journ. articles technol., social theory, human needs and environment; mem. Candn. Pol. Science Assn.; Candn. Communications Assn. (Pres. 1982–83); cons. on public policy issues; recreations: cooking, Great Danes, sports, wine, old furniture; Office: Simon Fraser Univ., Burnaby, B.C. V5A 1S6.

**LEITCH, John Daniel;** company chairman; b. Winnipeg, Man. 11 Jan. 1921; s. late Gordon Clifford and Hilda (Bawden) L.; e. Appleby Coll., Oakville, Ont.; Trinity Coll., Univ. of Toronto; m. Margaret Beatrice, (d. 8 Nov. 1979) d. Hon. Mr. Justice J. R. Cartwright, Ottawa, Ont., 14 June 1941; two d.; m. Catherine, d. Air Vice-Marshall D. Bradshaw 16 May 1985; CHAIRMAN, UPPER LAKES GROUP INC.; Dir. Emeritus, Canadian Imperial Bank of Commerce; Dofasco Inc.; American Airlines Inc.; Home: 61 St. Clair Ave. W., Toronto, Ont. M4V 2Y8; Office: 49 Jackes Ave., Toronto, Ont. M4T 1E2.

**LEITCH, Lorne Campbell,** LL.B., M.B.A.; business executive; b. Kerrobert, Sask. 6 Sept. 1925; s. Peter and Margaret Elizabeth (McLeod) L.; e. Pub. Schs., Winnipeg, Man. 1943; Univ. of Manitoba, LL.B. 1949; Univ. of Chicago, M.B.A. 1951; m. Kathleen Claire, d. R. B. McIntosh, 6 Sept. 1958; children: Christopher Lorne, Andrew Scott, Paul Robert; Extve. Dir., Edmonton Community Foundation 1990; read law with Parker, Parker, Hunter and Hamlin, Winnipeg, Man.; called to Bar of Man. 1952; with Great-West Life Assurance Co. as Mortgage Analyst 1951, Asst. Treas. 1957; joined Univ. of Alberta as Assoc. Prof., Faculty of Comm. 1961, Acting Chrmn., Div. Business Operations 1963, Acting Dean, Faculty Business Adm. and Comm. 1969, Assoc. Vice-Pres. (Finance and Adm.) 1970; Vice-Pres. (Finance and Adm.) 1972; Prof. of Finance 1972–90; Acting Dean, Faculty of Business 1988; Glenrose Hospital; Trustee, City of Edmonton Sinking Fund; recreations: swimming, golf, tennis; Clubs: University; Mayfair; Edmonton; Home: 14008 - 76 Ave., Edmonton, Alta. T5R 2Z5.

**LEITER, Lawrence A.,** M.D., F.R.C.P.(C), F.A.C.P.; b. Montreal, Que. 23 July 1951; e. McGill Univ. B.Sc. 1972, M.D.,C.M. 1976; DIR. LIPID CLINIC ST. MICHAEL'S HOSP. and Staff Endocrinol. 1990– ; Assoc. Prof. of Med. and of Nutritional Sci's Univ. of Toronto 1989– ; Staff Endocrinol. Toronto Western Hosp. 1980–89; Home: 569 Roselawn Ave., Toronto, Ont. M5N 1K6; Office: 30 Bond St., Toronto, Ont. M5B 1W8.

**LEITER, Michael P.,** M.A., Ph.D.; university professor; b. Hagerstown, Md 30 May 1947; s. Roy Allen and Minette (Patton) L.; e. Duke Univ. B.A. 1969; Vanderbilt Univ. M.A. 1972; Univ. of Oregon Ph.D. 1976; m. Franziska d. Karl and Helga Kruschen 8 Dec. 1980; children: Nicola, Alexander; DEAN OF SCIENCE 1992– and PROF., PSYCHOLOGY DEPT. 1977– ACADIA UNIV.; Adjunct Prof., Dalhousie Univ. 1990– ; Psychol., Kings Regl. Health & Rehab. Ctr. 1977–85; Cons. 1978–85; Rsch. Assoc., Psychol. Dept., Univ. of Calif. 1984–85; Psychol., Valley Health Serv. 1985; Cons. 1987–88; Head, Psychol. Dept., Acadia Univ. 1984– ; Cons./Adjunct Prof., Appalachian State Univ. 1987– ; Cons., N.S. Hosp. 1982–83, 1987– ; Candn. Employ & Immigr. Comn. 1982–83; co-author: 'Developing Community Service Networks' 1982; author of several articles; recreations: baroque flute and keyboard music; Home: 23 Orchard Ave., Wolfville, N.S. B0P 1X0; Office: Wolfville, N.S. B0P 1X0.

**LEITERMAN, Richard Mark,** R.C.A.; cinematographer; b. Dome Mines, Ont. 7 Apr. 1935; s. Douglas McGregor and Moynette (Stone) L.; e. W. Vancouver Sr. High Sch.; Univ. of B.C. 1 yr.; m. Margaret June d. Alfred Mansell, Edmonton, Alta. 10 Nov. 1960; children: Mark Julien, Rachel; DIR., WINDFORCE PRODUCTIONS LTD.; Newsreel and documentary cameraman London, Eng. and Toronto 1962–68; Cameraman and Co-dir. 'Married Couple' 1969; Dir. of Photography on more than 40 major Candn. and Am. feature films, mini-series, and T.V. movies for CBS, NBC, CBC, and ABC; Dir. various TV documentaries; rec'd Etrog Award 'Best Cinematography' for 'Far Shore' 1975; rec'd Genie Award and CSC Award 'Best Cinematography' for 'Silence of the North' 1981; rec'd Golden Sheaf Award and CSC Award for 'The Climb' 1986; nominated for two Emmy Awards for Best Cinematography; Address: #15 – 1019 Gilford St., Vancouver, B.C. V6G 2P1.

**LEITH, James Andrews,** M.A., Ph.D. F.R.S.C.; university professor; b. Toronto, Ont. 26 Oct. 1931; s. the late Matthew Andrews and the late Harriette Emily (Ball) L.; e. E. York Coll. Inst., Toronto, 1949; B.A. (Modern Hist.), Univ. of Toronto, 1953; M.A. (Hist.), Duke Univ., 1955; Ph.D. (Hist.), Univ. of Toronto, 1960; m. Carole May, d. late Marshall Peter Lang Wood, 16 June 1956; children: Margot, Marc; PROF., DEPT. OF HIST., QUEEN'S UNIV., since 1968 (Chrmn. 1968–73); Lectr. in Hist., Univ. of Sask., 1958–61; joined present Univ. as Lectr., 1961–62; Asst. Prof., 1962–64; Assoc. Prof., 1964–68; Visiting Prof., Cornell Univ., spring semester 1964 and St. Antony's Coll. Oxford 1970–71; Australian Nat. Univ. 1974–75; R. H. McLaughlin Research Professorship, 1965–66; has held maj. research grants from Royal Soc. of Can., Social Sciences and Humanities Research Council, Can. Council, the French Government, and the Killam Program; el. to Royal Soc. of Can., 1980 (Chrmn., Ctte. on Symposia 1987–90,

Editor 1990–91); author of 'The Idea of Art as Propaganda in France 1750–1799: A Study in the History of Ideas' 1965, 'Media and Revolution: Moulding a New Citizenry in France during the Terror' 1968; 'Space and Revolution: Projects for Monuments, Squares, and Public Buildings in France 1789–1799' 1991 (won the Raymond Klibansky Prize for the best book in humanities published 1991–92 in Canada); Ed. & Contbr.: 'Facets of Education in the Eighteenth Century' 1977, 'Images of the Commune/Images de la Commune' 1978, 'Symbols in Life and Art/Symboles dans la Vie et dans l'Art' 1987; (with Andrea Joyce) 'Face à Face: French and English Caricatures of the French Revolution and its Aftermath' 1989; (with Claudette Hould) 'Iconographie et Image de la Révolution Francaise' 1990; and numerous articles and reviews in scholarly journs.; mem. Soc. Française d'Etude du XVIIIe Siècle; Vice-Pres., Candn. Hist. Assn. 1993– ; Am. Hist. Assn.; Soc. for French Hist. Studies; Soc. d'Histoire Moderne; Candn. Soc. for Eighteenth Century Studies; recreation: oil painting; field naturalism; photography; Home: Apt. 206, The Landmark, 165 Ontario St., Kingston, Ont. K7L 2Y6.

**LEITH, James Clark,** B.A., M.S., Ph.D.; university professor; s. James Scott and Bertha Miriam (Clark) L.; e. Central Collegiate (Regina) Sr. Matric. 1955; Univ. Toronto, B.A. 1959; Univ. Wisconsin, M.S. 1960; Ph.D. 1967; m. Carole Ann, d. Leonard Harshaw and Ruby Mason, 29 Aug. 1964; children: James Douglas; Deborah Ann; Jonathan Gregory; PROF. OF ECON., UNIV. WESTERN ONT.; Foreign Service Officer, Govt. Can. Trade Commissioner Service 1960; posted Santo Domingo 1961; Chicago 1965; joined present univ. as Asst. Prof. Economics 1967; Assoc. Prof. 1971; Prof. 1978; Chrmn., Dept. Econ. 1972–76; Vice-Pres. (Academic) & Provost, U.W.O. 1980–86; author 'Foreign Trade Regimes and Economic Development; Ghana,' 1974; co-author (With P.T. Ellsworth) 'The International Economy,' 5th ed. 1975, 6th ed. 1984; co-editor (with Don Patinkin) 'Keynes, Cambridge and The General Theory,' 1977; Visiting Lectr., Univ. Ghana 1969–71; Sr. Research Assoc., Nat. Bureau Econ. Research (New York) 1971–75; Visiting Researcher, Inst. for Internat. Econ. Studies, Univ. Stockholm, 1976–77; Visiting Prof., Catholic Univ. Peru (Lima) 1979; Economic Cons., Min. of Finance & Development Planning, Botswana 1986–88; Visiting Scholar, Harvard Inst. for Internat. Development 1992–93; Dir. of Rsch., Bank of Botswana 1993– ; United Church; Office: Bank of Botswana, P.O. Box 712, Gaborone, Botswana.

**LeLACHEUR, Rick;** business executive; b. Edmonton, Alta.; e. Northern Alberta Inst. of Technology; m. Faye; children: Rob, Christine; PRESIDENT AND CHIEF EXECUTIVE OFFICER, ECONOMIC DEVELOPMENT EDMONTON 1992– ; joined Western Moving and Storage 1967; Pres. 1981–90 (revenues increased tenfold during tenure); company sold to NFC plc (U.K.) 1990 (remained for two years); Vice-Pres., 1978 Commonwealth Games; Chair, 1984 Grey Cup Organizing Ctte.; Pres., Edmonton Eskimo Football Club 1986–87; Bd. Mem., TELUS Corp., AGT Limited, Allied Van Lines Limited, Pickfords Canada; played hockey for Edmonton Oil Kings while attending N. Alta. Inst. of Technology; Home: St. Albert, Alta.; Office: 9797 Jasper Ave., Edmonton, Alta. T5J 1N9.

**LELAND, Vernon J.;** co-operative executive; b. Weldon, Sask. 23 Sept. 1936; m. Sylvia 24 August 1957; children: Kim Stuart, Lori Dawn, Tami Joanne; PRES. & DIR., FEDERATED CO-OPERATIVES LTD.; Consumers' Co-operative Refineries Ltd.; Chrmn., Co-Enerco Resources Ltd.; Chrmn., Elim Lodge; recreation: outdoor sports; Home: 903 – 620 Spadina Cres. E., Saskatoon, Sask. S7K 3T5; Office: 401 – 22nd Street E., Saskatoon, Sask. S7K 3M9.

**LELE, Jayant Khanderao,** M.A., Ph.D.; educator; b. Sinnar, India 25 May 1935; s. Khanderao Balwant and Laxmibai (Phanse) L.; e. Univ. of Poona B.A. 1956, M.A. 1958; Cornell Univ. Ph.D. 1964; m. Dorothy Joy d. Claude H. Vipond 14 Dec. 1973; children: Abhijeet Jayant, Amod Jayant; came to Can. 1965; PROF. OF SOCIOL., QUEEN'S UNIV. 1973– and Prof. of Pol. Studies 1969– ; Fellow, Ford Foundation 1960–62, Am. Inst. Indian Studies 1963–64; Assoc. Prof. of Pol. Studies Queen's Univ. 1968, Prof. and Head of Sociol. 1969–73; Visiting Prof., Center Internat. Studies Cornell Univ. 1969–70; Univ. of Poona 1974–75, also Indian Council Social Science Research Fellow; Sr. Fellow and Resident Dir. Shastri Indo-Candn. Inst. 1981–82 and Chrmn., Fellowship Comtes. 1982–83, 1983–84; Sr. Faculty Fellow, Shastri Indo-Canadian Inst. 1988–89; Convenor, Evaluation Group, Internat. Centre for the Advancement of Community-based Rehabilitation of the Disabled – ICACBR – (a CIDA Centre of Excellence) 1991– ; author: 'Local Government in India' 1965; 'Tradition and Modernity in Bhakti Movements' 1981; 'Elite Pluralism and Class Rule: Political Development in Maharashtra, India' 1981; 'Language and Society: Steps Towards an Integrated Theory' 1988; 'State and Society in India' 1990; various articles prof. journs.; Pres., Candn. S. Asian Studies Assn. 1973–74; Secy.-Treas. Candn. Asian Studies Assn. 1980–81; Life mem. Indian Sociol. Soc.; Indian Inst. of Public Admin.; Home: 283 Victoria St., Kingston, Ont. K7L 3Z2; Office: Kingston, Ont. K7L 3N6.

**LEMAN, Paul H.,** O.C. (1974), B.A., LL.L.; industrialist; b. Montreal, Que., 6 Aug. 1915; s. Beaudry & Caroline (Beique) L.; e. St-Mary's Coll., Montreal, B.A. 1934; Univ. of Montreal, LL.L. 1937; Harvard Bus. Sch. 1938; m. Jeannine, d. J. Alex Prud'Homme, Montreal, Que., 19 May 1939; children: Denise, Jacques, Nicole, Marc, Claire; Pres., Alcan Aluminium Ltd.; 1972–77; Vice-Chrmn 1977–79; called to the Bar of Que., 1937, but did not enter practice; joined Alcan in 1938; member, Royal Comn. on Banking & Finance (1962–64); Trustee, Nat. Museum of Can., 1979–83; Roman Catholic; recreations: golf, bridge; Clubs: University; Mt. Bruno Golf; Home: 6100 Deacon #L14, Montreal, Que. H3S 2V6.

**LeMAY, Jacques,** B.A., LL.L., D.E.S.; lawyer; b. Quebec City, Que. 10 July 1940; s. Gerard and Jacqueline (Lachance) LeM.; e. Seminaire de Que. B.A. 1959; Laval Univ. LL.L. 1962, D.E.S. 1965; Univ. of Toronto Law Sch. 1964; m. Denise d. Clovis Cardinal, Quebec City, Que. 15 March 1991; two d. Chantal, Diane; PARTNER, FLYNN, RIVARD & PARTNERS 1980– ; Dir., La St-Maurice Compagnie d'Assurance 1991– ; Candn. 88 Energy Corp. 1992– ; called to Bar of Que. 1963; law practice Prevost, Gagne, Flynn, Chouinard & Jacques 1963–66; Prevost, Gagne, Flynn, Gobeil, Rivard, Jacques, Cimon, Lessard & LeMay 1966–69; Flynn, Rivard, Jacques, Cimon, Lessard & LeMay 1969–79; mem. Assn. du Barreau Canadien (Secy. Div. de Que. 1981–82) (mem. of Council 1982–85); Soc. des Ajusteurs d'Assurances; R. Catholic; recreations: skiing, tennis; Club: Cercle de la Garnison Quebec; Home: 2342 Marie-Victorin, Sillery, Que. G1T 2W5; Office: 70 Dalhousie, P.O. Box 190, Stn. B, Quebec, Que. G1K 7A6.

**LEMAY, Jacques;** producer/director/choreographer; b. Montreal, Que. 27 June 1953; s. Guy Lionel and Rachel (Couture) L.; e. 3rd year, C.E.G.E.P.; m. Janis K. d. Eric Dunning 2 June 1978; children: Geneviève, Matthew; Dir. of Jazz/Choreographer, Royal Winnipeg Ballet 1977–89; appearances in over 125 TV shows; guest appearances with Les Grands Ballets Canadiens, The Royal Winnipeg Ballet, Les Ballets Jazz de Montreal, Winnipeg and Edmonton symphonies in major theatres across Can.; Mem., Les Feux Follets, 4 yrs.; choreography enjoyed by audiences across N. Am. & U.S.S.R.; prod./artistic dir./lectr., multi-cult. festival productions incl. Candn. Heritage Fest. (7); Art. Dir., Royal Visits (4); Creator, Sask Expo '86 live musical review; Candn. Heritage Fest. at Expo '86; Art. Dir./Choreographer, Opening Ceremonies, XV Winter Olympics; Dir./Choreog., Opening & Closing Ceremonies, Jeux Canada Summer Games Saskatoon 1989, and Canada Winter Games '91; Choreographer, 'Big Top', 'Anne of Green Gables' for the Royal Winnipeg Ballet; Choreographer, Grey Cup 1990; Producer/Artistic Dir., Experience Canada; Producer/Artistic Dir., 1994 Commonwealth Games Opening & Closing Ceremonies; Artistic Dir., Charlottetown Festival 1992– ; Home: 1660 Hampshire Rd., Victoria, B.C. V8R 5T6.

**LEMELIN, Louise,** Q.C., LL.L.; lawyer; b. St. Romuald, P.Q. 7 Oct. 1946; d. Hervé and Simone (Lemay) L.; e. Coll. Universitaire F.X. Garneau, B.A. 1966; Univ. Laval LL.L. 1969; called to Bar in 1970; m. Pierre s. Mr. and Mrs. Georges Hamel 1 May 1976; LEGAL COUNSEL, CORRECTIONAL SERVICE CANADA 1992– ; Sr. Consultant, Law Reform Comn. 1987; recipient Lacroix Prize in Criminal Procedure 1969; Assoc. Moisan, Bellavance, Aubert & Lemelin (Arthabaska, P.Q.) 1970–81; Chrmn. Bd. of Referees, Que. Div., Dist. of Victoriaville 1981; Comnr., Law Reform Commission 1981–86; Director General, Executive Services, Secretariat of the Solicitor General of Canada 1989–92; cr. Q.C. 1982; part-time educator and lectr.; mem., Que. Prov. Bar. 1970– ; IDEF; former mem. Arthabaska C. of C.; Soc. d'histoire d'Arthabaska (Vice-Pres.); Extve. Bar (Counsellor) 1979; Assn. des Diplômés de l'Univ. Laval (Vice-Pres.); Home: 4324 Meadowvale Lane, Gloucester, Ont. K1B 5A2; Office: 340 Laurier St. W., 12th Flr. B, Ottawa, Ont. K1P 0P8.

**LEMIEUX, Rév. Germain,** S.J., C.M., M.A., Ph.D., LL.D., Litt.D.; éducateur; né Cap-Chat, Que. 5 jan. 1914; f. Norbert et Augustine (Pelletier) L.; é. Ecole élémentaire Cap-Chat 1927; Séminaire de Gaspé 1935; Univ. Laval B.A. 1935, M.A. 1956, Ph.D. 1961; York Univ. LL.D. (hon. causa) 1977; Univ. Ottawa Litt.D. (hon. causa) 1978; Univ. Laurentienne Litt.D. (hon. causa) 1984; Prof. département de folklore, Univ. de Sudbury 1970–80; Prof. d'Humanités classiques Coll. Sacré-Coeur, Sudbury, Ont. 1941–44 et 1956–59, Prof. d'hist. et de français 1949–50; même emploi 1951–53; Prof. d'hist. médiévale et ancienne Univ. Laurentienne, Sudbury 1961–65; Prof. auxiliaire de Folklore Univ. Laval 1966–69; auteur 'Les Vieux M'Ont Conté' 32 vol. collection complétée en 1991, 'Chansonnier franco-ontarien' 2 vol. 1974 et 1976; divers articles; Ed. 'Les jongleurs du billochet' 1972; 'Le four de glaise,' 1982; 'La vie paysanne (1860–1900)' 1982; a reçu Prix Champlain du Conseil de la vie française en Amérique 1973; Médaille Luc-Lacourcière, 1980; Prix du Nouvel-Ontario 1983; Carnochan Award, Ont. Historical Soc. 1983; membre de l'Ordre du Canada 1984; Officier dans l'Ordre des Palmes Académiques (France) 1985; Médaille Marius-Barbeau (ACEF) 1986; Certificat de mérite, journal Le Voyageur 1991; Prix patrimonial, Ville de Sudbury 1992; membre de la Compagnie des Cents Associés francophones 1991; membre de l'Ordre de l'Ontario 1992; mem. de l'Ordre des francophones d'Amerique 1993; mem. de la Compagnie de Jésus depuis 1935, à sa retraite depuis 1980; Bureau: Maison d'Youville, 38, rue Xavier, Sudbury, Ont. P3C 2B9.

**LEMIEUX, Linda K.;** communications executive; VICE-PRESIDENT, MANAGEMENT INFORMATION SYSTEMS, TELEMEDIA INC.; Office: 500, 1411 Peel St., Montreal, Que. H3A 1S5.

**LEMIEUX, Marc,** B.A., B.Comm., M.Sc., C.A.; financial executive; b. Quebec 9 April 1931; s. Narcisse and Berthe (Simard) L.; e. Laval Univ. B.A. 1952, B.Comm. 1954, M.Sc. 1955; Ordre des C.A. de Qué. C.A. 1955; m. Diane d. Zita and Tancrède Sicard 20 April 1963; children: Sophie, Eric; FIRST VICE-PRES. & GENERAL MANAGER, FED. DES CAISSES POPULAIRES DESJARDINS DE QUEBEC 1986– ; Controller, Jos. E. Lemieux Enr. et Jean-Claude Lahaye, City Planner & Jean Ouellet, Arch. 1956–63; Analyst, Bélanger Comn. 1963–65; Treas. & Chief of Admin. Serv., Conseil de la Coop. du Qué. 1965–69; Mgr., Conf. des caisses populaires et d'écon. Desjardins du Qué. 1969–86; Mem., Bd. of Dir., Conf. des caisses populaires et d'écon. Desjardins du Qué. 1986– (Mem., Bd. of Gen. Dirs. 1986– ); Caisse Centrale Desjardins 1986– ; Desjardins Fed. Savings Bank 1992– ; Mem., Ordre des C.A. de Qué. 1955– ; Home: 294 de la Corniche, St-Nicolas, Qué. G0S 2Z0; Office: 95 ave. des Commandeurs, Lévis, Qué. G6V 6P6.

**LEMIEUX, Raymond U.,** O.C. (1968), B.Sc., Ph.D., D.Sc., F.R.S. (1967); chemist; university professor; b. Lac La Biche, Alberta; e. Univ. of Alta., B.Sc. (Chem); McGill Univ., Ph.D. 1946; Hon. D.Sc., Univ. of N.B. 1967; Laval Univ. 1970; Univ. de Provence, Marseille, France 1972; Univ. of Ottawa 1975; Hon. L.L.D., Univ. of Calgary, 1979; D.Sc.(Hon.c.) Univ. of Waterloo, 1980; Memorial Univ., Nfld. 1981; D.Sc. (hon.), Univ. de Qué. 1982; Queen's Univ. 1983; McGill Univ., 1984; McMaster Univ.; Univ. de Sherbrooke 1986; Hon. Ph.D., Univ. of Stockholm, 1988; Hon. D.Sc., Univ. of Alberta 1991; Don. D.L.L., Univ. of Saskatchewan 1993; UNIVERSITY PROFESSOR, 1980; after holding several posts in Candn. and U.S. universities, joined Univ. of Alberta in 1961; has made numerous important contrib. to study of general organic and carbohydrate chem. (main research related to methods for synthesis of complex carbohydrate structures); author of more than 200 publications; Pres., Chemical Inst. of Canada 1984–85; mem., Nat. Research Council of Can., 1976–79; Palladium Medal, Chem. Inst. of Can. 1964; C.S. Hudson Award, Am. Chem. Soc. 1966; Haworth Medal, Royal Soc. of Chem. 1978; Award of Achievement, Govt. of Alta., 1979; Issac J. Walton Killam Prize 1981; Univ. of Alta. Research Prize 1982; Sir Frederick Haultain Prize (Govt. of Alta.) 1982; Tishler Prize, Harvard Univ. 1983; Medal of Honour, Candn. Med. Assn. 1985; Gairdner Intl. Award 1985; Rhône-Poulenc Award, Royal Soc. of Chemistry 1989; King Faisal International Prize in Science 1990; mem. Alberta Order of Excellence 1990; Canada Gold Medal for Science and Engineering 1991; E.C. Manning National Award of Distinction 1992; PMAC Health Research Foundation Medal of Honour 1992; 'Albert Einstein' World Award of Science 1992; Hon. Fellow, Chem. Institute of Can. 1992; Great Canadian Award 1993; Home: 7602 119 St., Edmonton, Alta. T6G 1W3.

**LEMIRE, Andre,** B.Sc.; investment executive; b. Quebec City, Que. 15 March 1943; s. Adrien and Gabrielle

(Martel) L.; e. Univ. of Ottawa B.Sc. 1967; m. Ann d. Colin and Fern Chisholm 6 Sept. 1969; PRESIDENT & C.O.O., MARLEAU, LEMIRE INC. 1990– ; Extve. Vice Pres., Dir., & Mem. of Extve. Comte., Levesque, Beaubien & Co. Inc. 1972– ; Dir. of Invest. Rsch. 1973, Vice Pres. Internat. 1978, Dir. 1978; Financial Analyst, Bell Canada, Montreal 1967–68; Invest. Analyst, Jones Heward Co. 1969–72; Dir., Dalmys (Canada) Ltd.; Merfin Hygienics Products Ltd.; Transat Inc.; Virginia Gold Mines Inc.; author various articles Candn. and European financial publs.; R. Catholic; recreations: golf, squash, tennis; Clubs: Montreal Soc. of Financial Analysts; St. James's; Mount Royal; M.A.A.A.; Home: 174 Edgehill Rd., Westmount, Que. H3Y 1E9; Office: 1155 René-Levesque Blvd. W., Suite 2205, Montreal, Que. H3B 4T3.

**LEMIRE, Claude,** B.B.A.; investment management executive; b. Yamachiche, Qué. 6 March 1935; s. Raoul and Blanche (Desaulniers) L.; e. Portland (Ore.) Univ. B.B.A. 1964; m. Teresa d. Antonio and Dolores Guzman 23 Jan. 1960; two s. Richard, Jacques; Dir., Domco Industries; Acceuil Bonneau; Ensembles Urbains Ltée; Les Nouveaux Ensembles Urbains Ltée; Les Oeuvres de Keur-Moussa; Asst. Treas. Sun Life Assurance Co. of Canada 1964–72; Home: 237 avenue Clarke, Westmount, Que. H3Z 2E3.

**LEMIRE, Maurice,** B.A., L.Th., L.L., D.ès L., F.R.S.C., s.r.c.; educateur; né Saint-Gabriel-de-Brandon, Qué. 21 sept. 1927; f. Donat et Amilda (Bastien) L.; é. Coll. Jean-de-Brébeuf B.A. 1949; Univ. de Montréal L.Th. 1953; Sorbonne, Paris L.L. 1957; Univ. Laval D.E.S. 1962, D.ès L. 1966; PROF. DES LITTÉRATURES UNIV. LAVAL 1969– , Chrmn. Candn. Studies 1971–72; Univ. de Montréal 1960–64, chargé de cours; Univ. de Sherbrooke 1964–66, Chrmn. French Dept.; Univ. de Trois-Rivières, prof.; Fellow, Institut québécois de recherche sur la culture 1980–85; Centre de recherche sur le littérature québécoise 1985– ; Membre du conseil d'adm. de la Bibliothèque nationale du Québec 1989–92; recipient Cert. of Hon. Assn. Candn. Studies 1986; Lorne Pierce Medal Royal Soc. Can. 1989; Chief Ed.' Dictionnaire des oeuvres littéraires du Québec' 5 vols. 1971–85; 'Histoire littéraire du Québec' 1985; auteur 'Les grands thémes nationalistes du roman historique canadien-français' 1970; 'Charles Guérin de P.J.0. Chaveau' 1975; 'Les Contes de Louis Fréchette' 2 vol. 1976, 1978; 'Introduction à la littérature québécoise' 1980; 'L'Institution littéraire' 1986; 'Le poids des politiques culturelles' 1987; Membre, Soc. d'histoire du théâtre du Québec; Assn. des études canadiennes; Assn. pour l'étude de l'imprimé; Adresse: 1301 ave. Patenaude, Sillery, Qué. G1T 2J7; Bureau: Ste-Foy, Qué. G1K 7P4.

**LEMIRE, Robert,** B.A., M.D., CSPQ, FRCS(C); otalaryngologist; b. Montreal, Que. 16 Nov. 1939; s. Pierre and Theresa (Binda) L.; e. Univ of Paris B.A. 1957; Univ. of Montreal M.D. 1963; m. Michele d. René and Renée Gendron 7 Sept. 1963; children: Natalie, Anouc, Catherine, Louis-Robert; CHAIR, HUBBARD HOLDING INC.; Professor of Surgery, Univ. of Montreal 1967– ; Active Surgeon, Maisonneuve Rosemont and Gouin Rosemont hospitals; Pres., Conseil des Medecins 1985–93; recreations: golf, skiing; clubs: St. Denis, Laval sur le Lac, Indian Creek; Home: 416 Lockhart, Montreal, Que. H3P 1Y5; Office: 425 Marien, Montreal, Que. H1B 4V7.

**LEMM, Richard Dennis,** M.A., Ph.D.; writer; educator; b. Seattle, Wash. 7 Sept. 1946; s. Harvey Matthew and Gloria Aileen (Alexander) L.; e. Simon Fraser Univ. B.A. 1972; Queen's Univ. M.A. 1978; Dalhousie Univ. Ph.D. 1986; ASST. PROF. IN ENGLISH, UNIV. OF P.E.I. 1988– and CHAIRPERSON, ENGLISH DEPARTMENT; Therapeutic Tutor in Child Psychiatry Vancouver Gen. Hosp. 1972–74; Instr. Fraser Valley Regional Coll. 1975–76; Instr. Cariboo Regional Coll. B.C. and Teacher, Ashcroft Secondary Sch. B.C. 1978–79; Resident Instr. Summer Writing Prog. Banff Centre Sch. of Fine Arts 1977–87, Head of Poetry 1980–85, Acting Head 1986; Lit. Ed. Ragweed Press (P.E.I.) 1983–89; Research and writer Candn. Heart Found. P.E.I. Br. 1984–85; Writer-in-Community Truro, N.S. 1982; Coordinator Writer-in-Community Prog. Writers' Fedn. N.S. 1983; Coordinator Atlantic Poetry Project: Access Network Alta. 1985; Writer-in-Residence Northern Lights Community Coll. B.C. 1985, Goose Bay Labrador (Nat. Book Festival) 1984; Guest Lectr. Univ. Coll. of Cape Breton 1985–86; Lectr. in Eng., present univ. 1986–88; Poetry Instr., Maritime Writers Workshop 1987, 1989; Poetry Instr., Algoma Summer School of the Arts, Sault Ste. Marie 1990; recipient CBC Lit. Competition Third Prize Poetry 1983 and 1992; Candn. Heart Found. Award for Excellence of Publs. 1986; Candn. Authors' Assn. Award for Poetry 1991; Juror, Internat. Yr. of Youth Creative Writing Competition 1985; Judge, 1990 CBC Literary Competition, Poetry; mem. Pub. Lending Rights Comm. 1986–88; author (poetry) 'Dancing in Asylum' 1982; 'A Difficult Faith' 1985; 'Prelude to the Bacchanal' 1990; mem. League Can. Poets (Atlantic Rep. 1983–86; Pres. 1986–88); Writers' Fedn. N.S. (Extve. 1982–83); Amnesty Internat.; P.E.I. Council Arts (mem. Bd. 1985–87); recreations: tennis, cooking, cross-country skiing, music, travel; Home: 186 King St., Charlottetown, P.E.I. C1A 1C1; Office: Univ. of P.E.I., Charlottetown, P.E.I. C1A 4P3.

**LEMON, Kenneth William,** F.C.A. (Ont.); b. Orillia, Ont. 1 Oct. 1916; s. late Thomas Henry and Blanche Eva (Snoulten); e. Humberside Coll. Inst., Toronto, Ont. 1936; C.A. 1942; F.C.A. (Ont.) 1956; Hon. LL.D., Univ. of W. Ont. 1982; m. Honor Florence Eileen, d. late Reginald Shribbs, 4 July 1942; children: Richard Henry, Peter William Reginald, Patricia Ann; PARTNER, CLARKSON GORDON since 1949; joined the Co. as a Student in Accounts, Toronto 1936, Resident Mgr., London Br. 1948; past Chrmn. Extve. Bd., Huron Coll.; Past mem. Executive Comte., Synod of Diocese of Huron; Pres., Un. Appeal, Greater London 1955–57; YMCA-YWCA, London 1958; London Little Theatre 1961–63; mem. Inst. Chart. Accts. Ont. (mem. Council 1965–72, Pres. 1971–72); Chart. Accts. Assn. of W. Ont. (Pres. 1949–50); Adm. Mgmt. Soc. (Pres. 1952–53); mem. Vocational Adv. Comte., London Bd. of Educ. 1952–70 (Chrmn. 1961–70); Treas., St. James (Westminster) Church 1951–88; Chrmn., Mgmt. Avd. Bd., London Psychiatric Hosp. 1973–85; Chrmn., St. Joseph's Health Centre of London 1986–89; Freemason; Anglican; recreations: golf, fishing; Clubs: London Hunt & Country (Pres. 1972); London; Caughnawana Fishing & Hunting; National (Toronto); Home: 154 Commissioners Rd. E., London, Ont. N6C 2T1; Office: Suite 1601, 255 Queens Ave., London, Ont. N6A 5S7.

**LE MOYNE, Hon. Jean,** O.C.; former senator; author; b. Montreal, Que. 17 Feb. 1913; s. Médéric, M.D. and Albine (Geoffrion) Le M.; e. Coll. Ste-Marie (Jesuits) Montreal; m. Suzanne d. Antoine and Lucile Rivard 1970; Journalist 1941–59, La Presse, Le Canada (Asst. City Ed., Lit. Critic), Candn. Press, La Revue Moderne (Ed.-in-Chief); Researcher and Scenarist Nat. Film Bd. Can. 1959–69; Special Asst. and Sr. Adviser to Prime Min. of Can. 1969–78; summoned to Senate of Can. 1982; retired 1988; O.C. 1982; Gov. Gen.'s Award 1962; First Prize Les Concours Littéraires du Qué. (Prix David) 1962; Molson Prize 1968; author 'Convergences' (essays) 1961, Eng. transl. 1966; contrib. maj. French Candn. lit. jours., Radio-Can. (musical and lit. broadcasts); R. Catholic; Liberal; recreation: fish fancying; Home: 186 Latchford Rd., Ottawa, Ont. K1Z 5W2.

**LENCZNER, Alan John,** B.A., M.A., LL.B.; banker, lawyer; b. Bombay, India 5 Feb. 1943; s. Michael M. and Blanka (Jurgrau) L.; e. Upper Canada Coll. 1960; Univ. of Toronto B.A. (Hons.) 1964, M.A. 1965, LL.B. (1st class hons.) 1967; m. Joan d. Jack and Mary Marjory Hutchison 30 July 1970; children: Andrea, Erica, Matthew; Sr. Extve. Vice-Pres., Central Capital Corp. & Pres. & Chief Op. Offr., Central Capital Mngt. Inc. 1988; called to Bar 1969; Partner, McCarthy Tetrault 1975; Q.C. 1980; joined present firm 1987; Mem., Candn. Bar Assn.; The Advocates Soc. of Ont.; Dir., BGH Central Investment Mngt.; Candn. Gen. Insur. Cos.; Central Capital Corp.; Central Guaranty Trustco; Home: 42 Hudson Dr., Toronto, Ont. M4T 2J9.

**LENFESTY, Harold S.,** M.A.; importing executive; b. Vancouver, B.C. 14 Dec. 1952; e. York Univ. M.A. 1991; Candn. Inst. of Management P.Mgr.; m. Yvonne; children: Sean, Andrea; PRESIDENT & CHIEF OPERATING OFFICER, FRED DEELEY IMPORTS LTD.; formerly Asst. to Vice-Pres.; Mgr., Admin.; Vice-Pres.; Extve. Vice-Pres.; Dir., Motorcycle and Moped Industry Council; R.P. Eye Research Found.; Young President's Orgn. (Treas. 1992–93); Mem., Planning Forum; Candn. Inst. of Management; Office: 55 Penn Dr., Weston, Ont. M9L 2A6.

**LENNOX, Hon. Brian W.,** B.A., LL.B., D.E.S.; judge; b. Toronto, Ont. 16 Oct. 1946; s. Willliam J. and Marion E. (Landell) L.; e. York Univ. B.A. 1968; Univ. of Toronto LL.B. 1972; Univ. de Droit, d'Economie et de Sciences Sociales de Paris D.E.S. 1974; m. Susan d. James and Jean Paton 26 Sept. 1969; children: Britt, Jamie, Bess; REGIONAL SR. JUDGE (EAST REGION), ONTARIO COURT OF JUSTICE (PROVINCIAL DIV.) 1990– ; called to Bar of Ont. 1975; law practice Paris, Mercier, Sirois, Paris and Bélanger Ottawa 1975–78; Asst. Crown Atty. Ottawa 1978–86; Judge, Provincial Court (Criminal Div.) 1986–90; Part-time Prof. of Law 1981–92 and of Social Sci's (Criminol.) 1984– Univ. of Ottawa; Trustee Co. of Carleton Law Assn. 1982–83; recipient York Univ. Special Entrance Scholarship 1964; Candn. Pol. Sci. Assn. Parlty. Intern 1970; French Govt. Grad. Studies Scholarship 1972; mem. Assn. des juristes d'expression française de l'Ont.; Ontario Judges Assn.; Ontario Family Law Judges Assn.; anglican; recreations: cycling, basketball, sailing; Clubs: Ottawa Bicycle; Office: 161 Elgin St., Ottawa, Ont. K2P 2L1.

**LENNOX, John Watt,** B.A., M.ès A., Ph.D.; educator; b. Toronto, Ont. 14 June 1945; s. William James and Marion Elizabeth (Landell) L.; e. York Univ. B.A. 1967; Univ. de Sherbrooke M. ès A. 1969; Univ. of N.B. Ph.D. 1976; m. Jane d. Henry H. and Harriet Rooke 9 Oct. 1971; children: Mia Jane, Anna Barbara, Jeffers Landell; PROF. OF ENG., YORK UNIV. 1991– ; Lectr. in Eng. present univ. 1970–77, Assoc. Prof. in Eng. 1977–90, Dir. Graduate Programme in English 1987–90; Dir. Robarts Centre for Candn. Studies 1985–88; co-author (with Clara Thomas) 'William Arthur Deacon: A Canadian Literary Life' 1982; co-editor (with Michèle Lacombe) 'Dear Bill: The Correspondence of William Arthur Deacon' 1988; editor 'Margaret Laurence-Al Purdy: A Friendship in Letters' 1993; Pres. Assn. Candn. & Que. Lits. 1982–84; Pres., Assn. Candn. Studies 1992– ; Anglican; Home: 56 Highland Ave., Newmarket, Ont. L3Y 3H8; Office: 4700 Keele St., North York, Ont. M3J 1P3.

**LENNOX, Ronald Ian,** H.B.Sc., M.B.A.; business executive; b. Fort William, Ont. 18 Feb. 1953; s. Earl and Norma L.; e. Univ. of Western Ont. H.B.Sc. (Hons.) 1976; M.B.A. 1978; m. Barbara d. Gord and Jean Cunningham 21 Aug. 1976; children: Ryan, Craig, Derek, Blake; PRES. & CHIEF EXECUTIVE OFFICER, MONSANTO CANADA INC. 1991– ; Financial Analyst, Monsanto Canada Inc. 1978; various sales & mktg. admin. positions incl. Business Mgr., Specialty Chemicals, Monsanto Chem. Co. St. Louis, Mo. 1983; Regional Mgr., MCC Detergents & Phosphates Div. 1986; Dir., Latin Am. Countries & Bus. Devel.; Bd. Mem., Monsanto Canada Inc.; Candn. Chem. Producers' Assn. (Dir.); Internat. Ctr. for Agriculture, Sci. & Technology (Dir.); Jr. Achievement of Canada (Dir.); Jr. Achievement of Peel Region (Bd. of Gov.); United Way of Peel Leaders; Dir., Mississauga Hosp. Found.; Former Chair, Venezuela-U.S. Business Council, Council of Americas; clubs: The Boulevard, Mississauga Golf & Country; Home: 232 Indian Valley Trail, Mississauga, Ont. L5G 2K6; Office: P.O. Box 787, Streetsville P.O., 2330 Argentia Rd., Mississauga, Ont. L5M 2G4.

**LENNOX, William Craig,** B.A.Sc., M.Sc., Ph.D., P.Eng.; educator; b. Mount Forest, Ont. 22 May 1937; s. James Alex and Lila Agnas L.; e. Univ. of Waterloo B.A.Sc. (Engn. Physics) 1962, M.Sc. (Applied Math.) 1963; Lehigh Univ. Pa. Ph.D. (Applied Mechanics) 1966; m. Eileen d. Robert and Murial Hill June 1961; one child: Meghan; PROF. OF CIVIL ENGN., Univ. of Waterloo 1975– , Dean of Engineering 1982–90; Engr., NASA 1963–66; Asst. Prof. of Civil Engn. present Univ. 1966, Assoc. Prof. 1968, Chrmn. of Civil Engn. 1979–82; Visiting Prof., Lehigh Univ. 1967; Univ. of Petroleum and Minerals Saudi Arabia 1969–70; Visiting Prof. of Engn. Harvey Mudd Coll. Calif. 1977–79; Chrmn., Ctte. of Ont. Deans of Engn. 1986–87; Chrmn., Nat. Ctte. of Deans of Engn. & Applied Sci. 1986–87; Consultant, General Atomic, San Diego; Lockheed Aircraft; NASA; Dir., Waterloo Centre for Process Devel.; Candn. Industrial Innovation Centre; Manufacturing Research Corp. of Ont.; Industrial Development and Rsch. Inst.; Nat. Research Scholar 1963; Ford Foundation Engn. Residency; mem. Assn. Prof. Engrs. Prov. Ont.; Candn. Soc. Prof. Engrs.; Am. Acad. Mechanics; Sigma Xi; recreation: sailing; Home: 79 Rusholme Rd., Kitchener, Ont. N2M 2T5; Office: Waterloo, Ont. N2M 3G1.

**LENTON, Wayne Douglas,** B.Sc.; professional engineer; b. Vita, Manitoba 14 Dec. 1939; s. Henry Herbert and Martha M. (Scheibe) L.; e. Ridgeville H.S.; United College, Winnipeg; Montana School of Mines, B.Sc. (metallurgical engr.) 1964; m. Patricia C. d. Frank Lange 6 July 1963; children: Lori Ann, Donna Mae, Sydney Eugene; CHRMN., PRES., CHIEF EXTVE. OFFR., & DIR., CANAMAX RESOURCES INC. 1989– ; Plant Metallurgist, Molycorp (Questa, New Mexico) 1964–67; Staff Metallurgist, Chapman, Wood, Griswold & Evans Pty. Ltd. (Australia) then Mill Supt., Mount Gunson Mines Pty Ltd. 1967–70; Sr. Mill Engr., Climax Molybdenum Co. (Colorado) 1970–72; General Mill Foreman, Mill Prod. Supt., then Mill Mgr., Utah Mines Ltd. (Port Hardy, B.C.) 1972–78; Vice-Pres., Opns., AMAX of Can. Ltd. 1979–85; Pres., Chief Extve. Offr. & Dir., Can. Tungsten Mining Corp. Limited & Pres., AMAX of

Can. Limited 1985– ; Dir., Minerex Resources Ltd.; Mining Assn. of B.C. (Immediate Past-Chrmn.); Mining Assn. of Can.; Mem., Candn. Inst. of Mining & Metal.; Am. Inst. of Mining, Metal. & Petrol. Engrs.; Registered Profl. Engr., B.C. & Yukon Territory; club: Vancouver; Home: 565 Tralee Cres., Tsawwassen, B.C. V4M 3R9; Office: Ste. 1600 – 1066 West Hastings St., Vancouver, B.C. V6E 3X1.

**LÉON, Pierre R.A.,** D.èsL., FRSC; university professor, writer; b. Ligré, France 12 Mar. 1926; s. Roger and Marie-Louise (Cosson) L.; e. Paris, Sorbonne, L.èsL. 1952; doctorate de l'univ. of Besançon, 1960; Sorbonne, D.èsL. 1972; m. Monique d. Pierre and Simone Maury 18 Apr. 1949; one s.: Françoise; Prof., Founder & Dir., Experimental Phonetics Lab., Univ. of Toronto 1965–91; Asst. Prof., Inst. de Phonétique, Sorbonne 1950–58; French, Ohio State Univ. 1958–60, 1963–64; Dir., Ctr. Appl. Ling. Univ. of Besançon, Fac. Lettres 1960–63; Maître de Conf., Univ. of Besançon 1972–78; Prof. tit., Univ. de Pau 1978– ; Mem. dir. du Ctr. d'analyse du discours, Univ. de Paris XIII; Chroniqueur et reporter, l'Express de Toronto; artist; grants from Art Counc. of Can. & Ont. Arts Counc. 1978– ; Prix de l'acad. française, Paris 1966; Chevalier palmes acad. 1977; Officier palme acad. 1987; prix graphique loisirs-jeunes, Paris 1981; Bd. of Dir., Alliance Française 1978–90; Pres., Linguistics Assn. of Can. 1986–88; Fellow, Intern. Soc. Phonetic Sci. 1988; Mem. Permanent Council Phon. Sc. 1987– ; Doctor Honoris Causa, Univ. de Nancy II 1982; FRSC 1989; Mem., Soc. de Ling. de Paris 1960– ; Ling. Soc. of Can. 1970– ; Internat. Soc. of Phonetic Sci. 1960– ; Soc. des auteurs de l'Ont. 1986– ; author of 90 profl. articles & author & co-author of 35 books incl. most recently 'Le dialogue' 1985, 'Le conte' 1987, 'Prononciation du français standard' 1966, 72, 77, 86; 'Structure du français moderne' 1989; 'Phonétisme et prononciations du français' Nathan 1992; 'Traite de phonostylistique' Paris, Nathan, 1993; 'Grepotame' Nathan 1980; 'Crocogourou' 1990; 'Les mots d'Arlequin' (poems) 1983; 'Sur la piste des Jolicoeur' 1991 (novel), 'Le mariage du Petit Chaperon Rouge' (short stories) forthcoming, 'Pigou et compagnie, contes, Hurtubise, Montréal, et Les Cahiers Bleus' (short stories) 1986, 'Chants de la Toundra' La Découverte, Paris 1985; recreations: art work: drawing, painting & appliqué tapestry; juried exhibs. 1978– in various galleries nat. & internat.; Home: 150 Farnham Ave., #504, Toronto, Ont. M4V 1H5.

**LEONARD, Kevin John,** B.Comm., M.B.A., Ph.D., C.M.A.; university professor; b. Montreal, Que. 24 July 1957; s. John James and Barbara Rita (Nutter) L.; e. Concordia Univ. B.Comm. (magna cum laude) 1979, M.B.A. (Dean's Academic Honour List) 1980, Ph.D. 1988; Soc.of Mngt. Accountants of Ont. C.M.A. 1993; m. Sandra d. Kenneth and Adrian Dalziel 29 May 1982; Director, Research Centre for Management of Advancements in New Technology-Operations, Wilfrid Laurier Univ. 1993– ; Asst. Comptroller, Andrew Gilchrist Limited 1980; Lecturer, Fac. of Comm. & Admin., Concordia Univ. 1982–87; Research Analyst, Securities Dept., Bank of Can. 1987–89; Project Mgr for Fair, Isaac Companies (San Rafael, Calif.) 1989–90; Asst. Prof., Wilfrid Laurier Univ. 1990– ; consultant to financial institutions in use of credit statistical models for credit adjudication & fraud analysis 1990– ; Gen. Mgr., Risk Mngt. Div., CIBC 1991–93; Pres., Score Inc.; active consultant in design, devel., implementation & mngt. of statistical multi-media database Info. Systems for sports team; Founding Pres., Canadian Credit Risk Mngt. Assn. 1992– ; author: 'The Credit Scoring Manual: A Comprehensive Guide' 1992; playwright: 'Extensive Care' 1992, 'Adult Accompaniment' 1993; editor: 'For Score' (newsletter) 1992– ; prod., dir., writer: 'The Credit Scoring Video' 1993; Home: 1001 Bay St., Apt. 602, Toronto, Ont. M5S 3A6; Office: 75 University Ave. W., Waterloo, Ont. N2L 3C5.

**LEONARDI, C.W.,** F.C.A. (Eng. and Wales), C.A.; b. Sfax, Tunisia 27 May 1925; s. William and Beatrice May (Frost) L.; e. Finchley Grammar Sch., Eng.; Durham Univ.; 2 children: Stephen, Jane Frances (Mrs. Mason); Supvr., Geo. A. Touche & Co., London, Eng. 1951–54; Chief Acct. (Europe) Maple Leaf Services, Germany 1954–55; Secy.-Treas., Ottawa 1955–59; Gen. Mgr., Disston Div. H.K. Porter (Can.) Ltd., Acton, Ont. 1959–60; Treas., Trafalgar Investments Co. Ltd. Toronto, Pres. Venezuelan Power Co. Ltd. 1960–72; Extve. Vice Pres. Finance, Jannock Ltd. 1965–83; Group Vice Pres. Canada Development Investment Corporation 1983–84; Chrmn. ITL Industries Ltd. 1985–89; mem. Inst. of C.A. of Ont.; Fellow, Inst. of C.A. (Eng. and Wales); served with RAF as Flying Offr. 1943–47; rec'd. comm. RAF Coll., Cranwell; R. Catholic; recreations: woodworking; Home: P.O. Box 110, Dwight, Ont. P0A 1H0.

**LEPAGE, Yvan G.,** B.A., L.èsL., D.3e cycle; professeur; né. Sarsfield, Ont. 15 juin 1943; f. Albert et Gilberte (Lecomte) L.; é. Univ. d'Ottawa B.A. 1964, L.ès L. 1967; Univ. de Poitiers (C.E.S.C.M.), D.3e cycle 1969; ép. Françoise f. Marc et Marguerite Deguy 29 mars 1969; PROFESSEUR, UNIVERSITE D'OTTAWA 1977– ; professeur, Univ. d'Ottawa 1969–70; Univ. de Moncton 1970–77; dir., Etudes françaises 1973–76; dir., Lettres françaises, Univ. d'Ottawa 1981–82, 1986–89; secrétaire, Fac. des arts 1982–85, 1989– ; mem., Assoc. internat. des études françaises; auteur: 'Le Roman de Mahomet d'Alexandre du Pont' 1977, 'Les Rédactions en vers du Couronnement de Louis' 1978, 'L'Oeuvre lyrique de Richard de Fournival' 1981, 'Mémoires de Marie-Rose Girard' 1989, 'Le Survenant de Germaine Guèvremont' 1989, 'L'Oeuvre lyrique de Blondel de Nesle' 1994; rés.: 1502, 160 George, Ottawa, Ont. K1N 9M2; bureau: 60 Université, C.P. 450, Succ. A., Ottawa, Ont. K1N 6N5.

**LE PAGE, Yvon,** D.Sc.A.; crystallographer; b. Morlaix, France 7 Oct. 1943; s. Eugène and Jeannine (Morel) Le P.; e. Univ. of Lyon Eng. Physics Degree 1964; Ecole Polytechnique Montréal, M.Sc.A. 1970, D.Sc.A.; 1974; m. Colette d. Edmond and Dorothy Brochier 22 June 1965; children: Nathalie, Eric; RSCH. OFFR. CHEM. DIV., NAT. RSCH. COUNCIL CAN. 1977– ; Lectr. Ecole Polytechnique Montréal 1967–73; Postdoctoral Fellow McGill Univ. 1974–77; holds one patent; author or co-author over 80 sci. publs. internat. jours. geometrical crystallog., X-ray diffraction physics, diffractometry, structure & crystal chem. inorganic compounds; Home: 20 rue Lavandou, Touraine, Que. J8T 5M2; Office: Institute of Environmental Chemistry, Bldg. M-12, Rm B-9, Montreal Rd., Ottawa, Ont. K1A 0R6.

**LePAN, Douglas V.,** D. Litt., LL.D., F.R.S.C. (1968); writer; university professor; diplomat; b. Toronto, Ont. 1914; s. Lieut.-Col. Arthur D'Orr and Dorothy Lucinda (Edge) LeP.; e. Univ. of Toronto Schs.; Univ. of Toronto B.A., D.Litt. 1990; Oxford Univ. M.A.; Univ. of Man., D.Litt. 1964; LL.D. Queen's 1969; York, 1977; D.Litt. Ottawa 1972, Waterloo 1973; LL.D., Dalhousie, 1980; m. Sarah Katharine Chambers 1948 (separated 1971); two s., Nicholas, Donald; UNIVERSITY PROFESSOR EMERITUS, UNIV. OF TORONTO since 1979; Lectr., Univ. of Toronto 1937–38 and Harvard Univ. 1938–41; served in 2nd World War; Educ. Adviser to Gen. A.G. McNaughton 1942–43; enlisted in C.F.A. as a Gunner and saw service in Italian Campaign; discharged in 1945; joined Dept. of External Affairs and served on staff of High Commr. in London for three yrs.; attended Paris Reparations Conf. 1945, Paris Peace Conference 1946; studied writing under a Guggenheim Schol. (on leave of absence) 1948; Special Asst. to Min. of External Affairs 1950–51; attended Colombo Conf. and Sydney and London Confs. on aid for S. and S.-E. Asia; Counsellor and later Minister Counsellor at Canadian Embassy, Washington 1951–55; attended Commonwealth Economic Conf. 1952; Commonwealth Trade & Econ. Conf. 1958; Secy. and Dir. of Research, Royal Comn. on Canada's Econ. Prospects 1955–58; Asst. Under-Secy. of State for External Affairs 1958–59; Prof. of Eng. Lang. and Lit., Queen's Univ. 1959–64; Principal, Univ. College, Univ. of Toronto 1964–70; Principal Emeritus 1983– ; University Professor, U. of Toronto 1970–79; Sr. Fellow, Massey Coll. 1970–85, Sr. Fellow Emeritus 1985– ; author: 'The Wounded Prince' and 'The Net and the Sword' (poems); 'The Deserter' (fiction); 'Bright Glass of Memory' (memoirs); 'Something Still To Find' (poems); 'Weathering It' (poems); 'Far Voyages' (poems); rec'd. Gov. Gen. Lit. Award (poetry) 1953, (fiction) 1964; Lorne Pierce Medal, Roy. Soc. of Can. 1976; mem. Canada Council 1964–70; Pres., Academy of the Humanities and Social Sciences, Royal. Soc. of Can. 1978–79; Address: Massey College, 4 Devonshire Place, Toronto, Ont. M5S 2E1.

**LEPPER, Fred Daniel;** aviation & pilot supplies merchant, inventor; b. Toronto, Ont. 5 July 1955; s. Fred Robert and Marilyn Ruth (Whichello) L.; e. Malvern Coll. 1973; York Univ. 1974–76; Ryerson Polytechnical, aerospace engr. 1976–79; m. Imma d. Vito and Brigitte 1 Aug. 1981; children: Daniel, Laura; PRES. & SOLE OWNER, LEPPER AVIATION PRODUCTIONS 1979– ; started as propeller mfr. for custom & antique aircraft; branched out into var. lines of flight gear, aviation clothing, pilot supplies, aviation books & art; retail store & mail order; designed (invented) 'Weedwalker Airplane' – portable airboat motor; cert. acctg. software consultant; recreations: flying, cycling; Home: 193 Tansley Rd., Thornhill, Ont. L4J 2Y8.

**LEPPIK, John J.;** information systems executive; b. 10 Jan. 1938; e. Univ. of Toronto, B.A.Sc. 1961; m. Nancy M. Bissell 1961; children: Warren, Allan; PRES., KNOWLEDGE SYSTEMS INC. 1983– ; Vice Pres., Operations, Myrias Research Corp. 1988–90; Dir., Rsch. & Devel., IBM Canada 1977–83; Mem., Assn. of Profl. Engrs. of Ont.; speaker/lecturer; recreations: sports, boating, gardening; Office: 1 Swiftdale Pl., Don Mills, Ont. M3B 1M3.

**le RICHE, William Harding,** M.D., M.P.H., F.R.C.P.(C), F.A.C.P.; professor; b. Dewetsdorp, S. Africa 21 March 1916; s. Josef Daniel and Georgina Henrietta Guest (Harding) le R.; e. University of Witwatersrand, B.Sc. 1936, M.B., Ch.B. 1943, M.D. 1949; Harvard Univ. (Rockefeller Fellowship), M.P.H. (cum laude) 1950; m. Margaret Cardross, d. late Rev. Arthur Cardross Grant, 11 Dec. 1943; children: Jenny Harding, Robert Harding, Nicole Georgina Harding, Giles Harding, Claire Alison Harding; PROFESSOR EMERITUS, UNIV. OF TORONTO 1982; Interne, Zulu McCord Hosp., Durban 1944; apptd. by Union Health Dept. to Health Centre Service, firstly at Pholela, Natal, and later (1945) estbd. first Health Centre for Whites and Eurafricans at Knysna 1945–49; Epidemiologist, Union (Fed.) Health Dept. 1950–52; Consultant in Epidemiology, Dept. of Nat. Health & Welfare, Ottawa (worked on background report of Candn. Sickness Survey) 1952–54; Rsch. Med. Offr., Physicians Services Inc., Toronto, Ont. 1954–57; apptd. to Staff of Dept. of Public Health, Sch. of Hygiene, Toronto, Ont. 1957; apptd. Prof. of Pub. Health, Univ. of Toronto 1959; Prof. and Head, Dept. of Epidemiol., Univ. of Toronto 1962–75; Prof. of Epidemiol., Dept. of Preventive Med. and Biostatistics, Univ. of Toronto 1975–81; Prof. Emeritus 1982; received R.D. Defries Award 1981; publications: (with J. Milner) 'Epidemiology as Medical Ecology' 1971; 'A Complete Family Guide to Nutrition and Meal Planning' 1976; 'A Chemical Feast' 1982; over 130 articles; Delta Omega; Anglican; recreations: riding, photography.

**LERMER, George,** Ph.D.; educator; economist; consultant; b. Luck, Poland 18 Oct. 1939; s. Arthur and Miriam L.; e. Mass. Inst. Technol. B.Sc. 1960; McGill Univ. M.A. 1963, Ph.D. 1970; Wharton Sch. Univ. of Pa.; London Sch. of Econ.; m. Catherina Anna Mary d. Jan and Nellie Boon March 1963; children: Toby, Leonard, Noah, Eli; DEAN, FACULTY OF MGMT., UNIV. OF LETHBRIDGE 1981– ; Dir. Resources Br. Bureau Competition Policy Consumer Affairs Can. 1976; cons. on mergers, energy policy and trade law for govt. depts. and major corporations including Shell, Petro-Can., Gulf and Caterpillar; appeared as witness Restrictive Trade Practices Comn., Competition Tribunal, Ont. Securities Comn. and Candn. Import Tribunal; author and ed. several books and numerous articles prof. jours.; Office: Lethbridge, Alta. T1K 3M4.

**LERNER, Samuel,** C. St.J., C.D., Q.C., B.A., LL.B.; barrister; b. London, Ont. 27 Jan. 1916; s. Max and Minnie (Rosenthal) L.; e. Central Coll. Inst. London 1933; Univ. of W. Ont. B.A. 1936; Osgoode Hall Law Sch. 1939, LL.B. 1991; m. Frances d. Aaron Weinstein 20 Aug. 1944; children: Michael, Patricia Ann Klepic, Susan Johnston; Lerner & Associates (retired); called to Bar of Ont. 1939; Life Mem., L.S.U.C.; cr. Q.C. 1967; commenced law practice Lerner & Lerner 1939; Depy. Judge Small Claims Court; Arbitrator: Labour Relations Ont. Adjudicator; Canada Labour Code; Assessment Review Bd.; Hon. Counsel: Cong. Or Shalom; London Br. St. John's Ambulance; London Poppy Fund, Royal Candn. Legion; Past Pres., Vimy Br., R.C.L.; The Royal Candn. Regt. Assn. (Hon. Chrmn.); Past Pres., B'nai B'rith; N. London Kiwanis; Past Chrmn. London Pub. Lib. Bd. and Art Museum; Dir., Candn. Corps Commissionaires; Past Pres. Extve. Comte. London Dist. Council Boy Scouts; Hon. Mem., National Council Scouts Canada; Mem. Adv. Bd., London Un. Service Inst.; former mem. Bd. of Gov. Univ. of Western Ont.; served with The Royal Candn. Regt. 1940–46 Can., UK, Mediterranean, N.W. Europe, rank Maj.; Candn. Army Militia 1953–63, rank Lt. Col.; rec'd Queen's Silver Jubilee Medal; Associate Commdr. Order St. John; Bencher, Law Soc. Upper Can.; Past Pres. Middlesex Law Assn.; mem. Candn. Bar Assn.; Freemason; Sigma Alpha Mu (Prior); Liberal; Jewish; recreation: boating; Clubs: Royal Candn. Mil. Inst.; Baconian; Past Commodore Great Lakes Cruising Club; Home: 93, 607 Cranbrook Rd., London, Ont. N6K 2Y4.

**LERNER, Yale Howard,** LL.B.; lawyer; b. Winnipeg, Man. 31 July 1941; s. Arthur Isadore and Pearl (Staniloff) L.; e. Univ. of Man. LL.B. 1966; m. Reva d. Abraham and Jennie Rich 8 May 1966; children: Gabrielle, Jonathan Scott; Partner, Buchwald Asper

Hentelef 1970; Pres. YHL Associates Ltd. 1972– ; Chrmn. of the Bd., Specialty Foods Inc.; Vice Pres. Can-West Capital Corp.; Dir. CanWest Broadcasting Ltd.; Gemini Outerwear Ltd.; Global Ventures Western Ltd.; CanWest Financial Holdings Ltd.; Partner, Lerner and Klapman 1966–70; Isaac Pitblado Lectr. Continuing Legal Edn. 1975; mem. Law Soc. Man.; Candn. Bar Assn.; recreations: tennis, curling; Clubs: Winnipeg Squash Racquet; Maple Leaf Curling; Home: 221 Scotia St., Winnipeg, Man. R2W 3X2.

**LeROUX, Edgar Joseph,** B.A., M.Sc., Ph.D.; ecologist; Canadian public servant; b. Ottawa, Ont. 23 Jan. 1922; s. Dieudonné and Amanda (Beauchêsne) LeR.; e. Carleton Univ., B.A. 1950; McGill Univ., M.Sc. 1952, Ph.D. 1954, Ont. Inst. Prof. Agrologists, P.Ag. 1969; m. Ardis Myriam Andrew, Halifax, N.S., 30 June 1944; children: Estelle, Pierre, Elizabeth; Asst. Depy. Min., Research, Agriculture Canada 1978–87; Assoc. Prof. of Entom., Macdonald Coll., McGill Univ. 1962–65; Grace Griswold Lectr., Cornell Univ. 1971; mem. (and Vice-Chrmn. 1977–80) Agriculture Stabilization Board 1975–77; mem. (and Vice-Chrmn. 1977–80) Agricultural Products Board 1975–77; mem. Candn. Agric. Services Coordinating Comte (CASCC) 1975–87; Vice-Chrmn. Can. Agric. Research Council (CARC) 1977–87; Co-chrmn. Canada/USSR Agricultural Working Group 1981–87; Co-Chrmn. Can.-Romania Comte. on Cooperation in Agriculture 1981–87; Chrmn., OECD Comte. on Agric. 1978–80; mem. Interdepartmental Comte. of Asst. Depy. Mins. (Research), Can. Ministry of State for Science and Technol. 1978–84; mem. Interdepartmental Panel on Energy, R & D, Energy Mines and Resources Can. 1978–87; mem. Candn. Climate Planning Bd., Environment Can. 1978–87; Chrmn. Federal Interdepartmental Comte on Pesticides (FICP) 1978–87; mem. Bd. of Dir. of Public Works Land Co. Ltd. (to manage the Mirabel Peripheral Lands) 1978–79; Research Comte., Candn. Egg Marketing Agency 1980–84; mem.: Adv. Comte. on Inmate Employment (ACIE), Correctional Services of Canada (CSC) 1980–87; Nat. Rsch. Council of Canada 1980–86; Task Force on Sci. and Prof. Category Interdepartmental Adv. Comte. 1981–87; Ag. Can. Rep. Internat. Adv. Comte. on National Mineral Policy (IACNMP) 1983–87; National Biotechnology Adv. Comte. 1983–87; Program Eval. & Audit Comte., Agr. Can. 1984–87; Chrmn. NRC Associate Comte. on Biotechnology 1983–87; joined present Dept. as Rsch. Sci., Rsch. Br. 1950–62, Rsch. Co-ordinator, Rsch. Br. 1965–68, Asst. Dir. Gen. (Insts.), Rsch. Br. 1968–72; Asst. Dir. Gen. (Planning), Rsch. Br. 1972–75; Dir. Gen. (Ops.), Rsch. Br. 1975–78; served as Writer, RCN 1941–46 (service on high seas); Pres., Comité des Paroissiens, Paroisse St-Gérard Magella, St-Jean, Que. 1956–61; Pres. Navy League of Can., Qué. Div. 1961–64; Vice Pres., Nat. Council 1964–65 (awarded Cert. of Merit); author 'Population Dynamics of Agricultural and Forest Insect Pests' 1963; 'Recherches sur la Biologie et la Dynamique des Populations Naturelles *d'Archips argyrospilus* dans le sud-ouest de Québec' 1965; 'Population Dynamics and Biology of the Apple Leaf miner, *Lithocolletis Blancardella* in Quebec' 1970; 'Population Dynamics and Biology of the European Corn Borer, *Ostrinia nubilalis* in Quebec' 1986; other writings incl. over 75 research publs. on subject of insect ecol. and physiol.; Chrmn., Insect Ecol. Panel, Study of Basic Biol. in Can., Biolog. Council of Can. 1969–70; mem. Expert Panel, Integrated Pest Control, Food and Agric. Organ. of U.N.; official corr. in Entom., Commonwealth Inst. of Biol. Control; Candn. rep. (Plant Protection), Internat. Soc. for Hortic. Science; mem.: Can. Dept. Indust., Trade and Comm., Tech. Apple Mission to Japan, Australia, New Zealand and S. Africa 1971; Biol. Council Can. (Pres. 1970–71); Entom. Soc. Can. 1969– (Pres. 1969–70); Entom. Soc. Que. 1965– (Pres. 1965–66); Dir., Candn. Soc. Zools. 1968–70; mem.: Que. Soc. Protection Plants 1964– ; Agric. Inst. Can. 1962– ; Prof. Inst. Can. (Pres. St-Jean Que. Div. 1960–61); SCITEC (now AASC (the Assn. for the Advancement of Science in Can.); Hon. Treas. of Extve. Counc. 1970); Negotiated Grants Comte., N.R.C.; Publications Comte., Agric. Can.; Comte. for Internat. Plant Protection Congresses; Honorary D.Sc., McGill Univ. 1973; awarded Queen's Jubilee Medal by the Gov. Gen. of Can. 1977; Fellow, Entom. Soc. of Can. 1977; Armand Frappier Medal 1984; Fellow, AIC 1985; Hon. Degree, 'Doctor of the University' Ottawa Univ. 1986; Gold Medal, Entom. Soc. Can. 1986; Golden Award, Candn. Feed Indust. Assoc. 1986; Hon. Life Mem., Candn. Seed Growers' Assoc. 1986; Merit Award (Canada Agric.) Public Service of Canada 1987; invested as Officer of the Order of Canada 1988; awarded Sr. Officer Retirement Certificate, Public Service of Canada, by the Gov. Gen. of Can., Jeanne Sauve, 1989; Emeritus Mem., Entom. Soc. Que. 1989; awarded, Commemorative Medal of the Confederation of Canada 1992; Roman Catholic; recreations: fishing, golf, swimming, sailing, painting, wood sculpture; Home: 27 Keppler Cres., Nepean, Ont. K2H 5Y1.

**LEROY, Claude,** prof. titulaire, docteur en sciences, FRSC; university professor; b. Charleroi (Belgium) 30 Sept. 1947; s. Bernard and Renée (Jacobeus) L.; e. Math. Spéciale Saint-Louis Fac., Bruxelles, Belgium 1967; Univ. of Louvain, Lic. en Sciences 1971, Doctorat en Sciences 1976; PROFESSEUR TITULAIRE, UNIV. OF MONTRÉAL 1990– ; Dir., Nuclear Physics Laboratory, Univ. of Montreal 1991– ; Chercheur I.I.S.N., Univ. of Louvain 1971–77; Vis. Rsch. Fellow, Univ. of Southampton 1976–77; Rsch. Assoc. Physics McGill 1977–80; Attaché de Rech. Physique Univ. de Montréal 1978–80; Rsch. Assoc. Phys. N.W. Univ. 1980–81; Chercheur du Fonds du Développement Sci., Univ. of Louvain 1981–83; Rsch. Sci., Inst. of Particle Physics McGill 1983–90; Assoc. Prof. 1983–90; Sci. Assoc., Ctr. Eur. pour la Rech. Nucléaire, Switz. 1980– ; Mem., Inst. of Particle Physics of Can. 1983– ; Mem., Candn. Assoc. of Physicists 1992; Rutherford Prize for Physics 1988 (Royal Soc. of Can.); FRSC 1989– ; Killam Rsch. Fellowship 1993; Catholic; author/co-author of more than 200 sci. papers pub. in internat. sci. reviews; recreations: hieroglyph (Egyptian), history, fishing; Home: 5155 Blvd. Lasalle, Verdun, Que. H4G 2C1; Office: Lab. Nucl. Phys., U. of Montréal, C.P. 6128, Montréal, Qué. H3C 3J7.

**LE ROY, Robert James,** Ph.D.; university professor; b. Ottawa, Ont. 30 Sept. 1943; s. Donald James and Lillice Marie (Read) L.; e. North Toronto, C.I. 1961; Univ. of Toronto B.Sc. 1965, M.Sc. 1967; Univ. of Wisconsin Ph.D. 1971; m. Virginia d. Steponas and Elena Pusvaskis 22 July 1967; children: Alexander R., Sylvia M., Clara M., Monika A.; PROF., DEPT. OF CHEM., UNIV. OF WATERLOO 1982– ; NRC postdoct. fellow, Dept. of Physics, Univ. of Toronto 1971–72; Asst. Prof., Dept. of Chem., Univ. of Waterloo 1972–76; Assoc. Prof. 1976–82; Dir., Guelph-Waterloo Ctr. for Grad. Work in Chem. 1982–85; Vice-Chrmn., Div. of Atomic & Molecular Physics, Candn. Assn. of Physicists 1980–81; Chrmn. 1981–82; Sr. Vis. Fellow, Dept. of Theoretical Chem., Oxford Univ., Fall 1976; Prof. Invité, Univ. de Paris-Sud d'Orsay, Lab. Spectroscopie de Translation, April 1983; Alfred P. Sloan Found. Fellow 1974–76; John Simmon Guggenheim Found. Fellow 1979–80; Rutherford Medal in Chem., Royal Soc. of Can. 1984; Mem., Candn. Assn. of Physicists; Am. Physical Soc.; Fellow, Chem. Inst. of Can.; Ed. Adv. Bd. Mem., 'Chemical Physics Letters' 1981–89; author/co-author of 78 sci. papers in field of Theoretical Chem. Physics; recreations: squash, swimming; Home: 47 Thorndale Dr., Waterloo, Ont. N2L 5H6; Office: Waterloo, Ont. N2L 3G1.

**LESAUX, Peter Berkely,** B.A.; public servant; b. Ottawa, Ont. 30 Dec. 1934; s. Victor and Kathleen (Meagher) L.; e. St. Francis Xavier Univ. B.A. 1957; m. Joan d. William and Florence McCarron 7 Sept. 1959; children: Scott, Drew, Brent, Krista, Tara Lynn; Pres., Atlantic Canada Opportunities Agency 1989–93; joined Fed. Pub. Serv. (Treas. Bd.) 1957; Dept. of Northern Affairs & Nat. Resources 1963; Glassco Royal Comn., 2 yrs.; Asst. Dir., Nat. & Hist. Parks 1968; Dir., Econ. Devel. Br., Indian-Eskimo Affairs 1971; Asst. Dep. Min. 1972; Fitness & Amateur Sport 1977–85; Comnr., Public Serv. Comn. of Can. 1986–89; Bd. Dir., Waterloo Univ. Adv. Counc.; PARTICIPaction; Can. Sports Hall of Fame; The Ottawa Civil Serv. Recreation Assn.; Candn. Oldtimers Hockey Assn.; St. Francis Xavier Univ. Sports Hall of Fame; recreations: skiing, bridge; Address: P.O. Box 6051, Moncton, N.B. E1C 9J8.

**LESLIE, Donald A.,** FCA; chartered accountant; b. Winnipeg, Man. 11 Aug. 1942; s. Gregory and Matilda (Laas) L.; e. Burnhamthorpe C.I. 1961; C.A. 1966; m. Beverley d. Clifford and Mirabel Jones 10 Apr. 1964; children: Theodore, Gordon, Philip; PRES. & C.E.O., CANDN. INVESTOR PROTECTION FUND 1989– ; obtained C.A., Clarkson Gordon 1966; Chief Examiner, Investment Dealers Assn. of Can. 1967–70; returned to Clarkson Gordon 1971, Partner 1974–89; Partner, Woods Gordon 1984–89; Rsch. fellow, Univ. of Waterloo 1984– ; Mem., Adv. Counc., Ctr. for Audit. Rsch., Univ. of Georgia 1980–83; Lectr., Candn. Securities Inst. 1973–86; Am. Acct. Assn. Wildman Gold Medal 1980 and Distinguished Service in Auditing Award 1990; FCA 1982; Dir., Candn. Hearing Soc. (CHS) Found. (Founding Dir. 1979); CHS (Pres. 1979–82); Mississauga Assn. for the Mentally Retarded (MAMR) 1977–83 (Treas. 1977–79; Founding Dir., MAMR Found. 1982); Dir., N. Halton Assn. for the Developmentally Handicapped 1988– ; Mississauga S. Prov. Progressive Conservative Assn. 1976–85 (Vice-Pres. 1979–81); Mississauga S. Fed. Prog. Cons. Assn. 1978–84; Mem., Am. Acctg. Assn. (Sec. 1977–78; Audit. Standards Ctte. 1978–79, 1985–87; Vice-Chrmn., Audit. Section 1986–87); Candn. Acad. Acctg. Assn.; Am. Stats. Assn.; author: 'Materiality' 1985; co-author: 'Dollar-Unit Sampling' 1979; contbr.: 'Accountants Handbook' 1981; founding co-editor 1979 & ed. bd. mem. 1981–88: 'Auditing: A Journal of Practice and Theory'; former ed. bd. mem., four jours.; recreations: tennis, jogging; Clubs: Albany; Fitness Inst.; Meadows Country, Sarasota; Home: 7367 Appleby Line, Milton, Ont. L9T 2Y1; Office: 24th Flr., South Tower, P.O. Box 192, Royal Bank Plaza, Toronto, Ont. M5J 2J4.

**LESLIE, Peter Malcolm,** B.A., M.Sc. (Econ.), Ph.D.; educator; b. Montréal, Qué. 10 Apr. 1939; s. Angus Ogilvy and Kathleen Mary (Wilson) L.; e. Bishop's Univ. B.A. 1959; London Sch. of Econ. M.Sc. (Econ.) 1962; Queen's Univ. Ph.D. 1967; m. Kristina d. Ossi Hjelt and Elisabeth du Jardin 27 May 1967; children: Erik, Stefan, Adrian, Carl; PROF. OF POL. STUDIES, QUEEN'S UNIV. 1982– ; Lectr. in Pol. Studies 1965, Asst. Prof. 1967, Assoc. Prof. 1972, Dir. Inst. of Intergovernmental Relations 1983–88; Asst. Secy. to the Cabinet for Federal-Provincial Relations, Govt. of Can. 1988–90; author 'Canadian Universities 1980 and Beyond: Enrolment, Structure and Finance' 1980; 'Rebuilding the Relationship: Quebec and Its Confederation Partners' 1987; 'Federal State, National Economy' 1987; 'The European Community: A Political Model for Canada?' 1991; 'A Partnership in Trouble: Renegotiating Fiscal Federalism' 1993; ed. 'Canada: The State of the Federation' 1985, 1986, 1987/1988'; mem. Candn. Pol. Sci. Assn.; recreations: carpentry, swimming, skiing, boardsailing; Home: 254 Alfred St., Kingston, Ont. K7L 3S2; Office: Dept. of Political Studies, Queen's Univ., Kingston, Ont. K7L 3N6.

**LESSARD, Claude,** B.B.A.; communications executive; b. Québec, Qué. 29 July 1949; s. Jean-Luc and Carmen (Cerat) L.; e. Laval Univ. B.B.A.; m. Marie d. Lucien Lortie 18 Dec. 1971; three s. Jean-François, Michel-Alexandre, Pierre-Nicolas; CHRMN. AND CHIEF EXTVE. OFFR. COSSETTE COMMUNICATION-MARKETING INC.; Dir. Groupe Canam-Manac Inc.; Laurentienne Vie; Home: 1350 Patenaude St., Sillery, Qué. G1T 2J6; Office: 437 Grande-Allée E., Québec, Qué. G1R 2J5.

**LESSARD, Michel M.,** B.A., B.Com., M.Sc.Com., M.B.A., F.T.C.I.; financial executive; b. Quebec, Que. 31 Aug. 1939; s. Maurice and Jacqueline (Lacasse) L.; e. Laval Univ. B.A. 1958, B.Com. 1961, M.Sc.Com. 1962; Harvard Univ. M.B.A. 1967; Fellow, Trust Co.'s Inst. of Can. 1976; children: Eric, Christine; Pres. & C.E.O. SOGEXFI Inc. 1986– ; Chrmn., 2M Financial Inc.; Mildev, Real Estate Services Inc.; Pres. & C.E.O., Credit Foncier 1981–86; Chrmn., Pres. and C.E.O., Francana Real Estate Ltd. 1981–86; Dir. Jonergin Inc.; Boulanger Inc.; Sucana Investments Inc.; prior to Credit Foncier served as mgmt. cons. and with Domglass Ltd., Allied Chemical Canada Ltd. and Canadian Ingersoll Rand Ltd.; joined Credit Foncier as Vice Pres. Frandevcor Ventures Ltd. (subsidiary) 1970, Vice Pres. Francana Develop. Corp. 1972, Treas. Credit Foncier 1975, Asst. Gen. Mgr. and Treas. 1978, Sr. Asst. Gen. Mgr. 1979, Extve. Vice Pres. 1980, Dir., mem. Extve. Comte., Pres. and Chief Oper. Offr. 1981; Pres. & C.E.O. 1984; Clubs: Mount Royal; Winchester; Address: 279 Kenaston, Town of Montreal, Que. H3R 1M6.

**LESSARD, Pierre H.,** B.A., M.Sc.C., M.B.A., F.C.A.; executive; b. Quebec City, Que. 13 Feb. 1942; s. Maurice and Jacqueline (Lacasse) L.; e. Laval Univ. B.A. 1961, M.Sc.C. 1964, L.Sc.C. 1965; Harvard Univ. M.B.A. 1967; m. Andrée D. d. Philippe Dupuis, Quebec City, Que. 11 June 1966; children: Pierre Philippe, Stéphanie; PRES. & C.E.O., MÉTRO-RICHELIEU INC. 1990– ; Dir. Métro-Richelieu Inc.; Hydro-Québec; The Mutual Life of Canada; Fonds Croissance Quebec Inc.; Auditor, Touche-Ross & Partners, Montreal 1964–65; Asst. to Pres., Treas. and Controller Denault Ltée, Sherbrooke 1967–69; Treas. and Controller Provigo Inc. 1970, Vice Pres. Finance and Adm. 1972; Pres., Chief Oper. Offr., Dir. & mem. Extve. Comte. 1976–85; Vice-Chrmn., Pathonic Network Inc. 1985–88; Pres. & C.E.O., Aeterna Life Ins. Co. 1988–90; mem. Que. Inst. C.A.'s; Montreal Bd. Trade; St. Denis Club; The Hermitage Club (Dir.); Le Club Laval sur le Lac; Harvard Bus. School Assn. of Montreal; R. Catholic; recreations: tennis, golf, skiing; Home: 1515 Kenilworth Rd., Town of Mount Royal, Que. H3R 2S2; Office: 11011 Maurice-Duplessis, Montreal, Que. H1C 1V6.

**LESSER, Gloria,** B.F.A., M.F.A.; interior designer; b. Montreal, Que. 20 Dec. 1936; d. Harry and Sonia (Baylin) Lidsky; e. MacDonald Coll., McGill Univ. Perm. Teaching Dipl. (Class III) 1960; Chicago Sch. of Interior Decoration Dipl. 1963; Concordia Univ. B.F.A. 1977, M.F.A. 1983; m. Jack s. Morris and Lucy L. 29 June 1958; div. 1975; children: Mitchell Neil, Caroline, Diane; FOUNDER, GLORIA LESSER INTERIORS REG'D 1970– ; Elementary School Teacher 1956–60; Rsch. Asst., Candn. Art, Montreal Museum of Fine Arts 1979–80; Regional Contributor, *Canadian Collector*, News and Views Column 1982–84; Château Dufresne Montreal Mus. of Decorative Arts 1988–89, Guest Curator, Ecole du Meuble 1930–50: Interior Design & Decorative Art in Montreal 1989; frequent guest speaker 1969– ; freelance residential and commercial interior design, project mngt. & cons. 1970–93; initiated archives for Que. interior designers; Prof., Art Hist. & Interior Design, Champlain Regional College 1984–94; John Abbot Coll. Vanier Coll. 1976; 2 Canada Council grants; Grad. Fellowship Lectr., Art Hist., Concordia Univ. 1980–81; Mem., Interior Designers of Que.; Interior Designers of Can.; Candn. Soc. of Decorative Arts (Nom. Officer 1991–92; Special Ctte. Organizer, AGM 1992); author: 'Ecole du Meuble 1930–50' 1989 and approx. 45 articles; contbr.: 'Living in Style' 1994, 'The Homes and Furnishings of R.B. Angus, Montreal'; regional contbr., 'Canadian Collector' 1982–84; recreation: classical ballet; Office: 4870 Côte des Neiges, Suite E104, Montreal, Que. H3V 1H3.

**LESTER, Malcolm David,** M.A.; publisher; b. Toronto, Ont. 27 Aug. 1938; s. Lionel and Zelma Beatrice (Gorfinkle) L.; e. Univ. of Toronto B.A. 1959, M.A. 1962; Hebrew Union Coll. Bachelor of Hebrew Lit.; PRESIDENT, LESTER PUBLISHING LTD. 1991– ; President, Lester & Orpen Dennys Ltd. 1979–91; Gen. Mgr. Coles Publishing Co. Ltd. 1970–71; Mang. Ed. Holt Rinehart and Winston of Canada Ltd. 1964–70; Pres., Assn. Candn. Publishers 1980–82, 1985–86; Lectr., Ryerson Certificate Program in Publishing 1990–93; Home: Apt. 404, 50 Prince Arthur Ave., Toronto, Ont. M5R 1B5; Office: 56 The Esplanade, Ste. 507A, Toronto, Ont. M5E 1A7.

**LETARTE, l'hon. René,** B.A., LL.L., C.R.; juge; né Montréal, Qué. 4 sept. 1931; f. Louis-Philippe et Henriette (Asselin) L.; e. Séminaire St-Hyacinthe; Externat Classique St-Jean Eudes, Qué.; Séminaire de Qué. B.èsA. 1951; Faculté de Droit de l'Univ. Laval 1951–55; ép. Claire f. Léo Gilbert 25 mai 1957; enfants: Michel, Danièle; JUGE, COUR SUPÉRIEURE DE QUÉ. 1977– ; mem. du Comité général des juges de la Cour supérieure de Qué. (secrétaire) 1983– ; admission au Barreau de Qué. 1955; nommé C.R. 1973; Associé sénior de l'étude Letarte, Caron, Reinhardt; Dir. de la Comm. des Débats Interuniversitaires à Laval; chargé de cours à l'École d'entraînement professionnel du Barreau; enseignement du droit criminel à la licence à l'Univ. Laval 1963–70; membre du Conseil de la Faculté de droit; chargé de cours de droit criminel à l'Extension de l'enseignement de l'Académie de Qué.; conférencier invité pour traiter des aspects juridiques de la drogue, aux cours annuels de l'OPTAT; divers clubs sociaux de Qué.; Barreau de Québec 1964–66 (prés. du Service d'information 1970–72, Bâtonnier 1972–73); membre du Conseil général du Barreau de la province 1965–66 et 1972–73, membre du Comité exécutif; conseiller spécial du Comité interministériel du Qué. sur l'étude du Rapport LeDain; invité comme témoin expert par la Comm. Prévost chargée de l'enquête sur l'adm. de la Justice pénale et criminelle; Vice-prés. national, Société canadienne pour l'abolition de la peine de mort; administrateur, Société de Qué. de la Croix-Rouge canadienne; professeur invité à l'Univ. Laval pour l'année académique 1993–94 pour traiter de l'Indemnisation des victimes de blessures corporelles ou de décès; Religion catholique; récréation: ski, tennis, chasse, pêche; Club: Mount Stephen; Résidence: 2180, Brûlart, Sillery, Qué.; Bureau: Palais de justice, 300, boul. Jean-Lesage, R-342, Québec, Qué. G1K 8K6.

**LETENDRE, Rita,** R.C.A.; painter; b. Drummondville, Que. 1 Nov. 1928; d. Héliodore Letendre; e. Ecole des Beaux-Arts Montreal and with Paul-Emile Borduas Montreal; over 42 solo exhns. Can., N.Y., Los Angeles, Europe and Israel incl. Montreal Museum of Fine Arts 1961, Internat. Travel Exhn. 1977; Gallery Moos Toronto 1972, 1974, 1977, 1980, 1982, 1983, Calgary 1979; Musée d'Art Contemporain Montreal 1972, 1976; Arras Gallery N.Y. 1974, 1976; Palm Springs (Cal.) Museum 1974; Galerie Gilles Corbeil Montreal 1975, 1978, 1980, 1982, 1983, 1984; Equinox Gallery Vancouver 1976; West End Gallery Edmonton 1978; Arwin Galleries Detroit 1972, 1979; Art Gallery of Concordia, Montreal 1989; The Robert MacLaughlin Art Gallery 1990; Waddington & Gorce Montreal 1984, 1988; Concordia Art Gallery, Montreal 1989; Moore Art Gallery Hamilton 1988, 1989; Univ. of Toronto Erindale Art Gallery 1993; rep. in over 45 group exhns. Can., USA, Europe, Japan; rep. in perm. colls. maj. Candn. museums and galleries, USA, and various corporate colls.; comns. incl. 'Sunforce' (outdoor mural) Cal. State Univ. Long Beach 1965; 'Now' (acrylic on canvas) Berkshire House, Toronto 1971; 'Sunrise' (Outdoor mural) Ryerson Polytech. Inst. Toronto 1971; 2 paintings Exxon Bldg. N.Y. 1971; 'Tecumseth II' (indoor mural) Sheridan Mall, Pickering, Ont. 1972; 'Urta' (outdoor mural) Toronto 1972; 2 murals J.C. Penney H.O., N.Y. 1972; 'Summer Solstice' Dallas 1973; Toronto General Hosp. Main Lobby 1973; 2 murals Mountainville, N.Y. 1972; 'Irowakan' (acrylic on canvas) Royal Bank Plaza, Toronto 1977; 'Joy' skylight dome mural Glencairn Subway Stn. Toronto 1977; IBM (Canada) 1983; Via Rail Mural 1990; awards: Le Prix de la jeune Peinture Montreal 1959; Le Prix Rodolphe de Repentigny Montreal 1960; Le Prix de Peinture Concours Artistique du Qué. 1961; Can. Council Travel Grant 1962–63, Sr. Grant 1971, 1975; Bourse de Recherche Prov. Qué. 1967; Candn. Nat. Exhn. 1st Prize Painting 1968; Ont. Soc. Artists 1st Price Painting 1970; II Festival Internat. de Peinture Cagnes sur Mer (Prix Nat.) 1970; Address: 288 Sherbourne St., Toronto, Ont. M5A 2S1.

**LETKEMAN, Peter,** M.Sc., Ph.D., F.C.I.C.; educator; b. Winkler, Man. 12 Feb. 1938; e. Univ. of Man. B.Sc. (Hons.) 1960, M.Sc. 1961, Ph.D. 1969; Univ. of Cal. Riverside 1970; m. Mary Olfert 7 July 1940; children: Lorne Peter, Lloyd Myron, Leon David; PROFESSOR OF CHEMISTRY, BRANDON UNIV. 1976– ; High Sch. Teacher Vincent Massey, Brandon, Man. 1961–63; Lectr. in Chem. Brandon Coll. 1963–66; Asst. Prof. of Chem. Brandon Univ. 1966, Assoc. Prof. 1971, Chrmn. Chem. Dept. 1972–80, mem. Senate 1974–77 and 1982– , mem. Bd. Govs. 1974–76, Acting Dean of Science 1982–83, Dean of Science 1983–93; Visiting Prof. Texas A & M Univ. 1977–78; Rsch. Associate, Univ. of Arizona 1993–94; Chrmn. W. Man. Science Fair 1979, Awards Chrmn. 1973–76, Vice Chrmn. 1977–78; Judge-in-Chief Can.-Wide Science Fair 1976; mem. Man. Research Council 1979–83; author or co-author numerous publs.; mem. Science Teachers' Assn. Man.; Chem. Inst. Can.; Science Curriculum Council Man. 1974–77, 1978–85; Mem., Education Adv. Bd., Manitoba Govt. 1981–90; mem. Mennonite Found. of Can.; mem. Manitoba Round-Table on the Environment 1991– ; Fellow, Chem. Inst. Canada; recreations: philately, photography, music (guitar), numismatics; Home: R.R. 3, Box 95, Brandon, Man. R7A 5Y3; Office: Dept. of Chemistry, Brandon Univ., Brandon, Man. R7A 6A9.

**LETOURNEAU, Gilles,** B.A., LL.L., LL.M., Ph.D.; lawyer; university professor; b. St-Michel Cté Bellechasse, Que. 14 July 1945; s. Romeo and Marguerite (Thibault) L.; e. Coll. de Lévis, B.A. 1965; Laval Univ., LL.L. 1968; London Sch. of Econ. & Pol. Sci., LL.M. 1972, Ph.D. 1975; m. Claudette d. Gerard and Jeanne Tremblay 1 July 1971; children: Simon, Christian, Marie-Eve; JUDGE OF THE FEDERAL COURT OF APPEAL 1992– ; admitted to Qué. Bar 1969; private practice 1969–71, 1975–77; Assoc. Prof., Laval Univ. 1975–77; Dir., Undergrad. Studies & Vice-Dean of Fac. of Law 1975–77; Dir., Legal and Legis. Rsch., Que. Min. of Justice 1977–80; Assoc. Dir.-Gen., Legis. Affairs 1980–83; Spec. Adv. to Assoc. Dep. Min. for Criminal Affairs 1983–84; Assoc. Gen.-Sec., Extve. Ctte., Que. Govt. 1984–85; Vice Pres., Reform Commn. of Can. 1985–90; Pres., Law Reform Comn. of Can. 1990–92; Bd. of Dir., Min. of Justice; Fac. of Law, Laval Univ.; Legal Aid Regional Offices in Que.; Soc. Quebecoise d'information juridique; Mem., Exam. Bur., Que. Bar; Prof. of Criminal Law, Que. Bar Admission Course; Mem., Que. Bar; Candn. Bar Assn.; author: 'The Prerogative Writs in Canadian Criminal Law and Procedure' 1976; co-author; 'Report of the Committee on Violence in Amateur Hockey in Quebec' 1977; 'Loi annotée sur les poursuites sommaires' 1979, 1983; 'Code de procédure pénale du Québec annoté' 1990, 1992; recreations: skiing, ice hockey, theatre; Home: 2006 Woodglen Cr., Gloucester, Ont. K1J 6G4.

**LETOURNEAU, Jean-Paul,** C.R.I., Cert. Assoc. Mgmt.; consultant; b. St-Hyacinthe, Que. 4 May 1930; s. late Joseph Eugene and Annette (Deslandes) L.; e. Univ. of Montreal C.R.I. 1953; Syracuse Univ., N.Y. Cert. Assoc. Mgmt. 1962; m. Claire d. late Napoleon Paquin 24 Sept. 1956; Sec.-Tres. Munic. of Mont St-Hilaire 1950–53; Personnel Dir. Dupuis Freres Mail Order House 1953; Ed. weekly newsp. of Fed. des Chambres de Comm. des Jeunes du Qué. 1953–54; Extve. sec. La Chambre de Comm. des Jeunes du dist. Montréal 1954–56; Asst. Gen. Mgr. La Chambre De Comm. du Que. 1956–59, Gen. Mgr. 1959–71; Extve. V.P. La Chambre de Comm. du Quebec 1971–90; author 'Quebec, The Cost of Independence' 1969; 'Report on Corporate Social Responsibility' 1982; Dir. The Children's Broadcast Inst. Toronto 1980–84; La Fondation Crudem Canada-Haiti Inc. 1975–86; Pres. Chamber of Comm. Extves. of Can. 1982–83; Dir. Am. Chamber of Comm. Extves. (Washington D.C.) 1982–83; Dir. & Vice-Chrmn. of the Bd. of Dirs., Candn. Extve. Service Organization (Toronto) 1991– ; Dir., Office des personnes handicapées du Québec 1992– ; mem. La Corporation Prof. des Conseillers en Rel. Indust. Qué.; Candn. Foundation for Economic Education; apptd. Mem., Counc. of Excellence, Chamb. of Comm. Execs. of Can. 1986; Roman Catholic; recreations: reading, traveling; Office: 165 Cote Ste-Catherine, #202, Outremont, Qué. H2V 2A7.

**LETT, Patrick Fraser Kenyon,** B.Sc., M.Sc., Ph.D., LL.D.; business executive; b. 27 Sept. 1948; e. Ridley College; Univ. of Guelph B.Sc. (Hons.) 1971, M.Sc. 1974; Dalhousie Univ. Ph.D. 1978; Univ. of Toronto grad. studies 1983–84; m. Cynthia Jane (nee Depew); three children; CHAIRMAN, TRAFALGAR CAPITAL MANAGEMENT CORP. 1984– ; Pres., Pierrepont Financial Group 1988– ; Dir. & Prin. Shareholder, Arbitrage Risk Mngt. Limited 1988– ; Pres., Fraser Bancorp Limited 1989– ; Elora Mill Limited 1990– ; Mem., Chicago Board of Options Exchange and The Option Clearing Corp. 1991– ; Chair, Traser Investment Group 1992– ; Past Pres., Toronto Options & Futures Soc.; Mem., Aquatic Adv. Ctte., Univ. of Guelph; Trustee & Gov., Ridley College (extensive ctte. work); Mem., Investment Ctte., Upper Canada College; Finance Ctte., Dalhousie Univ.; Ont. Securities Comn. Registration: Investment Counsel, Portfolio Manager, Commodity Trading Manager, Limited Market Dealer; philanthropy: Dick Brown Scholarship, Univ. of Guelph; Patrick F. Lett Grad. Student Assistance Bursary, Dalhousie Univ.; Kenyon Lett House, Bishop Ridley Coll.; Patrick F. Lett Gym., Upper Canada Coll.; Bishop Strachan School; Oldfield School; Patron & Sponsor, Elora Festival; Sponsor, McMichael Gall.; Dalhousie Univ., LL.D. (Honoris Causa) 1992; recreations: squash, skiing, water skiing, swimming, sailing, power boating, tennis, fishing, jogging, walking, reading, travelling; Address: 178 Douglas Drive, Toronto, Ont. M4V 2B7.

**LETT, Tristram S.,** B.A., M.Sc.; investment executive; b. Geraldton, Ont. 29 Mar. 1947; s. Lt. Col. Stephen MacLeod, D.S.O. and Kathleen Audrey (Pierrepont) L.; e. Ridley College 1966; York Univ. B.A. 1970; London Sch. of Econ. M.Sc. 1971; m. Toni d. Ronald and Barbara Maskell 26 July 1976; children: Brittany K.M., Cambria S.Y.; PRESIDENT AND C.E.O., TRAFALGAR CAPITAL MANAGEMENT 1985– ; Dir., Pierreport Bancorp Limited 1991; Partner, Traser Investment Group 1992; Ont. Securities Registration: Investment Counsel, Portfolio Mgr., Commodity Trading Mgr.; Securities and Exchange Commission (Washington) Registration: Broker/Dealer; Chrmn., Bd. of Govs., Toronto Futures Exchange; joined Min. of Treasury and Econ. Ont. 1971–78, Sr. Budget Advr. Resp. for Pension Policy; contrib. columnist Oakville Beaver 1977–79; Vice Pres. N. Oakville, Halton P. Cons. Assn. 1978–80; Fed. P. Cons. cand. for Halton 1978; recreations: running, skiing, weight training, breeding & showing Old Engl. Sheepdogs and Smooth Fox Terriers (Am., Bda., Can. Ch. Raffles' Queen of the Colony, Top Herding Dog in Canada 1988; Am., Bda., Can. Ch. Proudfox Inspector Gadget, #1 Puppy in Canada (All breeds) and Top Terrier in Canada 1990; Am., Can. Ch. Raffles' Chelsea Buns, #1 Puppy in Canada (All Breeds) 1991, Winner of the Old English Sheepdog Club of America National Specialty 1992, Winner of the Old English Sheepdog Club of Canada National Specialty 1992, and Winner of Western Reserve Old English Sheepdog Club Speciality 1992); Office: 401, 277 Lakeshore Rd. E., Oakville, Ont. L6J 1H9.

**LETTE, Bernard,** B.A., B.C.L., LL.B., M.Bus.Law; lawyer; b. Montréal, Qué. 31 March 1957; s. Raymond and Maryrose (Fontana) L.; e. Coll. Stanislas Montréal B.A. 1974; McGill Univ. B.C.L. 1978, LL.B. 1981; Univ. Bordeaux (France) Lic. droit 1978, M.Bus.Law. 1979; m. Janis S. d. William and Edna Webster 5 June 1987; children: Fabienne, Danya; MNG. PARTNER, LETTE, WHITTAKER (Toronto Office law firm Lette Associates) 1984– ; Dir. & Chrmn., Potamine Potash Mining of Canada Inc.; Dir. & Pres., Manitoba Potash Corp.; Dir. & Vice-Pres., ASB Greenworld Ltd.; Dir., Vice-Pres. & Secy. Rondo Bakery Equipment Inc.; Dir. & Secy., API-PME Canada Inc.; Bestobell Canada Ltd.; Comus Electronics Canada Inc.; Dumez Real Estate North America Inc.; Dynamic & Proto Circuits Inc.; Grosfillex Inc.; Hazemag Canada Inc.; Hazemag USA Inc.; Helm Canada Chemicals Inc.; JAB Anstoctz Inc.; Osram Sylvania Ltd.; Rema Tip Top Canada Ltd.;

Schauenburg Industries Ltd.; Seb Canada Inc.; Sherman Supersonic Industries Inc.; Tractel North America Inc.; Dir., Hottinger Financial Corp.; Interforest Ltd.; Phoenix Contact Ltd.; Potash Co. of Canada Ltd.; Stellram Tool Company Ltd.; Swing Stage Ltd.; previously resident Montréal and Paris; admitted to Bar: Québec 1979, France 1979 and Ontario 1984; Conseiller du Comm. Exterieur de la France; Dir. and Pres., Swiss Candn. C. of C. Ont. Inc.; Dir. and Past Pres. French C. of C. Can. (Ont. Sect.); mem. and former Chrmn. Internat. Law Sect. Candn. Bar Assn. (Ont.); Vice-Consul Repub. of San Marino, Toronto; co-author column Internat. Bus. Law 'Action Canada-France' and 'The Link'; mem. Candn. Tax Found.; Internat. Lawyers Assn.; Consular Corps Assn. Toronto; Law Soc. Upper Can.; Que. Bar Assn.; Bar Assn. Paris; Candn. Inst. of Internat. Affairs; extr. mem. German Bar Assn.; recreations: golf, windsurfing, skiing, reading; Club: Ontario (Past Pres.); Home: 98 Wells St., Toronto, Ont. M5R 1P3; Office: 2800, 20 Queen St. W., Toronto, Ont. M5H 3R3.

**LETTE, Jean,** M.D., C.M., ABIM, ABNM, F.A.C.P., FRCPC (cardiology), FACC, FRCPC (nuclear medicine), FCCP; physician, university professor; b. Montreal, Que. 19 Dec. 1953; e. McGill Univ. M.D., C.M. 1977; L.M.C.C. 1977; U.S. Bd. of Med. Examiners 1978; NUCLEAR MED. & NUCLEAR CARDIOLOGY STAFF PHYSICIAN, MONTREAL HEART INST. & MAISONNEUVE HOSPITAL; Assoc. Prof. of Medicine, Fac. of Medicine, Univ. of Montreal; A.B.I.M. 1983; C.S.P.Q. 1983, 1986; F.R.C.P.(C) 1983 (cardiology), 1985 (nuclear medicine); F.A.C.C. 1986; F.C.C.P. 1986; A.B.N.M. 1985; Fellow, Am. College of Physicians 1988; Mem., Rsch. Ctte., Montreal Heart Inst. 1991– ; Clin. Rsch., Maisonneuve-Rosemont Hosp. 1991– ; Radiation Protection Ctte. 1986– ; Que. Nuclear Med. Assn. 1987–92; Quality Assur. & Practice Cert. Ctte., Am. Coll. of Nuclear Physicians 1987– ; Past Pres., Standards Practice Ctte., Candn. Nuclear Med. Assn. 1988–93; resp. for Dosimetry & Radiation Course, Nuclear Med. Fellowship Prog., Fac. of Med., Univ. of Montreal 1986– ; languages: English, French, German, Spanish (spoken & written), Japanese, Italian, Chinese, Russian (some proficiency); private pilot licence; recipient of several awards; presentor/co-presentor of num. scientific presentations; author of 50 articles and 10 book chapters; Office: 5415 Assomption Blvd., Montreal, Qué. H1T 2M4.

**LETTE, Philippe J.,** B.C.L., LL.B., LL.M.; lawyer; b. Paris, France 24 March 1948; s. Raymond and Maryrose (Fontana) L.; e. St. Malachy's Sch. and Coll. Stanislas Montreal; McGill Univ. B.C.L. 1968; Univ. of Bordeaux LL.B. 1969; Superior Studies Diploma in Comparative Law, Internat. Faculty of Comparative Law, Strasbourg 1970; Graduate Studies in Private Internat. Law, Univ. of Paris I, 1971; m. Chantal Jeanclos-Darcy 5 Dec. 1974; children: Alexander, Eleonore, Arthur; FOUNDER, LETTE & ASSOCIATES (Law firm) in Paris 1972; mem., Lette & Associates (offices in Montreal, Toronto, Ottawa, Paris, Geneva and Milan); mem., Paris and Montreal Bars; mem., Internat. Commission of Paris Bar 1987– ; Candn. Tax Found.; Candn. Bar Assn.; Assn. of Foreign Lawyers in Paris; Legal Counsel to the Candn. and Swiss Embassies; Apptd. by French Gov. decree: Conseiller du Commerce Extérieur de la France 1982– ; Vice-Pres. and then Pres. (1990), France-Canada Chamber of Commerce, Paris; Prof., I.E.P. of Paris; Visiting Prof., Univ. of Florida College of Law; Internat. Arbitrator (proceedings before the Court of Arbitration of the Internat. Chamber of Commerce and ad hoc procedures); Distinctions: Honoris causa scholar, Prov. of Quebec 1969; Canada Council Scholar 1969; Named by French Gov.: Chevalier de l'Ordre Nat. du Mérite de la France 1990; Pres., McGill Grads. Soc. Paris; recipient, Distinguished Service Award, McGill Grad. Soc. 1993; recreations: contemporary art, squash, tennis, golf, ski; Clubs: Jeu de Paume et Racquets; Standard Athletic; Saint Laurent; Maxim's Business (Paris & Geneva); Société Nautique (Geneva); Adresses: (France) 52 Bd. Malesherbes, 75008 Paris; Office: 3, rue du Boccador, 75008 Paris; (Canada) 27 McNider Ave., Montreal, Que. H2V 3X4; Office: 615 Blvd. René-Lévesque West, Montreal, Que. H3B 1P9.

**LETTE, Raymond,** Q.C.; counsellor at law; e. Univ. of Toulouse grad. 1946, doctoral studies in Law 1958; m. Maryrose Fontana 14 June 1947; children: Philippe, François, Jean, Bernard; SR. PARTNER, LETTE & ASSOCIATES 1962– ; Counsellor at Law, Paris France 1946– , Montreal Que. 1956– ; Vice Pres. and Dir., Reinforced Earth Co. Ltd.; Sopexa Canada Ltd.; Dir., Rubbermaid-Allibert Canada Inc.; Henkel Canada Ltd.; Interforest Ltd.; Schmidt Printing Inks Ltd.; Sulzer Canada Inc.; Stellram Tool Co. Ltd.; Legal Counsel to diplomatic and consular reps. in Can. of Austria, Fed. Repub. of Germany, France, Great Brit., Portugal, Spain, Switzerland; cr. Q.C. 1969; Chrmn. Drafting Comn. Treaty on Applicable Law in Maintenance Matters The Hague Conf. 1973; Chrmn. Del. to Universal Postal Union Cong. 1957; Hon. Consul Gen. San Marino; co-author draft Med. Act of Que. 1968; Del. Candn. Govt. to The Hague Conf. on Private Internat. Law 1972, 1973; Comte. Chrmn. Office of Revision Que. Civil Code 1965–77; Meredith Meml. Lectr. McGill Univ. 1982; Head of Delegation, Conf. of the States Signatories of the Helsinki Treaty on Security in Co-operation in Europe, Ottawa 1985; Past Pres., TDH (Terre des Hommes) Canada Inc.; Past Vice Pres.: Nat. Theatre Sch.; Internat. Law Assn. Montreal; Assn. Mems. Consular Corps Montreal; Past Dir.: Candn. Human Rights Foundation; French Chamber Comm. Can.; Candn. German Chamber Industry & Comm. Inc.; Swiss Candn. Chamber Comm. Inc.; Siemens Electric Ltd.; mem. German Bar Assn.; named Grand Offr. Equestrian Order Sant'Agata; recipient Queen's Silver Jubilee Medal 1977; Swiss Govt. Award for Services to Swiss Confed. 1982; recreations: swimming, skiing, cycling; Home: 27 McNider Ave., Outremont, Que. H2V 3X4; Office: 1010, 615 René-Lévesque Blvd. W., Montreal, Que. H3B 1P9.

**LEUNG, Kenneth P.;** chartered accountant; b. Hong Kong 11 Nov. 1944; married; former Senior Vice-Pres., Olympia & York Devel. Limited; Dir., Royal Trustco Limited.

**LEUTHEUSSER, Hans Joachim,** Dipl.-Ing., M.A.Sc., Ph.D., P.Eng.; b. Eisenach, Germany 1 Feb. 1927; s. Gustav and Elisabeth (Gonnerman) L.; e. Techn. Hochschule Karlsruhe Dipl.-Ing. 1952; Univ. of Toronto M.A.Sc. 1957, Ph.D. 1961; m. Gudrun E.P. d. Robert and Lore Bege 10 Jan. 1955; children: Michael John, Doris Elisabeth, Suzanne Marie; PROF. EMERITUS OF MECHANICAL ENGINEERING, UNIV. OF TORONTO 1992– ; Hydraulic Design Engr., Germany & Scandinavia 1952–54; joined Mech. Eng. Dept., U. of T. 1955; Asst. Prof. 1961; Assoc. Prof. 1965; Prof. 1970–92; Vis. Prof., Univ. d'Aix-Marseille 1966–67; Univ. of Karlsruhe 1975–76; Univ. de Santiago de Chile 1983; Aristotle Univ. of Thessaloniki 1983; Univ. of Victoria 1989; Shanghai Univ. of Technol. 1990; Univ. of Tokyo 1990; teaches contg. edn. courses in engineering; consultant; Mem., APEO, ASCE, IAHR, GAMM; Ed. Bd., 'Journal of Hydraulic Research' (IAHR) 1971– ; author/co-author of over 100 tech. & sci. pubns.; Home: 6 Kilchurn Castle Dr., Agincourt, Ont. M1T 2W2; Office: 5 King's College Rd., Toronto, Ont. M5S 1A4.

**LEVENE, Sam,** B.S.S., M.S.J.; television producer; director; writer; b. Kitchener, Ont. 6 May 1936; s. Jacob Morris and Beulah (Marlow) L.; e. Northwestern Univ. B.S.S. 1958; Medill Sch. of Journalism, N.W. Univ. M.S.J. 1962; m. Aasta Ingrid Hjertholm 11 Sept. 1960; children: Juliet Ann, Nancy Karin; PRODUCER, 'MAN ALIVE' CBC 1991– ; Extve. Prod., TV Drama, CBC 1978–91; Radio Prod./D.J., WNUR-FM, Chicago 1956–58; Staff writer, CKCO-TV, Kitchener, Ont. 1958–60; CFCF-TV, Montreal 1961; Assoc. Prod., 'The Pierre Berton Show' 1962–64; Story Ed., 'This Hour Has 7 Days' CBC 1964–65; series prod., 'The Public Eye,' 'The Way It Is,' 'The Day It Is' 1965–70; Prod./Writer (93 episodes), 'Telescope,' 'Gallery' 1970–75; CBC Olympics coverage; Nat. Ballet documentary 1976; Extve. Prod., 'Prime Time,' 'Our Fellow Americans' 1975–77; Drama series incl.: 'For the Record' 1978–82; 'Vanderberg' 1982–83; Prod., TV adaptations of Stratford Fest. (5) & Shaw Fest. stage prodns. (2) 1982–86; Production Extve., 'Joshua Then & Now' 1985; Extve. Prod., TV movies: '9B,' 'Murder Sees the Light' 1986–87; Producer-Director of Arts documentaries: 'Loreena McKennitt– '; 'Oliver Jones'; 'Veronica Tennant'; 'Eurovision Young Dancers' Competition'; 'Jazz Pianist Jon Ballantyne; 'Dancer Alexander Ritter' and others 1989–1992; 'Man Alive' documentaries include: 'The Crayon Man' (Robert Coles); 'Irrepressible Robert McClure'; 'Camille Paglia'; 'Take a Giant Step'; 'Médecins sans Frontières (in Bangladesh)'; 'AIDS at Work'; 'Gambling: Selling Hope' 1991–94; 'Generation X'; recipient of numerous TV/film awards incl.: T.V. Genie for 'Certain Practices' 1980; 'Rocky' Award, Banff TV Festival, 'Final Edition' 1981; Gemini Award nominations 1986, 1987, 1989, 1990; 'Freddie' Award, Internat. Health & Medical Film Festival 1994, 'Take a Giant Step'; Mem., Acad. of Candn. Cinema & TV (Bd. of Dir. 1985–88); recreations: playing piano, jazz music, canoeing; Home: 642 Shaw St., Toronto, Ont. M6G 3L7; Office: Box 500, Station A, Toronto, Ont. M5W 1E6.

**LEVENSON, Christopher René,** M.A.; educator; writer; b. London, Eng. 13 Feb. 1934; s. Maurice René and Ellen Ethel (Pinner) L.; e. Harrow Co. Grammar Sch. for Boys 1952; Downing Coll. Cambridge, B.A. 1957; Bristol Univ. Cert. in Edn. 1962; Univ. of Iowa, M.A. 1968; m. Ursula Fischer 12 Apr. 1958; children: Martin Roger, Michael Patrick, Sebastian Roderick, Sean Dominic; remarried 1977, 1986; PROF. OF ENGLISH, CARLETON UNIV. 1968– ; Teacher, Quakersch. Eerde, Netherlands 1957–58; Lektor in Eng. Univ. of Münster, German Fed. Repub. 1958–61; High Sch. Teacher Bristol 1962–64; recipient Eric Gregory Award for Poetry 1960; author (poetry) 'In Transit' 1959; 'Cairns' 1969; 'Stills' 1972; 'Into the Open' 1972; 'The Journey Back' 1978; 'Arriving at Night' 1986; 'The Return' 1986; ed. 'Poetry from Cambridge' 1958; ed. and co-founder ARC poetry mag.; transl. 'Seeking Heart's Solace' (17th Century Dutch love poetry) 1981; 'Light of the World' (17th Century Dutch religious & occasional poetry) 1982; 'Leavetaking' and 'Vanishing Point' by Peter Weiss 1966; mem. and Founder Candn. Assn. Advanc. Netherlandic Studies; mem. League Candn. Poets (Chrmn. Internat. Ctte. 1984–86); Lit. Transls. Assn.; recreations: travel, music, visual arts; Home: 40 First Ave., Ottawa, Ont. K1S 2G2; Office: (DT - 1907), 1125 Colonel By Dr., Ottawa, Ont. K1S 5B6.

**LEVER, Alfred Beverley Philip,** B.Sc., Ph.D.; educator; research scientist; b. London, Eng., 21 Feb. 1936; s. Reginald Walter and Rose (Verber) L.; e. Imp. Coll., London Univ., B.Sc., A.R.C.S. 1957, Ph.D., D.I.C. 1960; m. Bernice Ann, d. Albert Roth, Kelowna, B.C., 19 July 1963 (div.); m. 2ndly, Dr. Elaine S. Dodsworth d. Peter Dodsworth, Nottingham, U.K. 4 Apr. 1987; children: Gordon Joseph, Melanie Signe Anne, Janet Corinne, Nicholas David; PROF. OF CHEMISTRY, YORK UNIV. since 1972; Dir. of Grad. Programme in Chem. there 1969–76; Post-doctoral Fellow, Univ. Coll. London, 1960–62; Visiting Research Assoc., Univ. of B.C., summer 1962; Lectr., Univ. of Manchester Inst. of Science & Technol., 1962–66; Visiting Research Assoc., Ohio State Univ., 1967; joined present Univ. as Assoc. Prof. 1967–72; Visiting Prof., Univ. of B.C. summer 1963, 1965; Univ. of Florence, summer 1973; Calif. Inst. of Technology, Pasadena, 1976–77; Univ. of Sydney, June-Aug. 1978; Univ. of Calabria (Italy), April/May 1983; Contract Visiting Prof., Univ. of Pavia, spring 1988; Plenary Lectr. 'IX Congress in Coordination Chemistry' (Bratislava, Czechoslovakia) 1983; 'XIV European Congress on Molecular Spectroscopy' (Frankfurt) 1979; Sec. Lectr. 'XV Internat. Conf. on Coordination Chem.' (Moscow) 1973; XIX (Prague) 1978; author 'Inorganic Electronic Spectroscopy' 1968 (2nd ed. 1984); Ed., 'Coordination Chemistry Reviews'; other writings incl. over 180 research publs.; Am. Chem. Soc.; Chem. Inst. Can. (Chrmn. Inorganic Div. 1971–72); Alcan Lecture Award (Chemical Institute of Canada) 1981; Fellow, Japan Soc. for Promotion of Sci. 1984; Co-editor: (with H.B. Gray) 'Physical Bioinorganic Chemistry' series vol. 1, 2, 1983, vol. 3, 1986, vol. 4, 5, 1989; (with C.C. Leznoff) 'Phthalocyanines - Principles and Applications' series vol. 1, 1989, vol. 2 1992, vol. 3 1993; Editor: 'Excited States and Reactive Intermediates' 1986; Co-organiser (with D.V. Stynes and C.E. Holloway) 'Biennial Inorganic Chemical Symposium,' York Univ. 1985; Invited Keynote Speaker, Chem. Inst. of Can., National Meeting, Victoria, B.C. 1989 and Edmonton, Alta. 1992; Mem. Ed. Bd. 'Inorganica Chimica Acta' 1978–88; Bitnet Blever @ Sol.Yorku.Ca; recreations: chess, music, swimming; Home: 23 Royaleigh Ave., Etobicoke, Ont. M9P 2S4; Office: 4700 Keele St., Downsview, Ont M3J 1P3.

**LEVER, Allan Norman;** diplomat; b. Port Colborne, Ont. 22 Jan. 1933; s. Norman Leo and Minnie Alma (Bates) L.; e. Port Colborne H.S.; Ryerson Inst. of Technology; m. Nora d. Harvey Eaton and Marion Hazlewood 26 June 1954; children: John, David, Gillian, Christopher; CONSUL GENERAL, CHICAGO, ILLINOIS, USA 1994– ; Sec.-Treas. & Gen. Mgr., N.L. Lever Ltd. 1954–71; Pres., State-Lever Ltd. 1960–70; Vice-Pres., Humberstone Securities 1955–65; Extve. Asst. to Min. of Energy, Mines & Resources 1971–72; Sr. Project Mgr., Export Prog. & Serv., Industry, Trade & Commerce 1972–75; Sr. Departmental Asst., Industry, Trade & Commerce 1975–77; Extve. Asst. to Sec. of State for External Affairs 1977–79; Asst. Dir. Gen., Interchange Can. & Internat. Progs. 1979–83; Min.-Counsellor Pub. Affairs, Candn. High Comn. London 1983–85; Dir., Trade Devel. Div., W. Europe Bureau 1985–89; Ambassador to the Kingdom of Saudi Arabia and the Republic of Yemen 1985–93; Charter Pres., Mech. Contractors' Assn. 1967; Charter Chair, Construction Trades Apprenticeship Ctte. 1969; Dir., Niagara Construction Assn. 1967–71; mngt. rep. on labour arbitration bds. 1965–70; Mem., Port Colborne Gen. Hosp. (Chair, Property Ctte. 1968–71); Chair, Pub. Relns., Indus. Comn., City of Colborne 1967; Mem., Commonwealth War Graves Comn. (Ldn) 1983–85;

Past Pres., Jr. C. of C.; Charter Vice-Pres. & Past Pres., Port Colborne Club; Past Pres., P. Colborne Rotary Club; Elder, Presbyn. Ch. 1954– ; recreations: sailing, swimming; clubs: Reform (U.K.), Kingston Yacht, Trident Yacht; Address: P.O. Box 500, Station 'A,' Ottawa, Ont. K1N 8T7.

**LEVERE, Trevor Harvey,** M.A., D.Phil., F.R.S.C.; educator; b. London, Eng. 21 March 1944; s. Godfrey and Vicki (Mendes da Costa) L.; e. St. Paul's Sch. London; New Coll. Oxford, B.A. 1966, M.A. 1969, D.Phil. 1969; m. Jennifer d. Johan and Phyllis Tiesing 30 July 1966; children: Kevin Christopher, Rebecca Catherine; DIRECTOR, INST. FOR HIST. & PHILOS. OF SCI. & TECHNOL. UNIV. OF TORONTO 1993– ; Lectr. present Inst. 1968, Asst. Prof. 1969, Assoc. Prof. 1974, Prof. 1981, Dir 1981–86, Dir. Museum Studies Prog. 1981–83, Fellow, Victoria Coll. 1982; Visiting Scholar, Scott Polar Rsch. Inst. 1983–84; Visiting Fellow Clare Hall, Cambridge 1983; Killam Sr. Rsch. Fellow 1975–77; John Simon Guggenheim Meml. Found. Fellow 1983–84; Fellow, Royal Soc. of Can. 1980; author: 'Affinity and Matter. Elements of Chemical Philosophy 1800–1865' 1971; 'Poetry Realized in Nature: Samuel Taylor Coleridge and Early Nineteenth-Century Science' 1981; co-author: 'Martinus van Marum. Life and Work' vol. 4 'Van Marum's Scientific Instruments in Teyler's Museum' 1973; co-ed. 'A Curious Field-Book. Science and Society in Canadian History' 1974, 'Nature, Experiment, and the Sciences,' 1990; 'Science and the Canadian Arctic: A Century of Exploration 1818-1918' 1993; ca. 60 papers scholarly journs.; Pres. Victorian Studies Assn. Ont. 1982–84; Foreign mem. Dutch Soc. Sci's; Corr. mem. Internat. Acad. Hist. Sci. (Paris); Science for Peace (Dir. 1981–82); recreations: bird watching, music; Home: 649 Broadway Ave., Toronto, Ont. M4G 2S8; Office: 316 Victoria College, Toronto, Ont. M5S 1K7.

**LEVESON, Richard Cecil,** Ph.D., D.I.C., P.Eng.; entrepreneur; b. London, Eng. 25 Feb. 1941; s. Charles Ashton and Vera Maitland (Hogben) L.; e. Chelsea Coll. Univ. of London, B.Sc. 1963, Imp. Coll. Ph.D., D.I.C. 1973; m. Mei d. Henry and Claire Lam 24 March 1967; two s. Alexis Charles, Maxwell Conrad; PRES., CHIEF EXTVE. OFFR. AND FOUNDER, PHOTOVAC INCORPORATED 1975– ; Pres., Photovac International, Long Is., N.Y.; Managing Dir., Photovac Europa, Ringsted, Denmark; Vice Pres., Intra-Space International, Downsview, Ont. 1974–75; Cons. Johnson Space Center on Apollo prog. 1975; patents issued in 7 countries for ultra-sensitive analyser system and for specialized switching valve array for gas chromatography; Mem., Assn. Prof. Engs. Prov. Ont.; recreations: classical guitar, writing, swimming, music, travel; Office: 330 Cochrane Dr., Markham, Ont. L3R 8E5.

**LEVESQUE, Albert,** B.A., B.Bibl., M.L.S.; librarian; b. Campbellton, N.B. 3 June 1933; s. John and Laura (Parent) L.; two s., Pierre-Emmanuel, Jean-Sébastien; e. Univ. of Montreal, B.A. 1959, B.Bibl. 1962; Catholic Univ. of Am., M.L.S. 1970; m. Paulette, d. Roger T. Trudeau, Montreal, Qué. 17 Oct. 1970; HEAD-LIBRARIAN, UNIV. OF MONCTON since 1973; Asst. Lib., Sém. St. Hyacinthe, Que. 1962; Founding Dir. of Lib., Nat. Univ. of Rwanda, Africa 1964–69 and Founding Dir., Rwandan Bibliographic Centre there 1970–72; Pub'l Contrib. to the Nat'l Bibliography of Rwanda 1965–1970; Office: Moncton, N.B. E1A 3E9.

**LÉVESQUE, Benoît,** M.D., M.Sc., F.R.C.P.(C); physician; b. Québec City, Qué. 24 Feb. 1957; s. Marcel and Françoise (Fontaine) L.; e. Laval Univ. M.D. 1982, Master in Exper. Med. 1990; F.R.C.P.(C) 1990; m. Jeannette d. René and Eva Mercier; one d. Mylène; PHYS. IN ENVIRONMENTAL MED. COMMUNITY HEALTH DEPT. CENTRE HOSPITALIER DE L'UNIV. LAVAL 1990– ; internship in med. Laval Univ. 1983; Phys. in Occupational Med. Community Health Dept. Centre Hospitalier Régional de la Beauce 1986; recipient Outstanding Resident Presentation Award Cong. Prevention 90, Atlanta 1990; author or co-author numerous publs.; recreations: sports, reading; Home: 460, rue Dorval, Bernières. Qué. G7A 2L3; Office: 2050, Boul. St-Cyrille Ouest, Ste-Foy, Qué. G1V 2K8.

**LEVESQUE, Hon. Denis,** B.A., Ph.B., LL.L.; judge; b. Shawinigan, Que. 8 Sept. 1930; s. Georges and Antoinette (Lord) L.; e. Semy. Trois-Rivières, Que.; Univ. of Ottawa B.A., Ph.B.; Laval Univ. LL.L.; m. Françoise Dominique, d. François Guillaume Lahaise, 31 Aug. 1957; children: Martin, Rémy, Etienne, Agnès; JUSTICE, SUPERIOR COURT (QUE.); called to Bar of Que. 1956; R. Catholic; recreations: skiing, swimming, fishing; Home: 3830 Northcliffe, Montréal, Qué. H4A 3L1; Office: Court House, Room 12.39, Montreal, Que. H2Y 1B6.

**LEVESQUE, Donald Roger,** C.A.; financial executive; b. Timmins, Ont. 31 Oct. 1941; s. Andre Joseph and Lucienne Marie (Sainte-Marie) L.; e. Queen's Univ. C.A. 1965; m. Jeanne d'Arc d. Adolphe and Lorette Labelle 29 June 1969; children: Marc, Adèle, Nicole; TREASURER & VICE-PRES., IRWIN TOY LIMITED 1968–present; C.A. student (grad.), Ross-Pope & Co. 1960–67; Comptroller, Chempac 1967; Irwin Toy Limited 1968–94 (Controller 1968–75; Budget Dir. 1975–86; Vice-Pres., Treas. 1986–94); clubs: Millcroft Golf (Treas.), River Oaks Fitness Centre; Office: 43 Hanna Ave., Toronto, Ont. M6K 1X6.

**LEVESQUE, Mt. Rev. Georges-Henri,** C.C. (1979), F.R.S.C. (R.C.); b. Roberval, Que. 16 Feb. 1903; s. Georges and Laura (Richard) L.; e. Coll. de Chicoutimi, B.A. 1923; Dominican Theol. and Philos. Coll., Lector in Sacred Theol. 1930; Univ. Cath. de Lille (France), dipl. supérieur en Sciences sociales 1932; Hon. Doctorates: Univ. of B.C. 1948; Manitoba 1950; St-Francis Xavier 1951; Toronto 1952; Western 1953; St-Joseph 1954; Saskatchewan 1961; Ottawa 1961; Laval 1963; Sherbrooke 1967; McGill 1974; Montreal 1976; Rwanda 1977; Chicoutimi 1984; o. a priest (Dominican) 15 Apr. 1928; Prof. Social Philosophy, Dominican Theol. and Philos. Coll., Ottawa 1933–38; Prof. Social Philos., Montreal Univ. 1935–39 and Laval Univ. 1935–38; Organized a sch. of social sciences at Laval Univ. and was apptd Dir. and Prof. of Econ. Philos. 1938–55; on elevation of this sch. to the rank of faculty, apptd. Dean 1943–55; Rector of Montmorency House 1955–63; Founder and first Pres. Univ. Nat. du Rwanda, Africa 1963–71, and Hon. Pres. and Advisor since 1971; Founder and first Pres. of the Conseil sup. de la Cooperation de Que. 1939–44; Founder and first Dir., 'Les Cahiers de la Faculté des Sciences sociales' 1940–47; Founder and first Dir. of the periodical 'Ensemble') 1940–46; Co-Chrmn., Royal Comn. on National Development in the Arts, Letters and Sciences 1949–51; Candn. delegate, UNESCO Conf. on Adult Educ., Elsinore (Denmark) 1949; Co-Dir., Internat. Seminar, World University, Mysore (India) 1953; Vice-Chrmn., Canada Counc. 1957–62; Candn. delegate, Conf. on World Tensions, Bahia (Brazil) 1962; mem. Que. Labour Council; Que. Economic Council; Candn. Youth Commission; Candn. Assn. for Adult Educ.; World Brotherhood, Geneva (Switz.) since 1951; Can. Polit. Science Assn. (Pres. 1951–52); F.R.S.C. since '49 (Vice-Pres. 1962–63); Internat. Assn. of Non-Governmental Orgns., Brussels (Belgium) 1955– ; Inst. of Man and Science, N.Y. Univ. 1966– ; awarded 'Predicator Generalis,' Order of the Dominicans 1943; Chevalier de la Légion d'Honneur 1950; ACFAS, Archambault Medal 1959; Internat. Coop. Medal 1964; Molson Prize, Canada Council 1966; Commander, 'Order Nat. des Mille Collines' (Rwanda) 1977; Chevalier de l'Ordre internat. de La Pleiade 1980; Officer, Compagnie des Cent-Associés 1981; Royal Bank Award 1982; Pearson Medal for Peace 1983; Offr., Ordre national du Qué. 1985; Hon. prize 'Institut des Affaires internationales' Qué. 1986; 'Fondation Edouard-Montpetit' medal Qué. 1986; Prize 'Mérite canadien Jeunesse-éducation'; author: 'Souvenances I, II, III' and several other publications; recreation: music; Address: 2715 Côte Ste-Catherine, Montreal, Que. H3T 1B6.

**LEVESQUE, Gerald;** retired corporate executive; b. Woonsocket, R.I. 24 Feb. 1926; s. Georges-Etienne and Yvonne (Lambert) L.; e. m. Anita, d. Ernest Lajoie, 29 May 1950; three s. Daniel, André, Pierre; former Pres. & Dir. Gen., Meagher's Distillery Ltd. and Gillespies and Co. Ltd.; with Coca Cola Ltd. 1949–52; Canadian Breweries Ltd. 1952–64; Vice-Pres. Marketing, Dow Brewery (Que.) Ltd. 1964–66; Vice-Pres. Marketing, Pepsi-Cola Canada Ltd. 1966–68; recreations: golf, sailing, cooking, painting; Home: 12 Woodridge Cres., Beaconsfield, Que. H9W 4G7.

**LEVESQUE, Hector Joseph,** M.Sc., Ph.D.; educator; b. North Bay, Ont. 6 Aug. 1951; s. Antoine Joseph and Aileen Margaret (Meilleur) L.; e. Univ. of Toronto, B.Sc. 1975, M.Sc. 1977, Ph.D. 1981; m. Patricia d. William and Marie Hotten 24 Aug. 1974; children: Michelle, Marc; ASSOC. PROF. OF COMPUTER SCI., UNIV. OF TORONTO 1987– ; Computer Sci. Fairchild Lab. for Artificial Intelligence Rsch. Palo Alto, Cal. 1981–84; Asst. Prof. present Univ. 1984; Fellow, Candn. Inst. Advanced Rsch. 1984– ; Cons. AT&T Bell Labs, SRI International; co-ed. 'Readings in Knowledge Representation' 1985; mem. Adv. Council Internat. Jt. Confs. on Artificial Intelligence 1986–87, recipient Computers & Thought Award 1985; Extve. Council Am. Assn. Artificial Intelligence 1987–90; mem. Philip K. Dick Soc.; recreations: music, cinema, science fiction; Home: 49 Lorraine Dr., Willowdale, Ont. M2N 2E3; Office: Toronto, Ont. M5S 1A4.

**LEVESQUE, Jacques,** B.A., B.Sc., M.A., D.ét.Pol.; political scientist, university professor; b. St-Félicien, Qué., 2 Oct. 1940; s. Dr. Jean-Marie and Georgette (Dion) L.; e. Univ. Laval, B.A. 1960; Univ. de Montréal, B.Sc. 1962, M.A. 1965; Fondation Nationale des Sciences Politiques (Sorbonne, Paris), Doctorat en Etudes Politiques 1968; m. Ghislaine, d. Gérard and Berthe Sicotte, 5 Oct. 1966; children: Marianne, Catherine, Alexandra; PROF. OF POLITICAL SCIENCE, UNIV. DU QUEBEC A MONTREAL; sen. fellow, Rsch. Inst. on Communist Affairs, Columbia Univ. 1969; rsch. fellow, Russian Rsch. Center, Harvard Univ. 1972–73; visiting scholar, Inst. of the U.S.A. and Canada, Academy of Sciences, U.S.S.R. 1975; dir. d'études associé, Ecole des Hautes Etudes en Sciences Sociales, Paris 1977–78; Visiting Prof. of Pol. Sci., Univ. of Calif., Berkeley (and Rsch. Assoc., Center for Slavic and East European Studies, U.C. Berkeley) 1985–87; Vice-Pres., Royal Soc. of Can.; Pres., Academie des Lettres et Sciences Humaines, Soc. Royale du Can.; Pres. de la Société Québecois de Science Politique 1992–93; author: 'Le conflit sino-sovietique et l'Europe de l'est' 1970; 'Le conflit sino-sovietique' 1973, 1979; 'The U.S.S.R. and the Cuban Revolution' 1978; 'L'U.R.S.S. et sa politique internationale, de Lénine à Gorbatchev' 1987; '1979–89: L'URSS en Afghanistan' 1990; co-ed.: 'Socialism in the Third World' 1975; Home: 3750 Parc Lafontaine, Montreal, Que. H2L 3M4; Office: Dept. of Political Science, Univ. du Québec à Montréal, C.P. 8888, Montréal, Qué. H3C 3P8.

**LEVESQUE, Jacques,** F.C.A.; conseiller fiscalité; né. Amqui, Qué. 10 nov. 1946; f. Roger et Thérèse (Bérubé) L.; é. Univ. Laval, lic. en sci. de l'admin. et lic. en sci. compt. 1969; C.A. 1970; ép. Louise; enfants: Christine, Sébastien; ASSOC. EN FISCALITÉ ET CONSEILLER FINANCIER, CARON BÉLANGER ERNST & YOUNG 1974– ; se joint à la soc. Bélanger Dallaire Gagnon et Assoc. 1969 (devenue Caron Bélanger Ernst & Young); nommé assoc. spéc. en fiscalité 1974; cons., Loi anti-inflation édictée par le gouv. can. 1975–79; Prof. de fiscalité, l'Univ. Laval 1977–84; mem., Ordre des C.A.s du Qué. (Titre d'admin. 1970; Comité des C.A.s de Qué. 1977–81, 1985–90; Com. sur la fiscalité 1978–82, 1985–90; Com. organ. des Congrès 1987–88; Com. des finances 1985–87; du Bur. de l'Ordre 1985–91; Vice-Prés. 1989–90; Prés. 1990–91; Com. de planification strat. 1991– ); Inst. Can. des C.A. (Groupe de travail sur le bilinguisme 1990; Com. exécutif 1990–91; Com. de nom. à la Prés. 1990, 1991; Gouv. 1988–91); La C. de c. et d'indus. du Qué. métropolitain; Assoc. Can. d'études fiscales; Assoc. de planification fiscale et finan. (Admin. 1982–86); Orch. symph. de Qué. (mem. du Conseil et Admin. 1988–89 et 1993); mem., Conseil, Caisse Populaire Laurier de Qué. 1985–90; Membre du conseil d'administration du Club de Golf de Lorette Inc., depuis 1992; auteur d'articles et de confs. sur des sujets qui touchent la réorg. d'entreprise et la planification financière; Fellow, l'ordre des C.A.s du Qué. 1989; mem., Vie de l'Ordre des C.A.s du Qué. 1991; Émérite du Comité des C.A.s de Qué. et de la France 1969; loisirs: golf, pêche, natation, ski de fond, voyages, tennis, opéra, musique classique; clubs: Club de Golf de Lorette Inc.; rés.: 11850, rue Bellerose, Montchâtel, Qué. G2A 3L8; bureau: 140, Grande Allée Est, bureau 200, Québec, Qué. G1R 5M8.

**LEVESQUE, Most Rev. Louis,** (R.C.); retired archbishop; b. Amqui (Matapédia), Que. 27 May 1908; s. Philippe and Catherine (Beaulieu) L.; e. Laval Univ., B.A. 1928, Ph.L. 1930, Th.L. 1931, Th.D. 1932; Biblical Insts., Rome and Jerusalem, S.S.L. 1935; Inst. catholique, P.P.C. 1936; taught Holy Scripture, Rimouski, 1936–52; Bishop of Hearst, Ont. 1952–64; Archbishop of Rimouski, 1964–73 Pres., Candn. Cath. Conf. 1965–67; mem., Cath. Biblical Assn. of Am.; Assn. Cath. Etudes Bibliques au Can.; mem., Congregation of Bishops (Rome) 1968–73; Address: 300 Ave. du Rosaire, Box 2020, Rimouski, Que. G5L 3E3.

**LEVESQUE, René Jules Albert,** B.Sc., Ph.D.; retired; physicist; educator; b. St. Alexis, Qué. 30 Oct. 1926; s. Albert and Elmina Louisa (Veuilleux); e. Sir George Williams Univ. B.Sc. 1952; Northwestern Univ. Ph.D. 1957; m. 6 Apl. 1956 (divorced); children: Marc, Michel, André; Pres., Atomic Energy Control Bd. 1987–93; Professor Emeritus 1987, Prof. of Physics, Univ. de Montréal 1967–87; Research Assoc. Univ. of Md. 1957–59; Asst. Prof. Univ. de Montréal 1959, Assoc. Prof. 1964–67, Dir. Nuclear Physics Lab. 1965–69, Chrmn. of Physics 1968–73, Vice Dean Faculty of Arts & Science 1973–75, Dean 1975–78; Vice Pres. (Research) 1978–85, Vice Pres. (Research & Planning) 1985–87; mem. Comn. on Higher Educ. Qué. Ministry of Educ. 1972–78, Vice Pres. 1977–78; Vice Pres. Canada-France-Hawaii Telescope Corp. 1979, Pres. 1980; Vice Pres. Assn.

Scient. Engn. & Technol. Community Can. 1979, Pres. 1980; Vice Pres. Interciencia Assn. 1979–80; Vice Pres. Natural Sciences & Engn. Research Council Can. 1981–87; mem. Atomic Energy Control Bd. 1985–87 (Pres. 1987–93); mem. Candn. Assn. Physicists (Pres. 1976–77); author numerous publs. nuclear structure field; rec'd Queen Elizabeth Silver Jubilee Medal; recreations: cycling, skiing; Home: 190 Willowdale, Outremont, Qué. H3T 1G2.

**LEVINE, Allan G.,** B.A., M.A., Ph.D.; historian/teacher; b. Winnipeg, Man. 10 Feb. 1956; s. Marvin H. and Bernice (Kliman) L.; e. Univ. of Man., B.A. 1977; Univ. of Toronto, M.A. 1979, Ph.D. 1985; m. Angela d. Alexander and Edith Tenenbein 2 Sept. 1982; one s. Alexander Jonathon; one d. Mia Beth; TEACHER OF HISTORY, ST. JOHN'S-RAVENSCOURT SCH. 1984– ; Instr., Fac. of Edn., Univ. of Man. & Rsch. for Peter C. Newman 1983–84; Univ. of Man. Dean's Honour List 1976, 1977; Bd. Mem., Camp Massad; Mem., Candn. Hist. Assn. (participant, annual meetings 1984, 1986); Jewish Hist. Soc. of West. Can.; Writers' Union of Canada; author: 'The Exchange: 100 Years of Trading Grain in Winnipeg' 1987; 'Scrum Wars: The Prime Ministers and the Media' 1993 and num. articles & book reviews; editor: 'Your Worship: The Lives of Eight of Canada's Most Unforgettable Mayors' 1989; Home: 274 Queenston St., Winnipeg, Man. R3N 0W8.

**LEVINE, Boris G.,** F.C.A.; consultant; b. 1918; e. McGill Univ. C.A. 1943; married; two children; CONSULTANT, ZITTRER SIBLIN CARON BELANGER ERNST & YOUNG; Mem., Ordre des comptables agréés du Qué. (former Pres.); Allied Jewish Community Services of Montreal (Former Pres.); Dir., Sir Mortimer B. Davis Jewish Gen. Hosp.; Fellow, Ordre des C.A.s du Qué. 1984; Office: 1 Place Alexis Nihon, Montreal, Que. H3Z 3E8.

**LEVINE, Les;** artist; b. Ireland, 6 Oct. 1935; s. Charles Solomon and Murial (McMahon) L.; e. Central Sch. of Arts & Crafts, London, Eng.; came to Can. 1957; m. Catherine Kazuko, d. Alton Kanai, Honolulu, Hawaii, 26 Aug. 1973; Artist-in-Residence, N.S. Coll. of Art & Design, 1973; Assoc. Prof., N.Y. Univ. 1971, 1972; showings: 'Send Receive' Kinsthalle Wien, Vienna Billboard Campaign 1993; 'Lose Your Life' Stadtraum Remise, Vienna 1993; 'Lose Your Life' Schloss Pasternak, Stuttgart, Germany; 'Ease Pain' NYC Billboard Campaign 1992; 'Analyze Lovers' Centraal Museum, Utrecht, Holland 1990; 'Public Mind: Les Levine's Media Sculpture and Mass Ad Campaigns' Everson Museum of Art, Syracuse, NY 1990; 'Consume or Perish and Pray for More' (NY Subway) 1989; 'Brand New' (Art Frankfurt, W. Germany) 1989; 'Les Levine's Video: A Selection From Two Decades' (International Center of Photography, NY) 1989; 'Media Projects and Public Advertisement' Mai 36 Galerie, Luzern, Switzerland 1988; one-man traveling exhbn. 'Public Mind: Les Levine's Media Sculpture and Mass Ad Campaigns' (Everson Museum of Art, Syracuse, NY) 1990; 'Blame God' (Inst. of Contemp. Art, London, Engl.) 1985; 'Media Mass' Spectacolour Light Bd., Times Square, NYC June 1985; 'Committed to Print' Museum of Modern Art, N.Y. 1988; 'Forgive Yourself' Documenta 8, Kassel, W. Germany 1987; 'Content: A Contemporary Focus 1974–1984' (Hirshhorn Museum, Washington DC) 1984; 'New Media Projects' (Isaacs Gall., Toronto) 1983; 'Einstein: A Nuclear Comedy' (videotape shown at San Francisco Video Festival 1983 and Museum of Modern Art, NY 1983); 'Ads' (Marian Goodman Gal., NY) 1980; 'Deep Gossip' and 'I Am Not Blind' (Ronald Feldman Gal., NY) 1980; 'Peggy's Cove' (Isaacs Gallery, Toronto) 1973; 'Position' (Fischbach Gallery, NY) 1972; photomedia exhn. 'The Troubles' (Finch Coll.) NY 1973; mass media 'We Are Not Afraid' (NY Subway) 1982; collections incl. Metropolitan Museum of Art, NY; Museum Modern Art, NY; Whitney Museum, NY; Philadelphia Museum; NY Cultural Center; Nat. Gall. of Can. (Ottawa); Art Gall. of Ont. (Toronto); Vancouver Art Gall.; Assoc. Ed., 'Arts Magazine' 1973–74; author 'House' 1971; 'Media: The Bio-Tech Rehearsal for Leaving the Body' 1979; other writings incl. editorials and articles in various journs.; mem., Arch. League NY (Vice Pres. 1969–71); rec'd. 1st Prize, Candn. Sculpture Biennale 1967; rec'd. Nat. Endowment for the Arts Fellowship Award 1974 & 1980; NY State Council of Arts Video Award 1980; Address: Museum of Mott Art, Inc., 20 East 20th, New York, NY 10003.

**LEVINE, Martin David,** B.Eng., M.Eng., Ph.D., D.I.C.; educator; b. Montreal, Que. 30 Mar. 1938; s. Max and Ethel (Tauber) L.; e. McGill Univ. B.Eng. 1960; M.Eng. 1963; Imperial Coll. of Sci. and Technology, Univ. of London, England Ph.D. 1965; Diploma 1965; m. Deborah, d. Samuel Tiger 6 June 1961; children: Jonathan; Barbara; PROFESSOR, DEPT. OF ELECTRICAL ENG., Dir., Center for Intelligent Machines, MCGILL UNIV. 1986– ; Asst. Prof. there 1965; Assoc. Prof. 1969; Prof. 1977; mem. Technical Staff, Jet Propulsion Lab., Calif. Inst. of Tech. 1972–73; Visiting Prof. of Computer Sci., Hebrew Univ., Jerusalem 1979–80; consultant to various govt. agencies and industrial firms; mem. Order of Engrs. of Que.; Pattern Recognition Soc.; Fellow, Inst. for Electrical and Electronic Engrs. (FIEEE) 1988; I.E.E.E. Computer Soc.; Candn. Image Processing and Pattern Recognition Soc. (founding Pres.); McGill Assn. of Univ. Teachers; Internat. Assn. for Pattern Recognition, (Pres. 1988–90); Ford Found. Fellow, Amer. Soc. Eng. Educ. 1972–73; Scientific Exchange Canada/Japan 1977; Fellow, Candn. Inst. for Advanced Rsch. FCIAR (Artificial Intelligence & Robotics Section) 1984–90; CIAR/PRECARN Assoc. 1990– ; author 'Vision in Man and Machine' 1985; co-author (with P.B. Noble) 'Computer Assisted Analyses of Cell Locomotion and Chemotaxis' 1986; over 100 journal articles and conference presentations on Biomedical Image Processing, Computer Vision, Intelligent Robotics, Artificial Intelligence; Editorial Bd.: 'Computer Vision Graphics and Image Processing: Image Understanding,' 'IEEE Trans. on Pattern Analysis and Machine Intelligence' and 'Pattern Recognition'; Gen. Ed., 'Advances in Computer Vision and Machine Intelligence'; Jewish; Home: 306 Strathearn Ave. N., Montreal W., Que. H4X 1Y4; Office: 3480 University St., Montreal, Que. H3A 2A7

**LEVINE, Norman,** M.A.; writer; b. Ottawa, Ont. 22 Oct. 1924; s. Moses Mordecai and Annie (Gurevich) L.; e. York St. Sch. and High Sch. of Comm., Ottawa; Carleton Coll., 1945; McGill Univ., B.A. 1948, M.A. 1949; m. (late) Margaret, d. late Sydney Robert and late Christine (Eldered) Payne, London, Eng., 2 Jan. 1952; children: Cass, Kate, Rachel; m. 2ndly Anne, d. late Harold and Evelyn (Sharp) Sarginson 10 Aug. 1983; Head of Eng. Dept., Boys Grammar Sch., Barnstaple, N. Devon, 1953–54; first resident writer at Univ. of N.B. 1965–66; served Overseas, with RCAF 1942–45; rank Flying Offr.; CBC film 'Norman Levine Lived Here' made in 1970; BBC film 'Norman Levine's St. Ives' 1972; author: 'The Tightrope Walker' 1950; 'The Angled Road' 1952; 'Canada Made Me' 1958, 2nd ed. 1993; 'One Way Ticket' 1961; 'From a Seaside Town' 1970, 2nd ed. 1993; 'I Don't Want to Know Anyone Too Well and other stories' 1971; 'Selected Stories' 1975; 'I Walk by the Harbour' 1976; 'In Lower Town' (story with photographs) 1977; 'Thin Ice' 1979 (reviewed by Bernard Levin in Sunday Times); 'Why Do You Live So Far Away?' (novella and stories) 1984; 'Champagne Barn' (stories) 1984; 'Ein Kleines Stückchen Blau' (selected stories – transl. by Heinrich Böll) 1971; 'Der Mann mit Dem Notizbuch' (stories) 1975; enlarged ed. 1979; 'Django, Karfunkelstein & Rosen' (stories) 1987; 'The Beat and The Still' (Images by Ron Bolt) 1990; 'Something Happened Here' (stories) 1991; writings incl. in various anthologies such as The Penguin Book of Modern Canadian Short Stories; The Oxford Book of Canadian Short Stories; Canadian Classics; Vogue's Gallery; Winter's Tales; Saturday Night; Sunday Times; Encounter; Address: c/o Penguin Books Canada, 10 Alcorn Ave., Suite 300, Toronto, Ont. M4V 2B2.

**LEVINTER, Benjamin V.,** Q.C., B.S.A., P.Ag.; b. Toronto, Ont. 16 Dec. 1925; s. Isadore and Adeline (Miller) L.; e. Ont. Agric. Coll., Univ. of Guelph, B.S.A. 1947; Osgoode Hall Law Sch. 1952; m. Marion Elizabeth d. Frederick J. Fischer 1 March 1949; children: Dara Rebecca, Jan Fredericka, Shaun (Shoshana) Judith, Loretta Noreen, Samuel Lyon; PAST CHRMN., UNITY BANK OF CANADA (charter granted 1972) and Co-founder of Bank; Sr. Counsel law firm Levinter & Levinter, certified as a specialist in civil litigation by Law Soc. of Upper Canada, read law with Isadore Levinter, Q.C.; called to Bar of Ont. 1952; cr. Q.C. 1963; Past mem., Fac. of Law Soc. of Upper Can.; Fellow, Internat. Acad. Trial Lawyers; with William Atwell founded Advocates Soc.; Past Dir., York-Finch General Hosp.; mem. Candn. Bar Assn.; Medical-Legal Soc.; County of York Law Assn.; Advocates Soc.; Assn. of Trial Lawyers of America; Ontario Trial Lawyers Assn., Medico-Legal Soc.; Agric. Inst. Can.; B'nai B'rith; Toronto Board of Trade; Fellow, Royal Commonwealth Soc.; Hebrew; recreations: farming, horses, fishing, boating; Club: Candn. Mil. Inst.; Albany; Lawyers Club of Toronto; Home: R.R. #2, Woodbridge, Ont. L4L 1A6; Office: Levinter & Levinter, 130 Adelaide St. W., Suite 2520, Toronto, Ont. M5H 3P5.

**LEVITIN, Jordan Arthur,** B.E.S., M.B.A.; market rsch. executive; b. Ottawa, Ont. 8 Apr. 1959; s. Norman and Lil (Fireman) L.; e. Carleton Univ.; Univ. of Waterloo B.E.S. (Environmental Studies) 1981; McGill Univ.; Univ. of Toronto M.B.A.; VICE PRESIDENT, THE CREATIVE RESEARCH GROUP LTD. 1991– ; Sr. Associate, Environics Research Group 1985–91; Dir. Focus Canada Omnibus 1985–91; HOMES National 1990–91; Assoc. Dir. The CROP Report, CROP Inc. 1982–85; served as Cons. Nat. Museums Can., Canada Mortgage & Housing Corp., Rehabilitation Inst. Ottawa; Policy Analyst, Dept. Regional Econ. Expansion, Ottawa; C.D. Howe Rsch. Inst. Montréal 1982; recipient Alumni Gold Medal 1981; MediaCom Scholarship; mem., Am. Assoc. of Public Opinion Rsch. (AAPOR); Profl. Mktg. Rsch. Soc. (Chrmn. membership Montréal Chapter 1983–87); Bd. of Dirs., Public Affairs Assn. of Can.; recreation: outdoor sports; Office: 100 Sheppard Ave. E., Suite 700, Toronto, Ont. M2N 6N5.

**LEVITT, Brian Michael,** B.A.Sc., LL.B.; executive; b. Montreal, Que. 26 July 1947; s. Eric and Rya L.; e. Univ. of Toronto, B.A.Sc. 1969, LL.B. 1973; m. Claire Gohier; children: Marie Anne, Katherine; PRES. & CHIEF OPERATING OFFR., IMASCO LIMITED 1993– ; Special Asst. to Provost, Univ. of Toronto 1969–73; Dir. of Interpretation, Prices & Profits Branch, Anti-Inflation Bd., Govt. of Can. 1975–76; Assoc., Osler, Hoskin & Harcourt 1976–79; Partner, Osler, Hoskin & Harcourt 1979–91; Pres., Imasco Limited 1991–93; Dir., Imasco Limited; CT Finan. Serv. Inc.; Canada Trust Co.; Westbury Candn. Life Insur. Co.; Montcrest Sch.; First Federal Savings & Loan Assn., Rochester, NY; S.E.V.E.C.; Alpha Delta Phi (Pres., Toronto Chap. 1968–69); author of various articles on business law; recreations: skiing, riding, sailing; club: Toronto Club; Caledon Ski; Donalda Club; Mount-Royal (Mtl.); Home: 489 Victoria, Westmount, Quebec H3Y 2R3; Office: 600 de Maisonneuve Blvd. W., 20th Flr., Montréal, Qué. H3A 3K7.

**LEVITT, Howard A.,** B.A., LL.B.; lawyer; b. Hamilton, Ont. 23 Nov. 1952; s. Norman and Blanche (Rosenberg) L.; e. Univ. of Toronto B.A. 1974, LL.B. 1977; m. Erin O'Connor 13 June 1992; LAWYER, HOWARD LEVITT & ASSOC. 1985– ; articled at McCarthy, Tetrault 1977; Principal, Howard Levitt & Associates, Canada (largest employment law firm); Chrmn., Law Soc. of Upper Canada Symposium on Workplace Law; Lecturer, Univ. of Toronto 1986–88; regular guest lectr. to mngt. groups across Canada; Ontario Counsel, Chretien campaign 1990; active in var. capacities in Liberal Party of Canada; Chrmn., Grimsby Conference Policy; author: 'The Law of Dismissal in Canada' 1985, 1992; Editor-in-Chief, 'Dismissal & Employment Law Digest'; Columnist, 'Toronto Star'; monthly appearance CFRP; regular contbr. to academic legal journals; Home: 106 Roxborough Dr., Toronto, Ont.; Office: 401 Bay St., Ste. 1500, Toronto, Ont. M5H 2Y4.

**LEVITT-POLANYI, Kari,** B.Sc. (Econ.), M.A.; development economist; b. Vienna, Austria 14 June 1923; s. Karl Paul and Ilona (Duczynska) Polanyi; e. Bedales Sch. Petersfield, Hants. UK; London Sch. of Econ. B.Sc. 1947; Univ. of Toronto M.A. 1959; PROF. EMERITUS, McGILL UNIV.; Visiting Prof., Consortium Graduate School of Social Sciences, Univ. of the West Indies; Ex-tve. Dir. Karl Polanyi Inst. of Pol. Econ., Concordia Univ.; Cons. UN, World Bank, Govt. Trinidad & Tobago; author: 'Silent Surrender: The Multinational Corporation in Canada' 1970; 'Input-Output Study of the Atlantic Provinces' 2 vols. 1975; numerous articles, book chapters on Third World themes, structural adjustment, debt etc.; mem. Candn. Assn. Study Internat. Devel. (Pres. 1987–88); Home: 250 rue Ste-Anne, Senneville, Qué. H9X 1N8; Office: Dept. of Economics, Rm 443, Montréal, Qué. H3A 2T7.

**LEVY, Alan W.,** B.Sc., Ph.D.; executive; b. London, Eng. 29 Jan. 1948; s. Philip and Ann (Ariel) L.; e. Univ. of Kent, B.Sc. 1969; Zenith Radio Research Corp. (U.K.) Ltd., Ph.D. (C.N.A.A.) 1972) (Rsch. Offr. 1969–72); m. Ann d. Christopher and Maureen Prendergast 29 Aug. 1972; children: Zara Naomi, Philip Anthony; PRES. AND OWNER, ALAN W. LEVY CONSULTING 1989– ; Pres. and Dir., Rose Technology Group Ltd. 1984–89; Post-Doctoral Rsch. Sci. Clarendon Lab. Oxford Univ. 1972–75; Sci. Offr. Bldg. Rsch. Est. Dept. of Environment U.K. 1975–77; Head, Energy Services Sect. Div. Bldg. Rsch. Nat. Rsch. Council Can. 1977–80; Prin. and Dir. Mktg. & Devel. Engineering Interface 1980–84; holds Candn. Patent 1,156,308 'Timed Switch for an A.C. Load,' U.S. Patent 18,959; mem. Presidents Assoc., Am. Mgmt. Assoc.; Pres., Candn. Assoc. of Energy Service Companies; Address: 46 Lauralynn Cres., Agincourt, Ont. M1S 2H5.

**LEVY, Brian,** O.D., M.Sc.; optometrist; b. S. Africa 6 June 1951; s. Jack and Celia Marcia (Wainer) L.; e. Northview High Sch. Johannesburg 1969; Univ. of Cal. Berkeley O.D. (Dr. Optometry) 1976; Univ. of Waterloo, M.Sc. 1979; m. Dianne d. Harry and Jean Kalvin 17 Dec. 1973; children: Andrea, Gary, Nicole; ASSOC. PROF. AND DIR., CONTACT LENS SERVICE, DEPT. OPHTHALMOLOGY, CALIFORNIA PACIFIC MEDICAL CENTER, San Francisco, Ca. 1989– ; Asst. Prof., Univ. of California, Berkeley 1989– ; private practive 1979–89; Head, Cornea & Contact Lens Rsch. Optometric Inst. Toronto 1982–89; mem. Clin. Faculty, Sch. of Optometry Univ. of Waterloo 1976–89; Ophthalmic Cons. Metro Toronto Assn. for Mentally Retarded 1981–89; Clin. Investigator: Polymer Technology Corp. Boston, Mass.; Bausch & Lomb Rochester, N.Y.; Allergan Pharmaceuticals, Can.; Coopervision, Mountainview, Cal.; Alcon Pharmaceuticals Fort Worth, Texas; Syntex Pharmaceutical Phoenix, Ariz.; invited lectr. in cornea & contact lenses to sci. symposia Can., USA, Eur. and Africa; author over 25 publs. refered sci. jours.; Ed., International Abstracts in Corneal and Contact Lens Research; Fellow, Am. Acad. Optometry; mem. Candn. Assn. Optometrists; Assn. Rsch. Vision & Ophthalmol.; Internat. Assn. Vertebrate Morphologists; recreation: marathon running; Home: 60 Sanders Ranch Rd., Moraga, CA 94556; Office: 2340 Clay St., San Francisco, CA 94115.

**LEVY, Earl Joseph,** Q.C., LL.B.; barrister; b. Toronto, Ont. 1 July 1937; s. Oscar and Jean (Katz) L.; e. Forest Hill Coll. Inst. 1955; Univ. of Toronto 1956–57; Osgoode Hall Law Sch. LL.B. 1963; m. Avril d. Melbourne and Irene Walker 16 July 1971; children: Justin Benjamin, Annaliese Natasha; PRIN. EARL J. LEVY, Q.C. 1963– ; cr. Q.C. 1977; frequent lectr., panelist, teacher, demonstrator, criminal law various assns., govt. depts., univs.; author 'The Examination of Witnesses in Criminal Cases' 1987, 2nd ed. 1991; mem. Bench and Bar Council 1983–90; mem. Criminal Lawyers' Assn. Ont. (Pres. 1983–89); Bencher, Law Soc. of Upper Canada 1988– ; mem., Toronto Regional Courts Management Advisory Ctte.; mem. Attorney General's Adv. Ctte. on Charge Screening, Disclosure and Resolution Discussions; Certified by Law Society of Upper Canada as a Specialist in Criminal Litigation; recreations: reading, exercising, movies, theatre, classical music; Office: 250 Yonge St., P.O. Box 24, Suite 2600, Toronto, Ont. M5B 2M6.

**LEVY, Gary Edmund,** B.A., M.A., Ph.D.; editor, university professor; b. Saskatoon, Sask. 3 April 1946; s. Bernard and Rose (Mazer) L.; e. Univ. of Saskatchewan B.A. 1967; Carleton Univ. M.A. 1969; Laval Univ. Ph.D. 1974; m. Elena d. Alexei and Valentina Sazanova 1991; EDITOR, 'CANADIAN PARLIAMENTARY REVIEW' 1980– ; Researcher, Research Br., Library of Parliament 1971–80; Consultant & Advisor to cttes. of the House of Commons & Senate; Prof. of Political Science, Univ. of Western Ont. 1990–93; Visiting Prof., Univ. of B.C. 1977; Lecturer, Ottawa Univ. 1974–76, 1987–88; Visiting Fellow Americas Soc., Donner Foundation 1988–89; author: 'Speakers of the House of Commons' 1980; coeditor: 'Provincial and Territorial Legislatures in Canada' 1989, 'Making North America Competitive' 1989; Home: 1402 Lowen Dr., Ottawa, Ont. K1G 3N3; Office: P.O. Box 574, Stn. B, Ottawa, Ont. K2P 5P7.

**LEVY, Julia G.,** Ph.D., F.R.S.C.; educator; b. Singapore 15 May 1935; d. Guillaume Albert and Dorothy Frances (Brown) Coppens; e. Magee High Sch. Vancouver 1952; Univ. of B.C., B.A. (Hons.) 1955; Univ. Coll., Univ. of London Ph.D. 1958; m. Edwin s. Edwin and Marie Levy 13 June 1969; children: Nicholas Gerwing, Benjamin Gerwing, Jennifer; PROF., DEPT. OF MICROBIOL. 1973– and HEAD OF MICROBIOLOGY, UNIV. OF B.C.; Vice Pres. of Rsch. & Devel., Quadralogic Technologies Inc. 1986– (Prin. (Dir.) 1981– ); Instr. present Univ. 1958, Asst. Prof. 1962, Assoc. Prof. 1967, Prof. 1972; Pres., Candn. Soc. of Immunology 1980–82; Candn. Fed. of Biol. Sci. 1983–84; Cons., Monsanto Chem. 1978–80; Allied Chem. 1985–87; Triton Biosci. 1986–87; Dir., Helix Biosci. 1988– ; recipient Bieley Rsch. Award 1980; Fellow, Royal Soc. Can. 1980; B.C. Sci. Counc., Gold Medal for Med. Rsch. 1982; Killam Sr. Travel Fellowship 1982–83; Killam Sr. Rsch. Prize 1986; M.R.C. Indus. Professorship 1987–90; D.U. (Hon.), Univ. of Ottawa 1989; D.Lit. (Hon.) Mount St. Vincent's Univ. 1990; author over 120 sci. articles in peer reviewed journs., chaps. in scholarly texts & pub. symposium talks; recreations: tennis, camping, swimming; Club: Arbutus; Office: 6174 University Blvd., Westbrook Bldg., Rm 27, Vancouver, B.C. V6T 1Z3.

**LEVY, Kurt Leopold,** M.A., Ph.D., F.R.S.C.; educator; b. Berlin, Germany 10 July 1917; s. Anton and Toni (Moses) L.; e. Univ. of Toronto B.A. 1945, M.A. 1946, Ph.D. 1954; m. Enid d. Sidney and Ethelyn Gourlay 6 June 1947; children: Leslie, Judy, Andrew, Bruce, Jennifer; EMERITUS PROF. OF SPANISH & PORTUGUESE, UNIV. OF TORONTO 1984– ; Instr. in Spanish & Portuguese present Univ. 1945, Lectr. 1950, Asst. Prof. 1955, Assoc. Prof. 1961, Prof. 1965–84 (Assoc. Chrmn. of Dept. and Chrmn. Latin Am. Studies Prog. 1965–70, Chrmn. of Dept. 1978–83); Visiting Prof. Univ. of Ariz. summer 1962; Univ. del Valle, Cali, Colombia 1971–73; Instituto Caro Y Cuervo 1972, 1974; Visiting Prof. Shanghai International Studies Univ. Sept.-Dec. 1985; recipient Star of Antioquia, Prov. of Antioquia 1973; Symbolic Hatchet, City of Medellín, Colombia 1973; Nat. Distinguished Leadership Award in Foreign Lang. Edn. N.Y. Assn. Foreign Lang. Teachers 1982; Canada's Birthday Achievement Award 1983; Order of San Carlos, Colombia 1984; Order of Henry the Navigator, Portugal 1984; Distinguished Service Award 'in honour of unique contributions to the teaching of Spanish and Portuguese' Am. Assn. of Teachers of Sp. and Portug. 1985; Order of 'Pedro Justo Berrío', Prov. of Antioquia 1989; 'Culture Worker' Medal, Institute of Cultural Integration, Medellín 1991; author: 'Vida y obras de Tomás Carrasquilla' 1958; 'Tomás Carrasquilla' 1980; 'Efe Gómez' 1992; ed.: 'Book List on Latin America for Canadians' 1969; 'Kurt L. Levy - Benigno A. Gutiérrez, Correspondencia' 1989; 'Tomás Carrasquilla, La Marquesa de Yolombó' critical ed. 1974; co-ed.: 'El ensayo y la crítica literaria en Iberoamérica' 1970; 'Calderón and the Baroque Tradition' 1985; 'Camões and His Times' 1987; 1st Pres., Ont. Chapter Am. Assn. Teachers Spanish & Portuguese 1952–54; Pres. Intnl. Inst. Latin Am. Lit. 1967–69; 1st Pres., Candn. Assn. Latin Am. Studies 1969–71; Pres., Candn. Assn. Hispanists 1974–76; Home: 11 Rathnelly Ave., Toronto, Ont. M4V 2M2; Office: 21 Sussex Ave., Toronto, Ont. M5S 1A1.

**LEVY, Steven S.,** B.A., M.S.W., Ph.D.; promotion/marketing executive; b. Montreal, Que. 5 Apr. 1944; s. Lionel and Ann (Kerr) L.; e. McGill Univ., B.A. 1967, M.S.W. 1969; Univ. of Toronto, Ph.D. 1977; m. Laura Cope; children: Adam, Shauna; CO-FOUNDER (with Martin Rumack), FESTIVAL OF CANDN. FASHION 1985; Social Worker, sev. Mtl. agencies 1969–74; Co-founder (with Martin Rumack), 'The One of a Kind Canadian Craft Show' 1975; part-time Lectr., Univ. of Toronto 1991–93, York Univ. 1975–77, Ryerson 1979–83; Owner/op., The Levy-Coughlin Partnership 1979–85; Co-Founder (with Martin Rumack) The Schools and Skills Show 1992; Bd. Mem., Ontario Musical Arts Centre; Mem., City of Toronto, Fashion Indus. Liaison Ctte.; Past Mem., Candn. Nat. Exhib. Assn.; Past Bd. Mem., Chinese Translation & Interpreter Serv., The Jewish Community Ctr.; author of acad. articles; recreations: exercise, squash; Club: YMCA; Office: 66 Dupont St., Toronto, Ont. M5R 1V2.

**LEWIS, Andre Leon;** assoc. artistic director; b. Hull, Que. 16 Jan. 1955; s. Raymond Lincoln and Therese (Delisle) L.; e. Univ. of Ottawa, Kinanthropology; ASSOC. ARTISTIC DIRECTOR, ROYAL WINNIPEG BALLET 1990– ; joined Royal Winnipeg Ballet as Corps de Ballet 1979; Soloist 1982; Artistic Coordinator 1984; Interim Artistic Director, 1989; teaches in the Royal Winnipeg Ballet Sch. and has coached many of the ballets in the company repertoire; has guested extensively with Evelyn Hart around the world & notably at Tehoy Kovsky Hall in Moscow for a special gala in her honour; Office: 380 Graham Ave., Winnipeg, Man. R3C 4K2.

**LEWIS, Claude Wilson;** satellite broadcasting executive; b. Kemptville, Ont. 22 Jan. 1936; s. Amond A. and Dorothy M. (Wilson) L.; e. Kemptville High Sch. 1954; Ryerson Polytech. Inst. Radio & TV Arts Cert. 1957; Cert. Advtg. Agency Practioner; m. Barbara d. William and Gertrude Cox 27 Aug. 1960; children: Jeffrey, Douglas, Cheryl; EXTVE. VICE PRES. CANADIAN SATELLITE COMMUNICATIONS INC., Cancom Satellite Network Services Co. 1984– ; joined James Lovick Advertising 1957–64; Lesser Studio Ltd. and Film Art Corp. 1964–69; Dir. Pub. Affairs, Vice Pres. & Gen. Mgr. S.B. McLaughlin Associates Ltd., Caledon Mountain Properties Ltd. 1969–79; Pres. All-View Network One Inc. 1979–81; Extve. Vice Pres. Northstar Home Theatre Inc. and Mktg. Dir. Canadian Teleconference Network 1981–84; mem. Soc. Satellite Profls. Internat.; United Church; recreations: skiing, squash; Club: Albany; Home: 1385 Birchwood Rd. W., Mississauga, Ont. L5J 1T3; Office: 50 Burnhamthorpe Rd. W., Mississauga, Ont. L5B 3C2.

**LEWIS, David Andrew,** B.Com., S.M.; banker; b. Toronto, Ont. 26 Feb. 1937; s. George Dimmick and Kathleen Emma (Nettelfield) L.; e. Univ. of Toronto Schs. 1955; Univ. of Toronto B.Comm. 1959; Mass. Inst. of Technol. S.M. 1967; m. Penelope Anne d. Robert Christopher Dobson and Grace Pedlar (Northwood) Toronto, Ont. 12 June 1959; children: David Nettelfield, Jennifer Robinson, Christopher Dobson; Chrmn., Ontario Training Corp.; Depy. Chrmn., Key Publishers Co. Ltd.; Pres., Continental Bank of Can.; Chrmn., Books for Business Ltd.; Dir.: The Caldwell Partners International; Coscan Developments Corp.; The Consolidated Enfield Corp. Ltd.; Key Porter Books Ltd.; RCC Ltd.; Slough Estates Canada Ltd.; Quartex Corp.; Midland Walwyn Inc.; joined Imperial Bank of Canada, Toronto 1959; after management positions in Toronto and Alberta, became Senior Vice Pres. in 1973; joined Continental Bank of Canada as Dir., Extve. Vice Pres. and Chief Oper. Offr. 1981, Pres. & Chief Oper. Offr. 1982, Pres. & C.E.O. 1984, Chrmn. & C.E.O. 1986; Vice-Chrmn. & Dir., Lloyds Bank of Canada 1986; Chrmn. & Dir., Midland Doherty Financial Corp. 1989; Dir. & Past Chrmn., United Way of Canada; Trustee, Metropolitan Toronto Community Found.; The Tarragon Theatre; Adv. Counc., Salvation Army; Gov., Stratford Shakespearean Festival; Past Chrmn. Ctte., United Way of Greater Toronto, Harbourfront Centre; Anglican; recreations: skiing, golf, sailing; Clubs: Toronto; Toronto Golf; Badminton & Racquet; Home: 60 Warren Rd., Toronto, Ont. M4V 2R5.

**LEWIS, David James,** B.A., M.D., F.R.C.P.(C); psychiatrist; educator; b. Montreal, Que. 28 May 1920; s. David Sclater and Evelyn Doris (Ross) L.; e. Selwyn House Sch. 1934; Trinity Coll. Sch. Port Hope, Ont. 1937; McGill Univ. B.A. (Hons. English) 1941; Univ. of Toronto M.D. 1950; m. Catherine d. Wilson and Dorothy Jefferson 20 Dec. 1949; children: David W.R., Anne S., Peter J., Jane A. Squier, Naomi C.; Prof. Emeritus of Psych., Univ. of Calgary 1985; Internship Toronto Gen. Hosp. 1950–51, Sunnybrook Hosp. 1951–52; psychiatric residency Henry Phipps Clinic, Johns Hopkins Hosp. 1952–54; Sr. House Offr. and postgrad. student Bethlem Royal and Maudsley Hosp. 1954–56; Jr. Psychiatrist St. Michael's Hosp. Toronto 1956–65; Clin. Teacher to Asst. Prof. Psychiatry Univ. of Toronto 1956–65; Psychiatrist, Royal Victoria Hosp. Montreal 1965–71; Psychiatrist, Foothills Hosp., Calgary 1971–90; Assoc. Prof. of Psychiatry, McGill Univ. 1965–72, Co-ordinator Post Grad. Edn. in Psych. 1965–71; Clin. Dir. Allan Meml. Inst. Montreal 1965–71; Prof. of Psychiatry, Univ. of Calgary 1971–85, Acting Head of Psych. 1976–77, 1979–81; Dir. Affective Disorders Clinic, Foothills Hosp. 1978–84; served with RCNVR WWII, rank Lt.-Commdr. RCNR (retired), Mentioned in Dispatches 1942; Gov. Royal Humane Soc.; Cons. Montreal Rehab. Inst., St. Anne's Mil. Hosp., Ogdensberg State Hosp., Banff Mineral Spring Hosp., Orgn. Alberta Psychiatric Travelling Clinics; author or co-author 46 profl. and sci. publs., 65 profl. presentations; Guest, Candn. Psychoanalytic Assn.; M.R.C.(Psych.); LFAPA; recreations: bibliophile, visual arts, jogging, writing; Club: Candn. Alpine; Home: Serendip, P.O. Box 17, Site 3, R.R.l, Calgary, Alta. T2P 2G4.

**LEWIS, Donald Pryce,** B.Comm., C.A.; management consultant; b. Saskatoon, Sask. 17 July 1931; s. Llewelwyn Lawson and Hazel Irene (Sidle) L.; e. Univ. of Toronto, B.Comm. 1954; m. Beverley d. William and Alice Butler 18 Feb. 1955; children: Janet B., Peter B., William D.; PRINCIPAL, SIBSON & CO. 1985– ; Coopers & Lybrand to 1967; Vice-Pres., Johnson & Higgins Willis Faber 1967–73; Partner, Hay Mngt. Cons. 1974–85; Past Bd. Chrmn., Candn. Scholarship Trust Consultants; Past Bd. Chrmn., Candn. Scholarship Trust Found.; Anglican; recreations: tennis, golf, gymnastics, cross-country skiing; clubs: National; Rosedale Golf; Fitness Inst.; Home: 109 Munro Blvd., Willowdale, Ont. M2P 1C7; Office: P.O. Box 110, Scotia Plaza, 40 King St. W., Toronto, Ont. M5H 3Y2.

**LEWIS, Hon. Douglas Grinslade,** P.C., F.C.A., Q.C., M.P.; politician; b. Toronto, Ont. 17 Apr. 1938; s. Horace Grinslade and Brenda Hazeldine (Reynolds) L.; e. N. Toronto Coll. Inst. 1957; Univ. of Toronto, C.A. 1962; Osgoode Hall Law Sch., LL.B. 1967; m. Linda Diane Haggans 14 July 1962; children: Justin, Matthew, Penny, Gillian, Susan; Solicitor General of Canada 1991–93 & Govt. House Leader, Min.-Designate of Public Security 1993; el. Fellow, Inst. of C.A.'s 1982; cr. Q.C. 1984; el. to H. of C. for Simcoe North g.e. 1979, re-el. since; Parlty. Sec. to Min. of Supply & Services 1979, to Pres. of Treasury Bd. 1984, to Pres. of Privy Council 1985 and to Depy. Prime Min. and Pres. of the Queen's Privy Council for Can. 1986–87; Min. of State (Depy. House Leader) & Min. of State (Treasury Bd.) 1987–88; Min. of Justice, Attorney General, and Government House Leader, 1989–90; Min. of Transport 1990–91; Acting Pres. of the Treasury Bd. 1988; Dep. Opposition House Leader 1981, Opposition House Leader 1983; Pres., Toronto Jr. Bd. Trade 1967–68; Ont.

Jaycees 1970–71; Candn. Jaycees 1971–72; Vice pres. Simcoe East P.C. Assn. 1974–78, Pres. 1978; Vice Pres. Simcoe North P.C. Assn. 1975–78; United Church; Home: Box 535, Orillia, Ont. L3V 6K2.

**LEWIS, Fred A.;** farmer; b. London, Ont. 2 Sept. 1938; s. Clarence C. and Janet K. (Raycraft) L.; e. Ridgetown Coll. of Agricultural Tech.; m. Anne d. Charles and Gayle Cronyn 28 Dec. 1967; children: Julie, Brian; recreations: golf, boating; OWNERS, FRANS LIVESTOCK LTD.; Salesman, then territory manager for a livestock feed company after grad.; returned to farming in home county to build business up to 1500 acres of land with beef & poultry business as well; Chair, Farm Debt Review Panels 1987–92; Mem., Farm Drainage Tribunal (Ont.); Dir., Ont. Corn Producers; Ont. Chicken Producers Mktg. Bd.; Chair, Ausable Bayfield Conservation Authority 3 years; Chair, Ont. Farm Implements Bd. 1988– ; Roman Catholic; Reeve of London Twp. 1978–82; Warden, Co. of Middlesex 1980; Chair, Assn. of Conservation Authorities 1992–93; recreations: golf, boating; club: London C. of C.; Address: R.R. 2, Denfield, Ont. N0M 1P0.

**LEWIS, John Monk;** investment executive; b. Montreal, Que. 28 June 1924; e. McGill Univ. B.A. 1949; Khaki Coll. 1945–46; m. Joan Kalteissen Hart 7 Oct. 1978; children: Eve, Suzanne, Catherine, Duncan, Michelle, Nicole; stepchildren: Lisa and Christopher Hart; VICE-PRES., ROYAL BANK INVESTMENT MANAGEMENT INC.; Club: National; Home: 31 Winchester St., Toronto, Ont. M4X 1A6; Office: P.O. Box 70, Royal Bank Plaza, Toronto, Ont. M5J 2J2.

**LEWIS, Michael James,** B.Sc., M.B.A.; retail executive; b. St. Thomas, Ont. 18 Dec. 1950; s. Glen Patrick and Rose Catherine (Malik) L.; e. Queen's Univ. B.Sc. (Chem. Eng.) 1973; York Univ. M.B.A. 1977; m. Krystyna d. George and Margaret Ballantyne 6 May 1972; children: Shannon Nicole, Jessica Katherine; PRES., MANCHU WOK (div. of Scott's Food Service Inc.) 1993– ; Senior Consultant, CLC Candn. Mktg. Assoc. 1981–85; Vice-Pres., No Frills Division, Loblaws Supermarkets Ltd. 1985–89; Pres., Willson Stationers (div. of Federal Industries Ltd.) 1989–92; Mem., APEO; recreations: skiing (CSIA Level II Ski Instructor), squash; Home: 115 Melrose Ave., Toronto, Ont. M5M 1Y8.

**LEWIS, Raymond George;** executive; b. London, Eng. 15 Sept. 1931; s. Henry William and Alice Jane (Robertson); e. London, Eng.; m. Rosemary, d. Capt. Leslie C.M. Blackman, R.A., 28 Apr. 1955; children: Sandra Christine; Christopher Mark; CHRMN. & C.E.O., RACAL-CHUBB CANADA LIMITED 1978– ; Dir. & Sr. V.P., Racal Corp. (U.S.); Dir., Racal-Chubb Ltd. (U.K.); Engineer, Lucas Group (London, Eng.) 1953; Works Dir., Pyrene Can. Ltd. 1959; mem. Bd. 1970; Pres., Chubb Fire Security 1971; Vice-Pres., Chubb-Mosler & Taylor Holdings Ltd. 1973; Pres., Chubb-Mosler & Taylor Safes; Extve. Vice-Pres., Chubb Industries Ltd. 1976; Pres. 1977; served in R.A.F., attached to U.S. 5th Airforce (Korea) 1951–52; Assoc. Mem., Candn. Assn. Chiefs of Police; mem., Candn. Fire Equipment Mfg. Assn. (Pres. 1971–73); Club: Ontario; Home: Spring Rd., Clarkson, Ont. L5J 1M9; Office: 5201 Explorer Dr., Mississauga, Ont. L4W 4H1.

**LEWIS, Maj. Gen. Reginald William;** C.M.M., C.M., O.St.J., C.D.; public utility executive; b. London, Eng. 31 May 1930; s. George Edward and Aileen Lillian (Gladman) L.; e. Brixham 1942; S.E. London Tech. Coll. Eng. Dipl. 1948; Cert. Gen. Acct. 1962; Fellow, Chartered Inst. Secs. And Admin. 1965; Prof. Adm. 1982; m. Sheila Ethelyn d. Henry and Ethelyn O'Rourke 4 July 1959; PRES. AND C.E.O., TORONTO ECONOMIC DEVELOPMENT CORP. 1986– ; C.E.O., Parking Authority of Toronto 1974–90; Pres., Toronto New Business Centre 1989– ; Student in Accts. 1950–54; Lloyds Bank-Imperial Bank of Canada 1954–55; Parking Authority of Toronto 1955–90; Brit. Army Nat. Service 1948–50; UK, Greece, Turkey, Eritrea, Brit. Army Reserve 1950–54; Candn. Army Active Reserves 1954–90; Pres., Royal Candn. Ordnance Corps. Assn. 1968–69; Chrmn. Conf. Defence Assns. 1972; Pres., Candn. Forces Logistics Assn. 1974; Commdr., Central Militia Area 1975–78; Vice Chrmn. for Can., Interallied Confed. Reserve Offrs. NATO 1978–81; Special Projects Offr. Reserve Forces Counc. Nat. Defence HQ 1982–85; Chief of Reserves Candn. Armed Forces 1985–87; International Pres., Interallied Confed. Reserve Offrs. NATO 1988–90; Hon. Colonel, Royal Regiment of Canada 1991– ; Pres., Internat. Inst. & Mun. Parking Cong. 1979–80; Pres., Good Neighbours' Club Aged Men (United Appeal) 1979–81; Dir. and Treas. Ont. Charities' Lottery Group Inc. 1980–81; Treas., mem. Extve. and Chrmn. Finance Ctte. Easter Seals Soc. 1981–82; Pres. Imp. Offrs. Assn. Can. 1981–82; Pres. Toronto Sesquicentennial Bd. 1984; Chrmn., Home Care Metrop. Toronto 1985–88; Chrmn. Toronto Br., Royal Commonwealth Soc. 1987–88; Pres., Ont. Counc. Duke of Edinburgh Awards 1987–89; Finance Ctte. Ont. Counc. St. John Ambulance 1984– ; Vice Chrmn., Candn. Corps Commissionaires 1991– ; Vice-Pres., Atlantic Council of Canada 1991–93; Pres., Fort York Br. Royal Candn. Legion 1992–93; Chrmn. Empire Club of Canada Foundation 1992–94; Candn. Forces Decoration; Centennial Medal 1967; Queen's Silver Jubilee Medal 1977; recipient Commemorative Plaque City of Amsterdam 1980; Citation Merit Interallied Confed. Reserve Offrs. 1981; Kt. Order Lazarus; Kt. Grand Cross, Sovereign Mil. Order St. John Jerusalem; Special Commendation City of Toronto 1985; Order of St. John 1986; Member, Order of Canada 1986; Commander, Order of Military Merit 1986; Medal of Service City of Toronto 1991; recreations: sailing, skiing; Clubs: Empire (Pres. 1978–79); Canadian; Royal Candn. Mil. Inst. (Pres. 1983–84); Royal Candn. Yacht; Home: 21 Buckingham Ave., Toronto, Ont. M4N 1R3; Office: 50 Cumberland St., 4th Flr., Toronto, Ont. M4W 1J5.

**LEWIS, Robert,** B.A.; journalist; b. Montreal, Que. 19 Aug. 1943; s. Leon R. and Margaret (Horan) L.; e. Loyola Coll. B.A. 1964; m. Sara d. Dr. James H. and Madelene (Hersey) O'Neill 27 May 1967; children: Christopher Robert, Timothy O'Neill; EDITOR, MACLEAN'S MAGAZINE 1993– ; Gen. Reporter Montreal Star 1964–65; Ottawa Corr. Montreal Star 1965–66; Montreal Bur. Chief Time Magazine 1967–68, Ottawa Corr. 1968–70; Boston Corr. 1970–72, Toronto Bur. Chief 1972–74; Ottawa Bur. Chief Maclean's Magazine 1975–82; Managing Editor, Maclean's Magazine 1982–93; Home: 31 Brooke Ave., Toronto, Ont. M5M 2J5; Office: 777 Bay St., Toronto, Ont. M5W 1A7.

**LEWIS, Stephen;** b. Ottawa, Ont. 11 Nov. 1937; s. the late David, Q.C. (former Fed. Leader of New Democratic Party) and Sophie (Carson) L.; m. Michele Landsberg 30 May 1963; children: Ilana, Avram, Jenny; Candn. Ambassador to United Nations 1984–88; apptd. Special Advisor to UN Secretary-General on African Economic Recovery 1986–91; apptd. Barker Fairley Distinguished Visitor in Candn. Culture, University Coll., Univ. of Toronto 1988–90; apptd. Special Representative of UNICEF 1990; 1st el. to Ont. Leg., 25 Sept. 1963; Leader of Ont. N.D.P. 1970–78; became Leader of the official opposition in the Leg. 18 Sept. 1975; resigned seat 10 Nov. 1978; Address: 6 Montclair Ave., Toronto, Ont. M4V 1W1.

**LEWIS, Stephen M.,** B.Sc.; real estate executive; b. London, England 13 June 1954; s. Solly and Elizabeth Bessie (Lyons) Lewis; e. Univ. of Toronto B.Sc. 1976; m. Judith Shelley d. the late Saul and Florence (Cosman) Weinstein 10 June 1990; children: Jessie Rachel, Saul Adam; EXTVE. VICE PRES. & CHIEF FINAN. OFFR., LEHNDORFF GROUP 1988– ; Jr. Accountant, present firm 1976; Controller, Land Devel. Div. 1977; Controller Corp. Ownership Entities 1980; Vice Pres. Finan. 1987; Dir., Lehndorff 1988– ; recreations: tennis, golf; Home: 236 Deloraine Ave., Toronto, Ont. M5M 2B3; Office: 360 Bay St., Toronto, Ont. M5H 2V6.

**LEWIS, Victor Stanley George,** P.Eng., Hon. Maj.; retired executive; b. Birmingham, Eng. 10 June 1919; s. Mark George and Nellie (Webster) L.; e. Coll. Sch. Saltley 1924; Birmingham Tech. Coll. 1933 Higher Nat. Cert., Mech. Engn. with Endorsements 1939; m. Lucille Joan d. Nicholas Karlicki, Winnipeg, Man. 4 Feb. 1971; children: Mark Victor, Andrea Jodi; by previous marriage, Peter Noel, Simon Andrew, Julia Susan; joined Brit. Army 1939, served as Engr. with Armd. Divisions, N. Africa 1941–47, rank Maj., War Office 1947–50, Germany 1950–53, NATO Exchange Offr. Can. 1953–55, Depy. Asst. Dir. Mech. Engn. War Office 1955–57; resigned comn. and emigrated to Can. 1957; Partner Wilmac Construction 1957–58; Gen. Mgr. Calgary Suburban Developments 1958–59; Extve. Vice Pres. Engineered Homes 1959–66; Pres. Genstar Development Co. 1966–84; Pres. Urban Devel. Inst. Alta. 1960–62; Candn. Home Mfrs. Assn. 1967–69; Urban Devel. Inst. Can. and Urban Devel. Inst. Man. 1967–69; Urban Devel. Inst. B.C. 1973–75; Consultant to Govt. of B.C. on Privatization of B.C.E.C. Land 1988–90; presented papers Candn. Trade Mission France, Germany and U.K. 1964; Head, Candn. Trade Mission to Spain, France, Germany and U.K. 1965; honoured by City of Calgary for indust. expansion 1966 and by Prov. Man. for contrib. to planning econ. devel. of prov. 1969; rec'd Queen's Silver Jubilee Medal 1978; mem. Inst. Mech. Engrs.; Assn. Prof. Engrs. B.C.; Pres. Surrey Chamber of Comm. 1981–83; Pres. Arts Council of Surrey & District 1983–84; Pres., Surrey Symphony Soc. 1985–86; Anglican; recreations: music, gardening, swimming; Home: 14636 – 55A Ave., Surrey, B.C. V3S 1B1.

**LEXCHIN, Joel Raymond,** M.D., C.C.F.P.(E.M.), DABEM; physician; b. Toronto, Ont. 8 Jan. 1948; s. Edward and Ann (Greenspan) L.; e. Univ. of Toronto B.Sc. (Hons.) 1971, M.Sc. 1974; M.D. 1977; m. Catherine d. Laurence and Margaret Oliver 11 May 1984; one d. Esther, one s. David Oliver; ACTIVE STAFF, EMERGENCY DEPT., THE TORONTO HOSPITAL 1988– ; Family practice residency, Dalhousie Univ. 1977–79; Courtesy Staff, Dept. of Emergency Care, Hamilton Civic Hosps.; Certificant, Special Competence in Emergency Med., C.C.F.P. 1984; Diplomate, Am. Bd. of Emergency Medicine 1992; Mem., Med. Reform Group of Ont.; Health Action Internat./Can.; Candn. Coll. of Family Phys.; Candn. Assn. of Emerg. Phys.; N.Z. Med. Assn.; author: 'The Real Pushers: A Critical Analysis of the Canadian Drug Industry' 1984, 'Canadian Encyclopedia' 2nd ed., pharm. indus. entry 1988; Home: 121 Walmer Rd., Toronto, Ont. M5R 2X8; Office: 399 Bathurst St., Toronto, Ont. M5T 2S8.

**LEY, Dorothy Corinne Hobbs,** M.D., F.R.C.P.(C), F.A.C.P.; physician; b. Toronto, Ont. 4 Apl. 1924; e. Univ. of Toronto M.D. 1948, B.Sc. (Med.) 1951; Fellow, Royal Coll. of Physicians (Canada) 1956; Fellow, Am. Coll. of Physicians 1965; CHRMN. & PRES., THE DOROTHY LEY HOSPICE, Toronto 1990– ; Dir. Casey House Hospice for AIDS Toronto 1985–90; Chrmn. Ad Hoc Long Term Care Liaison Ctte.; Chrmn. Candn. Coalition on Medication Use and the Elderly; Vice Chrmn. Internat. Work Group on Death, Dying & Bereavement; formerly Attending Phys. and Dir. Hematol. Toronto W. Hosp.; Asst. Prof. of Med. Univ. of Toronto; Designer Lab. Proficiency Testing Prog. Sect. Lab. Med. Ont. Med. Assn. 1972–76, mem. Extve. Sect. Palliative Care; Founder and Pres. Toronto Med. Labs. Ltd. (now MDS Group); Founder, Pres. & Chief Extve. Offr. Palliative Care Found. 1981–86; Chrmn. Candn. Med. Assn. Ctte. Health Care Elderly 1984–87 and of Implementation Ctte. CMA Report Health Care Elderly 1988–89; recipient Queen's Silver Jubilee Medal 1977; CMA Medal of Service; Neville Hodson Walker Award Ont. Med. Assn. 1989; Commdr. Order St. Lazarus Jerusalem 1989; author numerous publs.; Alpha Omega Alpha; Chrmn., Coll. Bishops Task Force AIDS Diocese of Toronto Anglican Church Can., mem. Planning Ctte.; Mem., Diocesan Synod (Toronto) Anglican Church of Can.; Mem. Extve., Provincial Synod (Ont.) Anglican Church of Can.; Mem. Extve., Ont. Palliative Care Assn. 1991– ; Chair, Metro Toronto District Health Council Task Force on Palliative Care 1992– ; recreations: golf, gardening; Address: P.O. Box 430, Beaverton, Ont. L0K 1A0.

**LEYRAC, Monique,** C.C.; singer, actress; b. Montreal, Que. 26 Feb. 1928; m. Jean Dalmain, 1952; trained in elocution and studied theatre with Jeanne Maubourg, Montreal; made debut as actress (Le Chant de Bernadette) on Radio 1944; toured France, Switzerland, Belgium, 1950–1; joined Théâtre du Nouveau Monde 1955–66; performed in 'Three-Penny Opera,' 'Le Malade Imaginaire' and 'Bérénice' among others; rec'd 1st Prize Internat. Song Festival, Sopot, Poland 1965 and Ostend, Belgium; major role Paul Almond's 'Act of the Heart,' 1970; proclaimed 'best singer of year' twice, and 'woman of the year' twice in the Canadian Press' annual survey of women's editors; named an officer of the Order of Canada in 1968; received the 1978 Prix de musique Calixa-Lavallée; has made numerous radio and TV appearances and recorded for Columbia Records.

**LEYTON, Elliott Hastings,** M.A., Ph.D.; educator; writer; b. Leader, Sask. 21 Aug. 1939; s. Dr. Harry and Lilyan (Faibish) Levson; e. Lord Byng High Sch. Vancouver 1956; Univ. of B.C., B.A. 1961, M.A. 1963; Univ. of Toronto, Ph.D. 1972; m. Bonnie d. Louis and Betty Averbach 30 Dec. 1958; two s. Alan Marco, Jack Sean; one grands. Mark Sean; PROF. OF ANTHROP. MEML. UNIV. OF NFLD. 1979– ; Mem. Adv. Bd., Dept. of Psychology, Univ. of Surrey, England; Rsch. Fellow, Inst. of Irish Studies, The Queen's Univ. of Belfast, N. Ireland; Asst. Lectr. in Social Anthrop. Queen's Univ. Belfast 1964–66; Asst. Prof. of Anthrop. present Univ. 1967–70, Assoc. Prof. 1971; Visiting Lectr. in Anthrop. Univ. of Toronto 1970–71; homicide cons. CBS TV, NBC TV (U.S.), Channel Four (U.K.), CTV 'Canada AM,' CBC TV; internat. cons. to police especially serial killings; recipient Arthur Ellis Award Crime Writers Can. Best Book 1986; author 'The One Blood: Kinship and Class in an Irish Village' 1975; 'Dying Hard: The Ravages of Industrial Carnage' 1975; 'The Myth of Delinquency: An Anatomy of Juvenile Nihilism' 1979;

'Hunting Humans: The Rise of the Modern Multiple Murderer' 1986; 'Sole Survivor: Children Who Murder Their Families' 1991; co-author 'Bureaucracy and World View: Two Studies in the Logic of Official Interpretation' 1978; ed. 'The Compact: Selected Dimensions of Friendship' 1974; 'Violence and Public Anxiety: A Canadian Case' 1992; mem. Candn. Sociol. & Anthrop. Assn. (Pres. 1983); recreation: shooting; Club: St. John's Rod & Gun (Dir.); Office: St. John's, Nfld. A1C 5S7.

**LEYTON-BROWN, David Robert,** A.M., Ph.D.; educator; b. London, Eng. 11 Sept. 1946; s. Howard and Myrl Bernadette (Walker) L-B; e. Central Coll. Inst. Regina 1963; McGill Univ., B.A. 1967; Harvard Univ., A.M. 1969, Ph.D. 1973; m. Anne Carver d. Turbut and Aroline Wright 18 Dec. 1971; children: Kevin Eric, Allison Beth; DEAN, GRADUATE STUDIES, YORK UNIV. 1994– ; Assoc. Dir., Centre for Internat. & Strategic Studies, York Univ. 1986–92, Prof. of Pol. Sci. 1989– , mem. Senate 1985– (Chrmn. Ctte. Admissions, Recruitment & Student Assistance 1984–86, 1987–88), (Chrmn. Ctte. Academic Policy and Planning 1991–92), Acting Dean, Graduate Studies 1992–94; Asst. Sr. Tutor, Mather House Harvard Coll. 1970–73; Asst. Prof. of Pol. Sci. Carleton Univ. 1973–75, present Univ. 1975–78, Assoc. Prof. of Pol. Sci. 1978–89, Assoc. Dir. Rsch. Prog. Strategic Studies 1981–84, 1985–86, Acting Dir. 1984–85, Assoc. Dean, Graduate Studies 1988–92; Assoc. Dir. Rsch. Candn. Inst. Internat. Affairs 1981–85; Guest Lectr. Candn. Forces Staff Sch., Candn. Forces Coll., Nat. Defence Coll.; mem. Steering Ctte. Consultative Group Arms Control & Disarmament Dept. External Affairs 1984–92; Chrmn. Ctte. Rsch. & Publs. and mem. Nat. Extve. Ctte. Candn. Inst. Internat. Affairs 1979–84; author: 'Weathering the Storm: Canadian-U.S. Relations 1980–83' 1985; over 75 chapters, articles & other publs.; ed. 'Trade-offs on Free Trade: The Canada-U.S. Free Trade Agreement' (with Marc Gold) 1988; 'The Utility of International Economic Sanctions' 1984; 'The Canadian Strategic Review' 1984; ed. bd. 'International Journal'; Recording Steward Richmond Hill Un. Ch. 1984–86, Chrmn. Council 1987–90, Chrmn. Ministry & Personnel Ctte. 1991– ; recreations: badminton, music; Home: 35 Tomlin Cres., Richmond Hill, Ont. L4C 7T1; Office: 4700 Keele St., North York, Ont. M3J 1P3.

**LEZNOFF, Arthur,** M.Sc., M.D., C.M., F.R.C.P.(C); physician; b. Montréal, Qué. 7 Apr. 1930; s. Benjamin and Sybil (Braunstein) L.; e. McGill Univ. B.Sc. 1951, M.D., C.M. 1955, M.Sc. 1960; m. Ruth d. Hyman and Fannie Halperin 30 June 1954; children: Glenda, Fred, Joyce, Sandra; CHIEF, DIV. OF CLIN. IMMUNOL. ST. MICHAEL'S HOSP. 1972– ; internship Internal Med. Michael Reese Hosp. Chicago 1956–58; Fellow in Clin. Immunol. Royal Victoria Hosp. Montréal 1958–60; Staff Jewish Gen. Hosp. Montréal 1960–71; Staff Phys. present Hosp. 1971– ; Assoc. Prof. of Med. Univ. of Toronto; recreations: squash, tennis; Club: Hillcrest Tennis; Home: 57 Patina Dr., North York, Ont. M2H 1R3; Office: 215, 38 Shuter St., Toronto, Ont. M5B 1A6.

**LHÉRITIER, Régine,** B.A.; artist; b. Paris, France 18 Jan. 1935; d. Francis and Andrée (Raimbault) L.; e. Acad. des dessins, Paris B.A. 1953; Acad. Bonnier; Acad. la Grande Chaumière 1948–50; Saidye Bronfman Ctr., printing with Rosalind Shwartzman and painting with Chaki 1978–80; m. Jean Noel s. Laura and Zephirin Lavoie 6 Nov. 1954; children: Martine, Sophie; solo exhibns.: Saidye Bronfman Center Montreal 1980; Galerie Gilles St. Pierre Montreal 1981; Galerie Dresdnere Toronto 1982, '84, '86, '88, '90; Galerie Gilles Corbeil Montreal 1983; Galerie Joyce Goldman Montreal 1985; Galerie Daniel Montreal 1987, '89; Galerie Waddington & Gorce, Montreal 1991; Home: 4180 de la Loire, Laval, Que. H7W 2S4.

**L'HEUREUX, Willard J.,** Q.C., B.A., LL.B.; business executive; b. Ottawa, Ont. 25 May 1947; s. Dr. Willard Joseph and Viola L'H.; e. Kings Coll., Univ. of W. Ont. B.A. 1968; Univ. of Toronto LL.B. 1971; m. Janet Elizabeth d. Dr. John and June Button 1973; children: Willard John, Jocelyn Marie, Robert Malcolm; PRESIDENT & CHIEF EXTVE. OFFR., TRIZEC CORPORATION LTD. 1992– ; Dir.: Astral Communications Inc.; Hees International Bancorp Inc.; Trizec Corp. Ltd.; read law with Tory, Tory, DesLauriers & Binnington 1972, Assoc. 1973, Partner 1979–83; Mng. Partner Financial Services, Hees Internat. Bancorp Inc. 1983–88; Mng. Partner & Pres., 1988–92; called to Ont. Bar 1973; cr. Q.C. 1983; Chrmn. & Pres., Candn. Special Olympics; Hon. Chrmn., Intercollegiate Hockey Championships; Governing Council, Univ. of Toronto; Advisory Council, Candn. Canoe Museum; Hon. Chrmn., 1994 University Cup; Clubs: Royal Candn. Yacht; Ranchman's; Queen's Club (Tennis); Office: Suite 1700, 855 - 2nd St. S.W., Calgary, Alta. T2P 4J7.

**L'HEUREUX-DUBÉ, Hon. Claire,** B.A., LL.L.; judge; b. Québec, Qué. 7 Sept. 1927; d. Col. Paul H. and Marguerite (Dion) L'Heureux; e. Monastère des Ursulines, Rimouski; Coll. Notre-Dame de Bellevue, Qué. B.A.; Univ. Laval LL.L.; Hon. degrees: Dalhousie Univ., Doctor of Laws 1981; Univ. de Montréal, Doctorat 1983; Univ. Laval, Doct. en Droit 1984; Médaille du Barreau de Québec 1987; Univ. of Ottawa, LL.D. 1988; Doctorat honorifique, Univ. du Qué. à Rimouski 1989; m. Prof. Arthur Dubé 30 Nov. 1957; children: Louise, Pierre; PUISNE JUDGE OF THE SUPREME COURT OF CANADA, Ottawa, Ont. 1987– ; Pres., Assn. québécoise pour l'étude comparative du droit 1984–90; Vice-Pres., Internat. Soc. on Family Law 1981–88; Pres., Internat. Comm. of Jurists (Can. Sect.) 1981–83; Vice-Pres., Internat. Comm. of Jurists (Internat. Bd.) 1992– ; called to Bar of Qué. 1952; cr. Q.C. 1969; mem. law firm Bard, l'Heureux & Philippon 1952–69; Sr. mem. L'Heureux, Philippon, Garneau, Tourigny & St-Arnaud 1969–73; mem. Extve. Counc., Barreau de Qué. 1968–70; Lectr. in Family Law, Cours de formation professionnelle du Barreau de Qué. 1968–73; Puisné Judge, Superior Court of Qué. 1973; Commr. to investigate and report on certain matters relating to Dept. Manpower & Immigration Montreal 1973; Judge of the Court of Appeal, Que. 1979–87; Puisne Judge of the Supreme Court of Canada 1987; mem. Conseil consultatif de l'adm. de la justice de la Prov. de Qué. 1967–73, Vice Prés. 1973; Vice Pres., Can. Consumer Council 1970–73; The Vanier Inst. of the Family 1972–73; Chrmn. Human Rights & Family Law Comte. and Family Court Comte., Que. Civil Code Revision Office 1972–76; author various articles, book chapters; co-ed. (with Rosalie S. Abella) 'Family Law: Dimensions of Justice' 1983; R. Catholic; Office: Supreme Court of Canada, Ottawa, Ont. K1A 0J1.

**LIANG, Albert H.P.,** B.A., B.Comm., LL.B.; barrister and solicitor; b. Hong Kong 24 June 1957; s. Wai E. and Ying Ha (Lo) L.; e. Univ. of Hong Kong B.A. (Hons.) 1979; Univ. of Windsor B.Comm. (Hons.) 1981; Univ. of Ottawa LL.B. (Hons.) 1984; m. Grace C.T. d. Dr. C.M. Yeung 10 Aug. 1985; children: Samantha, Michael; BARRISTER AND SOLICITOR, LAW OFFICE OF ALBERT H.P. LIANG 1993– ; articled with Hocherg & Slopen Windsor, Ont. 1984–85; Assoc., Cobban/Mogan 1986–88; Partner, Cravit, Halman, Kanji & Liang 1988–91; Partner with Harry Cravit, Q.C. 1991–93; legal advisor and consultant, Chinese-Candn. Broadcasting Corp.; Mem., Canada Pension Plan Review Tribunal; Pres., Chinese Seniors Support Serv. Assn.; Bd. of Gov., Ryerson Polytechnic Univ.; Life Gov., Doctors Hosp. (resigned 1993); Pres., Toronto Tai Ping Shan Lions Club 1991; Executive Editor, 'University of Hong Kong: Review and Preview' 1978; Home: 134 Canongate Trail, Scarborough, Ont.; Office: 80 Acadia Ave., Suite 104, Markham, Ont. L3R 9V1.

**LIBA, Peter Michael,** C.M.; television executive; b. Winnipeg, Man. 10 May 1940; s. Theodore and Rose L.; e. Lord Selkirk Sch. 1957; m. Shirley Ann d. J.A. and Bertha Collett 4 May 1963; children: Jennifer Ann, Jeffrey Michael, Christopher Collett; EXEC. VICE PRES., CANWEST GLOBAL COMMUNICATIONS CORP. 1993– ; Reporter, 'The Daily Graphic' 1957; 'Winnipeg Tribune' 1959; City Ed. 1967; Communications cons. 1968–73; joined CanWest Group of Cos. 1974; Exec. Vice-Pres., CanWest Broadcasting Ltd.; Pres., CanWest Properties Ltd.; Pres. & C.E.O., CKND Television Inc. & Saskwest Television Inc. 1988–93; Dir., CanWest Communications Corp.; CanWest Broadcasting Ltd.; Global Communications Ltd.; CanWest Pacific Television Inc.; CKND Television Inc.; SaskWest Television Inc.; AltaWest Television Ltd.; CanWest Maritime Television Inc.; CanWest Productions Ltd.; CanWest Properties Ltd.; Pres. & Dir., Peli Ventures Inc. & Peli Mngt. Inc.; C.M. 1984; Chair, Bd. of Dir., St. Boniface Gen. Hosp.; Past Chair, Candn. Assn. of Broadcasters; num. past exec. posts; Charter Mem., Variety Club of Man. (former Chief Barker); Founding Chrmn., Variety Telethon, Man.; clubs: Manitoba, St. Charles Country; Home: 10 Dumbarton Blvd., Winnipeg, Man. R3P 2C7; Office: 31st Floor, TD Centre, 201 Portage Ave., Winnipeg, Man. R3B 3L7.

**LIBBY, Hon. Keith Jerome,** B.Com., M.B.A., LL.B.; judge; b. Regina, Sask. 26 May 1942; s. Harry William and Beatrice Helen (Young) L.; e. King George Elem. and Central Coll. Inst. Moose Jaw; Univ. of B.C., B.Com. 1965, LL.B. 1969; Univ. of Wash. M.B.A. 1966; m. Freya d. Gordon and Marion Genser 1 Sept. 1963; children: Robyn Pamela, Michael Jeffrey; ASSOC. CHIEF JUDGE, PROV. COURT OF B.C. 1989– , Judge 1980– ; Dep. Judge Y.T. 1984– ; called to Bar of B.C. 1970; gen. practice Buell, Ellis, Sargent & Russell, Vancouver 1970–73; criminal & family practice Libby, Libby, Blair & Moss 1973–80; Pres. Prov. Judges Assn. B.C. 1984–85; Prov. Rep. Candn. Assn. Prov. Court Judges 1984–85; Extve. Dir., Secy./Treas., Candn. Assoc. of Provincial Court Judges; recreation: golf; Club: Richmond Country; Home: 6049 Fremlin St., Vancouver, B.C. V5Z 3W8; Office: 222 Main St., Vancouver, B.C. V6A 2S8.

**LIBFELD, Al;** builder / developer; b. Chicago, Illinois 11 Apr. 1952; s. Morris and Rose L.; e. American Univ.; Univ. of Illinois; m. Sheila d. Robert and Loraine David 1 Sept. 1974; children: Steven, Rachel; PRES./PARTNER, TRIBUTE CORPORATION 1983– ; Pres./Owner, Brand Drywall 1974–82 (large residential & commerical drywall contractor); has built in excess of 5000 homes; has several indust. commercial projects underway and large tracts of land in various stages of devel.; Past Pres., Ont. Home Builders Assn.; Office: 1815 Ironstone Manor, Unit 1, Pickering, Ont. L1W 3W9.

**LIBMAN, Robert M.,** B.Sc., B.Arch., M.N.A.; architect, politician; b. Montreal, Que. 8 Nov. 1960; s. David Jack and Goldie Esther (Aronovitch) L.; e. Herzliah H.S. 1978; McGill Univ. B.Sc.(Arch.) 1984, B.Arch. 1985; m. Malia d. Eli and Simonne Azeroual 24 Aug. 1986; separated; one s.: Kevin Elliot; MEMBER, NATIONAL ASSEMBLY OF QUEBEC FOR DIST. OF D'ARCY MCGEE 1989– ; Student, Architect, Leonard Ostroff Design Assoc. 1983–84; Architect, T. Pringle & Sons Engineering 1985; Jacques Beique et Assoc. 1986; Tolchinsky & Goodz Architects 1986–89; Mem., Order of Architects of Que. 1987– ; Royal Arch. Inst. of Canada; Candn. Centre of Arch.; Council on Tall Buildings and Urban Habitat; Partner, architecture firm, 'Dimiele Libman Architects'; grad. McGill Sch. of Arch. with distinction & as a university scholar; Vice-Pres., B'Nai Brith Balfour Lodge; recreations: baseball, waterskiing, hockey; Home: 5765 Sir Walter Scott, Cote St. Luc, Que. H4M 2L9; Office: 5800 Cavendish, #403, Montreal, Que. H4W 2T5.

**LIDDLE, David Brian,** B.A., M.A.; insurance company executive; b. Hamilton, Ont. 11 Aug. 1944; s. Andrew Gerald and Eileen Constance (Jeffries) L.; e. Univ. of Toronto B.A. 1967, M.A. 1968; m. Kim d. John and Lorene Pauli 15 Sept. 1990; children: Steven Douglas, Donald Bruce, Heather Joanne; VICE-PRESIDENT & CHIEF OPERATING OFFICER, NATIONAL FRONTIER INSURANCE CO. 1989– ; Pres., Travel Algoma Ltd. 1971– ; Pres., Northern Frontier Insur. Co. 1979–89; Vice Chair, Nipissing Univ. Board of Governors; Candidate, Ont. Progressive Conservative Party, Algoma 1977; recreations: fishing, flying; clubs: Rotary of North Bay; Home: 129 Wallace Heights Dr., North Bay, Ont. P1C 1E7; Office: 373 Main St. W., North Bay, Ont. P1B 2T9.

**LIDSTER, Perry David,** B.Sc., M.Sc., Ph.D.; scientist; b. Peace River, Alta. 9 Aug. 1949; s. Morley Wilbert and Gertrude Edith (Senkiw) L.; e. Univ. of B.C. B.Sc. 1972, M.Sc. 1976, Ph.D. 1979; m. Carole d. John and Joan Payne 3 Apr. 1976; children: Amanda, Andrew, Caitlin, Harrison; PROGRAM DIR., WESTERN REGION, RESEARCH BR., AGRICULTURE CANADA 1990– ; Rsch. Sci for NRC – IRAP Project 1972–76; B.C. Tree Fruits Ltd. 1976–78; Agric. Can., Rsch. Station, Kentville N.S. 1979 (rsch. contributed to year round mktg. of Candn. apples); Head, Storage Section 1983; Asst. Dir. 1989; has served on internat. & nat. cttes. incl. Candn. delegate to Comms. B2 and D1, Internat. Inst. of Refrigeration & USDA N.E. 103 Rsch. & Planning Ctte.; invited speaker, Gordon Rsch. Conf. on Postharvest Physiology & Internat. Soc. for Horticultural Sci. Cong.; Hon. Rsch. Assoc., Acadia Univ.; Adjunct Prof., Technical Univ. of N.S.; Royal Soc. of Arts Silver Medal 1987 for contrib. to Agric. Rsch. in Atlantic Can.; author of over 100 sci. articles; recreations: antique auto & furniture restoration; Home: 1179 St. Therese Lane, Gloucester, Ont. K1C 2A5; Office: Room 7113, Sir John Carling Bldg., 930 Carling Ave., Ottawa, Ont. K1A 0C5.

**LIEBEL, Peter,** B.A., M.Sc.; Canadian public servant; b. Montreal, Que. 17 Apr. 1951; s. George and Greta (Nichols) L.; e. Montreal West H.S. 1968; McGill Univ., B.A. (Hons.) 1972; London Sch. of Econ., M.Sc. 1973; m. Margot d. Donald and Jean Montgomery Dec. 1983; one d.: Sarah; ASST. DEP. MIN., CONSULTATIONS & COMMUNICATIONS, DEPT. OF FINANCE, GOVT. OF CAN. 1988– ; Anti-Inflation Task Force 1975; Orgn. Analyst, Treas. Bd. Sec. 1974–76; Extve. Asst. to Min. of Fisheries & Environ. 1976–78; Dir. Gen., Min. of State for Econ. Devel. 1978–83; Dir. Gen., Indus. & Econ. Devel. Br., Dept. of Commun. 1983–88;

sessional lectr., Carleton Univ. 1976–77; Commonwealth Scholar 1972–73; Gold Medalist, McGill Univ. 1972; Alexander MacKenzie Scholar 1971; Contributor, 'Governing in An Information Society' (Steven A. Rosell et al) IRPP 1992; recreations: jogging, skiing, tennis, arts; clubs: Friends of the Nat. Gallery; Home: 69 Geneva St., Ottawa, Ont. K1Y 3N6; Office: 140 O'Connor St., 19th fl., Ottawa, Ont. K1A 0G5.

**LIEBEL-WECKOWICZ, Helen,** Ph.D.; university professor; b. New York, N.Y. 17 June 1930; d. Emil Frederick and Anna (Bonk) Liebel; e. Brooklyn Coll., B.A. 1952; Northwestern Univ., M.A. 1953, Ph.D. 1959; Fulbright scholar U. Marburg (BRD) 1955–56; Gasthörer U. Hamburg 1957; m. Thaddeus s. Waclaw and Sophie Weckowicz 11 July 1966; Asst. to full PROF. OF HISTORY, UNIV. OF ALBERTA 1962– ; Assoc. Ed., Consolid. Bk. Pub. 1954–55; Screener, Am. Hist. Assn. Project Microfilming Captured German War Documents 1958–59; Sessl. Lectr., Brooklyn Coll. 1959–62; Mem., Can. Ctte., Internat. Hist. Congress 1967–70, 1977–78, 1980; Can. Counc. grants 1969–71, 1973–74; Univ. of Alta. grants; Mem., Am. Ctte. Habsburg Studies; Conf. Orgnr., German Studies Assn.; Progr. Ctte., Pacific Coast AHA meeting 1985–86; Bd. Mem., Candn. Jour. of Hist. to 1989; Am. Biog. Inst.; Corr. ed., Europa; Mem., Candn. Hum. & Philos. Soc.; Am. Hist. Assn.; Candn. Soc. Cult. & Intell. Hist. (Pres. 1974–78, 1979–80, Prog. Chrmn. 1976–78, 1979–80, Treas. 1976–80); Candn. 18th Century Soc.; Gold Medal A.B.I. 1986; A.B.I. decoration 1990; participant Bi-Centenaire French Revol., Univ. René Descartes 1987; author & co-author of several titles in series 'Guides to Captured German War Documents' incl.: 'Records of the Reich Ministry f. Armaments & War Production' 1959–62; numerous papers, scholarly articles, book chapters, reviews & essays on diverse subjects; author: 'Enlightened Bureaucracy vs. Enlightened Despotism in Baden 1750–1792' 1965; contbr.: 'Historical Dictionary of Napoleonic France' 1984; (with T.E. Weckowicz) 'Hist. Ideas Abnm. Psych.' 1990; Office: Rm. 2-33, Tory Bldg., Univ. of Alta., Edmonton, Alta. T6G 2E1.

**LIEBERMAN, Hon. Samuel Sereth,** C.D., B.A., LL.B., LL.D.; judge; b. Edmonton, Alta. 14 Apr. 1922; s. Moses Isaac Lieberman; e. Garneau High Sch. Edmonton 1939; Univ. of Alta. B.A. 1947, LL.B. 1948, LL.D. (Hon.) 1990; m. Nancy d. late H.M. Berman, Chicago, Ill. 15 July 1950; children: David J., Jo Ann McLaughlin, Audrey G.; JUSTICE OF APPEAL OF THE COURT OF APPEAL OF ALBERTA (and Justice, Court of Appeal, N.W.T. and Depy. Judge, Supreme Court of N.W.T.) 1976– ; called to Bar of Alta. 1949; cr. Q.C. 1962; apptd. to Dist. Court of Alta. 1966; Trial Div. Supreme Court of Alta. 1970; Sessional Lectr. in Law, Univ. of Alta.; Past Chrmn. (1969–78) Alta. Adv. Bd. of Review; Alta. Legal Aid Soc.; mem. W. Bd., Candn. Council Christians & Jews; Hon. Dir. Can.'s Aviation Hall of Fame; Hon. Life mem. Bd. Govs., Technion-Israel Inst. of Technol. Haifa; served with RCAF 1940–45, pilot, rank Sqdn. Leader, RCAF Auxiliary 1949–56; RCAF Aide-de-Camp to Lt. Gov. of Alta. 1953–56; Jewish; recreations: fishing, golf, skiing; Club: Mayfair Golf & Country; Home: Apt. #202, 10010 – 119 St., Edmonton, Alta. T5K 1Y8; Office: The Law Courts, Edmonton, Alta. T5J 0R2.

**LIEW, Choong-Chin,** B.Sc., M.A., Ph.D., FCACB; university professor; b. Malaysia 2 Sept. 1937; e. Nanyang Univ., Singapore B.Sc. 1960; Univ. of Toronto, M.A. 1964, Ph.D. 1967; Fellow of Candn. Acad. of Clinical Biochemistry (FCACB) 1992; m. Eng. Ng 7 Oct. 1964; children: Gailina J.H., Allan L., Victor S.; PROF. OF CLIN. BIOCHEM. & MED. UNIV. OF TORONTO 1979– ; Hon. Prof. 10 Med. Schs. in China incl. Peking Union Med. Coll. and West China Univ. of Med. Sci's 1979– ; Hon. Prof. of Biochemistry, the Chinese Univ. of Hong Kong 1992– ; Dir. Clin. Molecular Biol. Unit Max Bell Rsch. Centre Toronto Gen. Hosp.; Asst. Prof. of Clin. Biochem. present Univ. 1970, Assoc. Prof. of Clin. Biochem. & Med. 1973; mem. Am. Soc. Cell Biol.; Candn. Biochem. Soc.; Soc. of Chinese Bioscientists in Am.; Biochem. Soc. UK; Home: 81 Millersgrove Dr., Willowdale, Ont. M2R 3S1; Office: 100 College St., Toronto, Ont. M5G 1L5.

**LIGHT, Walter Frederick,** O.C., O.Ont., B.Sc.; communications executive; b. Cobalt, Ont. 24 June 1923; s. Herbert and Rosetta Elizabeth (Hoffman) L.; e. Secondary Sch., Cobalt, Ont.; Queen's Univ., B.Sc. (Hons.) 1949; Hon. LL.D.: Concordia Univ. 1980; Queen's Univ. 1981; Dalhousie Univ. 1985; Hon. D.Ap.Sci.: Univ. of Ottawa 1981; Hon. D.Sc.: Laurentian Univ. 1984; Hon. D.Eng.: Univ. of Waterloo 1985; m. Margaret Anne Wylie, d. Dr. J.R. Miller, Iroquois, Ont. 8 July 1950; children: Elizabeth Jean, Janice Catherine; Dir., Air Products & Chemicals Inc.; Inco Ltd.; Northern Telecom Ltd.; Moore Corp. Ltd.; Royal Bank of Canada; Shell Canada Ltd.; NewTel Enterprises Limited; RockCliffe Research and Technology Inc.; The SNC Group Inc.; Transtream Inc.; joined Bell Canada, Toronto, Ontario as Engn. Asst. 1949, variety managing posts Toronto and Montreal 1952–67; apptd. Vice-Pres. (Engn.) 1967; Vice-Pres. (Operations) 1969; Extve. Vice-Pres. (Operations) 1970; Pres., Northern Telecom Ltd. 1974, Pres. & C.E.O. 1979, Chrmn. & C.E.O. 1982; Chrmn. 1984; retired as Chrmn. 1985; served with R.C.A.F. 1942–45; mem., Corp. of Engrs. of Que.; Assn. Prof. Engrs. (Ont.); Hon. Mem., Electrical Manuf. Club; Fellow, Engn. Inst. of Canada; Fellow, Candn. Acad. of Engn.; Fellow, Montreal Museum of Fine Arts; mem. Associates of Carleton Univ.; Officer, Order of Canada 1986; Order of Ontario 1988; Clubs: York; Mount Royal; Home: 7 Nanton Ave., Toronto, Ont. M4W 2Y8; Office: Bell Trinity Sq., Flr. 10, South Tower, Toronto, Ont. M5G 2E1.

**LIGHTBURN, Ronald Paul;** artist, illustrator; b. Cobourg, Ont. 24 June 1954; s. Thomas George and Mary Veronica (Scarisbrick) L.; e. Henry Wise Wood H.S. 1972; Alberta Coll. of Art; m. Sandra d. Conrad and Ethel Meyer 9 June 1975; illustrator since 1975 with comns for num. N. Am. pubns.; gallery exbns throughout N. Am. incl. The Soc. of Illustrators 33rd annual exbn (N.Y.) 1991; solo exbn: Fran Willis Gallery (Victoria) Nov. 1991; drawings and paintings are included in corp. and private collections incl. The Nat. Library; lecturer; Western Magazine Award for Graphic Illustration 1984; Mem., Soc. of Illustrators; Coloured Pencil Soc. of Am.; Children's Writers and Illustrators of B.C.; Island Illustrators Soc. (Founding Mem.); IBBY Canada (Internat. Board on Books for Young People); Children's Literature Roundtable (Victoria); illustrator (children's picture books): 'Waiting for the Whales' 1991 (Amelia Frances Howard-Gibbon Illustrators Award 1992, Elizabeth Mrazik-Cleaver Candn. Picture Book Award 1992, Gov. Gen. Literary Award for Children's Illustration 1992), 'I Can't Sleep!' 1992 (chosen by Candn. Children's Book Centre for inclusion in 1993 'Our Choice' list of recommended books), 'Eagle Dreams' 1994; recreations: film studies, travel; Address: 1034 Johnson St., Unit 803, Victoria, B.C. V8V 3N7.

**LIGHTFOOT, Gordon Meredith,** O.C., O.Ont.; singer; songwriter; b. Orillia, Ont. 17 Nov. 1938; s. Gordon Meredith and Jessie Vick (Trill) M.; student Westlake Coll. Music, Los Angeles 1958; m. 2ndly, Elizabeth (Moon); children: Fred, Ingrid, Eric (from previous marriage) Miles; singer, songwriter 1959– ; compositions incl. 'Early Morning Rain' 1965; 'Canadian Railroad Trilogy' 1967; 'If You Could Read My Mind' 1970; 'Sundown' 1974, 'Carefree Highway' 1974; 'The Wreck of the Edmund Fitzgerald' 1976; 'Race Among the Ruins' 1976; decorated Order Canada 1970; named Top Folksinger, Juno Gold Leaf Awards 1965, 66, 68, 69, 73, 74, 75, 76, 77; Top Male Vocalist 1967, 70, 71, 72, 74; Composer of Year 1972, 76; Juno 'Hall of Fame' Award 1986; recipient, Order of Ontario 1988; recipient awards for songs ASCAP 1971, 74, 76, 77; Pop Record of Year Award Music Operators Am. 1974; Vanier Award Canadian Jaycees 1977; numerous Gold albums Can., U.S., Australia; Platinum album for 'Sundown,' 'Summertime Dream' and 'Gord's Gold'; Gold record for 'Sundown'; Address: Suite 207, 1365 Yonge St., Toronto, Ont. M4T 2P7.

**LIGHTHEART, Kim;** ballet dancer; b. Strathroy, Ont. 30 May; d. Betty (Day) L.; e. Nat. Ballet Sch. 1979; Eur. studies 1979; Principal Dancer, The National Ballet of Canada 1987; joined The National Ballet of Canada 1980, 1st Soloist 1984; debut 'La Sylphide' 1982; debut in full-length ballet as Juliet 'Romeo and Juliet' 1983; title, leading and soloist roles incl. 'Giselle' 1984, 'The Nutcracker' (Snow Queen/Sugar Plum Fairy) 1984, 'Kettentanz,' 'Collective Symphony,' 'Etudes,' 'Nataraja,' 'La Bayaderka Act II,' 'Les Sylphides,' 'Raymonda Act III,' 'Transfigured Night'; created roles in 'L'Ile Inconnue,' 'Components,' 'Blue Snake,' created leading role world premiere 'Masada' by David Allan 1987; extensive repertoire incls. roles in 'Giselle' at Dance in Can. Conf. Halifax 1985, 'La Fille Mal Gardee' (Lise) 1985–86, 'The Merry Widow' (Valencienne) 1986, 'Coppelia' (Swanilda) 1987; Glen Tetley's new production of 'La Ronde' 1987; 'The Sleeping Beauty' (Aurora, Princess Florine) 1987; 'The Dream' (Hermia) 1988; 'Song of the Earth' (Third Song Girl) 1988; 'Onegin' (Olga); 'Don Juan' (Aminta); 'Don Quixote' (Mercedes); 'Diana and Acteon'; 'Symphony in C'; recipient Can. Council Grant 1979; Address: New York.

**LIGHTSTONE, Marilyn,** B.A.; actress; b. Montreal, Que. 28 June 1940; d. Manuel and Sophie (Shulman) Lightstone; e. McGill Univ. B.A. 1962; Nat. Theatre Sch. grad. 1965; films incl.: 'The Wild Pony' 1982; 'Love' 1980; 'Mary and Joseph' 1980; 'In Praise of Older Women' 1978 (Candn. Film Award Best Actress); 'Lies My Father Told Me' (Candn. Film Best Actress Award) 1976; plays incl. 'Refugees' (drama/opera) 1979; 'Miss Margarida' 1976; 'The Dybbuk' Mark Taper Forum (Los Angeles Drama Critics Award) Los Angeles 1975; 'Mary Queen of Scots' Charlottetown (P.E.I.) Festival 1974; 'King Lear' Lincoln Center, New York 1972; 'Electra Yard of the Sun' 1970; 'The Seagull' Stratford (Ont.) Festival 1968; numerous TV shows incl. 'Titans'; 'Witness to Yesterday'; 'Littlest Hobo'; King of Kensington'; 'The Adventurers.'

**LIIMATAINEN, Arvi John;** producer, director; b. Finland 31 Aug. 1949; s. John Oscar and Tynne Helena (Sepannen) L.; one child: Anja; Dir., 'Strange and Rich' TV Film 1993; Extve. Producer, 'Road To Saddle River' Th. Film 1993; Producer, 'Medicine River,' TV Film 1992; 'Angel Square' Th. Film 1990; 'Sylvan Lake' TV film 1989; 'Bye Bye Blues' Th. Film 1989; Bradbury Theatre (4 episodes) 1989; Line Prod., 'Cowboy's Don't Cry' TV film 1988; Prod./Dir., 'Moccasin Flats' TV pilot 1991; Dir., 'Down Came the Rain' TV 1989; 'Into the Fields' TV 1988; The Beachcombers (6 episodes) 1982–85; Co-Prod., 'Bridge to Terabithia "Wonderworks"' TV 1984; has worked in motion picture indus. since 1968; Office: Second Floor, 10022 – 103 St., Edmonton, Alta. T5J 0X2.

**LILL, John W.,** B.Sc.; resource executive; b. Calgary, Alta. 1 Oct. 1951; s. Robert George and Mary Livingston (Edgar) L.; e. Queen's Univ. B.Sc. (Hons.) 1973; m. Phyllis d. William and Mary Scandrett 23 March 1974; children: Mary, James, Marilyn; SENIOR VICE-PRES., U.S. OPERATIONS, AMERICAN BARRICK RESOURCES CORP. 1991– ; Mining Engr., Mine Captain, Roan Consolidated Mines, Mulfulira Div. Zambia 1973–76; Mining Engr., Palabora Mining Co. RSA 1976–78; Chief Mining Engr., Luscar Sterco Edson, Alta. 1978–80; Supt., Manager Mining, Palabora Mining Co. RSA 1980–88; Vice-Pres., U.S. Opns., Am. Barrick Resources Corp. 1988–91; Vice-Pres., Barrick Goldstrike Mines Inc.; Barrick U.S.A.; Dir., Candn. Mineral Indus. Edn. Found.; Mem., AIME, SME, CIMM, APEO, APEGGA; author: 'Palabora: Changing to Meet the Challenge of the 80s' 1987, 'Application of a Statistical Analysis Technique for Design of High Rock Slopes at Palabora Mine, S. Africa' 1987, 'Safety in trolley Assisted Truck Haulage' 1986, 'Operating Features and Control Aspects of the Palabora Copper Open Pit' 1987; recreations: running, tennis, boating; Home: 435 Russell Hill Rd., Toronto, Ont. M5P 2S4; Office: 24 Hazelton Ave., Toronto, Ont. M5R 2E2.

**LILL, Wendy Elizabeth,** B.A.; playwright, screenwriter; b. Vancouver, B.C. 2 Nov. 1950; d. Edwin Henry and Margaret Galbraith (Gordon) L.; e. York Univ. B.A. 1971; m. Richard s. George and Bainhi Starr 12 Sept. 1981; children: Samuel Edwin, Joseph Alexander; ACTRA awards for radio documentary progs. CBC; Golden Sheaf Award for Ikwe; Gov. Gen.'s Drama Award nominee for 'The Occupation of Heather Rose' author: 'The Occupation of Heather Rose' in 'NeWest Plays for Women' 1988, 'The Fighting Days' 1983, 'Memories of You' 1988, 'Sisters' 1991, 'All Fall Down' 1993 (plays performed widely in Canada); 'Ikwe' part of Daughters of the Country series; also author of TV adaptations of 'Sisters' and 'Passage To The Heart'; Home: 20 Summit St., Dartmouth, N.S. B2Y 3A2.

**LILLARD, Charles Marion,** B.A., M.F.A.; writer; b. Cal. 26 Feb. 1944; s. Donald George and Viola Katherine (Brooks) L.; e. Univ. of Alaska; Univ. of B.C., B.A. 1969, M.F.A. 1973; m. Rhonda d. Benjamin and Evelyn Batchelor 1983; children: Benjamin, Joanna; OWNER AND OPERATOR REFERENCE WEST 1988– ; self-employed writer since 1983; logging 1958–67; Environment Can. 1967–74; Lectr. Univ. of Victoria 1974–77; Mng. Ed. Gregson Graham 1978–79; Ed. Sound Heritage Series (Provl. Archives B.C.) 1982–83; columnist: 'Cut To' 1987–91; 'BC Bookworld' 1987– ; 'Times-Colonist' freelance book reviewer 1975–84, 1989–90, columnist 1990– ; 'Oak Bay Star' 1991–93; recipient McMillan Co. of Canada Poetry Award 1973; nominated Ethel Wilson Fiction Prize 1985; Lt. Gov.'s Medal 1986; Cert. of Merit B.C. Hist. Fedn. 1987; Dorothy Livesay Poetry Prize 1989; author (poetry) 'Cultus Coulee' 1971; 'Drunk on Wood' 1973; 'Jabble' 1975; 'Voice My Shaman' 1976; 'A Coastal Range' 1984; 'Circling North' 1988; 'Green Weather Country' 1991; (hist.) 'Paths Our Ancestors Walked' 1977; 'Seven Shillings A Year' 1986; (with John Ellis) 'Fernwood Files' 1989; 'The Certified General Accountants of British Columbia' 1991; 'Nanaimo' 1992; (with Michael Gregson)

'The Land of Destiny' 1991; (annotated eds.) 'Mission to Nootka' 1977; 'In the Wake of the War Canoe' 1981; 'Warriors of the North Pacific' 1984; 'The Nootka, Scenes and Studies of Savage Life' 1987; 'The Ghostland People' 1989; 'Fort Langley' 1991; 'Fort Victoria' 1993; (biog.) 'The Brother, XII' 1989; 'West Coast Wild' 1994; Address: 2450 Central Ave., Victoria, B.C. V8S 2S8.

**LILLES, Heino,** B.Sc., M.Sc., LL.B., LL.M.; judge; university professor; b. Sweden 13 Dec. 1944; s. Herbert and Hilda (Keek) L.; e. Queen's Univ., B.Sc. 1967, M.Sc. 1968, LL.B. 1971; London Sch. of Econ., LL.M. 1972; m. Sheila d. Keith and Irene Scott 1967; children: Eerik Matthew, Gregory Scott; CHIEF JUDGE, TERRITORIAL COURT, YUKON 1989– , Territorial Ct. Judge 1987– ; joined Queen's Univ. as Prof. of Law 1972–87; Extve. Asst., Vice-Principal (Services) 1981–86; Dir., Legal Services 1986–87; cons. to var. govt. mins.; mem. Task Force on Child Abuse, Min. of Community & Soc. Services 1978; Dir. & Past Pres. (1977–79), St. Lawrence Youth Assoc. 1974–80; Dir., Kingston & Frontenac Family Referral & Conciliation 1975–77; Dir. (1986) and Life Mem., Children's Aid Soc. of Kingston & Frontenac County; mem. Candn. Assn. of Univ. Teachers 1972– ; Law Soc. of Upper Can. 1974– ; Nat. Assn. of Councs. for Children 1980– ; Licensing Extve. Soc. 1983– ; Chrmn., Yukon Petroleum Pricing Inquiry 1988; co-author: 'Canadian Children's Law' 1982; 'The Young Offenders Act – Annotated' 1984; co-ed. 'The Young Offenders Service' 1984–87; recreations: cross-country skiing, camping; Home: 48 Firth Rd., Whitehorse, Yukon Y1A 4R6; Office: P.O. Box 2703, J-3E, Whitehorse, Yukon Y1A 5H6.

**LILLY, Augustus G.,** B.C.L., M.A.; lawyer; b. St. John's, Nfld. 11 Feb. 1948; s. Augustus and Jane (Conway) L.; e. St. Bonaventure's Coll. 1962; Brother Rice H.S. 1965; Meml. Univ. of Nfld. B.A. (Hons.) 1970; Oxford Univ. B.A. (Hons.) 1973, B.C.L. 1975, M.A. 1978; Rhodes Scholar (Nfld.) 1971; m. Janet d. M. Gordon and Edith McCannel 19 July 1975; children: Christine E., Stephen P.; PARTNER, STEWART MCKELVEY STIRLING SCALES; called to Bar of Nfld. 1976; joined Stirling, Ryan (predecessor to present co.) 1976; Prov. Secy. for Nfld., Rhodes Scholarship Trust; Bencher and Treasurer (Pres.), Law Soc. of Nfld.; mem. Candn. Bar Assn.; Home: 11 Primrose Place, St. John's, Nfld. A1B 4H1; Office: Cabot Place, New Gower St., P.O. Box 5038, St. John's, Nfld. A1C 5V3.

**LIMEBACK, Hardy,** B.Sc., Ph.D., D.D.S.; associate professor and dentist; b. Germany 15 Nov. 1951; s. George H. and Ursula (Lembcke) L.; e. Sir Wilfred Laurier Collegiate 1970; Univ. of Toronto B.Sc. 1975, Ph.D. 1979, D.D.S. 1983; m. Lynne d. William and Herdis Thompson 12 May 1984; children: Kurt William, Kevin Alexander; Faculty of Dentistry, Univ. of Toronto 1983; MRC (Canada) Scholar 1985; Assoc. Prof. with tenure & full mem., Sch. of Grad. Studies 1989; recognized worldwide for expertise in tooth enamel and dentin biochem., preventive & geriatric dentistry through grants, pubs. & presentations; Mem., Candn. Dental Assn. (spokesperson, interviewed by media on various dental topics); Consumer Products Recognition Ctte.; Chair, Assn. of Candn. Fac. of Dentistry; Fac. Mem., Devel. Ctte.; served MRC (Can.) Grants Ctt. 4 years; Chief, Dental Serv., Metro. Toronto Homes for the Aged; owns a part-time dental practice in Mississauga; helped organize Candn. workshop re use of flourides (endorsed by Candn. Dental Assn.); author/co-author of over 75 pubs.; recreations: T-ball coach, skiing, cycling; clubs: Beaver/Cub Scout leader; Owenwood Homeowners' Ass. (Dir.); Home: 946 Cristina Ct., Mississauga, Ont. L5J 4S1; Office: 124 Edward St., Toronto, Ont. M5G 1G6.

**LIMERICK, Jack McKenzie,** B.A., M.A., F.C.I.C. (1953); pulp, paper and container consultant; b. Fredericton, N.B.; s. Arthur Kerr and Lillian Ethel (McKenzie) L.; e. Fredericton, (N.B.) High Sch., 1924–27; Univ. of New Brunswick, B.A. (Hons. in Chem. and Math.) 1931; McGill Univ. and Univ. of N.B., M.A. (Chem.) 1934; Queen's Univ., Sch. of Comm. and Adm. (Extve. Training Course) 1957; m. Elsie Anderson, d. James P. Wetmore, Campbellton, N.B., 11 Sept. 1937; Research Chem., Fraser Cos., 1934–37; joined Bathurst Paper Co. Ltd. as Chief Chem., 1937; Supt. of Control Dept., 1941; Tech. and Research Dir., 1944–67; Assoc. Dir. Research and Devel., Consolidated-Bathurst 1967–71; set up own consulting practice 1971; consultant on estab. of pulp, paper & container indust. Iran, 1972–78; and in same capacity, Brazil, since 1973; built new bldgs. exclusively devoted to pulp & paper research (1944) & container research (1950); travelled extensively in Europe in interest of Pulp & Paper industry; lect. at Royal Tech. Inst., Stockholm, Sweden; Chrmn. of Tech. Section as a member of the Tech. Del. of the Pulp and Paper industry which made survey of mills and industry in Russia, 1959; made a study throughout the U.S. (for the U.S. Inst. of Paper Chem.) on the state of the art of using secondary fibre in the manufacture of kraft linerboard (now becoming standard practice thoughout the industry) 1976; Mem., Publications Ctte., Tech. Section, Candn. Pulp and Paper Assn. (Chrmn. 1959); appointed to Adv. Panel, Pulp and Paper Research Inst. of Can., 1961; Tech. Assn. of Pulp & Paper Industry (U.S.), Dir. 1962–65, Fellow 1968; mem. Alkaline Pulp Comte., Tech. Assn. of Pulp & Paper Ind. (U.S.) (Chrmn.-1st Candn.-1958–59), and rec'd. awards from Assn. 1959, 1982 for distinguished service (1st Candn. recipient) and 50 yrs. distinguished membership award 1990; Hon. Life Mem., Technical Sect., Candn. Pulp & Paper Assn. 1987, awarded 50 yrs. of distinguished membership award 1990; mem., Chem. Instit. of Can. Fellow 1953; Cdn. Soc. for Chemistry; Bd. Govs., Univ. of N.B., 1947–52; Pres. Univ. of N.B. Alumni Assn., 1955–56; Past Pres., Bathurst Community Concert Assn.; Past Pres., Bathurst Rotary Club; Publications: numerous, mostly in field of pulp, paper and containers incl. portion of 1955 ed. 'Pulp and Paper Manufacture'; Patents: a number on pulp, paper and container manufacture; Protestant; recreations: golf, fishing, music; Clubs: Bathurst (N.B.) Golf (Past Pres.); The Bath Club (Florida); Royal Montreal Golf; Oakville Golf; Address: 36 East St., PH 4, Oakville, Ont. L6L 5K2.

**LIMOGES, Camille,** Doct., F.R.S.C.; university professor; b. Montreal, Que. 31 May 1942; s. Alvarez E. and Louise B. (Brière) L.; e. Univ. de Montréal L.Phil. 1964; Univ. de Paris Doctorate 1968; PROFESSOR & DIR., CENTER FOR INTERUNIVERSITY RESEARCH ON SCI. & TECHNOL., UNIV. DU QUE. A MONTREAL 1987– ; Prof., Univ. of Montreal 1968–71, 1973–81; Johns Hopkins Univ. 1971–73; Visiting Prof., Johns Hopkins Univ. 1979; Harvard Univ. 1978; Rsch. Fellow, Humanities Rsch. Inst., Univ. of Calif. 1991; Founder & Dir., Inst. d'Hist. et de Sociopol. des sci., Univ. of Montreal 1973–77; Dep. Min. for Higher Edn. & Sci., Govt. of Que. 1985–86; for Science and Technol. 1983–85; Pres., ACFAS 1989–90; Mem., Acad. Internat. d'Hist. des Sciences; Fellow, Royal Soc. of Can.; author: 'La sélection naturelle' 1970; editor: 'L'équilibre de la nature'; co-editor: 'Studies in History and Biology' 7 vols. 1977–84 and over 100 scholarly articles; recreation: music; Home: 1206 Lajoie, Outremont, Que. H2V 1P1; Office: C.P. 8888, Succ. A., Montreal, Que. H3C 3P8.

**LIMOGES, Gérard-Antoine,** B.B.A., F.C.A.; management consultant; b. Montreal, Que. 5 July 1939; s. Théo and Blanche (Charbonneau) L.; e. Ecole des Hautes Etudes Commerciales, Univ. of Montreal B.B.A. 1966; C.A. 1967; m. Manon Beausoleil; children: Bertrand, Hélène, Antoine; PARTNER, ERNST & YOUNG 1971– ; joined Ernst & Young (formerly Clarkson Gordon) 1962; Auditing Prof., Ecole des Hautes Etudes Comm. 1967–70; Laval Univ. 1971–72; extensive ctte. work with Ordre des comptables agréés du Québec incl. most recent: Chair, Public Information Ctte. 1983–85; Chair, Audit Ctte., Candn. C. of C. 1975–78; Mem., Bd. of Dir. & Extve. Ctte., Sobeco Ernst & Young Inc. 1991– ; Treas., Que. Assn. for the Mentally Retarded 1973–74; F.C.A. Quebec 1984; C.A. 1966; Winner, Gov. Gen. Gold Medal; Gold Medal, Order des comp. agréés du Qué.; Edmund Gunn Award; Mem., Bd. of Dir., Hôp. St-Luc 1992– ; Candn. Council of Christians & Jews 1992– ; Vice-Pres., Ctr. de Rech. Hôp. Notre-Dame 1984–91; Mem., Strategic Planning Steering Ctte., The Arthritis Soc. 1990– ; author of articles & speaker on topics related to public auditing, finance & economics; recreations: nordic & alpine skiing, bicycling, opera, ballet, theatre, classical music; clubs: Canadian, Mount-Royal; Home: 311 Kensington Ave., Westmount, Que. H3Z 2H2; Office: 1 Place Ville Marie, Suite 2400, Montreal, Que. H3B 3M9.

**LIN, Tsung-yi,** M.D., F.R.C.P.(C); psychiatrist, medical educator; b. Taiwan 19 Sept. 1920; s. Bo-seng and Chaifan (Wong) L.; e. Tokyo Univ. Med. Sch. M.D. 1943, Grad. Training in Psychiatry 1943–46; Harvard Med. Sch. Training in Psychiatry 1950–52; Univ. of London 1956–57; m. Mei-chen Lee 8 Apl. 1946; children: Siongchi, Lillian Leng-bun, Elizabeth Hiok-bun, Joy Oat-bun, David Tat-chi; Prof. Emeritus, Univ. of B.C. 1986– ; Prof. and Head of Psychiatry Taiwan Univ. 1947–65; Dir. of Research in Social Psychiatry, World Health Organ. 1965–69; Prof. of Psychiatry and of Mental Health Univ. of Mich. 1969–73; Prof. of Psychiatry, Univ. of B.C. 1973–85; Visiting Prof. of Psychiatry Tokyo Univ. 1979–80; Hon. Pres. World Fed. for Mental Health; Adv. to Ministry of Pub. Health People's Repub. of China; Hon. Prof. Beijing Med. Coll.; Adv. to Dept. of Health, Extve. Yuan, Taiwan 1986– ; recipient Pacific Rim Coll. Psychiatrists Award; author or co-author numerous publs.; recreations: tennis, swimming, photography; Address: 6287 MacDonald St., Vancouver, B.C. V6N 1E7.

**LINCOLN, Hon. Clifford A.,** F.C.I.I. (London), F.C.I.Arb. (London); politician; b. Mauritius 1 Sept. 1928; s. Francis A. and Regina (de Baize) L.; e. Royal Coll. Mauritius and Mauritius Side Bar 1942–48; m. Lise d. Joseph and Marie Margéot 15 July 1953; children: Lawrence, Patrick, Denis, Michael, Micheline, Christine, Peter; Min. of the Environment, Que. 1985–88; articled with Robert & Perombelon, Attys., Mauritius; began ins. career with Hugh & McKinnon B.C. becoming Jr. Partner 1961; Vice pres. and Co-Founder Crosbie Manson McKinnon, Montréal 1964 becoming Pres. Lincoln Manson Ltd. and Lincoln Manson Inc.(USA); Vice Pres. and Co-Founder Dominican International Consultants; el. M.N.A. for Nelligan 1981, re-el. 1985; Dir. Emeritus Arbitrators' Inst. Can. and Co-Founder Qué. Chapter; Conf. Chrmn. and Lectr. Am. Mgmt. Assn. (N.Y.) and Candn. Mgmt. Centre (Toronto) 1960–70; Past Chrmn., The Center for the Great Lakes; Past Pres. Lakeshore Assn. Retarded Citizens; Child Care & Child Devel. Centres.; recreations: reading, sports; Home: 186 Westcroft Rd., Beaconsfield, Qué. H9W 2M3.

**LINCOLN, David Charles;** insurance executive; b. London, England 7 Sept. 1951; s. Ernest Edwin and June Pauline (Ward) L.; e. Eltham Green H.S. London, England; m. Donna d. Joyce and Ernest Baxter; one child: Candn. citizen; Keri; SENIOR VICE-PRES., CHIEF FINAN. OFFR. & SEC. TREAS., THE PERSONAL INSUR. CO. OF CANADA 1986– ; Silver Altman & Co. London, England (C.A.s) 1970–75; Wm. Eisenberg & Co. (C.A.s) 1975–77; Candn. Controller, Allstate Insur. Cos. of Canada 1977–86; Fellow, Inst. of C.A.s in England & Wales (admitted 1973); Mem., Candn. Inst. of C.A.s (admitted 1976); Mem., Un. Ch. of Can.; Markham Lions Club; United Way (Corp. Chrmn.); recreations: golf, skiing, jogging, personal computing; Home: 7 Reeve Dr., Markham, Ont. L3P 6B8; Office: 703 Evans Ave., Toronto, Ont. M9C 5A7.

**LIND, James Forest,** M.D., C.M., F.R.C.S.(C), F.A.C.S.; surgeon; educator; b. Fillmore, Sask. 22 Nov. 1925; s. James Forest and Isabella (Pringle) L.; e. Queen's Univ. M.D., C.M. 1951 (David Edward Mundell Prize in Surg. Anat. and Medal in surg.); m. Dorothy Anne d. late Cecil Henry Berlette 23 Aug. 1950; children: Heather Anne, James Forest, David Scott, Robbie Stuart, Gregory Jon; PROFESSOR, DEPT. OF SURG., EASTERN VIRGINIA MEDICAL SCHOOL; Surgeon-in-Chief, Sentara Hospitals; Dir. of Surg., Norfolk Gen. Hosp.; Active Staff, Medical Center Hosp.; Children's Hosp. of King's Daughters; Consultant, De Paul Hosp.; U.S. Public Health Serv. Hosp.; Veterans Admin. Med. Center; Naval Regional Med. Center; internship Hamilton Gen. Hosp. 1951–52, Resident in Pathol. 1952–53; Teaching Fellow in Anat. Queen's Univ. 1953–54, Fellow in Med. Queen's and Kingston Gen. Hosp. 1954–55 and Fellow in Surg. 1955–56; Registrar in Surg. Clatterbridge Hosp. Eng. 1956–58; Dept. Physiol. Liverpool Univ. 1957–58; Fellow in Physiol. Mayo Foundation, Rochester 1958–60; Lectr. in Surg. Univ. of Man. 1960, Asst. Prof. 1962, Assoc. Prof. 1964, Prof. 1966–72, Head of Surg. 1969–72; former Surg.-in-Chief Winnipeg Gen. Hosp.; former Prof. and Chrmn. of Surg., McMaster Univ., Phys.-in-Chief (Surg.) McMaster Univ. Med. Centre; rec'd John S. McEachern Fellowship Candn. Cancer Soc. 1956–57; George Christian Hoffman Award in Surg. Queen's Univ. 1957–58; John and Mary Markle Scholar in Acad. Med. 1960; Sir William Osler Award in Education 1981; Award for outstanding contributions to graduate education in Eastern Virginia 1986; Dean's Award for Outstanding Member of Faculty 1991; Visiting Prof. (Surg.) various univs. and hosps. Can. UK USA; author or co-author numerous publs.; served with RCAF 1943–45, Pilot Offr. Navig.; Surg. Lt. Commdr. RCN (R) since 1949; mem. Central Surg.; Candn. Assn. Gastroenterol. (Pres. 1972); Soc. of Surgical Chairmen; Soc. Univ. Surgs.; Soc. Surg. Alimentary Tract; Southeastern Surgical Congress; Virginia Med. Soc.; Virginia Surg. Soc.; Am. Med. Assn.; Soc. Amer. Gastrointestinal Endoscopic Surgs. (Chrmn. Membership Comte., Pres. Elect 1984); Am. Surgical Soc.; Southern Surgical Assn.; Soc. of Health and Human Values; Soc. for Surgical Education; Assn. of Academic Surg.; United Church; Home: 4044 Sherwood Lane, Virginia Beach, Virginia 23455; Office: Norfolk, Virginia 23507.

**LIND, Niels C.,** M.Sc., Ph.D., F.R.S.C., F.C.A.E.; educator; b. Copenhagen, Denmark 10 March 1930; s. Axel Holger and Karen (Larsen) L.; e. Tech. Univ. of Denmark M.Sc. 1953; Univ. of Ill. Ph.D. 1959; m. Virginia Patricia Cano Reynoso; children: Julie Wilhelmina, Peter Christian, Adam Conrad, Andreas; PROFESSOR EMERITUS, UNIV. OF WATERLOO 1992– ; Cons. to Atomic Energy Control Bd.; Design Eng.; Domina Ltd. Copenhagen 1953–54; Eng. I, Outside Plant Bell Telephone Co. Montreal 1954–55; Field Eng. Drake-Merritt, Labrador 1955; Design Eng. Fenco, Montreal 1956; Asst. Prof. Univ. of Ill. 1959–60; Assoc. Prof. Univ. of Waterloo 1960; Prof. of Civil Engineering, Univ. of Waterloo 1962–91; Dir. Inst. for Risk Research 1982–87; Visiting Appts. Cambridge Univ. 1964–65; Stanford Univ. 1967–68; Univ. Laval 1969; Laboratorio Nacional de Engenharia Civil Lisboa 1973–74; Instituto de Ingenieria UNAM, Mexico 1975; Tech. Univ. of Denmark 1977–78; Univ. of Canterbury, N.Z. 1979; Fundación Barros Sierra, Mexico 1981; Consejo Superior de Investigaciones Cientificas, Spain 1987–88 and 1992–93; Univ. of New South Wales 1988 and 1992; Univ. of Victoria 1992; ed. 'Risk Abstracts' journal, 'Technological Risk' 1982; co-author 'Methods of Structural Safety' 1986; 'Managing Risks in the Public Interest' 1991; 'Energy for 300 Years' 1992; Fellow, Am. Acad. Mechanics (Pres. 1971–72); mem., Soc. Risk Analysis; Internat. Assoc. for Civil Engr. Reliability and Risk Analysis (CERRA, Pres. 1987–91).

**LIND, Philip Bridgman,** M.A.; executive; b. Toronto, Ont. 20 Aug. 1943; s. Walter Heming and Susan (Bridgman) L.; e. Upper Can. Coll. Toronto; Ridley Coll. St. Catharines, Ont.; McGill Univ.; Univ. of B.C., B.A. (Pol. Science); Univ. of Rochester M.A. (Pol. Sociol.); m. Anne d. Alex G. Rankin, Toronto, Ont., 19 Aug. 1967; one d. Sarah Gay, one s. Jed Alexander; Vice-Chrmn., Communications Inc.; Chrmn. & Dir., Rogers U.S. Cablesystems Inc.: Dir., Rogers Broadcasting Ltd.; Multilingual Television (Toronto) Limited; St. Mary's Cement Co. Ltd.; Union Gas Ltd.; Canadian General Tower Ltd.; Focus National Mortgage Corp.; former Dir., Ont. Energy Corp.; Ontario Hydro; Asst. to Vice Pres. and Gen. Mgr. Taylor Pearson & Carson Ltd. (B.C.) 1966; Asst. to Nat. Dir. P. Cons. Party of Can. 1968; Dir. of Programming Rogers Cable TV 1970; Vice-Pres. and Secy. Rogers Cable Communications Ltd. 1973–79; Chrmn., Art Gallery at Harbourfront; Dir., Royal Candn. Geographical Soc.; mem., Arts & Cultural Industries Sectoral Advisory Group on Internat. Trade (SAGIT); former Dir. Conserv. Council Can.; Candn. Nature Fedn.; Dir. and former Chrmn. Candn. Cable Television Assn.; 1st Candn. el. to Bd. of Dir., National Cable Television Assn. (principal U.S. cable TV Assn.) 1984; Zeta Psi; P. Conservative; Anglican; recreations: outdoor sports; Clubs: Badminton & Racquet; Toronto; Albany; Home: 37 Warren Rd., Toronto, Ont. M4V 2R8.

**LINDEN, Allen Martin,** judge; b. Toronto, Ont. 7 Oct. 1934; e. Vaughan Rd. Coll. Inst., Toronto; Univ. of Toronto 1956; Osgoode Hall Law Sch., 1960; Univ. of Calif. at Berkeley, J.S.D. 1967; JUSTICE, FEDERAL COURT OF APPEAL 1990– ; read law with Levinter & Co., Toronto; called to Bar of Ont. 1960; Prof. of Law, Osgoode Hall Law School, York Univ., 1961–78; Justice, Supreme Court of Ont. 1978–90; Pres., Law Reform Commn. of Can. 1983–90; Exec. Dir., C.I.A.J. 1974–78; mem. Candn. Bar Assn.; Publications: 'Canadian Tort Law' 5th ed. 1993; 'Candn. Tort Law Cases, Notes and Materials' 9th ed. 1990; 'The Canadian Judiciary' (Ed.) 1976; 'Studies in Canadian Tort Law' (Ed.) 1968; also articles in Candn. Bar Review and other legal journs.; Office: Supreme Court Bldg., Ottawa, Ont. K1A 0H9.

**LINDEN, The Hon. Sidney B.,** Q.C., B.A., LL.B.; Chief Judge; b. Toronto, Ont. 9 Nov. 1938; s. Louis and Lily (Freedman) Lindenbaum; e. Univ. of Toronto B.A. 1961, LL.B. 1964; called to Bar of Ont. 1966; m. Beverley d. Thomas and Anne Hirschberg 2 June 1963; children: Cary Ian, Neil David, Jonathan Mark; CHIEF JUDGE, ONTARIO COURT OF JUSTICE, PROV. DIV. 1990– ; General Counsel & Extve. Dir., Candn. Civil Liberties Assn. 1966–68; Project Dir., 'Toronto Bail Project' 1968–69; private practice 1967–80; Public Complaints Comnr., Metro. Toronto 1981–85; Extve. Dir., Candn. Auto Workers Pre-Paid Legal Serv. Plan 1985–87; Information & Privacy Comnr. Ont. 1987–90; Past Mem., Candn. Bar Assn.; Criminal Lawyers Assn.; Law Soc. of U.C.; County of York Law Assn.; Internat. Assn. of Civilian Oversight of Law Enforcement; Internat. Ombudsman Assn.; Internat. Assn. of Data Protection Comnrs.; Council on Govt. Ethics, Laws; Am. Soc. of Access Profls.; recreations: basketball, sports; Home: Toronto, Ont.; Office: 1 Queen St. E., #2600, P.O. Box 91, Toronto, Ont. M5C 2W5.

**LINDER, Roger W.;** retired airline executive and company director; b. England, 1936; now Canadian citizen; served Royal Navy, 1953–55; Royal Air Force 1955–57; Leeds Univ., B.Sc. (Hons.) 1961; married Wendy Judd, 1961; joined Operational Rsch. Dept., Air Canada 1961; retired as Executive Vice-Pres. & Chief of Passenger Opns., Air Canada, 1989; Bd. Chrmn., Air Ontario 1989–92; sometime Cons. & educator in Mngt. Sci. & Mngt. Devel.; Address: Box 53064, C.P. Dorval, Dorval, Qué. H9S 5W4.

**LINDERS, James Gus,** B.A.Sc., M.A.Sc., Ph.D., FBCS; university professor; b. St. Catharines, Ont. 27 June 1936; s. Gus and Stratia (Nicholiades) L.; e. St. Catharines C.I. & V.S. 1955; Univ. of Toronto, B.A.Sc. 1960, M.A.Sc. 1961; Imperial Coll., London, England, Ph.D. 1969, D.I.C. 1969; m. Jean Elizabeth d. Richard and Dorothy Britton 12 Nov. 1965; children: John, Donald, Heather; PROF., COMPUTER SCI., UNIV. OF GUELPH 1977– ; Pres., GEOREF Systems Ltd.; Teaching Fellow, St. Michael's Coll., Univ. of Toronto 1960–64; Head, Comp. Section, Physics Dept., Ryerson Polytech. Inst. 1961–65; Lectr., Imperial Coll. 1965–69; Assoc. Prof., Univ. of Waterloo Computing Sci. 1969–76; Chrmn., Dept. of Comp. & Info. Sci., Univ. of Guelph 1977–81; cons., fed., prov. & mun. govt. agencies; seminar speaker; Fellow, British Computer Soc.; Mem., ACM, BCS, IEEE, AAAI; recreations: skiing, hiking; Home: 515 Colonial Dr., Waterloo, Ont. N2K 1Z7; Office: Guelph, Ont. N1G 2W1.

**LINDGREN, Charlotte,** B.Sc., R.C.A.; artist; b. Toronto, Ont. 1 Feb. 1931; e. Univ. of Mich. B.Sc. 1956; Haystack Sch. Me. (Scholarship) 1964; Canada Council Award (study) 1965; Garden Design with John Brookes in England 1985; has taught at: Univ. of Man. 1957–63; Haystack Sch. 1966; N.S. Coll. of Art & Design 1978, 1981–82, 1985; Banff Centre 1979; Roy. Coll. of Art, London, Eng. 1983; N.S. Rep. Candn. Artists Representation 1970; mem. Can Council Arts Adv. Panel 1971; Visiting Artist Pangnirtung, Baffin Island, N.W.T. 1978; Consultant for N.W.T. 1978–81; Consultant Nat. Capital Comn. Ottawa 1978; Founder, Halifax Friends of the Public Gardens 1983; rep. various exhns. incl. Confed. Centre Art Gallery Charlottetown 1965; Am. Fed. of Arts 'Threads of History' travel exhn. maj. USA galleries 1966; Montreal Museum of Fine Arts 1966; Nat. Gall. of Can. 1967; Art Gallery of Ont. 1967–74; Internat. Biennial of Tapestry Lausanne 1967, 1969; Expo '67 Art Gall.; Winnipeg Art Gall. 1967; Expo '70 Osaka 1970; Olympia Art Centre, Jamaica 1975; Can. House London, Eng. 1976; Centre Culturel Canadien Paris 1977; Harbourfront Toronto 1977 & 80; IV Triennale, Lodz, Poland 1981; Barbican Centre, London, Eng. 1982; Musée d'Art de d'Histoire, Belfort, France 1988; rep. in various pub. colls. incl. Assn. Pierre Pauli, Switzerland; Can. Council Art Bank; CBC Headquarters, Montreal; Dept. External Affairs Ottawa; Winnipeg Art Gallery, recipient Can. Council Arts Award 1965; Candn. Centennial Comn. Perspective Exhn. maj. prize 1967; Ont. Arts Counc. Award 1987; Vice Pres. R.C.A. 1978–86; Address: 1557 Vernon St., Halifax, N.S. B3H 3M8.

**LINDON, Paul Horace,** M.Sc., Ph.D., F.I.M., F.I.M.M., P.Eng., C.Eng.; educator; b. Birmingham, Eng. 17 July 1939; s. Horace William and Evelyn (Clark) L.; e. Univ. of Aston in Birmingham B.Sc. 1962, Ph.D. 1967; Univ. of Birmingham M.Sc. 1963; McMaster Univ. post-doctoral Fellow 1967–69; m. Kathleen d. James and Kathleen Mucklow 6 Aug. 1960; two s. Carl Paul William, Paul Joseph; PROF. OF METALL., LAURENTIAN UNIV. 1980– ; Dir., Sch. of Engineering 1981–85; Rsch. and Devel. Sect. Ldr., Foseco Intnl. Ltd. 1963–64; Falconbridge Nickel Mines Ltd. 1969–80 serving as Rsch. Metall., Sr. Rsch. Metall., Chief Metall. Sudbury Operations, and Head of Pyrometall., Corporate Rsch. Labs.; Fellow, Inst. Mining & Metall.; Inst. Metals.; mem., Assn. Prof. Eng. Ont.; Chartered Eng. U.K.; Am. Soc. Metals; Am. Inst. Mining & Metall.; recreation: music; Home: 1284 Drummond Ave., Sudbury, Ont. P3A 4Z6; Office: Ramsey Lake Rd., Sudbury, Ont. P3E 2C6.

**LINDORES, Douglas,** B.A., M.B.A.; association executive; b. Hamilton, Ont. 19 Feb. 1939; e. Univ. of Western Ont. B.A. 1965, M.B.A. 1967; married with three children; SECRETARY GENERAL, THE CANADIAN RED CROSS SOCIETY 1993– ; Aircrew Officer, Royal Candn. Air Force 1956–62; Asst. Personnel Mgr., Ex-Cell-O Corp. of Canada Ltd. 1964–65; Commercial Sec., Candn. diplomatic missions in Kuala Lumpur, Paris, Kinshasa 1967–73; First Sec., Perm. Mission of Canada to the U.N. N.Y. 1973–77; Dir., U.N. Programs, Candn. Internat. Development Agency (CIDA) 1977–79; Vice-Pres., Multilateral Programs 1979–87; Asst. Sec. to the Cabinet, Privy Council Office 1987–88; Sr. Vice-Pres., CIDA 1988–93; Procter & Gamble scholarship in Bus. Admin. 1965, '66; Robert W. Johnson Gold Medal 1967; Office: 1800 Alta Vista Dr., Ottawa, Ont. K1G 4J5.

**LINDQUIST, Robert John,** B.Comm., F.C.A., C.F.E.; chartered accountant and forensic financial investigator; b. Victoria, B.C. 8 Sept. 1945; s. George Albert and Lenore Rose (Assef) L.; e. Univ. of Windsor B.Comm. 1968; C.A. 1972; F.C.A. 1991; C.F.E. 1989; m. Angela d. Felix and Angela Janicki 29 June 1974; children: Justin, Aimee, Scott; CHARTERED ACCOUNTANT AND FORENSIC FINANCIAL INVESTIGATOR, LINDQUIST AVEY MACDONALD BASKERVILLE 1991– ; coined the phrase 'forensic accounting'; one of the most experienced & respected forensic & investigative accountants in the profession; started career in investigative acctg. Toronto 1972; he and his partners merged their highly successful business into a leading internat. acctg. firm 1985 and he served as Nat. Dir., Forensic & Investigative Acctg. Practice in Canada & Chair, Internat. Forensic Acctg. Network; Teacher / Developer of courses on fraud awareness, detection & investigation, Ont. Police College & num. other orgns. throughout Canada & U.S.; invesitgated hundreds of cases & testified in court on more than 70 occasions; F.C.A. 1991; Chrmn. of the Bd. of Regents, Assn. of Cert. Fraud Examiners 1993; co-author: 'Fraud Auditing & Forensic Accounting' 1987, 'The Accountant's Handbook of Fraud & Commercial Crime' 1992; subject of articles in several magazines; featured on CBC Radio & CBC TV's 'The Fifth Estate'; clubs: Fitness Inst., Albany Club, York Downs Golf & Country: Home: 11907 Parkside Dr., Fairfax, Virginia 22033 U.S.A.; Office: One Financial Place, One Adelaide St. E., 30th Floor, Toronto, Ont. M5C 2V9 and 805 - 15th St. N.W., Washington, D.C. 20005.

**LINDSAY, Doreen,** B.F.A., M.A.; artist; teacher; b. London, Ont. 29 Sept. 1934; d. Leonard Percy and Isabella Muir (Johnston) L.; e. Sir Adam Beck Coll. Inst. London 1953; H.B. Beal Tech. Sch. 1954; Instituto Allende, San Miguel de Allende, Mexico 1956; Sir George Williams Univ. B.F.A. 1965, M.A. 1969; m. Gabor s. Sandor and Erzabeth Szilasi 1962; one d. Andrea Doreen; HEAD OF PHOTOG. SAIDYE BRONFMAN CENTRE OF FINE ARTS 1989– , Photog. teacher 1974– ; Instr. in Non-Silver Photog. Concordia Univ. 1988–91; Instr. in Hist. of Photog. Coll. Marie-Victorin Montreal 1985– ; self-taught photog.; studied with Arthur Lismer Montreal Museum of Fine Art; during 1970's explored use of photog. images combined with hand printing processes of etching & lithog. (J'Existe Series 1977, Nourriture 1979); pioneered use of electrostatic copy art images, exhn. colour xerox prints (Galerie Powerhouse 1978); imagery family relations, feminist, yoga philos., exhn. Musée d'Art Contemporain Montreal 1982; during 1980's rsch. early alternative photog. processes; began cyanotype photograms (Indigenous vegetation series); Bd. of Dirs., Powerhouse Women's Gallery Montreal 1978–80; recipient Govt. Que. Cultural Affairs Grant 1979; Can. Council Project Grant 1986; Residency in Photography, Banff Centre for the Arts 1991; curator of photography exhibitions, Montreal, Que.; hand coloured photographs of Pacific Coast plants, San Francisco, CA 1993; co-author 'Women's Bookworks' 1979; 'A Posterior I: Women in Photography' 1989; ed. Self Portrayal 1988: A Photoetching Portfolio' 1988; contbr. 'La Gravure au Québec 1940–1980'; 'Canadian and Germain Copygraphy' 1987; Twenty Years of the Collection of the Contemporary Museum of Montreal 1985; Home: 483 Grosvenor Ave., Montreal, Que. H3Y 2S5; Office: 5170 Cote Ste. Catherine, Montreal, Que. H3W 1M7.

**LINDSAY, Robert Frederick,** Q.C., B.Com., M.A., LL.B.; lawyer; b. Toronto, Ont. 3 Oct. 1936; s. Frederick Robert and Olive Ann (Snowden) L.; e. Univ. of Toronto B.Com. 1958, M.A. 1959; Dalhousie Univ. LL.B. 1963; m. Anne d. Hugh and Marion Elliott 30 Dec. 1966; children: Jeffrey, John, Susan; PARTNER OSLER HOSKIN & HARCOURT; called to Bar of N.S. 1963, Ont. 1968, Alta. 1982; cr. Q.C. 1981; joined Fed. Justice Dept. serving Finance Dept. Fed. Tax Reform 1965–72; Partner present firm 1973; past Chrmn. Candn. Tax Found., mem. Extve. Ctte. and Gov.; former mem. Ont. Tax Adv. Ctte.; Revenue Can. Taxation Adv. Ctte.; mem. of Bd., Streethaven; mem. of Bd., The Wellesley Hospital; mem. Candn. Bar Assn.; (former Vice Chrmn.: Nat. Tax Sect., Candn. Bar-CICA Jt. Ctte. Taxation; former Chrmn. Ont. Jt. Ctte. Taxation); author numerous papers taxation; United Church; recreations: skiing, tennis, cottage; Clubs: Badminton & Racquet; Caledon Ski; Home: 22 Binscarth Rd., Toronto, Ont. M4W 1Y1; Office: P.O. Box 50, First Canadian Place, Toronto, Ont. M5X 1B8.

**LINDSAY, Roger Alexander,** K.S.J., C.A., F.I.Mgt., FInstD., F.S.A.(Scot.); financial executive; b. Dundee, Scot. 18 Feb. 1941; s. Archibald Carswell and Edith Paterson (Bissett) L.; e. Morgan Acad. Dundee; Queen's Coll. Univ. of St. Andrews; Inst. C.A.'s Scot. 1964; EXTVE. VICE PRES., WITTINGTON INVESTMENTS, LTD. 1981– , mem. Bd. and Sec.-Treas. 1971– ; Acct. and Adm. Andrew G. Kidd Ltd. (U.K.) 1964–66; H.O. Acct. Associated British Foods PLC ( U.K.) 1966–71; Dir. Luncheon Vouchers Ltd. (U.K.) 1969–71; Metrop. Toronto Convention Centre 1985–91; mem. Bd. The W. Garfield Weston Found.; Loblaw Companies Ltd.; United World Colleges Internat. of Canada Inc.; Intercon Security Ltd.; The National Club; The Charles H. Best Found.; The Oakah & Dorothy Jones Found.; Fellow, Brit. Inst. Mgmt.; Inst. Dirs.; Soc. Antiquaries Scot.; Trustee, The Presbyterian Church in Canada; Presbyterian (Elder); recreations: antique silver, heraldry; Clubs: National; RCYC; Royal Overseas League; Home: 150 Heath St. W., Toronto, Ont. M4V 2Y4; Office: 2001, 22 St. Clair Ave. E., Toronto, Ont. M4T 2S3.

**LINDSAY, T. David,** B.Com., M.B.A.; business executive; b. Can. 11 May 1940; s. Henry John and Edith Mary (Marrison) L.; e. Univ. of Windsor, B.Com. 1966; Univ. of Toronto, M.B.A. 1967; m. Bonnie d. Jack and Rita Taylor 18 June 1966; children: Michael, Stacey-Anne; VICE-PRES., ASIA PACIFIC, DURACELL INTERNATIONAL INC. 1992– ; Mktg. Mgr. Maple Leaf Mills 1977, Nat. Sales Mgr. 1979; Dir. Mktg. & Sales, Parker Pen Canada Ltd. 1980, Vice Pres. Mktg. & Sales 1981, Pres. and Gen. Mgr. 1983–85; Vice Pres. Health & Beauty Products Div. Chesebrough Ponds (Canada) Ltd. 1985; Vice Pres. Mktg. & Sales Duracell Canada Inc. 1985–87; Pres. & C.E.O. 1987–92; recreation: skiing, hiking, tennis, squash, canoe tripping, jogging; Vice Pres., Asia Pacific Jan. 1992– ; Office: Suite 2601-5 Shell Tower, Time Square, 1 Matheson St., Causeway Bay, Hong Kong.

**LINDSAY, William Kerr,** M.D., B.Sc., M.S., F.R.C.S.(C), F.A.C.S.; plastic surgeon; b. Vancouver, B.C. 3 Sept. 1920; s. James Arthur and Lottie Mary (Early) L.; e. Magee High Sch. Vancouver; Univ. of B.C.; Univ. of Toronto M.D. 1945, B.Sc.(Med.) 1949, M.S. 1959; m. Frances Beatrice d. Roland Ferris 15 Feb. 1945; 4 children; HEAD OF PLASTIC SURGERY, THE HOSP. FOR SICK CHILDREN 1958–86; Chrmn. Interhosp. Co-ordinating Comte. for Plastic Surgery, Faculty of Med. Univ. of Toronto 1965–86; Prof. Emeritus 1986; Chrmn. Med. Adv. Comte. (Ont. Soc. Crippled Children renamed) Hugh MacMillan Center 1957–65; Trustee, R. Samuel McLaughlin Found. 1986– ; recipient Lister Prize in Surgery (shared) 1959; Special Achievement Award in Plastic Surgery Am. Soc. Plastic & Reconstructive Surgeons Inc. 1979; served with R.C.A.M.C. 1943–46, RCN 1946–47, RCN (Active Reserve) 1949–51, rank Surg. Lt.; author or co-author numerous publs.; mem. Candn. Med. Assn.; Ont. Med. Assn.; Candn. Soc. Plastic Surgs. (Pres. 1963); Am. Assn. Plastic Surgs. (Pres. 1970); Am. Bd. of Plastic Surgs. Inc. (Dir. 1965–71); Am. Soc. Plastic & Reconstructive Surgs. Inc.; Am. Soc. Surgery Hand; Am. Cleft Palate Assn.; Brit. Soc. Surgery Hand; Phi Gamma Delta; United Church; recreations: conservation, farming, horseback riding, fishing; Clubs: Sydenham (Pres. 1971); York; Home: 44 Clarendon Ave., Toronto, Ont. M4V 1J1; Office: 555 University Ave., Toronto, Ont. M5G 1X8.

**LINDSETH, Roy Oliver,** F.R.S.C., LL.D., P. Geoph.; petroleum and computer services consultant; b. Calgary, Alta. 19 Aug. 1925; s. Ole Andrew and Etta (Sundquist) L.; e. W. Can. High Sch.; P. Geoph. Alta. 1969, Cal. 1974; m. Lucia M.B. Serrano d. Ramon Serrano Reyes 5 Feb. 1949; one s. Richard Raymond; CHRMN. & PRES., HPC HIGH PERFORMANCE COMPUTING CENTRE 1992– ; Dir., Det Norske Veritas Candn. Bd.; Party Chief United Geophysical Inc. Calgary 1945; Geophysicist, Richmond Exploration, Maracaibo, Venezuela, Cons. Caracas 1954; Vice Pres. EDP Engineering Data Processors Ltd. Calgary 1964; Vice Pres. and Dir. CDP Computer Data Processors Ltd. 1968; Chrmn., Teknika Corporation 1972–92; author over 175 techn. presentations, lectures & papers geophys. exploration petroleum & natural gas; Fellow, Royal Soc. of Can. 1987; Hon. Life mem. Assn. Prof. Engs., Geols. & Geophysicists Alta. (Centennial Award 1983; Past Pres.); J. Tuzo Wilson Medal Candn. Geophys. Union 1979; Univ. of Calgary LL.D. 1978; recipient Queen's Silver Jubilee Medal 1977; Hon. mem. Soc. Exploration Geophysicists (Kauffman Gold Medal 1970, Enterprise Award 1989, Past Pres.); Hon. mem. Can. Soc. Exploration Geophysicists (CSEG Medal 1989, Past Pres.); Fellow, Assn. Exploration Geophysicists; Sr. mem. Inst. Elect & Electronics Engrs.; Candn. Geoscience Coun. (Past Pres.); recreations: gardening, golf; Clubs: Ranchmen's (Pres.); Calgary Golf & Country; Calgary Petroleum; Canyon Meadows Golf & Country; Home: 241 Eagle Ridge Dr., Calgary, Alta. T2V 2V6; Office: #3408, 400 3rd Ave. S.W., Calgary, Alta. T2P 4H2.

**LINDSEY, Casimir Charles,** M.A., Ph.D., F.R.S.C.; educator; b. Toronto, Ont. 22 March 1923; s. Lt. Col. Charles Bethune, D.S.O. and Wanda Casimira (Gzowski) L.; e. Univ. of Toronto Schs. 1941; Univ. of Toronto B.A. 1948; Univ. of B.C. M.A. 1950; Cambridge Univ. Ph.D. 1952; m. Shelagh Pauline d. W.P.M. Kennedy, Toronto, Ont. 29 May 1948; EMERITUS PROF., DEPT. OF ZOOLOGY, UNIV. OF B.C. 1988– ; B.C. Game Dept. Div. Biol. 1952–57; Inst. of Fisheries and Dept. of Zool. Univ. of B.C. 1953–66; Prof. of Zool. Univ. of Man. 1966–79; Dir., Inst. Animal Resource Ecology, Univ. of B.C. 1980–85; Visiting Prof., Univ. of Singapore 1962–63 (organized Fisheries Training Unit); Fisheries Consultant to Univ. of S. Pacific for Candn. Internat. Devel. Agency 1972; Fisheries Adv. Reservoir Project, e. Pakistan 1964; Consultant on Fisheries Training to Papua-New Guinea inst. of Technol. 1972; External Assessor in Biol., Nanyang Univ., Singapore 1979–80; External Assessor in Zool., Univ. of Singapore 1980–81; Consultant of Fisheries Project in Bangladesh for Internat. Dev. Res. Centre 1981; Candn. Del. Pacific Science Congs. Thailand 1957, Japan 1966, Australia 1971, Vancouver 1975, Khabarovsk, U.S.S.R. 1979; Collecting Expdns. to Galapagos Islands 1953, S.E. Asia 1957, Malaysia 1962–63, Cocos Island, Costa Rica 1964, Bangladesh 1964, Revillagigedo Islands 1966, Hudson Bay 1967, Amazon Brazil 1976, N. Can. and Alaska 13 expdns. 1955–78; Wallace Mem. Lectr. Singapore 1963; rec'd Wildlife Soc. Publ. Award 1972; Nuffield Foundation Travel Award to Cambridge 1973; Saunderson Award for Excellence in Teaching, Univ. of Man. 1977; Killam Sr. Fellowship 1985–86; Rh. Inst. Award for Outstanding Contributions to Research, Univ. of Man. 1979; Gov., Vancouver Pub. Aquarium 1956–66, 1980– ; served with Candn. Armoured Corps and Candn. Intelligence Corps 1943–45; author or co-author 3 books and over 60 papers principally biol. of fishes; mem. Candn. Soc. Zools. (Vice Pres., Pres. 1975–78); Candn. Soc. Environmental Biols. (Vice Pres. 1974–75); Am. Soc. Ichthyols. & Herpetols. (Gov.); Royal Soc. of Can. (Fellow 1974, Convenor of Animal Biol. Subject Div. 1976–7); mem., Fisheries and Oceans Adv. Council to Federal Minister 1981–86; Home: 3757 W. 36th Ave., Vancouver, B.C. V6N 2S3; Office: Vancouver, B.C. V6T 1W5.

**LINDSEY, George Roy,** O.C., B.A., M.A., Ph.D.; b. Toronto, Ont. 2 June 1920; s. Late Charles Bethune and Wanda Casimira (Gzowski) L.; e. Univ. of Toronto Schs., 1938; Univ. of Toronto, B.A. 1942; Queen's Univ., M.A. 1946; Cambridge Univ., Ph.D. 1950; Nat. Defence Coll., 1965–66; Candn. Govt. Bilingual & Bicultural Course, Quebec City, 1970–71; m. June Monica, d. late Frederick W. Broomhead, 20 Aug. 1950; children: Charles Robin, Jane Casimira; SR. RESEARCH FELLOW, CANDN. INST. OF STRATEGIC STUDIES 1989– ; Military Operational Research, Defence Research Board, Ottawa, 1950–54; Senior Operational Research Officer, Air Defence Command, RCAF, 1954–59; Dir., Defence Systems Analysis Group, Ottawa, 1959–61; Head, Operational Research Group, SACLANT Antisubmarine Research Centre, Italy, 1961–64; Senior Operational Research Scientist, Defence Operational Research Establishment, Ottawa, 1964–67; Chief, Operational Research & Analysis Establishment 1968–87; Sr. Research Fellow, Candn. Inst. Internat. Peace & Security 1991–92; served with RCA 1942–45; Brit. Army Operational Research Group 1944–45; rank Capt.; Award of Merit, Candn. Oper. Res. Soc. 1984; Officer of the Order of Canada, 1989; mem. Adv. Bds. of Cdn. Def. Quarterly and Encyclopedia of Physical Science and Technology; author of 'The Dynamics of the Nuclear Balance' and 'Le Feu Nucléaire' (with A. Legault) and of various scientific and military papers; mem., Canadian Operational Research Society (Past Pres.); International Inst. Strategic Studies; Candn. Inst. Internat. Affairs; Operations Research Soc. Am.; Royal Candn. Mil. Inst.; Royal United Services Inst.; Zeta Psi; Home: 55 Westward Way, Ottawa, Ont. K1L 5A8.

**LINDZON, Andrew Stuart,** LL.B.; computer consultant; b. Toronto, Ont. 14 July 1961; s. Dr. Martin and Rose Rachelle (Kimel) L.; e. Univ. of Toronto Arts & Sci. 1979–81; Osgoode Hall, York Univ. LL.B.; MANAGER CONSULTING, QUIET TOUCH COMPUTER SYSTEMS INC. 1994– ; Pres., Ashlin Computer Consultants Ltd. 1979–87; part-time Instr. Career Learning Centre, Toronto 1980–81; profl. contrib. to Computing Canada 1985; Chrmn. TORPLUG (Digital equipment users group) 1985–86; Pres. St. Paul Young P.C. Party 1978–79; Vice-Pres. St. Andrew/St. Patrick Young P.C. Party 1978–79; Dir. St. Davids Young PC 1984; mem. Toronto/Eglinton Rotary 1984–85; recreations: tennis, skiing; Address: 550 Alden Rd., Markham, Ont. L3R 6A8.

**LING, Winston,** B.Comm., C.A., C.F.A.; financial executive; b. Shanghai, China 2 Aug. 1941; s. Edward and Ming-Hui L.; e. Univ of Toronto B.Comm. 1965; m. Stephanie Sam; children: Liana, Tina, Karina; EXECUTIVE VICE-PRESIDENT, CROWNX INC.; Ernst & Young 1965–68; Mem., Corp. Finance Dept. and Shareholder, Dominion Securities Corp. Limited 1969–78; C.F.O., Crownx Inc. 1978; Executive Vice-Pres., Crownx Inc. 22 April 1992; Vice-Pres., Devel., Crown Life Insurance Co. 1992– ; Mem., Candn. Inst. of C.A.s; Financial Extves. Inst. Can.; Inst. of Chartered Financial Analysts; Elder and Active Mem., Chinese Presbyterian Ch.; club: National; Home: 33 Rosemary Lane, Toronto, Ont. M5P 3E7; Office: 3000 Steeles Ave. E., Markham, Ont. L3R 9W2.

**LINGENFELTER, Dwain Matthew,** B.A.; politician, farmer; b. Shaunavon, Sask. 27 Feb. 1949; s. Robert Lewis and Mary Veronica (Harty) L.; e. Univ. of Sask., B.A.; children: Sacha, Matthew, Travis; Min. of Economic Development, Govt. of Sask.; Min. Responsible for Sask. Economic Development Corp.; Government House Leader 1991– ; Mem., Sask. Legislature (NDP, Regina Elphinstone Constituency 1988– ); Dept. of Revenue Can. 1970–76; active grain farmer, Shaunavon 1968– ; Mem., Sask. Legislature (NDP, Shaunavon Constituency 1978–86); Min. of Social Services, Sask. Cabinet 1980–82; Opposition House Leader 1982–86, 1988–91; recreations: skiing, running; Home: R.R. 2, Box 23, Regina, Sask. S4P 2Z2; Constituency Office: 1656 Albert St., Regina, Sask. S4P 2S6.

**LINGWOOD, Clifford Alan,** B.Sc., Ph.D.; university professor; b. England 2 Jan. 1950; s. Edward Frank and Joyce Evelyn (Baker) L.; e. Hull Univ. (U.K.), B.Sc. 1971; Univ. of London, Ph.D. 1975; m. Kathryn d. Joan and Kenneth Hall 28 Dec. 1974; children: James, Daniel, Samuel; RSCH. INST. STAFF, HOSP. FOR SICK CHILDREN & DEPT. OF CLIN. BIOCHEM., BIOCHEM. & MICROBIOL., UNIV. OF TORONTO 1987– ; post-doct. fellow with Dr. S. Hakomori, Seattle, USA & Dr. H. Schachter, Hosp. for Sick Children, Toronto; MRC Scholar 1981–86; Mem., Candn. Biochem. Soc.; Am. Soc. Cell Biol., Soc. Complex Carbohydrates; Am. Soc. Microbiology; Home: 116 Kingsway Cres., Toronto, Ont. M8X 2R9; Office: 555 University Ave., Toronto, Ont. M5G 1X8.

**LINHARES DE SOUSA, Hon. Maria,** B.A., M.A., LL.B.; provincial judge; b. Madeira, Portugal 20 Sept. 1949; d. José and Conceição L.; m. James s. John and Mary Lahey 26 May 1973; children: Sarah, Patrick, Daniel; JUDGE OF THE ONTARIO COURT OF JUSTICE (PROVINCIAL DIV.) 1989– ; Law Clerk to Chief Justice of High Court of Justice of Ont. 1978–79; Family Law Comnr., Supreme Court of Ont. 1979–89; Office: 161 Elgin St., Ottawa, Ont. K2P 2K1.

**LINT, David George,** B.Com. M.B.A.; entertainment industry executive; b. Montréal, Qué. 27 Apl. 1942; e. Burnhamthorpe Coll. Inst. 1960; Univ. of Toronto, B.Com. 1964, M.B.A. 1965; one s.: Christopher David; CHRMN., CINENOVA PRODUCTIONS INC. 1991– ; Mktg. Mgmt. Procter & Gamble 1966–70; Mgmt. Cons. McKinsey & Co. 1970–73; Pres. Office & TV Production, CBC 1973–82; Vice Pres. Corporate Devel., Telemedia Inc. 1982–83; Vice Pres. Devel. & Mktg., Cantel 1984; Devel. Head, Torstar Corp. 1984–86; Extve. Vice Pres., Famous Players Inc. 1986–90; mem. Bd., Acad. of Candn. Cinema & Television; Toronto Film Festival; Univ. of Toronto Press; Planned Parenthood; recreations: arts, tennis, film, scuba; Club: Queen's Quay Racquet; Home: 63 Woodlawn Ave. W., Toronto, Ont. M4V 1G6.

**LINTEAU, Denis;** business executive; b. Quebec City, Que. 1942; e. Inst. de Technologie de Québec 1962; m. Louise Pelletier; 2 children; PRESIDENT & BOARD OF DIRECTORS, ALMAX INTERNATIONAL INC. & LAMBERT SOMEC INC. 1985– ; Hervé Houde Ltée. Quebec City 1962–67; Tri-Bec Inc. 1967–71; various positions to Vice-Pres. & Dir., Electricity, Marcel Lambert Inc. 1971–85; Mem., La Corp. des Maîtres Electriciens du Qué.; Groupement Québécois des Entreprises; la Régie des Entreprises de construction du Qué.; Mem., Adv. Bd., Fac. of Sci. & Admin., Univ. Laval; Home 918-A ave. J.-C. Cantin, St-Augustin, Que. G3A 1A4; Office: 725 Lachance St., Quebec City, Que. G1P 2H3.

**LINTEAU, Paul-André,** L.ès L., M.A., Ph.D., F.R.S.C.; historian; educator; b. Montréal, Qué. 10 Jan. 1946; s. Paul-Emile and Gabrielle (Blais) L.; e. Coll. Saint-Viateur Outremont; Univ. de Montréal L.ès L. 1968, M.A. 1969, Ph.D. 1975; one s. Jean-Philippe; PROF. OF HIST. UNIV. DU QUÉBEC à MONTRÉAL 1969– ; recipient Sir. John A. Macdonald Prize Best Candn. Hist. Book 1981; Internat. Candn. Studies Award of Excellence 1990; Prix André-Laurendeau 1993; Prix Lionel-Groulx 1993; author: 'Maisonneuve' 1981, transl 'The Promoters' City' 1985; 'Histoire de Montréal depuis la Confédération' 1992; 'Brève histoire de Montréal' 1992; co-author: 'Histoire du Québec contemporain' 1979, transl. 'Quebec: A History 1867–1929' 1983; 'Nouvelle histoire du Québec et du Canada' 1985; 'Le Québec depuis 1930' 1986, transl. 'Quebec since 1930' 1991; 'Clés pour l'histoire de Montréal' 1992; ed. French version: 'Histoire générale du Canada' 1988, 'Atlas historique du Canada' vol. III 1990; ed.-in-chief Internat. Jour. Candn. Studies 1989–92; assoc. ed. Urban Hist. Review 1981–88; mng. ed. Revue d'histoire de l'Amérique française 1975–78; author or co-author over 45 articles; mem. Candn. Urban Hist. Assn. (Pres. 1984–86); Candn. Hist. Assn. (Council 1973–76); Institut d'histoire de l'Amérique française (Sec. Treas. 1970–72, 1973–74); Home: 10595 Laverdure, Montréal, Qué. H3L 2L6; Office: C.P. 8888 Succ. A, Montréal, Qué. H3C 3P8.

**LIPSEY, Richard G.,** O.C., M.A., Ph.D. F.R.S.C.; economist; b. Victoria, B.C. 28 Aug. 1928; s. Richard Andrew and Faith Thirell (Ledingham) L.; e. Oak Bay High Sch., Victoria, B.C., 1947; Univ. of B.C., B.A. (1st Class Hons.) 1951; Univ. of Toronto, M.A. 1953; London Sch. of Econ., Ph.D. 1958; LL.D.: McMaster Univ. 1984; Univ. of Victoria 1985; Carleton Univ. 1987; Queen's Univ. 1990; Univ. of Toronto D.Sc. 1992; Univ. of Guelph 1993; Univ. of Western Ont. 1994; m. Diana Louise, d. J.A. Smart, London, Eng. 17 Mar. 1960; children: Mark Alexander Daniels (step-s.), Mathew Richard, Joanna Louise, Claudia Amanda; Concurrently, ALCAN FELLOW, CANDN. INST. FOR ADVANCED RSCH. and PROF. OF ECONOMICS, SIMON FRASER UNIV. 1989– ; with B.C. Govt. as Research Asst. 1950–52; Asst. Lect., Lect., Reader and Prof., London Sch. of Econ., Eng. 1955–63; Visiting Prof. of Econ., Univ. of Calif. at Berkeley 1963–64; concurrently Prof. of Econ., Chrmn. Dept. Econ., Dean Sch. of Social Studies, Univ. of Essex, Eng. 1963–69; Visiting Prof., Univ. of B.C. 1969–70; Sir Edward Peacock Prof. of Econ., Queen's Univ. 1970–86; Irving Fisher Visiting Prof., Yale Univ. 1979–80; Sr. Economic Advisor, C.D. Howe Inst. 1983–89; Dir., Research into Obstacles to Growth in U.K., Nat. Econ. Devel. Council 1961–63; mem. Council, Brit. Social Sciences Research Council 1965–68; Governing Council and Adv. Council, Nat. Inst. for Econ. and Social Research (U.K.) 1964–70; Council, Royal Econ. Soc. (U.K.) 1967–70; Mang. Ed., Review of Econ. Studies 1961–65; Publications: 'An Introduction to Positive Economics' 1963 (8th ed. 1993); 'Economics' (with P.O. Steiner and D.D. Purvis) 1966 (10th ed. 1992); Candn. version with D. Purvis and P.O. Steiner (8th ed. 1993); 'An Introduction to a Mathematical Treatment of Economics' (with G.C. Archibald) 1967 (3rd ed. 1977); 'The Theory of Customs Unions: A General Equilibrium Analysis' 1971; 'An Introduction to the U.K. Economy' (with C. Harbury) 1983 (4th ed. 1993); 'Common Ground for the Canadian Common Market' (with F. Flatters) 1984; 'Canada's Trade Options' (with M. Smith) 1985; 'Global Imbalances and U.S. Policy Responses' (with M. Smith) 1987; 'Evaluating the Free Trade Deal' (with R.C. York) 1988; 'First Principles of Economics' (with C. Harbury) 1988 (2nd ed. 1992); other writings incl. numerous articles in prof. journs. on theoretical and applied aspects of econ.; Fellow, Econometric Soc.; Fellow, Royal Society of Can.; Officer of the Order of Canada; Pres., Cdn. Econ. Assoc. 1980–81; Pres. Atlantic Econ. Soc. 1986–87; recreations: skiing, ocean sailing; Home: 3248 West 1st Ave., Vancouver, B.C. V6K 1H5; Office: Simon Fraser Univ. at Harbour Centre, 515 West Hastings St., Vancouver, B.C. V6B 5K3.

**LISSON, Kathryn M.,** B.Sc., C.M.C.; managment consultant; b. Montreal, Que. 11 March 1952; d. George B. and Christine M. (MacNain) Johnstone; e. Carleton Univ. B.Sc. (Hons., Univ. medal) 1974; Inst. of Management Consultant C.M.C. 1980; m. James H. s. Muriel and Ron L. 21 June 1975; children: David, Karen; PARTNER RESPONSIBLE FOR NATIONAL FINANCIAL INSTITUTION CONSULTING, PRICE WATERHOUSE 1991– ; joined Finance Dept., Unemployment Insur. Canada 1974 and left as Senior Analyst, MIS 1976; Consultant, Computer Services Group, Price Waterhouse Management Consultants 1976 (progressed to Mgr. & qualified as a C.M.C.); Vice-Pres., Information Systems, Barclays Bank of Canada 1982–86; Dir., Financial Institution Consulting, Price Waterhouse 1986; Partner 1987; Mem. Bd. of Govs., Bishop Strachan School 1993– ; Mem., Inst. of Mngt. Cons. of Ont.; recreations: tennis, squash, skiing, reading; clubs: Toronto Cricket, Skating & Curling, Bd. of Trade; Home: 57 Colin Ave., Toronto, Ont. M5P 2V8; Office: 1 First Canadian Place, Suite 3300, Toronto, Ont. M5X 1H7.

**LIST, Michael H.,** B.Comm.; marketing, corporate development executive; b. Kingston, Jamaica 30 Nov. 1942; s. Sibrandt Henry and Cecille W. (Landale) L.; e. McGill Univ., B.Comm. 1967; Brighton Coll., England; m. Margot A. d. A.R. McMurrich 18 Nov. 1967; children: Michael, James, Julia; VICE-PRES., CORP. DEVEL., INTERNAT. SEMI-TECH MICROELECTRONICS INC. 1988– ; joined IBM Can. 1967, several sr. sales posts; joined Bank of Montreal 1979; Computel 1981 (later acquired by CSG); Pres., Teleride 1984–86; Security Card Systems 1986–88; joined Semi-Tech as Pres. of Datacrown 1988; Mem., Ontario Premier's Council on Economic Renewal; Chrmn., Task Force on Investment in Ontario; Mem. of Bd., Upper Can. Coll.; recreations: squash, rowing, tennis; clubs: Montreal Badminton & Squash, Toronto Racquet, Hanlan Boat Club; Granite; Home: 19 Birchwood Ave., Toronto, Ont. M2L 1M4; Office: 131 McNabb St., Markham, Ont. L3R 5V7.

**LIST, Roland,** Dr.sc.nat., F.R.S.C.; scientist and educator, former UN official; b. Frauenfeld, Switzerland 21 Feb. 1929; s. August Joseph and Anna (Kaufmann) L.; e. Swiss Fed. Inst. of Technol. Dipl. Phys. ETH. 1952, Dr.sc.nat. 1960; m. Gertrud K. d. Jean Egli-Schatt, Switzerland 9 Apl. 1956; children: Beat Roland, Claudia Gertrud; Prof. of Physics (Meteorology), Univ. of Toronto 1963–82, 1984– ; Depy. Sec.-Gen. World Meteorological Org., Geneva, Switzerland, 1982–84; Assoc. Chrmn. of Physics, Univ. of Toronto 1969–73; Sec. Head, Atmospheric Ice Formation, Swiss Fed. Inst. for Snow and Avalanche Research 1952–63; Visiting Prof. Swiss Fed. Inst. of Technol. 1974; Chrmn. Panel on Weather Modification and Working Group on Cloud Physics, Extve. Comte. World Meteorol. Organ. 1968–82, mem. Internat. Cloud Physics Comn., Internat. Assn. Meteorol. & Atmospheric Physics; Dir., Univ. Corp. of Atmospheric Research, Colo. 1974–77; mem. Science Council, Space Shuttle Program, Univ. Space Research Assn.; Chrmn., Italian Scientific Ctte. on Rain Enhancement (TECNAGRO) 1990– ; Certified Consulting Meteorologist; rec'd Sesquicentennial Medal Univ. of Leningrad; Plaque of recognition, Govt. of Thailand; Patterson Medal in meteorology; author over 200 articles; Fellow, Am. Meteorol. Soc.; Royal Soc. of Can.; Royal Meteorol. Soc.; mem., Candn. Meteorol. Soc.; European Geophys. Soc.; Am. Geophys. Union; Swiss Phys. Soc.; Cdn. Academy of Sciences; Swiss Acad. of Natural Sciences; R. Catholic; Home: 58 Olsen Dr., Don Mills, Ont. M3A 3J3; Office: Dept. of Physics, Univ. of Toronto, Toronto, Ont. M5S 1A7.

**LISTER, Richard Lloyd,** M.A.Sc., Ph.D.; executive; b. Toronto, Ont. 15 Nov. 1938; s. George and Shirley (Moldaver) L.; e. North Toronto Coll. Inst.; Univ. of Toronto B.A.Sc. 1961, M.A.Sc. 1962, Ph.D. (Metall. Eng.) 1964; DIRECTOR, PRESIDENT AND CHIEF EXECUTIVE OFFICER, ZEMEX CORPORATION and DIR. DUNDEE BANCORP. INC.; Rsch. Chem. National Lead Co. (now NL Industries) Sayreville, N.J. 1964–68; Tech. Dir., Candn. Titanium Pigments, Montreal 1968–74; Prodn. Adv. Titanium World Operations, NL Industries, Montreal and Sayreville 1971, Dir. Operations Metal Div. New York 1974, Gen. Mgr. Titanium Pigments Div. Sayreville 1975–78; Gen. Mgr. Pigments Div. Sun Chemical Corp. Cincinnati 1978–81; Pres. & C.E.O., Campbell Resources Inc., Toronto 1981–88, Chrmn. 1988–92; Hon. Chrmn. 1992–93; Affiliations: Candn. Inst. Mining & Metall.; Published several technical papers in the field of metallurgy, chemistry & thermodynamics; recreations: squash, sailing, horse breeding & racing; Home: 181 Forest Hill Rd., Toronto, Ont. M5P 2N3; Office: Scotia Plaza, 40 King St. W., 56th Floor, Toronto, Ont. M5H 3Y2.

**LISTON, Major-Gen. (Ret) Terrence,** M.B.E., C.D., B.A., M.P.A.; executive; b. Montreal, Que. 19 Nov. 1938; s. Stanley and Bertha (Leblanc) L.; e. D'Arcy McGee H.S. 1954; Queen's Univ., B.A. 1969; Candn. Army Staff Coll. 1971; Nat. Defence Coll. 1981; Ecole nat. admin. publique, MPA 1984; m. Louisette d. Louis-Philippe and Fabiola Desrosiers 24 April 1965; children: Catherine and Elisabeth; VICE-PRES., ADMINISTRATION, MIL-DAVIE 1988– ; joined Candn. Army 1957; commissioned into Royal 22e Regt.; served with parachute, mechanized & UN units 15 yrs. in Can., Fed. Rep. of Germany & former Belgian Congo (awarded M.B.E.); commanded 1st Bn. of his Regt. 1975–77; promoted Brig.-Gen. 1983 commanding 5th Brigade (Que.); Sr. Policy Analyst, Nat. HQ 1981–83; Head of Communications, Dept. of Nat. Def. 1985–87; promoted Maj.-Gen. 1987; Head of planning and operations for Dept.; headed UN mission to Western Sahara; Chrmn., Extve. Ctte., Royal 22e Regt. 1983–86; Mem., Ed. Bd. 'Canadian Defence Quarterly' 1985–86; Gov., Kidney Found. Campaign, Que. 1985; Pub. Relns. Offr., Ottawa-Hull Pub. Serv. Un. Way Campaign 1986; Dir., INNOVATECH, Que. 1994– ; Soc. dev. éco. du St. L. (SODES) 1993– ; Defence Assoc. Network 1989– ; Quebec Symphonic Orchestra 1989–93; Extve. Ctte., South Shore Chamber of Commerce 1990–93; Québec Chamber of Commerce 1993– ; Roman Catholic; Mem., Que. Garrison Club (Pres. 1984–85); Home: 1285 Gaspard-Fauteux, Sillery, Que. G1T 2E1; Office: 22 George-D-Davie, Lévis, Que. G6V 6N7.

**LITHERLAND, Albert Edward,** B.Sc., Ph.D., F.R.S.C., F.R.S.; educator; b. Wallasey, Eng. 12 March 1928; s. Albert and Ethel (Clement) L.; e. Wallasey Grammar Sch. 1946; Univ. of Liverpool B.Sc. 1949, Ph.D. 1955; m. Anne d. Elliott and Ruby Allen 12 May 1956; two d. Jane Elizabeth, Rosamund Mary; UNIVERSITY PROFESSOR EMERITUS 1993– , Dir. of ISOTRACE, Prof. of Physics, Univ. of Toronto 1966–79, University Professor 1979–93; Sci. Offr. Atomic Energy of Canada Ltd. 1953–66; Visiting Sci. Oxford Univ. 1960, 1973–74; recipient, Gold Medal for Achievement in Physics, Candn. Assn. Phys. 1971; Rutherford Medal, Inst. of Phys. (London) 1974; Henry Marshall Tory Medal, Royal Society of Can. 1993; author numerous publs. sci. jours.; Home: 3 Hawthorn Gdns., Toronto, Ont. M4W 1P4; Office: Physics Dept., Univ. of Toronto, Toronto, Ont. M5S 1A7.

**LITHWICK, Sidney,** B.Arch.; architect; b. Ottawa, Ont. 21 Aug. 1921; s. Abraham and Dora (Rosenberg) L.; e. Lisgar Coll. Inst., Ottawa, Ont.; McGill Univ. Sch. of Arch., B.Arch. 1943; m. Ida Irene, d. Sol Witchel, Sudbury, Ont., 21 Oct. 1945; children: Howard Alvin, Marilyn Elaine, Helene Ava; Pres., Aldow Holdings Ltd.; I.& S. Realty Corp. Ltd.; Sidal Holdings Inc.; Secy.-Treas., Dorwick Realty Ltd.; Arch. Asst., Dept. of Works and Bldgs. of Naval Service of Can. 1943–44; joined predecessor of Lithwick Johnston & Moy in 1945 as Chief Draughtsman and entered into Partnership in 1946; architects for sixteen high schools in Ottawa 1950–71 and for 40 million dollar Childrens Hosp. for E. Ont. (1972); firm completed joint venture with Zeidler Roberts Partnership as architects for 60 million dollar redevelopment of Ottawa Civic Hospital 1979–84; mem., Ottawa Bd. Trade (Chapter of Arch.); mem., Agudath Israel Cong.; Chrmn., National Property & Insurance Ctte.; Mem., O.A.A.; awarded Medal of Merit by Boy Scouts of Canada 1984; Jewish; Clubs: Kiwanis (Pres., Ottawa, 1967); B'nai Brith Lodge 885; Rideau View Golf; recreations: golf, reading; Home: 385 Island Park Dr., Ottawa, Ont. K1Y 0B1; Office: 1701 Woodward Dr., Ottawa, Ont. K2C 0R4.

**LITTLE, A. Hugh,** M.D., F.R.C.P.(C); physician; b. Tainan. Taiwan 15 Dec. 1933; s. John Llewellyn and Flora M. (Gauld) L.; e. Univ. of Toronto M.D. 1959; m. Donna d. Bill and Blanche Heineman 1 Sept. 1958; children: Adam, Martin, Allison, Kyrie; PHYS. SUNNYBROOK HEALTH SCI. CENTRE 1968– , mem. Bd. Trustees; postgrad. training Toronto, Halifax, London (Eng.); gen. practice Burin, Nfld.; author 'The Rheumatological Physical Examination' 1986; mem. Arthritis Soc., Ont. Div. Bd., Nat. Standing Cttes.; Home: 230 Stibbard Ave., Toronto, Ont. M4P 2C3; Office: 2075 Bayview Ave., Toronto, Ont. M4N 3M5.

**LITTLE, Alan Brian,** B.A., M.D., C.M., FRCS(C); physician; educator; b. Montréal, Qué. 11 March 1925; s. Herbert Melville and Mary Lisette (Campbell) L.; e. McGill Univ. B.A. 1948, M.D., C.M. 1950; Diplomate Am. Bd. Obstetrics & Gynecol. 1959; Advanced Cert. Reproduc. Endocrinol. 1974; m. Bitten, Ph.D. d. Knud and Astrid Stripp 31 March 1984; children: Michael (dec.), Susan, Deborah, Catherine, Jane, Lucinda; CHIEF OF OBSTETRICS & GYNECOL. ROYAL VICTORIA HOSP., Prof and Chrmn. of Obstetrics & Gynecol. McGill Univ. 1983– ; internship Montréal Gen. Hosp. 1950–51; residency Harvard Med. Sch. 1951–54, mem. Faculty Obstetrics & Gynecol. 1954–66; Asst. Prof. Case Western Reserve Univ. Cleveland, Prof. of Obstetrics & Gynecol. 1966–83; Visiting Prof. Harvard Med. Sch. 1982–83; Council mem. Nat. Inst. Child Health & Human Devel. 1983–87; Chrmn. Policy Data Monitoring Panel, Clin. Trial, Nat. Heart Lung & Blood Inst. 1977–82; mem. Fertility & Maternal Health Drugs Adv. Ctte. F.D.A. 1978–81; Dir. Am. Bd. Obstetrics & Gynecol.

1974–83; served with RCAF 1943–45, rank Flying Offr.; author or co-author over 100 sci. publs., mem. various ed. bds.; mem. Am. Gynecol. & Obstetrics Soc. (Pres. 1987–88); Am. Coll. Surgs. (Gov. 1981–87); Am. Gynecol. Soc. (Asst. Sec. and Sec. 1975–81), Assoc. Prof. Gynecol. & Obstet. (Council 1973–76); Prenatal Rsch. Soc. (Pres. 1982, Council 1973–76); Soc. Gynecol. Investig. (Pres. 1979, Council 1967–69, 1978–81); recreations: tennis, golf; Home: 3252 The Boulevard, Westmount, Qué. H3Y 1S3; Office: 687 Pine Ave. W., Montréal, Qué. H3A 1A1.

**LITTLE, Arthur John,** B.A., F.C.A. (1956); b. London, Ont. 17 Dec. 1913; s. late Arthur Thomas and late Lylian Edith (Hartson) L.; e. Public and High Schs., London, Ont.; Appleby Coll., Oakville, Ont. (1928–31): Univ. of Western Ont., B.A. 1935; m. Margaret Hunter, d. Dr. S. R. Moore, London, Ont., 28 Aug. 1939; children: Peter M., Elizabeth M.; Pres., Canadian Chamber Commerce, 1964–65; Past President, Toronto Board Trade (1956–57); Toronto Community Chest (1954); Past Chrmn. of Candn. Tax Foundation; Past Pres., St. John Ambulance Ontario Council; past mem. of Board of Trustees, Toronto General Hospital; mem. of Board of Governors, Appleby College, Oakville, Ont.; Bd. of Trustees, Metropolitan Toronto Community Found.; joined Clarkson Gordon Co. (then Clarkson, Gordon, Dilworth, Guilfoyle & Nash) after grad. from Univ. in 1935; C.A. in 1939, and was admitted to Partnership in the firm in 1945, retired 1974; Anglican; recreation: fishing; Clubs: University; Toronto Hunt; The Toronto; The York; Nekabong Hunting & Fishing; Home: Apt. 604, 70 Montclair Ave., Toronto, Ont. M5P 1P7.

**LITTLE, Charles Herbert,** C.D., M.A., F.R.C.G.S.; b. Larkspur, Calif. 11 Dec. 1907; s. Charles Herbert and Kara Elizabeth (French) L.; e. Mount Forest, Ont. pub. and high schs.; Upper Can. Coll. Toronto 1926; Univ. of Toronto Trinity Coll. B.A. 1930; Brasenose Coll. Oxford (Rhodes Scholar) B.A. 1932, M.A. 1937; m. Ruth B. d. Walter and Muriel Harrison 28 June 1934; children: Jennifer Paynter, Dr. C.H. Anthony, Maj.-Gen. W.E. Robert, H.A. Patrick; Modern Langs. and Games Master Upper Can. Coll. Toronto 1933–39; Royal Candn. Navy 1939–58 (retiring with the rank of Commander), first Candn. Dir. Naval Intelligence 1942–45; Brit. Intelligence Hong Kong 1945–46; organized Univ. Naval Training (UNTD) Can. 1946–52; prepared prog. Regular Offr. Training Plan (ROTP); Command Edn. Offr. Pacific 1953–56, Atlantic 1956–58; L'Ordre de Bon Temps, Candn. Pub. Service 1959–71 serving with Sec. of State, Min. Citizenship & Immigration, Emerg. Measures Orgn. nat. training plan 1960–64; bilingual Chief Ed. Royal Comn. on Pilotage 1964–71; recipient Queen's Silver Jubilee Medal 1977; Allan Sangster Award Candn. Authors Assn. 1981; Ottawa Branch CAA Achievement Award 1988; Admirals' Medal 1991; Chrmn. Maritime Museum of Esquimalt 1953–56; Dir. Maritime Museum Can. 1956–59; Supt. All Saints' Sandy Hill Ang. Ch. Sun. Sch. 1959–84, Warden 1970–83, Lay Reader 1973– ; Dir., Hospice of All Saints' 1986–88; former Dir. Ottawa Br. Candn. Red. Cross Soc.; former Vice Pres. Ottawa Br. Candn. Cancer Soc.; former mem. Editorial Ctte. Royal Candn. Geographical Soc.; Fellow RCGS 1969; author 'Influence of Sea Power on the Conquest of Canada' 1958; 'Battle of the Restigouche' 1962; 'The Rideau Club 1865–1965' 1965; 'Naval Reserves in Canada' 1973; 'All Saints' Church, Sandy Hill 1898–1975' (1974), '1975–85' (1985); 'The First Ninety Years 1900–1990' 1990; 'Rideau Curling Club 1888–1978' 1978; 'Rideau Curling Club Centennial' 1988; '18th Century Maritime Influences on the History and Place Names of British Columbia' 1991; mem. Ed. Bd. and columnist 'Canadian Author and Bookman'; ed. various publs.; Dir., Candn. Assn. of Rhodes Scholars 1982–87; mem. Candn. Authors Assn. (Pres. Ottawa Br 1966–68, Nat. Rep. and Vice Pres. 1968–72, Nat. Pres. 1972–75, Awards Chrmn. 1976–80); Candn. Writers' Found. (Dir. 1974– , Pres. 1978– ); Navy League of Can.; Hon. Life Mem., Naval Offrs.' Assn. of Can.; Hon. Pres., UNTD Assoc., Ottawa; Hon. Mem., UNTD Assoc. of Upper Canada; Trustee Can. Naval Memorial Trust; Hon. Life Mem., United Services Inst., Ottawa; Hon. Life Mem., Ottawa Valley Cricket Counc. 1953 (Pres. 1949–51); Zeta Psi; P. Conservative; recreations: nature study, walking, golf, curling; Clubs: Royal Ottawa Golf; Rideau Curling (Dir. 1968–72, Srs.' Pres. 1983–88, Hon. Life Mem. 1986); Rideau (former Dir. 1964–68 & Acting Pres. twice); Home: 905, 111 Wurtemburg St., Ottawa, Ont. K1N 8M1.

**LITTLE, Douglas I.;** marketing executive; b. Saint John, N.B. 3 Apl. 1948; s. Douglas Arthur and Anne Elizabeth (MacKinnon) L.; e. Simonds Regional High Sch. Saint John 1966; Univ. of N.B. one yr.; Perdue Univ. various extension courses; m. Roberta d. Roy and Roberteen Major 15 March 1969; one d. Melanie Jessica; FOUNDER AND OWNER LITTLE & ASSOCIATES 1986– ; Chrmn. and Founder Leacock Heritage Festival 1989– ; Pres. Festivals Ont. 1988–92; Vice-Pres., Candn. Assn. Festivals & Events 1990–91 (Dir. 1986–91, winner 4 Mktg. Awards Candn. Fantasy Festival 1987, winner 3 Mktg. Awards Leacock Heritage Festival 1991 and 4 Mktg. Awards Leacock Heritage Festival 1992); awarded Commemorative Medal for 125th Anniversary of Candn. Confederation; former journalist Timmins, Peterborough and London; Coordinator City of Timmins Diamond Jubilee 1972; Ed. Timmins Porcupine News 1976–77; owned and operated Little Services Public Relations 1977–82; Mgr. Huronia Tourist Assn. 1983–86; Mgr. Downtown Orillia Bus. Improvement Area 1989– ; Co-chair and Founder, Ship Orillia & Area First Ctte. 1991– ; Treas. & Founder, Orillia Winter Carnival 1993– ; Secretary, Ont. Downtowns Inc. 1993– ; Dir., Leacock Memorial Home Bd. 1991; Dir. Leacock Associates 1989– ; Mgr. 1987 Candn. Hot Air Balloon Championships; Official, 1988 Calgary Olympic Hot Air Balloon Festival; Home: 109 Maple Leaf Ave., Orillia, Ont. L3V 6Z1; Office: P.O. Box 2305, Orillia, Ont. L3V 6S3.

**LITTLE, George,** M.A.; teacher; author; b. Lanarkshire, Scot. 22 May 1937; s. George and Mary (Wyper) L.; e. Glasgow Univ. M.A. Hon. 1959; Jordanhill Coll. of Edn. Cert. Edn. 1960; m. Pearl d. John Bardsley and Flora Cassels 20 Sept. 1958; children: Jacqueline Ann (Stroud), Alison Joan; Leader New Democrat Party, New Brunswick 1980–88; Teacher Oban High Sch. 1960–62; Head Dept. Eng. R.A.F. Khormaksar Secondary Sch., Aden 1962–64; Teacher Saint John H.S., Saint John, N.B. 1964–67; Head Dept. Eng. Simonds H.S. Saint John N.B. 1967– ; author: 'The Many Deaths of George Robertson' (short story collection) 1990; author and broadcaster humorous commentaries on regional and national radio; poems publ. in various magazines; mem. New Brunswick Teachers' Assn.; Nat. Counc. of Teachers of Eng.; active volunteer for UNICEF (Dir. of annual campaign; N.B. Rep. Candn. Teachers' Tour of UNICEF Installations, Tanzania 1981); recreations: tennis, cross-country skiing, travel, camping, folk singing; Home: 64 Gibbon Rd., East Riverside, Saint John, N.B. E2H 1R2; Offices: 1490 Hickey Rd., Saint John, N.B.

**LITTLE, James Alexander,** M.D., M.A., F.R.C.P.(C); educator; b. Detroit, Mich. 8 Dec. 1922; s. John Burton and Beatrice Olive (Walker) L.; e. Parry Sound (Ont.) High Sch. 1941; Univ. of Toronto, M.D. 1946, M.A. 1950; m. Elizabeth d. Clifford and Florence Kempson 31 Jan. 1953; children: Ann Elizabeth, Roger Alexander; m. Barbara d. Leo and Gertrude Bradt 16 May 1985; PROF. OF MED., ST. MICHAEL'S HOSP., UNIV. OF TORONTO 1974– ; Dir. Lipid Rsch. Clinic Prog. Univ. of Toronto and McMaster Univ. 1972–92; mem. Univ. of Toronto Fac. of Med. Rsch. Ctte. 1988–91; Nat. Rsch. Council Fellow in Biochem. Univ. of Toronto 1947–49; Candn. Arthritis Found. Rsch. Fellow, Sunnybrook Hosp. Toronto 1951–52, Dir. Atherosclerosis Project 1952–67; Rsch. Assoc. & Clin. Teacher, Sunnybrook and St. Michael's Hosps. 1952–63; Assoc. in Med. St. Michael's Hosp., Univ. of Toronto 1963, Asst. Prof. of Med. 1966, Assoc. Prof. 1967–74; Dir. Diabetes Clinic, St. Michael's Hosp. 1954–70, Dir. Clin. Investig. 1964–72, Rsch. Coordinator 1964–91, Dir. Lipid Clinic 1966–89, Dir. Div. Endocrinol., Metabolism & Nephrol. 1970–72; mem. Health & Welfare Can. Adv. Ctte. Long Chain Fatty Acids 1973, Ctte. Nutrition & Cardiovascular Disease 1974–77; USA NHLI Ctte. Evaluation Lipid Rsch. Clinic Proposals 1971, MRFIT Centre Proposals 1973; Chrmn., Organizing Ctte., Candn. Consensus Conf. on Cholesterol 1988; mem. & Past Pres. Toronto Diabetes Soc.; Toronto Clin. Rsch. Soc.; Candn. Atherosclerosis Soc.; former mem., Gairdner Found. Med. Ctte.; Ont. Heart Found. Med. Ctte.; Univ. Toronto Rsch. Bd.; Candn. Heart Found. Profl. Edn. Ctte.; mem., Acad. Med. Toronto; Am. Diabetes Assn.; Am. Heart Assn.; Candn. Cardiovascular Soc.; Candn. Med. Assn.; Candn. Diabetes Assn.; Candn. Soc. Clin. Investig.; Candn. Soc. Endocrinol. & Metabolism; Internat. Atherosclerosis Soc.; Nutrition Soc. Can.; Candn. Fedn. Biol. Socs.; Pres., Candn. Lipoprotein Conf. 1990; Scientific publications 114, abstracts 85, invited lectures 118, principal investigator in 180 Lipid Research Clinic Program publications; recreations: skiing, curling, bowling, boating; Clubs: Osler Bluff Ski; Parry Sound Curling; Carling Trail Blazers; Home: R.R. 1, Nobel, Ont. P0G 1G0; Office: 1 Spadina Cres., Toronto, Ont. M5S 2J5.

**LITTLE, Jean,** C.M., B.A.; writer; b. Tainan, Taiwan 2 Jan. 1932; d. John Llewellyn and Flora Millicent (Gauld) L.; e. Guelph Elem. & High Schs.; Univ. of Toronto, B.A. 1955; author (juvenile fiction) 'Mine for Keeps' 1962; 'Home From Far' 1965; 'Spring Begins in March' 1966; 'Take Wing' 1968; 'One to Grow On' 1969; 'Look Through My Window' 1970; 'Kate' 1971; 'From Anna' 1972; 'Listen for the Singing' 1977; 'Mama's Going to Buy You a Mockingbird' 1984; 'Lost and Found' 1985; 'Different Dragons' 1986; 'Hey World, Here I Am!' 1986; 'Little by Little' 1987; 'Stars Come Out Within' 1990; co-author: (with Maggie DeVries) 'Once Upon A Golden Apple' 1991; 'Jess Was the Brave One' 1991; 'The Revenge of the Small Small' 1992; recipient Little Brown Candn. Children's Book Award 1961; Vicky Metcalf Award 1974; Can. Council Children's Book Award 1977; Candn. Lib. Assn. Children's Book of Yr. and Ruth Schwartz Children's Book Award 1985; Boston Globe 'Horn Book' Honour Book 1988; Mem., Order of Canada 1993; mem. Writers Union Can.; Candn. Soc. Children's Authors, Illus. & Performers; United Church; Home: R.R. 2, R.P.O., Elora, Ont. N0B 1S0.

**LITTLE, The Honourable Judge Judythe Patricia,** B.A., LL.B.; provincial court judge; b. Toronto, Ont. 31 Jan. 1946; d. Harold Merton and Shirley Elaine (Parliament) L.; e. Brampton Sec. H.S. 1964; McMaster Univ. B.A. (Hon.) 1968; Osgoode Hall Law Sch., York Univ. LL.B. 1974; m. Donald Gordon s. William and Marjorie Fraser 17 March 1976; children: Cameron Bruce, Ian Douglas; JUDGE, PROVINCIAL COURT, FAMILY DIV., PROV. OF ONT. 1986– ; Psychometrist & therapist, Queen St. Mental Health Ctr. 1968–71; Mng. Partner, Fraser & Little 1976–86; Mem., Bd. of Dir., Ont. Family Law Judges Assoc. 1987– ; Mem., Bd. of Dir., Inst. for the Prevention of Child Abuse, formerly Ont. Ctr. for Prevention of Child Abuse 1985–90; Reg. Mental Health Review Bd. (N.W. Reg.) 1985–86; Chrmn., Kenora Panel, Child Rep. Prog. 1984–86; Co-presentor 5th Internat. Cong. on Child Abuse 1984; Invited Participant, Bar Admission Curriculum Conf., Law Soc. of U.C. 1984; Extve. Mem. and/or Chrmn. of numerous cttes. & assns. 1972–84; several presentations on family law and first nations justice issues; Mem., Candn. Bar Assn.; Assn. of Family & Conciliation Courts; Ont. Judges Assn.; The Ont. Family Law Judges Assn.; Women's Law Assn.; recreations: reading, Scottish country dancing, gardening; Home: R.R. 1, Carlton Rd., Kenora, Ont. P9N 3W7; Office: 216 Water St., Kenora, Ont. P9N 1S4.

**LITTLE, Michael Victor,** B.A.; geophysical contracting executive; b. Vancouver, B.C. 29 Nov. 1951; s. Joseph Henry and Olga Perronne (Guichen) L.; e. Univ. of Victoria B.A. 1977; m. Elizabeth d. George and Joan Arnett 5 July 1980; children: Georgia, Zachary; PRESIDENT & CHIEF EXECUTIVE OFFICER, CAPILANO INTERNATIONAL INC. 1987– ; Alexco Geophysical 1978–79; Operations Supervisor, Home Oil Co. 1979–80; joined Capilano Geophysical 1981; Vice-Pres. 1983–87; Mem., Candn. Soc. of Exploration Geophysicists; Past Dir. & Vice-Pres., Candn. Assn. of Geophysical Construction; recreations: golf, skiing, hockey, squash; club: Calgary Winter; Home: Site 21, Box 1, S.S.1, Calgary, Alta. T2M 4N3; Office: 2615-22 St. NE, Calgary, Alta. T2E 7L9.

**LITTLE, Paul F.,** B.A., M.B.A., C.A.; merchant banker; b. Toronto, Ont. 29 May 1943; s. late Reginald Jack and Elizabeth Isabel (McCleary) L.; e. Univ. of Toronto B.A. 1965; Univ. of B.C. M.B.A. 1968; children: Katharine Anne, Peter Richard Gordon; Dir., Gornitzki Thompson & Little Company Ltd.; Pres., GTL Securities Inc.; Dir., Falvo Corp.; Pafco Insur. Co. Ltd.; Industrial Docks & Supplies Ltd.; C.A. student, Sr. Staff Acct., Clarkson Gordon & Co. 1967–70; Extve. Assist. Treasurer of Ont. 1971–74; Planning Analyst & Dir. Corp. Affairs, John Labatt Ltd. 1974–77; Vice-Pres., Finance, Allpak Ltd. 1977–80; Vice-Pres., Finance & Develop., Union Gas/Union Enterprises 1980–85; Clubs: Toronto Golf; Albany (Dir.); St. Catharines Rowing Club; Home: 401 Queen's Quay W., Toronto, Ont. M5V 2Y2; Office: 200 King St. W., Suite 2004, Box 86, Toronto, Ont. M5H 3T4.

**LITTLEJOHN, Edward L.,** B.A.Sc.; chemical engineer; b. Toronto, Ont. 21 Sept. 1927; s. Edward and Margaret Osborne (Lind) L.; e. Lawrence Park Collegiate Inst.; Univ. of Toronto B.A.Sc. Chem. Engrg. 1949; m. Margaret d. Robin M. Haultain 29 Sept. 1951; children: Edward James, David Haultain, Patricia Marnie; PRES. E.L. LITTLEJOHN & ASSOCIATES LTD. 1971– ; Publisher: 'The Canadian Free Trader and Directory'; 'Ottawa R & D Report and Directory'; 'Canadian Energy News'; Sales Mgr. Montreal Union Carbide Can. Ltd. 1953, Mgr. Publ. Relations Toronto 1958, Asst. to Pres. Visking Div. Lindsay 1962, Mgr. Ottawa 1966–71; Pres., E.L. Littlejohn and Assocs. Ltd. 1971– ;

author various tech. and mgmt. articles; mem. Assn. of Profl. Engrs. of Ont.; Chem. Inst. of Can.; Protestant; el. Fellow Chem. Inst. of Can. 1972; past Pres. and Chrmn. Soc. of Plastics Ind. of Can.; past Dir. Soc. of Plastics Ind. Inc., N.Y.; recreations: golf, fishing; Clubs: Royal Ottawa Golf; Rideau (past Dir.); Franklin; Home: 61 Park Rd., Rockcliffe Park, Ont. K1M 0C1; Office: 151½ Bank St., Ottawa, Ont. K1P 5N7.

**LITTLEJOHN, John Gordon,** B.Eng. LL.B., P.Eng.; lawyer; retired mining executive; b. Montreal, Que. 25 June 1925; s. John Campbell and Florence Lilian (Morbey) L.; e. McGill Univ. B.Eng. (Mining) 1951; Osgoode Hall Law Sch. LL.B. 1960; m. Maureen Patricia d. late George Terrance Hower 7 July 1956; children: Maureen Anne, Bruce Campbell; called to Bar of Ont. 1962; Partner, Mills, Cochrane & Littlejohn 1962–66; Assoc., Robertson, Lane, Perrett, Frankish & Estey 1966–69; Vice Pres. and Gen. Counsel, Rio Algom Ltd. 1969, retired 1990; Partner, Harris, Littlejohn 1990–91; Extve. Dir., Arbitration and Mediation Inst. of Ont. Inc.; Founding Dir. Centennial Nursery Sch.; served with R.C.N.V.R., W.W. II; mem. Law Soc. Upper Can.; Assn. Prof. Engrs. Prov. Ont.; Assn. Candn. Gen. Counsel; United Church; recreation: skiing; Clubs: Engineers (Pres. 1980); Lawyers; Home: 117 Lytton Blvd., Toronto, Ont. M4R 1L5; Office: Suite 602, 234 Eglinton Ave. E., Toronto, Ont. M4P 1K5.

**LITTLER, William,** B.A.; critic; educator; b. Vancouver, B.C. 12 July 1940; e. Univ. of B.C., B.A. 1963; also studied piano, theory, criticism; Conn. Coll. dance music, technique, composition and criticism 1971–72; freelance writer Vancouver Sun 1962 becoming Music and Dance Critic 1962–66; Music Critic Toronto Daily Star 1966 adding regular dance criticism 1971; reviews have been heard on various CBC radio series incl. 'Critically Speaking,' 'The Arts in Review,' 'Arts National,' 'Stereo Morning'; writer and host CBC TV 'Summer Concert' series Vancouver 1965; writer-host CBC TV specials on Nat. Arts Centre Orchestra and Toronto Symphony; began teaching courses in music and the theatre and in dance criticism York Univ. 1974; Guest Lectr. Univ. of Waterloo, Univ. of Calgary, McMaster Univ., Kent State Univ., Conn. Coll., Ohio State Univ., Peabody Conserv.; jury mem. CBC Talent Festival, Baldwin Nat. Piano and Organ Competition, Metropolitan Opera Auditions, Kennedy Center Friedheim Award for best US orchestral composition 1979; writings incl. articles, reviews and liner notes various publs.; Vice Pres. Music Critics' Assn. 1969–77; Founding Chrmn. Dance Critics' Assn. N. Am. 1974; directed first Critics' Inst. in Candn. Music Toronto, Ottawa, Montreal 1975; consultant Urwick, Currie & Partners for study and report 'An Assessment of the Impact of Selected Large Performing Companies upon the Canadian Economy' 1974; Address: c/o Toronto Star, 1 Yonge St., Toronto, Ont. M5E 1E6.

**LITTLETON, Sidney James;** producer; b. Montreal, Que. 17 Oct. 1941; s. Charles Theodore and Dorothy (Sloan) L.; e. Acadia Univ.; m. Cheryl d. Ralph and Jean Ozon 17 Sept. 1977; children: Susan Jean, Claire Elizabeth; PRODUCER, CANADIAN BROADCASTING CORP. 1980– ; Programme Dir., Company of Young Canadians 1966–69; Producer & Dir., National Film Bd. 1970–80; CBC producer in TV and radio current affairs depts. resp. for edit. devel., news & current affairs; Lectr., Pol. Sci., York Univ. Winner, Robert Weaver Award 1992; Mem., Nat. Radio Producers Assn.; Candn. Assn. for the Study of Intelligence & Security; author: 'Target Nation: Canada and the Western Intelligence Network' 1986; recreations: reading, hunting; Home: 888 Palmerston Ave., Toronto, Ont. M6G 2S2; Office: Rm 3A204, Cdn. Broadcasting Ctr., P.O. Box 500, Stn. A., Toronto, Ont. M5W 1E6.

**LITVAK, Isaiah A.,** B.Com., M.S., Ph.D.; educator; economist; b. Shanghai, China 1 Oct. 1936; s. Matthew S. and Basia (Daitch) L. (dec.); e. McGill Univ., B.Com. 1957; Columbia Univ., M.S. 1959, Ph.D. 1964; m. Marilyn, d. Coleman Kenigsberg, 21 Sept. 1958; one s, Matthew Kenneth; PROF. OF BUSINESS AND PUBLIC POLICY, FAC. OF ADMIN. STUDIES, YORK UNIV. 1978– ; Lectr. in Pol. Econ., McMaster Univ. 1961, Asst. Prof. 1962, Assoc. Prof., Faculty of Business, 1965, Prof. 1967–70; Prof. of Econ. and Internat. Affairs, Carleton Univ., 1970–77; Visiting Distinguished Prof., York Univ., 1973–74; Guest Lectr. univs. in U.S., Europe and Africa; Mgmt. Consultant to Fed. and Prov. Govts., United Nations and business; mem. McMaster Univ. Senate, Council Grad. Studies, Research Adv. Council and Extve. Council Sch. of Business; rec'd Research Grants and leave fellowships from Can. Council 1962, 1969, 1971, 1977, 1983, 1991–94; McMaster Univ. 1963–69; Candn. Donner Foundation, 1968 & 1979; McLean Foundation, 1970 and 1974; Fed. Depts. Indust., Trade & Comm. and Energy, Mines & Resources, 1971–88; Ford Foundation Workshop Grant, 1964; publ. grant Social Science Research Council, 1971; The Touche Ross Award, 1981; author, 'Marketing Management for the Middleman' 1967; co-author, 'An Annotated Bibliography on Canadian Marketing' 1967; 'Canadian Cases on Marketing' 1968; 'Dual Loyalty: Canadian-U.S. Business Arrangements' 1971; Ed. and co-author, 'Marketing: Canada' 1964 (rev. ed. 1968); 'The Nation Keepers' 1967; 'Foreign Investment: The Experience of Host Countries' 1970; 'Cultural Sovereignty' 1974; 'Corporate Dualism and the Canadian Steel Industry' 1977; 'Alcan Aluminum Ltd.: A Case Study' 1977; 'Plant Efficiency and Competition Policy' 1979; 'The Canadian Multinationals' 1981; 'Canadian Cases in International Business' 1984; 'Business Can Succeed' 1984; other writings incl. booklets, articles and reviews in various learned and prof. journs.; mem., Am. Econ. Assn.; Acad. of Mgmt.; Internat. Business Educ. Assn.; recreation: tennis; Home: 193 Dunvegan Rd., Toronto, Ont. M5P 2P1; Office: 4700 Keele St., Downsview, Ont. M3J 1P3.

**LITVAN, Gerard Gabriel;** research scientist; b. Vienna, Austria 17 May 1927; s. Charles and Amalia Grete (Birkenholz) Schaffer; e. Sr. Matric. 1945; Eotvos Lorand Univ., Dipl. in Chem. 1952; Univ. of Toronto Ph.D. 1962; m. Anna d. Arnold Stern 2 May 1964; one d.: Julia; CONSTRUCTION MATERIALS CONSULTANT; Demonstrator, Eotvos Lorand Univ. 1950–52; Asst. Prof. 1952–56; Rsch. Sci., Hungarian Acad. of Scis. 1956; Rsch. Chem., Candn. Indus. Ltd. 1957–59; Principal Rsch. Offr., Inst. for Research in Construction, National Research Council of Canada 1962–93; Vice-Pres., Am. Ceramic Soc. 1985–86 (Past Trustee & Chrmn.); Ctte. Mem., Candn. Standards Assn.; Am. Concrete Inst.; Reunion Internat. des Labs. d'Essais et de Rech. sur les Mater. et les Construc.; Fellow, Chem. Inst. of Can. 1981; recipient, Award in the General Area of Freezing and Thawing Concrete, Canada Centre for Mineral and Energy Tech./Am. Concrete Inst. 1990; Am. Ceramic Soc. 1981; author of numerous rsch. & tech. papers on freezing and thawing phenomena, corrosion of steel in concrete, and durability of building materials; co-editor: 'Durability of Building Materials and Components' (Proc. of 1st Internat. Conf., Am. Soc. for Testing and Materials) 1980; Jour. Ed.: 'Cement and Concrete Research'; co-author of patented process to render concrete frost-resistant; Address: 248 Range Rd., Ottawa, Ont. K1N 8J8.

**LIU, Fai,** O.Ont., M.D., DTM&H(Eng.), FACP, FRCP(C), FAGS; physician; b. Canton, China 25 Feb. 1919; s. Dr. Chun San and Suk Ching Liu (Wong) L.; e. Pui Ching Middle; Shanghai Med. Univ. M.D. 1944; London School of Hygiene & Tropical Med., Univ. of London DTM&H 1948; m. Edith d. the late Mr. du and Mrs. Sue Wong 26 Dec. 1953; children: Eleanor J., Barbara, Donna, William; postgrad. training Chungking, Tientsin & Shanghai China 1945–48; Victoria Hosp. London Ont., Jewish Gen. Hosp., Queen Mary Veterans Hosp.; 1949–54; Col., Chinese Red Cross Surg. Team, Chinese 52nd Army Corps 1944–45; private med. practice & affil. Toronto Western Hosp. 1954– ; Rsch. Asst., Lambert Lodge 1955–60; Cons., Prov. Geriatric Study Ctr. 1958–70; Captain, Royal Candn. Army Med. Corps. (Militia) 1961–65; Med. Dir., Castleview Wychwood Towers 1971–86; Mem., Ont. Adv. Council on Seniors, Ont. Min. of Citizenship 1989– ; Chair, Panel on Geriatrics, 5th Conf. on Health Problems Related to Chinese in N. Am. (Toronto) 1990– ; Mem., Toronto Maylr's Comn. on Aging & Chair, Subctte. on Health Wellbeing 1989– ; Bd. of Dir., Ont. Div., Canada Concerned Pensioners 1992– ; Co-chair, Chinese Comm. Fund Raising Ctte., Mt. Sinai Hosp. 1984– ; Pres. & Chair, Mon Sheong Found. 1975– ; Bd. of Gov., Mt. Sinai Hosp. 1976– ; several past extve. ctte. positions; FACP; FRCP(C); FAGS; Toronto Citizen of the Year 1967; Centennial Medal 1967; Cert. of Appreciation for Serv. to Seniors, Ont. Min. of Comm. & Social Serv. 1980; Leadership Cert., Mt. Sinai Hosp. 1985; Courvoisier Leadership Award 1989; Hon. Mem., Mon Sheong Found. 1989; Candn. Birthday Award 1989; Volunteer Service Award (15 years) Min. of Citizenship & Culture 1990; Order of Ont. 1991; Gardiner Award 1991; One of Ten Outstanding Overseas Chinese 1991, by Xinhua News Agency; mem., Candn. & Ont. Med. assns.; Candn. Public Health Assn.; Candn. Assn. on Gerontol.; Ont. Ger. Assn.; Chinese Candn. Med. Soc.; Fed. of Chinese Candn. Profls.; author: 'Acute Viral Pericarditis' 1954, 'The Elderly Chinese' 1975; co-author: 'Calcification of Motral Valve Annulus' 1953, 'Acute Parotitis' 1956; recreations: swimming, walking; clubs: Mandarin Club of Toronto, Royal Ont. Museum; Home: 30 Glenrose Ave., Toronto, Ont. M4T 1K4; Office: 407 – 360 Bloor St. W., Toronto, Ont. M5S 1X1.

**LIVERNOIS, John Richard,** M.A., Ph.D.; educator; b. Toronto, Ont. 3 Apr. 1953; s. Clifford Irving and Audrey Mae (Mulchey) L.; e. Univ. of Toronto, B.A. 1976; Univ. of B.C., M.A. 1978, Ph.D. 1984; m. Brenda d. John and Adele Dyack 9 June 1984; two d.: Alexandra, Rebecca; ASSOC. PROF. OF ECON. UNIV. OF GUELPH 1991– ; Visiting Fellow, Univ. of Southampton 1989–90; Owner Consulting Practice econ. of energy & natural resources; recipient SSHRC Doctoral Fellowship 1978–80; Killam Doctoral Scholarship 1980 (declined); Student Fellowship Prog. Dept. Energy, Mines & Resources Ottawa 1980–81; Asst. Prof. of Econ. Univ. of Alta. 1982–87, Assoc. Prof. 1988–90; author or co-author various jour. publs.; Book Review Ed., 'Candn. Public Policy' journal 1992– ; mem. Candn. Econ. Assn.; Am. Econ. Assn.; Assn. Environmental & Resource Econs.; recreations: golf, skiing; Home: 40 University Ave. W., Guelph Ont. N1G 1N4; Office: Dept. of Econ., Univ. of Guelph, Guelph, Ont. N1G 2W1.

**LIVESAY, Dorothy (Mrs. D.C. Macnair);** poet; journalist; social worker; professor; b. Winnipeg, Man. 12 Oct. 1909; d. J.F.B. and Florence (Randal) Livesay; e. Glen Mawr., Toronto, Ont.; Univ. of Toronto, B.A. 1931; Sorbonne, dipl. d'études supérieures 1932; Univ. of Toronto (Social Science) 1934; Univ. of B.C., M.Ed. 1966; m. Duncan Cameron Macnair 14 Aug. 1937; children: Peter Macnair, Marcia Hays; winner of Gov. Gen's. Medal for Poetry 1944 and 1947; Lorne Pierce Gold Medal for Lit., Roy. Soc. of Can. 1947; author: 'Green Pitcher' 1928; 'Signpost' 1932; 'Day and Night' 1944; 'Poems for People' 1947; 'Call My People Home' 1950; 'New Poems' 1955; 'Selected Poems 1926–56' 1957; 'The Unquiet Bed' 1967; 'The Documentaries' 1968; 'Plainsongs' 1970 and 1971 (revised ed.); 'The Two Seasons: Poems Collected and Uncollected' 1972; 'A Winnipeg Childhood' (fictional memoirs) 1973; 'Ice Age' 1975; 'Beginnings: A Winnipeg Childhood' (paperback edition) 1975; 'Right Hand Left Hand' (a collage of documents and writings from the 1930s) 1977; 'The Woman I Am' (selection of feminist poems) 1977, republished 1991; 'Room of One's Own' Vol. 5, No. 1/2 Dorothy Livesay Issue 1979; 'The Raw Edges' 1981; N.F.B. Film 'The Woman I Am' 1981; 'The Phases of Love' 1983, French translation 'Les Ages de L'amour' 1991; 'Feeling the Worlds' 1984; 'The Self-Completing Tree' 1986; (recent prose fiction) 'Beginnings' 1989; 'The Husband' (novella) 1990; ed., 'Collected Poems of Raymond Knister' 1949; founder and ed., 'Contemporary Verse (CV/II)'; 'Annotated Bibliography: Dorothy Livesay' 1983; 'The Livesay Papers: A Research Tool' Univ. of Manitoba Archives 1986; 'A Public and Private Voice: Essays on the Life and Work of Dorothy Livesay' 1986; 'Dorothy Livesay and Her Works' 1987; 'Dorothy Livesay Twayne World Authors' 1987; 'The Husband' 1990; 'Journey with My Selves' 1991; frequent contrib. to CBC programmes and talks; UNESCO Programme Asst. (Educ.) Paris 1959–60 and in N. Rhodesia 1960–63; Lectr. in Creative Writing, Univ. of B.C. 1965–66; Writer-in-Residence, University of N.B. 1966–68; Asst. Prof., Univ. of Alta. 1968–72; Univ. of Victoria 1973–74;, Writer-in-Residence, Univ. of Man. 1975, Univ. of Ottawa 1977, Simon Fraser Univ. 1979; Univ. of Toronto 1983; semi-retired but gives lectures and poetry readings across Can. and abroad; Hon. Fellow, St. John's Coll., Univ. of Man. and Trinity Coll., Univ. of Toronto; D. Litt. Univ. of Waterloo 1974; D. Litt. McGill 1985; LL.D. Simon Fraser Univ. 1987; D.Litt. Univ. of Toronto 1987; Hon. Degree, Athabasca Univ., Edmonton, Alta. 1983; Person's Case Award, Gov.-Gen. 1984; Officer, Order of Canada 1987; Hon. Degree, Univ. of B.C. 1990; Hon. Degree, Univ. of Victoria 1990; Order of B.C. 1992; Address: c/o Peter Macnair, Box 111, Merville, B.C. V0R 2M0.

**LIVINGSTON, William Ross,** B.Com.; insurance executive; b. Toronto, Ont. 8 Aug. 1922; s. Charles Wilmot and Gladys (Burton) L.; e. Univ. of Toronto Schs., 1935–40; Univ. of Toronto, 1940–42 and 1945–47; m. Joan, d. H. W. Vanstone, 25 Sept., 1948; children: Robert V., Brian W., Anne B.; VICE CHRMN. LAURENTIAN MUTUAL FUNDS 1987– ; Chrmn., Bellwood Health Services Inc.; Health Insur. Reciprocal of Canada; District Health Council, Toronto; Dir., Silcorp Limited; Abbey Life Insurance Co.; with Group Dept., Aetna Life 1947–50; New York Life at Toronto and New York as Regional Mgr., Dir. of Agencies and Asst. Vice-Pres. 1951–64; Vice. Pres., Pres. and Chrmn., Sovereign Life Assur. Co. and Sovereign General Insur. Co. 1964–78; Pres., Eaton Financial Services 1978–87; Chrmn. & Dir., West Park Hospital; Past Chrmn., Can. Safety Council; Candn. Red Cross; United Church; recreations: golf, curling, cottage; Clubs: Rosedale Golf; University; Granite; Home: 135 Stratford Cres., Toronto, Ont. M4N 1E1; Office: 310 Front St. W., 2nd Flr., Toronto, Ont. M5V 3B8.

**LIVINGSTONE, David Walker,** Ph.D.; educator; b. Vancouver, B.C. 13 Feb. 1943; s. Percy and Marjorie Fenwick (Paterson) L.; e. Lord Tweedsmuir High Sch. Cloverdale, B.C. 1961; Univ. of B.C., B.A. 1966; Johns Hopkins Univ., Ph.D. 1971; m. Angela Nall d. Stanley and Marjorie Nall 24 Dec. 1966; two d. Phaedra Janeen, Stephanie Kezia; PROF. OF SOCIOL. IN EDN., ONT. INST. FOR STUDIES IN EDN. 1984– ; Project Dir. Centre for Study of Social Orgn. of Schs. 1967–69; Lectr. present Inst. 1969; Asst. Prof. 1971, Assoc. Prof. 1974, Chairperson 1982–84; Project Dir., OISE Survey of Educational Issues 1977– ; Visiting Scholar, Centre d'Etudes Regionales Antilles Guyane, Fort de France, Martinique 1976; Univ. of B.C. 1979, Visiting Prof. 1985; Visiting Prof., Dept. of Behavioural Sci., Macquarrie Univ., Sydney, Australia 1989; cons. community groups & sch. bds. pub. opinion issues in edn. 1978– ; reviewer numerous Candn. & internat. scholarly jours. 1971– ; named Queen's Scout 1959; Surrey Athlete of Yr. 1961; Woodrow Wilson Fellow 1966; Can. Council Fellow 1967–69; Social Sci. & Humanities Rsch. Council Rsch. Grants 1974, 1979, 1983–85, 1987–89; author 'Public Attitudes Toward Education in Ontario' 1978, 1979; 'Class, Ideologies and Educational Futures' 1983; 'Social Crisis and Schooling' 1985; co-author 'Public Attitudes Toward Education in Ontario' 1980, 1982, 1984, 1986, 1988, 1990, 1992; ed. 'Critical Pedagogy and Cultural Power' 1987; co-ed. 'Working People and Hard Times' 1987; co-author 'Stacking the Deck' 1992; 'Recasting Steel Labour' 1993; mem. Editorial Cttee., 'Our Schools/Our Selves' 1988– ; mem. Editorial Bd., 'Two-Thirds: Journal of Underdevelopment Studies' 1977–80; assoc. ed. 'Sociological Inquiry' 1974–78; mem. Candn. Assn. Univ. Teachers; Candn. Sociol. & Anthrop. Assn.; Comparative & Internat. Edn. Soc.; Am. Sociol. Assn.; Soc. Socialist Studies; recreations: tennis, piano; Club: Credit Valley Lawn Tennis; Home: 1401 Carmen Dr., Mississauga, Ont. L5G 3Z2; Office: 252 Bloor St. W., Toronto, Ont. M5S 1V6.

**LLEWELLYN, Edward John,** B.Sc., Ph.D., D.Sc.; professor of physics and engineering physics; b. London, Eng. 17 Sept. 1938; s. Leonard Percy and Hilda May (Giles) L.; e. Univ. of Exeter B.Sc. (Hons.) 1960, Ph.D. 1963; Univ. of Saskatchewan D.Sc. 1987; m. Joan d. George and Teresa Richards 7 May 1988; PROF. OF PHYSICS AND ENGINEERING PHYSICS, UNIV. OF SASKATCHEWAN 1975– ; Rsch. Assoc. in Planetary Atmospheres, Norman Lockyer Observatory 1963–64; Asst. Prof. of Physics, Univ. of Sask. 1964–69; Assoc. Prof. 1969–75; Consultant, Barringer Rsch.; Lockheed Palo Alto Rsch. Lab.; Univ. Corp. for Astronomical rsch.; Defence Rsch. Establishment Valcartier; Excellence in refereeing, Am. Geophysical Union 1989; Edit. Adv. Bd., Planetary and Space Science; co-discoverer of upper ozone layer; of temperature effect on spacecraft glow; Principal investigator for experiments flown on the Space Shuttle; Mem., Assn. of Profl. Engrs. of Sask.; Am. Geophysical Union; Candn. Assn. of Physicists; author/co-author of num. sci. papers; Home: 455 Pinehouse Dr., Unit 13, Saskatoon, Sask. S7K 5X1; Office: Inst. of Space and Atmospheric Studies, Saskatoon, Sask. S7N 0W0

**LLOYD, Patrick D.,** B.A., M.B.A., LL.B.; utilities executive; b. B.C. 13 Oct. 1951; e. Univ. of Victoria B.A. 1975; York Univ. M.B.A., LL.B. 1979; m. Linda 1979; children: Nashlyn, Stephen, Leiland; EXTVE. VICE PRES., FINANCE & ADMINISTRATION, BC GAS UTILITY LTD. 1988– ; recreations: hiking, climbing, fishing, kayaking, skiing; Office: 1111 West Georgia St., Vancouver, B.C. V6E 4M4.

**LLOYD, Robert V.,** Q.C.; lawyer; b. Edmonton, Alta. 22 July 1938; s. Dr. Victor M. and Lloy M. (Greenfield) L.; e. Westglen H.S. 1956; Univ. of Alta. B.Comm. 1959, LL.B. 1962; m. Leah D., d. Harold and Gertrude Baker, 3 Sept. 1961; children: David, Jeffrey, Michael, Shelly; articled Ogilvie & Co. 1962; lawyer, commercial corp. prac. 1963– ; Dir., United Group of Funds; Canbra Foods Ltd.; Dir., Shock Trauma Air Rescue Soc. (STARS); mem., Alta. Law Soc.; Cdn. Bar Assn.; K-40 Club; Founding Mem., Minerva Found.; recreations: skiing, fishing; Club: Mayfair Golf & Country; Edmonton Centre; Home: 24 Westbrook Dr., Edmonton, Alta. T6J 2C9; Office: 1400 Metropolitan Place, 10303 Jasper Ave., Edmonton, Alta. T5J 3N6.

**LLOYD, Roy E.;** executive; b. Regina, Sask. 2 March 1941; s. late Timothy Ernest and Agnes (MacAlduff) L.; e. Fillmore (Sask.) Elem. and High Schs. 1959; Univ. of Sask. Coll. of Comm. 1963, grad. studies; m. Rose d. late George Dreher 7 Sept. 1963; children: Karen Louise, Leanne Rose; PARTNER, PEAT MARWICK STEVENSON & KELLOGG; Chrmn., Key Lake Mining Corp.; former Vice Chrmn., Cameco; Past Chrmn., Candn. Nuclear Assn.; mem. Chrmn., Uranium Inst.; R. Catholic; recreations: fishing, cross-country skiing, golf, reading; Club: Saskatoon; Home: 1003 Emerald Cres., Saskatoon, Sask. S7J 4J2.

**LLOYD, Trevor,** B.Sc., Ph.D., D.Sc., Hon. LL.D., Hon. M.A., F.R.S.C.; univ. prof. and geographical consultant; b. London, Eng., 4 May 1906; s. Jonathan and Mary (Gordge) L.; e. Sidcot Sch., Somerset, Eng.; Univ. of Bristol (Flounders Scholar), B.Sc. 1929, D.Sc. 1949; Teaching Cert., Bd. of Ed. 1930; Coll. teaching licence, Man., 1934; Clark Univ., Ph.D. 1940; Hon. M.A. Dartmouth Coll., 1944; LL.D. Windsor 1973; LL.D. Trent 1981; m. Joan, d. J. G. Glassco, 1936; divorced 1966; children: Mona Jean, Hugh Glassco; PROF. EMERITUS McGILL UNIV. 1977– ; Pres. Univ. of Bristol Students Union 1929–30; Delegate to Congress Cnfed. Internat. des étudiants: Budapest 1929, Bucharest 1930, Brussels 1931; Leader. Br. Universities Debating Team to Canada 1930; Pres. National Union of Students, U.K. 1930–31; Schoolmaster, Ravenscourt School, Winnipeg, Man. 1931–36; Chrmn. Bd of Inquiry into student affairs, Univ. of Man. 1932; mem., Royal Soc. of Teachers, London 1933; Candn. (Carnegie) Study Team on Adult Educ. in Scandinavia 1932; First Geography Specialist Winnipeg Public Schools 1936–42; Grad. Fellow, Geog., Clark Univ. 1938–40; Canadian Observer, 'Canol Project,' Mackenzie Valley 1942; Asst. Prof. of Geography, Carleton Coll., Northfield, Minn. 1942; Asst. Prof. of Geog., Dartmouth Coll. 1942–44, Prof. 1944–59, Chrmn. 1946–52; Sr. Rsch. Asst. (Study of Arctic U.S.S.R.), Wartime Info. Bd., Ottawa 1943; Consul for Canada in Greenland 1944–45; first Chief, Geographical Bureau, Ottawa 1947–49; Candn. Inst. of Internat. Affairs, Arctic Rsch. Project 1943–47; Prof. of Human Geography, McGill Univ. 1959–77 (Dir. Geog. Summer Sch. 1963–65; Chrmn. Dept. of Geog. 1962–66; Dir. Centre of North. Studies and Rsrch. 1973–77); Founding Extve. Dir., Assn. of Candn. Univs. for North. Studies 1977–80; publications: 'The Red River Valley: A Regional Study' 1940; 'The Geography and Administration of Northern Canada' 1947; 'Sky Highways' 1943; 'Canada and Her Neighbours' 1947, 1957; 'Canada et ses Voisons' 1953, 1956, 1957; 'Southern Lands' 1956; 'Lands of Europe and Asia' 1957, 1965; 'A Geographer's World' 1968; many tech. papers in geog., internat. affairs, educ., etc.; Founder, Fellow, Gov., Chrmn. 1967–70, Arctic Inst. N. Am.; Founding Ed. Journal 'Arctic' 1947–48; Am. Geog. Soc. (Fellow); Assn. of Am. Geog. (former mem. of Council); Am. Assn. for Advanc. of Science (Fellow, Vice Pres. and Chrmn. Sec. Geol. & Geog. 1964); mem., Candn. Assn. of Geogs. (Pres. 1957–58); Candn. Inst. Internat. Affairs; Greenland Soc., Copenhagen; Inst. of Current World Affairs (mem. since 1959, Chrmn. Bd. 1976); Project Offr. Royal (Glassco) Comn. on Govt. Organ. (reporting on government Research & Development) 1961–62; Pres. McGill Assn. of Univ. Teachers 1969–71; Hon. Corres. Mem., Geographical Soc. of Finland; Gov. and former Chrmn., Candn. Scandinavian Foundation; Hon. Pres., Candn. Nordic Soc.; Royal Soc. of Canada, Academy Two (elected Member Council and Nominating Ctte. 1991–94); Geographic Fieldwork: Alaska, Mackenzie Valley, Iceland, Greenland, N. Scandinavia, N. European Russia, Kola, North Eastern Siberia, Soviet Far East, Peru, Bolivia, Togo, Mali; Soc. of Friends; awarded Centennial Medal 1967; Silver Jubilee Medal 1977; Distinguished Service Award, Candn. Assn. of Geographers 1977; Jens Munck Medal, Candn.-Danish Soc., Copenhagen 1977; Massey Gold Medal, Royal Candn. Geog. Soc. 1982; Hans Egede Medal, Royal Danish Geographical Soc., Copenhagen 1984; Personal and Research papers on deposit, Public Archives Canada, File MG30B97; Arctic Library and Research papers deposited at Trent Univ. Bata Library; recreations: travel, out-of-doors activities, photography, amateur radio; Research Gorges-Gordge family XVIc-XVIIIc; field study of Norse North Atlantic Islands; Clubs: McGill Faculty; Address: 54 St. Andrew St. Apt. 1, Ottawa, Ont. K1N 5E9.

**LLOYD-JONES, Joseph,** M.A., M.B.A., Ph.D., CGA; university administrator and educator; management accounting, planning, program evaluation and accountability consultant; b. Karachi, Brit. India 23 Sept. 1944; s. Arthur Thomas and Mary Grace (De Souza) L.; e. Dalhousie Univ. B.A. 1971; Carleton Univ. M.A. 1974; Univ. of Iowa M.B.A. 1976, Ph.D. 1978; m. Joanne (M.D.) d. Jack and Lorna Walker 27 Oct. 1973; children: Michael, Adam; ASST. VICE-RECTOR, UNIV. OF OTTAWA 1987– ; Adjunct Prof. in Administrative Studies 1980– ; Visiting Prof., Sri Jawardenapura Univ., Sri Lanka 1986; Accountancy, Concordia Univ. 1989; Planning, Control systems and International Competitiveness, Univ. of Hawaii 1991; currently lecturing in Managerial Accounting, Strategic Planning, Program Evaluation and Accountability Methodologies; Mathematician, Weapons Release System, Litton Systems (Toronto) 1966–67; Corporate Planner, Robert Simpsons Ltd. (Toronto) 1968–69; Dir., Inst. Rsch. & Acad. Planning, Univ. of Ottawa 1978–87; Chrmn., Primary Care Bd., Ottawa-Carleton Dist. Health Counc. 1978–81; Human Resources Cttee., Ottawa-Carleton Bd. of Trade 1993; Dir./Treas., Shastri Indo-Candn. Inst. 1988–90; mem., Candn. Comprehensive Auditing Found.; Bd. of Dirs., CGA (Ottawa) 1989–92; Mem., CGA (Ontario) Education Ctte. 1991–93; Dir., Candn. Soc. for Studies in Higher Educ. 1991–93; Mem., Ont. Council for Univ. Planning and Analysis; COU Cttee. on University Accountability; co-author: 'Strategic Management in the Health Care Sector' 1988; co-editor: 'Marketing Strategies for the Health Administrator' 1990; 'L'enseignement postsecondaire en transition' 1993; Editor/Publisher: 'Helping Enhance Canada's Future: The Role of Institutional Researchers and Planners in Post-secondary Education' 1992; mem., Certified General Accountants' Assn. of Canada; Certified General Accountants' Assn. of Ont.; Am. Accounting Assn.; European Accounting Assn.; Home: 6078 Meadowglen Dr., Gloucester, Ont.; Office: 550 Cumberland St., Ottawa, Ont. K1N 6N5.

**LOAR, William Robert (Bill),** B.A., LL.B.; corporate executive; b. Okmulgee, Okla. 13 Aug. 1926; e. Univ. of Okla. B.A. 1949, LL.B. 1951; Harvard Advanced Mgmt. 1977; m. Jeanne Dubois 20 Dec. 1950; children: Jeanne Elizabeth, William Robert Jr., Carol Anne; PRES. & C.E.O., McDUFF DEVELOPMENTS INC., Austin, Texas 1989– ; joined Sun Oil Co. Tulsa, Okla. as Eng. 1951, held various positions Prodn. Dept. until 1966, Mgr. Sunray DX Candn. operations Calgary 1966, Regional Prodn. Mgr. Sun Oil Co. 1970, Group Vice Pres. Exploration & Prodn. 1974, Pres. Great Canadian Oil Sands Ltd. 1979 (above Co's amalgamated to form present Co. 1979); Pres. and C.E.O. Suncor Inc. 1983–84; Chrmn. and C.E.O., Suncor Inc. 1984–86; Clubs: Calgary Golf & Country; Home: 704 Rolling Green, Austin TX 78734.

**LOATES, Martin Glen;** wildlife artist; b. Toronto, Ont. 3 May 1945; s. Albert Arthur and Frona Maria (Rowe) L.; e. various schs. Toronto area; m. Sally d. Merritt and Margaret Harding 12 June 1971; children: Michael, Christopher; designed: Candn. Cancer Soc. daffodil 1956 (age 11); Christmas card, Fed. of Ont. Naturalists 1964; 1st full-colour Candn. stamps 1968; recipient Royal Philatelic Award 1968; Four Platinum Coins - Snowy Owls, Royal Candn. Mint 1991; films incl.: 'Colour It Living' 1971; 'Brush with Life' 1971; 'Paint It Wild' 1980; shows: Royal Ont. Museum 1965, 1975, 1985; Museum of Nat. Hist., Buffalo 1965; Jesse Besser Mus. of Nat. Hist. 1970; McMichael Candn. Coll. 1971, 1978; Leigh Yawkey Woodson Art Mus. 1974–77; Woodmere Art Museum, Philadelphia 1992; exhbns.: 'Canadian Nature Art' (Inst. of Zoological Rsch. & Alexander Koenig Mus., Bonn, W. Germany; Ctr. Cultural Canadien, Paris; British Mus., London; Kortright Conserv. Ctr.); presentations: to Pierre Elliot Trudeau, orig. lithographs & limited ed. book 1982; to HRH Prince Philip, limited ed. book (from Govt. of Ont.) 1982; to Pres. Reagan, from Candn. people to Am. people, painting 'Bald Eagle' 1982; Ambassador, Wildlife Cons. 1985; Pres., M.G.L. Fine Art; joined The Beebe Project 1987 (became the first artist to dive 1 mile below the ocean's surface); mem. The Explorers' Club; World Wildlife Fund; Nat. Audubon Soc.; Candn. Nature Fed.; Candn. Wildlife Fed.; Fed. of Ont. Naturalists; Life mem., Royal Ont. Mus.; Kortright Conserv. Ctr.; Nat. Wildlife Fed.; Royal Acad. of Arts; artist: 'Ontario Mammals' 1971; 'Mammals in Profile' Vol. I 1975, Vol. II 1976; 'The Art of Glen Loates' 1977; 'Birds of North America' 1979; 'A Coming of Winter' (folio) 1980; 'A Brush with Life' 1984; 'From the Wild' 1987; 'Owls' 1988; 'Birds at My Feeder' 1988; 'Animal Babies' 1988; 'Forest Mammals' 1988; recreations: nature walks, internat. travel; Home: Maple, Ont.; Office: 556 Edward Ave., Unit 68, Richmond Hill, Ont. L4C 9Y5.

**LOBAY, Mary,** C.M., B.Ed., M.Ed., LL.D. (Hon.); educator; community volunteer; b. Wasel, Alta. 24 June 1920; d. William and Anastasia (Strynadka) Hawrelak; e. Univ. of Alta., B.Ed. 1963, B.Ed.Dip. 1965, M.Ed. 1966; m. William s. John and Anastasia Lobay 23 June 1940; children: Gary, Carol, David; Sessional Lectr., Univ. of Alta. 1963–66; Fac. Cons. 1965–66; Coord. of Social Studies & Eng., Edmonton Pub. Sch. Bd. 1964–66; Asst. Prin., Victoria Composite High Sch. 1969–79; Dir., Heritage Savings & Trust Co. 1984–87; Dir.,

North West Trust Co. 1987– ; Mem. & (first woman) Chrmn., Edmonton Police Comn. 1979–85; Mem., Bd. of Govs., Univ. of Alta. 1986–92; Senate 1978–84 and 1986–92; Mem. & Extve., Bd. of Govs., Alta. Coll. 1984– ; Dir., Vanier Inst. of the Family 1986–91; Dir., Capital Care Hospital Group, & Royal Alexandra Hosp. Found. 1990– ; Dir. & Extve., Ft. Edmonton Hist. Found. 1974–91; Dir., Salvation Army Advisory Counc. 1988– ; Founding Pres., Friends of the Ukrainian Heritage Cultural Village 1984– ; mem. Candn. Ukrainian Women's Assn. 1954– ; mem., Candn. Multiculturalism Council 1985–88; rec'd City of Edmonton Award for outstanding service 1979; Alta. Achievement Award 1980; Hon. Life Mem., Ukrainian Candn. Profl. & Bus. Club 1982; Member, Order of Can. 1988; Hon. Life Mem., Vanier Institute of the Family; recipient, Les Carbot Award 1992; recreations: reading, writing rural histories, family dinners with grandchildren; Home: 638 Romaniuk Rd., Edmonton, Alta. T6R 1A6.

**LOBEL, Thomas Emanuel;** recycling executive; b. Leicester, England 4 Aug. 1942; s. Hugo Joseph and Alice (Synkova) L.; e. Bathurst Heights Coll. 1960; m. Madeline d. Dr. Maurice and Lilian Harris 9 July 1967; children: Amy, Aaron; OWNER, HOUSE OF METALS CO. LTD.; partner in 3 other recycling related ventures; Dir., Shoppers Trust Co.; Skylight Thetre, Inc. (free theatre); Toronto Leaside Rotary (past dir.); United Synagogue Day Sch. (past extve.); Candn. Assn. of Recycling Indus. (past extve.); recreations: golf; clubs: Maple Downs Golf & Country; Home: 22 Alexandra Wood, Toronto, Ont. M5N 2S1; Office: 45 Commercial Rd., Toronto, Ont. M4G 1Z3.

**LOCHAN, Frank Neville C.,** M.Sc., F.C.A., F.C.C.A., C.A., C.B.V.; financial executive; b. San Fernando, Trinidad 26 Sept. 1940; s. Ivan Hamilton and Nora Clarista (Laltoo) L.; e. London School of Econ. & Pol. Sci. M.Sc.(Econ.) 1969; articled with Pridie Brewster & Gold (U.K.) A.A.C.C.A. 1965, A.C.A. 1967, F.C.C.A. 1975, F.C.A. 1972; Alumnum, Banff Sch. of Advanced Mngt., 47th session 1980; Univ. of Toronto, Candn. Business Valuators Course 1982–84; m. Azniv d. Arthur and Florence Cook 15 April 1968; children: Carina, Amanda; SENIOR VICE-PRESIDENT & CHIEF FINANCIAL OFFICER 1983– ; Comptroller, Internat., Candn. Imperial Bank of Commerce 1969–74; Comptroller, Brascan Trading Group 1974; Special Projects, Corp. Devel., Brascan Limited 1976; Group Controller (Canada) 1977; Dir., Financial Serv. 1979; Vice-Pres., Corp. Planning 1982; Dir., Arteco Holdings Limited; Triathlon Leasing Inc.; Eurobrokers Internat. Inc.; Eurobrokers Investment Corp.; Mico Investments Ltd.; PSCO Fund; Royal LePage Holdings Limited; Trilon Bancorp Inc.; Trilon Equities Limited; Trilon Financial Corp.; Trilon Leaseco Inc.; clubs: Ontario Racquet, The Adelaide; Home: 2060 Tenth Sideroad, R.R. #1, Moffat, Ont. L0P 1J0; Office: BCE Place, 181 Bay St., Suite 4420, Box 771, Toronto, Ont. M5J 2T3.

**LOCHHEAD, Douglas Grant,** B.A., M.A., B.L.S., D.Litt., LL.D., F.R.S.C.; author and professor; b. Guelph, Ont. 25 Mar. 1922; s. Allan Grant and Helen Louise (VanWart) L.; e. McGill Univ., B.A. 1943, B.L.S. 1951; Univ. of Toronto, M.A. (English) 1947; m. Jean St. Clair, d. John Harold Beckwith, Sydney, N.S., 17 Sept. 1949; children: Sara Louise, Mary Elizabeth; PROFESSOR EMERITUS, CANADIAN STUDIES, MOUNT ALLISON and PRESIDENT, GOOSE LANE EDITIONS (FREDERICTON); Fellow Emeritus & Founding Librarian, Massey College; engaged in Advertising and Information work, Toronto and Ottawa 1947–50; Librarian, Victoria, (B.C.) Coll. 1951–52; Cataloguer, Cornell Univ. Lib. 1952–53; Univ. Lib., Dalhousie Univ., Halifax, N.S. 1953–60; Univ. Librarian & Asst. Prof. of Eng., York Univ. 1960–63; Librarian & Fellow, Massey Coll. 1963–75; Prof. of English, Univ. of Toronto 1965–75; Edgar and Dorothy Davidson Prof. and Dir., Candn. Studies, Mt. Allison Univ. 1975–87; Librarian in Residence, Dalhousie Univ. 1981, 1985; Visiting Prof. of Candn. Studies, Edinburgh Univ. 1983–84; Writer in Residence, Mount Allison Univ. 1987–90; served in the 2nd World War 1943–45 with Candn. Army, Inf. in Can. and Overseas, rank Lieut.; publications: 'The Heart is Fire' (poems) 1959; 'It is all around' (poems) 1960; 'Millwood Road Poems' 1970; 'Prayers in a Field' (poems) 1974; 'Collected Poems: The Full Furnace' 1975; 'High Marsh Road' (poems) 1980; 'Battle Sequence' (poems) 1980; 'A & E' (poems) 1980; 'The Panic Field' (poems) 1984; 'Tiger in the Skull: New and Selected Poems 1959–1986'; 'Upper Cape Poems' 1989; 'Dykelands', Jt. Author (poems) 1989; 'Black Festival' (poems) 1991; 'Homage to Henry Alline' (poems) 1992; compiler 'A Word Index of "In Parenthesis" by David Jones' 1983; Jt. Editor 'Made in Canada' (poems) 1971; '100 Poems of Nineteenth Century Canada' 1974; 'Windflower, Selected Poems of Bliss Carman' 1985; 'Powassan's Drum: Selected Poems of Duncan Campbell Scott' 1985; Ed., 'Bibliography of Canadian Bibliographies,' 2nd ed. 1972; 'Literature of Canada' series and Toronto Reprint Series; 'St. Ursula's Convent' 3rd ed. 1991; numerous articles in lib. prof. journs. and poems in many Canadian periodicals; mem., League of Canadian Poets (Vice-Chrmn. 1968–72); Bibliographical Soc. of Can. (Pres. 1974–76); recipient Marie Tremaine Medal in Candn. Bibliography 1985; Award of Merit, Assoc. of Candn. Studies 1987; Merit Award 1990, Atlantic Provinces Library Assn.; Psi Upsilon; Presbyterian; Address: P.O. Box 1108, Sackville, N.B. E0A 3C0.

**LOCHHEAD, Kenneth Campbell,** O.C.; painter; educator; b. Ottawa, Ont. 22 May 1926; s. Allan Grant and Helen Louise (Van Wart) L.; e. Barnes Found. Merion, Pa. Dip. 1948; Pa. Acad. of Fine Arts, Philadelphia Dip. 1949; m. 1stly Patricia Poole 23 May 1951; children: Colin, Allan, Merrill; m. 2ndly Joanne Bryers 1 Aug. 1973; children: Jennifer, Tessa, Pauline; Prof. of Visual Arts (Painting), Univ. of Ottawa 1975–89; Dir. Sch. of Art Regina Coll. 1950–64; Prof. in painting, Sch. of Art, Univ. of Man. 1964–73; Prof. in painting York Univ. 1974–75, Acting Chrmn. of Visual Arts 1974–75; exhns. maj. art galleries Can. since 1953; intnl. exhns. incl. Post-Painterly Abstraction Exhn. Los Angeles Co. Museum 1964, Can. 101 Edinburgh Intnl. Festival Exhn.; rep. maj. pub. and private colls. Can.; comns. incl. murals Regina Br. Royal Candn. Legion, Gander Intnl. Airport Terminal, York Univ. (also banner designs Winters Coll.), Candn. Chancery Bldg. Warsaw, Bank of Montreal Winnipeg, Dept. External Affairs Hdqrs. Bldg. Ottawa; banner designs incl. Pan-Am Swimming Pool Winnipeg, Confederation Centre P.E.I., Centennial Concert Hall Winnipeg, Sch. of Arch. Univ. of Man.; designer 1970 Man. Centennial Stamp; recipient O.C. 1970; Illustrator, 'Millwood Road Poems' 1970; Home: 35 Wilton Cres., Ottawa, Ont.; Office: Ottawa, Ont. K1S 2T4.

**LOCHNAN, Katharine Aileen,** M.A., Ph.D.; curator; b. Ottawa, Ont. 18 Aug. 1946; d. Carl Joseph and Barbara Fothergill (Duminy) L.; e. Prep. Schs. London, Eng. 1954–61; Nepean (Ont.) High Sch. 1964; Univ. of Toronto B.A. 1968, M.A. 1971; Univ. of London, Courtauld Inst. of Art Ph.D. 1982; Univ. of Cal. Berkeley Museum Mgmt. Inst. Cert. 1987; Ryerson Polytech. Inst. Cert. Bus. Adm. 1990; m. George Meier s. George and Frances Yost 24 Sept. 1983; step-children: John, Leslie; CURATOR OF PRINTS AND DRAWINGS (1st) ART GALLERY OF ONT. 1976– ; Curatorial Asst. Eur. Dept. Royal Ont. Museum 1968–69; Curatorial Asst. present Gallery 1969, Asst. Curator 1971, designed new Marvin Gelber Print & Drawing Study Centre, staged numerous exhns. incl. Turner, Blake, Picasso, Whistler and Morris; Volunteer Asst. Prints & Drawings Brit. Museum 1975–76; mem. Internat. Consultative Ctte. Nat. Gallery of Can. 1977; Guest Curator Metrop. Museum of Art N.Y. 1984; Consultant, Art Inst. of Chicago 1987–94; lectures, seminars, papers Univ. of Toronto, Univ. of Waterloo, Williams Coll. Mass., St. Andrew's Univ. Scot., Nat. Gallery of Art Washington, Museum of Fine Arts Boston, Minneapolis Inst. Arts, Bowdoin College; Ont. Scholar 1964; Prov. Ont. Grants 1966–68; Sec. of State Profl. Devel. Grant 1975–76; J.Paul Getty Trust Scholarship 1987; Award of Merit, Ryerson Polytechnical Inst. 1991; author 'The Etchings of James McNeill Whistler' 1984; 'Whistler's Etchings and the Sources of His Etching Style 1855–80' 1988; numerous articles, exhn. catalogues; mem. Toronto Historical Bd. (Vice-Chair 1993– ); mem. London House Assn. Can. (Pres. 1981–84); William Morris Soc. Can. (Vice Pres. 1984–85); Print Council of America (Bd. mem. 1980–82); recreations: arch. restoration, choral singing, gardening; Home: 21 Mackenzie Cres., Toronto, Ont. M6J 1S9; Office: 317 Dundas St. W., Toronto, Ont. M5T 1G4.

**LOCK, Colin J.L.,** B.Sc., A.R.C.S., D.I.C., Ph.D., D.Sc., F.C.I.C.; educator; b. London, Eng. 4 Oct. 1933; s. Lyne and Amy Hilda Irene (Howell) L.; e. Imperial Coll. London B.Sc., A.R.C.S. 1954, D.I.C., Ph.D. 1963; Univ. of London D.Sc. 1987; m. Helen d. John and Claire Howard 21 May 1960; two d. Nicola Elaine Simmons, Philippa Edlyne; PROF. OF PATHOL., McMASTER UNIV. 1984– , Prof. of Chem. 1974– , Assoc. Prof. 1966–74, Asst. Prof. 1962–66; Vice Pres. Howard Lock Associates Inc.; Asst. Exper. Offr. UKAEA, Harwell 1954–57, Sci. Offr. seconded to AECL Chalk River 1957–60; Asst. Lectr. 1961–63 and Eur. Rsch. Associates Fellow 1960–61 Imp. Coll.; Chrmn., Chem. Inst. Can. 1981–83; mem. Hamilton Philharmonic Orch.; Royal Bot. Gdns.; Hamilton Art Gallery; Hamilton & Dist. Rose Soc. (Pres. 1973–75); Candn. Rose Soc. (Vice Pres. 1977–78); Burlington Power Sqdn. (Commdr. 1983–84); recreations: sailing, gardening, choral singing, back room politics, classical music; Club: Faculty Club of McMaster Univ. (Pres. 1990–91); Royal Hamilton Yacht; United Church; Home: 138 Northshore Blvd. E., Burlington, Ont. L7T 1W4; Office: Labs. for Inorganic Med., ABB-266A, McMaster Univ., Hamilton, Ont. L8S 4M1.

**LOCKE, John Craig,** B.Sc., M.D., C.M., Med.Sc.D., F.R.C.S. (C), F.A.C.S.; ophthalmologist; university professor; b. Winnipeg, Manitoba, 7 Dec. 1918; s. William Francis and Margaret (Spence) L.; e. Selwyn House Sch., Montreal, Que. (1928–33); Upper Canada Coll., Toronto, Ont. (1933–35); McGill Univ., B.Sc., M.D., C.M. (1935–42); Univ. of Toronto Jan.-June 1944; New York Univ. Postgrad Sch., 1946–47; Columbia Univ., Med. Sc.D., 1951; m. Beatrice (dec.), d. late Dr. Charles Dillon, New York, 6 May 1950; children: James Edward Francis (dec'd.), Barbara Margaret Grace; m. Frances, d. late Arthur P. Earle 15 Sept. 1990; children: John Frederick, Gaylen Arthur, Gordon Alan, Jennifer Jane, James Douglas; PROF. (post-retirement) DEPT. OF OPHTHALMOLOGY, McGILL UNIVERSITY; Hon. Attending Opthalmologist, Royal Victoria Hospital, Montreal, Quebec; Diplomate of American Board of Opthalmology; Chairman and member of Examining Boards, Royal College of Physicians and Surgeons Can., 1954–61; Schneider Foundation Mem. Lect., Interstate Postgrad. Med. Assn., Milwaukee, 1955; awarded Certs. of Merit for scient. exhibit on 'Retrolental fibroplasia' by two Am. Assns. 1951 and 1952; annual Award in Med. of Royal Coll. of Phys. & Surgs. of Can. for essay 'Contributions to Retrolental Fibroplasia,' 1954; served in 2nd World War; Lieut., R.C.A.M.C., 1943–44, Capt., 1944–46, in Can.; author of a no. of original scient. publs. principally on opthal. subjects; mem., Candn. Med. Assn.; Candn. Opthal. Soc.; Am. Opthalmological Soc.; Jules Gonin Club; Soc. of Eye Surgeons (Ch. mem.); Fellow, Am. Acad. of Opthal. & Otolaryngol.; Hon. mem., Chilean Opthal. Soc. (1956); Delta Upsilon; Protestant; Clubs: Royal Montreal Golf; Montreal Badminton & Squash; Home: 2043 Graham Blvd., Town of Mount Royal, Que. H3R 1H5.

**LOCKE, Michael,** M.A., Ph.D., Sc.D., F.R.S.C.; educator; b. UK 14 Feb. 1929; s. Robert Henry and Kathleen N. (Waite) L.; e. St. Johns Coll. Cambridge (State Scholar and Foundation Scholar) M.A. 1955, Ph.D. 1956, Sc.D. 1976; m. J.V. d. Vincent Leopold and Josephine Louise Collins 3 May 1980; children: John, Timothy, Marius, Vanessa (by previous marriage); PROF. OF ZOOL. UNIV. OF W. ONT. 1971– , Chrmn. of Zool. 1971–85; Lectr. Univ. of W. Indies 1956–61; Assoc. Prof., Prof. Case Western Reserve Univ. 1961–71; Raman Prof. India 1969; served with RAF 1947–49; recipient Rockefeller Award 1960, Guest Investigator, Rockefeller Inst.; Carnegie Award 1961; Citation Classic 1987; Gold Medal Internat. Award in Morphol. & Embryol. 1988; Killam Fellow 1988–90; ed. 'Symposia of the Society for the Study of Development and Growth' Vols. 21–27 1963–68; 'Cell Ultra Structure' 7 vols. 1972–74; co-ed.' VBW 80 Insect Biology in the Future' 1980; over 200 articles sci. jours.; mem. various ed. bds.; Fellow, Am. Assn. Advanc. Sci.; Office: Zoology Dept., Univ. of W. Ont., London, Ont. N6A 3B7.

**LOCKE, Peter Charles;** general contractor; b. Port Arthur, Ont. 23 July 1956; s. Charles Edmund and Margaret Shirley L.; e. Stephen Leacock Coll. Inst. Agincourt, Ont. 1975; George Brown Coll. Toronto, Residential Constrn. Mgmt. Dip. 1979; m. Wendy d. Wayne and Dorothy Wood 15 May 1982; children: Jennifer Meaghan, Harry Charles, Stuart George; PRES. AND OWNER PETER C. LOCKE AND ASSOCIATES 1982– ; Vice Pres. and Partner Inverness Hotel Corp. (United States Virgin Islands); Vice Pres. & Partner L.S.H. Construction Inc., United States Virgin Islands; former Constrn. Supt. Bramalea Ltd., Rampart Enterprises Ltd. and Pronto Homes; mem. Adv. Ctte. George Brown Coll. Residential Constrn. Mgmt. Prog., Guest Lectr.; Jt. Constrn. Council rep. Urban Devel. Inst. and Metrop. Toronto Apt. Builders Assn.; Toronto Builders Assn. Renovation & Redevel. Council; Renovation Ctte. Part III Ont. Bldg. Code; video prodn. guest Bldg. Ind. Strategy Bd. to encourage student interest in constrn careers; guest speaker Ont. Min. of Housing Forum; recreations: downhill skiing, water sports; Home: 26 McRoberts Place, Aurora, Ont.; Office: 16, 110 Riviera Dr., Markham, Ont. L3R 5M1.

**LOCKER, (John) Gary,** B.Sc., M.Sc., Ph.D.; university professor and administrator; b. Kenora, Ont. 19 Nov. 1937; s. Lorne John and Gladys Sarah (Kirk) L.; e. Univ. of Manitoba B.Sc.(CE) 1961; Univ. of Alberta M.Sc. 1963, Ph.D. 1969; m. Elaine d. Eugene and Olga Letawasky 25 May 1963; children: Laura Lee, Tiffany

Dawn; DIRECTOR, SCHOOL OF ENGINEERING, LAKEHEAD UNIVERSITY 1976– & PROF. 1978– ; Lectr., Civil Engr., Royal Military College 1963–66; Asst. Prof. 1968–71; Assoc. Prof., Civil Engr., Univ. of Regina 1971–73; Lakehead Univ., Sch. of Engr. 1973–78; Mem., Ctte. of Ont. Deans of Engineering 1976– (Chair 1981–83); Nat. Ctte., Deans of Engineering & Applied Science 1976– (Chair 1990–91); Assn. of Profl. Engrs. of Ont. (Chair, Lakehead Chapter 1989–90; Admissions Ctte. Mem. 1991–92); Fisheries Adv. Council, Ministry of Natural Resources, Thunder Bay District; Fellow, Engineering Inst. of Canada; Mem., Order of Honour, Profl. Engrs. of Ont.; recreations: travel, fly tying & fishing; clubs: Thunder Bay Fly Fishing (Mem., Bd. of Dir.); Office: Thunder Bay, Ont. P7B 5E1.

**LOCKHART, Araby,** B.A.; actress; producer; b. Toronto, Ont. 4 Dec. 1926; d. James Watson and Beatrice Alma (Corsan) L.; e. Bishop Strachan Sch.; Univ. of Toronto B.A. 1948; m. John R. Gray Dec. 1952; children: John, Nicholas, Rebecca, Susannah, Felix; produced and starred in 'As I See It' 1955, 'Spare Rib' St. Lawrence Centre 1974; produced and appeared in 'Clap Hands' Hart House Theatre 1958, 1959, Prince Charles Theatre London, Eng. 1963–64, Old Angelo's Toronto 1974; has appeared as actress and comedienne most maj. Candn. theatres; radio and TV appearances CBC, CTV, BBC, Grenada, Southern; films incl. 'Little Gloria, Happy at Last' 1982; 'Police Academy' 1983; recipient, Silver Ticket Award for 'Outstanding Contribution to Theatre in Toronto' 1986; recipient, Brenda Donahue Award for distinguished contribution and achievement within the Toronto Theatre community 1992; Pres. Actors' Fund Can. 1984–92; recreations: hiking, travel; Address: 34 Howland Rd., Toronto, Ont. M4K 2Z6.

**LOCKHART, Kim Lawrence,** B.A.; magazine editor and writer; b. Toronto, Ont. 4 Sept. 1948; s. Lloyd Macdonald and Gertrude Louise (Moran) L.; e. Leaside H.S. Sr. Matric. 1966; Univ. of W. Ont. B.A. Bus. Admin. 1972; m. Renée d. André and Rolande Bonard 29 Sept. 1978; one s. Micah Bonard; Editor, Toronto Star 1992; Ed. Montreal Star 1976–77; Ed. and Feature Writer Globe and Mail 1977–83; Sr. Writer Global Television 1983–84; Extve. Ed., Canadian Lawyer Magazine 1984–87; Extve. Editor, Controlled Media Communications (publisher of Toronto Blue Jays magazine) 1988–92; mem. Extve. Bd., Toronto Studio Players; Port Stanley Summer Theatre, Port Stanley, Ont.; R. Catholic; mem. Kappa Alpha Soc.; Colombia South Am. Friendship Award 1984; recreations: golf, curling, tossing the caber; Club: Toronto Press; Home: 60 Pavane Linkway, PH 4, Don Mills, Ont. M3C 1A1.

**LOCKWOOD, Hon. George Hepworth,** M.A.; judge; b. Glasshoughton, Yorks., Eng. 18 Apr. 1923; s. George and Phoebe (Bradburn) L.; e. The King's School, Pontefract, Yorks; Univ. Coll. Oxford B.A. (Hons), M.A.; Lincoln's Inn London, Barrister-at-Law; m. Lissen Karen d. Ahlman and Ragnhild Eckhardt, Winnipeg, Man. 27 Jan. 1962; children: Mette Norma, Michael Hepworth, Martin Bradburn; Jonathan Connolly; JUDGE, COURT OF QUEEN'S BENCH, MAN. 1984– ; Chrmn. of Bd. of Inquiry into Boeing 767 Accident in Gimli, Manitoba July 1983; called to Bar of Man. 1958; cr. Q.C. 1975; Business Extve. and Mgr., London and Kenya 1950–53; Colonial Service Offr. Kenya 1953–57; mem. law firm Guy, Chappell, Guy, Wilson & Coghlin 1958–61; Pitblado & Hoskin 1961–66; Partner and Sr. Partner, Fillmore & Riley 1966–78; sometime Dir., Forum Art Inst.; Pres., John Howard Soc. Can.; Pres. Amnesty Internat. Can.; Pres., Internat. Comn. of Jurists (Candn. Sec.); Dir. Can. Judges Conf.; Bencher, Law Soc. Man.; mem. Nat. Council Candn. Bar Assn.; Dir. Legal Aid Man.; Part-time Judge of Prov. Judges Court (Criminal Div.); Judge, County Court and Surrogate Court of Man.; mem., Legal Rsch. Inst., Univ. of Man.; Comnr., Man. Law Reform Comn.; Dir., Royal Winnipeg Ballet; Prés., Alliance Française du Man.; currently Mem. The National Council, Royal Winnipeg Ballet; Nat. Councillor, Candn. Human Rights Foundation; Fellow, Foundation for Legal Rsch.; served with RAF 1943–47, Flying Offr.-Navig.; Chevalier of the Legion of Honour (France 1990); recreations: reading, golf, theatre; Home: 2602 - Eleven Evergreen Place, Winnipeg, Man. R3L 2T9; Office: The Law Courts, Winnipeg, Man. R3C 0V8.

**LOCKYER, Peter Robert,** LL.B., Q.C.; lawyer; b. Toronto, Ont. 18 Sept. 1943; s. Harry Roy and Alice (Jack) L.; e. Upper Can. Coll. 1962; Univ. of W. Ont. LL.B. 1967; Law Soc. of Upper Can. Bar Adm. Course 1969; m. Gail d. David Stewart 7 Oct. 1966; children: Lisanne, Kristen, Brooke; PARTNER, HARRISON, ELWOOD 1972– ; joined Harrison, Elwood 1969; Dir. & Chrmn. of the Bd., Pacific & Western Trustco Ltd.; Pacific & Western Trust Corp.; Dir., Ellis-Don Inc.; Trigen Energy Canada Inc.; Trigen-London District Energy Corp.; Past Chrmn., Extve. Bd., Huron Coll.; Mem. Bd. of Govs., Ridley Coll.; Mem. Bd. of Dirs., London Hunt and Country Club (President); Dir., London Found.; Dir., Siebens-Drake Rsch. Institute; Regional Pres., 500 Club P.C. Can. Fund; Chrmn., Candn. Nat. Srs. Tennis Championships 1985; recreations: tennis; skiing; Clubs: London; London Hunt & Country; Devil's Glen Country; Broken Sound Club; Home: RR 1, Arva, Ont. N0M 1C0; Office: 450 Talbot St., London, Ont. N6A 4K3.

**LODGE, Lorne Kenneth,** B.Com., F.C.A.; co. executive; b. Toronto, Ont. 17 Sept. 1930; s. Louis W. and Hilda (Thomas) L.; e. Bowmore Road Pub. Sch. and Riverdale Coll. Inst., Toronto, 1945–48; Victoria Coll., Univ. of Toronto, B.Com. 1952; C.A. 1955; F.C.A. 1973; m. Imbi Sepa, 23 June 1978; children: Lee James, Linda Diane, Wendy Ruth, Susan Marie; Chrmn., Security Pacific Bank Canada 1988–92; Dir., IBM Canada Ltd.; London Insur. Group Inc.; Shell Canada Ltd.; Royal LePage Ltd.; Spencer Stuart Advisory; Wellesley Hosp.; Gov., Olympic Trust of Canada; Auditor, Price Waterhouse & Co., 1952–56; joined IBM Canada as Data Processing Marketing Rep., Data Processing Marketing Mgr. 1962; Adm. Asst. to Pres. 1964; Mgr. of Budgets 1965; Assistant Controller 1966; Controller 1967; Extve. Vice Pres. 1968; Bd. of Dir., 1969; Pres. & C.E.O., 1972; Chrmn. and Pres. 1976; Chrmn. & C.E.O. 1982; Chrmn. 1986–88; Lieut. RCN(R); mem., Candn. Inst. C.A.s; Inst. of C.A.s, Ont.; Fellow Inst. of C.A.s of Ont.; Fellow, Ryerson Polytech. Inst.; Theta Delta Chi; Anglican; recreations: golf, skiing; Clubs: Toronto; Rosedale Golf & Country; Beacon Hall Golf; Loxahatchee Golf; Home: 524 Quail Ridge Dr., Aurora, Ont. L4G 3G8.

**LOEWEN, Charles Barnard,** B.A., M.B.A.; stockbroker; e. Winchester Coll. Univ. of B.C., B.A. 1954; Harvard Business Sch. M.B.A. 1956; VICE-CHRMN., LOEWEN, ONDAATJE, McCUTCHEON LIMITED; joined W.C. Pitfield & Co. Montreal 1956; Pitfield, Mackay Co. Inc. New York 1959; Pitfield, Mackay & Co. Ltd. (subsequently Pitfield, Mackay, Ross & Co. Ltd.) Toronto 1962, Dir. 1966, Vice Pres. 1968; Founding mem. of L.O.M. 1970 and Pres. 1970–87, Chrmn. 1987–92; Vice Chrmn., Loewen, Ondaatje, McCutcheon Limited 1993; Gov., Toronto Stock Exchange 1979–80; Dir. Investment Dealers Assn. 1983–85; mem. Gov., Vancouver Stock Exchange 1987–88; Chrmn., The Winchester Group Inc.; Dir., The Loewen Group Inc.; Internat. UNP Holdings; Clubs: National; Toronto Lawn Tennis; Tadenac; Osler Bluff Ski; Home: Boyne Mill House, 936414 Airport Rd., Mansfield, Ont. L0N 1M0; Office: 30A Hazelton Ave., Suite 200, Toronto, Ont. M5R 2E2.

**LOEWEN, William Herbert,** F.C.A.; payroll service executive; b. Elkhorn, Man. 28 July 1930; s. John Peter and Ada Sherwood (Howard) L.; e. Elkhorn High Sch. 1948; C.A. 1954; m. Shirley d. Charles and Zona Perret 22 Feb. 1958; children: Howard William, Ann Elizabeth, Louise May, Peter Charles, Jennifer Ada; FOUNDER & FORMER CHRMN. COMCHEQ SERVICES LIMITED; Dir. and former Pres., Winnipeg Symphony Orchestra; Pres., National Party of Canada; Pres., CTI-ComTel Inc.; Club: Manitoba; Home: 124 rue St. Pierre, St. Norbert, Man. R3V 1J8; Office: 298 Garry St., Winnipeg, Man. R3C 1H3.

**LOEWRIGKEIT, Wilfried O.A.,** FLMI, ISP, CSP; insurance executive; b. Anklam Saxony 20 Jan. 1945; s. Paul E. and Evelyn M. (Hempel) L.; m. Ilse M. d. Rudolf and Ilse Meyer 16 April 1967; VICE-PRESIDENT, NATIONAL LIFE ASSURANCE CO. OF CANADA 1988– ; Manager, National Life 1978; Manager, The Consumers' Gas Co. 1984; Dir., National Life 1985; Systems Vice-Pres. 1986; Mem., LOMA, ASM, ICCP, CIPS, LIIC (Past Chair); recreations: outdoors activities; Home: R.R. 1, Box 537, Kinmount, Ont. K0M 2A0; Office: 522 University Ave., Toronto, Ont. M5G 1Y7.

**LOEWY, Victor,** B.A.; film distribution executive; b. Bucharest, Roumania 8 May 1946; s. Adrian and Regina (Kramer) L.; e. German High Sch. Bucharest grad. 1963; McGill Univ. B.A. (Commerce & German) 1970; m. Irene d. Max and Lia Lobel 1972; children: Alexandra, Dan; PRES. ALLIANCE ENTERTAINMENT RELEASING CORP. 1987– ; Advtg. Mgr. McGill Daily 1971–72; Pres., Distributor Vivafilm Ltd. 1973, merged with Alliance Entertainment Corp. to form present Co. 1987; mem. Cinematheque Québeçois; rec'd., CFPTA Chetwyn Award for entrepreneurial excellence 1990; Golden Reel Award (Black Robe) 1992; Chrmn., Nat. Assn. Candn. Film Distributors (Dir.); Home: 467 Mount Stephen, Westmount, Qué. H3Y 2X8; Office: 920 Yonge St., Toronto, Ont. M4W 3C7 and 5 Place Ville Marie, Montreal, Que. H3B 2G2.

**LOGAN, Frank Henderson;** b. Montreal, Que. 19 May 1936; s. Frank Duncan and Mabel (Henderson) L.; e. Schs. of Westmount, (Que.); Princeton Univ.; m. Linda May, d. W. R. Hermitage, 26 Oct. 1962; two s.; VICE CHRMN. & DIR., CANADIAN IMPERIAL BANK OF COMMERCE 1981– ; Dir., Dofasco, Inc.; Thornmark Corporate Managment Inc.; Maple Leaf Foods Inc.; Candn. Chamber of Comm.; Mem. Bd. of Govs., McMaster Univ.; Clubs: Toronto; York; Granite; Goodwood; Mount Royal (Montreal); Princeton, New York; Ivy, Princeton, New Jersey; Office: Commerce Court, Toronto, Ont. M5L 1A2.

**LOGAN, Maurice Neil,** M.B.A.; banker; e. Univ. of Western Ont. M.B.A. 1971; m. Georgina 6 Sept. 1979; one child: Leslie; SENIOR VICE-PRESIDENT, THE BANK OF NOVA SCOTIA; Office: 44 King St. W., Toronto, Ont. M5H 1H1.

**LOGAN, Hon. Rodman Emmason,** C.D., B.A., B.C.L., D.C.L.; jurist; b. Saint John West, N.B. 7 Sept. 1922; s. Gilbert Earle, Q.C. and Emma Z. (Irwin) L.; e. Rothesay Coll. Sch. 1941; Univ. of N.B. B.A. 1949, B.C.L. 1951; St. Thomas Univ. D.C.L. 1974; Univ. of N.B. D.C.L. 1988; m. Evelyn Pearl d. C. Ray DeWitt, Woodstock, N.B. 19 June 1948; children: L/Col. John Bruce DeWitt, Ian David Alexander, Bruce Rodman Hans, Mary Jane Irwin; JUSTICE OF THE COURT OF QUEEN'S BENCH OF NEW BRUNSWICK since 1982; called to Bar of N.B. 1951, cr. Q.C. 1973; mem. Kings Co. Council 1952–54; el. to Leg. Assembly for Saint John Co. 1963, re-el. 1967, 1970, 1974, 1978 Saint John West; apptd. Min. of Labour and Prov. Secy. 1970, relinquished latter post 1972; re-apptd. Min. of Labour 1974 (subsequently Labour & Manpower 1975); Min. responsible for Housing 1974; Min. of Justice and Attorney-General, N.B. 1977–82; served with Carleton and York Regt. 1943–45 UK N.Africa Italy N.W. Europe, twice wounded, rank Lt.; served with Militia 1946–60; Hon. L/Col. 1 Royal New Brunswick Regiment (Carleton & York); Hon. Solr. Royal Candn. Legion 1953–70; Anglican; Home: Westfield, R.R.# 2, King's County, N.B. E0G 3J0; Office: 110 Charlotte St., Saint John, N.B. E2L 2J3.

**LOHANS, Alison Tacy,** B.A.; writer; b. Reedley, Cal. 13 July 1949; d. Walter Hermann and Mildred Eunice (Standing) Lohans; e. Reedley High Sch. 1967; Reedley Coll.; Whittier Coll.; Cal. State Univ. Los Angeles B.A. 1971; Univ. of Victoria postgrad. dip. in Elem. Edn. 1976; Univ. of Regina grad. studies 1984–88; m. Michael Alphonse Pirot 6 Dec. 1969 (dec.); m. (common law) Stewart Raby; two s. John Andrew, Christopher Thomas; teacher, Argenta (B.C.) Friends Sch. 1973–74; instrumental music teacher Regina Pub. Schs. 1976–79; rsch. asst. Sask. Instructional Devel. & Rsch. Unit Faculty of Edn. Univ. of Regina 1986–88; instructor, Univ. of Regina Extension 1990– ; maj. award winner Sask. Writers Guild Lit. competition 1989, 1991; Candn. Children's Book Centre 'Our Choice' awards (5); author (young adult novels) 'Who Cares About Karen?' 1983; 'Can You Promise Me Spring?' 1986, 1991; 'Foghorn Passage' 1992; 'Laws of Emotion' 1993; (children's books) 'Mystery of the Lunchbox Criminal' 1990; French edition 'Y a-t-il un voleur dans l'école?' 1990; 'Germy Johnson's Secret Plan' 1992; French ed. 'Le plan secret de Jérémie Jalbert' 1992; mem. Sask. Writers Guild (Bd. of Dirs. 1985–86, 1991–93); Candn. Soc. Children's Authors, Illus. & Performers (Prairie Rep. 1985–89); Writers' Union Can.; Soc. Children's Book Writers and Illustrators; Soc. of Friends; recreations: reading, music, gardening; Address: 76 Dolphin Bay, Regina, Sask. S4S 4Z8.

**LOISELLE, Gilles,** B.A.; former politician; b. Témiscamingue, Qué. 20 May 1929; e. classical studies with the Jesuits, Sudbury; Univ. Laval B.A. 1951; m. Lorraine Benoît; children: Anne, Frédéric; Minister of Finance 1993; Pres., Treasury Board 1990–93; Minister of State (Finance) 1989–93; Prof., Lycée Tafari Makonnen, Addis-Ababa, Ethiopia 1951–53; Reporter, 'Le Droit' & radio station 'CKCH' 1953–56; Dir., Inst. Berhane Zarie Neo & Prof., Lycée Haile Selassie, Addis-Ababa, Ethiopia 1956–62; Reporter/Line-up Ed., Téléjournal, Soc. Radio-Can. and then parliamentary correspondent in Quebec City 1962–65; Correspondent, Candn. Broadcasting Corp., Paris (French Network) 1965–67; First Counsellor, Quebec General Delegation, Paris 1967–72; Extve. Dir., Government Communications, Quebec Govt. 1972–76; Pres., Interministerial Ctte. for Olympic Year 1976; Dir., Interparl. Relns. for Pres. of Quebec Nat. Assembly 1977; Agent General for Quebec in Great Britain 1977–82; Asst. Dep. Min., Candn. Intergovernmental Affairs, Govt. of Qué. 1982–83; Cultural Affairs 1983–84; Delegate General of Qué. in Italy 1985–88; given the mandate of coordinating the participation of Québec for the 1st Sommet mondial de la francophonie 1986; elected Conservative M.P. for Québec 1989; Founder & Mem., L'Assn. France-Qué. (Paris) & L'Assn. Qué.-France (Qué.); Former Dir., L'Assn. franco-québécoise pour la jeunesse; Address: 602 - 135 Grand-Allée W., Québec, Qué. G1R 2H2.

**LOISELLE, Jean Ernest,** CJ, CLJ, MDF, BA; foundation executive; b. Montreal, Que. 14 Sept. 1931; s. Louis-Philippe and Jeanne (Dussault) L.; children: Anne, Sylvie; ADMINISTRATOR & VICE-PRES. EXTVE. DIR., JULES & PAUL-EMILE LEGER FOUNDATION 1985– ; TV Dir. & Prod., CBC 1958–63; self-employed scriptwriter, researcher, dir. & prod. 1963–65; Personal Advr. to P.M. of Que. 1965–68; Extve. Asst. 1970–73; resumed self-employment 1973; Advr. & Asst. to Pres. & Comnr. Gen., Montreal Olympics Orgn. Ctte. 1976; Extve. Dir., Oxfam-Qué. 1979–84; Extve. Dir., Jules & Paul-Emile Léger Fdn. 1984– ; City Counc., Outremont 1973–83; Mem., Internat. Fed. of Anti-Leprosy Assns. 1984– (Pres. 1990–92); Mem., Internat. Devel. Extve. Assn.; Candn. Counc. for Internat. Coop.; Que. Assn. of Internat. Co-op. Orgn.; Founding Mem., Montreal Counc. for Internat. Relns.; Commandeur de Bordeaux and Chevalier du Tastevin 1986; Hon. Mem., Régiment de Maisonneuve 1986; La Croix de Vermeil du Mérite et Dévouement Français 1988; Commander (1989) and Knight (1992) of the Military & Hosp. Order of St Lazarus of Jerusalem; Knight of the Patriarchal Order, Holy Cross of Jerusalem 1990; Chancellor & Chief of Protocol, Priv. Counc., Commanderie de Bordeaux de Montréal; Honorary Member, Officers' Mess of Les Fusiliers Mont-Royal 1991; Vice Pres., Internat. Leprosy Union for North America 1992; awarded Commemorative Medal for 125th Anniversary of Candn. Confederation; recreations: tennis; member of several tennis clubs in Montreal; Home: 1536 Summerhill Ave., #8, Montréal, Qué. H3H 1B9; Office: 130 de l'Epée Ave., Outremont, Qué. H2V 3T2.

**LOMAN, Judy;** see UMBRICO, Judy Loman.

**LOMAS, Jonathan,** B.A., M.A.; university professor; b. Swansea, U.K. 21 June 1952; s. Roy and Margaret (Williams) L.; e. Hitchin Boys' Grammar Sch.; Oriel Coll., Oxford Univ., B.A. 1973 (Duke of Beafort Exhibitioner 1971–73); Univ. of West. Ont., M.A. 1975 (Commonwealth Scholar 1973–75); m. Jean d. Robert and Elizabeth Porter; children: Ashley Claire, Cassandra Elizabeth; PROF., DEPT. OF CLIN. EPIDEMIOL. & BIOSTATISTICS, HEALTH SCI. CTR. 1982– , CO-ORDINATOR, CENTRE FOR HEALTH ECONOMICS AND POLICY ANALYSIS 1991– , MCMASTER UNIV.; psych. rsch. on functioning of the human brain 1975–78; Pol. Intern, Ont. Legisl. 1978–79; Cons., delivery of health serv. 1980–82; Extve. Dir., Ont. Health Coalition 1981–82; Cons., Justice Emmett Hall's 'Health Services Review '79' 1979–80; Spec. Policy Advr., Ont. Min. of Health 1982–83; Cons., Health Policy Devel., Sri Lanka 1984; Cons., Operative rates, WHO 1987; Cons., Health Manpower Development, World Bank/South Korea 1988; Mem., Ontario Premier's Council on Health, Well-being and Social Justice 1991– ; Ont. Prov. Career Sci. 1984– ; Candn. citizen 1979; Mem., Candn. Public Health Assn.; Candn. Health Econ. Rsch. Assn.; Am. Public Health Assn.; Internat. Soc. for Technol. Assessment in Health Care; author: 'First and Foremost in Community Health Centres' 1985, over 50 sci. articles & book chaps. and 150 sci. presentations; co-author: 'Physician Manpower Planning' 1986; recreations: canoeing, politics, woodworking; Home: 278 Charlton Ave. W., Hamilton, Ont. L8P 2E2; Office: McMaster Univ., Hamilton, Ont. L8N 3Z5.

**LOMBARDI, John Barba-Linardo,** C.M., O.Ont., SBStJ, CavUdR; broadcasting executive; impresario; b. Toronto, Ont. 4 Dec. 1915; s. late Leonardo and late Teresa L.; e. Pub. and High Schs., Toronto; Toronto Central Tech. Sch.; m. Antonia Lena, 4 July 1949; children: Leonard, Theresa Maria, Donina Antonia; PRES. & C.E.O., CHIN RADIO/TV INTERNATIONAL (Canada's largest Multilingual Broadcasting operation, establ. 1966) CHIN-AM/CHIN-FM (North America via satellite - Anik E-2, Transponder 3B(6), 6.84 MHz) Weekend Global Network TV/Weekend Channel 57 CITY-TV; Pres., Lombardi Italian Foods Ltd.; Bravo Records & Music Co. Ltd.; Carpejon Investments Ltd.; Italian Shows Ltd.; Originator of annual Johnny Lombardi Talent and Song Festival (establ. 1974 as Candn. Multicultural Songwriting Competition; name changed 1982); also CHIN International Picnic, Canada's largest free annual festival of ethnocultural music, song, dance and amusements; Annual Host: Variety Club Telethon 1983– ; Hospital for Sick Children Telethon 1985– ; Awards rec'd: B'nai Brith Can. Family of Man Award, 1977; The Howard Caine Mem. Award (Broadcasting) 1976; Broadcaster of the year Award, 1980; co-winner AM station of the yr. Award 1980; mem., Order of Canada 1981; Frederick C. Gardiner Award 1984; City of Toronto Civic Award of Merit 1986; recipient, Order of Ontario 1987; hon. award 'Cavaliere Ufficiale della Repubblica' 1987; admitted as Serving Brother of the Order of St. John 1988; recipient, Variety Club of Ont. Chief Barker's Award 1990; Paul Mulvihill Heart Award (bestowed by Broadcast Extves. Soc.) 1990; Beth sholom Brotherhood Humanitarian Award 1991; Canada's Birthday Achievement Award 1991; mem. of various organizations: Canada/Holland 1945 Liberation Soc.; Variety Club; Toronto Musicians' Assn. (Life Mem.); Pres. Candn. Assn. Ethnic (Radio) Broadcasters; Hon. Dir., Doctors' Hospital; Hon. Mem., Nat. Council of Boy Scouts of Canada; Candn. Italian Business and Profl. Assn.; Italian Candn. Benevolent Corp.; Hon. Dir., Candn.-Italian Amateur Hockey League; Trustee, Nat. Arts Centre Corp. 1982–85; Mem., President's Counc., Heart and Stroke Found. of Ont. 1987; subscribing mem., Toronto Gen. Hosp. Found.; recipient, Human Relations Award, Cdn. Counc. Christians & Jews 1989; Dir., Candn. Council of Christians and Jews 1990; Dir., Metro Toronto Police Community Projects Found. 1990; recipient, 125th Anniversary of the Confederation of Canada Medal, 1992; Famous People Players Star Award 1994; Home: 127 Grace St., Toronto, Ont. M6J 2S6; Office: 622 College St., Toronto, Ont. M6G 1B6.

**LONDON, Jack Reuben,** Q.C., LL.M.; lawyer; b. Winnipeg, Man. 7 Feb. 1943; s. Louise and Mary (Kab) L.; e. Luxton Elem. & Jr. High Sch. 1957; St. John's Tech. High Sch. 1959; Univ. of Man. Faculty Arts & Sci. 1959–62, LL.B. 1966 (Isbister Scholar); Harvard Univ. Law Sch. LL.M. 1971; m. Belva d. Eugene and Jean Weisz 23 Aug. 1964; two d. Larissa Beth, Rebecca Lee; PROF. OF LAW, UNIV. OF MAN. 1971– (Dean of Law there 1979–84); Of Counsel, Buchwald Asper Henteleff 1988– ; Chair, Man. Law Found. 1986–89; called to Bar of Man. 1966, cr. Q.C. 1983; Dir., Man. Hydro 1983–88; private law practice 1966– ; Adv. Counsel Tax Litigation Sect. Dept. of Justice of Can. 1967–69; law practice Asper & Co. Winnipeg 1969–70; Assoc. Prof. of Law present Univ. 1971; concurrently seconded as Dir. Legal Studies Law Soc. Man. 1975–77; studied comparative law aspects Candn. and French criminal justice systems, France 1977–78; consulting legal practice taxation and human rights advocacy 1971– ; mediator/arbitrator 1975– ; author weekly column 'London's Comments' Winnipeg Tribune 1968–73; regular broadcaster law, the legal system and its pol. implications CBC and CTV; regular contrb. 'Morningside,' 'The Journal,' 'Dayshift,' 'Canada AM'; mem., Canadian Human Rights Tribunal 1983–87; mem., Federal Task force on Child Care in Canada 1984–85; Dir., Winnipeg Health Sci's Centre 1974–77; Adv. Bd. Candn. Profs. Peace in Middle E. 1975– ; Extve. Ctte. Candn. Friends Hebrew Univ. 1979–85; Dir., Jewish Child & Family Service 1979–86; Candn. Human Rights Foundation 1980– ; Winnipeg Jewish Community Council 1981–90; Jt. Community Relations Ctte. B'nai Brith Anti-Defamation League & Winnipeg Jewish Community Council 1981–83; Adv. Bd. Candn. Law Teaching Clinic 1980– ; mem. Bd. Community Welfare Planning Council 1971–72; Children's House 1973–75, Chrmn. 1974; recipient Olive Beatrice Stanton Award for Excellence in Teaching Univ. of Man. 1973–74; 3M Teaching Fellow, Soc. for Teaching and Higher Learning (Can.) 1987; Campbell Outreach Award 1991; Eagle Feather 1991; 125th Anniversary of the Confederation of Canada Medal, 1992; author numerous law publs.; Bencher, Law Soc. Man. 1974–77, 1980–84; Pres., Assn. Candn. Law Deans 1983–84; host and writer, CBC-TV documentary 'Media Ethics: An Inquiry into News Morality in Canada'; originator, host and writer, CBC-TV series 'The Right Thing to Do – An Inquiry into Professional Ethics in Canada'; mem., Candn. Assn. Law Teachers; Candn. Bar Assn.; Candn. Tax Foundation; recreations: travel, tennis; Home: 203 Harvard Ave., Winnipeg, Man. R3M 0J9; Office: 2500 – 360 Main St., Winnipeg, Man. R3C 4H6.

**LONG, Benoît,** B.A., M.A.; senior manager; b. Edmundston, N.B. 12 May 1962; s. Lucien Ligori and Blanche (Albert) L.; e. Carleton Univ. B.A. (Hons.) 1984, M.A. 1985; various research and executive positions, Canadian govt. 1985–89; Special Asst., Econ. Policy, Min. of Finance 1989–90; Chief of Staff, Minister of Fisheries and Oceans 1990–91; Chief of Staff, Minister of Employment and Immigration 1991–93; Chief of Staff, Minister of Human Resources and Labour 1993; A.M. Sormany Medal 1980; Roman Catholic; Mem., P.C. Party; recreations: golf, music; Office: 1115e St-René ouest, Gatineau, Que. J8T 6L6.

**LONG, J. David,** B.A.; association executive; b. Toronto, Ont. 21 May 1946; s. Robert John and Cicely Maude (Waddington) L.; e. Richview Coll. Inst.; Univ. of Windsor; Univ. of Toronto, B.A.; m. Brenda d. Floyd and Lillian Kennedy 5 Sept. 1970; two s. Ryan Jeffrey, Andrew Jordan David; Pres. Candn. Ind. Transp. League 1984–90; Dir., Communications Carriers Br. Ont. Govt. 1978, Communications Policy 1980; Instr. in Transp. Econ. Univ. of Toronto Sch. Continuing Studies 1975–79; author 'Great Lakes Deckhouse Barge Study' 1974; 'Ontario Rail Task Force' 1980; 'Essays on Strategic Planning for Trnasport Ministers' 1981; 'Northern Ontario Freight Rate Studies' 1973; 'Transportation Industrial Requirements Study' 1976; mem. Assn. Am. Transp. Practicioners; Toronto Transp. Club; Thornhill Minor Hockey Assn. (Extve.); club: President's.

**LONG, John (Jack) W.;** architect and planner; b. Johnstown, Pa. 12 Dec. 1925; s. J.W. and Esther T. L.; e. Penna. State Univ., B.Arch., 1950; C.M.H.C. Fellowship, McGill Univ. 1967; m.; PRINCIPAL, JACK LONG AND THE NEW STREET GROUP; practised architecture in Philadelphia, New York City and Washington, D.C. prior to emigrating to Canada 1960; Partner, McMillan, Long and Assoc. 1964; Hon. Fellow, Royal Arch. Inst. Can.; recipient of numerous design awards; Address: 23 New Bow Lane S.E., Calgary, Alta. T2G 5J9.

**LONG, Tanya Carole,** M.A., M.Phil.; b. Sudbury, Ont. 13 Oct. 1944; d. Sulo and Jennie Marie (Niemi) Maenpaa; e. Laurentian Univ. B.A. 1966; Univ. of Toronto M.A. 1968, M.Phil. 1973; m. Stephen W. Long 1966, div. 1978; Lectr. in Eng. Scarborough Coll. Univ. of Toronto 1970, Asst. Prof. 1972–78; Ed.-in-Chief Macmillan-NAL 1978–81; Ed. Dir. Seal Books 1981–83; Sr. Ed. Methuen Publications 1984–87; Managing Ed., Prentice-Hall Canada Inc. 1988–93; mem. East York Chamber Choir; CAMMAC; Toronto Tai Chi Assn.; recreations: music, film.

**LONGHURST, Alan Reece,** Ph.D., D.Sc., F.R.S.C.; oceanographer; b. Plymouth, Eng. 5 March 1925; s. Eric Randall and Gladys Elsie (Hilton) L.; e. Epsom Coll. Eng. 1943; Chelsea Coll. London Univ. B.Sc. 1952, Bedford Coll. Ph.D. 1962, D.Sc. 1969; m. Françoise d. Helène and Jean Bergeret 21 Dec. 1963; children: Claire, Nicholas; RSCH. SCI. BIOL. OCEANOGRAPHY DIV. BEDFORD INST. OF OCEANOGRAPHY 1987– , Dir. Marine Ecol. Lab. 1977–79, Regional Dir-Gen. Ocean Sci. & Surveys Atlantic DFO 1979–87; mem. Adv. Ctte. Ocean Studies Prog. Dalhousie Univ. 1981– ; Sci. Offr. W. African Fisheries Rsch. Inst. Freetown, Sierra Leone 1954–57, Sr. Sci. Offr. Fishery Devel. & Rsch. Unit 1958–60; Marine Biol. Fisheries Lab. Wellington, N.Z. 1957–58; Prin. Sci. Offr. Fed. Fisheries Service Lagos, Nigeria 1960–63; Assoc. Rsch. Biol. Scripps Instn. of Oceanography La Jolla, USA 1963–67; Coordinator EASTROPAC 1967–70; Dir. Fishery-Oceanography Center (NOAA) labs. La Jolla and Honolulu 1967–71; Dep. Dir. NERC Inst. Marine Environmental Rsch. Plymouth, Eng. 1971–77; Professeur Associé Univ. of Aix-Marseille 1966; Rsch. Assoc. Univ. of Cal. San Diego, Scripps Instn. Oceanog. 1968–71; Vice Pres. ASLO Pacific Sect. 1968–70; Sec. ICSU Sci. Ctte. Oceanic Rsch. 1980–86; served with Royal Tank Regt. Italy, Austria, Egypt and E. Africa 1944–48, rank Lt.; mem. numerous nat. and internat. working groups, cttes. and dels. since 1960; Chrmn. Royal Soc. Can. Global Change Prog. Mar. W.G. 1987–90; Sec. Sci. Ctte. Oceanic Rsch. Internat. Council Sci. Unions 1979–86; author or co-author many sci. rsch. publs.; recipient, Gold Medal of Profl. Inst. of Canada 1991; Home: 6214 Regina Terrace, Halifax, N.S. B3H 1N5; Office: Dartmouth, N.S. B2Y 4A2.

**LONGSTAFFE, John Ronald,** B.A., LL.B.; executive; b. Toronto, Ont. 6 Apr. 1934; e. Upper Can. Coll., Toronto; Univ. of B.C., B.A. 1957, LL.B. 1958; one s., two d.; m. Jacqueline Slaughter 1978; CHRMN., VANCOUVER PORT CORPORATION; Dir., Canada Ports Corp.; Citizens Trust Co.; International Contour Technology Inc.; Mr. Jax Fashions Inc.; Pirelli Can. Ltd.; articled with Lawson, Lundell, Lawson & McIntosh; joined Canadian Forest Products Ltd. as Solicitor 1959 subsequently Secretary; leave of absence to serve Reed International Ltd., London, Eng. as Dir. of Corporate Planning 1969–72; rejoined Canadian Forest Products as Vice Pres. 1972; apptd. Extve. Vice Pres. 1975; resigned 1985; Dir., Royal Winnipeg Ballet; Past Vice-Chrmn., Nat. Museums of Can. 1968–69; mem., Vancouver Art Gallery (Pres. 1966–68); Past Chrmn., St. Paul's Hospital, Vancouver 1975–79; recreation: collecting contemporary Candn. art and internat. graphics; Club: Vancouver; Office: #8, 5760 Hampton Place, Vancouver, B.C. V6T 2G1.

**LONSDALE, Tanya Elise,** P.Eng., M.Sc., B.Sc.; consulting engineer, pricipal; b. Halifax, N.S. 15 July 1956; d. Ralph Duncan and Beverley Janette (Baxter) Mathieson; e. Seneca College, Resources Engineering Technologist 1979; Univ. of Guelph B.Sc. 1983, M.Sc. 1985; m. W. David s. William B. (dec.) and Nancy E. L. 28 Aug. 1982; one s.: Michael David; PRINCIPAL, BRAUN CONSULTING ENGINEERS LTD.; designated consulting engineer active in municipal & environmental engineering; present firm offers engineering services throughout Ontario to public & private sector; Mem., Bd. of Gov., Univ. of Guelph; Mem., Bd. of Dir., Guelph C. of C.; Co-chair, Guelph 2000 (not-for-profit orgn.); Home: 10 Laurelwood Court, Guelph, Ont. N1G 4E8; Office: 530 Willow Rd., Guelph, Ont. N1H 7G4.

**LOOMER, Diane Kolander,** B.A., B.Mus.; musician, conductor; b. White Bear Lake, Minn. 23 April 1940; d. Irwin and Viola (Knudsen) Kolander; e. White Bear Lake H.S. 1958; Gustavus Adolphus College B.A. 1962; Univ. of B.C. B.Musc. 1983; m. Richard s. Bernice and Leslie L. 28 Dec. 1963; one s.: Daniel McLeary; Founder, Douglas College Community Choir; Douglas College Children's Choir; Amabilis Singers (one of the foremost amateur choirs in B.C.); Conductor, Vancouver Bach Children's Chorus Organization 1988– ; Asst. Conductor, Vancouver Bach Choir 1990– ; Co-founder and Co-conductor 'Elektra' (women's choir; winner of 3 first prizes in CBC nat. choral competition & 1st prize, internat. choral festival); Healy Willan Award for outstanding contbns. to choral music in B.C.; 1st Canadian woman to conduct Vancouver Symphony Orch. in concert with the Vancouver Bach Choir 1991; frequent clinician, guest conductor, adjudicator & teacher throughout Canada and United States; Vice-Pres., B.C. Choral Fed. 1988–92; Treas., Assn. of Candn. Choral Conductors 1988–92; Chair, Nat. Youth Choir 1990–94; mem. Bd. of Dirs., International Symposium for Choral Music 1993; composer / arranger of : 'Soon ah will be Done wi' de Troubles of Dis World,' 'Ave Maris Stella,' 'A Fantasia on Oh Come Emanuel,' 'Away from the Roll of the Sea,' 'Blind Man,' 'I Saw Three Ships,' 'Song for Peace,' 'Four Canadian Folk Songs,' 'Yuletide Fires' (comns.); recreations: skiing, sea kayaking; Home: 7061 Cypress St., Vancouver, B.C. V6P 5M2; Office: Suite 102, 65 Richmond, New Westminster, B.C. V1L 5P5.

**LOOV, Robert Edmund,** M.S., D.Phil.; educator; b. Wetaskiwin, Alta. 29 Oct. 1933; s. Edvin Anders William and Augusta Charlotta (Svensson) L.; e. Univ. of Alta. B.Sc. (Civil Eng.) 1958; Stanford Univ. M.S. 1959; Cambridge Univ. D.Phil. 1973; m. Carrol d. Stead and Lolamae Hooper 17 Nov. 1979; two d. Nancy, Suzanne; PROF. OF CIVIL ENG. UNIV. OF CALGARY 1975– ; Design Eng. Kasten, Longworth & Associates, Edmonton 1958; Sales Eng. Con-Force Construction Ltd. Calgary 1959, Design Eng. and Chief Design Eng. 1960; Asst. Prof. present Univ. 1963, Assoc. Prof. 1969, half-time Asst. to Vice Pres. Services 1970–73, Acting Head of Dept. 1980–81, Head of Dept. 1984–89; cons. primarily fields reinforced concrete and prestressed concrete; author or co-author various publs.; recipient, Award of Merit, Candn. Standards Assn. (CSA); Killam Resident Fellowship, The Univ. of Calgary; Fellow, Candn. Soc. Civil Eng.; mem. Assn. Profl. Engs., Geols., Geophysicists Alta. (Bd. Examiners 1980–93); Am. Concrete Inst.; Candn. Soc. Civil Eng. (Chrmn. 1988 Conf.); Candn. Standards Assn.; Home: 6 Varal Place N.W., Calgary, Alta. T3A 0A7; Office: Calgary, Alta. T2N 1N4.

**LORCINI, Gino,** R.C.A.; sculptor; photographer; b. Plymouth, Eng. 7 July 1923; s. Luigi and Marie (Stride) L.; e. Boroughmuir Secondary Sch. Edinburgh, Scot.; Montreal Museum Sch. of Art 1952; came to Can. 1948; m. Marie Iosch 30 May 1953; children: Barrie, Anna, Nina, Gregory; solo exhns. incl. Galerie Agnes Lefort Montreal 1963, 1966; Gallery Moos Toronto 1966, 1969; Galerie Godard Lefort 1968, 1970; Atlantic Provs. Museums (tour) 1971–72; Marlborough Godard Gallery Toronto 1973, 1974; London (Ont.) Art Gallery 1976; McIntosh Gallery Univ W. Ont. 1977; Albert White Gallery Toronto 1979; Gallery Graphics Ottawa 1979; Thomas Gallery Winnipeg 1979; Art Expo N.Y. 1981; rep. in various group shows incl. Nat. Gallery Can. Candn. Sculpture 1964; Que. Prov. Competitions 1964–67; R.C.A. exhns. 1964–67; Art Gallery Ont. 1965 and Montreal Museum of Fine Arts; Univ. Vt. (Op from Montreal) 1965; Aspects Candn. Art Albright Gallery Buffalo 1974; rep. in variuos pub., corporate and private colls. Can., USA and Japan incl. Univ. Vt., Musée d'art contemporain Montréal, Nat. Gallery Can., Art Gallery Ont.; recipient Jessie Dow Award Montreal Museum Fine Arts; Can. Council Arts Award; comns. incl. Montreal Forum mural; Nat. Arts Centre Ottawa; Court House London, Ont.; City Hall Kingston; Dominion Plaza, Denver Col.; Bell Trinity Sq., Toronto; Canada's Capital Congress Centre, Ottawa; CFPL Broadcasting, London, Ont.; Asst. Prof. of Educ. McGill Univ. 1962–69; Resident Artist Univ. of W. Ont. 1969–72; served with R.A.M.C. 1942–46, Sgt./Instr. Educ.; recreations: exploring wilderness and ancient monuments; Address: 326 Old Brock Rd., Greensville, Ont. L9H 5H6.

**LORD, Michel,** B.A., M.B.A.; publication executive; b. St-Odilon, Qué. 28 Sept. 1941; s. J. Marius and Therese (Cloutier) L.; e. Laval Univ. B.A. 1960; Univ. du Québec (Montréal) M.B.A. 1981; m. Catherine (dec.) d. Louis-Martin Tard; children: Guillaume, Véronique; PRES. BUS. PUBLS. DIV. TRANSCONTINENTAL PUBLICATIONS 1982– ; Publisher, Les Affaires 1990– ; Publisher, Revue Commerce 1982– ; joined La Presse 1968–75; Publisher, Montreal-Matin 1975–78; Extve. CBC TV 1978–79; Mng. Partner Secor Inc. 1981–82; Dir. Theatre du Nouveau Monde; Office: 465 St-Jean, 9th Flr., Montréal, Qué. H2Y 3S4.

**LORD, Norman W.;** forest products, paper industry executive; VICE-PRES., CORPORATE DEVELOPMENT, CANADIAN PACIFIC FOREST PRODUCTS LTD.; m. Susan; children: Mike, Andy; Office: 1250 René Lévesque Blvd. W., Montreal, Qué. H3B 4Y3.

**LORD, Robert E.,** F.C.A.; b. Toronto, Ont. 16 May 1940; s. G. Ross and C. Nancy (Wilson) L.; e. Victoria Coll. Univ. of Toronto B.A. 1962; C.A. 1965; m. Patricia d. Edward and Gertrude Kernaghan 20 Sept. 1968; children: James, Jack, Vivian, Andrew; VICE CHAIRMAN, ERNST & YOUNG 1986– ; joined Toronto office present firm 1962, Audit Mgr. 1967, Partner 1971; Managing Partner, Edmonton Office 1976–86; Chrmn., Bd. of Govs., Royal Life Saving Soc., Canada; Past Chrmn. YMCA Edmonton; Past Pres.: Edmonton Art Gall.; Royal Life Saving Soc. Ont. Br.; Past Chrmn. Univ. Hosp. Found.; Mem., Bd. of Govs., Candn. Comprehensive Auditing Found.; Mem. Bd. of Govs., YMCA of Greater Toronto; Dir. Counc. for Candn. Unity; mem. Extve. Ctte. Univ. of Toronto Pres.' Ctte.; Past Pres., Osler Bluff Ski Club; Past Dir. Candn. Opera Co.; Past Chrmn. Corporate Fundraising Candn. Cancer Soc.; Past mem. Counc., Inst. C.A.'s Alta.; Past Dir., UTS Alumni Assn.; Clubs: Centre (Edmonton); Toronto; York (Toronto); University (Toronto); Badminton & Racquet (Toronto); Rosedale Golf; Osler Bluff Ski (Collingwood, Ont.); Ojibway (Pointe au Baril, Ont.); Nicholsons' Island Club; Home: 5 Cluny Ave., Toronto, Ont. M4W 1S4; Office: PO Box 251, Ernst & Young Tower, Toronto-Dominion Centre, Toronto, Ont. M5K 1J7.

**LORD, Ronald Daniel,** P.Eng., LL.D.; b. England 26 Dec. 1910; s. late Daniel Henry and Anne Mary (Chapman) L.; came to Can. 1912; e. Sydenham High Sch., Ont.; Queen's Univ. 1934–38, LL.D. 1972; m. Helen Dorothy, d. late Edwin Richards 7 Oct. 1939; children: Ronald Graham, Norman William, Ian James; Research Dir., Mining Indus. Rsch. of Canada, retired; employed by McIntyre-Porcupine Mines before and during univ. yrs.; from 1938–57 with Preston East Dome Mines in capacities of Mill Supt., Gen. Supt. and Mgr.; joined Rio Tinto Mining Co. of Canada in 1957 as Mang. Dir. of Mines and Vice Pres. R & D; Chrmn. Adv. Council on Engineering, Queen's Univ. 1969–70; Pres. (& mem.) Candn. Inst. Mining Metall. 1977–78 (Chrmn. Toronto Branch 1971–72); Pres. Ont. Mining Assn. 1968–69; Mem., Assn. Prof. Engrs. Ont.; Ontario Club (Toronto); Protestant; Home: 51 Heathcote Ave., Willowdale, Ont. M2L 1Y9.

**LORIMER, James,** Ph.D.; publisher; b. Regina, Sask. 27 July 1942; s. Wesley Crawford and Myrtle (Moore) L.; e. Univ. of Man. B.A. 1962; London Sch. of Econ. Ph.D. 1966; m. Carolyn MacGregor 1981; PUBLISHER, JAMES LORIMER & CO. LTD. 1969– ; Dir., Candn. Telebook Agency 1981–89; Pres., Formac Publishing Co. Ltd. 1983– ; Publisher, Canadian Forum 1988– ; Pres., Maritext Ltd. 1984– ; Publ., 'Atlantic Insight' magazine, 1985–89; Ed. Bd. mem. 'City Magazine' 1974–79; Cultural Policy Columnist, 'Quill and Quire' 1979–81; Asst. Prof. of Econ. York Univ. 1967–69; Founding Partner present Co. (then James Lewis & Samuel) 1969; Dir. Belford Book Distributing Co. Ltd. 1974–79; Trustee, Toronto Pub. Lib. 1974–79, Chrmn. 1976; former Visiting Lectr., Osgoode Hall Law Sch.; Univ. of Toronto Sch. of Arch.; Dalhousie Univ. Law Sch. and Sch. of Lib. Services; author 'The Real World of City Politics' 1970; 'Working People' 1971; 'A Citizen's Guide to City Politics' 1972; 'The Ex: A Picture History of The Canadian National Exhibition' 1973; 'The City Book' 1975; 'The Second City Book' 1976; 'The Developers,' 1978; 'After the Developers,' 1981; 'Book Reading in Canada,' 1983; City Hall Pol. Columnist, 'Globe and Mail' 1969–70; Founding mem. Assn. Candn. Publishers 1971, Pres. 1974; Office: 5502 Atlantic St., Halifax, N.S. B3H 1G4.

**LORIMER, Rowland Moore,** M.A., Ph.D.; professor, researcher, consultant; b. Regina, Sask. 17 March 1944; s. Wesley Crawford and Myrtle Isobel (Moore) L.; e. Churchill High Sch. 1961; Univ. of Man. B.A. 1964, M.A. 1966; Ont. Inst. Studies in Edn. Ph.D. 1968; m. Anne Carscallen d. Alan and Helen Carscallen 6 Dec. 1980; children: Stefan C., Conor R.J., Julia H.M.; Dir. Centre for Candn. Studies, Simon Fraser Univ. 1985–91, Dir. Candn. Centre for Studies in Publishing 1987– ; Prof. of Communication 1989– ; Asst. Prof. of Behavioral Sci. Founds. Simon Fraser Univ. 1968, Asst. Prof. of Communication 1973, Assoc. Prof. 1979; Candn. Visiting Fellow MacQuarie Univ. Australia 1981; rsch. cons. publishing; mem. Govt. Can. Awards (Social Sci.'s) 1982–88, Chair 1987–88; Can. Council (Book Promotion & Distbn. Panel) 1982–85; Mem. Adv. Bd., National Library of Canada 1989–93; author: 'The Nation in the Schools: Wanted, A Canadian Education' 1974; 'Book Publishing in British Columbia' 1989; 'Creating Ideas and Information' 1990; co-author 'Mass Communication in Canada' 1987 (2nd ed. 1991); 'A Harvest of Books: Book Publishing in Saskatchewan' 1992; ed. 'To See Ourselves/To Save Ourselves: Ecology and Culture in Canada' 1989; 'Communication Canada: Issues in Broadcasting and New Technologies' 1988; 'Canada and the Sea' 1979; 'The Other Guides to Language Patterns' Vols. I–III 1977; Producer and Host Video Series, Mass Communications in Canada 1986; Extve. Producer and Host Video 'Books and Water'; mem. Candn. Assn. Univ. Teachers; Candn. Communication Assn.; Assn. Candn. Studies (Extve. 1978–82, Pres. 1988–90, Past Pres. 1990–92); Home: 961 Lillian St., Coquitlam, B.C. V3J 5C6.

**LORRAIN, Paul,** M.Sc., Ph.D., F.R.S.C. (1967); physicist; b. Montréal, Qué. 8 Sept. 1916; s. Dr. Joseph Alphonse and Marie Ange (LeBel) L.; e. Univ. of Ottawa B.A. 1937; McGill Univ., B.Sc. 1940, M.Sc. 1941, Ph.D. 1947; m. Dorothée, d. Arthur Sainte-Marie, Outremont, Qué., 22 May 1944; children: François, Denis, Claire, Louis; Visiting Prof., Univ. of Grenoble (France) 1961–62; Univ. of B.C., Summer 1965; Univ. of Madrid (Spain) 1968–69; Visiting Fellow, Oxford Univ. 1981; Visiting Prof., École Polytechnique, Montréal, 1982–83 and McGill Univ. 1983– ; Visiting Prof. at 6 Chinese Univs. 1985; Univ. of Murcia, Spain 1986, 1987 and 1988; Visitor, Institut de Physique du Globe, Paris 1989, 1990; Visitor, Institut d'Astrophysique de Paris 1991, 1992, 1993, 1994; mem., Nat. Rsch. Counc. 1960–66; Dir., Dept. of Physics, Univ. de Montréal 1957–66; mem., Candn. Assn. Physicists; Am. Physical Soc.; Publications: co-author 'Electromagnetic Fields and Waves' (3rd ed.) 1988; co-ed. 'Nouvelles Tendances dans l'Enseignement de la Physique' 1972; co-author 'Electromagnetism: Principles and Applications' (2nd ed.) 1990; many recent papers on magnetohydrodynamics; Home: 777 Chemin des Vieux-Moulins, L'Acadie, Qué. J0J 1H0; Office: Dept. of Earth and Planetary Sciences, McGill Univ., Montréal, Qué. H3A 2A7.

**LORTIE, Jean-Paul;** executive; b. Quebec, Que. 5 Aug. 1927; s. Léon Joseph and Julia (Veilleux) L.; e. Ecole Sup. Notre-Dame de Grâces 1946; Univ. Laval 1950; m. Jeannine d. François-Xavier Lacroix 21 June 1954; children: Denise, Danielle, Jean; BD. CHRMN., PRES., & DIR., SICO INC. 1982– ; Pres., Parsico Inc.; Dir., I.P.L. Inc.; Janilo Inc.; Acct. Sico Ltd. 1946, Credit Mgr. and Office Mgr. 1949, Controller 1955, Asst. Gen. Mgr. 1971, Extve. V.P. 1973, Pres. and Gen. Mgr. 1977; Pres. & C.E.O. 1982; Bd. Chrmn., Pres. & C.E.O. 1986; Gov. Conseil du Patronat du Que.; mem. Que. and Montreal Chambers of Comm.; recreations: golf, fishing, chess, bridge, reading, music; Club: The Garrison of Que.; Home: 5070 Marie-Victorin, St.-Antoine de Tilly, Que. G0S 2C0; Office: 2505 de la Métropole St., Longueuil, Que. J4G 1E5 and 3280 Ste-Anne Boulevard, Beauport, Que. G1E 3K9.

**LORTIE, Pierre,** B.A.Sc., M.B.A., P.Eng.; executive; b. Giffard, Qué. 24 Jan. 1947; s. Raymond and Jeanne d'Arc (Turgeon) L.; e. Univ. Laval B.A.Sc. (Eng. Physics) 1970; Institut d'Adm. et de Gestion Univ. Louvain, Licence en Sciences Économiques appliquées 1974; Univ. of Chicago M.B.A. 1974; m. Michèle d. Louis A. Verreault 5 sept. 1970; PRES., BOMBARDIER REGIONAL AIRCRAFT DIVISION 1993– ; Sr. Partner Secor Inc. 1977–81; Pres. & C.E.O., The Montreal Stock Exchange 1981–85; Chrmn., C.E.O. & Pres., Provigo Inc. 1985–89; Chrmn. of the Royal Commn. on Electoral Reform and Party Financing 1989–92; Pres., Bombardier Capital Group 1990–93; Dir. and Mem. Extve. Comte., The National Bank of Can., Montreal, Que. 1986; Dir. & Mem. of Extve. Ctte., National Bank of Canada; Canam Manac Inc.; Dir., Working Ventures Economic Fund Inc.; CAI Capital Corp.; AKjuit Aerospace; Chrmn. of Bd., EDI-Wi Institure (Montreal); Chrmn., CITI (Centre for Information Technologies Innovation) Govt. of Canada; Mem., British North-Am. Ctte.; Mem., Bd. of Govs., McGill Univ.; Mem. Order of Engrs. of Que. 1986; Contbg. Ed., The Globe & Mail; author 'Economic Integration and the Law of GATT' 1975; various articles, reports, papers; Office: P.O. Box 6087, Stn. A, Montreal, Que. H3C 3G9.

**LOSEY, Nora Elizabeth,** Ph.D.; university professor; b. Toronto, Ont. 25 Mar. 1936; d. Robert Bell and Margaret (Burns) Lazier; e. Univ. Toronto, B.A. (Hons.) 1958; Univ. Wisconsin, M.Sc. 1959; Ph.D. 1963; m. Gerald Losey, 10 Aug. 1963; ASSOC. PROF. OF MATH., UNIV. MAN. 1970– ; Teaching Asst., Univ. Wisconsin 1958–64; Lectr., Univ. Wisconsin – Milwaukee 1963–64; Asst. Prof., Univ. Man. 1964–70; Visitor, Queen Mary Coll., Univ. London (Eng.) 1970–71; Assoc. Prof. Math., Univ. Man. 1970– , Assoc. Dean Sci., 1980–89; Visiting Fellow Math., Research Inst., Univ. Warwick (Eng.) 1977–78; co-author of several papers on mathematics published in professional journals; rec'd. Queen's Silver Jubilee Medal 1977; mem. Univ. Man. Faculty Assn. (Pres. 1974–75); Home: 50 Sandra Bay, Winnipeg, Man. R3T 0K1; Office: Dept. of Math & Astronomy, 438 Mackray Hall, University of Manitoba, Winnipeg, Man. R3T 2N2.

**LOSOS, Joseph Z.,** M.D., F.R.C.P.(C), F.A.C.P.M.; epidemiologist; b. Kulhapur, India 12 Dec. 1943; s. Marian and Gladys (Cieklinska) L.; e. Leaside High Sch. Toronto 1962; Univ. of Toronto, M.D. 1968, Dip. in Epidemiol. & Community Health 1977; m. Joanne Cameron d. Earnest and Phyllis Carr 24 July 1975; children: Andrew, Michelle, Craig; DIR. GEN., LAB. CENTRE FOR DISEASE CONTROL, HEALTH & WELFARE CAN. 1987– ; Adjunct Prof. of Community Med., Univ. of Ottawa 1980– and McGill Univ. 1987– ; internship Vancouver Gen. Hosp. 1968–69; Med. Offr. CUSO Min. of Health Uganda 1969–71; Clin. Teacher in Family & Community Med. Univ. of Toronto 1971–72; Med. Resident Toronto Gen. Hosp. 1975–76; Med. Offr., Prog. Offr. Internat. Devel. Rsch. Centre 1973–75, Assoc. Dir. Health Sci's Div. 1977–80, seconded to World Health Orgn. Tropical Disease Rsch. Centre, Zambia 1977–79; Dir. Bureau Communicable Disease Epidemiol. 1986; recipient various grants tropical med. & internat. health; co-author 'Travelling to the Tropics with Children' 1986; author or co-author numerous sci. publs., presentations; mem. Candn. Pub. Health Assn. (Epidemiol. Div.); Candn. Soc. Tropical Med. & Internat. Health (Pres. 1986–88); Candn. Hosp. Infection Control Assn. (Dir. 1983–84); recreation: athletics; Home: 175 Rothwell Dr., Ottawa, Ont. K1J 7G7; Office: Tunney's Pasture, Ottawa, Ont. K1A 0L2.

**LOSSING, Frederick P.,** M.A., Ph.D., F.R.S.C., F.C.I.C.; chemist; b. Norwich, Ont., 4 Aug. 1915; s. Frank Edgar and Evelyn (Pettit) L.; e. Public and High Schs., Norwich, Ont.; Univ. of W. Ont., B.A. 1938, M.A. 1940; McGill Univ., Ph.D. (Chem.) 1942; m. Frances Isabella, d. Sydney J. N. Glazier, 11 June 1938, three d., Wilda Evelyn, Patricia May, Catherine Louise; Research Chemist with Shawinigan Chemicals Ltd., Shawinigan Falls, Que., 1942–46; employed by Nat. Research Council of Can. at McMaster Univ., Hamilton, Ont., 1946–47; with N.R.C., Ottawa 1947–80; Assoc. Dir., Div. of Chem. 1969–77; retired 1980; presently Hon. Res. Scientist, Dept. of Chem., Univ. of Ottawa; research area: reactions and properties of ions and radicals by mass spectrometric techniques; mem. Royal Astron. Soc. Can.; recreations: music (cello), amateur astronomy; Home: 95 Dorothea Drive, Ottawa, Ont. K1V 7C6; Office: Dept. of Chem., Univ. of Ottawa, Ottawa, Ont. K1N 9B4.

**LOTTO, Victor George;** foreign service officer; b. Toronto, Ont. 19 Feb. 1935; s. Wallace Neil and Elizabeth Margaret (Saunders) L.; e. Univ. of Toronto B.A. 1958; Univ. of W. Ont. Dip. Adv. Mgmt. 1972; m. Margaret d. Nora and John Nixon 6 Apr. 1963; children: Andrew, Marc, John; DIR. GEN., INFORMATION SYSTEMS, EXTERNAL AFFAIRS AND INTERNAT. TRADE 1991– ; foreign assignments: Beirut 1963–66; Detroit 1966–69; Milan 1969–72; Asst. to Vice-Pres., John Labatt Ltd. 1972–76; Dir., Multilateral Prog., CIDA 1974–76; Counsellor, Dev. & Comm., Candn. High Comn. New Delhi, India 1976–79; Consul Gen., Sao Paulo, Brazil 1979–82; Depy. Chrmn., For. Serv. Restructuring Ctte. 1982–83; Dir. Gen. Export Prog. Bureau, External Affairs 1983–85; Candn. Ambassador to Venezuela & The Dominican Republic 1985–88; Extve. Dir., B.C.& Yukon, Industry, Science and Technology Canada 1988–91; Office: 125 Sussex Dr., Ottawa, Ont. K1A 0G2.

**LOUBERT, Patrick;** film producer; b. 7 March 1947; e. York Univ., B.A. (Eng. & Hist.); CO-FOUNDER & PRES., NELVANA LTD.; Selected credits include Extve. Prod., Animated Series 'The Care Bears (65), 'Inspector Gadget' (65), 'Ewoks' (26), 'Droids' (26), 'Babar' (65), 'Rupert' (39), 'The Adventures of Tintin' (39), 'Little Rosey' (13), 'Jim Henson's Dog City' (23); Producer, Animated Series, 'Fievel's American Tails' (13), 'Beetlejuice' (120), 'Eek the Cat' (26), 'Cadillacs and Dinosaurs' (13), 'Tales From the Cryptkeeper' (13); Extve. Prod., Live Action Series 'The Edison Twins' (78), 'T & T' (65), '20 Minute Workout' (120 - Co-Extve. Prod.); Extve. Prod., Animated Features 'The Care Bears Movie,' 'The Care Bears Movie II,' 'The Care Bears Adventure in Wonderland,' 'Rock and Rule,' 'Babar: The Movie'; Extve. Prod., Director, Writer, Live Action Feature '125 Rooms of Comfort', Golden Reel Award - 'The Care Bears Movie', Emmy Award 'Beetlejuice', Two time Gemini Award 'Babar', numerous others; Office: 32 Atlantic Ave., Toronto, Ont. M6K 1X8.

**LOUCKS, David H.,** B.Comm., M.B.A.; bank executive; b. Ottawa, Ont. 14 June 1941; s. Hugh Horatio and Laura Mary (Good) L.; e. Sir George Williams Univ. B.Comm. 1971; Concordia Univ. M.B.A. 1976; m. Madeleine d. Adjutor and Cecile Audet 8 July 1967; children: Kevin, Daniel; VICE-PRESIDENT, FINANCE & PLANNING, RETAIL BANKING, ROYAL BANK OF CANADA 1990– ; joined Royal Bank of Canada 1962; awarded Muir Scholarship 1968–71; Vice-Pres. & Comtroller, Product Mngt. & Mktg. 1986; Bus. Govt. Interchange Program 1988–90; Finance Canad, Special Advisor, Financial Sector Policy Br.; 3 assignments with Harvard Inst. for Internat. Devel. to assist with bank training in Indonesia 1985, '86, '88; Dir., Royal Bank Mortgage Corp.; Royal Bank Investor Trading; recreations: skiing, travel; club: Le Cercle Universitaire d'Ottawa; Home: 645 Grosvenor Ave., Westmount, Que. H3Y 2S9; Office: 1 Place Ville Marie, 3rd floor, East Wing, Montreal, Que. H3C 3A9.

**LOUCKS, Kenneth Edmun,** B.A., M.B.A., Ph.D.; Professor; b. Chatsworth, Ont., 15 Aug. 1937; s. Cecil R. and Blanche J. (Lougheed) L.; e. Univ. of W. Ont., B.A. 1960, M.B.A. 1965, Ph.D. 1974; m. Mary J., d. J. Manual Watson, St. Catharines, Ont., 5 Dec. 1959; children: Carolyn, Christopher, John, Jeffrey; PROF., FACULTY OF BUSINESS, BROCK UNIV. 1986– ; Adjunct Prof., Fac. of Business & Computing, Southern Cross Univ., Australia; Dir., Niagara Enterprise Agency; Pres., Entrepreneurial Educators Internat. Inc.; Past Pres., Niagara Region Development Corp.; Founding Dir., Burgoyne Centre for Entrepreneurship; High Sch. Teacher 1960–64; Lectr., Sch. of Business Adm., Univ. of W. Ont. 1965–67; consultant; Dir. & Assoc. Prof., Sch. of Comm. & Adm., Laurentian Univ. 1970–77, Prof. 1977–86; Dir., 1982–86; rec'd Xerox Centennial Fellowship 1967–68; Ford Foundation Fellowship 1968–69, 1969–70; External Collaborator, Internat. Labour Office, Entrepreneurship Development; Consultant, United Nations Devel. Prog., Bur. for Asia & the Pacific; Mgmt. Cons., Corporate Strategy and Entrepreneurship; Home: 66 Port Master Dr., St. Catharines, Ont. L2N 7H7.

**LOUCKS, Leon Frederick,** B.Sc., Ph.D.; university professor of chemistry; b. Minden, Ont. 12 March 1939; s. A. Vinton and Emily Letitia (Hunter) L.; e. Haliburton Co. Dist. H.S. 1957; Univ. of Toronto B.Sc. 1961; Univ. of Ottawa Ph.D. 1967; m. Susan d. Clifford and Viola Guthrie 17 Sept. 1960; children: Anita, Paul, Teresa; PROF. OF CHEMISTRY 1969– and CHRMN., DEPT. OF CHEMISTRY, UNIV. OF P.E.I. 1977–82, 1993– ; Rsch. Chemist, Hercules Rsch. Ctr., Wilmington, Delaware 1961–63; Asst. Prof., Prince of Wales College 1968–69; post-doctoral fellow, NRC 1967–68; P.E.I. Bd. Mem., Candn. Assn. of Univ. Teachers 1981–83; Pres., U.P.E.I. Fac. Assn. 1985–86; Mem., Maritime Prov. Higher Edn. Comn. 1974–80; Fellow, Chem. Inst. of Canada 1980; Excellence in Teaching Award, U.P.E.I. 1989; elected Councillor, Community of Sherwood 1979–90; Mem., Charlottetown Area Pollution Control Comn. 1983–89; Bd. Mem., P.E.I. Div., Candn. Cancer Soc. 1984–93; Charlottetown Area Devel. Corp. 1986–94; Nat. Mus. of Sci. & Technol. 1990–94; Mem., Roman Catholic Ch.; P.C. Assn. of P.E.I.; Chem. Inst. of Can.; Am. Chem. Soc.; Home: 26 MacMillan Cres., Sherwood, P.E.I. C1A 8G2; Office: Charlottetown, P.E.I. C1A 4P3.

**LOUCKS, Wallace John;** manufacturing executive; b. Tillsonburg, Ont. 12 Jan. 1931; s. Wallace Edward and Edith Doretta (McCord) L.; e. Port Burwell S.S.; m. Joan Irene d. Charles and Irene Bennett 29 Oct. 1952; children: Scot Edward, Craig Allen, Kurt Embry, Karen Elizabeth; PRES., KAUFMAN FOOTWEAR 1991– ; Branch Mgr., EDP Assoc. 1968; Chief Admin. Offr., Bata Industries 1969; Mgr., Information Services, Kaufman Footwear 1972; Vice-Pres., Mfg., Kaufman of Collingwood 1978; Vice-Pres., Admin., Kaufman Footwear 1986; Sr. Vice-Pres. 1990; recreations: curling, badminton, tennis, golf, antique cars; clubs: KW Granite Club; Home: 56 Thornridge Cres., Kitchener, Ont. N2M 4W1; Office: 410 King St. W., Kitchener, Ont. N2G 4J8.

**LOUCKS, Wilfrid Artley,** B.Sc.; natural resources executive; b. Invermay, Sask. 22 Apr. 1923; s. Harry Artley and Maude (Stephens) L.; e. Invermay (Sask.) High Sch. 1941; Univ. of Sask. B.Sc. (Geol. Engn.) 1949; m. Mary Anna Bernadette d. Thomas Daniel McNamee, Regina, Sask., 22 June 1946; children: Jacqueline Mollo, Maureen, Diane James, Ellen, David, Gregory; CHRMN. & DIRECTOR, RIFT RESOURCES LTD. 1993– ; Vice-Pres., Norcen Energy Resources Ltd. 1979–88; Operations Geol. Canadian Superior Oil Ltd. 1950–56; Sr. Geol. The Calgary and Edmonton Corp. 1956–62; Exploration Mgr. Medallion Petroleums Ltd. 1962–65; Vice Pres., Exploration Canadian Industrial Gas & Oil Ltd. 1965–73, Vice Pres. Finance 1974–75; Pres. Coleman Collieries Ltd. 1975–85; Pres. Prairie Oil Royalties Co. Ltd. 1983–85; Mng. Dir., Norcen International Ltd., Sydney, Australia, 1985–88; served with RCAF 1942–46; recreations: golf, music, sailing: Clubs: Calgary Golf & Country; Calgary Petroleum; Glencoe; Home: 2609 – 10th St. S.W., Calgary, Alta. T2T 3H1; Office: 715 – 5th Ave. S.W., Calgary, Alta. T2P 2X7.

**LOUGH, Donald K.,** B.Comm.; insurance executive; b. Montreal, Que. 9 April 1943; s. Kenneth P. and Enid (Stewart) L.; e. Sir George Williams Univ. B.Comm. 1969; m. Joan E. d. Marjorie and George Appleton 5 Aug. 1967; children: Michael, David; CHIEF EXECUTIVE OFFICER, HALIFAX INSURANCE CO. & CHRMN. & CHIEF EXTVE. OFFR., WESTERN UNION INSUR. CO. 1990– ; started career in insurance in Montreal as part of marketing dept. 1970; Branch Mgr. of a Greenfield opn. (Calgary) 1975; Vice-Pres. & Gen. Mgr., Canada, The Home Insurance (Toronto) 1985; Pres. & Chief Operating Offr., The Axa Home Insur. Co. 1989; The Halifax Isur. Co. 1990; Dir., Facility & Facility Assn. of Canada; Centre for Study of Insurance Operations; Insurance Inst. of Canada; Vehicle Information Centre for Canada; Office: 75 Eglinton Ave. E., Toronto, Ont. M4P 3A4.

**LOUGHEED, Jeanne Estelle,** B.A.; arts patron; b. Forestburg, Alta. 27 Oct. 1928; d. Lawrence Morrison and Estella Christena (Gunston) Rogers; e. Univ. of Alta. B.A. 1951; m. Edgar Peter s. Edgar and Edna Lougheed 21 June 1952; children: Steve, Andrea, Pamela, Joseph; Dir., Northwestern Utilites Ltd.; Sears Canada Inc.; former mem. Can. Council; served numerous local, prov. and nat. arts orgns.; Hon. Gov. Nat. Ballet of Can. (Past Dir.); mem. Adv. Counc., Dancer Transition Centre; former mem. Bd. Banff Television Festival Internat. Adv. Ctte.; former Hon. mem. Edmonton Opera; former mem. Adv. Bd. Alta. Ballet Co.; Prov. Ch. Alta. Heart Found. 1975, 1976; Hon. Pres. Tri-Bach Festival 1985; Member Calgary Art Gallery Found.; Hon. Gov. Calgary Real Estate Bd. Charitable Found.; Hon. Patron National Screen Inst., Can.; Mem. Bd. of Dirs., Calgary Philharmonic Orch.; Address: 805 Prospect Ave. S.W., Calgary, Alta. T2T 0W6.

**LOUGHEED, Hon. (Edgar) Peter,** P.C., C.C., Q.C., B.A., LL.B., M.B.A., LL.D.; lawyer; b. Calgary, Alta. 26 July 1928; s. late Edgar Donald and Edna Alexandria (Bauld) L.; e. public and high Schs., Calgary, Alta.; Univ. of Alta. B.A. 1950, LL.B. 1952; Harvard Univ. Grad. Sch. Business Adm., M.B.A. 1954; Hon. LL.D., St. Francis Xavier Univ.; Univ. of Alberta; Univ. of Calgary; Univ. of Lethbridge; Univ. of Windsor; m. Jeanne Estelle, d. late Dr. & Mrs. L.M. Rogers, Edmonton, Alta. 21 June 1952; children: Stephen, Andrea, Pamela, Joseph; PARTNER, BENNETT JONES VERCHERE, Barristers and Solicitors 1985– ; Mem. Bd. of Dir., ATCO Ltd.; Canadian Pacific Limited; Luscar Ltd.; Brascan Ltd.; CFCN Communications; Northern Telecom Ltd.; Princeton Developments; Royal Bank of Canada; Bombardier Inc.; Reed Stenhouse Companies Ltd.; Quorum Growth Inc.; Norcen Energy Resources Ltd.; PWA Corp.; Bechtel Canada Inc.; The DMR Group Inc.; Chrmn., Advisory Bd., Alberta Northeast Gas; Mem. Internat. Advisory Bd., Morgan Stanley Group Inc.; Co-Chrmn., Canada-Japan Forum 2000 – Partners Across the Pacific; read law with Fenerty, Fenerty, McGillivray & Robertson, Calgary, Alta.; called to Bar of Alta. 1955 and practised law with same firm 1955–56; joined Mannix Co. Ltd. as Secy. 1956, Gen. Counsel 1958, Vice-Pres. 1959, Dir. 1960; entered private legal practice 1962; el. Leader Prov. P. Conservative Party 1965; el. to Alta. Leg. for Calgary West in 1967; Leader of Official Opposition 1967; re-el. 1971, 1975, 1979, 1982; Premier of Alta. 1971–85; recreations: skiing, golf, hiking; Office: 4500 Bankers Hall East, 855, 2nd Street S.W., Calgary, Alta. T2P 4K7.

**LOUGHREY, Carol Elaine Ashfield,** B.B.A., M.B.A., F.C.A.; public servant; b. Fredericton, N.B. 13 July 1948; d. Vincent Evans and Marion Loretta (Thomas) Ashfield; e. Fredericton H.S. 1966; Univ. of N.B. B.B.A. 1970; N.B. Inst. of C.A.s C.A. 1972; Univ. of Maine (Orono) M.B.A. 1982; m. Ronald s. Dorothy and Carl T. 1970; children: Margaret, Katherine; COMPTROLLER, PROVINCE OF NEW BRUNSWICK 1988– ; public practice 1970–74; part-time consulting, stay-at-home mother 1974–77; various teaching & admin. functions, culminating as Assoc. Prof. & Asst. Dean (Graduate), Univ. of N.B., Faculty of Admin. 1977–88; inducted into Beta Gamma Sigma (nat. honour soc. for bus. students) 1982; U.N.B. President's Merit Award for outstanding contbn. in teaching, rsch. & univ. service 1987; Fellow, N.B. Inst. of C.A.s 1989; U.N.B. Fac. of Admin., Certificate of Achievement 1992; Pres., Muriel McQueen Fergusson Found. 1991–93; Vice-Chair, N.B. Law Found. 1981–88; YM-YWCA (Fredericton) Endowment Fund 1991–92; Mem., Candn. Inst. of C.A.s; N.B. Inst. of C.A.s; Finan. Mngt. Inst. of Can.; Inst. of Public Admin. of Canada; United Ch.; Bd. of Gov., Candn. Inst. of C.A.s 1985–87, 1992–95; 2nd Vice Chair 1992–93; 1st Vice Chair 1993–94; Chair 1994–95; Pres., N.B. Inst. of C.A.s 1986–87; numerous cttes. at prov. & nat. level for C.A.s; Pres., N.B. Regional Group, Inst. of Public Admin. of Canada 1991–92; volunteer work with various charitable orgns.; author/co-author various profl. & academic articles; Ed. Bd. Mem., 'F.M.I. Journal'; recreations: skiing, aerobics, walking; club: YM-YWCA; Home: 28 Eagle Court, Fredericton, N.B. E3B 5Y3; Office: P.O. Box 6000, Fredericton, N.B. E3B 5H1.

**LOUIE, Alexina Diane,** M.A., B.Mus., A.R.C.T.; composer; b. Vancouver, B.C. 30 July 1949; d. Alexander and Pansy L.; e. Assoc., Royal Conservatory of Toronto A.R.C.T. 1967; Univ. of B.C. B.Mus. 1970; Univ. of Calif. at San Diego M.A. 1973; m. Alex s. Alex and Jenny Pauk; children: Jasmine Sonia Ariana Alix Pauk, Jade Desirée Pauk; numerous performances worldwide incl. most important: 'The Ringing Earth,' Vancouver Symph., opening Gala concert, Expo '86; 'The Ringing Earth Fanfares,' opening Nat. Art Gallery; 'The Ringing Earth,' Montreal Symph. Orch. (Charlet Dutoit Conductor), Concert for United Nations Day, U.N. Gen. Assembly N.Y.; 'Scenes From a Jade Terrace,' Jon Kimura Parker, official opening of the Candn. Embassy, Tokyo 1991; frequent guest lecturer; Guest Composer, U.S.S.R. 1983, Toronto Symph. Eur. Tour 1986, Manhattan Sch. of Music 1988, Toronto Symph. Pacific Rim Tour 1990; numerous awards and commissions; Bd. Mem., The Esprit Orch. 1985– ; Composers Authors & Pubs. Assn. of Can. (CAPAC) 1988–90; Soc. of Composers, Authors, & Music Pubs. of Can. 1990– ; Toronto Arts Awards 1989–92; Roy Thompson Hall & Massey Hall 1992– ; has served on several juries; Mem., Canadian Music Centre (Assoc. Composer); CAPAC; has received extensive media coverage; Home: 323 Sunnyside Ave., Toronto, Ont. M6R 2R5.

**LOUIE, Brandt Channing,** B.Com., C.A.; business executive; b. Vancouver, B.C. 5 July 1943; s. Tong and Geraldine Maysien (Seto) L.; e. Univ. of B.C., B.Com. 1966; C.A. 1969; m. Belinda d. K.L. and Nancy Eu 30 June 1973; two s. Gregory, Stuart; PRES. AND CHIEF OPERATING OFFR., H.Y. LOUIE CO. LIMITED 1987– ; Dir., North American Life Assurance Co.; IGA Canada; Past Trustee & Past Chrmn., University Hosp.; Past Dir., Vancouver Symphony Soc.; Honorary Mem., Bd. of Dirs., Vancouver Community Coll. Education Found.; Vice Chrmn. & Dir., Vancouver Board of Trade; Pension Plan Trustee, H.Y. Louie Co. Limited; mem. Bd. of Dirs., Candn. Council of Grocery Distrib.; mem., Advisory Council, Food Research Centre, Faculty of Agriculture, Univ. of B.C.; mem., Inst. C.A.'s B.C.; Candn. Tax Found.; Bd. of Govs., Vancouver Maritime Museum; Dir., Hospital Foundations of B.C.; 1993 Hon. Chrmn., Timmy's Telethon (B.C. Lion's Soc.); Trustee, B.C. Sports Hall of Fame & Museum; Dir., Vancouver General Hosp. Foundation; recreations: skiing, tennis, golf; Clubs: Shaughnessy Golf & Country; Hollyburn Country (Dir.); The Vancouver; Home: 575 Southborough Dr., West Vancouver, B.C. V7S 1M5; Office: 2821 Production Way, Burnaby, B.C. V5A 3G7.

**LOUIE, Tong,** C.M., O.B.C., B.S.A., LL.D.; executive; b. Vancouver, B.C. 1 March 1914; e. Univ. of B.C. B.S.A. 1938; m. Geraldine 9 Apl. 1941; children: Brandt Channing, Kurt Harmon, Andrea Michele; CHRMN. & C.E.O., H.Y. LOUIE CO. LIMITED 1958– ; Chrmn., Pres. & C.E.O., London Drugs Ltd. (subsidiary of H.Y. Louie Co. ltd., wholesale food distributors) 1981– ; Vice Chrmn. and Dir., IGA Canada Ltd.; Hon. Chrmn., St. Paul's Hosp. Foundation of Vancouver; Dir., Pacific Otolaryngology Foundation; mem. Bd. of Gov., The Univ. of B.C.; B.C. Business Council; Hon. Dir., Candn. Diabetes Assn.; Hon. Dir., Crime Stoppers of Greater Vancouver; LL.D. (honoris causa) Univ. of B.C.; Clubs: Shaughnessy Golf & Country; Vancouver; Home: 6150 Southlands Pl., Vancouver, B.C. V6N 1N1; Office: P.O. Box 4000, Vancouver, B.C. V6B 3Z5.

**LOUIS, Robin J.,** B.Sc., M.Sc., Ph.D.; businessman; b. Victoria, B.C. 12 Dec. 1944; s. Benjamin and Mary Prudence (Smith) L.; e. Univ. of Victoria B.Sc. (Hons.) 1966, M.Sc. 1967; Univ. of B.C. Ph.D. 1971; m. Linda Mary d. John and Colette Tomczak 8 Jan. 1971; children: Aron John, Owen Benjamin; EXECUTIVE VICE-PRESIDENT & CHIEF OPERATING OFFICER, VENTURES WEST MANAGEMENT INC. 1990– ; Pres. & Chief Extve. Offr., Columbia Computing Services Ltd. 1985–90; Vice-Pres., Planning & Corp. Services, The Bentall Group Ltd. 1980–85; Dir., Ventures West Management Inc.; Ventures West Technologies Limited; Nissi Group Inc.; Chancery Software Ltd.; Simware Inc.; recreation: squash, running, reading, downhill skiing, cycling; clubs: Hollyburn Country, Evergreen Squash; Home: 5011 Howe Sound Lane, West Vancouver, B.C. V7W 1L3; Office: 250, 375 Water St., Vancouver, B.C. V6B 5C6.

**LOUNSBURY, Thornton Bendon,** B.E.; consultant; b. East Orange, N.J. 2 Jan. 1927; s. George and Jane Verne (Skelley) L.; e. McGill Univ. B.E.(E) 1950, Dip. Mgmt. & Bus. Adm. 1955; Harvard Univ. Dip. Advanced Mgmt. 1965; m. Helen d. Joseph and Catherine Flis 10 June 1978; children: Karen, Donna, Joanne, Steve; Pres. Assn. Maj. Power Consumers in Ont. 1989–91; retired; joined Canadian Westinghouse 1950, Vice Pres. & Gen. Mgr. Constrn. Group 1966, Vice Pres. Illumination & Dist. Apparatus Group 1968; Vice Pres. and Gen. Mgr. Canadian Westinghouse Internat. 1970–71; Vice Pres. Mktg. Westinghouse Canada Ltd. 1971–75; Vice Pres. Adm. Standard Brands Ltd. 1976–77; Vice Pres. Operations Canwest Investment Corp. 1978–79; Extve. Dir., Assn. Maj. Power Consumers in Ont. 1980–89; served with U.S. Navy 1944–46; mem. Assn. Profl. Engs. Prov. Ont.; Psi Upsilon; Phi Epsilon Alpha; Home: 1220 Cornerbrook Pl., Mississauga, Ont. L5C 3J4.

**LOVE, David Vaughan,** M.F.; university professor; b. Saint John, N.B. 25 Aug. 1919; s. Robert Alan and Elizabeth Louise (Davies) L.; e. Univ. of New Brunswick, B.Sc.F. 1941; Univ. of Mich., M.F. 1946; m. Ruth Geraldine, d. late Guy Welch, 9 Jan. 1943; children: Patricia Elizabeth, Peter Alan, Nancy Katherine; EMERITUS PROFESSOR, UNIVERSITY OF TORONTO, having joined Faculty of Forestry there as Lecturer, 1946; served in 2nd World War with R.C.N.V.R., 1942–45, Lieut:; mem., Candn. Inst. of Forestry (Pres., 1965–66, Fellow 1988); Pres. Conservation Council of Ont., 1975–76; Pres. Candn. Forestry Assn. 1975–76; United Church; recreations: reading, writing, swimming; Home: 16 Marchwood Drive, Downsview, Ont. M3H 1J8.

**LOVE, Gage Hayward,** B.A.; retired manufacturer; b. Toronto, Ont. 17 Sept. 1917; s. Harry Hayward and Eva Burnside (Gage) L.; e. Univ. of Toronto Schs.; Univ. of Toronto, B.A. 1939; m. Clara Elizabeth, d. Sir Ellsworth Flavelle, King, Ont. 20 Sept. 1941; children: Gage Ellsworth, David Hayward, Peter Flavelle, William Geoffrey; Dir., Bennett & Wright Ltd.; Dir., Custom Design Installations; Former Chrmn., Metropolitan Toronto Community Found.; Former Pres., Metrop. Toronto Bd. of Trade, 1967–68; served in 2nd World War, Lieut., R.C.N.V.R., 1942–45; Un. Church; Club: The National Club; Address: 'West Winds,' R.R. 2, King, Ont. L0G 1K0.

**LOVE, Hugh Morrison,** B.Sc., Ph.D.; educator; b. Downpatrick, N. Ireland 21 Aug. 1926; s. Hugh and Anna (Martin) L.; came to Canada 1950; e. Down High Sch., N. Ireland; Queen's Univ. of Belfast, B.Sc. (Hons.) 1946, Ph.D. 1950; m. Jean Claudia, d. H. Willis Hawkins, Cobden, Ont. 1954; children: Maureen, Norah, Denise, Robin; PROF., DEPT. OF PHYSICS, QUEEN'S UNIV. since 1976; Vice-Principal there 1976–1981; Lectr. in Physics, Univ. of Toronto 1950; joined present Univ. as Asst. Prof. 1952; research: Mass spectrometry, diffusion in solids and surface physics; mem. Candn. Assn. Phys.; Am. Phys. Soc.; Am. Vacuum Soc.; Am. Assn. Physics Teachers; Candn. Assn. Univ. Teachers; author of several scient. papers in learned and prof. journs.; Home: 185 Ontario St. #206, Kingston, Ont. K7L 2Y7; Office: Queen's University, Dept. of Physics, Stirling Hall, Rm 206A, Kingston, Ont. K7L 3N6.

**LOVE, James H.,** B.A., M.A., Ph.D.; university professor; b. Picton, Ont. 5 Oct. 1937; s. Malcolm Wallace and Carolyn Merilla (Kerr) L.; e. Prince Edward C.I. 1955; Queen's Univ., B.A. (Hons.) 1959; McMaster Univ., M.A. 1968; Univ. of Toronto, Ph.D. 1978; m. Shirley d. Thomas and Margaret Emmons 23 Apr. 1962; children: Sandra Marie, John Alexander; ASSOC. PROF., BROCK UNIV. 1980– ; Teacher, Hist. & Eng., Pelham Dist. H.S. 1959; Head, Hist. Dept., Thorold/Fonthill H.S. 1962; Co-ord., Social Studies, Pelham D.S.S. Bd. 1964; Lectr., Brainree Coll. of Further Edn. (U.K.) 1965–66; Instr., Fac. of Edn., Univ. of Toronto 1971–72; Rsch. Offr., O.I.S.E. 1972; Project Dir. 1973; Asst. Prof., Brock Univ. 1975; Vis. Prof., Univ. of Adelaide, S. Australia 1980; author of over 30 articles, monographs & reviews and 3 book chapters; editor 'History of Education in the Niagara Region' 1990; recreations: travel, fishing; Office: Faculty of Education, 500 Glenridge Ave., St. Catharines, Ont. L2S 3A1.

**LOVE, Jon E.;** real estate development executive; s. G. Donald and Marilyn R. (Duff) L.; e. Univ. of W. Ont. H.B.A. 1976; PRESIDENT & CHIEF EXTVE. OFFR., OXFORD DEVELOPMENT GROUP INC. 1980– ; Pres. & Dir., Oxford Properties Canada Ltd.; Retail Stockbroker McLeod Young Weir 1976–80; Office: #1700, 120 Adelaide St. W., Toronto, Ont. M5H 1T1.

**LOVEJOY, Paul E.,** M.S., Ph.D., F.R.S.C.; educator; b. Girard, Pa. 6 May 1943; s. Warren B. and Gertrude (Ells) L.; e. Clarkson Univ., B.S. 1965; Univ. of Wis., M.S. 1967, Ph.D. 1973; m. Elspeth d. Donald and Bertah Cameron 15 Apl. 1977; children: Beatrix, Hugo, Henry; PROF. OF HIST. YORK UNIV. 1983– , Assoc. Vice Pres. (Rsch.) 1986–90; joined present Univ. 1971, Chrmn. of Hist. 1983–86; Hon. Lectr. in African Econ. Hist. Ahmadu Bello Univ. Nigeria 1974–76; Fulbright-Hayes Fellow 1969–70; Social Sci. & Humanities Rsch. Council Leave Fellowship 1979–80, 1986–87; York Univ. Faculty of Arts Fellowship 1979–80; Council Mem., Social Science and Humanities Rsch. Council 1990–93; author 'Caravans of Kola. A History of the Hausa Kola Trade, 1700–1900' 1980; 'Transformations in Slavery. A History of Slavery in Africa' 1983; 'Salt of the Desert Sun: A History of Salt Production and Trade in the Central Sudan' 1986; 'Slow Death for Slavery. The Course of Abolition in Northern Nigeria, 1897–1936' 1993; ed. 'The Ideology of Slavery in Africa' 1981; 'Africans in Bondage: Studies in Slavery and the Slave Trade' 1986; co-ed. 'African Economic History' 1982–89, 1992– ; 'Workers of African Trade' 1985; 'Peculiar Substances: Anthropological and Historical Studies on Addictive Commodities' 1993; 'Pawnship in Africa' 1994; 'Slavery and Its Abolution in French West Africa' 1994; Series ed. 'African Modernization and Development'; mem. various ed. bds.; author over 30 chapters and articles learned jours.; Fellow, Royal Soc. of Can. 1989; mem. Candn. Assn. African Studies (Extve. Ctte. 1982–85; Pres. 1988–89); Candn. Hist. Assn.; African Studies Assn. (USA); Home: 28 Oriole Gardens, Toronto, Ont. M4V 1V7; Office: 4700 Keele St., Downsview, Ont. M3J 1P3.

**LOVELL, Paul John,** B.Sc., P.Eng.; executive; b. Eng. 16 May 1946; s. Ken John and Pearl June (Roberts) L.; e. Sir Joseph Williamsons Mathematical Sch. Rochester, Eng.; Imp. Coll. of Sci. & Technol. Univ. of London B.Sc. 1967; m. Sandra d. Ernest and Zillah Scott 13 Jan. 1968; two s. Simon, Peter; PRES., C.E.O. AND DIR., BANTREL INC. 1987– , Vice Pres. 1985–87; Trainee Eng. M.W. Kellogg London 1967–69; Project Eng. Ralph M. Parsons Co. London 1969–73; Project Mgr. J. Ray McDermott Inc. London 1973–81, Mgr. Eng. (North Sea); Mgr. Facilities Eng. Dome Petroleum Calgary 1981–82; Pres. Lavalin Offshore Calgary 1982–85; Fellow, Inst. Chem. Eng.; A.G.G.I.; recreations: golf, skiing; Clubs: Petroleum; Commerce; Home: P.O. Box 140, Site 7, R.R. 1, Calgary, Alta. T2P 2G4; Office: 703 – 6th Ave. S.W., Calgary, Alta. T2P 2M2.

**LOVESEY, Morris Roland Bazentin,** B.Sc., M.Th., M.A., D.D.(Bapt.); RET: educator; b. Watford, Eng. 8 Oct. 1916; s. late Roland and Winifred Hetty (Sparks) L.; e. Watford Grammar Sch. 1926–36; Birmingham Univ., B.Sc. 1939; Univ. of London, Spurgeon's Bapt. Theol. Coll., B.D. 1948, M.Th. 1953; Oxford Univ., Mansfield Coll., B.A. (Theol.) 1950, M.A. 1954;

McMaster Univ., D.D. 1970; m. Dorothy May, d. late Sidney Shone Surmon, Johannesburg, S. Africa, 4 Dec. 1943; children: Roland John Bazentin, Rosalind Edla May, Oliver Mark Bazentin; Shift Boss, Robinson Deep Gold Mining Co. (Johannesburg, S. Africa) 1939–44; Min., Kirby Muxloe Free Ch. (Leicester, Eng.) 1950–56; Assoc. Prof. of Biblical Lit., Sch. of Theol., Acadia Univ. 1956–58, Prof. 1958–68, Prof. Biblical Studies 1968–82 (ret.); served with 61st Tunnelling Co. (Mines Engrs. Bgde.), S. African Engr. Corps. Middle E., 1941–43; Wing Chaplain, Air Training Cadets, Eng., 1954–56; rec'd Am. Assn. Theological Schs. Theol. Faculty Fellowship for study in Britain 1966–67; Pres., Wolfville Inter-Ch. Council, 1972–74 and 1982–84; (Treas. 1970–72); Atlantic Ecumenical Council, 1970–72 (Vice Pres. 1968–70; Secy. 1972–74, 1976–78, 1986–88; Treas. 1982–84); Wolfville Br. Canadian Bible Soc. 1981–89 (Vice Pres. 1989–91); Wolfville Br., Humanities Assn. of Canada 1958–61; author 'The Pastoral Epistles' 1956; 'The Return from Exile' 1956; also numerous reports, articles and book reviews contrib. to various journs. and newspapers; Ed., 'Bulletin' of the Atlantic Baptist Fellowship 1985–92; former mem. Humanities Assn. Can. (Past Pres. and Secy., Wolfville Br.); Soc. Biblical Lit.; Candn. Soc. Biblical Studies; Candn. Soc. of Patristic Studies; Candn. Theol. Soc.; Chaplain, Dr. C.B. Lumsden Br. No. 74, Wolfville, Royal Candn. Legion since 1973; Baptist; recreations: sight-seeing, walking, reading; Home: 20 Westwood Ave., P.O. Box 68, Wolfville, N.S. B0P 1X0.

**LOW, Douglas John,** B.Com., F.C.A.; b. Toronto, Ont. 10 Feb. 1934; s. Douglas Andrew Graham and Florence Elizabeth (King) L.; e. Kent Pub. Sch. and Bloor Coll. Inst. Toronto 1951; Univ. of Toronto B. Comm. 1955; C.A. 1958; m. Jeanette Lynn d. late Rev. Dr. William John MacDonald, Bracebridge, Ont. 10 Sept. 1960; children: Douglas Andrew Graham, Jacqueline Candace; PARTNER, DELOITTE & TOUCHE, TORONTO; on secondment to the Institute of Chartered Accountants of Ont. as General Dir., Professional Standards and Self-regulation; joined Deloitte, Haskins & Sells, Toronto 1955, Audit Mgr. Montreal 1962, Partner Toronto 1966, transf. to Montreal 1971, Managing Partner, Montreal 1974–85, returned to Toronto 1985; past mem. Policy Board, DH & S, Canada; Past Pres. Tudor Singers of Montreal Inc.; mem. Candn. Inst. C.A.'s (Past Chrmn. Accounting Research Comte.; Past Chrmn., Auditing Standards Comte.; mem., Study Group on Financial Sector Reform and Study Group on Audit of Credit Losses; Chrmn., Study Group on Professional Judgment In Auditing; Ont. Inst. C.A.'s; Awarded F.C.A. 1988; Order C.A.'s Que. (mem. of Bureau 1978–80; past mem. Interpretations Comte., Education Comte., Profl. Inspection Comte., Adv. Comte to the Syndic.); awarded FCA 1984; mem. Financial Statements/Financial Reporting Task Force, Financial Accounting Standards Bd., U.S.A. 1978–79; Past Chrmn., Adv. Comte. of Bank Auditors to the Superintendent of financial Institutions; Past Mem. Adv. Ctte. of Pension Plan Auditors to the Superintendent of Financial Institutions; Chrmn. Bd. of Trustees, First Baptist Church, Montreal 1979–82, 1984–85; mem. and Past Chrmn., Finance Comte., Kingsway Baptist Church, Toronto; Chrmn. Audit Ctte., Baptist Convention of Ont. & Que.; Baptist; recreations: curling, tennis, bridge, philately, music; Clubs: Ontario (mem. membership Comte. 1988–91); Granite (Mem., Curling Ctte. 1993– ); St. James's of Montreal (mem. Gen. Comte. 1980–83; Treas. 1981–82); Royal Montreal Curling (Treas. 1979–83); Home: Suite 1606, 2010 Islington Ave., Weston, Ont. M9P 3S8; Office: Suite 1400, BCE Place, 181 Bay St., Toronto, Ont. M5J 2V1.

**LOW, Orian Edgar Beverly,** Q.C., B.A., LL.B.; b. Ottawa, Ont. 17 Oct. 1911; s. Archie Edgar and Jane Eva (Slinn) L.; e. Glebe Coll. Inst., Ottawa, Ont.; Queen's Univ., B.A. 1934; Osgoode Hall, Toronto, Ont. 1937; York Univ. LL.B. 1992; m. Ethel, d. Thomas Addison Hand, Ottawa, Ont., 22 June 1940; children: Dr. Sandra Ann, Bonnie Lynn, Orian, Jr.; former Counsel and founder Low, Murchison; Chrmn., Pres. Holo Investments Ltd.; Orbert Holdings Ltd.; former Chrmn. Extve. Comte. Ottawa Gas; former Vice-Pres. 161 Realty Ltd.; former Dir. Consumers Gas Co. Ltd.; Hiram Walker Resources Ltd.; Gen. Counsel and Secy. of Commodity Prices Stab. Corp. Ltd. and Wartime Foods Ltd. (Crown Cos.) 1942–46; served in N.P.A.M., 2nd Bn. Cameron Highlanders of Ottawa, 1941–46; Pres., Ottawa Jr. Bd. Trade, 1941–42; Ottawa Public Sch. Trustee, 1939–42 and 1945–52 (Chrmn. of Bd. 1942, Chrmn. of Property Comte. 1940–41, Chrmn. of Management Comte. 1949–51, Chrmn. of Finance 1946–47); former mem., Co. Carleton Bar Assn. (Past Trustee); Law Soc. Upper Can., called to the Bar of Ont., 1937; cr. K.C. 1951; Phi Delta Phi (Magister, 1936–37); Freemason (Scot. Rite; Consistory; Shrine); Anglican; recreations: photography, flying, travel, golf; Clubs: Laurentian (Pres. 1958); Ottawa Hunt & Golf; Kiwanis; Home: Apt. 2127, 200 Clearview Ave., Ottawa, Ont. K1Z 8M2.

**LOWDEN, James Arthur;** real estate consultant; b. Arden, Man. 17 Feb. 1916; s. Stuart and Christina (Anderson) L.; e. Regina Central Collegiate (Sr. Matric. 1933); m. Cecilia Agnes. d. David Simpson, St. James, Man., 23 March 1940; children: James David, Donald Blake; PRES. CEJAB Holdings and Investment Ltd.; formerly Pres. Canadian Interurban Properties Ltd., Montreal; formerly Vice Pres., Trizec Corp. Ltd.; Cummings Properties Limited; formerly Pres., Chrmn., Wilbr; & Devrin, NV; joined the Mfrs. Life Ins. Co. at Regina, 1933; trans. to Winnipeg as Inspector, 1939; moved to Montreal, 1947; apptd. Br. Mgr., Mortgage Lending Dept., 1948; apptd. Pres., United Principal Properties Ltd., 1961; Past Pres., Candn. Assn. of Real Estate Bds.; Past Pres., Candn. Inst. of Realtors (Fellow); Past Pres., Am. Soc. of Real Estate Counselors; Past Pres., Soc. of Real Estate Appraisers, Montreal & Winnipeg Chapters; Past Vice-Pres., Appraisal Inst. of Can.; mem., Am. Inst. of Real Estate Appraisers (Governing Council); Nat. Assn. of Real Estate Bds.; Real Estate Adv. Bd., National Capital Comn.; Conservative; Un. Church; recreations: reading, skating, sailing, swimming; Home: Apt. 1211, 10 The Driveway, Ottawa, Ont. K2P 1C7.

**LOWDEN, John Alexander,** M.D., Ph.D., FRCP, FCCMG; medical executive; b. Toronto, Ont. 21 Feb. 1933; s. John Alexander and Margaret Kathleen L.; e. Univ. of Toronto Schools 1951; Univ. of Toronto M.D. 1957; McGill Univ. Ph.D. 1964; FRCP 1976; m. Anne d. Horace and Edith Taylor 8 Sept. 1956; children: John, Eleanor, Jane, Thomas; VICE-PRES. AND CHIEF MEDICAL DIR., MEDICAL, CROWN LIFE INSUR. 1991– ; Pediatric Res., Hosp. for Sick Children 1958–60; Fellow, Montreal Neurol. Inst. 1960–64; Scientist, Rsch. Inst., Hosp. for Sick Children 1964–89 (Assoc. Dir. 1975–85; Physician, Dept. of Pediatrics 1966–89; Pres. Rsch. Devel. Corp. 1982–89); Dir. & Chrmn., Cyber Fluor Inc. 1985–89 (Dir. 1989–93); Dir. & Corp. Sec., Davstar Indus. Ltd. 1985– ; Dir., IAF Biochem Internat. Inc. 1988–89; Carolian Systems Internat. 1985–88; Fellow, Helen Hay Whitney Fdn. 1963–66; Kaplun Fdn. Award, Nat. Tay Sachs Assn. 1982; Dir., Metro. Toronto Assn. Mentally Retarded 1975–79; Dir., Bloorview Children's Hosp. Fdn. 1982–88; Nat. Sanitarium Assn. 1990–93; Queen Eliz. Hosp. Rsch. Inst. 1990–93; author of 90 pubns. in ref. sci. jours, 22 book chaps.; co-editor: 'Lysosomal Storage Diseases'; recreations: golf, sailing, travel; clubs: Toronto Hunt, Granite; Home: 303 Avon Dr., Regina, Sask. S4V 1L8; Office: 1901 Scarth St., Regina, Sask. S4P 3B1.

**LOWDEN, Stephens B.,** B.Comm., F.C.A.; b. Toronto, Ont. 26 Sept. 1938; s. late John Alexander and late Margaret Kathleen (Hartwick) L.; e. Univ. of Toronto Schs. 1951–1956; Univ. of Toronto, B.Comm. 1960; C.A. 1963; m. M. Linda d. Willard and Margaret Ruppel 15 July 1961; children: M. Laura, Stephen R.; EXTVE. PARTNER, ERNST & YOUNG 1990– and VICE CHRMN., SOBECO, ERNST & YOUNG 1993– ; with Ernst & Young (formerly Clarkson Gordon) 1960–87, Partner in Saint John Office 1968–70; Mng. Partner, Toronto Office 1982–86; Extve. Partner, 1984–87; Pres., Gardiner Group Capital Ltd. and Garbell Holdings Ltd. 1987–89; Vice Pres., Bd. of Trade of Metro. Toronto (Member of Council 1986– ); Dir. Kidder Foundation 1993– ; Past Chrmn., The Childrens Aid Soc. for Metro. Toronto Found. (Dir. 1985–93); Mem., Adv. Bd., York Univ. Fac. of Admin. Studies 1985– ; recreation: golf; Clubs: Lambton Golf & Country; Beacon Hall; Toronto; York; Caughnawana Fishing & Hunting; St. Andrew's (Delray Beach, Fla.); Residences: 70 Rosehill Ave., #704, Toronto, Ont. M4T 2W7 and R.R. 3, Port Carling, Ont. P0B 1J0; Office: Ernst & Young Tower, P.O. Box 251, Toronto, Ont. M5K 1J7.

**LOWE, David Graham,** B.Sc., Ph.D.; university professor; b. Loon Lake, Sask. 27 May 1956; s. Eric and Margaret W.S. (Bradshaw) L.; e. Univ. of B.C., B.Sc. 1978; Stanford Univ., Ph.D. 1984; m. Ruby Mawira 7 Nov. 1987; ASST. PROF. OF COMPUTER SCI. & SCHOLAR OF THE CANDN. INST. FOR ADV. RSCH., UNIV. OF B.C. 1987– ; Rsch. Asst., Artificial Intelligence Lab, Stanford Univ. 1978–84; Asst. Prof., Dept. of Comp. Sci., Courant Inst. for Math. Sci., New York Univ. 1984–87; Mem., Computer Profl. for Social Responsibility; author: 'Perceptual Organization and Visual Recognition' 1985; Home: 828 West 7th Ave., Vancouver, B.C. V5Z 1C1; Office: CICSR Bldg., Rm 111, 2366 Main Mall, Vancouver, B.C. V6T 1Z4.

**LOWE, Donald C.,** B.A.Sc., M.Sc.; b. Oshawa, Ont. 29 Jan. 1932; s. Samuel John and Corales Isobel (Cox) L.; e. Oshawa (Ont.) Coll. & Vocational Inst. 1950; Univ. of Toronto B.A.Sc. 1954; Univ. of Birmingham, Engl. (Athlone Fellowship) M.Sc. 1957; Harvard Internat. Sr. Mgrs. Program, Switzerland, grad. 1975; m. Susan Margaret Plunkett 22 July 1955; children: Michelle, Jeffrey, Steven; CHRMN., SEDGWICK LIMITED 1990– ; joined General Motors of Canada Ltd. as Mgr. Forward Planning, Oshawa 1957; Mgr. Indust. Engn. 1962–64; Project Engr. Ste. Therese Plant 1964–65; Plant Engr. St. Therese 1965–66 and Production Mgr. 1966–67; Plant Mgr. Body Assembly Oshawa 1967–69; Asst. Gen. Mgr. Ste. Therese 1969–70, Gen. Mgr. 1970–71; Dir. of Mfg. Vauxhall Motors Ltd., Gen. Motors Overseas Ops., Luton, Eng. 1971–75; Chrmn., Pres. & C.E.O., Pratt & Whitney Aircraft (Canada) Ltd. 1975–80; Pres. of Comml. Prods. Div., Pratt & Whitney, Hartford, Conn. 1980–82; Chrmn., C.E.O. & Pres., Allied Canada Inc., Mississauga, Ont. 1982–83; Pres. & C.E.O., Kidd Creek Mines Ltd., Toronto 1983–86; Pres. & C.E.O., Canadair Div., Bombardier Inc. 1986–89; Depy. Chrmn., Bombardier Inc. 1989–92; Dir., Bombardier Inc., Trilon Financial Corp., Canadian Tire Corp., Innocan Inc., Alberta Natural Gas, Scott's Hospitality, Airshow Canada; Bd. Chrmn., Sedgwick Limited; Mem. Adv. Bd., Ingersoll-Rand Canada; Dir., Fleet Aerospace; Haley Industries Ltd.; Devtek; mem., Conf. Bd. of Can.; mem., Aerospace Industries Assoc. of Can.; Montreal Bd. of Trade; Monteal Chamber of Comm.; Past Pres. Oshawa Jr. C of C.; Montreal Soc. Automotive Engrs.; Past Chrmn. Aerospace Industries Assn. of Can.; mem. Phi Gamma Delta; Protestant; recreations: skiing, squash, tennis, golf; Clubs: Les Ambassadeurs (London, Eng.); Donalda; Granite; Cambridge; Home: 47 St. Clair Ave. W., PH 4, Toronto, Ont. M4V 3A5; Office: Box 439, Toronto Dominion Centre, Commercial Union Tower, 8th Floor, Toronto, Ont. M5R 1M3.

**LOWE, James Frederick,** B.A., P.Ag.; corporate executive; b. Chicago, Ill. 15 Feb. 1922; s. Frank Arnold and Elsinore Burk (Conners) L.; e. Etobicoke H.S. 1939; Trinity Coll., Univ. of Toronto B.A. 1942; m. Iris Mary d. David Arthur and Dorothy Mary Pittis 10 Sept. 1949; children: Lynda Anne, Sandra Mary, Debora Jane, David Arnold, Patricia Eleanore; PRES. & CHIEF EXTVE. OFFR., BLATCHFORD FEEDS LTD. & EXCEL FEEDS LTD. 1969– ; Summer clerical work, Blatchford & Excel 1939–42; Pilot, RCAF 1942–45; Mngt. Trainee, Blatchford & Excel 1945–48; Gen. Supvr., Ont. Plant Opns. 1948–56; Asst. Gen. Mgr. 1956–64; Gen. Mgr. 1964–69; Mem., Candn. Feed Industry Assn. (Chrmn. 1962, 1963; Nutrition Ctte. 1964– ) 1949– ; Ont. Inst. of Agrol. (Chrmn. 1984–85) 1954– ; Candn. Mfrs. Assn. (Bus. Environ. Ctte.) 1949– ; Metro Bd. of Trade; Candn. Grains Counc.; Agric. Hall of Fame; Candn. Agri-Mktg. Assn.; Ont. Elevator & Dealers Assn.; Life Hon. Mem., Comml. Travellers Assn.; comnd. Flying Offr., RCAF 1944; organist/choirmaster, 3 Toronto chs. over 43–yr. period; Offr. & Dir., Kiwanis Music Festival Assn.; Mem. & Warden, St. James Cathedral 1979– ; recreations: travel, reading, music, walking, family, friends; Home: 378 The Kingsway, Islington, Ont. M9A 3V6; Office: 378 The Kingsway, Islington, Ont. M9A 3V6.

**LOWE, John Clifford;** banker; b. Bradford, Yorkshire, U.K. 6 Dec. 1945; s. Clifford Seddon and Winifred Mary (Bell) L.; e. grammar sch., Yorkshire, England; Univ. of B.C. & Calgary, extve. progs.; m. Shelagh d. Richard and Marion Carter 26 Sept. 1970; children: Christopher John, Kirsten Jane; EXTVE. VICE-PRES., NATIONAL WESTMINSTER BANK OF CANADA 1992– ; retail banking U.K. 1962–77; Midland Bank Can. 1978–82; Deputy Head, Mktg., present firm 1985–87; Head, Western Can. Bus. Devel. 1987–90; Sr. Vice-Pres., Marketing (Toronto) 1990–92; Home: 123 Triller Pl., Oakville, Ont.; Office: Ste. 2060, Royal Bank Plaza, South Tower, Toronto, Ont. M5J 2J1.

**LOWE, Mick (Michael Ellenwood);** writer; b. Omaha, Neb. 23 Sept. 1947; s. Jack Whiddon and Grace (Ellenwood) L.; e. Lincoln, Neb. S.E. High Sch. 1965; Univ. of Neb.-Lincoln 1965–69; Univ. of Calgary (Lyttik Cup for Journalism 1974); two d. Julia Kathleen, Melanie Nancy; Lectr., in Journalism, Cambrian Coll. 1988–90; staff writer Lincoln Daily Star 1967–68; staff writer and columnist Daily Nebraskan 1966–68, The Georgia Straight (Vancouver) 1970–72; co-founder The Grape (Western Voice) Vancouver 1972; ed. The Gauntlet 1973–74; freelance corr. Toronto Globe & Mail 1974–76, 1979–87; staff reporter CBC Radio News 1977–78; founding producer CBC radio Morning North Sudbury 1978; recipient Arthur B. Ellis Award best non-fiction crime Can. 1988; author: 'Conspiracy of Brothers: A True Story of Bikers, Murder and the Law'

1988, paperback 1989; 'One Woman Army: The Life of Claire Calhane' 1992; mem. Writers Union Can.; Address: 32 Onwatin Lake Rd. E., Hanmer, Ont. P3P 1J4.

**LOWE, Robert E.,** M.B.A.; chartered accountant; b. Winnipeg, Man. 31 Oct. 1940; s. Mark C. and Florence Irene L.; e. York Univ. M.B.A. 1975; m. Isabel d. William and Jean Liddell 1 Oct. 1965; children: Susan Patricia, Donna Jane, Mark William; DEPUTY CHRMN., COOPERS & LYBRAND 1991; C.A. 1965; Partner, Coopers & Lybrand 1971; Trustee in Bankruptcy 1971; Chrmn., Coopers & Lybrand Limited 1986; Home: 1500 Watersedge Rd., Mississauga, Ont.; Office: 145 King St. W., Toronto, Ont. M5H 1V8.

**LOWENSTEIN, Aubrey,** B.Sc., M.B.A.; business executive; b. Bulawayo, Zimbabwe 12 July 1946; s. Oscar and Lucia L.; e. Milton Sch. Zimbabwe 1958–64; London Sch. of Economics B.Sc. (Hons.) 1968; Univ. of Cape Town S. Africa M.B.A. 1969; m. Betty Ann d. Henry and Christine Greenfield 1968; children: Anthony Stewart, Robert John; PRESIDENT, GOLDLEASE LIMITED 1993– ; Administrative Manager, Edgar Stores 1970–71; Economist, Canadian National 1971–73; Vice-Pres., Unilease Inc. 1973–86; President, Shoppers Leasing 1986–93; Home: 2 Bannatyne Dr., North York, Ont. M2L 2N7; Office: 1131A Leslie St., Suite 210, North York, Ont. M3C 3L8.

**LOWENTHAL, Myra,** A.O.C.A., O.S.A.; artist; b. Belgrade, Yugoslavia 13 Jul. 1947; d. Leslie and Anne (Bem) L.; e. Central Tech. Sch., Toronto 1965; Ont. Coll. of Art, Toronto A.O.C.A. 1968; PAINTER, ILLUSTRATOR; worked in publishing and advtg. bus. while continuing portrait painting; freelance book and magazine illustration; painting and illustration, Toronto Star Advtg. Dept. 1970–73; exhbns.: Anamon Art Gall. Toronto 1976; McDowell Gall. Toronto 1981, 1982, 1983; Bonnie Kagan Gall. Toronto 1985–90; Edwards Gardens Toronto 1992; C'est What? Toronto 1993; group shows: Montreal Expo 67, 1967; display contrib. Aviva Art Show & Auction Toronto 1977, 1981, 1982, 1983, 1984; Pringle & Booth Art Show 1978–79; Gall. Moos Toronto 1979; McDowell Gall. Tor. 1980; Soc. of Illustrators N.Y., Japan 1981; C.A.P.I.C. Annual Exhbn. Tor. 1981; Women of The Ont. Soc. of Artists Toronto 1984; U.S. Consulate Exhibit 'Three' Toronto 1984; collections (Toronto): Noma Industries Canada, Toronto Star, Maclean Hunter, Eastern Construction Co. Ltd.; Paisley Products; Kennedy & Assoc.; (Que.) Michel Biguet Gall.; (Vancouver) C.P. Air; C.N. Hotels; Olympia & York; (Los Angeles, Calif.) Twentieth Century Fox; O.C.A. Scholarship 1965; Certificate of Merit, Soc. of Illustrators 1981; Address: 33 Rosehill Ave., #2502, Toronto, Ont. M4T 1G4.

**LOWERY, Richard,** O.C.; naval architect; b. Newcastle-on-Tyne, Eng., 26 Jan. 1910; s. James Beck and Mary (Ahern) L.; e. Heaton Tech. Sch., Rutherford Tech. Coll. and Armstrong Coll., Durham Univ.; Newcastle-on-Tyne; m. Dorothy, d. Thomas Heron, Eng., 22 Dec. 1937; children: Jane Margaret, Peter Richard; apprenticed to R. & W. Hawthorn Leslie & Co., Hepburn-on-Tyne, 1927–31; apptd. Asst. Naval Arch., 1931–36; Lectr. in Naval Arch. and Higher Math., Rutherford Tech. Coll., 1935–36; Asst. Naval Arch., Alfred Holt & Co., Liverpool, Eng., 1936–38; Naval Arch. and Asst. Gen. Mgr., Singapore Harbour Bd. Dockyards, 1938–42; Naval Arch. and Mgr., Melbourne Harbor Trust Shipyards and Advisor, Australian Commonwealth Salvage Bd., 1942–46; Naval Arch., Canadian Vickers Ltd., Montreal, becoming Vice-Pres., 1946–51; joined Canada Steamship Lines, 1951; as Vice Pres. & Pres. of Davie Ship-building Ltd., Kingston Shipyard, Candn. Shipbuilding Ltd., and Port Arthur Shipbuilding Ltd.; retired Jan. 1972; rec'd. Vice-Admiral 'Jerry' Land Gold Medal for 'Outstanding Achievement in the Marine Field,' Soc. Naval Archs. & Marine Engrs., 1964; Past Chrmn., Lloyd's Register of Shipping Candn. Comte.; Hon. Vice Pres. and Fellow, Soc. Naval Archs. and Marine Engrs. (1st Chrmn., E. Candn. Sec.); Past Pres., Canadian Shipbuilding and Ship Repairing Assn.; Fellow, Royal Inst. Naval Archs.; Officer, Order of Canada 1985; 125th Anniversary of the Confederation of Canada Medal, 1992; Anglican; recreations: golf, painting, reading; Homes: Apt 902 Ashby House, 114 Keith Rd. W., North Vancouver, B.C. V7M 3C9.

**LOWINGER, Katrina Esther,** B.A., M.Sc.; executive editor; b. Budapest, Hungary 14 March 1950; d. Ernest and the late Martha (Kalman) L.; e. Westdale Secondary Sch. and Hamilton (Ont.) Coll. Inst. 1967; Univ. of Toronto, B.A. 1971; Univ. of Cambridge, M.Sc. 1973; EXECUTIVE EDITOR, LESTER PUBLISHING LTD. 1991– ; Regional Cons. Ont. Assn. Mentally Retarded 1974–83; Supr. Community Services Easter Seal Soc. 1983–84; Extve. Dir. The Candn. Children's Book Centre 1984–89; Dir., Children's Division, Lester & Orpen Dennys 1989–91; Bd. Mem., New Israel Fund; Past Chair, Candn. Give the Gift of Literacy; Home: 61 Alexandra Wood, Toronto, Ont. M5N 2S6; Office: 56 The Esplanade, Ste. 507A, Toronto, Ont. M5E 1A7.

**LOWMAN, John,** B.A., M.A., Ph.D.; university professor; b. Dorking, Eng. 14 July 1950; s. Anthony and Edna (Watterson) L.; e. Sheffield Univ., B.A. 1971; York Univ., M.A. 1977; Univ. of B.C., Ph.D. (Geog.) 1983; m. Laura d. Ian and Kathy Fraser 1983; PROF., SCH. OF CRIMINOLOGY, SIMON FRASER UNIV. 1991– ; joined Simon Fraser Univ. 1982; consults and does rsch. in areas of soc. control systems, law, and prostitution; rec'd S.S.H.R.C. and Killam Doctoral Scholarships; co-ed. 'Regulating Sex: An Anthology of Commentaries on the Findings and Recommendations of the Badgley and Fraser Committees' 1986; 'Transcarceration: Essays in the Sociology of Social Control' 1987; 'Gambling in Canada: Golden Goose or Trojan Horse?' 1989; 'Realist Criminology: Crime Control and Policing in the 1990s' 1992; author 'Street Prostitution, Assessing the Impact of the Law: Vancouver' 1989; Home: 4116 Trinity St., Burnaby, B.C. V5C 1P1.

**LOWNSBROUGH, John Waldie,** B.A., M.A.; writer; b. Toronto, Ont. 15 Oct. 1946; s. Thomas Pattullo and Margaret Norval (Waldie) L.; e. Upper Can. Coll. 1965; Trinity Coll., Univ. of Toronto, B.A. (Hons.) 1969; London Sch. of Econ., M.A. 1970; freelance journalist 1977– ; work has appeared in Saturday Night, Toronto Life, Chatelaine, Macleans, Quest, Globe & Mail, Canadian Business, Report on Business Magazine, etc.; Contrib. Ed., Toronto Life; Columnist, 'City & Country Home' 1984–89; 'The Medical Post' 1977– ; Editor, New Press 1970–71; Hist. Rsch. Cons., Art Gallery of Ont. 1972–75; Copy Ed., Maclean Hunter Bus. Pubns. 1975–77; Nat. Mag. Award (Gold) 1988, (Hon. Mention) 1990; Finalist, City of Toronto Book Awards 1981; Mem., Bd. of Trustees, Art Gallery of Ont. (Extve. Ctte.) 1988–91; Assoc. Bd. of Trustees 1987–88; Oncology Endowment Sustaining Fund Ctte., Toronto Hosp. 1986–88; Bd. Mem., Candn. Rep. Theatre 1983–87; Mem., Bd. Candn. Soc. of Decorative Arts 1989–91; Mem. Bd. of Dirs., Arts Found. of Greater Toronto 1991–94 (Extve. Ctte. 1993–94); Gov., The Candn. Art Found.; Anglican; Kappa Alpha Soc. (Univ. of Toronto); author: 'The Privileged Few: The Grange and its People in Nineteenth Century Toronto' 1980; recreations: swimming, reading, movies; Club: Toronto Lawn Tennis; Home: 53 Woodlawn Ave W., Toronto, Ont. M4V 1G6; Office: Suite 504, 9 St. Nicholas St., Toronto, Ont. M4Y 1W5.

**LOWRY, Catherine Edna,** B.Sc., M.Ag., P.Ag.; agrologist; b. Carleton Place, Ont. 30 May 1955; d. Donald John and May Murray (Simpson) L.; e. Carleton Place H.S. 1974; Univ. of Guelph B.Sc.(Agr.) 1978, M.Ag. 1988; EXECUTIVE DIR., ONT. AGRICULTURAL TRAINING INST. 1991– ; Credit Advisor, Farm Credit Corp. 1978–86; Teaching & Rsch. Asst., Univ. of Guelph 1987–89; Mng. Dir., Ont. Agric. Training Inst. 1989–91; Pres., Ont. Inst. of Agrologists; Dir., Ont. Agric. College Alumni Found.; Mem., church cttes.; Ont. Agric. Leadership Alumni; Ont. Soc. for Training & Devel.; Home: 980 Avenue Rd., Toronto, Ont. M5P 2K8; Office: 405 – 491 Eglinton Ave. W., Toronto, Ont. M5P 1A8.

**LOWRY, Glenn David,** B.A., M.A., Ph.D.; art museum director; b. New York, N.Y. 28 Sept. 1954; s. Warren and Laure L.; e. Williams College B.A. 1976; Harvard Univ. M.A. 1978, Ph.D. 1982; m. Susan Chambers 1974; children: Nicholas, Alexis, William; DIRECTOR, THE ART GALLERY OF ONTARIO 1990– ; Curator, The Arthur M. Sackler Gallery & the Freer Gallery of Art, Smithsonian Inst. 1984–90; author: 'Timur and the Princely Vision: Persian Art and Culture in the Fifteenth Century' 1989, 'A Jeweler's Eye: Art of the Book from the Vever Collection' 1988, 'From Concept to Context: Approaches to Asian and Islamic Calligraphy' 1986, 'Fatehphur-Sikri: A Source Book' 1985, 'Fatehpur-Sikri: and the Age of Akbar' 1985; Office: 317 Dundas St. W., Toronto, Ont. M5T 1G4.

**LOWRY, The Honourable Mr. Justice Peter Donovan,** B.A., LL.B.; judge; b. Toronto, Ont. 25 April 1944; s. Donovan Johnson and Hope Evangeline (Smith) L.; e. Waterloo Lutheran Univ. B.A. 1967; Osgoode Hall Law School LL.B. 1970; m. Linda d. Olaf and Edith Alm 22 May 1971; children: Stephen, David; JUDGE, SUPREME COURT OF B.C. 1991– ; called to Bar of B.C. 1971; practiced, first in assoc., then in partnership with McRae Montgomery Spring & Cunningham 1971–79; Extve. Ctte. 1976–78; Partner, Campney & Murphy 1980–92; Extve. Ctte. 1985–89; Managing Partner 1987–89; practised primarily maritime litigation; recreations: sailing; clubs: Royal Vancouver Yacht; Office: 800 Hornby St., Vancouver, B.C. V6Z 2C5.

**LOWY, Frederick Hans,** B.A., M.D., C.M., FRCP (c) FACP, FAC Psy.; psychiatrist; educator; b. Grosspetersdorf, Austria, 1 Jan. 1933; s. Eugen and Maria (Braun) L.; e. McGill Univ., B.A. 1955, M.D., C.M. 1959; m. firstly Anne Louise (d. 1973), d. late Alexander G. Cloudsley, 25 June 1965; three s., David A., Eric B., Adam H.; m. 2ndly Mary Kay, d. late Michael O.Neil 1 June 1975; 1 d., Sarah E.; PROF. OF PSYCHIATRY, UNIV. OF TORONTO 1974– ; Dir., Ctr. for Bioethics, Univ. of Toronto 1989– ; Chrmn., Pharmaceutical Inquiry of Ont. 1988–90; prof. training Montreal and Cincinnati 1959–65; Demonst. Dept. Psychiatry McGill Univ. 1965, Lectr. 1966, Asst. Prof. 1968; Assoc. Prof. Univ. of Ottawa 1971, Prof. 1973; Chrmn., Dept. Psychiatry, present univ. 1974–80 and Prof. 1974– , Dean, Fac. of Med. 1980–87; Clin. Asst. in Psychiatry, Royal Victoria Hosp., Allan Mem. Inst., Montreal, 1965; Asst. 1967 and Assoc. Psychiatrist, Royal Victoria Hosp. 1969; Psychiatrist-in-Chief, Ottawa Civic Hosp. 1971; Dir., Psychiatrist-in-Chief, Clarke Inst. of Psychiatry 1974–80; Staff Psychiatrist, Toronto Gen. Hosp. 1988– ; mem. Adv. Bd. Ont. Mental Health Foundation, 1972–78; author and co-author numerous articles in learned and prof. journs.; Ed. Canadian Psychiatric Association Journal, 1973–77 (Assoc. Ed. 1971–72); Ed. Emeritus, Cdn. Journal of Psychiatry; mem. Canadian Med. Assn.; Candn. Psychiatric Assn.; Ont. Psychiatric Assn.; Internat. Psychoanalytic Soc.; Am. Psychiatric Assn.; Alpha Omega Alpha; Physicians for Social Responsibility; Home: 338 Inglewood Dr., Toronto, Ont. M4T 1J6.

**LOXLEY, John,** B.A., Ph.D.; university professor/economist; b. Sheffield, Eng. 12 Nov. 1942; s. John and Elizabeth (Antcliff) L.; e. Univ. of Leeds B.A. (Hons.) 1963, Ph.D. 1966; m. Zeeba Dawood 1967 (div. 1985); children: Salim John, Camille Elizabeth; m. 2ndly, Aurelie Mogan 1989; children: Raina Ilène, Matthew Reuben; PROF., DEPT. OF ECON., UNIV. OF MAN. 1977– ; Lectr., Makerere Univ. 1966–67; Rsch. Mgr., Nat. Bank of Comm., Tanzania 1967–69; Sr. Lectr., Dept. of Econ., Univ. of Dar es Salaam 1969–72, 1st Dir., Inst. of Fin. Mngt. 1972–73; UNDP Prof. of Econ. & Planning & Dept. Head 1973–74; Sec., Res. & Econ. Devel. Sub-Ctte. of Cabinet, Prov. of Man. 1975–77; Head, Dept. of Econ., Univ. of Man. 1984– ; Vis. Fellow, N.S. Inst., Ottawa 1982–83; past extve. positions in Tanzania & Can.; Advr./Cons. to Govts. of Tanzania 1981, 1981–84, 1989–90; Mozambique 1978, 1988; Uganda 1986–87; Central Bank of Madagascar 1985; Nevis 1991; St. Kitts 1992; ANC/COSATU (South Africa) 1991– ; Partner, HKL & Assoc. Ltd.; Mem., Bd. of Dir. (& Extve.), Soc. for Manitobans with Disabilities 1983–89; Chairperson, 'Choices' - a coalition for social justice 1990–93; Candn. Rehab. Counc. for the Disabled; Mem., Candn. Assn. for Study of Internat. Devel. (Past Pres.); Candn. Assn. of Afr. Studies; Pol. Econ. Network; Soc. for Soc. Studies; Mem., Candn. Commonwealth Scholarships and Fellowships Ctte. 1991– ; Mem., Ed. Bd. 'Canadian Dimension' 1976–81; 'Studies in Political Economy' 1979–92; 'Review of African Political Economy' 1985– ; Adv. Bd. and Editorial Bd., 'Canadian Journal of Development Studies'; author: 'The IMF and the Poorest Countries' 1984, 'Debt and Disorder' 1986, num. articles; co-editor: 'Towards Socialist Planning' 1971, 'Structural Adjustment in Africa' 1989; recreations: soccer, squash; Office: Winnipeg, Man. R3T 2N2.

**LOYER, Marie des Anges,** R.N., B.Sc.P.H.N., M.A., M.P.H., M.Ed., Ph.D., C.St.J., F.A.P.H.A.; university professor; b. Ottawa, Ont. 10 Oct. 1933; d. Paul Royal and Marie des Anges (Gour) L.; e. Univ. of Ottawa R.N. 1955, B.Sc.P.H.N. 1960; Columbia Univ. M.A. 1964, M.P.H. 1965; Univ. of Ottawa M.Ed. 1968; Univ. of W. Ont. dipl. Sr. Univ. Administrator 1976; Univ. of Ottawa Ph.D. 1982; m. Dr. Thomas s. Laura and Germano (Ribeiro) Da Silva 11 Aug. 1986; PROFESSOR, SCHOOL OF NURSING, FACULTY OF HEALTH SCIENCES, UNIV. OF OTTAWA 1965– ; Staff Nurse/Senior Nurse, Emergency Dept., Ottawa Gen. Hosp. 1955–57; Public Health Nurse, Prescott-Russell Health Unit & Ottawa-Carleton Health Unit 1958–63; Coord. of Continuing Edn., Univ. of Ottawa 1972–74; Dean, Sch. of Nursing 1974–78; Assoc. Dean, Fac. of Health Sci. & Dir., Sch. of Nursing 1978–80; Chairperson, Ctte. on the Status of Women, Member of the Senate, Mem. Ctte. on Bilingualism & Biculturalism, Mem. Bd. of Gov., Univ. of Ottawa 1992–95; Chair, Board of Dir., Can. Public Health Assn. 1980–82; Chair, Board of Dir., Royal Ottawa Hosp. 1982–85; several other past executive academic & assn. appointments; Mem., St. John Ambulance Canada 1974– (Chair, Nursing Adv. Ctte. 1990–92; Chief Nursing Offr., Canada 1985–89); Mem., NHRDP review committees; Candn. Forces Medical Council 1992–95; Fellow, Am. Public Health Assn. 1965; Officer, Venerable Order of St. John Canada 1978; Commander 1988; Hon. Life Mem., Candn. Public Health Assn. 1988; Kappa Delta Phi; Sigma Theta Tau; Roman Catholic; Mem., Liberal Party; Candn. Nurses Assn.; Candn. Assn. for the History of Nursing; Candn. Nursing Rsch. Group; Candn. Public Health Assn.; Am. Public Health Assn.; National League for Nursing; author: 'Leadership and the Effectiveness of Community Health Nursing Services' 1982 and over 40 articles and addresses in profl. journals & books on nursing; co-author: 'A Study of Nursing Satisfaction in the Ottawa General Hospital' 1985, 'Submission to the Task Force on Health Care Resources of the Canadian Medical Association' 1984, 'Survey of Library Resources in Canadian Schools of Nursing' 1971, 'Rector's Committee Report on the Status of Women Academics' 1976; recreations: gourmet cooking, mountain climbing; Home: The St. George, 1403 – 160 George St., Ottawa, Ont. K1N 9M2; Office: 451 Smyth Rd., Ottawa, Ont. K1H 8M5.

**LOZOWSKI, Edward Peter,** B.Sc., M.Sc., Ph.D., F.R.Met.S.; educator; meteorologist; b. Nottingham, Eng. 13 Apl. 1945; s. Stanislaw and Barbara Alice (Kirk) L.; e. Northview Hts. Coll. Inst. Toronto 1961; Univ. of Toronto B.Sc. 1965, M.Sc. 1967, Ph.D. 1970; m. Elizabeth d. George and Mary Tilden 20 July 1968; children: Sarah, Kenneth, Alexander, Augusta; PROF. OF GEOG. UNIV. OF ALTA. 1981– ; Sr. Visitor Cambridge Univ. 1970; Asst. Prof. present Univ. 1971, Assoc. Prof. 1976, Prof. 1981– ; Dir., Institute of Geophysics Meteorology and Space Physics 1993– ; author over 100 sci. papers & reports weather and climate; Cert. Consulting Meteorol. and Fellow Am. Meteorol. Soc.; mem. Candn. Meteorol. & Oceanographic Soc. (Pres. 1981–82); recreations: musician, gardener; Home: 3415 – 113 Street, Edmonton, Alta. T6J 3L7; Office: Edmonton, Alta. T6G 2H4.

**LUBA, Robert Walter,** F.C.A., M.B.A.; merchant banker; b. Edmonton, Alta. 6 Feb. 1942; s. Steve and Vera (Nakonechney) L.; e. C.A. Alta. 1964 (Gold Medallist); Univ. of W. Ont. M.B.A. 1967; F.C.A. 1988; m. Lorraine Ruth d. George and Matilda Heatherington 25 Aug. 1962; children: Robert Allen, Marcia Lorraine, Catherine Louise; PRESIDENT, LUBA FINANCIAL INC.; Dir., Franco-Nevada Mining Corp. Ltd.; T.G. Bright & Co. Ltd.; Pureplast Inc.; P.R.I.D.E. Canada; Dora Mavor Moore Awards; Financial Analyst, John Labatt Ltd. 1967; Comptroller Food Service Div. Ogilvie Flour Mills Co. Ltd. 1968, Controller and Treas., Ogilvie Flour Mills Co. 1970; Controller, John Labatt Ltd. 1971, Vice Pres. Finance 1972, Sr. Vice Pres. Development 1976, Sr. Vice Pres. Packaged Food Group 1978; Extve. Vice Pres. Corp. Finance and Invests., Crown Life Insurance Co. 1984–87; Pres., Crown Financial Services Inc. 1984–87; Pres. and C.O.O., Crown Life Insurance Co. 1987–88; Partner, Capital Canada Ltd. 1988–91; Pres. & C.E.O., Royal Bank Investment Mgmnt. Inc. 1991–93; Past Pres., Heart & Stroke Found. Ont.; mem. Chief Executives Orgn.; Financial Execs. Inst.; Inst. C.A. Ont.; Past Pres., Orchestra London; Clubs: Granite; Albany Club; London Hunt & Country; Home: 37 Sunnydene Cres., Toronto, Ont. M4N 3J5.

**LUCAS, Alec,** M.A., Ph.D.; university professor; b. Toronto, Ont. 20 June 1913; s. Bertie George and Emma (Crick) L.; e. Peterborough (Ont.) Normal Sch., 1935–36; Queen's Univ., B.A. (Hons. Eng. and Hist.) 1943, M.A. 1945; Harvard Univ., A.M. 1947, Ph.D. 1951; married; children: George Frederick, Suzanne Arbon, Roy Martin Ells; EMERITUS PROF., DEPT. OF ENGLISH, McGILL UNIV. 1981– ; Teaching Fellow, Harvard Univ. 1947–50; Assoc. Prof., Univ. of N.B. 1950–57; Asst. Prof. of Eng., McGill Univ. 1957–58; Assoc. Prof. 1958–64; Prof. 1964–81; Emeritus Prof., 1981– ; Publications: Assoc. Ed., 'Atlantic Anthology' 1961; 'Thoughts from the Learned Societies' 1961; Ed., 'Humanities Bulletin' 1958–62; Ed., 'The Last Barrier and Other Stories by Charles G.D. Roberts' 1958; Ed., 'The James Halliday Letters' 1966; Ed., 'The Best of Peter McArthur' 1967; 'Hugh MacLennan' 1970; Ed., 'Great Canadian Short Stories' 1971; 'Peter McArthur' 1975; 'Farley Mowat' 1976; 'The Otonabee School' 1977; many articles in popular and learned journs. and in books; mem., Assn. Candn. Univ. Teachers of English; Thomas Wolfe Soc.; Home: 853 Sherbrooke St. W., Montreal, Que. H3A 2T6.

**LUCAS, Douglas M.,** M.Sc., forensic scientist; b. Windsor, Ont. 5 May 1929; e. Victoria Pub. Sch., 1942 and Kennedy Coll. Inst., 1948, Windsor, Ont.; Univ. of Toronto, B.Sc. 1953, M.Sc. 1957; m. Marie Michener, d. Marion M. Macdonald, Toronto, Ont.; children: Eric, Brian, Kristen, Kelley, Paul; DIR., CENTRE OF FORENSIC SCIENCES, PROV. OF ONT., since 1967; Chemist, Atty.-Gen.'s Lab., Ont. 1957; Sec. Head, 1960; author of no. of publs. in field of forensic science; rec'd Centennial Medal; Silver Jubilee Medal; Past Pres., Internat. Assn. Forensic Sciences; Past Pres., Candn. Soc. Forensic Sciences; Past Pres., Am. Acad. Forensic Sciences; Past Pres., Am. Soc. Crime Lab. Dirs.; Past Chrmn., Comte. on Alcohol & Drugs, Nat. Safety Council, U.S.A.; Psi Upsilon; Protestant; recreations: sailing, golf, curling; Home: 55 Charles St. W., Toronto, Ont. M5W 2S9; Office: 25 Grosvenor St., Toronto, Ont. M7A 2G8.

**LUCAS, John Martin,** P.Eng., B.Sc., M.Sc., D.Phil.; scientist; b. Surbiton, England 19 Sept. 1942; s. Robert and Ida (Klamka) L.; e. St. Paul's School 1955–60; Bristol Univ. B.Sc. (Hons.) 1961–64; Sussex Univ. M.Sc. 1964–65, D.Phil. 1965–69; m. Helene d. Bluma and Anszel Klodawsky 4 May 1986; children: Simone, Yasmine; SENIOR SCIENTIST, CENTRE DE TECHNOLOGIE NORANDA; achievements incl. the invention of the 'Tuyere Pyrometer,' a fiber-optic instrument used worldwide for temperature measurement in copper converters & other metallurgical processes, the basis of Centre de Technologie Noranda's 1993 winning entry for the Quebec Chamber of Commerce Mercure R & D Award; an 'on-line smoothness sensor' used by the paper industry; the 'Eccentricity and Diameter Monitor' for medium & high voltage cable prodn. earned its sponsor, Canada Wire and Cable (now Alcatel Canada Wire), a Canada Award for Business Excellence 1991; present interests incl. geophysical instrumentation & sensors for the lumber indus.; Charles Babbage Award for the year's outstanding contbn. on electronic computers to the IERE Journal (U.K.); P.Eng., Que.; Mem., IEEE; Optical Soc. of Am.; holder of ten patents; author of num. rsch. pubs.; Home: 5385 Durocher, Outremont, Qué. H2V 3X9; Office: 240 Blvd. Hymus, Pointe Claire, Qué. H9R 1G5.

**LUCAS, Kenneth C.,** B.A.Sc.; executive; b. Vancouver, B.C. 8 June 1929; s. Kenneth Staples and Sydney Margarite (Maynard) L.; e. Kamloops (B.C.) High Sch. 1946; Univ. of B.C., B.A.Sc. (Civil) 1952; m. Anne-Marie d. Eugène and Thérèse Laurin 10 Nov. 1966; children: Janet Maureen, David James; PRES. AND DIR. AGRODEV CANADA INC. 1982– ; Pres. and Dir., SRD Sustainable Resource Development Inc., Ottawa 1985– ; Pres., Prince Edward International, Charlottetown 1991– ; Pres. & Dir., Envirocon Ltd. Vancouver 1982–88; Dir. Internat. Agri-Energy Roundtable; Visiting Prof., World Maritime Univ., Malmö, Sweden 1985– ; Fisheries & Environmental Protection Eng. Candn. Dept. Fisheries, B.C. 1952–62, Asst. Dir. Pacific Region 1963–65, Dir. of Resource Devel. Ottawa 1966–68, Dir. Gen. Environmental Quality Directorate 1969–70; Asst. Dep. Min. Environment Can. 1971, estbd. new Candn. Environment Protection Service 1971–72, Sr. Asst. Dep. Min. of new Fisheries & Marine Service 1973; Asst. Dir. Gen. Food & Agric. Orgn. (Fisheries Dept.) Rome 1978–82; former Gov. Internat. Center Ocean Devel. 1984–85; contbr. Ocean Yearbook 3, 1982; Keynote address Proceedings Nat. Aquaculture Conf. 1983; mem. Assn. Prof. Engs. B.C. (Council 1966); Assn. Prof. Engs. Prov. Ont.; Aquaculture Assn. Can.; Anglican; recreations: photography, outdoor recreation; Home: Unit 1A, 146 Waverley St., Ottawa, Ont. K2P 0V4; Office: 600, 222 Somerset St. W., Ottawa, Ont. K2P 2G3.

**LUCCISANO, Domenic J.,** B.Sc., M.B.A., A.I.B.; insurance executive; b. Montreal, Que. 30 March 1949; e. McGill Univ. B.Sc. 1971, M.B.A. 1979; m. Pierrette Boyer; one d.; EXECUTIVE VICE-PRES., ADMINISTRATION, DALE-PARIZEAU INC. 1993– ; Dir., Sogepar inc. 1981–84; Vice-Pres., Dale-Parizeau inc. 1984–87; Sr. Vice-Pres. 1987–92; Mem., Assn. for Systems Management; Am. Inst. of Industrial Engineers; Assn. of Insur. Brokers of the Prov. of Que.; Office: 1140 de Maisonneuve Blvd. W., Montreal, Que. H3A 3H1.

**LUCENTI, Gary Samuel,** B.Sc.; steel executive; b. North Bay, Ont. 16 Nov. 1939; s. James Leo and Dorothy May (Dugas) L.; e. Queen's Univ., B.Sc. 1962; m. Ruth d. Hilda and Russell Spencer 12 Sept. 1964; one d.: Stephanie; Pres., The Algoma Steel Corp., Limited 1991; Dir., Sault Marine Serv. Ltd.; Algoma Tube Corp. (& Vice-Pres.); Huron Steel; The Algoma Steel Corp., Ltd.; Jr. Engr., Iron Making Dept., Algoma Steel 1962; Asst. Supt. of Continous Casing 1969; Supt. of Steelmaking 1972; Asst. Div. Supt. of Primary Production 1974; Gen. Mgr. of Engineering 1980; Vice-Pres. of Opns. 1983; Vice-Pres., Mfg. 1987; Extve. Vice-Pres. & C.O.O., 1989–91; Bd. of Dir., Algoma Univ. Found.; P.Eng. (Ont.), AISI, AIME, AISE; Home: 140 Caddy Ave., Sault Ste. Marie, Ont. P6A 6H9.

**LUCIANI, Tony;** artist; b. Toronto, Ont. 1956; e. Central Tech. Sch. 1970–74; Sheridan Comm. Coll. 1974–75; Ont. Coll. of Art 1975–78 (incl. 1 yr post-grad study, Florence, Italy); solo exhibitions: Nancy Poole's Studio 1980, '84, 89; Rodman Hall Arts Ctr., Nat. Exhib. Ctr., St. Catharines 1984, 1990; Kitchener/Waterloo Art Gall. 1991; The Roberts Gallery, Toronto 1992; Homer Watson House and Gallery, Kitchener 1993; group exhibitions: 'Artitudes' 7th Internat. Art Comp., Art 54 Gall. N.Y. 1989; XVIIIthe Internat. Exhib. of Contemp. Art of Monte Carlo 1984; 'A Canadian Start in Art,' Canada House Gall., London, Eng. 1979 (internat.); Nancy Poole's Studio 1978, 80, 82, 83, 85–89; 'Personal Vision in Landscape,' The Gallery Cambridge 1987; 'Aspects of Contemporary Realism,' The McIntosh Art Gall. U.W.O. 1987; Art Gall. of St. Thomas-Elgin 1983; Gallery 1667 Halifax 1983; 'Toronto ... New Perspectives – Old Reflections,' City of Toronto Archives Market Gallery 1981; Univ. of Waterloo 1979; McLaughlin Lib. Univ. of Guelph 1978; The Cooley Gall., Conn. 1990; The Roberts Gallery, Toronto 1991, '92, '93, '94; 'Insights', Wellington County Museum Juried Exhib., 1st prize 1991, 2nd prize 1992; collections: Elizabeth Greenshields Found. Montreal, Rodman Hall Arts Ctr. St. Catharines, Corp. of the City of Toronto, Art Gall. of St. Thomas-Elgin, Canada House London (England), McColl Frontenace Inc. (formerly Texaco), Best Corp. Toronto; Office: c/o The Roberts Gallery, 641 Yonge St., Toronto, Ont. M4Y 1Z9.

**LUCIER, Gregory E.,** B.A., M.Sc., Ph.D.; university professor, medical biocommunication consultant; b. Chatham, Ont. 18 Oct. 1943; s. Gregory Burton and Cleo Bonita (Judson) L.; e. Univ. of Ottawa B.A. 1967, M.Sc. 1970; Univ. of Western Ont. Ph.D. 1974; m. Rita d. Assunta and Donato Egizii 28 Dec. 1983; children (from prev. m.): Laura Marie, Julia Ann; PROF., FAC. OF MED., UNIV. OF CALGARY, PHYSIOLOGY 1989– ; Demonstrator, Physiol., Univ. of Ottawa 1967–69; Tutor/Demonstrator, Univ. of West. Ont. 1969–73; Lectr., Centralia Coll. of Agric. Tech. 1973–74; Rsch. Asst., Dentistry, Univ. of Toronto 1975–76; Asst. Prof. 1976–80; Fac. of Med., Physiol., Univ. of Calgary, 1980–82; Assoc. Prof. 1982–89; tenure granted 1986; Dir., Med. Instruction Resources 1987–91; Adjunct Prof., Dept. of Med. Edn. 1990– ; Co-founder & Pres., Quick-draw Animation Soc.; Co-founder & Dir. of Devel., Triple I Productions 'Ideas for Images' Limited 1986– ; Pres., IMAGE Consulting 1989– ; Dir., Chromacolour North America 1993– ; $832,000 rsch. grants awarded incl. NIH, MRC, AHFMR & others; internat. lecturer; has served on var. cttes.; 1 yr. sabbatical at Nat. Film Bd.; has worked with R.O.M. & Royal Tyrrell Mus. of Paleontolgy; Mem., Candn. Physiol. Soc.; Soc. for Neurosci.; Candn. Assn. for Neurosci.; Candn. Pain Soc.; Univ. Film & Video Assn.; ASIFA Can.; Quick-draw Animation Soc.; Health Sci. Commun. Assn.; Am. Med. Writers' Assn.; co-author: 33 rsch. papers in ref. sci. jours., 4 book chaps. & 70 pub. sci. abstracts; author: 'Effective Visual Biocommunication' forthcoming; filmography: 14 video-films; recreations: animated film, special effects, sculpting, model-bldg., computer graphics, paleontol., early music appreciation, bonsai gardening, tai-chi and kendo; Home: 359 Scenic Acres Dr. N.W., Calgary, Alta. T3L 1T6; Office: 3330 Hospital Dr. N.W., Calgary, Alta. T2N 4N1.

**LUCIER, Hon. Paul;** senator; b. La Salle, Ont. 29 July 1930; s. Adolph and Claire (Laframboise) L.; e. Sacred Heart Sch. La Salle, Ont.; m. Grace Demchuk; children: Edward, Frances, Tom; summoned to the Senate 1975; Ald. City of Whitehorse 1964–65, 1970–74; Mayor 1974–75; Dir. Candn. Fedn. Mayors & Muns. 1973–74; Pres. Assn. Yukon Muns. and mem. Nat. Adv. Counc. on Fitness & Amateur Sports 1974–75; Hon. mem. Whitehorse C. of C.; Office: 163–S Centre Block, The Senate, Ottawa, Ont. K1A 0A4.

**LUCIUK, Lubomyr Yaroslav,** Ph.D.; university professor; b. Kingston, Ont. 9 July 1953; s. Danylo and Maria (Makalo) L.; e. Regiopolis Coll. 1971; Queen's Univ., B.Sc. (Hons.) 1976, M.A. 1979; The Univ. of Alta., Ph.D. 1984; one d. Kassandra Larysa; ASSOC. PROF., DEPT. OF POLITICS & ECONOMICS, ROYAL MILITARY COLL. OF CANADA; Editor, The Kashtan Press; Field Rsch. Asst., Royal Ont. Mus. 1967–71; Cataraqui Reg. Conserv. Authority 1971; Ont. Min. of Natural Resources 1973–77; Researcher & writer, Multicultural Hist. Soc. of Ont. 1978–90; Postdoct. fellow, Dept. of Geog., Univ. of Toronto 1984–88; Cons., major survey on multiculturalism, Queen's Univ. 1989; postdoctoral fellowships: SSHRCC, Edward Schreyer, Neporany (Candn. Inst. of Ukr. Studies); SSHRCC Canada Rsch. Fellowship; first recipient, The John Sopinka Award For Excellence in Ukrainian Studies (Chair, Ukr. Studies Found. at Univ. of Toronto) 1990; Fellow, Chair of Ukr. Studies and Ethnic & Immigration Studies Prog., Univ. of Toronto; Centre for Refugee Studies, York Univ.; Faculty Assoc., Centre for Internat. Relations, Queen's Univ.; Mem., Candn. Inst. of Internat. Affairs; Candn. & Am. Assn. of Geogs.; Candn. Ctte. for the Hist. of the Second World War; Chrmn., Rsch. Ctte., Ukrainian Candn. Civil Liberties Assn.; Chrmn., Refugee Atlas Project 1992–95; Mem., Candn. Ethnic Studies Assoc.; Candn. Assoc. of Slavists; Candn. Friends of Rukh; co-author: 'Creating a Landscape' 1989, 'A Time for Atonement' 1988; co-editor: 'The Foreign Office and the Famine' 1988, 'On Guard for Thee' 1988, 'Anglo-American Perspectives on the Ukrainian Question, 1938–1951' 1987, 'A Delicate and Difficult Question' 1986, 'Canada's Ukrainians: Negotiating An Identity' 1991; co-compiler: 'Memorial' 1989; articles & op-ed pieces pubd. in various newspapers; recreations: jogging, reading, travel, photography; Home: 22 Gretna Green, Kingston, Ont.; Office: Kingston, Ont. K7K 5L0.

**LUCKERT, Hans Joachim,** Dr. Phil.; scientist; b. Germany 26 Aug. 1905; s. Dr. Albert and Elisabeth (Wuenn) L.; e. Harvard Univ., A.M. 1929; Univ. of Berlin, Dr. Phil 1933; m. Ilse, d. late Robert Schwabedissen, Germany, 30 May 1953; one d. Doris Elizabeth: Tutor, Tech. Univ. of Berlin, 1925–27; Asst. to Prof. of Math., Bergakademie of Freiberg, Germany, and Research Scientist, Consultant to Finance Min. of Saxony, 1929–34; Aerodynamics Research, Henschel Aircraft Co., Germany, 1935–37; Sr. Group Leader, Aerodynamics Dept., Arado Aircraft Co., Germany, 1937–45; Scientist, Br. Min. of Supply, Brunswick-Voelkenrode, 1945–47; Consultant, Control Comn. for Germany, 1947–51; joined Canadair Ltd., Montreal, 1952; Sec. Chief, Tech. Sec., 1957–63; Missiles and Space Research Sec., 1963–64; Staff Scientist, Research and Devel. 1964–65; Chief, Aerodynamics and Analysis Sec., Space Research Inst., McGill Univ., 1965; transf. to Space Research Inst. Inc. 1968; Space Research Corp., 1969–80; Consultant, Potton Technical Industries Inc., Phoenix Engineering Inc., Space Research Corp., 1980–89; Fellow, Candn. Aero. and Space Inst. (Nat. Vice Chrmn., Astronautics Sec. 1959–60; Nat. Chrmn. 1962–63; Chrmn., Montreal Group of Sec. 1959–64; Chrmn., Montreal Br. 1965–66); Assoc. Fellow, Am. Inst. Aero. & Astronautics; Deutsche Gesellschaft für Luft-und Raumfahrt, Germany; N.R.C. Assoc. Comte. on Aerodynamics (1963–66) and on Space Research (1964–67); Chrmn., N.R.C. Research Co-ord. Group on Upper Atmosphere Research Vehicles, 1964–65; Hon. Research Assoc., McGill Univ., 1967–85; has publ. numerous papers and reports on various math. and aerodynamics subjects; Protestant; Home: 197–58th Ave., Laval des Rapides, Que. H7V 2A5.

**LUCKS, A. Stanley,** B.Sc., D.I.C., Ph.D.; engineering and construction industry executive; b. Blairgowrie, Scotland 10 March 1941; e. Heriot-Watt Univ. B.Sc. 1963; Imperial Coll. of Sci. & Technol. D.I.C. 1964; M.I.T. Ph.D. 1970; m. Marilyn C. Coupar 22 July 1966; children: Gillian, Alistair, Graham; PRESIDENT & CHIEF EXECUTIVE OFFICER, STONE & WEBSTER CANADA LIMITED 1993– ; Civil Engr, R.H. Cuthbertson & Assoc. 1964–66; Rsch. Asst., M.I.T. 1966–70; Geotech. Engr. Cons., T.W. Lambe & Assoc. 1970–72; Sr. Geotech. Engr., Stone & Webster Engr. Corp. (Boston) 1972; Asst. Chief Geotech. Engr. 1976; Chief Geotech. Engr. 1978; Project Engr. 1979; Project Mgr. 1982; Engr. Mgr. Stone & Webster Engr. Corp. (Denver) 1985; Vice-Pres. & Asst. Mgr. 1988; Vice-Pres. & Dir. of Engr. (Boston) 1990–93; Pres., Stone & Webster Civil & Transp. Services 1990–93; Mem., Am. Soc. of Civil Engrs.; Internat. Soc. of Soil Mechanics & Found. Engr.; Home: Toronto, Ont.; Office: 2300 Yonge St., Toronto, Ont. M4P 2W6.

**LUCKYJ, George S.N.,** M.A., Ph.D.; university professor emeritus; b. Janchyn, Ukraine 11 June 1919; s. Ostap and Irene Smal (Stocki) L.; e. Ukraine, 1929–37; Univ. of Berlin, 1937–39; Univ. of Birmingham, 1939–43, B.A., M.A.; Columbia Univ., Ph.D. 1952; m. Moira, d. J. J. McShane, J. P., 18 Feb. 1944; children: Natalie, Anna, Christina; PROFESSOR EMERITUS, DEPT. OF SLAVIC LANGUAGE AND LITERATURE, UNIV. OF TORONTO; Lectr., Univ. of Sask., 1947–49; Chrmn. of the Dept., 1954–61; Prof. of Slavic Studies, Univ. of Toronto, 1959–1985; Assoc. Dir., Candn. Inst. of Ukrainian Studies, Univ. of Toronto 1976–82; served with Brit. Army of the Rhine, 1943–47; Publications: 'Literary Politics in the Soviet Ukraine: 1917–34' 1956; 'Between Gogol and Shevchenko' 1971; ed., 'Shevchenko and the Critics' 1980; 'Panteleimon Kulish' 1983; co-author, 'Modern Ukrainian Grammar' 1949; mem., Candn. Assn. of Slavists; Ukrainian Acad. of Sciences in U.S.; Greek Catholic; recreation: skiing; Home: 5 Kendal Ave., Toronto, Ont. M5R 1L5; Office: 21 Sussex Ave., Toronto, Ont. M5S 1A1.

**LUDLAM, Mary Anne,** C.S.P.W.C., O.S.A., N.F.W.S.(USA), S.G.A.; artist; b. Oshawa, Ont. 19 Apl. 1931; d. Kennedy Campbell and Marion Lois (Germond) Mason; e. Leaside High Sch. 1950; Ont. Coll. of Art 1954 (Gordon C. Lietch Postgrad. Scholarship Interior Design & Arch.); Fontainebleau Sch. of Fine Art France 1955; m. Arthur W. s. Stewart and Gwyneth Ludlam 2 Apl. 1957; two d. Jennifer Anne, Pamela Jane; contract corporate interior designer 1955–77; freelance painter since 1978, exhns. Roberts Gallery Toronto, Horizon Gallery Vancouver and Edmonton, Brockst Gallery Kingston; exhibited over 50 Candn. and USA juried shows including San Diego Watercolour Soc., Adirondacks National Exhib. of Am. Watercolours 1989, 1991, 1992; Mem. & design advisor, Building Ctte., Nielsen Park Creative Centre (Etobicoke) 1991–92; winner 12 maj. awards; teacher and co-ord. workshops Sir Sanford Fleming Coll.; rep. 60 Candn. corporate colls., The Royal Collection of Drawing & Watercolour; Dir. Candn. Soc. Painters in Watercolour (Juror 1992); Retired Active Reg'd Interior Designers Ont.; Juror, Soc. of Candn. Artists 1992; United Church; Club: Arts & Letters; recreations: skiing, swimming, travel; Address: 63 Oldham Rd., Etobicoke, Ont. M9A 2B9.

**LUDMER, Irving;** business executive; b. Montreal, Que. 24 May 1935; s. Joseph and Tillie (Lapidus) L.; e. McGill Univ. B.Eng. 1957; m. Mona Vivian d. Lionel and Anna Azoulay 16 Aug. 1959; children: Brian, Cindy, David; PRES. & C.E.O., STEINBERG INC. 1985– ; various posns. beginning as Maintenance Engr., Steinberg Inc. 1957–71; Pres., Irving Ludmer & Assoc. Inc. 1971; Partner & V.P. Iberville Devel. Ltd. 1971; Owner/Pres., Ludco Enterprises Ltd. 1975; Pres. & C.E.O., Ivanhoe Inc. 1983, Pres. & Chief Op. Offr. Steinberg Inc. 1984; Office: 900, 2 Place Alexis Nihon, 3500 de Maisonneuve ouest, Montreal, Que. H1Z 3C1.

**LUDWICK, Arnold Martin,** C.A., B.A., M.B.A.; executive; b. Winnipeg, Man. 17 July 1937; s. the late Rube and Gertrude (Diamond) L.; e. Univ. of Man. C.A. 1962; B.A. 1963; Harvard Univ. M.B.A. 1965; m. Erna, d. late Earl and Lillian Shapera 16 July 1962; children: Heidi; Sheryl; Louis; PRES. & C.E.O., CLARIDGE INC. 1990– ; DEPY. CHRMN., JOSEPH E. SEAGRAM & SONS LTD. 1982– ; Vice Pres., The Seagram Company Ltd.; Dir., Du Pont Canada Ltd.; CRB Found.; Research Asst. and Doctoral Candidate, Harvard Univ. 1966; C.A., Price Waterhouse & Co., Winnipeg and Montreal 1957–62, 1966–67; Extve. Vice Pres. & Treas., CEMP Investments Ltd. 1967–82; recreations: golf; squash; tennis; skiing; bridge; Clubs: Pinegrove; M.A.A.A.; Montefiore; Office: c/o Claridge Inc., 1170 Peel St., Montréal, Qué. H3B 4P2.

**LUDWIG, Donald Alfred,** Ph.D., F.R.S.C.; university professor; b. New York, N.Y. 14 Nov. 1933; s. Daniel and Helen Emma (Herber) L.; e. New York Univ., B.Mus. 1954, M.S. 1957, Ph.D. (Math.) 1959; 1st m. W. Doris d. Winifred and George Stewart 1953; divorced 1986; 2nd m. Shirley Graystone 1986; children: W. Laurence, Stephen; PROF., DEPT. OF MATH. & ZOOL., UNIV. OF B.C. 1974– ; Instr., Princeton Univ. 1960–61; Asst. Prof., Univ. of Calif. at Berkeley 1961–64; Assoc. Prof. then Prof., New York Univ. 1964–69; Guggenheim Fellow 1969–70; F.R.S.C. 1982; Office: Vancouver, B.C. V6T 1W5.

**LUDWIG, Douglas L.,** H.B.A., C.A.; financial executive; b. Detroit, Michigan 27 Oct. 1953; s. Lloyd R. and Ruth L.; e. Univ. of Western Ont. H.B.A. 1977; Candn. Inst. of C.A.s C.A. 1980; m. Karen Rice 8 Oct. 1983; children: Victoria, Jonathan, Jillian; CHIEF FINANCIAL OFFR. 1993– and SENIOR VICE-PRES., FINANCE & TREASURER, FOUR SEASONS HOTELS LIMITED 1987– ; Senior Manager, Peat Marwick 7 years; Asst. Corp. Controller, Four Seasons Hotels Limited; Vice-Pres., Corp. Controller & Asst. Treasurer 1985; Treas. 1987; Chief Financial Offr. 1993; recreations: golf; clubs: National Golf; Office: 1165 Leslie St., Don Mills, Ont. M3C 2K8.

**LUDWIG, Jack,** Ph.D.; author; b. Winnipeg, Man. 30 Aug. 1922; s. Misha and Fanny (Dolgin) L.; e. St. John's High Sch., Winnipeg, 1940; Univ. of Man., B.A. 1944; Univ. of Cal. Los Angeles, Ph.D. 1953; m. Leya Geraldine, d. Louis Lauer, Edmonton, Alta. 9 March 1946; children: Susan, Brina; Emmy; PROF. OF ENGLISH, STONY BROOK UNIV., N.Y. 1961– ; Instr. and Lectr., Williams Coll., 1949–53; Asst. and Assoc. Prof., Bard Coll., 1953–58; Visiting Lectr., Univ. of Minn., 1958–61; Chrmn., Humanities Group, Harvard Univ. Internat. Seminar, 1963–66; Consultant, Comn. of Coll. Physics, 1965–66 and to mem. of Comn. on Automation, Tech. Econ. Progress; Visiting Prof. Contemp. Lit., Univ. of Cal., Los Angeles 1976; Prof. of English, Stony Brook Univ. 1961– ; Writer-in-Residence, Univ. of Toronto 1968–69; Assoc. of Stratford Shakespearean Festival 1969–70 (acting script for 'The Alchemist'); Jr. Stratford Co. Consultant, National Arts Centre 1970; CBC film on Joyceville minimum security facility 1970; Principal Writer Banff Centre for Performing Arts 1974; author: 'Confusions' (fiction) 1963; 'Above Ground' (fiction) 1968; 'A Woman of Her Age' (fiction) 1973; 'Recent American Novelists' (criticism) 1962; 'Hockey Night in Moscow' (non-fiction) 1972; 'The Great Hockey Thaw' (non-fiction) 1974; 'Games of Fear and Winning' (essays) 1976; 'The Great American Spectaculars' (non-fiction) 1976; 'Five Ring Circus' (non-fiction) 1976; 'Soundings' (new Candn. poetry) 1970; co-ed., 'Stories: British and American' 1953; 'The Noble Savage' 1960–62; 'Homage to Zolotova' (poetry) 1974; film script, 'Hedda Gabler' (CBC TV-Drama) 1978; and other writings incl. numerous short stories, part novels, essays and reviews in various Canadian and foreign publs. and anthologies; received 'Atlantic First' fiction award 1960; Longview Foundation (fiction) Award 1960; Best Am. Short Stories, 1961; O. Henry Prize Stories award, 1961, 1965; Can. Council Sr. Fiction Award, 1967–68, 1975–76; nominee Gov. Gen.'s Award in Lit. 1968; recreations: singing, swimming. Offices: P.O. Box 'A,' Setauket, N.Y. 11733; and in Can., c/o McClelland & Stewart, Toronto, Ont. M4B 3G2.

**LUDWIN, David,** M.B., B.Ch., F.R.C.P.(C), F.A.C.P., F.R.C.P. (London); physician/university professor; b. Johannesburg, S. Africa 11 Nov. 1949; s. Dorik and Genia (Glaser) K-Ludwin; e. King David H.S.; Univ. of the Witwatersrand M.B., B.Ch. 1972; m. Laura d. Fred and Naomi Metter 6 Jan. 1974; children: Adrian, Daniel, Ilana; ASSOC. PROF., DEPT. OF MED., MCMASTER UNIV. 1982– ; Intern, Univ. of Witwatersrand; training in internal. med., Royal Northern Hosp., London, England, Queen's Univ.; training in nephrology, Queen's Univ.; training in transplantation & rsch., Southwestern Univ., Dallas, Tx.; Staff Nephrologist, St. Joseph's Hosp. 1982–92; Office: Div. of Nephrology, Dept. of Med., St. Joseph's Hosp., 50 Charlton Ave. E., Hamilton, Ont. L8N 4A6.

**LUEDEKE, Raymond,** B.Mus., M.Mus., D.Mus.; musician, composer; b. New York, N.Y. 11 Nov. 1944; s. Otto Hans and Madeline Cecilia (Boesch) L.; e. Eastman School of Music B.Mus. 1966; Catholic Univ. of America M.Mus. 1971; Northwestern Univ. D.Mus. 1978; m. Jean d. Hector and Connie Darmanin 1969; children: Christine Angela, Ann Catherine; ASSOCIATE PRINCIPAL CLARINET, THE TORONTO SYMPHONY 1981– ; U.S. Air Force Band (Washington) 1967–71; Asst. Prof., Composition & Clarinet, Univ. of Wisconsin 1971–74; Dir., Univ. New Music Ensemble; Instr., Composition & Theory, Northwestern Univ. 1974–76; Dir., 'The Twittering Machine,' new music ensemble, Chicago Mus. of Contemporary Art 1975–76; Assoc. Prof. of Composition & Clarinet, Univ. of Missouri 1976–81; Dir., Univ. Contemp. Ensemble, Contemp. Chamber Players (profl. group, Kansas City, Mo.); Conductor, Univ. of Missouri Orch. & Kansas City Civic Orch. 1979–80; Fulbright Grant 1966–67; Fericy Award for Comp. (N.W. Univ.) 1976; Missouri Contemp. Music Comp. 1978, '80; Am. Composers Alliance, Recording Award (hon. mention) 1980; Internat. Horn Soc. Comp. Prize 1981; Orch. Fanfare Comp. for the opening of Thomson Hall 1982; Percussive Arts Soc. Composition Prize 1983; recordings: 'The Moon in the Labyrinth,' 'The Transparency of Time,' 'Shadow Music,' 'Brass Quintet'; major compositions: 'The North Wind's Gift,' 'Tales of the Netsilik,' 'Concerto' (Saxophone Quartet and Orchestra); 'String Quartet,' 'The Moon in the Labyrinth,' 'Nocturnal Variations' (chamber); over 60 compositions; recreations: bicycling; Home: 51 Arundel Ave., Toronto, Ont. M4K 3A3; Office: 60 Simcoe St., Toronto, Ont. M5J 2H5.

**LUKASIEWICZ, Julius,** B.Sc., D.I.C., D.Sc., F.A.I.A.A., F.C.A.S.I., F.I.Mech.E.; professional engineer; educator; b. Warsaw, Poland 7 Nov. 1919; s. Julius F. and Maria (Balukiewicz) L.; e. Univ. of London B.Sc. Engrg. 1943; Polish Tech. Univ., London Dip. Engrg. 1945; Imperial Coll., London D.I.C. Aero. Engrg. 1945; Univ. of London D.Sc. Engrg. 1966; m. Halina d. Halina and Tomir Drymmer 16 Dec. 1942; children: Peter Jan, Mark Julius; PROFESSOR, DEPT. OF MECHANICAL

AND AEROSPACE ENGINEERING, CARLETON UNIVERSITY 1971– ; Sr. Sci. Offr. Royal Aircraft Est., Farnborough, U.K. 1945–48; Head High Speed Aerodynamics Lab., National Rsch. Counc. of Can., Ottawa 1949–57; Chief, von Kármán Gas Dynamics Facility, ARO Inc., Arnold Engr. Devel. Center, USAF, Tullahoma, Tenn. 1958–68; Prof. Aerospace Engrg. and Assoc. Dean of Rsch. and Grad. Studies, Coll. of Engrg., Virginia Polytechnic Inst. and State Univ., Blacksburg, Virginia 1969–70; author 'The Railway Game: A Study in Socio-technological Obsolescence' 1976; 'Experimental Methods of Hypersonics' 1973; various papers on aeronautics and engrg.; Chrmn. Tech., Soc. and Environ. Studies Ctte.; Princ., Energy Rsch. Group, Carleton Univ.; Fellow and Founding Mem. Candn. Aeronautics and Space Inst.; Fellow Am. Inst. of Aeronautics and Astronautics; Fellow Inst. of Mech. Engrg.; recreations: skiing, sailing, tennis; Home: 46 Whippoorwill Dr., Ottawa, Ont. K1J 7H9; Office: Dept. of Mech. and Aeros. Engrg., Carleton Univ., Ottawa, Ont. K1S 5B6.

**LUMBER, Leslie R.;** real estate consultant; b. Cambridge (Galt), Ont. 20 Jan. 1937; s. Frank Leslie and Mary Georgina (Coleman) L.; e. Ryerson Inst. of Tech. Bus. Adm. Dip.; Internat. Counc. of Shopping Centres Univs. CSM (professional shopping centre mngmnt. degree); Ont. Real Estate Bd. licensed Real Estate Sales Rep.; m. Barbara Jane d. J. Stanley and Luella Overend 11 June 1960; children: Geoffrey, Heather; PRES., LUMBER & ASSOCS. INC. 1987– ; Dir. Hammerson Canada Inc.; Dir. Enterac; joined T. Eaton Co. serving as Store Mgr., Dept. Mgr.; Candn. Merchandise Mgr. American Optical; Regional Mgr. Cadillac-Fairview; Vice-Pres. Operations, Hammerson Canada Inc.; Lectr. in Retail, Internat. Counc. Shopping Centres Universities, Sheridan Coll.; comnd. Offrs. Highland Light Inf.; mem. Candn. Ctte., Internat. Counc. Shopping Centres, Chrmn. Shopping Centre Mgmt. Promotion Ctte.; mem. Intertnat. Counc. Shopping Centres CSM Admissions & Governing Bd.; author 'Cost Savings Through Energy Conservation'; recreations: jogging, tennis, skiing; Clubs: Cedar Highlands Ski; Home & Office: 1967 Delaney Dr., Mississauga, Ont. L5J 3L3.

**LUMLEY, Hon. Edward C.,** P.C., B.Com.; b. Windsor, Ont. 27 Oct. 1939; e. Univ. of Windsor; m. Patricia Arlene d. Robert Thomson, Windsor, Ont. 27 Jan. 1942; children: Robert Edward, Kelly Lynn, Dawn Marie, Cheryl Louise, Christopher James; VICE-CHRMN., BURNS FRY LIMITED; Chrmn. Noranda Manufacturing Inc.; Dir., Gendis Inc.; Sanivan Group Inc.; Intercan Leasing Inc.; Canada Wire & Cable Ltd.; Wire Rope Industries Inc.; DY-4 Systems Inc.; Mayor, City of Cornwall 1972–74; Chrmn., Cornwall Bd. of Police Commrs. 1973–74; el. to H. of C. for Stormont-Dundas 1974–84; Chrmn., Standing Comte. on Reg. Devel. 1975; Parlty. Secy. to Min. of Regional Econ. Expansion 1976 and to Min. of Finance 1977–78; Min. of Internat. Trade 1980–82; Min. of Industry Trade and Commerce 1982–84; Min. of Regional Economic Expansion 1982–83; Min. of Communications 1984; Min. of Science and Technology 1984; Liberal; United Church; Office: 500, 1 First Canadian Place, P.O. Box 150, Toronto, Ont. M5X 1H3.

**LUMSDEN, Allan Dale,** B.Com., F.C.A.; chartered accountant; b. Brockville, Ont. 8 Jan. 1941; s. Kenneth Lloyd and Catherine Agatha (McMillan) L.; e. S. Grenville Dist. High Sch. 1959; Carleton Univ., B.Com. 1963; C.A. 1966 (Gov. Gen.'s Honours List); F.C.A. 1991; m. Patricia d. Connor and Esme Pyke 12 Jan. 1963; children: Beverly, Judy, Bryan, Karen; MNG. PARTNER-OTTAWA, COOPERS & LYBRAND and mem. Mgmt. Ctte. 1985– ; joined McDonald, Currie & Co. Ottawa 1963 (subsequently present firm); Pres., The Perley Hosp. Corp.; Dir., mem. Extve. Ctte. and Chrmn., Ottawa-Carleton Bd. Trade; former Pres. C.A.'s Assn. Ottawa; recreations: fishing, farming; Club: Rideau; Home: 36 Parkridge Cres., Gloucester, Ont. K1B 3E7; Office: 1200, 55 Metcalf St., Ottawa, Ont. K1P 6L5.

**LUMSDEN, Ian Gordon,** B.A.; art gallery director; b. Montréal, Qué. 8 June 1945; s. Andrew Mark and Isobel Dallas (Wilson) L.; e. Tuxedo Sch. No. 2 Winnipeg; Beaconsfield High Sch. Montréal; McGill Univ. B.A. 1968; Museum Management Inst., Univ. of Calif., Berkeley 1991; m. Katherine Elizabeth d. James Douglas Carson 28 July 1979; one s. Craig Ian; DIR. BEAVERBROOK ART GALLERY 1983– ; Curator Art Dept. The New Brunswick Museum Saint John 1969; Curator present Gallery 1969–83; Programming Ctte., 49th Parallel Centre for Contemp. Candn. Art 1990–92; mem. Candn. Cultural Property Export Review Bd. 1982–85; ArtsAtlantic 1977– ; Candn. Art Museums Dirs.' Orgn. 1971– , (Pres. 1983–85, First Vice-Pres. 1977–83, Second Vice-Pres. 1975–77, Treas. 1973–75); mem. Material Hist. Steering Ctte. Univ. of N.B. 1984– ; Adv. Ctte. Atlantic Conserv. Centre, Candn. Conserv. Inst. (Sec. 1972–74); mem. Candn. Museums Assn. (Sec.-Treas. 1973–75); Atlantic Provs. Art Gallery Assn. (Chrmn. 1970–72); Am. Assn. Museums; author: 'Gainsborough in Canada' 1991; 'Drawings by Carol Fraser 1948–1986' 1987; '20th Century British Drawings in the Beaverbrook Art Gallery' 1986–87; 'New Brunswick Juried Exhibition' 1984; 'Recent Acquisitions 1978–1983' 1983; 'The Murray and Marguerite Vaughan Inuit Print Collection' 1981–83; 'Mexican Works from the Vaughan Collection' 1979–81; 'Fredericton Collects' 1979; 'Drawings By Jack Weldon Humphrey' 1977–1980; 'The Queen Comes to New Brunswick: Paintings and Drawings By Molly Lamb Bobak' 1977–79; 'Bloomsbury Painters and Their Circle' 1976–78; 'From Sickert to Dali: International Portraits' 1976; 'The Wallace S. Bird Memorial Collection' 1975–76; 'The First Decade' 1975; 'Esther Warkov' 1970; 'New Brunswick Landscape Artists of the 19th Century' 1969; mem., Union Club, Saint John; Anglican; Home: 725 George St., Fredericton, N.B. E3B 1K6; Office: P.O. Box 605, Fredericton, N.B. E3B 5A6.

**LUND, Kenneth Arden,** Q.C., B.A., LL.M.; lawyer; b. Sackville, N.B. 25 May 1930; s. Daniel Perrington and Gertrude Viola (Bird) L.; e. Sackville pub. and high schs. 1947; Mt. Allison Univ. B.A. 1951; St. Edmund Hall Oxford (Rhodes Scholar) 1951–53; Dalhousie Law Sch. LL.B. 1954; Osgoode Hall Law Sch. York Univ. LL.M. 1984; m. Anna Lois d. Charles Anderson and Annetta Murray 20 July 1957; children: Murray Arden, Allison Patricia, Kimberley Lois; PARTNER, DALE & DINGWALL 1993– ; called to Bars of N.B. 1954, Ont. 1955; cr. Q.C. 1976; law practice Millar, Hunter & Milne 1954–55; Daly, Thistle, Judson & Harvey 1955–70; Daly, Cooper, Guolla & O'Gorman 1970–80; Woolley, Dale & Dingwall 1980–93; mem. North York Counc. 1964–74; Metrop. Toronto Counc. 1970–73; Past Pres. Factory 77; former Chrmn. North York Social Planning Counc.; Credit Counselling Services Metrop. Toronto; Community Care Services Metrop. Toronto; North York Sr. Centre; Home: 16 Kenaston Gdns., Willowdale, Ont. M2K 1G8; Office: P.O. Box 65, Toronto-Dominion Centre, Toronto, Ont. M5K 1E7.

**LUND, Rolf Tonning,** B.PhE., M.A.; university professor; b. Edmonton, Alta. 30 Jan. 1937; s. Rolf Tonning and Thelma Elizabeth (Ueland) L.; e. Camrose H.S. 1956; Univ of Alberta B.PhE. 1959, M.A. 1970; m. Bonnie d. Fred and Grace Jones 6 July 1963; children: Rolf Frederick, Darren Andrew, Christine Sandra Anne; ASSOC. PROF., SCHOOL OF PHYSICAL & HEALTH EDUCATION, QUEEN'S UNIV. 1988– ; Comn. Officer, PPCLI, Dept. of Nat. Defence 1959–61; Sr. Instructor, Army School of Physical Training 1961–62; Physical Eduation Officer, Royal Military College 1962–63; Instr., Phys. & Health Edn., Queen's Univ. 1963–65; Lectr. 1965–69; Asst. Prof. 1970–74; Chair, Undergrad Prog. 1987–88; Chair, Athletics and Recreation 1988–93; Dir. of Athletics and Recreation 1994– ; Head Coach, Track & Field and Cross Country 1963–88; Head Coach Gymnastics 1963–65; Head Coack Skiing 1964–68; Pres., Ont. Track & Field Assn. 1982–93; Bd. of Dir. 1984–93; Bd. of Dir., Athletics Canada 1984–93; Bd. of Dir., World IAAF Indoor Track & Field Championships 1993; Special Achievement Award, Prov. of Ont., Fitness & Amateur Sport 1989; several past executive and coaching positions, World Univ. Games 1973–79, 1983–93 and World Cup 1985; Mem., Ont. Track & Field Assn. 1963–93; Athletics Canada 1967–93; Council Member, North Am. Central Am. & Carib. Athletic Assn. Track & Field 1985; Ont. Univ. Athletic Assn.; Ont. Women's Interuniv. Athletic Assn.; Candn. Interuniv. Athletic Assn.; Canada 125 Medal 1993; recreations: skiing, canoeing, hiking, aquatics; club: Kingston Track & Field, Lakeshore Swimming Pool Assn.; Home: 799 Ashley Cres., Kingston, Ont. K7M 4E2; Office: Kingston, Ont. K7L 3N6.

**LUNDELL, Anders G.,** M.D.; medical director; b. Karlstad, Sweden 18 Dec. 1936; s. Gunnar N. E. and Åslög A. (Ejuinsdotter) L.; e. Karolinska Inst. Stockholm M.D. 1971; common-law m. Diane D. d. Jack and Yvette Walsh; one s. Andreas E.L.; MED. DIR. MERRELL DOW PHARMACEUTICALS (CANADA) INC. 1978– ; Rsch. Pharmacol. Inst. Nat. Defence Stockholm 1966–68; med. practice gen. surgery Sweden 1967–74; Assoc. Med. Dir. Astra Pharmaceuticals Can. 1974–78; mem. Pharm. Mfrs. Assn. Can. (Vice Chrmn. Med. Rsch. & Devel. Sect.); Candn. Soc. Clin. Pharmacol.; Candn. Coll. Neuropsychopharmacol.; Drug Info. Assn.; YMCA; recreations: classical music, philosophy, fitness; Home: 23 Boulton Ave., Toronto, Ont. M4M 2J4.

**LUNEAU, Claude Pierre;** sculptor; b. Paris, France 9 Sept. 1935; s. René Marcel and Suzette Marie (Brets) L.; e. Ecole de Charenton Paris; Ecole des Arts Graphiques Paris; Ryerson Polytech. Inst.; Ont. Coll. of Art; m. Debra d. George and Eiko Machida 18 March 1983; children: Noël, Anton; Prodn. Asst. French Pub. Affairs CBC Ottawa 1966; CBC Toronto, CBFLT Radio Producer 1970; TV Dir. Channel 19 Toronto 1972; solo exhns. incl. Mira Godard Gallery Toronto 1982, 1984 (group 1983); Olga Korper Gallery Toronto 1986, 1988, 1991, 1993 (group 1986, 1988); Moosart Gallery Miami, Fla. 1986; Koffler Gallery Toronto 1993; group exhns. incl. Glenbow Museum Calgary 1983; Mendel Gallery Saskatoon 1983; Equinox Gallery Vancouver 1988; Robertson Gallery Ottawa 1988; 49th Parallel Gallery N.Y.C. 1989; Stratford Art Gallery, Stratford, Ont. 1990; rep. various pub., corporate and private colls. incl. Can. Council Art Bank, Windsor Art Gallery, Museum of Civilization; guest speaker sculpture techniques; recipient Candn. Art Council Awards 1984, 1985, 1988; Ont. Art Council Grant 1983; Visual Arts Ont. Grant 1987; recreation: travel; Home: 360 Bloor St. E., Suite 810, Toronto, Ont. M4W 3M3; Office: c/o Olga Korper Gallery, 17 Morrow Ave., Toronto, Ont. M6R 2H9.

**LUNGU, Dov B.,** B.A., M.Sc., Ph.D.; historian; research coordinator; b. Bucharest, Romania 23 March 1946; s. Mircea and Fanny (Blumenfeld) L.; e. Haifa High Sch. Israel 1965; Hebrew Univ. Jerusalem B.A. 1970; The London Sch. of Econ. & Pol. Sci. M.Sc. 1972; Queen Mary Coll. Univ. of London Ph.D. 1976; m. Claudia d. Meyer and Pearl Kaufman 25 Sept. 1977; two s. Michael, Anthony; Rsch. Fellow Inst. for Eur. Hist. Mainz, Germany 1977; Rsch. Assoc. Centre for Internat. Studies The London Sch. of Econ. & Pol. Sci. 1977–81; Rsch. Assoc. Centre for Russian & East Eur. Studies Univ. of Toronto 1982– , Lectr. in Internat. Hist. 1990–93; Co-ord. Jt. IBM-Univs. Rsch. Project Human-Computer Interaction, IBM Canada 1984– ; cons. E. Eur. affairs; recipient Social Sci. Rsch. Council (UK) Rsch. Grant 1977–81; Social Sci. & Humanities Rsch. Council (Can.) Rsch. Grant 1983–84; author 'Romania and the Great Powers: 1933–1940' 1989; numerous scholarly articles, conf. papers and book reviews E. Eur. hist. & politics; contbr. to Candn. newspapers, radio and TV; mem. Candn. Assn. Slavists; Am. Assn. Advanc. Slavic Studies; IEEE (Assn. for Social Implications of Computers); recreations: opera, kite flying; Home: 172 Ava Rd., Toronto, Ont. M6C 1W5; Office: CREES, Univ. of Toronto 130 St. George St., Suite 14335, Toronto, Ont. M5S 1A5.

**LUNN, Alice Jean Elizabeth,** M.A., Ph.D., B.L.S.; librarian; b. Montreal, Que.; d. Frederick William and Jean (Laughton) Lunn; e. McGill Univ., B.A. 1932, M.A. 1934, Ph.D. (History) 1942; McGill Univ. Library Sch., B.L.S. 1940; Royal Soc. of Can. Travelling Fellowship for Research in France, 1936–37; unm.; Cataloguer, McGill Univ., 1940–46; Librarian-in-Chief, Fraser Inst. Lib., Montreal, 1946–50; Dir. Cataloguing Br., Nat. Library of Can. and of nat. bibliog. 'Canadiana' 1950–1973; Dir. Office of Lib. Standards Nat. Lib. of Can. 1973–75; Chrmn. Candn. Advisory Comte. on ISO/TC 46 1973–75, Canadian Committee on Cataloguing 1974–75; mem., Standards Council of Can., 1975–81, and of its Adv. Comte. on Standards Inform. Service, 1976–81; Canadian del. to Internat. Conf. on the improvement of Bibliographical Services, Paris, 1950 and to other internat. confs. on standards and bibliog.; reported for Can. to UNESCO annual publ. 'Bibliographical Services Throughout The World'; dissertation, pub. on microfilm, 'Economic Development in New France, 1713–1760'; translated and publ. in book form 'Développement économique de la Nouvelle France 1713–1760'; nominated for the Prix François-Xavier Garneau, Candn. Hist. Assoc. 1990; has written articles in hist. and lib. journs.; in 'Encyclopedia Canadiana,' and in 'Dictionary of Canadian Biography' also papers for various prof. confs.; Anglican; Home: 119 Pineridge Rd., RR 3, Carp, Ont. K0A 1L0.

**LUNN, Janet Louise Swoboda;** writer; editor; b. Dallas, Texas 28 Dec. 1928; d. Herman Alfred and Margaretha Marie Hannah (Alexander) Swoboda; e. Montclair (N.J.) High Sch. 1946; Notre Dame Coll., Ottawa 1947; Queen's Univ. 3 yrs.; LL.D. (Hon.) Queen's Univ. 1992; m. Richard (dec.) s. William Herbert and Mary Ann L. 2 Mar. 1950; children: Eric, Jeffrey, Alexander, Katherine, John; WRITER, EDITOR, CRITIC OF CHILDREN'S LITERATURE; reviewer/critic of children's lit. for various papers and magazines 1953– ; in-house children's ed. Clarke Irwin & Co. Toronto 1972–75; freelance editor since 1975; co-author (with Richard Lunn) 'The County: A History of Prince Edward County, Ontario' 1967; author 'Double Spell' (children's fiction) 1968; 'Larger than Life' (hist./fiction) 1979; 'The Twelve Dancing Princesses' (picture book with Laszlo Gal) 1979 (winner Children's Book of the Year, Toronto Chapter IODE 1979; one of 10 Best Books of Yr. Candn. Library Assn. 1979); 'The Root Cellar' (children's fiction) 1981 (Vicki Metcalf Award for a body of work for children, Candn. Authors' Assn. 1981; runner up for Can. Counc. Children's Book Award 1981; runner up for Candn. Bookseller's Ruth Schwartz Award 1981; winner Candn. Library Assn. Children's Book of Yr. Award 1982; one of 12 best works of fiction for children, Am. Library Assn. Booklist 1983; Teacher's Choice, U.S. National Counc. of Teachers of English 1983; Honour list, Internat. Bd. of Books for Young People 1984; chosen Junior High Category, California Young Readers Medal program 1988; 'Shadow in Hawthorn Bay' 1986 (winner, The Can. Counc. Children's Lit. Prize; The Candn. Lib. Assoc. Book of the Year for Children Award; The Sask. Lib. Assoc. Young Adult Candn. Book Award; The National Chapter IODE Children's Book of the Year; chosen as one of forty books for the White Raven annual list in the internat. children's lib., Munich, Germany, 1986); 'Amos's Sweater' (picture book with Kim La Fave) 1988 (winner of Ruth Schwartz Award 1989); 'Duck Cakes for Sale' (picture book with Kim La Fave) 1989; 'One Hundred Shining Candles' (illus. Lindsay Grater) 1990; 'The Story of Canada for Children' (with Christopher Moore) 1992 (Christie Brown's Mr. Christie Award 1993; Toronto Chapter IODE 1993); 'The Hollow Tree' (historical novel) forthcoming; 'Umbrella Birthday' (picture book) forthcoming; 'Mr. and Mrs. Hat' (picture book) forthcoming; Chrmn. Writers' Union of Can. 1984–85 (Second Vice-Chrmn. and Treas. 1979–80; First Vice-Chrmn. 1983–84); Vice-Chair, Candn. Children's Book Centre; mem., Candn. Soc. of Children's Authors, Illustrators and Performers; P.E.N. Internat.; Writer-in-Residence, Regina Public Library 1982–83; Writer-in-Residence, Kitchener Public Library 1988 (six months); Writer-in-Residence, Ottawa Univ. Fall 1993; Lectr. on children's lit.; mem. Anglican Ch. of Can.; Home: R.R. #2, Hillier, Ont. K0K 2J0.

**LUNT, Wayne Edwin,** B.Sc., M.B.A.; financial executive; b. Grimsby, Ont. 30 Dec. 1949; e. Univ. of Western Ont. B.Sc. (Hons.) 1972, M.B.A. 1978; m. Enid Pearson 9 June 1973; children: Brian, Christopher, Adrienne; SR.VICE-PRESIDENT AND CHIEF FINANCIAL OFFICER, ALBERTA NATURAL GAS COMPANY LTD 1993– ; Geophysicist, Noranda Exploration Co. Ltd. 1972–76; Sr. Evaluation Analyst, Hudson Bay Oil & Gas 1978–82; Dir., Planning & Evaluations, 1981–82; Manager, Prod. Planning, Dome Petroleum 1982–85; Asst. to the Pres., TransCanada PipeLines Resources 1985–86; Extve. Asst. to Pres., TransCanada PipeLines 1986–87; Dir., Planning 1987–89; Vice-Pres., Econ. & Planning 1989–92; Home: 6719 Silverview Rd. N.W., Calgary, Alta. T3B 3L5; Office: 2900, 240 Fourth Ave. S.W., Calgary, Alta. T2P 4L7.

**LUNZ, Gerald;** director; actor; producer; b. Hamilton, Ont. 29 Oct. 1953; s. John Joseph and Mary Catherine (Mattice) L.; e. St. Patrick's Sch. Ottawa; Univ. of Ottawa; Creative Prod., CBC-TV 'This Hour Has 22 Minutes' 1993–94; Assoc. Prod., Codco TV Series, Salter St. Films 1990–91, 1992–93; Prod./Dir., Rick Mercer's 'Show Me the Button: I'll Push it or Charles Lynch Must Die', 1990–91 and 'I've Killed Before: I'll Kill Again' 1992 National Arts Centre, Factory Theatre, Resource Centre for the Arts Nfld.; Asst. Dir., Codco TV Series, Salter St. Films, Script Co-ordinator, Codco TV Series 1989–90; Tour Mgr., Codco 1987; Mgr. & Prod., Factory Theatre 1988–89; Writer, Actor, Prod., Codco 1988; Actor, Nat. Arts Centre 1988; Prod. Mgr., Resource Centre for the Arts, St. John's Nfld. 1988; Prod./Dir., 'Late Night Live' Nat. Arts Centre, Ottawa 1988; Office: 50 Freshwater Rd., St. John's, Nfld. A1C 2N4.

**LUPTON, John Anthony,** B.A., F.H.S.M., C.C.H.S.E., M.R.S.H.; hospital executive; b. London, Eng. 14 Nov. 1930; s. Gilbert and Hilda Artiss L.; e. Broadwater Manor House Sch.; Christ's Hosp; Manchester Univ. B.A. (Admin) 1950; Extve. Prog. in Health Policy & Mngt., Harvard Univ. 1981; m. Jean d. Frederick and Louis Edwards 25 Apr. 1964; children: Geoffrey Dickson, Paul Gilbert; EXTVE. DIR., THE PERLEY HOSP. 1985– ; U.K.: Admin. trainee, Royal Sussex Co. Hosp. 1951–52; Asst. Admin., Royal Alexandra Hosp. for Sick Children, New Sussex Hosp., Sussex Maternity Hosp. 1952–54; Asst. House Gov., King's Coll. Hosp. 1955–59; Can.: Asst. Admin., Royal Victoria Hosp. 1965–71; Extve. Dir., Trenton Mem. Hosp. 1972–85; Assoc. Mem., Inst. of Health Serv. Admins. (U.K.) 1954; Fellow 1970; Mem., Candn. Coll. of Health Serv. Extves.; Mem., Royal Soc. of Health; Bd. of Parks Mngt., City of Trenton 1980–83 (Chrmn. 1983); Secy., Bd. of Dirs., Ellwood House (Ottawa) Inc. 1987–89; Pres., Ottawa Academy of Hosp. Extves. 1990–92; Student Advr., Long Term Care Mngt. Prog., Candn. Hosp. Assn. 1986– ; Adjunct Prof., Fac. of Admin., Univ. of Ottawa; Home: 1394 Wesmar Dr., Ottawa, Ont. K1H 7T5; Office: 43 Aylmer Ave., Ottawa, Ont. K1S 4R5.

**LUSCOMBE, George,** C.M., LL.D.; actor; director; b. East York, Ont. 17 Nov. 1926; s. Edward and Annie (O'Donnell) L.; e. Chester Pub. Sch. E. York; Danforth Tech. Sch. Toronto grad. Art course; York Univ., LL.D. 1978; m. Mary Mona d. Hugh Maitland Walton 8 Aug. 1958; three d. Glenda, Nadine, Karen; Artistic Dir. Emeritus, Toronto Workshop Productions 1986–89; began profl. acting career with People's Repertory Theatre 1948; moved to Eng. 1950 to work in prov. repertory theatres; joined Joan Littlewood's Theatre Workshop, Manchester, Eng. 1952; played Theatre Royal, Stratford Atta-Bow, London, Theatre Workshop 1952–57; Founder & Artistic Dir., Toronto Workshop Productions 1959–86; recipient Drama Bench Award 1976; Chalmer's New Play Award 1980; Award of Merit City of Toronto 1980; Queen's Silver Jubilee Medal 1978; C.M. 1981; Royal Candn. Humane Assn. Cert. for Saving Life 1945; co-author, dir. and producer: 'Ain't Lookin'' 1980; 'The Mac-Paps' 1980; 'The Wobbly' 1982; 'Hey Rube!' 1961; co-author 12 additional plays; Hon. mem. Ont. Fedn. Labour; Candn. Theatre Hist. Soc.; Home: 23 Humewood Dr., Toronto, Ont. M6C 2W3.

**LUSIGNAN, Serge,** Ph.D., M.S.R.C.; university professor; b. Montreal, Que. 22 Oct. 1943; s. Florian and Germaine (Marsolais) L.; e. Univ. of Montreal, Ph.D. 1971; PROF., INSTITUTE OF MEDIEVAL STUDY, UNIV. OF MONTREAL 1983– ; faculty mem. since 1972; Chrmn., 1977–86; Pres., Rsch. Ctte., Univ. of Montreal 1983–86; Councillor, Med. Acad. of Am. 1979–82; Mem. of Counc. & Extve., Canadian Fed. for the Humanities 1985–87; Treas., Féd. internat. des Insts. et Centres d'études médiévales; Mem., Royal Soc. of Can. 1989– ; author: 'Préface au Speculum maius de Vincent de Beauvais: réfraction et diffraction' 1978, 'Parler vulgairement. Les intellectuels et la langue française aux XIII$^{e}$ et XIV$^{e}$ siècles' 1986, 1987, book chapter; Home: 3837 Kent St., Montreal, Que. H3S 1N4; Office: Box 6128, Station A, Montreal, Que. H3C 3J7.

**LUSSIER, André (Joseph-Alfred),** B.A., M.D., L.M.C.C., C.S.P.Q., C.S.C.R., F.R.C.P.(C), F.A.C.R.; professor of medicine; b. Sherbrooke, Que. 27 May 1933; s. Georges Joseph-Albert and Blanche Marie-Lucienne (Jetté) L.; e. Univ. of Montreal B.A. 1954; Internship, Notre-Dame Hosp. L.M.C.C. 1958–59; Med. Sch., Univ. of Montreal M.D. 1959; Residency (Internal Med. & Rheum.), Notre Dame Hosp. 1959–63; post-grad. studies 1961; Fellowship, Hosp. of The Univ. of Pennsylvania 1963–64; Internal Med. Cert., Prov. of Que. C.S.P.Q. 1964; Rheum. Cert. C.S.P.Q. 1970; Royal Coll. of Physicians of Can. S.C.R.C.(C) 1965; Internal Med. F.R.C.P.(C) 1972; Fellowship, Am. Coll. of Rheum. F.A.C.R. 1986; m. Denise d. Rosario and Lucienne (Dugal) Trudel 16 Sept. 1961; children: Yves, Sylvie, Isabelle; PROF. OF MEDICINE, FAC. OF MED. & CENTRE HOSPITALIER UNIV. OF SHERBROOKE (CHUS) 1975– ; Author of the Brief for the official recognition of Rheumatology as a specialty in the Province of Quebec 1970; Assoc. Prof. 1969; Founder & Dir., 1st Rheumatic Diseases Unit officialy recognized in Que., C.H.U.S. 1970–84; Pres., Musculoskeletal System Teaching Unit. 1978–78; Dir., Clinical Rsch. Ctr., CHUS 1980–84; Principal Investigator in basic & clin. rsch. studies on microcrystal synovites & hyperostosis in man & in animal with rsch. grants for past 20 years; involved in 56 clin. trials (principal investigator for 45); Annual Prize for Basic Med. Rsch. in Canada 1976; Member of Honor, Soc. of rheum. (France) 1980; Cert. of achievement, Am. Men & Women of Science June 1987; Pres., 1990 meeting, Assn. des Médecins de Langue Française du Canada; Mem., Med. Rsch. Council of Can. 1988–93; author/co-author of over 200 scientific pubs., four book chapters & three books; recreations: tennis, swimming, reading, computers, etc.; Home: 450 Montmagny, Sherbrooke, Que. J1L 1H3; Office: 3001, 12th Ave. N., Room 7423, Sherbrooke, Que. J1H 5N4.

**LUSSIER, Charles A.;** avocat, haut fonctionnaire; né Montréal, Qué., 18 août, 1920; f. Joseph Irénée et Marie-Louise (Patenaude) L.; é. Coll. St.-Jean de Brébeuf; Univ. de Montréal; Univ. McGill; ép. Monique, f. Léon Lortie et Rhea Labrosse, 14 sept. 1953; 2 fils, 2 filles; Greffier du Sénat et des Parlements 1982–89; Co-Président du 'Reseau sur la Constitution' 1991; reçu avocat (Montréal) 1945; avec spécialité en droit du travail, 1947–57; Dir. de la Maison des Etudiants canadiens à la Cité Univ. de Paris, 1957; Délégué général de la Prov. de Qué. en France, 1961; Sous-ministre adjoint (Citoyenneté) 1965; Détaché auprès du Ministère de l'Energie, des Mines et des Resources comme conseiller spécial au cours des négociations avec la France et les Etats-Unis sur le plateau continental, 1967; Sous-secrétaire d'Etat adjoint (Secrétariat d'Etat), 1968; Commissaire, Comm. de la Fonction publique du Canada, 1970–76; Dir., Conseil des arts du Canada 1976–82; sec.-gén. du Sénat et des Parlements du Can. 1982; retraite 1989; ancien Prés., Théâtre du Nouveau Monde, Montréal; Dir., Inst. canadien des Affaires Publiques; Conférencier invité à la Faculté de droit de l'Université de Paris et à l'Institut d'Etudes politiques de Paris sur le sujet du fédéralisme au Canada, 1957–64; Professeur à temps partiel à l'Université d'Ottawa Cours de maîtrise en droit civil, 1974–75 et 75–76; chef ou membre de délégations canadiennes de, 27ième Conférence internationale sur les Droits de l'homme à Genève, 1965; Mission minitérielle en Amérique latine (représentant le Secrétaire d'Etat), 1968; Mission canadienne à Niamey pour assister à la conférence sur la coopération multilatérale des pays de langue française, 1969; Conférence de l'Agence de coopération culturelle et technique à Lomé (Togo) sur 'L'Analyse comparative des structures de la Fonction publique des Etats-Membres de l'ACCT,' 1971; La Fédération du français universel à Liège (Belgique) en 1969, à Menton (France) en 1971, à Dakar (Sénégal) en 1973 et au Luxembourg en 1975; Membre de l'Institut d'administration publique du Canada; Directeur, Conseil canadien des Chrétiens et des Juifs; Membre de l'Institut scientifique franco-canadien (destiné à l'échange de professeurs subventionnés par le gouvernement); Directeur de l'Institut France-Canada; Membre et ancien vice-président, Alliance Française d'Ottawa; Directeur (à la fondation) du Centre de recherches en Relations humaines de l'Université de Montréal; Prés., Assoc. Internationale des secrétaires généraux des Parlements 1987; Catholique; sports: tennis, natation; golf; Clubs: Larrimac Golf; Rockcliffe Lawn Tennis; Cercle Universitaire; résidence: 211 River Rd., Ottawa, Ont. K1L 8B5.

**LUSSIER, Gaétan,** O.C. (1981), B.S.A., M.Sc., D.Sc.; b. Marieville (Rouville), Qué. 24 May 1941; e. Acad. Crevier, Marieville, Qué.; Mont St-Louis, Montréal; Univ. Oka B.S.A. 1962 (Lt. Gov.'s Gold Medal); Macdonald Coll. M.Sc. 1964; D.Sc. (Hon.) McDonald Coll., McGill Univ., 1979; Univ. Laval Adult Educ. courses 1965; PRES., LES BOULANGERIES WESTON QUÉBEC INC. 1988– ; Teacher, Inst. de Technol. Agricole, St-Hyacinthe, Qué. 1964–66, Head of Extension and Research 1965; Tech. Adv. and Dir. of Promotions E. Can., Am. Potash Inst. 1966–68; Agric. Co-ordinator for Richelieu Region 1968–70; Asst. Depy. Min., Qué. Ministry of Agric. 1970–71, DM 1971–77; DM Agriculture Canada 1977–82; Depy. Min. & Chrmn. of Employment & Immigration Canada 1982–88; Officer, Order of Canada 1981; DM/C CEIC 1982; Outstanding Achievement Award of Public Service of Canada 1982; mem. Ont. Inst. Agrols.; Agric. Inst. Can.; Corp. des agronomes du Qué.; Dir., Conf. Bd. of Can.; Montreal C. of C.; R. Catholic; recreations: reading, skiing; Office: 2700 Jacques-Cartier Blvd. E., Longueil, Que. J4N 1L5.

**LUST, Peter;** journalist; author; b. Nuremberg, West Germany 15 Jan. 1911; s. Arthur and Luise (Bloch) L.; e. Gymnasium Nuremberg; Le Rosey, Rolle, Switzerland 1928; Univ. of Geneva grad. in Hist. 1931; m. Evelyn d. George and Edith Heymannsohn 23 June 1953; children: Patricia, Arthur, Peter Jr.; journalist 'New York Sun' 1933; served with U.S. Forces during World War II; came to Can. as freelance journalist 1946; served CBC and CTV 1960–70; Candn. Corr. W. German weekly 'Der Spiegel' 1969; also became corr. for 'Der Stern' (Hamburg), Burda Publs. (Offenburg) and Springer publs.; weekly columnist 'The Suburban' Montreal 1969– ; author 'Two Germanies: Mirror of An Age' 1966 (non-fiction); 'The Last Seal Pup' 1967 (non-fiction; rec'd Que. Citation); 'Cuba: Time Bomb At Our Door' 1970 (non-fiction); Home: 13 Thompson Point, Beaconsfield, Qué. H9W 5Y8; Office: Box 824, Pointe Claire-Dorval Post Office, Pointe Claire, Qué. H9R 4Z5.

**LUSZTIG, Peter Alfred,** B.Com., M.B.A., Ph.D.; educator; b. Budapest, Hungary 12 May 1930; s. Alfred Peter and Suzanne (Szabo) L.; e. Univ. of B.C., B.Com. 1954; Univ. of W. Ont. M.B.A. 1955; Stanford Univ. Ph.D. 1965; m. Penny d. Ray and Margaret Bicknell Aug. 1961; children: Michael Peter, Cameron Byrn, Carrie Suzanne; PROF. OF FINANCE, UNIVERSITY OF B.C. 1968– ; Dir. Canfor; Royal Insurance (Canada); Public Gov., Vancouver Stock Exchange; Asst. to Vice Pres. Finance, B.C. Electric Co. 1955–57; Instr. Univ. of B.C. 1957–60, Asst. Prof. 1962, Assoc. Prof. 1964, Prof. of Finance 1968– , Dean of Commerce and Business Adm., Univ. of B.C. 1977–91; Visiting Scholar

London Grad. Business Sch. 1968–69; Prof. of Finance, IMEDE Switzerland 1973–74; Sr. Advisor, BC Ministry of Development, Trade and Tourism 1991; recipient Killam Sr. Faculty Fellowship; Ford Foundation Faculty Fellowship; named Hon. Cert. Gen. Acct.; mem. Royal Comn. B.C. 1966–68; Commnr., B.C. Tree Fruit Industry Inquiry 1990; co-author 'Report of the Royal Commission on Automobile Insurance' 1968; 'Report of the Commission of Inquiry - B.C. Tree Fruit Industry' 1990; 'Managerial Finance In A Canadian Setting' 5th ed. 1993; various journ. articles; Trustee Healthcare Benefit Trust; mem. Am. Finance Assn.; Delta Upsilon; Sigma Tau Chi; Lutheran; Home: 5589 Wycliffe Rd., Vancouver, B.C. V6T 1J4; Office: Vancouver, B.C. V6T 1Y8.

**LUTE, Graham E.,** B.A.; food industry executive; e. University of Western Ont. B.A. (Hons.); PRESIDENT, NESTLE CONFECTIONERY DIVISION 1991– ; management positions, Carnation Co. 1967–84; Vice-Pres., Sales & Mktg., Carnation Co. 1984–87; Gen. Mgr., Nutrition Div., Nestle Canada Inc. 1988–89; Pres., Clintec Nutrition Co. 1989–91; Dir., Confectionery Manufacturers Assn. 1992; Office: 1185 Eglinton Ave. E., Don Mills, Ont. M3C 3C7.

**LUTES, R.J.,** B.B.A., C.A.; financial executive; b. 1935; e. Univ. of New Brunswick B.B.A. 1958; m. Genevieve; 6 children; Sr. Vice-President, Finance and Administration, New Brunswick Power Corporation; Director, Audit Ctte., Crown Life Insurance Company; Past Pres., The Canadian Club; Mem., Inst. for Research on Public Policy (Extve. Ctte.; Dir.); Inst. of C.A.s of N.B. & Que.; Jr. Achievement of Canada; Founding Chair, Adv. Council, Sch. of Bus., Univ. of N.B.; Former Nat. Pres., Assn. for the Mentally Retarded; Address: 278 Woodlawn Lane, Fredericton, N.B. E3C 1J4.

**LUTHER, Hon. Donald S.,** LL.B.; judge; b. Deer Lake, Nfld. 30 Jan. 1951; s. Eric Reginald and Shirley Jean (Campbell) L.; e. S. Huron Dist. High Sch. Exeter, Ont. 1969; Univ. of W. Ont. LL.B. 1974; m. Helga d. Dietrich and Helen Neufeld 4 May 1974; children: Rachel May, Adam Martin; CHIEF JUDGE, PROVINCIAL COURT OF NFLD. 1988– ; Dep. Judge Yukon and N.W.T.; articled with Clyde Kirby Wells 1973–74; called to Bar of Nfld. 1975; apptd. to Provl. Court 1974; Sr. Judge Corner Brook, Nfld. 1981; mem. Gov. Gen.'s Study Conf. 1983; Chrmn. Salvation Army Territorial Adv. Council on Corrections (Can. & Bermuda) 1989– , Pres. Adv. Council Laymen W. Nfld. 1986–87, Corps Sgt.-Maj. of Temple Corner Brook 1987– ; Dir. Youth Adv. Council Nfld. & Labrador 1982–85; Pres. Corner Brook Br. Candn. Mental Health Assn. 1988; Nfld. Provl. Judges Assn. 1978–79; co-author 'Criminal Procedure and the Administration of Criminal Justice' 1979–87; recreations: music, chess, hockey; Office: P.O. Box 2006, Corner Brook, Nfld. A2H 6J8.

**LUTZ, The Hon. Mr. Arthur Morton,** B.Comm., LL.B.; judge; b. Grafton, N.S. 3 Feb. 1937; s. Morton Elwood and Reta May (Baltzer) L.; e. Acadia Univ. 1953–54; Mount Allison Univ. B.Comm. 1957; Dalhousie Univ. LL.B. 1960; m. Barbara Lynne d. David and Pauline Hunter 20 July 1963; children: James Morton, Marnie Lynne, Arthur Carson; JUSTICE, COURT OF QUEEN'S BENCH (& EX OFFICIO MEMBER OF COURT OF APPEAL) OF ALBERTA 1982– ; Clerk, Canada Packers summers of 1956, '57; Student at Law, Lindsay, Emery, Jamison (Edmonton) 1960–61; Assoc. 1961–62; German, Dinkel (Calgary) 1962–66; Partner, Lutz, Westerberg, O'Leary 1966–82; Deputy Judge, Supreme Court N.W.T. 1986– ; Supreme Court Yukon 1987– ; Mem., Kinsmen Club of Calgary; Sigma Chi Fraternity; recreations: antique auto restoration, skiing, golf; Office: Court House, 611 – 4th St. S.W., Calgary, Alta. T2P 1T5.

**LUUS, Rein,** B.A.Sc., M.A.Sc., A.M., Ph.D.; university professor; b. Tartu, Estonia 8 Mar. 1939; came to Can. 1949; s. late Edgar and Aili (Prakson) L.; e. Sault Ste. Marie Coll. Inst. 1952–57; Univ. of Toronto B.A.Sc. 1961, M.A.Sc. 1962; Princeton Univ. A.M. 1963, Ph.D. 1964; post-doctoral 1964–65; m. Hilkka d. late Fredi Jaakola 17 June 1973; children: Brian Markus, Kristina Annika; PROF. OF CHEMICAL ENGN., UNIV. OF TORONTO since 1974; Dir. Chem. Engn. Research Consultants Ltd.; came to the Univ. of Toronto as Asst. Prof. 1965–68; Assoc. Prof. 1968–74; consultant activities incl. Shell Can. 1966–70, 1979; Imperial Oil, 1974–77; Milltronics, 1967–71; Extve. Can. Society for Chem. Engn., Toronto, 1966–72 (Chrmn. 1969–70); co-author of 'Optimal Control of Engineering Processes,' 1967; articles in over 100 scientific publications; rec'd. E.W.R. Steacie Prize, 1976; ERCO Award, 1980; mem., Assn. of Prof. Engn. Ont.; Chem. Inst. of Can.; Candn. Society for Chem Engn.; Am. Institute for Chem. Engn. (AIChE); Sigma Xi; Lutheran; recreations; skiing, squash, swimming, tennis, sailing, violin; Home: 65 Laurentide Dr., Don Mills, Ont. M3A 3E1; Office: Univ. of Toronto, Toronto, Ont. M5S 1A4.

**LUXTON, Meg,** B.A., Phil.M., Ph.D.; university professor; b. England 28 Feb. 1946; d. Greg and Fenella (Earwicker) Macdiarmid; e. Univ. of Toronto B.A. (Hons.) 1969, Phil.M. 1973, Ph.D. 1978; children: Jan & Michelle Campbell-Luxton; PROF., YORK UNIV. & ATKINSON COLL. 1984– ; Prof., Univ. of Toronto 1970–79; Co-founder, Women's Studies Programme; Prof., McMaster Univ. 1980–84; Bd. Mem., The Candn. Women's Educational Press 1976–81; 'Canadian Women Studes/les cahiers de la femme' 1987– ; Mem., Nat. Action Ctte. on Status of Women; Employment & Econ. Ctte.; Organized Working Women; author: 'More Than a Labour of Love: Three Generations of Women's Work in the Home' 1980, 1984 (Postscript added); co-author: 'Through the Kitchen-Window: The Politics of Home and Family' 1986, 2nd ed. 1990; co-editor: 'Feminism & Political Economy: Women's Work, Women's Struggles' 1987; Office: 302 Atkinson Coll., York Univ., 4700 Keele St., North York, Ont. M3J 1P3.

**LUZ, Virginia Erskine,** R.C.A., O.S.A., C.S.P.W.C.; artist; b. Toronto, Ont. 15 Oct. 1911; d. G. John and Jessie (Minkler) L; e. Bloor Coll. Inst. 1929; Central Tech. Sch. Toronto Special Art Course 1932; McLane Art Inst. N.Y. City 1938; free-lance artist Toronto Studios 1932–38; Instr. of Illustration Art Dept. Central Tech. Sch. Toronto 1940–74, Asst. Dir. Art 1965–69, Dir. 1969–74; Exhns.: Royal Candn. Acad. 1952–88; Ont. Soc. Artists 1945–88; Candn. Soc. Painters in Water Colour 1947–88; Expo 1967; Candn. Group of Painters 1945–52; Candn. Women Artists Show New York 1947, Candn. Tour 1948–49; Montreal Museum of Fine Arts 1948–53; Candn. Nat. Exhn. Shows; one-man shows 1948, 1976, 1981, 1993; Two man shows 51, 53; Sisler Gallery Toronto 'Tribute to 10 Women' 1975; 'Artists Choice' Etobicoke Civic Centre 1981; rep. various pub. and private colls. incl. Dept. External Affairs Ottawa, J.S. McLean Coll., London (Ont.) Art Gallery, Robert McLaughlin Gallery Oshawa; mem. Roy. Candn. Acad. of Arts; Ont. Soc. Artists (Extve. Council 1963–65); Candn. Soc. Painters in Water Colour; Address: 113 Delaware Ave., Toronto, Ont. M6H 2S9.

**LYE, Brig.-Gen. William Kirby,** M.B.E., C.D., B.Sc., P.Eng.; retired army officer; b. Ottawa, Ont. 14 July 1918; s. Ossian Gardiner and Florence Hilda (Kirby) L.; e. Guelph (Ont.) Coll. & Vocational Inst., 1936; Royal Mil. Coll., grad. dipl. 1939; N.S. Tech. Coll. 1939–40; Queen's Univ., B.Sc. (Civil Engn.) 1947; U.S. Marine Corps Schs., Quantico, Va., 1949–50; m. Beverly Julia, d. late Joseph Henry Winteringham Bower, 3 Nov. 1943; children: Maj. Joseph William Kirby, Beverley Joan Blackwell Wicken, R.N.; commissioned in RCE 1939; served in Can., N.W. Europe and U.K. 1939–45; Depy. Dir. of Engr. Devel. and Asst. Dir. of Works, HQ Ottawa, 1951; Directing Staff. Candn. Army Staff Coll., 1954; Depy. Commdr., Candn. Base Units, Middle E., 1957; Asst. Adj. Gen., Directorate of Manning 1958; Commandant, Royal Candn. Sch. of Mil. Eng., Vedder Crossing, B.C., 1961; Commdr., Candn. Base Units Europe, 1964; Commdr., N.S. and P.E.I. area, 1965; Chief of Staff Adm., Mobile Command HQ Montreal, 1966; Dir. Gen. Land Forces, CFHQ Ottawa 1967; Dir. Gen. Ordnance Systems, CFHQ, 1968; Dir. Gen. Operations (Land), CFHQ, 1970; Commandant Royal Mil. Coll. of Can. 1970–73; Dir. Physical Plant Dept., Univ. of Toronto 1974–81; Mentioned in Despatches; mem. Prof. Engrs. Prov. Ont.; Anglican; Home: 2327 Bennington Gate, Oakville Ont. L6J 5N7.

**LYLE, John Kennett Christopher,** B.A., FRI.; real estate executive; b. Calgary, Alta. 4 March 1940; s. Kennett Irvin and Kathleen C. (Fewkes) L.; e. Pub. and High Schs., Calgary, Mt. Royal Jr. Coll., Univ. Western Ont., B.A. (Hons. Bus. Adm.) 1963; Univ. Alta., diploma, Advanced Real Estate Mang. 1969; m. Sydney, d. Bernie and Ada Tharp 17 Oct. 1987; one s. Mark Lawrence Kennett; three d. Catharine Elizabeth, Mary Jane, Karen Penny; SR. VICE PRES., GOVERNMENT SERVICES, ERS REAL ESTATE SERVICES LTD. 1986– ; joined family business, Lyle Bros. Ltd., Real Estate Brokers, Calgary, in 1963 (Co. acquired by The Royal Trust Co. 1966); Residential Sales Mgr., Royal Trust Co. 1966; ALTA. Area MGR., Real Estate, The Royal Trust Co. 1974–76; Pres., Lyle Real Estate Ltd. 1976–86; mem., Real Estate Inst. of Can. (Chrmn. Calgary Chapter 1972, National Chrmn., FRI Div., 1974; Dir., 1974–75;) Pres., Real Estate Inst. of Alta. 1979; Candn. Real Estate Assn.; Calgary Real Estate Bd. (Dir. 1971–72 & 1979–82; Pres. 1981); Alta. Real Estate Assn.; mem., City of Calgary Housing Comn. 1982–84; Calgary Chamber of Comm.; Calgary Tourist and Convention Bureau; Pres., Calgary Jr. Football Assoc. 1979 and 1980; Assoc. Dir., Calgary Stampeder Football Club 1975–85; Dir., Calgary Luge Club 1988; Chrmn., Corporate Relations Ctte., Canada Olympic Park, Calgary Olympic Winter Games 1988; Dir., P.C. Assoc. of Calgary Centre 1992; Conservative; recreations: skiing, water sports, hockey, photography; Clubs: Glencoe; Office: 220 Laurier Ave. W., Suite 300, Ottawa, Ont. K1P 5Z9.

**LYMER, John Arthur;** association executive, police officer; b. Liverpool, England 20 Aug. 1928; s. John Albert and Margaret (Brennan) L.; e. King Edward VII Nautical Coll. 2nd Mates Deep Sea cert. 1951; m. Audrey d. George and Lillian Bishop 3 Apr. 1950; children: Stephen, Gail, Gregg, Julie; PRES., METROPOLITAN TORONTO POLICE ASSN. 1988– ; Aberdovy Outward Bound Sea Sch. 1945; joined Brit. Merchant Marine as Deck Boy; sailed before the mast to obtain 2nd Mates cert.; 6 yrs. on cargo ships & oil tankers; joined City of Toronto Police 1952; served east end of Toronto #10 Div., Uniform Patrol, Motorcycle, Youth Bur.; promoted to Detective, Morality Bureau, 52 Crim. Investigations Bur. (CIB); promoted to Staff Sergeant, CIB; elected Dir., Metro. Toronto Police Assn. 1978; elected Evtve. Vice-Pres. 1980–84; elected Trustee, Metro. Toronto Police Benefit Fund 1978– ; Home: 222 Chine Dr., Scarborough, Ont. M1M 2L5; Office: 180 Yorkland Blvd., Willowdale, Ont. M2J 1R5.

**LYNCH, Andrew Burchill;** publishing executive; b. Toronto, Ont. 27 Dec. 1941; s. Charles Burchill and Mary-Elizabeth (Merkel) L.; e. King's College School 1957–60; Carleton Univ. 1960–61; Dalhousie Univ. 1962–64; m. Mary d. Alick and Anne Stockwood 31 May 1969; children: David Charles, Sarah Anne; PUBLISHER & PRESIDENT, MONDAY PUBLICATIONS LTD. 1976– ; var. advtg. agencies in Toronto 1965–69; 'Marketing' Magazine, Maclean Hunter Business Pubns. Div. 1969–72; Pres., Broughton Communications Group (mktg. cons. & trade typesetting firm); Monday Publications publishes 'Monday' magazine & 'Real Estate Victoria' (weekly pubs.) and 'Business Report' (a monthly journal); Pres., B.C. & Yukon Newspaper Assn.; Chrmn., The New Bastion Theatre Co. of B.C.; clubs: Victoria Entrepreneurial, Victoria C. of C. (Past Pres.); Home: 5178 Old West Saanich Rd., Victoria, B.C. V8X 3X4; Office: 1609 Blanshard St., Victoria, B.C. V8W 2J5.

**LYNCH, Charles B.,** LL.D., O.C.; journalist, radio and television commentator; b. Cambridge, Mass. 3 Dec. 1919; s. late Charles Victor and late Helen May (Burchill) L.; came to Canada 17 Dec. 1919; e. Saint John (N.B.) High Sch. 1932–35; Saint John Vocational Sch. 1935–36; m. the late Mary-Elizabeth, d. late Andrew D. Merkel, 16 Jan. 1941 (div.); children: Andrew B., C. Blake (dec.), Susan K., Daniel S., Lucinda E.; m. 2ndly Claudy Mailly, M.P. 1986; Freelance journalist and author 1985– ; began as Reporter, Saint John Citizen, 1936; Saint John Telegraph-Journal 1939; Candn. Press, Halifax, N.S. 1939; Bureau Chief, British United Press, Vancouver, B.C. 1940; trans. to Toronto 1941; Central Div. Mgr., Br. United Press, Toronto, 1942; joined Reuters and served in 2nd World War as War Corr. in Normandy, D-Day, 1944 to end of war; Chief of Team covering Nuremberg War Crimes Trial, 1945–46; Chief Corr. in S. Am. (Rio de Janeiro) 1946; in Canada, 1947; Editor, Reuters N. Am. Service (N.Y.C.) 1950; Corr. at U.N. for CBC 1956–57; Chief of Southam News 1958–84; won Bowater Award for Journalism, 1961 for series of dispatches from Latin Am.; Past Pres., Candn. War Corr. Assn.; Past Pres., Parlty. Press Gallery (Ottawa); Past Governor, Heritage Canada; won Nat. Newspaper Award for Staff Corr. 1965; Officer, Order of Canada 1977; named to National Newspaper Hall of Fame 1981; author of 'China: One Fourth of the World'; 'Our Retiring Prime Minister'; 'You Can't Print That!'; 'Race for the Rose'; 'A Funny Way to Run a Country'; 'The Lynch Mob'; 'Up From the Ashes - The Story of the Rideau Club'; 'Fishing With Simon'; Life mem., ACTRA, Am. Federation of Musicians; Anglican; recreations: skiing, fishing, music; Clubs: Rideau; National Press; Overseas Press (New York); Home: 36 Rue Cartier, Gatineau, Que. J8T 5L1; Office: Parliamentary Press Gallery, Ottawa, Ont. K1A 0A6.

**LYNCH, Gerald,** Ph.D.; university professor; b. Monaghan, Ireland 28 May 1953; s. Peter James and Brigid Ellen (Sheridan) L.; e. Univ. of Waterloo, B.A. 1976, M.A. 1978; Univ. of Western Ont., Ph.D. 1984; m. Mary Jo d. Cornelius and Joanna VandenHeuvel 8 Sept. 1978; children: Bryan, Meghan, Maura; ASSOC. PROF., UNIV. OF OTTAWA 1992– ; Asst. Prof., Univ. of West. Ont. 1984–85; Univ. of Ottawa 1985–92; Anthony Firetto Scholarship 1973–74, Newman Award 1974–75, Honours English Prize 1975–76 (all St Jerome's Coll., Univ. of Waterloo); 4 Prov. of Ont. grad. fellowships 1977–82; Nat. Magazine Award First Prize for Fiction 1982; Ont. Arts Counc. Grant 1982, 1986; Can. Rsch. Fellowship 1987–90; Okanagan Short Story Award 1989; Nepean Library Short Story Award 1990, 1992; Roman Catholic; mem., ACUTE; Leacock Assoc.; author: 'Stephen Leacock: Humour and Humanity' 1988, 'One's Company' 1989; 'Kisbey' 1992; editor: 'Oliver Goldsmith, The Rising Village' 1989; 'Bliss Carman' 1990; co-editor: 'Prose Models' 1989; 'The Canadian Essay' 1991; 'Short Fiction' 1992; 'Familiar Ground' 1993; 'Prose Models' 2nd ed. 1993; Home: 80 Westpark Dr., Blackburn Hamlet, Gloucester, Ont. K1B 3E8; Office: Ottawa, Ont. K1N 6N5.

**LYNDON, John L.,** B.A., LL.B.; insurance executive; b. 5 May 1934; e. Univ. of Alta. B.A., LL.B. 1961; m. Jane Mackie; children: Greg, Bruce, Charlene, Ian, Jacqueline & Jane Ayn; PRESIDENT, INSURANCE BUREAU OF CANADA; practiced law with Clement, Parlee 1961–64; Corporate Trust Offr. National Trust Co. Ltd. Toronto 1964; Vice Pres. Market Operations The Toronto Stock Exchange 1965–70; Dir. Cochran Murray Ltd. invest. dealers 1970; Depy. Min. of Consumer & Corporate Affairs, Alta. 1974–78; Sessional Lectr. in Law, Univ. of Alta. 1976–78; Public Gov., The Toronto Futures Exchange 1984–86; recreations: skiing, reading, music, theatre, equestrian riding and driving; Club: University; Home: R.R. #3, Caledon E., Ont. L0N 1E0; Office: 181 University Ave., Toronto, Ont. M5H 3M7.

**LYON, David,** B.Sc., Ph.D.; university professor; b. Edinburgh, Scotland 7 Dec. 1948; s. Harold Fullarton and Jean Mary (Laxton) L.; e. Univ. of Bradford B.Sc. 1971, Ph.D. 1976; m. Sue d. James and Rosalie Osborne 1 Jan. 1972; children: Timothy James, Abigail Sue, Joshua Thomas, Miriam Joy; ASSOC. PROF., SOCIOLOGY, QUEEN'S UNIV. 1990– ; Lecturer, Bingley College (U.K.) 1975–78; Asst. Prof., Wilfrid Laurier Univ. 1976–77; Sr. Lectr., Ilkley Coll. (U.K.) 1978–83; Rsch. Fellow, Calvin Coll. (MI) 1981; Bradford and Ilkley Coll., Bradford Univ. 1983–90; Rsch. Fellow, Univ. of Leeds 1983–84; Course Tutor, Open Univ. (U.K.) 1987–90; Consultant, Community Devel. Found. (U.K.); Mem., Candn. Soc. & Anthrop. Assn.; Brit. Soc. Assn.; Internat. Soc. Assn.; author: 'Karl Marx' 1979, 'Sociology and the Human Image' 1983, 'The Steeple's Shadow' 1985, 'The Information Society' 1988, 'The Electronic Eye' 1994, 'The Silicon Society' 1986, 'Future Society' 1984 (books translated into eight languages); lay reader, Anglican Church of Canada; recreations: canoeing, bicycling; Office: Kingston, Ont. K7L 3N6.

**LYON, Peyton,** M.A., D.Phil.; university professor, retired; b. Winnipeg, Man. 2 Oct. 1921; s. Herbert Redmond and Frederica Iveagh (Lee) L.; e. Kelvin High Sch., Winnipeg, Man.; Univ. of Manitoba, B.A. 1949; Oxford Univ. (Rhodes Scholar), B.A. 1951, M.A., D.Phil. 1953; m. Frances Marion (dec.), d. Frank B. Hazleton, Winnipeg, Man. 26 June 1943; children: Russell Vaughan, Stephen Lee, Barbara Jane; Prof. of Pol. Science, Carleton Univ. 1965–87 (Chrmn. of Dept. 1965–68); joined Dept. of External Affairs 1953–59; with Dept. of Pol. Science, Univ. of W. Ont. 1959–65; served with R.C.A.F. in U.K. & Africa 1940–45, rising to Flt. Lt.; author 'The Policy Question' 1963; 'Canada in World Affairs 1961–1963' 1968; 'NATO as a Diplomatic Instrument' 1971; 'Canada-US Free Trade and Canadian Independence' 1975; co-author 'Canada and the Third World' 1975; 'Canada as an International Actor' 1979; and numerous articles in journs., newspapers, mags.; mem., Candn. Inst. Internat. Affairs; Candn. Pol. Science Assn.; Home: 1 Church St., Appleton, Ont.; Mailing Address: R.R. #3, Almonte, Ont. K0A 1A0.

**LYON, The Hon. Mr. Justice Sterling Rufus Webster,** P.C.; provincial appeal court justice; b. Windsor, Ont. 30 Jan. 1927; s. late David Rufus and Ella Mae (Cuthbert) L.; e. Central Public Sch. and Portage la Prairie (Man.) Coll. Inst. (rec'd Gov. Gen.'s Medal and entrance scholarship to Univ. of Man.); United Coll. (Univ. of Manitoba), B.A. 1948; Manitoba Law Sch., LL.B. 1953; m. Barbara Jean, d. late John Garnet Howard and Maude (Wallace) Mayers, 26 Sept. 1953; children: Nancy, Andrea, Peter, Jennifer, Jonathan; JUSTICE, COURT OF APPEAL, MANITOBA 1986– ; called to the Bar of Manitoba 1953; cr. Q.C. 1960; with News Staff, Winnipeg Free Press, 1948–49; Pres., Manitoba Law Students Assoc. 1952–53; Univ. Officers Training, R.C.A.F. Reserve 1950–53; Crown Atty., Dept. of Atty.-Gen. 1953–57; Legal Consultant, The Man. Liquor Enquiry Comn., 1954–55; el. to Man. Leg. in g.e. June 1958; re-el. 1959, 1962, 1966; ret'd 1969; Atty.-Gen. 1958–63 & 1966–69; Min. of Munic. Affairs 1960–61; Min. of Publ. Utilities 1961–63; Min. of Natural Resources 1963–66; Min. of Tourism & Recreation 1966–68; Commr. of Northern Affairs 1966–68; Gov't. House Leader 1966–69; Corporate Counsel 1969–74; P. Cons. cand., Winnipeg S., fed. gen. el. 1974; Leader, Man. P.C. Party 1975–83; re-el. to Man. Leg. 2 Nov. 1976; re-el. 1977, 1981; ret'd March 1986; Premier of Manitoba (and Pres. of Extve. Council) 1977–81; Chrmn., Candn. Premiers Conf. 1980–81; Leader of Opposition 1976–77 and 1981–83; apptd. to Queen's Privy Council for Canada 1982; apptd. Court of Appeal (Man.) Dec. 1986; Chrmn., Candn. Counc. of Resource Ministers 1965–66; Chrmn., First Nat. Conf. on Pollution, Montreal 1966; Mem. Bd. of Regents, Univ. of Winnipeg 1972–76; Recipient of 25th Anniv. Outstanding Grad. Award, Univ. of Winnipeg Alumni Assn. 1973; Delegate, Commonwealth Parliamentary Assoc., Nigeria 1962, New Zealand 1979; Dir. & Officer, Ducks Unlimited (Canada) 1972–77; Hon. Life Mem., Winnipeg Trap & Skeet Club; Manitoba Wildlife Fedn.; Trustee, Delta Waterfowl Found.; Protestant; recreations: reading, hunting, fishing; Home: 705 South Dr., Winnipeg, Man. R3T 0C2; Office: The Law Courts, Winnipeg, Man. R3C 0V8.

**LYON, The Honourable Mr. Justice William Deneau,** B.A., LL.B.; judge; b. Toronto, Ont. 22 Oct. 1924; e. Vaughan Rd. C.I. 1943; St. Michael's Coll., Univ. of Toronto B.A. (Hon.) 1947 (Best All-Around Student SMC; U. of T. S.A.C. Gold Key Award); Univ. of Toronto Law Sch. LL.B. 1949; Osgoode Hall grad. 1950 (Gold Key Award); articled with John B. Hamilton, Q.C.; m. Margaret Mary Dandeneau 1949; six children; SUPERNUMERAY JUDGE, ONT. COURT OF JUSTICE (GENERAL DIV.) 1990– ; Lawyer, Hamilton, Torrance, Campbell and Lyon 1950–55; private practice 1955– ; Mem., County of York Law Assn.; Candn. Bar Assn.; Former Lecturer, Osgoode Hall; Judge, County and Distrit Courts of Ont. 1963; Pres., Ont. Co. Court Judges Assn.; Assoc. Chief Judge 1978; Chief Judge, County Court, Co. of York 1983; Chief Judge, Dist. Court of Ont. 1985; Mem., Municipal Council North York 1957–62 (retired) (Chair of all major cttes.); Former Mem., Candn. Judicial Council & Ont. Judicial Council; Chair, Oakville Police Comm. 1969–70; Chair, York Reg. Police Comm. 1971–78; several scholastic awards; Mem., Annunciation of Our Lady R.C. Ch.; Past Pres., Holy Name Soc.; Charter Mem. & Past Extve. Mem., Humber Valley Knights of Columbus; Former Mem., Adv. Sisters of the Good Shepherd; Mem., Bd. of Dir., Victorian Order of Nurses; Home: 112 Cassandra Blvd., Don Mills, Ont. M3A 1S9; Office: 361 University Ave., Toronto, Ont. M5G 1T3.

**LYONS, G. Jarvis;** real estate executive; b. Toronto, Ont. 13 Sept. 1922; s. Sigmund Elias and Fanny (Singer) L.; e. Univ. of Toronto Schs. (Grad. 1941); Univ. of Toronto, 1941–42; m. Elizabeth Ann, d. George Raymond Lehrer, Boston, Mass., 18 June 1955; children: Cynthia Lee, Gordon Raymond, Douglas Andrew; PRESIDENT, S.E. LYONS AND SON LTD. (Estbd. 1926) since 1959; joined the Co. in 1946 as a Salesman; subsequently apptd. Vice-Pres., served with R.C.N.V.R. retiring Jan. 1946 with rank of Lieut. R.C.N.(R); mem., Toronto Real Estate Bd. (Past Dir.); Jr. Bd. Trade, Toronto (Past Dir.); Soc. of Indust. and Office Realtors (Past Pres., S.I.O.R. Canada and V/P Dir., Internat.); Royal Candn. Mil. Inst.; Naval Offrs. Assn. Can. (Past Dir.); Reform Party; Unitarian; recreations: photography, travel, gardening, writing, music; Home: 1514 Kenneth Drive, Mississauga, Ont. L5E 2Y5; Office: 1515 Matheson Blvd. East, Ste. 205, Mississauga, Ont. L4W 2P5.

**LYONS, Jeffery Stephen,** Q.C., B.A., LL.B.; lawyer; b. Hamilton, Ont. 6 May 1940; s. Irwin and Frances (Agranove) L.; e. Hillfield Sch., Westdale Coll. Inst. Hamilton; Univ. of Toronto, B.A. 1961, LL.B. 1964; m. Sandra d. William and Dorothy Drevnig 4 July 1966; children: Heather, Stewart, Merrill; SR. PARTNER, FOGLER, RUBINOFF; Chrmn., KRG Management Inc. 1993– ; Chrmn. Toronto Transit Comn. 1987–89, Comnr. 1979–84, Vice Chrmn. 1984–87; Chrmn. Gray Coach Lines 1986–89; Chrmn. Trentway-Wagar (Properties) Inc. 1987–89; Dir., DeHavilland Aircraft Co. of Canada 1979–81; Dir., Eldorado Nuclear Ltd. 1985–88; Dir., Hanil Bank Canada 1991– ; Dir., Camvec Corp. 1992– ; Pres., Expo '98 Bid Consortium Inc. 1991–92; called to Bar of Ont. 1966; cr. Q.C. 1978; Bd. of Govs., North York General Hosp.; Bd. of Dirs., North York Performing Arts Centre 1992– ; Dir., World Film Festival Inc. 1991– ; Dir., Ontario Place Corporation 1992– ; Dir., Via Rail Canada Inc. 1993– ; Jewish; P. Conservative; Home: 2 Zaharias Court, North York, Ont. M2L 2H6; Office: Ste. 4400, P.O. Box 95, Royal Trust Tower, Toronto-Dominion Centre, Toronto, Ont. M5K 1G8.

**LYONS, Joseph Chisholm,** Q.C., B.A., M.B.A., LL.B.; barrister and solicitor; b. Halifax, N.S. 17 Oct. 1927; s. Dr. J. N. and Frances (Chisholm) L.; e. Pub. and High Sch., Halifax, N.S.; St. Francis Xavier Univ., B.A., 1948; Dalhousie Law Sch., LL.B. 1951; Harvard Grad. Sch. of Business Adm., M.B.A. 1953; m. Julianne, d. Mr. Justice W. D. Roach, 5 Oct. 1957; children: Julianne Frances; Catherine Ann, Patricia Gertrude, Joseph Chisholm, Elizabeth Chisholm, John Mark, Mathew; RESIDENT PARTNER IN HONG KONG, SMITH, LYONS, TORRANCE, STEVENSON & MAYER; Chrmn., Candn. Internat. School, Hong Kong; Vice-Chrmn. The Allen Group Inc. of N.Y.; Pres. Allan Group Canada Ltd.; Air King Ltd.; Dir. PPG Canada Inc.; Canadian Kawasaki Motors Ltd.; Browning-Ferris Industries Ltd.; Falk Canada Inc.; Chas. T. Main Canada Inc.; Prestonia Office Products Ltd.; read law with Stewart, McKeen & Covert, Halifax, N.S.; called to Bar of N.S., 1953; Bar of Ont., 1953; cr. Q.C. 1966; P. Conservative; R. Catholic; recreation: golf; Clubs: National; Toronto Golf; Discovery Bay Hong Kong; Office: 1218 Two Pacific Place, Queensway, Hong Kong.

**LYONS, Keiko Margaret,** B.A.; retired broadcasting executive; b. Mission City, B.C. 21 Nov. 1923; d. Yoshinobu and Teru (Tsuji) Inouye; e. McMaster Univ. B.A. (Econ.) 1949; m. Edward Ronald d. Seymour and Ethel L. 16 May 1949; children: Ruth Shizuka; Erskine Yoshio (dec.); News Clk., French News Desk, BBC European Service 1952; Program Asst. Japanese Service BBC 1953; Producer, BBC External Service 1954–60; Producer Publ. Affairs CBC 1960–63 (produced major radio biographies of J.S. Woodsworth, William Aberhardt, R.B. Bennett, Mitchell Hepburn, Frederich Philip Grove); Program Organiser 1964–68; Radio and TV Publ. Affairs and Extve. Producer Publ. Affairs Radio 1968–72; Head of Current Affairs 1972–76 (supervised introduction of As It Happens, This Country in the Morning, Quirks and Quarks); Program Dir. A.M. Radio Network 1976–80 (commissioned Sunday Morning and Daytime Radio Drama); Managing Dir. CBC Radio 1981–82; VIce Pres. English Radio Networks, Candn. Broadcasting Corp. 1982–86; Dir., CBC, London 1986–89; Mem., Toronto Planning Advisory Ctte. 1991–93; Home: 9 Buller Ave., Toronto, Ont. M4L 1B9.

**LYONS, Kenneth Lea,** B.Sc., P.Eng., M.B.A.; executive; b. Calgary, Alta. 12 Oct. 1938; s. Leslie John and Lillian Emily (Grainger) L.; e. Univ. of Alta. B.Sc. Mech. Engr. 1961; York Univ. M.B.A. 1971; m. Lynne d. Robert and Erma Clayton 3 Sept. 1960; children: Scott, Ian, David; PRES. & CHIEF OPERATING OFFR., LAIDLAW WASTE SYSTEMS INC. 1991– ; part-time Lectr. and Faculty Adv. York Univ.; Engr. Fin. and Mktg. positions Canadian General Electric 1961; Cons. Woods Gordon 1968; Lectr. York Univ. 1970; Sr. Mktg. Extve. Consumer Products Canadian General Electric 1971, Sr. Mktg. Extve. Lighting 1976, Sr. Mktg. Extve. Constrn. Products 1978, Gen. Mgr. Housewares & Audio 1982, Vice-Pres. 1983; Pres. and Gen. Mgr. Black and Decker Canada Inc. 1984; Pres. & C.O.O., Scott's Hospitality Inc. 1986–90; Pres., Passenger Services Group, Laidlaw Inc. 1990–92; recreations: golf, curling; Clubs: Lambton Golf & Country; Fitness Inst.; Home: 6 Woodvalley Dr., Islington, Ont. M9A 4H1; Office: 3221 North Service Rd., P.O. Box 5028, Burlington, Ont. L7R 3Y8.

**LYSYK, Hon. Kenneth Martin,** B.A., LL.B., B.C.L.; judge; b. Weyburn, Sask. 1 July 1934; s. Michael and Anna (Maradyn) L.; e. McGill Univ. B.A. 1954; Univ. of Sask. LL.B. 1957, Oxford Univ. B.C.L. 1960; m. Patricia Irene d. R.M. Kinnon, Lumsden, Sask. 2 Oct. 1959; three d. Joanne Rene, Karen Michele (d. Oct. 1979), Stephanie Patricia; JUDGE, SUPREME COURT BRITISH COLUMBIA Jan. 1 1983– , also Depy. Judge, Supreme Court of the Yukon Territory and Depy. Judge, Supreme Court of the Northwest Territories; formerly Dean and Prof. at Law, Univ. of B.C., 1976–82; Chrmn. Alaska Highway Pipeline Inquiry 1977 (on leave from Univ. of B.C.); Sole Commnr., Yukon Electoral Boundaries Commission 1991; called to Bar of Sask. 1959, B.C. 1965, Yukon 1977; cr. Q.C. 1973; Lectr. Faculty of Law, Univ. of B.C. 1960, Asst. Prof. 1962, Assoc. Prof. 1965, Prof. 1968–70; Adviser, Privy Council Office (Constitutional Review Sec.) Govt. of Can., Ottawa 1969–70 (on leave from Univ. of B.C.); Prof. of Law, Univ. of Toronto 1970–72; Depy. Atty. Gen. Govt. of Sask. 1972–76; mem., Internat. Comn. of Jurists, Can. Sec. (Vice-Pres. for B.C. 1992–93; Candn. Inst. for the Admin. of Justice (Pres. 1989–91); Candn. Bar Assoc.; Home: 3157 Point Grey Rd., Vancouver, B.C. V6K 1B3;

Office: The Law Courts, 800 Smithe St., Vancouver, B.C. V6Z 2E1.

# M

**MacADAM, Donald H.;** electronics executive; b. Spring Lake, N.J. 3 Nov. 1946; s. Hugh James and Gertrude Anna (Sack) MacA.; e. Rollins Coll.; Univ. of Fla.; m. Diane d. Edward and Helen Halliday 30 May 1967; children: Lenore Elizabeth, Lawrence Donald; CHAIRMAN & PRES., ANNULUS TECHNICAL INDUSTRIES, INC. 1986– : Salesman, Canadian Electronics Ltd. 1969–72; Sales Mgr. Vancouver, L.A. Varah Ltd. 1972–74; Gen. Mgr. Calgary 1975–77; Vice-Pres. Hamilton 1978–81; Chrmn. & Pres. 1982–86; Dir., CRS Plus Inc.; Q4 Instruments Inc.; Mt. Forest Investments Ltd.; inventor of stressed elliptical contact system for electronic switches – 5 issued patents; author numerous articles in various trade mags.; Home: 318 Grace St., Port Dover, Ont. N0A 1N0.

**MACAULAY, Hugh L.,** B.A.; executive; b. Toronto, Ont.; s. Leopold and Hazel Charlton (Haight) M.; e. Univ. of W. Ont. B.A. (Journalism) 1948; m. Dorothy Jean Taylor 11 Sept. 1946; children: Barbara (Mrs. F. W. Hacker), Robert James, Andrew Taylor; CHRMN., CANDN. TIRE CORP. 1984– ; joined Public and Industrial Relations Ltd. 1948–52; Ford Motor Co. 1952–54; Lawrence Motors Ltd. 1954–55; Owner, York Mills Pontiac Ltd. and York Mills Leasing Ltd. 1955–70; Vice Chrmn. Ont. Hydro 1979; Chrmn. Comte. on Organ. Ont. P. Cons. Party 1971–76; mem. and Chrmn. of Bd. Ryerson Polytech. Inst. 1964–71; mem. Comn. on Post-Secondary Educ. 1969–71; Chrmn., Ont. Hydro 1979–83; Chrmn. Candn. Tire Corp. 1984, C.E.O. 1985–87; Mem., Bd. of Govs., York Univ.; served with RCNVR 1943–45; recreation: golf; Clubs: Rosedale Golf; John's Island (Vero Beach, Fla.); Office: Box 770, Station K, Toronto, Ont. M4P 2V8.

**MACAULAY, I. Hamish,** B.Comm.; investment counsellor; b. England 18 July 1936; e. McGill Univ. B.Comm. 1963; children: Ian, Fiona; FOUNDER & PRESIDENT, MACAULAY ASSET MANAGEMENT 1989– ; 25 years of investment experience with expertise in both Candn. & U.S. consumer growth & natural resource related companies; Price Waterhouse 1963–66; Investment Analyst and Portfolio Mgr., Royal Securities 1966–69; CN Pension Fund 1969–72; founded Lank Roberton Macaulay 1973; recreation: tennis; clubs: Hillside Tennis, University Club of Montreal; Home: 1227 Sherbrooke St. W., Apt. 24, Montreal, Que. H3G 1G1; Office: 1155 Metcalfe St., Ste. 967, Montreal, Que. H3B 2V6.

**MACAULAY, James Archibald,** LL.B., Q.C.; barrister and solicitor; b. Montreal, Que. 30 Dec. 1928; s. Archibald Francis and Laura Seymour (McFadden) M.; e. Univ. of Brit. Columbia LL.B. 1956; m. Alice d. C.H. and Marie Locke 22 Nov. 1958; children: Hugh, Mary, Anne, Thomas, Sarah; FOUNDER & PARTNER, MACAULAY MCCOLL, BARRISTERS 1970– ; Lt. 2 Bn P.P.C.L.I., service in Korea 1951; called to B.C. Bar 1957; Partner, Cumming, Bird, Richards 1963–69; career in civil litigation incl. Sr. Counsel in the major B.C. Indian Land Claim Cases, med. malpractice & product liability litigation; Mem., Bd. of Dir., Air Canada 1985–88; Fellow, Am. Coll. of Trial Lawyers; Comnr., Internat. Joint Comn.; Chair, B.C. Campaign Ctte. (P.C. Party) 1984, '88; Mem., Candn. Bar Asn.; Q.C. B.C. 1983; Pres., Vancouver Art Gallery 1970–71 (Bd. Mem. several years); Roman Catholic; Mem., P.C. Party; Friends of Chamber Music (Bd. Mem. several years); Selden Soc.; clubs: Vancouver, Albion, Union; Office: 600-840 Howe St., Vancouver, B.C. V6Z 2L2.

**MacAULAY, John Blair,** B.A., LL.B.; b. Winnipeg, Man. 13 March 1934; s. John Alexander and Phyllis Ardelle (McPherson) MacA.; e. Pub. Schs. and Ravenscourt Sch., Winnipeg; Univ. of Man., B.A.; Man. Law Sch., LL.B.; m. Margaret Mary Elizabeth (Libby), d. W. Archie Bell, Winnipeg, Man. 10 June 1960; children: Alix Elizabeth, Robin Carol, John Christopher, Lesley Barbara; PARTNER, FRASER & BEATTY; Chrmn. & Dir., The Trust Company of Bank of Montreal; Dir., Bank of Montreal; The Great-West Life Assnce. Co.; Moffat Communications Ltd.; Fed. Industries Ltd.; Cambridge Shopping Centres Ltd.; Trustee, Art Gallery of Ontario; Mem. Adv. Bd., Sotheby's (Can.); read law with former Chief Justice R.G.B. Dickson; called to Bar of Man. 1960, Bar of Ont. 1977; recreations: reading, sailing, electronics; Club: Toronto; Home: 1126 Morrison Heights Dr., Oakville, Ont. L6J 4J1; Office: Box 100, First Canadian Place, Toronto, Ont. M5X 1B2.

**MacBAIN, John Howard,** B.A., M.A., M.B.A.; business executive; b. Niagara Falls, Ont. 13 Feb. 1958; s. Arthur Allister and Viola Rachel (Kennedy) M.; e. A.N. Myer S.S. 1977; McGill Univ. B.A. (Hons. Econ.) 1980; Oxford Univ. (Rhodes Scholar, Quebec and Wadham) B.A. (Law) 1982, M.A. (Law) 1986; Harvard Univ. M.B.A. 1984; Pres. A.N. Myer S.S. Student Govt. 1976–77; Principal's Cup 1977; Distinction Swimming Award 1977; activities at McGill Univ.: Chrmn. Welcome Week 1978; Gov. 1979–80; Senator 1979–80; Chrmn. Winter Carnival 1979; Pres., Students' Soc. 1979–80; Scarlet Key Award 1979; Grad. Soc. Student Award 1980; Valedictorian 1980; m. Louise Thérèse Viger Blouin; OWNER, PRES. & C.E.O., HEBDO MAG INC. 1987– , publisher of over 65 magazines and cable TV programmes in Canada, France, Sweden, Poland and the United States under the names Auto Trader, Auto Hebdo, La Centrale des Particuliers; Dir. and major shareholder: Bélanger Laminates 1989–92, Arpan 1989–92; Dir. of Mktg., Power Financial Corp. and Power Corp. of Canada 1984–87; Bus. Cons., The Boston Cons. Group (Paris) 1983; Extve. Asst. to Gen. Counsel, Candn. Gen. Electric 1982; Asst. Devel. Offr., Cadillac Fairview Corp. Ltd. 1980; Founder, Pres. and C.E.O., 391921 Ontario Inc. 1976–80; Vol., Boys' and Girls' Club of Niagara Falls 1974–77; Commercial Pilot License 1977; Shriners Hosp. for Crippled Children 1979; Captain Oxford Univ. Varsity Ice Hockey 1981–82; Hon. Sec. Jeunes Associés du Musée des Beaux Arts de Montréal 1984–87; Dir., Editorial Bd., McGill News 1986–88; Chrmn., Montreal YMCA Youth Enterprise Centre 1986–88; recreations: flying, skiing, swimming, ice hockey, tennis; Clubs: University (non-resident); Hillside; Badminton and Squash Club; Maxim's Business Club (Paris); Offices: 12 bis, ave. Bosquet, 75007 Paris, France and 130 de Liège East, Montréal, Qué. H2P 1J1.

**MACBETH, Robert Alexander Leslie,** B.A., M.D., M.Sc., D.Sc. (Hon.); F.R.C.S.(C), F.A.C.S.; academic surgeon and association executive; b. Edmonton, Alta. 26 Aug. 1920; s. late Alfred William and late Agnes DeLena (Lewis) M.; e. Westmount and Victoria High Schs. Edmonton 1938; Univ. of Alta. B.A. 1942, M.D. 1944; McGill Univ. M.Sc. 1947, Dipl. in Surg. 1952; Univ. of Alta. D.Sc. (Hon.) 1988; m. Monique Elizabeth d. late Philippe Filliol 10 Aug. 1949; children: Michèle Agnes (Cliff), Nicole Elizabeth (Curtis), Danielle Monique (Hawthorn), Joanne Leslie (Cameron); internship: Univ. of Alta. Hosp. and Royal Alexandra Hosp. Edmonton 1943–45; Fellow in Endocrinol. McGill Univ. 1946–47, Teaching Fellow in Anat. 1947–48; Surg. Residency: Montreal Gen. Hosp. and Royal Victoria Hosp. 1948–49, 1951–52; Children's Mem. Hosp. Montreal 1949–50; Postgrad. Med. Sch. Hosp. London, Eng. 1950–51; Instr. in Clin. Surg. 1953–54 and Clin. Lectr. in Surg. 1954–57 Univ. of Alta., Assoc. Prof. of Surg. 1957–60, Prof. and Chrmn. of Surg. 1960–75, Emeritus Prof. of Surg. 1986– Univ. of Alta.; Dir. of Surg. Services Univ. of Alta. Hosp. 1960–75; Assoc. Dean and Prof. of Surg. Dalhousie Univ. 1975–77; Dir. of Postgrad. Med. Educ. N.B. 1975–77; Extve. Vice Pres., Candn. Cancer Soc. and National Cancer Inst. of Can. 1977–85; Extve. Dir, Hannah Inst. for the History of Med. 1987–91; mem. Active Staff Royal Alexandra Hosp. 1953–57; Univ. of Alta. Hosp. 1953–75; Saint John (N.B.) Gen Hosp. 1975–77; Consulting Staff, Edmonton Gen. Hosp., Miseracordia Hosp. and Royal Alexandra Hosp. Edmonton 1957–75; Surg. Consultant Dept. Veterans Affairs Col. Mewburn Hosp. Edmonton 1957–75; mem. Bd. Examiners Med. Council Can. (Surg.) 1958–60; Bd. Surg. Examiners 1960–65, mem. Council 1972–76, Royal Coll. Phys. & Surgs.; Examiner in Surg. Trinity Coll. Dublin 1968; Visiting Prof. Am. Sch. for Classical Studies Athens 1972; Prof. Etranger, Service de Pathologie Experimentale, Institut Pasteur, Paris 1972–73; Visiting Prof. Polish Acad. of Sciences Warsaw 1975; External Examiner and Visiting Prof. of Surg. Univ. of W. Indies 1976; rec'd Mosher Mem. Medal and Harrison Prize Univ. of Alta. 1944; Nat. Research Council Can. Research Fellowship 1946–47; Nuffield Foundation Travelling Fellowship 1950–51; James IV Surg. Assn. Travelling Fellowship 1965; Distinguished Medical Alumnus Award, Univ. of Alta. 1985; Award of Merit, Int'l Union Against Cancer 1986; Hon. Mem., Can. Assn. Gen. Surgs. 1988; Hon. Life Mem., Can. Soc. Hist. Med. 1993; Dir.: Nat. Cancer Inst. Can. 1972–77; Candn. Council on Hosp. Accreditation 1977–82 (Pres. 1980–81); Associated Medical Services (Ont.) 1984–87; served with Royal Candn. Army Med. Corps 1943–46, rank Capt.; author over 70 articles, book chapters various publs.; mem. Ed. Bd. 'Canadian Journal of Surgery' 1960–80; Hon. mem. Flint Acad. of Surg. 1969; Corr. mem. Polish Acad. Surg. 1973; Pres. Edmonton Chapter 1968–69, mem. Bd. Govs. 1974–80, Chrmn. Alta. Adv. Bd. 1960–75 Am. Coll. Surgs.; mem. of Council, 1978–86, Chrmn., Cancer Educ. in the Workplace Project 1984– , Int'l Union Against Cancer; mem. Acad. Med. Toronto (Archivist 1986–89); Am. Assn. Hist. Med.; Am. Surg. Assn.; Can. Assn. Gastroenterol.; Can. Assn. Gen. Surgs.; Can. Oncology Soc.; Can. Soc. Hist. Med. (Sec. Treas. 1988–92); Can. Soc. Clin. Investigation (Pres. 1971, mem. Council 1966–72); James IV Assn. Surgs. (Dir. 1982–87, Vice-Pres. 1984–87); Internat. Surg. Group (Treas. 1982–88); Soc. Univ. Surgs.; Surg. Biol. Club II; W. Surg. Assn. (U.S.A.); Phi Kappa Pi (Past Pres.); Alpha Omega Alpha; United Church; recreations: medical history, philately; Home: 1 Concorde Place, Apt. 1506, Don Mills, Ont. M3C 3K6.

**MacBURNIE, Royden J.,** B.Com., F.C.A., F.T.I.; retired trust company executive; b. Halifax, N.S. 19 March 1929; e. Dalhousie Univ., B.Com. 1951; C.A. 1953; m. Marion 1956; four s. John, James, Craig, Stephen; Dir., Central Guaranty Trust Co. 1986–91; Auditor, Nightingale, Hayman & Co. 1951–55; Price Waterhouse & Co. 1955–60; Comptroller, Eastern Trust Co. 1960–64; Comptroller, Dep. Gen. Mgr. Central Trust Co. of Canada 1964–74; Regional Vice Pres. Central & Nova Scotia Trust Co. 1974–76; Vice Pres. Central and Eastern Trust Co. 1976–80; Extve. Vice Pres., Finance Central Trust Co. 1980–88; Vice Chrmn., Central Trust Co. 1988; Extve. Vice Pres., Finance Central Capital Corp. 1986–88; Extve. Vice Pres., Nova Scotia Savings & Loan Co. 1986–88; mem. Financial Extves. Inst. Can.; Ducks Unlimited; Inst. C.A.'s N.S.; recreations: golf, hunting, fishing; Clubs: Rotary; Halifax; Brightwood Golf & Country; Dartmouth Trap & Skeet; Home: 60 Kingston Cres., Dartmouth, N.S. B3A 2M2.

**MACCABÉE IQBAL, Françoise,** B.A., B.Ed., Ph.D.; writer; b. Quebec; d. Rodrigue and Hermance (Limoges) Maccabée; e. Univ. of Montreal B.A. 1962, B.Ed. 1963; Univ. of B.C. Ph.D. 1972; divorced; one d.: Isabeau Iqbal; Professor, Dept. of French, Univ. of B.C. 1975–86; Writing & Publishing Officer, The Canada Council 1987–90; Mem., ALCQ/ACQL (learned society), Administrator 1974–75, 1976–78, 1982–86; UNEQ 1990– ; author: 'Hubert Aquin Romancier' 1978, 'Desafinado. Otobiographie de Hubert Aquin' 1987; recreations: biking, yoga, travelling, creative dancing; Home: 454, Willowdale, #18, Outremont, Que. H3T 1H3.

**MacCONNELL, James MacLellan,** B.A.; business executive; b. New Glasgow 8 Apr. 1940; s. Thomas Cumming and Helen Sophia (MacLellan) M.; e. Pictou Acad. gr. 12 1957; Dalhousie Univ. B.A. 1961; m. Dorothy d. Archie and Ann Gillis 9 Nov. 1963; children: Diane, Kim, Nancy, Susan; PRES. & CHIEF EXTVE. OFFR., SCOTSBURN CO-OP. SERVICES LTD. 1973– ; Texaco Canada Ltd. 1961–64; joined present firm as Sales Mgr., later Asst. Gen. Mgr. and then Gen. Mgr.; Chrmn. & Pres., Brookfield Foods Ltd.; Pres., Braxco Ltd.; Chrmn., Brookfield Ice Cream; Dir., The Co-operators Group; National Dairy Counc.; Chrmn., Pictou Reg. Devel. Comn., Bd. Mem., Dalhousie Med. Rsch. Found.; Canadian Manufacturers (N.S. region); Elder, Bethel Presbyn. Ch.; recreations: golf, tennis; clubs: Abercrombie Golf, Scotsburn Recreation; Home: P.O. Box 354, Scotsburn, N.S. B0K 1R0; Office: Box 340, Scotsburn, N.S. B0K 1R0.

**MacCORMAC, Donald George,** B.Comm., M.B.A.; civil service commissioner; b. Summerside, P.E.I. 18 Dec. 1941; s. Wilfred Francis and Mabel Josephine (Noonan) M.; e. St. Dunstan's Univ. B.Comm. 1963; Queen's Univ. M.B.A. 1965; m. Katherine d. Dan and Agnes McGinn 27 Aug. 1966; children: Dan, Pamela (deceased); LECTURER, THE SCHOOL OF BUSINESS ADMINISTRATION, UNIV. OF P.E.I.; Mngt. Hawker Siddeley Ltd. 1965–68; Mgr. Personnel & Indus. Relns., Candn. Bridge Works 1968–70; Dir., Staff Devel. & Training, Civil Serv. of P.E.I. 1970; Vis. Lectr., Sch. of Bus., Univ. of P.E.I. 1972; Asst. Sec. Cabinet (Intergovt. Affairs), Govt. of P.E.I. 1980; Chrmn., Civil Service Commission, P.E.I. 1981; arbitrator / consultant / sessional university lecturer; Former Mem., Bd. of Gov., St. Dunstan's Univ; former elected mem., Unit 3 Sch. Bd.; former Vice-Chrmn., Queen Elizabeth Hosp. Found.; R.C.; Home: 12 Selkirk Cres., Charlottetown, P.E.I. C1A 3R6; Office: 550 Univ. Ave., Charlottetown, P.E.I. C1A 4P3.

**MacCORMACK, John Ronald,** B.A., M.A., Ph.D.; university professor/administrator; b. Halifax, N.S. 20th Jan. 1920; s. Allan John and Ida (Cameron) M.; e. Saint Mary's Coll.; Halifax Acad. 1933–39; Dalhousie Univ. B.A. 1948, M.A. 1949; Univ. of London 1952–55;

Univ. of Toronto Ph.D. 1960; m. Ann-Vibeke d. Stanley and Karen Bailey 17 Aug. 1957; children: Kirsten, Allan, Elizabeth, John; DIR., INST. OF HUMAN VALUES, SAINT MARY'S UNIV. 1975– ; enlisted Royal Candn. Artillery 1939; comnd. offr. 1941; 3rd Light Anti-Aircraft Reg., R.C.A. 1943–45 in England, France, Germany; Liaison Offr., H.Q. 2nd Candn. Inf. Div. 1944–45; Lectr., Saint Mary's Univ. 1956; Chair, Dept. of Hist., S.M.U. 1960–69; Prof. of Hist. 1969 (retired 1985); Mem., Acad. Senate 1971–74; Bd. of Gov. 1971–74; SSRCC fellowship 1954; Can. Counc. Leave Fellowship 1962, 1969, 1978 (SSHRC); Professor Emeritus 1988; Pres., S.M.U. Fac. Assn. 1963–65; Mem., Nat. Counc., C.A.U.T. 1963–66; SSHRC doct. fellowship ctte. 1978–83; Co-Founder, N.S. Conf. of Univ. Fac. Assn. 1965; nat. & internat. conf. organizer 1976– ; Roman Catholic; Mem., Candn. Hist. Assn.; Candn. Pol. Sci. Assn.; author: 'Revolutionary Politics in the Long Parliament' 1973; recreations: tennis, swimming; Club: Waegwoltic; Home: 1147 Dalhousie St., Halifax, N.S. B3H 3W5; Office: Inst. of Human Values, Saint Mary's Univ., Halifax, N.S. B3H 3C3.

**MacCRIMMON, Kenneth Robert,** B.S., M.B.A., Ph.D.; educator; b. Hamilton, Ont. 28 Dec. 1937; s. Archibald Robert and Dorothy Anna (Williams) MacC.; e. Univ. of Calif. Los Angeles B.S. 1959, M.B.A. 1960, Ph.D. 1965; m. Marilyn Louise d. Marion Francis Turner, Burbank, Calif. 3 Feb. 1962; children: Karyn Alene, Keith Stuart, Brian Cameron; PROFESSOR OF COMMERCE & BUSINESS ADMIN., UNIV. OF B.C.; Asst. and Assoc. Prof. Grad. Sch. of Indust. Adm. Carnegie-Mellon Univ. 1964–70; Prof. of Comm. and Business Adm. present Univ. 1970– , and Asst. Dean Fac. of Grad. Studies 1978–79; J.L. Kellogg Distinguished Prof. of Strategy & Decision, Grad. Sch. of Mgmt., Northwestern Univ. 1980–82; Earle Douglas MacPhee Prof. of Management, Univ. of B.C. 1981; Visiting Prof., Shanghai Jiao Tong Univ., China 1985; Can. Council Sabbatical Leave Fellow 1975–76, 1983–84; Fellow, Internat. Inst. of Mgmt., Berlin 1977; Consultant, The Rand Corp., Santa Monica 1962–70; rec'd McKinsey Foundation Research Design Award 1966; author 'Taking Risks' 1986; numerous articles various publs.; mem. Candn. Assn. Univ. Teachers; Econometric Soc.; Inst. Mgmt. Sciences; Am. Econ. Assn.; Operations Research Soc.; Beta Gamma Sigma; Home: 4593 West Sixth Ave., Vancouver, B.C. V6R 1V4; Office: David Lam Management Library, Rm 520, 2033 Main Mall, Vancouver, B.C. V6T 1Z2.

**MacCULLOCH, Patrick Campbell;** mining executive; b. Bedford, Engl. 11 Oct. 1928; s. James Campbell and Doris May (Hammond); e. Bedford Sch.; London Sch. of Econ.; m. Maureen d. James and Anne McMillan 9 Feb. 1957; children: Stephen, Gillian, Sarah, Ian; PRES., PEAK BUSINESS CONSULTANTS; Dir., Hemlo Gold Mines Inc.; Dir., Morgan Bank of Canada; Seaside Cable T.V. Ltd.; Brit. Army, Royal Signals, Lieut.; Dir. Selection Trust Ltd., London, Engl. 1967–80, served in U.K., Zambia, Australia, U.S.A., Can.; Pres. Selco Inc. 1970–83; Sr. Vice-Pres. & Dir., BP Canada Inc. 1983–89; Dir., Inst. of Corp. Dirs. in Can.; Fellow, Inst. of Corp. Dir., London, Engl.; Clubs: Ontario; Arts and Letters; Caledon Ski; Albany; Office: 77 St. Clair Ave. E., #2008, Toronto, Ont. M4T 1M5.

**MacDERMAID, Darryl Frederick,** B.Comm., M.B.A., U.E.L.; university administrator; b. Picton, Ont. 15 July 1940; s. Arthur Charles and Gena M.; e. Carleton Univ. B.Comm. 1966; Queen's Univ. M.B.A. 1973; m. M. Anne d. Roland and Grace Stalker 2 July 1966; one s. Dugal Arthur George; DIR. OF INVESTMENTS & INSUR., QUEEN'S UNIV. 1984– ; trainee, Candn. Imperial Bank of Commerce 1960–66; Asst. Mgr., Yonge & Bloor 1966–67; Finan. Analyst, Queen's Univ. 1967–73; Asst. Bursar 1973–78; Dir. of Resource Planning 1978–84; Mem., Investment Ctte., Queen's Theol. Coll.; Univ. Medalist in Commerce, Carleton Univ. 1966; Mem., Munic. Counc., Twp. of South Fred.; Bd. of Stewards, Conway Un. Ch.; Chrmn., Kingston & District United Way Campaign 1989; Bd. of Dirs. Kingston District United Way; author: 'Agricultural Bargaining Structures in Contemporary Ontario' 1973; recreations: skiing, sailing, travel, farming; clubs: District Commissioner of Scouts, Boy Scouts of Canada; Rotarian; Home: R.R. 1, Bath, Ont. K0H 1G0; Office: Rm. 316 Rideau Bldg., Queen's Univ., Kingston, Ont. K7L 3N6.

**MACDIARMID, William D.,** B.A., M.D., FRCPC, FACP; physician / professor (ret'd); consultant; b. Arcola, SK 22 June 1926; s. John Angus and Evaline (Reed) M.; e. Univ. of Sask., B.A. 1947; Univ. of Toronto, M.D. 1949; internship Grey Nun's Hosp., Regina, SK; postgrad. training, Internal Med., Endocrinol., Univ. of Utah (1958–62) & Human Gen., Univ. Coll. Hosp. Med. Sch., London (U.K.) 1962–64 (Rsch. Assoc.); m. Bette N. d. Mabel and Walter Brown 16 May 1953; children: John A., Margaret A., Donald G., Andrew L.; INDEPENDENT CONSULTANT IN HEALTH CARE SYSTEMS 1991– ; family physician, Regina, SK 1950–53; Shaunavon, SK 1953–58; Instr., Asst. then Assoc. Prof., Univ. of Utah 1964–69; Prof. of Med. & Head, Dept. of Med., St. Boniface Gen. Hosp. 1969–75; Memorial Univ. of Nfld. & Physician-in-Chief, St. John's Gen. Hosp. 1975–79; Univ. of Man. 1979–85; Vis. Prof. of Pediatrics, Univ. of Calif SF 1985–86; Prof. of Med., Human Gen. & Pediatrics, Univ. of Manitoba 1986–91; Pres., Swift Current & Dist. Med. Soc. 1956–57; Bd. Mem., Man. Med. Assn. 1981–83, 1987–91 (Chrmn. 1982–83; Hon. Treas. 1982–83, 1989–90; Hon. Sec. 1988–89; Chrmn., Ethics Ctte. 1987–91); Mem., CMA Ethics Ctte. 1987–91; Bd., Ctte. on Accreditation of Candn. Med. Schools (Chrmn. 1988–91); Rep. to Liaison Ctte. for Med. Edn. in U.S.A. 1988–91; Cons., Man. Dept. of Health 1988–89; Chrmn., Ethics Adv. Ctte., Health Sciences Centre of Winnipeg, 1989–91; Bd. Mem., various United churches 1955–83; Elder; Mt. Olympus Prebyn. Ch., Utah 1966–69; recreations: gardening, swimming, travel, volunteer work; Address: 4142 Cortez Place, Victoria, B.C. V8N 4R5.

**MacDONALD, Alan Hugh,** B.A., B.L.S.; librarian; b. Ottawa, Ont. 3 March 1943; s. Vincent C. and Hilda (Durney) MacD.; e. Saint Patrick's High Sch. Halifax; Dalhousie Univ. B.A. 1963; Univ. of Toronto B.L.S. 1964; DIR. INFORMATION SERVICES 1988– ; University of Calgary "Orator" 1989– ; joined Dalhousie Univ. 1964–78 serving as Documents Librarian, Asst. to Dir., Law Librarian, Asst. Univ. Librarian, Health Sciences Librarian; Lectr. Sch. of Lib. Service 1969–78; Visiting Lectr. South Australian Inst. of Technol. 1975; Librarian, N.S. Barristers' Soc. 1969–74; mem. Nat. Lib. Adv. Bd. 1972–76; Dir. of Libraries, Univ. of Calgary 1979–92; Min.'s Adv. Comte. on Univ. Affairs Alta. 1979–83; Pres. Teled Video Services 1972–74; mem. Univ. of Calgary Senate 1980–85; Fellow, Council on Lib. Resources 1975–76; Extve. Fellow, Univ. Microfilms Inc. 1986; mem. Bd. of Mgmt., Univ. of Calgary Press, 1981– ; Dir. Univ. of Calgary Press 1984–90; Chrmn., Alta Lib. Network Assembly, 1981–86; Mem., Editorial Bd., 'America: History and Life' (ABC-CLIO Press) 1985– ; Alberta Advanced Education Ctte. on Copyright Collectives, 1989– ; recipient Distinguished Academic Librarian Award, Candn. Assoc. of Coll. and Univ. Libraries 1988; President's Award, Library Assn. of Alberta 1992; author numerous papers, articles and addresses on libraries and information science; mem. Candn. Lib. Assn. (Treas. 1977–79, Vice Pres./Pres. 1979–81); Candn. Assn. Information Science (Pres. 1979–80); Assn. for Candn. Studies; Candn. Assn. of Rsch. Lib. (Extve. Bd. 1981–86; Vice-Pres. 1985–86); Atlantic Provs. Lib. Assn. (Pres. 1976–77); Candn. Health Libs. Assn. (Treas. 1976–79); Lib. Assn. Alta. (Vice-Pres. 1988–90); Australian Library and Information Assn. (Assoc.); N.Z. Lib. Assn.; Candn. Assn. Law Libs.; Candn. Civil Liberties Assn.; Alberta Found. for the Candn. Music Center (Bd. mem. 1985–92); Bibliographic Soc. of Canada; Vice-Pres., Candn. Inst. for Historical Microreproductions 1992– (Bd. mem. 1990– ); Home: 536 27th Avenue N.E., Calgary, Alta. T2E 2A6; Office: 2500 University Dr. N.W., Calgary, Alta. T2N 1N4.

**MACDONALD, Alan Roderic,** B.Sc., M.B.A.; senior banking officer; b. Saint John, N.B. 4 Feb. 1952; s. Dr. Roderic Glencross and Lois Barbara (Rising) M.; e. Bishops College School 1969; Dalhousie Univ. B.Sc. 1972; Univ. of Toronto M.B.A. 1987; m. Linda d. Arthur and Mary Hamm 29 Dec. 1973; children: Mahri Jane, Ryan Roderic; SENIOR VICE PRES., BANKING OPERATIONS, THE BANK OF NOVA SCOTIA 1990– ; joined Management Training Program, Scotiabank 1972; Branch Admin./Opns. positions in Saint John & Moncton, N.B. 1972–76; Extve. Office, Audit Dept. 1976–80; Regional Comptroller, Alta. 1980–82; Dir., Domestic Opns. 1982–86; Extve. Asst. to Extve. Vice-Pres. of Canada 1986–88; Asst. Gen. Mgr., Atlantic Canada Region 1988–90; recreations: golf, tennis, swimming; clubs: The Fitness Inst., Toronto Bd. of Trade; Home: 1191 Rushbrooke Dr., Oakville, Ont. L6M 1H8; Office: 44 King St. W., Toronto, Ont. M5H 1H1.

**MACDONALD, Hon. Alexander Barrett,** Q.C., M.L.A., B.A., LL.B.; journalist, author & broadcaster; b. Vancouver, B.C. 21 Oct. 1918; s. the late Chief Justice Malcolm Archibald and Ida (Williams) M.; e. Univ. of B.C., B.A.; Osgoode Hall Law Sch., LL.B.; m. Dorothy Anne, d. Collis Bower Lewis and Alix (Parrott), Ottawa, Ont. 4 Nov. 1944; one d. Christina Anne (Mrs. Adriaan de Jong); ADJUNCT PROF., POL. SCI., SIMON FRASER UNIV. 1987– ; speaker on CBC Radio; A.-G. for B.C. 1972–75; Min. Industry Trade and Commerce 1973; called to Bar of B.C.; cr. Q.C. 1972; former Parlty Secy. to Hon. M.J. Coldwell; el. to H. of C. for Vancouver-Kingsway; el. M.L.A. Vancouver-East in prov. g.e. 1960; re-el. in gen. el. 1963, 1966, 1969, 1972, 1975, 1979 and 1983; Opposition Critic on Intergovernmental Relations; NDP; presently Asst. Prof. in Political Science, Simon Fraser Univ.; author: 'My Dear Legs: Letters to a Young Social Democrat' 1985; 'Alex in Wonderland' 1993; Anglican; recreations: squash, tennis, badminton, fishing, classical music, reading; Home: 3461 Pt. Grey Rd., Vancouver, B.C. V6R 1A6.

**MacDONALD, Allan Sullivan,** M.D.; surgeon/university professor; b. Antigonish, N.S. 9 Apr. 1939; s. James Ronald Arthur and Laura (McNeil) M.; e. Aylmer H.S. 1955; St. Patrick's Coll. 1955–56; St. Francis Xavier Univ. 1956–58; Dalhousie Univ. M.D. 1963; m. Lorna d. Elizabeth and Earl Morrison 3 July 1965; children: Katriona, Sara, Neil; PROF. OF SURGERY, DALHOUSIE UNIV. 1986– ; Intern, N.S. & Nfld. 1962–63; Surgery Res., Victoria Gen. Hosp. 1963–67; Rsch. Fellow, Harvard Med. Sch. & Surg. Asst., P.B. Brigham Hosp. 1967–69; Asst. Prof. of Surg., present Univ. 1969–71; Surg. Cons., Addenbrooke's Hosp. & Physiol. Tutor, Trinity Hall, Cambridge Univ. U.K. 1971–72; Surg., Victoria Gen. Hosp.; N.S. Tumour Clinic; Visiting Surg., Halifax Infirmary; Surg. Cons., Camp Hill Hosp.; I.W.K. Hosp. for Sick Children 1972– ; Dir., Transplantation Lab. present Univ. 1969–82; Dir., Surg. Rsch. 1982–84; I.W.K. Med. Staff prize 1962; Sr. Intern, V.G. Hosp. 1962; Fellow, Royal Coll. of Physicians & Surg. of Can. 1967; I.W. Killam Scholar 1967; J.D. Tory Found. Sch. 1967–69; M.R.C. Cent. Fellow, Univ. of Cambridge 1971–72; Chrmn. & mem. numerous cttes.; recipient several rsch. grants; mem., N.S. Med. Soc.; Candn. Transp. Soc.; Candn. Oncology Soc.; Nat. Cancer Inst.; M.R.C.; R.C.P.S.C.; Candn. Assn. Gen. Surg.; Candn. Multi-Ctr. Transpl. Study Group; Kidney Found. of Can.; author or over 100 jour. articles & book chapters; guest ed.: 'Transplantation Proceedings' 1982, 1985; mem. Ed. Bd. 'Nova Scotia Med. Bulletin and Med. Post'; recreations: squash, sailing; Clubs: Dalhousie Faculty; Hist. of Med. Soc.; Dalhousie Med. Alumni; Alpha Omega Alpha Hon. Med. Sco.; St. Francis Xavier Alumni; Phi Rho Sigma Med. Frat; P.B. Brigham Surg. Alumni; Home: 5915 Emscote Dr., Halifax, N.S. B3H 1B3; Office: Rm. 4134 Dickson Centre, 5820 University Ave., Halifax, N.S. B3H 2Y9.

**MACDONALD, Andrew,** M.B.A., Ph.D.; federal civil servant; b. Regina, Sask. 28 Nov. 1941; s. Cyril Graham and Helen Maude (Draper) M.; e. RMC Kingston B.Eng. 1963; Queen's Univ. M.B.A. 1968; Stanford Univ. Ph.D. 1973; CHIEF INFORMATICS OFFR., TREASURY BOARD SECRETARIAT 1993– ; Telecommunications Offr. RCAF 1963–66; Asst. Prof. Sch. of Bus. and Asst. Dir. Candn. Inst. Guided Ground Transport Queen's Univ. 1973–76; Acting Dir., Pricing & Fin. Div., Strategic Planning Grp. Transport Canada 1976–77; Chief, Pricing & Financing Div. Strategic Planning Group Transport Can. 1977–80; Dir. Estimates Office Comptroller Gen. Can. 1980, Asst. Comptroller Gen. (Govt. Can. Reporting) 1981–83, Dep. Comptroller Gen. (Policy Devel.) 1983–87; Comptroller General of Canada 1988–93; Candn. repr., Public Sector Ctte., Internat. Federation of Accountants; Gov., Candn. Comprehensive Auditing Found.; mem. CICA, Public Sector Accounting and Auditing Ctte. 1982–86, Section Chrmn. 1983–85, Chrmn. 1985–86; recreations: swimming, cycling, skiing; Office: 300 Laurier Ave. W., L'Esplanade Laurier, 9 West Tower, Ottawa, Ont. K1A 1E4.

**MACDONALD, Col. Brian Scott,** C.D., B.A., M.B.A.; military executive; b. Sudbury, Ont. 6 June 1939; s. David Donald and Katherine Lillian (McKinnon) M.; e. Royal Military Coll., B.A. (Hons.) 1961; York Univ., M.B.A. with distinction 1980; m. Margaret d. Colin and Isobel Young 18 Aug. 1962; children: Heather Anne, David Colin, Michael Alexander; PRES., STRATEGIC INSIGHT PLANNING 1990– ; Extve. Dir., Candn. Inst. of Strategic Studies 1982–90; 4th Reg., Royal Candn. Horse Artillery 1961–64; N. York Bd. of Educ. 1967–80; Commanding Offr., 7 (Toronto) Reg. RCA 1972–75; Comm., Toronto Militia Dist. 1984–86; Sr. Vice-Pres., Atlantic Council of Canada 1991– ; Pres., Royal Candn. Artillery Assn. 1976; Vice Chrmn., Conf. of Defence Assns. 1975; Queen's Silver Jubilee Medal; Force Mobile Command Achievement Award; Hon. Aide de Camp to Gov. Gen. of Canada 1984–86; Hon. Gov., Candn. Corps of Commisssionaires 1984–86; Dir., Royal Candn. Mil. Inst. 1986–88; Atlantic Counc. of Can. 1986– ; Mem., Assn. of Political Risk Analysts; Candn. Operational Research Soc.; Internat. Soc. for Planning and Strategic Mgmt.; editor: 'Parliament and Defence Policy' 1982, 'War in the

Eighties' 1982, 'Canada's Strategies for Space ' 1983, 'The Grand Strategy of the Soviet Union' 1984, 'Defence and the Canadian Economy' 1984, 'Canada's Strategies for the Pacific Rim' 1985, 'High Tech and the High Seas' 1985; 'Canada, the Caribbean and Central America' 1986; 'Terror' 1986; 'Tactics and Technology' 1987; 'Soviet Military Challenge' 1987; 'A Grand Strategy for the United States' 1988; 'Airwar 2000' 1989; 'Canadian Strategic Forecast 1989' 1989; 'Space Strategy: Three Dimensions' 1989; Club: Royal Candn. Military Inst.; Home: 169 Newton Dr., Willowdale, Ont. M2M 2N6.

**MACDONALD, Bruce Ian,** B.A., C.G.A., F.B.A.; insurance executive; e. York Univ. B.A.; C.G.A. 1978; SR. VICE-PRES., ALLSTATE LIFE INSURANCE COMPANY OF CANADA 1990– ; Acctg. Mgr./Supervisor, Sentrol Systems Canada, Inc. 1978; Corp. Cont./Cont., Cdn. Computer Oper., Control Data Canada Ltd. 1978–83; Vice-Pres., & Gen. Mgr., Travel Management Services and Leisure Travel; Vice-Pres., Fin. & Planning, & CFO, American Express Canada, Inc. 1983–88; Vice-Pres., Fin. & Planning; Sr. Vice-Pres., Mktg.; Sr. Vice-Pres. & Gen. Mgr., Xerox Canada Finance Inc. 1988–90; Affil.: Financial Extves. Inst.; Certified General Accountants' Assn.; recreations: squash, hockey, skiing, golf; Office: 10 Allstate Parkway, Markham, Ont. L3R 5P8.

**MacDONALD, David G.,** B.Mus.Ed., M.M.A., Dipl.Mus.; organist, conductor, professor; b. Port Morien, Cape Breton 9 July 1952; s. George R. and Eleanor R. (MacIntosh) M.; e. Dalhousie Univ. B.Mus.Ed. 1974; McGill Univ. M.M.A. 1977; Conservatoire Rueil-Malmaison, France Dipl.Mus. 1977 (Prix d'excellence); m. Dr. Kathy d. Milton and Eva Schwartzentruber 23 Aug. 1986; one s.: Ian Alexander David; concert organist, played complete organ works of Bach in Halifax 1985–87 for Tercentenary of J.S. Bach; recitals Sweden, U.K., France, Germany, Holland, Switz.; Student of Maitland Farmer, Raymond Davelny, John Grew, Daniel Roth, Marie-Clâire Alain; concerts throughout Canada; Soloist, Roy Thomson & Jack Singer Halls, Man. Chamber Orch., Symphony Nova Scotia; Soloist & Guest Conductor, Symphony Nova Scotia; Organ & Ch. Music Teacher, Dalhousie Univ. & Atlantic Sch. of Theol.; recordings: J.S. Bach organ works CBC Enterprises; J.S. Bach Celebration organ works (spring 1994); Hosanna, Sing Lullaby, Choir of First Baptist Ch. Halifax; Adjucicator/Jury Mem., The Canada Council, Prov. of Que. Concours; over 100 CBC broadcasts; awards: N.S. Talent Trust; Canada Council Arts Award; Prov. of N.S.; Govt. of Que.; Nat. Competition Finalist; Past Chair, Royal Candn. Coll. of Organists; Mem., Un. Church of Canada (Faculty A.S.T.); recreations: golf; clubs: University (Halifax); Home: 602 Francklyn St., Halifax, N.S. B3H 3B4; Office: 1300 Oxford St., Halifax, N.S. B3H 3Y8.

**MacDONALD, Hon. David Samuel Horne,** P.C., B.A., LL.D.; b. Charlottetown, P.E.I. 20 Aug. 1936; s. John Gordon and Dr. Helen Alexandria (Mackie) MacD.; e. St. Peter's Church Private Sch., West Kent Sch., Prince of Wales Coll., Charlottetown, Dalhousie Univ., Pine Hill Divinity Hall Halifax; St. Mary's Univ. LL.D. 1980; Univ. of P.E.I. LL.D. 1981; D.D. Victoria Univ. 1986; m. Greta Sandra Belle d. Harris and Helene Rogers 11 July 1964; children: Helen, Kathryn, Sue Ann, Gordon; Member of Parliament for Rosedale 1988–93; Chrmn. of Standing Ctte. on Environment 1989– ; Chrmn. of the Parliamentary Ad Hoc Ctte. on AIDS 1989– ; Vice Chair, Special Ctte. on the Meech Lake Accord 1990; Candn. Ambassador to Ethiopia, Sudan and Djibouti with special responsibilities for the Orgn. of African Unity (OAU) and the Economic Comn. for Africa (ECA) 1986–88; apptd. Candn. Emergency Coordinator/African Famine by Secy. of State for External Affairs, the Rt. Hon. Joe Clark, Nov. 1984; led fact-finding missions to 10 African Countries: Ethiopia, Sudan, Mozambique, Zimbabwe, Botswana, Angola, Lesotho, Mauritania, Mali, Niger; Summer announcer, CFCY Charlottetown 1954–61, CBC Halifax 1956, CHNS 1958–60; o. Un. Ch. Min. 1961; Pastor in Alberton and Tignish 1962–65; Chrmn., N.A. Youth Del., Third Assembly, World Counc. of Churches, New Delhi, India 1961; mem. fact-finding mission during Biafra-Nigeria conflict 1968; Can. rep. to Anglo-North American Parl. Conf. on Africa 1974–79; Chrmn., Ctte. of Investigation into the Internat. Univ. Exchange Fund (precipitated by the South African spy infiltration) 1980; Co-chrmn. Nat. Conf. in support of the Liberation of South Africa 1982; M.P. (Prince & Egmont, P.E.I.) 1965–80; sworn of the Privy Counc. 1979; Min. of Communications, Sec. of State and Min. Responsible for Status of Women 1979; def. g.e. 1980; re-el. 1988; Fellow-in-Residence, Inst. for Rsch. on Pub. Policy, Ottawa 1980–82; Chrmn., Adv. Counc., Voluntary Resource Centre P.E.I.; Prog. Dir. and Special Adv. to Leader of Opposition 1982–83; Dir. of Logisitics, Papal Visit to Can. 1983–84; author 'Strong and Free' (coll. of articles concerning the War Measures Act); 1970; 'The African Famine and Canada's Response' 1985; 'No More Famine: A Decade for Africa' 1986; 'Canadians and Africa: What Was Said' 1986; 'Forum Africa: Canadians Working Together' 1986; co-author 'Canada and the Biafran Tragedy' 1969; 'One Gigantic Prison'; P.C.; Un. Church.

**MacDONALD, Donald C.,** B.A., M.A., LL.D.; public servant; b. Cranbrook, B.C. 7 Dec. 1913; s. Charles P. and Florence Gertrude Annie (Jennings) MacD.; e. Ormstown H.S. 1931; Macdonald Coll. Sch. for Teachers 1932; Queen's Univ. B.A. 1938, M.A. 1939; LL.D. York Univ. 1983; m. Simone d. Aimé and Victorine Bourcheix 20 Feb. 1942; children: Sandra, Joy, Brian; Lectr. Assn. for Anglo American Understanding 1939–40; journalist Montreal Gazette 1940–42; Royal Candn. Navy 1942–46; Educ. and Infor. Sec., CCF National Office 1946–49, Fed. Treas. and Organizer 1949–53, Ont. CCF Leader 1953–61; Ont. NDP Leader 1961–70; MPP York South 1955–82; Chrmn., Ont. NDP Caucus 1982–85; NDP Federal Pres. 1971–75; Chrmn., Comn. on Election Finances 1986–Apr. 1994; part-time Lectr. Pol. Sci. Dept. Atkinson and McLaughlin Coll. York Univ.; Dir.: Douglas-Coldwell Found.; Unitarian; NDP; mem.: John Howard Soc.; Candn. Civil Liberties Assn.; Royal Candn. Legion; Churchill Soc.; York Community Services; Learning Enrichment Foundation; Gen. Ed. 'Government and Politics of Ont.' 1975 (rev. eds. 1980, 1985); 'The Happy Warrior' (political memoirs) 1988; author articles and books reviews for periodicals; recreations: fishing, reading, writing; Home: 90 Burnside Dr., Toronto, Ont. M6G 2M8.

**MACDONALD, Hon. Donald Stovel,** P.C., B.A., LL.B., LL.M., LL.D. (Hon.), D. Eng. (Hon.); b. Ottawa, Ont. 1 March 1932; s. Donald Angus and Marjorie Isabel (Stovel) M.; e. Ottawa Schs.; Ashbury College, Ottawa; Univ. of Toronto; Osgoode Hall Law Sch.; Harvard Law Sch.; Trinity Hall, Cambridge Univ., B.A., LL.B., LL.M., Dipl. in Internat. Law; St. Lawrence Univ., LL.D. (hon. causa); D.Eng. (hon. causa) Colorado Sch. of Mines; Univ. of New Brunswick LL.D. (hon. causa) 1990; m. Ruth Hutchison (dec.), 1961; four children: Leigh, Nikki, Althea, Sonja; m. Adrian Merchant Lang 1988; seven step-children: Maria (dec'd), Timothy, Gregory, Andrew, Elisabeth, Amanda, Adrian; COUNSEL, McCARTHY TÉTRAULT 1991– ; Chrmn. & Dir., Siemens Electric Ltd.; Dir., Alberta Energy Company Ltd. 1992– ; Celanese Canada Inc.; Maclean Hunter 1992– ; Hambros Canada Inc. 1993– ; Slough Estates Canada Ltd.; Sun Life Assurance Co. of Canada; TransCanada PipeLines Ltd.; read law with Gowling, MacTavish, Osborne and Henderson, Ottawa 1953–54; called to Bar of Ont.; Associate, McCarthy & McCarthy, Toronto, 1957–68; Parlty. Secy. to Min. of Justice 1963–65; to Min. of Finance 1965; to Secy. of State for External Affairs 1966–68; to Min. of Industry 1968; Pres. of the Privy Council and Govt. House Leader, 1968–70; Min. of Nat. Defence, 1970–72; Min of Energy, Mines & Resources, 1972–75; Min. of Finance 1975–77; resigned as Min. of Finance Sept. 16, 1977; joined the law firm of McCarthy & McCarthy as a partner Dec. 1, 1977; Freeman of the City of London 1990; Mem., Law Soc. of Upper Canada; Candn. Bar Assoc.; Internat. Bar Assoc.; Chrmn., Internat. Development Research Centre, 1980–84; Chrmn., Royal Comm. on the Economic Union and Devel. Prospects for Can. 1982–85; Chrmn., Inst. for Research Public Policy 1991; High Commissioner for Canada to the United Kingdom of Gt. Britain and Northern Ireland 1988–91; Chrmn., Design Exchange, Toronto 1993– ; Chrmn., Candn. Friends of Cambridge Univ. 1993– ; Chrmn., Candn. Council for Public - Private Partnerships 1993– ; first el. M.P. for Toronto-Rosedale in g.e. 1962; re-el. g.e. 1963, 1965, 1968, 1972, and 1974; resigned Feb., 1978; awarded Insurance Prize, Law Soc. of Upper Can. 1955; Rowell Fellowship, Candn. Inst. of Internat. Affairs, 1956; mem., Delta Kappa Epsilon (Alphi Phi Chapter, House Mgr. and Alumni Secy.); Liberal; Baptist; recreations: tennis, cross-country skiing; Home: 27 Marlborough Ave., Toronto, Ont. M5R 1X5; Office: Suite 4700, Toronto Dominion Bank Tower, P.O. Box 48, Toronto-Dominion Centre, Toronto, Ont. M5K 1E6.

**MACDONALD, Douglas J.,** B.Eng.; b. Ormstown, Que.; s. Charles P. and Florence G.A.J. M.; e. Ormstown H.S.; McGill Univ. B.Eng. 1949; m. Suzanne Hirschmann; children: Heather, Susan, Patricia, Richard; PRESIDENT, CERTIFIED GENERAL ACCOUNTANTS ASSN. OF CANADA 1979– ; Pilot, RCAF 1943–45; joined Shawinigan Water & Power Co. 1949 and its subsidiary Quebec Power Co. 1950; Dir. of Operations 1958–65; Manager, Elecrical Div., Bédard Girard Ltd. Montreal 1966–69; Extve. Dir., Royal Victoria Hosp. 1969–78; Past Dir., Royal Victoria Hosp. 1974–78; Royal Victoria Hosp. Found. 1973–78; Que. Hosp. Assn. 1975–78; Montreal Joint Hosp. Inst. 1973–78; Gov., Que. Blue Cross Assn. 1975–78; Advisor to Council, Internat. Fed. of Accountants; Hon. C.G.A. 1983; Home: 1101 – 1575 Beach Ave., Vancouver, B.C. V6G 1Y5; Office: 700 – 1188 W. Georgia St., Vancouver, B.C. V6E 4A2.

**MacDONALD, The Hon. Madam Justice Edythe I.,** B.A. (Hons.), LL.B.; justice; b. Winnipeg, Man. 22 March 1931; d. Angus A. and I. Irene (Douglas) MacD.; e. Univ. of Man., B.A. (Hons.) 1953, LL.B. 1957; JUSTICE, ONTARIO COURT OF JUSTICE (GENERAL DIV.) 1982– ; called to Man. Bar 1957; Legal Adv., Dept. of Justice, Ottawa 1957–82, contbg. to devel. and drafting of the Candn. Charter of Rights and Freedoms, implementation of the Report of the Royal Comn. on the Status of Women, and subsequent proposals relating to the status of women; called to Ont. Bar 1982; apptd. Q.C. (Man.) 1970; Q.C. (Can.) 1972; Past Pres., Visiting Homemakers Assn. of Ottawa; Past Sec. & Dir., Civil Service Coop. Credit Soc.; Past Dir., Assn. of Family Conciliation Cts.; mem. Law Socs. of Upper Can. and Man.; Internat. Fedn. of Women Lawyers (Past Candn. Vice-Pres.); Candn. Conf. of Judges; Candn. Inst. for the Admin of Justice; author of var. articles in Candn. and internat. law jours.; recreations: photography, travel, handicrafts, theatre; Clubs: Chelsea; Larrimac Golf; Office: Court House, 102 East Main St., Welland, Ont. L3B 3W6.

**MACDONALD, The Hon. Madame Justice Ellen M.,** B.A., LL.B.; justice; b. Souris, P.E.I. 31 Dec. 1949; d. Donald Francis (dec'd) and Anne Rita (Howlett) M.; e. St. Dunstan's Univ.; Univ. of P.E.I., B.A. (Hons.) 1969; McGill Univ. LL.B. 1972; one child: Margaret Ashling Kavanagh; JUSTICE, ONTARIO COURT (GENERAL DIVISION) 1991– ; articled Gowling and Henderson; called to Bar of Ont. 1974; practice in comml. litigation Tory Tory Deslauriers and Binnington 1974; sole practitioner, family law and divorce 1976–81; Partner, Stapells & Sewell 1981–86; Partner, Borden Elliot 1986–91; Past Dir., Advocates Soc.; Past Chair, Holland Coll. Found.; Past Lectr., Bar Admission Course, Toronto; author various jour. articles; frequent Panel Mem., Candn. Bar Assn., Law Soc. of Upper Can.; Founding Dir., Ont. Assn. of Family Mediation; Past Dir., McGill Univ. Alumni; Past Dir., Dellerest Childrens Centre; R. Catholic; Clubs: Fitness Inst.; Royal Candn. Yacht; Residences: 38 Heathdale Rd., Toronto, Ont. M6C 1M6 and Caledon, Ont. L0N 1A0; Office: Court House, Judge's Chambers, 361 University Ave., Toronto, Ont. M5G 1T3.

**MacDONALD, Hon. Finlay,** O.C.; senator; broadcasting executive; b. Sydney, N.S. 4 Jan. 1923; s. F.M. and Olive (Guthrie) MacD.; e. St. Francis Xavier Univ.; Dalhousie Univ.; m. late Ann d. Colin and Christine MacKenzie 5 Aug. 1944; children: Finlay Jr., Mary, Ian; MEMBER, THE SENATE OF CANADA 1984– ; Dir. (and Past Pres.) ATV Ltd.; Founding Dir. CTV Television Network Ltd.; served with Candn. Army 1942–45; Nat. Campaign Chrmn. P. Cons. Party 1972; Chief of Staff, Hon. Robert L. Stanfield; Sr. Advr. to Rt. Hon. Joe Clark; Chrmn. Govt. Planning Ctte. Hon. Brian Mulroney; Past Pres. N.S. Prog. Cons. Party; Officer of the Order of Canada 1969; summoned to Senate of Can. 1984; Pres.: Candn. Assn. Broadcasters; Can. Games Soc.; Nat. Gov., Shaw Festival Bd.; Gov., St. Francis Xavier Univ.; R. Catholic; recreation: tennis; Clubs: Rideau; Rockcliffe; Tennis; Royal N.S. Yacht Squadron; Home: 73 Rideau Terrace, Ottawa, Ont. K1M 2A2; Office: 229 East Block, The Senate, Ottawa, Ont. K1A 0A4 and 36 Peninsula Rd., Chester, N.S. B0J 1J0.

**MACDONALD, Flora Isabel,** O.C., F.R.S.A.; executive; TV host; b. North Sydney, N.S. 3 June 1926; d. George Frederick and Mary Isabel (Royle) M.; e. N. Sydney High Sch.; Empire Business Coll.; Nat. Defence Coll. (first woman to complete one-year course in Cdn. & Internat. Studies); HOST, NORTH/SOUTH 1990– ; CHAIR, INTERNATIONAL DEVELOPMENT RESEARCH CENTRE (IDRC) 1992– ; Dir., Canada Trust Co.; Candn. Civil Liberties Assn.; Candn. Crafts Council; CARE Canada; Friends of the National Library; Queen's University Council; Centre for Refugee Studies, York Univ.; Refugee Policy Group, Washington, D.C.; Shastri Indo-Canada Institute; South African Education Trust Fund; Chair, Commonwealth Human Rights Initiative; Extve. Dir., Progressive Conservative National Headquarters 1957–66; Admin. Offr. & Tutor, Dept. of Political Studies, Queen's Univ. 1966–69; first el. to H. of C. g.e. 1972 (Kingston and the Islands); def. g.e. 1988; Secy. of State for External Affairs 1979–80; Min. of Employment and Immigration 1984–86; Min. of Communications 1986–88; as Opposition Mem. of Parliament: held Critic's Post for Indian Affairs and Northern Develop., Federal-Provincial Relations, External Affairs and Status of Women; Visiting Scholar, Centre for Candn. Studies, Univ. of Edinburgh 1989; Special Advr. to Pres. of the Commonwealth of Learning 1990–91; Past Extve Dir., Ctte. for an Independent Canada; Past Dir., Candn. Inst. Public Affairs; Past Dir. Candn. Civil Liberties Assn.; Past Pres., Elizabeth Fry Soc.; Fellow, Royal Society of Arts; Officer, Order of Canada; United Ch.; recreation: speedskating; Address: 502 - 350 Queen Elizabeth Driveway, Ottawa, Ont. K1S 3N1.

**MacDONALD, George Frederick,** B.A., Ph.D.; anthropologist; museum director; b. Cambridge, Ont. 4 July 1938; s. George and Jane (Gorton) MacDonald; e. Univ. of Toronto B.A. 1961; Yale Univ. Ph.D. 1966; m. Joanne d. Edgar and Cynthia Rice, 9th Sept. 1961; children: Christine, Grant; EXTVE. DIRECTOR, CANADIAN MUSEUM OF CIVILIZATION 1982– ; joined Archaeology Div. Nat. Museums of Can. as Atlantic Provs. Archaeol. 1964, W. Coast Archaeol. 1966, Head W. Can. Sect. 1968, Chief Archaeol. Div. 1969, Chief Archaeol. Survey of Can. 1972, Sr. Archaeol. of Museum 1978, Head New Accomodation Task Force 1982; Research Fellow Museum Fur Volkerkunde, Basel, Switz. 1977–78; Research Fellow, Florida State Museum, Gainesville, Florida 1980–81; Visiting Fellow, Museum of Anthrop. Univ. of B.C. 1981; lectr. Trent Univ., Univ. of Ottawa, Carleton Univ., Simon Fraser Univ.; mem., Nat. Historic Sites & Monuments Bd. Can.; mem. Bd., Can. Museums Construction Corp.; author or co-author numerous publs.; mem., Can. Archaeol. Assn. (Pres. 1968); Can. delegate drafting Ctte., UNESCO Convention on World Heritage, Paris 1972; Can. delegate Comm. of Experts, Mohenjo Daro, Pakistan 1973; Home: R.R.1, Cantley, Qué. J0X 1L0; Office: 100 Laurier St., P.O. Box 3100, Stn. B., Hull, Qué. J8X 4H2.

**MACDONALD, George Williston,** Q.C., P.Eng., LL.B., B.Eng.; barrister; b. Sydney, N.S. 13 Apr. 1939; s. Murdock and Mary E. (Williston) MacD.; e. Dalhousie Univ., LL.B. 1970; Nova Scotia Tech. Coll. (now Tech. Univ. Nova Scotia) B.Eng. (Elect.) 1966; m. Gina d. Carmen and Doris Stoddard, 22 May 1965; children: Kelly, Cindy, Katie; BARRISTER, MCINNES COOPER & ROBERTSON; Dir. Tie Telecommunications (Canada) Ltd.; RKO Steel Ltd.; Dir. several construction companies; prior to univ. spent 2 yrs. in Candn. Arctic as radio operator with Dept. Transport; worked with Candn. Gen. Electric (Peterborough, Ont.); admitted N.S. Bar 1970; taught Dalhousie Law Sch. and Tech. Univ. N.S.; partner in law firm 1977; Sir James Dunn Scholar (Dalhousie Law Sch.); winner Univ. Medal in Law 1970; Mem. Bd. of Govs., Dalhousie Univ.; Past Chrmn. Bd. Govs., Tech. Univ. N.S.; Past Pres., N.S. Gymnastics Assn.; Dir., Dalhousie Black & Gold Club; mem., N.S. Barristers Soc. (Past-Chrmn., Admin. of Justice Comm.); Candn. Bar Assn.; Assn. Professional Engineers N.S.; Protestant; Prog. Conservative; recreations: golf; jogging; skiing; hockey (old timer); Clubs: Ashburn Golf; Northumberland Golf; YMCA; Home: 107 Anchor Dr., Halifax, N.S. B3N 3B8; Office: P.O. Box 730, Halifax, N.S. B3J 2V1.

**MACDONALD, Hugh Ian,** O.C. (1977), K.L.J. (1978), B.Com., M.A., B.Phil., LL.D.; educator; economist; b. Toronto, Ont. 27 June 1929; s. Hugh and Winnifred (Mitchell) Macd.; e. Univ. of Toronto, B.Com. 1952; Balliol Coll. Oxford Univ. (Rhodes Scholar) M.A. 1954, B.Phil. (Econ.) 1955; LL.D. Univ. of Toronto 1974; m. Dorothy M. Vernon 1960; children: Gordon, Jill, Roy, Anne, Jennifer; PRES. EMERITUS, DIRECTOR OF THE DEGREE PROGRAMME IN PUBLIC MGMNT. and DIR., YORK INTERNATIONAL 1984– ; Prof. of Pub. Admin. and Econ., York Univ. 1974– , Pres. of Univ. 1974–84; Dir., The AGF Companies; CIBA-GEIGY Canada Ltd.; Aetna Canada, a group of cos. incl. Aetna Life Insurance Co. of Can.; McGraw-Hill Ryerson Ltd.; joined Teaching Staff, Univ. of Toronto 1955 becoming Dean of Men, Univ. Coll. 1956, Asst. Prof. of Econ. 1962; Chief Econ., Prov. Ont. 1965, Depy. Treasr. 1967, Depy. Treasr. and Depy. Min. of Econ. 1968; Depy. Treasr. and Depy. Min., Econ. & Intergovt'l Affairs 1972; Chrmn., Ont. Adv. Ctte. on Confederation 1965–71 and 1977–82; Chrmn., Comn. on Financing Elem. & Secondary Edn. Ont. 1984–86; Chrmn., IDEA Corp. 1982–86; Chrmn., Ont. Mun. Educ. and Training Adv. Counc. 1986–88; Chrmn., Hockey Can.; Chrmn., The Commonwealth of Learning; Chrmn., The Friends of the Internat. Assn. of Univs.; The Jewett Centenary Appeal in Canada of Balliol College, Oxford Univ.; Dir., Comite au Canada de la Maison des Etudiants Canadiens a Paris; Empire Club of Canada Foundation; NTCI Foundation; World Encyclopedia of Contemporary Theatre; Counc. for Candn. Unity; Gov. York Finch Hosp.; mem., Adv. Counc., CJRT-FM; Mem. Adv. Bd., Toronto Region Group, The Institute of Public Admin. of Can.; Candn. Olympic Assn.; The Internat. Master of Business Admin. Programme, York Univ.; Past Pres., Empire Club Can.; Ticker Club; Couchiching Inst. Pub. Affairs; Candn. Rhodes Scholars Found.; World Univ. Service of Can.; Past Chrmn., Toronto Men's Br. CIIA; Inst. Pol. Involvement; Founding Dir. (1981), Inter-American Organization for Higher Education, Vice-Pres. for Canada (1983–91) and Hon. Councillor 1992; former mem. Adm. Bd., Internat. Assn. Univs.; Atty. Gen.'s Ctte. Securities Leg.; Econ. Counc. of Can.; Adv. Ctte. on Confederation to the Ont. Govt.; mem., Candn. Econ. Assn.; Am. Econ. Assn.; Royal Econ. Soc. (London); Candn. Assn. Club of Rome; Inst. Pub. Adm. Can.; Am. Soc. Pub. Adm.; Lambda Alpha; recreations: hockey, tennis; Home: 7 Whitney Ave., Toronto, Ont. M4W 2A7; Office: 4700 Keele St., North York, Ont. M3J 1P3.

**MacDONALD, Ian,** MD, CM, MSc, FRCS(C), FCCMG; university professor and administrator; b. Montreal 5 Feb. 1951; CHAIRMAN, DEPT. OF OPHTHALMOLOGY, UNIV. OF ALBERTA; Office: 2 – 129 Clinical Sciences Bldg., Univ. of Alberta, Edmonton, Alta. T6G 2G3.

**MacDONALD, J. Barry;** business executive; b. Montreal, Que. 8 Oct. 1944; e. Univ. of Michigan; m. Dr. Wendy A. MacDonald 30 Sept. 1972; children: Jessica, John; PRES. & CHIEF EXTVE. OFFR., ROBCO INC.; Dir., Chrmn. & C.E.O. of subsidiaries, divisions & affiliated cos.: Albion Indus. Products Montreal, Anchor Packing Montreal, Ontario Rubber Toronto, Solidur Plastics and Robco Inc. Pittsburgh; Gov., Montreal Gen. Hosp.; Mem., Young President's Orgn.; Office: 630, 4150 St. Catherine St. W., Montreal, Que. H3Z 2Y5.

**MacDONALD, Jack Carnell,** B.Sc.; hospitality executive; b. Halifax, N.S. 23 Oct. 1945; s. Colin Michael and Belle Iris (Carnell) M.; e. Acadia Univ. B.Sc. 1971; m. Faye d. Mary and Lyle Allen 10 April 1987; children: Jennifer Ryan, Katherine Nicole; Pres., Marriott Corp. 1986; var. positions up to Dist. Mgr., Saga Corp. 1971–80; Vice-Pres., Clearwater Lobsters 1980–85; Pres., Saga Corp. 1985–86; Pres., Admin. Sogsabec Limitée 1989– ; Dir., Admin. Sogsabec Limitée; Marriott Candn. Mngt. Serv., Ltd.; Candn. Found. of Dietetic Rsch.; Mem., Adv. Counc., Ont. Restaurant News; Pres. Counc., Friends of We Care (Easter Seals); Mem., Corp. Serv. Ctte., Candn. Coll. of Health Care Extves.; Bd. Mem., AMPHI, Guelph Univ.; P.C. Party (500 Club); United Church; recreations: boating, golf; clubs: Fifty Point Yacht Squadron; Home: 1293 Monmouth Dr., Burlington, Ont. L7P 3N4.

**MacDONALD, Jake,** B.A.; writer; b. 6 Apl. 1949; s. Donald Ian and Peggy Christine (Monahan) MacD.; e. Univ. of Man. B.A. 1971; div.; one d. Caitlin Peggy-Jean; author (novel) 'Indian River' 1981, 2nd ed. 1987; (short stories) 'The Bridge Out of Town' 1986, 2nd and 3rd. eds. 1987, reprinted 1990; forthcoming 'Two Tickets to Paradise', 'Raised By the River'; numerous short stories various lit. mags., anthols.; CBC radio scripts incl. 'Becoming'(also stage play), 'Men Who Say No', 'The Highway is for Gamblers', 'The Longest Night of the Year', 'The Witch of Beacon Hill'; Nat. Hist. Sites dramatic prodns. 'The Siege of Batoche', 'Fort Prince of Wales'; videos 'Who is Responsible?' (hazardous waste), 'The People We Are' (Metis); various CBC dramatic readings; Instr. Man. Writers Guild Mentor Prog. 1986–90; participant various short term writing progs. Man.; recreation: part-time fishing guide; Home: General Delivery, Minaki, Ont. P0X 1J0; Office: 11, 165 Stafford St., Winnipeg, Man. R3M 2W9.

**MACDONALD, James Colin,** Q.C., LL.B.; barrister; b. Galahad, Alta. 19 Jan. 1934; s. James Percy and Marion Isobel (MacLeod) MacD.; e. Univ. B.C., LL.B. 1957; m. Elizabeth, d. Lewis and Fay Passman, 28 July 1965; children: Neil David; Mark Angus; INDEPENDENT PRACTITIONER IN FAMILY LAW; called to Bar B.C. 1958; Bar Ont. 1964; Q.C. 1972; Assoc., Clark Wilson & Co. 1958–63; Partner, MacDonald & Ferrier 1965–86; Partner, Osler, Hoskin & Harcourt 1986–92; Dir., Bar Ad. Course and Continuing Legal Ed., Law Soc. Upper Can. 1970–75; Head, Family Law Sect., Bar Ad. Course 1970–80; Founding Chrmn., Family Law Sect., Candn. Bar Assn.; Mem. Bd. Dirs. (for 3 terms), Assn. Family and Conciliation Courts; Pres., Family Mediation Service of Ont. 1982–92; Bd. mem., George Hull Centre for Families and Children 1986–92; co-author: 'Canadian Divorce Law and Practice' 1969 (a subscription service); 'Law and Practice under the Family Law Reform Act of Ontario' 1980 (a subscription service); 'Annotated Canadian Divorce Law and Practice' (published annually); 'Annotated Family Law Act of Ontario (published annually); ed.: ''Matrimonial Causes' Canadian Abridgment' (2nd ed.) 1970; recreations: swimming, canoeing, hiking, theatre, reading, mathematics, music; Clubs: University; Office: The Eaton Tower, 250 Yonge St., Suite 2600, P.O. Box 24, Toronto, Ont. M5B 2M6.

**MACDONALD, Most Reverend James H.,** C.S.C., D.D.; roman catholic archbishop; b. Wycocomagh, N.S. 28 April 1925; s. Alexander and Mary M.; e. St. Joseph's Univ. H.S. 1944–45; ARCHBISHOP OF ST. JOHN'S, NEWFOUNDLAND, ROMAN CATHOLIC EPISCOPAL CORP. OF ST. JOHN'S 1991– ; ordained to Priesthood Woodstock, Ont. 29 June 1953; to the Episcopate in Hamilton, Ont. 17 April 1978; apptd. Auxiliary Bishop of Hamilton 15 Feb. 1978; Bishop of Charlottetown, P.E.I. 13 Aug. 1982; Holy Cross Mission Bank 1954–56; Dir., Holy Cross Minor Seminary, St. Joseph's, N.B. 1956–62; Sec., Prov. Council, Holy Cross Fathers 1956–63; Dir. of Vocations 1962–63; Superior, Holy Cross House of Studies 1964–69; Asst. Provincial, Holy Cross Fathers 1966–72; Bursar 1969–72; Dir. of Personnel 1969–75; Pastor, St. Michael's Parish, Waterloo, Ont. 1969–77; Dean (V.F.) Waterloo County Priests, Diocese of Hamilton 1974–77; Mem., Permanent Council, Candn. Conf. of Catholic Bishops; CCCB Sexual Abuse Ctte.; CCCB Religious Edn. Comn. adult portfolio; Nat. Spiritual Dir., Catholic Women's League; State Chaplain, Knights of Columbus; Address: P.O. Box 37, St. John's, Nfld. A1C 5H5.

**MacDONALD, James Stuart Alexander,** B.A., M.B.A.; investment dealer; b. North Bay, Ont. 18 March 1945; s. Alexander Patrick and Ruth Margaret (Puckett) MacD.; e. Univ. of W. Ont. B.A. 1968; Northwestern Univ. M.B.A. 1969; m. Danielle d. Henry and Gloria Dusseault 16 Apl. 1971; two d. Katherine Margaret, Victoria Alexandra; DEPUTY CHRMN., SCOTIA McLEOD INC. 1991– ; Dir. Conwest Exploration Co. Ltd.; Adanac Mining Inc.; Invest. Rsch. McLeod Young Weir Ltd. 1969, Dir. 1973, Mng. Dir. Internat. 1976, Dir. Calgary 1979–86; Extve. Vice Pres. present Co. 1986; Deputy Chrmn. 1991; Club: National Golf; Home: 81 Hudson Dr., Toronto, Ont. M4T 2K2; Office: P.O. Box 433, T-D Centre, Toronto, Ont. M5K 1M2.

**MACDONALD, The Hon. John A.B.,** B.A., LL.B.; justice; b. Edmonton, Alta. 4 April 1944; s. Bruce Fraser and Lois Marie (Baker) M.; e. Univ. of Alberta B.A. 1965; Univ. of Toronto LL.B. 1968; JUSTICE, ONTARIO COURT OF JUSTICE (GENERAL DIVISION); Office: Court House, 361 University Ave., Toronto, Ont. M5G 1T3.

**MACDONALD, John Allister,** B.Sc., M.A. P.Eng.; consulting geologist; b. Brooklyn, NY 13 Nov. 1931; s. Francis Howard and Cecilia Elizabeth (Gorman) M.; e. St. Francis Xavier Univ., B.Sc. 1954, M.A. 1956; m. Cecelia d. Eva and Ralph Brennen 3 Apr. 1961; children: Teresa Ann, Eva Marie, Laura Joan, Mary Kathleen; PRES., TELMIN RESOURCES INC. 1988– ; Dir. & Vice Pres. Explor., Ontex Resources Limited 1991– ; var. pos. as explor. geol. 1956–58; joined Eldorado Mining & Refining 1958; Sr. Mine Geol., Ace Fay Mines, Sask. 1961–64; resumed grad. work, McGill Univ. 1964–68; Explor. Geochem., Imperial Oil Ltd. 1968–69; Pres., Sheba Mines 1969–70; Mgr., Mineral Explor., East. Can., Getty Mines Limited 1970–74; Dir., Pres. & Mgr., Candn. Minerals Prog. 1974–86; Dir. & Vice-Pres., Opns., Getty Resources Ltd. 1986–88; Pres., J.A. Macdonald & Assoc. 1988–90; Active duty U.S. Army 1957, reserve to 1963; Mem., Candn. Inst. of Mining & Metal.; Sigma Xi; Assn. of Profl. Engrs. of Sask.; Fellow, Geol. Assn. of Can.; recreations: cross country skiing, fishing, painting; Club: The Ontario Club; Home: 55 Lynngrove Ave., Etobicoke, Ont. M8X 1M7; Office: 1107 – 330 Bay St., Toronto, Ont. M5H 2S8.

**MACDONALD, Commdr. John Arthur,** B.A.; public servant (ret.); author; retired naval officer; b. Toronto, Ont., 26 Sept. 1912; s. late Duncan McGregor and Nellie Graham (Minns) M.; m. the late Catherine Mary Hilder, 29 Nov. 1939; m. Hylda Kathlyn Bateman 19 Jun. 1993; children: Catherine Muriel, Judith Ann (Panofsky), Margaret Duncan (Lamont); was Asst. Deputy Minister Health & Welfare Canada, responsible for national and international social welfare and development programs and National Fitness and Amateur Sport Programs; Special UN rapporteur, Canadian representative on UNICEF Extv. Bd., International Council on Social

Development and other health, welfare and sport/fitness bodies; currently mem., Amnesty International, NAACP, MATCH International, the Temagami Wilderness Assn. (so far as it still exists and its spirit fights on, with all others who strive to save our national heritage), Blissymbolics and other agencies concerned with making a better world and providing a decent life for all its inhabitants; author: 'Darkly the River Flows' (all Canada prize winning novel); Address: 130 Broadway Ave., Ottawa, Ont. K1S 2V8.

**MACDONALD, John Barfoot,** O.C., D.D.S., M.S., Ph.D., LL.D., D.Sc.; university professor; b. Toronto, Ont. 23 Feb. 1918; s. Arthur A. and Gladys L. (Barfoot) M.; e. Univ. of Toronto, D.D.S. (with Hons.) 1942; Univ. of Illinois M.S. (Bacteriol.) 1948; Columbia Univ., Ph.D. (Bacteriol.) 1953; Hon. degrees: A.M. (Harvard); LL.D. (Univ. of Man., Simon Fraser Univ., Wilfrid Laurier Univ., Brock Univ., Univ. of W. Ont.); D.Sc. (Univ. of B.C., Univ. of Windsor); m. Liba Kucera; children: Kaaren C., John Grant, Scott Arthur, Vivian Jane, Linda Rosemarie; Chrmn., Addiction Research Found. 1981–87; Pres., Addiction Research Foundation 1976–81; Extve. Dir., Council of Ont. Univs. and Prof. of Higher Educ., Univ. of Toronto 1968–76; Consultant, Nat. Insts. of Health; after war service, Instructor in Bacteriol., Faculty of Dent., Univ. of Toronto 1946–47; Research Asst., Univ. of Illinois, 1947–48; Kellogg Fellow, and Candn. Dental Assn. Research Student, Columbia Univ., 1948–49; Asst. Prof. of Bacteriol., Univ. of Toronto(Faculty of Dent.), 1949–53, and Assoc. Prof., 1953–56; Chairman, Div. of Dental Research, Univ. of Toronto, 1953–56 and apptd. (full) Prof. of Bacteriol., 1956; Consultant in Dent. Educ., Univ. of B.C., 1955–56; Dir., Forsyth Dental Infirmary, Boston, Mass., 1956–62; Prof. of Microbiol., Harvard Sch. of Dent. Med., 1956–62, and Dir. of Postdoctoral Studies there, 1960–62; Assoc. Ed. 'Journal of Dental Research' 1958–61; Regional Ed. 'Archives of Oral Biology' 1958–62; Ed. 'International Series on Oral Biology' 1958–63; Pres., Univ. of B.C. 1962–67; mem. Bd., Donwood Foundation 1966–79, Chrmn. 1972–75; mem. Bd., Banff School for Advanced Mgmt. 1962–67 (Chrmn. 1966–67); mem. Bd. Dirs., Assn. of Univs. and Colls. of Can. 1964–67; mem. Visiting Comte., Harvard Med. Sch. & Sch. of Dental Med. 1967–73; Consultant, Science Council of Can. and Can. Council on Support of Rsch. in Candn. Univs. 1967–69; Chrmn., Jt. Comte. of Candn. Dental Assn. and Candn. Med. Assn. on Fluoridation; mem., Candn. Nat. Research Council Comte. on Dental Rsch. 1950–60 (Chrmn. 1954–57); mem., Dental Study Sec., Nat. Insts. of Health; Chrmn. Comn. on Pharm. Services, Candn. Pharm. Assn. 1967; mem. Nat. Scient. Planning Council, Mental Health Assn. Can. 1969; mem. and Vice Chrmn. Ont. Counc. of Health 1981–84; served in 2nd World War with Candn. Dental Corps, 1944–46; released with rank of Capt.; Address: 1137 Royal York Rd., Apt. 1008C, Etobicoke, Ont. M9A 4A7.

**MacDONALD, John James,** B.Sc., M.A., Ph.D.; educator; b. New Glasgow, N.S. 30 Oct. 1925; s. John James and Margaret Jean MacD.; e. St. John's Acad. New Glasgow, N.S.; St. Francis Xavier Univ. B.Sc. 1945; Univ. of Toronto M.A. 1947, Ph.D. 1951; m. Mary Lou d. John E. McIntyre, Moncton, N.B. 7 June 1952; children: John James, Nancy Patricia, Anne Louise, Joan Elizabeth, Ronald Joseph, Margaret Ethel, Alan Roderick; Extve. Vice Pres., St. Francis Xavier Univ. 1978–91 (retired); Asst. Prof. of Chem. present Univ. 1949, Assoc. Prof. 1954, Dean of Science 1960, Prof. 1961, Acad. Vice Pres. 1970–78 and 1987–91; Visiting Scient. Naval Research Estab. Dartmouth 1955; Research Study Leave, Univ. of Ottawa 1959–60; Study Leave, Higher Educ. Group, Univ. of Toronto and Visiting Prof. Ont. Inst. of Studies in Educ. 1976–77; rec'd Centennial Medal 1967; selected 'Educateur exemplaire' Nova Scotia 1989; Dir. Maritime Telegraph & Telephone Co. Ltd. since 1973; Founding Dir. (and Pres. 1984), Adminet Inc.; Chrmn. Town Planning Bd. Antigonish 1962–68; Chrmn., St. Martha's Hospital Bd. 1984–91; War Supplies Agency E. N.S. Region; Chrmn., N.S. Northern Region Health Agency 1991– ; mem. Maritime Provs. Higher Educ. Comn. 1974–84; Science Council of Can. 1977–83; Chrmn., Sci. Council Transportation Study Comte. 1981; Nova Scotia Counc. of Applied Sci. and Technol. 1987–91; Mem., N.S. Task Force on Research and Technological Innovation; NRC Advisory Comm., Atlantic Region; NSERC, Adv. Comm. on Research Development and Task Force on Research Infrastructure; Mem.-at-Large, Candn. Nat. Comn. for UNESCO 1968–81; served as Pilot Offr. 1956 becoming Sqdn. Leader and C.O. 294 Univ. Sqdn. 1968; Mem. Extve. of Nova Scotia Assn. of Health Organisations, NSAHO; mem. Assn. Univs. & Colls. Can. (Dir. 1976–79); Chem. Inst. Can.; Chrmn., Program Ctte. & Moderator, 1986 World Exposition: Symposium Series Transportation and Telecommunications; Mem., Candn. Ctte. to World Union of Transport; Candn. Soc. Study Higher Educ.; Fellow, Royal Philatelic Soc. of Can.; Brit. N. Am. Philatelic Soc.; Postal History Society of Canada; Confrérie des Chevaliers du Tastevin, Commanderie d'Amerique; author: 'The Nova Scotia Post: Its Offices, Masters and Marks 1700–1867'; R. Catholic; recreations: fishing, golf, philately; Club: Antigonish Golf & Country; Home: 58 Hawthorne St., Antigonish, N.S. B2G 1A4; Office: Antigonish, N.S. B2G 1C0.

**MACDONALD, Hon. John Michael,** Q.C., M.A., LL.B.; senator; b. North Sydney, N.S. 3 May 1906; s. Joseph and Teresa Mary (MacDonald) M.; e. Sydney Acad.; St. Francis Xavier Univ. B.A. 1928, M.A. 1931; Dalhousie Law Sch. LL.B. 1934; Principal of Schs. Antigonish, N.S. 1928–30; called to Bar of N.S. 1934; cr. Q.C. 1957; law practice in assn. with father, Joseph Macdonald, Q.C. and Ronald J. Macdonald, Q.C.; mem., House of Assembly N.S. 1956–60; summoned to the Senate of Can. 1960; P. Conservative Whip in Chief Senate and Caucus Chrmn. 1962–84; part-time law practice 1960– ; served with RCEME Eng. and N.W. Europe World War II; mem., Royal Candn. Legion (mem. Extve. Br. 19 1945–60, Hon. Pres. 1960– ); R. Catholic; Home: 44 Beacon St., North Sydney, N.S. B2J 1R2; Office: Senate of Canada, Ottawa, Ont. K1A 0A4 and 321 Commercial St., North Sydney, N.S. B2A 1B9.

**MACDONALD, Joseph Albert Friel,** Q.C., LL.M.; lawyer; b. Halifax, N.S. 10 Dec. 1942; s. Charles F.H. and Mary E. (Friel) M.; e. elem. and high sch. Halifax; Dalhousie Univ. B.A. 1963, LL.B. 1966; N.Y. Univ. LL.M. 1967; m. Linda d. Lloyd and Georgette Bergstrom 15 Sept. 1967; children: Charles, Georgette; PARTNER, McINNES COOPER & ROBERTSON 1975– ; Chrmn., Nova Scotia Power Inc.; articled with above law firm becoming Assoc. 1967; cr. Q.C. 1983; Mem. Bd. of Govs., Mount Saint Vincent Univ.; Vice Chrmn. Bd. of Govs., IWK Hospital for Children, Halifax; mem., N.S. Barristers' Soc.; Candn. Bar Assn.; Internat. Bar Assn.; Candn. Tax Found.; R. Catholic; P. Conservative; Club: Halifax; Home: 2915 Somerset Ave., Halifax, N.S. B3L 3Z4; Office: 1601 Lower Water St., Halifax, N.S. B3J 2V1.

**MACDONALD, Judith Ann;** editor; b. Georgetown, Guyana 27 Sept. 1964; s. Alexander Sutherland and Lillian Ruth (Elder) M.; e. Ryerson School of Journalism; EDITOR, THIS MAGAZINE; Office: 16 Skey Lane, Toronto, Ont. M6J 3S4.

**MacDONALD, Lynn Mary,** B.A., B.J.; civil servant; b. Montreal, Que. 13 May 1951; d. Thomas and Betty Violet (Clark) MacD.; e. Carleton Univ. B.A. 1972, B.J. 1973; ASST. DEP. MIN. OF CORPORATE SERVICES, COMMUNITY AND SOCIAL SERVICES ONT. 1992– ; served Nat. Museums Corp., Privy Council Office; Dir. Gen. Cultural Policy & Progs. and Strategic Planning, Communications Can. 1983–86; Asst. Dep. Min. Policy/Progs. Min. of Citizenship and Citizenship & Culture Ont. 1986–88; Asst. Dep. Min. of Corporate Services, Community and Social Services Ont. 1988–92; mem. Niagara Inst.; Inst. Pub. Adm. Can.; recreations: boating, cross-country skiing; Office: 6F, 80 Grosvenor St., Toronto, Ont. M7A 1E9.

**MacDONALD, Myles J.,** B.A.; artist; b. New York City, N.Y. 17 Sept. 1941; s. Myles J. and Honorah Mary (McGrath) MacD.; e. Holy Apostles Semy. Cromwell, Conn. 1962; Hunter Coll. City Univ. of N.Y. 1963; Oakland Univ. Rochester, Mich. B.A. 1970; m. Mary Margaret d. Kahlil and Margaret (Forest) Shatilla 30 June 1972; children: Colin Alexander, Sarah Margaret, Peter Friedrich (dec.); exhns. incl. Nancy Poole Studio Toronto, Mendel Art Gallery Saskatoon, Prince Albert Winter Festival Open Juried Art Show (awarded Best of Show 1988, 1989, Mayor's Prize 1989), touring show Sask. and Alta.; rep. various W.Can. pub. colls. incl. Sask. Arts Bd. Perm. Coll., Mendel Art Gallery, Edmonton Art Gallery, Govt. Alta. Museums Coll., Lt. Gov.'s Mansion Edmonton, corporate colls. and numerous private colls.; taught short painting workshops Prince Albert and Emma Lake Art Camp since 1981; has lived and painted in Mich., Alta. and Sask.; served with USAF 1963–67; recipient Sask. Arts Bd. Visual Individual Assistance 'A' Grant 1988; adjudicator Orgn. Sask. Arts Councils; recreations: music, literature, history, archaeology, splitting wood, surviving the current economic recession; Address: P.O. Box 87, Spruce Home, Sask. S0J 2N0.

**MACDONALD, Nona Mary,** B.A.; public relations consultant; b. Saskatoon, Sask.; d. Ronald Hugh, D.S.O., M.C., F.R.C.S.(C), F.A.C.S. and Nona (Hutcheson) M.; e. Convent of Notre Dame de Sion and City Park Coll. Inst. Saskatoon; Univ. of Toronto B.A.; Accredited Pub. Relations (A.P.R.) Cert. 1978; m. William A. Heaslip 1983; Reporter, Saskatoon Star-Phoenix and Vancouver Province 1952–54; Radio and TV Pub. Affairs Programming CBC Vancouver, Montreal, Toronto 1954–63; United Nations Radio, UN, New York 1964–66; Radio-TV Publicity Dir. Time Inc. New York 1966–73; Pub. Relations Mgr. Ont. Place Corp. Toronto 1973–75; P.R. Mgr., Univ. of Toronto 1975–86; consultant, lectr. various groups pub. relations; recipient Council for Advanc. & Support of Educ. Award 1980 and 1984; Pres., Couchiching Inst. Pub. Affairs 1983–84 (Dir. 1980–87); Dir., Canadian Stage Company 1988–90; Dir., Candn. Pub. Relations Soc. 1979–82; Pres., John Graves Simcoe Assn. 1988– (Dir. 1977–88); Shaw Festival (Dir. 1991– ); Clubs: Empire (Pres. 1986–87, Dir. 1977–91); Badminton & Racquet; Toronto Hunt; Rosedale Golf; Office: Empire Club, Royal York Hotel, Toronto, Ont. M5J 1E3.

**MacDONALD, Peter Vincent,** B.A., LL.B., Q.C.; lawyer; writer; speaker; b. Halifax, N.S. 5 April 1934; s. Vincent Christopher and Emily Mary (O'Connor) M.; e. St. Francis Xavier Univ. B.A. 1954; Univ. of Toronto LL.B. 1960; called to Bar of Ont. 1962; Q.C. 1980; m. Catherine d. Michael and Mary Banaghan 20 Sept. 1958; children: Michael John, Peter Shaun, Mary Margaret; newspaper/mag. writer: Halifax 'Chronicle-Herald,' Toronto 'Globe and Mail,' Toronto 'Telegram,' Toronto 'Star Weekly,' to 1963; practicing lawyer, Hanover, Ont. 1963–88; legal-humour columnist for Candn. Bar Assn. newspaper 'National' 1984–92; 'Canadian Medical Association Journal' 1989–90; 'Toronto Star' and affiliates of Star Syndicate 1989– ; 'Punch Digest for Canadian Doctors' (later renamed 'STITCHES' magazine) 1990– ; 'The Comedy Magazine' (U.S.) 1993– ; Roman Catholic; Area Dir. of Legal Aid, Grey and Bruce Counties, Ont. 1984– ; former Pres., Bruce Co. Law Assn.; mem., Law Soc. of Upper Can.; Candn. Bar Assn.; Grey Co. Law Assn.; Bruce Co. Law Assn.; Writers' Union of Can.; contbr.: 'You and Your Rights' 1980; author: 'Court Jesters' 1985, 'More Court Jesters' 1987, 'Return of the Court Jesters' 1990, 'Court Jesters Cartoons' 1991; 'More Court Jesters Cartoons' 1993; narrator: 'Court Jesters' audio book 1993; international speaker on legal humour; recreations: golf, reading; Home/Office: 555 - 18th Ave., Hanover, Ont. N4N 3B2.

**MacDONALD, Pierre,** B.A., M.Com.; b. Quebec City, 19 June 1936; e. Laval Univ. B.A. 1957, B.Com. 1959, M.Com. 1960; children: Jean, Claude, Ann, Julie; VICE-PRES., TRANSPORTATION EQUIPMENT GROUP, TGV PROJECTS, BOMBARDIER INC. 1990– ; Dir., Paribas Participation Limited (PPL); Tandem Computers Canada Limited; Teleglobe Inc.; el. M.N.A. Dec. 1985; named Qué. Minister of Industry, Commerce and Technology June 1988; Vice Pres. Johnson & Higgins, Willis Faber Inc. 1965–68; Extve. Vice Pres. & Gen. Mgr. Les Industries L'Islet Inc. 1970–74; Vice Pres. and Dir. La Soc. d'énergie de la Baie James 1974–77; Chrmn. Canadian Arsenals Ltd.1977–1985; Sr. Vice Pres. Eastern Region, Bank of Montreal 1983–85; Qué. Min. of External Trade and Technology Dec. 1985; service Candn. Armed Forces (Reserve), rank Col.; Clubs: Cercle de la Garnison de Qué.; Le Club de Golf de Cap Rouge; Home: 80 Berlioz, Ile des Soeurs, Que. H3E 1N9; Office: 1101 Parent St., Saint-Bruno, Que. J3V 6E6.

**MACDONALD, R. Douglas;** insurance and real estate broker; b. Kentville, N.S. 14 June 1940; s. Ralph L. and E. Eileen (Burbidge) M.; e. Acadia Univ.; m. Fay d. Harold and Hazel Murray 1961; children: Susan, Bruce; CHAIRMAN, PRESIDENT & CHIEF EXECUTIVE OFFICER, MACDONALD CHISHOLM INC.; also Macdonald Chisholm Holdings Ltd. and Macdonald Chisholm Travel Ltd.; Pres., R.L. Macdonald Investments Ltd.; Vice-Pres., Auburn Investments Ltd.; Sec., Coldbrook Devel. Ltd.; Paul Haris Fellow, Rotary Club of Kentville 1990; Gen. Campaign Chair, Valley Reg. Hosp. Found. (successful $8 million fundraiser) 1985–89; Vice-Pres., Valley Health Serv. Assn. 1987–89; Comnr., Kentville Bd. of Police Comnrs. 1978–79; Mem., Insur. Brokers' Assn. of N.S. (Dir. 1965–67); Rotary Club (Pres. 1976–77); Kentville & Area Bd. of Trade (Pres. 1980–81); Kentville Devel. Corp. Ltd. (Pres. 1980–82); Annapolis Valley Real Estate Bd. (Pres. 1980–82); Annapolis Valley Affil. Bds. of Trade (Pres. 1981–82); N.S. Real Estate Assn. (Pres. 1983–84; Candn. Real Estate Assn. (Prov. Dir. 1986); Valey Reg. Hosp. Found. (Pres. 1985–89); Trustee, Un. Ch. of St. Paul & St. Stephen 1985–90; recreations: golf, curling; clubs: Ken-Wo Golf and Country, Glooscap Curling; Home: 126 Park St., Kentville, N.S. B4N 1M6; Office: 60 Aberdeen St., P.O. Box 880, Kentville, N.S. B4N 4H8.

**MacDONALD, R. Neil,** B.A., M.D., C.M., F.R.C.P.(C); b. Calgary, Alta., 6 Jan. 1935; s. Angus Neil and Florence (MacDonald) M.; e. St. Mary's Boy's High Sch., Calgary, 1952; Univ. of Toronto, B.A. 1955; McGill Univ., M.D., 1959; m. Mary Jane, d. James Frederick Whiting, Kingston, Jamaica, 30 June 1962; children: Cynthia, David, James, Gavin; DIRECTOR, CANCER BIOETHICS PROGRAM, INSTITUT DE RECHERCHES CLINIQUES DE MONTRÉAL and PROFESSOR OF ONCOLOGY, McGILL UNIV. 1994– ; Interne (1959–60) and Resident in Med. (1960–62), Royal Victoria Hosp., Montreal; Fellow in Hematol. there 1963–65; Fellow in Cancer Chemtherapy, Sloan-Kettering Inst., N.Y. 1962–63; joined McGill Univ. 1965, Assoc. Dean of Med. 1967–70; mem., Attending Staff, Royal Victoria Hospital, Montreal 1965–71; Dir., Cross Cancer Inst. 1971–87; Prof. and Dir., Div. of Oncology, Univ. of Alberta 1975–87; Alberta Cancer Found. Prof. of Palliative Care, Univ. of Alberta 1987–94; awards: Joseph Morley Drake Prize (Path.) 1958; Mosby Book Prize 1958; McGill Univ., James Eccles Schol. 1958; J. Francis Williams Med. Schol. 1959; Sir Edward Beatty Schol. (Post-Doctoral Studies) 1963; Queen's Jubilee Medal 1977; Alta. Achievement Award 1980; Co-Editor 'Oxford Textbook of Palliative Medicine' 1993; author or co-author of many med. reports; mem., Candn. Med. Assn.; Alpha Omega Alpha; Nu Sigma Nu; Amer. Soc. of Clinical Oncology (Secy-Treas. 1979–82); Edmonton Academy of Med. (Past Pres.); Candn. Oncology Soc. (Past Pres.); Candn. Cancer Soc. (Nat. Vice Pres. 1986–87); Nat. Bd., Candn. Palliative Care Found. 1987–88; Expert Adv. Panel on Cancer, World Health Orgn. 1986– ; Roman Catholic; recreations: squash; amateur historian; Office: The Centre for Bioethics, 110 Pine Ave. W., Montréal, Qué. H2W 1R7.

**MACDONALD, Ralph W.,** B.A.; business exective; b. Toronto, Ont. 27 Sept. 1945; e. Univ. of West. Ont., B.A. (Hons.) 1968; m. Carolyn Sloan 20 June 1972; two children; PRESIDENT, HILROY - DIV. OF ABITIBI-PRICE INC. 1993– ; Prod. Mgr., Health Care Div., Warner-Lambert Inc. 1968–75; Group Prod. Mgr., Confectionery Div., Warner-Lambert Inc. 1976; Dir., Prod. Mngt. 1977–78; Mktg. Mgr. 1970; Gen. Mgr. 1980–84; Pres. 1985; Pres. & C.O.O., Cooper Canada Ltd. 1986–93; Mem., Bus. Counc. on Nat. Issues 1985; Grocery Prod. Mfrs. Assn. 1982–85; Confectionery Mfrs. Assn. of Can. 1982–85; recreations: skiing, tennis, golf; Office: 250 Bowie Ave., Toronto, Ont. M6E 2R9.

**MACDONALD, Ramuna,** B.A., B.Sc.; film director; b. Vilkaviskis, Lithuania 17 Feb.; d. Dr. Anthony and Dr. Mary (Makauskas) Paplauskas-Ramunas; e. Univ. of Ottawa, B.A., B.Sc.; m. R. Douglas S. s. Ron and Mary M. 29 July 1969; children: Grazina, Bruce; PRES. & FOUNDER, DOOMSDAY STUDIOS LIMITED 1978– ; Founding Mem., Atlantic Film-makers Coop., Halifax; Bd. of Dir., mem. & interim Dir., Atlantic Film Fest. 1984; Founding Mem., Ottawa Feature Film Prod. Assn. 1988 (Sec. 1988–92); funded by Can. Counc., Nat. Film Bd., Saydie Bronfman Found., prov. of N.S., Telefilm Can., and Candn. Broadcasting Corp.; Dir., 'God's Island,' 'Spirits of an Amber Past,' 'Sarah Jackson,' 'Nobody's Perfect'; Prod., 'Perspectives,' 'Boundaries,' 'Nuclear War,' etc.; Co-prod., 'Spectrum' (with NFB); presently in post-production for 'Silent Conversations' and in development of 3 other feature films; recreations: nordic skiing; Office: 212 James St., Ottawa, Ont. K1R 5M7.

**MacDONALD, The Hon. Mr. Justice Robert,** LL.B., Q.C.; provincial supreme court justice; b. Westville, N.S. 4 Nov. 1920; s. Robert and Isabel Catherine (Ross) MacD.; e. New Glasgow H.S.; Roy. Mil. Coll.; Dalhousie Law Sch. LL.B. 1949; m. Jean d. Thomas and Doris Foster 14 Oct. 1950; children: Cathy, Maryl, Jane, Colla, Elizabeth, Stephen; JUSTICE, SUPREME COURT OF NOVA SCOTIA, TRIAL DIVISION 1985– ; armed service 1940–45; practiced law New Glasgow, N.S. 1950–84; Judge, Prov. Court of N.S. 1984–85; Dir., Maritime Steel and Foundaries Ltd.; Inter-City Gas; Office: Supreme Court, The Law Court Bldg., Trial Div., 1815 Upper Water St., Halifax, N.S. B3J 1S7.

**MACDONALD, Robert Edward Holmes,** B.A., LL.B.; lawyer; b. Oakville, Ont. 9 Dec. 1943; s. Robert Holmes and Lesley Asenath (Whittington) M.; e. Appleby College; Univ. of Western Ont. B.A. 1965, LL.B. 1968; m. Sharon d. Gilbert Kerrigan 11 Nov. 1972; children: Peter, David; PARTNER, BLAKE CASSELS & GRAYDON 1976– ; Chair, Practice and Business Devel. Ctte.; Counsel to major developers & major dept. store operators; Dir., EP Operations Ltd.; Dean's Honour List, Western 1968; recreations: biking, scuba diving; clubs: Cambridge, Granite; Home: 34 Buckingham Ave., Toronto, Ont. M4N 1R3; Office: Box 25, Commerce Ct. W., Toronto, Ont. M5L 1A9.

**MACDONALD, Roderick Alexander,** B.A., LL.B., LL.L., LL.M.; university professor/administrator; b. Markham, Ont. 6 Aug. 1948; s. Colin and Fern Gertrude (Kennedy) M.; e. York Univ., B.A. 1969, LL.B. 1972; Univ. of Ottawa, LL.L. 1974; Univ. of Toronto, LL.M. 1975; m. Shelley Margaret d. Brand and Kathleen Freeman 12 Oct. 1974; children: Madeleine Fern, Aidan Kennedy Bovill; PROF., FAC. OF LAW, MCGILL UNIV. 1984– ; Dir., Law and Society Programme, Candn. Inst. for Advanced Rsch. 1989– ; Asst. Prof., Fac. of Law, Univ. of Windsor 1975–77; Assoc. Prof. 1977–79; McGill Univ. 1979–84; Assoc. Dean 1981–83; Dean, 1984–89; num. speeches & seminars; Prix litt. du Barreau du Qué. 1983; SSHRCC sabbatical leave fellowship 1983; Mem., Law Soc. of Upper Can. 1977– ; Barreau du Qué. 1983– ; Home: 10 Windsor, Westmount, Que. H3Y 2L6; Office: 3644 Peel, Montreal, Que. H3A 1W9.

**MACDONALD, Ronald St. John,** O.C. (1984), B.A., LL.M.; judge; b. Montreal, P.Q. 20 Aug. 1928; s. Col. Ronald St. John and Elizabeth Marie (Smith) M.; e. St. Francis Xavier Univ., B.A. 1949; Dalhousie Univ., LL.B. 1952; Univ. of London (Eng.) LL.M. 1954; Harvard Law Sch., LL.M. 1955; McGill Univ., LL.D. 1988; Internat. Law Comn. Seminar, Geneva (Dipl.) 1952; SENIOR SCHOLAR IN RESIDENCE, FACULTY OF LAW, UNIV. OF TORONTO 1990– ; Lectr. in Law, Osgoode Hall 1955–57; Prof. 1957–59; Asst. Ed., Ont. Reports and Ont. Weekly Notes 1956–57; Prof. of Law, Univ. of W. Ont. 1959–61; Prof. of Law, Univ. of Toronto 1961–67, Dean of Law 1967–72; Dean of Law, Dalhousie Univ. 1972–79, Prof. of Internat. Law 1979–90; Judge at the European Court of Human Rights, Strasbourg 1980– ; mem. Permanent Court of Arbitration, The Hague 1984; Hon. Prof. in the Law Dept., Peking Univ. 1986– ; Pres., World Academy of Art and Science 1983–86; Offr., Order of Can. 1984; Gold Medal, Candn. Counc. Internat. Law, 1988; read law with McInnes, MacQuarrie & Cooper, Halifax, N.S.; called to the Bar of N.S. and of Ont. 1956; Consultant, Dept. of External Affairs, Prime Minister's Office (Ottawa) and Republic of Cyprus (1974–78); Candn. Rep. to U.N. Gen. Assembly 1965, 1966, 1968, 1977, 1990; Advisor, Am. Law Inst.; author of articles and essays in numerous prof. journs.; Sub-Lieut. R.C.N.V.R.(R), discharged 1946; mem., Inst. of Int. Law (Geneva); Bd. of Govs., African Soc. of I.L.; Candn. Bar Assn.; Candn. Inst. Internat. Affairs; Law Soc. Upper Can.; London Inst. World Affairs; Internat. Law Assn.; St. Andrew's Soc.; recreations: reading, walking, sailing, travelling; Home: 17 Leith Place, Toronto, Ont. M4N 2R9; Office: Toronto, Ont.

**MacDONALD, Stewart Ferguson,** M.A., Dr.rer. nat., F.R.S.C.; retired chemist; b. Toronto, Ont. 17 Aug. 1913; s. Mervil and Margaret Stuart (MacGregor) M.; e. Univ. of Toronto Schs.; Univ. of Toronto B.A. 1936, M.A. 1937; Technische Hochschule, Munich, Dr.rer.nat. 1939; m. Marian Katherine, d. late John Medley de Courcy O'Grady, 13 Oct. 1945; children: Peter, Lorna, Wanda, Constance, Sheila; Rsch. Assoc., Banting and Best Dept. of Med. Rsch., Toronto, Ont. 1939–40; Chemist, Welland Chemical Works, Niagara Falls, Ont. 1940–42; Asst. Prof., Banting and Best Dept. Med. Rsch., and Research Assoc., Connaught Labs., Toronto, Ont. 1942–48; on leave at Imp. Coll., London and Cambridge Univ. 1946–47; Univ. Chemical Labs., Cambridge, Eng. 1948–52; with Nat. Rsch. Council until 1978 (Div. of Pure Chem. 1952–68; Principal Research Offr., Biol. Sciences from 1968); Gertrude Davis Exchange Fellowship 1937; Wellcome Fellowship 1948–52; author of articles in tech. journs.; Protestant; Home: 2148 Beaumont Rd., Ottawa, Ont. K1H 5V3.

**MACDONALD, Walter Bruce,** B.A.; copywriter; b. New Westminster, B.C. 5 Dec. 1956; s. Walter Charles and Shirley Anne (Bowell) M.; e. Univ. of Victoria B.A. 1982; m. Janet d. Stanley and Jean Ellis 2 Dec. 1989; Sr. Vice-Pres./Assoc. Creative Dir., Goodgoll Curtis Advertising 1991; Senior Copywriter, Miller Myers Bruce Dalla Costa Advertising Toronto 1983–88; Partner, Ryan Macdonald Edwards Advertising 1989–91; Mem., Soc. for the Preservation of Wild Culture; Western Wilderness Ctte.; Greenpeace; editor: 'Journal of Wild Culture'; poet: various literary publications (e.g. Quarry, Malahat Review, Antigonish Review); recreations: tennis, golf, running; clubs: Waterfront Tennis & Squash; Home: 9 Fulton Ave., Toronto, Ont. M4K 1X6.

**MacDONALD, Wesley Angus Reginald;** retired; b. Prince Albert, Sask. 24 Oct. 1932; s. Harold Angus and Margaret Ada (Love) MacD.; m. Shirley Kathleen Ewart 7 May 1955; children: Nancy Lynn, Kathleen Anne, Christine Ada, Paula Joanne; Senior Extve. Vice Pres., Strategic Devel. - Retail, Royal Bank of Canada 1990–93, retired; Chrmn., Royal Bank Investment Management Inc.; Dir., The International Trust Co.; joined Royal Bank, 1949, occupying positions in several branches in Sask.; Inspection Asst., Candn. Credits Dept., Montreal 1960–61; Second Asst. Mgr., main Calgary Branch 1961–63; Sr. Asst. Mgr., Montreal 1963–66, Credit Insp., Candn. Credits Dept., Head Office 1966–67; Asst. Supvr., Dist. Gen. Mgr. Office, Regina 1967–69, Supvr. 1969–70; Asst. Gen. Mgr., Toronto 1970–73; Gen. Mgr., Manitoba District 1973–78; Vice-Pres. & Gen. Mgr., Ontario West District; Toronto 1978–80; Sr. Vice-Pres., Retail Banking, Canada (Montreal) 1980–86; Extve. Vice Pres., Banking Network 1986–87; Extve. Vice Pres., Retail Banking (Montreal) 1987–90; Clubs: Ontario; Manitoba; Cutten; Royal Montreal Golf; Office: 200 Bay St., Royal Bank Plaza, Toronto, Ont. M5J 2J5.

**MACDONALD, Wilbur Bernard,** M.L.A.; b. Orwell, P.E.I. 13 Sept. 1933; s. Leo R. and late Helen MacD.; e. Orwell Pub. Shc. and St. Dunstan's High Sch.; m. Pauline Mary d. late James A. Murphy 4 Aug. 1958; children: Dana, Helena, Laurena, Ronald, Bernard, Jaunita, Timothy, Andrew, Faber; mixed farm operator, Orwell Cove, P.E.I.; Opposition Critic of Industry, P.E.I.; el. H. of C. 1979; mem. Cttes. on Agric., Fisheries, Regional Ind. Expansion; mem. Nat. Beef Import Ctte. 1979; Chrmn. P.E.I. Land Use Comn. 1980; el. M.L.A. 1982; re-el. 1986; Chrmn. Prog. Conservative Caucus 1983–84; Chrmn. Legis. Cttes. on Agric., Fisheries, Tourism, Ind. 1983–84; el. M.L.A. for Dist. 4th Queens 1982; apptd. to Prov. Cabinet 1984; Min. of Industry, P.E.I. 1984–86; past Pres. Vernon River Lions Club; mem. Vernon Rive Counc., Knights of Columbus; Prog. Conservative; R. Catholic; recreation: owner/breeder standardbred race horses; Home: Orwell Cove, Vernon Bridge, R.R. 2, P.E.I. C0A 2E0.

**MACDONALD, William Atwood,** Q.C., B.A., LL.B.; lawyer; b. Montréal, Qué. 15 Dec. 1927; s. Charles A. and Anna H. (McLaughlin) M.; e. Rosedale Pub. Sch. and Westmount High Sc. Montréal 1945; McGill Univ., B.A. 1948; Osgoode Hall Law Sch., LL.B. 1951; m. Molly Anne d. Wray and Anne Patterson 17 Nov. 1951; children: Susan, David, Dougal, Alex; 4 grandchildren; PRESIDENT, W.A. MACDONALD ASSOCIATES INC. and PRINCIPAL ADVISOR CONSULTANT, McMILLAN BINCH (member of McMillan Bull Casgrain, Toronto, Mississauga, Vancouver, Montreal, Hong Kong, Taipei), joined firm 1951 and was Sr. Partner until 1993; Dir., Chrmn. & Mem., Environment Health and Safety Ctte.; Past Chrmn. (1978–90) and Mem., Audit Ctte., and mem. Extve. Resources, Nominations and Contributions Cttes. of Imperial Oil Ltd.; Trustee & Mem. Invst. Ctte., Imperial Oil Employee Pension Plans; Dir. & Mem., Extve. Ctte. & Mngmt. Resources and Compensation Ctte., Marathon Realty Co. Ltd.; Dir. and Mem. Extve. Ctte. & Audit Ctte., National Trust Co.; The National Victoria and Grey Trustco Ltd.; Dir. & Mem. of Audit and Environment, Health & Safety Cttes., Rio Algom Ltd.; Dir. & Mem. Extve. Ctte., Timminco Ltd.; Dir., Honda Canada Inc.; Dir., Frum Property Corp.; Chrmn., Founding Dir. & Mem. Extve. Ctte., The Japan Soc. in Canada; mem. Canada-Japan Bus. Ctte.; mem., British-North Am. Ctte.; Mem., The Leadership Council on the Americas, Center for Strategic & International Studies, Washington; mem., Candn. Ctte., Internat. Institute for Applied Systems Analysis, Vienna; mem. Adv. Ctte., Centre for Internat. Business, Faculty of Management, Univ. of Toronto; Chrmn., Adv. Ctte., Stratford Chefs Sch.; Robert L. Smith Memorial Fund; Board Mem., Royal Consv. of Music; and Dir. of Social Rsch. and Demonstration Corp.; Chrmn. Candn. Inst. C.A.'s Comn. to Study Public's Expectations of Audits 1988; Special Adv. on Fed. Tax Reform to Ont. Govt. 1970–72; Special Taxation Adv. to Bermuda Govt. 1971–73; Special Adviser, Ont. Govts. Min. of Consumer & Commercial Relations with respect to the Ont. Govt. action to take possession and control of three trust companies 1982–84; former Gov. Candn. Tax Found.; Offr. 8 yrs. and Chrmn. 2 yrs. Nat. Taxation Sect. Candn. Bar Assn.; mem. 10 yrs. and Co-Chrmn. 2 yrs. Jt. Ctte. on Taxation, CICA and Candn. Bar Assn.; mem., Quality of Working Life & Ont. Labour Mgmnt. Study Group 1977–85; mem., Premier of Ontario's Adv. Ctte. on the Economic Future 1977–84; author or co-author various studies, book chapters, articles taxation, competition law and other legal & econ. subjects; editor: 'Income Taxation in Canada' 10 vols.; frequent speaker Can. and abroad; Phi Gamma Delta; United Church; recreations: reading, swimming, fishing, theatre, movies, porcelain;

food; wine; Clubs: York; Rideau (Ottawa); National; Toronto Golf; Home: 48 Nanton Ave., Toronto Ont.; Office: Canada Trust Tower, BCE Place, P.O. Box 621, Suite 3720, 161 Bay St., Toronto, Ont. M5J 2S1.

**MacDONALD, William Brien,** B.A., M.D., M.S., F.R.C.P.(C); educator; b. Edmonton, Alta. 14 Dec. 1935; s. William Alexander and Margaret (O'Brien) MacD.; e. Luther Coll. Regina, Sask. 1953; Univ. of Sask. B.A. 1956, M.D. 1959; Univ. of Colorado M.S. (Health Care Admin.) 1988; m. Mary Donna d. Michael Frederick Tomilin, Kamsack, Sask. 24 May 1958; children: William Charles, Catherine Mary; MEM., ANAESTHETIC STAFF, PASQUA HOSPITAL 1992– ; Asst. Prof. of Anaesthesia, Univ. of Sask. 1964, Assoc. Prof. 1968–72, Prof. 1973, Prof. and Chrmn. of Anaesthesia 1977–84; Assoc. Prof. of Anaesthesia, Univ. of W. Ont. 1972–73; Asst. Dean of Medicine, Univ. of Sask. 1977–79, Assoc. Dean 1979–84; Prof. & Chrmn. of Anesthesia, Univ. of Alta. 1984–88; Principal Medical Advisor to Saskatchewan Health, 1989; Clinical Prof. of Community Medicine & Epidemiology, Univ. of Sask. 1989–92; Depy. Minister, Saskatchewan Health 1990–91; Extve. Dir., Alta. Medical Assoc. 1988; Pres., Sask. Div., Defence Medical Assn. of Can. 1973–1982, (Council mem. 1979–83, Second Vice-Pres. 1981–82); Pres., Defense Medical Assn. of Can. 1982–83; mem. Care-Medico (served in Malaysia 1966); served with Candn. Forces Med. Service Reserve, Commdr. Med. Co. Saskatoon, rank Lt. Col. on retirement 1971; mem. of Council, Royal Coll. Physicians and Surgeons, Can. 1978–84; mem. Candn. Anaesthetists Soc. (Chrmn., Sask. Div. 1980–83); Am. Soc. Anesthesiol.; Internat. Assn. Study Pain; Chrmn. of Council, Candn. Anaesthetists' Soc. 1982–84; P. Conservative; United Church; recreations: golf, boating, hunting; Office: 3666 Moffat Bay, Regina, Sask. S4V 2B5.

**MACDONELL, Harry Winsor,** Q.C., LL.B., B.Com.; b. Toronto, Ont. 19 July 1929; s. Charles Kenneth Sumner and Anita (Winsor) M.; e. Lakefield (Ont.) Prep. Sch., 1949; Carleton Univ., B.Com. 1952; Osgoode Hall Law Sch., LL.B. 1956; m. Marie Martine Malevez, d. late Eugene Nestor Malevez, 20 Feb. 1960; children: Nicole Marie, Ian Kenneth, Winsor James; PARTNER, McCARTHY TÉTRAULT; Chrmn. & Dir., Can. Niagara Power Co. Ltd.; Opinac Energy Corp.; Bonaventure Trust Inc.; The Standard Life Assurance Co. of Canada; Dir., Wajax Ltd.; The SNC-LAVALIN Group Inc.; Standard Life Assurance Co. (U.K.); 3M Canada Inc.; Woodbridge Foam Corp.; Canadian Tire Corp. Ltd.; The Caldwell Partners Intnl. Inc.; ICI Canada Inc.; Alcoa Internal. Canada, Inc.; read law with Fasken and Calvin; called to the Bar of Ontario 1956; cr. Q.C. 1967; Associate, Fasken and Calvin, Toronto, 1956; Partner 1962; Pres. Churchill Falls (Labrador) Corp. Ltd. 1972–75; mem., Candn. Bar Assn.; Co. York Law Assn.; Internat. Comn. Jurists (Candn. Sec.); Law Soc. Upper Can.; Candn. Tax Found.; recreations: skiing, tennis, sailing; Clubs: Toronto; York; Toronto Lawn Tennis; The New Club (Edinburgh); Home: 123 Winchester St., Toronto, Ont. M4X 1B3; Office: Toronto-Dominion Centre, Toronto, Ont. M5K 1E6.

**MacDOUGALD, J. Boyce;** travel company executive; b. Montréal, Qué. 11 Sept. 1931; s. Donald Robert and Maureen P. (Boyce) MacD.; e. Alexendria (Ont.) H.S. 1948; Sir George Williams Univ., McGill Univ. various night courses; m. Pat d. William and Margaret Scott 6 Oct. 1956; SR. VICE PRES. CORPORATE & INDUSTRY AFFAIRS, P. LAWSON TRAVEL 1980– ; Founding Partner and Pres. Voyages Bel-Air Inc., Montréal 1960– ; served Bell Canada 2 yrs.; B.O.A.C. (now British Airways) 9 yrs.; joined present co. 1967 with purchase of Voyages Bel-Air; Pres. Historic Banquets Montréal; Dir. Historically Speaking Montréal; Dir., Harvey's Travel Ltd.; Home: 56 Parfield Dr., Willowdale, Ont. M2J 1C3; Office: 3300 Bloor St. W., Centre Tower, Suite 1200, Toronto, Ont. M8X 2Y2.

**MacDOUGALL, Hartland M.,** C.V.O., O.C.; banker; b. Montreal, Que., 28 Jan. 1931; s. Hartland Campbell and Dorothy (Molson) MacD.; e. Lower Can. Coll., Montreal, 1937–41; Bishop's Coll. Sch., Lennoxville, Que., 1941–47; LeRosey, Switzerland, 1947–48; McGill Univ., 1949–53; Harvard '74; AMP '76; m. Eve, d. late J. Keith Gordon. M.D., 29 Oct. 1954; children: Keith, Cynthia, Wendy, Willa, Tania; DIR. & DEPY. CHRMN., TRILON FINANCIAL CORP., LONDON LIFE INSURANCE CO., LONDON INSURANCE GROUP, INC.; Past Chrmn., Trust Companies Assoc.; with Bank of Montreal 1953–84: Vice Chrmn. 1981–84; Dir. 1974–84; Past Chrmn., Royal Trust Group of Companies; Chrmn., Canada-Japan Business Ctte.; Founding Chrmn., The Japan Society, St. Michael's Hosp. Foundation; Heritage Can.; Gov. and Past Chrmn., Council for Cdn. Unity; Internat. Trustee & Chrmn., Duke of Edinburgh's International Council; Dir., Friends of the Youth Awards, Inc. (USA); Senator, Stratford Shakespearean Foundation; Gov., Olympic Trust; Dir., Cdn. Soc. for Weismann Inst.; Vice-Chrmn., Empire Club Found.; Vice-Pres., MacDonald Stewart Found.; Pres.-elect, Royal Agricultural Winter Fair; Mem., Canada-Japan Forum 2000; Int'l. Adv. Council, City Club of Tokyo; Canada's Sports Hall of Fame Advisory Council; Internat. Counc., Music Centre of Los Angeles and U.B.C. Faculty of Comn. Adv. Council; Trustee, The Candn. Robert T. Jones Jr. Foundation and former Trustee, Lester B. Pearson Coll. of the Pacific; Awarded Gabrielle Léger Medal 1978; Order of Can. 1981, promoted to Officer 1990; apptd. Commander of the Royal Victorian Order 1989; Knight Commander, Order of St. Lazurus of Jerusalem (KCLJ); Anglican; recreations: skiing, tennis, farming; Home: Belfountain, Ont. L0N 1B0; Office: Suite 1110, 70 York St., Toronto, Ont. M5J 1S9.

**MacDOUGALL, Hugh Andrew,** Ph.D.; educator; b. Christmas Island, N.S. 9 Nov. 1922; s. Donald Joseph and Mary Anne (Gillis) MacD.; e. St. Francis Xavier Univ. B.A. 1945; Cambridge Univ. Ph.D. 1960; m. Beverlee d. Donald and Dolores McIntosh 6 Sept. 1975; children: Alanna, Colin; PROF. OF HIST. CARLETON UNIV. 1976– , Dean St. Patrick's Coll. 1973–76; Dean, St. Patrick's Coll. Univ. of Ottawa 1961–67; author: 'Acton-Newman Relations' 1962; 'Lord Acton on Papal Power' 1973; 'Racial Myth in English History' 1982; recreations: skating, swimming; Home: 691 Highland Ave., Ottawa, Ont. K2A 2K5; Office: Ottawa, Ont. K1S 5B6.

**MACDOUGALL, James Colin,** M.A., Ph.D.; educator; b. Ottawa, Ont. 2 May 1942; s. Peter Henderson and Gladys Louise (Blais) MacD.; e. Lisgar C.I. 1960; Carleton Univ., B.A. 1964; McGill Univ., M.A. 1965, Ph.D. 1969; m. Michele d. Clark and Vesta Hayden 21 Nov. 1964; children: Stuart, Jennifer; ASSOC. PROF. OF PSYCHOL., MCGILL UNIV., PRES., CANDN. DEAFNESS RSCH. & TRAINING INST. & DIR. OF RSCH., THE REHAB CTR., OTTAWA 1988– ; Rsch. Fellow Inst. for Rsch. in Human Abilities & Asst. Prof. of Psychol., Meml. Univ. 1969–71; Rsch. Assoc. & Asst. Prof., Nat. Tech. Inst. for Deaf Rochester 1971–72; Psychol. & Dir. of Rsch., Mackay Ctr. for Deaf & Disabled Children Montréal 1972–75; Extve Dir. of Ctr. & Assoc. Prof. of Psychol., McGill Univ. 1976–87; Chrmn., US-Can. Adv. Ctte. Office of Demographic Studies on Deafness, Washington, D.C. 1977–79; Chrmn., Senate Ctte. on Disabled McGill 1984–88; Mem., Bd., Mackay Devel. Plan (Capital Campaign) 1985–87; named 'Man of the Year' Candn. Assn. Deaf 1986; author var. publs. & conf. presentations on deafness & physical disability; mem., Candn. Psychol. Assn.; Que. Corp. Psychols.; Am. Psychol. Assn.; N.Y. Acad. Sci's; recreations: camping, canoeing; club: University; Home: 230 Prince Albert Ave., Westmount, Que. H3Z 2N6; Office: Dept. of Psychology, McGill Univ., Montreal, Que. H3A 2T5.

**MacDOUGALL, William Philip,** B.B.A., C.A.; public servant; b. Port Hill, P.E.I. 15 Jan. 1945; s. Francis Joseph and Mary 'Patricia' (Callaghan) M.; e. Kinkora H.S.; St. Dunstan's Univ. B.B.A. 1968; c.a. 1971; m. Sharyn d. Reagh and Thelma Sudsbury 10 Oct. 1970; children: William 'Darcy,' Meghan Thelma Patricia; DEPUTY MINISTER, DEPT. OF ENVIRONMENTAL RESOURCES, PROV. OF P.E.I. 1993– ; Staff Acct., Clarkson, Gordon & Co. to 1972; Asst. Prov. Auditor, Prov. of P.E.I. 1972; Budget Dir., Treasury Bd. Secretariat 1976; Dep. Min., Dept. of Indus. & Comm. (renamed Dept. of Tourism, Indus. & Energy 1980) 1979; Sec., Treasury Bd. 1981; Deputy Min., Finance & Tourism 1983–93; Pres., Inst. of C.A.'s 1979; Belvedere Golf & Winter Club Inc. 1979; Past Pres., PEI Hostel Assn.; recreation: golf; Home: 45 Glencove Dr., Charlottetown, P.E.I. C1A 7T4; Office: P.O. Box 2000, Charlottetown, P.E.I. C1A 7N8.

**MACE, His Excellency Michael T.,** B.A.; diplomat; b. Dauphin, Man. 7 April 1942; s. the late Squadron Leader Roger M. (killed in 1944) and Margaret M. (Irwin) M. (stepfather: John G. Chance); e. Queen's Univ. B.A. 1964; m. Jane d. Kenneth and Patricia McIlraith 16 Dec. 1967; children: Roger, Alison; Canadian Ambassador to Chile with Concurrent Accreditation to Paraguay, Dept. of External Affairs 1990; joined Foreign Service 1967; Attache, Cairo 1968–70; 2nd Sec., Havana 1972–74; 1st Sec., Moscow 1977–79; Counsellor, Kuala Lumpur 1979–81; Head Soviet Affairs Section, Ottawa 1981–84; Dir., Pol./Econ. & Social Affairs, Personnel Div. 1984–87; Counsellor, Tel Aviv 1987–90; Naval Cadet UNTD 1961–65; Lt. RCN (R), retired 1967; recreations: golf, nordic skiing.

**MacEACHEN, Hon. Allan J.,** P.C. (Can.), M.A., LL.D.; senator; b. Inverness, N.S., 6 July 1921; s. Angus and Annie (Gillis) M.; e. St. Francis Xavier Univ., B.A. 1944; Univ. of Toronto, M.A. 1946 (Pol. Econ.); Univ. of Chicago (Econ.) 1948; Mass. Inst. Tech., Dept. Econ. and Social Science, 1951–1953; Hon. degrees; St. Francis Xavier, Acadia Univ., Loyola Coll. (Baltimore); LL.D. (Hon.), St. Marys Univ. 1973; Dalhousie Univ. 1974; Sir Wilfrid Laurier 1976; MEMBER OF THE SENATE OF CANADA; Leader of the Opposition in the Senate 1984–91; Prof. of Econ., St. Francis Xavier Univ., 1946–48 and subsequently Head, Dept. of Economics and Social Sciences; el. to H. of C. for Inverness-Richmond (now Cape Breton Highlands-Canso), g.e. 1953; re-el. g.e. 1957; def. g.e. 1958; apptd. Special Asst. and Consultant on Econ. Affairs to Hon. Lester Pearson, 1958; re-el. g.e. 1962 until and including 1980; Min. of Labour, 1963–65; Min. of Nat. Health & Welfare, 1965–68 (also Govt. House Leader 1967–68); Manpower and Immigration 1968–70; Pres. Privy Council and Govt. House Leader 1970–74; Secy. of State for External Affairs 1974–76; Pres. Privy Council 1976–77; Pres. Group of 10, 1980–81; Chrmn., Interim Ctte., Internat. Monetary Fund; Chrmn., Conf. on Internat. Economic Co-operation; Chrmn., GATT Ministerial 1982; Chrmn., Internat. Advisory Council of the Bank of Montreal 1986–91; Depy. Prime Min. and Pres. Privy Council 1977–79; Depy. Leader of the Opposition and Opposition House Leader, 1979; Depy. Prime Min. and Min. of Fin. 1980–82; Depy. Prime Min. and Secy. of State for External Affairs 1982–84; summoned to Senate June 1984; Leader of Govt. in Senate until Sept. 1984; Mem., Royal Ottawa Health Care Group's Bd. of Trustees 1987– ; Home: R.R. 1, Whycocomagh, N.S. B0E 3M0; Office: Room 381-S, Centre Block, The Senate, Ottawa, Ont. K1A 0A4.

**MACEROLA, François,** B.A., LL.L.; government film commissioner; cultural association executive; b. Montreal, Que. 31 Jan. 1942; s. Antonio and Yvette (Bayard) M.; e. Univ. of Montreal B.A. 1963, LL.L. 1970; children: Stéphanie, Louis; Candn. Govt. Film Commissioner and Chairman National Film Board of Canada 1984–89; called to Bar of Que. 1971; practiced law, Malouf, Pateras, Macerola 1971; Bds.: Telefilm Canada; National Arts Centre; Conservatoire d'art cinématographique de Montréal; National Screen Inst., Can.; Comité d'appui du centre de recherche et d'enseignement sur la francophonie des femmes (Inst. Simone de Beauvoir, Montréal); Jean-Talon Hosp. Found.; Bd. of Gov., Univ. of Montreal; recreations: tennis, racquetball, skiing; Club: social Canado-italien.

**MacEWAN, Douglas William,** M.D.; radiologist; consultant; b. Ottawa, Ont. 11 Nov. 1924; s. James Urquhart and Eleanor (Smith) MacE.; e. McGill Univ. B.Sc. 1948, M.D., C.M. 1952; m. Elizabeth d. Allan Turner Bone, Montreal, Que. 23 June 1951; children: Joanne, Elspeth, Eleanor, James; PUBLIC POLICY CONSULTANT, MANITOBA HEALTH 1990– ; Prof. of Radiology and Community Health Sciences, Senior Scholar, Univ. of Man. Health Sciences Centre 1990– ; served with RCAF 1943–45; rec'd Queen's Silver Jubilee Medal 1977; former Ed. 'Journal of the Canadian Association of Radiologists'; author 70 scient. articles in field of Radiology; Past Pres. and Gold Medalist Radiol. Soc. N. Am.; Candn. Assn. Radiols.; United Church; recreations: skiing, curling; Club: Winnipeg Winter; Home: 30 Aldershot Blvd., Winnipeg, Man. R3P 0C8.

**MacEWAN, Hon. John Walter Grant,** B.S.A., M.Sc., LL.D. (Hon.); agriculturist; historian; writer; b. Brandon, Man. 12 Aug. 1902; s. Alexander and Bertha (Grant) M.; e. Ont. Agric. Coll., B.S.A. 1926; Iowa State Coll., M.Sc. 1928; LL.D. (Hon.), Univ. of Alta. 1966; Calgary 1967; Brandon 1969; Guelph 1972; Sask. 1974; m. Phyllis, d. Vernon Cline, 1935; one d., Heather; Leader of Liberal Party in Alta. 1958–60; Mayor of Calgary 1963–65; former M.L.A. for Calgary; Lt. Gov. of Alta. 1965–74; former Chrmn., Calgary Community Foundation; former Dean, Faculty of Agric. & Home Econ., Univ. of Man.; co-author: 'Candn. Animal Husbandry' 1936; 'General Agriculture' 1939; author: 'Breeds of Farm Livestock in Canada' 1941;'Feeding of Farm Animals' 1945; 'Sodbusters' 1948; 'Agriculture on Parade' 1957; 'Between the Red and the Rockies' 1957; 'Eye Opener Bob' 1957; 'Fifty Mighty Men' 1958; 'Calgary Cavalcade' 1958; 'John Ware's Cow Country' 1960; 'Blazing the Old Cattle Trails' 1962; 'Entrusted to my Care' 1963; 'Hoofprints & Hitchingposts' 1964; 'Poking into Politics' 1965; 'Tatanga Mani' 1966; 'Harvest of Bread' 1967; 'West to the Sea' 1968; 'Portrait from the Plains' 1969; 'Sitting Bull' 1973; 'Power for Prairie Plows' 1972; 'Battle for the Bay' 1975; 'Mighty Women Too' 1975; 'Memory Meadows' 1976; 'Cornerstone Colony' 1977; 'The Rhyming Horsemen of the

Qu'Appelle' 1978; 'Pat Burns, Cattle King' 1979; 'Illustrated History of Western Canadian Agriculture' 1980; 'Métis Makers of History' 1981; (with R.H. MacDonald) 'Alberta Landscapes' 1982; 'Charles Noble, Guardian of The Soil' 1983; 'Wild Horse Jack' 1983; 'The Spirit of Marie Anne Lagimodiere' 1984; 'Highlights of Shorthorn History' 1983; 'Frederick Haultain, Frontier Statesman of the Canadian Northwest' 1985; 'Heavy Horses – Highlights of their History in Canada' 1986; 'Paddy Nolan Left Them Laughing When He Said Goodbye' 1987; 'James Walker, Man of the Western Frontier' 1989; 'Grant MacEwan's West: Sketches From the Past' 1990; 'Highlights of Sheep History in the Canadian West' 1991; 'Coyote Music, and Other Humorous Tales of the Early West' 1993; recreation: historical research; Home: Suite 1214, E. Calgary Village, 750 5th St. S.E., Calgary, Alta. T2G 5B4.

**MacEWEN, Don B.,** B.Eng., M.Eng.; professor of engineering; b. Charlottetown, P.E.I. 24 June 1950; s. Clarence and Alice M.; e. Univ. of P.E.I., eng. dipl. 1972; Univ. of N.B., B.Eng. (civil) 1974, M.Eng. (environ.) 1976; m. Arlene d. John and Doris Trainor 27 May 1972; children: Sidney J., Milisa D., Tasha D.; PROFESSOR OF ENGINEERING, UNIV. OF P.E.I. 1993– ; Cons. Engr., ADI Limited 1976–77; Asst. Prof. of Engr., Univ. of P.E.I. 1977–85, Assoc. Prof. of Engr. 1985–93; Chrmn., Engr. Dept. 1978–87; conducted extensive rsch., produced many reports & papers relating to environ. engr., engr. edn. & profl. practice as well as ethics in engr. in its relation to soc.; Pres., Candn. Counc. of Profl. Engrs. 1988–89; Assn. of Profl. Engrs. of P.E.I. 1982–83; Chrmn., P.E.I. Prov. Sci. Fair 1978–88; Mem., Assn. of Profl. Engrs. of P.E.I.; 1st recipient Assn. of Profl. Engrs. of P.E.I. Ralph Woodside Memorial Award for Outstanding Service to the Profession; Home: P.O. Box 178, Morell, P.E.I. C0A 1S0; Office: Charlottetown, P.E.I. C1A 4P3.

**MACFARLANE, Hon. Alan Brock;** judge; b. Victoria, B.C., 17 May 1924; s. late Justice Arthur Douglas and Myrtle Barnard (Sargison) M.; e. Oak Bay (B.C.) High Sch.; Victoria Coll.; Univ. of B.C., LL.B. 1949; m. Sheila Frances, d. late Frank Strachan, 22 Dec. 1945; JUSTICE, COURT OF APPEAL, B.C. 1982– ; read law with John L. Clay; called to Bar of B.C. 1949; Partner, Clay & Macfarlane, Victoria, 1949–51; Sr. Partner, Clay Macfarlane Ellis & Popham, 1951–68; Justice, Supreme Court of B.C., 1968–82; served with RCAF 1943–45; rank Flying Offr. (Pilot); el. M.L.A. for Oak Bay in B.C. g.e. 1960, 1963 and 1966; resigned to accept Supreme Court of B.C. appt.; Dir. and Past Pres., YM-YWCA of Victoria; Past Pres., Victoria Bar Assn. (1965–66); mem., Candn. Bar Assn.; Anglican; recreations: boating, travel; Clubs: Union; Victoria Golf; Home: Victoria, B.C. V8S 3P6; Office: Law Courts, 800 Smithe St., Vancouver, B.C. V6Z 2E1 and 850 Burdett St., Victoria, B.C. V8W 1B4.

**MacFARLANE, Andrew,** B.A., M.L.S.; b. Toronto, Ont. 18 Feb. 1928; s. late Joseph A., M.D. and late Marguerite (Walker) MacF.; e. Whitney Pub. Sch., Toronto; Univ. of Toronto Schs.; Univ. of Sask.; Univ. of Toronto, B.A. 1949; Univ. of Western Ont., M.L.S. 1977; m. Betty Doris Seldon; children: two d. Jeanie Andreas, Catriona Flora, Elizabeth Seldon (step-daughter); PROF. OF JOURNALISM, UNIV. OF W. ONT. 1981–91; PROF. OF MASS MEDIA STUDIES AND DIR. CENTRE FOR MASS MEDIA STUDIES, GRAD. SCH. OF JOURNALISM, UNIV. OF W. ONT. 1990– ; with Canadian Press, Toronto 1949; Reporter, 'Halifax Mail-Star' 1950; City Ed., 'Halifax Chronicle Herald' 1951; Reporter, 'Scottish Daily Express' 1951–52; Sub-ed., 'London Evening Standard' 1953–54; joined 'The Telegram' as Copy Ed., Toronto 1955; subsequently held positions of Night Ed., Feature Ed., Gen. Reporter, Daily Columnist, Asst. to Publisher, Mang. Ed. and Extve. Ed.; Dir., Citizens Inquiry Branch, Ont. Govt. Services 1971–73; Prof. & Dean, Sch. of Journ., Faculty Grad. Studies, Univ. of W. Ont. 1973–80; author: 'It Seemed Like a Good Idea at the Time'; 'Local Flavor'; ed.: 'Byline: The 1982 National Newspaper Awards'; 'Byline Canada: The 1984 National Newspaper Awards'; rec'd. National Newspaper Awards for Staff Corr. 1958 and Spot News Reporting 1959; Bowater Award, Commonwealth and Internat. Writing 1960; Southam Fellowship 1961; Bicentennial Medal for Public Service, Prov. of Ont. 1984; National Teaching Award, Poynter Inst. for Media Studies, St. Petersburg, Fla. 1987; Hon. Mention, Candn. Magazine Food Writer of the Year 1988; former Dir., Children's Aid Soc. Metrop. Toronto; Founder-Dir., Candn. Medic-Alert Foundation; mem. and former dir., Candn. Mang. Eds.' Conf.; Founding Dir. and later Pres. and Trustee Candn. Nat. Magazine Awards; Founder and later Chrmn., Advisory Council, Ont. Medal for Good Citizenship; Founding Pres., Commonwealth Assoc. for Educ. in Journalism and Comm.; recreation: riding; Clubs: University (London); Toronto Press; Trollope Hunt (Thorndale, Ont.); Home: 257 Bernard Ave., London, Ont. N6A 2M9; Office: Sch. of Journalism, Middlesex Coll., Univ. of W. Ont., London, Ont. N6A 5B7.

**MACFARLANE, Bruce Alexander,** B.A., LL.B., Q.C.; lawyer; author; b. Winnipeg, Man. 1 Sept. 1949; s. Gordon Alexander and Reta Merle (Thornton) M.; e. Univ. of Winnipeg, B.A. 1970; Univ. of Manitoba LL.B. 1973; m. Diane d. Ernest and Therese Meilleur 28 Aug. 1971; children: Cheryl, Kevin; Asst. Depy. Attorney General of Canada 1989; articled to A.A. Sarchuk, Q.C. 1973–74; called to Manitoba Bar 1974; Dir., Federal Prosecutions, Man. 1976; called to Sask. Bar 1979; Dir., Legal Serv., R.C.M.P. 1982; Dir., Dept. of Justice, Alta. 1986; called to Alta. Bar 1987; Q.C. 1987; has appeared in all levels of courts in Can., including the Supreme Ct. of Can. in numerous criminal & civil cases; lectures to numerous groups incl. bar assns., law socs., judges' assns., police academies, Internat. Prosecutors confs.; Chrmn., Criminal Justice Subsection, Candn. Bar Assn. (Man.); Commissioner, Uniform Law Conference; author: 'Drug Offences in Canada' 1979, 1986; Contbr.: 'Studies in Canadian Criminal Procedure' 1983; frequent contrb., Criminal Law Quarterly'; Former Editor-in-Chief, Manitoba Law Journal; recreations: hunting, photography, writing; Home: 1697 Place des Ravins, Ottawa, Ont. K1C 6H6.

**MACFARLANE, David,** B.A.; writer; b. Hamilton, Ont. 19 Aug. 1952; s. Edmond Blakely and Elizabeth Louise (Goodyear) M.; e. Trinity Coll. Sch. Port Hope 1971; Univ. of Toronto B.A. 1975; m. Janice d. Ian and Molly Lindsay 24 Oct. 1981; children: Caroline, Blakely; contbg. ed. Saturday Night mag. 1983–85, staff writer 1985–87, assoc. ed. 1987–88; ed. CBC Radio Guide 1983–85; producer and writer 'Where is Here?' (PBS-WTVS) 1986–87; sr. writer Toronto Mag. 1988–90; recipient 6 gold nat. mag. awards, 2 silver 1981–89; Sovereign Award Mag. Journalism 1987; author: 'The Danger Tree' published under the title 'Come From Away' in U.S. and U.K. 1992; recipient, The Canadian Author's Assn. Award for non-fiction 1992; nominated for the Trillium Award 1992; recreation: tennis; Club: The Dog; Home: Toronto, Ont.

**MACFARLANE, Donald A.,** B.Comm., C.A.; executive; e. Univ. of Toronto B.Comm. 1945; C.A. 1949; PRES. AND TREAS., CONSOLIDATED RAMBLER MINES LTD.; Atlantic Coast Copper Corp. Ltd., First Maritime Mining Corp. Ltd., Key Anacon Mines Ltd. and Northern Canada Mines Ltd.; prior to joining present co. Treas. Brunswick Mining & Smelting Corp. Ltd.; articled with Clarkson Gordon; Home: 114 Park Dr., Saint John, N.B. E2H 1A8; Office: P.O. Box 937, Saint John, N.B. E2L 4E3.

**MacFARLANE, J. Douglas,** M.B.E.; journalist; educator; b. Ottawa, Ont., 4 Oct. 1916; s. late Rev. James Phee and Annie Georgina (Nelson) M; e. Albert Coll., Belleville, Ont. (Grad.); m. Kathleen Kendrick, Chatham, Ont., 1940; COMMUNICATIONS CONSULTANT; entered newspaper work as Reporter, Windsor 'Star' 1934; Reporter, Toronto 'Star' 1940–41; enlisted with Candn. Inf., Commissioned in Essex Scottish 1942; Overseas 1943; Ed., Candn. Army newspaper 'Maple Leaf' 1944–45; joined staff of Toronto 'Globe & Mail' 1946 and apptd. City Ed. same yr.; City Ed., 'The Telegram' 1949, Asst. Mang. Ed. 1951, Mang. Ed. 1952, Vice-Pres. and Extve. Ed. 1954, Vice-Pres. and Ed.-in-Chief 1960–69; Chrmn., Dept. of Journalism, Ryerson Polytech. Inst. 1971–76; Fellow of Ryerson 1981; Ed. Dir., Toronto Sun 1976–81; Chrmn., Gordon Sinclair Foundation; Dir., Candn. War Correspondents Assn.; el. to Candn. News Hall of Fame 1985; author: 'Herbie'; 'Maple Leaf Forever'; Club: Mississaugua Golf; Home: 1945 Mississauga Rd., Mississauga, Ont. L5H 2K5.

**MacFARLANE, John Edward;** journalist; b. Montreal, Que. 28 Mar. 1942; s. William Stewart and Eileen Georgina (Easey) M.; e. Univ. of Toronto Schools; Western Canada H.S.; Univ. of Alberta; m. Pamela d. Eric and Margaret Purves 31 May 1987; children: Elizabeth Callon, Amy Victoria; EDITOR, TORONTO LIFE 1992– ; Editor, Toronto Life Magazine 1972–74; Pres., Analytical Communications Ltd. 1974–75; Extve. Ed., Maclean's Magazine 1975–76; Editor, Weekend Magazine 1976–80; Publisher, Saturday Night magazine 1980–87; Publisher & Editor-in-Chief, Financial Times of Canada 1987–90; Managing Dir., News, Features & Information Programming, CTV Television Network Ltd. 1990–92; Principal, MacFarlane Walter & Ross, Book Pubs.; Pres., Candn. Univ. Press 1964; Chrmn., YMCA of Metro. Toronto 1986–87; Bd. Mem., Ontario Arts Counc. 1985–87; co-author: 'The Death of Hockey' 1972; recreations: wilderness canoeing; club: Royal Candn. Yacht; Office: 59 Front St. E., 3rd Floor, Toronto, Ont. M5E 1B2.

**MacGILL, Neil Whyte,** M.A.; university professor; b. Manchester, England 12 April 1935; s. John Sylvanus and Dorothy (Bardsley) MacGill; e. Loretto School Musselburgh Scotland; Trinity College, Cambridge Univ. B.A. 1956, M.A. 1960; Univ. of Edinburgh M.A. 1960; Lincoln College, Oxford Univ. M.A. 1961; PROFESSOR OF PHILOSOPHY, UNIV. OF NEW BRUNSWICK 1975– ; Asst. Prof., Univ. of N.B. 1961–69; Assoc. Prof. 1969–75; Don of Neill House 1961–66; Resident Fellow, Bridges House 1966– ; Chairperson, Dept. of Philosophy 1971–82; Mem., Univ. Senate 1969– ; Bd. of Governors 1986– ; Mem., Candn. Philosophical Assn. 1961– (Dir. 1973–75); Extve. Council, U.N.B. Faculty Club 1983–90, 1992– ; Fredericton Ctte. for the Atlantic Symphony Orch. 1973–83; Fredericton Branch, Humanities Assn. of Can. (Sec.-Treas. 1979–81; Pres. 1981–84); Mind Assn. 1956– ; Atheist; Apolitical; recreations: plays and concert-going; clubs: Royal Overseas League; Home: Bridges House, U.N.B., P.O. Box 4400, Fredericton, N.B. E3B 5A3; Office: Philosophy Dept., U.N.B., P.O. Box 4400, Fredericton, N.B. E3B 5A3.

**MacGILLIVRAY, Peter Joseph;** real estate executive; b. Edmonton, Alta. 25 March 1955; s. Donald H. and Eileen Muriel (McCann) M.; e. Univ. of Victoria; Notre Dame Coll.; St. Michael's Sch.; Camoson Coll.; B.C. Coll.; EXTVE. VICE-PRES., RE/MAX PROMOTIONS (the Media and Public Relations arm of RE/MAX Ontario-Atlantic Canada) 1984– ; Admin., Strathcona Park Outdoor Edn. Ctr. 1976–77; Founder & Mgr., Handy Andy's Home Serv. 1977–79; Sales Rep., Monday Magazine 1979–81; Sales Mgr./Acct. Extve., Communications Concepts 1981; Acct. Extve. Internat. Sports Properties 1981–84; Sec.-Treas., Re/Max North Central Promotions 1987; Bd. of Dirs., 'Reach For The Rainbow'; Toronto Arts Awards; recipient: first RE/MAX Internat. Public Relations Award for outstanding achievement 1986; RE/MAX Ontario-Atlantic Canada Distinguished Service Award 1990; RE/MAX International Inc. Englewood, Colorado Distinguished Service Award 1992; Patron, Belfry Theatre; recreations: photography, sailing, theatre, travel; Office: 7101 Syntex Dr., Mississauga, Ont. L5N 6H5.

**MACGILLIVRAY, Royce Cooper,** Ph.D.; university professor; b. Alexandria, Ont. 13 May 1936; s. Rory and Penelope (MacLeod) M.; c. Alexandria H.S. 1955; Queen's Univ., B.A. 1959; Harvard Univ., A.M. 1960, Ph.D. 1965; LECTR., DEPT. OF HISTORY, UNIV. OF WATERLOO 1962– ; author: 'Restoration Historians' 1974, 'The House of Ontario' 1983, 'The New Querist' 1983, 'The Mind of Ontario' 1985; 'The Slopes of the Andes' 1990 (autobiog. essays); co-author: 'History of Glengarry' 1979; Editor, 'Ontario History' 1979–81; Home: 915 – 170 Erb St. W., Waterloo, Ont. N2L 1V4; Office: Waterloo, Ont. N2L 3G1.

**MacGIRR, C. Garth,** F.C.A., C.I.P.; chartered accountant, chartered insolvency practitioner; b. Niagara Falls, Ont. 25 April 1935; s. Albert Edward and Edna Isobel (Flummerfelt) M.; e. Riverdale Collegiate 1953; C.A. 1960; Trustee in Bankruptcy 1971; Western Bus. Sch. M.T.C. 1977; m. Mary d. Harry and Georgina Milanoff 31 May 1958; NATIONAL INSOLVENCY PARTNER, PRICE WATERHOUSE 1977– ; Peat, Marwick, Mitchell & Co. 1953–63; Group of Mortgage, Finance & Insurance Cos. 1963–67; joined Price Waterhouse 1967; Mgr., Trustee Dept. 1969; Partner 1973; Bd. Chair, Western Bus. Sch. Club of Toronto 1990– ; Fellow, Inst. of C.A.s of Ont. 1988; Past Pres., Insol Internat.; Candn. Insolvency Practitioners Assn.; Ont. Insolvency Assn.; recreations: tennis, travel, sports fan; clubs: Ontario, Royal Canadian Military Inst., Toronto Cricket, Skating & Curling; Home: 268 Lonsdale Rd., Toronto, Ont. M4V 1X1; Office: Box 190, Ste. 3200, 1 First Canadian Pl., Toronto, Ont. M5X 1H7.

**MACGOWAN, Kenneth Owen,** B.Com.; b. New Westminster, B.C. 11 Sept. 1921; s. Keith Campbell and Gertrude Augusta (Rand) M.; e. Herbert Spencer Pub. Sch.; Duke of Connaught High Sch.; Univ. of B.C., B.Com. 1946; m. Audrey Marion d., Douglas Churchill, 31 May 1946; children: John D., Patricia E., Peter J., Colleen M.; PRES., KENNETH MACGOWAN HOLDINGS LTD. 1967– ; Chrmn. & Dir., UT Technologies Limited 1989– ; Vice-Pres. & Dir., The K.C. Macgowan Co. Ltd.; joined William M. Mercer Ltd., 1946; spent 3 months in Montreal office; returned to Vancouver transferring to Toronto as Asst. Mgr., 1948; Mgr., Vancouver office and apptd. a Dir., 1950; Vice-Pres. (supervising operations for Winnipeg, Calgary and Vancouver offices) 1955; apptd. Mang. Dir. 1966, Pres. 1969; Chrmn. Extve. Comte. of firm and Marsh & McLennan Ltd. 1972; Sr. Vice Pres. Admin., and Secty. (both firms) 1975–80; served with Coastal Command 1943–45; Past Chrmn., New Westminster Pub. Lib. Bd.; No. 513 Sqdn. Royal Candn. Air Cadets; Pres., New Westminster Chamber Comm. 1968–69; mem. Urban Redevel. Comte. for New Westminster 1965–68; Past Gov., Pacific Nat. Exhn.; Pres. Multiple Sclerosis Soc. of Can. 1977–79; Vice Pres. for N. Am. I.F.M.S.S. 1985–89; mem. Bd. Trade Metrop. Toronto; Delta Upsilon; Anglican; recreations: golf, fishing; Clubs: Vancouver Golf; Terminal City; Vancouver (all B.C.); Toronto Hunt; National; Franklin; Home: 926–21 Dale Ave., Toronto, Ont. M4W 1K3; Office: 21 Dale Ave., Ste. 926, Toronto, Ont. M4W 1K3.

**MacGOWN, Magdalene (Madge) Coull,** M.A., B.L.S., M.Ed.; librarian; b. Campbeltown, Scotland 11 Jan. 1935; d. Robert MacCallum and Magdalene (Murray) M.; e. Univ. of Glasgow M.A. (Hons.) 1957; Jordanhill Coll. of Edn., teacher cert. 1958; Univ. of Toronto B.L.S. 1963, M.Ed. 1974; UNIVERSITY LIBRARIAN, UNIV. OF WINDSOR 1989– ; Teacher, Dunoon Grammar Sch. Scotland 1958–60 Library Asst., North York Public Lib. 1961–62; Librarian (Cataloguer), Imperial Oil Limited 1963–65; Tech. Serv. Librarian, Education Ctr., Toronto 1965–71; Tech. Serv. Supvr., Media Serv., Calgary Bd. of Edn. 1971–77; Collections Librarian, Edn. Lib., Univ. of Alta. 1977–81; Head 1981–89; Visiting Fellow, Nat. Lib. of Canada 1988–89; Dir., Legal Resource Ctr. of Alta. 1981–87; Mem., Candn. Assn. of Rsch. Libs.; Candn. Lib. Assn. (Counc. Mem. 1981–84; Bd. Mem. 1985–87); Candn. Assn. of Coll. & Univ. Libs. (Pres. 1985–87); Ont. Counc. of Univ. Libs.; Ont. Lib. Assn.; Am. Lib. Assn. (ACRL, LAMA); recreations: golf, travel, walking; clubs: Sutton Creek Golf & Country; Home: 351 Randolph Ave., Windsor, Ont. N9B 2T4; Office: Leddy Library, Univ. of Windsor, Windsor, Ont. N9B 3P4.

**MacGREGOR, David Edward Stephen,** M.A., Ph.D.; educator; b. Renfrew, Ont. 2 Jan. 1943; s. Edward Francis McGregor and Jean Mavis (née Love; formerly McGregor) Nethercote; e. Fisher Park High Sch. Ottawa; Carleton Univ. B.A. 1969, M.A. 1974; London Sch. of Econ. & Pol. Sci. Ph.D. 1978; m. Patricia d. John and Dorothy Bishop 11 May 1976; one s. Ethan MacGregor John David Bishop; PROF. OF SOCIOL. KING'S COLL. UNIV. OF W. ONT. 1988– ; Clk. Treasury Office Govt. Can. 1960–63; Prog. Evaluation Offr. (ESS) Manpower & Immigration Can. 1970–75; Asst. Prof. of Sociol. present Coll. 1978, Assoc. Prof. 1983, Chairperson 1983–88; recipient Ont. Grad. Scholarship 1969–70; Can. Council Fellowship 1975–78; SSHRRC Sabbatical Leave Grant 1984–85; John Porter Meml. Award (CSAA) 1985; SSHRCC Research Grant 1991–94; Dir. Raoul Wallenberg Centres London, Ont. 1985–89; author 'The Communist Ideal in Hegel and Marx' 1984, 1990; 'Hegel, Marx and the English State' 1992; various articles Hegel and Marx scholarly jours.; ed. bd. Candn. Review Sociol. & Anthrop. 1984–86; mem. Candn. Sociol. & Anthrop. Assn.; Am. Sociol. Assn.; Hegel Soc. Am.; Hegel Soc. of Great Britain; Center for Auto Safety; recreations: running, reading, films, travel, drawing; Home: 258 Seaton St., Toronto, Ont. M5A 2T4; Office: 266 Epworth Ave., London, Ont. N6A 2M3.

**MacGREGOR, Donald Chalmers,** B.A., F.R.S.C. (1954); retired university professor; b. Toronto, Ont. 31 Aug. 1905; s. Alexander, Q.C., and Alice M.; e. Univ. Coll., Univ. of Toronto, B.A. 1928; Harvard Univ. 1929–30; m. Dorothy Rosebrugh (died April, 1974) 19 Feb. 1938; one surviving s., Duncan Brec; m. 2ndly Eleanor Margaret, d. late Rev. Gordon Jones, 16 June 1975; Prof. of Economics, Univ. of Toronto 1953–72; Lect., Asst. and Assoc. Prof. 1931–53; Joint Editor, Bank of Nova Scotia Monthly Review, 1935–39; mem., Research Staff, Royal Comn. on Dom.-Prov. Relations 1937–38; Guggenheim Fellow, 1943–44; Dir. and co-author of 'National Income': A Study Prepared for Royal Comn. on Dom.-Prov. Relations (1939); Jt. Chrmn., Ont. Govt. Comte. on Portable Pensions 1960–62; Vice-Chrmn., Pensions Comn. of Ont. 1963–66; has contrib. many papers to prof. journs.; also submissions for publ. inquiries including studies in taxation (1970) and inflation (1974); collaborator in various works on Candn. econ. problems; Pres., The Harold Innis Found., Innis Coll., Toronto 1977–87; mem., Hart House; Clubs: Faculty; Madawaska Club (founded 1898–99); Address: Dept. of Political Science, Univ. of Toronto, Toronto, Ont. M5S 1A1.

**MacGREGOR, John;** artist; b. Dorking, Eng., 12 Jan. 1944; s. Wallace Robert and Joan Pearl (Barter) MacG.; came to Can. 1949; e. York Mem. Coll Inst. and Central Tech. Sch., Toronto; m. Melanie Ann Furse (div.); one d. Katherine Olivia; one-man exhns.: Hart House, Univ. of Toronto 1967; The Isaacs Gallery, Toronto 1968, 1970, 1971, 1972, 1973, 1974, 1975, 1977, 1979, 1981, 1982, 1984, 1986; Chatham Art Gallery 1972; Gallery III Montreal 1973; Gallery Graphics, Ottawa 1975; Time Tunnel Gallery, Windsor, Ont. 1981; North Bay Gallery 1982; 'John MacGregor: A Survey' Art Gallery of Greater Victoria (travelling) 1983–84; Thunderbay Art Gallery 1986; Moore Gallery, Hamilton 1986; other exhibitions incl.: The Isaacs Gallery 1966 and (two-man) 1967; Art Gallery of Ont. – Ont. Centennial Purchase Exhn. 1967, 'The Collector Chooses' 1967 and Candn. Artists '68; McIntosh Gallery, Univ. of W. Ont. 1967; Erindale Coll., Univ. of Toronto 1968; Winnipeg Show 1968, 1970; Montreal Museum of Fine Arts 1968; 'Art Sensual,' Hart House, Univ. of Toronto 1970; Survey 70, Art Gallery, Ont., and Montreal Museum Fine Arts 1970; 'Works on Paper,' Inst. Contemp. Art, Boston 1970; 22nd Annual Exhn., Hamilton Art Gallery 1971; 'Artario 72,' CNE Art Gallery 1972; Musée d'Art Moderne, Yugoslavia 1972; Bienal Am. de Arts Graphica, Columbia 1973; Trajectory, Paris 1973; Art Gallery of Ont., 'Contemporary Ontario Art' 1974, 'Chairs' 1975; 'Burnaby Print Biennial,' B.C. 1975; 'Six Artists,' Art Gallery of Ont. 1978–79; 'Twentieth Century Canadian Drawings' 1979; 'Old Techniques in New Hands,' Harbourfront Art Gallery 1981 Chromaliving, Chromazone, Toronto 1983; Lynwood Arts Centre 1984–85; Gallery Esperanza Montreal 1986 and many others; rep. in coll. of Nat. Gallery of Can., Art Gallery of Ont., Ministery of External Affairs and in many public and private colls.; rec'd. Can. Council Awards 1967, 1968, 1969, 1970, 1971, 1972; Sr. Arts Grant 1974, 1976; Canada Council Short Term Grants 1967, 1971, 1977, 1978, 1979, 1986; Ont. Arts Council Grants 1979–81; Winnipeg Biennial Purchase Award 1970; Teacher, Ont. Coll. of Art 1970–71; York Univ. 1971–72; New Sch. 1972–75 (Dir. 1977–78); Hart House, Univ. of Toronto, 1976, 1977; Anglican.

**MacGREGOR, Kenneth Robert,** E.D., B.Sc., F.S.A., F.C.I.A.; executive; b. Ottawa, Ont., 21 July 1906; s. Robert and Margaret (Goundrey) M.; e. Lisgar Coll. Inst., Ottawa, Ont.; Queen's Univ., B.Sc. (Hons. Mech. Engn.) 1929; m. Charlotte Jessie, d. late Dr. T.F. Donnelly, 29 June 1935; children: Jayne Ennis, Kenneth Robert; FORMER CHRMN. & PRES., THE MUTUAL LIFE ASSNCE. CO. OF CANADA; Hon. Dir., The Mutual Life Assnce. Co. of Canada; Economical Mutual Insurance Company; Missisquoi Insurance Co.; former Dir. and mem. Extve. Ctte., Canada Trustco Mortgage Co.; Canada Trust Co.; Lecturer, Queen's University, 1929–30; joined Federal Dept. of Ins., Ottawa, 1930; served in Actuarial & Examination Brs. and later in Adm. Br.; Chief Actuary 1947; Assistant Supt. of Ins. 1948; Assoc. Supt. of Ins. (with rank Depy. Min.), 1949–53; Supt. of Ins. 1953–64; Pres. Mutual Life Assurance Co. of Canada 1964–73, Chrmn. 1973–82, Chrmn. Extve. Ctte. 1982–83, Hon. Chrmn. of the Bd. 1983–89; former Vice Pres. and Gov., Soc. of Actuaries; served as Major, Gov. Gen's. Foot Guards (1923–45); E. D. 1945; mem., Candn. Bisley Rifle Team. 1926–27–28 (Commandant, 1957); Life Gov., Dom. of Can. Rifle Assn.; Pres., Candn. Life and Health Ins. Assn., 1968–69; Hon. Life mem., Candn. Cancer Soc.; Hon. Life mem., National Cancer Inst. of Can. (mem. and former Chrmn. Investment and Finance Cttes.); former Trustee, Queen's Univ.; Hon Life Mem., Univ. Council; mem. Investment Ctte.; Presbyterian; recreations: gardening, curling, golf; Clubs: Rideau (Ottawa); Rotary (Kitchener); Westmount Golf & Country (Kitchener); York (Toronto); Home: 125 John Blvd., Waterloo, Ont. N2L 1C4; Office: 227 King St. S., Waterloo, Ont. N2J 4C5.

**MacGREGOR, Roy,** B.A.; writer; b. Whitney, Ont. 4 June 1948; s. Duncan Fisher and Helen Geraldine (McCormick) MacG.; e. Huntsville (Ont.) Pub. and High Schs.; Laurentian Univ., B.A. 1970; Univ. of W. Ont., Dip. in Journalism 1972; m. Ellen d. Lloyd and Rosa Griffith 9 Sept. 1972; children: Kerry, Christine, Jocelyn, Gordon; currently daily columnist, Ottawa Citizen; Assoc. Ed. Maclean's mag. 1973–75, Sr. Writer 1978–82, Ottawa Ed. 1985; Sr. Ed. The Canadian Magazine 1975–78; Ottawa Ed. Today Magazine 1982; Columnist Toronto Star 1983–85; recipient Nat. Mag. Award 1977, 1980; ACTRA Award Best Candn. TV Writer-Drama 1979, 1980; co-winner Nat. Newspaper Award spot news reporting 1983; Citation Nat. Newspaper Award columnist 1986, 1988; Citation Nat. Newspaper Award feature writing 1990; Runner-up, Leacock Award for Humor 1990; winner, Southam President's Prize 1991; author: 'Shorelines' novel 1980; 'The Last Season' novel 1983 (also script CBC TV prodn. 1987); 'Tyler' drama 1979 (Grand Prix de la Presse Montréal World Film Festival 1979); 'Ready For Slaughter' drama 1983 (CBC 'For the Record' prodn. Drama Specials Award 1983 Banff Internat. TV Festival); 'Chief: The Fearless Vision of Billy Diamond' non-fiction 1989; 'Home Game,' with Ken Dryden, non-fiction 1989; 'Quantity Time: Words of Comfort for Imperfect Parents' non-fiction 1990; 'The Road Home: Images of The Ottawa Valley,' photographs by Steve Evans (non-fiction) 1992; 'Road Games: A Year in the Life of the NHL' non-fiction 1993; mem. ACTRA; recreations: hockey, outdoors; Home: 22 Banting Cres., Kanata, Ont. K2K 1P4; Office: 1101 Baxter Rd., Ottawa, Ont. K2C 3M4.

**MacGUIGAN, Hon. Mr. Justice Mark R.,** P.C., M.A., Ph.D., LL.B., LL.M., J.S.D., LL.D.; b. Charlottetown. P.E.I. 17 Feb. 1931; s. Hon. Mark R. (M.); e. Queen Square Sch.; Prince of Wales Coll., Charlottetown, 1946–49; St. Dunstan's Univ., B.A. 1951, summa cum laude; Univ. of Toronto, M.A. 1953, Ph.D. 1957; Osgoode Hall Law Sch. LL.B. 1958; Columbia Univ., LL.M. 1959, J.S.D. 1961; LL.D. Univ. of P.E.I. 1971; St. Thomas Univ., 1981; Law Society of Upper Canada 1983; Univ. of Windsor 1983; m. Judge Patricia D. Robinson 26 Dec. 1987; children: Ellen, Mark, Thomas; JUDGE, APPEAL DIVISION, FEDERAL COURT OF CANADA 1984– ; read law with Day, Wilson, Kelly, Martin & Morden 1956–58; called to Bar of Ont., Sept. 1958; to the Bar of Nfld. and of P.E.I. 1984; Queen's Counsel, Ont. 1982; Asst. Prof. of Law, Univ. of Toronto 1960–63, Assoc. Prof. 1963–66; Visiting Assoc. Prof. of Criminal Law, New York Univ. 1966; Prof. of Law Osgoode Hall Law Sch. 1966–67; Dean, Faculty of Law, Univ. of Windsor 1967–68; author of 'Jurisprudence: Readings and Cases' (2nd Ed. 1966); 'Cases and Materials on Creditor's Rights' (2nd Ed. 1967), and many articles in learned journals & press; mem. of Fed. Govt. Special Comte. on Hate Propaganda 1965–66; Adv. to Fed. Govt. Special Counsel on the Constitution 1967–68; Const. Adv. to Gov. of P.E.I. 1968; el. to H. of C. for Windsor-Walkerville in g.e. June 1968; re-elected 1972, 74, 79, 80; Chrmn., Special Comte. on Statutory Instruments 1968–69; Joint Chrmn., Spec. Joint Comte. on Const. of Can. 1970–72; Parliamentary Secty. to Min. of Manpower and Immigration 1972–74; Parliamentary Secty. to Min. of Labour 1974–75; Chrmn., Standing Comte. on Justice and Legal Affairs 1975–79; Chrmn., Sub-Comte. on Penitentiary System in Can. 1976–77; Chrmn., Spec. Joint Comte. on Const. of Can. 1978; Opposition Critic for Sol.-Gen. 1979; Sec'y of State for External Affairs 1980–82; Minister of Justice and Attorney General of Canada 1982–84; Pres., Candn. Section, International Commission of Jurists 1988–90; Catholic; recreations: running, skiing, tennis, swimming; Home: 23 Linden Terrace, Ottawa, Ont. K1S 1Z1; Office: Federal Court of Appeal, Supreme Court Bldg., Wellington St., Ottawa, Ont. K1A 0H9.

**MacINNES, Rev. John Murray,** B.A., M.Div., M.A.; minister; b. Musquodoboit Harbour, N.S. 23 Oct. 1927; s. Norman and Marybelle (Landells) MacI.; e. Dalhousie Univ. B.A. 1948; Atlantic Sch. of Theol. M.Div. 1951; Lisbon Univ. 1953; Andover Newton Theol. Sch. 1958–59; Am. Univ. Sch. of Internat. Serv. M.A. 1965; m. Innes d. George and Catherine Scherer 21 Apr. 1950; children: Stephen, Norman, Allan, Ainslie; Min., Apohaqui Norton, N.B. 1951–53; Dir. & Teacher, var. posts in Angola 1953–64; Consultant, Nat. Counc. of Churches (U.S.) 1965–67; Dir., S. Afr. Edn. Prod., NCCUSA 1967–72; Adjunct Prof., Maryknoll Coll. 1971–72; Min., St. Paul's Ave. Rd. 1972–75; Afr. Area Sec., Anglican Ch. 1975–83; Chaplain, Univ. of Windsor & Extve. Dir., Iona Coll. 1983–85; Principal, Iona College, University of Windsor 1986–89; Del., Anglican Ch. of Can. (consulting with S. Afr., Sudan, Burundi, etc.) 1972–83; Consultant, World Counc. of Chs. for Sodapa 1971; WCC Angola Relief & Devel. Prog. 1982 (Past Chrmn. two cttes.); o. 1951 Maritime conf., United Ch. of Can.; Observer elections of Namibia Nov. 1990, Zimbabwe first elections and the 1st Angolan elections 1992 for Candn. Council of Internat. Cooperation; Study of Angola Agriculture 1991 for CCIC; Apptd. Oct. 1991 by United Church of Canada to Angolan Council of Churches to organize a rural training centre in Huambo, República de Angola; Dir., Candn. Food Grains Bank 1994– ; recreations: raising beef cattle, cross-country skiing, sailing, curling; Club: Markdale Country; Home: R.R. 1, Maxwell, Ont. N0C 1J0.

**MacINNES, Norman J.,** M.A., LL.B.; lawyer; b. Hanover, Ont. 3 May 1952; s. Lauchlin and Anne Garrie (Tait) M.; e. Univ. of Toronto B.A. 1975, M.A. 1976, LL.B. 1980; called to Ontario Bar 1982; m. Pansy d.

Erris de Bellotte and Clementina Frederick 9 Oct. 1976; children: April Jasmine, Heather Lauren Anne; PUBLICATIONS EDITOR, THE LAW SOCIETY OF UPPER CANADA 1987– ; Richard De Boo Publishers 1983–87; Home: 103 Chester Ave., Toronto, Ont. M4K 2Z8; Office: 130 Queen St. W., Toronto, Ont. M5H 2N6.

**MacINNES, Ronald Jon,** B.J.; public relations executive; b. Toronto, Ont. 8 Oct. 1944; s. Charles Wellington and Doris (Wilcox) MacI.; e. R.H. King Coll. Inst.; Ryerson Polytech. Inst. B.J. 1969; Harvard Law School Program on Negotiation; m. Barbara d. Fred and Thelma Reid 31 May 1969; children: Scott, Sean, Shanna; Vice Pres. Corporate Communications and Pub. Affairs, Lawson Mardon Group 1990; Reporter Ottawa Journal 1969–70; Ed. Toronto Telegram 1970–71; Acct. Supr. Burson Marsteller Public Relations 1971–74; Copy Ed. Toronto Star 1974, Assignment Ed. 1976, Beats Ed. 1979, Sr. Assignment Ed. 1984–86; Dir. Pub. Affairs Kidd Creek Mines; Asst. Gen. Mgr. Corporate Communications Canadian Imperial Bank of Commerce 1986–88; Dir. Corporate Communications TransCanada PipeLines 1988–89; mem. Candn. Pub. Relations Soc.; Internat. Assn. Bus. Communicators; Pub. Affairs Assn. Can.; recreations: reading, writing; Club: Albany; Home: 28 Springwood Cres., Unionville, Ont. L3R 5Z7.

**MacINNIS, J. Lyman,** F.C.A., LL.D. (Hon.); chartered accountant; b. St. Peter's, P.E.I., 27 Sept. 1938; s. Joseph and Catherine (MacDonald) M.; e. Morell P.S.; Grade X 1953; C.A. 1965; m. Anne d. Walter and Georgina Affleck 9 Aug. 1969; children: Matthew Lyman, Alan Walter; MANAGING DIRECTOR, BALMUR LTD.; C.P.R. 1954–58; TransCanada Pipe Lines Ltd. 1958–61, 1965–68; H.R. Doane & Co. 1961–65; Partner, Coopers & Lybrand 1968–75; Sr. Partner, Deloitte & Touche 1975–90; Pres., Entertainment Group, John Labatt Ltd. 1990–91; Hoben Mem. Prize (C.A. finals) 1965; F.C.A. (Ont.) 1973, (P.E.I.) 1987; Nat. Bus. Writing Award 1976; Queen's Jubilee Medal 1977; Life Mem., Inst. of C.A.'s of Ont. 1984; Bd. mem., Balmur Ltd. 1992– ; Marson Productions Inc. 1992– ; Battery Technologies Inc. 1993– ; Bd. mem., Junior Achievement of Canada 1992–93; Bd. mem., Ontario Club 1991–92; Bd. mem., Candn. Scottish Heritage Found. 1986–88; Bd. mem., Hockey Canada 1987–90; Bd. mem., Sisters of St. Joseph Hospital Employees Pension Plan 1988–90; Bd. mem., U.P.E.I. Foundation 1991–92; Univ. of Waterloo Acctg. Adv. Counc. 1983–84; former mem. & advr. of num. community orgns.; Roman Catholic; Mem., Inst. of C.A.'s of Ont. (Pres. 1982–83), Candn. Inst. of C.A.'s (Pres. 1986–87) (num. past & present extve. & ctte. positions for both orgns.); Inst. of C.A.'s of P.E.I.; Candn. Tax Found.; Gov., Candn. Comp. Auditing Found. 1984–86; author: 'Get Smart, Make Your Money Count!' 1989 and 2 other books as well as numb. articles and tax courses; originator, 'The Gage Tax Report'; former columnist, ed. 'Check Mark' & CCH Ed. Bd.; co-author of 4 titles; frequent radio & TV commentator, past prod. & host; extensive public speaker; recreations: baseball, golf, hockey; Clubs: Granite; Rosedale; Office: Suite 2400, 4950 Yonge St., Toronto, Ont. M2N 6K1.

**MacINNIS, Jeff,** B.A. (hons.); author; business owner; b. Toronto, Ont. 9 March 1963; s. Joseph Beverly and Cynthia (Hare) M.; e. Univ. of Western Ont. B.Admin. (hons.) 1988; m. Andrea Una d. A. Fraser Isbester and Jacqueline Uni (Brennan) 5 Sept. 1993; skiing: raced on Canadian Nat. Downhill Ski Team 1982–83; competed in World Cup events; won Belgium Nat. Downhill Championships 1984; placed 7th, World Student Games Downhill Race, Cortina, Italy 1985; exploration: Breadlbane Expedition 1983 (140-year-old shipwreck, high Arctic); Polar Passage (creator & leader, 1st team to sail Northwest Passage; featured in May 1989 'National Geographic Magazine'); London to New York Overland Challenge 1994 (mem. 1st expedition to cross Bering Strait, driving from London, England to New York City, USA); lecturer: deliver human performance presentations to Fortune 500 companies and assns.; co-author: 'Polar Passage' (bestselling Random House book); author: 'North of Sixty (chapter on Polar Passage Expedition); 'Braving the Northwest Passage' and other mag. articles incl. 'National Geographic,' 'Canadian Geographic,' and 'Sail'; One-hour TV special 'Polar Passage' was televised in Canada, the U.K. & the U.S. (featured at World Ocean Film Festival, France); featured in Rolex Watch Co. advertisement; recipient, Paul Harris fellowship (Rotary Internat.); recreations: skiing, sailing, running, cycling; Office: 112 St. Clair Ave. W., Suite 401, Toronto, Ont. M4V 2Y3.

**MacINNIS, Joseph B.,** C.M., M.D., F.R.C.P., F.R.C.G.S.; LL.D. (Hon.); underwater research consultant and scientist; b. Barrie, Ont., 2 March 1937; s. Allistair and Beverley (Saunders) MacI.; e. Univ. of Toronto, M.D. 1962; Univ. of Calgary, LL.D. (Hon.) 1981; PRESIDENT, UNDERSEA RESEARCH LTD.; holds or has held consulting contracts with U.S. Navy; Canadian Government; Smithsonian Institution; IBM; Nat. Geographic; Oceaneering Internat.; Intern, Toronto Gen. Hosp. 1963; Instr. in Pharmacol., Univ. of Pa. (Link Foundation Fellowship) 1964; licensed to practice med. in State of N.Y., 1965; actively engaged in undersea research and diving med. since 1960; life support physician for Man-In-Sea project Phase II sponsored by Edwin A. Link, Nat. Geog. Soc. and Smithsonian Inst., 1964 directed over 75 exper. dives at Ocean Systems' pressure facility, Linde Research Lab., 1965; cert. by U.S. Navy as a Man-In-Sea Aquanaut for Sealab III program; observer at Sealab I and II projects and apptd. Consultant to Sealab III, 1967; Scient. Dir. of 700 ft. dive made from world's 1st lock-out submarine 1968; has travelled extensively for present Co. carrying out diving research in N.Sea, Grand Banks, Gulf of Mexico, Pacific, Bahamas, Gulf Stream and Caribbean; part of search team for nuclear submarine 'U.S.S. Scorpion' 1968; took part in search and salvage of flight wreckage, Caracas, 1969; conceived and constr. 'Sublimnos' (Can.'s 1st underwater habitat) to be placed in Georgian Bay for 2 yr. scient. study 1969; formed James Allister MacInnis Foundation for underwater research and educ. in Can. 1970; led ten scient. diving expeditions to Resolute Bay 600 miles N. of Arctic Circle 1970–74, establishing first ever polar dive stn. 'Sub-Igloo' under ice and leading first team diving scientists ever to N. Pole; discovered HMS Breadalbane (British barque sunk in 1853 off Beachey Island) 1980; first Canadian to dive three miles under the Atlantic in the Soviet 'Mir' re submersibles 1989; Co-leader, IMAX - Titanic Expedition 1991; guest lectr. at 10 univs. incl. Univs. of Toronto, Pa., Ind. and Calif., Los Angeles; author of 'Underwater Images' 1971; 'Underwater Man' 1974; 'Considerations for a National Ocean Policy' (Candn. govt. report); 'Coastline Canada' 1982; 'Shipwreck Shores' 1982; The Land that Devours Ships' 1984; 'Titanic: In a New Light' 1992; General ed.: 'Saving the Oceans' 1992; producer: 'The Land that Devours Ships' 1984; 'Comrades in the Deep' one hour TV special 1990; Co-Extve. producer of 'Titanica' (the story of the Titanic filmed in IMAX) 1991; articles for 'Scientific American' and 'National Geographic'; and over 30 papers on diving med.; contrib. to tech. and popular books incl. 'The Ocean Realm' (Nat. Geog. Soc.); apptd. Consultant, 'Journal of The American Medical Association' 1966; his underwater photographs have appeared in such publs. as 'National Geographic' and 'Sports Illustrated'; awarded Gold Medal of Excellence for film 'Deep Androsia,' Internat. Film Festival, Santa Monica 1965; his motion pictures have been presented on Candn. and Am. networks; Host CBC television series 'The New Wave' 1975–76; 'The Newfoundlanders: Voices from the Sea' 1978; Fellow, Royal Candn. Geog. Soc.; Hon. D.Sc., Queen's Univ. 1990; mem. Order of Can. 1976; mem. Candn. Council on Fitness and Health; 'Man-In-Sea Panel,' Nat. Academy Engineering, Washington; Canadian Environmental Adv. Council; Candn. and Am. Med. Assns. and 15 other prof. socs.; Consultant, Titanic Project 1985; First Canadian to dive to the Titanic 1987.

**MacINNIS, William Alexander,** B.Sc., D.D.S.; university professor and administrator; b. Montreal, Que. 10 April 1945; s. Alexander Archibald and Esther Marie (Weeks) M.; e. Dalhousie B.Sc. 1967, D.D.S. 1970; Madigan Army Medical Centre Tacoma Wash. general practice residency 1979; m. Robin d. Robert and Elizabeth Stedman 17 Aug. 1968; children: Carmen Elizabeth, Thomas Edward, Laura Marie; PROFESSOR, FACULTY OF DENTISTRY, DALHOUSIE UNIV. 1982– ; Clinician, Candn. Armed Forces in numerous locations rising to rank of Lt.-Col. following grad.; Base Dental Officer, CFB Halifax 1979–82; Head, Div. of General Dentistry, Dalhousie Univ. 1985–88; Acting Chair, Dept. of Restorative Dentistry 1988–91; Assoc. Dean, Clinical Affairs 1991–93; Dean 1993– ; Fellow, Internat. College of Dentists; research interests in field of edn. rsch. & dental epidemiology; active in organized dentistry: Past Pres., N.S. Dental Assn. & recently apptd. to Prov. Dental Bd. of N.S.; author: 'Amalcore Strength Recovery Following Refilling of Access Preparations' 1991, 'Placement and Replacement of Restorations in a Military Population' 1991, 'Analysis of an Institutionalized Geriatric Population' 1992; Home: 6241 Regina Terrace, Halifax, N.S. B3H 1N4; Office: Halifax, N.S. B3H 3J5.

**MacINTOSH, David Alan,** B.A., M.A.; insurance executive; b. Kitchener, Ont. 15 May 1940; s. Harold W. and Alice C. (Ebel) M.; e. McMaster Univ., B.A. (Hon.) 1963, M.A. (Econ.) 1968; m. Janice d. Lloyd and Ruth Fischer 8 Sept. 1962; children: Catherine, John, Susan; EXTVE. VICE-PRES., MUTUAL LIFE ASSURANCE CO. OF CAN. 1987– ; joined Mutual Life's Investment Div. in 1963; Extve. Offr., Investments 1973; Vice-Pres., Corp. Serv. 1975; Sr. Vice-Pres., Investments & Fin. 1985; Chrmn., Mu-Cana Investment Couns. Ltd.; The Mutual Trust Co.; Dir. of var. Mutual Life subs.; Lutheran; Home: 298 Roxton Dr., Waterloo, Ont. N2T 1R5; Office: 227 King St. S. Waterloo, Ont. N2J 4C5.

**MacINTOSH, Jeffrey Gordon,** B.Sc., LL.B., LL.M.; university professor; b. Toronto, Ont. 19 Jan. 1954; s. Robert Mallory and Mary Louise (Crippen) M.; e. Mass. Inst. of Technol. B.S. 1975; Univ. of Toronto LL.B. 1981; Harvard Univ. LL.M. 1982; ASSOC. PROF., FAC. OF LAW, UNIV. OF TORONTO 1987– ; Asst. Prof., Osgoode Hall Law Sch., York Univ. 1982–83; Univ. of Toronto 1983–87; John M. Olin Fellow in Law & Economics, Law Sch., Yale Univ. 1988–89; prof. of corp. law & securities regulation; Phi Beta Kappa; author of numerous publications in legal journals; recreations: squash, windsurfing; Home: 116 Edith Dr., Toronto, Ont. M4R 1Z2; Office: 78 Queen's Park, Toronto, Ont. M5S 2C5.

**MacINTOSH, Robert M.,** M.A., Ph.D. LL.D. (Hon.); banker, b. Stanstead, Que.; s. Gordon Leslie and Bernice Isabel (Mallory) McI.; e. Stanstead Coll.; McGill Univ., B.A. (Econ. and Pol. Science) 1947, M.A. 1949, Ph.D. 1952; Trinity Coll., Cambridge, post-grad. work 1949–50; LL.D. (Hon.), York Univ. 1976; m. 1stly Mary Louise Crippen; children Valerie, Jeffrey; 2ndly, Lynn Higgins Peers; children: John, Justine; Pres., The Canadian Bankers' Assn. 1980–89; Dir., Chemical Bank of Canada; United Corporations Ltd.; ONEX Corp.; Chrmn., Invest. Policy Comte., Ont. Mun. Employees Retirement Bd. 1974–90; Asst. Prof. Econ., Bishop's Univ., Que. 1950–53; Econ., Rsch. Dept., Bank of Nova Scotia 1953; Investment Dept. 1957; Supvr. Investments 1957; Asst. Gen. Mgr. Investments 1962; Jt. Gen. Mgr. 1966; Depy. Chief Gen. Mgr. 1968; Extve. Vice Pres. 1972–80; served in the 2nd World War with R.C.A., 1943–46; discharged with rank of Lieut.; author: 'Different Drummers: Banking and Politics in Canada'; formerly, Chrmn., Bd. Govs., York Univ.; recreation: tennis, golf; Clubs: Queen's; Toronto Lawn Tennis; Office: P.O. Box 348, 2 First Canadian Place, Toronto Ont. M5X 1E1.

**MacINTYRE, David Keith,** B.Mus., M.Mus.; composer, university professor; b. Yorkton, Sask. 26 June 1952; s. William Maurice and Betty Elizabeth (Tunnicliffe) Berry; adopted s. of Dr. J.A. MacIntyre 1963; e. Univ. of Sask., studied music comp. with Murray Adaskin 1970–73; Univ. of Victoria B.Mus. (with distinction) 1975 (studied with Rudolf Komorous), M.Mus. 1979; m. Catherine d. Walter and Anne Lubinsky 8 Aug. 1992; CO-FOUNDER OF MUSIC PROGRAM & PROF., SCHOOL FOR THE CONTEMPORARY ARTS, SIMON FRASER UNIV. 1979– ; Music Dir./Actor, var. theatre cos. summers 1970, '71, '72; formed 'Composers Group' (toured Europe) 1975; operas: 'Humulus the Mute' prem. 1979, 'Refrains' 1981 (co-creator), 'Aria da Capo' 1982, 'Heartland' 1987, 'The Architect' (comnd. by Vancouver Opera) 1993; creator (in collaboration with dancers/choreographers): 'Songs of the New Vaudeville' 1983, 'Sisyphus' and'Road Show' 1983–85, 'Highway 86 Event' for World Festival, Expo '86, 'Piazza' 1988 for First New York International Festival of the Arts, 'Sanctuary' 1989, 'Smudge' for Inde '90 Modern Dance Festival Toronto 1990, 'Gazebo' for Purcell String Quartet and 'Home' for CBC Vancouver Orch. 1991–92; Mem., Candn. League of Composers; Candn. Music Centre; Soc. of Composers, Authors & Pubs.; Home: 301 – 1465 Comox St., Vancouver, B.C. V6G 1N9; Office: Burnaby, B.C. V5A 1S6.

**MacISAAC, John A.,** M.L.A.; b. Inverness, N.S. 23 June 1939; s. John Archie and Dorothy (Kennedy) MacI.; e. New Victoria and Central High Schs. New Waterford; m. Evelyn d. William Chisholm 8 Apr. 1961; children: Heather, Ian, Ross; M.L.A. Pictou Centre 1991–93; Caucus Party Whip 1991–93; Min. Responsible for N.S. Power Corp. 1989–91; Min. of Mines and Energy, N.S. 1989–91; Min. Responsible for N.S. Communications & Information Act 1989; Chrmn., Senior Citizens Secretariat 1980–91; Great-West Life ins. agt.; served with Candn. Army 14 yrs (Militia), 1st and 2nd Btns. N.S. Highlanders, Sydney and New Glasgow; Pipe Maj. 1st Btn. 1965–69; el. M.L.A. for Pictou Centre prov. by-el. 1977, re-el. g.e. 1978, 1981, 1984, 1988 and 1991; Min. Responsible for Adm. Civil Service Act 1978; Min. of Social Services 1978–79; Min. of Municipal Affairs, 1979–81; Min. of Labour and Manpower 1981–83; Min. of Transportation 1983–84; Min. of Tourism 1984–87; Min. of Lands and Forests 1987–89;

mem. Br. #34, Royal Cndn. Legion, New Glasgow; mem. and Past Pres. New Glasgow Kinsmen; St. Andrew Soc. New Glasgow; Chrmn. Festival of Tartans Soc. 1972; Pres. N.S. Pipers & Pipe Band Assn. 1976; former Instr. and Dir. New Glasgow Ceilidh Pipe Band; P. Conservative; R. Catholic.

**MacISAAC, Ronald Francis Thérés,** LL.B.; lawyer/writer; b. Prince Albert, Sask. 29 Oct. 1925; s. John Francis and Mary (MacNair) M.; e. Univ. of Sask., LL.B. 1948; m. Jocelyn d. Edward and Eve Floyer; children: Carol, Dan, Elizabeth, Hugh, Melanie, Bruce; step children: Frank, Tara, Maria, Nicola, Bradley, Todd, Peter, Russell, Monique, Michele, Tami; trial lawyer; seminar speaker, Can., U.S.; Adjunct Prof., Internat. Coll. of Cayman Islands; Gov., Trial Lawyers Assoc. of B.C.; author of many legal articles in Candn. Bar Jour., Chitty's Law Jour. & num. others; journalist; travel & sports author; Hon. Life Mem., Alpine Club & Figure Skating Soc.; Roman Catholic; Mem., C. of C.; Hist. Assn.; Botany Club; recreations: bridge, riding, sailing, tennis, hiking; Home: 2946 Leigh Rd., Victoria, B.C.; Office: 560 Johnston St., Victoria, B.C. V8W 2R9.

**MacIVOR, Daniel;** writer, performer, director; b. Sydney, N.S. 23 July 1962; s. Buster and Lillian M.A.E. (MacLean) M.; e. Sydney Academy 1980; Centre for Actor's Study in Toronto; George Brown College grad. 1985; Dalhousie Univ.; ARTISTIC DIRECTOR, DA DA KAMERA 1985– ; Writer in Residence, Buddies in Bad Times Theatre 1986–87; Tarragon Theatre 1987–89; Mem., Banff Playwrights Colony 1988; writer and/or director of 21 plays since 1986; Dora Mavor Moore Awards 1990 (Best Production), 1992 (Best Design); Chalmer's Canadian Play nominations 1987, '90, '91 (in '91 3 noms. – an unprecedented event) Winner 91; author: 'See Bob Run' and 'Wild Abandon' 1990, 'House/Humans' 1992 (plays); co-author: 'Making Out' 1992; 'Never Swim Alone' 1994; 'This Is A Play' 1994; Home: 36 Maitland St., Apt. G6, Toronto, Ont. M4Y 1C5.

**MACK, Bruce Andrew,** B.Sc., Ph.D.; engineer; b. Ottawa, Ont. 12 Jan. 1962; s. Alexander Ross and Dorothy Shirley M.; e. Queen's Univ. B.Sc. 1983, Ph.D. 1993; m. Norma d. Norm and Claire Gould 15 June 1991; LEAD ENGINEER, SPDM GROUND TESTBED, MOBILE SERVICING SYSTEMS PROGRAM, SPAR AEROSPACE LTD. 1989– ; Lecturer & Research Asst., Queen's Univ. 1983–89; Automation & Robotics Engr., Adv. Technol. Systems Group, Spar Aerospace Ltd. 1989– ; Mem., Inst. of Electrical & Electronic Engineers; Office: 9445 Airport Rd., Brampton, Ont. L6S 4S3.

**MACK, Daniel G.,** B.Comm.; maintenance industry executive; b. Montreal, Que. 3 July 1932; s. Michael and Anna (Juzenko) M.; e. Concordia Univ. B.Comm. 1954; m. Danièle d. Jean-Marie Savignac 20 April 1963; children: Brigitte, Philippe; PRES., EMPIRE MAINTENANCE INDUSTRIES INC.; recreations: golf, skiing, tennis, jogging; Address: 180 Montée de Liesse, Montreal, Que. H4T 1N7.

**MACK, Maurice Michael,** B.E.; mechanical engineer; b. Montreal, Que., 30 Jan. 1931; s. Michael and Ann M.; e. Montreal High Sch.; McGill Univ., B.E. (Mech. Engn.) 1952; Chrmn., Empire Maintenance Industries Inc., since 1955; Engr., The Bell Telephone Co. of Can., 1952–53; joined present firm as Partner, 1953; Past Dir., Candn. Assn. of Family Enterprise; mem., XPO-graduates of Young Presidents' Organization; Phi Kappa Pi; recreations: golf, squash, fishing, tennis; Clubs: Rotary (Montreal); Summerlea Golf and Country; Canadian Club of Montreal; Home: 69 Lexington Dr., Beaconsfield, Que. H9W 5J5; Office: 180 Montée de Liesse, Montreal, Que. H4T 1N7.

**MACKASEY, Hon. Bryce,** P.C. (1966), LL.D.; b. Quebec City, Que., 25 Aug. 1927; s. Frank S. and Anne (Glover) M.; e. St. patrick's High Sch., Quebec, Que.; McGill Univ., Sir George Williams Univ., LL.D. 1970; m.; children: Bryan, Brenda, Michael, Susan; President, Air Canada, 1978–79; 1st elected to H. of C. for Verdun, Quebec in g.e. June 1962; apptd. Parlty. Secy. to Min. Nat. Health & Welfare, July 1965; Parlty. Secy. to Min. Labour, Jan. 1966; Min. without Portfolio, Feb. 1968; Min. of Labour, July 1968; Min. of Manpower and Immigration Jan. 1972; Min. of State Without Portfolio June 1974; Postmaster Gen. 1974–76; Min. of Consumer and Corp. Affairs 1976; resigned from Fed. cabinet in Sept. 1976 and resigned seat in H. of C., 27 Oct. 1976; el. to Que. Nat. Assembly for Notre Dame de Grace in g.e. 15 Nov. 1976; defeated in Federal by-election Oct. 1978; re-elected 1980; Delegate to U.N. 1963; Canadian Rep. on visit to the Republic of China 1965; Candn. Del., ILO, Geneva 1969, 1970; Gen. Chrmn., Nat. Tri-partite Conf. on Indust. Relations, Ottawa 1969; Past Chrmn., Nat. Lib. Caucus; Address: 1125 Moffat Ave, Verdun, Que. H4H 1Z1.

**MacKAY, Alexander Wayne,** B.A., M.A., B.Ed., LL.B.; university professor; b. Mount Thom, N.S. 23 May 1949; s. Alexander MacBeth and Evelyn Christina (MacCulloch) MacK.; e. West Pictou District H.S. 1962–67, Mt. Allison Univ. B.A. 1970, B.Ed. 1972; Univ. of Florida M.A. 1971; Dalhousie Law Sch. LL.B. 1978 (Gold Medalist and Smith Shield mooter); m. Laurie d. James R. Jordan 27 Dec. 1971; children: Erin Christina, Amanda Ruth, Alexa Mae, Andrew Jordan; PROFESSOR OF LAW, DALHOUSIE UNIVERSITY 1979– ; Lawyer and legal consultant associated with Pink-Larkin 1989– ; Law Clerk to late Rt. Hon. Bora Laskin, Supreme Court of Canada 1978–79; Teacher, History Dept., Prince Andrew H.S. 1972–75; called to Bar of N.S. 1980; media commentator & speaker at conferences, and consultant on Education Law, Human Rights and Discrimination, the Charter and Constitutional Law; mem. Tribunals Inquiry Panel (Candn. Human Rights Act) 1984–86; mem. Nova Scotia Pay Equity Commission 1989– ; Mem. Nova Scotia Human Rights Commission 1990–91 & mem. Tribunal Panel Inquiry under 'N.S. Human Rights Act' 1992– ; Labour Arbitrator; Research Co-ordinator, MacDonald Comn. 1984; Rsch. co-ord. & contbr.: 'Recurring Issues in Canadian Federalism' (vol. 57) and 'The Courts and the Charter' (vol. 58), of the research series of the Royal Comn. on the Econ. Union of Canada; editor 'The Canadian Charter of Rights' 1982; 'Charterwatch: Reflections on Equality' 1986; Assoc. Ed., 'Admin. Law Reports, Constitutional Law Journal, and Education Law Journal'; author 'Education Law in Canada' 1984; 'Rights, Freedoms and the Education System in Canada' 1989; 'Teachers and the Law: A Practical Guide for Educators' 1992; several articles for scholarly journals; several resch. reports for Govt. and the Candn. Bar Assoc.; Nat. Counc. of the Candn. Human Rights Found.; Lawyers for Social Responsibility (Halifax Chapter); First Dir., Dalhousie Law Programme for Indigenous Blacks and Micmacs 1989–91; Pres. Clan MacKay Soc. of N.S. 1980– ; recreations: hockey, jogging, geneology, writing; Home: 2584 Kline St., Halifax, N.S. B3L 2X5; Office: Dalhousie Law Sch., Halifax, N.S. B3H 4H9.

**MACKAY, Claire Lorraine,** B.A.; writer; b. Toronto, Ont. 21 Dec. 1930; d. Grant McLaren and (Anna) Bernice (Arland) Bacchus; e. Jarvis Coll. Inst. 1948; Univ. of Toronto, B.A. 1952; Univ. of B.C. postgrad. studies Social Work 1968–69; Univ. of Man. Cert. Rehab. Counselling 1971; m. Jackson Frederick s. Gordon and Ruby Mackay 12 Sept. 1952; three s. Ian, Scott, Grant; author (children's books) 'Minibike Hero' 1974; 'Minibike Racer' 1976; 'Exit Barney McGee' 1979; 'Minibike Rescue' 1982; 'The Minerva Program' 1984; 'Pay Cheques and Picket Lines' 1987; 'The Toronto Story' 1990; 'Touching All the Bases' 1994; co-author 'One Proud Summer' 1981; 'Bats About Baseball' 1994; Asst. Lib. Rsch. Dept. Polysar Corp. 1952–55; Med. Social Worker, Wascana Hosp. Regina 1969–71; Rsch. Lib. Un. Steelworkers of Am. Nat. Office 1972–78; freelance writer and ed. cons. since 1978; Feature Columnist 'Steel Labour' 1975–78; 'Kids Toronto' 1986–93; Writer-in-Libs. Metrop. Toronto 1987; Creative Artist in Schs. Toronto 1986; ed. CANSCAIP News 1978–83, assoc. ed. 1983–85; contbr. to various newspapers and mags.; Dir. Candn. Children's Book Centre Bd. 1985–89; Trustee, Vicky Metcalf Award 1979, 1985, 1989–93; recipient Arthur Cohen Scholarship in Eng., Latin, French & German 1948; Toronto Star Short Story Prize 1980; Hon. Mention Can. Council Children's Lit. Prize 1982; Ruth Schwartz Found. Award Best Children's Book 1982; Vicky Metcalf Award 1983; Vicky Metcalf Short Story Award 1988; Parenting Publications of North America Award of Excellence 1989, 1990; Finalist, City of Toronto Book Award 1991; City of Toronto Award of Merit 1992; Founding mem. Candn. Soc. Children's Authors, Illustrators & Performers (Sec. 1977–79, Pres. 1979–81); mem. Writers Union (Chair Grievance Ctte. 1979–80, 1984–85; Chair, Nominating Ctte. 1990–91); Internat. Bd. Books for Young People (Councillor, 1991–93); Internat. PEN; Candn. Authors Assn.; Friends Osborne & Smith Coll. Rare Children's Books; recreations: walking, birdwatching; Address: 6 Frank Cres., Toronto, Ont. M6G 3K5.

**MacKAY, Hon. Elmer MacIntosh,** P.C., Q.C., B.A., LL.B.; farmer; politician; lumberman; lawyer; b. Hopewell, N.S. 5 Aug. 1936; s. Gordon and Laura (MacIntosh) MacK.; e. Stellarton (N.S.) High Sch.; Acadia Univ. B.A. 1956; Dalhousie Univ. LL.B. 1959; m. 1stly 15 July 1961; children: Cethlyn Laura, Peter Gordon, Sheila Mary Louise, Andrew; m. 2ndly Laura d. Adrian MacAulay, Pictou, N.S. 17 July 1974; one d. Rebecca; Min. Responsible for Canada Mortgage & Housing Corp. 1991–93; called to the Bar of N.S. 1960; prior to entering politics practiced law in Pictou Co., N.S.; founded law firm MacKay, White, Stroud & Langley, New Glasgow, N.S.; 1st el. to H. of C. by-el. 1971, re-el since; Min. of Regional Econ. Expansion and Min. responsible for Central Mortgage & Housing Corp. 1979–80; Sr. Advr. to Brian Mulroney, Leader of Opposition 1984; Solicitor General of Canada 1984–85; Min. of National Revenue 1985–88; Min., Public Works, & Min. for Atlantic Canada Opportunity Agency 1989–91; P. Conservative; Presbyterian; Home: R.R. 1, Hopewell, Pictou Co., N.S. B0K 1C0.

**MacKAY, Harold Hugh,** Q.C., B.A., LL.B.; lawyer; b. Regina, Sask. 1 Aug. 1940; s. John Royden and Grace Madeleine (Irwin) MacK.; e. Weyburn (Sask.) High Sch. 1957; Univ. of Sask. B.A. 1960; Dalhousie Univ. LL.B. 1963; m. Jean Elizabeth d. James H. Hutchison, Sarnia, Ont. 27 Dec. 1963; children: Carol Anne, Donald Malcolm; PARTNER, MacPHERSON LESLIE & TYERMAN 1976– ; Dir. Ipsco Inc.; Vigoro Corporation; Uranerz Exploration and Mining Ltd.; Saskatoon Chemicals Ltd.; called to Bar of Sask. 1964; cr. Q.C. 1981; Assoc., MacPherson Leslie & Tyerman 1963–69, Partner 1969–75, 1976–89, Managing Partner 1989– ; mem. Candn. Bar Assn.; Law Soc. Sask.; Phi Delta Theta; United Church; Office: 1500 – 1874 Scarth St., Regina, Sask. S4P 4E9.

**MACKAY, James Clifford,** B.A., M.A., C.D.; industrial executive; b. North Vancouver, B.C. 15 March 1948; s. James Birch and Vivienne Lingwood (Clifford) M.; e. Univ. of New Brunswick B.A. (Hons.) 1970; McMaster Univ. M.A. 1971; m. Joan d. Allan and Alice Salstrom 12 April 1986; children: Daniel, Lisa, Christopher; SENIOR VICE-PRESIDENT RESP. FOR SPACE BUSINESS, SPAR AEROSPACE; joined Canadian Public Service 1971; held progressively sr. positions, Western Can. & Ottawa in indus. & econ. devel. fields; Sr. Asst. Dep. Min., Industry & Science Canada; worked on num. projects such as the privatization of Canada's airframe indus.; Dir., Radar Internat.; CD (Naval Reserve), C.D. Howe Award from CASI; Dir., AIAC; Ont. Aerospace Council; Anglican; recreations: walking, reading; club: Rideau; Office: 900 - 5090 Explorer Dr., Mississauga, Ont. L4W 4X6.

**MACKAY, John A.H.;** retired Candn. public servant; b. Hankow, Hupeh, China 27 Sept. 1928; s. John and Alys (Aiken) M.; e. Henley (Eng.) Tutorial Coll., 1947; Royal Tech. Coll., Manchester, Eng., Nat. Cert. Elect. Engn. 1952; McMaster Univ., (Cert. Indust. Mang.) 1957; m. Joan P., d. Lewis Hamer, 12 May 1951; children: Alyson, Anne; Former Depy. Min. of Public Works Canada and Pres. Canada Lands Co.; Dir., Canada Museums Construction Corp. since 1982; Harbourfront Corp. since 1984; Pres., Bd. of Dirs., Canada Lands Co. (Mirabel) Ltd. 1984– ; Pres., Bd. of Dirs., Canada Lands co. (Vieux-Port de Québec) Inc. 1984– ; interned as civilian in Japanese camp 1942–45; Student, Elect. Engn., Metropolitan Vickers, Manchester, Eng., 1947–52; Candn. Westinghouse Co., Production Supt., Motor Div., 1952–60; Pres., ITT Canada Ltd. 1961–69; Deputy Post Master Gen., Can. 1970; mem., Am. Inst. Indust. Engrs.; Candn. Indust. Management Assn.; recreations: tennis, photography, curling; Home: 722 Echo Dr., Ottawa, Ont. K1S 1P3.

**MACKAY, Hon. Kenneth Charles,** Q.C., B.C.L., M.C.L., F.S.A.(Scot); consultant; b. Montreal, Que. 29 Sept. 1920; s. Dr. Frederick H. and Marion Ferguson (Crowell) M.; e. St. Albans Sch., Brockville. Ont.; McGill Univ., B.C.L. 1950; M.C.L. 1951; m. Dawne d. C.A. Crosby 13 Aug. 1983; three d., Moragh, Meredith, Victoria; two s. (by a previous marriage), Charles, Iain; Justice of Superior Court, P.Q. 1969–92; read law with Hon. F. P. Brais, Q.C.; called to Bar of Que. 1950; cr. Q.C. 1965; Secy., Bar of Montreal, 1956–57; Dir., Legal Aid Bureau of Bar, 1956–61; Crown Atty., Dist. of Montreal, 1960–65; mem. Bar Examiners Comte., Bar of Que., 1964–67; Mun. Judge, Town of Hampstead, 1965–69; Lectr., Faculty of Law, McGill Univ., 1961–69; Meredith Lecturer, McGill Univ. 1969; Centre de Fonction Professionelle du Barreau 1970–72; Upper Canada Law Society 1979; served as Comn. Counsel for numerous shipping casualty inquiries, 1965–69, later as commissioner; formerly Partner, Paré, Mackay, Barbeau, Holden & Steinberg; Vice Pres., 1966–69, Que. Conf. Mun. Judges; mem. Council, Candn. Bar Assn., 1963–65, Chrmn., Maritime Law Sec. 1963–65; served with 1st Medium Batty., RCA, 1939–40; 1st Bn. Victoria Rifles of Can., 1940–42; Air Gunner in No. 424 Sqdn., 6 Bomber Group RCAF (Overseas) 1942–45; Hon. Col. 78th Fraser Highlanders; Compagnon, Fed. Nat. des

Combattants Voluntaires Alliées; Lib. Cand. for N.D.G. Montreal in g.e. 1958; Vice Pres., Que. Lib. Fed. 1960–63; Dir., Reform Club. 1964–69; mem., Nat. Policy Comte., Lib. Party of Can., 1961; Gov., Candn. Corps of Commisioners (Que. Div.); Mackay Centre for Deaf and Crippled Children; Queen Elizabeth Hospital; Spera Foundation, Trafalgar Sch.; Dir., Knights Hospitaller Foundation; David M. Stewart Military and Maritime Museum; Candn. Scottish Heritage Found.; Veterans Memorial Military Museum, Kensington (P.E.I.); Royal Commonwealth Soc. (P.E.I. Vice-Pres.); sometime mem., Jacques Viger Comn. for Old Montreal; Greater Montreal Arts Council; Past President, St. Andrews Society Montreal; N.D.G. Community Council Inc.; Past Vice-Pres., Montreal Parks and Playgrounds Assn.; Montreal Advocates Benevolent Assn.; Hon. life mem. Candn. Maritime Law Assn.; Life mem. Caledonian Society of Montreal; Kt. Cmmdr. of St. Lazarus of Jerusalem; mem., Internat. Comn. Jurists; Candn. Tax Foundation; Candn. Bar Assn.; Que. Bar Assn.; Royal Canadian Legion (Past Pres. No. 1 Br.); Presb. (Elder); Clubs: University; United Services; Home: Glenroy Farm, New London, P.E.I. C0B 1M0.

**MACKAY, Robert Murray, the Baron Strathnaver,** B.F.A., N.D.D.; auctioneering/fine art executive; b. Edinburgh, Scot. 28 May 1933; s. Edith Lillian (Webster) and late Cecil Thomson M.; e. George Heriot's Sch.; Cent. Sch. of Arts, London Univ., Nat. Design dip. 1954; Univ. of Calif. B.A. 1965; PRIVATE FINE ART CONSULTANT TO COLLECTORS AND CORPORATIONS; Dir., Fine Art Advisory Services Ltd. (London, Eng.); Dir., Fine Art Insurance Brokers Ltd. (London, Eng.); Lieut. R.N.V.R., Nat. Serv., Royal Navy; Fine Art appraiser and consultant 1953– ; accredited expert, Georgian decor. arts 1700–1835; Vice-Pres. Candn. Operations, Christie Manson & Woods International Inc. 1977–87; Retired Dec. 1987; Dir., Candn. Soc. of Decor. Arts; Vancouver Opera Assn. 1975–80; mem. Royal Naval Offrs.' Assn.; contrib. articles to several periodicals; listed in 'Who's Who in Fine Art'; recreations: opera, collecting, sailing; Clubs: Royal Navy, R.N.V.R.; Addresses: 805 - 1132 Haro St., Vancouver, B.C. V6E 1C9 and 'Glendevon Park', Midlothian, Scotland.

**MACKAY, (John) Ross,** O.C., M.A., Ph.D., D.Geog., D.Env. Studies, D.Sc., F.R.S.C.; b. Formosa, 31 Dec. 1915; s. Rev. George William, M.A., D.D., and Jean (Ross) M.; e. Clark Univ., B.A. 1939; Boston Univ., M.A. 1941; Univ. of Montreal, Ph.D. 1949; Univ. of Ottawa, D.Geog.; Univ. of Waterloo, D.Env. Studies; Univ. of Victoria, D.Sc.; Univ. of B.C., D.Sc.; m. Violet Anne, d. J.C. Meekins, China Lake, Cal., 19 Feb. 1944; children: Margaret Anne, Leslie Isabel; Prof. Emeritus of Geography, Univ. of British Columbia; Asst. Prof., Dept. of Geog., McGill Univ., 1946–49; served in 2nd World War; Pte. to Major, Candn. Intelligence Corps, 1941–46; numerous articles in scient. journs. on permafrost and cartography; rec'd. Award for Scholarly Merit, Candn. Assn. Geographers (1st recipient); Massey Medal, Roy. Candn. Geog. Soc.; Miller Medal, Roy. Soc. Can.; Biely Faculty Research Prize, U.B.C.; Kirk Bryan Award, Geol. Soc. Amer.; G.K. Gilbert Award, Assn. Am. Geographers (1st recipient); Centenary Medal for Northern Science, Gov't of Canada (1st recipient); Vega Gold Medal, Swedish Soc. of Anthropology and Geography; Roger J.E. Brown Memorial Award, Candn. Geotechnical Soc. (1st recipient); Distinguished Mentor, National Counc. for Geographic Education (U.S.A.); Distinguished Career Award, Assn. Am. Geographers; Rawson Award, Rawson Academy Aquatic Science; Logan Medal, Geol. Assn. Can.; Johnston Medal, Can. Quaternary Assn.; Officer, Order of Can.; Hon. mem., Geog. Soc. U.S.S.R.; Hon. mem. Chinese Soc. of Glaciology and Geocryology; Corresponding mem., Finnish Geog. Soc.; Fellow, Royal Society of Canada; Geol. Assn. Can.; Geol. Soc. of Am.; Arctic Inst. N. Am. (Past Chrmn., Bd. of Govs., Outstanding Fellow Award); Fellow (Foreign) Russian Acad. Natural Sciences; Fellow (Hon.) Internat. Assn. Geonorphologists; Past Pres., Candn. Assn. Geographers and Assn. Am. Geographers; Past Vice-Pres., Int'l. Geog. Union; Sec.-Gen., Int'l. Permafrost Assn.; Phi Beta Kappa; Presbyterian; recreations: camping, ornithology; Home: 4014 W. 37th Ave., Vancouver, B.C. V6N 2W7.

**MacKAY, Shane,** B.A.; retired journalist; b. Ottawa, Ont. 21 May 1926; s. Alice and Douglas D.; e. Ravenscourt Sch., Winnipeg, Man. (1933–42); Univ. of Manitoba, B.A. 1946; Harvard Univ. (Nieman Fellow, 1951–52); m. Shirley McDiarmid, Winnipeg, Man., 25 Sept. 1948 (dec'd 1990); 2ndly Isabelle Proctor 1 Sept. 1991; children: Douglas Charles, Sheila Athol (Brownscombe), Leslie Elizabeth (Chalke); Reporter, Winnipeg 'Tribune' 1942; with The Canadian Press, Winnipeg and Ottawa Bureaux, 1946–47; joined Winnipeg 'Free Press' as Leg. Corr. in 1948, and their Parlty. Corr., Press Gallery, Ottawa, 1952–53, and Washington Corr., 1953–54; Mang. Ed., Reader's Digest Assn. (Can.) Ltd., Montreal, P.Q., 1954–59; Extve. Ed., Winnipeg Free Press, 1959–67 when apptd. Dir. of Public Affairs of Internat. Nickel Co.; Vice Pres. Inco Ltd. 1972; Regional Vice Pres., 1976–80; Consultant, Inco Ltd. 1980–82; with R.C.A.F. 1943–44; Past Dir. or Gov., Winnipeg Free Press Co. Ltd.; St. John's Ravenscourt School; Man. Theatre Centre' Man. Heart Foundation; Man. Forestry Assn.; Winnipeg Chamber of Commerce; Canadian Club of Winnipeg; Home: 700 – 245 Wellington Cres., Winnipeg, Man. R3M 0A1 and 446 Pine Villa Dr., Atlantis, Fla. 33462.

**MacKAY, William Andrew,** B.A., LL.M., LL.D.; justice; b. Halifax, N.S., 20 March 1929; s. Robert Alexander and Mary Kathleen (Junkin) M.; e. Public Schs., Halifax, N.S. and Ottawa, Ont.; Dalhousie Univ., B.A. 1950, LL.B. 1953, LL.M. 1954; Harvard Univ., Ford Foundation Fellowship for grad. study by law teachers 1960–61, LL.M. 1970; LL.D., Memorial Univ. 1976, St. Francis Xavier Univ. 1986; m. Alexa Eaton, d. L. M. Wright, Riverside, N.S., 7 July 1954; one d. Margaret Kathleen; JUSTICE, FEDERAL COURT OF CANADA, TRIAL DIV. 1988– ; Foreign Service Offr. 1, 2, Dept. of External Affairs, Ottawa, 1954–57; Asst. Secy., Royal Comn. on Canada's Econ. Prospects, Ottawa, 1955–57; joined staff of Dalhousie Law Sch. as Asst. Prof., 1957; Assoc. Prof. 1959–61, Prof. 1961; George Munro Prof. of Constit. Law, 1963; Dean and Weldon Prof. of Law 1964–69; Prof. 1969–88; Vice-Pres. 1969–80; Pres. and Vice Chanc., Dalhousie Univ., 1980–86; Ombudsman, N.S. 1986–88; app'd Federal Court of Canada, Trial Div. and Judge, Court Martial Appeal Court of Canada, 1988; Chrmn., Assn. Atlantic Univ., 1981–83; Pres., Assoc. of Universities and Colleges of Canada 1983–85; Chrmn., N.S. Human Rights Comm. 1967–86; Chrmn. Comn. of Inquiry on Remuneration of Elected Provincial Officials (N.S.) 1974, 1978–79, 1981–82, 1983, 1984, 1985; Chrmn., N.S. Task Force on AIDS 1987–88; Dir., Bank of Nova Scotia 1984–86; Advisory Bd., Candn. Human Rights Foundation 1978–86; Bd., Candn. Civil Liberties Assoc. 1981–86; served in C.O.T.C., Lieut. R.C.I.C. (Contingent Reserve); read law with Stewart, Smith & MacKeen, Halifax, N.S.; called to the Bar of N.S. 1954, Q.C. 1973; mem., Candn. Inst. Internat. Affairs; Candn. Bar Assn.; formerly Assn. of Candn. Law Teachers (Pres. 1964–65); mem. Conf. of Gov. Bodies Legal Prof. in Can. 1964–69 (Pres. 1968–69); Dir., Halifax YMCA 1961–64; Bd. of Gov., Ambrae Academy 1976–82 (Chrmn. 1977–80); United Church; Clubs: Halifax; Home: 140 Rideau Terrace, Apt. 11, Ottawa, Ont. K1M 0Z2; Office: The Federal Court of Canada, Ottawa, Ont. K1A 0H9.

**MacKAY-LASSONDE, Claudette,** B.A.Sc., M.Sc., M.B.A., D.Eng., P.Eng.; engineer; b. Montréal, Qué. 2 July 1948; d. Raymond and Thérèse (Dufresne) MacKay; e. Ecole Polytechnique, Univ. de Montréal, B.A.Sc. (Chem. Engr.) 1971; Univ. of Utah, M.Sc. (Nuclear Engr.) 1973; Univ. of Toronto, M.B.A. 1983; Univ. of Windsor, D.Eng. (hon. causa) 1986; Carleton Univ., D.Eng. (hon. causa) 1987; Ryerson Fellowship 1989; St. Mary's Univ., D.Sc. (hon. causa) 1990; Technical Univ. of Nova Scotia, D.Eng (hon. causa) 1992; Guelph Univ., D.Sc. (hon. causa) 1992; m. Pierre s. Raoul and Juliette Lassonde 1 Aug. 1970; children: Julie-Alexandra, Christian-Pierre; VICE-PRESIDENT, CORPORATE AFFAIRS, XEROX CANADA LTD. 1993– ; Senior Fellow of Massey College, Univ. of Toronto 1990– ; Nuclear Eng. Bechtel Power Corp. San Francisco 1973–75; Nuclear Safety Compliance Eng. Atomic Energy of Canada Ltd. Mississauga 1975–76; Nuclear Design Eng., Ont. Hydro 1976–78; Specialist, Nuclear Design Studies 1978–80; Supervisory Planning Engr. 1980–81; Planning & Control Engr. 1981–84; Mgr. Load Forecasts Dept. 1984–87; Dir., Premier Accounts, Northern Telecom Canada 1988–91; Asst. Depy. Min., Trade and International Relations, Ont. Ministry of Industry, Trade and Technology 1991–92; Asst. Depy. Min., Communications, Ont. Ministry of Culture and Communications 1992–93; Mem. Bd. of Trustees 1988– , Vice Chrmn. 1990– Queen's Univ.; Mem. Ctte. of Ont. Deans of Engineering Advisory Council 1990– ; Mem. Bd. of Govs., Wellesley Hosp. Rsch. Inst. 1988–90; Chrmn., Canadian Engineering Manpower Bd. 1988– ; Mem. Bd., McMaster Management of Tech. Inst. 1988–90; Mem. Bd., Candn. Center for Creative Tech. 1987–89; Mem., Natural Sci's & Eng. Rsch. Council Can. 1985–88, Vice Pres. 1987–88; Mem., Bd. Innovation Ont. Corp. 1986–88; Mem., Nat. Adv. Bd. on Sciences and Technology 1987–88; Mem. Bd., Le Cercle Canadien (Toronto) 1987–88; Adv. Ctte. Chem. Eng. Technol. Prog. Ryerson Polytech. Inst. 1985–88; Selection Ctte. Elsie Gregory McGill Meml. Found. 1986; recipient of a Vanier Award (a Toronto Jr. Bd. of Trade Award) 1987; Founding mem. & Chrmn. 1989 Candn.Engr. Memorial Foundation; Founding mem. Women in Sci. & Eng. (Pres. 1977–79); Organizer First Candn. Convention Women Engs., Toronto 1981; mem. Assn. Women MBA; Assn. Prof. Engs., Prov. Ont. (first woman mem. Council 1981, first woman Pres. 1986); recreations: alpine skiing, reading, travel; Club: The Beaver; Home: 9 Old Forest Hill Rd., Toronto, Ont. M5P 2P6.

**MacKEIGAN, Hon. Ian Malcolm,** M.A., LL.D.; retired; b. Saint John, N.B., 11 April 1915; s. late Rev. John A. and Mabel (McAvity) M.; e. Moose Jaw, Sask. High Sch.; Univ. of Sask.; Dalhousie Univ. B.A. (Great Distinction) 1934, M.A. 1935, LL.B. 1938, LL.D. (Hon. Causa) 1975; Univ. of Toronto, M.A. (Public Adm.) 1939; m. Jean C., d. John D. Geddes, Halifax, N.S. 30 May 1942; children: John, Robert, Janet; Chief Justice of Nova Scotia 1973–85; Supernumerary Judge of Appeal Division of Supreme Court of N.S., 1985–90; admitted to N.S. Bar 1939, to P.E.I. Bar 1970; practised law with Rutledge, MacKeigan, Cox & Downie (and predecessor firms) 1950–73; created Queen's Counsel (N.S.), 1954; Depy. Enforcement Adm., W.T.P.B. and Depy. Comnr., Combines Investig. Comn. Ottawa 1940–50; Dir. John Labatt Ltd.; Gulf Oil Can. Ltd.; and other companies prior to 1974; Chrmn. Atlantic Devel. Bd. (Fed. Govt.) 1963–69; mem. Econ. Council of Can. 1965–71; Chrmn. Atlantic Research Centre for Mental Retardation 1968–73; Comnr. Victoria Gen. Hosp. 1970–73; Pres. N.S. Barristers Soc. 1959–60; Vice-Pres. Candn. Bar Assn. N.S. 1962–64; mem. Nat. Extve. Candn. Bar Assn. 1969–71; Pres., N.S. Div., Candn. Red Cross 1953–55; Gov. Candn. Tax Foundation 1963–64; Candn. Welfare Council 1961–64; Dir. N.S. Research Foundation 1970–73; Pres. Halifax-Dartmouth Welfare Council 1963; Lect. Dalhousie Law Sch. 1952–62; Chrmn., Research Ctee., Can. Judicial Council 1980–85; Fellow, Am. Coll. Trial Lawyers; Fellow, Foundation for Legal Research in Can.; Hon. mem. & Hon. Vice-Pres. Candn. Red Cross Soc.; awarded Centennial Medal 1967; Queen's Jubilee Medal 1977; Phi Kappa Pi; United Church; recreations: golf, fishing; Clubs: Halifax; Saraguay; Waegwoltic; Ashburn Golf; Home: 833 Marlborough Ave., Halifax, N.S. B3H 3G7.

**MacKELL, Peter Robert David,** B.A., B.C.L., Q.C.; lawyer; b. Ottawa, Ont. 23 Jan. 1927; s. Air Comdr. David Edward and Margaret Eileen (Kehoe) M.; e. St. Patricks Coll.; Royal Candn. Naval Coll., Royal Roads (1st class cert.); McGill Univ. B.A. 1948, B.C.L. 1951 (1st class Hons.); COUNSEL, MARTINEAU WALKER, ADVOCATES, BARRISTERS & SOLICITORS 1964– ; commenced practice with Duquet MacKay, Advocates Montreal 1952; joined present firm 1954; Chrmn. 1986–89; Dir., Goodfellow Inc.; Q.C. 1969; Roman Catholic; recreations: gardening, golf, life in the country; clubs: Mount Royal, University, Knowlton Country; Homes: 3470 Stanley St., Apts. 1503–4, Montreal, Que.; Spring Run Farm, Sutton, Que.; Office: P.O. Box 242, Tour de la Bourse, Montreal, Que. H4Z 1E9.

**MacKENDRICK, Louis King,** B.A., M.A., Phil.M., Ph.D.; university professor; b. Toronto, Ont. 1 Feb. 1941; s. William Harry and VeNorma Crown (DeGraff) M.; e. Appleby Coll. 1959; Huron Coll. B.A. (Hons.) 1963; Univ. of West. Ont. M.A. 1965; Univ. of Toronto Phil.M. 1966, Ph.D. 1971; m. Catherine d. Samuel and Miriam Anderson 13 Aug. 1966; children: Kenneth Gordon, Andrew Charles; PROF., DEPT. OF ENGLISH, UNIV. OF WINDSOR 1982– ; Instr., Univ. of Sask. 1967–70; Asst. Prof., Univ. of Windsor 1971–77; Assoc. Prof. 1977–82; Prov. of Ont. Grad. Fellowship 1963–67; Can. Counc. Doct. Fellowship 1970–71; Dir., Canterbury Coll. 1985–91; Senate, Univ. of Windsor 1984–86; Anglican (Bd. of Mngt., St. Matthew's Ch. 1981–83); Assn. of Candn. Univ. Teachers of English 1973– ; author of many reviews & articles in jours. & books, monographs on Robert Harlow 1989 and Al Purdy 1990 and 'Some Other Reality: Alice Munro's "Something I've Been Meaning to Tell You"' 1993; editor: 'Probable Fictions' 1983; 'God and Man in Modern Literature' 1987; guest editor: 'Essays on Canadian Writing 49'; contbr.: 'Profiles in Canadian Literature' 1982, 1991, 'Oxford Companion to Canadian Literature' 1983, 'The Montreal Story Tellers' 1985, 'Canadian Writers since 1960' 1986, 'Masterplots II' 1987, 'Writers in Aspic' 1988, 'Canadian Writers, 1920–1959' 1988, 1989; 'Canadian Writers, 1890–1920' 1990; recreations: camping, golf; Home: 2969 Skyline Dr., Windsor, Ont. N9E 3A6; Office: Dept. of English, Univ. of Windsor, Windsor, Ont. N9B 3P4.

**MACKENZIE, Cortlandt John Gordon,** M.D., C.M., D.P.H., F.R.C.P.(C); educator; b. Toronto, Ont. 6 Sept. 1920; s. John Gordon and Marjorie (Campbell) M.; e.

Queen's Univ. M.D., C.M. 1951; Univ. of Toronto D.P.H. 1955; m. Jean d. late Col. William Barker, V.C., 6 Jan. 1945; children: Alexander J.G., Ian B. G., David W. G.; PROF. OF HEALTH CARE & EPIDEMIOL. UNIV. OF B.C. since 1972; mem. Pollution Control Bd. of B.C. 1967–82, Chrmn. 1977–82; mem., Environmental Appeal Bd. of B.C. 1982–83; mem. Health Offrs.' Council of B.C. 1955–80; B.C. Inst. of Technol. Adv. Comte., Pub. Health Insprs. Option 1965–75, Chrmn. 1965–75; Chrmn. Royal Comn. on Herbicides & Pesticides, B.C.; Chrmn. Adv. Comte. to Min. of Environment B.C. on Control of Eurasian Milfoil; Visiting Prof., Univ. of Papua, New Guinea, 1976, 1981; mem. and Chrmn., C.P.H.A. Taskforce on Arsenic in Yellowknife, N.W.T. 1977; gen. med. practice Victoria 1952–54; Dir., Peace River Health B.C. 1954–55, West Kootenay Health Unit 1956–59, Selkirk Health Unit 1956–59, Central Vancouver Island Health 1959–63; Research Fellow, Dept. Health Care & Epidemiol. Univ. of B.C. 1961, Asst. Prof. 1963, Assoc. Prof. 1967, Acting Chrmn. 1969, Head of Dept. 1973–80, Emeritus Prof. 1986; served with RCNVR 1941–45, Lt. Commdr.; author various reports, articles prof. journs.; Fellow, Royal Soc. Health; mem. Candn. Med. Assn.; Candn. Pub. Health Assn. (Extve. B.C. Br. 1960–62); Candn. Assn. Teachers Social & Preventive Med. (Pres. 1976); Extve., Intl. Epidemiologic Assn., (IEA) 1981–84; awarded the C.P.H.A. Defries Medal 1986; Unitarian; Home: 3140 W. 55th Ave., Vancouver, B.C. V6N 3W9; Office: 5804 Fairview Ave., Vancouver, B.C. V6T 1W5.

**MACKENZIE, D. Murray,** B.A., M.A., D.H.A.; hospital administrator; b. Toronto, Ont. 5 June 1947; s. Donald Alexander and June Cameron (Mackie) M.; e. Univ. of Toronto, B.A. 1968, M.A. 1970, D.H.A. 1974; m. Marilyn d. George and Verna McNaughton 3 Jan. 1970; children: Jennifer, Katherine, Kenneth; PRES., NORTH YORK GENERAL HOSPITAL 1989– ; researcher & editor, 'History of Canadian Hospitals' by Dr. G.H. Agnew 1971–72; various positions, Mount Sinai Hosp. 1973–89 incl. Extve. Asst. to C.E.O. 1974–76; Asst. Extve. Dir. 1976–77; Assoc. Extve. Dir. 1977–84; Vice-Pres. 1984–89; Asst. Prof., Dept. of Health Admin., Univ. of Toronto; G. Harvey Agnew Award for highest acad. standing, Univ. of Toronto 1973; Award of Merit & Hon. Life Mem., Candn. Cancer Soc.; Bd. Mem., National Cancer Institute of Canada; mem., Candn. Cancer Soc. 1975– (many extve. posts, including Pres., Ont. Div. 1989–91); author/co-author of several articles; recreations: tennis, golf, skiing, travel; club: Bd. of Trade of Metro. Toronto; Home: 56 Doonaree Dr., Don Mills, Ont. M3A 1M6; Office: 4001 Leslie St., Willowdale, Ont. M2K 1E1.

**MacKENZIE, Gavin Alexander,** B.A., LL.B.; lawyer; b. Woodstock, Ont. 9 Nov. 1952; s. Alexander and Ruth (Fernie) M.; e. Univ. of Western Ont. B.A. 1972; Osgoode Hall Law Sch. LL.B. 1975; m. Rosemary d. Tony and Nan Legris 12 May 1984; children: Charlotte, Travis, Brooke; PARTNER, DAVIES, WARD & BECK 1993– ; articled to Claude R. Thomson Q.C. 1975–76; Lawyer, Campbell, Godfrey & Lewtas 1977–89; Fasken Campbell Godfrey 1989–90; Sr. Counsel, Discipline Dept., Law Soc. of U.C. 1990–93; cert. as specialist in civil litigation, Law Soc. of U.C.; Teacher, Ontario Bar admission course; Chair, Bd. of Dir., Rose of Sharon Services for Young Mothers 1992– ; author: 'Lawyers and Ethics: Professional Responsibility and Discipline' 1993 and num. legal articles; Home: 4444 Elgin Mills Rd. E., Markham, Ont. L6C 1L4; Office: P.O. Box 63, 1 First Canadian Pl., Toronto, Ont. M5X 1B1.

**MACKENZIE, George Alexander,** B.A., M.Phil.; economist; b. Halifax, N.S. 31 Mar. 1950; s. Charles Fogo and Sheila Mary (MacDonald) Mack.; e. Upper Can. Coll. Toronto 1967; Dalhousie Univ. B.A. 1970; Oxford Univ. (Rhodes Scholar) B.A. 1972, M.Phil. 1974; m. Carolyn Ann Medernach 18 Oct. 1986; daughter: Marjorie Gelsthorp; DIVISION CHIEF, FISCAL AFFAIRS DEPT., INTERNATIONAL MONETARY FUND 1993– ; Instr. in Econ. Univ. of W. Ont. 1974–75; Econ. Analyst Dept. Finance Ottawa 1975–78; Econ. Middle E. Dept., Internat. Monetary Fund 1978–79, European Dept., I.M.F. 1984–87, Economist, Fiscal Affairs Dept., I.M.F. 1979–84, 1987–88; Sr. Economist 1988–90, Depy. Div. Chief 1990–92, Advisor 1992–93; author of articles on public financial issues in 'IMF Staff Papers,' 'Finanzarchiv' and 'Public Finance/Finances Publiques'; contributor: 'Supply-Side Tax Policy - its Relevance to Developing Countries'; 'Public Expenditure Handbook'; Co-Chrmn. Choral Soc. World Bank and Internat. Monetary Fund 1982–84; recreations: tennis, hiking, choral singing, piano; Home: 6306 32nd St. NW, Washington, D.C. 20015; Office: Washington, D.C. 20431.

**MacKENZIE, Lt.-Gen. George Allan,** C.M.M., O. St.J., C.D., KLJ; b. Kingston, Jamaica 15 Dec. 1931; s. George Adam and Annette Louise (Maduro) MacK.; e. Beckford and Smith's High Sch. Jamaica; Jamaica Coll. 1944–48; RCAF Staff Coll. Toronto 1965–66; m. Valerie Ann d. Louis Marchand, Sedley, Sask. 30 June 1971; children: Richard Michael, Barbara Wynne; PRES. & C.O.O., GENDIS INC., 1989– and PRES. & C.O.O., SONY OF CANADA LTD. 1993– ; Dir., Gendis Inc.; Sony of Canada Ltd.; Tundra Oil and Gas Ltd.; St. Boniface General Hosp. Rsch. Found.; mem. Bd. Govs., Candn. Corps Commissionaires; began flying career with British West Indian Airways; enlisted RCAF 1950 and comnd. as pilot Centralia, Ont. 1951; assigned to 412 Transport Sqdn. Rockcliffe, Ont.; following tour on staff of Directorate of Postings & Careers HQ Ottawa trans. to 437 Transport Sqdn. Trenton, Ont. 1962–65; posted to HN Ottawa 1966 as staff mem. Dir. of Operations and Directorate of Equipment Requirements Air; promoted Col. and apptd. Base Commdr. CFB Greenwood, N.S. 1968; Depy. Chief of Staff, Operations, Maritime Command HQ Halifax 1971; promoted Brig.-Gen. and apptd. Chief of Staff Operations Maritime Command HQ 1974; apptd. Chief of Air Doctrine & Operations 1975, Maj.-Gen. 1976; Depy. Commdr., Air Command HQ Winnipeg 1977; Commdr., Candn. Armed Forces Air Command, 1978–80 (resigned 1 Apr. 1980); Extve. Vice Pres. & C.O.O., Gendis Inc., 1980–89; Past Hon. Nat. Pres., RCAF Assoc.; mem. Candn. Aeronautics & Space Inst.; Mem., Carleton Univ. Regional Advisory Bd.; Clubs: Rotary; Lakewood (Winnipeg); Manitoba Club; St. Charles Golf & Country; Home: 383 Christie Rd., Winnipeg, Man. R0G 2A0; Office: 1370 Sony Place, Winnipeg, Man. R3C 3C3.

**MacKENZIE, Gisèle (Marie Marguerite Louise Gisèle LaFleche);** singer; violinist; dramatic actress; b. Winnipeg, Manitoba Jan. 1927; d. Dr. George MacKenzie LaFleche, and Gabrielle Celine Oliva Marietta LaF.; began playing piano at an early age and violin at age seven; at age twelve made first appearance as a Violinist in recital at Royal Alexandra Hotel, Winnipeg, Man.; at age thirteen appeared as Concert Violinist with Que. Symphony Orchestra over C.B.C. network; studied violin under Kathleen Parlow at Royal Conservatory of Music of Toronto (won a no. of scholarships); while a student in 1946, contracted with C.B.C. for 15 min. show 'Meet Gisele' which ran for four yrs.; established her reputation in 'Gisele in Canada' with C.B.C.; chosen 'most popular female singer in Canada' by radio critics in Ottawa, Vancouver, Toronto, 1949; appeared on Bob Crosby's 'Club 15' (at this time changed surname from LaFleche to MacKenzie), 1951; sang on Mario Lanza Show, 1951; toured with Jack Benny playing violin duet, summers 1952–53; with 'Your Hit Parade,' weekly N.Y. TV show, 1953–57; appeared on 1st broadcast, 'The Woolworth Hour,' June 1955, and 100th broadcast, Apl. 1957; leading role in Dallas State Fair's production of 'South Pacific,' June 1955; Guest artist, Denver Symphony, July 1955; appeared at Flamingo Hotel, Las Vegas, Aug. 1955; has appeared at Las Vegas' Sahara Club with Bob Crosby and The Modernaires; voted 'top Candn. artist' in 2nd annual B.U.P. poll of Disk jockeys, 1955; star of 'Annie Get Your Gun,' Kansas Starlight Theatre, July 1956; presented with silver tray by Candn. Nat. Sportsman's Show for 'outstanding achievements in the TV and radio fields and for contrib. to the devel. of good-will between Can. and U.S.,' 1954; Hon. Mayor, Encino, Cal. 1962–63; m. Bob Shuttleworth 24 Feb. 1958; two children, Mac and Gigi; m. Robt. Francis Klein; hobby: cooking.

**MacKENZIE, Gordon,** B.A., B.Ed.; art educator, artist; b. New Liskeard, Ont. 1 March 1939; s. James (Jim) and Edna Viola (James) M.; e. North Bay Teachers' Coll. 1961; Algoma Univ. Coll. (Laurentian) B.A. 1973; Min. of Edn. Visual Arts Specialist; Nipissing Univ. B.Ed. 1966; m. Jane d. Wilfred and Laura McKague 1963; children: Barry, Sandra, Michael; art eduation/cons. with Sault Ste. Marie Bd. of Edn. 1964– ; Instructor, Min. of Edn. & Nipissing Univ. Art Edn. Courses 1967–94; self-taught watercolour artist 1970– ; 22 one-man shows in Can. & U.S.; works in private & corp. collections in Canada, U.S., U.K., Australia, Hong Kong, Japan, Finland, Germany, Italy and 2 Lt.-Gov. of Ont. Ont. Lottery Corp.; Mem., Michigan Art Ed. Assn.; Honours from Michigan Art Educators 1983; Detroit Inst. of Art 1979; Am. Artist Competition 1985; Rader's Digest Cover in 5 countries; Instr. of over 70 adult watercolour workshops 1972–94; Mem., Arts Adv. Ctte., Sault Coll.; Public Awareness Ctte., Art Gall. of Algoma; Arts in Edn. Adv. Ctte., Sault Ste. Marie Bd. of Edn.,; Edn. Ctte., Algoma Fall Festival; illustrator: 'Warriors & Statesman' 1986, 'The Real Bill Bannock Cookbook' 1987; Address: c/o The Gallery on the Lake, Box 10, Buckhorn, Ont. K0L 1J0.

**MACKENZIE, Hugh Sinclair,** Q.C.; b. Toronto, Ont. 2 Aug. 1911; s. Kenneth Ferns and Aileen (Sinclair) M.; e. Rosedale Public School and Upper Can. Coll., Toronto, Ont.; Univ. of Toronto (Trinity Coll.), B.A. 1932; Osgoode Hall Law Sch., Toronto, Ont.; m. Eleanor Smyth, d. William John Blair of Woodstock, Ont. and Provost, Alta., 20 Oct. 1934; one d., Jean Blair (Mrs. G. Rouse); COUNSEL, MACKENZIE, MAGILL and partner in predecessor firms 1935–77; Pres. Mackel Holdings Ltd.; Dir., Blair Estate Ltd.; Lockwood Geophysics Ltd.; and other Co's.; Osgoode Hall C.O.T.C. (R) 1939–42; served in World War 1942–47 as 2nd Lieut Candn. Inf. 1942, Lieut 1943 and Capt. (retired list) 1945; served in Can. 1942–44; with 8th Roy. Scots (15th Scot. Divn.) 1944 in England and Normandy; wounded Aug. 1944; rejoined firm on discharge from hosp. 1947; read law with Mackenzie & Saunderson; called to the Bar of Ont. 1935; cr. K.C. 1952; mem., Imp. Offrs. Assn. of Can. (Pres. 1958–59); Canloan Assn. (Pres., 1951–52); Delta Chi; Independent Conservative; Presbyterian; recreations: fishing, horses, bridge; Clubs; Royal Candn. Mil, Inst.; Royal Scots (Edinburgh); Home: Glencoile, RR 1, Terra Cotta Ont. L0P 1N0.

**MacKENZIE, Ian Alisdair;** retired newspaper publisher; b. Thunder Bay, Ont. 11 Oct. 1923; s. Jack and Annie (MacLeod) MacK.; e. Fort William Coll. Inst. 1941; s. Selkirk Vocational Tech. Sch. 1942; Publisher, Portage La Prairie Daily Graphic 1970–88; joined Advertising Dept. Times Journal Thunder Bay, RCAF 1943–45; joined Vopni Press Ltd. 1946 serving as Advertising Mgr., Assoc. Publisher, Publisher, Ed., Pres.; Sec. Treas. Portage Community Cablevision; Dir.: Dir. and Past Pres. Man. Community Newspapers; Past Pres. Candn. Community Newspapers; Hon. Dir. Scouts Can. (Comnr. Man.; recipient Silver Acorn); Vice-Chrmn. Man. Horse Racing Comn.; recipient Merit Award Yellowhead Hwy. Assn. (Past Pres.); Ald. City of Portage La Prairie 1992– ; Freemason; Elks; Presbyterian (Elder); recreation: horse racing; Club: Lions (Past Pres. Portage; Past Chrmn. Prairie Manor); Home: 2 Burns, Portage La Prairie, Man. R1N 3P3.

**MACKENZIE, John Price Sinclair,** B.Comm., LL.D.; investment consultant; b. Montreal, P.Q., 28 Dec. 1923; s. late Helen Margaret MacMillan (Price) and John Sinclair M.; e. Westmount (P.Q.) High Sch., Jr. Matric., 1941; McGill Univ., B.Comm., 1947; York Univ., LL.D. 1990; m. Lois Kernaghan, d. late Roy H. Parkhill, 3 Oct. 1970; Annette, d. late Harold A. Stevenson, 31 May 1947; children: John S.S., Alastair P. S., Carolyn M. S.; PRES., JPS MACKENZIE CONSULTANTS LTD.; Chrmn., Pente Investment Management Ltd.; Trustee, Canada Trust Income Investments; Acct., Bank of Montreal, 1947–49; with Barclays Bank group 1949–55; London, 1949–50, Barclays Bank D.C.O., London, 1950–51; Banque de Comm., Antwerp and Brussels, 1952, Barclays Bank (France), Paris, 1952, Barclays Bank D.C.O., West Indies, 1952–53, Barclays Bank (Can.), Toronto, 1953–55; Partner, Mgr. Inst. Sales and Mgr. Money Market Operations, Greenshields Inc., 1955–62; Vice Pres., Fullerton Mackenzie & Assocs. Ltd., 1962–67, business and assets acquired by International Trust Co. in Jan. (1967); apptd. Pres., International Trust Co. 1967; Vice Pres., Can. Permanent Cos. 1969–77; author: 'Birds of Eastern North America' 1975; 'Birds in Peril' 1977; 'Birds of Prey' 1986; 'Birds of the Oceans' 1987; 'Water Fowl' 1988; 'Game Birds' 1989; 'Song Birds' 1990; 'Wading Birds' 1991; served in war as Lieut., R.C.N.V.R., 1942–45; H.M.C.S. Brantford 1943, H.M.C.S. Thetford Mines (2nd in Command) 1944–45; Pres., Toronto ARTSCAPE Inc.; Past Pres., Toronto Arts Council; Anglican; recreations: sailing, fishing, shooting, skiing, tennis; Home: 16 Ancroft Place, Toronto, Ont. M4W 1M4; Office: 330 Bay St., Suite 1204, Toronto, Ont. M5H 2S8.

**MACKENZIE, Kenneth Claude (Kim),** B.A., Dip. U.R.Pl., M.A. (Oxon), M.C.I.P., A.C.P.; urban planning consultant; b. Sydney, N.S. 19 Sept. 1944; s. Walter Campbell and Dorothy Martin (Rosier) M.; e. Oliver Sch., Edmonton 1950–58; St. Johns-Ravenscourt Sch., Winnipeg 1958–62; Univ. of Alta. B.A. (Hons.) Geography 1966; Univ. of Toronto Dip. Urban and Region Planning 1967; Oxford Univ. B.A. Jurisprudence 1969, M.A. 1983; post-grad. studies, Athens Centre of Ekistics 1970, Univ. of Alberta Fac. of Law 1972; Delta Kappa Epsilon Fellowship 1966; Central Mortgage and Housing Corp. Fellowship in Planning 1967; Rhodes Scholar (Alta. and St. Peter's Coll.) 1967; Athens Centre of Ekistics Fellowship 1970; m. Linda-Lee d. Harding and Kathleen Brix 28 June 1969; children: Seanna Lee, Campbell Alexander, Karina Martin; PRINCIPAL, MACKENZIE ASSOCIATES CONSULTING GROUP LTD. 1969– ; formed K.C. Mackenzie Assoc. Ltd. 1969; Mackenzie Spencer Associates 1978–87; Lectr. Fac. of

Law, Univ. of Alta. 1972; mem. Land Use Planning Adv. Ctte., Fac. of Extension, Univ. of Alta. 1978–83; External Adv. Counc., Fac. of Environ. Design, Univ. of Calgary 1980; Planning and Production Ctte., Edmonton Commonwealth Games Found. 1973; City of Edmonton Citizens Zoo Advis. Ctte. 1982–85; Alta. Water Resources Comn. 1983–86; Trustee, Edmonton Art Gall. 1983–86; Univ. Hospitals Found. 1983–90; Dir. Edmonton Symphony Soc. 1978–84 (Vice-Pres. 1981–83); Edmonton Eskimo Football Club 1983–90 (Secy. 1987–90); mem. Candn. Inst. of Planners; Councillor Alta. Assn. Candn. Inst. of Planners 1973–78, Vice-Pres. 1976, Pres. 1977; mem. Edmonton Huskies Football Team, Candn. Jr. Champions 1963; Oxford Univ. Ice Hockey Club 1967–69; Club: Royal Glenora; Office: 10102 – 125 St., Edmonton, Alta. T5N 1S6.

**MACKENZIE, Landon,** B.F.A., M.F.A.; artist, artistic educator; b. Boston, Mass. 28 Nov. 1954; s. Michael A. and Sheila A. (Higgins) M.; e. N.S. College of Art & Design B.F.A. 1976; Concordia Univ. M.F.A. 1979; life partner, Donald MacPherson; children: Jeffryn, Georgia (daughters), Cluny (son); FACULTY MEM., EMILY CARR COLLEGE OF ART & DESIGN 1986– ; Extensive visiting lecturer across Canada since 1980; exhibiting artist through Canada with work in collections of Art Gall. of Ont., Montreal Mus. of Fine Arts, Musée d'art contemporain, Canada Council Art Bank, MacDonald/Steward Art Gall., univs. of Lethbridge & Concordia and several corps. incl. Nova Corp. (Calgary), Royal Bank (N.Y.), Osler, Hoskins & Harcourt (Toronto); painting exhibs. have been reviewed extensively since 1981; currently rep. by Wynick/Tuck Gallery of Toronto; several Canada Council grants & prov. grants from Ont. & B.C.; 1st prize, Que. Bienale of Painting 1981 Montreal; Home: 2206 Adanac St., Vancouver, B.C. V5L 2E8; Art College Office: 1399 Johnston St., Vancouver, B.C. V6H 3R9.

**MACKENZIE, Major General Lewis W.,** B.A., MSC, CD; Canadian forces officer; b. Truro, N.S. 30 April 1940; s. Eugene Murdock and Shirley Helene (Wharton) M.; e. Xavier Jr. Coll. 1960; Univ. of Manitoba, B.A. 1989; Canadian Army Staff College 1970; NATO Defence College Rome 1977; U.S. Army War College 1983; m. Dora d. Sarah and Ken McKinnon 2 Feb. 1967; one d.: Kimm Katheryn; Commander, Army of Ontario 1992–93; commissioned in Queen's Own Rifles of Canada (QOR) 1960; served with UN peacekeeping force Gaza Strip 1963, '64; with QOR Cyprus 1965; Army Staff Coll. 1969–70; 2nd tour Cyprus 1971; promoted to Major 1971; served with Internat. Comn. of Control & Supervision Viet Nam 1972; with UN peacekeeping Cairo 1973; promoted to Lt. Col. 1977; commanded IPPCLI 1977–79; 3rd tour Cyprus 1978; promoted to Col. 1982; to Brig. General 1987; conducted women in combat trials 1988; commanded UN observer mission Central America 1990; apptd. Chief of Staff UN Protection Force Yugoslavia 1992; assumed command of Sector Sarajevo 1992; Sr. Rsch. Fellow, Candn. Inst. of Strategic Studies; honorary degrees: Acadia, St. Mary's, St. Francis Xavier and Dalhousie universities 1993; Meritorious Service Cross with Bar; commanded 25 Nation Force which opened Sarajevo airport for humanitarian relief supplies in June 1992; Maclean's Honour Roll 1992; author: 'Road to Sarajevo, A Peacekeeper's Diary' forthcoming 1993; recreations: active in motor racing: National Sports Car Champion 1981, Ontario Sports Car Champion 1981, '82; club: British Automobile Racing Club Toronto; Address: 163 Holmwood Ave., Ottawa, Ont. K1S 2P3.

**MACKENZIE, Michael A.,** B.A., M.B.A., F.C.A.; public servant; b. Toronto, Ont. 18 Oct. 1926; s. Hugh and Alice M. (both dec.); e. Univ. of Toronto B.A. (Hons.) 1948; Inst. of C.A.s of Ont. C.A. 1953; Harvard Business Sch. M.B.A. 1955; C.A. Quebec 1969; m. June; children: Landon, Annabel, Hugh, D'Arcy; SUPERINTENDENT OF FINANCIAL INSTITUTIONS, GOVT. OF CANADA 1987– ; Accounting Partner, Clarkson Gordon Toronto 1957–68; Montreal 1969–79; Toronto 1979–87; Leave of Absence, Rsch. Fellow in Acctg., Fac. of Mngt., McGill Univ. 1968–69; Inspector General of Banks, Canada 1987; Fellow, Inst. of C.A.s of Ont. 1965; co-author: 'Interest Rate Futures in Canada: A Reporting Guide' 1984; Office: 255 Albert St., Ottawa, Ont. K1A 0H2.

**MacKENZIE, Norman Hugh,** D.Litt., M.A., Ph.D., F.R.S.C.; educator; b. Salisbury, Rhodesia 8 March 1915; s. Thomas Hugh and Ruth Blanche (Huskisson) MacK.; e. Rhodes Univ. S. Africa B.A. 1934, M.A. 1935, Ed. Dip. 1936; Univ. of London Ph.D. 1940; m. Rita Mavis Hofmann 14 Aug. 1948; children: Catherine Lynette, Ronald Philip; PROF. EMERITUS, QUEEN'S UNIV. 1980– ; Lectr. in Eng. Rhodes Univ. 1937; Univ. of Hong Kong 1940–41; Univ. of Melbourne 1946–48, Dir. Bd. Studies Journalism 1948; Sr. Lectr. in charge Dept. Eng. Univ. of Natal 1949–55, Dean of Men's Residence 1949–54; Prof. and Head of Eng. Univ. Coll. Rhodesia 1955–65, Dean of Arts 1957–60, 1963–64; Prof. and Head of Eng. Laurentian Univ. 1965–66; Prof. of Eng. present Univ. 1966–80, Dir. Grad. Studies in Eng. 1967–73, Chrmn. Counc. Grad. Studies & Research 1971–73; Vice-Chrm., Disraeli Project 1984– ; Martin D'Arcy lecturer, Oxford Univ. 1988; served with Hong Kong Volunteers Coastal Defence 1940–46, P.O.W. Hong Kong and Japan 1941–45; author 'South African Travel' 1955; 'The Outlook for English in Central Africa' 1960; 'Hopkins' 1968; 'Poems by Hopkins' 1974; 'Reader's Guide to Gerard Manley Hopkins' 1981; 'Early Poetic MSS and Note-books of G.M. Hopkins in Facsimile' 1989; 'Poetical Works of Gerard Manley Hopkins (Oxf. Engl. Texts)' 1990; 'The Later Poetic MSS of G.M. Hopkins in Facsimile' 1991; co-ed. 'The Poems of Gerard Manley Hopkins' 1967; various book chapters, articles; mem. Internat. Hopkins Assn. (Bd. of Scholars); Candn. Assn. Irish Studies (Treas. 1972–73); Hopkins Soc. (London, Pres. 1972–79); Modern Lang. Assn. (Life emeritus mem.); Yeats Soc. (Life mem.); recreations: book collecting, listening to music, ornithology; United Church; Home: 416 Windward Pl., Kingston, Ont. K7M 4E4.

**MACKENZIE, Suzanne Dale,** B.A., M.A., D.Phil.; university professor; b. Vancouver, B.C. 22 March 1950; d. Thomas Greer and Margaret Jean M.; e. Simon Fraser Univ. B.A. (Hons.) 1976; Univ. of Toronto M.A. 1978; Univ. of Sussex D.Phil. 1983; m. Alan E. s. Eric and Jessie Nash 29 May 1984; PROFESSOR, GEOGRAPHY, CARLETON UNIV. 1985– ; Asst. Prof., Geography, Queen's Univ. 1982–85; Co-Founder, Candn. Assn. of Geographers, Women and Geography Study Group; Inst. of British Geographers, Women & Geography Study Group; Mem., Candn. Assn. of Geographers 1975– (Nat. Extve. 1988–90; Internat. Geog. Union (Internat. Extve., Gender & Geog. Working Group 1989– ); author: 'Visible Histories: Gender and Environment in a Post-War British City' 1989; co-editor: 'Remaking Human Geography' 1989; Home: Ottawa, Ont.; Office: Ottawa, Ont. K1S 5B6.

**MACKEY, Robert Brian,** Bus.Adm., B.A., M.P.A., C.M.C.; writer; b. Toronto, Ont. 31 Mar. 1946; s. Ernest Edward and Elsie (Bates) M.; e. Ryerson Polytech. Inst. 1969; Carleton Univ., B.A. 1975, M.P.A. 1983, C.M.C. 1990; children: Craig, Kristin; Trustee, Ottawa Bd. of Education 1988–1991, 1991–94; PRES., THE WATERSHED MANAGEMENT GROUP; Lectr., Algonquin Coll.; Carleton Univ.; Ottawa Univ.; Founder, Graphic Arts Mngt. Inst.; Pres., Am. Mktg. Assn.; Mem., Inst. of Mngt. Cons.; author: 'Fire in Mouse Hamlet' 1983, 'Mystery in Mouse Hamlet' 1984, 'Ghost in Mouse Hamlet' 1986 (children's picturebooks); 'Red Sky at Morning' 1995 (children's novel); recreations: alpine & cross-country skiing, boating, guitar; Clubs: Independent Writers' Assn.; Kiwanis; Royal Candn. Legion; Address: 1212 Agincourt Rd., Ottawa, Ont. K2C 2J1.

**MACKIE, George Owen,** M.A., D.Phil., F.R.S.C., F.R.S.; educator; b. Louth, UK 20 Oct. 1929; s. Frederick Percival and Mary Elizabeth (Owen) M.; e. Vernon (B.C.) Prep. Sch.; Blundell's Sch. Tiverton, UK; Oxford Univ., B.A. 1953, M.A., D.Phil. 1956; m. Gillian d. Vera, Lady Aske and Roland Faulkner 6 Jan. 1955; children: Alexander, Christina, Richard, Rachel, Quentin; PROF. OF BIOLOGY, UNIV. OF VICTORIA 1968– ; mem. Faculty Univ. of Alta. 1956–68; joined present Univ. 1968, Chrmn. of Biol. 1971–74; Visiting Prof. Univ. of Wis., Stanford Univ., Univ. of Cal. Los Angeles; Killam Research Fellow, Can. Counc. 1986, 1987; awarded Fry medal Candn. Soc. of Zoologists 1989; author or co-author over 120 rsch. papers, book chapters, reviews invertebrate neurobiol.; ed. Candn. Jour. Zool. 1981–88; recreation: chamber music (cello); Home: 2173 Tryon Rd., R.R. 3, Sidney, B.C. V8L 3X9; Office: Dept. of Biology, Petch Bldg., P.O. Box 3055, Victoria, B.C. V8W 3P6.

**MACKIE, Gerald L.,** B.Sc., M.Sc., Ph.D.; university professor; b. Nakina, Ont. 20 July 1942; s. Einar Dominicus and Pearl June M.; e. Laurentian Univ. B.Sc. 1968; Univ. of Ottawa M.Sc. 1970, Ph.D. 1973; m. Catherine E. d. Kelly and Mary Thomas 26 Aug. 1967; children: Carolyn Louise, F. Einar; PROFESSOR, DEPT. OF ZOOLOGY, UNIV. OF GUELPH 1988– ; Nat. Museums of Canada postdoctoral work with Dr. Arthur Clarke 1973; Asst. Prof., Univ. of Guelph 1974–81; Assoc. Prof. 1981–88; Founder, Pres. & Co-owner (with Bruce Kilgour), Mackie and Associates Water Systems Analysts Inc. (environ. consulting) 1989– ; Mem., United Church; N. Am. Benthological Soc.; Candn. Soc. of Zoologists; Am. Malacological Union;p Soc. of Candn. Limnologists; Internat. Assn. of Great Lakes Rsch. and others; author/co-author of over 100 refereed journal pubns., 1 book, 6 book chapters, over 50 non-refereed reports, 20 ref. conf. proceedings & 5 magazine articles; recreations: woodworking, hockey; Home: 23 Avra Court, Guelph, Ont. N1H 7B2; Office: Guelph, Ont. N1G 2W1.

**MACKIE, Gilbert Richard,** B & E. Sc., M.B.A.; railway executive; b. Sudbury, Ont. 24 Dec. 1941; s. late Theodore H. and Isobel (Kilgour) M.; e. Univ. of Western Ont. B & E. Sc. 1964, M.B.A. 1970; m. Joyce d. late William and late Kathleen McTavish 16 July 1974; children: Lisa, Erin; EXECUTIVE VICE-PRESIDENT, CP RAIL 1990– ; Chrmn., Delaware & Hudson Railway Co., Inc.; Pres. & Dir., Incan Superior Limited; Dir., Aroostook River Railroad Company; Brunterm Ltd.; CNCP Niagara-Detroit Partnership; Houlton Branch Railroad Co.; Internat. Railway Co. of Maine; Niagara River Bridge Co.; Soo Line Corp.; The Canada Southern Railway Co.; The Detroit River Tunnel Co.; Transportation Assn. of Canada; TTX Company and Railbox Co.; Gen. Mgr. Mktg., CP Rail Montreal 1979; Gen. Mgr., Mktg. & Sales, Calgary 1984; Asst. Vice-Pres. Mktg. & Sales, Calgary 1986; Toronto 1987; Vice-Pres. Mktg. & Sales 1988; Home: 161 Wilder Dr., Oakville, Ont. L6L 5G2; Office: Room 354, Union Station, 65 Front St. W., Toronto, Ont. M5J 1E8.

**MACKIE, Iain Duncan Fyfe,** B.Sc., M.D., FRCPC; physician; b. Belfast, N. Ireland 8 Sept. 1953; s. William Henry and Mary Gault (Stirton) M.; e. Lorne Park S.S. 1972; Univ. of Toronto, B.Sc. (Hons.) 1976, M.D. 1979; Univ. of West. Ont. Teaching Hosps., FRCPC 1983; single; ASSOC. PROF. OF CLINICAL MED., ST. JOSEPH'S HEALTH CTR., UNIV. OF WEST. ONT. 1984– ; Residency in internal med. 1979–83; Assoc. Dir., Postgrad. Med. Edn. Ctte., U.W.O.; Chrmn., Div. of General Internal Medicine, U.W.O.; Dir., HIV Care Program, St. Joseph's Health Ctr.; Mem., Ont. Public Edn. Panel on AIDS 1986–88; Ont. Adv. Cttee. on AIDs 1989; Candn. AIDS Soc.; Pres., Main River Imports Ltd.; Bd. of Dir., AIDS Ctte. of London 1988–90 (Pres. 1986–88); Pres., London Regional AIDS Hospice Bd. of Dirs. 1992; Chair, Ont. HIV Clinic Directors; recreations: running, reading, music; Home: 712 Riverside Dr., London, Ont. N6H 2S4; Office: 268 Grosvenor St., London, Ont. N6A 4V2.

**MacKINNON, Hon. Angus Gordon,** LL.B.; judge; b. Regina, Sask. 12 Sept. 1921; s. Andrew G. MacK.; e. Univ. of Sask.; Univ. of B.C. LL.B.; m. d. M.T. O'Neil, Edmonton, Alta. 29 Dec. 1951; children: Anna Mary, Theresa, Graeme, David, Maureen, Cameron, Marguerite (Peggy); Judge, Supreme Court of B.C. 1978; called to Bar of B.C. 1949; cr. Q.C. 1971; served with RCAF 1940–45; R. Catholic; recreations: golf, bridge; Clubs: Vancouver Golf; Canadian; Lawyers' Inn; Home: 233 – 2nd St., New Westminster, B.C. V3L 2K5.

**MacKINNON, Archibald Alan,** B.A.Sc., M.B.A., P.Eng.; executive; b. Cranbrook, B.C. 13 Jan. 1937; s. C. Eric MacK.; e. Cranbrook Jr./Sr. High Sch.; Univ. of B.C., B.A.Sc. 1960; York Univ. M.B.A. 1969; PRES., CHIEF EXTVE. OFFR. AND DIR. ALTA-CAN TELECOM INC. 1983– ; Pres. and Dir. Assn. Candn. Venture Capital Co.'s; Dir. Alta. Microelectronic Centre; Candn. Centre Creative Technol. Waterloo, Ont.; Cybernex Ltd.; Idacom Elctronics Ltd.; Telematic Products Inc. Redmond, Wash.; Application Eng. Canadian General Electric Co. Ltd. Toronto 1961; Computer Systems Analyst, Ford Motor Co. Ltd. Oakville 1964; Founder and Dir. Decision Systems Inc. (mgmt. cons.) Toronto 1970; Vice Pres. CDC Ventures Inc. Toronto 1980; recipient Gold Medal in four-oared rowing Olympics, Melbourne 1956 and in eight-oared rowing Commonwealth Games, Cardiff 1958; Silver Medal eight-oared rowing Olympics, Rome 1960; mem. Dean's Honour List York Univ. 1968, 69; Litton Scholarship 1968; nominated Bronfman Scholarship 1968; recreation: jogging, hiking, skiing; Clubs: Ranchmen's; Bow Valley; Home: 728 Earl Grey Cres. S.W., Calgary, Alta. T2S 0N7.

**MacKINNON, Archie Roderick,** M.A., Ph.D., D.Litt.; university professor/administrator; b. Kincardine Twp., Bruce Co., Ont. 3 July 1927; s. Finnie George and Susan Christena (Thompson) M.; e. Queen's Univ. B.A. (Hons.) 1951, M.A. 1952; Univ. of Edinburgh Ph.D. 1957; Nipissing Univ. D.Litt. (Hon.) 1991; m. Gene Alison d. Gladys and Claude Lewis 23 Aug. 1952; children: Roderick (Rory), Hugh, Ian, Colum; Prof. & Dir., Ctr. for Internat. Programs, Univ. of Guelph 1985–91; Elem. Sch. Teacher/Principal, Waterloo Co. 1946–49; Master, Teachers' Coll., North Bay 1952–59; Dir. of

Rsch., Toronto Bd. of Edn. 1959–63; Prof., Grad. Sch. of Edn., Harvard Univ. 1963–64; Prof. & Dean of Edn., Simon Fraser Univ. 1964–70; Spec. Advr. & Sr. Edn. Specialist, CIDA 1970–85; Instr. Design Adviser: Brit. Counc., USAID, Internat. Inst. for Edn. Planning; Advr., UNESCO; Mem., Nat. Accreditation Cttes., Health Sci.; Adv. Group: Internat. Bur. of Edn.; Burton Lecture in Edn., Harvard 1961; Centennial Medal 1967; Gov., Donner Candn. Found.; Bd., Devel. Countries Farm Radio Network; W.H. Donner Found.; Vice-Chrmn., Burnaby Lib. Bd.; Adv. Voc. Ctte., Ottawa Bd. of Edn.; Mem., Phi Delta Kappa 1960– ; Candn. Soc. for the Study of Edn. 1971– ; author: 'How Do Children Learn to Read?' 1959, 'School and University' 1964, 'From International Aid to International Cooperation' 1979; co-author: 'Learning in Language and Literature' 1965; recreations: Scottish country dancing, gaelic folk culture, outdoor activities; Clubs: Royal Scottish Country Dance Soc.; Bruce Co. Hist. Soc.; Guelph Trail Club; Home: 693 Edinburgh Rd., Guelph, Ont. N1G 4H7.

**MacKINNON, David Cameron,** B.A., M.B.A.; public servant; b. Ottawa, Ont. 1 Sept. 1945; s. Frank P.T. and Daphne Margaret (Martin) M.; e. Dalhousie Univ., B.A. (Hons.) 1967; York Univ., M.B.A. 1969; m. Elisabeth d. Gar and Doris Hamblin 29 Dec. 1973; children: Kathleen Anne, Darcy Michael; PRESIDENT, ORTECH CORPORATION; Extve. Asst., Dep. Treas. of Ont. 1969–72; Dir., Rsch., Sask. Dept. of Indus. & Comm. 1973–75; Policy, Small Bus., Dept. of Indus., Trade & Comm. 1975–77; Planning & Econ., N.S. Dept. of Devel. 1977–81; Econ. Devel., Ont. Min. of Treas. & Econ. 1981–84; Sr. Mgr., Bank of Montreal 1984–86; Pres., Ont. Devel. Corporation 1986; Candn. Imperial Bank of Comm. Centennial Internat. Fellow 1967; Protestant; Mem., Inst. of Public Admin. of Can.; Am. Planetary Soc.; Club: Toronto Sailing and Canoe; Home: Village of Swansea, Toronto, Ont.; Office: 2395 Speakman Dr., Mississauga, Ont. L5K 1B3.

**MacKINNON, Frank,** O.C. (1969), M.A., Ph.D., LL.D.; university professor; author; b. Charlottetown, P.E.I. 24 Apr. 1919; s. Hon. Murdoch (former Min. of Agric. and later Lieut.-Gov., P.E.I.) and Perle Beecher (Taylor) M.; e. Prince of WalesColl., Charlottetown, P.E.I.; McGill Univ., B.A. (Hons. in Econ. and Pol. Science) 1941; Univ. of Toronto, M.A. (Pub. Adm.) 1942 and Ph.D. (Pol. Science) 1950; Univ. of New Brunswick, LL.D. 1950, Dalhousie 1964; m. Margaret Daphne, d. Prof. C. P. Martin, 27 Apr. 1943; children: Philip Murdoch, David Cameron, Robert Peter, Pamela Martin; Prof., Pol. Science, Univ. of Calgary 1968–84 and Head of Department there in 1971; Prof. Emeritus since 1984; Indust. Relations Offr. with Dept. of Labour, Ottawa 1942–45; Lectr. in Pol. Science, Univ. of Toronto. 1945–46; Head of the Dept. of Pol. Science, Carleton Univ., Ottawa 1946–49; Principal, Prince of Wales Coll., Charlottetown, P.E.I. 1949–68; mem. of The Canada Council, 1957–63; Pres., Atlantic Provs. Econ. Council, 1958–59; Pres., Inst . Pub. Adm. of Can. 1964–65; Pres., Fathers of Confed. Mem. Foundation; author 'The Government of Prince Edward Island' 1951 (rec'd. the Gov. Gen. Lit. Award for Non-Fiction 1951); 'The Politics of Education' 1960; 'Responsibility and Relevance in Education' 1968; 'Postures and Politics' 1973; 'The Crown in Canada' 1976; 'Honour the Founders! Enjoy the Arts!' 1990 and numerous articles; mem., Royal Comn. on Electoral Reform (P.E.I.) 1961–62; mem. Comte. of Enquiry into Post-Secondary Educ. (Alta.) 1970–72; winner, Stratford Medal for Civic Design, 1964; Canada Council Medal, 1982; Home: 1130 Crescent Rd. N.W., Calgary, Alta. T2M 4A8; Office: Dept. of Pol. Science, Univ. of Calgary, Alta. T2N 1N4.

**MacKINNON, Rev. Gregory A.,** B.A., S.T.L., S.T.D., Ph.D.; retired university president; b. Antigonish, N.S. 16 June 1925; s. William Francis, M.D. and Mary Patricia (Chisholm) MacK.; e. elem. and high schs. Antigonish, N.S.; St. Francis Xavier Univ. B.A. 1946; Holy Heart Semy. Halifax 1950; Univ. of Ottawa S.T.L. 1961, S.T.D., Ph.D. 1964; Asst. Pastor Mount Carmel Parish New Waterford, N.S. 1950–54; Spiritual Dir. St. Francis Xavier Univ. 1954, Prof. and Chrmn. of Theol. 1963–73; Assoc. Dean of Arts and Dir. Summer Sch. 1970–78; Pres. and Vice Chancellor, St. Francis Xavier Univ. 1978–90; mem. Acad. Council, Atlantic Inst. of Educ. 1975–78; Pres. Atlantic Ecumenical Coun. 1974–76; mem. Extve. Council, Assn. Atlantic Univs.; mem. Extve. Heads, Assn. Univs. & Colls. Can.; mem. Adv. Comte. to Internat. Devel. Office Can.; Counc. of Nova Scotia Univ. Presidents (Chrmn. 1985–89); Atlantic Assoc. for Continuing Univ. Educ. (hon. life mem.); Apptd. Comm., N.S. Roy. Comm. on Forestry, 1982–84; Chair, Nova Scotia Home Care Adv. Ctte. 1987–93; Past Mem., Commonwealth Standing Ctte. on Student Mobility and Higher Educ. Co-operation; Mem. of Bd. of Dirs., International Centre for Human Rights and Democratic Development 1992– ; Chrmn. Bd. of Dirs., Candn. Found. on Compulsive Gambling (Atlantic Branch) 1993– ; mem. Soc. Scient. Study Religion; Coll. Theol. Soc.; R. Catholic; recreations: sailing, swimming, gardening, woodworking; Address: P.O. Box 5000, Antigonish, N.S. B2G 2W5.

**MacKINNON, Hon. Janice,** B.A., M.A., Ph.D., M.L.A.; politician; b. Kitchener, Ont. 1 Jan. 1947; d. William John and Melinda (Ropp) Potter; e. Univ. of Western Ont. B.A. (Hons.) 1969; Queen's Univ. M.A., Ph.D.; m. Peter s. Dr. Frank and Daphne M. 20 April 1974; children: Alan Douglas, William Taylor; MINISTER OF FINANCE, GOVT. OF SASKATCHEWAN 1993– ; Univ. Prof., Univ. of Saskatchewan 1975–91; Min. of Social Services 1991–92; Assoc. Min. of Finance and Min. of Crown Investments Corporation 1992–93; Chairperson, Treasury Bd.; Investment Bd.; Municipal Financing Corp.; Sask. Development Fund Corp.; Sask. Pension Plan; Vice-Chairperson, Crown Investments Corp.; Public Sector Bargaining Ctte.; Mem., Planning and Priorities Ctte.; CIC Mineral Interests Corp.; Bd. of Revenue Commissioners; Municipal Employees Superannuation Commission; Provincial Auditor; Public Employees Superannuation Commission; Public Service Superannuation Bd.; Horse Racing Commission; Sask. Gaming Commission; Pres., Saskatoon Co-op.; author: 'The Liberty We Seek: Loyalist Ideology in Colonial New York and Massachusetts' 1983, 'While the Women Only Wept: Loyalist Refugee Women' 1994; Home: 605 Bedford Rd., Saskatoon, Sask. S7L 0E9; Office: Legislative Bldg., Regina, Sask. S4S 0B3.

**MacKINNON, John (Jack),** B.Com., B.A., M.A.,; economist; municipal councillor; b. Vancouver, B.C. 6 Apr. 1925; s. Donald and Theresa Elizabeth (Maloney) MacK.; e. Univ. of B.C., B.Com. 1950, B.A. 1952; Univ. of Toronto M.A. 1954; Univ. of Ottawa doctoral studies 1955–66; m. Leona Marie d. Orval and Lillian Mulligan 8 May 1954; children: Donald, Margaret, Ann, Robert, Patricia, Catherine; COUNCILLOR, CITY OF OTTAWA AND REGIONAL MUNICIPALITY OF OTTAWA-CARLETON 1991– ; served with Candn. Army 1944–46; Brit. Control Comn. for Germany 1946–48; Canadian Imperial Bank of Commerce 1951–53; Burroughs Business Machines 1953–56; Jr. to Sr. Econ. Govt. of Can. 1956–83; Pres., Economists', Sociologists' & Statisticians' Assn. 1983–91; Captain, then Major, Cameron Highlanders of Ottawa 1961–64; former Trustee & Past Chrmn., Ottawa R.C. Separate School Bd.; Extve. Sec. Candn. (Mil.) Intelligence & Security Assn.; Pres., Civil Liberties Assoc. (Nat. Capital Region); Home: 2190 Tawney Rd., Ottawa, Ont. K1G 1C5; Office: 111 Sussex Dr., Ottawa, Ont. K1N 5A1.

**MacKINNON, Victor S.,** M.A., LL.B., LL.M., S.J.D.; educator; b. Bradford, Eng. 2 Aug. 1928; s. Norman and Edith (Hirst) MacK.; e. Ayr Acad.; Hillhead High Sch. Glasgow; Univ. of Glasgow M.A. 1949, LL.B. 1952; Harvard Law Sch. LL.M. 1955, S.J.D. 1963; m. Ruth Ann d. Paul and Mildred Simmonds 29 June 1957; children: Gregor L., Aran S.; PROF. OF LAW IN ADM., YORK UNIV. 1969– , Master of Atkinson College 1992– ; Lectr., Sr. Lectr. Univ. of Edinburgh 1957–66; Prof. and Dean of Law, Dir. Inst. Adm. Ahmadu Bello Univ. Nigeria 1966–69; Prof. and Dean of Law Makerere Univ. Uganda 1971–72; Chrmn. Adm. Studies Atkinson Coll. 1975–92; Visiting Prof. Univ. of Zululand 1984, Univ. of Capetown 1985, Univ. of Malaya 1988; Dir. Captus Press Toronto; recipient Sir Godfrey Collins Travelling Fellowship Univ. Glasgow 1954–55; Special Commonwealth Award Min. Overseas Devel. (UK) 1966–69, 1971–72; author: 'Comparative Federalism' 1964; various articles scholarly jours.; Founding mem. Scot. Nat. Party Assn. Can.; recreations: walking, talking; Home: 10 De Vere Gardens, Toronto, Ont. M5M 3E5; Office: 4700 Keele St., North York, Ont. M3J 1P3.

**MACKIW, Vladimir Nicolaus,** D.Sc., FCIC; metals and chemicals consultant; b. Stanislawiw, W. Ukraine 4 Sept. 1923; came to Canada 1948, naturalized 1953; e. Univs. of Breslau and Erlangen, Dipl. Chem. 1946; Univ. of Louvain, Post grad. studies 1948; Univ. Alta., D.Sc. (Hon.) 1976; m. Bohdanna Irene Kebuz; CONSULTANT, SHERRITT INC.; Chem., Lingman Lake Gold Mines, Winnipeg 1948; Man. Prov. Bureau of Mines 1949; joined Sherritt Gordon Mines Ltd. as Research Chem. 1949, Dir. of Research 1952, Dir. Research & Devel. Div. 1955–68, el. a Dir. 1964, Vice-Pres. 1967, Vice-Pres. Technol. & Corp. Devel. 1968, Extve. Vice-Pres. 1972–88; Past mem., Nat. Adv. Comte. on Mining & Metall. Research, Min. Energy, Mines & Resources, Ottawa 1972–79; Past Co-Chrmn. 1975–79; Past mem., Nat. Research Council of Can., 1971–77; Past Chrmn., Nickel Development Inst. 1984–86; Fellow, Chem. Inst. Can.; Am. Inst. Mining & Metall. Engrs.; Hon. mem. Shevchenco Scientific Soc.; Assn. Prof. Engrs. Alta.; Fellow, Candn. Inst. Mining & Metall.; Fellow, Candn. Academy of Engineering; Awards and Hons. incl.: Inco Platinum Medal, Candn. Inst. Mining & Metall. 1966; Jules Garnier Prize, Metall. Society France (co-recipient) 1966; R. S. Jane Mem. Award, Chem. Inst. Can. 1967; Airey Award (Noranda) Metall. Soc. of Candn. Inst. Mining & Metall. 1972; Gold Medal, Inst. of Mining & Metall., London, U.K. 1977; CRMA R&D Management Award, Candn. Rsch. Management Assn. 1990; James Douglas Gold Medal Award, Am. Inst. of Mining, Metallurgical, Petroleum Engrs. 1991; ASM Internat., Canada Council Lectureship Award 1990–91, 1994 TMS Fellow Award, Lecture ASM Canadian Chapters; author or co-author over 50 publs. in numerous chem. and metall. journs. in field of extractive metall., hydrometall. and powder metall.; holder of over 45 patents; Ukrainian Catholic; Clubs: The Ontario Club; Home: 9 Blair Athol Cres., Etobicoke, Ont. M9A 1X6; Office: 5 Hazelton Ave., Toronto, Ont. M5R 2E1.

**MACKLEM, Michael Kirkpatrick,** A.M., Ph.D.; publisher; b. Toronto, Ont. 12 July 1928; s. Hedley Clark and Mary Eileen (Kirkpatrick) M.; e. Upper Can. Coll. 1946; Trinity Coll., Univ. of Toronto 1950; Princeton Univ. A.M., Ph.D. 1954 (Charles Scribner Fellow, Porter Ogden Jacobus Fellow); m. Anne Woodburne d. Francis Aubrey and Beatrix Mildred Hardy 30 Dec. 1950; children: Timothy Street, Nicholas Hardy; PRESIDENT, MICHAEL, HARDY LTD. 1972– ; Instr. in English, Yale Univ. 1954–55; Staff Ed., Encyclopedia Canadiana 1955–58; Asst. to the Dir., Humanities Rsch. Counc. 1958–60; Gen. Mgr., Oberon Press 1966–84; Royal Soc. of Can. Fellow; Can. Counc. Fellow; Pres. Medal, Univ. of West. Ont.; author: 'The Anatomy of the World' 1958, 'God Have Mercy' 1967, 'Cinderella' 1968, 'The Voyages of Samuel de Champlain 1615 to 1618' 1970, 'The Voyages of Samuel de Champlain 1599 to 1603' 1971, 'The Sleeping Beauty' 1973, 'Jacques the Woodcutter' 1974, 'Liberty & the Holy City' 1976, 'The Oberon Reader' 1991, 'The Oberon Poetry Collection' 1992; recreations: skiing, sailing, windsurfing, climbing; Home: 555 Maple Lane, Ottawa, Ont. K1M 0N7.

**MACKLEM, O. Richard,** B.Com.; retired foundation executive; b. Kingston, Ont. 5 Jan. 1930; s. Oliver Tiffany and Katherine Derby (Bermingham) M.; e. Trinity Coll. Sch. Port Hope, Ont.; Queen's Univ. B.Com. 1952; Centre d'Études Industrielles Geneva Dip. 1953; m. Janet d. E. Gray-Donald and Osla Gray-Donald 13 Mar. 1934; children: Richard Tiffany, Elizabeth Joy, Janet Mary Gaye; following grad. Geneva joined Bristol Aeroplane Co., Bristol, Eng. as Mgmt. Trainee; joined The Bristol Aeroplane Co. of Canada Ltd. Montreal 1954, Asst. Sec. 1960, Sec. 1964; following absorption of co. by Rolls-Royce apptd. Sec. Rolls-Royce Holdings North America Ltd. 1968; Corporate Sec. Henry Birks & Sons Ltd. 1973 becoming a Dir. and Vice Pres. until 1990, retired 1993; Vice Pres. & Extve. Dir., The Birks Family Foundation 1990–93; mem. Montreal Bd. Trade; Pres. Montreal Risk & Insurance Mgmt. Asssn. 1967; Dir. and Chrmn. Audit & Finance Ctte. St. Mary's Hosp. Centre; Chrmn. Sacred Heart Sch. Montreal; Founding Dir. Eng. Speaking Cath. Council Montreal 1982–88; recreations: golf, skiing, curling; Clubs: Hermitage (Dir. 1978–85, Pres. 1984–85); Royal Montreal Curling; Saint James's; Mount Bruno Golf & Country; Montreal Badminton & Squash; Home: 349 Metcalfe Ave., Westmount, Qué. H3Z 2J2.

**MACKLEM, Peter Tiffany,** O.C., M.D., C.M., F.R.C.P.& S.(C), F.R.S.C.; physician; b. Kingston, Ont. 4 Oct. 1931; s. Oliver Tiffany and Katherine Darby (Bermingham) M.; e. Queen's Univ. B.A. 1952; McGill Univ. M.D., C.M. 1956; m. Joy d. John and Hope Belcourt 19 June 1954; children: David, Katherine, Patrick, Jennifer, Anne; Massabki Prof. of Med. McGill Univ. 1985– ; Physician-in-Chief Dept. of Med. Royal Victoria Hosp. 1979–86, Sr. Phys. 1972– ; Dir. McGill Univ. Clinic 1979–86, Prof. of Med. McGill 1972– , Chrmn. of Med. 1980–85; Acting Phys.-in-Chief Montreal Chest Hosp. Centre 1984–86; Physician-in-Chief, Montreal Chest Hosp. Centre 1986– ; Pres. & Sci. Dir., Respiratory Health, Network of Centres of Excellence 1989– ; Cons. Specialist Dept. Med. Montreal Gen. Hosp. 1981– ; Hon. mem. Dept. Med. Queen Elizabeth Hosp. 1980– ; mem. Consulting Distinguished Adv. Bd. VENTECH CORP. 1985– ; internship and post grad. studies Royal Victoria and Queen Mary Veterans Hosps. 1956–64; Rsch. Fellow Harvard Sch. Pub. Health 1964–65; Dir. Meakins-Christie Labs. for Respiratory Rsch. 1972–79; Professeur Associé Univ. de Paris 1976–77; Visiting Prof., Università di Milano 1986–87; Université Libre de Bruxelles 1987; honours incl. Lederle Med. Student Rsch. Fellow 1955; Harrison Watson Scholar McGill Univ. 1961–62; Jonathan Meakins Meml. Fellow 1963; Medalist in Med. Royal Coll. Phys. 1964; McLaughlin Travelling Fellow 1964–65; Med. Rsch. Council Scholarship 1967–72 and Associateship 1972–79; Queen's Silver Jubilee Medal 1977; Medalist Am. Coll. Chest Phys. 1979; Doctor Honoris Causa, Université Libre de Bruxelles 1987; JB Stirling Medal, Queen's Univ. 1991; author or co-author numerous med. publs.; mem. various ed. bds.; mem. Corp. Professionelle des Medicins du Qué.; Candn. Soc. Clin. Investig. (Pres. 1983–84); Am. Soc. Clin. Investig.; Am. Physiol. Soc.; Candn. Thoracic Soc. (Pres. 1975–76); Am. Thoracic Soc. (Extve. Ctte. 1974–76); Peripatetic Club; Internat. Union Physiol. Sci's.; Internal Union Against Tuberculosis; Eur. Soc. Clin. Respiratory Physiol.; Am. Assn. Phys.; Alpha Omega Alpha; recreations: water sports, photography; Home: 206, 3470 Redpath St., Montréal, Qué. H3G 2G3; Office: Dept. of Medicine, Montreal Chest Hospital, 3650 rue St. Urbain, Montréal, Qué. H2X 2P4.

**MACKLIN, Arthur Wayne;** farmer, union executive; b. Grande Prairie 31 Aug. 1945; e. Grande Prairie H.S.; m. Donna Marlene Hickson; children: Sadie Catherine, Vance Arthur, John Laurence, Nathan Victor; PRESIDENT AND CHIEF EXECUTIVE OFFICER, NATIONAL FARMERS UNION 1993– ; operates mixed (barley, wheat, forage seeds & cattle) family farm 65 miles n.e. of Grande Prairie in Peace River Country; pedigreed seed grower; ; has served as local dir., local vice-pres., nat. bd. mem., nat. extve. mem., regional co-ord. and vice-pres., National Farmers Union; Mem., Candn. Seed Growers Assn. 1972– ; Elected Mem., Candn. Wheat Bd. Adv. Ctte. rep. Dist. 11 (northern Alta. & n.e. B.C.) 1987– ; Past Mem., Bd. of Dir., East Smoky Gas Co-op.; Sec.-Treas., Co-op Implement Depot Ctte.; Mem., St. Paul's Un. Ch.; Home: 10241 – 111 Ave., Grande Prairie, Alta. T8V 1T8; Office: 250C – 2nd Ave. S., Saskatoon, Sask. S7K 2M1.

**MACKLING, Hon. Alvin Henry,** Q.C., B.A., LL.B.; politician; b. Winnipeg, Man. 31 Dec. 1927; s. John and Anne Gertrude (Williams) M.; e. Univ. Coll., Univ. of Winnipeg B.A. 1953; Univ. of Manitoba LL.B. 1958; m. Patricia, Taeko Ono; children: Holly Naomi, Thomas Hal; Minister of Labour, Manitoba 1985; Min. of Consumer and Corporate Affairs, Manitoba 1986; Min. of Business Development and Tourism 1987; private law practice St. James, man. 1958–69; Alderman, City of St. James 1961–69; cr. Q.C. 1969; Atty.-Gen. Manitoba 1969–73; Min. of Consumer and Corp. Affairs 1969–73; Chrmn. Man. Motor Transport Bd. and Man. Traffic Bd. 1974–80; Min. of Natural Resources 1981–84; mem. New Democratic Party; United Ch.; recipient Lieut.-Gov.'s Gold Medal, Econ. and Hist., Univ. of Winnipeg 1951; Home: R.R. #1, Dugald, Man. R0E 0K0.

**MACKNESS, William,** B.Sc., M.A., C.L.J.; university administrator, economist, columnist; b. London, Ont. 28 April 1938; s. Samuel George and Olive Mary (Casey) M.; e. St. Jerome's Coll.; Univ. of Montreal B.Sc. 1961; Univ. of Western Ont. M.A. 1966; m. Denise d. Omer and Rita Préfontaine 30 June 1969; children: John, Elizabeth, Michelle, Sarah, Andrew; DEAN, FAC. OF MANAGEMENT, THE UNIV. OF MANITOBA 1988– ; Army Officer 1961–64; Sr. Advr., Dept. of Finance Ottawa 1966–74; Chief Econ., Burns Bros. & Denton 1974–76; Vice-Pres. & Dir., Pitfield Mackay Ross 1976–82; Sr. Vice-Pres., The Bank of N.S. 1982–88; Dir., Federal Indus. Ltd.; The Great-West Life Assur. Co.; UMA Group Ltd.; Crown Corp. Council; Trustee, The Fraser Inst.; Mem., Bd. of Dir., Winnipeg Symphony Orch.; Anglican Ch. of Can.; recreations: history, jogging, golf, salmon fishing; clubs: Cambridge, Canadian, Donalda, Manitoba, National, St. Charles Country; Home: 61 Waterloo St., Winnipeg, Man. R3N 0S3; Office: Univ. of Man., 314 Drake Centre, Winnipeg, Man. R3T 5V4.

**MACLACHLAN, Gordon A.,** M.A., Ph.D., F.R.S.C.; educator; b. Saskatoon, Sask. 30 June 1930; s. Hector R. and Eleanor May (Glass) M.; e. Univ. of Sask. B.A. 1952, M.A. 1954; Univ. of Man. Ph.D. 1956; Imp. Coll. London NRC Postdoctoral Fellow 1956–59; m. Sarah d. Alexandra and John Dangerfield 25 June 1959; children: Mary Alexandra, Anna Eleanor; Prof. of Biol. 1969– ; Asst. Prof. Univ. of Alta. 1959–62; joined present Univ. 1962, Chrmn. Biol. Dept. 1970–75; Dean of Grad. Studies & Research and Vice Princ. (Research), McGill Univ. 1980–90; Assoc. Ed. Candn. Journ. Biochem. 1971–75; Plant Physiol. (U.S.A.) 1980–86; Candn. Journ. Botany 1980–88; Plant & Cell Physiol. Tokyo 1982–87; Ed., Journ. Plant Mol. Biol. 1988–90; author various publs.; Pres. Candn. Soc. Plant Physiol. 1973; Candn. Soc. Cell Biol. 1982; Candn. Soc. Grad. Schools 1986; Candn. Assoc. Univ. Research Admin. 1987; Bd. of Dir., Pulp and Paper Rsch. Inst. Can. 1980–90; Can. Inst. Sci and Tech. Information 1985–90; Candn. Inst. Adv. Rsch. 1985– ; Plant Biotech. Inst. of N.R.C. 1991–93; Home: 561 Argyle Ave., Westmount, Que. H3Y 3B8; Biol. Laboratory, McGill Univ., 1205 Ave. Penfield, Montreal, Que. H3A 1B1.

**MacLACHLAN, Lachlan Patrick,** B.Arch., M.A.; educator; b. Salisbury, Rhodesia 16 Mar. 1928; s. Herbert Thomas and Muriel Maud (Mathews) MacL.; e. Plumtree Sch. Rhodesia 1945; Cape Town Univ. B.Arch. 1950; Exeter Coll. Oxford (Rhodes Scholar) M.A. 1954; m. Jocelyn d. Colwyn and Veronica Mary Vulliamy 21 July 1954; three s. Martin, Charles, Patrick; Founder & Dir., Independent Schools Service Ltd. 1972–94; Asst. Arch. R.S. and A.W. Parker, Salisbury, Rhodesia 1954–57, Partner in Nyasaland (Malawi) 1957–59; Asst. Arch. Anglo-American Corp. Salisbury 1959–61; Teacher Shawnigan Lake Sch., B.C. 1961–63, Asst. Headmaster 1963–67, Headmaster 1967–72; Oxford Univ. Rugby Blue 1953; Scot. & Barbarians Rugby 1954; recreations: golf, rugby; Clubs: Cowichan Golf & Country; Cowichan Rugby Football; Royal Hong Kong Golf; Hong Kong Football; Home: Haida Rd., R.R. 5, Duncan, B.C. V9L 4T6.

**MacLAREN, Alethea (Lee),** M.A.; economist; b. Memphis, Tenn.; d. Col. Americus and Charlotte Wardlaw Jackson Mitchell; e. Lausanne Sch. for Girls, Memphis; Vassar Coll. B.A.; Columbia Univ. M.A.; Carleton Univ. Candn. Pub. Admin. Course 1962–63; Univ. of Toronto Urban Studies; m. Roy MacLaren 25 June 1959; children: Ian, Vanessa, Malcolm; Dir. of Funding, Univ. of Toronto 1975–87; Consultant, Llewelyn-Davies Weeks Canada 1973–77; Foreign Service Offr. Dept. of State US 1954–59 serving in Cairo (Vice Consul), Khartoum (1954–55), Saigon Consul 1956, Second Secy. (Econ.) 1957; mem. US Del. to Colombo Plan Conf. 1957; reassigned to Dept. of State Washington evaluating econ. reporting from missions abroad 1958; Economist Candn. Govt. 1961–62; served Women's Comte. Nat. Gallery of Can.; Ang. Ch. groups, sch. comtes., fund-raising Candn. Cancer Soc., Candn. Red. Cross, and Lib. Party Ont.; mem. Extve. Comte. Un. Way Toronto; Leadership Chair, Campaign Cabinet, United Way 1989; Secy., Canada Memorial Foundation 1990– ; Huguenot Society, So. Carolina; Dir., Centrestage; Finance Chrmn., Liberal Party Ontario 1983–84; Standing Ctte. Finance, Liberal Party Canada; Dir., Dellcrest Childrens' Centre; Upper Canada College Foundation; Cdn. Inst. Internat. Affairs; Harbourfront Writers' Festival; Candn. Mediterranean Inst.; Pres. Candn. Assoc. University Development Officers 1985–86; Anglican; Liberal; Home: 425 Russell Hill Rd., Toronto, Ont. M5P 2S4.

**MacLAREN, James Wade,** B.A.Sc., S.M., P.Eng.; b. Toronto, Ont. 18 Oct. 1921; s. James Ferris and Dorothy (Wade) M.; e. Univ. of Toronto Schs., 1940; Univ. of Toronto, B.A.Sc. 1946; Mass. Inst. of Tech., S.M. 1947; m. Jessie Marie, d. Dr. Roy W. Simpson, 25 Sept. 1948; children: James, Ian, Andy, Thomas; Consulting Engineer – Sole Practitioner 1982– ; Chief Extve. Offr. MacLaren Engineers, Planners & Scientists, Inc. 1962–82; served as Jr. Project Engr. on Mun. Works, Gore & Storrie Ltd., 1947–50; joined father's firm, James F. MacLaren Associates in similar capacity, 1950; apptd. Jr. Partner 1956; served with Candn. Armoured Corps, 1942–44; rank 2nd Lt.; Pres. Assn. Consulting Engrs. Can. 1974–75; Dir., Erm Group (Exton P.A.); mem. Assn. Prof. Engrs. Ont.; Am. Acad. Environ. Engrs.; Fellow, Am. Soc. Civil Engrs.; Can. Soc. for Civil Engrs.; Trade Metrop. Toronto; Zeta Psi; Protestant; recreation: golf; Clubs: Granite; Bayview; Rideau; Home: Apt. 214, 4005 Bayview Ave., Willowdale Ont., M2M 3Z9; Office: Suite 900, 2 Sheppard Ave. E., North York, Ont. M2N 5Y7.

**MacLAREN, Hon. Roy,** P.C., B.A., M.A., M.Div.; executive; publisher; b. Vancouver, B.C. 26 Oct. 1934; s. Wilbur and Anne (Graham) MacL.; e. Univ. of B.C., B.A. 1955; Cambridge Univ., M.A. 1957; Harvard Univ., Grad. Sch. of Business Adm. Advanced Mang. Program, 1973; Univ. of Toronto M.Div. 1991; m. Alethea, d. Col. Americus Mitchell, 25 June 1959; children: Ian, Vanessa, Malcolm; MINISTER OF INTERNATIONAL TRADE, GOVT. OF CANADA 1993– ; Joined Dept. of External Affairs, Ottawa, as Foreign Service Offr., serving with Internat. Supervision and Control Comn. in Vietnam 1958–59; Second Secy., Prague, 1959–60; First Secy., Perm. Mission of Can. to UN, N.Y., 1964–68 and also served as mem. of Candn. del's to econ. conf's in Geneva, Vienna and New Delhi; Depy. Head, Aid and Devel. Div., Dept. of External Affairs, Ottawa, 1968–69; apptd. Dir. of Pub. Affairs, Massey-Ferguson Ltd., 1969; Pres. and Chief Extve. Offr., Ogilvy and Mather (Can.) Ltd. 1975–77; Chrmn., Fed. Task Force on Business-Govt. Relations 1977; Past Publisher, Candn. Business Magazine and Chrmn., CB Media Ltd., 1977–83 and 1984–93; former Dir., London Insur. Group Inc.; Deutsche Bank (Canada) Ltd.; Royal LePage Ltd.; Royal LePage Mortgage Co.; Broadview Press; elected M.P. for Etobicoke North, g.e. 1979, re-el g.e. 1980 and g.e. 1988; Parlty Secy. to Min. of Energy, Mines & Resources, 1980–82; Sworn to Privy Council and appointed Minister of State (Finance) 1983; Minister of National Revenue 1984; former Gov., Candn. Journalism Foundation; Gov., Etobicoke General Hosp.; Dir., Toronto School of Theology; Fellow, Royal Soc. of the Arts, UK; author 'Canadians in Russia, 1918–1919' 1976; 'Canadians on the Nile, 1882–1898' 1978; 'Canadians Behind Enemy Lines, 1939–1945,' 1981; 'Honourable Mentions' 1986; various articles in mags., newspapers, journs.; Liberal; Anglican; recreations: tennis, cross-country skiing; Clubs: R.C.Y.C.; Rideau (Ottawa); Home: 425 Russell Hill Rd., Toronto, Ont., M5P 2S4; Office: 70 The Esplanade, Toronto, Ont. M5E 1R2.

**MacLATCHIE, James Melvin,** B.A., M.S.W.; social worker; b. Montréal, Qué. 19 Mar. 1938; s. Arthur Nelson and Irene Isabel (Kollmar) M.; e. Carleton Univ., B.A. 1963; Maritime Sch. of Soc. Work, dipl.Soc.Work 1966; Acadia Univ., M.S.W. 1966; m. Susan d. Catherine and Otho Elliott 26 Aug. 1963; one s. Ian Christopher; EXTVE. DIR., THE JOHN HOWARD SOC. OF CAN. 1978– ; Dir., Rehab. Serv., Candn. Mental Health Assn. 1967–69; Dir., Soc. Serv. Worker Prog., Algonquin Coll. of Applied Arts 1967–71; Extve. Dir., The Elizabeth Fry Soc. of Ottawa 1971–78; Extve. Sec., Candn. Assn. of Elizabeth Fry Soc. 1974–78; Past Chair., Alliance of Candn. Prison Aftercare Soc. 1978–86; Vice Pres., Internat. Prisoners Aid Assn.; Founding Dir., Penal Reform Internat. 1989; Depy. Sec. General., Penal Reform Internat.; several Chairs with Fed. Govt.; Voluntary Assn. Cons.; Chair, National Assns. Active in Criminal Justice 1992– ; Chair, 1st Nat. Conf. on Violence in Candn. Soc.; Assoc. Dir., YM-YMCA of Ottawa; Ed. 'Insights Into Violence In Contemporary Canadian Society' 1987; recipient, Commemorative Medal for 125th Anniversary of Candn. Confederation; mem., Candn. Radio Relay League; Candn. Amateur Radio Fed.; recreations: amateur radio; Club: Toastmasters Internat.; Home: 1297 Pebble Rd., Ottawa, Ont. K1V 7R9; Office: 55 Parkdale Ave., Ottawa, Ont. K1Y 1E5.

**MacLEAN, Alistair William,** M.A., Ph.D.; university professor; b. Aberdeen, Scotland 24 Apr. 1943; s. Roderick Charles and Gladys (Calder) M.; e. Jordanhill Coll. Sch., Glasgow 1961; Aberdeen Univ., M.A. 1965; Queen's Univ., M.A. 1967, Ph.D. 1969; m. Helen d. William and Janet Seth 15 July 1967; children: Roderick William, Joanna Elizabeth, Janet Alice; PROF. OF PSYCHOL., QUEEN'S UNIV. 1984– ; Rsch. Assoc. & Postdoct. Fellow, Edinburgh Univ. 1969–71; Asst. Prof., Psych., present univ. 1971–75; Asoc. Prof. 1975–84; Asst. Prof. of Psychiatry 1978–82; Assoc. Prof. 1982–92; Prof. 1992– ; Clinical Asst., Dept. of Psychiatry 1973– ; Dept. of Med., Kingston Gen. Hosp. 1987– ; Staff Sci., The Toronto Hosp. (Western Div.) 1986– ; Registered Psych. (Ont.); Chartered Psych. (U.K.); Consultant Psych. 1972– ; past mem. of several cttes.; Commonwealth Scholar 1965–69; Alumni Award for Excellence in Teaching, Queen's Univ. 1988; Mem., Candn. & Ont. Psych. Assns.; Sleep Rsch. Soc.; Sleep Soc. of Can.; Soc. for Rsch. on Biol. Rhythms; Brit. Sleep Soc.; Assoc. Fellow, Brit. Psych. Soc.; Fellow, Candn. Psych. Assn.; recreations: reading, cross country skiing; Home: 207 Collingwood St., Kingston, Ont. K7L 3X7; Office: Kingston, Ont. K7L 3N6.

**MacLEAN, David B.,** B.Sc., Ph.D., F.R.S.C., F.C.I.C.; educator; b. Summerside, P.E.I. 15 July 1923; s. William and Lulu Adelaide (Stewart) MacL.; e. Acadia Univ., B.Sc. 1942; McGill Univ., Ph.D. 1946; m. (1) Helen Shirley d. Ross and Elsie Canning 1945; m. (2) Regina Lane Hutton d. Martin and Elizabeth Lane 1951; children: Susan, David, Richard, Robert, Gillian; stepchildren: Garry & Dariel Hutton; PROFESSOR EMERITUS OF CHEMISTRY, McMASTER UNIV. 1989– ; Rsch. Chem., Dominion Rubber Co. Guelph, Ont. 1946–49; Assoc. Prof., N.S. Tech. Coll., Halifax, N.S. 1949–54; Assoc. Prof. present Univ. 1954, Prof. of Chem. 1960–89, Chrmn. of Chem. 1959–62, 1973–79; Home: 394 Queen St. S., Hamilton, Ont.; Office: 1280 Main St. W., Hamilton, Ont. L8S 4M1.

**MacLEAN, David Robert,** M.D., M.H.Sc.; physician; b. Pictou, N.S. 17 Oct. 1944; s. George Sterling and

Irene Thorne (Gesner) MacL.; e. Dalhousie Univ. M.D. 1970; Univ. of Toronto M.H.Sc. 1982; m. Sandra d. Sidney and Jean Morrison 20 Dec. 1969; two d. Erin Elizabeth, Laura Alexandra; HEAD, DEPT. OF COMMUNITY HEALTH & EPIDEMIOLOGY, FACULTY OF MEDICINE, DALHOUSIE UNIV. 1991– and Assoc. Prof. of Med., Dept. of Community Health & Epidemiol., Dalhousie Univ. 1989– ; Med. Offr. Candn. Armed Forces 1970–73; private med. practice 1973–80; Med. Offr. of Health N.S. Dept. of Health and Dir. Atlantic Health Unit 1980–89; Lectr. in Community Health & Epidemiol. Dalhousie Univ.; mem. Pub. Health Assn. N.S. (Past Pres.); N.S. Med. Soc.; Candn. Pub. Health Assn.; Bd. of Dirs., Candn. Atherosclerosis Soc.; recreations: skiing, golf; Home: 56 Forest Rd., Dartmouth, N.S. B3A 2M5; Office: 10th Fl., Sir Charles Tupper Medical Bldg., University Ave., Halifax, N.S. B3H 4H7.

**MacLEAN, Guy Robertson,** M.A., Ph.D.; educator; b. Sydney, N.S. 21 Dec. 1929; s. (Charles) Whitmore and Mary Melinda (Nicholson) MacL.; e. Sydney (N.S.) Acad. 1948; Dalhousie Univ. B.A. 1951, M.A. 1953; Oxford Univ. (Rhodes Scholar N.S.) B.A. 1955, M.A. 1960; Duke Univ. Ph.D. 1958; m. (Mary) Judith d. late H. Murray Hunter 1963; children: Colin, Jocelyn; OMBUDSMAN, PROV. OF NOVA SCOTIA, 1989– ; Pres. Emeritus & Prof. of History, Mount Allison Univ. 1986– ; Pres., Mount Allison Univ. 1980–86; Vice Pres. (Acad.), Dalhousie Univ., 1974–80; and Prof. of Hist. since 1965; Asst. Prof. of Hist. Dalhousie Univ. 1957, Assoc. Prof. 1961, Dean of Residence 1960–64, Dean of Grad. Studies 1966–69, Dean of Arts & Science 1969–75; Lectr., N.S. Tech. Coll. 1960–61, Univ. of Alta. 1962; Dean of Men, King's Coll. 1958–60; served with C.O.T.C. 1949–51; Dir. and Chrmn. Opera East; Dir. Sport N.S.; Dir. and Past Pres. Soccer N.S.; Br. Chrmn. Candn. Inst. Internat. Affairs; Dir., Donner Candn. Foundation; Gov., Coll. of Cape Breton; Commr., Maritime Provs. Higher Educ. Comn.; mem. Extve. Comte. Social Sciences & Humanities Research Council Can.; mem. Nat. Extve. Council, Candn. Hist. Assn.; Gov. Canada Summer Games '86; rec'd Centennial Medal; Jubilee Medal; Malcolm Honour Award; Graeme Fraser Award; edited with introduction 'Life of A. T. Galt' 1966; author various articles Candn. and European hist.; United Church; Club: Waegwoltic; Home: Marlborough Woods, Halifax, N.S. B3H 1H9.

**MacLEAN, Heather,** B.Sc., Dip.Nutr., M.Sc., Ed.D.; university professor; b. Montreal, Que. 24 March 1947; d. Charles Howe and Margaret Hunter (Gilroy) M.; e. McGill Univ. B.Sc. 1968; Univ. of Toronto Dip.Nutr. 1972, M.Sc. 1973, Ed.D. 1979; one s.: David Bates; PROFESSOR, NUTRITIONAL SCIENCES, UNIVERSITY OF TORONTO; Mem., Candn. Public Health Assn.; Ont. Public Health Assn.; author: 'Women's Experience of Breast Feeding' 1990; co-author: 'Living with Diabetes' 1988; Home: 650 Merton St., Toronto, Ont. M4S 1B8; Office: 150 College St., Toronto, Ont. M5S 1A8.

**MacLEAN, Hon. J. Angus,** P.C., O.C., D.F.C., C.D., B.Sc., LL.D.; retired politician; b. Lewes, P.E.I. 15 May 1914; s. late George Allan and Sarah MacL.; e. Mt. Allison Acad.; Summerside High Sch.; Univ. of B.C.; Mt. Allison Univ., B.Sc. 1939, Hon. LL.D. 1958; Hon. LL.D., Univ. of P.E.I. 1985; m. Gwendolyn Esther Burwash 29 Oct. 1952; children: Sarah Jean, Allan Duart, Mary Esther, Robert Angus; served several yrs. Bd. of Regents, Mt. Allison Univ.; Past-Pres., R.A.F.E.S. (Candn. Br.); former Dir., R.C.A.F. Memorial Fund; former Vice-Pres., C.P.A. (Fed. Br.); served with R.C.A.F. (Reserve) 1939–47; Decorated with D.F.C. by H.M. King George VI, 1942; Mentioned in Dispatches 1942; commanded Test & Development Establishment 1943–45 and Missing Rsch. & Enquiry Unit, Europe 1945–47 (rank Wing Commdr.); mem.: United Services Officers' Club, Charlottetown; R.C.A.F. Assoc., Masonic Lodge, A.F. & A.M.; Royal Can. Legion; Greater Charlottetown Area C.C.; Can. Club, P.E.I.; Del. NATO Parl. Conf., Paris 1956; led Can. Delegation Colombo Plan Conf., Tokyo 1960; led F.A.O. Conf., Rome. 1961; mem. Candn.-Japanese Ministerial Del., Tokyo 1963; Del. Commonwealth Conf., Wellington, N.Z. 1965; Del. 18th Parl. Course, Westminster, Eng. 1969; led Can. Del., Inter-Parl. Conf. on European Co-operation and Security, Helsinki 1973; Del. Inter-Parl. Conf. on European Co-operation and Security, Belgrade 1974; Rep. P.E.I. Legis., 27th C.P.A., Fiji, Oct. 1981; rep. P.E.I. at First Ministers' Constitutional Conferences 1981; Cand. Fed. g.e. 1945 and 1949 and def.; 1st elected to H. of C. at by-elect., 25 June 1951; re-el. 1953, 1957, 1958, 1962, 1963, 1965, 1968, 1972 and 1974; sworn of the Privy Council 21 June 1957; resigned from H. of C. 20 Oct. 1976; first elected to P.E.I. Legislature at by-elect. 8 Nov. 1976; re-el. g.e. 1978, 1979; sworn in as Premier, Pres. of Extve. Counc. 3 May 1979; Min. Responsible for Cultural Affairs 1979–80; retired as Premier of P.E.I. 17 Nov. 1981, but retained seat in P.E.I. Legis. as Assemblyman for 4th Queens until dissolution of L.A. 31 Aug. 1982; installed as Officer, Most Venerable Order of St. John of Jerusalem Oct. 1982; mem.: P.E.I. Energy Corp. 1983–87; Sr. Adv. Bd., Maritime Provinces Education Foundn.; Mem., Sr. Adv. Bd., National Museum of Natural Sciences, Nat. Museums of Can. and P.E.I.'s Commnr. to EXPO '86; P.C.; Presbyterian; Address: Lewes, R.R. #3, Belle River, P.E.I. C0A 1B0.

**MacLEAN, James Alexander,** O.B.E. (1978), B.Sc., P.Eng.; b. Beauly, Scot. 3 Feb. 1913; s. John and Joanne (Cameron) M.; e. Dingwall Acad., Scot.; Univ. of Glasgow, B.Sc. (Elect. Engn.) 1936; Manchester Coll. of Tech., Dipl. in Indust. Adm.; m. Mary, d. late Sidney Furniss, 4 April 1941; children: Katherine Alison, Ian Michael; Chrmn., GEC Canada Ltd. 1969–80 (Dir. 1969–87); retired; with Metropolitan-Vickers Elec. Co. Ltd. 1937–59 (employed in Manchester, London, Nairobi and Toronto); Pres. and Dir., Associated Electrical Industries (Canada) Ltd. 1959–69; Pres. and Chief Extve. Offr., English Electric-AEI Can. Ltd., 1969; Assn. Prof. Engrs. Ont.; Presbyterian; Home: 2170 - 502 Marine Dr., Oakville, Ont. L6L 5V1.

**MACLEAN, John Dick,** M.D., FRCPC, MRCP(UK), DCMT, CCFP; university professor / physician; b. Flin Flon, Man. 22 Apr. 1940; s. Frank Willard and Isobel McLelland (Fleming) M.; e. Carleton Univ., B.A.; Queen's Univ., M.D. 1966; Univ. of London, DCMT; m. Meta d. Ronald and Geraldine Kitchen 10 Aug. 1971; children: Jennifer, Sara, James; DIR., MCGILL CTR. FOR TROPICAL DISEASE, MONTREAL GEN. HOSP. 1981– ; Dir., Faculty Program in Internat. Health; Program Dir., Div. of Infectious Disease and Medical Microbiology, McGill Univ.; worked in Zambia 1965, Malaysia 1968–70, Indonesia 1970, Kenya 1972–73, Japan 1974–5; trained in internal med., Montreal Gen. Hosp. 1966–68, 1970–72; joined staff, MGH and McGill Univ. 1975; Prog. Dir., Ctr. for Family Med. 1977–81; McGill Div. of Infectious Disease & Clin. Microbiol. 1987– ; Assoc. Prof., Dept. of Med. & Family Med.; Clin. Cons., Montreal Childrens Hosp.; Cons., Inst. of Parasitol. (Nat. Ref. Ctr.); Dir., McGill-Addis Ababa Med. Linkage Project 1981–92; Chrmn., Candn. Univ. Consortium for Health in Development; recreations: tennis, skiing; Home: 228 Lockhart Ave., Town of Mount Royal, Que. H3P 1Y4; Office: 1650 Cedar Ave., #787, Montreal, Que. H3G 1A4.

**MacLEAN, Lloyd Douglas,** O.C., B.Sc., Ph.D., M.D., D.Sc. (Hon.), F.A.C.S., F.R.C.S.(C), F.R.S.C.; surgeon; b. Calgary, Alta. 15 June 1924; s. Fred Hugh and Azilda (Trudell) M.; e. Univ. of Alberta, B.Sc., 1946, M.D., 1949; Univ. of Minnesota, Ph.D., 1957; D.Sc. (Hon.) Univ. of Alberta, McGill Univ.; m. Eleanor d. Alfred Colle, Minneapolis, Minn., 30 June 1954; 5 children; PROFESSOR OF SURGERY, McGILL UNIV. 1962– ; Surgeon-in-Chief, Royal Victoria Hosp. 1962–88, Sr. Surgeon 1988– ; Internship, 1949–50, Univ. of Alberta; Straight Internship in Surgery (1950–51), Residency (training surg.), Univ. of Minn., 1951–56; Instr., Dept. of Surgery there, 1956–58; Asst. Prof., 1958–59, Assoc. Prof., 1959–62; Surgeon-in-Chief, Ancker Hosp., St. Paul, Minn., 1957–62; apptd. Prof. of Surg., McGill Univ. 1962; Chrmn., Dept. of Surgery, McGill Univ. 1968–73, 1977–82, 1987–88; 2nd Lieut., R.C.A.M.C. (Reserve); Pres., Am. Surg. Assn. 1992–93; Pres., Am. College of Surgeons 1993– ; mem., Soc. Univ. Surg.; Am. Assn. for Thoracic Surg.; Soc. for Exper. Biol. & Med.; Am. Physiol. Soc.; Central Surg. Assn.; Officer, Order of Canada; Baptist; Home: #1402, 80 Berlioz, Montreal, Que. H3E 1N9.

**MacLEAN, Richard (Rick) Dale,** B.A., M.A.; newspaper editor; b. Newcastle, N.B. 12 Aug. 1957; s. Frederick Dale and Doris Marie (Johnston) M.; e. Miramichi Valley H.S. (Hons.) 1975; Mount Allison Univ., B.A. (1st class hons.) 1979; Univ. of West. Ont., M.A. 1984; m. Norma d. Frederick and Patricia Foran 26 May 1984; children: Alexandra Rae, Andrew Dale; EDITOR, 'MIRAMICHI LEADER'/'MIRAMICHI LEADER-WEEKEND' 1984– ; Fieldworker, Frontier Coll. summer 1978; Rsch., Mount Allison Univ. summers 1979, 1980, 1981; Reporter, 'Miramichi Leader' 1980–81 (6 mos.); Trade Comnr. Serv., Candn. Fgn. Serv. 1981–82; reporter/freelancer, 'Moncton Times-Transcript' & 'Miramichi Leader' 1983, 'Atlantic Insight Magazine' 1987; Maclean's 1989; Small Business Magazine 1989; weekly contbr., CBC Radio 1987– ; Legion bursary 1975; Renewable scholarship, Mount Allison Univ. 1975; scholarship & teaching asst., Carleton Univ. 1980 (left program after 2 mos.); winner, best news story, Atlantic Community Newspaper Assn. 1988; co-winner, best news story, Canadian Community Newspaper Assn. 1991; Pres., ACNA board 1992–93; co-author/editor: 'The Rebel Bureaucrat: Frederick John Shore (1799–1837) as Critic of William Bentinck's "India"' 1983; co-author: 'Terror's End: The Trial of Allan Legere' 1992; 'Terror: Murder and Panic in New Brunswick' 1990; recreations: distance running, tennis; Home: P.O. Box 35, Site 6, R.R. 1, Douglastown, N.B. E0C 1H0; Office: Box 500, 65 Jane St., Newcastle, N.B. E1V 3M6.

**MacLEAN, Ronald Stuart,** B.Sc., B. Ed., M.A.; retired diplomat; b. Camrose, Alta. 8 June 1928; s. Murdoch MacKenzie and Anabel Gladys (Ovendon) M.; e. Univ. of Alberta B.Sc. 1949, B. Ed. 1950; Grad. Studies 1951–52; Fletcher School of Law & Diplomacy, Medford, Mass., M.A. 1953, Grad. Studies 1953–55; m. Beverley d. C.J. Cobb 3 Jan. 1955; children: Christopher, Alyson, Thomas; Candn. Ambassador to Denmark 1991–92; Public Sch. Teacher, Killam, Alta. 1950–51; Instructor, Pol Sc. & Econ., M.I.T. 1955–56; External Affairs with postings in India, France, Japan, South Am. & Econ. Div. H.Q. (now C.I.D.A.) 1956–72; seconded to Treasury Bd. as Dir., External, Defence & Cultural Programs, Govt. of Can. 1972–75; Ambassador & Perm. Rep., Orgn. for Econ. Co-op. & Devel. (OECD) 1975–79; Candn. Ambassador, Brazil 1979–83; seconded to Dept. of Energy Mines & Resources as Dir.-Gen., Internat. Energy Relns. Br. 1983–86; Candn. Ambassador to the Rep. of S. Africa & High Comnr. to Kingdoms of Lesotho & Swaziland 1986–91; United Church; recreations: hiking, camping; Home: 2401 - 1480 Riverside Dr., Ottawa, Ont. K1G 5H2.

**MacLEAN, Rory Howe,** B.A.A.; writer; b. Vancouver, B.C. 5 Nov. 1954; s. Andrew Dyas and Joan (Howe) M.; e. Upper Canada College 1962–72; Ryerson Polytech. Inst. B.A.A. (Hons.) 1976; m. Katrin d. Stuart and Monika Latta 25 April 1992; freelance filmmaker & screenwriter 1976–89; awards at Los Angeles Filmex, Cannes & Candn. TV Commercials Festival; author: 'A Dead Czech' 1989 ('The Independent' Travel Writing Award), 'Stalin's Nose' 1992 ('Yorkshire Post' Best First Book Award, Publishing Marketing Assn. Award); recreation: his wife; Office: 55 Avenue Rd., Ste. 2900, Toronto, Ont. M5R 3L2.

**MacLEAN, Steven (Steve) Glenwood,** B.Sc., Ph.D.; Canadian astronaut; b. Ottawa, Ont. 14 Dec. 1954; e. York Univ. B.Sc. (Hons.) 1977, Ph.D. 1983; m. Nadie Wielgopolski; children: Jean-Philippe, Catherine, Michèle; CANADIAN ASTRONAUT; Sports Admin. & Public Relns. (incl. Olympic Liaison Officer), York Univ. 1974–76; Candn. Nat. Gymnastics Team 1976–77; Part-time Teacher, York Univ. 1980–83; Visiting Scholar, Stanford Univ. under Nobel Laureate A.L. Shawlow 1983; laser-physicist: research has included work on electro-optics, laser-induced fluorescence of particles & crystals & multiphoton laser spectroscopy; selected for Canadian Astronaut Program 1983; began astronaut training 1985; designated Canadian Payload Specialist, CANEX-2 set of Candn. experiments in Space 1985; his mission, STS-52 took place 22 Oct.–1 Nov. 1992; Astronaut Adviser, Strategic Technol. in Automation & Robotics Prog.; Program Mgr., Orbital Space Vision Systems and Advanced Vision Unit; Adjunct Prof., Univ. of Toronto Inst. for Aerospace Studies; Pres. Award, York Univ. (Murray G. Ross Award) 1977; NSERC postgrad. scholarship 1980, postdoctoral fellowship 1983; 2 Ont. grad. scholarships 1981, '82; Doctorate (honoris causa), Coll. militaire royal de Saint-Jean 1993; D.D.S. (honoris causa), York Univ.; Hon. Fellow, Norman Bethune Coll., York Univ. 1988– ; Pres., Bd. of Dir., Mont Megantic Observatory Project; rereations: hiking (March 1983, base of Mt. Everest), canoeing, gymnastics, flying, parachuting; Office: 6767, Route de l'aéroport, Saint-Hubert, Que. J3Y 8Y9.

**MACLEAR, Michael Patrick;** author/broadcaster/television producer; b. London, Eng. 19 Dec. 1929; s. Hugh and Carlyn M.; e. Westminster Cathedral Coll.; m. Yoko d. Fumiko and Shinzaburo Koide 10 Apr. 1963; one d. Kyo Iona; joined CBC 1955; was an originator of Candn. TV journalism; Writer & Extve.-Prod., 13–hr TV series 'Vietnam: The 10,000 Day War' (Nat. Edn. Ass. of Am. Best Documentary World Wide), 5–hr series 'American Caesar,' 6–hr series 'The American Century,' 4–hr series 'The Canadians'; Extve.-Prod., 6–hr. series 'Home Game'; Producer feature film, 'Beautiful Dreamers'; Writer-Extve. Prod. 'The Greenpeace Years' 2 hrs.; 'The Desert Wars' 3 x 60; Writer-Host, 60–episode series 'Maclear' (CTV 1974–8) (ACTRA best broadcaster); Fgn. Corresp. (reporting from 80 countries, incl. 1st N.A. TV reports from wartime N. Vietnam), CBC 1959–71; CTV 1971–74; Prod., Can. 1st live TV documentary series 'Newsmagazine' 1957– ; emigrated to Can. 1954; Candn. citizen 1959; Pres., Gallery Maclear, Specialists in Woodcuts; Cineworld Inc.; Informational TV Prod. Ltd.; Starplay Films, Inc.; author: 'Vietnam: The Ten Thousand Day War' 1981 (Military Book Club & Lit. Guild Selection); recreation: reading; Home: 85 Roxborough St. W., Toronto, Ont. M5R 1T9.

**MacLELLAN, Keith William,** M.A.; consultant; b. Aylmer, Que. 30 Nov. 1920; S. William David and Edith (Olmsted) MacL.; e. Montreal Schools, McGill Univ. 1939–42; New Coll. Oxford Univ. M.A. 1947; m. Marie Antoinette d. late Count Adelin Le Grelle, 12 Sept. 1946; children: Keith, Anne Marie, Janet, Andrew; Indust. Relations Imperial Oil H.O. 1948–52; joined Dept. of External Affairs 1952; posted to Berne, Los Angeles, Rome, London, and Brussels; Commissioner, ICSC Laos, 1965–66; Ambassador to Pakistan and Afghanistan, 1974–77; Ambassador to Yugoslavia and Bulgaria 1977–79; Ambassador to Jordan, 1982–85 and concurrently to Syria 1984–85; Delegate to various internat. meetings and confs. incl. ICAO, FAO, Atomic Energy, Vatican Ecumenical Council, Colombo Plan, World Bank Consortia, etc.; P.C. candidate, Ville La Salle, Que. 1979, St. Henri Westmount 1988; served with Royal Montreal Regt. 1940–43, Parachutist 1st Special Air Service Regt. 1944–45, N.W. European campaign; mem. CIIA; Sigma Chi; Cdn. Comprehensive Auditing Fdn.; Candn. Human Rights Found.; St. Andrew's Society of Montreal; Dir., Clan Maclellan in America; Anglican; Clubs: Ottawa Country; St. James's (Montreal); Address: 331 Island Park Dr., Ottawa, Ont., K1Y 0A6 and 630 Carleton Ave., Westmount, Que. H3Y 2Y2.

**MacLELLAN, Robert Simpson,** Q.C., B.A., LL.B.; b. Sydney, N.S. 2 July 1925; s. Robert Simpson and Sarah (Ferguson) MacL.; e. St. Francis Xavier Univ., B.A. 1945; Dalhousie Univ., LL.B. 1948; m. Mary Margaret, d. Frank H. MacDonald, Sydney, N.S., 15 Aug. 1953; children: Robert Francis, Kathryn Michelle, Ian Donald, Gordon Kenneth, Nancy Marie, Peter Gerard, Hugh Douglas; formerly Partner, MacLellan, Burchell, Sullivan & Matheson; read law with Donald M. Nicholson, Q.C.; called to Barof N.S., 1948; cr. Q.C. (Fed.) Dec. 1968; called to Bar of Ont. 1969; Del. to Atlantic Cong., NATO, London, Eng., 1959; Chrmn., Special Comte. of H. of C. Revision of Civil Service Superannuation Act, 1960, Revision of Civil Service Act, 1961; Del., NATO Parlty. Conf., Paris, 1960; Vice Chrmn., Candn. Del. to NATO Parlty. Conf., Paris, 1961; Chrmn., Candn. NATO Parlty. Assn., 1962; def. cand. to H. of C. for Inverness-Richmond, g.e. 1957; el. 1958; def. 1962; Chrmn., Restrictive Trade Practices Comn., 1963 till resigned June 1970; assoc. in law practice with Burke-Robertson, Urie, Weller & Chadwick; appt. mem., Restrictive Trade Practices Xomm., 1974; K. of C.; R. Catholic; recreations: sailing, skiing, fishing; Club: Gatineau Fish and Game; Home: 2060 Cabot St., Ottawa, Ont. K1H 6J9.

**MacLENNAN, David H.,** B.S.A., M.S., Ph.D., F.R.S.C.; scientist; educator; b. Swan River, Man. 3 July 1937; s. Douglas Henry and Sigridur (Sigurdson) MacL.; e. Swan River (Man.) Coll. Inst. 1955 (Gov. Gen.'s Medal 1954); Univ. of Man., B.S.A. 1959 (Lt. Gov.'s Gold Medal); Purdue Univ. M.S. 1961, Ph.D. 1963; m. Linda Carol, d. Laurence C. Vass, Sydney, Australia, 18 Aug. 1965; two s.: Jeremy Douglas, Jonathan David; UNIV. PROF. BANTING AND BEST DEPT. OF MED. RESEARCH, UNIV. OF TORONTO 1993– ; John W. Billes Prof. of Med. Rsch. 1987– ; Acting Chrmn. 1978, Chrmn. 1980–90; Asst. Prof. Univ. of Wis. 1964; Assoc. Prof. Univ. of Toronto 1969, Prof. 1974; Principal Investigator, Candn. Genetic Diseases Network 1991– ; rec'd Ayerst Award of Candn. Biochem. Soc. 1974; Isaac Walton Killam Mem. Scholar 1977–78; Fellow, Royal Soc. of Canada 1985; Internat. Lectr. Award of Biophys. Soc. 1990; Gairdner Foundation Internat. Award 1991; Fellow, Royal Soc. (London) 1994; author or co-author over 200 scient. research papers in the area of muscle membrane biochemistry; Assoc. Ed. 'Canadian Journal of Biochemistry' 1972–76; mem. Ed. Bd. 'Journal of Biological Chemistry' 1975–80, 1982–87; mem., Medical Adv. Bd., Muscular Dystrophy Assn. Can. 1976–87; MRC Scientist Review Panel 1988–90; mem. Univ. of Ottawa Heart Institute Rsch. Review Panel 1991– ; Consultant, Merck, Sharp and Dohme, West Point, PA 1992– ; Am. Soc. Biol. Chems.; Candn. Biochem. Soc.; Biophys. Soc.; Home: 293 Lytton Blvd., Toronto, Ont. M5N 1R7; Office: 112 College St., Toronto, Ont. M5G 1L6.

**MACLENNAN, William Edmund,** B.Sc.A.; dairy executive, retired; b. New Glasgow, N.S. 3 Apr. 1929; s. Murray and Muriel (Mosher) M.; e. Ont. Agric. Coll., B.Sc.A. 1951; m. Georgie d. George and Jean MacDonald 22 Nov. 1952; children: Donna, Susan; Foreman, Brookfield Dairy 1951–52; Plant Supt., Farmers Ltd. 1952–62; Asst. Mgr., Milk Div., Twin Cities Co-op. Dairy Ltd. 1962–67; Mgr., Producers Milk Products Ltd. 1967–68; Asst. to pres., Twin Cities Co-op. Dairy Ltd. 1968–71; Vice-Pres., Admin. 1971–79; Opns. 1979–80; Extve. Vice-Pres. 1980–81; Pres. & Gen. Mgr., Farmers Co-op. Dairy Ltd. (formerly Twin Cities Co-op.) 1981–88; Extve. Consultant, Farmers Co-operative Dairy Ltd. 1988–89; Chief Extve. Offr., Atlantic Inst. of Biotechnology 1989–93; Dir., Dover Mills Ltd.; Dir., NuPro Ltd.; Chair, Voluntary Planning Econ. Dev. Core Ctte.; Mem., Candn. Steering Group on Prosperity 1992; Mem., Victoria General Hosp. Bd. of Commissioners; Mem., Nova Scotia Counc. of Applied Sci. & Technology; Chair, Scottish Soc. Assoc. of N.S.; Past Chrmn., Victoria Gen. Hosp. Found.; Past Chrmn., Adv. Bd., Candn. Inst. of Fish. Technol.; Past Pres., Atlantic Dairy Counc.; North Brit. Soc. of Halifax; Former Dir., Nat. Dairy Council of Can.; N.S. Rsch. Found. Corp.; Candn. Co-operative Assn.; Past Commissioner, Victoria General Hosp.; Elder, St. Matthews Un. Ch.; recreations: sailing, gardening; Clubs: Rotary (Halifax); Halifax Extves. Assoc.; Home: 41 Litchfield Cr., Halifax, N.S. B3P 2N4.

**MacLEOD, Alistair,** B.Ed., M.A., Ph.D.; educator; writer; b. North Battleford, Sask. 20 July 1936; s. Alexander Duncan and Christene (MacLellan) MacL.; e. N.S. Teachers Coll. 1956; St. Francis Xavier Univ., B.A., B.Ed. 1960; Univ. of N.B., M.A. 1961; Notre Dame Univ. South Bend, Ph.D. 1968; m. Anita d. Lewis and Marion MacLellan 4 Sept. 1971; children: Alexander, Lewis, Kenneth, Marion, Daniel, Andrew; PROFESSOR, DEPT. OF ENGLISH, UNIV. OF WINDSOR 1969– ; Lectr. N.S. Teachers Coll. 1961–63; Notre Dame Univ. 1964–66; Univ. of Ind. Fort Wayne 1966–69; Banff Sch. of Fine Arts 1981–86; author (short stories) 'The Lost Salt Gift of Blood' 1976; 'As Birds Bring Forth the Sun' 1986; anthologized 'Best American Short Stories' 1969, 1975; 'Best Canadian Short Stories'; 'Best Modern Canadian Short Stories'; mem. Writers Fedn. N.S.; Writers Union Can.; Home: 231 Curry Ave., Windsor, Ont. N9B 2B4; Office: 401 Sunset Ave., Windsor, Ont. N9B 3P4.

**MacLEOD, Donald G.,** M.B.A.; manufacturer; b. Montreal, Que. 17 Sept. 1928; s. Edward Russell and Mary G. (Goulding) M.; e. Cambridge (Ont.) High Sch. 1946; Extension Dept., McMaster Univ. Cert. in Indust. Engn. 1952; Extension Dept., Waterloo Coll., Cert. in Indust. Mang. 1956; Harvard Business Sch., M.B.A. 1958; m. Beth A., d. A. Carman Anderson, 22 March 1951 (dec'd Jan. 1993); children: John A., Janet E., Mary K.; Pres., 429724 Ont. Ltd.; DGM Consulting Services; LeatherCam Technology Inc.; joined Savage Shoes Limited, Industrial Engineering Department 1951; Pres. and Mgr., Savage Shoes Ltd. 1971–88 (Retired); served in Candn. Army Militia, Capt. and Adjt. H.L.I. 1948–58; Past Pres., Waterloo P. Cons. Assn.; Pres., Shoe Mfrs. Assn. Can. 1976–79, Chrmn. 1980–81; Bd. Govs., Stratford Festival Found. 1977–1985; Past Dir. Conference Bd. of Can.; Life mem., Candn. Inst. Mang.; Conservative; recreations: curling, swimming; Clubs: National (Toronto); The London (Ont.); University Waterloo; Address: 7 Rosslinn Rd., Cambridge, Ont. N1S 3K2.

**MACLEOD, Gregory J.,** Ph.D.; university professor, priest; b. Sydney Mines, N.S. 24 Nov. 1935; s. John Thomas and Rose Mary (Turner) M.; e. Louvain, Belgium, Ph.D. 1969; member, Balliol Coll., Oxford; PROF. OF PHILOSOPHY, UNIV. OF CAPE BRETON, SYDNEY 1969– ; Founding Chairperson, New Dawn Enterprises; Ctr. for Community Econ. Devel.; Mem., OECD, Study Mission on Local Econ. Initiatives; Dir. of Study Tours to Spain; Dir., Tompkins Institute; author: 'New Age Business' 1986 as well as newspaper & mag. articles; commentator, Radio Canada (French) & CBC; club: Gaelic Soc.; Home: 37 Esplanade, Sydney, N.S. B1P 1A2; Office: Box 5300, Sydney, N.S. B1P 6L2.

**MacLEOD, John Peter,** B.A., M.D.C.M., FRCP(C), FCCP; physician, teacher; b. Montreal, Que. 14 Dec. 1939; s. John Wendell and Margaret (Wuerpel) M.; e. Univ. of Sask. B.A. 1960; McGill Univ. M.D.C.M. 1964; m. Margaret d. Lloyd and Mildred Slater 16 May 1964; children: Karen Lynne, Kenneth John; CHIEF OF UNIVERSITY RESPIRATORY DIVISION, OTTAWA CIVIC HOSPITAL 1988– ; Respirologist, Queen Mary Veterans Hosp. 1969–77; Ottawa Civic Hosp. (critical care, respiratory cons. and hosp. practice) 1977– ; Chief of Respiratory Div. 1979–92; Assoc. Prof., Med., Univ. of Otawa 1981– ; Acting Chief, Med., Ottawa Civic Hosp. 1988–89; FRCP(C) 1969; FACP 1971; Pres., Candn. Lung Assn. 1993–94; Mem., Candn. Thoracic Soc. (Pres. 1989–90); Ont. Thoracic Soc. (Pres. (1987–88); Am. Thoracic Soc.; Home: 2365 Whitehaven Cres., Ottawa, Ont. K2B 5H2; Office: 1053 Carling Ave., Ottawa, Ont. K1Y 4E9.

**MacLEOD, M. Joan,** B.A., M.F.A.; writer; b. Vancouver, B.C. 19 Jan. 1954; d. Frederick Campbell and Muriel Joan M.; e. Univ. of Victoria B.A. 1978; Univ. of Brit. Columbia M.F.A. 1981; Mem., Playwrights Union, P.E.N., ACTRA, CAEA; author: plays: 'The Hope Slide' 1992 (Chalmers Award), 'Amigo's Blue Guitar' 1990 (Governor General's Award), 'Toronto, Missippi' 1987 (15 prof. productions to date), 'Jewel' (Honourable Mention Prix Italia) 1987; libretto: 'The Secret Garden' 1985 (Dora Award); books: 'Toronto, Mississippi & Jewel' 1989, 'Amigo's Blue Guitar' 1991.

**MacLEOD, Malcolm Kenneth,** B.A., M.A., Ph.D.; historian, university professor, administrator; b. Lunenburg, N.S. 10 Oct. 1936; s. Ian Roderick and Sadie Bethune (Cameron) M.; e. Armdale H.S. 1954; Dalhousie Univ. B.A. 1958; Univ. of Toronto M.A. 1961; Univ. of Ottawa Ph.D. 1974; 1st m. Joan Misener 1961; divorced 1975; 2nd m. Heather d. Gerald and Enid Elliott 17 Aug. 1980; one stepson: Sean Williamson; PROFESSOR, HISTORY, MEMORIAL UNIV. OF NEWFOUNDLAND 1968–70, 1978– ; Teacher, Halifax Grammar School 1958; King's College School; Vaughan Rd. C.I.; Navigation School, Candn. Forces bases Stadacona & Cornwallis; summer sch., Univ. of Ottawa, Univ. de Moncton, St. Mary's Univ., N.S. Teachers College 1973–78; M.U.N.; Dep. Dir. Office of Research 1979–93; Former Mem., Un. Ch. of Can. (student min. & cand. for ordination); now believes in values of secular humanism; CCF-NDP; Pres., Campus Co-op. Residence, Inc. 1961; Colchester YMCA 1977–78; Nfld. Hist. Soc. (Pres. 1992– ); author: 'Nearer than Neighbours' 1982, 'Peace of the Continent' 1986, 'A Bridge Built Halfway' 1990, 'Kindred Countries' 1994; recreations: jogging, rough carpentry, birds; Home: 8 Hibbs Pl., Portugal Cove, Nfld. A0A 3K0; Office: Elizabeth Ave., St. John's Nfld. A1B 3X5.

**MACLEOD, R. Bruce G.,** B.Com., C.A.; business executive; b. Oshawa, Ont. 9 June 1952; s. John Murray and Mary Glendinning M.; e. Jarvis Coll. Inst. Toronto 1970; Univ. of Toronto B.Com. 1974; C.A. 1975; m. Willmot d. Blakeney and Georgina Woods 11 June 1976; four s. Christopher, Blakeney, Matthew, Peter; PRES., BEVERAGE AND BAKERY, QUAKER FOOD SERVICE 1993– ; joined Price Waterhouse 1974–78; AMF Canada Ltd. 1978–83, Controller 1978, Info. Services 1979, Warehouse & Distribution 1981, Human Resources 1982, Vice Pres. 1983; Vice Pres. Finance & Sec., The Quaker Oats Co. of Canada 1983, Vice Pres., Finance and Food Serv. Div. 1987–91; Pres. Richardson/Snyder and Ardmore Farms, Div. of the Quaker Oats Co. 1991–93; Past Vice Chrmn. St. Joseph's Hosp.; Gov. Trent Univ., Vice Chrmn. 'For Tomorrow' Campaign; mem. Ont. Inst. C.A.'s; Grocery Products Mfrs. Can.; Financial Extves. Insts.; Bd. of Advisors, Rochester Inst. of Technology's Food Service Faculty; recreations: skiing, tennis, biking, swimming; Club: RCYC; Office: The Quaker Oats Co., 321 North Clark St., Suite 21-4, Chicago, IL 60610-4714.

**MacLEOD, Robert Angus,** M.A., Ph.D., F.R.S.C.; marine bacteriologist and professor; b. Athabasca, Alberta, 13 July 1921; s. Norman John and Eleonora Pauline Bertha (Westerhoff) M.; e. Douglas Road School, Burnaby, B.C. 1927–35; Burnaby South High Sch. 1935–39; Univ. of B.C. B.A. 1943, M.A. 1945; Univ. of Wisc. Ph.D. 1949; m. Patricia Rosemarie, d. Edgar A. Robertson, Calgary, Alta. 1 Sept. 1948; children: Douglas J., Alexander R., Kathleen M., David G., Michael N., Susan J.; PROF. EMERITUS, DEPARTMENT OF MICROBIOLOGY, MACDONALD COLLEGE OF McGILL UNIVERSITY; Instructor, Dept. of Chem., Univ. of B.C., 1945–46; Asst. Prof., Dept., of Biochem., Queen's Univ. 1949–52; Head. Biochem. Sec., Technol. Stn., Fisheries Research Bd. of Can., Vancouver, B.C. 1952–60; Assoc. Prof., Dept. of Microbiology, Macdonald Coll. 1960–64 and subsequently Prof., Chrm. 1968, 1974–79; Prof. Emeritus 1986; Fellow, Royal Soc. of Canada; Harrison Prize 1960; mem., Am. Soc. Biol. Chem.; Am. Soc. Microbiol. (Honorary member 1992); Candn. Soc. Microbiol. (Pres. 1976–77, Hon. Mem. 1993), C.S.M. award for research 1973; Que. Soc. of Microbiol.; author or co-author of over 100 scient. papers; recreations: camping, fishing; Home: 448 Greenwood Dr., Beaconsfield, Que. H9W 4Z9.

**MacLEOD, William Brian,** B.Sc., D.H.A.; hospital president; b. Victoria, B.C. 12 June 1951; s. Jacob Eugene and Winnifred Joan (Beecher) M.; e. Univ. of Victoria B.Sc. 1973; Univ. of Toronto D.H.A. 1979; m. Lucy d. Joe and Doreen Scarbo; children: Magenta

Trishan, Collin Wilson, Andrew James; PRESIDENT, WOMEN'S COLLEGE HOSPITAL 1990– ; Comptroller, Kootenay Lake Dist. Hosp. 1973–76, 1979–80; Asst. Extve. Dir., St. Joseph's Hosp. 1980–85; Pres., Peel Memorial Hosp. 1985–90; Asst. Prof., Univ. of Toronto, Health Admin. Program; Robert Wood Johnson Award 1978; Mem., Candn. College of Health Service Extves.; clubs: YMCA (Toronto); Home: 740 Hurondale Dr., Mississauga, Ont.; Office: 76 Grenville St., Toronto, Ont. M5S 1B2.

**MacMARTIN, Donald C.,** B.S.S.; executive; b. Montreal, Que. 25 Oct. 1942; s. Arthur Edward and May Marie Dora (Legault) MacM.; e. St. Joseph Elem. Sch. 1955; Central Cath. H.S. Dip. 1959; St. Leo Coll., Assoc. Arts 1961; Loyola Univ. B.S.S. 1964; m. Laura d. Louis and Tina Michielini 28 Oct. 1967; children: Andrew, Tamra, David; Pres. & C.O.O. Canstar Sports Inc. 1992; Export Area Mgr. Robin Hood Multifoods Ltd. 1964–68, Product Mgr. Ind. Mixes 1968–71, Product Mgr. New Products 1972, Product Mgr. Frozen Foods 1972–74, Group Product Mgr. Frozen Foods 1974–75, Field Mktg. Mgr. 1975–76; Regional Sales Mgr. R.J.R. Foods Ltd. 1976–77, Dir. of Sales 1977–78, Vice-Pres. Sales 1979–80; Dir. of Sales and Mktg. Candn. Canners Ltd. 1980–83, Vice-Pres. Sales and Mktg. 1983–84; Extve. Vice-Pres. Corby Distilleries Ltd. 1984–89; Dir. 1988–92; Pres. & C.O.O. 1989–90; Pres. & C.E.O. 1990–92; Dir. Candn. Frozen Foods Assn.; Candn. Grocery Distributors Inst.; mem. Assn. Candn. Distillers; Address: 417 Roslyn Ave., Westmount, Que. H3Y 2T6.

**MacMILLAN, Ann Elizabeth,** B.A.; journalist; b. Tremadoc, North Wales 22 July 1946; d. Robert Laidlaw and Eluned Jane (Carey Evans) M.; e. Whitney P.S.; North Toronto Collegiate; Victoria College, Univ. of Toronto B.A. 1968; m. Peter s. John and Peggy Snow 15 May 1976; children: Daniel, Rebecca, Katherine; EUROPEAN CORRESPONDENT, CANADIAN BROADCASTING CORP. 1981– ; FM Program Supervisor, CHIN Radio 1970–72; Co-Host, 'New Directions,' CBLT Toronto 1972–73; TV Facilities Supvr., Commonwealth Heads of Govt. Meeting, Ottawa 1973; News Correspondent, Global TV News 1974; Toronto Correspondent, CTV Nat. News 1975; Montreal Bureau Chief, CTV News 1976; CTV News London Correspondent 1977–81; recreations: sailing, skiing, hiking; Home: 18 Ranelagh Ave., London SW13, U.K.; Office: 45 Great Titchfield St., London W1, U.K.

**MacMILLAN, Rev. Donald Neil,** M.A., B.D., Ph.D.; educator; b. Finch, Ont. 19 Dec. 1909; s. Neil and Sarah MacM.; e. McGill Univ. B.A., M.A.; Presb. Coll. Montreal B.D.; Edinburgh Univ. Ph.D.; Hon. D.D., Presb. Coll., Montreal 1979; m. Jean d. A. K. Maclean 14 Oct. 1936; two s. Donald K., Robert N.; Minister, Kenyon Church, Dunvegan 1935–59; Prof. of Theol., Presbyterian Coll. 1959–78 and Acting Princ. there 1973–78; served with RCAF as Chaplain, in Can. and overseas 1940–45; author 'Historical Sketch of Kenyon Church' 1940, 2nd ed. 1993; 'The Kirk in Glengarry' 1984; Pres., Glengarry Hist. Soc. 1988–90; Home: R.R. #2, Finch, Ont. K0C 1K0.

**MacMILLAN, Hugh P.,** D.Litt., U.E.; antiquarian, writer; b. Fitzroy Harbour, Ont. 12 Mar. 1924; s. Rev. John A. and Dulcie C. (Pearson) M.; e. Carleton Univ. Bus. Admin. 1946–47; Newspaper Inst. of Am. Journalism 1948; Ryerson Polytech. Inst. Pub. Relns. and Creative Writing 1963–64; D.Litt. (h.c.) Laurentian Univ. 1984; m. Muriel R. d. Gordon and Alice Diver 4 Oct. 1951; children: Malcolm, Ian, Neale, Jocelyn; Liaison Officer, Archives of Ont. 1964–89; a pioneer in the acquisition of manuscripts and pictorial material obtained by means of investigative genealogical research, field trips, lectures and publicity campaigns and now a collector/dealer in antiquities; Sgt. Candn. Army, S.D. and Glengarry Highlanders 1944–46; Mate on coastal ships and freelance writer for Vancouver newspapers 1947–52; Ins. Agt., farmer, logging contractor and writer 1952–64; founding mem., Glengarry Historical Soc.; The Dunvegan Museum; The NorWester-Loyalist Museum, in Williamstown; author, magazine articles for Beaver, Candn. Collector; book: 'The Manuscript Sleuth' forthcoming; mem. Ont. Hist. Soc.; Assn. Ont. Archivists; Genealogical Soc. of Ont.; Candn. Assn. Scottish Studies; United Empire Loyalist; The Manuscript Soc.; mem. Advisory Council, North American Fur Trade Conference; mem. Presbyterian Church History Ctte. Canada; recreations: canoeing, travel, reading, family history research; Club: Arts & Letters; Address: 21 Suffolk St. W., Guelph, Ont. N1H 2H9.

**MACMILLAN, Kathleen Ellen,** M.A.; economist; b. Karachi, Pakistan 1 Aug. 1956; d. William David and Helen Madeline (Lamon) Mills; e. Queen's Univ. B.A. 1978; Univ. of Alta. M.A. 1980; m. Graham C. s. Jack and Elizabeth Macmillan 23 Aug. 1980; two s. Thomas Jack, James William; VICE CHRMN. CANDN. INTERNAT. TRADE TRIBUNAL 1990– ; econ. specializing in rsch., writing & speaking on trade, regional & agric. policy; Econ. Council Can. 1978–79; Alta. Dept. Econ. Devel. 1980–82; Can. West Found. 1983–86; C.D. Howe Inst. 1987–89; apptd. mem. present Tribunal 1989; author 'Summary of Western Perspectives on the Crow' 1983; 'The Canadian Common Market: Interprovincial Trade and International Competitiveness' 1985; 'Women and Free Trade' 1988; co-author 'Focus on Follow-Through' 1988; 'The Next Agenda' 1989; ed. 'US-Canadian Agricultural Trade Challenges: Developing Common Approaches' 1988; Home: 313 Second Ave., Ottawa, Ont. K1S 2J1; Office: 365 Laurier Ave. W., Ottawa, Ont. K1A 0G7.

**MACMILLAN, Michael Iain MacKay,** B.A.; film and television producer; b. Scarborough, Ont. 31 Aug. 1956; s. John Hay Iain and Mary Margaret (MacKay) MacM.; e. Upper Can. Coll. Toronto 1974; Queen's Univ. B.A. 1978; m. A. Catherina d. Han and Mary Spoel 10 Oct. 1981; children: Claire Emma, Alison Mary; CHRMN. AND CHIEF EXECUTIVE OFFR., ATLANTIS COMMUNICATIONS INC. 1978– ; produced 600 films and TV progs. since 1978, won over 75 Candn. and internat. awards incl. an Oscar (Acad. Award) Best Short Film 'Boys and Girls' 1984 and an Emmy Award (Daytime) 'Lost In The Barrens' 1991; Dir. Candn. Film & TV Assn. 1983–89, Vice Pres. 1985–87; mem. St. Andrew's Soc. Toronto; recreations: squash, cooking; Office: 65 Heward Ave., Toronto, Ont. M4M 2T5.

**MacMILLAN, Thomas C.,** M.A.; trust company extve.; b. Toronto, Ont. 21 June 1948; s. Dr. Robert Laidlaw and Eluned Jane (Carey Evans) MacM.; e. Univ. of Toronto Schs. 1967; Princeton Univ. B.A. 1971; London Sch. of Econ. & Pol. Sci. M.A. 1973; m. Catharina d. Carl and Margaretta Leissner 26 Dec. 1974; children: Alexander, Megan; EXTVE. VICE-PRES., CORPORATE SERVICES DIVISION, MONTREAL TRUST 1992– ; joined Bank of Montreal 1973–84, various positions 1973–76, Adm. Offr. San Francisco Agency 1976, Rep. Houston Office 1977, Mgr. Denver Office 1982, Vice Pres. Corporate & Govt. Banking Toronto 1985; joined Chase Manhattan Bank of Canada 1986, Vice Pres. & Mgr.-Corp & Institutional Banking 1986–1987; Pres. & C.E.O., The Chase Manhattan Bank of Canada 1988–92; recreations: tennis, skiing, hockey; Clubs: Badminton & Racquet; Princeton Club of New York; Home: 29 Blythdale Rd., Toronto, Ont. M4N 3M3; Office: 3F, 15 King St. W., Toronto, Ont. M5H 1B4.

**MacMURRAY, James A.;** LL.D.; company president; b. Saint John, N.B. 1925; s. James and Ann Ogilvie (Peebles) M.; e. Pub. Schs. and Saint John High Sch.; Mount Allison Univ.; LL.D. Univ. of New Brunswick 1985; m. Jean F., d. Frank T. Palfrey, Vancouver, B.C., 19 May 1951; children: Ann F., Barbara J.; CHRMN., FUNDY CABLE LTD.; United Church; recreations: golf, Clubs: Union; Riverside Country; Home: 468 Pelton Rd., R.R. 1, Saint John, N.B. E2L 3W2; Office: Box 6399, Stn. A, Saint John, N.B. E2L 4R8.

**MacMURRAY, Stuart Brock,** M.D., F.R.C.P.(C); neonatal physician; b. Toronto, Ont. 7 May 1942; e. William Brock and Margaret Elizabeth (Christilaw) M.; e. Upper Can. Coll. 1960; Univ. of Toronto, M.D. 1966; F.R.C.P. (Paediatrics) 1971; m. Susan d. Colin and Mabel McRae 4 June 1965; children: Brenda, Bill; DIR., NEONATAL INTENSIVE CARE UNIT, CHILDREN'S HOSP. OF E. ONT. & ASSOC. PROF., DEPT. OF PAED., UNIV. OF OTTAWA 1976– ; Neonatal Physician, Hosp. for Sick Children & Asst. Prof., Dept. of Paed., Univ. of Toronto 1973–76; Cons. Perinatol., Ottawa Civic & Ottawa Gen. Hosps.; Med. Rsch. Counc. of Can. fellowship (Nuffield Inst. for Med. Rsch.) 1972–73; Mem., Candn. Paed. Soc.; Ont. Med. Assn.; recreations: squash, tennis; Club: Ottawa Athletic; Home: 1944 Camborne Cres., Ottawa, Ont.; Office: 401 Smyth Rd., Box 8010, Ottawa, Ont. K1H 8L1.

**MacNABB, Gordon Murray,** B.Sc., F.C.A.E.; b. Almonte, Ont. 13 July 1931; s. the late Keith Charles and the late Grace Marshall (Stevenson) MacN.; e. Carleton Place (Ont.) Pub. and High Schs.; Carleton Univ., Engn. Dipl. 1952; Queen's Univ. B.Sc. (Civil Engn.) 1954; D.Sc. (Hon.) Memorial Univ. 1979; Windsor 1980; LL.D. (Hon.) Concordia Univ. 1981; D.Sc. Univ. of Ottawa 1982; LL.D. Queens University 1982; LL.D. Dalhousie Univ. 1984; LL.D. McMaster Univ. 1985; D.Eng. Univ. of Toronto 1985; D.Sc. Univ. of Manitoba 1985; D.Eng. Carleton Univ. 1986; D.Sc. McGill Univ. 1986; m. Lorna Amelia, d. W. P. Clayton, Osbornville, N.J., 24 Apl. 1954; children: Charles Kevin, Stewart Clayton, Steven Andrew, James Duncan, Linda Gail, Barbara Heather; PRESIDENT, G.M. MACNABB & ASSOC. INC.; Hon. Vice Chrmn., World Energy Conf.; Hydraulic Engr., Columbia River Hydro-Elect. Investigations, 1954–57; Tech. Asst. to Columbia River Treaty Negotiators, 1958–62; Sr. Engn. Adviser to Candn. Treaty Negotiators, 1962–64; Asst. Depy. Minister (Energy Devel.), Dept. of Energy, Mines and Resources; 1967; Sr. Asst. Depy. Min. 1973; Depy. Min. 1975–78; Pres., Natural Sciences and Engn. Research Council 1978–86; Pres., Uranium Can. Ltd. 1975–85; Fellow & Pres., Candn. Acad. of Engrs.; mem., Assn. Prof. Engrs. Ont.; United Church; recreations: sports, gardening; Home: RR2 North Gower, Ont. K0A 2T0; Office: 30 Colonnade Rd., Suite 300, Nepean, Ont. K2E 7J6.

**MacNABB, Ian Carter,** B.Sc., P.Eng.; association executive; b. Carleton Place, Ont. 1929; e. Carleton Univ.; Queen's Univ., B.Sc. (Civil) 1952; Univ. of Toronto, Cert. in Pub. Adm. 1968; m. Susan Chapman; children: Nancy, Bruce, Elizabeth; PRES., CHIEF ADM. OFFR. AND DIR. CANDN. GAS ASSN. 1985– ; Dir., Gas Technology Canada 1992– ; Canadian Western Natural Gas Ltd. Calgary 1953–64; Ont. Energy Bd. Eng. 1964–66, Vice Chrmn. 1967–85; Pres., Candn. Gas Rsch. Inst. 1985–91; mem. Assn. Prof. Engs. Prov. Ont.; Perm. Candn. Del. to Internat. Gas Union Council; Clubs: Bd. Trade Metrop. Toronto; Bayview Country; Home: 36 Adencliff Rd., Scarborough, Ont. M1W 1N2; Office: 55 Scarsdale Rd., Don Mills, Ont. M3B 2R3.

**MacNAUGHTON, Hon. Alan,** P.C., Q.C., LL.D.; senator; b. Napanee, Ont. 30 July 1903; s. Donald Carmichael and Mabel Louise (Aylesworth) M.; e. Upper Can. Coll.; McGill Univ.; Univ. of London Grad Sch. of Econ. and Pol. Science (P.Q., I.O.D.E. Overseas Scholar.), B.A., B.C.L.; m. Mary Caroline, d. Fred Rollin White, 1 Aug. 1942; children: Elizabeth White, Alan Aylesworth, Jr., Laurence Robert Norton; Counsel, Martineau, Walker; Dir., Bendix Avelex Inc.; Saelectric Transmission Inc.; Federation Ins. Co. of Canada; read law with Brown, Montgomery & McMichael, Montreal, P.Q.; called to the Bar of Que. 1930; Crown Prosecutor, 1939–44; cr. K.C. 1944; Gov., Montreal General Hosp.; mem., H. of C. for Montreal-Mt. Royal, 1949–66; Speaker, H. of C. 1963–66 (Chrmn. Pub. Accts. Comte. First Opposition 1958–63 and Chrmn. Special Comte. on Procedure of Organ. 1963–65); Depy. Chrmn., Senate Banking Ctte. 1967–79; Candn. Alternate Del. to 8th Session of U.N., New York, Sept. 1953; summoned to Senate of Can., 8 July 1966; Depy. Chrmn. Candn. Del. to U.N. Conf. on Environment, Stockholm 1973; Past Pres., Jr. Board of Trade, Montreal; Past Vice-Pres., Nat. Candn. Jr. Chamber of Comm.; Hon. Life mem., Assemblée Nat. de la France; Founder and Hon. Chrmn., World Wildlife Fund (Can.), recipient of Internat. W.W.F. Mem. of Honour Award 1990; Hon. LL.D. (h.c.) McGill Univ. 1992; mem. 1001 'Nature Trust'; 200 Canadians for Worldlife – Conservation Trust; Past Chrmn., Roosevelt Campobello Internat. Park Comn.; Liberal; Anglican; Clubs: University; Montreal; Canadian (N.Y.); Royal Montreal Golf, Mount Royal, M.A.A.A. (Montreal); (London, Eng.); East India (London); Toronto (Toronto); Mill Reef (Antigua, W.I.); Home: 7 Redpath Row, Montreal, Que. H3G 1E6.

**MacNAUGHTON, Angus Athole;** financial company executive; b. Montreal, Que. 15 July 1931; s. Athole Austin and Emily Kidder (MacLean) MacN.; e. Lakefield Coll. Sch., 1941–47; McGill Univ. 1949–54; Que. Inst. C.A.'s; children: Gillian Heather, Angus Andrew; PRESIDENT, GENSTAR INVESTMENT CORPORATION 1987– ; Auditor, Coopers & Lybrand 1949–55; Acct., Genstar Ltd., Montreal 1955; Asst. Treas., Genstar Ltd. 1956–61, Treas. 1961–64, Vice Pres. 1964–70, Extve. Vice Pres. 1970–73, Pres. 1973–76, Vice Chrmn. & C.E.O. 1976–81, Chrmn. or Pres. & C.E.O. 1981–86; Dir., Canadian Pacific Limited; Stelco Inc.; Sun Life Assurance Co. of Can. Ltd.; American Barrick Resources Corp.; Varian Associates Inc.; Past Pres., Montreal chapter, Tax Executive Inst.; Bd. of Govs., Lakefield Coll. Sch.; Past Chrmn., San Francisco Bay Area Council, Boy Scouts of Am.; Clubs: Pacific Union; Villa Taverna; World Trade (San Francisco); Mount Royal (Montreal); Toronto (Toronto); Office: 950 Tower Lane, Suite 1170, Foster City, CA 94904–2121.

**MacNAUGHTON, John A.,** B.A.; investment dealer; b. Exeter, Ont. 6 March 1945; s. Charles S. and Adeline M. (Fulcher) MacN.; e. Univ. of W. Ont. B.A. 1967; m. Gail d. Keith and Agnes McKinnon 4 May 1973; children: Matthew, Adeline; PRES., C.E.O., AND DIR. BURNS FRY LTD. 1989– ; Pres. & C.E.O., Burns Fry Shareholders Holdings; Pres. Burns Fry Holdings Corp.;

joined Fry & Co. 1968; subsequent to merger with Mills Spence 1970 trans. to New York as Resident Mgr. Fry Mills Spence Inc.; after merger with Burns Brothers and Denton 1976 served Corporate Services Dept. Burns Fry specializing in Mergers & Acquisitions 1979; el. Dir. 1982, Mng. Dir. Mergers & Acquisitions 1986; subsequent to assn. Burns Fry and Security Pacific Corp. 1988 became Pres. and Chief Extve. Offr. Security Pacific Burns Fry and of Security Pacific Global Mergers and Acquisitions; Vice-Pres. & Dir., The Canadian Stage Company 1991– ; Vice Chrmn., Princess Margaret Hospital Council 1991– ; Past Pres. Spadina P. Cons. Assn.; Past Nat. Secy., Progressive Conservative Assn. of Can. 1974–77; recreations: skiing, tennis; Clubs: Alpine Ski; Albany (Dir. 1980–82, 1992– ); Bd. of Trade Metro. Toronto; Empire (Pres. 1979–80; Chrmn. Found. 1989–91); Toronto Club; Toronto Lawn Tennis; Home: 45 Garfield Ave., Toronto, Ont. M4T 1E8; Office: 5000, 1 First Canadian Place, Toronto, Ont. M5X 1H3.

**MacNAUGHTON, John D.,** P.Eng.; aeronautical industry executive; b. Moose Jaw, Sask. 10 April 1932; s. Francis Maurice and Grace Elizabeth Ellen (Moore) M.; e. deHavilland Aeronautical Tech. School & Hatfield Coll. (U.K.) aeronautical engr. degree 1954; m. Joy d. Gladys and William Spencer; children: Paul, Neil, Jane; PRESIDENT & CEO, SPAR AEROSPACE LIMITED 1989– ; Engineering Supvr., Guided Missile Div., deHavilland 1954; joined Garrett Mfg. Ltd. 1958; Chief Engr. 1961; Chief Mech. Engr., Special Products & Applied Rsch. (SPAR) Div., deHavilland 1962; SPAR became Spar Aerospace in 1968; major role in Canada's satellite projects incl. Alouette, Anik and Hermes; instrumental in creating Space Shuttle Remote Manipulator System project; estab. & managed Spar's Remote Manipulator Systems Div.; Vice-Pres., Spar Aerospace 1969–89; Bd. Chair & C.E.O., Commerical Telecomm. Corp. & Astro Aerospace Corp.; Boards incl.: Spar Aerospace Ltd. and its subsidiaries; Telesat Canada, Alouette Telecommunications and the National Quality Institute; Former Dir., Candn. Advanced Tech. Assn.; and former Mem. Extve. Ctte. and past Vice Chrmn., Aerospace Industries Assn. of Canada; Past Pres. & Winner, Casey Baldwin Award; McCurdy Award for Outstanding Achievements in the Arts, Sci. & Engr. relating to Aero. & Space; Profl. Engrs. of Ont. Engr. Medal 1965; Nat. Aero. & Space Admin. (NASA) Pub. Serv. Medal for Outstanding Performance 1982; RCAF Assn.'s McGregor Award 1983; Thomas W. Eadie Medal, Royal Soc. of Can. 1984; Invested with the Canada 125th Anniversary Commemorative Medal 1993; recreations: reading, tennis; clubs: Bd. of Trade, Rideau, Founder's, Mississauga Golf & Country; Office: Suite 900, 5090 Explorer Dr., Mississauga, Ont. L4W 4X6.

**MacNEIL, Most Rev. Joseph Neil,** B.A., J.C.D. (R.C.); archbishop; b. Sydney, N.S. 15 Apl. 1924; s. John Martin and Kate Alice (MacLean) MacN.; e. St. Joseph's Sch. and Sydney (N.S.) Acad.; St. Francis Xavier Univ., B.A. 1944; Holy Heart Semy., Halifax, o. 1948; Univ. of St. Thomas Aquinas, Rome, J.C.D. 1958; Univ. of Perugia, Inst. Catholique (Paris) and Univ. of Chicago, summers 1956, 1957, and 1964; Hon. LLD., St. Francis Xavier Univ. 1978, St. Thomas Univ. 1980, Univ. of Alta. 1982; ARCHBISHOP OF EDMONTON 1973– ; Chrmn., Alta. Bishops' Conf. 1973– ; Bd. Chrmn., Newman Theological Coll., Edmonton 1973– ; Bd. Chrmn., St. Joseph's Coll., Univ. of Alta., Edmonton 1973– ; Mem. Bd. of Mgmt., Edmonton Gen. Hosp. 1983– ; Mem. Bd. of Dir., Centre for Human Development, Toronto 1985– ; Mem. Comn. on Missions, Candn. Conf. of Catholic Bishops 1991– ; Bishop of St. John, N.B. 1969–73; Chancellor, Univ. of St. Thomas 1969–73; mem. of Extve., Candn. Council on Rural Devel. 1965–75; Dir. of Program & Planning Agency, N.S. Govt., 1969; Extve. Comte., Atlantic Provinces Economic Council, 1968–73; Vice Chrm, N.S. Voluntary Econ. Planning Bd. 1965–79; mem. Bd. Dirs., Candn. Assn. for Adult Educ. (Past Pres., N.S. Div.); Past Pres., Candn. Assn. Dirs., Univ. Extension & Summer Schs.; Vice-Pres. for Adult Educ. and Dir., Extension Dept., St. Francis Xavier Univ., 1961–69; honoured by Pope Paul for work in field of social action by being named Domestic Prelate with title of Msgr., 1964; founding mem., Inst. for Research on Public Policy 1968–80; mem., Nat. Comm. for Cdn. Participation in Habitat 1976; Pres., Cdn. Conf. of Catholic Bishops 1979–81; Mem., Bd. of Dir., Futures Secretariat 1981; Mem. Comn. on Ecumenism, Candn. Conf. of Catholic Bishops 1985–91; Address: 8421 - 101st Ave., Edmonton, Alta. T6A 0L1.

**MacNEIL, Robert Breckenridge Ware;** broadcast journalist; b. Montreal, Que. 19 Jan. 1931; s. Robert A.S. and Margaret Virginia (Oxner) M.; e. Dalhousie Univ. 1949–51; B.A. Carleton Univ. 1955; L.H.D. (hon.) William Patterson Coll., 1977, Beaver Coll., 1978, Bates Coll. 1979, Lawrence Univ., 1980; Bucknell Univ., 1982; Trinity Coll., 1983; Univ. of King's Coll., 1983; George Washington Univ., 1983; Univ. of Maine, 1983; Brown Univ. 1984, Colby Coll., Carleton Univ., Univ. of South Carolina, 1985; Franklin & Marshall Coll. 1987; Nazareth Coll. 1988; Washington Coll. 1988; Kenyon Coll. 1990; Univ. of Western Ont. 1992; m. Rosemarie Anne Copland, 1956 (Div. 1964); children: Catherine Anne, Ian B.; m. 2ndly Jane J. Doherty, 1965; (Div. 1983); children: Alison N., William H.; m. 3rdly Donna P. Richards 1984; MACNEIL/LEHRER NEWSHOUR, 1983– ; editor, co-anchor, MacNeil/Lehrer Report, Sta. WNET-TV, N.Y.C., 1975–83; Recipient awards, incl. Univ. of Missouri Medal of Honor, 1980; William Allen White Award, 1982; George Foster Peabody award U. Ga, 1977; Dupont award Columbia Sch. Journalism, 1977; Emmy award, 1974; 2 Emmy Awards 1984; Peabody Award 1987; Emmy Award 1987; Chrmn., The MacDowell Colony; Fellow, American Acad. of Arts & Scis.; mem. AFTRA, Assn. Radio and TV News Analysts; Clubs: Century, N.Y.C.; author: 'The People Machine: The Influence of Television on American Politics,' 1968; 'The Right Place at the Right Time,' 1982; 'Wordstruck' 1989; 'Burden of Desire' 1992; co-author: 'The Story of English' 1986; Ed., 'The Way We Were: 1963: The Year Kennedy Was Shot' 1988; Address: WNET/13 356 W. 58th St., New York, N.Y. 10019.

**MacNEIL, Teresa S.,** M.Sc., Ph.D.; educator; b. Richmond Co., N.S. 7 Jan. 1937; d. Joseph H. and Elizabeth F. (MacAdam) MacN.; e. St. Francis Xavier Univ., B.Sc. 1957; Univ. of Wis., M.Sc. 1964, Ph.D. 1970; m. Luke s. Harold and Elsie Batdorf 1973; DIR. EXTENSION DEPT. ST. FRANCIS XAVIER UNIV. 1982– , (1989 Rsch. leave: UCLA Visiting Scholar and review of Regional Development Policy in Europe; mem. Bd. Govs.; Chrmn. Cape Breton Development Corp. 1986–88 (Part-time); Acting Pres., Cape Breton Dev. Corp. 1987–88; Vice-Chrmn. Enterprise Cape Breton 1986–88; Prof. of Adult Edn. present Univ. 1970 (on leave), Chrmn. of Adult Edn. 1970–82; Mem. Bd. of Dirs., Candn. Cooperative Assn. 1992– ; former mem. Bd.: Henson Col.; Dalhousie Bureau of Industry; Dalhousie Univ.; former Dir. Can. World Youth; mem. Candn. Assn. Adult Edn. (Dir. & mem. Extve.; Pres. 1986–90); former Mem. Bd., Atlantic Council of Cooperatives; mem., Employment Initiatives Advisory Council, YMCA Canada; former mem. Extve. Ctte. Candn. Comn. for UNESCO; Atlantic Devel. Council; Past Gov. Atlantic Provs. Econ. Council; Past Gov. Frontier Coll. Can.; former Chrmn. Adv. Ctte. to Min. of DRIE and Premier of N.S. on Cape Breton Econ. 1985; Home: R.R. 1, Afton, Antigonish Co., N.S.; Office: Antigonish, N.S. B2G 1C0.

**MacNEILL, Hugh Gordon,** B.A., D.C.L.; executive; b. Sydney, N.S. 13 July 1925; s. late Hugh Archibald & Jean Campbell (Murray) MacN.; e. Sydney (N.S.) Acad.; Acadia Univ., B.A. (Econ.) 1948; D.C.L. 1987; m. Barbara, d. Capt. R. L. McLellan, 22 July 1950; children: Glenn Gordon, Janice Ellen, Scott Leston, Jesslyn Jean; CHRMN. & DIR., JANNOCK LTD. 1976– ; Chrmn., Interprovincial Pipe Line Inc.; Chrmn. & Dir., Wajax Limited; Dir., Aetna Life Ins. Co. of Canada; Bowater Inc.; Bowater Candn. Ltd.; Empire Company Ltd.; Hayes-Dana Inc.; Home Oil Co. Ltd.; Scott Paper Ltd.; The Toronto-Dominion Bank; Gov. and mem. Extve. Ctte. Acadia Univ.; Presbyterian; recreations: reading, music, collecting Candn. art & antiques; Clubs: Granite; Mississauga Golf; Toronto; Home: 62 Maple Ave., Toronto, Ont. M4W 2T7; Office: Suite 5205, Scotia Plaza, P.O. Box 1012, 40 King St. W., Toronto, Ont. M5H 3Y2.

**MacNEILL, James Joseph;** newspaper editor; b. Glasgow, Scot. 18 Jan. 1936; s. John and Christine (MacKinnon) MacN.; e. Salesian Coll. Eng.; m. Shirley d. Frank and Mary Ellen (Nellie) Nicholson 16 Aug. 1960; children: Sheila, Kevin, Jan, Paul, Gail; ED. AND FOUNDER, EASTERN GRAPHIC, ISLAND PRESS LTD. 1963– ; began newspaper career with The Journal-Pioneer, Summerside, P.E.I. 1960; estbd. The Island Farmer 1974 and The West Prince Graphic, Alberton, P.E.I. 1980, The Atlantic Fisherman 1985, Atlantic Fish Farming 1988; recipient Best News Story Award Candn. Community Newspapers Assn. 1979, 1981; Esso Award Reporter Initiative 1987, 1988; honorable mention, Michener Award 1987; Author, 'Ideas for A Newsier Newspaper' 1991; Pres., International Soc. of Weekly Newspaper Editors (1988–89); mem. Atlantic Community Newspapers Assn. (Pres. 1980–82); Candn. Community Newspaper Assn. (Dir. 1977–80, 1984–87, 1989– , Pres. 1991–92, Chrmn. of the Bd. 1992–93); Home: 117 Chestnut St., Montague, P.E.I. C0A 1R0; Office: P.O. Box 790, 9 Main St., Montague, P.E.I. C0A 1R0.

**MacNEILL, James William,** B.A., B.Sc., LL.D., D.Sc., D.Env.Sts.; international consultant; b. Mazenod, Sask. 22 Apl. 1928; s. William Leslie and Helga Ingaborg (Nohlgren) MacN.; e. Univ. of Sask. B.A. 1949, B.Sc. (Eng.) 1958, LL.D. 1988; Univ. of Stockholm Grad. Cert. in Pol. Sci. & Econ. 1951; McGill Univ. D.Sc. 1992; Univ. of Waterloo D.Env.Sts. 1993; m. Phyllis d. Herschel and Beryl Ferguson 30 Nov. 1953; two d. Catherine Anne, Robin Lynne; PRES., J.W. MacNEILL AND ASSOCIATES 1987– ; Comnr. Gen. UN Conf. on Human Settlements and Ambassador Extraordinary and Plenipotentiary 1975–76; Perm. Sec. (Dep. Min.) Min. of State for Urban Affairs Can. 1973–76; Dir. Environment, Orgn. Econ. Co-op. & Devel. Paris 1978–84; Sec. Gen. World Comn. Environment & Devel. Geneva 1984–87; Dir., Environment and Sustainable Devel. IRPP 1987–91; Dir. Woods Hole (Mass.) Rsch. Inst.; Candn. Inst. for Sustainable Devel. Winnipeg; Senior Advisor to Pres., Int. Dev. Rsch. Centre; recipient City of Paris Medal 1981; Prov. of Sask. Achievement Award 1984; Climate Inst. Award 1991; Swedish WASA Award 1991; author 'Environmental Management' 1971–73; co-author 'Our Common Future' 1987; 'Beyond Interdependence' 1991; mem. Assn. Profl. Engs. Sask.; Assn. Profl. Engs. Prov. Ont.; recreations: golf, skiing, photography; Office: 250 Albert St., Ottawa, Ont. K1P 5E6.

**MacNUTT, Cathy Marjorie Raymond,** B.A.; public servant; b. Digby, N.S. 14 Oct. 1949; d. Keith Orbin and Freda Grace (Condon) Raymond; e. Acadia Univ. B.A. 1970; Dalhousie & St. Mary's Univs., post-grad.; m. Michael s. Donald and Greta M. 24 Sept. 1970; children: Justin, Jessica, Alexandra, Nicholas; ASST. NATIONAL DIR., MNGMNT. SERVICES, CANDN. RED CROSS SOCIETY 1994– ; Econ., N.S. Dept. of Devel. 1971–75; Reg. Advr., Maritime Prov., Stats. Can. 1975–80; Deputy Min., Dept. of Consumer Affairs, Prov. of N.S. 1980–91; Deputy Min., N.S. Status of Women 1988–93; Deputy Min., Dept. of Health, Prov. of N.S. 1991–93; Interim Extve. Dir., N.S. Human Rights Comn. 1984–85; Chair, Bd. of Dirs., Halifax Harbour Clean Up Corp. 1989– ; Dir., King's Heritage Soc.; Trustee, N.S. Public Serv., Long Term Disability Plan Trust Fund; Mem., Atlantic Can. Econ. Assn.; recreations: tennis, aerobics, cooking; Clubs: YWCA, Waegwoltic; Home: Henry St., Halifax, N.S. B3H 3K2; Office: 1800 Alta Vista Dr., Ottawa, Ont. K1G 4J5.

**MacOWAN, William,** M.B.E.; manufacturer; b. Glasgow, Scotland 7 Jan. 1919; s. William and Elizabeth Williamson Niven M.; e. Queens Park High Sch., Glasgow, Scot. (1930–36); m. 1stly Mabel C. Henderson 1945 (dec.); one s. Brian Henderson; m. 2ndly Heather Alyson, d. Geoffrey and Marguerite Atkinson, 1978; VICE CHRMN., CORP. DEV. HOWDEN GROUP CANADA LTD.; joined James Howden and Co. in Glasgow as Apprentice Engr. 1936; Depy. Export Sales Mgr. 1949, Gen. Sales Mgr. 1955; Extve. Vice Pres. and Mang. Dir., James Howden & Co. of Canada Ltd. 1957–66; Pres., Howden Parsons Ltd. 1966–78; Pres., Brown Boveri Howden 1978–80; served in 2nd World War; Sgt., Cameronians, 1939–40; Royal Corps of Signals 1941–46; Major and G.S.O. 11; action Middle East, Italy; M.B.E.; Mentioned in Despatches; Anglican; recreations: gardening, skiing; Clubs: Granite; R.C.M.I.; Home: 64 Balmoral Heights, Queensville, Ont. L0G 1R0; Office: 1510 Birchmount Rd., Scarborough, Ont. M1P 2G6.

**MacPHAIL, Jannetta,** R.N., M.S.N., Ph.D., LL.D.; educ. administrator; b. Renfrew, Ont. 2 Mar. 1923; d. Donald M. and Emma Margaret (McNicoll) MacP.; e. Victoria Hosp. Sch. of Nursing London, Ont. R.N. 1949; Teachers' Coll. Columbia Univ. B.S.N. 1952; Wayne State Univ. M.S.N. 1960; Univ. of Mich. Ph.D. 1966; Hon. LL.D. McMaster Univ. 1986; Dean and Prof. of Nursing, Univ. of Alta. 1982–87; Prof. Emeritus, Univ. of Alta. 1987– ; Supr. Obstetric Nursing and Instr. Sch. of Nursing Kitchener-Waterloo Hosp. 1950–54; Lectr. and Coordinator Maternal-Child Nursing Univ. of Toronto Sch. of Nursing 1954–61; Asst. Prof. and Asst. in Adm. Coll. of Nursing Wayne State Univ. 1961–64; Dir., Nursing Demonst. Project, Assoc. Prof. and Asst. Dean Clin. Nursing Sch. of Nursing Case Western Reserve Univ. and Assoc. Dir. Nursing Univ. Hosps. of Cleveland 1966–71, Prof. and Assoc. Dean Nursing of CWRU and Clin. Assoc. Univ. Hosps. 1971–72, Prof. and Dean of Nursing, CWRU and Adm. Assoc. in Nursing Univ. Hosps. Cleveland 1972–82; cons. various Candn. and Am. Univ. Schs. of Nursing and Hosps.; Site Visitor Bush Foundation & Robert Wood Johnson Foundation grants; Visitor Nat. League Nursing Accreditation Service; Hon. mem. Nursing Alumni Assn., CWRU; recipient Am. Assembly Men in Nursing Award for Leadership in Nursing; Am. Assn. Colls.

Nursing, Distinguished Service Award; USPHS Special Nurse Fellowship; W.K. Kellogg Foundation Fellowship; Victoria Hosp. Alumnae Assn. Scholarship; co-author (with Dr. Janet Kerr) 'Canadian Nursing: Issues and Perspectives' 1988, 2nd ed. 1991; author or co-author numerous nursing publs.; Fellow, Am. Acad. Nursing 1978– (Gov. Council 1980–82); Hon. Life mem., Alumnae Assn. Teachers' Coll. Columbia Univ. 1982; Hon. Life mem., Alta. Assn. R.N.'s 1988; Treas. Am. Assn. Colls. Nursing 1975–77; Midwest Alliance Nursing (Gov. Bd. 1979–81); Am. Nurses Assn. (Chairperson Comm. Nursing Services 1976–80); Ohio Nurses' Assn. (Dir. 1971–77); Alta. Assn. R.N.'s (Prov. Council 1983–85); Candn. Nurses Assn. (1st Vice Pres. 1984–86); Alta. Found. Nsg. Research (Dir. 1982–87, Vice Chrmn. 1983–87, Chrmn., Scient. Review Comm. 1983–87); Candn. Nurses Found. (Chrmn, Research Comm. 1984–86); Am. Nurses Assn.; Florida Nurses Assn.; Am. Assn. Univ. Women (Pres., Vero Beach Branch 1991–94); Candn. Nurses Assn.; Alta. Assn. R.N.'s; Mem. Bd. of Trustees, Community Church, Vero Beach 1989–92; Mem. Bd. of Dirs., Vero Beach Choral Society 1992– ; Mem. Bd. of Dirs., Education Found. of Indian River County 1991–94; Sigma Theta Tau; Home: 325 Eugenia Rd., Vero Beach, Fla. 32963 U.S.A.

**MacPHAIL, The Hon. Lloyd George;** b. New Haven, P.E.I. 22 March 1920; s. Robert Archibald and Catherine C. (MacLean) MacP. (dec.); e. New Haven Pub. Sch.; Prince of Wales Coll. Charlottetown; m. Helen Mae d. the late Mr. & Mrs. John W. MacDougall, Argyle Shore, P.E.I.; children: Judith Anne, Lynn, Ferne, Robert; Lieutenant-Governor of P.E.I. 1985–90; retired; Min. of Industry and Natural Resources and of Tourist Dev. 1965–66; Min. of Devel., P.E.I. 1979–80; Min. of Finance & Chrmn. of the Treasury Bd. 1979–82; Min. of Finance and Tourism 1982–85; owner R.A. MacPhail & Son, Gen. Merchants; el. M.L.A. for 2nd Queens prov. by-el. 1961, re-el. since; Knight of the Most Venerable Order of Saint John of Jerusalem 1986; P. Conservative; Home: New Haven, Cornwall, R.R. 3, P.E.I. C0A 1H0.

**MacPHAIL, M(oray) S(t. John),** M.A., D.Phil., D.Sc., F.R.S.C.; university professor; b. Kingston, Ont. 27 May 1912; s. James Alexander and Agnes Mary (Macmorine) M.; e. Kingston Collegiate; Upper Can. Coll., Toronto, Ont.; Queen's Univ., B.A. 1933; McGill Univ., M.A. 1934; Oxford Univ., D.Phil. 1936; Carleton Univ., D.Sc. (Hon.) 1978; m. Frances Marian, d. Dr. F. W. Patterson, Wolfville, N.S., 17 Aug. 1939; one s. James Alexander; PROF. EMERITUS OF MATH., CARLETON UNIV. (former Dean of Grad. Studies 1963–69); Instr., Acadia Univ., 1937–39, Asst. Prof. 1939–41; Instr., Princeton Univ., 1941–42; Assoc. Prof., Acadia Univ., 1942–44, Prof. 1944–47; Visiting Lectr., Queen's Univ., 1947–48; Assoc. Prof. Carleton Univ., 1948–53, and Prof. 1953–77; Assoc. Dean, Faculty of Arts & Science, 1956–63; Dir., Sch. of Grad. Studies, 1960–63; Visiting Prof., Univ. of Toronto, 1967–68; mem., Candn. Math. Soc.; Am. Math. Soc.; Math. Assn. of Am.; United Church; Home: 165 Powell Ave., Ottawa, Ont. K1S 2A2.

**MacPHEE, Medrie,** B.F.A.; visual artist; b. Edmonton, Alta. 11 Sept. 1953; d. Douglas M. and Joan Irene (Tankard) MacP.; e. N.S. Coll. of Art & Design Halifax B.F.A. 1976; m. Harold Crooks s. Moses Sherback and Lilian Crooks 17 Nov. 1990; solo exhns. incl. Mira Godard Gallery Toronto 1980–92; The 49th Parallel N.Y. 1985, 1987; Concordia Univ. Gallery Montreal 1987; Phillipe Daverio Gallery N.Y. 1991; Baldacci - Daverio Gallery 1993; subject maj. articles 'Parnass' mag. Vienna 1990; 'Canadian Art' 1989; various catalogues incl. 'The Technological Muse' Katonah Museum of Arts; currently drawing teacher, N.Y. Studio School; summer studio head Banff Centre Alta. 1986; recipient Can. Council Arts Grant A, numerous Arts Grant B; Nat. Endowment Grant; Found. for Arts Grant; Greenshield Award; Address: 4F, 111 Bowery, New York, N.Y. 10002.

**MACPHERSON, Andrew Hall,** B.Sc., M.Sc., Ph.D., F.A.I.N.A.; private consultant; b. London, Eng. 2 June 1932; s. James Ewen and Dorothy Hall Macp.; e. London, Eng.; St. John's; Ottawa; Carleton Univ., B.Sc. 1954; McGill Univ., M.Sc. 1957; Ph.D. 1967; m. Elizabeth, d. Reginald and Lonia Menzer, 8 May 1957; children: David Thomas; Peter Andrew; Diana Elizabeth; mem. summer expeditions Candn. Arctic for various Govt. Depts. 1949–58; Asst. Curator Birds, Nat. Museum Can. 1957; Wildlife Biologist, Research Sci., Candn. Wildlife Service, Dept. Indian Affairs & Northern Development 1958–63; Sci. Advisor, Sci. Counc. Can. and Sci. Secretariat, Privy Counc. Office, 1967–69; Research Supervisor, Eastern Region, C.W.S. 1963–70; Dir., Western Region, C.W.S., Dept. Environment 1970–74; Regional Dir. Gen., Western and Northern Region, Environmental Mgmt. Service, Dept. Environment 1974–79; Reg. Dir. Gen., Dept. Environment for the Region 1979–86; Reg. Dir.-Gen., Northern Affairs, Northwest Territories, Dept. of Indian Affairs & Northern Development 1986–88; author numerous publications on arctic animals: taxonomy, population ecology, zoogeography, conservation; and on sport (particularly ice angling); former Mem. and Chrmn., I.U.C.N. Polar Bear Comte.; Former Gov., A.I.N.A.; Counsellor, Soc. Systematic Zoology; mem. Scientific Advisory Comte., World Wildlife Fund (Can.) 1979–84; currently on several boards, incl. True North Strong and Free Inquiry Soc. (Pres.); Trout Unlimited Canada (Western Vice-Pres.); Hon. Sec., Sustainable Population Soc.; rec'd. Centennial Medal, 1967; recreations: hunting, fishing; Address: 9619 96A St., Edmonton, Alta. T6C 3Z8.

**MACPHERSON, Donald Malcolm,** B.A., C.A.; consultant; b. Montreal, Que. 15 Dec. 1931; s. Hugh W. and Norma M. (McColl) M.; e. Acadia Univ. B.A. 1957; McGill Univ. C.A. 1961; m. Margaret d. T.P. Gladstone and Doris Shaw 5 July 1958; children: Barbara, Gordon, Janet; CONSULTANT, D.M. MACPHERSON & ASSOC. 1992– ; Dir., TD Trust Company; Audit Mgr. Clarkson, Gordon 1957–62; Greenshields Inc. Montreal 1962–66, Asst. Controller, Treas.; Yorkshire Securities Ltd. Vancouver 1966–67, Sec./Treas., Chief Financial Offr.; Comptroller of the Treasury Govt. Can. Ottawa 1967–72, Cons. Financial Control System; Post Office Dept. Ottawa 1972–74, Asst. Dir. Acctg. Br.; Asst. Inspector Gen. of Banks 1974–87; Depy. Superintendent of Financial Institutions 1987–92; mem. Inst. C.A.'s Ont.; Clubs: Rotary (Pres. Gloucester 1982–83); Kanata Lakes Golf & Country; Home/Office: 10 Catherwood Court, Kanata, Ont. K2K 2K1.

**MacPHERSON, Douglas William,** BSc, MD, MSc(CTM), FRCPC; medical doctor; b. Guelph, Ont. 19 June 1953; s. William Frederick and Nancy Roberta (Koshman) M.; e. Queen's Univ. BSc 1975; McMaster Univ. MD 1978; London Sch. of Tropical Medicine & Hygiene, Univ. of London MSc (Clinical Tropical Medicine) 1982; m. Mary Enid Haines d. Jean and Theodore Haines 9 Aug. 1980; children: Sarah Lindsay Alison, Stuart William Andrew; DIRECTOR, REGIONAL PARASITOLOGY LABORATORY, ST. JOSEPH'S HOSPITAL; Clinical consultant to Microbiologiy Services, St. Joseph's Hosp.; Consultant, Vector Biology and Control Project 1989– ; Asst. Prof., Dept. of Pathology, McMaster Univ.; Dir., Outpatient Services for Infectious Diseases & Tropical Med., Chedoke-McMaster Hospitals; Fellow, Royal College of Physicians & Surgeons of Canada Internal Medicine 1982, Med. Microbiol. 1985; active staff appts.: St. Joseph's Hosp., Chedoke McMaster Hosp.; social activist in the issues of planning, land use, health & safety & the environment in respect to non-ionizing radiation; Chrmn., Ctte. for Advise in Tropical Medicine & Travel; Chrmn. Sub-Ctte., Malaria;, Nat. Health Canada; Adv. Panel for Tropical Medicine and Parasitic Drugs, U.S. Pharmacopeial Convention 1990–95; Mem., Scientific Steering Ctte., Internat. Soc. for Travel Medicine and Am. Soc. Trop. Med. & Hyg.; mem. num. profl. assns. incl. assns. in medicine, med. microbiol., tropical med. & internat. health & public health; author/co-author of num. book chapters & sci. jour. articles in med.; referee for several medical journals; recreations: squash, travel, outdoor sports; clubs: Hamilton Thistle; Home: R.R. #1, Millgrove, Ont. L0R 1V0; Office: 59 Charlton Ave. E., Hamilton, Ont. L8N 4A6.

**MacPHERSON, Eric D.,** M.A., Ph.D.; educator; b. Hawkeye, Sask. 8 Apl. 1931; s. Duncan and Anna M. (Ohrn) MacP.; e. Univ. of B.C. B.A. 1952, M.A. 1960; Wash. State Univ. Ph.D. 1966; m. Fern d. Albert Bolger; 27 Dec. 1957; three s. James, Glen, Bruce; Dean of Education, Univ. of Manitoba 1974–84; Prof. of Ed. and Math, Univ. of B.C. 1959–73, Dept. Head 1964–72, Assoc. Dean 1972–74; has engaged in minor athletic coaching; author 'Contemporary Mathematics' 1964; 'Ginn Elementary Arithmetic' 1972; 'Mathematics in Modules' 1977; other writings incl. over 40 television programs and articles; mem. Nat. Council Teachers Math.; Phi Delta Kappa; recreation: chess; Home: 30 MacAlester Bay, Winnipeg, Man. R3T 2X5.

**MacPHERSON, George Roderick Ian,** B.A., .M.A., Ph.D.; university professor and administrator; b. Toronto, Ont. 6 July 1939; s. James Franklyn and Amelia (Reid) M.; e. South Grenville Dist. H.S.; Univ. of Windsor B.A. 1960; Univ. of W. Ont. M.A. 1966, Ph.D. 1971; m. Elizabeth Dawn d. Emily and Stanley Veinot 2 July 1966; children: Andrew, Jonathan; DEAN OF HUMANITIES, UNIV. OF VICTORIA; Teacher, Streetsville S.S. 1960–64; Asst. then Assoc. Prof., Univ. of Winnipeg 1968–76; Assoc. then Full Prof., Univ. of Victoria 1976– ; Chair, History 1984–91; Dean of Humanities 1992– ; Bd. Mem., local co-op. & credit union; Former Pres., B.C. Central Credit Union; Former Vice-Pres., Candn. Co-op. Credit Soc.; Co-op. Union of Canada; Co-op. College of Canada; Founding Pres., Candn. Co-op. Assn.; Mem., Extve. Ctte., Internat. Co-op. Alliance (Geneva); Dir., Pacific Coast Savings Credit Union; Victoria Peninsula Consumer Services Co-op.; Task Force for Reviewing Internat. Co-op. Principles, Internat. Co-op. Alliance; Chair, Pacific Coast Found.; Mem., Unitarian Ch.; author: 'Each for All' 1979, 'The Code of Brockville's Buells' 1982, 'The Story of Co-op Insurance Service' 1976, 'A History of Co-op Trust' 1978, 'Building and Protecting the Co-operation Movement' 1984; recreations: hiking; Home: 1646 Brousson Dr., Victoria, B.C. V8N 5M9; Office: Victoria, B.C. V8W 3P4.

**MACPHERSON, Gordon Clarke,** M.Mus.; educator; musician; b. Moose Jaw, Sask. 14 Nov. 1924; s. Douglas William and Jeannette (Newman) M.; e. Royal Conserv. of Music Toronto Licentiate Dipl. 1949; Univ. of Toronto Artist's Dipl. 1953; Ind. Univ. M.Mus. 1974; m. Billie d. Thomas and Helen Barry 1952; children: Sandra Jean, Stephen Ross; MEMBER, PIANO FACULTY, VICTORIA CONSERVATORY OF MUSIC; Music Adv. to CBC Maritimes 1955–66; Head Piano Dept. Maritime Conserv. 1964, Acting Dir. of Conserv. 1965; mem. Brandon Univ. Trio 1966– ; with Halifax Trio as Artists-in-Residence Brandon Univ. 1966; Acting Dir., School of Music, Brandon Univ. 1971–72, 1978–79, 1981–82; Dean 1982–87; Prof. of Music 1974–91; Prof. Emeritus 1992– ; W. Bd. Music Examiner and Adjudicator festivals in West and Maritimes; piano soloist in recital, with orchestra, Radio and TV; Chamber Music Player with Brandon Univ. Trio (formerly Halifax Trio) CBC broadcasts and concerts various Candn. provs. 1953–66; Conductor, CBC Halifax Strings, CBC Halifax Orchestra, Summer Promenade Concerts Halifax 1961–66; conductor and arranger several light music series CBC incl. TV series 'Reflections'; various recordings with present Trio; recipient Can. Council Sr. Arts Fellowship 1962–63, Touring Grant 1968, Doctoral Fellowship 1974; U.S. Internat. Communication Agency Grant 1979; Brandon Univ. Research Grants 1981, 1989; mem. Pi Kappa Lambda; Can. Music Council; Candn. Univ. Music Soc.; Fed. Candn. Music Festivals; recreation: reading; Address: 662 Sedger Rd., Victoria, B.C. V8Z 1S1.

**MACPHERSON, Hugh,** B.Eng.; professional engineer; b. Montreal, Que. 9 Apr. 1935; s. Hugh William and Norma MacGregor M.; e. McGill Univ., B.Eng. 1957; Carleton Univ., Dalhousie Univ., Royal Naval Coll., Greenwich, PSC, 1972; m. Jeanne Elliott d. Harry and Emma Callahan 27 Jan. 1968; one d.: Catherine Johanne; CHRMN., SEIMAC LIMITED 1986– ; Candn. Gen. Electric Co. 1958; Royal Candn. Navy 1959–78; Pres., Seimac Limited 1978–85; Pres., Oceanroutes Can. Inc. 1983; Dir., Nat. Optics Inst.; Past Pres., Bedford Bd. of Trade; Candn. Forces Decoration; Mem., Marine Tech. Soc.; Assn. of Profl. Engrs. of N.S.; Home: 36 First Ave., Bedford, N.S. B4A 1Z9.

**MacPHERSON, James Curry,** B.A., LL.B., LL.M.; judge; educator; b. Yarmouth, N.S. 11 June 1950; s. Donald Moland and Phyllis Elizabeth (Curry) MacP.; e. Acadia Univ., B.A. 1971; Dalhousie Univ., LL.B. 1974; Cambridge Univ., LL.M. 1976, Dip. Comparative Legal Studies 1977; m. Gladys d. Trevor and Kathleen Thompson 6 Oct. 1973; children: Blair, Jamie; JUSTICE, ONTARIO COURT OF JUSTICE (GENERAL DIVISION); Prof. of Law, Univ. of Victoria 1976–79, 1980–81; Visiting Prof. of Law, Osgood Hall Law School, York Univ. 1979–80, Dean 1988; Dir. Constitutional Br. Dept. Justice Sask. 1982–85; Extve. Legal Offr. Supreme Court of Can. 1985–87; mem. Candn. Bar Assn.; mem. Churchill Society; Office: Osgoode Hall, 130 Queen St. W., Toronto, Ont. M5H 2N5.

**MACPHERSON, Jean Jay,** M.A., Ph.D.; educator; author; b. London, Eng. 13 June 1931; d. James Ewan and Dorothy (Hall) M.; e. Maria Grey Prep., London; Convent of St. Francis de Sales, Tring; Bishop Spencer Coll., St. John's; Glebe Coll. Inst., Ottawa; Carleton Univ. B.A. 1951; McGill Univ. B.L.S. 1953; Univ. of Toronto M.A. 1955, Ph.D. 1964; PROF. OF ENGLISH, VICTORIA COLL. UNIV. OF TORONTO 1973– ; joined present coll. 1957; author 'The Boatman' poems 1957 (Gov. Gen.'s Award); 'Four Ages of Man' Grade 9 Textbook Classical Mythol. 1962; 'Welcoming Disaster' poems 1974; 'Poems Twice Told' collected poems 1981; 'The Spirit of Solitude: conventions and continuities in late romance' literary criticism 1982; various articles Candn. writers etc.; co-ed. 'The Hymn Book' Ang. and

Un. Chs. of Can. 1972; mem. Assn. Candn. Univ. Teachers Eng.; Candn. Soc. Eighteenth-Century Studies; NDP; recreation: research; Home: 17 Berryman St., Toronto, Ont. M5R 1M7; Office: 315 Northrop Frye Hall, Victoria College, Toronto, Ont. M5S 1K7.

**MacPHERSON, John Ian,** B.A.Sc., M.A.Sc.; research scientist, engineer; b. Redhill, Surrey, England 18 March 1942; s. John Austin and Margaret Aird White (McKail) M.; e. York Memorial C.I. 1961; Univ. of Toronto B.A.Sc. 1965; Univ. of Toronto, Inst. for Aerospace Studies M.A.Sc. 1966; m. Johanna d. Jacobus and Johanna Spaargaren 12 Nov. 1982; children: Andrew Graeme, Lisa Renée; RESEARCH SCIENTIST, FLIGHT RESEARCH LABORATORY, NATIONAL RESEARCH COUNCIL 1966– ; research conducted on water bombing of forest fires, atmospheric turbulence, aircraft accidents, cloud seeding, severe storms, airborne transport of atmospheric pollutants, acid rain & greenhouse gas measurement related to global warming issues; Sr. Rsch. Offr., Program Manager, Atmospheric Geoscience & Chief Scientist, NRC's Twin Otter atmospheric rsch. aircraft; Candn. Meteorology & Oceanographic Soc. Prize in Applied Meteorology 1977; Mem., Am. Meteorological Soc.; Am. Geophysical Union; Candn. Meteorological & Oceanographic Soc.; author/co-author of 28 articles in sci. journs., 98 reports & conf. papers; co-author of 3 book chapters; recreations: photography; Home: 1240 Plante Dr., Ottawa, Ont. K1V 9G2; Office: U-61, NRC, Ottawa, Ont. K1A 0R6.

**MACPHERSON, Marion Adams,** M.A.; retired diplomat; b. Moose Jaw, Sask. 16 May 1924; d. John Archibald and Anne Penelope (Adams) M.; e. Moosomin (Sask.) Pub. Sch. and Coll. Inst.; Univ. of Sask. B.A. 1946; Univ. of Toronto M.A. 1947; joined Dept. of External Affairs 1948; Third Secy. Washington 1950, Second Secy. 1953; Adviser Internat. Truce Comn. Indo-China 1957; Second Secy. Accra 1957, First Secy. 1958; Counsellor Candn. Perm. Mission to UN, N.Y. 1963–68; High Commr. to Sri Lanka 1973–76; Consul Gen. Boston 1977; Inspr. Gen. External Affairs 1977–79; Ambassador to Denmark 1979–83; Depy. Commandant, National Defence College 1983–85; High Commissioner to Zambia 1985–87; Presbyterian; Home: 215 Crichton St., Ottawa, Ont. K1M 1W3.

**MACQUARRIE, Heath Nelson,** M.A., LL.D.; political scientist., senator; b. Victoria, P.E.I., 18 Sept. 1919; s. late Wilfred and Mary (Mallard) M.; e. Prince of Wales Coll., Charlottetown, P.E.I.; P.E.I. Normal Sch. (1st Class Teachers Lic.) 1936; Univ. of Manitoba, B.A. 1947; Univ. of New Brunswick M.A. 1949; McGill Univ.; Univ. P.E.I., LL.D. (Hon.) 1978;m. Jean Isabel, d. late George Neil Stewart, 27 De. 1949; children: Heather Jean, Flora Mary, Iain Heath; Teacher in Public and High Schs., P.E.I., 1936–43; Secy., P.E.I. Teachers Fed., 1943; Asst. Boys Work Secy., Y.M.C.A., Winnipeg, Man., 1943–47; Asst. Prof. of Econ. and Pol. Science, Univ. of N.B., 1947–49, Lectr. in Pol. Science, McGill Univ., 1949–51; Instr., Asst. Prof. and later Prof. of Pol. Science and Internat. Relations, Brandon Coll., Man., 1951–55; Visiting Lect., Acadia Univ. Summer Sch., 1949 and 1952; Univ. of Man. Summer Sch., 1954; Mt. Allison Univ. Summer Sch., 1948 and 1955; News Analyst and Commentator, CKX, Brandon, Man., 1952–55; ResearchAssoc. in Pol. Science, Univ. of Toronto, 1957 (research grants); Instr. Internat. Relations, Carleton Univ. 1963–64; Assoc. Prof. Pol. Science, Mt. Allison Univ., 1978–79; Pres., Brandon P. Cons. Assn., 1955; Secy., Brandon-Souris Cons. Assn., 1954–55; 3rd Vice-Pres., P. Cons. Party of Can., 1955–58; mem.,Bd. of Sch. Trustees, City of Brandon, 1955; el. to H. of C. for Queens in g.e. 1957, and re-el. 1958, 1962, 1963, 1965, 1972, 1974; summoned to Senate of Can. Oct. 1979; Parlty. Secy. to Secy. of State for External Affairs, 1962–63; mem., Candn. Del. to U.N. Gen. Assembly, 1957, '58, '59, '62, '71; Candn. Observer del. to Inter-Am. Conf., Punta del Este, Uruguay, 1961; Chrmn., Can. branch, Commonwealth Parlty. Assn., 1961–62; deputy Chrmn., Senate Comte. on Foreign Affairs; Chrmn., H. of C. Comte. on Privileges and Elections, 1957–61; author 'The Conservative Party' 1965; 'Red Tory Blues' 1992 and of numerous articles on national and international politics; co-author 'Canada and the Third World'; a contrib. of articles to the press and learned journs.; Ed. (Carleton Library Edition) 'Robert Laird Borden, His Memoirs' 1969; awarded 'Grand Cordon (First Class) Order of Al-Istiqlal' by His Majesty King Hussein of Jordan; mem., Canadian Political Science Assn.; Nat. Council Canadian Human Rights Foundation; Chrmn., Foreign Affairs Ctte., Presbyterian Church in Can. 1979–84; Patron, Un. Nations Assn. Can.; Candn. Inst. Internat. Affairs; Freemason; Progressive Conservative; Presbyterian; recreations: swimming, walking, crossword puzzles, bird watching, cooking, reading; Home: Victoria, P.E.I. C0A 2G0.

**MacQUEEN, Very Rev. Angus James,** D.D., LL.D., B.A., L.Th., B.D. (Un. Ch.); retired minister; b. Port Morien, N.S. 3 JulY 1912; s. Duncan Archibald and Lillian Jane (Wadden) M.; e. Mount Allison Univ., B.A. 1933; Pine Hill Divinity Hall, L.Th. 1935, B.D. 1938, D.D. 1958; D.D., Victoria 1960; LL.D., Mount Allison 1959, W. Ont. 1959; m. Menetta May d. Calvin A. and Mary Anne MacFadyen, Sydney, N.S., 28 Oct. 1936; children: Marian (McNairn), Joan (Warren), Barbara, Heather (Pittas); Min., Zion Robertson, Port Hawkesbury, N.S., 1936–39; St. James,' Antigonish, N.S., 1939–42; Centenary-Queen Sq., Saint John, N.B., 1942–46; Robertson Ch., Edmonton, Alta., 1946–51; First-St. Andrew's Ch., London, Ont., 1951–64; St. George's Ch., Toronto, 1964–80; Special preacher & Lectr. Univs. in Canada & U.S.A., at conferences such as Chautauqua, New York & Berwick, N.S. and in cities: New York, Boston, Detroit, Vancouver, Montreal, Ottawa & Winnipeg; Chrmn. Bd. of Evangelism & Social Service, Un. Ch. of Can., 1954–58; el. Moderator, Un. Ch. of Can., 17 Sept. 1958–60; Chrmn., Bd. of Dirs. of 'United Church Observer' 1973–80; Chancellor, Mt. Allison Univ. 1977–85; author: 'Superman Is An Idiot' 1977; 'The Ten Commandments: New Light From Old Lamps' 1978; 'Memory Is My Diary' (memoirs) 2 vols. Lancelot Press, Hantsport, N.S. 1991; has written for publs. in Can., Br., U.S. and has contrib. chaps. for 6 bks.; since retirement has supplied, on an interim basis, at four churches in Toronto: Runnymede, Leaside, Forest Hill and Eastminster; has writtern articles for the Toronto Globe and Mail, MacLean's Magazine, Toronto Star, The Christian Century, The British Weekly, and the Reader's Digest; continues to do special preaching and lecturing; recreations: curling, swimming, golf, reading; Home: 326 Douglas Ave., Toronto, Ont. M5M 1H1.

**MacQUEEN, Kenneth John;** journalist; b. Galt, Ont. 9 July 1955; s. Daniel Alexander and Edna (Steckly) M.; e. Conestoga College, Journalism; m. Roswitha d. Hilde and Alfred Guggi 8 Oct. 1983; children: Daniel Scott Kenneth, Cameron Alfred John; NATIONAL AFFAIRS COLUMNIST, THE OTTAWA CITIZEN AND SOUTHAM NEWS 1992– ; Journlist, Kitchener-Waterloo Record 1976–79; The Ottawa Citizen 1980–81; Ottawa Bureau, Canadian Press 1982–85; Maclean's Magazine 1985–86; Legal and Political Correspondent, Southam News 1986–88; West Coast Correspondent 1988–92; Nat. Newspaper Award Citation for Internat. Reporting 1990; Presbyterian; Mem., Parliamentary Press Gallery; recreations: cycling, reading; Home: 475 Piccadilly Ave., Ottawa, Ont. K1Y 0H5; Office: 165 Sparks St., Sutie 805, Ottawa, Ont. K1P 5B9.

**MacRAE, Donald Alexander,** A.M., Ph.D., F.R.S.C., F.R.A.S.; astronomer; b. Halifax, N.S., 19 Feb. 1916; s. Donald Alexander and Laura (Barnstead) MacR.; e. Univ. of Toronto, B.A., 1937; Harvard Univ., A.M., 1940, Ph.D. 1943; m. Margaret Elizabeth, d. C. A. Malcolm, Chatham, Ont., 25 Aug. 1939; children: David M., Charles D., Andrew R.; PROFESSOR EMERITUS AND DIRECTOR EMERITUS, DEPT. OF ASTRONOMY, UNIVERSITY OF TORONTO; Chrmn., Dept. of Astronomy and Dir., David Dunlap Observatory 1965–78; mem., Am. Astron. Soc.; Candn. Astron. Soc.; founding mem. Bd. Trustees, Universities Space Research Assn. (operating Lunar and Planetary Inst., Houston, Texas) 1969–76; founding mem., Bd. Dir., Can.-Fr.-Hawaii Telescope Corp. 1973–79; founding mem., Bd. of Trustees, Cdn. Corp. for Univ. Space Sci. 1978–82; Address: David Dunlap Observatory, Box 360, Richmond Hill, Ont. L4C 4Y6.

**MACRAE, Herbert Farquhar,** C.M., B.Sc., M.Sc., Ph.D., F.A.I.C.; retired educational administrator; b. Middle River, N.S. 30 March 1926; s Murdoch John and Jessie Matheson (MacLennan) M.; e. N.S. Normal Coll., Teacher's license 1948; N.S. Agri. Coll. Diploma 1952; McGill Univ., B.Sc. 1954, M.Sc. 1956, Ph.D. 1960, D.Sc. (Hon.); m. Mary Ruth d. late Roderick K. Finlayson 24 Sept. 1955; children: Roderick John, Elizabeth Anne, Christy Margaret, Mary Jean; Principal, N.S. Agri. Coll. retired 1989; Fellow, Agricultural Inst. of Can. 1988; Member, Order of Canada 1992; mem., Candn. Soc. of Animal Science; N.S. Inst. of Agrologists; Agri. Inst. of Can.; Sigma Xi; Protestant; Club: Rotary, Truro; Home: 7 Hickman Dr., Truro, N.S. B2N 2Z2; Office: Truro, N.S. B2N 5E3.

**MACRAE, Marion Bell,** C.M. (1982); architectural and design historian; b. Apple Hill, Ont. 30 April 1921; d. John Donald and Hazel Ross (Carlyle) M.; e. Ont. Coll. of Art, A.O.C.A. 1947; Postgrad., Univ. of Illinois, 1951–54; Lectr. Hist. of Design, Ont. Coll. of Art 1969–86; Instr., Design and Museum Studies, Ont. Coll. of Art, 1949–69; Mem., Adv. Cmte. on Design, U.C. Village Restoration, 1957–61; Special Asst. to Design Consultant, Dundurn Castle Restoration, 1963–67; Lectr. (Part-time), Hist. of Candn. Arch., Univ. of Toronto, 1973–78; author of 'Settlement of the Old Eastern District,' R.A.I.C., 1959; 'MacNab of Dundurn,' 1971; co-author 'The Ancestral Roof,' 1963; 'Hallowed Walls,' 1975; 'Cornerstones of Order,' 1983; rec'd. Gov.-Gen. Literary Award (non-fiction), 1975; Soc. for the Study of Arch. in Can.; Natl. Trust. (U.K.); Natl. Trust for Scotland; Natl. Trust for Historical Preservation (USA); Arch. Conservancy of Ont.; Ont. Hist. Soc.; Liberal; Christian; recreations: travel; Home: 80 Lawton Blvd., Apt. 19, Toronto, Ont. M4V 2A2.

**MACVICAR, Sheila,** B.J.; journalist; b. Montreal, Que. 18 Mar. 1955; d. Alexander George and Elizabeth Jean (Sleeth) M.; e. Carleton Univ., B.J. (Hons.) 1977; m. John Owen; one d.: Tess Alexandra; Co-Host, 'The Fifth Estate,' CBC 1988; Reporter, CBC News, Montreal 1977–80; Actt. Extve., Palmer Jarvis Advtg., Calgary 1980–81; Reporter, CBC News, Calgary 1981–82; Correspondent, 'The National,' CBC TV News 1982–86; Fgn. Correspondent, CBC TV News based in London (covered Britain, Eastern & Western Europe, Middle East & N. Africa) 1986–88.

**MacWILLIAM, David Charles,** B.A., B.F.A.; artist, painting instructor; b. Halifax, N.S. 6 Jan. 1951; s. Herbert Dawson and Elizabeth Ruth (Jack) M.; e. Univ. of B.C. 1968–70; Univ. of Victoria 19701–72, B.A. 1975; Nova Scotia College of Art & Design B.F.A. 1976; one s.: Kent; PAINTING INSTRUCTOR, EMILY CARR COLLEGE OF ART & DESIGN 1988– ; selected one person & selected group exhbns.: 'David MacWilliam, Recent Paintings,' Costin & Klintworth Gall. Toronto 1991, Vancouver Art Gall. (catalogue) 1990; 'David MacWilliam, Paintings' Costin & Klintworth Gall. 1988, '89; 'David MacWilliam Paintings & Drawings 1985–87' Contemporary Art Gall. Vanc. (cat.) 1987; 'David MacWilliam,' Art Gall. of Greater Victoria (cat.) 1983; '6 Vancouver 6,' Harbourfront Art Gall. Toronto (cat.) 1984, 'Vancouver Art & Artists, 1931–1983,' Vanc. Art Gall. (cat.) 1983; 12th Paris Biennale, Musée d'Art Moderne, Paris (cat.) 1982; Founding Mem., Mercer Union, Toronto 1979; Vancouver Artists League 1982–83; Bd. of Trustees, Vanc. Art Gall. 1985–88 (Chair, Acquisitions Ctte. 1986–88); Bd. Mem., Contemporary Art Gall. Vanc. 1991– ; Asst. Prof., Ctr. for the Arts, Simon Fraser Univ. 1981–87; Canada Council Art Bank Jury 1992, 1985; 'B' Grant Jury 1987; collections: Art Gallery of Greater Victoria, Vanc. Art Gallery, Canada Council Art Bank & private collections; visiting artist presentations: Okanagan College 1993, Red Deer College 1992, Vanc. Art Gall. 1991, Cornish Inst. Seattle 1986, Univ. of Victoria 1983, Emily Carr College of Art & Design Vanc. 1980, Univ. of Manitoba, Sch. of Art 1979; author: 'David MacWilliam, Drawings' 1983 and five catalogues incl. most recent: 'Aspects of Drawing: Abstraction & Figuration,' Seattle Arts Comn., Public Art Space 1987, 'Michael Morris: Early Works 1965–72; The Problem of Nothing,' Art Gall. of Gr. Victoria 1985; Home: 2559 William St., Vancouver, B.C. V5K 2Y3; Office: 1399 Johnston St., Granville Is., Vancouver, B.C. V6H 3R9.

**MADDEN, Willard Edwin (Ted),** B.A.; business executive; b. Lashburn, Sask. 17 Aug. 1950; s. Frederick Ewart and Beatrice Stark (McBain) M.; e. York Univ. B.A. (Hons.) 1973; m. Shirley d. Roy and Elizabeth Taylor 25 Aug. 1973; children: Stephanie, Danielle; PRESIDENT, BULL HN INFORMATION SYSTEMS 1992– ; Sales & Mktg. Mngt., IBM Canada 1973–85; Director of Sales, Prime Computer of Can. 1986–90; Vice-Pres., Sales, Bull HN Information Systems 1990–92; Bd. Chair, Zenith Data Systems (Canada); Bd. Mem., Unionville Home Soc. (Seniors Campus in Unionville, Ont.); recreations: fitness, coaching children's sports, provincial and local politics; Office: 675 Cochrane Dr., Markham, Ont. L3R 0M3.

**MADILL, Shirley Jane-Raven,** B.A., M.A.; curator; b. Selkirk, Man. July 1952; d. Joseph and Marianne (Faseruk) Slipec; e. Univ. of Man., B.A. 1976, M.A. 1980; one d. Kassandra Kirsten; CURATOR OF CONTEMPORARY ART & PHOTOGRAPHY, THE WINNIPEG ART GALL. 1979– ; Asst. Prof., Univ. of Winnipeg 1984–85, 1987–90, 1990–92; Lectr., Sch. of Art., Univ. of Man. 1982 and var. other places incl. 'Creating Fictions,' Photo Conf. Banff, Alta. 1990; 'Talking Pictures' Conf., Toronto 1987; Ed., 'In/Versions' publication, MAWA, Winnipeg 1989– ; Cons., Man. Arts Counc. Visual Arts Bank; Founder, photography collection Winnipeg Art Gall.; Mem., Candn. Mus. Assn.; Art Adv. Ctte., Min. of Govt. Serv.; Bd.

Mem., Main Axis Gallery; Artspace; Reg. Adv., Jack Chambers Mem. Found. Project; author & curator: 'Suzanne Funnell' 1982, 'Dialogues: The Winnipeg Perspective' 1984, 'Illusion and Paradox' 1985, 'Esther Warkov' 1985, 'Tony Brown: Day Dreams' 1986, '1987: Contemporary Art in Manitoba' 1987; 'Theatre Tableaux' 1988; 'Identity/Identities' 1988; 'Eric Cameron: Divine Comedy' 1989; 'Marsha Whiddon' 1989; 'Robert Houle: Indians from A to Z' 1989; 'Private/Public: Galerie Art & Essai' Univ. of Rennes, France 1990; 'Kim Adams' Shedhalle, Zurich 1990; 'Janice Gurney: Sum Over Histories' 1992; 'Animals in Contemporary Art' 1991–92; 'Eleanor Bond: Social Centres' 1992; 'EDGE MANITOBA' 1992; Office: 300 Memorial Blvd., Winnipeg, Man. R3C 1V1.

**MADORE, Lina;** writer; b. St-Clément, Qué. 20 July 1929; e. N.B. Coll. Edmundston; m. 25 Aug. 1949; 15 children; author 'Petit Coin Perdu' autobiog. Vol. I 1979, Vol. II 1981 (Vermeil Prize Switzerland 1983); 'Poésie inachevée' poetry 1985; 'Joey Le Petit Pécheur de Lune' children's hist. 1985; (fiction):'Serpent Jaune' 1987; 'La Planèt Murat' 1990; 'Phosphorine la Girafe' 1990; recipient Gold Heart Prize 1989; mem. Acadian Writers; P.E.N.; recreations: reading, walking, tennis.

**MADSEN, Neil Bernard,** M.Sc., Ph.D., F.R.S.C.; educator; b. Grande Prairie, Alta. 8 Feb. 1928; s. Anders Kristian and Rose Priscilla (Broadbridge) M.; e. Univ. of Alta. B.Sc. 1950, M.Sc. 1952; Washington Univ. St. Louis Ph.D. 1955; m. Laura d. Blanche and Albert Kratky 31 Aug. 1970; children: Ian Christopher, Maureen Dorothy; Prof. of Biochem., Univ. of Alta. 1969; Instr. Washington Univ. 1955–56; Post-Doctoral Fellow Oxford Univ. 1956–57; Rsch. Offr. Agric. Can. Ottawa 1957–62; Assoc. Prof. of Biochem. present Univ. 1962; Visiting Sci. Molecular Biophysics Oxford 1972–73; Med. Research Council Can. grantee 1963– ; recipient Queen's Silver Jubilee Medal 1977; Del. XIth Intnl. Cong. of Biochem.; author or co-author over 90 sci. papers or intnl. symposium lectures since 1952; Assoc. Ed. 'Canadian Journal of Biochemistry' 1968–72; mem. ed. bd. 'Journal of Biological Chemistry' 1981–86; mem., Candn. Biochem. Soc. (Pres. 1969); Candn. Fed. Biol. Soc. (Pres. 1978); Am. Soc. Biol. Chems.; recreations: fishing, hunting, skiing.

**MAGAGNA, Lino,** C.M., M.A.Sc., Ph.D., M.B.A., P.Eng.; b. Trento, Italy 23 Jan. 1933; s. Giuseppe and Meri (Bertoldi) M.; e. Shurpass Pacific Coll., Vancouver, 1956; Vancouver Vocational Institute, Diesel Mech. 1954; Univ. of B.C., B.A.Sc. 1962; Univ. of Toronto, M.A.Sc. 1963, Ph.D. 1965, M.B.A. 1986; children: Mark Laurier, Marina Alice; MANAGING DIRECTOR, CANADIAN BRENTA MANAGEMENT LTD.; joined Finning Tractor of Vancouver 1954–56; D.C.F. Systems Ltd. 1965–71 Consulting Engr., Partner and Mgr. of Indust. Systems; Ontario Hydro - Engineering 1971–83, Finance 1983–92; Pres. Bd., COSTI 1970–1980; Vice Chrmn., Candn. Consultative Council on Multiculturalism 1973–78; Founder and First Vice-Pres., Nat. Congress Italian-Candns.; mem. Bd. Govs and Senate, York Univ.; mem. Bd. Trustees United Way Metro Toronto; mem. Bd. of Dirs., Ont. March of Dimes; Human Factors Assn. of Can.; mem. Ont. Council on Univ. Affairs; twice rec'd Ford Foundation Fellowship; Member, Order of Canada 1988; mem., Assn. Prof. Engrs. Ont.; Home: 1650 Lincolnshire Blvd., Mississauga, Ont., L5E 2S7.

**MAGARRELL, Gary William,** B.A., B.D., M.B.A., A.R.W.; institutional executive; b. St. Boniface, Man. 4 May 1943; s. Henry William and Doris Katherina (Manness) M.; e. Morris-Macdonald Coll. 1960; Univ. of Man., B.A. 1963; Univ. of Winnipeg, B.D. 1971; Simon Fraser Univ., M.B.A. 1983; Accredited Rehabilitation Worker; divorced; children: Darcy Jean, Paul Gary; EXTVE. DIR., CANDN. NAT. INST. FOR THE BLIND, ONT. DIV. 1985– ; Min., Vancouver Ch. for the Deaf 1966–69; Gilmore Pk. Un. Ch. 1969–74; Extve. Dir., West Inst. for the Deaf 1974–82; Extve. Dir., Candn. Nat. Inst. for the Blind B.C.-Yukon Div. 1982–85; Past Pres., Candn. Coordinating Counc. on Deafness; Candn. Representative to World Blind Union; H.S. & Univ. Valedictorian; Wesley Award; recreations: dancing, theatre, music; Home: 401 – 360 Bloor St. E., Toronto, Ont. M4W 3M3; Office: 1929 Bayview Ave., Toronto, Ont. M4G 3E8.

**MAGGS, Roger J.,** B.Sc., M.A.; business executive; b. Newport, Eng. 13 March 1946; s. Edgar George and Enyd May (Saddler) M.; e. Swansea Univ. B.Sc. 1967; Warwick Univ. M.A. 1972; div.; children: David, Alexandra, Huw; PRES. RAW MATERIALS & METAL MANAGEMENT, ALCAN 1992– ; Pres. Alcan Ingot & Recycling ( U.S.A.); Alcan Ingot Alloys (Can.); Extve. Vice Pres. Alcan Aluminum Corp.( U.S.A.); Dir. Alcan Australia Ltd.; Spar Aerospace Ltd.; joined Alcan 1967, Vice Pres. Personnel Rio de Janeiro 1980, Extve. Vice Pres. & Mng. Dir. Uruguay 1983, Vice Pres. Personnel Montreal and named Pres. & Gen. Mgr. Alcan Fiduciaires 1986, Pres. Metal Marketing & Recycling Alcan 1989; Vice Pres., Alcan Aluminium Ltd. 1993; recreations: show jumping; Clubs: East India (London); M.A.A.A.; Home: St-Lazare, Qué. J0P 1V0; Office: 1188 Sherbrooke St. W., Montréal, Qué. H3A 3GZ.

**MAGNET, Joseph Eliot,** B.A., LL.B., LL.M., Ph.D.; educator/lawyer; b. Springfield, Mass. 19 Aug. 1946; s. Isaac Harry, M.D. and Edith (Sahpiro) M.; e. Long Island Univ. B.A. 1968; McGill Univ. Ph.D. 1973, LL.B. 1976; Univ. of Ottawa LL.M. 1977; PROF. OF LAW, UNIV. OF OTTAWA 1984– ; Law Clk., Chief Justice Supreme Court of Can. 1976–77; Asst. Prof. present Univ. 1977, Assoc. Prof. 1980; Crown Attorney, Ottawa 1989–90; Distinguished Visiting Prof., Univ. of California, Berkeley 1990–91; Legal Counsel to Official Lang. Minority Assns., Aboriginal Assns., Religious Assns.; Cons. to Fed. Prov. and Territorial Govts. pub. law matters, and to various private law firms constitutional law matters; Chrmn. Select Ctte. on Constitution, Candn. Jewish Cong.; Past Dir. Nat. Legal Aid Rsch. Centre; Law Soc. Upper Can.; author 'Implementing Official Bilingualism in Manitoba' 1982; 'Constitutional Law of Canada' 1983, First Supplement 1984, 2nd ed. in 2 vols. 1985, 3rd ed. 1987, 4th ed. 1989, 5th ed. 1993; 'Withholding Treatment from Defective Newborn Children' 1985; Home: 306 Queen Elizabeth Driveway, Ottawa, Ont. K1S 3M7; Office: 57 Louis Pasteur, P.O. Box 450, Stn. A, Ottawa, Ont. K1N 6N5.

**MAGNUSSEN, Karen Diane,** O.C. (1973); world figure skating champion; b. Vancouver, B.C., 4 Apl. 1952; d. Alf John and Gloria (Johansson) M.; e Delbrook High Sch., N. Vancouver, 1968; Carson Graham Secondary High Sch., N. Vancouver, 1970; Simon Fraser Univ., 1971–72; m. Anthony R. Cella, 23 July 1977; children: Eric John, Kristopher Robert, Jennifer Marie; Olympic Silver Medallist 1972; Hon. Coach, Figure Skating, Special Olympic Winter Games, Vermont, U.S.A. 1981; Adv. Bd. mem., Calgary Devel. Comte. for the 1988 Winter Olympics; coaches figure skating at North Shore Winter Club, North Vancouver, B.C.; group & private instructor; founder, Karen Magnussen Foundation, 1973; founder, "Champions Way" Skating Schools; Owner & founder "Maggies Muffins" W. Vancouver, B.C., 2nd franchise Richmond, B.C.; past star skater with Ice Capades; named B.C. Jr. Athlete of Yr. 1967, Sr. 1971, 1972; B.C. Sports Special Merit Award 1970; N. Shore Jr. Athlete of Yr. and Hall of Fame, 1971; Can.'s Female Amateur Athlete of Yr. 1971, 1972; B.C. Overall Athlete of Yr. 1972; Vanier Award Can.'s Outstanding Young Candn. 1972; Special Achievement Award, Sons of Norway of Am., 1972; Award of Merit Candn. Figure Skating Assn. 1973; First Freeman Dist. of N. Vancouver 1973; Karen Magnussen Arena. Lynn Valley. N. Vancouver, named 1973; recipient: 'Good Skate Award' Vancouver Rotary Club & Ice Capades 1989; North Vancouver District 'Achievement Award of the Century' 1991; Dir., Lions Gate Hospital Foundation; Hon. Citizen Thunder Bay, Ont., 1973; Hon. Life mem., Pacific Nat. Exhn., 1973; Life mem. Vancouver Parks Bd. & Pub. Recreation, 1973; Internat. Hon. mem. Beta Sigma Phi; mem. B.C. and Candn. Sports Hall of Fame, 1973; named top female athlete of Can., Dec. 1972, 1973; biog. 'Karen' publd. 1973; United Church; recreations: figure skating, golf, tennis, swimming; Clubs: N. Shore Winter (Life Mem.); Swedish Candn.; Nordlandslaget; New Westminster Skating; B.C. Jockey (Life Mem.); Vancouver; Home: North Vancouver, B.C.; Office: 2852 Thorncliffe Dr., North Vancouver, B.C. V7R 2S8.

**MAGNUSSON, Warren Elmer Norris,** B.A., B.Phil., D.Phil.; educator; b. Toronto, Ont. 28 Jan. 1947; s. Norman Lawrence and Allene Elsie (Huhtala) M.; e. Univ. of Manitoba B.A. 1967; Oxford Univ. B.Phil. 1969, D.Phil. 1978; Rhodes Scholar 1967–69; Can. Counc. Doctoral Fellow 1971–73; m. Sharon d. Arch and Evelyn Walls 26 July 1974; one d. Rachel; ASSOCIATE PROFESSOR OF POLITICAL SCIENCE, UNIVERSITY OF VICTORIA 1986– , Asst. Prof. 1979–86; co-editor: 'City Politics in Canada' 1983; 'The New Reality' 1984; 'After Bennett' 1986; Home: 304 Robertson St., Victoria, B.C. V8S 3X7; Office: Dept. of Pol. Sci., U. of Victoria, P.O. Box 3050, Victoria, B.C. V8W 3P5.

**MAGUED, Mohammed H.,** B.Eng., M.Eng., Ph.D.; engineering executive; b. Cario, Egypt 29 July 1945; s. Hussein M. and Zeinab M. (Wahba) M.; e. Cairo Univ. B.Eng. 1967; Carleton Univ. M.Eng. 1971, Ph.D. 1975; m. Aida d. Ismail Magued and Attia Roshdy 22 May 1969; children: Ismail, Seba; Chairman & C.E.O., Morrison Hershfield Group 1991; Demonstrator, Cairo Univ. 1967–69; Teaching & Rsch. Asst., Carleton Univ. 1969–74; Engineer, Morrison Hershfield Limited 1974–86; Pres. & C.E.O. 1986–91; Chair, Morrison Hershfield Limited; Morrison Hershfield Project Managers Inc.; Morrison Hershfield Devel. Concepts Inc.; Morrison Hershfield Internat. Inc.; appt. by Lt.-Gov. of Ont. to Council of Assn. of Profl. Engrs. of Ont. 1991–93; Dir., Ont. Assn. of Learning Disabilities 1985–91; Dir. & Secty., Consulting Engrs. of Ont. 1992–95; Home: 2524 Maid Marion Place, Mississauga, Ont. L5K 2L9.

**MAGUIRE, Joyce O.,** G.R.S.M., L.R.A.M., A.R.C.M.; arts administrator, accompanist; b. London, Eng. 4 Nov. 1936; d. Ernest Edward and Olive Rhoda Florence (Hilton) Bailey; e. Notting Hill & Ealing H.S.; Royal Acad. of Music, Jr. Exhibitioner 1947–54; Royal Schools of Music grad. 1957; Licentiate, Royal Academy of Music (teaching, accompanying); Assoc., Royal Coll. of Music (piano performance); m. Gerald s. Sidney and Florrie M. 18 April 1960; children: John Fitzgerald, Mary Elizabeth; EXECUTIVE DIRECTOR, B.C. CHORAL FEDERATION 1983– ; Head, Music Dept., The Holt School (U.K.) 1957–60; Piano teacher, choral accompanist, church organist 1960–83; Joyce Maguire Arts Management: Manager, Vancouver Bach Children's Chorus 1984– , Vancouver Bach Youth Choir 1993– ; Agent for Jane Coop, pianist 1987– ; Bd. Mem., World Symposium on Choral Music 1990–93; Willan Award for Outstanding Service to the B.C.C.F. 1984; Home: 3526 W. 5th Ave., Vancouver, B.C. V6R 1R9; Office: P.O. Box 4397, Vancouver, B.C. V6B 3Z8.

**MAGUIRE, Sean Patrick,** B.A., M.A.; Ph.D. student; b. Granby, Que. 6 Sept. 1967; s. Edwin Michael and Marie Thérèse (Coiteux) M.; e. Massey-Vanier H.S. 1984; John Abbott College D.E.C. 1986; Concordia Univ. B.A. 1989; McMaster Univ. M.A. 1990; m. Jean Grundy d. George and Alice Grundy 5 Sept. 1992; MEM., BOARD OF GOVERNORS, UNIV. OF OTTAWA 1991– ; while at Concordia completed work terms at Royal Bank 1987, Transport Canada 1988, Nat. Transp. Agency 1988; Teaching Asst., Univ. of Ottawa 1990– ; McMaster Univ. Entrance Scholarship 1989; Senate, Univ. of Ottawa 1992– ; Mem., OPIRG-Ottawa 1993– ; Friends of the Environment Found. 1991–93; Catholic; Mem., Candn. Econ. Assn.; Candn. Assn. for Studies in Internat. Development; Candn. Assn. for Latin American and Caribbean Studies; recreations: running, squash, volleyball; clubs: National Capital Runners Assn.; Home: 101 Louis-Pasteur, No. 67, Ottawa, Ont. K1N 9N1; Office: Ottawa, Ont. K1N 6N5.

**MAGWOOD, John McLean,** Q.C., B.A., M.A., LL.B., S.J.D.; lawyer; author; b. Toronto, Ont. 26 Aug. 1912; s. Samuel John Newton and Susannah Maud (McLean) M.; e. Univ. of Toronto Schs. 1922–29; Univ. of Toronto B.A. 1933, M.A. 1937, LL.B. 1938, S.J.D. 1981; Osgoode Hall Law Sch. 1933–36; York Univ. LL.B. 1991; m. Doris Rose d. O.P. Johnston 18 June 1938; children: Beverley Dawn (Jamieson), Charles Johnston; RET. CHRMN., CANDN. EXTVE. SERVICE ORGANIZATION 1986; Ret. Dir. City of Toronto Non-Profit Housing Corp. 1989; Ret. Vice Chrmn. Ont. Workers' Compensation Appeals Tribunal 1988; called to Bar of Ont. 1936; Q.C. 1956; practiced law in Toronto since 1936– ; Snr. Partner Magwood, Frith, Pocock (and successor firms) 1950–80; served with Candn. and British army, SHAEF, 1942–45; Retired, Maj. GSO II, 1945; mentioned in dispatches; awarded Can. Centennial Medal 1967, Queen Eliz. II Jubilee Medal 1977; Past Pres. Natl. Council YMCA's of Can. (Hon. Vice-Chrmn.) and Companion Fellowship of Honour; Chrmn. Hon. Bd. Metro Toronto YMCA; Past Pres. Candn. Council for Intl. Cooperation; Former Prov. Candidate and Vice Pres Ont. Liberal Assn.; author of 'Competition Law of Canada,' 1981; Life mem. Law Soc. of Upper Canada; Candn. Bar Assn.; Past Pres. York County Law Assn. and Founding Area Legal Aid Dir.; Past Pres. Psi Upsilon, Nu Chapter; Chrmn. Trustees, Lawrence Park United Church, Toronto; Clubs: Lawyers; University; Badminton and Racquet; Rosedale Golf; Osler Bluff Ski; recreations: riding, harness driving, skiing, sailing, golf, tennis; Home: 2900 Yonge St., Suite 803, Toronto, Ont. M4N 2J7; Creemore and Ingoldsby, Ont.

**MAGYARODY, Thomas S.,** B.Eng. & Mgmt., M.B.A.; business executive; b. Hamilton, Ont 29 May 1956; e. McMaster Univ., B.Eng. & Mgmt. 1979, M.B.A. 1982; m. Dr. Christa M. Jeney; children: Nora, Katherine; Project Engr., Domglas Inc. 1979–83; various positions in Materials, M.I.S. & Human Resources ending as Director, Human Resources, McDonnell Douglas Canada Ltd. 1983–90; Sr. Vice-Pres., Admin., Commercial Union Assurance Co. of Canada 1990–92; Pres.,

Strategic Options 1993; Gen. Dir. Admin., Ont. Medical Assn. 1993– ; Board Dir., Institute for Clinical Evaluative Sciences; Mem., APEO; McMaster Univ. Indus. Adv. Counc.; recreations: sailing, skiing; clubs: Etobicoke Yacht; Home: 31 Abilene Dr., Etobicoke, Ont. M9A 2M7.

**MAHAFFY, Douglas William,** B.A., C.A., M.B.A.; executive; b. Toronto, Ont. 15 Mar. 1945; s. Howard William and Kirby Rhoda (Reynolds) M.; e. York Univ. B.A. 1966; Ont. Inst. of Chartered Accts. C.A. 1969; York Univ. M.B.A. 1971; m. Adrienne d. Lynal and Joyce Faust 7 Feb. 1969; children: Kirsten, Scott, Roy, Nicole, Michelle; CHRMN., PRES. AND C.E.O., MCLEAN, BUDDEN LIMITED 1989– ; Dir., Stelco Inc.; Gartmore Investment Mngmt. plc; Woodwards; Cons. Woods, Gordon & Co. 1971; Treas. Charterhouse Group Can. 1972; Controller Eli Lilly Canada 1975; Treas., Hudson's Bay Co. 1976–79, Divisional Vice Pres. Fin. 1979–85, Sr. Vice Pres. Fin. and Admin. 1985–87; Sr. Vice-Pres. & Dir., Merrill Lynch Canada Inc. 1987–89; mem. Fin. Extves. Inst.; recreations: skiing, golf, tennis; Clubs: Toronto; The Toronto Hunt; Beaver Valley; Home: 58 St. Andrews Gardens, Toronto, Ont.; Office: Suite 1000, 390 Bay St., Toronto, Ont. M5H 2Y2.

**MAHANT, Edelgard E.,** Ph.D.; university professor; b. Krobia, Poland 27 Nov. 1940; d. Friedrich W. and Margarethe A. (Pirang) P.; e. Univ. of B.C. B.A. 1962; Univ. of Toronto M.A. 1963; London Sch. of Econ. Ph.D. 1969; m. Ram Parkash Mahant s. the late Tulsi Das and Dawarki Mahant 8 May 1962; children: Paul, Sheila, Kamal; Prof. Laurentian Univ. 1969–90; Visiting Scholar, Univ. of Toronto 1990–91; Assoc. Prof., Glendon College, York Univ.; Liberal Candidate, Sudbury East 1985; Ed. Bd. Mem., 'Journal of European Integration'; co-author: 'An Introduction to Canadian-American Relations' 1989; author: 'Free Trade In American-Canadian Relations' 1992; Mem., Policy Ctte., Liberal Party of Can. (Ont.); Amnesty International; Home: 855 Logan, Toronto, Ont. M4K 3E2; Office: 2275 Bayview Ave., Toronto, Ont. M4N 3M6.

**MAHER, Peter Michael,** B.E., M.B.A., Ph.D., P.Eng.; educator; b. North Battleford, Sask. 4 March 1940; s. Hugh James and Florence Andrea (Showell) M.; e. Univ. of Sask. B.E. 1962; Univ. of W. Ont. M.B.A. 1965; Northwestern Univ. Ph.D. 1970; m. Illa d. Louise and Ralph Horning 5 Sept. 1938; children: Andrea, Allison, Jennifer; DEAN AND PROF. FACULTY OF MANAGEMENT, UNIV. OF CALGARY 1981– ; Mem., Univ. of Calgary Senate 1989–92; Dir., Calgary Airport Authority 1990– ; Dir., Nascor System 1988–92; Bd. Mem., Westronic Inc. 1991–92; Past Dir., Teknica Resource Development Ltd.; Nu-West Group Ltd.; SED Systems Inc.; Designex Building Ltd.; Premier's Council on Science and Technology; Subctte. on National Strategies on Science and Tech. 1990–91; Mem. Bd., Extve. Ctte. & Adv. Ctte., INTERMAN 1984– ; Devel. Engr., DuPont of Canada 1962–64, New Venture Analyst 1965–67; Teaching Asst., Sir George Williams Univ. 1966–67; Rsch. Engr., Dept. of Industrial Engr. & Management Sci., Northwestern Univ. 1968–76; Prof. and Research Coordinator, Faculty of Business Adm. & Comm. Univ. of Alta. 1970–76; Dean and Prof. of Adm. Coll. of Comm. Univ. of Sask. 1976–81; mem., Faculty Supply Ctte., Am. Assembly of Collegiate Schools of Business 1986–90, Continuing Accreditation Ctte. 1989–92; Candn. Fed. of Deans of Management and Administrative Studies: Vice-Chrmn. 1981–82, Chrmn. 1982–84, Repr. to INTERMAN (Internat. Labour Office, United Nations) 1985– , Secy. Treas. 1990– , Chrmn. Candn. Consortium of Management Schools 1990– ; Mem. of Corp., St. Thomas More Coll., Sask. 1983– ; Dir., Banff Sch. of Advanced Mang. 1976–84, 1990– (Chrmn. Acad. Council 1977–79, 1992– ); Dir., Banff Mountain Academy 1990– ; Mem. Selection Ctte. for Chair in the Management of Technological change, SSHRC/NSERC 1990– ; mem. Bd. of Dir., Canadian Chamber of Commerce 1984–85; Calgary Chamber of Commerce, 1982–86; Calgary Economic Development Authority 1983–90; mem., Small Business Consultative Ctte., Dept. of Trade & Commerce (Govt. of Can.) 1982–83; mem., Bd. of Dirs., Saskatoon Bd. of Trade 1977–81; Sr, Bd. Mem., Junior Achievement of Saskatoon 1979–81; mem., National Research Council of Canada 1981–86; consultant various business and govt. organizations; author or co-author numerous papers, monographs; Cabinet mem., The United Way of Calgary 1989–90; Chrmn., The United Way of Calgary Education Div. 1989–90; Mem. Bd. of Trustees, CNIB White Cane Found. 1989– ; Office: Scurfield Hall SH 339, 2500 University Dr. N.W., Calgary, Alta. T2N 1N4.

**MAHEUX-FORCIER, Louise;** C.M.; écrivain, née Montréal, Qué. 9 juin 1929; f. Louis-Alfred et Cécile (Giguère) Maheux; é. Diplôme cours Lettres-Sciences, Ecole Supérieure Sainte-Croix et Conservatoire de Musique et d'Art Dramatique de la P.Q. et Académie de Musique de Québec; Bourse du Gouvernement de la P.Q. pour séjour de deux ans au Conservatoire de Paris, époux Marcel Forcier, 8 Oct. 1955; auteur 'Amadou' (roman) 1963; 'L'Ile joyeuse' (roman) 1965; 'Triptyque' (nouvelle) 1965; 'Une forêt pour Zoé' (roman) 1969; 'Paroles et Musiques' (roman) 1973; 'Neige et Palmiers' et 'Le Violoncelle' (pièces en un acte) 1974; 'Un Arbre Chargé d'Oiseaux,' (téléfilm) 1976; 'Le Coeur Étoilé,' (téléfilm); 'Chrysanthème de Miroir de Nuit,' (textes-radio) 1977; 'Appassionata' (roman) 1978; 'En Toutes Lettres,' (nouvelles) 1980; 'Arioso' (teléfilm) 1981; 'Un Parc en Automne' (théâtre) 1982; 'Le Sablier' (journal intime) 1984; articles: La Presse, Le Devoir; Prix du Cercle du Livre de France, 1963; radio-diffusions: 'Neige et Palmiers' août 1970; 'Le Violoncelle' août 1973; 'Un ecrivain et son pays: Louise Maheux-Forcier et Huberdeau' 1975; 'Du monde entier au coeur du monde: La Grèce' 1975; 'Miroir de Nuit,' juin 1976; 'Chrysanthème' novembre 1976; 'Le papier d'Arménie,' 1979; 'Comme un oiseau,' 1980; 'Un Parc en Automne,' 1981; 'Auteurs de Notre Temps' (11 portraits d'écrivains) 1981–85; 'Préface pour la Radio' 1985; 'Eloge de l'Arbre' 1985; 'Eloge du Lit' 1985; téléthéâtre: 'Un arbre chargé d'oiseaux' mai 1975; 'Le Manuscrit (Le Coeur Étoilé)' 1977; 'Arioso,' 1980; 'Le piano rouge,' 1985; radio-diffusions et publication: 'Un Jardin Défendu' suivi de 'A la Brunante' 1988; attaché au CRCCF (Univ. d'Ottawa) 1972–73; écrivain résident l'Univ. d'Ottawa 1974; Prix du Cercle du Livre de France; Prix du Gouverneur Général, Canada, 1970; Bourse de travail libre du Conseil des Arts du Can. 1971; SOCAN, Soc. des Ecrivains; Membre du jury du Prix 'Jean Béraud' (Cercle du Livre de France); mem. du jury Canado-Belge; mem. du jury au Concours d'Oeuvres dramatiques de Radio-Canada; mem. de l'Académie canadienne-française; mem. de la Société Royale du Canada; mem. de l'Ordre du Canada; Adresse: 3450 Drummond #622, Montreal, Qué. H3G 1Y2.

**MAHLER, Richard T.,** B.Sc., M.B.A.; financial executive; b. Galt, Ont. 15 May 1943; s. Lawrence Herman and Therese Blanche (Trepanier) M.; e. Univ. of Waterloo B.Sc. 1966; McMaster Univ. M.B.A. 1976; m. Susan d. Peter and Jean Campbell 25 May 1968; children: Stephen, Katherine; VICE-PRESIDENT & CHIEF FINANCIAL OFFICER, FINNING LTD. 1990– ; various financial management positions, Ford Motor Co. & General Motors of Canada Ltd. prior to 1981; Vice-Pres. Finance & Chief Financial Offr., Amdahl Canada Ltd. 1981–90; Dir., Nat. Ballet School; Past Pres., Univ. of Waterloo Adv. Council; Chrmn., Simon Fraser Univ., Co-op Council; Mem., Conference Bd. Council of Financial Executives; Financial Executives Inst.; The Canadian Club of Vancouver; recreations: skiing, golf, boating, running; clubs: Hollyburn Country; Vancouver Lawn Tennis, Seymour Golf; Home: 4485 Piccadilly North, West Vancouver, B.C. V7W 1C8; Office: 555 Great Northern Way, Vancouver, B.C. V5T 1E2.

**MAHONEY, Hon. John William;** justice; b. St. John's, Nfld. 28 Dec. 1926; s. the late Thomas Gregory and Anne Victoria (O'Toole) M.; e. R.C. Acad. Conception Harbour, Nfld.; St. Bonaventure's Coll. St. John's; Mem. Univ. Coll.; m. Carmel J. d. late Denis and Katherine Galway 8 Sept. 1951; children: Karen, Erin, Lynn, Thomas, Denis, John; JUSTICE, COURT OF APPEAL, SUPREME COURT OF NFLD. 1982– ; called to Bar of Nfld. 1951; cr. Q.C. 1963; private law practice 1951–53; Crown Counsel Dept. of Justice Nfld. 1953–66; Partner, Curtis, Dawe, Fagan, Mahoney, Russell & Bonnell 1966–75; Judge, Supreme Court of Nfld Trial Div. 1975; Hon. Life mem., Benevolent Irish Soc.; R. Catholic; recreations: driving, reading; Home: 7 Somerset Pl., St. John's, Nfld. A1B 2G4; Office: Court of Appeal, Duckworth St., St. John's, Nfld. A1C 5M3.

**MAHONEY, Kathleen Elizabeth,** LL.M.; educator; barrister & solicitor; b. Trail, B.C. 23 Sept. 1947; d. Daniel Gerald and Patricia Margaret (Comerford) McGauley; e. Univ. of B.C., LL.B. 1976; Cambridge Univ., LL.M. 1979; Diploma, Strasbourg Inst. on Internat. Comparative Human Rights Law 1987; m. Bryan s. Gerald and Rita Mahoney 12 Sept. 1967; children: Bryan Jr., Meghan, Brendan, Tara, Conor; PROF. OF LAW, UNIV. OF CALGARY 1991– ; Sir Allan Sewell Visiting Fellow, Griffith Univ., Brisbane 1994; Distinguished Visiting Scholar, Univ. of Adelaide 1992; articled Ray, Wolfe & Co. Vancouver 1976–77; Asst. Prof. of Law present Univ. 1979–82, Assoc. Prof. of Law 1982–91; Founding Dir. and mem., Nat. Legal Ctte., Legal Edn. & Action Fund Can. 1984; Dir., Candn. Human Rights Found.; Calgary Civil Liberties Assn. 1981–85; Founding mem. Study Team Est. Candn. Inst. Law & the Family 1983–85; Dir. Nat. Congf. Women, the Law & the Econ. 1983; co-Dir. Nat. Conf. Judicial Neutrality 1986; Dir., Internat. Conf. 'Human Rights in the 21st Century: A Global Challenge' 1990; Founding Dir. & Chair Alta. Coalition Against Pornography 1983–86; mem., Ed. Bd., 'Canadian Women and the Law Journal'; mem., Ed. Bd., 'The National Journal of Constitutional Law'; recipient YWCA Woman of Yr. Award (Edn.) 1985; Independent Assessory Employment Equity Program, Employment & Immigration Canada; Chair, Human Rights Group for Rsch. & Education in Human Rights, Univ. of Calgary; Dir., Internat. Project to Promote Fairness in Judicial Processes; Mem., Mayor's Special Task Force on Urban and Family Violence, Calgary, Alta.; Academic Observer, Canadian Delegation Human Rights Commission, U.N. Geneva; Mem., 'Group of 22'; author: 'Daycare and 'Equality in Canada' Royal Comn. Report 1984; co-author 'Broadcasting and the Canadian Charter of Rights and Freedoms – Justifications for Limiting Freedom of Expression' comnd. report 1986; 'An Evaluation of Canada's International Obligations in Women's Employment Rights' comnd. report 1988; co-ed. 'Women, the Law and the Economy' 1985; 'Equality and Judicial Neutrality' 1987; 'Human Rights in the Twenty-First Century: A Global Challenge' 1993; 'Gender Bias in Judicial Decisions: International Strategies for Reforms'; mem. Alberta Bar 1989; numerous articles legal and other jours.; recreations: skiing, travel, reading, scuba diving, triathlon; Home: RR4, Site 33 Box 55, Calgary, Alta. T2M 4L4; Office: F5 Bio Sciences Bldg., Calgary, Alta. T2N 1N4.

**MAHONEY, Hon. Patrick Morgan,** P.C., Q.C., B.A., LL.B.; b. Winnipeg, Man., 20 Jan. 1929; s. Paul Morgan and Joan Ethel Tracy (Patrick) M.; e. Pub. and High Schs., Alta.; Mount Royal Coll., Calgary; Univ. of Alta., B.A. 1950, LL.B. 1951; m. Mary Alma, d. late George Homer Sneath, 28 June 1958; children: Michael George, Patrick Murray, Sheila Mary, D'Arcy Carole; called to Bar of Alta. 1952; cr. Q.C. 1972; JUDGE, FEDERAL COURT OF APPEAL since 1983; Judge, Federal Court, Trial Div., 1973; Chief Justice, Court Martial Appeal Court of Can., 1982; el. to H. of C. for Calgary S. in g.e. 1968; apptd. Parlty. Secy. to Min. of Finance 1970; Min. State 1972; Past Pres., Stampeder Football Club. Ltd.; Western Football Conf.; Candn. Football League; Senator, Univ. of Calgary (1966–72); Address: 3 Coltrin Place, Ottawa, Ont. K1M 0A5.

**MAIER, Gerald James,** B.Sc., P.Eng.; petroleum executive; b. Regina, Sask. 22 Sept. 1928; e. Notre Dame Coll, (Wilcox); Univ. of Man.; Univ. of Alta. B.Sc. (Petroleum Engn.) 1951; Univ. of W. Ont. Mang. Training 1969; m. Mary Isobel d. late Donald Byron Grant; CHRMN. & CHIEF EXTVE. OFFR., TRANSCANADA PIPELINES 1992– ; Petroleum Engr. Sun Oil Co. 1951–52 and Cactus Engineering Ltd. 1952–53; Chrmn. & Dir., Western Gas Marketing Ltd.; joined Hudson's Bay Oil & Gas Co. Ltd. 1953 as Petroleum Engr.; worked through various positions and three transfers to affiliates in the U.S.A., Australia and the United Kingdom before returning to Hudson's Bay Oil & Gas as Sr. Vice Pres. 1975; Extve. Vice Pres. 1977–80; Chrmn. & C.E.O., 1980–81, Chrmn. 1982; Pres. & C.E.O., Bow Valley Industries Ltd., 1982–85; Pres. & C.E.O., TransCanada PipLines 1985 and apptd. Chrmn. of the Bd. 1992; Dir., BCE Inc.; Bank of Nova Scotia; Du Pont Canada Inc.; Great Lakes Gas Transmission Company; TransAlta Corp.; Alberta Natural Gas Co. Ltd.; Hon. life mem., Assn. Prof. Engrs., Geols. & Geophysicists Alta. (Pres. 1978–79); recipient, Candn. Council of Professional Engineers Gold Medal Award 1990; Alberta Chamber of Resources 'Resource Man of the Year' Award 1990; Univ. of Alberta Distinguished Alumni Award 1992; mem., Cdn. Inst. Mining & Metall. (Past Dist. Chrmn.; rec'd Past Pres. Medal); Soc. Petrol. Engrs.; Chrmn., Candn. National Ctte. for the World Petroleum Congresses; Chrmn., Van Horne Institute; mem. Policy Ctte. of the Business Council on National Issues; Hon. Colonel of the King's Own Calgary Regiment; Clubs: Calgary Golf & Country; Canyon Meadows Golf & Country; Calgary Petroleum; Ranchmen's; Toronto Club; Office: 111 – 5th Ave. S.W., Calgary, Alta. T2P 3Y6.

**MAILHIOT, Gilles-Dominique,** O.P., B.A., S.S.L., S.T.M.; educator; b. Montreal, Que. 27 Sept. 1920; s. Adhémar and Virginie (Carey) M.; e. Ecole Notre-Dame de Grâce Montréal 1932; Coll. de Montréal et Séminaire de Philosophie B.A. 1941; Coll. Dominicain de Philosophie et de Théologie L.Th. 1950; Rome and Ecole biblique et arch. fr. de Jérusalem, S.S.L. 1955; Order of Friar Preachers, Rome S.T.M. 1965; PROF. OF HOLY SCRIPTURES, COLL. DOMINICAIN DE PHILOSO-

PHIE ET DE THEOLOGIE 1950–52, 1955– , Pres. and Regent of Studies 1960–88, Pres. of Coll. 1967–88; author various articles scient. journs.; Office: 96 Empress Ave., Ottawa, Ont. K1R 7G3.

**MAILLARD, Keith Lee;** author; b. Wheeling, W. Va. 28 Feb. 1942; s. Eugene Charles and Aileen (Sharp) M.; e. Linsly Mil. Inst. Wheeling, W. Va. 1960; W. Va. Univ. 1960–63; Vancouver (B.C.) Community Coll. Dept. Music 1975–77; m. Mary Jane Ward Skinner 1988; daughters: Elizabeth Alena, Mary Jane O'Grady (adopted); ASST. PROF., DEPT. OF CREATIVE WRITING, UNIV. OF B.C. 1989– ; author novels 'Two Strand River' 1976; 'Alex Driving South' 1980; 'The Knife in My Hands' 1981; 'Cutting Through' 1982; 'Motet' (winner, Ethel Wilson Fiction Prize 1990) 1989; 'Light in the Company of Women' 1993; contrib. to 'Instead of Revolution' 1971 (essays) and other publs.; Asst. Copy Ed. Porter Sargent Publisher, Boston 1968–69; writer and producer (pub. affairs) WBUR Boston 1969–70; free-lance writer CBC Radio (This Country in the Morning, Our Native Land, Five Nights) 1973–75, and (State of the Arts, Airwaves, Ideas) 1985–91; course designer, The Open Learning Inst., B.C. 1985–89; Teacher, novel writing The Literary Storefront 1979–80; lyric writing, screen writing, fiction, and poetry, Dept. Creative Writing, Univ. of B.C. 1984–86, 1988–89; and fiction Continuing Educ., Univ. of B.C. 1985; Screen writing Film Program, Centre for the Arts, Simon Fraser Univ. 1988–89; Recorder teacher Continuing Educ. Services Vancouver Community Coll. and Vancouver Sch. Bd. 1976–82; guest lectr. on publishing and copyright Capilano Coll. and Univ. of B.C., on 'magic realism' in fiction Univ. of Waterloo; rec'd Can. Council Grants 1974, 1982; writer and editor on 'The Riverside Anthology of Children's Literature,' Judith Saltman, ed. 1983–84; free-lance photographer 1983–89; Asst. Prof., Dept. of Creative Writing U.B.C. 1989– ; Address: c/o The Dept. of Creative Writing, Buchanan E-462, 1866 Main Mall, Univ. of B.C., Vancouver, B.C. V6T 1W5.

**MAILLET, Andrée,** O.C., G.O.Q.; author, journalist; b. Montreal, Que. 7 June 1921; d. Roger and Corinne (Dupuis), C.M., M.; e. private schools; post graduate studies N.Y. & Paris; m. Dr. L. Hamlyn Hobden 31 Dec. 1947; children: Roger, Alexandra, Christian (all M.D.s); Andrée Maillet published her first articles at age 11; Correspondent in Paris 1947–51 & Mem., Anglo-Am. Press Assn.; Journalist, Editorialist in Montreal ('Petit Journal,' 'Photo Journal'); Dir., 'Amérique Française'; recognized as the 'Dean of French-Canadian Letters'; Officer, Order of Canada 1978; 'A' Award, Canadian Arts Council; Prix David 1990 (at which time it was officially stated that Andrée Maillet marks the beginning of modern lit. in French Canada); Grand Officier, Order of Quebec 1991; Woman of the Year, Canadian Press 1967, Salon de la Femme 1975; Hon. Mem., PEN Internat.; Hon. Mem., Soc. des Ecrivains Canadiens; author: 'La Marquiset têtu' 1965, (Portuguese ed. 1972); 'Le Chêne des Tempêtes' 1965 (1st prize, Prov. of Que.), 'Ristontac' 1945, 'Storm Oak' 1972 (children's stories); 'Profil de L'orignal' 1953, '74, '90, 'Les Remparts de Québec' 1965, '77, '89, 'Le Bois-pourri' 1971, 'Le Doux Mal' 1972, '91, 'A la Mémoire d'un Héros' 1976, 'Lettres au Surhomme' 1976, '90, 'Miroir de Salomé' 1977, '90 (novels); 'Elémentaires' 1964, 'Le Paradigme de l'Idole' 1964, 'Le Chant de l'Iroquoise' 1967 (poetry); 'Les Montréalais' 1963, '87, 'Le Lendemain n'est pas sans amour' 1963, 'Nouvelles Montréalaises' 1966, 'Le Bois de Renards' 1967, 'Belle Gersende et l'Habitant' 1972 (short stories); theatre (live, radio & TV): 'Souvenirs en Accords Brisés' 1969, 'La Perdrière' 1971 (Radio Canada, TV), 'La Dépendance' 1973, 'Le Doux Mal' 1972, 'Belle Gersende et l'Habitant' (Radio-Canada, radio), 'Le Meurtre d'Igouille' (live, Québec) 1965, 'La Montréalaise' 1967; also innumerable articles; translated into Portuguese, Welsh, Slovak, Danish; Publisher, 'Amérique Française'; weekly column, 'Le Devoir'; Home: 28 Arlington Ave., Westmount, Que. H3Y 2W4.

**MAILLET, Antonine,** C.C., M.A., D.ès L., D.Litt., LL.D.; évrivain; née Bouctouche, N.B. 10 mai 1929; f. Léonide et Virginie (Cormier) M.; é. Coll. Notre-Dame d'Acadie, Moncton, B.A. 1950; Univ. de Moncton M.A. 1959, D.ès L. 1972; Univ. de Montréal L.ès L. 1962; Univ. Laval D.ès L. 1970; St. Mary's Univ., Halifax D.ès. L. 1980; Univ. of Windsor 1980; Acadia Univ. 1980; Univ. Laurentienne 1981; McGill Univ. D.Litt. 1982; Carleton Univ. 1978; Mt. Allison Univ. 1979; Univ. of Alta. LL.D. 1979; Dalhousie Univ. 1981; Univ. of Toronto 1982; Queen's Univ. 1982; St. Francis-Xavier Univ. 1984; St-Thomas Univ., Fredericton 1986; Univ. Ste-Anne N.E. 1987; Mount St-Vincent Univ., Halifax 1987; Recherches à Paris 1963–64, 1969–70; enseignement: Coll. Notre-Dame d'Acadie Moncton 1954–60; Univ. de Moncton 1965–67; Coll. des Jésuites Québec 1968–69; Univ. Laval 1971–74; Univ. de Montréal 1974–75; Prof. invité à l'Uni. de Berkeley 1983, SUNY-Albany 1985; publications: 'Pointe-aux-Coques' (novel) 1958, 1972; 'On a mangé la dune' 1962, 1977; 'Les Crasseux' (play) 1968, 1973 and new version 1974; 'La Sagouine' (monologues) 1971, 1973, 1974, 1976, 1986, English transl. 1979; 'Rabelais et les traditions populaires en Acadie' (doctoral thesis) 1971–80; 'Don l'orignal' (novel) 1972, English transl. 1978; 'Par derrière chez mon père' (tales) 1972; 'L'Acadie pour quasiment rien' (humoristic tourish guide) 1973; 'Mariaagélas' (novel) 1973, 1975, English transl. 1986; 'Gapi et Sullivan' (play) 1973, English transl. 1987; 'Emmanuel à Joseph à Dâvit' (novel) 1975; 'Evangeline Deusse' (play) 1975, English transl. 1987; 'Gapi' (play) 1976; 'Les Cordes-de-Bois' (novel) 1977; 'La Veuve enragée' (play) 1977; 'Le Bourgeois gentleman' (play) 1978; 'Pélagie-la-Charrette' 1979, English transl. 1982 and Slavic, Bulgarian and Romanian transl.; 'La Contrebandière' (play) 1981; 'Christophe Cartier de la Noisette dit Nounours' (children's story) 1981, English transl. 1984; 'Cent ans dans les bois' (novel) 1981; 'La Gribouille' (novel) 1982; 'Les drolatiques, horrifiques et épouvantables aventures de Panurge, ami de Pantagruel' (play) 1983; 'Crache-à-Pic' (novel) 1984; 'The Devil is loose' (English transl.) 1986; 'Le Huitième Jour' (novel) 1986, 1987, English transl. 1989; 'Garrochés en Paradis' (play) 1986; 'Margot la Folle' (play) 1987; 'Richard III' from Shakespeare (french translation) 1989; 'L'Oursiade' (novel) 1990, 1991; 'William S' (play) 1991; 'La Nuit des Rois' from Shakespeare (french translation) (play) 1993; 'Les Confessions de Jeanne de Valois' (novel) 1992, 1993; prix: Prix Champlain 1960; Prix de la meilleure pièce canadienne présentée au Festival de théâtre 1958; Prix du Conseil des Arts 1960; Prix du Gouverneur Gén. 1972; Grand Prix de la ville de Montréal 1973; Prix des Volcans (France) 1975; Prix France Can. 1975; Prix Littéraire de la Presse 1976; Prix des Quatre Jurys 1978; Prix Goncourt 1979; Chalmers Candn. Play Award 1980; Prix de la traduction pour 'La Nuit des Rois' décerné par l'assn. des critiques de théâtre 1992–93; bourses: Bourse du Conseil des Arts du Can. pour études à Montréal 1962–63, à Paris 1963–64, Bourse de travail aux écrivains 1974–75, Bourse de travail libre 1977; Subvention du Ministère des Affaires Culturelles du Qué. 1972–73; titres: O.C. 1976, C.C. 1982; Officier des Palmes académiques françaises 1980; Chevalier de l'Ordre de la Pléiade Frédéricton; Gloire de l'Escolle Univ. Laval 1981; Companion, Order of Canada 1982; Officier des Arts et des Lettres de France 1985; Grand Montréalais 1991; Chancellor, Moncton Univ. 1989; Officier, de l'ordre Nat. du Qué. 1990; Commandeur de l'ordre du mérite cultural de Monaco 1993; Guest of Michener Foundation, Queen's Univ. 1991; mem., Assn. des Ecrivains de Langue française; Soc. des Auteurs et Compositeurs Dramatiques de France; Soc. des Gens de Lettres de France; Soc. Royale du Can.; Académie canadienne-française; Ordre des francophones d'Amérique 1984; Membre du Haut Conseil de la francophonie 1987; Membre du Conseil Littéraire de la Fondation Prince Pierre de Monaco; Professeur associé d'Etudes françaises de l'Université de Moncton; membre du P.E.N. 1988; Chancelor, Moncton Univ. 1989; mem., Queen's Privy Council for Canada; Conseil des gouverneurs associés de l'Univ. de Montréal 1993; récréations: tennis, natation; Résidence: 735 Antonine Maillet Ave. Montreal, Qué. H2V 2Y4; Bureau: 355 rue Gilford, Montréal, Qué. H2T 1M6.

**MAILLOUX, Rev. Noel,** O.C. (1967), B.A., Ph.D., S,Th.L., F.R.S.C. (R.C.); psychologist; b. Napierville, P.Q. 25 Dec. 1909; e. Coll. Sainte-Marie, Montreal, P.Q., B.A. 1930; Angelicum, Rome, Ph.D. (Philos. and Psychol.) 1934 and S.Th.L. 1938; o. Priest 1937; Research Fellow, Univ. of Cincinnati, 1939; Prof. of Psychol. of Personality, l'Ecole Normale Secondaire, and mem. of the Council of the Sch. 1941–75; Dir., Centre of Research on Human Relations, Montreal; Director-Founder of Dept. of Psychol. and Prof. of Abnormal Psychol., Univ. of Montreal, 1942–75; Prof. Emeritus 1975; Prof. of Psychol., Coll. of Philos. and Theol., Dominican Order, Ottawa, 1938–41; author of 'Scientific Methods in Education' (4 vols.); numerous contrib. on psychol. and educ. subjects to journs.; Chief Ed., 'Contributions à l'Etude des Sciences de l'Homme'; Pres., Candn. Soc. of Criminology 1962–65; Pres., Candn. Psychol. Assn., 1954–55 (Hon. Life Fellow); mem. of Extve. Internat. Union of Scient. Psychology; mem. Am. Assn. for Advanc. of Science;Am. Assn. on Mental Deficiency (Fellow); Am. Psychol. Assn. (Fellow); Psychol. Assn. of Que. (Pres. 1945–46); Assoc. mem., La Soc. française de psychol.; Address: 2715 côte Sainte-Catherine, Montreal, Que. H3T 1B6.

**MAILLOUX, Terrance A.;** pharmaceutical executive; b. Montréal, Qué. 9 Apl. 1936; s. Alfred James and Gladys May (Jackson) M.; e. McGill Univ.; Dartmouth Coll.; Duke Univ.; children: Mark, Donna, Todd; VICE-PRES., PRO-PHARMA CONTRACT SELLING INC.; Pres., Mailloux Assocs. Reg'd.; Mem. of the Bd., Theratechnologies Inc. 1994– ; Inspiraplex Respiratory Center of Excellance 1993– ; Sales Rep. Witco Chem. 1956–60; Sales Rep. Hoechst Pharmaceuticals 1960, Sales Coordinator 1963, Mgr. Ind./Instl. Sales 1965, Sales Adm. Mgr. 1966, Extve. Asst. to Gen. Mgr. 1967, Mktg. Mgr. & Dep. Gen. Mgr. 1968, Gen. Mgr. Pharm. Dept. 1971–73; Corporate Vice Pres. & Gen. Mgr. Hoechst Canada 1973, Corporate Vice Pres. Govt. Relations 1984–85; Pres. and C.E.O., Pacific Pharmaceuticals and Br. Centre Ltd. 1985–87; C.E.O., Independent Scintillation Imaging Systems (ISIS) Inc. 1989–93; Pres., Internat. Diagnostics Ltd., Fla. 1989–93; Pres. Candn. Found. Advanc. Pharm. 1982; Chrmn. Candn. Found. Advanc. Clin. Pharmacol. 1980–83; Dir. Roussel Canada Ltd. 1979–86; Trustee, Terry Fox Med. Rsch. Found. 1985–87; Hon. Dir. Les Ballets Jazz de Montréal; mem. Pharm. Mfrs. Assn. Can. (Dir. 1973–78, 1979–83, 1985–87; Chrmn. 1976–77, 1981–82); Candn. Inst. Mgmt.; Soc. Chem. Ind.; Vancouver Bd. Trade; mem. Bd. Govs. Biotechnology Rsch. Inst. NRC; Founding mem. Candn. Ind. Biotechnol. Assn.; recreations: golf, tennis, racquetball; Clubs: Shaughnessy Golf & Country; Royal Montreal Golf; Home: 3274 Chevremont, Ile Bizard, Que. H9C 2A5.

**MAILVAGANAM, Noel Paul,** M.Sc.; construction materials scientist; b. Colombo, Sri-Lanka 30 June 1938; s. Joseph Arulappa and Josephine Lilian (Johnpulle) M.; e. Univ. of London B.Sc. (Chem) 1970; Polytechnic of North London M.Sc. (Inorganic Macromolecules) 1974; m. Nalini d. Alfred Ayathurai Ramanathan 20 Nov. 1964; children: Stefan R. N., Dimitri A.; HEAD POLYMER GROUP MATERIALS LABORATORIES, INST. FOR RSCH. IN CONSTRUCTION 1988– ; Chem. Research Tech. Polytechnic of Central London 1964–68; Research Chem. Charcon Tunnels Ltd. Ashford, Eng. 1969–73; Devel. Chem. Shell Composites Ltd. Uxbridge, Eng. 1973–75; Sr. Chem. Sternson Ltd. 1975–76, Mgr. Cement Products Div. 1976, Dir. Research & Devel. 1978; Vice-Pres. Research & Devel., 1983–87; Technical Dir., Master Builders Inc. Canada 1987–88; Secy. Comte. T-85 RILEM; Consultant: Connex Inc., Skokie, Ill.; Mascen Ltd. Toronto, Ont.; DEVS Pty, N.S.W. Australia; course Dir., 'Chemical Admixtures For Concrete' The Centre For Professional Advancement, NJ U.S.A.; co-author: 'Handbook on Chemical Admixtures' 1984; 'Chemical Admixtures for Concrete'; 2nd ed. 1984; 'New Developments in Admixtures' in Progress in Concrete Tech. Book 1992; author various articles on concrete in learned journals; editor 'Repair & Restoration of Concrete Structures' 1991; 'Handbook of Structural Grouts' forthcoming; reviewer for Canadian Jour. of Civil Eng., Jour. of American Concrete Inst., American Civil Eng. Jour.; Consulting Ed., Noyes Data Corp.; Consulting Ed. Auerbach Publications; mem. Task Force on Superplasticiser 1980– ; mem. Candn. Standards Assn. (Chrmn. various comtes.); Mem. Steering Ctte. on Solid Waste Managment; Am. Soc. Testing & Materials; Am. Concrete Inst.; Am. Ceramic Soc.; Review Comte. 1984, Nat. Research Council; RILEM Comte. on Hot Weather Concrete; RILEM Comte. on Repair of Reinforced Concrete Structures; Consultant, Intaco Group of Companies, Costa Rica, Puerto Rico, Equador; Inst. for Research in Construction best publication award 1989 & 1993; Candn. Standards Certificate of recognition for contribution to standards development; recreations: classical music, gardening; Office: National Research Counc., Ottawa, Ont. K1A 0R6.

**MAIN, Douglas Cameron;** b. Willow Bunch, Sask. 18 July 1946; s. Claude Bruce and Lillian Marie (Bellefleur) M.; e. Churchill High Sch. Winnipeg; Univ. of Winnipeg (Sci.); Athabasca Univ. (Adm.); m. Judith d. Joshua and Therese Sumner 25 Apl. 1970; two s. Joshua David, Jeremy Scott; Min. of Culture and Multiculturalism Alta. 1989; Broadcaster, Producer, Writer CITV News Edmonton 1975–88; Instr. in Journalism Grant MacEwan Community Coll. 1985–89; Vice Pres. CJIL Broadcasting Ltd. 1980–82; Pres. Adonai Productions Ltd. 1980–81; Extve. Producer Randy Lennon Productions Edmonton 1988–89; el. M.L.A. prov. g.e. 1989; Reform Party of Can. Cand. for Edmonton-Strathcona fed. g.e. 1988; recreations: golf, squash, tennis; Club: Royal Glenora; Home: 1511 Bearspaw Dr. E., Edmonton, Alta. T6J 5E2.

**MAIN, James Hamilton Prentice,** B.D.S., Ph.D., F.D.S.R.C.S. Edin., F.R.C.D.C., F.R.C. Path.; dentist; b. Biggar, Scot. 7 June 1933; s. George Prentice and Helen Hamilton (Stark) M.; e. Biggar (Scot.) High Sch., 1938–

50; Univ. of Edinburgh, B.D.S. 1955, Ph.D. 1964 (Carnegie Research Fellow 1960–61); Northwestern Univ., 1955–56 (King George VI Mem. Fellow); m. Patricia Ann, d. Robert Logan Robertson, London, Eng., 28 July 1961; children: Fiona Gillian, George Ian Prentice; HEAD, DEPARTMENT OF DENTISTRY, SUNNYBROOK MEDICAL CENTRE, 1971– , and Professor and Head of Oral Pathol., University of Toronto 1969– ; Pres., Roy. Coll. of Dentists (Can.) 1981–83; House Surg., Edinburgh Dental Hosp. 1956–57; Lectr. in Dental Surg. and Pathol., Univ. of Edinburgh, 1961–64; Internat. Research Fellow, Nat. Insts. of Health, Bethesda, Md. 1964–65; Sr. Lectr. and Consultant to S.E. Scot. Hosps. in Dental Surg. and Pathol. 1966–69; served with RAF, NATO HQ, Fontainebleau, France, 1957–60; rank Flight Lt.; rec'd Colgate Prize for Dental Research, 1966; Clark Prize for Cancer Research, 1968; author numerous scient. and prof. articles in various journs. and books; mem. Candn. Dental Assn.; Candn. Acad. Oral Pathol. (Pres. 1974–75); Am. Acad. Oral Pathol.; Internat. Assoc. of Oral Pathology (Secy. 1976–86, Pres. 1988–90); Presbyterian Church; recreations: golf, farming, reading; Home: 85 Dawlish Ave., Toronto, Ont. M4N 1H2; Office: 124 Edward St., Toronto, Ont. M5G 1G6.

**MAIN, Lorne Gordon,** B.A.; industrial executive; b. Smiths Falls, Ont., 4 April 1918; s. Halmer Judson and May Belle (Peachey) M.; e. Univ. of Man., B.A. 1941; m. Margaret Ruth, d. late Frank Wallar, 14 October 1944; three d.: Barbara Rasmussen, Shirley Domelle, Lorene Bodiam; Senior Marketing Consultant, after retirement from Urban Transportation Development Corporation; Sales Rep., Canadian Industries Ltd., 1946–47; Vice President, Northern Shirt Co., Winnipeg, 1948–51; Gen. Sales Mgr., Candn. Cottons Ltd., Montreal, 1952–57; Joined Hawker Siddeley Canada Ltd. as Coordinator of Merchandising, 1957–60; apptd. Product Devel. Mgr. 1960–63; Asst. Gen. Sales Mgr., Rly. Equipment, 1963–64; Gen. Sales Mgr., 1964–66; Vice-Pres., Exports, Dominion Steel & Coal Corp., 1966; Dir. of Marketing, Hawker-Siddeley Can. Ltd. 1969–74; Vice Pres., Marketing & Sales, and Dir., Export Sales U.T.D.C. 1974–1983; mem., and former Chrmn. Official Bd., Oriole York Mills United Church; Mem. Bd. of Govs., Metro Y.M.C.A.; Mem. Adv. Bd., North York Y.M.C.A.; served with R.C.N., Active Service, 1941–45; with R.C.N. Reserve to 1952; retired with rank Commdr.; Hon. Dir., North West Commercial Travellers Assn.; mem., Bd. Trade Metro. Toronto; Rotary Club of Toronto Eglinton; Phi Kappa Pi; Conservative; Un. Church; recreation: golf; Home: 1555 Finch Ave. E., Apt. 2403, Willowdale, Ont. M2J 4X9.

**MAIN, Oscar Warren,** M.A., Ph.D.; university professor; b. Hamilton, Ont., 10 Aug. 1916; s. Oscar and Rose Alberta M.; e. Delta Coll. Inst., Hamilton, Ont.; McMaster Univ., B.A. 1938; Univ. of Toronto, M.A. 1943, Ph.D. 1953; m. Marion, d. C. M. McConkey, Sudbury, Ont., 29 Dec. 1948; Prof., Fac. Mgmt., Univ. of Toronto 1960, Assoc. Dean (Academic) 1981–85 (Dean of Fac. 1960–71); Instr., Dept. of Pol. Econ., Univ. of Toronto, 1941–43, Lectr., 1945–48; Asst. Prof. of Commerce, Univ. of Sask., 1948–52, Assoc. Prof. 1952–53; Asst. Prof., Inst. of Business Adm., Univ. of Toronto, 1953–56; Assoc. Prof. 1956–59; Prof. since 1959; Prof. Emeritus 1987; served in 2nd World War with R.C.A.F. as Meteorologist, 1943–45; Publications: 'The Canadian Nickel Industry,' 1955; articles on econs. and adm. in various learned journs.; United Church; Home: 18 Lower Village Gate, Toronto, Ont. M5P 3M1.

**MAINGOT, (John Patrick) Joseph,** Q.C., B.Com.; lawyer / consultant; b Ottawa, Ont. 9 Apr. 1931; s. Albert Joseph and Dorothy Glynn (Gallagher) M.; e. Ecole Garneau, St. Patrick's Coll. High Sch. and Lisgar Coll. Inst. Ottawa; Univ. of Ottawa B. Com. 1956; Osgoode Hall Law Sch. grad. 1960; two s. Patrick, Peter; one daughter, Albani; Commissioner, Law Reform Commission of Canada 1982–89; law practice Fort Erie 1960–62; Hewitt, Hewitt & Nesbitt, Ottawa 1962–66; apptd. to staff Law Clk. & Parlty. Counsel, H. of C. 1967 becoming Law Clk. and Parlty. Counsel, H. of C. 1970; cr. Fed. Q.C. 1975; rep. H. of C. at meetings Soc. Clks.-at-the-Table in Commonwealth Parlts. and the Assn. of Secs. Gen. of Inter-Parlty. Union in Canada and abroad; Founding Sec., Assn. Clks.-at-the-Table Can., 1969; Adjunct Prof. of Law (Common Law) Univ. of Ottawa; author 'Parliamentary Privilege in Canada ' 1982, 'Le privilège parlementaire au Canada' 1987; various articles parlty. jours.; mem. Candn. Bar Assn. (Sec. Civil Liberties Sect. 1965–67); Law Soc. Upper Can.; Carleton Co. Law Assn.; St. Vincent de Paul Soc. Ottawa; Frontier Coll.; recreations: hockey, skiing, tennis, reading, cycling; Address: 3911-C Richmond Rd., Nepean, Ont. K2H 8T9.

**MAINGUY, Vice Admiral Daniel Nicholas,** CMM, CD, (Ret'd); Canadian armed forces; b. Victoria, B.C. 2 Dec. 1930; s. Edmond Rollo and Maraquita Frances Cynthia (Nichol) M.; e. Brentwood Coll. B.C.; Royal Roads 1950; m. Susan d. Gordon and Alice Wainwright 9 Jan. 1954; children: Sarah, Barbara, Nicholas; promoted to Midshipman 1950, Lt. 1953, Cdr. 1966, Capt. 1970, Cdre. 1974, Rear Admiral 1976, Vice Admiral 1982; Vice Chief of Defence Staff, Dept. of National Defence 1983–85; qualified Torpedo Anti-Submarine Br. 1956 and as Weapons Specialist 1960; served in variety of ships incl. command HMCS Annapolis 1966–67, rank Cdr. and HMCS Protecteur, rank Capt., served as Dir. of Strategic Plans Dept. Nat. Defence, Dir. Gen. Personnel Offrs., Chief Maritime Doctrine & Operations, Chief of Staff to Commdr.-in-Chief W. Atlantic, Dep. Chief of Defence Staff; Commanded NATO Standing Naval Force Atlantic, rank Commodore; Pres., Triton Strategies Inc. since 1986; Fellow, Royal Candn. Geographical Soc. 1992; Gov. RCGS 1993; Dir., Candn. Battle of Normandy Foundation 1993; recreation: canoeing; Clubs: Rideau; Chesapeake; Home: 66 Acacia Ave., Rockcliffe Park, Ont K1M 0P6.

**MAIR, Alexander;** record industry executive; b. Toronto, Ont. 29 Sept. 1940; s. Donald MacLean and Florence Lillian (Brobyn) M.; e. Harvard Bus. Sch., Owner/pres. Mngt. Course 1990; m. Virginia d. Walter and Hedwig Urbankiewicz 14 Dec. 1968; children: Sebastian, Jennifer; FOUNDER ATTIC MUSIC GROUP 1974– ; Sales & Promotion, Capitol Records 1962–64; Vice-Pres., Promotion, MCA/Canada 1964–68; Gen. Mgr., Early Morning Productions 1968–76; Attic Music Group comprises Attic Records Limited, Attic Music Limited, Attic Productions Limited, Music Consultants Limited; Past Chrmn., Candn. Independent Record Prodn. Assn. (CIRPA); Dir., Soc. of Composers, Authors & Music Pubs. of Canada (SOCAN); Candn. Musical Reproduction Rights Agency (CMRRA); Audio Video Licensing Agency (AVLA); Hon. Gov., Roy Thomson & Massey Halls; Dir., SOCAN Found.; recreations: Tai Chi, skiing; clubs: Baby Point; Office: 102 Atlantic Ave., Toronto, Ont. M6K 1X9.

**MAIR, Robert James,** Q.C.; lawyer; b. Vancouver, B.C. 17 Dec. 1935; s. Robert and Edith (Abrams) M.; e. Univ. of B.C., B.Comm. 1959, LL.B. 1960; Harvard Univ. LL.M. 1961; m. Merren d. Alexander and Lucy McKillop 31 Aug. 1960; children: Jane, Sarah, Geoffrey; LAWSON, LUNDELL, LAWSON & McINTOSH 1962– ; admitted to B.C. Bar 1962; Chrmn. of the Bd., Aetna Trust Co.; Dir., Cloverdale Paint Inc.; Savolite Corp.; Landex Properties Ltd.; CHC Helicopter Corp.; Aetna Life Ins. Co. of Canada; Aetna Casualty & Surety Co. of Canada; apptd. Q.C. 1986; Mem., Bd. of Govs., Crofton House Sch. 1979–84; mem. Law Soc. of B.C.; Candn. Bar Assn.; Candn. Tax Found.; recreations: skiing, golf, tennis; clubs: Shaughnessy Golf & Country; Vancouver; Home: 5716 Newton Wynd, Vancouver, B.C. V6T 1H5; Office: 1600 – 925 W. Georgia St., Vancouver, B.C. V6C 3L2.

**MAITLAND, Ron J.;** b. Vancouver, B.C. 10 Oct. 1946; s. John Douglas and Jeannie Ellis (McIntyre) M.; e. Magee H.S.; Univ. of B.C.; m. Diane Jean Sturdy; children: Sandy, Lindsey, Courtney; PRESIDENT, MAITLAND INSURANCE SERVICE LTD.; recreations: all sports, sailing, tennis, golf; Club: The Royal Vancouver Yacht Club; Home: 2677 Lawson Ave., W. Vancouver, B.C. V7V 2G3.

**MAITLIS, Peter Michael,** B.Sc., Ph.D., D.Sc., FCIC, FRS; university professor; b. 15 Jan. 1933; s. Jacob and Judith Maitlis; e. Univ. of Birmingham, (Eng.), B.Sc. 1953; Univ. of London, Ph.D., 1956, D.Sc. 1971; m. Marion Basco, 19 July 1959; 3 d.; PROF. OF INORGANIC CHEM., Univ. of Sheffield, England, 1972– ; researches in organometallic chem., catalysis and related subjects; author of 'The Organic Chemistry of Palladium,' (Vol. 1, Metal Complexes), (Vol. 2, Catalytic Reactions), 1971; numerous research publications in scientific journals; awarded Steacie Prize in Natural Sciences, 1970; Fellow, Alfred P. Sloan Foundation, 1967–69; Tilden Lecturer of the Chemical Soc., London, 1979; RSC Medal 1981 (London); el. Fellow of the Royal Society 1984; Royal Society Council Service 1991–93; Sir Edward Frankland Lecturer, RSC, 1984; Pres., Dalton Division, RSC (1985–87); Fellow, Royal Soc. of Chem. (London); Am. Chem. Soc.; recreation: swimming, travel, reading; Address: Dept. of Chemistry, Univ. of Sheffield, Sheffield S3 7HF, England.

**MAJOR, André;** écrivain; réalisateur; né à Montréal, Qué. 22 avril 1942; p. d'Arthur et d'Anna (Sharp) M.; m. Ginette Lepage juin 1970; enfants: Eric, Julie; auteur de 'Le Cabochon' roman 1964; 'La Chair de poule' nouvelles 1965; 'Le Vent du diable' roman 1968; 'Félix-Antoine Savard' essai 1968; 'Poèmes pour durer' (1960–69) 1969; 'Histoires de déserteurs' Vol. 1 'L'Epouvantail' 1974, Vol 2 'L'Epidémie' 1975, Vol. 3 'Les Rescapés' 1976 (Prix du Gouverneur général 1977); 'La Folle d'Elvis' nouvelles, 1981; 'L'hiver au coeur' novella 1987; 'Histoires de déserteurs', édition remaniée et augmentée 1991; Prix Belgique-Canada 1991; Prix David 1992; mem. l'Union des écrivains québécois; Home: 10595 Tanguay, Montréal, Qué. H3L 3G9; Office: Radio-Canada, 15e étage, 1400 boul. René-Lévesque, Montréal, Que. H2M 2L2.

**MAJOR, Jean-Louis,** L.Ph., M.A., Ph.D.; éducateur et essayiste littéraire; né Cornwall, Ont. 16 juillet 1937; p. Joseph et Noëlla (Daoust) M.; é. Univ. d'Ottawa B.A., B.Ph. 1959, B.A. (Hon.), L.Ph. 1960, M.A. 1961, Ph.D. 1965; Ecole Pratique des Hautes Etudes, Paris 1968–69; ép. Bibiane p. Rodolphe Landry, St-Isidore, Ont. 4 juin 1960; enfant: Marie-France; DOYEN ASSOCIÉ À LA RECHERCHE, FACULTÉ DES ARTS 1991– et PROFESSEUR TITULAIRE DEPT. DE LETTRES FRANCAISES, UNIV. D'OTTAWA 1971– ; Prof. de philosophie et de latin, Coll. Bruyère d'Ottawa 1960–61; Dépt. de philosophie, Univ. d'Ottawa (chargé de cours) 1961–65, prof. adjoint Dépt. de Lettres françaises 1965, prof. agrégé 1967; Visiting Prof. Univ. of Toronto 1970–71; auteur 'Saint-Exupéry, l'écriture et la pensée' 1968; 'Léone de Jean Cocteau' édition critique 1975; 'Anne Hébert et le miracle de la parole' 1976; 'Radiguet, Cocteau, Les Joues en feu' 1977; 'La littérature française par les textes théoriques: XIX siècle' 1977; 'Paul-Marie Lapointe: la nuit incendiée' 1978; 'Le jeu en étoile' (essais) 1978; 'Entre l'écriture et la parole' 1984; Henriette Dessaulles, 'Journal,' édition critique 1989; Ringuet, 'Trente arpents' édition critique 1991; co-auteur 11 livres; Rédacteur de la chronique 'Autobiographies' dans la revue 'Lettres québécoises' 1978–83; articles sur les littératures française et québécoise dans les revues en France et au Can.; critique littéraire 'Le Droit' 1963–65; co-dir. 'Cahiers d'Inédits'; 'Bibliothèque du Nouveau Monde'; coordonnateur 'Corpus d'Editions Critiques'; président du Academic Adv. Ctte. du Ont. Council on Univ. Affairs 1990–93; mem. de la Société Royale du Can.; Adresse: C.P. 357, St-Isidore, Ont. K0C 2B0; Bureau: Ottawa, Ont. K1N 6N5.

**MAJOR, The Honourable Mr Justice John Charles,** B.Comm., LL.B., Q.C.; justice; b. Mattawa, Ont. 20 Feb. 1931; s. William and Elsie (Thompson) M.; e. Loyola College B.Comm. 1953; Univ. of Toronto LL.B. 1957; m. Helene d. Paul Provencher 8 Aug. 1959; children: Suzan, Peter, Paul, Steven; PUISNE JUDGE OF THE SUPREME COURT OF CANADA 1992– ; JUSTICE OF THE COURT OF APPEAL OF ALBERTA 1991– ; articled to Bennett Jones Verchere 1957; admitted to Bar of Prov. of Alta. 1958; Partner, Bennett Jones Verchere 1966–91; Q.C. 1972; elected Fellow, Am. College of Trial Lawyers 1980; Vice-Chair, Bd. of Dir. & Extve. Mem., Compensation & Human Resources Ctte., PWA Corp. & Canadian Air Lines Internat. Ltd. 1981; Dir., Mem. of Extve. & Audit Cttes., Domtar Inc. 1982; Dir. & Mem., Compensation Ctte., Telus Corp. & A.G.T. 1990; Bd. of Management, Foothills Prov. Gen. Hosp. 1990; Mem., The Candn. Bar Assn.; Candn. Inst. for the Admin. of Justice; The Calgary Bar Assn.; recreations: golf, running; clubs: Calgary Golf & Country Club; Glencoe; Bankers Hall; Ottawa Hunt & Golf Club; Office: 530 – 7th Avenue S.W., Calgary, Alta. T2P 0Y3.

**MAJOR, Kevin Gerald,** B.Sc.; writer; b. Stephenville, Nfld. 12 Sept. 1949; s. Edward and Jessie (Headge) M.; e. Memorial Univ. B.Sc. 1972; m. Anne d. Andrew and Margaret Crawford 3 July 1982; children: Luke, Duncan; taught junior high and high sch. 1972–76; author (novels): 'Hold Fast' 1978 (Can. Counc. Award for Children's Lit.; Book-of-the-Year Award, Candn. Assn. of Children's Librarians; Ruth Schwartz Award; Honours List, Hans Christian Anderson Award); 'Far from Shore' 1980 (Candn. Young Adult Book Award); 'Thirty-Six Exposures' 1984; 'Dear Bruce Springsteen' 1987; 'Blood Red Ochre' 1989; 'Eating Between the Lines' 1991 (Book of the Year for Children Award, Candn. Library Assn. 1991 and Vicky Metcalf Award for body of work 1992); 'Diana: My Autobiography' 1993; mem. Writers' Union of Can.; Anglican; Address: 27 Poplar Ave., St. John's, Nfld. A1B 1C7.

**MAJOR, Leon,** C.M., B.A., LL.D. (Hon.); theatre director; b. Toronto, Ont. 3 Jan. 1933; s. Samuel and Sara (Soboloff) M.; e. Univ. of Toronto B.A. 1955; Dalhousie Univ. LL.D. (Hon.) 1971; m. Judith Ruth d. Robert and Sonia Strand 25 Feb. 1961; children: Joshua Strand, Rebecca, Rachel Sonia, Naomi; INTERIM CHAIR OF MUSIC & PROF. & DIR. OF OPERA, UNIV. OF MARYLAND 1989–91; Founder and First Artistic Dir.,

Neptune Theatre, Halifax 1963; Gen. and Artistic Dir., Toronto Arts Foundation (later Toronto Arts Productions) St. Lawrence Centre Toronto 1970; Dir. productions in opera and drama Can., USA and Europe; Prof. of Theatre, York Univ. 1984–87; Prof. & Dir. of Opera, Univ. of Maryland; mem., Order of Canada 1981; Address: 1751 New Hampshire Ave., N.W., Washington, D.C. 20009; Dept. of Music, Tawes Hall, Univ. of Maryland, College Park, MD, 20742 U.S.A.

**MAJOR-GIRARDIN, Judy,** B.F.A., M.F.A.; university professor, artist; b. Leamington, Ont. 2 March 1957; s. Peter Lawrence and Violete Roseline (Waites) M.; e. Univ. of Windsor B.F.A. 1980; Univ. of Alabama M.F.A. 1983; m. Robert d. Levi and Betty Girardin 18 May 1985; PROFESSOR, DEPT. OF ART & ART HISTORY, MCMASTER UNIV.; selected art exbns.: Staten Island Inst. of Arts & Science; Ariel Gall. N.Y.; World Print Exbn., Taipei Mus. of Fine Arts Taiwan; McMaster Univ. Art Gall.; Burlington Cultural Ctr.; Mississauga Civic Ctr.; Glenhyrst Art Gall. of Brant; Carnegie Gall. Dundas, Ont.; Pauline McGibbon Ctr. Toronto; juried exhbns. throughout Canada & U.S.; Extve. Mem., Art Hazards Resource Assn.; Mem., Acquisitions Ctte., McMaster Art Gall.; Home: 110 Concession St., Cambridge, Ont. N1K 2H3; Office: 330 Togo Salmon Hall, 1280 Main St. W., Hamilton, Ont. L8S 4L8.

**MAKIN, Andrew Julian,** M.A., M.C.I.T., F.R.Ae.S., F.N.Z.I.M., M.Inst.D.; b. London, Eng. 16 Apl. 1942; s. James and Mary (Morris) M.; e. Charterhouse 1959; Gonville & Caius Coll. Cambridge Univ. B.A. 1963, M.A. 1967; m. Maja Brigite Kucera 8 Feb. 1978; one d. Jessica Louise; CHIEF EXTVE. and MANAGING DIRECTOR, CLEAR COMMUNICATIONS LTD. 1993– ; Chief Extve., Airways Corp. of New Zealand 1990–93; Pres., B.C. Automobile Assoc. 1982–87; Past Dir., Sunny Hill Hospital; CMR Ltd.; joined McCann-Erickson Advertising Ltd. London, Eng. 1963–67; Advertising and Promotions Mgr. Europe, British European Airways 1967–72, Sales Mgr. USA 1972–74; Gen. Mgr. Scandinavia, British Airways 1974–78; Gen. Mgr. Can., Br. Airways, 1978–82; Pres., Argo Enterprises Internat. Inc. 1987–89; recreations: books, drama, boating, golf; Office: Auckland, New Zealand.

**MAKOSKY, Lyle Murray,** M.Sc.; federal civil servant; b. Windsor, Ont.; m. Michael and Elsie (Schmidt) M.; e. Univ. of W. Ont. B.Sc. (Physics) 1967; Univ. of B.C., M.Sc. (Nuclear Physics) 1969; Univ. of Toronto Ph.D. (courses completed) (Geophysics) 1971; ASST. DEP. MIN. OF FITNESS AND AMATEUR SPORT 1986– ; Lectr. in Physics Univ. of Toronto 1970–72; Extve. Dir. Nat. Assns. Diving, Synchronized Swimming & Water Polo 1972–75; Nat. Extve. Dir. Coaching Assn. Can. 1975–80, Dir. 1980–86, Chrmn. 1982–86; Vice Pres. The Niagara Inst. 1980–86, Extve. Vice Pres. 1986; Chrmn. NSRC Council Extve. Dirs. 1976–78; Adjunct Prof. Sport Adm. Prog. York Univ. 1982–86; Designer/Co-Dir. Olympic Acad. Can. 1983–86; Vice Pres. Candn. Olympic Assn. 1981–86; recipient Stan C. Reade Prize in Physics 1967; NRC Scholarship 1967; Ont. Grad. Fellowship 1970; author 'The Application of Managerial Roles in Amateur Sport' 1977; Univ. MVP Competitive Swimmer 1964–68; National Water Polo Team Roster 1972, 1973; mem. Candn. Automobile Sport Club; Candn. Amateur Photog. Soc.; recreations: photography, skiing, squash, jogging, cycling; Home: 24 Third Ave., Ottawa, Ont. K1S 2J6; Office: South Tower, Journal Bldg., 365 Laurier Ave. W., Ottawa, Ont. K1A 0X6.

**MALAREK, Victor Gregory;** journalist; b. Lachine, Que. 26 June 1948; s. Michael and Jennie (Yashan) M.; e. Sir George Williams Univ.; m. Anna d. Emilio and Ida Cipriani 11 July 1970; 1 d. Larissa; CO-HOST, THE FIFTH ESTATE, CBC 1990– ; Reporter, Montreal Star 1970–73; Press Aide, Secty. of State 1973–74; Media Relations Offr., Health & Welfare Can. 1974–76; Sr. Reporter, Social Policy Issues, The Globe & Mail 1976– ; rcvd. Michener Award 1985, 1988; author: 'Hey... Malarek: The True Story of a Street Kid' 1984; 'Haven's Gate: Canada's Immigration Fiasco' 1987; 'Merchants of Misery: Inside Canada's Illegal Drug Scene' 1989; 'Malarek' autobiography 1989; feature film, 'Malarek' based on autobiography; recreation: downhill skiing; Office: Box 500, Stn. A., Toronto, Ont. M5W 1E6.

**MALCOLMSON, Robert William,** B.A., M.A., Ph.D.; educator; b. Toronto, Ont. 8 Feb. 1943; s. Kenneth Witchall and Dorothy Jane (Mearns) M.; e. Univ. of Toronto, B.A. 1965; Univ. of Sussex, M.A. 1966; Univ. of Warwick, Ph.D. 1970; m. Patricia E. d. Ross and Eileen Kelly 7 Jan. 1967; one s. Stuart Grant; PROF. OF HIST. QUEEN'S UNIV. 1982– ; Chrmn., History Dept. 1989– ; joined present Univ. 1969; author 'Popular Recreations in English Society 1700–1850' 1973; 'Life and Labour in England 1700–1780' 1981; 'Nuclear Fallacies: How We Have Been Misguided Since Hiroshima' 1985; 'Beyond Nuclear Thinking' 1990; numerous articles; recreations: squash, hiking; Home: 100 Medley Court, No. 23, Kingston, Ont. K7L 5H6; Office: Kingston, Ont. K7L 3N6.

**MALCOLMSON, Samuel Alexander,** M.D., F.R.C.P.(C); psychiatrist; b. St. Catharines, Ont. 15 July 1938; s. Alexander and Eileen (Southcott) M.; e. Ridley Coll.; Univ. of Toronto M.D. 1964; m. Ann d. John and Elizabeth Osler 23 Dec. 1963; children: Sheila, Eric, Claire; PSYCHIATRIST-IN-CHIEF & CLINICAL DIR., QUEEN ST. MENTAL HEALTH CENTRE 1982– ; Staff Psychiatrist, Clark Inst. of Psychiatry 1972; Family Ct. Clinic, Div. of Child Psychiatry, Univ. of Toronto 1974; Dir. of Mental Health, Prov. of P.E.I. 1978; Assoc. Prof., Univ. of Toronto 1980– ; Consultant Psychiatrist to Clark Inst. of Psychiatry and Baffin Zone, N.W.T.; Community Resources Consultants of Toronto 1982–85; recreations: sailing, skiing; Home: 89 Clifton Rd., Toronto, Ont. M4T 2G1; Office: 1001 Queen St. W., Toronto, Ont. M6J 1H4.

**MALENFANT, J.E. Louis,** B.A., B.Ed., M.A.Ps.O., Ph.D.; educator; b. Montreal, Que. 18 Sept. 1941; s. Joseph Joffre and Rita (Bourque) M.; e. Univ. St. Joseph B.A. 1962, B.Ed. 1963; Univ. de Moncton M.A.Ps.O. 1968; Univ. of Kansas Ph.D. (psychol. & human devel.); VICE PRES., HUMAN RESOURCES AND STUDENT AFFAIRS UNIV. DE MONCTON 1985– ; Dean Faculté des sciences de l'éducation, Univ. de Moncton 1979–84, mem. Senate; part-time Prof. present Univ. 1963–77; Teacher, Ecole Ste-Thérèse Dieppe, N.B. 1963–64; Supervising Prin., Ecole Ste-Thérèse and Ecole Acadie Dieppe 1964–65, Ecole St-Anselme and Ecole Fox Creek, N.B. 1965–66; Sch. Psychol. Joliette, Que. 1967–68; Regional Dir. Pupil Personnel Services Moncton, N.B. 1968–76; Dir. Special Edn. Prov. N.B. 1976–79; Adjunct Asst. Prof., Dept. of Human Development, Univ. of Kansas 1990–91; Assoc., Law Enforcement Consultants Inc.; Founding Pres., N.B. Guidance Assn.; Founding Vice Pres. Assn. des spécialistes en modification du comportement; Sch. Bd. mem. Dist # 13 (Moncton-Shediac) 1983–86; Chrmn. 1985 Candn. Figure Skating Championships; Pres., Moncton Figure Skating Club 1983–84; Chrmn., Fund-Raising Ctte., Greater Moncton Art Centre Comn. 1987; author: 'Making Friends' 1975; 'Behaviour Management: A Course in Applied Psychology for High School Students' 1975; 'The Role of Punishment in Behaviour Modification: A Summary of the Literature and a Discussion on the Possible Negative Side Effects of Punishment' 1982; 'The Traditional Role of School Principals and How it Could be Changed if Approached Using an Applied Behaviour Analysis Viewpoint' 1982; co-author 'Etudes des régimes de l'éducation spéciale au Canada: définitions, financement et certification du personnel' 1977; Prin. author 'Increasing Driver Compliance at Crosswalks Using Feedback, Prompting, and Enforcement Techniques' 1984; 'The Effects of Nighttime Seat Belt Enforcement on Seat Belt Use By Tavern Patrons' 1986; (with Ron Van Houten) 'Courtesy Promotes Safety' The effects of a multi-faceted program to increase the safety of pedestrians at crosswalks, 1988; Other rsch. papers on traffic safety; Pres. & Extve. Dir., The Centre for Education and Rsch. in Safety; Office: Moncton, N.B. E1A 3E9.

**MALEY, John Patrick,** B.Sc.; mechanical engineer; b. Port Arthur, Ont. 11 March 1934; s. John Patrick and Mary (Belki) M.; e. Queen's Univ. B.Sc. 1956; m. Lorraine d. Edwin and Elsie Poole 24 Sept. 1955; children: Shelley, Margot, Pat, Jon; Pres., Repap-Ferrostaal 1988; Sr. Engr., Abitibi Paper, Mission Mill (Fort William, Ont.) 1964; Mill Mgr., (Sault Ste. Marie) 1972; Res. Mgr., Boise Cascade Can. (Fort Frances, Ont.) 1976; Vice-Pres., Opns., Midtec Paper Corp. (Kimberly, Wisc.) 1985; Extve. Vice-Pres., Mfg., Repap Enterprises (Montreal, Que.) 1987; Mem., C.P.P.A.; T.A.P.P.I.; P.I.M.A.; recreations: hunting, fishing; club: Butte Des Morts; Home: 13 Meadowbrook Ct., Appleton, Wisc. and 229 Binnacle Pt., Vero Beach, Fla.

**MALEY, Paul J.;** transportation executive; b. Estevan, Sask.; e. Estevan Coll. Inst. Sr. Matric. 1953; Univ. of B.C. Freight Traffic Mgmt. Cert. 1964; Red River Community Coll. Business Adm. Cert. 1972; Brit. Transport Staff Coll. Woking, Eng. Sr. Mgmt. Course 1978; m. Loretta; children: Grant, Janet; DIR. OF OPERATIONS, KINDERSLEY TRANSPORT LTD. 1990– ; Dir., Allied Van Lines Ltd.; Canadian Trucking Assn.; Traffic Injury Research Foundation; Gen. Clk. Estevan Soo-Security Motorways 1955, Audit Dept. Winnipeg 1958, Office Mgr. Vancouver 1960, Sales Rep. Vancouver 1963, Terminal Mgr. Vancouver 1964, Sales Mgr. Winnipeg 1966, Dir. of Mktg. Winnipeg 1970–72; Dir. of Terminals Toronto, Motorways (Ontario) Ltd. 1972, Dir. of Operations, Toronto 1973–74; Extve. Dir., Winnipeg, Canadian Motorways Ltd. 1974–77, Vice Pres. and Dir. 1979, Pres. and Dir., 1979–85; Pres. and Gen. Mgr. Winnipeg Hill Security Ltd. 1977–79; Sr. Manager, Parkside Ford Sales Ltd. 1985–90; Past Pres., Winnipeg Transp. Club; Past Chrmn., Winnipeg Business Devel. Corp.; Dir., Youth Business Learning & Devel. Centre; Jr. Achievement Man.; Vice Pres. Man. Trucking Assn.; Club: Rotary (Dir. W. Winnipeg); Address: 17 – 3415 Calder Cres., Saskatoon, Sask. S7J 5A3.

**MALHOTRA, Sudarshan K.,** M.Sc., M.A., Ph.D., D.Phil. D.Sc.; biologist; educator; b. India 20 June 1933; s. late Krishanlal and Vidyawati (Dhawan) M.; e. Panjab Univ., B.Sc. 1953, M.Sc. 1955, Ph.D. 1958; Oxford Univ., D.Phil. 1960, M.A. 1961, D.Sc. 1985; m. Kamini, d. late Bijai Krishan Dhaon, 30 Aug. 1963; two s. Shantanu, Atul; PROF. CELL BIOL. AND DIR., BIOL. SCIENCES ELECTRON MICROSCOPE LAB., UNIV. OF ALTA. since 1967 and Prof., Dept. of Zool. there; Research Fellow, New Coll., Oxford Univ., 1961–63; Research Fellow and Sr. Research Fellow, Div. of Biol., Calif. Inst. of Technol., 1963–67; Dean, Sch. of Life Sciences, Jawaharlal Nehru Univ. and Visiting Prof., All India Inst. of Med. Sciences, New Delhi, 1971–72; awarded Sr. Studentship, Royal Comn. for Exhn. of 1851, 1960–62; Del. E. Webb Visiting Assoc., Calif. Inst. Technol., 1980–81; McCalla Prof., Univ. of Alberta 1987–88; author: 'The Plasma Membrane' 1983; various articles for learned journs.; Series Ed., 'Advances in Structural Biology'; 'Advances in Neural Science'; Ed. 'Cytobios'; 'Microbios'; 'Biomedical Letters'; mem., Amer. Soc. Cell Biol.; Candn. British Soc. for Cell Biol.; Candn. Soc. of Zoologists; Soc. for Neurosci.; Microscopical Soc. of Can.; Home: 12916 – 63 Ave., Edmonton, Alta. T6H 1S1.

**MALKIN, David,** M.D., FRCP(C), FAAP; physician; b. Ottawa, Ont. 20 Jan. 1960; s. Aaron and Dina (Gordon) M.; e. Univ. of Toronto M.D. (Hons.) 1984; m. Karen d. Helen and Bernie Ceifets 18 Aug. 1991; PROJECT DIRECTOR, RESEARCH INSTITUTE, HOSPITAL FOR SICK CHILDREN 1991– ; Ped. Rsidency Program & Fellowship in Hematology-Oncology, Hosp. for Sick Children 1984–89; Postdoct. Rsch., Mass. Gen. Hosp. 1989–91; FRCP(C) 1988; FAAP 1988; Asst. Prof., Dept. of Ped., Univ. of Toronto 1991– ; Assoc. Staff Mem., Oncology, Hosp. for Sick Children; Scholarship, MRC 1992–97; Young Investigator Award, Abbot Pharm. 1992–94; research: devel. of genetic predictile testing in cancer-prone families & the identification of genes predisposing to cancer; Fellow, Candn. Ped. Soc.; Mem., Academy of Med.; Life Mem., Royal Candn. Inst.; author/co-author of over 25 sci. articles, abstracts, reviews & book chapters; recreations: classical music, outdoors; Home: 224 Delhi Ave., North York, Ont. M3H 1A8; Office: Division of Oncology, 6th Floor, 555 University Ave., Toronto, Ont. M5G 1X8.

**MALLEA, John Richard,** Ph.D.; university prof.; b. Liverpool, UK 17 Nov. 1936; s. John James and Mary (Smith) M.; e. De La Salle Coll. UK 1958; Carnegie Coll. UK 1959; Univ. of Manchester, D.A.S.E. 1963; Univ. Ore., M.S. 1964; Columbia Univ., Ph.D. 1971; m. Paula d. Chester and Margaret Wilson 27 May 1978; PRESIDENT & VICE-CHANCELLOR, BRANDON UNIVERSITY; Lectr. Loughborough Coll. 1964–66; Rsch. Assoc., Centre for Edn. in Ind. Nations, Teachers Coll. Columbia Univ. 1966–71; Co-ordinator B.Ed. Prog., Queen's Univ. Kingston 1974–75, Prof. of Edn. 1977; Professeur Invité Univ. Laval 1975–76; Visiting Prof. Univ. of B.C. 1977; Asst. Dir. (Acad.) Ont. Inst. for Studies in Edn. 1977–81, Prof. 1981–85; Pres. & Vice Chancellor, Brandon Univ. 1985–90; Pres., Candn. Bureau of Internat. Education 1989–91; Invited Visiting Prof. of Edn. Monash Univ. Melbourne, Australia 1982; recipient Fulbright Travel Scholarship USA 1963; SSHRC Travel Award China, Japan, Korea 1980; Brit. Council Award Acad. Links & Interchange Scheme 1982, 1983; Can.-Japan Bilateral Sr. Exchange Fellowship 1983; author 'Schooling in a Plural Canada' 1988; co-author, 'The National Case Study: An Empirical Comparative Study of Twentyone Educational Systems' 1976; comp. and ed., 'Quebec's Language Policies: Background and Response' 1977; 'Multiculturalism and Education: A Select Bibliography' 1979; co-ed., 'Handbook on Manpower Flexibility' 1984; 'Cultural Diversity and Canadian Education: Issues and Innovations' 1984; author or co-ed. various other publs. and papers; mem. various ed. bds.; mem. Candn. Soc. Study Higher Edn.; Candn. Sociol. & Anthrop. Assn.; Candn. Soc. Study Edn. (Nat. Extve. mem 1975–77); Candn. Asian Studies; Candn. Ethnic

Studies Assn.; Candn. Comparative & Internat. Edn. Soc. (Pres. 1975–77); Home: Box 520, Erickson, Man. R0J 0P0; Office: Faculty of Education, Brandon Univ., Brandon, Man. R7A 6A9.

**MALLEAU, Frederick Simon;** graphic arts executive; b. Massey, Ont. 8 Jan. 1944; s. Leo Allan and Anna Marie (Richer) M.; e. North Bay Teachers' Coll. 1963; Extve. Devel. Prog. Printing Industries of Am. grad. 1975; Extve. Program, Queen's Univ. 1988; m. Lynda d. Theodore and Ann Schoen 15 Aug. 1964; children: David Frederick, Anne Elizabeth, Timothy Frederick; VICE PRES. PRODUCT & DEVELOPMENT, TRI-GRAPHIC PRINTING (Ottawa) LIMITED 1993– ; joined Special Edn., Dept. of Indian Affairs & Northern Devel. 1964–66; Co-ordinator Pulp & Export Paper Sales Eddy Forest Products Ltd. Hull, Qué. 1967–70; joined John Deyell Co. Limited 1970, Gen. Mgr. 1976, Pres. 1977; Gen. Mgr. General Printers 1981; Pres. General Printers 1985–89; R. Catholic; recreations: golf, curling; Home: 60 Rice Dr., Whitby, Ont. L1N 7Z1; Office: 200 Consumers Rd., Suite 200, Willowdale, Ont. M2J 4R4.

**MALLESON, Andrew Graeme,** M.B., B.S., F.R.C.P.(C); psychiatrist; b. London, Eng. 3 Jan. 1931; s. Miles and Dr. Joan Graeme (Billson) M.; e. Leighton Park Sch., Reading, Eng.; Guy's Hosp. Med. Sch.; LRCP, MRCS 1954; M.B., B.S. 1954; MRCP (Eng.) 1960; DPM (Eng.) 1964; LMCC 1970; MRCPsych. (Eng.) 1972; came to Can. 1969; m. Dr. Donna Stewart; ASST. PROF., DEPT. OF PSYCHIATRY, UNIV. OF TORONTO; Assoc. Staff Psychiatrist, The Toronto Hosp.; Asst. Surg., SS Oronsay and Surg., SS Orsova, 1960; Scient. Offr., Med. Research Council Gt. Brit. 1963–65; Sr. Registrar in Biochem. and Psychiatry, Area Lab., West Park, Eng. 1965–66; author 'Need Your Doctor Be So Useless' 1973; 'The Medical Runaround' 1974; also assorted articles in various scient. journs. on biochem. of mental illness and on psychiatric subjects; served with RAMC 1955–56; rank Capt.; past Secy., Ont. Psychiatry Hosp. Assn. 1974; past mem., City of Toronto Bd. of Health; past Bd. mem., Planned Parenthood; past Pres., Med. Staff, Toronto Western Hosp.; Office: 25 Léonard Ave., Suite 303, Toronto, Ont. M5T 2R2.

**MALLING, Eric,** B.A., B.J.; journalist; b. Swift Current, Sask. 4 Sept. 1946; s. John and Anna (Stolhandske) M.; e. Univ. of Sask., B.A. 1967; Carelton Univ., B.J. 1968; m. Patricia d. Ed and Lydia Werner 1978; children: Leif, Paige; HOST, W-5 With Eric Malling, CTV 1990– ; pol. corr. Toronto Star 1969–74; Parlty. Bureau CTV News 1974–76; Host, The Fifth Estate, CBC-TV 1976–90; recipient Gemini award 1986; 6 ACTRA Awards incl. Best TV Interview, Documentary Writing and 3 Gordon Sinclair for Excellence in Broadcast Journalism; 2 Candn. Assn. of Journalists Awards (Tuna) 1986, (Fr. Larre) 1990; recreation: fishing; Office: W–5, P.O. Box 3000, Agincourt, Ont. M1S 3C6.

**MALLORY, James Russell,** M.A., LL.B., LL.D., D.C.L., F.R.S.C., (1964); university professor; b. St. Andrews, N.B. 5 Feb. 1916; s. late Charles Wesley and Eva Consuella (Outhouse) M.; e. Univ. of New Brunswick, B.A. (hons.) 1937, LL.D. 1968; Univ. of Edinburgh, LL.B. 1940; Dalhousie Univ., M.A. 1941; LL.D., Queen's Univ. 1978; LL.D. Univ. of Western Ont. 1987; D.C.L., Bishop's Univ. 1987; m. Frances Daniel, d. late Daniel S. Keller, Lancaster, Penn., 24 June 1940; two s. James Russell, Charles Daniel; EMERITUS PROF. OF POL. SCI., McGILL UNIV. 1982– ; (R.B. Angus Prof. of Pol. Sci. there 1977– ; Chrmn., Dept. of Econ. and Pol. Sci. 1959–69); Chrmn., Social Science Rsch. Counc. of Can. 1964–67; with Univ. of Sask. as Instr. in Pol. Science 1941–43; Univ. of Toronto, Lectr. in Pol. Econ. 1943–44; Asst. Prof. of Pol. Econ., Brandon Coll. 1944–46; apptd. Asst. Prof. Pol. Science, McGill Univ. 1946; Assoc. Prof. 1948; Nuffield Foundation Travelling Fellow 1953–54; Prof., McGill Univ. 1959–77; Can. Council Leave Fellowship 1969–70; Hon. Fellow, Faculty of Law, Univ. of Edinburgh 1969–70; Can. Council Leave Fellowship 1977–78; Visiting Fellow, Australian National Univ. 1977–78; Distinguished Visiting Prof., Univ. of Guelph, 1980; Timlin Lectr., Univ. of Sask. 1984; author: 'Social Credit and the Federal Power in Canada' 1954; 'The Structure of Canadian Government' 1970, rev. ed. 1984; mem., Candn. Pol. Science Assn. (Vice Pres. 1964–66); Inst. Pub. Adm. of Can.; Pres. (1973–74) Sec. II Roy. Soc. Can.; Candn. Study of Parliament Group (Vice Pres. 1986–87, Pres. 1988–89); Presbyterian; Home: 446 Gilmour St., Apt. 601, Ottawa, Ont. K2P 0R8.

**MALLORY, William Lloyd,** B.S.; manufacturer; b. Petoskey , Mich. 27 Jan. 1938; s. O. K. and Mabel A (Chellis) M.; e. Pellston High Sch. 1956; Mich. Technol. Univ. B.S. (Mech. Engn.) 1961; Extve. Devel. Inst. 1972; Mahler Advanced Management Course, 1981; m. Elaine Marie d. Lester Shorter, Pellston, Mich., 28 June 1958; children: Sheree Lee, Brian William, Leslie Kay; DIRECTOR, INGERSOLL-RAND CANADA INC.; joined Ingersoll-Rand 1961, trans. to Montreal as Sales Engr. 1962, Sales Mgr. E. Can.-Pulp & Paper Div. 1969, Product Div. Mgr. 1971, Gen. Mgr. Pulp & Paper Div. 1971 and Mining & Constr. Div. 1972, Vice Pres. Marketing 1973, Sr. Vice Pres. Marketing 1976, Pres. & C.E.O. 1976; served 8 yrs. with Mich. Nat. Guard; Gov., Stratford Festival; Chrmn., Machinery & Equipment Mfrs. Assn.; Internat. Business Rsch. Centre Adv. Counc.; Mem., Candn. Pulp & Paper Assn.; Candn. Inst. Mining; Candn. Soc. Mech. Engrs.; Construction Industry Develop. Counc.; Protestant; recreation: golf; Club: Whitlock Golf; Home: 2554 Gevrey Sq., St. Lazare, Que.; Office: 3501 St. Charles Blvd., Kirkland, Que. H9H 4S3.

**MALMO, Robert Beverley,** M.A., Ph.D., LL.D.; university professor; psychologist; b. Canal Zone, Panama 24 Oct. 1912; s. Robert H. and Mary Welby (Beverley) M.; e. Univ. of Missouri, B.A. (with distinction) 1935; M.A. 1937; Yale Univ., Ph.D. 1940; LL.D. Manitoba, 1970; m. Mary Rose Helen Pitts, d. Marjorie Louise Porter, 20 Mar. 1944; PROF. OF PSYCHOLOGY, McGILL UNIVERSITY; (retired) Medical Scientist, Royal Victoria Hosp.; mem., Scient. Adv. Council DISCUS; Psychologist, Norwich State Hospital, Conn., 1941–42; apptd. Psychophysiologist, 1942; Public Health Officer, National Inst. of Health, USPHS, Bethesda, Md., 1944–45; joined staff McGill Univ., 1945, as Dir., Lab. of Psychol., Allan Mem. Inst. of Psychiatry, Sch. of Med.; Hon. Life Fellow, Candn. Psychol. Assn. (Pres. and Hon. Pres.); Fellow, Am. Psychol. Assn. (and Council Mem.); Fellow, Am. Assoc. Advance. Sci.; Pres., Interam. Soc. of Psychol.; mem., Exper. Psychol. Study Sec., Nat. Insts. of Health., U.S. Pub. Health Service; mem., Assoc. Comte. on Exper. Psychol., Nat. Research Council; Bd. of Govs., Internat. Org. of Psychophysiology; rec'd. Centennial Medal; Citation of Merit, Univ. of Missouri; Lambda Chi Alpha; Phi Beta Kappa; Sigma Xi; Protestant; recreations: photography, squash; Clubs: McGill Faculty; Canadian Club of Montreal; Home: 814 Graham Blvd., Town of Mount Royal, Que. H3P 2E6; Office: 1033 Pine Ave. W., Montreal, Que. H3A 1A1.

**MALO, Nicole,** B.A., P.Péd., B.Sc., M.es A.; sous-ministre; née Joliette, Qué. 26 mars 1946; f. Bernard et Lucille (Rondeau) M.; é. Séminaire de Joliette, B.A. 1967; Univ. de Montréal, B.Péd. 1968, B.Sc. 1972; Univ. Laval, M.es A. 1976; ép. Bernard f. Raoul et Jeanne Ouimet 10 août 1968; enfants: Mathieu, Caroline; Sous-Ministre, Ministere de L'Energie et des Ressources 1991; Educatrice au préscolaire, Laval-des-Rapides 1968–72; Cons. Comn. des écoles cath. de Québec et au min. de l'Edn. du Qué. en Psychomotricité 1972–73; Agente de rech. et de planification, Serv. de garde à l'enfance et Serv. soc. à l'enfance, Min. des Affairs soc. du Que., Dir. gén. de la planification 1974–78; Chef du Serv. des pol. à l'enfance at à la famille, Dir. des pol. de serv. soc., Min. des Affaires soc. du Qué. 1978–81; Régie de l'assur. automobile du Qué., Dir. de la Réadaptation 1981–82; Dir. de l'Indemnisation 1982–84; Vice-prés. à la planification et à la promotion de la Sécurité routière 1984–86; Office des ressources humaines du Qué., Prés. 1986–88; Sousministre, ministère des Affairs culturelles 1988–91; mem.: Inst. d'adm. publique du Can.; CA de l'Ecole nat. d'adm. publique du Qué. 1987–88; co-auteur 'La Garderie, une expérience de vie pour l'enfant' 1977; nombreux articles; récreations: musique, ski, lecture.

**MALO, Paul-André,** F.I.C.B., F.C.G.A., Adm.A.; financial executive; b. Contrecoeur, Que. 10 April 1940; s. Lucien (dec.) and Antoinette (Gendron) M.; e. Univ. of Montreal F.I.C.B. 1968 (Inst. of Candn. Bankers); C.G.A. 1974; m. Lise d. the late Antoine and Flora Emma (Handfield) Cormier 4 Aug. 1962; children: Pierre, Josée, Maryse; VICE-PRESIDENT, AUDIT, NATIONAL BANK OF CANADA 1986– ; joined National Bank of Canada, Montreal 1959; Bank Mgr. 1968; Asst. District Mgr. 1974; District Mgr. 1978; Vice-Pres., Crédit 1984; Gov., The Candn. Comprehensive Auditing Foundation 1993; Mem., Cert. Gen. Accountants' Assn. of Can. (CGA-Canada) (Pres. 1986–87); Internat. Fed. of Accountants Council (Tech. Advr., Finan. Mngt. Acctg. Ctte.); Corp. prof. des comptables gén. licenciés du Qué. (Pres. 1982–83); Candn. Bankers' Assn. (Chief Inspectors' Ctte. 1986– ); Corp. Prof. des Admin. Agrees du Qué.; Hon. Fellow, CGA; Mérite 1992, Conseil Interprof. du Qué.; Mem., Candn. Numismatics Assn.; Assn. des num. et philatél. de Boucherville Inc. (Founder, Pres. 1967–70); Assn. des dipl. de l'Ecole des Hautes Etudes Comm.; C. de C. de la Rive-Sud; recreations: golf, numismatics; Home: 676 Augustin Quintal, Boucherville, Que. J4B 3E7; Office: 600 de la Gauchetière St. W., 7th Fl., Montreal, Que. H3B 4L2.

**MALONE, David Michael,** B.A., M.P.A.; diplomat; b. Ottawa, Ont. 7 Feb. 1954; s. Paul and Deirdre Lavalette (Ingram) Malone; e. Hautes Etudes Comm. B.A. 1975; Harvard Univ. M.P.A. 1982; AMBASSADOR AND DEPUTY PERMANENT REPRESENTATIVE OF CANADA TO THE UNITED NATIONS, NEW YORK 1992– ; joined Dept. of External Affairs 1975; assigned to Cairo Egypt 1976–80; Amman, Jordan 1984–86; Econ. Policy Bureau 1982–84; Visiting Prof., Pol. Sci., Univ. of Toronto & Guest Scholar, Brookings Inst. 1988–89; Dir., Internat. Econ. Relations, External Affairs 1989–90; Minister-Counsellor, Permanent Mission of Canada to the U.N., N.Y. 1990–92; Adjunct Prof. of Internat. Relations, Columbia Univ. 1991– ; Home: 425 E. 58th St., Apt. 30-E, New York, NY 10022; Office: 885 Second Ave., 14th fl., New York, NY 10017.

**MALONE, Thomas Paul;** retired diplomat; b. Edmonton, Alta. 8 Feb. 1915; s. Thomas Peter and Sarah (MacMillan) M.; e. Univ. of Alta., B.A. 1936; m. Deirdre Lavallette, d. Sefton Ingram and Margery (Metcalfe), Sydney, Aust., 9 July 1940; children: Anthony, Mark, Christopher, Patricia, David; Journalist, Edmonton Journal 1936–38; Commonwealth Press Union Exchange Journalist, Eng. and Aust. 1938–40; Rep., Candn. Wartime Information Bd., Aust. 1942–46; joined Dept. of External Affairs 1946; 2nd Secy., Canberra 1946–48; 1st Secy., Washington 1948–53; Dept. of External Affairs, Ottawa 1953–58; Counsellor, The Hague 1958–62; Ambassador to Iran 1962–67 (then concurrently to Iraq and Kuwait); High Commr. to Nigeria 1967–70 (Concurrently to Niger, Sierra Leone and Dahomey); Depy. Commandant, Nat. Defence Coll. Can. 1970–72; Ambassador to Israel and concurrently to Cyprus 1972–75; apptd. Ambassador to Finland 1975; retired from Foreign Service 31 Dec. 1979; Delta Upsilon; Roman Catholic; Club: Rideau; Home: Suite 506, 20 Driveway, Ottawa, Ont. K2P 1C8.

**MALONE, William James,** B.A.Sc.; consulting engineer; b. Toronto, Ont. 23 Sept. 1924; s. Charles Stuart and Charlotte Lamont (Davidson) M.; e. Davisville Public and Northern Secondary Schs., Toronto; Univ. of Toronto, B.A.Sc. 1949; m. Heidemarie, d. Wilhelm Wilmschen, Moers, Germany, 4 July 1968; four children (two by former m.); Chrmn. Mascon Engineering Limited; began as Jr. Rsch. Engr., HEPC, Toronto 1949; Resident Engr., De Leuw Cather & Brill, N.Y. 1952; joined De Leuw Cather & Co. of Can., Toronto 1954 as Design Engr.; Br. Mgr. Ottawa 1957; Pres. 1960; Chrmn. 1967–79 (ret.); served in R.C.A.F., pilot Offr. 1942–44; with Fleet Air Arm, R.N.V.R., Sub-Lt. 1944–45; mem. Assn. Prof. Engrs. of Ont.; Road & Transport. Assn. Can. (Past Chrmn., Tech. Council); Past Chrmn., Tech. Comte., Internat. Road Fed. Conf.; rec'd Distinguished Service Award, Candn. Good Roads Assn.; Centennial Medal 1967; author of numerous tech. papers dealing with transportation and housing; recreations: golf, curling; Home: 6 Tortoise Court, Brampton, Ont. L6T 3Z8.

**MALONEY, Aidan,** C.M., LL.D. (Hon.); executive; b. Kings Cove, Nfld. 12 Aug. 1920; s. Michael Edward and Alice Rose (Murphy) M.; e. R.C. High Sch., Kings Cove Nfld.; m. Eva M., d. William L. Wyse, 12 Aug. 1947; one d.; Maureen; Chrmn., Fisheries Prices Support Board of Can. 1979–85; Dir., Fisheries Development Corp of Nfld.; Canadian Saltfish Corp.; Regent, Meml. Univ. of Nfld.; Gov., Coll. of Fisheries of Nfld.; mem., Royal Comn. on Inshore Fisheries of Nfld. & Labrador; joined Royal Bank of Canada 1938–44; apptd. Chief Acct., John Penny & Sons Ltd. (fish processors) Ramea, Nfld. 1944; Mgr. 1946; Mang. Dir. 1949–57; served with Dept. of Fisheries, Nfld. as Asst. Depy. Min. 1957–66; el. M.H.A. for Dist. of Ferryland in Prov. g.e. 1966; apptd. Min. of Fisheries and Min. of Community & Social Devel., retired from Pol. Apr. 1970; Pres. and Gen. Mgr., Canadian Saltfish Corp. 1970–79; Chrmn., Nfld. and Labrador Arts Counc. 1979; Chrmn., Bd. of Gov. St. Clares Mercy Hospital Foundation 1985–1989; Chrmn., Bd. of Govs. St. Clares Mercy Hospital 1989– ; Dir., Newfoundland Hospital Assn.; Hon. Private Secy. to Lieut-Gov. of Nfld. 1986–91; Mem., Order of Canada 1992; Hon. Consul Gen. of Japan; Knight, Sovreign Military Order of Malta 1988; Hon. LL.D., Memorial Univ. of Nfld.; Mem. Bd., Nfld. Historic Parks; mem. Extve., K. of C.; mem., N.W. Rotary Club, St. John's; St. John's Bd. of Trade; Roman Catholic; recreation: painting; Home: 2 Laughlin Cres., St. John's, Nfld. A1A 2G2; Office: 2 Laughlin Cres., St. John's, Nfld. A1A 2G2.

**MALONEY, Hon. Anthony William;** b. Saskatoon, Sask. 12 May 1928; s. Leo and Katherine Jane (Shields) M.; e. St. Paul's Coll., Univ. of Man. B.A. 1949; Osgoode Hall Law Sch. grad. 1953; m. Marian Lucille Auringer 25 Nov. 1954; children: Patrick W., Michael L., James V.; JUSTICE, SUPREME COURT OF ONT.; REGIONAL SR. JUSTICE, ONTARIO COURT OF JUSTICE, NORTHWEST REGION (THUNDER BAY) 1990– and DEPY. JUSTICE, SUPREME COURT OF THE YUKON (WHITEHORSE) 1991– ; read law with Weiler, Maloney, Nelson; called to the Bar of Ont. 1953; cr. Q.C. 1964; practised law in N. Ont. for 23 years; mem. Council Candn. Bar Assn.; Former Trustee, Ft. William Bd. of Educ.; Past Dir., Advocates Soc.; Ont. Legal Aid Plan; R. Catholic; Delta Upsilon; recreations: skiing, swimming, hunting; Clubs: Caledon Mountain Trout, Fort William Gyro (Thunder Bay), K–40 (Thunder Bay), Thunder Bay Golf & Country; Home: 96 The Kingsway, Toronto, Ont. M8X 3T8; Office: 277 Camelot St., Thunder Bay, Ont. P7A 4B3.

**MALONEY, Sharon E.,** LL.B.; lawyer/association executive; b. Vancouver, B.C. 15 Feb. 1952; d. Douglas William and Alix (McPhail) M.; e. Miss Edgars & Miss Cramps H.S. 1969; Carleton Univ., B.A. 1973; McGill Univ., LL.B. 1979; m. William Patrick s. Eva Elin Rutsey 17 Dec. 1986; one d.: Alix Elin Rutsey; Pres., Candn. Shoe Retailers Assn. 1986; Litigation lawyer, Thomson Rogers 1980–81; Partner, Lilly, Goldman 1981–86; Extve. Vice-Pres., Coalition Against Open Sunday Shopping; Vice-Chair, Footwear Council of Canada; Mem., Legal Edn. Action Fund; Nat. Assn. of Women in Law; Ont. Coalition for Abortion Clinics; Royal Ont. Mus.; Art Gallery of Ont.; club: The McGill Club; Home: 799 Euclid Ave., Toronto, Ont. M6G 2V3.

**MALOUF, Hon. Albert-H.,** Q.C., B.A., B.C.L.; advocate; b. Montreal, Que. 19 Dec. 1916; s. Joseph H. and Emily (Kuzma) M.; e. McGill Univ., B.A. 1938, B.C.L. 1941; m. Mary, d. Elias N. Tabah, 23 Dec. 1961; two s. Paul, Marc; COUNSEL, MACKENZIE GERVAIS (active in arbitration, mediation and conciliation matters); read law with Sullivan & Johnson; called to Bar of Que. 1942; cr. Q.C. 1959; Sr. Partner, Malouf & Shorteno and in 1959 Malouf, Pateras & Macerola; named Judge, Court of Sessions of the Peace, Que., 1968; Justice, Superior Court Que. 1972; Justice, Court of Appeal, Que. 1981–91; presided over and granted the request presented by the Indians and Inuit of Quebec for the issue of an injunction against the Quebec Hydro-electric project in the James Bay area 1972–73; Chrmn., Commission of Inquiry into the Cost of the 21st Olympiad 1977–80; Chrmn., Royal Commission on Seals and the Sealing Industry in Canada 1984–86; Counsel, Mackenzie Gervais; served with RCA in Can., Italy and N.W. Europe 1942–46; rank Lt.; retired Hon. Col. 2nd Field Arty Regt.; Cmdr. Equestrian Order, Holy Cross of Jerusalem; mem. d'hon., Foundation de l'Université du Québec à Montreal; mem., Nat. Council, Candn. Human Rights Foundation; Gov., Cedars Home for Elderly; Lebanese Syrian Candn. Assn.; Hon. Life Gov., Arty. Offrs. Assn. Montreal; Hon. Patron, Montreal Assoc. for the Mentally Handicapped; mem., Quebec Adv. Council, University Scholarships of Canada; R. Catholic; recreations: skiing, swimming, tennis, golf, bridge; Club: Beaconsfield Golf & Country; Home: 240 Appin Ave., Town of Mount Royal, Que. H3P 1V8; Office: 770 Sherbrooke St. W., 13th Floor, Montreal, Que. H3A 1G1.

**MALUS, Avrum,** B.A., M.A., Ph.D.; university professor/writer; b. Montréal, Qué. 28 Dec. 1938; s. Louis Harry and Florence (Garmaise) M.; e. Strathcona Acad. 1956; McGill Univ. B.A. (Hons.) 1961; Rutgers Univ. M.A. 1966; Univ. de Montréal Ph.D. 1975; common-law wife: Monique d. Evelyn and Antonio Martin since October 1970; children: Jacob Martin-Malus, Sophie-Andrée Blondin, Philippe-Emmanuël Chartrand; PROF. OF ENGLISH, UNIV. DE SHERBROOKE 1969– ; Teaching Asst., Rutgers Univ. 1962–65; Prof. of English, McGill Univ. 1966–69; Dir., Dept. of English, Univ. de Sherbrooke 1985–87; Prof. of English 1969– ; Asst. Dir., Dept. of Letters & Commun. 1987–91; Poetry Ed., 'Matrix, New Canadian Writing' 1983–86; Researchist, FCAR, Prov. of Qué.; Organizer, 'The Seventh Moon' poetry readings 1975– ; translator: Bourse d'études supérieures, Prov. of Qué. 1964–65, 1965–66; 2 rsch. grants; author: 'I Set the Fire Which Destroyed Our Home' 1978 and poems pub. in lit. mags. & anthologies; Home: 17 Clough St., Lennoxville, Qué. J1M 1V7; Office: 2500 Université Blvd., Sherbrooke, Qué. J1K 2R1.

**MALYSHEFF, George Andrew,** B.Eng., LL.B.; lawyer, business executive; b. Ottawa, Ont. 10 Jan. 1951; s. Andrew George and Claudette M.; e. Carleton Univ. B.Eng. 1972; Ottawa Univ. LL.B. 1979; one s.: Andrew Vaughan; GENERAL COUNSEL & CORPORATE SECRETARY, TELUS CORP. 1990– ; Profl. Engr. working in civil engr. & construction 1972–76; law school, articles, bar admission course 1976–81; Corporate Solicitor, Nova Corp. / Foothills Pipelines Limited 1981–84; Sr. Corp. Counsel & Asst. Secretary, Norcen Energy Resources Limited 1984–90; Mem., Bar of Alta.; Bar of Ont.; recreations: golf, sailing, squash, running; clubs: Calgary Yacht, Britannia Yacht; Home: 9305 – 98th Ave., Edmonton, Alta.; Office: Floor 31, 10020 – 100 Street, Edmonton, Alta. T5J 0N5.

**MAMNGUQSUALUK, Victoria;** artist; b. Back River Area, N.W.T. 1930; medium: drawings, prints, wall-hangings, sculpture; 82 group exbns. incl. most recent: Winnipeg Art Gall. 1992, Marion Scott Gall. Vancouver 1992, Great Northern Arts Festival Inuvik, N.W.T. 1991, Nat. Gall. of Canada Ottawa 1991, Albers Gall. San Francisco, Ca. 1991; solo exbns.: Keeveeok, Awake! Mamnguqsualuk and the Rebirth of Legend at Baker Lake, Ring House Gallery, Edmonton 1986, Northern Images Whitehorse 1984, The Innuit Gall. of Eskimo Art Toronto 1983; works in 17 collections incl. art galleries of Kitchener-Waterloo and Winnipeg (Swartz, Swinton & Twomey colls.), Canada Council Art Bank Ottawa, Candn. Mus. of Civilization Hull, Que., Inuit Cultural Inst. Rankin Inlet, N.W.T., Prince of Wales northern Heritage Ctr., Yellowknife, N.W.T.; award for craftsmanship & design 'Crafts from Arctic Canada' exhbn. 1974; accompanied her mother Jessie Oonark to Ottawa for presentation of Sunday Missal of Roman Catholic Ch.; wallhanging presented on occasion of transfer of Candn. Arctic Producers' Ltd. share from Fed. Govt. to Arctic Co-op.; subject of several articles and catalogues; Home: Baker Lake, N.W.T.; Office: c/o Baker Lake Fine Arts and Crafts, Baker Lake, N.W.T. X0C 0A0.

**MANCHEVSKY, Norman;** Canadian public servant; b. Johannesburg, S. Africa 8 March 1942; s. Barnard and Ethel Miriam M.; e. Grey Sch. Port Elizabeth, S. Africa 1958; Rhodes Univ. Grahamstown, S. Africa 1965; m. Suzanne Massie; children: Jacqueline, Susan, Luke; CHIEF EXTVE. OFFICER, CANADA COMMUNICATION GROUP AND QUEEN'S PRINTER FOR CANADA 1984– ; served National Cash Register Co. S. Africa prior to emigration to Can. 1970; continued data processing career Toronto and Ottawa; apptd. Systems Adv. to Asst. Dep. Min. of Comm. Supply Service 1976 becoming Dir. Planning Analysis & Control Br. for above Service; Dir. Cdn. Govt. Expn. Centre 1979; recreations: sailing, microcomputer; Home: Ottawa, Ont.; Office: 45 Sacre-Coeur Blvd., Hull, Qué. K1A 0S7.

**MANCINI, Nick L.,** H.B.A., M.A.; business information executive; b. Toronto, Ont. 2 Sept. 1956; e. York Univ., H.B.A. 1979, M.A. 1980, Ph.D. candidate (economics); m. Gina; PRES. & C.E.O., DUN & BRADSTREET CANADA, MARKET DATA RETRIEVAL NORTH AMERICA, RECEIVABLES MNGMT. SERVICES NORTH AMERICA 1993– ; PRES. & C.E.O., DUN & BRADSTREET CANADA 1990– ; Co-Chrmn. and Dir., D&B Companies of Canada, Ltd.; Pres. & Dir., Dun & Bradstreet Canada Holding Ltd.; Dir., Primerica Financial Services - Canada; Corp. Planner, Traders Group/Guaranty Trust Company of Canada 1980–81; Sr. Finan. Economist, Toronto Stock Exchange 1982; Mgr., Finan. & Econ. Analysis, American Express Canada, Inc. 1982–83; Dir., Bus. Planning & Finan. Analysis 1983–85; Vice-Pres., Business & Strategic Planning & Finan. Analysis 1986–87; Vice-Pres. & Gen. Mgr., Finan. Services Group 1987–89; Sr. Vice-Pres. & Gen. Mgr., Finan. Services Group 1990; recreations: hockey, golf, theatre, reading; Office: 5770 Hurontario St., Mississauga, Ont. L5R 3G5.

**MAND, Martin G.,** B.Comm., M.B.A.; telecommunications executive; b. Norfolk, Virginia 26 Sept. 1936; s. Meyer J. and Lena S. (Sutton) M.; e. Maury H.S. 1954; Univ. of Virginia B.Comm. 1958; Univ. of Delaware M.B.A. 1964; m. Anita Rochelle 29 Aug. 1965; children: Gregory S., Michael E., Brian C.; EXTVE. VICE-PRES. & CHIEF FINANCIAL OFFICER, NORTHERN TELECOM LTD. 1990– ; various positons incl. Vice-Pres., Taxes & Financial Services / Vice-Pres. & Comptroller / Vice-Pres. & Treas., E.I. du Pont de Nemours & Co. 29 years; Bd. Mem., Bimcor Inc.; has served on committees for Financial Executives Inst.; Finance Council Mem., Mfrs. Alliance for Productivity & Innovation; American Mngt. Assn.; Conference Bd. of Canada; Adv. Bd., McIntire School of Commerce, Univ. of Virginia (Past Chrmn.); Past Trustee & Pres., FERF; Office: P.O. Box 458, Stn. A, Mississauga, Ont. L5A 3A2.

**MANDAGGIO, Eddie;** folk artist; b. Lorne, Muncman, Man. 4 May 1927; s. Joe Andrew and Gladys Alberta (Stewart) M.; former logger, guide, miner, railroader; lifelong woodsman; demonstrated carving Expo '86 Folk Life Pavilion; first solo exhn. Houston North Gallery Lunenburg 1985, exclusive agts. featuring large coll. sculptures, carvings, paintings primarily of animals; rep. Art Gallery of N.S.; TV appearances, newspaper and mag. interviews; carved flock of geese featured ads. across N.Am. for Tourism Can.; recreations: hunting, fishing, canoeing; Address: Italy Cross, Lunenburg Co., N.S. B0J 1V0.

**MANDEL, Lawrence H.,** Q.C., B.A., LL.B.; solicitor; b. Toronto, Ont. 25 Apl. 1936; s. Albert and Rose (Simlewitz) M.; e. Forest Hill Coll. Inst.; Univ. of Toronto B.A. 1958 (Tracey Award Philos.), LL.B. 1961; m. Marjorie d. Thomas and Mary Brown 21 June 1967; children: Sloan, Carrie; PARTNER, THOMSON, ROGERS 1970– ; called to Bar of Ont. 1963; cert. Litigation Specialist 1988; Counsel to Comte. Fair Action Ins. Reform; Lectr. Continuing Edn. Ctte. Law Soc. Upper Can.; Insight Ednl. Services; Instr. Trial Tactics & Procedures Bar Admission Course; Dir. Internat. Acad. Trial Lawyers; mem. Candn. Bar Assn. (Chrmn. Civil Justice Sect. Ont.); Advocates' Soc. (Dir., Prog. Chrmn., Treas.); N.Y. State Trial Lawyers' Assn.; Assn. Trial Lawyers Am.; Co. of York Law Assn.; recreations: music, sports, travel; Home: 6 Gilgorm Rd., Toronto, Ont. M5N 2M5; Office: 3100, 390 Bay St., Toronto, Ont. M5H 1W2.

**MANDER, Christine;** writer; b. Southey, Sask. d. Frank and Gertrude Patience (Cosham) Carter; e. St. Albans Grammar Sch.; Clark's Bus. Coll. (U.K.); m. Ronald s. Reginald and Ella M. 12 Aug. 1950; children: Susan, Paul; Sr. Sec., Brit. Cellophane Ltd. 1947–50; Admin. Sec., Alfred Pemberton Advtg. Ltd. 1950–52; Priv. Sec., Maj. R.G. Lloyd 1961–63; var. positions 1963–66; Admin. Sec., Oakville Public Lib. 1966–72; Admin. Sec., Comm. Relns. & Head, Prog. & Publicity 1972–86; Mem., Hamilton & Dist. Pub. Relns. Assn. (served on sev. cttes. & task forces); John Cotton Dana Lib. Public Relns. Award 1977; Buckerfield Award for Outstanding Lib. Serv. 1974; Town of Oakville Long Serv. Citation, 19 yrs. 1967–86; Bd. Mem., Lung Assn. of Halton 1984–87; Mem., Writers' Union 1982–83, 1987–91; Candn. Authors Assn. 1975– (Pres., Oakville Br. 1986–88); author: 'All You Need is Enough Rope' 1981 (Gov. Gen. award cand. 1982; selected for use in Alta. high sch. 1983), 'Emily Murphy: Rebel' 1985; 'A Bid for Murder' 1990; recreations: reading, swimming, furniture refinishing, book repairing; Home: 348 Sandhurst Dr., Oakville, Ont. L6L 4L2.

**MANGUEL, Alberto (Adrian),** A.S.; writer; b. Buenos Aires, Argentina 13 Mar. 1948; s. Pablo and Rosa (Finkelstein) M.; e. Colegio Nacional de Buenos Aires, AS. (Bac.) 1966; divorced; children: Alice Emily, Rachel Claire, Rupert Tobias; Reader for Gallimard, Denoël and les lettres nouvelles, Paris 1968–70; for Calder & Boyars, London 1971; Asst. Ed., Franco Maria Ricci Editore, Milan 1973–74; Asst. Ed., then Editor-in-Chief, Les Editions du Pacifique, Tahiti 1975–82; head, Arts Journalism Programme, Banff, Alta.; freelance writer & broadcaster, CBC TV & Radio; Contbg. Ed., Saturday Night Magazine; Fantastic Lit. Tutorial, Vanier Coll., York Univ., 1983–86; mem., PEN, Writers' Union; Internat. Assn. of Crime Writers; co-author (with Gianni Guadalupi): 'The Dictionary of Imaginary Places' 1980; anthologies: 'Black Water' 1983, 'Dark Arrows' 1985, 'Other Fires' 1986, 'Evening Games' 1986, 'The Oxford Book of Canadian Ghost Stories' 1990; 'Black Water II' 1990; 'Canadian Mystery Stories' 1991; 'The Gates of Paradise' 1993; author: 'News from A Foreign Country Came' (novel) 1991; recipient: McKitterick First Novel Award (UK) 1992; Candn. Authors' Assn. Fiction Award 1992; Harbourfront 1992 Award; Home: c/o The Lucinda Vardey Agency, 297 Seaton St., Toronto, Ont. M5A 2T6.

**MANIATES, Maria Rika,** A.R.C.T., B.A., M.A., Ph.D.; university professor and administrator; b. Toronto, Ont. 30 March 1937; d. Euripides and Sophia (Samaras) M.; e. Royal Cons. of Music (solo piano) A.R.C.T. 1958; Univ of Toronto B.A. 1960; Columbia Univ. M.A. 1962, Ph.D. 1965 (with distinction); PROFESSOR, MUSIC, UNIV. OF TORONTO 1965–95; Reader in Music, Columbia Univ. 1962–63; Fellow, Victoria Coll. 1979– ; Assoc. Dean, Div. I, Sch. of Grad. Studies 1990–91; Asst. Dean 1991–92; Acting Chair, Grad. Dept. of Music 1992; Vice Dean, Sch. of Grad. Studies 1992–93; Visiting Prof., Columbia Univ. 1967, '76; Former Consultant, Art Gall. of Ont., CBC-TV, Ont. Council for the Arts; Appraiser, Canada Council, SSHRCC, Killam Prog. 1969– ; Cons., GRE in Music,

Grad. Testing Serv., Princeton 1979– ; Pub. Ctte., Candn. Fed. for the Humanities 1991–94; awarded 6 scholarships, 6 fellowships, 3 grants; Mem., Am. Musicological Soc. (Council 1972–74, 1976–78; AMS 50 Fellowship Ctte. 1989–93; Chair, Einstein Award Ctte. 1978–79; Bd. of Dir. 1980–81); Internat. Musicological Soc. (Candn. Del. Bd. of Dir. 1972–82); Toronto Renaissance & Reformation Colloquium (Extve. Ctte. 1966–70); Candn. Assn. of Univ. Schools of Music; Renaissance Soc. of Am. (Council 1970, '90); Candn. Soc. for Renaissance Studies; Del., Internat. Music. Soc. on Gov. Council, Internat. Music Council, UNESCO; author: 'Don Nicola Vicentino' 1994, 'Music Discourse from Classical to Early Times' 1993/94, 'The Combinative Chanson' 1989, 'Music and Civilization' 1984 (ASCAP-DEEMS Taylor Award 1985), 'Mannerism in Italian Music and Culture, 1530–1630' 1979, 'Combinative Techniques in Franco-Flemish Polyphony' 1965; Home: 44 Charles St. W., Apt. 5003, Toronto, Ont. M4Y 1R8; Office: Northrop Frye Hall Room 313, Victoria College, Toronto, Ont. M5S 1K7.

**MANION, John Lawrence,** O.C.; retired public servant; b. Almonte, Ont. 27 June 1931; s. John Patrick and Catherine Anne (Mullins) M.; e. St. Patrick's Coll., Univ. of Ottawa, B.A. 1953; m. Sylvia d. Alderic and Ritha Beaudry 18 Sept. 1954; children: Laurie Anne, Ian Gregory, Bruce Patrick, Douglas Joseph; Immigration Serv. of Can. 1953–69; Dir. of Manpower Training, Dept. of Manpower & Immig. 1969–72; Asst. Dep. Min., Manpower 1972; Sr. ADM, Manpower & Immig. 1974; Dep. Min., Employment & Immig. & Chrmn., Employment & Immig. Comn. 1977–79; Sec. of the Treas. Bd. 1979–86; Assoc. Sec. to the Cabinet & Sr. Personnel Advisor 1986–89; Principal, Candn. Ctr. for Mngt. Devel./Ctr. Canad. de Gestion 1988–91; Fellow, Canadian Centre for Management Development 1991–92; Rsch. Fellow, Institute of Public Administration of Canada; Order of Canada 1984; Outstanding Achievement Award, Public Serv. of Can. 1986; Vanier Medal of the Inst. of Public Admin. 1989; Mem., Adv. Ctte., MBA Program for Public Extves., Queen's Univ.; Hon. Pres., Candn. Immig. Hist. Soc.; Dir., Digital Equipment of Canada; recreations: curling, cycling; Home: 900 Rand Ave., Ottawa, Ont. K1V 6X4.

**MANION, Robert C.,** B.S.; information technology consultant; e. Eastern Illinois Univ. B.S. (Business) 1966; m. Sally Gifford; children: Elizabeth, Charles; MANAGING PARTNER, ANDERSEN CONSULTING – CANADA 1989– ; joined Arthur Andersen & Co. Chicago 1966; Panama Canal Zone, Panama 1972; St. Louis, Missouri 1974; Partner 1976; Mng. Partner, Consulting, St. Louis Information Consulting Practice 1979; transferred to Germany as Mng. Partner of Information Consulting (Germany, Switz., Austria) 1985; Mng. Dir. of Practice Mngt. & Planning, Chicago World H.Q. 1988; Andersen Consulting management cttes.: Global Management Council, SC Executive, North Am. Operations; Chair, SAP Consulting (W. Germany); author of 10 business articles and one book chapter; Office: 185 The West Mall, Suite 500, Etobicoke, Ont. M9C 5L5.

**MANLEY, Hon. John Paul,** B.A., LL.B., M.P.; politician; b. Ottawa, Ont. 5 Jan. 1950; s. John Joseph and Mildred Charlotte (Scharf) M.; e. Carleton Univ. B.A.; Univ. of Ottawa LL.B.; m. Judith Mary Rae 21 April 1973; children: Rebecca Jane, David John, Sarah Kathleen; MINISTER OF INDUSTRY, GOVERNMENT OF CANADA 1993– ; 1st elected to House of Commons (Ottawa South) g.e. 1988; re-elected 1993; Law Clerk for Rt. Hon. Bora Laskin, Chief Justice of Can. 1976–77; Chair, Ottawa-Carleton Bd. of Trade 1985–86; Liberal; Anglican; Office: C.D. Howe Bldg., 235 Queen St., Ottawa, Ont. K1A 0H5; Riding Office: 211 – 1800 Bank St., Ottawa, Ont. K1V 0W3.

**MANN, Cedric Robert,** M.Sc., Ph.D., D.Eng., FRSC; oceanographer; b. Auckland, N.Z. 14 Feb. 1926; s. late Duncan and Winifred Mary (Hood) M.; came to Canada 1949; e. Univ. of N.Z., B.Sc. 1948; M.Sc. 1950; Univ. of B.C., Ph.D. (Physics) 1953; N.S. Tech. Coll., D.Eng. (hon. causa) 1972; m. Muriel Frances, d. late John May, Nanton, Alta. 18 Dec. 1950; one s. Robin Carl; retired Dir. Gen., Ocean Science and Surveys, Pacific Region 1979–86; Dir. Gen Ocean and Aquatic Sciences, Atlantic Region 1978–79; Dir., Atlantic Oceanographic Lab. 1975–78; Head, Ocean Circulation Div. 1965–75; Oceanographer, Bedford Inst. Oceanog. since 1961; Assoc. Prof., Dept. Physics, Dalhousie Univ. 1961–75; Del., Internat. Council for Exploration of Sea 1978–79; Chrmn., Scientific Advy. Bd., Integovernmental Oceanographic Comn. 1978–81; Chrmn., Sea Use Counc. U.S./Can. 1981–86; Physicist, Naval Research Estab., Defense Research Bd. 1953–61; Regional Rsch. Oceanographer, Bedford Inst. Oceanog. 1962–65; organized and dir. 'Hudson 70' Expdn.; mem. Candn. Meteorol. and Oceanog. Soc.; N.S. Inst. Science; author of numerous papers publ. in various journs.;elected Fellow of the Royal Soc. of Canada, 1979; Anglican; recreation: golf; Address: 9751 Ardmore Dr., R.R. #2, Sidney, B.C. V8L 3S1.

**MANN, Cy;** custom tailor; b. Toronto, Ont. 9 Apl. 1928; s. Louis and Freda (Wengle) Glicksman; e. Central Tech. Sch.; Ont. Coll. Art; m. Reta d. Samuel and Esther Wald 29 Jan. 1967; children: Paula Fox, Pamela Tuttelman, Freda; PRES. MR. MANN TAILOR AND SHIRTMAKER, Toronto 1977– ; cartoonist, artist, animator, Walt Disney Studios 1948; Co-Founder and Partner, Cy Mann Clothes Ltd. 1953–59 (no longer assoc.); estbd. The House of Mann Ltd. 1960; cons. men's wear; frequent guest speaker network and local radio and TV progs.; service with Royal Candn. Corps of Signals Trumpet Band; recreations: mem., Royal Canadian Military Institute, aviation and military hist., theatrical costumes, Candn. hist., Candn. furniture & glasss; Home: 2 Feldbar Court, Willowdale, Ont. M2N 4P8; Office: 41 Avenue Rd., Toronto, Ont. M5R 2G3.

**MANN, George Stanley;** b. Toronto, Ont. 23 Dec. 1932; s. David Philip and Elizabeth (Green) M.; e. Deer Park Public Sch., Toronto; N. Toronto Coll.; m. Saundra, d. Richard Sair of Montreal, 2 Jan. 1955; children: Michael, Tracy; CHRMN., PRESIDENT & DIRECTOR, LINCORP HOLDINGS, INC. NEW YORK; Dir., Unicorp Energy Corp.; Partner, Mann & Martel Co. Ltd. 1959–68, C.E.O. 1968–70; C.E.O., United Trust Co. 1970–76; Pres., Unicorp Canada Corp. 1972–76; Chrmn. Unicorp Canada Corp. 1976–90; Chrmn., Union Gas Limited and Union Energy Inc. 1986–93; Home: 18 Old Forest Hill Rd., Toronto, Ont. M5P 2P7; Office: 21 St. Clair Ave. E., Toronto, Ont. M4T 2T7.

**MANN, Kenneth Clifford,** O.B.E. (1946), B.Sc., B.Ed., M.A., Ph.D.; physicist; university professor; b. Swift Current, Sask. 2 Oct. 1910; s. William Beecher and Gertrude Amy (Mathews) M.; e. Univ. of Sask. B.Sc. 1931, B.Ed. 1933; Univ. of Toronto M.A. 1936, Ph.D. 1938; m. Iva Viola, d. Alex MacKenzie, Renfrew, Ont., 9 Sept. 1944; children: Shelley Anne; Asst. to Pres., Univ. of B.C. 1977–81; Lectr. in Physics, Univ. of B.C. 1938–39; Asst. Prof. 1939–41; on leave of absence 1941–45, with Radio Br., Nat. Rsch. Counc. as Rsch. Physicist on radar problems; Project Engr. on radar sets for Candn. Navy and Brit. Admiralty; sent to Eng. to test type '268' radar set 1943; loaned to Research Enterprises Ltd., Leaside, Ont., as Engr. in Charge of Production of this set; apptd. Brit. Admiralty Tech. Mission rep. there 1945; Assoc. Prof. of Physics, Univ. of B.C. 1945–46; Prof. 1946–76; joined staff, Chalk River Lab., Nat. Rsch. Counc. on Atomic Energy 1946; mem., Cdn. Assn. of Physicists; Am. Phys. Soc.; Kappa Sigma; Liberal; Anglican; recreations: golf, curling, swimming; Home: 1808 Acadia Rd., Vancouver, B.C. V6T 1R3.

**MANN, Kenneth Henry,** Ph.D., D.Sc., F.R.S.C.; scientist; b. Dovercourt, Essex, Eng. 15 Aug. 1923; s. Harry and Mabel (Ashby) M.; e. Univ. of London B.Sc. 1949, D.Sc. 1965; Univ. of Reading Ph.D. 1953; m. Isabella G. d. James and Annie Ness 18 Apl. 1946; children: Ian, Sheila, Colin; RESEARCH SCIENTIST EMERITUS, DEPT. OF FISHERIES AND OCEANS, BEDFORD INST. OF OCEANOGRAPHY 1993– ; Hon. Adjunct Prof. of Biol., Dalhousie Univ.; Asst. Lectr., Univ. of Reading 1949, Lectr. in Zool. 1951, Reader in Zool. 1965; Rsch. Sci. and Sr. Biol. present Inst. 1967; Prof. and Chrmn. of Biol. Dalhousie Univ. 1972; Dir. Marine Ecology Lab. Bedford Inst. of Oceanography 1980–87; Sr. Rsch. Scientist 1987–93; served with RAF 1942–46, rank Flying Officer; author 'Ecology of Coastal Waters: A Systems Approach' 1982; 'Leeches (Hirudinea): Their Structure, Physiology, Ecology and Embryology' 1962; co-author (with J.R.N. Lazier) 'Dynamics of Marine Ecosystems: Biological-Physical Interactions in the Oceans' 1991; co-author and ed. 'Fundamentals of Aquatic Ecosystems' 1980; 'Mathematical Models in Biological Oceanography' 1981; 'Network Analysis in Marine Ecology' 1989; 'Fundamentals of Aquatic Ecology' 1991; over 170 articles sci. jours.; mem., Brit. Ecol. Soc.; Am. Soc. Limnol. & Oceanog. (Extve. 1980–83); recreations: gardening, swimming, cross-country skiing; Home: 23 Woodward Cres., Halifax, N.S. B3M 1J6; Office: P.O. Box 1006, Dartmouth, N.S. B2Y 4A2.

**MANN, Ron,** B.A.; film maker; b. Toronto, Ont. 13 June 1958; s. Harold and Amy M.; e. Alternative Independent Study Prog. 1975; Bennington Coll. 1976; York Univ. 1977; Innis Coll., Univ. of Toronto, B.A. 1980; m. Patricia d. Ralph Barford 24 May 1986; has produced & direct award winning films ranging from shorts to theatrical features; short films: 'Flak,' 'The Only Game in Town,' 'Ssshhh!,' 'Feels So Good,' 'Echoes Without Saying,' 'Marcia Resnick's Bad Boys,' 'Depot'; feature length documentaries: 'Imagine the Sound,' 'Poetry in Motion,' 'Comic Book Confidential,' 'Twist'; feature drama: 'Listen to the City'; feature length screenplays: 'Hoods in the Woods,' 'Border Lives,' 'Who Am Us Anyway?' 'Electronic Press Kit: Making Legal Eagles'; television documentary: 'Dream Tower'; Extve. Prod. 'The New Cinema,' 'Special of the Day'; Pres., Sphinx Productions; many awards including Genie for best documentary 'Comic Book Confidential'; Office: 24 Mercer St., Toronto, Ont. M5V 1H3.

**MANN, Susan (Trofimenkoff),** Ph.D., LL.D., F.R.S.C.; university president/professor; b. Ottawa, Ont. 10 Feb. 1941; d. Walter Beresford and the late Marjorie Margaret (Diehl) Mann; e. Univ. of Toronto, B.A. 1963; Univ. of West. Ont., M.A. 1965; Univ. Laval, Ph.D. 1970; m. Nicholas s. Nicholas and Mary T.; one d.: Britt-Mari; PRESIDENT, YORK UNIVERSITY 1992– ; Prof. of History, York Univ. 1992– ; Prof., Univ. de Montréal 1966–70; Univ. of Calgary 1970–72; Univ. of Ottawa 1972–92; Chair, Dept. of History, Univ. of Ottawa 1977–80, Vice-Rector Academic 1984–1990; Founding Mem. (and Hon. Life Mem.), Candn. Rsch. Inst. for the Advancement of Women 1976; Pres., Candn. Hist. Assn. 1984–85; Chair, Nat. Archives of Can. Adv. Bd. 1989–91; Mem., Canada Post Corp. Stamp Adv. Ctte. 1989–92; Chair, Status of Women Ctte., Counc. of Ont. Univs. 1985–88; Concordia Univ., LL.D. (hon. doctorate) 1989; F.R.S.C. 1985; author: 'Visions nationales, Une histoire du Québec' 1986, 'Dream of Nation. A Social and Intellectual History of Quebec' cloth 1982, paper 1983, 'Stanley Knowles. The Man from Winnipeg North Centre' cloth 1982, paper 1986; 'Action Française. French Canadian Nationalism in the 1920s' 1975 and hist. articles in scholarly journals; co-editor: 'The Neglected Majority. Essays in Canadian Women's History' vol. 1 1977, vol. 2 1985; editor: 'Abbé Groulx, Variations on a Nationalist Theme' 1973, 'The Twenties in Western Canada' 1972; Office: Office of the President, York University, North York, Ont. M3J 1P3.

**MANN, William Edward,** B.A., M.A., Ph.D.; educator, author; b. Toronto, Ont. 4 Apr. 1918; s. Charles Edward and Laura Louise (Wainwright) M.; e. Univ. Toronto, B.A. 1942; M.A. 1943; Ph.D. 1953; Theology, Trinity Coll. Toronto 1949; m. 1stly Madeleine Helen, d. Frank and Margaret Bear, 15 Dec. 1951 (m. dissolved); m. 2ndly Elizabeth Dianne Hughes, d. George Douglas and Elizabeth Marie (Rosengren), 27 Aug. 1983; children: Jocelyn, Gwynneth, Christopher, Alison, Andrew, Portia; in business 1934–38; univ. teacher 1945–47; Anglican clergyman 1949–59 (Extve. Secy., Toronto Diocesan Counc. for Soc. Service 1953–58); Univ. Prof., Ont. Agricultural Coll. 1959; Univ. Western Ont. 1961; Prof. Sociology, York Univ. 1965–83; Chrmn. Dept. Soc. Atkinson Coll. 1965–68; author 7 books incl. 'Sect, Cult and Church in Alberta' 1955; 'Society Behind Bars' 1969; 'Orgone, Reich & Eros' 1973; 'Vital Energy & Health' 1989; 'The Quest for Total Bliss: A Sociological Interpretation of Rajneeshism' 1990; co-author (with John Lee) 'The RCMP vs the People' 1979; (with Ed Hoffman) 'The Man Who Dreamed of Tomorrow' 1980; editor 8 books incl. 'The Underside of Toronto; Social & Cultural Change in Canada'; 'Social Deviance in Canada' 1971; 'Canada: A Sociological Profile' (3rd ed. with Les Wheatcroft) 1976; rec'd. 6 Can. Counc. Awards, incl. Leave Fellowship 1972; 2 Candn. Soc. Scis. Rsch. Awards; Motoyama-Bentov Fellowship (for rsch.-study in Japan) 1985; served as Navigation instructor, Flying Offr., Royal Candn. Air Force 1943–45; Special Lectr., Trinity Coll, Univ. of Toronto 1945–46; 1947–49; Asst. Secy. Candn. Counc Churches 1948–49; Pres., Life Energy Action & Rsch. Network 1978–82; Ed., Internat. Journal of Life Energy 1978–81; Dir., Soc. Science Publishers 1967–69; Consultant, Community Relation Services 1968–72; Bioenergy researcher and facilitator 1973– ; Anglican; recreations: Squash, Volleyball, tennis, gardening; Home: 7 Pittypat Court, Aurora, Ont. L4G 6J6.

**MANN BORGESE, Elisabeth,** B.A., Ph.D., O.C.; university professor, author; b. Munich, Germany 24 Apr. 1918; d. Thomas Paul and Katharina (Pringsheim) Mann; e. Freies Gymnasium Zurich B.A. 1935; Conservatory of Music, Zurich dipl. 1937; Mount St. Vincent Univ. Ph.D. (h.c.) 1986; m. G.A. s. Giuseppe and Maria Borgese 23 Nov. 1939; children: Angelica, Dominica; PROF., POLITICAL SCIENCE DEPT., DALHOUSIE UNIV. 1979– ; Rsch. Assoc., Univ. of Chicago 1946–52; Editor, 'Common Cause' 1948–52; Intercultural Publications Inc. 1952–63; Extve. Sec., Bd. of Editors, Encyclopaedia Britannica 1964–65; Sr. Fellow, Ctr. for the Study of Democratic Institutions (Calif.) 1964–78; Killam Sr. Fellow, Dalhousie Univ. 1978–79; Chair, Internat. Ocean Inst. Malta 1972–92; Hon. Chair for Life 1992; Chair, Internat. Ctr. for Ocean Devel. 1986–92; Adviser, Delegation of Austria to the Law of the Sea 1974–84; decoration for High Merit, Govt. of Austria 1984; O.C. 1986; U.N. Environment Prize 1986; Gold Medal, Govt. of Malta; Medal of Merit, Govt. of Columbia 1992; St. Francis of Assisi Internat. Environment Prize 1993; Mem., World Acad. of Arts & Sci.; Third World Acad. of Sci.; author: 'To Whom It May Concern' 1963 (short stories), 'Ascent of Woman' 1964, 'The White Snake' (UK) 1966, 'The Language Barrier' (US) 1966, 'The Ocean Regime' 1968, 'The Drama of the Ocean' 1976, 'Seafarm' 1981, 'The Mines of Neptune' 1984, 'The Future of the Oceans' 1987, 'Ocean Frontiers' 1992; 'Chairworm and Supershark' 1992; editor: 'Pacem in Maribus' 1973, 'The Tides of Change' 1975, 'Ocean Yearbook' 10 vols. 1980– ; recreations: skiing, swimming, walking, caring for animals; Home: Sambro Head, Halifax, N.S.; Office: 1226 Lemarchant St., Halifax, N.S. B3H 3P7.

**MANNING, C(harles) Terrill,** Q.C., B.A., B.C.L.; b. Empress, Alta. 27 March 1925; s. N. Folsom and Mary Ethel (Terrill) M.; e. Huntingdon Acad. 1942; Bishop's Univ. B.A. 1946; McGill Univ. B.C.L. 1949; m. Hazel Joyce, d. late Andrew Stuart Johnson, 1946; children: A. Terrill, Timothy F., Heather J., Annabelle H.; ASSOCIATED MCMASTER MEIGHEN (MONTREAL) 1985– and CONSULTANT MEIGHEN DEMERS (TORONTO) 1990– ; read law with F. Winfield Hackett, K.C.; called to Bar of Que. 1949; cr. Q.C. 1968; law practice Hackett, Mulvena, Hackett 1949–56, Partner 1955; assoc. with Brinco 1956–69 serving latterly as Vice Pres. and Gen. Counsel; Vice Pres.-Legal, Churchill Falls Labrador Corp. Ltd.; Vice Pres. and Dir. Twin Falls Power Corp. Ltd. and British Newfoundland Exploration Ltd.; joined The Royal Trust Co. as Gen. Counsel 1970; Vice Pres. 1975; retired as Vice Pres., Sec. and Chief Legal Offr. Royal Trustco Ltd. 1978–84; served with RCNVR 1944–45; Chrmn. Special Corp's Div. Combined Appeal 1971; Pres. Nat. Comte. Bishop's Univ. Alumni Assn. 1965–67; active Montreal W. Boy Scouts 1955–65; Dir. Weston Sch. Inc. 1973–76; mem. Candn. Bar Assn.; Que. Bar Assn.; Liberal; Anglican; recreations: fishing, golf; Clubs: Bd. of Trade (Toronto); Home: 470 Copeland Crt., Oakville, Ont. L6J 4B9; Office: 11th Flr., PO Box 11, 200 King St. W., Toronto, Ont. M5H 3T4.

**MANNING, Eric,** B.Sc., M.Sc., Ph.D., F.IEEE, F.EIC, P.Eng.; university professor; b. Windsor, Ont. 4 Aug. 1940; s. George Gorman and Eleanor Katherine (Koehler) M.; e. Univ. of Waterloo, B.Sc. 1961, M.Sc. 1962; Univ. of Illinois, Ph.D. 1965; m. Betty d. Ken and Alberta Goldring 16 Sept. 1961; children: David, Paula; WIGHTON PROFESSOR, UNIV. OF VICTORIA 1993– ; various pos., MIT and Bell Telephone Labs. 1965–68; Prof., Computer Sci. 1968–86 and Dir., Inst. for Computer Rsch., Univ. of Waterloo 1982–86; Dir., Computer Commun. Networks Group 1973–82; Prof. & Dean, Faculty of Engineering, Univ. of Victoria 1986–92; IBM chair of Computer Sci., Keio Univ. Yokohama 1992–93; Mem., Natural Sci. & Engr. Rsch. Counc., 1981–86 (Past Chrmn., Ctte. on Strategic Grants); Dir., Science Counc. of B.C., 1988–91; Fellow, Inst. of Elect. & Elect. Engrs.; Dir., BC Microelectronics Soc. 1986–88; Trustee, BC Advanced Systems Found. 1986–93; Trustee, Candn. Soc. for Fifth Generation Rsch. 1987–88; Assn. Profl. Engrs. B.C. 1987– ; Soc. for Computer Simulation 1987– ; Nat. Adv. Counc. Mem., Candn. Advanced Technology Assoc. 1986– ; Bd. of Dirs., Candn. Microelectronics Corp. 1989–93; Dir., National Wireless Communications Rsch. Foundation 1991–92; Mem., Candn. Inst. for Advanced Rsch. Adv. Ctte. on Artificial Intelligence and Robotics 1986– ; Mem., Nat. Rsch. Counc. Adv. Ctte. on Artificial Intelligence 1987–91; various corporate boards; author or co-author of over 60 rsch. articles and one book; editor of various academic jours.; recreations: squash, scuba diving, trumpets, sailing, flying; Home: 2909 Phyllis St., Victoria, BC V8N 1Y8; Office: Faculty of Engineering, Univ. of Victoria, P.O. Box 3055, Victoria, B.C. V8W 3P6.

**MANNING, Frank Arthur,** M.D., M.Sc., F.R.C.S.(C), F.A.C.O.G.; obstetrician; educator; b. Virden, Man. 6 March 1946; s. Frank Russell and Florence Janet (Fletcher) M.; e. Brandon Univ. Pre-Med 1964–66; Univ. of Man. M.D. 1970; Oxford Univ. M.Sc.(Fetal Physiol.) 1976; m. Ann d. Peter and Iris Briggs 11 Feb. 1981; three d. Joanna Louise, Virginia Jane Helen, Alexandra Joy; CHRMN. OF OBSTETRICS, GYNECOL., REPRODUCTIVE SCIENCES, HEALTH SCIENCES CENTRE, UNIV. OF MAN. 1983– ; Asst. Prof. Univ. of S. Cal. Los Angeles 1976–80, estbd. first fetal assessment unit; described and reported concept 'fetal biophysical profile scanning' now universally applied fetal testing method; estbd. Can.'s first fetal assessment prog. 1980; performed first fetal surg. Can. and estbd. Candn. Fetal Surgery Prog. 1982; performed first fetal intravascular transfusion and estbd. Winnipeg as Candn. and N.Am. referral centre for this method; Registrar Internat. Fetal Surgery Registry; author 'Fetal Assessment: Current Concepts' 1986; 'Principles and Practice of Ultrasound in Obstetrics and Gynecology' 1990; 'Fetal Medicine Today and Tomorrow' 1990; over 140 sci. papers; numerous speaking engagements; mem. Soc. Obstetrics & Gynecol. Can. (Chrmn. Med. Legal Ctte.); Am. Gynecol. & Obstetrics Soc.; Soc. Gynecol. Investig.; Fetal Med. & Surg. Soc. (Past Pres.); Am. Inst. Ultrasound in Med.; Candn. Reproduction Investig.; recreations: golf, tennis, bridge; Club: St. Charles Country; Home: 119 Handsart Blvd., Winnipeg, Man. R3P 0C9; Office: 800 Sherbrooke St., Winnipeg, Man. R3A 1M4.

**MANNING, Jo (Joan Elizabeth);** artist; b. Sidney, B.C. 11 Dec. 1923; d. Frederick William and Elizabeth (Willcox) Manning; e. Gen Amherst Secondary Sch. 1941, Amherstburg, Ont.; Ont. Coll. of Art 1945; children: Paul, Peter, Ann and Mary Rothfels; solo exhns. incl. Pollock Gallery Toronto 1965, 1968; Gallery Pascal Toronto 1974, 1977, 1980; Univ. of Waterloo 1968; Mira Godard Gallery Montreal 1976; Mira Godard Calgary 1981; Gadatsy Gallery, Toronto 1984; Bishop's Univ., Lennoxville, P.Q. 1989; rep. numerous nat. and internat. (USA, Australia, Europe, S. Am.) group exhns. since 1966; rep. various pub., corporate and private colls. incl. Nat. Gallery Can.; Montreal Museum of Fine Art; Can. Council Art Bank; Dept. External Affairs; Nat. Lib. Can.; awards incl. Santiago, Chile 4th Am. Print Biennale First Prize 1970; Florence, Italy 2nd Print Biennale Gold Medal 1970; Norwegian Print Biennale Hon. Mention 1976; Medal, 6th Internat. Grafix Biennale, Frechen, Germany 1980; Address: R.R. 3, Blyth, Ont. N0M 1H0.

**MANNING, Morris,** LL.B., Q.C.; lawyer; b. Montréal, Qué. 6 Nov. 1940; e. Univ. of Toronto, LL.B. 1965; m. Linda Rapson 3 June 1965; children: Kathryn Jane, Rachel Elizabeth; Couns., Attorney Gen. for Ont. 1967–73; Sr. Crown Couns., Civil Litigation Legal Adv. Serv. 1973–76; priv. practice 1976– ; Special Couns., Metro Toronto Yonge Street problem, 1977; Special Couns., City of Toronto on drug problems; Couns., numerous groups & individuals with legal problems with govts. at all levels; Lectr., cont. legal edn., judicial seminars, other groups, on many aspects of law and constitutional rights; Certified as a Specialist in Criminal Litigation, Law Soc. of Upper Can.; cons. to Law Reform Comn. of Can.; Q.C. 1978; author: 'The Protection of Privacy Act' 1974, 'Wiretap Law in Canada' 1978, 'Rights, Freedoms and the Courts' 1982 and num. profl. articles in legal jours. and texts; co-author: 'Criminal Law' 1st ed. 1974, 2nd ed. 1978, 3rd ed. 1994; editor: 'Canadian Criminal Cases,' 'Dominion Law Reports,' 'Ontario Reports' 1969–72, 1981–83; listed in Who's Who in Canadian Law; recreations: cooking, classical music; Home: 125 Fallingbrook Rd., Scarborough, Ont. M1N 2T8; Office: 174 Avenue Rd., Toronto, Ont. M5R 2J1.

**MANNING, (Ernest) Preston,** M.P., B.A.; politician; b. Edmonton, Alta. 10 June 1942; s. Ernest Charles and Muriel Aileen (Preston) M.; e. Univ. of Alta. B.A. 1964; m. Sandra d. Gordon and Mary Beavis; children: Andrea, Avryll, Mary Joy, Nathan, David; LEADER, REFORM PARTY OF CANADA 1987– ; Owner/operator, Manning Consultants Limited 1968–88 (research and management consultant firm); has been interested in political reform for 25 years; key organizer, Western Assembly on Canada's Economic & Political Future, Vancouver May 1987; elected Leader at Founding Assembly, Oct. 1987, Reform Party of Canada; nominated Reform Party candidate, federal constituency of Calgary Southwest; elected Member of Parliament for Calgary Southwest, federal gen. election 1993; mandate: 'I want to help get federal spending under control. I want to help reform the Parliament so that MPs can more effectively represent the interests of the constituents who elect them. And I want to help rewrite the Canadian Constitution so that it provides for the equal treatment of the provinces and of all citizens regardless of race, language, or culture.' author: 'The New Canada' 1992; recreations: travelling, shopping, fishing, and horseback riding with family; Office: 600, 833 – 4 Ave. S.W., Calgary, Alta. T2P 0K5.

**MANNING, Randolph William,** F.C.A.; chartered accountant; b. Falmouth, N.S. 1 Aug. 1915; s. late Charles Randolph and late Mabel Vernon (Wilson) M.; e. Falmouth (N.S.) Sch. 1928; Windsor (N.S.) Acad. 1931; Kings Coll. Sch., Windsor, N.S. 1932; Maritime Business Coll., Halifax 1936; C.A. 1942; B.A. (Hist.) Univ. of P.E.I. 1986; m. Mary Kathleen, d. late W.G. Bauchman, 11 Sept. 1939; children: Terry Randolph (dec'd), Mrs. Carolyn Celeste Allworth; CONSULTANT, DOANE RAYMOND; Teacher, Maritime Business Coll. 1937; Student Acct., H.R. Doane and Co. 1938; became Partner 1942; opened firm's 1st br. office, Charlottetown, P.E.I. 1944; joined mgmt. comte. on formation of present firm 1959; Dir., P.E.I. Devel. Agency 1984–87; el. Pres., Candn. Inst. of C.A.'s 1967 (mem. Extve. Comte. 1954–56 and 1965–68); mem., Inst. of C.A.'s of P.E.I. (Pres. 1948); rec'd Queen's Silver Jubilee Medal 1977; Paul Harris Fellowship, Rotary Internat. 1977; Adjunct Prof., Univ. P.E.I. 1983–91; United Church; recreations: golf, gardening, music, history, travel; Club: Rotary; Home: 191 North River Rd., Charlottetown, P.E.I. C1A 3L4.

**MANNING, Travis Warren,** M.Sc., Ph.D.; educator; b. Okla. 17 June 1921; s. John and Ida (Young) M.; e. Univ. of Oklahoma 1947; Oklahoma State Univ. B.Sc. 1949; M.Sc. 1950; Univ. of Minn. Ph.D. 1954; m. Bobbie Jean, d. Robert Fulton, Hugo, Okla. 26 Jan. 1943; children: Barbara, Mary, Patricia, Nancy, John, Linda; PROF. EMERITUS OF AGRICULTURAL ECON., UNIV. OF ALTA. 1984– ; Instr., Univ. of Minn. 1950–53; Asst. Prof. to Prof., S.D. State Univ. 1953–59; Agric. Econ., Fed. Reserve Bank of Kansas City 1959–62; Prof. of Agricultural Econ., Univ. of Alta. 1962–84; Visiting Prof., Univ. of Cal. Berkeley 1967–68; served with U.S. Army 1941–45; author of articles for various prof. journs.; mem., Am. Agric. Econ. Assn.; W. Agric. Econ. Assn.; Phi Kappa Phi; Pi Gamma Mu; Fellow, Candn. Agricultural Econ. & Farm Management Soc.; Home: 3401 Galaway Bay Dr., Grand Prairie, TX 75052-8013; Office: Dept. of Rural Economy, Univ. of Alta., Edmonton, Alta. T6G 2H1.

**MANNION, Edward James;** publisher; b. Preston, Ont. 21 Sept. 1927; s. John and Elizabeth M.; e. St. Clements Sch. and Preston (Ont.) High Sch. 1943; Galt (Ont.) Coll. Inst. 1945; m. Marie Helene d. Oscar Messier, Montreal, Que. 22 Apr. 1950; children: James, Mary, Theresa, Kathleen; PRES., MANNION ENTERPRISES LTD.; Chrmn., The Bench Press Ltd.; Amalcon Corp.; Canadian Home Publishers Inc.; Creative Outdoor Advertising; Dir.: Children's Aid Soc. of Metrop. Toronto Foundn.; Advertising Salesman, Galt Evening Reporter 1948–50, Advertising Mgr. 1952–53; Advertising Mgr. Timmins Daily Press 1950–52; Dir. Retail Advertising, Thomson Newspapers Ltd. 1953–57, Dir. of Sales 1957–66; Gen. Mgr. Thomson Newspapers Inc. (U.S.) 1966–68; Pres., C.E.O. and Publisher, Southstar Publishers Ltd. 1968–78; Chrmn. & C.E.O., Southam Communications Ltd. 1978–84; Pres. & C.E.O., Jr. Achievement of Canada 1984–85; R. Catholic; recreations: golf, tennis; Clubs: National; Donalda; Canadian (N.Y.); Home: 17 Dempsey Cres., Willowdale, Ont. M2L 1Y4.

**MANOLAKOS, Demetrius,** B.A., LL.B.; notary; title attorney; b. Montreal, Que. 4 Mar. 1935; s. Nicholas and Panagiota (Konstiantou) M.; e. Strathcona Acad. 1952; Sir George Williams Coll. B.A. 1956; Univ. de Montréal LL.B. 1963; Dir., Equipex Ltd.; Secy., Metroplex Investments Ltd.; Dir. numerous cos.; admitted to practise as Notary Prov. Que. 1966; Past Dir., Hellenic Candn. Trust Co. (now National Bank of Greece (Canada); recipient Student Soc. 'Major Award' Sir George Williams Coll. 1956; Queen's Silver Jubilee Medal 1977; Commemorative Cross Patriarch Justinian I of Roumania; Patriarchal Cross of Constantinople; Councillor, City of Montreal 1978–82; Hon. Pres., Hellenic Candn. Solidarity Ctte. for Cyprus; Past Dir., Candn. Council Christians & Jews; Past. Pres., Montreal Citizenship Council; Hellenic Community Montreal; Order of AHEPA; past mem., Archdiocesan Council Greek Orthodox Archdiocese of N. and S. Am. 1971–88; Trustee, Holy Cross Theol. Semy. Hellenic Coll. Brookline, Mass.; mem., Candn. Concultative Council on Multiculturalism 1971–77; mem., Order Notaries Prov. Que.; Candn. Bar Assn.; Assn. Notaries Dist. Montreal; author numerous newspaper articles; recreations: music, hockey, skiing; Home: F–20, 1321 Sherbrooke St. W., Montreal, Que. H3G 1J4; Office: 1115 Sherbrooke St. W., Suite 1105, Montreal, Que. H3A 1H3.

**MANSON, Gen. Paul D.,** C.M.M., C.D., B.Sc., P.Eng.; executive; pilot; b. Trail, B.C. 20 Aug. 1934; s. late Robert E. and late Mary L. (McLeod) M.; e. Royal Roads Mil. Coll. 1954; Royal Mil. Coll. 1956; Queen's Univ. B.Sc. 1957; Candn. Forces Staff Coll. 1967; Nat. Defence Coll. 1974; Doctor of Mil. Sci. (hon. causa) Royal Roads 1990; m. Margaret d. Oscar and Marion

Nickel 11 May 1957; children: Robert, Catherine, Peter, Karen; PRES., PARAMAX SYSTEMS CANADA, INC. 1992– ; joined RCAF 1952; received Pilot's Wings 1957; served as fighter pilot in Germany and Can. flying CF–100, F–86, CF–104, CF–101; C.O. 441 Reconn. Squadron, Lahr, Germany 1960s; Base Comdr. CFB Chatham, N.B. 1974–76; Comdr. 1 Candn. Air Group, Germany 1980–81; Comdr., Air Command 1983–85; served in numerous staff positions: Extve. Asst. to the Chief of Defence Staff 1972–73, Prog. Mgr. for New Fighter Aircraft Prog. 1977–80, leading to selection of CF–18 Hornet; promoted Lt. Gen. 1983; ADM (Personnel), Dept. of Nat. Defence 1985–86; Chief of the Defence Staff 1986–89; Sr. Vice-Pres., Paramax Electronics Inc. 1990–92; Found. mem. Billy Bishop Heritage; Assn. of Profl. Engrs. of Ont.; Sword of Hon., Royal Mil. Coll. 1956; Comdr., Order of Mil. Merit 1981; C.D. Howe Award 1992; recreations: astronomy, golf, music, home computing; Home: 20 Lakeshore Dr., Dorval, Que. H9S 2A2; Office: 6111 Royalmount Ave., Montreal, Que. H4P 1K6.

**MANSOURI, Lotfollah (Lotfi),** A.B.; opera stage director; b. Tehran, Iran 15 June 1929; s. Hassan and Mehri (Jalili) M.; e. Univ. of Cal. Los Angeles A.B. 1953; m. Marjorie Anne Thompson 18 Sept. 1954; one d. Shireen Melinda; GENERAL DIR., SAN FRANCISCO OPERA 1988– ; Gen. Dir., Candn. Opera Co. 1976–88; Asst. Prof. Univ. Cal. Los Angeles 1957–60; Dramatic Coach Music Acad. West, Santa Barbara, Cal. 1959; Resident Stage Dir. Zurich Opera 1960–65; Dir. Dramatics Zurich Internat. Opera Studio 1961–65; Centre Lyrique Geneva 1967–72; Chief Stage Dir. Geneva Opera 1965–75; Artistic Adv. Tehran Opera 1973–75; Opera Adv. Nat. Arts Centre Ottawa 1977; Operatic Consulting Dir. MGM film 'Yes, Giorgio' 1981; Opera Sequence in Norman Jewison's Film 'Moonstruck' 1987; Guest Dir. various opera cos. incl. The Met, San Francisco Opera, La Scala, Vienna Staatsoper, Vienna Volksoper, Salzburg Festival, Covent Garden, Amsterdam Opera, Holland Festival, L'Opera de Nice, Festival d'Orange, Australian Opera, Lyric Opera Chicago, Dallas Opera; co-author 'An Operatic Life' 1982; with 'Surtitles TM' initiated above-stage projection of simultaneous translation of opera 1983; mem. Bd. Dirs., Opera Am. 1979–91; mem. Am. Guild Musical Artists; Candn. Actors' Equity Assn.; Office: War Memorial Opera House, 301 Van Ness Ave., San Francisco, CA 94102–4509.

**MANTSCH, Henry Horst,** Ph.D., F.C.I.C., F.R.S.C.; scientist; b. Mediasch, Transylvania 30 July 1935; s. Heinrich and Olga Augusta (Gondosch) M.; e. Univ. of Cluj-Napoca, Transylvania Dipl. Chem. 1958, Ph.D. 1964; m. Amy Emilia d. Ana and Francisc Kory 2 Nov. 1959; two d. Monica Ami, Marietta Liana; HEAD OF MOLECULAR SPECTROSCOPY SECT., NAT. RESEARCH COUNCIL OF CAN. 1977– ; Adjunct Prof. of Biophys. Chem., Carleton Univ. 1978–90; Ottawa Univ. 1990–93; Univ. of Manitoba, Winnipeg 1992– ; Rsch. Sci. Romanian Acad. Sciences 1958–65; Postdoctoral Humboldt Fellow Tech. Univ. Munich, W. Germany 1966–67; Postdoctoral Fellow, Div. of Pure Chem. present Council 1968–70, Visiting Rsch. Offr. Div. Biol. Sci. 1971–72; Prof. of Biochem. Univ. of Cluj-Napoca, Romania 1973–74; Prof. of Biophys. Chem. Liebig Univ., Giessen, W. Germany 1975–76; recipient Herzberg Award 1984; Humboldt Award and Medal for Intnl. Sci. Cooperation 1980; Medal for Sci. Merit 1972; author 350 sci. publs., patents, book chapters spectroscopy and biophys. chem.; mem., Chem. Inst. Can.; Cdn. Spectroscopy Soc.; Am. Biophys. Soc.; Soc. Applied Spectroscopy; recreations: mountain climbing, tennis, chess; Home: 2222 West Taylor Blvd., Winnipeg, Man. R3P 2J5; Office: 435 Ellice Ave., Winnipeg, Man. R3B 1Y6.

**MANU, Alexander H.;** industrial designer; b. Bucharest, Romania 1 Feb. 1954; s. Herman and Sabina (Schwartz) M.; e. Fine Arts High Sch. N.Tonitza Bucharest Dip. 1973; Univ. of Bucharest Inst. of Fine Arts Decorative Arts Div., Ind. Design Sect. Master of Decorative Arts 1978; FOUNDER, THE AXIS GROUP INC. 1980– ; came to Can. 1979; staff designer Creelman International Ltd.; Teacher Ind. Design Fanshawe Coll. London, Ont. 1981; mem. Adv. Bd. Humber Coll. Ind. Design Div. Toronto, part-time teacher; lectures and seminars design issues Ont. Coll. of Art, Toronto Design Conf., Osaka Univ., Sozosha Design Coll. Osaka, CETRA and BIPA Taiwan; mem. internat. design adv. group, design cons. Far E.; Cons. China Trade Devel. Council, CETRA Taiwan, R.O.C.; mem. Internat. Jury Taiwan Good Design Exposition 1988; Special guest Asian mems. Council Meeting Internat. Council Ind. Design Soc's 1988; frequent guest speaker design related subjects Can., Japan, Taiwan, R.O.C.; recipient Design Award Best of Show Ottawa High Tech. Sch. 1986; numerous speaking engagements on design related subjects; Dir., Assn. of Candn. Industrial Designers (ACID); mem., Design Advisory Boards active at governmental levels in Canada and the Far East; Consultant on Design Strategy for the Candn. Dept. of Candn. Heritage; mem. Extve. Bd., Internat. Council of Societies of Industrial Design 1992–93 (ICSID); Founding Dir., Humane Village Network 1993; mem., Assn. of Chartered Industrial Designers of Ont. (ACIDO), Pres. 1988–92; Assn. of Candn. Industrial Designers (ACID), Dir. 1989– ; Graphic Designers of Canada (MGDC); Industrial Design Soc. of Am. (IDSA); ; elected on Board, Internat. Council of Industrial Design Socs. (ICSID) 1992, re-elected 1993; Home: 369 Walmer Rd., Toronto, Ont. M5R 2Y4; Office: 65 Bellwoods Ave., Toronto, Ont. M6J 3N4.

**MANUCHA, Rajiv,** B.A.Sc., M.B.A., P.Eng.; computer hardware and software consulting; b. Kanpur, India 10 Jan. 1954; s. Raj Krishna and Radha (Sachdev) M.; e. Univ. of Toronto, B.A.Sc. 1975, M.B.A. 1976; PRES. MSR INC. 1982– and CHIEF EXTVE. OFFR., ESAS INC.; Chrmn. of the Board, EDI Customs Brokers Inc.; Financial Analyst Corporate Mfg. Control Area, International Business Machines 1976, Systems Eng. Atlanta, Ga. 1978, Toronto 1979–82; mem. Assn. Prof. Engs. Prov. Ont.; Liberal; recreations: canoeing, tennis, sailing, skiing; Clubs: Wychwood; Empire; Home: 325 Betty Ann Dr., Willowdale, Ont. M2R 1B4.

**MANZER, Alison Rosemary,** B.Sc., LL.B., M.B.A.; lawyer; b. Saint John, N.B. 1 July 1954; d. Turney Clarence and Audrey Elizabeth (Baird) M.; e. Dartmouth H.S. 1971; Dalhousie Univ. B.Sc. (Hons.) 1974, LL.B. 1977; Univ. of Toronto M.B.A. 1984; Candn. Securities Inst.: Candn. Securities Course 1984, Candn. Investment Finance I 1985, II 1986 (placed 5th in Canada); m. Glen s. Paul and Rita De La Franier 18 Sept. 1987; children: Amy Rose, Brian James; PARTNER, CASSELS, BROCK & BLACKWELL 1990– ; Lawyer, Burt, Burt, Wolfe and Bowman 1979–81; Robins, Appleby & Taub 1981–90 (Partner 1984–90); Dir. & Extve. Vice-Pres., Moyer Vico Corp. 1988–90; Special Advisor, Liptons Fashion Wear Limited 1987–88; Head, Law Soc. of U.C. Bar Admission Course Program on the Business of the Practice of Law, 1988, '89; Mem., Candn. Bar Assn. (Nat. & Prov. Council 1986– ); Candn. Bar Assn., Ont.; Mem., Prog. Ctte., Cont. Legal Edn., 1987–89; Chair 1989–91; Mem., Ctte. on Paralegals 1989– ; Extve. Business Law Section 1988– ; Special Ctte. on Paralegals, Mem. 1987–89; lecturer and author of num. articles specific to legal and business topics pub. in var. pubs. incl. 'The Nat. Banking Law Rev.,' Cont. Legal Edn. pubs. of Law Soc. of U.C. & Candn. Bar Assn., Ont.; Bank Act Annotated, May 1993 (Butterworths); recreations: horse-back riding, art collector; Office: 40 King St. W., Suite 2100, Toronto, Ont. M5H 3C2.

**MANZER, Ronald Alexander,** B.Ed., M.A., Ph.D.; educator; b. Fredericton, N.B. 8 July 1937; s. Ronald Wendell and Margaret Jean (McLean) M.; e. Smythe St. Sch. Fredericton; Fredericton H.S.; Univ. of N.B., B.A., B.Ed. 1959; Univ. Coll. Oxford (Rhodes Scholar) B.A. 1961, M.A. 1964; Harvard Univ. Ph.D. 1966; m. Kathryn d. John and Olive Hart 26 Aug. 1961; two d. Patricia, Jennifer; PROFESSOR OF POLITICAL SCIENCE, UNIVERSITY OF TORONTO 1975– ; Asst. Prof. present Univ. 1965, Assoc. Prof. 1968, Assoc. Chrmn. Pol. Econ. 1975–78, Asst. Dean Scarborough Coll. 1966–69, Gov. 1982–85; author 'Teachers and Politics' 1970; 'Canada: A Socio-Political Report' 1974; 'Public Policies and Political Development in Canada' 1985; 'Public Schools and Political Ideas: Canadian Educational Policy in Historical Perspective' 1994; co-editor 'Canadian Journal of Political Science' 1987–90; mem. Candn. Pol. Sci. Assn. (Dir. 1976–78); Inst. Pub. Adm. Can.; recreations: running, tennis, skiing; Home: 3 Donmac Dr., Don Mills, Ont. M3B 1N4; Office: Toronto, Ont. M5S 1A1.

**MAPLESDEN, Douglas Cecil,** D.V.M., M.S.A., Ph.D.; veterinarian; educator; writer; b. Sandhurst, Kent, Eng. 30 Oct. 1919; s. Cecil Walker and Frances (Pantry) M.; e. Ont. Veterinary Coll. D.V.M. 1950; Univ. of Toronto M.S.A. 1957; Cornell Univ. Ph.D. 1959; m. Joan Duda; children: Anne Elizabeth Hopkins, John Douglas, Mary Jane, Joann Margaret; stepchildren: Kelly and Joseph Kennedy; private practice Seaforth, Ont. 1950–51; Herd Veterinarian, Flat Top Ranch, Walnut Springs, Texas 1951–53; Assoc. to full Prof. Ont. Veterinary Coll. 1953–60; Veterinary Dir., V.P. Stevenson, Turner & Boyce Ltd. Guelph 1960–63; Dir. Animal Health R & D to Gen. Mgr. Animal Div., CIBA Pharmaceuticals, Summit, N.J. 1963–69; Dir. Animal Health R & D, Squibb Corp. Princeton, N.J. 1969–79; Pres., Hunterdon Co. Chamber Comm. N.J. 1971–72; Dean, Ont. Veterinary Coll., Univ. Of Guelph 1980–84; Writer/Consultant 1985–94; author: 'Handbook of Practical Feeding and Nutrition of Domestic Animals' 1962; 'The Universal Diet' 1986; 'Deadly Design' (novel) 1994; Ed.-in-Chief 'Canadian Veterinary Journal' 1962–64 (Business Mgr. 1960–62); mem., Am. Vet. Med. Assn.; Ont. Vet. Med. Assn.; recreations: swimming, boating; Home: 3117 N.E. 40th Court, Fort Lauderdale, FL 33308.

**MAR, Gary G.,** B.Comm., LL.B., M.L.A.; politician; b. Calgary, Alberta 26 July 1962; s. Barry George and Jean Ngwe (Mah) M.; e. Univ. of Calgary B.Comm. 1984; Univ. of Alberta LL.B. 1987; MINISTER OF COMMUNITY DEVELOPMENT ALBERTA 1993– ; Lawyer, MacKimmie Matthews 1987–90; Code Hunter 1990–92; private general law practice 1992– ; 1st elected M.L.A. for Calgary Nose Creek 15 June 1993; Dir., Sein Lok Soc. 1987–93; Vice-Pres., Chinatown Devel. Found. 1990–93; United Ch.; P.C.; co-author: 'The Law of Civil Procedure in Alberta'; Office: Room 227, Legislature Bldg., Edmonton, Alta. T5K 2B6.

**MARA, George Edward,** C.M.; executive; b. Toronto, Ont. 12 Dec. 1921; s. George Edward and Gladys (Franks) M.; e. Upper Can. Coll. Toronto; m. Margaret Mary d. late Margaret R. and late James O. Roddick 22 Mar. 1947; children: George Jr., Diane; VICE CHRMN. and DIR., JANNOCK LTD. 1975– ; Dir., Confederation Life Insurance Co.; Dir., The Conn Smythe Foundation; Gov., Olympic Trust of Can.; Hon. Mem., Candn. Olympic Assn.; Mem., Candn. Forces Sports Hall of Fame; Candn. Amateur Sports Hall of Fame; Canada's Sports Hall of Fame; Mem., Order of Canada 1976; Hon. Dir., Wellesley Hospital; served with RCN World War II, rank Lt.; Clubs: Toronto; York; Rosedale Golf; Badminton & Racquet (Toronto); Country Club of Florida; Gulfstream Golf; Delray Beach Yacht; Ocean Reef; St. Andrews, Florida; Home: 42 Park Lane Circle, Don Mills, Ont. M3C 2N2; Office: Scotia Plaza, Suite 5205, P.O. Box 1012, 40 King St. W., Toronto, Ont. M5H 3Y2.

**MARADEN, Marti;** actress; b. El Centro, Cal. 22 June 1945; d. Ole Woodrow and Mildred Genevieve (Wallin Fredrickson); e. Univ. of Minn.; Mich. State Univ.; joined Stratford Festival Theatre 1974–79: maj. roles incl. Juliet; Ophelia; Miranda; Cecily Cardew; Irina 'Three Sisters'; Sonya 'Uncle Vanya'; BAM Theatre Co., Off-Broadway 1979–80: maj. roles incl. Hermione 'Winter's Tale'; Anna 'The Barbarians'; Hudson Guild Theatre, Off-Broadway 1981, 1983: maj. roles incl. Janet 'Waiting for the Parade'; Actress/Lizzie 'Blood Relations'; Mark Taper Forum Los Angeles 1982: Bette Milner 'Number Our Days'; Shaw Festival Theatre Niagara-on-the-Lake 1982, 1983, 1985: maj. roles incl. Roxanne 'Cyrano'; Cleopatra; Ellie Dunn 'Heartbreak House'; Wendy 'Peter Pan'; numerous appearances CBC TV and Radio 1971–89; 'The Dining Room,' Gemstone Productions 1984; Dir.: (Shaw Festival) 'Breaking the Silence'; 'He Who Gets Slapped' 1988; 'Getting Married' 1989; (Stratford Festival) 'Home' 1990; 'Les Belles Soeurs' 1991; 'Homeward Bound' 1991; 'Love's Labour's Lost' 1992; 'The Two Gentlemen of Verona' 1992; 'The Illusion' 1993; (Candn. Stage Co.) 'Fallen Angels' 1992 (recipient, Dora nomination); recipient Tyrone Guthrie Award; Dir. 'Home' for Stratford Festival 1990; Home: 101 Geoffrey St., Toronto, Ont. M6R 1P2.

**MARANDA, Pierre,** L.Ph., M.A., Ph.D., F.R.S.C.; anthropologist; b. Québec, Qué. 27 March 1930; s. Lucien and Marie-Alma (Rochette) M.; e. Univ. Laval B.A. 1949; Univ. de Montréal M.A. 1952, L.Ph. 1955; Harvard Univ. M.A. 1966, Ph.D. 1966; m. Elli (dec.) d. Matti Köngäs, Tervola, Finland 12 March 1963; two s. Erik, Nicolas; PROF. OF ANTHROP. UNIV. LAVAL 1976– ; served as Prof. Harvard Univ., 1965–66; Sorbonne, 1968–70; Ecole des Hautes Etudes en Sciences Sociales Paris, 1968–70; Univ. of B.C., 1970–75; Coll. de France, 1975; Universidade Fed. do Rio de Janeiro; 1982; Bd. mem. several insts. and socs.; Pres. Comité des Citoyens de Belvédère 1976–83; recipient Médaille du Coll. de France 1975; Doctorate honoris causa, Memorial Univ. 1984; numerous fellowships and scholarships (Harvard, Nat. Inst. Health U.S.A., Sorbonne, Can. Council, Social Sciences & Humanities Research Council Can.); author 'Structural Models in Folklore and Transformational Essays' 1971; 'French Kinship: Structure and History' 1974; 'Soviet Structural Folkloristics' 1974; 'Mythology' 1972; 'Introduction to Anthropology: A Self-Guide' 1972; 'Structural Analysis of Oral Tradition' 1972; 'Dialogue Conjugal' 1985; 'DiscAn: A Computer System for Content and Discourse Analysis' 1989; 'L'Unité dans la diversité culturelle: Une Geste bantu' (with Fidèle Nze-Nguema) 1994, vol. 1: Le Sens des symboles fang, mbede, eshira; Fellow, Am. Anthrop. Assn.; mem. Counc., Candn. Inst. for Advanced Research; mem. Assn. Candn. Sociologie & Anthropologie (Pres. 1971); Candn. Ethnol. Soc. (Pres. 1975); Fellow, Royal Soc. of Can.; mem., Assoc. canadienne des sociologues et anthropologues de langue française; Candn. Semiotic Assoc.; mem. several internat. scientific bds., journals, and monograph series; recreations: swimming, skiing, music; Home: 25, Ave. Ste-Geneviève, Québec, Qué. G1R 4B1.

**MARATHÉ, Eknath V.,** B.Sc., M.Sc., Ed.D.; physicist; educator; b. Bombay, India 1 June 1923; s.Vyankatesh Vishwanath and Yamuna Vishnu (Agashé) M.; Bombay Univ. B.Sc. 1947; Poona Univ. M.Sc. 1955; SUNYB Ed.D. 1978; m. Godawari d. Mahadeo and Janaki Daté 5 June 1952; children: Aruna, Sanjay; Head of Science, Grantham High School 1965–88; Demonstrator, Physics, Ferguson Coll., Poona, India 1947–50; Research Physicist, Kaycee Industries Ltd., Poona 1950–52; Natnl. Chemical Lab. of India 1952–55; came to Can. 1955; Nuclear Res. Lab., McMaster Univ. 1955–56; Lecturer in Physics, Univ. of Guelph 1956–60; post-grad. work in Physics, Univ. of Manitoba 1960–61; Science Teacher, St. Catharines Collegiate 1961–65; teacher, Advanced Technical Courses, Niagara Coll. of A.A.&T.; Assoc., Althouse Coll. of Ed., Univ. of Western Ont.; Brock Univ., Coll of Ed.; Visiting Prof., Univ. of Poona, India, Sept.-Nov. 1984; Mem., Del. on Sci. & Technology Educ. to People's Republic of China, June 1987 and Australia and New Zealand June 1989; Pres., India-Canada Assn. of Niagara Region 1971–72, 1977–78; mem., Torch International, Pres. St. Catharines Club 1974–75; Bd. of Dir., Science Teachers Assn. of Ont. 1980–82; mem.-at-large, Extve. Ctte. of the Ont. Section of the Am. Assoc. of Physics Teachers, 1983–84; mem., Candn. Assn. of Physicists, Am. Physical Soc.; Am. Assn. of Physics Teachers; A.A.A.S; Life Mem., Natnl. Science Teachers Assn.; S.T.A.O.; Archaeol. Inst. of Am.; A.S.C.D.; A.E.T.S.; Fed. of Am. Scientists; has published 3 scientific research papers, 9 scientific articles and contributed 35 papers to national and international conferences Canada, U.S.A., Israel (twice), Australia, New Zealand (twice), West Germany, Philippines, U.S.S.R; UNESCO (Paris, France); Currently involved in development of Science, Technology & Society Course at an advance level; Mem., Ecological and Environmental Adv. Ctte. of the Regional Municipality of Niagara; recreations: reading, writing, gardening, classical music of India; Home: 25 King's Grant Rd., St. Catharines, Ont. L2N 2S1.

**MARCEAU, Hubert,** M.C.Sc., Adm.A.; business executive; b. Lac Mégantic, Qué. 13 Dec. 1933; s. Roland and Estelle (René de Cotret) M.; e. Laval Univ. B.Com.Sc. 1957, M.Com.Sc. 1958; m. Louise d. Paul and Rose Frescynet 30 Aug. 1958; children: Richard, Diane, Sylvie; PRESIDENT & CHIEF EXECUTIVE OFFICER, GENECAN FINANCIAL CORPORATION 1993– ; Mgr., Insur. Sales & Admin. for Caisses Populaires, Assurance-Vie Desjardins 1958–72; Pres. & Chief Extve. Offr., Polylab Inc. 1972–75; Min. des Consommateurs, Coop. et Inst. Finan. du Québec, Dep. Min. in Charge of Coop., Mng. Dir. of Finan. Insts. & Vice-Pres., Régie d'Assurance-dépôts du Québec 1975–77; Vice-Pres., Inspection & Verification, La Conféd. des Caisses Populaires d'écon. Desjardins du Qué. 1977–82; Sr. Vice-Pres., Opns., Laurentian Bank 1982–88; Pres. & C.O.O., Laurentian Trust of Canada 1988–89; Senior Vice-Pres., La Financière l'Industrielle-Alliance Inc. 1989–90; Extve. Vice-Pres. & C.O.O., General Trustco of Canada Inc. & General Trust of Canada 1990–92; Pres. & C.O.O., General Trustco of Canada Inc. & General Trust of Canada 1993; Dir., Genecan Financial Corp.; Fond. Armand-Frappier; Dir. & Extve. Ctte. Mem., IST; Mem., La Corp. profl. des admin. agréés du Qué.; Treas., Fond. Raymond Garneau; Past Pres., Candn. Assn. of Coop. Law Admin. 1976–77; Chrmn., Funding Campaign, Eye Bank 1986–87; recreations: swimming, fishing, hunting, reading; club: Saint-Denis; Home: 145, rue de Touraine, Saint-Lambert, Qué. J4S 1H3; Office: 2000, McGill College Ave., Suite 700, Montréal, Qué. H3A 3H3.

**MARCEAU, Hon. Louis,** LL.D.; judge; b. Quebec City, Que. 6 Feb. 1927; s. Paul-V. and Marie-Laure (Picard) M.; m. Suzanne d. Robert Duquette, Quebec City, Que. 8 Jan. 1972; children: Danièle, Marie-Odile, Patrice, Nathalie; JUDGE, FEDERAL COURT OF CAN.; called to Bar of Que. 1949; R. Catholic; Home: 211 Wurtemburg St., Ottawa, Ont. K1N 8R4; Office: Supreme Court Bldg., Wellington St., Ottawa, Ont. K1A 0H9.

**MARCH, Beryl Elizabeth,** B.A., M.S.A., D.Sc., F.R.S.C.; educator; b. Port Hammond, B.C. 30 Aug. 1920; d. James Roy and Sarah Catherine (Wilson) Warrack; e. Univ. of B.C. B.A. 1942, M.S.A. 1962; m. John Algot 31 Aug. 1946; one child, Laurel Allison; PROF. EMERITA OF ANIMAL SCIENCE, UNIV. OF B.C.; mem. Nat. Research Council Can. 1977–80; Nat. Acad. Sci., Nat. Research Council Comm. on Animal Nutrition 1980–82; Fellow, Agric. Inst. Can.; Poultry Science Assn.; author 160 scient. papers on nutrition & physiol. with particular reference to poultry and fish; rec'd Poultry Science Assn.'s Am. Feed Mfrs. Assn. Nutrition Research Award 1969; Queen's Silver Jubilee Medal 1977; Earle Willard McHenry Award (Candn. Soc. Nutr. Sci.) 1986; mem. Cdn. Soc. for Nutrition Sci.; mem. B.C. Agrols; Am. Soc. Exper. Biol. & Med.; Am. Inst. Nutrition; Candn. Soc. Animal Science; Aquaculture Assn. of Canada; Home: 5808 Wallace St., Vancouver, B.C. V6N 2A4; Office: Vancouver, B.C. V6T 1Z4.

**MARCHAK, Maureen Patricia,** B.A., Ph.D., F.R.S.C.; educator; author; b. Lethbridge, Alta. 22 June 1936; d. Adrian Ebenezer and Wilhelmina Rankin (Hamilton) Russell; e. Kitsilano Jr.-Sr. H.S. 1954; Univ. of B.C., B.A. 1958, Ph.D. 1970; m. William s. Dimitri and Maria Marchak 31 Dec. 1956; two s. Geordon Eric, Lauren Craig; DEAN, FACULTY OF ARTS, UNIV. OF BRITISH COLUMBIA 1990– ; PROFESSOR OF SOCIOLOGY 1980– ; Sessional Lectr. Anthrop. & Sociol. present Univ. 1965–72, Asst. Prof. 1973, Assoc. Prof. 1975; Head, Dept. of Anthropology and Sociology 1987–90; Dir. or mem. various rsch. studies incl. housing, forestry, fishing; numerous pub. lectures incl. Sorokin Lecture Univ. of Sask. 1982; John Porter Memorial Lecture, Candn. Sociology & Anthropology Assn. 1988; other major lectures at Canadian and U.S. Universities 1980– ; keynote addresses at public conferences on Fisheries, Forestry, Ecology, Women's Studies; Shastri Indo-Candn. Inst. Visiting Lectr. to India Feb. 1987; Visiting Prof., Carleton Univ., summer 1987; Cons.: Open Learning Inst. B.C. 1979, 1981–82; Ont. Counc. Grad. Studies, other univs.; Environment Can. and Candn. Forestry Services 1982; mem. Bd. of Dirs., Pacific Group Candn. Centre Policy Alternatives 1983–85, Open University Acad. Counc. (B.C.) 1988–90; Cedar Lodge Soc. 1988–92; mem. Bd. of Trustees and Chair Ethics Ctte., UBC Hospital 1992–93; mem. Ecotrust Advisory Council 1991– ; mem. Advisory Council, Academy II, Royal Soc. of Canada 1991– ; mem. Bd., Forest History Society 1991–92; Chair, Bd. of Dirs., B.C. Building Corp. 1992– ; recipient Rsch. Leave Fellowship SSHRCC 1977–78, 1984–85; Grants SSHRCC Rsch. 1977–78, 1981–84, 1988–90; NDP Cand. for Pt. Grey B.C. 1983, def.; author 'Ideological Perspectives on Canada' 1975, rev. ed. 1981, 3rd ed. 1987; 'In Whose Interests: An Essay on Multinational Corporations in a Canadian Context' 1979; 'Green Gold: The Forest Industry in British Columbia' 1983 (winner of John Porter Memorial Award 1986); ed. 'The Working Sexes' 1977; co-ed. 'Uncommon Property: The Fishing and Fish Processing Industries in British Columbia' 1987; author: 'The Integrated Circus: The New Right and the Restructuring of Global Markets' 1991; various book chapters, articles, rsch. reports, public speeches and keynote addresses; mem. Cecil Rhodes Scholarship Trust Selection Ctte. B.C. 1988–90; Chair, Candn. Ctte. of Shastri Indo-Candn. Inst. 1989–90; mem. various ed. bds. incl. Current Sociology, Studies in Political Economy; Candn. Journ. of Sociol., B.C. Studies; mem. Candn. Sociol. & Anthrop. Assn. (Pres. 1979); Life mem. Assn. Candn. Studies (Adv. Bd. 1978–80); Internat. Sociology Assn.; Candn. Pol. Sci. Assn.; Forest History Soc.; Fellow, Royal Soc. of Can. 1987; recreations: swimming, mountain hiking, skiing, painting; Home: 4455 W. First Ave., Vancouver, B.C. V6R 4H9; Office: 1866 Main Mall, Vancouver, B.C. V6T 1Z1.

**MARCHAND, Clément,** B.A., F.R.S.C.; journalist; poet; b. Ste-Geneviève de Batiscan (Champlain), P.Q. 12 Sept. 1912; s. Pierre and Paméla (Dessureault) M.; e. St. Joseph's Semy., Trois-Rivières, B.A. 1932; 1 s. Pierre; winner of Prix David de poésie, 1939 and Prix David de litt. 1942; hon. prés. Les Écrivains de la Mauricie, Trois-Rivières, PQ; hon. mem. L'Union des Écrivains québécois, Montréal, PQ; mem. Société royale du Canada 1947; mem. Académie des lettres du Québec 1989; author 'La Geste de la Croix' (sonnets) 1931; 'Courriers des Villages' (short stories) 1939; 'Vanishing Villages' (translated from the French by David Homel); 'Les Soirs Rouges' (poems) 1947; 'Nerée Beauchemin' (criticism) 1957; 'Le Choix de Clément Marchand dans l'oeuvre de Clément Marchand' (selected poems & novels) 1983; Prix Benjamin-Sulte de journalisme 1974; Prix. Ludger-Duvernay de litt. 1981; Décoré de L'Ordre des Francophones d'Amérique 1984; Prix litt. de Trois-Rivières 1985; Décoré de l'Ordre des Hebdos régionaux du Que. 1985; has also contributed to numerous literary journals and radio broadcasts; Home: 1637 Blvd. des Forges, Trois Rivières, Que. G8Z 1T7.

**MARCHAND, J.C. de Montigny,** Q.C., B.A., LL.L.; Canadian public servant; b. St. Jérôme, Qué. 19 March 1936; s. Jean-Charles, Q.C. and Françoise (Magnan) M.; e. Univ. de Montréal B.A. 1955, LL.L. 1959; Boston Univ. Sch. of Communications post-grad. studies; children: Julie, Charles, Emmanuelle; AMBASSADOR TO ITALY WITH ADDITIONAL ACCREDITATION TO MALTA AND SAN MARINO 1991– ; called to Bar of Que. 1960; cr. Q.C. 1978; Asst. to Dir. Pub. Relations Univ. de Montréal 1960, Asst. to Secy. Gen. 1964, Extve. Asst. to Pres. 1965, Secy. Gen. 1967; Dir. of Research and Co-Secy. of Telecommission Dept. of Communications, Can. 1969, Asst. Depy. Min. (Operations) 1971, Sr. Asst. Depy. Min. (Policy) 1974; Depy. Secy. to Cabinet (Operations) Privy Council Office 1975, special assignment to W. Europe, Paris 1979; Assoc. Under-Secy. of State for External Affairs, Dept. of External Affairs 1980; Depy. Min. for Political Affairs, Dept. of External Affairs, Can. 1982–85; Depy. Min. Dept. of Communications Jan.-Aug. 1985; Depy. Min. Dept. of Energy, Mines & Resources 1985–86; Sr. Adv., Privy Council Office 1986–1987; Ambassador and Permanent Representative to the U.N. in Geneva and to the Conference on Disarmament 1987–90; Under Secretary of State for External Affairs 1990–91; Head, Candn. Del. to Third Plenary Session Intelsat, Washington 1971 and to World Adm. Radio Conf. on Space Communications, Geneva 1971; also to Fourth, Fifth and Sixth Sessions UN Working Group Direct Broadcasting by Satellite New York and Geneva 1972, 1973, 1974; Depy. Head Candn. del. to ITU Plenipotentiary Conf. Malaga-Torremolinos 1973; Pres. Inst. canadien des Affaires publiques 1967–68; Dir.: Canadian Overseas Telecommunications Corp. 1971–75; Uranium Canada Ltd. 1975–79; Nat. Film Bd. 1978–79, 1982–85; Gov., Univ. of Ottawa 1980–83; Personal Rep. of Prime Min. for preparation of Versailles Summit (1982), Williamsburg Summit (1983) and London Summit (1984); Bd. Chrmn., Internat. Energy Agency 1986–87; recreations: fishing, tennis, reading; Club: Five Lakes Fishing; Home: Via di Porta Latina 11, 00179 Rome, Italy; Office: The Canadian Embassy, Via G.B. de Rossi 27, 00161 Rome, Italy.

**MARCHAND, Jean,** B.A., M.Sc.C.; insurance executive; b. 16 Jan. 1937; e. Académie de Qué. B.A. 1958; Laval Univ. B.Sc.C. 1960, M.Sc.C. 1961; C.L.U. 1963; I.D.A. 1964; NATIONAL PARTNER, CLIENT SERVICE & DEVELOP., SAMSON BÉLAIR / DELOITTE & TOUCHE since 1982; former Pres., l'Unique Assurance; Pres., Unigesco Inc.; Ins. Broker, Halle & Couture Ltée 1959, Mgr. 1961; Founder and Gen. Mgr. L'Unique Life Insurance 1967, Pres. and Gen. Mgr. 1972; Extve. Vice Pres. and Gen. Mgr. Unigesco Inc. Group 1972; Pres. and Gen. Mgr. L'Unique General Insurance Co. and Pres. Unigesco Inc.; mem. Chamber Comm.; recreations: boating, sailing, skiing, waterskiing, swimming; Clubs: Garrison; Nautique Fossambalut sur-le-Lac; Office: 5600 boul. des Galeries, Bureau 600, Quebec, Que. G2K 2H6.

**MARCHAND, Hon. Leonard Stephen,** P.C., B.S.A., M.S.F., P.Ag.; senator; b. Vernon, B.C. 16 Nov. 1933; s. Joe and Agnes (Robinson) M.; e. Okanagan Indian Day Sch.; Kamloops Indian Residential sch.; Vernon H.S. 1955; Univ. of B.C., B.S.A. 1959; Univ. of Idaho M.S.F. 1964; m. Donna d. Ben and Etta Parr 16 July 1960; children: Lori Anne, Leonard Stephen Jr.; CALLED TO SENATE OF CANADA 1984– ; Chrmn., Standing Senate Ctte. on Aboriginal Peoples 1990– ; Rsch. Scientist Fed. Dept. of Agric., Kamloops, B.C. 1960; Special Asst. to Hon. J.R. Nicholson 1965; Special Asst. to Hon. Arthur Laing 1966; el. to H. of C. for Kamloops-Cariboo riding 1968, re-el. 1972, 1974; Parlty. Secy. to Min. of Indian Affairs 1972–73; Parlty. Secy. to Min. of Environ. 1974; apptd. Min. of State (Small Bus.) 1976; Min. of State (Environ.) 1977–79; Admin. for Nicola Valley Indian Bands 1979–84; private cons. for agric., govt. and Indian questions 1979–84; Mem. Bd. of Dirs., Peace Hills Trust Co. Ltd.; Dir. Emeritus, Candn. Counc. for Native Bus.; Hon. National Patron of the Candn. Native Arts Found.; Hon. Chief of the Okanagans; author and co-author numerous agric. rsch. papers 1960–65; R. Catholic; mem. Liberal Party of Can.; Office: Rm. 307-VB, The Senate, Ottawa, Ont. K1A 0A4.

**MARCHANT, Edward D.,** C.A.; b. Winnipeg, Man. 6 Sept. 1927; s. late Cecil William Stanley and late Florence Maud M.; e. Winnipeg, Man. C.A. 1958; m. Irene Elliott d. late Robert Burton 18 June 1975; children: Diane, Joanne, Gregory, Ian, Daryl; PRESIDENT & C.E.O., MARCHANT SECURITIES INC. 1972– and

MARCHANT INVESTMENT INC. 1986– ; Shareholder, Dir., Barbican Properties Inc. 1985– ; Dir. and Chrmn. Audit Ctte. Midland Bank Canada 1983–88; Dir., Mississauga Hospital 1984–89; operated own C.A. practice 1958–62, 1966–67 Winnipeg; Tax Partner Deloitte, Haskins & Sells 1962–66 Winnipeg; Coopers & Lybrand, Toronto 1967–69; Vice Pres. Finance Bramalea Consolidated Developments Ltd. Toronto 1969–70; Great Northern Capital Corp. 1970–72; Pres. & C.E.O., Marchant and Co. Ltd. 1972–88; Pres. M.M. Builders Funds Ltd. (Marine Midland Bank in Can.) 1972–76; Exchequer Trust Co. 1976–79; Pres. & C.E.O., Exchequer Financial Corp. Ltd. 1979–90; mem. Man. Inst. Tax Comte. and Pub. Relations 1958–66; Life Underwriters Educ. Comte. 1962–66; Chrmn. Urban Devel. Inst. Tax & Accounting Comte. 1969–72, Financing of Real Estate Comte. 1974–76, mem. Fed. Comte. 1976; mem. Can. Inst. C.A.'s; Freemason; United Church; recreation; golf; Clubs: Jupiter Hills, Florida; Mississauga Country; National; Home: 1425 Elaine Trail,, Mississauga, Ont. L5G 3W9; Office: 55 University Ave., Suite 610, Toronto, Ont. M5J 2H7.

**MARCHANT, Murray Scott,** C.A.; business executive; b. Quebec, Que. 20 Aug. 1940; s. Bertram Joseph and Edith Cavell (Scott) M.; e. Coll. Militaire Royale 1960; m. Susan d. David and Peggy Savage 11 Oct. 1985; children: Kenneth, William, John, Sarah; VICE-PRESIDENT ADMINISTRATION, TREASURER & ASSISTANT SECRETARY, ASTRAL COMMUNICATIONS INC. 1993– ; Student & Public Accountant, Geo. A Welch & Co. 1962–68; Vice-Pres. Finance, Allan Crawford Assoc. Ltd. 1968–75; Asst. to the Gen. Mgr., The Globe and Mail 1975–78; Dir. of Opns., Infomart 1979–82; Vice-Pres. Finance, First Choice Pay TV 1982–88; Vice-Pres. Finance 1988–93, Vice-Pres., Administration & Treasurer, Astral Communications Inc. 1993– ; Home: 465 Clarke, Westmount, Que. H3Y 3C5; Office: 2100 Ste-Catherine St. W., Montreal, Que. H3H 2T3.

**MARCHESE, The Hon. Rosario,** M.P.P., B.A., B.Ed.; politician; b. Italy 10 May 1952; s. Giuseppe and Maddalena Bellissimo M.; e. Harbord C.I. 1972; Univ. of Toronto, St. Michael's Coll. B.A., B.Ed. 1977; shares life with partner Evelyn Murialdo; children: Vanessa, Stephanie, Michael; PARLIAMENTARY ASST. TO THE PREMIER & MIN. OF INTERGOVERNMENTAL AFFAIRS, GOVT. OF ONT. 1991– ; Elected Chair, Standing Ctte. on Admin. of Justice 1993; Mem., Cabinet Ctte. on the Constitution; Ont. delegate to Aboriginal Roundtable process & fed. govt.'s Multilateral Const. process; led Ontario's Social Charter consultations; Elected to Ont. Legislature as member for Fort York 1990; appt. Ont. Minister of Culture & Communications; Claims Adjudicator, Ont. Workers' Comp. Bd. 1978; French Teacher, Lady of Lourdes 1979, St. Nicholas of Bari 1982; Teacher, Applewood Heights; Vice-Pres., Nat. Congress of Italian-Canadians 1988–90; Chair, Multilingual Literacy Centre 1988–90; Bd. Mem., Toronto Public Library Bd. 1980–82; Public School Trustee (Wards 4 and 5) 1982–90; languages: fluent in English, French & Italian, conversant in Spanish; recreations: soccer, singing; Home: 391 Montrose Ave., Toronto, Ont. M6G 3H2; Offices: 854 Dundas St. W., Toronto, Ont. M6J 1V5 and Room 375, Legislative Bldg., Toronto, Ont. M7A 1A5.

**MARCHESSAULT, Victor,** M.D., FRCP(C); university professor/association executive; b. Prov. of Que. 16 Nov. 1929; s. Luc Sylvestre and Gertrude (Destroismaisons) M.; e. Coll. de Montréal B.A. 1950; Univ. of Montreal M.D. 1955; m. Louise Sheasgreen 7 Aug. 1971; children: Andrée, Jean Luc, Louis, Victor Jr.; PROF. OF PAEDIATRICS & INFECTIOUS DISEASES, DEPT. OF PAED., UNIV. OF OTTAWA & CHILDREN'S HOSP. OF EAST. ONT. 1983– ; DIR. OF AMBULATORY CARE, DEPT. OF PAEDIATRICS, CHILDREN'S HOSP. OF EAST ONT. 1991– ; spec. in paediatrics 1955–59; obtained Fellowship in paed., Royal Coll. of Physicians & Surg. of Can.; cert. of spec. in paed., Prov. of Que.; priv. practice, St. Lambert, Que. (affiliation with Montreal Children's Hosp. & McGill Univ.) 7 yrs.; Founding Chrmn., Dept. of Paed., Univ. of Sherbrooke 1967; Extve. Vice Pres., Candn. Paed. Soc. 1964– ; Ross Award, Candn. Paed. Soc. 1984; Hon. Mem., Australian Coll. of Paediatrics 1990; Mem., Am. Acad. of Pediatrics (Sci. Prog. Ctte.); Candn. Paed. Soc.; Treasurer, Candn. Infectious Disease Soc.; recreations: tennis, golf, skiing, hockey; Home 1382 Gerald St., Cumberland, Ont. K0A 1S0; Office: Children's Hospital of Eastern Ontario, 401 Smyth Rd., Ottawa, Ont. K1H 8L1.

**MARCHI, Sergio,** M.P.; politician; b. Argentina 12 May 1956; s. Ottavio and Luisa (D'Agostinis) M.; e. York Univ. Hon. B.A. 1979; m. Laureen d. Frank and Mariette Storozuk 1 Oct. 1983; MINISTER OF CITIZENSHIP & IMMIGRATION, GOVT. OF CANADA 1993– ; Extve. Asst. to Ron Irwin and Hon. Jim Fleming 1980–82; Alderman, City of North York and Mktg. Extve. 1982–84; el. H. of C. Sept. 1984; Critic portfolio: Immigration; re-el. 1988; Transport Critic and National Caucus Chrmn. 1990–93; elec. Ontario Caucus Chrmn. Oct. 3 1990; elec. Vice-Chrmn., Transport Ctte. 1991; Re-elected Chrmn., National Liberal Caucus 1991; Home: 1330 Talcy Cr., Orleans, Ont. K4A 3C3; Office: House of Commons, Ottawa, Ont. K1A 0A6.

**MARCHILDON, Pierre,** B.Eng.; engineer; b. Sorel, Que. 10 Dec. 1943; s. Jean and Solange (Landry) M.; e. Royal Military College of Canada B.Eng. 1965; m. Andrée d. Armand and Thérèse Pedneault 22 Oct. 1966; children: Claude, Annie, Vincent; DIRECTOR GENERAL, ADMIN., ATOMIC ENERGY CONTROL BOARD 1990– ; Royal Candn. Electrical & Mech. Engineers 1965–68; Shift Supervisor, NRX Reactor, Chalk River Nuclear Labs., Atomic Energy of Canada Ltd. 1968–71; Project Officer, Gentilly Nuclear Power Station, Atomic Energy Control Board 1971–83; Manager, Power Reactor Div. 1983–90; Mem., Assn. of Profl. Engrs. of Ont.; Home: 351 Lévis, Hull, Que. J8Z 1A5; Office: 280 Slater St., P.O. Box 1046, Ottawa, Ont. K1P 5S9.

**MARCHMENT, Alan Roy,** B.A., F.C.A., F.T.I.; b. Toronto, Ont. 29 May 1927; s. William Roy (dec'd) and Alice C. M. (dec'd); e. Univ. of Toronto, B.A. (Hons.) Philos.; Ont. Inst. C.A.'s (F.C.A.); m. Patricia Anne, d. late Frank S. Vanstone, 19 Jan. 1949; one s., one d.; CHRMN., C.E.O. AND DIR., WILTSHIRE GROUP LTD. 1989– ; Dir., Traders Group Ltd.; Cdn. General Ins. Co.; Levitt-Safety Ltd.; OSF Inc.; Algonquin Mercantile Corp.; Toronto General Ins. Co.; Traders General Ins. Co.; Scottish & York Ins. Co.; Victoria Ins. of Canada; Tintina Mines Ltd.; Clarkson Gordon 1950–55; Pacific Finance Corp. 1955–63; Transamerica International S.A. Paris, France, Pres. and Dir. 1963–65; The T. Eaton Co. Ltd. 1965, Vice-Pres. Finance & Admin. 1969–73; joined Guaranty Trust Co. of Can. as Pres. and Dir. 1973; C.E.O. 1975; Chrmn. 1979–85; Dir., Traders Group Ltd. 1977; Vice-Chrmn. 1978; Chrmn. and C.E.O. 1979; Pres., C.E.O. and Dir., Guaranty Trustco Limited 1985; Chrmn. 1987; Hon. Chrmn. & Dir. Central Guaranty Trustco 1987–92; Chrmn., Adelaide Capital Corp. 1993; Chrmn. Postal Service Review Bd. 1988–90; Dir., The Toronto Symphony 1965– (Pres. 1978–82); Trustee, The Toronto Symphony Foundation (Chrmn. 1983–86); Past Pres., The Bd. of Trade of Metro. Toronto (Pres. 1990–91); Dir., Metro Toronto Intnl. Caravan; Past Chrmn., Inst. of Corp. Dirs. 1988–91; Chrmn., Canada Post Review Ctte. 1985; Past Chrmn., Trust Companies Assoc. of Can. Inc. (1982–84); Past Chrmn., Ont. Provincial Courts Ctte. (1981–87); Past Chrmn., Bd. of Gov., Univ. of Guelph 1979–82; Past Pres., Nat. Club 1977; Gage Research Inst. 1976–79; C.M. Hincks Treatment Centre, 1972; Past Trustee, Toronto Western Hosp. 1969–78; Past Gov., Candn. Inst. of Chart. Accountants 1975–78; Hon. Life Mem., Cdn. Wildlife Fed.; Hon. Mem., Nat. Council, Boy Scouts of Can.; Fellow, Ryerson Polytechnical Univ.; Hon. Fellow, Univ. of Guelph; Knight, Order of St. Lazarus of Jerusalem; Anglican; Clubs: Toronto; York; Goodwood; National; Toronto Golf; Cambridge; Home: 18 Clarendon Ave., Toronto, Ont. M4V 1H9; Office: 105 Adelaide St. W., Toronto, Ont. M5H 4A4.

**MARCOTTE, Marcel Ernest,** M.Sc.Com.; communications executive; b. Sherbrooke, Qué. 2 May 1945; s. Gaston Arthur and Ernestine Leontine (Laventure) M.; e. Univ. of Sherbrooke M.Sc.Com. 1969; m. Ginette d. Jeanne-D'Arc Perusse 20 Sept. 1969; children: Marie-Claude, Phillippe; REGIONAL SALES MGR. BUSINESS MARKET, BELL CANADA 1992– ; Sales Rep. Office Products Div. IBM Canada, Sherbrooke 1969; Pricing and Mktg. Rsch. Analyst, Quebec-Telephone, Rimouski 1969–71, Budget Sales Analyst 1971–74, Market Rsch. Specialist 1974–76; Mktg. Services Mgr. Northern Telecom Div. Outside Plant Lachine 1976–77; Mktg. Dir., Paragon Business Forms Ltd. Montreal 1977–78; Pres., Centre de Gestion Rive-Sud Inc. St. Lambert 1978; Markets Mgmt. and Planning Dir. Telebec Ltd. Montreal 1979–82; Sales Mgr. Gen. Business Market Bell Canada Montreal 1982–83; Sales Mgr. Major Account, Bell Canada 1983–92; Lectr. Univ. du Qué. Rimouski 1971–73; CEGEP Rimouski 1971–73; author various articles prof. jours.; Dir., Laprairie Riding Lib. Party Que. 1982–85; mem., Prof. Corp. Chart. Administrators Que. 1968–92; K. of C.; recreations: golf, skiing, reading; Home: 115 Boul. des Champs Fleuris, La Prairie, Que.; Office: 700 La Gauchetiere W., Montreal, Que. H3B 4L1.

**MARCOTTE, Nancy Jean Sellars,** B.A.; freelance writer, editor; b. Selkirk, Man. 12 Apl. 1950; d. Walter Chesley and Roberta Henderson (Brown) Sellars; e. Univ. of Toronto B.A. 1971; Toronto Teachers' Coll. 1972; m. Brian Philip s. Philip and Dorothy Marcotte 26 June 1971; children: Chenoa Claire, Kyle Philip; lib. asst. various U of T Libs. and OISE 1968–74; teacher Langstaff Pub. Sch. Thornhill 1974–75; freelance writer 1975–81, freelance ed. 1981– ; teacher Univ. of Alta. Extension 1982– , Grant MacEwan Community Coll. 1988; book review columnist Edmonton Journal 1986–93; recipient Edmonton Jour. Lit. Award Short Story 1982; Vicky Metcalf Award Short Story Ed. 1989; runner-up, Three Day Novel Competition 1990; co-ordinator Alta. Book Fair 1986, 1988; Young Alta. Book Soc. 1989– ; contbg. author and ed. 'Ordinary People in Canada's Past' 1990; 'Ordinary People in Alberta's Past' 1993; ed. several books; Address: 7322 – 156 St., Edmonton, Alta. T5R 1X3.

**MARCOUX, Jules Edouard,** B.A.Sc., M.A., Ph.D.; retired; writer; b. Charny, Qué. 26 Jan. 1924; s. Joseph Roméo and Atala (Fontaine) M.; e. Coll. de Ste-Anne de la Pocatière (Laval Univ.) B.A. 1946; Laval Univ. B.A.Sc. 1952; Univ. of Toronto M.A. 1953, Ph.D. (Physics) 1956; m. Hermina d. Anton and Eva Manz 2 July 1955; children: Daniel, Edouard, Elise, Vincent, Pierre, Paul; Prof. of Physics, Coll. Militaire Royal de Saint-Jean 1957–62, 1964–90; Prof. of Physics Laval Univ. 1962–64; recipient Nat. Research Council Postgrad. Fellowship Univ. de Montréal 1956–57; author (in French) 'Astronautes et Astronautique' 1975; 'L'Energie, ses Sources, son Avenir' 1982; 'Mécanique à l'usage de l'Ingénieur' 1983; co-author 'Manuel de Physique' (coll. level) 6 vols. 1970–76; various articles physical constants in prof. publs.; Pres., Candn. Mil. Colls. Faculty Assn. 1980–82; mem. Extve. Comte. Conseil d'Administration CEGEP Saint-Jean sur Richelieu; mem. Am. Assn. Physics Teachers; Candn. Assn. Physics Teachers; Retired Sept. 1990; Home: 29 rue des Tilleuls, St-Luc, Qué. J2W 1B4; Office: Saint-Jean, Qué. J0J 1R0.

**MARCUS, Richard;** sculptor; designer; b. Barquisimeto, Venezuela 10 July 1951; s. Walter and Danuta (Sypniewicz) Miskiewicz; m. Rose d. Nick and Elaria Penzari 14 Feb. 1981; moved to Montréal 1956, Vancouver 1976; Sculptor/Designer in prehistoric ivory; Pres., Mammoth Enterprises Inc.; Sculpture & jewellery from prehistoric Mastodon/Mammoth ivory inlaid with semi-precious materials in mosaic form, distributed internationally; private royal coll.: Bagama Khan; museum collections: Museum Hauff, Wurttemberg, W. Germany; Medical Heritage Museum, Tulsa, OK; Exhbns. incl.: '94 Sculptures Soc. Can. 65th Anniversary touring show; N.Y. Art Expo 1989, 1990, 1991, 1992; LA Art Expo 1989, 1990, 1991, 1992; Jacobi Jewellers/Commerz Bank, Stuttgart 1989; Yokohama Japan 1989; Osaka World Fashion Fair, Japan 1989; subject numerous internat. interviews, 'The Financial Post, MoneyWise' 1987; ZDF Television, West Germany 1988; Home: 1286 E. 16th St., North Vancouver, B.C. V7J 1L3.

**MARCUSE, Judith Rose;** choreographer; dancer; teacher; b. Montreal, P.Q. 13 Mar. 1947; d. Frank Howard and Phyllis (Salomons) Margolick; e. Monklands High Sch., Montreal; Nat. Ballet Summer Sch. 1960; Royal Ballet Sch., London, England 1962–65; Sch. of Amer. Ballet; Banff Sch. of Fine Arts; m. Richard Frederick M. 28 Aug. 1972; one daughter, Rachel Katherine; ARTISTIC DIR., JUDITH MARCUSE DANCE PROJECTS SOCIETY 1980– , and JUDITH MARCUSE DANCE CO. 1984– ; danced with Les Grands Ballets Canadiens 1965–68; Ballet de Geneve 1969; Bat-Dor Dance Co., Israel 1970–72; Ballet Rambert, London, England 1974–76; has choreographed and directed numerous works, including: 'SpeakEasy' (Dennis Wayne's Dancers, N.Y. 1978; remounted for Dance Projects 1984 and the National Ballet of Canada 1979); 'Side by Side by Sondheim' (Belfry Theatre 1979); 'Mirrors, Masques and Transformations' (Shaw Festival and Dance Projects 1980); 'Spring Dances' (Les Grands Ballets Canadiens 1981); 'Cuts' (Dancemakers, Toronto 1981); 'H.M.S. Pinafore' (Stratford Festival, Ont. 1981; remounted for C.B.C.-TV); 'Playgrounds' (Dance Projects 1981); 'Transfer' (Nederlands Dans Theater, The Hague 1981); 'We Can Dance!' (Dance Projects 1982); 'Romeo and Juliette' (Vancouver Opera 1982); 'Reflections on Crooked Walking (Arts Club 1982, 1983, 1987, 1992); 'In Concert' (Dance Projects 1983); 'On Castle Rock' & 'Hors d'Ouevre' (Les Ballets Jazz de Montreal 1983); 'Seascape' (Les Grands Ballets Canadiens 1983; remounted for Dance Projects 1984 and the National Ballet of Portugal 1986); 'Currents' (Harbourfront Corp. 1983); 'Bartok Sonata' (Dance Projects 1984); 'Cole' (Theatre London 1984); 'Blue Skies' (Dance Projects 1985); 'Traces' (Dance Projects 1985); 'Time Out' (Dance Projects 1986); 'The Hopeful Return of the Flying Ferromanganese Players' (Dance Projects 1987); 'Moving Past Neutral' (commissioned by the Calgary Winter Olympics Arts Festival 1988); 'Threnody' (Royal Winnipeg Ballet 1988); 'Bach and Blue' (Dance Projects 1989); 'Madrugada' (Dance Projects 1990); 'Alcina' (Vancouver Opera 1990); 'Crooked Hearts' (A & M Films and MGM 1990); 'Tales from the Vaudeville Stage' (Dance Projects 1991); 'Room' (Royal Winnipeg Ballet 1992); 'Second Nature' (Conrad Films 1993); recipient of various awards and grants, including: Chalmers Award for Choreography 1976; Clifford E. Lee Award for Choreography 1979; YWCA Woman of Distinction 1985; Vancouver Award for Excellence in Theatre 1986; West Vancouver 75 Achiever Award 1987; awarded Commemorative Medal for 125th Anniversary of Candn. Confederation 1993; Silver prize, New York Dance Video & Film Festival; mem. Actors' Equity Assn.; Candn. Actors' Equity Assn. (mem. Equity Council 1981, 1982–85); British Actors' Equity Assn.; Dance Adv. Panel, Cultural Services Br. 1988–90; Dance in Can. Assn. (mem. Nat. Bd. 1978–80); A.C.T.R.A.; recreations: cooking, travel, literature; Address: 6754 Dufferin Ave., West Vancouver, B.C. V7W 2K2; Office: 106 - 206 E. 6th Ave., Vancouver, B.C. V5T 1J8.

**MARGARITIS, Argyrios,** B.A.Sc., M.S., Ph.D., P.Eng., F.C.I.C.; university professor and administrator; b. Kastoria, Greece 20 Dec. 1938; s. Demetrios and Kyriaki (Vlahos) M.; e. Univ. of Waterloo B.A.Sc. 1966; Univ. of Calif. at Berkeley M.S. 1968, Ph.D. 1975; F.C.I.C. 1985; Assn. of Profl. Engrs. of Ont. P.Eng. 1976; m. Mary d. Vaios Kambouris 6 Nov. 1976; children: Demetrios, Athena; PROFESSOR, DEPT. OF CHEMICAL & BIOCHEMICAL ENGINEERING, UNIV. OF WESTERN ONTARIO 1984– ; Rsch. Asst., Lawrence Berkeley Lab., Univ. of Calif. 1970–75; Mem., Honour Rsch. Soc. Sigma XI, Berkeley 1968; Pres., Epsilon PHI Sigma Soc. 1971; Asst. Prof., U.W.O. 1976; Assoc. Prof. 1980; Visiting Prof., Univ. of Calif. at Berkeley 1987; Dept. Chair, U.W.O. 1988–96; internat. collaboration with devel. countries through IDRC to promote & transfer biotechnol. for commercialization of bioprocesses (eg, prodn. of biodegradable & non-toxic bioinsecticides in Mexico, Nicaragua); Novel Biosensor Systems; Mem., New York Acad. of Sciences 1978; consultant to several chemical, food, & pharm. companies; 1991 Engineering Medal for Distinction in Rsch. & Devel., Assn. of Profl. Engrs. of Ont.; Fellow, Chem. Inst. of Canada 1985 for excellence in rsch.; Best Paper Award 1987 from Candn. Geotechnical Soc. (co-author); Chair, Chem. Inst. of Canada (London) 1985; Chair, Assn. of Profl. Engrs. of Ont. (London) 1991; Listed in Internat. Who's Who of Intellectuals 1983; Mem., Candn. Soc. for Chem. Engr.; Am. Inst. of Chem. Engr.; Austrian Assn. of Bioprocess Technology; Am. Assn. for the Advancement of Sci.; Nat. Geographic Soc.; Am. Soc. for Microbiol.; Am. Chem. Soc.; Teacher, Greek Orthodox Ch. Sunday Sch.; author of more than 100 sci. pubns.; recreations: Greek dancing, soccer, classical music; clubs: Macedonian Assn. of London and Vicinity, 'Aristotle' London, Ont. (Pres.); Hellenic Community London, Faculty Advr., Hellenic Soc. of U.W.O.; Home: 30 Rollingwood Circle, London, Ont. N6G 1P7; Office: Dept. of Chemical and Biochemical Engineering, Univ. of Western Ont., London, Ont. N6A 5B9.

**MARGESON, Hon. Theodore E.,** B.A., B.Ed., LL.B.; judge; b. New Glasgow, N.S. 15 Aug. 1938; s. Paul A.L. and Etta Mae (Cotter) M.; e. New Glasgow H.S. 1956; Mount Allison Univ. B.A. 1959, B.Ed. 1960, LL.B. 1965; m. Sandra Lee d. Stan and Lina Henderson 24 Oct. 1970; children: Jason, Andrew; JUDGE, TAX COURT OF CANADA 1990– ; High School Teacher 1960–62; general law practice 1965–90; Baptist; recreations: golf, hockey, fastball, squash, curling, tennis; Home: P.O. Box 13, Kings Head, R.R. 1, New Glasgow, N.S. B2H 5C4; Office: 200 Kent St., Ottawa, Ont. K1A 0M1.

**MARGESSON, Lynette Joan,** M.D., FRCPC; dermatologist; educator; b. Toronto, Ont. d. Maurice Philip and Pearl Lynette (Aikman) M.; e. St. Clement's Sch. Toronto 1964; Univ. of W. Ont., M.D. 1970; Univ. of Toronto, postgrad. training in Dermatol. 1975; m. Dr. Frederick William s. Dr. Charles and Lucy Danby 26 June 1975; children: Dawn Lynette, Claire Somerset; private practice in Dermatol. since 1975; Asst. Prof. in Dermatol. Queen's Univ.; supervised devel. Dermatol. Clinics several E. Ont. instns. for mentally & physically handicapped; cons. to 4 hosps.; recipient St. Clement's Sch. Alumnae First Gold Award 1985; Fellow, Am. Acad. Dermatol.; mem. Candn. Dermatol. Assn. (Past Dir.); Fedn. Med. Women Can.; recreation: skiing; Home: 234 Alwington Pl., Kingston, Ont. K7L 4P8; Office: 190 Wellington St., Kingston, Ont. K7L 3E4.

**MARGOLIS, Bernard,** M.Sc., Ph.D., F.R.S.C., F.A.P.S.; educator; physicist; b. Montreal, Que. 15 Aug. 1926; s. late John and late Esther (Flisfeder) M.; e. McGill Univ. B.Sc. 1947, M.Sc. 1949; Mass. Inst. of Technol. Ph.D. 1952; m. Barbara d. late Joshua and late Tillie Levin 29 Aug. 1954; children: Jared, Juley; PROF. OF PHYSICS, McGILL UNIV. 1963– , Dir. summer Inst. High Energy Physics 1967, 1969, 1973, 1975, 1976; Orgn. Ctte. IV European Antiproton Symposium Strasbourg, France 1978; Chrmn., Council Candn. Inst. Particle Physics 1971–76; mem. comité de Physique Jury de sélection Bourses de l'enseignement superior FCAC Qué. 1981–82, Chrmn. 1982–83; mem. Jt. NRC-AECL Grants Ctte. 1970–73; Visiting Sci., CERN Geneva, Switzerland 1967–68, 1970–78; DESY Hamburg, Germany 1969; Fermilab, Batavia, Ill. 1969–80; Lectr. Xth Cracow Sch. of Theoretical Physics, Poland 1970; author over 110 sci. papers nuclear and particle physics; co-ed. 'Nuclear and Particle Physics' 1968, various proceedings; mem., Candn. Assn. Physicists (Chrmn. Particle Phys. Div. 1978–79; Achievement Medal Physics 1980); mem., Council Acad. Sci. Royal Soc. Can. 1983–84; mem., Royal Philatelic Soc. Can.; Home: 28 Oakland Ave., Westmount, Que. H3Y 1P2; Office: Rutherford Bldg., 3600 University St., Montreal, Que. H3A 2T8.

**MARGOLIS, Leo,** O.C., M.Sc., Ph.D., F.R.S.C.; research scientist; b. Montreal, Que. 18 Dec. 1927; e. McGill Univ. B.Sc. 1948, M.Sc. 1950, Ph.D. 1952; m. Ruth Anne Lall, R.N.; Children: Rhonda Lee, Robert Allan, Murray Howard, Conrad Anton; SENIOR SCIENTIST, PACIFIC BIOL. STN., BIOLOGICAL SCIENCES BRANCH, DEPT. OF FISHERIES & OCEANS CAN. 1990– ; Research Scient. (Assoc. to Princ.) Pacific Biol. Stn. 1952–67, head various Research Divs. and Sections 1967–90; Canada-USSR Exchange Scientist 1971; Head, Fish Health and Parasitology Section, Pacific Biol. Stn., Biological Sciences Branch, Dept. of Fisheries & Oceans Can. 1981–90; Adjunct Prof., Simon Fraser Univ. 1983– ; Officer, Order of Canada 1990; recipient, Commemorative Medal for 125th Anniversary of Candn. Confederation 1992; Adv., Fed.-Prov. (B.C.) Fisheries Comte. 1969, 1970, 1972; Co-Chrmn. Candn. Comte. on Fish Diseases 1970–73; mem. National Tech. Ctte., Candn. Fish Health Protection Regulations 1990– ; mem. Comte. on Biol. and Rsch., Internat. N. Pacific Fisheries Comn. 1971–92 (Sr. Cdn. Sci. mem. 1976–92); Advr. Cdn. Sect., Internat. N. Pacific Fisheries Comm. 1956–93 (Sr. Sci. Advr. 1976–93); Dept. of Fisheries and Oceans Can. Sci. Subvention Comte. 1978–1981; Adv. Bd., Sci. Infor. and Pub., Dept. of Fisheries and Oceans Can. 1979–83; Science Council of B.C. Aquatic Resources Research Evaluation Comte. 1979–88 (Chrmn. 1986–88); Cons., Internat. Devel. Rsch. Centre 1986; Mem., Scientific Advisory Ctte., New Brunswick Aquaculture Consortium 1991– ; Mem., External Advisory Ctte., Biology Program, Malaspina College 1992– ; Chrmn., Ctte. on Scientific Rsch. and Statistics, North Pacific Anadromous Fish Commission 1993– (Mem. Candn. Delegation 1993– ); author Catalogue and synopsis of 'Caligus' 1975 and Synopsis of the parasites of fishes of Canada 1979; Sr. Co-editor 'Guide to the parasites of fishes of Canada, Part I' 1984, (Part II, 1988; Part III, 1989); Co-editor, 'Sockeye salmon (*Oncorhynchus nerka*) population biology and future management' 1987; 'Pacific Salmon Life Histories' 1991; over 170 articles on parasites and diseases of fish, shellfish, marine mammals and on biology of Pacific salmon; Assoc. Ed. 'Canadian Journal of Zoology' 1971–1981; mem., Ed. Referees Comm. 'Bulletin Internat. N. Pacific Fisheries Comm.' 1976–84; Ed. Board 'Journal of Parasitology' 1977–84, 1989–93 (Consultant to Ed. 1985–88); Assoc. Ed. 'Journal of the World Aquaculture Society' 1986– ; Pres. B.C. Amateur Hockey Assn. 1963–66, Hon. Vice Pres. 1968–88; Life Mem. since 1988 (Diamond Stick Award 1989); Candn. Amateur Hockey Assoc. Order of Merit Award 1990; Can. Soc. Zools. (2nd Vice-Pres. 1988–89, 1st Vice-Pres. 1989–90, Pres. 1990–91, Past Pres. 1991–92; Mem., Recognition Ctte. 1991–94 (Chrmn. 1991–93); Parasitol. Sec. Council mem. 1974–76, Vice-Chrmn. 1976–77, Chrmn. 1977–78, Past-Chrmn. 1978–79, mem. Recognition Ctte. 1985–88, 1993–95); Can. Soc. Zools. R. A. Wardle Invitational Lecture Award 1982; Bd. of Trustees, Zoological Education Trust, 1988–93, Chrmn. 1990–91; mem., Bd. of Dirs., Candn. Federation of Biological Socs. 1990–91; Am. Soc. Parasitols. (Transl. Comte. 1968–93, Chrmn. 1977–78; In Memoriam Comte. 1982–83; Public Responsibilities Ctte. 1988–89; Nominating Ctte. Chrmn. 1992–93); Wildlife Disease Assn.; Am. Fisheries Soc. (Awards Comte. 1975–76); Aquaculture Assn. Can.; World Aquaculture Soc.; Home: 200 Arrow Way, Nanaimo, B.C. V9T 1L1; Office: Nanaimo, B.C. V9R 5K6.

**MARGOSHES, Dave,** B.A., M.F.A.; writer; b. New Brunswick, N.J. 8 July 1941; s. Harry and Berte (Shalley) M.; e. Middlebury Coll.; Univ. of Iowa, B.A. 1963, M.F.A. 1969; m. Ilya d. Ira and Leah Silbar 29 Apr. 1963; Journalist, 'San Francisco Chronicle' 1963–64, 'New York Daily News' 1969, 'Colorado Springs Sun/Free Press' (City editor) 1969–70, 'Calgary Albertan' (City editor) 1974–75, 'Calgary Herald' 1972–74, 1977–81, 'Vancouver Sun' 1984–86 and others; taught journalism, Mount Royal Coll. & S. Alta. Inst. of Technol.; author: 'Discover Canada - Saskatchewan' 1992 (text), 'Nine Lives' 1991 (short stories), 'Northwest Passage' 1990 (poetry), 'Walking at Brighton' 1988 (poetry), 'Small Regrets' 1986 (short stories) and num. short stories & poems in mags. & anthols.; Address: 2922 19th Ave., Regina, Sask. S4T 1X5.

**MARIER, André,** M.Sc.Soc.; exécutif; né Québec, Qué. 15 août 1932; f. Joseph Albert et Antoinette (Desjardins) M.; é. Univ. Laval B.A. 1952, B.S.S. 1954, M.S.S. 1956; ép. Claire f. Aimé et Carméla (Morissette) Pettigrew 26 May 1956; enfants: Louis-Daniel, Christiane, Nicolas-Charles, Véronique; CONSEILLER POUR LA VILLE DE QUÉBEC; Bd. mem. Culinar Inc.; Caisse de dépôt et placement du Québec; Société des pêches de Newport; Centre d'insémination artificielle du Québec; Pêches Nordiques Inc.; Economiste, Canadian Industries Ltd. 1956–58; Economiste régional pour le Québec et les provs. de l'Atlantique, Société Centrale d'Hypothèques et de Logement 1958–61; Gouvernement du Québec 1961–76, Ministere des Richesses Naturelles: Chef, Div. de la mise en valeur des ressources, Direction générale de la Planification 1961–63, Directeur des Etudes économiques 1963–64, Directeur général de la Planification 1964–69; Ministere de l'Industrie et du Commerce, Conseiller économique, Délégation générale du Québec à Paris 1969–71; Ministère du Conseil Executif, Conseiller économique auprès du Conseil exécutif 1971–76; SOQUIP (Société québécoise d'initiatives pétrolières) 1976–77, Directeur des Activités industrielles et commerciales; CRIQ (Centre de Recherche industrielle du Québec) 1977–80, Président et Directeur général; Vice-prés. de SOQUIA 1980–81; Directeur Général SOQUIA (Société québécoise d'initiatives agro-alimentaires) 1981; pendant quelques années, membre du Conseil d'administration de la Régie de l'assurance-dépôt, de celui de l'Institut national de la Recherche scientifique (INRS), de celui de l'Office de Planification et du Développement du Québec (OPDQ), de la Société québécoise d'exploration minière (SOQUEM), de la Société minière Louvem Inc., de la Société québécoise d'initiatives pétrolières (SOQUIP), de l'Institut de Recherche et de Développement sur l'amiante (IRDA) et de l'Association canadienne de gestion de la recherche; Président (partie québécoise) du Groupe franco-québécois de Coopération industrielle 1975–76; auteur de plusieurs documents, rapports, publications ou articles; Adresse; 35 rue Sainte-Ursule, Québec, Qué. G1R 4E4; Bureau: 2 rue Desjardins, Québec, Qué. J1R 4S9.

**MARIER, Jean,** B.A., LL.M.; lawyer; b. Drummondville, Que. 1938; e. McGill Univ. B.A.; Sherbrooke Univ. LL.M.; Sir George Williams Univ. (Concordia); Ottawa Univ.; Geneva Univ.; Harvard Law Sch.; m. Hélène; 2 children; LAWYER, DESJARDINS DUCHARME STEIN MONAST; Dir., Industrial-Alliance Insur. Co.; Montel Inc.; Sani-Gestion Inc.; Tourbières Pearl Inc.; Caisse Populaire Laurier; Vetements Louis Garneau Inc.; Fibrocap Inc.; INFACC Inc.; & others; Gov., Candn. Tax Found.; Dir., Pavillon Robert Deschenes; Medal of Lt.-Gov. of Qué.; interests: mfg., business, commercial & securities law; Office: 1150 Claire-Fontaine, Ste. 300, Quebec, Que. G1R 5G4.

**MARIN, The Hon. René J.,** O.M.M., O.St.J., C.D., Comm. O.M.R.I., K.C.S.G., K.M., Q.C., B.A., B.Ph., LL.B., LL.D.; b. Moonbeam, Ont.; e. Univ. of Ottawa; Osgoode Hall; m. Thérèse Blondin; children: Michel, André, Danielle, Richard; CHAIRMAN, RCMP EXTERNAL REVIEW COMMITTEE 1987; Office of the Judge Advocate Gen., Fleet Esquimalt, B.C. 1960–61; Office of the Hon. Mr. Justice George Addy, Supreme Ct. of Ont. 1962; private practice 1962–66; apptd. mem. Ont. Municipal Bd. 1966; Magistrate for Prov. of Ont. and Judge of Juvenile and Family Ct. County of Renfrew 1968; Judge Prov. Ct. Criminal Div. 1968; apptd to Law Reform Comn. of Can. 1971; County and Dist. Ct. Judge, Prov. of Ont. and Local Judge High Ct. of Justice of Ont. 1973; Chrmn. of Commission of inquiry relating to pub. complaints, internal discipline and grievance procedure, Royal Candn. Mounted Police 1974; Depy. Solicitor Gen. (Can.) 1977; Comnr. of Commission of inquiry into Security and Investigation Services Br., Post Office Dept. 1980; Chrmn., Stamp and Nat'l Postal Museum Adv. Cttes., Canada Post Corp. 1981; Chrmn.,

Canada Post Corp. 1981; Chrmn. Special Ctte. to Study Procedures under the Pension Act 1984; Chrmn., RCMP External Review Ctte. 1987; Comnr. of Bd. of Inquiry on Activities of the RCMP related to Allegations made in the Senate of Canada 1990; Chrmn. of an External Review of the Cndn. Forces Spec. Investigation Unit - DND 1990; Mem., Canada Ports Corp. Police Ctte.; author 'Recevabilité des aveux extra-judiciaires' (1990) SOQUIJ; 'Admissibility of Statements' 7th ed., Canada Law Book; 'Police and Defence Counsel Interaction' 3rd ed.; 'The Police Function in Canada' Methuen; numerous articles on law and criminology; Lectr.: Comparative Law Programme, Univ. of Ottawa; Sch. of Criminology, Univ. of Ottawa; Criminal Law, Common Law Sect., Fac. of Law, Univ. of Ottawa; Law and Security, Algonquin Coll., Ottawa; Judicial Education Programme, B.C. Provincial Judges, (Criminal Div.), Univ. of B.C.; Judicial Education Programme, Ont. Prov. Judges (Criminal Div.), Univ. of Western Ont.; Sessional Lectr., Candn. Police Coll.; Health Protection Br., Dept. of Health and Welfare Can.; Environment Protection, Environment Can.; Bus. and non-bus. affiliations: mem. Candn. Armed Forces, (Reserve) Commodore (Navy); Candn. Bar Assoc.; Law Soc. of Upper Can.; County of Carleton Law Assoc.; Internat. Bd. of Consultants related to the Centre of Criminology, Univ. of Ottawa; Adv. Counc., Centre of Criminology, Univ. of Toronto; Bd. of Gov., Frontier Coll. (mem. Learning Foundation) Toronto; Bd. of Dir., Candn. Assn. for Mentally Retarded; Trustee, Marconi Celebration Trust Agreement; Co-Pres., Fundraising Campaign, Fondation franco-ontarienne; Chancellor and Mem., Extve. Counc., Candn. Assoc., Sovereign and Mil. Order of Malta; La Residence St. Louis; Ottawa Arts Centre Found.; Chrmn. Extve. Ctte., Bd. of Dirs., National Aviation Museum; Hon. Chrmn., Lodge Fund Raising Campaign, Candn. Cancer Soc.; Co-Chrmn., Task Force on Second Language Training for the Reserve (Candn. Armed Forces); Honours: Hon. Life Mem. Prov. Judges Assn. Criminal Div., Ont. 1973; Candn. Decoration 1973; Hon. LL.D.: Laurentian Univ. 1974; Fellow, Frontier Coll., Toronto 1977; Queen's Silver Jubilee Medal 1977; Offr., Order of Mil. Merit 1981; Q.C. (Fed.) 1981; Hon. Life Mem. Candn. Wildlife Fedn. 1982; Comdr. Order of Merit, Republic of Italy 1983; Officer, Order of Saint John 1984; Kt Sovereign and Mil. Order of Malta 1984; Kt Comdr. Order of St. Gregory the Great 1984; First Hon. Mem., Soc. for the Advancement of Pharmaceutical Sciences 1985; Hon. Life Mem., Cdn. Assoc. of Chiefs of Police 1988; Patron, Ronald McDonald House Rotel, Ottawa; Rotel Ottawa Heath Sci. Centre; Past Affiliations: Adv., Candn. Volunteers in Corrections 1971–79; Consultant, Law Reform Comn. of Can. 1971–76; Mem. Task Force of the Solicitor Gen. of Canada on the Selection and Training of Policemen, 1972–73; Chrmn., Task Force on Continuing Educ., Algonquin Coll., Ottawa 1972–73; Pres, Adv. Counc. Nat. Aviation Museum 1979–82; Vice-Chrmn. Bd. of Trustees, Nat. Museums of Can. 1979–83; Chrmn. Bd. of Trustees, Ottawa Gen. Hosp. 1982–86; Co-Pres. Extve. Ctee., Nat. Capital Papal Visit 1983–84; Pres., Assoc. of Science and Technology (AST) Inc.; mem. Bd. of Dirs. & Treasurer, Cercle Universitaire; Clubs: Rideau, Ottawa; Le Cercle Universitaire, Ottawa; Beaver, Montreal; Office: 365 Laurier Ave. W., Tower South, Suite 900, 9th Flr., P.O. Box 1159, Stn. B., Ottawa, Ont. K1P 5R2.

**MARKEN, Ronald Norman George,** M.A., Ph.D.; educator; writer; b. Camrose, Alta. 15 Jan. 1939; s. Edwin Fridtjof and Adelaide Constance (Lewis) M.; e. Camrose Lutheran Coll. (Gov. Gen.'s Medal 1954); Concordia Coll. Moorhead, Minn. B.A. 1960; Univ. of Alta. M.A. 1964, Ph.D. 1972; m. Patricia d. Albert and Mollie Mulford 3 May 1970; children: Erik, Siri, Kristian, Liv, Kari; CHAIR, DEPT. OF ENGLISH, UNIV. OF SASK. 1991– ; PROF. OF ENGLISH, UNIV. OF SASK. 1966– ; writing cons. to numerous Sask. acad., govt. and corporate instns.; Jury mem. Sask. Arts Bd.; Reviewer theatre and books CBC-FM Toronto, CBC-AM Saskatoon & Regina, Macleans mag.; theatre photog. Persephone Theatre (Chrmn. of Bf.), Twenty-Fifth Street Theatre, Saskatoon; Can. Council Doctoral Fellow 1968; Master Teacher Award Univ. Sask. 1985; author: 'Dark Honey' (poetry) 1976; 'Flights of Angels' (play) 1986; ed./author: 'The Easterner's Guide to Western Canada' (satire) 1985; co-author: '1919: The Love Letters of George and Adelaide' (fiction) 1987; ed. 'Don't Steal This Book' (poetry) 1974; 3 radio plays CBC 1980–84; 'Dancing in Poppies' (play) 1992; ed., 'Canadian Journal of Irish Studies' 1989– ; mem. Internat. Assn. Study Anglo-Irish Lit. (Candn. Rep. and Bibliog.); Candn. Assn. Irish Studies; Soc. Teaching & Learning in Higher Edn. (3M Nat. Teaching Fellow 1987); Candn. Assn. Univ. Teachers; Assn. Candn. Univ. Teachers Eng.; Thomas Hardy Soc.; Victorian Studies Assn. W. Can. (Treas.); recreations: cycling, photography, travel; Home: 1125 Temperance St., Saskatoon, Sask. S7N 0N7; Office: Saskatoon, Sask. S7N 0W0.

**MARKHAM, Charles Ian,** B.Sc., F.I.A., F.C.I.A.; actuary; b. Dar-es-Salaam, Tanzania 4 Feb. 1952; s. Robert Charles and the late Susanna (Liebert) M.; e. Clifton Coll. 1969; Univ. of Southampton B.Sc. (Hon.) 1973; m. Janet d. John and Mildred Bradshaw 14 Aug. 1976; children: Graham, Claire, Andrew; PARTNER, KPMG ACTUARIAL, BENEFITS & COMPENSATION INC. 1986– ; joined Life Actuarial Dept., Life & Gen. Assur. Co. 1973–77; joined present firm 1978; F.I.A. 1978; F.C.I.A. 1980; Mem., Can. Pension Conf. (Ont. Reg. Council) 1988–90; Bd. of Trade of Metro. Toronto (Chrmn., Employee Benefits Ctte. 1986– ); Candn. Inst. of Actuaries (Ctte. on Pension Plan Finan. Reporting 1985– ; Chrmn. 1993– ); co-author: 'Pensions and Retirement Income Planning' 1993; Mem., Ed. Bd., 'Benefits Canada' 1985–87; frequent lecturer & speaker; recreations: photography, trekking; clubs: Fitness Inst.; Home: 117 Grand River Blvd., Scarborough, Ont. M1B 1G4; Office: Box 31, 32nd floor, Commerce Court W., Toronto, Ont. M5L 1B2.

**MARKHAM, John;** industrial executive; b. London, England 12 June 1933; s. Sir Charles and Daisy Anne (Vanscolina) M. (both dec.); e. Eton; Gordonstoun; RMA Sandhurst; m. Elizabeth d. George and Norma Alexa (Von Langnau) Culling (both dec.) 26 Sept. 1987; children (by previous marriage): Toby John, Annalise; SPECIAL ADVISER, GOVT. PROGRAMMES - MPR TELTECH; Instr., Royal Artillery, Brit. Army 1953–67; retired as Major; Mgr., U.K. Military Systems, Sperry Div., Sperry Rand. 1967–70; Eur. Mgr., Bonn Frg-Def. Systems 1970–73; Mktg. Mgr., R & D., Dornier Gmbh-Internat. 1973–75; Vice-Pres., Mktg., Plessey Canada Inc. 1976–89; Mem., Ch. of England; Branch Chrmn., N.W. Surrey Cons. 1969–70; recreations: sailing, skiing, golf; Home: 37 Third Ave., Ottawa, Ont. K1S 2J5; Office: 2000 – 320 Queen St., Tower A, Ottawa, Ont. K1R 5A3.

**MARKLE, Clarke Wilson Jr.;** executive; b. Vancouver, B.C 2 Sept. 1938; s. Clarke Wilson and Dorothy Catherine (Mackin) M.; e. Montana State Coll. 1962; m. Kathryn d. Harry and Kathleen Parker 30 May 1981; children: Ashley Kathleen and Clarke Wilson III; EXTVE., TELESAT CANADA 1990– ; Hollyburn Film Studios 1962; Re-recording Mixer, Film House 1964; Producer, Westinghouse, Link Singer 1968; Found. Mem., Image Transform Inc. 1970; Vice Pres., Mktg., Film House 1972; Founder, Image Group 1981; Dir., Brandywine Investments Inc.; Variety Club Charitable Act 'Outstanding Contrib.' award 1977, 83, 85; C.S.C. 'Outstanding Contribution' 1980; UNIATEC Congress 'Prize of Excellence' 1984; The NATAS Emmy for 'Outstanding Engineering Achievement' 1987; Canada Award for Business Excellence 1987; Brit. Kinemographic Sound & TV Soc. 'Phil Berkely Award' 1988; SMPTE author 'Film for Television' 1981; 'Colorization Challenges' Los Angeles 1987; Montreal Que. SMPTE 'Speaker' 1984; SMPTE 'Fellow' 1985; Past Pres., Candn. Film & TV Assn.; Mem., Cdn. Soc. of Cinematographers; Variety Club; Brit. Kinemographic Sound & TV Soc. 'Fellow' 1988; Soc. of Motion Picture & TV Engrs.; author of articles in SMPTE jour.; recreation: sailing; Home: 364 Glengrove Ave. W., Toronto, Ont. M5N 1W4; Office: 100 Sheppard Ave. E., Suite 800, Toronto, Ont. M2N 6N5.

**MARKLE, Gower H.,** B.A.; b. Hamilton, Ont. 26 Nov. 1915; s. Hugh C. and Martha M. (Woelke) M.; e. Univ. of W. Ont. B.A. 1945 (Gold Medal-Econ.); Inst. of World Affairs 1946; m. Beatrice E. d. Frank Green, Hamilton, Ont., 8 Sept. 1942; three s. Glen H., Paul E., Ross A.; formerly Dir. of Education and Welfare, United Steel Workers of America; participant and lectr. internat. labour seminars Internat. Confed. of Free Trade Unions (Brussels) Calcutta 1954, Accra 1955, Banff 1957, Petropolis 1960; conducted survey and study labour educ. needs of W. Indies 1959 (sponsored by Fed. Gov. of W. Indies, Univ. of W. Indies, Candn. Assn. Adult Educ., Ford Foundation); Tech. Advisor to Internat. Labour Organ. Geneva 1972; Chrmn., 2nd Nat. Con. on Labour Educ., 1975; Co-ordr., Labour Educ., Labour Can. 1977–80; Dir., Employment Rel. & Cond. of Work 1980–82; Special Adv. to Depy. Min., Labour Can. 1982–83; mem. Educ. and Welfare Comtes. Candn. Labour Congress; served with RCNVR during World War II; Former Gov. McMaster Univ.; Labour Coll. of Can.; Trustee Toronto Gen. Hosp.; Nat. Museums of Can.; Former mem. Can. Manpower & Immigration Council; Past Pres. Ont. Welfare Council; former Dir. Ont. Mental Health Foundation; Past Gov. Can. Council for Social Devel.; Past Gov. and Vice Chrmn. George Brown Coll. of Applied Arts & Technol.; Past Chrmn. Educ. Comte. Ont. Fed. of Labour; Ottawa Repr. Intnl. Council for Adult Educ. 1984; Trustee Internat. Council for Adult Educ., mem. Candn. Assn. for Adult Educ. (Past Vice Pres.); Special Observer, I.L.O., Geneva, Switzerland 1985; Del., World Assembly of Adult Educ., Buenos Aires 1985; Apptd., Mississippi Valley Conversation Authority 1990; recreations: sports, music, reading; Home: 17 Bay Hill Ridge, Stittsville, Ont. K2S 1B9.

**MARKOTIC, Vladimir,** M.A., Ph.D.; university professor; b. Banjaluka, Bosnia 16 July 1920; s. Filip and Elizabeta (Weigl) M.; e. Indiana Univ., M.A. 1955; Harvard Univ., Ph.D. 1963; m. Margaret Becker 3 Dec. 1956; children: Lorraine, Nicole, Yvonne, Roland, Michelle; ASSOC. PROF. OF ARCHAEOL., UNIV. OF CALGARY 1969– ; Res. Asst., Air Force Res. Proj., Indiana Univ. 1952; Asst. Prof. of Anthrop., Ill. State Univ. 1962–65; Asst. Prof. of Archaeol., Univ. of Calgary 1965–69; Founder & Ed., Calgary Archaeologist 1973– ; Mem., Ed. Ctte., Candn. Ethnic Studies 1974–77; Hemenway Fellowship of Am. Archaeol. & Ethnol., Harvard Univ. 1957–58; Robert C. Winthrop Scholarship, Harvard Univ. 1957–58; Thaw Fellow, Peabody Mus. of Archaeol. & Ethnol., Harvard Univ. 1961–62; Assoc. and Fellow, Am. Anthrop. Assn. 1963– ; Pres., Croatian Lib. of Calgary Assn. 1985– ; Central Croatian Archives 1985– ; mem. Archaeol. Soc. of Alta.; Archaeol. Soc. of Croatia; Croatian Acad. of Am.; author: 'The Vinca Culture' 1984; ed.: 'Ancient Europe and the Mediterranean' 1978; 'The Sasquatch and Other Unknown Hominids' 1984; 'Symposium: Emigrants from Croatia and Their Achievements' 1987; compiler of various ethnic directories; Home: 2508 34th Ave. N.W., Calgary, Alta. T2L 0V5; Office: Calgary, Alta. T2N 1N4.

**MARKOWSKY, Martha A.;** artist; b. Lachine, Que.; d. John and Adele Louise (Chaikowsky) Markowski; e. Resurreciton of our Lord; solo exbns: MacDonald Club, Ottawa 1985; Algonquin College, Nepean 1988; Galerie Francis Alexandre, Vanier 1987, '88; Brock St. Gall., Kingston 1989; West End Gall., Westmount 1990; Art Mode Gall., Ottawa 1991; Gallery on the Lake, Buckhorn 1992; Victoria Art Gall., Toronto 1992, '93; Teacher, Algonquin College (painting); Earl of March H.S. (painting & drawing); First Prize Loeb's Mural Comp. 1991; Best Oil Painting in Show, Westboro Art Fest. 1991; MacDonald Club Scholarship 1984; Prog. Co-ord., Ottawa Art Assn. 1985; Visual Arts Ont. 1985–93; Confed. of Candn. Artists 1993; paintings in several corp. collections incl. Former Prime Min. Brian Mulroney, Ottawa Senators Hockey Assn., Ottawa City Hall, Candn. Mus. of Civilization, etc.; rep. by Art Mode Gall. I and II, Ottawa; Agnes Etherington Gall., Kingston; Brock St. Gall., Kingston; Gal. d'Art Vincent, Ottawa; Gallery on the Lake, Buckhorn; Studio 737, Tweed; Swann Gall., Stratford; Victoria Art Gall., Toronto; West End Gall., Westmount; Sheck Gall., Calgary; Burdette's Gall., Orton; publication: Guide Vallée III Edition 1993; recreations: reading, swimming, walking; Home: 216 Crichton St., Ottawa, Ont. K1M 1W4.

**MARKS, Gerald Samuel,** M.Sc., D.Phil.; educator; b. Cape Town, S. Africa 13 Feb. 1930; s. late Simon and Annie (Goodman) M.; e. Univ. of Cape Town B.Sc. 1950, M.Sc. 1951; Oxford Univ. D.Phil. (Organic Chem.) 1954; m. Marion Zoe d. late George Lewis Tobias 6 March 1955; children: Lynne Sorrel, Saul Ian; PROF. OF PHARMACOL., QUEEN'S UNIV. 1988– (and Head of Dept. 1969–88); mem. Candn. Heart and Stroke Foundation Grants Ctte. 1990–92; mem. Med. Adv. Bd. Muscular Dystrophy Assn. Can. 1971–79; Med. Research Council Grants Comte. for Metabolism, 1980–83, Program Grants Comte. 1986–87; Pharmaceutical Sciences 1972–75, Studentship Comte. 1969–70; Elected mem. extve. Internat. Union of Pharmacology 1990–94; rec'd Aesculapian Soc. Lectureship Award Queen's Univ. 1973, 1987, 1989; Queen's Univ. Alumni Award for Excellence in Teaching 1984; The Upjohn Award in Pharmacology for outstanding contributions to Pharmacology in Can. 1986; Faculty of Medicine, Queen's Univ., Education Award 1993; M.R.C. Visiting Prof. of Pharm. Dalhousie Univ. 1974, Univ. of Alta. 1976, Univ. of Sask., 1982; Chrmn., Gordon Res. Conf. on Pyrroles, 1982; Member of Task Force on Chemicals in the Environment and Human Reproductive problems in New Brunswick, 1983–84; Visiting Prof., Sch. of Pharmacy, Univ. of Calif., San Francisco 1984–85; author 'Heme and Chlorophyll: Chemical, Biochemical and Medical Aspects' 1969; book chapters and numerous publs. on biosynthesis of heme and porphyrins, pharmacology of organic nitrates; Assoc. Ed. 'Canadian Journal of Physiology and Pharmacology' 1970–75 (Coeditor 1981–86); mem., Editorial Bd., European Journal of Pharmacology 1991– ; Pres., Candn. Fedn. of Biol. Sci. 1988–89; Pres., Pharmacol. Soc. Can. 1984–85; Appt'd. Congress Chrmn. for Internat. Union of Pharmacology Congress to be held in Montreal in 1994; mem. Ont. Council of Graduate Studies Appraisals Ctte. 1990–93; mem. Pharmacol. Soc. Can.; Am. Soc. Pharmacol. & Exper. Therapeutics; New York Acad. Sci.; NPD; Jewish; recreations: swimming, squash, tennis, curling; Home: 15 Dickens Dr., Kingston, Ont. K7M 2M5; Office: Dept. of Pharmacology and Toxicology, Queen's Univ., Kingston, Ont. K7L 3N6.

**MARKS, Ross Gordon;** business executive; b. Toronto, Ont. 8 June 1927; s. Matthew Gordon and Emily Elizabeth (Connell) M.; e. Scarborough Collegiate 1945; Ontario Agricultural Coll. 1948; m. Marcia d. Bertha and Herbert Harvey 1954; children: Kenneth, Kevin, Barbara, Alison; MANAGING DIRECTOR, BRIDGE CREEK COMPANIES GROUP; Dir., Cariboo Reg. Dist. 1970–72, 1975–86; Mayor, Village of 100 Mile House 1965–86; Extve. Mem., Union of B.C. Municipalities 1967–75; Pres. 1972–74; Extve. Mem., Fed. of Candn. Municipalities 1973–75; Vice-Chrmn., Provincial Commission of Enquiry, Property Assessment and Taxation 1975–76; Dir., B.C. Assessment Authority 1977–86; Dir. & Trustee, Municipal Finan. Authority of B.C. 1980–86; Comnr., B.C. & Yukon, Fed. Task Force Candn. Unity 1977–79; Dir., Canada Mortgage and Housing Corp. 1985–91; Pres., Herald House Publications Ltd.; Dir., Red Coach Inn Ltd.; Pres., 100 Mile Lodge Holdings Ltd.; Paul Harris Fellow, Rotary Club; recipient, Centennial Medal 1967; Queen Elizabeth Silver Jubilee Medal; 125th Anniversary of the Confederation of Canada Medal, 1992; various former memberships such as Volunteer Fire Dept. (Chief), local Flying, Club, Dist. C. of C.; recreations: skiing, biking; Home: P.O. Box 1, 100 Mile House, B.C. V0K 2E0; Office 109 Cariboo Hwy N., 100 Mile House, B.C. V0K 2E0.

**MARKSON, Jerome,** B.Arch., F.R.A.I.C., R.C.A.; architect; b. Toronto, Ont.; s. Dr. Charles Albert and Etta (Levine) M.; e. Oakwood Coll, Inst., Toronto 1948; Cranbrook Acad. of Art 1952; Univ. of Toronto Sch. of Arch., B. Arch. 1953; m. Mayta Silver, Winnipeg, potter; children: Anna Fredda Markson, Nancy Dara Markson-McLellan; commenced private arch. practice 1955; mem. numerous architectural juries; winner of many arch. awards incl. Massey Medal for Arch., O.A.A. Design Awards, C.M.H.C. Design Awards, Ont. Masons Relations Council Awards, Can. Arch. magazine Design Awards, Stelco and Wood Design Awards; recreations: sailing and cruising, travel, music; Home: 11F Tranby Ave., Toronto, Ont. M5R 1N4.

**MARKWELL, Christopher Richard,** B.A.; insurance and banking executive; b. Rothesay, Isle of Bute, Scotland 22 Nov. 1944; s. Ian Bissett and Margaret (Irving) M.; e. York Univ. B.A. (Hons.) 1964; Univ. of Toronto, post grad. business studies; m. Hazel d. Walter and Lenore McFadyen 22 Nov. 1969; children: Jason, Adam; PRESIDENT, RBC INSURANCE HOLDINGS INC.; Chrmn., Voyageur Insurance Co.; Assured Assistance Inc.; RBC Underwriting Management Services; Royal Bank of Canada Insurance Co. Ltd. (Barbados); RBC Reinsurance (Cayman); Vice-Pres., Phoenix Insur. Co. 1968–84; Extve. Asst./Dep. Min. (Ont.) Consumer & Commercial Relns. 1973; Vice-Pres., Phoenix Continental Mngt. Ltd. 1984–86; Pres. & Chief Operating Offr., Crum & Forster of Canada Ltd. 1986–90; Sr. Vice-Pres., Insurance, Royal Bank of Canada 1990–92; monthly columnist, 'Canadian Underwriter Magazine' 1980–84 & articles in var. others; several honours & awards; Mem., Royal Candn. Military Inst.; Montreal Amateur Athletic Assn.; Summerlea G.C.; Toronto Bd. of Trade; recreations: travel, golf; Office: 44 Peel Centre Dr., Brampton, Ont. L6T 4M8.

**MARKWELL, Steve,** B.A.; sportswear executive; b. Bishop's Stortford, U.K. 7 Nov. 1946; s. Bryan Ernest Archibald and Gladys Esther (Haslen) M.; e. Bishop's Stortford College, Univ. of Keele B.A. (Hons.) 1970; m. Elizabeth d. Fred and Brenda Margaret Marsden 3 Aug. 1968; children: John, Candace, Georgia; PRESIDENT, MARKETING, THE JOHN FORSYTH COMPANY INC. 1989– ; Marketing Manager, Proctor and Gamble (U.K., France, Holland) 1970–83; Advertising Dir., Playtex U.K. then General Manager Playtext S. Africa then Canada 1983–89; recreations: tennis; clubs: Boulevard, Baby Point; Home: 104, Baby Point Rd., Toronto, Ont. M6S 2G3; Office: 215 Evans Ave., Toronto, Ont. M8Z 1J5.

**MARLATTE, George Ellis,** B.Comm., F.I.C.B.; banker; b. Saskatoon, Sask. 9 Oct. 1949; s. Clarence E. and Muriel M. M.; e. Univ. of Sask. B.Comm. 1973; Fellow, Inst. of Canadian Bankers; m. Donna; children: Thea, Read; SENIOR VICE-PRESIDENT, B.C. & YUKON REGION, THE BANK OF NOVA SCOTIA; various positions with The Bank of N.S. 1968– ; formerly Vice-Pres. Corporate Banking, Europe domiciled in London, U.K.; Trustee, Simon Fraser Univ. Found.; Dir., Jr. Achievement of B.C.; Office: 650 West Georgia St., 34th Floor, Vancouver, B.C. V6B 4N7.

**MARLEAU, The Hon. Diane Paulette,** B.A., P.C., M.P.; politician; b. Kirkland Lake, Ont. 21 June 1943; d. Jean-Paul and Yvonne (Desjardins) LeBel; e. Univ. of Ottawa 1960–63; Laurentian Univ. B.A. 1976; m. Paul s. Domina and Bernadette Marleau 3 Aug. 1963; children: Brigitte, Donald, Stéphane; MINISTER OF HEALTH IN THE CABINET OF THE RIGHT HONOURABLE JEAN CHRÉTIEN 1993– ; Accountant, Donald Jean Acctg. Serv. 1971–75; Receiver Mgr., Thorne Riddell 1975–76; Treas., Northern Reg. Recovery Home for Women 1976–80; apptd. by Fed. Govt. to Ctte. for Industry & Labour Adjustment Prog., Region of Sudbury 1983; Chair, Candn. Games for Physically Disabled 1983; Official Agent for re-election campaign for Hon. Judy Erola 1984; appt. by David Peterson as Northern Ont. Mem. of 10-member Transition Team 1984–85; Alderman 1980; Reg. Councillor, Sudbury Reg. Council 1980–85; Advisory Council on Women's Issues 1984; 1st elected Liberal M.P. for Sudbury 1988; 1989: Mem., Standing Ctte. on Fin. & Econ. Affairs; Vice-Chair, Nat. Liberal Party Standing Ctte. on Policy; Assoc. Critic for Energy, Mines & Resources & for Finan. Mngt.; 1990: Chair, Ont. Liberal Caucus; Liberal Party Nat. Extve.; Mem., Working Group on Fair Taxation; Assoc. Critic for Energy, Mines & Resources and for Govt. Operations; 1991: Deputy Opposition Whip; Mem., Standing Ctte. on House Mngt.; 1992: Assoc. Critic for Finance; Vice-Chair, Standing Ctte. on Finance; re-elected 1993; several past executive positions with Laurentian Hosp., Candn. Cancer Soc., Northern Devel. Council, Cambrian College and other orgns.; recreations: piano, gardening, reading, cooking; Home: S.S. 1, Site 13, Box 12, Sudbury, Ont. P3E 4S8; Offices: (constituency) 36 Elm St., Sudbury, Ont. P3C 5B4, (House of Commons) Room 256, Confederation Bldg., Ottawa, Ont. K1A 0A6.

**MARLEAU, Robert,** B.A.; b. Cornwall, Ont. 27 April 1948; s. Roland and Liliane (Hamilton) M.; e. Cornwall Classical College; Univ. of Ottawa B.A. 1969; m. Ann d. Louis and Freda Spilsbury 8 Aug. 1970; children: Stéphane, Kristian; CLERK OF THE HOUSE OF COMMONS 1987– ; French H.S. Teacher 1969; House of Commons 1970: Cttes. Branch, standing cttes. on Privileges & Elections, Health & Welfare and Social Affairs; Finance, Trade & Econ. Affairs & Penitentiary Reform 1970–74; Extve. Sec. Treas., Candn. Branch, 'Assemblée internat. des parlementaires de langue française' & Canada-France Interparl. Assn. 1974–81; Principal Clerk, Cttes. & Private Legisl. Branch & also Clerk of the Special Ctte. on Standing Orders & Procedure 1981–83; Clerk Asst. of the House of Commons 1983–87; Mem., Candn. Study of Parl. Group; Candn. Soc. of Clerks-at-the-Table; Found Pres., Assn. des sec. gén. des parl. mem. de l'A.I.P.L.F.; Commander, Ordre de la Pléiade; Knight of Magistral Grace, Sovereign Military Order of Malta; awarded Commemorative Medal for 125th Anniversary of Candn. Confederation 1992; Dir., Forum for Young Canadians; Office: Ottawa, Ont. K1A 0A6.

**MARLIN, Randal Robert,** M.A., Ph.D.; educator; b. Washington, D.C. 22 Jan. 1938; s. Ervin Ross and Hilda Gerarda (van Stockum) M.; e. Ampleforth Coll. York, Eng. 1955; Princeton Univ. A.B. 1959; McGill Univ. M.A. 1961; Trinity Coll. Oxford 1961–63; Univ. d'Aix-Marseille 1963–64; Univ. of Toronto Ph.D. 1973; m. Elaine Margaret d. Redmond and Margaret O'Brien 28 June 1969; children: Christine, Alexander, Gregory, Nicholas, Laura, Marguerite; ASSOC. PROF. OF PHILOS. CARLETON UNIV. 1977– ; Co-owner, E & R Marlin, Publishing; Visiting Lectr. Inst. Am. Univs. Aix-en-Provence, France 1963–64; Instr. Univ. of Toronto 1964–66, Don, New Coll. 1965–66; Lectr. Carleton Univ. 1966, Asst. Prof. 1968–77; Dow-Hickson Fellow in Philos. McGill Univ. 1960–61; Dept. of Nat. Defence Fellow 1979–80; Extve. mem. Glebe Community Assn. 1971–79, Pres. 1972; Lansdowne Devel. Adv. Ctte. City of Ottawa 1976; Ed. 'Ottawa Newspaper Review' 1970–73; 'Propaganda and the Ethics of Rhetoric' Canadian Journal of Rhetorical Studies Sept. 1993; Pub. 'Home Daycare Manual' 1976; transl. 'FLN Propaganda in France during the Algerian War' (Jacques Ellul) 1982; author: 'Logic and Rhetoric,' Internat. Journ. of Moral and Soc. Studies 1988; 'Propaganda and the Ethics of Persuasion,' Internat. Journ. of Moral and Soc. Studies 1989; 'Manufacturing Hate' Content 1991; mem. Candn. Philos. Assn.; Internat. Assn. Philos. Law & Social Philos. (Candn. Sect.); R. Catholic; recreations; chess, swimming, travel; Home: 22 Third Ave., Ottawa, Ont. K1S 2J6; Office: Colonel By Dr., Ottawa, Ont. K1S 5B6.

**MARLISS, Errol B.,** M.D., F.R.C.P.(C); university professor; physician; b. Edmonton, Alta. 6 Jan. 1941; s. Ben P. and Ethel A. (Segal) M.; e. Univ. of Alta., M.D. 1964; children: Stephan C., Karina B.; SR. PHYSICIAN, DEPT. OF MED., ROYAL VICTORIA & MONTREAL GEN. HOSPS. & DIR., MCGILL NUTR. & FOOD SCI. CTR. 1982– ; Intern, Univ. of Alta. Hosp. 1964–65; Res., Royal Victoria Hosp. 1965–67; post-doct. fellowships: Boston Univ. Sch. of Med. 1967–68, Harvard Med. Sch. 1968–70; Univ. de Geneve 1970–72; Staff Phys., Women's Coll. Hosp. 1972–76; Toronto Gen. Hosp. 1972–82; Hon. Cons., Hosp. for Sick Children 1977–82; Asst. Prof., Univ. of Toronto 1972; Assoc. Prof. 1977; Prof. 1982; Prof., McGill Univ. 1982– ; Garfield Weston Prof. of Nutrition, McGill Univ. 1984– ; extensive lectr.; num. awards rec'd in med. sch.; MRC scholarship 1972–77, fellowship 1967–72; Mem., Alpha Omega Alpha Hon. Med. Soc.; Am., Candn., Que., Eur. & Internat. Diabetes Assns.; Am. Fed. for Clin. Rsch.; Am. Physiol. Soc.; Am. & Candn. Socs. for Clin. Invest.; Am. Soc. for Clin. Nutr.; Am. Soc. for Parenteral & Enteral Nutr.; Candn. Soc. of Endocrinol. & Metabol.; Candn. Soc. for Nutr. Sci.; Club de Rech. Clin. du Que.; Endocrine Soc.; N.A. Soc. for Study of Obesity; author/co-author of 198 articles, 38 chapters, & 246 abstracts; Home: 2500 Pierre Dupuy, Apt. 903, Montreal, Que. H3C 4L1; Office: 687 Pine Ave. W., Montreal, Que. H3A 1A1.

**MARMET, Paul,** O.C., D.Sc.; physicien; éducateur; né Lévis, Qué. 20 mai 1932; f. Albert et Corinne (Filteau) M. (décédés); é. Univ. Laval B.Sc. 1956, D.Sc. 1960; CSIRO Melbourne, Australia Postdoctoral 1960–61; ép. Jacqueline f. Albert Côté (dé.) 6 juin 1959; enfants: Louis, Marie, Nicolas, Frédéric; PROFESSEUR INVITÉ, DEPT. PHYSIQUE UNIVERSITÉ D'OTTAWA 1991– ; enseignement en Physique, Coll. Univ. Laval 1958–60; Asst. de recherche CSIRO, Melbourne, Australia 1960–61; prof. auxiliaire, Univ. Laval 1961, prof. agrégé 1966, prof. chercheur 1974–77, prof. titulaire 1970–84; Agent de recherche senior, Institut Herzberg d'astrophysique, Conseil National des recherches 1984–91; Dir. du Lab. de Physique Atomique et Moléculaire 1967–82; année sabbatique au service de Chimie, Univ. de Liège, Belgique 1967; mem. co-fondateur de Centre de Recherche sur les Atomes et les Molécules,bureau de direction 1967–69; mem. du Comité de subventions du Gouvernement du Qué. 1975; Comité des Subventions-Physique du C.N.R.C. 1971–74, représentant Canadien, Union Internationale de Physique pure et appliquée 1976–79, Comité d'Organisation des ICPEAC Paris 1977 et Tokyo 1979 (organisateur du IV Congrès Internationale de la Physique des Collisions Atomiques et Ioniques, Qué. 1965); Officier de l'ordre du Canada, 1981; Médaille Herzberg de l'Assn. Canadienne des Physiciens 1971; Prix Rutherford de la Société Royal du Can. 1960; Médaille Pariseau (ACFAS) 1976; Service Award Soc. Roy. d'Astronomie du Can.; Prix Concours Scientifique de la Prov. de Qué. 1962; Bourse Post-doctorale du CNRC Melbourne 1960, 3 bourses graduées 1957–59; co-auteur 'High Resolution Electron Beams and their Applications' 1969; auteur 'A New Non-Doppler Redshift'; 'Absurdities in Modern Physics: A Solution' 1993; articles nombreux; mem. Conseil de Dir., Commn. de Control de l'Energie Atomique du Can. 1979–84; mem. Société Royale du Canada; Assn. Canadienne des Physiciens Vice Pres., 1979–81, Pres. 1981–82; Am. Phys. Soc.; Soc. Royale d'Astronomie du Can.; Résidence: 2401 Ch. Ogilvie, Gloucester, Ont. G1K 7P4; Bureau: Département de physique, Faculté des sciences, Université d'Ottawa, Ottawa, Ont. K1N 6N5.

**MARMURA, Michael E.,** B.A., M.A., Ph.D., F.R.S.C.; university professor; b. Jerusalem, Palestine 11 Nov. 1929; s. Elias and Anisah (Kawar) M.; e. Univ. of Wisconsin B.A. 1953; Univ. of Michigan M.A. 1955, Ph.D. 1959; m. Elizabeth d. Charles and Muriel Carscallen 30 June 1962; children: Heather, Stephen, Timothy; PROFESSOR, DEPT. OF MIDDLE EAST & ISLAMIC STUDIES, UNIV. OF TORONTO 1969– ; Lectr., Near Eastern Studies, Univ. of Toronto 1959–62; Asst. Prof., Middle East & Islamic Studies 1962–65; Assoc. Prof. 1965–69; Visiting Prof., New York Univ. summer 1969; cross-apptd. Univ. of Toronto, Centre for Medieval Studies, Dept. of Philos., Centre for Religious Studies; Department Chair 1978–83, 1988–93; Extve. Ctte., Soc. internat. pour l'étude de la philos. méd.; Adv. Bd. of Arabic, Science and Philos.; author: 'Der Islam II' 1985; editor: 'Ibn Sina fi Ithbat al-Nubuwwat (Proof of Prophecies)' 1968, '90, 'Islamic Theology and Philosophy Studies in Honor of G.P. Hourani' 1984; co-author: 'Refutation by Alexander of Aphrodisias of Galen's Treatise on the Theory of Motion' 1970; recreations: music, hiking; Home: 220 Clendenan Ave., Toronto, Ont. M6P 2X2; Office: 130 St. George St., Rm. 14087, Toronto, Ont. M5S 1A1.

**MAROTTA, Joseph Thomas,** M.D., F.R.C.P.(C); physician; educator; b. Niagara Falls, N.Y. 28 May 1926; s. Alfred and Mary (Montemurro) M.; e. Univ. of Toronto M.D. 1949; Columbia Presb. Med. Centre, Neurological Inst. post-grad. training 1952–55; Univ. of London 1955–56; m. Margaret Elizabeth Hughes 31 Aug. 1953; children: Maureen, Patricia Ann, Margaret, Frederick, Thomas, Jo Anne, Michael, Martha, John, Virginia; HON. PROF. OF NEUROLOGICAL SCIENCES, UNIV. OF WESTERN ONT. MEDICAL SCH. 1990– ; Lecturer in Medicine, Univ. of Toronto 1957; Prof., Faculty Med., Univ. of Toronto 1969– ; Prof. and Phys.-in-Chief, St. Michaels Hospital 1969–79; Prof. and Head Neurol Div. Wellesley Hosp. 1979–81; Assoc. Dean of Clinical & Institutional Affairs, Faculty of Med., Univ. of Toronto 1981–89; rec'd Queen's Silver Jubilee Medal; mem. Am. Acad. Neurol.; Ont. Med. Assn.; Candn. Med. Assn.; R. Catholic; Recreations: golf, gardening, furniture refinishing, reading, music, walking; Home: 46 Carnforth Rd., London, Ont. N6G 4P6.

**MARPLE, Allen C.,** B.A.; finance executive; b. Norwalk, Conn. 22 Nov. 1936; s. William Elwood and Jean (Sutherland) M.; e. Coll. Arts & Sci. Cornell Univ. B.A. 1959; Grad. Sch. Bus. N.Y. Univ.; m. Joan d. J. Arthur and Elsa A. Manson 20 Aug. 1960;; three s. William, David, Daniel; PRES., SPECTRUM BULLOCK FINANCIAL SERVICES, INC. 1990– ; Chrmn. & Pres., Calvin Bullock Ltd.; joined Chase Manhattan Bank 1959–83 holding various positions incl. Dep. Div. Extve. Aerospace Div., Mng. Dir. London, Eng., Dir. Chase Manhattan Capital Markets Group N.Y.; Bank of Montreal 1983–89, Sr. Vice Pres. Merchant Banking Div. Capital Mkts. Group; Dir. & Chair, Patron's Council; Nat. Ballet of Can.; Chair, IFIC; Gov. Invest. Funds Inst. Can.; Anglican; recreations: sailing, ballet, theatre, travel, skiing; Clubs: RCYC; Cambridge; Office: P.O. Box 160, Stn. A, Toronto, Ont. M5W 1B2.

**MARPLES, David Roger,** B.A., M.A., Ph.D.; university professor; b. Chesterfield, England 17 Oct. 1952; s. Joseph Neville and Ella Ivy (Stringfellow) M.; e. Shirebrook Gr. Sch. 1964–71; Univ. of London, B.A. (Hons.) 1975; Univ. of Alta., M.A. 1980; Univ. of Sheffield, Ph.D. 1985; m. Lan d. Jim and Mee Chan 28 Aug. 1982; children: Carlton, Keelan; ASSOC. PROF. OF RUSSIAN AND SOVIET HISTORY, UNIV. OF ALTA. 1991– ; Teaching Asst., Univ. of Alta. 1978–80; Mng. Ed., Candn. Inst. of Ukrainian Stud., Univ. of Alta. 1980–84; Rsch. Assoc. 1986–91; Adjunct Assoc. Prof., Dept. of Slavic & E. Eur. Studies, Univ. of Alta. 1987– ; Cons., Soviet Affairs, External Affairs Can., U.S. Dept. of State, Dept. of Sci. & Technol., The White House 1986–88; Cons. & contbr., Radio Liberty Rsch., RFE-RL Inc., Munich; CBC, CBS, BBC 1986–92; Dir., Stasiuk Program for the Study of Contemporary Ukraine, Candn. Inst. of Ukrainian Studies, Univ. of Alta. 1990–91; Skeel Essay Prize (London Univ. 1974); Brit. Counc. Exchange Fellowship to USSR 1977; Fellow, Salzburg Sem. on E.-W. Relns. 1985; World Opinion Leaders Tour of the Soviet Union 1987, 1988; Cleveland City Club Forum 1991; Hon. Trustee, Institute of Society and Humanity, Univ. of Saskatchewan 1993; Mem., Candn. Assn. of Slavists; Am. Assn. for the Advancement of Slavic Studies; Contributing ed.: 'Post-Soviet Geography' 1992–93; author: 'Chernobyl and Nuclear Power in the USSR' 1986, 1987, 'The Social Impact of the Chernobyl Disaster' 1988; 'Ukraine Under Perestroika' 1991; 'Stalinism in Ukraine in the 1940s' 1992; and num. newspaper & scholarly articles; co-author: 'The Chernobyl Commission Report' 1987; recreations: chess, music, soccer (playing & coaching); Club: Faculty (Univ. of Alta.); Hon. mem., The Washington Group, Washington, DC; Home: 10423–86 Ave., Edmonton, Alta. T6E 2M4; Office: Dept. of History, Univ. of Alberta, Edmonton, Alta. T6G 2H4.

**MARQUIS, Hon. Eugene;** retired judge; b. St. Alexandre, Kamouraska, P.Q. 11 Sept. 1901; s. Joseph and Eveline (Michaud) M.; e. St. Anne de Beaupré and Ste. Anne de la Pocatiere Colls.; Quebec Semy., B.A.; Laval Univ. LL.L.; LL.D. 1923; m. Veronique, d. Dr. J.A.N. Chabot, Ste. Claire de Dorchester, 14 Jan. 1931; children: Monique, Louise, Yves, Michel, Jean; Justice Superior Court P.Q. 1949–73; Sr. Assoc. Chief Justice 1973–76; Crown Atty. for Dist. of Que. 1931–36 and 1939–44; Hon. mem., Candn. Bar Assn. 1979; el. to H. of C. for Kamouraska, g.e. 1945; re-el. g.e. 1949; K. of C.; rec. Maltese Cross; Roman Catholic; Home: 650 Ave. Murray, Apt. 215A, Québec, Qué. G1S 4V8.

**MARQUIS, Hon. Jean,** B.A., LL.L.; judge; b. St-Césaire, Qué. 8 Nov. 1928; s. Roland Simeon and Florida Corrine (Brien) M.; e. Seminaire de St-Hyacinthe, B.A. 1949; Univ. de Montréal, LL.L. 1952; m. Claire d. Honorat and Antoinette Lussier 15 Sept. 1952; children: Robert, Isabelle, Lorraine, Charles, André; JUDGE, SUPERIOR COURT OF QUE. 1978– ; called to Bar of Qué. 1953; law practive Granby, Qué. 25 yrs.; Mun. Judge Granby 1960–78; Bencher, Bar of Bedford many yrs., Batonnier 1969–70; former Pres. De Ca Bois Inc.; Regional Sch. Bd. Meilleur 1969–71; R. Catholic; recreations: golf, gardening, reading; Home: 101, rue St-Michel, app. 307, Granby, Qué. J2G 9K9; Office: 15.51, 1 est, Notre Dame, Montréal, Qué. H2Y 1B6.

**MARR, Leon Grisha;** film-maker; b. Toronto, Ont. 26 May 1948; s. Abraham Grisha and Stephanie (Sloboda) M.; e. Leaside High Sch. 1967; Univ. of Toronto 1967–69; Ryerson Polytech. Inst. Dip. Photographic Arts 1974; PRIN. IKON KINO FILMS 1978–87; Dir. and Co-Producer half-hour dramatic films 'Clare's Wish' 1979, 'Flowers in the Sand' 1980; Dir. and Screenwriter feature film 'Dancing in the Dark' 1986 (Genie Award Best Adapted Screenplay 1987); Dir. and mem. Dirs. Guild Can.; Writer and mem. Alliance Candn. Cinema, TV & Radio Artists; Address: 47 Spruce Hill Rd., Toronto, Ont. M4E 3G2.

**MARR, Ronald James;** publisher; b. Caledonia, Ont 14 March 1933; s. Eldon Wray and Clara Muriel M.; e. Prairie Bible Inst. Three Hills, Alta. grad. dip. 1955; m. Ruth Viola d. Henry and Katherine Peters 2 July 1957; two d. Bonnie Lynne, Sherrie Colleen; PRES., CHRISTLIFE INC. 1991– ; CHRMN., WORLDWIDE REVIVAL PRAYER FELLOWSHIP 1986– ; Ed. and Publisher Christian Inquirer 1970–86; Founder and Pres.: Internat. Christian Communications Inc. 1971– ; Internat. Christian Alert Network 1983–86; Publisher: Prophecy Newsletter 1984–86; Freedom Alert 1984–86; o. Fellowship of Evangelical Bapt. Chs. 1964; Dir. Greater Winnipeg Youth For Christ 1955–60, Montreal Youth For Christ 1960–67; Interim Pastor Chomedy Bapt. Ch. Laval, Qué. 1965–66; Youth Ed. Evangelical Christian Mag. 1965–68; Dir. of Devel. Richmond Coll. 1968–69; Vice Pres. Christian Writers of Can. 1969–70, Pres. 1971–72; Vice Pres. Overseas Students Mission 1969–71; Pastor, Calvin Bapt. Ch. Toronto 1969–73; author: 'The Education Time Bomb' 1979; 'A Christianity That Really Works' 1993; Address: Box 508, Niagara Falls, Ont. L2E 6V2.

**MARR, William Lewis,** M.A., Ph.D.; educator; b. Hamilton, Ont. 25 March 1944; s. Frederick Lewis and Myrtle Elizabeth (Smith) M.; e. McMaster Univ. B.A. 1966; Univ. of W. Ont. M.A. 1967, Ph.D. 1973; m. Marion d. Ken and Jean Little 26 Aug. 1967; children: Jennifer Elaine, Peter William; PROF. OF ECON., WILFRID LAURIER UNIV. 1982– ; part-time Instr. King's Coll. Univ. of W. Ont. 1968–70; Lectr. in Econ. Waterloo Lutheran Univ. (now present Univ.) 1970, Asst. Prof. 1973, Assoc. Prof. 1975; Asst. Dean of Graduate Studies and Univ. Research, and Assoc. Dir. of Instruction Development, Wilfrid Laurier Univ. 1988–92, 1994– ; Visiting Scholar, Duke University; Visiting Prof. Univ. of W. Ont., McMaster Univ.; Cons. Employment & Immigration Can.; resource person Inst. Rsch. on Pub. Policy and Employment and Immigration Canada; author 'Labour Market and Other Implications of Immigration Policy for Ontario' 1976; co-author 'Canada, An Economic History' 1980; co-ed. 'How Economists Explain' 1983; various articles acad. jours.; recipient Ont. Grad. Fellowships; Can. Council Fellowships; Hurd Medal; rsch. grants Social Sci. & Humanities Rsch. Council, Ont. Econ. Council, Employment & Immigration Can., Inst. Rsch. Pub. Policy; Canada Mortgage and Housing Corp.; mem. Candn. Econ. Assn.; Candn. Population Soc. (Sec.-Treas. 1990–92); Econ. Hist. Assn.; Assn. Candn. Studies; Candn. Regional Sci. Assn.; recreations: golf, curling, reading; Home: 148 Albert St., Waterloo, Ont. N2L 3T3; Office: Waterloo, Ont. N2L 3C5.

**MARRON, Kevin Christopher Gerard,** B.A.; writer; b. London, Eng. 20 Oct. 1947; s. Desmond Francis Gerard and Evelyn Grace Rebecca (Harris) M.; e. Fitzwilliam Coll. Cambridge B.A. 1970; freelance writer and journalist crime, pol., social & environmental issues 1978– ; news stories and features for The Globe and Mail; Eng. teacher Algeria 1966; Grad. Teaching Fellow McMaster Univ. 1970–72; Teacher/Adm. Fairchild Free Sch. Paris, Ont. 1972–74; Ed. and Publisher The Brantford Free Press 1974–77; author: 'Ritual Abuse: Canada's Most Infamous Trial on Child Abuse' 1988; 'Witches, Pagans, & Magic in the New Age' 1989; recreations: walking, nature, photography, arts; Address: c/o Seal Books, 105 Bond St., Toronto, Ont. M5B 1Y3.

**MARRS, Douglas Charles;** retired executive; b. Hamilton, Ont. 27 Sept. 1913; s. late Mina Grace (Longhurst) and late Charles Hawkins M.; m. Hilda Elaine, d. late Robert W. Witherspoon, 8 June 1946; children: Robert Douglas, Pamela Anne (Vallance); Pres., C.E.O., and Dir., Westinghouse Can. Ltd. 1974–78; Chrmn. Westinghouse Canada Inc. 1978–84; Past Chrmn. Bd. Govs., McMaster Univ.; P. Conservative; United Church; recreations: golf, boating; Clubs: Hamilton Golf & Country; Hamilton; John's Island (Florida); Address: 2220 Lakeshore Rd., Burlington, Ont. L7R 4G7.

**MARRUS, Michael Robert,** B.A., M.A., Ph.D., F.R.S.C.; university professor; b. Toronto, Ont. 3 Feb. 1941; s. Elliott Lloyd and Lillian (Brenzel) M.; e. Univ. of Toronto, B.A. 1963; Univ. of Calif. at Berkeley, M.A. 1964, Ph.D. 1968; m. Randi d. Pinchas and Esther Greenstein 13 May 1971; children: Jeremy, Naomi, Adam; PROF. OF HIST., UNIV. OF TORONTO 1978– ; joined Univ. of Toronto 1968; Sr. Assoc. Mem., St. Antony's Coll., Oxford Univ. 1978–80; 1939 Club Vis. Prof. of Hist., Univ. of Calif. at Los Angeles 1982; Fellow, Inst. for Advanced Studies, Hebrew Univ. of Jerusalem 1984–85; Assoc., Massey Coll., Univ. of Toronto 1986– ; Fellow, Trinity Coll., Univ. of Toronto 1987– ; Bd. of Dir., Friends of Le Chambon-sur-Lignon 1983– ; mem. Academic Ctte., Internat. Centre for the Study of Anti-Semitism, Hebrew Univ. of Jerusalem 1983– ; Ed. Adv. Bd., Holocaust & Genocide Studies 1985– ; Internat. Adv. Ctte., Tauber Inst. 1987– ; Assoc. Ed., Jour. of Refugee Studies 1987– ; mem. Bd., International P.E.N. (Candn. section) 1989; mem. Bd., Canadian Friends of Peace Now 1982–92; mem. Governing Counc., Univ. of Toronto 1987– ; mem. Internat. Adv. Bd., Holocaust Series, Pargamon Press and the Institute for Contemporary Jewry 1988– ; Chrmn., Academic Bd. 1989– ; mem. Bd., Holy Blossom Temple 1986–90; Adv. Bd., Centre for Refugee Studies, York Univ. 1986– ; mem. Internat. Adv. Bd., Anti-Defamation League, Braun Center for Holocaust Studies 1990– ; Acad. Adv. Bd., Holocaust Education Found. 1992– ; Connaught Found. Fellowship 1977–79; Killam Sr. Rsch. Fellowship, Can. Counc. 1978–79; Guggenheim Fellow 1984–85; F.R.S.C. 1987; author 'The Politics of Assimilation' 1971, 1980; 'The Unwanted: European Refugees in the Twentieth Century' 1985; 'The Holocaust in History' 1987; 'Mr. Sam: The Life and Times of Samuel Bronfman' 1991; co-author 'Vichy, France and the Jews' 1981; ed., 'The Nazi Holocaust'; Home: 496 Markham St., Toronto, Ont. M6G 2L5; Office: Dept. of Hist., Univ. of Toronto, Toronto, Ont. M5S 1A1.

**MARS, Patrick J.,** B.Com., M.B.A.; b. Waterlooville, Hants, Eng. 19 April 1940; e. Cranleigh School, Surrey, Eng., McGill Univ. B.Com. 1962, M.B.A. 1965; Chart. Financial Analyst 1971; m. Robin 5 Nov. 1966; children: Anthea, Euan; PRESIDENT AND DIR., BUNTING WARBURG INC.; Dir., Investment Dealers Assn. of Canada; mem. Toronto Soc. of Financial Analysts; mem. Cdn. Inst. of Mining & Metallurgy; recreations: sailing, squash, skiing; Clubs: National; R.C.Y.C.; Toronto Ski; Home: 106 Mildenhall Rd., Toronto, Ont. M4N 3H5; Office: Suite 4100, P.O. Box 617, 161 Bay St., Toronto, Ont. M5J 2S1.

**MARSAN, André,** C.F.A.; portfolio manager; b. Montreal, Que. 1 July 1937; s. Jean-Marie and Pauline (Archambault) M.; e. Coll. Jean-de-Brébeuf, B.A. 1956; Univ. of Montreal, B.Phil. 1961, M.A. 1963; m. Ginette Pelletier; children: Geneviève, Nathalie, Marie-Josée, Jean-Philippe; PRES. & CHIEF EXTVE. OFFR., MONTRUSCO ASSOCIATES INC. 1984– ; Vice-Pres. & Dir. of Rsch., Levesque Beaubien Inc. 1969–74; Vice-Pres. & Dir., Rsch. Securities Inc. 1975–77; Vice-Pres. & Dir., Bolton, Tremblay Inc. 1977–81; Vice-Pres. & Dir., Timmins & Assoc. Ltd. 1981–84; Dir., Montgesco Inc.; Les Grands Ballets Canadiens; Camoplast Inc.; C.F.A. 1971; Office: 1501 McGill College, Suite 2800, Montreal, Que. H3A 3N3.

**MARSAN, Jean-Claude,** B.A., B.Arch., M.Sc., Ph.D., S.R.C., O.A.Q., C.P.U.Q.; university dean, architecture and planning critic, consultant; b. St-Eustache, Qué. 7 Oct. 1938; s. Aimé and Gertrude (Bolduc) M.; e. Univ. de Montréal, B.A. 1960, B.Arch. 1965; Univ. of Edinburgh, M.Sc. 1968, Ph.D. 1975; children: Jean-Sébastien, Marc-Aurèle; Dean, Fac. de l'Aménagement, Univ. de Montréal 1985–93; Assoc. Prof., Sch. of Arch., present univ. 1975–84; Dir. 1975–79; Rsch. Prof., Inst. québécois de rech. sur la culture 1980–82; Prof., Sch. of

Arch., present univ. 1984– ; Consultant, architecture & planning; Pres., Comn. to Study the Future of Olympic Installations 1977; Mem., Royal Soc. of Can. 1987; Prix Paul-Henri Lapointe, Ordre des Arch. du Qué. 1984, '85, '87; Prix Gerard-Morrisset 1992, Gouvernement du Québec; Bd. of Dir., Mus. of Fine Arts of Montréal 1975–87 (Vice-Pres. 1978–87); Pres., Héritage Montréal 1983–87; Mem., Ordre des Arch. du Qué. 1977– ; Corp. professionnelle des urbanistes du Québec 1990; author: 'Montréal en évolution' 1974, 'Montréal une esquisse du futur' 1983; 'Sauver Montréal' 1990; editor: 'Aménager l'urbain: de Montréal à San Francisco' 1987; recreations: hiking, travelling; Home: 4749 Roslyn, Montréal, Qué. H3W 2L3; Office: P.O. Box 6128, Stn. A., Montréal, Qué. H3C 3J7.

**MARSDEN, Lorna,** B.A., Ph.D.; senator; sociologist; b. Sidney, B.C. 6 Mar. 1942; d. John Ernest and Grace (Simister) Bosher; e. Univ. Coll., Univ. of Toronto B.A. 1968; Princeton Univ. Ph.D. 1972; Univ. of New Brunswick, Hon. LL.D. 1990; m. Edward s. Richard Harvey 1962; PRES. & VICE-CHANCELLOR, WILFRID LAURIER UNIV. 1992– ; Asst. Prof. of Sociology, Univ. of Toronto 1972; Assoc. Prof. 1976, Chair Dept. of Sociology 1977–79; Prof. 1979–92, Assoc. Dean Sch. of Grad. Studies 1979–82, Vice-Provost 1983–84; Dir. Air Canada 1978–84; Dir., Manulife Bank of Canada 1993; Dir., The Laidlaw Foundation 1993; Dir., Ont. Workers' Compensation Rsch. Inst. 1993; mem., Rsch. Council, Candn. Inst. for Advanced Rsch. 1982– ; Inst. for Hydrogen Systems 1982–83; Rsch. Ctte. German Marshall Fund of the U.S. 1978–81; Chair, Senate Standing Ctte. on Social Affairs, Science & Technology 1980–81; Adv. Ctte. on Women and the Econ., Econ. Counc. of Can. 1983; Scholar-in-residence, Technol. and Soc. Proj., Inst. for Rsch. on Pub. Policy 1983; Member, Senate of Canada 1984–92; Chair, Ed. Bd. Addiction Rsch. Found. 1984–1988; mem., Ont. Ctte. Status of Women 1971– ; Pres., Nat. Action Ctte. on the Status of Women 1975–77; Trustee, Elsie Gregory MacGill Meml. Foundn. 1984–90; mem. Liberal Party of Can. (Ont. Rep., Women's Liberal Comn. 1973–75, Vice-Pres. 1975–80, Chrmn. Standing Ctte. on Policy 1980–84); Princeton Univ. Fellow 1968–69; SSHRCC Doctoral Fellowship 1969–72; el. Sr. Fellow, Massey Coll. 1982– ; Sr. Fellow, Woodsworth Coll. 1983– ; Program Chair, Gov.-General's Study Conf. 1987; co-author: (with Charles Jones and Lorne Tepperman) 'Lives of their Own' 1990; (with Edward Harvey) 'The Fragile Federation: Social Change in Canada' 1979; 'Population Probe: Canada' 1972; Home: No. 1–62 Allen St. W., Waterloo, Ont.; Office: Wilfrid Laurier Univ., Waterloo, Ont. N2L 3C5.

**MARSDEN, Sandra L.,** RD, B.Sc., M.H.Sc.; association executive; b. Vancouver, B.C. 25 Feb. 1956; d. Ronald E. and Freda E. (Morel) M.; e. Univ. of Toronto B.Sc. 1978, M.H.Sc. 1982; St. Michael's Hosp. R.P.Dt. 1979; m. Bradley James s. Mary and the late Jim Kerr; PRESIDENT, CANADIAN SUGAR INST. 1992– ; Career: Rsch. Supervisor, York Univ. Inst. for Social Rsch. 1982; Nutrition Cons., Muskoka-Parry Sound Health Unit 1982–84; Halton Region Health Dept. 1984–85; Coord., High Risk Prenatal Program, City of Toronto Health Dept. 1985–87; Dir., Nutrition Affairs, Candn. Sugar Inst. 1987–91; Vice-Pres. 1991; Mem., Candn. Manufacturing Industries Forum 1992– ; Food Manufacturing Assn. Extves. 1991– ; Grocery Products Manufacturers Technical Council 1988–92; Dir., Candn. Dietetic Assn. 1992– ; (Chair, Ctte. on Endorsement and Legislative Review 1988–90); Hon. Pres., Ont. Dietetic Assn. 1993– (Dir., 1992–93; Vice-Pres. 1989–91; Dir. 1988–89); Dir., Ontario Public Health Assn. 1987–89; Pres., Ontario Soc. of Nutritionists in Public Health 1986–87; Honours: Univ. of Toronto Open Master's Fellowship 1982; Ont. Grad. Scholarship 1982; New College Admission Scholarship, Univ. of Toronto 1974; recreations: downshill ski instructor, squash, windsurfing; clubs: Bd. of Trade; Home: 1 Langmuir Gardens, Toronto, Ont. M6S 4Z3; Office: 10 Bay St., Suite 620, Toronto, Ont. M5J 2R8.

**MARSH, James Harley,** C.M.; editor; b. Toronto, Ont. 10 Sept. 1943; s. John Harley and Ada (Jenkins) M.; Oakwood C.I. 1963; Carleton Univ., B.A. (Hons.) 1974; m. Louise d. Joe and Grace Edwards 1975; one d.: Rebeccah Elizabeth; Editor-in-Chief, The Junior Encyclopedia of Canada 1987–91; Editor, Holt, Rinehart & Winston 1965–67; Collier Macmillan 1967–70; Extve. Editor, Carleton Library Series 1970–80; Editor-in-Chief, The Canadian Encyclopedia, The Junior Encyclopedia of Canada, The Concise Canadian Encyclopedia and The Canadian Encyclopedia: Multimedia Edition (1993); Spec. Adv., Book Policy, Dept. of Communications; Bd. Mem., Edmonton Concert Hall Assn.; author: 'Fishermen of Lunenburg' 1968, 'The Fur Trade' 1969, 'The Discoveries' 1970, 'The Canadian Encyclopedia' (352 entries) 1985; co-author: 'New Beginnings' 2 vols., 1981, 1982; rec'd Secy. of State Candn. Prize of Excellence 1986; Medal of the Royal Soc. 1986; Member, Order of Canada 1989; 125th Anniversary of the Confederation of Canada Medal, 1992; recreations: music, tennis, photography; Home: 9708 - 92 St., Edmonton, Alta. T6C 3S4.

**MARSHALL, (Patrick Oliver) Douglas,** B.A.; journalist; b. Cobourg, Ont. 25 Nov. 1937; s. William Porte and Beatrice Marion (Morgan) M.; e. Colborne P.S.; Upper Can. Coll. Prep. Sch. 1949; Highgate Sch. (U.K.) 1956; Univ. of Toronto, B.A. 1961; m. (1) Deborah d. Gilbert and Mary Pye 28 Feb. 1964 (2) Sarah d. Derrick and Felicite Murdoch 20 Aug. 1983; children: Barnaby, Benjamin; EDITOR AND WRITER; London, England bur. of The Candn. Press 1961–65; Staff Writer/Ed., Maclean's mag. 1965–71; Editor, Books in Canada mag. 1972–80; Entertainment Ed. The Toronto Star 1981–87; co-owner, Canadian Review of Books Ltd.; author: 'A Very Palpable Hit' (novel) 1992; recreations: swimming, debating; Club: Toronto Press; Home: 49 Tranby Ave., Toronto, Ont. M5R 1N4; Office: One Yonge St., Toronto, Ont. M5E 1E6.

**MARSHALL, Herbert Stanley,** B.A.Sc., LL.B.; lawyer, business executive; b. St. John's, Nfld. 27 June 1950; s. Thomas and Edith (Collins) M.; e. Memorial Univ. of Nfld.; Univ. of Waterloo B.A.Sc. 1972; Dalhousie Univ. LL.B. 1979; m. Elizabeth d. Dorman and Clara Foster 27 Dec. 1972; children: Krista, Keira, Darrin; VICE-PRESIDENT, CORPORATE AFFAIRS, FORTIS INC. 1987– ; engineer in mining industry in Ont. & N.B. 1972–76; Corp. Legal Counsel, Nfld. Light & Power Co. Ltd. 1979–90 (resigned as Vice-Pres. Regulatory Affairs & Gen. Council); Pres. & Dir., Fortis Trust Corp. 1989– ; Fortis Properties Corp. 1989– ; Dir., Maritime Electric Co. 1991– ; Dir., Nfld. Light & Power Co. Ltd. 1992– ; Profl. Engr. (Nfld.); Barrister & Solicitor (Nfld.); Home: 19 Conway Cres., St. John's, Nfld. A1A 2A8; Office: Box 8837, St. John's, Nfld. A1B 3T2.

**MARSHALL, Joanne Gard,** B.A., M.L.S., M.H.Sc., Ph.D.; university professor; b. England 19 Dec. 1945; d. Thomas Stanley Morris and Margaret Howes (Olson) Gard; e. Univ. of Calgary B.A. 1966; McGill Univ. M.L.S. 1968; McMaster Univ. M.H.Sc. 1978; Univ. of Toronto Ph.D. 1987; m. Victor William s. Victor George and Esther Marshall 13 June 1970; one d: Emily Gard Marshall; PROF., FAC. OF LIBRARY & INFORMATION SCIENCE, UNIV. OF TORONTO 1987– ; holds cross appointments in Dept. of Health Admin., Ctr. for Health Promotion & Ctr. for Studies of Aging; Librarian for 15 years; Cont. Edn. Instr., Med. Lib. Assn. 1977– ; Eliot Prize, Med. Lib. Assn. 1982, '93; Mem. of the Year Award, Special Libraries Assn. Toronto Chapter 1993; Award of Outstanding Achievement, Candn. Health Lib. Assn. 1991; Distinguished Mem., Acad. of Health Information Profls. 1991; Doctoral Fellowship, Inst. for Sci. Information 1987; Nat. Health Rsch. & Devel. Prog., Health & Welfare Can. 1985–87; Home: 63 Strath Ave., Toronto, Ont. M8X 1R4; Office: 140 St. George St., Toronto, Ont. M5S 1A1.

**MARSHALL, Lois C.,** C.C. (1967), LL.D.,; mezzo-soprano; b. Toronto, Ont. 1925; e. Wellesley Sch., Toronto; Royal Conservatory of Music, Toronto, where she studied under Weldon Kilburn and Emmy Heim; won notice as a singer at age 12; career highlights: 1947: profl. debut soprano soloist, Bach's St. Matthew Passion, Toronto (cond. Sir. Ernest MacMillan); 1948: first U.S. appearance Cleveland; 1949: first recital w. pianist Gerald Moore; 1950: Cdn. rep. Amer. Sesquicentennial celebration Washington DC; won Eaton Award upon grad. from Roy. Conservatory of Music, Toronto; Singing Stars of Tomorrow Grand Prize; 1951: Amer. premiere perf. Herbert Elwell's Pastorale for Voice and Orch. at US debut of Toronto Symph., Detroit; 1952: won Walter W. Naumburg Musical Foundation Award; N.Y. recital debut Town Hall; 1953: chosen by Arturo Toscanini to sing sopr. role, Beethoven's Missa Solemnis, Carnegie Hall (subsequently recorded work for RCA); 1954: began 20–year assn. with Columbia Artists, N.Y.; 1955: appeared in Mendelssohn's Elijah (w. Eduard Van Beinum), Hollywood Bowl; 1956: London debut (w. Sir Thomas Beecham and Roy. Phil. Orch. at Festival Hall) singing Mozart's Exultate Jubilate; began 2–month concert tour W. Can., Mid-W. U.S., England, Ireland, Netherlands, and Germany (incl. perfs. of Orff's Carmina Burana w. Chicago Symph. under Fritz Reiner); 1957: solo recital (accomp. Weldon Kilburn) 11th Edinburgh Internat. Festival; perf. Brahms' German Requiem (w. Heinz Rehfuss & Hallé Choir); Strauss' Four Last Songs (w. Eugen Jochum & Bavarian Radio Symph. Orch.); rec. role of Constanza, Mozart's Abduction from the Seraglio (w. Sir Thomas Beecham) and role of Queen of Sheba in Handel's Solomon; 1958: sang roles of Gabriel and Eve, Haydn's Creation (w. Nicolai Gedda & Montreal Symph. under Igor Markevitch); Italian deb. as sopr. in Beethoven's Missa Solemnis (w. Christa Ludwig under George Szell & Cleveland Orch.) La Scala, Milan; 1st Cdn. singer to tour USSR (has returned 8 times); perf. role of Mimi, Puccinni's La Bohème, inaug. season Boston Opera Co. (under Sarah Caldwell); 1959: sang Ellen Orford in world TV prem. Benjamin Britten's Peter Grimes (w. Richard Cassilly) CBC-TV; perf. before Queen Elizabeth II, Vancouver Internat. Festival; sang title role Verdi's Tosca, Boston Op. Co.; rec. Bach's Mass in B Minor (w. tenor Peter Pears and cond. Eugen Jochum & Bavarian Radio Symph.) for Epic; 1960: prem. perf. in Russia of Strauss' Four Last Songs (cond. Kiril Kondrashin & Leningrad Phil.; won Harriet Cohen Internat. Music Award; 1st World Tour incl. USSR, Europe, Australia and New Zealand; 1962: perf. Hindemith's Das Marienleben (w. pianist Glenn Gould), Stratford Festival; annual European Tour incl. Spain (perf. Haydn's Creation w. Hermann Scherchen, Palacio de la Musica, Barcelona); 1964: Cdn. prem. Benjamin Britten's War Requiem (w. tenor Peter Pears & Toronto Mendelssohn Choir), Massey Hall; 1965: replaced Eileen Farrell as sopr. soloist, Bach Aria Group of N.Y.; invited by Dmitri Shostakovich to join jury 3rd Internat. Tchaikovsky Music Competition; perf. Ravel's Scheherezade (w. Seiji Ozawa & Toronto Symph. in its European debut), Roy. Festival Hall London; Beethoven's Ah Perfido, La Salle Gaveau, Paris (during same TSO tour); awarded Hon. LL.D., Univ. of Toronto; 1967: several perfs. Expo 67 Montreal, CBC-TV live broadcast opening National Arts Centre Ottawa; 1968: perf. Mahler's 2nd Symph. (w. Lili Chookasian & San Francisco Symph. under Josef Krips); Bach's Wedding Cantata, Israel Festival, Caesarea; 1970: world prem. Oskar Morawetz' From the Diary of Anne Frank, Toronto; 1971: toured New Zealand (perfs. incl. Berlioz' Les Nuits d'Eté (w. Hein Jordans & NZBC Symph.); 1972: sang Almirena, NY prem. Handel's Rinaldo; 1973: sopr. soloist Bach's Mass in B Minor (w. Berlin Concert Choir & Orch. under Fritz Weisse) Carnegie Hall; recipient Award of Excellence, Cdn. Music Counc.; 1974: officially became mezzo-sopr.; 1976: rec. Schubert's Die Wintereisse (w. pianist Anton Kuerti); 1977: last tour of USSR (w. Elmer Iseler & Festival Singers of Can.; 1979: rec. Schubert's Die Schöne Mullerin (w. pianist Greta Kraus); 1980: won Molson Award; 16th and final N. Amer. tour w. Bach Aria Group; 1981–82: national farewell tour across Can. (w. pianist Stuart Hamilton), Dec. 1982 farewell benefit recital, Roy Thomson Hall, Toronto; 1983: Chairperson, Ont. March of Dimes; in July 1983 returned to opera stage after 23 yrs. to perf. role of Filipyevna, Tchaikovsky's Eugen Onegin (w. Thomas Allen and cond. Neeme Jarvi), National Arts Centre, Ottawa; 1984: made Hon. Pres. Toronto Mendelssohn Choir; 1985; Artistic Dir., TriBach Internat. Festival, Edmonton.

**MARSHALL, Marvin G.;** business executive; b. Linn County, Kansas 4 July 1937; m. Patricia J. Hellman 29 July 1978; children: Taylor Alexandra, Maxwell Giffin, Edwin, Morgan; PRESIDENT & CHIEF EXECUTIVE OFFICER, BRAMALEA LIMITED; Office: One Queen Street East, Suite 2300, Toronto, Ont. M5C 2Y9.

**MARSHALL, Paul Macklin,** B.C.L.; company executive; b. Toronto, Ont. 21 Sept. 1923; s. Griffith Macklin and Josephine Angela (Hodgson) M.; e. St. Leo's Acad., Westmount, P.Q.; St. Michael's Coll., Toronto, Ont.; McGill Univ., B.C.L. 1949; m. Carol Ann, d. Wm. H. Dickie, Toronto, Ont.; four s., Blake, Gregory, Jonathan, Kirk; CHRMN., WESTMIN RESOURCES LTD. 1978– ; Chrmn. & Pres., Brascade Resources Inc.; Depy. Chrmn., Norcen Energy Resources Ltd.; Vice-Chrmn, Brascan Ltd. 1987– ; Dir., Westinghouse Can. Inc.; Noranda Inc.; Journey's End Corp.; M.A. Hanna Co.; Legal Asst., Sun Life Assnce.Co., Montreal, P.Q., 1949–52 (on loan to Govt. as Extve. Asst. to Min. Nat. Defence, 1952–54); joined Celanese Canada Ltd. & predecessor companies as Asst. Secy., 1954, Secy. 1957, Secy.-Treas. 1958, Vice-Pres. 1959; Pres. and Chief Extve. Offr., Columbia Cellulose Co., Ltd., 1962; Chrmn. of the Bd., Celanese Canada Ltd. 1967–69; Pres., Hamilton Brothers Exploration Co., Vice-Pres. Hamilton Brothers Petroleum Corp., Extve. Vice-Pres. Hamilton Brothers Oil Co. June 1969–June 1972; Pres., Cdn. Hydrocarbons Ltd. 1972–76; Pres. Brascan Resources Ltd., 1978–80; Vice Chrmn. & Dir., Western Mines Ltd., 1978–80; served in 2nd World War with R.C.A. 1943–45; discharged with rank of Lieut.; called to the Bar of Que. 1949; Clubs: Toronto (Toronto, Ont.); Petroleum (Calgary); Home: 21 Elgin Ave., Toronto, Ont. M5R

1G5; Office: Box 762, BCE Place, 181 Bay St., Toronto, Ont. M5J 2T3.

**MARSHALL, Peter Frederick,** B.A., B.J.; public relations executive; b. St. John's, Nfld. 6 June 1946; s. Cyril Frederick and Ruth Elaine (Maunder) M.; e. Carleton Univ. B.A. 1968, B.J. (with distinction) 1969; m. Barbara d. Ted and Regina Rudolf 8 Aug. 1986; children: Lisa Parsons (Darrel, H.), Natalie, Jason; PUBLIC AFFAIRS ADVISOR, SYNCRUDE CANADA LTD.; Editor, Pulp & Paper Mag. of Canada, Southam Business Pubs. 1969–71; Supvr., Internal Communications, Inco (Sudbury) 1971–73; Special Projects Editor, Sudbury Star, Thompson Newspapers 1973–75; Co-ord., Coll. Info. Services, St. Lawrence Coll., then Supvr., Info. Serv., Ont. Fire Marshal, Govt. of Ont. 1975–81; Supvr., Public Affairs, then Supt., Community Relations, Falconbridge Ltd., Sudbury Operations 1981–85; Supvr., Communications, Sr. Benefits Administrator, Advisor, Corp. Communications and lastly Public Affairs Advisor, Synrude Canada Ltd. 1985–present; Mem., Athabasca Univ. Gov. Council 1989– ; Chair, Community Adv. Ctte., RCMP Fort McMurray 1993– ; Mem., Community Adv. Ctte. since 1990; Crimestoppers, Fort McMurray Bd. 1991– ; Chair, Promotions & Publicity, Alta. Winter Games 1992; Past Pres. (Nat.), Color Photographic Assn. of Can.; Former V.P., Fort McMurray & Dist. C. of C.; Mem., Internat. Assn. of Business Communicators (Past Pres. Fort McMurray; Former Dir., Dist. One Canada); Mem., Canadian Investor Relations Inst.; Former Dir., Sudbury Theatre Centre; Former Dir., Sudbury and Dist. C. of C.; author of num. articles on aeronautical topics in var. journals, reports & directories; recreations: aviation history: Home: 523 – 600 Signal Rd., Fort McMurray, Alta. T9H 3H5; Office: P.O. Bag 4023, M.D. 1000, Fort McMurray, Alta. T9H 3Z4.

**MARSHALL, Robert James,** B.Sc.; bank executive; b. Glasgow, Scotland 7 March 1939; s. James and Lilias Brown (Bissett) M.; e. London Sch. of Econ. B.Sc. (Hons.) 1960; m. Valerie d. John and Mary Vickers 30 July 1961; children: Iain, Susan, Joanna; EXTVE. VICE-PRES., RETAIL BANKING, THE BANK OF N.S. 1990– ; Dir., Scotia Mortgage Corp.; Scotia Securities Inc.; Investment Analyst, London Stock Exchange 1962–65; Bank Offr., Bank of London & S. Am. 1965–71; Bank Extve., Lloyds Bank Itnernat. 1972–79; Pres. & C.E.O. (Can.) 1980–83; Extve. Dir. (London) 1983–85; Sr. Gen. Mgr., Information Technol., Lloyds Bank Plc 1985–87; Dir., Support Serv. 1987–88; Extve. Asst. to Chrmn. & C.E.O., Bank of N.S. 1988–90; recreations: music, horticulture; clubs: The National; Home: 65 Harbour Sq., Queens Quay, Toronto, Ont. M5J 2L4; Office: Scotia Plaza, 44 King St. W., Toronto, Ont. M5H 1H1.

**MARSHALL, Rosalind Mary (Roz);** artist; b. Newport, Wales, U.K. 25 July 1947; d. Group Captain Harry Emlyn and Jeanne Patricia (Greenland) Bufton; e. 12 schools in England, U.S.A., Bahrain, Can.; Univ. of B.C. 1 yr.; Vanc. Sch. of Art, honours painting; children: Kate, Thomas; 25 one-woman shows across Canada; many group exhibitions incl. 'Vancouver Art and Artists 1930–83,' Vanc. Art Gall.; 20 years experience as an Art Educator; Canada Council travel grant (Italy) 1978; Can. Counc. 'B' grant 1978–79; presently represented by Buschlen/Mowatt Gallery, Vancouver, B.C.; Home: 3804 W. 30th Ave., Vancouver, B.C. V6S 1X1.

**MARSHALL, Hon. Thomas David Colbeck Hayden,** M.D., LL.B., L.M.C.C.; justice; b. Dunville, Ont. 23 Feb. 1939; s. Albert Hayden and Ora Ivadelle (Colbeck) M.; e. Univ. of Toronto M.D. 1963; Osgoode Hall Law Sch. 1970; Oxford Univ. postgrad. work in Law and Med. 1974; Candn. Forces Staff Coll. Kingston (Reserves) grad.; m. Jill d. Dr. Harold and late Mary Ann Smith, Barrie Ont. 1961; children: Jillian, Julia, Albert, Tom, David Jr.; EXTVE. DIR., NATIONAL JUDICIAL INSTITUTE, Ottawa; Past Chrmn., Ctte. of Law Reform of the Northern Territories; Past Chrmn., Conf. of Law Reform Comn. of Can. 1988–90; Hon. Prof., Univ. of Ottawa 1988–92; called to Bar of Ont. 1972; former Sr. Partner law firm Marshall, Thibideau and Rous, Cayuga, Ont.; med. practitioner Cayuga, Ont. 1964–82; served as Coroner many yrs.; Special Lectr. in Law and Med., Univ. of Toronto 1972; Asst. Prof. of Clin. Med. McMaster Univ. 1975–82; Prof. of Law, Univ. of Windsor 1982–83; Justice, Supreme Court of N.W.T. and Justice, Courts of Appeal, Y.T. AND N.W.T. 1983–92; Justice, Ontario Court, General Division 1992; named Hon. Chief Iroquois 6 Nations; Candn. Forces Reserve, rank Left.Col.; author 'Medical Law Handbook' 1985; 'Canadian Law of Inquests' 1980; 'The Physician and Canadian Law' 2nd ed. 1979; 'Patient's Rights' 1976; Past Pres. and Chrmn., Haldimand Assn. Mentally Handicapped; Pres. and Dir. (past) Ont. Assn. Injured Workmen; mem., Candn. Inst. Adm. Justice; Candn. Med. Assn.; Law Soc. Upper Can.; Candn. Bar Assn.; Candn. Inst. Intnl. Affairs; Ont. Med. Assn.; Oxford Soc.; Toronto and Ottawa Medico-Legal Soc.; Defence Med. Assn. Can.; Intnl. Comn. Jurists; Ont. Coll. Physicians & Surgs.; Chrmn., Standing Ctte. on Ethics in Human Experimentation, Med. Rsch. Counc. of Can.; Chair, Ethnic Ctte., Ottawa Heart Institute; recreations: canoeing, flying, tennis; Clubs: Empire; Home: R.R. #5, Cayuga, Ont. N0A 1E0.

**MARSHALL, Victor W.,** B.A., Ph.D.; university professor; b. Calgary, Alta. 11 April 1944; s. Victor George and Esther Adeline (Donlevy) M.; e. Univ. of Alberta B.A. (Hon.) 1966; Princeton Univ. Ph.D. 1973; m. Joanne d. Margaret and Tom Gard 13 June 1970; one d.: Emily; DIRECTOR, CENTRE FOR STUDIES OF AGING, UNIV. OF TORONTO 1990– ; Asst. Prof., Sociology, McMaster Univ. 1970–76; Assoc. Prof. 1976–81; Univ. of Toronto 1981; Prof., Dept. of Behav. Science 1984– ; Director, CARNET: The Canadian Aging Research Network 1990– ; Mem., Prog. Ctte., SSHRCC 1989– ; National Health Scientist 1978–87; Laidlaw Found. Award 1984–87; Fellow, Gerontological Soc. of Am. 1980; Bd. of Dir., Second Mile Club, Regional Geriatric Program; Mem., Panel on Health Goals for On. 1986–87; Chair, Social Sciences Div., Candn. Assn. on Gerontology 1982–85; Fellowhips Ctte., Gerontological Soc. of Am. 1980; Editor-in-Chief, 'Can. J. on Aging' 1985–90; author: 'Last Chapters: The Sociology of Aging and Dying' 1980; co-author: 'Nurses, Patients and Families' 1980; editor: 'Aging in Canada: Social Perspectives' 1980, rev. 1987, 'Later Life: The Social Psychology of Aging' 1986; Home: 63 Strath Ave., Etobicoke, Ont. M8X 1R4; Office: Toronto, Ont. M5S 2G8.

**MARSHALL, Victoria (Vicky);** artist; b. England 18 March 1952; d. neill Francis and Mary M.; e. Prince George (B.C.) Sr. Secondary Sch. 1969; Vancouver Sch. of Art grad. 1979; solo exhns. incl. Diane Farris Gallery Vancouver 1985, 1986; Grünwald Gallery Toronto 1987; group exhns. incl. Vancouver Art Gallery 1985, Gallery Optica Montréal 1986, Paul Kuhn Gallery 1987, Cologne Art Fair Germany 1987; Artist-in-Residence, Univ. of Man. 1986, Univ. of Lethbridge 1984; awarded Can. Council Art Grant B 1984, 1986; Home: c/o 165 Water St. Vancouver, B.C. V6B 1A7; Studio: 401, 310 Water St., Vancouver, B.C. V6B 1B6.

**MARSHALL, William Hext,** M.D., Ph.D., F.R.C.P.; educator; b. London, Eng. 10 Apr. 1933; s. Leslie Phillips and Catherine Mary (Hext) M.; e. Marlborough Coll. Eng.; Cambridge Univ. M.B., B.Chir. 1957, M.D. 1965; London Hosp. Med. Coll. M.R.C.S., L.R.C.P. 1957; Melbourne Univ. Ph.D. 1967; M.R.C.P. 1961; F.R.C.P. (Lond.) 1981; m. Ingeborg Constanze Luise d. Alfred Ristow, E. Germany 16 Sept. 1961; children: Alfred, Christopher, Mary-Anne; PROF. OF IMMUNOLOGY, MEMORIAL UNIV. OF NFLD. 1970– ; House Offr. and Sr. House Offr. The London Hosp. 1957–61; Jr. Lectr. in Physiol. The London Hosp. Med. Coll. 1961–63; Research Fellow and Asst. Phys. The Walter & Eliza Hall Inst. and The Royal Melbourne Hosp. 1963–66; Research Fellow N.Y. Univ. Med. Centre 1966–68; Assoc. prof. of Immunol. present Univ. 1968–70; author or co-author over 74 scient. papers on cellular immunology, clin. immunology and immunogenetics; mem. Candn., Australian and U.S. Socs. for Immunols.; Transplantation Soc.; Genetical Soc.; Anglican; recreations; cinema and theatre, gardening, outdoor sports; Office: Health Sciences Centre, St. John's, Nfld. A1B 3V6.

**MARSHMAN, Joan Anne,** Ph.D.; pharmacist; educator; b. London, Ont. 13 July 1939; d. Ernest Wilkinson and Winifred M. (Box) Smith; m. John Charles Marshman 17 Sept. 1966; Brantford Coll. Inst.; Univ. of Toronto B.Sc.Phm. 1961; Ph.D. 1966; d., Mary Elizabeth; Pres., Addiction Research Foundation 1981; Prof. (part-time), Fac. of Pharmacy, Univ. of Toronto 1980– ; Lectr., Fac. of Pharm., Univ. of Toronto 1966–67; Research Scientist, A.R.F. 1968–81; Asst. Prof. (part-time) 1968–73; Assoc. Prof. (part-time) 1973–80; Head, Pharmaceutical Sciences, Clinical Inst., A.R.F. 1975–81 (Head, Chemical Research 1978–81; Acting Head, Sociobehavioural Treatment Research 1979–80; Assoc. Dir. 1979–81); mem., Assoc. Staff, Sch. of Phys. and Health Educ., Univ. of Toronto 1980– ; mem. Ont. Coll. of Pharmacists; Candn. Pharmaceutical Assn.; Assn. of Faculties of Pharmacy of Can.; Candn. Soc. of Hospital Pharmacists; Ont. Pharmacists' Assn.; Div. of Medicinal Chemistry, Amer. Chemical Soc.; Candn. Coll. of Health Service Extves.; author 'Chemical and Biochemical Methods of Drug Detection and Measurement' (chapter in 'Research Advances in Alcohol & Drug Problems, Vol. I' 1974), and numerous scientific papers on topics related to street drugs; Anglican; Home: 64 Araman Dr., Agincourt, Ont. M1T 2P6.

**MARSKELL, V. Kenneth,** B.A.; publishing executive; b. Toronto, Ont. 4 March 1942; s. Victor Lorne and Etta May (Rabey) M.; e. Univ. of Toronto B.A. 1979 (Silver Medal & Dean's Scholarship 1979); Univ. of W. Ont. Mgmt. Training Course 1979; m. Diane d. James and Isabel 17 Jan. 1974 (separated); two s. Jeffrey, Sean; PRES. AND C.E.O., TOP EMPLOYERS GROUP and PUBLISHER TOP EMPLOYERS 1992– ; Publisher: 'Computers in Education' 1983–92; 'Computing Now!' 1987–92; 'Electronics & Technology Today' 1987–92; 'Business Computer News' 1988–92; 'Pets Magazine' 1988–92; 'Pets Today Magazine'; 'Government Purchasing Guide' 1988–92; 'Business Computer Reseller News' 1989–92; Pres. and Dir. P.J. Ward Press Ltd.; Dir. of Circulation, Vice Pres. Mktg. The Globe and Mail 1962–83; Pres. & C.E.O., Moorshead Publications Ltd. 1983–92; Man. of the Yr. Awards Inter-Frat. Cong. 1971, 1972; Circulation Mktg. Awards Internat. Circulation Mngrs. Assn. 1980, 1981; mem. Bd. Trade Metrop. Toronto; Pres., Etobicoke West P.C. Assn.; P. Conservative; recreations: golf, hockey; Clubs: Boulevard; Hot Stove; Home: 2 Valhalla Inn Rd., Suite 123, Etobicoke, Ont. M9B 6C3.

**MARTCHENKO, Michael,** AOCA; illustrator/art director; b. Carcassone, France 1 Aug. 1942; s. John and Mary (Jerchuk) M.; e. Glenview Pk. S.S. 1962; Ont. Coll. of Art AOCA 1966; m. Patricia Kerr; children: Holly, Susan, Janet; CREATIVE DIR., TDF ARTISTS LTD. 1972– ; Art Dir., Spitzer Mills & Bates 1066–69; Needham Harper & Steers 1969–70; Designer, Illus., Art Assoc. 1970–72; A.D. Club of Toronto, 3 awards of merit 1969, 1 in 1974; Graphica Show 1976, 2 awards of merit; Ruth Schwartz Award for Book Illust. 1986; Silver Medal Studio Magazine Awards Show 1990; Award of Merit A.D. Club of Toronto 1990; illustrator: 'The Paper Bag Princess' 1980; 'Jonathan Cleaned Up, Then He Heard A Sound' 1981; 'Murmel, Murmel, Murmel,' 'The Boy in the Drawer' 1982; 'David's Father,' 'The Fire Station,' 'Mortimer' 1983 (rep. 1985); 'I Have to Go,' 'Thomas's Snowsuit' 1986 (by R. Munsch); 'Matthew and the Midnight Tow Truck' 1984; 'Matthew and the Midnight Turkeys' 1986; 'Matthew and the Midnight Money Van' 1987 (by A. Morgan); 'Horray for the Dorchester' 1986 (by A. Fotheringham); Annikin's series #1, & #3; 'Moira's Birthday' (by R. Munsch) 1987; 'Pigs' (by R. Munsch) 1989; 'Something Good' (by R. Munsch) 1990; 'Jeremy's Decision' (by Ardyth Brott) 1990; 'Bird Feeder Banquet' (by M. Martchenko) 1990; 'Show and Tell' (by R. Munsch) 1991; 'The Magic Hockey Skates' (by A. Morgan) 1991; 'Portus Potter Was Loose!' (by Pat Seeley) 1992; 'Frogs' (by Andrea Wayne von Königslöw) 1992; 'Counting My Friends' (by Selma Hooge) 1992; Limited Edition Fine Art Aviation Prints ('Mosquito Day Rangers,' 'Friends Meet,' 'The Ruhr Express,' 'McKnights Hattrick,' 'Beaver One'); Mem., Am. Soc. of Aviation Artists; The Candn. Aircrew Assoc.; Ont. Aviation Hist. Soc.; The Candn. Airforce Assoc.; Club: Art Directors Club of Toronto; Home: 100 Airdrie Rd., Toronto, Ont. M4G 1M3; Office: 55 Barber Greene, Don Mills, Ont. M3C 2A1.

**MARTEINSON, Col. John Kristjan,** C.D., M.A.; editor; b. Langruth, Man. 14 Feb. 1939; s. Jon Edwin and Laura (Fjeldsted) M.; e. Univ. of Man. B.A. 1959; Univ. of N.B.; Army Staff Coll. Kingston 1972–73; NATO Defense Coll. Rome 1976; York Univ. M.A. 1987; m. Doreen d. George Harrington 14 Nov. 1964; two s. David John, Peter George; ED. CANADIAN DEFENCE QUARTERLY 1987– ; comnd. Fort Garry Horse 1959; regt'al duty Can., Germany, Cyprus tank and armoured reconnaissance sqdns. and helicopter pilot; staff offr. 4th Candn. Inf. Bgde. Group and Mobile Command HQ; commanded A Sqdn. 8th Candn. Hussars 1971–72; tactics instr. and chief standards offr. Combat Arms Sch. 1973–76; operations div. staff Central Army Group HQ Heidelberg 1976–79, Sr. Candn. Liaison Offr. 1979–80; instr. and sr. staff offr. Candn. Forces Staff Coll. Toronto 1980–85; plans and policy div. Internat. Mil. Staff NATO HQ 1985–87, rep. NATO Mil. Ctte. Mutual and Balanced Force Reduction Talks; External Fellow Centre Internat. & Strategic Studies York Univ.; Senior Vice-Pres., Atlantic Council of Canada; recipient, Candn. Centennial Medal 1967; Queen's Silver Jubilee Medal 1977; US Army Commendation Award 1979; German Order of Merit 1980; Commemorative Medal for 125th Anniversary of Candn. Confederation 1993; co-author 'The Gate: A History of The Fort Garry Horse' 1971; 'A Pictorial History of the 8th Canadian Hussars' 1973; 'We Stand on Guard: An Illustrated History of the Canadian Army' 1992; numerous articles defence issues; mem. Candn. Inst. Strategic Studies; Internat. Inst. Strategic Studies; Home: 30 Lescon Rd., Willowdale, Ont. M2J 2G6; Office: 310 Dupont St., Toronto, Ont. M5R 1V9.

**MARTEL, Jean Jacques;** consultant in business administration; agent; ancestors came to Can. around 1680, first settlers of Ville Marie; b. Baieville, Que. 3 Jan. 1927; s. Gérard and Irène (Simoneau) M.; e. Baieville Coll., Que.; Coll. of St. Frédéric, Amos Seminary; St-Simon Sch., Ellis Business Coll., Drummondville, Que.; m. Rolande Blais, Ste. Foy, Que., 10 Oct 1959; two s. Jean Claude, François; one d., Lucie; PRES. & C.E.O., EXPLORATIONS MINIÈRES DU NORD LTÉ 1990– ; Dir., Radio Nord Inc.; started with Canadian International Paper Co. as Clerk 1943; then Clerk, Amos Bureau of Mines 1944–46; Amos Woolen Mills Inc. 1947–48; Town of Amos 1948–49; estbd. J.J. Martel Inc. 1954 for gen. ins. business, operating as business consultant and private co. from 1973 to 1993; def. cand. to H. of C. 1957; el. to H. of C. for Chapleau 1958; def. in g.e. 1962 and 1979 for Abitibi; Extve. Secy. to Candn. Min. of Mines 1962–63; Extve. Secy. to Min. of Agric., Que. 1967–71; Indust. Del., Que. Dept. Industry, Comm. & for N.W. Que. 1971–87; Pres., Jr. Chamber of Comm., Amos, P.Q. 1953–54; Regional Pres., N.W. Que. Fed. 1955; Secy., Amos Br., N.W. Que. Prospectors Assn. Inc. 1946–57, Vice-Pres. 1957; Dir., Fondation de l'Université du Québec en Abitibi-Témiscaminque (Fondation de l'UQUAT) 1990; K. of C.; Conservative; Roman Catholic; recreations: fishing, part time prospecting; Office: (Box 276) 741 First St. W., Amos, Que. J9T 3A7.

**MARTEL, The Hon. Shelley Dawn Marie,** M.P.P., B.A.; politician; b. Sudbury, Ont. 8 Apr. 1963; d. Elie W. and Gaye (Fawcett) M.; e. Univ. of Toronto B.A.; La Sorbonne, Paris, cert. in French language; MINISTER OF NORTHERN DEVELOPMENT AND MINES, GOVT. OF ONTARIO 1993– ; Claims Adjudicator, Workers Comp. Bd., Sudbury; first elected M.P.P. for Sudbury East 1987; re-el. 1990; Home: 54 Hemlock St., Capreol, Ont. P0M 1H0; Office: 77 Grenville St., 11th Floor, Toronto, Ont. M5S 1B3.

**MARTENS, Harold;** politician; rancher; b. Herbert, Sask. 8 Sept. 1941; s. Eugene and Lydia Naiomi (Klassen) M.; e. high sch.; m. Sylvia d. David and Elizabeth Schroeder 21 Aug. 1966; children: Anthony, Chad, Joe; family farming and ranching; el. Councillor and Reeve 1972–78; former mem. Univ. of Regina Senate; served Sask. Assn. Rural Muns.; cand. provl. P. Cons. els. 1975, 1978, 1982, 1986, 1991; apptd. Legis. Sec. 1983; Assoc. Min. of Agric. and Food, Sask. 1989–91; recipient Queen's Silver Jubilee Medal 1977; Commemorative Medal for 125th Anniversary of Candn. Confederation 1992; Mennonite Brethern Ch.; recreations: hockey (Intermediate all-star goalie 4 yrs.), baseball, reading, football; Home: P.O. Box 155, Swift Current, Sask. S9H 3V6.

**MARTIN, Alexander Robert,** F.C.A.; executive, retired; b. Toronto, Ont. 23 Sept. 1928; s. late Alexander and late Janet Anderson Murray (McEwan) M.; e. Vaughan Rd. Coll. Inst. Toronto; Inst. C.A.'s Ont.; Univ. of W. Ont. Mang. Training Course; m. Dorothy Louise d. late William Brown, Toronto, Ont. 13 June 1953; two s. David Jeffrey, Peter George; Sr. Auditor, Peat Marwick Mitchell & Co. Toronto 1947–55; Hawker Siddley Canada Ltd. 1955–57; joined Emco Ltd. 1957; retired 1987; Fellow, Inst. C.A.'s Ont.; mem. Financial Extves. Inst. (Past Dir.); Madame Vanier Children's Services (Past Dir.); Un. Way London, Ont. (Past Dir.); Community Corrections of London (Past Dir.); Anglican; recreations: golf, music; Clubs: Sunningdale Country; Rotary (London) Dir. & Treas. 1990–94; Home: 217 Deer Park Circle, London, Ont. N6H 3C2.

**MARTIN, Andrew Jonathan,** M.A.; publisher; b. London, Eng. 4 Aug. 1952; s. Frederick and Cicely (Brown) M.; e. Cambridge Univ. B.A. 1974, M.A. 1978; Inns of Ct. Sch. of Law 1975; m. Sue d. David and Audrey Finnie 27 July 1974; children: Simon, Cassandra; EXECUTIVE DIRECTOR, CANCOPY 1992– ; Barrister, Middle Temple 1975; Freelance legal journalist and broadcaster 1975–88; Barrister in private practice 1976–79; Legal Correspondent, 'General Practitioner' 1976–81, 'Daily Express' 1977–80; Managing Ed. (Tax), Butterworth Law Pubs. Ltd. 1981–82; Dir. 1982–87; Dep. Managing Dir., Butterworths Tax Pubs. Ltd. 1987; Pres., Butterworths Canada Ltd. 1987–92; Dir., Butterworth & Co. (Pubs.) Ltd. 1987–92; Dir., Les Editions Yvon Blais Inc. 1989–92; Chrmn., Bottom Line Publications Inc. 1989–92; Chrmn., Octopus Publishing Group Canada 1990–92; co-author: 'You and Your Rights' 1979; 'Halsbury's Law of England,' Vol. 37 (Press & Printing) 1982; recreations: music, tennis, reading, swimming; Home: 174 Tomlinson Circle, Unionville, Ont. L3R 9J8; Office: 214 King St., Suite 312, Toronto, Ont.

**MARTIN, Freda Elizabeth,** M.D., FRCP(C); physician; educator; b. Niagara Falls, Ont. 11 Apl. 1932; d. Andrew William Fraser and Lily May (Coburn) McQueen; e. Stamford Coll. Inst. Niagara Falls; Univ. of Toronto M.D. 1956; D.P.M. Co-Jt. Examining Bd. for Eng. 1960; M.R.C. Psych. 1971; F.R.C. Psych. 1974; F.R.C.P.(C) 1978; m. Kenneth Charles s. Mervyn and Patricia Martin 26 Aug. 1961; two s. Andrew Kenneth Godfrey, Peter Charles Robert; EXTVE. DIR. C. M. HINCKS TREATMENT CENTRE and Assoc. Prof. of Psychiatry Univ. of Toronto 1984– ; Founding Dir. C. M. Hincks Inst. 1986– ; Rotating Intern Toronto Western Hosp. 1956; Clin. Asst., Sr. House Offr., Registrar, Royal Bethlehem and Maudsley Hosps. London, Eng. 1957–60; Registrar, Sr. Registrar and Cons., Tavistock Inst. of Human Relations and Clinic, Dept. for Children & Parents, London 1960–75; Chrmn. of Dept. 1972–75; Cons. Inner London Edn. Authority 1962–75; Assoc. Prof. (GFT) of Psychiatry Univ. of Ottawa, Dir. Psychiatric Out Patient Dept. Children's Hosp. E. Ont.; Founding Dir. Ottawa Family Therapy Training Prog. 1975–80; Assoc. Prof. of Psychiatry Univ. of Toronto, Chief of Service Child & Family Studies Centre Clarke Inst. of Psychiatry, Dir. Clarke Inst. Family Therapy Training Prog. 1980–84; Founding Extve. Candn. Assoc. for Treatment and Study of Families 1980–82; Professional mem., Soc. of Analytical Psychology, England 1971– ; Founding Chrmn. Ctte. for Child Analytic Training 1975; Extve. Child Section, Royal Medical Psychological Assn. 1968–69; Alpha Omega Alpha 1955; recreations: gardening, swimming, sailing; Home: Unit 1204, 278 Bloor St. E., Toronto, Ont. M4W 3M4; Office: 440 Jarvis St., Toronto, Ont. M4Y 2H4.

**MARTIN, Frederic S.,** LL.B., O.M.R.I., KCLJ; investment dealer; b. New Perth, P.E.I. 16 July 1922; s. George and Jennie (Shaw) M.; e. Prince of Wales Coll., Charlottetown, P.E.I.; Dalhousie Univ. (grad. Law); m. Ogden Frances, d. late Robert Lennox Blackburn, 8 Nov. 1956; children; Peter Charles Blackburn, Jane Lennox, Sarah Lennox, Caroline Mellish, Alexandra Mary; PRESIDENT, BLACKBURN PROPERTIES CORPORATION and VICE-PRES., RICHARDSON-GREENSHIELDS OF CANADA; Pres., Blackburn Properties Corp. Ltd; Stanley Lands Ltd.; Blackburn Bros. Ltd.; Culloden Investments Ltd.; Portree Investments Inc.; Dir., Kilmuir Holdings Ltd.; Macbar Investments Ltd.; Esstra Industries Ltd.; read law with McLeod and Bentley, Charlottetown, P.E.I.; called to the Bar of P.E.I. 1947; Clerk of Legislative Assembly P.E.I.; Legal Counsel to Central Mortgage and Housing Corp.; Extve. Asst. to Solr. Gen. and Leader of Govt. in Senate 1952–57; mem., Past Chrmn., Finance Comte., V.O.N.; Life Gov., Ashbury Coll.; Bd. Trustees, Confed. Centre of the Arts, Charlottetown; Gov., Children's Hosp. Foundn. E. Ont.; Trustee, Foundation for Legal Research in Can., Forum for Young Cans.; Comdr. Order of Merit, Republic of Italy; Vice-Chancellor and Secy.-Gen. Hospitaler Order of St. Lazarus of Jerusalem; Anglican; recreations: skiing, golfing, fishing; Clubs: Rideau; Royal Ottawa Golf; Ottawa Country; Maganassippi; Fish and Game; Lyford Cay, Bahamas; Home: 1449 Aylmer Rd., Aylmer, Que. J9H 5E1.

**MARTIN, Graham,** B.Sc.E.E., M.Sc.E.E., P.Eng.; university professor and administrator; b. Liverpool, England 5 May 1939; s. Donald Beattie and Olive Avril (Fitch) M.; e. Lower Canada College 1956; Univ. of N.B. B.Sc.E.E. 1961, M.Sc.E.E. 1962; m. C. Margaret H. d. Malcom and Elma Freeborough 6 June 1964; children: Heather, Catherine, Brian, Robert; PRINCIPAL, INSTITUTE FOR CO-OPERATIVE EDUCATION, CONCORDIA UNIV. 1991– ; joined Sir George Williams Univ. in Dept. of E.E. 1962; created Computer Centre 1965; Asst. Prof. of E.E. 1964; Assoc. Prof. E.E. & Comp. Sci. 1969; Dir., Computer Centre 1965–76; Assoc. Vice-Principal Communications 1971–76; Vice-Rector Admin. & Finance, Concordia Univ. 1976–85; Vice-Rector Services 1985–86; Past Pres., Data Processing Mngt. Assn. 1971–72; Mem., Order of Engineers of Que.; ASEE; IEEE; Candn. Assn. for Co-op. Edn.; Bd. of Gov., Concordia Univ. 1976–86; Pres., Quebec Easter Seals; Dir., Candn. Rehab. Council for the Disabled; Technical Aids & Systems for the Handicapped; Vice-Pres. Opns., Que. Prov. Council, Scouts Canada; Past Pres., Rotary Club of Montreal 1986–87; recreations: golf, model railroading, reading; Home: 188 Stonehenge Dr., Beaconsfield, Que.; Office: 1455, de Maisonneuve Blvd. W., Montreal, Que. H3G 1M8.

**MARTIN, Hugh A.;** company president; b. Los Angeles, Cal. 3 Feb. 1914; s. George Allen and Ruth (McDermid) M.; e. Public and High Schs., Vancouver, B.C.; Shawnigan Lake Sch., Vancouver Island, B.C.; m. Danae Maria, 15 June 1960; children: Melinda Jane, Hugh Gordon, Carol Ruth Martin; Pres., Road Builders & Heavy Constr. Assn. of B.C., 1953; formed Marwell Construction Co. Ltd. in partnership with R. D. Welch in 1936, acting as Extve. Vice-Pres.; el. Pres. in 1957; Patron, Lester B. Pearson Coll. of Pacific and United World Colleges (Can.) Inc.; Hon. Patron, Vancouver Oral Centre for Deaf Children Inc.; Protestant; recreations: golf, swimming, music; Clubs: The Vancouver and Terminal City; Shaughnessy Golf & Country; Home: 1870 S.W. Marine Dr., Vancouver, B.C. V6P 6B2.

**MARTIN, Hume,** B.A., M.S.W., M.H.Sc.; hospital administrator; b. Ottawa, Ont. 17 June 1947; s. Walter Ross and Norma Jacqueline (Hume) M.; e. Lisgar Coll. 1965; Univ. of Toronto, B.A. 1968, M.S.W. 1976, M.H.Sc. 1981; m. Sharon d. Douglas and Mary Mertens 12 June 1976; children: Sarah Alexandra, Stephanie Frances; EXTVE. DIR., BERMUDA HOSPITALS BOARD 1989– ; Sec. Sch. Teacher, CUSO, Sierra Leone 1968–70; Prog. Dir. 1971–73; Comm. Resource Offr., Indian Comm. Sec., Ont. Min. of Culture & Recreation, Kenora, Ont. 1976–77; Dir., Outreach Serv. & Acting Extve. Dir., Churchill Health Ctr. (Man.) 1977–79; Cons., Woods Gordon 1981–82; Pres. & C.E.O., North York General Hosp. 1982–89; Harvey G. Agnew Award; Johnson & Johnson Award; Burns Roth Book Award; recreation: bird watching, golfing; Home: 4 Southcote Rd., Paget, PG04; Office: King Edward VII Memorial Hospital, Hamilton, Bermuda.

**MARTIN, The Hon. J. Fraser,** B.A., B.C.L., J.S.C.; judge; b. Greenock, Scot. 5 Oct. 1939; s. John Grant and Anna Rhind (MacFarlane) M.; e. Greenock Acad., Rosemont H.S.; Sir George Williams Univ. B.A. 1960; McGill Univ. B.C.L. 1964; m. Anna Mai d. John & Barbara Norwell 28 Dec. 1963; children: Micheline, Derek, Francine, Colette; JUSTICE, SUPERIOR COURT OF QUE. 1983– ; Captain, Candn. Army Res. 1956–65; joined law firm of Chisholm, Smith, Davis, Anglin, Laing, Weldon & Courtois (now McCarthy Tétrault) 1966–67; Tansey, De Grandpré, Bergeron, Lavery & O'Donnell (now Lavery De Billy) 1967–83; Home: 79, chemin St-Henri, Ste-Marthe (Vaudreuil) Qué. J0P 1W0; Office: Court House #16.68, Notre-Dame St. E., Montréal, Qué. H2Y 1B6.

**MARTIN, Jane,** M.A.; artist; b. Montreal, Que. 31 March 1943; d. Robert John Douglas and Margaret Trenholme (Armitage) M.; e. Bishop's Univ. B.A. (Hons) 1965; Carleton Univ. M.A. 1966; m. Ewen Duncan s. Ewen and Helen McCuaig 26 June 1967; solo exhns. incl. Aggregation Gallery (now Wynick/Tuck) Toronto 1974, 1977, 1980; Meml. Univ. Art Gallery (touring) St. John's 1975; SAW Gallery Ottawa 1977, 1985; 'Contact' AGO Extension Div. Touring Show 1979–80; Whitewater Gallery North Bay 1985; 'Berkeley Castle Works 1984–1987' Toronto 1987; Gallery 101 Ottawa 1989; 'Wrapture' Open Space Victoria 1991; rep. numerous group exhns. since 1975 incl. AGO Toronto, Winnipeg Art Gallery, Harbourfront Art Gallery Toronto, Rideau Hall Ottawa, H. of C., Nat. Gallery Ottawa; rep. various touring exhns. 'On View' 13 Ont. centres 1976–77; 'Reflecting a Rural Consciousness' Can., USA, France 1978–79; 'Le Maison' internat. tour 1984–85; rep. various pub., corporate and private colls. incl. Art Gallery of Greater Victoria, B.C., City of Ottawa, Meml. Univ. Nfld., Robert McLaughlin Gallery Oshawa, Winnipeg Art Gallery, Can. Council Art Bank, Dept. External Affairs, Nat. Gallery Can.; Dir. SAW Gallery 1976–80, Co-ord. 1978; mem. Founding Bd. Candn. Reprography Collective (CanCopy) 1988–92; Co-founder CARFAC Copyright Collective and mem. Extve. 1988–91, Nat. Rep. and Dir. 1989–91; author: 'The Last Act' (play) first perform. 1966; 'F.R. Scott' (biog.) 1966; 'Women Visual Artists on Canada Council Juries, Selection Committees, and Arts Advisory Panels; and Amongst Grant Recipients from 1972–73 to 1977–78' (CARFAC 1978); 'Who Judges Whom?' Atlantis, vol 5, #1 1979; 'Women Visual Artists on CC Juries ... to 1979–80' (CARFAC and Status of Women Canada 1981); various articles; catalogues: 'Body Language' Susan Crean (1989); 'Wrapture' Joyce Nelson (1991); subject numerous newspapers and mag. articles; illus. various book covers; Address: 21 Rose Ave., Toronto, Ont. M4X 1N7.

**MARTIN, Jean-Claude,** B.Pharm., M.H.A.; association executive; b. Montreal, Que. 21 Dec. 1929; s. Lorenzo and Alice May (Baillargeon) M; e. Coll. Mont Saint-Louis 1950; Univ. de Montréal B.Pharm. 1956, M.H.A. 1962; Candn. Army Offr. Courses; m. Yvette d. Roméo Leclerc, Portneuf, Qué. 30 June 1956; children:

Denis, Diane, Benoit, Vincent; EXTVE. DIR., ASSOCIATION DES PHARMACIENS DE ÉTABLISSEMENTS DE SANTÉ DU QUEBEC 1992– ; Pharm., Dorval Shopping Centre, Qué. 1956; Pharm. Lt. Candn. Forces Med. Services, Camp Borden, Petawawa, Toronto and Ottawa 1957–60; Resident in Hosp. Adm. Montreal Children's Hosp. 1961, Adm. Asst. 1962, Asst. Extve. Dir. 1963–65, Adm. (Services) 1969–71; Sr. Lectr. Inst. Hosp. Adm. Univ. of Montreal 1965–69; in charge of Hosp. Adm. Course, Dept. Continuing Educ. 1965–69, Lectr. in Pharm., Continuing Educ. in Hosp. Adm. and Dept. Health Adm. 1969–74; Asst. Prof. of Epidemiol. and Health McGill Univ. 1971–75; Extve. Dir. Montreal Jt. Hosp. Inst. 1971–75; Extve. Dir. Hôpital du Sacré-Coeur, Montreal 1975–77; Pres., Candn. Hosp. Assn. 1977–89; Extve. in Residence, Faculty of Admin., Univ. of Ottawa 1990–92; mem. core comte. Nat. Health Grants and Sub-comte. on Analysis & Organ. Health Services 1971–75; Pres. Study Comte. on Out-patients Services & Emergency Services Montreal Region 1971; Adm. Centre St-Vallier 1971–73, Dir. 1973–74; mem. Sub-comte. on Health & Welfare Montreal Urban Community 1972–73; Study Comte. on Emergency Services Metrop. Montreal Regional Council on Health & Social Services 1973–74, Dir. on Council 1975–77; mem. Que. Research Council 1976–77; Chrmn. Health Computer Information Bureau 1977–80; Dir. Candn. Council Hosp. Accreditation 1977–88; Nursing Unit Adm. Program 1977–88; mem., Bd. of Dir., Internat. Hosp. Fed., 1981–89, Pres. 1989–91; author various med. publs.; Ed. 'Magazine Dimension in Health Services' 1977–89; Fellow, Am. Coll. Hosp. Adms.; mem., Bd. of Dir., Internat. Hosp. Fed.; mem. Candn. Coll. Health Service Extves.; Am. Hosp. Assn. (Hon.); R. Catholic; recreations: tennis, sailing, cross-country skiing; Home: 4874 Ave Grosvenor, Montréal, Qué. H3W 2M1; Office: 50 boul. Crémazie ouest, bureau 505, Montréal, Qué. H2P 2T2.

**MARTIN, John Rupert,** B.A., M.F.A., Ph.D., D.Litt. (Hon.); professor; b. Hamilton, Ont. 27 Sept. 1916; s. John Smith and Elizabeth (Hutchinson) M.; e. Central Coll. Inst., Hamilton, Ont.; McMaster Univ., B.A. 1938; Princeton Univ., M.F.A. 1941, Ph.D. 1947; McMaster Univ., D.Litt. (Hon.) 1976; m. Barbara Janet, d. Duncan Malcolm, Hamilton, Ont. 23 Aug. 1941; one d., Hilary Jane; Marquand Prof. of Art and Archeol., Princeton Univ. 1970–87; Prof. since 1961; Chrmn. Dept. 1973–79; Instr., Univ. Iowa 1941–42; joined present Univ. 1947; Bicentennial Preceptor 1952–55; McCosh Faculty Fellow 1964–65; Fellow, Am. Council of Learned Socs., 1965–66; Charles Rufus Morey Book Award, Coll. Art. Assn. Am. 1972; Visiting Prof., Williams College 1988; served with Candn. Army in Eng. & N.W. Europe 1942–46; rank Maj. on discharge; Mentioned in Despatches; author: 'The Illustration of the Heavenly Ladder of John Climacus' 1954, 'The Portrait of John Milton at Princeton and its Place in Milton Iconography' 1961; 'The Farnese Gallery' 1965; 'The Ceiling Paintings By Rubens for the Jesuit Church in Antwerp' 1968; 'Rubens: The Antwerp Altarpieces' 1969; 'Rubens' Decorations for the Pompa Introitus Ferdinandi' 1972; 'Rubens before 1620' 1972; 'Baroque' 1977; 'Van Dyck as Religious Artist' 1979; also numerous articles; Editor-in-Chief 'The Art Bulletin' 1971–74; Pres., College Art Assn. of Am. 1984–86; mem., Internat. Comte. for History of Art; Renaissance Soc. Am.; Am. Philos. Soc.; Democrat; Home: 107 Mercer St., Princeton, N.J. 08540.

**MARTIN, John William,** C.A., A.C.I.S.; reinsurance executive; b. Toronto, Ont. 18 Dec. 1945; e. C.A. 1969; EXTVE. VICE PRES. MUNICH REINSURANCE CO. OF CANADA 1986– ; joined Peat, Marwick, Mitchell & Co., C.A.'s Toronto 1964–77; present Co. 1977; Past Pres. Toronto Chapter Candn. Ins. Accts. Assn.; Office: 22F, 390 Bay St., Toronto, Ont. M5H 2Y2.

**MARTIN, Joseph E.,** B.A. (Hons.), F.C.M.C.; b. Kelvington, Sask. 13 Jan. 1937; s. late George Herbert and late Jakobeina Sigurlaug Margaret (Einarsson) M.; e. Un. Coll. (now Univ. of Winnipeg) (Sr. Stick 1957–58), B.A. (Hons.) 1959; m. Sally Ann, d. late W. Noble Dagg, 16 July 1960; children: Marian Michelle, Jon Noble George, Michael Reid, Meredith Ann; PARTNER, BRAXTON ASSOCIATES (the Strategy Consulting Div. of Deloitte & Touche) 1993– ; Chrmn., Deloitte Touche Tohmatsu International Mgmt. Consulting Ctte.; Invest. Analyst, The Monarch Life Assurance Co., 1959–61; served with Govt. of Man. 1961–66, Extve. Asst. to Premier Duff Roblin; joined present firm as Consultant, Winnipeg office 1966; transferred to Toronto 1968; Partner-in-Charge, Touche Ross Management Consultants 1978–90; Partner, Deloitte & Touche Mngmt. Consultants 1990–93; served with COTC, Univ. of Man., Prairie Command Personnel Selection Unit; retired with rank Capt. 1962; Past Pres., Man. Hist. Soc.; Manitoba YPC; Inst. of Certified Mgmt. Consultants of Ont.; Fellow, Inst. of Certified Mgmt. Consultants of Ont.; author of various articles for magazines and journals; Past Pres., Candn. Assn. of Mgmt. Consultants; Anglican; Clubs: Albany; Toronto Cricket Skating & Curling; North Toronto Tennis; Toronto Club; Home: 215 Glencairn Ave., Toronto, Ont.; Office: 1400, BCE Place, 181 Bay St., Toronto, Ont. M5J 2V1.

**MARTIN, Keith Anthony,** B.A., F.C.I.S., P.Adm.; banker; b. Bromley, Kent, England 3 June 1943; s. Alan Keith and D. Mary (dec.) M.; e. Trinity Sch. of John Whitgift (U.K.); Jamaica College 1960; York Univ. B.A. 1977; m. Maureen d. the late George and Elsie Hall 28 March 1970; children: Victoria, Bruce; VICE-PRES., CUSTODY AND INVESTMENT SERVICES, THE CHASE MANHATTAN BANK OF CANADA 1992– ; joined Chase Manhattan Bank, N.A. New York 1965; Trust & Custody Officer, The Chase Manhattan Trust 1968–78; joined Chase Manhattan Bank of Can. 1973; Vice-Pres., Admin. & Finance & Corp. Sec. 1978; Vice-Pres., Institutional Banking 1982; Electronic Banking 1986; Financial Insts. & Treas. Coord. 1988; Mem., Candn. Bankers Assn. (Securities Opns. Ctte.); Past Pres. & Dir., Treas. Mngt. Assn. of Toronto; Dir., Children's Aid Soc. of Metro. Toronto; Dir., Children's Aid Soc. of Metro. Toronto Found.; Mem., Islington Un. Ch.; Mem., Toastmasters Internat.; recreations: camping, gardening, hiking; clubs: Bd. of Trade of Metro. Toronto; Office: 150 King St. W., Box 68, Toronto, Ont. M5H 1J9.

**MARTIN, Patrick Allen,** LL.B.; journalist; b. Toronto, Ont. 10 Mar. 1951; s. Joseph Allen and Dorothy Adele (Falconer) M.; e. Univ. of West. Ont., LL.B. 1979; children: Gabriel, Samuel; MIDDLE EAST CORRESPONDENT, THE GLOBE AND MAIL 1991– ; freelance writer/broadcaster, The International Review, Financial Post, Saturday Night, The Globe and Mail/CBC Radio: Capital Report, Ideas, Sunday Morning 1972–78; Host/Prod., CBC Radio, Sunday Morning 1979–81; Writer/Editor, The Globe & Mail 1984–91; Editor, 'Focus,' The Globe and Mail 1986–89; Thomson Fellow, Massey Coll., Univ. of Toronto 1989–90; mem., The Globe and Mail (editorial Board) 1990–91; ACTRA Award, Best Radio Host 1981; Dean Ivan Rand Award, UWO Law Sch. 1979; author: 'Contenders: The Tory Quest for Power' 1983; Editor: 'U.W.O. Law Review' 1978–79; recreations: tennis, skiing; club: Cottingham Tennis (Pres. 1987–89); Office: 444 Front St. W., Toronto, Ont. M5V 2S9.

**MARTIN, Paul,** B.A., LL.B., b. Windsor, Ont. 28 Aug. 1938; s. the late Paul Joseph James and the late Eleanor Alice M.; e. Univ. of Ottawa; Univ. of Toronto, B.A. (Philos. & Hist.) 1962, LL.B. 1965; m. Sheila Ann, d. William A. and Sheila (Scott) Cowan, Windsor, Ont. 11 Sept. 1965; three s., Paul William James, Robert James Edward, David Patrick Anthony; MINISTER OF FINANCE, GOVT. OF CANADA 1993– ; Mem. of Parliament 1988– ; former Pres., C.E.O. & Dir., The CSL Group Inc.; former Chrmn. & C.E.O., Canada Steamship Lines Inc.; Former Corporate Dir., C.B. Pak Inc.; Redpath Industries Ltd.; Fednav Ltd.; The Manufacturers Life Insurance Co.; Canadian Shipbuilding & Engineering Limited; Imasco Corp.; read law with Osler, Hoskin & Harcourt, Toronto; called to the Bar of Ont. 1966; former Vice Pres., Power Corp. of Can.; Consolidated Bathurst Ltd.; prior to Bar admission worked as a merchant seaman on various salvage operations in Arctic; also served in Legal Dept., European Coal and Steel Community, Luxembourg and worked as a roustabout in Alta. gas fields; before being sworn in to Cabinet was member of the following Assns.: Vice-Chrmn. & Gov., Concordia Univ.; Founding Dir. (Emeritus), North-South Inst.; Candn. Counc. for Native Business; Dir., Candn. Counc. of Christians & Jews; Candn. Centre for Arms Control-Adv. Bd.; mem., Amnesty Internat.; Centre for Research and Action on Race Relations; British North American Comte.; R. Catholic; Law Soc. of Upper Canada; recreations: sports, reading; Clubs: Mount Bruno Country; University (Montreal); Mount Royal; Office: House of Commons, Ottawa, Ont. K1A 0A6.

**MARTIN, Paul-Louis,** B.A., M.A., Ph.D.; ethnologist, university professor; b. Trois-Rivières, Qué. 13 Jan. 1944; s. Henri-Paul and Madeleine (Dufresne) M.; e. Séminaire Saint-Joseph B.A. 1964; Univ. Laval M.A. 1972, Ph.D. 1980; m. Marie d. Charles and Pauline (Spénard) de Blois 7 May 1967; children: Philippe, Julie, Charles; PROF., UNIV. OF QUEBEC AT TROIS-RIVIERES 1990– ; Ethnologist, Que. Cultural Affairs Dept. 1969; Founder & Dir., Archaeological Mus. of Eastern Que., Rivière-du-Loup 1974–77; President, private group of consultants in history & human sciences 1977–79; Mem., Comn. des Biens Culturels (Cultural Properties) du Qué. 1979 (Vice-Pres., then Pres. 1983–88); Extve. Mem., Soc. des Musées Québécois 1976–77; Vice-Pres., Conseil de la culture de l'est du Qué. 1977–80; Hon. Mem., Soc. Québécoise des Ethnologues; recipient, 'Exceptional Career' Award, Soc. des Musées Québécois 1993; author of 9 books & 30 articles incl. 'La Berçante Québécoise' 1973, 'Les Maîtres – Potiers du Bourg Saint-Denis' 1978, 'Tolfrey, un Aristocrate au Bas-Canada' 1979, 'Rivière-du-Loup et son Portage' 1977; 'La Gaspésie de Miguasha à Percé' 1978, 'La Chasse au Québec' 1990; co-author & co-dir., 'Les Chemins de la Mémoire' 1990; recreations: farming (plum trees), hunting, tennis; Office: 1045 Ave du Parc, Québec, Qué. G1S 2W4; Office: C.P. 500, Trois-Rivières, Qué. G9A 5H7.

**MARTIN, Ray,** B.Ed., M.Sc.; politician; b. Delia, Alta. 8 Aug. 1941; s. James and Olive (Churchill) M.; e. Univ. of Alberta B.Ed.; Univ. of Calgary M.Sc.; m. Cheryl Matheson 1977; children: Barrett, Cathy, Matthew, Bruce, Dawn; LEADER, ALBERTA NEW DEMOCRATIC PARTY & LEADER OF THE OFFICIAL OPPOSITION, PROV. OF ALBERTA 1989– ; former school teacher; actively involved with N.D.P. since 1971; Prov. Sec. N.D.P. Edmonton 1975; Party Pres. 1979; 1st elected MLA for Edmonton, Norwood 1982; re-elected 1986, '89; recreations: squash, golf, curling; club: Edmonton Squash; Home: 11721-92 St., Edmonton, Alta. T5G 1A2; Office: Room 204, Legislative Bldg., Edmonton, Alta. T5K 2B6.

**MARTIN, Robert,** M.B.A.; financial executive; b. 10 Jan. 1951; e. McGill Univ. B.Comm. 1973; Univ. of West. Ont. M.B.A. 1975; VICE-PESIDENT, FINANCE & SECRETARY, UAP INC.; Vice-Pres. & Sec.-Treas., UAP Inc.; Director of Finance; Pres., Montreal Chapter, Financial Executives Inst.; Dir. & Treas., Internat. Edn. Sch. Found.; Office: 7025 Ontario St. E., Montreal, Que. H1N 2B3.

**MARTIN, Robert Ivan,** B.A., LL.B., LL.M.; educator; b. Toronto, Ont. 30 July 1939; s. Ivan Harold and Annette Joyce (McLaren) M.; e. Upper Can. Coll. Toronto 1957; Royal Mil. Coll. of Can. B.A. 1961; Univ. of Toronto LL.B. 1967; Univ. of London LL.M. with distinction 1971; m. Linda Margaret McNeilly, d. Georgina and James McNeilly 21 Jan. 1989; children: Ivan, Dawson Cabral; PROFESSOR OF LAW, UNIVERSITY OF WESTERN ONTARIO 1978– ; Lieut., Candn. Army 1961–63; Info. Offr. Dept. of National Health and Welfare 1964; Tutorial Asst. Univ. Coll. Dar es Salaam, Tanzania 1967–70; Lectr. in Law, Univ. of Botswana, Lesotho and Swaziland, Roma, Lesotho 1971–73; Sr. Lectr. in Law, Univ. of Nairobi, Kenya 1973–75; Assoc. Prof. of Law present Univ. 1975–78; Visiting Prof. of Law, Univ. of Dar es Salaam 1979–80; Visiting Fellow, Univ. of Mauritius 1988–89; Visiting Fellow, National Univ. of Lesotho 1989; Secy.-Treasr., Commonwealth Assn. for Education in Journalism and Communication 1985– ; Columnist, London Free Press 1985; The Lawyers Weekly 1986– ; author: 'Personal Freedom and the Law in Tanzania' 1974; Ed. 'Controls and the Canadian Media' 1978; 'Critical Perspectives on the Constitution' 1984; 'A Sourcebook of Canadian Media Law' 1989 (rev. ed. 1991, 2nd ed. 1994); articles in 'The Globe and Mail,' 'Toronto Star,' 'Ottawa Citizen,' 'Manchester Guardian Weekly,' 'Canadian Forum,' 'This Magazine' and 'Canadian Bar Review'; barrister and solicitor, Ont. 1978; cand. for NDP London East fed. el. 1979, 1980; faculty advisor, WUSC Zimbabwe Seminar 1987; Home: London, Ont.; Office: London, Ont. N6A 3K7.

**MARTIN, Robert William,** B.A.Sc., P.Eng.; corporate director; b. Toronto, Ont. 7 June 1936; s. William George and Evelyn Irene (Philips) M.; e. Leaside High Sch. Toronto 1954, Vaughan Rd. Coll. Inst. 1953; Univ. of Toronto B.A.Sc. (Civil Engn.) 1958; m. Patricia Lorraine d. Albert George Norris, Leaside, Ont. 27 June 1959; children: Stephen Gregory, Robert Scott, Adrienne Christine; CHRMN. & DIR., SILCORP LTD.; Retired Pres. & C.E.O., The Consumers' Gas Company Ltd.; Dir., Confederation Life Insurance Co. Ltd.; Inter Provincial Pipeline Ltd.; Peoples Jewellers Corp.; CC Telenterprises Ltd.; West Park Hospital; Toronto Symphony Orchestra; York University; mem., Assn. Prof. Engrs. Prov. Ont.; Candn. Gas Assn. (Past Chrmn.); Ont. Natural Gas Assn. (Past Pres.); Bd. Trade Metrop. Toronto; Protestant; recreations: racquet sports, fitness, bridge, golf; Clubs: Toronto; Mississauga Golf & Country; Mad River Golf; Home: 118 Farnham Ave., Toronto, Ont. M4V 1H4.

**MARTIN, Roger Lloyd,** B.A., M.B.A.; strategy consultant; b. Kitchener, Ont. 4 Aug. 1956; s. Lloyd M. and Delphine E. M.; e. Harvard College B.A. (Hons.) 1979; Harvard Univ. Graduate School of Business M.B.A. 1981; m. Nancy L. d. Senator Daniel and Mrs. F. Lang 24 Sept. 1983; children: Lloyd, Jennifer, Daniel; CHAIRMAN, MONITOR COMPANY CANADA LIMITED 1991– ; Principal, Canada Consulting Group 1981–85; Managing Director & Chief Extve. Offr., Monitor Company Canada Limited 1986–91; Dir., Monitor Company Inc. 1988– ; Extve. Ctte. Mem. 1991– ; Chrmn., Monitor Univ. 1993– ; Edit. Bd., Candn. Competition Policy Record; author of various magazine & newspaper articles; recreations: tennis, golf, basketball; clubs: Ojibway, Osler Bluffs Ski; Office: 152 King St. E., Toronto, Ont. M5A 1J3.

**MARTIN, Ronald Albert;** visual artist; b. London, Ont. 28 Apl. 1943; s. Albert Earl and Wanda E. (Hellopetter) M.; e. H. B. Beal Secondary High Sch. London Special Art; rep. by Carmen Lamanna Gallery 1971–91; rep. The complete works of Ron Martin represented by Christopher Cutts Gallery, Moore Gallery Ltd., Carmen Lamanna (Estate) since 1992; exhns. incl. XXXVIII Biennale di Venzia 1978; 'Ron Martin 1971–1981' Art Gallery of Ont. 1990–91; rep. pub. and private colls. incl. H. Laing and Kathlien Brown, Walter Klepac, Mr. and Mrs. Alan Schwartz, Dr. Shirley Thomson, Irving Zucker, Canada Council: Art Bank., Nat. Gallery of Can., Montreal Museum of Fine Arts, Musée D'Art Contemporain Montréal, Art Gallery of Ontario, Confederation Centre Art Gallery & Museum, Kitchener/Waterloo Art Gallery, Hamilton Art Gallery, Mackenzie Art Gallery, Vancouver Art Gallery; freelance curator, arts writer, Publ. Parachute, Volume 66, 1992 Apr., May, June; An Homage. CARMEN LAMANNA, The Person; curated 1988 Judd Red Room, Duchamp Room, Large American Room, Early Internat. Contemporary Room, Nat. Gallery Can.; Can. Council Sr. Arts Grant 'A' 1993; publisher Ron Martin; coauthor: (with Walter Klepac) 'Art and Knowledge', forward by Brydon E. Smith, launched at the Christopher Cutts Gall., Toronto 1993; distributed by Art Metropole, Toronto, Marginal Distributions, Peterborough; mem. Candn. Artists' Representation; Art Gallery of Ont.; Mackenzie Art Gallery, Regina, Sask.; recreations: reading, writing, history; Address: 692 St. Clarens Ave., Unit 3, Toronto, Ont. M6H 3X1.

**MARTIN, Sheilah Louise,** S.J.D.; educator; b. Montreal, Que. 31 May 1957; d. John William and Lillian Lucille M.; e. McGill Univ. B.C.L., LL.B. 1981; Univ. of Alta. LL.M. 1983; Univ. of Toronto S.J.D. 1991; m. John s. Jim and Mary Courtright 15 Dec. 1984; two s. Rory Patrick, Sean Thomas; DEAN OF LAW, UNIV. OF CALGARY 1992– and PROF. OF LAW 1992– ; Researcher Candn. Inst. Resources Law 1982–83; Asst. Prof. present Univ. 1983, Assoc. Prof. 1985 (tenured 1988); Visiting Assoc. Prof. of Law Osgoode Hall York Univ. 1986–87; Exchange Prog. Dept. of Justice Common Law/Civil Law summers 1986–89; recipient, Prov. Alta. Grad. Studies Award 1982; Superior Teaching Award Univ. Calgary Students Union 1985, Hon. Mention 1988; Fraser Beatty Fellowship Univ. Toronto 1987; SSHRC Doctoral Fellowship 1989; winner, YWCA 'Women of Distinction' award 1990; participant, Gov.-General's Study Conference of Can. 1990; frequent guest speaker; co-ed. 'Equality and Judicial Neutrality' 1987; numerous law publs. women & the law, the Charter, Can. Health Act; mem. Law Soc. Alta.; recreations: biking, swimming; Office: 2500 University Dr. N.W., Calgary, Alta. T2N 1N4.

**MARTIN, Hon. Shirley,** P.C.; b. 20 Nov. 1932; m. Jack Martin; two sons: John, Christopher; Min. of State for Transport 1991–93; former Business Service Mgr., Bell Canada; el. H. of C. g.e. (Lincoln) 1984; re-el. g.e. 1988; Vice Chair, P.C. National Caucus; Secy.-Treas., P.C. Ont. Caucus; Principal Del., U.N. 40th Gen. Assembly; Chair, National Parlty. Task Force on Child Care; Parlty Secy. to the Min. of Public Works; apptd. Min. of State for Transport and sworn to the Privy Counc. 1988; Min. of State (Indian Affairs & Northern Devel.) 1990–91; P.C.; United Ch.; Address: Unit 9, 44 King St. E., Stoney Creek, Ont. L8G 1K1.

**MARTINEAU, Mr. Justice Paul,** P.C. (Can.), J.C.S., Q.C., B.A., LL.L., K.C.S.G.; advocate; b. Bryson, Que. 10 Apr. 1921; s. Aphonse and Lucienne (Lemieux) M.; e. St. John's Sch., Campbell's Bay; Ottawa Univ., B.A. 1941; Univ. of Montreal, LL.L. 1949; m. Hélène, d. Richard Neclaw, Poland, 3 Jan. 1946; two d. Alice, Gabrielle; JUSTICE, QUE. SUPERIOR COURT 1980– ; former Dir., Morrison Lamothe Bakery Ltd.; Télécable Laurentian Inc.; Pres., Astra Research Centre Inc.; read law with Hon. Edouard Asselin, Q.C., and the late John Crankshaw, Q.C., called to the Bar of Que. 1949; cr. Q.C. 1966; practised for one year in Montreal with late John Crankshaw, Q.C.; private practice, Campbell's Bay 1950–66; Hull, Que. 1966–80; apptd. Crown Attorney for Pontiac District in 1950–58; Past Pres. and Founder of Campbell's Bay Chamber of Comm.; Past Pres., Candn. Legion No. 162; Pontiac Br.; served in 2nd World War with R.C.A.F. 1942–46; 1st el. to H.C. for Pontiac-Témiscamique, g.e. March 1958; re-el. 1962, 1963; def. cand. g.e. 1965; apptd. Parlty. Secy. to the Prime Minister, 1959; Depy. Speaker of the H. of C., Jan. 1962; Min. of Mines and Tech. Surveys, Aug. 1962–Apl. 1963; mem., Que. Royal Comn. of Inquiry on Adm. of Justice 1967–69; mem., Candn. Bar Assn.; Commonwealth Parlty. Assn.; Inter Parlty. Union; K. of C. (4th degree); P. Conservative; Roman Catholic; recreations: painting, travelling, prospecting; Home: 1204 Mountain Road, Aylmer, Quebec. Office: Palais de Justice, 1, Notre Dame St. E., Montreal, Que. H2Y 1B6.

**MARTINEAU, Richard;** journalist, author; b. Verdun, Que. 29 July 1961; s. Jacques and Huguette (Richer) M.; e. CEGEP Andre-Laurendeau, Ville Lasalle 1980; Concordia Univ., major in cinema 1983; COLUMNIST & DESK EDITOR, 'VOIR' 1988– ; began to write for magazines at the age of seventeen; has written for all major magazines in Quebec; works for radio, TV, etc.; author of TV series 'Playback' which was aired in 1987 (finalist for best screenplay, Gémeaux Awards 1988); Finalist for Best Text (Humour), 1991 Nat. Magazine Awards; author: 'La chasse à l'éléphant' 1990 (a cynical view of babyboomers' lifestyle & politics: an instant best-seller which stirred controversy among intellectuals); editor: 'Pour on finir avec ...' (a collection of pamphlets pub. by Boreal which criticize Quebec's edn. system, ecologist ideology, feminism, TV & the pop-psychology craze, etc.); Home: 662 Querbes, Outremont, Que. H2V 3W7.

**MARTINO, Michael John,** Q.C., B.A., LL.B.; franchise executive; b. Toronto, Ont. 9 July 1936; s. Michael Douglas and Olive Gertrude (Borman) M.; e. pub. and high schs. Montréal, Qué.; McMaster Univ. B.A. 1953; Osgoode Hall Law Sch. LL.B. 1960; m. Katherine Ann d. John and Eileen Murphy 4 July 1959; children: Michael, Terence, David, Kevin; PRES. & C.E.O, MBEC COMMUNICATIONS INC. MASTER LICENSEE, MAILBOXES ETC. 1990– ; private law practice 1962–80, Sr. Partner Corporate & Comm. Law Div. Hamilton firm; cr. Q.C. 1978; Co-Founder Home Savings and Loan Corp. 1978, Dir. 1978–87; Vice Pres. and Corporate Counsel Mother's Restaurants Inc. 1980, Extve. Vice Pres. 1981–83, Dir. 1974–83, Chrmn. & C.E.O. 1986–88; Sr. Mgmnt. Consultant, Little Caesar Internat. Inc. 1989–90; Dir. Big Brother Assn. Hamilton (Pres. 1972) 1970–74; Internat. Master Am. Contract Bridge League; N. Am. Men's Pair Championship 1969; Candn. Nat. Team and Men's Pair Championship 1969; R. Catholic; recreations: tennis, golf; Clubs: Hamilton Golf & Country; Burlington Racquets; Home: 1903 Pilgrim's Way, Ph2, Oakville, Ont. L6M 2X1.

**MARTITSCH, Karl;** consultant; b. Ratnitz, Austria, 19 Nov. 1917; s. late Josef and late Martha (Schaunig) M.; e. Univs. of Vienna and Graz, Dipl, Engr.-Master Civil Engn.; came to Can. 1951; m. Beverly, d. Dr. G. E. Westman, Sault Ste. Marie, Ont., 12 Sept. 1953; Children: Karl Nicholas, Franchesca; CONSULTANT TO STONE & WEBSTER CANADA LTD. 1988–91; with Foundation Co. of Canada 1951–63; served as Field Engr., Resident Engr., Supt., Project Mgr. and Constr. Mgr.; joined present Co. 1963 as Vice-Pres. and Constr. Mgr.; Vice Pres. and Gen. Mgr. 1972; Sr. Vice Pres. & Gen. Mgr. – Special Projects 1981–88; Dir., Nat. Constr. Indust. Devel. Foundation 1972–80; Candn. Construction Assn., 1972–76; Construction Labour Relations Assn., Ont., 1972–79; Toronto French School, 1973–78; mem. Construction Sector Comte., Economic Council of Can., 1973; mem., Assn. Prof. Engrs. Prov. Ont. (Citizenship Award 1973); Dir., Const. Safety Assn. Ont. 1970–88 (Pres. 1983–84; mem. Mgmt. Comte. 1979–85, Extve. Counc. 1979–87); Indust. Contractors' Assn. Can. 1968–88 (Past Pres. & Dir.); mem., World Ski (F.I.S.) Council 1979–92; Candn. rep. ski jumping & ski jump design; Olympic & F.I.S. ski jumping judge; awarded Commemorative Medal for 125th Anniversary of Candn. Confederation 1993; recreations: skiing, tennis; Club: RCYC; Home: 38A Whitehall Rd., Toronto, Ont. M4W 2C6.

**MARTLAND, Hon. Ronald,** LL.D.; retired judge; b. Liverpool, Eng. 10 Feb. 1907; s. John and Ada (Wild) M.; e. Univ. of Alta., B.A. 1926; LL.B. 1928, LL.D. 1964; Oxford Univ., B.A. 1930, B.C.L. 1931, M.A. 1935; m. Iris Euphemia Bury, 30 Mar. 1935; children: Patricia, John Gordon, Brigid Elizabeth; practised law at Edmonton, 1932 to 1958; Judge, Supreme Court of Canada 1958–82; Maj., 2nd Bn., Roy. Edmonton Regt. (Res.); read law with H.R. Milner, K.C., of Edmonton, Alta.; called to the Bar of Alta. 1932; cr. K.C. 1943; Hon. Prof., Faculty of Law, Univ. of Alta. and Univ. of Calgary; Hon. LL.D. Univ. of Alberta and Univ. of Calgary; Bencher, Alta. Law Soc., 1948–58; Hon. Bencher 1982; Hon. Fellow, Hertford College, Oxford; Companion Order of Canada; mem., Alta. Order of Excellence; Candn. Bar Assn.; Freemason; Anglican; Clubs: Edmonton; Kiwanis; Rideau; Royal Ottawa Golf; Home: 55 Placel Road, Rockcliffe Park, Ont. K1L 5B9; Office: Suite 300, 50 O'Connor St., Ottawa, Ont. K1P 6L2.

**MARTY, Dick,** LL.B.; management consultant; b. Ancaster, Ont. 9 May 1949; s. J. Kenneth and Elizabeth E. (Hogarth) M.; e. Univ. of Toronto LL.B. 1980; Managing Principal, ExecuCounsel Inc. 1984; Sales Rep. National Paper Goods Ltd. 1970–72; Sales Mgr. Arrco-Saxon Co. Ltd. 1972–74; Toronto Mgr. National Utility Service Inc. 1974–76; Pres. Marty Partners Inc. 1976–80; Cons. Price Waterhouse Associates 1980–81; Sr. Cons. Woods Gordon 1981–84; community service incls. Distress Centre, John Howard Soc.; recreations: classic cars, art; Home: 120 Rosedale Valley, Toronto, Ont. M4W 1P8.

**MARTYN, Maxwell Pearson,** C.D., B.A.; retired air force officer; b. Calgary, Alta. 29 June 1913; s. Angus Donald and Bernice Evelyn (Pearson) M.; e. Stanley Jones Pub. and Crescent Heights High Schs., Calgary, Alta.; Westmount and Victoria High Schs., Edmonton, Alta.; Univ. of Alta., B.A. (Hons.) 1936; m. 1stly late Eva Macpherson, d. late J.H. Johnson, Edmonton, Alta. 8 June 1940; m. 2ndly Virginia Helen Hopkirk, Montreal, Que. 25 Nov. 1967; children: Donald Macpherson, Heather Elizabeth; served with Candn. Mil. 1932–38; R.C.A.F. (Regular) 1938–65; awarded Sir John Siddley Trophy for Pilot Proficiency 1939; served in Battle of Atlantic commanding No. 10 and No. 11 Bomber Squadrons 1939–43; posted to Planning Staff of R.A.F. Transport Command 1944 and later apptd. Sr. Air Staff Offr. of No. 120 R.C.A.F. Transport Wing in European Theatre until June 1946; returned to Can. July 1946 to serve on staff of N.W. Air Command, operating N.W. Staging Route to Alaska; transfrd. to Air Force HQ 1947; attended Jt. Services Staff Coll. in Eng. 1949; Sr. Air Staff Offr., Tactical Air Command, Canada 1950; commanded R.C.A.F. Stn. Penhold, NATO Training Prog. 1953–54; awarded Hon. Pilot's Wings (by French Republic) for training French Air Force pilots; trans. overseas as Chief Staff Offr. and Asst. Air Attaché, Candn. Jt. Staff, London, Eng. 1955; Chief Staff Offr., Training Command, Winnipeg, Man. 1959; apptd. Chief of Training & Personnel Policy, Air Force H.Q. 1961; Air Mem. for Personnel, Air Council 1963; promoted Air Vice-Marshal & named Depy. Chief of Personnel in newly integrated Candn. Armed Forces 1964; ret. from service July 1965; Pres., Trans Air Ltd. 1965, Chrmn. & Pres. 1967; Special Rep. New Business Devel., Extve. Staff, Richardson Securities of Can., Wpg. 1968 until ret. July 1970; Home: #80, 1 Place d'Armes, Kingston, Ont. K7K 6S5.

**MARVY, Alain;** exploration and uranium mining executive; b. Dijon, France 5 Sept. 1947; e. Ecole Nat. Sup. de Geol. (Nancy France), grad. Mining Engr. & Geologist 1970; Inst. de Controle de Gestion, Inst. Français de Gestion (Paris France) grad. 1986; VICE-PRES., PROJECT, CIGAR LAKE MINING CORPORATION 1992– ; worked with French Collieries (U/G) 1972–74; basic metal mining opns. in Morocco 1974; var. uranium mining div. of Cogema (France & Niger: Somair – open pit opns. & Cominak – U/G opns.) 1974–89; formerly Vice Pres., Operations, Amok Ltd. 1990–92; Home: 53 Kirk Cres., Saskatoon, Sask. S7H 3B1; Office: 410 – 224 Fourth Ave. S., Saskatoon, Sask. S7K 5M5.

**MARWOOD, Maurice E.,** B.Sc., M.Sc., M.B.A.; business executive; b. Windsor, Ont. 23 Apr. 1941; s. Fred E. and Ruby M. (Mulcaster) M.; e. Univ. of Toronto B.Sc. 1964; Univ. of Guelph M.Sc. 1966; Univ. of Chicago M.B.A. 1974; married; children: Dale, Pamela, Andrew; VICE-PRES. and GENERAL MGR., ROBBINS & MYERS CANADA LTD.; Engr. & Product Support Mgmt. positions, Caterpillar Inc. USA 1966–76; Div. Mgr. Caterpillar Overseas S.A., Geneva, Switz. 1976–79; Dir., Caterpillar Far East Ltd., Hong Kong 1979–82; Gen. Mgr. Caterpillar Serv. Technology Group (USA) 1982–86; returned to Canada as V.P. Sales & Mktg. Canadian Kenworth Co. 1986–89; joined Canadian Foremost Ltd., Sr. V.P. & Chief Op. Offr. 1989, promoted to President 1990; joined Robbins & Myers Canada Ltd. 1992; Dir., Robbins & Myers Canada Ltd.; Dir., Brampton Board of Trade; Mem. Toronto Board of Trade; formerly Dir., Calgary Chamber of Commerce; Dir., Calgary Econ.

Dev. Authority; Dir., Canada-Arab Business Council; Dir., Candn. Inst. for Petroleum Ind. Dev.; Mem., Internat. Business Advisory Group to Univ. of Calgary; recreations: marathoner, squash, skiing; Home: 54 Madelaine Cres., Brampton, Ont. L6S 2Y9; Office: 8032 Torbram Rd., Brampton, Ont. L6T 3T2.

**MARX, The Hon. Herbert,** B.A., M.A., LL.L., LL.M.; judge; university law professor; lawyer; b. Montreal, Que. 16 Mar. 1932; s. Robert and Miriam M.; e. Concordia Univ., B.A. 1958; Univ. de Montréal, M.A. 1962, LL.L. 1967; Harvard Law Sch., LL.M. 1969; awarded Can. Counc. & Que. Govt. scholarships 1968–69; 1st place Que. Bar Exams, awarded Prix du Barreau de Paris 1968; m. Eva d. Eugene and Helen Felsenburg; children: Robert, Sarah; JUDGE, QUEBEC SUPERIOR COURT 1989– ; Vice-Pres., elect. light co. 1954–64; Prof., Const. Law, Univ. de Montréal 1969–79; Comnr., Que. Human Rights Comm. 1975–79; Adv. Counc. Mem., Inst. of Intergovt. Affairs, Queen's Univ. 1977–82; elected Que. Nat. Assembly for D'Arcy McGee 1979; Min. of Justice & Attorney Gen. of Que. 1985–88; Min. of Public Security 1987–88; author: 'Les grand arrêts de la jurisprudence constitutionnelle au Canada' 1974; co-author: 'Droit et Pauvreté au Québec' 1974; co-editor: 'The Law and the Poor in Canada' 1977, co-author 'Droit constitutionnel' 1982; Office: Palais de Justice, 1 rue Notre-Dame est., Montréal, Qué. H2Y 1B6.

**MARY-ROUSSELIÈRE, Rev. Guy,** B.ès L., M.A., o.m.i.; missionary priest; b. Le Mans (Sarthe), France 6 July 1913; s. René and Yvonne (Le Cardonnel) M-R.; e. Ecole du Sacré-Coeur, Univ. de Paris B.ès L. 1931; Séminaire St-Sulpice Paris 1931–33; Oblate Semy. La Brosse-Montceaux 1935–38; Univ. de Montréal M.A. 1965; came to Can. 1938; Missy. Chippewyan Indians (Déné) N. Man. until 1944; Missy. among Inuit since 1944; archaeol. work Arctic since 1958; mem. Hist. Sites & Monuments Bd. Can. 1981–84; recipient N. Sci. Award 1988; films incl. 'Light in the Darkness' 1957 (1st Prize Missy. Film Brussels 1964); 'Netsilik Series' 1963–67 (contbr.); author 'Les jeux de ficelle des Arviligjuarmiut' 1969; 'Qitdlarssuaq: L'histoire d'une migration polaire' 1980, English trans. by Alan Cooke 1991, German / Dutch / Greenlandic trans. by Univ. of Tübingen 1994; ed. 'Eskimo' mag. since 1953; Address: Catholic Mission, Pond Inlet, N.W.T. X0A 0S0.

**MARZARI, Hon. Darlene,** M.L.A., B.A., M.S.W.; politician; b. Toronto, On. 16 July 1943; d. William J. and Frances L. (Delrue) Smith; e. Univ. of Toronto B.A.; London Sch. of Economics, Dipl.Soc. Admin.; Univ. of B.C. M.S.W.; m. Dr. Stephen Straker s. Isabel and Robert Straker 8 April 1978; children: Francesca (Marzari), Robert and Daniel (Straker); MINISTER OF MUNICIPAL AFFAIRS, GOVERNMENT OF BRITISH COLUMBIA 1993– ; recreations: raising children; Office: Parliament Buildings, Victoria, B.C. V8V 1X4.

**MARZOLINI, Michael Joseph,** B.A.; pollster; b. Toronto, Ont. 20 Nov. 1957; s. Lou and Pamela (Kemp) M.; e. Univ. of Toronto, B.A. (Hons.) 1981; post-grad. studies: Kent State Univ.; Univ. of S. Calif.; Univ. of Michigan; CHAIRMAN, INSIGHT CANADA RESEARCH 1985– ; Computer Conceptualist, Multiple Access of Can. Ltd. (now Canada Systems Group) 1972–81; after apprenticing with both Republican & Democratic pollsters during 1980 U.S. election served as strategy advr. to 36 Candn. M.P.s 1980–84; pollster to the Premier of Ont. 1985; to the CTV Television Network 1988–92; to the Liberal Party of Canada 1993– ; frequent lectr. on public opinion, Univ. of Toronto, McMaster Univ., Kent State Univ.; frequent radio & TV commentator; holds record for fastest nation-wide public opinion poll taken in Can. (post-leaders debate – 1988 election); only pollster to accurately predict 1988 fed. election; Mem., Public Affairs Assn. of Can.; Candn. Assn. of Market Rsch. Orgns.; Profl. Market Rsch. Soc.; Toronto Bd. of Trade; author: 'Perspectives Canada' & numerous articles in popular & business mags.; co-author: 'Canadian Corporate Image Report'; recreations: cycling, studying political and military strategy, computers; Club: University; Office: 101 Yorkville Ave., Ste. 301, Toronto, Ont. M5R 1C1.

**MASCALL, Jennifer Wootton,** B.F.A.; choreographer; b. Winnipeg, Man. 11 Dec. 1952; d. David William Wootton and Elizabeth Mary (Blair) M.; e. York Univ. B.F.A. 1974; m. John Macfarlane 13 July 1984; children: Tobias, Matthew, Nicholas; ARTISTIC DIRECTOR, MASCALL DANCE 1989– ; Independent choreographer 1975–82; Co-founder & Co-Artistic Dir., EDAM 1982–89; Teacher, Stratford Festival 1975, EDAM 1982–89, Mount Allison summer school 1982, '83, S.F.U. 1986 (1 semester); national & internat. touring; choreography: 'The Shostakovich' 1993; 'I'll Leave The Back Door Open' 1992, 'The Lesson' 1992, 'Within These Four Walls' 1991, 'Cathedral,' 'New Material Only,' 'Carnival of the Animals' 1990, 'The Dumbfounding' 1989, 'Parade,' 'The Wash the Image and the Story' 1986, 'The Light at the End of the Tunnel May be the Other Train Coming Toward You,' 'Hurry Blurry' 'See Dot Quick' 1984, 'No Picnic, 'Acoustic Noose' 1981, 'All Flames are Waiting to Kill all Moths,' 'Smashed Carapace' 1979, 'Swank (Olors)', 'Unicycle Blues' 1978, 'Fatty Acids' 1977, 'Conduction' 1975; commissions: Van. New Music Soc.; Atlantic Dance, Nova Dance, Tamahnous, Autumn Angel theatres, Contemporary Dancers Can., Dancemakers, Expo 86 World Fest., Can. Dance Fest., World Council of Churches, Arts Umbrella Youth Dance Co.; Boards: BC. Status of the Artist Adv. Ctte. 1993–94; Dance Adv. Panel, Canada Council 1986–90; Can. Council Arts Awards Juries 1985–91; Vancouver Dance Ctr. Bd. 1986–87; Awards: Commemorative Medal for 125th Anniversary of Candn. Confederation 1992; Jesse Award 1988; Jacqueline Lemieux Award 1983; Dora Mavor Moore Award 1983; Ann O'Connor Award 1983; Clifford E. Lee Award 1982; var. grants, Ont. Arts Counc. & Can. Counc.; Editor: 'Footnotes' 1978; Russian Orthodox Church; Home: 1258 Haywood St., W. Vancouver, B.C.; Office: c/o St. Paul's Anglican Ch., 1130 Jervis St., Vancouver, B.C. V6E 2C7.

**MASHAAL, Victor,** B.Sc.; executive; b. Iraq 11 Sept. 1938; s. Menashi and Simha (Daniel) M.; e. Strathcona Acad. Montreal 1955; Mass. Inst. of Technol. B.Sc. 1959; m. Edna d. Albert Gareh 15 Apl. 1962; children: Robert, Richard, Joy; CHRMN. AND PRES. SENVEST CAPITAL INC. 1971– ; Vice Pres. and Dir. Yale Properties Group; Chrmn. Trenmore Printing; Office: 1140 Boul. de Maisonneuve W., Suite 1180, Montreal, Que. H3A 1M8.

**MASON, Alister Kenneth,** M.B.A., Ph.D., F.C.A., F.C.M.A.; chartered accountant; b. 29 Aug. 1939; e. Univ. of Toronto M.B.A. 1975; Univ. of Lancaster Ph.D. 1978; m. Susan d. Thomas and Edith McFadzean 7 June 1969; children: Janice, Craig; PARTNER, DELOITTE & TOUCHE 1978– ; articled with local firm 1957–61; var. positions Deloitte Haskins & Sells 1961–70; Assoc. Dir. of Rsch. then Rsch. Studies Dir., Candn. Inst. of C.A.s 1970–75; Rsch. Officer, Internat. Ctr. for Rsch. in Acctg., Univ. of Lancaster 1975–77; elected Fellow, Inst. of C.A.s of Ont. 1982; Soc. of Mngt. Accts. of Can. 1990; elected Life Mem., Candn. Bible Soc. 1993; Dir., Candn. Acad. Acctg. Assn. 1980–82 (Pres. 1981–82); Hon. Gen. Treas., Candn. Bible Soc. 1990–93; Presbyterian; Chair, Task Force on Not-for-Profit Orgns., Candn. Inst. of C.A.s 1989–94; author/co-author: 'The Development of International Financial Reporting Standards' 1978, 'Related Party Transactions' 1980, 'Guide to Accounting Pronouncements & Sources' 1985, '88, '91, 'Professional Judgment in Financial Reporting' 1988,'Excellence in Annual Reporting' 1991; Home: 23 Glenview Ave., Toronto, Ont. M4R 1P5; Office: 181 Bay St., Suite 1400, BCE Place, Toronto, Ont. M5J 2V1.

**MASON, Bryan Gordon,** B.A.; university administrator; b. Montreal, Que. 10 Nov. 1945; s. Robert Charles and Isabel Agnes (Smith) M.; e. Loyola H.S.; Loyola Coll., Univ. of Montreal, B.A. (Hons.) 1967; McGill Univ.; m. Maureen d. Arthur and Alice Bahen 5 Dec. 1964; children: Cynthia, Geoffrey; VICE-PRES., FINAN. & ADMIN., DALHOUSIE UNIV. 1986– ; Mngt. Training, Toronto-Dominion Bank 1964–65; Institutional Planner, Lakehead Univ. 1969–70; Extve. Asst. to Pres. 1970–72; Vice-Pres., Admin. 1973–86; Mem. Mngt. Ctte., Inter-Univ. Serv. Inc.; Mem. & Vice-Chair, Bd. of Dir., St. Joseph's Gen. Hosp. 1983–86; Mem. & Pres., Bd. of Dir., Thunder Bay Big Brothers 1978–82; Mem., Candn. Assn. of Univ. Bus. Offrs.; Atlantic Assn. of Univ. Bus. Offrs.; Counc. of Sr Admin. Offrs., Univs. of Ontario 1984–86; Home: 1225 Queen St., Halifax N.S. B3J 2H3; Office: Halifax, N.S. B3H 4H6.

**MASON, Douglas Laurence;** beverage industry executive; b. North Vancouver, B.C. 12 Sept. 1947; e. North Vancouver H.S. 1965; m. Carla Armstrong 15 Sept. 1991; e. North Vancouver H.S. 1965; CHAIRMAN, PRESIDENT & CHIEF EXECUTIVE OFFICER, CLEARLY CANADIAN BEVERAGE CORP. 1986– ; worked in food retailing 1965–76 incl. senior manager of one of Western Canada's leading grocery retail chains 1968–78; involved in two entreprenurial businesses 1978–85; partner in a consulting service that developed financing & mktg. plans for a variety of businesses in Texas, Illinios, B.C., Japan & Hong Kong 1984–85; Trustee, British Columbia Sports Hall of Fame; Dir., Clearly Candn. Beverage Corp.; Envirotech Systems Corp.; Commonwealth Gold Corp.; Vancouver's Financial Entrepreneur of the Year 1992; nominated Vancouver's Marketing Executive of the Year 1993; recreations: fishing, golf; Home: 3912 Marine Dr., West Vancouver, B.C. V7V 1N4; Office: 1900, 999 W. Hastings St., Vancouver, B.C. V6C 2W2.

**MASON, Gary Maclean;** journalist; b. Niagara Falls, Ont. 15 Aug. 1955; s. Jack Maclean and Norma Veronica (Burns) M.; e. St. Patrick's H.S. (Sarnia) 1974; Univ. of Waterloo, 2 yrs; Langara Coll. (Vancouver), 2 yr. journalism program; m. Barbara d. Dr. Struthers and Doris Gunn 10 Sept. 1983; children: Jordan, Geoffrey; CITY EDITOR, THE VANCOUVER SUN 1989– ; Reporter-editor, Canadian Press (Vanc.) 1982–84; Legislative Reporter, Victoria Times-Colonist 1985–86; Victoria Bureau Chief, present paper 1986–89; Columnist, Vancouver magazine 1985–86; recipient, Jack Webster Award for outstanding journalism (B.C.'s top journalism award) 1988; nominated for Southam President's award for reporting 1988; co-author: 'Fantasyland: Inside the Reign of Bill Vander Zalm' 1989; recreations: golf, basketball, tennis, squash; club: Vancouver Press; Home: 6471 Mara Cres., Richmond, B.C. V7C 2R1; Office: 2250 Granville St., Vancouver, B.C. V6H 3G2.

**MASON, Peter Leonard,** F.R.I., PLE, SIOR; real estate executive; e. Leaside H.S.; York Univ.; F.R.I.; Professional Land Economist (PLE); Soc. of Industrial & Office Realtors (SIOR). Dorothy; children: Sandra, Andrea, Joanna, Lesley; PRES., PETER L. MASON LIMITED REALTOR 1967– ; Branch Accountant, Royal Bank of Can. 1963; Industrial & Commercial Sales, Webb & Mason Limited 1965; numerous past executive positions with boards and associations incl. Past Pres. & Hon. Life Mem., Toronto and Ontario real estate boards; current: Mem., REBBA Task Force, Ont. Real Estate Asn. 1985– ; Pres., New America Network Canada; Adv. Bd., Salvation Army (Markham) 1991–94; Econ. Devel. Bd., Town of Markham 1994; Mem., Bd. of Trustees, Town of Markham Art Gall. Foundation; Hon. Life Mem., Ont. Real Estate Asn. 1982; Town of Markham Businessman of the Year 1989; Recipient of 1st Annual Anthony Roman Award for outstanding contributions to the Markham Business Community 1993/94; recreations: skiing, tennis; Office: 1 Valleybrook Dr., Ste. 200, Don Mills, Ont. M3B 2S7.

**MASON, Right Rev. Peter Ralph,** B.D., L.Th., M.A., D.Min., D.D. (Hon.); clergyman; educator; b. Brome, Qué. 30 Apr. 1943; s. Ralph V. and Dorothy Ida (Mullin) M.; e. Knowlton (Qué.) High Sch. 1960; McGill Univ. B.A. 1964, B.D. 1967, M.A. 1971; Princeton Theol. Semy. D. Min. 1983; Montreal Diocese Theol. College D.D. (Hon.) 1988; m. Carmen d. Stanley and Ella Ruddock 28 Aug. 1965; children: Patricia, Sarah, Paul; TENTH BISHOP OF THE DIOCESE OF ONTARIO 1992– ; o. Deacon and Priest Ang. Diocese Montréal 1967; Curate, St. Matthews Ch. Montréal 1967–69; Incumbent St. Luke's Ch. Hemmingford, Qué. 1969–71; Rector: St. Clement's Ch. Verdun, Qué. 1971–75; St. Peter's Ch. Town of Mount Royal, Qué. 1975–80; St. Paul's Ch. Halifax 1980–85; Principal, Wycliffe Coll. 1985–92; Lectr. in Homiletics and Liturgics, Atlantic Sch. of Theol. 1983–85; Prov. Chaplain, St. John's Ambulance (N.S.); recreations: golf, skiing; Home: Bishop's Lodge, 73 Seaforth Rd., Kingston, Ont. K7M 1E1; Office: 90 Johnson St., Kingston, Ont. K7L 1X7.

**MASON, R. Larry,** B.A.; banker; b. Winnipeg, Man. 12 June 1938; e. Univ. of Man. B.A. 1960; m. Diana 27 May 1967; children: Kelly, Stephen; Senior Vice-Pres., Retail Securities & Investments, The Bank of Nova Scotia 1989–93, retired; former Chrmn., Scotia Securities Inc.; former Dir., ScotiaMcLeod Inc.; Scotia Investment Management Ltd.; Supvr. Invests. The Bank of Nova Scotia 1967, Asst. Gen. Mgr. Invests. 1973, Gen. Mgr. Invests. 1977, Gen. Mgr. Comm. Banking 1978, Vice Pres. and Gen. Mgr. Man. and N.W. Ont. Region 1978, Sr. Vice Pres. and Gen. Mgr. B.C. & Yukon Region 1979; Sr. Vice Pres., Investment Banking North America 1984–89.

**MASSAM, Bryan Hazelwood,** B.Sc., M.A., Ph.D., F.R.G.S.; educator; social scientist; b. England 8 Apr. 1940; s. the late Richard William and the late Florence Hazelwood (Hunter) M.; e. Univ. of Liverpool, Cert. in Ed. 1961; Univ. of London, Cert. in Teaching of Geog. and Academic Dipl. in Geog., 1962; B.Sc. (Special), 1966; McMaster Univ., M.A. 1967; Ph.D. 1969; children: Alexandra Nicole; Laurent Nigel; PROFESSOR, YORK UNIV. 1980– ; Teacher, Kent, England 1962–66; World Friends Internat. Service for Youth (part-time), London, England 1963–67; Asst. Prof. of Geog., McGill Univ. 1969–73; Consultant, La Direction Scientifique, Soc. d'Economique et Mathematiques Appliquees, Paris 1970; Consultant, UN Develop. Progr., Seoul, Korea 1971; Assoc. Prof., McGill Univ. 1974–77; Consultant, Environment Canada 1974–75; joint appt. Geog. and Sch. of Urban Planning, McGill Univ. 1974–77; Short-term Visiting Lectr., Singapore Univ. 1976; Assoc. Prof., Geog. and Soc. Sci. Div., York Univ. 1977–80; Academic Visitor, Lent Term, London Sch. of Economics 1986; Academic Visitor, Michaelmas Term, London Sch. of Economics 1988; Visiting Prof., Inst. for Urban and Regional Studies, Hebrew Univ., Jerusalem; Dean of Research, York Univ. 1980–86; Chair, Dept. of Geography, York Univ. 1987– ; Visiting Prof., Centre of Urban Planning and Environmental Management, Univ. of Hong Kong Mar.-Apr. 1992; Ed., 'Progress in Planning' 1988– ; author 'Models of Urban Structure' 1970; 'The Spatial Structure of Administrative Systems' 1972; 'Location and Space in Social Administration' 1975; 'Spatial Search: applications to planning problems in the public sector' 1980; 'Multi-Criteria Decision Making (MCDM) Techniques in Planning' 1988; 'Environmental Assessment in Canada: theory and practice' 1989; 'The Right Place: Shared Responsibility and the Location of Public Facilities' 1993; author and co-author of numerous papers, chapters and reviews in journals and books; recreations: reading; painting; mountain-walking; Office: 4700 Keele St., North York, Ont. M3J 1P3.

**MASSE, Hon. Marcel,** P.C., B.Péd.; former politician; b. St. Jean-de-Matha, Qué. 27 May 1936; s. Rosaire and Angeline (Clermont) M.; e. École Normale Jacques-Cartier, Montréal B.Péd. 1958; Univ. de Montréal Comtemporary Hist. 1960; Inst. of Pol. Sci. Paris, France 1961; Sorbonne, Paris 1961; City of London Coll., London, Eng. Pol. & Econ. Hist. of Commonwealth 1962; Institut Européen d'Administration des Affaires, Fontainebleau, France Internat. Adm. & Mktg. 1978; m. Cécile d. René and Clémentine (Roch) Martin 30 Aug. 1960; children: Jean-Martin, Marie-Hélène; CONSEILLER PRINCIPAL, LE GROUPE CFC (Management et resources humaines); Hist. Teacher, Lanaudière Regional Sch. Bd. Joliette, Qué. 1962–66; el. M.N.A. 1966; Min. of State for Edn. Qué. 1966, Min. Responsible for Welcoming Heads of State, Candn. Corp. for 1967 World Exhn. Montréal 1967, Min. Responsible for Civil Service Qué. 1968–69, Min. for Planning & Devel., Min. for Intergovt'al Affairs, Qué. 1968–70, M.N.A. 1970–73; Project Mgr. Lavalin-UN Devel. Prog. 1974–76, Vice Pres. Lavalin-Econosult Inc. 1977–79, Vice Pres. Lavalin Services Inc. 1979–80, Corporate Vice Pres. Bus. Devel. & Mktg. Lavalin Inc. Montréal 1981–84; Min. of Communications, Can. 1984–86; Min. of Energy, Mines & Resources 1986–89; Re-Apptd. Min. of Communications 1989–91 and Min. Resp. for la Francophonie 1990; Min. of Defence 1991–93 (resigned); Apptd. Secy. to the Cabinet for Fed.-Prov. Relations 1993; served Lanaudière Summer Festival; Institut d'engagement politique; Candn. Found. Refugees; Found. Candn. Writers; Montréal Symphony Orch.; Théâtre du Nouveau Monde; Jeunesses Musicales du Can.; Wilfrid-Pelletier Found.; Sworn to the Privy Council 1984; recreations: reading, music, fishing, skiing; Office: 300, rue Léo-Pariseau, Bureau 800, C.P. 1086, Montréal, Qué. H2W 2P4.

**MASSÉ, Hon. Marcel,** P.C., O.C., Q.C., B.A., LL.B., B.Phil.; politician; b. Montreal, Que. 23 June 1940; e. Univ. of Montreal B.A. 1958; McGill Univ. LL.B. 1961; Univ. of Warsaw Dipl. in Internat. Law 1962; Oxford Univ. B.Phil. (Econ. 1966; Ecole des Hautes Etudes Commerciales de Montréal Dipls. in international affairs, Spanish, German, Italian & Econ.) m. Josée M'Baye 17 July 1965; four children; PRESIDENT, QUEEN'S PRIVY COUNCIL FOR CANADA; MINISTER OF INTERGOVERNMENTAL AFFAIRS and MINISTER RESPONSIBLE FOR PUBLIC SERVICE RENEWAL, GOVT. OF CANADA 1993– ; called to Bar of Que. 1963; served in Adm. and Econ., World Bank, Washington 1967–71; Econ. Advisor, Privy Council, Ottawa 1971–73; Depy. Min. of Finance, N.B. 1973–74, Chrmn. of Cabinet Secretariat N.B. 1974–77; Depy. Secy. to Cabinet for Fed.-Prov. Relations, Ottawa 1977–79, Depy. Secy. to Cabinet (Operations) 1979; Clerk of Privy Council and Secy. to Cabinet 1979–80; Pres., Candn. Internat. Devel. Agency (CIDA) 1980–82, 1989–93; Under-Secy. of State for External Affairs 1982–85; Candn. Extve. Dir., Internat. Monetary Fund 1985–89; recipient: World Univ. Service Scholarship in Internat. Law 1961; Rhodes Scholarship in Philosophy, History & Economics 1963; Nuffield Coll. Scholarship in Economics, Oxford 1966; published works: 'The International Law of Nationalization' (thesis in Internat. Law); 'The Development of the Manufacturing Industry in Senegal' (thesis in Indus. Econs. & Develop.); 'An Evaluation of Investment Appraisal Methods' (working paper published by World Bank); Office: Rm. 165, East Block, House of Commons, Ottawa, Ont. K1A 0A6.

**MASSÉ, Maurice A.;** financial executive; b. Windsor, Ont. 15 Mar. 1913; s. Joseph Jacob and Agnes Adele (Thibeault) M.; e. Acad. Provost; Aca. Piché; m. Gabrielle d. Angus and Clara Mickie 10 March 1945; one s.: Bernard Angus; PRES., MAURICE A. MASSÉ INC. FINAN. CONSULTANTS 1975– ; joined Bank of Montreal 10 Feb. 1929; Asst. Gen. Mgr., Que. Div. 1966; Vice Pres. 1967; Sr. Vice-Pres., Head Office 1968; Extve. Vice-Pres., Domestic Banking 1968; early retirement 1975; Chrmn., General Investment Corp. 1975; Timminco Ltd. 1981; Que. Blue Cross Group of Cos. (5) 1980– (Dir. 1973– ); Dir., Timminco Ltd.; Judo Investments Ltd.; Y.K.K. Canada Ltd.; Frisco Bay Indus. of Can. Ltd.; M.A. Massé Inc.; Timmins Investments Ltd.; Hon. Mem., Candn. Inst. of Internat. Affairs; Bd. Mem., Found. Montreal YMCA (also Chrmn., Endowment & Bequest Ctte.); Chrmn., Heritage Club, YMCA; Dir., McGill Assoc.; Fellowship of Honour Award, National Y.W.C.A.; recreations: golf; clubs: Mount Bruno Country, Laval-sur-le-Lac Golf & Country, Saint James's of Montreal; Home: 1212 Pine Ave. W., Apt. 1802, Montreal, Qué. H3G 1A9; Office: 1000 de la Gauchetiére West, Suite 3100, Montréal, Qué. H3B 4W5.

**MASSE, Yvon H.,** B.A., B.A.Sc., P.Eng.; transportation executive; b. Montreal, Que. 3 July 1935; s. Romeo and Gracia (Richard) M.; e. Univ. de Montréal Coll. Ste-Marie B.A. 1956, Ecole Polytechnique B.A.Sc. (Elec. Eng.) 1961; m. Adrienne d. Florian and Alice Habel 1 Aug. 1959; children: Jean-Yves, Sylvie; EXTVE. VICE PRES. & CHIEF FINANCIAL OFFICER, CANADIAN NATIONAL 1987– ; Chrmn., Pres. & Dir. CANAT Ltd.; Chrmn., E.I.D.S. Electronic Identification Systems Ltd.; Dir., Canac Consultants Ltd.; CANAPREV Inc.; Grand Trunk Corp.; Duluth, Winnipeg & Pacific Railway; The Toronto Terminals Railway Co.; mem. CN Investment Ctte.; CN Real Estate Ctte.; CN Exploration Inc.; C.N. (France) S.A.; Innotermodal Inc.; joined CN Rsch. and Devel. Dept. 1961, served in Analytical Services Winnipeg 1963–65 and Montreal 1965–70, Regional Mgr. Adm. and Tech. Services Montreal 1970, Gen. Mgr. Passenger Sales & Services 1972, Vice Pres. Mgmt. Services 1974, Vice Pres. CN Trucking and Express 1976, Vice Pres., St. Lawrence Region CN Rail 1977; Sr. Corporate Vice Pres. & Chief Financial Officer 1982; Sr. Vice Pres., Financial Planning & Admin. 1986; Sr. Vice Pres. and Chief Financial Officer 1987; Extve. Vice-Pres. and Chief Finan. Offr. 1993; mem., Corp. Que. Engs.; Clubs: Canadian Railway; St-Denis; Traffic; Royal Montreal Golf; Home: 169 Fairview, Dollard des Ormeaux, Qué. H9A 1V5; Office: (P.O. Box 8100) 935 de La Gauchetiere St. W., Montréal, Qué. H3C 3N4.

**MASSEL, Stephen W.,** B.B.A., C.A., C.M.A.; financial executive; b. Ottawa, Ont. 3 June 1958; s. William Joseph and Patricia Anne (Kelly) M.; e. Lakehead Univ. B.B.A. 1982; m. Rosetta. Edward and Eva DeBartolo 2 July 1983; children: Christina, Mark, Robert; CHIEF FINANCIAL OFFICER, IMUTEC CORPORATION 1992– ; joined Ernst & Young 1982; C.A. 1985; left as Audit Manager 1987; Manager, Taxation, Unisys Corp. 1987–88; Mgr. of Taxation & Treas., Baxter Corp. 1988–89; Dir. of Taxation & Treas. & Asst. Sec.-Treas. 1989–92; Mem., C.I.C.A., S.M.A.; recreations: golf, hockey; clubs: Board of Trade Country; Home: 137 Jackman Cres., Woodbridge, Ont. L4L 6N9; Office: 1285 Morningside Ave., Scarborough, Ont. M1B 3W2.

**MASSEY, Geoffrey,** B.A., M.Arch., F.R.A.I.C., A.I.B.C., R.C.A.; architect; b. London, Eng. 29 Oct. 1924; s. late Raymond and Margery (Fremantle) M.; came to Can. 1942; e. Harvard Coll. B.A. 1949; Harvard Graduate Sch. of Design M.Arch. 1952; m. Ruth Maud d. late Lawrence Killam 21 Sept. 1955; children: Raymond Hart, Vincent Lawrence, Nathaniel Killam, Eliza Ann; PRINCIPAL, GEOFFREY MASSEY ARCHITECT 1985– ; Partner, Coal Harbour Architectural Group 1975–85; Princ. private arch. practice 1956–63, 1972–75; Partner, Erickson/Massey 1963–72; Ald. City of Vancouver and mem. Greater Vancouver Regional Dist. Bd. 1973–75; Trustee, Vancouver Art Gallery 1973–80; mem. Granville Island Trust Vancouver 1975–84; rec'd numerous arch. awards; served with Candn. Army 1943–45; Fellow, Royal Architectural Inst. of Can.; Candn. Acad. of Arts; recreations: skiing, sailing; Clubs: Vancouver; W. Vancouver Yacht; Address: 1012 – 20th St., W. Vancouver, B.C. V7V 3Z1.

**MASSEY, Hart Parkin Vincent,** M.A. (Oxon.), B.Arch., R.C.A., F.R.A.I.C.; b. Toronto, Ont. 30 March 1918; s. Charles Vincent and Alice Stuart (Parkin) M.; e. St. Alban's Sch. Washington, D.C. 1929; Upper Can. Coll. Toronto 1935; Balliol Coll. Oxford Univ. M.A. 1939; Univ. of Toronto B.Arch 1951 (Pilkington Scholarship 1951, R.A.I.C. Arch. Guild Gold Medal); m. Frances Melodie d. Henry Willis-O'Connor 4 Aug. 1947; children: Lillias Caroline, Jonathan Hart; arch. practice Ottawa 1953–70; recipient Massey Medals for Arch. 1958, 1964; Ministry of Pub. Works Design Award 1968; Ont. Assn. Archs. Ottawa Chapter Design Awards (3); Chrmn. Massey Foundation; Sr. Fellow Massey Coll. Univ. of Toronto; craftsman (lost wax casting); author 'Travels with "Lionel"'; co-author, 'The Craftsman's Way'; served with RCAF Brit., France, Belgium, Holland 1939–45; Croix de Guerre (France); mem. Ont. Assn. Archs.; Fellow, Royal Architectural Institute of Can.; Royal Candn. Acad.; recreations: books, dogs, travel, European waterways; Home: Durham House, R.R.1, Port Hope, Ont. L1A 3V5.

**MASSEY, R. Bruce,** C.D.; management consultant; b. Montreal, Que. March 1933; s. Robert Neill and Irene Elizabeth (Hannaford) M.; e. McGill Univ. C.I.M.A. 1969; m. Carol (Bedard) 16 June 1956; children: Neill, Michelle, Nancy, Samantha; PRES. AND CHIEF EXTVE. OFFR., BRUCE MASSEY AND PARTNERS INC. 1988– ; joined Standard Electric Time Co. of Canada Ltd. 1955–65; Pres. and Chief Extve. Offr. Lab Volt Ltd. and Lab Volt (Quebec) Ltd. 1965–75; Corporate Vice Pres. Mktg. and Dir. Buck Engineering Co. Inc. Farmingdale, N.J. 1973–75; Founding Partner, Pres. and Chrmn. Massey Charbonneau Inc. 1975–88; served with Candn. Army Militia Royal Montreal Regt. 1955–65, rank Maj.; mem. Citizens Review Panel, Un. Way Oakville Halton Region; mem. Bd. Trade Metrop. Toronto; Bd. Trade Oakville; Nat. Assn. Corporate & Profl. Recruiters Inc.; recreations: sailing, squash; Clubs: Royal St. Lawrence Yacht; Oakville Club; Oakville Yacht Squadron; Home: 1138 Morrison Heights Dr., Oakville, Ont. L6J 4J1; Office: 1104, 330 Bay St., Toronto, Ont. M5H 2S8.

**MASSICOTTE, Guy,** L.ès L., M.A., Ph.D.; exécutif; né Montréal, Qué. 23 avril 1946; f. Maurice et Gabrielle (Daoust) M.; é. Coll. Ste-Marie Montréal B.A. 1966; Univ. de Montréal L.ès. L. 1969, M.A. 1970, Ph.D. 1974; ép. Jocelyne f. Ozani Pellerin 10 mai 1970; Vice-président à la planification, Univ. du Québec 1988– , Dir. de la recherche, Comn. Gauvin (Assces Automobile) 1971; Professeur, Univ. du Québec à Rimouski 1973, Dir. du Bureau Recherche et Développement 1976, Dir. des Communications et de la Planification 1980; Recteur, Univ. du Québec à Rimouski 1982–87; auteur (en collaboration avec Marie Beaupré) 'Edouard Lacroix Pionnier de l'entrepreneurship beauceron'; 'L'histoire-problème: La méthode de Lucien Febvre' 1981; Adresse: 990 blvd. St-Germain, Ouest, Rimouski, Qué. G5L 8Y9; Bureau: 2875 boul. Laurier, Sainte-Foy, Qué. G1V 2M3.

**MASSICOTTE, Paul J.,** B.Com., C.A.; real estate development executive; b. Ste. Anne, Man. 10 Sept. 1951; s. Louis and Armande (Tougas) M.; e. Univ. of Man. B.Com. 1974; C.A. Man. 1976, Que. 1977; m. Suzanne d. Rolande and Emile Mondor 3 June 1972; children: Melanie, Justin; PRES. ALEXIS NIHON CANADA INC. 1985– ; Dir. Candn. Inst. Pub. Real Estate Cos.; La Solidarité (a Qué. based Ins. Co.); Founding Dir. and Bd. Mem., The Urban Devel. Inst. Que.; joined Coopers & Lybrand Winnipeg 1974–76, Montreal 1976–77; Extve. Vice Pres. John A. Flanders Ltd. Winnipeg 1977–79; Extve. Vice Pres. and Chief Financial Offr. Marwest Group Winnipeg 1979–83, Duraps Corp. 1983–85; Vice Pres. Finance and Dir. Alexis Nihon Group 1985; recreations: golf, jogging, racquetball, skiing, reading; Club: Mount-Royal; Office: 6380 Côte de Liesse, Montreal, Que. H4T 1E3.

**MASSOBRIO, Giorgio;** mining executive; b. Genoa, Italy 15 Nov. 1927; s. Eugenio and Maria Emilia (Leumann) M.; e. Univ. of Genoa, electr. engr. degree 1951; Harvard Univ., adv. mngt. prog.; m. Carla Serra 18 Oct 1958; children: Simona, Alessandra; PRES., QUEBEC CARTIER MINING CO. 1980– ; various positions, Italsider 1951–77; Extve. Vice-Pres., Dir. & Mem., Mngt. Ctte. 1977; Vice-Pres., Met-Chem Can. Inc. 1977–79; Mem., Bd. of Dir., Mining Assn. of Can.; Bd. of Gov., Le Conseil du Patronat; Dir., Candn. Mining & Metall. Found.; Past Dir., Italian Metall. Assn.; Mem., Candn. Inst. of Mining & Metall.; Am. Iron & Steel Engrs.; Am. Mngt. Assn.; Am. Inst. of Mining, Metall. & Petrol. Engrs.; Clubs: The Royal St Lawrence Yacht, The Mount Royal; Home: 180 Geneva Cres., Town of Mt Royal, Que. H3R 2A8; Office: 1801 McGill Coll., Ste. 1400, Montreal, Que. H3A 2N4.

**MASSON, Henri L.,** LL.D.; artist; b. Spy (Namur), Belgium 10 Jan. 1907; s. Armand and Bertha (Solot) M.; e. Assumption Coll. Windsor, Ont. LL.D. 1954; came to Can. 1921; m. Germaine d. Arthur and Obeline St. Denis 27 Aug. 1929; children: Armande, Carl, Jacques; solo exhns. incl.; Picture Loan Soc. Toronto 1938;

Galerie Le Caveau Ottawa 1939; Galerie l'Art Français Montréal 1941, 1968, 1971; Contempo Studios Ottawa 1942; Laing Art Gallery Toronto 1943; Robertson Galleries Ottawa 1946; Galerie l'Atelier Québec 1952; Gallery Candn. Art Calgary 1954; Walter Klinkhoff Gallery Montréal 1964, 1974, 1976, 1980; Art Lenders Montréal 1967; Wallack's Gallery Ottawa 1967; Art Emporium Vancouver 1974, 1976; Downstairs Gallery Edmonton 1977; Kinsman Robinson Galleries Toronto 1981; Masters Gallery Calgary 1982; Galerie Vincent, Ottawa 1984; Kinsman Robinson Galleries, Toronto 1987; exhib. of pastels Galerie Vincent, Ottawa 1989; Mihausgalleries, Hudson 1990; rep. internat. exhns. incl.: New York World's Fair 1939, Aspects Contemporary Painting in Can. Andover, Mass. 1942, Internat. Water Colour Exhn. Brooklyn 1943, Biennale de Rio de Janeiro 1945, 1946, UNESCO Paris 1946, 6 Candn. Painters W. Palm Beach, Fla. 1947, nat. Gallery Arts Washington, D.C. 1950, London (Eng.) Museum 1950, Biennale de Sao Paulo 1951, Colombo Internat. Exhn. Modern Art New Delhi 1952, Osaka World's Fair 1970; rep. numerous perm. colls. incl. Nat. Gallery Can., Musée de la Prov. de Qué., Art Gallery Ont. and other Candn. galleries, Nat. Gallery Caracas, Museum Vinadelmar, Chile, Bezalel Museum jerusalem, Hirshorn Museum Washington, D.C.; art teacher various ednl. instns. 1945–65; rep. documentary Nat. Film Bd. 'Peintres du Québec' 1942; various TV appearances; Can. Post stamp issued 1974 'Skaters in Hull'; subject 4 books: 'Henri Masson' by Hughes de Jouvancourt 1969; 'La vision d'un Peintre' by Claude Bouchard' 1975; 'Henri Masson' by Marcel Gingras 1981; various book and mag. illustrations; rep. UNICEF Calendar 1972; mem. Candn. Group Painters; Candn. Soc. Painters in Water Colours; Candn. Soc. Graphic Arts; Ont. Soc. Artists; elected R.C.A. 1989; recreations: gardening, music, reading; Address: 1870 Ferncroft Cres., Ottawa, Ont. K1H 7B5.

**MASTERMAN, Jack Verner,** B. Com.; insurance executive; b. Calgary, Alta. 8 Aug. 1930; s. late Lawrence Arthur and late Mary Francis Georgina (Robinson) M.; e. Kelvin H.S., Winn.; Univ. of Manitoba B. Com. 1953; m. Theresa Ann Bezaire; children: Mary Christine (Murray), Lawrence Richard, Sheila Claire (Macdonald), Keith Charles, Derek Martin; CHRMN., THE MUTUAL LIFE ASSURANCE CO. OF CANADA 1993– ; joined Mutual Life Assurance in 1953; Actuarial Asst., 1957; Asst. Actuary, 1960; Assoc. Actuary, 1963; Actuary, 1966; Extve. Offr. (Individual Ins.), 1969; Vice Pres. Operations, 1972; Vice Pres. Individual Ins., 1975; Extve. Vice Pres. 1978; Dir. 1980; Pres. & Chief Oper. Offr. 1982; Pres. & C.E.O. 1985; Chrmn. & C.E.O. 1989; Fellow, Candn. Inst.of Actuaries; Fellow, Soc. of Actuaries; Clubs: National (Toronto); Rideau (Ottawa); Home: 2 Tweedsmuir Court, Kitchener, Ont. N2A 3K8; Office: 227 King St. S., Waterloo, Ont. N2J 4C5.

**MASTERS, Carlton A.;** banker; b. Jamaica 13 Sept. 1948; s. Theodore Augustus M.; e. St. Mary's Coll. Jamaica; Univ. of Miami (Fla.) Diploma Mngmt. Studies; Queen's Univ. Kingston postgrad. studies; Pace Univ. N.Y. postgrad. studies; m. Berjuhi d. Aksor Kassardjian 2 July 1983; one d. Vanessa; 2 step-sons: Rafique and Varoujan Symonette; Depy. Min. & Agent General for Ontario to the United States 1991; Life Underwriter National Life of Canada and Life of Jamaica; joined Bank of Montreal in 1974 serving Toronto, New York City, Bahamas, Kingston, Jamaica, Toronto and Hamilton, Ont.; apptd. Vice Pres. Bank of Montreal, Candn. Internat. Operations, former Chrmn. Candn. Nat. Mem. Group Soc. Worldwide Interbank Financial Telecommunications; former Dir. Stadium Corp. of Ontario Ltd.; former Chrmn. Hunger Project; Trustee Nelson Mandella Fund; former Dir. African Internat. Council; past Pres. Black Bus. & Profl. Assn.; former mem. Fed. Bus. Devel. Bank; Ethnocultural Adv. Ctte. Toronto; Bd. Trade Metrop. Toronto; Assoc. Chair 1990 Areawide Campaign Un. Way of Greater Toronto, Chrmn. 1990 Cricket Match, Depy. Campaign Chrmn. 1991; former Dir.: Toronto Pops Orch.; former Candn. Stage; former Oriole Community Centre; mem., Candn. Olympic Assn.; Hon. mem., Candn. Club of New York.

**MASTERS, Donald Campbell Charles,** M.A., Ph.D., D.C.L., F.R.S.C. (1953); university prof.; b. Shelburne, Ont. 8 Feb. 1908; s. Rev. Charles Keith, M.C., and Jean Campbell (Paterson) M.; e. Univ. of Toronto, B.A. 1930, M.A. 1931, MacKenzie Fellowship in Hist. 1931–32; Oxford Univ., Ph.D. 1935 (I.O.D.E. Overseas Scholarship); D.C.L. Bishop's Univ. 1975; m. Marjorie Winnifred, d. Frederick Harold Walker, 9 Sept. 1942; children: Margaret, Jane, Mary Ann, Lois, Charles; holder of post-doctorial Fellowship, Social Science Res. Council 1936–37; Lectr. in Hist., Queen's Univ., 1938–39; Un. Coll., Winnipeg, 1939–41; Asst. Prof. 1941–44; Prof. of Hist., Bishop's Univ., 1944–66; Prof. Candn. Hist. Univ. Guelph 1966–74; Visiting Prof. Simon Fraser Univ. 1974–75; Prof. Emeritus, Univ. of Guelph 1977; mem., Canadian History Association (mem. of Council 1956–59); Canadian Institute of Internat. Affairs (Chrmn., Sherbrooke-Lennoxville Br. 1947); author: 'The Reciprocity Treaty of 1854' 1937; 'The Rise of Toronto' 1947; 'The Winnipeg General Strike' 1950; 'Bishop's University: The First Hundred Years' 1950; 'A Short History of Canada' 1958; 'Canada in World Affairs' (Vol. VIII, 1953–1955) 1959; 'Protestant Church Colleges in Canada' 1966; co-author (with Marjorie W. Masters) 'Ten Rings on the Oak Mountain – Nicolls Family Story' 1987; del. to Ang. Gen. Synod, 1965, 1969, 1971, 1975, 1977, 1980, 1983; Anglican; Address: 19 Monticello Cres., Guelph, Ont. N1G 2M1.

**MASTERS, Jack G.;** mayor; b. Fort William, Ont. 27 Sept. 1931; s. John and Janet Mary (Winn) M.; e. Port Arthur Collegiate; m. Kathleen d. Charles and Emily Whatley 4 Sept. 1953; children: Susan, Diane, Gerald, Scott; Mayor, City of Thunder Bay 1985; Broadcaster 1952–77 (8 yrs. radio, 17 years TV); became vice-pres. & sales mgr., 2 local TV stations; Sales Mgr., 8-office general insurance agency 1977–80; Mem., H. of C. 1980–84 (served as Parlty. Sec. to two ministers; returned to insur. business 1984–85; Past Pres., Thunder C. of C.; Past Bd. of Dir., Confederation Coll.; extensive volunteer work; Mem., Liberal Party of Can.; Italian Mutual Benefit Soc.; Elks Lodge; Moose Lodge; Thunder Bay Twins Sr. Hockey Team; recreations: recreational hockey, bridge; club: Rotary (Hon. mem.); Home: 153 Whalen St., Thunder Bay, Ont. P7A 7H9.

**MASTERS, John Alan,** B.A., M.Sc.; geologist; petroleum executive; b. Shenandoah, Iowa 20 Sept. 1927; s. Alan Dunning and Maxine Lauretta (Day) M.; e. Yale Univ., B.A. 1948; Colo. Univ., M.Sc. 1951; m. lenora d. Don and Hilda Johnson 4 Nov. 1977; children: Charles, Barbara, Alan, Robert, James; Chrmn., Canadian Hunter Exploration Ltd. 1973; Dir. Biotechnica International; served U.S. Atomic Energy Comm. 1951–53; Kerr-McGee Corp. 1953–67, Mgr. Uranium Explor., Chief Geol. Oil & Gas, discovered Ambrosia Lake uranium deposit (largest in USA); Pres. Kerr-McGee of Canada 1967–73; discovered Elmworth (largest gas field in Can.); mem. Ind. Adv. Ctte. Earth Sci's Faculty Stanford Univ.; author 'The Hunters' 1980; various articles prof. jours.; mem. Am. Assn. Petrol. Geols.; Candn. Soc. Petrol. Geols.; recreations: skiing, windsurfing, reading; Home: P.O. Box 20 Site 20, R.R.2, Calgary, Alta. T2P 2G5.

**MASTERS, Roy George,** B.Sc., B.(Med.)Sc.; M.D., FRCSC (Gen. Surgery); FRCSC (Cardiothoracic Surg.); FACS; b. St. John's, Nfld. 8 Aug. 1953; s. Samuel James and Margaret Alice (Dicks) M.; e. Bishop's Coll. 1970; Meml. Univ. of Nfld., B.Sc. 1974, B.(Med.)Sc. 1976, M.D. 1978; CARDIAC SURG., UNIV. OF OTTAWA HEART INST. 1987– ; Asst. Prof. of Surgery, Univ. of Ottawa 1988– ; Intern, Univ. of Ottawa 1978–79; Chief Resident, Univ. of Ottawa 1984–85; Cons. Cardiac Surg., Children's Hosp. of E. Ont.; mem. Ottawa Heart Inst. Transplant and Artificial Heart Teams; Program Dir., Cardiovascular and Thoracic Surgery 1991– ; rec'd Govt. of Nfld. Scholarship 1974; Physicians' Services Inc. Found. Rsch. Grant 1987–89; Mosby Award 1978; mem. Candn. and Ont. Med. Assn.s; Candn. Cardiocascular Soc.; Am. Coll. of Chest Phys. (FCCP); American College of Surgeons (F.A.C.S.); author of var. publs. in sci. jours. of surg.; Home: 79 – 263 Botanica Priv., Ottawa, Ont. K1Y 4P9; Office: 1053 Carling Ave., Ottawa, Ont. K1Y 4E9.

**MATAR, Said E.,** B.Sc., M.Sc., P.Eng., Ph.D.; university professor, administrator; b. Alexandria, Egypt 2 Apr. 1934; s. Elsayed M. and Badria Korayem (Ramadan) M.; e. Alexandria Univ. B.Sc. 1957; Oklahoma State Univ. M.Sc. 1961; Northwestern Univ. Ph.D. 1966; m. Mary A. d. late, Bridget (Mackey) and Thomas Fennell 16 March 1973; children: Sidky Y., Nouri D.; PROF. OF MECHANICAL ENGINEERING, RYERSON POLYTECHNICAL UNIV. 1985– ; Asst. Prof., Univ. of Alexandria 1966–68; postdoctoral fellow, Univ. of Toronto 1968–70; Instr., Dept. of Mech. Engr., Ryerson 1970–85; Dir. of Tech. Studies 1980–82; Dept. Chrmn. 1989– ; Treas. & mem., Extve. Ctte., St. Lawrence Section of ASEE 1976–77; Representative, Continuing Engineering Studies Div., St. Lawrence Section of the ASEE 1977–80; Mem., Ryerson's Academic Council 1984–86 and 1992– ; Mem., Extve. Ctte., Ryerson Faculty Assn. 1986–87; Mem., Ryerson's Academic Standards Ctte. 1989– ; Mem., Engineering Accreditation Team, Tulane University 1989; Mem., Engineering Accreditation Team, Univ. of Regina 1993; Mem. Experience Requirement Ctte., Profl. Engrs. Ont. 1993– ; Mem., Academic Requirement Ctte., Assn. of Profl. Engrs. of Ont. (A.P.E.O.) 1984–93; Chrmn., Profl. Practice & Ethics Sub-Ctte. 1986–93; U.A.R. scholarship to study for Ph.D.; Mem., A.P.E.O.; Home: Scarborough, Ont.; Office: 350 Victoria St., Toronto, Ont. M5B 2K3.

**MATAS, David,** M.A., B.A.(Juris), B.C.L.; lawyer; b. Winnipeg, Man. 29 Aug. 1943; s. Harry and Esther (Steiman) M.; e. Univ. of Man. B.A. 1964; Princeton Univ. M.A. 1965; Oxford Univ. B.A.(Juris) 1967, B.C.L. 1968; Middle Temple UK Barrister 1969; called to Bar of Man. 1971; private law practice in refugee immigration and human rights 1979– ; Law Clk. Chief Justice Supreme Court of Can. 1968–69; mem. foreign ownership working group Govt. Can. 1969; articled with Thompson, Dorfman & Sweatman 1970–71; special asst. Solr. Gen. Can. 1971–72; assoc. Schwartz, McJannet, Weinberg 1973–79; mem. Candn. del. to UN Gen. Assembly 1980; Task Force Immigration Practices & Procedures 1980–81; Lectr. in Constitutional Law McGill Univ. 1972–73; Lectr.: Introductory Econ., Candn. Econ. Problems Univ. of Man. 1982, Internat. Law 1985, Civil Liberties 1986–88, Immigration & Refugee Law 1989– ; Dir. Internat. Defence & Aid Fund for S. Africa in Can. 1990–91; Co-chair Candn. Helsinki Watch Group 1985– ; Legal Co-ord. Eng. Speaking Candn. Sect. Amnesty Internat. 1980– ; Chair League for Human Rights, Bnai B'rith Can. 1983–85, Vice Pres. 1987–89, Sr. Counsel 1989– ; Chair Constitutional & Internat. Law Candn. Bar Assn. 1979–82; Dir. Man. Assn. Rights & Liberties 1983–87; Chair Legal Ctte. War Crimes Candn. Jewish Cong. 1981–84; Councillor Internat. Comn. Jurists Candn. Sect. 1983– ; Pres., Candn. Council for Refugees 1991– ; Dir., Canada-South Africa Cooperation 1991–93; author 'Canadian Immigration Law' 1986; 'The Sanctuary Trial' 1989; co-author 'Justice Delayed: Nazi War Criminals in Canada' 1987; 'Closing the Doors: The Failure of Refugee Protection' 1989; Home: 1146 Mulvey Ave., Winnipeg, Man. R3M 1J5; Office: 205 Edmonton St., Winnipeg, Man. R3C 1R4.

**MATE, Rt. Rev. Martin,** L.Th., M.A.; retired bishop; b. Port Rexton, Nfld. 12 Nov. 1929; s. John and Hilda (Toope) M.; e. Queen's Coll. St. John's L.Th. 1953; Bishop's Univ. Lennoxville B.A. 1966, M.A. 1967; m. Florence Mabel d. Carl and Elizabeth Hooper 12 Nov. 1962; children: Carolyn, Elizabeth, Phyllis, John, Carl; Bishop of E. Nfld. & Labrador 1980–92; o. Deacon 1952, Priest 1953; Curate, Cath. of St. John the Baptist, St. John's 1952–53; Rector, Pushthrough Parish, Nfld. 1953–58; Incumbent, St. Anthony Mission 1958–64; Rural Dean, St. Barbe 1958–64; Rector, Cookshire, Qué. 1964–67; Rector of Catalina, Nfld. 1967–72; Rural Dean Bonavista Bay 1970–72; Rector, Pouch Cove/Torbay Parish 1972–76; Treas. Diocesan Synod of E. Nfld. & Labrador 1976–80; author 'Pentateuchal Criticism' 1967; Anglican; recreations: carpentry, hunting, fishing, camping; Home: 42 Dundas St., St. John's, Nfld. A1B 1X1.

**MATEJCEK, Jan (Vladimir),** LL.D.; administrator; music editor; critic; b. Hamburg, Germany 29 Dec. 1926; e. studies composition, piano & musicology in Prague; Charles Univ., LL.D. 1951; m. Hanja Jindra 1950; EXECUTIVE DIRECTOR, SOCAN FOUNDATION 1992– ; Foreign Relns. Sec., Guild of Czechoslovak Composers 1954–61; Mgr., Prague Symphony Orch. 1961–62; Head, Music Dept., DILIA 1962–64; Gen. Mgr., Panton 1964–66; Dir. Gen. 1966–68; B. Schott's Sohne 1968; Cons., Candn. Music Ctr. 1969; Extve. Sec., Ont. Fed. of Symphony Orchs. & Ont. Choral Fed. 1970–71; Founder, Assn. of Candn. Orchs. 1971; Extve. Asst., Composer's, Author's & Music Publisher's Assn. of Canada (CAPAC) 1971–77; Asst. Gen. Mgr., Performing Rights Organization of Canada (PROCAN) 1977–80; Pres. & Gen. Mgr., PROCAN 1980–90; Chief Extve. Offr., SOCAN 1990–92; Founding Bd. Mem., Canada-Czech Republic Chamber of Commerce; Honorary Life Mem., Assn. of Candn. Orchestras; Mem., Extve. Bureau and Admin. Counc., CISAC 1986–92; author: '99 Tschechische Komponisten von Heute' 1957, 'Music in Czechoslovakia' 1967; editor: 'Contemporary Czechoslovak Piano Music, 2 vols' 1967, 'Catalogue of Canadian Music Suitable for Community Orchestras' 1971; Home: 28 Tarlton Rd., Toronto, Ont. M5P 2M4.

**MATHER, Derek H.,** B.Com.; management consultant; b. Calgary, Alta. 14 Jan. 1933; s. Thomas Herbert and Dorothy Lillian (Smith) M.; e. McGill Univ. B.Com. 1954; m. Maria Teresa d. Carlos and Luisa Demiguel 17 Dec. 1962; children: Ian, Luisa; SR. ASSOC., CORPORATE ASSOCIATES 1990– ; Dir. Paribas Participations Ltee.; Invest. Offr. Sun Life Assurance Co. of Canada 1954–62; Canadian Enterprise

Development Corp. Ltd. 1962–83, Extve. Vice Pres. on leaving; Pres. and Chief Extve. Offr. Westmills Carpets Ltd. 1978–81, Chrmn. 1981–83; Pres. & C.E.O., Vencap Equities Alberta Ltd. 1983–89; recreations: cross-country skiing, tennis; Address: 5385 Montiverdi Place, W. Vancouver, B.C. V7W 2W8.

**MATHERS, Andrew Sherlock,** B.arch.; architect; b. Toronto, Ont. 16 Sept. 1934; s. Alvin Sherlock and the late Nesta Prudhomme (Verner) S.; e. Oriole Park Pub. Sch.; Upper Can. Coll.; Univ. of Toronto, B.Arch. 1959; m. Suzanne Freemont, d. the late Freemont Whitfield Doan, 16 Sept. 1961; one s. Andrew Freemont; two d., Mary Verner; Jane Freemont; PARTNER, MATHERS & HALDENBY 1961– ; became Jr. Partner with present Co. 1961; York Univ. Residence (Glendon Campus) 1962; design and constr., Queen's Univ. Library Wing 1963; in charge design and constr., Can. Permanent Trust Co. Office Bldg., Ottawa, Ont. 1963; and Toronto-Dominion Bank Bldg., Sparks St., Ottawa, Ont. 1964; Faculty Club Bldg., Univ. of Waterloo; Athletic Complex, Wilfred Laurier Univ.; Royal Mil. Coll., Massey Library; Geology Bldg. and Mining Bldg., Queen's Univ.; Seneca Coll.; Humanities & Soc. Sci. Rsch. Library, Laidlaw Library, Balmer Neilly Library, Wycliff Coll., Univ. of Toronto; North York Bd. of Educ. Bldg.; mem., Ont. Assn. of Arch.; Fellow, Royal Arch. Inst. of Can.; Arch. Div., Metrop. Toronto, Un. Appeal; Anglican; Delta Upsilon; recreations: skiing, tennis; Clubs: Toronto Hunt; Badminton & Racquet; University; Home: 53 RiverView Dr., Toronto, Ont. M4N 3C8.

**MATHERS, John H.,** B.A.Sc., M.S.; executive; b. Penticton, B.C. 18 July 1923; s. Fred D. and Gladys C. (Robinson) M.; e. Pub. and High Schs., Vancouver; Univ. of B.C.; Univ. of Toronto, B.A.Sc.; Ore. State Univ., M.S.; m. Annamarie, d. A.S. Fumerton, Lethbridge, Alta. 22 June 1949; children: three; CHRMN. OF THE BOARD, ROYAL CITY FOODS LTD., since 1972; has served since 1949 in food processing indust. (buyer, production, production engr., sales and subsequently Vice Pres. Marketing); served with Candn. Army during World War II, rank Lt.; Past Pres., YM-YWCA and Kinsmen Club, New Westminster, B.C.; Anglican; recreations: golf, skiing, hunting; Clubs: Vancouver; Vancouver Golf; Home: 119 E. 8th Ave., New Westminster, B.C. V3L 4J6; Office: 3676 Bainbridge, Burnaby, B.C. V5A 2T4.

**MATHESON, David I.,** Q.C., B.Comm., LL.B.; lawyer; b. Moncton, N.B. 27 Sept. 1936; s. Rand Hector M.; e. Dalhousie Univ. B.Comm. 1958; Dalhousie Law Sch. LL.B. 1961; Univ. of Toronto Law Sch., post-grad. studies 1961–62; m. Dianne d. Frederick and Aileen Dawson 5 June 1965; children: Andrew Bruce, Christine Aileen; PARTNER, AIRD & BERLIS 1992– ; called to Bar of N.S. 1962, Ont. 1964; apptd. Q.C. 1978; Assoc. Lawyer, McMillan, Binch 1964; Partner 1968–92; Mem., Law Soc. of Upper Canada; Past Mem., Tax Ctte., Candn. C. of C.; Mem., Internat. Bar Assn.; Internat. Law Inst.; Candn. Tax Found.; Metro. Toronto Bd. of Trade; Dir., Ebasco Services of Canada Ltd.; Caulfeild Apparel Group Ltd.; Infa Corp. Canada Ltd.; Nfld. Capital Corp. Ltd.; LuCliff Company Limited; NIC International (Canada) Ltd.; Prima International Inc.; Rolins Hudig Hall of Canada Inc.; Past Chrmn., Ont. Tax Subsect., Candn. Bar Assn.; Queen's Jubilee Medal 1977; Malcolm Hon. Award, Dalhousie Univ.; Chrmn., The Candn. Bus. Hall of Fame Ctte. 1978– ; Dir., Hong Kong - Canada Business Assoc. & Past President, Toronto Section; Pres. & Dir., Candn. Scottish Heritage Found.; Junior Achievement of Canada; The Anne Murray Ctr.; Dalhousie Med. Rsch. Found.; Elder, St. George's Un. Ch. 1978–88; author of various pubns.; frequent speaker; recreations: sailing, skiing, tennis; clubs: Royal Candn. Yacht, The St. Andrew's Soc., Candn., Empire; Home: 201 Cortleigh Blvd., Toronto, Ont.; Office: BCE Place, Suite 1800, Box 754, 181 Bay St., Toronto, Ont. M5J 2T9.

**MATHESON, Edward Clay,** B.A.; publisher; b. Toronto, Ont. 24 Aug. 1931; s. William Bell and Anna (Pasika) M.; e. Queen's Univ. B.A. 1957; Indust. Relations Dipl. 1958; m. Eunice A., d. Frederick A. Thorne, 23 Apr. 1975; s. David Edward; PRES. AND DIR., AMPERSAND COMMUNICATIONS INC. 1973– ; Pres., FACS Records Centre, Ottawa 1987–92; Pres., Collier-Macmillan Canada 1971–73; Gen. Mgr., Methuen Publications 1964–71; Gen. Mgr., College Div., McGraw-Hill Co. of Canada Ltd. 1960–63; served with R.C.A.F., 1948–50, rank Flying Offr.; Adjunct Prof. of Journalism (Book Publishing), Univ. of W. Ont.; Dir. Publishing, Royal Commission on the Economic Union and Development Prospects for Can. 1984–86; recreations: golf, horses. Address: Robin Hill, 5606 Scobie Cr., Manotick, Ont. K0A 2N0.

**MATHESON, Hon. Joel Rand,** Q.C., M.L.A., B.Com., LL.B.; politician; b. 1930; e. Dalhousie Univ. B.Com. 1952, LL.B. 1954; m.; 3 children; Attorney General and Min. Resp. for Human Rights Act 1990 and Solicitor General 1991; Min. of Finance, N.S. 1979–1983; Min. of Mines & Energy Nov. 1983–87; Min. of Health & Fitness Dec. 1987–88; Min. of Advanced Education and Job Training 1988–91; read law with Barss & Hatfield; called to Bar of N.S. 1954; cr. Q.C. 1980; Pres., Hillis Oil Sales Ltd. 1955–79; el. M.L.A. for Halifax-Bedford Basin 1978; Pres. Bd. Govs. Izaak Walton Killam Hosp. for Children 1974–77, mem. Bd. 17 yrs.; Anglican; Home: 30 Robert Allen Dr., Halifax, N.S. B3M 3G8.

**MATHESON, Col. The Hon. John Ross,** O.C., K.St.J., C.D., Q.C., M.A., LL.M., LL.D.; retired judge; b. Arundel, Que. 14 Nov. 1917; s. Rev. Dr. Alexander Dawson and Gertrude (McCuaig) M.; e. Queen's Univ. B.A., Distinguished Service Award 1977, LL.D. (honoris causa) 1984; Osgoode Hall Law Sch. (President student body 1947–48), York Univ. LL.B.; Mount Allison Univ. M.A.; Univ. of W. Ont. LL.M.; The Royal Military College of Canada LL.D. (honoris causa) 1993; m. Edith May Bickley 4 Aug. 1945; children: Duncan, Wendy, Jill, Donald, Roderick, Murdoch; called to Bar of Ont. 1948; cr. Q.C. 1967; former law practice Matheson, Henderson & Hart, Brockville, Ont.; a judge of Judicial District of Ottawa-Carleton 1968–78; Judge, County Court of Lanark 1978–84; Judge, District Court of Ont. 1985–90; Justice, Ont. Court of Justice (General Division) 1990–92; served overseas 1940–44, First Regt. Royal Candn. Horse Arty., until wounded and invalided home; held hon. militia appts. with 30th Field Regt. RCA 1972–82; Registrar, Priory of Can. Most Venerable Order St. John of Jerusalem 1966–69, Genealogist 1969–93; el. to H. of C. for Leeds by-el. 1961, re-el. g.e.'s 1962, 1963, 1965; attended 16th Session UN Gen. Assembly; Chrmn. Commons Standing Comte. on External Affairs 1963–65; Parlty. Secy. to Prime Min. 1966–68; named Brockville Citizen of the Year 1967; Hons. incl. Officer, Order of Canada 1994; Kt. of Justice Order of St. John; Kt. Commdr. of Merit Order of St. Lazarus; Armigerous by Lyon Court and Coll. of Arms and Chief Herald of Canada; Awarded Centennial Medal, Jubilee Medal, 125th Anniversary of the Confederation of Canada Medal, Candn. Forces Decoration; Hon. Pres., United Empire Loyalists' Assn.; Hon. Pres., Heraldry Society of Canada; Honorary Secretary, Candn. Amateur Boxing Assn.; el. mem. Candn. Olympic Assn. 1968–89, Hon. Life Mem. 1989; el. Fellow: Royal Economic Society, Society of Antiquaries of Scotland, Heraldry Society of Canada, International Biographical Assn. (Deputy Director General); selected as an Internat. 'Man of the Year' 1992–93; Life member: Candn. Economics Assn.; Candn. Political Science Assn.; Candn. Bar Assn.; Candn. Institute for Admin. of Justice; Phi Delta Phi Legal fraternity; Nat. Trust for Scotland; Royal Candn. Arty. Assn; Hon. Life Mem.: Queen's Univ. Council; Bd. of Mgmt., Queen's Theological College; Faculty Club of Kingston; Life Gov.: Candn. Bible Society, Candn. Corps of Commissionaires; Deputy Gov., American Biographical Institute; Patron: Boy Scouts of Canada Trust; Member: The Law Society of Upper Canada; Candn. Inst. of Strategic Studies; Candn. Intelligence and Security Assn.; United Services Inst. of Ottawa; el. Life Member Royal Candn. Legion 1988; Paul Harris Fellow of Rotary International, Freemason, 33 degree, awarded William Mercer Wilson Medal for Meritorious Service 1988; Royal Order of Scotland, Grand Sovereign Order of Constantine 1989–90; author: 'Canada's Flag' 1980 and 1986; 'Sinews of the Heart' (poetry) 1982; recipient of: Commonwealth Heraldry Board Essay Prize 1980, Montreal Medal 1981, Chancellor Benidickson Award 1992 (latter two from Queen's Univ. Alumni); mem., United Church of Canada; Residence: Box 43, Rideau Ferry, Ont. K0G 1W0.

**MATHEWES, Rolf Walter,** B.Sc., Ph.D.; university professor; b. Berleburg, W. Germany 11 Nov. 1946; s. Walter Wilhelm and Anna Sofia (Bald) Mathewes; e. Simon Fraser Univ., B.Sc. 1969; Univ. of B.C., Ph.D. 1973; Cambridge Univ., postdoctoral fellow 1974; m. Donna d. Dorothy and Wilbur Worth 25 Mar. 1972; children: Kimberley Jean, (Alexandra) Brooke; PROF., BIOLOGICAL SCIENCES, SIMON FRASER UNIV. 1987– ; Environmental Consultant, Vancouver 1974–75; Asst. Prof., present univ. 1975–82; Assoc. Prof. 1982–87; Alexander von Humboldt Rsch. Fellow, W. Germany 1982 and 1991; Assoc. Ed., 'Canadian Journal of Botany' 1989–92; Excellence in Teaching Award, S.F.U. 1987; Pres., Candn. Assn. of Palynologists 1986; author of approx. 60 sci. pubs.; recreations: painting, fly fishing; Office: Burnaby, B.C. V5A 1S6.

**MATHEWS, Frederick Anthony John,** M.D.; physician-pathologist; b. Halifax, N.S. 17 Jan. 1933; s. Andrew Eusebius (Merchant) and Juanita Cox (Loomer) M.; a direct descendant of Cornwallis Planters (1761–64) in N.S. from New England and Economy Settlers (1779–1788) in N.S.; e. College St. Sch. Halifax 1947; St. Patrick's Boys' High Sch. 1950; Dalhousie Univ. 1950–56; Heidelberg Univ. 1958–59; Univ. of Marburg 1959–60; Univ. of Paris, Etudiant Libre 1960; Univ. of Bonn. 1960–62 (DM-Staataexam); Univ. de Montréal grad. studies (Research & Lab. Med. under Dr. Hans Selye) 1963; (summer) Lab technician, Imperial Oil (Burnside) 1949–50; private tutor Latin 1950–51; private tutor zoology 1952–53; Jr. Librarian, Dalhousie Med.-Dent. Library 1953–55; Nerve-muscle degeneration project, Anat. Dept., Dalhousie 1953–54; Clinical Rschr., Dal. Cancer Rsch. Grp. (under Dr. L.E. Steeves) 1954–56; Phys-Chem. Res. technician, Fisheries Research, Halifax 1956–57; Extern, Victoria Pub. Hosp. Fredericton, N.B. 1956; St. Clare's Hosp. NY. USA 1957; Hotel Dieu de St Joseph, Windsor, Ont. 1958; Asst. to Dir., Inst. of Path., Univ. of Köln 1962; Demonstrator in Pathology, Univ. of Pa. 1964, Univ. of Ottawa 1965–67, Univ. of Toronto 1967–68; Intern, Hotel Dieu de St. Joseph, Windsor, Ont. 1963–64, Halifax Infirmary 1965; Resident, Hosp. of Univ. of Pa. 1964, Ottawa Gen. Hosp. 1965–67, Toronto Gen. Hosp. 1967–68, New Mount Sinai Hosp. Toronto 1968–69, Winnipeg Gen. Hosp. 1969, Md. Gen. Hosp. Baltimore 1970–71; private practice Halifax 1971– ; partial regist. (1955), full regist. (1971) LMS PMB NS; Dipl. ECFMG 1965; LMCC 1969; Dipl. Am. Bd. Pathol. 1970; private practice: Locum pathol. Port Colborne 1969–70, Saint John, N.B. 1971; locum pathologist, Camp Hill Hosp. 1971; St. Rita's Hosp., Sydney 1971; St. Joseph's Hosp., Glace Bay 1971; Soldier's Mem. Hosp., Bridgewater, NS 1971; Pres./Dir. Casa Morgagni Enterprises (1971) Halifax; 16th Halifax Cubs and Boy Scouts (1944–1947); St Mary's Basilica Choir (1947–1951); Dal-Tech. COTC-Armoured Corp 1951–53; High Sch. Cadet, Halifax Rifles 1947–49; K. of C. (Council 1097; Recorder 1972–73); Adjunct Interim Judge, debating tournaments, N.S. jr. & sr. high schs. and N.S. Univ. 1980– ; mem. Royal N.S. Hist. Soc.; German Assn. Pathols.; Clan Donnachaidh Soc. in N.S. (Historian 1981–88, Secy. 1984–86); Inst. of Human Values (SMU); Immunology Club (Dalhousie); Dalhousie Alumni Assn.; Intl. Acad. of Pathologists; Kingsport Community Assn.; N.S. Inst. of Sci.; North British Soc.; Candn. Med. Assn.; Medical-Legal Soc. of Halifax 1975– ; N.S. Medical Soc.; N.Y. Acad. of Sci. 1987– ; P. Conservative; recreations: reading, outdoor sports, gardening; Address: 5784 Tower Terrace, Halifax, N.S. B3H 1R5.

**MATHIAS, Richard Gordon,** M.D., F.R.C.P.(C); physician; educator;. b. Agassiz, B.C. 22 July 1944; s. Douglas Gordon Browne and Winnifred Odetta (Hicks) M.; e. Penticton (B.C.) Sr. Secondary Sch. 1962; Univ. of Alta. M.D. 1968; Univ. of Calgary 1971–73, Univ. of Man. 1973–75 Residency Training in Med.; m. Barbara d. John and Margo Gordon 12 May 1973; children: Maureen, Gordon, Timothy; DIRECTOR, COMMUNITY MEDICINE RESIDENCY PROGRAM and PROFESSOR, DEPTS. OF HEALTH CARE & EPIDEMIOL., UNIV. OF B.C. 1983– ; gen. practice Cardston, Alta. 1969; Physician with Med. Assistance Progs. Kabul, Afghanistan 1970; Field Epidemiol. Bureau of Epidmiol. Lab. Centre for Disease Control, St. John's, Nfld. 1975–77; Med. Health Offr. Yorkton Melville Health Unit and Prov. Epidemiol. Sask. 1977–80; Cons. Epidemiol. Min. of Health B.C., Vancouver, 1980–83; Chrmn., Div. of Public Health Practice and Assoc. Prof. of Health Care & Epidmiol., Univ. of B.C. 1983– ; Visiting Prof., Inst. of Medical Res., Kuala Lumpur, Malaysia 1989–90; author various publs.; mem. Nat. Adv. Ctte. AIDS 1983–86; B.C. Pub. Health Assn. (Dir. 1981, Vice Pres. 1983–85, Pres. 1986–88); Nat. Immunization Policy Ctte. 1978–80; recreations: cycling, swimming; Home: 6280 Doulton Ave., Richmond, B.C. V7C Y4Y; Office: 5804 Fairview Ave., Vancouver, B.C. V6T 1Z3.

**MATHIEU, Jean,** M.D., F.R.C.P.(C); F.A.C.P.; physician; educator; b. Montreal, Que. 7 Aug. 1926; s. Dr. Emile and Marie Berthe (Larivière) M.; e. Coll. Stanislas Montreal B.A. 1944; Univ. de Montréal M.D. 1950; Univ. of Toronto postgrad. course Internal Med. 1951–54; m. Anne-Marie d. M. Marius Mouren, Tangiers, Morocco 16 Aug. 1956; children: Bernard, Yves, Nicolas; PROF. OF MED., UNIV. DE MONTREAL 1971, Professor Emeritus 1991; Physician Emeritus, Dept. of Med. Hôpital Maisonneuve-Rosemont 1992 (Physician 1956–91); Assoc. Dean, Faculté de médicine, Univ. de Montréal 1968–77; Chrmn., Dept. of Med., Univ. de

Montreal 1977–85; Cons. for health affairs, Internat. Assoc. of french-speaking Univ. (AUPELF) since 1986; Gov. Que. Coll. of Physicians and Surgs. 1966–74; Gov. for Que., Am. Coll. of Physicians, 1983–87; Adresse: 503 Perdriole Rd., Ste-Adèle, Qué. J0R 1L0; Bureau: AUPELF, Univ. de Montréal, CP 6128, Montréal, Qué. H3C 3J7.

**MATHIEU, Pierre;** poet; playwright; painter-artist (pseud. Duguay-Mathieu); b. Montréal, Qué. 28 July 1933; s. Jean Charles and Marguerite (Richard) M.; e. Univ. of Ottawa, Master in French Lit. 1972; sch. teacher; author 'Partance' poetry 1964; 'Midi de nuit' poetry 1966; 'Ressac' 1969; 'Stabat Mater' 1970; 'Interlune' 1971; 'Mots dits québécois' 1971; 'Toutes plaies balbutient ... d'étranges courage' 1977; 'Isis' 1980; 'Job' 1981; 'Cri ... Lumière' 1983, 2nd ed. 1983; 'Partage' 1983; 'La Pologne comme en nous-mêmes' 1983; 'Sous le Regard-Conscience'; 'La Guerre des Anges' 1987; 'Marie de Dieu' 1987; 'ABC poétique' 1987; 'Le Boulier Magique' poetry 1989; 'Les Oiseaux en liberté' poetry 1989; 'Les Dinosaures en fête' poetry 1989; 'Allo Allo Halloween' poetry 1993; 'Les insectes en parade' poetry 1993; 'D'est en Ouest' prose 1993; plays: 'Le Bleu et le Rouge' 1964; 'Evangeline ... qui donc?' 1973; co-author 'Mgr. ... La T.V.' 1980; 'Triptyque pour une église' 1981; 'Eminence ... Le code' 1981; 'Oh! Pape ... l'automate' 1981; 'La dernière scène' 1982; 'L'Ecole des langues' 1982; 'Le Miroir à deux faces' 1982; 'Le Zoo enchanté' poésie 1988; 'Sur La Pointe des mots' poésie 1988; 'Joseph de Marie' poésie 1990; Address: 4331 rue Christophe-Colomb, Montréal, Qué. H2J 3G2.

**MATHISON, William Arthur,** B.E., M.B.A.; executive; b. Vancouver, B.C. 7 Oct. 1940; s. Robert Arthur and Lola Alberta (Hunter) M.; e. City Park Coll. Inst. Saskatoon 1958; Univ. of Sask., B.E. (Chem.) 1962; Univ. of B.C., M.B.A. 1964; m. Loretta d. Arthur and Margaret Inkson 28 Dec. 1962; two s. Scott William, Cameron Arthur; PRES. & C.E.O., HARCROS CHEMICALS INC.; C.E.O. & Dir., Harcros Chemicals (Canada) Inc.; Savolite Chemical Ltd.; Linwo Industries; Laboratoire Orleans Ltée; Harrisons & Crosfield (America) Inc.; joined Dow Chemical of Canada 1964, Bus. & Mktg. Mgr. Organic Chems. 1969–72; Gen. Mgr. Canada Colors and Chemicals (Eastern) Ltd. 1972; Vice Pres., Gen. Sales Mgr. Canada Colors and Chemicals Ltd. 1978, Vice Pres. Mktg. 1981–86; Pres., C.E.O. & Dir., Harrisons & Crosfield (Canada) Ltd. 1986; mem. Chem. Inst. Can.; Soc. Chem. Ind. (Extve. Ctte.); Cand. Chem. Prod. Assn. (Communications Comm. 1984–85); recreations: golf, skiing, squash, jogging; Club: Donalda; Home: Chicago, Illinois.

**MATHUR, Dr. Brijesh,** B.Arch., M.P.L., Ph.D., M.C.I.P.; public servant; b. Shimla, India 16 Dec. 1947; s. Har Govind and Shiela Rani M.; e. Univ. of Bhopal B.Arch. 1971; Queen's Univ. M.P.L. 1977; Univ. of Sheffield Ph.D. 1991; m. Barbara Jean d. Dr. Malcolm J. McDonell 16 June 1990; stepchildren: Patricia, Robert, Margo Lane; ASSOC. DEP. MIN., SASK. EDUCATION, TRAINING & EMPLOYMENT 1993– ; freelance architect/planner 1971–75 (New Delhi & Toronto); Municipal Affairs, Govt. of Sask. 1977–79; Dir. of Planning & Programs, Meewasih Valley Authority Sask. 1979–84; Mgr. & Sec., Sask. New Careers Corp. 1984–85; Policy Advisor, Manitoba Extve. Council 1987–88; Sr. Rsch. Assoc. then Asst. Dir., leaving as Dir., Inst. of Urban Studies, Univ. of Winnipeg 1988–91; Assoc. Dep. Min to Premier & Sec., Planning & Priorities Ctte., Sask. Extve. Council 1991–93; Chair, Sask. New Careers Corp.; Edit. Bd. Mem., 'Can. J. of Urban Res.'; Nat. Recognition for Serv. to the Profession, Candn. Inst. of Planners 1991; Founding Mem., Western Inst. for Public Policy; widely recognized for playing key roles in creating new institutions, strategic direction plans & policies; Mem., Candn. Inst. of Planners; Inst. of Public Admin. of Can.; Editor-in-chief: 'Plan Canada' 1988–91, 'Planners Newsletter'; author of num. reports, monographs & articles; recreations: photography, cooking, travel; Home: 1329 Spadina Cres. E., Saskatoon, Sask. S7K 3J2; Office: 2220 College Ave., 5th fl., Regina, Sask. S4P 3V7.

**MATHYS, François Antoine,** B.A., LL.L., Ambassador; lawyer, diplomat; b. Timmins. Ont.; s. Joseph François and Helène (Baudouin) M.; e. Coll. Jean-de-Brébeuf, B.A. 1960; Univ. of Montreal, LL.L. 1965; Inst. Univ. des Hautes Etudes; Internat. Genève, internat. law; m. Elaine d. Claude and Françoise de Lorimier 20 Aug. 1966; children: Benoit, Antoine, Catherine; FIRST AMBASSADOR TO UKRAINE 1992– ; foreign serv. offr. & lawyer: 3rd & 2nd Sec., Candn. Perm. Mission to the U.N., N.Y. 1968–71; 1st Sec. & Consul, Candn. Embassy, Moscow 1974–76; Min.-Couns. 1981–83; Depy. Perm. Rep. & Min.-Couns., Candn. Deleg. to NATO, Brussels 1983–86; Sr. Dept. Asst. to Sec. of State of External Affaris, Joe Clark 1986–87; Dir.-Gen., Legal Affairs Bur., External Affairs 1987–89; Agent for Canada & Ambassador, Canada-France Maritime Boundary Arbitration 1989–92; Pres., Entreprises FIDO Inc.; Roman Cath.; Mem., Candn. Counc. of Internat. Law; Que. Bar; Am. Soc. of Internat. Law; author of 1 article; recreations: tennis; clubs: Rideau Tennis & Squash.

**MATKIN, James Grant,** B.A., LL.B., LL.M.; lawyer; executive; b. Cardston, Alta. 3 Dec. 1942; s. Grant and Clara (Ackroyd) M.; e. Univ. of Alta. B.A. 1967, LL.B. 1968; Harvard Law Sch. LL.M. 1969; m. Cheri d. Louis and Irene Belanger 16 Dec. 1966; children: Shauna Irene, Shelley Louise, Jennifer Cheri; Pres. & C.E.O., Business Council of B.C. 1983; lawyer Breed Abbott & Morgan New York 1969; Law Clerk, Justice Ronald Martland, Supreme Ct. of Can. 1970; Special Asst. to B.C. Chief Justice Nemetz, mediation of Longshore dispute; Prof. of Law Univ. of B.C. 1970–73; Special Advr. to Min. of Labour, Prov. of B.C. 1973; Depy. Min. of Labour, B.C.; mem. B.C. Negotiating team of Feasibility of Steel Mill with NKK, Japan 1975–77; Lectr. on Negotiations, Sch. of Public Admin., Univ. of Victoria 1982; Chrmn. Ind. Relns. Bd. of B.C. 1976–80; Negotiation Advr. to Premier of B.C. on patriation of Candn. Constitution 1981; Depy. Min. of Intergovernmental Relns., B.C. 1982–83; Lead Official on B.C.'s Compensation Stabilization Prog. 1982; Negotiation Advr. for B.C. on Internat. Hydro Agreement, Skagit Valley 1983; author: 'the Negotiation of the Charter of Rights: the Provincial Perspective' 1986; 'Government Intervention in Labour Disputes' in 'Collective Bargaining in the Essential and Public Service Sectors' 1975; Ed.-in-Chief Alta. Law Review 1967–68; Trustee Health Sciences Centre, Univ. of B.C.; mem. Adv. Bd. Simon Fraser Univ.; Pres. The Vancouver Inst.; mem. Bd. Asia Pacific Business Inst.; mem. Bd. Canada West Ventures Ltd.; Mormon Missionary, Cook Islands, S. Pacific 1962–65; mem. Candn. Bar Assn. 1970– ; Silver Medal in Law, Univ. of Alta.; Frank Knox Fellowship, Harvard Univ.; recreations: tennis, skiing, canoeing; Clubs: The University (B.C.); The Canadian (Vancouver); Office: Park Place, 2800 - 666 Burrard St., Vancouver, B.C. V6C 2Z7.

**MATLOW, Hon. Mr. Justice P. Theodore (Ted),** B.Comm., LL.B., LL.M.; judge; b. Kitchener, Ont. 14 Apr. 1940; s. Joseph Z. and Freda; e. Univ. of Toronto, B.Comm. 1962, LL.B. 1965; called to bar 1967; York Univ., LL.M. 1979; Q.C. 1979; children: Joshua, Rachel; JUDGE, THE ONTARIO COURT OF JUSTICE (GENERAL DIV.) 1990– ; Law Clerk, Chief Justice of Ont. 1967; sole practitioner 1968–72; Partner, Rosenberg, Smith, Paton, Hyman & Matlow, Toronto 1972–81; District Court Judge 1981–90; Founder, Candn. Soc. for the Abolition of the Death Penalty 1963; Mem., Nat. & Reg. Extves., Candn. Jewish Cong. 1986–92; Co-Chrmn., Soviet Jewry Ctte., Candn. Jewish Cong. 1989–92; Mem., Medico-Legal Soc. of Toronto; The Lawyers' Club; Jewish; Editor-in-Chief, 'The Advocates' Quarterly' 1977– ; recreations: tennis, other sports, music, theatre; clubs: York Racquets; Office: 361 University Ave., Toronto, Ont. M5G 1T3.

**MATTE, Bernard William,** B.Com., M.B.A.; manufacturer; b. Sherbrooke, Que. 31 March 1940; s. Joseph Osmond and Bertha (Lacoste) M.; e. Univ. of Ottawa B.Com. 1964; Univ. of W. Ont. M.B.A. 1966; m. Barbara Ida d. Dr. Harold E. Armstrong, Ottawa, Ont. 23 June 1962; children: John Cameron, Shelley Louise; PRES., BARCAM HOLDINGS LTD. 1989– ; Vice Pres. Greenshields Inc. 1966–74; Vice Pres. and Dir., G & H Steel Industries Ltd. 1974–77; Vice Pres. & Dir. Imasco Ltd. 1978–84; Vice Pres., Innocan Inc. 1984–87; Pres. & Dir., Wajax Ltd. 1987–89; Pres. & Dir., Fletcher Leisure Group Inc. 1991–92; R. Catholic; recreations: flying, golf, skiing, squash; Clubs: University; Lambton Golf & Country; Royal Montreal Golf; Home: #308 - 3460 Redpath, Montreal, Que. H3G 2G3.

**MATTE, Brigadier-General Michel,** C.D., B.A., M.Sc.; military officer, infantry; b. Trois-Rivières, Que. 26 May 1942; s. Jean-Paul and Yvette (Laroche) M.; e. Laval Univ. B.A. 1961; Royal Military Coll. B.A. (Hons.) 1965; Univ. du Qué. à Hull M.Sc. 1987; Carleton Univ., post-grad. work in Public Admin. 1966; m. Jeanne d. Philippe and Simonne Michaud 13 July 1968; Director General, Public Affairs, Dept. of National Defence, H.Q. 1991; joined Royal 22nd Regiment Sept. 1966 & served in regimental units to 1976; attended Army's Staff Coll. (Kingston) 1970–71; NATO Defence Coll. (Rome, Italy) 1976; following two years of service overseas in FRG commanded 3rd Battalion, Royal 22nd Regiment 1978; Comndr., Infantry School (Gagetown, N.B.) 1980; served on H.Q. staff in FMC HQ in Montreal & NDHQ Ottawa since 1982; during service with 22nd Regiment had three tours of duty with the U.N. Peacekeeping Forces in Cyprus 1968, '72, '79 as Commander, Nicosia Dist.; was also Chief of Staff Opns. for the Candn. Army during Oka crisis and the Gulf War; recreations: tennis, skiing, sailing; club: Nepean Sailing; Home: 176 Dunbarton Court, Ottawa, Ont. K1K 4L7.

**MATTE, Mimi (Madeleine R.),** B.F.A.; artist, painter; b. Regina, Sask. 10 Sept. 1929; d. Gedeon Joseph and Paule (Sasseville) M.; e. Central C.I. (Regina); Ottawa Univ.; Ottawa Tech. Sch.; McGill Univ. B.F.A. 1951; m. James s. James and Edith Packham 27 Dec. 1952; children: Christine Elizabeth, Blair James; commercial artist Montreal & Toronto prior to 1974; began exhibiting work at Marlborough-Godard Gall. Montreal & Toronto 1974; Bau-Xi Gall. 1979– ; work has been shown in many solo & group exhibitions incl. Bau-Xi Gall., Art Gall. of Ont., Hamilton, Kitchener-Waterloo, Gairdner Estate, Hart House, Shayne Gall. (Montreal), Rosemont (Sask.), Adley Gall. (Sarasota), More-Rubin (Buffalo, N.Y.); work incl. in major collections; recipient of awards for competitions; recreations: writing mystery novels, computer graphics; Home: 80 Front St. E., #418, Toronto, Ont. M5E 1T4.

**MATTE, Nicolas Mateesco,** O.C., Q.C., F.R.S.C.; lawyer; professor of law; b. Craiova, Romania 3 Dec. 1913; s. Ion and Maria (Dimitrescu) Matei; e. Univ. of Bucharest Licence en droit 1937, Docteur en droit 1939; Univ. de Paris Docteur en droit intnl. 1947; Inst. des hautes études internationales Paris Dip. 1948; m. Monica d. Lucretia and Alfred Berzeanu-Bunger 22 July 1943; children: Daniel, Anne-Karyne; DIR. EMERITUS, INSTITUTE OF AIR AND SPACE LAW and founder of the Centre for Research in Air and Space Law and the Annals of Air and Space Law; Counsel, Mackenzie Gervais; Dir., Inst. and Centre of Air and Space Law 1975–89; Dir., Centre for Research in Air and Space Law 1976–91; Hon. Consul of Guinea-Bissau 1988– ; Prof. of Law Inst. internat. d'études et de recherches diplomatiques de Paris 1948–50; Prof. of Law, Univ. de Montréal 1951–69; Visiting Prof. present Inst. 1962–75; Dir., Intnl. Inst. Space Law; named First Hon. Citizen Ville de Brossard (Quebec); Kt. Grand Priory Can., Mil. & Hosp. Order St. Lazarus Jerusalem; named Chevalier dans L'Ordre de la Légion d'Honneur; Officier de l'Ordre du Mérite Ivoirien; author 'Droit Aerospatial' 1969, Eng. Transl. 1969; 'Aerospace Law: From Scientific Exploration to Commercial Utilization' 1977, French transl. 1977; 'Space Policy and Programmes. Today and Tomorrow' 1980; 'Traité de droit aérien-aéronautique' 1980, Eng. transl. 1981; 'Droit aérospatial. Les télécommunications par satellites' 1982, Eng. transl. 1982; World Pres. Intnl. Law Assn. 1982–84; Life Vice Pres. Internat. Law Assn. 1984 (Pres., Candn. Br. 1976–82; Life Hon. Pres., Candn. Br. 1982); Vice Pres., Assn. Lawyers, Jurists and Experts in Air Law; mem., Internat. Acad. Astronautics; Home: 6111 ave. du Boisé, apt. 7M, Montreal, Que. H3S 2V8; Office: 3661 Peel St., Montreal, Que. H3A 1X1.

**MATTE, Pierre;** librarian; b. Shawinigan, Qué. 31 July 1918; s. late Auguste and late Joséphine (Gaillardetz) M.; e. Shawinigan-South Comm. Sch. 1935; St. Joseph Coll. Trois-Rivières 1942; Laval Univ. Faculty of Philos. 1942–43; Univ. of Montréal Faculty of Pharm. 1944–45, Statistics 1945–46, Sch. of Lib. Science 1947–48; m. Clothilde d. late Victor and late Clara (Constantin) Lessard 20 Oct. 1951; children: Johanne, Louise, Michèle; Dir., Que. Pub. Library Service and Secy. Que. Pub. Lib. Comn. 1975–83; now retired; Prof., St. Mary's Coll. Shawinigan 1943–44; Shawinigan Chemicals Ltd. classification of plans 1950; Maison Bellarmin Montréal 1950–51; Shawinigan Chemicals Ed. plant organ 1951–57; Chief librarian of the Shawinigan Public Library 1957–60; Service des bibliothèques publiques du Qué. and mem. of Comn. 1960; mem. Candn. Lib. Research and Devel. Council 1962–67; recipient Strathcona Medal; served with COTC 1942–45; author various papers; Pres. l'Assn. canadienne des bibliothécaires de langue française 1959–60; 2nd Vice Pres. Candn. Lib. Assn.1966–67, Vice Pres. Candn. Lib. Week; mem. Am. Lib. Assn. Council 1966–71; Hon. mem., Assn. pour l'avancement des sciences et des techniques de la documentation (ASTED) 1982– ; Commander, Equestrian Order of the Holy Sepulcher of Jerusalem 1985– ; R. Catholic; recreations: home work, handicrafts, skiing, skating, music; Home: 980, 125 St., Shawinigan, Qué. G9P 3V5.

**MATTEY, Viviane,** B.Comm., C.A.; financial executive; b. Montreal, Que. 6 Jan. 1957; d. Paul George and Anne (Milo) M.; e. McGill Univ. B.Comm. 1978; C.A. 1980; Vice-Pres., Investor Relations and Corporate Taxation, Dominion Textile Inc. 1991–93; Tax Accountant, Coopers & Lybrand 1978–82; Sr. Tax Accountant, Ernst & Whinney 1983–85; Mgr., Corp. Taxation, Dominion Textile Inc. 1985; Dir. 1987; Investor Relations, Corp. Taxation 1989; Lectr., Taxation, McGill Univ.; Home: 1100 Dr. Penfield, Montreal, Que. H3A 1A8.

**MATTHEW, Ian M.,** B.Com., C.A.; b. Glasgow, Scot. 10 Sept. 1951; s. John Lawson and Jean Ellen (MacLachlan) M.; e. Laurentian Univ. B.Com. 1976; C.A. Ont. 1978; m. Joanne D. Yvon and Jeannette Sauve 6 Oct. 1972; children: Jennifer, Kyle; PARTNER, MATTHEW & WARREN CHARTERED ACCOUNTANTS; Pres., Ram Tech; Vice-Pres., Aladdin Freightlines; joined Coopers & Lybrand, C.A.'s, Kitchener, Ont. 1976–80, Mgr. Insolvency & Bus. Investigs. 1980–82; Controller, Pop Shoppes International Inc. 1980; Pres. Aldershot Contractors Equipment Rental Ltd. Burlington 1983; Pres. & C.E.O., Beauty Counselors Internat. Inc., Toronto 1984–85; Mgr., Insolvency, Dunwoody; Pres. & Owner, Rolmaster Conveyors Ltd. 1987–90; P. Conservative; PC Candidate, Provincial Election 1990; recreation: golf; Home: 223 Blackhorne Dr., Kitchener, Ont. N2E 1Z2.

**MATTHEWS, BGen Beverley,** C.B.E., Q.C., B.A.; barrister; b. Toronto, Ont. 23 Feb. 1905; s. Frederick William and Elizabeth Mary (Leslie) M.; e. Univ. of Toronto Schs.; Univ. of Toronto, B.A. (Pol. Sci.); Osgoode Hall Law Sch. (Gold Medal); m. late Pauline Ritchie, 29 Apr. 1938; three s. and one d.; m. Kathleen Margaret Woods (née Baker) 21 Nov. 1970 (div.); m. Phyllis McKinnon (Cowie) 7 Sept. 1978; ASSOCIATE COUNSEL, McCARTHY TÉTRAULT; Hon. Dir.: Candn. Niagara Power Co. Ltd.; Opinac Energy Corp.; Bd. of Dir.: CGC Inc. (1962–90); W.H. Smith & Son (Canada) Ltd. (Chrmn. 1947–71); Gulf Oil Corp. 1957–77; Gulf Canada Ltd. 1950–77; Brascan Ltd. 1947–79; TransCanada PipeLines Ltd. 1961–76; The Canada Life Assurance Co. (Vice-Pres.) 1969–80; Westinghouse Canada Ltd. 1964–80; 3M Canada Ltd. 1951–80; Rheem Canada Ltd. 1946–76; Canada Permanent Trust Co. 1966–69, 1977–81; The Toronto-Dominion Bank (Vice-Pres.) 1955–76; Bd. of Govs., Univ. of Toronto 1946–71; Past Pres., Bd. of Trade of Metro. Toronto; called to the Bar of Ont. 1930; cr. K.C. 1945; joined 48th Highlanders of Can. 1939; served Overseas, 1940–45; appt. Commdr. of Order of Orange Nassau (Netherlands); BGen; Honours: O.B.E. and Mentioned in Despatches (Italy); C.B.E. and Mentioned in Despatches (Continent); Conservative; Anglican; recreations: shooting, fishing; Clubs: Toronto; York; University (Toronto); Ristigouche Salmon (Matapedia); White's (London); Home: 45 Ardmore Rd., Toronto, Ont. M5P 1V9; Office: Suite 4700, Toronto Dominion Bank Tower, Toronto-Dominion Centre, Toronto, Ont. M5K 1E6.

**MATTHEWS, Burton Clare,** B.S.A., A.M., Ph.D., D.U., LL.D., F.U.G.; b. Kerwood, Ont. 16 Dec. 1926; s. Clarence D. and Meryl (Freer) M.; e. Univ. of Toronto, B.S.A. 1947; Univ. of Missouri, A.M. 1948; Cornell Univ.,Ph.D. 1952; Nuffield Foundation Post-Doctorate Fellow, Oxford Univ., 1961–62; Univ. of Sherbrooke, D.U., 1979; University of Waterloo, LL.D. 1982; m. Lois Verna, d. Archibald Lewis, Ottawa, Ont., 23 June 1951; two s. David, Thomas; PRESIDENT EMERITUS and ADJUNCT PROF., UNIV. OF WATERLOO 1989– ; Dir., Mutual Life of Canada; Internat. Centre for Improvement of Wheat and Maize 1988– ; Pres., Kitchener Waterloo YMCA 1980–82; Dir., Ont. Educ. Communications Authority 1972–78; Assn. Univs. and Colls. Can. 1977–78 and 1984–86; Extve., Council of Ont. Univ. 1972–74 and 1979–81; Asst. Prof. of Soil Science, Ont. Agric. Coll., 1952–56; Assoc. Prof., 1956–58; Prof. 1958–62; Head, Dept. of Soil Science, 1962–66; V. Pres. (Acad.) Univ. of Guelph 1966–70; Pres. and Vice Chancellor, Univ. of Waterloo 1970–81; Chrmn., Ont. Council of Univ. Affairs 1982–84; Pres. & Vice-Chancellor, Univ. of Guelph 1984–88; Fellow, Univ. of Guelph (F.U.G.) 1989; mem., Agric. Inst. Can.; Ont. Inst. Agrologists; Can. Soc. of Soil Sci.(Past Pres.); Soil Conserv. Soc. Am.; Am. Soc. Agron.; Sigma Xi; Freemason; Anglican; Address: 245 Old Post Rd., Waterloo, Ont. N2L 5B8.

**MATTHEWS, Donald Charles,** M.Sc.; agrologist; company executive; b. Calgary, Alta. 24 Sept. 1918; s. Charles Curtice and Grace Miriam (Cathro) M.; e. Univ. of Alberta, 1937–39, 1945–47; B.Sc. (Agric.) with Distinction, 1947; Iowa State Coll., M.Sc. (Animal Breeding) 1948; m. Jean Lyndsay Lamaison, 1 Mar. 1941; children: Lyndsay Catherine, Robert Charles; CHRMN., HIGHLAND STOCK FARMS LTD., 1990– ; previously Farm. Mgr. and Vice-Pres. 1948–67, Pres. 1967–90; Dir., Canadian Pacific Ltd. 1975–89; Chrmn., Adv. Comte. (Calgary), Guaranty Trust Co. 1980–87, Ctte. mem., 1962–92; Hon. Pres. (1980) and past Pres., Alta. Aberdeen Angus Assn.; Past Pres., Candn. Jt. Beef Breeds Assn.; Hon. Chrmn., Candn. Beef Breeds Counc. 1991; Found. mem., Past Pres., Candn. Limousin Assn.; Dir., Alberta Cattle Commission 1974–78, Chrmn. 1976–77; Dir. Candn. Cattlemen's Assn. 1970–92; Past Pres., Canadian 4-H Council 1972; Charter Trustee and past Pres., Cdn. 4–H Foundation; past mem., Agric. Inst. Can. (Pres. Calgary Br. 1952–53); Am. Genetics Assn. (retired member); Candn. & Am. Soc. Animal Science (retired member); mem., Amer. Quarter Horse Assn.; Alta. Cattle Breeders Assn. (Past Pres. and Dir.); Past Pres. & Charter Dir., Candn. Agric. Hall of Fame; Past Pres., Calgary Exhibition & Stampede Co. Ltd. 1964–65 (Life Dir.); Past mem. Council and Past Chrmn., Agric. Bureau, Calgary Chamber of Comm.; Dir., Candn. Aberdeen Angus Assn. 1963–71, Extve. mem. 1967–68, Vice-Pres. 1968, Pres. 1969; Gov., Univ. of Calgary 1977–80 (and Senate 1974–80); Mgmt. Bd., Univ. of Calgary Press 1981–89; served in World War 1939–45 (Overseas 5 yrs.); discharged from 14th Candn. Armour. Regt. (K.O.C.R.) with rank Capt.; Centennial Medal 1967; awarded Commemorative Medal for 125th Anniversary of Candn. Confederation 1993; inducted into Candn. Agricultural Hall of Fame, Nov. 1984; Distinguished Cattleman (1st), Alta. Cattle Commission 1990; inducted into Alberta Agriculture Hall of Fame 1992; Delta Kappa Epsilon; Anglican; recreation: riding; Club: Ranchmens'; Address: Highland Stock Farm, R.R. 1, Calgary, Alta. T2P 2G4.

**MATTHEWS, Donald J.,** B.Sc., P.Eng.; business executive; b. Brantford, Ont. 11 Feb. 1926; s. John Henry and Florence Honora (Jeune) M.; e. Queen's Univ. B.Sc. 1950; children: Dona, Shelley, Deborah, Gini, Carole, Jack, Joseph, Cayleah, Gabrielle; CHAIRMAN AND C.E.O., MATTHEWS GROUP LTD. 1953– ; Dir. Weyerhaeuser Canada Ltd.; estbd. Matthews Construction Ltd. 1953 and subsequently 7 other co's during next 11 yrs. culminating in present co.; recreations: tennis, golf, mountain climbing, riding, skiing, scuba diving, swimming; Clubs: Albany; Beacon Hall Golf; Toronto Club; York Club; The Candn. Club of London; London Club; London Hunt & Country; Griffith Island; Sagemace Country; Sailfish Point, Fla.; Home: 1515 Killally Rd., London, Ont. N6A 4C1; London Office: P.O. Box 3055, 1091 Crumlin Rd. N., London, Ont. N6A 1J2; Mississauga Office: Suite 900 – 90 Burnhamthorpe Rd. W., Mississauga, Ont. L5B 3C3.

**MATTHEWS, Francis Richard,** Q.C., B.Com., LL.B.; b. Calgary, Alta. 19 Aug. 1920; s. Charles Curtice and Grace Miriam (Cathro) M.; e. W. Can. High Sch.; Univ. of Alta., B.Com. 1941, LL.B. 1948; m. Joyce Winter, d. J. Arthur Jarvis, Toronto, 10 Nov. 1944; children: James Richard, Michael John, Frances Elizabeth; COUNSEL, MacKIMMIE MATTHEWS, barristers and solicitors 1987– ; Dir., Ranger Oil Ltd.; Murphy Oil Co. Ltd.; called to Bar of Alta. 1949; cr. Q.C. 1963; Assoc., Mackimmie Matthews 1949–54; Partner 1954–87; served with RCNVR 1941–45; Lieutenant (S) on discharge; Pres., Calgary Philharmonic Orchestra Found. (Gov., Calgary Philharmonic Orchestra Soc. 1965–84; Pres. 1954–55, 1961–62; Dir. 1953–64); mem., Alta. Bar Assn.; Candn. Bar Assn.; Delta Kappa Epsilon (1938–41 and 1945–48); Anglican; Conservative; recreations: skiing, sailing, flying, golf, photography; Clubs: Calgary Petroleum; Ranchmen's; Cu-Nim Soaring; Home: #1810, 720–13 Ave. S.W., Calgary, Alta. T2R 2M5; Office: 700 Gulf Canada Square, 401–9th Ave. S.W., P.O. Box 2010, Calgary, Alta. T2P 2M2.

**MATTHEWS, Jack E.,** B.A., LL.D.; educator; b. Peterborough, Ont. 6 Apr. 1928; s. Gordon S. and Agnes (Eastwood) M.; e. Peterborough Coll. Inst.; Univ. of W. Ont. B.A. 1949, Business Dipl. 1950; Ont. Coll. of Educ. 1958; m. Jane d. John Lang Gillespie 6 Oct. 1951; children: Angus, Tam; Dir. Internat. Program, Trent Univ. 1982–89; joined Canada Packers 1951–52; Teacher, Lakefield Coll. Sch. 1953–60, Headmaster 1963–70; Gordonstoun Sch. Scot. 1961–62; Founding Dir. Lester B. Pearson Coll. of the Pacific 1971–81; Hon. Patron, Lester B. Pearson United World Colleges; Advisory Bd., Lakefield College Sch.; Bd. of Dirs., Quetico Foundation; recreations: canoeing, sailing, skiing; Clubs: University (Toronto); Home: 59 Clementi St., Lakefield, Ont. K0L 1H0; Office: Box 1338, Lakefield, Ont. K0L 2H0.

**MATTHEWS, John Pengwerne,** B.A., LL.B., Ph.D.; educator; b. Sydney, Australia 22 Oct. 1927; s. George Pengwerne and Rosalie Crossland (Pulsford) M.; e. The Scots Coll. Sydney 1945; Univ. of Melbourne B.A. 1951, Dipl. in Educ. 1952; Univ. of London LL.B. 1954; Univ. of Toronto Ph.D. 1957; n. Flora Jean Cameron d. James Gilchrist 11 June 1955; children: Peter Edmund Vashdye Pengwerne, Rosalie Elizabeth Jane Pengwerne, Christopher John Charles Pengwerne; EMERITUS PROF. OF ENGLISH, QUEEN'S UNIV. 1993– , Prof. 1962–93; Princ. Investigator (1974– ) and Sr. Ed. (1974–82), The Disraeli Project; Senior Ed. The Disraeli Letters Vols. I & II (1982), Ed. Vol. III (1987), Vol. IV (1989), Vol. V (1993); Asst. Prof. St. John's Coll. Univ. of Man. 1956, Prof. and Head of Eng. 1957, Dean of Arts & Science 1957–62; joined Queen's Univ. 1962, Dir. Inst. of Commonwealth & Comparative Studies 1962–67, Assoc. Dean of Grad. Studies & Research, Dir. of Research Adm. 1974–75; Hon. Fellow St. John's Coll. 1963; Visiting Fellow Oriel Coll. Oxford 1972–73; Nuffield Fellow 1972–73; served with RAAF 1950–53, Pilot Offr.; RCAF Auxiliary Flying Offr. 1953–56, Flight Lt. 1956–59; author 'Tradition in Exile' 1962; various book chapters, articles; Vice Pres. Kingston Symphony Assn.; Pres. Kingston Youth Orchestra 1968–74; Nat. Pres. Humanities Assn. Can. 1971–72, 1987–88 (Extve. 1973–92); mem. Acad. Panel, Social Sciences & Humanities Research Council 1978–81; Candn. Federation for the Humanities; Bd. of Directors 1979–82, Vice Pres. 1982–84, Pres. 1984–86, Past Pres. 1986–88; Anglican; recreations: chess, sailing, Great Danes; Home: 55 Watts Cres., Kingston, Ont. K7M 2P4; Office: Kingston, Ont. K7L 3N6.

**MATTHEWS, The Hon. Mr. Justice Kenneth M.,** LL.B.; supreme court justice; b. Millerton, N.B. 19 July 1922; s. Rev. W. McN. and Alena (Ward) M.; e. Truro Acad.; Dalhousie Univ., LL.B. 1949; m. Grace Yvonne d. Earl and Mabel Malloy 10 Aug. 1949; children: Douglas, Anne, Margaret, Sarah; JUSTICE, SUPREME COURT OF N.S., APPEAL DIV. 1985– ; Pilot, R.C.A.F. 1942–45; law practice, Patterson, Smith, Matthews & Grant & predecessor firms 1949–85; Q.C. 1964; Pres., N.S. Barristers' Soc. 1983–84; Fellow, Am. Coll. of Trial Lawyers; Former Candn. Chrmn., Internat. Soc. of Barristers; Former Pres., Sable Gas Systems, Limited; United Church; Home: 10 Smith Ave., Truro, N.S. B2N 1C1; Office: The Law Courts, P.O. Box 2314, Halifax, N.S. B3J 3C8.

**MATTHEWS, Linda,** B.A., F.I.I.C.; business executive; b. 1948; e. McMaster Univ. B.A. 1969; m. Al; DIR., CANADIAN CHAMBER OF COMMERCE 1990– ; var. mngt. positions, Bell Canada 1969–75; Extve. Asst. to Pres., Royal Insurance Can. 1975; var. positions with co. incl. Deputy Reg. Mgr. Ont. Personal Lines; Dir., Corp. Planning & Public Affairs 1988–91; Regional Vice-Pres., Ont. Personal Lines 1992– ; Mem., Ont. Chamber of Commerce (Pres. 1990, Chrmn. 1991); OBAC 1990– ; Queen's Park Liaison Comm. 1992–93; Insur. Inst. of Can. (Communications Ctte.); Board of Govs., McMaster University 1992– ; Candn. Chamber of Commerce (Bd. of Dir. 1990– ; Extve. Ctte. 1992– ); Clarke Institute Fundraising 1993; F.I.I.C. 1978; Jean Robitaille Employment Equity Award 1990; participant, 1987 Gov.-Gen.'s Candn. Study Conference; recreations: tennis, travel; Office: 405 The West Mall, 8th Floor, Etobicoke, Ont. M9C 5J1.

**MATTHEWS, Patrick J.,** B.Comm., C.A.; financial executive; b. Winnipeg, Man. 17 March 1942; e. Univ. of Manitoba B.Comm. 1968; C.A. (Manitoba) 1971; m. Clarice M. Carstens 1971; children: Brian, Richard; VICE-PRES., FINANCE, GENDIS INC. 1982– ; Branch clerical duties, Bank of Montreal 1960–65; Jr. Acct. to Audit Mgr., Peat, Marwick, Mitchell & Co. 1968–75; Partner 1975–79; Vice-Pres., Corp. Devel., Gendis Inc. 1979–82; Dir., Chauvco Resources Ltd.; Past Pres., Manitoba Theatre Centre; Trustee, Man. Theatre Ctr. Found.; Adv. Bd., St Boniface Gen. Hosp.; Mem., Inst. of C.A.s of Man.; Financial Extves. Inst.; clubs: Niakwa Country; Home: 110 Clearwater Rd., Winnipeg, Man. R2J 2T5; Office: 1370 Sony Pl., Winnipeg, Man. R3T 1N5.

**MATTHEWS, Robert Beverley,** B.A., M.A.(Oxon), LL.B., LL.M.; barrister & solicitor; b. Toronto, Ont. 12 June 1946; s. Beverley and Pauline (Ritchie) M.; e. Univ. of Toronto, B.A. (Hons.) 1968; Oxford Univ., M.A. 1971; Dalhousie Univ., LL.B. 1972; Osgoode Hall Law Sch., LL.M. 1982; m. Susan d. Gordon P and Nancy Osler 6 May 1978; children: Graham, Shannon, Trevor; PARTNER, McCARTHY TÉTRAULT, BARRISTERS & SOLICITORS 1986– ; called to Bar of Ont. 1974; articling student & assoc., Fraser & Beatty, Toronto 1973–75; Partner, McMaster Meighen, Toronto 1975–85; Dir., Rheem Canada Ltd.; World Wildlife Fund; Chrmn., Bus. Law Section, Candn. Bar Assn. (Ont.) 1983–85; recreations: wilderness canoeing, skiing, tennis; clubs: Toronto, Badminton & Racquet, Craigleith Ski Club; Home: 139 Roxborough Dr., Toronto, Ont. M4W 1X5; Office: Suite 4700, Toronto Dominion Bank Tower, Toronto-Dominion Centre, Toronto, Ont. M5K 1E6.

**MATTHEWS, Victor Bruce,** C.D., S.T.B., M.A., Ph.D.; educator; b. Toronto, Ont. 4 Jan. 1941; s. Albert Bruce and Victoria Corse (Thorne) M.; e. Upper Can. Coll. 1959; Acadia Univ. B.A. 1963; Oxford Univ. B.A. 1965, M.A. 1969; Trinity Coll. Univ. of Toronto, S.T.B. 1966; Univ. of Ceylon 1970; McMaster Univ., Ph.D. 1974; m. Pamela d. Edward and Geraldine Wright 28 Aug. 1965; two s. Mark Shirreff, Joshua Balfour; C.B. LUMSDEN PROF. OF COMPARATIVE RELIGION, ACADIA UNIV. 1983– ; Provost and Vice Chancellor, Thorneloe Coll. Laurentian Univ. 1972–76; Assoc. Prof. of Religion, Univ. of Toronto 1976–79, present Univ. 1979–83; served with Candn. Militia, retired 1978, rank Maj.; Priest, Ang. Ch. of Can. Diocese of N.S.; author: 'Craving and Salvation: A Study in Buddhist Soteriology' 1984; mem. Candn. Council S.E. Asian Studies (Pres. 1984–86); Candn. Assn. of Asian Studies (Pres. 1989–91); Assn. Asian Studies (USA); Clubs: University; Royal Candn. Mil. Inst.; Home: P.O. Box 73, 406 Main St., Wolfville, N.S. B0P 1X0; Office: Wolfville, N.S. B0P 1X0.

**MATTILA, Kerry Allan;** petroleum industry executive; b. Merrickville, Ont. 24 Aug. 1948; s. Olaf Alexander and Edith Leona (Knapp) M.; e. Algonquin College Civil Technology Dipl. 1969; m. Elizabeth d. Edgar and Pearl Gammon 30 Dec. 1983; one s.: Todd; VICE-PRESIDENT, OPERATIONS, CANADIAN PETROLEUM PRODUCTS INST. 1990– ; Oil & Gas Engr., National Energy Bd. 1970–72; Analyst, Oil Policy 1972–77; Real Estate Broker, A.H. Fitzsimmons 1977–79; Technical Co-ord., Petroleum Assn. for Conservation of the Cdn. Environment 1979–87; Manager 1987–90; Chair, Ministerial Adv. Cttee., Canada Gen. Standards Bd.; Cdn. Climate Change Adv. Cttee.; Dir., Major Indus. Accidents Council of Canada; Chair, Petroleum Refining Sector, Cdn. Indus. Prog. for Energy Conservation Council; Past Chair, Ottawa Valley Chap., Air & Waste Mngt. Assn.; Recreations: boating; Home: R.R. 4, Kemptville, Ont. K0G 1J0; Office: 1000 – 275 Slater St., Ottawa, Ont. K1P 5H9.

**MATUSICKY, Carol,** M.A., Ph.D.; educator, administrator; b. Vancouver, B.C. 7 April 1941; d. Joseph Atkinson and Caroline Mary (Stevens) Storrow; e. Mount Saint Vincent Univ. B.A., B.Sc. 1967; Univ. of Notre Dame M.A. 1972; Univ. of Toronto Ph.D. 1982; m. Leo s. Paul and Julia M. 1 March 1975; children: Catherine, Joseph; EXECUTIVE DIRECTOR, B.C. COUNCIL FOR THE FAMILY 1984– ; Elementary School Teacher; Rsch. Asst. to Vice-Pres. then Dir., Family Life Inst. 1972–75; Mem., several prov. adv. cttes. incl. Min. of Edn.; B.C. Task Force on Family Violence (Min. of Women's Equality); Min. of Attorney General's Community Policing; Rogers Cablevision Community Adv. Ctte.; Canada Council Award 1974–78; Dir., Public Legal Edn. Soc. 1983–90; McCreary Ctr. 1992– ; Vancouver Foundation's Child and Family Advisory Ctte. 1992– ; Mem., Vanier Inst. of the Family; Bd. Mem., Nat. Council on Family Relations; Family Services Canada (Nat. Steering Ctte. for Nat. Family Week 1984– and Nat. Steering Ctte. for Family Education Certification 1989– ); Internat. Union of Family Orgns. Paris (Mem. of General Assembly); keynote speaker in Canada and abroad; recreations: outdoors, music, theatre; Home: 1135 Eastlawn Dr., Burnaby, B.C. V5B 3G9; Office: 204, 2590 Granville St., Vancouver, B.C. V6H 3H1.

**MAURER, Armand,** M.A., M.S.L., Ph.D., F.R.S.C.; university professor; b. Rochester, N.Y. 21 Jan., 1915; s. Armand Augustine and Louise (Ribson) M.; e. Univ. of Toronto, B.A. 1938, M.A. 1943, M.S.L. (Pontifical Inst. of Mediaeval Studies) 1945, Ph.D. 1947; Post-doctoral studies, Univ. of Paris, 1948–49; Harvard Univ. and Italy (Guggenheim Fellowship), 1954–55; Fellow of Royal Soc. of Canada, 1966; PROF. EMERITUS OF PHILOS., PONTIFICAL INST. OF MEDIAEVAL STUDIES AND UNIV. OF TORONTO; Professor of Philosophy, Center for Thomistic Studies, Houston, Texas; Roman Catholic Priest of Congr. of St. Basil; Landed Immigrant in Canada 1957; author: 'Medieval Philosophy' 1962, 2nd rev. ed. 1982; co-author: 'Recent Philosophy' 1966; 'St. Thomas and Historicity' 1979; 'About Beauty: A Thomistic Interpretation' 1983; 'Being and Knowing: Studies in Thomas Aquinas and Later Medieval Philosophers' 1990; translator: 'St. Thomas Aquinas: On Being and Essence' 2nd rev. ed. 1968; 'Master Eckhart: Parisian Questions and Prologues' 1974; 'St. Thomas Aquinas: The Division and Methods of the Sciences' 4th rev. ed. 1986; 'St. Thomas Aquinas: Faith, Reason and Theology' 1987; Etienne Gilson, 'Christian Philosophy: An Introduction' 1993; editor: 'Siger of Brabant: Quaestiones in Metaphysicam' 1983; mem., Am. Cath. Philos. Assn. & President Am. Cath. Philos. Ass. 1979; Metaphysical Soc. Am.; Soc. internat. pour l'étude de la philosophie médiévale; recreation: walking; Address: 59 Queen's Park Cres., Toronto, Ont. M5S 2C4.

**MAURER, Janet R.,** M.D.; physician; associate professor of medicine; b. Great Falls, Mt. 26 Nov. 1947; d. Cedric Albert and Elfriede Emilie (Riebhoff) M.; e. Univ. of Montana, B.A. 1968; Univ. of Oregon, M.A. 1969; Univ. of Minn., M.D. 1976; m. David I. Kent s. Renee and Marvin Kent 27 Sept. 1980; children: Rachel, Jeremy; DIR., CLIN. RESPIRATORY SERV., TORONTO GEN. HOSP. 1986– ; Co-Dir., Lung Transplant Program 1991– (Med. Dir. 1988–91); Staff Physician, Bronx VA Hosp. 1981–84; Asst. Prof. of Med., Univ. of Toronto 1984–91; Assoc. Prof. of Med., Univ. of Toronto 1991– ; Mem., Am. Thoracic Soc., Am. Coll. of Physicians; Am. Coll. of Chest Physicians; Ont. Thoracic Soc.; Int. Soc. of Heart and Lung Transplant; author: 'How to Talk to Your Doctor, the Questions to Ask' 1986, 'Unilateral Lung Transplantation in Pulmonary Perspectives' 1987; Building a New Dream: 'A Guide for Families with Chronic Illness,' 1989; Home: 46 Yorkminster Rd., Willowdale, Ont. M2P 1M3; Office: 200 Elizabeth St., Toronto, Ont. M5G 2C4.

**MAURER, Kurt E.;** travel executive; b. Schiltach/Black Forest, Germany 13 Aug. 1921; s. Emil and Mina C. (Sola) M.; e. sr. matric. Germany; m. Else d. Max and Anna Petermann 28 May 1948; children: Lothar, Werner, Rolf, Helga, Horst, Ingrid; Apprentice, American Express Co. Germany 1948–51, in charge tour prog. Am. personnel in Germany 1951–52; immigrated to Can. 1952; Jr. Agt. Thomas Cook & Son 1952–54; Mgr. Royal City Travel Bureau, New Westminster, B.C. 1954–56; Mgr., Hagen's Travel Service 1956; Pres. 1962–89, Pres. Emeritus 1989– ; Pres. New Horizon Holidays 1968–78; Charter and Hon. Life mem.: Candn. Inst. Cert. Travel Counsellors (B.C.) and Inst. Cert. Travel Agts. (U.S.A.); Dir. World Assn. Travel Agencies (Geneva) 1967–73; Charter mem. and Past Pres.: Rotary Club Vancouver E. and German-Candn. Businessman's Assn. B.C. (Hon. Life Mem.); Dir. Edelweiss Credit Union 1964–81, 1989–91; recreations: flying, skiing, hiking; Club; Vancouver Alpen (Life mem.); Intern. SKAL Club (Past Pres. & Life Mem.); Home: 766 W. 39th Ave., Vancouver, B.C. V5Z 2M5.

**MAURER, Rolf,** B.A.; publisher; b. Vancouver, B.C. 13 April 1955; s. Kurt Emil and Else (Petermann) M.; e. Vancouver Coll. 1973; Univ. of B.C. B.A. 1978; PUBLISHER, NEW STAR BOOKS 1990– ; Reporter, Vancouver Province 1976–79; Co-editor, The Ubyssey 1976–77; Asst. Ed., B.C. Teachers' Fed. Newsletter 1979–81; Editor, New Star Books 1981–90; Pres., Assn. of Book Pubs. of B.C. 1986–88; Sessional Instructor, Communications, Simon Fraser Univ. (pub. prog.) 1989–90; Bertelsmann Stiftung (W. Germany) 1986; Bd. of Dir., Kootenay School of Writing; Office: 2504 York Ave., Vancouver, B.C. V6K 1E3.

**MAURICE, Hon. Gene Arthur Francis,** B.A., LL.B.; judge; b. Frontier, Sask. 25 July 1943; s. Arthur Joseph and Georgia, Elsie (Peterson) M.; e. Univ. Sask., B.A. 1965; LL.B. with distinction 1966; m. Elizabeth, d. Herbert and Anna Fenner, 22 Dec. 1963; JUSTICE, COURT OF QUEEN'S BENCH, SASKATCHEWAN since 1981; partner with law firm Wilson, McBean, Maurice & McIntosh 1968–81; Office: Court House, 2425 Victoria Ave., Regina, Sask. S4P 0S8.

**MAURO, Arthur V.,** O.C., Q.C., B.A., LL.B., LL.M., LL.D. (Hon.); financial executive; b. Thunder Bay, Ont. 15 Feb. 1927; s. Arthur George and Maria (Fortezza) M.; e. St. Andrews and Port Arthur (Ont.) Coll. Inst.; St. Patricks High Sch., Fort William, Ont.; St. Paul's Coll., Winnipeg, B.A. 1949; Univ. of Man., LL.B. 1953, LL.M. 1956; m. Nancie June, d. late H. Tooley, 1 Sept. 1951; children: Barbara, Christine, Jennifer, Gregory; CHANCELLOR, UNIV. OF MANITOBA; Dir., Investors Group Inc.; Investors Syndicate Ltd.; Investors Group Trust Co. Ltd.; Investors Syndicate Property Corp.; I.G. Investment Management. Ltd.; PWA Corp.; Canadian Pacific Hotels Corp.; United Grain Growers; Andersen Consulting, Atomic Energy of Canada Ltd.; read law with Andrews, Andrews, Thorvaldson & Co.; called to Bar of Man. 1953; cr. Q.C. 1964; Special Counsel to Prov. of Man. 1958–69; Chrmn., Royal Comn. on N. Transport. 1967–69; Lectr. in Transport. and Communication Law, Univ. of Man. Law Sch. 1967–69; named Kt. of St. Gregory 1967; mem., Man. Bar Assn.; P. Conservative; R. Catholic; Home: 1034 Wellington Cres., Winnipeg, Man. R3M 0E1; Office: 447 Portage Ave., Winnipeg, Man. R3C 3B6.

**MAUS, Dr. John Hall,** M.D., F.R.C.P.(C), F.A.C.R.; physician; radiation oncologist; b. Ayr, Ont. 28 Mar. 1918; s. Jairus Wilton and Elizabeth Ann (Baxter) M.; e. pub. and high schs. S. Dumfries, Ayr and Paris, Ont. 1936; Univ. of Toronto M.D. 1942; Wayne State Univ. Coll. of Lib. Arts 1952–53; m. Shirley Sloan d. Kenneth and Anna Foster 30 Oct. 1943; children: Jairus Roger, Elizabeth F. Snider, LindaAnn, Natalie J. Maus-Fisher, Margaret H. Thorne, K. Laurie Maus; RADIATION ONCOLOGIST ONTARIO CANCER TREATMENT & RESEARCH FOUNDATION, WINDSOR REGIONAL CANCER CENTRE 1954– ; retired 1985; served RCAMC Canada and Overseas 1943–46; discharged with rank Capt.; Intern, Metrop. Gen. Hosp. Windsor 1942, 1946, joined Neoplastic Service there 1947, also private practice; Dir. Ont. Cancer Treatment & Rsch. Found. Windsor Clinic 1963–84; served various positions Metrop. Gen. Hosp. incl. Chief of Staff, mem. Bd. 1984; served Bd. Windsor Med. Services; Past Pres. Essex City Med. Soc.; mem. Bd. Willistead Manor Inc. Windsor; Adv. Bd. Hospice Windsor Inc.; Pres., Unicom Sr. Resources Centre, Univ. of Windsor 1987–89; Mem. of Bd., Unicom Sr. Resources Centre, Univ. of Windsor 1989– ; author numerous med. publs.; Life mem. Essex Co. Med. Soc.; Life Mem. Ont. Med. Assn. 1986; Assoc. mem. Royal Soc. Med.; mem. Am. Radium Soc.; Radiological Soc. N. Am.; Candn. Med. Assn.; Am. Soc. for Therapeutic Radiology & Oncology; Candn. Assn. Radiols., and other med. assns.; Emeritus Mem., College of Physicians & Surgeons of Ont. (1993); Hon. D.Sc.: Univ. of Windsor 1985; recreations: golf, woodworking, bridge; Club: Rotary (Pres. Windsor 1979–80); Summer Address: 'Four Winds,' Portland-on-The-Rideau, Ont. K0G 1V0; Home: 269 Reedmere Rd., Windsor, Ont. N8S 2L3.

**MAVALWALA, Jamshed,** B.Sc., M.Sc., Ph.D.; university professor; b. Quetta, India 1 Sept. 1933; e. Panjab Univ. B.Sc. 1953; Delhi Univ. M.Sc. 1955, Ph.D. 1960; postdoc. Fulbright & Smith-Mundt Fellow at Harvard 1960–63; PROFESSOR OF ANTHROPOLOGY, UNIV. OF TORONTO 1969– ; postdoctoral fellow, Harvard Univ. 1960–63; Asst. Prof. of Anthropology, Univ. of Manitoba 1963–64; Rsch. Offr., Ctr. for Sci. & Indus. Rsch. India 1964–65; Anthropology, Univ. of Calif. Riverside & Santa Barbara 1965–69; Visiting Prof., Univ. of Santiago 1967; Sec., Internat. Dermatoglyphics Assn. 1974–78; Pres. 1978–84; Editor, 'Dermatoglyphics' bulletin 1974– ; Ont. Confed. of Univ. Faculty Assn., Excellence in Teaching Award 1974; Govt. of Ont., Volunteer Serv. Award 1986; N. Am. Zoroastrian Cong., Life Excellence Award 1992; Mem., Council of Christians & Jews 1977– ; Pres., Zoroastrian Soc. of Ont. 1974–75, 1976–77; Chair, World Conf. on Religions for Peace 1980–81, 1984–85; Mem., Extve. Ctte. & Chair, Edn. Ctte., Ont. Adv. Council on Multiculturalism 1975–81; Chair, 81st Group Ctte., Boy Scouts of Canada 1978–79; Co-chair, North American InterFaith Network 1992– ; editor: 'Dermatoglyphics: An International Perspective' 1978, 'Dermatoglypics: An International Bibliography' 1977; author of over 80 articles, films & TV programmes (multiculturalism); extensive lecturer; Founding Bd. Mem., Vision-TV; recreation: travel, reading; Office: Toronto, Ont. M5S 1A1.

**MAVRINAC, Joseph (Joe);** mayor; retired hotelier; b. Croatia, Yugoslavia 20 Mar. 1924; s. Ivan B. and Danica (Blazevic) M.; emigrated to Can. 1929; e. Kirkland Lake Collegiate Vocational Inst.; Rehab Sch. (Post Navy) 1946; Univ. of Toronto 1946–47; m. Millie Podnar 26 Oct. 1952; children: Diane Elizabeth, Mary Ann; MAYOR, TOWN OF KIRKLAND LAKE 1981– ; R.C.N.V.R. 1942–45, discharged AB Offrs. cand.; served N. Atlantic Convoy Duty Corvettes 'Trail' & 'Battleford'; Life Member-at-Large, The Royal Canadian Naval Assoc.; Hotel/Motel Owner/Mgr. 1948–85; Councillor, Town of Kirkland Lake 1959–61; Past Pres., 3 hotel/motel assns.; Vice-Pres., Hotel Assn. of Can. 1983–85; Dir., Am. Hotel Assn. 1984–85; Pres., Fed. of N. Ont. Municipalities 1987–88; Chrmn. Northern Section, Assoc. Municipalities of Ont. (AMO) 1988–89, Dir., AMO 1989–90, Vice-Pres. AMO 1990–91, 1st Vice-Pres. AMO 1991–92, Pres. AMO 1992–93; Past Pres. AMO 1993– ; Chrmn., N.E. Ont. Action Group 1980–81, 1988–91; Dir., Federation Candn. Municipalities 1992–93; Founding Dir., Candn. Assn. of Single Indus. Towns; Chrmn., Timiskaming N. Devel. Counc. 1986–88; Municipal Spokesman, Save The Flow Thru Share Ctte.; Pres., Kirkland Lake & Dist. C. of C. 1966–68, 1974–76; Royal Candn. Legion: Pres., Br. 87 1958–59; Dist. Comndr. (K) 1959; Vice-Pres., Prov. Comnd. 1960; Life Member, 48 years service; P.C. Candidate, Timiskaming, Fed. 1962, Prov. 1967; awarded The Rotary Foundation of Rotary Internat. Paul Harris Fellow; Fifty-year Pin - Croation Fraternal Union; recreations: skiing, travel; clubs: Variety Club, Tent 28; Home: 37 Porteous Ave., P.O. Box 1014, Kirkland Lake, Ont. P2N

3L1; Office: P.O. Box 1757, 3 Kirkland St., Kirkland Lake, Ont. P2N 3P4.

**MAVROS, Constantin A.,** M.A., Ph.D.; health care services administrator; b. Athens, Greece 13 Oct. 1941; s. Anargyros and Sophia (Kouthouridou) M.; e. Concordia Univ. M.A. 1978; Univ. of Montreal Dipl. in Inst. Adm. 1980; Pacific Western Univ. Ph.D. 1988; m. Marie-Louise d. Heinrich and Martha Sichtig 12 Dec. 1966; children: Myriam, Sylvia, Aris; National Dir. of Emergency Services, Ministry of Health, Greece 1986–88; American Medical Internat. (A.M.I.) Extve. Dir., 'Hygeia' Hospital, Athen's Greece; Dir. Candn. Citizens' Rights Assn. 1966–73; Extve. Dir. Community Health Center Pilote A 1973–76; mem. Fed. Social & Health Adms. Qué.; Candn. Council on Social Devel.; Internat. Relations Club; recipient Lifestyle Award Govt. Can.; Cert. of Merit, D.I.B. Cambridge and Men of Achievement Cambridge; mem. U.S.A. Biog. Roll of Honor; Gov., Centraide Montréal; St. Mary's Hosp.; Pres. St. Louis Community Center; Vice Pres. Contact Conserv.; Fellow, Internat. Biog. Assn.; Am. Biog. Inst.; A.B.I.R.A.; mem. UN Assn. Can.; Dawson College Board of Governors; Amnesty Internat.; St. James Lit. Soc.

**MAW, James Gordon,** B.A., B.Comm., M.B.A.; financial executive; b. Hamilton, Ont. 2 June 1936; s. John Lawrence and Holly Alexandra M.; e. Queen's Univ. B.A. 1957, B.Comm. 1958; Harvard Univ. M.B.A. 1960; m. Ann McCaghey 23 Dec. 1961; children: Sean, Jay; CONSULTANT 1993– ; Corporate Planner, Abitibi Price Inc. 1970–73; Manager, Financial Planning 1973–80; Treasurer 1980–84; Vice-Pres. & Treas. 1984–87; Vice-Pres. Finance 1987–88; Senior Vice-Pres., Finance (C.F.O.) 1988–90; Sr. Vice-Pres. & Chief Financial Offr., Lac Minerals Ltd. 1991–93; Mem., The National Club; Bd. of Trade; Financial Executives Inst.; author: 'Return on Investment: Concept and Application' 1968; recreations: riding, skiing, sailing; clubs: Port Credit Yacht, Claireville Riders; Home: 132 Oakes Drive, Mississauga, Ont. L5G 3M1; Office: Royal Bank Plaza, North Tower, Box 156, Toronto, Ont. M5J 2J4.

**MAWANI, Al W.,** M.B.A., C.A.; financial executive; b. Tanzania 2 Oct. 1951; s. W.M. and S.K. (Merali) Mawani; e. Karimjee S.S. 1968; Univ. of Dar es Salaam; Univ. of Toronto M.B.A. 1988; C.A. (England) 1972–76; C.A. (Ont.) 1976–77; m. Arzina A. d. A.R. Hussein 29 Dec. 1975; children: Salim Aladin, Yasmin Jenny (Mawani); SENIOR VICE-PRES. & CHIEF FINANCIAL OFFICER, OXFORD DEVELOPMENT GROUP INC. 1989– ; Account Mgr., Walter Heller Financial Corp. 1976–78; Staff C.A., Thorne Riddell & Co. 1978–79; joined Oxford Development Group Inc. 1979; Dir. of Accounting 1980; Vice-Pres. & Controller 1984; Senior Vice-Pres. & Controller 1988; Dir., Oxford Development Group Inc.; The Edmonton Centre Limited; Calford Properties Ltd.; Mem., Accounting Practices Cttee., Candn. Inst. of Public Real Estate Cos. 1987– ; Dean's List, M.B.A. Prog., Univ. of Toronto 1987–88; Shell Prize for Chemistry (1st yr. univ.), Univ. of Dar es Salaam 1970–71; Mem., Inst. of C.A.s in Ont. 1976– ; Fellow Mem., Inst. of C.A.s in England & Wales 1975– ; recreations: foreign travel, reading, information technology; Club: Toronto Bd. of Trade; Home: 19 Pining Road, Thornhill, Ont. L3T 5N5; Office: #1700 – 120 Adelaide St. W., Toronto, Ont. M5H 1T1.

**MAWHINNEY, Harold Stevenson,** B.A.; financial services executive; b. Winnipeg, Man. 11 May 1938; s. Andrew Thomas M.; e. Univ. of Manitoba B.A. 1978; m. Judith Moon 23 June 1989; children: Colleen, Gordon, Thomas; SR. VICE-PRES., INFORMATION TECHNOLOGY, INVESTORS GROUP INC. 1982– ; Manitoba Hydro 1956–64; Univ. of Manitoba 1964–72; Alberta Wheat Pool 1972–82; Pres., Alzheimers Soc. 1989–91; Bd. Mem. 1986– ; recreations: golf, racquets; club: Emlhurst; Home: 7 – 341 Westwood Dr., Winnipeg, Man. R3K 1G4; Office: One Canada Ctr., 447 Portage Ave., Winnipeg, Man. R3C 3B6.

**MAWHINNEY, J. Donald,** LL.B., Q.C.; lawyer; e. Univ. of B.C. LL.B. 1954; VICE CHRMN., FRASER & BEATTY; Partner law firm Ladner Downs, Vancouver 1955–78; President, Bancorp Financial Ltd. 1979–80; Sr. Partner, Mawhinney & Kellough 1980–90; Clubs: Vancouver; Rotary; Canadian; Home: 6016 Alma St., Vancouver, B.C. V6N 1Y4; Office: 15th Fl., 1040 W. Georgia St., Vancouver, B.C. V6E 4H8.

**MAXWELL, The Hon. Colin C.D.,** B.Ed.; provincial minister; b. Tillicoultry, Scotland 16 Dec. 1943; s. Colin and Molly (Drummond) M.; e. Scottish Sch. of Phys. Edn., dipl. 1965; Jordanhill Coll. of Edn., grad. dipl. edn. 1966; Univ. of Regina, B.Ed. 1975; m. Cherry Harvey 6 July 1966; children: Ashley, Kirstin, Brigham; EXTVE. VICE-PRES., CANDN. WILDLIFE FEDERATION; Min. of Culture, Multiculturalism & Recreation, Govt. of Sask. 1989; Teacher, Phys. Edn. 1967–74; Spec. Lectr., Univ. of Regina 1974–76; Prin., Spiritwood H.S. 1976–82; elected to Sask. Legisl. Assembly (Turtleford) 1982; re-elected 1986; Min. of Advanced Education & Manpower 1983–85; Min. of Parks & Renewable Resources 1985–87 and Min. of Culture & Recreation 1986–87; Min. of Parks, Recreation & Culture 1987–89; Mayor, Town of Spiritwood, two terms; Mem., Sask. Wildlife Fed.; Natural History Soc.; Ducks Unlimited; World Wildlife Fund; Lions; Freemason; Office: 2740 Queensview Dr., Ottawa, Ont. K2B 1A2.

**MAXWELL, James Douglas,** B.A., Dip.H.A., Ph.D.; university professor; b. Chesley, Ont. 18 Mar. 1938; s. John Harvey and Ora Marjorie (McCannel) M.; e. Chesley & Dist. H.S. 1956; Univ. of Toronto, B.A. (Hons.) 1960, Dip.H.A. 1963; Cornell Univ., Ph.D. 1969; m. Mary d. Peter F.W. and Dorothy (Warren) Percival 7 Sept. 1963; children: Peter-John, Kim Elizabeth; PROF., DEPT. OF SOCIOLOGY, QUEEN'S UNIV. 1969– ; employed for short periods by Ont. Hosp. Assn., Agnew Peckham & Assoc. and Toronto General Hosp. 1960–63; employed by Univ. of B.C. 1967–69; co-author (with Mary Percival Maxwell): 'Occupational Therapy: The Diffident Profession' 1977 and numerous articles & papers; Home: 'Glen Warren,' Box 1, R.R. #2, Shanty Bay, Ont.; 22 Kensington Ave., Kingston, Ont. K7L 4B5; Office: Queen's Univ., Kingston, Ont. K7L 3N6.

**MAXWELL, John Alfred,** M.Sc., Ph.D., F.R.S.C.; s. John Harold and Florence Lillian (Miller) M.; e. McMaster Univ., B.Sc. 1949, M.Sc. 1950; Univ. of Minn., Ph.D. (Geol. and Analytical Chem.) 1953; m. Helen Catharine, d. late Rev. S.H. Moyer, 20 Nov. 1953; Research Fellow, Rock Analysis Laboratory, Univ. of Minn. 1951–53; joined Geological Survey of Canada 1953–86; Head, Analytical Chem. Sec. 1957–67; Dir., Central Labs. & Tech. Services 1974–84; Spec. Advisor to Dir. Gen. 1984–86; rec'd Ont. Rsch. Foundation Scholarship 1949, 1950; author 'Rock and Mineral Analysis' 1968, 2nd ed. (with W.M. Johnson) 1981; other writings incl. scient. papers on analysis of rocks and minerals, mercury cathode and its applications, laser microprobe, lunar sample analysis; Protestant; Home: 672 Denbury Ave., Ottawa, Ont. K2A 2P3.

**MAXWELL, Judith,** B.Com., LL.D.; economist; b. Kingston, Ont. 21 July 1943; d. the late James Ruffee and Marguerite Jane (Spanner) McMahon; e. Dalhousie Univ., B.Com. 1963, LL.D. 1991; London Sch. of Econ. 1965–66; Queen's Univ. LL.D. 1992; Concordia Univ. LL.D. 1992; m. Anthony Stirling s. V. Elizabeth and H. Stirling M. 8 May 1970; children: David, Elizabeth Jane; ASSOC. DIR., SCHOOL OF POLICY STUDIES, QUEEN'S UNIV., KINGSTON and EXTVE. DIR., QUEEN'S-UNIVERSITY OF OTTAWA ECONOMIC PROJECTS 1992– ; Researcher, Combines Investigation Br., Fed. Dept. of Consumer and Corporate Affairs 1963–65; Econ. Writer, Financial Times of Can. 1966–72; Dir., Policy Studies, C.D. Howe Inst. 1972–80; Cons., Esso Europe Inc. 1980–82; Cons. Econ., Coopers & Lybrand 1982–85; Chrmn., Economic Council of Canada 1985–92; Past Pres., Candn. Assn. for Bus. Econ.; Montreal Econ. Assn.; Mem., Nfld. and Labrador Science and Technology Adv. Counc. 1988–90; Member, Ontario Premier's Counc. 1988–90; co-author 'Partnership for Growth: Corporate-University Education in Canada' 1984; 'Economic Realities of Contemporary Confederation' 1980; author: 'Energy from the Arctic' 1973 and numerous articles; author & editor: Annual 'Policy Review and Outlook' C.D. Howe Inst. 1974–80; recreations: skiing, gardening; Office: P.O. Box 1503, 350 Sparks St., 5th Floor, Ottawa, Ont. K1P 5R5.

**MAXWELL, Michael P.,** M.A., Ph.D.; educator; b. Eng. 8 Sept. 1933; s. John P. and Phoebe Laura (Cherry) M.; e. Eton; Concordia Univ. B.A.; McGill Univ., Macdonald Coll. Dipl. in Agric. 1954, M.A. 1961, Ph.D. 1966; m. Maria d. Janos de Holtzer 20 Aug. 1960; children: Shaun, Dylan; PROF. OF HIST., McGILL UNIV. 1979– ; Dean of Arts there 1981–86, 1989– ; joined Canada Packers' and Merk Sharpe and Dohme 1954–59; Teacher, Montreal Inst. of Technol. 1959–60; Lectr. in Hist. McGill Univ. 1963, Asst. Prof. 1966, Assoc. Prof. 1969, Chrmn. of Hist. 1972–75; named Woodrow Wilson Fellow 1960; author 'The Scottish Migration to Ulster in the Reign of James I' 1973; recreations: tennis, skiing; Office: 855 Sherbrooke St. W., Room 625, Montreal, Que. H3A 2T6.

**MAXWELL, Robert D.,** B.Eng., M.B.A.; business executive; b. St. Jean, Que. 22 June 1941; e. McGill Univ. B.Eng. 1963; Univ. of West. Ont. M.B.A. 1965; m. Christine (Ross) Oct. 1970; children: Andra, Ian; VICE-PRESIDENT, BUSINESS DEVELOPMENT AND GOVERNMENT RELATIONS, HONEYWELL LIMITED 1972– ; I.C.I. Canada 1965–68; Celanese Canada 1968–72; Information Systems, Honeywell Limited Montreal 1972–77; Ottawa 1977–82; Home: 67 Hemingway Cr., Unionville, Ont. L3R 2S4; Office: 155 Gordon Baker Rd., North York, Ont. M2H 3N7.

**MAY, Arthur William,** M.Sc., Ph.D.; b. St. John's, Nfld. 29 June 1937; s. William James and Florence (Dawe) M.; e. Mem. Univ. of Nfld. B.Sc. (Hons.) 1958, M.Sc. 1964; McGill Univ. Ph.D. 1966; m. Sonia d. Alfred and Violet Streeter 18 Aug. 1958; children: Stephen, Heather, Maria, Douglas; PRES., MEMORIAL UNIVERSITY OF NFLD. 1990– ; Research Scient. Nfld. Biol. Stn. St. John's 1958–71, Dir. 1973–75; Scient. Adviser Internat. Fisheries Ottawa 1971–73; Dir-Gen. Resource Services Fisheries and Marine, Ottawa 1975–78; Asst. Depy. Min. Atlantic Fisheries, Ottawa 1978–82; Depy. Min. of Fisheries and Oceans, Canada 1982–86; Pres., Natural Sciences and Engineering Research Council 1986–90; Vice Pres. Internat. Council for Exploration of the Sea 1978–80; Pres. NW Atlantic Fisheries Organ. 1979–81; Candn. Rep. NATO Science Cttee. 1990– ; recipient Gov. Gen.'s Medal 1954 and 1958; Alumnus of the Yr. Award, Meml. Univ. of Nfld. 1983; D.U. (h.c.), Univ. of Ottawa 1988; D.Sc. (h.c.), Meml. Univ. of Nfld. 1989; LL.D. (h.c.), Brock Univ. 1992; author or co-author numerous research papers Atlantic fishery resources; Home: 20 Baker St., St. John's, Nfld. A1A 5A7; Office: Elizabeth Ave. West, St. John's, Nfld. A1C 5S7.

**MAYBIN, John Edwin,** M.Sc.; b. Regina, Sask. 14 Feb. 1925; s. John and Gertrude (Hinton) M.; e. Calgary (Alta.) Pub. and High Schs.; Univ. of Alta.; Princeton Univ., B.Sc., M.Sc.; m. Ella Joy Louise, d. Dr. R.M. Parsons, Red Deer, Alta., 21 Dec. 1964; Dir., Alta. Energy Co.; Chieftain International, Inc.; joined Cdn. Western and Northwestern as prof. engr. 1949; Pres., Cdn. Western Natural Gas Co. and Northwestern Utilities Ltd. 1968–69; Chrmn. and C.E.O., Cdn. Utilities Ltd. 1969–72; Group Vice Pres., Utilities; IU International Corp. 1972–74; Chrmn. and C.E.O., Cdn. Utilities Ltd. 1974–81 (ret.); served with RN 1944–46; Pres., Candn. Gas Assn. 1971–72; Treas. & Dir., Calgary Centre for Performing Arts 1985–90; Chrmn., Alta. Children's Hosp. 1985–87; recreation: golf; Clubs: Ranchmen's (Calgary); Calgary Golf & Country Club; Home: 6 – 3315 Rideau Place S.W., Calgary, Alta. T2S 2T1.

**MAYER, Hon. Charles James,** P.C., B.S.A. (Agric. Econ.); farmer, former politician; b. Saskatoon, Sask. 21 Apr. 1936; s. Roy Fred and Anna Viola (Anderson) M.; e. Nutana Coll. H.S. Saskatoon; Univ. of Sask. B.S.A. 1964; m. Muriel Elaine d. Dr. and Mrs. A.B. Van Cleave 27 Dec. 1963; children: Holly Louise, Cheryl Anne, Judith Lenore; Minister of Agric., Small Communities & Rural Areas, Min.-Designate of Agric. & Agri-Food 1993; el. to H. of C. for Lisgar-Marquette 1988 and for Portage-Marquette 1979, 1980, 1984; Min. of State for the Candn. Wheat Bd. and Fed. Min. responsible for liaison with Canada's cooperative sector 1984; Min. of State (Grains and Oilseeds) 1987–92; Min. of Western Economic Diversification 1989–92; Min. of Western Econ. Diversification & Min. of State (Grains & Oilseeds) 1989–92; Min. of Agriculture 1993– ; former Chrmn., Manitoba P.C. Caucus; farmed in Sask. and presently Carberry, Man.; Past Pres. Man. Beef Growers Assn. 1975–78; mem. Manitoba Inst. Agrologists; Agricultural Inst. of Can.; Presbyterian; P. Conservative; Home: Carberry, Man. R0K 0H0.

**MAYER, Guy L.,** B.A.; business executive; b. Ottawa, Ont. 8 Nov. 1951; s. Adolphe Joseph and Germaine Mayer (Paquette) M.; e. Univ. of Ottawa, B.A. 1983; m. Marie d. Louis and Gabrielle Labrosse 10 May 1975; children: Julie Josee, Danielle Christine, Annick Diane; VICE PRES., BRISTOL-MYERS SQUIBB K.K.; SR. VICE PRES., ZIMMER INTERNATIONAL; and PRES. ZIMMER JAPAN 1992– ; Biomed. Product Mgr., American Hospital Supply 1974–78; Sales Mgr. 1978–79; Regional Mgr. 1979–83; Nat. Sales & Mktg. Mgr., Picker Internat. 1983–84; Pres., Zimmer of Can. Ltd. 1984–87; Vice Pres., Zimmer Internat. and Managing Dir., U.K. & Ireland, Zimmer Ltd. 1988–90; Vice Pres., Corporate Planning & Development, Zimmer Inc. 1990–91; Sr. Vice Pres., Corporate Planning and Development, Zimmer Inc. 1991–92; Vice-Chrmn., Candn. Assn. of Mfrs. of Med. Devices; Address: Arisugawa Homes #103, 5-5-14, Minami-Azabu, Minato-ku, Tokyo 106, Japan.

**MAYHEW, Elza Lovitt,** B.A., M.F.A., R.C.A.; sculptor; b. Victoria, B.C. 19 Jan. 1916; d. George and Alice (Bordman) Lovitt; e. Univ. of B.C., B.A.; studied with Jan Zach Victoria 1955–58; Univ. of Ore. M.F.A. 1963; m. Charles Alan Mayhew (d. 1943) 10 Sept. 1938; children: Anne Lovitt, Garth Alan; solo exhns. incl. The Point Gallery Victoria 1960, 1962; Art Gallery of Greater Victoria 1961, 1964, 1971 (Retrospective); Fine Arts Gallery Univ. of B.C. 1961; Lucien Campbell Plaza Univ. of Ore. 1963; Venice Biennale Candn. Pavilion 1964; Dorothy Cameron Gallery Toronto 1965; EXPO 67, Montreal (two sculptures); The Backroom Gallery Victoria 1978; Burnaby (B.C.) Art Gallery 1979; Equinox Gallery Vancouver 1980; Albert White Gallery Toronto 1980; Wallack Gallery, Ottawa 1981; EXPO 86, Vancouver, 'ZONG I,' and 'Supplicant,' both bronze; Port Angeles Fine Art Center 1988; rep. in nat. and internat. group exhns.; rep in various perm. colls. incl. Nat. Gallery Can., Nat. Capital Comn. 'Meditation Piece' Rideau Canal Ottawa; comns. incl. B.C. Archives and Museum Victoria 1967; Expo '67 2 sculptures; Bank of Can. Vancouver bronze mural 1968; Confed. Centre Charlottetown 'Column of the Sea' Centennial Project 1973; Univ. of Victoria 'Bronze Priestess' 1988; rec'd Sir Otto Beit Medal Royal Soc. Brit. Sculptors 1962; B.C. Centennial Sculpture Exhn. Purchase Award 1967; Honorary Doctorate, Univ. of Victoria 1989; Dir. Internat. Sculpture Center Kansas 1968–79; Consultant, B.C. Comte on Art 1974–76; work subject of film 'Time Markers' 1985; cited various bibliogs.; work in progress 'Moon Piece' 8 ft.; Address: 698 Beaver Lake Rd., Victoria, B.C. V8Z 5N8.

**MAYNARD, John C.,** B.A., F.S.A., F.C.I.A.; actuary; b. Toronto, Ont. 30 July 1919; s. late Dr. John C. and Anne Marjorie (Wilson) M.; e. Univ. of Toronto Schs.; Lakefield Coll. Sch.; Trinity Coll., Univ. of Toronto, B.A. 1940; m. Margaret S. McClelland, 1948; children: Jennifer, John, Judith; served in RCNVR 1940–45; on loan to RN for duties in naval radar, serving as radar offr. in HMS Revenge, HMS Victorious, HMS Implacable; rank Lt. Commdr. on discharge; joined Actuarial Div., Canada Life Assurance Co. 1945, Sr. Vice Pres. and Chief Actuary 1977–81; mem., Soc. of Actuaries (Fellow 1949, Vice Pres. 1974–76); Candn. Inst. Actuaries (Pres. 1972–73); Pres., T. Holders Assn. of Univ. of Toronto 1980–82; Chrmn., Ont. Pension Comm. 1982–86; Gov., Candn. Corps. of Commissionaires (Toronto and region) 1964–89; Dir., Canada Life Insur. Co. of New York 1972– ; Pres., Navy League of Canada (Ont. Div.) 1991–93; mem. Harcourt Lodge, AF & AM; Alpha Delta Phi; Anglican; recreations: tennis, golf; Clubs: Badminton & Racquet, Toronto Hunt; Home: 500 Avenue Rd., Apt. 1103, Toronto, Ont. M4V 2J6.

**MAYNE, Seymour,** Ph.D.; writer; professor; b. Montreal, Qué. 18 May 1944; s. Henry and Doris (Minkin) M.; e. McGill Univ., B.A. (Hon.) 1965; Univ. of B.C., M.A. 1966, Ph.D. 1972; PROF. UNIV. OF OTTAWA 1985– ; Lectr., Univ. of B.C. 1972; Univ. of Ottawa 1973; Asst. Prof. 1973–78; Assoc. Prof. 1978–85; Vis. Prof., Hebrew Univ. of Jerusalem 1979–80, 1983–84; Concordia Univ. 1982–83; Writer-in-residence, Prog. of Candn. Studies, Hebrew Univ. 1987–88; Chester Macnaghten First Prize in Creative Writing 1962; J.I. Segal Prize for Eng.-Fr. Lit. 1974; York Poetry Workshop Award 1975; ALTA (Am. Literary Translators Assn.) Poetry Translation Award 1990; Can. Counc. Arts Grants 1969, 1973, 1977, 1979, 1984; Mng. Ed., Very Stone House 1966–70; Ed., Ingluvin Pubns. 1970–73; Mosaic Press 1974–82; Ed. & Contrib. Ed., var. lit. & acad. jours. 1960– ; author: 'Tiptoeing on the Mount' 1965, 'Mouth' 1970, 'Name' 1975, 'Diasporas' 1977, 'The Impossible Promised Land' 1981, 'Vanguard of Dreams' 1984, 'Children of Abel' 1986; 'Diversions' 1987; 'Simple Ceremony' 1990; 'Killing Time' 1992; 'Locust of Silence' 1993; transl.: 'Burnt Pearls' 1981; co-transl.: 'Genealogy of Instruments' 1974; ed. & co-transl.: 'Generations' 1982, 'Crossing the River' 1989; 'Jerusalem as She Is' 1991; 'Night Prayer and Other Poems' 1993; editor: 'Essential Words' 1985, 'Irving Layton' 1978, 'The A.M. Klein Symposium' 1975, six other titles; Office: Dept. of English, Univ. of Ottawa, Ottawa, Ont. K1N 6N5.

**MAYRAND, Hon. Albert,** LL.D.; né Longueuil, Qué. 19 février 1911; f. Oswald et Orphise (Gadbois) M.; é. Univ. de Montréal; Univ. d'Ottawa LL.D. 1965; Univ. de Montréal LL.D. 1978; Dalhousie Univ. LL.D. 1983; ép. Lucienne f. Louis A. Boyer 30 juin 1940; enfants: Cécile, Nicole, Lise, Yves, Louis, Chantal; admis au barreau 1934; Q.C. 1955; avocat 1934–48, étude Mayrand, Deslauriers et Trépanier; prof. Faculté des sciences sociales Univ. de Montréal 1940–48, Faculté de droit 1948–65, prof. émérite 1965; dir. Revue du Barreau prov. de Qué. 1955–65; juge, Cour supérieure 1965; prés. du Comité du droit de la famille et du Comité du droit des obligations, Office de révision du Code civil 1969–74; juge, Cour Supérieure du Qué. 1965–74; juge, Cour d'Appel du Qué. 1974–86; Wainwright Sr. Rsch. Fellow, McGill Univ. 1986–1988; conseil LEDUC, LeBel depuis 1989; jurisconsulte de l'Assemblée nationale depuis 1986; auteur 'Les successions ab intestat' 1971; 'Dictionnaire de maximes latines' 1972, 2ème éd. 1985; 'L'inviolabilité de la personne humaine' 1975; 'The Influence of Spousal Conduct on the Custody of Children' 1983; 'The Quebec Civil Code: New Steps Towards Equality in Family Law' 1985; co-auteur 'Quelques aspects du droit de la prov. de Québec' 1963; 'Mélanges B. Bissonnette' 1963; 'Mélanges R. Savatier' 1965; 'Mélanges M.-L. Beaulieu' 1967–68; 'Lois nouvelles' 1965 et 1970; catholique; Adresse: 21 ave. Péronne, Outremont, Qué. H3S 1X7.

**MAYRAND, Hon. Yves;** juge; né Montréal, Qué. 14 nov. 1935; f. Emilien et Lucia (Hamelin) M.; é. Coll. de Montréal 1948–54; Philosophie Coll. Ste-Marie de Montréal 1955–56; Droit à l'Univ. de Montréal 1957–59; Année du stage à l'Univ. McGill 1960; ép. Lucille f. Lucien et Germaine (Dussault) Mongrain 21 dec. 1961; JUGE, COUR SUPERIEURE DU QUE. 1985– ; Admis au Barreau 1960; Procureur de la Commission Raynault 1968; Procureur de la Commission de Police 1969–71; nommé juge de la Cour des Sessions de la Paix 1972; Juge en chef par intérim de cette cour 1977; Juge en chef en titre 1978–85; Adresse: 1977 Des Ormes, St-Bruno, Qué. J3V 4G6; Bureau: 16.53 Palais de Justice, 1 Notre-Dame est, Montréal, Qué. H2Y 1B6.

**MAYRS, Charles A.;** advertising agency executive; b. Winnipeg, Man. 18 April 1940; s. William Black and Marjorie Tinsdale Henry M.; e. Magee Sr. H.S. (hons. art/graphic design) 1957; Vanc. Sch. of Art, Hons. grad. 1961 (scholarship winner 1958, 1959, 1960, 1961); m. Mary Lou d. Don and Velma Forester 3 June 1961; children: Coreen, Kathleen, Paul, Andrew, Sara; PRES., DOME ADVERTISING LTD. 1986– ; Dir., Corporate Strategies Group; Instr., Vanc. Sch. of Art (nights) 1962–64; Graphic Designer, James Lovick Ltd. 1961; Art Dir. 1963; Assoc. Creative Dir. 1969; Creative Dir., Baker Lovick Ltd. 1979; Vice-Pres. 1981; designed & executed advtg. campaigns for CP Air, B.C. Govt., Bridgestone Tires, Expo '86, CN Rail, Tourism Vancouver & others; Lectr., 'Communications in the 20th Century' Douglas Coll.; Capilano Coll.; Emily Carr Coll. of Art; Mem., Vanc. Art Dir. Club; Vanc. Creative Club; affiliated Advtg. Agencies Internat.; 1992 Georgie Awards, Best Advertising Campaign; 1992 Billi Awards, Bronze, Vancouver Aquarium; 'Bessie' Gold Award & Hollywood TV & Radio Internat. Broadcast Award (B.C. Tel) 1986; AAAI Gold Award (Pharmasave Drug Stores) 1985, (Province Newspaper) 1984, (Yellow Pages) 1983; BBDO Internat. Award of Merit (B.C. Govt.) 1985; Award of Excellence, Graphex '84 (Vancouver Aquarium) 1984; Internat. Award (Sweden & USA) for Calgary Albertan TV campaign 1977; 'Best in North America' award for Vancouver Sun newspaper, outdoor bd. advtg. 1974; 'Best in Canada' for Toronto Telegram Public Serv. campaign 1971; Roland Paper Student Award 'Best in Canada' 1961; Exhib. of paintings: Vancouver Art Gall. Annual Exhib. 1959–60; Group Show, Winnipeg Art Gall. 1960; Montreal Museum of Fine Arts 1960; Presentation House, N. Vancouver 1978; Diane Farris Gall., Vancouver 1990; Ferry Gallery, W. Vancouver 1991; Seymour Gallery, N. Vancouver 1993; Pres., Nor-westers Track & Field Club 1974–76; recreation: running; Clubs: North Shore Nomads (Pres., Nomad Silver Fund 1981– ); Capilano Golf and Country; Home: 5447 Monte Bre Place, W. Vancouver, B.C. V7W 3A8; Office: 666 Burrard St., Ste. 770, Vancouver, B.C. V6C 2X8.

**MAYRS, David Blair;** artist, teacher; b. Winnipeg, Man. 2 May 1935; s. William Black and Marjorie Tinsdale (Henry) M.; e. Magee H.S. 1953; Vancouver Sch. of Art 1957; m. Mary d. John and Margaret Crysdale 21 Dec. 1968; children: Marjorie, Katherine; TEACHER, VANCOUVER SCHOOL OF ART & EMILY CARR COLL. OF ART & DESIGN 1966– ; Jey Studios, Vanc. 1959; James Lovick Advtg. Agency 1959–60; Crane Advtg. Agency 1960–61; Kelly Douglas (Advtg. Dept.) 1962–66; Leon & Thea Korner Travelling Scholarship 1957 (travelled through Eur. & British Isles); Purchase Award, Burnaby Print Show, Burnaby Art Gall. 1971; one-man shows incl.: Bau-Xi Gall. Vanc. 1977, '79, '81, '85, '89; Bau-Xi Gall. Toronto 1991; Douglas Art Gall. Vanc. 1968; Studio Art Gall. Vanc. 1965; Tempus Gall. Vanc. 1964; group exhibitions incl.: Diane Farris Gall. (Four Brothers - Bill, Frank, David & Charles) 1990; SFU Art Gall. 1989; Eye Centre Gall. Vanc. 1988; Mus. of Modern Art Japan 1987; Vanc. Art & Artists 1983; West Coast Surrealists, Gall. Move Vanc. 1980; Other Realities, the Legacy of Surrealism in Canadian Art, Ctr. Cult. Can., Paris & Canada House, London 1978 and others; Home: 440 Ellis St., North Vancouver, B.C. V7H 2G6; Office: 1399 Johnston, Granville Island, Vancouver, B.C.

**MAZANKOWSKI, The Right Hon. Donald Frank,** P.C.; former politician; b. Viking, Alta. 27 July 1935; s. late Frank and late Dora (Lonowski) M.; e. Pub. and High Schs. Viking, Alta.; D.Eng. (Hon.), Technical Univ. of N.S. 1987; LL.D. (Hon.) Univ. of Alberta 1993; m. Lorraine Effie d. late Lawrence James Poleschuk 6 Sept. 1958; three s. Gregory, Roger, Donald; first elected Mem. of Parliament for Vegreville, Alta. 1968; apptd. Min. of Transport, Govt. of Can. and Min. responsible for Candn. Wheat Bd. 1979–80; Min. of Transport and Acting Min. of Industry, Science & Technology 1984–86; Deputy Prime Minister 1986–93; Government House Leader and Pres. of the Queen's Privy Council 1986–91; Pres. of the Treasury Bd. 1987–88; Minister responsible for Privatization & Regulatory Affairs 1988; Min. of Agriculture 1988–91; Min. of Finance 1991–93; retired from politics June 7, 1993; Chrmn., Action Ctte. on Western Low Sulphur Coal to Ontario & responsible for Northern Pipeline Agency; Home: P.O. Box 1350, Vegreville, Alta. T9C 1S5.

**MAZER, Brian Michael,** B.A., LL.B., LL.M.; professor of law; b. Saskatoon, Sask. 21 Feb. 1952; s. Oscar and Doris (Krauss) M.; e. Univ. of Sask., B.A. 1975, LL.B. 1975; Univ. of Alta., LL.M. 1977; m. Candice L. Schachter d. Sarah and Joseph Schachter; PROF. OF LAW, UNIV. OF WINDSOR 1985– ; Asst. Prof., present univ. 1978–81; Assoc. Prof. 1981–85; Assoc. Dean of Law 1982–88; Home: 648 Sunset Ave., Windsor, Ont.; Office: Fac. of Law, Univ. of Windsor, Windsor, Ont. N9B 3P4.

**MAZINKE, Harvey Gordon,** B.Sc.ME, P.Eng.; business executive; b. Altona, Man. 6 Apl. 1937; s. Henry and Bertha (Schroeder) M.; e. Morris (Man.) High Sch. 1955; Univ. of Man. B.Sc.ME 1959; m. Marian d. John and Edythe Dickson 1959; children: Scott, DeEtta; MNG. PARTNER PLAINS EQUIPMENT LTD. 1965– ; Pres. Mazco Holdings Ltd.; Chief Design Eng. Strong-Scott Ltd. Winnipeg 1959–63; Prodn. Mgr. Greensteel Industries Ltd. 1963–64; Partner Philmaz Services Ltd. 1963–65; mem. Adv. Bd. Labatt's Sask. Brewery 1972–87; Nat. Chrmn. Massey-Ferguson Candn. Dealer Council 1972–76; Chrmn. Bd. Govs. and Presidential Search Ctte. Univ. of Regina 1989–92; Bd. mem. Sask. Literacy Council 1988–91; Chrmn. Curl Can. 1987–88; Chrmn. Olympic Ctte. Curling Internat. Curling Fedn. 1985–88; Pres. Adm. Centre Sask. Sports & Recreation 1985–86; mem., Regina Economic Development Council 1993– ; Bd. mem., Ranch Erhlo Soc.; four times men's provl. curling champion; Candn. curling champion and world finalist 1973; numerous curling awards and competitions; inductee Sask. Sports and Candn. Curling Halls of Fame; Hon. Life mem. Candn. Curling Assn. (Pres. 1987–88, Nat. Players Rep. 1978–82); mem. Assn. Profl. Engs. Sask.; Lutheran; recreations: curling, golf; Clubs: Wascana Country; Tartan Curling; Home: 30 Green Meadow Rd., Regina, Sask. S4V 0A5; Office: P.O. Box 967 Regina, Sask. S4P 3B2.

**MAZUMDAR, Pauline Margaret Hodgson,** B.S., M.Tech., Ph.D.; university professor; b. Northumberland, Eng. 14 Nov. 1933; d. Hugh Hodgson and Lucie Rosalie (Calazel) Davidson; e. Univ. of London, Royal Free Hosp. Sch. of Med., M.B., B.S. 1958; Brunel Univ., M.Tech. (Immunology) 1973; Johns Hopkins Univ., Ph.D. 1976; m. Dipak s. Dwijendra Lal and Lakshmi M. 25 April 1959; PROFESSOR OF HISTORY OF MEDICINE, UNIV. OF TORONTO 1987– ; practiced med. 1958–72; Asst. Physician, Blood Grouping Lab., Children's Hosp. (Boston) 1961–62; Asst. Pathologist, North London Blood Transfusion Ctr. (U.K.) 1972; Hannah Prof. of History of Med., Univ. of Toronto 1977–87; Dir., Peebles Hotel Hydro, Peebles, Scotland; Editor, 'Sigerist Circle Newsletter' 1991– ; Mem., Royal Soc. of Med. (London) 1962– ; mem., N.D.P. 1978– ; Fellow, Eugenics Soc. (London) 1976– ; mem., Am. Assn. for History of Med. 1972– ; (Council 1979–81; Garrison Lecture Ctte. 1987; Chair, Osler Medal Ctte. 1988); Fellow, Academy of Medicine, Toronto 1978– ; (Chair, Section on History of Med. 1977–87; Council 1983–84, 1988–89; Nom. Ctte. 1988, '92; Mus. Ctte. 1979–92); mem., Henry E. Sigerist Circle 1991– ; conducting historical rsch. on: 'League of Nations Health Section, Commission for Standardization of Sera, Serological Tests & Biol. Products 1919–1940'; author: 'Eugenics, Human Genetics & Human Failings' 1992 (Jason A. Hannah Medal, Royal Soc. of Canada 1993), 'Species & Specificity' 1994; also papers on the history of eugenics, genetics & immunology; editor: 'Immunology 1930–

1980' 1989 (proceedings); recreations: history of art & architecture, painting, photography, breeding maine coon cats; Home: The Kent House, 368 Sumach St., Toronto, Ont. M4X 1V4; Office: Univ. of Toronto, Institute for History & Philosophy of Science & Technology, Victoria College, Toronto, Ont. M5S 1K7.

**MAZZA, Antonino,** B.A., M.A.; poet, literary translator, editor, publisher, guest lecturer; b. 10 Jan. 1949; e. Carleton Univ. B.A. (Hons.) 1972, M.A. 1975; Univ. of Toronto, Ph.D. cand. 1985–87; studied Romance Philology with G. Contini, Scuola Normale Sup. Pisa Italy 1975–76 and Semiotics with Umberto Eco, Univ. of Bologna 1976; Lecturer, Modern Lang. & Lit., Univ. of Ottawa 1978–81; Spanish & Italian, Queen's Univ. 1983–85; Teaching Asst., Italian Studies, Univ. of Toronto 1985–87; Mem., P.E.N. Internat. 1990– ; League of Candn. Poets 1988– ; Literary Translators' Assn. 1984– (Vice-Pres. 1985–87); SOCAM 1983– ; Editor: 'Vice Versa' 1985; Co-editor: 'Gamut International' 1987–89; Co-Founder & Assoc. Ed.: 'Anthos' 1978–87; Italo Calvino Translation Prize, Columbia Univ. 1992; ItalCanada Prize for Poetry 1978; author: 'Shifting Terrains' 1995; 'The City Without Women' (translated with an essay) 1993, 'The Way I Remember It' (book) 1992 (poetry album) 1988, 'Pier Paolo Pasolini: Poetry' (selected & translated with an afterword) 1991, 'The First Paradise, Odetta ...' (poetry recording) 1987 (book: translated) 1985, 'The Bones of Cuttlefish' (translated) 1983, 'Structures of Chaos' 1979 and others; works pub. in several anthologies; contributor to other books and theatre; Producer 'Renga' (Kaleidoscope TV Ottawa) 1981; author of numerous magazine, journal & newspaper articles; participant in several readings, lectures, conferences & radio interviews; listed in 'The Canadian Encyclopedia,' 'Canadian Literary Translators' Directory,' 'Who's Who in the League of Canadian Poets'; Address: 1 Palace Pier Court, Suite 1908, Etobicoke, Ont. M8V 3W9.

**McADAM, Rhona Margaret,** B.A., M.L.S.; writer; b. Duncan, B.C. 20 May 1957; d. Duncan Kennedy and Ruth Isabel (Cooper) McA.; e. Univ. of Alta. B.A. 1980, M.L.S. 1982; Univ. of Wolverhampton M.A. 1994; author (poetry) 'Life in Glass' 1984; 'Hour of the Pearl' 1987 (Alta. Poetry Award 1987); 'Creating the Country' 1989; 'Old Habits' 1993; poetry pub. anthols. and mags. Can., Eng., USA & Ireland; poetry readings across Can., UK; joined Records Mgmt. Govt. Alta. 1982–87 becoming Pub. Records Offr. Solr. Gen.'s Dept.; freelance writer 1987–92; Info Offr., Spencer Stuart 1992– ; mem. Writers Union Can.; PEN Internat.; League of Candn. Poets; Soc. of Authors; recreations: cooking, reading, cinema; Address: c/o Writers Union of Canada, 24 Ryerson Ave., Toronto, Ont. M5T 2P3.

**McAFEE, Jerry,** B.S., Sc.D.; oil company executive (retired); b. Port Arthur, Texas 3 Nov. 1916; s. Almer McDuffie and Marguerite (Calfee) McA.; e. Univ. Texas, B.S. (Chem. Engn.) 1937; Mass. Inst. Tech., Sc.D. (Chem. Engn.) 1940; Univ. Pittsburgh, Mang. Problems for Extves., 1952; m. Geraldine, d. William H. Smith, 21 June 1940; children: Joe R., William M., Loretta M., Thomas R.; Dir., Am. Petrol. Inst.; Mass. Inst. of Tech. Corp.; joined Universal Oil Products Co., Chicago as Rsch. Chem. Engr. 1940–43; Operating Engr. 1944–45; Tech. Specialist, Gulf Oil Corp., Port Arthur, Texas 1945–50; successively Dir. Chem., Asst. Dir. Rsch., Vice-Pres., Assoc. Dir., Gulf Rsch. & Development Co., Harmarville, Pa. 1950–55; Vice-Pres. Engn. Mfg., Gulf Oil Corp. 1955–60; Vice-Pres. Extve. Tech. Advisor 1960; Dir. of Planning and Econ. 1962–64; Sr. Vice-Pres. of Corp. and Coordinator of Gulf Eastern Co. 1964–67; Extve. Vice Pres. & Dir., Gulf Oil Can. Ltd. 1967–69; Pres. and C.E.O. 1969–76; Chrmn. and C.E.O., Gulf Oil Corp. 1976–81; mem., Am. Inst. Chem. Engn. (Vice-Pres. 1959, Pres. 1960); Nat. Acad. Engn.; Am. Chem. Soc.; Presbyterian; recreations: tennis, golf, music; Clubs: Duquesne (Pittsburgh); Fox Chapel Golf; Rolling Rock; John's Island (Vero Beach, Fla.); Bent Pine (Vero Beach, Fla.); Address: 1150 Beach Rd., Apt. 3L, Vero Beach, FL 32963.

**McALDUFF, Edward J.,** Ph.D.; university professor; b. Alberton, P.E.I. 3 Dec. 1939; s. Charles Augustin and Dorothy Sarah (Gillis) M.; e. St. Francis Xavier Univ. B.Sc. 1961; Univ. of Toronto Ph.D. 1965; m. Kathleen d. Sarto and Gwen Bradshaw 19 Dec. 1973; children: David, Michael, Ann; DEAN OF SCIENCE 1981–87, 1993– and PROF. OF CHEMISTRY, ST. FRANCIS XAVIER UNIV. 1982– ; Rsch. Instr., Univ. of Washington 1965–67; Asst. Prof., present Univ. 1967–72; Visiting Assoc. Prof., Univ. of B.C. 1973; Rsch. Assoc., Louisiana State Univ. 1975–76; Assoc. Prof. of Chem., present Univ. 1972–82; Assoc. Dean of Sci. 1980–81; Dean 1981–87; Chair of Grad. Studies 1989–93; Chair, Dept. of Chemistry 1992–93; mem., Chem. Inst. of Can.; Am. Chem. Soc.; Home: 26 Hillcrest St., Antigonish, N.S.; Office: Nicholson Hall, St. Francis Xavier Univ., Antigonish, N.S. B2G 1C0.

**McALEER, William J.;** insurance executive; b. Toronto, Ont. 17 Oct. 1934; s. William J. and Effie J. (Davis) M.; m. Doreen d. Norman and Clara Kinsman 5 Oct. 1957; children: Diane, Lynn, William; CHAIRMAN, CHIEF EXTVE. OFFR. & DIR., JOHNSON & HIGGINS LTD. 1993– ; Extve. Vice-Pres. & Dir., Trillium Insur. Serv. Ltd. 1970–85; Sr. Vice Pres. present company 1985–91; Extve. Vice-Pres., C.O.O. & Dir. 1991–92; Chrmn., Pres. & C.E.O., Harbourfront Corp. 1990– ; Pres., Creditbrae Investments Inc. 1978–91; Chrmn., Bd. of Dir., Federal Business Devel. Bank 1986–90; The Ontario Place Corp. 1977–87; Pres., Toronto Insur. Conf. 1984; Dir., Extve. Vice-Pres. & Pres., The Albany Club 1982–94; recreations: tennis, bridge; club: The Albany; Home: 215 Riverside Dr., Toronto, Ont. M6S 4A8; Office: P.O. Box 1010, Scotia Plaza, 40 King St. W., Toronto, Ont. M5H 3Y2.

**McALISTER, Daniel F.,** B.Arch., M.O.A.A., M.R.A.I.C.; architect; b. Windsor, Ont. 9 Sept. 1947; s. George Alexander and Mary Carolyn (McDonald) McA.; e. Lawrence Park C.I., Toronto; Queen's Univ. 1966; Univ. of Toronto B.Arch. 1972; m. Frances G. d. Dr. A.F.W. Peart 7 Oct. 1971; children: Suzanna, Teddy, Margo, Ariel; PARTNER, BREGMAN & HAMANN ARCHITECTS; Design Arch. Prof. Rolf Gutbrod, Stuggart, W. Germany 1972–75; Vice Pres., Crang and Boake Inc. 1978–89; Extve. Arch. Metro Toronto Convention Centre Complex 1980–84 (commissioned to design expansion 1993); Guest Lectr. Univ. of Toronto; Chrmn. Toronto Soc. of Arch.; mem. Ont. Assn. of Arch.; Roy. Arch. Inst. of Can.; recipient Alpha Ro Chi Medal, Univ. of Toronto; Queen's Univ., Campus Planning and Development Ctte.; recreations: windsurfing, cooking, skiing, squash, sailing; Clubs: Cambridge; Beaver Valley Ski; Home: 37 Playter Blvd., Toronto, Ont. M4K 2W1; Office: 481 University Ave., Toronto, Ont. M5G 2H4.

**McALLISTER, David Andrew,** B.Comm.; marketing executive; b. Wolfville, N.S. 15 May 1956; s. Francis Charles and Helen Emma (Edwards) M.; e. Mt. Allison Univ. B.Comm. 1978; m. Margaret d. Daniel and Mona Macmillan 5 Dec. 1981; children: Alicia Ann Marie, Klye Andrew; VICE-PRES., MARKETING, SABIAN LTD. 1984– ; Sales Rep., McCain Foods Ltd. 1978; Sales Supvr. 1979; Asst. Product Manager 1980; Product Manager 1981–82; Sr. Product Manager 1983–84; Mem., Consumer Products Sectorial Advisory Group on International Trade (S.A.G.I.T.), Govt. of Canada; Advisory Bd., Ctr. for Internat. Marketing & Entrepreneurship, UNB & UDEM; Bd. of Dirs., Music Industry Assn. of Can.; recreations: jogging, golf, skiing, reading; Home: 154 Connell St., Box 1802, Woodstock, N.B. E0J 2B0; Office: Meductic, N.B. E0H 1L0.

**McALLISTER, Don E.,** B.A., M.A., Ph.D.; museum biodiversity advisor and curator/adjunct professor; b. Victoria, B.C. 23 Aug. 1934; s. Ken and Clare (MacQuarrie) M.; e. Univ. of B.C., B.A. 1955, M.A. 1957, Ph.D. 1964; m. the late Nancy Anne d. Gertrude and William Mahoney 10 Aug. 1956; m. Elisabeth Janssen 9 Jan. 1992; children: Fern, Wendy Anne, Sylvia Kathleen, Jean Heather, Bruce Douglas; RESEARCH CURATOR IN ICHTHYOLOGY 1986–94 and SR. BIODIVERSITY ADVISOR, CANDN. MUS. OF NATURE 1991–94 (EMERITUS positions 1994– ); Curator of Fishes, Nat. Mus. of Natural Sci. 1958–86; specialist: smelts, sculpins, eelpouts, snailfishes, Arctic fishes; rsch. on mus. computer applications & biogeog.; active conservationist, esp. in biodiversity issues and in trying to halt destruction of world's coral reefs; built nat. collection to 1 million fish specimens & over 3000 species; Adjunct Prof., Univs. of Ottawa & Carleton; Ctte. Mem., Status of Endangered Wildlife in Can.; editor: 'Sea Wind', 'Global Biodiversity' / 'La biodiversité mondiale'; Hon. Mem., Chinese Soc. of Ichthyology; author of over 200 sci. papers, monographs, books & book chapters; using GIS to study global biodiversity of coral reef fishes; Hon. Mem., Ottawa Field-Naturalist's Club; Gov., Am. Soc. of Ichth. & Herpetol.; Co-founder, Editor & Pres., Ocean Voice Internat. Inc.; Chairperson, IUCN SSC coral reef fish ctte.; recreation: cross-country skiing; Home: 2883 Otterson Dr., Ottawa, Ont. K1V 7B2; Office: P.O. Box 3443, Stn. D, Ottawa, Ont. K1P 6P4.

**McALLISTER, Robert Ian,** M.A.; university professor; b. London, Eng. 29 March 1937; s. Charles and Margaret (Towell) McA.; e. St. John's Sch. Leatherhead, Eng.; Oxford Univ., B.A. 1959, M.A. 1963, Dip. Econ. Devel. 1968; Cambridge Univ., B.A. 1962, M.A. 1968; m. Jeanette d. John and Rita Hudson 2 July 1963; children: Karen, Lara, Kirsten; PROF. OF ECONOMICS, DALHOUSIE UNIV. 1971– ; Prof. of Resource & Environmental Studies 1986– and Prof. of International Development Studies 1991– ; Chrmn., Dalhousie Senate Ctte. on Internat. Development 1992– ; Chrmn. Bd. Dirs. Lester Pearson Inst. for Internat. Devel. 1985–87; Chrmn. of Econ. Dept. Dalhousie Univ. 1976–78; Econ. Advs., Premier Nfld. 1962–65; Sec. Royal Comn. Nfld.'s Econ. Prospects 1966–67; Chief, Regional Devel. Unit, Dept. of Finance Can. 1968–71; mem. Bd. Econ. Advs. to Premier N.S. 1977–79; Dir. Regional Devel. Prog. Inst. Rsch. Pub. Policy 1980–82; mem. Micmac Indian Devel. Council 1980–84; Advs., CIDA Projects Training Pub. Servants Ghana 1974–81, Zimbabwe 1981–84, Nepal 1988–89; Mem., Royal Comn. Seals & Sealing Ind. Can. 1984–86; mem. Adv. Group to Min. of External Relations on Africa 2000, 1986–89; Sr. Adviser on Development to the Internat. Federation of Red Cross and Red Crescent Societies, Geneva 1989–91; mem. Mayor's Task Force on Development of Halifax 1993– ; cons. various Candn. govt. depts. on energy, ind., econ., social, rural program and projects; author: 'Regional Development and the European Community' 1982; 'Projects for Relief and Development' 1991; 'Sustaining Relief with Development: Strategic Issues for the Red Cross and Red Crescent' 1993; co-author (with Tom Kent) 'Management for Development' 1985; ed. 'Newfoundland and Labrador: The First Fifteen Years of Confederation' 1966; 'Six International Development Projects' 1982; 'Windows on the World' 1993; and various articles; Home: 4 Armshore Dr., Halifax, N.S. B3N 1M5; Office: Dalhousie Univ., Halifax, N.S. B3H 3J5.

**McALPINE, Lt. Gen. Duncan Alastair;** C.M.M., K.St.J., C.D., M.A.; b. Montreal 23 July 1922; s. Angus and Sarah (Cooper) McA.; e. Sir George Williams Univ., B.A. 1952; Univ. of Ottawa, M.A. 1961; L'Institut des Etudes Politiques, Univ. de Paris, 1962; Univ. of N.B., doctoral studies 1966; 2 Lt. to Lt. Col., Black Watch (RHR) of Can.; Nat. Defence Coll., 1967; m. Barnelle Alice, d. Stanley Maurice and Florence (Barnes) Chatham; children: Lynn Carole, Bruce Duncan, Keith Andrew, Craig Alastair; Vice-Pres., Corp. Affairs, Brascan Ltd. 1977–87; Dir., Intertel Ltd.; Blue Cross Life Insurance Co. of Canada; C.O. 2nd Bn. Black Watch of Can. in Germany, Can. and Cyprus 1963–66; Commdr., Combat Training Centre 1970; Dir. Gen. Postings and Careers 1971; Assoc. Asst. Depy. Min. (Personnel) Dept. Nat. Defence 1972; Commdr. Candn. Mil. Component ICCS Vietnam 1973; Chief Personnel Devel. 1974; Commdr. Candn. Forces Europe 1975–76; Vice-Pres., National Defence College Assn.; Pres., Ont. Council St. John Ambulance 1987–89; Chrmn., Ont. Hospital Assn. 1989–90; Chrmn., Industrial Adv. Bd., Univ. of Waterloo, Office of Tech. Transfer and Licensing; United Church; recreations: sailing, tennis; Home: Portland, Ont. K0G 1V0.

**McANDLESS, F.W. Douglas,** C.D., B.A., M.Ed., F.O.T.F.; association executive; b. London, Ont. 7 Jan. 1935; s. Fred Watson and Helene Victoria (Woollatt) McA.; e. Univ. of W. Ont., B.A. 1964; Wayne State Univ., M.Ed. 1974; m. Jacki d. Fred and Marge Keene 2 July 1955; children: Patricia Lee, William Douglas, Jane Elizabeth; Pres., Ont. Teachers' Fedn. 1986; Teacher, Northdale, Northridge and Ealing Pub. Schs. 1954–66; Vice Prin. Ryerson Pub. Sch. 1966–75; Prin. Lord Roberts, Ecole Alexandra and Chippewa Pub. Schs. 1975–79, 1981–86; Pres. Ont. Pub. Sch. Teachers' Fedn. 1979–81; served as C.O. Service Btn. (London) 1975–80 and Elgin Regt. (RCAC, St. Thomas) 1981–85; named Teacher of Yr. (London 1976; recipient Queen's Silver Jubilee Medal 1977; Candn. Forces Decoration; Past Pres. and Founding Dir. Stoneybrook Sports; Fellow, Ont. Teachers' Fedn.; United Church; recreation: tennis; Club: Royal Candn. Mil. Inst.; Home: 679 Clermont Ave., London, Ont. N5X 1N3.

**McARTHUR, (George) Arnold,** C.M., O.S.M., F.C.C.T., M.A., D.C.L.; education and management consultant; b. Howick, Que. 21 June 1909; s. Peter Daniel and Marion Wilhelmina (Wright) McA.; e. Bishop's Univ. B.A. (Hons.) 1930, M.A. (Hons.) 1931, D.C.L. 1980; 1st Class High Sch. Dipl. (C.B.) 1931; Que. Educ. Dept. 1st Class Inspr.'s Cert. 1938, 1st Class Superior High Sch. Dipl. 1962; m. Audrey Jean d. Lt. Col. Norman C. and Elizabeth (Maclean) MacKay, N.B. 19 Aug. 1933; two s. Donald Norman Wright, Peter Arnold; Asst. Princ. and Athletic Dir. Laurentide High Sch. Grand'Mere, Que. 1931–33; Math. and Science Specialist, Westmount High Sch. 1933–34; Princ. Arvida (Que.) High Sch. 1934–38; Inspr. of Schs. Que. 1938–40; Supt. of Consolidated Paper Co. Schs. 1940–49, Shawinigan Falls High Sch. 1949–63, Rosemere High

Sch. 1963–65; Dir. Gen. N. Island Regional Sch. Bd. 1965–68; Educ. Consultant to Gaspe Regional Sch. Bd., Dawson Coll.1969–70, John Abbott Coll., Jewish Peoples' Schs., Manitou Coll. (Native N. Am. Culture Center) 1970–72, Vanier Coll.; Charter Pres./Chrm. Bd. Govs. Vanier Coll. 1970–73, Socio-Econ. mem. Bd. Govs., Vanier College 1973–77); mem. Prof. Staff, McGill Univ. 1970–73; Candn. Teachers Fed. Rep. to Kellogg Leadership Course, Univ. Alta. 1955; Dir., Jr. Red Cross Leadership Training Center for E. Can. 1957; mem. Adv. Comte. to Grand'Mere City Council 1946–49; Dir., Les Loisirs de Shawinigan 1958–63; Gov., Internat. Rotary 779, 1959–60; Candn. Rep. Rotary Internat. Consultative Comte. 1962–63, 1975–76; Chrmn. Foundation Comte. Dist. 779, 1977–78; Paul Harris Fellow since 1977; Mem., Protestant Ctte. of the Council of Educ. for Prov. of Que. 1960–64; Charter mem. Que. Superior Council Educ. 1964–68; Pres. and Dir., PAPT Credit Union 1968–91; rec'd Queen's Coronation Medal 1953; Order Scholastic Merit Que. 1957; Distinguished Service Award, Que. Assn. Sch. Adms. 1979; Order of Canada 1979; Fellow, Candn. Coll. Teachers; D.C.L. (Hon. Causa), Bishop's Univ. 1980; 125th Anniversary of the Confederation of Canada Medal, 1992; Past Pres., Prov. Assn. Prot. Teachers; Que. High Sch. Princ.'s Assn.; Past Dir., Candn. Teachers' Fed.; Assn. Candn. Community Colls.; Fed. des CEGEPS de la Prov. de Que.; mem., McGill Univ. Faculty Club; past Gov., Laurentide Men's Club; Governeur, Fondation Centre d'Acceuil Vaudreuil; recreations: curling, golf, tennis, badminton, theatre, music; Presbyterian; Clubs: Whitlock Golf and Country; Hudson Heights; Town of Mount Royal Country; Town of Mount Royal Curling; Hudson Yacht; Address: 85 Oakland Ave., PO Box 303, Hudson Heights, Que. J0P 1J0.

**McARTHUR, Donald Russell,** B.A.; business executive; b. Beamsville, Ont. 25 June 1931; s. Angus Russell and Grace Helen (McDonnell) McA.; e. Univ. of W. Ont. Sch. Bus. Adm., B.A. 1955; m. Rosemary d. Clayton and Emma Collins 2 June 1956; children: Stephen Russell, Catherine Grace; PRES., CANDN. IMPORTERS ASSOC. INC. 1988– ; Regional Mgr. Canadian General Electric 1957–68; Vice Pres. and Gen. Mgr. Clairtone Sound Corp. 1968–70; Sr. Vice Pres. Toyota Canada Inc. 1970–79; Pres. Peter Dennis Motor Corp. 1979–84; Pres., Yucan Motor Corp. 1985–88; Dir., Assn. of Internat. Automobile Manufacturers of Canada; Trade Facilitation Office of Canada; Candn. Automotive Repair and Service Council; Candn. Importers Assn.; recreations: curling, boating, skiing; Clubs: Dixie Curling, Royal Canadian Military Institute, World Trade Centre; Home: 31 Rainbow Creekway, Willowdale, Ont. M2K 2T9; Office: 210 Dundas St. W., Suite 700, Toronto, Ont. M5G 2E8.

**McARTHUR, Herbert Kimberley,** F.C.A.; chartered accountant; b. Sault Ste. Marie 11 May 1942; s. Herbert Kimberley and Florence Mary (Saunders) M.; e. C.A. 1965; elected Fellow 1991; m. Barbara d. Wilbert and Betty Evans 6 Dec. 1962; children: Stephen, Nancy; MANAGING PARTNER, BDO DUNWOODY WARD MALLETTE C.A.s SAULT STE. MARIE OFFICE; joined Tessier, Massicotte & Company 1960; Partner, Tessier, Smith and Partners 1967; merged with Dunwoody 1983; Pres., Sault Ste. Marie C.A. Assn. 1983–84; Mem., Sault Ste. Marie Police Services Bd. 1988–92 (Vice Chair 1990–92); Dir., Childrens Aid Soc. 1979–80; Treas. 1980; Pres., Mental Health Sault Ste. Marie 1976; Chair, Finance Ctte., C. of C. 1978–79; Mem., St. Andrews United Ch. (Treas. 1985–91; Chair, Extve. Bd. 1972–73); recreations: fishing, YMCA; club: YMCA; Home: 531 MacDonald Ave., Sault Ste. Marie, Ont. P6B 1H8; Office: P.O. Box 1109, Sault Ste. Marie, Ont. P6A 5N7.

**McARTHUR, John C.,** F.I.I.C.; insurance executive; b. Durham, Ont. 16 June 1939; s. Donald Duncan and Ruth Isobel (Dingwall) M.; e. Univ. of Waterloo, F.I.I.C. 1966; m. K. Adair d. Gordon and Mattie Hartwick 13 Jan. 1962; children: Karen Maureen, Heather Adair, Donald Allan John; PRESIDENT, ITT HARTFORD CANADA 1992– ; Pres. & C.E.O., Hartford Insurance Co. of Canada 1992– ; Chief Agent & General Mgr., Hartford Fire Insurance Co. 1992– ; Chief Agent, Hartford Life Insurance Co. 1992– ; Baillie, Nelson & Wark Ltd. 1961–64; Dist. Claims Mgr., North Western Mutual, Unigard Group 1964; Claims Mgr. for Can. 1970; Ont. Mgr. 1973; Ont. Br. Mgr., Safeco Insur. Cos. 1974; Can. Div. Mgr. 1975; Resident Vice Pres. 1978–91; Vice-Pres., Business Development, Dominion of Canada General Insurance Co. 1991–92; Pres., Northern Chap., Alta. Assn. of Ins. Adjusters 1967–68; Pres., Ins. Inst. of Ont. 1978–79; Vice-Pres., Ins. Inst. of Can. 1978–79; Dir., Vehicle Information Centre of Canada; Extve. Dir., Insur. Bur. of Can. (Chrmn., Claims Ctte.; Past Chrmn., Pub. Relns. & Prov. Leg. Liaison Cttes.); Dir., Ctr. for Study of Insur. Opns.; Depy. Chrmn., Facility Assoc.; Chrmn., Bd. of Dir., Insur. Crime Prev. Bur.; Candn. Automobile Theft Bur.; recreations: golf, curling; Club: Burlington Golf & Country; Home: 1292 Fairway Court, Burlington, Ont. L7P 1M4.

**MCAULAY, James Boyd;** retired hospital administrator; b. N. Cobalt, Ont. 29 June 1927; s. Angus and Margaret (McKee); e. Runnymede Coll. Inst., Toronto; m. Jeanne d. Hubert Woolfrey 10 Apr. 1953; children: Nancy Kim (Low), Kathryn Irene, Carol Jeanne (Weldon), Sharon June (Merchan), James Boyd; G.H. Woods Co. Ltd. 1946; Shanahan Cartage 1949; joined Toronto Western Hosp. 1950 and served in various positions, incl. Assoc. Extve. Dir. 1965–69, Extve. Dir. 1969–84; Asst. Dean, Institutional Affairs, Faculty of Med., Univ. of Toronto 1984; Special Adv. to the Vice-Provost, Health Sci., Univ. of Toronto 1984; Hon. Trustee, Toronto Western Hosp.; Toronto Western Hosp. Found.; Assoc. Prof. (Hon.), Fac. of Med., Univ. of Toronto; Past Pres., Assn. of Candn. Teaching Hospitals; Past Pres., Ont. Council of Administrators of Teaching Hospitals; mem., Amer. Coll. of Hosp. Adminrs.; Candn. Coll. of Health Service Extves.; Roy. Candn. Inst.; Conservative; Un. Church; Club: Bd. of Trade of Metro. Toronto; recreations: golf, curling; Home: 18 Aquila Ct., Rexdale, Ont. M9W 5J2.

**McAULEY, Alexander,** B.Sc., Ph.D., D.Sc., C.Chem., MRSChem., FCIC; university professor and administrator; b. Glasgow, Scotland 13 June 1936; s. Alexander and Susan Theresa (Haveron) M.; e. St. Aloysius College; Glasgow Univ. B.Sc. (Hons.) 1958, Ph.D. 1962, D.Sc. 1977; m. Sarah d. William and Maureen McGinley 22 Aug. 1962; children: Claire, Iain, Laura, Monica, Julie; ASSOCIATE VICE-PRESIDENT, RESEARCH, UNIV. OF VICTORIA 1993– ; Fulbright Fellowship, Michigan State Univ. 1962; ICI Fellowship, Strathclyde Univ. 1963; Lecturer 1964–70; Lecturer-Sr. Lecturer, Univ. of Glasgow 1970–75; Prof., Univ. of Victoria 1975– ; Chair, Chem. 1979–84; Dean, Grad. Studies 1986–91; Visiting Prof., Carleton Univ. 1981–82; Visiting Scientist, NRC Ottawa 1982; Visiting Rsch. Fellow, Australian Nat. Univ. 1991; Mem., Bd. of Gov., Univ. of Victoria 1984–90; Dir., Discovery Found.; Mem., Bd. of Mngt., Triumf Lab.; Edit. Bd., 'Coordinaton Chemistry Reviews'; Royal Soc. of Chem.; Fellow, Chem. Inst. of Canada; Dir., Victoria Business & Econ. Devel. Comn.; Pres., Candn. Assn. for Co-op. Edn. 1979–80; Mem., Chemistry Grants Selection Ctte., NSERC 1984–86, Chair 1986; Group Chair, Scholarships, Fellowships Ctte. 1988–91; Vice-Pres., Candn. Soc. for Chem. 1993–94; Pres. 1994; author/co-author of over 140 sci. articles; Editor, 'Specialist Chemical Reports' Royal Soc. of Chem. 1975–84; recreations: music, Scottish country dancing; club: Faculty; Office: P.O. Box 1700, Victoria, B.C. V8W 2Y2.

**McAULIFFE, Jane Dammen,** B.A., M.A., Ph.D.; university professor; b. Madison, Wisc., 16 April 1944; d. Arnold Hendrick and Margaret Anne (McDonald) Dammen; e. Trinity College (Washington, D.C.) B.A. 1968; Univ. of Toronto M.A. 1979, Ph.D. 1984; m. Dennis s. Leo and Ethel McAuliffe 8 June 1968; children: Dennis, Margaret, Katherine, Elizabeth; CHAIR, DEPT. FOR THE STUDY OF RELIGION & DIR., CENTRE FOR THE STUDY OF RELIGION, UNIV. OF TORONTO 1992– ; Asst. & Assoc. Prof., Hist. of Religions & Islamic Studies, Emory Univ. 1986–92; Assoc. Dean, Candler Sch. of Theol., Emory Univ. 1990–92; Assoc. Prof., Dept. for the Study of Religion & Dept. of Middle East & Islamic Studies, Univ. of Toronto 1992; NEH and SSHRC fellowships; Mem., Am. Acad. of Relgion; Am. Oriental Soc.; Candn. Soc. for the Study of Religion; Soc. for Values of Higher Education; author: 'Qur'anic Christians' 1992, 'Abbasid Authority Affirmed' 1993; Home: 180 Sherwood Ave., Toronto, Ont. M4P 2A8; Office: 123 St. George St., Toronto, Ont. M5S 2E8.

**McAUSLAN, Peter Gould,** B.A.; brewery executive; b. Lachine, Que. 6 Jan. 1946; s. William Martin and Elizabeth Mary (Snasdell-Taylor) M.; e. Sir George Williams Univ. B.A. 1972; m. Ellen Frances Bounsall; children: Taylor William, Todd Russell; PRESIDENT, McAUSLAN BREWING INC., MONTREAL 1988– ; Director of Admissions, Dawson College 1973–75; Registrar 1976–84; Secretary General 1985–87; Pres., Quebec Microbrewers Assn. 1992; Mem., Bd. of Advisors, Inst. for Brewing Studies, Boulder, Colorado; author: 'Brewing under Adversity' in 'The Marketing of Draft Versus Bottled Beer' 1991; clubs: Montreal Badminton and Squash, Hudson Yacht; Home: 92 Upper Whitlock Rd., Hudson Heights, Que. J0P 1J0; Office: 4850 St. Ambroise, Suite 100, Montreal, Que. H4C 3N8.

**McAVITY, Lieut.-Col. James Malcolm,** D.S.O., M.B.E.; retired executive; b. Westmount, Que. 20 Nov. 1909; s. late Allan Getchell and Amy Fellows (Adams) M.; e. Ridley Coll., St. Catharines, Ont. (1920–27, Sr. Matric.); Royal Mil. Coll., Kingston, Ont. 1927–31 (Dipl.); m. Margaret Audrey, d. Trevor H. Temple, Toronto, Ont., 30 Jan. 1937; children: Virginia Temple, Ian Malcolm; Sales Rep., Toronto office Consumers Glass Co. Ltd. 1932–40; Asst. to Gen. Sales Mgr., Jan.-Nov. 1946; apptd. Gen. Sales Mgr. of Jos. E. Seagram & Sons Ltd. 1946; Vice-Pres. 1951; Pres. and Dir., The House of Seagram Ltd. 1956; Chrmn. 1958; Pres., Candn. Export Assn. 1963–79; Founding Pres., Candn.-South African Soc., 1979–86; joined Candn. Armoured Corps Jan. 1940; attached 1 British Armoured Div. 1940–41 in U.K.; development of A 33 Training Centre in Camp Borden, purchase and development of Meaford Tank Range 1941–43; posted to Lord Strathcona's Horse (R.C.) in 1943, with rank of Major, promoted to Lt.-Col. in command in Italy 1944; brought Regt. back to Winnipeg, Jan. 1946; awarded D.S.O., M.B.E.; Col. of the Regiment, Lord Strathcona's Horse (R.C.) 1965–70; Gen. Chrmn., Welfare Fed. of Montreal (Red Feather) fund campaign 1959; Past Pres., Seigniory Club, Montreal Thistle Curling Club, Eagle River Salmon Club, Candn. Lawn Tennis Assn., Sir Arthur Currie Br. (Que. No. 1) Royal Candn. Legion, Assn. of Candn. Distillers, Candn. Tourist Assn.; Anglican; recreations: golf, fishing; Clubs: Toronto Golf; Vineyards Golf Club (Naples, FL); Royal Candn. Mil. Inst.; Home: c/o General Delivery, Maitland, Ont. K0E 1P0.

**McAVITY, John G.,** B.A.; association executive; museologist; b. Saint John, N.B. 30 Oct. 1950; s. J. Patrick H. and Catharine A. (MacNeill) M.; e. Univ. of N.B., B.A. 1972; Certified Assoc. Extve. 1981; EXTVE. DIR., CANADIAN MUSEUMS ASSOC. 1981– ; Researcher, Candn. Inventory of Hist. Bldgs. 1968–72; Asst. Curator, King's Landing Hist. Settlement 1972–73; Prov. Mus. Advr., N.B. Museum 1973–76; Extve. Sec., Carleton Martello Tower; Extve. Dir., Ontario Museum Assoc. 1976–81; Mem., Bd. of Dir., Ont. Assn. of Art Galls. 1986–88; Mem., Bd. of Dirs., Assn. of Cultural Extves. (Dir. 1986–92); Dir. National Bd., Candn. Soc. of Assn. Extves. 1993– ; Dir., Ottawa Chap., Candn. Soc. of Assn. Extves. 1985–90; Dir., Tourism Industry Assoc. of Canada 1990– ; Dir., Candn. Soc. of Copyright Consumers, 1990– ; Hon. Life Mem., Quaco Lib. & Hist. Soc.; Life Mem., Heritage Can.; Vice-Pres., Saint John Heritage Trust 1975–76; Dir., Centertown Citizens Corp. 1986–87; Am. Assn. of Mus.; Am. Assn. for State & Local Hist. (Awards Ctte. & Regl. Chrmn., 1981–85; Nom. Ctte. 1985–87); Kidney Found. of Can. (volunteer mem., Shefford Heritage Co-op Inc.); Home: 41 – 300 Cooper St., Ottawa, Ont. K2P 0G7; Office: 306 Metcalfe St., Ottawa, Ont. K2P 1S2.

**MCBAIN, Raymond Stuart;** industrialist; b. Quebec City, Que. 30 Sept. 1935; s. Vernal Lewis and Henrietta Jane (Kack) M.; e. Bishop's Coll. Sch. 1954; Sir George Williams; Laval Univ.; m. Barbara Ann d. Patrick and Jennifer Lamontagne 10 June 1961; children: Sandra-Lee, Curtis, Joanna-Lynn; PRES., VER-MAC INC. 1963– ; Pres., Maritime Road Signals Ltd. 1989– ; Pilot, R.C.A.F. 1957–60; Private Investigator 1960–63; manufactures electronic road safety devices; Bd. Mem., Port of Quebec 1985–88; Vice-Pres./Chrmn., Port of Quebec Corp. 1988– ; Past Vice-Pres., Quebec Jaycess; Past Pres., Quebec Kiwanis Club 1986–87; Mem., P.C. Party; Pres. of Finan., Quebec East Co.; recreations: tennis, golf, skiing; clubs: Club Advantage, Club Loretteville, Stoneham Ski Centre; Home: 1575 Ranvoyzé, Ste-Foy, Que. G1W 3J8; Office: 2520, Watt St., Ste-Foy, Que. G1P 3T4.

**MCBAIN, Hon. Ross Thomas George,** B.A., LL.B.; judge; b. Montreal, Que. 31 May 1926; s. Stanley Thomas and Gladys Florence Helen (Baker) M.; e. McGill Univ. and Univ. of Manitoba B.A. 1948; Univ. of Man. Law Sch. LL.B. 1952; m. Rosemary d. John and Mary Matilda Jobb 31 May 1954; children: Maureen Shelagh, Hugh John, Scott Thomas; JUSTICE, COURT OF QUEEN'S BENCH, ALBERTA 1983– ; Sr. Partner Barron-McBain law firm Calgary, Alta. 1958–81; Chrmn. Alta. Labour Rlns. Bd. 1981–83; cr. Q.C. 1970; Senator, Univ. of Calgary; recreation: sailing; Club: Glenmore Yacht (Commodore); Home: F101, 500 Eau Claire Ave. S.W., Calgary, Alta. T2P 3R8; Office: 611–4th St. S.W., Calgary, Alta. T2P 1T5.

**McBRYDE, William Arthur Evelyn,** M.A., Ph.D.; university professor; b. Ottawa, Ont. 20 Oct. 1917; s. Edwin Brooks and Evelyn Agnes (Riddick) M.; e. Univ. of Toronto Schs.; Univ. of Toronto, B.A. (Chem.) 1939, M.A. (Chem.) 1940; Univ. of Virginia, Ph.D. (Chem.) 1947; m. Marion Eleanor, d. John Robertson, Toronto,

Ont., 28 May 1949; children: Ian Douglas, Sheila Kathleen; EMERITUS PROFESSOR, UNIV. OF WATERLOO 1986– ; Teaching Asst., Univ. of Toronto 1939–42; Chemist, Welland Chemical Works, Niagara Falls 1942–44; Asst. Prof., Univ. of Toronto 1948–57; Travelling Fellowship, The Nuffield Foundation, Oxford Univ. 1954–55; Assoc. Prof., Univ. of Toronto 1957–60; Prof., Univ. of Waterloo 1960–86; Chrmn., Dept. of Chem. 1960–64, 1971–77; Dean, Faculty of Science 1961–69; Visiting Fellow, Aust. Nat. Univ. 1969–70; served in 2nd World War 1944–45, R.C.N.V.R., Sub-Lieut. (Special Br.) 1945; publications: 'Elementary Experimental Chemistry' (with M.W. Lister) 1950, 4th ed. 1959; 'The Outlines of Chemistry' (with R.P. Graham) 1966, 2nd ed. 1978; articles and papers to scient. journs.; mem., Chem. Inst. Can. (Councillor 1958–61; Dir. 1960–63); Chem. Soc. (London); Presbyterian; recreations: golf, gardening, curling; Address: 502 – 4 Willow St., Waterloo, Ont. N2J 4S2.

**McBURNEY, Margot B.,** B.A., M.Sc.; librarian; b. Lethbridge, Alta.; d. Ronald L. M. and R. Blanche (Lott) Hart; e. Principia Coll. Elsah, Ill. B.A.; Univ. of Ill. M.Sc.; m. 4 Sept. 1954 (divorced); children: Margot Elisabeth (Lisa) (Mrs. Walter Critchett Lane), James Ronald Gordon; 4 grandchildren; Reference Librarian, Principia Coll. 1969; Systems Analyst Trainee, Univ. of Alta. 1970–71; Undergrad. Reference Librarian 1971–72; Ed., Periodicals Holdings List 1972–73; Serials Cataloguer 1973–74; Head of Acquisitions 1974–77; Chief Librarian, Queen's Univ. 1977–90; mem. Am. Soc. Information Science (Councillor 1976–79); Assn. Rsch. Libs. (Dir. 1978–81); Candn. Assn. Rsch. Libs.; Candn. Lib. Assn.; Am. Lib. Assn.; Ont. Council Univ. Libs. (Secy. 1982–83); P. Conservative; Christian Scientist; recreations: dressage riding, tennis, swimming, skiing; Home: 32 Clarissa Dr., #917, Richmond Hill, Ont. L4C 9R7.

**McBURNEY, Air Vice Marshal Ralph Edward,** C.B.E., C.D.; b. Montreal, P.Q. 1906; s. Irvile Albert M.; e. Univ. of Sask.; Univ. of Man. B.Sc.E.E., 1930; m. Gertrude Elizabeth, d. William Bate, Saskatoon, Sask.; children: Peter, Kay, David; Cadet, R.C.A.F. 1924; Govt. flying operations Northern Canada 1927–31; Sch. of Army Co-operation, Old Sarum 1931; Staff Pilot, Winnipeg Air Stn. 1932; Instructor, R.C.A.F. School of Army Co-operation, Camp Borden 1933–34; R.A.F. Wireless Sch., Cranwell 1935; R.A.F. Staff Coll. 1939; Dir. of Signals, R.C.A.F. Hdqrs., Ottawa 1935–39 and 1939–43; commanded R.C.A.F. Stn., Trenton, Ont. 1943; Overseas 1943–45 as Stn. and Base Commdr., No. 6 R.C.A.F. Bomber Group, and as S.A.S.O., No. 6 Group Hdqrs.; apptd. A.O.C. Maintenance Command, R.C.A.F. 1945; Chrmn., Candn. Joint Liaison Office, London, Eng. 1946–48; apptd. A.O.C., Air Materiel Command 1948 before retiring from the forces in 1952; Mgr., Defence Equipment Div., Philips Industries Ltd. 1952–59; Indust. Consult. 1959–60; Chief, Tech. Information Svce., Nat. Rsch. Counc. Can. 1960–72; Secy., Indust. Rsch. Assistance Program 1962–72; Chrmn. Comte. for Information for Indust., Internat. Fed. for Documentation (F.I.D.) 1960–68; Pres., F.I.D. 1968–72; recreation: curling; Home: 2022 Sharon Avenue, Ottawa, Ont. K2A 1L8.

**MCCAFFERY, Daniel Edward;** newspaper reporter; b. Sarnia, Ont. 15 July 1952; s. James Cyril and Veronica (MacDonald) M.; e. St. Patrick's H.S. 1971; Lambton Coll., dipl. in journalism 1973; m. Valerie Roberts 29 June 1974; REPORTER, SARNIA OBSERVER 1989– ; Reporter, Sarnia Gazette 1974; News Editor 1984; Mayor's Honour List, City of Sarnia 1988; mem., Internat. Soc. of World War One Aero Historians; author: 'Billy Bishop: Canadian Hero' 1988; 'Air Aces: The Lives and Times of Twelve Canadian Fighter Pilots' 1990; recreations: travel, photography, reading, hockey; Home: 703 Grove Ave., Sarnia, Ont. N7V 2y2; Office: 140 St. Front St., Sarnia, Ont. N7T 7M8.

**McCAFFERY, Steve,** B.A., M.A.; poet and critic; b. Sheffield, England 24 Jan. 1947; s. Edwin and Kathleen (Gallagher) M.; e. Hull Univ. B.A. (Hons.) 1968; York Univ. M.A. 1969; Contbg. Ed., 'Open Letter'; Diploma of Merit, Universita delle Arti, Salsomaggiore, Italy 1982; Lectr., Dept. of English, Queen's Univ.; Guest Lectr., Cambridge Univ. 1989; Co-Founder, Toronto Rsch. Group; Mem., Modern Language Assn.; Candn. Coll. of 'Pataphysics; author: 'Dr. Sadhu's Muffins' 1974, 'Ow's Waif' 1975, 'Intimate Distortions' 1978, 'Knowledge Never Knew' 1983, 'Panopticon' 1984 (fiction), 'North of Intention' 1986 (criticism), 'Evoba' 1987, 'The Black Debt' 1989, 'Theory of Sediment' 1991; co-author: 'Horse d'Oeuvres 1976, 'In England Now that Spring' 1978, 'The Prose Tattoo' 1983, 'Rational Geomancy: Collected Reports of the Toronto Research Group' 1992; recreations: bibliomania, music, paleontology; Office: English Dept., Queen's Univ., Kingston, Ont. K7L 3N6.

**McCAFFREY, D'Arcy Charles Henry,** B.Comm., LL.B., Q.C.; trial & appellate lawyer; b. Winnipeg, Man. 2 Feb. 1936; s. Charles Joseph and Leana May (Harris) McC.; e. Univ. of Manitoba B.Comm. 1958, LL.B. 1963 (recipient Alexander Morris Exhbn. Award for highest aggregate standing in law sch.); children: Shaun, Michelle, Wendy, Hillaine, Tamara; SENIOR PARTNER TAYLOR, MCCAFFREY; read law with Walsh, Micay & Co. 1959–63; called to Bar. of Man. 1963; Counsel to Churchill Forest Ind. Inquiry; Counsel to Northern Flood Ctte., an assn. of 8,000 Cree people (negotiated compensation agreement with Fed. and Prov. Govt.); rep. Four Nations Confederacy in Constitutional Reference to the Supreme Court 1981; cr. Q.C. 1974; Counsel in Manitoba Language Reference, Supreme Court 1984; Guest Lectr., Univ. of Manitoba Law Sch.; Bencher, Manitoba Law Soc.; former Chrmn., Judicial Ctte.; mem. Am. Trial Lawyers Assn.; Sask. Law Soc.; Alberta Law Soc.; Anglican; Candn. Bar Assn.; recreations: running, swimming, cross-country skiing, cycling, wind-surfing; Clubs: Blackstone; Reh-Fit Running; The Manitoba Club; YMCA; Office: 400 St. Mary Ave., 10th Flr., Winnipeg, Man. R3C 4K5.

**McCAFFREY, Dennis E.,** B.Sc.E.E., C.B.M.; telecommunications executive; b. Sudbury, Ont. 5 March 1946; s. Jessie Irene (Haines) M. (father dec.); e. Univ. of Manitoba B.Sc.E.E. 1968, C.B.M. 1973; m. Anne d. Iris and Lawson Carter 16 July 1981; children: Michael, Christopher; DIR. OF MARKETING, MANITOBA TELEPHONE SYSTEM 1989– ; Dir. of Information Systems, Manitoba Telephone System 1985–89; Mem., Winnipeg Chamber of Commerce; recreations: squash, tennis, sailing, skiing; clubs: Carleton Club; Home: 2740 Assiniboine Ave., Winnipeg, Man. R3J 0B1; Office: 12th Floor, 360 Main St., Box 6666, Winnipeg, Man. R3C 3V6.

**McCAGUE, George Raymond;** b. Alliston, Ont. 5 Dec. 1929; s. John Joseph Edward and Lillian Mae (Meek) McC.; e. Burns Pub. Sch. and Banting Mem. High Sch. Alliston, Ont.; Ont. Agric. Coll. 1952; ELECTED MAYOR, TOWN OF NEW TECUMSETH 1991– ; operated family farm to 1953; Owner McCague General Insurance 1953–56; Owner and Broker McCague Real Estate 1953–62; Secy. Glenafton Farms Ltd. 1960–69; Pres. McCague Merion Sod Ltd. since 1962; Chrmn. Niagara Escarpment Comn. 1973–75; Dir. Farmers' Central Mutual Fire Ins. Co. 1968; Chrmn. Allied Hortic. Trades Cong. 1972; Councillor Town of Alliston 1960, 1961, Depy. Reeve 1962, 1964, Co. Councillor 1962, 1964–66, Reeve 1965–66, Warden Simcoe Co. 1966, mem. Alliston Pub. Sch. Bd. 1967–68, Mayor 1969–73, mem. Pub. Utilities Comn. 1969–73; Chrmn. Bd. Govs. Georgian Coll. 1967–74; mem. Extve. Assn. Muns. Ont. 1970–73; Nottawasaga Valley Conserv. Authority 1970–73; Alliston Planning Bd. 1972–73; el. to Ont. Leg. 1975, re-el. 1977, 1981, 1985 & 1987; Parlty. Asst. to Min. of Treasury, Econ. and Intergov'tal Affairs 1977; Min. of Govt. Services 1977; Min. of the Environment 1978; Chrmn. of Cabinet 1979–85; Chrmn., Mgmt. Bd. 1978–85; Min. of Transp. & Communications 1985; Chrmn., Standing Ctte. on General Govt. 1985; Standing Cttes. on Finance and Economic Affairs, and Regulations and Private Bills, 1988; former M.P.P. Simcoe West; Pres. Beeton Agric. Soc. 1959–60; Nursery Sod Growers Assn. Ont. 1969; mem. Ont. Nursery Trades Assn.; Ont. Landscape Contractors Assn.; Ont. Garden Maintenance & Landscape Assn.; Alliston Chamber Comm.; Royal Candn. Legion (Hon. mem.); Grey & Simcoe Foresters (Hon. mem.); P. Conservative; United Church; Clubs: Lions (Secy. 1974–75); Kinsmen (Hon. mem.); Alliston Curling (Secy. 1956–68); Home: P.O. Box 489, Alliston, Ont. L9R 1V7.

**McCAIG, Jeffrey J.,** A.B., LL.B., M.Sc.; corporate executive; b. Moose Jaw, Sask. 5 July 1951; s. John Robert and Anne Shorrocks (Glass) McC.; e. Candn. Jr. Coll. Lausanne, Switzerland 1970; Harvard Coll. A.B. 1973; Osgoode Hall Law Sch. LL.B. 1976; Leland Stanford Jr. Univ. Cal. M.Sc. (Mgmt.) 1984; m. Marilyn d. George and Grace Graves 7 July 1983; children: Robbert Angus, Scott Thomas, Christa Mae; PRES., TRIMAC LTD. 1990– ; Dir. Trimac Limited; Alberta Special Waste Management System; Bovar Inc.; Greyhound Lines of Canada Ltd.; 20/20 Financial Corp; Conference Bd. of Canada; ATA Foundation; Assoc. MacKimmie Matthews 1976–81; Owner & Sr. Offr. Jeffrey J. McCaig Professional Corp. 1981–83; Vice Pres. Planning & Corporate Devel. Trimac Ltd. 1983–87; Exec. Vice Pres., Trimac Ltd. and Pres., Trimac Transp. Group Ltd. 1987–90; mem. Law Soc. Alta.; Young Pres. Orgn.; Jr. Achievement; Clubs: 400 Club; Calgary Golf & Country; Calgary Petroleum; Glencoe; Home: 1201 Riverdale Ave. S.W., Calgary, Alta. T2S 0Z1; Office: P.O. Box 3500, Calgary, Alta. T2P 2P9.

**McCAIG, John Robert;** business executive; b. Moose Jaw, Sask. 14 June 1929; s. John Waters and Stella May (Cook) McC.; e. Moose Jaw (Sask.) Tech. High Sch. 1946; m. Ann; children: Jeffrey James, JoAnn, Melanie; CHRMN. & C.E.O., TRIMAC LTD. since 1972 and Dir. of all Trimac subsidiaries; Dir.: Pan-Alberta Gas Ltd.; Banister Inc.; Montreal Trust; Foothills Provincial General Hosp.; Bovar Inc.; Brookfield Development Corp.; Chauvco Resources Ltd.; Computalog Ltd.; Vencap Equities Alberta Ltd.; Dispatch/Operations, Maccam Transport Ltd., Moose Jaw, 1947–52; Gen. Mgr. 1952–60; Pres., HM Trimble & Sons, Calgary, 1961–68; Pres., Westburne International Industries Ltd., 1969–70; Pres. and Chief Extve. Offr. Trimac Ltd. 1970–72; Chrmn. & C.E.O., Trimac Limited 1981– ; Protestant; recreations: golf, skiing; Clubs: Glencoe; Calgary Golf & Country; Petroleum; Ranchmen's; Home: 5909 Elbow Dr. S.W., Calgary, Alta. T2V 1H7; Office: 800–5th Ave. S.W., 21st Floor, Calgary, Alta. T2P 2P9.

**McCAIN, G. Wallace F.;** B.A., LL.D., D.C.L.; company president; b. Florenceville, N.B. 9 April 1930; s. the late A.D. McCain (a pioneer in the export of seed potatoes from Canada) and the late Laura B. (Perley) McC.; e. Florenceville public schs.; Mt. Allison Univ., B.A. 1951, LL.D. (Hon.) 1973; Univ. of King's Coll., D.C.L. (Hon.) 1987; m. Margaret L.A. Norrie; four children: Scott, Michael, Martha, Eleanor; PRESIDENT, McCAIN FOODS LTD., Florenceville, N.B.; Chrmn. of the Bd.: Thomas Equipment Ltd., Centreville, N.B.; McCain Foods Inc., Rosemont, IL.; McCain Foods (Aust) Pty. Ltd., Wendouree, Australia; McCain Refrigerated Foods Inc., Oakville, Ont.; McCain Citrus Inc., Chicago, IL; McCain USA Inc., Chicago, IL; Pres.: Valley Farms Limited, Florenceville, N.B.; Director of other associated companies within the McCain Group; Dir., Royal Bank of Can.; Dir., Alliance for a Drug Free Canada; Bd. of Advisors, Internat. Assn. for Students of Economics and Commerce (AIESEC); Hon. Dir., Save Our Northwest Atlantic Resources (SONAR); Gary Wright Humanitarian Award from Friends of We Care Inc. 1992; Hon. Life Mem., Potato Assn. of Am. 1992; Candn. Business Hall of Fame 1993; Anglican; recreations: skiing, swimming, hunting; Address: Florenceville, N.B. E0J 1K0.

**McCAIN, H. Harrison,** O.C., B.A., LL.D.; executive; b. Florenceville, N.B 3 Nov. 1927; s. late A.D. and late Laura B. (Perley) McC.; e. Florenceville (N.B.) Pub. and High Schs.; Acadia Univ., B.A.; m. Marion McNair; children: Mark, Peter, Laura, Ann, Gillian; CHAIRMAN OF THE BOARD, McCAIN FOODS LTD., Florenceville, N.B.; Bd. Chrmn.: McCain Foods (GB) Limited, Scarborough, England; McCain Alimentaire SARL, Harnes, France; McCain Holland B.V., Hoofddorp, Netherlands; McCain Europa B.V., Hoofddorp, Netherlands; Day & Ross Inc., Hartland, New Brunswick; Multipatat Inc., Florenceville, New Brunswick and McCain Frima N.V., Grobbendonk, Belgium; Dir.L McCain Espana S.A., Burgos, Spain; McCain Foods (Aust) Pty. Limited, Ballarat, Australia; McCain Foods Inc., Easton, Maine, U.S.A.; McCain Refrigerated Foods Inc., Oakville, Ont.; Bilopage Inc., Quebec City, Que.; Thomas Equipment Ltd., Centreville, N.B.; Britfish Ltd., Hull, Eng.; McCain Citrus Inc., Chicago, Illinois; Beau Marais SARL, Bethune, France; Valley Farms Limited, McCain Foods Western Inc., Othello, Washington, U.S.A.; McCain Sunnyland B.V. Turnhout, Belgium, and other associated companies within the McCain Group; Dir., Bank of Nova Scotia; Beaverbrook Art Gall., Fredericton, N.B.; Izaak Walton Killam Children's Hosp., Halifax, N.S.; Officer, Order of Canada 1984; Candn. Business Statesman Award, Harvard Bus. Sch., Toronto 1988; Life Mem., Agricultural Inst. of Can. 1986; LL.D. (Hon.), Univ. of New Brunswick 1986; D.C.L. (hon. causa), Acadia Univ. 1991; Presbyterian; recreation: skiing; Address: Florenceville, N.B. E0J 1K0.

**McCALL, Christina,** B.A.; writer & editor; b. Toronto, Ont. 29 Jan. 1935; d. Christopher Warnock and Orlie Alma (Freeman) McCall; e. Jarvis Coll. Inst. Toronto, 1952; Victoria Coll., Univ. of Toronto, B.A. 1956; m. 1. Peter Charles Newman, 1959, divorced 1977; 2. Stephen Hugh Elliott Clarkson 1978; children: Ashley McCall, Kyra Clarkson, Blaise Clarkson; Ed. Asst., Maclean's 1956–58; Assoc. Ed., Chatelaine Mag. 1958–63; freelance writer and broadcaster 1963–67; Ottawa Ed., Saturday Night 1967–70; Assoc. Ed., Maclean's 1971–74; National Reporter, The Globe & Mail (Newspaper) 1974–1976; Extve Ed., Saturday Night 1976; Contrib. Ed., Saturday Night 1980–88; received several Press Club Awards for mag. writing; Pres.'s Medal for Best

Mag. Article, Univ. of Western Ont. 1970; Southam Fellowship in Journalism, Univ. of Toronto 1977; Nat. Magazine Award Gold Medal 1981; 'Book of the Year' Award, Candn. Authors' Assn. 1983; nominated for Gov. Gen.'s Literary Award for Non-Fiction 1983; awarded Gov. Gen.'s Literary Award for Non-Fiction 1990; has served on Can. council juries and comtes. and as jurist for the Toronto Book Award and Toronto Arts Foundation Award; Dir., Telecanada; Mengen Inst.; mem. Chancellor's Comte., Victoria Univ.; Hon. Degree Comte., Univ. of Toronto; Comte. for 1994 (Pres. 1986–87), Tarragon Theatre Bd.; author: 'The Man from Oxbow' 1967; 'Grits: An Intimate Portrait of the Liberal Party' 1982; 'Les Rouges: un portrait intime du parti libéral' 1983; co-author: 'Trudeau and Our Times, Vol. 1: The Magnificent Obsession' 1990; 'Trudeau: l'homme, l'utopie, l'histoire'; Home: 44 Rosedale Rd. Toronto, Ont. M4W 2P6.

**McCALL, Ronald Storrs,** D.Phil.; educator; b. Montreal, Que. 5 Nov. 1930; s. George Ronald and Frances Storrs (Stocking) McC.; e. Lower Can. Coll. Montreal; McGill Univ. B.A. 1952; New Coll. Oxford (Rhodes Scholar) B.Phil. 1955, D.Phil. 1964; m. Ann d. Anthony G.S. Griffin 6 June 1964; children: Ronald Mengo, Homer Kai Mackenzie, Sophie Storrs; PROF. OF PHILOSOPHY, MCGILL UNIVERSITY; Asst. Prof. of Philos. present Univ. 1955–63, Assoc. Prof. 1974; Assoc. Prof. Univ. of Pittsburgh 1963–65, 1971–74; Visiting Prof. of Philos. Makerere Univ. Kampala, Uganda 1965–71; author 'Aristotle's Modal Syllogisms' 1963; 'A Model of the Universe' 1994; ed. 'Polish Logic 1920–39' 1967; Founder and Co-Chrmn. Positive Action Ctte. Montreal 1976–83; mem. Candn. Philos. Assn.; Am. Philos. Assn.; Home: 509 Argyle Ave., Montreal, Que. H3Y 3B6; Office: Montreal, Que. H3A 2T7.

**McCALLA, Peter Douglas Whitby,** M.A., D.Phil.; historian; educator; b. Edmonton, Alta. 4 Sept. 1942; s. Peter Douglas Ralston and Lois (Whitby) McC.; e. Strathcona Composite High Sch. Edmonton 1960; Queen's Univ. B.A. 1964; Univ. of Toronto M.A. 1965 (Woodrow Wilson Fellowship); Oriel Coll. Oxford Univ. (Rhodes Scholar) D.Phil. 1972; m. Anna Maria d. W. B. Skorski, Peterborough, Ont. 25 July 1970; PROF. OF HISTORY, TRENT UNIV. 1981– ; Chair, History Dept. 1988–92; Acting Dir., Administrative & Policy Studies Prog. 1983–84; Assoc. Prof. of Hist. 1973–81; Principal Lady Eaton Coll. 1976–81; Asst. Prof. of Hist. Trent Univ. 1968–73; author 'The Upper Canada Trade 1834–1872: A Study of the Buchanans' Business' 1979; 'Planting the Province: The Economic History of Upper Canada, 1784–1870' 1993; editor: 'Perspectives on Canadian Economic History' 1987, rev. ed. 1994; 'The Development of Canadian Capitalism' 1990; various articles 19th century Candn. business, social and econ. hist.; Ed., Ont. Series, Champlain Soc. 1979–89; Ed. 'Canadian Historical Review' 1983–86; mem. Candn. Hist. Assn.; Econ. Hist. Assn.; Ont. Hist. Soc.; Am. Hist. Assn.; Econ. Hist. Soc.; Address: Peterborough, Ont. K9J 7B8.

**McCALLION, David John,** M.A., Ph.D., M.R.E.; university professor; b. Toronto, Ont. 25 Sept. 1916; s. John and Elizabeth (Service) M.; e. York Mem. Coll. Inst. (1938); McMaster Univ., B.A. 1942, M.A. 1947; Brown Univ., Ph.D. 1949; m. Norah Jean, d. late James Moore, 1 Sept. 1944; children: Kathryn, Sharon, Janet, James, Thomas, Margaret; PROF. EMERITUS OF ANATOMY, McMASTER UNIV. 1982– ; Lectr. in Zool., McMaster Univ. 1945–47; Teaching Fellow, Brown Univ. 1947–49; Asst. Prof., Acadia Univ. 1949–51; Prof. there 1951–55; Asst. Prof., Univ. of Toronto 1955–58; Assoc. Prof. 1958–62; Prof. 1962–68; Prof. of Anat., McMaster Univ. 1968–82; Rsch. Assoc., Hist. of Med., McMaster Univ. 1986– ; o. Anglican Deacon, May 1978; Priest, Dec. 1979; Hon. Asst., St. James (Anglican) Dundas, Ont.; mem. Internat. Inst. for Embryology; Teratology Soc.; N.Y. Acad. of Sciences; Candn. Assoc. Anat.; Am. Assn. of Anat.; Sigma Xi; P. Conservative; Anglican; recreations: golf, cooking; Home: 722 Hiawatha Blvd., Ancaster, Ont. L9G 3A7.

**McCALLION, Kathryn Elizabeth,** B.A.; diplomat; b. Toronto, Ont. 19 June 1945; d. David John and Norah Jean (Moore) McC.; e. St. Mildred's Coll.; Jarvis Coll. Inst.; Univ. of Waterloo, B.A. 1972; DIRECTOR GENERAL, WESTERN EUROPE, EXTERNAL AFFAIRS OTTAWA 1990– ; Second Sec. Mexico 1973–75, Consul & Trade Comnr. Boston 1975–78, Extve. Asst. to Dep. Min. Internat. Trade Ottawa 1981–82, Dir. Food Policy Div. Ottawa 1982–83, Counsellor Perm. Del. to OECD Paris 1983–87; High Comnr. to Jamaica, Bahamas, and Belize 1987–90; Pres. Profl. Assn. Foreign Service Offrs. 1980–81; recreations: sports, reading; Clubs: Ottawa Athletic; Office: 125 Sussex Dr., Ottawa, Ont. K1N 7T7.

**McCALLUM, Ian Armstrong Campbell,** LL.B.; trust company executive; b. Vancouver, B.C. 27 July 1936; s. Arthur Howard, M.B.E., and Jane McGee (Armstrong) McC.; e. Univ. of B.C. LL.B. 1959; m. Mary d. John and Maida Stephen 3 May 1962; children: Jane, Susan, Elizabeth; MNG. PARTNER ROYAL TRUSTCO LTD. 1990– ; joined Bank of Montreal 1953–83, various positions Treasury & Internat. Banking Divs.; present Co. 1983– , Sr. Vice Pres., dir. various subsidiaries; Dir. Dacks Williams Inc.; Clubs: Hamilton Golf & Country; Canadian (N.Y.); Home: 83 Brentwood Rd., Oakville, Ont. L6J 4B7; Office: Box 7500 Stn. A, Toronto, Ont. M5W 1P9.

**McCALLUM, John Stuart,** B.Sc., B.A., M.B.A., Ph.D.; educator; columnist; b. Prescott, Ont. 2 Feb. 1944; s. Donald Robinson and Margaret Louise (Hoeschen) McC.; e. Univ. de Montréal B.Sc. 1965, B.A 1968; Queen's Univ. M.B.A. 1968; Univ. of Toronto Ph.D. 1973; m. Deborah Joan d. R.M. and E.M. Howe, Winnipeg, Man. 7 Nov. 1985; children: Pamela Anne, James Andrew; PROF. OF FINANCE, UNIV. OF MAN. 1973– ; Chrmn., Manitoba Hydro 1991– (Vice-Chrmn. 1988–91); Dir., Toromont Industries Ltd. 1984– , Manitoba Energy Authority 1988– , Investors Group Mutual Funds 1991– , Investors Syndicate Ltd. 1991– ; Cons. various Candn. co's 1977– ; Columnist, Financial Post 1979– , Business Quarterly 1978– ; joined Bank of Montreal 1965–68; Sr. Analyst Shell Canada, Toronto 1968–70; author 'The Term Structure of Interest Rates' 1974; 'The Canadian Chartered Banks and the Bond Market' 1976; 'The Changing Face of Canadian Finance ' 1980; 'Canadian Finance and the Federal Deficit' 1983; 'Canada and Technological Change' 1985; recipient Stanton Award for Teaching Excellence 1975; Graduate Award for Teaching Excellence 1978; Deloitte Touche Business Writing Award 1985, 1986, 1987, 1991 and 1992; mem. Am. Finance Assn.; R. Catholic; recreations: jogging, reading; Home: 26 Lake Lindero Rd., Winnipeg, Man. R3T 4P3; Office: Winnipeg, Man. R3T 2N2.

**McCALLUM, Kenneth James,** M.Sc., Ph.D., F.C.I.C., F.R.S.C.; retired university dean; b. Scott, Sask. 25 Apr. 1918; s. James Alexander and Alice (Fines) M.; e. Univ. of Sask., B.Sc. 1936, M.Sc. 1939; Columbia Univ., Ph.D. 1942; m. Erika Connell, 16 Aug. 1974; children (by prev. m.); Patricia, Douglas; Dean of Grad. Studies, Univ. of Sask. 1970–85; Jr. Rsch. Offr., N.R.C. of Can. 1942–43; Asst. Prof. Chem., present Univ. 1943; Assoc. Prof. 1946; Prof. 1953; Assoc. Dean of Grad. Studies 1967; Pres., Chem. Inst. Can. 1968–69; United Church; Home: 1622 Park Ave., Saskatoon, Sask. S7H 2P3.

**McCAMBLY, James Alexander,** O.C.; union representative; b. Airdrie, Alta. 24 July 1933; s. Rockliff Leslie and Winnifred Gladys (Molyneaux) M.; e. Mount Royal College, Calgary (Labour Economics); m. Dorene E. d. James Gilbert and Evelyn D. Wright 12 Nov. 1955; children: Diane, Scott, Dawna; PRESIDENT, CANADIAN FED. OF LABOUR 1982– ; Heavy Equipment Operator until 1956; Union Rep. & Business Mgr., Local 955 Alberta Internat. Union of Operating Engrs. 1970; Alderman, Calgary City Council 1967–69, 1971–82; selected to open Candn. Office Bldg. & Construction Trades Dept. AFL-CIO 1982; Chair, Working Ventures Candn. Fund Inc.; Co-chair, Nat. Apprenticeship Ctte., Candn. Labour Force Devel. Bd.; Bd. Mem., Candn. Found. for Econ. Edn.; Bd. & Extve. Mem., Candn. Labour Market & Productivity Ctr.; Public Policy Forum 1993; Ctte. Mem., Candn.-Am. Ctte.; Mem., Bd. of Dir., Nat. Quality Inst.; Member, Order of Canada 1994; recreations: golf, sailing; Home: 651 Tubman Cres., Ottawa, Ont.; Office: No. 300, 107 Sparks St., Ottawa, Ont. K1P 5B5.

**McCAMUS, David Robert;** business executive; b. Walkerton, Ont., 18 July 1931; s. William Roswell and Margaret Irene (Moore) M.; e. Univ. of Toronto, B.Com. 1956; m. Inez, d. Lorne Tracy, 17 Sept. 1955; children: Gregory, Jane, Carolyn, Bradley; President, Xerox Canada Inc. 1982–92 (retired); ten years with IBM; Nat. Sales Mgr., Xerox 1971; Vice-Pres., Marketing, Xerox Canada 1973; Mgr., Multinat. Bus. Planning, Xerox Corp. 1976; Vice-Pres. & Regional Gen. Mgr., Mid-West Region, Xerox Corp. 1978; Vice-Pres., Marketing and Planning, Xerox Canada 1980; Chrmn., United Way of Metropolitan Toronto 1983; Chrmn., Information Tech. Assoc. 1987; Chrmn., Corporate Higher Education Forum 1990; Dir., Confederation Life; Campbell Soup Co.; mem. B.C.N.I.

**McCAMUS, John Douglas,** M.A., LL.M.; educator; b. St. Catharines, Ont. 3 Apr. 1941; s. William Roswell and Margaret Irene (Moore) McC.; e. Univ. of W. Ont. B.A. 1963; Univ. of Toronto M.A. 1965, LL.B. 1968; Univ. of London LL.M. 1969; m. Wendy d. Harvey Clare 31 Jan. 1980; two s. Matthew William, Simon Daniel; PROFESSOR OF LAW, OSGOODE HALL LAW SCHOOL, YORK UNIV. since 1985; read law with Fasken & Calvin 1969–70; called to Bar of Ont. 1973; Legal Secy. to Chief Justice Laskin, Supreme Court of Canada 1970–71; Asst. Prof. Osgoode Hall Law Sch. 1971, Assoc. Prof. 1974, Prof. 1985, Asst. Dean 1975, Assoc. Dean 1976–78, Dir. Grad. Program in Law 1981–82, Dean 1982–87; Visiting Prof., Université d'Aix-Marseille III (Aix-en-Provence) 1987–88; Rsch. Dir. Ont. Comn. on Freedom of Information & Individual Privacy 1977–80; Dir., Candn. Civil Liberties Assn. 1986– ; mem. Ont. Law Reform Comn. 1990–92, Chair 1993– ; recipient, Mundell Medal for Distinguished Contributions to Letters and Law 1991 (A.G. Ont.); Walter Owen Book Prize for 1990–91 (Candn. Bar Assn.); Editor-in-Chief, Osgoode Hall Law Journal 1989– ; ed., 'Freedom of Information: Canadian Perspectives' 1981; 'National Security: Surveillance and Accountability in a Democratic Society' 1989; co-author, 'The Law of Restitution' 1990; author numerous rsch. monographs and law review articles; mem. Candn. Bar Assn.; Candn. Assn. Law Teachers; Nat. Stats. Counc. 1987–92; Home: 190 Montclair Ave., Toronto, Ont. M5P 1P9; Office: 4700 Keele St., Downsview, Ont. M3J 2R5.

**McCARDLE, James Joachim,** B.A.; diplomat; b. Stratford, Ont. 27 Apr. 1922; s. John Patrick and Mary (Keegan) McC.; e. Univ. of Toronto, B.A. 1943; m. Lannie Roth, d. Benjamin Harrison, Weyburn, Sask., 27 Nov. 1948; one d., Bennett; joined Candn. Foreign Service 1946; Candn. Liaison Mission, Tokyo, 1947–49, Ottawa 1949–53, 1956–59, 1962–69; Secy. to Candn. Del. to Peace Conf. with Japan, San Francisco, 1951, Washington, D.C. 1953–56; Secy. to Canadian Sec., Canada-U.S.A. Permanent Joint Board on Defence 1956–59; Delegate to North Atlantic Council, Paris 1959–62; Ambassador to Ireland 1969–72; High Commissioner to Australia and Fiji 1972–77; Dir. Gen. of Defense and Arm, Control Bureau, Dept. of Ext. Affairs 1977–80; Special Negotiator (Nuclear Safeguards) 1980–81; Consul Gen. of Can. in San Francisco, 1981; served with Candn. Army 1943–46; rank Lt.; R. Catholic; recreations: golf, bridge; Clubs: Rideau; Commonwealth (California).

**McCARTER, John Alexander (Alex),** M.A., Ph.D., F.R.S.C.; educator; b. Eng. 25 Jan. 1918; s. Alexander and Helen Turnbull (McKellar) McC.; e. Dawson Pub. Sch. Dawson City, Y.T.; King Edward High Sch. Vancouver; Univ. of B.C. B.A. 1939, M.A. 1941; Univ. of Toronto Ph.D. 1945; m. Patricia d. Oliver and Winifred St. John 27 Dec. 1941; children: David G., Robert M., Patricia L., William A.; Jr. and Asst. Rsch. Offr. Nat. Rsch. Council Atomic Energy Project Chalk River, Ont. 1945–48; Assoc. Prof. of Biochem. Dalhousie Univ. 1948, Prof. and Head of Biochem. 1950–65; Prof. of Biochem. and Dir., Cancer Rsch. Lab. Univ. of W. Ont. 1965–80; Rsch. prof., Nat. Cancer Inst. Can., Prof. Univ. of W. Ont. 1980–83; Visiting Prof. Univ. of Victoria, B.C. 1983–85, Adjunct Prof. 1985–90; Exchange Fellow Brit. Empire Cancer Campaign 1959–60; recipient Queen's Silver Jubilee Medal 1977; author or co-author over 60 sci. publs.; mem., Candn. Biochem. Soc. (Pres. 1967); recreations: gardening, painting, ornithology; Home: 3171 Henderson Rd., Victoria, B.C. V8P 5A3.

**McCARTHY, Barry Raymond Joseph,** B.A., B.Ed.; b. Deep River, Ont. 11 Aug. 1951; s. Raymond and Melvina (Fournier) Mc.; e. Univ. of Guelph B.A. 1975; Univ. of W. Ont. B.Ed. 1976; m. Deborah d. Arthur and Marian Frey 15 June 1979; children: Erin, Rachel, Andrew; art teacher Waterloo Coll. Inst. 1976– ; sessional instr. Univ. of Waterloo 1987, 1988; art instr. 15 yrs.; art exhns. 18 yrs.; solo exhns. since 1978; solo exhns. Quan-Schieder Gallery Ltd. since 1986; 4 retrospect/surveys Centre in the Square 1985, Waterloo Pub. Lib. Gallery, Tom Thomson Gallery Owen Sound 1985, Macdonald Stewart Art Centre Guelph 1986, Wellington Co. Museum 1990–91, Nancy Poole Studio, Toronto 1991– ; mem. several jurys; curator Percy Runells Exhn. 1990, Corbett Gray Exhn. 1991; recipient several awards, recognitions; R. Catholic; recreations: antiques, vintage cars; Home: 245 Bridge St., Fergus, Ont. N1M 1T7; Office: 300 Hazel St., Waterloo, Ont. N2L 3P2.

**MCCARTHY, Don;** food processing executive; b. Hornepayne, Ont. 19 Sept. 1930; s. William Allan and Mildred (Brown) M.; e. Imede, Lausanne, Switzerland;

m. Ann d. Tom and Sybil Casey 17 Oct. 1959; children: Suzanne, Jennifer; CHRMN., BEATRICE FOODS 1985– ; various pos., Nestlé 1952–75; George Weston Limited 1975–84; Club; Granite; Home: 43 Wilket Rd., Willowdale, Ont. M2L 1N9; Office: Ste. 600, 295 The West Mall, Etobicoke, Ont. M9C 4Z4.

**McCARTHY, Doris,** C.M., R.C.A. (1951), O.S.A. (1945), CSPWC (1952), FOCA (1990); artist; teacher; b. Calgary, Alta. 7 July 1910; e. Ont. Coll. of Art, Toronto; London, Eng. 1935–36; teacher, Art Dept., Central Tech. Sch. Toronto 1932–72; Univ. of Toronto B.A. (Hons.) 1987; regular exhibitor juried and invitation group shows from 1933; over 90 solo exhbns.; world wide study and painting 1950–51, 1961–62; painting on location and research for studio work across Canada incl. ten trips to High Arctic; subject of award-winning docudrama 'Doris McCarthy, Heart of a Painter'; calligrapher; liturgical artist: wood sculpture, fabric wall-hangings and banners; rep. by Wynick/Tuck Gallery, Toronto; Canadian Art Galleries, Calgary; rep. in public coll. of A.G.O., Toronto, A.G. of Hamilton, London A.G., Robt. McLaughlin Gall. Oshawa etc., also in many corporate and private collections; subject of retrospective exhbn. 'A Feast of Incarnation' 1991–94; retrospective exhbn. of mountain paintings'Crown of Time' 1992; author: 'A Fool in Paradise' 1990 and 'The Good Wine' 1991 (parts 1 and 2 of autobiography); Member, Order of Canada 1987; Order of Ontario 1992; Fellow, Ontario College of Art 1990; Pres. OSA 1964–67; Pres. CSPWC 1956–58; Anglican; Home: 1 Meadowcliff Dr., Scarborough, Ont. M1M 2X8.

**McCARTHY, George F.,** B.Sc., M.B.A.; business executive; b. Detroit, Mich. 1 Dec. 1936; e. Univ. of Detroit B.Sc. 1962; Univ. of Chicago M.B.A. 1964; m. Virginia Ann Jones 28 Jan. 1961; children: Marie Ann, Kevin Justin, George Mark; PRESIDENT, NORTH AMERICA, HIRAM WALLKER GROUP 1993– ; sales & mktg. positions, E&J Gallo Winery 1964–67; Vice-Pres., Marketing, Imported Brands, Hublein Inc. 1967–74; Extve. Vice-Pres., The Pillsbury Co. 1974–85; Pres., Seagram Overseas Sales co. 1986; Seagram Far East 1988 (located in Hong Kong); Pres., Joseph E. Seagram & Sons, Limited 1991–93; Dir., Assn. of Canadian Distillers; Mem., Business Council on Nat. Issues; recreations: sailing; Home: 29 Pheasant Lane, Greenwich, CT 06830; Office: 2072 Riverside Dr. E., Windsor, Ont. N8Y 4S5.

**McCARTHY, Grace Mary,** O.C., M.L.A.; politician; b. Vancouver, B.C. 14 Oct. 1927; d. George and Allrietta (McCloy) Winterbottom; e. Vancouver Grade 12 Cert.; m. Raymond McCarthy 23 June 1948; children: Mary Grace, Calvin G.R.; LEADER, B.C. SOCIAL CREDIT PARTY 1993– ; Honorary Advisor, Vancouver Japanese School 1993– ; Dir., Western Internat. Communications, Vancouver 1993– ; Dir., Health-Mor Inc., Cleveland 1993– ; Founder & Pres., Grayce Florists Ltd. 1944–75; Commr. Parks Bd. 1961–66; Vice Chrmn. 1966 City of Vancouver; el. M.L.A. 1966, re-el. since; Min. Without Portfolio 1966–72; Pres., B.C. Social Credit Party 1973–75; Prov. Secy., Depy. Premier and Min. of Recreation & Travel 1975–76; Prov. Secy., Depy. Premier and Min. of Travel 1976–78; Min. of Human Resources, B.C. (and Min. Responsible for B.C. Transit) 1978–86; Prov. Sec. & Min. of Govt. Services B.C. 1986; Min. of Economic Devel. B.C. 1986–88; resigned from Cabinet to sit as Caucus Mem., Legislative Assembly 1988; retired from B.C. politics 1991; elected Leader, B.C. Social Credit Party 1993; Pres., Candn. Chamber of Commerce (Hastings Chamber of Commerce) (first woman president of any 1950–51); Gov., Vancouver Aquarium Assn. 1960– ; Active Volun., Variety Club, Tent 47 1966– ; Hon. Mem. 3-H Soc. (Help for Homebound Hanidcapped) 1970– ; mem. Adv. Bd. Salvation Army 1985– ; Dir., Candn. Paraplegic Assn., B.C. Div. 1990– ; Chrmn., Vision 20/21 (fundraising for eye rsch., Univ. of BC) 1991– ; Chrmn., Cultural Heritage Ctte., Salvation Army 1991– ; Patron, Worldsphere Found. 1991– ; Hon. Patron, 411 Seniors' Centre Soc. 1992; Hon. Citizen, Dist. of W. Vancouver 1992; Hon. Chrmn., 'Jail & Bail Fundraiser' Candn. Cancer Soc. 1992; Community Adv. Council, Vancouver Holocaust Centre Soc. 1992/93; Hon. Patron, Ronald McDonald House Soc. 1993; Hon. Advr., Vancouver Japanese Language Sch. 2000 Project 1993; Ctte. Mem., 'Friends of Grace' Grace Hosp. Found. 1993; Patron, Internat. Found. for the Arts 1993; Chrmn., Steering Ctte. 'Doormen of the World' 1994 Internat. Convention; Mem., Miss Vancouver Chinatown Lions Pageant (fundraising for children in crisis) 1993; Mem., Candn. Paraplegic Assn., Chrmn. fundraising 1993– ; Hon. Mem.: Van. A.M. Tourist Assn.; B.C. Soc. of Landscape Architects; Victoria A.M. Tourist Assoc.; B.C. Chef's Assoc.; Honours: Award for 'Most Outstanding Contrib. in Assisting the Mentally Handicapped' B.C. Assn. of Retarded Children 1969; Service award, 'Outstanding Contrib. to B.C. Handicapped Citizens as Hon. Chief Marching Mother' Kinsmen's Mothers' 1972, 1973; Harold J. Merilees Award of the Year, Greater Vancouver Convention and Visitors' Bureau 1977; 'Marketer of the Year Award' Northwest Council of Sales and Mktg. 1977, Internat. Sales & Mktg. Extves. 1978, B.C. Chapter of the Am. Mktg. Assn. 1979; Pres. Award for Outstanding Contrib. to Tourism in Greater Victoria 1977; Commendation 'Outstanding Service in the Public Interest' Lieutenant-Gov., State of Calif. 1977; 'Appreciation of Service' plaque, B.C. Aviation Council 1978; Heart Award, Variety Club Tent 47 1981 and Golden Heart Community Achievement Award (first woman recipient) 1992; Medal of Distinction, Internat. Assn. of Lions Club 1982; Canada's First Woman Barker, Variety Clubs Internat. 1982; Govt. of Canada Silver Medal 1982; 'Man of the Year' Award, Brotherhood Interfaith Assn. 1987; Service Award, Restaurant & Food Services Assn. of B.C. 1992; Community Achievement Award, Vancouver Bd. of Trade 1992; Jewish Nat. Fund Honoree 1993; Officer, The Order of Canada 1993; Negev Award 'for providing a bridge for brotherhood and sisterhood between Christian and Jew by her fair play, tolerance and justice' Jewish National Fund 1993; Life Achievement Award, Vancouver A.M. Tourist Assn. 1993; Commemorative Medal for 125th Anniversary of Candn. Confederation 1993; Mem., Order of Saint Lazarus; Native Daughters of B.C.; Daughters of the Nile; Mem., Lamda Alpha Internat. 1993; Anglican; recreations: swimming, interior decorating; Home: 4610 Beverly Cres., Vancouver, B.C. V6J 4E6.

**McCARTHY, Michael J.,** M.A., Ph.D., F.S.A.; university professor/author; b. Dublin, Ireland 27 April 1939; s. Michael J. and Mary E. (Burke) M.; e. Cambridge Univ. B.A. 1964, M.A. 1968; London, Courtauld Inst. of Art Ph.D. 1972; PROF., DEPT. OF FINE ART, UNIV. OF TORONTO 1980– ; Lectr., Queen's Univ. 1967–69; Asst. Prof., Fac. of Edn., Univ. of Toronto 1970–77; Assoc. Prof., Dept. of Fine Art 1977–80; Fellow, Soc. of Antiquaries of London; Trinity Coll., Univ. of Toronto 1979–92; Dir., Soane Mus. Assn.; author: 'Introducing Art History: A Guide for Teachers' 1978, 'The Origins of the Gothic Revival' 1987; Home: 177 Martin St., Milton, Ont. L9T 2R3; Office: 100 St. George St., Sidney Smith Hall, Toronto, Ont. M5S 1A1.

**MCCARTHY, Paul Wigmore,** M.B., F.R.C.Psych.; medical doctor; psychiatrist; university professor; b. Galway, Ireland 13 Aug. 1938; s. Cornelius Wigmore and Mary Kathryn (Ryan) M.; e. St. Mary's Coll.; Nat. Univ. of Ireland, M.B., BCh., B.A.O. 1961; m. Carmel d. Edward and Theresa Cumiskey 15 Aug. 1964; children: Odette, Natasha, Cormac, Samara; Psychiatrist-in-Chief, Whitby Psychiatric Hosp.; pediatrics postgrad. training, Univ. of Maryland Hosp. 1962–63; postgrad. psych., Edinburgh Univ. 1964, '65, '66; child psych., Hosp. for Sick Children, Glasgow 1967; Fellow in Psych., Harvard Univ. Med. Sch. 1968; Counc. of Europe Fellowship 1970; Clin. Dir. of Child Psych. Serv., Dublin City & Region, Ireland 1970–86; Asst. Prof. of Psych., Univ. of Toronto 1986– ; part-time staff psych., Hosp. for Sick Children, Toronto; F.R.C.Psych; Mem., Candn. Acad. of Child Psych.; Roman Cath.; numerous pubs. in med. & psych. jours.; recreations: golf, watercolouring, music; clubs: Portmarnock Golf (Dublin, Ire.), Thunderers (Toronto); Home: 66 Birch Ave., Toronto, Ont. M4V 1C8.

**McCARTHY, Walter J.,** B.Com.; investment consultant; b. Albany, N.Y. 20 Feb. 1923; s. J. Earle (dec.) and Katherine (Maxwell) McC.; e. St. Mary's Acad. (N.Y.) 1941; McGill Univ. B.Com 1950; Harvard Univ. Grad. Sch. Business Adm.-Advanced Mang. Program 1968; children: Sheila Anne (Mrs. H. Haddad), James, Susan (Mrs. D. Ternlund), John; Sr. Vice Pres., Investments, Sun Life Assurance Co. of Canada 1979–88; Dir., New Growth Corporation; TransAlta Utilities Corp.; TransAlta Resources Corp.; Rostland Corporation; served with R.C.A.F. 1941–46, rank Flight Lt.; recreation: flying; sailing, skiing.

**McCARTNEY, William G.;** business executive; b. Vancouver, B.C. 7 June 1934; s. William John and Florence Mary (Robson) M.; e. Vancouver Technical School 1952; children: Katherine, Janet, Nancy, Victoria; PRESIDENT, TSC SHANNOCK CORP. 1984– ; Mgr., Vancouver Br., WEA Music 1967–72; Owner, Spran Enterprises Ltd. (Doodleart Posters) 1972–76; Pres., Shannock Sales Ltd. 1977–84; Pres., Candn. Assn. of Video Distributors; Bd. of Gov., Video Software Dealers Assn.; Bd. of Trustees, Motion Picture Found. of Canada; Dir., B.C. Special Olympics; recreations: sailing, bicycling, badminton; Home: 5552 Westhaven Rd., West Vancouver, B.C. V7W 3E9; Office: 4222 Manor St., Burnaby, B.C. V5G 1B2.

**McCAUGHEY, Andrew Gilmour,** B.Com., C.A.; b. Montreal, Que. 8 Dec. 1922; s. Andrew Gilmour and Mary Doris (Sheldon) McC.; e. McGill Univ. B.Com. 1949; C.A. Inst. 1950; m. Lorraine Baltera; children: Jennifer H., Andrew John, Matthew James; Chrmn., Scott's Hospitality Inc. (retired 30 Apr. 1992); Dir., Toromont Industries Ltd.; Global Government Plus Fund Ltd.; Aquaterra Corp.; The Canadian Insurance Group Ltd.; Capel-Cure Myers Capital Mngmt. Ltd. (London, Eng.) 1993– ; Former Pres. & C.E.O. North American Life Assurance Co.; Former Dir., The Molson Companies Ltd.; Monac International Inc.; served with RCAF as Pilot 1941–45 attached to RAF Europe and Mediterranean Theatres; mem. Inst. C.A.'s Que. and Ont.; Financial Extves. Inst. Toronto (Past Pres. Montreal Chapter); Dir., Tim Horton Children's Foundation; Anglican; Clubs: Toronto; York; Royal Candn. Mil. Inst. Toronto; Royal Air Force (London, Eng.); Goodwood Club; Lambton Golf & Country; York Skeet; Home: 87 Valecrest Dr., Islington, Ont. M9A 4P5.

**McCAUGHEY, Lorraine B.,** B.A.; public relations executive; e. City Univ. of N.Y.C. Hunter Coll. B.A. 1972; m.; Pres. & C.E.O., Burson-Marsteller Canada 1990; former Sr. Vice Pres. and Dir. Burson-Marsteller International; Dir. BCE Mobile Communications Inc.; Extve. Consultants Ltd.; The Conference Bd. of Canada; Reporter Fairchild Publications New York 1971–72; Assoc. Ed. Advertising Age, N.Y. 1972–77; Sr. Vice Pres. The Rowland Co. N.Y. 1977–79; joined present Co. as Acct. Supr. 1980, Vice Pres. and Gen. Mgr. Toronto 1985, Sr. Vice Pres. 1987; Dir., W. Park Hosp. Found.; Gov., Jr. Achievement Metro Toronto & York Region; Dir., Bd. Trade Metrop. Toronto (Council); Mem., Candn. Pub. Relations Soc.; Candn. Clubs of Toronto and Montreal; Young Presidents' Organization; recreation: trap shooting; Home: 87 Valecrest Dr., Islington, Ont. M9A 4P5.

**McCAULEY, William Alexander,** A.T.C.M., Mus.B., M.M., A.M.D., composer; conductor; performer (music); b. Tofield, Alta. 14 Feb. 1917; s. Alexander James Henry and Barbara Ann (Sinclair) McC.; e. Tofield (Alta.) Pub. and High Schs.; Royal Conserv. of Music of Toronto, A.T.C.M. (Piano); Univ. of Toronto, Mus.B.; Ont. Coll. of Educ., High Sch. Teachers Specialist Cert. (Music); Eastman Sch. of Music, M.M., A.M.D.; m. late Elaine Patricia, d. late C. Leslie McFarlane, Whitby, Ont., 2 Dec. 1950; m. Patricia Maud McCauley 16 Oct. 1987; children (from previous m.): Brian Matthew, Timothy John, Julie Megan; Dir. of Music, O'Keefe Centre, Toronto 1960–87; Dir. of Music, York Univ., 1961–69; formed McCauley Music Ltd. 1966; apptd. Dir. of Music, Ottawa Tech. High Sch., 1947 and played 1st Trombone in Ottawa Philharmonic and Nat. Film Bd. Orchestras; Dir. of Music for Crawley Films, Ottawa, 1949–60; wrote scores for over 125 films incl. winners of over 60 nat. and internat. awards; compositions incl.: 'Concerto for Horn' (Alta. Centennial Comn. Award, 1967); 'Newfoundland Scene'; 'Saskatchewan Suite'; 'Quebec Lumber Camp'; 'Theme and Variations for Orchestra'; 'Five Miniatures for Flute, Strings and Harp'; 'Five Miniatures for Bass Trombone, Strings and Harp; 'Five Miniatures for Six Percussionists'; 'Five Miniatures for Ten Winds'; 'Contrasts for Orchestra'; 'Metropolis' for Concert Band; 'Fantasy on Canadian Folk Songs' (performed on Parlt. Hill, May, 1967); 'Centennial Suite' for Concert Band; 'Plus One' for C.P.R. Cominco Bldg. at Expo; 'International Anthem' (words by Wilson McDonald); 'How Do I Love Thee' (for Soprano); has conducted over 200 recording sessions for film, T.V. and records (incl. Columbia Records, Capitol Records and Mercury); Children's Concert with Toronto Symphony Orchestra; Variety Series for Screen Gems; Concert Series at York Univ.; Irish Radio Orchestra; Dublin (programme of own music); under his direction York Univ. Choir won Lincoln Trophy (highest honour for choral groups competing across Can.); composed music for Christopher Chapman film 'Festivals' 1970 for Osaka World's Fair; for C.B.C. film series 'Whiteoaks of Jalna'; arranged and conducted music from 'Jalna' for Capital records; composed music for C.B.C.'s 'Louis Riel,' recorded sound track album; Dir. Music, Seneca Coll, 1970–78; Conductor, North York Symphony 1973–88; conducted series of Children's Concerts with North York Philharmonic 1978–79; recent works: 'The Flute Family'; 'Miniature Overture for Brass Quintet' (recorded by Candn. Brass); 'Five Miniatures for Brass Quintet' (comnd. & recorded by C.B.C.); 'Kaleidescope Québecoise' (comnd. by Canada Council); 'Concerto Grosso' (comnd. by Can. Council, recorded by Canadian Brass); 'Piano Concerto #1' and 'String Quartet #2' (comnd. by Ont. Arts Council);

'Five Miniatures for Four Trombones'; 'Hand Gliding' for two harps (for Intnl. Harp Congress); 'Rhapsody for Alto Flute & Orchestra,' 'Holiday in Brazil' (perf. North York Symphony); 'Five Miniature' (for four saxophones); film score 'Sunday in the Country'; 'It Seemed like a Good Idea at the Time'; 'City on Fire' (co-composer); 'The Last Bar for Eddy Miles' (new musical) 18 songs with lyrics by Kevin Gilbert 1992; mem., Toronto Musicians Assn.; Ottawa Mus. Assn.; Candn. Assn. Publ. & Composers; Canadian League Composers (mem. Bd.); Past Pres., Guild of Candn. Film Composers; recreations: golf, tennis, curling, reading; Address: 2006 - 75 Wynford Hts. Cres., North York, Ont. M3C 3H9.

**McCAUSLAND, Ian,** B.A., B.Sc., M.Sc., Ph.D., P.Eng.; educator; b. Lisbellaw, N. Ireland 10 Apr. 1929; s. Joseph and Edith Ellen (McLean) McC.; e. Coleraine (N. Ireland) Acad. Inst. 1946; Queen's Univ. Belfast, B.Sc. 1949, M.Sc. 1950; Univ. of Toronto, Ph.D. 1958, B.A. 1991; Churchill Coll. Cambridge, Ph.D. 1964; m. Joan d. James and Jessie Lees 9 July 1965; children: William James, Janet Patricia; PROF. OF ELECT. ENG. UNIV. OF TORONTO 1971– , Assoc. Chrmn. Grad. Studies Elect. Eng. 1985–90, 1991– , Chrmn. Devonshire House Ctte. 1987–89; Transformer Designer, Ferranti Ltd. Hollinwood Eng. 1950–52; Distbn. Eng. Electricity Supply Bd. Dublin 1952–53; Eng. Canadian General Electric 1953–55; Lectr. present Univ. 1958–60, Asst. Prof. 1960–61, 1964–65, Assoc. Prof. 1965–71, Chrmn. Control Systems Group Elect. Eng. 1970–71, Assoc. Chrmn. of Elect. Eng. 1972–76, Co-ordinator Grad. Studies Elect. Eng. 1982–85, Founding mem. Sch. Grad. Studies Alumni Assn. (Pres. 1979–81); NATO Sci. Fellow 1961–63; Visiting Sci. Dept. Eng. Cambridge 1971–72; recipient, George Sinclair Award 1992; author: 'Introduction to Optimal Control' 1969; various articles sci. and eng. jours.; Ed., Candn. Electrical Engr. Journ. 1979–80; Dir. Metrop. Toronto Br. UN Assn. 1976–77; mem. Assn. Profl. Engs. Prov. Ont. (Bd. Examiners 1970–71); Home: 32 Helendale Ave., Toronto, Ont. M4R 1C4; Office: 10 King's College Rd., Toronto, Ont. M5S 1A4.

**McCAWLEY, Deborah Joan,** Q.C., B.A., LL.B.; association executive; b. Winnipeg, Man. 2 Feb. 1951; d. James Comrie and Mona Rosamond (Lee) McC.; e. Univ. of Man. B.A. 1972; Osgoode Hall Law Sch. LL.B. 1975; m. Hon. Otto Lang, P.C., Q.C. s. Otto and Maria Lang 6 May 1989; children: Andrew and Rebecca Parkinson; Maria, Timothy, Andrew, Elisabeth, Gregory, Adrian and Amanda Lang; CHIEF EXTVE. OFFR. LAW SOC. OF MAN. 1988– ; law practice Aikins, MacAulay & Thorvaldson 1976–78; Houston & McCawley 1978–80; Dep. Chief Extve. Offr. present Soc. 1981–88; cr. Q.C. 1988; sessional and guest lectr. in Law Univ. of Man.; lectr. Bar Admn. Course Law Soc. Man.; mem. Extve. and Bd. Govs. Candn. Law Info. Council 1981–91; Sec. Man. Law Sch. Found.; Extve. and Bd. mem. River Hts. Learning Centre 1983–85; Bd. mem. Man. Med. Services Found. 1987– ; Bd. Mem., Royal Winnipeg Ballet 1992– ; co-ed. 'Legal Education in Canada' 1987; United Church; Home: 680 Wellington Cres., Winnipeg, Man. R3M 0C2; Office: 201, 219 Kennedy St., Winnipeg, Man. R3C 1S8.

**MCCAWLEY, Peter Edward;** service management executive; b. Montreal, Que. 13 Dec. 1946; s. Gilbert Michael and Mary (Hayden) M.; e. St. Thomas Aquinas H.S.; Sir George Williams Univ.; Adv. Mgmt. Prog. for the Hospitality Ind., Univ. of Guelph 1983; m. Judith d. Edmund and Alice Stefani 16 Sept. 1972; children: Christopher Paul, Jonathan Scott, Crystal Laura, Jessica Alice; PRES. & C.O.O., MODERN BUILDING CLEANING INC. 1989– ; Buyer, Americal Hosp. Supply 1965; Office Mgr., La Soc. VS Ltée., VS Services Ltd. 1970; Admin. Asst. to Vice Pres. 1974; Div. Mgr., Diplomat Coffee System 1976; Extve. Asst. to Pres., VS Services Ltd. 1978; Vice Pres., Opns. Major Foods Ltd. 1981; Extve. Vice Pres. 1982; Group Vice Pres., Versa Services 1984; Extve. Vice Pres., Versa Services 1985; Dir., Versabec Inc.; recreations: coaching baseball, swimming, reading; Home: 1201 Queen Victoria Ave., Mississauga, Ont. L5H 3H2; Office: Box 950, Stn. U, Toronto, Ont. M8Z 5Y7.

**McCLEAN, William James,** B.Sc., M.B.A., P.Eng.; business executive; b. Toronto, Ont. 4 Dec. 1940; s. Robert Joseph and Letitia (Hewitt) M.; e. North Toronto C.I. 1958; Univ. of Toronto B.Sc. 1962, M.B.A. 1966 (outstanding scholastic achievement for grad. class); m. Vesta d. Sam and Marjorie Hambly 30 May 1970; children: Robert Joseph, Andrea Jane, Christine Marjorie; VICE-PRES., MFG. & DEVEL., IBM CANADA LTD. 1982– ; joined IBM Canada Ltd. 1962; var. mgmt. roles to Opns. Mgr., Mfg. & Devel. 1970; Dir., IBM Can. Lab. 1973; Datacentre Serv. 1977; Plant Mgr., Toronto Mfg. 1978; Extve. Ctte. Mem. 1986; Chrmn. of Bd. of Dirs., Mfg. Research Corp. of Ont.; Bd. of Govs., Ortech Internat. 1988; Adv. Counc. of Ont. Deans of Engineering; Mem. Repr., Candn. Microelectronics Corp.; Member of IAPA of Ontario; Adv. Mem., Centre for Adv. Tech. Edn., Ryerson Polytech Inst. 1984; Jnt. Policy Review Bd. Mem., Workmen's Compensation Bd. 1988; Bd. of Dirs., Candn. Manufacturers' Assn. 1993– ; Bd. mem., Ontario Safety League; clubs: Granite, Leaside Tennis; Home: 45 Sutherland Dr., Toronto, Ont. M4G 1H4; Office: 3E/426, 1150 Eglinton Ave. E., North York, Ont. M3C 1H7.

**McCLEAVE, Robert Jardine,** Q.C., B.A., LL.B., D.C.L.; retired judge; b. Moncton, N.B. 19 Dec. 1922; s. Robert David and Marjorie Doherty (Jardine) M.; e. Dalhousie Univ., B.A. 1943, LL.B. 1946; D.C.L. University King's Coll. 1973; m. Ruth Loughead James, 31 August 1946, (d. June 7, 1994); children: Christine Mary, Nicola Ruth, Melissa Hope, Robert James, Sarah Yuill; m. Sylvia Swan Jan. 26, 1985; read law with J. McG. Stewart, Q.C.; called to Bar of Nova Scotia 1950; cr. Q.C. Jan. 1968; with British United Press as Radio News Editor 1946; Maritime Mgr. 1947, W. Mgr. 1948, Ottawa Mgr. 1949; assoc. with Messrs. Stewart, Smith, MacKeen, Covert, Rogers, Sperry & Cowan, Halifax, 1950–53; first Chief News Editor, Stn. CJCH, Halifax, 1954–57; Dean, Maritime Sch. of Journalism 1955–64; first Pres., Halifax Broadcasting Club, 1963–64; el. to H. of C. for Halifax, 1957, 1958 and 1962; Parlty. Secy. to Min. of Public Works, 1962–63; def. in g.e. Apl. 1963, re-el. 1965, 1968, 1972 and 1974; Depy. Speaker 1973–74; Co-Chrmn. Comte. on Statutory Instruments 1974–77; resigned 8 Dec. 1977 and apptd. a judge of the Prov. Court, retired 1987; Chrmn., N.S. Labour Relations Bd. 1980–90; Commr. to conduct uranium inquiry 1982; Lectr. and Assoc. Fellow, Sch. of Journalism, Univ. of King's College 1979–89; Presbyterian; recreations: cryptic crosswords; golf; Home: 14 Merrill Dr., Halifax, N.S. B3M 2M3 and Tyn-Y-Maes, Rexton, N.B. E0A 2L0.

**McCLELLAN, Ross,** B.A., M.S.W.; social worker; b. Toronto, Ont. 8 Oct. 1942; s. Lorne Alexander and Raffaela Maria (Costabile) M.; e. Univ. of Toronto B.A. 1964, M.S.W. 1967; m. Patricia d. Lawrence and Maude O'Dowd 27 Dec. 1965; children: Maura, Ian; SPECIAL ADVISOR, POLICY AND ISSUES, PREMIER OF ONTARIO 1990– ; Social Worker, Min. of Community & Social Services and the Social Planning Council of Metro. Toronto 1964–75; Faculty of Social Work, Univ. of Toronto 1973–75; elected M.P.P. for Bellwoods 1975–87 (served as NDP Whip 1982–85; NDP House Leader 1985–87); Dir., Political Edn. & Legislation, Ont. Fed. of Labour 1988–90; Vice-Pres., Ont. NDP 1989–92; chaired NDP team which negotiated the NDP-Liberal Accord ending 42 years of Conservative govt. in Ont.; as member of NDP Election Planning Ctte. 1989–90 co-ord. labour participation in successful 1990 prov. election; Home: 896 Manning Ave., Toronto, Ont. M6G 2X4; Office: Room 267, Main Building, Queen's Park, Toronto, Ont. M7A 1A1.

**McCLELLAN, Hon. Shirley,** M.L.A.; politician, farmer; b. Hanna, Alta.; m. Lloyd; children: Mick, Tami; MINISTER OF HEALTH and MINISTER responsible for ALBERTA ALCOHOL AND DRUG ABUSE COMMISSION 1993– ; 1st. el. M.L.A. Chinook in by-election 23 Nov. 1987; Mem., Agric. & Rural Affairs Caucus, Rural Affairs Caucus, & Irrigation Caucus cttee.; apptd. to Water Supply Action Ctte. during 1988 drought; re-elected 20 Mar. 1989; Assoc. Min. of Agric. 1989–93; Min. resp. for the Land Compensation Bd. 1991; Min. resp. for Rural Development 1992; Min. of Health & Min. resp. for the Wild Rose Foundation 1992; serves on Agric. & Rural Econ. Cabinet, Economic Planning Cabinet & Legis. Review cttes.; currently resp. for Alta. Hail & Crop Insur. Corp., Irrigation Counc., Irrigation & Resource Mngt. Div. & Irrigation Secretariat, Alta. Agric. Rsch. Inst., Surface Rights Bd., Land Compensation Bd., Rsch. Div. & Field Services Sector; farms with husband & son in New Brigden; Past Dir., Alta. Agric. Rsch. Inst. Bd.; Alta. Wheat Pool Adv. Ctte.; Alta. Assn. of Continuing Edn.; Candn. Assn. for Cont. Edn.; Co-ord., Big Country Furth Edn. Counc. 12 yrs.; Rep., Min. Adv. Ctte., Further Edn. 5 yrs.; Mins. Adv. Ctte. on College Affairs 2 yrs.; Office: 127 Legislative Bldg., Edmonton, Alta. T5K 2B6.

**McCLELLAN, The Hon. William Arthur,** B.Com.; retired judge; b. Moose Jaw. Sask. 1 Sept. 1912; s. George Brinton and Elizabeth Anne (Cunnington) McC.; e. Elem. Schs. and High Sch., N. Vancouver, B.C.; Ridley Coll., St. Catharines, Ont.; Univ. of B.C., B.Com. 1934; Vancouver and B.C. Law Schs., 1943–46; m. Mildred Marie, d. Frank Pollock, 27 May 1939; children Jane Leslie, Michael; Judge, Co. Court of Vancouver 1967–87; retired 1987; read law with Lawrence and Shaw, Vancouver; called to Bar of B.C. 1946; began practice of law in Dawson Creek, 1946; formed firm of McClellan, Lundeen and Clancy 1958; practiced in Peace River area till 1967; prior to legal career served 9 yrs. with Canada Packers in Toronto and Vancouver; mem. Dawson Creek, B.C., Village Council 1954–57 (Chrmn. 1955); def. Lib. cand. for South Peace in Prov. g.e. 1964 and for Cariboo in Fed. g.e. 1965; former Gov., Ang. Theol. Coll., Univ. of B.C.; former Chancellor, Ang. Diocese of Caledonia; mem., Candn. Bar Assn.; Freemason; Psi Upsilon; Anglican; recreations: fishing, gardening; Home: 902 – 2155 W 44th Ave., Vancouver, B.C. V6M 2G4.

**McCLELLAND, Jack;** O.C. (1976), LL.D.; publisher; b. Toronto 1922; s. Jack McC.; e. St. Andrew's Coll., UTS; Trinity Coll. Univ of Toronto, grad. 1946; m.; four d. and one s.; former Publisher, McClelland & Stewart Ltd. (resigned 1987); Pres. Seal Books; joined the Co. (co-founded by father 1906) 1946; served in 2nd World War, R.C.N. 1945, skipper of motor torpedo boat; Mentioned in Dispatches; awarded LL.D., Carleton Univ. 1984; Banff Medal 1984; Molson Award 1984.

**McCLINTOCK, Margaret Louise;** publisher; b. Jonquière, Que. 4 Mar. 1954; d. George Bernard and Elizabeth Louise (Long) M.; e. Univ. of Toronto; m. James N. s. James MacCammon and Elizabeth Stieneker 1978; PUBLISHER, COACH HOUSE PRESS 1990– ; Editor, 'Books for Everybody' 1980–83; Assoc. Pub., 'Canadian Art' magazine 1984–85; Literature Offr., Ontario Arts Council 1987–90; Home: Toronto, Ont.; Office: #307 - 50 Prince Arthur Ave., Toronto, Ont. M5R 1B5.

**McCLUNG, Hon. John Wesley,** B.A., LL.B.; judge; b. Edmonton, Alta. 15 July 1935; s. John Wesley and Lillian Mae (Johnston) McC.; e. Univ. of Alta. B.A. 1957, LL.B. 1958; m. Eda d. Waldemar Matiisen 26 Oct. 1973; Justice of Appeal, Court of Appeal of Alta. since 1980; called to Bar of Alta. 1959; cr. Q.C. 1973; Sr. Partner, McClung Frohlich & Rand, Edmonton until apptd. Judge, Dist. Court of Alta. 1976; Judge, Supreme Court of Alta. (Trial Div.) 1977–80; United Church; recreations: golf, hunting waterfowl; Club: Edmonton Country; Home: 14631 Mackenzie Dr., Edmonton, Alta.; Office: Law Courts, Edmonton, Alta. T5J 0R2.

**McCLYMONT, Hamilton,** B.A.; entertainment executive; b. Montreal, Que. 20 March 1944; s. Hamilton and Zoe A. (Cook) McC.; e. John Rennie High Sch. Pointe Claire, Que. 1960; Lower Can. Coll. Montreal 1961; Dalhousie Univ. B.A. 1969; m. Torill Samuelsen, 1990; children: Alexander Hamilton, Laura Christine; Gen. Mgr., Canadian Stage Company 1990; Sales Adm., Drummond McCall & Co. Ltd. Montreal, Halifax, Toronto 1963–69; Adm. Dir. Toronto Arts Productions 1969–74; Adm., Neptune Theatre Foundation, Halifax 1974–76; Music Offr. Finance, Can. Council 1976–78; Gen. Mgr., Vancouver Opera Assn. 1978–82; Pres., Prof. Opera Co's of Can. 1980–82; Chrmn., Candn. Comte. Opera Am. 1979–82; Producer, Special Events, Expo 86, 1983–85; Vice Pres., Entertainment, EXPO 86, 1986; Pres., Alpha Projects Internat. Ltd. 1987–90; served with UNTD 1961–63; HMCS Scotian, HMCS Cornwallis, HMCS Buckingham; mem. Assn. Cultural Extves.; ACTRA; Candn. Owners & Pilots Assn.; Phi Delta Theta; recreation: flying; golf; sailing.

**McCOMB, Eleanor Grace,** A.O.C.A.; artist, homemaker; b. Toronto, Ont.; d. Harry Douglas and Eva Gladys (Campbell) Woodcroft; e. Ont. College of Art A.O.C.A. 1937; m. Robert s. Madge and Thornton McComb 10 May 1947; children: Carolyn, Susan, David; exbns: Eaton's Art Gall. Toronto 1968–76, The Shayne Gall. Montreal 1974–80, Montreal Mus. of Fine Art 1978–83; Ziska Gall. Bracebridge, Ont. 1983– , Cobblestone Galleries, St. Catharines 1984– , Gallery on the Lake Buckhorn, Ont. 1985– , Fawcett-Langdon Gall. Burlington 1989–93, Artworld, Sherway Gardens West Mall Etobicoke, Ont. 1993– ; Protestant; Home: 6 Orchard St., Markham, Ont. L3P 2T1.

**McCOMBE, Brian George,** B.A., LL.B.; lawyer; b. Winnipeg, Man. 6 May 1935; s. Joseph and Jean J. (Winning) M.; e. Univ. of Manitoba B.A. 1956, LL.B. 1961; m. Irene d. Joseph and Nora Davey 25 July 1959; children: Robert, Cameron, Shawn; PRES., MEGIN MANAGEMENT LTD. 1988– ; Underwriter, GWL 1957; Landman, California Standard & Partner, Prothroe, Gibbs, McCruden, Hilland & McCombe 1963; Partner, McLaws & Co. 1967; McCombe, Cameron & Cormie 1975; retired from law practice 1988; Dir., Drake Petroleums Ltd.; recipient of more than 15 scholarships; Gold Medal winner 1961; Fellow, Found. for

Legal Research; Mem., Alberta Law Soc.; author: 'Helium and Its Place in the Petroleum and Natural Gas Leases' 1963 and several papers on Securities Act; clubs: Calgary Petroleum, Earl Grey Golf; Address: 427 Lake Placid Green, Calgary, Alta. T2J 5A4.

**McCONICA, James K.,** M.A., D.Phil., LL.D., D.Litt., F.R.H.S., F.R.S.C.; research fellow; b. Sask., 24 Apl. 1930; s. Thomas Henry and Edith Wilma (Crates) McC.; e. Univ. of Sask., B.A. 1951; Oxford Univ. (Rhodes Scholar), B.A. 1954, M.A. 1957, D.Phil. 1963; Univ. of Toronto, M.A. 1964; LL.D. Univ. of Sask. 1986; Univ. of Windsor, D.Litt. 1989; RSCH. FELLOW, ALL SOULS COLLEGE, OXFORD, ENGLAND 1990– ; Academic Dean 1990–92; Emeritus Prof. of Hist., Pontifical Inst. of Mediaeval Studies and Centre for Medieval Studies, Univ. of Toronto; Priest, Cong. of St. Basil; Chaplain, Sovereign Order Knights of Malta; Fellow, Royal Historical Society 1964; Fellow, John Simon Guggenheim Foundation, 1969–70; Visiting Fellow, All Souls Coll. 1969–71, 1977 and Corpus Christi Coll. 1972; James Ford Special Lectr., Oxford Univ. 1977; Fellow, All Souls Coll., Oxford 1980–84; Pres., Univ. of St. Michael's College, Toronto 1984–90; Fellow, Royal Soc. of Can. 1987; Foreign mem., Royal Belgian Academy 1988; author: 'English Humanists and Reformation Politics' 1965; 'Thomas More: A Short Biography' 1977; 'The Collegiate University' (vol. 3 of the History of the University of Oxford) 1986; 'Erasmus' 1991; Chrmn. of Ed. Bd., 'Collected Works of Erasmus' (Annotator vols. 3 and 4); mem., Conseil Internat. pour l'édition des oeuvres complètes d'Erasme of the Koninklijke Nederlandse Akademie van Wetenschappen; Am. Soc. for Reformation Rsch.; Oxfordshire Architectural and Historical Soc.; Oxford Archaeological Advisory Ctte.; Renaissance Soc. Am.; Candn. Soc. for Renaissance Studies; Exeter Coll. (Oxford) Assn.; Candn. Assn. Rhodes Scholars; Clubs: Athenaeum Gridiron; R. Catholic; Address: All Souls College, Oxford, England OX1 4AL.

**McCONKEY, Edward Bruce,** C.A.; b. Barrie, Ont. 9 April 1924; s. Robert and Rita (Webb) M.; e. Private and High Schs., Barrie, Ont.; Inst. Chart. Accts., C.A.; children: David Bruce, Gregory Michael, Paul Andre, Brian James, Mary Diane, Janet Marie, Angela; Vice Chrmn., Denison Mines Ltd. 1981–91, retired; with Peat, Marwick, Mitchell & Co., Chart. Accts. 1943; J. Arthur Rank Organisation of Canada 1951; joined Denison Mines Ltd. as Asst. Treas. 1955; Comptroller 1958, Treas. and Comptroller 1964; Vice-Pres., Finance, and Treas. 1966; Vice Pres., Finance and Dir. 1967; former Chrmn. & Dir., Quintette Coal Ltd.; former Dir., Standard Trust Co.; mem., Inst. Chart Accts. Ont.

**McCONNELL, Edward J.,** OBE, LL.B., LL.D.; investment counsellor; b. Belfast, N. Ireland 3 June 1931; s. late Edward and late Sarah (Maguire) McC.; e. St. Mary's Belfast; Queen's Univ. Belfast, LL.B. 1955, LL.D. 1988; m. Pauline B. Murphy, 31 May 1958; children: Eamonn, Stephen, Michael, David, Eileen; VICE CHRMN., BARCLAYS McCONNELL LTD. (formerly E.J. McConnell & Associates Ltd.) estbl. 1976; Vice Chrmn. & Dir., Ireland Fund of Can.; Candn. Observer International Fund for Ireland; joined Crown Trust Co. Montreal 1959; Asst. to Pres. Guardian Trust Co. Montreal 1962, Vice Pres. 1964; Gen. Mgr. Internat. Trust Co. Montreal 1965, Vice Pres. Toronto 1967, Extve. Vice Pres. 1969, Dir. 1970, Pres. and C.E.O. 1971; Gov., St. Michael's Coll., Univ. of Toronto; recreations: golf, tennis; Clubs: RCYC; National; Toronto Golf; Ballybunion Golf, Ireland; Malone Golf, Ireland; Royal Portrush, Ireland; Gator Creek, Fla.; Homes: 65 Highland Ave., Toronto, Ont. M4W 2A2 and Longboat Key, FL USA.

**McCONNELL, Frank E.,** B.S.E., M.B.A.; executive; e. Princeton Univ. B.S.E. 1962; Harvard Business Sch. M.B.A. 1964; Dir., Chart Industries Ltd.; Mountain Spring Vineyards Inc.; Clubs: University; Address: 71 Charles St. E., Toronto, Ont. M4Y 2T3.

**McCONNELL, John Charles,** B.Sc., Ph.D.; educator; b. Belfast, N.Ireland 11 Sept. 1945; s. John Douglas and Margaret Mary (Johnston) McC.; e. Annadale Grammar Sch. Belfast 1963; Queen's Univ. Belfast B.Sc. 1966, Ph.D. 1969; m. Joan Sinclair d. John and Margaret Harris 24 Oct. 1986; children: Deirdre Louise, Alison Joyce, Andrew Padraigh Sinclair; PROF. OF EARTH AND ATMOSPHERIC SCI. YORK UNIV. 1981– ; Rsch. Asst.: Kitt Peak Nat. Obs. Ariz. 1969–70, D.E.A.P. Harvard 1970–72; Asst. Prof. of Phys. present Univ. 1972, Assoc. Prof. 1975, Prof. of Physics 1980–81, Chair of Earth & Atmospheric Sci. 1982–86; mem. NSERC Strategic Grants Panel on Environmental Quality 1990–93; mem. U.V.S. team Voyager space craft 1972–90; mem. MOPITT Team; Assoc. Editor of Journal of Geophysical Research - Atmosphere Section; author over 70 publs. sci. jours. mem. Candn. Meteorol. & Oceanog. Soc.; Am. Geophys. Union; Div. Planetary Sci. of Am. Astron. Soc.; Royal Scot. Country Dance Soc.; recreations: Scottish country dancing, hiking, cross-country skiing, running; Club: Trakkers; Office: 4700 Keele St., North York, Ont. M3J 1P3.

**McCONNELL, Rob,** (Robert Murray Gordon); musician; b. London, Ont. 14 Feb. 1935; began career with Don Thompson's band, Edmonton 1954; a trombonist with Bobby Gimby, Toronto; formed own rehearsal band; performed with Maynard Ferguson's big band, New York 1964; returned to Toronto becoming leading studio player, also an arranger and composer; mem. Nimmons 'N' Nine Plus Six 1965–69; formed Boss Brass 1968; performs in clubs and on CBC Radio with smaller groups incl. quintets with Rick Wilson and Ian McDougall; has recorded with Guido Basso, Ferguson, Moe Koffman, Nimmons and others; Boss Brass has recorded his compositions 'My Man Bill'; 'It's Hard to Find One'; 'That's Right'; 'Tribute to Art Fern'; 'Runaway Hormones'; '4,389,165th Blues in B Flat'; 7 Grammy nominations, 5 for best performance by Big Band; Grammy Winner, Best Big Band Jazz 'All in Good Time' 1983; Grammy Nominee, Best Arrangement Instrumental 'I Got Rhythm' 1983; winner 3 Juno Awards; arranger music sung by Singers Unlimited and Hi-Lo's; mem. SOCAN.

**McCONNELL, William Howard,** LL.M., Ph.D.; professor of law; b. Aylmer, Que. 2 July 1930; s. Miles Conrad and Valeria (Tait) M. (both dec.); e. Carleton Univ. B.A. 1955; Univ. of N.B. B.C.L. 1958; Univ. of Toronto Ph.D. 1968; Univ. of Sask. LL.M. 1970; m. Nadage d. Capt. Ralph (dec.) and Marjorie (Underhill) Neville 4 Oct. 1963; children: Richard, Conrad (dec.); PROFESSOR OF LAW, UNIV. OF SASKATCHEWAN 1975– ; F/L, Judge Advocate General's Br., R.C.A.F. 1959–63; Lectr., Pol. Sci., Bishop's Univ. 1966–69; Asst. Prof., present univ. 1970; Assoc. Prof. 1973; Lectr., summer programs at Sherbrooke, Dalhousie, & Sask. univs.; frequent commentator on legal & constitutional affairs in media; Gov.-Gen's Medal, Carleton Univ. 1955; Mackenzie King Fellowship, Univ. of Toronto 1965–66; Dir., Soc. for the Advancement of Voter Equality; Chrmn., Independent Schools Review Bd., Prov. of Sask.; Ed. Bd., 'Can. J. of Irish Studies'; author: 'Commentary on the British North America Act' 1977, 'Prairie Justice' 1980 and num. articles in law reviews; recreations: chess; club: Faculty; Home: 1328 Osler St., Saskatoon, Sask. S7N 0V2; Office: Saskatoon, Sask. S7N 0W0.

**MCCORMACK, Andrew Ross;** B.A., M.A., Ph.D.; university professor; b. Winnipeg, Man. 8 June 1943; s. Andrew George and Agnes Penny (Ross) McC.; e. United Coll., Winnipeg, B.A. 1964; Univ. Man., M.A. 1966; Univ. Western Ont., Ph.D. 1973; m. Carolyn, d. Clarence and Anne Carson, 27 Aug. 1965; children: Carolyn Jane; Rebecca Kathleen; Vice-Pres. (Acad.), Univ. of Winnipeg 1982; Extve. Asst. Deputy Min., Man. Dept. Labour 1966; Lectr., present Univ. 1968–70; Asst. Prof. 1972; Adjunct Prof., Univ. of Man. 1974; Assoc. Prof., present Univ. 1977; Asst. Dean Arts & Sci. 1979; Sr. Univs. Officer, Inter-Univs. North 1982; Prof. present Univ. 1983; author 'Reformers, Rebels and Revolutionaries: The Western Canadian Radical Movement 1899–1919,' 1977; co-ed. (with Ian MacPherson) 'Cities in the West: Papers of the Western Canada Urban History Conference' 1975; Can. Counc. Leave Fellowship 1977–78; Visiting Fellow, Inst. Commonwealth Studies, Univ. of London 1977–78; Internat. Travel Fellowship, Social Sciences and Humanities Rsch. Counc. Can. 1979; mem. Bd. Dirs.: Health Sci. Centre, Sch. Nursing; Man. Record Soc. (Pres. 1981–82); mem.: Mayor's Comte. on Race Relations; Candn. Hist. Assn. (Counc. Mem. 1981–82); Univ. of Man. Press (Bd. Dirs. 1980–82); Man. Hist. Sites Bd. (Chrmn. 1979–82); Commonwealth Labour Hist. Conf. (Co-Chrmn. 1978–81); Assn. Candn. Labour Historians (Pres. 1977–82); mem. Delta Upsilon; clubs: Reh-Fit Running; Victoria Beach Yacht; recreations: running; squash; canoeing; sailing; photography; Home: 467 Kingston Cres., Winnipeg, Man. R2M 0V1.

**McCORMACK, Eric Patrick,** M.A., Ph.D.; writer; b. Scotland 20 Sept. 1938; s. John and Joan M.; e. Glasgow Univ. M.A. 1962; Univ. of Manitoba Ph.D. 1973; m. Nancy d. Rudy and Johanna Helfinger 22 Dec. 1987; children (by prev. marriage): Michael, Jody; ASSOC. PROF. (ENGLISH), ST. JEROME'S COLLEGE 1970– ; came to Canada 1966; Candn. citizen 1970; Commonwealth Writers Prize 1988; Scottish Council Book Award 1990; author: 'Inspecting the Vaults' 1987 (short stories), 'The Paradise Motel' 1989, 'The Mysterium' 1992 (novels); Home: 578 Westvale Dr., Waterloo, Ont. N2T 1K2; Office: Waterloo, Ont. N2L 3G3.

**McCORMACK, Thomas William,** M.A.; economist; b. St. Thomas, Ont. 4 March 1946; s. Thomas Henry and Annie Amelia (Wright) McC.; e. Univ. of W. Ont., B.A. 1968, M.A. 1970; m. Barbara d. Chester and Pauline Campbell 13 Sept. 1969; children: Jeffrey Campbell, Morgan Victoria; PRES., STRATEGIC PROJECTIONS INC. 1989– ; Sr. Econ. Econ. Analysis Div. Finance Can. Ottawa 1970–74; Sr. Cons. Econ. Dept. Woods Gordon Management Consultants Toronto 1974–76; Dir. Econ. Rsch. Br. Anti-Inflation Bd. Ottawa 1976–79; Special Adv. Econ. Policy Finance Can. 1979–80; Dir. Econ. Intelligence Br. Ind., Trade & Comm. Can. 1980–82; Dir. Econ. Data Resources of Can. 1982–86; Principal, Economics Practice, Coopers & Lybrand Consulting Group 1986–87; Vice Pres. of Research, Compusearch Market & Social Research Ltd. 1987–89; mem. Candn. Assn. Bus. Econs. (Treas. 1981–85); Toronto Assn. Bus. Econs. (Pres. 1985–87); Nat. Assn. Bus. Econs.; Pres. Ottawa Assn. Applied Econ. 1980–81, Treas. 1977–79, 1992– ; recreations: reading, music; Office: P.O. Box 775, Oakville, Ont.

**McCORMACK, William Charles,** M.A., Ph.D., F.R.A.I.; educator; b. Sutherland, Iowa 31 March 1929; s. late Dan Bicknell and late Wilna (Plager) McC.; e. Univ. of Chicago B.A. 1948, Ph.D. (Anthrop.) 1956; Stanford Univ. B.A. 1949, M.A. 1950; Univ. of Calif. Berkeley 1950–51; Univ. of Mich. Summer Inst. Linguistics 1956; Univ. of Toronto Internat. Summer Inst. Semiotic & Structural Studies 1980, 1982, 1984, 1986 and 1990; m. Anna Mary d. late John Charles Pikelis 9 June 1962; EMERITUS PROF. OF ANTHROP. UNIV. OF CALGARY 1988– ; Assoc. Research Anthrop. Modern India Project Univ. of Calif. Berkeley 1958–59; Visiting Lectr. in Indian Anthrop. Sch. of Oriental & African Studies Univ. of London, Eng. 1959–60; Asst. Prof. Univ. of Wisc. Madison 1960–64; Assoc. Prof. Duke Univ. 1964–69; Prof. of Anthrop. & Linguistics, Univ. of Calgary 1969–87; Head of Linguistics 1972–73; ed. consultant various univ. presses; mem. and chrmn. numerous grants evaluation comtes.; consultant on Kannada lit. Univ. Texas 1958, Univ. of Wisc. Lib. 1960–64; univ. external consultant; various pub. service lectures on India; participant numerous confs./congs.; recipient many scholarships, fellowships, grants incl. Ford Foundation, Rockefeller Foundation, Am. Council Learned Socs., U.S. Office of Education, Duke Endowment Foundation, Can. Council, Wenner-Gren Foundation, Social Sciences and Humanities Resch. Counc. of Can.; author 'Kannada: A Cultural Introduction to the Spoken Styles of the Language' 1966; co-editor 'Language and Man' 1976; 'Language and Thought' 1977; 'Approaches to Language' 1978; 'Language and Society' 1979; 'The Sixth LACUS Forum 1979' 1980; author various book chapters, articles prof. journs.; Fellow, Am. Anthrop. Assn.; Current Anthrop.; Life mem. Folklore Fellows India; Mythic Soc.; mem. various Candn. and foreign anthrop. assns.; Sigma Xi Scient. Research Soc.; Beta Theta Pi; recreation: music, travel; Home: 340–40 Ave. S.W., Calgary, Alta. T2S 0X4; Office: Dept. of Anthropology, Univ. of Calgary, Calgary, Alta. T2N 1N4.

**McCORMICK, William Ormsby,** M.A., M.B., F.R.C.P.(Lond.), F.R.C.P.C., F.R.C.Psych., DPM; professor of psychiatry; b. Dublin, Ireland 4 Mar. 1929; s. Victor Ormsby and Margaretta Tate (Stevenson) M.; e. The Leys Sc., Cambridge; Cambridge Univ., B.A. 1950, M.B. 1953; London Univ., DPM 1962; m. Aileen d. John and Mary Kirby 17 July 1954; children: Charles William Ormsby, Catherine Louise; PROF., DIR. OF POSTGRAD. PSYCH. EDN., DEPT. OF PSYCH., DALHOUSIE UNIV. 1982– ; Med./Clin. Dir., The Nova Scotia Hospital, Dartmouth N.S. 1989– ; Internal Med. & Psych. Training, London, Eng.; Sr. Lectr., Dept. of Mental Health, The Queens Univ. of Belfast, N. Ireland 1965–76; Assoc. Prof. then Prof., Dept. of Psych., Univ. of Toronto 1976–82; Dir., Psych. Day Hosp., Camp Hill Hosp. 1982–86; Med. Dir., Mental Health Div., Valley Health Serv. Assn. 1985–89; Breeder, Owner, Trainer & Handler, Irish Nat. Champion Retriever 1973: Tappanzee Phaedra; Dir. at Large, Bd. of Dir., Candn. Psych. Assn. 1984–87 and Pres.-Elect 1993–94; Pres., N.S. Psych. Assn. 1985–86; Pres., Atlantic Prov. Psych. Assn. 1985–86; author/co-author, var. sci. pubs.; co-editor: 'Evaluation of Quality of Care in Psychiatry' 1980, 'Disturbed Behaviour in the Elderly' 1987; recreations: fishing, hunting, retriever training, tennis; Office: Camp Hill Hosp., 1763 Robie St., 4th Fl., Abbie Lane Bld., Halifax, N.S. B3H 3G2.

**McCORRISTON, James R.,** B.A., M.D., C.M., M.Sc., F.R.C.S.(C), F.A.C.S.; surgeon; b. Ridgedale, Sask. 27

July 1919; s. Tolbert James and Grace (Peter) M.; e. Ridgedale (Sask.) High Sch. (1936); Univ. of Sask., B.A. 1939; Queen's Univ., M.D., C.M. 1943; McGill Univ., M.Sc. 1948, Dipl. in Surg. 1951; F.R.C.S.(C) 1951; F.A.C.S. 1953; widower; children: Colin, Pamela, Janet; PROF. EMERITUS OF SURGERY, QUEEN'S UNIV. 1985– ; Surgeon, Kingston Gen. Hospital; Clinical Asst. in Surgery 1951, Assoc. Surgeon 1959, Royal Victoria Hospital, Montreal, Que.; Lectr. in Surgery, McGill Univ. 1951; Assoc. Prof. 1959; Prof. of Surgery, Queen's Univ.; Head of Dept. 1963–73; Publications: numerous articles and chapters in several medical books and journs.; United Church; Home: PO Box 370, Sharbot Lake, Ont. K0H 2P0.

**MCCOSHEN, John Adrian,** B.Sc., M.S., Ph.D.; university professor; b. Port Arthur, Ont. 27 May 1941; s. Cleveland Lawrence and Ida Mary (Arnot) M.; e. St. Francis Xavier Univ., B.Sc. 1968; State Univ. of N.Y., M.S. 1971; McMaster Univ. Med. Ctr., Ph.D. 1976; post-doct. fellow, McGill Univ. 1976–78 (MRC); m. Jeanette d. Frederick and Dorothy Warner 28 Aug. 1965; children: Sean, Sonya; PROF. OF OBSTETRICS/GYNECOLOGY, UNIV. OF MANITOBA 1989– ; Instr., State Univ. of N.Y. 1970–71; Curriculum Specialist 1972–73; Instr., McGill Univ. 1977–78; Asst. Prof. of Anatomy, Univ. of Man. 1978–79; Adjunct Prof. 1979– ; Asst. Prof. of OB/GYN 1979–84; Head, Reproductive Sci. 1981– ; Staff Sci., Women's Hosp., Health Sci. Ctr. 1981– ; Assoc. Prof. of OB/GYN 1984–89; Dir., In Vitro Fertilization Lab. 1986–88; invited visiting prof. to numerous univs. in Can., U.S., Eur. & Asia; established first Clin. Androl. Lab., Prov. of Man.; Editor, 'Trophoblast Research'; Cons. (Infertility), Women's Hosp. & St. Boniface Gen. Hosp.; Mem., Med. Staff Counc., Health Sci. Ctr.; Grants Reviewer (Endocrinology), MRC; State Univ. of N.Y. Fgn. Student Scholarship 1969; Sigma Xi Sci. Award 1971; David Russell Mem. Scholarship 1973; Yates Scholarship 1974; MRC post-doct. fellowship 1976; Upjohn Award, Am. Assn. of OB & GYN 1984; Mem., Soc. for GYN Investigation; Candn. Fertility & Androl. Soc. (Reg. Dir. 1985–87); Am. Fertility Soc.; Am. Soc. of Androl.; author of numerous sci. articles & book chapters; recreations: 3D computer imaging, astronomy; Home: 864 Ash St., Winnipeg, Man. R3N 0R8; Office: Respiratory Bldg., 4th Floor, 810 Sherbrook St., Winnipeg, Man. R3A 1R8.

**McCOUBREY, R. James,** B.Com.; media and advertising executive; b. Grand Mere, Que. 1 Sept. 1944; s. Dr.James Addison and Margaret Genevieve Fernio (Scarratt) McC.; e. Lower Can. Coll. Montreal; McGill Univ. B.Com. 1966; m. Annette d. Marcel and Therese Hebert 16 Sept. 1972; two s. James Andrew, Matthew Alexander; PRES. & C.E.O., TELEMEDIA INC. 1990– ; Chrmn., Magazines Canada; Dir., Telemedia Inc.; Telemedia Communications U.S.A.; Blount Group of Companies; Greyhound Lines of Canada; The Council for Business and the Arts in Canada; joined The Procter and Gamble Co. Toronto 1967–69; Asst. Mgr. Young & Rubicam Ltée Montreal 1970–71; Dir. of Client Services Young & Rubicam Ltd. Toronto 1972–73, Gen. Mgr. 1974–76, Pres. and C.E.O. 1977–82; Chrmn. & C.E.O. 1982–90; Sr. Vice Pres., Area Dir. Can./Latin Am., Young & Rubicam International, N.Y. 1980–82, Extve. Vice Pres., Gen. Mgr. Europe and Dir. Young & Rubicam International, London 1982–84, Extve. Vice Pres., Group Dir. and Area Dir. Young & Rubicam Advertising, N.Y. 1983–90; Dir., Young Presidents Orgn.; Immed. Past Chrmn., Young Presidents' Orgn., Ont. Chapter; Past Chrmn. Inst. Candn. Advertising; Zeta Psi; P. Conservative; Anglican; Clubs: Mount Royal Club; RCYC; Home: 54 Bernard Ave., Toronto, Ont. M5R 1R5; Office: 50 Holly St., Toronto, Ont. M4S 3B3.

**McCOURT, William Kenneth,** B.Comm., M.B.A.; insurance executive; b. Vancouver, B.C. 26 July 1935; e. Univ. of B.C. B.Comm. 1958; Univ. of Maryland and George Washington Univ. M.B.A. 1959; m. Joan; children: Kelly, Craig; PRESIDENT AND CHIEF EXECUTIVE OFFICER, INSURANCE CORPORATION OF BRITISH COLUMBIA 1993– ; started in marketing consulting; various positions leaving as Vice-President for the Pacific Div., Eaton's 1964–81; Sr. Vice-Pres. of Merchandising Toronto 1982; returned to west coast lifestyle after a few months; various positions leaving as Executive Vice-Pres., BC Tel 1982–91; Office: 151 West Esplanade, North Vancouver, B.C. V7M 3H9.

**MCCOY, Hon. Elaine J.,** Q.C., B.A., LL.B.; executive; b. Brandon, Man. 7 Mar. 1946; d. John Frederick and Jean Stewart (Hope); e. Univ. of Alta., B.A., LL.B. 1969; Univ. of B.C., grad. studies 1978; m. Miles H. Patterson, Q.C. 19 Apr. 1988; PRES., THE MCCOY GROUP; elected MLA, Calgary West 1986; re-elected 1989; Min. of Labour with resp. for Human Rights & Personnel Admin., Alta. Govt. 1989–92; Min. responsible for Women's Issues 1987–92; and Min. of Consumer and Corp. Affairs 1986–89; admitted Alta. Bar 1970; Former Sr. Legal Couns., Alta. Public Utilities Bd.; Former Barrister & Solicitor, Black & Co.; Head of Course, Admin. Advocacy, Bar Adm. Prog., Law Soc. of Alta.; Found. Trustee, Angela Cheng Musical Found.; United Church; Pres., Sir Winston Churchill Soc.; Pres., The Brock Institute; Mem., Calgary Economic Development Authority Adv. Council; Mem., Univ. of Calgary Faculty of Mngmt. Adv. Council; mem., Environmental Rsch. Centre Advisory Bd.; Home: 223, 20 Coachway Rd. S.W., Calgary, Alta. T3H 1E6; Office: 830, 407 - 2nd St. S.W., Calgary, Alta. T2P 2Y3.

**McCOY, Richard Hall,** B.Comm., M.B.A.; investment banker; b. Montreal, Que. 3 July 1942; e. Loyola College B.Comm. 1964; Univ. of Western Ontario M.B.A. 1968; m. Susan DuBois 1965; DEPUTY-CHAIRMAN, WOOD GUNDY INC.; Dir., CIBC Wood Gundy Corp.; First Australia Prime Income Investment Co. Ltd.; The First Australia Fund Inc.; Wood Gundy Pacific Limited; club: The York Club; Office: BCE Place, P.O. Box 500, Toronto, Ont. M5J 2S8.

**McCRACKEN, Archie Ross,** M.A., F.S.A. (1948) F.C.I.A.; retired insurance executive; b. Melbourne, Ont. 14 Feb. 1917; s. late Ross and Laura Belle (Sutherland); e. Univ. of Western Ont. (Hon. Math. and Physics), B.A. 1938, Gold Medalist; Univ. of Toronto M.A. (Meteorol.) 1944; m. Jocelyn Marie, d. late Arthur Jones, Belleville, Ont., 21 Dec. 1942; one s. Douglas R.: Sr. Vice Pres., North American Life Assurance Co. 1975–80; Asst. Actuary 1950, Assoc. 1958; Vice Pres. and Actuary 1964; Vice Pres. and Chief Actuary 1969; mem., Soc. of Actuaries; Candn. Inst. Actuaries (Pres. 1967–68); Internat. Actuarial Assn. (Vice Pres. for Can. 1973–76); Protestant; recreations: golf, bridge; Clubs: St. George's Golf & Country; Bd. of Trade, Toronto; Home: 30 Bemersyde Drive, Islington, Ont. M9A 2S8.

**McCRACKEN, Grant David,** Ph.D.; curator; b. Vancouver, B.C. 27 March 1951; s. John Stanley and Isabel (McQuade) McC.; e. Univ. of Chicago Ph.D. 1981; m. Judy d. Morley and Diana Globerman 10 Aug. 1990; HEAD AND FULL CURATOR INST. OF CONTEMPORARY CULTURE ROYAL ONT. MUSEUM 1990– ; Visiting Scholar Cambridge Univ. 1978–80; Killam Postdoctoral Fellow Univ. of B.C. 1981–83; Asst.-Assoc. Prof. Univ. of Guelph 1983–89; Sr. Resident Massey Coll. 1989–90; cons. to Chrysler Corp. USA, Saatchi and Saatchi Advertising USA, Winterthur Museum, Un. World Colls., Denver Art Gallery; recipient 'most distinguished contribution' award Jour. Consumer Rsch. 1984–87; author 'Culture and Consumption: New Approaches to Consumer Goods and Activities' 1988; 'The Long Interview' 1988; frequent contbr. 'Facts and Arguments' page Globe and Mail; Home: 92 Langley Ave., Toronto, Ont. M4K 1B5; Office: Toronto, Ont. M5S 2C6.

**McCRACKEN, Kathleen Luanne,** M.A., PhD.; poet; literary critic; lecturer; b. Dundalk, Ont. 26 Oct. 1960; d. Robert Ivan and Shirley Marguerite (Hardy) McC; e. Grey Highlands Secondary Sch. Flesherton, Ont. (Ont. Scholar 1979); York Univ. B.A. 1983, M.A. 1984; Univ. of Toronto Ph.D. 1989; author: (poetry) 'Reflections' 1978; 'Into Celebration' 1980; 'The Constancy of Objects' 1988; 'Blue Light, Bay and College' 1991 (nominated for Gov.-Gen.'s Award for Poetry 1992); co-author: 'Reflections: A Creative History of the One-Room Schoolhouse in Proton Township' (poetry/hist.) 1977; poetry and lit. criticism pub. various Candn., Am., Irish and Brit. jours.; Teaching Asst., Course Dir., Lectr. Univ. of Toronto, Ryerson Polytech. Inst. 1985–89; Course Dir., Dept. of English, York Univ. 1988–89; Social Sci. & Humanities Res. Council Postdoctoral Fellowship, University College, Dublin, Ireland 1989–91; Tutor, Trinity College, Dublin 1991; Lectr., Univ. of Ulster, Belfast 1991– ; acad. papers given confs. Can., Ireland and USA; recipient Ont. Arts Council Writers Grants (4); Univ. of Toronto Open Fellowship; Ont. Grad. Scholarships; mem. League Candn. Poets; Modern Lang. Assn.; Candn. Assn. Irish Studies; Internat. Assn. Study Anglo-Irish Lit.; recreations: swimming, sailing, travel, horseback riding, painting; Address: Dept. of English, Univ. of Ulster at Jordanstown, Newtonabbey, Co. Antrim, Northern Ireland BT37 0QB.

**McCRACKEN, Michael Clark,** B.A., M.A.; economist/executive; b. Tulsa, OK 24 June 1940; s. Austin Ralph and Athanell (Hall) M.; e. Rice Univ., B.A. 1961; Southern Methodist Univ., M.A. 1964; m. Catherine Doyle 1960; children: Mary Margaret, George, Catherine Mary; FOUNDER & PRES., INFORMETRICA LIMITED 1972– ; Staff Econ., Econ. Counc. of Can. 1965–67; U.S. Govt. 1967–70; CANDIDE Proj. Mgr., Econ. Counc. of Can. 1970–72; member of var. adv. bds.; mem., Candn. Assn. for Bus. Econ.; Mem., National Assn. of Business Economists (US) and Conference of Business Economists (US); author: 'CANDIDE Model 1.0' 1972; recreation: golf; Home: 15 Madawaska Dr., Ottawa, Ont. K1S 3G5; Office: 130 Slater St., 11th Floor, Ottawa, Ont. K1P 6E2.

**McCRANK, Ernest William Thomas,** M.D., F.R.C.P.(C).; psychiatrist; b. Val D'Or, Que. 4 April 1940; s. Ernest and Anna Mary (Amyotte) McC.; e. Queen's Univ., M.D. 1964; F.R.C.P.(C)., Spec. in Psychiatry 1970; m. Janice d. Dawson and Merlein MacDowall Aug. 1964; children: Colleen Louise, Ernest Dawson; CHIEF, DEPT. OF PSYCHIATRY 1991– and DIR., ANXIETY DISORDERS UNIT 1992– , UNIV. HOSPITAL, LONDON; Assoc. Prof. of Psychiatry, Univ. of W. Ont. 1976– ; Pres., Medical Staff, University Hosp. 1994–95; Bd. Mem., University Hosp. 1993–96; Fellow, Internal Med., Cleveland Clinic, 1965–66; Res., Psychiatry, Queen's Univ. 1966–70; Staff Psychiatrist, Community Psychiatric Clinic & Homewood Sanitarium, Guelph 1970–76; Dir. of Med. Edn., St. Joseph's Hosp., London 1977–80; cons. psychiatrist, St. Joseph's Hosp. and London Psychiatric Hospital, London; awarded Candn. Patent 1,209,959 1986; Dir., Affective Disorders Rsch. Devel. Fund; Progressive Supranuclear Bulbar Palsy Rsch. Devel. Fund; Univ. Hosp. Found.; R. Catholic; Hon. Mem., Am. Med. Assn.; mem. London Acad. of Med.; Ont. and Candn. Med. Assns.; Candn. Diabetic Assn.; Academy of Psychsomatic Medicine; author of var. articles and abstracts in med. jours.; recreations: athletics, guitar, woodworking; Home: 1670 Louise Blvd., London, Ont. N6G 2R3; Office: Univ. Hosp., P.O. Box 5339, Stn. A, London, Ont. N6A 5A5.

**McCRANK, M. Neil,** Q.C., B.Sc., LL.B.; prosecutor, public servant; b. Bourlamaque, P.Q. 9 May 1943; s. Ernest Martin and Anna Mary (Amyotte) M.; c. Queen's Univ. B.Sc. 1966, LL.B. 1969; m. Susan d. Jack and Mary Vincent 26 Aug. 1967; children: Jason, Kelly, Darren, Matthew; DEPUTY ATTORNEY GENERAL OF ALBERTA 1989– ; articled and practice with Lang, Michener et al. Toronto 1969–73; Asst. Crown Attorney Oshawa Ont. 1973–79; Special Prosecutor, Edmonton 1979–83; Dir. of Special Prosecutions Edmonton 1982–84; Asst. Deputy Minister (Criminal Justice) Alberta 1984–89; Q.C. Alberta 1990; Dir., Catholic Social Services Edmonton 1988–92; Chair, Bd. of Dir., Catholic Social Serv. 1992–93; Mem., Law Soc. of U.C. 1971– ; of Alta. 1980– ; Candn. Bar Assn. 1980– ; Nat. District Attorney's Assn. 1982– ; recreations: sports, camping, backpacking; club: Crestwood Tennis; Home: 13711 – 90 Ave., Edmonton, Alta. T5R 4T3; Office: 9833 109 St., Edmonton, Alta. T5K 2E8.

**McCREADY, Douglas Jackson,** B.A., M.Sc., Ph.D.; educator; b. Ottawa, Ont. 20 July 1943; s. Grant Roland and Margaret Anne (Jackson) McC.; e. Univ. of Windsor B.A. 1965; London Sch. of Econ. & Pol. Sci. M.Sc. (Econ.) 1966; Univ. of Alta. Ph.D. 1973; m. Catherine Lucille d. Ross and Grace Hatch 3 Sept. 1966; three s. Bryan Douglas, Mark Edward, Trevor Scott; PROF. OF ECON. WILFRID LAURIER UNIV. 1986– ; Core Faculty, Walden Univ. (Minneapolis MN USA) 1990– ; Part-time Instr. in Econ. Univ. of Alta. 1968–69; Asst. and Assoc. Prof. present Univ. 1969–86, Dir. of Instructional Devel. 1977–79, Pres. Faculty Assn. 1978–79; Assoc. Cons. Abt. Associates; mem. Waterloo Region Dist. Health Council 1979–81; Ont. Health Council, Ad Hoc Ctte. on Aging & Costs 1980–82; author 'The Canadian Public Sector' 1984; ed. 'Health Care in Canada: Looking Ahead' 1989; co-ed. and mem. ed. bds. various profl. jours.; elected mem., Mngmt. Bd., Internat. Institute of Public Finance 1992–95; mem. Candn. Evaluation Soc.; Candn. Econ. Assn.; Candn. Health Econ. Rsch. Assn.; E. Econ. Assn. (Ont. Area Rep. 1984–94); mem. Nat. Extve. P.Cons. Party 1964–65; Home: 344 Craigleith Dr., Waterloo, Ont. N2L 5B7; Office: Waterloo, Ont. N2L 3C5.

**McCREADY, Kenneth F.,** B.Sc., P.Eng.; utilities executive; b. Edmonton, Alta. 9 Oct. 1939; s. Ralph and Lillian McC.; e. Crescent Hts. High Sch. Calgary; Univ. of Alta. B.Sc. (Elect. Eng.) 1963; m. Margaret E. d. John Randall 2 Sept. 1961; children: John, Brian, Janet; PRES., CHIEF EXTVE. OFFR. AND DIR., TRANSALTA UTILITIES CORP. and TRANSALTA ENERGY CORP.; Pres. & C.E.O. May 1989, Pres. & Chief Operating Offr. 1985–88, Sr. Vice Pres. 1980; Dir.: Hewlett Packard (Canada) Ltd.; Keyword Office Technologies Ltd.; Marigold Foundation Ltd.; PanCanadian Petroleum Ltd.; The Conference Board of Canada; Calgary International Organ Festival; Chrmn., Alta. Round

Table on Environment and Economy; Chrmn., Advanced Computing Technologies Inc.; Pres., Northwest Electric Light & Power Assn.; Engineer in Training Comm. Dept. Calgary Power Ltd. 1963, Supr. Data Processing & Systems 1965, Supr. Rates & Contracts 1967, Adm. Asst. to Extve. Vice Pres. 1968–72, Asst. Mgr. Mgmt. Consulting Div. 1972–75, Mgr. Mgmt. Systems Dept. Montreal Engineering Co. Ltd. and Gen. Mgr. Monenco Computing Services Ltd. 1975–76, Vice Pres. Adm., Calgary Power Ltd. 1976–80; Past Dep. Chrmn. Bd. Govs. S. Alta. Inst. Technol.; mem., Business Council on National Issues; Internat. Business Council for Sustainable Development; Asea Brown Boveri Environment Advisory Bd.; CESO Advisory Council; Canada West Foundation Council; Past Pres. Men's Candn. Club Calgary; Past Pres., Constrn. Owners' Assn. Alta.; Calgary C. of C.; Past Dir., Candn. Elect Assn.; mem., Assn. Profl. Engs., Geols. & Geophys. Alta.; recreations: computers, cycling, photography; Club: Ranchmen's; Home: 1332 – 16A Street N.W., Calgary, Alta. T2N 2E1; Office: (P.O. Box 1900) 110 – 12 Avenue S.W., Calgary, Alta. T2P 2M1.

**MCCREADY, Warren Thomas,** M.A., Ph.D.; university professor; b. New York, N.Y. 8 Feb. 1915; came to Canada 1954; s. Thomas Burns and Louise Harriet (Rudolph) M.; e. Univ. of Chicago M.A. 1949, Ph.D. 1961; Instr. Univ. of Indiana, 1950–53; Lectr. Queen's Univ., Kingston 1954–56; Lectr., Univ. of Toronto 1956–60; Asst. Prof. 1960–64; Assoc. Prof. 1964–69; Prof. 1969; Prof. Emeritus 1980, Dept. of Spanish & Portuguese; merchant seaman 1933–40; served with U.S. Air Force 1940–45, rank Sgt.; author 'La hera'ldica en las obras de Lope de Vega y sus contempora'neos' 1962; 'Bibliografi'a tema'tica de estudios sobre el teatro espanol antiguo' 1966; 'El mejor mozo de Espana by Lope de Vega' 1967; other writings incl. bibliographical supplement to J.P.W. Crawford: 'Spanish Drama before Lope de Vega' 1967; articles on Spanish Golden Age Lit., cryptography; Ed., Bulletin of the Comediantes, 1967–72; mem., Internat. Assn. of Hispanists; Candn. Assn. of Hispanists; Am. Assn. of Teachers of Span. and Port.; recreations: reading, painting, traveling, cryptogram solving; Home: P.O. Box 122, Greenbank, Ont. L0C 1B0.

**McCREATH, Peter Leith,** B.A., M.A.(Hist.), B.Ed., M.A.(Ed.); businessman; b. Halifax, N.S. 5 July 1943; s. Peter M.; e. Univ. of Toronto B.A. 1966; Dalhousie Univ. M.A. 1967; St. Mary's Univ. B.Ed. 1971, M.A. (Ed.) 1979; m. Judy Elizabeth d. Hilda Duncan 5 July 1982; children: Jefferson, Adam; Lt., Royal Candn. Naval Reserve Regiment 1962–71; writer/broadcaster; High School Teacher, N.S.; Rsch. Assoc., Atlantic Inst. of Edn.; Comnr. of Oaths, Prov. of N.S. 1982– ; num. past extve. positions incl. Mem., N.S. Human Rights Comn. 1986–88; Member of Parliament (South Shore), House of Commons 1988–93; Min. of Veterans Affairs 1993; Dir. of Rsch., P.C. Party Nat. H.Q.; recreations: sailing, gardening; clubs: Chester Yacht; Home: Shore Rd., Hubbards, N.S. B0J 1T0.

**McCRORY, Colleen;** conservationist; b. New Denver, B.C. 5 Jan. 1950; d. Patrick M. (mother dec.); children: Sean, Rory, Shea; CHAIRPERSON, VALHALLA WILDERNESS SOCIETY 1976– ; leader of an 8-year campaign for the establishment of the 49,600 hectare Valhalla Prov. Park in 1983; Co-founder, National Save South Moresby Ctte. 1984–87 (instrumental in helping with creation of Nat. S. Moresby Park Reserve, Queen Charlotte Islands 1987); Co-ord., B.C. Environmental Netowrk 1987–89 (set up B.C. Environ. Hotline, a 1-800 number for environ. groups); work on a number of forest and park issues incl. stopping the mining in Strathcona Park (oldest park in B.C.) 1984– ; travelled across Canada in a van for six months, speaking to the public & gathering information on the Candn. logging (pulp & paper) industry 1989–90; Founder, Canada's Future Forest Alliance (an umbrella coalition of grassroots orgns. rep. 1 mill. Candns.) 1990; Legislative Asst., NDP Environ. Critic, Jim Fulton 1990–91; key focus at present is on exposing the Forest Crisis of Canada nationally & internationally; assists grassroots, environmental & native organizations; key media spokesperson for wilderness & forest issues in Canada; Fred M. Packard International Parks Merit Award; Gov. Gen. Award for Conservation 1984; Equinox Citation Award for outstanding achievements in saving Canada's Environment 1989; Office: c/o Valhalla Wilderness Society, Box 224, New Denver, B.C. V0G 1S0.

**McCUBBIN, Neil;** consulting engineer; b. Scot. 1 Sept. 1943; s. Archibald Cook and Isabel Anderson (McDonald) McC.; e. Univ. of Glasgow B.Sc. Eng. (1st Hons.), A.R.C.S.T. (Hons.) 1964; m. Helen d. Herbert and Edna Irwin 30 Dec. 1970; two s. Michael James, Derek Irwin; FOUNDER, N. McCUBBIN CONSULTANTS INC., pulp & paper environmental issues 1973– ; after grad. served in missile devel. for defence contractor Scot. then emigrated to Can.; engineer for various capital projects in pulp mills Woodfibre, B.C. and Hinton, Alta.; project eng. turnkey chem. plant mfr. Montreal 1968; joined BEAK Consultants (specialists enviromental eng.) 1970; entered private practice 1973; projects with present firm incl. provision expert testimony various hearings incl. U.S. Supreme Court case, analysis eng. and econ. aspects numerous paper ind. projects related to environment, eng. design air and water pollution control systems; mem. Nat. Rsch. Council Review Bd.; recipient Duke of Edinburgh Award 1959; Doug Jones Award Candn. Pulp & Paper Assn. 1978; Nat. Award Soc. Tech. Communications 1984; Tasman Fellowship 1988; author 'Technology of the Pulp and Paper Industry and its Environment Practices' 1984; 'State of Art of the Pulp and Paper Industry and its Environmental Practices' 1984; co-author 'Kraft Mill Effluents in Ontario' 1988; 'Best Available Technology for Ontario Pulp and Paper Industry' 1992; author or co-author numerous sci. papers, trade jour. & mag. articles; mem. Candn. Pulp & Paper Assn.; Assn. Profl. Engs. Que.; recreations: sailing, mountaineering, skiing; Clubs: Alpine; Trans-Atlantic; Home: 136 Fisher's Point, Foster, Que. J0E 1R0; Office: 140 Fisher's Point, Foster, Que. J0E 1R0.

**McCULLOCH, Arthur Ronald,** B.Sc., CMC; computer industry executive; b. Moose Jaw, Sask. 12 July 1942; s. Thomas Arthur and Gladys Bernice (McCracken) M.; e. Univ. of Manitoba B.Sc. 1968; PRESIDENT, U.S. DIVISION, DMR GROUP, INC. 1989– ; various positions in systems engineering, marketing, & management leaving as Regional Systems Marketing Manager for the West, IBM 1968–80; joined DRM Group, Inc. 1980; Managing Dir. Vancouver Office 1983; Vice-Pres., Western Region & Mem., Extve. Mngt. Ctte. 1985; V.P. & Sales Managers' Award for Outstanding Marketing Management Jan. 1979; Golden Circle Award for Outstanding Marketing Success Jan. 1974; Mem., Inst. of Management Consultants; Home: 11 Vista Clara Rd., Sausalito, CA 94965; Office: 450 - 404 Wyman St., Waltham, MA 02154-1264.

**McCULLOCH, Ernest Armstrong,** O.C., M.D., F.R.C.P.(C) F.R.S.C.; b. Toronto, Ont. 27 Apr. 1926; s. Dr. Albert Ernest McCulloch; e. Univ. of Toronto M.D. 1948; m. Ona Mary Morganty 21 July 1953; children: James A., Michael E., Robert E., Cecelia E., Paul A.; UNIVERSITY PROFESSOR EMERITUS, UNIV. OF TORONTO 1991– ; Phys. Head, Division of Cellular and Molecular Biology, Ont. Cancer Inst. 1989–91; Phys. Toronto Gen. Hosp. 1960–67; Prof. of Med. Biophysics, Univ. of Toronto 1966, Prof. of Med. 1970; Dir. Inst. of Med. Science 1975–1979; Asst. Dean, Sch. of Grad. Studies, Univ. of Toronto 1979–82; Head, Div. of Biol. Rsch., Ont. Cancer Inst. 1982–89; Univ. Prof. 1982–91; Univ. Prof. Emeritus 1991– ; Pres., The Acad. of Sci., The Royal Soc. of Can. 1987–90; numerous univ. nat. and internat. adv. comtes. on med. rsch.; rec'd Starr Medal in Anat. 1957; William Goldie Prize in Med. 1964; Annual Gairdner Award 1969; Queen's Silver Jubilee Medal 1977; Officer of the Order of Canada 1988; Honorary Prof., Shanxi Cancer Institute, People's Republic of China 1991– ; awarded Commemorative Medal for 125th Anniversary of Candn. Confederation 1992; author over 250 scient. articles in fields of cancer research and hematology; mem. several ed. bds.; mem. Am. Assn. Cancer Rsch.; Am. Soc. Pathol.; Candn. Soc. Clin. Investigation; Internat. Soc. Hematology; Internat. Soc. Exper. Hematol.; Soc. Exper. Biol. & Med.; Royal Soc. Can.; Am. Soc. Hematol.; Candn. Hematol. Soc.; Candn. Inst. of Academic Med.; recreations: sailing, golf; Club: Badminton & Racquet; Home: 480 Summerhill Ave., Toronto, Ont. M4W 2E4; Office: 500 Sherbourne St., Toronto, Ont. M4X 1K9.

**MCCULLOUGH, Colin David,** B.A.; newspaper publisher; b. Windsor, Ont. 11 Oct. 1929; s. Samuel and Elizabeth (Jamison) M.; e. Detroit Inst. of Technol., B.A. 1951; m. Regina M. d. Adele and Stanislas Ratinskas 12 Feb. 1958; one d.: Katharine Regina; PUB., TIMES-COLONIST 1981– ; Asst. Dir., Personnel Relns., Hiram Walker & Sons 1952–53; Reporter, Feature Ed., Asst. Ed., Asst. Pub., Globe and Mail 1954–78; Fgn. Corr., Peking, China 1968–69; London, Eng. 1971–73; Pub., Victoria Times & Vice-Pres., Victoria Press 1978–81; Trustee, Art Gall. of Greater Victoria 1982–86; Mem., Candn. Daily Newspaper Pub. Assn. (Dir. 1980–81, 1988–92); Candn. Press (Dir. 1980–81; 1992– ); United Appeal (Dir. 1981); Trustee, B.C. Government House Found. 1988– ; 1994 Commonwealth Games (Dir., 1989– ); B.C. Press Council (Dir. 1991– ); author: 'Insider's London' 1971, 'Stranger in China' 1972; recreations: golf, fishing; Clubs: Victoria Golf; Union; Home: 194 Denison Rd., Victoria, B.C. V8S 4K3; Office: 2621 Douglas St., Victoria, B.C. V8W 2N4.

**McCULLY, Leonard Douglas,** F.C.A.; chartered accountant; b. Debert, N.S. 2 Aug. 1929; s. Sidney Douglas and Lillian Margaret (Geldart) McC.; e. Colchester Co. Acad. Truro, N.S. 1947; Mount Allison Comm. Coll. Sackville, N.B. Bus. Adm. Dip. 1948; Queen's Univ. Corr. Courses 1948–53; C.A. 1953; m. Doreen Jean d. Raymond and Hilda Dixon 13 Nov. 1954; children: Catherine, Michael, John, Lynn, Nancy; VICE PRES. FINANCE AND CORPORATE SEC. SCOTIA INVESTMENTS LTD. 1984– ; Dir. Minas Basin Pulp & Power Co. Ltd.; Ben's Holdings Ltd.; Minas Basin Holdings Ltd.; Minas Basin Investments Ltd.; Minas Group Ltd.; Dir. and/or Offr. over 50 subsidiary and related co's present firm; joined H.R. Doane & Co. 1949–53; Chief Acct. Cleland Co. Ltd. Newcastle, N.B. 1953–56; Acct., Corporate Sec. Minas Basin Pulp & Power Co. Ltd. Hantsport 1956–84; Mayor Hantsport Town Council 1974–76, 1986–91; former Councillor and mem. Sch. Bd.; Boy Scout Leader 1957–67; Freemason; Baptist (Past Treas. Hantsport); recreations: golf, reading, orchard farming; Home: 33 Holmes Hill, Hantsport, N.S. B0P 1P0; Office: 50 Main St., Hantsport, N.S. B0P 1P0.

**McCURDY, Howard Douglas Jr.,** M.Sc., Ph.D.; b. London, Ont. 10 Dec. 1932; s. Howard Douglas and Marion Bernice (Logan) McC.; e. St. George Pub. Sch., London, Ont. 1937–42; Amherstburg (Ont.) Pub. Sch. 1942–45; Gen. Amherst High Sch., Amherstburg 1945–50; Assumption Coll., Univ. of W. Ont., B.A. 1953; Assumption Univ. of Windsor, B.Sc. 1954; Mich. State Univ., M.Sc. 1955, Ph.D. 1959; m. Dr. Brenda Wright McCurdy; children: Leslie Lorraine, Linda Louise, Cheryl Lauralyn, Brian Douglas Howard; VICE-PRESIDENT, FEDERAL NEW DEMOCRATIC PARTY 1991– ; joined Univ. of Windsor as Lectr. 1959, Asst. Prof. 1962, Assoc. Prof. 1965, Prof. 1969–84, Acting Head of Biology 1971–72, Head, 1974–79; mem., Senate, Univ. of Windsor 1966–67, 1969–72, 1973–77 and 1978–81; Bd. of Govs., Univ. of Windsor 1972–75; Academic Planning Ctte., Univ. of Windsor 1978–81; Vice Pres., Ctte. of Chairs of Univ. Biology Depts. in Ont. 1978–79; elected Windsor City Council 1979, re-el. 1971–84; elected M.P. for Windsor-Walkerville 1984; re-el. Windsor-St. Clair 1988; Pres. Michigan State Univ. Chapter, National Assn. for the Advancement of Colored People (NAACP) 1957–58; Chrmn., Conf. of Univ. Chapters of the NAACP; Pres., Guardian Club (Civil Rights) 1962–69; Founding Pres., National Black Coalition of Canada 1969–70, Past Pres. 1972, mem. of Interim Extve. Ctte. 1978–90, First Vice Pres. 1979–80; Vice Chrmn., Windsor Unitarian Fellowship 1962–69; mem. Windsor & District Human Rights Institute 1964–65; Dir., Candn. Civil Liberties Assn. of Windsor 1968–70; mem., Windsor Adv. Ctte., Ont. Human Rights Commission on Employment Opportunities 1968–69; mem. Bd. of Govs., St. Clair Coll. of Applied Arts and Technol. 1968–76, Extve. Ctte. 1968–76, Chair, Curriculum Ctte. 1968–76, Bd. Vice Chair 1972, Chair 1973–75; Chair, Assn. of Colleges of Applied Arts and Tech. 1972, 1973–75; Chair, Essex County Task Force on Diploma Nursing 1968–69; rec'd. Centennial Medal 1967; Queen's Silver Jubilee Medal 1977; author: 'Myxobacterales' (Bergey's Manual of Determinative Bacteriology); also various articles in scient. journs.; Mem. Editorial Bd., Bacteriological Reviews 1973–76; Section Editor, Candn. Journal of Microbiology (Assoc. Ed. 1977–78) 1978–84; mem., Am. Soc. for the Advancement of Sci.; Am. Soc. for Microbiology (Science Policy Ctte. 1976–80; Extve. Council 1976–78); Candn. Soc. of Microbiologists; Am. Inst. for Biological Sci.; Candn. Fed. of Biological Sciences; Candn. College of Microbiologists (Pres. 1976–80); Faculty Assn., Univ. of Windsor (Vice-Pres. 1964–65; Pres. 1965–66); Candn. Assn. of Univ. Teachers (Nat. Vice Pres. 1966–67; Pres. 1965–66); Sigma Xi; Phi Kappa Phi; Kappa Alpha Psi; NDP; Unitarian; recreations: golf, dance, cooking, reading, coaching track & field; Club: University.

**McCURDY, Sherburne G.,** M.A., Ph.D., D.D., LL.D.; educator; b. Old Barns, Colchester Co., N.S. 30 March 1924; s. Raymond and Margaret Agnes (Crowe) McC.; e. Elem. and High Schs. Colchester Co. N.S.; Dalhousie Univ. B.A. 1949, M.A. 1950; Mem. Univ. of Nfld. undergrad. teacher training; Univ. of Alta. Ph.D. 1964; m. Elizabeth Blois d. late William Evans Jefferson and Erna Belle Clarke, Halifax, N.S. 8 Dec. 1943; children: Margaret Mackey, Earle, David (d), Bruce, Janet Horwood; PRESIDENT EMERITUS, ALBERTA COLL. 1985– ; Princ. Prince of Wales Coll. St. John's, Nfld. 1950–62; Supvr. of Instr. St. John's Un. Ch. Sch. Bd. 1964–67; Extve. Secy. Nfld. Teachers Assn. 1967–71; Pres., Alberta Coll. 1971–85; served with RCAF Can. and Europe 1942–45; Pres. St. John's W. Dist. Lib. Assn. 1967–69; Del. to Fed. Lib. Leadership Convention 1968; Past Chrmn. and mem. Edmonton Assn. for Continuing Educ. and Recreation: Past Pres. Educ. Soc. Edmonton; Leader Candn. Del. Annual Meeting of World Confed. Organs. Teaching Prof. Stockholm 1962; Del. Third Internat. Curriculum Symposium Oxford 1967; rec'd Centennial Medal 1967; Pres. St. John's Br. Nfld. Teachers' Assn. 1955–57 (Pres. Assn. 1957–59); Pres. Candn. Teachers' Fed. 1961–62; Dir. Candn. Educ. Assn. 1961–63; mem. Nat. Comte. Candn. Conf. on Educ. 1961–63; Founder, Pres. and Extve. Dir., Bach Terecentenary Festival Fdn. 1985; Fellow, Candn. Coll. Teachers; mem. of Senate, Univ. of Alta. 1979–85, Chrmn. Senate Second Languages Task Force; author 'The Legal Status of the Canadian Teacher,' 1968; Awarded Candn. Teachers' Federation 1983 Special Recognition Award; Liberal; United Church; recreations: travel, classical music, spectator sport, family antiques; Club: Edmonton; Home: 4807 - 122 A St. Edmonton, Alta. T6H 3S8.

**McDANIEL, Roderick Rogers,** B.Sc.; P.Eng.; b. High River, Alta. 18 Mar. 1926; s. Dorsey Patton and Daisy (Rogers) McD.; e. Central High Sch. Calgary, Alta.; Univ. of Alta. Engn. Sch.; Univ. of Okla. B.Sc. (Petroleum Engn.); m. Marilyn d. late Dr. Charles Bouck, 16 Oct. 1948; children: Nancy, Leslie; CHAIRMAN, McDANIEL & ASSOCIATES CONSULTANTS LTD. 1955– ; Dir., Prudential Steel Ltd.; Honeywell Canada Ltd.; Petroleum Reservoir Engr. Creole Petroleum Corp. Venezuela 1947; Imperial Oil Ltd. 1948, Chief Reservoir Engr. 1952; Chrmn. Parking Authority City of Calgary 1968–74; Chrmn., PWA Corp. 1974–91; Chrmn., Candn. Regional Airlines 1991–92; Hon. Life Dir., Calgary Exhbn. and Stampede (Dir. 1977–86); Past Vice Chrmn. Strathcona Tweedsmuir Private Sch.; Pres. Calgary Chamber Comm. 1973–74; Calgary Petroleum Club 1973–74; Dir., Candn. Chamber Comm. 1974–75; mem. Calgary Research & Development Authority (C.R.D.A.); mem. Assn. Prof. Engrs. Alta.; Candn. Inst. Mining & Metall.; P. Conservative; Protestant; recreations: golf, skiing, fishing, horse racing; Clubs: Calgary Petroleum; Ranchman's; Calgary Golf & Country; Outrigger, Honolulu; Mission Hills Golf & Country - Rancho Mirage; Home: 11–3231 Rideau Place, Calgary, Alta. T2S 2T1; Office: Ste. 2200, Bow Valley Square III, 255 - 5th Ave. S.W., Calgary, Alta. T2P 3G6.

**McDANIEL, Susan Anderson,** B.A., M.A., Ph.D.; university professor, sociologist-demographer; b. New York, N.Y. 4 May 1946; d. Frank Theodore and Lola Ethel (Reynolds) Anderson; e. Univ. of Mass. B.A. (cum laude) 1968; Cornell Univ. M.A. 1970; Univ. of Alberta Ph.D. 1977; m. Douglas Wahlsten; PROFESSOR OF SOCIOLOGY, UNIV. OF ALBERTA 1989– ; Research Offr., Dept. of Health & Social Devel., Prov. of Alta. 1970–73; Lectr., Sociology, Univ. of Waterloo 1976–77; Asst. Prof. 1977–83; Assoc. Prof. 1983–88; Prof. 1989; Chair, Adv. Ctte. to Chief Statistician of Canada on Demographic Stats. & Studies 1990–93; Pres., Candn. Population Soc. 1990–92; Mem., Nat. Orgn. Corp., Internat. Union for the Sci. Study of Pop. 1991–92; Adv. Ctte. on 1991 Census Analytical Studies 1992; on Family Policy Project, Vanier Inst. of the Family 1992–93; on the Demographic Review, Royal Soc. of Canada 1987; Apptd. to National Statistics Council 1992– ; Apptd. Canada Ctte., Internat. Year of the Family 1993–94; Mem., Edit. Bd., 'J. of Women and Aging' 1987– , 'Can. J. of Health and Soc.' 1990– , 'Atlantis' 1991– , 'Can. J. of Soc.' 1989–91; Editor, 'Canadian Journal of Sociology' 1994– ; Keynote Speaker, Candn. Assn. on Gerontology Ot. 1992; 23rd Annual Sorokin Lecture, Univ. of Sask. 1992; Fed.-Prov. Conf. on Family Regina 1989; Francoise Ricour-Singh Mem. Census Lecture 1989; Woman of the Year (Profl.), Kitchener-Waterloo, Ont. 1988; 1st recipient, Therese Casgrain Rsch. Fellowship 1987–88; Univ. of Waterloo Disting. Teacher Award 1981; elected mem., Internat. Union for the Sci. Study of Pop.; Mem., Candn. Pop. Soc.; Candn. Soc. & Anthrop. Assn.; Pop. Assn. of Am.; Candn. Assn. on Gerontol.; Candn. Women's Studies Assn.; Candn. Rsch. Inst. for the Advancement of Women; Vanier Inst. of the Family; Internat. Council on Women's Health Issues; author: 'Canada's Aging Population' 1986 and over 100 articles in learned jours. & book chapters; co-author: 'Social Problems Through Conflict and Order' 1982; clubs: Faculty; Home: 5432 114B St., Edmonton, Alta. T6H 3N5; Office: Edmonton, Alta. T6G 2H4.

**McDAVID, James Colin,** B.A., M.A., A.M., Ph.D.; university professor and administrator; b. Stettler, Alta. 18 July 1947; s. David Mason and Olga Germaine (Kolenosky) M.; e. Univ. of Alta. B.A. (Hons.) 1969, M.A. 1970; Indiana Univ. A.M. 1972, Ph.D. 1975; m. Barbara d. Ernst and Gertrud Grafe 11 May 1968; one d.: Kristina; PROF., SCHOOL OF PUBLIC ADMIN., UNIV. OF VICTORIA 1990– ; Asst. Prof., Public Admin., Pennsylvania State Univ. 1974–80; Assoc. Prof. 1980–90; Dean, Fac. of Human & Social Devel. 1990– ; Rsch. Fellow, Univ. of Auckland 1986–87; Mem., Acad. Council, Open Univ. of B.C. 1988– ; Dir., Ctr. for Public Sector Studies, Univ. of Victoria 1987–90; Cons. to U.S. & Candn. govts. on program evaluation & mngt. issues; Francis F. Reeve Scholarship (Univ. of Alta.); Canada Council Doctoral Fellowship; Univ. of Victoria Alumni Teaching Award 1993; author: 'Police Cooperation and Performance' 1979; co-author: 'Applied Program Evaluation in Local Government' 1979, 'The Victoria Community Police Stations' 1992; co-editor: 'The Well-Performing Government Organization' 1991; Home: 1405 Wende Rd., Victoria, B.C. V8P 3T6; Office: P.O. Box 1700, Victoria, B.C. V8W 2Y2.

**McDERMID, Hon. John Horton,** P.C.; b. 17 Mar. 1940; s. Rev. John Andrew and Nora Margaret (Horton) McD.; e. Brampton (Ont.) Pub. and High Schs.; Albert Coll. Belleville, Ont.; Ryerson Inst. of Technol. (Radio & TV Arts); York Univ.; m. Sandra Post 24 Dec. 1992; radio and TV announcer 1957–65; Asst. Extve. Dir. Ont. Real Estate Assn. 1965–73; Extve. Asst. to Min. of Industry & Tourism, Ont. 1973–77; Dir., Pub. Relations & Planning Ont. Place Corp. 1977–79; el. to H. of C. for Brampton-Georgetown g.e. 1979, re-el. 1980, 1984 and (riding of Brampton) 1988; former Min. of State (International Trade) and (Housing); Min. of State, Privatization and Regulatory Affairs 1989–90; Minister of State, Finance & Privatization 1991–93; Fellow, Real Estate Inst. Can.; Freemason; United Church; Home: Caledon, Ont.

**McDERMOTT, Dennis,** O.Ont.; diplomat; b. Portsmouth, Eng. 3 Nov. 1922; s. John and Beatrice (Sutton) McD; m. Mary Claire Elizabeth d. Adelard Caza 22 Oct. 1976; children: Michael, Mark, Patrick, William, Maureen; Candn. Ambassador to Ireland 1986–89; mem. Extve. Bd., Inter-American Regional Organ. of Workers; Internat. Confed. Free Trade Unions; Assembler and Welder, Massey-Ferguson 1948–54; Internat. Rep., Un. Automobile Workers Am. 1954–68, Candn. Dir. 1968–78; Pres., Candn. Labour Congress 1978–86; served with RN 1939–46; rec'd Candn. Centennial Medal 1967; Queen's Silver Jubilee Medal; Order of Ontario 1988; awarded Commemorative Medal for 125th Anniversary of Candn. Confederation; mem. Ont. Labour Relations Bd.; Chrmn. Bd. Govs. Labour Coll. Can.; Chrmn. Bd. Dirs. CLC Labour Educ. & Studies Centre; Dir., Candn. Inst. for Internat. Peace and Security; recreations: golf, gardening, oil and acrylic painting; Address: 1663 Kudu Court, Lakefield, Ont. K0L 2H0.

**McDERMOTT, Michael Albert,** B.A.; federal civil servant; b. Harpenden, Eng. 28 Sept. 1939; s. Albert and Maud Louise (Garnet) McD.; e. Owen's Sch. London, Eng. 1959; Univ. of Hull (Eng.) B.A. 1962; Carleton Univ. 1962–63; L'Ecole nationale d'adm. Paris 1972; m. Sandra d. Stewart and Madeleine Bell 8 Apl. 1971; children: Sarah, Jonathan; SENIOR ASST. DEPUTY MINISTER, LABOUR PROGRAM, HUMAN RESOURCES DEVELOPMENT CANADA 1993– ; archivist Pub. Archives of Can. 1964; trans. to Internat. Labour Affairs Br. Labour Can. 1965, Extve. Asst. to Dep. Min. 1969–71, Asst. Dir. Conciliation & Arbitration Br. 1974–76, Ind. Relations Adv. Fed. Mediation & Conciliation Service 1981–83, Dir. Gen. Policy and Liaison 1983–84, Mediation & Conciliation Fed. Mediation & Conciliation Service 1984–89; Head Fed. Mediation & Conciliation Service 1989–93; Sec. Food Prices Review Bd. 1973–74; Counsellor (Labour) Candn. Embassy Brussels and Candn. Mission to Eur. Communities 1976–79; Labour Relations Secretariat Privy Council Office 1979–80; Head, Candn. dels. Annual Internat. Labour Conf. Geneva 1983, 1984; Mem., Extve. Bd., Assn. of Labour Relations Agencies, (Canada & USA); recreations: fitness, music, reading; Home: 12 Claret Court, Ottawa, Ont. K1V 9C4; Office: Ottawa, Ont. K1A 0J2.

**McDERMOTT, William Barrie,** B.A., M.B.A.; management consultant; b. Hamilton, Ont. 31 May 1939; s. Wilfred James and Margaret Laverne (Kidd) M.; e. Lakehead Univ. B.A. 1976, Grad. Dipl. in Bus. Admin. 1979; Univ. of Toronto M.B.A. 1980; Internat. Mngt. Inst. (Switz.) Cert. in Internat. Finance 1983; m. Ruby, d. George and Dorothy Moffatt, 10 Oct. 1975; children: Rhonda, Lynda, Trevor; PRESIDENT, THE McDERMOTT GROUP INC. 1992– ; Mngt. Trainee, Hudson's Bay Co.; Supvr., Data Processing, Great Lakes Power Co.; Supvr., Computer Ctr., Eaton's 1966–68; Asst. Registrar Systems & Records & Mgr., Computer Ctr., Lakehead Univ. 1968–79; var. sr. mngt. positions, Commercial Banking Group & Human Resources, Bank of Montreal 1980–87; Partner, Peat Marwick Stevenson & Kellogg Mngt. Cons. 1987–90; Partner, Financial Institutions Practice, Price Waterhouse Management Consultants 1990–92; Mem. Bd. of Govs., Lakehead Univ.; Campaign Cabinet, Share Our Northern Vision, Lakehead Univ.; Sec. Toronto Chap., IMD Alumni Assn.; Mem., The Empire Club of Canada; Candn. Information Processing Soc.; Thunderers; The Candn. Club; recreations: golf, fishing, running; clubs: Markland Wood Golf & Country (Dir.); Mississauga Golf & Country; Home & Office: 4307 Bacchus Cres., Suite 201, Mississagua, Ont. L4W 2Y2.

**McDIARMID, Ian Bertrand,** M.A., Ph.D.; scientist; b. Carleton Place, Ont. 1 Oct. 1928; s. John and Lillian (Campbell) McD.; e. Queen's Univ. B.A. 1950, M.A. 1951; Univ. of Manchester Ph.D. 1954; m. Dorothy May Folger 16 Aug. 1951; children: John, Leslie; ASSOC. DIR. HERZBERG INST. OF ASTROPHYSICS, NAT. RESEARCH COUNCIL since 1975; Dir., Can. Centre for Space Sci. since 1980 Research Offr. Nat. Research Council 1955–64, Head Cosmic Ray Sec. 1964–69, Asst. Dir. Div. of Physics 1969–75; author over 100 scient. papers; mem. Royal Soc. Can.; Am. Geophys. Union; Candn. Assn. Physicists; Home: 1106 – 60 McLeod St., Ottawa, Ont. K2P 2G1; Office: Ottawa, Ont. K1A 0R6.

**McDONALD, Arthur Bruce,** B.Sc., M.Sc., Ph.D.; educator; b. Sydney, N.S. 29 Aug. 1943; s. Arthur Bruce and Valerie Mildred (DeRoche) McD.; e. Dalhousie Univ. B.Sc. 1964 (Gov. Gen.'s Gold Medal 1964), M.Sc. 1965; Cal. Inst. Technol. Ph.D. 1969; m. Janet d. Gladstone and Catherine Macdonald 16 July 1966; children: Bruce, Heather, Ross, Fraser; PROF. OF PHYSICS QUEEN'S UNIV. 1989– ; Dir. Sudbury Neutrino Observatory Project 1989– ; Rutherford Fellow Chalk River Nuclear Labs. 1969–70, Rsch. Offr. 1970–82; Visiting Sci.: Univ. of Wash. Seattle 1978; Los Alamos Nat. Lab. 1981; Prof. Princeton Univ. 1982–89; mem. Nuclear Sci. Adv. Ctte. U.S. Dept. Energy & Nat. Sci. Found. 1986–89; Exper. Evaluation Ctte. TRIUMF Accelerator 1986–88; Subatomic Physics Grant Selection Ctte. NSERC 1978–80, 1986–89; Adv. Ctte., Lawrence Berkeley Laboratory Nuclear Science Div. 1992– ; author over 100 articles sci. jours.; mem. Candn. Assn. Physicists (Councillor 1978–80); Fellow, American Physical Soc.; recreations: skiing, swimming; Home: 830 Sandringham Pl., Kingston, Ont. K7P 1N2; Office: Stirling Hall, Queen's Univ., Kingston, Ont. K7L 3N6.

**McDONALD, Bruce Eugene,** M.Sc., Ph.D.; educator; b. Chailey, Alta. 30 Apl. 1933; s. Matthew and Mary (Hawryluk) McD.; e. Mannville (Alta.) High Sch.; Univ. of Alta. B.Sc. 1958, M.Sc. 1960; Univ. of Wis. Ph.D. 1963; m. Judith d. James and Ruth Ahern 30 June 1962; children: Mary Ellen, Mark, Anne, Ruth, Jane; PROF. OF FOODS & NUTRITION, UNIV. OF MAN. 1971– ; Rsch. Assoc. in Biochem. Univ. of Ill. 1963–64; Asst. Prof. of Animal Sci. Macdonald Coll. McGill Univ. 1964–68; Assoc. Prof. of Foods & Nutrition present Univ. 1968–71; Rsch. Prof. Inst. of Nutrition Univ. of Uppsala, Sweden 1976–77; Dean of Human Ecology, present Univ. 1977–85; Visiting Scientist, Fac. Sci. & Technol., Univ. Western Sydney, Australia; Visiting Scientist, Nutrition & Food Science, Univ. of Arizona 1992–93; Public Trustee, Bd. of Trustees. Nat. Inst. of Nutrition 1984–92; mem., Tech. Missions on Canola to Taiwan, Japan and South Korea 1988; Egypt and Israel 1987; Columbia and Peru 1985; Egypt 1984; S. Korea 1983; USSR 1983; Algeria 1982; Morocco, Algeria and Tunisia 1980; Candn. Del. to Gen. Assembly Intnl. Union Nutritional Sciences Kyoto, Japan 1975; Chrmn. Ctte., Revision Candn. Dietary Standard 1973–75; co-author 'Fundamentals of Nutrition' 2nd ed. 1978; recipient, CSP Canola Research Award 1989; Fellow, Candn. Inst. Food Sci. & Technol.; mem., Candn. Soc. Nutritional Sciences (Pres. 1974–75); Candn. Inst. Food Sci. & Technol.; Candn. Dietetic Assn.; Am. Inst. Nutrition; Am. Oil Chems. Soc. (Vice-Pres., Candn. Section 1993–94); Home: 95 Acadia Bay, Winnipeg, Man. R3T 3J1; Office: Winnipeg, Man. R3T 2N2.

**McDONALD, Graeme Donald,** C.D., A.M., Ph.D.; foundation executive; b. Edmonton, Alta. 17 July 1944; s. Earle George and Mae Florence (Sorensen) McD.; e. Univ. of Alta. B.A. 1965; Harvard Univ. A.M. 1967, Ph.D. 1978; m. Susan d. Charles and Mary-Elizabeth Lynch 25 Aug. 1988; children: Graeme Jr., Perry, Sarah; PRES. AND CHIEF EXTVE. OFFR. ASIA PACIFIC FOUND. OF CAN. 1990– (on secondment from Northern Telecom); served Candn. Forces 1960–78, rank Maj.; First Sec. Peking 1975–77; Dir. Mkt. Analysis Northern Telecom Ltd. 1979; Dep. Mng. Dir. Northern Telecom Asia 1983; Mng. Dir. Northern Telecom

Asean 1985; Asst. Vice Pres. Maj. Accts. Northern Telecom Canada 1987, Div. Gen. Mgr. Telecom Services Div. 1988; recipient Gov. Gen.'s Medal Alta. and Woodrow Wilson Fellowship 1965; Dir.: Asian Develop. Bank Business Seminar Soc.; Ex-Terra Found. Edmonton; Canada Pacific Publ. Soc.; Laurier Inst., Vancouver; Pacific Basin Economic Counc., Toronto; Vancouver Dragon Boat Festival Soc.; mem. Canada-ASEAN Ctr. Adv. Council; mem. Advisory Council, Asian Society, NY; Office: 666, 999 Canada Place, Vancouver, B.C. V6C 3E1.

**McDONALD, H. John,** B.A.Sc., P.Eng.; business executive; b. Toronto, Ont 21 March 1928; s. William J. and Ida L. (Langdon) McD.; e. pub. and high schs. Toronto; Univ. of Toronto B.A.Sc. 1951; m. Barbara E. d. Richard J. Ellis 8 Nov. 1963; three d. Robyn, Gaye, Kimberly; CHAIRMAN, BLACK & McDONALD LTD. 1977– ; Chrmn., BML Leasing Ltd. Toronto; Black & McDonald International N.V.; Dir. CARE Canada; Placer Dome Inc.; United Dominian Industries Ltd.; Pres. present co. 1956–77; Pres. Rotary Club Toronto 1969; former Dir. Nat. Ballet Guild Can.; former Council mem. Bd. Trade Metrop. Toronto; Chevalier de Confrerie du Tastevin; mem. Assn. Prof. Engs. Prov. Ont.; recreations: golf, tennis, fishing; Clubs: Lambton Golf & Country; York; Rosedale Golf; Caledon Mountain Trout; Ristigouche Salmon Club; Lost Tree (Fla.); Home: 65 Binscarth Rd., Toronto, Ont. M4W 1Y3; Office: 2800, 2 Bloor St. E., Toronto, Ont. M4W 1A8.

**McDONALD, Norman J.;** communications executive; b. North Bay, Ont., 29 Sept. 1924; s. John James and Mary Ida (Cullen) McD.; e. Scollard Hall, North Bay, Ont., 1936; Inst. of C.A.'s; m. Anne Isobel (dec.), d. late I. E. Godin, 22 Nov. 1947; one d., Elizabeth Anne PRES., NORMAN J. McDONALD & ASSOC. INC., 1983– ; Pres., Candn. Tobacco Manufacturers Council 1982–87; Officer & Partner, Public & Industrial Relations Ltd. 1965–82; private business, North Bay, 1946–52; served in various adm. appts. with RCN, Naval HQ, Ottawa, 1952–57; joined PIR as Sr. Account Extve., Montreal, 1957–61; held various extve. positions, Cyanamid of Canada Ltd., Montreal, incl. Extve. Asst. to Pres. and Secy. and mem. Mang. Comte., 1961–65; served with RCN, in N. Atlantic during World War II; rank Commdr.; Gov., St. Mary's Hosp., Montreal; mem. Candn. Chamber Comm.; mem., Candn. Pub. Relations Soc.; R. Catholic; recreations: golf; Clubs: Royal Montreal Golf; Mount Royal; Rideau (Ottawa); Home: 239 Kensington Ave., Apt. 804, Westmount, Montreal, Que. H3Z 2H1; Office: 1808 Sherbrooke St. W., Suite 401, Montreal, Que. H3H 1E5.

**McDONALD, Peter Ward,** B.Comm.; financial executive; b. Vancouver, B.C. 16 Feb. 1941; s. the late John Ward and Ida Jane M.; e. Univ. of B.C. B.Comm. 1964; divorced; children: Michael, Ryan; CHAIRMAN & CHIEF EXTVE. OFFR., TUCKAHOE LEASING INC. 1982– ; Sr. Vice-Pres., Candn. Dominion Leasing 1968–77; Pres., First City Capital 1977–82; Dir., Tuckahoe Finan. Corp.; recreations: golf, skiing, squash, tennis; clubs: Capilano Golf, Islington Golf, Toronto Lawn & Tennis; Home: 346 Fairlawn Ave., Toronto, Ont. M5M 1T6; Office: 425 Bloor St. E., Toronto, Ont. M4W 3R4.

**McDONALD, Russell James,** D.V.M.; veterinarian; b. Woodstock, Ont. 25 Sept. 1922; s. William James and Sarah Jean (McMillan) McD.; e. Woodstock Coll. Inst. 1941; Ont. Veterinary Coll. Univ. of Guelph D.V.M. 1945; m. Margot Helen Whyte 7 Apl. 1945; children: Margot Jean, Catherine Anne, John Lachlan; EXTVE. DIR., CANDN. ASSOC. OF ANIMAL BREEDERS 1989– ; Gen. Veterinary practice Waterloo, Ont. 1945–46; Mgr., Oxford Holstein Breeders Assn., Woodstock 1946–52; Gen. Mgr., Oxford & Dist. Cattle Breeding Assn. 1952–69; Gen. Mgr., Western Ont. Breeders Inc. 1969–89; served with COTC Univ. Guelph 1941–45; mem. Agric. Research Inst. Ont. 1962–74 (Chrmn. 1966–74); rec'd Ont. Agric. Coll. Centennial Medal 1974; Univ. of Guelph Alumnus Honour Award 1979; author 'Reproduction in the Cow' 1957; various articles; Ont. Veterinary Assn. (Pres. 1959); Ont. Inst. Prof. Agrols.; Candn. Veterinary Med. Assn.; Am. Dairy Science Assn.; Woodstock Agric. Soc. (Pres.); Ont. Agric. Hall of Fame Assn. (Chrmn.); Woodstock YMCA (Pres.); Woodstock Hosp. Bd. of Trustees (Chrmn.); Candn. Assn. of Animal Breeders, Pres. 1982–83; Omega Tau Sigma; United Church; recreations: golf, skiing, curling; Clubs: Oxford Golf & Country; Woodstock Curling; Farmers' (London, Eng.); Home: R.R. 3, Woodstock, Ont. N4S 7V7; Office: P.O. Box 457, Woodstock, Ont. N4S 7Y7.

**McDONALD, Wendy Burdon;** engineering executive; b. North Vancouver, B.C. 13 June 1922; d. Howard Burdon and Marie Scott (Archibald) Stoker; e. St. Anthony's College; Vancouver H.S.; widowed 3 times; 1st m. Robt. S. MacPherson 21 Jan. 1942 (4 children); 2nd m. Wm. D. Dix 2 April 1954 (3 children: 2 adopted from Wm.); 3rd m. Sydney A. McDonald 16 Jan. 1960 (3 stepchildren); children: Roberta Sandra, Robert Sinclair, Wendy Penelope, Scott Alexander (MacPherson), William Maurice Dix (natural mother); Kerry Douglas, Robin Melinda (Dix) (adopted); Sherry, Candy, Brooke (McDonald) (stepchildren); CHRMN. & CHIEF EXTVE. OFFR., B.C. BEARINGS 1950– ; took over B.C. Bearings which had branches in Vancouver, Calgary & Edmonton when 1st husband died; B.C. Bearings now has 26 branches in Western Can., 10 in Western U.S.A., 1 in Mexico & 1 in Singapore; Dir., Sandwell; Zurich Canada; Past Dir., B.C. Bancorp; Westcoast Energy; recipient, Veuve Cliquot Award (1st for Canada), Canadian Business Woman 1982; Gov., Vancouver Bd. of Trade (1st woman) 1987–94; mem., Internat. Trade Adv. Council; Dir., Canada West Found. (Calgary); Chrmn., Candn. Council of the Americas (BC Chapter); Dir., Pacific Corridor Enterprise Council (PACE); Bd. of Govs., B.C. Institute of Tech. (B.C.I.T.); Gov., Swan-E-Set Golf and Country Club; recreations: gardening, tennis; clubs: Capilano Golf, Sunshine Coast Golf, BC Club, Vancouver Bd. of Trade, Washington Athletic (Seattle), Terminal City Club; Office: 8985 Fraserwood Court, Burnaby, B.C. V5J 5E8.

**McDONALD, William H.;** executive; b. Ottawa, Ont. 8 Sept. 1924; s. late Joseph and late Constance Mary (Gordon) McD.; e. Lord Selkirk High Sch. Winnipeg, Man. 1942; m. Dorothy Gwen d. late John Lorne Selkirk 8 July 1950; one d. Barbara Elaine Irwin; Pres. and C.E.O., Boyd Stott & McDonald Technologies Ltd.; Pres. Thornton McDonald Associates Inc.; Pres., Marlcourt Books; Administrative Offr. Dept. Finance Ottawa 1949–55; Asst. Gen. Mgr. Bank of Nova Scotia Toronto 1955–66; Dir. and Offr., Boyd Stott & McDonald Ltd. Toronto 1966–80; Dir. and Extve. Offr. Morguard Trust Co. 1966–76; Chrmn. of the Bd., Canadian Commercial Bank 1976–81, Chrmn. Extve. Comte. 1981–84; ; Dir. and mem. Extve. Comte. Mortgage Insurance Co. of Canada, Central Covenants Ltd. and Markborough Properties Ltd. 1963–66; Chrmn. Bd. Govs. J. Douglas Ferguson Hist. Research Foundation; Hon. Pres., Candn. Paper Money Soc.; Life Mem., Internat. Bank Note Soc.; Extve. Secy., Classical & Medieval Numismatic Soc.; served with RCNVR 1943–45; P. Conservative; Anglican; recreations: books, photographs, numismatics; Club: Ontario; Office: P.O. Box 956, Stn. B, Willowdale, Ont. M2K 2T6.

**McDONELL, Wayne Norman,** D.V.M., M.Sc., Ph.D., D.V.A., Dipl. ACVA; university professor; b. Edmonton, Alta. 1 Feb. 1943; s. Angus G. and Agnes M. (Borle) M.; e. Camilla Dist. H.S.; St. Anthony's Coll. 1980; Univ. of Guelph, D.V.M. 1965, M.Sc. 1969; Univ. of Cambridge, Ph.D. 1974; m. Iva d. Herb and Lorna Orr 22 Oct. 1966; children: Brent, Daniel, Sarah; PROF., ONT. VET. COLL., DEPT. OF CLIN. STUDIES, UNIV. OF GUELPH 1974– ; priv. practice 1965; MRC Fellowship 1971–74; Pres., Am. Coll. of Vet. Anesthesiol. 1981; Chief of Staff & Hosp. Dir., Vet. Teaching Hosp., Univ. of Guelph 1982–86; D.V.A. (UK) 1973; Charter Diplomate, Am. Coll. of Vet. Anesthesiol. 1976; author of over 70 sci. pubs. & 9 chapters in texts & review periodicals; recreations: hockey, curling, slow pitch baseball; Club: Guelph Curling; Home: 9 Graham St., Guelph, Ont. N1G 2B6; Office: Guelph, Ont. N1G 2W1.

**McDONOUGH, Christopher James,** B.A., M.A., Ph.D.; university professor; b. Carmarthen, Wales, U.K. 10 Apr. 1942; s. James and Elizabeth Mary (Thomas) M.; e. Queen Elizabeth Grammar Sch.; Univ. Coll., London Univ. B.A. 1963, M.A. 1965; Univ. of Toronto Ph.D. 1968; m. Hanna d. Stephen and Charlotte de Heinrich 20 May 1967; children: Geoffrey Cameron and Christian Paul; VICE-PROVOST, DEAN OF ARTS AND PROGRAMME DIR., TRINITY COLL., UNIV. OF TORONTO 1991– ; Lectr., Trinity Coll., Univ. of Toronto 1967; Asst. Prof. 1968; Assoc. Prof. 1975; Prof. 1988; Assoc. Chrmn., Dept. of Classics, Univ. of Toronto 1985–89; Commonwealth Scholar 1965–68; Mem., Medieval Academy of Am.; Classical Assn. of Can.; author of articles on late Latin & med. lit.; editor: 'The Oxford Poems of Hugh Primas and the Arundel Lyrics' 1984; review editor: 'The Journal of Medieval Latin' 1991; recreations: tennis, cross country skiing; Home: 81 Crescent Rd., Toronto, Ont. M4W 1T7; Office: 329 Larkin Bldg., Trinity Coll., Hoskin Ave., Toronto, Ont. M5S 1H8.

**McDONOUGH, James Maurice;** Canadian public servant; b. Moose Jaw, Sask. 21 Aug. 1933; s. late James and Winnifred (Lowe) McD.; m. Anna Marie, d. late Basil Hersche, Regina, Sask., 25 July 1953; three d., Debra, Jean, Joan; Dir., Radisson Rental Properties Ltd., Calgary; Mem. Canadian Transportation Education Found., Candn. Inst. of Traffic & Transp.; Hon. mem., Candn. Inst. of Traffic & Transp. 1989; Mem. Chartered Inst. of Transp., London, Eng. 1989; Pres., Arbitration & Mediation Assoc. of Saskatchewan, Candn. Transp. Research Forum; Mem. of Bd., Candn. Livestock Feed Bd. (Ottawa) 1967–78; Mem. of Bd. of Dirs., Central Western Railway Corp. 1989; Mem. of Bd., The Multiple Sclerosis Soc. of Canada (Saskatoon Chapter); Dir., Grain Handling & Transportation Can. Grains Council (Winnipeg) 1973–75; Hall Comn. on Grain Handling & Transportation 1975–77; appoint. Commisr., Candn. Transport Comm. (Ottawa) 1977; Sr. Comnr., Candn. Transport Comm., Western Canada 1979–87; inducted into Transportation Hall of Fame, by Min. of Transp., Saskatchewan 1989; Home: 113 - 306 La Ronge Rd., Saskatoon, Sask. S7K 8B9

**McDOUGALL, Hon. Barbara Jean,** P.C., B.A.; former politician; financial analyst; b. Toronto, Ont. 12 Nov. 1937; d. Robert James and Margaret Jean (Dryden) Leamen; e. Leaside H.S.; Univ. of Toronto B.A. 1960; m. late Peter McDougall 6 Sept. 1963; Secretary of State for External Affairs, Govt. of Canada 1991–93; formerly Extve. Dir. Candn. Counc. Financial Analysts; Vice Pres. Dominion Securities Ames Ltd.; Vice Pres. A.E. Ames and Co. Ltd.; Mgr. Portfolio Invest. Northwest Trust Co.; Invest. Analyst Odlum Brown Ltd.; Market Rsch. Analyst The Toronto Star Ltd.; Econ. Analyst Candn. Imperial Bank of Commerce; served as Financial Columnist Chatelaine mag.; Financial Commentator CBC 'Take 30'; Business Columnist City Woman mag.; Business Journalist CITV Edmonton; Business Journalist Vancouver Sun; Past Pres. Rosedale P. Cons. Assn.; Campaign Mgr. Hon. David Crombie 2 fed. g.e.'s, Policy & Press Adv. by-el.; el. to H. of C. g.e. 1984; Min. of State for Finance 1984–86; Min. of State (Privatization) 1986–88; Min. responsible for Regulatory Affairs 1986–88; Min. resp. for The Status of Women 1986–90; Min. of Employment & Immigration 1988–91; Chrmn. City of Toronto Salvation Army 1984 Red Shield Appeal; Dir. Community Occupational Therapy Associates (Chrmn. 1982–84); Dir. Second Mile Club, United Way Agy.; Dir. Enoch Turner Schoolhouse; Counsellor, Oakhalla Prov. Prison for Women; Vice Chrmn. Elizabeth Fry Soc.; Club: Albany; Home: 1 Clarendon Ave., Apt. 401, Toronto, Ont. M4V 1H8; Office: c/o Sharwood & Co., 8 King St. E., Suite 300, Toronto, Ont. M5C 1B5.

**McDOUGALL, Donald Blake,** B.A., B.Ed., B.L.S., M.L.S.; retired administrator and librarian; b. Moose Jaw, Sask. 6 March 1938; s. Daniel Albert and Donela (McRae) McD.; e. Regina Central Coll. Inst. 1956; Univ. of Sask. B.A. 1966, B.Ed. 1966; Univ. of Toronto B.L.S. 1969; Univ. of Alta. M.L.S. 1983; m. Norma Rose d. John Wesley Peacock 19 May 1962; Asst. Depy. Min./Legislature Librarian, Legislative Assembly of Alberta 1987–93, retired; Teacher and Vice Princ. Regina Bd. Educ. 1960–68; Chief Librarian, Stratford Pub. Lib. 1969–72; Head of Pub. Services, Edmonton Pub. Lib. 1972–74; Legislature Librarian, Prov. of Alta. 1974–87; C.O., Rosetown Legion Cadet Corps (Master Cadet, Nat. Award Camp); comnd. R.C.A.; rec'd Queen's Silver Jubilee Medal 1977; Hon. Clerk-at-the-Table, Legislative Assembly of Alta. 1987; Ed. 'Alberta Scrapbook Hansard (Microfilm)' 1976; 'A History of the Legislature Library,' 1979; 'Princess Louise Caroline Alberta' 1988; 'Lieutenant-Governors of the Northwest Territories and Alberta, 1876–1991' 1991; 'Premiers of the Northwest Territories and Alberta, 1897–1991' 1991; mem. Bd. Mang. St. Andrew's Presb. Ch. Stratford and Elder, First Presb. Ch. Edmonton; mem. Edmonton Art Gal.; Edmonton Opera Soc.; Edmonton Soc. for the Prevention of Cruelty to Animals; Cracker Barrel (Debating) Club Stratford (past Pres.); Ft. Edmonton Voyageurs; Friends of the Univ. of Alta.; Alta. Gov't. Libraries' Council (past Chrmn.); Assn. Parlty. Librarians Can. (past Pres.); Greater Edmonton Lib. Assn.; Lib. Assn. Alta.; Candn. Lib. Assn.; Friend of Glenbow; Hist. Soc. Alta. (past Vice Pres. Edmonton Chapter); Heritage Can.; Intnl. Library Sci. Honorary Soc.; Friends of the National Library of Canada; Presbyterian; recreation: automobiles; music; travel; reading; Clubs: Edmonton Scottish Soc.; Edmonton Jaguar Drivers; Home: 209 Rhatigan Rd. W., Edmonton, Alta. T6R 1A2.

**McDOUGALL, Donald Joseph,** B.Com., M.B.A., LL.D.; management consultant; b. Charlottetown, P.E.I. 15 Dec. 1937; s. Frank and Patricia (Callaghan) McD.; e. Bloomfield Elem. Sch.; St. Dunstan's High Sch.; St. Dunstan's Univ. B. Com. 1958; Univ. of W. Ont.

M.B.A. 1961; Univ. of P.E.I. LL.D. 1978; m. Marion d. Henry MacDonald 26 Aug. 1961; children: Brian, Donna, Neil, Colin, Anne; PRESIDENT AND CHIEF EXTVE. OFFR., NOVATRONICS INC.; Chrmn., Slemon Park Corp.; Pres., Burlington Investments Inc.; St. Joseph's Health Care Society; Accuform Golf Corp.; Chrmn., Clark Davis Medical Systems Inc.; Founding Dir., Toronto Blue Jays; Teacher, Summerside Sch. Bd. 1958–59; Sales Rep. John Labatt Ltd. 1961; Sales Rep. Lucky Lager Breweries Lt. Vancouver 1962, Asst. to Gen. Mgr. 1962, Personnel Mgr. 1964; Toronto Sales Mgr. Labatt's Ontario Breweries ltd. 1964, Ont. Sales Mgr. 1965; Vice Pres. and Gen. Mgr. Labatt's Alberta Brewery Ltd. 1968, Labatt Breweries of B.C 1970; Pres. Labatt Breweries of Canada Ltd. London, Ont. 1973–79; Chrmn. Task Force Privatization Petro Canada 1979; Past Chrmn., Holland Coll. Found., Charlottetown; Dir., St. Joseph's Health Centre Foundation; R. Catholic; P. Conservative; recreations: golf, skiing, tennis, reading; Clubs: Founders (Toronto); London Hunt & Country; London Club; Innisbrook Golf & Country (Tarpon Springs, Fla.); Home: 1556 Gloucester Rd., London, Ont. N6G 2S6; Office: 677 Erie St., Stratford, Ont. N5A 6V6.

**McDOUGALL, Douglass G.,** B.A., M.B.A.; distribution industry executive; b. Montreal, Que. 31 Dec. 1946; s. Allan Houlistan and Elizabeth Ann (Kerr) M.; e. McGill Univ. B.A. 1967; Univ. of Western Ont. M.B.A. 1971; m. Sally d. Chipman and Janet Drury 23 May 1969; children: Todd, John, Reid, Peter; PRESIDENT, SODISCO GROUP & PRESIDENT & CHIEF OPERATING OFFICER, UNIGESCO INC. 1989– ; various positions John Labatt Ltd. 1971–89 incl. Pres., Miracle Feeds, Commercial Vice-Pres., Zymaize Ltd., Vice-Pres. Devel., Ogilvie Mills Ltd., Pres., Lactantia, Pres., Indus. Milk Div. of Ault Foods Ltd.; primary focus on definition of strategic direction for businesses and implementation of that plan; recreation, school & community volunteer work; Home: 671 Grosvenor Ave., Montreal, Que. H3Y 2S9; Office: 1250 Réne Lévesque Blvd. W., Room 4200, Montreal, Que. H3B 4X1.

**McDOUGALL, Ian Walter,** B.Mus., M.Mus.; university professor, trombonist, composer, arranger; b. Calgary, Alta. 14 June 1938; s. George and Olive Myrtle (Freeman) M.; e. Univ. of B.C. B.Mus. 1965, M.Mus. 1971; m. Barbara d. Nelson and Elaine Allen 4 June 1969; PROF., SCHOOL OF MUSIC, UNIV. OF VICTORIA; played professional trombone since age 12; played & toured with John Dankworth, Ted Heath, Vancouver Symphony, Woody Herman, Boss Brass, Brass Connection, Ian McDougall Trio, Brasswest (U. of Victoria Brass Quintet); soloed with Toronto Symphony, Victoria Symphony; many works performed & recorded by CBC Radio & TV; CBC Chamber Orch. (Vanc.), Lafayette String Quartet; wrote & conducted hundreds of 'Jingles' in Toronto; Mem., Candn. Music Centre; Candn. League of Composers; SOCAN; composer: String Quartet, Clarinet Concerto, Bass trombone Concerto, Brass Quintet, num. jazz compositions; Musical Dir., 1994 Commonwealth Games (opening and closing ceremonies); recreations: sailing, fishing, cryptic crosswords; clubs: Royal Victoria Yacht, Univ. of Victoria Faculty; Home: 3030 McAnally Rd., Victoria, B.C. V8N 1T4; Office: Sch. of Music, Univ. of Victoria, Victoria, B.C. V8W 2Y2.

**McDOUGALL, James Thomas,** M.T.C.I.; banking executive; b. Hearst, Ont. 5 Jan. 1942; s. John Malcolm and Rose Isobel (Hawkins) M.; e. Ryerson Polytechnical Inst. bus. admin. 1965; m. Marie d. Greg and Bernice Murphy 27 Dec. 1986; children: Linda Ann, Marion Rose; VICE-PRES., SALES MANAGEMENT, CANADA TRUST (LONDON) 1993– ; joined Canada Trust 1967; Asst. Vice-Pres., Product Group, Personal Trust (London) 1976–82; Asst. Vice-Pres. & Mgr., Calgary Main Branch 1982–85; Vice-Pres., S.W. Ont. Reg. (London, Ont.) 1986–88; Vice-Pres., Personal Trust & Private Banking, Toronto-Hamilton Region (Toronto) 1988–93; Fundraiser, McMichael Candn. Gallery; recreations: golf, skiing; Home: 1 - 10 Mackellar Ave., London, Ont. N6H 5C5; Office: 22nd Floor, 380 Wellington St., London, Ont. N6A 4S4.

**McDOUGALL, John Frederick,** M.Sc., P.Eng.; b. Edmonton, Alta. 16 Nov. 1907; s. John Charles and Sophie Bernice (Tait) M.; e. Univ. of Alta. (Civil Engn.), B.Sc. 1930; McGill Univ. (Civil Engn.) M.Sc. 1931; m. Phyllis Eirene, d. Roland Sladden, Edmonton, Alta., 10 Sept. 1940; children: John Roland, Lori Jane, Eirene Bernice, Eleanor Phyllis Anne; CHAIRMAN, McDOUGALL & SECORD, LTD. (Real Estate Devel. & Mang.) since 1990; Hon. Dir., Royal Trustco Ltd.; mem. Friends of the Univ. of Alberta; with Highways Dept., Prov. of Alta., in various engn. positions, 1931–37; joined present firm in 1937 as Asst. Mgr. becoming Mgr. in 1951 and Vice-Pres. 1948–52; Pres. 1952–90; on leave of absence to work with Poole Construction Co. Ltd. on wartime constr. projects in W. Can. in 1943–45; mem., Bd. of Examiners in Prof.Engn. for Alta., 1953–59; mem., Interim Devel. Appeal Bd. (Town Planning), Edmonton, for 11 yrs. (Chrmn. final yr.); Pres. Candn. Council Prof. Engrs. 1964–65; mem., Engn. Inst. Can.; Edmonton Chamber Comm.; Alta. Chamber of Resources; Assn. Prof. Engrs. Alta. (Registrar for 12 yrs., Councillor for 3 yrs.); Edmonton Chamber Music Soc.; Hist. Soc. Alta.; Fellow, Royal Commonwealth Soc.; Conservative; Presbyterian; recreations: music, photography; Clubs: Edmonton; Home: 8915 Saskatchewan Dr. W., Edmonton, Alta. T6G 2B1; Office: 1101 – 10080 Jasper Ave., Edmonton, Alta. T5J 1V9.

**McDOUGALL, John Roland,** B.Sc., P.Eng., FCAE; business executive / university professor; b. Edmonton, Alta. 4 April 1945; s. John Frederick and Phyllis Eirene (Sladden) M.; e. Univ. of Alta. B.Sc. 1967; m. Susan d. Cecil and Monah Carley 2 July 1971; children: John C., Jordan P., Michael T.; POOLE CHAIR IN MANAGEMENT FOR ENGINEERS, UNIV. OF ALBERTA 1991– and PRES., McDOUGALL & SECORD, LIMITED 1990– ; Imperial Oil Limited 1967–75; Secretary-Treas., McDougall & Secord, Limited 1970–77; Vice-Pres. 1977–90; Founder & Mng. Partner, Dalcor Companies 1976–80, 1982–84; Chief Extve. Offr. 1984– ; Dir., Edmonton Northlands; D.B. Robinson & Assoc.; Adv. Bd., Royal Trust; Mem., Premiers' Council on Sci. & Tech.; Construction Indus. Devel. Council; Internat. Trade Adv. Ctte.; Fellow, Candn. Acad. of Engrs.; Hon. Mem., Loyal Edmonton Regiment; Pres., Edmonton C. of C. 1989; Vice-Pres., World Trade Centre Edmonton; Pres., Candn. Council of Profl. Engrs. 1990–91; Assn. of Profl. Engrs., Geol. & Geophysicists of Alta. 1980–81; recreations: skiing, squash; clubs: Edmonton, Royal Glenora; Home: 39 Westridge Cres., Edmonton, Alta.; Office: 4-8 K Mechanical Engr. Bldg., Univ. of Alta., Edmonton, Alta. T6G 2E5.

**McDOUGALL, Robert Law,** M.A., Ph.D., D.Lit.; professor emeritus; b. North Vancouver, B.C. 28 July 1918; s. Richard Irving and Catherine Henderson (Law) McD.; e. Univ. of B.C. B.A. 1939; Univ. of Toronto M.A. 1948, Ph.D. 1950; Carleton Univ. D.Lit. 1988; m. Phyllis Brenda Goddard (dec.); m. Anne MacDermot 19 June 1971; children: Richard, Ian, Christine (dec.); PROF. EMERITUS OF ENG. CARLETON UNIV. 1985– ; early specialist in Candn. lit. and pioneer in promoting Candn. studies in schs. and univs.; mem. Faculty Univ. Coll. Univ. of Toronto 1950–57; Founding Dir. Inst. Candn. Studies Carleton Univ. 1958–67, Gen. Ed. Carleton Lib. Series Candn. reprints and new compilations 1960–67, mem. Ed. Bd. and Chief Cons. Centre for Editing Early Candn. Texts 1982– ; Founding mem. Leeds Univ. Assn. for Commonwealth Lit. & Lang. Studies 1963, Internat. Chrmn. 1968–71; Visiting Prof. of Candn. Lit. Univ. of Mysore, India, Univ. of Victoria, B.C., Australian Nat. Univ. Canberra, Univ. of Edinburgh; served overseas with Seaforth Highlanders of Can. 1940–45; author 'The Poet and the Critic' 1985; 'Totems: Essays on the Cultural History of Canada' 1990; co-author 'The Undergraduate Essay' 1958/1976; ed. 'Our Living Tradition' 1959, 1962–65; 'The Clockmaker' by T.C. Haliburton 1958/1989; 'Life in the Clearings' by Susanna Moodie 1959/1976; Anglican; recreations: gardening, bird watching, cross-country skiing, music; Home: 24 Glen Ave., Ottawa, Ont. K1S 2Z7.

**McDOULETT, C.D. Jr.,** B.B.A., LL.B.; business executive; b. Duncan, Oklahoma 28 Dec. 1944; e. Univ. of Oklahoma B.A. 1967, LL.B. 1970; m. Elizabeth; children: Anthony, Scott; PRES. & DIR., NORTH AMERICAN PALLADIUM LTD. 1991– ; Vice-Pres., Falcon Seaboard, Inc. & Falcon Coal Co., Inc.; various positions, Diamond Shamrock Corp.; Partner, Jackson McDoulett Assoc.; Pres. & Chief Extve. Offr., Spendthrift Farm Inc.; Dir., Bank of Oklahoma; Mgr., Strategic Ventures, Kaiser-Francis Oil Co.; Trustee, Univ. of Oklahoma Foundation, Inc.; Mem., Oklahoma & Am. Bar assns.; Oklahoma Soc. of C.P.A.'s; Candn. Inst.of Mining & Engr.; Home: 6656 E. 107th St., Tulsa, OK 74133; Office: P.O. Box 21468, Tulsa, OK 74121-1468.

**McDOWALL, Duncan Lovatt,** B.A., M.A., Ph.D.; historian; professor; b. Victoria, B.C. 15 June 1949; s. John William and Grace Kelso (Lovatt) M.; e. Cranbrook Sch., Engl. 1965–68; Queen's Univ. B.A. 1972, M.A. 1973; Carleton Univ. Ph.D. 1978; m. Sandra Campbell d. Cornelius and Barbara Van Orden 28 Aug. 1976; PROF. OF HISTORY, CARLETON UNIV. 1987– ; Corp. Hist., Brascan Ltd. 1978–80; Sr. Rsch. Assoc., The Conf. Bd. of Can. 1980–87; Corp. Hist., Royal Bank of Canada 1989–93; Organizing Secy., Cdn. Business Hist. Conf. 1983– ; mem. Anglican Ch.; author: 'Steel at the Sault' 1984; 'The Light: Brazilian Traction, Light & Power Co. Ltd. 1899–1945' 1988; 'Quick to the Frontier: Canada's Royal Bank' 1993; various publications on business hist., corp. governance and foreign investment; contrib. to Candn. and foreign business and hist. jours. and encyclopedias; recreations: squash and sailing; Home: 187 Hopewell Ave., Ottawa, Ont. K1S 2Z4; Office: Carleton Univ., Ottawa, Ont. K1S 5B6.

**McDOWELL, Charles Alexander,** D.Sc., M.Sc., F.R.S.C.; University Professor; b. Belfast, Ireland 29 Aug. 1918; s. Charles and Mabel (McGregor) McD.; e. Municipal High Sch., Belfast, Ireland; Queen's Univ. of Belfast; Univ. of Liverpool, B.Sc. (1st class Hons.), 1941, M.Sc. 1942, D.Sc.1955; Univ. of B.C. D.Sc. (Honoris causa) 1984; m. Christine Joan, d. W. C. Stoddart, London, Eng., 10 Aug. 1945; children: Karen Mary Anne, Christina Anne, Avril Jeanne; Asst. Lectr., Queen's Univ. of Belfast, Ireland, 1941–42; Scient. Offr. U.K. Min. of Supply, 1942–45; Lectr. in Inorganic & Physical Chem., Univ. of Liverpool, 1945–55; Prof. & Head, Dept. of Chem., Univ. of B.C., 1955–81; awarded Letts Gold Medal in Theoretical Chem., Queen's Univ. of Belfast, 1941; Medal, Univ. de Liège, 1955; Chem. Inst. Can. Medallist 1969; Killam Sr. Research Fellow 1969–70; Centennial Medal 1967; Queen's Jubilee Medal 1978; Chem. Inst. Can. Montreal Medal, 1982; Gov. and Mgr., Sefton Park Modern Secondary Sch., Liverpool, 1949–55; Fellow, Royal Soc. of Can., 1962; mem. Churchill Coll., Cambridge, 1963–64; Nat. Research Council Sr. Research Fellow and Visiting Prof., Univ. of Cambridge, 1963–64; Science Council of Japan Visiting Prof., Kyoto Univ. 1965, 1969; Distinguished Visiting Prof., Univ. of Fla., Gainesville 1974; Distinguished Visiting Prof., Univ. of Cape Town 1975; Frontiers of Chemistry Lecturer, Wayne State Univ 1978; mem. Bd. of Gov., Univ. B.C. 1977–78; Pres. Chem. Inst. of Can. 1978–79; appointed Univ. Prof., Univ. B.C., 1981; Chrmn., Int. Union Pure and Applied Chem., Vancouver, 1981–84; John Simon Guggenheim Fellow 1984, 1985; University Prof. Emeritus 1984; Fellow, European Acad. of Arts, Sciences and Humanities, Paris 1986; Hon. Fellow, Candn. Soc. for Chemistry 1986; served in the 2nd World War in U.K. Civil Defence as Gas and Bomb Identification Officer; Publications: numerous scient. publ. on chem. kinetics, mass spectrometry, molecular structure, electron and nuclear magnetic resonance spectroscopy, heterogeneous catalysis; mem. Faraday Soc.; Royal Society of Chem. U.K. (Fellow); Am. Chem. Soc.; Am. Physical Soc. (Fellow); Mass Spectrometry Soc. of Japan; Combustion Inst.; Chem. Soc. of Can.; Royal Inst. Chem. of G.B.; Anglican; recreations: gardening, walking; Home: 5612 McMaster Rd., Vancouver, B.C. V6T 1J8.

**McDOWELL, Frederick G. (Ted),** F.I.C.B.; business executive; b. 12 Aug. 1929; joined The Toronto-Dominion Bank, Assiniboia, Sask. 1947, progressing through a variety of postings and responsibilities in Western and Eastern Canada culminating in being named a Dir. and Vice-Chrmn. of the Bank in 1981, which position he held until retirement in Jan. 1990; Dir., Atlantic Shopping Centres Ltd.; Dynacare Inc.; Goodwill Industries of Toronto; Jim Pattison Group Inc.; Kellogg Canada Inc.; Mobil Oil Canada Ltd.; Pan Pacific Development Corporation; Revenue Properties Co. Ltd.; The Toronto-Dominion Bank; Vicathgord Investments Ltd.; Zurich Canadian Holdings Ltd.; Zurich Life Insurance Co. of Canada; Zurich Indemnity Co. of Canada; Office: Suite 3300, Toronto-Dominion Tower, P.O. Box 1, Toronto-Dominion Centre, Toronto, Ont. M5K 1A2.

**McEACHERN, Hon. Allan,** B.A., LL.B.; judge; b. Vancouver, B.C. 20 May 1926; e. Vancouver and Penticton Pub. Schs.; Kitsilano Jr. High Sch.; Lord Byng Sr. High Sch.; Univ. of B.C. B.A. 1949, LL.B. 1950; m. Gloria 17 July 1953; two d. Jean, Joanne; CHIEF JUSTICE OF B.C. since 1988; law practice Russell & DuMoulin 1950–78; Chief Justice, Supreme Court of B.C. 1979–88; Pres., Kats Rugby Club 1953–64; B.C. Lions Football Club 1967–69; W. Football Conf. 1964; Candn. Football League 1967 (Commr. 1967–68); Dir. Vancouver Bar Assn.; Council, Candn. Bar Assn.; Pres., Legal Aid Society of B.C. 1977–78; Bencher 1971–79; recreations: sailing, walking, cottage, gardening; Office: Law Courts, 800 Smithe Street, Vancouver, B.C. V6Z 2E1.

**McELHERAN, Brock,** B.A., Mus.B.; conductor and music professor; b. Winnipeg, Man. 6 Jan. 1918; s. The Rev. Principal Robert B. and Irene B. (Brock) B.; e. Winnipeg, Man. Pub. Schs.; Univ. of Toronto Schs.; Univ. of Toronto, B.A. 1939, Mus.B. 1947; Royal Conservatory of Music of Toronto, 1934–47; Berkshire Music Centre,

Lenox, Mass. 1947; L'Ecole Monteux 1953; faculty member, Crane Sch. of Music, State Univ. Coll. of Arts and Science, Potsdam, N.Y. 1947–88, now Professor Emeritus and Senior Fellow; Cond. Montreal Elgar Choir 1972–79; Cond. Chorale Nouvelle de Montréal 1987– ; Dir., Saratoga-Potsdam Choral Institute (assoc. with The Philadelphia Orchestra) 1970–85; Guest Cond., The Philadelphia Orchestra 1983 & 1984 at the Saratoga Performing Arts Center; has collaborated with Stockhausen, Kagel, Foss, William Schuman & Robert Washburn in premieres of their vocal works; author: 'Conducting Technique' 1964 (rev. ed. 1989); composer of works for chorus, all in new notations; Meteorol. with the Canadian Dept. of Transport, 1940–42; R.C.N. (R), 1942–45; retired from the service with rank of Lieut; awarded, Honorary Doctorate of Music, State Univ. of New York 1993; Anglican; recreation: scuba diving; Address: 17 Spring St., Potsdam, NY 13676 and State University College, Potsdam, NY 13676.

**McELLIGOTT, Paul J.,** M.B.A., B.A.; transportation and communications executive; b. Montreal, Que. 3 Mar. 1953; married; 3 children; e. Concordia Univ., M.B.A. 1978; PRES. & CHIEF EXTVE. OFFR., BRITISH COLUMBIA RAILWAY GROUP OF COMPANIES (incl. BC Rail Ltd., Westel Telecommunications Ltd., BCR Properties Ltd.and Vancouver Wharves Ltd.) 1989– ; Mktg. Cons., Secor 1977; Sr. Corp. Planner, CSL Group Montreal 1978; Dir. of Mktg., Voyageur Enterprises Ltd. 1979; Vice-Pres., Mktg. 1982; Sr. Vice-Pres. 1985; Pres. 1988; Dir., BC Rail Ltd.; BCR Properties Ltd.; Westel Telecommunications Ltd.; Vancouver Wharves Ltd.; Westac; Gov., Business Council of B.C.; Dir., The Canadian Club of Vancouver; Dir., Railway Assn. of Canada; Canada Japan Soc. 1993– ; Capilano College Found. 1993– ; Past Pres., Candn. Bus. Assn. 1986—89; Mem., Chartered Inst. of Transp.; Am. Mktg. Assn.; Office: Box 8770, Vancouver, B.C. V6B 4X6.

**McELMAN, Hon. Charles Robert;** senator (retired); b. South Devon, N.B. 18 June 1920; s. late Frank E. and Amanda G. (Dunphy) M.; e. Fredericton (N.B.); LL.D. St. Thomas Univ.; m. Jessie Faye Douglass, 22 Nov. 1941; children: James D., Barbara Jean (Mrs. Jock Jardine), Frederick C., Mary Faye (Mrs. DonaldSmith); with Candn. Bank of Commerce, 1937–40; Secy., N.B. Liquor Control Bd., 1946–51; Private Secy. to Premier John B. McNair, 1951–52; with Dept. of Nat. Defence, 1953–54; Extve. Secy., N.B. Lib. Assn. 1954–60; Extve. Asst. to Premier Louis J. Robichaud, 1960–66; summoned to Senate of Canada Feb. 1966; retired 1990; served with R.C.A.F., 1941–46; Liberal; Anglican; Home: 324 King's College Rd., Frederiction, N.B. E3B 2E9.

**McELVAINE, Christopher H.,** FSA, FCIA; insurance executive; b. Buenos Aires 7 June 1936; s. Andrew Floyd and Hazel (Knapp) M.; e. St. George's College Buenos Aires 1954; FSA 1972; FCIA 1972; m. Marie d. Frank and Ruby Lashley 4 Sept. 1961; children: Timothy, Suzanne, Scott, Penny; PRESIDENT & CHIEF EXECUTIVE OFFICER, EMPIRE LIFE INSURANCE COMPANY 1991– ; Actuarial Asst., M & G Reinsurance 1959; Gen. Mgr., M & G Computer Systems Ltd. 1969; Senior Consultant, SDI Assoc. 1971; Asst. Actuary, Dominion of Canda Gen. Insur. Co. 1973; Vice-Prs., Individual Opns., Empire Life Insur. Co. 1974; Individual & Group Opns. 1982; Insurance Opns. 1984; Senior Vice-Pres. 1987; Executive Vice-President 1988; Chrmn., C.E.O. & Dir., Connecticut Nat. Life Insur. Co.; Extve. Vice-Pres. & Dir., E-L Financial Corp.; Pres. & Dir., E-L Financial Services Ltd.; Dir.: The Empire Life Insur. Co.; The Dominion of Canada General Insur. Co.; Dir., Kingston Symphony Assn.; Jeanne Mance Fdn.; Past Chrmn., Hotel Dieu Hosp.; Past Dir., C. of C.; recreations: sailing; clubs: Albany, Kingston Yacht; Home: R.R. 1, Kingston, Ont. K7L 4V1; Office: 259 King St. E., Kingston, Ont. K7L 3A8.

**McELWAIN, John David,** B.A., LL.B., Q.C.; lawyer; b. Toronto, Ont. 9 May 1938; s. Fred Alexander and Mary Agnes (Harvie) M.; e. Upper Canada Coll. 1956; Univ. of Toronto B.A. 1959; Osgoode Hall Law Sch. LL.B. 1962; called to Ont. Bar 1964; Q.C. 1974; m. Janice d. Roy and Elisabeth Broadfoot 1 Aug. 1985; children: David Christopher, Laura Christine; SENIOR PARTNER, McELWAIN & ASSOC., BARRISTERS & SOLIICTORS 1981– ; Solicitor, Wright and McTaggart 1964–67; Partner 1967–69; MacKinnon, McTaggart 1969–75; Sr. Partner, Seabrook, Outerbridge McElwain & Burk 1975–77; McElwain, Burk & Elliott 1977–78; McElwain, Burk 1978–81; Dir., Via Rail Canada Inc.; Candn. Business Machines Ltd.; Tackla Can. Inc.; Gen. Couns., YMCA of Metro. Toronto; Chrmn. & Dir., The MacLachlan Sch. Edn. Found.; Dir. & Sec., The Dr. Page Harshman Memorial Found.; United Ch. of Can.; Extve. Vice-Pres., Etobicoke Ctr. Fed. P.C. Assn.; Dir., Internat. Wine & Food Soc., Toronto Br.; Hon. Solicitor, Royal Commonwealth Soc., Toronto Br.; Mem., Candn. Bar Assn.; Internat. Tax Assn.; Naval Officers Assn. of Can.; Lieutenant, Royal Candn. Navy Reserve (retired); recreations: skiing, tennis, sailing, badminton; clubs: Royal Candn. Yacht, Albany of Toronto, Craigleith Ski; Home: 349 St. Clair Avenue W., Toronto, Ont. M5P 1N3; Office: 41 Hazelton Ave., Toronto, Ont. M5R 2E3.

**McEWEN, Alexander Campbell,** LL.M., Ph.D., F.R.G.S.; university professor; b. Eng. 22 Aug. 1926; e. Univ. of London; Univ. of E. Africa; m. Patricia Stuart Richards; divorced 1988; married Sherry Lee Wilson 13 June 1993; three d. Ann, Sheila, Laura; PROF., DEPT. OF GEOMATICS ENGINEERING, UNIV. OF CALGARY 1991– ; Canada Lands Surveyor; mem. Council, Candn. Inst. of Surveying 1977–81; Director of Lands and Surveys, Government of Newfoundland, 1972–1976; Candn. Commr., Internat. Boundary Comn. 1976–1991; posted Sabah, Malaysia (Colombo Plan) 1954–1956; Seychelles (UN) 1958–1961; Tanzania (CIDA) 1964–1970; Jamaica (CESO) 1981; Ecuador (CESO) 1986; Nigeria (External Affairs) 1989–90; mem. Bd. Examiners, Assn. Nfld. Land Surveyors 1975–1976; Secy.-Treas. Assn. Ont. Land Surveyors 1963–1964; author of 'International Boundaries of East Africa,' 1971, 'In Search of the Highlands,' 1988; has written many reports, professional articles and book reviews; mem., Can. Inst. of Geomatics; Writers' Union of Canada; Western Candn. Bd. of Examiners for Land Surveyors 1991– ; Writers Guild of Alberta; Internat. P.E.N.; Mensa; recreations: legal and historical research, writing; Home: 2129 - 2nd Ave. N.W., Calgary, Alta. T2N 0G8; Office: 2500 University Drive N.W., Calgary, Alta. T2N 1N4.

**McEWEN, Jean Albert,** R.C.A.; artist (painter); educator; b. Montreal, Que., 14 Dec. 1923; s. William and Eliane (Renaud) M.; e. Univ. of Montréal, Professional Degree in Pharmacy 1948; m. Indra d. Yvette Kagis 18 Sept. 1976; children: Isabelle, Dominique, Jean, Sabin, Marianne, Jeremie; Prof. of Art, Concordia Univ.; worked in Paris till 1953 (travelled to Spain, Italy, Holland); first one-man show in Montréal at Galerie Angès Lefort, since when has had more than ten, chiefly at Montréal, Ottawa, Toronto, New York and Paris; since 1961 a continuous exhibitor at Spring Exhn., Museum of Fine Arts, Montréal; among other exhibits incl. 3rd Candn. Biennial, Ottawa (1959), Candn. Coll. Musée de Bordeaux, France (1962), 25 Painters from Qué., Stratford Festival, Ont. (1962), Candn. Artists, Albright-Knox Gallery, Buffalo, N.Y. (1962), Commonwealth Art, Commonwealth Inst., London (1962), Contemp. Candn. Painting, Johannesburg, S.A. (1962), Dunn Internat. Exhn., Fredericton, N.B. and London, Eng., (1963), Five Candn. Painters, Musée Galliera, Paris (1963), Fifteen Candn. Artists, travelling exhn. organ. by Museum of Modern Art, N.Y. (1963), Sao Paulo Biennial, Brazil (1963), A quarter of a century of Candn. Painting, Tate Gallery, London (1964); solo exhns. incl. Walter Moos Gallery Toronto 1960–67; Mira Godard Gallery Toronto 1963–87; Martha Jackson Gallery N.Y.C. 1964; Mayer Galerie Paris 1965; Waddington Galerie Montreal 1987–90; Moore Gallery Hamilton 1989; retrospectives incl. 'Jean McEwen 1953–63' Musée d'art comtemporain 1963; maj. retrospective Musée des Beaux-Arts Montréal 1987–88; rep. various publ. colls. incl. Musée de Montréal, Musée d'art contemporain, Winnipeg Art Gallery, Edmonton Art Gallery, Art Gallery of Ont., Nat. Gallery Can., Museum of Modern Art N.Y., Walker Art Center Minneapolis, Albright Knox Buffalo, Smithsonian Inst. Washington; completed mural for Toronto Internat. Airport, 1963; designed stained glass window mural for Sir George Williams Univ. 1966; completed mural for Place des Arts Montreal 1967; Mural, Bank of Nova Scotia Headquarters 1991; awarded a Can. Council Grant 1961; awarded First Prize, Que., 1961, Jessie Dow Award, 1964, both at Spring Exhn., Montréal Museum of Fine Arts; Pres., Assn. of Non-Figurative Artists of Montréal, 1959–62; Vice Pres., Roy. Acad. of Arts since 1970; R. Catholic; recreation: music; Address: 3908 rue de Parc Lafrontaine, Montreal, Que. H2L 3M6.

**McEWEN, John Alan;** sculptor; b. Toronto, Ont. 28 Aug. 1945; s. John Ronald James and Francis Elizabeth (Benham) McE.; e. McMaster Univ. 1964–65; Ont. Coll. of Art 1966–70; George Brown Coll. Applied Arts & Technol. 1972–73; Co-founder, 'A Space,' Toronto 1970; comns. inc.: 'Western Channel' Performing Arts Centre Lethbridge, Alta. 1980–81; 'Boat Sight' Nat. Capital Comn. Hull, Qué. 1983–85; 'Stelco's Cabin' Banff Sch. of Fine Art 1984–85; 'Patterns for the Tree of Life' Asquith Green, Toronto 1987–88; 'The RCAF Hall of Tribute' Nat. Aviation Museum Ottawa 1987–88; 'Still Life and Blind' Gairloch Gdns. Oakville, Ont. 1988; rep. various colls. incl. Art Gallery of Ont., Nat. Gallery Can., Utsukuishi-Ga-Hara Open Air Museum Japan; Address: General Delivery, Hillsdale, Ont. L0L 1V0.

**McEWEN, Michael Lawrence,** B.A.; broadcasting executive; b. Winnipeg, Man. 5 May 1945; s. Lawrence James and Hope Mary (Anstie) McE.; e. Henry Wise Wood High Sch. Calgary 1963; Univ. of Calgary, B.A. 1967, 2yrs. grad. studies Candn. politics; m. Luci d. Lillian Zwolak 29 Aug. 1981; two d. Kathryn Lindsay, Julia Michelle; SR. VICE-PRES., RADIO SERVICES, CBC 1992– ; joined CFAC Calgary after grad.; Radio Current Affairs Producer CBC Calgary 1970; subsequently trans. to Ottawa as Producer 'CBO MORNING' later serving as Extve. Producer local progs. Ottawa area; joined CBC Radio Current Affairs Dept. Toronto 1973 producing 'As It Happens,' 'Five Nights' and other progs.; named Dep. Head Radio Current Affairs and later apptd. Dir. Radio Man. 1979; Dir. Prog. Operations Eng. Radio 1982; Vice Pres., CBC Radio 1986–89; Extve. Vice Pres., CBC 1990–92; rep. CBC Radio on Eur. Broadcasting Union Prog. Council and other internat. forums;Office: P.O. Box 8478, Ottawa, Ont. K1G 3J5.

**McFADDEN, David;** author; b. Hamilton, Ont. 11 Oct. 1940; author 'A Trip Around Lake Huron' novel 1981; 'A Trip Around Lake Erie' novel 1981; 'Animal Spirits' short stories 1983; 'Tha Art of Darkness' poetry 1984; 'Canadian Sunset' novel 1986.

**McFARLAND, James Douglas,** M.Sc.; petroleum executive; b. Toronto, Ont. 17 Dec. 1946; s. Harold Douglas and Moira Elizabeth (McCaskill) McF.; e. Queen's Univ. B.Sc.(Chem.Eng.) 1970; Univ. of Alta. M.Sc.(Petrol.Eng.) 1974; Cornell Univ. Advanced Mgmt. Prog. 1981; m. Valerie C. d. Irvine and Rose Hanson 21 Apl. 1973; three d. Heather Anne, Jennifer Lynn, Gillian Elizabeth; VICE PRES., OIL SANDS, IMPERIAL OIL LTD. 1993– ; Eng. Prodn. Dept. Calgary present Co. 1972; Sr. Prodn. Adv. Esso Europe Inc. London, Eng. 1983; Operations Mgr. Esso Exploration and Production U.K. Ltd. 1985; Mgr. Communications & Planning Esso Resources Canada Ltd. Calgary 1986, Cold Lake Operations Mgr. 1988; Dir., Environment and Safety, Imperial Oil Ltd. 1990; Bd. Syncrude Canada Ltd.; Bd. Alberta Chamber of Resources; Past Chair, Adv. Bd. Conf. Bd. Can.'s Bus. & Environment Prog.; Past Mem. Advisory Ctte. on Environmental Protection, Govt. of Canada; Alumnus 1987 Gov. Gen.'s Candn. Study Conf.; Past mem. Extve. Council Alta. C. of C.; Past Bd. mem. Calgary City Ballet; Founding mem. UK Friends Queen's Univ. Can. Trust; mem. Assn. Profl. Engs., Geols. & Geophysicists Alta.; Soc. Petrol. Engs. AIME; recreations: golf, downhill skiing; Clubs: Calgary Golf & Country; Calgary Petroleum Club; Calgary Chamber of Commerce; Office: 237 - 4 Ave. S.W., Calgary, Alta. T2P 3M9.

**McFARLANE, James Ross,** O.C., C.D., B.Sc., M.Sc., D.Eng., P.Eng.; engineer; b. Winnipeg, Man. 20 June 1934; s. John Ross and Francis Opal (Angus) McF.; e. Chilliwack High Sch. 1952; Univ. of N.B. B.Sc. (Mech. Eng.) 1960; Mass. Inst. of Technol. M.Sc. 1965, Naval Eng. 1965; Royal Mil. Coll. D.Eng. 1988; Univ. of Victoria D.Eng. 1988; Dr. Military Sci., Royal Road's 1991; Dr. Science, Univ. of N.B. 1992; m. Noreen d. George and Mary Wood 31 Aug. 1957; one s.: James Arthur Ross; FOUNDER AND PRES. INTERNATIONAL SUBMARINE ENGINEERING LTD. 1974– ; Adjunct Prof. Simon Fraser Univ.; joined RCN as Ordinary Seaman 1952; served as Staff Offr. Constrn. Can.'s Oberon submarines 1966–68; retired rank Lt. Commdr. 1971; Vice Pres. International Hydrodynamics 1971–74; Robert Bruce Wallace Speaker Mass. Inst. Technol. 1986; IEEE Oceanic Eng. Soc.'s Distinguished Tech. Achievement Award 1987; Ernest C. Manning Award 1987; Profl. Engs. Meritorious Achievement Award 1987; BC Science & engineering Gold Medal 1989; Officer of the Order of Canada 1989; Julian C. Smith Medal 1990; mem. Candn. Acad. Eng.; Soc. Profl. Engs. B.C.; Sigma Xi; Home: 2900 Glen Dr., Port Coquitlam, B.C. V3B 2P5; Office: 1734 Broadway St., Port Coquitlam, B.C.

**McFARLANE, Lawrie,** B.A., M.Litt., Ph.D.; public servant; b. Scotland 3 Nov. 1947; s. John and Maisie (Haliday) McF.; e. Univ. of Dundee B.A. 1970; St. Andrews Univ. M.Litt. 1972; Queen's Univ. Ph.D. 1976; m. Anne d. Michael and Ruth Feger 1 March 1986; one d.: Julia Marie; European Trade Comnr., Saskatchewan 1989; joined Govt. of Sask. as Policy Analyst, Dept. of Finance 1976; Dir. of Budget Bureau, Dept. of Fin. 1980; Assoc. Dep. Min. Fin. 1983; Dep. Min. of Adv. Edn. 1985; Dep. Min. of Edn., Sask. 1986.

**MCFARLANE, Peter A.;** writer; b. Thunder Bay, Ont. 17 Sept. 1954; s. John Peter and Alma Margaret (Boyce) M.; e. St. Mary's Univ.; m. Betsy d. Gilbert and Helma Schwartz 21 Oct. 1978; freelance writer/broadcaster 1978– ; regular contbr., CBC radio 'Our Native Land' 1982–84; Contbg. Ed., Goodwin's Magazine; has written for Candn., Am. & Brit. mags. & newspapers; author: 'Northern Shadows' 1989; 'Brotherhood to Nationhood' 1993; Pres., Federation of English Writers of Quebec 1993; Home: 974 Gouin Blvd. W., Montreal, Que. H3L 1K8.

**MCFARLANE, Ross William,** Q.C., B.A., LL.B.; barrister and solicitor; b. Toronto, Ont. 29 Sept. 1937; s. George Brading and Jane Louise Ann (Ross) M.; e. Upper Can. Coll. 1956; Univ. of West. Ont., B.A. 1959; Osgoode Hall Law Sch., LL.B. 1962; Columbia Univ., Extve. Program, Bus. Admin. 1981; m. Margaret Ann d. the late Marguerite and Ab Barr 25 Aug. 1962; children: David, Brian, Lynda; Vice-Pres., Gen. Counsel & Sec., General Motors of Canada Limited 1984, retired; articled with Faskin Calvin, Toronto 1963; called to Bar of Ont. 1964; Phi Delta Phi Legal Fraternity; lawyer & counsel, IBM Canada Limited 1965–76; Dir., General Motors of Canada Limited; Candn. Mfrs. Assn. (Extve.); Mem., Law Soc. of U.C.; Candn. Bar Assn.; Computer Law Assn.; Bd. of Trade of Metro. Toronto; Assn. of Candn. Gen. Counsel; recreations: golf, cottage (Muskoka); club: Bd. of Trade; Home: 30 Lonsdale Rd., Toronto, Ont. M4V 1W5.

**McFARLANE, Sheryl Patricia,** B.Ed.; writer; b. Pembroke, Ont. 20 Jan. 1954; d. Patrick Martin and Constance Vivian (Brunette) M.;e. Univ. of B.C. B.Ed. 1985; m. John Hewitt s. Tony and Dorothy H. 27 Sept. 1977; children: Alexandra, Claudette, Katherine Ann; Preschool teacher/daycare worker 1972–78; Rsch. Technician, Agric. Canada and U.B.C. 1978–84; Teacher 1985–86; writer, readings (public, school, library), workshops; Mem., B.C. College of Teachers; Candn. Soc. of Children's Authors, Illustrators & Performers; B.C. Fed. of Writers; Candn. Children's Book Centre; Literature Roundtables; author: 'Waiting for the Whales' Can. 1991, U.S. 1993 (Our Choice Award, Children's Book Centre; Candn. Nat. Lib. 'Notable Book'; IODE Nat. Chapter Award for Text), 'Jessie's Island' 1992 (Our Choice Award), 'Eagle Dreams' and 'Moonsnail Song' forthcoming (children's books); recreations: gardening, reading, kayaking, hiking; clubs: Victoria Horticulture Society; Home: 168 Beechwood Ave., Victoria, B.C. V8S 3W5.

**McFAULL, Jack Young,** LL.D.; estate management consultant; b. Philadelphia, Pa. 21 June 1916; s. William and Sarah J. (Young) McF.; e. Zealandia (Sask.) High Sch.; Univ. of Sask. Cert. in Agric. 1944, LL.D. 1981; Prof.ag.; m. Muriel I. d. late Herbert L. and Helen J. Morrison 14 Sept. 1946; children: Daniel M., Terry J., Eldeen J., Herbert W.; CONSULTANT, J.E.M. CONSULTING SERVICES INC. 1981– ; Dir., Innovation Place; Protein, Oil & Starch Corp.; J.E.M. Consulting Services Inc.; Instr. Agric. Engn. Coll. Univ. of Sask. 1945–55; Estate Mang. Consultant Manufacturers' Insurance Co. 1955–81; lectr. in Financial and Estate Planning Univ. of Sask.; recipient Distinguished Agrologist Award 1979; named Citizen of the Yr. Saskatoon 1979; Dr. of Laws Degree Univ. of Sask. 1981; author various articles agric. mags.; mem. Usadian Extve. Assn.; Sask. Inst. Agrols.; Agric. Inst. Can.; Life Underwriters Assn.; Million Dollar Round Table; Protestant; recreations: tennis, curling; Home: 1202, 510 – 5th Ave. N., Saskatoon, Sask. S7K 2R2; Office: 999, 119–4th Ave. S., Saskatoon, Sask. S7K 5X2.

**McFEE, Oonah;** writer; b. Newcastle, N.B. 11 Sept. 1919; d. Cecil George Watson and Marie (White) Browne; e. Model Sch., Ottawa; Lisgar Coll. Inst., Ottawa; Instituto Allende, San Miguel, Mexico; Royal Conservatory of Music (piano); m. Allan s. Allan and Amy McFee 16 Aug. 1941; author (novel) 'Sandbars' 1977; sequel 'Silent Eyes' forthcoming; various short stories publ.: 'Redbook'; 'Chatelaine'; 'The University of Texas Quarterly'; short story broadcast CBC Anthology; invited contbr. Breadloaf Writers' Conf. Vt.; guest lectr. and readings Univ. of Toronto, Univ. of W. Ont., Trent Univ., Univ. of PEI; Writer-in-Residence Trent Univ. 1979–80; recipient Books in Can. First Novel Award 1978; various Can. Council and Ont. Arts Council grants; Address: 2005, 44 Jackes Ave., Toronto, Ont. M4T 1E5.

**McFEETERS, Paul J.,** B.B.A., C.M.A., M.B.A.; b. Lindsay, Ont. 1 Sept. 1954; e. Wilfrid Laurier Univ. B.B.A. (Hons.) 1977; C.M.A. 1980; York Univ. M.B.A. 1984; m., 4 children; PRESIDENT & CHIEF OPERATING OFFR., THE MUNICIPAL TRUST COMPANY AND THE MUNICIPAL SAVINGS & LOAN CORPORATION 1991– ; Career: Pres. & Chief Operating Offr., Municipal Trust and The Municipal Savings & Loan Corporation 1991– ; Vice Chrmn. of the Board, Municipal Financial Leasing Corporation 1991– ; Chief Financial Offr. & Chief Operating Offr., Municipal Financial Corporation 1989– ; Sr. Vice Pres. Finance, MSL Properties Ltd. 1985– ; Sr. Vice Pres. Finance and Chief Financial Offr., Municipal Financial Corporation 1985–89; Vice Pres. Finance, The Municipal Savings & Loan Corporation 1982–85; Controller, The Municipal Savings & Loan Corporation 1981–82; Internal Audit/Finance Mgr., Hepcoe Credit Union Ltd. 1979–81; Acctg. Supervisor, Ward Mallette 1977–79; Office: 70 Collier St., P.O. Box 147, Barrie, Ont. L4M 4S9.

**McFEETORS, Raymond Lindsay,** B.A., C.F.A.; insurance executive; b. 23 May 1944; e. Univ. of Winnipeg B.A. 1968; Chartered Financial Analyst 1978; m. Lynne-Anne; children: Leah, Marshall, Holly, Drew; PRESIDENT & CHIEF EXECUTIVE OFFICER, THE GREAT-WEST LIFE ASSUR. CO. 1992– ; Trainee, Group Div., Great-West Life 1968; trans. to Bond Investments 1971; Mgr. 1976; Bond Investment Officer 1978; Investment Offr., Private Placements 1980; Vice-Pres., Private Placement Investments 1984; Bond & Private Placement Investments 1984; Sr. Vice-Pres., Private Placement Investments Canada 1986; Sr. Vice-Pres. & Chief Investment Officer 1991; recreations: cottage at Lake of the Woods, boating; Home: 112 Barker Blvd., Winnipeg, Man. R3R 2E1; Office: 1000 Osborne St. N., Winnipeg, Man. R3C 3A5.

**McGARRY, Brian William;** funeral director; b. Wakefield, Que. 25 Sept. 1943; s. William Patrick and Lyla A. (Cross) McG.; e. Ottawa Tech. High Sch.; Carleton Univ.; Univ. of Toronto, Funeral Service Edn.; m. Sharon d. Norman and Myrtle Moore 4 June 1966; one s. Brett; one d. Erin; PRES., HULSE, PLAYFAIR & McGARRY FUNERAL HOMES, Ottawa 1987– , Partner 1973– ; Chrmn. Ont. Bd. Funeral Services 1986 and Discipline Chrmn. 1987; mem. Humber Coll. Adv. Ctte. Funeral Service Edn. 1977–80; Ont. Govt. Select Cttes. reviewing Funeral Service Legis. 1984, 1986 and 1987; Charter Mem. Bd. Crime Stoppers Ottawa; Past Vice Pres. Bereaved Families Ont.; mem. Internat. Fedn. Thanatols.; Associates Carleton Univ.; Candn. Institute of Internat. Affairs; elected to Ottawa Bd. Edn. 1985, re-el. 1988, 1991, elected Vice-Chair 1991, Chair 1993; mem. World Federalists Can.; Hist. Soc. Gatineau; Ottawa Carleton Bd. Trade; TV appearances incl. 'The Fifth Estate' and 'Marketplace'; Pres. Funeral Service Assn. Can. 1985; Ont. Funeral Service Assn. 1981; Past Lt. Gov. Kiwanis Internat.; Past Adm. Kiwanis Youth Prog. E. Can. & Caribbean; recipient, B'nai Brith's Ottawa Citizen of the Year 1991; 125th Anniversary of the Confederation of Canada Medal, 1992; Ottawa-Carleton Bd. of Trade 1993 Business Person of the Year Award; recreation: skiing; Clubs: Rideau; Hunt; Canadian; Office: 315 McLeod St., Ottawa, Ont. K2P 1A2.

**McGARRY, Michael Edmund,** B.A. (Lond.), M.A. (Oxon), M.A., LL.B.; lawyer; b. Rhodesia (Zimbabwe) 18 Feb. 1940; s. Thomas James and Thelma (Sarney) McG.; e. St. George's Coll. Salisbury; Univ. Coll. of Rhodesia B.A. 1963; St. Peter's Coll. Oxford (Rhodes Scholar) M.A. 1966; Univ. of W. Ont. LL.B. 1982; m. Jacqueline A. d. Alec and Mollie Wood 5 Aug. 1967; children: Gavin, Craig, Nicola; Lawyer, Judson, Kennedy 1984; called to Bar of Ont. 1984; Secondary Sch. Teacher 1966–79, Shawnigan Lake (B.C.) Sch., Oriel Boys Sch. Salisbury, Rhodesia, Garth Hill Sec. Sch. Bracknell, Eng., KLO Secondary Sch. Kelowna, B.C.; Past Pres. Central Okanagan Teachers' Assn. Kelowna; Dir. Girls Group Home, London, Ont.; recreations: tennis, soccer, travel; Clubs: Oakridge Optimist; Greenhills Tennis; Home: 45 Wychwood Park, London, Ont. N6G 1R4; Office: 12 - 515 Richmond St., London, Ont. N6A 3T4.

**McGAVIN, Gerald Allan Bell,** B.Com., M.B.A., F.C.A.; property company executive; b. Vancouver, B.C., 29 July 1937; s. late Allan Morton and Beatrice W. (Bell) McG.; e. Shawnigan Lake (B.C.) Schs.; Univ. of B.C., B.Com. 1960; C.A. 1963; Univ. of Calif. M.B.A. 1965; m. Sheahan Beale, d. late Elmer Stephen Glaspie, 8 Sept. 1962; children: Catharine Sheahan, Alexia Russell; CHRMN. & C.E.O. BRITISH PACIFIC PROPERTIES LTD. 1988– ; Pres. & Dir., McGavin Properties Ltd.; Dir., Candn. Western Bank; Dir., Seaboard Life Ins. Co.; Dir., Discovery Enterprises Ltd.; Dir., Chateau Montlabert Inc.; Audit Clk. Peat Marwick Mitchell, Vancouver 1960; Wood Supply Comptroller B.C. Forest Products Ltd. Vancouver 1965; Secy.-Treas. Ancore International Ltd. Vancouver 1969; Pres. & C.E.O., Yorkshire Trust Co. Vancouver 1972; Pres. & C.O.O. B.C. Hydro & Power Authority 1986–88; joined present co. Dir., 1979; served with RCNVR 1955–60, rank Sub. Lt.; Past Pres., Vancouver Symphony Soc.; Past Pres., Vancouver Art Gallery; Chrmn., Wesbrook Soc. of U.B.C.; Former Chrmn., B.C. Sports Hall of Fame; Fellow, Inst. C.A.'s B.C.; Protestant; recreations: squash, golf, tennis; Clubs: Vancouver; Vancouver Lawn Tennis & Badminton; Shaughnessy Golf & Country; Home: 1675 Laurier Ave., Vancouver, B.C. V6J 2V5; Office: 520 - 1100 Melville St., Vancouver, B.C. V6E 4A6.

**McGAVIN, Robert J.,** B.P.E., M.Sc., Ph.D.; banker; b. Calgary, Alta. 21 Aug. 1942; e. Univ. of B.C., B.P.E. 1965; Univ. of Wash. M.Sc. 1966, Ph.D. 1969; Univ. of Oslo 1966; Northeastern Univ. Mgmt. Devel. Prog. 1985; SENIOR VICE PRESIDENT, PUBLIC AFFAIRS & ECONOMIC RESEARCH DEPT., TORONTO DOMINION BANK 1981– ; joined Cdn. Foreign Service, Dept. Ind. Trade & Comm. 1968–79, Australia – Trade 1969–72, Cdn. Inst. Internat. Affairs Govt. Interchange Prog. Toronto 1972–73, Israel – Trade, Gen. Relations 1973–75, Washington, D.C. – Press, Info. 1975–79; Dir. of Communications Bank of Montreal Toronto 1979–81; Chrmn., Donations Ctte., T-D Bank; Past Chrmn., Governing Council, Univ. of Toronto; Chrmn., Olympic Trust of Canada; Extve. Ctte., Cdn. Olympic Assoc.; Toronto Hosp.; Jr. Achievement of Can.; Canada U.S. Business Assoc.; mem., Candn. Public Relations Society; Conf. Bd. Council Pub. Affairs Extves.; Clubs: Badminton & Racquet Club (Toronto); Albany Club; Office: P.O. Box 1 Toronto-Dominion Centre, Toronto, Ont. M5K 1A2.

**McGEACHY, Duncan Donald Cameron,** B.Sc., P.Eng.; executive; b. Hazelton, B.C. 12 Dec. 1918; s. Edwin C. and Clara (Cameron) M.; e. Queen's Univ., B.Sc. (Mech. Engn.); Univ. of Western Ont. (Post Grad. course in Business Adm.); m. Joan Catherine Macdonald, 30 January 1982; children by previous marriage: Edithe Lynn, Joan Margaret, Neil Wallace, Ruth Ann; Dir., Gore Mutual Insurance Co.; Trimac Ltd.; Unit Drop Forge Inc. (Milwaukee); Impact Industries; Past Pres., Stratford Shakespearean Festival Foundation; served with British Admiralty and R.C.N.V.R.; mem., Assn. of Prof. Engrs. of Ont.; Un. Church; recreation: golf; Clubs: London Hunt & Country; London; Caledon Mountain Trout; Home: 1607 Gloucester Road, London, Ont. N6G 2S5.

**McGEE, Hon. Frank C.,** P.C. (Can.) 1963; b. Ottawa, Ont. 3 Mar. 1926; s. late Walter Robert and Frances (McCool) M.; e. Carleton Coll.; St. Patricks Coll., High Sch., Ottawa; served in R.C.A.F. 1943–45; m. Moira, d. Late Senator M. Grattan O'Leary, Ottawa, Ont., 16 June 1951; children: Maureen, Sheilagh, Owen; 1st el. to H. of C. for York-Scarborough, g.e. 1957; re-el. 1958, 1962; apptd. Minister without Portfolio in Diefenbaker Cabinet, 11 March 1963; def. g.e. 1963 1965 and 1972; served on Security Intelligence Review Cttee. 1984–89; Apptd. Judge of the Citizenship Court 1990; Conservative; Clubs: Albany; The Toronto Hunt; Home: 330 Spadina Rd., Apt. 407, Toronto, Ont. M5R 2V9.

**McGEER, Edith G.,** Ph.D., D.Sc. (Hon.); professor emerita; b. New York City 18 Nov. 1923; d. Charles and Charlotte Annie (Ruhl) Graef; e. Swathmore Coll. B.A. 1944; Univ. of Virginia Ph.D. 1946; m. Patrrick L. s. James A. M. 15 Apr. 1954; children: Patrick Charles, Brian Theodore, Victoria Lynn; PROF. EMERITA, UNIV. OF B.C. 1989– ; Rsch. Chem., E.I. DuPont de Nemours & Co. (Wilmington, Delaware) 1946–54; Rsch. Assoc., present univ. 1954–74; Assoc. Prof. 1974–76; Prof. & Acting Head 1976–83; Prof. & Head 1983–88; Mem., Ed. Adv. Bd., 'Neurology of Aging,' 'J. of Devel. Neurosci.,' 'Brain Research,' 'Neurosci. Letters,' 'Alzheimer's Disease and Assoc. Disorders'; 'Neurodegeneration'; Extve. Ctte., World Fed. for Neurol. Rsch., Group on Dementias; Can., Internat. & U.S. Biochm. socs.; Soc. for Neurosci.; Candn. Fed. Biol. Soc., etc.; Sigma Xi 1943; Phi Beta Kappa 1944; DuPont Fellow 1945, '46; Lychnos Soc. 1946; Citation, Delaware Section, Am. Chem. Soc. 1958; Hon. Fellow, N. Pacific Soc. of Neurol. & Psych.; Teaching Award, 1st Yr Residents in Psych., UBC 1982; Distinguished Sci. Lectr., UBC 1982; Eccles Lectureship, 1st Candn. Symp. on Organic Dementias 1986, etc.; Hon. D.Sc.; recipient, Clarke Institute of Psychiatry Rsch. Award 1992; co-author: 'The Molecular Neurobiology of the Mammalian Brain' 1978, 1987; editor of 2 books; author: 91 book chaps. & 291 papers in refereed sci. journals; 4 patents; Home: 4727 West 2nd Ave., Vancouver, B.C. V6T 1C1; Office: 2255 Westbrook Mall, Vancouver, B.C. V6T 1Z3.

**McGEER, Patrick L.,** Ph.D., M.D., F.R.C.P. (Can.), LL.D. (Hon.); former politician; medical neuroscientist; b. Vancouver, B.C. 29 June 1927; s. James Arthur McG.;

e. Univ. of B.C., B.A. 1948, M.D. 1958; Princeton Univ. Ph.D. 1951; m. Edith d. Charles Graef, New York City 15 Apl. 1954; children: Patrick Charles, Tad, Victoria L.; PROFESSOR EMERITUS, UNIV. OF B.C. 1993– ; Prof. Faculty of Med. Univ. of B.C. 1960–92 (leave-of-absence 1975–86); M.L.A. 1962–86; Min. of Educ. 1976–79; Min. of Educ., Science & Technol. 1979; Min. of Univs., Science & Communications, B.C. 1979–86; Min. of International Trade Science and Investment 1986; Min. of International Trade, Science & Communications, B.C., 1986; Nat. lectureships for Research Soc. of Am.; Soc. for Neuroscience, Green Scholar; recipient, Clarke Institute of Psychiatry Rsch. Award 1992; author 'Politics in Paradise' 1972; 'Molecular Neurobiology of the Mammalian Brain' 1978, 1987; ed. 'Methane: Fuel for the Future' 1982; over 400 papers scient. journs.; Protestant; recreations: tennis, skiing; Clubs: Vancouver Lawn Tennis; Home: 4727 W. 2nd Ave., Vancouver, B.C. V6T 1C1; Office: Faculty of Med., Univ. of B.C., Vancouver, B.C. V6T 1Z3.

**McGEORGE, Ronald Kenneth,** B.Sc., D.H.A.; hospital b. Fredericton, N.B. 7 June 1944; s. Hubert Oswald and Ruth Johanna (Kolding) McG.; e. Houghton (N.Y.) Coll. B.Sc. 1966; Univ. of Toronto Dipl. Hosp. Adm. 1969; m. Gail F. d. Millard and Marion Mitchell 17 July 1970; children: Scott, Dacia; PRESIDENT & CHIEF EXTVE. OFFR., REGION 3 HOSPITAL CORPORATION, FREDERICTON, N.B. 1992– ; Counsellor in Adm., N.S. Hosp. Ins. Comn. 1969–70; Asst. Extve. Dir. Izaak Walton Killam Hosp. for Children, Halifax 1970–72; Vice Pres. (Patient Services) Greater Niagara Gen. Hosp. Niagara Falls, Ont. 1972–74; Extve. Dir. Halifax Infirmary 1974–79; Pres. & C.E.O., Kingston Gen. Hosp. 1980–90; Chief Extve. Offr., Dr. Everett Chalmers Hosp. 1990–92; Pres., Region 3 Hospital Corp. 1992– ; author numerous articles, papers hosp. adm.; Dir., N.S. Hosp. Assn.; Dir. Ont. Hosp. Assn. & Chrmn. Rsrch. Ctte.; Chrmn., Council of Teaching Hosps.; Candn. Coll. Health Service Extves. (Dir. of Foundation); Past Chairman Canadian College of Health Service Executives; Business Alumnus of the Year, Houghton Coll. 1988; Vice Chrmn. Kingston Youth for Christ; mem. W.D. Piercey Mem. Soc. Bd.; Surveyor, Canadian Council on Hospital Accreditation; Pres., Ont. Council of Admins. of Teaching Hosps.; Mem., Bd. of Dir., and Executive Ctte., Ontario Hosp. Assoc., Chrmn. Research Ctte.; Graduate Literary Award, Univ. of Toronto, Fac. of Health Admin. 1985; Business Alumnus of the Year, Houghton Coll., Houghton, N.Y. 1988; Wesleyan Church; recreation: hockey, basketball, fishing; Club: Rotary; Home: 182 Springwater Lane, Fredericton, N.B. E3B 5W9; Office: Priestman St., Fredericton, N.B. E3B 5X8.

**MCGHEE, Robert John,** Ph.D., F.R.S.C.; archaeologist; b. Wiarton, Ont. 27 Feb. 1941; s. John Douglas and Marie (MacBeth) M.; e. Univ. of Toronto, B.A. 1964, M.A. 1966; Univ. of Calgary, Ph.D. 1968; m. Patricia d. Donald and Helen Sutherland 1980; one s.: John Ross; CURATOR OF ARCTIC ARCHAEOLOGY, ARCHAEOLOGICAL SURVEY OF CAN., CANDN. MUS. OF CIVILIZATION 1976– ; Arctic Archaeologist, Nat. Mus. of Can. 1968–72; Assoc. Prof., Mem. Univ. of Nfld. 1972–76; Pres., Candn. Archaeological Assn. 1987–90; Fellow, Royal Soc. of Can.; Arctic Inst. of N. Am.; author: 'Canadian Arctic Prehistory' 1978, 'Ancient Canada' 1989, 'Canada Rediscovered' 1991 and over 100 other books & articles on the subject of archaeology & history; Home: 1154 Bayview Rd., R.R. #1, Woodlawn, Ont. K0A 3M0; Office: Hull, Que. J8X 4H2.

**McGIBBON, Donald Walker,** B.A., KStJ, KCLJ; b. Sarnia, Ont. 13 Jan. 1910; s. Donald Archibald and Margaret Agnes (Collier) McG.; e. elem. and high sch. Sarnia; Univ. of Toronto B.A. 1932; Harvard Business Sch. Advanced Mgmt. Course 1948; m. Pauline d. Alfred William and Ethel Selina Mills 26 Jan. 1935; joined Imperial Oil Sarnia Refinery 1932 becoming Budget Controller, trans. to Comptroller's Office Toronto 1940, Asst. to Treas. 1948, Treas. 1950, Vice pres. 1974–75; Past Chrmn. Bd. Victoria Univ. Toronto; former Trustee, Canada Permanent Income Investments; Past pres., Ont. Chamber Comm., Dom. Drama Festival; Gov. Nat. Theatre Sch. Can. 10 yrs.; Vice Chrmn., Ont. Arts Council 1979–82; Chrmn. 1982–85; former Bd. Mem., College of Art; former Chrmn., Coll. of Art Found.; Past Vice Pres. and Treas. Ont. Council Order of St. John; Past Chrmn., Investment Ctte., Candn. Priory of St. John; recreations: reading, music, art; Clubs: York; Granite; Home: 2004, 20 Avoca Ave., Toronto, Ont. M4T 2B8.

**McGIBBON, (James) Ian,** B.Eng.; executive; b. Montreal, Qué. 15 Jan. 1927; s. late Roy H., M.D., and late Alice (Armitage) McG.; e. Royal Candn. Naval Coll., Royal Roads, B.C. 1946; McGill Univ., B.E. 1951; Univ. of W. Ont. Grad. Sch. of Business Adm. 1953–54; Harvard Business Sch. Advanced Mang. Program 1976; m. Catherine d. late George S. Veith, D.D.S. 13 Sept. 1957; children: Catherine, Jamie, Alexandra, Nicolas; Group Vice-Pres., Abitibi-Price Inc. 1982–87; Vice-Pres. Finance, The Price Co. Ltd. 78–82; Gen. Mgr. Bldg. Materials present Co. 1963, Dir. of Planning 1969, Vice-Pres. Corp. Devel. 1974, Vice-Pres. (Finance), 1978–80, Group Vice-Pres., (finance) 1980–82; served with RCN and RCN(R) 1944–53, rank Lt.; mem. Ont. Forestry Assn.; Anglican; recreations: tree farming, tennis, cross-country skiing; Club: University; Home: R.R. 2, Erin, Ont. N0B 1T0.

**McGIBBON, Hon. Pauline M.,** O.C. (1967), C.C. (1980), O.Ont. (1988), B.A., LL.D., D.U., D. Hum. L., D. Litt. S., B.A.A. (Theatre), Hon. F.R.C.P.S.(C.); b. Sarnia, Ont. 20 October 1910; d. Alfred William and Ethel Selina (French) Mills; e. Pub. and High Schools, Sarnia, Ontario; University of Toronto (Victoria Coll.), B.A. (Modern Hist.) 1933; LL.D., Alta. 1967, Western 1974, Queen's 1974, Toronto 1975; D.U. Ottawa 1972; Laval 1976; D. Hum. L. St. Lawrence Univ., Canton N.Y. 1977; D. Litt. S. Univ. of Victoria, Toronto 1979; B.A.A. (Theatre) Ryerson Polytech. Inst. 1974; Hon. F.R.C.P.S. 1977; LL.D. McMaster Univ., 1981; LL.D. Carleton Univ., 1981; LL.D. Univ. of Windsor 1988; D.Admin. Northland Open Univ. 1990; m. Donald Walker, s. late Donald McGibbon, 26 Jan. 1935; Lieut.-Governor of Ont. April 1974–Sept. 1980; (former Chancellor, 1st woman, Univ. of Toronto 1971–74); first Woman Chancellor Univ. of Guelph 1977–83; first woman Gov. of Upper Canada College, 1971–74; Chrmn. Ont. Selection Comte. for Rhodes Scholarships 1984–90; Hon. Chrmn. du Maurier Council for Arts (Chrmn. 1980– ); Life Mem. Bd. of Govs., Nat. Theatre Sch. (Chairman Bd. Govs. 1966–69); Hon. Vice-Pres., National Chapter, I.O.D.E. (Nat. Pres. 1963–65); Hon. Pres. of the Municipal Chapter of Toronto; Past Pres., Dom. Drama Festival 1957–59; 1st woman Pres., Candn. Conf. of the Arts 1972–73; Hon. Secy., Women's Adv. Comte. to Expo '67; Past Pres. (1st woman) Univ. of Toronto Alumni Assn. 1952–53; Past Pres. Victoria Coll. Alumnae Assn.; Hon. Colonel (1st Can. Woman), 25 Toronto Service Battalion 1975–83; Hon. Life Member, Royal Canadian Military Inst.; Mem., Fort York Branch of the Canadian Legion; 1st Pres., Children's Film Lib. of Can. 1948–50; Vice-Pres., Candn. Assn. for Adult Educ. 1958–63; Past Chrmn., Ont. Theatre Study 1966–69; Chrmn. Women's Coll. Hosp. 1970–74; Dir., Mt. Sinai Inst. 1981–86; Dir., Donwoods Inst. 1973–85; First Woman Director, IBM Canada (ret'd 1974); First Woman Dir., George Weston Ltd. 1981– ; First Woman to be Director, Imasco Limited (ret'd 1974); Dir., Mercedes-Benz Canada Inc. 1983–91; Hon. mem., Toronto Symphony Women's Comte; Senate. Univ. of Toronto 1952–61; 1st woman Chrmn. of Bd. of Trustees, Nat. Arts Centre (Ottawa) 1980–84; Chrmn. Toronto International Festival (June 1984); Dir., Massey Hall – Roy Thomson Hall, Oct. 1980–90 (Vice Pres. 1988–90); Hon. Patron of Volunteers of Roy Thomson Hall; mem. Extve., Candn. Scene 1951–59; Can. Council 1968–71; mem. Bd. Elliot Lake Centre for Continuing Educ. 1965–71; Governor, Candn. Centenary Council 1963–67; Hon. fellow, Heraldry Soc. of Can.; Hon. mem: Royal Candn. Yacht., National (first woman mem.), Granite, Toronto Ladies Golf, Boulevard Club, Albany, Toronto Ladies,' Business & Professional Women's Club; Executive Women's Club; Zonta; University Women's Club of Toronto; recipient: Canadian Drama Award 1957; Centennial Medal; Civic Award of Merit, City of Toronto 1967; Award of Merit, Candn. Public Relations Society, 1972; Queen's Jubilee Medal 1977; Paul Harris Fellowship Award, Rotary Club of Toronto-Forest Hill, 1977; Eleanor Roosevelt Humanities Award, State of Israel Bonds 1978; Human Relations Award, The Can. Council of Christians and Jews; Ont. Teachers' Federation Fellowship 1979; Humanitarian Award, B'nai Brith 1980; Diplome d'honneur, Can. Conf. of the Arts 1981; Prix au mérité, J-Louis Lévesque Foundation 1982; Fellowship Award, Rotary Club of Sarnia 1989; Arbor Award, U. of T. Alumni 1990; 125th Anniversary of the Confederation of Canada Medal, 1992; honours: $7,000 medal named in her honour (Pauline McGibbon Hon. Award in Theatre Arts) presented annually by Govt. of Prov. of Ontario since 1980; Pauline McGibbon Lifetime Award in the Arts 1991– ; Dame, Order of St. Lazarus of Jerusalem 1967; Member, Order of Ontario 1988; First Hon. Life mem., Ontario Chamber of Commerce 1980; Hon. Reeve, Black Creek Pioneer Village 1982–84; Dame of Grace of the Order of St. John of Jerusalem, 1974; Grand Prior of the Order of St. Lazarus, 1982–85; Dame Grand Cross 1982, Order of Sr. Lazarus; An Hon. Nat. Co-Chrmn., Candn. Counc. of Christians & Jews 1986–93; Member-at-large, Board of Trustees, Toronto School of Theology 1984–87; Protestant; Clubs: University Women's; Toronto Ladies; Home: Twenty Avoca Ave., Apt. 2004, Toronto, Ont. M4T 2B8.

**McGILL, Donald Gordon,** B.A.; retired; b. Toronto, Ont. 30 March 1918; s. Harold Linton and Lillian (Ireland) M.; e. Malvern Coll. Inst., Toronto, Ont.; Univ. of Western Ont., B.A., and Mang. Training course (1948); m. Margaret Naomi, d. Kenneth C. Greene, London, Ont., 21 Nov. 1942; children: Donald Gordon, Jr., Patricia Anne, Robert Bruce; Pres., Donmar Investments Ltd.; joined John Labatt Ltd., 1940; Vice-Pres., Western Can. Reg. 1965–78; R.C.N.V.R., 1940–45; Gov., Vancouver Board Trade 1987; mem., Adv. Bd., Fraser Inst.; Anglican; recreations: golf, fishing; Clubs: Vancouver; Capilano Golf & Country; Home: 1410 Sandhurst Place, West Vancouver, B.C. V7S 2P3.

**McGILL, John Williamson,** B.Comm.; executive; b. Montreal, Que. 17 Mar. 1932; s. Frank and Margaret (Williamson) M.; e. Trinity Coll. Sch. 1949; McGill Univ. B.Comm. 1954; Centre d'Etudes Industrielles 1958; Harvard Advanced Mgmt. Prog. 1982; children: Jennifer, Colleen, Sandra; VICE CHAIRMAN, CANADIAN LIQUID AIR LTD. 1983– ; Chrmn., Innocan Inc.; Dir., Air Liquide America; Sales Mgr. Canadair 1959–63; Founding Pres. and Managing Dir. Air Jamaica 1968–71; Chrmn. Air Transit 1973; Vice-Pres. Sales and Service, Vice-Pres. Mktg., Extve. Vice-Pres. Air Canada 1963–83; Pres., Montreal General Hospital; recreations: golf, fishing, shooting; Clubs: Mount Royal; Mount Bruno Country; Forest & Stream; University Club; Office: 1155 Sherbrooke W., Montreal, Que. H3A 1H8.

**McGILL, Stuart Michael,** BPHE, M.Sc., Ph.D.; university professor; b. Richmond Hill, Ont. 24 July 1957; s. John Stuart and Elizabeth Marie (Nicholson) M.; e. Univ. of Toronto, BPHE 1980; Univ. of Ottawa, M.Sc. 1982; Univ. of Waterloo, Ph.D. 1986; m. Kathryn A. d. David and Margaret Barr 11 Aug. 1990; one son: John David; research in area of spinal biomechanics; developed a sophisticated computer model of lumbar spine for which he was awarded Volvo Bioengr. Award for low back pain rsch. 1986; extensive presentations worldwide; rsch. & lectr., Kinesiology Dept., Univ. of Waterloo; Founder, S.M. McGill and Assoc., consultants; Alumni Gold Medal 1986 (top grad. Ph.D. Waterloo); Julian Christensen Award, Human Factors Assn. of Can. 1986 (top grad. stud.); Univ. of Toronto Alumni Award 1978 (top male stud. in class); author of over 70 scientific publications; Home: R.R. 2, Elora, Ont. N0B 1S0; Office: Dept. of Kinesiology, Univ. of Waterloo, Waterloo, Ont. N2L 3G1.

**McGILLIS, The Honourable Madam Justice Donna Catherine,** B.A., LL.B., Q.C.; judge; b. Peterborough, Ont. 23 Dec. 1951; d. Donald Edward and Joan Teresa (Donnelly) M.; e. Queen's Univ. B.A. 1972; Univ. of Windsor LL.B. 1975; m. Jean-Claude (Q.C.) s. Charles and Georgette Demers; children: Jean Léandre; JUDGE, FEDERAL COURT OF CANADA, TRIAL DIVISION 1992– ; called to Bar of Ont. 1977; private practice 1977–80; various positions in Dept. of Justice 1980–92 incl. criminal prosecutions in Toronto 1980–86; Sr. Counsel, Legal Serv., Royal Canadian Mounted Police 1986–88; Sr. General Counsel, Legal Serv., Dept. of Indian Affairs & Northern Devel. 1988–92; Q.C. 1990; Office: Ottawa, Ont. K1A 0H9.

**McGILLIVRAY, Barbara Carol,** M.D., F.R.C.P.(C), F.C.C.M.G.; associate professor/clinical geneticist; b. Nova Scotia 13 Dec. 1948; d. George William and Beatrice (Underhill) Wagstaff; e. Univ. of B.C. B.Sc. 1970; Univ. of Calgary M.D. 1974; m. Robert John s. Margaret and William M. 22 Dec. 1972; children: Karen, Andrea; ASSOC. PROF., UNIV. OF B.C. 1987– ; Fellow, Royal Coll. of Physicians & Surg. (Paed.) 1978 and (Med. Genet.) 1993; Candn. Coll. of Med. Geneticists 1979; Clinical Geneticist, Dept. of Med. Genetics, Univ. of B.C. with interests in prenatal diagnosis, biomedical ethics, intersex problems, mental retardation; teaches Med. Genetics 440, plus other univ. classes, resident, student, lay teaching; Chair, UBC Rsch. Ethics Ctte.; Mem., Am. Soc. of Human Genetics; Am. Soc. for Clin. Rsch.; Pacific N.W. Paed. Soc.; B.C. Med. Legal Soc.; author of various med. articles on genetic conditions, prenatal diagnosis; recreations: camping, Girl Guides, home crafts; Home: 657 West 53rd Ave., Vancouver, B.C. V6P 1K2; Office: Dept. of Med. Genetics, BC Children's Hospital, 4480 Oak St., Vancouver, B.C. V6H 3V4.

**McGILLIVRAY, Donald G.,** B.A.; journalist; b. Moose Jaw, Sask, 21 June 1927; s. Malcolm and Mary

(Riddel) McG.; e. Univ. of Sask. B.A. 1951; m. Julietta (dec. 1979) d. Albion and Addie Kepner 4 Sept. 1950; children: Murray, Peigi Ann, Neil, Fionna; NAT. POL. COLUMNIST, SOUTHAM NEWS 1985– ; Reporter, The Leader-Post, Regina, 1951–55; Leg. Reporter, Columnist Winnipeg Tribune 1955–62; Parlty. Corr. Southam News, Ottawa 1962–66, Nat. Corr. Washington, D.C. 1966, Bureau Chief London, Eng. 1967–70; Assoc. Ed. Edmonton Journal 1970–72; Ed. Financial Times of Canada 1972–75; Nat. Econ. Ed. Southam News, Ottawa 1975–84; Adjunct Rsch. Prof. of Journalism, Carleton Univ. Ottawa 1979– ; recipient Nat. Bus. Writing Award 1976, 78; Distinguished Service Award 1984; Pres., Centre for Investigative Journalism 1986–87; mem. Nat. Press Club; Dir., Parlty. Press Gallery; Bd. Deacons Westmount Bapt. Ch. 1976–85; Home: 63 Glendale Ave., Ottawa, Ont. K1S 1W5; Office: 512, 151 Sparks St., Ottawa, Ont. K1P 5E3.

**MCGINNIS, Lloyd R.,** B.Sc., M.Sc., P.Eng.; engineering consultant; b. Roblin, Man. 30 July 1933; s. Walter Patrick and Clementine Bertha May (Rosevear) McG.; e. Univ. of Man., B.Sc. (Civil Eng.) 1956; Georgia Inst. of Technol., M.Sc. 1967; m. Vera-Anne; d. William Roy Spencer 13 Aug. 1955; children: Brock Lee, Grant Robert; CHRMN. & C.E.O., WARDROP ENGINEERING INC. 1991– ; Cons. 1956– ; Project Engr., W.L. Wardrop & Assoc. 1956–62; Engr. Dir. 1962–70; Transport Advr., Govt. of Tanzania 1970–73; Vice-Pres. & Dir., Internat. Div. 1973–79; Chrmn., Internat. Inst. for Sustainable Develop. 1990–91; Dir., RoyFund Mutual Funds Services Inc.; Past Mem., Prime Minister's National Advisory Bd. on Sci. and Tech.; National Task Force on the Environment and Economy; Past Chrmn., Candn. C. of C.; Project Bus., Jr. Achievement; Past Chrmn., World Community Serv. for Rotary Dist. 555; Past Pres., Rotary Club of Winnipeg; Past Advr., Royal Trust Bd.; Past Dir., Flyer Indus.; Past Dir., Micro Electronics Ctr.; Winnipeg Convention Centre; Past Chrmn., Winnipeg Bus. Devel. Corp.; Past Mem., Science Council of Canada; Chrmn., Canada/USA Business Relations Ctte.; mem. and Past Pres., Winnipeg C. of C.; Fellow, Soc. of Civil Engrs.; Life Elder, Presbyn. Ch. of Can.; Mem., Assn. of Consulting Engrs. of Can.; Assn. of Profl. Engrs. of Man.; Globe '92 Internal Advisory Bd.; recipient Gold Medal Award, Candn. Council Profl. Engs. 1986; Man. Export Award; author of num. tech. & econ. articles; frequent pub. speaker; advocate of Candn. small bus. competition in global marketplace; recreations: golf, cycling, skating, skiing, sailing; Clubs: St. Charles Golf and Country; Manitoba; Home: 703 – 160 Tuxedo Blvd., Winnipeg, Man. R3P 1B2; Office: 400 - 386 Broadway, Winnipeg, Man. R3C 4M8.

**McGIVERIN, Donald S.,** B.Com., M.B.A.; merchant; b. Calgary, Alta. 4 April 1924; s. late Alfred Chester & late Ella (Scott) McG.; e. Toronto, Ont. Schs.; Univ. of Manitoba, B.Com.; Ohio State Univ., M.B.A.; m. Margaret Ann (dec.), d. late Harold Falconar Weld, 9 Sept. 1950; one s. Richard Weld (dec.), one d. Mary Edith Daniher; GOVERNOR AND CHAIRMAN, HUDSON'S BAY CO. since 1982; Dir., Dupont of Can. Ltd.; Manufacturers Life Ins. Co.; Manufacturers Capital Corp.; Noranda Inc.; joined present Co. as Mang. Dir. Retail Stores 1969; Phi Kappa Phi; recreation: golf; Clubs: Rosedale Golf; The Toronto; York; Granite; Loxahatchee (Jupiter, Fla.); Home: Apt. 4802, 44 Charles St. W., Toronto, Ont. M4Y 1R8; Office: 401 Bay St., Toronto, Ont. M5H 2Y4.

**MCGONIGAL, The Hon. Pearl;** b. Melville, Sask.; d. Frederic and Catherine Marie (Lay) Kuhlman; e. Melville H.S.; Univ. of Man. LL.D. (Hon.); d., Kimberley; Lieut.-Gov. of Manitoba 1981–86; Dir., Candn. Imperial Bank of Commerce; Dir., Mediacom Inc.; early career comprised of 9 years in banking, followed by 7 years as Merchandising Rep.; el. to City Council, Winnipeg 1969; Grter. Winnipeg City Counc. 1971; Depy. Mayor and Chrmn. Extve. Policy Comte. 1979–81; Comnr., Manitoba Law Reform Comn.; Chrmn., Bd. of Mgmt., Grace Gen. Hosp.; Campaign Chair, United Way Campaign 1990; Vice-Chair, Grey Cup '91; Bd. of Dirs., Red River Exhbn., Rainbow Stage; ex-officio mem., Man. Theatre Centre; Bd. of Mgmt., Winnipeg Home Improvement Prog.; Chrmn., Adv. Comte., Sch. of Nursing & Chrmn., former mem. Manitoba Environmental Council; former mem., Manitoba Blue Cross; Bd. of Dirs., Winnipeg Convention Centre; Man. Aviation Counc.; Wpg. Convention and Visitor's Bureau; Mediacom Inc.; Western Adv. Bd., Royal Trustco; Selection Comte., Fac. of Dental Hygiene, Univ. of Man.; Hon. Col., 735 Communications Regt. 1982–86; Hon. Colonel 402 City of Winnipeg Squadron 1992– ; recipient Internat. Toastmistress Award, Benevolent and Protective Order of Elks of Can.; Man. Parks and Recreation Assn. Award; invested in the Order of St. John as Dame of Grace; Recipient of the 1984 B'Nai Brith National Humanitarian Award and the Candn. Corps of Commissionaires' Corps Silver Medal; Citizen of the Year, Knights of Columbus 1987; Paul Harris Fellow 1989; The Salvation Army Order of Distinguished Auxiliary Service 1991; Hon. Col., 402 City of Winnipeg Squadron 1992; author: 'Frankly Feminine' 1975; 'Bringing It All Together' 1990; Anglican; recreations: fishing, cooking; Club: Winnipeg Winter; Home: 51, 361 Westwood Dr., Winnipeg, Man. R3K 1G4.

**McGOURTY, Brian Michael,** P.Eng.; executive; b. Saint John, N.B. 17 Nov. 1937; s. Michael John and Stella (Moran) McG.; e. St. Francis Xavier Univ.; Tech. Univ. of N.S. E.Eng. 1960; Harvard Business Sch. A.M.P. 1984; m. Anne d. Jim and Alma Bishop 14 Sept. 1963; children: Michael, James, Sean; CHRMN. OF THE BOARD, HONEYWELL INC.; Mgr. Quality, Scarborough Mfg. Facility present firm 1969, Operations Mgr. Residential Div. 1974; Vice-Pres. and Gen. Mgr. Honeywell Amplitrol Inc. 1976; Dir. Info. Systems Operations 1982; Extve. Vice-Pres. and Group Dir. Computer and Automation Systems Grup 1983; Pres. & C.O.O. 1984; Chrmn., Pres. & C.E.O. 1986; mem. Business Council on National Issues; Bd. of Govs. & Chrmn. Governors Circle, The Wellesley Hosp. Rsch. Inst.; mem. Candn. Mfrs.' Assn.; Toronto Bd. of Trade; Ont. Assn. of Profl. Engrs.; recreations: jogging, swimming, boating; Office: Honeywell Plaza, Minneapolis, Minn. 55408-1792, USA.

**McGOWAN, Christopher,** B.Sc., Ph.D.; museum curator; educator; b. Beckenham, Eng. 30 March 1942; s. Wilfred Clarence and Daisy Gwendoline (Morphew) McG.; e. The Polytechnic, London, B.Sc. (Zool.) 1965; Birkbeck Coll. Univ. of London, Ph.D. 1969; m. Elizabeth d. George and Daisy Gregory 4 Sept. 1965; two d. Claire, Angela; CURATOR IN CHARGE, DEPT. VERTEBRATE PALAEONTOL. ROYAL ONT. MUSEUM 1980– ; Asst. Prof. of Zool. Univ. of Toronto 1972–78, Assoc. Prof. of Zool. 1978–90, Prof. 1990– ; Asst. Master Biol. & Chem. Robert Clack Tech. Sch. 1965–66; Asst. Master Biol. Westminster City Sch. 1966–69; Curatorial Asst. present Museum Dept. 1969, Asst. Curator 1970, Assoc. Curator 1974, Assoc. Curator in Charge 1975–80; author: 'The Successful Dragons: A Natural History of Extinct Reptiles' 1983; 'In the Beginning: A Scientist Shows Why the Creationists Are Wrong' 1983; 'Dinosaurs, Spitfires and Sea Dragons' 1991; 'Discover Dinosaurs' 1992; recreation: brewing; Office: 100 Queens Park, Toronto, Ont. M5S 2C6.

**McGOWAN, J. William,** D.Sc. F.A.P.S.; F.A.A.A.S. physicist; educator; b. Pittsburgh, Pa. 5 July 1931; s. James William and Margaret Eleanor (Campion) McG.; e. St. Francis Xavier Univ., B.Sc. 1953; Carnegie-Mellon Univ., M.S. 1958; Univ. Laval, D.Sc. 1961; divorced; children: Maura, Liam, Laurie, Colin, John, Michelle; Pres., Associates of Science and Technology (AST), Ottawa; Dir., National Museum of Science and Technology, Ottawa 1984–88; Instr., St. Francis Univ. 1955–56; Research Assoc., Westinghouse Research 1957; Instr., St. Lawrence Coll., Univ. Laval 1958–59; Staff mem. General Atomic, San Diego 1962–69; Visiting Fellowship, Jt. Inst. for Lab. Astrophysics, Univ. of Colo. 1966; joined staff of Univ. of Western Ont. as Prof. and Chrmn., Dept. of Physics 1969; Prof. of Physics, Univ. of Western Ont. and Founding Chrmn., Centre for Interdisciplinary Studies in Chem. Physics there 1972–76; visiting Prof., Centro Atomico, Bariloche, Argentina 1973; Facultés Universitaires, Namur Belgium 1976–77; Libera Universita di Trento, Trento, Italy 1976–77; Université de Louvain, Louvain la Neuve, Belgium 1978 to present; N.R.C. Exchange Fellowship USSR 1975; Lecturer for COSTED, India, 1977–79; Research Associate Lawrence Berkley Labs, Univ. of Calif. Berkley 1978–82; James Chair of Science, St. Francis Xavier Univ., Antigonish N.S., 1983; has served as Advisor to Advanced Research Projects Agency; Nat. Science Foundation; Defence Research Bd.; Nat. Bureau Standards; Atomic Energy Comn.; Past Chrmn. Div. of Atomic and Molecular Physics, Canada Assn. Physics 1972–73; Chrmn., CAP Div., Physics and Society, 1981–83; Past mem. Organ. Comte., Gaseous Electronics Conf. for Internat. Conf. on Physics of Electron & Atomic Collisions; Past Secy., Gaseous Electronics Conf.; Council mem., Electron & Atomic Physics Div., Am. Physical Soc. 1970–73; Co-Chrmn., NATO Adv. Study Inst. on Physics of Ion-Ion and Electron-Ion Collisions, Baddeck, N.S. 1981; Co-Chrmn., NATO Adv. Study Inst. on New Methods for Examining the Micro World, Baddeck, N.S. 1984; mem., Am. Phys. Soc. Panel on Pub. Affairs 1978–83; Founding Chrmn. POPA Subcomte. on Internat. Scientific Affairs (S.I.S.A.); Organizing Chrmn., A.P.S. Workshop on Focus of Physics on Sci. & Technol. for Development (Baddeck, Oct. 1980); Dir., A.P.S. Asian Summer Seminar, Antigonish and Baddeck, N.S. 1983; Secy. IUPAP Internat. Comm. on Physics for Devel. 1980–84; Coordination Ctte., I.U.P.A.P. General Assembly, Trieste, Italy 1984; apporteur for Global Seminar of Scientific and Eng. Socs. for Devel., (New Delhi, Dec. 1980); em., Council, Internat. Centre for Theoretical Physics Trieste, Italy, 1982–84; Pres. El., Assn. for Adv. of Sci. in Can. 1984; Founding Bd. Mem. and Pres., Assocs. of Sci. and Tech. 1984– ; Chrmn., Council Ont. Physics Depts. 1972–73; founding Chrmn., V.L.S.I. Study Group (Univ. of Western Ont.) 1980–82; Sr. Research Fellow, Northern Telecom Research Labs 1981; Co-organizer of V.L.S.I. Implementation Workshop (Ottawa) 1980; Founding Chrmn., V.L.S.I. Implementation Group, 1981–83; mem., NRC and NSERC Nat. Comtes for Development of a National Microelectronics Facility, 1982; mem. NSERC Comte., Indst. Post Doc. 1984–88; holds patent for 'Method and Apparatus for Sensing Gases,' USA 1968; rec'd Bart Griffen Mem. Award, St. Francis Xavier Univ.; mem. Organ. Committee, Gaseous Electronics Conf. 1973; Co-Ed., 'Gaseous Electronics – Some Applications,' 1974; 'The Excited State in Chemical Physics' Vol. 1 (1976), Vol 11 (1981); Electron-Ion and Ion-Ion Collisions (1983); author of over 150 published papers and books on Physics of Collisions of Atoms, Electrons, Ions, Positrons, Photons with Atoms, Ions, and Molecules and Solids, Science for Development and Science Policy; Development of VLSI microcircuits; Synchrotron Radiation Studies of Cells; Light Interaction with the Retina; mem., Amer. Physical Soc. (Fellow); Candn. Assn. Physicists; Am. Assn. Physics Teachers; Am. Assn. Advanc. Science (Fellow); Chem. Inst. of Can.; Amer. Vacuum Soc.; mem. of Pugwash Group; mem. and Vice Pres., Can. Comte. of Scientists & Scholars, 1980– ; mem. of Bd., Science for Peace, 1981– ; Pres., Assoc. for Advancement of Science in Can. 1984– ; Organizing Ctte., Nat. Conf. on Tech. and Innovation 1988; Bd. mem., Centre Bras d'Or, Baddeck NS 1984–88; Founding Chrmn., Sci. Tech. and You (STAY) London; Dir., London Symphony Orch.; London Regional Children's Museum; Ont. Science Centre; K. of C.; R. Catholic; recreations: singing, sailing, skiing; Home: 80 Waverley St., Ottawa, Ont. K2P 0V2.

**McGOWEN, Kenneth Cameron;** business executive; b. Toronto, Ont. 27 June 1935; s. Geoffry and Juliette (Roberge) M.; e. Toronto, Ont.; children: Kelly, Janice, David, Drew, Michelle; worked in the automobile bus. 1956–61; Founder Mac's Milk 1961 (Pres. 1961–72); Cloverlawn Investment 1972–81; Founder, Hasty Market Inc. 1981 (Pres. 1981–89); Dir., Mcdonald's Restaurants; Income Trust; Ont. Sci. Centre; received awards from Variety Club of Ont.; Variety Village; recreations: handball, scuba diving, skiing; Home: Apt. 5009, 44 Charles St. W., Toronto, Ont. M4Y 1R8.

**McGRAIL, John Simon,** M.D., M.Sc., Ph.D., M.S., D.L.O., F.R.C.S. (C); physician-surgeon; educator; b. Wakefield, Yorkshire, U.K. 28 May 1931; s. William Anthony and Dorothy (John) M.; e. Univ. of Manchester M.D. 1955; Univ. of Mich. M.S. 1964; D.L.O. (London, U.K.) 1957; F.R.C.S.(C.) 1964; m. Terry d. Aidan Jenkins 4 Apr. 1959; children: Susan, Mark, Christopher, Justin; PROFESSOR OF OTOLARYNGOLOGY, UNIV. OF TORONTO: Chief, Dept. of Otolaryn., Wellesley Hosp.; Consultant in Otolaryn. to Ont. Cancer Inst. and Princess Margaret Hosp.; Consultant Throat Specialist to Toronto theatres; Physician, Toronto Maple Leafs and Team Canada; Capt., R.A.M.C. 1956–58; came to Can. 1960; author various articles on head-and-neck and reconstructive surgery; Dir., Candn. Inst. of Facial Plastic Surgery; mem. Candn. Acad. of Sports Med.; Med. Comte., Internat. Ice Hockey Fedn.; Royal Soc. of Med. (London, U.K.); Candn. Med. Assn.; Acad. of Med.; Amer. Acad. of Facial Plastic and Reconstructive Surgery; Dir., Nat. Bd. of Candn. Counc. of Christians and Jews; Conservative; Roman Catholic; recreations: tennis, soccer, theatre; Home: 111 Harrison Rd., Willowdale, Ont. M2L 1W3; Office: 160 Wellesley St. E., Toronto, Ont. M4Y 1J3.

**McGRATH, Brian C.,** B.E., P.Eng.; executive; b. St. John's, Nfld. 12 Sept. 1928; s. Thomas David and Alice I. (Cron) McG.; e. Memorial Univ. of Nfld.; McGill Univ. B.E. (Mech. Eng.) 1950; m. Joyce d. Walter and May Dawe 6 Jan. 1955; children: John Desmond, Deborah Jane; Pres., Churchill Falls (Labrador) Corp. Ltd. 1979; Pres. and Dir., Twin Falls Power Corp. Ltd.; Vice Pres., Newfoundland Hydro; Vice pres. and Dir., Gull Island Power Co. Ltd.; Asst. to Chief Eng., Bowater Newfoundland Ltd. 1950–55; Plant Eng., Bowater Power Co. Ltd. 1955–64; Project Eng., Beothuk Engineering Co. Ltd. 1964–66; Mgr. Concrete Div., Lundrigans ltd. 1966–77; Vice Pres., Eng. and Constrn. Newfoundland Hydro 1977–79; mem., Candn. Elec.

Assn. (Dir.); Assn. Prof. Engs. Nfld. (Pres. 1971–72); recreations: yachting, fishing; Club: St. John's Rotary; Home: (P.O. Box 448) R.R.1, Paradise, Nfld. A0A 2E0.

**McGRATH, Edward Joseph,** LL.B.; lawyer; b. London, Ont. 19 Apl. 1942; s. Edward Stanislaus and Veronica Catherine (McConnell) McG.; e. Univ. of W. Ont. LL.B. 1968; Osgoode Hall Bar Admission 1970; m. Nancy C. d. Reginald and Barbara Lamon 19 Apl. 1969; three s. Jonathan, Simon, Nicholas; PARTNER, McGRATH BRAIDEN 1990– ; Dir. Suncor Inc. 1986–91; articled with John Labatt Ltd. (Corporate Counsel) and Judge David G. Humphrey, Toronto 1968–69; Sessional Lectr. Univ. of W. Ont. Law Sch. 1973–90, named Adjunct Prof. of Law 1991; Lamon, McGrath & Braiden 1985–90; Special Asst. Legal Affairs, Solr. Gen. of Ont. 1987–89; Asst. Dir. Bar Admission and Continuing Edn. Progs. Law Soc. Upper Can. 1985–91; Campaign Chrmn. Premier David R. Peterson 1975–90; Publications (Donelly's London) 1990; Home: 1346 Sprucedale Ave., London, Ont. N5X 2N8; Office 4 Covent Market Pl., London, Ont. N6A 1E2.

**McGRATH, Hon. James Aloysius,** P.C., K.St.J., LL.D. (Hon.); b. Buchans, Nfld. 11 Jan. 1932; s. Patrick Bernard and Mary Agnes (Cole) McG.; e. St. Patrick's Hall St. John's, Nfld.; St. Francis Xavier Univ. LL.D. (Hon.) 1979; Memorial Univ. of Nfld. LL.D. (Hon.) 1992; m. Margaret Smart, Westmount, Qué. 24 Sept. 1960; children: Kathleen, Caroline, Margaret-Moira, Joanna, Sean, Sheliagh; Lieutenant-Governor of Newfoundland 1986–91; served with RCAF; Radio and TV Extve. Nfld. 1953–56; Sec. P. Cons. Assn. Nfld. 1955–57; Candn. Nfld. Prov. 3. 1956; el. to H. of C. for St. John's E. gen. el. 1957, defeated 1963, re-el. 1968, re-el. since; Parlty. Sec. to Min. of Mines & Tech. Surveys 1962–63; Extve. Asst. to Leader of Opposition in Senate and Prov. Pres. Nfld. P. Cons. Assn. 1965–67; Official Opposition Spokesman for: Consumer & Corporate Affairs, Regional & Econ. Expansion 1968–72; Labour, Consumer Affairs 1972–74; Consumer Affairs, Housing & Urban Affairs 1974–79; Min. of Fisheries & Oceans 1979–80; Official Spokesman for: Health & Welfare, Housing Employment & Immigration, mem. Jt. Senate & H. of C. Ctte. on Constitution 1980–84; Chrmn. Special Ctte. on Reform of House of Commons 1984–85; mem. Trilateral Comn. and Internat. Council Parliamentarians for World Order 1984; Vice Chrmn. Candn. Br. Commonwealth Parlty. Assn. 1984; awarded Queen's Jubilee Medal; Knight, Order of St. John of Jerusalem; Knight, Grand Cross, Sovereign Mil. Order of Malta; Officer of the Order of the Red Cross; Humantarian award, Boys and Girls Clubs of Can.; Hon. Life Mem., Commonwealth Parliamentary Assoc.; awarded Churchill Soc. Award for Advancement of Parliamentary Democracy; el. Hon. Mem., Churchill Soc.; Hon. Chief of the Royal Newfoundland Constabulary; Founder, The Lt. Gov.'s Inst. on Family Life; mem. Royal Candn. Legion; Benevolent Irish Soc., Nfld.; R. Catholic; Residence: 5 Morris St., Ottawa, Ont. K1S 4A6.

**McGRATH, Malcolm Frederick,** B.A.Sc., P.Eng.; university administrator; b. Toronto, Ont. 29 Aug. 1932; s. Frederick William and Florence Sarah (Organ) M.; e. Univ. of Toronto, B.A.Sc. 1954; m. Joy d. William and Ivy Perry 2 Oct. 1954; children: Anne, Malcolm Jr., Michael, Amy; ASST. DEAN, FAC. OF APPL. SCI. & ENGR., UNIV. OF TORONTO 1982– ; Field Engr., Armstrong, Kingston & Hanson 1954–55; Project Mgr., & Vice-Pres., W.S. Perry Constr. 1956–61; Pres., McGrath Engr. Ltd. 1962–82; Citizenship Award, Assoc. of Prof. Engrs. of Ont. 1988; Dir., Dray Holdings Inc.; Muskoka Lakes Navigation Co.; Chrmn. (retired), Toronto Br., Royal Sch. of Church Music; Organist (retired), Timothy Eaton Mem. Ch.; Organist, Lake Joseph Community Church; Mem., Archit. Adv. Ctte., Un. Ch. of Can.; author: 'A Song for the Nation' 1972, 6 operettas composed for Arts & Letters Club (Libretto by J.G. Parr) & unpub. sacred solos & anthems; recreation: antique boats; Clubs: Royal Candn. Yacht; Arts & Letters; Home: 11 Thorncliffe Pk. Dr., Toronto, Ont.; Office: 35 St. George St., Toronto, Ont. M5S 1A4.

**McGRAW, Richard D.,** B.Com.; transportation executive; b. Vancouver, B.C. 12 Oct. 1943; s. John and Jean (Buckham) McG.; e. Univ. of B.C. B.Com. 1966; m. Gayle d. Jack and Shirley West 16 Apl. 1982; children: Lara, Ryan, Tyler, Morgan; PRES. AND CHIEF EXTVE. OFFR. VITRAN CORP. INC. 1983– ; Pres. and Chief Extve. Offr. Parkway Automotive Investments; Chrmn. and Chief Extve. Offr. Griffin Development Corp.; Dir., Exco Technologies Ltd.; recreation: skiing, tennis; Club: Toronto Lawn Tennis; Home: 22 Edgar Ave., Toronto, Ont. M4W 2A9; Office: 24 Mobile Dr., Toronto, Ont. M4A 1H9.

**McGREGOR, Michael H.,** B.A.Sc., P.Eng.; utilities executive; b. Chatham, Ont. 21 April 1936; s. Cameron McPherson and Edna Muriel (Rogers) McG.; e. Univ. of Toronto B.A.Sc. 1958; m. Penny d. Harry and Marjorie Dagley 27 Dec. 1965; children: Robert, Colin, Alexander; SR. VICE PRES. UNION GAS LTD. 1988– ; Vice Pres. Operations Fram Canada Inc. 1975–78, Extve. positions 1978–83, Vice Pres. and Gen. Mgr. 1983–85; Vice Pres. and Dir. of Operations Bendix Electronics Ltd. (previous co.) 1985–88; Mem. Bd. of Govs., Stratford Festival Theatre 1992– ; Trustee, Pub. Gen. Hosp. Chatham; mem. Assn. Profl. Engs. Prov. Ont.; recreation: golf; Club: Maple City Country (Chatham); Home: 900 Charing Cross Rd., Chatham, Ont. N7M 5H4; Office: 50 Keil Dr. N., Chatham, Ont. N7M 5M1.

**MCGREGOR, Stewart Donald,** B.A., LL.B.; petroleum executive; b. Calgary, Alta. 9 Feb. 1945; s. William Stewart and Verona Almeda (Rolls) M.; e. Univ. of Alta., B.A. 1966, LL.B. 1969; m. Barbara Louise d. E.K. (Bud) Upstone 24 June 1967; children: William Scott, Marla Louise; CHAIRMAN, NUMAC ENERGY INC. 1993– ; lawyer, Cormie Kennedy 1969–80; Partner 1973–80; Vice-Pres., Corp. Affairs, Numac Oil & Gas Ltd. 1980–84; Extve. Vice-Pres., 1984–92; Pres., C.O.O. & Dir., Giant Reef Petroleums Ltd. 1987–90 (company amalgated with Numac Oil & Gas Ltd.); Pres. & C.E.O., Numac Oil & Gas Ltd. 1992–93; Dir., Numac Oil & Gas Ltd. 1974– ; Northwestern Utilities Ltd. 1986– ; Bellanca Developments Ltd.; recreations: golfing, fishing; Club: Mayfair Golf and Country (Past Pres. & Gov.); Home: 4808 – 154 St., Edmonton, Alta. T6H 5K7; Office: 1400, 9915 – 108 St., Edmonton, Alta. T5J 2G8.

**McGREGOR, William Duncan,** broadcasting executive; b. Toronto, Ont. 3 June 1922; s. Duncan and Louise (Cook) McG.; e. elem. and high schs. Toronto and London, Ont.; Univ. of Toronto (Engineering); m. Ellen Eileen d. Ernest E. and Victoria McDonald 30 Dec. 1950; one d. Kelly; PRES. & DIR., C A P COMMUNICATIONS LTD. 1972– ; Radio Operator, CFRB Toronto 1947–50; Chief Engr. CKFH Toronto 1950–51; TV Instr. CBC Toronto 1951–53; Operations Mgr., Central Ontario Television Ltd. (now present Co.) Kitchener, Ont. 1953, Gen. Mgr. 1955, Vice Pres. and Gen. Mgr. 1965; Vice Chrmn. & C.E.O., Sunwapta Broadcasting Edmonton; Pres., Electrohome Communications; Vice-Pres., Electrohome Ltd. 1977– ; Chrmn. of Bd. CTV Television Network Ltd.; Dir., Economical Mutual Insurance Co.; The Missisquoi Insurance Co.; Rogers Communications Inc.; Rogers Canada Inc.; Rogers Cablesystems Ltd.; Rogers Broadcasting Ltd.; Sunwapta Broadcasting; Paul Mulvihill 1989; named CCBA Broadcaster of Yr. 1971; recipient Canada Medal 1972; CAB Howard Caine Mem. Award 1977; CAB Broadcast Hall of Fame 1990; Past Pres., Central Can. Broadcasters' Assn.; Past Pres., Candn. Assn. Broadcasters; Past Pres. & Dir., Kitchener Chamber Comm. (Pres. 1972–73); Chrmn., Kitchener Urban Renewal Comte. 1973–76; Mem. Bd. of Gov., Wilfrid Laurier Univ.; recreations: flying, travel; Clubs: Westmount Golf & Country; Waterloo-Wellington Flying; Rotary (Kitchener-Conestoga); University; Home: 36 Farmbrook Place, Kitchener, Ont. N2M 4K8; Office: 809 Wellington St. N., Kitchener, Ont. N2G 4J6.

**MCGUIGAN, Thomas J.,** B.A.Sc., P. Eng.; business executive; b. Toronto, Ont. 3 Jan. 1942; s. Thomas F. and Priscilla M. (Robitaille) M.; e. De La Salle Coll.; Univ. of Toronto, B.A. Sc. 1963; m. Ileana Petri 3 Aug. 1968; two children; PRESIDENT, LITTON SYSTEMS CANADA LIMITED 1986– ; Vice Pres., Litton Industries 1988– ; var. positions, Litton Systems Canada Limited 1963–71; Project Engr., Dir. Adv. Progs. 1971–81; Vice Pres., Mktg., Litton Systems Can. Ltd. 1981–86; Mem., APEO 1963; Office: 25 Cityview Dr., Etobicoke, Ont. M9W 5A7.

**McGUIRE, Daniel Malcolm;** video post-production consultant; b. Montréal, Qué. 5 Apr. 1936; s. Roy and Avis McRae Kapuskasing (Ont.) High Sch. 1954; Ryerson Polytech. Inst. 1954–57; m. Joan d. Harold and Mattie Leask 11 Sept. 1958; three s. Reginald Roy, Gordon Douglas, Brian Kenneth; Pres. & C.E.O., The Magnetic Enterprises Corp. consisting of The Magnetic North Corp., The Magnetic Fax Corp., The Master's Workshop Corp.; joined CHAT-TV Medicine Hat, Alta. 1957–60; Tech. Dir. CHCH-TV Hamilton, Ont. 1960–72; Operations Supr. Global Television Network 1972–82; mem. Adv. Bd. Radio & TV Arts Dept. Ryerson Polytech. Inst.; Adv. Ctte. Broadcasting-Radio & TV Dept. Niagara Coll. of Applied Arts & Technol.; mem. Soc. Motion Picture & TV Engs.; Home: 39 Peppertree Cres., Ancaster, Ont. L9G 4L8.

**McGUIRE, Frank Oliver;** university professor and administrator; b. Glasgow, Scotland 10 Aug. 1931; s. John and Elizabeth (McLeod) M.; e. Stowe College of Printing Glasgow Scotland Gold Medalist 1955; m. Katherine d. Jean and Stanley Dougal 30 May 1957; children: Sheila, Lesley, Ian; CHAIR, SCHOOL OF GRAPHIC COMMUNICATIONS MANAGEMENT, RYERSON POLYTECHNIC UNIV. 1987– ; Assoc. Dir., Communications, Nat. H.Q., Anglican Ch. of Canada; Salvation Army Printing & Pub. House 7 years; Dir., Printing & Pubs., McMaster Univ. 1969–75; Queen's Printer and Extve. Dir. of Communications Production, Prov. of Alta. 1975–80; Managing Director, The Canadian Encyclopedia, 1st ed. (largest pub. project in history of Candn. pub.) 1980–85; Pres., Frank McGuire and Assoc., Management Consultants 1985–87; Dir., Toronto Br., Candn. Printing Indus. Assn. 1987– ; Mem., Nat. Adv. Bd., National Atlas of Canada 1986–89, reapptd. 1989; Past Pres., Queen's Printer Assn. of Can. 1978; Past Chair, Graphic Arts Indus., Govt. Joint Apprenticeship Ctte., Prov. of Alta.; Mem., Steering Ctte., Alta. Heritage Learning Resources Project; Univ. of Alta. Pub. Adv. Ctte. 1984–86; Distinguished Service Award, Candn. Printing Indus. Assn. for contbns. over a 35-year period 1991; Hon. Life Mem., Alta. Printing Indus. Assn.; Chair, Steering Ctte., Keyano Swim Club 1982–83; Bd. Chair, St. Paul's Un. Ch. Edmonton 1980–81; recreations: tennis, golf, travel; clubs: Sherwood Forest Tennis, Aldershot Winter Tennis; Home: 1160 Augustus Dr., Burlington, Ont. L7S 2K5; Office: 350 Victoria St., Toronto, Ont. M5B 2K3.

**McHALE, John Joseph,** B.A.; retired sports executive; b. Detroit, Mich. 21 Sept. 1921; s. John M. and Catherine (Kelly) McH.; e. Cath. Central High Sch. 1939; Univ. of Notre Dame B.A. 1947; Central Mich. Coll.; Univ. of Detroit; Northwestern Univ.; m. Patricia Anne d. Raymond Cameron 15 Feb. 1947; children: John Jr., Patricia Cameron II, Kevin K., Anne F., Brian F., Mary M.; PRESIDENT, JAPAN SPORTS SYSTEMS NORTH AMERICA; Depy. Chrmn. & C.E.O., Montreal Baseball Club Ltd. 1987–92; Gen. Mgr. Detroit Tigers 1957–58; Pres. and Gen. Mgr., Milwaukee Braves 1959–65, Atlanta Braves 1966; Asst. Baseball Commr. New York 1967–68; Pres. & C.E.O. Montreal Baseball Club Ltd. 1968–86; Depy. Chrmn. & Dir., Montreal Baseball Club Ltd. 1988– ; Dir., Perini Corp.; RCM Mutual Fund; St. Mary's Hosp., West Palm Beach, Fla.; Baseball Hall of Fame; Monogram Club Univ. Notre Dame; mem. Adv. Bd. Coll. Arts & Letters Univ. Notre Dame; Trustee, Jacksonville Univ. FL; major league playing experience incls. games with Detroit Tigers 1945, 1947, 1948; pinch hitter 3 occasions during 1945 World Series; served with U.S. Navy 1943–45; R. Catholic; recreations: reading, music, handball, boating; Address: Harbour Ridge, 2014 Royal Fern Ct., Palm City, FL 34990 U.S.A.

**McHUGH, John Laurence,** M.A., Ph.D.; oceanographer (fisheries); university professor emeritus; b. Vancouver, B.C. 24 Nov. 1911; s. John and Annie Margaret (Woodward) McH.; e. Pub. and High Schs., New Westminster and Vancouver, B.C., 1928; Univ. of B.C., B.A. 1936, M.A. 1938; Univ. of Cal. (Los Angeles) and Scripps Inst. of Oceanography, Ph.D. 1950; m. Sophie Kleban 30 Mar. 1979; children (by former marriage): Peter Chadwick, Heather, Jan Margaret; PROF. EMERITUS OF MARINE RESOURCES, MARINE SCIENCES RESEARCH CENTER, STATE UNIV. OF N.Y. 1982– (Prof. of Marine Resources there 1970–82); Scient. Asst., Fisheries Rsch. Bd. of Can. 1938–41 and 1945–46; Rsch. Asst., Scripps Inst. of Oceanography 1946–48; Rsch. Assoc. 1948–51; Dir., Va. Fisheries Lab. and Prof. of Marine Biol., Coll. of William and Mary 1951–59; Chief, Div. of Biol. Rsch., U.S. Dept. of Interior, Bureau of Comm. Fisheries 1959–63; Asst. Dir for Biol. Rsch. 1963–66; Depy. Dir. of Bureau 1966–68; Acting Dir., Office of Marine Resources, Dept. of Interior 1968–70; Head, Office for Internat. Decade of Ocean Exploration, Nat. Science Foundation 1970; Consultant, Nat. Council on Marine Resources & Engn. Devel. 1970–71; served with Candn. Scot. Regt. 1940–44; Queen's Own Cameron Highlanders of Winnipeg 1944–45; rank Capt. on discharge; U.S. Commr., Inter-Am. Tropical Tuna Comn. 1960–70; Chrmn., Internat. Whaling Comn. (Vice-Chrmn. 1968–71, Chrmn. 1971–72 and Commr. 1961–72); mem. Adv. Comte. on Marine Resources Rsch. to Dir.-Gen., Food and Agric. Organ. of U.N. 1965–69; mem. Nat. Rsch. Council (USA) 1965–70 and U.S. Nat. Comte. Internat. Biol. Program 1967–70; mem. Comte. on Internat. Marine Science Affairs Policy of Ocean Bd., Nat. Acad. Sciences; Mid-Atlantic Fishery Mgmt. Council 1976–79; Scientific and Statistical Comte. of Council 1980–84; Fellow, Woodrow Wilson Internat. Centre for Scholars 1971; M.S.R.C. Distinguished Teaching Award 1977; Head or mem. of U.S. dels. to numerous internat. fishery meetings; Emeritus mem. Bd. of Trustees, Internat. Oceanographic Foundation, Coral Gables, Fla.; citation for exceptional service, cert. of Hon. Membership, Nat. Shellfisheries Assn. 1984; Award of Excellence and bronze medal, Am. Fisheries Soc. 1984; consultant at various times to Smithsonian Institution, Riverside Research Institute (N.Y.), Town of Islip (LI.); author of 181 scient. papers, tech. articles, and one book; mem., Am. Inst. Fishery Research Biols.; Am. Fisheries Soc.; Nat. Shellfisheries Assn.; Va. Acad. Science (Past Chrmn., Biol. Sec.); Atlantic Estuarine Rsch. Soc. (Past. Pres., Hon mem.); Beta Theta Pi (Past Secy.); Sigma Xi; Home: 150 Strathmore Gate Dr., Stony Brook, N.Y. 11790; Office: Stony Brook, N.Y. 11794-5000.

**McHUGHEN, Alan G.,** B.Sc. (Hons.), D.Phil., MIBiol, CBiol; research scientist/educator; b. Ottawa, Ont. 13 Apr. 1954; s. Gordon Patrick and Olive Blanche (Urquhart) M.; e. Dalhousie Univ., B.Sc. (Hons.) 1976; Oxford Univ. (Magd. Coll.), D.Phil. 1979; m. P. Jane d. Patrick and Ann B. Billinghurst 12 July 1980; children: Stephanie Alexandra, Nicola Amy; ADJUNCT PROF., UNIV. OF SASKATCHEWAN 1984– and RSCH. SCI., BIOTECHNOL. 1985– ; Rsch. Fellow/Lectr., Yale Univ. 1979–82; Rsch. Fellow, Royal Comn. for the Exhib. of 1851; NATO; Robert B. Anderson Fellow in Biochem.; Profl. Rsch. Assoc., Crop Devel. Ctr., Univ. of Sask. 1982–85; mem., Candn. Bot. Assn.; Internat. Assn. Plant Tissue Culture; Candn. Soc. Plant Molecular Biol.; Genetics Soc. Can.; Soc. Exper. Biol.; Cons. to var. firms on genetic manipulation in plants; 1st Candn. to patent higher life form created through biotechnol. methods (US 4,616,100); co-developed Canada's first Somaclonal variant crop cultivar (Andro flax); author of sci. articles & reviews; recreations: outdoor sports, family activities; Home: 659 Whiteswan Dr., Saskatoon, Sask. S7K 8A2; Office: Crop Development Centre, Univ. of Saskatchewan, Saskatoon, Sask. S7N 0W0.

**McINNES, David Leslie,** B.S.F.; forest industry executive; b. Nelson, B.C. 19 May 1928; s. Malcolm Leslie and Grace (MacPherson) McI.; e. Univ. of B.C., B.S.F. 1953; m. Winifred Marie, d. J. Archie Millar, 2 May 1953; 4 children; CHRMN. AND DIR., WEYERHAEUSER CANADA LTD.; employed in coastal region of B.C. for 2 yrs. following graduation; moved to interior 1966 and worked in lumber business acquired by present firm 1965; Vice-Pres. & Dir., Wood Products & Timberlands 1970; Pres. 1973; Pres. & Chief Extve. Offr. 1976–93; Past Chrmn., Pulp and Paper Rsch. Inst. of Canada; Past Chrmn., Council of Forest Indus. of B.C.; Past Chrmn., Candn. Pulp & Paper Assn.; Forest Engr. Rsch. Inst. of Can.; B.C. Forestry Education Found.; Dir., Pulp & Paper Indus. Relns. Bur., COFI, CPPA; Mem., Forest Sector Adv. Counc., Govt. of Can.; Past Chair, Dean's Adv. Ctte., U.B.C. Fac. of Forestry; recreations: boating, fishing,; Clubs: Vancouver; Home: 1378 Chartwell Dr., W. Vancouver, B.C. V7S 2R5; Office: 11th Flr., 1100 Melville St., Vancouver, B.C. V6E 4A6.

**McINNES, Donald,** O.C., Q.C., LL.D., D.C.L.; b. Halifax, N.S. 4 Apr. 1904; s. Hector and Charlotte (MacNeill) M.; e. Ashbury Coll., Ottawa; Dalhousie Univ.; m. Constance, d. E.L. Rowan-Legg, 18 June 1932; children: Hector, Stewart, Roderick, Ann; Retired Sr. Partner, McInnes, Cooper and Robertson 1946–92; Hon. Director, The Bank of Nova Scotia; read law with Hector McInnes, K.C.; called to the Bar of N.S. 1926; cr. K.C. 1941; Pres., Candn. Bar Assn., 1960–61; Conservative; Un. Church; Clubs: Saraguay; Halifax; Office: 1601 Lower Water St., Halifax, N.S. B3J 3P6.

**McINNES, Donald P. (Peter),** M.L.A.; politician; b. Pictou, N.S. 19 Dec. 1933; s. J. Logan and Jennie M.; e. Pictou Academy; Nova Scotia Agric. Coll.; m. Jennie 1956; children: Carol, Karen, Teri, Lynn; Min. of Agriculture & Marketing, Prov. of N.S. 1992; owned and operated dairy farm RR 2 Pictou; 1st el. to N.S. legis. 19 Sept. 1978; re-el. 1981, 1984, 1988, 1993; apptd. Min. of the Environment & Min. resp. for the Status of Women 22 Apr. 1988; appt. Min. of Fisheries 5 Jan. 1989; reappt. Min. resp. for the Status of Women 5 Jan. 1989; Min. of Transportation & Communications 1990–91; Min. of Consumer Affairs 1991–92; Former Chrmn., Scotsburn Co-op. Serv. Limited; Past Pres., N.S. Holstein Assn.; Dir. & Former Mgr., Pictou Exhib.; Past Dir., Dairy Farmers of Can.; Past Sec., Pictou Co. Fed. of Agric.; Chrmn., N.S. Govt. Caucus 23 Jan. 1984; Chrmn., Bd. of Stewards, Lyons Brook Uc. Ch.; Past Master, New Caledonia Lodge No. 11; Past Chrmn., Municipal Sch. Bd.; Past Leader, 4-H Orgn.; Past Pres., Pictou West P.C. Assn.; Assoc. Mem., Royal Candn. Legion, Br. 16; Mem., Scottish Cultural Soc.; recreations: golfing; clubs: Pictou Golf & Country; Home: Lyons Brook, R.R. #2, Pictou, N.S. B0K 1H0; Office: Province House, P.O. Box 1617, Halifax, N.S. B3J 2Y3.

**McINNES, Douglas Norman,** B.A., B.L.S.; librarian (retired); b. Melita, Man. 22 Sept. 1933; s. Norman and Clarice (McKinney) M.; e. Univ. of B.C. B.A. 1955, Professional Teaching Certificate 1957, B.L.S. 1963; Sorbonne, Paris, Certificat 1956; m. Emily d. Clarence Gordon and Marion Campbell 16 Aug. 1957; children: Alison, Scott; Biomedical Librarian, Univ. of B.C. 1989–91 (retired); Secondary School Teacher 1957–62; Librarian, Special Collections Div., U.B.C. 1963–64, Biomedical Librarian, 1964–67, Asst. Univ. Librarian for Pub. Services 1967–81, Acting Univ. Lib. 1981–82, Univ. Librarian 1982–89; mem., Can Lib. Assn. Council 1967–70; Chrmn., Candn. Lib. Assn. A.C.B.L.F. (Assn. Canadienne des Bibliothecaires de Langue Française) Liaison Comte. 1969–70; Dir., Candn. Assn. of Coll. & Univ. Libraries 1976–77; Chrmn., C.L.A. Structural Comte. 1970–72; Dir., Candn. Assn. of Rsch. Libraries 1983–89; Pres., Candn. Assn. of Rsch. Libraries 1987–89; Mem., Adv. Bd. for Sci. & Tech. Infor. (CISTI) 1986–89; Adv. Bd. to Centre for Chinese Rsch. Materials 1983–85; co-author 'A Survey and Interpretation of the Literature of Interlibrary Loan' 1975; 'Interlibrary Loan in Canada: A Report of a Survey' 1975; recipient French Govt. Scholarship 1955–56; Vancouver Sun Scholarship 1951–55; Mary Stewart McInnes Memorial Schol. 1953–54; Dorothy M. Jefferd Schol. 1962–63; Gold Medal, U.B.C. School of Librarianship 1963; recreation: golf; Club: Sudden Valley Golf; Home: 3171 W. 26 Ave., Vancouver, B.C. V6L 1V9.

**MCINNES, The Hon. Stewart D.,** P.C., Q.C., B.A., LL.B.; politician; lawyer; b. Halifax, N.S. 24 July 1937; s. Donald and Constance B. (Rowan-Legg) M.; e. Ashbury Coll.; Dalhousie Univ., B.A. 1958, LL.B. 1961; m. Shirley d. Robert and Thelma Bowness 29 Dec. 1984; children: Donald, Janet, Edward, Sarah, Constance; MIN. OF PUBLIC WORKS AND MIN. RESPONSIBLE FOR CMHC 1986; Partner, McInnes, Cooper & Robertson 1961–84; el. to House of Commons 1984; apptd. Parliamentary Sec., Min. of Internat. Trade 1984; Min. of Supply & Services 1985–86; Dir., Arbitration and Mediation Institute of Can.; Former Mem., Security Intelligence Review Ctte.; Dir., Care Canada; Chrmn., Mayor's Task Force on Drugs for the City of Halifax; Dir., Halifax Foundation; Pres., North British Soc. of Halifax; Trustee, St. Matthews Church; Pres., The Halifax Club; Pres., Iona Resources Ltd.; Dir., First Mortgage Nova Scotia Funds I, II, III; Dir., Western Keltic Mines Ltd.; Former Pres., Candn. Bar Assn. (N.S.); Mem., N.S. Bar Soc.; Former Dir., Law Found. of N.S.; Halifax Bd. of Trade; Mem., Bd. of Former Gov., Dalhousie Univ.; Former Bd., Grace Maternity Hosp.; Past Pres., School for Blind; Former Pres., Hearing & Speech Clinic; Former Dir., Duke of Edinburgh Award Prog. in N.S.; Former Dir., Pan Am. Wheelchair Games; Chrmn., United Way Annual Campaign 1976; Past Pres., Halifax P.C. Assn.; recreations: squash (former N.S. champ.), tennis (prov. ranked player), skiing, gardening; Home: 490 Francklyn St., Halifax, N.S. B3H 1A9.

**McINNIS, Douglas George,** C.A., B.Comm.; financial executive; b. Owen Sound, Ont. 7 June 1956; s. George Herbert and Margaret Ruth (Alcox) M.; e. McMaster Univ. B.Comm. 1979; m. Deborah d. Charles and Shirley Statham 20 July 1991; children: Steven; VICE-PRES., FINANCE & CHIEF FINANCIAL OFFICER, CORPORATE FOODS LIMITED 1990– ; Audit Sr., Coopers & Lybrand 1979–83; Chief Financial Offr., Jannock Imaging Companies Limited (& predecessor cos.) 1983–88; Chief Financial Offr., Corporate Foods Ltd. 1988–90; Mem., Candn. Inst. of C.A.s; Home: 52 Beaver Bend Cres., Etobicoke, Ont. M9B 5R3; Office: 10 Four Seasons Place, Etobicoke, Ont. M9B 6H7.

**McINNIS, Nadine Patricia,** B.A., M.A.; writer, poet; b. Belleville, Ont. 20 Sept. 1957; d. Charles Everett and Corinne (Connor) M.; e. Univ. of Ottawa B.A. (Hons.) 1981, M.A. 1992; m. Tim d. William and Laura Fairbairn 12 July 1982; m. Nadia, Owen; author: 'Shaking the Dreamland Tree' 1986, 'The Litmus Body' 1992 (poetry); Winner, 1st place, 1992 Nat. Poetry Context; Co-editor, 'Arc' (a literary journal devoted to poetry, reviews & articles about poetry); Mem., League of Canadian Poets; Home: 230 Mart Circle, Ottawa, Ont. K1K 2W9.

**McINNIS, Robert Francis Michael (R.F.M.);** artist; b. Saint John, N.B. 11 March 1942; s. Frank E. and Phillis Mary Florence (Groves) McI.; e. Saint John Vocational Sch. Dip. in Fine & Applied Arts 1961; one s. Duncan Angus Robert; joined RCAF as Photographer 1962–66; Graphic Illustrator, Transport Can. 1966–67; Artist-in-Residence and Head of Art Dept. Prince George (B.C.) Coll. 1968–70; painting career since 1970; one-man exhns. incl. Kinsman-Robinson Gallery (Toronto), Roberts Gallery (Toronto), Masters Gallery (Calgary), Wallacks Gallery (Ottawa), Walter Klinkhoff Gallery (Montréal), West End Gallery (Edmonton), Canadian Art Gallery (Calgary), Rodman Hall (St. Catharines, Ont.); rep. in numerous private and pub. colls. incl. Hart House Univ. of Toronto, Edmonton Art Gallery, H. of C. Ottawa, Rideau and Petroleum Clubs; comns. incl. copies Tom Thompson paintings for Joyce Wieland movie 'The Far Shore'; Peter Pocklington portrait; portraits of Fed. P. Cons. leaders to hang in nat. Hdqrs. bldg.; oil rig paintings Alta. Govt.; paintings presented by Prime Min. to Premier of Rumania and Prime Min. of Japan; author 'The Renegade's Lament' poetry 1974; co-author 'Toronto We Love You' drawings & poems 1974; 'Steel and Steam' series train paintings, text by Pierre Berton (presented to HRH Prince Charles and Lady Dianne by the Prime Minister as Canada's gift during Expo in Vancouver) 1986; 10 mth. Sabbatical to paint in Comte Charlevoix, Qué., winter 1991–92; moved to Southern Alta. to paint landscapes of area 1993; mem. various Candn. hist. railway assns.; Address: Box 658, Nanton, Alta. T0L 1R0.

**McINNIS, Robert John;** association executive, airline captain; b. Port Arthur, Ont. 15 May 1949; m. Denise A. d. John W. and Patricia McDevitt Aug. 1993; children: Jason Christopher, Amy Louise, Scott Andrew, Robert Daniel; PRES., CANDN. AIR LINE PILOTS ASSN. 1990– ; Capt. Canadian Airlines 1986– ; Flying Instructor London Flying Club 1968; Second Offr. Cdn. 1971, First Offr. 1976; 1st VP present assn. 1988–90; recreations: private flying, skiing; Home: R.R.2, Keene, Ont. K0L 2G0; Office: 1300 Steeles Ave. E., Brampton, Ont. L6T 1A2.

**McINTIRE, Carl Thomas,** B.A., M.A., M.Div., Ph.D.; professor of history; b. Philadelphia, Pa. 4 Oct. 1939; s. Charles Curtis and Fairy Eunice (Davis) M.; e. Shelton Coll. B.A. (magna cum laude) 1961; Univ. of Penn. M.A. 1962, Ph.D. 1976; Faith Theol. Sem., M.Div. 1966; m. Rebekah d. Elmer and Jane Smick 7 June 1980; children: Gabrielle, Eliot, Matthias, Olivia; PROF. OF THE HIST. OF CHRISTIANITY, TRINITY COLL., UNIV. OF TORONTO 1988– ; T.A., Univ. of Penn. 1964–65; Instr., Shelton Coll. 1965–67; Instr. then Asst. Prof., Trinity Christian Coll. 1967–71 (Chair 1970–71); Sr. Mem., Inst. for Christian Studies 1973–84 (Chair 1977–80, 1982); Assoc. Prof., Trinity Coll., Univ. of Toronto 1984–88 (Mem., Extve. Ctte. of Corp. 1986–88, 1989–92; Chair, Sesquicentennial Ctte. 1987–92, Chair, Institutional Self-Study, 1989–91, Dir. of Advanced Degree Studies 1992–93); Mem., Dept. of History, Univ. of Toronto 1984– ; Mem., Centre for Religious Studies/Centre for the Study of Religion, Univ. of Toronto 1982– ; Vis. Scholar, Cambridge Univ., (Emmanuel Coll.) 1971–73; (Peterhouse) 1977, 1980, 1986; Jawalharlal Nehru Univ. 1980–81; Univ. di Firenze 1988–89; Vis. Prof., Univ. Can. en France 1988–93; Mem., Inst. of Hist Rsch., Univ. of London 1981; Chair., Hist. Dept., Toronto Sch. of Theol. 1985–88, 1989–90; Mem., Extve. Ctte., Ctr. for Religious Studies, Univ. of Toronto 1986–88, 1991–92; Assoc. Dir. for Graduate Studies, Centre for the Study of Religion, Univ. of Toronto 1992– ; Mem., Extve. Ctte. 1992– ; fellowships: Weaver 1967–68; Nat. Endowment for the Humanities 1967–68; recipient of 10 rsch. grants; Anglican; NDP; Mem., Candn. & Am. Socs. of Ch. Hist., Am. Hist. Assn.; Victorian Studies Assn. of Ont.; Candn. Ch. Hist. Soc.; author: 'The Ongoing Task of Christian Historiography' 1974; 'England Against the Papacy, 1858–61' 1983; 'Christian Views of History' 1987; 'Butterfield as Historian' forthcoming; ed./co-ed. of six scholarly books; recreations: travel, tennis, basketball; Home: 321 Carlton St., Toronto, Ont. M5A 2L8; Office: Toronto, Ont. M5S 1H8.

**McINTOSH, David Norman,** B.A.; writer; b. Sherbrooke, Que. 24 Aug. 1921; s. Gordon Leslie and Bernice Isabella (Mallory) M.; e. Wesleyan Coll. 1939; Univ. of Toronto, Victoria Coll., B.A. 1942; m. Jean d. John Margaret MacKinnon 1950; children: Kirk, Ian; Royal Candn. Air Force 1942–45; Def., Fgn. & Pol. Corr., Candn. Press News Agency 1946–72; writer, filmmaker, Nat. Capital Comn. 1972–80; Dept. Hist., Customs & Excise 1980–87; Distinguished Flying Cross; author: 'Terror in the Starboard Seat' 1980, 'The Seasons of My Youth' 1984, 'The Collectors: A History of Canadian Customs and Excise' 1984, 'Ottawa Unbuttoned' 1987; 'When the Work's All Done This Fall' 1989; 'High Blue Battle' 1990; 'Visits' 1990; 'Lots of Guys My Age Are Dead' forthcoming 1994; Home: 856 Iroquois Rd., Ottawa, Ont. K2A 3N2; Office: Parliamentary Press Gall., House of Commons, Ottawa, Ont. K1A 0A6.

**McINTOSH, Duncan Charles;** director/actor; b. Cornwall, Ont.; s. Duncan Ambrose and Patricia Marion (Cameron) McI.; e. Gen. Vanier Secondary Sch. Cornwall; Ryerson Theatre Sch. Ryerson Polytech. Inst. 1978; ARTISTIC DIRECTOR, THEATRE PLUS TORONTO 1990– ; Dir., Vancouver Playhouse: 'Much Ado About Nothing'; Dir., Theatre Plus Toronto: 'Martin Guerre,' 'Old Times,' 'Le Bal,' 'Summer and Smoke,' 'The Marriage of Figaro' (Co-adapted), 'Jack Scapino!' (Co-adapted with Richard Binsley from Molier's 'Les Fourberies de Scapin'); Shaw Festival: (Director) 'Peer Gynt,' 'Peter Pan,' 'Once in a Lifetime,' 'Fanny's First Play,' 'Marathon 33,' 'Holiday,' 'The Women,' 'Roberta'; (Co-Director) 'War and Peace,' 'Girl Crazy'; (Co-Dir. & Choreographer) 'Cavalcade'; (Choreographer) 'Naughty Marietta,' 'The Vortex,' 'The Skin of Our Teeth'; (Ass't. to Denise Coffey) 'Simpleton of the Unexpected Isles'; Dir., The Royal Alexandra Theatre/Shaw Production 'The Women'; Dir., The Candn. Opera Co.: 'The Marriage of Figaro'; Dir., Theatre New Brunswick 'Scapino'; Dir., Tarragon Theatre: 'Farther West' (recipient, Chalmers Award), 'Being At Home With Claude'; Dir., Factory Theatre 'Souvenirs'; Dir., Press Theatre 'Special Occasions'; Dir. & Actor, Film & TV (7 episodes) 'Hangin' In'; Actor, Theatre Plus Toronto: 'Jack Scapino!,' 'Saint Joan'; Actor, Shaw Festival: 'Back to Methusaleh,' 'Madwoman of Chaillot,' 'Androcles & The Lion,' 'Cyrano de Bergerac,' 'Caesar & Cleopatra,' 'Pygmalion,' 'Camille,' 'Saint Joan,' 'The Suicide'; Actor, Theatre Calgary 'Cloud 9'; Actor, Theatre London: 'Gwendoline,' 'The Proudfoot Papers'; Actor, Charlottetown Festival: 'Anne of Green Gables,' 'Windsor,' 'Legend of the Dumbells'; Actor, Young Peoples Theatre: 'Really Rosie'; Actor, Film & TV: 'Zero Patience,' 'Ticket to Heaven,' 'Incubus,' 'The Calling,' 'Dead Lines,' 'Double Negative'; Co-founder with C. Newton, The Academy of the Shaw Festival, Principal of the Acad. 1984–89; Dramaturge, The Candn. Opera Co., New Candn. Operas 'Realitillusion' and 'An Expensive Embarrassment'; Acting Coach, The Candn. Opera Co. Ensemble 1987, 1988; Teacher, Ryerson Theatre School, Niagara College, Maggie Bassett Studio; Bd. of Dirs., Toronto Theatre Alliance; mem. Candn. Actors Equity; Profl. Assn. Candn. Theatres; Home: 99 Harcourt Ave., Toronto, Ont. M4J 1J3.

**McINTOSH, H. Ian,** B.A., F.S.A., F.C.I.A.; retired insurance executive; b. Toronto, Ont. 25 June 1930; s. Harvey E. and Marion (Williams) M.; e. Lawrence Park C.I. 1948; Univ. of Toronto B.A. 1952; m. Frances d. Harold and Elsa Rothaermel 12 Sept. 1953; children: Kathryn, Carol, David, John; Vice Chrmn. Bd. of Dirs., Equitable Life Insur. Co. of Canada 1992, retired; joined Equitable Life Insur. Co. of Canada 1952; Asst. Actuary 1955; Vice-Pres. & Actuary 1968; Sr. Vice-Pres. & Chief Actuary 1981; Sr. Vice-Pres. & Chief Mktg. Offr. 1985; Pres. & C.E.O. 1987–92; Mem., Candn. Inst. of Actuaries (former Counc. Mem., Vice-Pres.); Bd. of Dirs., Freeport Hosp.; recreations: golf, curling, travel; clubs: Westmount Golf & Country (Past Pres.); Home: 555 Leighland Dr., Waterloo, Ont. N2T 2H4.

**McINTOSH, Hilton Alexander,** Q.C., LL.M.; b. Saskatoon, Sask. 8 Sept. 1930; s. Ranzo and Mary (Rennie) McI.; e. Caswell Hill Pub. Sch. and Bedford Rd. Coll. Inst., Saskatoon, 1948; Univ. of Sask., B.A. 1951, LL.B. 1953; Dalhousie Univ. (Sir James Dunn Scholar), LL.M. 1955; DIR., LEGISLATIVE DRAFTING PROGRAMME, FACULTY OF LAW, COMMON LAW SECTION, UNIV. OF OTTAWA 1986– ; read law with W.B. Francis, Q.C.; called to Bar of Sask. 1954; cr. Q.C. 1971; Lectr. in Leg., Univ. of Ottawa (Common Law) 1961–75; Secretary, Nat. Council on Adm. of Justice in Can. 1967–76; mem. Leg. Sec., Dept. of Justice 1956–70; Jr. Adv. Counsel 1956; Sr. Adv. Counsel 1959; Dir., Dept. of Justice, Privy Council Sec. 1970–75; Asst. Depy. Min. (Leg. Programming), Dept. of Justice 1975–86; mem. Conf. of Commrs. on Uniformity of Leg. 1959–66; Chrmn., Statute Revision Comm. of Can. 1976–86; served with COTC, Univ. of Sask. 1948–53; rank Lt.; Gov. Gen.'s Foot Guards 1956–58; rank Capt.; mem., Law Soc. Sask.; Commonwealth Assoc. of Legislative Counsel; Candn. Assoc. of Law Teachers; Internat. Comn. Jurists; Protestant; recreations: reading, travel, tennis; Club: Faculty (Univ. of Ottawa); Home: 111 Wurtemburg St., Apt. 1103, Ottawa, Ont. K1N 8M1; Office: 57 Louis Pasteur Priv., Ottawa, Ont. K1N 6N5.

**McINTOSH, Lawrie Gandier,** B.A.Sc., M.S.; product design consultant; b. Clinton, Ont. 24 June 1924; s. Rev. William Donald and Margaret Almina (Nicholson) McI.; e. Univ. of Toronto B.A.Sc. (Mech. Engn.) 1946; Ill. Inst. of Technol. M.S. (Product Design) 1951; Mass. Inst. Technol. various summer courses; m. Helen Kathleen d. Frederick William Cameron 17 Sept. 1949; children: Cameron Lawrie, Wanda Lee; PROP., LAWRIE McINTOSH DESIGN LTD. 1951– ; completed projects incl. products in indust., agric., comm. and inst., consumer fields; Dir., Cameron Enterprises Ltd.; winner various competitions and awards incl. N.D.C. Chair Competition 1952; Dipl. Di Medaglia D'oro Milan 1956; Stainless Steel Competition 1961; Candn. Souvenir Competition 1966; Citation by the National Design Council, Design Canada and the Assoc. of Candn. Industrial Designers, in recognition of outstanding achievement and contribution to the practice of design and the profession of design in Canada, 1981; Consulting Tech. Ed. 'Product Design and Engineering' 6 yrs.; occasional lectr. various univs. and community colls. Can.; mem. Assn. Prof. Engrs. Prov. Ont.; United Church; recreations: fishing; Home: 12 – 1330 Mississauga Valley Blvd., Mississauga, Ont. L5A 3T1; Office: Box 1436 Stn. B, Mississauga, Ont. L4Y 4G2.

**McINTOSH, Robert Lloyd,** M.B.E., B.A., Ph.D., D.Sc., F.R.S.C., F.C.I.C.; educator; b. Montreal, Que. 16 Feb. 1915; s. Alexander Douglas and Bella (Marcuse) McI.; e. Halifax (N.S.) Pub. Schs. and Halifax Co. Acad. (Harris Gold Medallist); Dalhousie Univ., B.A. 1935, M.Sc. 1936; McGill Univ., Ph.D. 1939, D.Sc. (Hon. Causa) 1972; m. Margaret Jean, d. late Harcourt V. Callaghan 31 March 1966; children: Sharon (Mrs. J.T. Lamb), Janet (Mrs. P.T. Truant), Alec; EMERITUS PROFESSOR OF CHEMISTRY, QUEEN'S UNIV. 1979– ; Offr. i/c Extramural Rsch., Directorate Chem. Warfare & Smoke 1940–45; Assoc. Prof. and Prof., Univ. of Toronto 1948–54; Prof. and Head Dept. of Chem. present Univ. 1961; Assoc. Dean (Sciences) Faculty of Arts & Science present Univ. 1969; Dean, Sch. of Grad. Studies, Queen's Univ. 1970–79; Dir., Off. of Occupational Health and Safety, Queen's Univ. 1982–83; mem. Scient. Adv. Comte., Candn. Soc. for Weizmann Inst. Science; awards incl. Royal Exhn. of 1851 Scholar. 1939; Chem. Educ. Award, Chem. Inst. Can. 1972; author of 'Dielectric Behavior of Physically Adsorbed Gases' N.Y. 1966 and over 60 articles in scient. journs. in field of physical chem.; recreation: sailing; Clubs: Kingston (Ont.) Yacht; Home: 185 Ontario St., Unit 607, Kingston, Ont. K7L 2Y7.

**McINTYRE, Colin James;** dance administrator; b. Edinburgh, Scot. 18 Oct. 1944; s. George Gibson and Edna May McI.; e. George Watson's Coll. Edinburgh 1960; Rose Bruford Coll. Sidcup, Kent 1963–64; m. Suzanne Lavigne 21 June 1980; one s. Philippe George; Tutor in Tech Theatre Rose Bruford Coll. 1964–67; Stage Mgr. London Festival Ballet Eng. 1967–70; Stage Dir. and Prodn. Mgr. Calouste Gulbenkian Found. Lisbon, Portugal 1970–74; Adm. and Dir. Prodns. present ballet co. 1974, Dir. Gen. 1975–84, 1988, mem. Artistic Direction 1978– ; Pres. Candn. Assn. Profession Dance Orgns. 1981–84, 1990– ; Head of Policy Secretariat Can. Council 1986–88; author: 'Road Signs: A Guide to Foreign Touring' 1986; Address: 751 Chemin du Lac St-Louis, Ville de Léry, Qué. J6N 3B8.

**McINTYRE, Hon. J. Roger,** B.A., LL.B.; judge; b. Charlo, N.B. 8 Feb. 1941; s. Donat and Victoria (Des-Rosiers) McI.; e. Charlo Elem. Sch. 1956; Bathurst (N.B.) Coll. 1959; St. Dunstan's Univ. P.E.I., B.A. 1964; Dalhousie Univ. Law Sch., LL.B. 1968; m. Mariette d. Amédée and Claire Paulin 27 Feb. 1979; children: Ryan Patrick, Dominique Andrée, Marie Claude; JUDGE, COURT OF QUEEN'S BENCH OF N.B. 1990– ; called to Bar of N.B. 1968; gen. law practice Dalhousie, N.B. 1969–85; Founder and Sr. Partner, McIntyre & McIntyre 1969–85; Judge, Provincial Court of N.B. 1985–90; mem. Barristers Soc. N.B.; Candn. Bar Assn.; R. Catholic; Home: 1150 Ocean Ridge Dr., Bathurst, N.B. E2A 4R6; Office: (P.O. Box 5001) Court of Queen's Bench, Bathurst, N.B. E2A 3Z9.

**McINTYRE, John George Wallace,** B.Com., M.B.A.; executive; b. Toronto, Ont. 26 July 1920; s. late Dr. George Crerar and late Gwendolyn Alberta (Wallace) McI.; e. Univ. of Toronto Schs., 1937; Univ. of Toronto, B.Com. 1941; Harvard Grad. Sch. of Business Adm., M.B.A. 1947; m. late Ruth Elizabeth; children: Angus, Heather, Robert, Anne; CONSULTANT ON MANAGEMENT, BUSINESS PLANNING, REAL ESTATE, AND PROJECT DEVELOPMENT; Budget Acct., Abitibi Paper Co. 1947; Budget Mgr., Ford Motor Co. of Canada Ltd. 1951 subsequently becoming Asst. Controller and Extve. Asst. to Vice Pres. Overseas Operations; Asst. Gen. Mgr., Windsor Mfg. Operations 1958, Gen. Mgr. 1963–65; Asst. Mang. Dir., Ford Australia 1958, Mang. Dir. 1959–63; Extve. Vice Pres., Columbia Cellulose Ltd., Vancouver 1965, Pres. 1966; joined Hudson's Bay Company as Pres., Ruperts Land Trading Co. and Gen. Mgr. Retail Devel. 1967, Vice Pres., Retail Development and Distribution, Pres., Hudson's Bay Developments Ltd.; Dir., Markborough Properties Ltd. to 1984; Vice Pres. and Gen. Mgr., The Broadcast Centre Development Project, CBC 1984–88; served with Royal Candn. Ordnance Corps in Can. and overseas during World War II; rank Capt.; has served as Dir., CNIB; Un. Appeal; Jr. Achievement; Chrmn., Australian Productivity Council; Australian Indust. Adv. Bd. (mem.); Gov., Univ. of Windsor; Balmoral Hall, Winnipeg; United Church; recreations: urban planning, business concepts and strategy, management policies & projects, ICSC trade assoc.; Home: 53 Widdicombe Hill Blvd., Suite 401E, Etobicoke, Ont. M9R 1Y3.

**McINTYRE, John Sidney,** M.A., Ph.D.; educator; b. Turner Valley, Alta. 3 Jan. 1941; s. John Earl and Kathleen Clara (Webb) McI.; e. Univ. of Alta. Calgary B.A. 1962, M.A. 1964; Univ. of Ill. Ph.D. 1969; m. Beverley d. Thomas and Edith Ogden 27 Dec. 1961; children: Stacey Lyn, Michael John; ASSOC. PROF. OF PSYCHOL. UNIV. OF MAN. 1973– , Asst. Prof. 1968, Head of Psychol. 1978–83; Visiting Scholar San Diego State Univ. Rsch. Found. 1975–76; Cons. Man. Dept. Edn. 1972–75, Great West Life Assurance Co. 1980–83; Dir. Acupuncture Rsch. Found. Man.; mem. Candn. Soc. for Brain Behaviour and Cognitive Science; Psychonomic Soc.; recreations: hockey, golf, jogging; Home: 50 Gillingham Ave., Winnipeg, Man. R3T 3S9; Office: Psychology Department, Univ. of Manitoba, Winnipeg, Man. R3T 2N2.

**McINTYRE, Hon. Joseph G.,** E.D., LL.B.; judge; b. Glace Bay, N.S. 25 Feb. 1920; s. Peter Joseph and Jessie (MacNeil) McI.; e. elem. and high schs. Glace Bay 1937; St. Francis Xavier Univ. 1946–47 pre-law; Dalhousie Univ. LL.B. 1950; m. Rita M. d. Daniel J. Nicholson 16 Sept. 1946; children: Peter, Vaughan, Alan, Paul, James, Mary, Maggie, Martha; JUDGE, COURT OF QUEEN'S BENCH, SASK. 1981– ; called to Bar of N.S. 1950, Sask. 1953; cr. Q.C. 1965; joined Thompson & Sutherland Hard ware, Glace Bay 1937–39; law practice Glace Bay 3 yrs.; Sr. Partner MacPherson, Leslie & Tyerman, Regina prior to appt. as Judge, Dist. Court, Sask. 1974; Rep. Sask. on Conf. Uniformity Legis. (Criminal Side) 1965–73; served with Cape Breton Highlanders 1939–45, Eng., Italy, N.W. Europe; Past Zone Cmdr. Royal Candn. Legion; Past Chrmn. Regina Cath. Sch. Bds.; Past Pres., Cath. Sec. Sask. Sch. Trustees 1960–63; Candn. Cath. Sch. Trustees Assn. 1965; Law Soc. Sask. 1967; mem., Candn. Judges Conf.; Candn. Bar Assn.; R. Catholic; recreation: walking; Home: 281 Leopold Cres., Regina, Sask. S4T 6N8; Office: 107 Court House, Regina, Sask. S4P 0S8.

**McINTYRE, Keith L.,** B.A.Sc., M.B.A., C.I.M., LL.D.; college president; b. St. Thomas, Ont. 11 Oct. 1935; s. Keith Malcolm and Josephine Dorothy (Honsinger) M.; e. Univ. of Toronto B.A.Sc. 1957; McMaster Univ. M.B.A. 1968; Univ. of Waterloo LL.D. 1993; m. Beverly M. d. Ben and Margaret Lindberg 29 June 1957; children: Margaret, Keith; PRESIDENT, MOHAWK COLLEGE OF APPLIED ARTS & TECH. 1976– ; Project Engr., Dept. Mgr., Div. Mgr., Plant Mgr., Procter & Gamble Co. of Can. 1957–68; Teacher, Chairman, Dean, Canadore College 1968–76; Hamilton-Wentworth Engr. of Year Award 1992; Candn. Coop. Edn. 'Bill Poole' Award 1991; Chair, Council of Ont. Coll. Pres. 1991–92; Chair, Hamilton Auto Club Bd. of Dir. 1993–95; Bd. Mem., Candn. Auto. Assn. 1991–94; Pres., Candn. Club of Hamilton 1981–82; Bd. of Dir., Joseph Brant Mem. Hosp. 1977–85; Pres., World Assn. for Coop. Edn. 1989–92; Burlington Amateur Softball Assn. 1959–60; recreations: squash, curling, golf, cottage; clubs: Hamilton Thistle, Hamilton, Hamilton Dist. C. of C.; Home: 602 Northshore Blvd. E., Burlington, Ont.; Office: Box 2034, Hamilton, Ont. L8N 3T2.

**McINTYRE, (Lucy) Lynn,** M.D., M.H.Sc., FRCPC; university professor and administrator; b. Peterborough, Ont. 29 Sept. 1956; d. (Thomas) Gordon and (Marie Françoise Yolande) Michelle (Couture) M.; e. Univ. of Toronto Med. School M.D. 1980, M.H.Sc. 1984; Royal College of Physicians of Canada, Fellowship in Community Med. 1986; DEAN, FACULTY OF HEALTH PROFESSIONS, DALHOUSIE UNIV. 1992– ; Staff Physician, Sioux Lookout Zone Hosp. 1982–83; Hosp. Epidemiologist, Izaak Walton Killam Children's Hosp. 1986–91; current provides admin. & acad. leadership for a large faculty that includes 8 profl. schools; also Assoc. Prof. jointly in Schools of Health Serv. Admin. & Recreation, Physical and Health Edn.; Mem., Nat. Advisory Council on Sucrulose, Redpath Industries; Advisory Panel, Organon Canada Ltd.; total research grant funding to date: $1.6 million; Founding Mem., N.S. Health Council 1990–93; Current Past

Pres., Public Health Assn. of N.S.; Extve. Mem. & Dir., Candn. Soc. for International Health; author of 56 conf. presentations, 29 pub. reports, 55 peer reviewed pubs.; recreations: running, travel; Home: 633 Purcell's Cove Rd., Halifax, N.S. B3P 2G4; Office: 5968 College St., 3rd Floor, Burbidge Bldg., Halifax, N.S. B3H 3J5.

**McINTYRE, Norman F.,** B.Sc., M.S.; petroleum industry executive; b. Pangman, Sask. 21 Oct. 1945; e. Univ. of Wyoming B.Sc. 1971; M.I.T. M.S. Management 1991; m. Lana Jean; children: Jason Lee, Spencer James; PRESIDENT, PETRO-CANADA RESOURCES 1991– ; var. engr. & operating positions in Canada & U.S., Mobil Oil 1967–82; joined Petro-Canada 1982; Group Mgr., Engineering, Offshore Div. 1982–83; Gen. Mgr., Frontier Devel. 1983; Vice Pres. Production Development 1983–86; Sr. Vice Pres., Production 1986–89; Sr. Vice Pres. Western Region, Petro-Canada Products 1989–90; Dir., PanArctic Oils Ltd.; Petroleum Transmission Co.; Mem., Assn. of Profl. Engrs., Geol. & Geophysicists of Alta.; clubs: Glencoe Golf & Country, Calgary Petroleum; Home: 68 Massey Place S.W., Calgary, Alta. T2V 2G8; Office: P.O. Box 2844, 150 – 6th Ave. S.W., Calgary, Alta. T2P 3E3.

**McINTYRE, Paul,** D.Mus., A.R.C.T.; musician; university professor; b. Peterborough, Ont. 1 Oct. 1931; s. (John) Vincent and Mary H. (Poirier) M.; e. Royal Conservatory of Toronto, A.R.C.T. (Piano; Gold Medal for highest mark in Can.) 1950; Univ. of Toronto, B.Mus. 1951; Artist Dipl. of Royal Cons. (1st Class Hons. in Comp. and Piano) 1952; Univ. of Toronto, D.Mus. (1st Class Hons.) 1958; studied under Dr. Arnold Walter for Comp., Béla Böszörmènyi-Nagy and Alexander Uninsky for Piano, and others; Nicholas Goldschmidt for Conducting; awarded a Canada Foundation Scholarship for study in Europe, 1953; studied Comp. with Tony Aubin and Olivier Messiaen at Cons. Nat. in Paris; Conducting with Igor Markewitch and Wolfgang Sawallisch at Mozarteum in Salzburg and with Pierre Monteux, Hancock, Maine 1960–61; m. Phyllis Runge, 26 Dec. 1959; children: John Francis; Stephen Paul, Moira Clare, Lenore Therese, Judith Eva; Carnegie Visiting Assoc. Prof.,and Head, Music Dept., Univ. of Alaska 1961–64; Asst. Prof., Music Dept., Univ. of Minnesota, 1964–67; Assoc. Prof. and Head, Music Dept., College of St. Catherine, St. Paul, Minn. 1967–70; PROFESSOR OF MUSIC, UNIVERSITY OF WINDSOR since 1970; Head of the Department and Dir. of Sch. of Music 1970–80; Compositions: 'Trio in E minor' 1949; 'Sonatina for Piano' 1950; song cycle 'Four Poems of Walter de la Mare' 1950; 'String Quartet' 1951; 'Concerto for Piano and Orchestra' 1952; song cycle 'Three Poems of Arthur Symons' 1953; 'Song of Autumn' (a poem for string orchestra) 1953; 'Deux Etudes Poetiques' for piano 1954; 'Judith' (a melodrama-cantata) 1957; 'Symphonia Sacra' for Voices and Orchestra 1956; 'Death of the Hired Man' (opera) 1960; 'Jean de Brebeuf' (symphony) 1963; 'Out of the Cradle Endlessly Rocking' (Chamber cantata) 1966; Permutations on a Paginini Caprice' (string quartet) 1967; 'This Is Not True' (opera) 1967; 'Encounters' for violin and piano 1970; 'The Little Red Hen' (Cantata for voices &orchestra) 1976; 'Fantasy for Organ' 1977; 'Song of Renewal' 1977; 'Five Sonnets of Archebald Lampman' for Voice and Piano 1978; 'Commedia' for orchestra 1978; 'Three Preludes' for organ; comp. performed over CBC, Eaton Auditorium, Massey Hall, National Arts Centre, Orheum Theatre (Vancouver), Art Gallery of Windsor etc.; piano soloist on many occasions; Asst. Conductor Opera Festival Co. of Toronto, 1953 and 1955, and at Opera Summer Sch., Univ. of B.C. 1955; mem., Candn. League of Composers (Council 1956–57, and Vice Pres., 1980–81); Past Pres., Alumni Assn., Univ. of Toronto Faculty of Music; Roman Catholic; recreations: bridge, swimming; Home: 4285 Mitchell St., Windsor, Ont. N9G 2G1.

**McINTYRE, Hon. William Rogers,** C.C., B.A., LL.B., Q.C.; judge; b. Lachine, Que. 15 March 1918; s. Charles Sidney and Pauline May (Sifton) McI.; e. Univ. of Sask. B.A., LL.B. 1941; m. Hermione Elizabeth d. late Alexander Reeves, Newmarket, Eng. 12 Dec. 1944; children: Elizabeth Pauline, John Stuart; Judge, Supreme Court of Can. 1979–89; called to Bar of Sask. 1947, B.C. 1947; apptd. Judge, Supreme Court of B.C. 1967 and Court of Appeal B.C. 1973; Bencher, Law Soc. B.C. 1965–66; served with Candn. Army 1941–46, UK, Sicily, Italy and NW Europe; named Companion of the Order of Canada 1991; Clubs: Union (Victoria, B.C.); Rideau; Vancouver; Home: Ste. 801 - 2075 Comox, Vancouver, B.C. V6G 1S2; Office: 15th Floor, 1075 W. Georgia St., Vancouver, B.C. V6E 3G2.

**McIVER, Susan Bertha,** B.A., M.Sc., Ph.D.; writer; educator; b. Hutchinson, Kans. 6 Nov. 1940; d. Ernest Dale and Thelma Faye (McCrory) McI.; e. San Bernardino High Sch. 1958; Univ. of Cal. Riverside, B.A. 1962; Wash. State Univ. M.Sc. 1964, Ph.D. 1967; Woods Hole Marine Biol. Lab. Cert. 1965; cross appt. Dept. of Microbiol. Faculty of Med. Univ. of Toronto 1984–89; Asst. Prof. of Parasitol. Univ. of Toronto 1967, Assoc. Prof. of Microbiol. & Parasitol. 1972, Prof. of Zool. and of Microbiol. 1980–84; Prof. & chair of Environmental Biol., Univ. of Guelph 1984–89; Coroner, Province of B.C. 1993– ; Cons., Surg. Gen. US Army Med. Entomol. 1975–79, 1986–89; Cons. Study Group Tropical Med. & Parasitol. Nat. Insts. Health USA 1983–85, Inter. Am. Fellowship 1973; Meml. Lectr. Am. Mosquito Control Assn. 1988; Visiting Sci. Award Med. Rsch. Council Can. 1978–79; Von Hofsten Meml. Lectr. Univ. of Uppsala, Sweden 1983; Melville DuPorte Meml. Lectr. McGill Univ. 1984; C. Gordon Hewitt Award Entomol. Soc. Can. 1979; awarded Commemorative Medal for 125th Anniversary of Candn. Confederation; Dir. Women-in-Crisis Guelph 1980–87, Vice Chair, Chair 1988–89; Secy., Hospice Salt Spring 1993– ; author: 'Cat's Tail' 1992; and over 80 sci. rsch. papers, review articles, textbook; Fellow, Entomol. Soc. Can. (Pres. 1984–85); mem. Entomol. Soc. Ont. (Pres. 1980–81); Biol. Council Can. (Extve. 1982–85); Entomol. Soc. Am. (Chair Med. Entomol. Sect. 1983–84); Candn. Soc. Zool.; Am. Soc. Parasitols.; Candn. Microsc. Soc.; Mosquito Control Assn.; Amnesty International; West Coast Women and Words Soc.; recreations: literature, theatre, hiking, cross-country skiing; Home: C95 Reynolds Rd., R.R. 1, Fulford Harbour, B.C. V0S 1C0.

**McIVOR, Donald K.,** B.Sc.; retired petroleum executive; b. Winnipeg, Man. 12 April 1928; e. Univ. of Man. B.Sc. (Geol.) 1950; Nat. Defence Coll. 1972–73; m. Avonia Isabel Forbes 1953; children: Gordon, Deborah, Duncan, Donald, Daniel; joined Imperial Oil as geophysical trainee seismic crew Alta. 1950, held various operational and research positions in exploration 1950–58; held various positions incl. Asst. to Exploration Mgr., Supvr. Exploration Planning, Mgr. Exploration Research, Calgary 1958–68, also held assignments Angola, France and Tulsa, Okla. (Jersey Production Research Co.); Asst. Mgr. and Mgr. Corporate Planning, Toronto H.O. 1968–69, Exploration Mgr. 1970–72, Sr. Vice Pres. and Dir. 1973, Extve. Vice Pres. 1975, Vice Pres. Oil & Gas Exploration & Production, Exxon Corp. 1977–81; Depy. Chrmn. and Dir. Imperial Oil Ltd. 1981; Chrmn. and C.E.O., Imperial Oil Ltd. 1982–85; Dir. & Sr. Vice Pres., Exxon Corp., Dallas, TX 1985–92; Extve.-in-Residence, Queen's Univ. Business School; Office: 111 Hemlock Hill Rd., New Canoon, CT 06840.

**McIVOR, Gordon K.,** B.A., M.A., Ph.D., KHS; public affairs executive; b. Regina, Sask. 13 Oct. 1954; s. Donald Kenneth and Avonia Isobelle (Forbes) M.; e. Glendon Coll., York Univ. B.A. (Hons.) 1977; Univ. Paul Valéry (France) M.A.ès hon. 1978, Ph.D. cum laude 1980; single; VICE-PRES., PUBLIC AFFAIRS, CN REAL ESTATE 1988– ; Dir. of Communications, Lavalin Inc. 1982–84; Sr. Mgr. Corp. Commun., The Bank of N.S. 1984–87; Group Dir., Burson-Marsteller 1987–88; Pres., The Couching Inst. on Public Affairs 1992– ; Nat. Sec., The Candn. Public Relns. Soc. 1991–92; Bd. Mem. & Chair, Special Events Ctte., Harbourfront Reading Series 1989–92; Bd. Mem., The Downtown Business Council 1991–92; Knights of the Holy Sepulchre of Jerusalem (KHS) Papal Knighthood; Accredited Public Relations Practitioner; Founding Mem. & Past Dir., The Wilfred-Pelletier Found.; Dir. of Media, Yes/Oui Ont./Can. Ctte. 1992; Founder, The CEO Award of Excellence in Public Affairs 1990; Policy Advisor, St.-Jacques Riding Montreal 1984; author: 'Jean Carrière, la quintessence des Cévennes' 1979, 'Les Cévennes: une banlieue de luxe' 1980; recreations: religious doctrine; Home: 7 Hambly Ave., Toronto, Ont. M4E 2R5; Office: 200 King St. W., Suite 1509, Toronto, Ont. M5H 3T4.

**McKAY, Alexander Gordon,** O.C., K.St.J, B.A., M.A., A.M., Ph.D., LL.D. (h.c.), D.Litt. (h.c.), F.R.S.C.; educator; editor; b. Toronto, Ont. 24 Dec. 1924; s. Alexander Lynn and Marjory Maude Redfern (Nicoll) McK.; e. Upper Can. Coll. Toronto 1942; Trinity Coll. Univ. of Toronto B.A. (Hons. Classics) 1946; Yale Univ. M.A. 1947; Princeton Univ. A.M. (1948), Ph.D. 1950; Univ. of Manitoba LL.D. (h.c.) 1986; Brock Univ. LL.D. (h.c.) 1990; Queen's Univ. LL.D. (h.c.) 1991; McMaster Univ. D.Litt. (h.c.) 1992; Waterloo Univ. D.Litt. (h.c.) 1993; m. Helen Jean d. Gustav Walter Zulauf 24 Dec. 1964; step-children: Julie Anne Stephanie Brott, Danae Helen Fraser; Distinguished Visiting Lecturer, Classics, Concordia Univ. 1992–93; Adjunct Prof. of Humanities, York Univ. 1990– ; Emeritus Prof. of Classics, McMaster Univ. 1990– ; Dir. Classical Summer Sch. Italy, Vergilian Soc. Am. 1955–92; Instr. Princeton Univ. 1947–49; Wells College, 1949–50; Univ. of Pa. 1950–51; Univ. of Man. 1951–52; Asst. Prof. Mount Allison Univ. 1952–53; Waterloo Coll. 1953–55; Univ. of Man. 1955–57; McMaster Univ. 1957–59, Assoc. Prof. 1959–61, Prof. of Classics 1961–90, Prof. Emeritus 1990– , Chrmn. of Classics 1962–68, 1976–79, Dean of Humanities 1968–73, Senate 1968–73, 1985–87; Visiting mem. Inst. Advanced Study Princeton, N.J. 1979, 1981; Prof.-in-Charge Intercollegiate Center Classical Studies in Italy 1975; Extve. Dir. McMaster Univ. Archaeol. Survey Team Sacco-Liri Valleys, Italy 1977–79; Visiting Scholar, Dept. of Classics, Univ. of Texas at Austin 1987; Fondation Hardt, Vandoeuvres, Geneva 1988; Visiting Fellow, Trinity Coll., Univ. of Cambridge 1988; Rockefeller Foundation Study and Rsch. Centre, Bellagio (Como) 1993; Princ. Lectr. Royal Ont. Museum Mediterranean Cruises 1981, 1982; Historian, Christ's Ch. Cath. Hamilton; Dir. Hamilton Foundation 1970–73; Pres. Hamilton Philharmonic Orchestra, Hamilton Chamber Music Soc.; Sir Ernest MacMillan String Ensemble, Hamilton; Vice Pres., Bach Elgar Choir Soc., Hamilton; Chrmn. Candn. Comte. Lexicon Iconographicum Mythologiae Classicae; Acad. Adv. Comte. Candn. Archaeol. Inst. Athens; Candn. Acad. Centre Italy; recipient Queen's Silver Jubilee Medal 1977; Centenary Medal, Royal Soc. Can. 1982; 125th Anniversary of the Confederation of Canada Medal, 1992; Award of Merit Classical Assn. Middle W. and S.; Woodrow Wilson Fellowship; Killam Sr. Rsch. Fellowship; author 'Naples and Campania' 1962; 'Victorian Architecture in Hamilton' 1967; 'Vergil's Italy' U.S. 1970, Eng. 1971; 'Ancient Campania' Vols. I and II 1972; 'Houses, Villas, and Palaces in the Roman World' 1975; 'Vitruvius, Architect and Engineer' 1978, 1985; 'Römische Haüser, Villen, und Paläste' 1980; 'Roma Antiqua, Latium & Etruria' 1986; co-author 'Roman Lyric Poetry; Catullus and Horace' 1969, 1974; 'Roman Satire: Horace, Juvenal, Persius et al.,' 1976; 'Selections from Vergil's Aeneid, Books I, IV, VI, (Dido and Aeneas)' 1988; 'The Two Worlds of the Poet: New Perspectives on Virgil' (Festschrift volume) 1992; 'Tragedy, Love, and Change: Roman Poetic Themes and Variations' 1994; articles, reviews, reports; Councillor, Royal Soc. Can. 1967–84, Hon. Ed. 1970–84, Pres. 1984–87, Past Pres. 1987–90, Councillor, Acad. Humanities & Social Sciences; Pres., Classical Assn. Can. 1978–80; Classical Assn. Middle W. & S. 1972–73; Vergilian Soc. 1972–73 (Hon. Pres. for Life 1989– ); Dir. Internat. Acad. Union 1980–83, 1986–90, Vice Pres., 1983–86; Knight Cmdr. of Merit, Order of St. John of Jerusalem, 1986; Officer, Order of Canada 1988; Liberal; Anglican; recreations: pianoforte, reading, travel; Clubs: Arts & Letters (Toronto); X-Club (Toronto); Tamahaac (Ancaster); Yale (New York); University Club (Pittsburgh); Canadian (Pres. Hamilton 1972–73); McMaster Faculty; Home: One Turner Ave., Hamilton, Ont. L8P 3K4.

**McKAY, (Robert) Bruce,** B.Eng., M.A., Ph.D., P.Eng.; television producer and executive; systems engineer; b. Stratford, Ont. 15 May 1944; s. James John and Helen Smith (Oman) McK.; e. Stratford Coll. Inst. 1962; McMaster Univ. B.Eng. (Elect.) 1966 (Chancellor's Gold Medal); Stanford Univ. M.A. 1971, Ph.D. 1976; DIRECTOR OF PLANNING AND POLICY, CBC TELEVISION NETWORK 1989– ; Systems Eng. IBM Canada Ltd. Hamilton, Ont. 1966–67, Product Mktg. Specialist HQ Don Mills 1968–69; Cons. Stanford Univ. Controller's Office 1969–71; Producer CBC Ottawa radio and TV Current Affairs 1970, Producer/Dir. 'Hourglass' TV Vancouver 1971, Mgr. Strategic Planning Eng. Services Div. 1977–78, Asst. Prog. Dir. of Network 1979, Co-devel. and Sr. Producer 'The Journal' 1980–84, Dir. TV Facilities Planning Toronto Broadcast Centre Devel. Project 1984–88; Can. Council Doctoral Fellow 1970–74; co-author 'The Financing of Public Television' 1972; 'The Future of Public Broadcasting' 1976; 'The CBC: A Perspective' 1978; mem. Assn. Profl. Engs. Prov. Ont.; Inst. Elect. & Electronics Engs.; Soc. Motion Picture and TV Engs.; Home: 233 Milan St., Toronto, Ont. M5A 4C3; Office: 1255 Bay St., P.O. Box 500 Stn. A, Toronto, Ont. M5W 1E6.

**McKAY, Donald Douglas,** F.I.I.C.; executive; b. Kildonan, Man. 20 Apr. 1920; s. Douglas and Isabel (MacDonald) M.; e. St. John's and United Coll. (1939), Winnipeg, Man.; m. Thelma M., d. Walter G. Draper, 20 June 1947; children: Donald Douglas, Jr., Ross George, Nancy Jane; Past Chrmn. & Dir.: Facility Assn. of Can., Toronto; General Manager, Facility Assn. 1984–90; Assn. of Independent Insurers, Toronto; Underwriters Adjustment Bureau, Montreal; Past Chrmn.: Canada Safety Council, Ottawa; Past Pres. & Dir.: United Way of Cambridge & N. Dumfries; Past Pres.: Heritage Cambridge; Past Dir.; Ins. Bureau of Can., Toronto; Architectural Conservancy of Ont., Toronto; Grand River Conservation Authority, Cambridge;

Grand Valley Conservation Foundation, Cambridge; Cambridge Chamber of Commerce; Cambridge Public Library; Hon. Dir., South Waterloo Vocational Centre; past Dir., Ont. Heart Foundation, Waterloo County Chapter; joined W. Can. Insurance Underwriters Assn. 1938; Underwriting Mgr., Federated Mutual Insurance 1948–59; Br. Mgr., Prudential of England 1960–63; Auto. and Property Mgr., Canadian Surety Co. 1964, Pres. and Gen. Mgr. 1969, Chrmn. 1974; Pres. & C.E.O., The Gore Mutual Insurance Co. 1974–84; served as Lieutenant RCNR 1940–45; United Church; Home: 176 Old Orchard Grove, Toronto Ont. M5M 2E5.

**McKAY, Donald Douglas Jr.,** B.Arch.; educator; designer; b. St. Boniface, Man. 19 Nov. 1948; s. Donald Douglas and Thelma Mary (Draper) McK.; e. Univ. of Toronto B.Arch. 1973 (Alpha Rho Chi Medal); PRES., DONALD MCKAY AND CO. LTD. 1989– ; Assoc. Prof. of Arch. Univ. of Waterloo 1987– ; Asst. Prof. of Arch.; studio teacher and design critic in arch. & urban design, Univ. of Waterloo, Head of Design 1981, Head of Thesis Prog. 1981, 1983–84, 1986–88, lectr. in hist. and theory of arch., Head of Alzheimer's Working Group, Founder Working Papers in Arch., 1979– ; frequent lectr. Candn., U.S. and Eur. univs.; Visiting Prof. Univ. of Toronto Sch. of Arch. 1983; Rhode Island Sch. of Design 1987; Planning Cons. to Toronto Pub. Lib. Bd., Town of Aurora, Cambridge Hist. Bd., Heritage Properties Ltd., National Archives of Canada; designer and mfr. exper. furniture designs, various exhns.; recipient, Citation for Architectural Design, Progressive Architecture Magazine 1991; Founding Dir. Neighbourhood Renewal Corp. 1972; author: 'Sanctuary' 1988; co-author: 'Metropolitan Mutations' 1989; Office: Waterloo, Ont. N2L 3G1 and Suite 200, 515 Queen St. W., Toronto, Ont. M5V 2B4.

**McKAY, Donald Fleming,** B.A., M.A., Ph.D.; writer, university teacher, editor; b. Owen Sound, Ont. 25 June 1942; s. John Brown and Margaret Janet (Fleming) M.; e. Univ. of Western Ont. B.A. 1965, M.A. 1966; Univ. of Wales Ph.D. 1971; divorced; children: Sarah, Joseph; EDITOR, THE FIDDLEHEAD 1991– and EDITOR & PUBLISHER, BRICK BOOKS 1976– ; Teacher, Dept. of English, Univ. of N.B.; Candn. Authors' Assn. Award for Poetry 1983; Governor General's Award nominee 1983; National Magazine Award for Poetry 1991; Winner, Governor General's Award for poetry 1991; Mem., Writer's Union of Can.; League of Candn. Poets; P.E.N.; author: 'Air Occupies Space' 1973, 'Long Sault' 1975, 'Lependu' 1978, 'Lighting Bait Bait' 1980, 'Birding, or Desire' 1983, 'Sanding Down This Rocking Chair on a Windy Night' 1987, 'Night Field' 1991 (all books of poetry); Office: Dept. of English, Univ. of N.B., Box 4400, Fredericton, N.B. E3B 5A3.

**McKAY, Ian,** M.A., Ph.D.; educator; b. Cornwall, Ont. 20 Apl. 1953; s. John B. and Margaret (Fleming) McK.; e. Dalhousie Univ. B.A. 1975, Ph.D. 1983; Univ. of Warwick M.A. 1976; m. Sally d. Sam and Hilda Sharpe 25 June 1971; children: David Alexander, J. Naomi; ASSOC. PROF. OF HIST. QUEEN'S UNIV. 1988– ; Postdoctoral Fellow St. Mary's Univ. 1985–87; Asst. Prof. and Can. Rsch. Fellow Dalhousie Univ. 1987–88; author: 'The Craft Transformed: An Essay on the Carpenters of Halifax 1885–1985' 1985; 'The Quest of the Folk: Antimodernism and Cultural Selection in Nova Scotia' 1994; editor: 'New Maritimes' 1983– ; 'The Challenge of Modernity' 1992; co-editor: 'People, Resources and Power: Critical Perspectives on Underdevelopment and Primary Industries in the Atlantic Region' 1987; 'Toward A New Maritimes' 1992; various articles and monographs labour & cultural hist.; Home: 208 King St. E., Kingston, Ont. K7L 3A4; Office: History Dept., Queen's Univ., Kingston, Ont. K7L 3N6.

**McKAY, Kenneth Neil,** B.Math., M.A.Sc., Ph.D.; educator; b. Stratford, Ont. 14 May 1953; s. Neil Alexander and Mary Erb (Worden) M.; e. Univ. of Waterloo B.Math. 1978, M.A.Sc. 1987 (Alumni Gold Medal for Outstanding Acad. Achievement; Fac. of Engr. Award for Outstanding Master of Appl. Sci. degree), Ph.D. 1992; m. Emily Agnes d. Angus Walter and Agnes Theresa (Richard) 17 Sept. 1986; ASST. PROF., FACULTY OF BUSINESS ADMIN., MEMORIAL UNIV. OF NEWFOUNDLAND, INFORMATION SYSTEMS AND PRODUCTION MANAGEMENT 1992– ; Visiting Scholar, Sloan School of Management, MIT 1991; Systems Analyst/Sr. Systems Analyst/Cons. Analyst/Sr. Systems Arch., NCR Canada Ltd. 1978–85; Assoc. Dir., Mntg. of Integrated Mfg. Systems (WATMIMS) Rsch. Group, Fac. of Engr., Univ. of Waterloo 1985–91; Faculty Mem., Dept. of Management Sciences, Univ. of Waterloo 1991–92; has developed a variety of systems incl. real time cheque proc., job shop scheduling, mfg. simulations, relational database, search & rescue simulation, software devel. tool box, accounting; Pres., Kenneth N. McKay & Assoc. Inc.; Cons., Govt. of Can., NCR Can., IBM Can., Gen. Motors, John Deere Ltd., Northern Telecom, Allen-Bradley; co-author: 'Modula–2' (text & ref.) 1987; Office: St. John's, Nfld. A1B 3X5.

**McKAY, Michael John,** B.A., M.A.; Canadian astronaut; b. Bracebridge, Ont. 10 May 1963; e. Royal Military College of Canada B.A. 1985, M.A. 1991; single; CANADIAN ASTRONAUT; Software Support Officer, Aircraft Maintenance & Engr. Div., Candn. Forces Base Cold Lake Alta. 1986–87; Mechanical Support Officer and later CF5 Repair Officer 1987–91; Lecturer, Coll. Militaire de St. Jean; selected for Canadian Astronaut Program 1992; currently involved with a shuttle payload that will fly in early 1994, providing Space Vision System support to Wake Shield Facility and preparing for Mission Specialist Training, NASA; Postgrad. Scholarship, Royal Military Coll.of Canada 1989–91; presented papers in Monterey at 34th Midwest Symposium on Circuits & Systems and to the Flight Dynamics Group, NASA Ames Flight Rsch. Ctr.; Guest Speaker, Couchiching Conf. on Public Affairs 1993; Space Week Conf. (Vandmberg, Calif.) 1993; private pilot licence 1993; open water scuba diver 1992; 1st freefall parachute jumps 1992; recreations: flying, gliding, weight lifting, cycling, swimming, sailing, skiing, hiking, photography, reading, chess, astronomy and many other leisure pursuits; Office: 6767 Route de l'aéroport, Saint-Hubert, Que. J3Y 8Y9.

**McKAY, Paul Douglas,** B.A.; investigative reporter, author; b. Toronto, Ont. 19 Jan. 1953; s. Henry H. and Margaret F. (McCulloch) M.; e. Sir John A. MacDonald Collegiate 1971 (Winner of Centennial Award); Trent Univ. B.A. 1978; m. Emily Louise d. Gerrit and Harriet Conger 7 June 1986; FOUNDER AND PRES., THE WILDSIDE FOUNDATION 1991– ; Staff Dir., Ontario Public Interest Research Group 1978–82; Reporter, 'Kingston Whig-Standard' newspaper 1985–88; Sr. Policy Advisor, Ont. Minister of Energy (Personal Staff) 1991–92; Former Dir., Centre for Investigative Journalism; 1st Prize, Enterprise Reporting, National Newspaper Award 1985, 1st Prize, National Business Writing Award 1986; 1st Prize (Magazines), Ctr. for Investigative Journalism Award 1987; Silver, Nat. Magazine Writing Award 1989; Radical Democrat; author: 'Electric Empire: The Inside Story of Ontario Hydro' 1983, 'A Citizen's Guide to the Ontario Legislature' 1984, 'The Pilgrim and the Cowboy' 1989, 'The Roman Empire: The Life and Times of Stephen Roman' 1990; recreations: jazz and folk guitar, wilderness canoeing.

**McKAY, Robert James,** B.Sc., F.S.A., F.C.I.A.; pension and benefits consultant; b. Brandon, Man. 31 May 1949; s. Robert Neil and Shirley Edna (Coupar) M.; e. Bishop's Univ. B.Sc.; m. Nancy d. John and Harriett Pope 30 July 1977; children: Neil Alexander, Andrew Robert, Heather Elizabeth; PRINCIPAL, HEWITT ASSOC. 1984– ; Standard Life Assur. Co. 1972–77; Unit Mgr., present firm (Lincolnshire, Ill.) 1978–84; 1971 Gov. General's gold medal Bishop's Univ.; F.S.A. 1976; F.C.I.A. 1976; Gen. Chrmn., Edn. & Exam. Ctte. 1989–90; elected Bd. of Govs., Soc. of Actuaries 1991; editor: 'Canadian Handbook of Flexible Benefits' 1990; recreations: sailing, windsurfing, travelling; Office: 4110 Yonge St., Toronto, Ont. M2P 2B7.

**McKAY, Sharon,** B.A., M.S.W.; university dean; b. Edmonton, Alta. 06 Oct. 1940; d. David Thomas and Marion Elizabeth (Rendall) Forster; e. Univ. of Alberta B.A. 1961; Smith College, Mass. M.S.W. 1964; m. Bruce s. Ross and Marion M. 23 Dec. 1963; children: Kelsie Beth, Lindsey Colleen, Ashley Meghan; DEAN, FACULTY OF SOCIAL WORK, UNIV. OF REGINA 1990– ; Social Worker, Sask. Dept. of Child Welfare 1961–62; Halifax Family Counselling Agency 1964–65; Peterborough Civic Hosp. 1969–70; Toronto East Gen. Hosp. 1971–72; Thunder Bay Children's Aid Soc. 1972–73; also worked in the U.S. and England as social worker; Sessional Lectr./Field Instr., Lakehead Univ. 1974–75; Dept. of Social Work 1975–90; Life Mem., Ont. Assn. of Profl. Social Workers; Mem., Candn. Assn. of Schools of Social Work (Individual Assoc.); Candn. Council on Social Devel.; Internat. Council on Social Welfare (Can.); Internat. Network on Unemployment and Social Work; Bertha Reynolds Soc.; Home: 2723 Angus Blvd., Regina, Sask. S4T 2A8; Office: Regina, Sask. S4S 0A2.

**McKAY, Verne Gordon,** B.Comm., M.B.A.; banker; b. Calgary, Alta. 4 Oct. 1942 s. Gordon James and Edna Redmen (Winters) M.; e. Univ. of Alberta B.Comm. 1964; Univ. of Toronto M.B.A. 1966; Queen's Univ. 1967; Fellowship Canadian Bankers; m. Patricia d. David and Ellen Nicol 21 Dec. 1963; children: Kathleen Mary, Margaret Anne, Susan Ellen; SR. VICE-PRES. & GENERAL MANAGER, ASIA, ROYAL BANK OF CANADA; various positions leaving as Agent, N.Y. Agency, Toronto Dominion Bank 1966–72; various positions leaving as Extve. Vice-Pres. & Chief Operating Offr., Export Development Corp. 1972–81; joined Royal Bank of Canada 1981; former Pres., Candn. C. of C., Japan; Dir., Inst. of Foreign Bankers'; Chair, Coaching Assn. of Canada; recreations: athletics; member of various clubs; Home: 107B Dalvey Rd., Villa d'Este, Singapore 1025; Office: 140 Cecil St. #01-00, PIL Building, Singapore 0106.

**MCKAY, Winfield Cleland;** customs broker; b. Toronto, Ont 6 Nov. 1930; s. Winfield George and Jessie May (Cleland) M.; e. Jarvis Coll.; Upper Canada Coll.; PRES., W.G. MCKAY LTD. 1965– ; Mgr. 1953–65; Dir., Levitt-Safety Ltd.; Besser Canada Ltd.; Freight Consolidators of Canada Ltd.; Federated Customs Brokers Ltd.; Dir., Candn. Automobile Assn. Toronto Div.; Collections Ctte. R.O.M.; Former Mem., Metro Toronto Police Comm. 1972–82; Ont. Police Comm. 1985–88; Past Pres., Downtown Kiwanis Club; Past Chrmn., Young Pres. Orgn.; Former Dir., Arthritis Soc.; Boys & Girls Clubs of Canada; Adv. Bd. Salvation Army; Bishop Strachan School; Fed. candidate P.C. Party High Park 1968; recreations: golf, hunting, dog training, trap & skeet shooting, fishing, art, antiques; Clubs: Toronto, Badminton & Racquet, Rosedale Golf, Caledon Mountain Trout, Lost Tree (Florida); Home: 100 Ardwold Gate, Toronto, Ont.; Office: Main Flr., 40 University Ave., Toronto, Ont. M5J 1J9.

**McKEAG, Dawn Rue'ann Campbell,** R.N., O.St.J.; investment executive; b. Portage La Prairie, Man. 15 Aug. 1927; d. Douglas Lloyd and Margaret Gladys Victoria (Crampton) Campbell; e. Kelvin High Sch.; Winnipeg Gen. Hosp. Sch. of Nursing 1949; Red River Community Coll. Creative Communications Dip. 1977; Univ. of Winnipeg part-time studies gen. arts; m. W. John (Lt. Gov. of Man. 1970–76) s. George H. and Elizabeth McKeag 28 Dec. 1950; children: Janis Dawn, Darcy Elizabeth Crawford, Kelly Ann Rees, Douglas George; PRESIDENT, WALFORD INVESTMENTS LTD.; Dir., Royal Bank of Canada; Hudson's Bay Co. Ltd.; Assiniboine Travel Service; GoodYear Canada Inc.; Robarts Research Inst.; Spruce Developments Ltd.; Dir. & Secy., Manitoba Heart Foundn.; served specialized nursing areas, active volunteer, community, ch. and pol. orgs.; Life mem., Royal Winnipeg Ballet; mem., Winnipeg Art Gallery; Council Christians and Jews; Liberal; Protestant; recreations: skiing, curling, needlework, writing; Clubs: St. Charles Golf & Country; Manitoba; Elmwood (Toronto); Home: 510 Kelvin Blvd., Winnipeg, Man. R3P 0J4; Office: 400, 717 Portage Ave., Winnipeg, Man. R3G 0M8.

**McKEAG, T.B. Oliver,** Q.C., LL.B., B.L.; retired barrister and solicitor; b. Belfast, N. Ireland 21 March 1928; s. Thomas and Margaret (McCaffrey) McK.; e. St. Malachys Coll. Belfast; Queen's Univ. Belfast LL.B. 1948; Inn of Court N. Ireland B.L. 1950; m. Marie Cooper 8 Dec. 1956; children: Maura, Ellen, Siobhan, Kevin; Counsel, Fasken Campbell Godfrey 1980–93, retired; Solr. Law Dept. Shell Canada 1956, Gen. Solr. 1969, Gen. Counsel 1973–80; called to Bar of Ont. 1956; cr. Q.C. 1971; mem. Bd., St. Joseph's Health Centre 1972–88 (Chrmn. 1980–85); Pres. St. Joseph's Rsch. Foundn. 1975–84; Dir., St. Joseph's Hospital Employees Pension Plan 1988–93; Pres. Armour Heights Ratepayers Assn. 1970–71; mem. Candn. Bar Assn. (Pres. Ont. Br. 1973–74, mem. Nat. Extve. 1979–81); mem. Ed. Bd., Canadian Bar Review 1980–86; Law Soc. Upper Can.; Dir. Candn. Mfrs. Assn. 1978–80; Assoc. Mem. Conference Bd. of Canada 1987–93; P. Conservative; R. Catholic; recreations: sailing; Club: R.C.Y.C.; Hope Town Sailing Club (Treas. 1993– ); Home: 1902 - 65 Spring Garden Ave., Willowdale, Ont. M2N 6H9; Winter residence: Dun Lough, Hope Town, Abaco, Bahamas.

**McKEAG, Col. The Hon. William John,** KSTJ, KLJ, CD, B.Com., LL.D.; b. Winnipeg, Man. 17 March 1928; s. George Hammill and Elizabeth (Biggar) McK.; e. Univ. of Man. B.Com. 1949, LL.D. 1977; Univ. of Winnipeg LL.D. 1976; m. Dawn Rue-Ann d. Hon. D. L. Campbell 28 Dec. 1950; children: Janis, Darcy, Kelly, Douglas; PRES., McKEAG REALTY LTD. 1960– ; The Investors Group; Greater Winnipeg Cablevision Ltd.; Lt. Gov. of Man. 1970–76; Dir., Norcen Energy Resources Ltd. 1980– ; Hollinger Inc. 1985– ; Chrmn., Ducks Unltd. (Can.); Hon. Counsellor, Winnipeg Chamber Comm. 1976; Dist. Gov. W. Can. Kiwanis 1967; mem. The 1001 (Nature Trust); rec'd Univ. of Man. Alumni Jubilee Award 1973; apptd. Hon. Col. Fort

Garry Horse 1973; Hon. Life mem. Winnipeg Rotary; Man. Curling Assn.; rec'd Queen's Silver Jubilee Medal 1978; Knight, Order of Saint Lazarus 1980; Knight of Justice, Order of St. John 1986; Zeta Psi; United Church; recreations: golf, curling, skiing, hunting; Clubs: Manitoba; St. Charles Country; Lakewood Country; Bent Tree, Fla.; Home: 510 Kelvin Blvd., Winnipeg, Man. R3P 0J4; Office: 400–717 Portage Ave., Winnipeg, Man. R3G 0M8.

**McKEAN, Michael H.,** B.A., M.B.A.; confectionary industry executive; b. Toronto, Ont. 16 Sept. 1950; s. Roger Pearson and Theresa (Malloy) M.; e. Univ. of Guelph B.A. 1974; Univ. of Toronto M.B.A. 1977; m. Nancy d. Sinclair and Amy Abell 14 Aug. 1982; children: Sean, Amber; PRESIDENT, WRIGLEY CANADA INC. 1990– ; Trade Acct. Mgr., Brand Mgr., Canada Packers 1974–77; Product Dir., Johnson & Johnson 1977–80; Group Product Dir., McNeil Consumer Products/J&J 1980–82; Dir., Consumer Div., Johnson & Johnson Hong Kong 1983–85; Dir., Marketing & Sales Brazil 1985–88; Task Force Chair New Jersey U.S.A. 1988–89; Home: 60 Olsen Dr., Don Mills, Ont. M3A 3J3; Office: 1123 Leslie St., Don Mills, Ont. M3C 2K1.

**McKEE, Eric Arthur,** B.A., M.A.; university administrator; b. Toronto, Ont. 8 July 1944; s. Arthur David and Nora Elsie (Worsdall) M.; e. De La Salle College Oaklands 1963; St. Michael's College, Univ. of Toronto B.A. 1966, Sch. of Grad. Studies M.A. 1968; m. Marie Colleen d. Lester and Blanche McCarthy 23 May 1972; one s.: Lester James; VICE-PRESIDENT STUDENT SERVICES, DALHOUSIE UNIVERSITY 1988– ; Sales Planning, Procter & Gamble 1968–69; International Student Centre, Univ. of Toronto 1969–75; Ombudsman 1975–81; Dir. of Student Services 1981–84; Asst. Vice-Pres. Student Affairs 1984–88; Chair, N.S. Student Aid Advisory Ctte.; recreations: sailing; clubs: Bedford Basin Yacht (Sec.); Home: 91 Millrun Cres., Bedford, N.S. B4A 3H9; Office: Halifax, N.S. B3H 3J5.

**McKEE, James Stanley Colton (Jasper),** B.Sc., Ph.D., D.Sc., F.Inst.P., C.Phys.; university professor and administrator; b. Belfast, U.K. 6 June 1930; s. Capt. James and Dorothy (Colton) M.; e. Campbell College Belfast 1937–48 (jr. & sr. scholarships); Queen's Univ. Belfast B.Sc. 1952, Ph.D. 1956 (Capt. 1st XI Hockey; Research studentship 1953–55); Birmingham Univ. D.Sc. 1968 (Fulbright Scholar 1967–68); m. Christine d. Wilfred and Sylvia Savage 16 June 1961; children: Conor, Siobhan; PROFESSOR AND DIRECTOR OF ACCELERATOR CENTRE, UNIV. OF MANITOBA 1974– ; Asst. Lecturer, Queen's Univ. 1954–56; Lecturer, Birmingham Univ. 1956–64; Sr. Lecturer 1964–74; Visiting Prof., Univ. of Calif. at Berkeley 1966–67, 1972; Fulbright Scholar 1966–67; CBC Science Correspondent Manitoba 1979– ; Newsworld 1988–91; Editor, 'Physics in Canada' 1990– ; Pres., Candn. Assn. of Physicists 1988; Mem., Rotary Club of Winnipeg West; Univ. Senate 1976– ; Bd. of Gov. 1984– ; Past Mem., NSERC cttes. & Science Culture Canada 1988–91; Runner up as Best Broadcaster, ACTRA Awards Manitoba 1981; Univ. Outreach Award 1984; Cabinet Mem., United Way of Winnipeg 1989–94; Westminster Un. Ch.; Liberal Party of Canada; Past Candidate, Prov.: Tuxedo 1988, Kirkfield Park 1990; editor: 'Fourth International Cluster Conference' 1978; co-editor: 'First Int. Conference on the Three Body Problem' 1969; author of over 200 rsch. papers in sci. journals; recreations: tennis, pontificating; clubs: Winnipeg West Rotary; Home: 1443 Wellington Cres., Winnipeg, Man. R3N 0B2; Office: 223 Allen Physics Bldg., Univ. of Man., Winnipeg, Man. R3T 2N2.

**McKEE, John Angus;** executive; b. Toronto, Ont. 31 Aug. 1935; s. John William and Margaret E. (Phippen) McK.; e. Upper Can. Coll. Toronto; Trinity Coll. Sch. Port Hope, Ont.; Univ. of Toronto; m. Susan Elizabeth Harley 30 May 1970; children: John Andrew, Mary Susan; PRES. & C.E.O., CANADIAN OCCIDENTAL PETROLEUM LTD. 1983– ; Chrmn., Cansulex; Dir., Canadian Occidental Petroleum Ltd.; Stone & Webster Canada; Stone & Webster, Inc. (U.S.A.); Gerling Global; Sultran Ltd.; Pacific Coast Terminals Co. Ltd.; Rsch., Dominion Securities Corp. 1958–61; Asst. to Pres. and later Vice-Pres., The Patino Mining Corp. 1962–64; Mng. Dir., Consolidated Tin Smelters Ltd., British Tin Investment Corp. and Amalgamated Metal Corp. (London, England) 1964–71; owner, J. Angus McKee & Assocs. Ltd. 1971–83; joined present company as Extve. Vice-Pres. July 1983, Pres. & C.E.O. Nov. 1983; Dir., Candn. Petroleum Assn.; mem. Alpha Delta Phi (Gov. and Dir. of Foundation); Anglican; recreations: skiing, shooting; Clubs: York; Toronto; Toronto Lawn & Tennis; Badminton & Racquet; Craigleith Ski; Knickerbocker (N.Y.); Ranchmans (Calgary); Petroleum (Calgary); Office: 1500, 635 - 8th Ave. S.W., Calgary, Alta. T2P 3Z1.

**McKEE, John Robert,** B.A., M.F.A.; artist (landscape painter); b. Sudbury, Ont. 11 Jan. 1941; s. Percy and Enid (Owen) McK.; e. Univ. of Alberta B.A. 1962; Arizona State Univ. M.F.A. 1969; married with three children; Faculty Assoc. in Art, Arizona State Univ. 1968–69; Asst. Prof. of Art, Findlay Coll. (Ohio) 1969–71; Columbus Coll. (Georgia) 1971–75; Admin. Cons., Alberta Culture, Visual Arts Br. 1976–79; full time artist 1979– ; represented in Gallery Moos Toronto; Patrick Doheny Gallery, Vancouver; Pat Henning Representative, Edmonton; Masters Gallery, Calgary; Melnychenko Gallery, Winnipeg; Home: Box 58, Canyon, B.C. V0B 1C0.

**McKEE, Michael George,** B.A., B.S.T., LL.B.; politician; b. Bouctouche, N.B. 22 March 1940; s. J. Killeen and Juliette (Michaud) M.; e. Saint Thomas Univ. B.A. 1962; Holy Heart Seminary, B.S.T. 1966; Univ. of N.B., LL.B. 1978; m. Winnie d. Robert Shaw 27 Nov. 1982; children: Sheila, Robbie; Min. of Labour & Min. resp. for Multiculturalism, Govt. of N.B. 1987; parish priest, 5 yrs. in Moncton, N.B.; chaplain, Dorchester Fed. Penitentiary, 4 yrs.; practising lawyer 1979–87; elected to N.B. Legis. Assembly for the riding of Moncton North 1974, 1978, 1982, 1987 (obtained largest majority of all 58 ridings); Mem., Moncton Barristers' Soc.; N.B. Law Soc.; Candn. Bar Soc.; Coach, Moncton Minor Hockey Assn., 18 yrs.; Mem., Moncton Minor Football Assn.; involved with Moncton Boys & Girls Club Inc., East End Boys & Girls Club Inc., St. Patrick's Family Ctr., YMCA, United Way, Beauséjour Curling Club, and Knights of Columbus; Home: P.O. Box 2393, Stn. A, Moncton, N.B. E1C 8J3.

**MCKELVEY, E. Neil,** O.C., Q.C., LL.B., D.C.L.; barrister, solicitor; b. Saint John, N.B. 1 May 1925; s. Fenwick M. and Margaret L. (Holder) McK.; e. Saint John (N.B.) High Sch. 1943; Khaki Univ. of Can. 1946; Dalhousie Univ. LL.B. 1949; m. Joan B. d. John C. and Norah Belyea 14 Aug. 1948; children: Peter F., P.Eng.; Dr. J. Roger; COUNSEL, STEWART MCKELVEY STIRLING SCALES 1991– ; Dir. BCE Inc.; Canadian Pacific Forest Products Ltd.; New Brunswick Power Corp.; mem. N.B. Adv. Bd., Royal Trust Corp. of Can.; Chrmn., Saint John Port Devel. Comn. 1981–84; called to Bar of N.B. 1949; Partner Ritchie, McKelvey, Mackay 1949–55; Sr. Partner, McKelvey, Macaulay, Machum 1955–90; cr. Q.C. 1960; Partner, present company 1990; Pres. Candn. Bar Assn. 1973–74; Internat. Bar Assn. 1978–80; Mem., Law Soc. of N.B.; Candn. Council for Internat. Business (Arbitrators Panel); Arbitration & Mediation Inst. of Can.; Am. Arbitrators Assn.; Fellow, Am. Coll. of Trial Lawyers; apptd. Officer of the Order of Canada 1986; awarded Hon. D.C.L. Univ. of N.B. 1980; Jubilee Medal 1977; C.D. 1992; awarded Commemorative Medal for 125th Anniversary of Candn. Confederation 1993; Assoc. Mem. of Bd. of Govs., Dalhousie Univ.; Clubs: Union (Saint John); Royal Kennebecasis Yacht (Commodore 1964–65) Saint John; Riverside Country (Saint John); Home: 14 Beach Cres., Saint John, N.B. E2K 2E3; Office: 44 Chipman Hill, P.O. Box 7289, Station A, Saint John, N.B. E2L 4S6.

**McKELVEY, John Gowans Kent,** B.Com., C.A., C.F.A.; investment counsellor; b. Toronto, Ont. 19 July 1930; s. Dr. Alexander Dunbar and Margaret Oliver (Kent) McK.; e. Univ. of Toronto Schs. 1947; Univ. of Toronto B.Com. 1951; C.A. 1954; C.F.A. 1967; m. Anna Margaret (Peggy) d. Murray and Eleanor Stewart 3 Dec. 1960; children: Mary, Karen Hurd, John; CHRMN. WINDCROFT FINANCIAL COUNSEL LTD. 1979– ; joined Price Waterhouse & Co. 1951–56; McLeod, Young, Weir Ltd. 1956–62; Lindsay, McKelvey & Co. Ltd. 1962–79, Co-founder and Pres.; joined present firm 1979; Gov. and Treas. Frontier Coll. 1978–90; Treas. Columbus Un. Ch. 1976–90; author/ed. 'Your Personal Money Manager' 1980; 'Take Charge!' 1980; 'General Trust Tax Review' (Quarterly 1982–89); mem. Toronto Soc. Financial Analysts; Inst. Chart. Financial Analysts; Ont. Inst. C.A.'s; Candn. Assn. Financial Planners; Candn. Tax Found.; Dir. and Pres. Invest. Counsel Assn. Ont. 1974–76; recreation: gardening; Home: 4200 Grandview St. N., R.R.1, Oshawa, Ont. L1H 7K4; Office: 1040, 67 Yonge St., Toronto, Ont. M5E 1J8.

**McKELVIE, Donald;** public utilities executive; b. New Liskeard, Ont., 14 Apr. 1913; s. Angus Alexander and Jessie Marjorie (Dowzer) M.; e. Queen's Univ.; m. Aileen Laura, d. late R.H. Wright, Apr. 1941; children: Peter, Julie; served in 2nd World War as Pilot Offr., R.C.A.F., in Can. & U.K. 1942–44; Un. Church; recreations: golf; Home: 91 Niven St., New Liskeard, Ont. P0J 1P0; Office: Paget St., New Liskeard, Ont. P0J 1P0.

**McKELVIE, James H.,** B.Sc., C.A.; financial executive; b. Toronto, Ont. 9 Aug. 1951; s. James A. and Margaret M. (Achesion) M.; e. York Univ. B.Sc. 1975; m. Glenys U.R. d. Ann and Edward Wilkings 19 Oct. 1973; one s.: Cameron Brandon Chris; EXECUTIVE VICE-PRESIDENT, ROY-L CAPITAL CORPORATION 1991– ; Manager, Tax Dept., Deloitte & Touche; Corp. Controller, Carma Ltd.; Vice-Pres., Lakeview Estates Ltd. 1984–87; Vice-Pres. Finance and only employee Tarragon Oil & Gas Limited 1987–90; Dir.: Tarragon Oil and Gas Limited; National Rubber Inc.; Clairvest Group Inc.; A.G. Simpson Co. Limited; C.A. Ont. 1977, Alberta 1979; recreations: running, squash, reading; clubs: Mayfair Squash and Tennis; Office: 22 St. Clair Ave. E., Suite 1701, Toronto, Ont. M4T 2S3.

**McKENDRY, David John,** B.Com., B.J., C.A.; director; b. Montreal, Que. 9 Feb. 1944; s. Blake Ault and Ruth (McLeod) McK.; e. Carleton Univ. B.Com. 1966, B.J. 1972; C.A. 1969; m. Nancy d. Harry and Violet Nelles 18 July 1968; children: Ian Andrew, Martin James; DIRECTOR OF CONSUMER AFFAIRS CONSULTING, PRICE WATERHOUSE 1989– ; Dir., (Regulated Industries Prog.) Consumers' Assn. of Can. 1982–89; articled with Coopers & Lybrand, Toronto becoming Audit Supr., 1967–70; self-employed cons. and writer Ottawa, Vancouver 1970–74; Fed. Pub. Servant 1975–82, Dept. Indian Affairs & N. Devel., Auditor Gen. of Can., Dept. Communications, Min. of State for Social Devel., Kenora, Ottawa; author various articles, newspapers and mags.; Co-editor: 'Consumer Insight'; ed. cons. 'In the Children's Aid' 1981; Dir., Public Interest Advocacy Centre; Chrmn., Privacy Ctte., Candn. Standards Assn.; Mem., Steering Ctte. on Telecommunications, Candn. Standards Assn.; recreations: running, cross-country skiing; Club: National Press; Home: 159 Ivy Cres., Ottawa, Ont. K1M 1X7; Office: 1100, 180 Elgin St., Ottawa, Ont. K2P 2K3.

**MCKENNA, Frank Joseph,** M.L.A.; politician; lawyer; b. Apohaqui, N.B. 19 Jan. 1948; s. Durward and Olive (Moody) M.; e. St. Francis Xavier Univ., B.A. (Hons.) 1970; Grad. work, Queen's Univ. 1970–71; Univ. of N.B., LL.B. 1974; Ellis Charters Award as Outstanding Sophomore, St. Francis Xavier Univ.; Paul Blizzard Award as Outstanding Jr.; Birk's medal for outstanding contrib. to student govt.; recipient, Vanier Award 1988; D.Sc.Pol. (Hon.), Univ. de Moncton 1988; LL.D. (Hon.) Univ. of N.B. 1988; m. Julie (Friel); children: Toby, Tina, Jamie; PREMIER, PROV. OF NEW BRUNSWICK 1987– ; Leader, N.B. Liberal Party 1985– ; Spc. Asst. to Pres., Privy Counc. 1971; Rsch. Asst., Const. Law Unit, PMO 1973; Vice Pres., Univ. of N.B. Fac. of Law Liberal Assn. 1974; York-Sunbury Fed. Liberal Assn. 1974; Mem., Orgn. & Policy Cttes., N.B. Liberal Party 1974–81; Pres., Chatham Const. Liberals 1981–82; Chief Returning Offr. & Mem., Steering Ctte., Leadership Convention 1982; el. M.L.A., Chatham 1982; re-el. MLA, Chatham 1987, 1991, sworn in as 27th Premier of N.B. 1987; Mem., N.B. Bar Assn.; Candn. Bar Assn. (Counc. Mem., N.B. Br.); extensive trial & appellate experience in Candn. courts; Founder & 1st Pres., Chatham Downtown Merchants; Former Pres., Chatham C. of C.; author of journal articles; recreation: jogging, baseball; Office: P.O. Box 6000, Fredericton, N.B. E3B 5H1.

**McKENNA, Kenneth J.;** florist; b. Montreal, Que. 31 Aug. 1931; s. late Edward Philip and Kathleen Clare (McGrory) M.; e. Loyola Coll., Montreal (1950) and Macdonald Coll. (1951); m. Margaret Anne, d. late Robert Berry, 29 May 1954; children: Kathleen Jean, Kenneth Robert, Mary Martha, Josephine Anne, Brigid Rose; PRES. AND GEN. MGR., McKENNA INC. 1957– ; Dir., Mòd-Ontario; joined present firm 1951 in Greenhouse Department, working successively in various depts.; served in R.C.A.F. (Reserve) 1948–52; el. to Montreal City Council, 1960, re-el. 1962 (Pro-Mayor 1961); mem., Montreal Mil. and Maritime Museum; Founding mem., Glenfinnan Assn.; Pres., Glengarry Highland Soc.; mem., Glengarry Hist. Society (Life); Caledonian Soc. of Montreal (Life); Highland Soc. of Montreal; Past Pres., St. Patrick's Soc., Montreal; mem., St. Andrew's Soc.; Canada Celtic Cong.; Hon. mem., Pipes and Drums, Black Watch (R.H.R.); recreations: music, literature; Club: University; Office: 4509 Côte des Neiges, Montreal, Que. H3V 1E8.

**McKENNA, Marianne,** B.A., M.Arch.; architect; b. Montreal, Que. 25 Sept. 1950; d. Richard D. and Anna M. (Lohr) McK.; e. The Study Montreal 1969; Swarthmore Coll. B.A. 1972; Yale Univ. M.Arch. 1976; m. Ian C. s. Alan H. and Erie M. Tudhope 24 Aug. 1985; children: Cameron Lohr, Portia McKinley; PARTNER, KUWABARA PAYNE McKENNA BLUMBERG ARCHS. 1987– ; Asst. Arch. Bobrow & Fieldman

Montreal 1976–78; Arch. Denys Lasdun, Redhouse & Softley, London 1978–79; Barton Myers Associates 1980–87, Assoc. 1981 (selected projects Unionville Lib. Toronto 1982, Hasbro Toy Co. N.Y. City 1984); selected projects present firm York Univ. Centre Fine Arts 3 1987, Tudhope Associates Design Studios Toronto 1989, 35 E. Wacker Addition Chicago 1989; Kitchener City Hall 1991, Royal Conservatory of Music Master Plan 1991; Canadian Imperial Bank of Commerce (Pickering) 1992; Visiting Tutor Univ. of Toronto Sch. of Arch. 1982–84, Guest Critic there and Waterloo Univ., McGill Univ., Yale Univ. 1975–87; Extve. Dir. Toronto Arts Found.; mem. Ont. Assn. Archs.; Ordre des architectes de Québec; Royal Arch. Inst. Can.; Home: 74 Roxborough St. E., Toronto, Ont. M4W 1V7; Office: 3F, 322 King St. W., Toronto, Ont. M5V 1J2.

**McKENZIE, Alan;** banker; b. Chester, Eng. 22 Sept. 1936; s. Major William Alexander and Ada Ethel May (Cross) McK.; e. Sutton High Sch. Plymouth, Eng. 1953; m. Jill d. Charles and Flora Leach 16 Aug. 1958; children: Duncan Stuart, Fiona Juliet, Ian Bruce, Catherine Alison; SR. VICE-PRES. AND SEC. BARCLAYS BANK OF CANADA 1978– ; Dir., Barclays Canada Leasing Corp.; Barclays de Zoete Wedd Canada Holdings Ltd.; joined Barclays Bank Ltd. Eng. 1953–75, Asst. Dist. Mgr. (Staff) Exeter Local H.O.; Bank of Montreal, Montréal 1975–76, Com. Acct. Mgr.; Cosmopolitan Properties & Securities Ltd. Hong Kong 1976–78, Jt. Mng. Dir.; Dir.: Scottish Studies Found. Inc.; Comnr., Clan MacKenzie Soc. in the Americas; Fellow, Inst. Candn. Bankers (Gov.); Assoc., Chartered Inst. Bankers (UK); Fellow Inst. Corporate Dirs. Can. (Past Pres.); recreations: chess, philately; Clubs: Carlton (London, Eng.); World Trade Centre (Toronto); Home: 580 Rebecca St., Oakville, Ont. L6K 3N9; Office: 304 Bay St., Toronto, Ont. M5K 2P2.

**McKENZIE, Douglas Graeme,** B.Sc., P.Eng.; executive; b. Winnipeg, Man. 9 May 1934; s. Alexander and Clementina Margaret (McLeod) McK.; e. Univ. of Man. B.Sc. (Mech. Eng.) 1956; m. Mary d. Edward and May Dewar 1966; two s. James, Gordon; Pres., Canadian Blower/Canada Pumps Ltd. 1982; joined Canadian Blower, Kitchener 1956, Sales Eng. Toronto 1959, Sales Mgr. Kitchener H.O. 1976, Vice Pres. Sales 1978; Pres. 1982; mem. Kitchener YMCA; Assn. Prof. Engs. Prov. Ont.; United Church; recreations: golf, curling, jogging; Clubs: Rotary; Westmount Golf & Country (Kitchener); Home: 78 McCarron Cr., Waterloo, Ont. N2L 5N1.

**McKENZIE, Garth Reid;** executive; b. Winnipeg, Man. 10 June 1929; s. Daniel and Nancy McCullough (Brown) McK.; e. Daniel McIntyre Coll. Inst. Winnipeg 1946; m. Phyllis d. Philip and Hanna Orestes 6 Oct. 1956; two d. Nancy Elizabeth, Susan Jennifer; Pres. & Dir., Bonar Inc. 1986– ; Pres., C.E.O. & Dir., Low & Bonar Canada Inc.; Chrmn. & Dir., Bonar Plastics Inc.; Vice Pres. & Dir., The Prince Edward Island Bag Co. Ltd.; Chrmn., Pres., & Dir., Bonar U.S. Inc.; Chrmn. & Dir., Bonar Packaging Inc.; Chrmn., Pres., & Dir., Bonar Industries Inc.; Sales Trainee Bonar Packaging Ltd. 1953, Alta. Rep. Calgary 1956, Plant Mgr. Fredericton 1964, Sales Mgr. Paper Div. Burlington 1967, Asst. Plant Mgr. Paper Div. 1970, Dir. of Mktg. All Products 1973, Vice Pres. and Dir. of Mktg. 1979; United Church; P. Conservative; recreations: golf, walking, gardening; Clubs: Burlington Golf & Country; The Hamilton; Home: 4199 Spruce Ave., Burlington, Ont. L7L 1L1.

**MCKENZIE, Geoffrey Gordon,** B.Comm., F.C.A., F.C.M.C.; b. Trinidad, W.I. 11 Mar. 1931; s. Rupert Bertram and Violet Louise (Lewis) M.; e. Lodge Sch. 1948; McGill Univ., B.Comm. (Hons. Econ.) 1952; C.A. 1954; m. Margery Georgina d. Jessie and Edward Gourlay 8 Oct. 1955; children: Morag Louise, Laurie Anne, Geoffrey Alexander; PARTNER, KPMG MANAGEMENT CONSULTING 1990– ; Auditor, McDonald, Currie & Co. 1952; Ch. Internal Auditor, Atomic Energy of Can. 1954; Controller, Am. Machine & Foundry Co. 1956; The Coopers & Lybrand Consulting Group 1962–89 (Mng. Partner 1984–89, Ont. Reg. Partner 1971–83, Partner 1966, Cons., 1962); Chief Operating Offr., McCarthy Tétrault 1989–90; Pres., Phi Gamma Delta 1952; Mem., Inst. of C.A.s of Que. 1955– ; Inst. of C.A.s of Ont. 1969– ; (F.C.A. 1985); Inst. of Mngt. Cons. of Ont. 1966– (Pres. 1979–80, F.C.M.C. 1981); Candn. Assn. of Mngt. Cons. 1984–89 (Pres. 1988–89); The Toronto Symphony 1975– (Pres. & Bd. Chrmn. 1987–89, Past-Pres. 1989–91); Bd. of Govs., Roy Thomson Hall 1987– ; Bd. of Govs., Ortech International 1988–91; Dir. & Treas., Council for Business & The Arts in Can. 1990– ; recreations: sailing, classical music, reading; Clubs: Toronto; Mississauga Golf; Home: 1524 Wateska Blvd., Mississauga, Ont. L5H 2R2; Office: 2300 Yonge St., Toronto, Ont. M4P 1G2.

**McKENZIE, Kenneth Albert,** Q.C., B.A., LL.B.; b. Calgary, Alta. 29 March 1917; s. John Aldrid and Aveline Irene (Laws) McK.; e. Univ. of Alta., B.A. 1938, LL.B. 1939; m. Doris Vivian, d. Walter Grierson, 30 May 1942; children: Donald G., Mrs. Heather Nilsen, Gordon, Keltie; Partner, Bishop & McKenzie 1952–86; Chrmn. Bd. Life Insurance Co. of Alberta; Dir., Toronto Mutual Life Ins. Co.; The Western Life Assurance Co.; Coronet Leaseholds Ltd.; Campbelltown Sewer Services Ltd.; Conjuring Estates Ltd.; Counsel, Judge Comn. on Prov. and Mun. Taxation; Counsel, McNally Royal Comn.; Chrmn., Gasoline Marketing Enquiry, Alta. Govt.; Chrmn., West Edm. Mall Roller Coaster Enquiry; called to Bar of Alta. 1940; cr. Q.C. 1955; Solr., Atty.-Gen's Dept., Alta. 1940–42; Crown Prosecutor, Edmonton 1946; Sessional Lect., Univ. of Alta. Law Sch. 1946; Leg. Counsel, Govt. of Alta. 1946–52; served in 2nd World War, R.C.A. 1942–46; Capt., Calgary Highlanders; Governor of Alberta and Terr. Br., Royal Life Saving Soc. Can. 1970–75; Public Mem. of Practice Review Bd. of The Assn. of Professional Engineers, Geologists and Geophysicists of Alberta 1987–92; Secy. Bd., St. Stephens Coll.; Secy. and Dir., Rundle's Mission Inc.; mem. Edmonton Bar Assn.; Law Soc. Alta.; Candn. Bar Assn.; Phi Kappa Pi; United Church; recreations: sailing, skiing, mountaineering; Clubs: The Edmonton; Itaska Yacht; Kiwanis; Home: 8, 14812 – 45 Ave., Edmonton, Alta. T6H 5M5.

**McKENZIE, Hon. Lloyd George,** B.A., LL.B., LL.D. (Hon.); retired judge; b. Penticton, B.C. 20 Aug. 1918; s. William Alexander McK.; e. Monterey Sch., Oak Bay High, Victoria High and Victoria Coll. B.C.; Univ. of B.C. B.A., LL.B.; Univ. of Victoria LL.D.; m. Dorothy Elizabeth d. late Andrew Amos Meharey 6 Jan. 1943; INFORMATION OFFR., B.C. COURT OF APPEAL and SUPREME COURT; apptd. Chrmn., Electoral Boundaries Commission (Federal) 1993; Judge, Supreme Court of B.C. retired 1993; Judge, Court Martial Appeal Court, retired; called to Bar of B.C. 1948; cr. Q.C. 1960; practiced primarily in civil and criminal litigation; served 19 yrs. as Gov. and Chrmn. Univ. of Victoria; Pres. Victoria Bar Assn.; Bencher, Law Soc. B.C.; mem. Am. Coll. Trial Lawyers; served with Candn. Army 1942–45, UK, Italy and NW Europe, rank Capt.; Clubs: Union; Lawyers' Inn; Home: 755 Fairmile Rd., West Vancouver, B.C. V7S 1R1.

**McKENZIE, Ross Kenneth,** B.A.; entrepreneur; business executive; b. Winnipeg, Man. 28 Mar. 1936; s. Merrill Wood and Charlotte Ann (Polson) M.; e. Kelvin H.S. 1953; Univ. of Man., B.A. 1957; m. Donna Anne d. Earl and Monica MacDonald 21 May 1960; children: Monica Anne, Laura Diane, Ross Andrew; Chairman, Owner & Dir., Triathlon Leasing Inc. 1981–94; Salesman, 3M Co. 1958–62; Sales Mgr., Can., Dayco Corp. 1962–64; Pres., Can. 1964–73; Sr. Vice Pres., Mktg. (World HQ) 1973–74; Dir., N.M. Davis Corp. Ltd. 1974–92; Pres., Owner & Dir., Parkwood Central Ltd. 1974–91; Westwood Chevrolet Oldsmobile Ltd. 1988– ; Chrmn. & Dir., Barrymore Furniture 1983–91; DiTrani Ski Wear 1985–88; Kingmac Holdings Ltd. 1988– ; Triathlon Computer Leasing 1987–92; Trexar Inc. 1988–93; Deilcraft Furniture Co. Ltd. 1987–90; Deerhurst Resorts Ltd. 1986–87; Vice-Chrmn. & Dir., Scarborough Automotive Centre Ltd. 1988– ; Dir., Trilon Fin. Corp.; MFP Technology Services Ltd.; Ross K. McKenzie & Assoc. Ltd.; Chrmn. Ont. Corp. Campaign, Diabetes Canada 1988, 1989, 1990, 1991 and Candn. Diabetes Assn. 1992, 1993; Past Chrmn. & Dir., National Golf Club; recreations: golf, hunting, fishing; Clubs: Mississauga Golf & Country; Home: 1896 Will Scarlett Dr., Mississauga, Ont. L5K 1J8; Office: 2300 Yonge St., Ste. 3000, Toronto, Ont. M4P 2Z2.

**McKEOUGH, Patrick,** B.A.; executive editor; b. Jamestown, N.Y. 15 Apr. 1947; s. John and Alice M.; e. Univ. of Buffalo B.A. 1969; m. Gisele d. Wilfred and Jeanette Coulombe 13 Apr. 1977; children: Patricia, Andrew; EXTVE. ED., MPL COMMUNICATIONS 1985– ; Tech. analyst, writer/rsch., Coordinator Reports 1969–71; Tech. analyst, Gairdner & Co. 1971–73; Editor, 'The Investment Reporter,' Marpep Pub. 1974–80 & 1990– ; launched 'The Commodity & Currency Reporter' 1980; 'The Personal Wealth Reporter' 1984; 'The Low Priced Stock Analyst' 1985; 'Canadian PennyMines Analyst' 1986; author: 'Riding the Bull - How You Can Profit from the Coming Stock Market Boom' 1993; 'The Mutual Funds Investor' 1994; Mem., Newsletter Assn.; recipient, Newsletter Assn. Editorial Excellence In a Finan. Adv. Pub. competition, 1st prize 1979, 1980; 2nd prize 1986, Hon. mention 1988; Mem., Mensa; Extve. ed.: above publications plus 'The CBC Blue Book of Stock Reports'and 'The Money Reporter'; Home: 157 Northwood Dr., Willowdale, Ont. M2M 2K2; Office: Ste. 700, 133 Richmond St. W., Toronto, Ont. M5H 3M8.

**McKEOUGH, William Darcy,** O.C., B.A., LL.D.; company executive; b. Chatham, Ont. 31 Jan. 1933; s. Florence Sewell (Woodward) and late George Grant McK.; e. Cedar Springs (Ont.) Pub. Sch.; Ridley Coll., St. Catharines, Ont.; Univ. of W. Ont., B.A., 1954; LL.D., Univ. of Western Ont., 1979 (Hon. Causa) LL.D., Wilfrid Laurier Univ., 1980 (Hon. Causa); m. Margaret Joyce, d. Senator the Hon. D.J. Walker, P.C., Q.C., LL.D.; 18 June 1965; two s., Walker Stewart, James Grant; CHAIRMAN, MCKEOUGH INVESTMENTS LTD.; Dir., Canada Development Investment Corp.; Cameco; Candn. General Tower Ltd.; Matthews Group Ltd.; Candn. Imperial Bank of Commerce; McKeough Sons Co. Ltd.; Noranda Mines Ltd.; Numac Energy Inc.; Varity Corp. Inc.; Canada Hibernia Holdings Ltd.; Queens Quay West Land Corp.; Member, Chatham City Council 1960–61 and 1962–63; 1st el. to Ont. Leg. for Kent West 1963; re-el., 1967, 1971, 1975 and 1977; apptd. Min. without Portfolio, Nov. 1966; Min. Municipal Affairs, Nov. 1967; Treas., Min. of Econ. and Chrmn. Treasury Bd. 1971; re-apptd. Min. of Municipal Affairs 1972; Treas., and Min. of Economics and Intergov. Affairs 1972; resigned as Treas. & Min., 1972; Parlty. Asst. to Premier 1973; Min. of Energy 1973–75; Treasr. and Min of Econ. and Intergovernmental Affairs 1975–78; resigned from Cabinet and as M.P.P. 1978; Pres. and C.E.O., Union Gas Ltd. 1979–86, Chrmn. & C.E.O. Union Enterprises Ltd. 1985; Pres. & C.E.O., Redpath Industries Ltd. 1988–89; Past Chrmn. and Pres., Ridley Coll.; Chrmn., The John P. Robarts Rsch. Inst.; Officer, Order of Canada 1994; P. Conservative; Anglican; recreations: tennis, swimming, gardening; Clubs: Toronto; Albany (Toronto); Address: P.O. Box 940, Chatham, Ont. N7M 5L3.

**McKEOWN, Peter Lewis Austin,** B.Com., C.A.; petroleum executive; b. Plattsburgh, N.Y. 9 May 1955; s. Lewis Austin and Marjorie (McHenry) McK.; e. Ashbury Coll. Rockcliffe Park, Ont. 1972; Carleton Univ., B.Com. 1977; C.A. 1980; PRES. AND DIR., SENEX PETROLEUM CORP.; Dir. New Jordan Petroleum Ltd.; Vice Pres. Bedford Petroleum Ltd. 1983–85; recreations: skiing, cycling, reading, fishing; Club: 400 Club; Home: 105, 220 – 26th Ave. S.W., Calgary, Alta. T2S 0M4.

**MCKEOWN, Robert Duff,** B.A.; journalist; b. Ottawa, Ont. 10 Oct. 1950 s. Robert and Vaida (Tischler) M.; e. Yale Univ., B.A. 1971; m. Sheilagh D'Arcy d. Frank and Moira McGee 25 Aug. 1984; children: Robert Emanuel, Alexander Kenneth, Grattan D'Arcy; Host-Reporter, 'The Fifth Estate,' CBC TV 1981; Mem., Ottawa Rough Riders, CFL 1971–76; Freelance print & broadcast journalism 1971–76; Host, 'CBO Morning,' CBC Radio 1976–79; Host-Reporter, 'Quebec Report,' CBC TV & Host, 'Daybreak,' CBC Radio 1979–81; Pres., McKeown/McGee Films 1983– (releases incl. 'The Boys on the Bus' 1987 (Gemini Award for Best Sports Program 1988), 'Les Canadiens' 1986, 'Cleared for Take-Off' 1984, 'Strangers in a Strange Land' 1988, 'The Boys are Back' 1988); Finalist, Gordon Sinclair Award for Outstanding Broadcast journalism 1984; Gemini Award for Best Direction in a Television Documentary 1988; Candn. Football League All-Star 1974; Mem., Grey Cup Champ. Team 1973.

**MCKERCHER, Robert Hamilton,** Q.C., B.A., LL.B., LL.M.; barrister and solicitor; b. Saskatoon, Sask. 6 May 1930; s. Stewart and Etta Marie M.; e. Univ. of Sask., B.A., LL.B. 1952; Harvard Law Sch., LL.M. 1953; m. Margaret Louise Wilton 1952; children: Duncan, Malcolm, Nancy (Bell); SR. PARTNER, MCKERCHER, MCKERCHER, LAING & WHITMORE 1961– ; Bencher, Law Soc. of Sask. 1972–78; Pres., Law Soc. of Sask. 1976–77; Vice-Chrmn., Candn. Bar Assn. (Sask.) 1966–68; Pres., Candn. Bar Assn. 1983–84; practised law with Gowling & Henderson (Ottawa) 1955–61; practice is largely civil litigation (commercial, contract, profl. liability & med. malpractice suits); Dir., Bank of Montreal and various Saskatchewan corporations; formerly part-time lectr., Univ. of Ottawa Law Sch., Univ. of Sask. Law Sch., Bar Adm. Course, Law Soc. of Sask.; Mem., Bd. of Govs., Candn. Law Schoalrship Found.; clubs: Riverside Golf & Country, Carmel Valley Ranch Golf, The Saskatoon; Home: Crossmount Farms, R.R. 5, Saskatoon, Sask. S7K 3J8; Office: 374 Third Ave. S., Saskatoon, Sask. S7K 1M5.

**McKERRACHER, Keith B.,** M.B.A.; advertising executive; b. Central Butte, Sask. 4 Apr. 1929; s. John Burgess and Helen Mary (Samuel) M.; e. Ridgetown Dist. High Sch. 1949; Univ. of W. Ont. Bus. Admin. 1953; m. Helen Jean d. John and Mamie Carey 25 July 1953; children: Nancy Jane, Lisa Joan, Sandra Lynn,

Krista Lee; PRES., MANAGEMENT INSIGHTS LTD.; Trainee Canadian General Electric 1953–55; Project Dir., Vice-Pres., Extve. Vice-Pres. and Partner Gruneau Research Ltd. 1955–61; Dir. of Rsch., Internat. Mktg. Co-ordinator, Canadian Breweries Ltd. 1961–66; Dir. of Mktg. Devel. and Rsch. Carling Brewing Co., Cleveland, Ohio 1967–68; Pres. Canada Dry Corp. 1968–70; Founding Extve. and Pres. Participacion 1971–78; Pres. & C.E.O., Inst. of Canadian Advertising (Retired) 1978–92; Former Treas. and Dir. Candn. Advertising Found.; Bd. mem., Fred Victor Mission; mem. Royal Ontario Museum; recreations: tennis, classical guitar, cabinet making, flying, skiing; Club: University; The Boulevard; The Mandarin; Home/Office: 29 Inglewood Dr., Toronto, Ont. M4T 1G7.

**McKILLOP, John Harvey,** M.Sc.; retired geologist, civil servant; b. Detroit, Mich. 21 Sept. 1927; s. Angus Hugh and Helen (Harvey) M.; came to Canada 1930; e. High Sch. Judique, N.S.; St. Francis Xavier Univ., B.Sc. 1951; Memorial Univ., M.Sc. 1961; m. Teresa, d. James Penney, Holyrood, Nfld., 26 Dec. 1954; one d. Sheri Elizabeth Helen; one s. Andrew Robert Joseph; with Geol. Survey of Can., 1951; joined Nfld. civil service as Asst. Govt. Geol. 1951 and later became Chief Staff Geol.; apptd. Dir. Mineral Resources 1964; Depy. Min. Mines & Energy, Nfld. 1973–87; Channing Sr. Fellow, Memorial Univ. of Nfld. 1987–88; Fellow, Geol. Assn. Can. (former Chrmn. Nfld. sec.); mem., Candn. Inst. Mining & Metall. (former dist. Vice Pres.); Roman Catholic; recreations: distance running, Mem. Candn. Masters Athletic Assn., antique automobiles, lapidary art; Home: 17 Dublin Rd., St. John's, Nfld. A1B 2E7.

**McKINLAY, Ronald A.,** B.A.Sc., M.Com., P.Eng.; C.M.A., F.S.M.A.C., F.I.C.B. trustee-in-bankruptcy; b. Toronto, Ont. 22 Nov. 1924; s. Archibald Stewart and Ruth Mildred (Hambly) McK.; e. Lawrence Park Coll. Inst. Toronto; Univ. of Toronto B.A.Sc. 1949, M.Com. 1952; m. The Hon. Madam Justice Hilda M. McKinlay (nee Galbraith) Supreme Court of Ont., Court of Appeal 29 June 1951; children: Henry Archibald, Mildred Anne, Ronald Galbraith, James Stuart; Chrmn., Canada Deposit Insurance Corp. 1985–92 (Retired); Dir., Champion Road Machinery Ltd., Goderich, Ont.; former Dir., Nu-West Group Ltd., Calgary; H & K Equipment Ltd., Toronto; with The Clarkson Co. Ltd. 1966–85 (Chrmn. 1982–85); Indust. Engr. Canadian Kodak Co. Ltd.; Engr. Reliance Electric (Canada) Ltd.; Indust. Adviser Bank of Montreal; mem. Senate Univ. of Toronto 8 yrs.; Past Chrmn., Bd. Stewards and Trustee, Metrop. Un. Ch.; C.M.A.; Fellow, Inst. Candn. Bankers; Fellow Soc. Mgmt. Accts. Can. (Pres.); Pres., Soc. Mgmt. Accts. Ont.; mem. Bd. Trade Metro. Toronto; served as an officer in Candn. Navy during World War II; Liberal; recreations: camping, duck hunting, boating; Clubs: Ontario; Toronto; Bd. of Trade (Toronto); Rideau (Ottawa); Home: 2045 Lakeshore Blvd. W., Suite 4201, Toronto, Ont. M8V 2Z6.

**McKINNA, Alfred John,** M.D., C.M.; educator; b. Alida, Sask. 16 Apl. 1921; s. John and Maude Alice (Farr) McK.; e. Oxbow (Sask.) High Sch. 1940; Univ. of Sask. B.A. (Biol.) 1948; McGill Univ. M.D., C.M. 1952; m. Lois Patricia d. late Ernest George Saunders 3 Sept. 1955; children: John Saunders, Patricia Jane, Andrew James; PROF. EMERITUS, UNIV. OF W. ONT. 1986– , Prof. and Chrmn. of Ophthalmol. 1975–86; Dir. Dept. Ophthalmol. Univ. Hosp.; Intern, Montreal Gen. Hosp. 1952–53, Resident Ophthalmol. 1957–59, Staff Ophthalmol. 1962; Resident Med. & Surg. Montreal Children's Hosp. 1953–54, Fellow 1961–62, Dir. of Ophthalmol. 1964; Fellow in Ophthalmol. Univ. of Cal. San Francisco 1959–60; Fellow of Wilmer Inst. Johns Hopkins Hosp. Baltimore 1960–61; Asst. Prof. of Ophthalmol. McGill Univ. 1964, Assoc. Prof. 1968; Assoc. Prof. Ophthalmol. Univ. of W. Ont. and Dir. Ophthalmol. Univ. Hosp. 1972; Prof. of Ophthalmol. Univ. of W. Ont. and Chrmn., Dept. of Ophthalmol. 1975; mem. Candn. Med. Assn.; Ont. Med. Assn.; Candn. Ophthalmol. Soc.; Am. Acad. Ophthalmol.; Wilmer Residents Soc.; F.C. Cordes Residents Soc.; McGill Alumnae Assn.; Univ. of Sask. Alumnae Assn.; served with RCAF 1942–45; United Church; recreations: sport, travel; Home: 69 Green Acres Dr., London, Ont. N6G 2S4; Office: #209 - 450 Central Ave., London, Ont. N6B 2E8.

**McKINNEY, James Russell,** B.Com.; retired diplomat; b. Summer Hill, N.B. 28 June 1925; s. George Melbourne and Margaret Jane (Russell) McK.; e. Saint John (N.B.) High Sch., 1940; Dalhousie Univ., B.Com. 1949; Nat. Defence Coll., 1956–57; m. Chloë Constance, d. Col. George W. MacLeod, D.S.O. and Bar, Edmonton, Alta., June 1955; children: Jane, Mark, Nicholas; joined Dept. of External Affairs, 1949; Second Secy., Candn. Embassy, Belgrade, Yugoslavia, 1951–53; Ottawa and Nat. Defence Coll. 1954–57; First Secy., Djakarta, Indonesia 1957–59; First Secy. and later Counsellor, Copenhagen, Denmark 1959–62; Depy. Head, Econ. Div., Dept. of External Affairs, Ottawa 1962–66; High Commr. for Can. in Trinidad and Tobago and in Barbados, Candn. Commr. to W. Indies Assoc. States, 1966–69; Perm. Rep. and Ambassador to O.E.C.D. 1969–72; Minister, Candn. Embassy, Washington 1972–77; Dir. Gen., Bureau of U.S. Affairs and subsequently Asst. Under Secty. Dept. of External Affairs, Ottawa 1977–82; Ambassador to Mexico 1982–85; retired 1985; served with RCAF 1943–45; rank Flying Offr.; Phi Kappa Pi; Anglican; recreations: sailing, skiing, fishing; Club: White Pine Fishing; Address: 762 Eastbourne Ave., Ottawa, Ont. K1K 0H7.

**MCKINNON, Alastair Thomson,** B.A., M.A., Ph.D., B.D., F.R.S.C.; university professor; b. Hillsburgh, Ont. 25 May 1925; s. late Arnold Thomson and late Mary Ella M.; e. sec. sch. Erin, Ont. 1942; Guelph Coll. 1943; Vict. Coll. Univ. of Toronto B.A. 1947; Univ. of Toronto M.A. 1948; Univ. of Edinburgh Ph.D. 1950; McGill Univ. B.D. 1953; m. Mildred Mae d. late Wilson Bousfield Sutton 13 Sept. 1947; children: Mary Catherine (Pfaff), Frances Christine, Angus Thomson; PROF. EMERITUS OF PHILOSOPHY, MCGILL UNIV. 1990– ; Visiting Prof., Søren Kierkegaard Forskningscenteret, Univ. of Copenhagen 1994– ; apptd. Prof. McGill Univ. 1969; Macdonald Prof. of Moral Phil. 1971; Chrmn. of Dept. 1975–83; served with RCNVR, 1944–45; rec'd Rockefeller Travelling Fellowship 1961–62; author of 'Falsification and Belief' 1970, 1978; 'Kierkegaard in Translation en Traduction in Übersetzung' 1970; 'Fundamental Polyglot Konkordans til Kierkegaards Samlede Vaerker' 1975; 'Index Verborum til Kierkegaards Samlede Vaerker' 1973; 'Computational Analysis of Kierkegaard's Samlede Vaerker' 1975; 'Concordance to Wittgenstein's Philosophische Untersuchungen' 1975; 'Dating Kierkegaard's Battles with Fate' 1986; Co-ed. 'revue CIRPHO review' 1973–76; (with N.J. Cappelorn), Kierkegaard Critical Editions Project 1990– ; Ed., 'The Kierkegaard Monograph Series,'; 'The Kierkegaard-Malantschuk Collection'; other writings incl. Kierkegaard, Wittgenstein, Philosophy of religion, moral phil., the use of computers and statistics as aids in the interpretation of philosophical and literary texts; mem. Comité de Redaction, 'Laval theologique et philosophique' 1982–85; Redaktions kommite, 'Kierkegaardiana' 1983– ; Dir., Candn. Fed. for the Humanities 1979–82; named charter mem. Kierkegaard Akademiet 1977–82; Fellow, Roy. Soc. of Canada 1981; mem., Candn. Theol. Soc. (Pres. 1959–60); Sören Kierkegaard Selskabet 1968– ; CIRPHO International (Pres. 1973– ); Candn. Phil. Assn. (Pres. 1979–80); Assn. for Lit. and Ling. Computing; Assn. for Computers and the Humanities; United Church; Club: McGill Univ. Faculty; recreations: carpentry, sailing; Home: 3005 Barat Rd., Montreal, Que. H3Y 2H4; Office: 855 Sherbrooke St. W., Montreal, Que. H3A 2T7.

**MCKINNON, Colin Donald Angus,** Q.C., B.A., LL.B.; barrister & solicitor; b. Montreal, Que. 13 Nov 1944; s. Ronald Angus and Mafalda Maria (Di Paolo) M.; e. St. Patrick's Coll., B.A. 1965; Univ. of Ottawa Law Sch., LL.B. 1968; called to Bar of Ont. 1970; m. Nicole d. Jean Paul and Marcelle Lemieux 14 June 1969; children: John Angus, Caroline Elizabeth, Veronica Christine; PARTNER, BEAMENT GREEN DUST 1972– (certified by the Law Soc. of Upper Canada as a specialist in civic & criminal litigation); Asst. Crown Attorney Ottawa-Carleton 1970–72; Part-time 1972–81; Spec. Agent for Crim. Prosecutions for Att.-Gen. Canada 1972–75; Spec. Counsel, Govt. of Gt. Brit. 1973– ; Counsel to Marin Commission of Inquiry into R.C.M.P. activities ('Cogger Inquiry') 1990–91; Law Soc. of Upper Canada 1975–87; various lecturing & instructing pos., Law Soc. of U.C. 1974– ; Asst. Prof., Univ. of Ottawa Law Sch. 1983–87; Offr. & Trustee, County of Carleton Law Assn. 1974–82 (Pres. 1981) Chrmn., County and District Law Presidents Assn. of Ont. 1983–85; el. Bencher, Law Soc. of Upper Canada 1987; Chair, Professional Standards Ctte.; Vice-Chair, Legal Education Ctte.; mem., Discipline, Equity in Legal Profession, Insurance, Certification of Specialists; Bencher Election Reform, Complaints Procedure Reform, Court Reform, Reform Implementation Cttes.; former Chair, Communications and French Language Services Cttes.; Law Soc. Delegate to Federation of Law Societies of Canada and Court of Appeal Civil Rules Ctte.; Mem., Ont. Counc. Candn. Bar Assn. 1983–85; Founding Dir., Thomas More Lawyer's Guild of Ottawa 1983– ; Dir., Med.-Legal Soc. of Ottawa-Carleton 1984–90; Housing & Urban Devel. Assn. of Canada 1976–79; Pres., Common Law Students Soc., Univ. of Ottawa Law Sch. 1968; Pres., St Patrick's Coll. Student Union 1965; author, numerous published articles; R. Catholic; recreations: squash, tennis, skiing; Clubs: Laurentian, Ottawa Athletic; Home: 2224 Bowman Rd., Ottawa, Ont. K1H 6V5; Office: 1400 - 155 Queen St., Ottawa, Ont. K1P 6L1.

**McKINNON, Douglas J.,** C.M.A.; paperboard industry executive; b. Worthing, England 3 Nov. 1943; e. C.M.A. 1971; m. Maureen Mynett 20 June 1981; children: Randy, Barbara, Adam, Cory; PRESIDENT & CHIEF OPERATING OFFICER, CPL PAPERBOARD INDUSTRIES 1993– ; Vice-Pres. & Chief Finance Officer, Belkin Inc. 1976–87; Sr. Vice-Pres., Finance, Paperboard Industries Corp. 1987–90, Pres. & Chief Oper. Offr. 1990–93; recreations: golf, cycling; Home: 2654 - 133 St., Surrey, B.C. V4P 1X9.

**MCKINNON, Gordon Arthur,** LL.B.; lawyer; b. Winnipeg, Man. 13 June 1953; s. Donald Taylor and Margaret Elizabeth Sproule (Robinson) M.; e. Univ. of Man. Law Sch., LL.B. 1978; m. Lori d. Sidney and Mira Spivak 9 Aug. 1984; children: Sarah, Andrew, Daniel; PARTNER, THOMPSON, DORFMAN, SWEATMAN 1987– ; called to Bar of Man. 1979; practiced with Scarth Simonsen & Co. 1979–84; Partner 1984–87; Trustee, St. James-Assiniboia Sch. Div. 1974–80; Mem., Bd. of Regents, Univ. of Winnipeg 1981– (Chrmn. 1988–90); Home: 664 Ash St., Winnipeg, Man.; Office: 2200 – 201 Portage Avenue, Winnipeg, Man. R3B 3L3.

**McKINNON, Hon. John Kenneth (Ken),** B.A.; commissioner; b. Winnipeg, Man. 20 Apl. 1936; s. Alexander and Catherine (Luce) McK.; e. Holy Cross Sch. Norwood, Man.; Saint Paul's Coll. Winnipeg; Univ. of Man., B.A. 1966; m. Judy d. David and Annie Steven 1970; children: Craig, Alexia; COMNR. OF Y.T. 1986– ; el. M.L.A., Y.T. 1961, re-el. 1967, 1970, 1974; mem. Financial Adv. Ctte. 1962–64, Chrmn. 1968–70; Mgr. Northern Television Systems Ltd. (WHTV) 1972–74, Vice Pres. and Gen. Mgr. 1984–86; Min. of Local Govt. 1974–78; Min. of Highways & Pub. Works 1976–78; Yukon Adm. Northern Pipeline Agency 1979–84; mem. Task Force on N. Conserv. 1983–84; Co-Chrmn. Alaska Highway Gas Pipeline Hearings 1979; Pres. First Arctic Winter Games Corp. 1970–72; Yukon Pres., Counc. for Candn. Unity; Dir., Arctic Inst. of North Am.; Chrmn.: Northern Resources Conf. Scholarship Ctte.; Patron: Yukon/B.C. Scout Counc.; St. John's Ambulance; Whitehorse Cadet Camp; Yukon/B.C. Red Cross; Hon. Mem.: Yukon Chamb. of Comm.; Whitehorse Chamb. of Comm.; Yukon Arts Council; Hon. Chief Yukon Native Brotherhood; former Athlete of Yr. St. Paul's Coll,; K. of C. Debating Award 1961; Internat. Travel Bursary study in Japan Rotary Club 1970; nominated Jaycees Outstanding Young Candn. 1974; Candn. Centennial Medal 1967; Queen's Silver Jubilee Medal 1977; awarded Commemorative Medal for 125th Anniversary of Candn. Confederation 1992; recreations: sports, camping, fishing; Clubs: Rotary (Hon. Mem.); Yukon Order Pioneers; Candn. Cable TV Pioneers; Home: 4 Kluhini Cres., Whitehorse, Y.T. Y1A 3P3; Office: 211 Hawkins St., Whitehorse, Y.T. Y1A 1X3.

**McKNIGHT, Linda Elizabeth,** A.B.; literary agent; b. Kirkland Lake, Ont. 22 Apl. 1942; d. Charles E.V. and Helen B. (Garver) McK.; e. Glebe Coll. Inst. Ottawa 1959; Radcliffe Coll. Cambridge, Mass. A.B. 1963; VICE PRES., STERLING LORD ASSOC. CANADA 1993– ; Ed., Copp Clark 1965; Ed., McClelland and Stewart Ltd. 1969 becoming Mang. Ed., Dir. of Publishing, Vice Pres. Publishing; Pres. and Publisher, 1982–85; Publisher, Macmillan of Canada 1986–89; Pres., MGA Inc. 1989–93; Address: 10 St. Mary St., Toronto, Ont. M4Y 1P9.

**McKNIGHT, William Hunter;** b. Elrose, Sask. 12 July 1940; s. Robert and Jean (Hunter) McK.; e. Elrose, Sask.; m. Beverley Rae d. Harry and Eunice Ogden 4 Nov. 1961; children: Robert Ogden, Torrie Shawn; AGRA-BUSINESS; el. to H. of C. for Kindersley-Lloydminster g.e. 1979, re-el. till retirement 1993; Min. of Labour & Min. Responsible for C.M.H.C. (Canada Mortgage & Housing Corp.), Can. 1984–86; Min. of Indian Affairs and Northern Development 1986–89; Min. of Western Economic Diversification 1987–89; Min. of National Defence 1989–91; Min. of Agriculture 1991–93; Min. of Energy, Mines and Resources 1993; Chrmn., NAFTA Trade Consultants Inc. 1993; Dir., Anvil Range Mining Corp. 1994; Pres. P. Conservative Party Sask. 1974–77; Home: Saskatoon, Sask.; Office: McKnight Commercial Centre, 103B Packham Ave., Saskatoon, Sask. S7N 4K4.

**McLACHLAN, Lt. Gen. (Ret'd) Hugh,** C.M.M., D.F.C., C.D.; retired; b. Gourock, Scot., 19 Sept. 1922; s. late Hugh and Margaret (Campbell) McL.; e. Coalhurst, Alta., Sr. Matric. 1940; RCAF Staff Coll. 1953–54; Nat.

Defence Coll. 1967–68; m. Sybil Ellen, d. late William George Naylor, 17 Aug. 1946; two d. Rhonda Ellen, Patricia May; comnd. as Pilot in RCAF. 1941; served in Middle E. and Greece with R.A.F. fighter sqdns. 1941–45; attained rank Sqdn. Leader; Customs & Excise Div., Lethbridge, Alta. 1945–46; re-enlisted in RCAF 1947; various staff and flying assignments 1947–53; various staff positions, Ottawa 1954–57; C.O. 441 Fighter Sqdn. Marville, France 1958–61; Directing Staff, RCAF Staff Coll. 1961–64; Staff, CFHQ 1964–67; Commdr., 36 NORAD Div., Brunswick, Maine 1968–69; Staff CFHQ 1969–71; promoted Maj. Gen. and mem., Min. of Nat. Defence Mgmt. Review Group 1971; Commdr., Air Transport Command, Trenton 1972–74; Chief of Air Operations, NDHQ 1974; promoted Lt. Gen. and Depy. Chief of Defence Staff 1975–77; Vice-Pres., Government Relations, Rolls Royce Industries Canada Inc. 1977–1991; Anglican; recreations: golf, farming; Club: Royal Ottawa Golf; Home: Apt. 306, 20 Driveway, Ottawa, Ont. K2P 1C8.

**McLACHLAN, William Ian,** M.A.; author; educator; b. London, Eng. 20 Oct. 1938; s. William Nicol and Oonagh (McMartin) M.; e. Ryde Sch., Isle of Wight, 1956; Oxford, Eng. M.A. 1960; m. Dominique Francoise d. Marc Isabelle 20 Sept. 1960; children: Stephane Marc, Jerome Neil, Gavin Matthew; came to Can. 1970; Chrmn., Cultural Studies Program, Trent Univ. 1981; Prof. of English & Cultural Studies 1976– ; Lectr. in English, Univ. of Hong Kong 1960–66, Sr. Lectr. and Chrmn., Dept. of Comparative Lit. 1967–70; Assoc. Prof. of English, Trent Univ. 1970–76; Chrmn., Comparative Lit. Program 1971–75; Master, Peter Robinson College 1977–82; author 'The Seventh Hexagram' 1976; 'Helen in Exile' 1980; 'Shanghai, 1949' 1990; various articles and book chapters; mem., Writer's Union of Can.; Nat. Steering Comte. Cultural Workers Alliance; Chrmn., Bd. of Dirs., Artspace, Peterborough; Emergency Press; Dir. 'border/lines' magazine; winner of Books in Canada Best 1st Candn. Novel Award 1977; was curator 'Arts Against Repression' exhibition, Artspace, Peterborough 1982; Brock Univ., St. Catharines 1982; Hamilton Artists' Inc. Hamilton 1982; Marxist; recreations: work, cars, politics, travel; Home: R.R. 1, Ennismore, Ont. K0L 1T0.

**McLACHLIN, The Hon. Madam Justice Beverley,** B.A., M.A., LL.B.; justice; b. Pincher Creek, Alta. 7 Sept. 1943; d. Ernest and Eleanora Marian (Kruschell) Gietz; e. Univ. of Alta. B.A. 1964, M.A. (Philosophy) 1968, LL.B. 1968; Univ. of B.C. LL.D. 1990; m. late Roderick A. s. Angus and Sheila McLachlin 8 July 1967; m. Frank E. McArdle Feb. 1992; one s. Angus; JUSTICE, SUPREME COURT OF CANADA, 1989– ; called to Bar of Alta. 1969, Bar of B.C. 1971; practised law with Wood, Moir, Hyde & Ross, Edmonton 1969–71; Thomas, Herdy, Mitchell & Co., Fort St. John, B.C. 1971–72; Bull, Housser & Tupper, Vancouver 1972–75; Lectr., Assoc. Prof. and Prof. with tenure, Univ. of B.C. 1974–78; author of numerous publications; mem. Editorial Advisory Bd., Family Law Restatement Project 1987–88 and Civil Jury Instructions 1988; Apptd. to County Court of Vancouver 1981; Apptd. to Supreme Court of B.C. 1981 and to the Court of Appeal of B.C. 1985; Apptd. Chief Justice of the Supreme Court of B.C. 1988; Apptd. to the Supreme Court of Canada 1989; Office: Supreme Court Bldg., Wellington St., Ottawa, Ont. K1A 0J1.

**McLAREN, Angus,** Ph.D.; educator; b. Vancouver, B.C. 20 Dec. 1942; s. Thomas Smiles and Lillian (Brown) McL.; e. Gladstone High Sch. Vancouver 1961; Univ. of B.C., B.A. 1965; Harvard Univ. M.A. 1966, Ph.D. 1971; m. Arlene d. Lloyd and Margaret Tigar 1 July 1965; one child: Jesse; PROF. OF HIST. UNIV. OF VICTORIA 1983– ; Asst. Prof. Univ. of Calgary 1970–71, Grinnell Coll. 1971–73; Sr. Assoc. Fellow, St. Antony's Coll. Oxford 1973–75; Assoc. Prof. present Univ. 1975–83; Visiting Hannah Prof. of Hist. of Med. Univ. of Toronto 1985; author: 'Birth Control in Nineteenth Century England' 1978, 'Sexuality and Social Order' 1983, 'Reproductive Rituals' 1984; 'Our Own Master Race' 1990; 'A History of Contraception' 1990; 'A Prescription for Murder' 1993; co-author: 'The Bedroom and the State' 1986; mem. Soc. Social Hist. of Med.; Candn. Soc. Hist. Med.; Candn. Hist. Assn.; recreation: squash; Home: 4187 W. 11th Ave., Vancouver, B.C. V6R 2L5; Office: Victoria, B.C. V8W 2Y2.

**McLAREN, Digby Johns,** O.C., M.A., Ph.D., F.R.S., F.R.S.C.; geologist; b. Carrickfergus, N. Ireland 11 Dec. 1919; s. James and Louie (Kinsey) McL.; e. Sedbergh Sch. Eng. 1933–37; Queens Coll. Cambridge B.A. 1940, M.A. 1948 (Foundation Scholar 1948, Harkness Scholarship 1949); Univ. of Mich. Ph.D. 1951; Univ. of Ottawa, D.Sc. (h.c.) 1980; Carleton Univ., D.Sc. (h.c.) 1993; m. Phyllis Mary d. Charles Matkin, Lavenham, Eng. 25 March 1942; children: Ian Johns, Patrick, Alison Mary; Visiting Professor, University of Ottawa 1981–88; joined Geol. Survey of Can. as Scient. 1948, Head of Paleontol. 1959–67; Dir. Inst. Sedimentary & Petroleum Geol. 1967–73; Dir. Gen., Geol. Survey of Can. 1973–80; Sr. Advr., Dept. Energy, Mines and Resources 1981–84; Chrmn., Comn. on Stratigraphy, Internat. Union of Geol. Sciences 1972–76; Chrmn. of Bd., Internat. Geol. Correlation Prog (IUGS-UNESCO) 1976–80; Convenor, 2 Dahlem Conferences on Resources and World Development, Berlin 1986 and editor of report publ. 1987; recipient Gold Medal (Pure or Applied Sci.), Profl. Inst. of the Public Service of Can. 1979; Leopold-von-Buch Award, German Geological Soc. 1982; Edward Fitzgerald Coke Medal, Geological Soc. of London 1985; Logan Medal, Geological Assoc. of Can. 1987; President's Award, Candn. Soc. Petrol. Geols. 1988; served with RA 1940–46, Iraq, Iran, Palestine, Syria, Egypt, Italy, rank Capt.; author over 100 publs.; mem. Am. Paleontol. Soc. (Pres. 1969); Candn. Soc. Petrol. Geols. (Pres. 1971); Fellow, Geol. Soc. of America (Pres., 1982); Fellow, Royal Soc. of London; Foreign Assoc., Geol. Soc. France; Foreign Assoc., Nat. Acad. Sci. U.S.A.; Foreign Fellow, European Union of Geosciences; Pres., Royal Soc. of Can. 1987–90; Officer of the Order of Canada; research area: stratigraphy and paleontology, western and northern Canada; past extinctions and asteroid impacts; world development, population and global change; recreations: gardening, orchid culture, cross-country skiing, flute; Home: 248 Marilyn Ave., Ottawa, Ont. K1V 7E5.

**McLAREN, Richard Henry,** H.B.A., LL.B., LL.M., ACI.Arb. (U.K.); C.ARB. (Can.); university professor, lawyer; b. Toronto, Ont. 7 Aug. 1945; s. Richard Evatt and Dorothy Edith (Bastedo) M.; e. Univ. of Western Ont., Sch. of Bus. Admin. H.B.A. 1968; Faculty of Law LL.B. 1971; Univ. of London, LSE, LL.M., 1972; Osgoode Hall, Barrister & Solicitor 1974; children: Joshua Murray, Zachary Kenneth; PROFESSOR, FACULTY OF LAW, UNIV. OF WESTERN ONT. 1972– ; Assoc. Dean, Faculty of Law 1979–82; Visiting Scholar, Stanford Univ., Palo Alto, CA 1986–87; Univ. Lectr. for 22 yrs. & author of several Candn. legal texts; labour arbitrator for 20 yrs.; has been consultant to the Min. of Consumer & Comm. Relations (Ont.); worked as consultant to Anti-Inflation Bd. (Ont.); directed major research proj. on Electronic Funds Transfer systems for Ministries of Att-Gen., Consumer & Comm. Rel., and Transport (all Ont.); currently on Ministerial Adv. Comte. on Personal Property Security Act; Mem. Bankruptcy & Insolvency Act Ctte.; Research Consultant, Ont. Law Reform Comm. (Law of Mortgages Project); Vice-Chrmn., The Grievance Settlement Bd. Ont.; Arbitrator for Ont. Police Arbitration Comm.; Assoc., Chartered Inst. of Arbitrators (U.K.); National Panelist, Am. Arbitration Assn. (U.S.); Panelist, B.C. Internat. Commercial Arbitration Centre; mem., Natl. Academy of Arbitrators (U.S.); Arbitrators' Inst. of Can.; Euro-Arab Arbitration System; Designated Chartered Arbitrator, Arbitrators' Inst. of Canada Inc.; Soc. of Professionals in Dispute Resolution (SPIDR) USA; Corp. of Huron Coll.; Dir., Royal Candn. Humane Assn.; Consumer Debt Counselling Service (London); Dir., Ont. Arbitration & Mediation Inst.; Gov., Trinity Coll. Sch.; author 4-vol. 'Secured Transactions in Personal Property in Canada' 1979, 2nd Ed. 1989; 'Annotations: Personal Property Security Act' 1993; 'Insolvency Law in Canada' 1994; 'Innovative Dispute Resolution: The Alternative' 1994; co-author 'Falconbridge on Mortgages (4th Ed.)' 1977; 'Law and Practice of Commercial Arbitration in Canada' 1982; contr. author 'Personal Property Security Law' 1976; assoc. ed., 'Ont. Law Reports' 1980–82; Ed. 'The Personal Property Security Act Cases Law Reports' 1977– ; holder of McKenzie King Scholarship for study of law at Lond. Sch. of Econ.; recreations: sailing, squash, tennis, stamps; Clubs: University Club of Toronto; London; London Hunt & Country; London Squash Racquets; Alpine Hills Tennis & Swimming (Portola Valley, CA); Home: 383 Huron St., London, Ont. N6A 2K3; Offices: Fac. of Law, Univ. of W. Ont., London, Ont. N6A 3K7.

**McLAREN, Robert Wallace,** B.A.; b. Hamburg, Germany 22 Jan. 1927; s. late Robert Wallace and late Marjorie (Brunton) M.; came to Canada 1932; e. Assumption Coll., Windsor, B.A. 1948; Univ. of W. Ont. B.A. (Hons. Hist.) 1950; Postgrad. studies in Econs., St. Johns Coll., Cambridge 1972–73; m. Marion J., d. late Angus Urquhart Meikle, 30 June 1951; children: Margot (Mrs. D. Moore), Andrea (Mrs. C. McWhinnie), Robert; with Nat. Research Council, Ottawa 1950–56; Attaché, Candn. Embassy, Washington, D.C. 1956–69; Nat. Research Council, Ottawa 1959–62; with Min. Transport, Ottawa 1962–65; Sr. Planner (Asia Program), Dir., Advisers Div., Dir. Educ. Div., Dir. Asia Div. with External Aid Office (later Candn. Internat. Devel. Agency) 1965–72; former Candn. High Commr. to Peoples' Republic of Bangladesh 1973–75; Candn. High Commr. to Tanzania Seychelles, and Mauritius, Candn. Ambassador to Somalia, Madagascar and Comoro Islands 1975–78; Candn. High Commr. to Zimbabwe & Botswana 1980–84; Candn. Ambassador to Mozambique 1980–84; Asst. Sec.-Gen. of the Commonwealth 1984–88; Manager of Change, Commonwealth Secretariat, London 1993; currently Prop., Robert McLaren and Associate (B.C.); served as Pte., Candn. Army (AF) 6th Div. 1945; Hon. Secy., Holothurian Soc.; Un. Church; recreations: swimming, underwater photography boating; Address: 4513 Edgewood Pl., Victoria, B.C. V8X 2N8.

**McLARTY, Donald William;** executive; b. Newcastle, Eng. 21 May 1922; s. Donald and Helen (Groundwater) McL.; e. Woodville Sch. and St. Alban's Coll. Argentina; Univ. of Toronto; m. Hope d. Ivan and Oswald McSloy 12 Apl. 1948; children: Judith, Douglas, Susan, Christine; PRINCIPAL, D.W. MCLARTY CONSULTING 1988– ; Pres. Candn. Assn. of Aerial Surveyors 1968–88; Pres. Hobrough Ltd. Vancouver; Dir. Sulmac Exploration Services Ltd.; Velocity Services Ltd.; Spartan Air Services, S.A., Argentina; Spartan Air Services (Eastern) Ltd. Kenya; Meridian Airmaps Ltd. UK; Aerotechnica de Mexico, S.A.; Gen. Mgr. Aerofoto, Bogota, Colombia and Mng. Dir. Photographic Surveys (Western) Ltd. Vancouver 1946–51; Vice Pres. Genaire Ltd. St. Catharines, Ont. 1951–53; Vice pres. Mktg. Spartan Air Services Ltd. Ottawa 1954–66, Pres. and Chief Extve. Offr. 1966; Vice Pres. Bristol de Mexico, S.A. Mexico, D.F. 1954–66; recipient Queen's Silver Jubilee Medal 1977; served with RCAF 1940–46, Fighter Pilot W. Desert, P.O.W. 1942, escaped 1943; Mentioned in Despatches; mem. Royal Air Forces Escaping Soc. (Pres. 1974–76); Candn. Inst. Surveying; Candn. Aeronautics & Space Inst.; Candn. Adv. Ctte. on Remote Sensing; Inst. Assn. Extves.; Clubs: Royal Ottawa Golf; Royal Candn. Mil. Inst. (Toronto); Home: 306, 1833 Riverside Dr., Ottawa, Ont. K1G 0E8.

**McLATCHIE, William,** B.Sc., Ph.D.; university professor and administrator; b. New Cumnock, Scotland 22 March 1940; s. John and Agnes (Reid) M.; e. Central S.S. (Hamilton); McMaster Univ. B.Sc. 1962, Ph.D. 1966; m. Laureen d. Donald and Violet Snider June 1990; children: William John, David Michael, Joanne (McLatchie) and Cameron, Carolina (McDonald); VICE-PRINCIPAL (RESEARCH) AND DEAN OF GRADUATE STUDIES, QUEEN'S UNIVERSITY AT KINGSTON 1989– ; Nuclear Physics Lab., Univ. of Oxford 1966–68; Chalk River Nuclear Labs. summer 1974, 1975–76; Dept. of Physics, Queen's Univ. 1968– ; Dir., Queen's Nuclear Physics Lab. 1977–83; Associate Dean (Arts & Science) 1984–88; Vice-Principal (Research and Academic Serv.) 1988–89; Bd. of Dir., TRIO 1988– ; CITR 1990– ; Insect Biotech. 1990– ; NSERC-NRC Agency Review Ctte. for Sudbury Neutrino Observatory 1990– ; Bd. of Dir., PARTEQ 1991– ; McMaster University Athletic Hall of Fame 1989 (Soccer); Mem., Candn. Assn. of Physicists; Am. Physical Soc.; author of 75 peer reviewed scientific pubns.; recreations: golf, reading; Home: 100 Cliff Crescent, Kingston, Ont. K7M 1A8; Office: Kingston, Ont. K7L 3N6.

**McLAUCHLAN, Murray Edward;** musician; b. Paisley, Scot. 30 June 1948; came to Can. 1953; HOST, SWINGING ON A STAR, CBC RADIO 1990– ; began career Toronto's Yorkville coffeehouses at 17; first maj. appearance Mariposa Folk Festival 1966; LPS incl. 'Song from the Street' 1971; 'Murray McLauchlan' 1972; 'Day to Day Dust' 1973; 'Sweeping the Spotlight Away' 1974; 'Only the Silence Remains' 1975; 'Boulevard' 1976; 'Hard Rock Town' 1977; 'Greatest Hits' 1978; 'Whispering Rain' 1979; 'Into a Mystery' 1980; 'Storm Warning' 1981; 'Windows' 1982; 'Timberline' 1983; 'Heroes' 1984; 'Midnight Break' 1985; songs recorded by various performers and used in films 'Rip-Off' 1971, 'Partners' 1976, BBC-TV Ont. co-production 'Reflections of Toronto' 1975; CBC Radio series 'Murray McLauchlan's "Timberline"' 1984; CBC TV appearances incl. Gordon Lightfoot's Olympic Benefit; special 'On the Boulevard'; 'Floating over Canada' 1985; song 'If the Wind Could Blow My Troubles Away' chosen as theme for Internat. Yr. of Disabled Persons 1981; Christmas Seals Chrmn., Candn. Lung Assn. 1984; participated in benefits for Barrie, Ont. tornado victims 1985; contrib. to Northern Lights for African Relief Aid record 'Tears Are Not Enough' 1985; Juno awards: Composer of Yr. (for 'Farmer's Song') 1973; Folk Singer of Yr. 1973, 1974; Country Male Artist of Yr. 1975; Country Male Vocalist of Yr. 1976, 1984; Folk Artist of Yr. 1978; RPM Big Country Award: Male Vocalist of Yr. 1985; mem. SOCAN; Office: c/o Swinging on a

Star, CBC Radio, Box 500, Stn. A, Toronto, Ont. M5W 1E6.

**MCLAUGHLIN, Hon. Audrey,** M.P., P.C., B.A., M.S.W.; b. Dutton, Ont. 7 Nov. 1936; d. Wm. and Margaret Brown; e. Univ. of West. Ont., B.A.; Univ. of Toronto, M.S.W.; children: David, Tracy; FEDERAL LEADER, NEW DEMOCRATIC PARTY 1989– ; Career: small business operator, administrator and community worker; operated consulting business, Whitehorse, Yukon; Extve. Dir., Metro Toronto Branch, Candn. Mental Assn.; Caseworker, Children's Aid Soc. of Toronto; taught at Adisadel College, Ghana, W. Africa; has been active member of many organizations within the women's movement of the arts, environment community and anti-poverty groups; el. to H. of C. for the Yukon by-election 20 July 1987; re-el. g.e. 1988, 1993; NDP critic for Northern Development, Health, the Constitution and Women; Apptd. to Privy Council 1991; Honours: Awarded rank of Knight by L'Assemblée internationale des parlementaires de langue française 1991; author: 'A Woman's Place: My Life and Politics' 1992; Offices: 6 - 210 Lambert St., Whitehorse, Yukon Y1A 1Z4 and 531-S Centre Block, House of Commons, Ottawa, Ont. K1A 0A6.

**MCLAUGHLIN, Hon. Bruce,** MLA, B.Sc.; businessman; former politician; b. Edmonton, Alta. 15 Jan. 1946; s. Roy David and Dorothy (Burness) M.; e. Ross Sheppard Comp. H.S.; Univ. of Alta., B.Sc. 1969; Min. of Health and Social Services, Govt. of the N.W.T. 1984; elected Pine Point Town Counc. 1972; re-elected 1973–74, 1979–80, 1983–84; elected N.W.T. Legisl. Assembly for Pine Point 1979; re-elected 1983; Resp. for Highway Transp. Bd. 1984–85; Resp. for Workers' Comp. Bd. 1985; P.C. volunteer worker fed. elections N.W.T. 1972, 1974, 1979, 1980; Alta. 1963, 1967; elected Dir., Nat. Extve., P.C. Party of Can. 1981; Vice-Pres. (Rep. NWT) 1983, 1986; apptd., P.C. Party 1984 Nat. Campaign Ctte.; staff, Cominco 1970–74; Sec.-Treas. & Public Works Supt., Town of Pine Point 1974–76; operated local freight agency 1975–80; Owner, M.B. Holdings Ltd. & Pineridge Enterprises Ltd. 1978– ; Mem., Delta Kappa Epsilon; recreations: coach/mgr., amateur hockey & fastball; Home: P.O. Box 555, Pine Point, N.W.T. X0E 0W0.

**McLAUGHLIN, Edward T.,** B.S.A.; association executive; b. Iroquois, Ont. 9 April 1916; s. Harvey Peter and Annie Margaret (Colquhoun) M.; e. Morrisburg (Ont.) Coll. Inst.; Ont. Agric. Coll., B.S.A. (Agron.); m. Margaret Ruth, d. Alfred Earl Merkley, 14 July 1938; two s. Ian Edward, Peter Ross; Mgr., A.E. McKenzie Ltd., Toronto, Ont. 1950–62; Vice-Pres., Rudy-Patrick Seed Co., Kansas City, Mo., 1963–64; Past Pres., Assn. of Official Seed Certifying Agencies 1977–79; Secy. & Gen. Mgr., Candn. Seed Growers' Assn. 1964–81; Past Pres. The Candn. Seed Trade Assn. 1958–59; inducted Candn. Agricultural Hall of Fame 1984; Anglican; recreations: golfing, fishing; Address: 2 Nanaimo Dr., Nepean, Ont. K2H 6X5.

**McLAUGHLIN, John Douglas,** B.Sc., M.Sc., Ph.D., P.Eng.; professor of engineering; b. Fredericton, N.B. 14 March 1947; s. Archie William and Lois (Mackenzie) M.; e. Univ. of N.B. B.Sc. 1969, M.Sc. 1971; Univ. of Wisconsin Ph.D. 1975; m. Margaret d. Freeman and Aurore Graham Aug. 1971; children: Heather, Katherine, Andrew; PROFESSOR OF ENGINEERING, UNIV. OF NEW BRUNSWICK 1972– ; Pres., Champlain Inst. 1988–92; Principal, Path to Property Foundation 1992– ; Bd. of Dir., N.B. Geographic Information Corp.; Fellow, Inst. for Liberty & Democracy; Bd. of Gov., Univ. of N.B. 1991–94; Past Pres., Candn. Inst. of Geomatics; Candn. Council of Land Surveyors; author of over 200 publications incl. 'Land Information Management' (Oxford U.P.) 1989; Home: 25 Elgin St., Fredericton, N.B. E3B 5P5; Office: Box 4400, Fredericton, N.B. E3B 5A3.

**McLAUGHLIN, Kathryn D.,** B.A.; executive; b. Vancouver, B.C. 21 Sept. 1956; d. Thomas and Nancy Carol Baird; e. Magee S.S. 1973; Univ. of B.C. B.A. (Hons.) 1977; m. Rob s. Robert E. and Arden M. 27 Dec. 1983; children: Conor William Baird, Madison Le Sar; VICE-PRES. & G.M., B.C. ROGERS CANTEL INC. 1991– ; Gen. Mgr., Burson-Marsteller Ltd. 1982–83; Group Mgr., Client Services Dir. 1983–84; Dir. of Marketing, Rogers Cantel Inc. 1984–87; Asst. Vice-Pres., Mktg. 1987–88; Vice-Pres., Mktg. 1988–90; Vice-Pres., Mktg. & Merchandising, Rogers Cantel Retail Div. 1990–91; Dale Carnegie Grad. Asst. 1988–89; 1990 nominee, Marketer of the Year, Toronto Chap., American Mktg. Assn.; Communications Chair, 1991 United Way of Metro. Toronto; club: Royal Vancouver Yacht; Home: 878 Anderson Cres., West Vancouver, B.C. V7T 1S7; Office: 4710 Kingsway, Burnaby, B.C. V5H 4M5.

**McLAUGHLIN, Mary F.;** insurance executive; b. Saint John, N.B. 13 Sept. 1944; e. Ryerson Polytechnical Inst., radio & TV grad 1966; VICE-PRES., PUBLIC AFFAIRS, THE MUTUAL GROUP (INSURANCE); National Vice-Pres., Council for Candn. Unity 1993– ; Dir., Festival of Festivals 1990–93; Mem., Public Affairs Council, Conf. Bd. of Canada 1985– ; Chairperson, Univ. of St. Jerome's 1991–93; Honorary Chairperson, Waterloo Recreation Complex; Office: 227 King St. S., Waterloo, Ont. N2J 4C5.

**MCLAUGHLIN, Terrence Peter Aurèle,** KCSJ; public servant; writer; b. Montreal, Que. 31 Oct 1941; s. Lawrence Peter and Isabelle Evangeline (Valade) M.; e. Loyola H.S.; Sir George Williams Univ.; SENIOR COMMUNICATIONS ADVISOR (SCIENCE & HABITAT), DEPT. OF FISHERIES AND OCEANS, GOVT. OF CANADA 1992– ; Copyboy, then Reporter, The Gazette 1959–61; Asst. Ed., Lakeshore News Ltd. 1961–64; Mng. Ed., Bahamian Rev. Group of Pubs. & 'Newsweek' Rep. Bahamas 1964–67; Assoc., McDermott Assoc. Ltd., a mktg. and public relns. agency, Nassau, Bahamas 1967–71; Infor. Offr., Indian & North. Affairs, Ottawa 1972–73; Dir., PR, Cdn., Construction Assn. 1973–75; Founding Ottawa Mgr., Canada NewsWire 1975–77; Dir. Communications & Nat. Prog. Co-ord., Cdn. Cable TV Assn. 1977–79 (Prod., 'On the House' 1970); priv. practice 1979–89; Communications Advisor to two Special Cttes. of House of Commons (Disabled Persons, 1979–81, and Alternative Energy 1981); Co-ordinator of the joint Federal/Provincial National Seat-Belt Campaign 1981; Pres. Immedia Communications Assoc. Ltd., a property mgmt. co., Ottawa 1984–92 (Dir. 1982–92); Pres., PCC Public Communications Cons. Ltd. 1981–92; Information Offr., Dept. of Communications, Govt. of Canada 1989–92; Prof. communications co-ordinator, Children's Hospital Campaign 1984; Founder, Nat. Capital Livery and Limousine Assn. 1986– ; Official Representative of the Holy See (Vatican) June 5-10, 1989, to the Intl. Symposium on Museology, Hull, Que.; Volunteer communications advisor, Thomas More Lawyers' Guild, Ottawa (re-opening of the Courts and "Red Mass" Service, 1988 and 1989; House of Commons Award of Merit 'for outstanding service to the cause of Freedom of Information' 1975; Knight, Order of St. John of Jerusalem, Knights Hospitaller 1982; Knight of Grace 1985; Commander of Grace 1986; awarded the 'Pontifical Medal' by the Vatican 1989; Pres., The Capital List Ltd. 1976–80; Founding Pres., ACCESS (A Cdn. Ctte. for the Right to Public Information) 1975–76; The New Providence Club, Nassau 1968–71; Founding Pres., The Capital List Ltd., publishers, 1976–80 and Co-editor: 'The Capital List' 1978; Writer/Rsch.: 'Disabled Persons in Canada' 1980 (rev. 1981); author of numerous press articles, pamphlets, papers, ministerial and corporate speeches, etc.; Roman Catholic; Dir., Canada–Argentine Institute (Ottawa) 1991–93; candidate, aldermanic election 1985; Dir., Centretown Citizens' Community Assoc. 1986–89, Heritage Ctte. Chrmn. 1988–89; mem., National Press Club of Can.; Vice-Pres. (Policy) 1992–93, (ISI) Information Services Institute, Ottawa; Past mem., Candn. Pub. Relns. Soc.; Men's Canadian Club; Internat. Food & Wine Soc.; Royal Commonwealth Soc.; Past Ctte. mem. CANSAVE Gala; Heart Fund of Ottawa; and of the Fort Charlotte Ctte., Kiwanis Club of Nassau; author: 'Sir Thomas Summerfield' (fictional autobiography) and 'Miss Piaf Does Not Sit With the Customers' (a collection of short stories) forthcoming; Residence: 402 – 235 Somerset St. W., Ottawa, Ont. K2P 0J3.

**McLAWS, Brig.-Gen. Derek James,** C.D., CF(retd.); NATO executive; b. London, England 19 Aug. 1928; s. James and Doris Norah (Crisfield) M.; e. U.K.; RCAF Command & Staff Coll. 1960–61; Laval Univ. 1972–73; adv. military training courses; m. Margaret M. d. James Arthur Drysdale and Elizabeth Jane Goode 7 July 1951; children: Bruce, Elizabeth, Ian; Chief of Personnel and Admin., NATO Undersea Rsch. Centre 1984–93; comnd. RCAF 1950; var. opn. & staff posts assoc. with Maritime Patrol Aviation to 1966; Depy. Dir. Cadets, NDHQ Ottawa 1969–73; Depy. Dir.-Gen. Bilingualism & Biculturalism 1973–76; Dir., Candn. Forces Exchange System 1976–78; Base Comdr., St. Jean, Qué. 1978–80; Dir.-Gen. Recruiting, Edn. & Training, NDHQ Ottawa 1981–84; Project Mgr., Military Language Training Improvement Prog. 1984; retired 1984; Centennial Medal 1967; Queen's Jubilee Medal 1977; Candn. Forces decoration (2 clasps); Former Mem., Bd. of Trustees, Riverside Hosp., Ottawa; Peoples Warden, Ch. of St. Thomas Apostle, Ottawa; recreations: jogging, bridge; Clubs: Garrison, Quebec City; Circolo San Giorgio, La Spezia, Italy; Circolo Ufficiale di Marina, La Spezia, Italy; RCAF Assn.; Home: 32 Varley Dr., Kanata, Ont. K2K 1G2.

**McLAY, Alan Drummond,** B.A., M.A., Ph.D.; university professor; b. Hamilton, Ont. 31 Aug. 1931; s. Alexander Boyd and Catherine Lucy (Drummond) M.; e. Westdale S.S. 1950; McMaster Univ. B.A. 1954; Univ. of N.B., M.A. 1960; Univ. of Wisconsin, Ph.D. 1969; m. Mary d. William and Antonina Matkowsky 24 Oct. 1959; children: Alexander, Anne, Carol, Sonia, Eric; ASSOC. PROF., DEPT. OF ENGLISH, CARLETON UNIV. 1969– (Chrmn. 1985–88); Lt., Royal Candn. Navy Res. (retd); Modern Lang. Teacher, Pickering Coll. 1955–58; Lectr., Dept. of Eng., Carleton Univ. 1963–65; Asst. Prof. 1965–69; Assoc. Prof. 1969– ; Asst. to Dean of Arts 1967–71; Supr., Grad. Studies, Dept. of Eng. 1978–81; Chrmn., Dept. of English 1985–88; Co-Chrmn., Children's Lit. Assn. Conf. May 1987; mem., United Ch. of Can.; Assn. of Candn. Univ. Teachers of English; Candn. Soc. for Renaissance Studies; Children's Lit. Assn.; recreations: reading, boating; Clubs: Faculty Club; Carleton Univ.; Home: 83 Ossington Ave., Ottawa, Ont. K1S 3B5; Office: Ottawa, Ont. K1S 5B6.

**McLEAN, Alexander,** B.Sc., Ph.D., A.R.C.S.T., F.I.B.F., F.I.Ref.E., C.Eng., P.Eng; university professor; b. Hamilton, Scotland 21 Aug. 1936; s. Thomas and Agnes Gibson (Mackie) M.; e. Royal Coll. of Sci. & Technol. (Scotland) A.R.C.S.T. 1958; Univ. of Glasgow B.Sc. 1958, Ph.D. 1963; Univ. of Miskolc Doctorem Honoris Causa 1992; m. Elizabeth d. Elizabeth and John McGill 17 June 1961; children: Thomas Alexander, Elizabeth Helen; DIR., FERROUS METALLURGY RESEARCH GROUP, UNIV. OF TORONTO 1984– ; postdoctoral fellow then Assoc. Prof., McMaster Univ. 1963–68; Supvr., Deoxidation & Casting Group, Graham Rsch. Lab., Jones & Laughlin Steel Corp. 1968–70; Prof., Dept. of Metallurgy, Univ. of Toronto 1970– ; Dept. Chair 1992– ; Cons. Prof., Wuhan Iron & Steel Univ., People's Rep. of China; Adjunct Prof., Chiba Inst. of Technol., Japan; several past extve. positions with CIMM & AIME; Hon. Mem., AIME; Hon. Mem., OMBKE (Hungary); F.I.B.F.; F.I.Ref.E.; Mem., ASM Internat.; Am. Foundrymen's Soc.; Iron and Steel Soc., and T.M.S.; AIME; CIM; Inst. of Materials (UK); Iron & Steel Inst. of Japan; Assn. of Profl. Engrs. (Ont.); Engineering Council (UK); consultant to a number of cos. in N. Am.; served on boards of several Candn. companies & Mngt. Bd., Am. Iron & Steel Inst.; Sc. and Tech. Council, Inland Steel Co.; Gov., Candn. Nazarene Coll. (Winnipeg); Trustee, ISS Found., Iron & Steel Soc. of AIME (Pittsburgh); recipient of several awards & honours; Bd. Mem. & Trustee, Oakville Ch. of the Nazarene; author of over 170 tech. papers & co-author of 5 books, most recent: 'Continuous Casting Vol. 6' 1992; co-holder of U.S. patent 4,738,719; recreations: music, painting, reading, walking, driving, swimming; club: Royal Scottish Auto.; Home: 104, Solingate Dr., Oakville, Ont. L6L 3S6; Office: Toronto, Ont. M5S 1A4.

**MCLEAN, Allan K.,** M.P.P.; politician; dairy farmer; b. Barrie, Ont. 20 Mar. 1937; s. Edgerton and Mamie (Caldwell) M.; e. secondary; m. Marjorie d. Albert and Doris Blythe; children: Gary, Nancy, Sandra, Patsy, Angela, Darrin; M.P.P., SIMCOE EAST, GOVT. OF ONTARIO 1981– ; Chrmn., Standing Ctte. on Gen. Govt. & Deputy Whip 1983–85; Min. without Portfolio & Chief Govt. Whip Feb. 1985; Minister without Portfolio, Min. of Municipal Affairs & Housing May 1985; Deputy Whip Nov. 1985; Chrmn., Standing Ctte. on Govt. Agencies; on Gen. Govt.; on the Ombudsman; Critic for Tourism & Rec. & Dep. Critic, Agric. & Food Oct. 1987; Critic for Natural Resources and Mines 1990; first elected to local govt. in 1963; served as Deputy Reeve then Reeve of Oro Twp.; Warden of Simcoe Co. 1980; owner of 200-acre dairy farm in Dalston, Ont. Past Dir., Simcoe Co. Holstein Assn.; Past Chrmn., Conservation Authority of Ont. (Central Reg.); Nottawasaga Conservation Authority; Shriner; recreations: boating, hockey, fishing; Home: Orillia, Ont.; Office: Rm 122, North Wing, Legislative Bldg., Toronto, Ont. M7A 1A8.

**McLEAN, Reverend Canon Bradley Halstead,** B.Sc., M.Div., M.Th., Ph.D.; university administrator; b. Toronto, Ont. 8 May 1957; s. Bevis Leonard and Gayle Hedley (Halstead) M.; e. McMaster Univ. B.Sc. 1979; Univ. of Toronto M.Div. 1979, M.Th. 1987; Univ. of St. Michael's College Ph.D. 1989; m. Shauna J. Pugsley 7 May 1983; children: Hudson B., Merrill D.; DEAN OF THEOLOGY, ST. JOHN'S COLLEGE, UNIV. OF MANITOBA 1992– ; Sessional Lecturer, Toronto Sch. of Theology summer 1991; Fac. of Divinity, Trinity College, Univ. of Toronto 1991–92; Curate,

St. Giles' Ch., Diocese of Durham England 1983–85; Curate, St. Paul's Ch., Diocese of Toronto 1984–85; Incumbent, Parish of Mono 1985–87; Hon. Asst. St. Peter's Ch., Diocese of Toronto 1989–91; Assoc. Priest 1991–92; Canon, Diocese of Rupert's Land 22 Oct. 1992; Priest, Diocese of Toronto, Anglican Ch. of Can. 6 Jan. 1985; Deacon, Diocese of Durham, Church of England 3 July 1983; Mem., Soc. of Biblical Literature; Candn. Soc. of Biblical Studies; Assn. Internat. d'Epigraphie Grecque et Latine; Brit. Inst. of Arch. in Ankara; author: 'The Cursed Christ' forthcoming, 'Citations and Allusions to Jewish Scripture in Early Christian and Jewish Writings through 180 C.E.' 1992; editor: 'Origins and Method' 1993; Home: 38 Tweedsmuir Rd., Winnipeg, Man. R3P 1Z1; Office: 400 Dysart Rd., Winnipeg, Man. R3T 2M5.

**McLEAN, Brian L.;** media executive; b. Calgary, Alta. 19 May 1943; s. Daniel Lloyd and Florence Alberta (Lindsay) M.; e. North Toronto Coll.; Ryerson P.I.; York Univ.; m. Deborah d. Thomas and Ellenor Fry 18 Oct. 1969; children: Peirson, Meredith; PRES. & C.E.O. MEDIACOM IND. 1987– ; Mgr., Mall Poster Advtg. Sales, Mediacom 1972–74; Vice-Pres., Nat. Sales (Toronto) 1974–76; Media Sales 1976–78; Sr. Vice Pres. 1978–80; New Products 1980–82; Business Devel. 1982–84; Pres., Mediacom West. Reg. (Winnipeg) 1984–86; Pres., Mediacom Prod. Group 1986–87; Dir., Winnipeg Art Gallery; mem., United Way Commun. Ctte.; Candn. Red Cross Liaison Ctte.; Home: 18 Snowdon Ave., Toronto, Ont.; Office: 250 Bloor St. E., Toronto, Ont. M4W 1G6.

**McLEAN, Bruce,** C.A.; utilities executive; b. 19 Feb. 1943; e. C.A. 1966; VICE PRES., CUSTOMER ACCOUNTING SERVICES, CENTRA GAS MANITOBA INC.; assoc. with Inter-City Group of Companies 1967–90; Westcoast Energy Inc. 1990– ; Home: 49 Mager Dr. W., Winnipeg, Man. R2M 0S1; Office: 444 St. Mary Ave., Winnipeg, Man. R3C 3T7.

**McLEAN, David George Alexander,** B.A., LL.B., LL.D.(Hon.); business executive; b. Calgary, Alta. 25 June 1938; e. Univ. of Alberta B.A. 1959, LL.B. 19 62; m. Brenda 28 April 1972; children: Jason David Duncan, Sacha Rutherford Franklin; CHAIRMAN & CHIEF EXECUTIVE OFFICER, MCLEAN GROUP 1985– ; Founding Partner, McLean Hungerford & Simon, Barristers & Solicitors until 1985; Dir., Canadian National 1979–86; DeHavilland Aircraft 1976–80; Nu-West Devel. Corp.; Bd. Chair, Westech Information Systems Inc.; Achievement Award, Downtown Vancouver Assn. 1987; Dir., Candn. C. of C. 1986–93 (Bd. Chair 1992–93); Bd. Chair, Vancouver Bd. of Trade 1992–93; U.B.C. 1983–85; Honorary Doctor of Laws U.B.C. 1994, U. of A. 1994; recreations: skiing, golf; clubs: Vancouver, Royal Vancouver Yacht, Shaughnessy Golf & Country, Faculty Club (UBC); Home: 4721 Drummond Dr., Vancouver, B.C. V6T 1B3; Office: 375 Water St., Ste. 400, Vancouver, B.C. V6B 5C6.

**McLEAN, David Ian,** B.Sc., M.D., FRCP(C); physician, university professor; b. Brandon, Man. 8 June 1947; s. Ian Arthur L. and Marjory Nina (Wilding) M.; e. Univ. of Manitoba B.Sc. 1971, M.D. 1971; m. Siu-Li d. Nyuk Lin Yong; children: Lianne, Robert; ASSOC. PROF., UNIV. OF BRITISH COLUMBIA 1989– ; Resident in Dermatology, U.B.C. 1973–75; McGill Univ. 1975–76; Fellow, Harvard Univ. 1976–77; Asst. Prof., U.B.C. 1977–89; Head, Div. of Dermatology UBC and Vancouver General Hospital 1989– ; Head, Div. of Dermatologic Oncology, B.C. Cancer Agency 1978– ; Trustee, Vancouver Art Gallery 1989–92; Co-Chair, Benefactor Program Vancouver Art Gallery 1989–92; Trustee, Friends of Chamber Music 1992– ; Chair, Grant Ctte., Candn. Dermatology Found. 1993– (Vice Pres. 1989–93); Pres., Candn. Professors of Dermatology 1993– ; Secy.-Treas., Candn. Soc. of Investigative Dermatology 1993– ; Sr. Assoc. Ed. 'Canadian Journal of Dermatology' 1988–92; Editor, 'Dermatology Times of Canada'; Mem. Editorial Bd. 'Journal of the American Academy of Dermatology'; 'Journal of Dermatologic Treatment'; Pres., Candn. Melanoma Found. 1991– ; author of 48 publications; Clubs: Vancouver Club; Royal Vancouver Yacht Club; Office: 855 West 10th Ave., Vancouver, B.C. V6T 1Z4.

**McLEAN, Donald Millis,** B.Sc., M.D., F.R.C.P.C.; educator; m. Melbourne, Australia 26 July 1926; s. late Donald and Nellie Victoria (Millis) McL.; e. Univ. of Melbourne, B.Sc. 1947, M.B., B.S. 1950, M.D. 1954; m. Margaret Joyce d. late Charles Hicks 29 Dec. 1976; PROF. EMERITUS OF MED. MICROBIOL. UNIV. OF B.C. 1991– ; Consultant Microbiol. to University Hosp., UBC Site, Vancouver 1967–91; Assoc. Prof. of Microbiol. Sch. of Hygiene Univ. of Toronto and Virologist Hosp. for Sick Children 1958–67; author 'Virology in Health Care' 1980; 'Immunological Investigation of Human Virus Diseases' 1982; 'Same-Day Diagnosis of Human Virus Infections' 1984; 'Virological Infections' 1988; "Medical Microbiology Synopsis" 1991; 'Recognition, Identification and Prevention of Acute Viral Infections' 1991; various articles in Candn. and U.S. prof. journs.; mem. Candn. Med. Assn.; and other prof. socs. Can., USA and UK; Presbyterian; Home: 6 - 5885 Yew St., Vancouver, B.C. V6M 3Y5.

**McLEAN, (Alexander) Duncan;** fine art auctioneer and appraiser; b. Keswick, Eng. 22 June 1954; s. Ronald and Nancy Margaret (Clough) McL.; e. Rosseau Lake Coll. Ont. 1974; Trent Univ. anthrop. studies; m. Tess d. Gunnar and Noreen Saare 20 July 1989; joined family bus. Waddington, McLean & Co. Ltd. 1978; estbd. Inuit Art Dept. and held first maj. auction N.Am. Inuit Art (The William Eccles Coll.); apptd. Head Candn. Art Dept. 1980; auctioneer most maj. charity groups Toronto; recreations: native culture & art, travel, arch. design; Club: National; Office: 189 Queen St. E., Toronto, Ont. M5A 1S2.

**McLEAN, Eric Donald,** O.C. (1975); retired; b. Montreal West, Que. 25 Sept. 1919; s. William Ernest and Emma Alice (Keillor) Mcl.; e. Montreal West (Que.) High Sch.; McGill Univ. Arts and Music 1945; studied composition privately with Claude Champagne; joined The Standard (Montreal), first as Entertainment Critic 1945–47, then as Editor of Standard magazine 1947–49; Music Critic, The Montreal Star 1950–79; Music Critic, The Gazette, Montreal 1979–90; consultant restoration and conserv., City of Montreal 1963–64; Gov. McGill Univ. 1970–80; mem. Can. Council 1971–77; mem. Metrop. Arts Counc. 1957–77 (Vice Pres. 1975); Charter Mem. Jacques Viger Comn. (Vice Pres. 1984, Pres. 1988– ); Dir., Montreal Mus. of Fine Arts 1979–82; McCord Museum 1980– ; served as Wireless Operator RAF Transport Command during World War II; rec'd Candn. Music Council Award 1973; author 'The Living Past of Montreal' 1964; Eng. Transl. Jean Palardy's 'The Early Furniture of French Canada' 1963; mem. Internat. P.E.N.; Fellow, Royal Soc. Arts; Music Critics' Assn. (Pres. 1964); Liberal; Protestant; recreation: restoration of historic bldgs.; Club: McGill Faculty; Home: 440 rue du Bon-Secours, Montreal, Que. H2Y 3C4.

**McLEAN, George Elson,** R.C.A.; artist, painter; b. Toronto, Ont. 18 Sept. 1939; s. William Gordon and Violet Winona (Sanders) M.; e. Northern Vocational Inst.; m. Helen d. William and Gertrude Wills 24 Aug. 1963; painter, wild animal portraits since 1957; exhibited in Britain, Europe, Japan, U.S.A.; his works are in several museums & private collections; major show at Royal Ontario Museum 1990–91; subject of 'George McLean, Paintings from the Wild' (David Lank author); Home: R.R. 1, Bognor, Ont. N0H 1E0.

**McLEAN, Guy Scott,** M.A.; headmaster; b. London, Ont. 1 Feb. 1949; s. Ian Merritt and Felicity Ann (Brown) McL.; e. Sedbergh Sch. Montebello, Qué. 1965; Atlantic Coll. Wales 1967; Swarthmore (Pa.) Coll., B.A. 1970; Univ. of Wis., M.A. 1971; m. Joanne d. William and Frances Whiting 28 June 1969; one d. Jennifer; HEADMASTER, APPLEBY COLL. 1987– ; Teacher present Coll. 1971– , Athletic Dir. Jr. Sch. 1976–83, Asst. Dir. Jr. Sch. 1977–83, Dir. of Studies 1983–87; Trustee, Toronto Children's Chorus; Trustee Sedbergh Sch.; Club: University; Address: 540 Lakeshore Rd. W., Oakville, Ont. L6K 3P1.

**McLEAN, Hugh John,** C.M. (1988), Stern der Völkerfreundschaft, German Democratic Republic (1990), Mus.B. (Cantab), M.A. (Cantab), F.R.C.O. (1953), F.R.S.C. (1977), F.R.C.C.O. hon. causa (1988), F.R.C.M. (1985); musician; educator; b. Winnipeg, Man. 5 Jan 1930; s. Robert and Olive May (Smallwood) McL.; e. Pub. and High Schs., Winnipeg; studied music privately Winnipeg and Vancouver 1937–49; Univ. of Man., Assoc. of Music 1947; Assoc. Bd., Royal Schs. of Music, Lic. 1948; Royal Coll. of Music, Assoc. 1951; Univ. of Cambridge, B.A. 1954; Mus.B. 1956, M.A. 1958; m. Gunlaug Julie Gaberg, 8 Jan. 1951, d. 1978; children: Robert Andreas, John Stuart, Hugh Dundas; m. Florence Anne Stillman 18 Aug. 1979; children: Ross Alan, Olivia Anne; PROF. FACULTY OF MUSIC, UNIV. OF WESTERN ONT.; Dean, Fac. of Music there 1973–80; Founder (1958) and Music Dir., Hugh McLean Consort; CBC Vancouver Singers 1963–73; Music Consultant, Ang. Ch. and Un. Ch. of Can. Jt. Comte. on Preparation of Hymn Book; Organist, St. Luke's Ang. Ch., Winnipeg 1945–47; Cdn. Mem. Ch., Vancouver 1947–49; Organ Scholar, King's Coll., Univ. of Cambridge 1951–55; Organist and Choirmaster, Ryerson Un. Ch., Vancouver, B.C. 1957–73; St. John's Angl. Ch., London, Ont. 1977– ; toured Switzerland as organist 1952, 1955, 1972, 1985; Finland 1975; Japan 1976, Germany 1980; England 1980–81; U.S.S.R. 1988; organ performances with Vancouver and Toronto Symphonies and Nat. Arts Centre Orch. (Ottawa); various CBC and BBC broadcasts; solo recitals in major Cdn. and Amer. cities; Founder and Music Dir., Vancouver Cantata Soc. 1958–67; toured W. Europe for CBC recording music on famous pipe organs 1963; Asst. Prof. of Music, Univ. of Victoria 1967–69; Assoc. Prof. of Music, Univ. of B.C. 1969–73; rec'd various scholarships, prizes and awards incl. Arnold Bax Commonwealth Medal 1954; Harriet Cohen Bach Medal 1955; Can. Council Grants 1960, 1965, 1972, 1980, 1983, 1985; compositions incl. incidental music for CBC radio dramas 'Much Ado About Nothing' 1962; 'Antony & Cleopatra' 1964; transcriptions & eds. for CBC Festival of Music 1966, 1973; Ed., 'Organ Works' (by Henry Purcell) 1957 (2nd ed. 1967); 'Andante in F for Mechanical Organ' (by W.A. Mozart) 1957; 'Concerto in B Flat for Organ and Orchestra' (by William Felton) 1957; 'Two Voluntaries for Organ from the Nanki Manuscript' (by John Blow) 1971; 'Collected Works for Solo Instrument and Organ' (by J.L. Krebs) 1981; 'Suite in D for violin and harpsichord' (Anon. Eng., 18th cent.) 1987; author various articles, incl. 19 for New Grove Dictionary of Music (1980), reviews and papers; life mem., AFMUSC Vancouver local; Royal Musical Assn.; recreation: collecting antiquarian music and books; Home: 1020 Maitland St., London, Ont. N5Y 2X9; Office: Faculty of Music, Univ. of W. Ont., London, Ont. N6A 3K7.

**McLEAN, Leslie C.,** M.Sc., Ph.D., P.Eng.; executive; b. St. Catharines, Ont. 7 Feb. 1941; e. McMaster Univ. B.Sc. 1965, M.Sc. 1966, Ph.D. 1969; m. Nadine L. LeBlanc 1973; 2 children; PRESIDENT, STELTECH LTD. 1994– ; Dir., Hatchcos Ltd.; Steltech Ltd.; Manufacturing Rsch. Corp. of Ont.; mem. Min.'s Nat. Adv. Council to CANMET; Canadian Academy of Engineering; Gov. McMaster Univ.; Premier's Council on Economic Renewal; Office: 2800 Speakman Dr., Sheridan Science and Technology Park, Mississauga, Ont. L5K 2R7.

**McLEAN, Marianne Louise,** B.A., M.A., Ph.D.; historian; b. Winnipeg, Man. 18 Nov. 1949; d. Louis Raymond and Renée Marie (Lovatt) M.; e. Univ. of Montreal B.A. (Hons.) 1970; Carleton Univ. M.A. 1972; Univ. of Edinburgh Ph.D. 1982; m. Philip s. Charles and Jean Goldring 13 Dec. 1969; children: Dmitri, Hugh, Alexander, Colin; ARCHIVIST, MSS DIV., NATIONAL ARCHIVES 1982– ; author: 'The People of Glengarry: Highlanders in Transiton, 1745–1820' 1991; recreations: cycling, hiking; Home: 53 Pooler Ave., Ottawa, Ont. K2B 5A3; Office: 395 Wellington St., Ottawa, Ont. K1A 0N3.

**MCLEAN, Ronald,** F.R.I.C.S.; fine art auctioneer and appraiser; b. Penrith, England 25 Aug. 1924; s. Joseph Robert and Eleanor Teresa (Little) M.; e. Trinity Sch.; Coll. of Estate Mngt.; m. Nancy; d. James and Elizabeth Clough 4 Oct. 1950; children: Alastair J., A. Duncan, Donald P.; OWNER & PRES., WADDINGTON, MCLEAN & CO. LTD. 1960– ; Articled pupil, Penrith, Farmers & Kidds Auctioneers & Estate Agents 1939–42; served Royal Engrs. 1942–47; Mgr., Lake Dist. Area of England, Penrith, Farmers & Kidds 1947–57; emigrated to Can. 1957; joined Ward, Price Ltd. 1957–60; Dir. 1958–60; Fellow, Chartered Auctioneers & Estate Agents Inst. 1955; Royal Inst. of Chartered Surveyors 1970; recreations: gardening, travel, the arts; Club: Bd. of Trade; Home: 106 Briar Hill Ave., Toronto, Ont. M4R 1H9; Office: 189 Queen St. E., Toronto, Ont. M5A 1S2.

**McLEAN, Seaton S.,** B.A.; television producer; b. Clearwater, Fla. 19 Feb. 1955; s. Allan and Lily (Seaton) M.; e. Queens Univ. B.A. 1978; TELEVISION PRODUCER, ATLANTIS FILMS LIMITED; Spv. Prod., 'Maniac Mansion' 44 eps (Can., U.S.) 1990–91; Prod., 'Glory Glory' 2 eps (Can., U.S.) 1988, 'The Twilight Zone' 30 eps (Can., U.S.) 1988, 'Ray Bradbury Theatre' 18 eps (Can., U.S.A., France, U.K.) 1985–88 (Gemini 1986), 'A Child's Christimas in Wales' (Can., U.S., U.K.) 1987 (Gemini 1988), 'Really Weird Tales' 3 eps (Can., U.S.) 1986 (CFTA); Co-Prod., 'Journey into Darkness: The Bruce Curtis Story' 1990, 'Magic Hour' 8 eps 1989–90, 'Bell Canada Playhouse' 25 eps 1984–85, 'Sons and Daughters' 11 eps 1982–83 (Bijou, CFTA); Co-Prod. & Ed., 'Brothers By Choice' 6 eps 1985 (CFTA, Oscar), 'The Olden Days Coat' 1981 (Bijou, CFTA); Dir., 'Airwaves' 1 eps 1985; Office: 65 Heward Ave., Toronto, Ont. M4M 2T5.

**McLEAN, Stuart,** B.A.; educator; journalist; b. Montréal, Qué. 19 Apr. 1948; s. Andrew Thompson and Margret Patricia (Godkin) McL.; e. Lower Can. Coll. 1965; Sir George Williams Univ., B.A. 1971; m. Linda d.

Margaret and Ed Read 10 July 1983; children: Andrew, Robert, Christopher Trowbridge (step-son); DIR. OF BROADCAST JOURNALISM, RYERSON POLYTECHNICAL INST. 1984– ; Prof. 1987– ; Adm. Dawson Coll. Montréal 1971–74; Extve. Producer CBC Radio 'Sunday Morning' 1981–83; began series weekly essays CBC Radio 'Morningside' 1984; co-writer 'Looking for Miracles' (feature film); author 'The Morningside World of Stuart McLean' 1989; 'Welcome Home: Travels in Small Town Canada' 1992 (Best Non-fiction Award, Candn. Authors Assn. 1993); contbr. 'The New Morningside Papers' 1987; 'The Latest Morningside Papers' 1989; recipient 3 nominations best documentary ACTRA; ACTRA Award best documentary 1979; B'nai Brith Award Human Rights Broadcast Journalism 1985; nominated Gordon Sinclair Award 1985; Office: 350 Victoria St., Toronto, Ont. M5B 2K3.

**McLEAN, Hon. Walter Franklin,** P.C., B.A., M.Div.; politician; b. Leamington, Ont. 26 Apr. 1936; e. Victoria Coll. B.C.; Univ. of B.C., B.A. 1957; Knox Coll. Univ. of Toronto M.Div. 1960; Univ. of Edinburgh; m. Barbara Scott 1961; four s. Scott, Chima, Duncan, Ian; el. to H. of C. for Waterloo 1979, re-el. 1980, 1984, 1988; sworn to Privy Council 1984; Secretary of State, Canada 1984–85; Min. Responsible for the Status of Women 1984–85; Min. of State (Immigration) 1985–86; Candn. del. to 41st, 42nd, 43rd, 44th, 45th, 46th, 47th and 48th Gen. Assembly of the U.N. in New York 1986–93; attended 3rd UN Special Session on Disarmament (UNSSOD III) 1988; Appt. Special Representative on Southern African and Commonwealth Affairs 1989; Candn. Rep. at Southern Africa Development Co-Ordination conference (SADCC) 1987, 1988, 1989, 1990, 1991, 1992, 1993; Joint Human Rights Delegation to Guatamala & El Salvador 1993; led Candn. Del. to South Pacific Forum 1993; Candn. Rep. at the Commonwealth Foreign Ministers' Conferences in 1987, 1988, 1989 and 1991; Chrmn. of Internat. Council, (PGA) Parliamentarians Global Action (co-founder 1981); Mem., Standing Ctte., External Affairs & International Trade - Chair, Sub-Ctte. on Internat. Debt. - Chair, Sub-Ctte. on Development & Human Rights; attended joint conf. Assoc. of West European Parliamentarians for Action Against Apartheid (AWEPPA) 1988; former mem., Standing Cttes. on Communications & Culture; Human Rights and Status of Disabled Persons; External Affairs and Nat. Defence; Can.'s Rlns. with Latin Am. & Caribbean; Led Parliamentary Delegation to observe the pre-election process and attended Namibian Independence March 21, 1990; Accompanied Rt. Hon. Joe Clark to welcome Nelson Mandela to Lusaka, Zamibia, Feb. 1990; Visits to Russia & Ukraine 1990, 1992; co-founder of CUSO and first Nigerian Co-Ordinator, Chaplain Univ. of Nigeria; Presbyterian Missionary 1962–67; joined staff Candn. Centennial 1967, pioneering 'Miles for Millions' walks; apptd. Extve. Dir., Man. World Devel. Assn.; Extve. Dir., Man. Centennial Corp.; Min., Knox Presbyn. Ch. Waterloo 1971–79; twice elected Ald. City of Waterloo; former Dir., Candn. Council Chs.; Comm. on World Concerns; Mem., The Group of 78, Padre RCAF Assn. 404 Wing; Club: Rotary; Address: 122 Avondale Ave. S., Waterloo, Ont. N2L 2C3.

**McLEAN, William Alexander,** B.A., M.Sc.; conservation executive; b. Toronto, Ont. 4 Sept. 1935; s. Alexander and Beatrice Levina (Moffat) M.; e. Earl Haig Coll.; McMaster Univ., B.A. (Hons.) 1959; Michigan State Univ., M.Sc. 1962; m. Margaret d. Lee and Mary Begg 19 Aug. 1961; children: Barbara, Deborah, Angela; C.A.O., The Metro. Toronto & Region Conservation Authority 1983–92 (Retired); Planner & Conservation Area Admin. 1959–70; Admin. of Lake Ont. Waterfront Devel. for Metro. & Region waterfront projects 1970–76; Policy Dir. & Dep. Gen. Mgr. 1976–83; Queen's 25th Anniv. Medal; Mem., Bd. of Trustees, Humbercrest Un. Ch.; Mem., Candn. Parks/Rec. Assn. (Past Pres.); Club: Bd. of Trade of Metro. Toronto; Vice-Pres., Conservation Found. of Greater Toronto 1993– ; Home: 41 Langmuir Cres., Toronto, Ont. M6S 2A8.

**McLEAN, William Flavelle;** b. Toronto, Ont. 1916; s. late James Stanley and Edith (Flavelle) McLean; e. Univ. of Toronto Schools; Univ. of Toronto B.Sc. (Honours in Chemical Engineering) 1938; m. June McClure, Toronto, Ont.; two s. and one d.; Home: 32 Whitney Ave., Toronto, Ont. M4W 2A8; Office: Suite 1008, 2 St. Clair Ave. W., Toronto, Ont. M4V 1L5.

**McLELLAN, A. Anne,** B.A., LL.B., LL.M.; politician, university professor, lawyer; b. Hants County, N.S. 31 Aug. 1950; d. Howard Gilmore and Joan Mary (Pullan) M.; e. Dalhousie Univ. B.A. 1971, LL.B. 1974; Univ. of London (King's College) LL.M. 1975; MINISTER OF NATURAL RESOURCES, GOVERNMENT OF CANADA 1993– ; admitted to Bar of N.S. 1976 (currently holds status of non-practicing member, N.S. Bar); Asst. Prof. of Law, Univ. of N.B. 1976–80 (Acting Assoc. Dean 1.5 years); Assoc. Prof. of Law, Univ. of Alta. 1980–89; Assoc. Dean 1985–87; Prof. 1989–93; Acting Dean 1991–92; 1st elected M.P. for Edmonton Northwest g.e. 25 Oct. 1993; Home: 10332 – 135 St., Edmonton, Alta. T5N 2C3.

**McLELLAN, Edward R.,** B.Sc., M.Eng., P.Eng.; public servant; b. Fredericton, N.B. 17 April 1938; s. William Wilkinson and Dorothy Mildred (McDonald) M.; e. Fredericton H.S. 1956; Univ. of N.B., B.Sc. 1961; Univ. of Alta. M.Eng. 1968; Banff Sch. of Adv. Mgnt. 1982; m. Phyllis d. Peter and Alexandra Pawliuk 16 June 1962; children: Katherine, William; DEPUTY MIN., ALTA. PUBLIC WORKS, SUPPLY & SERV. 1987– ; Engr., Northern Affairs & Natural Resources, Yellowknife, N.W.T. 1961–62; Struct. Eng. & Sr. Struct. Eng., Alta. Public Works 1962–72; Project Mgr. 1973–76; Dir., Construction Br., Alta. Housing & Public Works 1977–81; Asst. Dep. Min., Design & Constr. Div. 1981–83; Asst. Dep. Min. Properties, Alta. Public Works, Supply & Serv. 1983–87; Mem., Assn. of Profl. Engrs., Geophys. & Geol. of Alta.; recreations: golf, hockey, gardening; Home: 4232 Whitemud Rd., Edmonton, Alta. T6H 5S8; Office: 6950 – 113th St., Edmonton, Alta. T6H 5V7.

**McLELLAN, Nora;** actress; singer; b. Vancouver, B.C. 29 Oct. 1954; d. Godfrey and Jeanne (Viaud) McClelland; e. Univ. of B.C.; HB Studio, New York (with Uta Hagen); profl. stage debut at age 9, in 'La Boheme,' Vancouver Opera Assn.; Candn. Theatre 1972–87: Shaw Festival: Bride in 'A Respectable Wedding,' Mrs. Lunn in 'Overruled,' Charlotte in 'The Magistrate,' Joan in 'Saint Joan,' Ida in 'See How They Run,' Albert in 'The Singular Life of Albert Nobbs' (Candn. premiere), Proserpine in 'Candida,' Mrs. Hyerling in 'The Simpleton of the Unexpected Isles,' Sabine in 'Skin of Our Teeth,' Mary Haines in 'The Women,' Jane Marryott in 'Cavalcade,' Louka in 'Arms and the Man,' Parlor Maid/Mrs. Lutestring in 'Back to Methuselah,' Mrs. Darling/Tiger Lily in 'Peter Pan,' Reno Sweeney in 'Anything Goes'; Vancouver Playhouse: 'Julius Caesar,' 'Scrooge,' 'A Doll's House,' Maggie in 'Lovers'; independent productions: Lucy in 'You're a Good Man, Charlie Brown,' 'Godspell,' 'What's a Nice Country Like Your Doing in a State Like This?,' 'Jacques Brel is Alive and Well and Living in Paris,' 'A Bistro Car'; Arts Club, Vancouver: Kathy in 'Vanities,' 'Starting Here Starting Now,' 'The Club'; Theatre London: 'Godspell,' 'The War Show,' How the Other Half Loves,' 'Jubilay'; Manitoba Theatre Centre: Amy in 'Company'; Citadel Theatre: 'Joseph and his Amazing Technicolor Dreamcoat,' Maria in 'Twelfth Night'; Toronto theatres: 'Harry's Back in Town,' Ellen/Mrs. Saunders in 'Cloud Nine' (Bayview Playhouse), 'Jennie's Story' (St. Lawrence Centre), Sonya in 'Uncle Vanya,' May in 'Farther West' (Tarragon Theatre; both Dora Mavor Moore award nominations); Belfry Theatre, Victoria: Jessie in ''night Mother,' Barbara in 'Children'; National Arts Centre: Eve in 'A History of the American Film,' Blue Fairy in 'Pinocchio'; Persephone Theatre, Saskatoon: '18 Wheels'; Alberta Theatre Projects, Calgary: Eva in 'Absurd Person Singular'; Royal Gala for Queen Elizabeth II (Roy Thomson Hall, 1984); U.S. Theatre: Seattle Repertory Theatre: Glady Bump in 'Pal Joey,' Billie Dawn in 'Born Yesterday' Julia in 'Two Gentlemen of Verona,' Susannah in 'Bedroom co-founder (with Michael Dobbin), A.R.F. (AIDS Relief Fundraising), for the Actors' Fund of Can. 1987; recreations: travel, reading; Club: Elmwood.

**McLELLAN, Susan,** B.A., M.A., Ph.D.; provincial public servant; b. UK 5 Feb. 1947; d. William and Phyllis Louise (Marw) McL.; e. King's Coll. Cambridge B.A. 1978; Univ. of Leeds Post Grad. Cert. in Edn. 1979; McMaster Univ. M.A. 1981, Ph.D. 1986; DIR., SASKATCHEWAN INTERGOVERNMENTAL AFFAIRS 1989– ; joined UK Diplomatic Service 1967–73 serving Kuala Lumpur 1967–70, Prague 1970–72, Foreign & Commonwealth Office London 1972–73; lectr. social sci's and devel. studies Eng. and Can. 1979–85; cons. 1982–86, Univ. of Malaya 1982–83, CIDA 1986; Policy Analyst Govt. Sask. 1987; Extve. Asst. to Dep. Min. to Premier of Sask. 1988– ; mem. Candn. Ambassador for Disarmament – Consultative Group Arms Control & Disarmament 1986; various govt. reports, articles, monographs; contbr. Candn., US, UK, Australia & Malaysia jours. and books.; mem. Adv. Bd. Candn. Jour. Devel. Studies; mem. Candn. Assn. Study Internat. Devel.; recreations: water sports, skiing; Address: Suite 608, Heritage Place, 155 Queen St., Ottawa, Ont. K1P 6L1.

**McLELLAND, Rev. Joseph Cumming,** M.A., B.D., Ph.D., D.D.; educator; b. Port-Glasgow, Scot. 10 Sept. 1925; s. David and Jessie (Cumming) McL.; e. Wentworth St. Pub. Sch. & Central Coll. Inst. Hamilton, Ont.; McMaster Univ. B.A. 1946; Knox Coll. Toronto B.D. 1951, D.D. 1976; Univ. of Toronto M.A. 1949; New Coll. Edinburgh Ph.D. 1953; Montreal Diocesan Theol. Coll. D.D. 1973; m. Audrey Mary d. Alexander Brunton 23 Aug. 1947; children: Jonathan Paul, Peter Joseph, Andrew David, Margaret Dorothy; Moderator, 111th General Assembly (1985), Presbyterian Church in Canada; McConnell Prof. Philos. of Religion, McGill Univ. 1964–91; Emeritus Prof. 1992; Dean of Religious Studies there 1975–85; o. 1949; Prof. of Hist. & Philos. of Religion & Christian Ethics, The Presb. Coll. Montreal 1957–64; Assoc. Prof. Philos. of Religion present Univ. 1959–64; mem. Reformed-Lutheran Consultation (N. Am.) 1963–67; Co-Chrmn. Reformed-Orthodox Consultation (N.Am.) 1968–71; mem. Orthodox-Reformed Consultation (Internat.) 1979–85; sometime mem. Faith & Order Comn. (Candn. Council Chs.) and dialogue groups; author 'The Visible Words of God' 1957; 'The Other Six Days' 1959; 'The Reformation and its Significance Today' 1962; 'Toward a Radical Church' 1967; 'The Clown and the Crocodile' 1970; 'God the Anonymous' 1976; 'Peter Martyr Vermigli and Italian Reform' ed. 1980; 'Celebration and Suffering' 1984; 'Prometheus Rebound' 1988; General Ed., 'The Peter Martyr Library' 1993– ; over 60 articles philos. religion and hist. theol.; former Book Review Ed. and Ed. 'Studies in Religion/Sciences Religieuses'; mem. Candn. Theol. Soc. (Past Pres.); Candn. Soc. Study Religion; Presbyterian; recreation: Scottish country dancing; Home: 121 Alston Rd., Pointe Claire, Que. H9R 3E2.

**McLENNAN, Hugh,** B.Sc., Ph.D., F.R.S.C.; retired educator; b. Montreal, Que. 22 Oct. 1927; s. William Durie and Gyneth Maud (Wanklyn) McL.; e. Trinity Coll. Sch. Port Hope; McGill Univ. B.Sc. 1947, Ph.D. 1951; m. Hilda d. Thomas and Enid Connell 2 June 1949; children: Catriona Isabelle, Neil Stewart; Prof. of Physiol. Univ. of B.C. 1965–90; Asst. Lectr., Univ. Coll. London 1952–53; Rsch. Fellow Montreal Neurol. Inst. 1953–55; Asst. Prof., Dalhousie Univ. 1955–57; Asst. Prof., present Univ. 1957, Assoc. Prof. 1959; Visiting Prof., Univ. of Ottawa 1973, Laval Univ. 1977, Australian Nat. Univ. 1970, 1978, Univ. of Calgary 1982; Killam Foundation Sr. Fellow 1977–78; mem. Extve. Council, Med. Rsch. Council Can. 1971–77; author or co-author over 200 sci. papers; author 2 sci. monographs 1963, 1970; mem., Candn. Ski Assn. (Pres. W. Div. 1971–74, Nat. Vice Pres. 1972–75); Candn. Physiol. Soc. (Sec. 1965–69, Pres. 1972–73); Physiol. Soc. (UK); Intnl. Brain Rsch. Orgn.; recreations: skiing, golf; Club: Whistler Mountain Ski; Home: 2961 W. 49th Ave., Vancouver, B.C. V6N 3T1; Office: Dept. of Physiol., U.B.C., Vancouver, B.C. V6T 1Z3.

**McLENNAN, John T.,** B.Sc., M.Sc.; business executive; b. Sydney, N.S. 15 April 1945; s. Philip Walter and Laura Mae (MacDonald) M.; e. Clarkson Univ. B.Sc. 1968, M.Sc. 1969; m. Claudette McHugh 23 Nov. 1968; children: Jennifer, Mark; PRESIDENT & CHIEF EXTVE. OFFR., BELL CANADA 1994– ; Executive Vice-Pres., Operations, Mitel Corp. 1976–83; Pres. & Chief Extve. Offr., Cantel Inc. 1985; Pres., Founder, Owner, Jenmark Consulting Inc. (specialized in strategizing, financing & managing growth technol. cos. in Canada and US with primary focus on telecommunications; worked with more than 30 cos. in this capacity) 1983–90; Pres., Bell Ontario and Chrmn. of the Bd., BCE Mobile 1990–93; University Trustee, Clarkson Univ.; recreations: golf, Old Timers hockey, boating; Home: 34 Pentland Cres., Kanata, Ont. K2K 1V5; Office: 1050 Beaver Hall Hill, FL919, Montreal, Que. H2Z 1S4.

**McLEOD, Alex(ander) N(orman),** Ph.D.; university professor; economist; b. Arcola, Sask. 6 May 1911; s. Norman Roderick and F. Mable (Baragar) McL.; e. Queen's Univ., B.A. (Math.) 1933, B.A. (Hons., Econ.) 1940; Harvard Univ., Master in Pub. Adm., 1946, Ph.D. (Econ.) 1949; m. Rosalind, d. late Rev. Robert A. Biggerstaff, 29 Sept. 1941; children: Norman Robert, Donald Bruce, Duncan Keith, Ronald Allan; PROF. EMERITUS, YORK UNIV.; prior to Second World War with Office of Auditor Gen., Ottawa, and subsequently with Dept. of Finance; joined staff of Internat. Monetary Fund, 1947; seconded to U.N. Missions to Haiti, 1948, and Libya, 1950–51; I.M.F. missions to Honduras and Costa Rica (1949), Nicaragua (1952) and Guatemala (1954–55) dealing with monetary and central-banking problems; Dir. of Rsch., Saudi Arabian Monetary Agency 1952–54; apptd. Chief Econ., The Toronto-Dominion Bank, 1955 and also served as Chrmn. of Econs. Comte., Candn. Bankers' Assn.; Gov., Central Bank of

Trinidad and Tobago 1966–69; Prof. of Economics, Atkinson Coll., York Univ. 1969–77; Monetary Consultant to Govt. of Botswana (1973–74); rec'd. several scholarships & Littauer Fellowship, Harvard Univ. 1945–47; author 'The Principles of Financial Intermediation' 1984; 'The Fearsome Dilemma: Simultaneous Inflation and Unemployment' 1985; 'The Practice of Economics' 1992; numerous tech. articles for learned journs.; mem., Am. Econ. Assn.; United Church; recreations: sailing, photography; Home: 8111 Yonge St., #607, Thornhill, Ont. L3T 4V9.

**McLEOD, Hon. George Malcolm,** M.L.A., B.Ed.; politician; teacher; b. Meadow Lake, Sask. 5 Jan. 1946; s. Stanley Malcolm and Lena Rose (Code) McL.; e. Univ. of Sask. B.Ed. 1969; m. Karen d. Philip and M. Grace Bird 17 July 1971; children: Natasha, Trevor; Depy. Premier of Saskatchewan 1990–91; Teacher, Meadow Lake Sch. Unit 1970–72; Vice Prin. Jonas Samson Jr. High Sch. 1972–74, Prin. 1974–82; el. M.L.A. prov. g.e. 1978, re-el. 1982 & 1986, cabinet min. 1982– ; Min. of Tourism and Renewable Resources 1982–83; Min. of Northern Sask. 1982; Min. of Supply and Services 1983–85; Min. Resp. for Sask. Liquor Bd. 1983–86; Min. Advanced Education and Manpower, Sask. 1985–86; Min. of Health, Sask. 1986–90; Sask. Forests Products Corp. 1983– and Prince Albert Pulp Co. Ltd. 1985–86; Sask. Archives Bd., Sask. Research Counc. and Advanced Technology Training Centre 1985–86; Town Councillor Meadow Lake 1973–77; Founding mem. and Chrmn. Meadow Lake Recreation Assn.; Nat. Jr. Football Championship Regina Rams football Club 1966; Freemason; Presbyterian; Club: Lions.

**McLEOD, Ian Bruce,** B.A., C.A.; senior financial executive; b. Windsor, Ont. 19 Oct. 1946; s. Hubert B. and Gladys E. (Dowling) M.; e. Univ. of Windsor B.A. 1975; C.A. 1982; m. Sandra d. Art and Helen Radu 6 Aug. 1977; CHIEF FINANCIAL OFFICER, CITIBANK CANADA 1993– ; Audit Student to Manager, Coopers & Lybrand 1976–82; Gen. Mgr., Treasury Opns., Continental Bank of Canada 1982–86; Vice-Pres. Finance, Mutual Trust Co. 1986–88; Sr. Vice-Pres. Finance & Treas., Investors Group Inc. Winnipeg 1988–92; Vice-Pres. & C.F.O., Ontario Teachers Pension Plan 1991–92; Dale Carnegie Training, Grad. Asst.; Former Vice Chair, Manitoba Jr. Achievement; Former Dir., Children's Hosp. Rsch. Found. of Manitoba; Toronto Football Officials Assn.; Mem., Kingsway-Lambton Un. Ch.; recreations: golf, swimming; clubs: Adelaide Club of Toronto, Weston Golf & Country; Home: 94 Chestnut Hills Parkway, Islington, Ont. M9A 3R3; Office: 123 Front St. W., Toronto, Ont. M5J 2M3.

**McLEOD, Ian Hadley,** B.A., M.B.A.; retired executive; b. Bronxville, N.Y. 17 Jan. 1929; s. Ronald Norman and Dorothy (Buchanan) McL.; e. Culver (Ind.) Mil. Acad.; Wesleyan Univ., B.A.; Harvard Grad. Sch. of Business Adm., M.B.A.; m. Jane Anne, d. Lou B. Jordan, 2 Aug. 1952; children: Kim F., Laurie W.; Vice Chrmn. & C.E.O., Ivest Corp., Pres. & C.E.O. 1978–88; Dir., Arrow Electronics Inc.; Asst. to Vice Pres., Finance, Carling Brewing Co., Inc., Cleveland, Ohio, 1955, Asst. to Pres. 1956; Financial Co-ordinator, Blackhawk Manufacturing Co., Inc., Milwaukee, Wisc. 1958, Controller 1959; joined McKinsey & Co., Inc. as Assoc. Chicago and Cleveland 1961, Princ. Cleveland and Toronto 1967; Managing Dir. 1974–78; served with U.S. Marine Corps 1951–53 (Korea); rank Capt.; Dir., The Stratford Shakespearean Festival (former Pres.); former Pres. & Dir., National Ballet of Canada; London Sanctuary Theatre; former Dir., London Regional Art Gallery; O'Keefe Centre for the Performing Arts; former Mem., Ontario Arts Council; recreations: gardening, furniture refinishing; Address: 35 Rosedale Rd., Apt. 4, Toronto, Ont. M4W 2P5.

**McLEOD, John Tennyson,** (Jack *Mac*Leod), M.A., Ph.D.; polymath; writer; splendid person; b. Regina, Sask. 2 Oct 1932; s. John Lorne and Dorothy Mary (Tennyson) McL.; e. Univ. of Sask. B.A., 1954; M.A. (Econ.) 1955; Univ. of Toronto Ph.D. (Pol Sci) 1964; m. Barbara d. William and Elizabeth Sampson 1964 (div.); one d. Heather Jocelyn; m. 2ndly Cynthia McKay Thomas Smith d. Judge Douglas C. and Margaret L. Thomas 12 Apr. 1986; stepchildren: Andrew T.P. and Adrienne F.P.; PROF. OF POLITICAL SCIENCE, UNIV. OF TORONTO, 1972– ; Research Economist, Econ. Advisory and Planning Bd., Govt. of Sask., 1955–56; Lecturer, Dept. of Pol. Econ., Univ. of Toronto, 1959–64; Asst. Prof., 1964–67; Assoc. Prof., 1967–72 (a keen political observer, he has predicted the outcome of every Canadian election since 1867 – unsuccessfully); author, 'Going Grand' (novel) 1982; 'Zinger and Me' (novel) 1979; ed. (with T. Lloyd) 'Agenda 1970' 1968; ed. (with K.J. Rea) 'Business and Government in Canada' 1969, revised 1974; ed. (with R.S. Blair) 'The Canadian Political Tradition' 1986; ed. 'Oxford Book of Canadian Political Anecdotes' 1988; principal author, Report, Ont. Committee on the Healing Arts, 3 vols. 1970; co-ed., 'Essays on the Left' 1971; 'Sir John A. - An Anecdotal Life,' (with Cynthia Smith) 1989; misc. journalism: CBC, Saturday Night, Maclean's, Canadian Forum, Quest, Books in Canada, etc.; Research and Ed. Dir., Ont. Committee on the Healing Arts 1967–69; Ed. Dir., Ont. Comm. on Post-Secondary Educ. 1971–72; Consultant, Min. of Health, Govt. of Sask. 1972; Consultant, Health Security Project Report, Govt. of B.C. 1973; Trustee, Tor. General Hospital 1974–81; Dir., 'Trivial Pursuit'; City of Toronto Medal of Service 1982; Hon. L.W.T. (Leader of Western Thought) Prince Albert College of Journalism and Upholstery, 1979; recreations: buying and restoring antique cars and selling them at a loss; laughing, joking, fantasizing; Clubs: Bookman's Club (Toronto); P.O.E.T.S. Corner (Founding Pres.); The Reform (London); Address: Dept. of Political Science, University of Toronto, Toronto, Ont. M5S 1A1.

**McLEOD, Lyn,** B.A., M.A.; b. 1942; e. Univ. of Man.; Lakehead Univ.; m. Dr. Neil McLeod; four children: Dana, Robin, Dara, Kristen; LEADER OF THE OFFICIAL OPPOSITION, ONTARIO LIBERAL PARTY 1992– ; el. g.e. 1987; re-el. g.e. 1990; apptd. Min. of Colleges and Univs. 1987; Min. of Energy and Min. of Natural Resources 1989–90; apptd. mem., Bd. of Gov., Lakehead Univ. 1987; Chair, Thunder Bay Bd. of Ed. 7 yrs.; Liberal; Office: 223, Legislative Bldg., Toronto, Ont. M7A 1A4.

**McLEOD, Malcolm Edward Wills,** B.A., B.C.L.; lawyer; b. Fredericton, N.B. 26 June 1941; s. Norman James Millar and Mildred Seward (Wills) M.; e. Lower Can. Coll. 1958; McGill Univ., B.A. 1961, B.C.L. 1964; m. Joan d. Robert and Theodosia Dawes Bond Thornton 20 June 1975; children: Rebecca, Rachel, Miriam; called to Bar Prov. of Que. 1965; senior partner in law practice of Ogilvy, Renault & predecessor firms spec. in intellectual property law 1965– ; called to Bar, Prov. of Alta. 1978; reg. patent agent; reg. trade mark agent; Past Sec., Chargex Ltd.; Asst. Secy., VISA Canada Assoc.; Treas. Tradau Inc.; Lectr., McGill Univ. 1971–78; Mem., Candn. Bar Assn.; Patent-Trademark Inst. of Can. (Past Pres.); Internat. Assn. for Protection of Indus. Property; Am. Intellectual Property Law Assn.; Am. Bar Assn.; Intellectual Property Ctte., Candn. C. of C.; Candn. Patent Agents Exam. Bd. 1974–76; Nat. Adv. Bd. of Sci. & Tech. 1987–88; Gov., Montreal Gen. Hosp.; Past Chrmn., The Study Sch.; First Vice-Pres., St. Andrew's Soc. of Montreal; Presbyn.; Mem., Metro. Mus. of Art; Montreal Mus. of Fine Art; Am. Museum of Natural History, McCord Museum; editor: 'Intellectual Property Journal'; Am. Bar Assn. 'Canadian Law Letter'; Chrmn., Copyright Legislation Ctte. of Candn. Bar Assn.; recreations: swimming, golf; Clubs: Univ. Club of Montreal; Montreal Amateur Athletic Assn.; Home: 4085 Gage Rd., Montreal, Que. H3Y 1R6; Office: 1981 McGill College Ave., Montreal, Que. H3A 3C1.

**McLEOD, Philip Robert;** newspaper editor; b. Winnipeg, Man. 4 May 1943; s. Donald Gordon and Phyllis (Brown) M.; e. Nanton Cons. H.S. 1961; Baptist Leadership Training Inst. 1962; Univ. of Toronto 1971; m. Cheryl Amy Stewart 25 Sept. 1965, div. 1992; m. Virginia Mary Corner 6 Nov. 1992; children: Shawn Robert, Erin Dawn; THE EDITOR, LONDON FREE PRESS 1987– ; Reporter, copy ed., mng. ed., ed., The Grande Prairie (Alta.) Herald-Tribune 1963–70; pub., The Truro (N.S.) Daily News 1971–76; reporter, copy ed., nat. ed., dep. mng. ed., The Toronto Star 1976–87; Winner, Southam Newspapers Fellowships for Journalists 1970–71; Office: P.O. Box 2280, London, Ont. N6A 4G1.

**MCLEOD, Roderick Morrison,** B.Comm., LL.B., Q.C.; lawyer; b. Toronto, Ont 1 June 1942; s. Norman and Mary (Johnston) M.; e. Queen's Univ., B. Comm. 1964; Univ. of Toronto, LL.B. 1967; m. Mary Anne d. E.E. Tieman 25 June 1966; children: Andrew, Carolyn, Katie; LITIGATION AND ENVIRONMENTAL LAWYER, MILLER THOMSON 1987– ; articled G. Arthur Martin, Q.C. 1968; called to Ont. Bar 1969; Couns., Min. of the Attorney Gen. 1969; Dir., Criminal Appeals & Spec. Prosecutions 1974–77; Asst. Dep. Attorney Gen. (Crim. Law) 1977–82; Q.C. 1979; Dep. Solictor Gen. 1982–85; Dep. Min., Ont. Min. of the Environment 1985–87; Partner, McLeod, Takach & Co. Legal Pubs.; author: 'Breathalyzer Law in Canada,' 'The Canadian Charter of Rights & Freedoms'; 'Criminal Code Driving Offences'; Office: 60 Columbia Way, 6th Floor, Markham, Ont. L3R 0C9.

**McLEOD, Terry D.,** B.Math., M.B.A.; trust company executive; b. Niagara Falls, Ont. 14 May 1950; s. Douglas A. and Harriet H. (Laird) M.; e. Univ. of Waterloo B.Math. 1973; York University M.B.A. 1979; m. Joanna Wong 23 Dec. 1985; children: Nancy, Adam; VICE-PRESIDENT, OPERATIONAL EFFECTIVENESS, MONTREAL TRUST 1992– ; computer & actuarial positions, Mutual Life of Canada 1973–77; Pension & Benefits Consultant, Peat Marwick & Partners 1977–79; various positions, Montreal Trust 1979–92; Pauline McGibbon Award, Trust Companies Inst.; Chair, Ont. Region, Candn. Pension Conf. 1991–92; Mem., Trust Companies Inst.; recreation: fitness, golf, reading; clubs: Fitness Inst., Markham Golf & Country; Home: 126 Timberbank Blvd., Scarborough, Ont. M1W 2A1; Office: 15 King St. W., Toronto, Ont. M5H 1B4.

**McLEOD, Wayne Malcolm Ernest,** F.C.A., M.B.A.; business executive; b. Winnipeg, Man. 28 June 1939; s. Malcolm Ewen and Lily Dorothy (Cameron) M.; e. Univ. of Manitoba C.A. 1961; Harvard Business School M.B.A. 1965; m. Beverley d. James and Hazel Black 11 June 1960; children: Heather, Pamela; PRESIDENT & CHIEF EXTVE. OFFR., CCL INDUSTRIES INC. 1990– ; Partner, Thorne Riddell & Co. 1967–79; Vice-Pres., Corp. Planning, CCL Industries Inc. 180; Vice-Pres. Finance & Chief Financial Offr. 1981; Extve. Vice-Pres. 1982; Pres. 1983; Past Chair, North York Gen. Hosp.; Dir., Seeing Eye Inc.; Metropolitan Toronto Bd. of Trade; recreations: golf, exercise, reading; clubs: Toronto, Rosedale, Granite; Home: 2 Sagewood Dr., Don Mills, Ont.; Office: 105 Gordon Baker Rd., Willowdale, Ont. M2H 3P8.

**McLEOD, William Emiry,** B.A., M.B.A.; professor; b. Chapleau, Ont. 24 April 1941; s. William Borden and Georgina Isadora (Emiry) M.; e. Chapleau H.S.; Waterloo Lutheran Univ. B.A. (Hons.) 1964; Michigan State Univ. M.B.A. 1966; m. Sheryl Margaret d. Phyllis and Clarence Ade 21 Dec. 1968; children: Heather, David, Neil; PROFESSOR OF BUSINESS, CAMBRIAN COLLEGE OF APPLIED ARTS & TECHNOLOGY 1969– ; Industrial Relations, Ford Motor Co. 1966–67; Prof. of Business, St. Clair College of Applied Arts & Technology 1967–69; Chair, Sch. of Business, Cambrian College 4 years; Visiting Prof. of Mktg., Laurentian Univ. 1980–81; commentator, CBC Radio, northern Ont. on business & financial matters; Consultant for a variety of public & private orgns.; Dir. and Vice-Pres., Lakeside Centre; author: 'Personnel Management for Canadians' 1970, 'Tax Shelters' 1974–87, 'Ripoff: Canadian Buyers' Guide to Life Insurance' 1988, '89, '92 (Prentice-Hall, Canada); several articles in newspapers & consumer magazines; resource person on life insurance for govts. of Canada & US, most major newspapers & magazines, CBC Radio and CBC's 'Marketplace'; club: Idylwylde Golf & Country (Dir.); Home: 15 Eden Pt., Sudbury, Ont. P3E 4V6; Office: 1400 Barrydowne Rd., Sudbury, Ont. P3A 3V8.

**McLEOD-STRINGHAM, Alberta J.,** B.A., B.Ed.; market research executive; b. Saskatchewan 19 June 1950; d. John Clinton and Elizabeth Marjorie (Ellis) McLeod; e. Univ. of Manitoba B.A. 1971, B.Ed. 1973; m. Peter E. s. Dr. Elwood Stringham 24 March 1984; children: J.P. (John Peter) and Wells (James Wellington Ellis) Stringham; VICE-CHRMN., INFOGROUP INC. (one of the Blackburn Marketing Services Inc. companies, London Ont.) 1992– ; Social Worker, Manitoba Dept. of Health & Social Devel. 1973–76; Teacher, Tuxedo Shaftesbury H.S. 1976–79; Market Research, Angus Reid & Assoc. 1979–81; S+GT Advertising 1981–83; Pres., Infogroup Inc. 1984–93; Bd. Mem., C.P.A. Winnipeg 1976–80; Mem. Steering Committee for Fundraising, Children's Aid (Toronto) 1992–94; Mem., Grace Church Day Care Board 1993; Mem. & Marketing Advr., O.A.D.C. Board (Ont. Assn. of Distress Centres) 1993; recreations: golf, tennis, swimming, boating; clubs: Royal Canadian Yacht; Windermere Golf Club, Lake Rousseau; Homes: 42 Russell Hill Rd., Toronto, Ont.; (Summer) Malvern Island, Windermere, Lake Rosseau; Office: 4th Floor, 330 Front St. W., Toronto, Ont. M5B 3V7.

**McLURE, John D.,** C.D., B.Sc.; federal civil service; b. Melita, Man. 10 July 1942; s. late Malcolm Alexander and late Rachel (Simpson) M.; e. Univ. of Man., B.Sc. 1963; Royal Mil. Coll. of Sci. Shrivenham, England, Tech. Studies a.t.o. 1964, a.s.c. Div. I, 1970; ASST. DEP. MIN., FINANCE, DEPT. OF NATIONAL DEFENCE 1989– ; Asst. Dep. Min., Finance, Personnel & Admin; Regional Industrial Expansion Canada 1987–88; Industry, Science and Technology Canada 1988–89; served with Candn. Forces 1963–75, rank Maj.; joined Fed. Civil Service 1975 serving various positions up to Asst. Sec. in Treas. Bd. Secretariat 1975–83; Asst. Dep. Min.

for Atlantic Fisheries Restructuring, Fisheries & Oceans 1983–84; Asst. Dep. Min. Small Business & Special Projects 1984–85; Asst. Dep. Min. Crown Invests. & Special Projects 1985–86; Asst. Dep. Min. Native Econ. Programs 1986–87; Dir., Defence Construction Ltd. 1990– ; recreations: boating, alpine & water skiing; Office: 101 Colonel By Drive, Ottawa, Ont. K1A 0K2.

**McMANUS, John Gerald,** B.Sc., P.Eng.; engineering executive; b. Ottawa, Ont. 2 Feb. 1937; s. John Gerald and Ethel (Garside) M.; e. Queen's Univ. B.Sc. 1960; Royal Military College, Dipl. Military Studies; m. Sandra d. Donald and Norma Blaine 6 Jan. 1961; children: Douglas, Sean, Drew, Donald, Meghan; SECRETARY GENERAL & SEC. TO THE ATOMIC ENERGY CONTROL BOARD 1989– ; Royal Canadian Navy 1955–63; Reactor Operations & Equipment Devel., Atomic Energy of Canada Ltd. 1963–67; Sci. Advisor, Div. Chief & Asst. Dir. in Safeguards Operations & Dir. Planning & Admin., Atomic Energy Control Board 1967–84; Dir., Safeguards Operations for European Community, Internat. Atomic Energy Agency (Vienna) 1984–89; recreations: skiing, woodworking; Home: P.O. Box 92, Almonte, Ont. K0A 1A0; Office: P.O. Box 1046, Station B, 280 Slater St., Ottawa, Ont. K1P 5S9.

**McMASTER, Juliet Sylvia,** M.A., Ph.D., F.R.S.C.; educator; b. Kisumu, Kenya 2 Aug. 1937; d. Sydney Herbert and Sylvia (Hook) Fazan; e. Kenya Girls' High Sch. Nairobi Higher Sch. Cert. 1955; St. Anne's Coll. Oxford Univ. B.A. 1959, M.A. 1962; Mt. Holyoke Coll. Mass. 1959–60; Univ. of Alta. M.A. 1963, Ph.D. 1965; Alberta Woman Athlete of the Year 1965; m. Rowland Douglas McMaster 10 May 1968; children: Rawdon Joseph, Lindsey Sylvia; UNIVERSITY PROF., UNIV. OF ALTA. 1986– , Asst. Prof. 1965, Assoc. Prof. 1970, Prof. 1976; author 'Thackeray: The Major Novels' 1971; 'Trollope's Palliser Novels: Theme and Pattern' 1978; 'Jane Austen on Love' 1978; 'Dickens the Designer' 1987; co-author 'The Novel from Sterne to James'; 60 articles on Eng. novel in learned journs.; ed. 'Jane Austen's Achievement' 1976; ed. & illustr. Jane Austen's 'The Beautifull Cassandra' 1993; rec'd Can. Council Post-doctoral Fellowship 1969–70; Guggenheim Fellowship 1976–77; McCalla Professorship 1983–84; Killam Research Fellowship 1987–89; recreations: hiking, ceramic sculpture, riding; Home: 7815 – 119 St., Edmonton, Alta. T6G 1W5; Office: English Dept., University of Alberta, Edmonton, Alta. T6G 2E5.

**McMASTER, Susan,** B.A.; poet, editor; b. Toronto, Ont., 11 Aug. 1950; d. Gordon George McClure and Betty Isabel Emily Page; e. Lisgar C.I. 1966; Carleton Univ., B.A. 1970, Master of Journalism studies 1975–80 (a.b.t.); Ottawa Teachers' Coll., elem. teaching cert. 1971; m. Ian s. Eric and Nancy M. 5 July 1969; children: Sarah Aven, Sylva Morel; EDITOR, NATIONAL GALLERY OF CANADA 1989– ; Teacher, Edmonton P.S. Bd. 1971–73; Founding Ed. 'Branching Out' 1973–75, Assoc. 1975–80; freelance editor & writer Edmonton 1973–75, Ottawa 1975–89; Founding Mem., 'FIRST DRAFT' (intermedia performance group) 1980–90; word music performed by 'Open Score,' 'Exposure,' etc.; music-theatre performed at Great Candn. Theatre Co., NAC Atelier etc.; Mem., League of Candn. Poets (co-ed. 'Living Archives' series); P.E.N. Internat.; Mem., Religious Soc. of Friends (Quakers); author: 'Learning to Ride' 1994; 'The Hummingbird Murders' 1992; 'Dangerous Graces: Women's Poetry on Stage' 1987 (ed.); 'Dark Galaxies' 1986; co-author: 'North/South' 1987, 'Pass this way again' 1983, 'Wordmusic' 1986 (audiotape); recreations: canoeing, guitar, horse riding; Home: 43 Belmont Ave., Ottawa, Ont. K1S 0T9; Office: National Gallery of Canada, Publications, 380 Sussex Dr., P.O. Box 427, Stn. A., Ottawa, Ont. K1N 9N4.

**McMICHAEL, Robert,** C.M. (1974), D.Litt., LL.D.; founder dir.-emeritus, The McMichael Canadian Collection; b. Toronto 27 July 1921; s. Norman & Evelyn May (Kennedy) McM.; e. Runnymede Pub. Sch. and Humberside Coll. Inst., Toronto, 1941; York Univ., D.Litt. 1970; LL.D., Univ. of Waterloo, 1983; Order of Canada (C.M.) 1974; Fellow, ont. Coll. of Art, 1979; Univ. of Waterloo, Doctor of Laws 1983; m. Signe Kirstin, d. late Soren Christian Sorensen, 9 Feb. 1949; Co-founder 'Canadian High News' 1940; Founder 'Robert McMichael Studios' 1946; Founder and Pres. Travel Pak Ltd. 1952 and Robert McMichael Inc. (New York) 1959; Dir. The McMichael Canadian Collection, Kleinburg, Ont. 1964–81; mem. B. McMichael Candn. Collection; author: 'One Man's Obsession: a History of the McMichael Canadian Art Collection 1986; served with RCN during World War II; recipient (with wife Signe) Connie Award, Soc. of Amer. Travel Writers 1978; first recipients award Contrib. to Candn. Art, Ont. Soc. of Artists 1981; Hon. Patron, Sculptor's Soc. of Can. 1982; Anglican; Club: Arts & Letters; Address: 40 Caledon Mountain Dr., Belfountain, Ont. L0N 1B0.

**McMILLAN, Carl Henry,** M.A., Ph.D.; educator; b. San Diego, Cal. 9 Jan. 1930; s. Carl Henry and Marian Alice (Olley) McM.; e. Yale Univ. A.B. 1952, M.A. 1953; Johns Hopkins Univ. Ph.D. 1972; PROF. OF ECON. CARLETON UNIV. 1980– , Dir. East-West Project 1973– ; served naval and dipl. service; joined present Univ. 1968, Dir. Inst. Soviet & E. Eur. Studies 1975–82; cons. bus., govt. and internat. orgns.; recipient Ford, Carnegie, SSHRC Fellowships; author 'Multinationals from the Second World: Growth of Foreign Investment by Soviet and East European State Enterprises' 1987; co-ed. 'Planned Economies: Facing the Challenges of the 1980s' 1988; Home: 23 Woodlawn Ave., Ottawa, Ont. KlS 2S8; Office: 1125 Colonel By Drive, Ottawa, Ont. K1S 5B6.

**McMILLAN, Charles J.,** B.A., M.B.A., Ph.D.; professor of international business; b. Charlottetown, P.E.I. 15 Oct. 1945; s. the late Joseph Alexander and Dorothy Eileen (McQuaid) M.; e. St. Dunstan's Univ. B.A. 1967; M.B.A. 1969; Ph.D. 1976; m. Kazuyo d. Dr. & Mrs. Tokuma Yokohata 28 June 1975; children: Aya Chantal, Mari Christine; PROF., FAC. OF ADMINISTRATIVE STUDIES, YORK UNIV. 1974– ; Lectr., Fac. of Business, Univ. of Alta. 1969–71; Rsch. Fellow, Mngt. Ctr., Univ. of Bradford (U.K.) 1971–74; Visiting Prof., Univ. Laval 1979; Ecole Supérière de Lyons 1981; Chrmn., Policy Analysis Group, Office of the Leader of the Opposition (Fed.) 1973–74; Senior Policy Advisor, Prime Min. of Canada 1984–87; Mem., Candn. delegation, G-7 Economic Summit: Bonn 1985, Tokyo 1986, Venice 1987; Dir., Boeing Canada 1988–90; Yamaichi Internat. (Can.) Limited 1988– ; Prince Edward Internat. 1988–91; Global Capital Group 1988– ; P.E.I. Heritage Award for 'Duncan House' restoration 1976; rsch. grants from Canada Council, SSHRCC, Japanese Rsch. Council; Royal Comn. on Corp. Concentration; Nat. Adv. Council, Candn. Advanced Technol. Assn. 1988– ; Nat. Co-Chair, Nat. Forum of Sci. & Technol. Adv. Councils (Halifax) 1989; Dir., Asia Pacific Found. 1990– ; Dir., Nat. Ballet School 1990– ; Mem., Council of Applied Sci. & Technol., Govt. of N.S. 1989– ; Candn. Children's Foundation 1991– ; Advr., Gordon Found.; Arctic Council; Mem., North American Institute; Mem., Internat. Ctte. for Economic Reconstruction, Kyrgystan; P.C. Catholic; author: 'Entrepreneurship and Corporate Growth: An Organizational Study of the Irving Group' 1976; 'The Japanese Industrial System' 1983, 2nd ed. 1989; 'Bridge Across The Pacific: Japan and Canada In The 1990's' 1988; 'Investing in Tomorrow: Japan's Science and Technology Organization and Strategies' 1990; 'Services: Japan's 21st Century Challenge' 1991 and num. articles & reviews appearing in texts, books, & journals; co-author: 'Productivity and the Urban Transit Industry' 1981; co-editor: 'Organization and Nation' 1981; recreations: skating, cooking, gardening, Candn. antiques, P.E.I. history, Japanese economic history, Arctic development; Home: 209 Glenayre Rd., Toronto, Ont. M5P 3C4; Office: 212, ASB-FAS, 4700 Keele St., North York, Ont. M3J 1P3.

**McMILLAN, Colin James,** M.A., M.D.C.M., F.R.C.P.C.; F.A.C.P.; physician; b. Charlottetown, P.E.I. 5 July 1942; s. Joseph Alexander and Dorothy Eileen (McQuaid) M.; e. Charlottetown City Schools; St. Dunstan's Univ. B.A. 1964; Oxford Univ. B.A. 1966, M.A. 1970; McGill Univ. Med. Sch. M.D.C.M. 1972; Gold medalist Birchwood H.S., Charlottetown 1958; Rhodes Scholar (N.B. and Oriel Coll., Oxford) 1964; dip., Am. Bd. of Internal Med. 1975; F.R.C.P. Internal Med. 1976, Cardiology 1977; F.A.C.P. 1990; m. Sandra d. James and Joan Flintoft 4 June 1976; children: Andrew, Alexandra, James, Victoria, Virginia; PHYSICIAN, RIVERSIDE MEDICAL CENTRE 1991– ; Physician, Charlottetown Clinic 1977–91; Chief of Staff, Queen Elizabeth Hosp., Charlottetown 1989–91; Vice Chief of Staff, 1987–89; Head, Dept. of Medicine, 1981–87; Intern and Resident, Internal Med., Royal Victoria Hosp., McGill Univ. 1972–75; Resident and Fellow, Joint Cardiorespiratory Unit, Royal Vic. and Montreal Children's Hosps., McGill Univ. 1975–77; Cons. internal med. and cardiology, Charlottetown Clinic 1977–91; internal med. Charlottetown and P.E.I. Hospitals 1977–81; Cons. staff King's Co. Meml. Hosp., Montague, P.E.I 1979– ; Sessional Lectr. Dept. of History, St. Dunstan's Univ. 1967–68; Clinical Instr., Dept. of Medicine, Dalhousie Univ. 1991– ; Dir. Fathers of Confederation Centre Mem. Bldg. Trust 1980–82 and 1991– , Chrmn. 1982–86, Gov. & Chrmn. of Long Range Planning Ctte. 1986–91; mem. Univ. Naval Training Div. 1960–64; Sub-Lieut. Roy. Candn. Navy Reserve 1963; Liaison Offr. HMCS Queen Charlotte 1964; retired to study in U.K.; Candn. Heart Found.: Med. Advr. P.E.I. Div. 1978– , mem. Med. Advy. Ctte. (Chrmn. 1990–91), Vice Pres. (Medical) & Chrmn., Pharmaceutical Roundtable 1991– , Chrmn. Subctte. on Emergency Cardiac Care 1978–84; Dir., Heart and Stroke Research Found. of Canada 1991– ; Liaison mem. Emergency Cardiac Care Ctte., Am. Heart Found. 1982–84; mem. Candn. Cardiovascular Soc. (Mem. of Council 1991– ); Am. Coll. of Physicians; P.E.I. Medical Soc.: mem. 1977, Dir. Public Information Ctte. 1979–82 (Chrmn. Tariff Ctte. 1981–85), Pres. 1986–87; Candn. Medical Assn.: mem. Economics Counc. 1981–89 (Chrmn. 1985–89), Political Action Ctte. 1980–86, Chrmn. 1989–93; Bd. of Dirs. 1989–93, Chrmn. 1993– ; Dir. Hillsborough P.C. Assn. 1979– ; Gov. National Theatre Sch. of Can. 1984– ; mem. Rhodes Scholarship Selection Ctte., Maritimes 1985– ; Bd. of Dirs., P.E.I. Arts Counc. 1987–90; Mem., Univ. of P.E.I. Found. 1987– , Vice Chrmn. 1988– ; Mem., P.E.I. Govt. Confederation Birthplace Commission 1990–91; recreations: bridge, reading, public affairs, Newfoundland dogs; Club: Rotary Internat.; Home: 'Balechin,' Keppoch, R.R. #1, Charlottetown, P.E.I. C1A 7J6; Office: Riverside Medical Centre, 1 Garfield St., Charlottetown, P.E.I. C1A 6A4.

**McMILLAN, John Clark;** retired banker; b. Glasgow, Scot. 4 Jan. 1920; s. Thomas Paton and Lily (Clark) McM.; m. Orma Margaret, d. late Charles Lacheur, 17 Apr. 1946; Extve. Vice Pres. Royal Bank of Can. 1979–82; Dir., RoyNat. Inc.; Chateau Stores of Canada Ltd.; Bellwood Health Services Inc.; served with RCAF 400 City of Toronto Sqdn. during World War II; rank Flight Lt.; Past Pres., Candn. Heart Foundation; Presbyterian; recreations: hunting, fishing, golf; Clubs: Toronto; Lambton Golf & Country; Home: 57 Widdicombe Hill Blvd., 1803W, Weston, Ont. M9R 1Y4.

**McMILLAN, Very Rev. Kenneth George,** C.M., O.C. (1984), B.A., M.Div., D.D. (Presb.); b. Mount Forest, Ont. 28 Mar. 1916; s. George Henry and Gertrude Elizabeth (Watson) M.; e. Palmerston and Listowel, Ont. High Schs.; Univ. Coll., Univ. of Toronto, B.A. 1939; Knox Theol. Coll., Toronto, Grad. 1942, M.Div. 1946, D.D. 1961, Wycliffe Coll. D.D. 1974; Acadia Univ. D.D. 1978; apptd. mem. Order of Can. 1984; rec'd. 125th Anniversary of the Confederation of Canada Medal, 1992; m. Isobel Islay, d. Alexander McCannel, Port Elgin, Ont. 3 Aug. 1942; two d., Catherine Isobel, Barbara Jean; MINISTER-AT-LARGE, WORLD VISION CANADA 1983– ; Candn. Patron, Global Cooperation for a Better World 1988; Gen. Secy., Candn. Bible Society, 1957–83; Chrmn. Gen. Comte. of Un. Bible Socs. of the World 1976–80; Minister, Burgoyne and Dunblane 1942–43; Drummond Hill Church, Niagara Falls, Ont. 1944–50; St. Andrew's Church, Guelph, Ont. 1950–57; Beguin Mem. Lectr., Australia 1974; Reserve Chaplain, R.C.N.; Past Moderator, Presby. Synod of Toronto and Kingston; Moderator, Presb. Church in Can. 1979–80; author: 'What But Thy Grace'; 'Against the Tide'; recreations: camping, woodwork; Home: Apt. 604, 80 Inverlochy Blvd., Thornhill, Ont. L3T 4P3.

**McMILLAN, The Hon. Thomas Michael,** M.A.; diplomat; b. Charlottetown, P.E.I. 15 Oct. 1945; s. Dr. Joseph A. and D. Eileen (McQuaid) McM.; e. Queen's Square Sch. and Birchwood High Sch. Charlottetown; St. Dunstan's Univ. B.A. 1967; Queen's Univ. M.A. 1970; m. Katherine d. W.L. Hambly 2 Aug. 1980; three daughters, Kelly Eileen, Rebecca Jean, Emily Kathleen; Canadian Consul General to New England 1989; el. to H. of C. for Hillsborough g.e. 1979, re-el. 1980, 1984; Environment Critic P. Conservative Party 1980–83; Depy. Opposition House Leader 1983–84; Min. of State (Tourism) 1984; Min. of the Environment 1985–88; Lectr., Environmental and Resource Studies Program, Special Advisor to the Pres., Trent Univ. 1988; Chair, task force on the environment, Candn. Chamb. of Comm.; Extve. Offr. Ont. Human Rights Comn. 1975–78; Sr. Rsch. Assoc. Comn. on Candn. Studies Assn. Univs. & Colls. 1973–79; Extve. Sec. to Policy Adv. Ctte. Hon. R.C. Stanfield, Sec. Policy Co-ordinating Ctte. P. Conservative Party Can. 1970–74; Part-time Inst. Faculty of Arts Sir Sanford Fleming Coll. Peterborough 1971–72; Rsch. Asst. in Pol. Sci. Queen's Univ. 1969; Chrmn. Nat. Book & Periodical Devel. Council Can. 1973–79; mem. Candn. Heritage Foundation; P.E.I. Heritage Foundation (recipient Special Award and Prize Restoration Duncan House, Keppoch 1976); Officer (Brother) Order St. John 1983; Gov. Gen.'s Conservation Award for his role in creating South Moresby Nat. Park Reserve 1988; Hoyt Fellow (annual Graves Lectr.), Yale Univ. 1988; Edgar Wayburn Award for outstanding environmental work by a political leader, U.S. Sierra Club 1988; co-author 'To Know Ourselves' 1975; 'Life Together' 1977; author numerous articles on Candn. environmental studies, human rights and Candn. heritage subjects; mem. Candn. Pol. Sci. Assn.; recreations:

Candn. and Am. antiques, early Candn. arch., landscaping, athletics; Home: Keppoch Beach, P.O. Box 2590, Charlottetown, P.E.I. C1A 8C3.

**McMILLEN, Grant Ralph Arnold,** B.A., M.B.A., C.M.A.; food industry executive; b. Hamilton, Ont. 5 June 1946; s. Charles Ralph and Dorothy Roberta (Barbour) M.; e. Univ. of Western Ont. B.A. 1968; McMaster Univ. M.B.A. 1970; Cert. Management Accountant 1976; m. Sharron d. Jack and Elsie Hill 16 Aug. 1969; children: Kelly Michelle, Matthew Grant; PRES. & CHIEF EXTVE. OFFR., PRIMO FOODS LIMITED 1990– ; increasingly sr. finan. positions, General Foods, Inc. 1970–88; Vice-Pres., Finance & Admin., Primo Foods Limited 1988; Extve. Vice-Pres. 1989; Mem., Grocery Products Mfrs. of Canada; Finan. Extves. Inst.; Cert. Mngt. Accountants; club: The Bd. of Trade; Home: 17 Palace Arch Dr., Islington, Ont. M9A 2R9; Office: 3700 Steeles Ave. W., Woodbridge, Ont. L4L 8M4.

**MCMILLIN, Robert Selby,** B.P.H.E., M.D., C.C.F.P.; physician; b. Toronto, Ont. 4 Apr. 1927; s. Robert Andrew and Helen Rezin (Clark); e. Malvern C.I.; Univ. of Toronto, Sch. of Phy. & Health Edn. 1947; Fac. of Edn. 1948; Fac. of Med. 1954; m. Judith d. Ronald and Wilda Cosburn 28 June 1977; children: Mary, Carolyn, Lorna, Andrew, Janice, Meredith, Allison; Chief of Staff, Humber Memorial Hospital 1965–91; priv. med. practice, Weston, Ont. 1955; appt. to staff, Humber Meml. Hosp. 1955; Chief, Family Practice 1961–65; Clin. Teacher, Univ. of Toronto, Dept. of Family Med. 1979–92; Gov., Humber Meml. Hosp. 1965–91; Dir., Humber Meml. Hosp. Found.; Racing Dir., Craigleith Ski Club 1975–83; recreations: skiing, sailing, canoeing, tennis; Clubs: Weston Golf, Craigleith Ski, Craigleith Tennis; Home: 12 Paddinton Place, Weston, Ont. M9R 2T1; Office: 2160 Weston Rd., Weston, Ont. M9N 1X6.

**McMONAGLE, Frederick Duncan;** journalist; b. Winnipeg, Man. 24 Nov. 1949; s. Daniel Brown and Mary (Shapansky) M.; m. Verena d. Erhard and Ursula Unger 24 Jan. 1979; children: Ethan Alastair, Andrew Fraser; EXECUTIVE EDITOR, WINNIPEG FREE PRESS 1993– ; Reporter and Editor, Winnipeg Free Press 1970–75; Asst. City Editor, Asst. Nat. Editor, News Dir., Globe and Mail 1975–92; Home: 333 Oakdale Dr., Winnipeg, Man. R3R 0Z6; Office: 1355 Mountain Ave., Winnipeg, Man. R2X 3B6.

**MCMORDIE, Michael John,** B.Arch, Ph.D.; professor of architecture; professor of general studies; b. Toronto, Ont. 23 Apr. 1935; s. Robert Campbell and Ena May (Helwig) M.; e. Allenby P.S. 1948; Univ. of Toronto Schools 1953; Univ. of Toronto, B.Arch. 1962; Univ. of Edinburgh, Ph.D. 1972 (Brit. Counc. Scholar); m. Claire d. John and Claire Howard 7 Sept. 1963; children: Benjamin (d. 1982), Margaret Jenny, David; DEAN, FACULTY OF GENERAL STUDIES, THE UNIV. OF CALGARY 1990– ; worked with Thompson, Berwick & Pratt prior to B.Arch. grad.; with Gordon S. Adamson & Assoc. 1962–65 (seconded to UPACE); Lectr., Edinburgh Univ.; joined present univ. 1974 as Assoc. Prof.; Prog. Dir., Arch. 1979–82; Co-founder & Acad. Advr., Candn. Arch. Archives, The Univ. of Calgary (approx. 750,000 items); wide range of arch. rsch. interests; Cons. on history & theory of arch. for public & private clients incl. cities of Calgary & Edmonton and the Candn. Parks Serv.; Cons., 'The Canadian Encyclopaedia'; Charter Mem. & Pres., Soc. for the Study of Arch. in Can. 1977–80; Candn. Arch. Archives rep. at found. of Internat. Confed. of Arch. Museums Helsinki 1979 & subsequent meetings; Vis. Assoc., Clare Hall, Univ. of Cambridge 1974–75; The Martin Ctr., Univ. of Cambridge 1974–75; Life Mem., Clare Hall 1976– ; Adv. Ctte., Candn. Ctr. for Arch. Montreal 1987–89; Mem., Soc. for the Study of Arch. in Can. (Dir. 1975–77; Pres. 1977–80); Assn. for Candn. Studies; Soc. of Arch. Historians (USA and UK); Calgary Soc. for Mediterranean Studies; Ed. Bd., 'TRACE' 1979–82; 'Urban History Review 1983– ; Ed. Ctte., The Univ. of Calgary Press 1988–91; author of numerous articles & reports; 19 articles in 'Canadian Encyclopaedia' 2nd ed. 1988; recreations: hiking, skiing, music, travel; clubs: University (Calgary), Hart House (U. of Toronto); Office: Calgary, Alta. T2N 1N4.

**McMORLAND, Donald,** B.Sc., P.Geo.; gas industry executive; b. Winnipeg, Man. 18 Dec. 1927; e. Univ. of Manitoba B.Sc. 1954; m. Barbara Joan; children: Janice, Todd, Gordon, Marjorie-Jean; CHAIRMAN, ALBERTA & SOUTHERN GAS CO. LTD. 1991– ; Bd. of Dirs., Alberta & Southern Gas Co. Ltd.; Belfast Petroleum Inc.; Dekalb Energy; West of Five, Inc.; joined Stekoll Petroleum Corp. (Sask.) 1958–60; joined present company as Geologist in 1960, subsequently achieving Extve. Vice-Pres. & C.O.O.; Pres., & C.E.O. to 1993; clubs: Ranchmen's, Calgary Petroleum, Calgary Golf & Country, Glencoe; Office: 2900, 240 – 4th Ave. S.W., Calgary, Alta. T2P 4L7.

**McMORRAN, The Hon. Mr. Justice Allen Stewart,** B.A.; b. Vancouver, B.C. 12 Aug. 1919; s. Oscar Stewart and Sarah Louisa Parfitt (Mullett) McM.; e. Florence Nightingale and Cecil Rhodes Pub. Schs., King Edward High Sch., Vancouver, 1937; Univ. of B.C., B.A. 1941; Vancouver Law Sch., grad. 1946; m. Mary Adele, d. late Francis Augustus Whitfield, 31 Aug. 1951; children: Vanessa Lee, Lisa Anne, William Eric, Allen Steven; JUDGE, SUPREME COURT OF BRITISH COLUMBIA 1990– ; City Prosecutor, Vancouver, since 1953; read law with Tiffin Russell Dumoulin and Brown; called to Bar of B.C. 1946; cr. Q.C. 1964; joined Office of City Prosecutor as Asst. City Prosecutor, 1947; apptd. County Court Judge, Co. of Cariboo, B.C. 1974; Judge of County Court of Westminster, B.C. 1975– ; served with 1st Bn. Irish Fusiliers 1942–44; rank Lt.; Adj. Capt. No. 11 Vocational Training Sch. Pacific Command, 1944–45; Past mem., Special Comte., Detoxification Soc. of B.C.; Vancouver Traffic & Safety Council 1947–73; Vancouver Official Traffic Commission 1953–74; Dir., Alcoholism Foundation of B.C. 1958; Narcotic Addiction Foundation of B.C. 1956–74 (Pres., Chrmn. & mem. Extve. Comte 1963–65); Past Dir. Legal Aid Soc. 1970–74; Dir. Candn. Council Christians & Jews; Pres., Irish Fus. of Can. (Vancouver Regiment) Trustees; Pres., Royal Westminster Regt. Historical Soc. 1987– ; mem. Shaughnessy Hts. Property Owners Assn. 1954–74; mem., Vancouver Bar Assn. (Extve. 1965–67); Past mem. Law Soc. B.C. (Head of Criminal Law Tutorials 1956–74); Candn. Bar Assn. (Council B.C. Sec. 1961–65; Council 1961–65; Chrmn. B.C. Criminal Justice Sec. 1961–63, Nat. Chrmn. of Sec. 1963–65); el. Bencher, Law Soc. B.C. 1969, 1971, 1973; Commr. (Legal Adviser), Vancouver Basketball Comn.; Past Dir., Shaughnessy Little League Baseball; Past Chrmn. Archbishop's Comte. Diocese of New Westminster Eccl. Matrimonial Comn.; mem. Vancouver Mil. Inst.; Mem. Provincial Council of St. John Ambulance 1989– , serving brother 1992; Commander, Order of St. Lazarus 1991– ; mem., Royal Westminster Regt. Council 1987– ; Kappa Sigma (Grand Master 1941; Alumnus Advisor); Anglican; recreation: fishing; Clubs: Point Grey Golf & Country; Westminster; B.C. Regt. Offrs.' Mess; Royal Can. Mil. Institute; Home: 722 - 666 Leg in Boot Sq., Vancouver, B.C. V5Z 4B3; Office: Law Courts, Begbie Sq., New Westminster, B.C. V3M 1C9.

**McMORRAN, Sydney Robert,** B.A., M.B.A.; bank executive; b. Lachine, Que. 12 Oct. 1939; s. Sydney Dixon and Jean Katherine (McLaughlin) M.; e. Bishop's Univ. B.A. 1960; Univ. of Western Ont. M.B.A. 1963; m. Yvonne May d. George and Pauline LePage 15 Aug. 1964; children: Alison Lea, Tracy Elizabeth, Thomas Sydney; VICE CHAIRMAN, THE TORONTO-DOMINION BANK 1992– ; various positions in Montreal & Toronto, Toronto-Dominion Bank 1963–77; Vice-Pres. & Gen. Mgr., Metro East Div. 1977; Sr. Vice-Pres., Commercial Devel. Div. 1980; Extve. Vice-Pres., Operations Div. 1983; Dir., Toronto Dominion Securities Inc.; TD Mortgage Corp.; TD Pacific Mortgage Corp.; Gov., Bishop's Univ.; Pres., Toronto East Gen. Hospital Foundation; recreations: golf; clubs: Lambton Golf & Country, Bellaire Country; National Club; Home: 132 Mona Dr., Toronto, Ont. M5N 2R6; Office: P.O. Box 1, Toronto-Dominion Centre, Toronto, Ont. M5K 1A2.

**MCMULLAN, Wallace Edward,** B.A., M.B.A., Ph.D.; university professor; b. Ottawa, Ont. 28 Aug 1944; s. Wallace Davis and Louise Sarah N.; e. Univ. of B.C., B.A. 1967, M.B.A. 1968, Ph.D. 1975; m. Carol Anne d. Allen and Lavina Huber; 1 s.: Benjamin; PROF., NEW VENTURE DEVELOP. PROG., UNIV. OF CALGARY 1981 to present; author of numerous articles on creativity, innovation & entrepreneurship; Home: 419 – 11th St. N.W., Calgary, Alta.; Office: New Venture Office, Scurfield Hall, Univ. of Calgary, Calgary, Alta. T2N 1N4.

**McMULLEN, Robert Michael,** M.Sc., Ph.D., F.G.S.; retired science manager; b. Toronto, Ont. 20 Nov. 1935; s. Robert Gascoigne and Kathleen Mary (Holt) McM.; e. Upper Can. Coll. Toronto 1954; Univ. of Toronto 1954–55; Univ. of Alta. B.Sc. 1957, M.Sc. 1959; Reading (UK) Univ. Ph.D. 1965; m. Patricia d. Henry and Ethel Brinkler 9 June 1962; one d. Catriona Jane; Retired 1993; Regional Dir. Science, Central and Arctic Region, Dept. of Fisheries and Oceans, Canada 1986–93; Mem., Great Lakes Water Quality Bd. 1987–93; Dir.-Gen., Oceanographic Sciences, Dept. of Fisheries and Oceans, Can. 1986; Acting Asst. Depy. Min., Ocean Sci. & Surveys, Dept. of Fisheries & Oceans, Canada 1985–86; Dir., Policy & Program Coordination Br., Ocean Sci. & Surveys, Dept. of Fisheries and Oceans, Can. 1973–85 (formerly Dept. of Environment 1973–79); Dir., Information Retrieval Services Br. Dept. of Communications, Can. 1970–73; Head, Scient. Information Services and Lib., Bedford Inst. of Oceanography, Dept. Energy, Mines & Resources, Dartmouth 1967–70, Marine Geol. 1966–67; mem. Ed. Bd. 'Maritime Sediments' 1966–70 (Mang. Ed. 1967–70); Subsurface Geol. Hudson's Bay Oil and Gas and Imperial Oil Enterprises 1964–65, Calgary; Information Specialist (Exploration), Imperial Oil Ltd. Calgary 1959–61; recipient Shell Oil Grad. Fellowship in Geol. Univ. of Alta. 1958–59; author or co-author various papers geol. and information science scholarly and prof. journs. 1959–73; Fellow, Geol. Soc. London; Fellow, Geol. Assn. Can.; mem. Am. Assn. Petroleum Geols.; Inst. Information Scientists (UK) 1972–91; Candn. Assn. Information Science 1969–75 (Dir. Ottawa Chapter 1971–75, Pres. 1973–74, Nat. Secy. 1974–75); mem. and Treas. Pinecrest-Queensway Citizens Comte. Ottawa 1971–74; recreations: fishing, photography, philately; Home: 215 - 1 Snow St., Winnipeg, Man. R3T 2M4.

**McMULLIN, Neil Francis,** B.A., S.T.B., Th.M., Ph.D.; university professor; b. Sydney, N.S. 3 July 1940; s. Daniel Francis and Barbara Iris (Petrie) M.; e. St. Francis Xavier Univ. B.A. 1960; St. Michael's College, Univ. of Toronto S.T.B. 1965; Nihongo Gakuin, Tokyo, dipl. in Japanese Studies 1967; Harvard Univ. Th.M. 1971; Univ. of B.C. Ph.D. 1977; m. Sheila K. d. William and Gertrude Foley 27 Aug. 1971; children: James F., S. Irene, Heather J., Neil F.; ASSOC. PROF., RELIGIOUS STUDIES, UNIV. OF TORONTO 1986– ; Asst. Prof., Religious Studies, Univ. of Rochester 1974–83; Assoc. Prof., Religion, Sweet Briar College (Virginia) 1983–86; Dir., Graduate Center for Religious Studies, Univ. of Toronto 1990–92; Co-ord., Yehan Numata Prog. in Buddhist Studies 1989– ; Rsch. Assoc., East-West Center (Honolulu) 1983–84; Japan Found. Fellow, Kyoto, Japan 1981–82; Vice-Pres., Soc. for the Study of Japanese Religions (Can. & U.S.) 1987–92; Mem., Am. Acad. of Religion; Assn. for Asian Studies; Candn. Asian Studies Assn.; Japan Studies Assn. of Can.; Soc. for the Study of Japanese Religions; author: 'Buddhism and the State in Sixteenth-Century Japan' 1985, two book chapters & a number of articles in acad. jours.; recreations: reading, skiing; club: Oriental Soc. of Toronto; Home: 2189 Sunnyvale Dr., Oakville, Ont. L6L 1W6; Office: 118 North Building, Erindale College, Univ. of Toronto, Mississauga, Ont. L5L 1C6.

**McMURRAY, MacKenzie,** B.A.Sc., M.Com., P.Eng.; retired manufacturer; b. Toronto, Ont. 7 Apr. 1915; s. Samuel and Helen (MacKenzie) McM.; e. Harbord Coll. Inst., Toronto; Univ. of Toronto, B.A.Sc. 1939, M.Com. 1954; m. Helen Bernice, d. Samuel Wilson, 24 May 1951; Imperial Windsor Group Inc.; joined Dominion Bridge Co. Ltd. 1940; apptd. Asst. to Vice Pres. and Mang. Dir., Montreal, 1956; Vice Pres., Finance, Montreal, 1957; Vice Pres., Ont. Region, Montreal, 1959–62; Vice Pres., Finance and Dir., 1962; Pres. and Chief Extve. Offr. 1963; Chrmn. Bd. 1974–77; mem., Engn. Inst. Can. (Toronto Br. Chrmn. 1954; Councillor 1954–57); Assn. Prof. Engrs. Ont.; Corp. Engrs. Que.; Presbyterian; recreations: golf, curling; Clubs: University; Montreal Thistle Curling; Forest & Stream; Kanawaki Golf; Home: 4066 Gage Rd., Montreal, Que. H3Y 1R5; Office: Suite 2912, 1155 René-Lévesque Blvd. W., Montreal, Que. H3B 2L5.

**McMURRAY, Robert David;** retired; b. New Westminster, B.C. 26 June 1926; s. Murdoch and Lillian Ethel (Wray) McM.; e. Burnaby S. High Sch. 1944; m. Kathryn d. Colin and Ada McMillan 5 Aug. 1955; children: Mark, Janet, Grant; Copy Boy, Reporter 'The Province' newspaper 1945, Asst. City Ed. 1956, Business Ed. 1961, City Ed. 1976, Asst. Mng. Ed. 1978, Mng. Ed. 1984, Editor 1985–89; Home: 6, 3980 Canada Way, Burnaby, B.C. V5G 1G7.

**McMURRICH, Arthur R.,** B.Com.; retired company executive; b. Toronto, Ont. 21 May 1917; s. Arthur R. and Muriel Logie (Smellie) McM.; e. Brown Public Sch., Toronto, Ont.; Upper Can. Coll.; McGill Univ., B.Com. 1939; m. 1stly, Carol Jean Roy, 14 June 1941 (d. 1967); children: Mrs. Margot Anne List, A.R., R.D.R., A.L.; m. 2ndly, Bridget Wendy Crutchlow, d. Burrell Page, Norfolk, Eng. Dec. 1969; joined Stelco, Inc. 1940, retired Vice Pres., Marketing and Corp. Planning, 1982; Pres., Candn. Steel Serv. Centre Inst. 1983–87; served in 2nd World War, Royal Highland Regt. Can. Black Watch (N.P.A.M.) Montreal; Royal Rifles Can., Quebec City; H.Q. 1st Candn. Army, Eng. 1943; H.Q. 4th Candn. Armd. Div. – GSO III, Eng., France, Belgium, Holland 1943–44; Past Pres., Bd. of Trade of metro. Toronto,

1976–77; Alpha Delta Phi; Anglican; recreations: golf, tennis; Clubs: St. James's (Montreal); The Hamilton; Badminton & Racquet, Toronto; Toronto Golf; Home: 40 Rosehill Ave., Toronto, Ont. M4T 1G5.

**McMURRICH, Norman Hay,** B.Arch.; b. Toronto, Ont. 2 June 1920; s. Arthur Redpath and Muriel Logie (Smellie) M.; e. Upper Canada Coll.; Univ. of Toronto (Sch. of Arch.) B.Arch. 1946; m. (late) Mary, d. late Robert G. Armour, M.D. 1 June 1947; children: Marilyn, Sheila, Edward (Ted), Donald (deceased), Anne (deceased); m. 2ndly, Nancy Gwendoline (widow late William Dafoe) d. Charles M.D. and late Christobel Stogdill; step-children, William and Catherine Dafoe; CONSULTANT, NORR PARTNERSHIP LIMITED, Architects Engineers 1987; former Partner, McMurrich & Oxley: Architects (joined firm as Assoc. 1946; firm terminated operations 1987); main large projects which have been under his personal guidance are: Pembroke Gen. Hosp., additions to Candn. Approach Plaza at the Peace Bridge; York Co. Hosp., and St. Mary's Hosp., Kitchener, Ont.; Acad. and Residence Bldgs., George Ignatieff Theatre, Trinity Coll., Toronto; Medical Sciences Bldg., Univ. of Toronto; extensions to Havergal College; restoration of St. Andrews Presbyterian Church, Toronto; Huronia District Hosp. (Midland); Prince Edward Communinity Centre, Picton; firm was apptd. architects for the Law Soc. of Upper Canada in joint venture with Neish, Owen, Roland and Roy, Architects & Engineers 1985; served in 2nd World War; Lieut., 48th Highlanders (R) 1941; on active service Overseas with 48th Highlanders in Eng. 1943, Italy 1943–45, Holland and Belgium 1945; Pres., Arts & Letters Club (until May 1982); Chrmn., Commemorative Services of Ont.; Past Chrmn. Toronto Unit, Cdn. Cancer Soc.; Fellow, Royal Arch. Inst. Can. 1963; Pres., Royal Arch. Inst. Can. 1969; Past Treas., Ont. Assn. of Archs. (and Past Chrmn., Toronto Chapter); el. Hon. Fellow, Am. Inst. of Arch. 1969; Kappa Alpha; Presbyterian; recreations: squash, sketching; Clubs: University; Arts & Letters; Home: 1 Knightswood Road, North York, Ont. M4N 2G9.

**MCMURTRY, Robert Younghusband,** M.D., FRCS(C), FACS; orthopedic surgeon; b. Toronto, Ont. 6 Mar. 1941; s. Roland Roy and Doris Elizabeth M.; e. Forest Hill P.S.; Univ. of Toronto Sch. 1959; Univ. of Toronto, M.D. 1965; m. Jane d. Robert and Patricia Macdougall 6 May 1979; children: Angus, Abbey, Sean, Meaghan; DEAN, FACULTY OF MEDICINE, UNIV. OF WESTERN ONTARIO 1992– ; Specialist, Royal Coll. of Phys. & Surgs. 1972; Head, Emergency Serv., Sunnybrook Med. Ctr. 1975, Orthopedic Surgeon 1975–88, Dir., Trauma Prog. 1976; Chrmn., Trauma Ctte., Univ. of Toronto 1984; Assoc. Prof. of Surgery; Prof. & Chrmn., Dept. of Surgery, Univ. of Calgary, Alta. 1988–92; Chief Surgeon, Foothills Hosp., Calgary 1988–92; Founder, Regl. Trauma Unit, Air Ambulance Prog. & Paramedic Prog., Sunnybrook Med. Ct.; Past Pres. & Found. Mem., Trauma Assn. of Can.; Chrmn., Prov. Ctte. on Trauma; Am.-Brit.-Candn. Travelling Fellowship 1981; Pres., Candn. Assoc. of Surgical Chairmen 1990; Regent, Am. College of Surgeons 1992– ; mem., 16 med. assns.; recreations: sports; Home: Office: Faculty of Medicine, Univ. of Western Ont., Health Sciences Addition, Room 112, London, Ont. N6A 5C1.

**McMURTRY, (Roland) Roy;** chief justice; b. Toronto, Ont. 31 May 1932; s. Roland Roy and Doris Elizabeth (Belcher) McM.; e. St. Andrew's Coll. Aurora, Ont.; Trinity Coll. Univ. of Toronto; Osgoode Hall Law Sch.; Hon. LL.D.: Univ. of Ottawa 1983; Law Soc. of Upper Can. 1984; Leeds Univ. 1988; York Univ. 1991; m. Ria Jean d. Dr. Harry Macrae, Toronto, Ont. 18 Apr. 1957; children: Janet, Jim, Harry, Jeannie, Erin, Michael; CHIEF JUSTICE, ONT. COURT OF JUSTICE 1994– ; rec'd the Freedom of the City of London, 23 Sept. 1986; called to Bar of Ont. 1958; cr. Q.C. 1970; Partner, Benson, McMurtry, Percival & Brown 1958–75; el. to Ont. Leg. 1975, re-el. 1977 and 1981, ret'd 1985; Atty. Gen. for Ont. 1975–85; Sol. Gen. for Ont. 1978–82; High Comnr. for Can. to Britain 1985–88; Partner, Blaney, McMurtry, Stapells 1988–91; Chrmn. & C.E.O., Candn. Football League 1989–91; Assoc. Chief Justive, Ont. Court of Justice 1991–94; Hon. Gov., Frontier Coll.; mem. Advocates Soc.; Zeta Psi; Phi Delta Phi; United Church; recreations: painting, skiing, tennis; Clubs: Albany; Office: Ontario Court of Justice, Osgoode Hall, 130 Queen St. W., Toronto, Ont. M5H 2N5.

**MCNABB, Ernest Ian;** C.S.C.; filmmaker; b. Viking, Alta. 15 Sept. 1939; s. Peter and Stella Marie (Froehler) M.; e. Loyola H.S.; Montreal Inst. of Technol. 1958; Loyola Coll.; m. Susan d. Frank and Eileen McCormack 23 June 1962; one d. Heather Ann; Engr. Dept., Nat. Film Bd. of Can. 1960; Sci. Film Unit 1965; involved in var. rsch. & design projects 1965– incl. USSR (1973), diving & photography under ice North Pole Arctic IV expedition (1974), prototype 3D IMAX system (design & test 1982–83; construction supvr. 1984–86); Camera Operator, 'XXIst Olympiad' 1976; Tech. Advr., 3D Cons. & Designer on loan from NFB: 'Sea Dream' (Marineland, Florida) 1977; 'Magic Journeys' (Walt Disney Prodns.) 1981; 'Spacehunter' (Columbia Pictures) 1982–83; 'Sudbury Science Centre' film 1983–84; Dir., 'The Mystery of Bay Bulls' 1978; Wesscam Opr., 'Top of the Hill' 1979; Co-Dir., 'Atmos' 1980; Dir. of Photo. & Post-Prodn. Supvr. 'Transitions,' world's 1st 3D IMAX film made for Can. Pavillion, Expo '86; Dir. of Photo. 'Urgence/Emergency' 1988; D.O.P. on the China/Canada co-production 'The First Emperor' filmed in Imax (1989); Dir. of Photo. 'Momentum' for Seville World's Fair, Candn. Pavillion (filmed in Imax H.D., world's first 48 frame per second Imax film) 1992; author and co-author of papers & articles; awarded special recognition by the C.S.C. (Candn. Soc. of Cinematographers) 'for outstanding service to the motion picture industry, especially with development of 3D processes for Imax in particular' 1987; recreations: scuba diving, skiing, sailing; Home: 4540 King Edward Ave., Montreal, Que. H4B 2H7; Office: Nat. Film Bd., P.O. 6100, Stn. 'A,' Montreal, Que. H3C 3H5.

**MCNAIR, The Hon. John Caldwell,** Q.C.; retired judge; b. Fredericton, N.B. 24 Jan. 1923; s. John Babbitt and Marion M. (Crocket) M.; e. Univ. of N.B., B.A. 1944, M.A. 1947; Lord Beaverbrook Overseas Scholar, Univ. of London 1947–48; Dalhousie Univ., LL.B. 1951; called to N.B. bar 1951; apptd. Q.C. 1968; m. Marion M. d. Joseph H. and Jean Gorman Morrison 1 Aug. 1950; children: Jean, John, Kathleen; 2nd Lt., Candn. Army, W.W. II; Lectr., Univ. of N.B. 1946–47; Asst. Prof. 1948–49; began law practice 1952; Mem., Candn. Bar Assn.; apptd. Judge, Fed. Court of Can.; Trial Div. Judge, Court Martial Appeal Court of Canada 1983–90 and Mem., Ex-officio, Fed. Court of Appeal 1983–90; Mem., Hiram Lodge No. 6, F. & A.M.; Fredericton Shrine Club; Luxor Temple, A.A.O.N.M.S.; Fredericton Soc. of St. Andrew; Fredericton Br. 4, Royal Candn. Legion; recreations: hunting, fishing, outdoor pursuits; Home: Fredericton, N.B.

**McNALLY, Alan G.,** B.Sc., M.Eng., M.B.A.; banker; b. Québec City, Qué. 3 Nov. 1945; e. Cornell Univ. B.Sc., M.Eng. 1963–67; York Univ. M.B.A. 1969; Harvard Grad. Sch. Bus.; Oxford Univ. Centre Mgmt. Studies; Institut Eur. D'Adm. des Affaires, Fontainebleau; m. Ruth MacFadden; children: Lisa, Graham; CHIEF EXECUTIVE OFFICER, HARRIS BANKCORP, INC. and HARRIS TRUST AND SAVINGS BANK 1993– ; Career: Aluminum Co. of Canada, Montréal & Arvida, Qué. 1969–75; Computer Sciences Canada 1969; joined Bank of Montreal, 1975; Vice Pres. & Comptroller, Montréal 1978; Vice Pres. Treasury Operations, Toronto 1980; Vice Pres. Internat. Banking 1981; Vice Pres. and Mgr. London Branch, England 1982; Sr. Vice Pres. & Mgr. London Branch 1984; Sr. Vice Pres. & Deputy Group Extve., Treasury Group, Toronto 1985; Sr. Vice Pres. & Deputy Group Extve., Commercial Banking 1986; Extve. Vice Pres. Personal Banking 1987–90; Vice Chrmn., Personal & Commercial Financial Services 1990–93; Past Chrmn., MasterCard International; former Managing Dir., First Candn. Financial Services (U.K.); former Dir.: Trust Company of Bank of Montreal; Nesbitt Thomson; Bank of Montreal Investment Management Ltd.; Bank of Montreal Investor Services Ltd.; Candn. Payments Assn.; Banque Transatlantique; Candn. Council for Aboriginal Business; Candn. Children's Foundation and Kids' Help Phone; Former Mem. Bd. of Govs., York University; MBA Advisory Bd., York Univ.; Domestic Banking Policy Ctte., Candn. Bankers Assn.; Former Treasr., Queen Elizabeth Hosp. Found.; has been active in coaching young people's hockey and baseball Toronto; Office: 111 West Monroe St., Chicago, IL 60603 USA.

**McNALLY, Edward Elliott,** B.A., LL.B.; brewery executive; b. Lethbridge, Alta. 18 July 1925; s. Alfred and Margaret Elliot (Thompson) McN.; e. Univ. of B.C., B.A. 1947, LL.B. 1951; m. Linda M. d. W.N. (Bill) and Sybil Graburn June 1958; children: William Elliot, Sybil M., Kathleen M., Shelagh Sue; PRES. AND FOUNDER, BIG ROCK BREWERY LTD. 1985– ; farmer and rancher 1975– ; lawyer Calgary 1955–81; Office: 6403 35 St. S.E., Calgary, Alta. T2C 1N2.

**MCNALLY, Joseph L.,** B.Sc.; space agency executive; b. Calumet Island, Que. 28 July 1930; s. Lawrence and Mary (Ryan) M.; e. Univ. of Ottawa B.Sc. 1953; m. Carmen d. Vincent and Germaine Petitclerc 19 April 1954; children: Marguerite, Michael, Stephen, Christopher, George, Lawrence, Lisa; DIRECTOR GENERAL, RADARSAT PROJECT OFFICE, CANADIAN SPACE AGENCY 1990– ; joined RCA Limited Montreal 1955; Payload Engineer, Alouette II Spacecraft 1963; Project Mgr., ISIS Project 1968; seconded to Dept. of Communications as Dep. Project Mgr., CTS Hermes Communication Satellite 1973; Project Mgr. on two heavy route satellite ground stations for Peoples Rep. of China 1971; Project Mgr., Mobile Satellite Program, Dept. of Communications 1981; Merit Award, Public Serv. of Canada 1990; Award of Excellence, Treas. Bd. of Can. 1991; Mem., Candn. Astronautic & Space Inst.; co-author: 'The ISIS Scanning Auroral Photometer' 1984; 'A Mobile Satellite System: A Review' 1986; author/co-author of 35 technical papers; recreations; violin, flying; Home: 1048 William Mooney Rd., R.R. 3, Carp, Ont. K0A 1L0; Office: 6767 route de l'Aéroport, Saint-Hubert, Que. J3Y 8Y9.

**McNALLY, Joseph Martin,** B.Sc., B.E.E.; energy engineer, administrator; b. New Waterford N.S. 1 Oct. 1938; s. Joseph Francis and Georgina Frances (Flynn) M.; e. St. Francis Xavier Univ. B.Sc. 1958; N.S. Technical College B.E.E. 1960; m. Jeannine d. Dona and Irma Byrns 24 Aug. 1974; children: Andrew, Donna; VICE-PRES., MAJOR CLIENT ACCOUNTS, HYDRO-QUEBEC 1990– ; Vice-Pres., Manicouagan Region, Hydro-Quebec 1979–86; Mauricie Region 1986–90; Mem., Bd. of Dir., Candn. Nuclear Assn.; Northshore (Quebec) Conservation Soc.; Pres., Financial Campaign, Musée Pierre-Boucher of Trois-Rivières, Qué.; Patron of Honour, 1993–94 Financial Campaign, Les Petits Violons, Montreal; Vice-Pres., Financial Campaign 1992/3, 1993/4 Montreal Museum of Fine Arts; Home: 37 Place d'Auvergne, Candiac, Que. J5R 5R2; Office: 1010 Ste-Catherine St. W., Dominion Sq., 8th Fl., Montreal, Que. H3C 4S7.

**McNALLY, William J.,** B.Sc., M.A., M.B.A.; pulp and paper executive; b. Chicago, Ill. 27 Sept. 1941; s. William Joseph and Anne Marie McN.; e. DePaul Univ. B.Sc. 1964, M.A. 1977; Harvard Univ. M.B.A. 1969; m. Lorraine 5 Aug. 1972; three d. Katie, Megan, Susan; PRES. AND CHIEF EXTVE. OFFR. QUNO CORPORATION 1991– ; C.P.A. Price Waterhouse, USA 1961–71; Development Offr. Mid-America Internat. Development Group USA 1971–72; Extve. Vice Pres. Manufactured Product Group Hartmarx USA 1972–82; Vice Pres. Planning & Control Tribune Co. USA 1982–84; Extve. Vice Pres. and Chief Operating Offr. present Co. 1984–89; Pres. & C.O.O. 1989–91; Extve. Bd., Candn. Pulp & Paper Assn. (Dir.); Chrmn., Ont. Forest Ind. Assn.; Quebec Forest Ind. Assn. (Dir.); Home: 26 Woodmount Dr., St. Catharines, Ont. L2T 2X9; Office: 80 King St., St. Catharines, Ont. L2R 7G1.

**McNAMARA, Kevin David,** B.Com., C.H.E., C.F.R.E.; health care administrator; b. Sydney, N.S. 15 Apr. 1947; s. David Robert and Margarita (Cogswell) McN.; e. St. Mary's Univ. B.Com. 1969; Cert. Health Extve. 1984; Cert. Fund Raising Extve. 1987; VICE-PRES., HUMAN RESOURCES CAMP HILL MEDICAL CENTRE 1988– ; Social Service Worker, Mun. Co. of Halifax 1970–73; Adm. Ocean View Manor 1973–79; Spring Garden Villa 1979–80; Dir., Personnel Adm. & Labour Relations Villa Centres Ltd. 1980–82; Extve. Dir., Cobequid Multi-Service Centre 1983–88; Pres. Assoc. Homes for Special Care 1975; 1st Vice Pres., Candn. Long Term Care Assn. 1978; mem., Candn. Coll. Health Service Extves. 1977– ; Commr. Supreme Court of N.S. 1972– ; Chrmn., Dartmouth Housing Authority 1973–79, Dartmouth Community Contact 1977–79; Founding Pres., N.S. Assn. Housing Authorities 1977–79, Hon. Life mem. 1980; Mem., Big Brothers and Sisters of Dartmouth, Halifax N.S. 1969–89; Gen. Chrmn. Dartmouth Winter Carnival 1975–76; Vice Chrmn. Cape Breton Un. Appeal 1979; Pres. N.S. Drama League 1979–80; Chrmn. Cultural Fed. of N.S. 1980–82, 1989–91; 1st Vice Pres. Nat. Multicultural Theatre Assn. 1980–87; Pres. Stage East Prof. Theatre Assn. 1982–85; Pres., Dartmouth Ward 4 Residents' Assn. 1984–86; Chrmn., Dartmouth Recreation Adv. Bd. 1986–88; Mem., Dartmouth Municipal Planning Strategy Review Ctte 1986–88; Mem., N.S. Symphony Bd. 1986– , Pres. 1988–91; Pres., Candn. Soc. of Fund Raising Extves., Nova Scotia Br. 1987–89; Pres., Diabetes Care Program of N.S. 1991– ; Bd. Mem., Canadian Healthcare Human Resource Assn. 1991– , Treas. 1993– ; mem., Citizens Advisory Board - Halifax Herald and Mail Star; recipient, President's Award for community service, Metro United Way 1988; Fund Raising Executive of the Year, Candn. Soc. of Fund Raising Extves., N.S. Chapter 1988; Home: 6049 Pepperell St., Halifax, N.S.; Office: 1763 Robie St., Halifax, N.S. B3H 3G1.

**McNAUGHT, Kenneth,** M.A., Ph.D.; university professor; b. Toronto, Ont. 10 Nov. 1918; s. William Carlton and Eleanor Mildred (Sanderson) McN.; e. Upper Can. Coll., Toronto, 1936; Univ. of Toronto, B.A. 1941, M.A. 1946, Ph.D. 1950, D.S.Litt., Thorneloe Coll., 1990; m. Beverley Eileen, d. late S.W. Argue, 13 June 1942; children: Christopher, Allison, Andrew; served with Candn. Army (RCOC) 1942–45; Prof. of Hist., Univ. Coll., Winnipeg 1947–59; Prof. of Hist., Univ. of Toronto 1959–84; Contrib. Ed., 'Saturday Night' 1959–69; Ed., 'Canadian Studies in History and Government' 1959–66; 'Canadian Welfare' 1961–65; 'Canadian Forum' 1968–78; Chrmn. CBC TV panel 'Round Table' 1953–57; rec'd Can. Council Sr. Fellowships, 1963, 1969; Killam Award 1975; Rockefeller Foundation Fellow, Bellagio 1981; inaugural Lectr., Candn. Studies, Free Univ. of Berlin 1982; Messecar Prof. of Hist., McMaster Univ. 1984; Visiting Sr. Lectr., Univ. of Warwick 1985; Visiting prof., York Univ. 1989–90; author 'A Prophet in Politics' 1959; 'Manifest Destiny' 1981; 'The Pelican History of Canada' 1982, revised and expanded as 'The Penguin History of Canada' 1988; 'The Winnipeg Strike: 1919' 1974; co-author 'A Source-Book in Canadian History' 1959; 'Canada & the United States' 1963; co-editor: '"English Canada" Speaks Out' 1991; other writings include numerous articles in various journals; mem., Canadian Hist. Association; Organ. Am. Historians; NDP; Anglican; recreations: sailing, golf, sketching; Home: 39 Glengowan Rd. Toronto, Ont. M4N 1G1.

**MCNAUGHTON, Lt.-Gen. Donald Malcolm,** CMM, CD; (retired) Canadian forces pilot; b. Perth, Ont 7 March 1934; s. Wallace John and Margaret Jean (Wilson) M.; e. Perth Coll. 1951; m. Frances Jean d. William and Fanny Finkle 12 Oct. 1957; children: Jean (Dabros), Ian; joined Royal Candn. Air Force 1952; recd. pilot wings 1953; flying instr., fighter & helicopter pilot 1953–89; attended Candn. Army Staff Coll. & R.A.F. Air Warfare Coll.; commanded 427 Tactical Helicopter Squadron, Petawawa, Candn. Forces Base Winnipeg & 10 Tactical Air Group, St. Hubert; Brigadier-General 1978; Dir., Gen. Air Doctrine & Opns. NDHQ 1978–81; Major-Gen. 1982; Dep. Commander, Air Command 1982–85; Lt.-Gen. 1985; Commander Air Command 1985–86; Depy. Commander in chief, NORAD 1986–89; Commander, Order of Military Merit 1983; U.S. Legion of Merit 1989; recreations: golf, skiing; Home: Glen Eyrie Farm, R.R. 6, Perth, Ont. K7H 3C8.

**McNAUGHTON, Donald William;** industrialist; b. Montreal, Que. 18 July 1926; s. Edmund Moore and Mildred Agnes (Caven) McN.; e. St. Leo's Acad., Westmount; Loyola Coll.; Sir George Williams Univ., Montreal; m. Barbara Ann, d. late William J. Little 24 Apr. 1954; children: Tim, John, Susan, Ann; PRES., D.W. MCNAUGHTON ASSOCS.; Account Extve., McKim Advertising Ltd., Montreal 1947–50; Adv. Supvr., Canadian Liquid Air, Montreal 1951–53; Gen. Supvr., Display Adv., Air Canada 1953–57; Adv. Mgr. and later Mktg. Mgr., Carling Breweries, Montreal and Que. City 1957–63; Dir. of Adv. and Co-ordinator, Schenley Football Awards 1963–66; Gen. Mgr., Canadian Park & Tilford Distilleries Ltd. Vancouver (a Schenley subsidiary) 1966, Pres. 1967–69; re-joined Schenley Canada Inc. as Pres. 1969, Pres. and C.E.O. 1972–85, Chrmn., 1986–89; Dir., Central Guaranty Trust Co., Halifax; Vice Chrmn., Que. Adv. Bd., Central Guaranty Trust Co., Montreal; Dir., Loto-Quebec; mem. & immed. past Chrmn., Bd. of Govs., Concordia Univ.; Immed. Past Chrmn., Can. Safety Counc.; Vice-Pres., St. Mary's Hosp. Found.; Immediate Past Chrmn., Bd. Govs., St. Mary's Hosp.; Past Pres. and Dir., St. Mary's Hospital Center; Past Chrmn. Assn. of Candn. Distillers; Immed. Past Pres. and Hon. Life Mem., St. Patrick's Soc. of Montreal; Dir., Candn. Arthritis Soc. (Que. Div.); Dir.: Loyola Foundation (Past Pres.); Loyola Alumni Assn. (and Past Pres.); Hon. Vice Pres., Que. Prov. Counc., Boy Scouts of Can.; Baden-Powell Fellow, World Scout Federation; Clubs: Mt. Royal; Montreal Badminton & Squash; recreations: boating, winter sports; Home: Montreal West, Que.; Office: Suite 1215, 770 Sherbrooke St. W., Montreal, Que. H3A 1G1.

**McNAUGHTON, John Craig,** B.A., M.A.; association executive; b. Halifax, N.S. 19 July 1951; s. John William and Verna Marjorie (Craig) M.; e. Queen's Univ. B.A. 1975; Carleton Univ. M.A. 1980; m. Ann d. Charles and Joan Dodman 16 Aug. 1980; one s.: Timothy John; EXECUTIVE DIRECTOR, CANDN. FEDERATION FOR THE HUMANITIES 1990– ; Rsch. Asst., Centre for Internat. Relations, Queen's Univ. 1977–78; Extve. Asst., Candn. Soc. for the Prevention of Cruelty to Children 1978–79; Asst. Ed., Dir. of Pubns. & Ed., 'Northern Perspectives,' Cdn. Arctic Resources Ctte. 1979–82; Policy Analyst, Advisor, Northern and Native Affairs, Corp. Planning Group, Environment Can. 1982–88; Rsch. Assoc., Candn. Fed. for the Humanities 1988–90; Medal in Religion, Queen's Univ. 1975; Ont. Grad. Scholarship 1976–77; recreations: wine-making, public speaking, swimming, gardening; Home: 54 Appleby Private, Ottawa, Ont. K2C 3P4; Office: Suite 407, 151 Slater St., Ottawa, Ont. K1P 5H3.

**McNEIL, John D.,** M.A., C.F.A.; insurance executive; b. Southampton, Eng. 17 Feb. 1934; s. Spencer Ewart and Janet (Scott) McN.; e. Univ. of Edinburgh M.A. 1956; Chart. Financial Analyst 1966; m. (Isobel) Esther Spence 24 Dec. 1956; children: Spencer, Claire, John, Alison, David; CHRMN., C.E.O. & DIR., SUNLIFE ASSURANCE CO. OF CANADA 1988– ; Chrmn. and Dir., Sun Life Assurance Co. of Canada (U.S.); Sun Life Insurance & Annuity Co. of New York; Sun Life Assurance Co. of Canada (U.K.) Ltd.; Sun Life Financial Holdings Inc.; Chrmn. Bd. Mgrs. Compass II Variable Annuity Funds; Pres. & Dir., Sun Growth Variable Annuity Fund Inc.; Dir., Shell Canada Ltd.; Massachusetts Financial Services Co.; Sun Life Trust Co.; Sun Life Savings and Mortgage Corp.; Sun Life of Canada Home Loans Limited; Sun Life of Canada Investment Management Ltd.; Sun Benefit Services Co.; Sun Investment Services Co.; Marathon Realty Co. Ltd.; Canadian Pacific Limited; Life Office Management Assn.; Spectrum Bullock Holdings Corp.; Spectrum Bullock Financial Services, Inc.; Chrmn. & Dir., Candn. Life and Health Insurance Assn. (CLHIA); Chrmn., CLHIA Task Force on Tax Policy and Ctte. on Par Policy Holders Protection; CLHIA Task Force on Bilateral and Multilateral Trade and CLHIA Standing Ctte. on Government Relations; Mem., CLHIA Standing Ctte. on Resources; Joint CLHIA-LUAC Ctte. on Marketing; Chrmn. & Dir., C.D. Howe Inst., Mem., British North Am. Ctte. and Mem., Candn.-Am. Ctte.; Trustee, MFS/Sun Life Series Trust; Mem., Business Counc. on Nat. Issues; Mem., Ontario Business Advisory Council; joined Sun Life of Canada Invest Dept. 1956; Asst. Treas. 1962–66; Mutual Funds Management Corp. Ltd. and Grouped Funds Distributors Ltd. (Vice-Pres., Investments 1966–72, Pres. 1972–73); Principal, Morrison, Krembil Ltd. 1974–75; Bank of Montreal 1975–79; Vice Pres. Invests 1977–79; rejoined Sun Life of Canada 1979; Vice Pres. Securities Invests. 1979–82; Sr. Vice Pres. and Gen. Mgr. for USA 1982; Extve. Vice Pres. 1985; Depy. Chrmn. 1987–88; Dir., Candn. Ditchley Foundation; S.S. Huebner Foundation; Canadian Club of Toronto; Trustee, Hospital for Sick Children; mem. Inst. Chart. Financial Analysts; Toronto Soc. Financial Analysts; The Ticker Club; Mem. Advisory Bd., Salvation Army; Clubs: Royal Candn. Yacht; Toronto; York; Office: Sun Life Centre, 150 King St. W., Toronto, Ont. M5H 1J9.

**McNEIL, Michael Stewart,** B.A., D.P.A., M.A.; business and association executive; b. Toronto, Ont. 22 Sept. 1951; s. Alexander James and Eunice May (Hampson) M.; e. McMaster Univ. B.A. 1975; Carleton Univ. D.P.A. 1976, M.A. 1977; m. Charlyne d. Alderic and Jeanette Leger 1 July 1978; PRESIDENT, CANADIAN AUTOMOBILE ASSOCIATION 1988– ; Dir. of Rsch. & Policy, Intercounsel Ltd. & Rideau Public Policy Rsch. Group 1976–77; Extve. Asst., Leader of the Official Opposition's Office 1977–79; Extve. Asst. to Principal Sec., Prime Minister's Office 1979–80; Special Asst. & Tour Mgr., Leader of the Official Opposition 1980–81; Consultant, government & industry relns. 1981–83; Dir. of Govt. & Public Affairs, Candn. Auto. Assn. 1982–88; Chair & Pres., Club Auto Roadside Serv. Ltd. 1991– ; Vice-Pres., Transportation Assn. of Canada 1993–94; Extve. Bd. Mem., Tourism Industry Assn. of Canada 1990– ; Pres., Region III, Alliance Internat. de Tourisme (Geneva) 1992–95; Council Mem., Fed. Internat. de l'Auto. (FIA, Paris) 1990– ; TAC Award of Merit, Honour 'M' Award McMaster Univ.; Anglican; recreations: golf, skiing, court sports, reading, writing; Home: 631 Hunt Club Place, R.R. 5, Ottawa, Ont. K1G 3N3; Office: 1775 Courtwood Cres., Ottawa, Ont. K2C 3J2.

**McNEILL, John,** B.Sc., Ph.D.; museum administrator; b. Edinburgh, Scot. 15 Sept. 1933; s. Thomas and Helen Lawrie (Eagle) McN.; e. George Heriot's Edinburgh 1951; Univ. of Edinburgh B.Sc. 1955, Ph.D. 1960; m. Bridget Winterton 29 July 1961; two s. Andrew Thomas, Douglas Paul; m. Marilyn James 6 Apl. 1990; DIR. ROYAL ONT. MUSEUM 1991– ; Prof. of Bot. Univ. of Toronto 1990– ; Asst. Lectr. and Lectr. in Agric. Bot. Univ. of Reading 1957–61; Lectr. in Bot. Univ. of Liverpool 1961–69; Rsch. Sci. Plant (later Biosystematics) Rsch. Inst. Agric. Can. 1969–77, Chief Vascular Plant Taxonomy Sect. 1969–72, Sr. Rsch. Sci. 1977–81; Prof. and Chrmn. of Biol. Univ. of Ottawa 1981–87; Regius Keeper Royal Botanic Gdn. Edinburgh 1987–89; Hon. Prof. Univ. of Edinburgh 1989; Assoc. Dir. Curatorial, Royal Ont. Museum 1989–90; Acting Dir., Royal Ontario Museum 1990–91; Pres. Biol. Council Can. 1986–87 (Vice Pres. 1984–86); Candn. Council of Univ. Biol. Chrmn. (Pres. 1984–85, Vice Pres. 1983–84); Extve. mem. Internat. Union Biol. Sci. 1985–88, 1991– ; Adm. of Finance Internat. Assn. Plant Taxonomy 1987–93 (Councillor 1981–87, 1993– ); mem. 15 sci. soc's; co-author 'Grasses of Ontario' 1977; 'Preliminary Inventory of Canadian Weeds' 1988; co-ed. 'Phenetic and Phylogenetic Classification' 1964; 'International Code of Botanical Nomenclature' 1983, new eds. 1988 & 1994; author or co-author numerous book chapters, articles sci. rsch. jours.; Office: 100 Queen's Park, Toronto, Ont. M5S 2C6.

**McNEILL, John H.,** M.Sc., Ph.D.; educator; b. Chicago, Ill. 5 Dec. 1938; s. John and Agnes Margaret (McLean) McN.; e. Univ. of Alta B.Sc. 1960, M.Sc. 1962; Univ. of Mich. Ph.D. 1967; m. Sharon d. Allan and Merril Keneffly 27 July 1963; two d. Sandra Lynn, Laurie Ann; DEAN AND PROF. OF PHARMACEUTICAL SCIENCES, UNIV. OF B.C. 1985– ; Lab. Asst. Univ. of Alta. 1959–62, Lectr. in Pharm. 1963; Lectr. in Pharm. Dalhousie Univ 1962–63; Rsch. Assoc. Univ. of Mich. 1963, Teaching Fellow 1965–66; Asst. Instr. Mich. State Univ. 1966, Asst. Prof. 1967–71; Assoc. Prof. present univ. 1971, Prof. 1975– , Chrmn. of Pharmacol. & Toxicol. 1972–81, Dir. Rsch. & Grad. Studies Faculty Pharm. Sci's 1977–78, Asst. Dean 1978, Assoc. Dean 1982–84; Med. Rsch. Council Visiting Sci. Montpellier, France 1981, Visiting Prof. Univ. of Toronto 1981, Univ. Sask 1983, Laval Univ. 1984, Rsch. Prof. 1981–82; Cons.: Gov.'s Office Drug Abuse State of Mich. 1969–71; Alcohol & Drug Comn. Prov. B.C. 1974; Sci. Review Panel Am. Pharm. Assn. Drug Interaction Project 1974– ; frequent radio and TV commentator drugs, heart disease and diabetes; recipient Alta. Pharm. Scholarship 1959 and Gold Medal 1960; Zeta Psi Ednl. Found. Award 1961; Upjohn Award 1983; McNeil Award 1983; named Outstanding Teacher Pharm. Sci's 1977; Outstanding Pharmacol. Rsch. Paper 1980 (Candn. Jour. Physiol. & Pharmacol.); author or co-author numerous publs.; ed./ed. bd. various learned jours.; mem. B.C. Heart Adv. Bd. 1981– ; Chrmn. Sci. Review Ctte. Candn. Heart Found. 1984–86; mem. Am. Fedn. Clin. Rsch.; Pharmacol. Soc. Can. (Pres. 1980–81, Council 1975–83); Am. Soc. Pharmacol. & Therapeutics; N.Y. Acad. Sci's; Internat. Soc. for Health Rsch.; W. Pharmacol. Soc. (Pres. 1979–80, Council 1977–81); Am. Assn. Advanc. Sci.; Internat. Soc. Heart Rsch.; B.C. Coll. Pharmacists (Council 1985– ); Am. Pharm. Assn.; Candn. Cardiovascular Soc.; Candn. IUPHAR Rep. 1982–87; CNC/IUPHAR 1981–87; Candn. Counc. Animal Care 1985–88 (Chrmn. 1986–87); Assoc. Deans of Pharmacy of Canada 1985– (Chrmn. 1986–87); Home: #54 - 5880 Hampton Place, Vancouver, B.C. V6T 2E9; Office: Vancouver, B.C. V6T 1Z3.

**McNEILL, Kenneth Gordon,** B.A., M.A., D.Phil.; medical physicist; b. Cheshire, Eng. 21 Dec. 1926; s. Ferguson and Elizabeth (Stevenson) McN.; e. B.A. Oxford Univ. 1947, M.A. 1950, D.Phil. 1950; m. J. Ruth S. Robertson 6 Nov. 1959; one d. Diane E.S.; Harmsworth Sr. Scholar Merton Coll. Oxford 1948–50; Sir John Dill Meml. Fellow Yale Univ. 1950–51; Nuffield Rsch. Fellow Glasgow Univ. 1951–52; Lectr. 1952–57; mem. Faculty Univ. of Toronto 1957; Prof. Physics 1963–92; Prof. Medicine 1969–92; Spec. Staff Mem. Toronto Gen. Hosp. 1974; Fellow, Trinity College 1963–92; Prof. Emeritus 1992; mem. Adv. Ctte. Radiation Protection, Min. Nat. Health and Welfare 1964–68; Nuclear Accident Contingency Planning Bd. Govt. of Ont. 1974– ; Technical Advr. to Sol. Gen. of Ont. for Nuclear Contingencies 1983– ; Sir Thomas Lyle Fellow, Univ. of Melbourne 1984; Visiting Research Fellow, Univ. of Melbourne 1986–87; Hon. Prof., Monash Univ., Melbourne 1988; Pres., Kishmul Resources Inc.; Kishmul Kitchen Inc.; co-author (with J. MacLachlan, P.T. Spencer, J. Bell) 'Matter and Energy' 1963 (2nd ed. 1978; French ed. 1981; 3rd ed. 1987); contrib. numerous articles to profl. jours.; mem. Governing Counc. Univ. of Toronto 1980–86, 1989–92; Fellow, Inst. Nuclear Engrs. (U.K.); Candn. Assn. of Physicists; Candn. Radiation Protection Assn.; engaged in rsch. on low-energy nuclear physics and med. physics; Home: 70 Rathnelly Ave., Toronto, Ont. M4V 2M6.

**McNEILL, Ronald Gordon,** B.A., F.C.A.; chartered accountant; b. Owen Sound, Ont. 16 June 1940; s. Gordon Alexander and Gertrude Adeline (Anderson) M.; e. Univ. of Western Ont. B.A. (Hons.) 1963; Inst. of C.A.s C.A. 1966; m. Janis d. Thelma Wauthier 3 Aug. 1984; children: John, Andrew, Carolyn, Neil; PARTNER, DELOITTE & TOUCHE 1973– ; Council Mem., Inst. of C.A.s of Ont. 1982–89; Extve. Ctte. 1984–89; Pres. 1988–89; Chair, Building Ctte. 1987–90; Final Appeal

Ctte. 1989–91; Discipline Ctte. 1981–82; Education Ctte. 1977–80; Bd. of Govs., Candn. Inst. of C.A.s 1986–90; Extve. Ctte. 1988–89; Mem., Assn. of Kinsmen Clubs: Mississauga, Erin Mills, Windsor; Windsor C. of C. (Chair 1985–86); Ont. C. of C. (Dir. 1985–86, 1990–92); Markham Bd. of Trade (Vice-Pres. 1990–91; Pres. 1991–92); Group Managing Partner, South Western Ont. 1990–93; F.C.A. 1985; active in community affairs: clubs: Windsor Yacht; Home: 29 Calderbridge Cres., Unionville, Ont. L3R 9M9; Office: One City Centre Dr., Suite 1100, Mississauga, Ont. L5B 1M2.

**McNIE, John Duncan,** B.A., M.Ed.; retired advertising executive; b. Toronto, Ont. 24 July 1920; s. John and Ann (Duncan) M.; e. Pub. Schs. and York Mem. Coll. Inst., Toronto, Ont.; Western Tech. School, Toronto, Ont.; B.A. McMaster Univ.; M.ed., Univ. of Toronto; m. late Mary Kathleen, d. Alfred John Skeans, Q.C., Toronto, Ont., 8 Dec. 1951; m. Bernice Mackay (Sosulski) 10 Sept. 1988; children: Frances Ann, Heather Kathleen, Duncan Scott, John Thorp, Mary Alice; PAST CHRMN., R.T. KELLEY INC. (Advertising Agency, Estbd. 1913); employed Salada Tea Co. Ltd., Toronto, Ont. 1938–43; served in 2nd World War with R.C.A.F. 1943–45; el. to Ont. Leg. for Hamilton W., Oct. 1971; apptd. to Cabinet Oct. 1972–75; United Church; Club: Rotary; Home: 66 Forsyth Ave. North, Hamilton, Ont. L8S 4E3.

**McOUAT, John Frederick,** B.A.Sc., P. Eng., D. Eng. (Hon.); executive; b. Toronto, Ont. 4 May 1933; s. James Harold and Muriel Gertrude (Benn) McO.; e. Univ. of Toronto Schs. 1952; Univ. of Toronto, B.A.Sc. (Geol. Engn.) 1956; m. Vodrie Jo-Anne, d. late Charles Miller, 12 Dec. 1959; children: Leslie Jo-Anne, Lindsey Dianne, Morrie Cathryn; John Gavin; PRES., WATTS, GRIFFIS AND McOUAT LIMITED; Dir., Cominco Ltd.; Echo Bay Mines; Euro-Nevada Mining Corp. Ltd.; mem. Candn. Inst. Mining & Metall.; Australian Inst. Mining & Metall.; Assn. Prof. Engrs. Ont.; mem. Amer. Inst. of Prof Geol. (U.S.); Lt. Gov. in Council appt. to Council of Assoc. of Prof. Engrs. of Ont. 1981–87; mem. Nat. Adv. Ctte. on the Mining Industry to Min. of State for Mines, Ottawa; awarded Hon. degree, Doctor of Engineering 1987; Officer of the Order of the Sons of Martha Engineering Award; author of numerous articles publd. in leading prof. journs.; P. Conservative; Protestant; recreations: hockey, children, reading; Club: Granite; Home: 24 Danville Drive, Willowdale, Ont. M2P 1J1; Office: Suite 400, 8 King St. E., Toronto, Ont. M5C 1B5.

**McPHAIL, Donald Sutherland,** M.A.; b. Halifax, N.S., 26 May 1931; s. late Donald and Ruby (Sutherland) McP.; e. Univ. of N.B., B.A. 1952, M.A. 1953; Univ. of the Netherlands 1952; London Sch. of Econ. 1953–54; m. Ruth Elizabeth, d. late Herbert and Hughena Tracy 27 May 1953; children: Kim Tracy, Jocelyn Nan, Donald Alexander; PARTNER, THE OSPREY GROUP 1990– ; Econ., DuPont Co. of Canada Ltd., 1955; Dept. of External Affairs 1956; Paris, 1957; Ottawa 1961; Candn. Del. to 1964–65 GATT Negotiating Conf. Geneva 1966; Ambassador to Venezuela and to Dominican Republic 1970; Dir. Gen. Bureau of Econ. and Sci. Affairs, Ottawa 1972; Asst. Depy Min., Dept. of Regional Econ. Expansion (Atlantic Region) Moncton 1978; Asst. Under Sec. of State for External Affairs, Ottawa 1976; Ambassador and Permanent Representative to the Office of the United Nations at Geneva, to GATT and to the Committee on Disarmament, Geneva 1979–83; Chrmn. GATT Contracting Parties 1982; Canadian Ambassador to Federal German Republic, Bonn and Head, Canadian Military Mission, Berlin 1983–87; Pres., Atlantic Canada Opportunities Agency, Moncton 1987–89; Senior Advisor, Privy Council Office, Ottawa 1989–90; recreations: golf, gardening, bridge; Address: Murray Corner, R.R. 2, Port Elgin, N.B. E0A 2K0.

**McPHEDRAN, Marilou,** C.M., B.A., LL.B., LL.D.; lawyer; b. Neepawa, Man. 22 July 1951; e. Univ. of Winnipeg 1969–72; Univ. of Toronto B.A. 1973; York Univ. Osgoode Hall Law Sch. LL.B. 1976; Univ. of Winnipeg LL.D. (honoris causa) 1992; two s. Jonathan and David McPhedran Waitzer; CORPORATE DIR., HEALTHY CITY TORONTO; private law practice since 1988; Chair and Founding mem. LEAF Found.; Founding Dir. METRAC; Dir. Gerstein Crisis Centre; Nat. Feminist Legal Inst. Osgoode Hall; active Women's Coll. Hosp.; Chairperson, Task Force on Sexual Abuse of Patients, College of Physicians & Surgeons of Ont. 1991; Founding Advisory Council of Democracy Watch 1993; recipient: Special Citation, YWCA Women of Distinction 1981; Mem., Order of Canada 1985; 'Women of the Year' 1993, B'nai Brith; Club: McGill; Office: 20 Dundas St. W., Box 22, Suite 1036, Toronto, Ont. M5G 2C2.

**McPHEE, W.R. (Bob),** B.Ed.Mus.; arts executive; b. Winnipeg, Man. 22 Jan. 1956; s. William Ross and Iona (Chisholm) M.; e. Univ. of Man., B.Ed.Mus. 1978; Grant MacEwan Coll., cert. Arts Admin. 1982; Sch. of Mngt., Banff Sch. of Fine Arts 1984; m. Sandra d. Douglas and Kathleen Brown 29 Aug. 1981; MANAGING DIRECTOR, EDMONTON SYMPHONY ORCHESTRA and EDMONTON CONCERT HALL FOUNDATION 1992– ; Devel. Offr., Royal Wpg. Ballet 1982–83; Dir. of Devel. 1983–84; Calgary Phil. Orch. 1984–85; Dir. of Devel. & Mktg. 1985–86; Asst. Gen Mgr. 1986–88; Gen. Mgr., Orchestra London Can. 1988–89; Gen. Mgr., Edmonton Symphony Orchestra 1989–92; Clin. & Lectr., Grant MacEwan Coll., Mt. Royal Coll., Assn. of Candn. Orch., Performing Arts Publicist Assn. & others; many music awards incl. 'Rose Bowl' Man. Music Fest.; finalist, Candn. Music Comp.; Prov. of Alta. Achievement Award (for work on Olympics); Chair, Edmonton Professional Arts Council; Special Adv., Edmonton Concert Hall Foundation; Mem., Olympic Arts Fest. Ctte. 1984–88; Music Art Admin. Adv. Ctte., Grant MacEwan Coll.; Mem., Un. Ch. of Can.; recreations: music; Home: 14011 – 91 Ave., Edmonton, Alta. T5R 4Y1; Office: 10160 - 103 St., Edmonton, Alta. T5J 0X6.

**McPHERSON, Ian Edward,** D.F.C., Q.C., B.A., LL.B., LL.M., K.L.J.; b. Victoria, B.C. 8 June 1920; s. late Thomas and Maude (Hyatt) McP.; e. Victoria (B.C.) Coll. 1941; Univ. of Brit. Columbia, B.A. 1948, LL.B. 1949; Inst. Internat. Air Law, McGill Univ., LL.M. 1955; m. Mary Alexa Anne, d. Gordon McLeod Pitts, 21 Feb. 1959; children: Mary Margot Ann, Ian Andrew, Thomas Alexander Gordon; read law with late Mr. Justice George Gregory; called to Bar of B.C. 1949, of Que. 1968–83; practised law in Victoria, B.C. 1949–51; Solr., Canadian National Railways, Montreal 1952; Gen. Atty., Air Canada 1961; Gen. Counsel Air Canada, 1966; Vice Pres., Law, Air Canada 1979–83 (retired); served in 2nd World War, R.C.A.F. 1941–45; Pilot R.A.F. Bomber Command; awarded D.F.C.: R.C.A.F. Auxiliary 1952–60; mem. Law Soc. B.C.; Candn. Bar Assn. (Past Chrmn., Air Law Section); Mem. Emeritus, Assn. Candn. Gen. Counsel (Pres. 1979–80); Past Chrmn., Internat. Air Transport Assn. Legal Comte.; Past Pres. Inst. Air and Space Law Assn.; Alderman, Westmount, P.Q. 1983–84; Co-ordr. Official Visits, EXPO 86 World Exposition Vancouver 1984–86; Dir., Victoria Foundation; comn. a Kentucky Col. 1988; Protestant; Clubs: Victoria Golf; Union (Victoria); recreations: golf, swimming, travel; Home: 24 Sylvan Lane, Victoria, B.C. V8S 2K8.

**McPHERSON, Dr. Ruth,** B.Sc., M.Sc., M.D., Ph.D., F.R.C.P.(C); physician, scientist; b. Seaforth, Ont. 26 March 1949; d. Kenneth Bruce and Catherine Durkin (Dwyer) M.; e. Univ. of Toronto B.Sc. 1971; Univ. of London (UK) M.Sc. 1974, Ph.D. 1976; Univ. of Toronto M.D. 1984; 1st m. Peter William Kay 1971–84; 2nd m. Yves Louis s. Louis and Angelina Marcel 22 June 1991; 1 d. Gabrielle; DIR., LIPID CLINIC & LIPID RESEARCH LAB., UNIV. OF OTTAWA HEART INST. 1992– ; Asst. Prof., Surgery, Univ. of Toronto 1977–80; clinical training leave 1980–88; Asst. Prof., Medicine, Univ. of Toronto 1988–89; Asst. Prof., Med. & Dir., Lipid Clinic & Lipid Rsch. Lab., McGill Univ. 1989–92; Assoc. Prof., Med., Univ. of Ottawa 1992– ; research focus: 'reverse cholesterol transport' in man; Ctte. Mem., Med. Rsch. Council Adv. Ctte. on Science 1993; Med. Edn. Consultant, Marion Merrell Dow (US), Merck Frosst Canada; Ctte. Mem., World Health Orgn. Expert Ctte. on Carbohydrates in Human Nutrition 1979; Alpha Omega Alpha Hon. Med. Soc. 1982; F. Colling OBE Memorial Scholarship, Univ. of Toronto 1982, '83; FRSQ Chercheur-Clinicien Award 1990; Mem., Am. Coll. of Physicians; Am. Fed. for Clin. Rsch.; Am. Heart Assn.; RCPS; author of 30 sci. articles; editor: 'Medical Aspects of Dietary Fibre' 1980; recreations: running, gardening, classical music; Home: 155 Sherwood Dr., Ottawa, Ont. K1Y 3V5; Office: H441, Heart Inst., 1053 Carling Ave., Ottawa, Ont. K1Y 4E9.

**McQUAID, Hon. Melvin J.,** B.A., LL.B.; retired judge; b. Souris, P.E.I. 6 Sept. 1911; s. John and Annie (Mullally) McQ.; e. Souris High Sch.; St. Dunstans Univ. B.A. 1934; St. Francis Xavier Univ. B.A. 1936; Dalhousie Univ. LL.B. 1939; m. Catherine E. d. Austin Handrahan, Tignish, P.E.I., 16 Sept. 1947; children: John, Mary-Jo, Peter; Mem., National Parole Bd. 1985–87; Justice, Supreme Court of P.E.I. 1976–81; called to Bar of P.E.I. 1940; cr. Q.C. 1953; Town Clk. Souris 1940–58; mem. Leg. Assembly P.E.I. 1959–62 holding portfolios Min. of Finance and Min. of Justice, Leader of Official Opposition 1973–76; mem. H. of C. for Cardigan 1965–72; mem. Bd. of Govs. Souris Hosp. (Secy. 1945–58); mem. Atlantic Devel. Bd. 1963–65; Pres. P.E.I. Cons. Assn. 1956–59; Past Pres. Eastern King's Bd. Trade; mem., K. of C.; mem. Law Soc. P.E.I. (Past Pres.); Candn. Bar Assn.; R. Catholic; recreations: baseball, swimming; Home: Souris, P.E.I. C0A 2B0.

**McQUAIG, Linda Joy,** B.A.; journalist; b. Toronto, Ont. 5 Sept. 1951; d. Jack Hunter and Audrey Joy (Lyons) McQ.; e. Univ. of Toronto, B.A. 1974; m. Fred Fedorsen; daughter: Amy Joy Margaret; Reporter, Globe and Mail 1973–76, 1984–90; Assoc. Producer CBC Radio 1977–80; Sr. Writer Maclean's mag. 1981–84; author: 'Behind Closed Doors: How the Rich Won Control of Canada's Tax System... and Ended Up Richer' 1987; 'The Quick and the Dead: Brian Mulroney, Big Business and the Seduction of Canada' 1991; 'The Wealthy Banker's Wife: the Assault on Equality on Canada' 1993; National Newspaper Award 1989; Office: 551 Gerrard St. E., Toronto, Ont.

**McQUARRIE, John Robert;** photographer; b. Sudbury, Ont. 28 June 1946; s. John Lawson and Mary Elise (Young) M.; e. Eastern Ont. Inst. of Technol., Bus.Admin. 1967; single; author/photographer: 'Canadian Wings' 1990; 'Till We Meet Again' 1991; 'Canadian Fighter Pilot' 1992; 'Between the Lines, Canadians in the Service of Peace' 1993; 'Canadian Cowboy' forthcoming; recreations: tennis, skiing, parachuting; Home: 192 Bruyere St., Ottawa, Ont. K1N 5E1.

**MCQUEEN, Catherine Margaret (Trina);** broadcaster; b. Belleville, Ont. d. Anthony D. and Frances Janitsch; e. Carleton Univ., B.J. prog.; Univ. of B.C., B.A. prog.; m. Donald M. 1970; one d.: Jennifer; Vice-President and General Mgr., Discovery Channel 1993– ; Reporter/Host: Ottawa Journal, CTV W-5 1965–68; Reporter, Host, Prod. CBC 1968–76; Executive Producer, National TV News 1976–80; Network Program Director 1980–84; Director Network Television 1984–88; Director/Vice-President News, Current Affairs, Newsworld 1988–1992; Vice-President, Regional Broadcasting Operations, CBC 1992–93; Executive Board: Canadian Women in Radio and Television 1991– ; Banff Television Foundation 1987– ; Canadian Stage Company 1988– ; Member Board of Governors Canadian Journalism Foundation 1990– ; Member Board of Directors: Broadcast Executives Society 1982– ; Visnews Inc. 1989– ; Advisory Board Ryerson Journalism School 1978–82; University of Regina 1980–89; Presidents Council, Carleton University 1991– ; Home: 47 Wanless Cres., Toronto, Ont. M4N 3B8; Office: Box 8478, Ottawa, Ont. K1G 3J5.

**McQUEEN, David Lisle,** M.A., Ph.D.; educator: b. Saskatoon, Sask. 25 Dec. 1926; s. late Robert and Monica (Lisle) McQ.; e. Univ. of Man. B.Com. 1947; Queen's Univ. M.A. (Econ.) 1948; London Sch. of Econ. Ph.D. (Econ.) 1952 (IODE Overseas Scholarship 1948–50); m. Janet Mary (divorced), d. late Maj. Arthur Gorham, 6 Sept. 1952; two s., Robert John, Martin Alexander; m. 2ndly Nancy Ker (divorced), d. Bruce and Molly Lawrence, 15 Dec. 1978; one d. Alison Elizabeth Jennifer; PROFESSOR EMERITUS OF ECON. GLENDON COLL., YORK UNIV.; Econ. and subsequently Rsch. Offr., Asst. Chief, Rsch. Dept. Bank of Can. 1952–65; Econ. subsequently Dir., Vice Chrmn. Econ. Council Can. 1965–69; Chrmn. Dept. Econ. present Coll. 1969–75; Prof. of Econ. 1969–93; Senate rep. Bd. Govs. York Univ. 1973–75; Principal, Glendon Coll. 1975–80; rec'd. Univ of Man. Alumni Assn. Jubilee Award 1947; co-author 'Canadian Competition Policy – An Economic and Legal Analysis' 1987; author various book chapters, articles, conf. papers; mem. Candn. Econ. Assn.; Amer. Econ. Assn.; Nat. Statistics Council; Ont. Environment Network; Dir., Family Service Assn. Toronto 1984–90; recreations: photography, hiking, swimming; Office: 2275 Bayview Ave., Toronto, Ont. M4N 3M6.

**McQUEEN, Jennifer Robertson;** retired federal public servant; b. Saskatoon, Sask.; d. Robert and Monica Lisle (Holdsworth) McQ.; e. Univ. of Manitoba 1951; Former High Commnr. for Canada to Jamaica, Commonwealth of the Bahamas and Belize; Retired from Public Service of Canada 1994; T. Eaton Co., London, Eng. 1951–53; Economic Rsch. & Inform. Services Branch, Canada Mortgage & Housing Corp., Ottawa 1953–57; asst. prod. 'Canadian Art' magazine for National Gallery of Canada; Ed., 'Community Planning Review'; Asst. Nat. Dir., Community Planning Assoc. 1957–64; Candn. Corp. for the 1967 World Exhbn., Montreal 1965–67; staff mem. Roy. Comn. on Status of Women 1968; Spec. asst. to Min. of Consumer & Corporate Affairs; Chrmn., Citizen's Cultures Dept. of Sec. of State, resp. for devel. of multiculturalism policy

1971; Chief of Manpower Policy Grp. in Personnel Policy Br., Treasury Bd. 1974; Asst. Sec.-Gen. to National Museums of Can. 1974, Acting Sec.-Gen. 1977; Sr. Advr. Fed.-Prov. Relns. Office 1978; Asst. Sec. to the Cabinet 1978–79; mem. Royal Coll. of Defence Studies, London, Eng. 1980; Dir. Gen. Internat. Affairs for Agric. Can. 1981; Comnr., Public Service Comn. of Can. 1982–85; Deputy Min., Labour Canada 1985–90; Commnr. for Canada, Cayman Islands & Turks and Caicos Islands 1990–93; Address: Pond House, Lydeard St. Lawrence, Taunton, Somerset, U.K. TA4 3SE.

**McQUEEN, Roderick Moir,** B.A.; author/journalist; b. Guelph, Ont. 29 June 1944; s. Duncan Roderick and Jean Moir (Work) M.; e. Univ. of West. Ont. B.A. (Hons.) 1967 (Univ. Students' Counc. Gold Key Award for contrib. to campus publications); m. Sandra Illingworth; children: Mark Roderick, Alison Jane; Reporter/Feature Writer, The London Free Press 1964–67; Ed., Maclean Hunter Ltd. 1967–70; Press Sec., The Hon. R. Stanfield, Leader, P.C. Party 1970–76; Dir., Pub. Affairs, Bank of N.S. 1976–78; Bus. Ed. (1978–79) then Mng. Ed. (1979–82) Maclean's Mag.; freelance writer/broadcaster 1982–88; Editor, Vista Mag. 1989; Washington Bureau Chief, The Financial Post 1989– ; written extensively on bus. fin. & pol. in many U.S., U.K. & Candn. mags. & papers incl.: Canadian Business, Toronto Life, Saturday Night, The Financial Post, Fortune, Financial Times of London, Business; Sr. Contrib. Ed., 'Canadian Business' 1983–88; Contrib. Ed., 'Toronto Life' 1985–88; City of Toronto Book Award 1984 finalist; Nat. Bus. Writing Award for distinguished regular column 1985; City & Reg. Mag. Assn. of N. Am. bronze award for commentary 1986; Silver Nat. Mag. Award for Pol. 1986; Mem., National Press Club of Washington; author: 'The Moneyspinners' 1983, 'Risky Business' 1985, 'Leap of Faith' 1986, 'Both My Houses' (in collaboration with Father Sean O'Sullivan) 1986; 'Blind Trust' 1987; recreations: country walks, composting; Office: 1225 Eye St. NW, Suite 810, Washington, D.C. 20005 USA.

**McRAE, Bruce Alexander Henry,** C.L.U., CHFC; insurance executive; b. Vancouver, B.C. 4 May 1934; s. Hector Albert and Nellie May (Henry) McR.; e. Kitsilano High Sch.; Univ. of B.C.; C.L.U. 1965, C.H.F.C. 1989; m. Janice A. d. Dawson and Minnie Gordon 24 June 1961; children: Alison Louise, Cameron Alexander; PRES., McRAE INSURANCE & ANNUITY SERVICES LTD. 1981– ; began life ins. career 1958; Vice Pres. Bd. Govs. Vancouver Metrop. YMCA 1984–89; Pres. Life Underwriters Assn. Vancouver 1969; B.C. Mainland Chapter Inst. C.L.U.'s Can. 1976; Chrmn. Ins. Council B.C. 1975, 1980; Chrmn. and Chief Extve. Offr. Life Underwriters Assn. Can. 1988–90; Life & Qualifying mem. Million Dollar Round Table; mem. Estate Planning Council Vancouver; recreations: raquetball, tennis, golf; Home: 4027 West 29th Ave., Vancouver, B.C. V6S 1V4; Office: 339 - 1275 West 6th Ave., Vancouver, B.C. V6H 1A6.

**McRAE, Kenneth Douglas,** B.A., A.M., Ph.D., F.R.S.C.; university professor; b. Toronto, Ont. 20 Jan. 1925; s. Douglas Archibald and Margaret Constance (Dingle) M.; e. Univ. of Toronto Schs. 1937–42; Univ. of Toronto, B.A. 1946; Harvard Univ., A.M. 1947, Ph.D. 1954; m. Dorothea A. d. Sir Francis and Lady Charlotte Simon 4 Aug. 1950; daughters: Patricia, Sandra, Karen, Susan; PROF., CARLETON UNIV. 1964– ; Lectr., Univ. of Toronto 1950–52; Asst. Prof., Carleton Univ. 1955–57; Assoc. Prof. 1957–64; Rsch. Supvr., Royal Comn. on Bilingualism & Biculturalism 1964–69; Killam Rsch. fellowships 1977–79, 1982–83; Pres., Candn. Pol. Sci. Assn. 1978–79; F.R.S.C. 1977 (Hon. Sec. of the Soc. 1980–83); Foreign Mem., Societas Scientiarum Fennica 1992; author: 'Switzerland' 1964, 'Conflict and Compromise in Multilingual Societies' vol. 1, Switzerland, 1983, vol. 2, Belgium, 1986; co-author: 'The Founding of New Societies' 1964; editor: Jean Bodin, 'The Six Bookes of a Commonweale' 1962, 'The Federal Capital' 1969, 'Consociational Democracy' 1974; Office: Dept. of Pol. Sci., Carleton Univ., Ottawa, Ont. K1S 5B6.

**McRAE, Robert Forbes,** M.A., Ph.D.; university professor (emeritus); b. Winnipeg, Man. 27 June 1914; s. Duncan and Susan Helena (Rodgers) M.; e. Univ. of Toronto, B.A. 1936, M.A. 1938; Johns Hopkins Univ., Ph.D. 1946; m. Nora Frances. d. V. A. Beacock, Toronto, Ont., 1 Sept. 1950; children: Kiloran, Alison, Ellen; Prof. of Philos., Univ. of Toronto 1960–79 (retired); Instr., Lectr., Asst. Prof., Assoc. Prof. there 1945–1960: Nuffield Fellow 1951–52; served in 2nd World War;Ordinary Seaman and Lieut. in R.C.N.V.R. 1940–45 on loan to Royal Navy; taken prisoner at Dieppe 1942: Commndg. Offr., U.N.T.D., Univ. of Toronto 1947–54, rank Lieut-Commdr.; author: 'The Problem of the Unity of the Sciences: Bacon to Kant' 1961; 'Leibniz: Perception, Apperception, and Thought' 1976; Home: 29 Dunbar Rd., Toronto, Ont. M4W 2X5.

**McSHERRY, James Andrew,** T.D., M.B. Ch.B., C.C.F.P., F.C.F.P., F.R.C.G.P., F.A.A.F.P., F.A.B.M.P., D.Obst., R.C.O.G.; family physician & educator; b. Comrie, Scotland 20 May 1942; s. James and Margaret (Brown) M.; e. St. Aloysius' College and Univ. of Glasgow M.B., Ch.B. 1965; m. Helen d. Dr. Walter and Joan Weetch 3 Feb. 1968; children: Peter, Stephen, Audrey; PROFESSOR OF FAMILY MEDICINE, THE UNIV. OF WESTERN ONTARIO; CHIEF OF FAMILY MEDICINE, VICTORIA HOSPITAL CORP.; MEDICAL DIRECTOR, VICTORIA FAMILY MEDICAL CENTRE 1993– ; sometime Major, RAMC(V), R.M.O. 71 (Scottish) Engineer Regiment (V); postgrad. training, Glasgow Southern Gen. & Royal Maternity Hosps. Scotland 1965–67; family physician in Glasgow 1967–73; e. to Canada 1973; family physician in Sarnia, Ont. 1973–81; Active Staff, Sarnia Gen. & St. Joseph's Hosp. 1973–81; Chief, Dept. of General Practice, St. Joseph's Hosp., Sarnia 1978–81; Medical Dir., Sarnia-Lambton Home Care Program 1975–81; Professor, Depts. of Family Medicine & Psychology, Director of Student Health Service, Queen's Univ., Kingston, Ont. 1981–93; Attending Staff, Kingston General and Hotel Dieu Hosps. 1981–93; Attending Staff, Victoria Hosp. Corp. & Parkwood Hosp., London 1993– ; Past Pres., Candn. College Health Services Assn., Ont. College Health Assn., John Austin Soc. of Queen's Univ., St. Andrew's Soc. of Kingston, Sarnia-Lambton Community Girls' Home Assn.; Hon. Pres. Queen's Univ. Aesculapian Soc. 1985–88; Pres., London and District Eating Disorders Assn. 1993– ; Territorial Decoration 1973; Canada Volunteer Award and Medal of Honor 1986; Officer Brother, Order of St. John of Jerusalem 1989; Fellow, Royal Soc. of Arts, Royal Soc. of Health, Royal Soc. of Medicine, Soc. of Antiquaries of Scotland, Am. Geriatrics Soc.; Ont. College Health Assn.; author, chapters in medical textbooks, articles in medical journals, popular press, etc., on health care, clinical medicine, med. humour, history of med., Scottish history; Roman Catholic; recreations: Scottish country dancing, choral singing; Home: 1355 Brookline Rd., London, Ont. N5X 2L1; Office: Victoria Family Medical Centre, 60 Chesley Ave., London, Ont. N5Z 2C1.

**McSWEENEY, Michael Benjamin,** B.A., M.P.A.; executive; b. Ottawa, Ont. 13 July 1957; s. Michael Albert and Marion Daisy (Chapman) M.; e. Carleton Univ. B.A. 1980; Harvard Univ. M.P.A. 1992; CHIEF EXECUTIVE OFFICER & EXTVE. DIR., STANDARDS COUNCIL OF CANADA 1992– ; elected City and Regional Councillor, Ottawa 1982–85; re-elected 1985–88, 1988–91; Special Asst. to Brian Mulroney 1983–84; Deputy Mayor, City of Ottawa 1985–86; Comnr., Ottawa-Carleton Transit Authority 1985–91; Special Asst. to the Assoc. Min. of Nat. Defence 1986–87; Comnr., Ottawa Police 1988–91; Anglican; recreations: skiing, squash, tennis; clubs: Ottawa Athletic; Home: 102 Sai Cres., Ottawa, Ont. K1G 5P1; Office: 45 O'Connor St., Ottawa, Ont. K1P 6N7.

**McTAGGART, Douglas Graham,** B.A., L.I.M.I., C.L.U.; b. Toronto, Ont. 30 Sept. 1931; s. the late Donald Harrison, Q.C. and Hazel G. (Defoe) McT.; e. Rawlinson Pub. Sch. and Forest Hill Coll. Inst., Toronto, 1950; Univ. of Toronto, Victoria Coll., B.A. 1954; Inst. of Ins. Marketing, School of Business Administration, Southern Methodist Univ., Dallas, 1956; m. the late Mary Eleanor Hunter; children: Pamela, Kimberly, Douglas Gregory; PRESIDENT AND DIR., PLANNED INSURANCE PORTFOLIOS CO. LTD., since 1969; Chrmn. and Dir., Estate and Corporate Funding Programmes Co. Ltd.; Chartered mem., Sports Coll. Testing Group (founded by the late Lloyd Percival), competed in Madison Square Gardens N.Y., Chicago, Montreal and Hamilton 1946–48; Muskoka Lakes Sales Rep., Swift Canadian Co. as summer employment while attending univ. 1951–55; Sales Agt., Canada Life Assurance Co., 1956; Mgr., Field Training Research, 1957–58; Agency Mgr., Toronto, 1958–63; conducted own agency for a Candn. life insurance co., Toronto 1963–69; Past Chrmn., Ins. Sec., Un. Appeal; fellow, Royal Ont. Museum; mem., Art Gallery of Ont.; Candn. Tax Foundation; mem., Edinburgh Language Foundation; Royal Candn. Military Inst.; Life Ins. Mang. Assn.; Life Underwriters Assn. (Past Dir. and Offr.); Bd. Trade Metrop. Toronto; mem., Candn. Institute of Mining, Metallurgy and Petroleum; Founding Benefactor and Past Dir., Lake of Bays Heritage Found.; Life & Qualifying Mem., Million Dollar Round Table; Life Mem., St. Andrew's Lodge; Officer in 78th Regiment, Fraser's Highlanders; mem. Chancellor's Counc. of Victoria Univ. 1988–94; Freemason; United Church; recreations: golf, skeet shooting, boating, skiing, curling, military history; Club: Granite; Empire; Delray Beach Club (Delray Beach, Fla.); Home: 222 Walmer Rd., Toronto, Ont. M5R 3R7; Rolling Rock North, Burnt Island Bay, Lake of Bays, Ont.; 1091 Bel Lido Dr., Highland Beach, Fla.; Office: Suite 105, P.O. Box 2213, Postal Station P, Toronto, Ont. M5S 2T2.

**McTAGGART-COWAN, Ian,** O.C. (1970), O.B.C. (1991), Ph.D., LL.D., D.Env.Sc., D.Sc., F.R.S.C.; retired university professor; b. Edinburgh, Scot. 25 June 1910; s. Garry McTaggart and Laura Alice (Mackenzie) C.; came to Can. 1913; e. Univ. of B.C., B.A. 1932; Univ. of Cal., PhD. 1935; LL.D. Univ. of Alta. 1971, Simon Fraser Univ. 1980; D. Env. St., Univ. of Waterloo 1975; D. Sc., Univ. of B.C. 1977, Univ. Victoria 1985; m. Joyce Stewart, d. Kenneth Racey, Vancouver, B.C. 21 Apr. 1936; children: Garry, Barbara Ann; PROF. OF ZOOLOGY, UNIV. OF B.C. 1945–75; Head of the Dept. 1953–64; Asst. Dean of Arts & Sciences 1957–63; Dean of Grad. Studies 1964–75; Dean Emeritus since 1975; mem., Fisheries Research Bd. of Can.; Nat. Research Council of Canada; Wildlife Adv. Comte. to U.S. Secy. of Interior; IUCN (V. Pres. 1970–76); Arctic Institute (Past Chrmn.); Pres., Biol. Council of Can. 1967–68; Asst. Biol., B.C. Prov. Museum, 1936–38; Asst. Dir. 1938–40; Consulting Biol., Nat. Parks of Can., 1943–46; mem. and Chrmn., Canadian Environmental Adv. Council 1972–79; Chrmn., B.C. Academic Bd. 1977–78; Chrmn. Academic Council (B.C.) 1978–82; Chrmn. Canadian Comte. on Whales and Whaling 1981–93; Chrmn. Habitat Conserv. Fund Adv. Bd., B.C. 1981– ; Dir., Nature Trust of B.C.; National Audubon Soc. (USA); Chancellor, Univ. of Victoria, 1979–85; Can. Centennial Medal, 1967; Fred Fry Medal, Can. Soc. Zoologists, 1977; Queen Elizabeth Jubilee Medal, 1978; awarded Commemorative Medal for 125th Anniversary of Candn. Confederation 1993; mem., Am. Ornithologists Union; Am. Soc. of Mammologists; Am. Wildlife Soc. (Past Pres.; Leopold Medal 1970, Wallmo Award 1993); has contrib. many books and papers on mammals, birds, parasites and diseases of mammals, and on conservation topics to various tech. jours.; Sigma Xi; Anglican; Home: 3919 Woodhaven Terrace, Victoria, B.C. V8N 1S7.

**McTAGGART-COWAN, Patrick Duncan,** O.C., M.B.E., LL.D., D.Sc.; b. Edinburgh, Scotland 31 May 1912; s. G. and Laura Alice (MacKenzie) M-C; e. Univ. of B.C. (Grad. with 1st Class Hons. in Math. and Physics) 1929–33. D.Sc. 1961: LL.D. St. Francis-Xavier 1970; Simon Fraser 1972; Lakehead 1974; D.Sc. McGill 1974; Univ. of N.B. 1976; Univ. of Guelph, 1981; Corpus Christi, Oxford (B.C. Rhodes Schol.), Grad. with Hons. deg. in Natural Sciences; Atlantic Training School, British Meteorol. Office, Croydon, Eng.; m. Margaret Lawson, d. late J. T. E. Palmer, 17 Oct. 1939; children: Gillian Hope, James Duncan; Offr. in charge, Meteorol. Office at Botwood and then Gander, Nfld., 1937–42; Chief Meteorol. Offr., R.A.F. Ferry Command, 1942–45 (mem. of Jt. Control Bd. for delivery of aircraft across the N. Atlantic 1943–45); loaned to the Candn. Preparatory Comte. for the Provisional I.C.A.O. as Tech. Secy., 1945; awarded M.B.E. 1944; Coronation Medal 1953; Patterson Medal 1965; Centennial Medal 1967; Officer of Order of Can. 1979; 125th Anniversary of the Confederation of Canada Medal, 1992; Asst. Dir., Meteorol. Div., Dept. of Transport 1946–57; Assoc. Dir. 1958–59: Dir. 1959–64: Pres., Simon Fraser Univ. 1963–68; Head Task Force, Operation Oil 1970–73; Gov. Arctic Inst. of N. Am. 1963–65 and 1968–74; Extve. Dir., Science Council of Can. 1968–75; non-viable farmer and consult. since retirement; rec'd. Robert M. Losey Award 1959; Hon. Mem., Assn. for Advancement of Sci. in Can.; mem. Candn. Meterological & Oceanographic Soc., Hon. Life Mem. 1986; mem., American Meteorol. Soc. 1938, Fellow, 1967, Hon. Life mem. 1978, Charles Franklin Brooks Award 1965, Cleveland Abbe Award 1976; Fellow, Am. Geophys. Union; mem., Candn. Assn. of Physicists (Charter mem.); Oxford Soc. (Life); Am. Assn. Advanc. Science; Fellow Arctic Inst. N. Am.; Dir., Bracebridge Agric. Soc., 1979–86; Anglican; recreations: skiing, golf, gardening; Club: Raleigh; Diamond University (S.F.U.); Home: High Falls Rd., R.R. 2, Bracebridge, Ont. P1L 1W9.

**MCTEER, Maureen Anne,** B.A., LL.B.; barrister and solicitor; author; political activist; b. Ottawa, Ont. 27 Feb. 1952; d. John Joseph and Beatrice Ella (Griffith) M.; e. Notre Dame H.S.; Univ. of Ottawa, B.A. 1973;, LL.B. 1977; m. Right Hon. Charles Joseph s. Charles and Grace Clark 30 June 1973; one d. Catherine Jane; called to Ont. Bar 1980; P.C. Candidate, 1988 federal election; Mem., Candn. Bar Assn.; Chair, CBA Eastern European Internship Program; Mem., Federal Royal Commn. on the New Reproductive Technologies 1989–92; Bd. mem., Candn. Native Arts Foundation; Progressive Conservative; Roman Catholic; author: 'Residences' 1981, 'Des maisons qui ont une histoire' 1982, 'Parliament: Democracy in Canada and how it works' 1987 (Fr. & Eng. versions); 'Ottawa Report' in 'Chatelaine' (monthly column) 1984–88; 'The Tangled Womb: Politics of Human Reproduction' 1992; Club: Le Cercle Univ.; Home: 122 Lasalle Ave., Piedmont, CA 94610 USA.

**McVICAR, Barry Marshall,** B.Sc., P.Eng.; executive; b. Winnipeg, Man. 25 Feb. 1927; s. John Archibald and Beth Ecce (Billington) McV.; e. Gordon Bell High Sch.; Univ. of Man. B.Sc. (Elect. Eng.) 1949; m. Pauline Allison d. Sam and Sylvia Broadfoot 9 Dec. 1950; children: Marcia L., David B., Jamie M., Tara L.; Chrmn., Beta Monitors & Controls Ltd.; former President and Chrmn., Consolidated Natural Gas Ltd. 1980–87, Consolidated Pipe Lines Co., Consolidated Gathering Systems Ltd.; Consolidex Gas and Oil Ltd.; Consoligas Management Ltd.; former Dir., Camlin Consulting Corp.; Div. Mgr., Gen. Mgr. Sales, Schlumberger of Canada 1949–66; Pres. (Geophys. Data Analysis) Allison-Marshall Development Co. Ltd. 1966–72; Mgr. Planning & Scheduling, Mgr. Eng. Adm. Candn. Arctic Gas Study Ltd. 1972–75; Mgr., Mgr. Business Devel. Lummus/Crest, Mgr. Pengalta Rsch. & Development Ltd. 1976–80; Past Dir. & Hon. mem., Calgary Olympic Devel. Assn.; Olympic 72; Founding Dir., Jr. Achievement, Calgary; Co-founder, Intnl. Oilmen's Ski Soc.; author various publs.; Gov., Candn. Petrol. Assn. (Chrmn. Pipeline Div.); Past Chrmn., Southern Alta. Sect., Inst. Elect. & Electronic Engs.; Hon. Mem., Candn. Well Logging Soc.; Mem., Candn. Inst. Mining & Metall.; Petrol. Soc.; Am. Radio Relay league (VE6BMM); (Life) Assoc. of Professional Engrs. Geologists & Geophysicists of Alta.; Past Chrmn., Post Polio Awareness and Support Soc. of Alta.; Chrmn., River Valleys Ctte., Parks Found. Calgary; United Church; recreations: skiing, paddling, hiking, photography; Clubs: Calgary Petroleum; Glencoe; Glencoe Golf & Country; Revellers; Home: 7832 Calla Donna Pl. S.W., Calgary, Alta. T2V 2R1.

**McWHINNEY, Edward Watson,** Q.C., LL.M., S.J.D., M.P.; professor; governmental advisor; writer; b. Sydney, Australia, 19 May 1924; s. Matthew Andrew and Evelyn Annie (Watson) M.; e. Yale Univ., LL.M. 1951, Sc.Jur.D. 1953; Acad. de Droit Internat., The Hague, Dipl. 1951: m. Emily Ingalore, d. late Hugo Sabatzky, Berlin, Germany, 27 June 1951; MEMBER OF PARLIAMENT (VANCOUVER-QUADRA) 1993– ; PROF. EMERITUS INTERNAT. LAW, SIMON FRASER UNIV.; Bursar, Carnegie Corp.; Fellow, Rockefeller Foundation (Div. of Social Sciences); mem., Prime Min. of Ont.'s Adv. Comte. on Confederation 1965–71; Lecturer in Constitutional Law, Yale University Law Sch., 1951–53; Asst. Prof. of Pol. Science, Yale Grad. Sch., 1953–55; Fellow of Silliman Coll., Yale Univ., 1953–55: Prof. of Internat. and Comparative Law, Univ. of Toronto, 1955–66; Prof. of Law and Dir., Inst. of Air and Space Law, McGill Univ. 1966–71; Prof. of Law and Dir. Internat. and Comparative Legal Studies, Univ. of Indiana 1971–74; Legal Consultant, United Nations, 1953–54; Consultant (Internat. Law), U.S. Navy, 1961–68; Royal Commr., Comn. of Enquiry on the French Language and Language Rights in Quebec 1968–72; Special Counsel, Government of Quebec 1969–70, 1974–75; served in 2nd World War with Air Force, enlisting in 1943 as Flying Trainee; service from 1943–45; discharged with rank of Flying Offr.; Publications: 'Judicial Review' 1956 (2nd ed. 1960, 3rd ed. 1965, 4th ed. 1969); 'Canadian Jurisprudence: The Civil Law and Common Law in Canada' 1958; 'Föderalismus und Bundesverfassungsrecht' 1961; 'Constitutionalism in Germany' 1962; 'Comparative Federalism, States' Rights and National Power' 1962, 2nd ed. 1965; 'Peaceful Coexistence and Soviet-Western International Law' 1964; 'Law, Foreign Policy, and the East-West Détente' 1964; 'Federal Constitution-Making for a Multi-National World' 1966; 'International Law and World Revolution' 1967; 'Conflit idéologique et ordre public mondial' 1970; 'The Freedom of the Air' (with M.A. Bradley) 1968; 'New Frontiers in Space Law' (with M.A. Bradley) 1969; 'The International Law of Communications' 1970; 'Aerial Piracy and International Law' 1971; 'Federalism and Supreme Courts and the Integration of Legal Systems' (with Pierre Pescatore) 1973; 'The Illegal Diversion of Aircraft and International Law' 1975; 'The International Law of Détente' 1978; 'The World Court and the Contemporary International Law-Making Process' 1979; 'Quebec and the Constitution' 1979; 'Municipal Government in a New Canadian Federal System,' 1980; 'Conflict and Compromise: International Law and World Order in a Revolutionary Age' 1981; 'Constitu-

tion-Making: Principles, Process, Practice' 1981; 'Mécanismes pour une nouvelle Constitution' (with E. Orban et al.) 1981; 'Canada and the Constitution: Patriation and the Charter of Rights' 1982; 'United Nations Law Making: Cultural & Ideological Relativism and International Law-Making for an Era of Transition' 1984; 'Supreme Courts and Judicial Law-Making: Constitutional Tribunals and Constitutional Review' 1986; 'Les Nations Unies et la Formation du Droit' 1986; 'Aerial Piracy and International Terrorism' 1987; 'The International Court of Justice and the Western Tradition of International Law' 1987; (with Nagendra Singh) 'Nuclear Weapons and Contemporary International Law' 1988; 'Judicial Settlement of International Disputes' 1990; 'From Coexistence to Cooperation. International Law and Organization in the Post-Cold War Era' (with G.I. Tunkin & V.S. Vereshchetin) 1991; 'Federalism-in-the-Making. Contemporary Canadian and German Constitutionalism, National and Trans-national' (with J. Zaslove & W. Wolf) 1992; 'Judge Shigeru Oda and the Progressive Development of International Law' 1992; Special Commr. of Inquiry, Leg. of B.C. 1974–75; Chrmn., Research Task Force on Constitution, Fed. of Cdn. Municipalities 1977–82; Chief Adv., Pepin-Robarts Comm. 1978; Commr. of Enquiry, Gov't. Structure in City of Vancouver 1979; Constitutional Advisor, Indian Assn. (Treaty Indians) of Alta. 1980–82; Special Advisor to Cdn. Delegation, 36th, 37th and 38th Annual Sessions, U.N. Gen. Assembly 1981, 1982 and 1983; Depy Chrmn., Federal Electoral Boundaries Commission, B.C. 1982–83; mem., Permanent Court of Arbitration, The Hague 1985–91; articles, essays, etc., in Am., German, Spanish, French, Russian, Chinese, etc. journs. and learned soc. pubs.; contrib. to 'Encyclopedia Britannica'; 'International Encyclopaedia of the Social Sciences'; cr. Q.C. 1967; Visiting Prof. Ecole Libre des Hautes Etudes 1952; New York Univ. 1954; Inst. Univ. du Luxembourg 1959–60, 1972, 1974, 1976; Max Planck-Inst. and Univ. of Heidelberg, 1960–61 and 1990 (Max Planck-Inst.); Universidad Nacional Autónoma de México 1965; Univ. Laval 1967; Univ. de Paris 1968; Univ. da Madrid 1968; Univ. d'Aix-Marseilles 1969; Acad. Internat. Law, The Hague 1973 and 1990; Aristotelian Univ. Thessaloniki 1974, 1978, 1985; Univ. de Nice 1976–77; Jagellonean University of Cracow 1976; Université de Paris I (Panthéon – Sorbonne) 1982; Collège de France, Paris 1983; Univ. de Paris I (Sorbonne) 1985; Paul Martin Prof. of Internat. Relations and Law, Univ. of Windsor 1986; Meiji Univ., Tokyo 1987; Inst. International Relations, Beijing 1987, 1992; el. an Assoc. of Inst. de Droit Internat. (1st lawyer from Canada) Sept. 1967; el. Membre titulaire (Inst. de Droit Internat.) 1975; el. Membre-Associé, Académie Internationale de Droit Comparé 1986; Mem. de l'Inst. Grand-Ducal de Luxembourg 1985– ; Dir., Instituto Interamericano de Estudios Juridicos Internacionales; Pres. Toronto and Montreal Brs., Internat. Law Assn. (Chrmn. Extve. Comte. Candn. Br. 1972–75); Yale Law School Assn. Can.; mem., Nat. Rsch. Comte., Candn. Inst. Internat. Affairs; Un. Nations Assn., Toronto Br. (Extve.); Candn. Bar Assn. (former mem. Council, Ont. Sec.); Internat. Comn. of Jurists (Candn. Br.), Mem. of Counc. 1988– ; Fellow Am. Soc. of Internat. Law. (mem. Council); mem. Ed. Bd., Candn. Yearbook of Intnl. Law 1963– ; Ed. Bd., Journal of Media Law & Practice 1980–85; Ed. Adv. Comte., 'Encyclopedia Britannica' 1985– ; Editorial Ctte. 'Annuaire International de Justice Constitutionnelle' (France) 1987– ; Hon. Mem., (Knight) Mark Twain Soc. (U.S.); Hon. Mem., Deutsche Gesellschaft für Völkerrecht 1992– ; recreations: tennis, swimming, walking, golf; Address: House of Commons, 555-D, Centre Block, Ottawa, Ont. K1A 0A6.

**McWHIRTER, George,** M.A.; author; educator; b. Belfast, N. Ireland 26 Sept. 1939; s. James and Margaret (McConnell) McW.; e. Grosvenor High Sch., Belfast; Queen's Univ. Belfast, B.A. Dipl. in Educ.; Univ. of B.C., M.A.; m. Angela Mairead, d. late William Coid, 1963; children: James Liam Yates, Grania Gema Louise; PROF. & FORMER HEAD (1983–93), CREATIVE WRITING DEPT., UNIV. OF B.C.; Eng. Teacher, Kilkeel Secondary Sch. and Bangor Grammar Sch., N. Ireland; Escuela de Idiomas, Univ. of Barcelona; Alberni Dist. Secondary Sch., Vancouver Island, B.C.; winner of Macmillan Poetry Prize 1969; author 'Catalan Poems' 1971 (awarded Commonwealth Inst. and Nat. Book League Jt. 1st Prize 1972); 'Bodyworks' (short stories) 1974; 'Columbuscade' (poetry) 1974; 'Queen of the Sea' (poetry) 1976; 'Twenty-five' (poetry) 1978; 'Ties' (pamphlet, League of Candn. Poets) 1980; 'The Island Man' (poetry) 1981; 'God's Eye' 1981; 'Coming to Grips With Lucy' (stories) 1982; 'Fire Before Dark' (poetry) 1984; 'Paula Lake' (novel) 1984; 'Cage' (novel) 1987 (awarded Ethel Wilson Fiction Prize, the B.C. Book Prizes, 1988, by the West Coast Book Prize Soc.); 'Selected Poems of José Emilio Pacheco' (translation) 1987 (awarded F.R.

Scott Translation Prize by F.R. Scott Found. and League of Candn. Poets); 'The Voyeur and the Countess Wielopolska' (poetry) 1988; 'The Listeners' (novel) 1991; 'A Bad Day To Be Winning' (short stories) 1991; 'A Staircase of All Souls' (poems) 1993; anthologized in 'Penguin Book of Canadian Verse' and 'Stories of Pacific and Arctic Canada'; Assoc. Ed., 'Contemporary Poetry of British Columbia' 1970; Ed., 'Words from Inside' (Prison Arts Mag.) 1974, 1975; Adv. Ed., 'Prism International' 1978–89; recreations: swimming, dogs; Home: 4637 West 13th Ave., Vancouver, B.C. V6R 2V6.

**McWILLIAM, Hon. David Laurence,** B.A., LL.B.; judge; b. Newcastle, N.B. 29 June 1933; s. George Roy and Mary Catherine (Richard) McW.; e. St. Francis Xavier Univ. B.A. 1955; Oxford Univ. (Rhodes Scholar) B.A. (Jurisprudence) 1957; Univ. of Ottawa LL.B. 1964; m. Yvonne d. Robert and Patricia Bayliss 25 Feb. 1961; three d. Moyra, Rosalind, Cicely; JUSTICE, ONTARIO COURT OF JUSTICE (GENERAL DIVISION) 1976– ; Reporter, Ottawa Citizen and Ottawa Journal 1960–64; called to Bar of Ont. 1966; mem. Law Soc. Upper Can.; R. Catholic; recreation: golf; Club: Carleton (Manotick, Ont.); Home: 247 Crocus Ave., Ottawa, Ont. K1K 6E7; Office: 161 Elgin St., Ottawa, Ont. K2P 2K1.

**MCWILLIAM, Joanne Elizabeth,** M.A., Ph.D.; educator; b. Toronto, Ont. 10 Dec. 1928; d. Cecil Edward and Edna Viola (Archer) McW.; e. Oriole Park Sch., Loretto Abbey, Toronto; Univ. of Toronto B.A. 1951, M.A. (Philos.) 1953; Univ. of St. Michael's Coll. Toronto M.A. (Theol.), Ph.D. (Theol) 1968; m. C. Peter s. Robert and Alys Slater 6 June 1987; children: Leslie Mary de la Giroday, Elizabeth McEwen, Sean Dewart, Colin Dewart; PROF. OF RELIGIOUS STUDIES, UNIV. OF TORONTO 1987– and CHAIR, DEPT. OF RELIGIOUS STUDIES 1990– ; Assoc. Dir. Centre for Religious Studies 1987–90; Lectr. in Philos. Univ. of Detroit 1951; o. Ang. Ch. Can. 1988; Lectr., Asst. Prof. 1968, Assoc. Prof. 1973 Religious Studies present Univ.; Dir. Advanced Degree Studies Toronto Sch. of Theol. 1980–85; author: 'The Theology of Grace of Theodore of Mopsuestia' 1971; 'Death and Resurrection in the Fathers of the Church' 1986; editor: 'Augustine: From Rhetor to Theologian' 1992; various articles, book chapters; Pres. Candn. Theol. Soc. 1980–81; Candn. Soc. Patristic Studies 1987–91; recreations: walking, reading; Home: 59 Duggan Ave., Toronto, Ont. M4V 1Y1; Office: 6 Hoskin Ave., Toronto, Ont. M5S 1H8.

**MEADE, Ronald Michael Guy,** B.A.; merchant banker; b. Lausanne, Switzerland 17 Sept. 1938; s. Gerald Charles and Beatrix Francoise (Audibert) M.; e. Summer Fields Oxford England; Wellington College Berkshire England; Heidelbert Univ., Germany; McGill Univ. B.A. 1961; divorced; children: Kelly Ann, Christine Louise; CHAIRMAN & CHIEF EXECUTIVE OFFICER, ALTAMIRA MANAGEMENT LTD. 1986– ; Institutional Sales, Greenshields Inc. 1961–67; Vice-Pres., Investments, Internat. Trust Co. 1967–69; Merchant Bankers, Kauser, Lowenstein & Meade Ltd. 1969–78; Pres., Investment Counsellor, Altanational Limited 1978–86; Vice-Pres., Merchant Bankers, Almiria Capital Corp. (formerly Altamira Capital Corp.) 1986– ; Chrmn. & Dir., Merchant Bankers, Miralta Capital Inc. 1992– ; Dir., Altacap Investment Inc.; Centric Systems Corp.; Chrmn., Male Health Centres 1993– ; recreations: golf, squash, boating, tennis; clubs: Beacon Hall Golf, Cambridge; Home: 43 Elgin Ave., Toronto, Ont. M5R 1G5.

**MEADOW, Charles T.,** B.A., M.S., FIInfSc; university professor; b. Paterson, N.J. 16 Dec. 1929; s. Abraham and Florence Lillian (Troub) M.; e. Univ. of Rochester B.A. 1951; Rutgers Univ. M.S. 1954; 1st m. Harriet d. Leo and Rose Reiss 1956; 2nd m. Mary Louise d. Burt and Eugenia Shinskey 1972; children: Debra Lynne, Sandra Lee, Alison Maria, Benjamin Niland; PROF. EMERITUS, FACULTY OF LIBRARY & INFORMATION SCIENCE, UNIV. OF TORONTO 1994– ; served as 1st Lt., US Marine Corps 1951–53; Unit Mgr., General Electric Co. 1956–60; Sr. Systems Analyst, IBM Corp. 1960–68; var. positions, U.S. Civil Service 1968–74; Prof., College of Information Studies, Drexel Univ. 1974–82; Project Mgr. & Mgr. of Customer Serv., Dialog Information Serv. 1982–84; Prof., Fac. of Library & Information Science, Univ. of Toronto 1984–94; Assoc. Dean 1990–94; Visiting Prof., Univ. of Sheffield 1980–81; West Indies 1991–92 Washington 1993; Pres., Meadow Information Systems Ltd. 1985– ; Dir. of Pubn., Candn. Soc. for Info. Sci. 1987–94, President 1994; Hon. Mention, N.Y. Acad. of Sci., Children's Science Book Awards 1975; Fellow, Inst. of Information Scientists 1980; Distinguished Lectureship Award, N.J. Chapter, Am. Soc. for Info. Sci. 1986; Lazerow Lecturer, Columbia Univ. 1986, Drexel Univ. 1988; Mem.,

Candn. Assn. for Info. Sci.; Am. Soc. for Info. Sci.; Assn. for Computing Machinery; The Inst. for Info. Scientists; Sigma Xi; The N.Y. Acad. of Sci.; author: 'The Analysis of Information Systems' 1967, 1973, 'Man-Machine Communications' 1970, 'Applied Data Management' 1976, 'Text Information Retrieval Systems' 1992; 'The Story of Computers' 1970, 'Sounds and Signals: How We Communicate' 1975 (juvenile non-fiction); co-author: 'Basics of Online Searching' 1981, 'Telecommunications for Management' 1985, 'Measurement in Information Science' 1994; Editor, 'Can. J. of Info. Sci.' 1985–86; Edit. Bd. Mem., 'J. of the Am. Soc. for Info. Sci.' (Editor 1977–84), 'Online and CD ROM Review'; recreations: photography; Home: 66 Tyrrel Ave., Toronto, Ont. M6G 2G4; Office: 140 St. George St., Toronto, Ont. M5S 1A1.

**MEADOWS, Donald Frederick,** B.A., B.L.S.; librarian; b. Regina, Sask. 13 Jan. 1937; s. late Frederick John and Doris Eileen M.; e. elem. & high schs. Regina; Univ. of Sask. B.A. 1962; Univ. of B.C. B.L.S. 1968; m. Ruth d. late George and Susan Cochrane 10 June 1960; two s. Scott Frederick, George Edward; DIR., VANCOUVER ISLAND REGIONAL LIBRARY 1986– ; Pharm. Sales 1962–63; Reference Lib. Govt. Sask. 1963, Lib. Cons. 1968, Asst. Prov. Lib. 1968, Prov. Lib. 1970–81; Dir., Metrop. Toronto Library Bd. 1981–86; Pres. Sask. Lib. Assn. 1972; mem. B.C. Lib. Assn.; Candn. Lib. Assn. Am. Lib. Assn.; recreations: gardening, reading; Home: 859 Beach Dr., Nanaimo, B.C. V9S 2Y4; Office: Box 3333, Nanaimo, B.C. V9R 5N3.

**MEADOWS, George Lee,** C.A., B.A.; communications executive; b. Toronto, Ont. 17 Nov. 1938; e. Univ. of Toronto, B.A. 1963; C.A. 1966; m. Donna McKay 26 Sept. 1964; children: Lee Ann, Shelly; PRESIDENT & PUBLISHER, UNIVERSITY OF TORONTO PRESS 1990– ; Clarkson Gordon & Co., C.A. 1963; Project Group of Can. Ltd 1973; Sec.-Treas., Southam Commun. Limited 1974; Vice Pres. & Sec. Treas. 1976; Asst. to the Pres., Southam Inc. 1977; Vice Pres. Corp. Devel. 1978–84; Sr. Vice Pres., Communications Group, Southam Inc. 1984–87; Mng. Dir. & C.E.O., Selkirk Communications Ltd. 1987–88; Pres. & C.E.O., Selkirk Communications Ltd. 1988–89; Vice Commodore, Royal Candn. Yacht Club; Mem.: C.I.C.A.; recreations: sailing, squash, badminton, tennis, skiing; Clubs: R.C.Y.C.; University Club; Home: 2 Ivor Rd., Toronto, Ont. M4N 2H4; Office: 10 St. Mary St., Ste. 700, Toronto, Ont. M4Y 2W8.

**MEAGHER, Blanche Margaret,** O.C. (1974), M.A.; diplomat (ret.) b. Halifax, N.S. 27 Jan. 1911; d. John Nicholas and Blanche (Seals) M.; e. St. Patrick's High Sch., and Mount St. Vincent Coll., Halifax, N.S.; Dalhousie Univ., B.A. 1932, M.A. 1935; Post-grad. studies in Political Science, 1937–38; D.C.L. (H.c.) Dalhousie Univ., 1970; St. Francis Xavier 1974; St. Mary's Univ. 1975; Governor for Canada, Bd. Govs., Internat. Atomic Energy Agency 1962–66 (el. Chrmn. Policy-making Bd. 1964); Junior High Sch. Teacher, Halifax, N.S. 1932–42; joined Dept. of External Affairs 1942; Third Secy., Candn. Embassy, Mexico 1945–47 and Second Secy. there 1947–49; First Secy., Canada House, London 1953–55, and Counsellor there 1955–56: Chargé d'Affaires, Israel 1957 and Ambassador there 1958–61; High Commr. to Cyprus 1961, concurrently with Israel assignments; Ambassador to Austria 1962–66: subsequently High Commr. to Kenya and Uganda 1967–69; Ambassador to Sweden 1969–73; Diplomat in Residence, Dalhousie Univ. 1973–74; Trustee, Nat. Museums of Can. 1975–78; Gov., Atlantic Sch. of Theology 1976–82; Nova Scotia Coll. of Art and Design 1984–89; R. Catholic; Address: 6899 Armview Ave., Halifax, N.S. B3H 2M5.

**MEAGHER, George Vincent,** B.Sc., B.Eng., F.E.I.C.; engineer; b. Halifax, N.S. 23 Apr. 1919; s. John Nicholas and Blanche Margaret (Seals) M.; e. Dalhousie Univ. B.Sc. 1940; McGill Univ. B.Eng. 1942; m. Evelyn Margaret d. Abraham and Margaret Hamm 2 June 1942; children: Maureen, Lindsey, Lise, Shelagh; PRES., GEORGE V. MEAGHER INC.; Engn. and Mgmt. positions Candn. industry 1945–56; joined Dilworth, Secord, Meagher & Assoc. 1957; Pres. and C.E.O. 1977; Chrmn. 1987; Vice-Chrmn., Tata-Dilworth, Secord, Meagher & Assoc., Bombay, India; Dir. State Bank of India (Canada); Past Chrmn., Canada-India Bus. Coun.; former mem. Counc. and Chrmn. Publ. Ctte., Engn. Inst. of Can.; mem. Assoc. of Cons. Engrs. of Can.; Assn. of Profl. Engrs. of Ont.; Clubs: National; St. George's Golf & Country; Willoughby Golf Club (Florida); Home: 15 Edenbridge Dr., Islington, Ont. M9A 3E8; Office: 6655 Airport Rd., Mississauga, Ont. L4V 1V8.

**MEAGHER, Louise,** LL.B.; lawyer; b. Ottawa, Ont. 14 Oct. 1955; d. Louis E. and Winnifred T. (Ryan) Lefaive; e. Notre Dame de Lourdes H.S.; Univ. of Ottawa LL.B. 1977; called to Law Soc. of U.C. 1979; m. Robert s. Morgan and Peggy M. 30 June 1979; children: Daniel, Liam; DEPUTY REGISTRAR, SUPREME COURT OF CANADA 1991– ; Asst. to Parly. Counsel to the Senate 1980–82; Counsel, Acting Asst. Gen. Counsel & Sec. to the Board, Nat. Energy Bd. 1982–91; Mem., Law Soc. of U.C.; Candn. Bar Assn.; Assn. of Candn. Court Administrators; club: Kent; Home: 6050 Forest Glen Cres., Gloucester, Ont. K1C 5N5; Office: Kent & Wellington Sts., Ottawa, Ont. K1A 0J1.

**MEARNS, William Clark,** B.A.; company president; b. Victoria, B.C. 19 Aug. 1909; s. William Hunter and Mildred (Baker) M.; e. Stanford Univ., B.A. (Elect. Engn.) 1932; Univ. of Washington, post-graduate work in Engn. and Business Adm., 1933; Harvard Business Sch., Advanced Management Program, 1954; m. Loula Cary, d. D.O. Cameron 27 Jan. 1940; children: Craig Cameron, Dale Donnelly, Marily Ann, Lindsay J.; PRES., ROCKCLIFFE ESTATES LTD.; Past Dir., Bank of B.C.; Metropolitan Estates Property Co.; Labatt Breweries; Past Chrmn., B.C. Harbours Bd.; began as Meterman, B.C. Electric Co. Ltd. 1934; Sales Engr. 1946; Operations Mgr. 1948; Acting Dir. of Rsch., Vancouver 1955; special assignments, Western Devel. and Power Ltd., Vancouver 1957; Vice-Pres., V.I. Div., B.C. Electric Vice-Pres. Devel. 1961–62; Extve. Dir., B.C. Hydro and Power Authority 1962–69; Past Mem., National Harbours Bd.; Canada Trust Adv. Bd.; Mem. of Adv. Bd., Y.M. and Y.W.C.A., Victoria; Hon. Gov., Candn. Assn. for Retarded Children; Dir. of Armed Services Centre, Victoria; Past Pres., B.C. Natural Resources Conf.; Past Vice-Pres. and Dir., Victoria Rotary Club; Past Dir., Queen Alexandra Solarium, Community Chest YMCA, Victoria; mem. Assn. of Prof. Engrs. B.C.; Inst. Elect. & Electronics Engrs.; Victoria Electric Club (Past Pres.); Pacific Northwest Trade Assn. (Past Vice-Pres. and Dir.); mem., Vancouver Bd. of Trade; Victoria Chamber of Commerce (Past Vice-Pres. and Dir.); Protestant; recreation: golf; Clubs: Union; Victoria Golf; Royal Colwood Golf & Country; Home: 303 – 1211 Beach Dr., Victoria, B.C.; Office: 1239 Beach Dr., Victoria, B.C. V8S 2N4.

**MECREDY-WILLIAMS, Robin de Breton,** B.A., LL.B.; barrister; b. Toronto, Ont. 14 March 1951; s. Frederick Warren Williams of Washington, D.C., and Katharine Gordon Mecredy, M.B.E., of Monte Vista, Dalkey, Co. Dublin, Ireland; e. Univ. of Toronto B.A. 1974; Osgoode Hall Law Sch. LL.B. 1980; CORPORATE COUNSEL, WOOD GUNDY INC. 1994– ; Principal, Montevista Assoc. 1979– ; read law at Cassels, Brock 1980–81; called to Bar of Ont. & admitted as Solicitor 1982; Counsel, Market Policy, The Toronto Stock Exchange 1982–84; Policy Counsel, The Securities Indus. Ctte. on Take-over Bids 1983; Corp. Finance Solicitor, Ont. Securities Comn. 1984–87; Acting Sec. 1985; Assoc., Shibley, Righton & McCutcheon 1987–90; Lectr., Law Soc. of U.C. Bar Admission Course 1990; Corp. Counsel & Sec., Loewen, Ondaatje, McCutcheon Inc. 1990–92; Dir., Corp. Counsel & Sec., Loewen, Ondaatje, McCutcheon & Co. Ltd. 1990–92; Consulting Editor, CCH Canadian Ltd. 1993–94; Anglican; Mem., Candn. Inst. of Internat. Affairs; World Wildlife Fund Canada; Candn. Found. for Ileitis & Colitis; Co-author: 'The Regulation of Take-over Bids in Canada: Premium Private Agreement Transactions' 1983; recreations: sailing, tennis, art history, photography, editing; Clubs: The Bessborough; Mayfair Racquet; Home: 603 Roehampton Ave., Toronto, Ont. M4P 1S7; Office: P.O. Box 500, BCE Place, Toronto, Ont. M5J 2S8.

**MEDER, William John,** B.Comm., M.B.A.; executive; b. Thunder Bay, Ont. 5 June 1942; s. William Joseph and Ruth Catherine (Zoller) M.; e. Concordia Univ., B.Comm. 1965; McMaster Univ., M.B.A. 1968; m. Sally d. Jack and Eva McFetrick 25 March 1967; children: Robert, Jennifer; EXTVE. VICE PRES. & CHIEF OPERATING OFFR., HENRY BIRKS AND SONS LTD.; Extve., IBM 1965–78; Imperial Mfg. 1978–82; Pres., Travel Connections Inc. 1982–1990; Chrmn., Young Pres. Orgn.; recreations: golf, skiing, squash; Clubs: Royal Montreal Golf; Montreal Amateur Athletic Assn.; Home: 438 Lake Shore Rd., Beaconsfield, Que. H9W 4H9; Office: 1240 Phillips Square, Montreal, Que. H3B 3H4.

**MEDHURST, David Hardwick,** B.Comm., C.A.; chartered accountant; b. Bristol, England 11 Apr. 1948; s. Dr. John David and Barbara Joan (Hardwick) M.; e. Hillcrest H.S. 1966; Carleton Univ., B.Comm. (Hons.) 1970; C.A. 1972; m. Beth M. d. Thomas and Catherine Phair 13 May 1978; MNG. DIR., YORK HANNOVER HOLDING AG, LUCERNE SWITZERLAND 1990– ; Partner, Peat Marwick Thorne (formerly Thorne Riddell) 1980–90; joined Thorne Gunn Helliwell & Christenson 1970; Mem., Ont. & Candn. Insts. of C.A.'s; Univ. Club of Toronto (Hon. Treas. 1987, 1988); Royal Candn. Yacht Club (Hon. Treas. 1984–86; Commodore 1989, 1990); Past Pres., Ont. Sailing Assn.; Past Dir., Candn. Yachting Assn.; recreations: sailing, skiing, badminton; clubs: RCYC, Univ. Club of Toronto; Office: Bahnhofstrasse 21, CH-6000 Lucerne 7, Switzerland.

**MEDINA, Ann Hillyer,** M.A.; film producer; news anchor and correspondent; b. New York, N.Y. 9 May 1943; d. Harold Raymond Jr. and Janet Williams M.; e. The Spence Sch., Dip. 1961; Wellesley Coll., B.A. 1965; Fellow, Univ. of Edinburgh 1964; Univ. of Chicago, M.A. (philosophy) 1967; Hon. D.C.L., Univ. of King's College; Independant Producer; Producer Resident, Cdn. Centre for Adv. Film Studies 1988; Senior Producer Resident, Cdn. Centre for Adv. Film Studies 1989; teacher Philos. Univ. of Ill. 1967–68; Researcher, WMAQ-TV NBC Chicago 1969–70; Reporter, WKYC-TV NBC Cleveland 1970–72, Network prod. NBC News 1972; Network Corr. ABC News, New York 1972–75, produced & reported 2 hour-long documentaries for 'Close-Up'; Reporter, CBC Newsmagazine 1975–80, Extve. Prod. 1980–81, Sr. Foreign Jour. The Journal 1981–86; Beirut Bureau Chief 1983; Sr. Nat. Corr. The Journal and News Anchor, The National, CBC-TV 1986–87; reported from China, Nicaragua, the Sahara, Syria, Beirut, Uganda, W. Bank, Israel, Jordan, Egypt, Spain, Bhopal, Philippines; Herschel Fellow, Univ. of Chicago; Emmy Award 1973; Gold Hugo, Chicago Film Fest. 1988; 'Golden Sheaf' Yorkton Film Festival 1985; 2nd Prize, N.Y. Film Festival 1986; Chair, Acad. Candn. Film & TV; Bd. of Dir., Calmeadows Foundation; Dir. Extve. Ctte., ACTRA 1988–91; Bd. of Dir., CANFAR 1990–92; Bd. of Dirs., TWIFT 1991–92; CFTPA; recreations: sailing, ornithology; Address: 112 Alcina Ave., Toronto, Ont. M6G 2E8.

**MEDJUCK, Ralph Marven,** Q.C.; executive; b. Halifax, N.S., 26 Sept. 1932; s. Irving and Blanche (Pascal) M.; e. Pub. Schs., Halifax, N.S.; Dalhousie Univ., LL.B. 1954; m. Shirlee Arron, 4 Jan. 1955; one s. Brian; three d. Pamela, Lynda, Beth; CHRMN. & C.E.O. THE CENTENNIAL GROUP OF COMPANIES LIMITED; PRES. & C.E.O. CENTENNIAL HOTELS LIMITED; Chrmn. & C.E.O. Scotia Energy Resources Limited; founding Gov., Candn. Internat. Devel. Research Centre; Dir., Central Guaranty Trustco Ltd.; called to Bar of N.S., Nov. 1954, member of N.S. and Canadian Bar; since 1959 has been responsible for major real estate devels. in Atlantic Provs., Alta. and Ont.; Clubs: Royal Nova Scotia Yacht Squadron; Home: 5956 Emscote Dr., Halifax, N.S. B3H 1B3; Office: 1601 Lower Water St., Halifax, N.S. B3J 3P6.

**MEDLAND, Charles Edward,** B.A.; private investor; b. Toronto, Ont. 6 July 1928; s. Robert Charles and Winnifred (Parker) M.; e. St. Andrew's Coll., Aurora, Ont.; Univ. of Toronto, B.A. 1950; m. Julia Winsor Eby, 1 Feb. 1973; two d. Virginia, Zoe; two step s. Brian, Stephen; PRESIDENT, BEAUWOOD INVESTMENTS INC. 1989– ; Dir., C.T. Financial Services Inc.; Irwin Toy Ltd.; The Thomson Corp. Ltd.; Quorum Growth Inc.; The Seagram Co. Ltd.; Abitibi-Price Inc.; Ontario Teachers Pension Plan Bd.; Canadian Tire Corp.; Teleglobe Inc.; Former Chrmn. & C.E.O., Wood Gundy Inc.; Former Chrmn., Investment Dealers Association; Past Chrmn., Wellesley Hospital; Alpha Delta Phi; Anglican; recreations: golf, tennis, skiing, bridge; Clubs: Toronto Golf; The Toronto; Badminton & Racquet; Craigleith Ski; Rosedale Golf; York; Beacon Hall Golf; Home: 30 Glenallan Rd., Toronto, Ont. M4N 1G8; Office: 150 King St. W., Suite 1505, P.O. Box 5, Toronto, Ont. M5H 1J9.

**MEDLEY, Sue (Susan G.);** recording artist, singer/songwriter; b. Nanaimo, B.C. 19 Aug. 1962; d. Fred Charles and Leona May (Smith) M.; signed to Polygram Records 1989; released debut album 'Sue Medley' 1990 (5 singles and 4 videos were released from that album); released 2nd album 'Inside Out' 1992 (4 singles and 3 videos released); awards incl. 5 West Coast Music Awards, 2 Junos and 2 SOCAN Songwriter Awards, as well as a Gold Album Award for first album (sales of 50,000 in Can.); has toured extensively, incl. dates with Bob Dylan, Dwight Yoakam, Steve Earle, Tom Cochrane, etc.; National Spokesperson, 'The Ride for Sight' (nationwide motorcycle rally that raises over $1 million per annum for research into cures for eye diseases); Mem., SOCAN, CARAS, AFM; songwriter/lyricist: 'Dangerous Times,' 'That's Life,' 'Love Thing' 1990, 'Maybe the Next Time,' 'Queen of the Underground' 1991, 'When the Stars Fall,' 'Inside Out,'

'Jane's House' 1992, 'Forget You' 1993 (singles/release dates); Address: 107 Grenadier Rd., Toronto, Ont. M6R 1R1.

**MEDOVY, Harry,** O.C., B.A., M.D., D.Sc., FRCP(C), FAAP; physician, university professor; b. Russia 22 Oct. 1904; came to Canada 1905; s. Esrael and Molly (Levertawsky) M.; e. Univ. of Manitoba B.A. 1923, M.D. 1928, D.Sc. 1976; m. Mary d. Michael and Ida Rosenblat 28 Oct. 1934; children: Elinor Ruth, Nancy Anne; PROFESSOR EMERITUS, PEDIATRICS, FAC. OF MEDICINE, UNIV. OF MANITOBA 1976– ; Major, RCAMC 1942–45; Resident, Children's Hosp. of Wpg. 1928; Univ. of Pennsylvania 1929–30; Fac., Pediatrics, Fac. of Med., Univ. of Man. 1932–54; Prof. & Dept. Head 1954–70; Prof., Post-Retirement 1970–76; Consultant in Ped., Children's Hosp. of Wpg. 1954–70; Consultant, Child Care Serv., City of Wpg. 1952–88; Man. Tech. Adv. Ctte. on Infectious Diseases 1965– ; served in many other executive positions for several assns. & socs. incl. (most recent) Prov. Chair, Internat. Congress on Health Edn. 1975; lectured widely in Canada, U.S., Hawaii, Israel, England & Sweden; num. visiting professorships esp. post-retirement on Senior Med. Teachers Program; Bronze Medal in Pathology 1926; Chown Prize in Me. 1928; Prowse Prize in Med. 1933; Miles Award, Candn. Public Health Assn. 1971; Simon Flexner Club 1974; Distinguished Serv. Award, Man. Medical Assn. 1975; Queen Elizabeth II Jubilee Silver Medal 1978; Ross Award, Candn. Ped. Soc. 1980; Teddy Award, Children's Hosp. of Wpg. Rsch. Found. 1984; Parim Award (Profl. Assn. of Residents & Interns of Man.) Distinguished Med. Educator Award 1985; Founders Award, Man. Heart Found. 30th Anniversary 1986; Officer, Order of Canada 1990; Annual Harry Medovy lecture Series on Social Ped. est. 1971; Harry Medovy Fellowship, est. by Children's Hosp. Rsch. Found. 1987; Bd. of Dir., Winnipeg Symphony Orch. 1959; Bd. Mem., Eckhardt-Grammate Musical Competition 1975; author: 'Early Jewish Physicians of Manitoba' 1972, 'A Vision Fulfilled: The Story of the Children's Hospital of Winnipeg' 1979; editor: 'Pediatric Clinics of North America' 1965; contbr. to four textbooks; Journals: numerous contbns. to leading medical journals, the most important of which were: 'Western Equine Encephalomyelitis in Infants,' J. Pediat. 1943; 'Well-Water Methemoglobinemia in Infants: Its Occurrence in Rural Manitoba and Ontario,' Lancet 1948; 'A Plea for Vitamin C Fortified Milk,' Candn. Med. Assoc. J. 1959 (work in this area resulted in infant scurvey in Nfld. virtually disappearing) and 'Smoking Habits of Winnipeg School Children,' Candn. Med. Assoc. J. 1961; Ed. Board, 'J. of Pediatrics' 1964–71; recreations: music, medical history, baseball enthusiast, walking; Home: 2A - 221 Wellington Cres., Winnipeg, Man. R3M 0A1.

**MEDWID, Nicholas M.,** FRI, CMR; real estate executive officer; b. Foam Lake, Sask. 19 Dec. 1938; s. Mike and Rose M.; e. Foam Lake H.S. 1959; Mount Royal College and Univ. of Calgary FRI, CMR 1985; m. Doreen d. Aime and Yvonne Marchand 27 June 1964; children: Daryn, Dean, Terra; EXECUTIVE OFFICER, THE RED DEER & DISTRICT REAL ESTATE BOARD CO-OP LTD. 1992– ; Retail Clerk, McLeod's Limited 1959; Royal Bank of Canada 5 years; Household Finance until 1968; Sales Manager, Qualico Devel. until 1974; Owner & Operator, Heritage Properties until 1981 (sold business); Manager & Consultant to Bucar Realty 1981–82; Owner & Operator, Horsehoe Realty 1982–84; Manager & Agent for Prov. of Alta., Canada Trust Real Estate 1984–88; Owner & Operator, Heritage Properties 1988–92; Jaycees Public Relns. 1965; director of several community assn.; Mem., Edn. Ctte., Calgary Real Estate Bd. 5 years (Chair 1 yr.; lectr. 11 yrs.; marked exams for 9 yrs.); sat on 12 cttes. with Calgary Real Estate Bd. (Dir. 2 yrs.; 2nd Vice-Pres. 1 yr.; 1st Vice-Pres. 1 yr., Pres. 1991– ); Alta. Real Estate Assn. Edn. Ctte. 2 yrs. (Chair, Ctte. on Adv. Edn. 1 yr.); several recognitions for coaching junior hockey & junior competitive curling; recreations: curling, hiking, golf; clubs: Calgary Curling; Address: Box 1048, Blackfalds, Alta. T0M 0J0.

**MEDWIDSKY, Wolodymyr,** B.A., M.D., FRCP(C); dermatologist; b. Ukraine 1 Sept. 1941; s. Konstantyn and Natalia (Lebedowych) M.; e. Univ. of West. Ont. B.A. 1963, M.D. 1967; Univ. of Toronto FRCP(C) 1972; m. Switlana Benesh 1967; children: Jaroslaw, Tanya, Tamara, Yurij; Lecturer, Fac. of Med., Univ. of Toronto 1973; Asst. Prof. 1978; Active Staff/Consulting Staff, St. Michael's Hosp., Riverdale Hosp., Orthopedic & Arthritic Hosp.; extensive lecturer, Canada, US, Ukraine; Mem., Underserviced Health Care Program, Ont.; Coord. for Ukraine, Office of Internat. Relns., Fac. of Med., Univ. of Toronto; Past Pres. & Med. Dir., Children of Chornobyl Candn. Fund; author of medical articles; Past Chief Editor of newsletter of internat. news, World Fed. of Ukrainian Med. Assn.; recreations; hunting, fishing; Home: 82 Wells Hill Ave., Toronto, Ont. M5R 3A8; Office: Box 37, Commerce Court East, Toronto, Ont. M5L 1A1.

**MEECH, Richard C.,** Q.C., B.A., LL.B., LL.M.; b. Portsmouth, Hampshire, Eng. 16 Sept. 1921; s. late Richard George and late Elizabeth (Campbell) M.; e. Ridley Coll., St. Catharine's, Ont.; Univ. of Toronto, B.A. 1946; Osgoode Hall Law Sch., Toronto, Ont. LL.B. 1950; Harvard Law Sch., LL.M. 1951; m. Carol, d. late Charles and late Helen (Williams) Crockett, 6 Oct. 1951; children: Susan Crockett, Richard George, Peter Campbell, Sarah Elizabeth, Nancy Bingham; PARTNER, BORDEN & ELLIOT 1956– ; Dir. & Vice-Pres, Textron Can. Ltd.; Dir. and mem. Extve. Comte.; Personal Insurance Co. of Canada; Bd. Chrmn., Howden Group P.L.C. 1983–87; Director, Barclays Bank of Canada; Budd Canada Inc.; Canabam Limited; Eskofot Canada Ltd.; JBA Software Canada Ltd.; R. C. Cola Canada Ltd.; Secy., Candn. Securities Inst.; Candn. Investor Protection Fund 1969–90; Dir. and Secy., Canabam Ltd.; Hon. Consul of Thailand at Toronto 1967; Hon. Consul General 1983; Apptd. Commander of the Most Exalted Order of the White Elephant (Thailand), 1986; made Knight Commander of the Most Noble Order of the Crown of Thailand 1990; Chrmn., Business Section, Internat. Bar Assn. (1982–84); Chrmn. Bd. of Trustees, Havergal Coll. Fdn. (1972–74); Pres., Harvard Law Sch. Assn. of Ont. 1971–75; Trustee, Sunnybrook Medical Centre, Toronto 1966–81; Queen's Univ. 1980–92; Trustee Emeritus, Sunnybrook Health Science Centre; read law with Daly, Thistle, Judson & McTaggart, Toronto, Ont.; called to Bar of Ont. 1950; joined Borden, Elliot, Kelley, Palmer & Sankey (predecessor firm) 1951; cr. Q.C. 1960; served as Pilot during 2nd World War with R.C.A.F. and R.A.F. 1942–46; discharged with rank of Flying Offr.; mem. Adv. Council, Ridley Coll. (Gov. 1971–77); Gov., Havergal Coll. (1971–77); Chrmn. of the Bd. of Trustees, Havergal College Found. 1972–74; Nat. Chrmn., Queen's Univ. Parents' Assn. 1975–85; mem. Adv. Bd., Salvation Army; mem., Internat. Bar Assn. (Chrmn. Section on Business Law 1982–84); Candn. Bar Assn.; Candn. Tax Foundation; Co. York Law Assn.; Kappa Alpha; Anglican; recreations: golf, skiing, tennis, fishing; Clubs: Badminton & Racquet; National (Pres. 1980–81); Toronto; York; Toronto Golf; Canadian; (Pres. 1974–75); Harvard (N.Y.); Coral Beach & Tennis (Bermuda); Garden of the Gods (Colo.); Office: Scotia Plaza, 40 King St. W., Toronto, Ont. M5H 3Y4.

**MEEHAN, Eugene,** LL.B., LL.M., LL.B., D.C.L.; lawyer; b. Baillieston, Scotland 26 April 1952; s. Hugh and Bernadette (Doig) M.; e. Univ. of Edinburgh LL.B. 1975; McGill Univ. LL.M. 1976; Univ. of Ottawa LL.B. 1977; McGill Univ. D.C.L. 1984; m. Anne (M.D.) d. Alan and Marie Rankin 19 Aug. 1978; children: Marc, Mélanie, Morgan; PARTNER, LANG MICHENER, OTTAWA; called to Bar of Alta. 1982, to Bar of Ont. 1988; articled with Parlee McLaws (Edmonton) 1981–82; Counsel, Lang Michener Honeywell Wotherspoon 1988–90; Extve. Legal Officer, Supreme Court of Canada 1990–92; Prof. of Law, Univ. of Alta. 1978–86; Univ. of Ottawa 1986–90; co-author: 'Alberta Corporations Law Guide' 1983, 'Law of Criminal Attempt' 1984; co-author: 'Creditors' Remedies in Alberta' 1987, 'Creditors' Remedies in Ontario' 1994; 'Constitutional Law in a Nutshell' forthcoming; 'Charter of Rights Annotated' forthcoming; num. periodical articles; Home: 33 Russell Ave., Ottawa, Ont. K1N 7W9; Office: 300 – 50 O'Connor St., Ottawa, Ont. K1P 6L2.

**MEEROVITCH, Eugene,** B.Sc., M.Sc., Ph.D.; university professor (retired); parasitologist; biologist; b. Vladivostok, Russia 11 July 1919; came to Can. 1953; s. late Boris and late Zoreva R.; e. St. John's Univ., Shanghai, China, B.Sc. 1947; McGill Univ. M.Sc. 1955; Ph.D. 1957; m. d. late Francisco Pedroso 16 May 1961; children: Karen Ray Kellner, Sandra Fay Langleben; Prof. of Parasitology, McGill Univ. 1971–85 (and Dir. of Inst. of Parasitology and National Reference Centre for Parasitology there 1978–84); apptd. McGill Univ. as Asst. Prof. of Parasitology 1961; Assoc. Prof. 1965; Prof. 1971; author of chapts. in several books on technical subj. and of more than 100 scientific papers; held positions on extve. boards of prof. societies; Jewish; Home: 6980 Côte St. Luc Rd., Apt. 710, Montreal, Que. H4V 3A4.

**MEGARRY, A. Roy,** O.C.; executive; b. Belfast, N. Ireland 10 Feb. 1937; s. Andrew Blain and Barbara (Bennett) M.; e. Annadale Grammar Sch. N. Ireland; C.M.A. degree; Princeton Univ. Mgmt. Devel. Course; m. Barbara Todd Bird d. Charles C. Bird, 31 May 1958; children: Andrew Roy, Kevin Charles, Lianne Jean; Publisher and C.E.O., The Globe and Mail 1978–92; Controller, Honeywell Canada, Toronto 1957–62; Daystrom (Heathkit) Ltd. Toronto 1962–64; Sr. Consultant, Coopers, Lybrand Toronto 1964–68; Vice Pres. Finance International Syscoms Ltd. Toronto 1968–72; Vice Pres., Corp. Development, Torstar 1972–78; mem., Bd. of Dir., Inter Am. Press Assn.; The Ireland Fund of Canada; Officer, Order of Canada; R. Catholic; recreations: sailing, skiing; Clubs: Toronto; Granite; Home: R.R. 2, Uxbridge, Ont. L9P 1R2.

**MEGAW, William James,** D.Sc., F.Inst.P., C.Phys.; educator; scientist; b. Belfast, N. Ireland 8 July 1924; s. William Alexander and Agnes (Munn) M.; e. The Royal Sch. Armagh; Queens Univ. Belfast; Univ. of Liverpool B.Sc. 1951, D.Sc. 1973; m. Anne-Maureen d. William and Catherine Russell 5 Oct. 1946; children: Michael William James (dec'd 1992), Maura Patricia, Timothy John; PROF. EMERITUS, YORK UNIV. 1989– ; Principal Investigator Aerosol Project, Inst. for Space and Terrestrial Science 1989–93; served with Royal Engrs. mainly Far E. 1942–47; scient. research Atomic Energy Research Estab. Harwell 1951–71, responsible for radiological protection Harwell site 1969–71; Prof. of Physics, York Univ. 1971–89, Chrmn. of Physics 1979–89; sometime consultant Danish Atomic Energy Comn., Atomic Energy Control Bd., Ont. Ministry of Environment and various firms Can. and USA; participant 4 scient. expeditions to Greenland 1971–76; Dir., Centre for Research on Environmental Quality, York Univ. 1974–84; Mem. Advisory Ctte. on Nuclear Safety (Atomic Energy Control Bd.) 1994– ; author or co-author over 80 scient. papers; ed. 'Prospects for Man' 1976; 'Prospects for Man: Communication' 1977; 'Prospects for Man: The Quality of Life' 1982; 'Prospects for Man: Economics, Inflation and Employment' 1983; 'Prospects for Man: Science, Technology and The Economy' 1984; author 'How Safe? Three Mile Island, Chernobyl and Beyond' 1987; mem. Ed. Bd. Journal of Aerosol Science 1981–88; recreations: reading, skiing, swimming, walking; Office: 4700 Keele St., Downsview, Ont. M3J 1P3.

**MEICHENBAUM, Donald,** Ph.D., F.R.C.S.; educator; b. New York City, N.Y. 10 June 1940; s. Max and Florence (Karp) M.; e. City Coll. of New York B.A. 1962; Univ. of Ill. Ph.D. 1966; m. Marianne d. Louis and Lillian Pizzo 1 July 1964; children: Lauren, Michelle, David, Daniel; PROF. OF PSYCHOL. UNIV. OF WATERLOO; joined present univ. 1966; recipient Izaak Killam Fellowship 1989; Distinguished Service Award Candn. Psychol. Assn. 1990; named one of 10 most influential psychotherapists of century by 'American Psychologist'; author 8 books incl. 'Cognitive Behavior Modification: An Integrative Approach' 1977; 'Pain and Behavioral Medicine' 1983; 'The Unconscious Reconsidered' 1984 'Stress Inoculation Training' 1985; 'Facilitating Treatment Adherence' 1987; recreations: tennis, swimming; Home: 292 Shakespeare Dr., Waterloo, Ont. N2L 2V1; Office: Waterloo, Ont. N2L 3G1.

**MEIER, Max;** banker; b. Zurich, Switzerland 26 Feb. 1947; s. Walter Karl and Gertrud (Schlegel) M.; e. Mercantile Soc. Sch. Zurich, Switz. commerce degree 1965; Univ. of B.C. dipl. in urban land economics, mortgage lending 1980; m. Margrit d. Robert and Margrith Hess July 1972; children: Monica, Miriam; PRESIDENT & CHIEF EXTVE. OFFR., PACIFIC INTERNAT. SECURITIES INC. 1983– ; Accountant, Clariden Bank Zurich 1969–70; various positions, C.I.B.C. Montreal & Vancouver 1970–78; Sr. Asst. Mgr., C.I.B.C. Vancouver 1978–80; Sr. Asst. Inspector Credit 1980; Controller, Bond St. Internat. Securities Ltd. 1981–82; Extve. Vice-Pres. & Gen. Mgr., DJ Hall & Co. 1982–83; Vice Chrmn., Vancouver Stock Exchange; Dir., Internat. Finan. Ctr. Vancouver; recreations: skiing; clubs: Whistler Mountain Ski, Hollyburn Country; Home: 6077 Gleneagles Dr., West Vancouver, B.C. V7W 1W1; Office: P.O. Box 10015, Pacific Centre, 1500 – 700 West Georgia St., Vancouver, B.C. V7Y 1G1.

**MEIGHEN, The Hon. Michael Arthur,** Q.C., B.A., LL.L.; senator; lawyer; b. Montréal, Qué. 25 Mar.1939; s. Theodore Roosevelt and Margaret deLancey (Robinson) M.; e. Selwyn House Sch. Montréal; Trinity Coll. Sch. Port Hope, Ont.; Univ. de Genève Cértificat d'études françaises 1957; McGill Univ. B.A. 1960; Univ. Laval LL.L. 1963 (cum laude); m. Kelly d. Richard and Elizabeth Dillon 8 Apr. 1978; three s. Theodore Richard, Hugh Arthur Kennedy, Max Talbot deLancey; COUNSEL, MEIGHEN DEMERS, Toronto; Mem., Candn. Que. & Ont. Bar Assocs.; Co-Counsel, Comm. of Inquiry on War Criminals 1985–86; Dir., Laurentian Group Inc.; UAP Inc.; Cundill Value Fund (Chrmn.); Participations Paribas Ltée; Conwest Exploration Co.

Ltd.; Sodarcan Inc.; CamVec Corp.; called to Bar of Que. 1964, Ont. 1981; apptd. Q.C. 1983; apptd. to the Senate of Canada 1990; P. Cons. Cand. for Montréal-Westmount Fed. g.e. 1972, 1974; Nat. Pres. P. Cons. Assn. Can. 1974–77; Co-Chrmn. P. Cons. Nat. Leadership Convention 1976; Vice Pres. and Dir. Mktg., TV Guide Inc. Toronto 1978–80; Life Mem., Counc. for Candn. Unity (Chrmn. 1985–87); Chrmn. Ont. Cancer Treatment & Research Foundation 1982–93; Dir., Ont. Cancer Inst. Princess Margaret Hosp. 1982–93; Themadel Foundation (Chrmn.); Stratford Shakespearean Festival (Vice-Pres.); Salvation Army Metro. Toronto Advisory Bd. (Vice-Chrmn.); Atlantic Salmon Federation; Jules and Paul-Emile Leger Found.; Life Gov. Trinity Coll. Sch.; recreations: fishing, golf, tennis, skiing; Clubs: Albany (Dir.); Toronto Lawn Tennis; Caledon Ski; Mount Bruno Golf (Montréal); Hillside Tennis (Montréal); University (Montréal); Home: 4 Lamport Ave., Toronto, Ont. M4W 1S6; Office: 11th Flr. 200 King St. W., Toronto, Ont. M5H 3T4.

**MEIGS, Mary;** writer, painter; b. Philadelphia, Penn. 27 April 1917; d. Edward Browning and Margaret (Wister) M.; e. Bryn Mawr College 1939; Instr., English Comp. & Creative Writing, Bryn Mawr College 1940–42; Mem., Women's Auxiliary Volunteer Emergency Serv. (WAVES), U.S. Navy 1942–45; studied painting 1945–47 and subsequently had one-woman shows in Boston, Wellfleet, Mass, New York City, Paris, St. Sauveur, Quebec, Montreal; Q Spell Award, Que. Soc. for the Promotion of English-Language Literature 1992; author: 'Lily Briscoe: A Self-Portrait' 1981, 'The Medusa Head' 1983, 'The Box Closet' 1987, 'In "The Company of Strangers"' 1991; Address: 427 Grosvenor Ave., Westmount, Que. H3Y 2S5.

**MEILEN, Wilm-Artur (Bill),** F.T.C.L.; university professor/dialects specialist; co-ordinator of playwriting; novelist; screenwriter; actor; director; b. Cardiff, Wales 16 Sept. 1932; s. William Thomas and Lillian Nancy Georgina (Poole) Mudd; e. Heswall Naut. Training Sch. 'Akbar'; Cardiff Coll. of Music & Drama; Fellow, Trinity Coll. of Music, London; 1st. m. Rhuanedd (James); children: Lisa Angharad, Lara Myfanwy; 2nd m. Patricia d. Enid (Harrisson) and Francis McKenzie 28 Jan 1978; PROF., DEPT. OF DRAMA, UNIV. OF ALTA. 1980– ; Merchant Navy deckhand then military serv., 5 yrs. (French army, Indo-China; Brit. army, Korean War); freelance actor 1954; novelist/screenwriter 1963; Asst. Prof., Univ. of Alta. 1969; Assoc. Prof. 1974; active writer; actor; dir.; prod.; speaker; Founder, Welsh Artists' Workshop; Pres., Meilen Productions Ltd.; Cons., Telefilm & Alta. Motion Picture Devel. Corp.; Banff Sch. of Fine Arts (Dialects); Immed. Past Pres., TV & Film Inst., Immed. Past Sec./Treas., Writers Guild of ACTRA Alta.; Mem., ACTRA; Candn. & Am. Actors Equities; Writers Guild of Canada; Writers Guild of America (W.); Internat. Platform Assn.; Welsh Acad.; Writers Union of Wales; Andrew Allan Award, Best Radio Actor 1986; Nellie Finalist 1988; 7 ACTRA nominations as Actor/Writer; author: 'The Division' 1967, 'Moving On' 1968, 'The Bullpen' 1968, 'Eyes of Grass' 1969, 'Delta Two' 1970 (novels) as well as short stories, poetry, screenplays, TV drama ('Beachcombers' CBC TV, 'The Beyond' series CBC TV, 'Song for the Eyes of Tovah' Allarcom, CBC Radio Dramas and medical inst. films; 4 new novels forthcoming: 'Gim San,' 'The Armorer,' 'Hexenhammer,' 'Acting Without Orders'; student of all religions; extensive traveller; recreations: writing, poetry, martial arts; Home: 9517 – 87 Ave. Edmonton, Alta. T6C 1K4; Office: 3 – 122 Fine Arts Ctr., Univ. of Alta., Edmonton, Alta. T6G 2C9.

**MEINCKE, Peter Paul Max,** B.Sc., M.A., Ph.D.; educator; b. Winnipeg, Man. 21 Jan. 1936; s. Paul Henry and Marie (Winther) M.; e. Royal Mil. Coll. 1958 (Sword of Honour); Queen's Univ. B.Sc. 1959; Univ. of Toronto M.A. 1960; Ph.D. 1963; m. Donna Pauline d. the late Albert Mallinson 28 June 1958; children: Thomas, Carolyn; PROF., UNIV. OF P.E.I.; RCAF Offr. teaching at Royal Mil. Coll. 1962–65; mem. Tech. Staff Bell Telephone Labs. Murray Hill, N.J. 1965–67; Asst. Prof. Erindale Coll. Univ. of Toronto 1967, Assoc. Prof. 1969, Assoc. Dean of Coll. 1970–72, Vice Provost of Univ. 1972–76; Prof. of Physics 1977; Pres., Univ. of P.E.I. 1978–85; Chrmn. and Pres., Inst. Of Man and Res. 1979–82; Chrmn., Assn. of Atlantic Univ. 1979–81; Chrmn., Nat. Library Adv. Bd. 1982–85; Can. Environmental Adv. Council 1980–83; Vice Chrmn., Min. Adv. Bd. on Can. Military Coll. 1984–86; Chrmn., Group of 78 1988–90; Bd. of Imapro Inc.; Secy./Treas. of Carratech 1990– ; Pres., Pro-Teck 1988– ; Pres. PEI Branch, Royal Commonwealth Soc. 1993– ; Chair, Candn. Council of the Univ. of the World; author over 40 papers in physics, information science, computing and computer assisted learning, also conf. papers; Protestant; recreations: swimming, skiing; Office: Charlottetown, P.E.I. C1A 4P3.

**MEINIG, Walter Paul;** banker; b. 25 Aug. 1932 Davidson, Sask.; e. Shellbrook, Sask. H.S.; m. Jessie Eddleston 21 May 1956; children: Elaine, John, Dianne, Sandra; SENIOR VICE-PRESIDENT AND EXTVE. ASST. TO THE CHRMN., BANK OF NOVA SCOTIA 1989– ; Gen. Mgr. Adm. present Bank 1974, Gen. Mgr. W. & N. Ont. Region 1976, Vice Pres. & Gen. Mgr. Candn. Regions 1977, Sr. Vice Pres. Candn. Regions 1979; Sr. Vice Pres. and Gen. Mgr., Ont. Div. 1980; Senior Vice-Pres., Investment and Corporate Banking 1983; Chrmn., The Riverdale Hosp.; Clubs: St. George's Golf & Country; National; Home: 18 Butterfield Drive, Don Mills, Ont. M3A 2L8; Office: 44 King St. W., Toronto, Ont. M5H 1H1.

**MEINZER, Gerhard Emil;** executive; b. Karlsruhe, Germany 25 Apr. 1936; e. Dip., Bus. Adm.; separated; one s. Robert; PRES., MEINZER HOLDINGS LTD. 1977– ; PARTNER, PMP ASSOCIATES INC.; Chrmn., Tritech Financial Systems Inc.; L & L Computer Systems Internat. Inc.; Newlogic Data Systems Ltd.; Infoscan Canada Inc.; Chief Extve. Offr., Real Time Datapro Ltd. 1970–89; Past Pres., Metro Toronto Bd. of Trade; ten years with IBM Canada; W.R. Grace of Canada; Past Pres. German-Candn. Congress; Home: #608, 251 Queens Quay West, Toronto, Ont. M5J 2N6.

**MEISEL, John,** O.C., M.A., Ph.D., F.R.S.C., LL.D., D.Sc.Soc., D.U.; educator; political scientist; b. Vienna, Austria 23 Oct. 1923; s. Fryda S. and Anne (Heller) M.; e. Elem. and Secondary Schs. Czechoslovakia, Gt. Brit., Haiti, Pickering Coll. Newmarket, Ont.; Univ. of Toronto Victoria Coll. B.A. 1948, M.A. 1950; London Sch. of Pol. Science & Econ. Ph.D. 1959; LL.D.: Brock Univ.; Carleton Univ.; Univ. of Guelph; Univ. of Toronto; D.U.: Univ. of Ottawa; D.Sc.Soc.: Laval Univ.; SIR EDWARD PEACOCK PROFESSOR OF POLITICAL SCIENCE, QUEEN'S UNIV. 1983– ; former Chrmn., Candn. Radio-Television and Telecommunications Comm.; former Head of Pol. Studies, Queen's Univ. and Hardy Prof. of Pol. Science; Past Pres. Social Science Research Council Can.; Data Clearing House; joined Queen's Univ. 1949; Visiting Prof. Yale Univ. 1976–77; Commonwealth Distinguished Visiting Prof. Gt. Brit. 1978; served various Royal Comns., Task Forces and Inquiries incl. Biculturalism & Bilingualism, Nat. Unity, Status of Women, bias in newscasting; sometime adviser to Candn. and Ont. govts.; mem. Premier Robarts' Adv. Comte. on Confederation; expert witness Que. govt.'s ctte. on electoral reform; participated in inquiries conducted on behalf of La conf. des recteurs et des principaux des univs. du Qué.; guest lectr. Can., U.S.A. and Europe; past mem. Inter-Univ. Consortium for Pol. Research; rec'd Can. Council Killam Award 5 yrs.; Officer of the Order of Canada 1989; recipient, Northern Telecom Internat. Candn. Studies Award of Excellence 1991; author 'The Canadian General Election of 1957' 1962; ed. 'Papers on the 1962 Election' 1964; 'L'évolution des partis politiques canadiens' 1966; 'Working Papers on Canadian Politics' 1972, 1973, 1975; 'Cleavages, Parties and Values in Canada' 1974; numerous articles; Ed. 'International Political Science Review' 1979– ; former Co-Editor 'The Canadian Journal of Political Science'; Pres., The Royal Soc. of Canada 1992–95; mem. Adv. Bds. several pol. science journs. N. Am. and Europe; mem. Internat. Pol. Science Assn.; Candn. Pol. Science Assn. (Past Pres.); recreations: music, skiing, swimming, literature, nature; Clubs: Cercle Universitaire d'Ottawa; Cave Reginam; Home: Colimaison, R.R. 1, Tichborne, Ont. K0H 2V0; Office: Dep. of Pol. Studies, Queen's Univ. Kingston, Ont. K7L 3N6.

**MEISELS, Alexander,** B.Sc., M.D., F.R.C.P.(C), F.I.A.C.; physician; educator; pathologist; b. Berlin, Germany 18 Feb. 1926; s. Bruno and Elisabeth (König) M.; e. Universidad Nacional Autonoma de Mexico B.Sc. 1944, M.D. 1951; m. Lillian d. Ricardo and Maria de la Luz Wille 11 July 1953; children: Monica, Felix, Victor, Susana, Isabelle; HEAD OF PATHOL. ST. SACREMENT HOSP. 1978– ; Prof. of Pathol. Laval Univ. 1968– , Dir. Sch. of Cytotechnol. 1960– ; Cythopathol. Nat. Cancer Inst. Mexico 1952–60; Asst. Prof. of Pathol. present Univ. 1960, Assoc. Prof. 1965, Head of Cythopathol. 1960–70, Residency in Pathol. 1970–73; Head of Cytopathol. Service present Hosp. 1970–78; recipient Maurice Goldblatt Award 1975; City of Paris Silver Medal 1977; Queen's Silver Jubilee Medal 1977; George N. Papanicolaou Award 1982; author: 'Cytopathology of the Uterine Cervix' 1991; and over 110 publs. cytopathol.; Pres. Internat. Acad. Cytol. 1986–89, Sec.-Treas. 1971–86, Treas. 1989– ; Pres. Candn. Assn. Pathols. 1988–89; Vice Pres., Am. Soc. of Cytology 1989–90; Pres. elect. 1990–91; Pres. 1991–92; recreation: computers; Home: 1221 ave. du Ravin, Sillery, Que. G1S 3K5; Office: 1050 ch. Ste-Foy, Quebec, Que. G1S 4L8.

**MEISEN, Axel,** Ph.D., P.Eng., Eur.Ing.; university professor and administrator, engineer; b. Hamburg, Germany 17 Oct. 1943; s. Paul and Emmi C. (Schaaf) M.; e. Imperial College of Sci. & Technol. B.Sc. 1965; Calif. Inst. of Technol. M.Sc. 1966; McGill Univ. Ph.D. 1970; m. Judith Anne d. Philipe and Nora Gonzales 6 June 1987; children: Nadine Ramona, Kai Noel; DEAN OF APPLIED SCIENCE, UNIV. OF B.C. 1985– ; Lectr., McGill Univ. 1967–68; Asst. Prof., Univ. of B.C. 1969–74; Environmental Engr., Imperial Oil Enterprises Ltd. 1974–75; Assoc. Prof., Univ. of B.C. 1975–79; Prof. of Chem. Engr. 1979– ; Bd. of Dir., Candn. Soc. for Chem. Engr. 1983–86, 1992– (Pres. 1993–94); Bd. of Dir., Candn. Univ. Consortium, Asian Inst. of Technol. 1988– (Chair 1989–90); Candn. Council of Profl. Engrs./Nat. Ctte. of Deans of Engr. & Applied Sci. Task Force 1988–90 (Co-chair 1990– ); Trustee, Advanced Systems Inst. of B.C. 1990– ; Candn. Univ. Consortium, Nepal Engr. Edn. Project 1989– (Chair 1990–91); Govt. of B.C. Adv. Ctte. on Coop. Edn. 1991–92; Intelligent Mfg. Systems Ctte., Industry, Sci. & Technol. 1991–93; Fellow, Chem. Inst. of Canada 1981; Profl. Serv. Award, Assn. of Profl. Engrs. of B.C. 1985; ERCO Award, Candn. Soc. for Chem. Eng. 1986; Fellow, Inst. of Engrs. of Ireland 1990; Fellow, Can. Acad. of Engr. 1993; Mem., Bd. of Dir., Vancouver Inst. 1986– ; Mem., Candn. Soc. for Chem. Engr. 1969– ; Assn. of Profl. Engrs. & Geoscientists of B.C. 1977– ; Am. Soc. for Engr. Edn. 1978– ; Euro Engineer 1991– ; author of 104 technical & 22 non-technical pubns.; Home: 3080 W. 42nd Ave., Vancouver, B.C. V6N 3H2; Office: 2006 - 2324 Main Mall, Vancouver, B.C. V6T 1Z4.

**MEKJAVIĆ, Igor Bonifacij,** B.Sc., M.Sc., Ph.D.; university professor; b. London, England 10 Sept. 1956; s. Vojko and Breda (Pretnar) M.; e. Šentvid Gimnazija, Yugoslavia; Salford Univ. B.Sc. 1977, M.Sc. 1978; Simon Fraser Univ. Ph.D. 1983; PROF., DEPT. OF KINESIOLOGY, SIMON FRASER UNIV. 1983– ; rsch. interests in human temp. regulation, hypothermia, hyperthermia, altitude & diving physiol., exercise physiol. & ergonomics; evaluates thermal protective garments & surv. suits for indus. & regulating agencies (Can. & U.S.); instrumental in devel. of thermal gear used in 'Man in Motion World Tour'; Chrmn., 2nd Internat. Environ. Ergonomics Conf.; Assoc. Ed., 'Annals of Physiol. Anthrop.'; Sci. Cons.; Chrmn., Candn.-Yugoslav Ethnic Expo. Ctte.; Mem., Candn.-Yugoslav Community Assn.; Mem., IEEE; Undersea Biomed. Soc.; N.Y. Acad. of Sci.; Candn. Physiol. Soc. (pending); author: 'Experiments in Human Performance' 1986, 'Environmental Ergonomics' 1988; recreations: scuba diving, sailing, skiing; Office: School of Kinesiology, Burnaby, B.C. V5A 1S6.

**MELADY, John Flynn,** B.A., M.Ed.; educator; writer; b. Seaforth, Ont. 12 Sept. 1938; s. Maurice Patrick and Mary Catherine (Flynn) M.; e. Univ. of W. Ont. B.A. 1962; Ont. Coll. of Edn. Toronto 1963; Univ. of Toronto M.Ed. 1973; m. Mary d. William and Helen Lemaire 25 Aug. 1962; three s. Paul, Mark, Timothy; High Sch. Vice Prin. Hastings County Board of Education 1967–94; Elem. Teacher Prescott, Ont. 1959–60; High Sch. teacher Trenton, Ont. 1962–65; High Sch. Dept. Head 1965–67; magazine feature writer 1980– ; book reviewer Globe and Mail 1983–90; Quill & Quire 1991– ; columnist, 'The Catholic Register' 1980–86; author 'Explosion' 1980, 'Escape from Canada!' 1981, 'Korea: Canada's Forgotten War' 1983, 'The French In Ontario' in The Shaping of Ontario 1985; 'Cross of Valour' 1985, 'Overtime, Overdue: The Bill Barilko Story' 1988, 'The Little Princes' 1988 (novel); 'Pilots' 1989; 'About the Artist' in Keirstead's Canada 1991; Workshop Leader - Student Writing 1980– ; mem. Writers Union Can.; Ont. Secondary Sch. Teachers Fedn.; Offrs. Mess Candn. Forces Base Trenton; R. Catholic; recreations: skiing, travel, golf, photography; club: Royal Candn. Mil Inst.; Home: R.R. 3, Brighton, Ont. K0K 1H0.

**MELANCON, Robert,** B.A., M.A., Ph.D., FRSC; university professor, writer; b. Verdun, Que. 12 May 1947; s. Horace and Madelaine (Beaulieu) M. e. Collège Sainte-Marie (Montreal) B.A. 19 66; Univ. de Tours, France M.A. 1970, Ph.D. 1972; m. Charlotte d. Gaëtan J. and Madeleine Côté 20 Sept. 1969; children: Bernard, Paul; PROFESSOR OF FRENCH LITERATURE, UNIV. DE MONTREAL 1972– ; Governor General's Award for Poetry in French 1979, for Translation from English to French 1990; elected Mem., Royal Soc. of Canada 1992; Mem., Candn. Soc. for Renaissance Studies (Vice-Pres. 1982–84; Pres. 1984–86); La Soc. Internat. des

Amis de Montaigne; author: 'Peinture aveugle' 1979, 'Territoire' 1982 (poetry), 'Paul-Marie Lapointe' 1987 (essay), 'L'Avant-printemps à Montréal' 1994 (poetry); co-author: 'Au petit matin' 1993; Assoc. Ed., 'Renaissance & Reformation' 1976–84; Ed., 'Etudes françaises' 1987–91; Home: 5782, Côte St-Antoine, Montréal, Qué. H4A 1S2; Office: Box 6128, Station A, Montréal, Qué. H3C 3J7.

**MELCHER, Antony Henry,** B.D.S., H.D.D., M.D.S., Ph.D., D.Sc.; educator; b. Johannesburg, S. Africa 1 July 1927; e. A. Robert and Anne (Lewis) M.; e. King Edward VII Sch., Johannesburg, 1934–45; Univ. of the Witwatersrand, B.D.S. 1949, H.D.D. 1958, M.D.S. 1960; Univ. of London, Ph.D. 1964, D.Sc. 1984; m. Marcia Ruth, d. Max Marcus, Pietersburg, S. Africa, 15 Nov. 1953; children: Rowena, Lindsay; PROFESSOR EMERITUS OF DENTISTRY, UNIV. OF TORONTO 1993– ; private dental practice 1950–61; Demonst., Faculty of Dent., Univ. of Witwatersrand 1952–61 and mem. Jt. Dental Research Unit of Univ. and of C.S.I.R. 1956–61; Research Fellow, Inst. of Dent. Surg., Univ. of London 1961–62; Leverhulme Research Fellow, Royal Coll. of Surgs. Eng., 1963–69; Prof. of Dentistry, Univ. of Toronto 1969–93; Dir., Med. Research Council Group in Periodontal Physiology 1973–83; Chrmn. Grad. Dept. of Dentistry and Dir. Postgrad. Dental Educ. Univ. of Toronto 1983–84; Assoc. Dean, Life Sciences, Sch. of Grad. Studies 1984–88; Vice-Provost, Univ. of Toronto 1988–92; author 'Biology of the Periodontium' 1969; also numerous publs. in scient. journs.; mem. Counc. Sci. Advisors, N.I.D.R., N.I.H. 1978–82; mem. Medical Rsch. Counc. of Can. 1984–89 and Extve. 1986–89; Chrmn. MRC Dental Sciences Ctte. 1985–89; Sci. Adv. Counc., Alta. Heritage Fund for Medical Rsch. 1985–90; Candn. Dental Assn.; Royal Soc. Med.; Internat. Assn. Dental Rsch. (Pres. 1982–83); Fellow, Am. Assn. Advanc. Science; Am. Soc. Cell Biol.; recreations: music, theatre; Home: 278 Bloor St. E., Apt. 708, Toronto, Ont. M4W 3M4.

**MELDRUM, Wendell Wynn,** Q.C.; b. Simpson's Corner, Lunenburg Co., N.S. 27 June 1924; s. Hazen Hibbert and Bernice Beatrice (Simpson) M.; e. Bridgewater (N.S.) Elem. and 2ndary Schs., 1930–42; Dalhousie Law Sch., LL.B. 1948; Univ. N.B., D.C.L. (Hon.) 1969; m. Dorothy Ferne, d. Sterling L. Downey and Aggie Beatrice (Steeves) D., R.R. 3, Moncton, N.B., 4 Nov. 1944; children: Wynn Wendell, Kirk Walter; called to Bar of N.S. and N.B. 1948; cr. Q.C. 1965; Lectr. in Comm. Law, Mount Allison Univ., 1956–65; Town Solr., Sackville, N.B., 1952–65, 1970–77; Attorney-Gen. N.B. 1965–66; Judge of the Co. Court 1977–79; Judge of Court of Queen's Bench 1979–87, retired; el. M.L.A. for Westmorland Co. in by-el. 1965; Min. of Educ. 1966–70; served with R.C.A.F. as Flying Offr., 1942–45; Pilot with R.A.F. Ferry Command Dorval; served in U.K., N. Africa, India; United Church; recreations: golf, reading; Clubs: Sackville Golf (Past Pres.); Sackvill Candn. Legion (Past Pres.); Home: P.O. Box 38, Sackville, N.B. E0A 3C0.

**MELHUISH, Thomas Duggan,** B.Com.; organization and human resource management consultant; writer and editor; b. Brampton, Ont. 20 March 1930; s. Ivan Roy and late Dorothy (Duggan) M.; e. Brampton High Sch.; Victoria Coll. Univ. of Toronto B.Com. 1953 (Honours Award); m. Alistair Ruth d. late Judge Erastus W. Grant 10 Aug. 1953; children: Duggan Grant, Ian Alexander, Bruce Fraser, Kenneth Gordon Warren; former Operations Mgr. Sears Canada; joined Deloitte & Touche as Sr. Cons. Montréal office 1966; trans. to Winnipeg 1968; Dir. of Operations Prairie practice 1975–78; Partner 1976–92; Partner-in-Charge Human Resource Mgmt. practice Toronto 1985–88; Chrmn., National H.R. Strategy Ctte. 1986–88; Human Resource Mgmt. Consultant to Metro. Toronto, Deloitte & Touche 1988–92; editor, 'Cognashene Cottager' 1993; 'Cognashene Cottagers Assn. Magazine' 1992; Publisher/editor, 'A History of the Cognashene Area, Georgian Bay, Ont.'; served as Bus. Mgr. Victoria Coll. Dir. Winnipeg Art Gallery; Man. Opera Soc.; Inst. Mgmt. Cons. Man. and Ont.; various journal articles, speaking engagements; Past Pres. Cognashene Cottagers Assn. Georgian Bay; Past Chrmn., CentreStage Co. for the Arts (now Canadian Stage); Un. Church; P. Conservative; Clubs: RCYC; Waterfront Tennis & Squash; Home: 118 Roxborough Dr., Toronto, Ont. M4W 1X4.

**MELLA, Patricia Janet,** B.A., B.Ed., M.A.; politician; educator; b. Port HIll, P.E.I. 29 Aug. 1943; d. Frank Joseph and Patricia Mary Hilda (Callaghan) MacDougall; e. Kinkora H.S. 1961; St. Dunstan's Univ. B.A. 1965; Univ. of P.E.I. B.Ed. 1973; Catholic Univ. of America M.A. 1967; m. Angelo s. Silvio and Josephine M. 27 June 1970; children: Andrew, Michael, Nancy; LEADER OF THE OFFICIAL OPPOSITION OF PEI and LEADER, PROGRESSIVE CONSERVATIVE PARTY OF P.E.I. 1990– ; Mem. of the Legislative Assembly, District of 3rd Queen's, elected 29 Mar. 1993; Sec., Cardigan Riding Assn., P.C. Party 1985–88; Co-chair, Nat. Orgn. Ctte. 1987; P.C. Candidate, 3rd Queen's Prov. Election 1989; Teaching Asst., Catholic Univ. of Am. 1966–67; Lectr., Carleton Univ. 1967–70; Queen's Univ. 1970–72; Teacher, Jr. & Sr. High, Charlottetown area schools 1979–87; Charlottetown Rural H.S. 1987–90; Mem., Economic Welfare Ctte., P.E.I. Teacher's Fed. 1985–86; Local Adv. Council, Employment & Immigration Canada 1988; Pres., Charlottetown Christian Council 1985–86; Mem., Southport Recreation Comn., Community of Southport, P.E.I.; recreations: golf, jogging; clubs: Stanhope Golf; Home: 15 Ferguson Dr., Charlottetown, P.E.I. C1B 1B5; Office: P.O. Box 338, Charlottetown, P.E.I. C1A 7K7.

**MELLEMA, Andries Willem,** B.Sc., M.I.M.; manufacturing executive; b. Utrecht, Netherlands 23 May 1947; s. Andries Willem and Johanna (van der Meer) M.; e. Netherlands Sch. of Bus. Dipl. 1972; Univ. of Ore. B.Sc. 1973; Am. Grad. Sch. Internat. Mgmt. Glendale, Ariz. Masters Degree Internat. Mgmt. 1974; m. Angelika d. Josef Schwerzler and Ingeborg Freuis 18 Sept. 1976; children: Johan Andries, Robert Freerk, Tatiana Angelique; PRES. AND CHIEF OPERATING OFFR. CANADIAN KENWORTH CO. 1989– ; Dir. Paccar of Canada; Mgmt. Trainee Firestone Tire & Rubber Co. France and Akron, Ohio 1974–76, Prodn. Mgr. Portugal 1976–79, Factory Mgr. Tunisia 1979–80, Dir. Mfg. N.Z. 1980–83, Vice Pres. Operations Joliette, Que. 1984–86; Sr. Vice Pres. Onex Packaging Toronto 1986–88; mem. Motor Vehicle Mfrs. Assn. (Dir. 1989– ); Bd. Trade Metrop. Toronto; Anglican; recreations: sailing, skiing, golf; Club: Royal Netherlands Rowing & Yachting 'De Maas'; Home: 476 Russell Hill Rd., Toronto, Ont. M5P 2S7; Office: 6711 Mississauga Rd. N., Mississauga, Ont. L5N 4J8.

**MELLING, O.R.,** B.A., M.A.; writer & critic; b. Dublin, Ireland 2 Dec. 1956; d. Kevin and Georgina (Craney) Whelan; e. Loretto Coll.; Malvern Collegiate; Trinity Coll., Univ. of Toronto, B.A. 1976; Sch. of Grad. Studies, M.A. 1984; one daughter: Findabhair Columba O'Faoláin; professional highlights: Critical contbr., 'Books Ireland' & 'The Irish Times' 1993, 1994; panelist, Summer School on Children's Literature, Dublin Writers' Museum 1993; Harbourfront Reading Series March 1989; Writer-in-Residence, Tyrone Guthrie Centre for the Arts, Annaghmakerrig, Co. Monaghan, Ireland 1987, 1988; Children's Book Fest., Touring Author (Nfld. & Lab.) 1987; CBC Morningside with P. Gzowski Jan. 1987; Nat. Sch. & Library Tour, Central & West. Can. 1987; author: 'The Druid's Tune' (Young Adult Book of the Year Award 1984; short-listed, Ruth Schwartz Award 1985) 1983; 'The Singing Stone' (short-listed, R. Schwartz Award 1986) 1986 (young adult novels); 'Falling Out of Time' 1989 (adult novel); 'The Hunter's Moon' 1993 (young adult novel); recreations: travelling, hiking, dancing, rock music, gardening, reading, day-dreaming; Office: c/o HarperCollins Publishers Ltd., Hazelton Lanes, Suite 2900, 55 Avenue Rd., Toronto, Ont. M5R 3L2.

**MELLORS, Clint Stuart;** private consultant; e. Univ. of Alta. Personnel Adm.; Candn. Hosp. Assn. Cert. Health Care Orgn. & Mgmt.; m. Carol; children: Neil, Charlene, Ross; MANAGEMENT CONSULTANT 1991– ; Plant Personnel Supt., Supt. Mgmt. Salaries & Orgn. Alberta Government Telephones 1960–68; Plant Personnel Supr., Chemcell Ltd. 1968–70; Dir. Personnel Services Royal Alexandra Hosp. 1974–81; Bd. Mem. Labour Relations Bd. Alta. Labour 1979–81; Vice Chair, Labour Relations Bd. 1981–83; Asst. Dep. Min. Alta. Labour 1983–84; Dep. Min. of Alta. Labour 1984–90; Sec. Candn. Nat. Inst. for Blind (CNIB); Mem. Bd. CNIB Alta.-N.W.T.; recreations: reading, gardening, carpentry, sports; Address: 8723 – 64 St., Edmonton, Alta. T6B 1R1.

**MELMAN, Anthony Ronald,** B.Sc., M.B.A., Ph.D.; business executive; b. Johannesburg, S. Africa 1 June 1947; s. Jack and Frances Josephine (Jochelson) M.; e. Univ. of The Witwatersrand, B.Sc., 1969, Ph.D. 1976; Cape Town Univ., M.B.A. 1971 (Gold Medalist); m. Valerie d. Jill and Lionel Rayne 21 Dec. 1969; children: Vanessa, Justine, Jason; VICE-PRES., ONEX CORP. 1984– ; Sr. Mgr., Union Acceptances Limited 1972–77 (concurrently held positions in other parts of company incl. Sr. Investment Rsch. Analyst for a trust co.; seconded to Charterhouse Group (U.K.) 1973–74); Emigrated to Canada 1977; joined Candn. Imperial Bank of Commerce as Manager, Special Projects Div. 1977; Vice-Pres., Corporate Banking Div. 1981; Sr. Vice-Pres., Merchant Banking, Project & Acquisition Financing 1983; Bd. Dir., various Onex companies incl. Purolator & ProSource Distribution Services, Inc.; Office: 161 Bay St., BCE Place, Toronto, Ont. M5J 2S1.

**MELNIK, David,** Q.C., B.A., LL.B.; management consultant; b. 26 Oct. 1931; e. McMaster Univ. B.A. 1954; Fac. of Law, Univ. of Toronto LL.B. 1957; Osgoode Hall Law School LL.B. 1959; Harvard Business School, graduated S.C.M.P. 1982; m. June Ann Grant, 1970; children: Andrew Grant, Christy Elizabeth; Counsel, Turkstra, Mazza; Sessional Lectr. Univ. of Toronto, Fac. of Mgmt. Studies, MBA Program; Dir.: Shirmax Fashions Ltd., Montreal; Cdn. Nat. Sportmen's Shows, Toronto (Vice-Chrmn.); U-Store & U-Move Inc., Toronto; Marshall McLuhan Programme in Communications & Tech., Univ. of Toronto; Plasticolors, Inc., Ashtabula, Ohio; Cowan & Lobel Inc., Albany NY; Vector Systems Inc. (Chrmn.); Outdoor Canada (Chrmn.); The Innovision TMA Group, Toronto; First Comm Cato Johnson, Toronto; Club: University; Homes: 350 Lonsdale Rd., Toronto, Ont. M5P 1R6; R.R. #1, Orangeville, Ont. L9W 2Y8.

**MELNUK, Paul D.,** B.Com., C.A.; executive; b. Winnipeg, Man. 24 May 1954; s. Martin William and Rita Clarice (Cochrane) M.; e. Univ. of Man. B.Com. 1976; C.A. Man. 1979; m. Donna d. Lawrence and Patricia Sturko 21 Oct. 1989; children: Jillian, Andrew, Bryan, Kevin; PRESIDENT AND CHIEF OPERATING OFFR., THE HORSHAM CORP. 1993– ; Pres. and Chief Extve. Offr. Clark Refining & Marketing Inc. (St. Louis, Mo); joined Touche Ross & Co. 1976–80; Vice Pres., Controller Canadian Commercial Bank 1980–86; Corporate Finance Rep. Pemberton Securities Inc. 1986–87; Pres. WFL Capital Corp. 1987–88; Home: 37 Countryside Lane, St. Louis, Mo. 63131; Office: 24 Hazelton Ave., Toronto, Ont. M5R 2E2 and 8182 Maryland Ave., St. Louis, MO 63105 USA.

**MELOCHE, Pierre;** insurance executive; b. Montreal, Que. 15 Jan. 1940; s. Jean and Marcelle (Pelland) M.; e. Coll. Jean de Brébeuf Montreal 1958; Ecole des Hautes Etudes Commerciales 1960; Sir George Williams Univ. 1961; m. Danielle Archambault 15 Sept. 1962; children: Eric, Nathalie; DEPUTY CHRMN., C.E.O. AND DIR., MELOCHE MONNEX INC. (formerly The Optimum Financial Corporation) 1991– ; Security National Insurance Co.; Primmum Insurance Co.; Meloche Insurance Management Inc.; Monnex Insurance Management Inc.; Monnex Insurance Brokers Ltd.; J. Meloche Inc.; Sr. Partner, Meloche Monnex Insurance Brokers Inc.; London Ins. Group; Bd. Mem., Wellington Insurance Co.; Longroup Insurance Co.; Pres. & Dir. Denmel Investments Ltd.; joined J. Meloche Inc. 1960, Vice Pres. & Dir. 1961, Extve. Vice Pres. 1969, Pres. & C.E.O. 1974; Dir., Reed Stenhouse Ltd. 1973–83;Managing Dir. for Europe, Stenhouse Reed Shaw Management Serv. Ltd., Glasgow, 1976–78; Mem. of the Directoire, 1977–78 and Mem. Conseil de Surveillance, 1978–80, Soc. Générale de Courtage d'Assurances, Paris; Pres. & C.E.O., Monnex Insurance Brokers Ltd. 1973–83; Pres., C.E.O. and Dir., Reed Stenhouse Services Ltd. 1983–87; Vice Chrmn. & Dir., Société de Courtage Meloche Ltée 1978–87; Cantrek Insurance Mgmt. Ltd. 1983–87; Chrmn. & Dir., Sonef Insurance Mgmt. Ltd. 1983–87; Reed Stenhouse Personal Insurance Ltd. 1983–87; Pres., C.E.O. and Dir., The Optimum Financial Corp. Ltd. 1987–91; Chrmn., C.E.O. and Dir., The Optimum Financial Services Ltd. 1987–91; Lectr. on Ins. Coll. Maisonneuve, Montreal 1968–70; Past Pres. Research & Orientation Comte.; Past Dir. and Secy. N. Sector Montreal Regional Comte.; Past Dir., Ins. Brokers Assn. Prov. Que.; Past Chrmn. Quebec Div., The Arthritis Soc. and Past mem. National Bd.; Past Board Mem., Fonds de Recherche de l'Institut de Cardiologie de Montréal; R. Catholic; recreation: riding; Club: St-Denis; Offices: 50 Pl. Cremazie, 12th Floor, Montreal, Que. H2P 1B6.

**MELOSKY, Louis Clement,** C.M., B.Sc., D.D.S., M.S.D., F.I.C.D.; orthodontist; b. Oakburn, Man. 14 July 1930; s. John Walter and May (Luhowy) M.; e. St. Joseph's Coll. Yorkton, Sask.; Univ. of Man. B.Sc. (Pharm.) 1955; Univ. of Alta. D.D.S. 1959; Univ. of Wash. M.S.D. 1966; m. Helen Mary d. Panteloman and Sarafina Orysiuk 3 Sept. 1955; children: Cynthia, Diane, Barbara, Cheryl; ORTHODONTIC SPECIALIST (private practice) 1966– ; Dir., Adv. Bd., Central Trust 1986– ; Assoc. Prof. (part-time) of Dentistry, Univ. of Man. 1966, Chrmn. Bd. Govs. of Univ. 1980–83; Chrmn., Candn. Multiculturalism Counc. 1985–88; Chrmn., Universities Grant Commission Province of Man. 1989– ; Pres., Ukrainian Canadian Profession and Business Federation 1993– ; Past Pres., Candn. Found. for Ukrainian Studies 1987– ; Past Pres., Ukrainian

Prof. and Business Club Winnipeg 1975; Candn. Assn. Orthodontics; Man. Orthodontic Soc.; Dir. Mid Western Soc. Orthodontics (USA) 1972–75; mem., Pierre Fauchard Academy 1990; Mem., Order of Canada 1990; Office: 1511 Medical Arts, 233 Kennedy St., Winnipeg, Man. R3C 3J5.

**MELTZ, Noah Moshe,** B.Comm., A.M., Ph.D.; university professor; b. Toronto, Ont. 16 Aug. 1934; s. Jack Henry and Lena (Gang) M.; e. Univ. of Toronto, B.Comm. 1957; Princeton Univ., A.M. 1960, Ph.D. 1964; (Fellowships: Indus. Relns. 1957, Theodore Culyer Jr. 1959, Can. Counc. Pre-doct. 1963); m. Rochelle d. Aaron and Frances LaPorter 23 June 1963; children: David Ari, Jonathan Zev, Toba Sarah, Hillel Levi; PRINCIPAL, WOODSWORTH COLLEGE, UNIV. OF TORONTO 1991– ; var. rsch. & lectr. positions summer 1957–59; Econ., Can. Dept. of Labour 1960–64; Asst. Prof., Univ. of Toronto 1964–65; Assoc. Prof. 1965–71; Prof. 1971– ; Asst. Dean, Grad. Studies 1985–87; Acting Dean, Grad. Studies 1988; Cons., Fed. Dept. of Manpower & Immigr. 1967–68; Acting Chrmn., Div. of Soc. Sci., Scarborough Coll., Univ. of Toronto 1968–69; Assoc. Chrmn., Dept. of Pol. Econ. 1974–75; Dir., Ctr. for Indus. Relns. 1975–85; Adv., Cent. Bur. of Statistics Israel summers 1975, 1981, 1989 and 1993; Vis. Prof., Beit Berl College Israel summer 1975; Technion-Israel Inst. of Technol. 1981 (Lady Davis Fellowship); Vis. Scholar, M.I.T. (summer) 1982; Pres., Candn. Indus. Relns. Assn. 1978–79; Mem., Rsch. Adv. Ctte. 1980–85; mem., National Statistics Council 1992– ; Chair, Advisory Ctte. on Labour Statistics to the Chief Statistician of Canada 1988– ; Co-Chair, Study Group on Industrial Relations Theory, Internat. Industrial Relations Assn. 1988– ; Can. Dept. of Labour-Univ. Rsch. Ctte. 1976–85; SSHRCC, Selection Ctte., Doct. Fellowships comp. 1981–82, 1982–83; past mem. of numerous other cttes. & task forces; author: 'An Economic Analysis of Labour Shortages: Tool and Die Makers' 1982; co-author: 'Human Resource Management in Canada' 1993, 'Taking Charge: Career Planning for Canadian Workers' (with wife Rochelle) 1992; 'The Shortage of Registered Nurses' 1988, 'Sharing the Work' 1981; co-editor: 'Industrial Relations Theory: Its Nature, Scope, and Pedagogy' 1993; 'The State of the Art in Industrial Relations' 1988; 'Unemployment: International Perspectives' 1987; 'Lagging Productivity Growth' 1980; plus five earlier authored, co-authored and co-edited books, and more than 90 monographs, book chapters, scholarly articles, conf. proc. & tech. reports; Mem., Ont. Region Extve., Candn. Jewish Congress 1989– ; Bd. Mem., B'Nai Akiva Sch. of Toronto 1981– ; recreations: tennis, squash; Club: Trinity Coll. Tennis; Home: 237 Sandringham Dr., Downsview, Ont. M3H 1G2; Office: Woodsworth College, 119 St. George St., Toronto, Ont. M5S 1A9.

**MELTZER, Susan R.,** B.A., C.R.M., F.I.I.C.; communications executive; b. Toronto, Ont. 30 June 1954; d. Samuel Harry and Lena (Slotnick) M.; e. Carleton Univ. B.A. 1975; Ins. Inst. Can. Fellow in Risk Mgmt. 1987; one s. Jeremy Shane; ASSOC. DIR. RISK AND INS. BELL CANADA 1987– ; Ins. Broker Morris & Mackenzie Ltd. 1975–81; Co-ordinator Risk & Ins. Canada Development Corp. 1982–85; Risk Mgmt. Offr. Prov. Ont. 1985–87; Instr. in Risk Management, Univ. of Toronto; Chair, 1994 RIMS Conference Programming Ctte.; mem., Editorial Adv. Bd., 'Risk Management' Magazine; frequent speaker risk mgmt.; Vice-Pres. & Secy. Extve. Council, Risk & Ins. Mgmt. Soc.; Past Pres. Ont. Risk & Ins. Mgmt. Soc.; mem. Soc. of Fellows; recreations: travel, reading, music; Home: 1214, 155 Antibes Dr., Willowdale, Ont. M2R 2G7; Office: 9N, 483 Bay St., Toronto, Ont. M5G 2E1.

**MELVILLE, Robert D.,** B.S.M.E., M.B.A.; manufacturer; b. Montreal, Que. 28 Sept. 1937; s. Douglas Reid and Millicent (Hudson) M.; e. Sir George Williams Univ., Cert. in Engn. 1959; McGill Univ., B.S.M.E. 1962, M.B.A. 1969; m. Joyce Marie d. late Douglas Gunn, 16 Sept. 1961; children: Douglas William, Susan Lynn, David Hudson, John Ramsey; PRESIDENT - GLOBAL BUSINESS AREA - INDUSTRIAL DRYING, ASEA BROWN BOVERI since 1992; joined present organization as Project Engr. 1962, Project Mgr. 1964, Sales Mgr. 1966, Vice-Pres. 1969, Pres., ABB Flakt Ltd. 1973; Dir., ABB Flakt Industri A.B.; ABB Flakt Ross Inc.; mem., Corp. Engrs. Que.; Assn. Prof. Eng. of Ont.; Assn. Prof. Eng. Geol. & Geophys., Alta.; Assn. Prof. Engrs. B.C.; Clubs: St. James's; The Country; Office: 1410 Blair Place, Suite 600, Gloucester, Ont. K1J 9B9.

**MELVIN, James Rae,** B.Sc., M.A., Ph.D., F.R.S.C.; economist, university professor; b. Deloraine, Man. 8 July 1938; s. Andrew and Mary Elizabeth (LeBarron) M.; e. Univ. of Man., B.Sc. 1959; Univ. of Alta., M.A. 1963; Univ. of Minnesota, Ph.D. 1966; m. Barbara, d. Harvey and Maude Minnikin, 28 Mar. 1964; children: Mary Elizabeth, Robert James, Richard Brian; PROFESSOR OF ECONOMICS, UNIV. OF WATERLOO 1990– ; work includes projects for Economic Counc. of Can., Ont. Economic Counc., Inst. for Rsch. on Public Policy and Environment Canada; author: 'The Effect of Energy Price Increase on Commodity Prices, Interprovincial Trade, and Employment' 1976; 'The Tax Structure and Canadian Trade' 1976; 'Trade in Services: A Theoretical Analysis' 1989; and numerous articles in prof. journals; co-author: 'Effective Protection in the Canadian Economy' 1969; 'The Effect of Energy Prices on the Structure of Urban Areas' 1983; 'The Theory of International Trade' 1988; Home: 144 Candlewood Cres., Waterloo, Ont. N2L 5T4; Office: Dept. of Economics, Univ. of Waterloo, Waterloo, Ont. N2L 3G1.

**MELZACK, Ronald,** Ph.D., F.R.S.C.; psychologist, university professor; b. Montreal, Que. 19 July 1929; s. Joseph and Annie (Mandel) M.; e. McGill Univ., B.Sc. 1950, M.Sc. 1951, Ph.D. 1954; m. Lucy, d. Nahum and Celia Birch, 7 Aug. 1960; children: Lauren, Joel; E.P. TAYLOR PROFESSOR OF PSYCHOLOGY, McGILL UNIV. 1963– ; lectr., McGill Univ. 1953–54; rsch. fellow, Univ. of Oregon Medical Sch. 1954–57; lectr., Univ. Coll., London, U.K. 1957–58; rsch. fellow, Univ. of Pisa, Italy 1958–59; assoc. prof., M.I.T. 1959–63; Fellow of Am. and Can. Psychol. Assns.; Fellow, Royal Soc. Can.; Past Pres., Internat. Assn. for the Study of Pain; rec'd Canada Council Molson Prize 1985; author: 'The Day Tuk Became a Hunter, and other Eskimo stories' 1967; 'Raven, Creator of the World' 1970; 'The Puzzle of Pain' 1973; 'Why the Man in the Moon is Happy, and other Eskimo stories' 1978; ed. 'Pain Measurement and Assessment' 1983; co-author: 'The Challenge of Pain' 1982, 2nd ed. 1988; co-editor: 'Textbook of Pain' 1984, 2nd ed. 1989, 3rd ed. 1994; 'Handbook of Pain Assessment' 1992; recreations: bicycling, skiing, writing children's books; Home: 51 Banstead Rd., Montreal W., Que. H4X 1P1; Office: Dept. of Psychology, McGill University, 1205 Dr. Penfield Ave., Montreal, Que. H3A 1B1.

**MÉNARD, L. Jacques,** B.A., B.Comm., M.B.A.; investment dealer; b. Chicoutimi, Que. 29 Jan. 1946; s. Joseph N. and Aline (Lasanté) M.; e. Coll. Ste-Marie B.A. 1966; Loyola Coll. of Montreal B.Comm. 1967; Univ. of W. Ont. M.B.A. 1970; m. Marie-José Ratelle 7 June 1975; children: Louis-Simon, Anne-Valérie; VICE-CHRMN., BURNS FRY LIMITED (and CHRMN., EXTVE. CTTE.); Inst. Equity Salesman present firm 1972; Mgr. Inst. Sales Dept. 1973–75; Dir. 1975; Dir. Corp. Serv. 1976; Corp. and Inst. Serv. 1977; Managing Dir., Qué.; Dir., Société générale de financement 1992– ; Mem., Economic Council of Canada 1991–92; Chrmn., Montréal Expos Baseball Club 1991– ; Pres., Chamber of Commerce of Metropolitan Montreal, 1989–90, Chrmn. 1990–91; Chrmn. Montreal Exchange 1984–86, Vice-Chrmn. 1983–84, Gov. 1979–81; Chrmn. & Pres., Trans Canada Options Inc. 1987–88, Dir. 1985–88; Dir.: Investment Dealers Assn. 1984–86; National Contingency Fund 1984–86; Internat. Options Clearing Corp. 1985–88; Internat. Financial Centers Organisation of Montreal 1986– ; Centraide 1990–93; Fondation Ressources-Jeunesse 1990– ; R. Catholic; recreations: golf, tennis, skiing; Clubs: Le Club Saint-Denis; Mount Royal Club; Royal Montreal Golf and Country; Home: 104 Jasper Ave., Town of Mt-Royal, Qué. H3B 1J9; Office: 1501 McGill College Ave., Suite 3200, Montréal, Qué. H3A 3M8.

**MÉNARD, Mario F.,** LL.L.; lawyer; b. Granby, Que. 16 Jan. 1952; s. Jean-Marc and Bernadette (Dumoulin) M.; e. Univ. of Sherbrooke LL.L. 1974; m. Nicole Mohr May 1990; children: Isabelle, David, Nicolas, Frédéric; PARTNER, SPIEGEL SOHMER 1992– ; Tax Counsel, Justice Canada 1975–76; Tax Counsel & Partner, Verchère, Noël Eddy 1976–84; Founding Mem. & Managing Partner, Ménard, Allard 1984–91; Tax Lectr., Masters Program, Univ. of Sherbrooke 1983–87; Quebec Bar Assn. 1978–84; Dir., Lemmerz Canada; Mngt. Ctte., Reynolds-Lemmerz Industries; clubs: St. James's; Montreal Hunt; Home: Chemin Ménard, St-Joachim de Shefford, Qué. J0E 2G0; Office: 5, Place Ville Marie, Suite 1203, Montréal, Qué. H3B 2G2.

**MENARD, Michel R.,** B.Com., M.B.A., M.P.A., C.M.A., C.G.A.; exexutive; b. Halifax, N.S. 12 Aug. 1949; s. Robert and Georgette (Boulet) M.; e. Univ. of Ottawa B.Com. 1971; York Univ. M.B.A. 1974, M.P.A. 1975; C.M.A. 1977; C.G.A. 1978; PRES. AND CHIEF OPERATING OFFR. VOLCANO ENERGY SYSTEMS INC. 1989– ; Chrmn., Internat. Boiler Works 1989– ; Operations & Control Review Group Analyst Northern Telecom 1976–78; Mill Controller, Dir. Cash Mgmt., Sr. Financial Analyst C.I.P. Inc. 1979–86; Div. Controller Domtar 1986–87; Chief Financial Offr. Manson Group 1987–89; Home: 3794 Côte des Neiges, Montreal, Que. H3H 1V6; 2045 Lakeshore Blvd. W., Suite 1006, Toronto, Ont. M8V 2Z6; Office: 4300 Beaudry, St-Hyacinthe, Que. J2S 8A5.

**MENDELSOHN, Nathan S.,** M.A., Ph.D., F.R.S.C.; university professor; b. Brooklyn, N.Y. 14 Apl. 1917; s. Samuel and Sylvia (Kirschenbaum) M.; came to Canada, 1917; e. Univ. of Toronto, B.A. 1939, M.A. 1940, Ph.D. 1942; m. Helen, d. Abraham Brontman, Toronto, 26 Oct. 1940; two s. Eric, Alan; PROF. OF MATH., UNIV. OF MANITOBA 1946– , and Head of Dept. 1963– ; Rsch. Scient., Nat. Rsch. Council and Inspection Bd. of U.K. and Can. 1942–45; Lectr. in Math., Queen's Univ. 1945–46; Candn. Del. to Internat. Math. Union, Saltjobaden, Sweden 1962; Del. to Univ. of Man. to Internat. Cong. of Math., Stockholm 1962; mem., Assoc. Comte. of Pure and Applied Maths., Nat. Rsch. Counc. 1963– ; Candn. rep. to Internat. Math. Union, Dubna, U.S.S.R., Aug. 1966; author of over 100 papers in prof. journs.; winner, Roy. Soc. of Can. 'Henry Marshall Tory Gold Medal' 1979; named distinguished Prof. 1981; Dir., Computing and Data Processing Soc. Can.; mem., Candn. Math. Cong. (Pres. 1970–71); Am. Math. Soc.; Math. Assn. Am.; Soc. Indust. and Applied Math.; Jewish; recreations: chess, bridge, music; Home: 364 Enniskillen Ave., Winnipeg, Man. R2V 0J3.

**MENDELSON, Michael,** B.A., M.A.; public servant; b. Winnipeg, Man. 22 Nov. 1948; s. Israel and Zetta (Kurnarsky) M.; e. Univ. of Man., B.A. (Hons.) 1971; Univ. of Toronto, M.A. 1976; m. Marsha d. Barney and Rose Cohen 15 Apr. 1979; DEPY. SECRETARY OF THE CABINET, GOVT. OF ONT. 1990– ; ASST. DEPY. MIN., OFFICE OF THE BUDGET AND INTERGOVERNMENTAL FINANCE, MIN. OF TREASURY AND ECONOMICS, GOVT. OF ONT. 1990– ; var. positions, Govt. of Man. 1971–74; Rsch. Staff, Ont. Econ. Counc. 1977–81; Acting Chief, Intergovt. Transfers, Min. of State for Soc. Devel., Govt. of Can. 1981–83; Depy. Min. of Community Serv., Govt. of Man. 1983–87; Sec. to Treas. Bd., Govt. of Man. 1987–88; Asst. Depy. Min., Min. of Community and Social Services and Min. of Health, Govt. of Ont.; Rsch. Staff, Parliamentary Task Force on Fed.-Prov. Fiscal Arrangements; Rsch. Dir., Interprov. Task Force on Soc. Security; Cons., Man. Basic Annual Income Experiment; and other cons. positions; former Asst. Prof., Fac. of Med., Univ. of Man.; Mem., Candn. Health Econ. Rsch. Assn.; author: 'Administrative Cost of Income Security Programs: Canada and Ontario' 1979, 'Universal or Selective? The Debate on Reforming Income Security' 1981 & num. articles; recreations: cycling, reading; Home: 703 – 62 Wellesley St., Toronto, Ont. M5S 2X3; Office: Cabinet Office, 4th Floor – Whitney Block, 99 Wellesley St. West, Toronto, Ont. M7A 1A1.

**MENDES, Errol P.;** professor; b. Fort Hall, Kenya March 1956; s. Francis Xavier and Olivia Esperanca (Pinto) M.; e. Univ. of Exeter, LL.B. (Hons.) 1977 (Gold Medalist); Univ. of Illinois, LL.M. 1979; ASSOC. PROF., FACULTY OF LAW, THE UNIVERSITY OF WESTERN ONTARIO, 1984– and DIR., HUMAN RIGHTS RSCH. AND EDUCATION CENTRE, UNIV. OF OTTAWA 1993–96; Visiting Professor, Faculty of Law, Univ. of Ottawa, Common Law Section 1992–93; Barrister and Solicitor, Law Society of Upper Canada; Teaching Fellow, Univ. of Illinois 1978–79; Asst. Prof., Univ. of Alta. 1979–84; Panel Mem., Bd. of Inquiry Under Ontario Human Rights Code; Cons., Internat. Comm. Arbitration; Editor-in-Chief, The National Journal of Constitutional Law; Mem., Panel of Arbitrators, Am. Arbitration Assn., NY; Internat. Chamb. of Commerce, Paris; Found. Dir., Minority Advocacy Rights Council of Can.; Mem., Candn. Counc. on Internat. Law; mem., Cdn. Council on Internat. Business; recreations: creative writing (poetry), public speaking, speech writing, politics, travel; Club: University; Home: 37 Glen Ave., Ottawa, Ont. K1S 2Z6; Office: Univ. of Ottawa, Ottawa, Ont. K1N 6N5.

**MENDES da COSTA, The Hon. Derek,** Q.C., LL.B.(Hons.) LL.M., S.J.D., LL.D., F.K.C.; judge; b. London, Eng. 7 March 1929; s. Judah and Esther (Ellis) M.; e. King's Coll. Univ. of London LL.B. 1955; Univ. of Melbourne LL.M. 1965; Harvard Univ. S.J.D. 1972; Univ. of London LL.D. 1980; m. Barbara Helen d. David Prevost, Stanmore, Eng. 26 June 1950; children: Virginia Sara (Murdoch), Philip Charles; JUSTICE, ONTARIO COURT OF JUSTICE (General Division) 1990– , assigned to Unified Family Court; Dir., Candn. Inst. for the Admin. of Justice 1983–87; Bencher, The Law Soc. of Upper Canada 1983–84; Vice-Chrmn., Legal Education Ctte. 1983–84; Chrmn. Bd. Dirs. Ont. Prov.

Court (Family Div.) Conciliation Project 1976–81; Chrmn. Atty. Gen.'s Comte. on Representation of Children 1977–84; mem. Statutory Powers Procedure Rules Comte. 1977–84; Commr. for Ont. Uniform Law Conf. of Can. 1977–84; Chrmn., Comte. on Sale of Goods of the Uniform Law Conf. of Canada 1979–81; Co-Chrmn., Products Liability Ctte. of the Uniform Law Conference of Canada 1982–84; Judge of the District Court of Ont. 1984–90, assigned to Unified Family Court 1984; Chrmn., Ont. Law Reform Commission 1977–84; Spec. Lectr., Faculty of Law, Univ. of Toronto 1977–84; Asst. Lectr. in Law, King's Coll. Univ. of London 1955–58; Sr. Lectr in Law, Univ. of Melbourne 1958–65; Prof. Osgoode Hall Law Sch. 1965–68; Univ. of Toronto, Prof. of Law 1968–77, mem. Council Sch. Grad. Studies 1971, 1975–77, Chrmn. of Counc., Sch. of Continuing Studies 1977–80; Fellow Victoria Coll. 1975–78, Fellow, Kings College London 1986; Citation, Sch. of Continuing Studies, Univ. of Toronto 1986; Visiting Prof. Ariz. State Univ. 1972; Univ. of Texas 1972; Gov., Candn. Inst. Advanced Legal Studies 1978–82; mem. Senate York Univ. 1966–68, Vice Chrmn. 1967–68; Internat. Faculty of Comparative Law (Strasbourg) since 1966; Special Comte. on Legal Educ. Law Soc. Upper Can. 1970–72; Solr. Supreme Court Judicature Eng. (Hons.) 1955; Barrister & Solr. Supreme Court Victoria, Australia 1963, Solicitor of Supreme Court Ont. 1966; cr. Q.C. 1972 (Ont.); Notary Public (Ont.) 1982; Intermediate Laws Scholarship, 1952; John Mackrell Prizeman and City of London Solrs.' Co.'s Grotius Prizeman 1955; served with R.A.M.C. 1948–49; Research Assoc. Ont. Law Reform Comn. Family Law Project 1965–68; Law of Property Project 1968–71, 1973–76; co-author 'Matrimonial Causes Jurisdiction' 1961; author various articles Candn. Commonwealth, and foreign law journs.; ed. and contrib., 'Studies in Canadian Family Law'; ed., 'The Cambridge Lectures' 1979; co-author, 'Property Law'; mem. Law Soc. Upper Can. 1966; Nat. Council (1977–84) & Ont. Council (1981–84) of the Candn. Bar Assn.; Law Soc. (Eng.); Selden Soc.; Soc. Pub. Teachers Law; Candn. Assn. Law Teachers; Medico-Legal Soc. Toronto; American Foreign Law Assn. Inc.; Internat. Soc. Family Law; Harvard Law Sch. Assn.; The British Inst. of International and Comparative Law; Club: The Athenaeum; The Hamilton; Empire; Phi Delta Phi (Hon. mem.); Recreation: Walking my Dog; Home: Hamilton, Ont.; Office: 55 Main St. West, Hamilton, Ont. L8P 1H4.

**MENKE, Ursula,** B.Sc., B.C.L.; public servant; b. Bielefeld, Germany 12 Sept. 1947; d. Heinrich Joseph and Ann Olga (Kleinemeier) M.; e. McGill Univ. B.Sc. 1968, B.C.L. 1976; Univ. of Alta. teaching dipl. 1969; m. Konrad Winrich Graf Finck s. Ottfried and Eva von Finckenstein 23 July 1986; children: Konrad Christopher, Alexis Veronica; VICE PRESIDENT, COUNSEL & CORPORATE SECRETARY, METLIFE 1993– ; High School Teacher (Sci. & Math.) 1969–73; Lawyer, Federal Dept. of Justice 1977–88; Public Policy Cons., Strategico Inc. 1989–90; Sr. Corp. Advr., Office of the Supt. of Finan. Insts. 1990–92; Inspector General, Candn. Security Intelligence Service 1992–93; Bd. Mem., St. Matthew's Harmony House; author/co-author of 4 book chapters; Home: 1362 Whippoorwill Dr., Gloucester, Ont. K1J 7J2; Office: 340 Laurier Ave. W., Suite 8F, Ottawa, Ont. K1A 0P8.

**MENKES, René,** A.R.I.B.A.; architect; b. Paris, France 10 Feb. 1932; e. Lower Can. Coll., 1944–49; McGill Univ., 1949–55; m. Ann Wallace Sullivan; PARTNER, WEBB, ZERAFA, MENKES, HOUSDEN; Partner, Webb, Zerafa, Menkès, Toronto and Kitchener, Ont.; firm won Massey Medal, Nat. Design and Nat. Steel Design Awards in 1964; designed and supv. constr. of most major type bldgs. incl. schs. and univs., hotels, commercial offices, shopping, indust. and residential centres and Govt. projects; also projects in Toronto, Montreal, Calgary, Lancaster, N.B., etc.; mem., Prov. Que. Assn. Archs.; Royal Arch. Inst. Can.; Home: 38 Belvedere Rd., Westmount, Montreal, Que. H3A 2L1; Office: 1801 McGill College Ave., Suite 501, Montreal, Que. H3A 2N4.

**MENSES, Jan,** R.C.A., A.I.A., A.E., A.N., LL.D.; painter; draughtsman; printmaker; muralist; b. Rotterdam, Netherlands 28 Apl. 1933; s. Jan and Elisabeth Wilhelmina (Schwarz) M.; e. Willem de Zwijger H.B.S. Rotterdam 1951; Degrees in Eng. lang. and Dutch lang. Rotterdam 1952, 1956; Royal Air Force Offrs.' Acad. Breda, Holland grad. 1954; Rotterdam Art Acad. Etching & Lithography 1959; study trips Europe, N. Africa 1956–58, Israel 1971, 1984, 1985, 1986, 1989; m. Rachel Régine d. late Rabbi Shlomo Kadoch, Morocco, 7 Dec. 1958; children: Solomon, Hnina Sarah, Nechama Elisabeth Halo; Rsch./work trips to Israel 1992– ; solo exhns. France, Holland, Spain, Morocco to 1960; Jewish Pub. Lib. Montreal 1960; McGill Univ. 1961; Penthouse Gallery Montreal 1962; Montebello Gallery, Montreal 1962; Tifereth Jerusalem Cong. Montreal 1963; Isaacs Gallery Toronto 1964; Jason Teff Gallery, Montreal, 1964; Delta Gallery Rotterdam 1965; Galerie Godard Lefort Montreal 1966; Gallery Moos Toronto 1967; Galerie Martal Montreal 1971, 1972; Rotterdamse Kunststichting 1974; Galerie Mira Godard Toronto 1977, Montreal 1978; Montreal Museum of Fine Arts 1976 (retrospective); Studio Gravure G Ottawa 1979; Elca London Gallery Montreal 1979; Seasons Galleries The Hague 1980; Univ. of B.C. Fine Arts Gallery 1981; Galerie Don Stewart, Montreal, 1981; Mead Art Museum, Amherst, Mass., 1983; Galerie Michel Tetreault Art Contemporain, Montreal 1983; Saidye Bronfman Centre Museum 1984; Agnes Etherington Art Centre, Queen's Univ. Kingston 1984; Blom & Dorn Gallery, New York 1985, 1987–88, 1989–1991, 1994; Marywood College Museum, Scranton, Pa. 1985; Congregation Shaar Hashomayim, Westmount Que. 1986–87; Wolfson Community Ctr., Safed, Israel 1987; Mayanot Gallery, Jerusalem 1987, 1988; Esperanza Gall., Montreal 1988, 1989; Young Israel of Montreal, 1989; Gallery Hamaayan Haradum-Safed, Israel 1989–94; Blom & Dorn Gallery, Los Angeles, U.S.A. 1990; Galerie Kô-Zen, Montreal 1992; Galerie La Magie D'Art, Toronto 1991; Blom & Dorn Gallery, Hartford, Conn. 1992; Gallery Har Nof, Jerusalem, Israel 1994; Haags Gemeenklyk Museum, Holland; Safed Gallery/Museum: Menses Hamaayan Haradum; Tel Aviv Museum T.A. (in preparation); two-man shows Montreal Museum of Fine Arts 1961, 1965, Philadelphia Art Alliance 1969; Concordia Univ. Montreal 1985; Blom & Dorn Gall. N.Y. 1986; rep. over 250 group exhns. Can., USA, Europe, most recent: R.C.A. 'Tableaux du Quebec,' Academy House Gallery, Toronto 1991; Permanent Exhibition of Safed Artists, Artist's Colony, Safed, Israel; 'Ora Group of 8 - Israel' Art Gallery of Ont. (Toronto) 1990; rep. major permanent collections incl.: Olympia & York Collection, Toronto; McGill Univ. Collection, Montreal; Israel Museum, Jerusalem; Candn. Jewish Congress Museum, Montreal; Esperanza Gallery Collection, Montreal; Holocaust Remembrance Centre, Toronto; City of Safed, Israel; Museum of Modern Art New York, Philadelphia Museum of Art, Solomon R. Guggenheim Museum New York, Brooklyn Museum, N.Y.; Art Inst. of Chicago; Cleveland Museum of Art, Detroit Inst. of Arts, Yale Univ., New Haven; Yivo Inst., N.Y.; Mead Art Museum, Amherst (Mass.); Jonathan Edwards College, New Haven; Museum of Art, Univ. of Arizona, Tucson, AZ, U.S.A.; Nat. Gallery Can., Can. Council Art Bank, Dept. of External Affairs, Ottawa; Thomas More Inst. Montreal, Universite de Montreal, CBC Collection Montreal; Montreal Museum of Fine Arts, Musée d'Art Contemporain, Montreal; Concordia Univ. Montreal, Lavalin Collection Montreal; The Gallery, Stratford; The Robert McLaughlin Gallery, Oshawa; Holocaust Mem. Centre Montreal (Mural.); Quebec Prov. Museum; Agnes Etherington Art Centre, Kingston; C.I.L. Collection, Montreal; Cadillac-Fairview Collection, Montreal; Loto Québec Collection, Montreal; Owens Art Museum, Sackville (N.B.); Rijksmuseum Amsterdam; Stedelijk Museum, Amsterdam; Boymans-Van Beuningen Museum, Rotterdam; David Giles Carter Collection, New Haven (Conn) U.S.A.; Bar Ilan Univ. Collection, Tel Aviv, Israel; Museo Ciani di Villa Caccia Lugano; Yad Vashem Holocaust Mem. Jerusalem; Hebrew Univ. Jerusalem; Victoria and Albert London; The Currier Gallery of Art, Manchester, New Hampshire, U.S.A.; Worcester Art Museum, Worcester, U.S.A.; The New York Public Library; Art Gallery of Hamilton, Ont. Canada; as well as private colls. Can., USA, Europe, N. Africa, Australia & New Zealand, Japan, USSR; Haifa Museum of Modern Art, Haifa; Vatican Museum, Rome; Banque d'Oeuvres d'Art du Québec, Québec; Ministère des Communautés Culturelles et de l'Immigration du Québec, Québec; Shalom Hartman Inst., Jerusalem; Collection Rishon Lezion, Jerusalem; Jewish Public Library, Montreal; Cemp Collection, Montreal; Museum of Art, Rhode Island School of Design, Providence, R.I. USA; University Art Galleries, Univ. of New Hampshire, USA; Halifax Museum of Fine Arts, Halifax; Rose Art Museum, Brandeis Univ. (Waltham, Mass. U.S.A.); recipient 5 First Prizes Nat. Art Exhn. Que. 1960–64; Concours Artistiques de la Prov. de Qué. Grand Prize 1965; 5th, 10th and 11th Winnipeg Shows 1961, 1966, 1968; IX Internat. Exhn. Drawings & Engravings Lugano 1966; Official Centennial Art Competition Toronto 'Perspective' Prize 1967; Hadassah Prizes Montreal 1967, 1969, 1970, 1971, 1982; Reeves of Can. Award Ont. Soc. Artists Toronto 1969, Tigert Award 1970, Loomis & Toles Award 1972; Lauréat Concours Artistiques Prov. Qué. 1971; J.I. Segal Arts Award Montreal 1975; Accademia Italia delle Arte e del Lavoro Italy Gold Medal 1980; First Prize, Third Quebec Biennale, 1981; Hon. degree, Universita Delle Arti, Italy 1981; Image 81 Award, Ont. Soc. Artists, 1981; Gold Medal Intnl. Parliament U.S.A. 1982; Image 82 Award Montreal, Ont. Soc. Artists, 1982; Gran Premio delle Nazione, Italy 1983; World Culture Prize for Letters, The Arts and the Sciences, Italy 1984; Oscar d'Italia 1985; European Banner of Arts with Gold Medal 1984; Hon. degree, Maestro Academico, Accademia Bedriacense, Italy 1984; Golden Flame Award, Italy 1986; Ish Shalom Award, Jerusalem 1994; various Can. Council grants and Sr. Arts Fellowships 1969–70, 1971–72, 1981–82; 4 purchase awards; CBC Film Documentary 'Jan Menses: Exile and Redemption' (on Klippoth, Kaddish & Tikkun Cycles) 1985; participated Internat. Art Fairs Paris, France & Cologne, Germany 1986; Lectr. in Fine Arts Concordia Univ. 1973–76; Visiting Artist Mount Allison Univ. 1978–90; maj. cycles of work: 'Diabolica Series' 1961–62, 'Victors Series' 1963, 'Kaddish Series' 1965–80, 'Klippoth Series' 1963–78, 'Tikkun Series' 1978– ; illustrated vol. of poetry based on Exodus 1960; 'Staub un Ebigkeit' 1981; served with Royal Dutch Air Force 1953–55; Officer's Academy; mem., President's Council, Univ. of New Hampshire, U.S.A.; mem., Accademia Italia delle Arte e del Lavoro; Soc. des Artistes en Arts Visuels du Qué.; Royal Canadian Academy of Arts (R.C.A.); Accademia D'Europa; Accademia Delle Nazioni; Jewish Amer. Acad. of Arts and Sciences, USA; Israeli Artists Assoc., Tel Aviv; Assoc. of Professional Artists, Safed, Israel; Ora Group of 8, Safed, Israel; elected to Israel Assn. of Visual Art, Jerusalem 1994; Address: c/o Solomon Menses, 74 Invermay Ave., Toronto, Ont. M3H 1Z5.

**MENZIE, Elmer L.,** B.S.A., M.S.A., Ph.D.; educator; b. Saskatoon, Sask. 7 Jan. 1923; s. Ross Hamilton and Margaret Anne (Gay) M.; e. Univ. of B.C., B.S.A. 1952, M.S.A. 1955; Univ. of Cal. Berkeley, Ph.D. 1961; m. Emily d. Emil Bidin 16 May 1953; children: Keith L., Anne L.; Prof. of Agric. Econ. & Bus., Univ. of Guelph 1986–88; retired 1988; Instr. in Agric. Econ. Univ. of B.C. 1955–57; Asst. Prof. of Agric. Econ. Mont. State Coll. 1960–61; Prof. of Agric. Econ. Univ. of Ariz. 1961–75; Dir. Sch. of Agric. Econ. and Extension Edn. present Univ. 1975–85, Chrmn. of Agric. Econ. & Bus. 1985–86; Adv., Univ. of Ceara, Fortaleza, Brazil 1964–67; mem. Candn. Agric. Econ. Soc. (Pres. 1978–79); Am. Agric. Econ. Assn.; Internat. Assn. Agric. Econs.; W. Agric. Econ. Assn.; Home: 83 Rickson Ave., Guelph, Ont. N1G 3B6.

**MENZIES, Arthur Redpath,** M.A.; consultant; retired diplomat; b. Changte-Ho, Honan, China 29 Nov. 1916; e. Univ. of Toronto, B.A.; Harvard Univ., M.A.; m.; has two children; Consultant & Lectr. on Foreign Affairs; joined Dept. of External Affairs in 1940; Second Secy., Havana 1945–46; apptd. Head of the Candn. Liaison Mission in Japan, Nov. 1950, and following the conclusion of the Peace Treaty with Japan, became Chargé d'Affaires a. i. of Canadian Embassy, Tokyo in Apr. 1952; on return to Ottawa in July 1953, apptd. Head of the Far Eastern Divn. of the Dept.; High Commissioner to Fed. of Malaya and concurrently Ambassador to Burma 1958–61; Head of Defence Liaison (1) Div., Ottawa 1962–65; High Commr. to Australia 1965–72, High Commr. concurrently to Fiji 1970–72; Permanent Rep. and Ambassador to North Atlantic Council 1972–76; Ambassador to People's Republic of China, 1976–80 concurrently, to Socialist Republic of Vietnam 1976–79; Ambassador for Disarmament 1980–82; Address: 445 Maple Lane, Rockcliffe, Ottawa, Ont. K1M 1H8.

**MENZIES, John,** B.Sc., Ph.D.; university professor; b. Alyth, Scotland, U.K. 29 June 1949; s. John Alexander and Winifred Collier (Findlay) M.; e. Univ. of Aberdeen B.Sc. (Hons.) 1971; Univ. of Edinburgh Ph.D. 1976; m. Teresa d. James and Gerardina Cameron 22 July 1972; children: Erica, Fiona, Rebecca; PROFESSOR OF GEOGRAPHY & GEOLOGICAL SCIENCES, BROCK UNIV. 1990– ; H.S.O. Dept. Soil Survey, Macaulay Inst. Soil Rsch., U.K. 1975–77; Asst. Prof., present univ. 1977–84, Assoc. Prof. 1984–90; Mem., Internat. Glaciological Soc.; Geol. Assn. of Can.; Candn. Geographic Assn.; INQUA; Candn. Quaternary Rsch. Assoc. Geol. Soc. of Am.; Mem., Ed. Bd., 'Sedimentary Geology'; editor: 'Drumlin Bibliography' 1984, 'Drumlin Symposium' 1987; author of academic articles; recreations: reading, travel; Home: 9 Fern Gate, Fonthill, Ont. L0S 1E4; Office: St. Catharines, Ont. L2S 3A1.

**MERBIS, Eduard;** banker; b. Hilversum, Holland 18 Feb. 1943; e. Hilversum H.S.; Nijenrode Coll. of Business Admin. 1962; m. Nienke E. Jorg 22 May 1971; children: Merijn A.E., Roland C.; Pres., ABN AMRO Bank Canada 1988; joined Algemene Bank Nederland N.V. 1962; had overseas assignments in Singapore, Uganda, Italy, & Indonesia; Dept. Mgr., Head Office,

Internat. Directorate 1977–82; Country Mgr. in Turkey & Mem., Bd. of Dir. of the Bank's Saudi Arabian affiliate 1982–88; Past Mem., Bd. of Gov., Internat. Schools in Jakarta, Istanbul & Holland; Dir., Toronto Symphony Orchestra; Chrmn., Ont. Chapter of Canada–Netherlands Chamber of Commerce; recreations: reading, travel, photography; clubs: The National, The Toronto Hunt.

**MERCALDO, Edward L.,** B.Sc.; director; b. Baltimore, Md. 19 Aug. 1941; e. Georgetown Univ. B.Sc. 1963; Harvard Univ. Advanced Mgmt. Prog. 1984; VICE PRESIDENT & DIRECTOR, FIRST MARATHON SECURITIES LTD. 1992– ; Mgr. Internat. Operations Wachovia Bank & Trust Co. Winston-Salem, N.C. 1963–65, Vice Pres. Internat. Banking 1968–70; Export Devel. Co-ord. State of N.C. 1966–67; Equibank N.A. 1970–76 serving as Vice Pres. and Sr. Vice Pres. Internat. Banking, Extve. Vice Pres. Funds Mgmt.; Bank of Montreal 1976–85 serving as Vice Pres. Loan Syndication, Sr. Vice Pres. Internat. Banking, Sr. Vice Pres. and Dep. Group Extve. Corporate & Govt. Banking; Pres. and Chief Extve. BT Bank of Canada 1985–87; Partner, Gordon Capital Corp. 1988–92; former lectr. Univ. of Pittsburgh; author various articles profl. subjects; Address: 565 Robin Hood Rd., Vancouver, B.C. V7S 1T4.

**MERCER, David William,** B.A., M.A.; hydro executive; b. St. John's, Nfld. 11 July 1940; s. Roy Cavendish and Phyllis Gertrude (Cousens) M.; e. Bishop Field Coll. 1958; Meml. Univ. of Nfld., B.A. (Hons.) 1963 (Gov. Gen. Gold Medal for Acad. Excellence); Queen's Univ., M.A. 1966; m. Stella Regina d. Reginald F. Martin 16 Oct. 1963; children: Susan Regina, Stephen Geoffrey, Donald Christopher, Andrew Paul; PRES. & C.E.O., NFLD. & LABRADOR HYDRO 1992– ; Pres. & Chief Extve. Offr., Lower Churchill Devel. Corp.; Dir., Nfld. & Labrador Hydro; Lower Churchill Devel. Corp.; Gull Island Power Co. Ltd.; Econ., Govt. of Can. 1963–66; Econ. Rsch. Unit., Fed. Dept. of Trade & Comm. 1966–67; Econ. Policy Advr., Royal Comn. on Nfld.'s Econ. Prospects 1966–67; Dir. of Econ. Analysis, Dept. of Fin., Govt. of Nfld. 1968–71; Extve. Dir., Planning & Priorities Sec., Extve. Counc. Office, Govt. of Nfld. 1971–74; Vice-Pres., Corp. Planning, Nfld. & Lab. Hydro 1975–83; Extve. Vice-Pres. 1984–85; Pres., 1986–92; recreations: sailing, photography; Clubs: Royal Nfld. Yacht; Rotary of St. John's; Home: 25 Fagan Dr., St. John's, Nfld. A1A 3N2; Office: P.O. Box 12400, Hydro Place, St. John's, Nfld. A1B 4K7.

**MERCER, Keith James Harold;** b. St. John's, Nfld. 4 Dec. 1945; s. Malcolm James and Mary (Godden) M.; e. Memorial Univ. of Nfld. B.A. 1966; Oxford Univ. B.A. 1969, B.C.L. 1970; m. Harriet Anne. d. Cdr. & Mrs. E.B. Pearce 18 July 1973; children: Lesley Anne, Nicholas James Edward; JUDGE, SUPREME COURT OF NFLD. (TRIAL DIV.) 1992– ; called to Bar of Nfld. 1971; Asst. Clerk and Law Clerk, House of Assembly 1972–75; Dept. of Justice (Nfld.) 1974–80; Asst. and Assoc. Depy. Min. 1977–80; private practice 1981; former Partner, Stewart, McKelvey, Stirling, Scales; cr. Q.C. 1984; Apptd. Judge 1992; Anglican; mem. Law Soc. of Nfld.; Candn. Bar Assn.; Home: 79 Circular Rd., St. John's, Nfld. A1C 2Z4.

**MERCER, Peter Philip,** LL.M., Ph.D.; educator; b. St. John's, Nfld. 29 July 1953; s. William Douglas and Pauline (Collier) M.; e. Univ. of W. Ont. Huron Coll. 1971–73, Faculty of Law LL.B. 1976; Cambridge Univ. LL.M. 1977, Ph.D. 1986; m. Cydna d. Charles and Carman Carmichael 9 Aug. 1975; children: Ryan, Imogen; PROF. AND DEAN OF LAW UNIV. OF W. ONT. 1989– ; Asst. Prof. of Law Univ. of Windsor 1979–82, Dir. LL.B./M.B.A. Prog. 1981–82; Assoc. Prof. of Law Univ. of Calgary 1982–85, Law Co-ord. Grad. Prog. in Communications Studies; Assoc. Prof. and Assoc. Dean (Student Affairs) present Univ. 1985–88; Adjunct Prof. Univ. of Detroit Law Sch. 1981–82; Dir. of Rsch. Lerner and Associates 1987–89; recipient Superior Teacher Award Univ. Calgary 1984; Rotary Grad. Fellowship 1977; Dean Ivan C. Rand Honour Soc. Univ. W. Ont. 1976; Hon. Fellow, Huron College 1992; Dir.: Children's Hosp. of W. Ont. Found. 1989– ; Pres., Children's Hosp. of Western Ont. Found. Bd. of Dir. 1992– ; Dir., Victoria Hosp. Corp. 1993– ; Mem. Bd. of Govs., Univ. of Western Ont. 1993– ; Legal Edn. Soc. Alta. 1983–85; co-author 'An Introduction to Business Associations in Canada' 1984; 'Products Liability in Canada' 2nd ed. 1988; numerous articles and govt. studies; assoc. ed.: Ont. Reports 1981–82; Administrative Law Reports 1983– ; mem. Law Soc. Upper Can.; Anglican; recreations: cooking, golf, tennis; Home: R.R.2, Ilderton, Ont. N0M 2A0; Office: London, Ont. N6A 3K7.

**MERCER, Ruby,** A.B., BM, Mus.D.; writer and editor; b. Athens, Ohio 26 July 1906; d. Leslie L. and Iva (McElhinny) M.; e. Ohio Univ., A.B.; Cincinnati Conserv. BM; Ohio Univ., Mus.D.; grad. Juilliard Sch. of Music, N.Y. 1934; m. Theo Haig 1942–54; G.G. Por 1958; widowed; Founder & Editor Emeritus, 'Opera Canada' magazine 1960– ; Founder, Candn. Children's Opera Chorus 1963; Singer, 2 seasons as leading soprano, Met. Opera, N.Y., leading role in 3 Broadway shows, summer operettas in St. Louis, Birmingham, Ala., Vancouver, B.C.; opera in San Francisco, Mexico City, Philadelphia, Montreal, Chicago, Cincinnati and on tour as leading soprano, Salvatore Baccaloni Opera Co.; 'Mrs. Opera' on WNYC's 'Mr. & Mrs. Opera' 1948–58; Ruby Mercer Show, Mutual Network WOR 1955–58; moved to Toronto 1958; Hostess, CBC 'Opera Time' and 'Opera in Stereo' 1962–85; Roman Catholic; author: 'The Tenor of His Time' (biography of Edward Johnson); 'The Quilicos - Louis, Lina, and Gino - an Operatic Family' (biography); rec'd. Canada Council grant 1993; Clubs: Arts & Letters; Heliconian; and others (opera and musical); Recipient: 1983 Candn. Music Council Medal; The Ohio Governor's Award 1986; 1988 Lifetime Achievement Award, Toronto Arts Awards Found.; Home: 400 Walmer Rd., 1710 W.T., Toronto, Ont. M5P 2X7; Office: 366 Adelaide St. E., Suite 433, Toronto, Ont. M5A 3X9.

**MERCER, Stanley,** M.B., B.Ch., D'OBST, R.C.O.G., F.A.A.P., F.R.C.S.(C); paediatric surgeon; university professor; b. Belfast, N. Ireland 25 Apr. 1924; s. Malcolm and Mary Jane (Crossley) M.; e. Queen's Univ. of Belfast, M.B., B.Ch., B.A.O. 1947; Royal Coll. of Obstetr. & Gynaecol. (Eng.), B'OBST, 1949; post-grad. training: Dudley Rd. Hosp., Royal Victoria Hosp., Hosp. for Sick Children, Belfast Univ. of St. Andrews Scot., Royal Coll. of Surgs. (Eng.), Univ. of Sask. 1948–54; Chief Res. & Fellow in Surg., Hosp. for Sick Children, Toronto 1954–56; m. Sylvia d. Chalmers and Geraldine MacKenzie 30 May 1953; children: Malcolm, Kevin, Brian; F.R.C.S.(C) 1956; Cert. Spec. Competence Ped. Surg., R.C.P.S. 1976; Surg. Staff, Ottawa Civic Hosp. 1957–74, Cons., Ped. Surg. 1974; Lectr. in Surg. (Ped.), Univ. of Ottawa 1962; Prof. 1980–89; Prof. in Pediatrics (Hon.) 1989; Programme Dir., Gen. Paediatric Surgery, Univ. of Ottawa 1986–89; Visiting Prof., Queen's Univ. 1986; Visiting Prof., Univ. of Montreal 1987; Mem., Interim Bd. of Trustees, Children's Hosp. of East. Ont. 1968–74; Chief of Staff 1971–74; Surg. in Chief, 1972–89; Founding Mem., Ottawa Health Sci. Ctr. Planning Bd. 1969–76; Con. Surgery, Childrens' Hospital of Eastern Ontario; Ont. Cancer Found.; Mem., Extve. Ctte., Univ. of Ottawa, Fac. of Health Sci. 1978–81; Dept. of Surgery 1979–89; Queen's Silver Jubilee Medal 1977; awarded Commemorative Medal for 125th Anniversary of Candn. Confederation 1993; Mem., Candn. Assn. of Ped. Surg. (Pres. 1985–86); Brit. Assn. of Ped. Surg.; Am. Ped. Surg. Assn.; Royal Coll. of Surg. of Can. (Chief Exam. in Ped. Surg. 1985–88; Mem., Speciality Ctte. 1985–87, Chrmn. 1988–90); co-author: 'Basic Surgery' 2nd ed. 1986; 'Thoracic Surgery Management of Pleural Diseases' Vol. 6 1st ed. 1990; author & co-author of num. pubs. in ped. surg.; Gov., Foundation Childrens Hospital of Eastern Ont., Ottawa; recreations: skiing, golf, music, reading; Club: Royal Ottawa Golf; Home: 210 Buena Vista Rd., Rockcliffe Park, Ont. K1M 0V7.

**MERCIER, Claude Y.,** F.I.I.C.; insurance executive; b. Montréal, Qué. 4 Dec. 1942; s. Arnaud and Cécile (Juneau) M.; e. Fr. McDonald High Sch. Montréal 1961; Fellow, Ins. Inst. Can. 1971; m. Diane d. Guy and Daisy Goudreau 22 Aug. 1964; children: Sylvie, Michèle; PRES. & C.E.O., SEABURY & SMITH INC., New York 1991– ; Chrmn., ENCON Insur. Managers Inc., Ottawa; Dir. ENCON Holdings Inc., Dallas; Victor O. Schinnerer & Co. Inc., Washington, D.C.; Seabury & Smith Inc., NY; The Frizzell Group and Schinnerer & Co. (U.K.) Ltd., London, Eng.; began ins. career 1961; Co-founding Partner ENCON Insur. Managers Inc. 1974, Pres. 1982, Chrmn. 1990; author 'Professional Liability and the Canadian Design Consultant' 1984, reprinted 1986; numerous tech. bulletins ins. & loss prevention for Candn. archs. & engs.; numerous ins. articles various trade publs.; recreations: skiing, squash, cycling; Home: 35 Emery Dr. E., Stamford, Ct. U.S.A. 06902; Office 1166 Avenue of the Americas, New York, N.Y. 10036.

**MERCIER, Denis,** B.A., B.Sc.; telecommunications executive; b. L'Islet, Qué. 15 May 1934; s. Maxime and Géraldine (Coulombe) M.; e. Coll. La Pocatière B.A. 1956; Laval Univ. B.Sc.(EE) 1961; m. Ghislaine d. Alphonse Lamontagne 10 Sept. 1960; children: Louise, Claude, Gilles, Charles; VICE PRES. QUE. NORTHERN TELECOM CANADA LTD. 1988– ; joined Quebec Telephone 1961–81 becoming Vice Pres. Planning & Eng.; joined present Co. 1981 serving as Gen. Mgr., Vice Pres. Operations (Internat.), Vice Pres. Mktg., Vice Pres. Operations Cable Group; Chrmn. Promotion & New Fund Raising Projects Un. Way; mem. Que. Tel Co's Assn. (Past Pres.); Que. Ind. Relation Inst. (Past Chrmn.); Telecommunication Extve. Mgmt. Inst. Can. (Past Chrmn.); Prov. Que. C. of C. (Pres.); recreations: golf, skiing, hunting; Club: Richelieu (Past Pres., Gov.); Home: 458 Jubilee Cres., Beaconsfield, Qué. H9W 5S2; Office: 380 St. Antoine Ouest, 8è étage, Montréal, Qué. H2Y 3Y4.

**MERCIER, Eileen Ann,** M.A., M.B.A.; financial executive; b. Toronto, Ont. 7 July 1947; d. Thomas S. and Frances K. Falconer; e. Waterloo Lutheran Univ., B.A. 1968; Univ. of Alta., M.A. 1969; York Univ., M.B.A. 1976; m. Ernest C. Mercier 8 Feb. 1980; one s. Stuart; SENIOR VICE-PRES. & CHIEF FINAN. OFFR., ABITIBI-PRICE INC. 1990– ; joined The Toronto-Dominion Bank 1972–78; Canwest Capital Corp. 1978–81; Gulf Canada Ltd. 1981–86; The Pagurian Corp. Ltd. 1986–87; Vice-Pres., Corporate Develop., Abitibi-Price Inc. 1987–90; Bd. of Dirs., John Labatt Limited; Candn. Institute of Internat. Affairs; Bd. of Govs., The Toronto Hosp. Found.; Fin. Extve.'s Council Conf. Bd.; Fellow, Inst. Cdn. Bankers; Home: 77 Strathallan Blvd., Toronto, Ont. M5N 1S8; Office: 207 Queen's Quay West, Suite 680, P.O. Box 102, Toronto, Ont. M5J 2P5.

**MERCIER, Ernest,** O.C.; retired agrologist; b. Rosaire (Montmagny), Qué. 1 Mar. 1914; s. Georges and Williamine (Dion) M.; e. Laval Univ., B.A. 1939, B.Sc.Agr. 1943; Cornell Univ., M.S. 1944, Ph.D. 1946; Dale Carnegie & other improvement courses; m. Marcelle d. Joseph and Anna (Leclerc) Normand 6 Oct. 1945; children: Pierre, Alain, Suzanne, Louis, Christine, Charles; CO-FOUNDER & DIR., ARDA INC. (formerly Agrovet Inc.) 1979– ; Public Servant, Govt. of Qué. 1943–50, Govt. of Can. 1950–60, Govt. of Qué. 1960–79; Prof. & Dir., Animal Sciences Dept., Faculty of Agriculture, McGill Univ. 1960; Depy. Min. of Agriculture and Colonization for Québec 1960–66; initiator & administrator of the main policies involving the modernization of Québec agric. 1960–66 & the implemention of Joint Can.-Qué. projects in the fields of rural & agric. devel. at the internat. level 1967–79; Assoc. Mem., 'Le Conseil D'Orientation Économique du Québec' 1961–1966; spec. advr. to CIDA 1972–76; Fellow, Agric. Inst. of Can.; Comdr., l'Ordre du mérite agron. du Qué.; l'Ordre du Mérite agricole du Qué.; l'Ordre équestre du Saint-Sépulcre de Jérusalem; Mem., La Fond. Mgr. de Saint-Vallier; Life Mem.; Candn. Extve. Services Organization (CESO); Officer, Order of Canada 1989; Mem., Canadian Agricultural Hall of Fame Assn. 1991; Mem. of the Quebec Agricultural Hall of Fame Assn. 1992; Founder and Life Pres., L'Association des Mercier D'Amérique du Nord (AMAN); author: 'Le Chemin des Anglais' 1981; 'N.D.-du-Rosaire, étape de l'amitié' 1983; 'Mercier depuis des siècles' 1987 and 3 other titles; Address: 910, ave des Braves, Québec, Qué. G1S 3C6.

**MERCIER, Ernest Cochrane,** B.Sc.; banker; b. Dublin, Ireland 13 Jan. 1933; e. Univ. of Glasgow B.Sc. 1954; m. Eileen Falconer 1980; children: Jenny, Sheelagh, Peter, Michael, Stuart; Extve. Vice Pres. Corporate & Investment Banking Group, The Toronto Dominion Bank 1984; Chrmn., Toronto Dominion Securities Inc.; Dir. Oxford Properties Canada Ltd.; Dir., Art Gallery of Ont.; Club: Toronto Golf; Home: 77 Strathallan Blvd., Toronto, Ont. M5N 1S8.

**MERCIER, François,** O.C. Q.C.; b. Paris, France, 13 April 1923; s. Dr. Oscar and Jeanne (Bruneau) M.; e. (came to Canada in 1927) Loyola Coll., B.A. 1942; Univ. of Montreal, LL.L. 1945; called to the Bar of Que., July 1945; C.R. Q.C. 3 Jan. 1961; m. Lucile, d. Avila Rouleau, Town of Mount Royal, Que., 25 May 1946; children: Genevieve, Jean-Francois, Madeleine, Hélène; PARTNER, STIKEMAN ELLIOTT; Pres., La Libraire Fernand Nathan, Can. Ltée.; Vice Pres., MeridienCan. Ltée.; Dir., Popular Industries Ltd.; Chrmn., The General Accident Assurance Co.; Chrmn. Bd.Trustees, Place des Arts, Montreal 1964–68; National Art Centre, Ottawa, Nov. 1969–77; Chrmn. Bd., Hôtel-Dieu Hospital, Montreal 1976–85; actively engaged in trial law since 1945 (Fleury Hosp. Royal Enquiry 1963; Regina vs. Reader's Digest 1961; Regina vs. Hal C. Banks 1964; Asbestos Corp. vs. Att. Gen. of Que. 1979; Sun Life Assur. Co. of Can. vs. Domglas Inc. 1980; Roger Taillibert vs Régie des Installations Olympiques (R.I.O.) et Ville de Montréal); Lectr. in Ins. Law, Univ. of Montreal 1950–63; mem., Montreal Bar Assn. (Secy. 1954, Dir. 1963–64); Candn. Bar Assn.; Liberal; Catholic; recreations: skiing, gardening; Club: Mount Royal; Home:

1 Spring Grove Crescent, Outremont, Montreal, Que. H2V 3H8; Office: 3900 - 1155 René Levesque Blvd. W., Montreal, Que. H3B 3V2.

**MERCIER, Jean Claude,** M.Sc.; public servant; b. Lévis, Qué. 23 July 1940; s. Roland and Fernande (Aubert) M.; e. Laval Univ., B.Sc. 1961; N.Y. State Coll. of Forestry, M.Sc. 1973; m. Lisette d. Pauline and Armand Carrier 3 July 1965; one d.: Stephanie; SPECIAL ADVISOR, NATURAL RESOURCES CANADA; Forest Eng., Domtar Inc. 1963–70; Economist, Laurentian Forest Res. Ctr., C.F.S. 1970–74; Mgr., Res. Prog. on Forest Resources, L.F.R.C. 1974–75; Dir., Groupe Conseil en Gestion des Forêts 1975–80; Assoc. Dep. Min., Lands & Forestry Sector, Dept. of Energy & Resources, Govt. of Québec 1980–85; Assoc. Dep. Min., (Forestry), Candn. Forestry Serv., Govt. of Canada 1985–88; Deputy Minister, Forestry Canada 1988; Dir., Forintek Corp.; PAPRICAN, FERIC; mem., Candn. Inst. of Forestry; Ordre des Ingénieurs Forestiers du Québec; Quebec Forestry Assoc.; Candn. Pulp and Paper Assoc.; Soc. of Am. Foresters; Inst. of Public Admin. of Canada; Bd. of Dir., Forest History Soc.; Home: 898 Explorer Lane, Ottawa, Ont. K1C 2S2; Office: 580 Booth St., 21st Floor, Ottawa, Ont. K1A 0E4.

**MERCIER, Jean-Jacques;** b. Joliette, Que. 4 Sept. 1918; s. J-Honoré & Atala (Gibeault) M.; e. Jardin de l'Enfance, Montreal; Coll. de l'Assomption, Cours classique; children: Claude, Pierre, Louise, Jean-Honoré, Louis; Founder, La Voix Populaire 1946– ; Reporter for La Presse, Montreal 1941–42; Reporter, Le Devoir, Montreal 1942–44; Head of French Sec., Information Service, Nat. Film Bd., Ottawa 1944; Pub. Relations Offr. for Que. 1945; Co-founder (1954) with Pierre Peladeau and Paul Desormiers, Imprimerie Hebdo Printing (now Quebecor); Life Gov., Centre de Santé Saint–Henri; Prés. 1966–68, Hebdos du Canada, Gouverneur et Membre de l'Ordre des Hebdos du Canada; Union Nationale; Cand. for St. Henry Riding, Que. g.e. 1962 and for La Prairie-Napierville Riding, Que. g.e. 1966, 1970; Union Canadienne des Journ. de Lang. Français; Soc. Hist. de Montréal; Soc. Hist. de Saint-Heuri; Conseil Expansion Econ.; Fed. Candn. Advertising & Sales Club; Assoc. mem., Internat. Conf. of Weekly Newspaper Eds.; mem., Conseil d'administration, Soc pour les Enfants Handicapés du Que.; Cofoundateur et mem., conseil d'administration, La Fondation Yvon Lamarre Inc.; mem., conseil adminstration Hopital Maisonneuve-Rosemont; mem., La Corporation de l'Etincelle; Societé St Jean-Baptiste de Montréal; Mem. Associe, Candn. Wildlife Federation; Pres.-founder, Les Amis du Père Armand Inc.; founder Aide Sociale Anonyme; Assist. to prés. (communications), City of Montreal Extve. Comte. 1979–86; Chevalier de l'Ordre de Cein Clou; K. of C.; awarded Commemorative Medal for 125th Anniversary of Candn. Confederation; Roman Catholic; Clubs: Optimiste St. Paul; Home: 5916 MacDonald Ave., Hampstead, Que. H3X 2X1.

**MERCIER, Jean-Louis;** executive; b. Trois-Rivières, P.Q. 27 Apr. 1934; s. Gustave and Jeanne (Décarie) M.; e. Ecole Supérieure Montcalm; McGill Univ.; m. Diane, d. Fernand and Alice Morrissette, June 1961; children: Guy; Eric; Chrmn. & C.E.O., Imperial Tobacco Ltd. 1985–92; joined present firm responsible for mktg. acct. 1961; then profit planning; Comptroller profit planning; Vice-Pres. Finance and Comptroller 1970; Extve. Vice-Pres. 1976; Pres. & C.E.O. 1979; Vice-Chrmn., Imasco 1988; mem. Candn. Industrial Mgmt. Assn.; Candn. Mfrs.' Assn.; named Tobacco Man of the Year (1982) by Nat. Assn. Tobacco and Confectionery Distributors (NATCD); recreations: reading; swimming; skiing.

**MERCIER, Laurent;** agricultural executive, farmer; b. St-Roch de l'Achigan, Que. 9 March 1928; s. Joseph Télesphore and Louise Marie (Renaud) M.; e. Cécile d. Hildère and Honorine Brouillette 9 Sept. 1954; children: Claude, Martine, Richard, Nathalie, Laurent, Jean-François; VICE-CHAIRMAN, NATIONAL FARM PRODUCTS COUNCIL 1992– ; family farm includes 500,000 kg broiler chicken, 9,000-tap maple sugar bush and 100-hectares prod. cereal crops; Chair, Syndicat des prod. de volailles, Dist. de Lanaudière 1969–90; Extve. Mem., Féd. des prod. de volailles du Qué. 1969–89; Chair 1976–89; Extve. Mem., Union des prod. agricoles (Que.) 1977–81; Chair, Candn. Chicken Marketing Agency 1989–91; Mem., Com. aviseur du com. de médiation de la prod. laitière au Qué. 1991; Mem., Nat. Poultry Task Force 1990; Dir., Caisse Populaire, St-Esprit, Que. (14 years); Chair, Soc. d'agric. du Qué., Region 10 (2 years); recipient, Prix du développement économique Raoûl Charette, Société nationale des Québecois de Lanaudière 1993; recreations: swimming, cross-country skiing; Home: 189, Rang Montcalm, St-Esprit, Qué. J0K 2L0; Office: 270 Albert St., 13th floor, P.O. Box 3430, Stn. D, Ottawa, Ont. K1P 6L4.

**MERCIER, The Hon. Pierre,** B.A.; judge; b. Ottawa, Ont. 18 Dec. 1927; s. Raoul and Jeanne (Gauthier) M.; e. Univ. d'Ottawa H.S. 1945; Univ. d'Ottawa, B.A. 1949; Osgoode Hall Law Sch. 1953; m. late Lucienne d. Arthur and Gratia Bissonnette 29 May 1954; children: Paul, Adèle, Lise, Louis; JUDGE, ONT. COURT OF JUSTICE (GENERAL DIVISION) 1990– ; Séguin & Mercier 1954–1960; Vincent, Addy, Mercier & Sirois 1960–64; Paris Mercier Sirois 1964–82; Dir., 'Le Droit' 1975–82; Judge, Dist. Court of Ont. & Local Judge, High Court of Ont. 1982–90; Comnr., Nat. Capital Comn. 1977–78; Dir. & Legal Advr., La Féd. des Assns. de Parents-Inst. de Langue Fran. d'Ont.; Trustee, Ottawa Roman Catholic Sep. Sch. Bd. 1963–72 (Chrmn. 1965–67, 1969–70, 1972; Delegate, Ont. Trustees Counc. 1965); Ottawa Gen. Hosp. 1977–78, 1979; Elizabeth Bruyère Health Ctr. 1980–81; Gov. & Founding Mem., Samuel Genest S.S. of Ottawa; Mem., Co. of Carleton Law Assn.; Candn. Bar Assn.; l'Assn. des Juristes d'Expression Fran. de l'Ont.; Ont. Dist. Court Judges Assn.; Candn. Judges Conf.; Award of Merit, Ont. Sep. Sch. Trustees Assn. 1973; Man of the Year, La Jeune C. of C. d'Ottawa-Vanier 1966; Past Pres., Richelieu Club of Vanier; Internat. Richelieu Soc.; Ligue d'Action Civique d'Ottawa; Lower Town East Ratepayers Assn.; Past Dir., Assn. Candn.-Fran. d'Ont.; recreations: golf; Club: Rivermead Golf (Past Pres.); Home: 781 Mooney Bay Place, Ottawa, Ont. K1V 9X1; Office: 161 Elgin St. 6th Fl., Ottawa, Ont. K2P 2K1.

**MERCREDI, Ovide;** Assembly of First Nations National Chief, lawyer, politician; b. Grand Rapids, Manitoba 1946; s. George and Louise M.; e. Univ. of Manitoba LL.B. 1977; m. Shelley Buhay; four children; NATIONAL CHIEF, ASSEMBLY OF FIRST NATIONS 1991– ; main message to Canada: 'Aboriginal people, as the land's original inhabitants, have inherent rights to self-government'; involved in Crees of Northern Quebec movement to stop the Great Whale hydroelectric project; Co-author (with Mary Ellen Turpel) 'In the Rapids: Navigating the Future of First Nations' 1993; Former Labourer, Manitoba Hydro; Past Mem., Manitoba Human Rights Comn.; Former Vice-Chief, Assembly of First Nations; languages: Cree, English; has earned the privilege of wearing a Cree headdress made of the tail feathers of the bald eagle; Roman Catholic; deeply devoted to native spirituality; Home: 596 Brookridge Cres., Orleans, Ont. K4A 1Z4; Office: 5th Floor, 55 Murray St., Ottawa, Ont. K1N 5M3.

**MERCURE, Monique,** C.C., B.Mus.; actress; b. Montreal, Que. 14 Nov. 1930; d. Eugene and Yvonne (Williams) Emond; e. l'Ecole Superieure de Musique d'Outrement (Vincent d'Indy) B.Mus. 1949; Ecole Jacques Le Coq, Paris; Montreal Drama Studio 1958–60; m. Pierre s. L.P. and Eva M. (Dupré) Mercure Sept. 1949; children: Michèle, Daniel, Christian; principal theatre roles incl. Gherda 'Le Pelican' 1959, Rosa Gonzales 'Summer and Smoke' 1960, the aunt 'Une Femme Douce' 1960, Sybilla 'Magie Rouge' 1961, Ernestine 'Les Maxibules' 1964, all at Theatre de l'Egregore; Polly 'Opera de 4 sous' 1961 Theatre du Nouveau Monde (T.N.M.); Helena 'La Paix du Dimanche' 1962 Comedie Canadienne and Prairie Theatre; Claire 'The Maids' La Poudriere 1964; Marguerite 'Un Simple Soldat' 1967, 1968 La Nouvelle Compagnie Théâtrale (N.C.T.); Dona Isabelle 'Le Soulier de Satin' 1967 T.N.M.; widow Begbick 'Man for Man' 1968 T.N.M., Man. Theatre 1970; Eurydice 'Orphee' Nat. Arts Centre Ottawa 1969, Stratford Festival 1975; Andromaque 'The Trojan Women' N.C.T. 1970; Rose Ouimet 'Les Belles Soeurs' Rideau Vert 1971, Place des Arts and in Paris 1973, T.N.M. 1974, Toronto 1973, CBC TV; Anne 'Quatre a Quatre' Theatre de Quatre Sous 1973; Esther Solomon 'Equus' T.N.M. 1976; Lady U 'Le Pere Humilie' T.N.M. 1976; Madame Irma 'Le Balcon' T.N.M. 1977; Marie Lou 'For Ever Yours Marie Lou' Lennoxville 1977; solo performance after 'Le Journal d'un Fou, Patriote 1975; performed 'Le pays du Dragon' and 'Toi et tes nuages' 1972 Theatre de Quatre Sous; 'Total Eclipse' and 'The Maids' 1972, 1975 Centaur; participated opening 'Les Richesses Naturelles' Theatre Nat. de Strasbourg 1974; recent performances incl. 'The Saga of the Wet Hens' Tarragon Theatre and 'Memoir' (Sarah Bernhardt) Free Theatre, Toronto; 'Night of the Iguana' Alliance Theatre, Atlanta; televised theatre prodns. incl. 'Le Dialogue des Carmelites' 1956; 'La Cellule' 1969; 'Quand nous serons heureux' 1968; 'Le Paradis Perdu' 1969; 'Napoleon Unique' 1972; 'Chin Chin' 1977; 'Coup de Sang' 1977 and recently 'Monsieur le Ministre'; performed in over 20 films incl. 'Felix Leclerc Troubadour,' 'Ce n'est pas le temps des romans' (Prix de la critique Tours Festival), 'Mon Oncle Antoine,' 'J.A. Martin Photographe' (Cannes Festival Golden Palm for Best Actress, Candn. Film Etrog Award), 'The Third Walker, 'La Chanson de Roland,' 'Quintet,' 'La quarantaine,' 'The Naked Lunch,' 'Montréal vu par...,' 'Dans le ventre du dragon,' Nat. Film Bd.; invited lectr. l'Ecole Nationale de Theatre 1978, 1980, 1983 (Dir. since 1981); Dir. Gen., National Theatre Sch. of Canada since 1991; apptd. Companion, Order of Canada 1993; recipient, Governor General Award for Performing Arts 1993; Québec's Denise-Pelletier Award for Performing Arts 1993; TNM's Gascon-Roux Award for Best Actor 1993; Address: 1, 440 Bonsecours, Montreal, Que. H2Y 3C4.

**MEREDITH, Griffith Thomas;** farmer, agricultural executive; b. Ellesmere Port, England 9 March 1932; s. Griffith Thomas and Gladys May (Parker) M.; e. primary & high school Ellesmere Port, Cheshire; Cheshire School of Agriculture; m. Valerie d. Florence and Joseph Jinks 22 Feb. 1956; children: Griffith Thomas, Stanley Paul, Richard John, Rosemary Florence May, Valerie Jane; CHAIRMAN, CANADIAN LIVESTOCK FEED BOARD; farmed in Herefordshire, England 1956–69; moved to N.S. 1969 and has farmed there since; Meredith Farms consists of over 2000 acres (incl. woodland) and produces hogs, cattle, carrots, grain, cabbage, sweet corn, cauliflower & broccoli; Chrmn., Farm Credit Corp. Appeal Bd. for N.S.; Sec.-Treas., Cobequid Grain Centre; Pres., Candn. Pork Council 1977–82; Chrmn., N.S. Hog Marketing Bd. 1979–81; Chrmn., Adv. Ctte., Livestock Feed Board 1985–87; Mem., Livestock Feed Bd. of Can. 1987– ; Mem., Italian Wine Soc.; German Wine Soc.; recreations: wine tasting, bird watching; Home: R.R. #1, Great Village, N.S. B0M 1L0; Office; 5180 Queen Mary Rd., Room 400, Montreal, Que. H3W 3E7.

**MEREDITH, Harry A.,** B.A.; management consultant; b. Toronto, Ont. 26 March 1931; s. late Allen Osler and Jean Grahame (Wright) M.; e. Univ. of Toronto, B.A. 1953; m. Marie (Mimi), d. late Charles-Auguste Drouin; 5 children: DIRECTOR HUMAN RESOURCES, DELOITTE TOUCHE TOKMATSU INTERNATIONAL; retired partner, Samson Bélair Deloitte & Touche; served Dept. Citzenship and Immigration Winnipeg and Ottawa; became Partner present firm 1969; on loan to fed. govt. through Extve. Interchange Program (Treas. Bd., Ministry of Sol. Gen.) 1972–74; participated in Royal Comm. Govt. Org. (Glassco), Royal Comm. Gov't Admin (Sask.), Operation Productivity (Man.), Etude des rouages administratifs (Que.), Comte. on Govt. Productivity (Ont.), Royal Comm. on Financial Mgmt. & Accountability (Lambert); mem. Inst. Mgmt. Consultants (Que.); Candn. Inst. Pub. Adm.; Clubs: Rideau; Royal Ottawa Golf; Home: 34 Chemin Beakie, Ste Anne des Lacs, Que. J0R 1B0; Office: 90 Sparks St., Ottawa, Ont. K1P 5B4.

**MEREDITH, Lindsay Norman,** B.A., M.A., Ph.D.; university professor; b. Vancouver, B.C. 15 June 1947; s. Norman James and Anne Catherine (Prechtl) M.; e. Simon Fraser Univ. B.A. 1969, M.A. 1974, Ph.D. 1981; m. Susan d. Carl and Helen McKay 25 Aug. 1978; PROF., DIRECTOR OF GRADUATE PROGRAMS, FAC. OF BUSINESS ADMIN., SIMON FRASER UNIV. 1981– ; Management, Simpson Sears 1969; Lumber Trader & Sales Analyst, Weldwood of Canada & Cariboo Pulp & Paper 1970–73; Prof., Memorial Univ. of Nfld. 1978; President's Task Force, Simon Fraser Univ. 1989; Dir., Graduate Prog., Fac. of Bus. Admin. 1992; Program Advisor & Lecturer, Inst. of Candn. Bankers Fellowship Program; Adv. Mem., Min. of State for Small Business; 25 years consultancy to major multinat. corps. & all levels of govt. incl. Sr. Fed. Govt. Staff; over 130 interviews using all media since 1991; Program Chair, 32nd Annual World Conf. of the Internat. Council of Small Business; Co-Chair, Macromarketing Conf. UBC 1985; Committee Chair, Eagle Ridge Hosp. Foundation; editorial reviewer for 11 journals incl. 'J. of Mktg.' & 'Rev. of Econ. & Statistics'; textbook reviewer for 3 pubs.; co-author: 'International Business Marketing' 1993; co-editor: 'The Spirit of Entrepreneurship' 1987; author of num. cases currently used in N. Am. univ. textbooks; author of num. marketing & economics journal articles; recreations: skiing, biking, squash, hiking; Home: 973 Seaforth Way, Port Moody, B.C. V3H 3T6; Office: Simon Fraser Univ., Fac. of Business Admin., Burnaby, B.C. V5A 1S6.

**MERGLER, Donna,** B.Sc., Ph.D.; professeure; née. Montréal, Qué. 7 June 1944; f. Bernard S. and Rose (Helfield) M.; é. McGill Univ. B.Sc. 1965, Ph.D. 1973; enfants: Genevieve, Sébastien; PROFESSEURE DE PHYSIOLOGIE, DEP. DES SCI. BIOL., UNIV. DU QUEBEC A MONTREAL 1980– ; Prof. de biol., Westbury College 1967–68; Prof. de physiol., CEGEP de

Maisonneuve 1968–70; Univ. du Qué. à Montréal 1970– ; Dir. du dép. des sci. biol. 1982–84; Co-dir. du Groupe de rech.-action en biol. du travail 1985– ; Dir. 1990– ; Dir. intérimaire du Centre pour l'étude des interactions biologiques 1990–91; mem., com. sci., l'assn. internat. de neurotoxicol. 1991– ; Comn. internat. en santé au travail 1990– ; com. neurotocicol & psychophys., ICOH 1991– ; Dir. du Doctorate en sci. de l'environ. 1993– ; Visiting Scholar: Univ. of Calif. at Berkeley; N. Calif. Occupational Health Ctr. 1987–88; mem., Am. Public Health Assn.; Internat. Neurotox. Assn.; Assn. can.-française pour l'avancement des sci.; Internat. Epidemiology Assn.; Soc. can. de toxicologie; Internat. Comn. on Occupational Health; nombreux prix, distinctions et nominations: Elue femme de l'année en Environ., Salon de la Femme 1991, Prix Muriel Duckworth 1990, mem. com. d'experts, Min. des affaires soc. 1989– ; mem. Conseil d'admin. de l'Inst. de rech. appliqueée sur le travail 1988– etc.; auteur/co-auteur de nombreux articles, comptes rendus de confs. publies in extenso, chapitres de livres, monographies, articles sollicités, confs. avec résumés publiés, posters, conf. invitée, et rapports' récipient de nombreaux subventions; bureau: Montréal, Qué. H3C 3P8.

**MEROLA, Mario,** R.C.A.; sculptor; educator; b. Montreal, Que. 31 March 1931; s. Nicola and Octavie (Filteau) M.; e. Ecole des Beaux-Arts Montréal 1946–52; Ecole Supérieure des Arts Décoratifs Paris 1952–53; m. Nicole Goyette 5 Aug. 1961; children: Caroline, Colette, Eleonora, Domenica, Nicola; PROF D'ART, UNIV. DU QUE. 1969– ; Prof., Ecole des Beaux Arts Montréal 1960–69; Founding Dir. Le Module Arts d'Environnement Univ. du Qué. 1969–70, Dir. Module Arts Plastiques 1973–74; has created over 100 sculptures and murals integrated to arch. environment since 1951; rep. in over 150 solo and group exhns. Montreal, Ottawa, New York, Paris, Brussels, Brest, Osaka, Vancouver, Milan; recent solo exhbns.: Galerie Uqam 1984; Grand Théatre de Qué. 1985; Galerie D'Art Contemporain, Montréal 1989; Muvezsetek haza Pècs, Hungary 1991; Ady Andre Gimnazium, Nagyatad, Hungary 1992; rep. in pub., corporate and private colls. incl. Nat. Gallery Can., Montreal Museum of Fine Arts, Musée du Qué., Musée D'Art Contemporain, Can. Council Art Bank, Musée de Brest (France), Won Kwang Univ. (South Korea), City of Cortina d'Ampezzo (Italy), The Nagyatàd Sculpture Symposium (Hungary) 1989; recipient First Prize mural Hôtel de LaSalle Montreal 1951; French Govt. Grant 1952; First Prize mural Candn. Pavillion Brussels Internat. Exhn. 1957; Can. Council Grant 1963, 1968; 5 Hon. Mentions Montreal 'Monuments-Fontaine Contest' 1965; Ministère des Affaires Culturelles du Qué. Grant 1972; First Prize several murals Institut d'Hôtellerie 1973, mural CEGEP du vieux Montréal 1975; Pierrefonds mural exhibited Milan Biennal 1968; First Prize Sculpture, Recontre Internat. de Sculpture Saint-Jean-Port-Joli 1984; Pres., Soc.des Artistes Prof. du Qué. 1967–68; Assn. des Sculpteurs du Qué. 1971–72; Hon. citizen, City of Iri, South Korea; bibliographies written by J. De Roussan, Lidec 1970, L.Letocha, Formart 1972 and A. Metchnikov, Fini-Infini 1992; R. Catholic; Home: 216 rue Somerville, Montréal, Qué. H3L 1A3; Office: Univ. Du Qué. Dept. Art Plastique, C.P. 8888, Succ. A, Montréal, Qué. H3C 3P8.

**MERREDEW, His Honour Charles Russell,** LL.B.; judge; b. Kenora, Ont. 15 June 1932; s. Charles Read and Elsie Elizabeth (Russell) M.; e. Royal Roads, Candn. Serv. Coll.; Univ. of Man. Law Sch.; m. Elva d. Herman and Irene Remus 2 Aug. 1958; children: Charles, Mark, Maria, Paul; JUDGE, ONT. PROV. COURT 1977– ; Office of the Judge Advocate Gen., Candn. Forces 1956–60; Private practice, Pembroke, Ont. and Deep River, Ont. 1960–77; Home: R.R. 7, Pembroke, Ont.; Office: 415 Pembroke St. W., Pembroke, Ont. K8A 6X3.

**MERRENS, H. Roy,** B.A., M.A., Ph.D.; university professor; b. Salford, England 21 July 1931; s. Alec and Dora (Nachman) M.; e. Univ. Coll. London, B.A. (Hons.) 1954; Univ. of Maryland, M.A. 1957; Univ. of Wisconsin, Ph.D. 1962; m. Colleen d. Al and Eileen Kelly 1 Aug. 1985; PROF., DEPT. OF GEOGRAPHY, YORK UNIV. 1968– ; Instr., Rutgers Univ. 1960–61; Univ. of Wisc. 1961–62; Asst. Prof., Calif. State Univ. 1962–65; Assoc. Prof. 1967–68; Vis. Lectr., Univ. of Wisc. 1965–66; Bd. Mem. (Chrmn. 1 yr.), Toronto Harbour Comn. 1973–78; Adv. Bd. & Corr. Ed., Waterfront Ctr. (Washington DC) 1981– ; Dir., Can. Ports Project, York Univ./Univ. of Toronto Joint Prog. in Transp. 1978–80; Fulbright Travel Award 1955–57; Guggenheim Fellowship 1966–67; Fac. of Arts Fellowship 1978–79; Medal of Service, City of Toronto 1980; Rsch. Fellowship, Inst. of Southern Studies, Univ. of S. Carolina 1981–82; var. publishing awards; past extve. mem. of num. socs.; author: 'Colonial North Carolina in the Eighteenth Century' 1964, 'Regions of the United States' 1970, 'Urban Waterfront Redevelopment in North America' 1980 & many articles; editor: 'The Colonial South Carolina Scene' 1977, York Univ., Dept. of Geog., Discussion Paper series 1974–85; recreation: running; Office: York Univ., North York, Ont. M3J 1P3.

**MERRIAM, Thomas G.,** B.Comm.; public servant; b. Parrsboro, N.S. 11 Feb. 1948; s. Donald St. Clair and Evelyn Mary (Thorne) M.; e. Saint Mary's Univ. B.Comm. 1974; m. Barbara d. Joseph and Elizabeth Morrow 26 July 1969; one d.: Courtney Allison; Dep. Min., Dept. of Economic Development, Govt. of N.S. 1987; Mktg., N.S. Power Comn. 1969–71; Econ. Devel. Profl., Indus. Estates Limited 1971–83; Indus. Devel., N.S. Dept. of Devel. 1983–87; Dir., Halifax-Dartmouth Indus. Limited; N.S. Rsch. Found. Corp.; Cert. Econ. Devel., designated by Econ. Devel. Assn. of Can.; Clubs: World Trade Ctr., Halifax Bd. of Trade; Home: 26 Mountain Ash Ct., Dartmouth, N.S. B2Y 4J8.

**MERRICK, Paul M.,** B.Arch., FRAIC, MAIBC, RCA; architect; b. Vancouver, B.C. 20 Nov. 1938; s. Charles James and Charlotte Marjorie (Roberts) M., Elizabeth Emilyne Copeland, step-mother; e. W. Vancouver H.S. 1956; Univ. of B.C., B.Arch. 1964; divorced; children: Natasha, Kim, Nika, Maya, Nathaniel; PRINCIPAL, PAUL MERRICK ARCHITECTS LIMITED 1984– ; R.J. Thom, Toronto 1966–69; Thompson Berwick Pratt & Partners 1969–1979 (Chrmn. 1976–79); Dir. of Arch., Project Planning Internat. Ltd. (UK) 1976–79; Partner, Merrick Chandler Kennedy Arch. Group 1979–84; Past lectr. & design tutorial mentor, Sch. of Arch., Univ. of B.C.; elected Royal Candn. Acad. of Arts 1978; Fellow, Royal Arch. Inst. of Can. 1989; Bd. Mem., Candn. Craft Mus.; Downtown Vancouver Assn.; principle representative projects: Trent Univ.: Sciences, Bridge, Library; Vancouver: CBC consolidation; Orpheum Theatre, False Creek redevel.; Saudi Arabia: King Abdulaziz Univ.; Calgary: Mount Royal Coll. expansion; Vancouver: The Village of Port Moody, Riverway Golf Course, Westwood Village, City Square, Tudor Manor, Marine Bldg. restoration, Cathedral Place, Westwood 9-Hole Golf Club, The Victoria, Bridgeview Place, Canadian Craft Museum; Victoria: St. Ann's Academy, Sussex Place, The Victoria Accord; recreations: sailing, yacht design; Office: One Gaolers Mews, Vancouver, B.C. V6B 4K7.

**MERRIL, Judith;** writer; anthologist; broadcaster; b. New York City, N.Y. 21 Jan. 1923; d. Samuel Solomon and Ethel (Hurwich) Grossman; e. City Coll. of New York 1939–40; Rochdale Coll. Toronto 1968–71; children: Merril Allen, Ann Pohl; Work-in-progress: 'Better to Have Loved' a volume of memoirs; author (novels) 'Shadow on the Hearth' 1950; 'The Tomorrow People' 1960; (short story colls.) 'The Best of Judith Merril' 1976; 'Daughters of Earth' 1969; 'Out of Bounds' 1963; 'Survival Ship' 1977; 'Daughters of Earth and other Stories' 1985; co-author (novels) 'Gunner Cade' 1952; 'Outpost Mars' 1952; ed. (anthols.) 'SF: The Year's Greatest Science Fiction and Fantasy' vols. 1–12, 1956–68; 'SF: The Best of the Best' 1967; 'Shot in the Dark' 1950; 'Beyond Human Ken' 1952; 'Beyond the Barriers of Space and Time' 1954; 'Human?' 1954; 'Galaxy of Ghouls' 1955; 'England Swings SF' 1968; 'Tesseracts' 1985; various radio and TV documentaries, commentaries incl. 108 mini-documentaries for TV Ont. 'Doctor Who' and radio-documentaries for CBC 'Ideas'; Founder and Resource Person, The Merril Collection of Science Fiction, Speculation and Fantasy; cross Can. lectr. since 1968; teacher, Rochdale Coll., Univ. of Toronto, SEED Sch., Wesleyan Univ., Trent Univ., First Annual Candn. Sci. Fiction Writers' Workshop; Writer-in-Residence, Centennial Coll.; Writer-in-Residence, Toronto Public Libraries 1987; Brampton Pub. Libs. 1989; University of Toronto 1991–92; mem. ed. bd. The Proceedings of the Inst. of Twenty-first Century Studies (PITFCS); Dir. Stafford Beer Found.; recipient 4th Annual Candn. Sci. Fiction & Fantasy Award 1983; CASPER Award (Eng. Can.) 1986; 1990 Milford Award for Lifetime Achievement in Science Fiction and Fantasy Editing; mem. Writers Union Can.; ACTRA; PEN; World SF; SF Canada; The Council of Canadians; recreations: conversation, reading, jazz, reggae, dancing, water sports, grandchildren; Office: 40 St. George St., Toronto, Ont. M5S 2E4.

**MERRITHEW, Hon. Gerald S.,** P.C., M.P.; retired politician; educator; b. Saint John, N.B. 23 Sept. 1931; e. Rothesay Consol. Sch., Grad., Teacher's Coll., Fredericton; B.A., B.Ed. Univ. of N.B.; m. Gloria (Bobbie) McLean; six children; el. to Saint John City Council 1971; resigned following el. to N.B. Leg. as M.L.A. for East Saint John, Dec. 1972; re-el. 1974, 1978, 1982; Min. of Education 1974–76; Min. of Comm. and Development 1976–82; apptd. Min. of Nat. Resources, responsible for Energy Policy, Nov. 1982; Govt. House Leader for 6 yrs.; el. to H. of C. in g. e. of 1984; Min. of State (Forestry) 1984–88, (Forestry & Mines) 1986–88; Minister of Veterans Affairs 1988–93; retired from political life Oct. 1993; a sch. teacher and principal for over 25 years in Saint John area; former Pres., Saint John Teachers' Assn.; el to Candn. Coll. of Teachers 1962; served in Candn. Army Mil. 16 yrs. attaining rank Lt.-Col.; former C.O., Royal N.B. Regt.; Former Hon. Lt. Col., First Battalion, Royal N.B. Regt. 1977–87; recipient, Medal of Honour, National Council of Veterans Assn.; Nat. Past Pres. (Past Pres. N.B. Br.) Candn. Inf. Assn.; Dir. Army Cadet League N.B.; Mem., Royal Candn. Legion, Jervis Bay Meml. Br. #53; Hon. Vice Pres. Red Cross Youth Adv. Bd.; Dir. United Fund; charter mem., Social Services Council of Saint John; Hon. Vice Pres., N.B. Rifle Assn.; Life Mem., Army Cadet League of Canada (New Brunswick); Hon. Life Mem., Army, Navy & Air Force Veterans in Canada; Hon. Mem., Royal Marine Command Assn. (Canada); 1st Hon. Pres., and Life Mem., Korea Veterans Assn. of Canada; Hon. Life Mem., Hong Kong Veterans Assn. of Canada; Hon. Patron, Black Powder Assoc.; Past Pres., Depy. District Gov., Lions; Home: R.R. 1, Norton, N.B. E0G 2N0.

**MERTA de VELEHRAD, Jan;** B.Sc., Ph.D., D.G., FIBA, psychologist; artist; reverend; scientist; diving systems and production engineer; accredited safety and marine auditor; safety offr.; civil servant; international lecturer; b. (Stare Mesto), Czechoslovakia 24 Apr. 1944; s. Jan and Marie (Sebkova) Merta; brother of Marta; e. Tech. Trade Sch. (Slusovice), Trade Dip. 1962; Coll. of Social Law (Prague), 1964–68; McGill Univ., (Montréal) B.Sc. 1971; Univ. of Aberdeen (Scotland), Ph.D. (expr. psych.) 1978; Univ. of Edinburgh (Scotland), Cert. Stylometrics 1984; Carleton Univ. (Ottawa) Fire Eng. Course 1985; Internat. Loss Control Inst. (Atlanta, USA), Diplomas in Risk Management and Safety Auditing 1992; Advanced Loss Control; Modern Safety Mgmnt. 1993; m. Margaret; one d. Iveta; CHIEF INSPR. OF DIVING, GOVT. OF CAN. 1981– ; army service 1962–64; Publisher & Ed.-in-Chief Sign and Market Place mags. 1972–74; co. pres., guest lectr., deep sea diver and diving supvr. offshore oil platforms N. Sea, Middle E., Africa and N. Am. 1974–78; Dir. of R and D maj. diving co's UK, Kuwait and Am. 1978–81; Project Mgr. over 24 R and D projects, investig. Ocean Ranger Oil Rig disaster 1982; provided diving expertise maj. deep sea diving & salvage operations incl. gold recovery from H.M.S. Edinburgh 1981, salvage Ocean Ranger 1984, M.V. Trans Pac 1987, Piper Alpha 1988, Captain K 1990, and Nadine 1991; as scientist participated in a majority of ULTRA-DEEP diving exper. progs. conducted during the past 20 yrs. incl. record dives to 1600 feet, Univ. of Pa. 1976; to 2250 feet, Duke Univ. 1982 (world record); Diplomate certified in speciality of Hyperbaric Medicine (USA) 1989; holds two Brit. patents, various patents pending; recipient H.S.H. Prince of Armavir, Duke of Melk, Captain, Legion de 'L Aigle de Mer 1985; Chevalier and Baron, Ordre Royal de la Couronne de Boheme 1986; Knight Commander of Lofsensic Ursunius Order (Germany) 1993; Special Merit Award Candn. Diving Ind. 1985; Commemorative Medal of Honour (USA) 1988; Medallon de L'Etoile Celeste (Holland) 1989; Noble Order of Gran Cruz de Justicia (Spain) 1991; Order of Knights Templars of Jerusalem 1993; Internat. Leadership Hall of Fame (USA) 1988; International Cultural Diploma of Honour (UK) 1989; World Biographical Hall of Fame (USA) 1989; The International Hall of Leaders (USA) 1988; Certificate of Merit for distinguished service to community (UK) 1988; Charter recipient of The '20th Century Award of Achievement' (UK) 1992; Am. Biographical Inst. 'Man of the Year' 1990 and 'The Most Admired Man of the Decade' 1992; 'International Man of the Year' (UK) 1991; 'One in a Million' (UK) 1992; 'World Intellectual' 1993; Internat. Biographical Centre (U.K.); nominated for 'Frank Dearman Award of Merit' (UK) 1991; Galletti Memorial Award (USA) 1993; 'Lifetime Achievement Academy' (USA) 1991 and as 'The Most Accomplished Man' The Guinness Book of World Records (UK) 1992; apptd. pursuivant Flanders-at-Arms Spanish Heraldic Soc. 1990; Dragon Vert Pursuivant, State College of Arms (Albania) 1992; Plaque of Distinction as well as Roll of Honor Plaque 1989; Internat. Hall of Leaders 1988; Silver Shield of Valor (USA) 1992; listed in: Internat. Who's Who of Intellectuals; Man of Achievement; Who's Who in the World; The Internat. Directory of Distinguished Leadership; The Five Hundred Leaders of Influence; Dictionary of Internat. Biography; 5000 Personalities of the World; Internat. Registry of Profiles; Book of Dedications; The First Five-Hundred; Who is Who in Internat. Hyperbaric Medicine; Who's Who in Science and Engineering; Internat. Book of Honor; Internat. Leaders of Achievement; Hon. appt. Adv. Ctte. Seneca Coll. 1983; Chrmn. Candn. Standard Bd. Ctte. Survival Suits 1983– ; Chrmn. Candn. Assn. Ctte. on Diving competency 1993– ; Depy. Gov., Am. Biographical Inst. 1988– ; Hon. mem., Adv. Council Internat. Biographical Centre (U.K.) 1990; first Hon. Life mem., Candn. Assn. Diving Contractors 1993; Bd. Adv., Stroke Centre, Fort Lauderdale 1990; mem. of Bd., Medical Technologies Management (Florida) 1990; Vice-Pres., Institute of Mentalphysics (California) 1994; Vice-Pres., Internat. Soc. of Hyperbaric Medicine (Switzerland) 1990; Senator and Mem. of High Chamber, Internat. Parliament for Safety and Peace (Palermo) 1990; ordained as Preceptor and Church Minister-at-Large (USA) 1993; co-author: 'Exploring the Human Aura' 1976; 'Candn. Oil and Gas Diving Regulations' 1988; and 14 National Safety and Technical Standards; author various news articles and tech. papers; interviewed numerous internat. TV and Radio shows, cited various books, mags. & news articles; guest speaker internat. symposiums, confs. & seminars; Founder Fellow, Inst. Diagnostic Engrs. (UK) 1981; Fellow, Inst. Petrol. (Scot.) 1981; Fellow, Inst. Intern. Biographic Assn. (UK) 1988; Founder, Candn. Soc. Psychic Rsch. 1973; Candn. Assn. Diving Contractors 1982; Chrmn. Czechoslovak Assn. Can. Ottawa Br. 1986–91; Founder and Chief Spokesman, Internat. Movement Let's Help Democracy in Eastern Europe 1990, Co-founder and Extve. Ctte. Mem. for International Day of Democracy 1990; Assoc., Inst. Mech. Engrs. (UK) 1982; Inst. Marine Engrs. (UK) 1988; Mem., Undersea Med. Soc. (USA) 1978; Am. College of Hyperbaric Medicine 1989; Dinshah Health Soc. (USA) 1992; Inst. Patents & Patentees (UK) 1981; Ancient Astronaut Soc. (USA) 1982; Candn. Standards Assn. 1982; Brit. Psychol. Soc. 1983; Soc. Fire Protection Engrs. (Can.) 1985; Marine Tech. Soc. (USA) 1989; Internat. Inst. of Accredited Safety Auditors (USA) 1992; Soc. of Petroleum Engrs. (USA) 1992; Inst. Marine Safety Auditors (Can.) 1992; Professional Inst. of Public Service of Can. 1993; recreations: book collecting, lit. investig., music, film making; Home: Box 22244, Bankers Hall, Calgary, Alta. T2P 4J6; Office: National Energy Board, 311–6th Avenue S.W., Calgary, Alta. T2P 3H2.

**MES, Hans Johannes Antoine François,** B.Sc., Ph.D.; physicist; b. Eindhoven, Netherlands 1 July 1944; s. John J.J.A.F. and Margaret (van Dinther) M.; e. Univ. of Ottawa H.S. 1960; Univ. of Ottawa, B.Sc. (summa cum laude) 1965, Ph.D. 1968; m. Lynne d. Harry and Germaine Crouch 6 Aug. 1966; children: Ian, Derek; DIR., CENTRE FOR RSCH. IN PARTICLE PHYSICS 1990– ; post-doct. fellow, Inst. de Physique Theorique, Univ. de Geneve 1968–69; Dept. of Physics, Carleton Univ. 1969–70; Profl. Assoc. & Instr. 1970–71; Profl. Assoc. & Sess. Lectr. 1971–72; Rsch. Assoc. 1972–73; Asst. Rsch. Offr., Nat. Rsch. Counc. 1973–77; Assoc. Rsch. Offr. 1977–82; Sr. Rsch. Offr., 1982–91; Adjunct Prof., Carleton Univ. 1985– ; Univ. of Ottawa 1986–92; recipient of num. fellowships, bursaries, scholarships & acad. awards; author/co-author several sci. jour. articles; Address: CRPP, Carleton Univ., Hertzberg Bldg., Rm 216, 1125 Colonel By Drive, Ottawa, Ont. K1S 5B6.

**MESLEY, Wendy,** B.A.A.; journalist; b. Montreal, Que. 4 July 1957; d. Gordon and Joan (Pearson) M.; e. Ryerson Polytechnical Inst. B.A.A. 1979; HOST, 'SUNDAY REPORT,' CBC-TV 1992– ; Reporter, CFRB, CKFM, CHIN Radio Toronto 1976–79; CFCF-TV Montreal 1979; Co-Host, 'As It Is,' CFCF-TV 1980; Quebec Correspondent, CFTO-TV 1981; Reporter, CBC-TV 1982; Quebec National Assembly Correspondent 1983; Parliamentary & National Affairs Correspondent for 'The National' 1986; recreations: skiing, windsurfing; Office: Box 500, Station A, Toronto, Ont. M5W 1E6.

**MESSING, Karen,** B.A., M.Sc., Ph.D.; researcher in genetics and occupational health; b. Springfield, Mass. 2 Feb. 1943; d. Edgar and Pauline (Stiriss) M.; e. Harvard Univ. B.A. 1963; McGill Univ. M.Sc. 1970, Ph.D. 1975; children: Daood and Mikail Al-Aidroos; PROF. DES SCIENCES BIOLOGIQUES, UNIV. DU QUÉ. À MONTRÉAL 1976– ; Dir., Center for the Study of Biological Interactions between Health & the Environment 1990– ; Co-Dir. Associated Rsch. Team Qué. Inst. Rsch. in Occupational Health 1985–90; Chercheure associée Institut du Cancer de Montréal 1985– ; Post-doctoral Rsch. Boyce Thompson Inst. for Plant Rsch. Cornell Univ. 1975–76; mem. Editorial Bd. 'Recherches féministes'; mem. Qué. Council Social Affairs 1984–89; Dir. Montréal Museum of Sci. & Technol. 1984–85; author: 'Occupational Health and Safety of Canadian Women' 1991; author or co-author numerous book chapters, articles, presentations; "Women of the Year

(Environment)" Québec salon de la femme 1991; Duckworth Award, Canadian Rsch. Inst. for the Advancement of Women 1991; Jacques Rousseau Prize for Interdisciplinary Rsch., Assn. canadienne-française pour l'avancement des sciences 1993; mem. Candn. Genetics Soc.; Environmental Mutagenesis Soc.; Home: 4456 Christophe-Colomb, Montréal, Qué. H2J 3G5; Office: C.P. 8888, Succ. Centre-Ville, Montréal, Qué. H3C 3P8.

**MESSNER, Joseph Anton;** association executive; child welfare executive; b. Solbad Hall Tirol, Austria 1 March 1924; s. Josef Franz and Marianne (Kiniger) M.; e. Gymnasium Innsbruck, Matura 1942; Ferdinand Franzens Universität Innsbruck, Akademisch geprüfter Übersetzter 1948; Diplom Dolmetscher 1949; Philosophikum 1950; m. 1stly Magdalene d. Johann and Elisabeth Schreder (d); m. 2ndly Herlinde d. Gustav and Maria Maier 28 March 1952; children: Peter, William (dec'd), Patricia; Extve. Dir., Children's Aid Soc. Ottawa/Carleton 1965–86; Treas. and Extve. Dir. Friends of SOS-Children's Villages Can. Inc. 1969–91; SOS Kinderdorf Internat. Order of Merit; Mgr. and Owner, Mesle Canada Reg'd; Consulting Services; Sports-Recreation Instructions; holder 17 Sports Achievement Awards; Candn. Record Holder in all Waterski disciplines; Multiple Nat. Champion; Bd. mem. SOS-Nova Scotia; Investigator-Interpreter, U.S. Displaced Persons Screening Mission 1950, Austria; Sec. Head, Internat. Refugee Organ. Austria 1951; lectr. U.S. Information Centre Austria 1952; emigrated to Can., Social Worker Cath. Welfare Bureau Hamilton, Ont. 1952; Extve. Dir. Cath. Children's Aid Soc. 1954–65; Special Lectr. Scient. German McMaster Univ. 1954–65; Coach McMaster Ski Team; Founder Hamilton Winter Sports Park (Chedoke); mem. Ont. Hang-Gliding Assn.; Windsurfing Can.; Pres., Ottawa Paragliding Club; recreations: skiing, waterskiing, windsurfing, Hang-Gliding, Paragliding, golf; Home: 7 Rapidsview St., Gloucester, Ont. K1G 3N3.

**METCALF, Frederick Thomas,** C.D.; communications executive; b. Toronto, Ont. 17 March 1921; s. Charles and Mabel (Atkinson) M.; e. N. Toronto Coll. Inst.; m. Kathleen May d. Arthur C. Adams 3 Oct. 1940; children: Douglas, David, Charles, Diane, Cheryl; Hon. Chrmn., Maclean Hunter Cable TV; Bd. of Govs., Finsco Family of Funds; Sales Rep. Dunn Sales Toronto 1946–47; Vice Pres. and Gen. Mgr. CJOY Ltd. Guelph 1947 Pres. Neighbourhood Television Ltd. 1952; Mang. Dir. Maclean-Hunter Cable TV Ltd. Toronto 1967, Pres. 1968; Pres. and C.O.O., Maclean Hunter Ltd. 1977–84; served with Candn. Army 1942–46, N.W. Europe; joined Militia 1948 retiring as C.O. 11th Field Regt., Royal Regt. Candn. Arty. 1961; apptd. Hon. Lt. Col. 1972, promoted Col. and apptd. Hon. Col. 1974; Founding Pres. Candn. Cable Television Assn.; Founding Pres., 'Candn. Cable Pioneers'; mem. Candn. Assn. Broadcasters; recreations: swimming, hiking, reading, travel; Clubs: Guelph Country; Royal Candn. Mil. Inst.; Home: 21 Stuart St., Guelph, Ont. N1E 4S3; Office: Maclean Hunter Bldg., 777 Bay St., Toronto, Ont. M5W 1A7.

**METCALF, John Philip,** B.Mus.; composer; artistic director; b. Swansea, Wales 13 Aug. 1946; s. Graeme Molyneux and Audrey May (Fry) M.; e. Dean Close Sch. Cheltenham; Univ. Coll. Cardiff, B.Mus. 1967; m. Gillian d. Duncan and Evelyn Alexander 14 Sept. 1972; children: Alexander, Harriet, Thomas; ARTISTIC DIR., VALE OF GLAMORGAN FESTIVAL, WALES 1969– ; Dir. of Music, Un. World Coll. of the Atlantic, S. Wales 1971–81; Artistic Dir., St. Donats Arts Centre Wales 1975–86; Assoc. Artistic Dir., Music Theatre, Sch. of Fine Arts, Banff Centre 1990–93; UK/USA Bicentennial Arts Fellow 1977–78; Creative Arts Fellow, Univ. of Wales 1984; composer (Opera) PTOC 1972; 'The Journey' 1981; 'The Crossing' 1984; (chorus & orch.) 'Tornrak' (1989); 'The Boundaries of Time' 1985; (orch.) 'Horn Concerto' 1973; 'Music of Changes' 1981; 'Orchestra Variations' 1990; 'Marimba Concerto' 1991; (choral) 'Ave Maria' 1977; 'Two Carols' 1981; (chamber music) 'Flute Quartet' 1982; 'Brass Quintet' 1983; comns. incl. Gulbenkian Found., London Sinfonietta, BBC and Festivals of Bath, Cardiff, Frankfurt, Swansea; recreations: fishing, hiking; Home: Tŷ Yfory, Llanfair Rd., Lampeter, Dyfed SA48 8JZ, Wales, UK.

**METCALF, John Wesley;** writer; b. Carlisle 12 Nov. 1938; s. Thomas and Gladys (Moore) M.; e. Bristol Univ., B.A. 1960; m. Myrna d. Leon and Annie Teitelbaum; children: Ronald, Elizabeth, Daniel, Rangidam; English teacher, var. high schs. & univs. 1960–75; freelance writer 1975– ; Writer-in-Residence, Univ. of N.B. 1972–73; Loyola Coll. 1976; Univ. of Ottawa 1977; Concordia Univ. 1980–81; Univ. of Bologna 1985; Canada Council Arts Awards 1968, 69, 71, 74, 76, 78, 80,

83, 86; author: 'New Canadian Writing' 1969, 'The Lady Who Sold Furniture' 1970, 'The Teeth of My Father' 1975, 'Selected Stories' 1982 (stories); 'Going Down Slow' 1972, 'General Ludd' 1980 (novels); 'Girl in Gingham,' 'Adult Entertainment' 1986 (novellas); 'Shooting the Stars' (novellas) 1992; 'Kicking Against the Pricks' 1982, 'Freedom From Culture' 1987, 'What is a Canadian Literature?' 1988, 'Volleys' (with Sam Solecki and W.J. Keith) 1990 (essays); co-editor: 'Best Canadian Stories 1976,' '1977,' '1978,' '1979,' '1980,' '1981,' 1982,' 'The New Press Anthology; Best Canadian Stories 1984,' '1985'; 'The Macmillan Anthology' (I) 1988 and (II) 1989 (literary anthology) edited with Leon Rooke; ed.: 'The Bumper Book,' 'Carry on Bumping' 1988, 'Writers in Aspic' 1988 (critical essays on Canadian Literature); Co-ed. (with Kent Thompson) 'The Macmillan Anthology' (3) 1990; 'How Stories Mean' (with J.R. 'Tim' Struthers) 1991; Home: 128 Lewis St., Ottawa, Ont. K2P 0S7; Office: P.O. Box 2700, Stn. D, Ottawa, Ont. K1P 5W7.

**METCALFE, Robin Douglas,** B.A.; writer, editor, curator, broadcaster; b. Chester, N.S. 23 May 1954; s. David Douglas and Marguerite Marie (Comeau) M.; e. Dalhousie Univ. B.A. (Hons.) 1980; N.S. College of Art & Design; freelance writer since 1976 pub. journalism, fiction, poetry, art criticism & essays in ca 50 periodicals and anthologies worldwide; independent curator since 1982 with exbns in N.S., P.E.I. and Ont.; Curator, 'Subject/Matter: Contemporary Painting & Sculpture in Nova Scotia' Art Gallery of N.S. 1992–93; prepares independent commentaries, documentaries & visual arts reports, CBC 1976– ; visual & audio artist with exbns in N.S. and N.B.; Mem., Canada Council Jury, Jean A. Chalmers Fund for the Crafts 1992; Co-ord., Nat. Gay & Lesbian Conf. Halifax 1978; Canada Council Nonfiction Writing Grant 1992; Writers' Fed. of N.S. Literary Comp. 1st Prize, Adult Poetry 1984; Mem., Writers' Council; Writers' Fed. of N.S. (Standards Ctte. 1992; Freedom of Expression Ctte. 1993); Periodical Writers Assn. of Can. (Nat. Chair, Freedom of Expression Ctte., 1985) 1983– ; var. Bd. & Ctte. positions, Gay Alliance for Equality 1976–78; Gay and Lesbian Assn. of N.S. 1983, '87, '90; Delegate, Internat. Lesbian & Gay Assn. World Confs. 1985, '90, '92; editor: 'Making Waves' 1981–82, 'Imprint' 1987–91; Co-ed/Co.-pub., Pottersfield Portfolio 1986–87; author of numerous articles; contbr.: 'Hot Living' 1985, 'Themes for All Times' (poetry) 1989, 'Hometowns' (essay) 1991, 'Flesh and the Word' 1992; recreations: dancing, reading, films, clubs: Tightrope; Address: 1472 Tower Rd., Apt. 709, Halifax, N.S. B3H 4K8.

**MÉTHÉ, Pierrette,** B.Sc., P.dt.; administrative dietitian; b. Montreal, Que. 5 May 1933; d. Joseph Aimé and Marie Germaine (Brosseau) M.; e. Laval Univ. B.Sc. 1955; Toronto Western Hospital P.dt. 1956; Univ. of Montreal, Italian Studies 1985; S.M.B.D. Jewish Gen. Hosp., Hebrew Studies 1987–88; m. Reginald s. Helena and Dr. Côme Hamel 26 Oct. 1958; children: Julie, Sonia; DIRECTOR OF DIETETICS, S.M.B.D. JEWISH GENERAL HOSPITAL 1962– ; Clinical and Teaching Dietitian, Chicoutimi, P.Q. to Sept. 1957; Clin. Dietitian, Ottawa Civic Hosp. 1957–58; Dir. of Dietetics, St. Vincent Hosp. 1958–61; Nutrition & Research, Nat. Health & Welfare 1961–62; Achievements, Exceptional Performance Awards at Jewish Gen. Hosp. 1987–89; Outstanding Performance & Leadership in Food Serv. Management Award 1989 (Bernard & Assoc.); Mem., Profl. Corp. of Dietitians of Quebec 1956– (Pres., Profl. Inspection Ctte.; Management Standards Ctte. 1986– ); Canadian Dietetic Assn. 1956– (Pres. 1978–79; Life Mem. 1979– ; Strategic Planning Task Force 1982–85; Auxiliary Edn. Task Force 1989–90); Am. Soc. for Food Service Administrators 1963– ; Quebec-Italy Assn. 1984–85; co-author: 'Dictionary on Alexandre Dumas' (Italian section) 1990; recreations: photography, music, languages, skiing, swimming, reading; Home: 219 Springdale, Pointe Claire, Que. H9R 2R4; Office: 3755 Côte Ste. Catherine Rd., Montreal, Que. H3T 1E2.

**METZGER, The Honourable Robert William,** LL.B.; judge; b. Thunder Bay, Ont. 8 Jan. 1941; s. William Rhienholdt and Lydia (Wutzke) M.; e. Ryerson Inst. of Technol. Toronto Dip. Bus. Adm. 1963; Simon Fraser Univ.; Univ. of B.C., LL.B. 1973; m. Susan Phillips, B.Ed., M.Ed., Ed.D. 31 Dec. 1981; PROV. COURT JUDGE, B.C. 1980– ; Extve. The Hudson's Bay Co. Vancouver 1963–68; articled with Lawrence & Shaw, Vancouver 1973–74; private law practice 1974–80; Resident Judge Courtenay, B.C. 1980–81, Duncan, B.C. 1982–86, Victoria 1986– ; Assoc. Chief Judge, Prov. of B.C. and Administrative Judge Vancouver Island; Judge Victoria, B.C. 1989– ; Office: 213 - 850 Burdett Ave., Victoria, B.C. V8W 1B4.

**MEWETT, Alan W.,** Q.C., B.C.L., LL.M., S.J.D.; educator; b. Southampton, Eng. 25 Sept. 1930; s. Stanley Arthur and Kathleen (Mew) M.; e. King Edwards Sch., Eng., 1949; Birmingham Univ., LL.B. 1952; Hertford Coll., Oxford Univ., B.C.L. 1954; Univ. of Mich., LL.M. 1956, S.J.D. 1959; PROF. OF LAW UNIV. OF TORONTO 1967– ; formerly taught at Chicago Univ., Univ. of Sask., Queen's Univ.; Acting Dean and Assoc. Dean, Osgoode Hall Law Sch. 1966–67; called to Bar of Ont. 1961; co-author 'Philosophy of Sentencing' 1970; 'Criminal Law' 1985; Ed., 'Criminal Law Quarterly' 1966– ; 'Martin's Criminal Code of Canada' 1965–68; 'Introduction to the Criminal Process'; 'The Law of Witnesses in Canada' 1990; other writings incl. numerous periodical articles; mem., Assn. Candn. Law Teachers; York Co. Law Assn.; Hertford Soc. Oxford; Phi Delta Phi; recreations: bridge, backgammon, crosswords; Home: 179 Madison Ave., Toronto, Ont. M5R 2S6.

**MEYBOOM, Peter,** M.Sc., Ph.D.; mediator; geologist; b. Barneveld, The Netherlands 26 Apl. 1934; s. Petrus and Maria Catherina Jacoba (v. Wel) M.; e. State Univ. Utrecht, B.Sc. 1956, M.Sc. (Geol.) 1958, Ph.D. (Geol) 1960; first m. Elisabeth, d. J.P. Janssen, 19 Dec. 1957; children: Jan Peter, Joost, Alexander; second m. Jane Elizabeth d. D.H. McIndoe; children: Julia Christina; ENVIRONMENTAL MEDIATOR 1992– ; Rsch. Scient., Alta. Rsch. Council, Edmonton 1958–61; Geol. Survey of Can. 1961–66; Head, Groundwater Subdiv., Inland Waters Br., Dept. Energy Mines & Resources 1967–69; Science Advisor, Can. Dept. of Finance 1970–72; Dir., Science Policy, Can. Dept. Environment 1972–73; Dir. Gen., Science Procurement Sec., Can. Dept. of Supply & Services 1973–75; Asst. Secy. (Indust.), Can. Min. of State Sci. and Technol. 1975–77; Depu. Secy., Adm. Policy, Can. Treasury Bd. Secretariat 1977–84; Public Sector Adv., Min. Task Force on Prog. Review, Office of the Depy. Prime Minister of Canada 1984–86; Depy. Min., Fisheries and Oceans, Govt. of Canada 1986–90 (retired); Vice-Pres. for Environmental Affairs, Hill and Knowlton (Canada) Ltd. 1991–92; rec'd Candn. Centennial Medal 1967; mem., Prof. Engrs. Alta.; The Network: Interaction for Conflict Resolution; Home: 55 Bristol Ave., Ottawa, Ont. K1S 1P6; Office: 200 MacLaren St., Suite 300, Ottawa, Ont. K2P 0L6.

**MEYER, Perry,** Hon. Mr. Justice;b. Montreal, Que., 6 May 1928; s. Philip, Q.C., and Queenie (Klineberg) Meyerovitch; e. High Sch. of Montreal; McGill Univ., B.A. 1949 (1st Class Hons. Math.; Univ. Scholar), B.C.L. 1952 (1st Class Hons.; Eliz. Torrance Gold Medal; MacDonald Travelling Scholar); post-grad work at Univ. of Grenoble (France) 1952–53; m. Joy, d. David Ballon, M.D., Westmount, Que., 25 June 1952; children: Vicki Anne, Linda Ruth, Sarah Jane; PUISNE JUDGE, SUPERIOR COURT OF QUE. 1975– ; Depy. Judge, Supreme Court of Yukon Territory 1982– ; ad hoc judge, Que. Ct. of Appeal 1988; Prof. of Law, McGill Univ. 1968–75; mem. Bd. Govs., McGill till 1975; former Prof. Faculté Internat. pour l'Enseignement du Droit Comparé (Strasbourg); Chrmn., Nat. Extve., Candn. Jewish Congress 1974–77; Adjudicator for Federal public service 1970–75; mem., Superior Council of Education of P.Q. 1964–71; Chrmn. (1967–70) Comn. of Higher Education of P.Q.; Que. Council of Univs. 1972–75; Que. Human Rights Comn. 1975; Pres. (later Hon. Pres.), Cercle Juif de Langue Française; Pres., Hampstead Mun. Assn. 1964–66; read law with Meyerovitch & Levy, Montreal; called to the Bar of Que. 1954 (awarded gold medal of Paris Bar for highest standing civil law in Que. Bar exams); practised law actively in partnership with father, Philip Meyerovitch, Q.C. till 1963; Lectr., Faculty of Law, McGill Univ., 1960–63; Assoc. Prof. 1963–68; cr. Q.C. 1973; Publications: Editor for Quebec, Canadian Bankruptcy Reports 1962–65; shared $30,000 grand prize in 1967 Canadian Centennial writing competition 'Canada-2000 A.D.' for work on future of Canadian legal system; articles and book reviews in various publs.; recipient, 'Mérite du Barreau' Quebec Bar 1993; mem., Candn. Judges Conference; Candn. Bar Assn.; Candn. Assn. of Comparative Law; l'Assn. internat. du droit comparé; Hebrew; Home: 9 Thurlow Rd., Hampstead, Montreal, Que. H3X 3G4; Office: 1 Notre Dame East, Montreal, Que. H2Y 1B6.

**MEYERHOF, George Geoffrey,** B.Sc., M.Sc., Ph.D., D.Sc., D.Eng., LL.D., Dr. Ing., D.ès Sc., F.R.S.C. (1969); professor; b. Kiel, Germany 29 May 1916; s. late Prof. Otto, M.D., LL.D., F.R.S., and late Hedwig (Schallenberg) M.; e. Gymnasium, Berlin and Heidelberg; University Coll., London Univ., B.Sc. (1st Class Hon.) 1938 and Dipl. in Civil and Mun. Engn. with Distinction, also Vernon Harcourt Civil Engn. Prize; London Univ., M.Sc. 1944, Ph.D. 1950; D.Sc. 1954 (Eng.; for contrib. to soil mech. and study of foundations and structures); Dr. Ing. Aachen 1973; D.èsSc. Ghent 1975; D.Eng. Tech. Univ. of N.S. 1982; D.Sc. McMaster 1982; D.Sc.Queen's 1982; LL.D. Concordia 1985; m. Elisabeth (dec.), d. late Hans Meyerhof, 22 Feb. 1947; two s., Thomas Paul, Peter George; m. 2ndly. Ingrid, d. late Dr. Reinhard Goering, 1 Dec. 1984; RESEARCH PROF. CIVIL ENGN., TECH. UNIV. OF N.S. 1981– ; Engr. with consultants for design of various bldgs., bridges, indust. structures and pub. works in Britain, 1938–43; supervised design of various civil engn. works in connection with 2nd World War, and in charge of soil mech. lab. for design of earthworks, earth retaining structures, foundations and aerodromes 1943–46; Sr. Scient. Offr. at Brit. Govt. Bldg. Rsch. Stn., Garston 1946–50; Principal Scient. Offr. and Head of Foundation Sec. at Bldg. Rsch. Stn. 1950–53; mem. of Staff of Foundation Co. of Canada and Supervising Engr. in Foundation of Canada Engineering Corp. 1953–55; Prof. and Head, Dept. Civil Eng. 1955–81 (Dir. Sch. Grad. Studies 1962–64; Dean of Engn. 1964–70); awarded Rsch. Medal, Inst. of Structural Engrs. (Eng.) 1953; Duggan Medal, Engn. Inst. Canada 1958, 1963; Julian C. Smith Medal, Engn. Inst. Canada 1982; el. Fellow, Candn. Acad. of Engn. 1987; Fellow, Engn. Inst. Can. (Vice-Pres. 1972–74); Am. Soc. Civil Engrs.; Inst. of Civil Engrs. (England); Inst. of Structural Engrs. (Eng.; Overseas Rep. for E. Can.); mem., Am. Concrete Inst.; Council for Can. of Institution of Civil Engrs. (Eng.); Internat. Assn. Bridge and Structural Engn.; Internat. Soc. Soil Mech. & Foundation Engn.; Hon. Life Mem., Assn. Prof. Engrs. N.S.; Hon. mem. N.S. Consult. Engn. Assn.; Pres. (1972–74) Candn. Geotech. Soc. (R.F. Legget Award 1974; R.M. Hardy Lectr. 1994); Terzaghi Lecturer, Am. Soc. of Civil Engrs. 1975 (rec'd. Karl Terzaghi Award 1991); Fellow, Roy. Soc. of Can.; N.Y. Acad. of Sciences; Gov., N.S. Tech. Coll. 1964–77; Candn. Accreditation Bd., Can. Council of Prof. Engrs. 1971–74; rec'd. Can. Centennial Medal 1967; Queen's Silver Jubilee Medal 1978; Engineering Award, Assn. Prof. Engrs. N.S. 1977; life mem., Engn. Inst. Canada and Am. Soc. Civ. Engrs.; author of over 150 papers on structural engn. and soil mech. subjects; selected papers in book 'The Bearing Capacity and Settlement of Foundations' 1982; Protestant; recreations: travelling, photography, music; Home: 889 Beaufort Ave., Halifax, N.S. B3H 3X7; Office: Spring Garden Road, Halifax, N.S. B3J 2X4.

**MEYERMAN, Harold J.,** B.Comm., LL.B.; bank executive; b. Deventer, Netherlands 3 Sept. 1938; s. Evert and Rita M.; e. Univ. of B.C., B.Comm. 1967, LL.B. 1970; m. Dorothy C. Harris 30 Sept. 1978; PRES. & CHIEF EXTVE. OFFR., FIRST INTERSTATE BANK LTD. 1986– ; Candn. Imperial Bank of Comm. 1957–68; Pres., University Prod. Corp. 1968–73; Sr. Vice Pres., Bankers Trust Co. 1973–84; Extve. Vice Pres., First Interstate Bank of Calif. 1984–85; Dir., Los Angeles Philharmonic; Royal Philharmonic (London); Pasadena Symphony; Extve. Dir., Japan West. US Assn.; Asia Society, Council on Foreign Relations; Clubs: California; Annandale Golf; River Club (NY); Office: 707 Wilshire Blvd., Los Angeles, Calif. 90017.

**MICHAEL, The Hon. Cliff;** politician; b. Lashburn, Sask. 5 Oct. 1933; s. Milton H. and Barbara G. M.; e. Mount View H.S.; Nat. Inst. of Labour Edn.; Univ. of Michigan; Banff Sch. of Adv. Mngt.; m. Dilys; four children; Min. of Tourism, Prov. of B.C. 1989–91; Min. resp. for B.C. Pavilion, Pacific National Exhib., Pacific Rim Inst. of Tourism & Prov. Tourism Adv. Ctte. 1989–91; industrial relations manager; entered politics as School Trustee, Shuswap School Bd. 1978, (Chrmn. of Bd. 1980–83); elected Social Credit M.L.A. for Shuswap-Revelstoke 1983, 1986; Min. of Transp. & Highways, Min. resp. for B.C. Ferry Corp., and Min. resp. for B.C. Rail Ltd. 1986–87; Min. of Govt. Mngt. Services 1988–89; Min. resp. for B.C. Bldgs. Corp., B.C. Enterprise Corp., B.C. Pavilion Corp., B.C. Systems Corp., Pacific Nat. Exhib., Purchasing Comn., and Superannuation Comn. 1988–89; mem. of Cabinet Cttes: Regional Economic Develop.; Environment and Land Use; Treasury Bd.; and Privatization; active in minor hockey, Boy Scouts, baseball, societies & serv. groups; Past Pres., Salmon Arm Rotary Club; Home: 6 - 111 Harbour Front Dr., Salmon Arm, B.C. V1E 1A3.

**MICHAEL, T.H. Glynn,** B.A., C.A.E., F.C.I.C., F.R.S.C. (UK); b. Toronto, Ont. 20 May 1918; s. John Hugh and Hilda (Clarke) M.; e. Upper Canada Coll.; Victoria Coll., Univ. of Toronto, B.A. (Chem.) 1940; m. Ruth Vivien Dexter, 1942; children: Margaret Vivian (Dr. M.V. Tait), Barbara Elizabeth (Mrs. B.E. Drew), John Hugh; CONSULTANT IN ASSOCIATION MANAGEMENT 1985– ; with Nat. Rsch. Council, Ottawa 1941–46; Chief Chemist, Woburn Chemicals Ltd., Toronto 1946–53; Dir. of Rsch., Howards & Sons (Can.) Ltd., Cornwall, Ont. 1953–58; Extve. Dir. and Secy., Chemical Inst. of Can. 1958–85; Treas., Youth Science Foundation 1961–71; mem., Chem. Inst. of Can. (Chrmn. of Toronto Sec. 1951; Chrmn. of Protective Coatings Divn. 1950–51; Dir. and Treas. 1953–56); Am. Chem. Soc.; Candn. Soc. of Assn. Extves (Pres. 1971–72, C.A.E. 1982); Council of Engn. & Scient. Soc. Extves. (Pres. 1969–70); Roy. Soc. of Chemistry (Fellow); United Church; Home: 370 Dominion Ave. Apt. 702, Ottawa, Ont. K2A 3X4.

**MICHAELS, Anne,** B.A.; writer; b. Toronto, Ont. 15 April 1958; e. Univ. of Toronto B.A. (Hons.) 1980; Creative Writing Teacher, Univ. of Toronto 1988– ; Former freelance writer for daily radio broadcasts, two major Toronto radio stations 1986–90; Epstein Award for Poetry 1980; Commonwealth Poetry Prize for the Americas 1986; Canadian Authors' Assn. Award for Poetry 1991; National Magazine Award (Gold) for Poetry 1991; Mem., League of Canadian Poets; Writers' Union of Canada; author: 'The Weight of Oranges' 1986, pub. as talking book 1989, 'Miner's Pond' 1991 (poetry) nominated for the Governor-General's Award for Poetry (1991) and the Trillium Award (1991); anthologized in 'Poetry by Canadian Women' 1988, 'Poets 88' 1988, 'Sudden Miracles' 1991, 'Worst Journeys' 1992 (UK); poems translated into Hebrew and Gujarati for pub. in anthologies in Israel & India; workshops and readings across the country 1980– ; poems, articles, reviews & interviews appear in many magazines incl. 'Saturday Night,' 'Poetry Canada Review,' 'Performing Arts in Canada,' 'Brick,' 'Malahat Review,' 'Quarry,' 'Event,' 'Arc,' etc.; Office: c/o McClelland & Stewart Inc., 481 University Ave., Ste. 900, Toronto, Ont. M5G 2E9.

**MICHAELS, Joel Bialys;** motion picture producer; b. Buffalo, N.Y. 24 Oct. 1938; s. Alexander Bialys and Doris (Prais) M.; e. Buffalo Bennett High Sch. 1956; m. Diana Maddox 24 Aug. 1964; one child: Carey Drusilla; emigrated to Can. 1962; PRES., CINEPLEX ODEON FILMS 1988– ; joined Robert Vaughn's independent prod. co. at MGM 1967; producer: 'The Peace Killers' 1971; 'Bittersweet Love' 1975; 'The Philadelphia Experiment,' 'Black Moon Rising' (New World Pictures) 1983–85; 'Courage' a CBC three-hour TV special (Highgate Pictures, Inc./New World TV) 1986; consulting Prod., 'Harem' ABC mini-series 1986; co-producer (with Garth Drabinsky): 'The Silent Partner' 1977; 'The Changeling' 1978; 'Tribute' 1980; 'The Amateur' 1983; 'Losin' It' 1983; Sr. Vice Pres., Cineplex Odeon Films 1986–88; Producer, Michaels/Drabinsky Productions; mem. Screen Actors Guild; Actors Equity Assn.; ACTRA; AFTRA; MPPA; Jewish.

**MICHALS, George Francis,** B.Com., C.A.; executive; b. Hungary 14 Sept. 1935; s. Todor and Ilona (Sinkovich) Mihalcsics; e. Sir George Williams Univ. B.Com. 1961; McGill Univ. C.A. 1963; came to Can. 1956; m. Patricia Elizabeth d. George Henry and Bertha Hoffman, Vancouver, B.C. 18 June 1971; children: Katherine, Julie, Elizabeth, Georgina; PRES. BAYMONT CAPITAL RESOURCES INC. 1990– ; C.A. with Coopers & Lybrand, Montreal 1963–68; Treas., Dominion Textile Co. Ltd. 1969–70, Vice Pres. Subsidiaries 1970–71, Div. Extve. Vice Pres. 1971–74; Vice Pres. Finance, Genstar Ltd., Montreal 1974–76, Sr. Vice Pres. 1976–79; Extve. Vice Pres. Genstar Corp., San Francisco 1979–87; Vice-Pres., Finance and Acctg., Candn. Pacific Ltd. 1987–88; Extve. Vice Pres. & C.F.O. 1988–90; Dir., Adv. Bd., Center for Real Estate Urban Economics, Berkeley, CA; mem. Urban Land Inst.; Candn. Inst. of C.A.'s; Ordre des Comptables Agrées du Qué.; Clubs: Mount Royal (Montreal); Bankers (San Francisco); Home: R.R. 5, Orangeville, Ont. L9W 2Z2.

**MICHAUD, Alphee Martial,** M.D.; physician; executive; b. St. Quentin, N.B. 13 Nov. 1938; s. Napoleon and Alpheda (Deschenes) M.; e. Laval Univ. M.D. 1965; McGill Univ. postgrad. studies econ. 1973; m. Claudette Gingras 4 July 1964; children: Marie Claude (d), Harold, Isabelle; PRES., OMNIMAGE (Film distribution & production) 1991– ; Pres., Les Entreprises Ami Ltd. 1972– ; Radio-Acadie Ltd. 1976–77, Secy. 1977– ; Intern. Hotel-Dieu and Hosp. St. Sacrement, Quebec City 1964–66; Resident in Internal Med. Hosp. St. Sacrement 1966–67; gen. med. practice Caraquet, N.B. 1968–71; Pres. & Owner, Les Pharmacies Populaires Ltd. 1971–88; med. ed. Le Voilier 1972–76, Publisher 1977–88; Publisher Le Point 1977–88, Laviron 1978–80; Publisher Week-End (weekly newspaper) 1984–88; Dir. N.B. Devel. Corp.; Tracadie Assn. Mental Disease 1973–77; N.B. Indust. Devel. Bd. 1976–84; Chrmn. Econ. Adv. Council Maritime Premiers 1982–85; Pres. Le Festival Acadien Caraquet 1974–76; mem. Candn. and N.B. Med. Assns.; Candn. Chamber Comm. (Dir. 1981–2); Assn. Med. de Langue Française; Caraquet Bd. Trade; N.B. Chamber Comm. (Pres. 1979–81); Atlantic Chamber Comm.

(Vice Pres. 1978–80); R. Catholic; Home: 316 A Boulevard St. Pierre Ouest, Caraquet, N.B. E0B 1K0.

**MICHAUD, Patrick G.,** B.Eng., M.B.A.; merchant banker; b. Windsor, Ont. 15 Jan. 1952; s. Gerard G. and Dorothy R. (Young) M.; e. Royal Mil. Coll. B.Eng. (Civil) 1974; Univ. of W. Ont. M.B.A. 1980; m. Michele Singleton 2 July 1977; children: Andrew, Corina; Vice Pres. and Chief Financial Offr., Roy-l Merchant Group Inc. 1987; Dir. Continental Pharma Cryosan Inc.; Conpharma Vaccines Ltd.; Trentway-Wagar (Properties) Inc.; served with Cdn. Forces 1969–78; Dominion Securities 1980–81; Asst. Gen. Mgr. CIBC 1981–87; Office: 1625 Sherbrooke W., Montreal, Que. H3H 1E2.

**MICHAUD, Paul-André,** C.A.; b. St. Juste du Lac, Temiscouata, Que. 9 Apl. 1935; s. Louis-Philippe and Simone (Dubé) M.; e. École de Commerce, Rimouski, Que.; Laval Univ.; m. Liliane, d. Henri Buisson, 24 Sept. 1960; children: Suzanne, Helene, Eric; Managing Partner, Quebec office (& Mem. Bd. of Dir. & Mem. Extve. Ctte.), SAMSON BELAIR/DELOITTE & TOUCHE; apptd. Auditor of Bank of Canada 1975; apptd. Auditor Canadian Mortgage and Housing Corp. 1984; Chrmn. Federal Liberal Agency of Can. 1986; Pres. Loto Quebec 1976–77; Gov., Laval Univ. Fondation; mem. of Prof. Assns.; recreations: squash, skiing, sailing; Clubs: Quebec Yacht Club; Mess des Officiers de la Citadelle de Que.; Tennis Montcalm; Home: 2680 Plaza, Sillery, Que. G1T 2V3; Office: 5600 boul. des Galeries, Quebec City, Que. G2K 2H6.

**MICHAUD, Hon. Pierre A.,** B.A., LL.L.; judge; b. Port-Alfred, Que. 17 Apr. 1936; s. J. Adolphe and M. Lucile (Gravel) M.; e. Coll. St. Laurent B.A. 1957; Univ. de. Montréal LL.L. 1960; m. Louise d. Charles and Florence Painchaud 8 Sept. 1962; two s. Jacques, Jean-François; ASSOCIATE CHIEF JUSTICE, QUEBEC SUPERIOR COURT 1992– ; called to Bar of Que. 1961; cr. Q.C. 1976; private law practice Desjardins Duchame, Montreal 1961–83; Judge, Superior Court of Que. 1983–92; Lectr. in Trial Tactics Que. Bar; Secy. Montreal Bar Assn. 1970; recreations: skiing, golf; Club: Laval-sur-le-Lac; Home: 195 Côte Ste. Catherine, Outremont, Que.; Office: Rm. 16.60, 1 est Notre-Dame, Montreal, Que. H2Y 1B6.

**MICHAUD, Yves;** executive officer; b. St-Hyacithe, Que. 13 Feb. 1930; s. Jean-Baptiste and Roberta (Robert) M.; e. Univ. de Strasbourg, journalism deg. 1960; m. Monique d. Aimé and Alida Morrissette 26 Mar. 1951; children: Luc, Anne; PRESIDENT, SELECTIONS YVES MICHAUD 1987– ; Pres. & C.E.O., Montreal Convention Ctr., 1984– ; Pub. & Ed.-in-Chief, Le Clairon 1952–60; La Patrie 1960–66; M.P. Que. Nat. Assembly 1966–70; High Comnr., Qué. External Coop. & Spec. Adv. to Prime Min. 1970–73; Pub. & Ed.-in-Chief, Le Jour 1973–76; Qué delegate to internat. orgn. 1977–78; Dipl. couns., Prime Min. of Qué 1978–79; Chief, Qué. dipl. mission, France 1979–80; Adv. for Pub. relns. & external affairs, UNESCO 1984– ; Pres., Cons. qué. du tourisme; Comdr. of the Legion of Honour (France); Founder Mem., Montréal Counc. of Internat. Relns.; author: 'Je conteste' 1969; recreation: tennis; Home: 4765 Meridian, Montréal, Qué. H3W 2C3; Office: 5344 Boul. St. Laurent, Montréal, Qué. H2T 1S1.

**MICHEL, Bernard,** B.A.Sc., Dr.Eng., F.E.I.C., F.R.S.C., F.C.S.C.E.; educator; b. Chicoutimi, Que. 31 May 1930; s. Joseph-Williams and Jeanne (Tremblay) M.; e. Laval Univ. B.A.Sc. 1954; Grenoble Univ. Dr.Eng. 1962; m. Mariette Boivin 7 Sept. 1954; children: Marianne, François, Luc, Jacques, Charles, Christine; PROF. OF CIVIL ENG., UNIV. LAVAL 1958– , Dir. of Civil Eng. 1960–63; Pres., Recherches Bermic Inc. 1983– ; Vice Pres., Arctec Canada Ltd. 1973–78; intnl. expert cons. hydraulic and ice eng.; holds 4 patents; recipient Gzowski Medal Eng. Inst. Can. 1963; Keefer Medal 1977, 1981; Camille A. Dagenais Award 1983 Candn. Soc. Civil Eng.; author 'Eléments de la physique de la neige et de la glace' 1964; 'Ice Pressure on Engineering Structures' 1970, transl. Russian; 'Ice Mechanics' 1978; 'Hydraulique appliquée' 1982; over 100 rsch. papers maj. field floating ice mechanics; Pres. Ctte. Snow and Ice nat. Rsch. Council 1968–76; Fellow, Royal Soc. of Can. 1982; Fellow, Candn. Soc.of Civil Engrs. 1982; Fellow, Eng. Inst. of Canada 1983; Pres. Ctte. Ice Problems Intnl. Assn. Hydraulic Rsch. 1970–76; mem. over 10 nat. and intnl. assns. 1954– ; recreations: salmon fishing, hunting; Home: 739 rue des Vignes, Ste-Foy, Que. G1V 2Y1.

**MICHEL, Bernard M.;** business executive; b. Paris, France 1938; e. Ecole Polytechnique, Paris, Eng. 1960; m. Suzy; 2 children; CHAIR, PRES. & CHIEF EXECUTIVE OFFR., CAMECO CORPORATION 1991– ; 2nd Lieut., French Navy 1960–62; Production & Design Engr., Entreprise Minière et Chimique, Paris 1962–67; Vice-Pres., Alwinsal Potash of Canada 1967–76; Pres., Amok Ltd. 1977–88; Sr. Vice-Pres. of Operations, Cameco Corp. 1988–90; Chief Operating Offr., Cameco 1990; Pres. (mem. Bd. of Dirs.) Cameco 1990, C.E.O. 1991, Chair 1993; Mem. Bd. of Dirs., Candn. Nuclear Assn.; Conference Bd. of Canada; Producer Extve. Mem., Uranium Institute; Chair of Bd. of Dirs., Uranium Sask.; Honorary Consul of France; Office: 2121 – 11th St. W., Saskatoon, Sask. S7M 1J3.

**MICHEL, Dominique;** artiste; commedienne; née Sorel, Qu., 24 septembre 1932; f. Jean-Noel et Emerentienne (Dupuis) Sylbestre; ép. 25 mai 1957; divorcee; é. course universitaire, Bacheliere en Musique (piano); TV: plusieurs émissions et séries à succès dont: 'Le Petit Café,' 'Moi et l'Autre,' 'Dominique'; animatrice et co-animatrice de différent galas; co-animatrice du 'Festival Juste Pour Rire'; emission spéciale intitulée 'La Petite Sylvestre' sur la vie et la carrière de Dominique Michel; plusieurs 'Bye, Bye,' revue humoristique de fin d'année; scène: co-animatrice du 'Festival Juste Pour Rire,' Théâtre Saint-Denis; deux spectables sur scène (solo) qui ont tenu l'affice pendant deux ans chacun: 'Showtime – Showtime' et 'Ben Yoyons Donc'; présentatrice de plusieurs trophées lors de galas; productrice et comédienne pièces de théâtre; disques: enregistrement de 9 disques 33 tours; filmographie: 'Tiens Toi Bien Après les Oreilles à Papa'; 'J'Ai Mon Voyage'; 'Y'A Toujours Moyen de Moyenne'; 'Les Aventures d'une Jeune Veuve; 'Les Tisserans du Pouvoir'; 'Le Declin de l'Empire Americain'; Un Zoo la Nuit'; merites: Decourverte de l'Année 1958; Actrice de l'Année 1967, 1972, 1983–86; Femme de l'Année 1978–80; gala excellence de la presse 1987; auteur 'Dominique en Forme'.

**MICHELMANN, Hans J.,** B.A., Ph.D.; university professor; b. Osterburg, Altmark, Germany 22 Feb. 1944; s. Ernst Paul 'Joachim' and Marie Luise 'Gertraude' (Braemer) M.; e. Niton Central H.S. 1962; Univ. of Alta., B.A. 1970; Indiana Univ., Ph.D. 1975; m. Martha Johanna d. Christoffel and Martha Jacobs 25 Nov. 1967; HEAD, DEPT. OF POLITICAL STUDIES 1991– and PROF. OF POL. STUDIES, UNIV. OF SASKATCHEWAN 1985– ; Asst. Prof. of Pol. Sci. & Rsch. Assoc., Ctr. for Internat. Studies, Univ. of Missouri-St.-Louis 1975–77; Asst. Prof., Univ. of Sask. 1977–79, Assoc. Prof. 1979–85; Dir. Gen., Candn. Counc. for Eur. Affairs 1984– ; Co-ed., 'J. of European Integration' 1984– ; Woodrow Wilson Fellow 1970–71; Can. Counc. Grad. Fellow 1971–75; F.A. Scherrer Gold Medal in Pol. Sci., Univ. of Alta. 1970; Mem., Candn. Pol. Sci. Assn.; author: 'Organisational Effectiveness in a Multinational Bureaucracy' 1978 and numerous articles & book chapters; co-author: 'The Canada-European Communities Framework Agreement' 1984; co-editor: 'Federalism and International Relations' 1990; 'The Political Economy of Agricultural Trade and Policy' 1990; 'Politik und Politikstile in Kanada' 1991; recreations: scuba diving, underwater photography, photography; Home: 318 Wakaw Cres., Saskatoon, Sask. S7J 4E2; Office: Saskatoon, Sask. S7N 0W0.

**MICHENER, Gail R.,** B.Sc., Ph.D.; university professor; b. Wisbech, England 25 Feb. 1946; d. Harold Albert Stony and Grace Mitchell; e. Univ. of Adelaide B.Sc. (Hons.) 1967; Univ. of Sask. Ph.D. 1972; m. Daniel s. Charles and Mary M. 6 Aug. 1971; one s.: Rory Marcel; PROF., BIOLOGICAL SCI., UNIV. OF LETHBRIDGE 1985– ; Lectr., Univ. of Ghana 1972–74; Killam Post-doct. fellow, Univ. of Alta. 1974–76; NSERC Univ. Rsch. Fellow, Univ. of Lethbridge 1981–85; Pres., Candn. Counc. on Animal Care 1988–89; Wildlife Soc. Award for editorship 1986; Mem., Animal Behavior Soc. (Extve. Mem. 1985–88, 1990–92, Pres. 1992–93); Assoc. Ed., 'Journal of Mammalogy' 1983–87; Ed. Bd. Mem., 'Canadian Journal of Zoology' 1987–93; co-editor: 'The Biology of Ground-Dwelling Squirrels' 1984; author of over 30 sci. pubs.; recreation: Scottish country dancing; club: Lethbridge Scottish Country Dance (Pres. 1988–94); Home: Box 99, Picture Butte, Alta. T0K 1V0; Office: Lethbridge, Alta. T1K 3M4.

**MICHOLS, Dann M.,** B.Comm.(Hons.), M.B.A.; federal public servant; b. Calgary, Alta. 4 July 1947; s. L. Murray and Jean A. M.; e. Univ. of Calgary B.Comm. 1969; Harvard Grad. Sch. of Bus. Admin. M.B.A. 1975; ASST. DEPUTY MINISTER, NATIONAL PHARMACEUTICAL STRATEGY & DRUGS DIRECTORATE, HEALTH CANADA 1992– ; Mgr. Prog. Planning System, Dept. of Secy. of State, Ottawa 1972–73; Dir. Museum Assistance Prog., Nat. Museums of Can., Ottawa 1975–79; Dir. of Policy Analysis, Min. of State for Social Devel., Ottawa 1980–82; Asst. Secy.-Gen., National Museums of Can. 1982–88; Mgmt. Advisor to UNESCO 1987–89; Special Advisor, Candn. Centre for Management Develop., Ottawa 1989; Dir., Royal Commission on New Reproductive Technologies 1990–92; Home: 139 Patterson, Ottawa, Ont. K1S 1Y4; Office: Rm. 107, Health Protection Building, Tunney's Pasture, Ottawa, Ont. K1A 0K9.

**MICKELSON, Norma I.,** B.Ed., M.A., Ph.D.; educator; b. Victoria, B.C. 5 Nov. 1926; d. Ambrose Seymour and Iva Matthews; e. Univ. of B.C. B.Ed. 1963; Univ. of Victoria M.A. 1968; Univ. of Wash. Ph.D. 1972; m. Harvey Mickelson 12 Aug. 1946; children: Richard Paul, Irene Ann; PROFESSOR EMERITUS, UNIV. OF VICTORIA 1992– ; Teacher 1945–60; Supvr. 1960–66; Professor, Univ. of Victoria 1967–92; Dean, Faculty of Education 1975–80; mem. P.E.O.; Chair, B.C. Assessment Authority Bd. 1992– ; Charter Mem. of Bd., Whole Language Umbrella; mem. B.C. Education Advisory Council 1994– ; recreation: bridge; Home: 3000 Spring Bay Rd., Victoria, B.C. V8N 1Z3.

**MICKLEBOROUGH, Lynda L.,** B.Sc., M.D.C.M., F.R.C.S.(C); cardiac surgeon, university professor; b. Regina, Sask. 26 Oct. 1947; d. Herbert Wallace and Dorothy Winogene (Taylor) M.; e. McGill Univ., B.Sc. 1969, M.D.C.M. 1973; FRCS(C) Gen. Surg. 1978; Cardiovascular & Thoracic Surg. 1981; m. William B. s. Bruce and Ethel Ferguson 8 July 1989; children: Lisa, Christopher, Stephen, Jennifer; CARDIAC SURGEON, TORONTO GENERAL HOSP. 1981– & ASSOC. PROF. OF MED., UNIV. OF TORONTO 1989– ; Editorial Bd. of Journal of Thoracic and Cardiovascular Surgery 1990– ; Sr. Rsch. Fellow, Ont. Heart & Stroke Found. 1981–88; Mem., Am. Assn. of Thoracic Surg.; Soc. of Thoracic Surg.; Candn. Cardiovascular Soc.; N. Am. Soc. of Pacing & Electrophysiology; Cardiovascular Soc., Young Investigation Award 1967; author of numerous sci. papers; clin. & basic lab. rsch. related to coronary artery disease, ventricular arrhythmias & surg. treatment of heart failure; recreations: music, boating, skiing, windsurfing; Home: 10 Whitney Ave., Toronto, Ont.; Office: 200 Elizabeth St., Toronto, Ont. M5G 2C4.

**MIDDAUGH, Stanley A.;** banker; VICE-PRES., CORP. BANKING, ATLANTIC PROVINCES, ROYAL BANK OF CANADA 1987– ; joined Royal Bank Cooksville, Ont. 1951; Sr. Asst. Acctnt. Sarnia 1960; Acctnt. 1961; Asst. Mgr. Brantford 1962; Mgr. Preston 1964; Personnel Mgr., Asst. Inspector & Sr. Asst. Inspector, Gen. Mgr.'s Dept. Toronto 1967; Mgr., Spadina & College Br. Toronto 1973; Inspector, Ont. dists. 1975; Dist. Mgr., Br. Banking, Atlantic Dist. H.Q. Halifax 1978; promoted to extve. rank 1979; Office: 5161 George St., Halifax, N.S. B3J 2Y1.

**MIDDLETON, Alexander Lewis Aitken,** M.Sc., Ph.D.; educator; b. Banchory, Scot. 20 May 1938; s. Charles Harper Davidson and Agnes Hamilton Letham (Aitken) M.; e. Univ. of W. Ont. B.Sc. 1961, M.Sc. 1962; Monash Univ. Ph.D. 1966; m. Ann d. Carl and Lena Manore 6 Oct. 1962; children: Catherine, Moira, Ian; PROF. OF ZOOL. UNIV. OF GUELPH 1991– , Asst. Prof. 1966–71, Assoc. Prof. 1971–91, Coordinator for Instrnl. Devel. 1985–87; Asst. Master, Southend High Sch. for Boys, Southend-On-Sea, Eng. 1965–66; Visiting Sci. Oxford Univ. 1975–76; Univ. of Canterbury, Christchurch, N.Z. 1990–91; recipient OCUFA Award for Teaching 1984; 3M Teaching Fellow 1989; John Bell Award, Univ. of Guelph 1993; Trustee, Baillie Fund; Dir. Long Point Bird Observatory 1971–77; co-ed. 'The Encyclopedia of Birds' 1985; mem. Guelph Chamber Music Soc. (Past Pres. & Ctte. mem.); Am. Ornithols. Union; Cooper Soc.; Royal Australasian Ornithols. Union; Candn. Soc. Ornithol.; recreations: music, gardening; Home: 61 Forest St., Guelph, Ont. N1G 1J2; Office: Guelph, Ont. N1G 2W1.

**MIDDLETON, Gerard Viner,** B.Sc., Ph.D., D.I.C., F.R.S.C.; geologist; educator; b. Capetown, S. Africa 13 May 1931; s. Reginald Viner Cecil and Doris May (Hutchinson) M.; e. Mt. St. Mary's Coll. Spinkhill, Eng. 1949; Imp. Coll. Univ. London B.Sc., A.R.C.S. 1952, Ph.D., D.I.C. 1954; m. Muriel Anne d. William Zinkewich, Brantford, Ont. 4 Apr. 1959; children: Laurence, Teresa, Margaret; PROF. OF GEOL. McMASTER UNIV. since 1967; Geol. California Standard Oil Co. Calgary and Regina 1954–55; Dept. of Geol. McMaster Univ. 1955, Chrmn. 1959–62, 1978–84, Prof. 1967– ; co-author 'Origin of Sedimentary Rocks' 1972 (2nd ed. 1980); author over 80 scient. articles various aspects geol. (sedimentol.); Fellow, Roy. Soc. of Canada; mem. Geol. Assn. Can. (Ed. 1972–74; Pres. 1987–88); Internat. Assn. Sedimentols. (Vice Pres. 1978–82); Am. Assn. Petrol. Geols.; Soc. Econ. Paleontols. & Minerals.; Candn. Assn. Univ. Teachers; R. Catholic; Home: 90 St.

Margaret's Rd., Ancaster, Ont. L9G 2K9; Office: Hamilton, Ont. L8S 4M1.

**MIDDLETON, Peter J.H.,** A.C.A., F.C.A., C.A.; financial executive; b. Southend-On-Sea, Essex, England 1 July 1947; s. Norman W.H. and M. Peggy M.; e. A.C.A. U.K. 1969; F.C.A. U.K. 1975; C.A. Ontario 1977; m. Halina B. d. Irene and Aleksander Sandig 23 April 1988; children: Sarah Dawn, Katie Alexandra; SENIOR VICE-PRES., MARKET RISK MANAGEMENT, CANADIAN IMPERIAL BANK OF COMMERCE (CIBC) 1992– ; Audit Sr., Touche Ross & Co. (U.K.) 1969–71; Financial Analyst, Phillips 1971–74; Financial Consultant, Mktg., Ford Motor Co. 1974–76; Manager, Financial Control, CIBC 1976–84; Vice-Pres., Asset Liability Mngt. 1984–88; Sr. Vice-Pres. & Treasurer 1988–92; Office: Commerce Court N., 23rd Floor, Toronto, Ont. M5L 1A2.

**MIDDLETON, William Edgar Knowles,** D.Sc., F.R.S.C.; b. Walsall Eng. 23 June 1902; s. Richard Edgar and Margaret Jane (Knowles) M.; e. Purdue Univ.; Univ. of Sask., B.Sc. 1927, M.Sc. 1929; D.Sc., Boston Univ. 1957; D.Sc., McGill Univ. 1976; m. Dorothy, d. Rev. D.C. Day, Saskatoon, Sask., 1 Feb. 1930; children: John, Diana; Hon. Lect., Dept. of Physics, Univ. of Toronto 1933–39; with Meteorol. Service of Can. 1930–46; Rsch. Offr., Nat. Rsch. Labs. 1946 till retirement; Fellow, Optical Soc. of Am. (Ives Medal 1959); Roy. Meteorol. Soc. (Pres., Candn. Br. 1944–46); Hon. mem., Amer. Meteorol. Soc.; Hon. Lectr., Dept. of Hist. of Med. & Science, Univ. of B.C. 1967–78; author of 'Visibility in Meteorology' 1935, 2nd ed. 1941; 'Meteorological Instruments' 1941, 2nd ed. 1943; 'Vision Through the Atmosphere' 1952; 'The History of the Barometer' 1964; 'A History of the Theories of Rain' 1965; 'A History of the Thermometer' 1966; 'Invention of the Meteorological Instruments' 1969; 'The Experimenters: a Study of the Accademia del Cimento' 1971; 'Physics at the National Research Council of Canada, 1929–1952' 1979; 'Lorenzo Magalotti at the Court of Charles II' 1980; 'Radar Development in Can.' 1981; 'Mechanical Engineering at the National Research Council of Canada 1929–1951' 1984; has written about 100 scient. papers in fields of meteorol., optics, history of science and articles for 'Encycl. Brit.'; recreation: music; Address: Apt. 603, 11007 83 Ave., Edmonton, Alta. T6G 0T9.

**MIDGHALL, William Paul,** B.Eng., M.Sc.; executive; b. Toronto, Ont. 20 May 1935; s. Ernest J. and Teresa (O'Donohue) M.; e. Riverdale Coll.; Rensselaer Polytechnic Inst. B.Eng. 1959; Union Coll. M.Sc. 1965; m. Marianne d. Joseph Barco 1960; children: Gregory, Nancy, Mary Jo, Margaret; PRESIDENT, W.P. MANAGEMENT/TAIWAN CONNECTION INC. 1990– ; Mfg. Engr., Norton Co. 1959, Product Mgr. 1962, Mgr. Mktg. Rsch. 1965; Mgr. Distrib., Norton International Inc. 1968, Business Planning Mgr. 1970; Pres. and Mng. Dir., Norton de Mexico 1972; V.P. and Gen. Mgr. Coated Abrasive Div. Norton Co. 1975;, Pres. and Mng. Dir. Norton Canada Inc. 1978; Pres., Ortech International 1983; mem. Business Adv. Counc. and Inteface Rsch. Ctte., McMaster Univ.; Dir., Mgmt. of Technology Inst., McMaster Univ.; Dir., Candn. Plastics Inst.; Mem., Am. Soc. For Metals; Candn. Rsch. Mgmt. Assn.; Pres. Rensselaer Club of Greater Toronto; recreations: golf, tennis, fitness; Club: Burlington Racquet; Home: 2144 Canterbury Dr., Burlington, Ont. L7P 1P1.

**MIDWINTER, James Robert,** M.A.; retired diplomat; b. Brandon, Man. 27 Sept. 1929; s. Harold Kitchener and Florence Myra Jean (Cliffe) M.; e. Univ. of B.C., B.A. 1951; Oxford Univ. (Rhodes Scholar) B.A. 1953, M.A. 1957; Bicultural & Bilingual Prog. Que. 1969; m. Sally d. Albert and Kathleen Heard 26 June 1954; children: Stewart, James, Jenny; Foreign Service Offr. Dept. Trade & Comm. Ottawa 1953; Asst. Trade Comnr. Guatemala 1954 and Detroit, Mich. 1957; Second Sec. (Comm.) New Delhi 1959; First Sec. (Comm.) Santiago, Chile 1961; Asst. Chief Commonwealth Div. Ottawa 1964; Chief Financing & Aid Div. 1965; Dir. Internat. Financing Br. and Alternate Dir. Export Credits Insurance Corp. 1967; Gen. Dir. Wood Products Br. 1970 and Resource Inds. & Constr. Br. 1973 Dept. Ind., Trade & comm.; Asst. Sec. to Cabinet (Govt. Operations) 1974 and Sr. Asst. Sec. (Operations) Privy Counc. Office 1975; Insp. Gen. Foreign Operations 1979; Ambassador to Venezuela and to Dominican Republic 1983; comnd. Lt. COTC 1950, served with 27th Candn. Inf. Bgde. Germany 1952; Pres. Tradex Invest. Fund. 1968–70; Founding mem., Treas. and Vice Pres. Profl. Assn. Foreign Service Offrs. 1965–67; mem. Candn. Yachting Assn.; recreations: sailing, golf, reading; Club: Trident Yacht (Gananoque, Ont.); Home: 9 Carlyle Ave., Ottawa, Ont. K1A 4Y1.

**MIECZNIKOWSKI, Anita,** B.A.; publisher; b. Buffalo, N.Y. 15 June 1943; d. Jacob E. and Lucille G. (Schmitt) Pfohl; e. St. Mary's H.S. 1960; Rosary Hill College (now Damien College) B.A. 1964; m. Adolf E. s. Adolf and Mary M. 5 June 1965; children: Alicia, Alexei; PUBLISHER, BOOKS IN CANADA 1991– ; various positions ending as Managing Editor, College Div., Methuen Publications 1981–87; Co-ord. Editor, College Div., Nelson Canada 1987–88; Marketing Manager, College Div., McClelland & Stewart 1988–89; Assoc. Publisher, Books in Canada 1989–91; Home: 48 Galley Ave., Toronto, Ont. M6R 1G8; Office: 130 Spadina Ave., Suite 603, Toronto, Ont. M5V 2L4.

**MIFFLIN, Hon. Arthur Samuel,** LL.B.; judge; b. Catalina, Nfld. 19 June 1920; s. Samuel William and Jane Blanche (Manuel) M.; e. St. Peter's Sch. Catalina; Meml. Univ. Coll. Nfld.; Univ. of King's Coll. Halifax; Dalhousie Univ. LL.B. 1947; m. Millicent d. Frederick and Louisa Seymour 28 Nov. 1957; children: Jane, Keith, Neil, Victoria; SUPERNUMERARY JUSTICE, COURT OF APPEAL 1986– ; Bank of Nova Scotia 1937–42; called to Bars of N.S. and Nfld. 1947; cr. Q.C. 1958; M.H.A. for Trinity N., Nfld. 1956–62; law practice St. John's, Nfld. 1947–64; Judge, Supreme Court of Nfld. 1964; Chief Justice Trial Div. 1975–79; Chief Justice of Nfld. 1979–86; recipient Centennial Medal 1967; Queen's Silver Jubilee Medal; sometime mem. St. John's Ang. Sch. Bd.; Extve. Ctte. Diocesan Synod Nfld.; Gen. Synod Can.; Bd. Mgmt. Grace Gen. Hosp.; Home: 68 Smithville Cres., St. John's, Nfld. A1B 2V2; Office: P.O. Box 937, Court of Appeal, Court House, Duckworth St., St. John's, Nfld. A1C 5M3.

**MIFFLIN, Rear Admiral Fred J.,** P.F.S.C., N.W.C., N.D.C., C.D., M.P.; b. Bonavista, Nfld. 6 Feb. 1938; e. Naval Coll. Esquimalt Weapons Eng. 1963; Candn. Forces Staff Coll. Toronto 1968; U.S. Naval War Coll. Newport, R.I. 1973; Nat. Defence Coll. Kingston 1982; m. Gwenneth Elizabeth Davies 19 Dec. 1959; children: Mark, Cathy, Sarah; first sea command 1969; during naval career commanded 10 destroyers; served 11 yrs. in Ottawa various sr. govt. positions related to law of the sea, fisheries protection, procurement maj. mil. systems and internat. relations; Head of Nat. Defence Secretariat during early 1980's; promoted Rear Adm. 1985; el. to H. of C. for Bonavista Trinity Conception 1988, re-el. 1993; recipient Oland Trophy 1962; Herbert Lott Award 1964; Past Dir.: Candn. Automobile Assn.; Candn. Paraplegic Assn.; mem. Royal Candn. Legion; Kinsman; recreations: jogging, country music, gourmet cooking, raising golden retrievers; Home: Church St., Bonavista, Nfld. A0C 1B0 and 2102 Grafton Cres., Gloucester, Ont. K1J 6K8; Office: House of Commons, Ottawa, Ont. K1A 0A2 and P.O. Box 159, Bonavista, Nfld. A0C 1B0.

**MIGHTON, John Stephen,** H.Ba., M.A.; playwright, tutor; b. Hamilton, Ont. 2 Oct. 1957; s. Albert Kenneth and Marion Olivia (Swent) M.; e. Univ. of Toronto H.Ba. 1978; McMaster Univ. M.A. 1982; m. Raegan d. Brien and Elizabeth Hornby 27 Aug. 1988; one d.: Chloe Elizabeth; Teaching Asst., McMaster Univ. 1978–81; Lecturer in Philosophy 1981–83; Playwright 1983– ; Tutor in Math. & Physics 1986– ; Writer-in-Residence, Caribbean Am. Repertory Theatre; Theatre Pass Muraille; plays have been produced across Canada, N.Y., Edinburgh & London; Founder of environmental collective Citizens' Group; author: 'Scientific Americans' (play) 1989 (Dora Mavor Moore Award 1989; Finalist, Governor General's Award), 'Possible Worlds and A Short History of Night' (plays) 1992 (Chalmers Award 1992; Dora Mavor Moore Award 1992; Governor General's Award 1992); recreations: cycling, swimming; Home: 49 Pendrith St., Toronto, Ont. M6G 1R6.

**MIGUÉ, Jean-Luc,** M.A., Ph.D., F.R.S.C.; economist; educator; b. St-Jacques, Qué. 13 Apl. 1933; s. Joseph Alfred and Laurence (Venne) M.; e. Univ. de Montréal B.A. 1953, M.A. 1956; London Sch. of Econ. 1958–60; Am. Univ. Ph.D. 1968; m. Renée d. Gaston Caron 13 Sept. 1958; children: Elizabeth Paule, Philippe Pascal, Sébastien Nicolas; PROF. OF ECON., NAT. SCH. OF PUB. ADM. 1970– ; Rsch. Offr., Bank of Canada 1957–58, Dept. of Educ. Qué. 1961–62; Prof. of Econ. Laval Univ. 1962–70; staff mem. Econ. Council of Can. 1973–74; author: 'Nationalistic Policies in Canada' 1979; 'L'Economiste et la Chose Publique' 1979; 'The Public Monopoly of Education' 1989; 'Institutionalizing Competition Between Governments' 1991; 'Federalism and Free Trade' 1994; co-author 'The Price of Health' 1974; 'Le Prix du Transport' 1978; Ed. 'Le Québec D'Aujourd'hui' 1971; various articles; mem. Candn. Econ. Assn. (Extve. Council 1975–78); Am. Econ. Assn.; Pub. Choice Soc.; R. Catholic; recreation: greenhouse gardening; Home: 3181 de Galais, Québec City, Qué. G1W 2Z7; Office: 945 Wolfe, Québec City, Qué. G1V 3J9.

**MIHALCHEON, George J.;** artist, educator; b. Boian, Alta. 29 Nov. 1924; s. John and Pearl (Darda) M.; e. Hairy Hill H.S. art program; Prov. Inst. of Technol. & Art (now Alta. Coll. of Art); m. Jean Marie d. Joseph and Georgina Lapointe 1952; children: George James, Jane Mary Gina, Gail Patricia, Daniel Grant; Lecturer Emeritus, Alberta College of Art 1991; Graphic Designer & Art Dir., Stewart, Bowman, McPherson Advtg. Agency 1950–56; Palmer, Mihalcheon, Freelance Studio 1956–57; Art Dir., McConnell Eastman Advtg. Agency 1957–60; Art Faculty, Alta. Coll. of Art 1960–87 (Co-ord., Cont. Edn. Prog. 1966–71; Prog. Co-ord., Found. Core Prog. 1974–79; Opns. Supvr. 1979–80); Mem., Calgary Allied Arts Found. 1980–88 (Chrmn. 1987–88); Extve. Mem., Visual Arts Bd. 1986, 1988; Mem., Alta. Soc. of Artists 1951–76 (Sec. Calgary Br. 1967–70); Alumni., Alta. Coll. of Art; Hon. Mem., Calgary Allied Arts Found. 1989– ; collections incl.: Fathers of Confed. Gall. Charlottetown; N.B. Mus. of Art; Univ. of Calgary; Alta. Coll. of Art; T-D Bank Calgary & Edmonton; Alta. Art Found.; Heinz Jordon Toronto; Nat. Trust Calgary; Dept. Consumer Affairs Edmonton; Students Union, Univ. of Alta. Edmonton; Civic Art Coll. Calgary; Ballem McDill MacInnes Calgary; most recent painting exhib., Visions Gallery, Edmonton 1990; & private collections in Toronto, San Francisco, Winnipeg, Edmonton & Calgary; recreations: hiking, fishing; Home: 15 Silvergrove Crt. N.W., Calgary, Alta. T3B 5A3.

**MIKALACHKI, Alexander,** B.Com., M.B.A., Ph.D.; educator; b. Montréal, Qué. 13 Sept. 1933; s. Dina and Sela (Biremac) M.; e. Sir George Williams Univ. B.Com. 1958; Univ. of W. Ont. M.B.A. 1960, Ph.D. 1964; m. Dorothy Ruth d. Thomas and Louise Martin 14 Aug. 1959; children: Jodi, Sandy, Robert; PROFESSOR, SCHOOL OF BUSINESS ADMIN., UNIV. OF WESTERN ONT. 1972– ; Instr. present Univ. 1960, Asst. Prof. 1964, Assoc. Prof. 1967, M.B.A. Prog. Chrmn. 1971–72, Rsch. Dir. 1980–82, Assoc. Dean - Programs 1981, Acting Dean, Sch. of Bus. Adm. 1989–1990; Dir., Helix Circuites; Maclean Hunter; author: 'Group Cohesion Reconsidered' 1969; co-author: 'Management's View of Union – Management Relations at the Local Level' 1978; 'Managing Absenteeism' 1982; Home: 34 Longbow Pl., London Ont. N6G 1Y3; Office: Western Business School, Rm 144A, Univ. of Western Ont., London, Ont. N6A 3K7.

**MIKI, Roy Akira,** B.A., M.A., Ph.D.; university professor; b. Winnipeg, Man. 10 Oct. 1942; s. Kazuo and Shizuko (Ooto) M.; e. Univ. of Manitoba B.A. 1964; Simon Fraser Univ. M.A. 1969; Univ. of B.C. Ph.D. 1980; m. Slavia d. Ann and Robert Knysh 10 June 1967; children: Waylen, Elisse; FULL PROF., DEPT. OF ENGLISH, SIMON FRASER UNIV. 1986– ; taught in Japan and travelled in Asia 1969–71; joined Dept. of English, Simon Fraser Univ. 1977; rsch. & teaching specialization in Am. & Can. lit.; Editor, 'West Coast Line: Contemporary Writing and Criticism'; active in Japanese-Candn. movement to seek redress for injustices suffered during 1940s; joined Nat. Assn. of Japanese Candns. (which successfully negotiated a redress settlement 1988) as publicist, researcher & negotiator; 3rd-generation Japanese-Candn. (a sansei, born shortly after family was relocated from Haney BC to a sugar beet farm in Manitoba); SSHRC grants 1985, '88; Dr. William Black Award, Vanc. Multicultural Soc. 1985; President's Award, Simon Fraser Univ. 1989; Renata Shearer Human Rights Award, Un. Nations Assn. & BC Human Rights Coalition 1990; author: 'The Prepoetics of William Carlos Williams: Kora in Hell' 1983, 'A Record of Writing: An Annotated and Illustrated Bibliography of George Bowering' (Gabriel Roy Award for best book on Candn. literature, Assn. of Candn. and Que. Literatures 1991) 1990, 'Saving Face: Selected Poems 1976–1988' 1991; co-author: 'Justice in Our Time: The Japanese Canadian Redress Settlement' 1991; editor: 'This Is My Own: Letters to Wes and Other Writings on Japanese Canadians, 1941–48' by Muriel Kitagawa 1985, 'Tracing the Paths: Reading & Writing the Martyrology' by bp Nichol 1988; Office: Burnaby, B.C. V5A 1S6.

**MIKUSKA, Vincent,** B.F.A.; visual artist; b. Winnipeg, Man. 8 May 1956; s. Frank Peter and Shirley Mabel (Stevens) M.; e. Univ. of Manitoba B.F.A. 1985; Univ. of Winnipeg; Univ. of Alta.; m. Janice d. Edwin and Anita Sorobey 20 Apr. 1985; children: Alaina, Stefan; exhibitions (one-man): Bau-Xi Gall. Vanc. 1990, 1992, 1994; Ace Art Winnipeg 1984; Ctr. Culturel Franco-Manitobain Winnipeg 1982; (two-person): Boss/Mikuska Janet Ian Cameron Gall. 1985; Surrey

Theatre Gall. 1989; Richmond Art Gallery 1992; (group): Ace Art, The First Decade, Winnipeg 1993; Fraser Valley Juried, Abbotsford 1993; Figuratine, Bau-Xi, Vancouver 1993; Fraser Valley Juried, Chilliwack Arts Center 1991; Images and Objects IX, North Vancouver 1991; Mikuska, Brown, Toews, Thomas Gallery Winnipeg 1991; Bau-Xi 25th anniv. show 1990; Arts 90, Surrey Art Gall., Surrey Art Gall. Silent Auction 1988–90; Manitoba Soc. of Artists juried show 1983–85; Under Thirty, Janet Ian Cameron Gall. 1982; Head Age Group Coach, Spartan Swim Club, Chilliwack B.C.; Bd. of Dir., Janet Ian Cameron Gall. 1983–84; Home: 6960 Centennial Dr., Sardis, B.C. V2R 1J7; Office: Box 101, Vedder Crossing, B.C. V0X 1Y1.

**MILAVSKY, Harold P.,** B. Comm., F.C.A.; executive; b. Limerick, Sask. 25 Jan. 1931; s. Jack and Clara (Levitsky) M.; e. Bedford Collegiate, Sask.; Univ. of Sask. B.Comm. 1953; children: Charlene, Roxanne, Gregory, Abbie, Carrie; GROUP CHRMN., REAL ESTATE ED-PER-BRASCAN; Former Bd. Chrmn. & C.E.O., Trizec Corp. Ltd.; Bd. Chrmn. and Dir., Carena Bancorp-Inc. (Toronto); Dir., Trizec Corp. Ltd.; Brascan Ltd. (Toronto); London Life Insurance Co. (London); London Insurance Group (Toronto); Hees Internat. (Toronto); Coscan Development Corp. (Toronto); Wascana Energy Inc. (Regina); Nova Corp. of Alta. (Calgary); Amoco Canada (Calgary); Telus Corp. Ltd. (Edmonton); joined Loram Internat. Ltd. (Mannix Co. Ltd.) Calgary 1956, served as Chief Acct. and Treas./Controller; Vice Pres. & Chief Financial Offr., Power Corp. Developments Ltd. 1965; Dir. & Extve. Vice Pres., Great West International Equities Ltd. 1969 (taken over by Trizec Corp Ltd. 1971); Pres. & C.E.O., Trizec Corp. 1976; Bd. Chrmn. & C.E.O. 1986; mem. Inst. C.A.'s Sask. & Alta. 1956; Fellow, Inst. C.A.'s Alta. 1984; Past Chrmn., Candn. Chamber of Commerce; Past Dir. & Past Pres. Candn. Inst. Pub. Real Estate Co's.; Past Dir., Conf. Bd. of Can.; Past Dir., Founding Gov., Acctg. Education Found. of Alberta (sponsored by the Inst. of C.A.'s of Alta.); past mem. Bd. of Gov., Univ. of Calgary; recreations: skiing, tennis, horseback riding; Clubs: Calgary Petroleum; The Ranchmen's; Univ. of Calgary Chancellor's; Glenmore Racquet; Office: 1700, 855 - 2nd St. S.W., Calgary, Alta. T2P 4J7.

**MILBERRY, Lawrence Joseph,** B.A., M.Ed.; teacher; author; publisher; b. Haileybury, Ont. 30 Oct. 1943; s. Basil Emerson and Julia Helen (Brown) M.; e. Univ. of Toronto B.A. 1968, M.Ed. 1971; div.; children: Matthew Stephen, Mary Kathleen, Simon Patrick, Stephanie Anne; FOUNDER AND PUBLISHER, CANAV BOOKS 1980– ; Teacher Metrop. Separate Sch. Bd. 1961–80; author: 'Aviation in Canada' 1979; 'The Avro CF-100' 1981; 'The Canadair North Star' 1982; 'Sixty Years: The RCAF and CF Air Command 1924–1984' 1984; 'Austin Airways: Canada's Oldest Airline' 1985; 'The Canadair Sabre' 1986; 'Canada's Air Force Today' 1987; 'AIR-COM: Canada's Air Force' 1991; 'Air Transport in Canada' 1992; also publ.: 'The De Havilland Canada Story' (Fred Hotson) 1983; 'Helicopters: The British Columbia Experience' (David Parker & Peter Corley-Smith) 1985; 'And I Shall Fly' (G/C Z.L. Leigh) 1985; 'A Formidable Hero: Lt. R.H. Gray' 1987; 'Woody: A Fighter Pilot's Album' 1987; 'Power: The Pratt and Whitney Canada Story' (Kenneth Sullivan & Larry Milberry) 1989; 'The Royal Canadian Air Force at War 1939-1945' 1990; 'Typhoon and Tempest: The RCAF Story' (H. Halliday) 1992; cons. to authors and publishers; mem. Candn. Aviation Hist. Soc.; recreations: writing, photography, cycling, gardening; Address: 51 Balsam Ave., Toronto, Ont. M4E 3B6.

**MILBORNE, C. Hunter,** B.Comm.; business executive; b. Hamilton, Ont. 4 Sept. 1950; s. the late William Henry and Dorothy Eugene (Taylor) M.; e. Univ. of Toronto, B.Comm. 1972; m. Kornelia d. Edit Fabenyi 12 Aug. 1983; CHRMN. & CHIEF EXTVE. OFFR., MILBORNE REAL ESTATE CORP.; recognized as 'Dean of the Condominium Industry,' specializing in the marketing and sale of condominium ownership; Office: One Yonge St., Suite 1010, Toronto, Ont. M5E 1E5 and 1122 Mainland St., Suite 360, Vancouver, B.C. V6B 5L1.

**MILBOURNE, Robert J.,** B.A.Sc.; steel industry executive; b. Vancouver, B.C. 7 Sept. 1941; s. William James Frederick and Margaret (Galloway) M.; e. Univ. of B.C. B.A.Sc. 1963; m. Sharon Patricia d. Arthur H. and Helen B. Chandler 6 July 1963; one d.: Mercedes Elaine; PRESIDENT & CHIEF OPERATING OFFICER, STELCO INC. 1991– ; Asst. Gen. Supt., Lake Erie Works, Stelco Inc. 1980–82; Gen. Supt. 1982–84; Gen. Works Mgr. (Hamilton) 1984–87; Vice-Pres., Mfg. 1988–90; Pres. 1991; Dir. & Co-Chair, Projet Bessemer 1989– ; Dir., Baycoat 1989– ; Candn. Heat Treaters 1989– ; Cont. Colour Coaters 1989– ; Iron & Steel Soc. of AIME Awards: NOH-BOSC Conf. Award 1968, McKune Award 1969, Robert W. Hunt Silver Medal 1969; Dir., Occupational Health Clinic, Ont. Works 1989; Comnr., Ont. Human Rights Comn. 1992; Mem., Assn. of Profl. Engineers of Ont.; Mem., Candn. Inst. of Mining & Metallurgy 1988; Iron & Steel Soc. of AIME 1979; Am. Iron & Steel Inst. 1988; Hamilton & Dist. C. of C. 1984; Candn. Rep. to the I.I.S.I., Ctte. on Technology 1991; recreations: fishing, antiques, Canadiana; clubs: Hamilton; Home: 2180 Marine Dr., Oakville, Ont. L6L 5V2; Office: 100 King St. W., P.O. Box 2030, Hamilton, Ont. L8N 3T1.

**MILBURN, John Alexander,** B.Comm., C.A., Ph.D., F.C.A.; professional accountant; b. Toronto, Ont. 4 Aug. 1938; s. Henry Henshaw and Isabelle Louise (Green) M.; e. Carleton Univ. B.Comm. 1959; Ont. Inst. of C.A.s C.A. 1962; Univ. of Illinois Ph.D. 1977; m. Joan d. William and Una Faulds 21 Oct. 1961; children: James Alexander, Robert Henry, Christopher Bruce; PARTNER, NATIONAL ACCOUNTING AND AUDITING SERVICES GROUP, ERNST & YOUNG; joined Clarkson, Gordon (now Ernst & Young) 1959; Manager 1965; Univ. of Illinois 1969–72; Partner, Clarkson, Gordon 1972; currently resp. for accounting research; Dir., Clarkson Gordon Found.; Chrmn., Acctg. Standards Bd. of Candn. Inst. of C.A.s; Past Pres., Candn. Academic Accounting Assn.; Ont. Inst. of C.A.s F.C.A. 1982; author: 'Incorporating the Time Value of Money Within Financial Accounting' 1988; co-author: 'Research to Support Standard Setting in Financial Accounting' 1982; author/co-author of numerous articles and papers on finan. accounting topics; recreations: skiing, cottage; Home: 1630 Stone Haven Dr., Mississauga, Ont. L5J 1E7; Office: P.O. Box 251, Toronto-Dominion Centre, Toronto, Ont. M5K 1J7.

**MILES, Gary Lawrence;** broadcasting executive; b. Regina, Sask. 7 Feb. 1939; s. Geoffry Lawrence and Dorthey (Field) Miles; e. Scott C.I. 1957; divorced; children: Gary Lee, Galen Brett; EXTVE. VICE-PRES., ROGERS BROADCASTING LIMITED, WESTERN DIV. 1989– ; began broadcasting career in Regina - Announcer, CKCK Radio Regina 1957–61; became Sales Extve. at CKCK 1961–65; Sales Mgr. 1965–69; Gen. Mgr. 1969–77; moved to Winnipeg as Gen. Mgr., CKRC-AM Winnipeg 1972–84; In 1979 launched FM station CKWG-FM; moved to Toronto, Pres. Radio Bureau of Canada 1984–87; Vice-Pres., Radio Selkirk Communications Ltd. 1987–89; served many civic organizations in Regina including Past Chrmn. of Sask. Roughrider Annual Dinner; in Winnipeg: member of board United Way, Winnipeg Symphony Orchestra, Contemporary Dancers; served for 6 yrs. Chrmn. of the Alcoholism Foundation of Manitoba and 4 yrs. on the Winnipeg Grace Hospital Bd.; in Toronto: Bd. Mem., Broadcast Extves. Soc. and the Toronto Grace Hospital; In the broadcast industry: Dir., Radio Bureau of Can.; Past Chrmn., Radio Bureau of Canada; Past Chrmn., Bureau of Broadcast Measurement; Past Chrmn., West. Assn. of Broadcasters; Past Chrmn., Man. Assn. of Broadcasters; Past Dir., Candn. Assn. of Broadcasters; 5 Year Judge, Internat. Broadcast Awards Assn. serving U.S., Can., Eur. & Asia; in Vancouver currently Dir., Vancouver Museum; Trustee, Vancouver Grace Hosp.; Dir., First Night, Vancouver; Home: 4435 West 6th Ave., Vancouver, B.C. V6R 1V2; Office: 2440 Ash St., Vancouver, B.C. V5Z 4J6.

**MILES, James Edward,** B.A., M.D.C.M., D.P.M., F.R.C.P.(C); university professor/administrator; b. Victoria, B.C. 6 Nov. 1928; s. James Edgar and Winona Ruth (Parsell) M.; e. Univ. of Sask. B.A. (cum laude) 1949, Med. 1 & 2 1951; McGill Univ., M.D.C.M. 1953; m. Gail d. Peter and Gwen Cromie 2 May 1970; children: Stephanie, Peter, Hilary, Brent, Michael; PART-TIME PRIVATE PRACTICE (PSYCHIATRY) 1990– ; intern, Vancouver Gen. Hosp./Royal Jubilee Hosp. 1953–54; House Officer, Prov. Mental Hosp., Essondale, B.C. 1954–55; family physician, Quesnel 1955–56; N. Vancouver 1956–64; Psych. Res., Univ. B.C. Dept. of Psych. 1964–66; Maudsley Hosp., Univ. of London (U.K.) 1966–67; Instr., Univ. B.C. Dept. of Psych. 1967; Asst. Prof. 1968; Assoc. Prof. 1976; Prof. 1982; Clin. Supr. & Clin. Dir., Health Sci. Ctr. Hosp. 1969–76; Head, Dept. of Psych., Shaughnessy Hosp. 1976–85; Prof. & Head., Dept. of Psychiatry, Univ. of B.C. 1985–90; Co-ord., Outreach Mental Health Project, Dawson Creek, B.C. 1977–80; Dawson Creek Comm. Award 1980; extensive acad./profl. ctte. involvements; Mem., Med. Assns.; Candn. Psych. Assn. (Dir. at Large 1977–78; Founding Mem., Forensic Section); Founding mem., Nat. Bds. of Review (and editor of proceedings 1976); author of num. articles, book chapters & papers; recreations: racing/breeding thoroughbred horses, sailing; Home: 2176 Nelson Ave., W. Vancouver, B.C. V7V 2P7; Office: 407–125 East 13th Ave., North Vancouver, B.C. V7L 2L3.

**MILES, John Frederick,** B.Sc.; retired steel industry executive; b. Fredericton, N.B. 13 Aug. 1926; s. Ralph Edward and Hazel Jean (Young) M.; e. Univ. of N.B. 1943–44; Queen's Univ., B.Sc. 1948; m. Frances d. John and Frances Power 2 Oct. 1950; children: John F., Robert Douglas, Dalyce J., Leytha J.; DIRECTOR & MEM. CAPITAL CTTE., SLATER INDUSTRIES INC. 1992– ; Pres. & C.E.O., Hamilton Sp. Bar Div., Slater Indus. Inc. 1991–92; joined Dominion Steel & Coal Corp. 1948; Asst. Works Mgr., Sydney, N.S. 1960–62; Gen. Mgr., Etobicoke Works 1962–65; Prodn. Mgr., Burlington Steel Div., Slater Steel Indus. Ltd. 1965; Works Mgr. 1966; Vice-Pres., Mfg. 1971; Pres., Hamilton Sp. Bar Div. 1986–91; Home: 3472 Spruce Ave., Burlington, Ont. L7N 1K3.

**MILES, Simon Richard,** M.A.; public policy and international development consultant; b. London, England 10 Mar. 1939; s. Richard and Henrietta (Geller) M.; e. Univ. of Edinburgh, M.A. (Hons.) 1962; joined Herts Co. Counc. Planning Office (Eng.) 1962–63; emigrated to Can. 1963; Rsch. Assoc., Bur. of Mun. Rsch. 1963; Asst. Dir. 1965–69; Assoc. Dir., Centennial Study & Training Prog. on Metro. Problems 1965–69; Extve. Vice-Pres. & Extve. Dir., Internat. Assn. for Metro Rsch. & Devel. 1969–76; Cons., public policy and internat. devel. 1977– ; Lectr., Atkinson Coll., Geog. Dept., York Univ. 1966–68; Fac. of Environ. Studies 1970–71; Asst. Prof. 1971–74; Cons., U.N., New York 1978; Geneva 1979; Orgn. for Econ. Coop. & Devel., Paris 1979–80; Rsch. Assoc., Ctr. for Urban & Comm. Studies, Univ. of Toronto 1977– ; Assoc., Devel. Planning Unit, Univ. of London 1980– ; Inst. for Environ. Studies, Univ. of Toronto 1986– ; Mem., The Conserv. Counc. of Ont. 1977– (Pres. 1984–86); Mem., Toronto Population Group 1986– (Chrmn. 1990– ); Dir., Lake of Bays Heritage Found. 1985– (Pres. 1987– ); Mem., Bd. of Adv., Inst. for Studies in Policy, Ethics & Law, Carleton Univ. 1982– ; Counc. on Mun. Performance, New York 1976– ; Cdn. Correspondent, National Civic Review, New York 1988– ; Mem., Salzburg Cong. on Urban Planning & Devel., Austria 1966– ; World Futures Studies Fed., Hawaii 1981– ; Fellow, Royal Soc. of Arts, U.K. 1987– ; co-author: 'Developing a Canadian Urban Policy' 1973; editor: 'Metropolitan Problems: International Perspectives' 1970; author of num. chapters, articles & reports based on work in over 50 countries on econ., soc., environ., tech. & pol.-admin. aspects of societal devel.; recreations: tennis, swimming; Home and office: 62 Hampton Ave., Toronto, Ont. M4K 2Y6.

**MILES-PICKUP, Arnold E.,** B.A.; banking executive; b. Calcutta, India 8 Oct. 1944; e. Univ. of B.C., B.A. 1967; m. Alison Stewart 9 Oct 1982; children: Warren, Lindsay; PRES., AETNA TRUST 1986– ; Royal Candn. Navy 1962–65; Branch Acct., Bank of Montreal 1967–69; Sr. Vice-Pres. & Treas., Bank of B.C. 1969–86; Dir., Boys & Girls Clubs of British Columbia; Boys & Girls Clubs of Greater Vancouver; Home: 1875 26th St., West Vancouver, B.C. V7V 4K2.

**MILIC-EMILI, Joseph,** C.M., M.D., F.R.S.C.; educator; b. Sezana, Slovenia 27 May 1931; s. Joseph and Ivanka (Perhavec) M-L.; e. Univ. of Milan M.D. 1955; m. Ann d. Leslie and Kathleen Harding 2 Nov. 1967; children: Claire, Anne-Marie, Alice, Andrew; PROF. OF PHYSIOL. McGILL UNIV. 1969– ; Dir., Meakins-Christie Lung Rsch. Labs. 1979– ; Cons. Brookhaven Nat. Lab. Long Island, N.Y. 1974–90; Columbia Univ. 1977–90; Asst. Prof. of Physiol. Univ. of Milan 1955–60, Univ. of Liége 1958–60; Rsch. Fellow Harvard Sch. of Pub. Health Boston 1960–63; Asst. Prof. of Physiol. present Univ. 1963, Assoc. Prof. 1965, Chrmn. of Physiol. 1973–78; author over 400 sci. papers; co-author 20 books; ed. one book; corr. mem. Slovenian Acad. Arts & Sci.; Doctor Honoris Causa, Université Catholique de Louvain, Belgium; Order of Canada 1990; Home: 4394 Circle Rd., Montreal, Que. H3W 1Y5; Office: 3626 St. Urbain St., Montreal, Que. H2X 2P2.

**MILJAN, Toivo,** B.A., M.A., Ph.D.; university professor; b. Tallinn, Estonia 14 Nov. 1938; s. Jaan and Aime-Ive (Kasak) M.; e. Jarvis C.I. 1958; Univ. of Toronto, B.A. (Hons.) 1962, M.A. 1963; Univ. of London, Ph.D. 1976; m. Aina d. Emilia and Ernest Pludums 30 Oct. 1962; children: Carl Andre Arthur, Erik Armand Jaan; DIRECTOR, EURO FACULTY (LATVIA) 1993– and PROF., WILFRID LAURIER UNIVERSITY 1980– (on leave 1993–96); joined WLU 1963; Rsch. Offr., Royal Comn. on Bilingualism & Biculturalism 1965–67 (on leave); co-Dir., Centre on Foreign Policy & Federalism; Vis. Prof., Helsinki 1977, 1987; Adjunct Prof., Pol. Sci., Swedish Sch. of Bus. & Econ., Helsinki 1988– ; Cons.,

UN Inst. on Training & Rsch.; Ctr. des Estudos Econ. y Soc. del Tercer Mundo, Mexico 1979–81; Chrmn. of Bd., FRC Composites Ltd.; Mem., Internat. Economic Adv. Bd. to the Prime Minister of the Republic of Estonia 1990– ; Counsellor to the Foreign Minister of Estonia 1991– ; Mem. Advisory Council to the Rector of Tartu Univ. 1991– ; Vice-Pres., Assn. for the Advancement of Baltic Studies 1990– ; Dir., Tartu Inst.; Founding Dir., K-W Br., CIIA; Waterloo Br., UNAC; Mem., Candn. Assn. of Univ. Teachers; Candn. Pol. Sci. Assn.; Assn. for Advancement of Baltic Stud.; Deutsche Gesellschaft f. Kan. Stud.; author: 'Bilingualism in Finland' Vol. I 1966, Vol. II 1967, 'The Reluctant Europeans' 1977, 'Food and Agriculture in Global Perspective' 1980; editor: 'Culture and Legitimacy' 1982, 'Energy in the Eighties' 1984, 'L'Energie et les annes 80' 1985, 'The Political Economy of North-South Relations' 1987; co-editor: 'Unity in Diversity' 1980; extensive recent articles on Soviet Union and the Baltic States; recreations: swimming, hunting, sailing; Clubs: Korp! Rotalia (Toronto, NY, Stockholm, Sydney); Tallinn; Tartu; Home: 46 Combermere Cres., Waterloo, Ont. N2L 5B1; Offices: 75 University Ave. W., Waterloo, Ont. N2L 3C5 and Euro Faculty, Raina blvd. 25, Riga LV - 1050, Latvia.

**MILL, William Arthur;** retired executive; b. Kensington, P.E.I. 2 May 1924; s. W. Roy and B. Irene (Semple) M.; e. Kensington (P.E.I.) High Sch.; Northwestern Univ., Marketing Course (2) 1963; Univ. of W. Ont., Mang. Course, 1970; m. Hazel L., (dec'd) d. Gordon Elliott, 27 Sept. 1952; served in various Maritime Brs., Bank of Nova Scotia 1941–44; joined Swift Cdn. Co. Ltd. Accounting & Provision Depts., Moncton 1945–58; Asst., Gen. Provision Dept., Toronto 1958–59; Provision Mgr., Calgary 1959–61; Gen. Provision Mgr., Toronto 1961–64; Asst. to Pres., Toronto 1964–65; Business Planning Div., Swift & Co., Chicago 1965–66; Plant Mgr., St. Joseph, Mo. 1966–68; Gen. Mgr., Presswood Bros. Ltd. 1968–69; Executive Vice President of Swift Can. Co. 1969–73; Pres. and Dir. 1973–78; Chrmn. Bd. and Dir. 1978; Past Pres., Meat Packers Council Can.; Freemason; Shriner; Protestant; recreation: fishing, golf; Club: Moncton Golf & Country; Address: 36 Woolridge Dr., Riverview, N.B. E1B 4G3.

**MILLAIRE, Albert,** O.C.; actor/stage director; b. Montreal, Que. 18 Jan. 1935; s. Albert and Laura (Rollet) M.; e. Coll. de l'Assomption; Prov. of Que. Dramatic Art Conservatory; m. Michèle d. Rodolphe Marchand 22 Aug. 1983; children: (from prev. marriage): Anne, Catherine, Frédérique; for the past 38 years has performed on the main stages of Montreal and Can. in French as well as in English; most recent work: Actor and Dir., Stratford Shakespearean Festival; directed in Can. & U.S.; winner of several Que. awards; Mem., U.D.A.; A.C.T.R.A.; Can. Equity; recreations: horse riding; Club: Commanderie de Bordeaux; Home: 439 Mount Pleasant, Westmount, Que. H3Y 3G9.

**MILLAR, Margaret Ellis (Mrs. Kenneth);** novelist; nature writer; b. Kitchener, Ont. 5 Feb. 1915; d. Henry William and Lavinia (Ferrier) Sturm; e. Kitchener-Waterloo (Ont.) Coll. Inst., 1933; Univ. of Toronto, 1933–36; m. Kenneth Millar (dec.) 2 June 1938; one d., Linda Jane Pagnusat (dec.); author of following novels: 'The Invisible Worm' 1941; 'The Weak-Eyed Bat' 1942; 'The Devil Loves Me' 1942; 'Wall of Eyes' 1943; 'Fire Will Freeze' 1944; 'The Iron Gates' 1945; 'Experiment in Springtime' 1947; 'It's All in the Family' 1948; 'The Cannibal Heart' 1949; 'Do Evil in Return' 1950; 'Vanish In An Instant' 1952; 'Rose's Last Summer' 1952; 'Wives and Lovers' 1954; 'Beast in View' 1955; 'An Air That Kills' 1957; 'The Listening Walls' 1959; 'A Stranger In My Grave' 1960; 'How Like An Angel' 1962; 'The Fiend' 1964; 'The Birds and the Beasts Were There' (nature book) 1968; 'Beyond This Point Are Monsters' 1970; 'Ask For Me Tomorrow' 1976; 'The Murder of Miranda' 1980; 'Mermaid' 1982; 'Banshee' 1983; 'Spider Webs' 1986; rec'd Edgar Allan Poe Award for Best Mystery of the Yr. 1956; Grandmaster Award, Mystery Writers of Am. 1983; mem., Mystery Writers Am. (Pres. 1957); Crime Writers of Canada; Democrat; Clubs: Coral Casino; University Club of Santa Barbara; Sierra; Greenpeace; Home: 87 Seaview Dr., Santa Barbara, Cal. 93108.

**MILLAR, Marjorie E.,** B.A., M.Ed.; university administrator; b. Rome, N.Y. 3 Nov. 1938; d. Stanley D. and Evelyn A. (Hall) Putman; e. Pacific Univ. B.A. 1960; Oregon State Univ. M.Ed. 1971; m. Herbert M. 7 Feb. 1960 (dec. 1972); children: Suzanne, Sandra; VICE-PRES. (EXTERNAL), THE UNIV. OF WESTERN ONT. 1988– ; Educator (U.S.) 1960–73; Dir., Placement & Career Serv., Wilfrid Laurier Univ. 1979–85; Univ. Devel. & Alumni Affairs 1982–85; Alumni Affairs & Devel., Univ. of Guelph 1985–88; Candn. Assn. of Edn. Devel. Officers (Past Pres.); Mem., Council for the Advancement and Support of Edn. (CASE); Candn. Coun. for the Adv. of Edn. (CCAE); frequent fac. mem. & seminar leader at CASE & CCAE; Award of Excellence for Outstanding Leadership & Serv., Edn. Adv. in Canada 1991; Hon. Fellow, Wilfrid Laurier Univ. 1993 (Hon. Alumnus 1988); author of 2 book chapters & 3 articles; co-author of 1 manual; directed 3 successful capital campaigns for Candn. Higher Edn. raising nearly 200 mill. dollars; recreations: sailing, skiing, golf; clubs: Board of Trade; Home: 34 Medway Cres., London, Ont. N5X 3S8; Office: Rm. 108A, Stevenson-Lawson Bldg., London, Ont. N6A 5B8.

**MILLAR, Wayne Jordan,** B.A., M.A., M.Sc.; public servant; b. Sydney Mines, N.S. 26 April 1942; Alexander and Gertrude Elizabeth (Crowley) M.; e. Guelph C.V.I. 1960; Univ. of Waterloo B.A. 1967; Univ. of Toronto M.A. 1970; London Sch. of Economics M.Sc. 1977; m. Laura d. Robert and Patricia (Apted) Knowles 31 May 1969; children: Erin Elizabeth, David Keith; HEALTH ANALYST, CANADIAN CENTRE FOR HEALTH INFORMATION, STATISTICS CANADA 1990– ; Medical Services Br., Health & Welfare Can. 1972–81; Health Serv. & Promotion Br. 1981–90; Edit. Ctte., 'Chronic Diseases in Canada'; consultant to World Health Orgn. United Nations; United Church; Mem., Candn. Population Soc.; author of over 60 analytical papers; recreations: photography, hiking, fishing, camping; Home: 1944 Navaho Dr., Ottawa, Ont. K2C 0T6; Office: R.H. Coats Bldg., 18th fl., Tunney's Pasture, Ottawa, Ont. K1A 0T6.

**MILLAR, William John,** B.A., LL.B., LL.M.; lawyer; b. Edmonton, Alta. 13 Jan. 1948; s. James Lea and Margaret Anna (Smathers) M.; e. Univ. of Alberta B.A. (hons.) 1970; McMaster Univ. M.A. 1971; Univ. of Toronto LL.B. 1978; Osgoode Hall Law School LL.M. 1984; m. Barbara d. David and Eva Vininsky 22 Dec. 1974; children: Daniel, David; PARTNER, THORSTEINSSONS 1991– ; called to Bar of Ontario 1980, Bar of British Columbia 1993; joined Blake, Cassels & Graydon 1981; Partner 1986; Mem., Sales Tax Ctte., Dept. of Finance 1987; Vice-Chrmn., National Sales and Commodity Tax Section, Candn. Bar Assn. 1992– ; Deputy Min. Adv. Cttes., Revenue Canada (GST implementation 1989–91; GST administration 1992– ); frequent lectr., Tax Extves. Institute, Candn. Bar Assn., Candn. Tax Found., Candn. Institute of Chartered Accountants; Mem., Taxation Ctte., Toronto Bd. of Trade; Co-Editor, DeBoo GST & Commodity Tax newsletter; Mem., Editorial Adv. Bd., Canada GST Serv.; author: 'The Goods and Services Tax: Basic Concepts and Issues' 1989; 'Cross-Border/Non-Resident Issues Under the GST' 1991; 'GST Implications of Doing Business in Canada' 1993; 'The Canadian International Trade Tribunal' 1989, 'Seizures, Forfeitures and Offences under the Customs Act' 1990 (course); 'How to Deal With a Contentious Customs Valuation Issue' 1992; 'The Canada–U.S. Free Trade Agreement: A Canadian View' (speech) 1988; 'Dispute Settlement Under NAFTA' 1992; clubs: Albany; Board of Trade; Home: 14 Cuthbert Cres., Toronto, Ont. M4S 2H8; Office: Canada Trust Tower, BCE Place, 161 Bay St., Toronto, Ont. M5J 2S1.

**MILLARD, Michael A.,** P.Eng.; engineer; b. Montreal, Que. 26 Oct. 1939; s. James Harold and Muriel Mae (Fyfe) M.; e. Loyola Coll. 1960; McGill Univ. B.Civil Eng. 1962; m. Lynda d. Charlotte and Owen Watt 23 Sept. 1977; children: Scott, Brett; PRESIDENT, SCOBRE LIMITED; PRINCIPAL, MILRAN DEVELOPMENTS CONSULTANTS 1986– ; City Engr., Pointe Claire, Que. 1966–74; Depy. Comnr., Eng. and Works, Mississauga 1974–76; V.P. Devel., Mascan Corp. 1976–84; Pres., Traders Assoc. 1984–86; recreations: skiing, golf; Clubs: Mississauga Golf & Country; Horseshoe Valley Golf; Heights of Horseshoe Ski; Home: 4 Pine Point, R.R. 1, Barrie, Ont. L4M 4Y8; Office: Mississauga Executive Centre, Suite 250, Four Robert Speck Parkway, Mississauga, Ont. L4Z 1S1.

**MILLARD, Peter Tudor,** B.A., D.Phil.; university professor; b. Treorchy, Wales 21 July 1932; s. Percival and Catherine (Davies) M.; e. Bath Tech. Coll. 1947; McGill Univ. B.A. 1959; Oxford Univ. B.A. 1961, D.Phil. 1970; Chrmn., Dept. of Eng., Univ. of Sask. 1985–91; joined Univ. of Sask. as Spl. Lectr. 1964; Asst. Prof. 1970; Assoc. Prof. 1974; Prof. 1986; Pres., Saskatoon Art Centre 1970–71; Trustee, Saskatoon Art Gallery & Civic Conserv. 1971–74; Pres., Sask. Assn. on Human Rts. 1980–83; Pres., Univ. of Sask. Fac. Assn. 1987–88; mem. ACUTE; author: 'Dmytro Stryjek: Trying the Colors' 1988; var. articles and reviews; short stories in The Malahat Review; ed. 'Roger North: General Preface and Life of Dr. John North' 1984; Contbg. Ed., Border Crossings 1977–87; contrib. ed., Inuit Art Quarterly 1992– ; recreations: art, friends; Home: 308 Skyline Dr., Box 1372, Gibsons, B.C. V0N 1V0.

**MILLER, Alistair,** B.Sc., Ph.D., F.C.I.C.; chemical engineering executive; b. Edinburgh, Scotland 6 July 1940; s. Ian and Jean Forbes (Watson) M.; e. Univ. of Glasgow B.Sc. 1962; Imperial Coll., Univ. of London (U.K.) Ph.D. 1966; m. Margaret d. John and Winifred Walker 29 July 1964; children: Ian James, Alison Fiona, Peter Richard, Susan Margaret; CHEMICAL ENGINEERING BRANCH MGR., AECL RESEARCH, CHALK RIVER LABORATORIES 1982– ; joined AECL 1966; specialized in isotope separation, esp. of hydrogen isotopes & production of heavy water; resp. for process re-design details of Glace Bay Heavy Water Plant 1971; Team Leader, Process Analysis Team, Ont. Hydro's Bruce Heavy Water Plant 1975–76; designed process for Laprade Heavy Water Plant 1979; Fellow, Chem. Inst. of Can.; Co-Founder & Vice-Chrmn., Deep River Science Acad. 1986– ; Mem., Candn. Soc. for Chem. Engr. (Chrmn., Pubns. Ctte. 1986–90; Dir. 1991–94); recreations: cycling, nordic skiing, walking; Home: P.O. Box 1212, Deep River, Ont. K0J 1P0; Office: Chalk River, Ont. K0J 1J0.

**MILLER, Anthony Bernard,** B.A., M.B., F.R.C.P.(C); university professor; epidemiologist; b. Woodford, Eng. 17 Apr. 1931; s. Thomas Henry and Elsie Alice (Hamlet) M.; e. Friends' Sch., Saffron Walden 1948; Univ. of Cambridge B.A. 1952; St. Bartholomew's Hosp. Med. Sch. M.B., B.Ch. 1955; m. Sheena d. Daniel and Isobel McCulloch 18 Oct. 1952; children: Richard, Naomi, Alison, Peter, Fiona; PROFESSOR, DEPT. OF PREVENTIVE MED. & BIOSTATISTICS, UNIV. OF TORONTO 1976– (CHRMN. 1992– ); Med. Registrar, Luton and Dunstable Hosp. 1958–61; mem. Sci. Staff, Med. Rsch. Counc. Tuberculosis and Chest Diseases Rsch. Unit 1961–71; Dir. Epidemiology Unit, National Cancer Inst. of Canada 1971–86; Nat. Health Scientist 1988–93; Dir., M.Sc./Ph.D. Programme in Epidemiology, Univ. of Toronto 1986–91; author over 200 papers on cancer epidemiology; Ed. 'Screening for Cancer' 1985; 'Diet and the Aetiology of Cancer' 1989; 'Cancer Screening' 1991; mem. and Chrmn. (1984–85) Sci. Counc., Internat. Agy. for Rsch. on Cancer, Lyon, France 1981–85; Chrmn. UICC Project on Screening 1982–93; Chrmn., U.S. Nat. Res. Council Ctte. on Environmental Epidemiology 1990– ; mem. U.S. Nat. Acad. of Sci. Ctte. on Diet, Nutrition and Cancer 1980–83; Oversight Ctte. on Radio Epidemiological Tables 1983–84; Ctte. on Diet and Health 1985–88; Ctte. on Dietary Guidelines Implementation 1988–90; Internat. Epidemiology Assn.; Mem. Royal Coll. of Physicians of London 1964; Fellow Royal Coll. of Physicians of Can. 1973; Fellow Fac. of Community Med., U.K. 1977; Fellow, Am. Coll. of Epidemiology 1985; Fellow, Royal Coll. of Physicians of London 1987; Pres. Candn. Oncology Soc. 1980–81; Am. Soc. of Preventive Oncology 1983–85; recreations: sailing, furniture making; Clubs: National Yacht, Toronto; Faculty, Univ. of Toronto; Athenaeum, London; Home: 575 Avenue Rd., Apt. 304, Toronto, Ont. M4V 2K2; Office: McMurrich Bldg., 4th Flr., 12 Queen's Pk. Cres. W., Toronto, Ont. M5S 1A8.

**MILLER, Bernard Francis Jr.,** B.A., B.Comm., M.Sc.; educator and management consultant; b. Halifax, N.S. 25 Feb. 1935; s. Dr. Bernard Francis and Mary Barbara (Currie) M.; e. St. Francis Xavier Univ., Pre-Med. 1956; Dalhousie Univ., B.Comm. 1961; Concordia Univ., B.A. 1967; Cornell Univ., M.Sc. 1970; m. Susan d. Fisher and Ellen MacLennan 28 July 1960; children: Carole Ann, Bernard Francis, Mary Joanne, Robert Alexander; DIRECTOR, ADVANCED MANAGEMENT CENTRE, DALHOUSIE UNIV. 1993– ; Prof., Henson College of Public Affairs and Continuing Education; Pres., Masters of Industrial & Labour Relations Inc. (MILR); Dir., Atlantic Council for Organizational Excellence; Dir., Halifax Airport Privatization Study Group; Dir., Walnut Properties Ltd.; Lilac Investments Inc.; Offr., Royal Candn. Ordnance Corps 1954–56; Passenger Agent, Trans.-Can. Airlines (now Air Canada) 1957; Econ. Analyst 1963; var. positions in Personnel and Admin. 1963–80; Vice-Pres., Personnel 1980; Vice-Pres., Atlantic Can. 1983; Vice-Pres., Cargo 1985; Vice-Pres., In-Flight Service 1988; Sr. Associate, Advanced Management Centre, Dalhousie Univ. 1991; Vice Chrmn., Halifax Industrial Commission; Dir., Victoria General Hospital Foundation; mem., Arbitration and Mediation Institute of N.S.; mem., Royal United Services Institute; author: 'Collective Bargaining in the Canadian Airline Industry' 1970; 'Productivity or Perish' 1981; 'Collective Bargaining in Transition' 1984; 'Labour Relations in the Era of Deregulation Mergers Bankruptcies and Layoffs' 1992; recreations: reading, travel, summer cottage; Clubs: Royal N.S. Yacht Squadron; Pictou Golf & Country; Home: 51 Downs Ave., Halifax, N.S. B3N 2Z1; Office: Advanced Mgmnt. Centre, Dalhousie Univ., 6100 University Ave., Halifax, N.S. B3H 3J5.

**MILLER, Danny,** B.Comm., M.B.A., Ph.D.; university professor; b. Montreal, Que. 15 Nov. 1947; s. Morris and Maria Louisa (Verbruggen) M.; e. Sir George Williams Univ., B.Comm. (distinction) 1968; Univ. of Toronto, M.B.A. 1970; McGill Univ., Ph.D. 1976; single; PROF., ECOLE DES HAUTES ETUDES COMM., UNIV. OF MONTREAL 1986– ; VISITING PROF., McGILL UNIV. 1986– & UNIV. OF ALTA. 1989–91; Sr. Project Analyst, Bank of Montreal 1970–72; Rsch. Assoc., Fac. of Mngt., McGill Univ. 1976–80; Assoc. Prof., Rsch., Ecole des Hautes Etudes Comm., Univ. of Montreal 1980–86; Dean's List 1967–68; fellowships: SSHRCC 1972–75; Govt. of Que. Doct. 1972–75; Central Mortgage & Housing 1973; Outstanding Rsch. Award, Ecole des Hautes Etudes Comm. 1981; Best Paper Award, Acad. of Mngmt. 1993; Mem., Awards Ctte. (& Ed. Bd.), 'Academy of Management Journal' 1987; Ed. Bd. Mem., 'Journal of Management,' 'Administrative Science Quarterly,' 'Journal of Management Studies,' 'Strategic Management Journal,' 'Organization Science,' 'Industrial Crisis Quarterly' and 'Canadian Journal of Administrative Sciences'; author of over 60 acad. papers; author: 'The Icarus Paradox' 1990; co-author: 'Organizations: A Quantum View' 1984, 'The Neurotic Organization: Diagnosing and Changing Counterproductive Styles of Management' 1984, 'Unstable at the Top: Inside the Troubled Organization' 1988; recreation: hiking; Office: 4642 Melrose Ave., Montreal, Que. H4A 2S9.

**MILLER, Douglas Wilfred,** B.A.; executive; b. Vancouver, B.C. 13 July 1928; s. Jenny Josephine (Stifler) Spicer and late Wilfred Earle M.; e. Univ. of B.C., B.A. 1950; m. Margery Elaine d. late Archdeacon S. Williams 21 May 1954; children: D.Scott, Nancy J., Laura J.; PRES., DWM PETROLEUM MANAGEMENT CORPORATION; Dir. & Chrmn. Greypower Resources Ltd.; Dir., RTER Holding Corp.; Dir., Northstar Energy Corp.; Phi Gamma Delta; Anglican; recreations: swimming, bridge; Clubs: Calgary Petroleum; Ranchmen's; Office: 606 Bank of Canada Bldg., 404–Sixth Ave. S.W., Calgary, Alta. T2P 0R9.

**MILLER, Frank,** B.Eng., P.Eng.; b. Toronto, Ont. 14 May 1927; s. Percy Frank and Margaret Stuart (McKean) M.; e. Regal Road Public School and Oakwood Coll. Inst., Toronto, 1942; Gravenhurst (Ont.) High Sch., 1945; McGill Univ., B.Eng. 1949; m. Ann McArthur, d. William M. Norman, Montreal, 13 May 1950; children: Lawrence, Ross, Norman, Mary; CHRMN., DISTRICT MUNICIPALITY OF MUSKOKA 1991– ; Chrmn., Algoma Central Corp. 1991– ; Dir., National Trust; Algoma Central Railway; John Forsyth Co. Ltd.; Rsch. Engr., Rubberset Co. Ltd., Gravenhurst 1949–52; Production Engr., Alcan, Arvida, Que. 1952–53; Chem. Teacher, St. Andrew's Coll., Aurora, Ont. 1953–56; Sales Engr. and Br. Mgr. Scarfe & Co., Brantford and Montreal 1956–60; Resort Owner, Patterson Kaye Lodge, Bracebridge, Ont. 1960–71; Pres., Gordon Motor Sales Muskoka Ltd. 1962–69; Councillor, Bracebridge 1967–70; el. Ont. Prov. Parliament, for Muskoka prov. g.e. 1971; Parlty. Asst. to Min. of Health for Ont. 1972–74; Min. of Health for Ont. 1974–77; Min. of Nat. Resources 1977–78; Min. of Treasury & Econ. 1978–83; Min. of Industry and Trade 1983–85; Min. of Intergovernmental Affairs 1985; Premier of Ont. 1985; Chrmn. Ontario International Corp. 1987–92; mem., Assn. Prof. Engrs. Ont.; P. Conservative; United Church; recreations: skiing, boating, golf; Club: Albany, Rotary; Home: Box 2198, Bracebridge, Ont. P1L 1W1; Office: 10 Pine St., Bracebridge, Ont. P1L 1N3.

**MILLER, (Charles) George,** M.Sc., D.Phil., P.Eng.; b. Winnipeg, Man. 1 Nov. 1932; s. Rossel Lorne and Mary Christine (Cornelius) M.; e. West Ward Pub. Sch. and Napanee (Ont.) Coll. Inst. 1950; Queen's Univ. B.Sc. (Engn. Chem.) 1954, M.Sc. (Phys. Chem.) 1955; Balliol Coll. Oxford Univ. D.Phil. (Phys. Chem.) 1957; children: Peter George, Patricia Margaret, David Lorne, Stephen James; PRESIDENT & C.E.O., THE MINING ASSOCIATION OF CANADA 1984– ; Post Doctorate Fellow Nat. Research Council 1957; Research Group Leader Imperial Tobacco Co. Ltd. Montreal 1958; served with Celanese Canada Ltd. (formerly Chemcell Ltd.) successively as Devel. Sec. Head Edmonton, Supt. Chem. Devel., Supt. Process Systems, Dir. Manpower Planning Montreal, Mang. Dir. Chemcell S.A. Switzerland, Plant Mgr. Edmonton, Gen. Mgr. Chem. Div. 1960–72; Vice Pres. Operations, Stanley Associates Engineering Ltd. Edmonton 1972; Extve. Dir., Centre for Resource Studies, Queen's Univ. 1974–81; Asst. Depy. Min., Mineral Policy, Energy Mines & Resources, Canada 1981–84; Past mem. Adv. Council on Engn. Queen's Univ.; Past Dir., Orphans Home and Widows Friend Soc. of Kingston; Past Dir. and Treas. Child Devel. Centre Edmonton; Past mem. Alta. Bd. Engn. Educ.; Past Chrmn. Science Adv. Comte. Alta. Environment Conserv. Authority; author or co-author various scient. papers; Gen. Ed. of series of monographs on mineral policy; CIMM distinguished lecturer, 1979/80; Gen. Chrmn., CIMM Annual General Meeting 1984; mem., Prof. Engrs. Assn. Ont.; Candn. Inst. Mining and Metall.; recreations: travel, hiking; Home: 275 Charlotte St., #1, Ottawa, Ont. K1N 9L1; Office: 350 Sparks St., Suite 1105, Ottawa, Ont. K1R 7S8.

**MILLER, Ian Douglas,** B.A.; commercial credit specialist; b. Edmonton, Alta. 19 Dec. 1950; s. John Beattie and Marie-Louise (Grunert) M.; e. Carleton Univ. B.A. (Hons.) 1976; m. Kathryn d. Herbert Darrell and Mary Elizabeth Biggs 7 Sept. 1974; children: Laura Elizabeth, Grady John Darrell; VICE-PRESIDENT, UNDERWRITING AND RISK MANAGEMENT, TRADE INDEMNITY plc 1989– ; Supervisor, Commercial Credit Operations, Export Development Corp. 1976–81; Manager, Commercial Lending, Royal Bank of Canada 1981–83; Mgr., Short Term Credit Analysis Div., Export Devel. Corp. 1983–89; recreations: fly-fishing, golf, fitness; Home: 240 Spring St., Almonte, Ont. K0A 1A0; Office: 331 Cooper St., Ste. 707, Ottawa, Ont. K2P 0G5.

**MILLER, Jack David Raoul,** B.Sc., M.B., B.Ch., F.R.C.P.(C), F.A.C.R.; neuroradiologist; b. Johannesburg, S. Africa 15 Apr. 1930; s. Harold and Inez Gwynneth (Behrman) M.; e. Parktown Boys' High Sch. Johannesburg 1946; Univ. of Witwatersrand B.Sc. (Mech. Engn.) 1950, M.B., B.Ch. 1956; F.R.C.P.(C) 1968; F.A.C.R. 1984; children: Richard Keir, Nina Kathleen, Gavin Keith; m. Miriam Sheckter 28 Dec. 1988; Clin. Prof. and Chrmn. of Radiology, Univ. of Alta. 1971–1983; Chrmn. Dept. Radiology, Univ. of Alta. Hosp. 1971–1983; interned Cornation Hosp. Johannesburg; residency Northwestern Univ. Med. Sch. Chicago 1959–63; Clin. Instr. Univ. of Alta. 1963, Clin. Lectr. 1967, Asst. Clin. Prof. 1968, Assoc. Clin. Prof. and Acting Chrmn. of Radiology 1970–71; author or co-author numerous articles diagnostic radiology; mem. Candn. Med. Assn.; Am. Coll. Radiol.; Am. Neuroradiol. Soc.; Assn. Univ. Radiols.; Candn. Assn. Radiols.; Hebrew; recreations: reading, swimming; Clubs: Royal Glenora; Nucleus Ambiguous; Home: #501, 11826 – 100 Ave., Edmonton, Alta. T5K 0K3; Office: 112 St. & 83 Ave., Edmonton, Alta. T6G 2B7.

**MILLER, Joanna Elizabeth,** B.A.; peace, international development, human rights and environmental activist; b. Vancouver B.C. 18 May 1926; d. William Roger and Irene Mabel (Martin) Green; e. North Vanc. H.S. 1943; Univ. of B.C. B.A. 1948; m. Leonard Gordon s. Dorance and Louise M. 25 June 1949; children: Jeffrey Stephen, Leslie Anne, Gary Andrew, David Matthew; 30 years of intensive involvement on local, nat. & internat. level in orgns. & activities related to peace, internat. devel., human rights & the environment; Saskatoon Woman of the Year for Community Serv. 1983; Candn. Rsch. Inst. for the Advancement of Women, Muriel Duckworth Award 1985; Dir., The Muttart Found. (Edmonton) 1981–86, 1988– ; Mem., UNICEF Canada (Dir. 1974–84; Vice-Pres. 1976–78; Pres. 1978–80); Dir., U.N. Assn. in Canada 1980–83; Dir., Project Ploughshares 1983–85; Dir., Candn. Inst. for Internat. Peace & Security 1984–86; Dir., Arms Control Centre 1987– ; Dir., Group of 78 1988–89; Dir., Science for Peace 1989– ; Mem., Consultative Group on Arms Control & Disarmament of the Candn. Ambassador for Disarmament 1984–86; Spec. Advr. on Disarmament to Candn. Del. at 39th & 40th sessions, U.N. Gen. Assembly 1984, 1985; recreations: wilderness canoeing; Home: 913 University Dr., Saskatoon, Sask. S7N 0J9.

**MILLER, John A.,** M.A.; arts and cultural affairs executive; b. Guelph, Ont. 13 Oct. 1943; s. William and Agnes (Morrison) M.; e. Univ. of Waterloo B.A. 1966; Niagara (N.Y.) Univ. M.A. 1975; Educator, Adm. Orchard Park Secondary Sch. Stoney Creek and Central Secondary Sch. Stratford, Ont. 1966–79; Chief of Staff to Min. of Fed./Prov. Relations Can. 1979–80; Arts Adm. Stratford Festival and Stratford Summer Music 1980–81; Extve. Dir. Candn. Music Centre 1981–86; Internat. Sec. World Body of Music Info. Centres 1984–86; Pres., Cultural Support Services Inc., Toronto 1986– ; co-author 3 texts on Candn. govt. studies for schs.: 'Gaining Power,' 'Exercising Power,' 'The Challenge of Power' 1976, 1979; Office: 206 Gerrard St. E., Toronto, Ont. M5A 2E6.

**MILLER, Meier,** B.A., C.M.A., M.B.A.; business executive; b. 10 May 1947; e. C.M.A. 1972; Univ. of Toronto B.A. 1973, M.B.A. 1982; SR. VICE-PRES. FINANCE AND ADMINISTRATION, RESIDENTIAL GROUP, BRAMALEA LIMITED 1992– ; Accountant, Acres Ltd. 1971; Cost Accountant, Coscan Devel. Corp. 1971; Chief Accountant 1974; Controller, Operations 1976; Sr. Controller 1980; Dir. of Fin., Commercial Div. 1981; Vice-Pres. & Treas. 1981–89; Sr. Vice-Pres. & Treas. 1989–92; Mem., CIPREC Accounting Practices Comn.; Financial Extves. Inst.; Office: 20 Richmond St. E., Toronto, Ont. M5C 2Z4.

**MILLER, Michael Chilcott d'Elboux,** B.A., M.A.; aluminum industry executive; b. Northampton, England 26 Feb. 1929; s. Douglas Owen d'Elboux and Marian Chilcott (Lander) M.; e. Clifton Coll. Bristol, England 1942–47; Oxford Univ. B.A. 1952, M.A. 1956; Centre d'études indus. (Switz.), dipl. in bus. admin. 1958; m. Valerie d. Tetley and Beryl Tetley-Jones 16 Sept. 1967; children: Charlotte d'Elboux, Antonia Lea d'Elboux, Hugo Tetley d'Elboux; VICE-PRES., CORPORATE AFFAIRS, ALCAN ALUMINIUM LIMITED 1987– ; joined Alcan in U.K. 1952; held a number of sales & mktg. positions; apptd. Dir. of Sales, Alcan Indus. Ltd. 1968; Mng. Dir., Alcan Foils Ltd. 1972; Chrmn., Alcan Foils & Mng. Dir., Alcan's U.K. Foil Div. 1974; Commercial Mgr., Alcan Alum. (U.K.) Limited & Dir., Alcan Booth Indus. 1977; Dir., Corp. Relns., Alcan Alum. Limited Montreal 1981; Dir., Montreal Neurological Hosp.; Dir. and Vice Pres., Candn. Club of Montreal; recreations: golf, tennis, sailing; clubs: Mount Bruno Country, Hillside Tennis, Lake Brome Boating, University Club of Montreal, Hurlingham (U.K.); Home: 4325 Montrose Ave., Westmount, Que. H3Y 2A8; Office: 1188 Sherbrooke St. W., Montreal, Que. H3A 3G2.

**MILLER, Michael Coogan,** B.Arch., OAA, FRAIC; architect, university professor; b. Vancouver, B.C. 25 March 1939; s. Sidney Wilfred and Jessie Evelyn (Coogan) M.; e. Magee H.S. 1957; Univ. of B.C. B.Arch. 1965; m. Margit d. Ejner and Inger Sorensen 27 Dec. 1965; children: Mila-Christine, Patrick Coogan, Stephen Coogan; PROFESSOR, RYERSON POLYTECHNIC UNIV. 1992– ; Architect, Erickson Massey Arch. 1965–67, 1970–72 (Project Arch., 2 pavilions at Expo '67 Montreal); Architect & Partner, The Thom Partnership 1972–79; Principal, Michael Miller Arch. Inc. 1979–93 (exhibit designer, Ont. Pavilion, Expo '86 Vancouver); Lecturer (part-time), Ont. College of Art 1972–93; Lecturer & Design Critic, RAIC Syllabus Program 1979–83, '86; Guest Lecturer & Design Critic, Univs. of Waterloo, Manitoba, Guelph, York, McGill, B.C., Carleton, Copenhagen, Texas, Ryerson, and Humber and Sheridan colleges 1968–93; Principal & Dir. Design Coordinates Ltd. Toronto 1989–93, Dallas 1981–93; Mississauga Urban Design Award 1984, '87; Cdn. House and Home & OAA Award 1990, '92; Citation Expo '86; Mem., Capital Projects Ctte., Bd. of Trustees, Royal Ont. Museum; author: 'The Canadian Guide to Home Renovation' 1979, 'Guide to Home Renovation' 1981; Home: 103 Sutherland Dr., Toronto, Ont. M4G 1H6; Office: 350 Victoria St., Toronto, Ont. M5B 2K3.

**MILLER, Michael Joseph,** D.A.U., O.C.; oilfield firefighter; b. Black Diamond, Alta. 19 Oct. 1944; s. Kenneth Joseph (Smokey) and Jeanne Josephine (Wilson) M.; 1st m. Sandra Lea Langston; 2nd m. Sharie Lynn Jones; children: Stacy Jeanne, Tanis Ann, Lindsay Tyler (from 1st m.); Logan Jose Hurricane (from 2nd m.); CHIEF EXECUTIVE OFFICER, SAFETY BOSS LTD.; one of the world's foremost well control experts; active in oilfield fire fighting & well control 1956– ; contracted by Kuwait Oil Co. in early 1991 to extinguish fires & control wells damaged during 1991 Gulf War: 180 wells capped in 200 days (last well capped 6 Nov. 1991); Dir., Fire Boss Ltd.; Emir of Kuwait's Award Nov. 1991; U.S. Cong. Fire Serv. Inst. Award 1991; Oilweek Mag. Oilman of the Year Award 1991; Maclean's Magazine 1991 Honor Roll of Canadians Who Make A Difference 1991; Candn. Energy Inst. Cert. of Recognition 1992; Emerald Award, Alta. Found. for Environ. Excellence 1992; Canada Day Ctte. Great Candn. Award 1993; D.A.U. (Honoris Causa), Univ. of Athabasa 1992; Mem., Order of Canada 1994; Petroleum Serv. Assn. of Can. (Past Dir.); Candn. Assn. of Drilling Engrs.; Soc. of Petroleum Engineers; author of num. tech. papers; recreations: diving, sailing, skiing; Home: c/o P.O. Box 11560, Dubai, U.A.E.; Office: 707 – 425 First St. S.W., Calgary, Alta. T2P 3V7.

**MILLER, Peter,** B.A., M.A., Ph.D.; university professor; b. Chicago, Illinois 20 Nov. 1936; s. William Whipple and Helen (Robbins) Miller; e. Yale Univ. B.A. 1958, M.A. 1966, PH.D. 1967; m. Carolyn Garlich d. William and Lydia Garlich Aug. 1960; children: Joel Garlich-Miller, Dr. Maria Miller, Micah Garlich-Miller; PROF., DEPT. OF PHILOSOPHY, UNIV. OF WINNIPEG 1967– ; Chair, present dept. 1975–78, 1990– ; Acting Chair 1981–82; Treas., Internat. Soc. for Environ. Ethics 1989–93; Extve., Candn. Soc. for the Study of Practical Ethics 1988– (Pres. 1990– ); Vice-Pres., Time to Respect Earth's Ecosytems (TREE) 1990– ; Mem., Manitoba NDP Environ. Task Force 1989–91 (authored report 'The Place of Recycling in Sustainable Development'); Bd. Mem., Manitoba Model Forest; author of a variety of papers; Home: 133 Riley Cres., Winnipeg, Man. R3T 0J5; Office: 515 Portage Ave., Winnipeg, Man. R3B 2E9.

**MILLER, Peter J.,** B.Sc., M.Ed., Ph.D.; university professor and administrator; b. London, England 15 Feb. 1934; s. Frederick and Florence (Shepherd) M.; e. London Sch. of Econ. B.Sc. (Hons.) 1957; Univ. of Alberta B.Ed. (Hons.) 1962, M.Ed. 1965, Ph.D. 1969; m. Angela d. Sebastian and Rosina Cuomo 12 Jan. 1957; children: Terrence, Susan, Christine, Catherine; Pilot Offr., Royal Air Force 1952–54; Teacher, Sarah Robinson Sch. (U.K.) 1958–60; Teacher, Edmonton Public Sch. Bd. 1960–65; Univ. Prof., Fac. of Edn., Univ. of Alta. 1969–75; Chrmn., Dept. of Educational Foundation 1975–83; Dean of Student Services, Univ. of Alberta 1983–93; editor: 'Education in Canada: An Interpretation' 1985; author of over 40 articles in scholarly & profl. jours.; recreations: golf, tennis; clubs: Glendale Golf & Country, Michener Park Tennis; Home: 64 Glenhaven Cres., St. Albert, Alta. T8N 1A5; Office: 245 Athabasca Hall, Edmonton, Alta. T6G 2E8.

**MILLER, Richard Graham,** B.Sc., M.Sc., Ph.D.; university professor; scientist; b. St. Catharines, Ont. 2 Oct. 1938; s. Richard Birnie and Lillian Frances (Harkness) M.; e. Univ. of Alta., B.Sc. 1960, M.Sc. 1961; Calif. Inst. of Technol., Ph.D. 1966; m. Beverley d. George and Dorothy Barnhouse 6 Sept. 1963; children: Graham Birnie, George Moore; Founding Chrmn., Dept. of Immunology, Univ. of Toronto 1984–90; Chrmn., Dept. of Med. Biophysics 1992– ; post-doct. work, Ont. Cancer Inst. 1966–67, Sr. Sci. 1967– ; Asst. Prof., Univ. of Toronto 1967, Assoc. Prof. 1971, Prof. 1976; Dept. of Med. Biophysics 1967– , Inst. Med. Sci. 1970– , Inst./Dept. Immunol. 1973– ; developed physical methods for characterization & separation of living cells (one such method became a science citation classic); rsch.: stem cells, T cell differentiation, autoreactivity & tolerance; regular lectr. to grad. students & undergrad. med. students; has served on local, prov. & nat. grant review panels of numerous agencies incl. Nat. Cancer Inst., Min. of Health, Ont.; Med. Rsch. Counc.; Mem., Adv. Ctte., MS Soc.; Arthritis Soc.; Fellow, Trinity College; Charles Gould Easton Prof. of Immunology; Mem., Candn. & Am. Socs. for Immunol.; Soc. for Anal. Cytology; author or co-author of over 150 sci. pubs.; recreations: bird watching; Home: 415 Heath St. E., Toronto, Ont. M4G 1B4; Office: Ontario Cancer Institute, Toronto, Ont. M4X 1K9.

**MILLER, Robert Carmi,** M.Sc., Ph.D.; educator; b. Elgin, Ill. 10 Aug. 1942; e. Trinity Coll. Hartford, Conn. B.Sc. 1964; Pa. State Univ., M.Sc. 1965; Univ. of Pa. Ph.D. 1969; VICE-PRESIDENT, RESEARCH, UNIV. OF B.C. 1988– , Prof. of Microbiol. 1979– ; U.S. Pub. Health Service Trainee 1966–69; USAEC Postdoctoral Fellow 1969–70; Postdoctoral Fellow Am. Cancer Soc. 1970–71; Asst. Prof. present Univ. 1971, Assoc. Prof. 1975, Head of Microbiol. 1982–85, Dean of Science 1985–88; Med. Rsch. Council Grants Ctte. on Genetics 1980–82; Nat. Cancer Inst. Grants Panel A (Molecular Biol., Virol. & Genetics) 1981–85; NSERC Strategic Grant Ctte. for Biotechnol. 1985–87; MRC Univ./Ind. Prog. Grant Ctte. 1987–89; co-recipient, Science Council of B.C. Gold Medal for Natural Sciences 1993; author or co-author various sci. publs.; Assoc. Ed. 'Virology' 1974–85; 'Journal Virology' 1975–84; Mem. Bd. of Dirs.: Discovery Foundation (Chrmn.); Discovery Parks, Inc. (Pres.); Vancouver General Hospital; PAPRICAN; LIST (Chrmn.); Past Mem. Bd. of Dirs.: Science Council of B.C.; Forintek; BC Rsch. Inc.; BC Cancer Agency; Office: 6328 Memorial Rd., Vancouver, B.C. V6T 2B3.

**MILLER, Hon. Tevie Harold,** B.A., LL.B.; judge; b. Edmonton, Alta. 1 Jan. 1928; s. Abe William and Rebecca (Griesdorf) M.; e. Univ. of Alta. B.A. 1949, LL.B. 1950; m. Arliss June d. late Louis Toban, Vancouver, B.C. 24 June 1951; children: Catherine Dolgoy, Joshua, Lisa, Shadlyn; Assoc. Chief Justice, Court of Queen's Bench Alta. 1984–93, retired; Justice of the Court with Supernumary Status; called to Bar of Alta. 1951; cr. Q.C. 1968; joined in partnership with father 1951; Sr. Partner, Miller, Miller, Witten 1964; Chrmn. Jt. Law Soc. Alta. and Candn. Bar Assn. Comte. Kirby Comn. Prov. Court System; apptd. Judge, Dist. Court Alta. 1974; Depy. Judge N.W.T. 1976; apptd. to Trial Div. Supreme Court Alta. 1976; Depy. Judge Y.T. 1978; Judge, Court of Queen's Bench, Alta. 1979–84; Chancellor, Univ. of Alta. 1986–90; service as mem. Senate and Bd. Govs., Univ. of Alta., Sessional Lectr. in Law, Pres. of Gen. Alumni Assn.; Chrmn. Prof. Div., Three Alta. Univs. Fund Raising Campaigns; Bd. Govs. Alta. Coll.; Chrmn. of Bd., Banff Sch. Advanced Mang., Lectr. in Business Law; Pres. Un. Way of Edmonton, Campaign Chrmn. Prof. Div.; Chrmn. Bd., Banff Sch. of Adv. Mgmnt.; Pres., Edmonton Symphony Soc.; mem. Bd. Edmonton Assn. Retarded Children; mem., Bd. of Gov., Universiade '83; Past Pres. Edmonton Jewish Community Council; Chrmn. Edmonton Un. Jewish Appeal; Pres., N.W. Candn. Council B'Nai Brith; Honoree, Edmonton Jewish Community Negev Dinner 1972; Pres. Edmonton Lib. Assn.; Convention Chrmn. Alta. Lib. Assn.; Lib. Cand. for Edmonton W. Fed. g.e. 1968; Dir. Edmonton Eskimo Football Club; Vice Pres. Bd. Dirs. Eleventh Commonwealth Games (1978) Foundation; Dir. YMCA; Sub-Lt. R.C.N. (R) retired; Past Pres. Edmonton Bar Assn.; mem. Council, Candn. Bar Assn. Alta. Div.; Hebrew; recipient, Hon. LL.D. Univ. of Alberta 1991; recipient, Torch of Learning Award from Hebrew Univ. of Jerusalem 1992; 'Integrity Award' Rotary Club 1993; recreations: sailing, travel; Clubs: Univ. of Alta. Faculty; Centre; Home: 34 Riverside Cres., Edmonton, Alta. T5N 3M5; Office: Law Courts Bldg., Edmonton, Alta. T5J 0R2.

**MILLER, W.R.,** C.A.; oil and gas executive; b. Dunnville, Ont. 5 Feb. 1935; s. Roy B. and Ruby Lillian (Pollock) M.; e. Dunnville H.S.; Ont. Inst. of C.A.; m. Carroll Elizabeth d. Clarence and Violet Martin 10 Oct. 1959; children: Andrew, Timothy, Roderick; VICE-PRES. & CHIEF FINANCIAL OFFR., HUSKY OIL LTD. 1984– ; Student to Audit Mgr., Clarkson Gordon & Co. 1953–65; Vice-Pres. Finance, United Financial Management Ltd. 1965–74; Sr. Vice-Pres. Finance, Brascan Limited 1974–81; Vice-Pres., Dir. & Chief Finan. Offr., Wood Gundy Corp. 1981–84; Dir., Candn. Liquid Air Ltd.; Dir., Alberta Theatre Projects; Office: P.O. Box 6525, Stn. D, Calgary, Alta. T2P 3G7.

**MILLET, Nicholas Byram,** M.A., Ph.D.; museum curator; educator; b. Richmond, N.H. 28 June 1934; s. Charles Sumner Jr. and Frances Ina (Williamson) M.; e. Wesley Coll. Melbourne, Australia; Univ. of Chicago A.B. 1955, M.A. 1959; Yale Univ. Ph.D. 1968; m. Saralaine d. Charles and Sarah Evans 8 May 1965; children: Lydia, Joshua Evans, Amanda Ruth; CURATOR AND HEAD OF EGYPTIAN DEPT., ROYAL ONT. MUSEUM 1974– ; Prof. of Egyptian Archaeol. Univ. of Toronto 1981– ; Dir., Am. Research Centre in Egypt, Cairo 1960–63, Dir. of Excavations 1963–65, mem. Bd. Govs. 1973– ; Asst. Prof. of Egyptology Harvard Univ. 1968–70; Curator and Head Egyptian Dept. present Museum 1970– ; Dir. Gebel Adda Project, Nubia 1962–66; Dir. Dongola Reach Project N. Sudan 1976–84; Dir., Lahun Expedition 1988– ; Soc. for Study Egyptian Antiquities 1970– , Pres. 1982–89; co-author 'Mummies, Disease and Ancient Cultures' 1980; Home: 524 Castlefield Ave., Toronto, Ont.; Office: 100 Queen's Park W., Toronto, Ont. M5S 2C6.

**MILLETTE, Yves,** B.A., LL.L.; insurance executive; b. Drummondville, Que. 22 July 1948; e. Univ. of Sherbrooke B.A. 1969; Univ. of Montreal LL.L. 1972; SR. VICE-PRES., CANADIAN LIFE & HEALTH INSUR. ASSN. 1990– ; Mem., Que. Bar 1974; Legal Counsel, Govt. of Que. 1974–80; Deputy Supt. of Insur., Que. 1980–86; Vice-Pres., Francophone Dept, CLHIA 1986–89; Assoc., Sobeco Group (Pension & Benefit Cons.) 1989–90; Mem., Quebec Bar; Canadian Bar; Home: 1245 Place Ste Croix, St-Laurent, Que. H4L 4Y6; Office: 1 Queen St. E., Suite 1700, Toronto, Ont. M5C 2X9.

**MILLEY, Fred March;** executive; b. St. John's, Nfld. 22 Dec. 1921; s. Jordan and Beatrice Mary (March) M.; e. Prince of Wales Coll. St. John's 1939; Univ. of W. Ont. Bus. Mgmt. courses 1964, 1975; m. Margaret d. T.A. and Dorothy MacNab June 1950; children: Peter, Douglas, Ian, Janet; CHRMN. ST. JOHN'S PORT CORP.; Mgr. St. John's Airport 1946–49; Canadian General Electric Co. Ltd. 1949–55; joined soft drink and brewing firms Nfld. 1955 (acquired by John Labatt Ltd. 1962), Vice Pres. and Gen. Mgr. Nfld. Div. 1976; Trustee Blue Cross Atlantic Can.; Past Pres. Jaycees; Dir. Kiwanis Music Festival Assn. St. John's; United Church (Past Chrmn. Bd. Mgmt.); recreation: golf; Club: Bally Holy Golf & Curling; Home: 30 Roche St., St. John's, Nfld. A1B 1L7; Office: P.O. Box 6178, St. John's, Nfld. A1C 5X8.

**MILLGATE, Jane,** B.A., M.A., Ph.D., F.R.S.C.; university professor; b. Leeds, England 8 June 1937; d. Maurice and Marie (Schofield) Barr; e. Leeds Girls' H.S.; Univ. of Leeds, B.A. (Hons.) 1959, M.A. 1963; Univ. of Kent at Canterbury, Ph.D. 1970; m. Michael s. Stanley and Marjorie M. 27 Feb. 1960; PROF., DEPT. OF ENGLISH, VICTORIA COLL., UNIV. OF TORONTO 1977– ; Instr., 1964–65; Lectr. 1965–70; Asst. Prof. 1970–72; Assoc. Prof. 1972–77; Vice-Dean, Fac. of Arts & Sci., Univ. of Toronto 1982–87; Ed. Bd., 'English Studies in Canada' 1979–82, 1987–93; 'Victorian Review' 1989– ; 'Dalhousie Review' 1991– ; Adv. Bd., Edinburgh Ed. of the Waverley Novels 1984– ; Fellow, Inst. of Adv. Studies in the Humanities, Edinburgh Univ., Fall 1974; F.R.S.C. 1986; Rose Mary Crawshay Prize, British Acad. 1988; Bd. of Regents, Victoria Univ. 1981–86; mem., Assn. of Candn. Univ. Teachers of Eng. (Pres. 1980–82); Candn. Fed. for the Humanities (Bd. Mem. 1980–83, 1987–90; extve. 1981–83); Victorian Studies Assn. of Ont. (Pres. 1978–80); Assn. for Scottish Lit. Studies; author: 'Macaulay' 1973, 'Walter Scott: The Making of the Novelist' 1984, 'Scott's Last Edition: A Study in Publishing History' 1987; editor: 'Editing Nineteenth-Century Fiction' 1978; Home: 75 Highland Ave., Toronto, Ont. M4W 2A4; Office: Toronto, Ont. M5S 1K7.

**MILLGATE, Michael (Henry),** M.A., Ph.D., F.R.S.C., F.R.S.L.; educator; b. Southampton, Eng. 19 July 1929; s. Stanley and Marjorie Louisa (Norris) M.; e. St. Catharine's Coll. Cambridge B.A. 1952, M.A. 1956; Univ. of Mich. 1956–57; Univ. of Leeds Ph.D. 1960; m. Jane d. Maurice and Marie Barr 27 Feb. 1960; UNIVERSITY PROFESSOR, UNIV. OF TORONTO 1987; Tutor-Organizer, Workers' Ednl. Assn., S. Lindsey, Eng. 1953–56; Lectr. in Eng. Univ. of Leeds 1958–64; Prof. and Chrmn. of Eng. York Univ. Downsview, Ont. 1964–67; Prof. of English, Univ. of Toronto 1967– ; Can. Council Leave Fellow 1968–69; S.W. Brooks Fellow Univ. of Queensland, Australia 1971; Killam Sr. Rsch. Scholar 1974–75; John Simon Guggenheim Meml. Fellow 1977–78; Carpenter Lectr. Ohio Wesleyan Univ. 1978; Connaught Sr. Fellow in Humanities 1979–80; SSHRCC Leave Fellow 1981–82; Killam Research Fellow 1986–88; University Professor 1987; author 'William Faulkner' 1961; 'American Social Fiction' 1964; 'The Achievement of William Faulkner' 1966; 'Thomas Hardy: His Career as a Novelist' 1971; 'Thomas Hardy: A Biography' 1982; 'Testamentary Acts: Browning, Tennyson, James, Hardy' 1992; ed. 'Selected Poems' Tennyson 1963; 'Sister Carrie' Dreiser 1965; 'The Life and Work of Thomas Hardy' Hardy 1985; 'New Essays on Light in August' 1987; 'William Faulkner Manuscripts' 20 (4 vols.), 21 (2 vols.), 22 (4 vols.), and 23 (2 vols.) 1987; 'Selected Letters' Thomas Hardy 1990; co-ed. 'Transatlantic Dialogue' 1966; 'Lion in the Garden: Interviews with William Faulkner 1926–1962' 1966; 'The Collected Letters of Thomas Hardy' I 1978, II 1980, III 1982, IV 1984, V 1985, VI 1987, VII 1988; 'Thomas Hardy's "Studies, Specimens &c." Notebook' 1994; mem. adv. bd. 'Nineteenth–Century Fiction' 1978–86; ed. bd. 'Journal of American Studies' 1979–82; mem. Brit. Assn. Am. Studies (Extve. Ctte. 1961–64); Victorian Studies Assn. Ont. (Pres. 1970–72); Modern Lang. Assn. (Adv. Ctte. Center for Eds. Am. Authors 1971–74; Chrmn. Am. Lit. Sect. 1972; Chrmn. Methods of Literary Rsch. Div. 1984; Ctte. on Scholarly Editions 1985–89; Chrmn. Victorian Div. 1988); Thomas Hardy Soc. (Vice Pres. 1973– ); Soc. Study S. Lit. (Extve. Council 1972–76, 1981–85); Home: 75 Highland Ave., Toronto, Ont. M4W 2A4; Office: 7 King's Coll. Circle, Toronto, Ont. M5S 1A1.

**MILLIGAN, Andrew Frank Barnett,** M.B.E. (mil.), M.A.; b. Glasgow, Scot. 5 Dec. 1924; s. Francis Marshall and Elise Adrienne (Barnett) M.; e. Ayr. (Scot.) Acad., 1929–38; Fettes Coll. 1938–41; Univ. of Glasgow, 1941–42 and 1947–51; m. Linda Culter, 14 Feb. 1975; children: Bruce, Clive, Michele, Kate; Chrmn., Lysander Gold Corp.; Pres. & Dir., Cornucopia Resources Ltd.; Dir.: Advanced Projects Ltd.; Goldstack Resources Ltd.; Rare Earth Resources Ltd.; joined Bristol Aeroplane Company as Economist, 1951; appointed Assistant Overseas Contracts Mgr., 1954; Asst. Secretary, Bristol Aero Engines Limited, Montreal, 1956. Secy. 1958; Secy., The Bristol Aeroplane Co. of Can. Ltd. and Bristol Aero-Industries Ltd., 1958; Vice-Pres. and Dir., Bristol Aero-Industries Ltd. 1961; Vice-Pres. and Gen. Mgr., Power Machinery Div., 1964; established own mang. counselling business 1967; Pres. TRV Group 1981–83; Pres. Glamis Gold Ltd. 1984–86; Chrmn., Cornucopia Resources Ltd. 1986–89; served with Royal Scots Fusiliers 1942–47; seconded to Somaliland Scouts 1944–47; served in U.K. and Africa; discharged with rank Maj.; recreations: swimming, scuba diving, marathon running, reading; Club: The Vancouver; Home: 5811 Marguerite St., Vancouver, B.C. V6M 3K7.

**MILLIGAN, Frank D.,** B.A., M.A., Ph.D.; museum director; b. Toronto, Ont. 7 April 1952; s. Frank J. and Doris M. (McParland) M.; e. Univ. of Guelph B.A. (Hons.); Univ. of Western Ont. M.A. 1987; Univ. of Alta. Ph.D. 1988; m. Nancy d. David and Catherine Nicolson 21 Aug. 1976; children: Julie, Carrolyn, Heather; DIRECTOR, NEW BRUNSWICK MUSEUM 1992– ; Lecturer, Univ. of Alta. 1987–91; Historic Site Mus. Dir., Historic Naval & Miliary Establishments, Penetanguishene 1977–81; Alberta Culture 1981–92; lectured in Candn. history & Eur. history; Cert. in Museum Studies, Ont.; Home: 43 Queensbury Dr., Rothesay, N.B.; Office: 277 Douglas Ave., Saint John, N.B. E2K 1E5.

**MILLIKEN, John A.,** M.D., C.M., F.R.C.P.(C); physician; b. Saskatoon, Sask 15 May 1923; s. Robert Handside and Ethel May (McIntosh) M.; e. Queen's Univ., M.D., C.M. 1946; F.R.C.P.(C) 1954; m. Catherine Margaret, d. Dr. C. H. McCuaig, Kingston, Ont., 9 Feb. 1946; seven children; Prof. Emeritus of Medicine, Queen's Univ.; Hotel Dieu Hosp., Kingston, Ont.; Fellow, Royal Coll. of Physicians Can.; Am. Coll. Cardiol.; Am. Coll. Phys. Am. Coll. Chest Phys.; mem., Candn. Cardiovascular Soc.; Candn. Med. Assn.; Ont. Med. Assn.; Kingston Acad. of Med.; N.Y. Acad. Sciences; United Church; recreation: golf; Clubs: Cataraqui; Royal Ottawa; Imperial (Naples, Fla.); Home: R.R. #2, Kingston, Ont.; Office: Hotel Dieu Hospital, Kingston, Ont. K7L 5G2.

**MILLIKEN, Peter Andrew Stewart,** M.P.; barrister and solicitor; b. Kingston, Ont. 12 Nov. 1946; s. John Andrew and Catherine Margaret (McCuaig) M.; e. Kingston C.&V.I. 1964; Queen's Univ., B.A. (Hons.) 1968; Oxford Univ., B.A. 1970, M.A. 1978; Dalhousie Univ., LL.B. 1971; M.P. FOR KINGSTON & THE ISLANDS 1988– and PARLIAMENTARY SECRETARY TO THE LEADER OF THE GOVERNMENT IN THE HOUSE OF COMMONS 1993– ; called to Bar of Ont. 1973; practiced with Cunningham Swan Carty, Little & Bonham 1973– ; Dir., Kingston Symphony Assn. 1984–89; Mem., Coroners' Counc., Ont. 1985–88; Gov., Kingston Gen. Hosp.; Le Royer Patron, Hotel Dieu Hosp.; Past Pres., Kingston & The Islands Lib. Assn.; Mem., Chalmers United Ch.; recreations: white water canoeing; clubs: University Club of Toronto, Cave Reginam; Home: Quaker Valley, R.R. #1, Elginburg, Ont. K0H 1M0; Office: House of Commons, Ottawa, Ont. K1A 0A6.

**MILLMAN, Allan David,** B.Sc., M.B.A.; appliance industry executive; b. Kingston, Ont. 13 Dec. 1947; s. Harvey Lawrence and Edythe Rae (Zacks) M.; e. Queen's Univ., B.Sc. 1970, M.B.A. 1972; m. Natalie d. Fred and Marjorie Walker 9 Mar. 1984; children: Ian Jeremy, Heather Lauren, Joanna Kathryn; PRES. & CHIEF EXTVE. OFFR., IONA APPLIANCES INC. 1984– ; var. mktg. & gen. mngmt. positions, Warner Lambert Can. Inc. 1972–75; Am. Can Can. 1976–83; Pres., General Signal Appliances Div. (Iona) Jan.-June 1984; completed buyout of Iona from Gen. Signal 1984; Past Chrmn., Portable Appliance Mfrs. Assn.; recreations: tennis, skiing, jogging; Clubs: Island Yacht; Mayfair Racket; Home: 25 Braeside Rd., Toronto, Ont. M4N 1X8; Office: 1 Eva Rd., Toronto, Ont. M9C 4Z5.

**MILLMAN, Thomas Reagh,** Ph.D., D.D., D.C.L.; b. Kensington, P.E.I. 14 June 1905; s. James Borthwick and Lottie Everett (Smith) M.; e. Prince of Wales Coll., P.E.I.; Univ. Coll., Toronto, B.A. 1931, M.A. 1933; Wycliffe Coll., L.Th. 1933, B.D. 1938; McGill Univ., Ph.D., 1943; Univ. of W. Ont., D.D. 1953; Wycliffe Coll. 1974; Trinity Coll. 1977; D.C.L. Univ. King's Coll. 1974; m. Colena Margaret (dec'd 16 Sept. 1991) d. J.A. McLeod, Lennoxville, Que., 1 Aug. 1944; o. Deacon 1933, Priest 1934; Tutor and Dean of Residence, Montreal Diocesan Theol. College 1935–41; Rector of Dunham and St. Armand East, Que. 1941–49; Prof. of Ch. Hist., Huron Coll., London, Ont. 1950–54; Archivist of Gen. Synod of Anglican Church of Can. 1956–75; Prof. Church Hist., Wycliffe Coll. 1954–74; Canon, St. James' Cathedral, Toronto 1969– ; Publications: 'Jacob Mountain, First Lord Bishop of Quebec' 1947; 'The Life of the Hon. the Rt. Rev. Charles James Stewart' 1953; 'A History of the Parish of New London, Prince Edward Island' 1959; 'Atlantic Canada to 1900: A History of the Anglican Church' 1983; contribs. Dict. Candn. Biog.; Home: 27 Brookdale Ave., Toronto, Ont. M5M 1P2.

**MILLMAN-FLOYD, Cynthia Gray,** A.R.C.T.; musician, university professor; b. Toronto, Ont. 13 March 1938; d. Peter MacKenzie and Margaret Bowness (Gray) Millman; e. Glebe Collegiate 1958; Royal Conserv. of Toronto A.R.C.T. 1958; State Academy for Music and the Performing Arts (Vienna, Austria), Pedagogical Dipl. with distinction 1963; Concert Dipl. with distinction 1968; principal teachers: Frederick Karam, Erwin Ratz (theory); Gladys Barnes, Bruno Seidlhofer, Dieter Weber, Malcom Frager (piano); m. Rowland Winslow s. Beulahree and Willis Floyd 25 July 1970; one d.: Margaret Elise; ASSOCIATE PROF., DEPT. OF MUSIC, UNIV. OF OTTAWA 1980– ; Lectr., Univ. of Ottawa 1970–73; Asst. Prof. 1973–80; Chair, Dept. of Music 1983–89 and 1990–91; Vice-Dean, Faculty of Arts 1991–93; concerts in Canada, Austria & China as soloist & chamber musician, specializing in Viennese Classical Period esp. Haydn & Schubert; Masterclasses & Adjudication in Canada & China (Tianjin 1988); research in piano pedagogy & classical period perf. practice; played major role in preparation of master's program, Univ. of Ottawa (approved 1988); fundraiser for new music bldg., Perez Hall (compl. in 1988); private piano teacher & coach; Abgangspreis (Grad. Prize), State Academy Vienna 1968; Can. Counc. grants 1964, '66; Candn. Nat. Exhib., Gold Medals, Piano 1958; Mem., Candn. Univ. Music Soc. (Chair, Council of Member Schools 1985–87); Am. Fed. of Musicians; recreations: reading, walking, swimming; Home: 584 Manor Ave., Ottawa, Ont. K1M 0J7; Office: 50 University, Ottawa, Ont. K1N 6N5.

**MILLS, Anthony John,** B.A., F.R.G.S., F.S.A.; egyptologist; b. Hamilton, Ont. 8 Sept. 1937; s. Wilfrid Laurier and Lydia Irene (Morwick) M.; e. McMaster Univ. B.A. 1959; Univ. of London, postgrad. dipl. in Egyptology 1963; m. Lesley Fiona d. Graham and Florence Murray 24 Oct. 1964; children: Heather Elizabeth, David Patrick, Andrew Graham, Thomas Trevelyan; RSCH. ASSOC., ROYAL ONT. MUSEUM 1983– ; UNESCO Arch. Expert, Sudan Antiquities Serv. (Dir., Arch. Survey of 2nd Cataract area of Nile Valley) 1963–72; Dir., Dakhleh Oasis Proj., Egypt 1978– ; Curator, Egyptian Dept., Royal Ont. Mus. & Asst./Assoc. Prof., Dept. of Near Eastern Studies, Univ. of Toronto 1972–83; Rsch. Fellow, Univ. Coll., London, Dept. of Egyptology; Rsch. Fellow, Centre for the Evolution of Human Environments, Univ. of Durham; Mem., Soc. for the Study of Egyptian Antiquities; Fellow, Royal Geog. Soc.; Fellow, Soc. of Antiquaries of London; Mem., Am. Rsch. Ctr. in Egypt; Arch. Soc. of Alexandria, Egypt Expl. Soc.; Internat. Assn. of Egyptologists; author: 'The Cemeteries of Qasr Ibrim' 1978 and num. reports on arch. rsch. in scholarly journals; Home: 34 Dennis Rd., Padstow, Cornwall, England; Office: Egyptian Dept., Royal Ont. Mus., 100 Queens Pk., Toronto, Ont. M5C 2C6.

**MILLS, Dennis Joseph,** M.P.; politician; b. Toronto, Ont. 19 July 1946; s. Alfred and Alice (Dalgleish) M.; e. St. Michael's Coll.; St. Thomas Univ.; York Univ.; m. Victoria Upper 3 Jan. 1971; children: Stephanie Monica, Jennifer Catherine, Craig Alfred Arthur, Andrea Elizabeth; PARLIAMENTARY SECRETARY TO THE MINISTER OF INDUSTRY; el. to H. of C. for Broadview-Greenwood g.e. 1988; Liberal; Catholic; mem., The National Club; The Ontario Jockey Club; Home: 2 Hawthorne Ave., Toronto, Ont. M4W 2Z2; Office: House of Commons, Ottawa, Ont. K1A 0A6.

**MILLS, Douglas Grant,** B.Sc., LL.B.; lawyer; b. Calgary, Alta. 15 Jan. 1956; s. James Grant and Rhoda Nancy (Kirkby) M.; e. Crescent Heights High Sch. 1973; Univ. of Calgary B.Sc. 1978, LL.B. 1983; m. Caroll d. Helmut and Eugenia Vollmer 20 Aug. 1977; children: Lindsay Rae, Laura Alexandra, Julia Crystal; PARTNER, BURNET DUCKWORTH & PALMER 1990– ; called to Bar of Alta. 1984; part-time contracts adm. Dome Petroleum Ltd. 1980–82; articled with present firm 1983–84, Assoc. Litigation practice 1984–90; Office: 1400, 350 7th Ave. S.W., Calgary, Alta. T2P 3N9.

**MILLS, Eric L.,** B.Sc., M.S., Ph.D.; university professor; b. Toronto, Ont. 7 July 1936; s. Leonard James and Evelyn (Barraclough) M.; e. Fisher Park H.S. 1955; Carleton Univ. B.Sc. (Hons.) 1959; Yale Univ. M.S. 1962, Ph.D. 1964; m. Anne d. Howard and Laura Glen 25 Aug. 1962; children: Christopher, Karen; Lectr., Carleton Univ. summer 1960; Asst. Prof., Zool., Queen's Univ. 1963–67; Instr. Marine Biol. Lab., Mass. summers 1963–67; Assoc. Prof., Dalhousie Univ. 1967–71, Prof. Dept. of Oceanography & Biol. 1971– ; Prof. of History and of Science 1994– ; Instr. Huntsman Marine Lab. 1971–78; Vis. Fellow, Corpus Christi Coll., Cambridge Univ. 1974–75; Instr. Bamfield Marine Stn. 1977; Nuffield Fellow, Univ. of Edinburgh 1981–82; Guest Prof., Inst. f. Meereskunde, Univ. Kiel, W. Germany 1984, 1988; H. Burr Steinbach Visiting Scholar, Woods Hole Oceanographic Inst. 1988; Ritter Memorial Fellow, Scripps Institution of Oceanography 1990; Chrmn., Dept. of Oceanography, Dalhousie Univ. 1990–92; Mem., Animal Biol. Grant Selection Ctte., NRC 1975–78; Adv. Ctte., Maritime Mus. of the Atlantic 1978– ; Steering Ctte., Maritimes Breeding Bird Atlas 1985–88; Gov. Gen's Medal, Carleton Univ. 1959; Woodrow Wilson fellow, Yale Univ. 1960–61; Fellow, Linnean Soc. of London 1975; Mem., N.S. Bird Soc. (Pres. 1969–71); Am. Soc. of Limnol. & Oceanography; Hist. of Sci. Soc.; Soc. for the Hist. of Nat. History; editor & author: 'One Hundred Years of Oceanography' 1975; 'Biological Oceanography: An Early History' 1989; approx. 70 sci. articles; recreations: bird watching, amateur radio; Home: R.R. 1, Rose Bay, Lunenburg Co., N.S. B0J 1R0; Office: Halifax, N.S. B3H 4J1.

**MILLS, J.M. (Jack),** B.Mus.; arts administrator; musician; b. Montague, P.E.I. 10 Jan. 1948; s. Donald Franklin and Mary Doreen (Murdock) M.; e. Univ. of Toronto, B.Mus. 1973; m. Rhonda d. Alonzo and Andrewine Armitage 28 Dec. 1971; one s.: John Michael; ACTING DIRECTOR GENERAL 1994– and MANAGING DIRECTOR PROGRAMMING, NATIONAL ARTS CENTRE 1993– and MANAGING DIRECTOR, NATIONAL ARTS CENTRE ORCHESTRA 1989– ; freelance musician Toronto 1968–71; Prod. Mgr., freelance prod. & Concert Mgr. var. contemporary music orgns. in Toronto incl. New Music Concerts 1971–73; Bldg. & Concerts Coord., Univ. of Toronto (Edward Johnson Bldg.) 1973–74; Founding Mgr., Toronto Symphony Youth Orch. 1974; Asst. Orch. Mgr., Toronto Symphony 1975; Orchestra Mgr. 1978; Extve. Dir., Winnipeg Symphony 1980; Denver Symphony Orch. 1985; Finan. Offr., Music Section, Can. Counc. 1986; Co-acting Head, Music & Opera 1988; Music Producer, National Arts Centre 1989–93; Acting Dir. of Operations, NAC 1992–93; Presbyterian; recreations: skiing, bicycling; Office: Box 1534, Stn B, Ottawa, Ont. K1P 5W1.

**MILLS, (Howard) John (Edwin),** B.A., M.A.; educator; writer; b. London, Eng. 23 June 1930; s. Albert William and Dorothy May (Blakeway) M.; e. Sutton Grammar Sch. Eng.; Univ. Coll. of N. Wales Bangor 1947–49; Univ. of B.C., B.A. 1964; Stanford Univ. M.A. 1965; Vancouver School of Theology, Master of Theological Studies 1989; m. Elaine d. Norman and Ivy Davies 10 Dec. 1983; step-children: Adam, Emma; PROF. OF ENG., SIMON FRASER UNIV. 1980– ; served with Brit. Army 1950–52; Labourer, Fisherman 1949–50, 1952–55; came to Can. 1953; tech. writer 1955–56; Radar Tech. Mid Can. and DEW Lines 1956–59; Teacher 1959–61; Instr. present Univ. 1965; Woodrow Wilson Fellow 1964; author (novels): 'The Land of Is' 1972; 'The October Men' 1973; 'Skevington's Daughter' 1978; 'Runner in the Dark' 1992; (essays) 'Lizard in the Grass' 1981; 'Thank Your Mother For the Rabbits' 1993; Anglican; NDP; recreations: hiking, cycling; Home: 248 W. 16th Ave., Vancouver, B.C. V5Y 1Y9; Office: Burnaby, B.C. V5A 1S6.

**MILLS, Ralph Shaw,** Q.C., B.A., LL.B., D.Litt.S.; b. Toronto 23 Oct. 1903; s. Alexander (K.C.) and Minnie L. (Shaw) M.; e. Rosedale Pub. Sch., Toronto; Univ.of Toronto Schs. (Sch. Capt. 1921); Victoria Coll., Univ. of Toronto, B.A. 1925; Osgoode Hall Law Sch., Toronto, Ont., LL.B. 1928; Victoria Univ. D.Litt.S. 1974; m. Thora Rosalind, d. late Rev. W.A. McIlroy, 11 May 1929; five s., Alex, Donald, Howard, James, Paul; COUNSEL, MILLS AND MILLS; Pres. and Dir., Anson Securities Corp. Ltd.; former Pres. Toronto United Church Council, Toronto; former mem., of Judicial Comte., Un. Ch. of Can.; former Chrmn., Board of Regents, Victoria Univ., Toronto, Ont.; former Pres., and life mem., Roy. Can. Inst.; former Pres., Big Brothers; Silver Jubilee Medal 1977; read law with Sir Wm. Hearst, K.C.; called to the Bar of Ont. 1928; cr. K.C. 1950; since entering upon the practice of law, has had extensive corp. and litigation experience, incl. Supreme Court of Can. and one successful appearance before the P.C. (1948); Lieut., Q.O.R. of Can. 1926–29; C.O.T.C. of Osgoode Hall, Toronto 1940–41; sports career incl. Quarterback and Captain, Victoria Coll. Interfaculty football 1921–23; Quarterback, Univ. of Toronto Intercoll. football 1924; played hockey successively with Univ. of Toronto Schs., Victoria Coll., Varsity Jrs., Varsity Intermediates and Osgoode Hall Intermediates; played baseball with Toronto Fastball League, etc.; United Church; recreation: golf; Clubs: Lawyers of Toronto; York Downs Golf; Muskoka Lakes Golf; Home: 505 - 278 Bloor St. E., Toronto, Ont. M4W 3M4; Office: 2500 - 145 King St. W., Toronto, Ont. M5H 3T6.

**MILLS, Russell Andrew;** newspaper publisher; b. St. Thomas, Ont. 14 July 1944; s. Gerald Armond and

Phyllis Marie (Hulse) M.; e. Univ. of W. Ont., B.A. 1967, M.A. 1968; m. Judith d. Kenneth and Marjorie Zimmerman 25 March 1967; children: Lara, Colin, Patrick; PUBLISHER, THE OTTAWA CITIZEN 1992– ; Reporter, The London Free Press 1964–67; City Editor, The Oshawa Times 1970; Asst. City Ed., Night Ed., Asst. Mng. Ed., The Ottawa Citizen 1971–85; Extve. Ed. 1975–76; Editor 1977–84; Gen. Mgr. 1984–86; Publisher, 1986–89; Pres., The Southam Newspaper Group 1989–92; Home: 325 Fairmont Ave., Ottawa, Ont. K1Y 1Y6; Office: 1101 Baxter Rd., Ottawa, Ont. K2C 3M4.

**MILLS, Wallace George,** B.A., M.A., Ph.D.; university professor; b. Essex, Ont. 31 Dec. 1939; s. Milo Everett and Mary Murell (Barnett) M.; e. Queen's Univ. B.A. (Hons.) 1965, M.A. 1967; Univ. of Calif., Los Angeles Ph.D. 1975; m. Margaret d. Allan and Janet Sparling 22 Aug. 1959; ASSOC. PROF., ST. MARY'S UNIV. 1977– ; Lectr., St. Mary's Univ. 1968; Asst. Prof. 1971; Can. Council Fellowship, South Africa 1971–72; author of scholarly articles; Home: 35 Purcell's Cove Rd., Halifax, N.S. B3N 1R3; Office: Halifax, N.S. B3H 3C3.

**MILLS-COCKELL, John Lewis;** composer; b. Toronto, Ont. 19 May 1943; s. John Horace and Cynthia Jean (Kimble) Cockell; e. Malvern Coll. Inst.; Faculty of Music Univ. of Toronto; Royal Conserv. Music; div.; children: Julian, Juno; first pub. performance of compositions Toronto 1966; teaching asst. in electronic music Royal Conserv. Music 1967, scored 2 short films NFB, 10 electronic pieces as part of Environmental Installation for 'Perception '67' Univ. of Toronto; numerous concerts Can. and U.S.; first live performance in the world using electronic music synthesizer Art Gallery of Ont.; composed and performed score 'Party Day' Nat. Arts Centre Ottawa; comns. Nat. Ballet (2) and Toronto Dance Theatre 1971; scoring for film and theatre incl. 'The Stag King' Tarragon Theatre and 'Carnivals' CBC; guest lectr. Fanshawe Coll. London, Ont.; moved to UK and scored music TV series 'A Third Testament' hosted by Malcolm Muggeridge, performed and recorded in London, Copenhagen and Toronto 1973; rtn'd Can. 1975 scoring film music TV dramas, theatrical features, documentaries; arranging and session work recording artists incl. Anne Murray, Bruce Cockburn, Murray McLauchlan 1978; guest composer/musical dir. Nat. Theatre Sch. Montreal 1979; scoring for theatre and film incl. Toronto Free Theatre, Stratford Festival, CentreStage & Candn. Stage Company 1980–90; co-writer 'The Brass Ring' opera 1988; 'Marco', 'Donut City' CBC musicals 1989; hons. incl. best orch. score BMI student composers award 1965; best original film score CFTA awards 1978; nominated best original score Genie Awards 1983, Am. ACE Awards 1986; nominated best new musical Dora Awards 1989; Pro-Can Award 'outstanding contribution to music in film' 1989; jr. and sr. grants Can. Council; bursaries Ont. Arts Council; mem. Am. Fedn. Musicians; SOCAN; Musikverlage (Munich), Candn. Guild Film Composers.

**MILLWARD, Robert E.,** B.A., M.U.P.; urban planner; b. Saratoga Springs, N.Y. 24 June 1942; s. Wilton P. and Velma G. M.; e. Univ. of Rochester B.A.; New York Univ. M.U.P.; m. Denise D. d. Alex and Ann Mossey 10 July 1983; children: Michael Philip, Nicole Claire; COMMISSIONER, PLANNING & DEVEL. DEPT., CITY OF TORONTO 1987– ; Dir. of Planning, City of Toronto Housing Dept. 1974–79; Deputy Comnr./Dir. of Central Core & Waterfront, Planning & Devel. Dept., City of Toronto 1979–84; seconded to Toronto Harbour Comn. 1984–86; Acting Comnr. 1986–87; Office: City Hall, Toronto, Ont. M5H 2N2.

**MILNE, Arthur Gordon,** B.A., LL.B.; lawyer; b. Montreal, Que. 19 Sept. 1954; s. late Thomas Beattie and Clasina Grietje (Boland) M.; e. Ernest Manning H.S., Calgary; Univ. of Calgary Hons. B.A. 1976; Magdalen Coll., Oxford Univ. (Rhodes Scholar, Alberta 1976); Univ. of Toronto LL.B. 1984; LAWYER; Parliamentary Intern, House of Commons 1979–80; Asst. to Ombudsman of Prov. of B.C. 1979–81; Admin. Trainee, Dept. of Nat. Revenue Customs & Excise 1981; Cons. Ont. Min. of Revenue 1982; Law student, Ont. Securities Comn. 1983; Student-at-Law, McMillan, Binch Barristers and Solicitors 1984–85; Burnet Duckworth & Palmer, Barristers & Solicitors 1986; author various articles scholarly jours.; recreations: skiing, travel, running, chess; Address: 1500 - 400 Third Ave. S.W., Calgary, Alta. T2P 2H4.

**MILNE, David Alvin,** B.A., M.A., Ph.D.; professor; b. Bowmanville, Ont. 28 Sept. 1941; s. Bruce William and Helen Lorraine (Virtue) M.; e. Bowmanville H.S. 1961; Queen's Univ., B.A. (Hons.) 1965; Univ. of Toronto, M.A. 1966, Ph.D. 1975; m. Dr. Frances Gray d. Nesbit and Fanny Gray 9 Oct. 1976; one d.: Kyla Margaret Gray Milne; PROF. OF POL. STUDIES, UNIV. OF P.E.I. 1970– ; Bd. of Dirs., Candn. Assn. of Univ. Teachers 1983–85; Candn. Pol. Sci. Assn. 1977–78; Mem., Maritime Prov. Higher Edn. Comn. 1980–83 and Chrmn., Acad. Adv. Ctte. 1982–83; Mem., Centre for Constitutional Studies, Univ. of Alberta 1988– ; Institute of Intergovernmental Relations, Queen's Univ. 1990– ; Advisory Bd., Candn. Journal of Political Science 1991– ; Chrmn., Dept. of Pol. Studies, U.P.E.I. 1972–74, 1984–90; Constitutional Advr., P.E.I. Cabinet 1980–83, New Brunswick Commission on Canadian Federalism 1991, and the Government of Canada 1991; author: 'The New Canadian Constitution' 1982 (2nd rev. ed. 1989, 3rd rev. ed. 1991), 'Tug of War' 1986 and many articles on archit. & pol. theory, federalism, and constitutional law; 'New Brunswick - Aboriginal Relations' essay for Royal Commission on Aboriginal Peoples 1993; co-editor: 'The Garden Transformed' 1982; Mem., Candn. Pol. Sci. Assn.; SSHRCC rsch. grant awards 1974, 1979, 1983; Fellowships: Can. Counc. Doctoral 1969–70, Prov. of Ont. Grad. Scholarships 1965–70; Central Mortgage and Housing Corp. 1969–70; Univ. of Toronto Open 1967–68; recreations: swimming, tennis, music; Home: 14 Harbour Lane, Charlottetown, P.E.I. C1A 2G9; Office: Dept. of Pol. Studies, Univ. of P.E.I., Charlottetown, P.E.I. C1A 4P3.

**MILNE, Rev. Donald William,** B.A., LL.B., M.Div., M.R.E.; b. Toronto, Ont. 31 March 1938; s. Jack Donald and Olive Bernice M.; e. Univ. of Toronto Schs. 1956; Univ. of W. Ont. B.A. 1960; Univ. of Toronto LL.B. 1963; Emmanuel Coll. Toronto M.Div. 1990; and M.R.E. 1993; m. Sylvia Janet Swinden 3 July 1964; div. 1988; m. Doris Jean Dyke 9 Sept. 1989; children: Douglas Gordon, Catherine Janet; MINISTER, PARKVIEW UNITED CHURCH 1993– ; called to Bar of Ont. 1965; Partner, Blake, Cassels & Graydon 1965–85; Real Estate Counsel, Blott Fejer 1986, Paroian/Raphael 1987; o. 1990; Min. Iondale Hts. United Church 1990–92; service RCNR, rank Lt.; Comnr. 32nd Gen. Council Un. Ch.; Past Pres. Toronto Un. Ch. Council; former pub. sch. Trustee Toronto Bd. Edn.; mem. Law Soc. Upper Can.; Can. Bar Assoc.; recreations: arts, skiing, travel; Home: 82 Admiral Rd., Toronto, Ont. M5R 2L6.

**MILNE, Eleanor Rose,** C.M.; sculptor; b. Saint John, N.B. 14 May 1925; d. William Harold and Irene Eleanor Mary (Gilhooly) M.; e. Saint Pauls Acad., Montreal; Sacred Heart Convent, Athunsic; Montreal Museum Sch. of Fine Art and McGill Lab. of Anatomy 1944–45; Central Coll. Arts & Crafts, London, Eng. 1945–46; L'Ecole des Beaux Arts, Montreal 1946–48; Syracuse Univ. 1950–52; OFFICIAL SCULPTOR, CANADA 1961– ; formerly free-lance sculptor, stained glass window builder, engraver in wood, painter in water colors; makes her own bronze castings; has designed and built statues in wood, bronze and stone for both outdoor and indoor uses; many low relief panels in wood, stone and bronze; designed and carved (with assists.) high relief frieze 'History of Canada' in Lobby, H. of C., Ottawa; designed and built (with assists.) 12 stained glass windows for Chamber of H. of C.; designed and built (with assists.) 12 stones for Chamber of H. of C. in theme of North Amer. Act; designed the series 'The Origins of Life: Prehistoric Life' for House of Commons, Ottawa; designed and made carvings and mosaic for 1st Speaker's chair for Yellowknife, N.W.T.; designed 1st Speaker's table and carved bronze mace cradle for Leg., Whitehorse, Yukon; Visiting Lecturer, Carleton Univ. Ottawa; lecturer to various groups in Can. & England; work has been seen in Montreal, Vancouver, Ottawa, N.Y.C., London, etc.; metal work sculpture in private collection, China; bronze and watercolours in Eng.; woodcarvings in private collections, Montreal, Ottawa; series of oils and watercolours in the Public Works Canada Collection; awarded Centennial Medal; D.Litt. (hon. causa) Carleton Univ.; Member, Order of Canada 1989; mem. and adjudicator, The Centennial Coins and Medallions Ctte.; Bd. Judges, Fine Arts, City of Ottawa; mem. and adjudicator, The Diefenbaker Memorial Ctte.; The L.B. Pearson Memorial Ctte.; mem., The Elizabeth II, equestrian bronze monument Ctte.; mem. of jury, The Peacekeeping Monument; mem., The Visual Arts Ctte. for the National Capital Comn.; The Conservation of Bronze Sculptures and Architectural Bronze Ctte.; mem., Que. Sculptors Assn.; Smithsonian Inst.; Candn. Wildlife; mem., CARC (Candn. Arctic Resources Ctte.); recreations: modern history, landscape gardening, pursuit of fractals; Home: 229 Powell Ave., Ottawa, Que. K1S 2A4; Office: Box 162, House of Commons, Ottawa, Ont. K1A 0A6.

**MILNE, Lorus Johnson,** M.A., Ph.D.; naturalist; university professor; author; b. Toronto, Ont.; s. Charles Stanley and Edna Shepard (Johnson) M.; e. Humberside Coll. Inst., Toronto; Univ. of Toronto, B.A. (Biol.; Gold Medal) 1933; Harvard Univ., M.A. 1934, Ph.D. 1936; m. Margery Joan, Ph.D., d. S. Harrison Greene; PROF. OF ZOOLOGY, UNIV. OF NEW HAMPSHIRE; author and co-author (chiefly with wife) of over 55 books incl. many receiving literary awards and many in several foreign eds., 2 selected for perm. White House Lib., 2 for 'Books Across the Sea' program whereby Am. ambassadors provide books to rep. USA in foreign countries and 4 on long-play records for blind; other writings incl. over 200 pub. articles and reports and numerous book reviews in natural hist. field in Am. and foreign journs.; served with Office of Naval Research and Office of Scient. Research Devel., Univ. of Pa. Hosp., on night vision problems of armed services, 1942–47; exchangée on U.S.-S. Africa Leader Exchange Program for 3 months; National Geographic Soc. grant to study fresh water (global); Consultant-Leader for U.N. Educ. and Scient. Organ., in N.Z. for 3 months; taught Semester at Sea aboard SS Universe (100 days around world) under auspices of Univ. of Pitts. (Inst. for Shipboard Education) 1984; Fellow, Am. Assn. Advanc. Science; mem., Am. Behaviour. Soc.; Am. Soc. Zools.; Conserv. Foundation; Explorers Club; N.H. Audubon Soc.; Sigma Xi; Republican; United Church; recreations: exploring, photography, natural history; Home: 1 Garden Lane, Durham, N.H. 03824; Office: 241A Spaulding Bldg. Durham, N.H. 03824.

**MILNE, Robert Stephen,** M.A., F.R.S.C.; educator; b. Paisley, Scot. 20 June 1919; s. Robert Stephen and Flora Margaret (Campbell) M.; e. Glasgow Acad. 1937; Queen's Coll. Oxford B.A. 1937, M.A. 1946; m. Diane d. Charles and Agnes Mauzy 20 May 1975; two s. Robert Stephen, Charles Roderick Cameron; PROF. EMERITUS UNIV. OF B.C. 1984– ; Lectr. Bristol Univ. 1947–55; Prof. Univ. of Wellington, N.Z. 1955–59; Visiting Rockefeller Prof. Univ. of the Philippines 1959–60; Prof. Inst. of Social Studies The Hague 1960–61; Prof. Univ. of Singapore 1961–65; Prof. of Pol. Sci. Univ. of B.C. 1965–84; served with Brit. Army 1940–46, rank Maj., R.A.; Gov., Intnl. Devel. Rsch. Center 1974–78; author 'Political Parties in New Zealand' 1966; 'Concepts and Models in Public Administration' 1966; 'Government and Politics in Malaysia' 1967; 'Politics in Ethnically Bi-polar Societies: Malaysia, Guyana and Fiji' 1981; co-author 'Straight Fight' 1954; 'Marginal Seat' 1955; 'The Malayan Parliamentary Election of 1964' 1967; 'New States in a New Nation: Political Development in the Borneo States of Malaysia' 1974; 'Politics and Government in Malaysia' 1978, 2nd ed. 1980; 'Malaysia: Tradition, Modernity, and Islam' 1986; 'Singapore: The Legacy of Lee Kuan Yew' 1990; ed. and contbr. 'Bureaucracy in New Zealand' 1957; 'Planning for Progress, the Administration of Economic Planning in the Philippines' 1960; mem. Assn. Asian Studies; Candn. Assn. Asian Studies; Candn. Pol. Sci. Assn.; recreations: bridge, wine; Home: 3223 W. 33rd Ave., Vancouver, B.C. V6N 2G8; Office: Vancouver, B.C. V6T 1W5.

**MILNER, Eric Charles,** M.Sc., Ph.D., F.R.S.C.; educator; b. London, UK 17 May 1928; s. Frederick Charles and Ann Elizabeth (Kluth) M.; e. Askes Haberdashers Sch. London 1939–46; Kings Coll. London B.Sc. 1949, M.Sc. 1950, Ph.D. 1962; m. 1stly Estelle Lawton (dec.); children: Suzanne, Mark, Paul, Simon; m. 2ndly Elizabeth d. James and Edith Borthwick 2 July 1979; son: Robert; PROF. OF MATH., UNIV. OF CALGARY 1967– , Head of Math. 1976–80; Lectr. Univ. of Malaya, Singapore 1952–61; Univ. of Reading, UK 1961–67; author numerous papers on set theory and combinatorial math.; mem., Candn. Math. Soc. (Vice Pres. 1975–78); London Math. Soc.; Am. Math. Soc.; N.Y. Acad. Sciences; recreations: walking, tennis, squash, go; Home: 3020 Underhill Dr., Calgary, Alta. T2N 4E5; Office: 2920 – 24th Ave. N.W., Calgary, Alta. T2N 1N4.

**MILNER, Morris (Mickey),** B.Sc.(Eng.), Ph.D., P.Eng., F.I.E.E.; biomedical rehabilitation engineer; educator; b. Johannesburg, S. Africa 7 May 1936; s. Hyman and Rachel Florence (Israel) M.; e. Johannesburg Tech. and High Trade Sch. 1953; Univ. of Witwatersrand B.Sc. (Elect. Engn.) 1957, Ph.D. (elect. engn./biomed. engn.) 1968; m. Maureen d. Meyer and Rose Maltz 20 Sept. 1959; children: Michelle (d.), Joanne, Alan Sean; VICE PRES., RSCH. & DEVEL., HUGH MACMILLAN REHABILITATION CENTRE (operated by ONT. CRIPPLED CHILDREN'S CENTRE) 1989– ; Dir., Rehabilitation Engn. Dept. Hugh MacMillan Rehabilitation Centre 1978– ; Dir., Rsch. Dept. Hugh MacMillan Rehabilitation Centre 1983– ; Dir., Ontario Rehabilitation Technology Consortium 1992– ; Mem., International Centre for Advancement of Community Based

Rehabilitation 1991– ; Adjunct Prof. Depts. Mech. Engn. and Surg., Prof. Inst. of Biomed. Engn. & Prof. Dept. Rehabilitation Med. Univ. of Toronto; Jr. to Sr. Lectr. in Elect. Engn. Univ. of Witwatersrand 1958–68; joined Associated Electrical Industries Ltd. Eng. 1961–62; Visiting Scient. Div. Mech. Engn. Nat. Research Council Ottawa 1967, Assoc. Research Offr. 1969–70; Princ. Specialist, Sr. Lectr. and Head Bio-Engn. and Med. Physics Dept. Groote Schuur Hosp. and Univ. of Cape Town 1970–72; Sr. Research Assoc. Dept. Phys. Med. Emory Univ. and Visiting Assoc. Prof. Sch. Elect. Engn. Ga. Inst. Technol. 1973–74; Assoc. Prof. Depts. Med. and Elect. Engn., Coordinator of Biomed. Engn. Program, McMaster Univ. 1974–78, also Dir. Biomed. Engn. Dept. Chedoke Hosp.; Prof. and Chrmn., Dept. Rehabilitation Med., Univ. of Toronto 1985–88; Chrmn. Adv. Comte. Tech. Assistance for Handicapped NRC 1978– , mem. NRC Adv. Comte. on Biomed. Engn., Assoc. Comte. Research & Devel. for Disabled 1982– , Chrmn. 1990– ; Dir., Candn. Rehabilitation Council for Disabled Persons 1981–90, mem. Tech. Aids Comte., Chrmn. Nat. Prof. Assns. Comte. 1982–85; recipient Engn. Medal Assn. Prof. Engrs. Prov. Ont. 1982; Isabelle and Leonard Goldenson Award for Technological Rsch. and Devel. for Disabled Children 1985; Presidential Citation, Variety Clubs Internat. 1985; Presidential Citation, Rehabilitation Internat. 1989; Merit Award Canadn. Assoc. Occupational Therapists 1989; recipient, Wiegand Award for Canadian Excellence 1992; Eminent Visiting Speaker, Inst. of Engrs., Australia Aug./Sept. 1985; Visiting Prof., Paediatrics Dept., Univ. of Ottawa 1988; Visiting Lectr., Regency Park Ctr. for Young Disabled, Adelaide, Australia 1988; mem. Candn. Bd. Examiners for Clin. Engn. 1979–81; Chrmn. Candn. Standards Assn. Comte. Technol. for Handicapped 1977–82; Fellow, S. African Inst. Elect. Engn. 1971–76; mem. Candn. Med. & Biol. Engn. Soc. (Vice Pres. 1980–82, Chrmn. Prof. Affairs Comte. 1975–78); Rehabilitation Engn. Soc. N. Am. (Dir. 1980– , Pres. 1982–83, apptd. Fellow 1987); Sr. Mem., Inst. of Electrical and Electronic Engrs.; Gov. Physiotherapy Found. of Can. 1984–88; Chrmn., Internat. Comn. on Technical Aids, Building and Transportation (Rehabilitation Internat.) 1984–88; Chrmn. Assistive Devices Program Adv. Ctte., Ont. Ministry of Health 1987–90; Chrmn., Adv. Ctte. on Rehabilitation, Ont. Ministry of Health 1991–93; Mem., Bd. of Govs., Lyndhurst Hosp., Toronto 1985– ; Mem., Rick Hansen Man in Motion Legacy Fund Advisory Panel 1990–92; Mem., Grant Review Ctte., Hosp. for Sick Children Found. 1991– ; Mem., Editorial Bd., International Journal of Rehabilitation; Consulting Editor, Candn. Journal of Rehabilitation; Mem., Bd. of Dirs., The Hugh MacMillan Children's Foundation 1992– ; Mem., Research Ctte., Am. Cong. Rehabilitation Med. 1992–94; co-author 'Understanding the Scientific Bases of Human Movement' 2nd ed. 1980, 3rd e. 1988; Fellow, American Academy of Cerebral Palsy and Developmental Medicine 1990; recreations: cycling, swimming, photography; Home: 395 Sutherland Dr., Toronto, Ont. M4G 1K1; Office: 350 Rumsey Rd., Toronto, Ont. M4G 1R8.

**MILNER, Peter,** M.Sc., Ph.D.; neuroscientist; b. Silkstone Common, Eng. 13 June 1919; s. David William M.; came to Can. 1944; m. Susan Walker; one s. David Elliot; PROF. EMERITUS, DEPT. OF PSYCHOLOGY, MCGILL UNIVERSITY; Address: 1205 Dr. Penfield Ave., Montreal, Que. H3A 1B1.

**MILNES, John Herbert;** executive; b. Toronto, Ont. 9 Aug. 1912; s. James Herbert and Isabel Gertrude (Sinclair) M.; e. Ridley Coll. St. Catharines, Ont. 1929; Upper Can. Coll. Toronto 1932; Univ. of Toronto 1933–34; PRESIDENT, MILNES FUEL OIL LTD. 1967– ; Pres., Milnes Holding Co. Ltd. 1971– ; served with Candn. Intelligence Corps. 1941–46; Standard Fuel Co. Ltd. 1948–74, Extve. Vice Pres. 1960–71, Pres. 1971–74; mem. Bd. Trade Metrop. Toronto; YMCA; Anglican; recreations: swimming, skiing, history; Clubs: Granite; Empire; Home: 22 Deer Park Cres., Toronto, Ont. M4V 2C2; Office: 1815 Yonge St., Toronto, Ont. M4T 2A4.

**MILORD, Yves,** DEC, B.A.A.; retail executive; b. Montreal, Que. 24 Feb. 1951; s. Rosaire and Simone (Ladouceur) M.; m. Lynda Langis 20 April 1970; children: Claudia, Veronique, Pierre-Luc; EXTVE. VICE-PRES., RETAIL, METRO-RICHELIEU INC. 1991– ; Quebec Group Dir., Campeau Corp. 1975–78; Gen. Mgr., Cooprix 1978–85; Provigo 1985–89; Vice-Pres. 1989–91; recreations: skiing, tennis; club: St-Denis; Office: 11011 Maurice Duplessis Blvd., Montreal, Que. H1C 1V6.

**MILOT, Louise,** B.èsA., L.èsL., M.A., Ph.D.; vice-rectrice aux études; née. Asbestos, Qué. 13 sept. 1942; f. Charles et Lina (Richard) M.; é. Univ. de Sherbrooke B.èsA. 1965; Univ. Laval L.èsL. 1968, M.A. 1972; Univ. de Paris VIII Vincennes Ph.D. 1976; ép. Fernand f. Hilaire Roy 8 sept. 1966; enfant: Valérie; VICE-RECTRICE AUX ÉTUDES, UNIVERSITÉ LAVAL 1992– ; Directrice adjointe, Dép. des littératures, Univ. Laval 1977–80; Directrice de la Revue 'Etudes littéraires' 1982–86; Directrice par intérim, Dép. des littératures 1985–86; Vice-doyenne aux ressources, Fac. des lettres 1986–88; rés.: 5, rue Hamel, Apt. 102, Québec, Qué. G1R 4J6; bureau: Pavillon des sciences de l'éducation, bureau 1534, Québec, Qué. G0R 1P0.

**MILTON, (John Charles) Douglas,** B.Sc., M.A., Ph.D., F.A.P.S., F.R.S.C.; physicist; b. Regina, Sask. 1 June 1924; s. William and Frances Craigie (McDowall) M.; e. Greenway Elem. Sch., Gen. Wolfe Jr. High and Daniel McIntyre Coll. Inst. Winnipeg 1943; Univ. of Man. A.M.M. (Piano) 1944, B.Sc. 1947; Princeton Univ. M.A. 1949, Ph.D. 1951; m. Gwendolyn Margaret d. late Forrest Linden Shaw, O.B.E., Victoria, B.C. 10 Oct. 1953; children: Bruce Forrest, Leslie Jean Frances, Neil William Douglas, Theresa Marie; RESEARCHER EMERITUS 1990– ; joined present Labs. as Asst. becoming Sr. Rsch. Offr. Physics 1951–67; Head of Nuclear Physics 1967–82; Visiting Physicist, Lawrence Berkeley Labs. (Cal.) 1960–62, Bruyères-le-Châtel (France) 1975–76; Directeur de Recherche, CRNS Strasbourg, France 1975; Chrmn. Nuclear Physics grant Selection Comte. of Nat. Sci. & Eng. Research Council (NSERC) 1978–82, (& 3 other grant selection comtes.); Dir. Physics Division 1982–85, Acting Dir. of Rsch. 1985, Chalk River Nuclear Labs., Atomic Energy of Can. Ltd. 1985; Vice-Pres., Physics & Health Sciences 1986–90; Researcher Emeritus 1990– ; author over 50 scient. papers and reviews; Pres., Candn. Assn. Physicists 1992; Phi Kappa Pi; Sigma Xi; recreations: gardening, piano, boating; Club: Deep River Yacht & Tennis; Home: 3 Alexander Pl., Deep River, Ont. K0J 1P0; Office: Chalk River, Ont. K0J 1J0.

**MILTON, Gerald Ralph Friesen;** publisher, writer; b. Altona, Man. 23 Dec. 1934; s. Henry Friesen and Marie Reimer; e. Lord Selkirk H.S., Winnipeg; m. Rev. Beverley J. d. Norman and Barbara Ingledew 25 Aug. 1956; children: Mark, Kari, Lloyd, Grace; PUBLISHER, WOOD LAKE BOOKS INC. 1983– ; commercial radio broadcaster 10 years; United Church missionary, Philippines 5 years; media consultant, Nat. Council of Churches of U.S.A. 5 years; TV producer, Un. Ch. of Can. 10 years; Mem., Un. Ch. of Can.; author: 'Gift of Story' 1981, 'This United Church of Ours' 1982, '92, 'Through Rose-colored Bifocals' 1984, 'Commonsense Christianity' 1986, 'Living God's Way' 1993 (religion, humour) and 5 other books plus several hundred mag. articles; frequent public speaker; clubs: Okanagan Women's Sewing Circle and Terrorist Society; Address: Box 700, Winfield, B.C. V0H 2C0.

**MINCHOM, Clive Alan,** B.A.; economist; b. London, England 18 Dec. 1945; s. Daniel and Rosalind M.; e. Balliol College, Oxford Univ. B.A. (Hons.) 1968; divorced; children: Sarah, Simon; VICE-PRES., MERIDIAN TECHNOLOGIES INC. 1987– ; Economics Dept. Courtaulds (U.K.) 1968–71; Extve. Asst. to Chair, BPC Publishing 1972–74; Analyst, Alcan Internat. Montreal1975–76; Asst. Treas., Brascan Toronto 1976–79; Manager, Investment Policy, Cadillac Fairview 1980–82; Treasurer, Crowntek 1983–84; Real Estate Analyst, McLeod Young 1985–87; Dir., Accurcast Limited; Magnesium Products Limited; Richmond Die Casting Ltd.; Clemmer Industries Limited; Magnesium Products of America Inc. (all Meridian subs.); Jr. Achievement, Volunteer Teacher; recreations: tennis, skiing, music; Home: 54 Ava Rd., Toronto, Ont. M5P 1Y8; Office: 2 St. Clair Ave. W., Ste. 1700, Toronto, Ont. M4V 1L5.

**MINDSZENTHY de deaki et zavar, Bartholomew (Bart) Joseph,** Ph.B., APR; public relations executive; b. Bavaria, W. Germany 12 June 1946; s. Bartholomew A. and Lenke C. (de Köszegi) M.; e. Wayne State Univ., Ph.B. 1968; children: Andrea, Nicole, Andrew; PARTNER, MINDSZENTHY & ROBERTS, COMMUNICATIONS COUNSEL 1991– ; Extve. Dir., The Center for Crisis Communications and Management 1993– ; Mng. Dir., MPI Communications (Detroit) 1968–69; Cons. and lastly Vice-Pres., PIR Communications (Toronto) 1969–83; Dir., Corp. Pub. Affairs, C-I-L Inc. 1983–88; Extve. Vice-Pres., The Beloff Group Inc. 1988–90; Chrmn., Corp. Commun. Prog., Seneca Coll.; Canadian Public Relations Extve. of the Year 1988; CPRS (Candn. Public Relns. Soc.) Award of Recognition 1988; of Excellence 1985, 1986, 1987; IABC (Internat. Assn. of Business Communications) Award of Merit 1983, 1986; President's Medal 1991; Pres., CPRS, Toronto 1987–88 (Ctte. Chrmn. 1988–91); Chrmn., CPRS National Ctte. on Professionalism 1991– ; Dir., The Empire Club of Can. 1988– ; Mem., CPRS; co-author: 'No Surprises: The Crisis Communications Management System' 1988; contbr.: 3 books & several mags.; frequent guest speaker; recreations: golf, swimming, Chinese waterbrush painting; clubs: Emerald Hills Golf & Country; Office: 92 Isabella St., Toronto, Ont. M4Y 1N4.

**MINER, David Bruce,** B.Sc., M.B.A., F.C.S.I.; financial executive; b. Port Colborne, Ont. 22 Feb. 1953; s. Murray Bruce and Ruth Eloise (Byers) M.; e. Univ. of Toronto B.Sc. 1975, M.B.A. 1979; m. Meena Rajpatee 20 Dec. 1986; children: Amelia, Victoria; PARTNER, HODGSON ROBERTON LAING LIMITED 1988– ; Asst. Mgr., Toronto Dominion Bank 1975–77; Manager, Marketing Administration, Paul Revere Life 1978–81; Mgr., Marketing Admin., Colonial Life 1982–83; Stockbroker, Burns Fry 1983–88; Arbor Award, Univ. of Toronto; Past Pres., Fac. of Mngt. Alumni Assn., Univ. of Toronto; Past Vice-Pres., Alumni Assn., Univ. of Toronto; recreations: skiing, classical guitar; Home: 257 Friendship Ave., Scarborough, Ont. M1C 4E8; Office: 1 Queen St. E., Suite 1920, Toronto, Ont. M5C 2Y5.

**MINER, Frederick C., Jr.,** B.A., M.B.A., Ph.D.; university administrator; b. Lewes, Delaware 23 May 1946; s. Frederick C. and Nola Bell (Ohlwein) M.; e. Gettysburg College B.A. 1968; Univ. of Utah M.B.A. 1971; Univ. of Minnesota Ph.D. 1976; children: Kier Frederick, Colin Enric; VICE-PRESIDENT (SAINT JOHN), UNIV. OF NEW BRUNSWICK 1994– ; Management Professor, Saint Mary's Univ. 1976–93; Chairperson, Business Admin. 1977–78; M.B.A. Dir. 1978–81; Dean of Commerce 1982–87; Visiting Prof., Univ. of Toronto 1987–89; Dir., Canada/China Language & Cultural Prog., Saint Mary's Univ. 1989–93; private management consultant 1976– ; Dir., Radio Canada, SMU Language Program for China 1990–91; Candn.-ASEA Fac. Devel. Prog. 1988–89; Candn.-ASEA Mngt. Devel. Prog. 1985–87; Global Mngt. Network Project 1986–87; CIDA Professional Award 1993; Saint Mary's Univ. Service Award 1987; Mem., Internat. Div. Ctte., Assn. of Univ. & Coll. of Canada; Acad. of Mngt.; Admin. Sci. Assn. of Can. (Chair 1981, Program Chair 1980, Academic Reviewer, Organizational Behaviour Div. 1979) author of over 50 academic papers; co-author: 'Canadian Personnel Management and Human Resources' 1st ed. 1982, 2nd ed. 1985; co-editor: 'Canadian Asean Management Development: A Technology' 1987; receations: jogging, travel; Office: P.O. Box 5050, Saint John, N.B. E2L 4L5.

**MINGAY, Arthur Hammond;** corporate director; b. Windsor, Ont. 26 Nov. 1919; s. John and Esther (Rodgers) M.; e. Windsor (Ont.) Pub. Sch.; Walkerville (Ont.) Coll. Inst.; m. Florence d. Henry Carmichael 15 Feb. 1947; children: Cameron, Mary Jane, Margo; CHRMN., FINSCO SERVICES LIMITED; Chrmn., Bd. of Govs., Finsco Investment Management Corp.; Dir. Loblaw Cos. Ltd.; joined The Canada Trust Co. Windsor, Ont. 1938, Estates Offr. London, Ont. 1945, Trust Offr. Chatham, Ont. 1948, Mgr. Pension Trust Div. 1954, Asst. Gen. Mgr. Toronto Area 1959, Dir. 1964, Vice Pres. and Gen. Mgr. 1968, Pres. and Gen. Mgr. 1973, Pres. and Chief Extve. Offr. 1973, Chrmn. and Chief Extve. Offr. 1978; Chrmn. of Bd. & Extve. Comte., The Canada Trust Co. 1979–1985; served with RCAF 1941–45, rank Flight Lt.; Trustee, Sunnybrook Medical Science Centre and Foundation; United Church; recreations: golf, swimming; Clubs: Toronto; Granite; Rosedale Golf; Home: 35 Daneswood Rd., Toronto, Ont. M4N 3J7.

**MINGAY, Lieut.-Col. J. Donald,** D.S.O., M.B.E.; b. Barrie, Ont. 2 Feb. 1915; s. John and Esther (Rodgers) M.; e. Public and High Schs., Windsor, Ont.; m. Mary, d. late Walter L. McGregor, 4 Nov. 1939; children: John, Jill, Esther, Robert; Chrmn., Creemore Springs Brewery Ltd.; served with Candn. Army, with rank of Lt.-Col. 1934–46; Un. Church; recreations: gardening, skiing; Clubs: Toronto; Badminton & Racquet; Mad River Golf; Homes: Box 295, Creemore, Ont. L0M 1G0 and 20 Avoca Cres., Toronto, Ont. M4T 2B8.

**MINGO, J. William E.,** Q.C., B.A., LL.B., LL.M., LL.D. (Hon); b. Halifax, N.S. 25 Nov. 1926; s. late Edgar Willard and late Lila Theresa (McManus) M.; e. Dalhousie Univ., B.A. 1947, LL.B. 1949; Columbia Univ., LL.M. 1950; St. Mary's Univ., LL.D. (Hon) 1981; m. Edith Peppard, d. late Hon. C. G. Hawkins, Milford, N.S., 6 July 1953; children: Sally (Mrs. J.P. Camus), James, Johanna, Nancy, Charles; PARTNER, STEWART MCKELVEY STIRLING SCALES (Chrmn., Extve. Ctte. 1990–92, predecessor firm 1979–90); Pres. & Dir., Canning Investment Corp. Ltd.; Dir., Royal Bank of Canada; Sun Life Assur. Co. of Can.; Minas Basin

Holdings Ltd.; Minas Basin Pulp and Power Co. Ltd.; Maritime Telegraph & Telephone Co. Ltd.; Eastern Telephone & Telegraph Co.; The North Eastern Corp. Ltd.; The Great Eastern Corp. Ltd.; Onex Corp.; Oxford Frozen Foods Ltd.; Riversdale Lumber Ltd.; Crossley Carpet Mills Ltd.; read law with Stewart, Smith, MacKeen, Covert and Rogers; practised law with successor firms 1950–90; called to Bar of N.S. 1950; cr. Q.C. 1966; N.S. Barristers' Soc. (Pres., 1975–76); Candn. Bar Assn. (mem., Nat. Extve. Comm. 1973–76); Gov., Law Foundation of N.S.; Trustee, Foundation for Legal Research; Forum for Young Cdns.; Dir., Bank of Canada 1975–83; Chrmn., Halifax-Dartmouth Port Comn. 1960–83 (mem. 1955–59); mem., Halifax Port Authority 1972–84; Chrmn., Nat. Treasy. Comte., Lib. Party of Can. 1976–85; mem., N.S. Legal Aid 1977–80; Chrmn., Halifax Grammar Sch. 1971–73; mem., CBA Spec. Comm. on Legal Ethics 1969–75, 1985–87 and 1991–93; mem., MRC Working Group on Human Experimentation 1977–78; Liberal; United Church; recreations: tennis, skiing; Clubs: Halifax; Saraguay; RNSYS; Home: 5860 Chain Rock Dr., Halifax, N.S.; Office: P.O. Box 997, Halifax, N.S. B3J 2X2.

**MINICH, Edward A.,** B.Sc., M.B.A.; business executive; b. Hamilton, Ont. 1950; e. McMaster Univ. B.Sc. 1972, M.B.A. 1974; m.; two sons, one d.; PRESIDENT, CHIEF EXECUTIVE OFFICER & DIRECTOR, OTIS CANADA 1993– ; joined Otis Canada 1974; served in a variety of positions in Ont. incl. sales, dist. mgr., service mgr.; nine years in Boston in a variety of increasingly responsible mngt. positions most recently as Regional General Manager for New England; Pres., Nat. Elevator and Escalator Assn.of Can. 1993– ; Office: 710 Dorval Dr., Oakville, Ont. L6J 5B7.

**MINION, D. Wayne,** B.Sc., M.Sc.; petroleum executive; b. Magrath, Alta. 19 July 1928; s. Everett Laverne and Isabel (Rollingson) M.; e. Lethbridge C.I.; Univ. of Alta., B.Sc. 1950; M.I.T., M.Sc. 1964; m. Marion d. John and Mary Julak 17 May 1950; children: Douglas Shayne, Laurie Beth, Robin Leigh, Tracy Lynne (d. 1956), Cory Ann, Erin Joan, Daurel Michelle, Joel Todd; CHRMN., NORTHRIDGE CANADA 1993– , NORTHRIDGE EXPLORATION INC. 1987– and NORTHRIDGE PETROLEUM MKTG. LTD. 1984– ; Mgr., Gas Dist., B.C. Hydro & Power Authority 1959–64; Asst. Chief Engr. 1964–70; Dir. Adjunto, Light Serv. de Electridade (Brazil) 1970–73; Chrmn., Alta. Petrol. Mktg. Comm., Govt. of Alta. 1974–84; Pres., D.W. Minion Cons. Ltd. 1984; Dir., Candn. Montana Gas Co. Ltd.; Candn. Montana PipeLine Co.; Entech; Roan Resources Ltd.; Office: 1200, 421 7th Ave. S.W., Calgary, Alta. T2P 4K9.

**MINNS, Geoffrey Roger,** F.I.A., F.C.I.A., A.S.A.; insurance executive; b. Carshalton, Surrey, England 9 May 1937; s. Arthur Jesse and Gladys May (Muggeridge) M.; m. Joyce McKenzie 26 Sept. 1963; children: Lisa, David; PRESIDENT, MUNICH LIFE MANAGEMENT CORP. LTD. 1974– ; Actuary, present firm 1966; Vice-Pres. & Actuary 1972; Dir., Munich Life Management Corp.; Munich Reinsurance Co. of Canada; Munich Canada Management Corp.; Vice-Pres. & Dir., Munich Holdings Ltd.; clubs: Mississauga Golf & Country, Ontario; Home: 1525 Chasehurst Dr., Mississauga, Ont. L5J 3A8; Office: 26th floor, 390 Bay St., Toronto, Ont. M5H 2Y2.

**MINSHALL, William Harold,** B.S.A., M.Sc., Ph.D.; research scientist; b. Brantford, Ont. 6 Dec. 1911; s. David William and Mary Etta (Kirkpatrick) M.; e. Ont. Agric. Coll., B.S.A. 1933; McGill Univ., M.Sc. 1938; Ph.D. 1941; m. Reta Elizabeth, d. George J. McBride, Ottawa, 17 June 1939; children: Gaye Carol (Mrs. M. R. Sinclair), Bruce William; Sr. Plant Physiologist, Research Inst., Agric. Can., London, 1951–75; Hon. Lectr., Dept. of Plant Science, Univ. of W. Ont., 1952–76; joined Dept. of Agric., 1933 as Grad. Asst., Div. of Botany, Ottawa; Jr. Botanist there, 1941–45, Assoc. Botanist, 1945–48, Botanist, 1948–51; mem. Senate, Univ. of Guelph 1969–72; mem. Ont. Geneal. Soc. (Pres. 1971–72); Internat. Soc. for Br. Genealogy and Family History (Pres. 1981–83); Ont. Agric. Coll. Alumni Assn. (Pres. 1969–70); Prof. Inst. Pub. Service of Can. (Chrmn., London Br. 1957–58); Ont. Inst. Prof. Agrol. (Pres. 1963–64; recipient Distinguished Agrologist Award 1983); Agric. Inst. Can. (mem. Extve. Council 1950–51; Fellow); Can. Weed Comte. (Pres. E. Sec. 1969); Candn. Soc. Plant Physiologists; McIlwraith Field Naturalists (Pres. 1968–69); Am. Soc. Plant Physiols.; Bot. Soc. Am.; Fellow (1980) Candn. Pest Mgmt. Soc. (Secretary-Treasurer 1955–72); English-Speaking Union of the Commonwealth in Can. (Pres. London Br. 1977–78); Fellow, Am. Assn. Advanc. Science; Fellow, Weed Science Soc. of Am. (mem. extve. comte. 1960–66); rec'd. Centennial Plaque, Ont. Agric. Coll. 1974; Alumnus of Hon., Univ. Guelph 1977; publications: numerous articles in scient. journs.; Comnr. from London Conference to 30th General Counc., Un. Ch. of Can.; Chrmn. Finance Comte., Middlesex Presbytery, Un. Ch. of Can. 1982– ; recreations: genealogy, phenology, stamps; Home: 91 Huron St., London, Ont. N6A 2H9.

**MINTO, Clive,** B.Sc.; retail and consumer products executive; b. Cardiff, Wales 17 Aug. 1945; s. Clifford and Doris (Parkhouse) M.; e. Univ. of Birmingham B.Sc. (Hons.) 1966; m. Frances B. d. Frank and Ilene Lloyd 23 Sept. 1967; children: Anna, Emma; EXECUTIVE VICE-PRESIDENT, DIVERSIFIED BUSINESSES GROUP, CANADIAN TIRE CORPORATION, LIMITED 1987– ; Mktg. Extve., Internat. Mktg. Planning, Rank Xerox (Eur.) 1966–69; Acct. Extve., Maclaren Advtg. 1969–70; Mktg. Mgr., Personal Prod. Div., Lever Brothers 1970–77; Dir. of Mktg., Pepsi-Cola Canada Ltd. 1977–80; Managing Dir. & C.E.O., Pepsi-Cola Africa (Pty) Ltd. 1980–81; Reg. Vice-Pres. & C.E.O., Pepsi-Cola Northern Eur. 1981–83; Pres. & C.E.O., Pepsi-Cola Canada Ltd. 1983–87; Bd. of Dir., Nominating Ctte., National Ballet of Canada 1990– ; recreations: scuba diving (certified scuba diver), alpine skiing, travel, water sports, fitness; Office: P.O. Box 770, Stn. K, Toronto, Ont. M4P 2V8.

**MINTZ, Eric Phillip,** B.A., M.A.; university professor; b. Vancouver, B.C. 29 Aug. 1950; s. Charles Sydney and Sally (Woolfson) M.; e. Univ. of B.C. B.A. 1971; York Univ. M.A. 1972; Univ. of Toronto; m. Diane d. Milton and Beatrice Koffman 19 Dec. 1981; children: Kaila, Aaron; COORDINATOR, POLITICAL SCIENCE DEPT., SIR WILFRED GRENFELL COLLEGE 1977– ; Teaching Asst., Univ. of Toronto 1971–75; Visiting Lecturer, Memorial Univ. of Nfld. 1976–77; rep. faculty in negotiating 1st collective agreement 1986–89; involved in devel. plans for expansion of Sir Wilfred Grenfell College 1987– ; public affairs commentator on radio & TV; Jewish; Candidate, Nfld. House of Assembly 1979; Mem., Candn. Political Sci. Assn. (Head, Political Behaviour/Soc. section 1991–92); Atlantic Prov. Political Studies Assn.; author of various articles; recreations: nordic skiing, orienteering; Home: 28 Stuart St., Corner Brook, Nfld. A2H 6R7; Office: Corner Brook, Nfld. A2H 6P9.

**MINTZ, Jack Maurice,** M.A., Ph.D.; educator; b. Edmonton, Alta. 6 March 1951; s. David Benjamin and Clara (Abramovitch) M.; e. Univ. of Alta. B.A. 1973; Queen's Univ. M.A. 1974; Univ. of Essex Ph.D. 1980; m. Eleanor d. Sam and Vera Schwartz 31 Aug. 1975; children: Avi, Gaela; ARTHUR ANDERSEN PROF. OF TAXATION and ASSOC. DEAN (ACADEMIC), UNIV. OF TORONTO, FACULTY OF MANAGEMENT 1989– ; Asst. Prof., Queen's Univ. 1978–84; Assoc. Prof. of Econ. 1984–89; Dir. John Deutsch Inst. Kingston 1987–89; Special Adv. Tax Policy Br. Dept. Finance 1984–86; Cons.: World Bank, OECD, IMF, Govt. Sask., Alberta and Ontario, Peat Marwick - Wash., D.C.; Auditor General Depts. Finance & Energy, Mines & Resources Can.; Extve. mem. John Deutsch Inst.; recipient Alexandor MacGibbon Award Univ. of Alta. 1973; Commonwealth Fellowship 1975–77; mem. Ontario Candn. Jewish Congress and Jewish Federation of Greater Toronto Extve.; author: 'Measure of Rates of Return in Canadian Banking' 1979, and over 50 published papers; co-author: 'Taxes on Capital Income in Canada: Analysis and Policy' 1987; editor: 'International Tax and Public Finance'; co-ed. 'Economic Impacts of Tax Reform' 1988; 'Impact of Taxation on Business Activity' 1988; co-author 'Dividing the Spoils: Federal-Provincial Allocation of Taxing Powers'; mem. Candn. Econ. Assn.; Am. Econ. Assn.; recreations: running, squash; Home: 59 Robingrove Rd., Willowdale, Ont. M2R 2A1; Office: 246 Bloor St. W., Toronto, Ont. M5S 1V4.

**MINTZBERG, Henry,** F.R.S.C.; university professor; b. Montreal, 2 Sept. 1939; s. Myer and Irene (Wetzler) M.; e. McGill Univ., B.Eng. 1961; Sir George Williams Univ., B.A. 1962; M.I.T., S.M. 1965, Ph.D. 1968; children: Susie, Lisa; PROFESSOR OF MANAGEMENT, McGILL UNIV. 1982– ; with McGill Faculty of Mgmt. since 1968; vis. prof. at Carnegie Mellon Univ. 1973, Univ. d'Aix-Marseille 1974–76, H.E.C. Montreal 1976–77; London Business Sch. 1990–91; INSEAD 1991, 1993–94; has also served as cons. and lectr. to bus. and govt. around the world; hon. degree, Univ. of Venice 1983, Univ. of Lund 1989, Univ. of Lausanne 1991; Université de Montréal 1992; McKinsey Prize (Harvard Bus. Review) 1975, second 1987; author 'The Nature of Managerial Work' 1973; 'The Structuring of Organizations' 1979; 'Power In and Around Organizations' 1983; 'The Strategy Process' 1988; 'Mintzberg on Management: Inside our Strange World of Organizations' 1989; 'The Rise and Fall of Strategic Planning' 1994; also 80 articles about mgmt., strategy, structure, power and role of orgs. in soc.; Pres., Strategic Management Soc. 1988–91; recreations: hiking, canoeing, cross-country skiing, bicycling, short story writing; Office: Fac. of Mgmt., McGill Univ., 1001 Sherbrooke St. W., Montreal, Que. H3A 1G5.

**MIQUELON, Dale Bernard,** M.A., Ph.D.; educator; historian; b. Wetaskiwin, Alta. 27 Sept. 1940; s. Hector Bernard and Margaret Belsheim (Gullekson) M.; e. Univ. of Alta., B.A. 1963; Carleton Univ., M.A. 1966; Univ. of Toronto, Ph.D. 1973; m. Patricia d. James and Kathleen Finnigan 6 July 1968; HEAD, DEPT. OF HISTORY, UNIV. OF SASK. 1990– ; Hist. Researcher, Nat. Hist. Sites Div. N.A. & N.R. Ottawa 1963–64; Asst. prof. present univ. 1970, Assoc. Prof. 1975; Prof. of History 1979– ; recipient Can. Council Pre-doctoral Fellowship 1966–70, Leave Fellowship 1976–77, Doctoral Thesis Prize 1975; SSHRCC Released Time Fellowship 1982–83; Assoc. Dean of Humanities and Fine Arts, Univ. of Sask. 1984–89; author 'The First Canada: to 1791' 1994; 'New France 1701–1744: "A Supplement to Europe"' 1987; 'Dugard of Rouen: French Trade to Canada and the West Indies 1729–1770' 1978; numerous articles and reviews; Ed. 'Society and Conquest: The Debate on the Bourgeoisie and Social Change in French Canada 1799–1850' 1977; Home: 822 – 14th St. E., Saskatoon, Sask. S7N 0P8; Office: Saskatoon, Sask. S7N 0W0.

**MIRABELLI, Alan,** B.A., M.A.; administrator; b. Egypt 11 April 1948; s. Robert and Lysette (Haim) M.; e. Loyola College B.A. 1970; Fairfield Univ. M.A. 1971; Eastman Sch. of Music 1973; m. Anne d. Clive and Vivienne Mason 17 Oct. 1981; one s.: Michel; DIR. OF ADMINISTARTION AND COMMUNICATION, VANIER INSTITUTE OF THE FAMILY 1983– ; Lecturer, Loyola Coll., Concordia Univ. 1971–75; Coord. of Communication & Information, Vanier Inst. of the Family 1975–83; Dir., Photo-Electric Arts Foundation 1980–84; Family Recreation Adv. Ctte., Candn. Parks & Rec. Assn. 1982–84; Bd. Mem., Children's Broadcast Inst. 1986–90; Treas. 1989–90; Vice-Chair 1990–91; Chair, Alliance of Children & TV 1991–93; Dir., Candn. Ctte., Internat. Union of Family Orgns. & Family Horizons 1992– ; Mem., Econ. Devel. Ctte., Ramsay Twp. 1992–93; author: 'Families in the 1990s: In control or out of control? 1990, 'Canadians Seem to Need Television' 1989; co-author: 'A Choice of Futures: Canada's Commitment to its Children' 1989; recreations: cabinet-making, hiking; Home: R.R. 3, Almonte, Ont. K0A 1A0; Office: 120 Holland Ave., No. 300, Ottawa, Ont. K1Y 0X6.

**MIRRLEES, A.,** A.I.B., F.I.C.B.; banking executive; b. Newton Stewart, Scotland 20 May 1939; s. George B.M. and Anne L.P. (Brown) M.; e. Douglas Ewart H.S.; Assoc. of Scottish Inst. of Bankers A.I.B. (Scot) 1961; Fellow, Candn. Inst. of Bankers F.C.I.B. 1973; m. Helen d. Peter and Eileen Kropman 5 June 1969; one d.: Shelagh; VICE-PRES., CREDIT POLICY - TREASURY, ROYAL BANK OF CANADA 1989– ; joined Royal Bank in London, England 1962; subsequently served at offices in Jamaica, Bahamas, Montreal, Hong Kong, Singapore & Portland, Oregon before moving to Toronto as Manager, Trading, Treasury Div. 1982; Vice-Pres., Capital Markets, Treasury 1987; Office: 7th Floor, South Tower, 200 Bay St., Toronto, Ont. M5J 2J5.

**MIRUCKI, Jean,** Ph.D., C.D.P.; university professor; b. Quiévrechain, Nord, France 19 May 1943; s. Pierre and Rosalie (Hulewicz) M.; e. Concordia Univ. B.A. (with distinction) 1976; Univ. of Bordeaux, D.E.A. (with distinction) 1977; Ph.D. (with great distinction) 1980; Rsch. Asst., Univ. of Toronto 1965–66; Computer Operator, CIBC 1966–67; Programmer-Analyst & Project Leader, N.C.R. 1968–70 Systems Analyst, Royal Trust 1970–71; Sr. Mmgt. Cons., S.G.I. 1971–76; Asst. Prof., Univ. of Que. at Montreal 1979–84; Assoc. Prof. 1984–88; Adjunct Prof. of Econ., Concordia Univ. 1987–88; Maître de Conférences (Econ.), Univ. of Valenciennes 1988– ; Cons., Bell Canada; Dept. of Commun. (Ottawa); Min. of Culture & Commun. (Paris); French Ed. Corr., 'Journal of Economic Literature'; Zellidja Foundation Award (Paris) 1961; Dir., Inst. of Mngt., Econ. & Law, Univ. of Valenciennes 1980– ; Soc. des Ecrivains Can. (Dir. 1981–88; Vice Pres. 1982–84); Mem., Am. Econ. Assn. 1976– ; Assn. Française de Sci. Econ. 1978– ; P.E.N. Centre Francophone canadien 1984– ; author: 'Les Chemins de la Nuit' 1972, 'Comportement de l'Entreprise Réglementée' 1980, 'Le Marché du Livre au Canada' 2 vols. 1986; and several scholarly articles; recreations: tennis, classical music, collecting books & stamps; club: Mensa (Can. & France);

Home: 41 - 4660 Bourret Ave., Montreal, Que. H3W 1K8; Office: 82 avenue Faidherbe, 59300 Valenciennes, France.

**MIRVISH, Edwin,** C.B.E., O.C., C.M., LL.D.; entrepreneur; b. Colonial Beach, Va. 24 July 1914; s. David and Annie (Kornhauser) M.; came to Can. 1923; e. King Edward Pub. Sch. and Central Tech. Sch. Toronto; Trent Univ. LL.D. 1967; Univ. of Waterloo LL.D. 1969; York Univ. LL.D. 1992; Ryerson Technical Institute (Hon. Fellowship); m. Anne d. Jack Maklin, Columbia, Md. 29 June 1940; one s. David; OWNER, HONEST ED'S LTD.; Ed Mirvish Enterprises; Royal Alexandra Theatre; Princess of Wales Theatre; Old Vic, London, England; Ed's Theatre Museum; operates six large restaurants, Ed's Warehouse, Old Ed's, Ed's Seafood, Ed's Follies, Ed's Chinese and Ed's Italian Restaurant; recipient of many Awards including: Telegram Theatre Award; Award of Merit City of Toronto; B'Nai Brith Award; C.B.E. (Commander of the British Empire); Order of Canada; Marketing Award, Seneca Coll.; Gold Star Award Metropolitan Toronto Assn. for Retarded Children; Hon. Mem. Billy Bishop Heritage Candn. Hearing Soc.; author: (biography) 'How to Build an Empire on an Orange Crate' 1993; Jewish; recreation: ballroom dancing; Clubs: Toronto Press; Arts & Letters; Empire; Variety; Canadian; Friars; Office: 581 Bloor St. W., Toronto, Ont. M6G 1K3 and 260 King St. W., Toronto, Ont. M5V 1H9.

**MISKA, John P.,** B.A., B.L.Sc.; librarian; author; translator; editor; bibliographer; b. Nyirbéltek, Hungary 20 Jan. 1932; s. Mihály and Teréz (Kovács) M.; e. Bocskay Gymnasium; Univ. of Budapest; McMaster Univ.; Univ. of Toronto B.A., B.L.Sc.; m. Maria von Brockhausen; VISITING SCHOLAR, UNIVERSITY OF VICTORIA at work on memoirs 'Life is A Novel' and other writings (essays, review articles, short stories) published in Toronto and Budapest; Head Engn. Lib. Univ. of Man. 1962–66; Head Acquisitions, Agric. Can. Ottawa 1969–72; Head Librarian, Agric. Can., Lethbridge Res. Stn., 1972–83; Area Coordinator, Agric. Can. Libraries, National Capital Region and Ont. 1983–92; author 'Best Short Stories from English' 1965; 'A Mug of Milk: Short Stories' (Hungarian) 1968; 'Mending Our Fences: Selected Essays 1963–73' 1974 (Hungarian), rec'd. Silver Medal Arpad Acad. Cleveland; Ed. 'Antologia: Canadian-Hungarian Authors 1969–72' 3 vols. (Hungarian); 'The Sound of Time: Anthology of Canadian-Hungarian Authors' 1974; biographies incl.; 'Agriculture: A Bibliography of Research' 1973 5 vols.; 'Solonetz Soils of the World: A Bibliography' 1975; 'Potato Seed Piece Decay 1920–1975: A Bibliography'; 'Irrigation of the World: An Annotated Bibliography' 1977 4 vols.; 'Hungarian-Canadian Literature: A Preliminary List of Creative Works'; 'Bibliography of the Pea Aphid'; 'Ethnic & Native Canadian Literature 1850–1979: A Bibliography of Primary & Secondary Materials' (2,960 references on microfiche) 1980; 'Canadian Prose Written in English 1833–1980' (3,360 citations on microfiche) 1980; 'Cold Hardiness & Winter Survival of Plants: An Annotated Bibliography' (4,000 references) 1980; 'P.F. Grove: A Bibliography of Primary and Secondary Material' 1984; 'Canadian University Studies on Hungarians: A Bibliography' 1984; 'Canadian Studies on Hungarians 1885–1984: An Annotated Bibliography' (1300 refs) 1985; 'Crossroads: An Anthology of Hungarian Canadian Writing' 1989 under grant from Secretary of State received Gold Medal, Arpad Acad., Cleveland; 'Kanadából szeretettel/From Canada with Love: A Book of Essays 1975–85' 1986 under grant from Secretary of State; 'Ethnic and Native Canadian Literature: A Bibliography' (5,500) references) 1990; 'Literature of Hungarian-Canadians: Essays and Bibliography' 1991; more than 200 review articles in lit. and prof. journs.; recipient SSHRCC grant to prepare a comprehensive research tool on Candn. literature in the non-offical languages; recipient Queen's Jubilee Medal 1977; Alta. Achievement Award for Literature 1978; Home: 903 - 139 Clarence St., Victoria, B.C. V8V 2J1.

**MISSEN, Ronald William,** M.Sc., Ph.D., F.C.I.C., P.Eng.; educator; b. St. Catharines, Ont. 26 Feb. 1928; s. Edward Lionel and Helen Harrison (Miller) M.; e. Alexandra Pub. Sch. St. Catharines, Ont. 1940; Ryerson Sr. Pub. Sch. and Westdale Secondary Sch. Hamilton, Ont. 1946; Queen's Univ. B.Sc. 1950, M.Sc. 1951; Cambridge Univ. Ph.D. 1956 (Athlone Fellow 1953–55); m. (Elizabeth) Barbara d. late Norman E. Ward 28 July 1951; four d. Nancy Elizabeth, Kathryn Margaret, Brenda Carol, Lynne Patricia; PROFESSOR EMERITUS OF CHEM. ENGN., UNIV. OF TORONTO 1993– ; Chem. Engr. Polysar, Sarnia, Ont. 1951–53; Dir., Chemical Engineering Rsch. Consultants Ltd. 1963–93; Asst. Prof. of Chem. Engn., Univ. of Toronto 1956, Assoc. Prof. 1961–68, Prof. 1968–93, Pres. Faculty Assn. 1970–71, mem. Gov. Council 1975–77, Assoc. Dean (Phys. Sciences) Sch. of Grad. Studies 1976–77, Vice Provost (Prof. Faculties) 1977–81; rec'd Plummer Medal Engn. Inst. Can. 1962; author (with W.R. Smith) 'Chemical Reaction Equilibrium Analysis: Theory and Algorithms' 1982; 50 articles mainly in Applied Chem. Thermodynamics various scient. and engn. journs.; Fellow, Chem. Inst. Canada; Candn. Soc. Chem. Engn.; mem. Assn. Prof. Engrs. Prov. Ont.; Am. Inst. Chem. Engrs.; Anglican; Home: 19 Didrickson Dr., Willowdale, Ont. M2P 1J7; Office: Toronto, Ont. M5S 1A4.

**Mitch.** See Keirstead, Walter Mitchell.

**MITCHELL, Claude Leslie;** retired executive; b. Southampton, Eng. 6 July 1914; s. Charles Archibald and Edith Lucy (Newman) M.; came to Can. 1 Dec. 1914; e. Bloomfield High Sch., Halifax, N.S., grad. 1930; m. Ruth Margaret, d. late Harold Willard Tingley, 14 Oct. 1938; one d. Mrs. Corinne Andrea Walsh; with Bank of N.S. 1930–37; apptd. Salesman of H.J. Heinz Co. of Can. 1937–49; Dist. Supv., N.B. Sales 1949–53; Sales Br. Mgr., Saint John, N.B. 1953–56; Mgr., Atlantic Region 1956–61, Ont. Region 1961–62; Mang. Dir., Netherlands 1962–64; Vice Pres. Sales, 1964–79 (ret.); Past Pres., Sun Parlour Nature Club; mem., Maritime Comm. Travellers' Assn.; I.O.O.F.; Club: Bd. of Trade, Metro. Toronto; Conservative; Protestant; recreation: spectator sports; Home: 16 Lyon Ave., Leamington, Ont. N8H 3Z4.

**MITCHELL, David Alexander,** M.A., Ph.D.; educator; b. Regina, Sask. 9 Mar. 1930; s. Alexander and Morag (Irwin) M.; e. Univ. of Sask. B.A. 1952; Oxford Univ. (Rhodes Scholar) M.A. 1962; Stanford Univ. Ph.D. 1967; PROFESSOR OF HUMANITIES, FRENCH, DAWSON COLL. 1973– , Chrmn. of Humanities and Philos. 1975–76; lecteur d'anglais Ecole Normale Supérieure, Paris 1955–56; Instr. Univ. of Sask. 1956–58; Lectr. Univ. of Man. 1958–60; Instr. Stanford Univ. 1962–63; Asst. Prof. Univ. of Chicago 1964–67; Asst. Prof. York Univ. 1967–69; mem. Parti Québécois; Parti Nationaliste; Soc. St-Jean Baptiste; recreations: water-colour, sailing; Clubs: Junior Carleton (Oxford); Adelphi (Oxford); Home: 1029 blvd. Saint-Joseph est, Montréal, Qué. H2J 1L2; Office: 3040, rue Sherbrooke ouest, Westmount, Qué. H3Z 1A4.

**MITCHELL, David J.,** M.A.; writer; businessman; b. Montreal, Que. 15 March 1954; s. Michael and Margaret (Lalonde) M.; e. Simon Fraser Univ. B.A. 1975, M.A. 1976; B.C. Legislative Intern 1978; Banff Sch. Advanced Mgmt. 1988; m. Marlene d. Charles and Helen Layton 6 Dec. 1975; two d. Madeleine Anne, Jane Elizabeth; MEMBER OF THE LEGISLATIVE ASSEMBLY OF B.C. (W. VANCOUVER-GARIBALDI) 1991– ; Teaching Asst. Simon Fraser 1976, Univ. of B.C. 1977; Archivist, Prov. Archives of B.C. 1977–80; Dep. Clk. Legis. Assembly of Sask. 1981–84; Mgr. Govt. Relations B.C. Resources Investment Corp. 1984–85; Gen. Mgr. Ind. Relations Westar Timber Ltd. 1985–86, Vice Pres. Adm. 1987–90; Vice Pres. Export Mktg. 1990; Independent Consultant and Media Commentator 1991; author 'W.A.C.: Bennett and the Rise of British Columbia' 1983; 'Succession: The Political Reshaping of British Columbia' 1987; Address: 1424 Briarlynn Cr., North Vancouver, B.C. V7J 3G5.

**MITCHELL, David Malcolm;** fine art consultant and art historian; b. Exeter, Devon, England 30 May 1938; s. William and Doreen (Barwick) M.; e. Bromley Grammar Sch.; co-vivant Tanya d'Anger; children: Alycen Catherine Grace, Joanna Louise, Xenia Laurene, Fitzroy (adopted); INDEPENDENT FINE ART CONSTULTANT AND ART HISTORIAN 1979– ; Sales & Media Relns. Extve., Sotheby & Co. London 1958–68; Gen. Mgr. 1968–70; Sotheby & Co. Canada; Founded nat. market for sale of Candn. fine art at auction; Pres., The Mitchell Gallery 1970–72 ; Central (Nat.) Buyer, Inuit Art, Dec. Art & Accessories, Hudson's Bay Co. 1973–78; specialist fields: Candn. 19th & 20th century art, Inuit & Native Indian art; Ont. Arts Council grant 1986; Anglican; contbr.: 'Ivory Hammer' 1966, 'Antiques Collector' 1965, 'Kennedy Quarterly' 1965–68, 'Canadian Collector' 1966–68 and to articles & books by English & French art writers; author of several articles; recent rediscoverer of painting & drawings by Ottilie Palm Jost; organized retrospective exbn., Beckett Gallery Hamilton 1992; subject of CBC documentary about Ottilie Palm Jost 1994; describes himself as an art 'detective' and a catalyst in the Candn. art world; recreations: gardening, travel; clubs: Arts and Letters of Toronto, The Daguerreian Soc. (Founding Mem.); Home: 358 Berkeley St., Toronto, Ont. M5A 2X7.

**MITCHELL, Dawn,** B.A.; foundation executive; b. St. John's, Nfld. 4 Dec. 1969; d. Joan E. and Henry C. Mitchell; e. Memorial Univ. of Newfoundland B.A. 1992; Pres., John H. Mcdonald Journalism Foundation 1992– ; News editor, 'The Muse,' Memorial Univ. 1989–90; Editor 1990–91; Atlantic Reg. Bureau Chief, Canadian Univ. Press 1991–92; Pres. 1992–93; Chair, Candn. Univ. Press Media Serv. Limited, Campus Plus 1992–93.

**MITCHELL, Hon. Gerard Eugene,** B.A., LL.B.; judge; b. Charlottetown, P.E.I. 25 Aug. 1943; s. Harold Edward and Margaret Mary (Macdonald) M.; e. Grand Tracadie Consolidated 1958; St. Dunstan's High Sch. 1960; St. Dunstan's Univ., B.A. 1964; Univ. New Brunswick, LL.B. 1970; m. Mary, d. Arthur and Mildred Kelly, 25 Aug. 1973; children: Erin Trinity; John Nathanael; JUDGE, SUPREME COURT, APPEAL DIV., P.E.I. 1987– ; School Teacher 1964–67; admitted to P.E.I. Bar 1970; practiced law Charlottetown 1970–75; appointed Prov. Court Judge 1975; returned to private practice with Campbell, Mitchell, Lea and Cheverie 1977; Judge, Supreme Court, P.E.I. 1981– ; Home: 125 North Rd., Charlottetown, P.E.I. C1A 7K7; Office: Law Courts Bldg., Box 2000, 42 Water St., Charlottetown, P.E.I. C1A 7N8.

**MITCHELL, James Gordon,** B.B.M.; business executive; b. Brantford, Ont. 26 Nov. 1949; s. Gordon Mitchell and Alice (Montaque) M.; e. Paris Dist. H.S. 1969 (valedictorian); Ryerson Polytech Inst. 1972, Marketing/Finance Program 1978 B.B.M.; York Univ., Mktg. Mngt.; m. Maureen Cunningham 14 July 1973; children: Jonathan, David; Group Vice-Pres., North America, Tambrands Inc.; Mktg. Mgr. & Div. Mgr., Miles Labs. 1977–84; Vice-Pres. & Gen. Mgr., Gaines Pet Foods 1984–87; C.O.O., Chieftain Products 1987–89; Pres., Tambrands Canada 1989–91; mem., Alumni Assn.; Ryerson Polytch.; recreations: golf, hockey, coaching; Club: Beacon Hall Golf & Country (Aurora, Ont.); Home: 125 Norrans Ridge Dr., Ridgefield, CT 06877.

**MITCHELL, Janet,** R.C.A.; artist; b. Medicine Hat, Alta. 24 Nov. 1912; d. John and Janet (McLellan) Mitchell; e. Pub., High and Business Schs. Calgary; Calgary and London, Eng. art schs.; LL.D. (Hon.), Univ. of Calgary 1988; paintings exhibited across Can., Brit., Japan and USA since 1946; recipient several awards in maj. shows; rep. in many private colls.; mem. Adv. Purchasing Comte. Alta Art Foundation; 1975–77; Calgary Regional Foundation of Arts 1976–1978; subject of documentary on CBC TV; book publication, 'Janet Mitchell: Her Life and Art' (by Peggy Armstrong) 1990; painting reproduced on a postage stamp for the special edition issued by Canadian Post Corp. to celebrate Canada's 125 birthday; mem. Council R.C.A.; mem. Candn. Soc. Painters in Watercolour; Alta. Soc. Artists; Address: 1240 – 20 St. N.W., Calgary, Alta. T2N 2K4.

**MITCHELL, John Kirkman,** B.Comm., C.A.; banker; b. South Africa 30 Dec. 1935; s. William Henry and Mary Ida (Kirkman) M.; e. Univ. of Witwatersrand B.Comm. 1964; m. Meryl d. Alan and Kathleen Watt 18 April 1959; children: Roger, Robin, Kim, Merianne; SENIOR VICE-PRES. & CHIEF ACCOUNTANT, THE BANK OF NOVA SCOTIA; qualified as C.A. Ernst and Whinney 1958; Gen. Mgr., Industrial Devel. Corp. of S. Africa 1959–79; joined Bank of N.S. 1979; Dir., Scotia Mortgage Corp.; recreations: golf, sailing; Home: 1171 Colborne Ct., Oakville, Ont. L6J 6B9; Office: Scotia Plaza, 40 King St. W., Toronto, Ont. M5H 1H1.

**MITCHELL, John Marvin,** Ph.D., F.A.B.I., F.W.L.A., F.I.B.A., H.E.; internat. management and financial services executive; b. Toronto, Ont. 10 July 1948; s. the late John Campbell and late Catherine Mary (Bonazza) M.; e. Pacific Western Univ. Los Angeles Ph.D. 1988; m. Bernadette d. Raymond and Elizabeth Hay 13 Nov. 1971; children: Nicole, J.R. Scott, Monique; PRES., C.E.O. & DIR., CANDN. FINANCIAL INVESTMENTS INC. 1990– ; joined IAC Ltd., Continental Bank 1969–79, Mgr. Training & Devel.; designed, conducted, management, marketing, finance, credit programs for Univ. Graduates in Banking (co-author 'Professional Selling Program' 1977; Bank of Nova Scotia 1979–81, Regional Mgr. Man., Ont., Scotia Leasing Ltd.(Co-Founder Scotia Leasing Plan 1980); Canadian Financial Investments Inc. 1981–86, Pres.; C.E.O. & Dir., Operating Divisions - Phillips Parkway, Lifestyle Books, Heritage LifeStyles International; Beneficial Canada Inc. 1986–88, Gen. Mgr. Beneficial Income Tax Service, Dir. of Human Resources and of Govt. Relations; Sr. Vice Pres., Gen. Mgr. & Dir., Bentax Ltd., I/G Tax Services, Investors Group Inc. 1988–90; Dir. Candn. Council Better Bus. Bureaus 1989–91; Mem., Disciplinary and Ethics Ctte.

1989–91; designed fund raising progs. Easter Seals Soc. 1986–90, IWK Hosp. N.S., N.B., P.E.I. 1988–90; author 'Fathers of Motivation' 1988; 'How To Design Effective Management Training Programs' 1988; 'How to Plan and Conduct Effective Staff, Sales Meetings 1992; 'Face to Face Communications' 1993; 'Face to Face Negotiations' 1993; mem. Bd. Trade Metrop. Toronto; Assn. Candn. Financial Corps.; apptd. Comnr. Province of Ont. 1989–90; listed in: Dictionary of International Biography (22nd ed.); International - Men of Achievement (15th ed.); International Who's Who of Intellectuals (10th ed.); Grand Ambassador of Achievement Internat.; Internat. Directory of Distinguished Leadership, Volume 3, 4th ed.; Mem., World Institute of Achievement; Fellow, Am. Biographical Institute; Fellow, Internat. Biographical Assn.; Fellow, World Literary Academy; Advisory Council, Internat. Biographical Centre; awarded 'International Man of the Year' 1991/92; 'One in a Million' I.B.C.; 'Most Admired Man of the Decade', A.B.I.; Internat. Silver Shield of Valor; named 'World Intellectual' I.B.C. 1993; recipient, Internat. Cultural Diploma of Honor 1993; to be published in five hundred Leaders of Influence 1993; Roman Catholic; recreations: golf, tennis, baseball, gardening, hockey; Home: 41 Humber College Blvd., Etobicoke, Ont. M9V 1P2.

**MITCHELL, Joni (Roberta Joan Anderson);** singer, songwriter; b. Ft. McLeod, Alta. 7 Nov. 1943; d. William A. and Myrtle M. (McKee) A.; student Alta. Coll.; m. Chuck Mitchell, 1965, (div.); m. 2ndly, Larry Klein 1982; albums incl.: 'Song to a Seagull'; 'Clouds'; 'Ladies of the Canyon'; 'Blue'; 'For the Roses'; 'Court and Spark'; 'Miles of Aisles'; 'The Hissing of Summer Lawns'; 'Hejira'; 'Don Juan's Reckless Daughter'; 'Mingus' (Jazz Album of Year and Rock-Blues Album of Year, Downbeat mag. 1979); 'Shadows and Light'; 'Wild Things Run Fast' 1982; 'Dog Eat Dog' 1985; 'Chalk Mark In A Rain Storm' 1988; 'Night Ride Home' 1991; Juno award for special achievement, 1981; Address: c/o Peter Asher Mgmt., 644 North Doheny Dr., Los Angeles, CA 90069.

**MITCHELL, Kenneth Ronald,** B.A., M.A.; university professor; novelist; playwright; b. Moose Jaw, Sask. 13 Dec. 1940; s. Colin McIntyre and Eileen Reid (Howe) M.; e. Central Coll. 1958; Univ. of Sask., B.A. 1965, M.A. 1967; m. Jeanne d. Fred and Rolande Shami 23 Aug. 1983; children: Kevin Edward, James Alexander, Colin Paul, Andrew Kenneth, Julia Yvonne; PROF., UNIV. OF REGINA 1984– ; English Instr., Univ. of Regina 1967–70; Scot.-Candn. Exchange Fellow 1979–80; Vis. Prof., Univ. of Nanjing, China 1980–81; Fgn. Affairs Coll., Beijing, China 1986–87; author: 'Wandering Rafferty' 1972, 'The Meadowlark Connection' 1975, 'The Con Man' 1979, 'Stones of the Dalai Lama: a Novel' 1993 (novels); 'Everybody Gets Something Here' 1977 (short stories); 'The Shipbuilder' 1990; 'Davin' 1979, 'Gone the Burning Sun' 1985 (Candn. Authors Assn. Award for Best Candn. Play 1985), (co-author) 'Cruel Tears' 1977 (plays); 'Sinclair Ross' 1981 (criticism); 'Ken Mitchell Country' 1984 (selected works); 'Witches and Idiots' 1990; 'Through the Nan Da Gate' 1986 (poetry); editor: 'Horizon, Writings of the Canadian Prairie' 1977 (anthology); Ottawa Little Theatre Prize for Best One Act Play in Can. for 'Heroes' 1971; Genie nom., Best Candn. Screenplay for 'The Hounds of Notre Dame' 1981; Mem., St. Paul's Greek Orthodox Ch.; Playwrights Union of Can.; Sask. Writers Guild; Candn. Assn. of Univ. Teachers; club: Sask. Cultural Exch. Soc.; Home: 209 Angus Cres., Regina, Sask. S4T 6N3; Office: English Dept., Univ. of Regina, Regina, Sask. S4T 6N3.

**MITCHELL, Margaret Thomas (Meg),** B.A.; business executive; b. Baltimore, Md. 17 May 1946; d. F.W.B. and Priscilla H. Thomas; e. Centenary Coll. for Women 1966; Univ. of Ky. B.A. 1969; PRES. THE THOMAS-MITCHELL ASSOCIATES INC. (executive recruitment firm) 1982– ; previously educator and staff mem. Nat. Geog. Soc.; Assoc. E.L. Shore & Associates 1975–79; Partner The Caldwell Partners 1979–82; Past Dir. Candn. Assn. Women Extves.; Office: 18A Hazelton Ave., Toronto, Ont. M5R 2E2.

**MITCHELL, Maurice Stephen,** B.Sc.; civil engineer; b. Cardiff, Alta. 10 May 1919; s. Hugh John and Agatha (Lillijord) M.; e. Garneau (Alta.) HighSch.; Univ. of Alta., B.Sc. (C.E.) 1942; m. Molly, d. W. D. Browning, 6 July 1946; children: Marda, Kurt Davison; with Aluminum Co. of Can., 1942–43; Hamilton Bridge Co. (Western) 1944; Univ. of Alta., Civil Engn. Staff, 1943–46; Founding partner, Meech Mitchell & Meech 1946–72; served C.O.T.C., Lieut., Reserve Signals, 1938–42; Cub Master, 1959–69, Boy Scouts of Can. and Pres. of S. Alta. Region 1971 (rec'd 15 yr medal 1975); Councillor, Lethbridge Chamber of Comm.; Senator, Univ. Lethbridge 1973–79; Budget Dir., United Way of Lethbridge 1975–81, Campaign Chrmn. 1978–79; Lethbridge Housing Authority 1977–85; Ch. 1983–85; Pres., United Way of Alta., 1979–80; Hon. Life mem. Assn. Prof. Engrs. Alta.; Kappa Sigma (Alumnus Advisor 1945–46); Conservative; Anglican; recreations: tennis, golf; Clubs: Country; Kiwanis (Vice-Pres. 1955–56, Pres. 1958, Lt. Gov. 1964); Address: 33 – 135 Jerry Potts Blvd., Lethbridge, Alta. T1K 6H2.

**MITCHELL, Michael Frederick (Fred),** B.A.; executive; b. Los Angeles, Ca. 1 Dec. 1946; s. Cameron and Johanna (Mendel) M.; e. pub. and high schs. Los Angeles; Univ. of Ariz. B.A. (Econ.) 1969; m. Lu-Anne Gingara, Aug. 1986; PRESIDENT since 1976 AND C.E.O. since 1983, INTERCONTINENTAL PACKERS LTD.; joined Intercontinental Packers part-time 1965, full-time as Mang. Trainee 1969, subsequently serving as Salesman, Asst. to Pork and Beef Dept. Heads, Marketing Coordinator, Vice Pres. Marketing 1973, Pres. 1976; mem., Young Presidents Organization; Past Pres., Candn. Meat Council (Past Chrmn. of Western Section); Dir., Intercontinental Packers Ltd.; Intercontinental Packers Inc. (U.S.A.); Mitchell's Gourmet Meats; Save The Planet Holdings Inc.; Arthritis Found. of Sask.; Saskatchewan Chamber of Commerce; M.F.M. Holdings; A.L.S.E. Holdings; F. Mendel Holdings Ltd.; Past Mem., SAGIT 1985–88; Mem. Bd. of Govs., Univ. of Sask.; Co-Chrmn., Univ. of Sask. Centre for Agricultural Medicine, Founding Chairs Development Council; Past Bd. of Govs. Trustee, Univ. of Sask.; Mem., Ctte. on U.S. Canada Trade Relations; Past Pres., Mendel Art Gall; Bd. Mem. & Dir., Arthritis Soc., Sask. Div.; Sr. Mem., Conference Bd. Inc. New York; Hon. Mem., Boy Scouts of Canada, Nat. Counc.; Mem., Advisory Council on Science, Technology and Innovation; Former mem. Sask. Chamber of Commerce; recreations: fishing, skiing, art, music; Clubs: Saskatoon; Riverside Golf & Country; Office: 3003 – 11th Street W., P.O. Box 850, Saskatoon, Sask. S7K 3V4.

**MITCHELL, Paul D.;** executive; b. Niagara Falls, Ont. 1 Jan. 1942; s. David and Marjorie Barbara (Banwell) M.; e. Univ. of Windsor, Bus. Adm.; m. Lucille d. Armand and Irene Poitras 18 Jan. 1964; children: Merilee, David, Megan; Pres. & Dir., McNeil Consumer Products Co.; Dir. Johnson & Johnson Inc.; Air Canada; Junior Achievement of Canada; joined Johnson & Johnson 1966, Product Dir. Montréal 1966, W. Regional Sales Mgr. Vancouver 1969, Product Group Dir. Montréal 1971, Dir. Mktg., Consumer 1972, Vice Pres. Consumer Div. and mem. Bd. Dirs. 1973; Executive Vice Pres. and Gen. Mgr. present Co. 1978; Dir. Koffler Inst. Pharm. Mgmt.; Past Chrmn. of Bd., Nonprescription Drug Manufacturers Assoc. of Canada; Chrmn., Bd. of Govs., Univ. of Waterloo; Past Dir. Kitchener-Waterloo Symphony; Confedn. Club Kitchener-Waterloo; Mem., Advisory Bd., Candn. Cosmetic, Toiletry & Fragrance Assn. (Past Dir. and Chrmn.); recreations: bridge, reading, sports; Clubs: Albany; Westmount Golf & Country; Office: 890 Woodlawn Rd. W., Guelph, Ont. N1K 1A5.

**MITCHELL, Richard Morden,** E.D., B.Sc., M.B.A., P.Eng.; b. Clarksburg, Ont 2 Nov 1911; s. George Herbert and Caroline Cartwright (Carthew) M.; e. Queen's Univ. B. Sc. (Mech.) 1935; Harvard Bus. Sch. M.B.A. 1948; m. Helen d. Ernest and Leila Chapman 24 March 1945; children: Peter, Graham, Lynn; Canadian Ingersoll Rand Co. Ltd. 1935–39; Carrier Engineering Ltd. 1948–54; Dunham-Bush Canada Ltd. 1954–65; Lake Ontario Cement Ltd. 1966–78; served Overseas 1939–45, Royal Candn. Engs. UK, N. Africa, Italy and N.W. Eur., rank Maj.; Lt. Col. commdg. 2nd field Eng. Regt.(M) 1949–52, Hon. Lt. Col. 1975–82; Hon. Col. 1982–86; Nat. Pres. Candn. Refrigeration & Air Conditioning Assn. 1964–65; mem. Mil. Engs. Assn. Can. (Pres. Toronto Br. 1958); Anglican; recreations: golf, sailing, curling; Clubs: Weston Golf & Country; Home: 7 Lambeth Cres., Islington, Ont. M9A 3A6.

**MITCHELL, Robert Ian,** M.D., F.R.C.S.(C), F.R.A.C.S., F.R.C.S., F.A.C.S., F.C.C.P; surgeon/health care consultant/corporate director; b. Sydney Australia 13 Oct. 1927; s. William Robert and Lillian (Coram) M.; e. Sydney Ch. of Eng. Gr. Sch.; Sydney Univ. Med. Sch., M.B., B.S. (Hons.) 1950; post-grad. training in surgery, Australia, Eng. & U.S.; m. Barbara E. d. Garfield and Reta Weston 10 Aug. 1957; children: Garfield, Eliza, Mark, Emma, Sarah, Serena; MEDICAL CONSULTANT; commenced spec. surg. practice Toronto joining active staff, Wellesley Hosp. & fac., Univ. of Toronto 1960; appt. Cons. Surg., Princess Margaret Hosp., Sr. Surg. & Chief of Thoracic Surg., Wellesley Hosp. & Assoc. Prof., Dept. of Surg., Univ. of Toronto; retired from active surg. practice 1982; Sr. Med. Cons., Workers Compensation Bd. of Ont. 1987–91; Bd. of Dir., Wellesley Hosp. 1986– ; George Weston Limited 1987– ; Chrmn. of Bd. of Trustees, Eye Research Institute of Canada 1992– ; invited speaker, Internat. Cong. of Gastro-Enterology, France 1970 and Harvard Med. Sch. 1974; Mem., Bd. of Examiners, Royal Coll. of Surg. of Can. 1972–80; Mem., Central Surg. Soc.; Soc. of Thoracic Surg.; Candn. Assn. of Clin. Surg.; author of numerous pub. sci. articles; awarded Commemorative Medal for 125th Anniversary of Candn. Confederation 1992; recreations: tennis, swimming; Club: Granite; Home: 3 High Point Rd., Don Mills, Ont. M3B 2A3.

**MITCHELL, Robert Wayne,** Q.C., B.A., LL.B.; lawyer; b. Preeceville, Sask. 29 March 1936; s. Charles Stuart and Beda Annette (Abrahamson) M.; e. Sturgis Comp. H.S. 1954; Univ. of Sask. B.A. 1957, LL.B. 1959; m. Sandra Gail d. Stolie and Bertha Stolson 18 Oct. 1968; children: Janet, Roberta, Shannon, Stephanie, Donna, Alison; MINISTER OF JUSTICE, GOVERNMENT OF SASKATCHEWAN 1991– ; Assoc., Salloum & Hagemeister 1961–64; Partner, Pierce, Hleck, Kanuka, Mitchell & Thuringer 1964–70; Dir., Legal Serv. & Legis. Rsch., Labour Can. 1970–72; Dir. Legal Serv., Dept. of Reg. Econ. Expansion 1973; Labour Relns. Expert, Internat. Labour Orgn. 1973–74; Dep. Min., Sask. Labour 1974–79; Sr. Partner, Mitchell Taylor Mattison Ching 1979–91; M.L.A., Sask. Fairview 1986– ; Opposition Critic, Trade & Investment; Chrmn., Key Lake Bd. of Inquiry 1979–81; Chief Fed. Negotiator, Inuit Land Claim 1980–82; Cons., Labour Legis., Govt. of Yukon 1981–84; Prov. of Man. 1984; Auditor Gen. Adv. Ctte., Lab. Can. 1984; cr. Q.C. 1989; Mem., Un. Ch.; NDP; Law Soc. of Sask.; co-author: 'Mega Projects' 1981; recreations: golf, canoeing; Home: 70 Degeer Cres., Saskatoon, Sask. S7H 4P7.

**MITCHELL, Robert William,** B.Sc., M.Sc., Ph.D., C.Eng.; oil company executive; b. Woking England 11 Feb. 1945; s. Harry Albert and Elsie Kate (Preston) M.; e. Univ. of Hull B.Sc. (Hons.) 1966, Ph.D. 1969; Queen's Univ. 1971; m. Dorothy d. Lillian and Ronald Hunt 10 Sept. 1966; children: Timothy Derek, Katherine Susannah; VICE PRES. OPERATIONS, TALISMAN ENERGY 1985– ; var. of engineering positions, 1970–77; Head, Production Technology, BP Exploration 1978; Manager, Petroleum Engineering 1980; Vice-Pres., Oil Sands, BP Canada 1984; extensive internat. oil & gas experience working in U.S., Canada, Europe, Middle East & Africa for BP & Shell; Dir., Fortuna Petroleum Inc.; Mem., Candn. Petroleum Soc.; Mem., Soc. of Petroleum Engrs.; Fellow, Inst. of Mining & Metallurgy; Chartered Engineer; Baptist; recreations: hiking, boating, model engineering; clubs: Calgary Model Engineering Soc.; Petroleum Club; Home: 903 Edinburgh Rd. S.W., Calgary, Alta. T2S 1L7; Office: Suite 2100 – 855 2nd Street S.W., Calgary, Alta. T2P 4J9.

**MITCHELL, William Ormond,** O.C. (1972), B.A.; author; b. Weyburn, Sask. 13 Mar. 1914; s. Ormond S. & Margaret Letitia (MacMurray) M.; e. St. Petersburg High Sch., Fla.; Univ. of Man., 1932–34; Univ. of Alta., B.A. 1942; m. Merna Lynne, d. Spurgeon M. Hirtle, Vancouver, B.C., 15 Aug. 1942; children: Ormond Skinner, Hugh Hirtle, Willa Lynne; Hon. mem., Eugene Field Soc.; author 'Who Has Seen the Wind' 1947; 'The Kite'; 'The Devil's Instrument' 1973; 'Jake and the Kid' 1974; 'The Vanishing Point' 1973; 'The Black Bonpiel of Wullie MacCrimmon' 1974; 'Back to Beulah' 1978; 'How I Spent My Summer Holidays' 1981; 'Since Daisy Creek' 1984; 'Ladybug - Lady Bug' 1988; 'According to Jake the Kid' 1989; 'Roses Are Difficult Here' 1990; 'For Art's Sake' 1992; contrib. to 'Maclean's,' 'Liberty,' 'Atlantic Monthly,' 'Queen's Quarterly,' 'Canadian Forum,' 'Ladies' Home Journal'; incl. in 'Best American Short Stories' 1946; author of a number of radio scripts for CBC since 1947; awarded Leacock Medal for Humour (collected ed. of 'Jake and the Kid') 1962; former Writer in Residence Massey College, U. of Calgary, U. of Alta., U. of Windsor; Delta Kappa Epsilon; Liberal; Presbyterian; recreations: angling, orchid culture, dramatics; Address: McClelland & Stewart, 481 University Ave., Suite 900, Toronto, Ont. M5G 2E9.

**MITCHELSON, The Hon. Bonnie,** M.L.A.; politician; b. Winnipeg, Man. 28 Nov. 1947; d. Henry Alfred and Millie Christine (Leslie) Bester; e. Sisler High Sch. Winnipeg 1964; Winnipeg Gen. Hosp. Sch. of Nursing R.N. 1968, I.C.U. Course 1969; m. Donald s. Richard and Margaret Mitchelson 30 Aug. 1969; children: Michele, Scott; MIN. OF FAMILY SERVICES 1993– ; intensive care and recovery room nursing Health Sciences Centre, Toronto Gen. Hosp., Etobicoke Gen. Hosp. Toronto, Grace Hosp. Winnipeg, Concordia Hosp. Winnipeg 1968–86; el. M.L.A. Man. 1986, Dep.

Health Critic, Urban Affairs Critic 1987; Min. of Culture, Heritage & Citizenship, Man. and Min. responsible for Lotteries 1988–93, Min. responsible for Multiculturalism 1990–93, Min. responsible for Status of Women 1990–93; Dir. Man. Heart Found.; recreations: downhill skiing, boating, reading; Home: 51 Uxbridge Rd., Winnipeg, Man. R2G 1Z7; Office: 357 Legislative Building, 450 Broadway, Winnipeg, Man. R3C 0V8.

**MITCHINSON, James Alfred,** B.Comm.; b. Oshawa, Ont. 21 Mar. 1934;s. Thomas Moffat Herbert and Emily May (Wells) M.; e. Westmount & Ritson Rd. Elem. Schs.; Oshawa Collegiate; Concordia Univ., B.Comm. 1968; m. Mary Josephine, d. Ferdinand and Eva Spragar, 1 Oct. 1955; children: Laureen Mary (Mrs. Steven Park), Gayle Eva May (Mrs. Larry Houle); Extve. Dir., Halton Work Programme; Pres.-Elect, Oakville Civitan Club Inc.; began investment training Toronto General Trust, Toronto 1954; Supervisor Mortgages & Real Estate, Winnipeg 1955; joined Great-West Life Assurance Co., Winnipeg 1956; Montreal 1959; Vice-Pres., Real Estate Investments, Winnipeg 1968–81; Pres., Dir. & C.E.O. Rostland Corp. Toronto 1981–86; mem. Concordia Alumni Assn.; Anglican; Clubs: Oakville Golf; Civitan (Oakville); recreations: golf; travel; Home: 16 Birch Hill Lane, Oakville, Ont. L6K 2N9.

**MITROVIĆ, Boidar,** M.Sc., Ph.D.; university professor; b. Belgrade, Yugoslavia 2 July 1952; s. Petar and Bogdanka (Bubalo) M.; e. Univ. of Belgrade, dipl. physicist 1977; McMaster Univ. M.Sc. 1979, Ph.D. 1981; ASSOC. PROF. OF PHYSICS, BROCK UNIV. 1987– ; Postdoctoral Research Fellows, Dept. of Physics, SUNY at Stony Brook 1981–83; Asst. Prof. of Physics, Brock Univ. 1983–87; Mem., Bd. of Trustees, Brock Univ.; Edit. Bd. Mem., 'Brock Review'; Home: 56 Royal Oak Dr., St. Catharines, Ont. L2N 6K7; Office: St. Catharines, Ont. L2S 3A1.

**MITTON, Rev. Harold Logan,** B.A., B.D., D.D. (Bapt.); Retired; b. Moncton, N.B. 20 Dec. 1919; s. Clifford John and Eva Isabelle (Logan) M.; e. Acadia Univ. B.A. 1944, B.D. 1946, D.D. 1966; special study and reading Princeton Theol. Semy., Fuller Theol. Semy. and Inst. for Advanced Pastoral Study 1970; m. Marguerite McKay d. late Burtt Rideout 9 Aug. 1944; children: Ronald Burtt, Ruth Christine; Professor Emeritus and Dir. of Supervised Field Education, Acadia Divinity Coll. 1986–92 (Principal and Dean there 1975–85; mem. Bd. of Trustees and Senate there); mem. Bd. of Govs. and Senate Acadia Univ.; held pastorates Aylesford and Windsor, N.S., Charlottetown, Brunswick St. Un. Bapt. Ch. Fredericton, First Bapt. Ch. Calgary; mem. of Faculty Acadia Univ. 1975; Pres. Atlantic Un. Bapt. Convention 1962; 1st Vice Pres. Bapt. Fed. of Can. 1968; Atlantic Bapt. rep. Candn. Council Chs.; apptd. to Candn. Bapt. Overseas Mission Bd. 1971; numerous speaking engagements; Field Assoc. 'Faith at Work' and frequent leader Ch. Renewal Confs.; served as Chaplain with Candn. Army (Reserve) 1952–62, rank Maj.; author 'Facing Today's World'; contrib. to various denominational journs.; syllabus and cassette lectures 'The Psalms and Modern Man'; mem., Acad. of Homiletics of U.S. and Can.; recreation: swimming; Address: 20 Grandview Dr., Wolfville, N.S. B0P 1X0.

**MITTON, Ronald B.,** B.A., LL.B.; barrister; b. Berwick, N.S. 23 Oct. 1947; s. Dr. Harold Logan and Marguerite Mackay (Rideout) M.; e. Acadia Univ. B.A. 1969; Dalhousie Law School LL.B. 1972; m. Susan d. John K. Young 20 June 1981; children: Julia Jane, John Logan; FOUNDING PARTNER, FRANKLIN BURKE 1976– ; Associate, Macleod Dixon 1972–76; specialist in civil litigation & trial practice; Mem., Law Soc. of Alta.; Law Soc. of N.S.; Candn. Bar Assn.; Dir., Writers' Development Trust; Mem., First Baptist Church; recreations: sailing, golf; clubs: The Halifax (Past Dir.), Royal N.S. Yacht Squadron (Past Vice Commodore); Home: 6053 Jubilee Rd., Halifax, N.S. B3H 2E3; Office: 5162 Duke St., Halifax, N.S. B3J 2N7.

**MIX, Catherine Lillian;** food industry executive; b. Toronto, Ont. 4 Nov. 1928; d. Frederick and Winnifred Florence (Meek) Hotrum; e. Etobicoke C.I. 1948; Dominion Business Coll. 1949; m. Ronald MacFarlane s. Edwin and Mary Susan M. 3 May 1952; children: Steven, Nancy, Jennifer; FOUNDER & PRES., CATHERINE'S FOODS LTD. 1983– a family owned & operated business; Charter Bd. Dir., Candn. Assn. of Specialty Foods; Lecturer, Univ. of Toronto & Ryerson Polytech. Univ.; Consultant to startup business personnel; Mem., Culinary Guild; Women in Food Management; Dist. Dir., UNICEF Etobicoke 1965–75; Mem., I.O.D.E. 1955–65; Temagami Lakes Assn. 1938– ; Kingsway Lambton Un. Ch. 1940– ; Bermuda Nat. Trust 1984– ; recreations: yoga, ice skating, summer home; Clubs: St. Georges (Bermuda); Home: 385 Sackville St., Toronto, Ont. M5A 3G5; Office: 3952 Chesswood Dr., Downsview, Ont. M3J 2W6.

**MIZGALA, Henry Frank,** B.A., M.D., C.M., FRCPC, FACC; professor of medicine, physician; b. Montreal, Que. 28 Nov. 1932; s. Louis and Mary M.; e. Loyola Coll. B.A. 1953; McGill Univ., M.D., C.M. 1957; m. Pauline Barbara d. William J. and Pauline Delaney 26 Oct. 1957; children: Paul Stephen, Dr. Cynthia Louise, Dr. Liane Mary, Melanie Frances (Dressler), Nancy Elizabeth (Lewis); PROF. OF MED., UNIV. OF B.C. 1980– ; Physician, St. Mary's Hosp. Montreal 1963–66; Montreal Gen. Hosp. 1964–74; Cardiologist, Montreal Heart Inst. 1974–80; Head, Div. of Cardiol., Univ. of B.C. & Head, Cardiol., Vanc. Gen. Hosp. 1980–87; Consultant Cardiol., Univ. Hosp., Campus Site 1980– & Cancer Control Agency of B.C.; Asst. Prof., McGill Univ. 1970–74; Clinical Prof., Univ. of Montreal 1974–80; Ed. Bd., 'Can. J. of Cardiol.' 1980– and 'J. of the Am. Coll. of Cardiol.; Mem., Examining Bd. in Cardiol., Royal Coll. of Physicians, Canada 1985–89; Mem., Candn. Cardiovascular Soc. (Treas. 1974–90); Dir., Que. Heart Found. 1968–80; B.C. & Yukon Heart & Stroke Found. 1988–90; Mem., Am. Heart Assn. Counc. on Clinical Cardiol.; Fellow, Am. Coll. of Cardiol.; Alpha Omega Alpha Hon. Med. Soc.; author of num. articles & several book chaps.; recreations: fishing, golf, gardening; clubs: Richmond Golf & Country Club; Home: 4217 Staulo Cres., Vancouver, B.C. V6N 3S1; Office: 326 – 2775 Heather St., Vancouver, B.C. V5Z 3J5.

**MLADENOV, Philip Vassil,** M.Sc., Ph.D.; educator; b. Toronto, Ont. 5 Nov. 1951; s. Stilian Vassil and Margaret Ula (Algar) M.; e. Univ. of Toronto B.Sc. 1974; McGill Univ. M.Sc. 1977; Univ. of Alta. Ph.D. 1981; m. Gwendolin d. Horst and Oda Nowrath 5 July 1980; children: Alisha, Daniel; PROF. OF MARINE SCI. UNIV. OF OTAGO 1989– ; Head, Dept. of Marine Science, Univ. of Otago 1992– ; Dir., Cray Corporation Limited 1991– ; Dir., of Marine Science Postgraduate Prog., Univ. of Otago 1989– ; Dir., Marine Science & Aquaculture Research Centre, Univ. of Otago 1990– ; Asst. Prof. of Biol. Mount Allison Univ. Sackville 1980, Assoc. Prof. 1986–89; Hon. Rsch. Assoc. in Biol. Dalhousie Univ. 1985–88; Visiting Sci. in Biol. Univ. of Victoria 1986–87 and various rsch. instns. incl. Univ. of N.H., Bellairs Rsch. Inst. McGill Univ., Discovery Bay Marine Lab. Univ. of W.Indies, Bermuda Biol. Stn. for Rsch., Univ. of the South Pacific, James Cook Univ. of North Queensland 1981–93; Marine Biol. LGL Ltd., Environmental Rsch. Associates Toronto 1977–80; Cons. Fisheries Div. Min. of Agric., Food & Consumer Affairs Barbados 1985–86; Mem. of Review Team (for the New Zealand Min. of Rsch., Science & Tech.) reviewing Marine and Freshwater Sciences in New Zealand 1991; Mem. Review Team, New Zealand Min. of Rsch., Science & Tech. (reviewing rsch. vessel needs for New Zealand) 1992–93; Co-founder Underwater Optics mfr. of 'Aqualens' 1986; recipient rsch. grants Nat. Sci's & Eng. Rsch. Council Can., NATO, Nat. Geog. Soc., Donner Can. Found., New Zealand Ministry of Agriculture & Fisheries, Found. of Rsch., Science & Tech. New Zealand; recipient, Assn. of Commonwealth Universities Development Fellowship for the development of cooperative programmes in Marine Science between New Zealand and Australia 1993; co-ed. 'Echinoderm Biology' 1988; over 48 jour. articles; mem., Editorial Advisory Bd. 'Journal of Experimental Marine Biology and Ecology' 1992– ; Trustee, New Zealand Whale and Dolphin Trust 1992– ; Advisory Trustee, The New Zealand Centre for Marine Studies 1992– ; mem. Am. Assn. Advanc. Sci.; W. Soc. Naturalists; Candn. Soc. Zools.; Internat. Soc. Invertebrate Reprodn. & Devel., New Zealand Marine Sciences Soc.; Council Mem., New Zealand Marine Sciences Soc. (Vice-Pres. 1991–92) 1992–93; recreations: scuba, swimming, skiing, squash, windsurfing, photography, travel; Office: Dept. of Marine Science, Univ. of Otago, P.O. Box 56, Dunedin, New Zealand.

**MODRY, Dennis L.,** M.D., B.M.Sc., M.Sc., F.R.C.S.(C), F.A.A.C.P., F.A.C.S.; cardiovascular and thoracic surgeon; b. 27 Dec. 1948; e. Univ. of Alta., B.M.Sc. 1971, M.D. 1973; LMCC 1974; U.S. Nat. Bd., dipl. 1974; McGill Univ., M.Sc. 1976; training in gen. surg., McGill Univ. hosps. 1973–78; in cardiovascular & thoracic surg. 1978–80; Gen. Sur., cert., FRCS(C) & Profl. Corp. of Phys. of Que. 1978; Cardio. & Thor. Surg., cert. 1980; Am. Bd. of Surg., cert. 1978; Am. Bd. of Thor. Surg., dipl. 1981; m. with 4 children; DIR., HEART & LUNG TRANSPLANTATION SERV., UNIV. OF ALTA. HOSPS. 1986– ; Asst. Surg., Montreal Gen. Hosp., Royal Victoria Hosp., The Montreal Childrens Hosp. 1980–83; Surgeon, Univ. of Alta. Hosp. 1984; Dir., Cardiac Intensive Care Unit 1984– ; Dir., Heart & Lung Transp. Serv. 1985– ; Demonstrator, McGill Univ. 1974–75; Asst. Prof. 1980–83; Clin. Asst. Prof., Univ. of Alta. 1984; Clin. & Rsch. fellow, Dept. of Med., Stanford Univ. 1981–82; Dept. of Cardio. Surg. 1982–84; Clin. Assoc. Prof., Dept. of Surgery, Div. CVT Surgery 1986– , Acting Dir., Div. of CVT Surgery 1986–87; Dir., Div. of CVT Surgery 1987–91; Vanier Award for Outstanding Young Candn. 1985; Hon. mention, 1985 Edmonton Citizen of the Year; Travelling fellowships: 1983 Alta. Heritage Found.; 1981 & 1982 Frank McGill; 1983 McLaughlin; 1981 W.C. MacKenzie/Ethicon; 2nd prize, 1971 Alfred A. Richman Essay Contest; extensive contributions to fed., prov., internat. task forces & cttes.; Ed. Bd. Mem., 'The Journal of Heart Transplantation' 1986– ; author or co-author of 40 articles, 3 book chapters & 10 abstracts; author of 15 sci. presentations & 114 lectures; Fellow, Am. Coll. of Surg.; McGill Cardio. & Thor. Surg. Soc.; Que. Med. Assn.; Coll. of Phys. & Surg. of Que. & Alta.; Fed. of Med. Specialists of Que.; Candn. Med. Protective Assn.; Candn. Assn. of Gen. Surg.; Candn. Cardio. Soc.; Am. Heart Assn.; Royal Coll. of Phys. & Surg. of Can.; Alberta Med. Assn.; Candn. Soc. for Vascular Surgery; Soc. for Critical Care Med.; Candn. Critical Care Soc.; Alta. Soc. of Critical Care Med.; Alpha Omega Alpha Hon. Med. Soc.; Am. Coll. of Chest Phys.; Candn. Transplantation Soc.; Edmonton Thoracic Soc.; Office: 3H210, Walter Mackenzie, Univ. of Alberta Hosp., #8440, 10012 St., Edmonton, Alta. T6G 2B7.

**MOENS, H. Peter B.,** B.Sc.F., M.A., Ph.D., F.R.S.C.; b. Sukabumie, Indonesia 15 May 1931; s. H. Peter B. and A. D. M. Ritsema van Eck M.; e. Univ. of Toronto B.Sc.F. 1959, M.A. 1961, Ph.D. 1963; m. Marja d. Jakob Schröder 8 May 1953; children: Richard, Theodore, Vivian, Cecilia, Francis; DISTINGUISHED RESEARCH PROFESSOR OF BIOLOGY, YORK UNIV. (Chrmn. of Dept. 1981–84); author over 90 articles cytogenetics; mem. Genetics Soc. Can. (Pres. 1978–79); Editor, Genome (1983– ), Chromosoma (1988– ), Candn. Soc. Cell Biol.; Am. Soc. Cell. Biol.; recreations: sailing, tennis; Home: 217 Northwood Dr., Willowdale, Ont. M2M 2K5; Office: Dept. of Biology, York University, Downsview, Ont. M3J 1P3.

**MOESER, Diana R.E.,** B.A., M.A., MHSC; hospital administration; b. Toronto, Ont. 24 March 1944; d. John Frederik and Ruth Alice (Griffin) M.; e. St. Clements Sch. 1963; Trinity Coll., Univ. of Toronto B.A. 1967; M.A. 1970 (political science), MHSC, Health Admin. 1984; completed all requirements for PH.D. except thesis; VICE-PRES., AMBULATORY SERVICES AND COMMUNITY HEALTH, THE WELLESLEY HOSPITAL 1992– ; Vice-Pres., Ambulatory and Community Health Services, Doctors Hospital 1984–91; Business Mgr., Graduate Assistants Assn.; E.A. Faculty Association, U. of T.; Benefit Concert Organizer, Oxfam Canada; consultant, freelance reporter, writer & editor; Cons., Rehab. through Edn. Program; York Community Services; Assoc., Ctr. for Health Promotion, Fac. of Med., Community Health Div., Univ. of Toronto; Univ. of Toronto T holder, Badminton 1964; Head Girl, Valedictorian, St. Clements School 1963; Mem., The Multicultural Health Coalition; Bd. Mem., Gerstein Ctr. for Crisis Intervention; mem. OXFAM, Ont. Regional Council; Chair, Advisory Bd., 'Womens Own'; first detox centre for women in Metro. Toronto 1991; author: 'Community Involvement in Hospital-Based Ambulatory Care Programmes' 1990; presentor at major health care conferences across Canada; recreations: canoeing, hiking, bicycling, drawing; Home: 18 Follis Ave., Toronto, Ont. M6G 1S3; Office: 160 Wellesley St. E., Toronto, Ont. M4Y 1J3.

**MOESER, William Alan,** B.A.Sc.; corporate director; b. Toronto, Ont. 8 Feb. 1921; s. Frederick William and Estelle (Stanger) M.; e. Oakwood Coll. Inst. (Toronto); Univ. of Toronto, B.A.Sc. 1943, Business Adm. Dipl., 1950; m. May, d. W.W. Lindsay, 8 Feb. 1944; children: Mrs. Sheila Jean Roy, Douglas William, Mrs. Lindsay Ann McLaughlin; Dir., Budd Canada Inc.; with Massey-Harris Co. in various mfg. capacities in Toronto 1945–52; trans. to Lille, France with Cie Massey-Harris S.A. as Works Mgr. 1952–55; became Mfg. Mgr., H.V. McKay-Massey-Harris Prop. Ltd. (Melbourne, Australia) 1955–61; el. Dir., Massey-Ferguson (Australia) Ltd. 1958; returned to Can. in 1961 as Asst. Gen. Factory Mgr., Massey-Ferguson Ltd. until Apr. 1962; joined Studebaker of Can. Ltd. as Production Mgr. May 1962; Dir.-Mfg. Oct. 1963; Vice-Pres. Mfg. July 1964; Vice-Pres. Operations and Dir., General Spring Products Ltd. (predecessor to Lear Siegler Ltd.) 1966; Pres. 1969; ret'd 1986; served in 2nd World War with R.C.N.V.R. as Lieut. (E), 1943–45; Mem. Bd. of Govs., Conestoga College; Past Pres. Rotary Club of Kitchener; member,

Assn. Prof. Engrs. Ont.; Soc. Auto. Engrs.; Delta Upsilon; United Church; recreations: golf, travel, photography; Clubs: Royal Candn. Mil. Inst. (Toronto); Westmount Golf; Home: 208 Roxton Dr., Waterloo, Ont. N2T 1N8.

**MOFFAT, Anthony Frederick John,** B.Sc., M.Sc., Dr.rer.nat., Dr.Habil.; educator; b. Toronto, Ont. 30 Jan. 1943; s. Bryce Fulford and Margaret Esther (Boorman) M.; e. Univ. of Toronto, B.Sc. 1965, M.Sc. 1966; Ruhr-Universität Bochum Dr.rer.nat. 1970, Dr.Habil. 1976; m. Ann d. Donald and Helen Huntley 10 Sept. 1966; children: Bryce Anton, Lesley Ann; PROFESSEUR TITULAIRE, UNIV. DE MONTREAL 1981– ; Wissenschaftliche Hilfskraft Univ. Bonn 1967–69; Wissenschaftlicher Assistent Ruhr-Univ. 1970–76; Professeur agrégé present Univ. 1977–80; mem. NSERC Grant Selection Ctte. Space & Astron. 1985–88, Pres. 1988–89; mem. FCAR Centre Program Ctte. 1992–94; Dir., Centre 'Observatoire du mont Mégantic' 1990–94; recipient Silver Medal in Physics & Math. Victoria Coll. Univ. Toronto 1965 and tuition waiver 1961–65; Royal Astron. Soc. Can. Gold Medal 1965; NRC Bursary 1965–66; Imperial Oil Fellow 1966–69; Alexander von Humboldt Fellow 1982–83 and June-July 1989; author or co-author over 150 publs. refereed sci. jours., over 100 articles and various popular articles and conf. abstracts; mem. Editorial Bd. 'Astrophysics and Space Science'; mem. Candn. Steering Ctte. for 8m telescope project 1989–93; mem. Herzberg Inst. of Astrophysics Advisory Bd., NRC 1990–92; mem. Candn. Steering Ctte. for Lyman FUSE Project 1993– ; mem. Royal Astron. Soc. Can. 1977– (mem. Montréal Center Bd. 1985–90, 1992– , Vice-Pres., 1988–90); Candn. Astron. Soc. 1977– (Councillor 1981–83); Am. Astron. Soc. 1967– ; Astronomische Gesellschaft 1970– ; Internat. Astron. Union 1973– ; recreations: music, philately, canoeing, tennis, travel; Home: 82 Sunnyside Ave., Westmount, Qué. H3Y 1C5; Office: Département de physique, Univ. de Montréal, C.P. 6128, Succ. A., Montréal, Qué. H3C 3J7.

**MOFFAT, Donald Ormond,** B. Arch.; architect; b. Hamilton, Ont. 11 Nov. 1933; s. Ormond George and Anne Mitchell (Souter) M.; e. Hamilton Pub. Schs., Westdale Secondary Sch. Hamilton; Univ. of Toronto B.Arch.; m. Jane Ann d. Harold Freeburne 9 Sept. 1961; one d. Mary Elizabeth; PRINCIPAL, MOFFAT KINOSHITA ASSOCIATES INC.; present firm estbd. mid-sixties with offices Hamilton and Toronto; projects incl. major library expansions at Univ. of Toronto, UWO and McMaster Univ.; Sir Frederick Banting Research Centre; Royal Ont. Museum; firm recipient over thirty-six design awards; Pres., Hamilton Dist. Chamber Comm. 1979–80; Dir. 1974–81, mem Standards Council of Can. 1981–85; Chrmn., Ont. Region Comm. College of Fellows RAIC 1986–90; Dir., Ina Grafton Gage Home; Chrmn., Etobicoke Municipal Arts Commn.; Fellow, Royal Architectural Inst. of Canada 1976; Academician, Royal Candn. Acad. of the Arts 1978; recreations: tennis, skiing; Club: Badminton & Racquet; Beaumaris Yacht; Home: 104 The Kingsway, Toronto, Ont. M8X 2T8; Office: 124 Merton St., Toronto, Ont. M4S 2Z2.

**MOFFAT, Donald Paul,** B.Comm., C.A.; utilities executive; b. Toronto, Ont. 8 May 1938; e. Upper Canada College; Univ. of Toronto B.Comm. 1962; C.A. 1966; m. Cathie Graydon 14 Sept. 1963; children: Graydon, Julie; VICE-PRES., FINANCE and SECRETARY, CANADIAN NIAGARA POWER COMPANY LIMITED 1992– and TREASURER & SECRETARY, OPINAC ENERGY CORPORATION 1993– ; Price Waterhouse 1962–68; Deloitte Touche 1968–74; Partner, Bregman & Hamann, Arch. & Engrs. 1974–85; Vice-Pres. Finance, Lac Minerals Limited 1985–87; Vice-Pres. Finance, The Citadel Assurance 1987–92; Dir., Fort Erie Economic Development Corp.; Dir., Camp Oochigeas (a camp for children with cancer); Mem., Insurance Institute of Canada, Institute of Chartered Accountants of Ontario, Confrerie des Chevaliers du Tastevin; recreations: tennis, golf; clubs: Granite, Big Bay Point Golf & Country; Home: 12 St. Margaret's Dr., Toronto, Ont. M4N 3E5; Office: 1130 Bertie Rd., P.O. Box 1218, Fort Erie, Ont. L2A 5Y2.

**MOFFAT, John Harris,** M.D., F.R.C.S. (C); surgeon; b. Hamilton, Ont. 3 Sept. 1930; s. John Albert and Mary Regis (Harris) M.; e. De LaSalle Coll. 'Oaklands' (Toronto) 1948; Faculty Medicine, Univ. Toronto, 1954; Gallie Course in Surgery, Univ. Toronto, 1960; m. Dolores, d. William and Dolores Sprowls, 13 July, 1957; children: Lorie; Christine; John; Michael; Stephen; Robert; SURGEON, CAMBRIDGE MEM. HOSP.; Fellow, Royal Coll. Surgeons Can. 1960; Surgical Consulting Staff, Dept. Surg., Cambridge Mem. Hosp. 1960; Pres. Med. Staff 1965–66; Bd. Dirs. 1965–66; Chief, Dept. Surg., 1969–72; 1977–79; Citizenship Award, City of Cambridge 1973; Benita & Don Rope Sports Contributor Award 1988; Pres., The Janes Surg. Soc. 1985–86; Pres., Southern Ont. Surg. Soc. 1983–86; Candn. Assn. Gen. Surgeons; Rotary Club of Galt (Founding Mem. 1965), (Paul Harris Fellow 1989), (Pres. 1991–92); Beta Theta Pi; Bd. Govs. Wilfrid Laurier Univ. (Chrmn. 1982–85); Parks and Recreation Comte., City of Galt, (1971); Riverbank Comte., City of Cambridge 1977–78; Dir., Assn. for the Mentally Retarded 1962–65; Chrmn., Easter Seal Campaign, City of Galt, 1970; Chrmn. Can-Amera Games 1972–75; awarded Commemorative Medal for 125th Anniversary of Candn. Confederation 1993; Roman Catholic; Home: 40 Charles St., Cambridge, Ont. N1S 2W8; Office: 564 Coronation Boulevard, Cambridge, Ont. N1R 5Y3.

**MOFFAT, John William,** Ph.D., D.Sc.; educator; b. Copenhagen, Denmark 24 May 1932; s. George William McKay and Esther (Winther) M.; e. Trinity Coll. Cambridge Ph.D. 1958; Univ. of Winnipeg D.Sc. 1989; two d. Sandra, Christina; m. Patricia Dietterle Ohlendorf 8 May 1986; PROF. OF PHYSICS, UNIV. OF TORONTO 1967– ; came to Can. 1964; author over 140 publs. theoretical physics internat. journs.; mem. Cambridge Philos. Soc.; Cdn. Astron. Soc.; mem. Internat. Astron. Union; N.Y. Acad. Sciences; recreations: jogging, travel, painting; Home: 293 Crawford St., Toronto, Ont. M6J 2V7; Office: 60 St. George St., Toronto, Ont. M5S 1A7.

**MOFFITT, Emerson Amos,** M.D., C.M., M.Sc., F.R.C.P.(C); educator; anaesthetist; b. McAdam, N.B. 9 Sept. 1924; s. Amos Alexander and Ellen Selena (Wilson) M.; e. High Sch. McAdam, N.B. 1942; Univ. of N.B. 1942–44, 1945–46; Dalhousie Univ. M.D., C.M. 1951; Mayo Foundation, Specialist Training 1954–57; Univ. of Minn. M.Sc. (Anesthesiol.) 1958; m. 1stly Helen Gertrude MacDonald (dec. 1971) 19 May 1951; children: Eric Emerson, Mary Celene, Laurie Anne; m. 2ndly Phyllis Isabel Redden (dec. 1987) 25 April 1973; 3rdly Isabel A. MacDonald 20 Jan. 1989; EMERITUS PROFESSOR OF ANAESTHESIA, DALHOUSIE UNIV. 1993; gen. practice North Sydney, N.S. 1951–54; Consultant in Anesthesiol. Mayo Clinic, Rochester 1957–72, Instr. to Assoc. Prof. Mayo Grad. Sch. 1959–72; Research Prof. of Anaesthesia present Univ. 1972–73; Prof. and Head of Anaesthesia 1973–80; Assoc. Dean of Medicine, Dalhousie Univ. 1980–86; Prof. of Anaesthesia 1986–93; served with RN Fleet Air Arm 1944–45; rec'd U.S. Nat. Inst. of Health Grant 1966–72, Candn. Heart Assoc. Grant 1981–91; Assoc. Ed. 'Survey of Anesthesiology' 1970–84; 'Anesthesia and Analgesia' 1973–77; mem. Ed. Bd. 'Canadian Anaesthetists' Society Journal' 1976–82; author or co-author numerous publs.; Bd. Trustees, Internat. Anesthesia Research Soc. 1973–90 (Chrmn. 1977–79, Extve. Secretary 1983–90); Assn. Candn. Univ. Depts. Anaesthesia (Chrmn. 1977–78); Acad. Anesthesiol. (Pres. 1978–79); Candn. Med. Assn.; N.S. Med. Soc.; Candn. Anaesthetists' Soc. (Gold Medal 1990); Am. Soc. Anesthesiol.; Sigma Xi; Alpha Omega Alpha; Protestant; recreations: golf, skiing, photography; Clubs: Ashburn Golf; Home: 2 Turnberry Lane, Halifax, N.S. B3M 4E5.

**MOGFORD, Mary,** B.A.; corporate director; b. Plymouth, U.K. 29 April 1944; d. Alfred George and Audrey Phyllis (Ashton) M.; e. Plymouth H.S. for Girls; Univ. of Wales (Hons.) B.A. 1966; Coll. of William & Mary, Williamsburg, Virginia (Lady Astor Scholar); m. Thomas s. Thomas and Elizabeth Campbell 30 Dec. 1984; stepchildren: John Stuart, Alexandra; MOGFORD CAMPBELL ASSOCS. INC. 1989– ; Dep. Min. of Natural Resources 1985–87; Dep. Treasurer of Ont. & Dep. Min. of Economics 1987–89; Dir., Niagara Inst. 1989– ; mem., Economic Council of Canada 1990–92; Gov., Trent Univ. 1990– ; Bd. mem., Credit Suisse Canada 1990– ; Bd. Member: Hemlo Gold Mines Inc. 1992– ; Ontario Blue Cross 1992– ; Humber College Educational Foundation 1992– ; Toronto Symphony Foundation 1992– ; Teranet 1993– ; Nature Conservancy of Canada 1994– ; Trustee, Hospital for Sick Children 1991– ; Address: 43 Sunnydale Dr., Toronto, Ont. M8Y 2J4.

**MOGGRIDGE, Donald Edward,** B.A., M.A., Ph.D.; university professor; b. Windsor, Ont. 25 May 1943; e. Univ. of Toronto B.A. (Hons.) 1965; Univ. of Cambridge M.A. 1968, Ph.D. 1970; m. Janet d. Sydney and Margaret Skelton 29 July 1967 (dissolved 1977); PROF. OF ECONOMICS, UNIV. OF TORONTO 1974– ; Rsch. Fellow/Fellow, Clare Coll., Cambridge 1967–75, 1979–81; Jr. Rsch. Offr., Dept. of Applied Econ., Univ. of Cambridge 1968–69; Asst. Lectr./Lectr. in Econ., Univ. of Cambridge 1971–75; Assoc. Dean, Social Sci., Sch. of Grad. Studies 1985–87; Fac. of Arts & Sci. 1987–92; editor: 'Collected Writings of John Maynard Keynes' 1969–89; joint mng. editor 1977–89; Ford Found. Vis. Prof., Pontifical Catholic Univ. of Rio de Janeiro 1987; Benians Fellow, St. John's Coll., Cambridge 1988–89; Mem., Hist. of Econ. Soc. (Pres. 1988–89); Royal Econ. Soc. (Keynes Ctte. 1977–89); Am. Econ. Assn.; Candn. Econ. Assn.; Econ. Hist. Soc.; Econ. Hist. Assn.; author: 'The Return to Gold 1925: The Formulation of Economic Policy and its Critics' 1969, 'British Monetary Policy 1924–1931: The Norman Conquest of $4.86' 1972, 'Keynes' 1976, 2nd ed. 1980, 3rd ed. 1993; 'Maynard Keynes: An Economist's Biography' 1992; editor: 'The Collected Writings of John Maynard Keynes' 24 of 30 vols (1971–89); 'Keynes: Aspects of the Man and His Work' 1974; 'Editing Modern Economists' 1988; (with P.L. Cottrell) 'Money and Power' 1988; (with S. Howson) 'The Collected Papers of James Meade, Vol. IV, The Cabinet Office Diary 1944–1946' 1990; (with S. Howson) 'The Wartime Diaries of Lionel Robbins and James Meade 1943–45' 1990; recreations: squash, wine, walking; Club: United Oxford and Cambridge (London); Home: 11 Woodstock Place, Toronto, Ont. M4X 1T7; Office: Dept. of Economics, 150 St. George St., Toronto, Ont. M5S 1A1.

**MOHER, Francis (Frank) Anthony Peter;** writer; b. Edmonton, Alta. 14 Sept. 1955; s. Stanley Edward and Dorothy Antoinette (Prausa) M.; e. Univ. of Alta.; m. Diana d. Richard and Edith Hart 2 Oct. 1982; children: Aidan Hart, Nathaniel Francis, Conor Douglas; Assoc. Playwright & Lit. Mgr., Northern Light Theatre 1977–82; Co-founder & Dramaturg, Alta. Playwriting Centre 1981–82; Lectr., Univ. of Alta. 1982–83, 1986; Sr. Ed., Alberta Report Newsmagazine 1983–86; Dramaturg & Playwright-in-Res., Workshop West Theatre 1984–86; Sr. Ed., Western Report Newsmagazine 1986; Assoc. Dir., Workshop West Theatre 1987–88; Vice Chair, Playwrights Union of Canada 1988–89; Lectr., Univ. of B.C. 1990–91; Malaspina College 1991–93; 'Distinguished Visitor', Univ. of Alberta 1993; Dir., New Play Development, Nanaimo Festival 1991–93; Stage plays: 'Pause' 1974; 'The Broken Globe' 1975; 'Stage Falls' 1978; 'Down for the Weekend' 1980; 'Odd Jobs' 1985; 'Sliding for Home' 1987; 'The Third Ascent' 1988; 'Prairie Report' 1988; 'At Sea' 1990; 'Kidnapping the Bride' 1991; 'Farewell' 1991; 'Brother 12' 1991; 'Blue Trumpeter' 1993; also author of var. plays for radio, television, and film; rec'd. Alta. Culture Playwriting Award; Edmonton Journal Playwriting Award; Clifford E. Lee Found. Scholarship; Elizabeth Sterling Haynes Award; City of Edmonton Cultural Achievement Award; Alberta Achievement Award; Los Angeles 'Drama-Logue' Award; Home: R.R. 2, Site 57, Gabriola Island, B.C. V0R 1X0; Office: c/o Great North Artists Management, 350 Dupont St., Toronto, Ont. M5R 1V9.

**MOHER, William P.,** B.A.; business executive; b. Toronto, Ont. 2 Oct. 1926; s. M. Harry and Laura M. (Parker) M.; e. St. Michael's H.S.; St. Michael's Coll., Univ. of Toronto, B.A.; m. Joan Marie d. Redvers and Rita Brown 11 Oct. 1952; children: Suzanne, Catherine, Michael, Barbara, Kevin, Brian (dec'd.); CHRMN., ADDICTION RESEARCH FOUND. 1988– ; Dir., National Addiction Prevention Fund; St. Michael's College Foundation; Indus. Relns., Dayton Rubber Can. 1947–49; Employee Relns. (Toronto, Regina, Edmonton), Imperial Oil Limited 1949; Mktg. (Que.) 1961; Mgr., Nat. Accts. & Planning (Toronto) 1968; Extve. Devel. Mgr., Corp. 1975; Employee Relns. 1977; Mngt. Devel. & Orgn. 1979; Vice-Pres., Human Resources & Extve. Development 1986, retired from co. 1988; Past Chrmn., Human Resources Adv. Group to Pres., Conf. Bd. of Can.; Past Chrmn., Counc. of Human Resources Extves; Past Chrmn., Compensation Rsch. Counc.; Mem., Univ. of Toronto Hosp. Univ. Bd.; Past Mem. of Collegium, Past Chrmn., Fin. Ctte. & Past Mem. of Senate, Univ. of St. Michael's Coll.; author: 'Moher Report on Managing Human Resources in the Ontario Public Service' 1986; Cons.; recreations: farming, skiing, water sports; Home: 78 Treegrove Circle, Aurora, Ont. L4G 6M2; Office: 33 Russell St., Toronto, Ont. M5S 2S1.

**MOHIDE, Thomas Patrick,** LL.B., J.D.; b. Bristol, Eng. 22 July 1921; s. Patrick Joseph Thomas, D.C.M. and Christina May (Lloyd) M.; e. St. Brendan's Coll., Clifton, Eng., 1936; Merchant Venturers' Tech. Coll., Bristol, grad. 1948; Blackstone Sch. of Law, Chicago, LL.B. 1970, J.D. 1972; m. Jean Dorothy; d. late William Joseph Dudbridge, 2 Sept. 1942; children: Patrick Thomas, M.D., F.R.C.S.(C), Deirdre Siobhan, B.Sc.; Consultant, Precious Metals; Dir., Renzy Mines Ltd.; Sr. Asst. for Continental Sales, Internat. Nickel Co. of Can. (Inco), London, Eng., 1950; Mgr. Overseas Sales, Falconbridge Nickel Mines Ltd., Toronto, Ont., 1956–66; Mgr. Gold and Silver Bullion Sales, Purchases and

Inventory Control, Engelhard Industries U.S.A., 1967–72; Pres. & C.E.O., Winnipeg Commodity Exchange 1972–73; Dir., Mineral Resources, Govt. of Ont., 1973–86; Special Advisor to Deputy Min. 1986; Adv., Delegation of Gov. of Can. to U.N. Conf. on the Law of the Sea 1975–82; Adv. Delegation of Gov. of Can. to Intergov. Study Group on Nickel 1979–85; has travelled widely throughout world in marketing & purchasing Candn. & other metals & commodities; rec'd. Territorial Efficiency Medal; 'Million Miler' Award in recognition of world business travel beyond that figure 1967; served with Irish Guards Regt., Household Brigade of Guards (Buckingham Palace), Guards Armoured Division, 1939–46; rank Capt.; el. Town Councillor, Merton and Morden, Eng. 1949–51; Vice-President Grenadier Guards Assn.; Past Vice Pres., Household Bgde. Assn. N. Am.; Past Dir., Rapeseed Assn. Can.; author 'Platinum Group Metals: Ontario and the World' 1979; 'Gold' 1981; 'Silver' 1985; 'The World Silver Trade' 1991; co-author 'Towards a Nickel Policy for Ontario' 1978; 'The Future of Nickel and the Law of the Sea' 1980; 'Report of the Interministerial Committee on Commodity Futures Trading'; 'On Gold' 1982; 'World Precious Metals Survey' 1983; 'Platinum Group Metals, 1988–2000' 1988; co-author and ed. 'Precious Metals 1984'; Editorial Adv., 'Gold Stocks Advisory' monthly, U.S.A.; Monthly Columnist, 'Northern Miner' weekly, Toronto; Chevalier, Grand Commander, Ordre Souverain et Militaire de la Milice du Saint Sepulcre, Confederation of Chivalry; Home: Apt. 2213, 44 Jackes Ave., Toronto, Ont. M4T 1E5.

**MOHR, Lionel Charles,** A.B., M.B.A.; management consultant; b. New York City, N.Y. 18 Dec. 1927; s. Lionel Charles and Emma Anne (Stohldrier) M.; e. Mayflower Pub. Sch. 1941; New Rochelle (N.Y.) High Sch. 1946; Wesleyan Univ. A.B. 1950; Harvard Univ. M.B.A. 1959; m. Anne Crosby Tredwell 1955 (dec. 1965); m. Patricia Margaret d. late Clive Martin Sinclair 24 Aug. 1968; children: Lionel Thomas, Deborah Susan, Sharon Patricia, Deborah Anne, Douglas Tredwell, John David Edward; PRES., BOYDEN ASSOCIATES LTD. 1986– ; Salesman, Scott Paper Co. New York 1950, Retail Dist. Sales Mgr. Binghamton, N.Y. 1954, Advertising Staff Asst. Philadelphia 1959, Asst. Merchandising Mgr. 1960; Mgr. Consumer Products Div. E. B. Eddy Co. Ottawa 1961; Product Mgr. General Foods Ltd. Toronto 1962, Sales Promotion Mgr. 1963, Product Planning Mgr. Birds Eye & Inst. Products Div. 1964, Sr. Product Mgr. 1965; Consultant, Stevenson & Kellogg, Toronto 1966, Princ. 1967, Princ.-in-Charge-Marketing Function 1969; Dir. of Marketing and Corp. Planning, Toronto Star Ltd. 1971, Dir. of Marketing 1971, Vice Pres. Marketing 1974, Dir. 1974–76; Vice Pres. Toronto Star Newspapers Ltd. 1976, Dir. 1976–77; Vice Pres. and Dir., Torstar Corp. 1977–79; Dir., Comac Communications Ltd. (Chrmn. 1974–79); Pres. L. Mohr & Assoc. 1979–82; Vice Pres., Boyden Assoc. Inc. 1982–85, Sr. Vice Pres. 1985– ; Pres. Boyden Consulting Group 1983–86; Adjunct Prof., Bus. Admin., Niagara Univ. 1981– ; Past chrmn. Div. Cong. Life & Work and Dept. Planning Assistance, Un. Ch. of Can.; Elder, First Presbyterian Church, Lewiston, N.Y.; Founding Dir. Peel Family Services 1970; past Pres., mem. Bd. Govs. Candn. Opera Co.; Dir. Shaw Festival Theatre Foundation 1981–86; Bd. of Govs., Candn. Daily Newspaper Publishers Assn. 1975–79; mem. Newspaper Readership Council (N.Am.) 1978–79; Chrmn. Canadian Plans Bd. Newspaper Advertising Bureau 1978–79; Chrmn. Marketing Comte. Internat. Newspaper Advertising Extves. 1977–79; mem. Internat. Circulation Mgrs. Assn. 1971–79; Am. Marketing Assn. (Dir. Toronto Chapter 1965–69); Beta Theta Pi; Tau Pi; Freemason served with U.S. Army Transport. Corps 1950–52; Presbyterian; recreations: golf, fly fishing, cross-country skiing; Clubs: National; Niagara Falls (N.Y.) Country; Rotary; Empire; Harvard Business of Toronto (Dir., Past Chrmn., Past Pres.); Harvard Business of Buffalo.

**MOISAN, Clement,** Ph.D., F.R.S.C.; educator; b. Lyster, Qué. 26 July 1933; s. Adolphe and Noella (Boisvert) M.; e. Coll. de Levis 1954; Laval Univ. B.A. 1959; La Sorbonne Univ. de Paris Ph.D. 1963; m. Renate d. Heinz and Emilie Hildebrand 6 June 1964; one child; Ariadne; PROF. OF FRENCH, LAVAL UNIV. 1972– , Chrmn. of French 1967–70, joined present Univ. 1964; Visiting Prof., Univ. of Mannheim 1971, Univ. of Strasbourg 1971–73, Univ. of Kiel 1991; Lectr. in Qué. and Candn. Lit. Can., U.S.A., Japan, Europe; Fellow, The Royal Society of Canada 1980; Killam Scholarship 1989–91; author: 'Henri Bremond et la poésie pure' 1967; 'L'Age de la littérature canadienne' 1969; 'Anatole France, L'Ile des Pingouins, coll. 'l'Univers des Lettres'' 1971; 'Poésie des frontières' 1979, Eng. transl. 'A Poetry of Frontiers' 1983; 'Qu'est-ce que l'histoire littéraire?' 1987; 'Comparaison et raison' 1987; 'Que sais-je? l'Histoire Littéraire' 1990; co-author: 'Le discours d'une didactique. La formation littéraire dans l'enseignement classique au Québec (1852–1967)' (co-authors Joseph Melançon and Max Roy) 1988; author numerous articles various jours.; ed. 'Livres et Auteurs Québécois' 1973–76; 'L'histoire littéraire. Théories, méthodes, pratiques' 1989; mem., Candn. Comparative Lit. Assn.; Assn. Candn. & Que. Lits.; Candn. Assn. Univ. Teachers French; Home: 9 Jardin Mérici, App 1404, Quebec, Que. G1S 4S8.

**MOL, Marten A.;** management consultant; b. Bussum 5 Dec. 1943; s. Marten and Aleida Mol (Brands) M.; e. York Univ.; Seneca Coll.; m. Anne Oussoren 22 June 1968; children: Yolanda, Kevin, Allison; PRESIDENT & CHAIRMAN OF THE BOARD, DUCA COMMUNITY CREDIT UNION LTD. 1980– ; Systems Engr., Motorola Can. 1961– ; Pres., Marten A. Mol & Assoc. Ltd. 1966–93; Mgr., Information-Communication, Honeywell Information Systems Inc. 1968–74; Vice-Pres., Versatel Corp. Serv. 1974–80; Pres., Martech Corporate & Personal Advisory Ltd. 1980–86; Pres., DCA Travel Services Inc. 1986– ; Dir., Altai Resources Inc.; Dir. & Sec., Royal Yorkfield Inc. 1990–93; Founder, Candn. Netherlands Business Profl. Assn. Inc. (Toronto & Amsterdam) 1981; Christian Centred Homes Inc. (Senior Citizen Centre); Chair, Dutch-Canadian Alliance Foundation Fund; member of several societies, associations, etc.; recreations: travel, golf, tennis; Home: 7 Cedar Cres., Aurora, Ont. L4G 3J7; Office: 5290 Yonge St., Willowdale, Ont. M2N 5R1.

**MÖLDER, Sannu,** B.A.Sc., M.A.Sc., M.Eng., A.F.AIAA, F.CASI; professor of aerospace engineering; b. Tallinn, Estonia 1 Sept. 1935; s. Aleksander and Helmi Renate (Eisenschmidt) M.; e. Univ. of Toronto B.A.Sc. 1958, M.A.Sc. 1960, M.Eng. 1978; m. Susan d. Carl and Edith Wright 7 Oct. 1989; children: Triina, Mikk, Markus; PROFESSOR OF AEROSPACE ENGINEERING, RYERSON POLYTECHNIC UNIV. 1971– ; Asst. Prof., Mech. Dept., McGill Univ. 1960–62; Assoc. Prof. 1962–68; Chrmn. 1969–71; Ryerson Polytechnical Inst. 1972–78; Visiting Prof., Unif. of Sydney 1971–72; Johns Hopkins Univ. 1985–86; Consultant, Dept. of Nat. Defence; Australian Min. of Supply & Services; Canadair Ltd.; USAF; The Johns Hopkins Univ.; Visiting Scientist, Deutsche Forschungsanstalt für Luft und Raumfahrt / Göttingen 1992–93; 3 directorships in Candn. corps.; Air Cadet League of Canada, 1st Yr. Engr. Scholarship 1953; Flying Scholarship; RCAF Pilot (wings awarded 1958); Assoc. Fellow, Am. Inst. of Aeronautics & Astronautics; Fellow, Candn. Aeronautics & Space Inst.; Dir., Candn. Soc. for Mech. Engrs.; Mem., NRC Assoc. Ctte. for Aerodynamics; recreations: flying, scuba diving; Home: 177 Ellerslie Ave., North York, Ont. M2N 1Y3; Office: 350 Victoria St., Toronto, Ont. M5B 2K3.

**MOLGAT, Hon. Gildas L.,** C.D., B.Comm.; b. Ste. Rose du Lac, Man. 25 Jan. 1927; s. Louis and Adele (Abraham) M.; e. Ste. Rose Sch.; St. Paul's Coll.; Univ. of Man. B.Comm. (Hons.) 1947 (Gold Medallist); m. Allison d. Wilbert G. Malcom & Mary (Greig) 31 July 1958; children: Anne Marie, Mathurin Paul; several years business in Winnipeg; now a business cons.; el. M.L.A. Man. 1953; re-el. g.e. 1958, 1959, 1962, 1966 and 1969; Leader of Lib. Party in Man. and Leader of Opposition 1961–68; summoned to the Senate of Can. 1970; Joint Chrmn., Special Joint Ctte., Senate and H. of C., on the Constitution of Canada (MacGuigan-Molgat Report) 1971; and on the Reform of the Senate of Canada (Molgat-Cosgrove Report) 1982; el. Depy. Speaker of Senate 1983–84; re-el. Depy. Speaker 1989–91; apptd. Deputy Leader of the Opposition in the Senate 1991; apptd. Deputy Leader of the Government 1993; Chrmn. of Senate Ctte. of the Whole on Meech Lake Constitutional Accord 1987–88; Chrmn. Senate Task Force on Meech Lake Constitutional Accord and Yukon and the N.W. Territories 1987–88; Chrmn., Submissions Group on the Meech Lake Constitutional Accord 1988; Chrmn. Man. Lib. Fed. Campaign 1972; Government Whip 1973; el. Pres., Lib. Party in Can. 1973; served with the Royal Winnipeg Rifles 1946–66, Hon. Lt. Col. 1966; Hon. Col. 1985; Hon. Pres., Royal United Services Inst. of Manitoba 1990; Hon. Pres., Army, Navy & Air Force Veterans in Canada, Winnipeg Unit No. 1, 1992; Founding Pres. Manitoba Army Cadet League 1971; Pres., Army Cadet League Can. 1977–79 (and Gov.); Founding Chrmn., St. Boniface Hosp. Rsch. Foundation 1971; Dir., Parliamentary Centre for Foreign Affairs & Foreign Trade; Candn. Corps Commissionaires; mem. Royal Candn. Legion; Société Franco-Manitobaine; St. Andrew's Soc.; Liberal; Catholic; Address: 463 Kingston Cres., Winnipeg, Man. R2M 0V1.

**MOLLER, Dr. George,** Dr. Juris; F.S.M.A., C.M.A., C.A., F.M.A., business consultant b. Prague, Bohemia 19 Oct. 1903; s. Ernest and Laura (Klepetar) M.; e. Univ. of Vienna (Dipl. in Comm. 1921); Univ. of Prague (Law and Pol. Science), Dr. Juris 1925; C.A. (Ont.) 1946, F.C.A. 1965 (Life mem. 1986); R.I.A. (Ont.) 1952 (Life mem. 1971); F.S.M.A. 1979; m. Edith R. (dec.), d. late Rudolph Berger, 5 Oct. 1931; Hon. Dir., Hamilton & District Sheet Metal Contractors Inc.; with Bohemian Union Bank, Prague (H.O.), 1928–39; came to Canada, 1939; Office Manager, Tru-Lite Ltd., and Armco Ltd., Toronto and Acton, Ont., 1939–42; articled with George A. Touche & Co., C.A.'s, Toronto, Ont., 1942 (Supervisor of Taxation Dept. 1946); joined Robertson-Irwin Ltd., Hamilton, Ont., 1949 as Asst. Controller; Controller, 1950, Treas. 1951, Dir. and Treas. 1955; Vice-Pres. 1958–70; In-house Mngmnt. Consultant, Dominion Auto Accessories Ltd. 1971–87; Lectr. at McMaster University, 1949–56 and 1961–68; Lectr. University of Toronto 1973–74; served in Queen's York Rangers (Reserve), 1940–46; Fellow, Society Mgmt. Accts. (Life); Fellow, Inst. Chart. Accts. Ont. (Life); Fin. Extves. Inst. (Life); Adv. Council Internat. Assn. Fin. Extves. Institutes; Gov. Hamilton Philharmonic; Dir., Hamilton Opera Guild; Unitarian; recreations: walking, swimming; Clubs: Hamilton; Canadian (Burlington) (Past Pres.); Roseland Park Country; Address: 3164 Princess Blvd., Burlington, Ont. L7N 1G4.

**MOLNAR, Edward L.,** B.Sc.; petroleum executive; b. Saskatoon, Sask. 23 Aug. 1936; e. Univ. of Sask. B.Sc. (Chem. Eng.) 1958; PRES. AND CHIEF EXTVE. OFFR., DORSET EXPLORATION LTD. 1990– ; Mgr. Prodn. Pacific Petroleums 1975; Vice Pres. Prodn. Voyager Petroleums Ltd. 1976–78, Extve. Vice Pres and Chief Operating Offr. 1979–84; Pres. & C.O.O., Voyager Energy Co. 1984–89; Office: 3600, 205 – 5th Ave. S.W., Calgary, Alta. T2P 2V7.

**MOLNAR, George Dempster,** B.Sc., M.D., Ph.D., F.A.C.P., F.R.C.P.(C); physician, educator, researcher; b. Szekesfehervar, Hungary 30 July 1922; s. Eugene Frank and Clara Bertha (Becker) M.; e. Westdale Coll. Inst. Hamilton, Ont. 1940; Mount Royal Coll. Calgary, Alta. 1941; Univ. of Alta. B.Sc. 1949, M.D. 1951; Univ. of Minn. Ph.D. 1956; m. Gwendoline Esther McGregor; children: Gwendoline Jane, Charles McGregor; EMERITUS PROF. OF MEDICINE, UNIV. OF ALTA.; Co-Dir., Muttart Diabetes Rsch. and Training Centre, Univ. of Alta.; Consultant in Endocrinol. and Internal Med. Mayo Clinic 1956–75; Instr. in Med. Mayo Grad. Sch. 1956, Asst. Prof. 1963, Assoc. Prof. 1966, Prof. 1971; Prof. of Med. Mayo Med. Sch. 1973; Chrmn., Dept. of Med., Univ. of Alta 1975–86; served with Candn. Army 1942–45, rank Capt.; named Kt. Offr. of Netherlands Order of Orange-Nassau (with swords); mentioned in despatches; mem. Candn. Soc. Clin. Invest.; Royal Coll. Phys. & Surgs. Can.; W. Assn. Phys.; Am. Coll. Phys.; Am. Diabetes Assn.; Am. Fed. Clin. Research; Candn. Diabetes Assn. (Past Chrmn., Rsch. Counc., Past Chrmn., Clinical and Scientific Sect.); Candn. Diabetes Adv. Bd.; Candn. and Alta. Med. Assn.; Endocrine Soc.; Candn. Assn. Profs. of Med. (Pres. 1982–83); United Church; Home: 7216 - 114 A St., Edmonton, Alta. T6G 1N2; Office: 458 Heritage Medical Research Centre CW, Edmonton, Alta. T6G 2S2.

**MOLSON, Eric H.,** A.B.; company executive; b. Montreal, Que. 16 Sept. 1937; s. Thomas Henry Pentland and Celia Frances (Cantlie) M.; e. Selwyn House Sch. Montreal 1948; Bishop's Coll. Sch. Lennoxville 1954; Le Rosey Switzerland 1955; Princeton Univ. A.B. 1959; McGill Univ. 1962–63; U.S. Brewers Acad. N.Y. 1960; m. Jane d. Hon. William Mitchell 16 Apr. 1966; 3 children; CHRMN., THE MOLSON COMPANIES LTD.; served as Apprentice Brewer, Chem., Asst. Brewmaster, Asst. to Pres., Mkt. Rsch. Analyst, Brewmaster, Tech. Dir., Vice Pres. Operations, Vice Pres. Corporate Devel., Pres. Molson's Ontario, Extve. Vice Pres. and subsequently Pres., Molson Breweries of Canada Ltd.; Depy. Chrmn., The Molson Companies Ltd.; Chancellor, Concordia Univ.; Dir. Montreal Gen. Hosp. Foundn.; Bank of Montreal; Candn. Arctic Resources Comte.; Candn. Princeton Alumni Fund; Vie des Arts; Selwyn House Sch. Endowment Fund; Olympic Trust of Can.; Anglican; Clubs: York; Mt. Royal; North Hatley Sailing; University; Office: 1555 Notre Dame E., Montreal, Que. H2L 2R5.

**MOLSON, Hon. Hartland de Montarville,** O.B.E., K.St.J., C.A., F.C.I.S., D.Sc.C. (Montreal), D.C.L. (Calgary), D.C.L. (Bishop's), LL.D. (R.M.C.); LL.D. (McGill); D.Adm. (C.M.R.); b. Montreal, Quebec, 29 May 1907; s. Lieutenant-Colonel Herbert, C.M.G., M.C., and Elizabeth Zoë (Pentland) M.; e. Bishop's Coll. Sch., Lennoxville, Que.; Charterhouse, Eng.; Royal Mil.

Coll., Dipl. 1928; C.A. 1933 m. Margaret de Lancey Meighen (née Robinson) 3 May 1990; one d. Zoë Anne (Mrs. C.M.H. Murray); served in Militia as Lt., 27th Field Batty. 1928–33; joined the R.C.A.F. in 1939; served Overseas with No. 1 Fighter Sqdn. 1940; retired 1945 with rank of Group Capt., O.B.E. 1946; Senator, Canada 1955–93; mem., Canadian Club of Montreal (Past Pres.); Soc. of Chart. Accts. of Que.; Inst. of Ch. Secretaries and Administrators; Anglican; Clubs: Mount Royal; St. James's; University (Montreal); Montreal Racket; Forest and Stream; Mount Bruno; Racquet and Tennis (N.Y.); Toronto; Rideau (Ottawa); Home: 21 Rosemount Ave., Westmount, Que. H3Y 3G6; Office: 1555 Notre Dame St. E., Montreal, Que. H2L 2R5.

**MOLZAHN, Anita E.,** R.N., B.Sc.(N), M.N., Ph.D.; university professor and administrator; b. Edmonton, Alta. 8 Feb. 1955; d. August and Leonie (Brenner) M.; e. Royal Alexandra Hosp. School of Nursing R.N. 1974; Univ. of Alta. B.Sc.(N) 1980, M.N. 1986, Ph.D. 1989; m. Nigel F. s. Frank and Barbara Scott 16 March 1985; children: Wesley David, Laurel Barbara; DIRECTOR, SCHOOL OF NURSING, UNIV. OF VICTORIA 1992– ; Staff Nurse, Nurse Educator, Nurse Clinician, Univ. of Alta. Hosp. 1974–84; joined faculty, Univ. of Alta. 1987; granted tenure 1990; Assoc. Prof., Fac. of Nursing 1991; research focus: quality of life in relation to chronic illness; recipient of num. research grants; Adjunct Prof., Nursing, Univ. of Alta. 1992– ; Univ. of B.C. 1992– ; Am. Nephrol. Nurses Assn. awards: Nephrology Nurse Researcher Award, 1992, Research Abstract Award 1993; Bd. Mem., Kidney Found., N. Alta. Chapter 1975–83; Edit. Bd. Mem., Am. Nephrology Nurses Assn. Journal 1992– ; Co-Chair, Research Ctte., Am. Neph. Nurses Assn. 1992– ; author/co-author of 21 peer-reviewed articles; author of 7 non peer-reviewed articles & 2 book chapters; recreations: skiing, hiking; Home: 4193 Thornhill Cres., Victoria, B.C. V8N 5E6; Office: P.O. Box 1700, Victoria, B.C. V8W 2Y2.

**MOMOTIUK, Hon. Harry,** B.B.A., LL.B.; judge; b. Windsor, Ont. 20 Aug. 1934; s. Andrew and Anne (Turchyn) M.; e. Univ. of Detroit, B.B.A. 1960; Univ. of Ottawa, LL.B. 1964; Osgoode Hall Law Sch. 1966; m. Irene d. Dr. Frank and Lillian Martyniuk 14 Sept. 1968; children: Karen, Gregory, David; REGIONAL SENIOR JUDGE, ONTARIO COURT OF JUSTICE, PROVINCIAL DIVISION 1990– ; called to Bar of Ont. 1966; various positions Chrysler Canada 1955–60; Asst. Crown Atty. Windsor 1966–69; law practice 1969–76; Regional Sr. Judge, Southwestern Ont., Prov. Court of Ont. (Criminal Div.) 1976–90; apptd. Provincial Court Judge 1976; Regional Sr. Judge, Prov. Div. for S.W. Ont. 1989; Lectr. in Bus. Law, Univ. of Windsor 1968–88; Lectr. in Co. Law, St. Clair Coll. Windsor 1972– ; Lectr. in Comm. Crime RCMP Coll. Ottawa 1977– ; in Extremism / Terrorism RCMP Coll. 1988; Pres. Ukrainian Grads. Windsor-Detroit 1969; Vice Pres. Ukrainian Bus. & Profl. Assn. 1969; Legal Adv. & mem. St. Vladimir's Ukrainian Greek Othrodox Cath., Pres. 1978; mem. Candn. Bar Assn.; Essex Law Assn.; Club: Beach Grove Golf; Home: 107 Rutland Rd., St. Clair Beach, Ont. N8N 1E8; Office: City Hall Square, P.O. Box 607, Windsor, Ont. N9A 6N4.

**MONAHAN, Patrick J.,** B.A., M.A., LL.B., LL.M.; university professor; b. Ottawa, Ont. 10 June 1954; s. Gordon John and Victorine Gertrude (Hachey) M.; e. Univ. of Ottawa B.A. 1976; Carleton Univ. M.A. 1977; Osgoode Hall Law School, York Univ. LL.B. 1980; Harvard Univ. LL.M. 1982; m. Monica d. Thomas and Dorene Feeney 18 June 1977; children: Brendan Patrick Feeney Monahan, Sean Gordon Feeney Monahan; ASSOC. PROF., OSGOODE HALL LAW SCHOOL OF YORK UNIV. 1990– ; Law Clerk, Mr. Justice R.G.B. Dickson, Supreme Court of Canada 1980–81; Asst. Prof., Osgoode Hall Law Sch. 1982–86; Sr. Policy Adv., Office of the Attorney Gen., Govt. of Ont. 1986–89; Office of the Premier 1989–90; Dir., York Univ. Centre for Public Law and Public Policy 1990–93; Scholar-in-Residence, Davies, Ward and Beck (Barristers & Solicitors) 1993–94; Editor-in-Chief, 'Canada Watch' (newsletter); Legal Cons., Inuit Tapirisat during 'Canada Round' of constitutional negotiations 1992; frequent commentator, nat. media; Gold Medalist, Osgoode Hall Law Sch. 1980; Frank Knox Scholar, Harvard Univ. 1981–82; Barrister & Solicitor, Law Soc. of U.C.; Mem., Candn. Assn. of Law Teachers; author: 'Meech Lake: The Inside Story' 1991, 'Politics and the Constitution: The Charter, Federalism and the Supreme Court of Canada' 1987; co-author: 'An Agenda for Constitutional Reform: Final Report of the York University Constitutional Reform Project' 1992; editor: 'The Rule of Law: Ideal or Ideology?' 1987; recreations: golf, tennis, skiing; Home: 348 Brookdale Ave., Toronto, Ont. M5M 1P8; Office: 4700 Keele St., North York, Ont. M3J 1P3.

**MONAHAN, Pierre,** B.Comm.; business executive; b. Montreal, Que. 1946; e. Univ. de Montréal B.Comm. 1968; m. Diane; three children; SENIOR VICE-PRESIDENT, TEMBEC INC. 1988– ; various oper. mngt. positions incl. Plant Manager, Quebec City, Domtar Inc. 1968–73; Asst. Treas., Tembec Inc. 1973; Vice-Pres. Finance & Treas.; Chair, Tembec Forest Products Inc.; Chair & C.E.O., Patriot Paper; Former Chair, Forintek Canada 1991–93 (Bd. Mem. & Mem., Extve. Ctte.); Dir., Que. Forest Industries Assn.; Montreal C. of C.; Bd. of Trade of Canada; 1989 Laureate, Les Nouveaux Performants, Que. Bus. Award; Office: 2790, 800 René Lévesque Blvd. W., Montreal, Que. H3B 1X9.

**MONCEL, Lt.-Gen. Robert William,** O.C. (1967), O.B.E. (1944), D.S.O. (1945), C.D., LL.D.; Canadian Army (retired); b. Montreal, Que. 9 Apr. 1917; s. Rene Edward and Edith (Brady) M.; e. Selwyn House Sch., Montreal; Bishop's Coll. Sch., Lennoxville, Que.; McGill Univ. 1934–35; Staff Coll. 1940; National War Coll. (U.S.A.) 1949; Mt. Allison Univ., LL.D. 1968; m. Nancy Allison, d. Ralph P. Bell, N.S., 11 Nov. 1939; one d., Renée; served in World War II 1939–45, with Roy. Candn. Regt., 1st Armoured Bdge., 5th Armoured Divn.; 4th Armoured Divn.; Hdqrs., 2nd Candn. Corps; Commanded 18th Candn. Armoured Car Regt., 4th Candn. Armoured Bgde. 1945; promoted Capt. 1941, Maj. 1942, G.S.O.1 and Lt.-Col. 1943, Brig. 1944; Mentioned in Despatches; Chevalier, Legion d'Honneur; Croix de Guerre avec Palme; Dir., Roy. Candn. Armoured Corps 1946; Dir. of Mil. Training, Army Hdqrs., Ottawa 1947–49; attended Nat. War Coll., Wash., D.C. 1949–50; Sr. Candn. Army Liaison Offr., England 1951–53; Depy. Chief of Gen. Staff 1954–56; Sr. Candn. Mil. Offr., Internat. Truce Comn., Indo China 1957–58; Commdr., 3 Candn. Inf. Bgde., Gagetown, N.B. 1958–59; Quarter Master Gen. 1959–62; G.O.C. Eastern Command 1962–64; Vice Chief of the Defence Staff 1965–66; retired 1966; Co-ordinator for Visits of Heads of State 1967; Recipient, Canada Medal 1967; Queen Elizabeth II Silver Jubilee Medal 1977; Past Chrmn. of Bd., The Fisherman's Memorial Hosp., Lunenburg, N.S. 1980; mem. Bd. of Regents, Mt. Allison Univ. 1983; mem. Roy. Astronomical Soc. of Can.; Dir., N.S. Rehabilitation Centre; Delta Upsilon; Anglican; recreations: golf, sailing, fishing; Club: Royal N.S. Yacht Sqdn.; Home: 'High Head,' Murder Point, Mahone Bay, N.S. B0J 2E0 and Summer Gardens 1470 Summer St., Halifax, N.S. B3H 3A3.

**MONCUR, Robert H.,** B.Com., M.A.,; municipal executive; b. 7 March 1944; e. Univ. of Sask. B.Com. 1965; Oxford Univ. (Rhodes Scholar) M.A. (jurisprudence) 1968; Stanford Univ. 1973; m. Regina Louise Dishaw 1970; DIR., ADMIN. & COMMUNITY SERVICES, Burnaby, B.C. 1986– ; Niagara Inst. Niagara-on-the-Lake 1981–86; Senate, Univ. of Regina 1984–86; Instr. in Business Adm. Univ. of Sask. 1968–69, summer 1970; Asst. Prof. of Business Adm. Queen's Univ. 1973–76; Policy Planning & Research Adm. Ministry of Solr. Gen. Can., Ottawa 1975–77; Depy. Min. of Mineral Resources, Sask. 1977–81; Chrmn. Interprov. Adv. Council on Energy 1978–80; Pres., Sask. Power Corp. 1981–83; Asst. City Mgr., Regina 1983–86; recipient 4 Can. Council Doctoral Fellowships 1969–73; Stanford Univ. Tuition Fellowship 1969–73; named Outstanding Grad. Coll. of Comm. Univ. of Sask. 1965; co-author 'Some Effects of Participative Budgeting Systems on Managerial Behavior' 1971; various articles, reviews; recreations: curling, wine collecting, gourmet cooking, philately; Home: 6224 Gordon Ave., Burnaby, B.C. V5E 3M1.

**MONET, Jacques,** s.j., Ph.L., Th.L., M.A., Ph.D.,; éducateur; né Saint-Jean, Qué. 26 jan. 1930; f. Fabio et Anita (Deland) M.; é. Univ. de Montréal, B.A. 1955; Immaculée Conception, Ph.L. 1956, Th.L. 1967; Univ. de Toronto, M.A. 1961, Ph.D. 1964; PRES., UNIVERSITÉ DE SUDBURY 1992– ; Dir., Canadian Inst. of Jesuit Studies 1988– ; o. prêtre Montréal, 9 juin 1966; derniers voeux dans la Cie de Jesus (Jésuites) Montmartre, 15 août 1971; Prof. (hist.) Saint Mary's Univ. High Sch. 1956; Loyola Coll. 1964–67; Asst. Prof. Univ. Toronto 1968; Prof. Agrége, Univ. d'Ottawa 1969–80; Dir., Dept. d'Histoire 1972–77; Prof., Titulaire, 1980–82, 1982–92; Prés., Regis Coll., Toronto 1982–88; Prés. (1975–76), Soc. hist. du Can.; mem. comité internat. des. hists. et des géogs. de langue française; comité de la politique de la Féd. candnne des sciences sociales 1976–78; Dir. de Recherche auprès du Gouv. gén. du Can. 1976–78; Conseiller spécial en politique culturelle, Secrétariat d'État 1978–79; Conseiller, Centre d'études du Qué., Sir George Williams Univ. 1966–70; mem. Conseil, Soc. hist. du Can. 1969–72 (Sec. 1969–75); Bureau de dir. French Can. Studies Programme 1965–70; comité consultatif d'Hist., gouvernement du Qué. 1964–67; mem. du Bureau des Gouverneurs, Univ. d'Ottawa 1974–77; élu à la Soc. royale du Can. 1978; mem. du Comité consultatif sur les Timbres-postes, Société Canadienne des Postes, 1978–87; mem. du conseil Nat. pour l'évaluation des Archives 1979–83; mem., Queen Elizabeth Scholarship Comm.; comité des Bourses Killam, conseil des Arts, 1982–1985; auteur 'The Last Cannon Shot: A Study of French Canadian Nationalism' 1969; 'The Canadian Crown' 1979; 'La Monarchie au Canada' 1979; 'La Première Révolution Tranquille' 1981; aussi plusieurs articles de revue spécialisée et chapitres de volumes; Catholique r.; bureau: Univ. de Sudbury, Sudbury, Ont. P3E 2C6.

**MONET, Jean,** Q.C., B.A., LL.L.; lawyer; b. Saint-Jean, Que. 31 March 1932; s. Fabio and Anita (Deland) M.; e. Univ. of Ottawa B.A. 1953, LL.L. 1956; COUNSEL, COLBY, MONET, DEMERS, DELAGE & CREVIER; Lectr. in Corporate and Tax Law McGill Univ., Univ. de Montréal, Univ. Laval, Univ. de Sherbrooke, Que. Bar Sch.; Lectr., Continuing Edn. Prog. Candn. Bar Assn., Candn. Inst. C.A.'s; Gov., Candn. Tax Foundation 1983; author 'Vos biens, Votre deces et les impots' 5 publs. 1967–74; 'Your Assets, Death and Taxes' 1971; 'Estate Planning for Canadians' 1975; 'La Soutane et la Carronne' 1993; numerous papers tax and corporate topics various prof. jours.; mem., Quebec Bar; Candn. Bar Assoc.; Candn. Tax Foundation; Intnl. Fiscal Assn.; recreations: swimming, cycling, skiing, tennis; Office: 2900 McGill College Tower, 1501 McGill College Ave., Montreal, Que. H3A 3M8.

**MONEY, Maj. Kenneth,** C.D., M.A., Ph.D.; physiologist; b. Toronto, Ont. 4 Jan. 1935; s. late Walter John and June Bradnee (Bate) M.; e. Whitney Pub. Sch. Toronto 1947; Noranda (Que.) High Sch. 1953; Univ. of Toronto B.A. 1958, M.A. 1959, Ph.D. 1961; Nat. Defence Coll. 1971–72; m. Sheila Mary d. late Wilfred Donnelly, Kirkland Lake, Ont. June 1958; one d. Laura Ann; Physiol., Dept. of Nat. Defence (defence and med. research); Assoc. Prof. Dept. of Physiol. Univ. of Toronto; discovered physiol. action of alcohol in inner ear 1974; rec'd. NASA contract for experiments on motion sickness and inner ear 1977; apptd. to Candn. Astronaut Corps. 1983–92; discovered role of inner ear in vomiting response to poisons 1983; Air Reserve (pilot) 400 Sqdn. 1956–83; Olympic Athlete 1956 (high jump); United States Masters badminton champion 1989; invented surgical operation to cure certain kinds of dizzy spells since 1990; author over 90 scient. publs.; World Book encyclopedia author for five topics; Fellow, Royal Soc. Health; mem. Canadn. Physiol Soc.; Barany Soc.; Fellow, Aerospace Med. Assn.; Bd. of Dirs., Interquest Technologies Inc.; Academician and Chrmn. of Human Factors Cttee. for the Mars Mision, Internat. Acad. of Astronautics; recreations: badminton, aerobatic flying, skiing, fishing; Home: 12 Audubon Court, Willowdale, Ont. M2N 1T9; Offices: Senior Scientist, DCIEM, DND, Box 2000, Downsview, Ont. M3M 3B9.

**MONEY, Peter Lawrence,** M.Sc., Ph.D.; economic and regional geologist; b. Montreal, Que. 8 Feb. 1935; s. late Lawrence Charles and Phyllis Freeman (Bullock) M.; e. McGill Univ. B.Sc. 1956; Univ. of B.C. M.Sc. 1959; Univ. of Alta. Ph.D. 1967; Queen Mary Coll. London (UK), NRC Post-doctoral Fellow 1968–69; m. Frances Margaret d. late Edward Albert Munro and late Frances Emily (Davies) M. 8 Sept. 1962; children: the late David, Katherine; CONSULTING GEOLOGIST 1991– ; Regional Mapping Geol. Sask. Dept. of Mineral Resources 1960; Resident Geol. Uranium City 1965; Asst. Prof. Carleton Univ. Ottawa 1969–70; Sr. Staff Geol. Texasgulf Inc. 1970; Chief Geol. Can. Exploration 1975; Regional Mgr., Can. Exploration 1979; Vice Pres., Exploration, Kidd Creek Mines Ltd. 1982; Vice Pres., Exploration Planning 1985; Geological Cons. 1986; Sr. Geoscientist, Ont. Geological Survey 1987–91; author or co-author various geological reports and papers; Home: 195 Stibbard Ave., Toronto, Ont. M4P 2C4.

**MONGRAIN, André C.,** M.B.A., B.Comm.; financial executive; b. Cap de la Madeleine 11 Mar. 1942; s. Charles Emile and Simone (Loranger) M.; e. Univ. Laval, M.B.A. 1965, B.Comm. 1964; m. Georgette d. Gerard and Mariette Heroux 4 Sept. 1965; children: Sophie, Julie; Regional Vice-Pres., Médis Services Pharmaceutiques et de Santé Inc. 1992; Group Controller, Celanese Can. 1965–67; Dir. of Admin., Atlas Steel Co. 1967–69; Gen. Mgr., Tricots Excel Inc. 1969–70; Controller, SNC Inc. 1970–74; Vice-Pres., Finan. & Admin., SNC Inc., Div Canaton 1974–78; Vice-Pres., Finan., U.A.P. Inc. 1978–82; Vice-Pres. Finan. & Corp. Store 1982–88; Extve. Vice-Pres., Sodisco Inc. 1988–90; Pres. & C.E.O.,

Groupe Pharmaceutique Focus Inc. 1990–92; mem., Finan. Extves. Inst.; recreations: skiing, boating; Home: 1056 Emile Nelligan, Boucherville, Que. J4B 2L4.

**MONK, Lorraine Althea Constance,** O.C. (1983), C.M. (1973), M.A.; D.Litt.; author; b. Montreal, Que.; d. Edwin and Eileen Marion (Nurse) Spurrell; e. McGill Univ., B.A. 1944, M.A. 1946; D.Litt.: York Univ. 1982; Carleton Univ. 1985; m. John McCaughan Monk; children: Leslie Ann, Karyn Elizabeth, John Spurrell, David Chapman; rec'd. Centennial Medal 1967; Excellence of Service Award, Fed. internat. de l'art photographique; Nat. Assn. Photographic Art Gold Medal for 'outstanding contribution to photography'; author, 'Canada: A Year of the Land' 1967; 'Ces Visages qui sont en pays' 1967; 'Stones of History' 1967; 'Call Them Canadians' 1968; 'A Time to Dream – Reveries en Couleurs' 1971; 'Canada' 1973; won Silver Medal at Leipzig Book Fair 1975 in 'Most Beautiful Book in the World' competition; 'The Female Eye' 1975; 'Between Friends/Entre Amis' 1976 won many awards, including 'Best Printed Book' award at Int. Gallery of Superb Printing (U.S.A.) and 1st recipient of Gold Medal 1977 at Internat. Book Fair in Leipzig, Germany 'in honour of her extraordinary achievement in the art of book creating'; other writings incl. 10 books in 'Image' series; 3 books in 'Signature' series; 'The Robert Bourdeau Monograph' 1980; 'Canada with Love/Canada avec amour' (patriation of the Constitution of Canada), 1982; awarded first prize Intnl. Craftsman Guild, 1983; 'Celebrate our City' (150th Anniv. of Toronto), 1983; 'Ontario: A Loving Look' 1984; 'Photographs that Changed the World' 1989; Extve. Dir., Candn. Museum of Photography; prod. first major exhbn. ''The Incredible Journeys' photographs from the Canadian Far North 1947–1952' by Richard Harrington, Toronto 1987; Home: 176 Balmoral Ave., Toronto, Ont. M4V 1J6.

**MONNIN, Hon. Alfred Maurice,** B.A., LL.B.; retired judge; b. Winnipeg, Man. 6 Mar. 1920; s. Alphonse Louis and Adèle (Sperisen) M.; e. Provencher Coll. Inst., St. Boniface, Man.; St. Boniface Coll., B.A. (Latin Philos.) 1939; Univ. of Manitoba Law Sch., LL.B. 1946; m. Denise, d. late J.D. Pelletier, 30 Jan. 1943; children: Michel, Pierre, Bernard, Marc, Jean-Paul; Chief Justice of Manitoba 1983–90; Justice, Court of Appeal, Man. 1962– ; called to Bar of Man. June 1946; read law with F.T. Taylor, Q.C., T.M. Long and H.G.H. Smith, Q.C.; Police Magistrate 1956; cr. Q.C. Jan. 1957; apptd. Justice, Court of Queen's Bench, Man. 1957; served in 2nd World War 1942–45 (in Canada 1942–43; U.K., France, Holland, Belgium, Germany 1943–45); Capt., Royal Regt. of Can.; Sr. Liaison Offr., 4th Candn. Infantry Brigade; hon. degrees: Univ. of Winnipeg, Univ. of Ottawa, Univ. Laval, Univ. of Man.; past Pres.: Public Sch. Comn. of St. Boniface; l'Assn. d'éducation des canadiens français du Man.; Hist. Soc. of St. Boniface; Winnipeg Symph. Orch.; Alliance française de Winnipeg; Centre culturel franco-manitobain; Candn. Catholic Orgn. for Development and Peace; former Chrmn. Sch. Divisions Boundaries Comn.; Adv. Bds. St. Boniface Coll., St. Amant Centre, Taché Centre; former Vice-Pres. Counc. for Higher Learning in Man.; Man. Centennial Corp.; Man. Centennial Cultural Centre; former mem. National Centennial Conference; Comte. for the Creation of Bilingual Districts in Can.; decorated French Legion of Honour; mem. Candn. Bar Assn.; Man. Bar Assn.; Home: 608 Aulneau St., Winnipeg, Man. R2H 2V4.

**MONSAROFF, Adolph,** B.A.Sc., F.C.I.C.; retired company executive; b. Russia 21 Feb. 1912; s. Boris and Sonya (Green) M.; e. Univ. of Toronto, B.A.Sc. (Chem. Engn. with Hons.) 1934; m. Marion Mink, 15 Jan. 1937; after grad. from Univ. joined Mallinckrodt Chemical Works Ltd., Toronto, Ont., as Chem. Engr.; Plant Supt., 1936–44; joined Monsanto Can. Ltd., 1945; Vice-Pres., 1951–59; Extve. Vice-Pres., 1959–62; el. Dir. 1960; Vice-Pres., Marketing & Devel., Domtar Chemicals Ltd., 1963; Vice-Pres. and Mang. Dir., 1964–68; Pres. 1968–76; Dir., Office of Indust. Research, McGill Univ. 1977–82; Dir., Candn. Human Rights Foundation; Dir., Fraser Hickson (Library) Inst. of Montreal; served with C.O.T.C. 1940; Fellow, Chem. Inst. of Can. (Chrmn., Bd. of Dirs., 1954–55, Vice Pres. 1973–74, Pres. 1974–75); mem., Soc. of Plastics Industry (Can.) Inc. (Pres. 1960–62); Bd. Dirs., Mfg. Chemists' Assn. (U.S.) 1974–77; Soc. of Chem. Industry; Am. Inst. Chem. Engrs.; Order Engrs. Que.; Am. Assn. Advanc. Science; recreation: literature; Clubs: University Club of Montreal; Montreal Badminton and Squash; Faculty Club (McGill Univ.); Home: 255 Bamburgh Circle, Apt. 401, Scarborough, Ont. M1W 3T6.

**MONTAGNES, (Edward) Ian,** B.A., M.A.; publishing consultant; b. Toronto, Ont. 11 Mar. 1932; s. James and Rose (Cornblat) M.; e. Univ. of Toronto Schools; Univ. of Toronto B.A. 1953; M.A. 1956; m. Anne, d. Selwyn and Mary Franks, 1956; children: David, Joan; m. Elizabeth Wilson, 1984; Assistant Director and Editor-in-Chief, University of Toronto Press 1982–92; Editor, 'Scholarly Publishing: A Journal for Authors and Publishers' 1969–93; taught journalism, Ryerson Inst. of Technology 1957–59; Information Officer, Univ. of Toronto 1959–63; Information Officer, Royal Ontario Museum 1963–66; joined Univ. of Toronto Press 1966; on leave to direct training program for editors associated with research centres in the Third World, based at International Rice Research Institute, Los Baños, Philippines 1985–88; led training courses in China and Kenya 1987, Malaysia and Thailand 1988, Nigeria 1989, China 1991, Pakistan 1992 and 1993, Zimbabwe 1993; advised similar course in Indonesia 1986; publishing consultant in Netherlands 1991, Guyana 1992, Zambia and England 1993; lecturer, Faculty of Library Science, Univ. of Toronto 1989– , and Ryerson Polytechnical Inst. 1990; author 'An Uncommon Fellowship: The Story of Hart House' 1969; co-editor (with Robin Harris) 'Cold Iron and Lady Godiva: Engineering Education at Toronto 1920–72' 1972; (with Eleanor Harman) 'The Thesis and the Book' 1976; author: 'The University of Toronto: A Souvenir' (with photographs by Rudi Cristl) 1984; 'Editing and Publication: A Training Manual' 1991; 'Publishing Management' 1993, and of various articles, mostly on book publishing; Secy., Assn. of Candn. Univ. Presses/Assn. des Presses Universitaires Canadiennes 1972–84; various comte. offices and board, Assn. of Amer. Univ. Presses 1975–91; Advisory Bd., Internat. Fed. Science Editors 1991– ; Assoc. Fellow, Massey College 1989– ; Club: Arts & Letters, Toronto, Toronto Lawn Tennis; Home: 130 Carlton St., Toronto, Ont. M5A 4K3.

**MONTAGUE, George Hastings,** B.A., LL.B.; investment company executive; b. Winnipeg, Man. 22 March 1928; s. Furry F. and Margaret Helen (Hastings) M.; e. Univ. of Man. B.A. 1949 LL.B. 1953; London Sch. of Econ. Cert. in Business Adm. 1954; m. Donna Lambert 7 Jan. 1959; children: Price John, Michael Hastings; PRES., MARMONT LTD. 1988– ; law practice Pitblado, Hoskin & Co. Winnipeg 1954–56; Underwriting Dept. Equitable Securities of Canada Ltd. 1956–59; law practice (latterly as a Partner) Blackwell, Hilton, Treadgold & Spratt, Toronto 1959–66; Rothschild Bank, Paris, France 1966–67; Unas Investments of Toronto 1967–72, latterly as Vice Pres.; Vice pres. and Secy. Merban Capital Corp. 1972–76; Vice Pres. & Secy., Consolidated Talcorp Ltd. 1976–88; Past Pres., Metrop. Toronto Region Boy Scouts of Can.; Past Pres. and Dir. Shaw Festival; recreations: music, sailing, hobby farming, astronomy; Club: Arts and Letters (Toronto); Home: Suite 15B, 66 Collier St., Toronto, Ont. M4W 1L9.

**MONTCALM, Sister Mary Beth,** M.A., Ph.D.; b. Cochrane, Ont. 11 Apl. 1946; d. William Albert and Dorothy Kathleen (McManus) M.; e. York Univ. B.A. 1972; Carleton Univ. M.A. 1976, Ph.D. 1983; GEN. SUPERIOR, SISTERS OF ST. JOSEPH OF TORONTO 1990– , mem. since 1965; Asst. Prof. of Pol. Studies Univ. of Man. 1983, Assoc. Prof. 1989; recipient Dr. and Mrs. H.H. Saunderson Award for Excellence in Teaching Univ. of Man. 1989; Dir. St. Michael's Hosp. and St. Joseph's Health Centre; co-author 'Beyond The Quiet Revolution' 1990; author or co-author several articles Que. and Candn. politics; R.Catholic; recreations: jogging, gardening; Home: 18 Sawley Dr., Willowdale, Ont. M2K 2J1; Office: 3377 Bayview Ave., Willowdale, Ont. M2M 3S4.

**MONTCALM, Ronald,** B.A., LL.L.; lawyer; b. Trois Rivières, Que. 26 Dec. 1939; s. Aimé and Alida (Filion) M.; e. St. Sacrement Sch. Trois Rivières; Loyola High Sch. 1958; Loyola Coll. B.A. 1962; Univ. de Montréal LL.L. 1966; PARTNER, LAFLEUR BROWN law firm; Dir. Univers Info Inc.; municipal judge Roxboro; called to Bar of Que. 1967; served with Univ. Naval Training Div. 1959–66, rank Capt.; mem. Montreal Bar Assn.; Que. Bar Assn.; Candn. Bar Assn.; R. Catholic; recreations: jogging, squash, golfing, skiing; Clubs: Montreal Amateur Athletic Assoc.; Club Laval sur le Lac; Home: 4005 Redpath Ave., Apt. 103, Montreal, Que. H3G 2G9 Office: 1 Place Ville Marie, Suite 3700, Montreal, Que. H3B 3P4.

**MONTESANO, John,** B.Sc.; foundation executive; b. Toronto, Ont. 28 June 1966; s. Antonio and Maria M.; e. York Univ. B.Sc. (Chem.) 1989; Pres., John H. McDonald Journalism Foundation 1991; Production Mgr., Lexicon Newspaper, York Univ. 1988–89; Editor-in-Chief 1989–90; Candn. Univ. Press Fundraiser/Conf. Organizer 1990–91; Pres., Candn. Univ. Press; Chair, Candn. Univ. Press Media Serv. – Campus Plus; Home: 343A Elgin St., Ottawa, Ont. K2P 1M7.

**MONTGOMERY, Charles R. (Chuck);** aviation executive; b. Simcoe, Ont. 23 July 1947; s. Edward G. and Laurena E. M.; e. Chippewa S.S. 1966; children: Darryl, Gregory; PRESIDENT, ODESSEY AVIATION LTD. 1989– ; Pilot, Falconbridge Ltd. 1979–82; Dir. of Training, Flight Safety Canada Ltd. 1982–86; Dir. of Operations, Magna Internat. 1986–89; Dir., Hamilton Internat. Airshow; Mem., Royal Candn. Air Force Assn.; Royal Canadian Legion 1980– ; Board of Trade of Metro Toroto; recreations: tennis, boating; clubs: Regency Racquet, Hot Stove; Home: 20 Paradise Gardens, Brampton, Ont. L6S 5C7; Office: 2450 Derry Rd. E., Hangar 9, Mississauga, Ont. L5S 1B2.

**MONTGOMERY, Donald;** trade unionist; b. Canora, Sask. 8 June 1920; s. Milton Templeton and Margaret Geneva (Culbert) M.; e. elem. and high schs. Hamilton, Ont.; Turner Business Coll.; m. Lu Eirene d. Thomas Huggard, 20 May 1954; children: Charmiene, Donald Kirk; PARTNER, PRES. & C.E.O., METROLABOUR CONSULTANTS INC. 1989– ; Consultant on Industrial Relations and Govt. Policy 1984– ; youngest man ever apptd. to staff of Steelworkers' Organ. Comte. (predecessor to United Steelworkers of Am.) at age 20; toured E. Ont. on variety of organ. drives for 10 yrs. from 1943; trans. to Toronto 1953 and apptd. Steelworkers Area Supvr. for Toronto-Barrie Area until present apptd.; Mem., Bd. of Dirs., GSW Water Products; el. Secy.-Treas. Toronto and Lakeshore Labour Council 1953 and re-el. to same position on merged Labour Council of Metrop. Toronto, el. Pres. 1964–74; Secy.-Treas. Candn. Labour Congress 1974–84 (decided not to seek a 6th term); Founding mem. Labour Council Devel. Foundation and served as Dir., Nat. Inst. for Social Assistance; former Dir. Social Planning Council Metro Toronto; served gov. bd. Un. Appeal; Adv. Vocational Comte. Borough York Bd. Educ.; John Howard Soc.; Riverdale Hosp. (Dir.); founding mem. Zool. Soc.; former mem. Aeronautics Adv. Bd.; served on AFL-CIO-CLC Liaison Comte. and Candn. Labour Congress Internat. Affairs Comte., Maritime Comte.; Organ. and Pub. Relations Adv. Comtes.; Council for Performing Arts; White Collar Organ. Comte.; served Export Development Bd.; recreation: woodwork; Home: 19 Baby Point Rd., Toronto, Ont. M6S 2E8; Office: Box 98546, 873 Jane St., Toronto, Ont. M6N 5N6.

**MONTGOMERY, Eldon Maurice,** B.A., B.Ed.; educator; b. Maryfield, Sask. 27 Sept. 1943; s. James Maurice and Rachel Marion M.; e. Brandon Univ. B.A. 1969, B.Ed. 1971; m. Joan d. James and Isabel Gilmour 26 Aug. 1967; children: Jodi, Mark (deceased), Jillian, Jonathan; Elementary Teacher, Russell Central School 1963–66; Grade 7 Teacher, Dept. of Nat. Defence, CFB Shilo 1967–68; taught Special Edn., was Vice Principal (1973–90), taught high school and has been part-time counsellor at Major Pratt School (Russell, Man.) 1968– ; Mem., Man. Assessment Ctte. for Gr. 9 Social Studies 1986; Man. Grade 9 Adv. Ctte. for Social Studies assisted Prentice-Hall with 'Canada Today' 1991; Educators Study Tour Program of Japanese Schools 1991; Bd. of Gov. Rep. to Brandon Univ. 1988– (Vice Chair 1991–92); Mem., United Ch.; Conservative Party of Man.; recreations: hockey, golf, volleyball; clubs: Russell & District Lions (Pres. 1986–87, 1992–93), Russell & Area Swimming Pool Ctte. (Pres.); Address: Box 723, Russell, Man. R0J 1W0.

**MONTGOMERY, J. Ross;** management consultant; b. Melfort, Sask. 15 Sept. 1940; s. James and Nellie Rachel (Young) M.; e. Princess Margaret H.S. 1958; C.G.A. 1967; m. Maureen d. J. Robert and Dorothy Bonshor 28 July 1962; children: James Allan, Christopher John; CHIEF EXTVE. OFFR., CUE DATAWEST LTD. 1993– ; Asst. Gen. Mgr., C.U. & C. Health Serv. Soc. 1967–71; Admin., Op. Engrs. Pension Plan, B.C. Central Credit Union 1971–73; Asst. to Gen. Mgr. 1973–76; Pres., Credit Union Deposit Ins. Corp. of B.C. 1976–86; Principal, Montgomery Thornton Management Services Inc. 1987–88; Principal, Ross Montgomery & Associates Ltd. 1989–93; Trustee, Credit Union Found. of B.C.; Past Chrmn., Credit Union Stabilization Funds of Can.; Club: Mensa Canada; Address: 82 Richmond St., New Westminster, B.C. V3L 5N1.

**MONTGOMERY, The Honourable Judge Leonard Thorburn,** Q.C., B.A., LL.B.; provincial court judge; b. Orillia, Ont. 28 May 1932; s. James Reid and Dorothy Edith (Thorburn) M.; e. Orillia Dist. H.S. 1950; Queen's Univ. B.A. 1954; Osgoode Hall Law Sch., LL.B. 1958; m. Stefanie d. William and Anastasia Bachorski 20 Apr. 1963; children: Christopher Andrew, Tracy Nadine; ONTARIO COURT OF JUSTICE, PROVINCIAL DIVI-

SION 1975– ; lawyer, City of Orillia 1958–75; Q.C. 1971; attained 32 degree Masonic Lodge; mem., St. James Anglican Ch. (Past Mem., Adv. Bd.); Past Pres., Ontario Judges Assn.; mem. Delta Chi Fraternity; mem. Canadian Bar Assn.; Am. Judges Assn.; Ontario Rep. to the Canadian Assn. of Provincial Court Judges; recipient Solicitor General's Award for Crime Prevention 1991; recreations: tennis, swimming, nature walks, cross country skiing; Clubs: Kiwanis; Shrine; Home: 20 Lowther Ave., Toronto, Ont. M5R 1C6; Office: 19 Front St. N., Orillia, Ont. L3V 6J3.

**MONTGOMERY, Ronald,** M.Sc.; business executive; b. Belfast, Northern Ireland 28 March 1935; s. Edward Bryce and Margaret Ann (McConnell) M.; e. College of Aeronautics, Cranfield Inst. of Technology M.Sc. 1958; m. Elizabeth Threlfall 7 Oct. 1961; children: Deborah, Don, Kelly; PRESIDENT & CHIEF EXECUTIVE OFFICER, HAEFELY-TRENCH GROUP, BBA CANADA LIMITED 1974– ; Scientist, Defence Research Board Canada 1958–64; Dir., Research & Technology and Vice-President, Marketing, Computing Devices of Canada, Control Data Corp. 1965–73; Pres. & Chief Extve. Offr., Collins Radio Co. of Canada 1973–74; recreations: tennis, skiing, windsurfing; clubs: Bayview Golf & Country; Home: 33 Normandale Rd., Unionville, Ont. L3R 4J8; Office: 71 Maybrook Dr., Scarborough, Ont. M1V 4B6.

**MONTGOMERY, William Harp,** LL.M.; diplomat; b. Vancouver B.C. 11 Oct. 1933; s. William and Hazel (Hutcherson) M.; e. Univ. of B.C., B.A. 1956, LL.B. 1959; London Sch. of Econ. and Pol. Science LL.M. 1961; m. Julia, d. of late E. J. Meilicke 16 Dec. 1960; children: Andrea Claire, Ian Donald; joined Dept. of External Affairs 1961; Extve. Asst. to Secy. of State for External Affairs 1962–63; New Delhi 1963–66; Bangkok 1968–70; Geneva 1973–77; Dir. Legal Adv. Div. Ottawa 1977–79; Ambassador to Indonesia 1979–82; Dir. Gen., Internat. Relations, Dept. of Communications 1982–85; Dir. Gen. East Asia Bureau 1985–86; Extve. Dir. Gen. Asia and Pacific Branch 1986–87; Assistant Secretary General, Commonwealth Secretariat, London, Eng. 1987–93; mem. Candn. Inst. Internat. Affairs; Candn. Council Internat. Law; Office: Dept. of External Affairs, Ottawa, Ont. K1A 0G2.

**MONTIGNY, Richard Warren,** B.B.A., C.M.A., C.M.C.; municipal administrator; b. Charlottetown, P.E.I. 20 Aug. 1948; s. Louis Alfred andRuth Frances (Hood) M.; e. Birchwood High Sch. 1964; Prince of Wales Coll. 1966; Univ. of P.E.I. B.B.A. 1971; Cert. Municipal Admin., Inst. of Public Affairs, Dalhousie Univ. 1984; Cert. Municipal Clerk, Internat. Inst. of Municipal Clerks 1987; m. Marion d. Austin and Winnifred Campbell 16 Apr. 1976; one daughter; ADMINISTRATOR, COMMUNITY OF CORNWALL 1980–87, 1989– ; Office Mgr. Bruce Stewart Ltd. 1971–73; Extve. Dir., Atlantic Cerebral Palsy Assn. 1973–76 and P.E.I. Council of the Disabled 1976–80 (Pres. 1974–76); Coordinator of Special Projects, Prince Edward Island Civil Service Comn. 1987-89; Dir., Maritime Municipal Training and Development Bd. 1985–88; Trustee, Queen Elizabeth Hosp. 1981–90; Dir., Metro Credit Union Ltd., 1983–91; mem. Inst. of Public Admin. of Canada - P.E.I. Regional Group (Treas. 1983–86, Chrmn. 1986–87); mem. Univ. of P.E.I. Senate 1969–70; Pres., P.E.I. Cerebral Palsy Assn. 1976–80, Secy.-Treas. 1969–73; Treas. 1985– ; Pres., Assoc. of Municipal Administrators - P.E.I. 1987–88, 1989–90; Pres., Credit Union Deposit Insurance Corp. 1992– ; First Vice Pres. Candn. Cerebral Palsy Assn. 1978–80, 1981–82, Dir. 1969–78; Pres., Wheels Inc. 1975–91; Dir. and Secy.-Treas. P.E.I. Recreation & Sports Assn. for Disabled 1975–79; Dir. P.E.I. Un. Way 1969–81; P.E.I. Epilepsy Assn. 1979–81; Past Pres. Charlottetown Lions (Lion of Yr. and 100% Pres. 1976); Past Secy. and Vice Pres. Charlottetown Jaycees; Dir. Occupational Training Centre for Handicapped 1971–79; Pres. Voluntary Resource Council 1980–81; mem. Internat. Cerebral Palsy Soc.; recipient Cecil Hart Award Atlantic Cerebral Palsy Assn. 1981; mem. P.E.I. Numismatic Assn. (Secy.-Treas. 1967.71, 1976–78); Atlantic and Candn. Numismatic Assns.; Pres., P.E.I. NDP 1974–76; Presbyterian; recreations: reading, gardening, music; Home: 13 Linden Ave., Parkdale, P.E.I. C1A 5Y5; Office: 29 Cornwall Rd., P.O. Box 430, Cornwall, P.E.I. C0A 1H0.

**MONTMINY, Pierre Daniel,** B.Sc., M.Sc.; b. St-Agapit, Que. 16 June 1958; s. Georges Etienne and Madeleine (Rousseau) M.; e. classical course, Levis, Que. 1978; Laval Univ., B.Sc. 1982, M.Sc. 1992; Revenue Programs Manager, IBM Canada 1984; Pres., Pierdon Inc. 1988– ; FCAC Scholarship for postgrad. studies 1982, 1983; Mem., Assn. of Profl. Engr. 1987; recreations: volleyball, tennis, sailing, skiing, reading; Clubs: Cedar Springs Athletic Club; Home: 1242 Hedgestone Cres., Oakville, Ont. L6M 1X8.

**MONTSION, Rollande,** M.A.; auditor; executive; b. Hull, Que. 8 Apr. 1949; d. Joseph Roland and Jeanne Irma (Savard) M.; e. Ottawa Univ. B.A. (Hons.) 1970, M.A. 1975; SPECIAL ADVISOR FOR ADMINISTRATIVE REFORM FOR THE PRESIDENT OF THE REPUBLIC OF BENIN, WESTERN AFRICA 1994– ; Vice-Pres. & Auditor General, Hydro-Quebec 1986–94; French lang. teacher & counsellor 1970–75; Couns. & Mgr., fed. govt.; Sr. Advr. & Teacher; Principal in comprehensive auditing, Auditor General of Canada; cons. in standards of internal auditing, C.I.C.A.; Extve., Que. Ctte. resp. for internal audits; Trainer, Candn. Comprehensive Auditing Found.; First woman on Hydro-Québec's President's mngt. ctte.; Dir., Montréal Sect., Inst. of Internal Auditors; Candn. Standards Assn.; Pres. of the Bd., Internat. Development Center in Audit and Controls; recreations: music, travel; Address: Bureau de la Présidence, Cotonou, Bénin, Afrique de l'Ouest.

**MOOALLEM, Jack,** B.Comm., M.Comm., B.C.L., C.A.; financial executive; b. 1943; m. Suzanne; 2 children; e. McGill Univ. B.Comm. 1966, M.Comm. 1967, C.A. 1968, B.C.L. 1970; Harvard Univ. Internat. Lawyers' Program 1978; DIRECTOR & HEAD OF DOMESTIC PRIVATE BANKING, SWISS BANK CORP. 1992– ; Taxation & Auditing, Peat, Marwick, Mitchell & Co. Toronto 1966–67; Sr. Tax Analyst, General Motors Corp. Detroit 1968; Vice-Pres., Finance & Law, Alcan Aluminium Ltd. 1970–84; Dir., M.&A., Varity Corp. (formerly Massey-Ferguson) 1984–87; Vice-Pres. & Dir., Steinberg Inc. 1987–88; Vice-Pres. & Head, M.&A., Citibank-Citicorp 1988–92; Mem., Insts. of C.A.s of Ont., Que. & Canada; Candn. & Que. Bar Assns.; Canadian Tax Found.; Toronto Bd. of Trade; Practicing Law Inst.; Corp. Finance Inst.; clubs: Granite, University; Office: Suite 780, P.O. Box 103, 207 Queen's Quay W., Toronto, Ont. M5J 1A7.

**MOODY, Norman F.;** B.E., F.I.E.E., S.M.I.E.E.E., F.C.M.B.E.S., F.R.S.C.; b. England; Prof. Emeritus, Univ. of Toronto 1977– ; former Prof. of Elect. Engn. & Biomed. Eng. and Dir. Inst. Biomed. Engineering, Univ. of Toronto; during war was research worker at Telecommunications Rsch. Estab.; came to Canada 1948 to head Electronics Division, Atomic Energy of Canada Ltd., Chalk River; became Sr. Principal Scient. Offr. with a High Explosive Rsch. Estab. in Eng. 1951; Head Basic Circuit Rsch., Defence Rsch. Bd., Govt. of Can. to 1959; subsequently apptd. Head, Dept. Elect. Engn., Univ. of Sask.; Address: 1334 St. Patrick St., Victoria, B.C. V8S 4Y4.

**MOOGK, Peter Nicholas,** Ph.D.; university professor; b. West Chiltington, England 5 Oct. 1943; s. Willis John and Grace Elizabeth (Shuttleworth) M.; e. Univ. of Sask., Univ. of Toronto (Trinity), B.A. (hons.) 1965; Univ. of Toronto, M.A. 1966; McGill Univ., Univ. of Toronto, Ph.D. 1973; m. Susan Rosa d. Freeman and Rosita Tovell 30 Mar. 1965; children: Jonathan, Benjamin, Anna; ASSOC. PROF. OF HIST., UNIV. OF B.C. 1977– ; Rsch. Asst., French Can. Studies Prog., McGill Univ. 1966–67; Asst. Prof., present univ. 1970–77; Vis. Scholar, Darwin Coll., Cambridge Univ. 1982–83; Ste-Marie Prize for History 1975; Candn. Numismatic Assn. Rsch. Awards 1976, 1988; Daughters of Colonial Wars Prize for early Am. hist. 1980; Museum Dir., 15 Fd. Artillery Regt.; Unitarian; Army Reserve (Major); Mem., Candn. Numismatic Soc.; Candn. Hist. Assn.; French Colonial Historical Soc.; Dominion Councillor, United Empire Loyalists' Assn. of Canada; Vice-Pres., Vancouver Numismatic Soc.; author: 'Building a House in New France' 1977 (architectural hist.); 'Vancouver Defended' 1978 (military hist.); co-author: 'Berczy' 1991 (art hist.); recreations: numismatics, antique collector; clubs: UBC Fac., 15 Fd. Regt. Offrs. Mess; Home: 4645 West 6th Ave., Vancouver, B.C. V6R 1V6; Office: Vancouver, B.C. V6T 1Z1.

**MOON, Barbara Ethel,** B.A.; writer, editor; b. St. Catharines, Ont. 28 Oct. 1926; d. Clifford Graham and Ethel Harriet (Ward) M.; e. Univ. of Toronto B.A. 1948; m. D. Wynne s. Llewellyn and Florence Jane (Stevens) Thomas; EDITOR-AT-LARGE, SATURDAY NIGHT MAGAZINE 1990– ; Asst. Ed., Staff Writer, Maclean's magazine 1948–52, 1956–64; Asst. Ed., Mayfair mag. 1953–56; Feature Writer, The Globe and Mail 1964–66; Editor, Toronto Calendar mag. 1980–82; Sr. Ed., Saturday Night mag. 1986–90; Faculty, Arts Journalism Prog., The Banff Centre for the Arts 1992– ; Life Mem., ACTRA, Writers Guild of Can.; 1st Prize, Maclean Hunter Edit. Achievement 1961–62; President's Medal, Univ. of W. Ont. 1962; Award for Outstanding Achievement, The Nat. Mag. Found. 1993; freelance writer of num. arts and sci. TV documentaries; author of books incl. 'The Canadian Shield' 1970, reviews, newspaper & mag. columns, mag. articles, etc.; broadcaster; performer; Office: 184 Front St. E., Ste. 400, Toronto, Ont. M5A 4N3.

**MOONEN, Fred Hubert,** B.A., LL.D.; retired forest industry executive; b. Saskatoon, Sask. 27 Aug. 1928; s. Peter Hubert and Alida Wilhelmina (Van Winsen) M.; e. St. Louis College; Victoria College; Univ. of B.C. B.A. 1949; m. Elaine d. Henry and Edna Boon 14 Feb. 1953; children: Peter N., John F., Alida J.; SENIOR CONSULTANT, CORPORATE STRATEGIES GROUP LTD. 1992– ; Public Relations Supervisor, BC Tel 1949–62; Public Relations Mgr., Community Chest 1962; Vice-Pres., Council of Forest Industries of B.C. 1962–78; Vice-Pres., Govt. Affairs, MacMillan Bloedel Ltd. 1979–93; Part-time Lecturer, Univ. of B.C.; Nat. Pres., Candn. Public Relations Soc. (Shield of Public Service 1978); Hon. Deg. (LL.D.), Simon Fraser Univ.; Chair, Simon Fraser Univ. Bd. of Gov. 1982–88, 1990–94; Chair, SFU Foundation 1988–90; Roman Catholic; Chair, St. Anthony's Parish; Mem., St. Paul's Hosp. Bd. 1976–83; St. Paul's Hosp. Found. 1982–83; Chair, Grey Cup Parade 1960; Chair, Ad & Sales Bureau of Vanc. Bd. of Trade 1962; sundrey other volunteer agencies 1962–94; recreations: reading, cooking, carpentry; clubs: Vancouver, Diamond Univ.; Address: 3945 Viewridge Place, W. Vancouver, B.C. V7V 3K7.

**MOONEY, Patrick Roy;** researcher; b. Brandon, Man. 24 Feb. 1947; s. Joseph Lorne and Barbara Isabelle (Marlatt) M.; e. Kelvin H.S.; m. Marilyn d. Aubrey and Beryl McGregor 4 May 1974; children: Robin, Kate, Sarah, Jeff, Nicholas; RESEARCHER, RURAL ADVANCEMENT FOUNDATION INTERNAT. 1984– ; Youth Liaison Offr., Man. Govt. 1966–67; Miles for Millions Nat. Walk Comn. (Ottawa, Winnipeg, Calgary) 1967–71; Nat. Co-ord., DEAP/CCIC 1971–75; Rsch. Dir., SCIC 1977–79; Seeds Campaign Dir., ICDA 1979–84; Cons., Man. Govt. 1987; Food & Agric. Orgn. of U.N.; Agric. Lectr., Brandon Univ.; 'The Right Livelihood Award' (Sweden) 1985; 'The Order of the Buffalo Hunt,' Man. Govt. 1986; author: 'The Law of the Seed' 1983, 'Seeds of the Earth' 1979; co-author: 'The Community Seed Bank Kit' 1986, 'The Laws of Life' 1988, 'Shattering' 1990; Office: 504 – 71 Bank St., Ottawa, Ont. K1P 5N2.

**MOONEY, William John;** B.Sc.; geologist; petroleum executive; b. Regina, Sask. 27 Feb. 1929; s. William Joseph and Esther Ellen (Murphy) M.; e. Notre Dame of Can. Wilcox, Sask., 1952; Colo. Coll. B.Sc. (Geol.) 1957; Banff Sch. Advanced Mang. 1971; m. Lois Carol d. Louis Marvin Larson, Los Angeles, Ca., 7 Nov. 1953; children: William Joseph, Michael Marvin, Timothy Stephen, Melissa Anne, Barbara Ellen; CANDN. REPRESENTATIVE, PACIFIC GAS TRANSMISSION CO.; Pres. & C.E.O., Millepede Energy Ltd. 1989– ; Adv. Board, Cutting Internat. Ltd.; Dir., Noble Drilling; Surface Search; Signal Energy; Bd. of Govs., Glenbow Museum 1988–91; Dir., Syncrude Can. Ltd. 1973–78; Pres. and Dir. Canada-Cities Service Ltd. 1975–78; Pres. Cities Service Europe-Africa-Middle East Petroleum Corp. 1978–80; Pres., C.O.O. & Dir., Harvard Intnl. Resources Ltd. 1980–89; Gov., Candn. Petroleum Assn. 1975–78; Vice Chrmn. Alta. Enviromental Research Trust 1976–78; Co-Chrmn. Energy Zoo Fund; Bd. of Govs. & Bd. of Regents Athol Murray Coll. of Notre Dame; Bd. of Regents Candn. Oldtimers Hockey Assn.; Camp Cadicasu Bd. of Dir. & Chrmn. 1962–68; Am. Assn. Petrol. Geols.; Candn. Soc. of Petrol. Geols.; Am. Internat. Petroleum Negotiaters; R. Catholic; recreation: golf; Clubs: National Press; Canyon Meadows Golf & Country; Calgary Petroleum; A.H.S.T.C.; Home: 1110 Crescent Rd. N.W., Calgary Alta. T2M 4A8; Office: 3000, 240 Fourth Ave. S.W., Calgary, Alta. T2P 4L7.

**MOORADIAN, Ara John,** M.Sc., Ph.D., D.Sc., D.Eng. F.C.I.C., F.R.S.C.; engineer, scientist; b. Hamilton, Ont. 21 May 1922; s. John Hogop and Nazen (Papertzian) M.; e. Univ. of Sask., B.Sc. (Chem. Engn.) 1945, M.Sc. (Phys. Chem.) 1948; Univ. of Mo., Ph.D. 1950; Univ. of Man., Hon. D.Sc. 1972; Univ. of Toronto, Hon. D.Eng. 1982; m. Alice C., d. late Charles C. Clerkson, 19 May 1945; children: Jo-Anne, Carol, Peggy, Diana; SR. V.P., ATOMIC ENERGY OF CAN. LTD. 1982– ; Assoc. mem., Science Council of Can. 1972–73; Plant Tester, Alta. Nitrogen Div., Consol. Mining & Smelting Co. 1945–46; Asst. Rsch. Offr., Chalk River Nuclear Labs., Nat. Rsch. Counc. 1950; Br. Head, Devel. Engn. of present labs. 1955, Fuel Devel. 1959; Dir., Devel. Eng. Div. 1964; Mang. Dir., Whiteshell Nuclear Rsch. Lab., Pinawa, Man. 1966; Vice Pres.-in-charge of WNRE, Atomic Energy of Canada Ltd. 1969; Vice Pres. i/c Chalk River Nuclear Labs.

1971; Extve. Vice Pres., Rsch. and Devel. 1977; Corp. Vice Pres., Research and Devel. 1978; maj. contrib. to devel. of low cost nuclear fuel of CANDU nuclear power generating stns.; Trustee, Improvement Dist. Deep River; First Mayor, Town of Deep River; rec'd Can. Medal; rec'd. W.B. Lewis Award; author of over 40 papers and publs.; mem., Chem. Inst. of Can. (Pres. 1980–81); Am. Nuclear Soc.; Anglican; recreations: furniture design, golf, skiing; Home: Box 1542, Deep River, Ont. K0J 1P0.

**MOORE, Brian,** F.R.S.L.; author; b. Belfast, N. Ireland 25 Aug. 1921; s. late James Bernard and late Eileen (McFadden) M.; e. Ireland; m. Jean Denney, 1967; served with Brit. Ministry of War Transport (Civilian Overseas), 1943–45, N. Africa, Italy, France; author: 'The Lonely Passion of Judith Hearne' 1956 (Author's Club Gt. Brit. Best First Novel Award 1956, Que. Lit. Award 1956, Beta Sigma Phi First Novel Award 1956); 'The Feast of Lupercal' 1957; 'The Luck of Ginger Coffey' 1960 (Gov.-General's Lit. Award for Fiction 1960); 'An Answer From Limbo' 1962; 'The Emperor of Ice-Cream' 1965; 'I am Mary Dunne' 1968; 'Fergus' 1970; 'The Revolution Script' (non-fiction) 1971; 'Catholics' 1972; 'The Great Victorian Collection,' 1975; 'The Doctor's Wife' 1976; 'The Mangan Inheritance' 1979; 'The Temptation of Eileen Hughes' 1981; 'Cold Heaven' 1983; 'Black Robe' 1985; 'The Colour of Blood' 1987; 'Lies of Silence' 1990; 'No Other Life' 1993; Recip. U.S. Nat. Arts & Letters Award 1958; Gov.-General's Award 1960, 1975; W.H. Smith Award 1973; James Tait Black Mem. Award 1975; Heinemann Award, Royal Soc. of Literature 1986; Sunday Express Book of the Year Award, U.K. 1987, 1989; Guggenheim Fellow 1959; Can. Council Sen. Fellow 1962, 1976; Writer-in-Residence, Univ. of Toronto 1982; Scottish Arts Counc. Internat. Fellowship 1983; Hon. D.Litt., The Queens Univ. of Belfast 1987; The National Univ. of Ireland (U.C.D.) 1991; Address: 33958 Pacific Coast Hwy., Malibu, Calif. 90265 U.S.A.

**MOORE, Brian L.,** B.Sc., F.F.A., F.C.I.A., C.F.A.; actuary; executive; b. London, Eng. 4 Aug. 1944; s. George and Ivy (Berry) M.; e. Univ. of Sheffield B.Sc. 1965; m. Anne d. Dennis and Margaret Hudson 19 Aug. 1967; children: Patrick, Nicola; PRES., THE NORTH AMERICAN GROUP INC. and CHRMN. & C.E.O., NORTH AMERICAN LIFE FINANCIAL SERVICES INC.; Chrmn., Edgecombe Group Inc.; Elliott & Page Ltd.; First North Am. Life Assurance Co.; Grayrock Shared Ventures Ltd.; NAL Resources Ltd.; NAL Resources Management Ltd.; NASL Series Trust; North Am. Life Financial Services Inc.; North Am. Security Life Insurance Co.; North Am. Security Trust; Vice-Chrmn. & Dir., North Am. Life Assurance Co.; Depy. Chrmn., North Am. Trust Co.; Dir., FNA Financial Inc.; Institute of Corp. Dirs.; NAL Mortgage Co.; NAL Trustco Inc.; NASL Financial Services Inc.; National Club; Seamark Asset Mgmt. Ltd.; Sunnybrook Foundation; TI Remnaco Inc.; Wood Logan Associates, Inc.; Wood Logan Distributors, Inc.; Systems Analyst, Standard Life Assurance Co. Edinburgh, Scot. 1965; Vice Pres. and Actuary, Dir. Life of Jamaica Ltd. Kingston, Jamaica 1972; Actuary, Corporate Actuarial Dept. North American Life Assurance Co. 1977, Vice Pres. Acctg. & Control 1981, Vice Pres. Finance & Control 1982; Sr. Vice Pres. Elliott and Page 1983; Pres. & C.E.O. Elliott and Page 1985; Extve. Vice-Pres. & C.F.O., North Am. Life Assurance Co. 1988; Pres. & C.E.O. North Am. Life Financial Services Inc.; Assoc. Soc. Actuaries; mem. Am. Acad. Actuaries; Financial Extves. Inst. Toronto; Clubs: Donalda, National; Home: 28 Heathview Ave., Willowdale, Ont.; Office: 151 Yonge St., Toronto, Ont. M5C 2W7.

**MOORE, Carole Rinne,** A.B., M.S.; librarian; b. Berkeley, Calif. 15 Aug. 1944; e. Stanford Univ. A.B. 1966; Columbia Univ. M.S. 1967; CHIEF LIBRARIAN, UNIV. OF TORONTO 1986– ; Ref. Lib., Columbia Univ. Libs. 1967–68; joined Univ. of Toronto Lib. as Ref. Lib. 1968; Asst. Head, Ref. Dept. 1973–74; Head, Ref. Dept. 1974–80; Head, Bibliog. Processing Dept. 1980–86; Assoc. Lib., Tech. Services 1986–87; rec'd Columbia Univ. Sch. of Lib. Service Centenary Distinguished Alumni Award 1987; mem. Candn. Lib. Assn.; Am. Lib. Assn.; Assn. of Rsch. Libs.; Candn. Assn. of Rsch. Libs. (Pres., 1989–91); National Library of Canada Adv. Bd. 1991– ; Univ. of B.C. President's Adv. Council on the Univ. Library 1992; ed. 'Labour Relations and the Librarian' 1974; 'Canadian Essays & Collections Index 1972–73' 1976; Office: 130 St. George St., Toronto, Ont. M5S 1A5.

**MOORE, Christopher Hugh,** B.A., M.A.; writer, historian; b. Stoke-on-Trent, England 9 June 1950; s. M. Vincent and Kathleen A. (Lennox) M.; immigrated to Canada 1954; e. Vancouver College (H.S.) 1967; Univ. Laval cours d'été 1970; Univ. of B.C. B.A. 1971; Univ. of Ottawa M.A. 1977; m. Louise d. Joseph and Rita Brophy 7 May 1977; children: Elizabeth, Kate; HISTORICAL CONSULTANT AND WRITER 1978– ; Staff Historian, Parks Canada 1972–75; Sec. to Bd. of Gov., Heritage Canada Found. 1977–78; historical columnist, 'The Beaver' 1991– ; frequent contbr., CBC Radio 'Ideas' 1981– ; consultant on historical films, NFB, CBC TV, Baton Broadcasting 1979– ; Ed., 'History and Social Science Teacher' 1985–90; Part-time Lectr., Univ. of Guelph 1985; Univ. of Toronto 1989–91; Visiting Scholar, Univ. of Guelph 1990; Gov. Gen. Literary Award 1982; Riddell Award, Ont. Hist. 1984; Sec. of State, Prize for Excellence in Candn. Studies 1985; IODE Toronto Book Award 1993; Mr Christie's Children's Book Award 1993; Mem., Writers' Union of Canada (Chair, Contracts Ctte. 1990–94); author: 'Louisbourg Portraits' 1982, 'The Loyalists' 1984, 'M & S Guide to Ontario Colleges' 1993; co-author: The Illustrated History of Canada' 1987, 'The Story of Canada' (juvenile) 1992; recreations: squash, literature, family; Home: Toronto; Office: 396 Pacific, No. 202, Toronto, Ont. M6P 2R1.

**MOORE, Donnie M.,** B.S., M.B.A.; financial executive; b. Oklahoma, U.S.A. 14 June 1948; e. Univ. of Oklahoma B.S. 1971; Univ. of Houston M.B.A. 1973; m. Sherrill 7 Feb. 1981; CHIEF FINANCIAL OFFICER, COGNOS INC. since 1986; various positions in MIS and Finance in U.S., N.Z. & Canada, Burroughs Corp. 1973–86; Office: 3755 Riverside Dr., Box 9707, Ottawa, Ont. K1G 3Z4.

**MOORE, Francis T. (Tim),** C.A.; financial executive; b. Corbridge, England 30 Dec. 1942; s. Thomas Oswald and Nancy Agnes (Campbell) M.; e. Royal Grammar Sch., Newcastle upon Tyne 1960; C.A.; m. Susan d. Dan and Margaret Coffield 3 Dec. 1983; children: Stephen James, Andrew Paul; VICE-PRES., FINAN. & CHIEF FINAN. OFFR., PHILLIPS CABLES LIMITED 1988– ; Peat Marwick, UK 1961–68; Procter & Gamble Ltd., UK & Scandinavia 1968–73; Seagram UK Ltd. 1973–75; Northern Telecom Ltd. 1975–83; Philips Electronics Ltd. 1983–88; Dir., BICC - Phillips Inc.; Electrak Canada Ltd.; Pyrotenax USA Inc.; Mem., Finan. Extves. Inst.; Toronto Cash Mngt. Soc.; Fellow, Inst. of C.A.'s in England & Wales; recreations: golf, bridge, running; clubs: Credit Valley Golf & Country, Agincourt Raquet; Office: 200, 300 Consilium Pl., Scarborough, Ont. M1H 3G2.

**MOORE, Gerald Wayne,** M.Sc.; agriculture executive; b. Stonewall, Man. 14 Sept. 1940; s. Lionel H. and Elizabeth (Fisher) M.; e. Univ. of Man. B.Sc.A. 1969, M.Sc. 1970; m. Carol d. George and Katherine Pritchard 4 Aug. 1962; children: Candace, Darren, Melanie; Extve. Vice Pres. and Chief Operating Offr. United Grain Growers Ltd. 1988–90; Retired; Extve. Asst. Devel. & Planning United Grain Growers 1971, Asst. Area Mgr. Saskatoon 1976, Asst. to Mgr. Elevator Operations 1978 and Mgr. 1980, Asst. Gen. Mgr. and Gen. Mgr. 1983–88; Co-Chrmn. 'Drive for Excellence' Univ. of Man. Faculty of Agric. 1988; mem. Mgmt. Bd. Jt. Venture: United Grain Growers and Allelix Crop Technologies devel. new canola cultivars; Agripro Biosciences Inc. and United Grain Growers for devel. new wheat varieties; mem. Nat. Biotechnol. Adv. Ctte. 1989; Chrmn. Agri-Business & Food Ctte.; Canola Task Force 1990; Man. Govt. Econ. Adv. Council; Past mem. Sr. Grain Transp. Ctte.; Chrmn. S.I.R. Fund Ctte.; Past Chrmn. Bd. Govs. Winnipeg Commodity Exchange; Past Dir. Chamber Maritime Comm.; Past Chrmn. W. Grain Elevator Assn.; mem. Man. Inst. Agrols.; Candn. Inst. Agrols.; Home: P.O. Box 803, Stonewall, Man. R0C 2Z0.

**MOORE, J. Sherrold,** B.Sc.; petroleum executive; b. Winnipeg, Man. 1 July 1929; s. William Stewart and Grace Evelyn M.; e. Montana Sch. of Mines B.Sc.(Petrol.Eng.) 1956; m. Patricia Meirion 2 July 1955; one d. Cynthia Patricia; SR. VICE PRES. SPECIAL PRODUCTS and DIR. AMOCO CANADA PETROLEUM CO. LTD. 1986– ; Dir. Welchem Canada Ltd.; joined present Co. 1956; Chrmn. Alta. Sport Council; mem., Alta. Round Table on Environment & The Economy; Advisory Ctte., Alta. Energy Min. Rick Orman; Dir., Alta. Theatre Projects (Govt. Liaison & Fundraising Comm.); Candn. Mental Health Assn. Alta. S. Central Region; Petroleum Research Institute (Financial Comm.); mem. CPA – APIGEC Ctte.; Candn. Chamber of Commerce, Ottawa Liaison Ctte.; Candn. Major Projects Assn.; Conference Bd. of Canada, Business and the Environment Rsch. Program; Calgary Chamber of Commerce; Calgary Educational Partnerships Foundation (Fundraising Ctte.); Glenbow Museum Soc., Acquisitions Soc. (sponsorship); Governors Club, Mount Royal College; Calgary Centre PC Assn. (Finance Ctte., Chrmn. and Advisory Ctte. to H. Andre); Calgary Elbow PC Assn.; mem. Special Adv. Ctte. to Govt. House Leader 1984– ; recipient Distinguished Service Award Petrol. Soc. of CIM 1977; Special Award APEGGA 1990; CCPE Meritorious Service Award for Community Service, Ottawa 1991; P.Conservative; Club: Calgary Petroleum; Office: P.O. Box 200 Station M, Calgary, Alta. T2P 2H8.

**MOORE, James Doran;** retired manufacturing executive; b. Winnipeg, Man. 20 Feb. 1917; s. Patrick Joseph and Virginia Agnes (Rice) M.; e. St. Mary's Coll. (High Sch.) Calgary, grad. 1935; m. Patricia Anne, d. Rupert Henry A. Lacey, 10 Oct. 1975; children: Marcia Jane, James Patrick, Margaret Suellen, Barbara Lynne, Nancy Ann, Michael Doran, Sarah Marie; on grad. began in jr. positions with Searle Grain Co., Calgary; three yrs. in sales with Heintzman & Co. Ltd.; after war service joined Firestone Can. Inc. at Calgary as Wholesale Terr. Salesman, 1945; Mgr., Truck Tire Sales for Alta. Dist., 1946; Alta. Dist. Mgr., 1949, W. Ont. Dist. 1951; W. Can. Div. Mgr., 1954; Candn. Trade Sales Mgr., 1963; Candn. Gen. Sales Mgr., 1964; Vice-Pres., 1966; el. a Dir., 1967; Pres., Jan. 1969; Chrmn. 1978–81 (ret.); Pres., Rubber Assn. of Can. 1981–85 (Chrmn. 1969–70 and 1977; Dir. 1969–81); served with R.C.N., July 1941 to Oct. 1945; loaned to R.N. (motor torpedo boats) for 1 yr., after which saw service in Atlantic theatre (commanded Corvette 1944–45); Past Pres. & Dir., Opera Hamilton; C.L.J., Commander, Order of St. Lazarus of Jerusalem; R. Catholic; recreation: golf; Club: Hamilton Golf & Country; Home: 5087 Ashland Dr., Burlington, Ont. L7L 3H3.

**MOORE, John Henderson,** LL.D., F.C.A.; retired executive; b. London, Ont. 27 Dec. 1915; s. late John McClary and late Phyllis E. Moore; e. Public Sch., London, Ont.; Ridley Coll., St. Catharines, Ont.; Royal Mil. Coll., Kingston, Ont. (four yrs.); m. S. Elizabeth, d. late S. F. Wood, London, Ont., 11 Dec. 1939; two s.and three d.; Partner, Clarkson, Gordon & Company, London, Ontario, 1950; Director of Finance and Treas., John Labatt Ltd., 1953; apptd. Extve. Vice-Pres. and Mang. Dir., 1957; Pres., 1958; Chrmn. Bd. and Pres. 1967; retired 1981; apptd. Pres., Brascan Ltd., 1969; Chrmn., 1976; retired 1979; served in 2nd World War; 2nd in Command, 15th Field Regt., R.C.A., N.W. Europe; attended Staff Col., Camberley, 1944; Anglican; Clubs: London Hunt & Country; The London (Ont.); York; Toronto; Address: P.O. Box 758, Stn. B., London, Ont. N6A 4Y8.

**MOORE, Keith Leon,** B.A., M.Sc., Ph.D., F.I.A.C., F.R.S.M.; medical educator and author; b. Brantford, Ont. 5 Oct. 1925; s. late Rev. James Henry and Gertrude Myrtle (McCombe) M.; e. Elem. Sch., Wallacetown, Ont.; High Sch., Stratford, Ont.; Univ. of W. Ont., B.A. 1949, M.Sc. 1951, Ph.D. 1954; m. Marion Edith, d. late William and Ishbel (Foster) McDermid 20 Aug. 1949; children: Warren, Pamela, Karen, Laurel, Joyce; PROF. EMERITUS OF ANATOMY AND CELL BIOLOGY, UNIV. OF TORONTO 1991– ; Chrmn. of Anatomy Dept. 1976–85; Assoc. Dean, Basic Sciences 1984–89; Consultant in Anat., Health Sciences Centre, Winnipeg 1965–76; Lectr. in Anat., Univ. of W. Ont. 1954–56; joined Univ. of Man. as Asst. Prof. of Anat. 1956, Assoc. Prof. 1959, Prof. and Head of Anatomy 1965–76, and mem. Senate 1958–76; Prof. of Anatomy, Univ. of Toronto 1976–91; served with RCNVR 1944–46; author: 'The Sex Chromatin' 1966; 'The Developing Human' 1973, 2nd ed. 1977, 3rd ed. 1982, 4th ed. 1988, 5th ed. 1993 (with T.V.N. Persaud); 'Before We Are Born' 1974, 2nd ed. 1983, 3rd ed. 1989, 4th ed. 1993 (with T.V.N. Persaud); 'Study Guide and Review Manual of': 'Human Embryology' 1975, 2nd ed. 1982, 3rd ed. 1988, 4th ed. 1993 (with T.V.N. Persaud); 'Human Anatomy' 1976, 2nd ed. 1982; 'Human Nervous System' 1978, 2nd ed. 1985; 'Clinically Oriented Anatomy' 1980, 2nd ed. 1985, 3rd ed. 1992; 'An Atlas of the Human Brain and Spinal Cord' (with E.G. Bertram) 1982; 'Study Guide and Self-Examination Review for Clinically Oriented Anatomy' 1986; 'Essentials of Human Embryology' 1988; 'Color Atlas of Clinical Embryology' 1994 (with K. Shiota and T.V.N. Persaud); 'Highlights of Reproduction and Prenatal Development' (16 mm. movie) 1978; 'Formation of Sex Cells and Chromosomal Abnormalities' parts I & II (16 mm. movie) 1980; 'Reproductive Cycles in the Human Female,' parts I & II 1981; 'Fertilization, Cleavage and Implantation,' 1982; also book chapters and over 60 publs. in scient. journs.; Fourth Annual Raymond C. Truex Distinguished Lectr. Award 1983; J.C.B. Grant Award, Candn. Assn. Anats. 1984; Fellow, Internat. Acad. Cytol.; Roy. Soc. of Med.; mem. Candn. Assn. Anats. (Pres. 1969–70); Candn. Fed. Biol. Socs. (Chrmn. 1970–71); Amer. Assn. Anats; Am. Assn. Clin. Anats. (Vice Pres. 1986–

87; Pres. Elect. 1987–89, Pres. 1989–91, Hon. Mem. 1994); Assoc. ed., Clin. Anat. 1988– ; Pres., Xth Internat. Symposium on Morphological Sciences 1990–91; Panamer Assn. Anats.; Teratology Soc.; Internat. Ctte. on the Morphological Sciences; Scient. Club Winnipeg (Secy. 1970–73); United Church; recreations: curling, golf, swimming; Clubs: Mississauga Golf & Country; Home and Office: 55 Harbour Sq., Ste. 3513, Toronto Ont. M5J 2L1.

**MOORE, Linda;** artistic director; b. Winnipeg, Man. 2 July 1950; d. Thane William and Marion Elizabeth (Barkwell) Smith; m. Victor (Sandy) s. Mary and Herbert M. 28 Oct. 1973; one d.: Lorca; ARTISTIC DIRECTOR, NEPTUNE THEATRE (HALIFAX) 1990– ; freelance stage director since 1980; Assoc. Artistic Dir., Manitoba Theatre Ctr. 1984–86; Asst. Dir., Stratford Festival 1985; Guest Instr./Dir., National Theatre Sch. of Canada 1987–90; Home: 2125 Brunswick St., Halifax, N.S.; Office: 1593 Argyle St., Halifax, N.S. B3J 2B2.

**MOORE, (James) Mavor,** O.C. (1973), B.A., D.Litt., LL.D.; playwright, actor, producer, critic, university professor; b. Toronto Toronto, Ont., 8 March 1919; s. Francis John and Dora (Mavor) M.; e. Univ. of Toronto Schs.; Univ. of Toronto, B.A. (1st Class Hons. in Philos. and English) 1941; D.Litt. (Hon.) York 1969; LL.D. (Hon.) Mt. Alison, 1982; m. 1stly, Darwina, d. Charles Faessler, Toronto, Ont., 14 Oct. 1943; four d., Dorothea, Rosalind, Marieli, Charlotte; 2ndly, Phyllis (Langstaff) Grosskurth, Toronto, Ont. 1969; 3rdly, Alexandra (Browning) 1982; one d., Jessica; Former Chairman, Canada Council; Gov., Nat. Theatre Sch.; Pres., Mavor Moore Productions, Ltd.; C.B.C. Feature Producer 1941–42; C.B.C. Internat. Service 1944–45; C.B.C. Pacific Region, Sr. Producer 1946; Chief Producer, Television 1950–54; U.N. Information Divn. 1947 and 1949 (New York); Chrmn., Radio Sec. UNESCO World Seminar on Educ., New York 1948; Producer-Dir. of over 50 stage plays incl. several first performances, some Candn.; served in2nd World War as Capt., Candn. Army Intelligence, Psychol. Warfare Offr.; winner of three Peabody Awards; author: 'And What Do YOU Do!' (verse) 1960; 'Reinventing Myself' (autobiography) 1994; author and composer of many plays incl. 'Who's Who' (stage) 1943; 'The Great Flood' (radio) 1947; 'Inside Out' (television) 1974; 'The Roncarelli Affairs' with Frank R. Scott (television) 1976; 'Six Plays by Mavor Moore' 1989; 'Customs, in Clues and Entrances' 1993; plays in translation: 'Yesterday the Children Were Dancing' (from the French of Gratien Gélinas) 1967; 'The Puppet Caravan' (from the French of Marie-Claire Blais) 1968; opera librettos: 'Lois Riel' music: Harry Somers, text with Jacques Languirand 1967; 'Abracadabra' music: Harry Freedman 1979; musicals: 'The Optimist' (radio 1952, stage 1956, television 1968); Sunshine Town' (radio 1954, stage 1956, television 1957); 'Belinda' music: John Fenwick (stage 1969, television 1976); 'A Christmas Carol' 1988; also author of numerous articles (Maclean's, The Arts in Canada) etc.; Producer-Dir. record breaking annual revue 'Spring Thaw' 1948–57, 1961–65; 'The Roncarelli Affair' 1973; mem. (1st) Bd. of Govs., Stratford Shakespearean Festival; Drama Critic and Columnist, Toronto 'Telegram' 1959–60; founding Chrmn., Can. Theatre Center 1960; founding Dir., Charlottetown Festival 1964; Chrmn., Cultural Comte., Nat. Centennial Conf. 1966–67; Gen. Dir., St. Lawrence Centre, Toronto 1965–69; founding Chrmn., Guild of Can. Playwrights 1977; apptd. mem. of Can. Council 1974; awarded Centennial Medal; mem. Candn. Actors Equity; Assn. Candn. TV & Radio Artists; recreation: music; Club: Arts and Letters; Address: 2826 Arbutus Rd., Victoria, B.C. V8N 5X5.

**MOORE, Richard E.;** marketing communications executive; b. Buffalo, N.Y. 25 March 1936; s. Jackson F. and Isabel E. M.; e. Lawrenceville Sch. 1954; m. Jane d. M.H. Ewing 28 Nov. 1958; children: Andrew, Jonathan, Mitchell; Internat. Vice-Pres., Internat. Management Group 1973–94; Acct. Extve., Ted Bates Advtg. (N.Y.) 1958–59; Mgr., TV Prod. & Advtg., Colgate Palmolive 1960–70; Pres., Century Broadcast Commun. 1971–72; Sr. Vice-Pres., TV, Ted Bates Advtg. 1972–73; Vice-Pres., Internat. Mngt. Group, New York/Toronto 1973–94; recreations: golf, music, painting; Clubs: Spring Island Old Tabby Links, Ahmic Lake Golf; Home: R.R. 6, Spring Island, Ridgeland, SC 29935 USA and Rocky Reef, Magnetawan, Ont. P0A 1P0.

**MOORE, S. Donald;** oil and mining company executive; PRESIDENT & DIRECTOR, PHOENIX CANADA OIL COMPANY LTD.; Pres. & Dir., Starrex Mining Corp. Ltd.; InterStar Mining Group Inc.; Dir., Parkland Industries Ltd.; Office: 70 York St., Ste. 1240, Toronto, Ont. M5J 1S9.

**MOORE, Sean,** M.B., B.Ch., B.A.O., F.R.C.P.(C); pathologist; educator; b. Belfast, N. Ireland 24 Nov. 1926; s. James Bernard and Eileen (McFadden) M.; e. elem. sch. Belfast 1940; St. Malachy's Coll. Belfast 1944; Belfast Tech. Coll. 1944–45; Queen's Univ. of Belfast M.B., B.Ch., B.A.O. 1950 (Hutchison Stewart Scholarship, Adami Medal in Pathol.); m. Cynthia d. Reginald Ernest Balch, Fredericton, N.B. 19 Oct. 1957; children: John Brian, Martha Ailish, Patrick Balch; CHRMN., DEPT. PATHOL., McGILL UNIV. 1984– ; Strathcona Prof. of Pathology 1985– ; internship Mater Infirmorum Hosp. Belfast, Royal Victoria Hosp. Montreal, Montreal Gen. Hosp. and St. Mary's Hosp; Asst. Prosector, Autopsy Service, Pathol. Inst. McGill Univ. 1953–54, Prosector 1956–57, Demonst. in Pathol. McGill 1955–56, Asst. Pathol. Montreal Gen. Hosp. and McGill 1958–61, Demonst. in Cytol. 1958, Lectr. 1959, Asst. Prof. 1964, Assoc. Prof. 1969–71, Assoc. Pathol. Montreal Gen. Hosp. 1961–69; Pathol.-in-Chief Jewish Gen. Hosp. Montreal 1969–71; Co-ord. Anatomic Pathol. and Prof. of Pathol. McMaster Univ. 1971–72, Chrmn. of Pathol. 1972–78; Dir. of Labs. McMaster Univ. Med. Centre 1972–84; mem. Senate McMaster Univ. 1982–84; McEachern Fellow Candn. Cancer Soc., Mem. Center for Cancer & Allied Diseases, Strang-Depew Clinic, New York 1957–58; mem. Prov. Lab. Adv. Comte. to Ministry of Health Ont.; mem. Task Force on Laboratory Services, Ont. Council of Health; Fellow, Council on Arteriosclerosis, Am. Heart Assn.; Ont. Assn. Pathols. (Council); Assn. Pathol. Chrmn. Can. (Secy.-Treas. 1974–77); Am. Assn. Pathols. & Bacteriols.; Fed. Am. Socs. Exper. Biol.; Internat. Acad. Pathol.; Candn. Cytology Council; Candn. Assn. Pathols. and other Candn. and Am. med. assns.; author numerous publs., presentations; Mng. Ed., Exp. Mol. Pathol.; recreations: reading, skiing; Home: 522 Clarke Ave., Westmount, Que. H3Y 3C9; Office: Lyman Duff Bldg., 3775 University St., Montreal, Que. H3A 2B4.

**MOORE, Thomas Charles,** B.A.(Hons.); transportation executive; b. Montreal, Que. 7 Dec. 1944; s. Thomas Albert and June (Howell) M. e. Michael Power H.S. 1965; St. Augustine's Seminary 1967; Laval Univ. 1968; Waterloo Lutheran Univ. B.A. (Hons.) 1971; McGill Univ. 1971–72; m. Bernardine d. Joseph and Rita Bohan 21 May 1977; children: Timmy, Jason, Matthew, Christopher; PRESIDENT, CAMVEC CORP. 1992– ; Jr. H.S. Teacher, Sudbury, Ont. 1967–69; Pres., T.C. Moore Transport 1971–77; Pres., AMJ Campbell Van Lines (Canada's largest moving company) 1977– ; Pres., AMJ Campbell Holdings; Mid-Vader Developments; Partnership with Subach Ltd. (Swiss Chalet franchises: Dartmouth and Truro); Dir., Healthview Ltd.; Venture Inn; 8161238 Nova Scotia Ltd.; Guaranteed Real Estate Partnership; misc. real estate investments; Certificate of Merit for Entrepreneurship, Canada Awards for Business Excellence; Mem., Jr. Achievers of Canada (Volunteer Teacher); Bd. of Trade of Metro Toronto; subject of Canadian Business Mag. May 1989 and 'The New Entrepreneurs: 80 Canadian Success Stories' by Allan Gould; recreations: skiing, racquetball; clubs: Canadian Ski Instructor; Office: 1190 Meyerside Dr., Mississauga, Ont. L5T 1R7.

**MOORE, Tracey;** actress; b. Edmonton, Alta. 17 Jan. 1963; d. David John and Barbara Jean M.; e. Univ. of Toronto; Univ. of Calgary; Univ. of Victoria; Banff School of Fine Arts; one d.: Eleanora; professional actress in Canada for more than 10 years; featured vocalist on five Candn. recording albums, the last of which 'Mozart's Magic Fantasy' won 1 1990 Juno; stage credits incl.: 'Dorothy,' Wizard of Oz (Kansas), 'Anne,' Anne of Green Gables (Charlottetown), 'Jenny,' Shenandoah (Broadway, NYC), 'Gilda,' Rigoletto (Theatre Passe Muraille), 'Polly Reachum,' Three Penny Opera (Candn. Stage), 'Gooch Mame,' Rainbow Stage; Artistic Dir., Fishnet Players (Alta.); film roles incl.: 'Defy Gravity' & 'The White Room'; has been referred to as Canada's most popular voice having done leading voices on more than 50 cartoon series; Dora nominee, best actress in musical 1987, '89, '90; Juno Award 1990; Teacher, Music Theatre, Dalton College (NYC); recreations: horsebackriding, music; Home: 604 Shaw St., Toronto, Ont. M6G 3L6; Office: c/o Jordan Associates, Suite 401, 615 Yonge St., Toronto, Ont. M4Y 1Z5.

**MOORE, Victor Alan,** B.A.Sc., P.Eng.; professional engineer; b. East York, Ont. 24 Aug. 1930; s. Victor Gordon and Ruby Agnes (Brown) M.; e. Univ. of Toronto B.A.Sc. 1953; m. Leona d. Alvin and Elizabeth Moore 31 Aug. 1957; children: Carole, Susan, Jennifer; Manager, Generator Engineering, G.E. Hydro, General Electric Canada 1971–93, retired 1993; joined C.G.E. 1953, test course, Mechanical Eng. Design – Hydro Generators 1954–61, Seconded to AEG – Berlin 1958–59; Design Engineering, Turbine Generators 1961–69, Chief Design Engineer 1969–71; mem., C.S.M.E.; A.S.M.E.; A.P.E.O.; Chrmn., E.I.C., Peterborough Branch 1979–81; technical papers relating to generator tech. for various industry and learned societies; Candn. Representative for CIGRE Study Ctte. II, Rotating Machines 1979–91; recipient, A.P.E.O. Engineering Medal 1982; Elder, St. Andrew's Church, Peterborough; recreations: skiing, reading, music appreciation; Home: 490 Gordon Ave., Peterborough, Ont. K9J 6G8.

**MOORE, Victor Campbell,** B.A.; diplomat; b. Victoria, B.C. 25 Jan. 1918; s. Lt. Col. Frederick William Louis and Ruby Ermine (Jackson) M.; e. Cloverdale Pub. Sch. and Mount View High Sch., Saanich, B.C.; Victoria (B.C.) Coll.; Univ. of B.C., B.A. 1940; Georgia Augusta Univ., Germany, 1947–48; m. Kerstin Margaret, d. Ing. Cyrus and Margit (Hedberg) Odemar, Sweden; children: Yan Paul, Mrs Catherine A.V. Keet; joined Dept. of External Affairs, Ottawa, as Foreign Service Officer 1948; 3rd Secy. Candn. Embassy, Bonn, 1951; 2nd Secy. 1952; Chargé d'affaires, a.i., Vienna, 1954; Advisor, ECOSOC Session, N.Y., 1956; 2nd Secy., Moscow, 1956; 1st Secy. 1958; 1st Secy., Stockholm, 1958; Acting High Commr., Karachi 1960–62; Canadian Rep. Indus Waters Agreement, Karachi 1960; charge d'affaires/Counsellor, The Hague 1962–65; World Politics Conf., Holland, 1965; Ambassador, Head of Candn. Del. to Internat. Comn. for Supervision and Control in Viet Nam, (Saigon and Hanoi) 1965–67; Depy. Head, Office of Econ. Affairs, Ottawa, 1967–68; Advisor to Candn. Dels. to Commonwealth Finance Mins. Mtgs. 1967, 1971, 1974; Heads of Gov't Mtgs. 1973, 1975 and 1979; Sr. Officials Mtgs. 1972, 1974, 1976, and to World Bank/IMF Conf. 1967, to Carribean Devpt. Bank 1970 and 1971; Chrm., Interdepartmental Comte. on Commonwealth Caribbean-Canada Relations, 1967–68; Candn. Rep. to 5th Session of UNDP Governing Council, N.Y., Jan. 1968; Cdn. Del. to Maputo Conf. on Zimbabwe and Namibia 1977; Advisor to organizing comte. of Conf. on Comwel and NG bodies, Dalhousie Univ. 1976; High Commr. to Jamaica 1968–72 and Commissioner to Belize and to Bahamas; Dir., Commonwealth Div., Ext. Affairs, Ottawa, 1972–76; 1976–79, High Commr. to Zambia and Malawi and Amb. to Mozambique; Bd. of Gov., Commonwealth Africa Youth Devel. Centre; Cdn. rep. to Conference of NATO Defence Coll. Commandants, Rome, 1981, 1982 and 1983; NATO Symposium, Nat. Def. Univ., Washington, D.C., 1982 and 1983; Depy. Commandant & Dir. of Studies, Nat. Defence Coll., Kingston. Ont. 1979–83; IISS Annual Conf. (East-West Relations in the 1980's), Ottawa 1983; Consultant, Internat. Relations, Trade, Develop. Co-op. 1983–89; served with The Candn. Scottish Regt. (Princess Royals) NPAM 1938–39; C.O.T.C., Univ. of B.C.; Candn. Scottish Regt. (AF), Can., Eng., 1940–43; Seaforth Highlanders of Can., Italy 1943–44; Candn. Scottish (RF); Mentioned in Despatches; mem., Nat. Gallery Assn.; Nat. Council; Royal Commonwealth Society; Arch. Soc. of Jamaica; Zambia Wildlife Conservation Society; Malawi Fauna Preservation Society; Candn. Inst. of Intnl. Affairs; Anglican; recreations: swimming, literature, music, art; Clubs: Fort Frontenac Officers' Mess, Kingston, Ont.; Address: 185 William St., Kingston, Ont. K7L 2E1.

**MOOS, Walter Anton;** art dealer; b. Germany 6 Sept. 1926; s. Frederick and Clara (Kadisch) M.; e. Ecole Superieure de Comm. Geneva 1946; New Sch. for Social Rsch. New York 1948–51; m. Martha Wegmuller 1962; two s. Michel Andre, David Alfred; OWNER, GALLERY MOOS 1959– (contemporary Candn., Am. and Eur. painting and sculpture); introduced many artists incl. Karel Appel, Sorel Etrog and Ken Danby; pioneered ltd. ed. art book 'Ken Danby' by Paul Duval; mem. Candn. Eskimo Arts Council 1974–82; Trustee, Gershon Iskowitz Found. 1986–90; mem. Profl. Art Dealers Assn. Can. Inc. (Pres. 1971–78); Office: 622 Richmond St. W., Toronto, Ont. M5V 1Y9.

**MORAN, Michael Francis,** B.Sc., Ph.D.; university professor, scientist; b. Toronto, Ont. 9 July 1960; s. John Henry and Mary Katherine (Halladay) M.; e. G.S. Vanier S.S. 1978 (Ontario Scholar); Univ. of Western Ont. B.Sc. 1982, Ph.D. 1987; m. Mary Kay d. Felix and Joan Quinn 28 Feb. 1987; children: Joan Katherine, Kathleen Margaret, Abigail Quinn; ASST. PROF., BANTING & BEST DEPT. OF MEDICAL RESEARCH, UNIV. OF TORONTO 1990– ; Grad. Student of Biochem. & Ont. Grad. Scholar, Cancer Research Lab., Univ. of Western Ont. 1982–86; Postdoctoral Fellow, Mt. Sinai Hosp. Research Inst., Div. of Molecular & Devel. Biology 1986–90; Fellow, Nat. Cancer Inst. 1987–90; Asst. Prof., Dept. of Molecular & Medical Genetics, Univ. of Toronto 1991– ; Research Scientist, National Cancer Inst. of Canada 1991– ; Mem., Candn. Biochem. Soc.; Am. Soc. for Microbiol.; Am. Assn. for the Advancement of Science; New York Acad. of Sciences; author/co-author of num. pubns. on molecular mechanisms of DNA damage & repair, oncogenes & signal transduction; Home: 1806 Gerrard St. E., Toronto, Ont. M4L 2B4; Office: C.H. Best Inst., 112 College St., Toronto, Ont. M5G 1L6.

**MORAND, Peter,** B.Sc., Ph.D.; research executive; b. Montreal, Que. 11 Feb. 1935; s. Frank and Rose Alice (Fortier) M.; e. Bishop's Univ. B.Sc. (Hons.) 1956; McGill Univ. Ph.D. 1959; m. Dawn d. Dorothy and Donald McKell 10 Oct. 1957; children: Clifford, Tanya; PRES., NATURAL SCIENCES & ENGINEERING RESEARCH COUNCIL 1990– ; NATO Postdoct. Fellow, Imperial College (U.K.) 1959–60; Sr. Rsch. Chemist, Ayerst Labs. 1961–63; Asst. Prof., Univ. of Ottawa 1963–67; Asst. Vice-Rector, Academic & Assoc. Prof. 1968–71; Dean, Fac. of Science & Engr. 1976–81; Dir., Rsch. Services & Prof. of Chemistry 1984–87; Vice Rector, Univ. Relations & Devel. & Prof. of Chem. 1987–90; Dir. & Vice-Pres. of Bd., Ottawa Virology Inc. 1990; Mem., Fisher Scientific Biotechnology Council 1989–90; Scientific Adv. Ctte., ARTEC Canada 1988; Bd. Dir., IDEA Corp. 1982–86; D.C.L. (Honoris Causis), Bishop's Univ. 1991; Trustee, B.C. Applied Systems Inst. 1990– ; Bd. Mem., Ottawa-Carleton Econ. Devel. Corp. 1988– ; Ottawa-Carleton Rsch. Inst. 1987–90; Inst. for Chem. Science & Technology 1989–90; Bd. Chrmn., Ottawa Life Sciences Technology Park 1989–90; Bd. Dir., Ottawa Health Sciences Centre Inc. 1987–90; author of over 80 articles in refereed journals & 20 patents; recreations: tennis; clubs: Rideau, Cercle Universitaire; Home: 26 Central Ave., Ottawa, Ont. K2P 0M9; Office: Suite 501, 200 Kent St., Ottawa, Ont. K1A 1H5.

**MORANIS, Stephen M.,** B.Comm., M.B.A., FRI, CMR; real estate executive; b. Kitchener, Ont. 22 Feb. 1950; s. Jules and Sadie (Smith) M.; e. Univ. of Toronto, B.Comm. 1973, M.B.A. 1974; PRES., SADIE MORANIS LIMITED, REALTOR; Dir., Faculty of Management Alumni Assn., Univ. of Toronto; Past Pres., Toronto Real Estate Bd. 1990; Dir., Canadian Real Estate Assn. 1991, '93, '94; Clubs: Toronto Cricket Skating & Curling Club; National Golf; Midland Golf & Country; Great Lakes Cruising Club; Office: 801 York Mills Rd., Suite 101, Don Mills, Ont. M3B 1X7.

**MORASH, Frederick Douglas,** C.M.A., F.C.M.A.; communications executive; b. Halifax, N.S. 5 May 1947; s. Arnold Cameron and Elizabeth Shirley (Kidston) M.; e. B.C. Silver H.S. 1965; Dalhousie Univ.; Certified Management Account, C.M.A. 1972; m. Carole d. John and Delories Mahoney 15 Aug. 1970; children: Karen, Jennifer; PRESIDENT & C.E.O., THE ISLAND TELEPHONE CO. LTD. 1992– ; Accounting Trainee, Maritime Telegraph & Telephone Co. Ltd. (MT&T) 1966; progressed through var. junior & mid-mngt. positions & apptd. Gen. Mgr., Admin. 1984; Comptroller, MT&T & Island Telephone 1987; Vice-Pres., Finance, MT&T Mobile 1990; Vice-Pres., Island Telephone Co. Ltd. 1991; Dir., Schneider Corporation; Dir., Stentor Resource Centre Inc.; Fellow, Soc. of Mngt. Accountants of Canada 1991; Vice-Chrmn., Holland College Found., Inc.; Former Dir., Camp Hill Medical Ctr.; Soc. of Management Accountants of Canada; Home: 105 England Circle, Charlottetown, P.E.I. C1E 1V7; Office: P.O. Box 820, Charlottetown, P.E.I. C1A 7M1.

**MORAWETZ, Oskar,** C.M., D.Mus.; composer; professor; b. Czechoslovakia 17 Jan. 1917; s. Richard and Frieda (Glaser) M.; e. High Sch., Prague (1927–35); Univ. of Prague, 1935–37; came to Canada, June 1940; Univ. of Toronto, B.Mus. 1944, D.Mus. 1953; PROF. OF MUSIC, UNIV. OF TORONTO; his works performed on trans-Can. concerts of CBC; with conductors abroad such as Zubin Mehta, Seiji Ozawa, Andrew Davis, Charles Dutoit, Rafael Kubelik, William Steinberg, Sir Adrian Boult, Walter Susskind, Karel Ancerl, Kazuyoshi Akiyama, Kurt Masur, Sir Charles Mackerras; and with Canadian conductors; his orchestral compositions are played by Candn. orchestras and by orchestras in Europe, N. & S. America, Australia and Asia; his 'Divertimento for Strings' was conducted by Dr. Boyd Neel at Brussels World Fair (1958), 'Overture to a Fairy Tale' conducted by Walter Susskind and his 'Fantasy for Piano,' played by Glenn Gould have been premiered at Stratford Music Festival; his choral comp. 'Keep Us Free' chosen to precede (on CBC) the Queen's speech at state dinner in Ottawa; 'Memorial to Martin Luther King' commissioned by Mstislav Rostropovich and recorded by Zara Nelsova and performed by 16 other cellists incl. Yo Yo Ma; with New York Philharmonic under baton of Kurt Masur 1993; 'Psalm 22' for voice and orchestra commissioned and premiered by Maureen Forrester in 1984 with Andrew Davis conducting the Toronto Symphony; first composer to receive a Can. Council comn. for a work premiered by Toronto Symphony Orchestra; has written works for full orchestra, string orchestra, piano, voice, violin, viola, cello and string quartet, flute, oboe, clarinet, bassoon, french horn, trumpet, tuba and harp; also music for several motion pictures; many recordings on Columbia, Capitol, Melodiya and RCA records, C.B.C., and Candn. Center Discs; awards incl. Canada Council Fellowships 1961, 1967, 1974; SOCAN Award (String Quartet No. 1) 1944, (Sonata Tragica) 1945; Zubin Mehta Award (Piano Concerto No. 1) 1961; Critics Award, Internat. Competition Contemporary Music, Cava di Tirreni, Italy (Sinfonietta for winds and percussion) 1966; Segal Foundation Special Award (From the Diary of Anne Frank) 1971; for his great contribution to Canadian music, the CBC paid tribute to him in 1983 by issuing an anthology of his music on seven records; Candn. Acad. of Recording Arts & Sciences "Best Classical Composition in 1989" Award ('Harp Concerto') 1990; Juno Award for 'Harp Concerto' 1990; first composer to receive the Order of Ontario 1987; Member, Order of Canada 1989; mem., Candn. League of Composers; Composers, Authors & Publ. Assn. Can.; Home: 59 Duncannon Dr., Toronto, Ont. M5P 2M3.

**MORCOS, Gamila,** Ph.D., university professor emeritus; b. Assiout, Egypt 8 Jan. 1928; d. Tawfik Nan Roweis and Nuzha Yassa Boulos; e. Bryn Mawr Summer Inst. for Women in Higher Education Admin., Certificate, 1978; Univ. Paris (Sorbonne), Ph.D., 1954; Ecole Normale Supérieure de St-Cloud, France, Diploma, 1954; children: Chaker; Nagui; Sameh; PROFESSOR EMERITUS, FACULTÉ SAINT-JEAN, UNIV. OF ALBERTA 1993– (Prof. 1980–93 and Dean of Faculté 1980–85); High Sch. Teacher 1950; Asst., then Assoc. Prof., Ain-Chams Univ. (Cairo) 1957; Asst., then Assoc. Prof., Laurentian Univ. 1967; Dean of Humanities, Laurentian Univ. 1975–80; author books and several articles on European lit. and on Education published in scholarly journals; awarded APFUCC Prize in Literature 1984, 1990; Officer, l'Ordre des Palmes Académiques 1984; recipient, Commemorative Medal of Honor, Am. Biographical Inst. 1987; mem., The Internat. Order of Merit; Assn. francophone internat. de recherche scientifique en éducation; Assn. internat. de Docteurs des Univ. de France; Assn. Internat. des Critiques Littéraires; Intnl. Comparative Literature Assn.; World Assn. for Educ. Rsch.; Assn. Candnne.-Française pour l'Avancement des Sciences; Assn. des professeurs de français des Univs. et Colls. du Canada; Life Fellow, Internat. Biographical Assn.; Home: #2, 9529 – 87th Ave., Edmonton, Alta. T6C 1K4.

**MORDEN, Ven. John Grant,** D.D., D.Th., LL.D. (Ang.); professor and college principal emeritus; b. London, Eng., 17 Aug. 1925; s. Lt. Col. Walter Grant, J.P., M.P. and Doris (Henshaw) M.; e. Royal Masonic Schs., Bushy, Herts., Eng., 1940; Univ. of Toronto, B.A. 1949; Wycliffe Coll., Toronto, L.Th. 1952, B.D. 1953, D.D. 1963; Union Theol. Semy., New York, S.T.M. 1954; Gen. Theol. Semy., New York, D.Th. 1961; Huron Coll., London, D.D. 1985; Trinity Coll., Toronto, D.D. 1986; St. John's Coll., Winnipeg D.D. 1989; Univ. of Western Ont. LL.D. 1992; m. Elizabeth Grace, d. James A. Tannahill, 7 Sept. 1949; children: Ann, Margaret, James (deceased), Mary, Peter; ARCHDEACON EMERITUS, DIOCESE OF HURON 1990– ; Archdeacon, Diocese of Huron 1968–90; Prof. of Theology, Huron Coll. 1962–90; Principal 1962–84; Principal Emeritus, 1984– ; mem. Corp. and Extve. Bd., Huron Coll. 1961–90; Lifetime Hon. Mem., Corporation of Huron Coll. 1990– ; mem. Gen. Synod, Anglican Ch. of Can. 1961–88 (and mem. Sub-Comte. World Religions 1980–90); with Cassidy's Ltd. as Clerk, 1940–43; Asst. Curate, Annunciation and All Soul's Parish, Toronto, 1951–53; St. Bartholomew's, White Plains, N.Y., 1953–56; Rector of St. Matthews, Toronto, 1956–57; Registrar and Asst. Prof. of Theol., Huron Coll., 1957; Prof. of Theol. and Vice Prin., 1961; served with R.C.A.F. 1943–46; Address: 286 Steele St., London, Ont. N6A 2L1.

**MORDEN, John Reid,** B.A.; public servant; b. Hamilton, Ont. 17 June 1941; s. Warren Wilbert and Isabelle Gemmell (Reid) M.; e. Monklands H.S. 1958; McGill Univ. 1958–59; Dalhousie Univ., B.A. 1962; Dalhousie Univ. Law Sch. 1962–63; m. Margaret d. James and Elizabeth Keens 27 June 1964; two s.: Michael J.W., Geoffrey R.; DEPUTY MINISTER OF FOREIGN AFFAIRS, GOVT. OF CANADA 1991– ; various assignments, Dept. of External Affairs incl. Karachi, New York, Geneva, Tokyo 1963–84; Min. and Dep. Permanent Rep. to the U.N., N.Y. 1980–82; Asst. Under-Secy., Sector Policy & External Affairs 1982–83; Asst. Dep. Min., Native Claims, Dept. of Indian & N. Affairs 1984–85; Trade Policy & Econ. Affairs, External Affairs 1985–86; Asst. Sec. to the Cabinet, Fgn. & Defence Affairs 1986–87; Dir., Candn. Security Intelligence Service 1987–91; Bd. of Dir., Candn. Gen. Standards Bd. 1985–86; International Advisory Council, York Univ.; Commander, Order of St. Lazarus of Jerusalem; recreations: photography, music, ballet, reading; Clubs: Rideau, Five Lakes; Home: Ottawa, Ont.; Office: Ottawa, Ont. K1A 0G2.

**MORDEN, Hon. John W.,** B.A., LL.B.; judge; b. Toronto, Ont. 26 July 1934; s. Hon. Kenneth Gibson and Elizabeth Helen (Marquis) M.; e. Upper Can. Coll. Toronto 1952; Univ. of Toronto, Trinity Coll. B.A. 1956, Faculty of Law LL.B. 1959; m. Joyce Gillies, d. late Hon. G. Peter Campbell 6 Sept. 1958; two d., Mary Catherine, Martha Elizabeth; ASSOC. CHIEF JUSTICE OF ONTARIO 1990– ; called to Bar of Ont. 1961; practiced law Day, Wilson, Campbell 1961–73; Counsel Royal Comn. Inquiry Civil Rights 1964–71; Mem., Senate, Univ. of Toronto, 1968–72; Asst. Counsel H. of C. Special Comte. on Statutory Instruments 1969; mem. Faculty Council Faculty of Law Univ. of Toronto since 1971; Editor, Land Compensation Reports, 1971–73; Bencher Law Soc. Upper Can. 1971–73; Justice, High Court of Justice, Supreme Court of Ont. 1973–78; Justice, Court of Appeal for Ont. 1978–90; mem. Statutory Powers Procedure Rules Comte (Ont.) 1975–83; Mem., Adv. Panel, Consultative Group on Research and Education in Law apptd. by the SSHRC, 1980–82; Bd. of Knox Coll. 1980–86; Bd. of Trustees, Toronto Sch. of Theology 1986–92; Kappa Alpha; Presbyterian; Clubs: University; Toronto Hunt; Home: 12 Garfield Ave., Toronto, Ont. M4T 1E7; Office: Osgoode Hall, 130 Queen St. W., Toronto, Ont. M5H 2N5.

**MORDEN, Larry,** B.A.; food industry executive; b. Sudbury, Ont. 16 Aug. 1944; s. Walter Rowland and Catherine (Pigeau) M.; e. Univ. of Windsor B.A. 1967; m. Beverley d. Russ and Mary Richards 28 June 1985; children: Matthew, Jennifer; CORPORATE VICE-PRESIDENT, AULT FOODS LIMITED 1985– ; Retailing Management, Hudson's Bay Co. 1967–69; Compensation Mngt., Internat. Nickel 1969–73; Dir., Org. Planning Compensation, Canada Permanent 1973–76; Dir., Admin., Reed Paper 1976–81; Senior Consultant / Partner, Pioneer Steel, Wm. M. Mercer 1981–85; Mem., Bd. of Trade, Metro. Toronto; H.R.; P.A.O.; Internat. H.R. Planning Assoc.; associated with 'Kid's Help Phone' Canada; recreations: tennis, skiing; clubs: Boulevard; Office: 405 The West Mall, Toronto, Ont. M9C 5J1.

**MORE, David John;** painter; muralist; cartoonist; b. Aberdeen, Scot. 11 Sept. 1947; s. Charles George Robb and Helen Barbara (Mackenzie) M.; e. Alta. Coll. of Art Dip. in Painting 1972; m. Yvette d. Hilaire and Grace Brideau 7 Apl. 1984; Med. Graphics Artist, Univ. of Calgary 1973–74; Can. Council Arts Grant in Painting 1974; part-time Instr. in Painting, Design and Drawing, Alta. Coll. of Art, Calgary 1975–77; full-time painter, illustrator Calgary and Cobble Hill, B.C. 1978–84, Red Deer, Alta. 1984– , also part-time instr. Red Deer Coll.; outdoor murals: Chemainus, B.C. 1983; Bashaw, Alta., 1987; Welland, Ont., 1988; Stony Plain, Alta., 1990; Fort Macleod, Alta. 1993; National Museum Tour Exhib. of Oil Paintings (titled) 'Forest - Fade to Silent' 1990–93; co-author (with Eric Nicol) and illustrator (satire) 'Joy of Hockey' 1978; 'Joy of Football' 1980; 'Golf: The Agony and the Ectasy' 1982; 'Tennis: It Serves You Right' 1984; 'The U.S. or Us/What's the Difference, eh?' 1986; author and illustrator (satire) '101 Ways to Recycle a Hockey Stick' 1992; illustrator (young readers) 'Chinook Christmas' (by Rudy Wiebe) 1992; Address: 5708, 47 A Ave., Red Deer, Alta. T4N 6M2.

**MORE, Roger Allan,** B.Sc., M.B.A., Ph.D., P.Eng.; university professor; b. Edmonton, Alta. 19 March 1942; s. Albert Alexander and Irene Goodman (Jones) M.; e. Univ. of Alberta B.Sc. 1964; Western Bus. Sch., Univ. of Western Ont. M.B.A. 1970, Ph.D. 1974; m. Nancy Carolyn d. Lester and Margaret Brown 15 June 1985; one d.: Mary Kate; FACULTY, WESTERN BUSINESS SCH., UNIV. OF WESTERN ONT. 1975– ; Process Engr., Celanese 1964–68; Faculty, Harvard Bus. Sch. 1974–75; Pres., Roger More & Assoc., Mngt. Cons.; Dir., GSW Inc., Construction Products & Heating Products divs.; Former Dir., Laurier Life Insur.; consultant to num. opns. worldwide; Holder, Hewlett-Packard Chair, Univ. of Western Ont.; author: 'Improving the Adoption of New Technology' 1990; Ed. Bd. Mem., 'J. of Product Innovation Management'; recreations: golf, tennis; Office: The National Centre for Management Rsch. & Development, Western Business School, Univ. of Western Ont., London, Ont. N6A 3K7.

**MOREHOUSE, Ralph Ernest,** P.Ag., B.S.A., M.S.A.; agrologist/public servant; b. Centreville, Digby Co., N.S. 29 March 1928; s. Frederick A. and Lillian B. (Graham) M.; e. Central H.S., New Waterford, N.S.; N.S. Agric. Coll., Assoc; Univ. of B.C., B.S.A. 1953, M.S.A. 1968; m. Pauline d. Archibald and Pearl Nauss 10 July 1954; children: Sheri, Kathryn; Deputy Minister, N.S. Dept. of Agric. & Mktg. 1986–91; Agric. Rep., N.S. Dept. of Agric. & Mktg. 1953–64; Reg. Agric. Rep. 1964–74; Reg. Extension Supvr. 1974–75; Chief Dir. of Opns. 1975–86; Mem., Atlantic Agric. Hall of Fame; Candn. Agric. Hall of Fame; several past extve. posts; Mem., United Ch. of Can.; recreations: barbershop quartet singing; Home: 27 Rockmanor Dr., Bedford, N.S. B4A 2V3.

**MORENCY, Pierre,** B.A., L.ès L.; writer; b. Lauzon, Qué. 8 May 1942; s. Louis and Laurette (Croussett) M.; e. Coll. de Lévis B.A. 1963; Univ. Laval L.ès L. 1966; profl. writer since 1967; freelance writer and animator CBC since 1967; author numerous publs. poetry, theatre, radio progs., nature and bird documentaries; most recent books incl. 'Effets Personnels' poetry 1986; 'Quand Nous Serons' poetry 1988; 'Les Passeuses' theatre 1976; 'L'Oeil Americain' récits 1989; 'Lumière des Oiseaux' récits 1992; 'A Season for Birds' selected poems 1991; 'The Eye is an Eagle' short stories 1992; recipient numerous awards incl. Québec-Paris 1988; Alain-Granbois 1988; François-Sommer' 1990; Duvernay 1991; Address: 2435 rue Adolphe-Chapleau, Sillery, Que. G1T 1M5.

**MOREY, Carl Reginald,** A.R.C.T., Mus.Bac., M.M., Ph.D.; musicologist and educator; b. Toronto, Ont. 14 July 1934; s. Reginald Donald and Julia Beatrice (Mabey) M.; e. Oakwood Collegiate 1953; Univ. of Toronto Mus.Bac. 1957; Indiana Univ. M.M. 1961, Ph.D. 1965; m. late Lorna Dalton 2 June 1960; one d., Rachel Adriana; JEAN A. CHALMERS PROF., FACULTY OF MUSIC, UNIV. OF TORONTO 1991– ; Dir., Inst. for Canadian Music (Faculty of Music); Assoc. Prof. and founding Head Dept. of Music, Univ. of Windsor 1964–70; Prof. of Musicology present Univ. 1970– ; Dean, Faculty of Music and Chrmn. Grad. Dept. of Music, Univ. of Toronto 1984–90; Visiting Prof. Colorado Coll. 1966, 1969 and Indiana Univ. 1970; Vice-Pres., Candn. Music Council 1988–90; broadcaster CBC Stereo/Radio; author: articles in 'Music and Letters'; 'Acta Musicologica'; 'Opera Canada'; 'U. of T. Quarterly'; 'New Grove Dictionary of Music and Musicians'; 'Encyclopedia of Music in Canada'; 'Célébration'; 'Musical Canada'; mem. Candn. Univ. Music Soc.; Internat. Musicological Soc.; Am. Musicological Soc.; recreations: sailing, swimming; Home: 540 Palmerston Blvd., Toronto, Ont. M6G 2P5; Office: Faculty of Music, Univ. of Toronto, Toronto, Ont. M5S 1A1.

**MORFITT, George Lyell,** B.Comm., F.C.A.; chartered accountant; b. West Vancouver, B.C. 11 May 1936; s. Wilson George and Eleanor May (Darling) M.; e. West. Vanc. H.S. 1953; Modesto Jr. Coll., Calif.; Univ. of B.C., B.Comm. 1958; m. Peggy d. Ruby and Clint Wilson 24 May 1959; children: Graham, Russell, Gillian, Angela; AUDITOR GEN. OF B.C. 1988– ; articled student/audit supvr., Clarkson Gordon & Co. 1958–67; Extve. Vice-Pres. & Chief Fin. Offr., Diamond Group of Cos. 1967–87; Mem., B.C. Sports Hall of Fame & Mus.; Cadboro Bay Un. Ch.; Beta Theta Pi Fraternity; former Chrmn., Universities Council of B.C., Univ. of B.C. Bd. of Govs.; former Pres., Inst. of Chartered Accountants of B.C.; author of numerous reports; recreations: sports (squash, jogging), stamp collecting; clubs: Hollyburn Country, Evergreen Squash, The Nautilus; Home: 2380 Queenswood Dr., Victoria, B.C. V8N 1X3; Office: 8 Bastion Sq., Victoria, B.C. V8V 1X4.

**MORGAN, Alan Vivian,** B.Sc., M.Sc., Ph.D.; educator; b. Barry, Glamorgan, Wales 29 Jan. 1943; s. George Vivian Williams and Sylvia Nesta (Atkinson) Morgan and (by adoption) Nicholas Gregory Morgan (deceased); came to Can. 1964; e. Univ. of Leicester, Eng. B.Sc. 1964; Univ. of Alta., Calgary M.Sc. 1966; Univ. of Birmingham, Eng. Ph.D. 1970; Univ. of W. Ont. and Univ. of Waterloo Post-Doctoral Fellow 1970–71; m. Marion Anne d. Henry James Medhurst 14 June 1966; children: Siân Kristina, Alexis John; PROF., DEPT. OF EARTH SCIENCES, UNIV. OF WATERLOO 1985– ; Asst. Prof. 1971–78, Assoc. Prof. 1978–85; Visiting Prof., Univ. of Seattle 1978; Visiting Scientist, U.S. Geol. Survey 1979; Assoc. Prof. Earth Sciences & Dept. of Man-Envt. Studies, Univ. of Waterloo, 1978–82; Visiting Prof., Univ. of Kiel, Germany 1982; Visiting Prof., Univ. of Canterbury, N.Z. 1986; Sec.-Gen. XII INQUA Congress 1983–87; Pres., Candn. Quaternary Assoc. 1987–89; Scientific Co-ordinator, Global Change, Geological Survey of Can. 1990–92; Extve.-Dir., Candn. Geoscience Counc. 1988–94 (mem. 1977–83); Co-chair, Proxy Data Resource Group; Roy-Soc. Canada Global Change Programme 1988–92; Mem., Roy-Soc. Canada Ctte. on Public Awareness of Sci. 1989– ; author over 60 scientific papers and book chapters on Quaternary geol.; dir. and producer 'The Heimaey Eruption: Iceland, 1973' (short documentary film); mem., Geol. Assn. of Can. (Secy-Treas., Councillor, mem. Extve. Comte.) 1975–83; Sigma Xi; Brit. Quaternary Assn.; Pres., Amer. Quat. Assn. 1990–92 (Pres.-elect 1988–90); recreations: travel, natural hist., photography; Office: Waterloo, Ont. N2L 3G1.

**MORGAN, Alison,** B.Com., M.A.; university administrator; b. Kingston, Ont. 13 Apl. 1939; d. William Archibald and Jean Isobel (Easton) Mackintosh; e. Kingston Coll. & Vocational Inst. 1956; Neuchatel Jr. Coll. Switzerland; Queen's Univ. B.Com. 1961; Univ. of W. Ont. M.A. 1969; Univ. of Chicago 1970–72; m. Ieuan s. Edward and Nina Morgan 17 June 1961; children: Karen Sian, Owen William Rhys; REGISTRAR, QUEEN'S UNIV. 1988– ; joined present Univ. as Supr. Instr. Profl. Courses Sch. of Bus. 1961–63, Instr. in Econ. 1978– , Sr. Adm. Asst. in Econ. 1979–84, Sec. of Univ. and of Bd. Trustees 1985–88; National Ctte., Queen's Campaign 1989–93; Rsch. Asst. in Econ. McGill Univ. 1965–67, Harvard Univ. 1963–65; Agent de recherche et de planification, Ministère de l'agric. gouvernement du Qué. 1974–75, Office de planification et du développement Qué. 1975–78; Visiting Asst. Prof. of Econ. Univ. of B.C. 1984–85; Cons. Gouvernement du Qué. 1978–79; mem. Community Ed. Bd., Whig Standard, Kingston 1988–89; mem. Bd. of Dirs., Ban Righ Centre 1988– ; Kingston Tai Chi Assn. 1993– ; author several publs. applied econometrics and income distribution; recreation: skiing; Office: Kingston, Ont. K7L 3N6.

**MORGAN, Brian Gerald,** B.A., M.A., LL.B.; lawyer; b. Lethbridge, Alta. 27 Apr. 1950; s. Frederick John and Audrey (Boyd) M.; e. Univ. of Toronto B.A. 1973; Oxford Univ. (Rhodes scholar) B.A. 1976, M.A. 1979; Dalhousie Univ. LL.B. 1977; m. Ann d. Glen and Marjory Wilton 12 July 1974; three s. Andrew, Eric, Colin; one d. Catherine; PARTNER, OSLER, HOSKIN & HARCOURT 1983– ; articled as law clk. to Mr. Justice Dickson 1977–78; called to Bar of Ont. 1979; Assoc. Lawyer with present firm 1979; sec. Cand. Found. for Legal Rsch. 1982–85; Special Lectr. in Law Univ. of Toronto 1980–87; Trustee, Candn. Rhodes Found. 1981– (Vice Pres. 1986–92, Pres. 1992– ); author various legal articles, papers and chapters legal publs. particularly constitutional, adm. and comm. law; United Ch.; recreations: squash, tennis, sailing, golf, swimming; Clubs: RCYC; Muskoka Lakes Golf and Country; Home: 167 Douglas Dr., Toronto, Ont. M4W 2B6; Office: (P.O. Box 50) Suite 6600, First Canadian Pl., Toronto, Ont. M5X 1B8.

**MORGAN, E. Louise;** investment executive; b. P.E.I. 10 March 1929; d. Edson White and Annie Florence (Larkin) Dalzell; e. Summerside Comm. Coll. Dipl.; div.; children: Maxwell Scott, Vanessa Louise, Jonathan Andrew; CHRMN. CANADIAN GENERAL INVESTMENTS LTD. and THIRD CANADIAN GENERAL INVESTMENT TRUST LTD. 1989– ; Pres. Maxwell Meighen & Associates Ltd., Corporate Sec. 1955–88; Sec., T.L. Linkletter, Q.C. Summerside, P.E.I. 1947–49; Pentagon Construction Lac St. Jean, Que. 1952–53, Niagara Falls, Ont. 1953–55; Corporate Sec. Canadian General Investments Ltd. Toronto and present Co. 1955–88, Vice Chrmn. 1988; Pres., The Catherine & Maxwell Meighen Found.; mem. Autism Soc. Ont. (Chrmn. Fund Raising and Dir. 1973–77); recreations: cross-country skiing, hiking, fishing, boating, reading, miniaturist; Home: 407 Walmer Rd., Toronto, Ont. M5R 3N2; Office: 1601, 110 Yonge St., Toronto, Ont. M5C 1T4.

**MORGAN, G. Carl;** retired newspaper editor; b. Toronto, Ont. 12 Nov. 1931; s. Thomas and Christine (Genier) M.; e. Earl Haig C.I.; m. Gloria Ann d. Henry and Julia Plexman 14 July 1956; children: Jocelyn, Scott, Julie; The Windsor Star 1956–92; Editor 1977–92, retired; Reporter, Trenton Courier-Advocate 1950–52; Sudbury Star 1952–55; 3 awards in Western Ont. Newspaper Awards comp.; author/illustrator: 'Early Woodenware in Canada' 1977; 'Birth of a City' (early years of Windsor, Ont.) 1991; co-author & publisher 'Pioneering The Auto Age' 1992; Club: Beachgrove Golf & Country; Home: 12402 Riverside Dr. E., Windsor, Ont. N8N 1A3.

**MORGAN, Gwyn,** B.Sc., P.Eng.; oil and gas executive; b. Didsbury, Alta. 4 Nov. 1945; s. Ian and Margaret (Hergenhein) M.; e. Univ. of Alta. B.Sc. (Mech. Eng.) 1967; Univ. of Calgary, Cornell Univ. post-grad bus. progs.; m. Jill d. Al and Gwen Park; PRESIDENT AND CHIEF EXTVE. OFFR., ALBERTA ENERGY COMPANY LTD.; Dir., Gwil Industries Inc.; prior to 1970 served as Petrol. Engr. Alta. Energy Resources Conserv. Bd.; Mgr. Operations and Eng. Consolidated Natural Gas Ltd., Consolidated Pipelines Ltd., Norlands Petroleums Ltd. 1970–75; joined Alta. Energy Co. Ltd. 1975; Pres. Independent Petrol. Assn. Can. 1984–85; Bd. of Mgmt., Calgary Foothills Gen. Hosp.; Bd. of Govs., Candn. Assn. of Petroleum Producers; Hon. Col., 410 Tactical Fighter Squadron, Candn. Forces; recreations: sailing, horse raising, riding; Club: Calgary Petroleum; Ranchman's; Office: 3900, 421 - 7th Ave. S.W., Calgary, Alta. T2P 4K9.

**MORGAN, Hon. H.B.,** M.A.; judge; b. Harbour Deep, Nfld. 11 June 1919; s. late Jacob and Florence S. (Osborne) M.; e. Bishop Feild 1935; Mem. Univ. Coll. 1937; Dalhousie Univ. B.A. 1939; Pembroke Coll. Oxford Univ. (Rhodes Scholar) B.A. 1949, M.A. 1953; m. Betty Gradidge d. late Harold and Mary Maude Smith, 18 Oct. 1950; children: Christina, Christopher, Timothy; JUSTICE, COURT OF APPEAL, NFLD. since 1975; Chrmn. Nfld. Crimes Compensation Bd. 1972–75; Dist. Pensions' Advocate (Part time) Bureau of Pension Advocates 1963–75; Hon. Solr. Prov. Command Royal Candn. Legion 1963–75; Gov. Candn. Corps of Commissionaires; called to Bar of Eng. and Wales 1950; Bar of Nfld. 1950; cr. Q.C. 1972; served with RAF 1940–46, rank Flight Lt. (Pilot); rec'd Coronation Medal 1953; Confederation Medal; Jubilee Medal; Past Pres. RCAF Assn.; former Bencher Law Soc. Nfld.; Anglican; recreation: fishing; Home: 6 Rendell Place, St. John's, Nfld. A1B 1L3; Office: Court House, St. John's, Nfld. A1C 5M3.

**MORGAN, Rev. Ivan Clifford,** B.A., B.D., Th.M., D.D. (Bapt.); b. Paris, Ont. 14 Aug. 1912; s. Henry Thomas and Sarah Elizabeth (Benedict) M.; e. Pub. Sch. and Sir Adam Beck Coll. Inst., London, Ont.; McMaster Univ., B.A. 1938 and The Divinity Sch. there, B.D. 1942; Union Theol. Semy., Virginia, Th.M. 1963; D.D. Acadia 1968; m. Ruth Eleanor, d. Rev. Wm. Raithby, Strathroy, Ont., 30 Aug. 1939; children: Franklin William, Mary Ruth; Prof. Emeritus and Princ. Emeritus, McMaster Divinity Coll. since 1978; Prof. 1960–78; Princ. 1966–78; Pres., Bapt. Convention of Ont. and Que., 1953–54; o. 1939; Min., MacNeill Mem. Ch., Hamilton, Ont. 1938–46; Murray St. Ch., Peterborough, Ont., 1946–56; Temple Ch., Windsor, Ont. 1956–60; Dir., Children's Aid Soc., Hamilton 1941–46, Peterborough 1948–56; mem., Bapt. Convention of Ont. & Que. (mem., Bd. of Religious Educ. 1930–33, 1940–43; Bd. of Evangelism & Social Service 1939–45 and Chrmn. 1942–45; Candn. Bapt. Foreign Mission Bd. 1946–49; Pres., Probus Club (Dundas, Ont.) 1992–93; recreations: golf, fishing; Address: 7 Underhill Ave., Dundas, Ont. L9H 1S2.

**MORGAN, J. Graham,** M.A., D.Phil.; retired college president; b. Barrow-in-Furness, England 11 Aug. 1940; s. Stanley and Winifred (Richie) M.; e. St. Pauls Sch., Barrow-in-Furness, Eng., 1945–50; Sebright Sch., Worcestershire, Eng., 1950–59; Univ. of Nottingham, B.A. 1962; McMaster Univ., M.A. 1963; Balliol Coll., Oxford Univ., D.Phil. 1966; m. Marilyn Revell, d. Charles Ward, Amherst, N.S. 21 June 1968; three children; ASSOC. PROF. OF SOCIOL., DALHOUSIE UNIV. 1970– ; Tutor in Sociol., Oxford Univ. 1965–66; Asst. Prof. of Sociol., Dalhousie 1966–70; Pres., Univ. of King's Coll. 1970–77; Pres., Univ. of King's Coll. (ret.) writings incl. many journ. articles, book reviews and tech. reports; mem., Internat. Sociol. Assn.; Internat. Soc. for History of Soc. Sci.; Candn. Sociol. & Anthrop. Assn.; Anglican; recreation: music; Address: Dalhousie Univ., Halifax, N.S. B3H 3J5.

**MORGAN, James Evans;** retired banker; b. Ottawa, Ont. 23 July 1916; s. Arthur Llewellyn and Ella Victoria (Evans) M.; e. Montreal West (Que.) High Sch.; McGill Univ. (Econ. & Pol. Science), B.A. (Hons.) 1937; m. Barbara Anne, d. late William A. Newman, 21 Dec. 1940; children: David James, Beverly Anne; Depy. Gen. Mgr., The Royal Bank of Canada and Corporate Planning Offr. (ret.); served in 2nd World War with 5 Candn. Armoured Div. Signals (1943–46); discharged with rank of Capt.; Sigma Chi; Anglican; recreations: gardening, travel, reading; Club: University; Home: 36 Benoit, P.O. Box 517, Knowlton, Que. J0E 1V0.

**MORGAN, John D.,** M.A., Ph.D.; educator; b. San Francisco, Cal. 8 Sept. 1933; s. John Francis and Shirley Marie (Wright) M.; e. Loyola of Los Angeles B.A. 1958; Univ. of S. Cal. M.A. 1959, Ph.D. (Philos.) 1966; m. Mary Ann d. A. J. Constantin 8 June 1968; two s. David, Brian; PROF. OF PHILOS., KING'S COLL.

1976– ; Assoc. Prof. of Philos. Loyola of Montreal 1969–75; Assoc. Prof. of Philos. and Acad. Dean, King's Coll. 1975–76; Principal, King's Coll. 1976–87; author various articles and papers on death educ. and ethics; mem. Forum for Death Educ.; Internat. Work Group on Death, Dying & Bereavement; Candn. Soc. Study Higher Educ.; Home: 1167 Royal York Rd., London, Ont. N6H 3Z8; Office: 266 Epworth Ave., London, Ont. N6A 2M3.

**MORGAN, John Dinham,** B.Comm.; investment dealer; b. Montreal, Que. 16 Aug. 1930; s. Theodore Gold and Margaret Dinham (Molson) M.; e. Trinity College Sch. 1948; McGill Univ. B.Comm. 1952; Univ. of Western Ont., bus. admin. 1953; m. Norma d. Calvin and Donna Dewitta 17 June 1955; children: Scott, Victoria, James; CHRMN., CIBC TRUST, and VICE-PRES., MIDLAND WALWYN CAPITAL INC. 1990– ; Cockfield Brown 1953–67; Dir., Collier Norris & Quinlan 1967–69; Chrmn., Mead & Co. 1969–80; Vice-Chrmn., Walwyn Stodgell 1980–89; Chrmn., Morgan Bancorp 1980–85; Mem., Investment Dealers Assn. (Chrmn., Que. 1973–74); Gov., Montreal Exchange 1983–84; Gov., Montreal Gen. Hosp. Found.; Royal Victoria Hosp. Found.; recreations: sailing, skiing, tennis; clubs: Royal St. Lawrence Yacht, Hillside Tennis; Home: 32 Edgehill Rd., Westmount, Que. H3Y 1E9; Office: 1250 Rene Levesque Blvd. W., Suite 3100, Montreal, Que. H3B 4W8.

**MORGAN, John Frederick,** B.A., M.B.A.; brewery executive; b. Toronto, Ont. 29 Nov. 1943; s. Frederick Thomas and Mary Isobel (Gray) M.; e. Univ. of Man., B.A. 1967; Queen's Univ. M.B.A. 1971; m. Lynne d. Jack and Vonda Kennedy 22 Aug. 1970; children: Jennifer, Kathryn, Heather; Pres., Labatt Breweries of Canada 1990; Product. Mgr., Warner Lambert Can. Ltd. 1971–74; Acct. Supr., Leo Burnett Adv. 1974–76; Dir. of Mktg., Labatt's Man. 1976–79; Vice Pres. & Gen. Mgr., Labatt's Alta. 1979–82; Prairie Reg. 1982–83; Ont. Reg. 1983–86; Pres. & Mng. Dir., Labatt Breweries of Europe 1986–90; Chrmn., Brewers Assn. of Canada 1991– ; Dir., Toronto Blue Jays; Dir., Market Art of Can. Inc.; Fallis Turf (B.C.) Ltd.; Moretti Brewing Spa - Italy; Clubs: Port Credit Yacht; Royal Lymington Yacht; The National; Office: 2115 Commissioner St., Vancouver, B.C. V5L 1A6.

**MORGAN, Rev. John Hanly,** B.D., M.A., Ph.D.; Unitarian minister emeritus; b. New Albany, Ind. 28 Nov. 1918; s. John Sidney and Vada Elizabeth (Dorn) M.; e. New Albany Sr. High Sch. 1938; Ball State Univ. B.A. 1943; Harvard Divinity Sch. B.D. 1946; Univ. of Mich. M.A. 1955; Univ. of S. Fla. Ph.D. 1979; m. Jeannette d. Wayland and Mae Mutzfeld 6 Sept. 1942; children: Lois, David, Lee, Ann; HON. PRESIDENT, CANDN. PEACE CONGRESS 1986; served as Min. Unitarian chs. Mass., N.C., Mich., Ind. and Ont.; First Unitarian Congregation Toronto 1959; Minister Emeritus 1973; Pres., Thomas Jefferson Unitarian Conf. 1950–51; Mich. Area Council Lib. Chs. 1954–55; Sec. Unitarian Mins. Assn. 1956–60; Vice Pres. Unitarian Fellowship for Social Justice 1958–59; Past mem., Metro Toronto Unitarian Council and Candn. Unitarian Council; Instr. in Philos. Flint, Mich. Community Coll. 1952–56, Ind. Univ. Extension Center 1956–59; mem. Bd. Flint Urban League 1952–56; Vice Pres. Flint Chapter Nat. Assn. for Advanc. Colored People 1952–56, mem. Bd. South bend Chapter 1956–49; mem. Prog. Comte. S. Bend Counc. Social Agencies 1956–59; Candn. Ctte. of Concern S. Africa 1960–64; Chrmn. Toronto Ctte. for Survival 1960–64; Co-Chrmn. Candns. for Middle E. Understanding 1968–70; Pres., Candn. Peace Congress 1972–86; Vice-Pres. World Peace Counc. 1983–87; author poetry 'Strange Return' 1941; 'Lifetime' 1957; 'Kangaroo City' 1980; poetry and prose 'Hands of Friends' 1977; 'Receive These Hands' 1984; 'That We Shall Live' 1985; 'Journeys from Breakfast' 1987; recipient Intnl. Lenin Peace Prize 1983; Joliot-Curie Gold Medal for Peace 1984; Home: R.R. 11, Peterborough, Ont. K9J 6Y3.

**MORGAN, Moses Osbourne,** C.C. (1973), C.D., D.C.L., LL.D.; b. Blaketown, Trinity Bay, Nfld. 28 Aug. 1917; s. Jacob and Flora Susannah (Osbourne) M.; e. Bishop Feild Coll., St. John's, Nfld.; Memorial Univ. Coll.; Dalhousie Univ., B.A. 1939, M.A. 1946; Oxford Univ., B.A. 1948, M.A. 1951; LL.D. Mount Allison Univ., Univ. of N.B., St. Francis Xavier, Dalhousie, Queen's and Univ. of Toronto.; D.C.L. Univ. of King's College; m. 1stly Margaret d. Michael Fitzpatrick, 31 Aug. 1945; 2ndly Margaret Grace, d. William John Weymark, 6 July 1968; Pres. and Vice Chancellor, Memorial Univ. of Nfld., 1973–82, Pres. Emeritus 1983; served with Candn. Army 1942–45; N. N.S. Highlanders European Theatre; served as Commdr. #1 Militia Group; present rank Brig. (Retired); Pres., Assn. of Univs. and Colleges of Can., 1977–78; served as Chrmn., Adv. Bd. Candn. Services Coll.; Chrmn., Mil. Studes Comte., A.U.C.C. (Dir.); Chrmn. many arbitration and conciliation bds.; apptd. Royal Comm. on Ocean Ranger Disaster and on Royal Comm. on Unemployment Insurance; writings incl. numerous articles; Anglican; recreations: fishing, gardening, reading, travelling; Home: 117 Nagles Place, St. John's, Nfld. A1B 2Z2.

**MORGAN, Nicola;** writer/illustrator/painter; b. Victoria, B.C. 25 Jan. 1959; d. Peter Charles and Sidney Elizabeth (Woodward) M.; e. Langara Coll.; Banff Sch. of Fine Arts; Emily Coll. of Art, 4 yr. dip.; m. David W. s. Harold and Lillian Tupper 26 May 1984; one d.: Sophia Mabel; author: 'The Great B.C. Alphabet Book' 1985, 'A Pride of Lions' 1986, 'Temper Temper' 1988; one-man painting exhib., Richmond Arts Ctr. 1985; Art Instr., Richmond Arts Ctr. 1984; Arts Umbrella 1985; Instr., Vanc. Sch. Bd. 1986–88; Images & Objects exhibit award winner 1985; Childrens' Book Counc. Choice 1985; Sheila Egoff Award 1988; Mem., Canscaip; Fed. of Writers; Office: c/o Oxford University Press, 70 Wynford Dr., Don Mills, Ont. M3C 1J9.

**MORGAN, Nicole Anne Elisabeth,** M.A., Ph.D.; professor and consultant; b. France 23 March 1945; d. Louis and Lucie (Friedrich) Schwartz; e. Dijon M.A. 1968; Aix-en-Provence M.A. 1971; Univ. of Ottawa Ph.D. 1993; m. Alan s. David and Jenny Morgan 11 Oct. 1975; children: Ingrid, Eric; taught philos. in France 1966–69; began forecasting career Futuribles, Paris; pioneered application integrated forecasting methodology Candn. Fed. Pub. Service; Queen's National Scholar 1991; Asst. Prof. of Public Admin., Queen's Univ., Kingston, Ont.; frequent guest speaker seminars and confs.; author 'Nowhere To Go' 1981, French pub. 'Où Aller!'; 'Implosion, An Analysis of the Growth of the Federal Public Service 1945–1985' 1986, French pub. 'Implosion, une analyse de la croissance de la fonction publique fédérale'; 'The Equality Game, Advisory Council on the Status of Women' 1988, French pub. 'Jouer à l'égalité'; recreation: painting; Address: 377 Maple Lane, Ottawa, Ont. K1M 1H7.

**MORGAN, Paul James,** B.Sc., Dip.Min.Econ., F.Aus.I.M.M.; geologist; b. Melbourne, Austr. 21 Oct. 1946; s. Albert Henry George and Fay Rae (Witt) M.; e. Univ. of Queensland B.Sc. 1968; MacQuarie Univ. Dip.Min.Econ. 1983; m. Glenda Jean d. Norm and Marion Whitehead 25 Jan. 1986; children: Jodi Lee, Nicholas James, Daniel Christopher; CHIEF EXECUTIVE OFFICER & MANAGING DIRECTOR., GOLDBELT RESOURCES LTD. 1991– ; joined Mt. Isa Mines Ltd. 1968; worked as a geol. cons. in Australia and Papua New Guinea 1969–72; various positions, U.S.A. & Australia, Chevron Oil Co.; Gen. Mgr., Australmin Holdings Ltd. 1987; career highlights: resp. for devel., construction & opns. of Mt. Wilkinson Mine 1986, Tuckabianna Mine 1988, Newyrbar Dredge & Concentrator and Woodburn Dry Plant 1990; Freeman of the City of London 1990; Fellow, Australasian Inst. of Mining & Metallurgy; Guild of Air Pilots & Air Navigators; Mem., Prospectors & Developers Assn. of Can.; author/co-author of 8 sci. papers; recreations: golf, flying, motor racing; clubs: Royal Freemantle Golf, Toothill Golf; Home: Waterlees, Harlow Common, Harlow, Essex, CM17 9JD U.K.; Office: 1200, 885 W. Georgia St., Vancouver, B.C. V6C 3E8.

**MORGAN, Peter F.,** B.A., M.A., Ph.D.; university professor; b. Uttoxeter, England 1 Sept. 1930; s. Frederick John and Kathleen May M.; e. Univ. of Birmingham, B.A. 1951; Univ. of London, M.A. 1955, Ph.D. 1959; divorced; m. Alice Y. Morgan 28 Aug. 1993; children: Peter, Martin, Alison, Katharine; PROF. OF ENG., UNIV. OF TORONTO 1974– ; Lectr., Victoria Coll., B.C. 1959–60; joined Univ. of Toronto as Lectr. 1960; Pres., Ont. Counc. of Teachers of Eng. 1977–79; Pres., Soc. for the Study of Human Ideas on Ultimate Reality and Meaning 1993; N.D.P.; author: 'Literary Critics and Reviewers in Early Nineteenth Century Britain' 1983; 'Poetic and Pictorial' 1992; editor: 'Thomas Hood: Letters' 1973; 'Francis Jeffrey: Criticism' 1983; Office: University College, Univ. of Toronto, Toronto, Ont. M5S 1A1.

**MORGAN, William John;** journalist and television executive; b. Geelong, Australia 24 Jan. 1940; s. William Henry and Josephine (Ryan) M.; e. Geelong High Sch.; Univ. of Melbourne; Victoria Coll. Advanced Edn.; m. Sheelagh Dillon; d. Dean and Tessie (Sadlier-Brown) Whittaker; children: Abigail, Emily, Nicholas Whittaker M.; step-children: Meghan, Matthew, Daniel; OMBUDSMAN, CBC 1991– ; Trustee, Visnews London, UK, 1990– ; Actor, stage, including work with John Alden Shakespearean Company and, in film, leading role in 'The Pudding Thieves' 1962–63; Teacher, Victoria Dept. of Edn. Australia and Inner London Edn. Authority UK 1963–67; Columnist, Editorial Page Ed. The Brandon Sun 1968–69; Radio Public Affairs Producer CBC Winnipeg, Extve. Producer 'Information Radio' 1969–70; TV Producer, Extve. Producer '24 Hours' 1970–74; Dir. of Television, CBC Winnipeg 1974–76; Television Network Prog. Dir., CBC Toronto 1976–79; Head of Television Current Affairs CBC 1980–82; Dir. of Television News & Current Affairs, CBC 1982–89; Dir., Office of Journalism Policy & Practices, CBC 1989–91; Dir., Visnews London, UK 1982–89; Royal Television Soc.; Internat. Institute of Communications; Assn. of News Ombudsmen; Home: Apt. 2810, 65 Harbour Square, Toronto, Ont. M5J 2L4; Offices: Canadian Broadcasting Centre, P.O. Box 500, Station A, Toronto, Ont. M5W 1E6 and 1500 Bronson Ave., P.O. Box 8478, Ottawa, Ont. K1G 3J5.

**MORGANTINI, Luigi Emanuele,** D.Sc., M.Sc., Ph.D.; wildlife biologist consultant, adjunct professor; b. Rome, Italy 24 July 1948; s. Paolo and Valeria M.; e. Univ. of Rome D.Sc. 1974; Univ. of Alberta M.Sc. 1979, Ph.D. 1988; m. Raffaella d. Guglielmo and Lucia Ubaldi 14 March 1974; children: Christine, David; PRES., WILDLIFE RESOURCES CONSULTING LTD. 1979– and ADJUNCT PROF., DEPT. OF FOREST SCIENCE, UNIV. OF ALBERTA 1989– ; Asst. to Gen. Sec., World Wildlife Fund, Italy 1972–74; Rsch. Asst., Dept. of Animal Science, Univ. of Alta. 1974–80; advised several private cos. & govt. agencies on various aspects of wildlife ecology & management and directed 13 long-term research studies on impact of resource devel. on wildlife 1980–91; Wildlife Expert witness, var. public hearings 1980–91; Cons., Cenex & Meridian Oil (U.S.) on impact of resource devel. and bighorn sheep in N. Dakota 1991; developed one of the 1st N. Am. Univ. courses on the Impact & Mitigation of Resource Devel. on Wildlife 1991–92; Dir., Alta. Chapter, Wildlife Soc. 1991; Western Canada Wilderness Ctte., Wildlife Soc.; author of more than 30 scientific pubs. on wildlife ecology, behaviour & mngt.; recreations: hiking, swimming; Home: Site 3, Box 9, R.R. 2, Spruce Grove, Alta. T7X 2T5; Office: Edmonton, Alta. T6G 2H1.

**MORGENSTERN, Norbert Rubin,** B.A.Sc., D.I.C., Ph.D., F.R.S.C., D.Eng, D.Sc.; educator; consulting engineer; b. Toronto, Ont. 25 May 1935; s. Joel and Bella (Skornik) M.; e. Harbord Coll. Inst. Toronto 1952; Univ. of Toronto B.A.Sc. 1956; Imp. Coll. of Science and Technol. D.I.C. in Soil Mechanics 1964; Univ. of London Ph.D. 1964; Univ. of Toronto D.Eng. 1983; Queen's Univ. D.Sc. 1989; m. Patricia Elizabeth d. Ronald M. Gooderham, Terra Cotta, Ont. 29 Dec. 1960; children: Sarah Alexandra, Katherine Victoria, David Michael Gooderham; UNIV. PROF., UNIV. OF ALTA. since 1983; Pres., Norbert R. Morgenstern Consultants Ltd.; Consulting Engr. to various private and pub. agencies on problems in engn. earth sciences since 1961; Engr., Geocon Ltd. Toronto 1956; grad. student and research asst. Imp. Coll. of Science & Technol. 1957–60, Lectr. in Civil Engn. 1960–68; Prof. of Civil Engn. Univ. of Alta. 1968–83; rec'd Athlone Fellowship 1956; Brit. Geotech. Soc. Prize 1961, 1966; Huber Rsch. Prize, Am. Soc. Civil Engrs. 1971; Cdn. Geotech. Soc. Prize 1977, 1985; Legget Award, Cdn. Geotech. Soc. 1979; Rankine Lecture, Br. Geotech. Soc 1981; Boase Lecture, Univ. of Colorado 1981; Engr. Alumni Award, Univ. of Toronto, 1981; Pres. Can. Geosci. Council 1983; Rsch. Prize, Univ. of Alta. 1984; Centennial Award, Assoc. Prof. Eng. Alta. 1984; Fellow, Engineering Inst. of Can. 1985; Sir Frederick Haultain Prize in Science 1987; Roger J. Brown Memorial Award, Cdn.-Geotech-Soc. 1987; Thomas Roy Award, Cdn. Geotech. Soc., 1987; Fellow, Candn. Acad. of Engr. 1988; Distinguished Lectr., Mem. Univ. of Nfld. and Colorado State Univ., 1988; Manuel Rocha Lecture, Portugese Geotechnical Soc. 1989; Honorary Research Fellow, Institute of Water Conservancy and Hydroelectric Research, Beijing, PRC 1990; Geotechnical Soc. of Edmonton Award 1991; Mem., Alberta Order of Excellence 1991; Terzaghi Lectr., Am. Society of Civil Engrs. 1992; Foreign Assoc., U.S. National Academy of Engr. 1992; Pres., Candn. Geotechnical Soc. 1989–91; Vice-Pres., Engineering Inst. of Can. 1989–91; Pres., Intnl. Soc. for Soil Mech. & Foundation Engr., 1989–94; Dir. Young Naturalists Foundation 1975–81; Edmonton Symphony Soc. 1978–86; author over 240 articles; mem. ed. bd. various scient. Journs.; mem. Assn. Prof. Engrs. Alta.; Engn. Inst. Can.; Candn. Geotech. Soc.; Candn. Soc. Civil Engrs.; Candn. Inst. Mining & Metall.; Am. Soc. Civil Engrs.; Geol. Soc. London; Brit. Geotech. Soc.; Assn. Engn. Geols.; Internat. Soc. Rock Mechanics; Internat. Assn. Eng. Geol.; Internat. Soc. Soil Mechanics and Foundation Engrg.;

recreations: tennis, skiing; Clubs: Royal Glenora; Athenaeum (London); Home: 106 Laurier Dr., Edmonton, Alta. T5R 5P6; Office: Edmonton, Alta. T6G 2E1.

**MORIMANNO, Paul P.J.,** C.A., M.B.A.; financial executive; b. Montreal, Que. 28 May 1939; s. Frank A. and Cécile (Donato) M.; e. Hautes Etudes Commerciales Montreal B.Comm. 1959; C.A. 1961; McGill Univ., dipl. in mngt. 1970; Columbia Univ. M.B.A. 1972; VICE-PRES. & TREASURER, POWER CORPORATION OF CANADA 1985– ; various responsibilities in Controller's office, Bell Canada 1962–70; Asst. to Vice-Pres., Finance, Royal Trust Co. 1970–71; Asst. Treas., Power Corp. of Canada 1975–80; Treas. 1980–83; Sec.-Treas. 1983–85; Governor General Gold Medal for Uniform Examination for C.A.s 1961; Mem., Phi Beta Kappa; Mem., Financial Executives Inst.; recreations: alpine & nordic skiing; Home: 10195 ave D'Auteuil, Montreal, Que. H3L 2K2; Office: 751 Victoria Sq., Montreal, Que. H2Y 2J3.

**MORIN, Jacques-Yvan;** professor of law; b. Québec, Qué. 1931; s. Arsène M.; e. Univ. of Montréal; McGill Univ.; Harvard Univ.; Cambridge Univ.; m. Elisabeth Gallat; children: 2; PROF., CONSTITUTIONAL LAW AND PUBLIC INTERNAT. LAW, UNIVERSITÉ DE MONTREAL 1957–73 and 1984– ; Ed.-in-Chief, McGill Law Journal, 1952 and Revue québécoise de droit international 1984–90; Vice-Premier ministre et min. de l'Education, Qué. 1976–80; Vice-Premier ministre et Min. d'Etat au développement culturel et scientifique 1981–82; Vice-Premier Min. et Min. Affaires intergouvernementales 1982–84; el. M.N.A. for Sauvé prov. g.e. 1973; Leader of the Opposition 1973–76; Office: 3101 Chemin de la Tour, PO Box 6128, Succ. Centre Ville, Montréal, Qué. H3C 3J7.

**MORIN, Jean-Marie,** né Rivière-Ouelle, Qué. 19 fév. 1929; f. François et Emilia (Lafrance) M.; é. La Pocatière (coll. classique) et pédagogie et psychol., litt. française, initiation à l'enseignement dans les labs. de langues aux univs.; ép. Pauline Turcotte, 15 juin 1959; Prof. de langues, Coll. de Lévis, Que. 1948–66 (Dir. du Lab. de Langue 1962–66, Trésorier prov. des profs. de l'enseignement classique 1962–63); Député du comté de Lévis à la Législature prov. (Qué.) 1966–70; Secrétaire parlementaire au P.M. 1966–68; Ministre délégué au Haut-Commissariat à la Jeunesse, aux Loisirs et aux Sports 1968; Min. d'Etat à l'Educ., Min. d'Etat aux Affaires intergouvernementales, Min. responsable de l'Office franco-qué, pour la Jeunesse 1968–70; Rep. le Qué. aux Jeux panam., Winnipeg 1967, aux Jeux olympiques de Grenoble 1968, de Mexico 1968; Dirige la Mission de la Jeunesse en France 1967; la Délég. candn. à la Conf. des mins. de l'Educ. des Etats d'Afrique et de Madagascar au Congo-Kinshasa, et à Paris 1969, Nouakchott en Mauritanie 1970; Min. délég. du Qué. à la Conf. des mins. candn. siégeant sur la Comité des langues officielles 1969–70; nommé Sous-Commissaire au bureau du Commissaire aux langues officielles, Ottawa, juin 1970 – août 1980; nommé Conseiller spécial en relations internat. et Chargé de mission de l'Agence de cooperation culturelle et technique près des Nations-Unies, sept. 1980; détaché en qualité de Conseiller auprès des autorités de la République de Vanuatu 1984; détaché auprès du Secrétariat d'Etat (Hull-Ottawa) à la promotion des langues officielles; se mérite une bourse donnée par la Fondation Nuffield de Londres, mars 1971; président de l'Association Canada-France de la région de la Capitale Nationale, 1989– ; Chev. de Colomb; Club: Lions du Lauzon (membre-fondateur); adresse: R.R. #1 – C.P. 792, 32 Place Neufbourg, Cantley, P.Q. J0X 1L0.

**MORIN, The Hon. Mr. Justice Lawrence R.,** B.A., LL.B.; justice; b. Windsor, Ont. 15 Aug. 1940; s. Roland Arthur and Gilberthe (LaMarre) M.; e. Univ. of Windsor B.A. 1962; Univ. of W. Ont. LL.B. 1967; m. Wendy E. d. Robert and Marjorie Barbeau 28 June 1969; two s. Kevin Robert, Kyle Lawrence; JUSTICE, ONTARIO COURT OF JUSTICE (GENERAL DIVISION) 1990– ; Judge, Dist. Court of Ont. 1989–90; Home: R.R.1, Belle River, Ont. N0R 1A0; Office: 245 Windsor Ave., Windsor, Ont. N9A 1J2.

**MORIN, Normand,** B.Sc.A., M.Sc., Ph.D.; business executive; b. Drummondville, Que. 6 March 1942; s. Charles and Lina (Lachapelle) M.; e. Univ. of Sherbrooke B.Sc.A. 1964; Univ. of London (U.K.) M.Sc. 1965; Mass. Inst. of Technology Ph.D. 1970; m. Claudette d. Laurette and Georges Leclair 24 June 1967; children: Marie-Andrée, Isabelle, Sophie; PRES. GENERAL ENGINEERING GROUP, SNC–LAVALIN INC.; Assoc. Prof., Univ. of Sherbrooke 1970–72; Engineer, LAVALIN 1971; responsibilities at SNC-Lavalin range from tech. to admin. & extve.; major projects: highrise bldgs., highways, bridges, James Bay 735kV Transmission Lines, Que. City Sewage Treatment Plant; corp. responsibilities for div. in Winnipeg, Regina, St. John's, Halifax, Frederiction, Que. City & Montreal; Athlone Fellow 1964; Performer Award 1990; Fellow, Cand. Soc. of Civil Engr.; Candn. Acad. of Engr.; Mem., Order of Engrs. of Que.; Candn. Soc. of Civil Engr.; recreations: ski, golf, sailing; club: Montreal Country Club; Home: 75 Courcelette, Outremont, Que. H2V 3A5; Office: 2 Place Félix-Martin, Montreal, Que. H2Z 1Z3.

**MORIN, Yves,** O.C., B.A., M.D., F.R.C.P.(C), F.A.C.C.; cardiologist; b. Québec, Qué. 28 Nov. 1929; s. Lucien and Marcelle (Samson) M.; e. Univ. Laval, B.A. 1948, M.D. 1953; Nat. Inst. of Cardiology, London, Eng. (Rotary Internat. Foundation Fellow), 1954–55; m. Marie, d. Jean Sénécal, Québec, Qué., 15 Aug. 1959; children: Suzanne, François, Philippe, Frédéric; CHEF, SERVICE DE CARDIOLOGIE, HOTEL DIEU DE QUEBEC 1980– ; Vice-Doyen 1971, Dir. Dept. de Méd. 1970, Prof. titulaire 1970, agrégé 1966, Prof. adjoint Univ. Laval 1961, agrégé 1966, Prof. titulaire and Dir. Dept. de Méd. 1970, Vice-Doyen 1971, Doyen Fac. de Méd. 1975–80; Internship, L'Hôtel-Dieu de Québec, Sunnybrook Hosp. Toronto, Toronto Gen. Hosp., 1952–58; Asst. Service de Méd., Hôtel-Dieu de Qué. 1960, Dir. Lab. de Cardiol. 1961; Dir. Inst. de Cardiol. de Qué. 1966; Dir. Dépt. de Méd., C.H.U.L. 1971; author or coauthor of over 200 publs.; mem., Soc. canadienne de cardiol. (Vice-Prés.); N.Y. Acad. Sciences; Soc. de cardiol. du Qué.; Soc. de cardiol. de Montréal; Club de recherches clinqiues du Québec (secy. scient. 1971); Soc. candnne. de recherches cliniques; Candn. Heart Foundation; Coll. Royal des méds. et chirurgiens du Can. (Vice Pres. 1986–88); mem. Internat. Study Group for Research in Cardiac Metabolism (Am. Sec.); Council on Cardiomyopathies, Internat. Soc. of Cardiol.; Fellow, Am. Coll. Cardiol.; Candn. Founding Fellow, Am. Heart Assn.; Officier de l'Ordre du Canada; Home: 1280 Pelletier, Sillery, Québec City, Qué. G1T 2H4; Office: 11 Cote du Palais, Québec, Qué. G1R 2J6.

**MORINIS, Alan,** D.Phil.; film producer; b. Toronto, Ont. 8 Dec. 1949; s. David and Bess (Lapides) M.; e. Bathurst Heights H.S. 1968; York Univ. B.A. 1972; Oxford Univ. M.Litt. 1974, D.Phil. 1980; Rhodes Scholar (Ont. and Magdalen) 1972; Canada Counc./S.S.H.R.C. Fellow 1977–79; recipient S.S.H.R.C. Resch. grant 1983–84; m. Beverly d. Nathan & Myrle Spring 8 Aug. 1973; two d. Julia Beth Spring, Leora Evelyn Spring; World Health Orgn., India, Global Smallpox Eradication Prog.; various teaching positions at Univ. of Alta., Simon Fraser Univ., Univ. of Victoria, Univ. of B.C.; currently active in entertainment industry; Pres., Ark Films Inc. 1989– ; former Pres., Meta Communications Group Inc.; former Dir., Northern Lights Media Corp. 1984–88; Dir. & Co-Chrmn., Seva Service Soc.; Dir. Seva Foundation; mem., City of Vancouver Economic Adv. Comn.; Executive producer: 'The Healing Journey' (documentary film); Producer: 'Harmony Cats' (feature film); author: 'Pilgrimage in the Hindu Tradition' 1984; co-ed., 'Pilgrimage in Latin America' 1991; editor: 'Sacred Journeys: the Anthropology of Pilgrimage' 1992; Address: 4537 Marguerite St., Vancouver, B.C. V6J 4G7.

**MORIYAMA, Raymond,** O.C., O.Ont., B.Arch., M.Arch., LL.D., D. Eng., F.R.A.I.C., M.C.I.P., R.C.A., F.R.S.A., D.Sc.; architect and planner; b. Vancouver, B.C. 11 Oct. 1929; e. Pub. and High Schools, Vancouver, B.C., Hamilton, Ontario and one year Public School, Tokyo, Japan; Univ. of Toronto, B.Arch.; McGill University, M.Arch.; LL.D. Brock University, York University, Trent University, Univ. of Saskatchewan; Fellowship, Ryerson Polytech. Inst.; D. Eng. Tech. Univ. of N.S.; D.Sc. McGill Univ.; m. Sachi Miyauchi, 17 September 1954; children: Mark-Michi, Murina-Lei, Selena-Midori, Jason-Jun, Adrian-Keiju; commenced practice in May 1958, Raymond Moriyama, Architects and Planners; has wide range of experience ranging from Vancouver, U.S.A., Nassau, Bahamas, Hong Kong, Japan, Germany to Pakistan; PRINCIPAL, MORIYAMA AND TESHIMA – ARCHITECTS 1980– ; Awards incl. Ont. Assn. Arch (Arch. Design); Toronto Guilds (Medal for Arch. Design); Presb. Ch. of Can. (First Prize, Ch. Design, Competition); Nat. Indust. Design Council (Hon. Award. Silver Tea Set Design); Massey Medal (Arch., 1961 and 76); Can. Archs. Award of Excellence for Centennial Baptist Ch. 1968 and Meewasin Valley Project, a 100 yr. conceptual Master Plan, 1979; Pre-Stressed Concrete Inst. Award for Ont. Science Centre 1969; Ont. Masons' Relation Council Award, Minota Hagey Residence, Univ. of Waterloo 1969; Burnhamthorpe District Library 1977; Malton Community Centre & District Library 1978; Whitby Municipal Bldg. 1979; Award of Excellence, Peterborough Public Library, 1982: Gov. Gen. Medals for Arch., Goh Ohn Bell and Metro Toronto Library, 1982 and Science North, Sudbury, 1986; Louisiana State Award of Excellence 1986; Award of Excellence, State of Illinois Engr. Assoc. 1987; Art Directors' Club of Toronto Gold Award for Canadian Embassy, Tokyo, Redevelopment' Report, 1988; Progressive Architecture Awards Citation, 'Ontario's Niagara Parks: Planning the Second Century,' 1989; Candn. Soc. of Landscape Architects' Awards, Buffalo's Main Street Mall and 'Ontario's Niagara Parks: Planning the Second Century' 1989; Excellence on the Waterfront Award (Washington, D.C.) for the Meewasin Valley Project, 1990; Lifetime Achievement Award, Arts Foundation of Greater Toronto 1990; Excellence on the Waterfront Award (Washington, D.C.) for the Niagara Parks, 1991; Ottawa Architectural Conservation Award of Excellence 1991; Waterfront Award (Washington, D.C.) 1992; Top Honour, Japan Architects' Assn. Award (Tokyo, Japan) 1992; Arch. Institute of Japan Award 1992; Award of Excellence, North York Design Awards 1993; Top Honour, Scarborough Urban Design Awards 1993; Civic Award of Merit, Toronto & City of Scarborough, & other civic award and citizen's awards; has lect. in universities and to organizations in Can., Japan, and U.S.A.; mem., Ont. Assn. Arch.; Cdn. Inst. of Planners; Fellow, Royal Arch. Inst. Can.; Officer, Order of Canada 1985; Order of Ontario 1992; Founding Dir. Asia Pacific Found. of Can.; recreations: sailing; Office: 32 Davenport Road, Toronto, Ont. M5R 1H3.

**MORLEY, J. Fred,** B.Sc., B.A, M.A.; economist; b. Sydney, Cape Breton 13 Oct. 1954; s. Charles S. and Mary M. (MacKinnon) M.; e. Dalhousie Univ. B.Sc. 1976, B.A. 1978; Saint Mary's Univ. M.A. 1988; m. Denise d. Raymond and Joan Burton 9 Oct. 1981; children: Claire, Colleen; SENIOR POLICY ANALYST & RESEARCH COORDINATOR, ATLANTIC PROVINCES ECONOMIC COUNCIL 1989– ; Economics Professor, Saint Mary's Univ. 1988– ; Consulting Economist 1980– ; media commentator and public speaker on regional economic analysis, federal-prov. relations & economic forecasts; Pres., Atlantic Assn. of Applied Economics; Roman Catholic; author of over 50 articles and reports mainly on the Atlantic economy; Office: 5121 Sackville St., Suite 500, Halifax, N.S. B3J 1K1.

**MORLEY, John Terence,** B.A., Ph.D.; educator; b. Toronto, Ont. 22 March 1943; s. John N. and Ruth G. (Hetherington) M.; e. pub. and high schs. West Vancouver, Saskatoon, Toronto; Dalhousie Univ. B.A. 1966; Queen's Univ. Ph.D. 1978; m. Jane d. Andrew and Margaret Brewin 7 Sept. 1968; children: Gareth, James, Simon; ASSOC. PROF. OF POL. SCI. UNIV. OF VICTORIA 1985– ; Staff Rep. Candn. Labour Cong. 1967–68; Extve. Asst. to Leader of NDP Ont. 1969–71; Instr. in Pol. Sci. Queen's Univ. 1972–74; Lectr. in Pol. Sci. present Univ. 1974, Asst. Prof. 1978; pol. columnist, Victoria Times-Colonist 1987–92, Vancouver Sun 1989–92; Managing Partner, Coastal Policy Planners 1991; author: 'Secular Socialists: The CCF/NDP in Ontario' 1984; co-author: 'Reins of Power: Governing British Columbia' 1983; several book chapters, jour. articles; mem. Candn. Pol. Sci. Assn.; Pacific N.W. Pol. Sci. Assn. (Co-Pres., 1992–93); Inst. Pub. Adm. Can.; Anglican (Bd. mem. Ednl. Trusts Bd. Diocese B.C. 1985–92); recreations: golf, boating; Clubs: Pender Island Golf & Country; Home: 1203 Port Washington Rd., Pender Island, B.C. V0N 2M0; Office: Dept. of Political Science, Univ. of Victoria, Victoria, B.C. V8W 3P5.

**MORLEY, Lawrence Whitaker,** Ph.D., D.Sc., F.R.S.C., P.Eng., F.C.A.S.I.; b. Toronto, Ont. 19 Feb. 1920; s. George Whitaker and Mary Olive (Boyd) M.; e. Brown Sch., Toronto; Victoria Sch., Collingwood, Ont.; Owen Sound (Ontario) Collegiate Institute; Lakefield (Ont.) Coll. Sch., 1938; Univ. of Toronto, Ph.D. 1952; m. former Beverly Anne Beckworth; children: Lawrence, Patricia, Christopher, David; stepchildren: Sandra, Stephen, Richard Burdett; PRES., TELEDETECTION INTERNATIONAL 1982– ; Founding Dir., Inst. for Space & Terrestrial Science 1987–88; Adjunct Prof., Fac. of Sci., CRESS/York Univ. 1985–87; Founding Dir., Exploration Geophysics Div., Geol. Survey of Can. 1957–69; propounded theory of magnetic imprinting of ocean floors by earth's reversing magnetic field 1963 which led to the Theory of Plate Tectonics; instigated Fed./Prov. Aeromagnetic Survey Plan for Can. 1962; instigated plans for Resource Satellite Planning for Can. 1970, then founding Dir. Gen. Can. Centre for Remote Sensing, Dept. Energy Mines & Resources; Counsellor (Scientific), Can. High Commission, London, Eng. 1980–82; Ed. 'Mining Geophysics' 1967; 'Economic Geology Series'; many papers on geophys. exploration and remote sensing; Hon. D.Sc. York Univ. 1974; past Pres., Can. Aeronautics & Space Inst. (McCurdy Medal 1974);

Fellow, Roy. Soc. of Can.; Founding Pres., Candn. Remote Sensing Soc.; Gov., Imperial Coll. of Sci. 1980–82; Soc. Exploration Geophysicists; Candn. Geophys. Union; Am. Geophys. Union; Anglican; Home: 767, 2nd Ave. W., Owen Sound, Ont. N4K 4M2.

**MORLEY, Patricia,** M.A., Ph.D., D.S.Litt. (Hon.); writer; educator; b. Toronto, Ont. 25 May 1929; d. Frederick Charles and Mabel Olive (Winsland) Marlow; e. Univ. of Toronto Trinity Coll. B.A. 1951; Carleton Univ. M.A. 1967; Univ. of Ottawa Ph.D. 1970; Thorneloe Univ., Sudbury D.S.Litt. (Doctor of Sacred Letters) 1992; m. Lawrence W. s. George W. Morley 17 June 1950, div. 1975; children: Lawrence Charles, Patricia Kathleen, Christopher George, David Boyd; freelance writer 1968– ; Lectr. Univ. of Ottawa 1971–72; Asst. Prof. Sir George Williams Univ. 1972–75; Assoc. Prof., Concordia Univ. 1975–80, Prof. of English & Candn. Studies 1980–89; Professor Emerita 1992; Fellow, Lonergan Univ. Coll. 1979–84; Fellow, Simone de Beauvoir Inst. 1979–88, Assoc. Fellow 1988–89, Lifetime Hon. Fellow 1989– ; book reviewer The Ottawa Journal 1971–80, The Ottawa Citizen 1980– , The Birmingham News (USA) 1982–87; recipient The Ottawa Citizen Award for Non-fiction 1987; The Ottawa-Carleton Lit. Award 1988; Japan Foundation Fellow 1991–92; Ottawa-Carleton Lit. Award 1991; Canada Council Non-Fiction Award 1991; SSHRCC Rsch. Grants 1982–86, Leave Fellowships 1978–79, 1985–86; Can. Council Doctoral Fellowship 1969; Can. Council Travel Grant 1993; author 'The Mystery of Unity: Theme and Technique in the Novels of Patrick White' 1972; 'The Immoral Moralists: Hugh MacLennan and Leonard Cohen' 1972; 'Robertson Davies' 1976; 'The Comedians: Hugh Hood and Rudy Wiebe' 1977; 'Morley Callaghan' 1978; 'Margaret Laurence' 1981; 'Kurelek. A Biography' 1986; 'Margaret Laurence: The Long Journey Home' 1991; 'As Though Life Mattered: Leo Kennedy's Story' 1994; ed. 'Ernest Thompson Seton. Selected Stories' 1978; mem. Manotick Art Assn.; Writers Union Can.; Assn. Candn. & Que. Lits.; Candn. Assn. Commonwealth Lang. & Lit. Studies; recreations: gardening, travel; Address: P.O. Box 137 Manotick, Ont. K4M 1A2.

**MORLEY, Thomas Paterson,** F.R.C.S.C.; university professor emeritus; b. Manchester, Engl. 13 June 1920; s. John and Mary Ogilvie (Simon) M.; e. Dragon Sch.; Rugby Sch.; Oxford Univ., B.M., B.Ch. 1943; m. Helen d. Donald Henry and Elizabeth Currer Briggs 17 Apr. 1943; children: Jane, Rosamund, David; PROF. EMERITUS OF NEUROSURGERY, UNIV. OF TORONTO 1985– ; F./Lt., Royal Air Force 1944–46; F.R.C.S. (England) 1949; F.R.C.S.C. (Neurosurgery) 1953; Teaching Staff, Toronto Gen. Hosp. & Univ. of Toronto 1953; Head, Div. of Neurosurgery 1963; Prof., Univ. of Toronto 1973; Pres., Toronto Acad. of Med. 1961; Medicolegal Soc. of Toronto 1969–70; Candn. Neurosurg. Soc. & Candn. Congress of Neurol. Scis. 1971; Charter Pres., Med. Staff Assn., Toronto Gen. Hosp. 1963–66; Pres. 1983–85; Senate Mem., Univ. of Toronto 1964–68; Governing Counc. 1979–82; Counsellor, Workers' Compensation Appeals Tribunal, Ont. 1987–92; Dir., Ont. Med. Assn. 1968–69; Chrmn., Ctte. on Neurosurg., R.C.P.S.C. 1970–76; Vice Pres., Neurosurg. Soc. of Am. 1970–71; Soc. of Neurol. Surgs. 1976; Examiner, Am. Bd. of Neurol. Surg. 1973; Ed., Hannah Inst. of Hist. of Medicine; Life Mem., Ont. Med. Assn. 1985– ; Sr. Mem., Candn. Med. Assn. 1986; author of numerous articles in neurosurg. lit.; editor: 'Current Controversies in Neurosurgery' 1976, 'Moral, Ethical and Legal Issues in the Neurosciences' 1981; 'Canadian Medical Lives' series 1989– ; 'Medical Specialty Societies of Canada' 1991; recreations: silviculture, wilderness canoeing; Club: Glen Major Angling; Home: P.O. Box 5058, Claremont, Ont. L1Y 1A4.

**MORNEAU, William Francis, Jr.,** B.A., M.Sc., M.B.A.; business executive; b. Toronto, Ont. 7 Oct. 1962; s. William Francis and Helen Therese (Lynch) M.; e. Univ. of Western Ont. B.A. (Hons.); London Sch. of Econ. M.Sc.; INSEAD Bus. School (Fontainebleau, France) M.B.A.; PRESIDENT, W.F. MORNEAU & ASSOC. 1991– and PRESIDENT, MORNEAU COOPERS & LYBRAND 1992– ; Consultant, Lloyd's of London; Godwins; joined W.F. Morneau & Assoc., Inc. Chicago 1987; W.F. Morneau & Assoc., Ltd. Toronto 1989; Dir., INSEAD Alumni Assn.; author of num. articles on employee benefits; recreations: skiing, sailing, tennis, squash; clubs: Granite, Royal Candn. Yacht, Craigleith Ski; Office: 1500 Don Mills Rd., Suite 500, Don Mills, Ont. M3B 3K4.

**MORNEAULT, J. Philippe,** B.A., LL.B.; labour relations executive; b. New Brunswick 28 Feb. 1948; s. Henri J. and Annette M.S. (Bouchard) M.; e. St. Thomas Univ. B.A. 1969; Univ. of N.B. LL.B. 1977; m. Jeanne d'Arc d. Ronald and Marie Jeanne Cloutier 22 June 1968; children: Lynne, Richard, Anne; VICE CHAIRMAN, CANADA LABOUR RELATIONS BOARD 1991– ; Industrial Relations, Fraser Inc. 1969–71; Human Rights Officer, N.B. Human Rights Comn. 1971–74; Asst. Supvr. of Political Financing, Prov. of N.B. (part-time) 1978–84; private practice of Law, Edmundston, N.B. 1977–91; Mem., Law Soc. of N.B.; recreations: fly fishing, hunting, skiing; Home: 906 – 230 Brittany Dr., Ottawa, Ont. K1K 0R6; Office: C.D. Howe Bldg., 240 Sparks St., 4th Fl. W., Ottawa, Ont. K1A 0X8.

**MOROCHOVE, Richard James,** B.Comm., F.C.A.; computer consultant; writer; speaker; b. Toronto, Ont. 26 May 1953; s. Max and Victoria (Mironchuk) M.; e. Univ. of Toronto, B.Comm. 1975; Inst. of Chartered Accts. of Ont., C.A. 1977, Fellow 1994; single; PRES., MOROCHOVE & ASSOC. INC. 1988– ; Audit Mgr., Arthur Andersen & Co. 1975–84; Dir., Computer Serv., Wm. Eisenberg & Co. 1984–88; columnist, The Toronto Star Syndicate 1991– ; The Bottom Line 1985– ; The Financial Post 1983–91; Reviewer, PC World (San Francisco, CA) 1990– ; Contrib. Ed./Reviews, InfoWorld (Menlo Park, Calif.) 1985–90; Ed., Computer Acctg. Letter 1988– ; Extve. Ed., 'The Bottom Line Guide to Business Software' 1990–93; contbr.: 'The Handbook of Information Technology' 1987; co-author: 'The Electronic Law Office' 1986; Office: 390 Bay St., Ste. 2000-W, Toronto, Ont. M5H 2Y2.

**MOROSOLI, Joëlle,** B.F.A.; sculptor (art in motion), writer; b. Strasbourg, France 17 Nov. 1951; d. Erwin and Gisèle (Talbot) M.; e. Coll. Notre-Dame-de-Bellevue, phil. & lit. coll. cert. 1971; Laval Univ. B.F.A. 1975; Univ. of Que., 1st grade cert. in edn. 1980; thirteen solo exhibs. incl. Maison de la culture Frontenac, Montréal, Galerie Horace, Sherbrooke 1993; Saint Mary's Univ. Art Gall. Halifax, Ctr. des arts contemporains du Qué. Montreal, Pierre Boucher Mus. Trois-Rivières, Low-St-Laurent Mus. Rivière-du-Loup 1991; Mus., City of Lachine 1990; Reg. Mus. of Rimouski 1989; 28 juried exhibs; 1989: Galerie Daniel, Galerie d'art Lavalin, Leo Kamen Gall. Toronto & 9 internat. exhibs.; 1988: Hotel Drouot Paris; 1987: Centre Georges Pompidou Paris; 1986: La Chartreuse, Villeneuve-lez-Avignon France etc.; eight monumental sculptures in public bldgs., Congress Hall Hull 1981; Rsch. Centre, Fernand Séguin, Montréal 1992; Asst. Dir. & Co-founder, Espace mag. 1987– ; Art Teacher, Univ. of Que. 1977–80; Outaouais Reg. H.S. Bd. 1983–86; Co-mgr., 'Galerie Comme' 1975–77; recipient of several art grants; Vice-Pres., Cons. de la Sculpture du Que. 1985–87; sculpting work in collaboration with Rolf Morosoli; author: 'Le ressac des ombres' 1988 (novel), 'Traînée rouge dans un soleil de lait' 1984 (misc. poetry); 1986, 2nd Robert Cliche Award for the novel 'Avec l'angoisse pour sablier'; Home: 3385 rue Geoffrion, Ville Saint-Laurent, Que. H4K 2V1.

**MORRIS, Hugh Clough,** B.Sc., Ph.D.; mineral industry consultant; b. Rangoon, Burma 24 June 1932; e. Univ. of Witwatersrand B.Sc. 1953, Ph.D. 1962; m. Pat; children: Katherine, Rosalind, Susan; PRESIDENT, PADRE RESOURCES CORPORATION 1993– ; Exploration / Mine Geologist, Project Manager, various companies S. Africa & Canada 1953–58; Lectr., Univ. of Witwatersrand 1958–62; var. positions incl. Dir., Exploration, Cominco Ltd., Canada 1962–79; Pres. & Chief Extve. Offr., Geomex/E & B Group 1979–83; Chrmn. & Chief Extve. Offr., Imperial Metals Corp. 1983–93; Chrmn. & Dir., Anglesey Mining plc (U.K.), Colony Pacific Exploration Ltd.; Dir., Imperial Metals Corp., Cathedral Gold Corp., Sedona Industries Ltd., Soranzo Internat. Spirits Inc., Pacific Northern Gas Ltd.; Chrmn. & Dir., Lithoprobe (NSERC); Dir. & Extve. Ctte. Mem., Candn. Global Change Program (Royal Soc. of Can.); Treas. & Dir., Candn. Geol. Found.; Mem., Geol. Soc. of London; Geol. Soc. of America; Geol. Assn. of Canada; Assn. of Profl. Engrs. of B.C., Canada; The Inst. of Mining & Metallurgy, London, U.K.; Candn. Inst. of Mining, Metallurgy & Petroleum; Home: 5326 – 4A Ave., Delta, B.C.; Office: P.O. Box 1205, Stn. A, Delta, B.C. V4M 3T3.

**MORRIS, Ian Thomas,** B.Comm., C.A., C.B.V.; financial executive; b. Yellowknife, N.W.T. 12 Nov. 1953; s. Alexander Paterson and Ernestine Georgine (Smith-Harris) M.; e. Univ. of Alta. B.Comm. 1975; m. Brenda d. George and Roberta Chorney 1 June 1974; children: Steven, Brian; SR. VICE-PRES. & CHIEF FINAN. OFFR., VENCAP EQUITIES ALBERTA LTD. 1994– ; Auditor, Price Waterhouse Edmonton 1975–80; Valuator Toronto 1981; Mgr., Valuation & Audit Edmonton 1982–85; Controller, present firm 1985–89, Chief Finan. Offr. 1989–94; Dir., Mountain Minerals Co. Ltd.; Peters & Co. Ltd.; C.A. Alta. 1978; Chartered Bus. Valuator 1985; Finance Ctte., Univ. of Alta. Bd. of Gov.; Chrmn., Jr. Achievement of N. Alta.; Extve. Mem., Riverbend Community League; Dir., S.W. Edmonton Minor Soccer Assn.; Tax Ctte., Assn. of Candn. Venture Capital Coop.; recreations: jogging, squash, skiing; clubs: Centre; Home: 5507 – 142 St., Edmonton, Alta. T6H 4B7; Office: 1980, 10180 – 101 St., Edmonton, Alta. T5J 3S4.

**MORRIS, James Victor,** M.Sc., P.Eng.; consulting engineer; b. Crieff, Scot. 18 Sept. 1930; s. Thomas Brown and Mary Steedman (Watt) M.; e. Falkirk High Sch. Scot. 1948; Strathclyde Univ. Scot. Higher Nat. Cert. 1953; Univ. of Minn. M.Sc 1962; m. Elizabeth d. Alexander and Mary Findlay 9 June 1956; children: Tom, Ann Rogers, Moira; VICE-PRES., SENES CONSULTANTS LIMITED 1989– ; Design Eng. Proctor and Redfern Ltd. 1953–55; Project Eng. James F. MacLaren Ltd. 1956–70, Gen. Mgr. S.W. Ont. and Dir. 1970–78, Sr. Vice Pres. 1978–80; Extve. Vice Pres. MacLaren Engineers Planners and Scientists Inc. 1980–81; Pres., MacLaren Plansearch Inc. 1981–89; Lectr. (Extension) Univ. of W. Ont. 1966–67; Dir. Un. Way York Region 1982–85; Capt. Mil. Engs. Assn. Can.; Diplomate, Am. Acad. Environmental Engs. Dir. Ont. Chapter Candn. Water Resources Assn. 1982–84; Pres. London Chapter Assn. Prof. Engs. Prov. Ont. 1975–76; Elder, Thornhill Presb. Ch.; recreations: golf, squash; Clubs: Thornhill Golf & Country; Mayfair Racquet; Sunningdale Golf & Country, London; Home: 77 Royal Orchard Blvd., Thornhill, Ont. L3T 3C7.

**MORRIS, Joe,** C.C.; labour executive; b. Lancashire, England 1913; s. of a British Trade Unionist; m. Margaret Cameron, in Ladysmith V.I. July 1942; has four children; Pres., Canadian Labour Congress, 1974–78; began career as a logger in forest products industry & cont. till 1948; joined Lumber & Sawmill Workers' Union in 1934; on organ. of I.W.A. on Vancouver Is. in 1936, became an active member, later becoming Chairman of the Unions Plant Comte. within the operations of the Comox Logging & Rly. Co. Ltd. with hdqrs. at Ladysmith, B.C.; on the frustration of a secessionist movement in 1948, his leadership in the struggle brought about his el. as Pres. of the re-organ. local Union (1–80, I.W.A. Duncan), and a mem. of the Staff of the Internat. Union as Field Rep.; el. Vice-Pres. of the I.W.A. Dist. Council in 1949, 1st Vice-Pres. in 1951, Pres. 1953–62; Extve. Vice-President, Candn. Labour Congress 1962–74; Regional Vice-Pres., C.L.C., 1956–62; elected for 5 successive 3 year terms as worker/member of I.L.O. Gov. Body 1966, 69, 72, 75, 78; Chrmn. of worker's group and Vice Chrmn. Gov. Body I.L.O. 1970–80; Chrmn. of I.L.O. Gov. body 1977–78; mem. Bd. Trustees, Queen's Univ. 1974–80; mem. Nat. Sci. and Egn. Research Council 1978–80; Dir., Bank of Canada 1984–87; B.C. Ferry Corporation 1984– ; Chrmn., Candn. Labour Adjustment Review Board 1982– ; Mem., Independant Comn. on Internat. Development Concerns; awarded Oficer of the Order of Canada, 1979, Companion of Canada, 1984; Hon. Deg. (Doctor of Laws), Univ. of Victoria, 1982; served in Candn. Army, commissioned in 1944; recreations: music, sports; Address: 4257 Thornhill Cres., Victoria, B.C. V8N 3G6.

**MORRIS, John F.,** B.A., M.A., Ph.D.; university educator; b. Windsor, Ont 17 Feb. 1940; s. J. Frank and Gladys M.; e. Assumption H.S. 1959; Kennedy Collegiate 1960; Univ. of Windsor B.A. (Hons.) 1965; Univ. of Windsor M.A. 1966; Univ. of Toronto Ph.D. 1977; m. Claire M. d. Raymond and Margaret Labarge 2 Aug. 1969; children: Jeremy W., Regan R.; DIRECTOR OF EXTENSION & SUMMER SESSION, UNIV. OF N.B. 1970– ; Tutor, Writing Lab., Division of Univ. Extension, Univ. of Toronto; 1967–70; Consultant, Youth and Recreation Branch, Dept. of Edn., Prov. of Ontario 1969–70; Assoc. Ed., 'Canadian Journal of University Continuing Education'; Sec.-Treas., Internat. Congress of University Adult Education; Bd. of Dir., Candn. Assn. for Adult Edn. 1989– ; Mem., Candn. Cancer Soc. N.B. Div. (various prov. & nat. cttes.; currently Pres. N.B. Div.) 1985– ; Bd. of Dir., Junior Achievement Fredericton 1989– ; co-author: 'A Selected Bibliography of Library Holdings in New Brusnwick for Labour Education' 1978, 'Continuing Education in Canadian Universities: A Summary Report of Policies and Practices' 1985; recreations: cycling, tennis, nordic skiing; Home: 786 Burden St., Fredericton, N.B. E3B 4C4; Office: Box 4400, Fredericton, N.B. E3B 5A3.

**MORRIS, Ralph D.,** Dip.Ed., Ph.D.; university professor and administrator; b. Humboldt, Sask. 13 Feb. 1940; s. Stanley T. and Margaret M. M.; e. Univ. of Colorado Dip.Ed. 1963; Univ. of Saskatchewan Ph.D. 1969; m. Carole d. Eileen and George Ward 21 Dec. 1963; children: Kimberly Teresa, Richard David; PROFESSOR OF BIOLOGY, BROCK UNIVERSITY 1985– ; Assoc. Vice-President, Academic, Brock Univ. 1992– ; Adjunct Prof., York Univ. 1988– ; primary acad. rsch. interests in behavioural & evolutionary ecology, using colonial nesting seabirds as the rsch. organism; numerous research grants from a variety of funding sources; Dir., Owl Research & Rehabilitation Foundation; mem. of num. profl. societies, Extve. memberships; editor of profl. journals; author of over 50 papers in fully refereed journals 1970– ; also num. articles in popular journals; Home: 275 Foss Rd., Fenwick, Ont. L0S 1C0; Office; St. Catharines, Ont. L2S 3A1.

**MORRIS, Richard;** fire protection specialist; b. New Glasgow, N.S. 30 Oct. 1929; s. Rowland and Marguerite (Waldren) M.; e. John Ross Robertson Pub. Sch. and Lawrence Park Coll. Inst. Toronto; Haileybury (Ont.) Sch. of Mines; Univ. of W. Ont.; m. the late Pauline Morissette 10 Sept. 1955; three s. James Rowland, Patrick John, David Michael; CHRMN., CERBERUS PYROTRONICS INC. 1973– ; Sales Rep. Qué. Pyrene Canada Ltd. 1954, Nat. Sales Mgr. 1957–71, also served as Mktg. Mgr. and Dir.; Candn. Regional Mgr. present Co. 1971–73; pioneered introduction & acceptance of smoke detectors in Can.; Dir. & 2nd Vice-Chrmn., National Fire Protection Assn.; Treas. and Trustee Learn Not To Burn Found.; Chrmn., Main Fire Alarm Ctte. of the Underwriter Laboratories of Canada; Dir. of Fire Prevention Canada; Mem., Candn. Commission on Buildings and Fire Codes; Mem. Inst. for Rsch. in Constr.; Nat. Rsch. Counc.; Past Pres. and Founding Dir. Candn. Fire Safety Assn.; Past Pres. Candn. Fire Alarm Assn.; Hon. mem., Candn. Assn. Fire Chiefs; Vice-Pres., Fire Prevention Can.; recipient, Society of Fire Protection Engineers 'Man of the Year' Award 1992; recreations: golf, curling, swimming; Club: Granite; Home: 41 Brownstone Circle, Thornhill, Ont. L4J 7P5; Office: 50 East Pearce St., Richmond Hill, Ont. L4B 1C9.

**MORRISEY, Rev. Francis G.,** O.M.I., M.A., Ph.L., S.T.L., Ph.D., J.C.D.; educator; b. Charlottetown, P.E.I. 13 Feb. 1936; s. E.J. Hodgson and Lucy Rita (Coady) M.; e. Univ. of Ottawa B.A., B.Ph. 1955, Ph.L. 1957, S.T.B. 1960, S.T.L. 1962, M.A. 1963; J.C.B. 1965, M.D.C. 1966, Ph.D. (C.L.) 1971; J.C.D. (St. Paul Univ., Ottawa) 1971; PROF. OF CANON LAW, SAINT PAUL UNIV. 1970– ; o. 1961; Sec. Eccl. Faculties Univ. of Ottawa 1963–65; Registrar present univ. 1965–71; Vice-Rector, St. Paul Univ. Seminary 1971–83; Lectr., Fac. of Canon Law, St. Paul Univ. 1970–72, Assoc. Prof. 1972–77, Titular Prof. 1977– ; Dean of Canon Law 1972–84; internat. lectr. on Canon Law and Candn. Religious Hist.; author numerous articles nat. and internat. jours.; Ed., 'Studia Canonica' 1967– ; Sec.-Treas. Candn. Canon Law Soc. 1966–73, Pres. 1973–75, Consultor 1975–77, Extve. Sec 1977–83, Hon. Life mem.; Cons., Pontifical Council for the Interpretation of Legislative Texts (Vatican City) 1985– ; Hon. Life mem. Canon Law Soc. Gt. Brit. & Ireland, Australia & N.Z., Am.; recreation: philately; Home: 175 Main St., Ottawa, Ont. K1S 1C3; Office: 223 Main St., Ottawa, Ont. K1S 1C4.

**MORRISH, Allan Henry,** B.Sc., M.A., Ph.D., FRSC, F.Inst.P., FAPS; educator; b. Winnipeg, Man. 18 Apl. 1924; s. Stanley and Agnes (Payne) M.; e. Univ. of Man., B.Sc. 1943; Univ. of Toronto, M.A. 1946; Univ. of Chicago, Ph.D. 1949; N.R.C. Postdoctoral Fellow, Bristol Univ., 1950; Guggenheim Fellow, Oxford Univ., 1957; two s. John Stanley, Allan Richard; DISTINGUISHED PROF. OF PHYSICS 1984– ; HEAD OF DEPT.,UNIV. OF MANITOBA 1966–87; Prof. of Elect. Engn., Univ. of Minn. 1953; joined present Univ. 1964 as Prof. of Physics; has served on comtes. of Nat. Research Council, Natural Sciences and Engineering Rsch. Council and Defence Research Bd., Ottawa; served as Meteorol., RCAF, 1943–44; RCNVR 1944–45; rank Lt.; convenor several confs. in physics; contrib. new knowledge in magnetic materials; author, 'The Physical Principles of Magnetism' 1965 (transl. Polish); article on Ferromagnetism in 'Encyclopaedia Britannica' 1974; book chapter 'Crystals' in 'Problems in Solid State Physics' Vol. 2; author or co-author of over 200 papers in prof. physics journs'; Co-ed. 'Magnetic Materials Digest' 1964; mem. Candn. Assn. Physics (Pres. 1974–75); Candn. Assn. Physicists' Gold Medal for Achievement in Physics 1977; Queen's Jubilee Medal; Sigma Xi; United Church; recreations: travel, swimming, hiking; Home: 71 Agassiz Dr., Winnipeg, Man. R3T 2K9; Office: Winnipeg, Man. R3T 2N2.

**MORRISH, John Herbert,** B.A.Sc., P.Eng.; b. Cherrywood, Ont. 6 Aug. 1930; s. late Albert Roy and late MaryElla (Milroy) M.; e. Cherrywood (Ont.) Pub. Sch., 1943; Scarborough (Ont.) High Sch., 1948; Univ. of Toronto, B.A.Sc. 1952, Degree in Civil Engn. 1953; m. Elizabeth Anne; d. late Ernest Lunn, Bowmanville, Ont. 7 March 1953; children: Catherine, David; CHRMN. & DIR., FORDING COAL LIMITED 1990– ; Dir., NYCO Minerals Inc.; GWIL Industries Inc.; joined Engineering Department, Canadian Pacific Rly. Co. 1949, Asst. Engr. Toronto 1953, Asst. Div. Engr. Montreal 1957, Div. Engr. Schreiber, Ont. 1959, Moose Jaw, Sask. 1963, Winnipeg, Man. 1964, Mgr. Freight Devel. Vancouver 1966, Freight Sales and Devel. 1968, System Mgr.-Planning, Montreal 1969, Mgr. Market Devel. 1970; Vice Pres., Marketing and Sales, C.P. Rail 1974–77; Pres. & C.E.O., Fording Coal Ltd. 1977–90; Chrmn., Coal Assn. of Can. 1981 and 1988; Chrmn., World Coal Inst.; mem. Internat. Energy Agency; Coal Ind. Adv. Bd; Assn. Prof. Engrs. Prov. Ont.; Univ. of Toronto Alumni Assn.; Mem., Canada Taiwan Business Assn.; Mem. & Vice-Chrmn., Canada-Japan Businessmen's Assn.; Canada-Korea Business Counc.; Office: 205 Ninth Ave. S.E., Calgary, Alta. T2G 0R3.

**MORRISON, Alex,** M.S.C., C.D., M.A.; executive director ; b. Sydney, N.S. 23 Jan. 1941; s. Alexander Joseph and Agnes Marie (Nicholson) M.; e. elem. and secondary schs. N.S.; Mount Allison Univ. B.A. 1968; Royal Mil. Coll. Can. M.A. 1980; m. Janice d. Everett and Viola Woodman 1962; one d. Margo; EXTVE. DIR. CANDN. INST. OF STRATEGIC STUDIES 1989– ; served Candn. forces 1956–90; trans. from Black Watch to PPCLI 1970; Chrmn. Candn. Ctte. Hist. Second World War 1983; served Perm. Mission Can. to UN 1983–89; promoted to Min.-Counsellor 1988; mem. Security Council Del. , Rapporteur-Gen. 1987 Conf. Relationship between Disarmament & Devel., Pres. Internat. Yr. Peace Pledging Conf., Vice Pres. Special Ctte. Peacekeeping Operations, mem. Indian Ocean Ctte.; 43rd session UN Gen. Assembly 1988, Chrmn. Barton Group; Mem., Internat. Assn. of Univ. Presidents Commission on Arms Control Education; retired regular army 1990, rank Lt. Col.; lectr, Candn. Mil. Hist. Royal Mil. Coll. 1982–83; Columbia Univ. N.Y. 1988; Glendon Coll., York Univ. 1987– ; author 'The Voice of Defence; The History of the Conference of Defence Associations' 1982; ed. several books and periodicals incl. 'Peacekeeping and International Relations'; 'The McNaughton Papers (The Canadian Journal of Strategic Studies); 'The Canadian Strategic Forecast Annual'; 'Peacekeeping, Peacemaking or War: International Security Enforcement' 1991; 'Divided We Fall: The National Security Implications of Canadian Constitutional Issues' 1992; 'A Continuing Commitment: Canada and North Atlantic Security' 1992; 'The Changing Face of Peacekeeping' 1993; Decorated with Meritorious Service Cross by Gov.-Gen. Sauve 1989; recipient, Award of Merit from Secretary of State for External Affairs 1991; Club: Royal Candn. Mil. Inst.; Office: 76 St. Clair Ave. W., Suite 502, Toronto, Ont. M4V 1N2.

**MORRISON, Alexander B.,** B.Sc., M.Sc., Ph.D., M.S.; church official; b. Edmonton, Alta. 22 Dec. 1930; s. Alexander S. and Christina G. (Wilson) M.; e. Univ. of Alta. B.Sc. 1951, M.Sc. 1952; Cornell Univ. Ph.D. 1956; Univ. of Michigan M.S. 1966; m. Shirley d. Leonard and Winnifred Brooks 23 Dec. 1950; children: David, Barbara, Howard, Sandra, Allen, Jeffrey, Heather, Mary; General Authority, Church of Jesus Christ of Latter-Day Saints, 1987– ; Chemist Mead Johnson & Co., Evansville, Ind. 1956–59; various tech. and managerial positions Dept. of National Health & Welfare, Ottawa 1959–72, Asst. Depy. Min. in charge of Health Protection Br. 1972–84; Prof. and Chrmn., Dept. of Food Science, Univ. of Guelph 1984–87; frequent cons. to World Health Orgn. on human health in developing countries, tropical diseases, nutrition, essential drugs; author of a number of tech. reports and papers on nutrition, biochemistry, toxicology, public health; former Dir. Connaught Laboratories; CDC Life Sciences (resigned 1987); Visiting Prof. of Pharmacology, Univ. of Toronto; Church of Jesus Christ of Latter-day Saints; Fellow Royal Soc. of Med.; Chem. Inst. of Can.; recipient Queen's Jubilee Medal; David M. Kennedy Internat. Service Award, Brigham Young Univ.; recreation: family; Home: 3852 South Monarch Dr., Bountiful, Utah 84010; Office: 47 East South Temple, Salt Lake City, Utah 84150.

**MORRISON, Cathleen,** B.A.; association executive; b. Brantford, Ont. 17 Apl. 1943; d. late Judge James E. Brown and Elizabeth Eedy Brown Frye; e. Brantford Coll. Inst. 1961; Univ. of Toronto B.A. 1965 (Walter Massey Scholarship Victoria Univ. 1961); m. Ian s. Rev. Dr. George and Robina Morrison Aug. 1966; two s. Patrick, Colin; EXTVE. DIR. CANDN. CYSTIC FIBROSIS FOUND. 1981– ; Teacher of Eng. Lang. & Lit. Prog. W. German Min. of Culture Staatliches Nicholaus Cusanus Gymnasium Bonn/Bad Godesberg 1965–66; Teacher of

Eng. Nat. Ballet Sch. 1966–69; Extve. Dir. Ont. Assn. Children's Mental Health Centres 1976–81; Chrmn. Ctte. Nat. Voluntary Health Agencies 1988–90, mem. since 1981; Dir. J.D. Griffin Adolescent Centre 1982–85; Social Planning Council Metrop. Toronto 1975–82, Chrmn. Extve. Ctte. 1978–80; Bd. Mgmt. Nat. Action Ctte. Status Women 1974–78, Extve. Offr. 1975–78, Adv. 1978–79; Steering Ctte. Ont. Ctte. Status Women 1973–80; Home: 184 Moore Ave., Toronto, Ont. M4T 1V8; Office: 601, 2221 Yonge St., Toronto, Ont. M4S 2B4.

**MORRISON, Claudia C.,** M.A., Ph.D.; educator; writer; b. Galveston, Texas 17 Nov. 1936; d. Joseph Arthur and Edna Lorene (Crawford) Christopherson; e. American Univ. B.A. 1957; Univ. of Fla. M.A. 1958; Univ. of N.C. Ph.D. 1964; div.; two d. Barbara Lynette, Laura Elaine; PROF. OF ENG. JOHN ABBOTT COLL. 1971– ; Prof. Sweetbriar Coll. 1965, Youngstown State Univ. 1966–68, Univ. of Waterloo 1969–71; recipient 3rd Prize CBC Lit. Competition Memoir Div. 1980; author 'Freud and the Critic' 1968; 'From the Foot of the Mountain' novel 1990; Home: 169 Fairhaven Ave., Pointe Claire, Que. H9S 4A6; Office: P.O. Box 2000, Ste Anne de Bellevue, Que. H9X 3L9.

**MORRISON, George Hamilton,** M.D., F.R.C.P.(C); physician, internist; b. Kincardine, Ont.; s. John George and Agnes Isabel (Hamilton) M.; e. Univ. of Toronto M.D. 1952; m. Mary d. Marwood and Marion Parish 10 Aug. 1957; children: George William, John Robert Gordon, Gillian Mary, Catherine Elizabeth; PAST PRES., COLLEGE OF PHYSICIANS & SURGEONS OF ONTARIO 1991–92; practice of Internal Medicine, Fort William Clinic, Thunder Bay 1958– ; Home: 2720 Silles Court, Thunder Bay, Ont. P7C 1R1; Office: 117 S. McKellar St., Thunder Bay, Ont. P7E 1H5.

**MORRISON, Rev. George Matthew,** B.Com., F.C.A., M.Div., D.D. (Un. Ch.); b. Toronto, Ont. 7 June 1913; s. George William and Hattie Euphemia (McCrimmon) M.; e. Univ. of Toronto Schs. 1931; Univ. of Toronto B.Com. 1936, Emmanuel Coll. M.Div. 1956; Inst. C.A.'s, C.A. 1939; D.D. Victoria Univ. (Toronto); St. Andrew's Univ. (Scot.); m. Robina Douglas, d. late Andrew B. and Jessie M. (Bell) Taylor 2 Sept. 1940; children: Ian George, Janet Robina Carey; Acct. Fur Trade, Hudson's Bay Co. 1939–40, Partner Henry Barber Mapp & Mapp 1944–49; Controller IBM World Trade Corp. 1949–53; Secy. Div. Finance Un. Ch. Can. H.Q. 1958; Min. Ryerson Un. Ch. Vancouver 1966, Secy. Gen. Council 1971–75; Sr. Min., Timothy Eaton Mem. Ch., Toronto, 1975–78 (ret.); served with RCAF 1941–44, observer; author various books and articles; Inst. C.A.'s Ont. and Can.; Home: #8 - 7130 Ash Cres., Vancouver, B.C. V6P 3K7.

**MORRISON, Harold Lavell,** B.Sc.; retired; b. Edmonton, Alta. 2 Jan. 1928; s. Ibrahim F. and Kathleen B. (Lavell) M.; e. Univ. High Sch., Edmonton; Univ. of Alta., B.Sc. (Civil Engn.) 1950; m. Norma, d. Edward S. Forsyth, Regina, Sask., 5 March 1955; children: Nancy Gail, Ian Forsyth; PRES. & DIR., H.L. MORRISON CONSULTANTS INC.; Sessional Demonst., Univ. of Alta., 1950–51; Staff Engr., Brown & Root Ltd., Edmonton, 1951–58; Chief Engr. 1958–63; Gen. Mgr. Hardy Associates Ltd. 1963–75; Pres. & C.E.O. 1975–86; Life mem., Assn. Prof. Engrs. Alta. (Council 1961–63; Vice Pres. 1963–64); Engn. Inst. Can.; Cdn. Soc. for Civil Eng., (Fellow 1983); Candn. Council Prof. Engrs. (Dir. 1965–71; Pres. 1971–72); Treas., Consulting Engineers of Alta., 1978–80; Dir., Assn. of Consulting Engrs of Can., 1980–84; Technical Serv. Council 1981–86; Gov., Alberta College 1982–90; mem., Univ. of Alta. Hosps. Bd. (Vice-Chrmn. 1990–93); City of Edmonton Rapid Transit Advisory Board (Vice-Chrmn. 1992–93); City of Edmonton Devel. Appeal Bd. 1987–92 (Chrmn. 1992– ); mem. United Church; Club: Rotary (Pres. 1984–85); Home: 14004 – 88 Ave., Edmonton, Alta. T5R 4J3; Office: 1790 – 10405 Jasper Ave., Edmonton, Alta. T5J 3N4.

**MORRISON, Hugh Whitney,** B.A., M.A.; retired; b. Vegreville, Alta. 15 May 1908; s. Judge Frederic Augustus (Getchell) and Mabel (Wood) Whitney M.; e. Strathcona H.S. 1926; Univ. of Alberta, B.A. 1930; Oxford Univ. B.A. (Hons.) 1932, post-grad. study 1933, M.A. 1964; Rhodes Scholar (Alta.) Merton Coll., Oxford 1930; Sir James Aikins Scholarship; Samuel R. Hosford Mem. Prize in Shakespeare; m. Florentine St. Clair Sherman, Patricia LeMoine FitzGerald (d. 1976), Marita LaFlèche (d. 1992); one s. Hugh Peter St. Clair; reporter, Evening Standard 1933; rep. and ed., Toronto Star, Star Weekly 1934–37; Dir., Talks & Public Affairs, C.B.C. 1938–42; produced war-effort series 'We Have Been There' (more than 35,000 copies sold) 1941–42;

wartime assignment Asst. to Pres. for a Central American airline (T.A.C.A.) and Br. W. Indian Airways 1943–47; Head, Latin Amer. Overseas ShortWave Broadcasting Serv., C.B.C. 1948; first pub. rel. dir., United Way of Gter. Toronto 1952; retired 1972; teacher, Humber Coll.; retired 1983; Apptd. Gen. Editor, Ben-Simon Publications, Brentwood Bay, B.C. 1993; Centennial Medal 1967; Queen's Jubilee Medal 1977; Cit. for Meritorious Serv.: Canadian Welfare Council 1972, United Way of America 1972; Volunteer Serv. Medal, Canadian Red Cross Soc. 1973–83; Sec.-Treas., Canadian Assoc. of Rhodes Scholars 1969–77; Vice-Pres. 1977–79; Pres. 1979–81; Bd. mem., Volunteer Soc. of Metro Toronto 1983–85; Merton Soc. Oxford; former mem., Canadian Player's Found.; Theatre Toronto; Arts & Letters Club 1962–76; Toronto Press Club 1952–77; Dir., Oxford Univ. Found. of Canada; mem., Canadian Rhodes Scholar Found.; author: 'Water,' 'Valse Triste'; short stories in Star Weekly, 'Oxford Today and the Canadian Rhodes Scholarships' 1958, 'Shakespeare, His Daughters & his Tempest' 1963, numerous feature articles; contrib.: 'Public Relations in Canada' 1984, oral history of C.B.C. for P.A.C.; has made numerous donations of original art, books and ms. to various univs., archives and art galleries; recreation: bicycling; Home: 1211 - 50 Inverlochy Blvd., Thornhill, Ont. L3T 4T6.

**MORRISON, Ian,** B.A., M.Sc.; association executive; b. Toronto, Ont. 11 July 1944; s. George and Robina (Taylor) M.; e. Univ. of Toronto B.A. 1965; London Sch. of Econ. M.Sc. 1966; m. Cathleen d. James and Elizabeth Brown 6 Aug. 1966; children: Patrick, Colin; PRES., COALESCENCE INC. 1993– ; Nat. Programs Dir., Frontier College 1966–70; Pres. 1971–74; Extve. Dir., Candn. Assn. for Adult Education 1975–93; Chair, Coalition of Nat. Voluntary Orgns. 1976–84; Spokesperson, Friends of Candn. Broadcasting 1985– ; Managing Dir., Friends of Ontario Universities 1992– ; Citation for Citizenship 1989; Dir., Candn. Ctr. for Philanthropy; The Donwood Inst.; Internat. Counc. for Adult Edn.; Theatre du P'Tit Bonheur; Trillium Found.; United Ch. of Can.; YMCA; Mem. of the Bd. of Regents, Victoria Univ. (Univ. of Toronto); co-author: 'Human Resources Development and a Competitive Economy' 1990; Home: 184 Moore Ave., Toronto, Ont. M4T 1V8; Office: 29 Prince Arthur Ave., Toronto, Ont. M5R 1B2.

**MORRISON, James A.,** F.C.A.; accounting executive; b. Goderich, Ont. 18 July 1934; s. Patrick Daniel and Anne (McLeod) M.; e. Toronto schools; C.A. 1959; m. Kathryn d. Francis and Gertrude Connolly 17 June 1961; children: Terese, Ian, Stuart, Michael, Sean; CHRMN., DELOITTE & TOUCHE INC. and PARTNER, DELOITTE & TOUCHE; Dir. Prof. Standards, Touche Ross International 1979–82; former Treas. and Dir. United Way of Metro. Toronto; former Dir., Candn. Red Cross; mem. Auditing Standards Ctte., Candn. Inst. of C.A.s; Profl. Conduct Ctte., Ont. Inst. of C.A.s; Fellow, Inst. of C.A.s of Ont. 1979; author: 'Report of the Special Examination by James A. Morrison, F.C.A. of Crown Trust Company, Greymac Trust Company, Seaway Trust Company, Greymac Mortgage Corporation and Seaway Mortgage Corporation' 1983; recreations: swimming, golf; Clubs: National; Weston Golf and Country; Metropolitan; Home: 55 The Kingsway, Toronto, Ont. M8X 2T3; Office: 95 Wellington St. W., Toronto, Ont. M5J 2P4.

**MORRISON, Ken J.,** B.Comm.; management consultant; e. Sir George Williams Univ. (now Concordia) B.Comm. 1972 (Royal Bank Muir Medallion; Froost Medal as highest ranking grad.); PRESIDENT, KEN MORRISON CONSULTING INC. 1993– ; Financial Extve., Royal Bank of Canada 1960–93; joined Royal Bank in North Bay, Ont. 1960 and held banking posts in various branches until 1965; accelerated training program 1965; Systems Officer 1966; apptd. to task force to devel. long-range systems plan 1967; attended univ. 1968–72; Vice-Pres., Systems Devel., Royal Bank 1981; Planning, Technol. & Finan. Mngt. 1985; Information Technol. Strategy 1987; Technol. & Distribution 1988; Network Planning & Automation 1990–92; Quality Serv. & Planning, Retail Banking 1992–93; involved in a broad range of special bank & external cttes.; Mem., Candn. Bankers Assn.; Candn. Payments Assn.; regular speaker on topics such as technology, security, privacy & edn.; has held posts in a number of community, sports & local govt. orgns.; Chair, Bd. of Gov., John Abbott College 1975–82; Office: Montreal, Que. H9W 5Y3.

**MORRISON, Robert Neil,** B.Eng., M.A.; educator; b. Trois Rivières, Qué. 21 July 1931; s. Thomas W. and Alison H. (McQueen) M.; e. McGill Univ. B.Eng. 1953 (Ernest Brown Gold Medal in Eng.); Oxford Univ. B.A.

1956, M.A. 1959 (Rhodes Scholar 1953–56; Jenkins Prize in Philos., Politics & Econ.); m. H. Doreen d. Wallace R. Henry, Q.C. 6 June 1959; children: Neil, Ian, Cynthia; PROF. OF MGMT. McGILL UNIV. 1968– ; Pres. Rodnic Holdings Inc. 1980– ; Dir. Manecon Associates Ltd.; Peacock Inc. 1981–92; Innotech Aviation Ltd. 1974–80; Cons. Eng. Racey, MacCallum & Assoc. 1956–59; Asst. to Pres. Dupont of Canada Ltd. 1959–62; Associate Prof. present Univ. 1962, Dir. Mgmt. Inst. 1967–82; author 'Corporate Adaptability to Bilingualism and Biculturalism ' 1970; 'The Use of French and the Employment of Francophones in Business in Québec' 1973; co-author 'Business and Economic Forecasting for Microcomputers' 1984; ed. 'Pipeline Regulation and Inflation: An Evaluation of Tariff Levelling' 1983; Mem. Senate & Mem. Bd. of Govs., McGill Univ.; Pres.: McGill Assn. Univ. Teachers 1984–85; Sixteen Island Lake Assn.; Senator, Presb. Coll. Montréal 1983–86; Elder, Montréal W. Presb. Ch.; Chrmn., United Church Montreal Homes for Elderly People; St. Andrew's Presbyterian Homes Found.; mem. Order Engs. Qué. recreations: travel, golf, reading; Home: 341 Ballantyne Ave. N., Montréal West, Qué. H4X 2C4; Office: Faculty of Mgmt., McGill Univ., 1001 Sherbrooke St. W., Montréal, Qué. H3A 1G5.

**MORRISON, (Stanley) Roy,** Ph.D.; professor emeritus; b. Saskatoon, Sask. 24 Sept. 1926; s. Latto McKechnie and Lilian Sarah (Prowse) M.; e. Univ. of B.C., B.A. 1948, M.A. 1949; Univ. of Pennsylvania, Ph.D. 1953; post-doctoral work, Univ. of Illinois 1953–55; m. Phyllis d. James and Sheila Parkinson 27 Aug. 1949; children: Catherine, Deborah, Barbara; PROFESSOR EMERITUS, SIMON FRASER UNIV. 1992– ; Staff Sci. to Asst. Dir. Rsch., Honeywell Rsch. Ctr. 1955–64; Sr. Sci. to Mgr., Surface Group, Stanford Rsch. Inst. 1964–82; Prof. of Physics & Dir., Energy Rsch. Inst., Simon Fraser Univ. 1982–92; Vis. Sci., Univ. of Gottingen; U.S. Army Rsch. Labs, Fort Monmouth, N.J.; numerous cons. contracts; awarded two certs. of merit from NASA; Fellowship, Japan Soc. for Promotion of Sci.; Mem., Candn. Assn. of Physicists; Candn. Inst. of Chem.; Am. Phys. Soc.; Surface Group of Am. Chem. Soc.; author: 'The Chemical Physics of Surfaces' (also translated into Chinese); 'Electrochemistry at Semiconductor and Oxidized Metal Electodes' (also transl. into Chinese and Russian); co-author: 'Adsorption,' 'Chemical Sensing with Solid State Devices'; recreations: tennis, boating; Office: Physics Dept. Simon Fraser Univ., Burnaby, B.C. V5A 1A6.

**MORRISON, Roy Alexander;** aviation executive; b. Hamilton, Ont. 10 Dec. 1940; s. Roy Buckley and Rosemary (Tulk) M.; e. Lisgar Coll. Inst., Ottawa, Ont.; Univ. of W. Ont.; m. Donna Justine, 31 May 1973 (deceased); children: Bruce John, Deborah Lynn, Tara Justine; VICE-PRES., CORPORATE COMMUNICATIONS, GOVERNMENT & INDUSTRY RELATIONS, AIR CANADA since 1992; Reporter, CFRA, Ottawa, 1960; Correspondent, United Press International, Parliamentary Press Gallery, Ottawa 1963; Nat. Ed., CTV Nat. News, 1965; Extve. Asst., Min. of Transport, Ottawa, 1966; Vice-Pres. Transair Limited, Winnipeg 1969; Extve. Vice Pres. Transair Limited 1973; Extve. Vice-Pres. Northwest Territorial Airways Ltd., Yellowknife and Calgary 1977; Vice-Pres., H.B. Nickerson & Sons Ltd., Sydney, N.S. 1980; Pres. & CEO, Brewers Assn. of Canada 1984; recipient: Centennial Medal 1967; Mem. Bd. of Dirs., Transport Assn. of Canada; Mem. Bd. of Trustees, Alcoholic Beverage Medical Research Foundation, Johns Hopkins Univ., Baltimore, Md. since 1985; Anglican; recreations: golf, skiing, fishing; Clubs: Rideau Club (Ottawa), Royal Ottawa Golf, National Press (Ottawa); Home: 153 Dunbarton Court, Ottawa, Ont. K1K 6L4; Office: 20th Floor, 275 Slater St., Ottawa, Ont. K1P 5H9.

**MORRISON, Scot,** B.Sc., M.F.A.; writer; b. Edmonton, Alta. 8 Sept. 1957; s. Robert Malcolm and Laurie Joanna M.; e. Univ. of Alta. B.Sc. 1980; Univ. of B.C. M.F.A. 1988; m. Karen d. Moneer and Patricia Hamdon 29 Aug. 1981; children: Anissa Jenny, Geordie Moneer; Writers Cons. Film & Lit. Arts Br. Alta. Culture & Multiculturalism Edmonton 1990; coll. instr. in Eng. & Creative Writing Grant MacEwan Community Coll. Edmonton 1988–90; freelance jour. since 1980; recipient Alta. New Fiction Competition Award 1988; Alta. TV Script Writing Competition Award 1986; author 'Noble Sanctuary' (novel) 1990; Address: c/o Doubleday Canada Ltd., 105 Bond St., Toronto, Ont. M5B 1V3.

**MORRISON, Stuart John Innes;** publisher; b. Croydon, Surrey, Eng. 6 April 1949; s. Alexander Innes and Geraldine Mary M.; e. Eltham Coll.; children: Alexander, Andrew; PUBLISHER, CANADIAN LAWYER mag. 1984– ; Vice Pres. Canada Law Book 1984– ; Jus-

tice of the Peace B.C. 1973–77; Courts Planning Atty.-Gen. B.C. 1977–80; Gen. Mgr. Western Legal Publications 1980–82; P. Conservative; recreations: motorcycling, hunting; Club: Albany; Home: 10 Sumach St., Toronto, Ont. M5A 3J4; Office: 240 Edward St., Aurora, Ont. L4G 3S9.

**MORRISON, William Douglas,** B.S.A., M.Sc., Ph.D., F.A.I.C.; university professor; b. Provost, Alta. 16 Oct. 1927; s. Duncan and Eleanor (Ferrier) M.; e. Waterdown H.S. 1944; Univ. of Toronto, B.S.A. 1949; Univ. of Ill., M.Sc. 1954, Ph.D. 1955; m. Barbara-Jean d. Walter and Kathleen Frid 28 May 1949; children: Jo-Anne, Jacqueline, Douglas, Scott; PROFESSOR EMERITUS, DEPT. OF ANIMAL & POULTRY SCI., UNIV. OF GUELPH 1993– ; Territory Mgr., Master Feeds 1949–52; Nutritionist 1955–61; Dir., Nutrition & Rsch., Agric. Div., Maple Leaf Mills Ltd. 1961–71; Prof. & Chrmn., Dept. of Animal & Poultry Sci., Univ. of Guelph 1971–82, Prof. 1982–93; Fellow, Agric. Inst. of Can.; Dir., Shantymen's Christian Assn.; Mem., Am. Soc. of Animal Sci.; Candn. Soc. of Animal Sci.; Poultry Sci.; Candn. Sci. & Christian Affiliation; Home: R.R. #4, Fergus, Ont. N1M 2W5.

**MORRISON, William Robert,** B.A., M.A., Ph.D.; university professor; b. Hamilton, Ont. 26 Jan. 1942; s. William Robert and Elizabeth Louise (Ward) M.; e. Westdale S.S. 1959; McMaster Univ., B.A. 1963, M.A. 1964; Univ. of West. Ont. Ph.D. 1973; m. Linda d. Ronald and Clair Deacon 1 May 1976; children: Catherine, John, Claire, Ruth; DEAN OF RESEARCH AND GRADUATE STUDIES, UNIV. OF NORTHERN BRITISH COLUMBIA 1992– ; joined faculty, Brandon Univ. 1969; Prof., Dept. of History, Brandon Univ. 1985–89; joined faculty, Lakehead Univ. 1989; Dir., Centre for Northern Studies, Lakehead Univ. 1990–92; author: 'A Survey of the History and Claims of the Native People of Northern Canada' 1984; 'Showing the Flag' 1985; co-author 'Land of the Midnight Sun: A History of the Yukon' 1988; 'The Sinking of the Princess Sophia: Taking the North Down With Her' 1990; 'The Alaska Highway in World War II: The U.S. Army of Occupation in Canada's Northwest' 1992; 'The Forgotten North' 1992; 'Working the North: Labor and the Northwest Defense Projects' 1994; co-editor 'For Purposes of Dominion: Essays in Honour of Morris Zaslow' 1989; 'Interpreting the North: Selected Readings' 1989; 'My Dear Maggie: Letters from a Western Manitoba Pioneer' 1991; Office: U.N.B.C., P.O. Bag 1950, Prince George, B.C. V2L 5P3.

**MORRISSETTE, Gaëtan C.;** retired company executive; b. Quebec, Que. 9 May 1910; s. Achille and Augusta (Kerstius) M.; e. Mount St. Bernard Coll.; m. Lillian, (deceased), d. late J. A. Bilodeau, 18 Feb. 1933; children: Lise, Paul, John, Peter; m. Françoise Stringer, 7 March 1971; joined Standard Brands Limited as Acct., 1930; Comptroller and Asst. Secy., 1943; el. a Dir., 1944; Secy.-Treas., 1945; Vice-Pres., 1954; Vice-Pres.-Adm., 1958; Chrmn. of the Bd. & C.E.O., Nabisco Brands Ltd. 1961–75, Chrmn. 1975–83; Hon. Chrmn., Nabisco Brands Ltd. 1983–88; R. Catholic; recreations: fishing; Clubs: Saint-Denis; The Mount Royal Club; Kataska F&G; Home: Apt. 301, 100 Hall St., Nun's Island, Que. H3E 1P3.

**MORRISSETTE, Jean F.;** business executive; b. Montreal, Que. 3 Sept. 1942; s. Gaetan C. and Lilliane (Bilodeau) M.; m. Margot Michaud 1965; children: Sylvie, Natalie; CHRMN. OF THE BOARD & CHIEF EXTVE. OFFR., PARCAP MNGT. INC., Chrmn., Parcap Elect. & Elect. Inc., Parcap Technol. Inc. (incl. subsidaries & companies); Man of the Month, Electrical Indus. 1976; clubs: Mount Royal; St. Denis; Office: 800 René Lévesque Blvd., Suite 2450, Montréal, Qué. H3B 4V7.

**MORRISSETTE, Pierre L.,** B.A., M.B.A.; communications executive; b. Montreal, Que. 15 Mar. 1947; s. Gaetan C. and Lillian (Bilodeau) M.; e. Loyola H.S. 1964; Loyola of Montreal B.A. Econ. 1968; Univ. of W. Ont. M.B.A. 1972; PRES. & C.E.O., PELMOREX COMMUNICATIONS INC., DIR. OF M-CORP. INC. & CANTEL INC. 1989– ; Commercial Lending, Canadian Imperial Bank of Commerce 1968–70; Br. and Regional Mgmt. Commercial Lending, Royal Bank of Canada 1972–77; Vice-Pres. Fin., Telemedia Communications Inc. 1977–79; Sr. Vice-Pres. and Chief Financial Officer, Telemedia Inc. 1979–83; Pres. Telemedia Ventures 1983; Pres. & C.E.O., Candn. Satellite Communications Inc. (Cancom) 1983–89; R. Catholic; recreations: skiing and water sports; Home: R.R. 3, Collingwood, Ont.; Office: 186 Robert Speck Parkway, Suite 200, Mississauga, Ont. L4Z 3G1.

**MORRISSEY, Kim,** B.A.; writer; b. Canada 8 March 1955; d. Leslie Dales; e. Mount Royal College, Radio Broadcasting 1975; Univ. of Saskatchewan B.A. (Hons.) 1979; m. the late Prof. L.J. s. Edith and Edward M. 16 Oct. 1980; Step-children: Timothy Edward, Kathleen Marie, Sean Henry; Founding Mem., Sask. Playwrights' Centre; Robert Kroetsch Prose Scholarship, Fort San Summer Sch. of the Arts 1988; Mem., Playwrights Union of Can.; League of Candn. Poets; Writers Union of Can.; PEN Internat.; Sask. Writers Guild; author: 'Batoche' (3rd Prize, CBC Nat. Poetry Contest 1987; shortlisted, Gerald Lampert Award (Best First Book: League of Candn. Poets); taught in univs. in Canada, Britain & Germany) 1989, '90, 92; 'Poems For Men Who Dream Of Lolita' 1992; 'Dora: A Case of Hysteria' (stage play) produced in Regina 1987, Kentucky '90, Victoria '92, St. John's '92, London, England '93, (radio adaptation) produced on BBC Radio 3 1991, (book) published by Nick Hern Books 1994; recreations: reading, riding, travelling; Office: c/o Coteau Books, 401 – 2206 Dewdney Ave., Regina, Sask. S4R 1H3.

**MORRISSEY, Hon. Robert J.,** M.L.A.; politician; b. Alberton, P.E.I. 18 Nov. 1954; s. the late Bernard C. and Marie Joan (O'Connor) M.; e. Sea Cow Pond Elem.; Tignish Regional High Schs.; Holland Coll.; Univ. of P.E.I.; MIN. OF ECONOMIC DEVELOPMENT & TOURISM, P.E.I. 1993– ; Minister resp. for Enterprise P.E.I.; Mem., Management Board; Mem., Cabinet Ctte. on Rural Development; Mem., Cabinet Ctte. on Govt. Reform; el. M.L.A. for First Prince prov. g.e. 1982, re-el. 1986, 1989, 1993; Min. of Industry, P.E.I. 1989–93; Min. of Transp. and Public Works, P.E.I. 1986–89; Past Mem., Treasury Bd., Policy Bd.; Former Trustee, Unit One Sch. Bd.; Chrmn. W. Prince Adv. Bd.; Orgn. mem. Tignish Irish Moss Festival; mem. St. Simon and St. Jude Cath. Ch.; Home: Sea Cow Pond, Tignish, P.E.I. C0B 2B0; Office: P.O. Box 2000, Charlottetown, P.E.I. C1A 7N8.

**MORRISSON, J. Norman;** business executive; b. Montreal, Que. 27 April 1943; s. J. Albert and Yvette (Cantara) M.; e. Univ. of Montreal H.E.C.; m. Lucie Dufresne 26 April 1986; one s.: Steven B.; CHAIRMAN & CHIEF EXECUTIVE OFFICER, CABANO TRANSPORTATION GROUP INC.; var. positions ending as Vice-Pres. Quebec & Dir., Pitfield Mackay Ross Ltd. 1967–84; Vice-Pres. & Dir., F.H. Deacon Hodgson 1984–87; Founder & Chief Extve. Offr., Saumier & Morrisson & Assoc. (merged with Midland Doherty 1989); Founder & Chairman, Alpha Capital Inc. 1990– ; Dir., Capital Trust Inc.; Premier CDN Enterprises Ltd.; Groupe SECPRO Inc.; recreations: golf, reading; clubs: Le Club Saint-Denis, Le Club Laval Sur Le Lac, Le Club de Golf de la Vallée du Richelieu; Home: 1024 Emile Nelligan, Boucherville, Que. J4B 2L4; Office: 6600 chemin St-François, St-Laurent, Que. H4J 1B7.

**MORROW-GIGANTES, Joanne,** B.A.; arts administrator; b. Ithaca, N.Y. 27 Sept. 1949; d. John David and Edith Patterson (Whicher) Morrow; e. Univ. of Toronto Trinity Coll. B.A. 1971; m. Terry s. Christodoulos and Mary Gigantes 6 March 1976; children: Christos Alexander, Adèle Marie; ASST. DIR. and DIR. OF THE ARTS DIVISION, THE CANADA COUNCIL 1993– ; Grants Adm. Touring Office Can. Council Ottawa 1973–76; Prodn. Mgr. Les Productions Internationales Albert Sarfati, Paris 1978–80; Music Adm. Nat. Arts Centre of Can. Ottawa 1981, Music Producer 1985–89; Head of Music and Opera, The Canada Council 1989–93; Office: P.O. Box 1047, Ottawa, Ont. K1P 5V8.

**MORSE, Barry;** actor; director; writer; b. London, Eng. 10 June 1918; s. Charles Hayward and Mary Florence (Hollis) M.; e. London, Eng. Schs.; Royal Acad. of Dramatic Art, London, Eng. (scholarship) 1935–37; m. Sydney, d. late Archibald Richard Sturgess, 26 March 1939; children: Melanie Virginia Sydney, Hayward Barry; first prof. stage appearance in London, Eng., Dec. 1936; first radio, BBC, London, 1936; first film, England, 1940; first television, Eng., BBC 1938; came to Canada, 1951 since when has appeared on radio and television for CBC in Can., BBC and ITV in England, and CBS, NBC and ABC in U.S. as well as many film and stage productions in all three countries as actor and director; to date has played over 2,000 roles in various media; five times winner of award for Best Actor in Candn. television (1954, 1956, 1959, 1960, 1961); dir., 'Staircase,' Broadway 1968; starred in title role of 'Hadrian VII' on Broadway and in Australia 1969; Scrooge in 'A Christmas Carol' – Canadian theatres 1980–83; devised and presented one-man stage show 'Merely Players,' Canadian tours 1983 and 1987–88; World première of Shaw's 'The Philanderer' Hampstead Theatre, London, England 1991; television series include 'The Fugitive' 1963–67; 'The Golden Bowl' 1972; 'The Adventurer' 1973; 'The Zoo Gang' 1974; 'Space 1999' 1975–76;; 'The Winds of War' 1981; 'Whoops Apocalypse' 1981–82; 'Strange but True' (Host) 1983; 'Master of the Game' 1984; 'The Covenant' (Series pilot) 1985; 'War and Remembrance' 1986–87; 'Tekwar' 1993; feature films and films for TV include 'Power Play' 1977; 'The Changeling' 1978; 'The Shape of Things to Come' 1978; 'Klondike Fever' 1979; 'Cries in the Night' 1979; 'The Hounds of Notre Dame' 1980; 'A Tale of Two Cities' 1980; 'Bells' 1980; 'The Legacy of Mark Rothko' 1981; Mark Twain's 'Innocents Abroad' 1982; 'Sadat' (Menachem Begin) 1983; 'A Woman of Substance' 1984; 'Reunion' 1985; 'The Return of Sherlock Holmes' 1986; 'The Race for the Bomb' 1986; 'Fight for Life' 1987; 'Hoover vs. the Kennedys' 1987; 'Glory! Glory!' 1988; 'Ray Bradbury Series' New Zealand 1990; 'Al Lupo, lupo' Italy 1992; 'J.F.K.: Reckless Youth' 1993; Artistic Dir.-Shaw Festival Niagara-on-the-Lake, Ont. 1966; Adjunct Prof. (1968) Drama Dept., Yale Univ.; Vice Pres. Shaw Soc. of U.K., 1976; Pres. Planet Productions Ltd., Ont.; Address: Apt. 506, 71 Charles St. E., Toronto, Ont. M4Y 2T3.

**MORSE, Bradford W.,** B.A., LL.B., LL.M.; professor of law; b. Orange, N.J. 17 Sept. 1950; s. Donald Richard and Martha (Ruesch) M.; e. Rutgers Univ. B.A. 1972; Univ. of B.C. LL.B. 1975; York Univ. LL.M. 1981; m. Deirdre d. Cecil and Frances Lyons 3 Oct. 1987; PROF., FAC. OF LAW, UNIV. OF OTTAWA 1976– (on leave) and EXTVE. ASST. TO MINISTER OF INDIAN AFFAIRS AND NORTHERN DEVELOPMENT; Rsch. Offr., Royal Comn. on Family & Children's Law of B.C. 1974; Extve. Dir., Task Force on Delivery of Legal Serv. to Native People of B.C. 1974–75; Asst. Prof., Fac. of Law, Univ. of Ottawa 1976–83; Assoc. Prof. 1983–86; Vice Dean 1983–85; Dir., Graduate Studies in Law 1990–92; Candn. Vis. Fellow, Macquarie Univ. 1987; Hon. Vis. Lectr., Univ. of Hong Kong 1983; Cons., Dept. of Justice, Solicitor Gen. of Can., Candn. & Australian Law Reform Comns., Aboriginal Development Comn. of Australia, Min. of Comm. & Social Serv. of Ont., Candn. Sentencing Comn., Native Counc. of Can., Assembly of First Nations and numerous other Indian & Metis orgns.; Dir. of Rsch. & Planning, Aboriginal Justice Inquiry of Manitoba 1988–91; Supreme Ct. of Can., Duff-Rinfret LL.M. Fellowship; SSHRCC Internat. travel grants; Dir., Comn. on Folk Law and Legal Pluralism 1984– ; Mem., Candn. Assn. of Law Teachers (Section Chair 1984– ); Candn. Bar Assn. (Spec. Ctte. on Native Justice 1986–88); mem. of Extve. of Native Justice Section of Candn. Bar Assn. and Native Law Section of Candn. Bar Assn. Ont. 1988– ; author: 'Indian Tribal Courts in the U.S.' 1980; 'Self Government in Australia and Canada' 1985; 'Providing Lands and Resources for Aboriginal Peoples' 1987; co-author: 'Native Offenders' Perceptions of the Criminal Justice System' 1988; editor: 'Aboriginal Peoples and the Law' 1985, 1989; co-editor: 'Indigenous Law and the State' 1987, 'Law and the Citizen' 1981; numerous articles and chapters in books; recreations: squash, tennis; Office: 10 Wellington St., Room 2100, Hull, Que. K1A 0H4.

**MORSE, Hon. Peter Scott,** B.A., LL.B., D.C.L.; b. Winnipeg, Man. 29 May 1927; s. Harry Dodge and Tena Bell (Scott) M.; e. Ravenscourt Sch., Fort Garry, Man., 1944; Royal Candn. Naval Coll., Royal Roads, B.C., 1944–46; Univ. of Man., B.A. 1948, LL.B. 1952; m. 1stly, late Marjorie Jane 19 September 1954; 2ndly Margaret Elizabeth Chown 30 June 1983; children: David Scott, Stephen Flanders, Ruth Elizabeth; JUSTICE, COURT OF QUEEN'S BENCH, MAN. since 1975; read law with D. A. Thompson, Q.C.; called to the Bar of Manitoba 1952; practised law with Aikins, MacAulay & Thorvaldson 1952–75; Chancellor, Diocese of Rupert's Land 1980–92; Anglican; Clubs: Manitoba; Home: 17 Oakdale Dr., Winnipeg, Man. R3R 0Z3; Office: Law Courts, Winnipeg, Man. R3C 0P9.

**MORSON, Alan Ernest,** B.Comm., F.S.A., F.C.I.A., M.A.A.A.; insurance executive; b. Toronto, Ont. 23 July 1934; s. Alfred Errol and Emo Alexandra (Gilmour) M.; e. Univ. of Toronto Schs. Sr. Matric. 1953; Trinity Coll. Univ. of Toronto B.Comm. 1957; m. Florence Jane Dempster Middleton 28 Dec. 1957; children: Stephen, Scott, Beth; VICE-CHAIRMAN (AND DIR.) CROWN LIFE INSURANCE CO. 1987– ; Vice Chrmn. Am. Crown Life Ins. Co., N.Y.; Dir., Crown Financial Management Ltd., U.K.; Crown Life (Caribbean) Limited, Trinidad; Am. Counc. of Life Insurance, Washington; Life Office Mgmt. Assoc., Atlanta; joined present firm 1957, Asst. Actuary 1966, Assoc. Supt. Systems 1967, Supt. Data Services 1969, Admin. Vice-Pres. 1972, Sr. Admin. Vice-Pres. 1975, Vice-Pres. and Dir. of Admin. 1976, Vice-Pres. and Dir. Individual Ins. 1981, Extve. Vice-Pres. Ins. Operations 1982; Pres. 1984; Trustee Cedar Glen Endowment Fund; mem. Trinity Coll. Corp.; recreations: golf, squash, travel; Clubs: Granite; Muskoka Lakes Golf and Country; Rosedale Golf; Office: 1 Queen St. E., Suite 1700, Toronto, Ont. M5C 2X9.

**MORTIMER, Alan John,** B.Sc., M.Sc., Ph.D.; research scientist; b. Kingston, Ont. 7 Jan. 1950; s. Donald Charles and Mary Katherine (Robertson) M.; e. Carleton Univ. B.Sc. 1972, M.Sc. 1974; Guys Hosp. Medical Sch. Ph.D. 1990; m. Patricia Adelaide d. late Sanford Stratton Burley 1 May 1976; children: Sandra Irene, Colleen Adel; CHIEF, SPACE LIFE SCIENCES, CANADIAN SPACE AGENCY 1991– ; Avionics Engr., Computing Devices of Can. 1974–75; Rsch. Offr., Nat. Research Council of Can. 1975–91; invented Echo-Oculometer 1977; ongoing studies of therapeutic uses of ultrasound for heart disease, of ultrasound bioeffects and medical care in space; Chrmn. A.I.U.M. Bioeffects Ctte.; Chrmn. Candn. Ctte. Internat. Electrotechnical Ctte., Ultrasound; Chair, Space Station Life Sciences Ctte.; Mission Scientist, Candn. Life Sciences Space flights; author 'Characteristics of Ultrasound' 1982; sci. publications on ultrasound safety and instruments, Space Biology and Medicine; mem., Candn. Med. and Biol. Eng. Soc.; Amer. Inst. of Ultrasound in Med. and Biol.; Radiation Research Soc.; Alpine Club of Can.; Nat. Capital Runners Assn.; recreations: cycling; running, whitewater canoeing, mountaineering, music performance; Home: 828 Explorer Lane, Ottawa, Ont. K1C 2S2; Office: Ottawa, Ont. K1A 0R8.

**MORTIMER, David,** B.Sc., Ph.D.; educator; b. Huddersfield, Yorks., Eng. 29 Apl. 1953; s. Keith and Dorothy (Lindley) M.; e. King James's Grammar Sch. Huddersfield 1971; Bristol Univ. B.Sc. 1974; Edinburgh Univ. Ph.D. 1977; m. Sharon d. Allan and Lorraine Gellert 21 March 1987; children: Caitlin Alyssa, Sara Louise; SCIENTIFIC DIR., SYDNEY I.V.F. 1991– ; Visiting Principal Scientific Offr., Royal Prince Alfred Hospital, Sydney; Asst. Prof. Univ. of Calgary 1983–88, Sci. Dir. Diagnostic Semen Lab. 1983–91, In Vitro Fertilization Prog. 1988–91, Assoc. Prof. of Obstetrics & Gynaecol. and of Med. Physiol., 1988–91, Assoc. Prof. of Pathology 1990–91; prin. author Canadian Fertility and Andrology Society 'Guidelines for Therapeutic Donor Insemination' 1988 & 1992; author: 'Practical Laboratory Andrology' 1994; author or co-author over 100 sci. papers and other publs.; ed. bd. Human Reprodn.; Andrologie; Fertility Digest; mem. Am. Soc. of Andrology; Am. Fertility Soc.; Brit. Andrology Soc.; Candn. Fertility & Andrology Soc.; Eur. Soc. Human Reprodn. & Embryol.; Fertility Soc. Australia; Galton Inst.; Soc. Study Fertility; Soc. Study of Reproduction; recreations: downhill skiing, reading, computers, movies, travel; Office: 187 Macquarie St., Sydney, NSW 2000, Australia.

**MORTON, Brian Christopher,** B.Sc., M.D., C.M., FRCP(C); cardiologist; b. Montreal, Que. 2 Feb. 1942; s. Nelson Whitman and Barbara Maxwell (Robertson) M.; e. McGill Univ. B.Sc. 1964, M.D., C.M. 1966; Univ. of Toronto FRCP(C) Cardiology 1973; children: Alan, Pamela, Sheila; DIRECTOR, ADULT CONGENITAL HEART CLINIC, UNIV. OF OTTAWA HEART INST. 1986– ; Prof. of Medicine (Cardiology), Univ. of Ottawa; Dir., Cardiac Catheterization Labs., Univ. of Ottawa Heart Inst. 1975– ; Head of Research, Ottawa Civic Hosp. 1980–84; Consultant in Cardiology, Ottawa Gen. Hosp.; Mem., Candn. Cardiovascular Soc.; Am. Coll. of Cardiology; Royal Soc. of Med.; clubs: Nepean Sailing, The Country Club (Aylmer, Que.); Home: 537A Hilson Ave., Ottawa, Ont. K1Z 6C9; Office: Ottawa, Ont. K1Y 4E9.

**MORTON, Colin Todd,** B.A., M.A.; writer/poet; b. Toronto, Ont. 26 July 1948; s. Arthur Norman M. and Jean Laverne (Hicks) Clarke; e. Univ. of Calgary B.A. (Hons.) 1970, profl. teaching cert. 1975; Univ. of Alta. M.A. 1979; m. Mary Lee d. Norman and Rachel Bragg 30 Aug. 1969; one s.: Jeffrey; author: 'In Transit' 1981; 'Printed Matter' 1982; 'This Won't Last Forever' 1985; 'The Merzbook: Kurt Schwitters Poems' 1987; 'Two Decades' 1987; 'The Cabbage of Paradise' (play) 1988; 'How to Be Born Again' 1992; co-author: 'North/South' 1987; editor: 'The Scream: First Draft, the third annual group show' 1984; 'Capital Poets: An Ottawa Anthology' 1989; also poetry, fiction, reviews & criticism in num. periodicals & anthol. incl. 'Anthology of Magazine Verse and Yearbook of American Poetry' 1985, 1988, edn. film scripts for ACCESS Alta. 1979–80; co-produced poetry animated film 'Primiti Too Taa' 1986 (won awards at 4 film fests.); Pub., Ouroboros Press 1983–91; Ed., Can. Dept. of Labour 1982–93; Teaches writers' workshops, Algonquin College 1993– ; Spec. edn., Sylvan Lake H.S. 1975–77; CBC Lit. Award 1984; A. Lampman Poetry Award 1986; Mem., First Draft intermedia arts group 1983–91; recorded 'Wordmusic' 1986; Mem., ACTRA; League of Candn. Poets (Extve.

Ctte. Ont. 1986–89); Home: 40 Grove Ave., Ottawa, Ont. K1S 3A6.

**MORTON, David,** M.A.; executive; b. Devonport, Eng. 31 Oct. 1929; s. Leslie and Mary (Webber) M.; e. Pembroke Coll., Cambridge Univ. M.A. 1954; Centre d'Études Industrielles, Geneva, Switzerland 1960–61; m. Bess d. Aldred and Ellen Townsend 24 July 1954; children: Sarah, James; CHAIRMAN, ALCAN ALUMINIUM LTD. 1989– ; Dir., Bank of Nova Scotia; Industrial-Alliance Life Insurance Co.; McCain Foods Ltd.; began career with Alcan, Banbury, England 1954; worked in various mgmt. and staff posts with Alcan in the U.K. till 1974; Mng. Dir., Alcan Booth Industries Ltd. (Alcan's fabricating co. in U.K.) 1974–77; Vice Pres., Corporate Planning, Alcan Aluminum Ltd. (Montreal) 1977–79; Mng. Dir. and Chief Extve. Offr., Alcan Aluminum (U.K.) Limited, London 1979–81; Pres. & C.E.O., Aluminum Co. of Canada Limited 1981–84; Extve. Vice Pres., North & South American Operations, Alcan Aluminium Limited 1984–87, Bd. mem. 1985, Pres. & C.O.O. 1987–89, Chrmn. & C.E.O. 1989–93; Chrmn., Internat. Primary Aluminium Institute; Mem., IMD Foundation Bd., Lausanne, Switzerland; Lafarge Coppée International Advisory Bd.; Home: 1 Wood Ave., Apt. 301, Westmount, Que. H3Z 3C5; Office: 1188 Sherbrooke St. W., Montreal, Que. H3A 3G2.

**MORTON, Desmond Dillon Paul,** M.A., Ph.D., F.R.S.C.; educator; author; b. Calgary, Alta. 10 Sept. 1937; s. Brig. Ronald Edward Alfred and Sylvia Cuyler (Frink) M.; e. Rothesay (N.B.) Consolidated Sch. 1946; Herchmer Sch. Regina 1949; St. John's Ravenscourt Sch. Winnipeg 1951; Kingston (Ont.) Coll. & Vocational Inst.; Candn. Acad. Kobe, Japan 1954; Coll. Militaire Royal de St-Jean 1957; Royal Mil. Coll. Can. B.A. 1959; Keble Coll. Oxford Univ. (Rhodes Scholar) B.A. 1961, M.A. 1966; London Sch. of Econ. Univ. of London Ph.D. 1968; m. the late Janet Lillian d. the late William Herbert Smith, North Bay, Ont. 7 July 1967; children: David William Edward, Marion Catherine; PRINCIPAL OF ERINDALE COLL. 1986– and PROF. OF HIST., UNIV. OF TORONTO 1975– ; Asst. Prof. of Hist. Univ. of Ottawa 1968–69; Univ. of Toronto 1969, Assoc. Prof. 1971; Visiting Asst. Prof. Univ. of W. Ont. 1970–71; Visiting Assoc. Prof. Mich. State Univ. 1975; Assoc. Dean Erindale Coll. 1975–79, Vice Princ. (Acad.) 1976–79; joined Candn. Army 1954, comnd. Lt. 1959, Capt. 1962, trans. to Supplementary Reserve 1964; Asst. Prov. Secy. NDP Ont. 1964–68 , Fed. Council 1968–72, Cand. Mississauga N. (fed.) 1978, resigned 1979; Jt. Winner City of Toronto Book Prize 1973; Univ. of Toronto Alumni Award 1983; former Pres. and Dir. Canada Hamble Ltd.; mem. Ed. Bd. 'History and Social Science Teacher'; author: 'Ministers and Generals: Politics and the Canadian Militia' 1970; 'The Last War Drum: The North-West Campaign of 1885' 1972; 'Mayor Howland: The Citizens' Candidate' 1973; 'The Canadian General: Sir William Otter' 1974; 'NDP: The Dream of Power' 1974; 'A Peculiar Kind of Politics: Canada's Overseas Ministry in the First World War' 1982; 'A Short History of Canada' 1983; 'Winning the Second Battle: Canadian Veterans and the Return to Civilian Life' 1987; 'Marching to Armageddon: Canada in the First World War' 1989; 'Working People: An Illustrated History of the Canadian Labour Movement' 1990; 'A Military History of Canada' 1990; 'Silent Battle: Canadian Prisoners of War in Germany, 1914–19' 1992; 'When Your Number's Up: The Canadian Soldier in the First World War' 1993; various articles scholarly journs., newspapers, mags.; mem. Candn. Hist. Assn. (Pres. 1978–79); Candn. Comn. Mil. Hist. (Chrmn. 1976–84); NDP; Anglican; Home: 362 Queen St. S., Streetsville, Ont. L5M 1M2; Office: 3359 Mississauga Rd. N., Mississauga, Ont. L5L 1C6.

**MORTON, Douglas Gibb,** R.C.A. (1968); university professor; academic administrator; artist; b. Winnipeg, Man. 26 Nov. 1926; s. James Marshall and Mary Murdoch (Dickie) M.; e. Kelvin High Sch. and Un. Coll., Winnipeg, 1946; Univ. of S. Cal. and Art Centre Sch., L.A. 1947–48; Ecole desBeaux Arts, Acad. Julian and Studio of André L'Hote, Paris, 1949; Camberwell Sch. and Studio of Martin Bloch, London, 1950; m. Edna Eileen, d. late William Henry Morgan, 23 April 1949; children: Mary Ruth, Nadene, Jocelyn, Cynthia, Taron, Douglas William; PROF. EMERITUS, UNIV. OF VICTORIA 1992– ; Curator, Calgary Allied Arts Centre, 1951–53; Mgr. Sask. Br. and Vice Pres., MacKay-Morton Ltd. (mfrs. agts.), 1954–67; Dir., Sch. of Art, Univ. of Sask., Regina, 1967–69; Prof. & Chrmn. of Visual Arts, Fac. of Fine Arts, York Univ., 1969–71; Assoc. Dean, 1972–75; Prof. & Dean of Fine Arts, Victoria Univ. 1980–85; Pres., Alberta Coll. of Art, Calgary, Alta. 1985–87; Chrmn. & Prof., Dept. of Visual Arts, Univ. of Victoria 1988–92 (Retired); Can. Council Sen. Arts Grant 1975–76; Western Reg. Vice Pres., Royal Candn. Acad. of Arts 1983–85; created mural Regina Pub. Lib. and York Univ.; rep. in colls. of Nat. Gallery of Can., Art Bank, Vancouver Art Gallery, Mendel Gallery (Saskatoon), Norman Mackenzie Gallery (Regina); Beaverbrook Gallery (Fredericton), Univ. of Alta. & York Univ., Toronto, Art Gall. of Greater Victoria, Univ. of Victoria and many major corporate collections across Can.; served with Candn. Army 1945; mem., Candn. Conf. of Arts; Univ. Art Assn. Can. (Dir. 1967–69); Internat. Counc. of Fine Arts Deans 1980–87; Residence: Victoria, B.C.

**MORTON, Francis William Orde,** D.Phil.; business executive; b. Winnipeg, Man. 6 Sept. 1940; s. William Lewis and Guinevere Margaret M.; e. Kelvin H.S. 1957; Univ. of Manitoba (Gold Medalist) B.A. 1961; Univ. of Toronto 1962; Oxford Univ. 1962–64, 1970–75, D.Phil. 1975; Woodrow Wilson Fellow 1961; Rhodes Scholar (Man.) 1962; Canada Counc. Post-Doctoral Fellow 1975; MANAGER, POLICY ANALYSIS, BANK OF MONTREAL 1989– ; cons. and speaker on Brazilian affairs; joined Dept. of External Affairs 1964; Third Sec., Candn. Embassy Rio de Janeiro 1965, Second Sec 1967; Sec., Task Force for Review of Policy toward Latin Am. 1968–70; Visiting Asst. Prof., Univ. of Calgary 1974–75; Prof. Grad. Sch. of Hist., Univ. Federal Fluminense, Niterói, Rio de Janeiro 1975–78; Associate Secretary, Brascan Ltd. 1978–89; Sr. Visitor, St. Antony's College, Oxford, 1985; Dir., Brazil-Canada Chamb. of Comm.; Hon. Citizen of Rio de Janeiro 1986; Anglican; author articles in newspapers and scholarly jours.; recreations: history, politics, international affairs; Home: 40 Homewood Ave., Apt. 2414, Toronto, Ont. M4Y 2K2; Office: 3rd Floor Podium, First Canadian Place, Toronto, Ont. M5X 1A1.

**MORTON, Frederick Lee (Ted),** B.A., M.A., Ph.D.; university professor; b. Los Angeles, Calif. 28 Mar. 1949; s. Warren Allen and Katharine Allen M.; e. Colorado Coll. B.A. (Phi Beta Kappa) 1971; Univ. of Toronto M.A. 1975, Ph.D. 1981; m. Patricia d. Robert and Patricia Lathrop 16 June 1973; children: Sara, Peter, Callary; PROF. OF POLITICAL SCIENCE, UNIV. OF CALGARY 1981– ; rsch. on law, politics, courts & civil liberties; charter-related consulting for fed. & prov. govts.; Co-Dir., Rsch. Unit for Socio-Legal Studies, Univ. of Calgary 1985– ; Mem., Candn. Pol. Sci. Assn.; Am. Pol. Sci. Assn.; Candn. Law & Soc. Assn. (Sec. Treas. 1985–89); author: 'Morgentaler v. Borowski: Abortion, the Charter and the Courts'; co-author: 'Charter Politics' 1992; editor: 'Law, Politics, and the Judicial Process in Canada' 1985, 2nd ed. 1992; co-editor: 'Federalism and the Charter' 1989; recreations: skiing, tennis, hunting, coaching baseball; Home: 3319 Upton Place N.W., Calgary, Alta. T2N 4G9; Office: Calgary, Alta. T2N 1N4.

**MORTON, Harry Stafford,** O.B.E., C.D., B.A., M.Sc., M.B., B.S., F.R.C.S.(Eng.), F.R.C.S.(C), F.A.C.S., F.R.C.O.G.; consultant surgeon; b. Port Greville, N.S. 18 Aug. 1905; s. Charles S., M.D. and Maie Howard (Stafford) M.; e. St. Andrews Coll. Toronto 1918–21; Dalhousie Univ., B.A. 1925, M.Sc. 1927; Univ. of London, M.B., B.S., M.R.C.S., L.R.C.P. 1927–32; Hon LL.D., Mount Allison 1976; m. Rachel Perot, d. late Gregor Wainwright, July 1937; Pres., Haramo Investments Ltd.; Hon. Dir., Equitable Life Insurance Co. of Canada 1983; mem., Bd. Regents, Mt. Allison Univ. 1964–83; Hon. Attending Surg., Royal Victoria Hosp. Montreal, Que. 1970; Chief of Surg., Queen Mary Veterans' Hosp., Montreal 1960–69; Consultant in Surg., Fishermen's Mem. Hosp., Lunenburg, N.S. 1970–75; Chrmn. and Examiner in Surg., Royal Coll. Surgs. Can.; Founder and Chrmn. of Programme, Royal Victoria Hosp. Surgical Fellowship Course 1946–64; Examiner in Surg., Med. Council Can. and McGill Univ. 1949–64; Past Pres. and Founder, Quebec Tumour Registry 1963–70, Nat. Cancer Registry, Ottawa 1966; Hunterian Prof. of Surgery, Royal College of Surgeons, Eng. 1954; Founder of Tumour Registries, Royal Victoria and Queen Mary Veterans' Hosps. 1949; Chrmn. Cancer Comte., Que. Med. Soc.; Sr. mem., Past Dir., Candn. Med. Assn.; Titular mem. Internat. Surg. Soc. (Sr. mem. Central Surg. Soc.); mem. Candn. Assn. of Clinical Surgeons; Past Pres. Bd. of Governors, Pan-Canada Foundation 1976–78 (Past Pres. Bd. of Trustees, 1974–76); sometime Extve. Cancer Comn. and Chrmn. Local Programme Comte., Am. Coll. Surgs.; mem. Comte. of Assessment, Nat. Cancer Inst. Can.; Past Treas., Montreal Medico-Chirurgical Soc.; mem. A.Y.R.S. (Britain); mem. Naval Officers Assn. of Nova Scotia; former Candn. Med. Assn. Rep., D.N.D. S.A.B.; served in R.C.N.V.R. 1938–51; 2nd World War 1939–45; O.B.E., C.D.; promoted Surg. Capt., R.C.N.(R) 1949; Phi Rho Sigma; United Church; Hon. Med. Offr. H.M.C.S. Sackville and Naval Med. Historian 1986; recreations: dialing, gardening, photography; Clubs: University Club of Montreal; In & Out, London, Eng.; Montreal Power Squadron; Fellow, Roy. Soc. Med. (Eng.); Life mem., Lunenberg Yacht (N.S.); London Hospital Medical (U.K.); Home: R.R. #1, Lunenburg, N.S. B0J 2C0.

**MORTON, John;** retired construction executive; b. Newcastle, Eng. 9 Jan. 1927; s. Thomas Milton and Mary (Gourley) M.; e. Heaton Grammar Sch. Newcastle; m. Elizabeth H. M. d. late W. A. Edgeworth 1940; children: Bruce Milton, Mark John; Dir., E.G.M. Cape & Co. Ltd. 1992– (Pres. 1981–89, Chrmn. & C.E.O. 1990–92); Chrmn., BCM Cape Ltd. 1990–92 (Pres. 1981–89); Vice Pres. Robertson Yates Corp. Ltd. 1966–70; Dir. Intercon Ltd. Bermuda 1970–74; joined present Co. 1974; served with R.E. then Glider Pilot A.A.C.; Pres. Ont. Gen. Contractors Assn. 1980–81; Chrmn. of Bd., Candn. Construction Assn. 1993/4; recreations: tennis, sailing; Home: Box 4159, 572 The Oxbow, Collingwood, Ont. L9Y 4T9.

**MORTON, John Kenneth,** Ph.D., D.Sc., F.L.S.; educator; b. Tamworth, U.K. 3 Jan. 1928; s. Ernest and Evelyn Hodgson (Brewer) M.; e. Bede Coll. Grammar Sch. for Boys Sunderland, U.K. 1946; King's Coll. Univ. of Durham B.Sc. 1949, Ph.D. 1953; Univ. of Newcastle upon Tyne D.Sc. 1987; m. Doreen d. William Ernest Freeman 16 June 1951; children: David John, Eileen Heather; PROF. OF BIOL., UNIV. OF WATERLOO 1968– ; Lectr. Univ. Coll. of Ghana 1951–58, Sr. Lectr. 1958–61, Curator Ghana Herbarium 1951–61; Lectr. Birkbeck Coll. Univ. of London 1961–63; Prof. and Head of Botany, Fourah Bay Coll. Univ. of Sierra Leone 1963–67, mem. Bd. Govs. 1965–67, Dir. Botanic Garden & Arboretum 1963–67, Assoc. Dir. Inst. Marine Biol. & Oceanography 1963–67; Acting Princ. of Univ. 1967; Chrmn. of Biol. present Univ. 1974–80; rec'd Candn. Bot. Assn. Mary E. Elliot Award 1978; author 'The Flora of Islay and Jura' 1959; 'West African Lilies and Orchids' 1961; co-author 'An Atlas of Pollen of Trees and Shrubs of Eastern Canada and the Adjacent United States' Parts 1–4 1972–79; 'The Flora of Manitoulin Island' 2nd ed. 1984; over 100 publs. Brit., W. Africa and N. Am. Bot.; mem. Candn. Bot. Assn. (Pres. 1974–75, Extve. Comte. 1970–80); Bot. Soc. Brit. Isles; Am. Soc. Plant Taxonomists; Bot. Soc. Scotland; Internat. Assn. Plant Taxonomists; recreations: natural history, outdoors; Home: 501 Cedarcliffe Dr., Waterloo, Ont. N2K 2J2; Office: Waterloo, Ont. N2L 3G1.

**MORTON, Ross Albert,** B.A., FLMI; insurance executive; b. Harriston, Ont. 18 Jan. 1947; s. James Wright and Isabel (French) Morton; e. Univ. of Toronto B.A. 1969; Life Management Inst. F.L.M.I. 1972; m. Susan d. William and Marjorie Stonehouse 12 July 1969; children: Garth William, Emily I.M.; VICE-PRES., LIFE REINSURANCE, MANULIFE FINANCIAL 1992– ; Underwriter, Mercantile & General Reinsur. Co. Ltd. 1970–72; Asst. Mgr., Underwriting 1972–74; Vice-Pres., Mktg. & Underwriting 1977–82; Extve. Vice-Pres. & Chief Agent for Canada, Storebrand Reinsur. Co. Ltd. 1982–88; Vice-Pres. & Gen. Mgr., New Bus. & Systems, Nat. Life Assur. Co. 1988–89; Sr. Vice-Pres., CAPSCO Software Canada Limited 1989; Reinsur. Vice-Pres., Manulife Financial 1990–92; Gov., Holy Trinity Schools (Vice-Chrmn., Mem., Extve. Ctte. & Corp. Sec.); Past Chair, Candn. Reinsur. Conference; Counter Holy Trinity Ch.; Mem., Candn. Inst. of Underwriters; Home Office Life Underwriters Assn.; Extve. Candn. Reinsur. Conf.; author of magazine articles; recreations: carpentry, reading, writing; Home: Thornhill, Ont.; Office: 200 Bloor St. E., Toronto, Ont. M4W 1E5.

**MOSCO, Vincent,** Ph.D.; educator; b. New York, N.Y. 23 July 1948; s. Frank A. and Rose (Di Pilato) M.; e. Georgetown Univ. B.A. 1970; Harvard Univ. Ph.D. 1975; m. Catherine d. Douglas and Dorothy McKercher 17 May 1980; two d. Rosemary, Madeline; PROF. OF JOURNALISM, CARLETON UNIV. 1989– and RSCH. ASSOC., HARVARD UNIV., PROG. ON INFORMATION RESOURCES POLICY; Prof. of Sociol. Univ. of Lowell 1975–77, Georgetown Univ. 1978–81, Queen's Univ. 1984–89; Prof. of Communication Temple Univ. 1981–84; Rsch. Fellow Harvard Univ. Prog. Info. Resources Policy 1975–77; Postdoctoral Fellow White House Office of Telecommunications Policy 1977–78; Rsch. Fellow U.S. Nat. Acad. Sci.'s 1981–82; Cons. Dept. Communications Can. 1985–88, Labour Can. 1985–87, Finance Can. 1985; author 'Broadcasting in the United States' 1979; 'Pushbutton Fantasies' 1982; 'The Pay-Per Society' 1989; ed. 'Policy Research in Telecommunications' 1984; co-ed. 'Labor, The Working Class and the Media' 1983; 'Changing Patterns of Communication Control' 1984; 'Popular Culture and Media

Events' 1985; 'The Political Economy of Information' 1988; 'Democratic Communication in the Information Age' 1992; 'Illuminating the Blindspots'; Corr. ed. Media, Culture & Soc. (UK); Contbg. ed., Science as Culture (US); mem. various ed. bds.; over 60 scholarly articles, reports and book chapters; Founding mem. Union for Democratic Communication; mem. Internat. Council and Pres. of the Political Economy Section, Internat. Assn. Mass Communication Rsch.; Phi Beta Kappa; recreations: running, basketball, Boston Red Sox; Home: 1 Lakeview Terrace, Ottawa, Ont. K1S 3H3; Office: Ottawa, Ont. K1S 5B6.

**MOSCOVITCH, Allan Stanley,** B.A., M.A.; university professor; b. Montreal, Que. 29 Dec. 1946; s. Samuel and Sally (Granofsky) M.; e. Carleton Univ. B.A. 1969; Univ. of Essex M.A. 1970; m. Julie d. George and Molly White Nov. 1977; children: Hannah, Noah; PROF., SCHOOL OF SOCIAL WORK, CARLETON UNIV. 1975– ; Policy Analyst, Planning Branch, Treas. Bd., Fed. Govt. 1970–71; Rsch. Asst., Assn. of Scientific Tech. & Managerial Staffs (U.K.) 1973–74; Visiting Prof., Univ. of Sydney 1982; Visiting Researcher, Centre nat. de rech. scientifique, laboratoire en écon. et sociologie de travail, Aix-en-Provence, France 1988; Dir. of Planning, Social Serv. Dept., Regional Mun. of Ottawa-Carleton 1988–89 (executive exchange); Chair, Minister's Adv. Group on New Social Assistance Legislation, Govt. of Ont. 1990–92; Co-Founder & Mem. of Ed. Bd., 'Studies in Political Economy' 1977–85; Co-ordinator Ed. Bd. 'Canadian Review of Social Policy' 1991– ; Dir., Planned Parenthood of Ottawa 1989– ; co-editor: 'Inequality: Essays on the Political Economy of Social Welfare' 1981; 'The Welfare State in Canada: A Selected Bibliography, 1840–1978' 1983; 'The Benevolent State' 1987; Chair of Ctte. producing Ont. govt. reports 'Back on Track, Time for Action'; Hebrew; recreations: running, bicycling; Home: 165 Holmwood Ave., Ottawa, Ont. K1S 2P3; Office: Ottawa, Ont. K1S 5B6.

**MOSER, Marie L.,** B.A., B.Sc.; writer; b. Edmonton, Alta. 2 Oct. 1948; d. Arthur Joseph and Lucienne Marie (Pagé) Cantin Sr.; e. Univ. of Alta. B.Sc. 1969, B.A. 1976; m. Jerry P. s. Michael and Lena M. 24 Aug. 1968; children: Michael, Christopher, Genevieve, Gabrielle; author: 'The Storm' 1984, 'The Fire' 1986 (short stories); 'Counterpoint' 1987 (novel: 1st prize New Alta. Novelist Competition 1986); 2nd prize Alta. Short Stories competition 1984 for 'Foxtails' broadcast on CKUA radio and published; 'Characteristics of the French-Canadian Community in the Edmonton Area' 1981 (essay); Broadcasts on CBC's 'Alberta Anthology': 'The Long Gravel Road,' 'All the Fallen Sparrows,' 'A Christmas Story' 1984, 1986; 'Two Photographs in an Antique Shop' 1989; 'Battlefields' 1990; 'The Last Lullaby' short story in 'The Road Home' (an anthology of Alberta Writing) 1992; bilingual; Home: Edmonton, Alta.

**MOSER, William Oscar Jules,** B.Sc., M.A., Ph.D.; educator; b. Winnipeg, Man. 5 Sept. 1927; s. Robert and Laura (Fenson) M.; e. Univ. of Man. B.Sc. 1949; Univ. of Minn. M.A. 1951; Univ. of Toronto Ph.D. 1957; m. Beryl Rita d. Sidney Pearlman 2 Sept. 1953; children: Marla, Lionel, Paula; PROF. OF MATH., McGILL UNIV. 1966– ; Teaching Asst. Univ. of Minn. 1949–51; Teaching Fellow Univ. of Toronto 1953–55; Instr. Univ. of Sask. 1955, Asst. Prof. 1957–59; Assoc. Prof. Univ. of Man. 1959–64; Assoc. Prof. present Univ. 1964; mem. Senate 1970–72; recipient Isbister Scholarships 1946–48; Nat. Research Council Fellowships 1951–53; Univ. of Toronto Fellowship 1954–55; Can. Council Leave Fellowship 1971–72; invited lectr. numerous Candn., Am. and UK univs.; co-author 'Generators and Relations for Discrete Groups' 1957, 4th ed. 1980; Ed.-in-Chief Candn. Math. Bulletin 1961–70; Assoc. Ed. Candn. Journ. Math. 1981–85; mem. Candn. Math. Soc. (Pres. 1975–77); Am. Math. Soc.; Math. Assn. Am.; Fibonacci Assn.; London Math. Soc.; Sigma Xi; Hebrew; recreations: chess, billiards; Home: 2333 Sherbrooke St. W., Apt. 501, Montreal, Que. H3H 2T6; Office: 805 Sherbrooke St. W., Montreal, Que. H3A 2K6.

**MOSES, Robert,** B.Sc., M.D.; entrepreneur; b. Romania 4 Feb. 1948; s. Alexander and Agnes (Coller) M.; e. Bathurst Hts. Coll. Inst. Toronto 1966 (Ont. Scholar); Univ. of Toronto B.Sc. 1970, M.D. 1973; m. Ruth d. Irvine and Anne Glass 24 May 1970; children: Sandra, Alan, Lisa; C.E.O. and DIR., PCI INC. 1990– and CHIEF EXTVE. OFFR. & DIR., TYDAC TECHNOLOGIES INC. 1994– ; Dir., Institute of Space & Terrestrial Science 1993– ; gen. med. practice specializing in emergency med. 1974–80; C.E.O., Syntronics Group 1980–87; Dir., PCI Inc. 1988–90; recipient Design Can. Award of Excellence for McLeyvier Computer Music System 1982; recreations: philosophy, history, watching baseball; Home: 5 Ormsby Cres., Toronto, Ont.; Office: 50 West Wilmot St., Richmond Hill, Ont. L4B 1M5.

**MOSHANSKY, The Hon. Virgil Peter,** B.A., LL.B.; Justice; b. Lamont, Alta. 14 Sept. 1928; s. Peter and Victoria (Figol) M.; e. Univ. of Alta., B.A. 1951, LL.B. 1954; m. June L. d. Leo and Mary Kerchinsky 1953; children: Blair, Karen, Marla, Lynn; JUSTICE, COURT OF QUEEN'S BENCH OF ALBERTA 1979– ; Justice, Supreme Court of Alta. 1976–79; apptd. Commissioner of Inquiry into Air Ontario crash at Dryden, Ont. (1989–92); Mayor, Town of Vegreville 1970–76; Sr. Partner, law firm, Vegreville, Alta. to 1976; Dir., sev. cos. to 1976; recipient, Candn. Centennial Medal 1967; Ambassador of Goodwill Award, Lions Internat. 1968; Aerospace Laurel Award 1993; B.C. Aviation Council Award of Honour 1993; Melvin Jones (Founders) Fellowship, Lions Internat. 1993; apptd. Q.C. 1976; Mem., Bd. of Trustees, St. Joseph's Gen. Hosp. 1971–75; Bencher, Law Soc. of Alta. 1975–76; Mem., Candn. Bar Assn. Nat. Counc. 1975–76; Vegreville Flying Club 1964–76 (Past Dir.); Edmonton Flying Club; Candn. Owners & Pilots Assn.; Alta. Aviation Counc.; Sec., Northeast. Alta. Bar Assn. 1960–75 (Chrmn., Legal Aid Ctte. 1965–75); Life Mem., Vegreville Lions Club (Pres. 1960–61); Vegreville C. of C.; Chrmn., Counc. of Govs. Dist. 37, Lions Internat. 1962–63; Internat. Dir. Lions Internat. 1966–68; Chrmn., Vegreville Airport Development Commn. 1972–76; mem., Extve. Comm., Alberta Urban Municipalities Assoc. 1974–76; recreations: aviation; Clubs: Royal Glenora; Pinebrook Golf & Country; Calgary Flying; Office: Court House, 611 – 4th St. S.W., Calgary, Alta. T2P 1T5.

**MOSHER, Christopher Terry (nom de plume Aislin);** cartoonist; b. Ottawa, Ont. 11 Nov. 1942; s. Jack and Norma (Fogg) M.; e. Ecole des Beaux-Arts Québec City 1967; m. Carol d. Frank and Mary Devlin 16 Jan. 1965; two d. Aislin, Jessica; ED. CARTOONIST, THE GAZETTE 1972– ; pol. cartoonist The Montreal Star 1967 and later present newspaper, also sports cartoonist; syndicated by The Toronto Star and by New York's Cartoonists and Writers' Syndicate throughout the world; appeared most maj. Candn. newspapers and mags. and has freelanced in USA and abroad for such publs. as The New York Times, Time mag., The National Lampoon, Harper's, The Atlantic and London's Punch mag.; recipient Can. Council Grant 1971 for study abroad (resulting in NFB film 'The Hecklers' 1976); numerous citations incl. 2 Candn. Nat. Newspaper Awards, Quill Award and 5 individual prizes Internat. Salon of Caricature; mem. Candn. News Hall of Fame; Baseball Writers' Assn. Am.; author 'Aislin–100 Caricatures' 1971, 'Aislin–150 Caricatures' 1973, ''Ello, Morgentaler? Aislin–150 Caricatures' 1975, 'O.K. Everybody Take A Valium! Aislin–150 Caricatures' 1977, 'Aislin–180 Caricatures' 1980, 'Stretchmarks' 1982, 'Where's the Trough' 1985, 'Old Whores' 1987; 'The Lawn Jockey and other Aislin cartoons' 1989; 'Drawing Bones: Fifteen Years of Cartooning Brian Mulroney' 1991; co-author 'Hockey Night in Moscow' 1972, 'The Great Hockey Thaw' 1974, 'The Retarded Giant' 1977, 'The Hecklers: A History of Canadian Political Cartooning' 1979, 'The Year the Expos Almost Won the Pennant' 1979, 'The Year the Expos Finally Won Something' 1981, 'The First Canadian Sports Trivia Quiz Book' 1981, 'The Anglo Guide to Survival in Quebec' 1983, 'Tootle: A Children's Story' 1984; Office: c/o Key Porter Books, 3rd Floor, 70 The Esplanade, Toronto, Ont. M5E 1R2.

**MOSHER, Edith Mercy;** writer/housewife; b. Summerville, N.S. 19 Jan. 1910; d. Lewis Eldon and Mildred May (Mosher) Dodge; e. primarily self taught; h.s. plus 1 yr. journalism Acadia Univ.; m. Raymond Fraser, adopted son of George DeWolfe and Amelia M. 21 Jan. 1931; children: Frederick George, Hazel Rita, Ernest Eldon; began writing plays as a child; personal care worker (nurse) 1950s; several prizes for poetry; Baptist; Past Mem., N.S. Author's Assn., Writers' Fed. at Halifax; author: 'The Sea and the Supernatural' 1974, 'Haunted' 1982 (ghost stories); 'Farm Tales' 1976 (humour); 'North Along the Shore' 1975, 'White Rock' 1979, 'From Howe to Now' 1981, 'Old Time Travel in Nova Scotia' 1984 (historical); 'Lost' 1988; 'There's a Hostile World Out There' 1989; author of 'Lookout' column in 'Atlantic Co-operator 1960s–70s; numerous articles, short plays & one 3–act musical (prod. locally); co-author: 'Land of a Loyalist' 1988; Address: Hants County, N.S. B0N 2K0.

**MOSKOVITS, Martin,** B.Sc., Ph.D.; university professor; b. Braila, Romania 13 April 1943; s. Emanuel and Ana (Moise) M.; e. Harbord C.I. 1961; Univ. of Toronto B.Sc. 1965, Ph.D. 1970; m. Linda d. Albert and Anne Burke 8 July 1976; children: Allyson, Joshua, Leslie; stepson: Steven; PROFESSOR, CHEMISTRY, UNIVERSITY OF TORONTO 1982– ; Research Scientist, Alcan Research & Devel. 1970–71; Asst. Prof., Chem., Univ. of Toronto 1974; Assoc. Prof. 1978; Chair 1993; Gov. 1993; Bd. Mem., Ont. Laser and Lightwave Research Ctr.; Centres of Excellence for Molecular & Interfacial Dynamics; Chair, Grants Selection Ctte. NSERC; Pres., OHM Distributors & Mfrs. Ltd. 1966–68; Killam Fellowship 1989–91; Guggenheim Fellowship 1986–87; Gerhard Herzberg Award (Spectroscopy Soc. of Can.) 1993; Unilever Award, Royal Soc. of Chem. (U.K.); Mem., Am. Chem. Soc.; Optical Soc. of Am.; Materials Research Soc.; AAAS; author of over 150 articles and more than a dozen book chapters; editor of 3 books; club: Orpheus Choir; Office: Univ. of Toronto, Chair, Dept. of Chemistry, Toronto, Ont. M5S 1A1.

**MOSQUIN, Theodore (Ted),** B.Sc., Ph.D.; environment consultant; b. Brokenhead, Man. 8 July 1932; s. William and Anastasia (Kushnir) M.; e. Beasejour Coll. 1951; Univ. of Man. B.Sc. 1956; Univ. of Cal. Los Angeles Ph.D. 1961; m. Linda Ruth d. Theodore and Ruth Lideen 11 June 1961; children: Alexandra Marie, Paul Lideen; PRES. ECOSPHERICS INTERNAT. INC. 1992– and PRES. MOSQUIN BIO-INFORMATION LTD. 1981– ; Asst. Prof. of Bot. Univ. of Calgary 1961–62; Rsch. Sci. Plant Evolution Agric. Can. Ottawa 1962–72; Visiting Prof. of Systematic Bot. Univ. of Cal. Berkeley 1968–69; Extve. Dir. Candn. Nature Fedn. Ottawa 1973–77 (Pres. 1971–72); Biol. Environment Can. Ottawa (devel. Ont.'s wetland evaluation system) 1983–84; recipient Queen's Silver Jubilee Medal 1977; Co-founder and Candn. Co-Chrmn. Can./U.S. Environmental Council 1975–77; ed. 'Canadian Field-Naturalist' quarterly 1967–72; 'Nature Canada' quarterly 1971–77; 'Canada's Threatened Species and Habitats' 1977; assoc. ed. 'Legacy; The Natural History of Ontario' 1989; co-author 'On the Brink; Endangered Species in Canada' 1989; author over 28 sci. papers evolution & ecology, 60 popular articles conserv., biol., ecology; Pres. Candn. Parks & Wilderness Soc. 1987–90, Trustee and Vice Pres. 1984–87; Dir. Candn. Wildflower Soc. 1985–87; Chrmn. Candn. Audubon Soc. 1971; Pres. Ottawa Field-Naturalists Club 1970–71; Address: P.O. Box 279, Lanark, Ont. K0G 1K0.

**MOSS, Brian John Gordon,** B.E.S., M.C.I.P.; real estate developer; b. Kitchener, Ont. 12 Dec. 1955; s. Gordon Scott and Betty Lorraine (Davidson) M.; e. Waterloo C.I. 1974; Univ. of Waterloo B.E.S. 1978; m. Donna Lee d. Don and Marilyn Post 10 Dec. 1977; children: Rebecca, Emily, Jordan; PRESIDENT, BRIAN MOSS AND ASSOCIATES LTD. 1992– ; positions in planning & real estate consulting firms in Alta. & Ont. 1978–85; Project Manager, Herity Corp. 1985–90; Vice-Pres., Planning, Herity Corp. 1990–92; Extve. Ctte., Pragma Council, Univ. of Waterloo; Mem., Candn. Inst. of Planners; Ont. Profl. Planners Inst.; Mem., Deacons Bd., Forestbrook Bible Chapel, Pickering; Chrmn., Building Ctte., Forestbrook Bible Chapel; recreations: squash, hiking, skiing; Home: 1192 Maple Gate Rd., Pickering, Ont. L1X 1R9; Office: 245 Yorkland Blvd., Suite 100, Willowdale, Ont. M2J 4W9.

**MOSS, Edward John,** Q.C., LL.B.; b. Sussex, Eng. 26 Apl. 1917; s. Henry John and Alice (Turner) M.; e. Brighton Grammar Sch. Eng.; London Univ. LL.B. 1939; m. Anne d. George Hodkinson, 21 Sept. 1946; one d. Sally Anne; Retired Counsel, Balfour Moss (Regina, Sask.); admitted solicitor Eng. 1939, Bar of Sask. 1954, Bar of Alta. 1966; cr. Q.C. 1967; law practice London, Eng. after war; emigrated to Sask. 1954; former Lectr. in Oil and Gas Univ. of Sask. (part-time) and Bar Admission Course for Sask.; joined Sussex Yeomanry (Territorials) 1939, Active War Service 1939–46, comnd. RA 1944; Past Dir. Candn. Law Petroleum Foundation; Past Pres. Roy. Un. Services Inst. Regina; Emeritus Fellow Am. Coll. Trial Lawyers; Past Pres. Regina Bar Assn. and Regina Men's Candn. Club; mem. Law Soc. Sask. (Past Pres. and Bencher); Law Soc. Eng.; Law Soc. Alta.; Candn. Bar Assn.; Anglican; P. Conservative; recreations: natural history, gardening, motoring; Home: 4 - 919 Pemberton Rd., Victoria, B.C. V8S 3R5.

**MOSS, John Errington,** M.A., M.Phil., Ph.D.; university professor, literary critic; b. Galt, Ont. 7 Feb. 1940; s. George Francis and Mary Margaret (Clare) M.; e. Preston S.S. 1958; Univ. of West. Ont. B.A. 1961, M.A. 1969; Univ. of Waterloo, M.Phil. 1970; Univ. of N.B. Ph.D. 1973; m. Virginia d. Howard and Enid Lavin 29 May 1965; children: Julia Clare Zillah, Laura Frances Errington; PROF. OF ENGLISH (CAN. LIT.), UNIV. OF OTTAWA 1980– ; Concordia Univ. 1973–76; Univ. of B.C. 1977–78; Queen's Univ. 1978–80; Vis. Prof. in Germany 1980, England 1983, India 1984; lectured in Italy, Norway, the United Kingdom, Greenland, Canary

Islands, India & the U.S.; author of 16 books incl.: 'Arctic Landscape and the Metaphysics of Geography'; 'A Reader's Guide to the Canadian Novel' 2 eds., 'Invisible in the House of Mirrors,' 'Sex and Violence in the Canadian Novel,' 'Patterns of Isolation' (lit. criticism); 'Bellrock' (memoir); 'Enduring Dreams: An Exploration of Arctic Landscape' (creative non-fiction); contrib. ed., 'Arctic Circle' magazine; editor, co-author, contrib. numerous other books; Mem., Assn. of Candn. Univ. Teachers of English, The Writers Union of Canada & other profl. orgns.; awards: Ont. Arts Counc., Can. Counc., SSHRCC (academic); Ironman 1987, CSM Coureur de bois, Gold 1989, 1991, Boston Marathon 1986, '87, '88, '89, '91, '92, '93 Nanisivik Ultra 1987, '88, '91, London to Brighton 1991, Sri Chinmoy Internat. 24 Hour Race 1990, '93 (sports); mem., various sports orgns.; recreations: endurance sports, the Arctic, wine, literary criticism; clubs: Canadian Ski Marathon, Roadrunners, Triathlon, etc.; Home: R.R. 1, Verona, Ont. K0H 2W0; Office: Ottawa, Ont. K1N 6N5.

**MOSS, Peter,** M.A.; artistic director; b. Montreal, Que. 10 Oct. 1947; s. Archie and Anne (Tchaikofsky) M.; e. Nat. Theatre Sch. of Can.; Michigan State Univ., M.A.; m. Joan d. Abe and Florence Kirshner 1 Sept. 1969; children: Jessica, Nadia; CREATIVE HEAD, T.V. CHILDREN'S PROGRAMS, ARTS & ENTERTAINMENT, C.B.C.; Assoc. Dir., Crewe Theatre 1972–74; Phoenix Theatre 1974–76; Dir., Third Stage & Assoc. Dir., Stratford Festival 1977–80; Artistic Dir., Young People's Theatre 1980–91; extensive freelance assignments; Teacher, Nat. Theatre Sch.; Maggie Bassett Studio; Arts Counc. of Great Britain, Assoc. Dir. Award 1974; Home: 164 Walmer Rd., Toronto, Ont. M5R 2X9.

**MOSSMAN, Mary Jane,** B.A., LL.M.; educator; b. Halifax, N.S. 6 Sept. 1946; d. Harris Vernon and Mary Estelle (Murley) M.; e. McGill Univ. Hons. B.A. 1967; Queen's Univ. LL.B. 1970; Univ. of London, LL.M. 1971; m. Brian s. Delby and Jean Bucknall 22 Sept. 1979; PROF. OSGOODE HALL LAW SCH., YORK UNIV. 1990– ; Visiting Prof., Columbia Univ., NYC 1992, Univ. of Sydney Law School 1992 and Queen's Univ. 1990–91; Lectr. and Sr. Lectr. Univ. of New South Wales, Sydney, Australia 1972–76; Assoc. Prof., present Univ. 1977–89, Asst. Dean 1983–85, Assoc. Dean 1986–87; Clinic Funding Mgr. Ont. Legal Aid Plan 1979–82; Mem. of Bar N.S.W. 1975; Ont. 1977; Jr. Counsel, Appeal to Privy Council from NSW 1979; mem. Extve. Jane-Finch Community Legal Clinic 1983–85; Dir., Metro Toronto Action Ctte. on Violence 1986–89; Advocacy Centre for the Elderly 1987–90; Adv. Bd. Psychiatric Patient Advocacy Office 1986– , Chrmn. 1987–88; Bd. Vanier Inst. of Family 1988–91; Adv. Ctte., Social Assistance Legislation (Min. Comm. and Soc. Servs.) 1990–91; author numerous law articles and govt. reports; mem. various law jour. adv. bds.; Elder, Bloor St. Un. Ch. 1986–88; mem. Candn. Assn. Law Teachers (Extve. 1984–85, 1986–87); Candn. Bar Assn. (Ont. Council 1986–87); recipient Human Rights Award (ARCH) 1988; CBAO Service Award 1988; Law Society Medal 1990; recreations: swimming, hiking, cycling, reading; Home: 14 Weybourne Cres., Toronto, Ont. M4N 2R3; Office: 4700 Keele St., North York, Ont. M3J 1P3.

**MOSSOP, Glenn Christopher Stephenson,** B.A., B.Mus.; conductor; b. Calgary, Alta. 13 May 1951; s. Cyril Stephenson and Freida Evelyn (Dilworth) M.; e. Univ. of Calgary B.A. 1971, B.Mus. 1975; State Coll. of Music Stockholm Dip. in Conducting 1982; m. Anna d. Tomas and Margareta Brundin 16 Aug. 1989; one d. Frieda Anna Maria; CONDUCTOR AND MUSIC DIR. THUNDER BAY SYMPHONY ORCH. 1989– ; Prin. Conductor Sundsvall Chamber Orch. 1988–90; freelance opera and orchestral conductor Can., Sweden, Finland, Czechoslovakia; guest conductor various orchs. incl. Stockholm Philharmonic, Örebro Chamber Orch., Helsingborg Symphony Orch., Norrköping Symphony Orch., Umeå Sinfonietta, all Sweden; Kuopio City Orch. Finland; Calgary Philharmonic, Edmonton Symphony, Victoria Symphony, Hamilton Philharmonic, CBC Vancouver Orchestra, Windsor Symphony, Orchestra London Canada; Conductor, Stockholm Folkopera 1982–88 (appearances Edinburgh Festival 1986, 1988); Värmland's Opera and Norrland's Opera; Nordic Youth Orchestra 1985, 1986; Asst. Conductor, World Youth Orchestra 1988; winner orch. prize 2nd Internat. Grzgorz Fitelberg Conducting Competition Katowice, Poland 1983; mem. Conductors Guild; Assn. Candn. Orchs.; recreations: hiking, mountaineering; Homes: 291 College St., Thunder Bay, Ont. P7A 5K2; Körsbärsvägen 19, 114 23 Stockholm, Sweden; Office: P.O. Box 2004, Thunder Bay, Ont. P7B 5E7.

**MOTHERWELL, Cathryn Mary,** B.J.; journalist; b. Victoria, B.C. 10 June 1957; d. John Loudon and Gladys Muriel (Finlay) M.; e. Univ. of Victoria; Carleton Univ., B.J. 1979; m. Gary d. Rudy and Hilde Loewen 30 May 1981; CALGARY BUREAU CHIEF, THE GLOBE & MAIL 1991– ; started as Sports Reporter, Calgary Sun; joined Globe & Mail Report on Business 1984; apptd. Assoc. Ed. of the Dept. 1987; Assoc. National Editor 1989–91; Business Writing Finalist, National Newspaper Awards 1987; author: 'Smart Money: Investment Strategies for Canadian Women' 1989; has presented seminars on personal finance for women; mem. CBC Morningside business panel; Office: 444 Front St. W., Toronto, Ont. M5V 2S9.

**MOTYER, Arthur John,** M.A., D.C.L., F.R.S.A.; educator; b. Bermuda 15 Dec. 1925; s. William Ernest and Edith Alice (Brunning) M.; e. Saltus Grammar Sch., Bermuda; Mt. Allison Univ. B.A. 1945; Univ. of Toronto Grad. Sch. 1945–46; Christ Church, Oxford B.A. 1948, M.A. 1951; Bermuda Scholarship 1942; Rhodes Scholarship 1946; m. Janet d. Arthur and Mary Speid 25 June 1955; children: Michael Ian and Gillian Mary; Purvis Chair in English, Mount Allison University 1970–93; Dean of Arts and Science there 1971–75, Academic Vice-Pres. 1973–75, First Dir. of Drama 1975–93; Chrmn. Performing Arts Series 1975–93; Mem., Maritime Provinces Higher Education Comn. 1988–91; Chrmn., Debut Atlantic Soc. 1988– ; F.R.S.A.; Lectr. Univ. of Manitoba 1948–50; Bishop's Univ. 1950–70: Dir. of Drama 1963; Prof. 1965; planned Bishop's Centennial Theatre 1967; Dir., N. Hatley (Que.) Playhouse; Summer Sch. Drama (Univ. of N.B.); Stephenville (Nfld.) Festival; Pres. N.B. Drama League; Gov. Theatre Canada; Adjudicator, N.B. High School Drama; mem. Rhodes Schol. Selection Ctte. for Que., N.B., Maritimes; National Counc., Duke of Edinburgh Awards; Dir. H.R.C.C.; Cdn. Fed. of the Humanities; Academic Adv. Ctte. for Atlantic Univs.; Chrmn. Academic V.P.s of Atlantic Univs.; mem. Ch. of England; author: 'Pillars of Modern Drama' 1973; 'Directions in Modern Theatre' 1978; recreations: swimming, gardening, cooking; Home: P.O. Box 1153, Sackville, N.B. E0A 3C0; Office: Sackville, N.B. E0A 3C0.

**MOTZ, Paul J.,** B.A.; executive; b. Kitchener, Ont. 25 Jan. 1950; s. John E. and Mary (Stoody) M.; e. Univ. of W. Ont.; Univ. of Waterloo; Wilfrid Laurier Univ. B.A. 1971; Univ. of Cambridge, England 1990; m. Catherine Meechan 1992; two d. Mary Helen, Jane Ann; PRES., FIRST ECHO GROUP INC. 1990– ; Co-ordinating Supvr., Jemcom Inc. 1971, Asst. to Pres. 1973, Vice Pres. 1975, Pres. 1978, Pres. & Gen. Mgr. 1980–89; Dir., Inland Daily Press Assn.; K-W Community Foundation; St. Mary's Gen. Hosp. Foundation; Stratford Festival; R. Catholic; recreations: music, reading, fishing, golf, tennis, handyman; Home: 57 Heins Ave., Kitchener, Ont. N2G 1Z7; Office: 279 King St. W., Kitchener, Ont. N2G 3X9.

**MOULDEN, H. Julia;** writer; b. Toronto, Ont. 2 April 1956; d. Howard Jeffrey and Dollie Helen Pauline (Ritchie) M.; e. Univ. of Toronto; OWNER, MOULDEN COMMUNICATIONS 1985– ; serves clients in corp., govt. & arts sectors; Bd. Dir., Digimation Incorporated; Dir., Charles Hastings Housing Co-operative 1990–94; Ctte. Mem., Candn. Outward Bound Wilderness Sch.; co-author: 'Green is Gold: Business Talking to Business about the Environmental Revolution' 1991; recreations: outdoors, travel, opera; Office: 175 Elm St., Suite 602, Toronto, Ont. M5T 2Z8.

**MOULTON, Mary E.C.;** university administrator; b. Montreal, Que. 25 May 1948; d. Melville Allison and Jessie Helen (MacIntyre) Ross; Codrington H.S., Barbados W.I., 0 levels; Univ. of Kings Coll., 1 year; m. Maxwell s. Charles and Ann M. 10 Sept. 1966; children: Allan Ross, Brian Douglas; DIRECTOR OF UNIV. RELATIONS, MOUNT SAINT VINCENT UNIV. 1990– ; Asst. Vice-Pres., Systems Devel. 1989–90; Asst. Vice-Pres., Mktg. 1986–89; Mktg. Mgr. 1983–85; Deposit Serv. Mktg. Mgr., Central Trust Co. 1981–83; Supvr., Credit Card Services, Central Trust Co. 1980–81; Speaker-Presenter, Internal Training Capacity & Management seminars; Guest Speaker, Univ. Devel. Seminar; Candn. Soc. of Fund Raising Extves.; Chair, Allocations Ctte., United Way; Lectr., Adult Edn., Halifax; Mem., St. Margaret of Scotland Ch. (Spiritual Devel. Ctte. 1989– ); The Rotary Club of Halifax 1993– ; Candn. Information Processing Soc. 1989–90; Bank Marketing Assn. 1985–89; recreations: skiing, golf, travel, family; Home: 29 Braemount Dr., Halifax, N.S. B3M 3P3; Office: Halifax, N.S. B3M 2J6.

**MOUNFIELD, William K.,** B.Com., M.B.A.; retired. industrialist; b. Toronto, Ont. 30 March 1924; s. William Mark and Emily Caryl (Jaques) M.; e. Queen Victoria Public Sch., Toronto 1937; Univ. of Toronto Schs. 1942; Univ of Toronto, B.Com. 1948, M.B.A. 1960; m.Marion Helen, d. John Beaton Macmillan, 15 Nov. 1968; retired Vice Pres. Administration, Massey-Ferguson Ltd. since 1980; Former Chrmn. & Dir. Massey-Ferguson Ind. Ltd.; President and Dir. Massey-Ferguson Finance Co. of Canada Ltd.; Dir. Perkins Engines Canada Ltd.; chrmn. of Bd., Sunar Ltd. joined the Co. 1948, Sales and Adm. positions France and U.K. incl. Secy. MF U.K. and Br. Mgr. France 1952–59; Asst. to Mang. Dir. MF Italy 1960; Asst. Secy. Massey-Ferguson Ltd. 1960, Secy. and Dir. Legal Services 1972; Pres. Massey Ferguson Ind. Ltd. 1973–77; served in 2nd World War R.C.A. 1943–45, rank Lt.; Presbyterian; recreations: golf, tennis, skiing; Clubs: University; Granite; Caledon Ski; Rosedale Golf; Toronto Lawn Tennis; Home: 15 Glengowan Rd., Toronto, Ont. M4N 1E9.

**MOUNSEY, Joseph Backhouse,** M.A.; financial services executive; b. Lisburn, U.K. 27 Mar. 1949; s. Colin Anthony and Helen (Roake) M.; e. Leighton Park Sch., Reading, U.K.; New College, Oxford Univ., M.A. 1970; m. (Elizabeth) Anne d. Peter and Barbara Burton 18 Nov. 1978; one d.: Elizabeth Helen; SR. VICE-PRES., INTERNATIONAL INVESTMENTS, MANULIFE FINANCIAL 1991– ; joined present firm in U.K. Internat. Investment Office 1970; Investment Mgr. 1978; Vice-Pres., Internat. Investments 1981; Vice-Pres. & Gen. Mgr., U.K. Opns. 1986; Sr. Vice-Pres. & Gen. Mgr., U.K. Opns. 1988; Extve. Vice-Pres., Insurance Opns. 1988–91; Dir., numerous subsidiary companies of Manulife Financial; Mem., Inst. of Dir.; recreations: travel, reading, gardening; club: The Reform (U.K.); Home: 'West Mount,' 29 Prospect Lane, Harpenden, Herts. AL5 2PL U.K.; Office: 200 Bloor St. E., Toronto, Ont. M4W 1E5.

**MOUNT, Graeme S.,** Ph.D.; professor of history; b. Montreal, Que. 26 July 1939; s. Frederick Stewart and Josephine Margaret Weir (Brown) M.; e. h.s. 1958; McGill Univ. B.A. (Hon.) 1961; Univ. of Toronto M.A. 1967, Ph.D. 1969; m. Joan Eva Janet; d. Allan and Freda Biggar 27 June 1964; children: Fraser Robert, Andrew Duncan; PROF., LAURENTIAN UNIV. 1985– ; author: 'Presbyterian Missions to Trinidad and Puerto Rico' 1983, 'The Sudbury Region: An Illustrated History' 1986; 'Canada's Enemies: Spies and Spying in the Peacable Kingdom' 1993; author of several articles; co-author (with E.E. Mahant): 'An Introduction to Canadian-American Relations' 1984 and 1989 (2nd. ed.); Home: 150 Walford Rd., Sudbury, Ont. P3E 2G9; Office: Sudbury, Ont. P3E 2C6.

**MOUNTAIN, Sir Denis Mortimer,** Bart.; insurance executive; b. London, Eng. 2 June 1929; s. Sir Brian Edward Stanley, Bart. and Doris Elsie (Lamb) M.; e. Eton, Eng. 1946; m. Helene Fleur Mary d. John William Kirwan-Taylor, Switzerland 18 Feb. 1958; children: Georgina Lily Fleur, Edward Brian Stanford, William Denis Charles; Dir. Allied London Properties; Bank of Nova Scotia; Bank of Nova Scotia Trust Co. (Bahamas) Ltd.; Bank of Nova Scotia Trust Co. (Cayman) Ltd.; Bank of Nova Scotia Trust Co. (Caribbean) Ltd.; Bank of Nova Scotia International Ltd. (Bahamas); served with Royal Horse Guards, rank Lt.; mem. Winchester Div. Cons. Assn.; Inst. Dirs.; Chelsea Cons.Assn.; recreations: shooting, fishing; Clubs: National Sporting; Blues & Royals; Home: 12 Queens Elm Sq., London S.W. 3, England.

**MOURÉ, Erin;** writer; poet; freelance editor; b. Calgary, Alta. 17 Apr. 1955; d. William Benito and Mary Irene (Grendys) M.; e. Univ. of Calgary; Univ. of B.C.; author: 'Empire, York Street' 1979 (Gov. Gen. Award short list), 'The Whisky Vigil' 1981, 'Wanted Alive' 1983, 'Domestic Fuel' 1985; 'Furious' 1988 (Gov. Gen. Award for Poetry 1988); 'West South West' 1989; 'Sheepish Beauty, Civilian Love' 1992; works incl. in many anthologies incl. 'The New Canadian Poets' 1985; poems, book reviews, essays and articles pub. in several literary jours.; Nat. Mag. Award for poetry 1983, 1993; Mem., League of Candn. Poets; Mem., Writers' Union of Canada; Specialist, Customer Services, Via Rail 1976– ; recreations: bike-riding, skiing; Home: Montréal.

**MOURTON, Maurice Reginald;** banker; b. London, England 21 Feb. 1939; s. Harry R. and Grace M. M.; e. Univ. of Toronto, advanced mngt.; m. Anne d. Jack and Betty Foster 6 May 1961; one d.: Michelle Lien; EXTVE. VICE-PRESIDENT, HONGKONG BANK OF CANADA 1990– ; Barclays Bank Ltd. 1955–62; joined Bank of Montreal 1962; Dir., Mastercard Div. 1977; Vice-Pres., Human Resources 1978–80; Western Ont. Div. 1980–83; B.C. Div. 1983–87; Senior Vice-Pres., Retail

Banking, Hongkong Bank of Canada 1987–89; Dir., Hongkong Bank Securities Inc.; Hongkong Bank Mortgage Corp.; James Capel Canada Inc.; Wardley Canada Inc.; Dir.: Dragon Boat Fest.; B.C. Children's Hosp. (Past Telethon Chair); Vancouver Foundation; Internat. Finance Center; Chrmn., Candn. Bankers Assn., B.C.; recreations: rowing, skiing, swimming; clubs: Arbutus, Terminal City; Home: 25 - 5760 Hampton Place, Vancouver, B.C. V6A 4B3; Office: 300, 885 W. Georgia St., Vancouver, B.C. V6C 3E9.

**MOVAT, Henry Zoltan,** M.D., M.Sc., Ph.D., F.R.C.P.(C); scientist & educator; b. Temesvar, Romania 11 Aug. 1923; s. Erwin Karl and Piroska (Kubitschka) M.; e. Univ. of Vienna; Univ. of Innsbruck, Austria, M.D. 1948; Queen's Univ., M.Sc. 1954, Ph.D. 1956; m. Ilse Adeline, d. Franz Hirselandt, Germany, 29 Dec. 1956; three s., Ronald, Kenneth, Douglas; PROF. EMERITUS OF PATHOL. UNIV. OF TORONTO; Fellow in Pathol., Univ. of Innsbruck, 1948–50; Interne, Ottawa Civic Hosp., 1950–51, and Res. in Pathol. there, 1951–53; Fellow in Pathol., Queen's Univ., 1953–56; Mem. Center for Cancer, New York, 1956–57; Asst. Prof. of Pathol., Univ. of Toronto, 1957–60; Assoc. Prof. 1960–66; Prof. 1966–89; Career Investigator of the Med. Res. Council of Can. 1961–89; Disting. Service Award, Pathol., Univ. of Toronto 1987; Ed., 'Inflammation, Immunity and Hypersensitivity' 1979; 'Leukocyte Emigration and its Sequelae' 1987; author 'The Inflammatory Reaction' 1985; over 200 scient. articles and book chapters; mem., Am. Assn. Pathols.; Internat. Acad. Pathol.; Am. Assn. Immunol.; Candn. Assn. Immunol.; Soc. Exper. Biol. Med.; recreations: oenology, music, gardening, history; Home: 17 Truxford Rd., Parkway Woods, Don Mills, Ont. M3A 2S5.

**MOWAT, Farley,** O.C., B.A., D.Litt.; author; b. Belleville, Ont. 12 May 1921; s. Angus McGill and Helen E. (Thomson) M.; e. Pub. Schs., Trenton, Belleville, Windsor, Ont., and Saskatoon, Sask.; High Schs., Saskatoon, Sask., Toronto and Richmond Hill, Ont.; Univ. of Toronto, B.A. 1949; D.Litt. (Hon.) Laurentian 1970, Univ. of Victoria 1982, Lakehead Univ. 1986; D. Laws. Lethbridge, Toronto (both 1973) P.E.I. 1979; m. 1st, Frances Elizabeth, d. H. R. Thornhill, Toronto, 20 Dec. 1947; children: Robert Alexander, David Peter; 2ndly, Claire Angel Wheeler 1963; began writing as Free-Lance author after return from two yrs. in Arctic (1947–48) at Palgrave, Ont.; has written for 'Atlantic Monthly,' 'Saturday Evening Post' (regular contrib.), 'Reader's Digest,' 'Maclean's Mag.' etc.; author of: 'People of the Deer,' 1952 (Anisfield-Wolf Award, U.S.A. 1954 for outstanding work in field of race relations); rec'd. Pres. Medal, Univ. of W. Ont. for best short story publ. by a Candn. in 1952; 'The Regiment' (story of a Candn. Inf. Regt. in World War II), 1955; 'Lost in the Barrens,' 1956 (Gov. Gen. Award for Juvenile Lit.); 'The Dog Who Wouldn't Be,' 1957 (Candn. Women's Club Award (Candn.) 1958); 'The Grey Seas Under,' 1958; 'Coppermine Journey,' 1958; 'The Desperate People,' 1959; 'Ordeal by Ice,' 1960; 'Owls in the Family,' 1961 (Boys' Clubs of America Junior Book Award (U.S.A) 1962); 'The Serpents Coil,' 1961; 'The Black Joke,' 1962; 'Never Cry Wolf' 1963 (Disney/Ballard Film Prodn. 1983; Bantam/Seal Audio recording by author 1988); 'Westviking,' 1965; 'Curse of the Viking Grave,' 1966 (TV Production, Atlantis Films Ltd., Canada 1991); 'The Polar Passion,' 1967; 'Canada North,' 1967; 'The Rock Within the Sea,' 1968; 'The Boat Who Wouldn't Float,' 1969 (winner 1970 Stephen Leacock Mem. Medal for Humour; L'Etoile de la Mer, Honours List (France) as 'Fleur de Passion' 1972); 'Sibir,' 1970; 'A Whale for the Killing' 1972; 'Wake of the Great Sealers,' 1973; 'Tundra,' 1973; 'The Snow Walker,' 1975; 'Canada North Now,' 1976; 'And No Birds Sang,' 1979 (Author's Award (Candn.), Periodical Distributors of Canada Best non-fiction book of 1981); 'The World of Farley Mowat,' 1980; 'Sea of Slaughter,' 1984 (Author's Award (Candn.), Periodical Distributors of Canada 1985; CBC 'The Nature of Things' documentary 1990); 'My Discovery of America,' 1985; 'Virunga' 1987; 'The New Founde Land' 1989; 'The New North' (Norwolf/Noralpha, CTV documentary, 1989); 'Rescue The Earth' 1990; 'Lost in the Barrens' (television production, Atlantis Films Ltd., Canada) 1990; 'My Father's Son' 1992; 'Born Naked,' 1993; served in 2nd World War, 1940–46 mostly with Hastings and Prince Edward Regiment (Infantry) as Platoon Commander and Intelligence Officer through Sicily, North West Europe; rec'd Book of the Year Medal, Candn. Lib. Assn. 1958; Hans Christian Andersen Internat. Award 1958; National Assn. of Independent Schools Award (U.S.A.) for juvenile books 1963; Hans Christian Anderson Honours List (Internat.) for juvenile books 1965; Canadian Centennial Medal 1967; Vicky Metcalfe Award (Candn. Authors Assn.) for contribution to Candn. writing 1970; Mark Twain Award (U.S.A.) 1971; Curran Award (Candn.) for contributions to understanding wolves 1977; Book of the Year (Candn.), Candn. Assn. of Children's Librarians 1976; Queen Elizabeth II Jubilee Medal 1978; Knight of Mark Twain 1980; Officer, Order of Canada 1981; Author of the Year (Candn. Booksellers Assn.) 1988; Book of the Year (Cdn.), Periodical Marketers of Canada ('Virunga') 1988; Gemini Award ('The New North') 1989; Torgi Talking Book of the Year Award (Candn. Nat. Inst. of the Blind), Toronto, (Virunga) 1989; Award of Excellence, Atlantic Film Fest., Halifax, NS ('Sea of Slaughter') documentary 1990; 1990 Canadian Achievers Award, Toshiba Canada; Nominated for Conservation Film of the Year, Wildscreen Internat. Film Festival, Bristol, England ('Sea of Slaughter') documentary 1990; Finalist, American Cable Entertainment Awards ('Sea of Slaughter') documentary 1990; Take Back the Nation Award (first annual), Council of Canadians 1991; Address: c/o Key Porter Books Ltd., 70 The Esplanade, 3rd Floor, Toronto, Ont. M5E 1R2.

**MOWLING, J. Keith;** executive; b. Montreal, Que. 25 Apl. 1944; s. Robert Jack and Helen Lilias (Chalmers) M.; e. Lorne Park (Ont.) Pub. and High Schs., 1964; Waterloo Univ. Coll., 1964–65; m. Ruth Anne, d. late Walter Grierson, Waterloo, Ont., 11 Nov. 1967; children: Robert H. Stephen, Christine Anne; PRESIDENT, K. MOWLING & ASSOCS. INC. 1988– ; joined Border Brokers Ltd. as Customs Rater, Halifax, 1965; joined father's co. Jacksons Chinaware Ltd. 1965, served in Sales, E. Can. (co. subsequently amalgamated with present cos.), served as Mgr. Toronto Sales, Montreal Sales and Atlantic Regional Mgr. 1968–73; Nat. Marketing and Sales Mgr., Wedgwood Ltd., March-Oct. 1973; Pres., Waterford Wedgwood Canada Inc. 1973–88; Dir., Candn. Gift and Tableware Assn.; mem. Brit. Candn. Trade Associates; United Church; recreations: golf, hockey, home decorating, philately; Club: York Downs Golf; Home: 2916 Vivian Rd., Newmarket, Ont. L3Y 4W1; Office: 135 East Beaver Creek, Unit 9, Richmond Hill, Ont. L4B 1E2.

**MOWLING, (Robert) Ray,** B.Comm.; business executive; b. Toronto, Ont. 10 Oct. 1942; s. Robert Jack and Helen M.; e. Appleby Coll. Oakville, Ont. 1954; Lorne Park Secondary Sch. 1961; Carleton Univ. B.Comm. 1965; m. Gerlinde Herrmann Sept. 1981; children: 5; VICE PRES., LEGAL AND PUBLIC AFFAIRS, MONSANTO CANADA INC. 1990– , Dir. 1986– ; joined Shell Canada 1965–69, Ford Canada 1969–71, present Co. 1971, Sr. Vice Pres. Monsanto Canada Inc. 1983–90; Dir., Junior Achievement (Metro Toronto & York Region); recreations: golf, hockey; Club: Mississauga Golf & Country; Office: P.O. Box 787 Streetsville P.S., Mississauga, Ont. L5M 2G4.

**MOYER, Janice Mary,** B.Sc.; computer industry and assn. executive; b. Hamilton, Ont. 28 Aug. 1952; d. Richard Henry and Veronica Marie (Howard) Holt; e. Bishop Ryan H.S.; McMaster Univ. B.Sc. 1974; m. Wesley D. (David) s. Lawrence and Amelia M. 19 May 1973; PRES. & C.E.O., INFORMATION TECHNOLOGY ASSN. OF CANADA (ITAC) 1990– ; various positions with IBM Canada Ltd. incl. Location Sales Mgr., Hamilton (1981–82); Extve. Asst. to Chrmn. of Bd. (1983); Mgr., Corp. & Sci. Programs (1984–85); ending as Branch Mgr., Retail & Serv. Indus. Sales Branch 1974–87; Pres., McCormack & Dodge Systems Can. Ltd. 1987–90; recreations: swimming, scuba diving; Home: 111 Manitou Dr., King City, Ont. L0G 1K0; Office: 2800 Skymark Ave., Suite 402, Mississauga, Ont. L4W 5A6.

**MOYLS, Benjamin Nelson,** B.A., M.A., A.M., Ph.D.;educator; b. Vancouver, B.C. 1 May 1919; s. Benjamin James and Jessie Catherine (Walker) M.; e. Univ. of B.C. B.A. 1940, M.A. 1941; Harvard Univ. A.M. 1942, Ph.D. 1947; m. 1stly Ina Elizabeth Barbour (dec.); children: Gregory Nelson, Peter William; m. 2ndly Toby Claire d. Nathan Buller 7 May 1976; PROF. EMERITUS, UNIV. OF B.C. 1984– ; joined Univ. as Lectr. 1947, Asst. Prof. 1948, Assoc. Prof. 1954, Professor of Math., 1959–84; Asst. Dean of Grad. Studies 1967–76; Head of Math. Dept., 1978–83; R.C.N.V.R. 1943–45 (retired as Elect. Lt.); author various research papers in linear and multilinear algebra; Vice-Pres., Can. Math Soc. 1981–1982; mem. Candn. Math. Soc.; Amer. Math. Soc.; Math. Assn. of Amer.; Soc. for Industrial and Applied Math; Anglican; recreations: music, swimming; Home: 2016 Western Parkway, Vancouver, B.C. V6T 1V5; Office: 1984 Mathematics Rd., Univ. of B.C., Vancouver, B.C. V6T 1Y4.

**MOYSEY, A. Warren,** B.Com., M.A., FICB; b. Toronto, Ont. 16 Jan. 1939; e. Univ. of Toronto B.Com. 1961; Univ. of Chicago M.A. Economics, 1962; FICB 1965; m.; 3 children; Dir., The General Accident Assurance Co. of Can.; Gentra Inc.; Candn. Internat. Group; Sceptre Investment Counsel Ltd. 1986–91; joined CIBC 1962; Vice Pres. and Gen. Mgr., Internat. 1978; Sr. Vice Pres., Systems 1979; Extve. Vice Pres. 1980; Sr. Extve. Vice Pres. 1982; Pres., Individual Bank, CIBC 1986–90; Dir., CIBC 1989–90; Chrmn., Extve. Council, Candn. Bankers Assn. 1988–90; Pres., Central Guaranty Trust 1991–92; Pres. & C.E.O., Aetna Life Insurance Co. of Can. 1992–94, Chrmn. & C.E.O., Candn. Internat. Group 1994– ; Hon. Dir., Dellcrest Children's Centre; Clubs: Toronto Golf; Mad River Golf; Mid Ocean Club (Bermuda); Badminton & Racquet; Cambridge; Toronto; Osler Bluff Ski (Dir.); Office: 151 Yonge St., 8th Floor, Toronto, Ont. M5C 2Y1.

**MOZERSKY, Dan,** B.A.; bookstore executive; b. Winnipeg, Man. 22 July 1945; s. Myer and Lillian (Soudack) M.; e. Carleton Univ. B.A. 1969, B.A. (Hons.) 1970; m. Joy d. Morris and Sabine Amsel 1 Jan. 1967; children: Joshua, Lolly, Jessica; BOOK INDUSTRY CONSULTANT 1989– ; ASSOC., ERNST & YOUNG, OTTAWA 1991; Teacher of Eng. as second lang. Fed. Govt. Ottawa 1971–72; Co-Founder Prospero Books, Ottawa 1972; Pres. & C.O.O., Prospero Books Ltd. 1975–89; Acting Managing Editor, Carleton Univ. Press 1991; recipient Book Publishers' Prof. Assn. 'Bookseller of the Year' Award 1985; Co-Founder and Chrmn. Ottawa Regional Booksellers Assn. 1974–75; Chrmn. Ottawa Regional Booksellers Trade Fair 1975–87; Judge, Books in Can. First Novel Award 1983–84; Dir. Candn. Booksellers Assn. 1985–87 (Vice Pres. 1987–88; Chrmn., Supplier Relations Ctte. 1987–88); Bd. mem., Ctte. of Mgmt., Carleton Univ. Press 1988– ; mem. Canadian Telebook Agency Bd. of Management 1991; mem. Founding Bd. & Treasurer, Friends of the National Library 1991– ; mem. Book Industry Task Force on GST; mem. Candn. Booksellers Assn.; Am. Booksellers Assn.; recreations: book collecting; Address: 286 Roger Rd., Ottawa, Ont. K1H 5C6.

**MRAZEK, Margaret L.,** B.Sc.N., MHSA, LL.B.; lawyer; e. Misericordia Hosp. Sch. of Nursing (Edmonton) RN 1960; Univ. of Alta. B.Sc.N. 1962, M.H.S.A. 1970, LL.B. 1986; m. late Norbert M.; one d.: Monique; PARTNER, REYNOLDS, MIRTH, RICHARDS & FARMER (EDMONTON) 1987– ; Nursing Instructor, Misericordia Hosp. Sch. of Nursing 1962–65; Asst. Extve. Dir. 1967–76; Vice Pres., Patient Care Serv. 1977–83; Trustee, Alta. Heritage Found. for Medial Research 1990– , Vice Chair 1992–94; Chair of Health Rsch. Ctte.; Adjunct Prof., Fac. of Med., Univ. of Alta. 1990–93; Vice-Chrmn., Health law subsection, Candn. Bar Assoc. 1990–92; Candn. Nurses' Found. Fellow 1969–70; Misericordia Nurses' Alumni Assn. Bursary 1961; Misericordia Hosp. Women's Aux. Scholarship 1960; Chrmn., Midwifery Services Review Ctte. (1991) providing advice to the Alberta Govt. regarding midwifery; Mem. of Advisory Ctte., St. Joseph's Coll., Catholic Bioethics Centre 1991– ; Bd. of Dirs. Extve. Ctte., Catholic Social Services 1992– ; Mem., Am. Coll. of Healthcare Extves; cert. mem., Candn. Coll. of Health Serv. Extves.; Personal Mem., Catholic Health Assn. of Alta.; Mem., Alta. Assn. of Registered Nurses; Candn. Bar Assn.; Medico-Legal Soc.; frequent public speaker; author of many published articles; Home: St. Albert, Alta.; Office: 3200 – 10180 – 101 St., Edmonton, Alta. T5J 3W8.

**MRKICH, Dan Dušan,** B.A.; writer, diplomat; b. Bud Rijeka, Krajina, Yugoslavia 11 Dec. 1939; s. Ignatia and Milica (Boić) Mrkić; e. Karlovac, Croatia H.S.; Carleton Univ. B.A. (Hons.) 1971; m. Susan d. Arthur and Dorothy Cooke 10 Nov. 1973; children: Alexander, Soren, Astrid; TRADE COMMISSIONER FOR MOLDOVA, ROMANIA, HUNGARY, BULGARIA, ALBANIA, SLOVENIA, CROATIA, BOSNIA & HERZEGOVINA, MACEDONIA and YUGOSLAVIA, FOREIGN AFFAIRS CANADA 1993– ; Officer, Dept. of Sec. of State 1964–74; Regional Econ. Expansion 1975–81; joined External Affairs 1982; temporary duties abroad in Yugoslavia 1984; Korea 1988; Hong Kong, China, Mongolia and Macau 1989; Mem., Serbian Orthodox Ch.; author: 'No Morning Can Restore What We Have Forfeited' (TV drama) 1973, 'Mountain Laurel' (play, transl. of P.P. Nyegosh) 1985, 'Kosovo' (epic poem) 1989, 'Redemption' (novel) 1990, 'Inheritance' (short stories in Serbian) 1991, 'The White Spectre and Other Poems' (collected shorter poems) 1991; 'Passengers to Points North' (novel) 1993; recreation: gardening; Home: 618 Golden Ave., Ottawa, Ont. K2A 2G1; Office: 125 Sussex Dr., Ottawa, Ont. K2A 0G2.

**MROZEWSKI, Andrzej Henryk,** M.A., M.L.S.; librarian; b. Paris, France, 25 Feb. 1930; s. Stefan and

Irena (Blizinska) M.; e. High Sch. and Coll., Poland and France; Univ. de Montréal; M.A. (Slavic Studies) 1954; Univ. of Ottawa, B.L.S. 1960; McGill Univ., M.L.S. 1972; Ecole du Louvre, Paris; m. Janina, d. late Maj. Witold Karolewski and late Zofia (Bilinska) Poland, 21 Aug. 1954; children: Monika-Marta, André Witold Jr., Jan Stefan; REFERENCE LIBRARIAN, LAURENTIAN UNIV. OF SUDBURY; Chief Librarian, Coll. de Rouyn, 1960–64; Med. Librarian (part-time), Hôpital Youville, Noranda, 1962–64; Head of Acquisitions, Univ. de Sherbrooke, 1964, Head, Tech. Services 1965–68, Asst. Chief Librarian 1965–71, Acting Chief Librarian 1970–71; Chief Librarian, Laurentian Univ. of Sudbury 1972–86; mem. Comité de coordination de la documentation dans les univs. du Qué., 1966–71; Comité de coordination des bibliothèques univs. du Qué., 1967–71; Ont. Council Univ. Libraries since 1972 (Chrmn. 1974); Lectr. Lib. Sch. summers 1962–64 and in Polish Lit. summers 1961–62, Univ. of Ottawa 1980; invited scholar at Katolicki Uniwersytet Lubelski (KUL) Lublin, Poland, also guest lectr. at PAN (Polish Acad. of Sciences) Inst. for Studies on Poles Abroad, Poznan; Warsaw Univ. Grad. Sch. of Librarianship and Scientific Documentation; Maria Curie-Sklodowska Univ. Lublin; Krzyz Armii Krajowej (Home Army Cross) and Medal Wojska (Polish Army Medal) for service in Polish Underground W.W. II; Médaille d'argent de l'Univ. du Sherbrooke; working on book on life and art of Stefan Mrozewski and catalogue raisonnée of his works; publ. articles and notes in field of librarianship, bibliog.and graphic art; Candn. Lib. Assn.; Candn. Assn. Coll. & Univ. Libs.; A.C.B.F. (Pres., Sec. des bibliothèques univs., gouvernmentales et spécialisées, 1967); Assn. des bibliothécaires du Qué. (Pres. 1967–68, Ed. Newsletter 1967–71); Corp. des bibliothécaires professionnels du Qué. (Dir. 1969–70); Polish Candn. Librairies Assn.; mem. Polish Combattants Assn. (S.P.K.); mem Adv. Comte., Library Technician Program, Cambrian College (1972–80); mem. Stowarzyszenie Bibliofilow Polskich (Polish Soc. of Bibliophiles); Ont. Assn. of Archivists; Friends of the Catholic Univ. of Poland; Vice-Pres., Candn.-Polish Congress, Sudbury Dist.; mem. Bd. of Dirs., Sudbury & Dist. Multicultural and Folk Arts Assn.; R. Catholic; recreations: nature, collecting prints and books; Home: 27 Nepahwin Ave., Sudbury, Ont. P3A 2H5.

**MUCCI, Daniel Charles,** B.A., P.Eng.; manufacturing executive; b. Toronto, Ont. 1 Apr. 1936; s. James V. and Mary Rose (Gray) M.; e. Univ. of Toronto, B.A. 1958; m. Eileen d. Charles and Mary Matthews 26 July 1958; children: Lynn, David, Steven; Pres. & C.O.O., Fleck Mfg. Inc. 1986; Opns. Mgr., Sangamo Co. Ltd. 1958–68; Vice-Pres., Engr. Serv., Olivetti Can. Ltd. 1968–75; Vice-Pres., On Line Systems Div. 1975–78; Vice-Pres. & Gen. Mgr., Fleck Mfg. Inc. 1978–85; Pres. 1986; Sons of Martha Apeo; Dir., Tillsonburg Meml. Hosp.; Tillsonburg Indus. Comn.; recreations: golf, sailing.

**MUCHNICK, Howard F.,** B.B.A., M.A.; executive; b. New York City, N.Y. 27 March 1944; s. Charles and Esther (Greenberg) M.; e. The City Coll. of N.Y. B.B.A. 1965; Hofstra Univ. N.Y. M.A. 1969; m. Lisa d. James and Elaine Slater 20 Nov. 1980; children: Joanna, Alexander; Teacher N.Y.C. Sch. System 1965–71; Prin. Keene, N.H. 1971–73; joined Chase Manhattan Bank, N.A. (N.Y.C.) 1973–75; Citibank (N.Y.) 1975–81; Bank of Montreal, Montreal and Toronto 1981–83; Goodhost Foods Ltd. Toronto 1983–85; Casa Loma, Toronto 1985–89; Pres., CN Tower Ltd. 1989–92; mem. Holy Blossom Temple (teacher since 1981); recreations: running, reading; Home: 412 Russell Hill Rd., Toronto, Ont. M4V 2V2.

**MUELLER, John Charles,** B.A., C.A.; insurance executive; b. Toronto, Ont. 21 Feb. 1938; s. Norbert Edward and Violet Jean (Hill) M.; e. Univ. of Toronto C.A. 1959; York Univ. B.A. 1974; m. Margaret d. Margaret and John Scott 7 Sept. 1962; children: John Charles, Margaret Dunning; MANAGING DIR., MARSH & MCLENNAN LIMITED 1985– ; Controller, William M. Mercer Ltd. 1971; Marsh & McLennan Limited (sister co.) 1972; Treas., both companies 1974; resigned as Cont. & Treas., William M. Mercer Ltd. 1979 but retained duties for Marsh & McLennan Ltd.; Vice-Pres. Finance & Admin. 1979; Sr. Vice-Pres. & Dir. 1981; Presbyterian; P.C.; recreations: golf, tennis, bridge, music; clubs: Granite, Rosedale Golf (Dir. & President), National, Board of Trade, Big Bay Point Golf; Home: 58 Lympstone Ave., Toronto, Ont. M4N 1M7; Office: 161 Bay St., P.O. Box 502, Toronto, Ont. M5J 2S4.

**MUGGAH, Henry Forman,** B.A., M.D., F.R.C.S.(C); physician; educator; b. Halifax, N.S. May 1942; s. Henry F. and Ella K. (Philpot) M.; e. Dalhousie Univ. B.A. 1963, M.D. 1968; F.R.C.S.(C) 1975; m. Betty Crookshank 1968; children: Sean, Elizabeth, Robert, Alexander; CHIEF OF OBSTETRICS AND GYNECOL. ST. JOSEPHS HOSP. 1988– ; Prof. of Obstetrics & Gynecol. McMaster Univ. 1988– ; Assoc. Prof. of Obstetrics & Gynecol. Univ. of Ottawa 1975–88; recreations: hiking, sailing; Home: 120 Chedoke Ave., Hamilton, Ont. L8P 4N9; Office: 50 Charlton Ave., Hamilton, Ont. L8N 4A6.

**MUIR, David Charles Fraser,** Ph.D., F.R.C.P.(C), F.R.C.P.(L), F.R.C.P.(E), F.F.O.M.; physician/professor of medicine; b. Hull, U.K. 1 Nov. 1931; s. David Charles and Annie Rennie M.; e. Repton Sch. (U.K.); Middlesex Hosp. (U.K.); m. Gisèle d. William and Jeanne de Lane Lea 6 June 1959; children: Angus, Roderick, Tamsin; PROF., DEPT. OF MED. & DIR., OCCUPATIONAL HEALTH PROG., MCMASTER UNIV. 1977– ; Dir., Inst. of Occup. Med. and Cons., Physician City Hops. (U.K.); author of sci. pubs. in field of occup. diseases & epidemiol., properties of aerosols; Home: 353 Lodor St., Ancaster, Ont. L9G 2Z5; Office: 1200 Main St. W., Hamilton, Ont. L8N 3Z5.

**MUIR, Hon. Robert;** senator; b. Edinburgh, Scot. 10 Nov. 1919; s. James and Helen (Clark) M.; e. Sydney Mines, N.S.; m. Mary Melina d. Angus King, Sydney Mines, N.S. 22 Feb. 1944; children: Robert Munro, Gary Stuart, Ruth Lenora; came to Can. 1921; worked in coal mines at early age and was seriously injured 1940; held numerous positions local union of Un. Mine Workers of Am. and el. as del. to 3 dist. conventions and 3 internat. conventions; joined London Life Insurance Co. as salesman 1949; Sales and Credit Mgr. Moores Electric, North Sydney 1953; Town Councillor Sydney Mines 1948–58; Dir. Harbour View Hosp. 1944–58, Pres. of Bd. 1951–58; Chrmn. Cape Breton Regional Hosp. Assn. 2 terms; el. to H. of C. g.e. 1957 (M.P. for Cape Breton N. and Victoria), re-el. to 1974 (constituency changed to Cape Breton The Sydneys 1967); Parlty. Observer to UN Cen. Assembly 1960 and mem. Candn. Del. 1979; Head Del. N. Atlantic Treaty Organ. Cong. Washington 1962; Candn. Del. to Internat. Labour Cong. Geneva 1966; Del. Inter-Parlty. Conf. New Delhi 1969, Bonn 1978, E. Berlin 1980; organized and headed del. of Mems. and Sens. to Vatican 1969; Del. Commonwealth Parlty. Assn. Assembly Sri Lanka 1974; Del. N. Atlantic Assembly Brussels 1976; named Hon. Grand Chief MicMac Tribe 1977; mem. All Party del. to Repub. of China (Taiwan) 1977 and People's Repub. of China 1978; All Party del. to Rep. of Korea 1981; Canada-Arab World Parliamentary Group; Canada-Taiwan Parliamentary Friendship Group; Observer to U.N. Special Conf. on Nuclear Disarmament 1982; Candn. Delegation, 40th Anniv. of the Dieppe Raid, Aug 1982; delegate from Canada Latin America Parliamentary Assoc. to Buenos Aires and other centres in Argentina 1983; delegate to the Commonwealth Parliamentary Assoc. Assembly in the U.K. 1984; All Party delegation with Min. of Defense on a Military and Ind. tour of Egypt, Thailand, People's Rep. of China, Singapore, Australia, S.E. Pacific Command, U.S.A. Pearl Harbour; Delegate, Inter-Parlty. Union Conf., Mexico City 1986; Mem., Trade Delegation – All Parties to Japan; former Vice Chrmn. P. Cons. Party Caucus Comte. on Labour; summoned to the Senate 1979; Hon. mem. B'nai Brith Confed. Lodge Ottawa; Dir. Candn. Council Christians & Jews; Hon. mem. Royal Candn. Legion; Sydney Mines Fire Dept.; Hon. Pres., Brigade Canada; mem. Nat. Press Club Can.; Candn. NATO Parlty. Assn.; Commonwealth Parlty. Assn. (Candn. Br.); Candn. Group Inter-Parlty. Union; Can.-U.S. Inter-Parlty. Group; Can.-Japan Friendship Assn.; Hon. Pres., Royal Cdn. Legion, Br. #8, Hon. Patron & mem., Eighth Army Veterans Assoc., Candn. Chapter; named Hon. Principal, Canada Sch., Buenos Aires, Argentina; Mem., Can.-Korea Parliamentary Group; Can.-Israel Parliamentary Friendship Group; Can.-German Friendship Assn.; Can.-Europe Parliamentary Group; Can.-Greece Friendship Assn.; Can.-Latin-America Parliamentary Assn.; Pres. Candn.-Argentine Inst.; Mem., Senate Standing Cttes.: Internal Economy, Budgets and Admin.; Transport & Communications; Foreign Affairs; Internat. Affairs Ctte., Presbyterian Church in Canada; Dir., John G. Diefenbaker Memorial Fdn., Inc.; Hon. by the Rabbinical College, Kiryas Tash, Montreal, Que., 1980; P. Conservative; Presbyterian; Club: Northern Yacht (Hon. mem.); Home: 40 Birchwood Dr., Sydney Mines, N.S. B1V 3G6; Office: The Senate, Ottawa, Ont. K1A 0A4.

**MUIR, Robert;** banker (retired); b. Co. Durham, Eng. 8 Feb. 1925; s. Robert and Margaret Miller Ferguson M.; e. Consett (Co. Durham, Eng.) Grammar Sch.; Univ. of Glasgow 1942–43; m. Stella Margaret d. Prof. E. A. Allcut, Toronto, Ont. 10 June 1950; children: Margaret, David, Peter, Alexander, Douglas, Stanley, Andrew; Vice Pres. and Secy. Bank of Montreal 1973–86; joined present Bank 1948; Dir., Denbridge Capital Corp. 1987–93; Dir., Denbridge Gas Corp. 1994– ; served with RNVR 1943–46, rank Sub-Lt.; Fellow, Chartered Inst. Bankers (London, Eng.); Fellow, Inst. Candn. Bankers; Prof. Admin., Inst. of Chartered Secretaries and Administrators in Canada; Presbyterian; Home: 57 Beaconsfield Court, Beaconsfield, Que. H9W 5G5.

**MULCAHY, Sean,** B.A.; director; actor; b. Bantry, Republic of Ireland; s. John and Mary (Barry) M.; e. The North Monastery, Cork; The Sch. of Art Cork; Univ. of Bristol, B.A.; Dir. and Teacher, Drama Div., Banff Sch. of Fine Arts (Sr. Drama Instr. & Dir. 1969–70); Former Dir. Citadel Theatre; Drama Dir. and Lectr. at Univs. of Toronto, N.B., Alta., W. Ont., McMaster and Ryerson Coll.; Artistic Advisor, Sudbury Theatre, Sudbury, Ont.; TV panelist on CBC and CTV; has performed on most maj. CBC TV and radio series since 1957 and for Nat. Film Bd. since 1958; Assoc. Dir., The Shaw Festival, 1963–65; Artistic Dir., Instant Theatre, Montreal, 1964–66; Dir., Beaverbrook Playhouse, Fredericton, 1966–67; Artistic Dir., Georgian Foundation for Performing Arts, Barrie, Ont. and The Press Theatre, St. Catharines, Ont. 1974–76; narrated and starred in 'Horseman Pass By' (documentary film in Ireland for CBC's 'Camera Canada') 1965; Dir. 'The Picture of Dorian Gray' (Columbia Pictures TV) 1974;'The Electric Gospel' (Candn. Electronic Ensemble) 1981; starred in world premieres 'Step-Dance' and 'The Second' 1981; Dir., world premieres of Wiesels' 'The Madness of God' and 'Educating Rita' 1983; starred as H.G. Wells in CBC's 'The Panther and the Jaguar' 1983 (and received Andrew Allan Award 1984 for that role); starred as Cervantes in C.B.C.'s 'Life & Times of Cervantes' nominated for ACTRA Award 1986, and in C.B.C's 'Philadelphia, Here I Come!' (1985), winner of ACTRA Nellie Award 1986; starred in Global TV's 'Trial of Evelyn Dick' and 'The Vanishing Point' 1987, 'The Mask' and 'Dedication' 1988; starred in 'Dear Liar' Neptune Theatre (1989); starred in CBC's 'The Last Romantic' as W.B. Yeats (1989); Apptd. Artistic Dir., The Stephenville Festival, 1989; Directed '1949', 'Cold Storage' 'Dear Liar' and 'Step Dance' 1989; starred in 'Brass Rubbings' 1990; Dir.: 'Stepping Out' UK 1991; 'Educating Rita' Grand Bend 1991; 'Don't Dress for Dinner,' 'Jitters,' and played 'Merlin' in 'Camelot' Grand Bend 1992; 'Educating Rita' Keswick 1992; Dir. & Starred, 'Come Into The Parlour' New Brunswick Celtic Festival 1991 (Fredericton, St. John, Moncton); starred as G.B.S., Arthur Rubinstein and Gerald Moore for 'Arts National' CBC 1991; starred in 'Return to the Hill' San Diego 1992; commentator on CBC's 'Arts National' and 'Infotape' 1992; Host of C.B.C. Arts Nationals' 'Music Library' 1993; CTV 'Counterstrike' 1993; starred in Anna Livia Productions 'Bloomsday' 1993; served with RAF 1948–52; rank Flight Lt.; Silver Jubilee Medal 1977; mem., Alliance of Candn. Cinema, Television and Radio Artists (Vice-Pres. 1960–61); mem. of Bd., Alliance of Candn. Cinema, TV and Radio Artists 1978; Chrmn., Performer's Guild; ACTRA 1978 (Nat. Vice Pres. 1988–89, Acting Nat. Pres. 1989); elected to ACTRA Fraternal Board of Govs. 1990; Extve. mem. Council, Cdn. Actors' Equity Assn. 1978; Edmonton Chamber of Comm.; Liberal; R. Catholic; recreations: rowing, travel, talking; Club: Arts and Letters; Variety; Toronto Press Club; Home: 34 Heydon Park Rd. #37, Toronto, Ont. M6J 2C8; Office: C/O Canadian Actors Equity Assn., 260 Richmond St. E., Toronto, Ont. M5A 1P4.

**MULCAIR, Thomas J.,** B.C.L., LL.B.; attorney; b. Ottawa, Ont. 24 Oct. 1954; s. Harry Donnelly and Jeanne Marie (Hurtubise) M.; e. McGill Univ. B.C.L. 1976, LL.B. 1977; m. Catherine d. Raphaël and Lydia Pinhas 31 July 1976; children: Matthew, Gregory; PRES., OFFICE DES PROFESSIONS DU QUÉBEC 1987– ; Legis. Counsel, Que. Justice 1978–80; Dir. des Affaires juridiques, cons. de la langue française 1980–83; Dir. of Legal Affairs, Alliance Québec 1983–85; Partner (Nom.), Donald & Duggan 1985–87; Prof., Champlain Coll. 1979–82; Univ. du Qué. à Trois-Rivières 1982–87; Legal Revisor, Attorney Gen. of Man. 1985–87; Comr., Comn. d'appel sur la langue d'enseignement 1986–87; Pres., Law Students Assn., McGill Univ. 1974–75; Pres., English-Speaking Cath. Coun. 1987 (Bd. Mem. 1984–86; Vice-Pres. 1986); Bd. of Dir., 'Opération Enfant Soleil' Children's Hosp. Telethon 1991–93; R.C.; Mem., St. Patrick's Soc. of Montreal; author: 'Bibliographie sur la rédaction et l'interprétation des textes législatifs' 1979; recreations: swimming, ice hockey, skiing, golf; club: Lac Marois Country; Home: 109 Lynwood Dr., Beaconsfield, Que. H9W 5L9; Office: 276, rue St-Jacques O., bureau 728, Montreal, Que. H2Y 1N3.

**MULCHEY, Ronald Douglas,** B.A., M.Div.; health care executive; b. Toronto, Ont. 11 Aug. 1937; s. William and Rena Katherine (Hilts) M.; e. Riverdale Coll. 1956; Univ. of Sask., B.A. 1960; Univ. of Toronto, Knox Coll., M.Div. 1963, Sch. of Hygiene, grad. studies in hosp. admin. 1973–75 (G. Harvey Agnew Award 1974); m. Heather d. George and Ruth Spence 12 Aug. 1967; PRES. & CHIEF EXECUTIVE OFFR., ST. PAUL'S HOSPITAL, Vancouver, B.C. 1987– ; Cong. Min. (Man., Sask., Ont.), Presbyterian Ch. in Can. 1963–70; Nat. Cons. in Ch. & Univ. 1970–73; past mem. num. bds. & cttes.; Dir., Support Serv., Sunnybrook Med. Ctr. 1975–80; Asst. Admin. 1980–83; Acting Extve. Dir. 1983; C.O.O., 1984–87; Preceptor, Univ. of Toronto 1983– ; Lectr. 1986– ; Clinical Asst. Prof. (U.B.C.) 1988– ; Bd. Mem., St. Andrew's Hall, U.B.C. 1988– ; Former Clerk of Presbytery, Assiniboia Presbyn. Ch. of Can. 1966–67; Former Dir., Knox Coll. 1970–72; Dir., B.C. Health Assoc. 1987– ; Past Chrmn., BC Health Assn. (Chrmn. 1989–91); Bd. Mem. Health & Labour Relations Assn. 1991– ; Mem., Candn. Coll. of Health Serv. Extves. 1978– ; Former Mem., Rotary Club; Kinsmen Club; recreations: golf, tennis; Clubs: Shaughnessy Golf and Country; Candn. Club of Vancouver; Home: 1281 20th St., West Vancouver, B.C. V7V 3Z4; Office: 1081 Burrard St., Vancouver, B.C. V6Z 1Y6.

**MULDER, Nicodemus (Nick) G.,** B.A., M.A.; government executive; b. Deventer, The Netherlands 6 Nov. 1939; s. Johannus H. and Everdina J. (Boerkamp) M.; e. Univ. of N.B. B.A. 1962, M.A. 1965; grad. studies: Sweden, Univ. of Illinois; m. Claudette d. Arthur and Doris Richard 8 June 1968; children: Nathalie, René, Nicole; Deputy Min., Environment Canada 1993; Pres., Candn. Commercial Corp.; Economist, Govt. of Canada, Govt. of N.B. 1962–69; Economic Advisor, Premier of N.B. 1969–71; Dir. Gen., Regional Economic Expansion 1971–75; Asst. Deputy Min., Transport Canada 1975–87; Assoc. Deputy Min. and Vice Chairperson, Employment & Immigration 1987–90; Deputy Min., Supply and Services and Deputy Receiver General for Canada 1990–93; Deputy Min. and Chairperson, Employment and Immigration Feb. 1993–June 1993; Bd. of Dir., United Way Canada; Mem./Extve., Inst. of Public Admin.; Kidney Found.; Little League Baseball; Transport Assn. of Canada; Home: 297 Clemow Ave., Ottawa, Ont. K1S 2B7.

**MULDOON, Hon. Mr. Justice Francis Creighton,** B.A., LL.B.; b. Winnipeg, Man. 3 Aug. 1930; s. William John and Laura Grace (Meredith) M.; e. Grosvenor Sch., Robert H. Smith Sch., Kelvin High Sch. (Winnipeg); Univ. of Man., B.A. 1952; LL.B. 1956; m. Lucille, d. Lewis and Stella Shirtliff, 6 Aug. 1955; two children; JUDGE, FEDERAL COURT TRIAL DIV. & COURT MARTIAL APPEAL COURT, 1983– ; admitted to Man. Bar 1956; joined firm Monnin, Grafton, Deniset & Dowhan (Winnipeg), which became Grafton, Dowhan, Muldoon, Lafrenière & Walsh; cr. Q.C. 1970; Chrmn. Man. Law Reform Commission 1970; Man. Commissioner, Uniform Law Conf. Can. 1971; Vice-Pres., Law Reform Commission Can. 1977; Fed. Delegate, Uniform Law Conf. Can. 1977; Can. Delegate, Commonwealth Law Reform Conf. London, Eng. 1977; Pres., Law Reform Comm. of Canada, 1978–83; author numerous articles pub. law journals and contrib. 'Civil Liberties in Canada – Entering the 1980s,' 1982; Bencher, Law Soc. Man, 1968–71; part time Prof. Const. Law, Faculty of Law, Univ. Man., 1971–72; engaged by Man. Govt. to review Toal Enquiry Commission Report on Race Relations in Brandon 1973; Sec'y., Candn. Assn. Law Teachers Study Group on the Candn. Constitution 1975; mem. City of Winnipeg Commission on Conflict of Interest 1976; recipient Manitoba Bar Assn. Award for Distinguished Service to the Legal Profession 1987; conferred Hon. Mem., St. Paul's College, Univ. of Manitoba 1991; Mem., Law Soc. Sask.; Medico-Legal Soc. Ottawa-Carleton; Candn. Bar Assn.; Pres., Children's Aid Soc. Winnipeg; Manitoba Medico-Legal Soc.; Chrmn., Bd. of Mgmt., St. Paul's Coll., Univ. Man.; Chrmn., Adv. Bd., Marymound Sch. (Winnipeg); Pres., Catholic Sch. Trustees Assn. Man.; recreations: bicycling; reading; public speaking; Office: Federal Court of Canada, Ottawa, Ont. K1A 0H9.

**MULGREW, Ian;** journalist; b. Dumbarton, Scotland 4 Feb. 1957; s. Edward and Marion (Harper) M.; e. O'Neill C.I.; Oshawa Cath. H.S.; Simon Fraser Univ.; York Univ.; children: Christopher, Deanna, Paul; HOST, CBC Television Program 'FORUM'; Thomson Newspapers Ltd. 1977–80; The Globe and Mail 1980–85; Asst. City Ed., The Province 1985–89; Journalism Instr., Kwantlen Coll., Richmond, B.C.; R. Cath.; author: 'Unholy Terror: The Sikhs and International Terrorism' 1988; 'Final Payoff: The True Price of Convicting Clifford Robert Olson' 1990; 'Who Killed Cindy James' 1991; co-author: 'The Expo Story' 1986; recreations: chess, reading, skiing, sailing; Home: 1 – 2531 Pt. Grey Rd., Vancouver, B.C. V6K 1A1.

**MULHALLEN, Karen Ann,** M.A., Ph.D.; educator; writer; editor; publisher; b. Woodstock, Ont. 1 May 1942; d. H.J. Thomas and Edna Anne (Aziz) Naylor; e. Waterloo Lutheran Univ. B.A. 1963; Univ. of Toronto M.A. 1967, Ph.D. 1975; m. 27 Dec. 1967; divorced; PROF. OF ENGLISH, RYERSON POLYTECHNIC UNIV. 1969– ; Ed. and Publisher Descant mag. 1970– ; Poetry Review Ed. The Canadian Forum 1974–76, Arts Features Ed. 1976–88; author 'Sheba and Solomon' (poetry) 1984; 'Modern Love' (poetry) 1990; 'In the Era of Acid Rain' (prose) 1993; numerous articles William Blake; Candn. letters and culture for Canadian Diary column The Literary Review, Edinburgh and London; Ed. 'Views From the North' 1984 travel anthol.; co-ed. 'Tasks of Passion, Dennis Lee at Mid-career' 1982; Dir. Survival Found.; Womenspeak; Descant Arts & Letters Foundation; Adv. Bd. Cocoleria Umbrella; Judge CBC Poetry Competition 1986; National Magazine Awards 1989; recipient various Can. Council, Ont. Arts Council and Social Sci. & Humanities Rsch. Council Awards since 1970; mem. Candn. Magazine Publishers Assn.; PEN International; The Writers' Union of Can.; Home: 245 Markham St., Toronto, Ont. M6J 2G7; Office: 350 Victoria St., Toronto, Ont. M5B 2K3.

**MULHOLLAND, William David,** A.B., M.B.A., LL.D. (Hon.); banker; b. Albany, N.Y. 16 June 1926; s. William David and Helen E. (Flack) M.; e. Christian Brothers Academy, Albany, N.Y.; Harvard Coll., B.A.; Harvard Graduate School of Business Administration M.B.A.; m. Nancy Louise Booth, New Scotland, N.Y.; five s. and four d.; DIR., BANK OF MONTREAL (Mem. Extve. Ctte.); The Upjohn Co.; Candn. Pacific Ltd.; Brooks Fashion Stores Inc. N.Y.; joined investment banking firm of Morgan Stanley & Co., New York, 1952, becoming a Partner in 1962; Pres. and Chief Extve. Offr. Brinco Ltd. and Pres. and Chief Extve. Offr., Churchill Falls (Labrador) Corp. Ltd. 1970; Dir. (1970), Pres. (1975), C.E.O. (1979) and Chrmn. (1981), Bank of Montreal; served in U.S. Army in 2nd World War 1944–46, A.P.T.O. commissioned in the Infantry; mem., Candn. Inst. of Internat. Affairs; Council on Foreign Relations Inc.; Dir., Atlantic Salmon Fedn., Can.; decorated Knight Commander's Cross with Star, Order of Merit, Federal Republic of Germany 1989; Trustee, Queen's Univ., Kingston; St. Michael's College Found.; mem., Adv. Ctte., Ecole des Hautes Etudes Commerciales, Montreal; mem., Adv. Counc. for the Center of Candn. Studies at the Sch. of Advanced Internat. Studies, The Johns Hopkins Univ.; Life Gov., Douglas Hosp., Montreal; Hon. Vice-Pres., Boy Scouts of Can., Que. Prov. Counc.; Nat. Co-Chrmn., Candn. Counc. of Christians and Jews; recreations: fly fishing, shooting, riding; Clubs: Mount Royal; Toronto; York; Chicago; Eglinton & Caledon Hunt; Home: RR 1, Georgetown, Ont. L7G 4S4; Office: 302 Bay St., Suite 400, Toronto, Ont. M5X 1A1.

**MULLER, Robin Lester;** children's book author & illustrator; b. Toronto, Ont. s. Fredrick Walter and Sarah Ada (Thomas) M.; Ontario Soc. of Artists 'Best Painting' 1980; Toronto Art Dir. Award, Illustration 1981; N.Y. Art Directors Award, Art 1983; I.O.D.E. Book Award, Toronto Chapter for 'The Sorcerer's Apprentice' 1986; I.B.B.Y., Ezra Jack Keats Memorial Award, Medalist 1986; The Governor General's Award 1990 for 'The Magic Paintbrush'; Mem., Canscaip; The Writers' Union; author/illustrator: 'Mollie Whuppie and the Giant' 1982, 'Tatterhood,' 1984, 'The Sorcerer's Apprentice' 1985, 'The Lucky Old Woman' 1987, 'Little Kay' 1988, 'The Magic Paintbrush' 1989, 'The Nightwood' 1991, 'Hickory Dickory Dock' 1992, 'Row, Row, Row Your Boat' 1993, 'Little Wonder' 1994; Home: 26 Wardell St., Toronto, Ont. M4M 2L5.

**MULLER, Thomas Edward,** L.I.R.I., L.N.C.R.T., M.B.A., Ph.D.; university professor; b. Nairobi, Kenya 13 Dec. 1939; s. Bohuslav and Marie Claire (Yfrah) M.; e. London Acad. (England) 1957; Bata Tech. Coll. (U.K.) 1959; Nat. Coll. of Rubber Technol. London L.N.C.R.T., L.I.R.I. 1960; Simon Fraser Univ. M.B.A. 1975; Univ. of B.C. Ph.D. 1982; m. Edith d. Viktor and Anna Saatkamp 22 Nov. 1966; divorced 1994; one d.: Monica Silvie; PROF. OF MKTG., SCH. OF BUSINESS, MCMASTER UNIV. 1993– ; Rubber Technol., British Bata Shoe Co. 1959; Melli Shoe Co. 1959–60; Private, Imperial Iranian Army 1960–62; Clerk, Khuzestan Water & Power Auth. 1962–63; Mng. Dir., internat. mfrs.' agency 1963–71; Sub-editor, Kayhan Internat. (Engl. lang. daily newspaper) Tehran 1971; came to Canada 1971; Salesman, Arbutus Buscombe Co. Vanc. 1971–73; Sales Supvr., Home Oil Dist.-Sr. Analyst, Imperial Oil Ltd. 1973–75; Instr., B.C. Inst. of Tech. 1975; Candn. Inst. of Mngt. 1977; Lectr., Univ. of B.C. 1977–78; Asst. Prof. of Mktg., Concordia Univ. 1979–84; Assoc. Prof. of Mktg., Univ. of Guelph 1984–86; Assoc. Prof. of Mktg., McMaster Univ. 1987–92; Dir., Internat. Soc. for Quality-of-Life Studies 1994– ; Dir., Tourism Rsch. & Edn. Ctr., Univ. of Waterloo 1988–92; Mem., Mktg. Ctte., Opera Hamilton 1991– ; Ed. Rev. Bd., 'Service Industries J.' 1986– ; 'North American Business Journal' 1991– ; 'Journal of Public Policy & Marketing' 1992–94; Regional Coordinator (Canada), Fourth Symposium on Cross-Cultural Consumer and Business Studies, Univ. of Hawaii 1993, Third Symposium 1990; Programme Ctte., 21st Annual Conference of the European Marketing Academy, Aarhus, Denmark 1992; Chrmn., Acad. Panel, Selection Bd. 1989–90 Ont. Graduate Scholarship Competition; Mem. Acad. Panel, Selection Bd. 1988–89; 1986–87 Div. Chrmn. (Mktg.), Administrative Sciences Assn. of Canada; 1985–86 Program Chrmn. (Mktg.), Administrative Sciences Assn. of Canada Annual Conference; Fac. Advr., Am. Mktg. Assn., McMaster Univ. Coll. Chap. 1987–91; Assoc. Mem., Faculty of Graduate Studies, Univ. of Guelph 1992– ; Co-winner, Candn. Studies Writing Award 1986–88; Admin. Sci. Assn. of Can. Award of Excellence 1982; Foster Advtg. Ltd. Award of Distinction 1982; Faculty Finalist Award, McMaster Students Union Teaching Awards 1991–92; Mem., Admin. Sci. Assn. of Can.; Am. Mktg. Assn.; Assn. for Consumer Rsch.; Czech. & Slovak Business Council of Can.; Czech. Soc. of Arts & Sci.; Decision Sci. Inst.; Innovation Rsch. Working Group, McMaster Univ.; Soc. for Consumer Psych.; World Future Soc.; co-author: 'Consumer Behaviour: The Canadian Perspective (2nd ed.) 1994; 'Consumer Behaviour in Canada' 1989; 'Le comportement du consommateur au Canada' 1991; co-editor: 'Proc. of 4th Symp. on Cross-Cultural Consumer & Business Studies' 1993; 'Proc. of 3rd Symp. on Cross-Cultural Consumer & Business Studies' 1990; editor: 'Marketing 1986'; author/co-author 65 pub. sci. articles & papers; recreations: alpine skiing, astronomy, aviation, bodysurfing, disco dancing, languages, mountaineering, movies, opera, scuba-diving, travel, underwater photography; Home: 112 Finley Forest Dr., Chapel Hill, NC 27514-8624 U.S.A.; Office: Hamilton, Ont. L8S 4M4.

**MULLIN, Peter Christopher,** B.A.; real estate development industry executive; b. Ottawa, Ont. 2 Nov. 1945; s. Francis Elmore and Margaret MacMillan (Trueman) M.; e. Lawrence Park Coll. Inst. 1966; Wilfred Laurier Univ., B.A. 1969; m. Nancy d. Horace and Dorothy Kuehnbaum 31st May 1969; children: Robert, Jennifer, Christopher; Prin., Penta Stolp Corp. 1986– ; Prin., Stolp Homes 1983– ; Pres., Toronto Home Builders' Assoc. 1990–91; Mktg. Dir., Polysar Bldg. Systems Ltd. 1974–76; Monarch Construc. Ltd. 1976–79; Mktg. Mgr., Costain Group 1979–82; Dir., Nat. Home Show 1984– ; Candn. Home Builders' Assn. 1983–84; Toronto Home Builders' Assn. 1982– ; Pres., Robert Christopher Mktg. Limited 1982– ; P.M.A. Award Winner for contrib. to real estate mktg. 1981; C.H.B.A. Nat. Riley Brethour Award 1982; Anglican; Mem., Toronto Speakers' Bureau 1979–81; Columnist, 'Magic of Marketing,' Toronto Globe & Mail 1984; Home: 94 Lord Seaton Rd., North York, Ont. M2P 1K5.

**MULLIN, Ronald Cleveland,** B.A., M.A., Ph.D.; university professor; b. Guelph, Ont. 15 Aug. 1936; s. William Cleveland and Edna Mae (Rachar) M.; e. Univ. of West. Ont., B.A. 1959; Univ. of Waterloo, M.A. 1960, Ph.D. 1964; m. Janet d. Howard and Elizabeth Simpson 12 Aug. 1971; children: Kimberley Janine, Jaime Anne; PROF., UNIV. OF WATERLOO 1969– ; Asst. Prof., Univ. of Waterloo 1964–66; Assoc. Prof. 1966–67; Prof., Florida Atlantic Univ. 1967–69; Pres., Watcrypt Corp. 1985–90; Dir., Descartes Found.; Fellow, Inst. for Math. & Applications; co-author: 'Mathematical Theory of Coding'; recreations: boating, watersports; Home: 533 Twin Oaks Cres., Waterloo, Ont. N2L 4R9; Office: Dept. of C. & O., Univ. of Waterloo, Waterloo, Ont. N2L 3G1.

**MULLINGTON, Hugh J.,** B.Com., M.A.; executive; b. Cairo Twp., Ont. 10 Aug. 1935; s. Walter J. and Hannah (Horan) M.; e. St. Patrick's Coll. High Sch.; Carleton Univ. B.Com. 1964, D.P.A. 1967, M.A. 1969; m. Ina Jeanne d'Entremont 12 May 1956 (divorced); m. Gayle Alexandra McNeill 12 Jan. 1980; children: Christopher James, Janet Marie, Kevin Joseph; PRES. & CHIEF EXTVE. OFFR., INTERNATIONAL DATACASTING CORPORATION (OTTAWA); Supr. Eng. Services, Eldorado Nuclear 1956–64; Econ. St. Lawrence Seaway Authority 1964–69; Asst. Sec. and Dir. of Adm. Telesat Canada 1969–74; Dir. Transp., Communications & Sci. Div. Prog. Br. Treasury Bd. Secretariat 1975–79, Asst. Sec. Prog. Br. 1979–85; Pres. and Chief Extve. Offr.,

Canadian Commercial Corp. 1985–91; Treas., Dir. and mem. Extve. Ctte. Queensway-Carleton Hosp. 1974–79; Pres. and Dir. Civil Service Co-operative Credit Soc. Ottawa 1974–80; Mem. Advisory Bd., Queen's Univ. Executive M.B.A. Program 1991– ; recreations: cross-country skiing, skating, gardening, travel, reading; Club: Rideau Club; Home: 11 Cowichan Way, Nepean, Ont. K2H 7E6.

**MULLINS, Sister Patricia,** B.A., M.Sc., Ph.D.; educator; b. Boston, Mass. 25 Jan. 1930; d. Paul and Yvonne Marie (Melanson) M.; e. elem. and sec. schs. N.B.; Mount St. Vincent Coll. Halifax B.A. 1951; Univ. of Notre Dame M.Sc. 1963, Ph.D. 1968; GENERAL ASSISTANT/TREASURER, SISTERS OF CHARITY 1988–1996; high sch. teacher N.S. 1951–65; Asst. Prof. of Chem. Mount St. Vincent Univ. 1968, Assoc. Prof. 1972, Prof. of Chem. 1978–88; Chairperson of Chem. Dept. 1977–79, NRC, NSERC Univ. Operating Research Grant Recipient 1969, 1970, 1972–79; Dean of Humanities and Sciences, Mount St. Vincent Univ. 1979–88, Prof. of Chem. 1978–88; Visiting Prof. Univ. of W. Ont. summer 1974; Visiting Post-doctoral Research Assoc. Univ. of Notre Dame Radiation Lab. 1975–76; author or co-author various articles chem. publs.; mem., Sisters of Charity Halifax 1951– ; recreations: reading, music; Address: Mount St. Vincent Motherhouse, 150 Bedford Highway, Halifax, N.S. B3M 3J5.

**MULRONEY, Rt. Hon. M. Brian,** P.C., M.P., B.A., LL.L., LL.D.; b. Baie Comeau, Que. 20 March 1939; s. Benedict and Irene (O'Shea) M.; e. St. Francis Xavier Univ. B.A.; Univ. Laval LL.L.; L.L.D. (Hons) Memorial Univ.; St. Francis Xavier Univ.; m. Mila d. Dr. D. Pivnicki, Montreal, Que. 26 May 1973; children: Caroline Ann, Benedict Martin, Robert Mark, Daniel Nicholas Dimitri; Prime Minister of Canada 1984–93 (resigned) and Leader, Progressive Conservative Party of Canada 1983–93; called to Bar of Que. 1965; joined Ogilvy, Cope, Porteous, Montgomery, Renault, Clarke & Kirkpatrick remaining as Partner until 1976; apptd. to Cliche Royal Comn. 1974; joined Iron Ore Co. of Canada as Extve. Vice Pres. Corporate Affairs 1976, Pres. & Dir., 1977–83; Cand. for Nat. Leader P. Cons. Party Can. 1976; el. to H. of C. (Central Nova) 1983; el. to H. of C. (Manicouagan) 1984; el. to H. of C. (Charlevoix) 1988; Resigned as Leader of Progessive Conservative Party March 1993; mem. Bar Prov. Que.; Candn. Bar Assn.; Conservative; R. Catholic; recreation: tennis; Clubs: Mount Royal; University; Garrison; Mount Royal Tennis; Albany; Address: 47 Forden Cres., Westmount, Que. H3Y 2Y5.

**MULVIHILL, Dennis Patrick,** B.A.; investment executive; b. Winnipeg, Man. 22 July 1948; s. Kevin Patrick and Fernande Rita (Frechette) M.; e. Campion College 1964; Univ. of Saskatchewan B.A. 1969; m. Vicki Anne d. Harvey and Sybil Coleman 30 Aug. 1969; children: Sara Anne, Daniel James; VICE-PRES. & DIR., INVESTMENT BANKING, RBC DOMINION SECURITIES 1989– ; Investment Mngt. & Mortgage Devel., Royal Trust Co. 1970–74; Vice-Pres. & Dir., Houston Willoughby Limited 1977–82; Sr. Vice-Pres. & Dir., Govt. Finance, Inst. Equity & Fixed Income, Pemberton Houston Willoughby Ltd. 1983–89; Dir., Optimists Club; Univ. of Regina Alumni Assn.; Regina United Way; recreations: golf, skiing; clubs: Assiniboia, Wascana Country; Home: 2670 Dorsey Pl., Regina, Sask. S4V 2B9; Office: 2103 11th Ave., 6th fl., Regina, Sask. S4P 3Z8.

**MULVIHILL, John Paul,** B.A., C.F.A.; financial executive; b. Belleville, Ont. 5 June 1947; s. John Patrick and Ethel Margaret (Townend) M.; e. Loyola H.S.; Univ. of Toronto, B.A. (Hons.) 1971; C.F.A. 1977; m. Nancy d. John and Julia Roche 16 Aug. 1974; children: Jennifer Anne, Ashley Meredith, John Paul; CHRMN. & CHIEF EXTVE. OFFR., CT INVESTMENT COUNSEL INC. 1994– ; Investment Analyst, Crown Life Insur. Co. 1971–75; Dir. of Rsch. 1975–79; Asst. Treas. of Common Stocks 1979–82; Vice-Pres., Equity Investments 1982–85; Sr. Vice-Pres., CT Investment Counsel Inc. 1985–89, Chrmn. 1989–94; Former Dir., Accel Capital Partnership Ltd.; Derlan Indus. Ltd.; Helix Investments Ltd.; ICIC Holdings Ltd.; Medokrisp Food Systems Ltd.; Current Dir., CT Investment Counsel; Mem., The Investors & Issues Adv. Ctte. of the Toronto Stock Exchange; recreations: golf, skiing, sailing, squash, computers; clubs: Royal Candn. Yacht, The Cambridge Club, Kingsway Platform Tennis; Home: 75 Strath Ave., Etobicoke, Ont. M8X 1R6; Office: 110 Yonge St., Toronto, Ont. M5C 1W2.

**MUMEY, Glen,** M.A., B.Sc., Ph.D.; university professor; b. Hallock, Minnesota 5 Dec. 1933; s. Leo and Olga (Nelson) M.; e. Univ. of North Dakota M.A. 1955, B.Sc. 1957; Univ. of Washington Ph.D. 1965; m. Lois d. George and Lillian Simpson Dec. 1966; children: Brendan M., Sol T.; PROFESSOR OF FINANCE, UNIV. OF ALBERTA 1970– ; Chair, Dept. of Finance & Management Science, Univ. of Alta.; Adjunct Prof., Agric. Econ.; Past Pres., Admin. Science Assn. of Canada; author: 'Theory of Financial Structure' 1969, 'Personal Economic Planning' 1971, 'Canadian Business Finance' 1976; recreations: hiking, bridge; club: Alpine Club of Canada; Home: 8743 117 St., Edmonton, Alta. T6G 1R6; Office: Edmonton, Alta. T6G 2E5.

**MUMFORD, John Edwin (Ted);** journalist; b. Whitehorse, Yukon 16 Aug. 1955; s. John George (Peter) and Mary Evelyn (Thornhill) M.; e. Bell H.S. Nepean, Ont.; York Univ.; m. Denise Louise d. Peter and Betty Droescher 15 Sept. 1978; children: Nicole Louise, Michelle Holly; EDITOR/CO-PUBLISHER, 'QUILL & QUIRE' 1991– ; Managing Ed., York Univ. 'Excalibur' 1977–78; Newmarket Ed., 'The Banner' (Aurora, Ont.) 1978–79; Writer/editor, Ont. Workers Comp. Bd. 1979–81; Trade Ed., James Lorimer & Co. 1981–86; Staff Writer, 'NOW' Magazine 1986; Assoc. Ed. 1987; Editorial Coordinator 1988–89; Editor, Quill & Quire 1989; Contbg. Ed., 'NOW' Magazine 1990–93, Books Ed. 1993– ; 'Toronto Life' magazine 1992–93; Art Directors Club of Toronto Merit Award 1989; Office: 4th floor, 70 The Esplanade, Toronto, Ont. M5E 1R2.

**MUMMÉ, Carla Lipsig,** B.A., M.A., Ph.D.; educator, labour specialist; b. New York City, N.Y. 26 Jan. 1946; d. James and Frances (Katz) Lipsig; e. Brandeis Univ., B.A. 1966; Boston Univ., M.A. 1968; Univ. of Montreal, Ph.D. 1979; m. John s. Colin and Nina Mummé. 30 Nov. 1973; one d.: Claire-Isobel; DIR., CENTRE FOR RSCH. ON WORK & SOCIETY, PROF. OF LABOUR STUDIES AND CO-ORD., LABOUR STUDIES PROG., YORK UNIV. 1990– ; Union Organizer, United Farm Workers of Am. 1968; Orgn., Internat. Ladies Garment Workers' Union 1969–70; Advr. on Minority Workers, Conseil Central de Montréal, Confed. des syndicats nationaux 1980–85; Prof. of Indus. Relns., Laval Univ.; Advisor, Office of the Pres. 1989–90; Negotiator, Féd. nat. des enseignants du Qué. 1972–77; Advr., Extve., Centrale de l'Enseignement du Qué. 1985–87; radio & TV commentator on labour issues; Cons. for union orgns. in Can., the U.S. & Australia; Prof., Labour Coll. of Can. 1976; Polaroid Fellowship in Human Relns.; Edward P. Morgan Award in Labour Econ.; SSHRCC rsch. grants; Extve. Mem., Candn. Indus. Relns. Assn. 1986–87; Mem., l'Assoc. d'Econ. pol.; l'Assoc. des sociol. et anthropol. de la langue française; N.D.P.; Montreal Citizens' Movement; Home: 23 Hewitt Ave., Toronto, Ont. M6R 1Y4; Office: Univ., 4700 Keele St., North York, Ont. M3J 1P3.

**MUNCASTER, J. Dean,** B.A., M.B.A., LL.D.; executive; b. Sudbury, Ont. 23 Oct. 1933; s. W. Walter and Beatrice M. (Vance) M.; e. Sudbury (Ont.) High School; Univ. of W. Ont., B.A. (Business Adm.) 1956; Northwestern University, M.B.A. 1957; Laurentian Univ., LL.D. 1976; children: Robert Dean, Bernard Walter, David Arthur; PRESIDENT & C.E.O., ENVIRONMENTAL TECHNOLOGIES INTERNATIONAL, INC. 1993– ; Dir., Stelco, Inc.; Black & Decker Mfg. Co. (U.S.); Renaissance Energy Ltd.; joined Canadian Tire Corp. as Financial Analyst, Toronto, Ont., 1957; Retail Store Mgr., Sudbury, Ont., 1960; Vice-Pres., Toronto, 1963; Pres. & C.E.O. 1966–85; Consultant & Corp. Dir., 1985–90; Chrmn., Bargain Harolds Discount Ltd. 1990–92; Past Chrmn., Retail Council of Canada; Task Force Hydro; mem., Adv. Bd., Univ. Western Ont. Bus. Sch.; Sr. Mem., Business Counc. on Nat. Issues; recreations: skiing, sailing; Home: Box 4363, Collingwood, Ont. L9Y 4T9.

**MUNCASTER, Russell Walter,** B.A., M.A., Ph.D.; educator; b. Sudbury, Ont. 30 June 1935; s. William Walter and Beatrice Mary (Vance) M.; e. Waterloo Lutheran Univ. B.A. 1966; Clark Univ. Worcester, Mass. M.A. 1968, Ph.D. 1972; m. Carol Ann d. J. Kenneth and Marion Ault 30 March 1957; children: Marion Elizabeth Melse, Penelope Ann, Russell Paul; PROF. OF GEOG., WILFRID LAURIER UNIV. 1984– ; Canadian Tire Associate Store, Sudbury 1956–59, Deep River 1959–62; Asst. Prof. Waterloo Lutheran Univ. 1969–73; Chrmn. of Geog. Wilfrid Laurier, 1973–76, 1979–80; Dean of Arts and Sci., Wilfrid Laurier Univ. 1980–83, Assoc. Prof. of Geog. 1973–84; Vice-Pres. Academic, Wilfrid Laurier Univ. 1983–89; mem. Candn. Assn. Geogs.; Assn. Am. Geogs.; Regional Science Assn.; Candn. Regional Science Assn.; Office: Waterloo, Ont. N2L 3C5.

**MUNDY, David Beatty,** B.Com., K.C.L.J., M.M.L.J., K.S.J.; retired executive; b. Edmonton, Alta. 20 Aug. 1919; s. Christopher Gordon and Irene (Tardrew) M.; e. Public and High Sch., Edmonton, Alta.; Univ. of Alberta, B.Com. 1940; m. Denise Michell Shirley, d. late Capt. Desmond FitzHarry Dolphin, R.N., 29 May 1943; children: Roderick David, Louise Anne, John Michell, Georgina Denise; joined Trade Commr. Ser., Dept. of Trade & Comm., 1945; Asst. Trade Commr., Liverpool, Eng., 1946–48; Comm. Secy., Candn. Leg., Stockholm, 1948–49; on loan to Dept. of Fisheries as Chief Statistician, Vancouver, B.C., 1949–50; on loan to Dept. of Defence Production as Special Asst. to Co-ordinator of Production, 1951–52; Production Adviser to Candn. Del. to N.A.T.O., Paris, 1953–54; joined Dept. of Defence Production as Dir., Ammunition Br., Nov. 1954; apptd. Assoc. Dir., Electronics Br., Apl. 1956; Dir., Aug. 1956; Asst. Depy. Min. 1962; Asst. Depy. Min., Depts. Defence Production & Industry 1963; Asst. Depy. Min (External Services) Dept. Industry, Trade & Comm. 1968; Pres. Air Industries Assn. of Can. 1970–79; served in 2nd World War; enlisted as 2nd Lieut., 5 July 1940 with Loyal Edmonton Regt.; served Overseas in U.K., France, Belgium, Holland and Germany, 1941–45; retired to Reserve with rank of Capt.; Kappa Sigma; Order of St. Lazarus; Order of St. John; Anglican; recreations: skiing, canoeing, sailing, back packing; Clubs: Royal Victoria Yacht; Union Club of B.C.; Home: The Last Hurrah, 130 Mariner's Lane, Salt Spring Is., B.C. V8K 1S6.

**MUNDY, Thomas A.,** B.Com., C.A.; business executive; b. Bashaw, Alta. 2 Dec. 1925; s. William Lory and Lillian Belle (Ainsley) M.; e. Victoria High Sch. Edmonton 1944; Univ. of Alta., B.Com. 1947; C.A. Alta. 1950; m. Laura d. Gladstone and Martha Walker 13 Aug. 1949; children: Brian Thomas, Laura Lillian, Richard Walker; joined Muttart Organization 1951–56; Chief Financial Offr. Candn. Phoenix Steel & Pipe Ltd. 1956–72; Sr. Vice Pres. Comm. Activities, Western Cooperative Fertilizers Ltd. 1972–83; Pres. and C.E.O. Frigstad Manufacturing 1983–84; Chief Financial Offr., Credit Union Deposit Guarantee Corp. 1984–86; Pres. & C.E.O. 1986–92 (Retired); Chrmn. Candn. Fertilizer Inst. 1982–83; Financial Extve. Inst.; Club: Ranchmen's (Calgary); Office: 127 Wakina Dr., Edmonton, Alta. T5T 2X4.

**MUNGALL, Constance Vivian,** B.A.; writer; b. Los Angeles, Calif.; d. Denis and Joyce Vivian (Coates) Taylor; e. Univ. of B.C.; Univ. of Toronto, B.A. 1954; children: Robert Taylor, John Alexander; Econ., Govt. of Ont. 1953–55; housewife & mother 1955–77; freelance writer & CBC documentary maker 1961–77; Ed., GEOS 1977–86; Founder, Super School, Toronto 1969; mem. BeSpoke Co-op. Enterprises; Quaker; editor, 'Planet Under Stress: The Challenge of Global Change' 1990; 'La Terre en Péril, Metamorphose d'une planète' 1990; author: 'Probate Guide for British Columbia' 1974, 1977, 1980, 1982–91, 1993; 'Changing Your Name in Canada' 1977; 'More Than Just a Job' 1986; co-author (with Elizabeth Amer): 'Yes We Can! How to Organize Citizen Action' 1980; 'Taking Action, Working Together for Positive Change in Your Community' 1992; recreations: hiking, bicycling, swimming, talking; Address: 946 Wilmer St., Victoria, B.C. V8S 4B7.

**MUNK, Peter,** O.C., B.A.Sc., LL.D.; resource executive; b. Hungary 8 Nov. 1927; s. Louis L. and Katherine (Adler) M.; e. Univ. of Toronto B.A.Sc. 1953; m. Melanie d. David and Hazel Bosanquet 1973; children: Anthony, Nina, Natalie, Cheyne, Marc-David; FOUNDER, CHRMN. & C.E.O., AMERICAN BARRICK RESOURCES CORP. 1984– and THE HORSHAM CORP. 1987– ; previously Chrmn. and Chief Extve. Offr. Southern Pacific Hotel Corp. Sydney, Australia; Dir. World Gold Council; mem. The Toronto Hosp. Bd. Trustees; Trustee, Univ. of Toronto Crown Found.; recreations: skiing, tennis; Home: 19 Highland Ave., Toronto, Ont. M4W 2A2; Office: 24 Hazelton Ave., Toronto, Ont. M5R 2E2.

**MUNN, R.E.,** Ph.D., FRSC; 'nominally' retired; b. Winnipeg, Man. 26 July 1919; s. Bernard Aubrey and Melita Catherine (Jenkins) M.; m. Joyce d. Earl and Agnes Rodgers 10 Sept. 1944; children: Eric, Elspeth, Sheila, Robert; ASSOC., INST. FOR ENVIRONMENTAL STUDIES, UNIV. OF TORONTO 1977–85, 1989– ; Chief Sci., Air Quality Rsch. Br., Environ. Can. 1972–77; Depy. Dir. 1987–88 & Leader, Environ. Prog. 1985–88, Internat. Inst. for Applied Systems Analysis, Laxenburg, Austria (el. Hon. Scholar 1988); rsch. interests: air pollution, environ. impact assessment; optimization of monitoring systems; environ. mngt.; Ed.-in-Chief, 'Int. J. of Boundary-Layer Meteorology' 1971– ; ICSU-SCOPE 1969– (Ed.-in-Chief, 1979– ); FRSC 1986; Hon. Life Mem., Inst. for Environ. Studies, Univ. of Toronto 1985; Frank A. Chambers Rsch. Award, Air Pollution Control Assn. 1984; Fellow, Am.

Assn. for Adv. of Sci. 1982; Fellow, Am. Meteor. Soc. 1977; J. Paterson Medal 1975; Applied Meteor. Prize, Am. Meteor. Soc. 1974; Pres. Prize, Candn. Meteor. Soc. 1960, 1972; author: 'Descriptive Micrometeorology' 1966 (in 5th prtg.), 'Biometeorological Methods' 1970 & 6 other monographs; editor/co-editor of 7 monographs; author/co-author of about 150 sci. papers; Home: 64 Glencairn Ave., Toronto, Ont. M4R 1M8; Office: Toronto, Ont. M5S 1A4.

**MUNRO, Alice;** writer; b. Wingham, Ont. 10 July 1931; d. Robert Eric and Anne Clarke (Chamney) Laidlaw; e. Wingham (Ont.) Pub. and High Schs.; Univ. of W. Ont.; m. James Armstrong Munro 29 Dec. 1951, div. 1976; children: Sheila, Jenny, Andrea; m. 2ndly, Gerald Fremlin 1976; author 'Dance of the Happy Shades' 1968 (winner Gov.-Gen.'s Award for Lit. 1968); 'Lives of Girls and Women' 1971; (Candn. Booksellers Award 1971); 'Something I've Been Meaning to Tell You' 1974; 'Who Do You Think You Are? ('The Beggar Maid - U.S., U.K.) 1978; 'The Moons of Jupiter' 1982; 'The Progress of Love' 1986; 'Friend of My Youth' 1990; Winner, Canada-Australia Literary Prize; Address: c/o Writers' Union of Canada, 24 Ryerson St., Toronto, Ont. M5T 2P4.

**MUNRO, Alistair,** M.D., F.R.C.P.(C); educator; psychiatrist; b. Glasgow, Scot. 6 Apl. 1933; s. David and Elizabeth Hosie (Clubb) M.; e. Allan Glen's Sch. Glasgow 1950; Univ. of Glasgow M.B.,Ch.B. 1956, M.D. 1965; Univ. of Edinburgh Rsch. Training Psych. Epidemiol. 1962–65; Univ. of Liverpool M.Psy.Med. 1981; m. Mary d. George and Anna Stewart 26 March 1959; two d. Sharon Christian, Kirsten Jane Clark; PROF. OF PSYCHIATRY, DALHOUSIE UNIV. 1994– , mem. Senate; Staff Psychiatrist various Halifax hosps.; postgrad. training Psychiatry & Internal Med. various Glasgow hosps.; joined Univ. of Leeds 1965–67; Univ. of Birmingham 1967–69; Prof. and Head of Psychiatry Univ. of Liverpool 1969–75, Staff Psychiatrist privileges Liverpool Royal Infirmary; came to Can. 1975 becoming Psychiatrist-in-Chief Toronto Gen. Hosp. until 1982, Chrmn. Med. Adv. Bd. 1978–80, mem. Bd. Trustees 1977–80; Prof. of Psychiatry Univ. of Toronto until 1982; Prof. & Head of Psychiatry, Dalhousie Univ. 1982–94; Hoenig Lectr. Meml. Univ. of Nfld. 1990; Visiting Prof./Examiner Univs. Birmingham, Leeds, Aberdeen, Belfast, Malaysia; author 'Delusional Hypochondriasis' 1982; co-author 'Psychiatry for Social Workers' 1969, 1975; ed. 6 psychiatric texts; over 70 sci. articles, several book chapters, articles and essays; adv. to work in progress 'Diagnostic and Statistical Manual of Mental Disorders' 4th ed. Am. Psych. Assn.; F.R.C.P.Ed.; F.R.C.Psych; mem. Candn. Med. Assn.; Candn. Psychiatric Assn.; recreations: family, music, walking, writing; Home: 1759 Connaught Ave., Halifax, N.S. B3H 4C9; Office: Dept. of Psychiatry, Camp Hill Hospital, Halifax, N.S. B3H 3G2.

**MUNRO, Donald Wallace,** M.A.; b. Regina, Saskatchewan 8 April 1916; s. Fenton and Nellie (Ellis) Wallace M.; e. Model Sch., Regina; Lord Byng High Sch., Vancouver; U.B.C., B.A. (Hons. French) 1938; Teaching Cert. 1939; awarded French Govt. Scholarship for study at Sorbonne, 1939; U. of T., M.A. (Pol. Sc.) 1946; m. the late Evelyn May, Cape Town, S. Africa d. late Capt. Arthur (IASC) and Louise Secombe, Bursledon Hants 7 Sept. 1944; High Sch. Teacher, Coquitlam, B.C. 1939–40; joined Dept. of Ext. Affairs, 1946; served in Paris 1947–49; Ankara 1949–51; Dublin 1954–55; Brussels 1955–57; Beirut 1960–63; Head of Candn. Del., Internat. Supervisory Comn., Vientiane, Laos, 1964–65; Nat. Defence Coll., Kingston, 1965–66; Advisor to Candn. Del., XIVth Session, Gen. Assembly UNESCO 1966; Acting Head, Cultural Affairs Div., Ottawa, 1967; Head, Commonwealth Div., 1967–68; Ambassador to Costa Rica, Nicaragua, Honduras, El Salvador and Panama, 1968–70; Foreign Service Visitor, Centre for Pol. Studies, Dalhousie Univ. 1971–72; while in Ottawa, also served in European Div., D.L. II (Security), American Div.; M.P. for Esquimalt-Saanich 1972–84; retired, undefeated, Sept. 4, 1984; Chrmn., H. of C. Standing Comte. on External Affairs and Defense, 1979; mem., Candn. Delegation to U.N. Gen. Assembly, 1979; attended Law of the Sea Conferences, N.Y., Caracas, Geneva; served in 2nd World War, RCAF (F'Lt. Nav.) 1940–45; N., E. and S. Africa – Coastal Command and Instr.; author, 'Abortion and the Charter' 1985; 'A Search for Origins, An Enquiry into the Canadian Origins of Canada's Constitution' 1986; mem., CIIA; Monarchist League; Royal Commonwealth Soc.; R.U.S.I.; P. Conservative; recreations: reading, history, biography, philosophy, philately, cartography; Home: 7 – 9901 Third St., Sidney, B.C. V8L 3B1.

**MUNRO, John A.;** transportation executive; b. Birmingham, U.K. 1948; e. Vancouver City Coll.; m. Paddy 1970; children: Aaron, Sean, Shannon, Terri; EXTVE. VICE-PRES., GREYHOUND LINES OF CANADA 1989– (led customer service and quality service initiatives; introduced intermodal travel such as one way bus and one way air); num. positions in domestic & internat. opns., sales & mktg. ending as Vice-Pres., Mktg., CP Air 1967–85 (specialized in internat. negotiations and launched Canada's first travel bonus program); Pres. & C.E.O., Internat. Sav-On Financial Serv. 1986; Extve. Dir., Tourism Vancouver 1987–88 (increased funding from $865,000 to over $7 million and initiated marketing initiatives that resulted in Vancouver being first City in history of world expositions to enjoy better post-Expo level of tourism than pre-Expo year – up by 23%); Dir., Tourism Indus. Assn. of Can.; W.M. Helijet Ltd. (Mem., Finan. Ctte.); Vancouver-Yokohama Sister City Soc.; Calgary Convention & Visitors Bureau; Japan-Canada Businessman's Assn.; Tourism Mktg. Council; recreations: travel, tennis; clubs: Glencoe, Calgary; Richmond Country Club, Richmond, B.C.; Home: 1515 – 21 Ave. S.W., Calgary, Alta. T2T 0M8; Office: 877 Greyhound Way S.W., Calgary, Alta. T3C 3V8.

**MUNRO, John McCulloch,** B.A.; insurance executive; b. Toronto, Ont. 27 Sept. 1913; s. late Archibald and late Margaret (McCulloch) M.; e. Jarvis Coll. Inst., Toronto; Queen's Univ., B.A. (Jenkins Trophy); Univ. of Toronto, Post-grad. studies; m. Bette M., d. C. R. Gilmour, 24 May 1941; children: Michael John, Brian, Elizabeth Ann (Mrs. J. M. Pigott III); SR. VICE-PRES. AND DIR. OF AGENCIES (RET.), THE CANADA LIFE ASSURANCE CO. 1978– ; joined Co. as Salesman, 1946; Mgr., Field Training and Research, 1951; Mgr., Toronto Bayview Br., 1953; Asst. Supt. of Agencies H.O., April 1957 and of Ont. Brs., Dec. 1957; Agency Supt. 1960; Supt. of Agencies 1962; Dir. of Agencies, Canada, 1965; Vice-Pres. and Assoc. Dir. of Agencies, 1968; apptd. mem., Mang. Comte., Canada Life 1968; Vice Pres. and Dir. of Agencies 1969; Sr. Vice Pres. and Dir. of Agencies 1976; served with Candn. Grenadier Guards, 22nd Armoured, during World War II; rank Maj.; Past Trustee, Candn. Schenley Football Awards; former Candn. Prof. Football League player with Toronto Argonauts; former Sr. Field Official, Candn., Football League; Chrmn., Canada Sport's Hall of Fame; Charter Mem., Queen's Univ. Football Hall of Fame; Chrmn. Bd., Life Ins. Marketing and Research Assn. 1975–76; Chrmn., Agency Offrs. Round Table, L.I.M.R.A., 1974–75; Candn. Comte., L.I.M.R.A.; Past Chrmn., Extve. Comte., Sr. Marketing Offrs. Sec., Candn. Life Ins. Assn.; mem., Pedlars; Life Underwriters Assn. Can.; Bd. mem. (ret.), Queen's Univ. Trustee Bd.; Chrmn., Ted Reeve Memorial Scholarship Award, Queen's Univ.; Former Bd. Trustee, Toronto Gen. Hosp.; Chrmn., Canada Sports Hall of Fame 1988; Clubs: Rosedale Golf; Granite; Argonaut 'A'; Pedlars; Home: 2106 - 65 Skymark Dr., Willowdale, Ont. M2H 3N9.

**MUNRO, June E.,** B.J., M.L.S.; librarian; b. Echo Bay, Ont. 20 June 1921; d. late Neil and late Agnes (MacLeod) M.; e. Sault Ste. Marie (Ont.) Coll. Inst. 1939; Carleton Univ. B.J. 1961; Univ. of Toronto B.L.S. 1962, M.L.S. 1972; SESSIONAL LECTURER, SCHOOL OF LIBRARIANSHIP, UNIV. OF B.C., 1983; Head, Children's Lib. Services Sault Ste. Marie Pub. Lib. 1941–51; Children's Librarian;, London Pub. Lib. 1951–53; Head Children's Lib. Services Leaside Pub. Lib. 1953–56; Asst. to Extve. Dir. and Publs. Production Ed. Candn. Lib. Assn. 1956–61; Supvr. Extension Service and Ed. 'Ontario Library Review,' Ont. Prov. Lib. Service 1961–70; Book Acquisition Adv., Coll. Bibliocentre, Toronto 1970–72; Chief, Pub. Relations Div. Nat. Lib. of Can. 1972–73; Dir., of Lib. Services, St Catharines Pub. Lib. 1973–82; rec'd St. Catharines Y.W.C.A. Award to Women in Business and Professions category 1986; rec'd Librarian of Yr. Award Ont. Lib. Trustee Assn. 1971; author various publs.; Extve. mem., Shaw Festival Guild; mem. Am. Lib. Assn.; Candn. Lib. Assn.; Ont. Lib. Assn.; Protestant; recreations: dance, theatre; Clubs: University Women's; Home: Apt. 710, 35 Towering Hts., St. Catharines, Ont. L2T 3G8.

**MUNRO, William G.,** B.Com., FLMI; insurance executive; b. Toronto, Ont. 9 July 1926; s. late H. Elmer and late Hazel (Gourlay) M.; e. Univ. of Toronto B.Com. 1949; m. Mary Patricia d. late George D. Fleming, Owen Sound, Ont. 25 June 1949; one s., two d.; DIR. THE IMPERIAL LIFE ASSURANCE CO. OF CANADA since 1977, Past-Pres., retired Oct. 31st 1983; Dir., National Trustco Ltd.; joined H.O. Imperial Life 1949, Asst. Treas. 1959, Assoc. Treas. 1964, Asst. to Adm. Vice Pres. 1967, Extve. Offr.-Adm. 1969, Adm. Vice Pres. 1971, Extve. Vice Pres. 1974; Fellow, Life Office Mang. Inst.; Past Pres., Greater Toronto Region, Boy Scouts of Can.; United Church; recreations: Tennis, squash; Club: Badminton & Racquet (past Pres.); Home: 27 Oriole Rd., Toronto, Ont. M4V 2E6.

**MUNROE, Eugene G.,** M.Sc., Ph.D., F.E.S.C., F.R.S.C. (1966); Self-emp. consultant and research scientist; b. Detroit, Michigan 8 Sept. 1919; s. Donald Gordon and Helen Grace (Carroll) M.; e. Westmount (Que.) High Sch.; McGill Univ., B.Sc. 1940, M.Sc. 1941; Cornell Univ., Ph.D. 1947; m. Isobel Margaret, d. David Douglas, Toronto, Ont., 1944; children: Janet Gordon (Wilson), Donald Douglas (deceased), Susan Margaret, Elizabeth Anne; HON. RESEARCH ASSOC., LYMAN ENTOMOLOGICAL MUS. & RESEARCH LAB., MACDONALD CAMPUS, MCGILL UNIV.; RSCH. ASSOC., BISHOP MUS., Honolulu; Rsch. Assoc. Biosystematics Rsch. Centre, Agric. Canada, Ottawa; Commr., Internat. Comn. on Zool. Nomenclature, 1963–75; Lecturer and Research Assistant, Institute of Parasitology, Macdonald College, Quebec, 1946–50; Research Scientist, Canada Dept. of Agric., 1950–65, 1968–79; Chief, Taxonomy Sec., Entom. Research Inst. 1962–65; Science Adviser, Science Secreatriat, Privy Council Office, 1965–67; Princ. Scient. Adv. and Head of Studies, 1967–68; Visiting Prof., Univ. of Cal., Berkeley, 1960–61; Hon. Lectr., Carleton Univ., Ottawa, 1966; served with R.C.A.F.1942–45, rank Flying Offr.; Dir. Wedge Entomol. Research Foundation since 1974; Vice pres. & Mang. Dir., 1979–84; Chrmn. Bd. of Eds. 'The Moths of America North of Mexico' 1974–84; Ed., 'The Canadian Entomologist,' 1957–60; author of some 260 scient. papers and books; mem., Entom. Soc. Am.; Entom. Soc. Can. (Past Pres., Hon. Life Mem.); Entom. Soc. Washington; Hawaiian Malacol. Soc.; Conchologists of Am.; Lepidopterists' Soc. (Past Pres. and Hon. mem.); Ottawa Field-Naturalists' Club (Hon. Life Member; Past Dir.); Soc. Hosp. Lus Am. de Lepidopterol. (Socio de Hon.); Dir., Assoc. for Tropical Lepidoptera 1992– ; Candn. mem., Standing Comte. on Pacific Entom., Pacific Science Assn.1947–65; Sigma Xi; Anglican; Home: 3093 Barlow Cres., R.R. 1, Dunrobin, Ont. K0A 1T0.

**MUNROE, Roderick Allison,** B.B.A.; banker; b. Sydney, N.S. 21 Sept. 1942; e. Candn. Inst. of Management, Coll. of Cape Breton 1976; Credit Union Inst. Fellows Prog., Co-op Coll. 1984; Univ. Coll., Cape Breton B.B.A. 1988; m. Judith 15 April 1967; children: Laurel Ann, Alyson; GEN. MGR., SYDNEY CREDIT UNION LIMITED; Dir., The CUMIS Group Limited; Dir., CUMIS Life Insur. Co.; CUMIS Gen. Insur. Co.; Candn. Northern Shield Insur. Co.; Mem., Cape Breton Antique & Custom Car Club; Home: Dutch Brook, P.O. Box 775, Sydney, N.S. B1P 6J1; Office: 95 Townsend St., P.O. Box 1386, Sydney, N.S. B1P 6K3.

**MUNSCH, Robert N.,** B.A., M.A., M.Ed.; writer; b. Pittsburgh, Pa. 11 June 1945; s. Thomas John and Margaret (McKeon) M.; e. Fordham Univ. B.A. Hist. 1969; Boston Univ. M.A. Anthrop. 1971; Tufts Univ. M.Ed. Child Studies 1973; m. Ann d. Metta and Robert Beeler 20 Jan. 1973; children: Julie, Andrew, Tyya; WRITER-CHILDREN'S BOOKS; Daycare Teacher Boston and Coos Bay, Ore. 1972–75; Lectr. Dept. of Family Studies, Univ. of Guelph 1975–80, Asst. Prof. 1980–84; Full time writer 1984– ; 25 books in print, the best known books are: 'The Paper Bag Princess' 1980; and 'Love You Forever' 1986; Candn. Booksellers Assn. Author of the Year 1991; mem. Writer's Union of Canada; Candn. Assn. of Children's Authors, Illustrators and Performers; Candn. Authors' Assn.; Contact: Writers's Union of Canada.

**MUNSCHE, Peter Bernard,** Ph.D.; university administrator; b. New York, N.Y. 13 Sept. 1947; s. Richard C. and Lucille (Brady) M.; e. Reed Coll. (Portland, Oregon), B.A. 1969; Univ. of Toronto, M.A. 1971, Ph.D. 1978; m. Brigid d. Mary and William H. O'Reilly 9 June 1973; ASST. VICE-PRES., RESEARCH SERVICES, UNIV. OF TORONTO 1992– ; Asst. Prof. of History, Univ. of Toronto 1979–80; Extve. Asst. to Dean of Grad. Studies, Univ. of Toronto 1981–82; Asst. to Pres., Candn. Inst. for Advanced Rsch. 1982–84; Extve. Dir. 1984–88; Asst. Vice-Pres., Research Relations and Tech. Transfer, Univ. of Toronto 1988–92; Phi Beta Kappa; Dir., VOICE for Hearing Impaired Children 1987– (Chrmn. 1991– ); Dir., Toronto New Business Develop. Centre 1990– ; Dir., Candn. Inst. for Telecommunications Rsch. 1991– ; Dir., Candn. Inst. of Biotechnology 1991– ; author: 'Gentlemen and Poachers: The English Game Laws, 1671–1831' 1981; Home: 217 Albany Ave., Toronto, Ont. M5R 3C7; Office: 27 King's College Circle, Toronto, Ont. M5S 1A1.

**MURASUGI, Kunio,** D. Sc., F.R.S.C.; educator; b. Tokyo, Japan 25 March 1929; s. Kiyoshi and Torae (Nakatani) M.; e. Tokyo Higher Normal Sch. 1949; Tokyo Univ. of Educ. B.Sc. 1952, D.Sc. 1961; Univ. of Toronto M.Sc. 1961; m. Yasue d. late Jisuke Kuwahara 30 Oct. 1955; children: Chieko, Kumiko, Sachiho; PROF. OF MATH. UNIV. OF TORONTO 1969– ; Research Assoc. Princeton Univ.1962–64; Asst. Prof. Univ. of Toronto 1964, Assoc. Prof. 1966; Visiting mem. Inst. Advanced Study Princeton 1974; Visiting Prof. Univ. of Southwestern La. 1978; Tsukuba Univ. Japan 1979; Univ. of Geneva, Switzerland 1985; author 'On Closed 3–Braids' 1974; various articles learned journs.; Ed. 'Canadian Journal of Mathematics' 1969–71; Assoc. Ed., 'Journal of Knot Theory and its Ramifications' 1991– ; awarded Fall Prize, Mathematical Soc. of Japan 1993; mem., Am. Math. Soc.; Japanese Math. Soc.; Anglican; recreation: go (Japanese game); Home: 611 Cummer Ave., Willowdale, Ont. M2K 2M5; Office: 100 St. George St., Toronto, Ont. M5S 1A1.

**MURATA, Taketo,** B.Sc., M.S., M.A.; business executive; b. Vancouver, B.C. 21 Sept. 1937; s. Kiyoshi and Matsue (Ota) M.; e. McGill Univ. B.Sc. 1958; Yale Univ. M.S. 1960, M.A. 1962; m. Vija d. Alfred and Alma Raminsh 27 June 1970; children: Alfred, Theodore, Ariana; PRESIDENT, ConAGRA GROCERY COMPANIES INTERNAT. and ConAGRA LTD. 1993– ; PRESIDENT, INTERNAT. HUNT-WESSON INC. 1992– ; Vice-Pres., Hunt-Wesson Inc. 1990– ; Chrmn., V-H Foods Inc. 1986– ; Pres., Hunt-Wesson Canada 1973– ; Dir.: ConAgra Ltd. 1993– ; Food Producers Europe B.V. (Holland) 1990– ; Hunt Universal Robina Corp. (Philippines) 1990– ; Banquet Foods (Canada) Corp. 1992– ; Maple Leaf Mills Inc. 1992– ; Nippon B-K Foods, Ltd. (Japan) 1992–93; Mktg. Rsch. Supr., Leo Burnett Co. of Canada 1964–65; Mktg. Rsch. Assoc., Product Mgr., Controller of Grocery Products Div., General Foods Inc. 1965–73; Dir. Food Inst. of Canada 1989–92 (and mem. Extve. 1989–92); Dir. Candn. Food Processors Assn. 1980–89 (and mem. Extve. 1981–89; Chrmn. 1983–84; Treas. 1986–88); Dir. Candn. Frozen Food Assn. 1983–84; Dir., Candn. Children's Opera Chorus 1992– ; Home: 648 Broadway Ave., Toronto, Ont. M4G 2S7; Office: 1 Concorde Gate, Don Mills, Ont. M3C 3N6.

**MURCHISON, Myles Francis;** writer, novelist, playwright; b. Cheltenham, England 3 June 1942; s. Thomas Gordon and Barbara Daisy (Churchyard) M.; e. Churchill H.S.; m. Ada Gabriel d. Lillian and Richard Haughian 14 Feb. 1977; first novel pub. by Ballantine Books N.Y. 1989; Contbr., 'Globe and Mail,' 'TV Guide,' 'Royal British Columbia Museum'; Nat. Syndication for Radio incl. news retrospective series 'The Day Before' 1977–78; Radio Documentary Writer & Prod. 1969–77; Advtg. Writer & Extve. 1962–69, 1979–89; winner of several Candn. Assn. of Broadcasters News & Programming Awards 1969–72; Documentary work written & co-prod. in 1971, Edward R. Murrow Award for Best Radio Documentary in N. Am.; Former Dir., Presentation House 1986; author: 'The Deathless' 1989 (novel), 'Jump' (Great Britain Tour) 1968; co-author: 'Gilliam' (Centennial Award 1967 for Best New Play in Western Canada;) 1967; Address: 2280 152A Street, White Rock, B.C. V4A 4R1.

**MURENBEELD, Martin,** M.Sc., Ph.D.; consulting economist; b. Amsterdam, The Netherlands 6 Feb. 1944; s. William Hendrik and Ans (Ladde) M.; e. Univ. of Alta. B.Sc. 1966, M.Sc. 1969; Univ. of Cal. Berkeley, Ph.D. 1974; m. Helen d. Jacob and Peggy Ladde 16 Dec. 1977; two s. Steven William, Michael Jacob; PRIN. M. MURENBEELD & ASSOCIATES INC. 1978– ; Prof. of Mgmt. Studies Univ. of Toronto 1972–78, presently Lectr.; commentator media, confs., forums; recipient Can. Council Doctoral Fellowships 1972–74 inclusive; author various acad. papers; ed. corporate publs.; mem. Acad. Internat. Bus.; Am. Econ. Assn.; recreations: boating, skiing, swimming; Clubs: Ducks Unlimited; Home: 3969 Juan de Fuca Terrace, Victoria, B.C. V8N 5W9; Office: P.O. Box 6187, Depot 1, Victoria, B.C. V8P 5L5.

**MURPHY, Brian Patrick,** B.Sc., Dip.Meteorology; meteorologist; b. Windsor, Ont. 4 Aug. 1958; s. Terence Patrick and Dolores Marie (Boussey) M.; e. Assumption College H.S. 1976; Univ. of Windsor B.Sc. 1982; Univ. of Toronto, dipl. in Meteorology 1983; m. Angela d. James and Rita Keelan 4 April 1987; son: Brendan James; METEOROLOGIST (SEVERE WEATHER SPECIALIST), ATMOSPHERIC ENVIRONMENT SERVICE, ONT. WEATHER CENTRE 1989– ; Meteorolgist, Atmospheric Environ. Serv. 1983– ; posted to Nfld. Weather Centre, Gander, Nfld. 1984–86; transferred to Ont. Weather Centre 1986– ; developed lake effect snow forecast methodology 1989–90; participant, L. Ont. Winter Storms Program 1990; Environment Canada Citation of Excellence 1991; Atmospheric Environ. Serv., Ont. Region Award of Excellence 1990; U.S. Nat. Weather Serv. Commendaton 1990; Roman Catholic; Mem., Am. Meteor. Soc.; Candn. Correspondence Chess Assn.; Cambridge Humane Soc.; Toronto Humane Soc.; Dir., Scarlet Brigade Youth Marching & Concert Band (Windsor); author/co-author various papers in meteorological journs.; conducts profl. workshops pertaining to weather forecasting; recreations: chess, trombone, clock making; Home: 193 Ironstone Dr., Cambridge, Ont. N1P 1A8; Office: Pearson Internat. Airport, Box 159, Toronto AMF, Ont. L5P 1B1.

**MURPHY, C. Francis,** Q.C.; lawyer; b. Calgary, Alta. 27 April 1929; s. William Joseph and Josephine C. M.; e. Univ. of B.C. LL.B. 1950; m. Jean Marie d. John A. McDougall 29 Jan. 1955; children: Caroline Jean, Elizabeth Joan, Adrienne Mary, John McDougall, Frances Rose, Sarah Louise; FARRIS, VAUGHAN, WILLS & MURPHY 1959– ; articling student, Campney Owen Murphy & Owen 1950–51; Assoc. 1951–58; Assoc., present firm 1958–59, partner 1959–92; of counsel 1992– ; Dir. of several Candn. corps.; Q.C. 1984; Bd. of Trustees, St. Paul's Hospital; Mem., Candn. Bar Assn. (Former Chair Comm. Law Section; Former Rep. to Internat. Bar Assn.); recreations: skiing; clubs: Vancouver, Shaughnessy; Home: 6050 Athlone St., Vancouver, B.C. V6M 3A4; Office: P.O. Box 10026, Pacific Centre South, Toronto Dominion Bank Tower, 700 W. Georgia St., Vancouver, B.C. V7Y 1B3.

**MURPHY, Charles Terrence,** B.A.; judge; b. Sault Ste. Marie, Ont. 19 Oct. 1926; s. Charles Joseph and Monica (Walsh) M.; e. Sault Ste. Marie (Ont.) Coll. Inst., 1943; Assumption Coll.; Univ. of W. Ont. B.A. 1946; Osgoode Hall Law Sch.; m. Dorothy Anne, d. Lloyd Jenkins, 30 Aug. 1952; children: Sean Terrence, Karen Anne, Mary Lynn, Michaela Marie, Timothy Robert; JUDGE, ONTARIO COURT OF JUSTICE, GENERAL DIVISION 1990– ; called to Bar of Ont. 1949; cr. Q.C. 1960; Ald., Ward One, Sault Ste. Marie City Council, 1965–66; el. M.P. for Sault Ste. Marie in g.e. 1968; District Court Judge, Dist. of Manitoulin 1980–90; Past Pres., N. Atlantic Assembly; R. Catholic; recreations: golf, swimming, curling; Club: Kiwanis (Hon. mem.); Home: 1170 Ramseyview Ct., Apt. 1006, Sudbury, Ont.; Office: Judge's Chambers, Court House, 155 Elm St. W., Sudbury, Ont. P3C 1T9.

**MURPHY, David Ridgeway,** B.A., C.A.; transportation company executive; b. Ottawa, Ont. 10 July 1945; e. Univ. of B.C. B.A. 1968; C.A. 1971; m. Cheri June 1968; children: Shannon, Christine; SENIOR RESTRUCTING OFFR., PWA CORP./CANADIAN AIRLINES 1993– ; Article Clerk – Supervisor, Price Waterhouse (Vanc.) 1968–73; Head, Internal Audit, Canadian Pacific Air Lines 1973–79; Dir., Internal Audit 1979–83; Treas. 1983–84; Treas. & Sec. 1984–87; PWA Corp./Candn. Airlines (Calgary) 1987; Vice-Pres. & Treas. 1987–88; Vice-Pres. Finance, 1988–89; Sr. Vice-Pres. Finance 1989–93; Mem., Candn./B.C. Inst. of C.A.s; Conf. Bd. of Canad (Finance Counc.); Financial Extves. Inst.; recreations: squash, travel; Home: 48 Midpark Cres. S.E., Calgary, Alta. T2X 1P2; Office: Suite 2800, 700 Second St. S.W., Calgary, Alta. T2P 2W2.

**MURPHY, His Hon. Judge Henry,** B.A., B.C.L.; provincial court judge; b. Moncton, N.B. 9 Feb. 1921; s. Francis Patrick and Elizabeth Ann (Carey) M.; e. St Thomas Univ.; Univ. of N.B., B.A., B.C.L.; m. Joan d. John A. and Julia Barry 19 Apr. 1945; children: Francis Patrick, Julia, Henry Jr., Michael Barry; JUDGE, PROVINCIAL COURT OF N.B. (now Supernumerary) 1960– ; Merchant Navy 1942; Candn. Army 1943–46; law practice, Moncton 1946–60; elected to Parliament (Liberal) 1953; re-elected 1957; defeated in Diefenbaker Sweep 1958; defeated cand. for N.B. Liberal leadership; Former City Counc.; Pres., Moncton Lib. Assn.; Former Prov. Prosecutor; Sr. Judge of N.B. Prov. Court; Former Pres., N.B. Prov. Court Assn.; Chrmn., New Brunswick Harness Racing Comn. 1989; Roman Catholic; Liberal; Mem., Candn.-Irish Cultural Assn.; U.S. Trotting Assn.; recreations: harness racing; Club: Moncton City; Home: R.R. #10, Moncton, N.B. E1C 9J9; Office: Box 5001, Moncton, N.B. E1C 8R3.

**MURPHY, J. Elmer;** retired newspaper publisher; b. Summerside, P.E.I., 27 Jan. 1914; s. late Patrick Alphonsus and Josephine Frances (Power) M.; e. Summerside High Sch. 1930; St. Dunstan's Univ. 1930–32; m. Mary Pearl, d. late Daniel F. McNeill, 7 Oct. 1947; children: Mary Maureen, John Michael; PUBLISHER EMERITUS, THE JOURNAL-PIONEER; Summerside Citizen of the Year 1970; past mem. Candn. Mang. Eds. Conf.; mem., Candn. Daily Newspapers Publishers Assn.; R. Catholic; recreations: walking, photography; Clubs: Rotary (past Pres.); Kinsmen (Life mem.); K. of C. (Past Grand Kt.); Home: 186 Hanover St., Summerside, P.E.I. C1N 1E6; Office: Water at Queen Sts., Summerside, P.E.I.

**MURPHY, J. Wayne,** B.B.A., C.A.; public servant; b. Mount Stewart, P.E.I. 5 July 1950; s Clarence James and Elizabeth (Kneebone) M.; e. Univ. of P.E.I., B.B.A. 1972; C.A. 1974; m. Elaine d. John and Ida Ostridge 1 July 1972; children: Christa, Jonathan; AUDITOR-GENERAL, PROV. OF P.E.I. 1986– ; Mem. Rsch. Ctte., Candn. Comprehensive Auditing Found. 1992– ; Public Sector Acctg. & Auditing Ctte., Candn. Inst. of C.A.'s 1987–89; Mem. Bd. of Govs., Candn. Comp. Auditing Foundation 1991– ; Home: 14 Marjorie Crescent, Charlottetown, P.E.I. C1A 7T9; Office: P.O. Box 2000, Charlottetown, P.E.I. C1A 7N8.

**MURPHY, James F.;** retired; b. Windsor, Ont. 26 Apr. 1933; s. James H. and Estelle M. (McPharlin) M.; e. Assumption H.S.; Univ. of Windsor; m. Marion Blanche Bechard 8 May 1954; children: Mary, Cathy, Vicki, Jim, Chris; Pres., North America, The Hiram Walker Group 1992–93, retired; various sales & mktg. positions, Hiram Walker Inc. (Detroit) 1953–78; Pres., W.A. Taylor & Co. (Miami) 1978–83; Extve. Vice-Pres., Hiram Walker & Sons Inc. (Detroit) 1983–87; Pres. 1987–88; Extve. Vice-Pres., Hiram Walker-Allied Vintners 1988– ; Chrmn., Hiram Walker-Allied Vintners Inc. (Detroit) 1988–90; Chrmn., Hiram Walker-Allied Vintner (Canada) Ltd. 1989–90; Chrmn., N. American Sector, Hiram Walker-Allied Vintners 1990–91; Chrmn., N. American Sector, The Hirom Walker Group 1991–92; Dir., Corby Distilleries Ltd. (Montreal) 1989– ; Laird & Company (N.J.) 1985– ; Domecq & Co. (N.Y.) 1989– ; Dir., The Century Council; Trustee, Childrens Hosp. of Michigan; Sky Ranch Found., S. Dakota; recreations: sailing, golfing; clubs: Orchard Lake Country; Home: 26565 Willowgreen Rd., Franklin, Mich. 48025.

**MURPHY, John Joseph,** C.M.; Mayor of City of St. John's 1993– ; businessman; b. St. John's, Nfld. 24 Sept. 1922; s. John and Gertrude M.; e. St. Bonaventure's Coll. 1929–40; m. the late Marjorie d. Patrick and Alice Halley 4 June 1951; children: Karen, Patricia, Paul, Jane; PRES. JOHN J. MURPHY LTD. 1966– ; PRES. HALLEY & CO. 1956– ; Chrmn. of the Bd., Cabot Celebrations (1997) Corp. 1992–93; worked in advtg. and ins. investigation 1943; freelance broadcaster 1948; former Mayor, St. John's, Nfld. 1981–90; mem. Adv. Bd. Royal Trust; Pres. (and later Senator) Jr. C. of C.; Nfld. Bd. of Trade; Nfld. Cancer Soc.; National Campaign Chrmn. (and Life Mem.) Candn. Cancer Soc.; mem. Capital Comm.; Chrmn. New Building Fund, Candn. National Inst. for the Blind; mem. Royal Comn. on Edn. 1968–71; Campaign Chrmn.: New Building Fund, Salvation Army; St. John Ambulance; mem. Bd. of Regents, Meml. Univ. of Nfld.; Officer, Order of Canada 1985; recreations: sailing, archives; Clubs: Royal Nfld. Yacht; Home: 36 Smithville Cres., St. John's, Nfld. A1B 2V2.

**MURPHY, Michael Joseph G.;** writer; b. Kingston, Ont. 1 Nov. 1927; s. George Dominic and Kathleen (Freeman) M.; e. Regiopolis Coll., Kingston (5 yrs.); single; constr. labourer; reporter, Smith's Falls, Ont.; Locomotive Fireman, C.P.R. (working on steam locomotives 10 yrs.); moved to Toronto 1961; worked as clerk, taxi driver, building supt., etc.; spent 10 years on skid row living in flop houses & park benches; Mem., Alcoholics Anonymous (12 yrs.); Roman Cath.; author: 'My Kind of People' 1987, 'I Met Them at the Track' forthcoming, and several published short stories; recreations: attending horse races regularly; Club: Writers' Union of Can.; Home: 416 – 1684 Victoria Park Ave., Scarborough, Ont. M1R 1R1.

**MURPHY, Rae Allan,** B.A.; educator; writer; b. Blairmore, Alta. 20 Nov. 1935; s. Harvey and Isabel Agnes (Rae) M.; e. Britannia High Sch. Vancouver; York Univ. B.A. 1972; m. Elsie 1 June 1957; one s. Michael; LECTR. IN JOURNALISM AND CANDN. STUDIES CONESTOGA COLL: 1972– ; reporter, ed. and former mem. ed. bd. Last Post; contbr. various publs., CBC Radio, film scripts; co-author 'Your Place Or Mine' novel 1979; 'Winners Losers' 1976; 'Brian Mulroney, Boy From Baie Comeau' 1984; 'Selling Out' 1988; 'Canada: The Unmaking' 1990; 'Canada in the Global Economy' 1993; co-ed. 'Corporate Canada' 1972; 'Let Us Prey' 1974; author: 'Essentials of Canadian History: Post Confederation' 1993; mem. YMCA; recreations: swimming, hiking; Home: 903, 3650 Kaneff Cres., Mississauga, Ont. L5A 4A1; Office: 299 Doon Valley Rd., Kitchener, Ont. N2G 4M4.

**MURPHY, Sean Buller,** C.M., S.B., M.D.; ophthalmologist; b. London, Eng. 25 Jan. 1924; s. late John Joseph Aloysius and late Cecil Tremaine (Buller) M.; e. Downside Sch., Stratton-on-the-Fosse, Eng.; Worcester (Mass.) Acad., 1940; Harvard Univ., S.B. 1943; McGill Univ., M.D., C.M. 1947; m. Elizabeth Anne, d. Hollis H. Blake, Westmount, Que., 8 Aug. 1950; children: Elizabeth Gaill, Brian Buller, Carolyn Anne; Intern, Royal Victoria Hosp. 1947–48; Attending staff 1955, Ophthalmol. 1966, Ophthalmologist-in-Chief 1970–86; Sr. Ophthalmologist 1986; research, Montreal Neurol. Inst., 1948–49; Asst. Resident 1950–52 and Resident 1952; Inst. of Ophthalmol., Presb. Hospital, New York; Asst. Prof., Dept. of Ophthalmol., McGill Univ., 1966; Assoc. Prof. 1970, Prof. and Chrmn. 1975–87; Acting Chrmn. 1992–93; Prof. Emeritus 1989; served with RCAF 1953–55; rank Wing Commander; Pres., The Montreal Museum of Fine Arts, 1968–79 (Councillor 1959–79; Chairman Acquisition Committee 1966–79; Vice President 1968–79; Hon. Pres. 1979); mem. Can. Council 1977–79, Extve Comte. 1978–79, Investment Comte. 1978–79, Council Rep. to Arts Panel 1978–79; Chrmn., Nat. Museums of Can. 1979–84, 1987–90; Nat. Museum of Sci. and Tech., Bd. of Trustees 1990– , Extve. Ctte. 1990– ; Nat. Gallery of Canada Aquisition Ctte. 1990– ; Harvard Club of Montreal President 1981–84; Visual Arts Center, Montreal, Board member; Bd. of Trustees, Bishop's Univ.; Bd., Canadian Mediterranean Inst.; Bd. Arts Club of Montreal 1988; Bd. Arts Sutton 1988; writings include several articles for prof. journals; mem., Candn. Med. Assn.; Que. Med. Assn.; Que. Fed. Specialists; Eye Study Club; Candn. Ophthalmol. Soc. (council mem. 1975–77; Pres. 1978); Que. Assn. Ophthalmol. (Extve. Comte. 1970–73; Pres. 1973–76); Montreal Ophthalmol. Soc.; Am. Acad. Ophthalmol.; Candn. Museums Assn.; Am. Assn. Museums; mem. Order of Can. 1976; Queen's Jubilee Medal 1977; Candn. Ophthalmological Soc. Medal 1987; mem. Zeta Psi; Alpha Kappa Kappa; Alpha Omega Alpha; R. Catholic; recreation: painting, travel; Home: 3001 Sherbrooke St. W., Apt. 904, Montreal, Que. H3Z 2X8; Office: 687 Pine W., Montreal, Que. H3A 1A1.

**MURRAY, Anne,** O.C. (1974); C.O.C. (1985); singer; b. Springhill, N.S. 20 June 1945; d. Carson, M.D. and Marion (Burke) M.; e. Springhill (N.S.) High Sch., 1962; Mount St. Vincent Coll., Halifax; Univ. of N.B., B.P.E. 1966; Univ. of N.B., D.Litt. (Hon.); St. Mary's Univ., D. Litt. (Hon.), 1982; taught phys. educ., Athena Regional High Sch., Summerside, P.E.I., 1966–67; entered full-time music career 1967; named Top Candn. Female Vocalist of 1970 (R.P.M. Award); Top Candn. Female Entertainer of the Yr. 1970 (Candn. Press); Best Female Newcomer of the Yr. 1970–71 (Record World Mag., U.S.); Top Newcomer Female Vocalist of the Yr. 1970–80 (Cashbox Mag., U.S.); 1st Candn. female to win Gold Record in U.S., 1970; Juno Award (Canada's Top Country Female Vocalist) 1970–86; Grammy Award (U.S.) Best Female Vocal Performance (Country) 1974; incl. in Nashville's Country Music Hall of Fame 'Walkway of Stars' 1974; Vanier Award, Outstanding Young Canadian; voted Cdn. Female Recording Artist of Decade by C.R.I.A. and C.A.R.A.S.; 'own star' placed in Hollywood's 'Walkway of Stars' June 1980; Grammy Award, Best Female Vocal Performance (Pop) 1978, 1979, 1980 & (country) 1983; 3 CMA awards 1984–1985; winner of ACTRA Nellie Award, 1986 for Best Variety Performance (Anne Murray's Sounds of London); U.S. television specials (CBS) CBC: 'Anne Murray's Christmas Special' 1981; 'Anne Murray's Caribbean Cruise' 1983; 'Anne Murray's Winter Carnival from Quebec' 1984; 'Sounds of London' 1985; 'Anne Murray's Family Christmas' 1988; 'Anne Murray's Greatest Hits Volume II' (CBC) 1989; 'Anne Murray in DisneyWorld' 1991; 'Anne Murray in Nova Scotia' 1993; Roman Catholic; recreation: sports; Address: c/o Balmuir, Suite 2400, 4950 Yonge St., Toronto, Ont. M2N 6K1.

**MURRAY, David Logan,** M.A.Sc., P.Eng.; executive; b. Windsor, Ont. 8 May 1945; s. Nigel Bruce and Norma Mary (Saunders) M.; e. W.F. Herman Coll. Inst. Windsor 1959; Univ. of Windsor, B.A.Sc. (Elect.) 1969, M.A.Sc. 1970; one d. Janet Lynn; DIR., DMR GROUP INC. 1989– ; Sci. Service Offr. Defence Rsch. Bd. Can. 1970–73; Design Eng. Digital Equipment of Canada Ltd. 1973, becoming Applications Eng., Mktg. Mgr., Eng. Mgr. 1981; Founder, Pres. & C.E.O., Taurus Computer Products Inc. 1981–88; Gen. Mgr., Taurus Division of DY-4 Systems Inc. 1988–89; mem. Exper. Aircraft Assn.; recreations: skiing, sport aviation; Home: 84 Bujold Ct., Kanata, Ont.

**MURRAY, David Robert,** M.A., Ph.D.; educator; b. Saskatoon, Sask. 21 March 1940; s. Robert Allan and Margaret Beattie (Stone) M.; e. Bishop's Univ. B.A. 1962; Univ. of Edinburgh M.A. 1964; Univ. of Cambridge Ph.D. 1968; m. Ann Elizabeth d. Hermann and Maud Stockwell 17 Aug. 1963; children: Heather Elizabeth, Robert Bruce, Deborah Ann; PROF., DEPT. OF HISTORY, UNIV. OF GUELPH 1982– ; Asst. Prof. of Hist. present Univ. 1967–72, Assoc. Prof. 1972–82, Prof. 1982–92, Acting Dean Coll. of Arts 1980–81, Dean, Coll. of Arts 1981–92; mem. Bd. Govs. 1979–82; Resident Historian Dept. External Affairs 1971–72; Fellow-Commoner Churchill Coll. Univ. of Cambridge 1977–78; mem. Queen Elizabeth Scholarship Comte. 1979–81 (Chrmn. 1980–81); I.O.D.E. Ont. Scholarship Comte. 1980–82; Dir. Community Service Council Guelph 1975–77, 1978–82 (Treas. 1976–77, 1978–80; Pres. 1980–82); recipient Bishop's Univ.; Pres.'s Prize in Eng.; Lt. Gov.'s Bronze Medal Hist.; Hon. G. Howard Ferguson Cup; Chancellor's Prize; Univ. Corp. Prize; mem. Golden Mitre Hon. Soc.; Commonwealth Scholarship 1962–64; Can. Council Predoctoral Fellowship 1964–66; I.O.D.E. War Mem. Scholarship 1966–67; author: 'Odious Commerce; Britain, Spain and the Abolition of the Slave Trade to Cuba' 1980; 'Hatching the Cowbird's Egg: The Creation of the Univ. of Guelph' 1989; co-author, 'The Prairie Builder: 'Walter Murray of Saskatchewan,' 1984; ed. 'Documents on Canadian External Relations' Vol. 7 1939–41 part 1 1974, Vol. 8 1939–41 part 2 1976; Home: 126 Palmer St., Guelph, Ont. N1E 2R3; Office: Univ. of Guelph, Guelph, Ont. N1G 2W1.

**MURRAY, Heather,** B.A., M.A., Ph.D.; university professor; b. Toronto, Ont. 26 July 1951; d. Donald Wellesley and Eunice Ethel (Futerall) M.; e. Univ. of Toronto B.A. 1973; York Univ. M.A. 1977, Ph.D. 1984; m. David s. Doris and James Galbraith 1 May 1991; one d. Sarah Cate Galbraith-Murray; ASSOC. PROF. OF ENGLISH & DIR., WOMEN'S STUDIES PROGRAMME, UNIV. OF TORONTO; Office: Trinity College, Univ. of Toronto, Toronto, Ont. M5S 1H8.

**MURRAY, J. Alex;** university professor; e. Univ. Illinois Ph.D. 1967; DEAN, SCH. BUSINESS & ECONOMICS, WILFRID LAURIER UNIV. since 1982; Visiting Prof. of Internat. Marketing at Univ. of Southern California, Los Angeles, CA 1987; Dir., Inst. for Candn.-Am. Studies, Univ. Windsor 1971–82; Visiting Prof., U.C.L.A. 1977, 1980, 1992; author: 'Transnational Executives: A Study of Japanese Executives' 1985; 'International Countertrade and Offset Management' 1988; 'Project 1992: Confronting the Unified Market in Europe' 1991; 'Benchmaking: A Tool for Excellence' 1993; Office: Wilfrid Laurier Univ., Waterloo, Ont. N2L 3C5.

**MURRAY, James Ronald,** B.S., M.A.; television producer; b. Toronto, Ont. 17 July 1932; s. Charles Paul and Emma Louise (Veit) M.; e. Runnymede C.I. 1946–48; New Albany H.S. 1950; Indiana Univ. B.S. 1954; Northwestern Univ. M.A. 1957; m. Nancy d. Ernest and Gladys Archibald; children: Linda Joan, Carol Louise; EXECUTIVE PRODUCER, 'THE NATURE OF THINGS WITH DAVID SUZUKI' 1979– ; Radio Producer, CBC Toronto 1957–60; Television Producer 1960–61; Producer, 'The Nature of Things' 1961–68; Extve. Prod. 1968–72; 'The National Dream' 1972–74; 'Science Magazine with David Suzuki' 1974–79; 'A Planet for the Taking' 1983–85; Candn. Sci. Film Assn. Award 1970; Fed. of Ont. Naturalists Disting. Serv. Award 1979, Conservation Award 1986; N. Am. Assn. for Environ. Edn. Disting. Serv. Award 1988; Wildscreen Fest., Great Britain, Outstanding Achievement Award 1990; Gemini Awards for best documentary series on Candn. TV (James Murray, Extve. Prod., 'The Nature of Things' 1987, '88, '91, '92); awards for individual programs produced for 'The Nature of Things': The Alexandria Prize 1965; 'Diplôme D'Honneur,' Internat. Sci. Film Fest. 1967; 'The Wilderness Medal' 1967; 'The Wilderness Award' 1972; 'Best of Festival,' N. Am. Assn. for Environ. Edn. Comp. 1988; 'Blue Ribbon,' Am. Film & Video Fest. 1992; Soc. of Motion Picture and Television Engrs. (SMPTE) John Grierson Gold Medal, Achievement in Film 1992; Past Pres., Assn. of TV Prod. & Dir., CBC, Toronto; recreations: birdwatching, photography, music; Home: 30-A Victoria Park Ave., Toronto, Ont. M4E 3R9; Office: CBC - TV, Box 500, Station A, Toronto, Ont. M5W 1E6.

**MURRAY, Joan,** B.A., M.A.; arts executive; curator; author; artist; b. 12 Aug. 1943; d. Sidney Arnold and Lucia Grace (de Castro) Charlat; e. Univ. of Toronto, B.A. 1965, Columbia Univ., M.A. 1966; Univ. of Toronto 1967–68; m. W. Ross s. Chesley M. 20 June 1959; children: Laura, Victoria, Adam; DIR., THE ROBERT McLAUGHLIN GALLERY 1974– ; Curator of Candn. Art, Art Gall. of Ont. 1970–73; Acting Chief Curator, Art Gall. of Ont. 1973; Advr., Toronto Western Hosp. Art Ctte. 1973; Ont. Cancer Inst., Princess Margaret Hosp. 1977–78; Cons., Ont. Arts Counc. 1972–75, and others; Adv. Counc., Bata Shoe Mus. Found. 1980– ; Bd. of Gov., Candn. Conf. of the Arts 1975–76; Candn. Art Mus. Dir. Orgn. 1975– ; Counc., Candn. Mus. Assn. 1974–76; Extve. Counc., Ont. Assn. of Art Galls. 1974–76; Bd. of Dir., Ont. Heritage Found. 1975–78; Adv. Ctte. on Art, Fine Arts Prog., Dept. of Pub. Works Can. 1976–78; Art Ed.: 'The Canadian Forum' 1970–74; Contbg. Ed.: 'Canadian Art' 1984–86; Contbr.: 'The Art Post' 1984–87; Mem., Adv. Bd.: 'Artmagazine' 1974–78; elected Fellow, Royal Candn. Academy 1992; recipient, Assn. of Cultural Executives Award for outstanding contribution in field of cultural management 1993; author: 'Letters Home: 1859–1906, The Letters of William Blair Bruce' 1982; (with Robert Fulford) 'The Beginning of Vision: The Drawings of Lawren S. Harris' 1982; 'Kurelek's Vision of Canada' 1983, 'Frederick Arthur Verner: The Last Buffalo' 1984, 'Daffodils in Winter: The Life and Letters of Pegi Nicol MacLeod' 1984, 'The Best of the Group of Seven' 1984, 'The Best of Tom Thomson' 1986; 'The Best of Contemporary Canadian Art' 1987 and 100 catalogues & 200 articles on Candn. art; Broadcaster, Arts Nat., CBC 1976–79; Lectr., York Univ. 1970–71, 1973–75, Scarborough Coll. 1975–76 and nationally on Candn. art; also an artist with numerous one-person shows since 1983; recreations: swimming; Home: 400 Saint John St. W., Whitby, Ont. L1N 1N7; Office: Civic Centre, Oshawa, Ont. L1H 3Z3.

**MURRAY, John Bruce,** B.Comm., M.B.A.; public servant; b. Belleville, Ont. 2 June 1936; s. Gregor and Jean Isobel (Wallbridge) M.; e. St. Mary's Univ. B.Comm. 1968; Univ. of Western Ont. M.B.A. 1973; m. Barbara d. Harry and Dorcas Jones 1 Aug. 1959; children: Karen, Michael; Asst. Deputy Minister, Indian and Northern Affairs, Govt. of Canada 1988–93; Royal Candn. Navy-Candn. Armed Forces, retired as Commander 1954–78; Treas. Bd. of Can. 1978–83; Supply & Serv. Can. 1983–88; Dir., then Pres. of Bd. of Dirs., Civil Serv. Co-op. Credit Soc. 1988– ; Home: 789 Hemlock Rd., Ottawa, Ont. K1K 0K6.

**MURRAY, John W.,** M.A.; retired executive; b. London, Ont. Sept. 1920; s. K. D. and Mrs. H. S. (Simpson) M.; e. Public and High Schs., London, Ont.; Ridley Coll., St. Catharines, Ont.; Univ. of Western Ont., B.A., M.A.; m. Marion, d. D. F. Hassel, Oct. 1942; children: John, Kenneth, Anne; Dir., St. Joseph's Health Centre Found.; Adv. Bd., St. Joseph's Health Centre; Bd. mem., Ont. Labour Relations Bd.; Chrmn. & Dir., Finance Ctte., Physicians Services Inc. Foundation; joined John Labatt Limited in Purchasing Department, 1956; Director of Purchasing, 1957, Export Sales Mgr., 1958; Vice-Pres. and Dir. of Marketing, Lucky Lager Breweries Ltd., Vancouver, B.C. 1958–61; Dir. of Marketing, John Labatt Limited, Ontario Div., Toronto, 1961–64; Pres., Labatt's Ontario Breweries Ltd., 1964–67; Vice-Pres., Planning & Devel., John Labatt Ltd., 1968–71; Vice President, Maritime Region, 1971–74; Vice Pres., Corp. Affairs, Labatt Breweries of Can., 1974–79; former Extve. Vice Pres., Intnl., Labatt Breweries Canada Ltd.; served in the 2nd World War with R.C.N. 1941–45; discharged with rank of Lieut.; Anglican; recreation: golf; Clubs: Lambton Golf; London Hunt & Country; The London (Ont.); Longboat Key Club; Home: 306, 250 Sydenham St., London, Ont. N6A 5S1; and 1701 Gulf of Mexico Dr., Longboat Key, Fla.

**MURRAY, Kenneth Sherwood,** H. Bus. Ad., B.A.; merchant; b. London, Ont. 3 June 1916; s. Kenneth Donald and Hazel Kirke (Simpson) M.; e. Pub. Schs., London, Ont.; Ridley Coll., St. Catharines, Ont.; Univ. of Western Ont., B.A. 1937, with Hons. in Business Adm.; m. Anne Elizabeth, d. Alexander Harvey of London, Ont., 1 June 1940; two d., Allison Ann, Martha Elizabeth; DIR./SALES, P. LAWSON TRAVEL, London; Chrmn. Rusetravel Agency Ltd. 1976–83; since 1971 Pres. & Managing Dir., Hobbs Hardware Co. Ltd. 1960–71; Past Mem. & Hon. Vice Pres. University Hosp., London, Ont.; Past Mem. Extve. Comte., London Health Assn.; Past Pres. Boy Scouts Assn.; Past Mem., Bd. Govs. and Senate, Univ. of W. Ont.; Past Mem. of Bd., Huron College; Past Mem. & Bd., Ont. Golf Assn.; recipient Univ. of W. Ont. Alumni Award; Past Pres., Univ. of W. Ont. Alumni Assn. & Great Artists Concerts; Past Pres., Can. Wholesale Hardware Assn.; Jr. Extve. with Murray Selby Shoe Co. London, Ont., 1937–42; served in World War 1939–45, with C.O.T.C. 1939–42, and Lieut., Royal Candn. Navy 1943–45; Delta Upsilon (Past Pres.); Conservative; Anglican; recreations: golf, hockey; Clubs: London; London Hunt and Country (Past Pres.); London Univ.; Home: 1 Grosvenor St., Apt. 1214, London, Ont. N6A 1Y2.

**MURRAY, Laurence Corbett Michael,** F.C.A., B.Comm.; chartered accountant; b. Toronto, Ont. 29 Sept. 1944; s. Frank Patrick and Jean Margaret (Corbett) M.; e. Univ. of Toronto, B.Comm. 1966; m. Nancy d. Frank and the late Catherine Wilson 25 June 1970; children: Catharine Louise, Lawren Wilson; PARTNER, PEAT MARWICK THORNE 1989– ; Coopers & Lybrand 1966–75; Thorne Riddell 1975–86; Thorne Ernst & Whinney (successor to Thorne Riddell) 1986–89; C.A. 1969; F.C.A. designation 1991; Dir. & Past Treas., The Candn. Centre for Philanthropy; Dir. & Mem. of Executive Ctte., The Candn. Hearing Soc. Foundation; Dir., Chrmn. Provincial Grants Review Ctte.; Treas., Ont. Trillium Found. 1984–91; Dir., Peat Marwick Thorne Educational Found. 1984–90; Roman Catholic; clubs: National, Granite; Home: 55 Ridge Dr., Toronto, Ont. M4T 1B6; Office: Peat Marwick Thorne Bldg., One Toronto St., Suite 1200, Toronto, Ont. M5C 2V5.

**MURRAY, Hon. Lowell,** P.C., M.A.; senator; b. New Waterford, N.S. 26 Sept. 1936; s. late Daniel and late Evelyn (Young) M.; e. St. Francis Xavier Univ., B.A.; Queen's Univ., M.A. (Public Admin.); m. Colleen Elaine d. Mr. and Mrs. John D. MacDonald, 19 Dec. 1981; two sons: William, Colin; GOVERNMENT LEADER IN THE SENATE 1993– ; Mem., Senate of Canada since 1979; former Chief of Staff to Hon. E.D. Fulton, Min. Justice and Min. Public Works; to Hon. Senator M. Wallace McCutcheon; to Hon. R.L. Stanfield, Leader of Opposition; Deputy Min. to Hon. Richard B. Hatfield, Premier of N.B.; Chrmn., National Campaign Ctte., Progressive Conservative Party of Canada 1977–79, and 1981–83; Summoned to the Senate, Sept. 13, 1979; Co-Chrmn. Joint Senate House of Commons Ctte., on Official Languages 1980–84; Chrmn. Standing Senate Ctte. on Banking, Trade & Commerce 1984–86; mem. Bd. of Trustees, Inst. for Research on Public Policy 1984–86; mem. Trilateral Comn. 1985–86; Sworn of the Privy Council & apptd. Leader of the Govt. in the Senate 30 June 1986, re-apptd. 1993; Min. of State (Fed.-Prov. Relations) 1986–91; Min. Responsible for the Atlantic Canada Opportunities Agency 1987–88; Progressive Conservative; Roman Catholic; Office: The Senate of Canada, Room 502, Victoria Bldg., Ottawa, Ont. K1A 0A4.

**MURRAY, Nickolas Richard,** M.P.A.; public administrator; b. Campbellton, N.B. 19 Nov. 1938; s. Leo Richard and Greta Anne (Morrison) M.; e. Dalhousie Univ., M.P.A.; Chairperson - G.S.T. Consumer Information Office 1990–91; Pres., Consumers' Assoc. of Can. 1989–90; Chairperson - Candn. General Standards Bd. (CGSB) Standards Ctte. 1985–91; Public administrator, City of Halifax; recreations: skiing, tennis, swimming, hockey; Club: Saraguay; Home: 5682 Inglis St., Halifax, N.S. B3H 1K3; Office: P.O. Box 1749, Halifax, N.S. B3J 3A5.

**MURRAY, Paul J.,** B.A.; businessman, consultant; b. Toronto, Ont. 7 Dec. 1946; s. Edward Joseph and Eleanor Marie (Doyle) M.; e. Markham Dist. H.S.; Carleton Univ., B.A. 1969; m. Colleen Mary d. Thomas J. and Eva M. Coghlan 3 Oct. 1973; children: Erin M., Jennifer K., Anne M., Brendan J.; CORPORATE COMMUNICATIONS CONSULTANT 1989– ; Investment Broker, member firms of Toronto Stock Exchange 1969–75; Policy Analyst, Bus.-Govt. Relations, Govt. of Can. 1976–78; Dept. Asst. to Min. of Indus. Trade & Comm. 1978–79; Pres., Paul J. Murray & Assoc. 1980–85; Pres., Ottawa Valley Brewing Co. Ltd. 1985–89; club: National Press Club of Canada; Home: 53 Grange Ave., Ottawa, Ont. K1Y 0N8; Office: 302 – 120 Holland Ave., Ottawa, Ont. K1Y 0X6.

**MURRAY, Robert Daniel;** C.M.; manufacturing executive; b. La Tuque, P.Q. 4 Sept. 1921; s. William Reginald and Louise Marie (Lord) M.; e. Acad. David (Drummondville, P.Q.): Commissioners' H.S. (Quebec City); Sir George Williams Univ., Montreal; m. Irene DeLery; d. Albert and Yvonne Demers 23 Jan. 1971; children: Louise Emilie; Louis; PRESIDENT, CONSULTANTS ROBERT D. MURRAY AND ASSOCIATES; Chrmn., Laidlaw (Quebec) Advisory Board; Chrmn. Bd. of Govs. and Vice-Pres., Quebec Manufacturers' Assn.; Chrmn., Hydrogen Industry Counc.; Vice-Chrmn. Canadian Armed Forces D.N.D. Candn. Forces Liaison Council; Pres., Durand Medical Rsch. Foundation; Les Immeubles Murray Inc.; Dir., Candn. Manufacturers Assn.; Corporation Financiere Canassurance; Assoc. d'hospitalisation du Québec, Quebec Blue Cross; Extve. Ctte. Mem. & Dir., Montreal Museum of Fine Arts; Mem., Order of Canada 1991; recipient, 125th Anniversary of the Confederation of Canada Medal, 1992; R. Catholic; recreations; golf, skiing; Clubs: Saint-Denis (Montreal); Club de Golf Laval sur-le-Lac; Home: 14 Ramezay Rd., Westmount, Que. H3Y 3J6; Office: 630 Dorchester Blvd. West, P.O. Box 10, Montreal, Que. H3C 2R3.

**MURRAY, Robert George Everitt,** M.A., M.D., C.M., F.R.S.C. (1958), D.Sc. (h.c.); bacteriologist; university professor; b. Ruislip, Middlesex, Eng. 19 May 1919; s. late Everitt George Dunne, O.B.E. and late Winifred Hardwick (Woods) M.; e. Summer Fields, Oxford, Eng., 1927–30; Lower Can. Coll., Montreal, Que., 1931–36; McGill Univ. (1936–38) and (1941–43), M.D., C.M.; Cambridge Univ., Eng., B.A. 1941 and M.A. 1945, D.Sc. (h.c.) Univ. of Western Ontario 1985; D.Sc. (h.c.) Univ. of Guelph 1988; m. Doris (deceased), d. late Richard Werner Marchand, 1944; two s. and one d.; m. Marion, d.late Frederic Winnett Luney, 1985; PROFESSOR EMERITUS, UNIV. OF W. ONT. 1984– ; mem. Ed. Bd., 'Microbiological Reviews' (formerly 'Bacteriological Reviews') 1967–79 and Ed. 1969–79; mem., Gov. Bd. Biol. Council Can. 1966–72; Editor, 'Canadian Journal of Microbiology,' 1954–60; mem. of Ed. Bd., 'Journal of Bacteriology,' 1951–56 and 1980–86; Assoc. Editor 'International Journal of Systematic Bacteriology' 1982–90, Editor 1991– ; Lect., Dept. of Bacter. and Immunology, University of Western Ontario, 1945; Professor and Head of Dept. 1949–74; Professor (of Microbiology and Immunology) until 1984; Acting Dean of Sci. 1973–74; Capt., R.C.A.M.C. 1944–45; mem., Candn. Pub. Health Assn. (Chrmn., Lab. Sec., 1951); Candn. Assn. Clin. Microbiol. and Inf. Diseases (Hon. Mem. 1992– ); Am. Soc. for Microbiol. (Vice-Pres. 1971–72, Pres. 1972–73, J. Roger Porter Award 1987, Hon. mem. 1988– ); Chrmn., Internat. Comm. for Systematic Bacteriology 1982–86 and 1986–90; Candn. Soc. Microbiol. (Org. Chrmn. 1951–52 and Pres. 1952–3 Hon. Mem. 1983– ); Soc. for Gen. Microbiol.; Soc. for Appl. Bacteriol. (Hon. mem. 1988– ); Cdn. and Amer. Socs. for Cell Biol.; Electron Microscope Soc. Am.; Pathol. Soc., Gt. Brit. and Ireland; rec'd. Coronation Medal 1953; Harrison Prize, Roy. Soc. Can., 1957; Fellow, Roy. Soc. Ca. 1958; Roy. Soc. Can. Travelling Award, 1961; Candn. Soc. Microbiols. Prize, 1963; Centennial Medal 1967; Fellow, Am. Acad. of Microbiol. 1974; Queen's Jubilee Medal 1978; Flavelle Medal, Roy. Soc. Can. 1984; mem. Bd. of Govs. Am. Acad. of Microbiol. 1980–83; mem., Bd. Trustees, Bergey's Manual Trust 1964–91, Chrmn. 1976–90; Bd. of Dirs., Candn. Bacterial Diseases Network 1989–94; recreation: fishing, flying; Address: Dept. of Microbiology & Immunology, Univ. of Western Ont., London, Ont. N6A 5C1.

**MURRAY, Roy Victor,** C.D., P.S.C., B.Eng., M.Eng., P.Eng.; education administrator; b. North Sydney, N.S. 30 July 1940; s. Roy Stanley and Olive Eileen (Amey) M.; e. Acadia Univ., Applied Sci. cert. 1961; N.S. Tech. Coll., B.Eng. 1963, M.Eng. 1969; m. Anita d. James W. and Rita Rogerson 5 Sept. 1980; children: Stephen, Elizabeth; PRES., CONFEDERATION COLLEGE 1989– and CHAIR, NORTHWEST ENTERPRISE CENTRE BOARD 1992– ; Bd. mem., Ont. Training Corp. 1990–93; Mem., OTC Training Investment Ctte. 1990–93; Mem., ACAATO, Council of Presidents Extve. Ctte. 1989– ; Mem., ACAATO, Council of Presidents 1989– ; Bd. mem., Thunder Bay Exonomic Development Corp. 1991– ; Mem., B.C. Premier's Adv. Counc. on Sci. and Technol. 1987–89; Candn. Armed Forces 1963–70; Asst. Prof., Lakehead Univ. 1970–73; Dean of Technol., Confederation Coll. 1973–76; Bus. & Technol. 1976–80; Pres., Lakeland Coll. 1980–85; Pres., B.C. Inst. of Technol. 1985–89; Chrmn. Postsecondary Internat. Network, Can./U.S./U.K. 1987–91; Assn. of Candn. Community Colls.; Alderman, City of Thunder Bay 1979–80; PSC, Candn. Land Forces Comm. & Staff Coll.; Candn. Decoration; Mem., Making Canada Productive Task Force; Home: P.O. Box 398, Thunder Bay, Ont. P7C 4W1; Office: P.O. Box 398, Thunder Bay, Ont. P7C 4W1.

**MURRAY, Sandy James,** B.Sc., M.D.; physician; association executive; b. Red Deer, Alta. 15 March 1951; s. James Robert and Mildred Ruth (Sinclair) M.; e. Univ. of Alta. B.Sc. 1973, M.D. 1977; CCFP 1980; m. Dorothy d. Alfred and Alberta Swainson 5 May 1972; children: Fraser, Kolin; rotating internship Rotorua, N.Z. 1977–78; family practice residency Calgary Gen. Hosp. 1978–80; mem. Active Staff Red Deer Regional Hosp. 1980– , Pres. Med. Staff 1983; mem. Bd. Alta. Press Council 1985–87; Fedn. Alta. Naturalists 1987; Pres. Red Deer River Naturalists Soc. 1985–86; Central Alta. Med. Soc. 1982–84; Dir., Alta. Med. Assn. 1984–91, Pres., 1988–89; Dir., Candn. Medical Assn. 1989–91; Chrmn. Ctte. Environmental Health 1989–91; Pres., Medical Alumni Assn., Univ. of Alta. 1993– ; recreation: tuba; Office: 240, 5201 – 43 St., Red Deer, Alta. T4N 1C7

**MURRAY, Susan,** B.Sc.; government relations consultant; b. Hamilton, Ont. 2 Feb. 1953; d. Alec Walter and Ruth Andrea (Pilgrim) M.; e. Univ. of Western Ont. B.Sc. 1976; PRES. & OWNER, S.A. MURRAY CONSULTING INC. 1982– ; S.A. Murray Consulting has 23 employees based in Toronto, Ottawa and Vancouver and is one of the country's leading lobbying/govt. relns. firms rep. domestic & multi-nat. companies to Candn. govts.; Bd. Chrmn., Nat. Ballet School; Vice-Pres., Candn. Inst. for Strategic Studies; Dir., Counc. for Candn. Unity; Mem. of Advisory Bd. to the Extve. MBA Program for Queens Univ.; Mem., Candn./U.S. Business Assn.; former Mem. of Bd., Candn. Opera Co.; Metro. Bd. of Trade; clubs: Rideau, Albany; Office: 49 Jackes Ave., 1st Fl., Toronto, Ont. M4T 1E2.

**MURRAY, T. Jock,** O.C., M.D., LL.D. (Hons.), D.Sc. (Hons.), F.R.C.P.(C), F.A.C.P.; b. Halifax, N.S. 30 May 1938; s. George Carson and Nora Kathleen (Wallace) M.; e. Pictou Acad.; St. Francis Xavier Pre-Med. 1958, LL.D. (Hons.) 1989, D.Sc. (Hons.) 1991; Dalhousie Univ. M.D. 1963, postgrad. training Neurol. 1965; Univ. of London & Nat. Hosp. Queen Sq. (Commonwealth Scholar) 1967; m. Janet d. Frank and Kathleen Pottie 27 Aug. 1960; children: Shannon, Bruce, Suellen, Brian; PROF. OF MEDICAL HUMANITIES, DALHOUSIE UNIV. 1992– ; gen. practice N.B. 1963–65; further training in Toronto returning to Dalhousie as Neurol. Cons. and Teacher; became Chief of Med. Camp Hill Hosp. and later Div. Head of Neurol. and Royal Coll. Prog. Dir.; named Prof. of Yr. 1984; Dean of Medicine, Dalhousie Univ. 1985–92; Dir. N.S. Art Gallery, Dalhousie Art Gallery, Tourette Soc., Dalhousie Med. Rsch. Found., Epilepsy Soc., N.S. Heart Found.; mem. Strategic Adv. Bd. Searle Canada; Discovery Centre; St. Francis Xavier Univ.; Dalhousie Bd. of Govs.; co-author 'Essential Neurology' neurol. textbook 4th ed. 1992; over 200 med. publs. and papers; mem. Candn. Neurol. Soc. (Pres.); Am. Acad. Neurol. (Vice Pres.); Am. Coll. Phys. (Gov.& Chrmn. Bd.; Regent); MS Soc. Can. (Chrmn. Med. Adv. Bd.); Founding Pres., Dalhousie History of Medicine Soc.; Assn. of Canadian Medical Colleges (Pres.); Officer, Order of Canada; recipient, 125th Anniversary of the Confederation of Canada Medal, 1992; Cutter Medal; recreations: marathon running, ragtime piano, kayaking, writing & rsch. Samuel Johnson, Chaucer, Lewis Carroll; Home: 16 Bobolink St., Halifax, N.S. B3M 1W3; Office: 5849 University Ave., Halifax, N.S. B3H 4H7.

**MURRAY, Timothy Vincent,** F.R.I.B.A., F.R.A.I.C., F.R.I.A.I., M.C.D.; architect; b. Dublin, Ireland 6 May 1930; s. T.J. and M.T. (Purcell) M.; e. Rockwell Coll., Cashel, Ireland; Univ. Coll., Dublin; Liverpool Univ.; m. Juliet d. Horace and Rachel Taylor 1958; children: Thady Basil, Sean Patrick, Sarah Jane; PARTNER, MURRAY & MURRAY; Archit. & Planner, Lord Holford 1953–55; London County Counc. 1955–57; Fed. Govt. of Can. 1957–58; Prin. & Founding Partner, Murray & Murray Assocs. 1959– ; Former Chrmn., Design Ctte., Nat. Capital Comn. 1985–89; Life Gov., Ashbury Coll. (former Chrmn. 1985–87); Kt. of St. Gregory; Kt. of St. Lazarus of Jerusalem; author var. articles in profl. jours.; Address: 444 Springfield Rd., Ottawa, Ont. K1M 0K4.

**MURRAY, Victor Vereker,** B.A., M.A., Ph.D.; educator; b. Winnipeg, Man. 27 Dec. 1932; s. Victor Vereker and Jean Moore (Kirk) M.; e. Univ. of Manitoba B.A. 1953; Univ. of Minnesota M.A. 1957; Cornell Univ. Ph.D. 1965; m. Shelagh d. Ronald and Leslie Swaine 12 Sept. 1959; children: David, Alison, Tamara; CHRMN. SENATE 1984–85 AND PROF. OF ADMIN. STUDIES, YORK UNIVERSITY 1966– ; Admin. Offr. Dept. of Citizenship & Immigration 1955–56; Personnel Offr. Imperial Oil Ltd. 1957–59; Asst. Prof. Univ. of B.C. 1962–66; Chrmn. Dept. of Sociology present Univ. 1976–79, Assoc. Dean Fac. of Admin. Studies 1979–82; Mem. Bd. of Governors 1992–94; author 'Improving Corporate Donations' 1991; co-author 'Grievance Procedures in Theory and Practice' 1975; 'Personnel Management in Large and Middle-Sized Canadian Businesses' 1978; Ed. 'Theories of Business-Government Relations' 1985; Home: 10 Hartfield Ct., Islington, Ont. M9A 3E3; Office: Downsview, Ont. M3J 2R6.

**MURRAY, Walter Ross,** B.A., LL.B., Q.C.; barrister and solicitor; b. Toronto, Ont. 30 Dec. 1930; s. Chesley Edmund and Mary Rebecca (Stone) M.; e. Humberside Collegiate; Etobicoke Collegiate Institute; Univ. of Toronto B.A. 1955, LL.B. 1958; m. Joan d. Dr. Sydney A. and Lucia (de Castro) Charlat 20 June 1959; children: Laura, Victoria, Adam; PARTNER, BORDEN & ELLIOT 1969; called to Ontario Bar 1959; Assoc. Lawyer, Borden & Elliot 1959–69; Q.C. 1974; heads real property litigation section of firm; lecturer; instructor, Bar

Admission Course; extensive past ctte., conf., panel & symposia work; speaker incl. Law Soc. Special Lectures on Aboriginal Title Litigation 1991; Mem., Candn. Bar Assn.; Advocates Soc.; Champlain Soc.; Am. Bar Assn.; Standing Ctte. on Lawyers Profl. Liability; recreations: skiing, farming; clubs: University Club, Psi Upsilon Alumnae Assn.; Home: 400 St. John St. W., Whitby, Ont.; Office: 40 King St. W., Toronto, Ont. M5H 3Y4.

**MURRAY, Warren James,** Ph.D.; educator; b. St. Paul, Minn. 3 Dec. 1936; s. James Bernard and Louise (Bilodeau-Robertson) M.; e. Wisc. State Univ. B.Sc. (Chem.) 1962; Univ. Laval B.Ph. 1964, Ph.L. 1965, Ph.D. 1966; m. Mary Ann McAulay 18 July 1959; children: Mark, Anne, Kathleen; PROF. OF PHILOS. OF SCIENCE, UNIV. LAVAL 1966– , Vice Dean 1979–81; Analytical Chem., 3M Co. 1957, Research Chem. 1961–63; Invited Prof., Paris 1969, 1972, 1975, 1982; Foreign Exchange Teaching Grantee Prov. Que. 1969; Invited Prof., Univ. of Tucumán, Argentina 1991; author various publs.; mem. Soc. Aristotelian Studies (Pres.); Candn. Soc. Hist. & Philos. of Science; R. Catholic; Home: 716 Carré d'Anjou, Ste-Foy, Qué. G1X 2X7; Office: Cité Universitaire, Qué. G1K 7P4.

**MURRAY-WEBER, Kathleen (Kay) Nichol,** R.C.A.; artist; b. Ayr, Ont. 5 Nov. 1919; d. John and Annie Fulton (Carswell) Murray; e. Ayr Continuation Sch.; Galt Coll. Inst. 1935; Ont. Coll. of Art 1959; Printmaking Monitor 1960–62; Univ. of Calgary summer Lithography workshop 1969; George Brown Coll. Toronto photographic screen workshop 1971–77; m. L. George Weber, D.V.M. 31 Aug. 1946; children: Mark Frederick, Krista Nichol; mem. Bd. of Dirs., Visual Arts Ont. 1973–74; organized silk screen workshop and taught serigraphy Centennial Coll. Scarborough 1968–70; serigraphy workshops Ont. Dept. of Culture & Recreation; Visiting Artist Dept. of Art & Environment Fanshawe Coll. London, Ont. 1973; solo exhns. Merton Gallery Toronto 1977; Gallery Moos Toronto 1980; Print shows, Pascal Gallery, Toronto 1982, 1983; Solo shows, Rosedale United Church 1984, 1990; Dual Exhib., Merton Gallery, Toronto 1971; Thomas Gallery, Winnipeg 1981; Dual Print Exhib., Latcham Gallery, Stouffville 1984; rep. in numerous group exhns. incl. Internat. Graphics Montreal Museum of Fine Arts 1971; Contemporary Candns. Albright-Knox Gallery Buffalo 1971; 9th and 10th Internat. Exhns. Graphic Art Ljubljana, Yugoslavia 1971, 1973; 4th Internat. Print Biennial Cracow, Poland 1972; Survey Contemporary Candn. Prints Pratt Graphic Center N.Y. 1972; The Mall Galleries London, Eng. 6 Candn. Artists with Soc. Wood Engravers & Relief Printers (invitational) 1973; World Print Competition San Francisco Museum 1973; 1st Internat. Biennial Graphic Art & Multiples Segovia, Spain (invitational) 1974; 2nd Vienna Graphic Biennale (invitational) 1975; travel exhn. Ont. 1975–77; exchange Print exhn. Chelsea Sch. Art Eng. and Ont. Coll. Art 1975; 100 Yrs. Evolution Ont. Coll. Art, Art Gallery Ont. 1976; RCA Centennial Contemporary Exhn. 1980; 'Masters of Their Media,' part of 3 person show, Miriam Perlman Inc. Chicago U.S.A. 1985; rep. in pub., corporate and private colls. incl. Albertina Art Museum Vienna; Nat. Gallery Can.; Le Service de la Culture du Conseil Municipal de Cracovie, Poland; Ont. Arts Council; Purchase Awards: Internat. Print Biennial Cracow 1972; Graphex I Brantford, Ont. 1973; Toronto-Dominion Bank 1975, 1978; Crown Life Insurance Co. 1978; Dofasco 1978; recipient Metrop. Award Candn. Soc. Graphic Art Robert McLaughlin Gallery Oshawa 1969; Hon. Mention Art Gallery of Brant Annual Exhn. Brantford 1970; Print & Drawing Council Can. Award 'Imprint '76' Montreal 1976; Juror's Award 9th Burnaby (B.C.) Biennial Print Show 1977; Editions Award Graphex 6 Art Gallery of Brant 1978; O.S.A. Award for Mixed Media 1978; Award of Merit 'Pressure 79' O.S.A. Print Exhn. Toronto 1979; Collectors Choice Award 'Image "79"' St. Catharines, Ont. 1980; elected to Royal Candn. Academy of Arts 1977; mem., Arts and Letters Club, Toronto 1987; Candn. Soc. Graphic Art (Extve. 1964–65, Treas. 1966–67); Candn. Painter-Etchers & Engravers; Print & Drawing Council Can.; O.S.A.; Candn. Artists' Representation; N.D.P.; Protestant; recreation: photography; Address: 11 Linden St., Toronto, Ont. M4Y 1V5.

**MURRELL, David,** B.Soc., M.A., Ph.D.; university professor; b. Pittsburgh, Pa. 29 Dec. 1948; s. Wilbur Reed and the late Carmen Zaragosa M.; e. Univ. of Ottawa B.Soc. (Hons.) 1973, M.A. 1975; Queen's Univ. Ph.D. 1988; ASSOC. PROF., DEPT. OF ECONOMICS, UNIV. OF N.B. 1990– ; Research Econ., Conf. Bd. of Canada 1975–82; Adjunct Lectr. in Econ., Queen's Univ. 1983–85; Asst. Prof., Univ. of N.B. 1985; specialization: regional economics & public finance; SSHRCC Doctoral Scholarship 1983–85; SSHRCC Rsch. grants 1987, '90;

Policy Dir., the Reform Party of Canada, Fredericton-York-Sunbury Constituency Assn., N.B.; Mem., Reform Party of Canada; Conf. of Regions Party N.B.; author: 'A Balanced Overall View? Media Reporting of th Labrador Low-Flying Controversy' 1990; recreations: music; Home: 247 Leeds Dr., Fredericton, N.B. E3B 4S7; Office: P.O. Box 4400, Fredericton, N.B. E3B 5A3.

**MURTA, Jack Burnett;** b. Carman, Man. 13 May 1943; s. John James and Jean (Burnett) M.; e. Graysville elem. and high schs.; Univ. of Man. Agric. 1964; m. Lynda E. d. Dr. Charles E. and Elizabeth Morris 27 May 1977; two d. Meaghan, Shevaughn; one s. Liam; farmer; HON. CANADIAN GRAIN COMMISSIONER; el. to H. of C. for Lisgar (Man.) by-el. 1970, re-el. since; Min. of State (Multiculturalism) 1984–85; Min. of State (Tourism) 1985–86; Conservative; Protestant; Home: 1188 Wellington Cres., Winnipeg, Man. R3N 0A4; Office: Canadian Grain Commission, Winnipeg, Man.

**MURTON, Kenneth Gow,** B.Com.; executive; b. Toronto, Ont. 6 Apr. 1930; s. Kenneth Sidney and Marion Lavinia (Gow) M.; e. Scarborough Coll. Inst., 1948; Univ. of Toronto, B.Com. 1952; m. Marilyn Julia, d. Roy Angus McLeod, Vancouver, B.C., 5 Oct. 1964; children: Dana Laurel, Dr. Andrew Grant, Christy Elizabeth (all from previous marriage), Kenneth John; PRES., CANUC RESOURCES INC.; joined A. E. Ames & Co. Ltd., Toronto, 1952; Rep. of firm in London, Ont., 1954–57; returned to Toronto 1958–61; joined A. E. Ames & Co. Inc. (New York City subsidiary) 1962, becoming Pres., Treas. and Dir. 1965; returned to Toronto 1969–71 as Vice Pres. & Dir., A.E. Ames & Co. Ltd.; Sr. Extve. overseas operations, First Boston Corp. (London & Zurich) 1971–74; Extve. Vice-Pres. and Dir., Basic Resources Internat. New York 1974–78; Chrmn., Petrotech, Inc. 1978–86; Vice-Chrmn., Jones, Gable & Co. Ltd. 1986–89; Pres., The BCB Technology Group Inc.; Adv. Bd. The Skin Cancer Foundation, New York City; rec'd. Centennial Medal; Former Gov. Bd., Midwest Stock Exchange, Chicago.

**MUSGRAVE, Susan;** writer; b. Santa Cruz, Calif. 12 Mar. 1951 of Canadian parents; d. Edward Lindsay and Judith Bradfield (Stevens) M.; Oak Bay H.S., gr. 10; m. Stephen Douglas Reid 1986; two d.: Charlotte Nelson Musgrave (by previous marriage), Sophie Alexandra; first pub. in Malahat Review at age 16; author: (fiction) 'The Charcoal Burners' 1980; 'Hag Head' 1980; 'The Dancing Chicken' 1987; (poetry) 'Songs of the Sea-Witch' 1970; 'Entrance of the Celebrant' 1972; 'Grave-Dirt and Selected Strawberries' 1973; 'Gullband' 1974 (theatre prodn. by Theatre Pass Muraille & Touchstone Theatre); 'The Impstone' 1974; Kiskatinaw Songs' 1977; 'Selected Strawberries and Other Poems' 1977; 'Becky Swan's Book' 1978; 'A Man to Marry, a Man to Bury' 1979; 'Tarts and Muggers' 1982; 'Cocktails at the Mausoleum' 1985; 'The New Canadian Poets 1970–85' 1985; 'The Norton Anthology of Modern Poetry' 2nd ed. 1988; 'Kestrel and Leonardo' (juvenile) 1990; 'Forcing the Narcissus' 1994; (non-fiction) 'Great Musgrave' 1989; 'The Embalmer's Art' 1991; 'Musgrave Landing: Musings on The Writing Life' 1994; and many others; columnist, Toronto Star; Vancouver Sun; numerous pamphlets & broadsides; extensive mag. publ. in Can. & abroad incl. 'Saturday Night,' 'New Orleans Review,' 'Second Aeon,' 'Helix'; presented over 250 poetry readings across Can. & the U.S., incl. radio & TV broadcasts & interviews; Second Prize, Nat. Mag. Award 1981; Third Prize, R.P. Adams Short Fiction Award, Mobile, Alabama 1988; First Prize bp nichol Poetry Chapbook Award 1991; writer-in-Res., Univ of Waterloo 1983–85; Univ. of New Brunswick (summer) 1985; Univ. of Western Ont. 1992–93; archives: McMaster Univ.; Address: P.O. Box 2421, Sidney, B.C. V8L 3Y3.

**MUSSALLEM, Helen K.,** C.C., D.St.J., B.N., M.A., Ed.D., F.R.C.N., LL.D, D.Sc., M.R.S.H.; b. Prince Rupert, B.C.; d. late Annie (Bassette) and Solomon M.; e. Vancouver Gen. Hosp., Sch. of Nursing, Dipl.; Univ. of Washington., Dipl. – Teaching, Supvn. and Adm.; McGill Univ., B.N.; Teachers Coll., Columbia Univ., M.A.; Columbia Univ., Ed.D.; Memorial Univ. D.Sc.(Hon.); Univ. of N.B., LL.D.(Hon.); Queens Univ. LL.D.(Hon.) 1983; McMaster Univ. LL.D.(Hon.) 1989; Univ. of B.C. LL.D.(Hon.); SPEC. ADV., NAT. AND INTERNAT. HEALTH AGENCIES, 1981– ; Pres., Victorian Order of Nurses for Canada 1989–92; mem., Bd. of Dir., Internat. Council of Nurses, 1981–85; Active Service 1943–46, Lieut., R.C.A.M.C., Can. and overseas; Staff Nurse, Head Nurse and Supv., Vancouver Gen Hosp.; Instr., Sr. Instr., Dir. Nursing Educ., Vancouver Gen. Hosp., Sch. of Nursing, 1947–57; Dir., Pilot Project for Evaluation of Schs. of Nursing in Can., Candn. Nurses Assn., 1957–60; Dir. of Special Studies, Candn. Nurses Assn. 1960–63; (Seconded to Roy. Comn. on

Health Svces. for Study of Nursing Educ. in Can., 1962–63); Extve. Dir., Candn. Nurses Assn., 1963–81; Secy.-Treas., Candn. Nurses Found. 1966–81; mem. of and/or adv. to many nat. and internat. organs. incl. World Health Organization; Commonwealth Foundation (London); Commonwealth Nurses Fed.; Roy. Soc. of Health; Candn. Internat. Devel. Agency; Internat. Red Cross Soc.; St. John Ambulance; Victorian Order of Nurses for Can.; Candn. Pub. Health Assn.; CUSO; Candn. Nurses Found.; Human Rights Inst. of Can.; Candn. Fed. of Univ. Women; Candn. Assoc. of History of Nursing in Canada; Centre for Days of Peace; Friends of Rideau Hall; The Lung Assn.; Can. Nurses Respiratory Soc.; major publications: 'Spotlight on Nursing Education' 1960; 'Path to Quality' 1964; 'Trends in Research in Nursing' 1963; 'Social Change and Nursing Education' 1964; 'Nursing Education in Canada' 1965; 'Studies on Nursing in Canada' 1966; 'Nursing Fifty Years Hence in 2020,' 1970; 'Changing Patterns in Nursing Practice,' 1971; 'A Glimse of Nursing in Cuba,' 1973; 'Nurses and Political Action,' 1977; 'Through the Eyes of Continuing Education in Canada, 1980; 'Succeeding Together,' 1983; 'Continuing Education: An Essential to Nursing Strategy and Network in Primary Health Care,' 1983; 'Professional Associations and Political Action' 1985; 'Changing Roles of Professional Organizations' 1986; 'Preventable and non-preventable conditions today; Prospects and research directions in the future' 1988; 'Professional Nurses Associations' ch. 25 in Nursing Faces the Future 1992; over 40 articles in prof. journs.; chaps. in bks. on nursing; Offr. Order of Can. 1969; Companion, Order of Can. 1992; Award for Distinguished Achievement in Nursing Research & Scholarship, Columbia Univ., N.Y. 1966; Centennial Medal 1967; Dame of Grace, Order of St. John of Jerusalem 1983; Hon. mem. Assn. of Reg. Nurses in provinces of P.E.I. 1970, Sask. 1979, Alta. 1980, Man. 1980, N.B., NWTRNA 1982, Ont. 1988; Hon. mem., Indian & Inuit Nurses Assn. of Canada; Candn. Student Nurses Assn. 1992; Jeanne Mance Award of Candn. Nurses Assn.; Award of Merit, Reg. Nurses Assn. of B.C.; Special Citation of Recognition, Candn. Red Cross Soc., 1974; Certificate of Recognition, Ont. Occup. Health Nurses Assoc.; Fellow, Roy. Coll. of Nurses of U.K. 1976; Awarded Internat. Red Cross Florence Nightingale Medal, 1981; National Nursing Library named Helen K. Mussallem Library 1981; Queen's Jubilee Medal 1977; Medal for Distinguished Service, Teacher's College, Columbia Univ., 1979; 125th Anniversary of the Confederation of Canada Medal, 1992; VON Canada Volunteer Award for 30 years service 1993; St. John Ambulance Long Service Award 1993; awarded Commonwealth Foundation Lectureship to West Africa, Malta & Cyprus, 1981; Miembro de Honor, Sociedad Cubana de Enfermeria 1984; Life mem., Candn. Coll. of Health Serv. Extve., 1982; Candn. Nurses Found. Award for Leadership in Candn. Nursing 1991; Mem., Candn. Soc. of Assoc. Extves.; Nursing Officers Assoc. of Canada; Office: Suite 1706, 20 The Driveway, Ottawa, Ont. K2P 1C8.

**MUSTARD, James Fraser,** C.C., M.D., Ph.D., F.R.S.(C.); b. Toronto, Ont. 16 Oct. 1927; s. Alan Alexander and Jean Ann (Oldham) M.; e. Whitney Pub. Sch., Toronto; Univ. of Toronto Schs., Sr. Matric 1946 (Nesbitt Silver Medal); Univ. of Toronto, M.D. (Hons.) 1953; Cambridge Univ. Ph.D. Biology 1956; m. Christine Elizabeth, d. Harry S. Sifton, London, Ont., 4 June 1952; children: Cameron Alexander, Anne Elizabeth, James Sifton, Duncan Mowbray, John Fraser, Christine MacFarlane; PRES., CANDN. INST. FOR ADVANCED RESEARCH, 1982– ; Mem., The Premier's Council on Economic Renewal, Government of Ontario 1991– ; Chrmn., Bd. of Dirs., Ont. Workers' Compensation Inst. 1990– ; Bd. of Dirs., Atomic Energy of Canada Ltd. 1990– ; Mem., Royal Comm. on Matters of Health and Safety Arising from the use of Asbestos in Ont. 1980–83; Chrmn., Task Force on Health Planning for Ont., Min. Health and Govt. Ont. 1973–74; Bd. of Trustees, Aga Khan Univ., Karachi, Pakistan 1985– ; Aga Khan Chancellor's Commission 1992– ; Bd. of Dir., Steel Co. of Canada Inc. 1985– ; Alcoholic Beverage Med. Rsch. Found., Baltimore, MD.; Bd. of Trustees 1988– , Vice-Chrmn. 1992– ; Prof., Dept. of Pathology, McMaster Univ., Hamilton 1966–88, Chrmn. 1966–72; Dean, Faculty of Health Sciences, 1972–80; Vice Pres. Health Sciences, 1980–82; and Professor Emeritus 1988– ; Consultant to Dept. of Physiol. Sciences, Univ. of Guelph, 1957–66; Sr. Research Assoc., Heart and Stroke Foundation of Canada, 1961–63; Research Assoc., Med. Research Council 1963–66; rec'd Medal in Med., Roy. Coll. Phys., Can. 1958; Fellow, Royal College of Physicians of Canada (F.R.C.P.(C)) 1965; James F. Mitchell Award for Heart and Vascular Rsch. 1972; Gairdner Foundation Internat. Award for Med. Research 1967; Fellow, Royal Soc. of Canada

1976; Officer, Order of Canada 1986; Izaak Walton Killam Prize in Health Sciences, Can. Counc. 1987; Robert P. Grant Award, Int. Society on Thrombosis and Haemostasis 1987; Distinguished Service Award, Candn. Soc. for Clinical Investigation 1988; J. Allyn Taylor Internat. Prize in Med. 1988; Intnl. Soc. of Thrombosis & Haemostasis, Distinguished Career Award for Contributions to Haemostasis, 1989; The Candn. Advanced Tech. Assoc. (CATA), Private Sector Leadership Award in Advanced Tech., 1989; Candn. Rsch. Mngmt. Assoc. (CRMA) R&D Mngmt. Award, 1989; Candn. High Tech. Person of the Year Award, 1989; Xerox Canada-Forum Award 1990, Corporate-Higher Education Forum; Mem., Order of Ontario 1992; Royal Bank Award 1993; Companion, Order of Canada 1994; author of over 450 scient. articles; recreation: skiing, farming; Office: Suite #701, 179 John St., Toronto, Ont. M5T 1X4.

**MUTTON, Ross Edward,** B.A.A.; educator; b. Cobourg, Ont. 11 Nov. 1948; s. Clarence John and Martha Amy (Ross) M.; e. E. Northumberland Secondary Sch. 1966; Ryerson Polytech. Inst. Dip. Radio & TV Arts 1969, B.A.A. 1975; m. Gail d. Gerald and Marjorie Harmer 30 May 1987; DIR. INSTRUCTIONAL MEDIA SERVICES, CARLETON UNIV. 1982– ; Audio Visual Tech. Microsystems International Ottawa 1969–70; Prodn. Adv., Media Operations Instructional Aids present Univ. 1971–75, Mgr. 1975–82, Instr. in TV Prodn. Sch. of Continuing Edn. 1972– , Co-ordinator TV Prodn. Course Prog. 1981–93; Columnist – weekly commentary on broadcasting 'Iroquois Post' 1975–81; weekly radio commentator TV broadcasting 1980–86; author various articles; mem. Soc. Motion Picture & TV Engs. (Co-Founder and first Chrmn. Ottawa Sect. 1981–84); Pres., Assn. for Media & Technol. in Education in Canada (AMTEC) 1993–94; Chair AMTEC '91 Conference 1990–91; Awarded AMTEC Leadership Award in Recognition of Outstanding Service in the Field of Educational Media 1991; Active on various cttes. of Bells Corners United Church 1984– ; recreations: photography, philately, skating, gourmet cooking; Home: 43 Florizel Ave., Nepean, Ont. K2H 9R1; Office: 623 Southam Hall, Ottawa, Ont. K1S 5B6.

**MYERS, Barton,** FRAIC, FAIA; architect; b. Norfolk, Virginia 6 Nov. 1934; s. Barton and Meeta (Burrage) M.; e. Norfolk Academy 1952; U.S. Naval Academy B.Sc. 1956; Univ. of Pennsylvania M.Arch. (Hons.) 1964; m. Victoria d. Frank and Suzanne George 7 March 1959; one d.: Suzanne Lewis; PRESIDENT, BARTON MYERS ASSOCIATES INC., LOS ANGELES 1984– ; U.S. Air Force 1956; resigned 1961; Architect, Louis I. Kahn Philadelphia 1964–65; Bower, Fradley 1967–68; Principal, Diamond & Myers Toronto 1968–75; Barton Myers Associates (Toronto) 1975–86; Barton Myers Architect Inc. (Toronto) 1986– ; Sr. Prof., Grad. Sch. of Arch. & Urban Planning, Univ. of Calif.; recipient, Governor General's Medal for Arch. 1986, 1992; Architectural designs include: Seagram Museum (Waterloo, Ont.); Woodsworth College (Toronto); UCLA NW Commons & Housing (Los Angeles); Art Gallery of Ont. (Toronto); Portland Performing Arts Center (Portland, OR); Cernitos Performing Arts Center (Cerritos, CA); New Jersey Performing Arts Center (Newark, NJ); Fellow, Royal Arch. Inst. of Canada; Fellow, Am. Inst. of Archs.; Soc. of Arch. Historians; Urban Design Adv. Ctte. Bd. Mem.; co-author: 'The Car and the City' 1992, 'Vacant Lottery' 1978; contbr.: 'Designing in Car Oriented Cities'; recreations: travelling, reading; Home: 6900 Los Tilos Rd., Los Angeles, Ca. 90068; Offices: 9348 Civic Center Dr., Beverly Hills, CA 90210, USA and 50 Park Rd., Toronto, Ont. M4W 2N5.

**MYERS, Glen George,** B.Sc.; petroleum industry executive; b. Lethbridge, Alta. 29 Aug. 1936; S. Thomas Elden and Margaret Anne M.; e. Univ. of Alta. B.Sc. 1958; m. Janet d. George and Ethel Thompson 27 Dec. 1965; children: Paul, David; VICE-PRESIDENT, REFINING & MARKETING, CANADIAN PETROLEUM PRODUCTS INST. 1991– ; refinery, chemical and gas plant management, planning, design, construction & chem. processing, Shell Canada Ltd. 1958–90; served on var. boards such as Lambton Industrial Soc.; Ont. Petroleum Assn.; Candn. Industry Program for Energy Conservation; Candn. Centre for Occupational Health & Safety; Dir., Prairie Region Oil Spill Containment & Recovery Advisory Corp.; Anglican; Mem., Assn. of Profl. Engineers of Ont.; recreations: golf, nordic skiing; Home: 159 Palisbriar Park S.W., Calgary, Alta. T2V 5H6; Office: Ste. 2860, Bow Valley Square 2, 205 – 5 Ave. S.W., Calgary, Alta. T2P 2V7.

**MYERS, Glenn S.;** computer company executive; b. Scot. 4 Dec. 1945; s. Charles E. and Marion M. (Smith) M.; m. Valerie d. Norman and Lois Glover 7 Aug. 1965; children: Grant, Kyle, Amy; C.E.O. & DIR., US VIDEOTEL, HOUSTON, TX 1990– ; Chrmn. & C.E.O., Encode Internat. 1991– ; Pres. & Dir., Canadian Video Net 1990– ; Pres. & Dir., Willow Associates International 1988– ; Dir., Transfluid Inc. 1991– ; Computer Programmer Control Data Canada 1968–69; Mktg. Operations Micr Systems Ltd. 1969–75; Vice Pres. Mktg. Incoterm Canada 1975–76; Dir. Mktg. TRW Data Systems 1976–79; Pres. Data Point Canada 1980; Vice Pres. and Gen. Mgr. Telecommunications Terminal Systems 1981–83; Vice Pres., Meridian Technologies 1983–88; Pres. and Dir. Cemcorp 1983–86; Dir. Cemcorp International 1984–86; Meridian 1985–86; Pres., C.E.O. & Dir., Education Systems Technology Canada Inc. 1986–88; Pres., C.E.O. & Dir., Amberon Inc. 1988–89; mem. Data Processing Mgt. Assn.; Soc. Applied Learning Technol.; recreations: riding, skiing; Home: Northlands Farm, R.R.5, Cookstown, Ont. L0L 1L0 and 14E Rivercrest, Houston, TX.

**MYERS, John A.,** B.Comm., M.B.A., F.I.C.B.; executive; b. Toronto, Ont. 13 June 1942; s. Benjamin Hubert and Doris Brownridge (Muir) M.; e. McGill Univ., B.Comm. 1965; Univ. of Toronto, M.B.A. 1967; Queen's Univ., F.I.C.B. 1968; m. Dawn d. Edward and Minola Davie 12 Nov. 1966; children: Laurie, David; PRES. & C.O.O., AGF MANAGEMENT LTD., TORONTO 1991– ; joined CIBC 1965; Br. Mngt. 1967–78; Regl. Mgr., Corp. Banking 1978–80; Vice Pres., Corp. Banking 1980–83; Sr. Vice Pres., Special Loans 1983–86; Extve. Vice Pres., 1986–90; Mem., Internat. Naval Rsch. Orgn.; U.S. Naval Inst.; Club; Ontario; Home: 5 Princess of Wales Court, Etobicoke, Ont.; Office: 31st Floor, Toronto Dominion Bank Tower, Toronto, Ont. M5K 1E9.

**MYERS, Martin,** M.A.; author; b. Toronto, Ont. 7 Dec. 1927; s. Max and Esther (Friedman) M.; e. Harbord Coll. Inst. Toronto 1945; Univ. of Toronto B.A. 1951; Johns Hopkins Univ. M.A. 1969; m. Colleen Croll 25 June 1955; children: Lori, Bradley; Partner, Myers & Bruce & Myers & Bruce Inc.; author 'The Assignment' 1971; 'Frigate' 1975; 'Izzy Manheim's Reunion' 1977; Writer-in-Residence and Visiting Assoc. Prof. Scarborough Coll. Univ. of Toronto 1972–74; Lectr. Writers Workshop, York Univ. 1971–73 and New Coll. Univ. Toronto 1974–75; mem. ACTRA; Address: 160 Frederick St., Unit 804, Toronto, Ont. M5A 4H9.

**MYERS, Martin Gregory,** M.D., F.R.C.P.(C); cardiologist; educator; b. Toronto, Ont. 22 March 1945; e. Univ. of Toronto M.D. 1968; children: Carla, Rebecca; CONS. CARDIOL. SUNNYBROOK HEALTH SCIENCE CENTRE 1975– , estbd. Div. Clin. Pharmacol. 1985; Prof. of Med., Univ. of Toronto, Past Coordinator Clin. Pharmacol., estbd. Can.'s first residency training prog. Clin. Pharmacol. 1983; Dir. of Cardiology Rsch., Univ. of Toronto 1990–92; recipient William Goldie Prize Univ. Toronto 1982; Co-founder Candn. Hypertension Soc. 1977, Pres. 1987–88, rec'd Young Investigator Award 1984; author various articles med. jours.; recreations: skiing, sailing; Club: Mimico Cruising Club; Home: 145 Bessborough Dr., Toronto, Ont. M4G 3J7; Office: 2075 Bayview Ave., Toronto, Ont. M4N 3M5.

**MYERS, Michael F.,** M.D., F.R.C.P(C); psychiatrist; b. Chatham, Ont. 31 Jan. 1943; s. Reginald Joseph and Agnes Gertrude M.; e. Chatham Coll. Inst. 1960; Univ. of W. Ont. M.D. 1966; Univ. of S.Cal. Los Angeles 1966–67, 1968–69; Wayne State Univ. Detroit 1967–68; Univ. of B.C. 1969–72; m. R. Joice d. Molinda and Jake Aronson 1 May 1969; children: Briana, Zachary; Clin. Prof. of Psychiatry Univ. Hosp. Shaughnessy Site, Univ. of B.C. 1972–93, Dir. Undergrad. Edn. in Psychiatry at Univ. 1986–87; Dir., Marital Discord Clinic, Dept. of Psychiatry, Univ. Hosp. Shaughnessy Site 1991–93; Dir., Marital Discord Clinic, Dept. of Psychiatry, St. Paul's Hosp. 1993– ; private practice adult psychiatry; recipient Teacher-of-the-Yr. Award Univ. B.C. Psychiatry Residents 1984; Vancouver Med. Assn. Lit. Contest 1990; nominee Vestermark Award (teaching excellence) Am. Psychiatry Assn. 1989, 1991; recipient, Excellence In Teaching Award, Faculty of Medicine, Univ. of B.C. 1991; recipient, Nancy CA Roeske Cert. of Excellence in Medical Student Educ., Am. Psychiatric Assn. 1993; elected to Membership, Am. College of Psychiatrists 1991; author 'Doctors' Marriages: A Look at the Problems and their Solutions' 1988, 2nd ed. 1994; 'Men and Divorce' 1989; 8 book chapters; numerous jour. articles, book reviews; teaching videotapes; Fellow, Am. Psych. Assn.; Fellow, Am. Orthopsych. Assn.; mem. Candn. Psych. Assn.; Jewish Family Services Assn. (Dir. 1989–92); Ctte. on HIV/AIDS of Union of American Hebrew Congregations, Central Conference of American Rabbis; Candn. Med. Assn.; B.C. Med. Assn.; recreations: swimming, skiing, piano, writing; Office: 405 - 2150 W. Broadway, Vancouver, B.C. V6K 4L9.

**MYERS, William;** business executive; CHRMN. OF THE BOARD, SANCELLA INC.; Office: 6 – 2300 Bristol Circle, Oakville, Ont. L6H 5S2.

**MYKLE, Rodney Harold,** B.A., LL.B.; judge; b. Portage la Prairie, Man. 13 Sept. 1945; s. Halvdan Sigurd and Gudrun Amelia (Nordal) M.; e. Brandon Coll., B.A. 1966; Univ. of Man., LL.B. 1969; m. Lori d. Richard and Margaret McBeth; children: Christopher, Jonathan, Jennifer; JUDGE, MANITOBA COURT OF QUEEN'S BENCH (GENERAL DIVISION) 1991– ; admitted to Man. Bar 1970; Partner, Clement, Pearson, Williams & Mykle, Brandon Man. 1971–75; apptd. to Man. Prov. Ct. (Family Div.) 1975; Dep. Judge, N.W.T. 1981–82; Candn. rep., U.N. Conf. on Juvenile Law, London, Eng. 1976; Judge, Man. Prov. Ct. (Criminal Div.) 1976–89; Judge, Man. Court of Queen's Bench (Family Div.) 1989–91; Nat. Ed.-in-Chief, Candn. Prov. Judges Jour. 1978–83; Lectr., Nat. New Judges Ednl. Prog., Ottawa 1981–82, 1988–94; mem. Brandon Univ. Alumni Assoc. (Pres. 1972–74); U.N. Assn. in Can. (Dir. 1979–83); Chrmn., W. Can. Prov. Judges Conf. 1981; United Church; Fellow, Royal Commonwealth Soc.; mem. Candn. Judges Conference; Candn. Bar Assn.; Man. Law Soc.; recreations: skiing, music; Club: Royal Commonwealth (London); Home: R.R. 3, Brandon, Man. R7A 5Z4; Office: 1104 Princess Ave., Brandon, Man. R7A 0P9.

**MYLES, John,** B.A., B.Ph., B.Th., M.A., Ph.D.; educator; b. South Porcupine, Ont. 17 Sept. 1943; s. Clifford J. and Erminia (Paolini) M.; e. Univ. of Ottawa B.A., B.Ph. 1965; Gregorian Univ. B.Th. 1967; Carleton Univ. M.A. 1970; Univ. of Wis. Ph.D. 1977; m. Monica d. George and Valbourg Boyd 6 May 1972; one d. Jennifer; PROF. OF SOCIOLOGY AND DIR., INSTITUTE ON AGING, FLORIDA STATE UNIV. 1992– ; Foreign Service Offr. External Affairs 1971–73; Asst. Prof. Carleton Univ. 1977, Assoc. Prof. 1980, Prof. of Sociol. 1985–92; Visiting Fellow: Dept. of Sociol. and Center for Eur. Studies Harvard Univ. 1980–81; Stats. Can. 1986–88; Mem., Advisory Council on Labour Statistics, Statistics Canada 1991– ; Dir. Gerontol. Rsch. Inst. Nat. Capitol Region; recipient, Distinguished Scholar Award, American Sociological Assn. (ASA) section on the Sociology of Aging; author 'Old Age in the Welfare State: The Political Economy of Public Pensions 1989' 1984; co-author 'Wages and Jobs in the 80's: Changing Youth Wages and the Declining Middle' 1988; (with W. Clement) 'Relations of Ruling: Class and Gender in Postindustrial Societies' 1994; ed. 'Comparative Political Economy' 1988; co-ed. 'States, Labor Markets and the Future of Old Age Policy' 1991; over 40 articles, book chapters; mem. ed. bds. various profl. jours.; Mem., National Academy of Social Insurance (U.S.); Home: 4004 Roscrea Dr., Tallahassee, FL 32308, USA.

**MYSAK, Lawrence Alexander,** A.Mus., B.Sc., M.Sc., A.M., Ph.D., F.R.S.C.; educator; b. Saskatoon, Sask. 22 Jan. 1940; s. Stephen and Anastasia (Trojan) M.; e. Univ. of Alta. A.Mus. 1960, B.Sc. 1961; Univ. of Adelaide, Australia M.Sc. 1963; Harvard Univ. A.M. 1964, Ph.D. 1967; m. Mary d. Joseph and Elsie Eeles 15 Aug. 1974; children: Paul Alexander, Claire Anastasia; AES/NSERC PROF. OF CLIMATE RSCH. McGILL UNIV. 1986– , Dir. Climate Rsch. Group 1986–89, Can. Steamships Line Prof. of Meteorol. 1989– , Founding Dir. Centre for Climate & Global Change Rsch. 1990– ; Rsch. Assoc. Harvard Univ. 1966–67; Asst. Prof. of Math. Univ. of B.C. 1967, Assoc. Prof. of Math. & Oceanog. 1970, Prof. 1976–86; Convenor Interdisciplinary Sect. Acad. Sci. Royal Soc. Can. 1988–90; mem. Bd. Candn. Global Change Prog. 1989– ; Vice-Pres., Academy of Science, Royal Society of Canada 1991–93, Pres., 1993– ; Rotary Found. Fellow Internat. Understanding 1962; Sr. Visitor Cambridge Univ. 1971–72; Visiting Sci. Nat. Center Atmospheric Rsch. Boulder, Colo. 1977; Visiting Prof. Naval Postgrad. Sch. Monterey, Cal. 1981; Swiss Fed. Inst. Technol. Zurich 1982–83; guest lectr. over 300 seminars sci. confs., univs., labs. and pub. meetings; served 3 Grant Selection Cttes. NSERC 1981–89; co-author 'Waves in the Ocean' textbook 1978; over 150 jour. articles, book chapters, atlases, phys. oceanog., climate, meteorol. & fisheries; assoc. ed. Climatological Bulletin; Geophys. & Astrophys. Fluid Dynamics; Fellow, Royal Society of Canada 1986; mem. Candn. Meteorol. & Oceanographic Soc. (Pres.'s Prize 1980); Am. Meteorol. Soc.; Am. Geophys. Union; Am. Oceanographic Soc.; recreations: squash, tennis, hiking, cross-country skiing, reading, theatre, music, gourmet dining; Home: 119 Strathearn Ave. N., Montreal West, Que. H4X 1X8; Office: Dept. of Atmospheric and Oceanic Sciences, 805 Sherbrooke St. W., Montreal, Que. H3A 2K6.

# N

**NACHMAN, Gabriel,** B.A., C.A.; chartered accountant; b. Bucharest, Romania 27 Feb. 1948; s. Hascal and Betty (Frankl) N.; e. Bathurst Hts. Secondary Sch. 1967; Univ. of Toronto New Coll. B.A. 1970; C.A. 1973; m. Rochelle d. Joe and Jenny Pifko 21 June 1970; children: Barbara Kelly, Eric Wesley; PARTNER-IN-CHARGE COOPERS & LYBRAND, North York 1988– ; Partner present firm 1979, Chrmn., Retail & Distribution Ind. Services Group 1986; Pres., B'nai Brith Can. 1992– ; Chrmn., B'nai Brith Found. 1989–92; Bd. of Dirs., B'nai Brith Found., B'nai Brith Canada, B'nai Brith Internat., Canada-Israel Ctte.; recipient, Commemorative Medal for 125th Anniversary of Candn. Confederation; mem. Inst. C.A.'s; Jewish; recreation: golf; Club: Aurora Highlands Golf; Home: 45 Lunau Lane, Thornhill, Ont. L3T 5N1; Office: 5160 Yonge St., North York, Ont. M2N 6L3.

**NADAL, Miles Spencer;** communications executive; b. Toronto, Ont. 28 Feb. 1958; s. Irwin Allan and Renee (Silverman) N.; e. Forest Hill Coll. Inst. (Ont. Scholar) 1977; Univ. of Toronto 1977–78; Univ. of W. Ont. 1978–79; York Univ. 1979–81; m. Joanne d. Lloyd and Gladys Fogler 7 March 1987; children: Sarah Jennifer, Samantha Faith; FOUNDER, CHRMN., PRES. AND CHIEF EXTVE. OFFR. MDC CORPORATION 1980– ; Dir. affiliated co's; Gov. Mount Sinai Hsop.; Dir. Candn. Weizmann Inst. Sci; Jr. Achievement Can.; mem. Young Pres. Orgn.; recreations: yachting, tennis, golf, reading; Clubs: Founders National; Island Yacht; Oakdale Golf & Country; York Racquet; Home: 82 Kilbarry Rd., Toronto, Ont. M5P 1K7.

**NADASDI, Miklos,** M.D., Ph.D.; physician; b. Budapest, Hungary 29 Jan. 1932; s. William and Kornelia (Werner) N.; e. Budapest M.D. 1956; Montreal Ph.D. 1961; m. Ria d. Michael and Julia Simon 27 July 1964; children: Heidi, Tom; VICE-PRES., MEDICAL, WYETH-AYERST CANADA 1989– ; worked in medical research with Dr. Hans Selye 1957–60; trained in clin. pharm., Univ. of Toronto 1966–67; Med. Dir. & Vice-Pres., Glaxo Can. 1964–87; active staff mem., North York Gen. Hosp. 1967– ; Consultant, Hazleton Labs. 1988; Research Fellow, N.Y. City Rsch. Council 1960–61; acted as panelist on several health-related TV programs in Toronto; Mem., Coll. of Physicians & Surg. of Ont.; Candn. Med. Assn.; Candn. Clin. Pharm. Soc.; Candn. Hypertension Soc.; Am. Soc. of Clin. Pharm.; Pharm. Mfg. Assn. of Can. Med. Section (ex-council mem.); author:'All about the Pill' 1969 and 30 sci. pubns and one book chapter; recreations: swimming, graphic arts, literature, travel; Home: 407 Lawrence Ave. W., Toronto, Ont. M5M 1C1; Hosp. Address: 6227 Bathurst St., North York, Ont. M2R 2A5; Office: 110 Sheppard Ave. E., North York, Ont. M2N 6R5.

**NADEAU, Allan J.,** B.Sc., M.A.; business executive; b. Portland, Maine 22 Mar. 1935; e. Kennebunk H.S. 1954; Univ. of Maine, B.Sc. 1958, M.A. 1959; Univ. of Chicago, Cert. of Bus. Admin. 1962; m. Judith Bennis 9 Feb. 1963; children: Charles Scott, Remy Lyn; PRES. & CHIEF OP. OFFR., ROLLAND INC. 1989–90; Project Engr., Beloit Iron Works 1959–67; Asst. Sup., Internat. Paper Co. 1967–68; Sales Engr., Mt. Hope Machinery 1968–69; V.P., Mfg., Penntech Papers 1969–75; Co-ord. of Mfg., N.E. Div., Georgia-Pacific Corp. 1975–78; Dir., Tissue Mfg. 1978–81; Pres. & Chief Op. Offr., G-P Inveresk Corp. (U.K.) 1981–84; Vice-Pres., Northern Pulp & Paper Div., Georgia-Pacific Corp. 1984–87; Southern Pulp & Paper Div. 1987–88; Mem., TAPPI; Univ. of Maine Pulp & Paper Found.; Candn. Pulp & Paper Assn.; recreations: golf, woodworking, collecting antiques; club: Webnannet Country; Home: 1227 Sherbrooke W., Apt. 112, Montreal, Que. H3G 1G1; Office: Ship Locke Pointe, Ship Locks Dr., Kennebunk, Maine 04043.

**NADEAU, Bertin F.,** B.A., L.Sc.Com., D.B.A.; business executive; b. N.B. 26 May 1940; s. Docithe and Irène (Daigle) N.; e. Coll. St-Louis, Edmunston, N.B. B.A. 1961; École des Hautes Études Commerciales de Montréal L.Sc.Com. 1964; Harvard Univ. Grad. Sch. of Business; Ind. Univ. Grad. Sch. of Bus. D.B.A. 1969; Queen's Univ. (Hon.) LL.D. 1987; Moncton Univ. (Hon.) D.F.Sc. 1989; Ste-Anne Univ. (Hon.) D.B.A. 1990; Bishop's Univ. Honorary D.C.L.; m. Juliette Angell 24 July 1971; children: Eric, Shahn, Stéphanie; CHRMN. & C.E.O., UNIGESCO INC. 1982– ; Dir. DMR Group Inc.; Lafarge Corp.; National Bank of Canada; Sun Life Assurance Co. of Canada; Prof. École des Hautes Études Commerciales de Montréal 1969–76; Pres. La Société Nadeau Ltée 1976–81; co-author 'Le Management - Textes et Cas' 1973; Office: 1250 René-Lévesque Blvd., Suite 4200, Montréal, Qué. H3B 5A6.

**NADEAU, Laurent A.;** executive; b. St-Evariste, Que. 8 Feb. 1934; s. Honorius and Anna (Plante) N.; e. McGill Univ., Comm.; C.M.A.; two d. Julie, Brigitte; PRES., CITec 1990– ; Dir., Zavitz Technology Inc., Montreal; Mgr. Gen. Acctg. Pratt & Whitney of Canada 1954–64; Controller, Central Dynamics Ltd. 1964–67, Vice Pres. Finance 1967–78; Pres. and C.E.O., Comterm Inc. 1978–84, Chrmn. 1984–85; Pres. & C.E.O., Xicom Technologies, Ottawa 1986–89; Dir., Canadian Advanced Technology Assn., Ottawa; Dir., Centre Canadien de recherche sur l'informatisation du travail, Laval, Quebec; recreation: golf; Club: Summerlea Golf, Dorion; Home: Tropiques Nord, 2500 Pierre Dupuy, Apt. 505, Montreal, Que. H3C 4L1.

**NADEAU, Leopold Maurice,** B.A.Sc., D.Eng. (Hon.), P.Eng., F.C.A.E., F.E.I.C.; consulting engineer; b. Montreal, Que., 29 Nov. 1913; s. Joseph-Alphonse and Marie-Louise (Lavoie) N.; e. Querbes Acad., Outremont, Que., 1919–28; St. Louis High Sch., Montreal, Que., 1929–30; Ecole Polytechnique of Montreal, B.A.Sc. 1936 (Civil Engn.); m. Huguette, d. late Joseph Emery Lavigne, 3 Dec. 1942; children: Jacques, Pierre, Louise, Gilles, Marie; began career as Asst. Plant Engr. at Port Alfred mill of Consolidated Paper Corp., then as Resident Engineer, Que. Dept. of Highways, subsequently joining Tech. Staff of Candn. Underwriters' Assn. as Fire Protection Engr.; joined staff of Corp. of Prof. Engrs. of Quebec in 1946 as Asst. Gen. Secy. and became Gen. Secy. in 1949; in 1954, joined Racey MacCallum and Associates Ltd., Consulting Engrs., where he held the position of Dir. and Extve. Engr. in charge of Montreal Div.; Gen. Mgr., Cdn. Council of Professional Engineers 1959–79 and 1984; Gen. Co-ord., Cdn. Engineering Centennial Celebrations 1987; Vice-Pres., World Fed. of Engn. Organizations 1974–79; Dir. for Can., Pan Am. Union for Engn. Societies; Fellow, Engn. Inst. Can.; Fellow, Extve. Dir., Secy. & Treas., Candn. Acad. of Engn.; Order Engrs. Qué.; Ass'n Prof. Ont. Engrs.; Cercle Universitaire, Ottawa; Roman Catholic; recreations: fishing, golf, Home: 25 Acadie St., Aylmer, Que. J9J 1H7; Office: 25 Acadie St., Aylmer, Que. J9J 1H7.

**NADEAU, Michel,** M.B.A.; executive; b. Québec City, Qué. 8 Nov. 1946; s. Louis-André and Lucie (Goupil) N.; e. Coll. de Victoriaville B.A. 1967; Univ. Laval bacc. pol. sci. 1970, M.B.A. 1972; m. Geneviève Gallouet 1978; children: Maëlle, Philippe; SR. VICE PRES., INVEST. PLANNING AND STRATEGIC AFFAIRS, CAISSE DE DEPOT ET PLACEMENT DU QUÉBEC 1984– ; Dir., Mutuelle S.S.Q.; Gen. Sec. Candn. C. of C. France 1972; Financial Ed. Le Devoir 1974–84; recipient Southam Fellowship 1977; ed. 'L'Industrie des Métiers d'Art au Québec' 1971; mem. Pension Investment Assn. of Canada; Trustee, City of Montréal Pension Fund, Université Laval Pension Fund; recreations: travel, tennis; Home: 242 Av. McDougall, Outremont, Qué. H2V 3P2; Office: 1981 Av. McGill College, Montréal, Qué. H3A 3C7.

**NADON, Jean-Claude,** B.A.; public servant; b. Montreal, Que. 30 Jan. 1935; s. Oscar and Germaine (Miron) N.; m. Anita d. Oscar Sauvageau 8 Nov. 1958; children: Dominique, Marie-Claude; DEPUTY COMMISSIONER OF OFFICIAL LANGUAGES, GOVERNMENT OF CANADA 1992– ; Dir. of Personnel, Secretary of State 1972–76; Sr. Financial Officer, Treasury Board 1976–79; Dir. of Operations 1979–86; Dir. General, Complaints & Audits, Office of the Comnr. of Official Languages 1986–92; Teaching Certificate (Que.) 1966; Pres., Collège St-Alexandre; Sec. Gen., Public Management Assn.; recreations: oil painting, travelling, music; Home: 1952 Marquis St., Ottawa, Ont. K1J 8J4; Office: 110 O'Connor St., Ottawa, Ont. K1A 0T8.

**NAHIRNY, Michael,** B.Comm., C.A.; financial executive; b. Bolton, England 26 June 1948; s. Walter (dec.) and Maria (Iwancio) N.; e. Thomas D'Archy McGee H.S. 1965; Loyola College (Concordia) B.Comm. 1969; McGill Univ. C.A. 1971; m. Mary Elizabeth d. Sarah (McLeod) and Alphonsus Ryan (dec'd.) 26 June 1976; one s.: Stephen Joseph; SR. VICE-PRES. & CHIEF FINANCIAL OFFR., CARA OPERATIONS LIMITED 1990– ; Auditor, Peat Marwick Mitchell & Co. 1969–74; Internal Auditor, RJR MacDonald Inc. 1974–76; Mfg. Controller 1976–80; Corp. Comptroller, Foodcorp Limited (CARA subs.) 1980–83; Vice-Pres., Finance 1983–84; Treas., CARA Operations Limited 1984–85; Vice-Pres. Finance & Admin. 1985–90; Dir. CARA Operations Limited; Grand and Toy Limited; Beaver Foods Limited; Summit Food Distributors Inc.; Mem., Financial Executives Inst.; Ont. & Que. Insts. of C.A.s; Roman Catholic, St. Leonard's Brampton 1987– ; recreations: landscaping, nordic skiing, swimming, walking, carpentry; Home: 44 Inder Heights Drive, Brampton, Ont. L6Z 3N4; Office: 230 Bloor St. W., Toronto, Ont. M5S 1T8.

**NAIMARK, Arnold,** O.C., M.D., B.Sc.Med., M.Sc., F.R.C.P.(C), F.R.S.C., LL.D.; educator; b. Winnipeg, Man. 24 Aug. 1933; s. Harvey and Lisa N.; e. St. John's High Sch. Winnipeg; Univ. of Man. M.D. 1957, B.Sc.Med. 1957, M.Sc. 1959; m. Barbara Jean d. Ellis David Alder, Q.C. 28 Feb. 1960; children: David, Mila; PRESIDENT AND VICE CHANCELLOR, UNIV. OF MAN. 1981– , mem. Bd. Govs.; Asst. Prof. of Physiol. present Univ. 1963, Assoc. Prof. 1965, Acting Head 1966–67, Prof. and Head 1967–71, Dean of Med. 1971–81; Vice-Pres. (Canada) Inter-American Organization for Higher Education 1994– ; mem., Candn. Council Animal Care; Cons. Nat. Inst. of Health U.S.; Adv. Council Nat. Cancer Inst.; mem., Biol. Council Can.; Chrmn., A.C.M.C. Standing Ctte. on Rsch.; Past Pres., Council W. Candn. Univ. Pres.; mem., Rsch. Council Inst. for Adv. Rsch.; Dir., Candn. Assocs. Ben-Gurion Univ. of Negev; St. Boniface Gen. Hosp.; Inst. Cell Biol.; Man. Health Rsch. Council; Chrmn. North Portage Develop. Corp.; Past Chrmn., Assn. of Commonwealth Universities; Dir., Corporate-Higher Education Forum; Bd. of Dirs., Inspiraplex; Patron of the Friends of the Child Protection Centre; Nat. Hon. Bd. of Dirs, Juvenile Diabetes Found. Internat., Can.; Bd. of Dirs., Candn. Imperial Bank of Commerce 1987– ; North American Life Assurance Co.; Bd. of Trustees, National Inst. of Nutrition; author or co-author over 60 sci. books and papers physiol. and med.; mem. various ed. bds.; Isbister Scholar 1950–56; Medal in Physiol. 1954–55; Stefansson Meml. Prize 1957; Prowse Prize in Clin. Rsch. 1959; Queen's Silver Jubilee Medal 1977; Ben Gurion Univ., Distinguished Service Medal 1981; Doctor of Laws (hon. causa), Mt. Allison Univ. 1986; Fellow, Royal Soc. of Can. 1987; Am. Assn. Adv. Sci.; Hon. mem. Candn. Soc. Orthopaedic Rsch.; Past Pres., Assn. Univs. & Colls. Can.; Mem.: Candn. Med. Assn.; Candn. Physiol. Soc.; Am. Physiol. Soc.; Can. Soc. Clin. Investigation; Med. Rsch. Soc. Gt. Brit.; Assn. Chrmn. Depts. Physiol.; Candn. Tuberculosis & Respiratory Disease Assn.; recreations: tennis, other racquet sports; Home: 37 King's Dr., Winnipeg, Man. R3T 3E6; Office: Winnipeg, Man. R3T 2N2.

**NAIRN, John Graham,** B.Sc.Phm., Ph.D.; scientist; educator; b. Toronto, Ont. 23 Aug. 1928; s. Lawrence Graham and Aileen Euphemia (McAlpine) N.; e. Humewood Pub. Sch. and Vaughan Rd. Coll. Inst., Toronto, 1946; Ont. Coll. of Pharm., Univ. of Toronto, B.Sc.Phm. 1952; Univ. of Buffalo, Ph.D. 1959; m. Mary Kathleen F., d. late Robert Pollock, 2 Aug. 1954; children: Dawn Kathleen, David Graham, Diane Aileen, Debra Margaret; PROF. OF PHARMACY, UNIV. OF TORONTO since 1973; joined present Univ. as Asst. Prof. 1958, Assoc. Prof. 1965–72; author various research and prof. publs.; mem., Pharm. Examining Bd. of Can.; Assn. Faculties Pharm. Can.; Ont. Coll. Pharm.; Royal Candn. Geog. Soc.; Univ. of Toronto Faculty Association; United Church; recreations: camping, canoeing, skiing; Office: Faculty of Pharmacy, Univ. of Toronto, Toronto, Ont. M5S 1A1.

**NAIRNE, Michael Edwards,** B.Comm., C.M.C., C.F.P., R.F.P.; financial services executive; b. Winnipeg, Man. 25 Oct. 1952; s. Harvey Cameron and June Elizabeth (Wilcock) N.; e. Silver Heights C.I. 1969; Univ. of Man. B.Comm (Hons., Gold Medallist) 1973; Inst. of Mngt. Cons. of Ont. C.M.C. 1980; Chartered Finan. Planner, Candn. Inst. of Finan. Planning 1985 (first in Can., CFP prog., Fall 1985 grad. class); m. Joanne E. d. John and Anne Swystun 1979; children: James Richard, Anastasia Michelle, Alexander Daniel; Pres., The Equion Group 1986; Brand Asst., Procter & Gamble 1973–74; Mngt. Cons., Laventhol & Horwath 1974–76; Partner, Nairne, Nicholson & Assoc. 1976–77; Mgr., Laventhol & Horwath 1978–81; Vice-Pres., The Equion Group 1981–86; Dir., 2100 Bloor St. W. Limited Partnership; Jarvis Mutual Limited Partnership; Centre St. Limited Partnership; Ont. Chap., Candn. Assn. of Finan. Planners; Mem., Internat. Assn. of Finan. Planning Inc.; author of numerous articles; recreations: swimming, reading, karate; Home: 21 Edenbrook Hill, Etobicoke, Ont. M9A 3Z7.

**NAKAGAWA, Patrick T.,** B.Comm.; business executive; b. Osaka, Japan; e. Loyola of Montreal (Concordia) B.Comm. 1974; m. Agnes 19 Sept. 1959; children:

Carol, Michael, Mark; Managing Partner, Enterprise Capital Partnership, Royal Trustco Limited & Vice-Pres., Royal Trustco Limited 1988; Chief Accountant, Nat. Drug & Chem. Co. of Canada Ltd. 1965; Mgr. of Acctg., Smith Kline & French 1969; Dir., Corp. Planning, Abbott Labs. 1974; Dir., Planning, Acquisitions, Northern Telecom 1977; Dir., Acquisitions, Domtar Inc. 1979; Vice-Pres., Corp. Dev., Harlequin Enterprises Limited 1980; Vice-Pres., Brinco Limited 1981; Vice-Pres. & Dir., Firan Corp. and Pres. of subsidiary, Graphico Electronics Inc. 1988; Dir., Great Lakes Investments Inc.; Votek Systems Limited; Assayers Corp. Inc.; Mem., Planning Extves. Inst.; Home: 2083 Shawanaga Trail, Mississauga, Ont. L5H 3Z3.

**NAKAHIRA, Noboru;** diplomat; b. Kochi, Japan 11 Jan. 1930; s. Kuniaki and Toyoki (Fujita) N.; e. grad. from Tokyo Univ. Fac. of Law 1952; studied at Univ. of Oregon; m. Sumiko d. Shigehiro and Hideko Mori 21 May 1960; children: Shigeru, Kaoru; AMBASSADOR TO CANADA FROM JAPAN 1993– ; served in various capacities (Japan and abroad), Ministry of Foreign Affairs Japan 1953–78; Dir., General Affairs Div., Minister's Secretariat 1979; Dep. Dir. General, General Affairs, Minister's Secretariat 1980; Ambassador to the United Arab Emirates 1980; Extve. Dir., Japan Internat. Co-op. Agency 1983; Dir. Gen., U.N. Bureau 1985; Ambassador to Malaysia 1987; Ambassador (Rep.) to Japan-North Korea Normalization Talks 1991; recreations: golf; clubs: Rideau, Royal Ottawa Golf; Office: 255 Sussex Dr., Ottawa, Ont. K1N 9E6.

**NAKAJIMA, Takashi,** M.Arch., Ph.D., P.Eng.; b. Japan 10 July 1941; s. Tatsuo and Yachi (Ina) N.; e. Waseda Univ. Tokyo B.Arch. 1965, M.Arch. 1968; Univ. of Ill. Ph.D. (Civil Engn.) 1972; m. Renee d. Roger and Therese Tremblay 8 Dec. 1974; children: Mariko, Claude; DEAN OF THE FACULTY OF ARCHITECTURE, LAVAL UNIV.; Prof. of Architecture 1982– ; Arch., Taisei Construction Co. Ltd. Tokyo 1965; Lectr., Univ. of Ill. 1969; Asst. Prof., Laval Univ. 1971, Assoc. Prof. 1976; Dir., Sch. of Arch. 1981–84; Arch., Seibu Real Estate Co. Ltd. Tokyo 1977; Fellow IBM Japan, Tokyo Scient. Center 1977; recipient Arch. Inst. Japan 1st Prize; Fulbright-Hay Grant; author 'Modeling and Optimization of the Building Process for Systems Building' 1982; co-author 'Simulation of Human Behaviour in Architectural Space' 1979; mem., Royal Inst. Candn. Archs.; Order Que. Engrs.; Arch. Inst. Japan; recreations: skiing, flute; Home: 1299 Belleterre, Ste-Foy, Que. G1W 3M8; Office: Un Cote de la Fabrique, Laval Univ., Quebec City, Que. G1K 7P4.

**NAKAMOTO, Ian K.,** B.Sc., B.Comm., M.B.A., C.F.A.; investment manager; b. Toronto, Ont. 28 May 1955; s. Jim S. and Massie (Ito) N.; e. Univ. of Toronto B.Sc. 1977; Univ. of Windsor B.Com. 1978; McMaster Univ. M.B.A. 1980; C.F.A. 1983; m. Terry Au-Yeung 16 Sept. 1989; VICE PRES. CANDN. EQUITIES, CANADA LIFE INVESTMENT MANAGEMENT LTD. 1982– ; joined A.G.F. Management 1980–82; Lectr. C.F.A. Analyst Study Prog.; mem. Toronto Soc. Financial Analysts; recreations: tennis, golf, swimming, skiing; Office: 804, 130 Adelaide St. W., Toronto, Ont. M5H 3P5.

**NAKAMURA, Kazuo;** artist; b. Vancouver, B.C. 13 Oct. 1926; s. Toichi and Yoshiyo (Uyemoto) N.; e. Central Tech. Sch., Toronto, Ont. (Grad. 1951); m. Lillian Y. Kobayakawa, 1967; children: Elaine Y., Bryan K.; rep. in following public collections: Nat. Gallery Can.; Museum Modern Art, N.Y.; Art Gallery of Ontario; Hirshhorn Museum, Washington, D.C.; British Museum; Musee D'art Contemporain, Montreal; Hart House, Univ. of Toronto; Univ. of W. Ont.; R. McLaughlin Gallery, Oshawa; Hamilton Art Gallery; Lugano Coll., Switzerland; Hallmark Collection, U.S.A.; Dept. of External Affairs, Can.; Winnipeg Art Gallery; has exhibited in Group Shows since 1952 in Canada and abroad, and in Candn. Paintings, Polish Tour 1962; Candn. Biennials, Nat. Gallery Can.; Contemp. Candn. Paintings, London, Eng. (1963), World Show, N.Y. (1964), Canada '68 Exhbn., Toronto 1968; Painters Eleven in Retrospect, 1979–81; Ontario Heritage Foundation's Firestone Collection, European Tour 1983–85; 20th Century Canadian Paintings, Florida U.S.A. 1984; Opening Exhbn., (New) National Gall. of Can. 1988; The 1950s, National Gallery of Canada and Candn. Tour 1992–94; Home: 3 Langmuir Cres., Toronto, Ont. M6S 2A6.

**NAKATSU, Grace Fukuyo;** theatre technician; b. Toronto, Ont. 19 Dec. 1958; d. Kichinosuke and Tsuruyo (Hamade) N.; e. Humberside Coll. Inst.; Ryerson Polytech. Inst.; theatre tech. numerous prodns. Stratford Festival, Nat. Ballet of Can., Candn. Stage/Centre Stage during 1980's; Theatre Plus 1980, 1990; Candn. Opera Co., Phantom of the Opera, Tarragon Theatre and others; part-time teacher George Brown Coll.; mem. Staff Banff Centre for Continuing Edn. 1986, 1987 seasons; recipient Pauline M. McGibbon Award 1989; Address: 20 Brockton Ave., Unit 9, Toronto, Ont. M6K 1S5.

**NAKHLEH, Faraj M.,** B.Sc.; business executive; b. Haifa, Palestine 9 June 1945; s. Mueen Faraj and Salma Gabriel; e. Robert Coll. Istanbul, Turkey, B.Sc. 1968; McGill Univ. course requirements M.Eng.; Harvard Bus. Sch. Dip. Strategic Mktg. Mgmt. 1986; m. Carolle d. Denis and Nina Charlebois 28 Aug. 1982; children: Karen Nyssa, Marc Charles, Paul Eric; CHRMN., PRES. & C.E.O. NAKHLEH HOLDINGS INC. and NAKHLEH & ASSOCIÉS 1991– ; Dir., Nakhleh Holdings Inc.; Nakhleh & Associés; AVL Vision Inc.; Alex Recherche Inc.; Extve. Dir., Candn. Advanced Technology Assn. (CATA); Pres., Conseil de L'Industrie Électronique du Québec (CIEQ); Adviser, Innocentre Québec; NRC Teaching Fellow McGill Univ. 1969–70; Systems Eng. IBM Canada, 1970–72; mem. Sci. Staff Bell Northern Research 1973; Mktg. Sales & Sales Mgmt. Xerox Canada Inc. 1973–79; Mktg. Mgr. becoming Br. Mgr. AES Data 1979; Dir. Internat. Sales Comterm Inc. 1983, Vice Pres. Internat. Sales 1984, Vice Pres. Mktg. & Internat. Sales 1985; Pres. of Operations, Mux Lab Inc. 1987; Pres. and Dir., Comterm Inc. 1987–89; Pres., Dir., & C.E.O., Coreco Inc. 1989–91; mem. Order Engs. Qué., Assn. of Candn. Venture Capital Companies (ACVCC), Réseau Capital; recreations: tennis, badminton, flying, skiing; Club: Montreal Badminton & Squash; Office: 217 Northcliff, Beaconsfield, Qué. H9W 6C3.

**NAKONECHNY, Victor Peter,** B.Sc., B.Ed., b. Boyle, Alta. 28 Aug. 1932; s. late Steve and Sally (Ryl) N.; e. Univ. of Alta. B.Ed. 1957, B.Sc. 1963; m. Geraldine Marie, d. late N. A. Melnyk 3 June 1960; two s. Lorne, Gregory; PRES. & OWNER, TRINAX MARKETING LTD. 1988– ; Edmonton Savings Bd., 1967–83; Pres. Bd. of Dirs. Edmonton Savings & Credit Union 1972–80, Vice Pres. 1969–72; Princ. Hardisty Sch. 1974–81, Asst. Princ. 1967–69; Princ., Londonderry School, 1981–88; Pres. NST Enterprises Ltd. since 1975; Teacher Highlands Sch. 1959–64; Asst. Princ. Westglen Sch. 1964–67; Princ. Rosslyn Sch. 1969–74; Pres. Nigon Investments Ltd. 1971–72, Dir. 1970–75; mem. Extended Practicum Comte. Univ. of Alta.; Vice Pres. Northmount Community League 1977–82; served in various adm. positions teaching field since 1960; Pres., Order of St. Andrew 1985–87 (Vice-Pres. 1981–85); Pres., Sr. Citizens Home of St. John, 1985–88 (Treas. 1981–85); Pres., St. John's Cathedral Ch. Bd., 1982–85; Vice Pres. St. John's Cath. Ch. Bd. 1967–72 (Chrmn. Finance 1968–72); Chrmn. Bldg. Ctte., St John's Cath. 1984– ; Pres., Edmonton Glengarry Liberal Assn. 1988– ; mem. Alta. Teachers Assn. (held various extve. positions); Edmonton Pub. Sch. Adm. Assn.; Phi Delta Kappa; Ukrainian Orthodox; Home: 9528 – 142 Ave., Edmonton, Alta. T5E 6A5.

**NALDRETT, Anthony James,** Ph.D., F.R.S.C., F.G.S.A., F.M.S.A.; educator; b. Hampstead, Eng. 23 June 1933; s. Anthony George and Violet Ethel (Latham) N.; e. St. George's Coll. Weybridge; St. Paul's Sch. London; Trinity Hall Cambridge Univ. B.A. 1956, M.A. 1962; Queen's Univ. M.Sc. 1961, Ph.D. 1964; m. Sylvia d. Gordon and Jean Clark 23 Apl. 1960; three d. Anne, Jennifer, Penelope; divorced 1991; m. Galina d. Stanislav and Rimma Miasnikova 6 July 1991; UNIVERSITY PROFESSOR, GEOL., UNIV. OF TORONTO 1984– ; Mine Geol. Falconbridge Nickel 1957–59, Exploration Geol. 1959–63 (summers); Postdoctoral Fellow Geophys. Lab. Carnegie Inst. of Washington 1964–67; Asst. Prof. present Univ. 1967, Assoc. Prof. 1968, Prof. 1972; Sr. Prin. Rsch. Offr. CSIRO Perth, W. Australia 1972–73; Visiting Prof. and Sr. Rsch. Fellow Bushveld Rsch. Inst. Univ. of Pretoria 1979–80; Chercheur Associé, CNRS, Orleans, France 1986–87; Stagiere, BRGM, Orleans, France 1993–94; served with RAF 1951–53, Pilot Offr.; recipient Barlow Gold Medal Candn. Inst. Mining & Metall. 1974; Duncan Derry Medal Geol. Assn. Can. 1980; Soc. Econ. Geols. Medal 1982; Bownocker Gold Medal, Univ. of Ohio 1986; Mineralogical Assn. Canada Past Pres. Medal 1991; Geological Assn. Canada Logan Medal 1994; ed. 'Journal of Petrology' 1974–82; Hon. Foreign Fellow, European Union Geosci's.; Fellow, Geol. Assn. Can.; mem. Mineral Assn. Can. (Pres. 1982–83); Soc. Econ. Geols. (Vice Pres. 1982–83, Pres. 1991–92); recreations: sailing, skiing, carpentry; Home: 1210 - 33 Harbour Square, Toronto, Ont. M5J 2G2; Office: Toronto, Ont. M5S 1A1.

**NANJI, Amin Akbarali,** M.D., F.R.C.P.(C); physician/university professor; b. Mombasa, Kenya 21 Feb. 1954; s. Akbarali Nanji and Gulbanu (Velji) Ebrahim; e. Agakhan H.S. 1972; Univ. of Nairobi, M.D. 1977; Univ. of B.C., F.R.C.P.(C) 1982; m. Zenobia d. Sherali and Gulbanu Jaffer 10 June 1978; children: Azra, Afshan; DIR., CLIN. BIOCHEM., NEW ENGLAND DEACONESS HOSP. & ASSOC. PROF. OF PATHOL., HARVARD MED. SCH. 1988– ; Med. Biochem., Vancouver Gen. Hosp. & Asst. Prof. of Pathol., Univ. of B.C. 1981–84; Dir., Clin. Biochem., Ottawa Gen. Hosp. and Assoc. Prof. of Pathol., Med. & Biochem., Univ. of Ottawa Sch. of Med. 1984–88; Vis. Prof. & Cons., Agakhan Univ., Karachi, Pakistan 1986; Cons. to Crown & Reg. Coroner 1986; invited speaker worldwide conf. & symposia; external examiner, King Saud Univ., Riyadh 1987; Award for Excellence in Rsch., Candn. Assoc. of Pathologists 1989; recipient of sev. acad. awards, grants & contracts from N.A. agencies for rsch. into lab. & drug testing and experimental alcoholic liver disease; US Patent for method of drug detection 1991; Chrmn., Internat. Fed. Clin. Chem. working group on testing nearer the patient; Ismaili Moslem; Mem., Am. Fed. of Clin. Rsch.; Am. Soc. for Investigative Pathology; Am. Assn. for Study of Liver Diseases; Soc. for Experimental Biology and Medicine; Am. Assn. for Clin. Chem.; Acad. Lab. Phys. Scient.; Am. Assoc. for the Advancement of Sci.; Chrmn., Assn. of Ismaili Health Profls. 1981–83; author/co-author of over 200 profl. articles and several symposia proceedings; Club: Harvard Faculty; recreations: swimming, hiking, tennis; Home: Wellesley, Mass. USA; Office: Dept. of Pathol., Harvard Med. Sch., New England Deaconess Hosp., 185 Pilgrim Rd., Boston, MA 02215 USA.

**NANKIVELL, Neville John,** B.A., M.Comm.; editor; b. Cottesloe, W. Australia 8 Dec. 1934; s. John Penn and Ivy Savage (Smith) N.; e. Scotch Coll. Swanbourne, W. Australia 1951; Univ. of W. Australia B.A. (Econ.) 1955; Univ. of Toronto M.Comm. 1960; m. (late) Joan d. late Clive B. Davidson 13 Sept. 1958; two s. William Penn, Jeffery John; m. 2ndly Margret Rose Brady, d. P.E.H. Brady 4 May 1985; SENIOR EDITOR, OTTAWA BUREAU, FINANCIAL POST; Dir., Financial Post Advisory Board; joined The Financial Post 1960, Invest. Ed. 1964, Assoc. Ed. 1968, Mang. Ed. 1972, Ed. 1977; Ed.-in-Chief 1981; Publisher 1986; Publisher & Editor-in-Chief 1988–91; Vice-Pres. & & Editor-at-large (Europe) 1991; mem. Accounting, Res. Adv. Bd. (of Canada) 1983–87; mem., National Adv. Counc. on Entrepreneurship 1986–87; mem., Dean's Adv. Counc., Faculty of Mgmt. Studies, Univ. of Toronto 1987–92; mem. Adv. Counc., Faculty of Mgmt., Univ. of B.C. 1988–92; Metrop. Toronto Dist. Health Council 1981–83; Council mem., Canada-U.K. Chamber of Commerce; Chrmn., Task Force on Specialized Medical Imaging (for Metrop. Toronto Dist. Health Council) 1983–84; Trustee, Candn. Outward Bound Wilderness Sch. 1980–82; Pres. Univ. of Toronto Schs. Parents Assn. 1979–81; Dir. Toronto Free Theatre 1977–81; Canada World Youth, 1982–85; Office: 150 Wellington St., Suite 704, Ottawa, Ont. K1P 5A4.

**NANTES, Hon. Gerald David,** B.Sc., B.Eng., P.Eng.; engineer; politician; b. Charlottetown, P.E.I. 6 June 1945; s. Gerald Terrance and Mary (Hogan) N.; e. St. Dunstan's H.S., Charlottetown; St. Dunstan's Univ. B.Sc. 1968; Tech. Univ. of N.S. B.Eng. (Civil Engn.); m. Dianne d. Edward and Clarisse LaRose 27 Mar. 1967; children: Darren Scott, Christopher Shawn, Heather Andrea; Min. of Health and Fitness, N.S. 1988–90; Cons. Engr. 1970–83; Pres. and C.E.O. N.S. Tidal Power Corp. 1979–84; mem. N.S. Legis. 1978– ; Min. of Labour and Manpower, N.S. 1983–85; Min. of Municipal Affairs 1985–87; Min. of Small Business Development 1987–88; Assn. of Profl. Engrs. of N.S.; recreations: golf, baseball, racquetball; Clubs: Cole Harbour – Westphal Kiwanis; Home: 30 Fireside Dr., Dartmouth, N.S. B2V 1Z1.

**NARANG, Saran A.,** O.C., M.Sc., Ph.D., D.Sc. (Hons.), F.R.S.C.; research scientist; b. Agra, India 10 Sept. 1930; s. Sant Dass and Kirpal Devi N.; e. Panjab Univ. B.Sc. 1951, M.Sc. 1953; Calcutta Univ. Ph.D. 1960; m. Sandhya d. Babu Ram Dheer, New Delhi, India 7 Oct. 1959; one d. Monica Ajoo; PRINCIPAL RESEARCH OFFR., NAT. RESEARCH COUNCIL OF CANADA 1973– ; Adjunct Prof. of Chem., Carleton Univ., The Johns Hopkins Univ.; Mem. of Panel of Sci. Advisors, Internat. Centre for Genetic Engineering and Biotechnology (UNIDO); Research Assoc., The Johns Hopkins Univ. 1962–63; Project Assoc. Enzyme Research Inst. Univ. of Wis. 1963–66; Asst. Research Offr. present Council 1966, Assoc. Research Offr. 1967–73 Sen. Research Officer, 1973–82; rec'd Coochbihar Professorship Mem. Award 1973; Johns Hopkins Scholar

Medal 1979; Ottawa Biol. & Biochem. Soc. Award 1979; appointed Officer of the Order of Canada 1985; awarded D.Sc. (Hons.) Carleton Univ. 1985; Rice-Belanger Lectureship Award 1990; 125th Anniversary of the Confederation of Canada Medal, 1992; Vice Pres., XV Internat. Congress of Genetics; author over 140 research papers; achieved the Synthesis and Cloning of Human Proinsulin Gene and Antibody Genes; Fellow, Royal Soc. of Canada 1979; mem. Fed. Am. Socs. Exper. Biol.; Hindu; recreations: Indian classical music, chess, sculpture, painting; Home: 30 Higgins Rd., Ottawa, Ont. K2G 0R5; Office: 100 Sussex Dr., Ottawa, Ont. K1A 0R6.

**NARBONNE, Guy Michael,** B.Sc., Ph.D.; university professor; b. Montreal, Que. 19 Jan. 1954; s. Jean-Guy and Margaret Ann (Good) N.; e. Brock Univ. B.Sc. 1975; Univ. of Ottawa Ph.D. 1981; m. Roslyn d. Harry and Mildred Schwartz March 1977; children: Daniel, Rachel, Melody; ASSOC. PROF., DEPT. OF GEOLOGICAL SCIENCES, QUEEN'S UNIV. 1987– ; NSERC postdoctoral fellow, Dept. of Geology, Univ. of Montreal 1981–82; Asst. Prof., present univ. 1982–87; Voting Mem., Internat. Precambrian-Cambrian Boundary Working Group 1986–92; Voting Mem. & Secy., Internat. Terminal Precambrian System Working Group 1989– ; Assoc. Ed., 'Palaios' 1988– ; Co-discoverer, oldest known fossil animals 1990; Journal of Paleontology, Best Paper Award 1989; Proposer of global stratotype for the Precambrian-Cambrian boundary (1987); author of num. sci. pubs. on the origin & early evolution of animals; recreations: photography, theatre; Home: 171 College St., Kingston, Ont. K7L 4L9; Office: Miller Hall, Queen's Univ., Kingston, Ont. K7L 3N6.

**NARVESON, Jan,** Ph.D.; educator; b. Erskine, Minn. 15 June 1936; s. Carl Robert and Sophie Helen (Krbechek) N.; e. Moorhead State Teachers Coll. Sch. and Moorhead High Sch. Minn.; Univ. of Chicago B.A. 1955, 1956; Harvard Univ. Ph.D. 1961; children: Kaja Lee, Jascha Wallace, Julia Amadea; PROF. OF PHILOSOPHY, UNIV. OF WATERLOO 1963– ; Visiting Prof., Johns Hopkins Univ. 1966; Stanford Univ. 1968; Univ. of Calgary 1976; Bowling Green State Univ., Social Philosophy and Policy Center 1990; Dir., Kitchener-Waterloo Symphony Orchestra Assn.; Kitchener-Waterloo Chamber Music Soc. (Pres.); K-W Community Orchestra; mem. of Ed. Bd., 'Ethics,' 'Dialogue,' 'Journal of Social Philosophy,' 'Philosophy Research Archives,' 'International Journal of Applied Philosophy,' 'Social Philosophy & Policy,' 'Journal of Value Inquiry'; author 'Morality and Utility' 1967; 'The Libertarian Idea' 1989; 'Moral Matters' 1993; recipient honorary D.Litt. (hon. caus.), Wilfred Laurier Univ. 1989; numerous papers primarily on Ethics in professional philosophical journals; weekly columnist (music) 'University of Waterloo Gazette'; commentaries and musical selections weekly radio program (chamber music); Ed., 'Moral Issues' 1983; Fellow, Royal Society of Canada; mem. Candn. Philos. Assn.; Am. Philos. Assn.; Secy.-Treas., Candn. Assn. Publishing in Philos.; recreation: music; Home: 57 Young St. W., Waterloo, Ont. N2L 2Z4; Office: Waterloo, Ont. N2L 3G1.

**NASGAARD, Roald,** M.A., Ph.D.; museum curator; art historian; b. Denmark 14 Oct. 1941; s. Jens Larsen and Petra (Guldbaek) N.; e. Univ. of B.C., B.A. 1965, M.A. 1967; Inst. of Fine Arts, N.Y. Univ. Ph.D. 1973; m. Susan Ursula d. Eric D. Watterson 8 Sept. 1967; Lectr., Dept. of Fine Art, Univ. of Guelph 1971–74, Asst. Prof. 1974–75; Curator of Contemporary Art, A.G.O. 1975–78; Deputy Dir. & Chief Curator, Art Gallery of Ont. 1978–93; Visiting Lectr., Univ. of Guelph 1976; York Univ. 1976–77; Univ. of Toronto 1983–92; Adjunct Prof., Univ. of Toronto 1992– ; exhns. Art Gallery of Ont. incl. Ron Martin; World Paintings 1976, Peter Kolisynk 1977, Structures for Behaviour (new sculptures by Robert Morris, David Rabinowitch, Richard Serra and George Trakas) 1977, Garry Neill Kennedy: Recent Work 1978, Yves Gaucher: A Fifteen Year Perspective 1978, 10 Candn. Artists in the 1970's (1980); The Mystic North: Symbolist Landscape Painting in N. Europe and N. America, 1890–1940 (1984); Co-ordinator of The European Iceberg: Creativity in Italy and Germany Today (1985); Gerhard Richter: Paintings (1988); Individualités: 14 Contemporary Artists from France (1991); Free Worlds: Metaphors and Realities in contemporary Hungarian Art (1991); author various articles (Artscanada, Vie des Art, Arts Magazine (New York), Northward Journal); Mem., Toronto Public Art Comn. 1986–88; mem. Coll. Art Assn.; Univ. Art Assn. Can.; Internat. Art Critics Assn. (Secy. 1976–78); Address: 196 Pape Ave., Toronto, Ont. M4M 2V8.

**NASH, Frank Thomas William,** B.Comm., M.B.A., C.A.; chartered accountant; b. Penarth, Wales 10 Aug. 1919; s. Thomas A. and Amy B. N.; e. Queen's Univ. B.Comm. 1943; Univ. of Wash. M.B.A. 1946; Ont. Inst. of C.A.s, C.A. 1949; m. Patricia 26 Oct. 1946; children: Robert G., David W., J. Graham; Dir., Selkirk Communications Limited 1966–87; with Price Waterhouse 1946–54; Vice Pres. W.L. Ballentine Co. Ltd. 1954–65; Club: Oakville Golf; The Meadows Country (Sarasota, FL); Home: 1073 Cedar Grove Blvd., Oakville, Ont. K6J 2C2.

**NASH, (Cyril) Knowlton,** O.C. (1989); journalist; broadcasting executive; author; b. Toronto, Ont. 18 Nov. 1927; s. Cyril Knowlton and Alys (Worsley) N.; e. Forest Hill Village Pub. Sch. and Coll. Inst., Toronto; Univ. of Toronto, 1 yr.; m. Lorraine Thomson; one d. Anne; SR. CORRESPONDENT, C.B.C. TELEVISION NEWS; Chief Correspondent and Anchor, CBC-TV 1978–88; Dir., Television News and Current affairs C.B.C.; sports writer, 'Globe and Mail,' Toronto, 1946; fiction mag. editing, Toronto, 1946; Ed. of weekly newspaper, Toronto, 1947; Bureau Mgr., Brit. United Press in Halifax, Vancouver and Toronto, 1947–51; Dir. of Information, Internat. Fed. of Agric. Producers, Washington and Paris, 1951–58; writer/broadcaster (CBC Washington Corr., Financial Post, various Candn. newspapers) 1958–69; apptd. Dir., News & Public Affairs, C.B.C. 1969; Rapporteur various U.N. Comtes., 1951–58; author: 'History on the Run' 1984; 'Times to Remember' 1986; 'Prime Time at Ten' 1987; 'Kennedy and Diefenbaker' 1990; 'Visions of Canada' 1991; former Pres., CBC Corrs. Assn.; former Pres., Candn. Corrs. Assn. (Washington); and White House Correspondents Assn.; Overseas Writers Club; Chrmn., CODE, Candn. Orgn. for Devel. through Educ.; Chrmn., Candn. Journalism Found.; Hon. Chrmn., Arts Found. of Greater Toronto; Bd. mem., Gordon Sinclair Found.; Developing Countries Farm Radio Network; Official 'Friend,' Candn. Cystic Fibrosis Found.; mem., former chrmn., Toronto Branch, Candn. Mental Health Assn.; apptd. Officer, Order of Canada 1989; recreations: books, jogging; Clubs: National Press, Washington; Toronto Press; Home: 29 Whitehall Rd., Toronto, Ont. M4W 2C5; Office: Box 500, Terminal 'A,' Toronto, Ont. M5W 1E4.

**NASH, Peter Hugh John, Sr.,** M.A., M.C.P., M.P.A., Ph.D.; educator; consultant; b. Frankfurt-on-Main, Germany 18 Sept. 1921; s. John Hans Joseph and Alice (Heuman) N.; e. Lindisfarne Coll., Essex, Eng. 1937; Los Angeles City Coll., A.A. 1941; Univ. of Cal. (Los Angeles) B.A. 1942 (Gruen Fellow), M.A. (Geography) 1946; Univ. of Grenoble, Cert. d'Etudes 1945; Harvard Grad. Sch. of Design (Holtzer Fellow) M. City Planning 1949; Harvard Grad. Sch. of Pub. Adm. M.P.A. 1956; Architectural Sciences Ph.D. Harvard 1958; Univ. of Cincinnati Law Sch., 1961–63; m. late Inez Mae Frost (dec. 21 Apr. 1988), d. late Bertram Frost, 30 July 1955; children: Carina Frost, Peter Hugh Jr.; PROFESSOR EMERITUS OF ARCHITECTURE, GEOGRAPHY AND PLANNING, UNIV. OF WATERLOO; (Prof. 1970–87, Adjunct Prof. 1987–93); and Dean of Faculty of Environmental Studies 1970–75; Princ. Planning Asst., Boston City Planning Bd. 1949; Sr. Planner, Planning Dept., City of Worcester, Mass. 1950; Asst. Chief. Urban Redevel. Div., Boston Housing Authority 1951; Dir., Planning Dept., City of Medford, Mass. 1952–56; Visiting Critic, Harvard Grad. Sch. of Design 1955–1957 and Asst. Prof. of Geog., Boston Univ. 1956–57; Assoc. Prof. of City & Regional Planning and Research Assoc., Inst. for Research in Social Science, Univ. of N.C. 1957–59; Prof. and Head, Dept. of Geog. and Regional Planning, Univ. of Cincinnati 1959–63; Dean of Grad. Sch. and Prof. of Geog. & Regional Planning, Univ. of Rhode Island (Kingston) 1963–70; Visiting Prof., Inst. of Human Sciences, Boston Coll. 1969–70; Sr. Mgmt. Consultant, Battelle Mem. Inst., Columbus, Ohio, 1969–74; served with U.S. Army in N.W. and Central Europe 1942–45; rec'd Purple Heart with Oak Leaf Cluster; Bronze Star; Croix de Guerre; recipient numerous research (U.S.S.S.R.C.), foreign travel grants (N.S.F.) and faculty leave fellowships (S.S.H.R.C.), acad. and civic honours and awards in Canada, U.S. and other countries; including Univ. of Liège; Aligarh Muslim Univ., India; and Cities of Yokohama, Japan and Recife, Brazil; mem. various bds., comns. and councils; author of three books and over 180 articles, chapters and reviews in books and prof. or learned journs., all listed in 'Abstract Thoughts: Concrete Solutions; Essays in Honour of Peter Nash' (Festschrift published on his retirement, Dept. of Geography Publication Series No. 29, Univ. of Waterloo) 1987; Bd. of Dir., K/W Philharmonic Choir (Chrmn. 1977–79); mem. Kitchener Rotary Internat. (Paul Harris Fellow); Am. Assn. Geogs. (Life); Am. Planning Assn. (A.I.C.P.); Am. Soc. Pub. Adm.; Am. Geographical Society (Life); Assn. Coll. Schs. Planning (Treas. 1967–70); Candn. Assn. Geogs.; Harvard Grad. Sch. Design Alumni Assn. (Pres. 1966–70); Harvard Kennedy Sch. of Gov't. Extve. Council 1981–87 (Secy.-Treas. 1985–87); Inst. Alpine Geog. (Hon.); Internat. Geog. Union Comm. Appl. Geog. (W. Hemisphere Rep. 1960–84); Internat. City Managers. Assn.; Regional Science Assn.; Candn. Inst. Planners; World Soc. Ekistics (Delos Symposion Participant: 1967, 1970, 1974); Alpha Mu Gamma; Kappa Delta Pi; Phi Kappa Phi (Hon.); Pi Gamma Mu; Sigma Nu; Sigma Xi; Freemason (K.T.); Unitarian; recreations: skiing, swimming; Home: 588 Sugarbush Dr., Waterloo, Ont. N2K 1Z8.

**NASH, Roger Laurence,** B.A., M.A., Ph.D.; university professor, poet, farmer; b. Maidenhead, Berkshire, England 3 Nov. 1942; s. Lawrence and Margaret Ellen (Davis) N.; e. Univ. of Wales B.A. 1965; McMaster Univ. M.A. 1966; Univ. of Exeter Ph.D. 1974; m. Bronwen d. David and Florence Harrhy 28 May 1966; children: Piers, Caedmon; ASSOC. PROF., LAURENTIAN UNIV. 1982– ; Lectr., Thorneloe Univ. Coll. 1966–67; Tutor, Univ. of Exeter 1967–69; Asst. Prof., present univ. 1969–82; Lectr., O.I.S.E. 1973–74; Visiting Prof., Athabasca Univ. 1991–93; Public Relns., Publicity & Membership Cttes., Stratford Shakespearean Festival Found. of Can.; Dir., Fine Arts Task Force, Laurentian Univ. 1983–85; Language Arts Resource Consultancy 1986–88; 1st Prize, Prism Internat. Poetry Contest 1986; Mem., League of Candn. Poets; Candn. Philos. Assn.; Assn. of Candn. Univ. Teachers of English; author: 'Settlement in a School of Whales' 1983; 'Psalms from the Suburbs' 1986; 'Night Flying' 1990 (poetry); 'The Poetry of Prayer' 1991; 'Ethics, Science, Technology and the Environment: A Study Guide' 1993; 'Ethics, Science, Technology and the Environment: A Reader' 1993; recreations: music, canoeing, hiking; Home: #5 - 1848 Paris St., Sudbury, Ont. P3E 3C7; Office: Philosophy Dept., Laurentian Univ., Sudbury, Ont. P3E 2C6.

**NASH, Terre,** B.A., M.A., Ph.D.; freelance filmmaker; b. Nanaimo, B.C.; d. Charles W. and Mary Bernadette (Corcoran) N.; e. Simon Fraser Univ. B.A. 1969, M.A. 1973; McGill Univ. Ph.D. 1983 (Dean's List); FREELANCE FILMMAKER, NASHFILM INC. 1977– ; Teaching Asst., Simon Fraser Univ. Behav. Sci. & Commun. 1970–71, Interpersonal Commun. 1971–72, Mass Media & Soc. Psych. 1972–73; and other teaching positions 1971–73; Distrib. Rep., Studio D., Nat. Film Bd. of Can. 1976–77; films: 'Mother Earth/La Terre Notre Mère' 1991, 'Russian Diary' 1990, 'A Love Affair with Politics' 1988, 'Nuclear Addiction' 1986, 'A Writer in the Nuclear Age' 1985, 'Speaking Our Peace' 1984–85, 'If You Love This Planet' 1982–83, 'It's No Yolk' 1975, 'The Fish That Ate the World' 1969; Academy Award (Oscar) for Best Documentary Short Subject ('If You Love This Planet') 1983; Blue Ribbon 1st Prize, N.Y. Am. Film Fest.; Golden Sheaf nom., Yorkton Internat. Short Film & Video Fest.; Leipzig Peace Prize; Atom Award, Brazil Sci. Film Fest.; Karlovy Vary Dipl. Prague; Silver Medal Melbourne Film Fest. John Muir Med. Film Fest. 1st Prize 1986 & Hon. Mention, 2nd Vermont World Peace Film Fest. 1987 ('Speaking Our Peace'); 2nd Prize, 2nd Vermont World Peace Film Fest. 1987 (nuclear disarmament: 'Nuclear Addiction'; internat. relns.: 'A Love Affair with Politics); Bronze Plaque, Columbus Internat. Film Fest. 1990 ('Russian Diary'); Award for Best Editing at the 1st Ecocine Film Festival, Brazil, June 1992 ('Mother Earth'); Can. Counc. Doct. Fellowship, McGill Univ. 1974–77; Fonds F.C.A.C. 1979–83; Alumni Award, Simon Fraser Univ.; Pres. Grad. Award, SFU; six undergrad. acad. scholarships, SFU; co-author: 'Women at the National Film Board/Les femmes à l'Office national du film au travail' 1978; author: 'Images of Women in N.F.B. Films During World War II and the Post War Years: 1939–1949'; Address: 2024, avenue Grey, Montreal, Que. H4A 3N4.

**NASTICH, Milan M.,** B.A., B.A.Sc., P.Eng.; business executive; b. Vancouver, B.C. 27 Feb. 1926; s. Midzor and Rose (Snihur) N.; e. Drumheller High Sch. Alberta; Univ. of B.C. B.A. 1947, B.A.Sc. (Elect. Engn.) 1948; m. Mary Hudson 15 May 1954; one s. Jeffrey; DIR., AGF MANAGEMENT LTD. 1988– ; joined Ontario Hydro 1949, Comptroller 1964, Dir. of Computing Services 1967, Dir. of Property 1970, Asst. Gen. Mgr. Finance 1972, Vice Pres. Resources 1974, Extve. Vice Pres. Planning & Adm. 1978; Chrmn., Pres. and Dir., Ontario Hydro 1980–85, (Chrmn. 1983–84); Past Pres. Arthritis Soc.; Kennedy House for Boys 1971–73; Mem. Bd. of Dir., Hardit Corp.; Honey Well Ltd.; Acres Internat.; Opinac Energy Inc.; Sumitomo Bank Canada Ltd.; Cochrane Power; Kirkland Lake Power; mem. Soc. Ont. Hydro Prof. Engrs. (Pres. 1956–57); Assn. Prof. Engrs. Prov. Ont.; Pres., Candn. Electrical Assoc. 1983–84; Greek Orthodox; recreations: curling, cross-country skiing, target shooting, chess, farming, wine tasting; Clubs: Toronto; Ticker (Past Pres.); Past Grand Pilier General Confrerie des Chevaliers du Tastevin; Franklin Fishing; Home: 259 Yonge Blvd., Toronto, Ont. M5M 3J1; Office: 31st Flr., TD Bank Tower, Toronto, Ont. M5K 1E9.

**NATHANSON, Hon. Hilroy Selig,** B.A., LL.B.; judge; b. New Glasgow, N.S. 15 May 1932; s. Joseph and Fania Rebecca (Marcus) N.; e. Morrison H.S. (Glace Bay, N.S.) 1950; Univ. of King's Coll. B.A. 1955; Dalhousie Univ. LL.B. 1958; m. Fannie d. Nathan and Fannie David 10 Jan. 1960; children: Kendall Eve, Peter David, Jan Aviva; JUDGE, TRIAL DIVISION, SUPREME COURT OF NOVA SCOTIA 1982– ; practised law at Sydney, N.S. 1959–82; Gov. Univ. of King's Coll.; mem. Maritime Div. Bd. of Mgmt., Candn. National Inst. for the Blind; Temple Sons of Israel, Sydney, N.S.; Home: 141 Shandwick St., Sydney, N.S. B1P 4V7; Office: The Law Courts, 1815 Water St., Halifax, N.S. B3J 3C8.

**NATTIEZ, Jean-Jacques André René,** C.M., D.de l'Un., M.S.R.C.; professeur; né à Amiens, France, 30 décembre 1945; f. Jean et Jacqueline (Lancelle) N.; e. Univ. de Paris VIII, Doctorat de 3e cycle 1973; séparé; enfants: Florence, Muriel; PROF. DE MUSICOLIGIE, UNIV. DE MONTRÉAL 1970– ; Professeur invité au Collège de France (Paris) en octobre-novembre 1993; y dirige le Groupe de Recherches en Sémiologie Musicale 1974–80; est considéré comme le pionnier de cette branche de la musicologie; en 1979, le compositeur et chef d'orchestre Pierre Boulez lui propose de co-diriger avec lui une collection de livres 'Musique/passé/présent', consacrée à la musique du XXe siècle et à la théorie musicale; auteur (essais): 'Fondements d'une sémiologie de la musique' 1975; 'Tétralogies (Wagner, Boulez, Chéreau) 1983; 'Proust musicien' 1984; 'Musicologie générale et sémiologie' 1987; 'Wagner androgyne' 1990; 'Le combat de Chronos et d'Orphée' 1993; Disques: 'Chants et jeux des Inuit' 1979 et 'Collection universelle de musique populaire enregistrée' 1987 (Grand prix internat. du disque pour les deux, Académie Charles-Cros); 'Jeux voceaux des Inuit' 1989; membre: Soc. internat. de musicologie; Am. Musicol. Soc.; Soc. for Music Theory; Soc. for Enthnomusicol.; Assn. canadienne des profs. univs. de musique; Adresse: 4845 Rosedale, Montréal, Qué. H4V 2H3; Bureau: C.P. 6128 Succ. A, Montréal, Qué. H3C 3J7.

**NAULT, Heather Jean,** B.Sc., C.M.A.; telecommunications executive; b. Winnipeg, Man.; e. Univ. of Manitoba B.Sc. 1964; C.M.A. 1979; VICE-PRESIDENT, MANITOBA TELEPHONE SYSTEM; Office: P.O. Box 6666, Winnipeg, Man. R3C 3V6.

**NAUMOVSKI, Ljupco Lou,** M.A.; international public servant; b. Bitola, Yugoslavia 17 Nov. 1956; s. Mihajlo and Olivera (Gligorovska) N.; e. Univ. of Toronto B.A. 1978; Carleton Univ. M.A. 1980; m. Sylvia d. Alexander and Joan Toogood 7 March 1981; one s. Stefan Alexander; RESIDENT REPRESENTATIVE, MOSCOW, RUSSIA, EUROPEAN BANK FOR RECONSTRUCTION AND DEVELOPMENT 1992– ; Second Sec. (Comm) Moscow 1982–84; Consul and Trade Comnr., Candn. Consulate Gen. Atlanta, Ga. 1984–86; First Sec. (Comm.) Baghdad 1986–88; Dep. Dir. USSR and E. Eur. Trade Devel. Div. Dept. External Affairs & Internat. Trade Ottawa 1988–90; Extve. Dir., Canada-USSR Business Council 1990–92; mem. Adv. Bd. York Univ., Enterprise York, East-West Exchange Prog. 1990–92; mem., Adv. Bd., Centre for Candn. Soviet Studies, Carleton Univ. 1991–92; frequent guest speaker and commentator Can.-USSR relations; Macedonian Orthodox; recreations: tennis, golf; Home: 75 Rossburn Dr., Etobicoke, Ont. M9C 2P9; Office: c/o EBRD, (Moscow) One Exchange Square, London EC2A 2EH, England.

**NAYAR, Baldev Raj,** M.A., Ph.D.; educator; b. Gujrat, Punjab, India 26 Oct. 1931; s. Jamna Das and Durga Devi (Marwah) N.; e. Punjab Univ. B.A. 1953, M.A. 1956; Univ. of Chicago M.A. 1959, Ph.D. 1963; m. Nancy Ann d. Durward A. Skinner 27 Aug. 1961; children: Sheila Jane, Kamala Elizabeth, Sunita Maria; PROF. OF POL. SCIENCE, McGILL UNIV. 1971– ; Asst. Prof. of Pol. Science Calif. State Coll. Hayward 1963–64; Asst. Prof. present Univ. 1964, Assoc. Prof. 1966, Assoc. Chrmn. 1990–93; author 'Minority Politics in the Punjab' 1966; 'National Communication and Language Policy in India' 1968; 'The Modernization Imperative and Indian Planning' 1972; 'Violence and Crime in India: A Quantitative Study' 1975; 'American Geopolitics and India' 1976; 'India's Quest for Technological Independence' (2 vols.) 1983; 'India's Mixed Economy' 1989; 'The Political Economy of India's Public Sector' 1990; 'Superpower Dominance and Military Aid' 1991; mem., Candn. Asian Studies Assn.; Candn. Pol. Sci. Assn.; Assn. Asian Studies; Home: 441 Lansdowne Ave., Westmount, Que. H3Y 2V4; Office: 855 Sherbrooke St. W., Montreal, Que. H3A 2T7.

**NAYLOR, Bruce Gordon,** B.Sc., Ph.D.; museum administrator/university professor; b. Midale, Sask. 19 Aug. 1950; s. John R. and Mary Lynn (Frisby) N.; e. Weyburn C.I. 1968; Univ. of Sask., B.Sc. (High Hons.) 1972; Univ. of Alta., Ph.D. 1978; m. Marlene Johnstone 18 Dec. 1981 (dec'd. 1992); DIR., ROYAL TYRRELL MUSEUM 1992– ; Senator, Univ. of Calgary 1989–90; NSERC post-doct. fellowship, Univ. of Toronto 1978–80; Sess. Lectr., Univ. of Calif., Berkeley 1979; Asst. Prof. & NSERC Rsch. Fellow, Univ. of Alta. 1980–82; Curator of Vertebrate Palaeontol., Tyrrell Mus. 1982–86; Asst. Dir., Royal Tyrrell Museum 1986–92; Adj. Prof. of Geol. & Zool., Univ. of Alta.; Fellow, Geol. Assn. of Can.; Mem., Soc. of Vertebrate Paleontol.; Candn. Mus. Assn.; author/co-author, 20 sci. pub.; editor: 'Dinosaur Systematics Symposium, Field Trip Guidebook to Dinosaur Prov. Park' 1986; recreation: horses; Clubs: Appaloosa Horse Club of Can.; Am. Quarter Horse Assn.; Home: Box 2706 Drumheller, Alta. T0J 0Y0; Office: Box 7500, Drumheller, Alta. T0J 0Y0.

**NAYLOR, Bruce Russell,** B.Sc.A.; transport executive; b. Toronto, Ont. 24 Oct. 1935; s. H. Russell and Norah (Cross) N.; e. Lawrence Park Coll. 1955; Univ. of Toronto, Ont. Agric. Coll., B.Sc.A. 1959; m. Maureen d. Jack and Irene Hinz 11 Sept. 1959; children: Stephen, Ruth, Barbara, Patricia; PRES., TIPPET-RICHARDSON LIMITED 1986– ; Mgr. (Beaverton then Belleville), United Co-operatives of Ont. 1959–64; Mgr. (Hamilton), Tippet-Richardson Limited 1964–70; Mgr., Warehousing (Toronto) 1970–76; Vice-Pres. & Gen. Mgr. 1976–86; Chrmn., Bd. of Dir., Allied Van Lines Ltd. 1987–92; Pres., Candn. Overseas Movers Assn. 1979–80; Ont. Movers Assn. 1975–77; Service to Indus. Award, Ont. Trucking Assn. 1974; Home: 20 Fairway Heights Cres., Thornhill, Ont. L3T 1K2; Office: 79 East Don Roadway, Toronto, Ont. M4M 3J8.

**NAYLOR, Bryan,** C.G.A.; manufacturing executive; b. Oldham, England 2 Aug. 1949; s. Alan and Doreen Mary (Crabtree) N.; Cert. Gen. Acct. 1984; m. Krystyna Anna d. Irena Marta Kleniewski and the late Antoni Kleniewski; one d.: Julia Allison; PRES., GEN. MGR. & DIR., COLUMBUS MCKINNON LIMITED 1986– ; Controller, Sec.-Treas. & Dir., Columbus McKinnon Limited 1979– ; Mem., Cert. Gen. Accts. Assn. of Can.; Conf. Bd. of Can.; Counc. Internat. Business Rsch.; Counc. for Econ. Relns. between Canada and the USA; Standards Counc. of Can. (CAC Chrmn., ISO/TC 111); Mem., Pres. Assn., A.M.A.; Dir., Jr. Achievement, Cobourg 1984–86; Dist. C. of C. 1987–88; Home: 828 Lavis St., Oshawa, Ont.; Office: P.O. Box 1106, Cobourg, Ont. K9A 4W5.

**NAYLOR, Christopher David,** M.D., D.Phil., F.R.C.P.(C); physician; b. Woodstock, Ont. 26 Oct. 1954; s. Thomas and Edna Anne (Aziz) N.; e. Woodstock Coll. Inst. 1972; Univ. Coll. Univ. of Toronto, Faculty of Med. M.D. 1978; Hertford Coll. Oxford (Rhodes Scholar) D. Phil. 1983; m. Dr. Ilse (Rhodes Scholar) d. Pieter and Eline Treurnicht, Johannesburg, S. Africa 1 June 1985; 2 daughter, 2 sons; DIR., CLINICAL EPIDEMIOLOGY, SUNNYBROOK HEALTH SCIENCE CENTRE 1990– ; Chief Extve. Offr., Institute for Clinical Evaluative Sciences in Ontario 1992– ; specialty training, Univ. of West. Ont. teaching hosps. 1983–85; Chief Med. Resident, Victoria Hosp. 1985–86; Medical Research Coun. Fellow, Toronto Gen. Hosp. 1987–88; Staff Physician, Toronto Western Hosp. 1988–90; Asst. Prof., Dept. of Med., Univ. of Toronto 1988–92, Assoc. Prof. 1992– ; author: 'Private Practice, Public Payment: Canadian Medicine and the Politics of Health Insurance, 1911–1966' 1986; co-author: 'Detection and Management of Asymptomatic Hypercholesterolemia' 1989; 'Asymptomatic Hypercholesterolemia: A Clinical Policy Review' 1990; 'Managed Care in Canada' 1991; editor: 'Canadian Health Care and the State' 1992; mem. Candn. Health Econ. Rsch. Assn.; Candn. Soc. Hist. Med.; Oxford Soc.; Ont. Med. Assn. (Ctte. on Hosps. 1984–86; Ctte. on Manpower 1987); Home: 123 Glencairn Ave., Toronto, Ont. M4R 1N1.

**NEALE, Ernest Richard Ward,** O.C., B.Sc., M.S., Ph.D., LL.D., D.Sc., F.R.S.C.; geologist; b. Montreal, Que. 3 July 1923; s. Ernest John and Mabel Elizabeth (McNamee) N.; e. McGill Univ. B.Sc. 1949 (Logan Gold Medal); Yale Univ. M.S. 1950, Ph.D. 1952; Univ. of Calgary LL.D. 1977; Memorial Univ. D.Sc. 1989; m. Roxie Eveline d. late Arthur Ernest Anderson 3 June 1950; children: Richard Ward, Owen Curtis; CONSULTING GEOLOGIST 1988– ; Asst. Prof. Univ. of Rochester 1952–54; Head of Appalachian Sec. Geol. Survey of Can. 1959–63, Head of Precambrian Sec. 1965–68; Commonwealth Geol. Liaison Offr. London, UK 1963–65; Prof. and Head of Geol. Mem. Univ. of Nfld. 1968–76; Head of Geol. Information Subdiv. Inst. of Sedimentary And Petroleum Geol. 1976–81; Adjunct Prof. 1976–80 (mem. of Senate 1979–81) Univ. of Calgary; Vice-Pres. (Academic), Memorial Univ. of Newfoundland 1982–87; rec'd Bancroft Award, Royal Soc. Can. 1975; Queen's Silver Jubilee Medal 1977; R.T. Bell Medal, Can. Mining Journal 1977; Distinguished Service Award, Geol. Assn. Can. 1981; Ambrose Medal, Geol. Assoc. Can. 1986; Officer, Order of Canada 1990; 125th Anniversary of the Confederation of Canada Medal, 1992; served with RCN 1943–45; Dir. Candn. Geol. Foundation 1973–78; author 'Some Guides to Mineral Exploration' 1965; 'Geology of the Atlantic Area' 1967; 'The Earth Sciences in Canada' 1968; 'Geology and Geophysics in Canadian Universities,' 1980; various articles geol., popular science, geo-politics; editor, Can. Journal of Earth Sciences 1974–80; elected Fellow, Royal Soc. Can. 1965 (Councillor 1972–74); Geol. Assn. Can. (Pres. 1972–73); Candn. Geoscience Council (Pres. 1976); Assoc. of Geoscientists for Intnl. Dev.; Chrmn., Review Ctte. on Chemical Biological Defence (DND) 1990–93; Chrmn., Nat. Adv. Bd. on Scientific Publications (NRC) 1983–88; Chrmn., Royal Soc. Can. Ctte. on Public Awareness of Science 1987–90; Calgary Science Network (Pres. 1989); Geol. Soc. Am.; Unitarian Church of Calgary (Bd. 1993– ); recreations: cross-country skiing, golf, hiking, canoeing; Home: 5108 Carney Rd. N.W., Calgary, Alta. T2L 1G2.

**NEALE, Gladys Emily;** publisher; b. Toronto, Ont.; d. William George and Annie Louisa (Wright) N.; e. Malvern Coll. Inst. Toronto; Teacher's Coll. Toronto; Columbia Univ. Teacher's Coll.; Mng. Editor, Maritext Ltd. 1984–87; Consultant, Educational Publishing 1984– ; Secy. Macmillan Co. of Canada Ltd. 1959, Dir. 1961, Vice Pres. 1967, Sr. Vice Pres. 1977; Dir. of Educ. Div., Clarke Irwin & Co. 1979–83; Dir. Educ. Dept., Irwin Publishing Co. Inc. 1983–84; Hon. Dir. Candn. Scholarship Trust Foundation; Past Chrmn. Soroptimist Foundation Can.; mem. Soroptimist Internat.; Past Pres. World Literacy Can.; Dir., Laubach Literacy of Canada 1980– ; Dir., Laubach Literacy Internat. 1988– ; Chrmn., Book Distributorship and Publications Ctte., Laubach Literacy of Canada; Chrmn. Book and Periodical Devel. Counc. 1985–87; Chrmn., Candn. Give the Gift of Literacy Found. 1987–90; recipient, Eve Orpen Award for excellence in publishing 1985; Gladys Neale $10,000 annual post-graduate scholarship established by Canadian Scholarship Trust Foundation 1992; Home: 84 Main St., Toronto, Ont. M4E 2V7.

**NEASE, Alfred Stuart,** B.A., M.A., F.C.C.T.; university professor and administrator; b. Calgary, Alta. 26 Aug. 1922; s. Frederick George and Margaret (Jewitt) N.; Univ. of Toronto B.A. 1944, M.A. 1949; Ont. Coll. of Education 1947; m. Barbara d. John and Esther Scott Sept. 1951; children: Scott, Christopher, Robyn, Timothy, Stephanie; PROFESSOR EMERITUS, UNIV. OF WINDSOR 1992; Teacher of Latin & Greek and Dept. Head, Malvern C. I., Toronto 1947–55 and Oakwood C.I., Tor. 1955–60; Vice-Principal, Northview Heights C.I., North York 1960–64; Principal, Saltfleet H.S. 1964–65; Prof. of Education, and Chrmn., Dept. of Admin. & Program Devel., Faculty of Ed., Univ. of Tor. 1965–72; Dean, Faculty of Education, Univ. of Windsor 1972–83; Professor of Education, Faculty of Education, University of Windsor 1972–88; educational consultant; author of reversal educational articles; co-author: 'Porta Est Aperta,' 1953; 'An Introductory Handbook on School Law and Administration in Ontario, 1964; 'The Professional Teacher in Ontario' 1970; co-editor: 'The School and the Individual Student,' 1970; Bd. of Dir., Ont. Educational Research Council; mem., Assn. of Deans of Ed. in Ont. Universities; Editorial Comte. of 'Comment on Education'; Classical Assn. of Can.; Classical Assn. of Ont.; Candn. Soc. for Study of Ed.; Candn. Educational Assn.; The Vergilian Soc. of Am.; Am. Assn. of School Administrators; Am. Ed. Research Assn.; Ont. Assn. of Ed. Administrative Officials; Phi Delta Kappa; mem. and Chrmn., Early Childhood Ed. Comte., St. Clair Coll. of Applied Arts and Tech.; 1980– ; mem., John Howard Soc. of Ont. Bd. of Dirs.; Pres. and mem., John Howard Soc. of Windsor and Essex County Bd. of Dir.; Pres., UNI-COM Senior Resource Centre; Mem. Bd. of Dirs., Capitol Theatre and Arts Centre (Windsor); Fell., Candn. Coll. of Teachers; Home: 5265 Riverside Dr. E., Windsor, Ont. N8A 1A1; Office: Faculty of Education, University of Windsor, Windsor, Ont. N9E 1A5.

**NEATBY, H. Blair,** M.A., Ph.D.; educator; b. Renown, Sask. 11 Dec. 1924; s. Walter B. and Margaret (MacKay) N.; e. Univ. of Sask. B.A. 1950; Oxford Univ. M.A. 1955; Univ. of Toronto Ph.D. 1956; m. Jacqueline Côté 15 Apl. 1961; children: Nicole, Pierre, Jacques; PROF. OF HIST. CARLETON UNIV.; author 'W.L. MacKenzie King' Vol. 1 1923–32, 1963, Vol. II 1932–39, 1976; 'Laurier and a Liberal Quebec' 1972; 'The Politics of Chaos' 1972; Home: 220 Patterson Ave., Ottawa, Ont. K1S 1Y6; Office: Carleton Univ., Ottawa, Ont.

**NEDDEAU, Donald Frederick Price,** A.O.C.A., O.S.A., F.I.A.L. (1960), R.C.A.; artist, painter, designer, teacher; b. Toronto, Ont. 28 Jan. 1913; s. Frederick Price and Pearl Franklin (Bland) N.; e. Ont. Coll. Art, A.O.C.A. (Hons.) 1936; post grad. work in fine art, 1937; Ont. Coll. Educ., Univ. of Toronto, grad. 1954; m. Elizabeth Bryce Elder one d. Barbara Ann Neddeau McNulty; has exhibited with major art socs. and galleries in Can. and U.S.A.; one-man shows in Can., U.S.A., New Zealand; Diamond Jubilee Collection 1986 Gt. Britain; Head of Art, Princ. of Art Summer School; Emeritus, 1978, Central Technical School, Toronto; served in 2nd World War with R.C.A.F. and Canadian Army, 1942–45; Life mem., Ont. Soc. of Artists 1955 (O.S.A.); Canadian Soc. Painters in Water Colour (Pres. 1964–66; Life mem. 1987); Candn. Artist Representation Ont. (C.A.R.O.); Fellow, Intnl. Inst. Arts & Lett. (F.I.A.L.); el. Roy. Candn. Acad. of Arts, 1976; Life mem., Councillor 1983 R.C.A.; Anglican; recreations: swimming, golf, tennis; Club: Arts & Letters; Address: 609 Avenue Rd., Suite 202, Toronto, Ont. M4V 2K6.

**NEDZELA, Michel,** B.Eng., M.S.; university professor; b. Paris, France 3 Aug. 1946; s. Louis and Jeanne (Strouf) N.; e. Ecole Centrale des Arts et Manufactures Paris France B.Eng. 1969; Stanford Univ. M.S. 1971; m. Jennifer d. John and Cora Ward 28 Oct. 1979; children: Claire, Marc; PROFESSOR OF MANAGEMENT SCIENCE, FACULTY OF ADMINISTRATION, UNIV. OF OTTAWA 1973– ; Dir., Dept. of Management Sci., Univ. of Ottawa 1978–79; Asst.-Dean, Undergrad. Programmes 1979–83; Vice-Dean 1985–88; Dir., Internat. Exchange Programmes 1981–92; Dir., Internat. MBA Prog. 1991–92; Visiting Prof., Ecole Sup. de Commerce de Paris 1983–84; Ecole Sup. de Commerce de Grenoble 1992–93; Dir., P.E. Logic Inc. 1981– ; Aleph Consultants Ltd. 1974–81; Univ. of Ottawa Award for Excellence in Teaching 1978; Harkness Fellow, Commonwealth Fund of New York 1969–71; Mem., Candn. Operational Rsch. Soc.; Inst. of Mngt. Science; author: 'Introduction à la science de la gestion' 1979, '83, '86, '90, 'Modèles probabilistes d'aide à la décision' 1987; Home: 100 Lisgar Rd., Rockcliffe, Ont. K1M 2G5; Office: Ottawa, Ont. K1N 6N5.

**NEEDHAM, Michael J.,** B.A., M.B.A.; business executive; b. Manchester, Engl. 15 July 1941; s. Peter Thomas and Margaret Victoria (Power) N.; e. Univ. of Leeds, Yorks. B.A. Geography 1962; Univ. of W. Ont. M.B.A. 1968; m. Roberta d. Garfield Taylor 30 July 1965; children: Elizabeth, Catherine, Richard; CHRMN. & PRES., INTERACTIVE SIMULATION INC.; Dir., Novametrix Medical Inc.; Standard Chartered Bank of Canada; Mem. of Adv. Ctte., Univ. of Western Ont. Business Sch.; Fin. Planning Dept. Rio Tinto Zinc Corp., London 1962–64; Mktg. Dept. Atlas Steels Welland 1964–66; Pres., Helix Investments Ltd. 1968–91; recreations: tennis, squash; Clubs: Toronto Lawn Tennis; Cambridge (Toronto); Home: 6 Warren Rd., Toronto, Ont. M4V 2R5; Office: 511 King St. W., Suite 130, Toronto, Ont. M5V 2Z4.

**NEEDLER, Alfred Walker Holinshead,** O.B.E., C.M., Ph.D., D.Sc., F.R.S.C.; biologist; b. Huntsville, Ont. 14 Aug. 1906; s. George Henry and Mary Winifred (Chisholm) N.; e. Upper Can. Coll. Toronto; Univ. of Toronto Schs.; Univ. of Toronto B.A. 1926, Ph.D. 1930; Univ. of N.B. D.Sc. 1954; Univ. of B.C. D.Sc. 1969; m. lstly Alfreda Alice (dec. 1951) d. Cyril and Edith Berkeley 30 May 1930; children Mary Elizabeth, George Treglohan, Edith Chisholm; m. 2ndly Nina Mae d. Martin and Mabel Parker 20 March 1953; children: Joan Claire, John Duncan, David Henry; joined Fisheries Rsch. Bd. Can. in charge Oyster Rsch., Adm. Oyster Farming P.E.I. Biol. Stn. 1929–41, Dir., St. Andrews Biol. Stn. 1941–54, Dir., Nanaimo Biol. Stn. 1954–63; Asst. Depy. Min. of Fisheries Can. 1948–50, Depy. Min. 1963–68, Depy. Min. of Fisheries & Forestry Can. 1968–71; Extve. Dir., Huntsman Marine Lab. St. Andrews, N.B. 1971–76; Candn. Adv. or Rep. numerous meetings FAO bodies, 1st Chrmn. Adv. Ctte. Marine Resources Rsch. 1963–65, 1st Chrmn. Ctte. on Fisheries 1966–67; Chrmn. FAO Tech. Conf. Marine Pollution & Its Effects on Fisheries, Rome 1970, Fisheries Mgmt. & Devel. Vancouver 1973; Sr. Sci. Adv. to Candn. Del. meetings leading to est. Intnl. Comn. Northwest Atlantic Fisheries and to Candn. Del. to ICNAF 1951–54, Candn. Comnr. ICNAF 1965–77, Chrmn. 1970–71; Sr. Sci. Adv. to Candn. Del. Intnl. N. Pacific Fisheries Comn. 1954–63, Comnr. 1963–67, Chrmn. 1963, 1966; Sr. Fisheries Adv. Candn. Del. UN Conf. Law of Sea 1974–78; mem., Fisheries Rsch. Bd. Can. 1972–77; Sci. Council Can. 1968–71; Grand Banks Panel Fed. Environmental Assessment Review Office 1980–85; recipient Prof. Inst. Pub. Service Can. gold Medal 1973; Am. Fisheries Soc. Award Excellence 1976; named Chief Pacific Native Indian Brotherhood 1977; author numerous sci. and tech. papers; recreations: sailing, hunting; Address: (P.O. Box 481) St. Andrews, N.B. E0G 2X0.

**NEEDLER, George T.,** B.Sc., M.Sc., Ph.D., FRSC; research oceanographer; b. Summerside, P.E.I. 2 Feb. 1935; s. Alfred Walker Holinshead and Alfreda Alice (Berkeley) N.; e. St. Andrews Gram. Sch., St. Andrews, N.B. 1952; Univ. of N.B. 1952–53; Univ. of B.C., B.Sc. 1958, M.Sc. 1959; McGill Univ., Ph.D. 1963; m. Catherine d. Christiane (de Badrihaye) and Robert Lebedoff 11 June 1984; children: Mary Catherine, Kirstie, Ian, Peter, Frederik; RESEARCH SCIENTIST, PHYSICAL AND CHEMICAL SCIENCES BRANCH, BEDFORD INSTITUTE OF OCEANOGRAPHY 1992– ; Rsch. Sci., Atlantic Oceanogr. Lab., Bedford, Inst. of Oceanogr. 1962–74; Div. Head, Ocean Circ. Div. 1975–79; Dir. 1979–85; Scientific Dir., World Ocean Circulation Experiment (Wormley, U.K.) 1985–89; Chief Scientist 1989–92; Rsch. Assoc., Dalhousie Univ. 1967–85; Mem., Sci. Ctte., Candn. Meteorol. & Oceanogr. Soc. 1977–80 (Soc. Mem. 1970– ); Candn. Nat. Ctte. for SCOR 1978–79; for IUGG 1979–83 (Chrmn. 1983–85); Mem., GESAMP 1980–85; Rossby Mem. Fellow, Woods Hole Oceanogr. Inst. 1970; F.R.S.C. 1985; recreations: golf, squash; Office: Bedford Institute of Oceanography, P.O. Box 1006, Dartmouth, N.S. B2Y 4A2.

**NEEDLES, Raymond Daniel,** B.A.; writer; b. Toronto, Ont. 27 July 1951; s. George William and Dorothy-Jane (Goulding) N.; e. Lakefield Coll. Sch.; Univ. of Toronto B.A. 1974; m. Heath d. John and Patricia Matthews 26 Sept. 1987; children: Madeline, Hart; PLAYWRIGHT & FREELANCE WRITER 1988– ; Editor, Shelburne Free Press 1974–76; Minister's Asst., Ont. Govt. 1976–81; Dir. of public Affairs, Canada Life Assur. 1981–88; author: The Wingfield Trilogy: 'Letter from Wingfield Farm,' 'Wingfield's Progress,' 'Wingfield's Folly' (one-man stage plays which have appeared across Canada & on CBC Morningside Drama), 'Perils of Persephone' 1989, 'Letters from Wingfield Farm' 1989, (paperback) 1990; nominated for Leacock Medal for Humour 1990; recreations: farming, fishing, gardening; clubs: Arts & Letters Toronto; Home: R.R. #1, Nottawa, Ont. L0M 1P0.

**NEELANDS, Donald Grant,** Q.C.; retired trust company executive; b. Toronto, Ont. 21 March 1916; s. Ernest Victor and Jessie Margaret (Easson) N.; e. Cobalt (Ont.) Public and High Schs.; Upper Canada Coll., Toronto, Ont. (1934); Trinity Coll., Univ. of Toronto, B.A. 1938; Osgoode Hall Law Sch., Toronto, Ont.; m. Christine Martin, d. Arthur E. MacGregor, Toronto, Ont., 16 April 1942; three d., Nancy, Margaret, Patricia; Trustee, Nat. Sanitarium Assn.; called to the Bar of Ont. 1941; Legal Asst., Candn. Tax Foundation, 1946–49; joined Toronto Gen. Trusts Corp. (predecessor Co.), 1949 as Trust Offr.; Corp. Trust Offr., 1956, Estates Mgr. 1959; Asst. Gen. Mgr. 1960; Depy. Gen. Mgr. and Asst. to Pres., Can. Permanent Mortgage Co. and Can. Perm. Trust Co. 1968, Extve. Vice-President February 1969; President 1969; Chrmn., Canada Permanent Mortgage Corp. and Canada Permanent Trust Co. 1975–81; Captain, Canadian Intelligence Corps. 1941–45; Phi Kappa Pi; Presbyterian; Clubs: Toronto Hunt; York; Empire; Home: 170 Inglewood Drive, Toronto, Ont. M4T 1H7.

**NEELANDS, William David,** M.A., M.Div., Th.D.; university administrator; b. Brampton, Ont. 30 Oct. 1943; s. William Gordon and Lillian Marguerite (Judge) N.; e. Brampton H.S.; Trinity Coll., Univ. of Toronto, B.A. 1965, M.A. 1966, M.Div. 1978, Th.D. 1988; Pembroke Coll., Oxford; m. Mary d. Denne and Joan Bosworth 28 June 1975; children: William Andrew Denne, Peter Gordon Bosworth; ASSISTANT VICE-PRES. – STUDENT AFFAIRS, UNIV. OF TORONTO 1988– ; Lectr., Dept. of Philos., Trinity Coll., Univ. of Toronto 1969–72; Registrar, Trinity 1973–88; Dean of Men 1975–80; Special Lectr., Dept. of Religious Studies & Fac. of Divinity, Trinity; Fellow, Trinity; Hon. Fellow, Woodsworth Coll.; Home: 372 Markham St., Toronto, Ont. M5S 1A1.

**NEILL, Robert D.;** consulting engineer/executive; b. Fredericton, N.B. 8 Aug. 1932; s. Wallace Raymond and Marjorie Haines (Fletcher) N.; Univ. of N.B., B.Sc. 1954; D.Sc. honoris causa 1985; m. Joey J. d. Leonard and Aida Coates 25 June 1954; children: Katherine Josephine, Kimberly Robert; CHRMN., NEILL AND GUNTER LIMITED 1984– ; Design Engr., N.B. Power 1954–56; Sr. Mech Engr. 1957–61; Chief Design Engr. 1962–64; Extve. Vice Pres., Neill and Gunter Limited 1964–78; Pres. & Chief Extve. Offr. 1979–84; Pres., Neill and Gunter Incorp. 1976–84; Chrmn. & Chief Extve. Offr. 1984– ; Pres., NGM Internat. 1978– ; Vice Pres., Manufacturing Technology Center of N.B.; Vice Pres., CADMI Microelectronics Ctr., Univ. of N.B.; Chrmn., Wood Science Technology Inst.; Bd. of Govs., Univ. of N.B.; Beaverbrook Art Gallery; Bd. of Dirs., NBTEL; Candn. Nuclear Assn.; Mem., Assn. of Profl. Engrs. of N.B.; Am. Soc. of Mech. Engrs.; Forest Prod. Rsch. Soc.; recreations: skiing, tennis, golf; Club: Fredericton Garrison Club Inc.; Fredericton Golf & Curling; Home: 505 Golf Club Rd., Fredericton, N.B. E3B 5Z5; Office: 191 Prospect St., P.O. Box 713, Fredericton, N.B. E3B 5B4.

**NEILSON, Keith Erick,** B.Sc., B.A., M.A., Ph.D.; university professor; b. Red Deer, Alta. 29 June 1948; s. Frederick William and Agnes Marietta (Farewell) Neilson; e. Univ. of Alta. B.Sc. 1969, B.A. 1971, M.A. 1974; Univ. of Cambridge Ph.D. 1978; m. Joan d. George and Mary Grinde 7 Aug. 1971; children: Beverley Anne, David Walter Andrew, Susan Mary; PROFESSOR, HISTORY, ROYAL MILITARY COLLEGE OF CANADA 1990– ; Teacher, Royal Roads Military College 1978–79; Asst. Prof., Royal Military College 1979–84; Assoc. Prof. 1984–90; Head of History Dept. 1993; specialist in Brit. fgn. policy & Brit. military history with particular interest in Anglo-Russian/Soviet relations; author: 'Strategy and Supply' 1984 and journal articles; co-editor:'Coalition Warfare' 1983, 'Men, Machines and War' 1988, 'The Cold War and Defense' 1990, 'Go Spy the Land' 1992; recreations: squash, coaching basketball; Home: 893 Percy Cres., Kingston, Ont. K7M 4P3; Office: Kingston, Ont. K7K 5L0.

**NEILY, Wayne Patrick,** B.Sc., B.Ed.; environmentalist, naturalist; b. Middleton, N.S. 17 March 1946; s. Earle Balcom and Vivian Elizabeth (Barkhouse) N.; e. West Kings Dist. H.S. 1963; Acadia Univ. B.Sc. 1966; Univ. of Winnipeg & Coll. Univ. de Saint-Boniface B.Ed. 1986; Mem., Manitoba Environ. Council 1980– ; Chair of Council 1989–91; Co-ordinator & Executive Offr., Manitoba Environ. Council 1991; pioneer in environ. interpretation/edn. in Canada, estab. programs of on-site interpretation in Nat. Parks incl. 1st bilingual prog., Cape Breton Highlands N.P. 1967–72, Kluane N.P. 1973–76; interpretation planning, Nahanni & Wood Buffalo N.P.s 1977–78; estab. 1st interpretive programs, Oak Hammock Marsh Wildlife Mngt. Area 1979; Fort Whyte Nature Centre, Winnipeg 1980–84; Life Elective Mem., Am. Birding Assn.; Nat. Dir., Candn. Nature Fed. 1974–76; Cape Breton Br., N.S. Bird Soc. 1970–72; Yukon Conserv. Soc. (Dir., Vice-Pres., Acting Pres. 1973–76); Am. Birding Assn. (Dir. 1975–84, Reg. Co-ord., W. Can. 1975–84); Man. Naturalists' Soc. [Dir. 1980–83; Vice-Pres., (Environ. Action) 1982–83]; Internat. Council for Bird Preserv. (Candn. Sec.-Treas. 1973–74); regional editor: 'American Birds' (Atlantic Prov.) 1972–73, (N.W. Canada) 1974–76; editor: 'Branta' 1982–84, Problem Corner in 'Generations'; co-author: 'Birder's Guide to S.E. Manitoba' 1980, '88, 'Birds of Nahanni National Park, N.W.T.' 1985, 'Field Checklist of the Birds of Manitoba' 1986; author of articles on natural history & genealogy in var. pubs.; recreations: birding, nature study, genealogy, philately; Home: Box 1856, Winnipeg, Man. R3C 3R1.

**NELDNER, H.M. (Hal);** telecommunications executive; b. Lodz, Poland 22 Oct. 1938; e. Univ. of Alta. B.Com. 1964; Harvard Advanced Mgmt. Prog. 1984; m. Marion Riske; PRESIDENT & C.E.O., TELUS CORPORATION 1990– and Depy. Chrmn. & C.E.O., AGT Limited (formerly Alberta Govt. Telephones); Dir., Canadian Utilities; Suncor Inc.; joined AGT 1964 assuming progressively more senior financial positions; two-year assignment Telecom Canada 1975–77; returned to AGT as comptroller 1977; Vice Pres. Finance & Chrmn., AGT Pension Bd. 1980; Vice Pres. Corp. Planning & Engineering 1983; President 1984; Chief Extve. Offr. 1987; Mem. Faculty of Business Adv. Council, Univ. of Alta.; K40 Fort Edmonton; Office: 31st Flr., 10020 – 100 St., Edmonton, Alta. T5J 0N5.

**NELLES, Henry Vivian,** Ph.D., F.R.S.C.; university professor; b. (Galt) Cambridge, Ont. 9 Nov. 1942; s. the late Henry Stuart and Dorothy Margaret (McCrow) N.; e. Paris Dist. H.S., Univ. of Toronto, B.A. 1964, M.A.

1965, Ph.D. 1970; m. Diane d. the late Leslie Claremont and Phyllis Dilworth 2 Sept. 1967; children: Jennifer Leslie, Geoffrey Andrew; PROF., DEPT. OF HIST., YORK UNIV. 1970– ; Chrmn., Ont. Council on Univ. Affairs 1988–92; Univ. of Toronto 1967–68; Univ. of B.C. 1968–70; Vis. Candn. Studies Prof., Tsukuba Univ. Keio Univ. Internat. Christian Univ. 1976–77; W.L.M. King Prof. of Candn. Studies, Harvard Univ. 1981–82; Co-editor 'Canadian Historical Review' 1988–92; active in Candn. Hist. Assn.; Newcomen Award 1973; Toronto Book Award 1977; Fellow, Royal Soc. 1985; Sir John A. Macdonald Prize 1986; Gen. Ed.: 'Social History of Canada series' 1978–88; author: 'Politics of Development ' 1974; co-author: 'The Revenge of the Methodist Bicycle Company' 1977, 'Monopoly's Moment' 1986; 'Southern Exposure' 1988; editor: 'The Philosophy of Railroads' 1972, 'Nationalism or Local Control' 1972, 'But This Is Our War' 1981; Clubs: Internat. House of Japan, Tokyo; Home: 301 Jedburgh Rd., Toronto, Ont. M5M 3K5; Office: Dept. of Hist., York Univ., 4700 Keele St., North York, Ont. M3J 1P3.

**NELLIGAN, John P.,** Q.C., L.S.M.; lawyer; b. Hamilton, Ont. 22 July 1921; m. Marion Sirdevan 1946; children: Margaret Greb, Jack, Kathleen Britt; SR. PARTNER NELLIGAN POWER 1963– ; Home: 40 Pond St., Rockcliffe Park, Ottawa, Ont. K1L 8J3; Office: 1900, 66 Slater St., Ottawa, Ont. K1P 5H1.

**NELSON, (Dewart) Erle,** B.Sc., Ph.D.; university professor; b. Antler, Sask. 11 Oct. 1943; s. Paul C. and Astrid (Larsen) N.; e. Univ. of Sask. B.Sc. 1966; McMaster Univ. Ph.D. (Physics) 1972; m. Gitte d. Aksel and Helga Nørgaard 10 June 1965; children: Torben P., Leif B.; PROF., ARCHEOL. DEPT., SIMON FRASER UNIV. 1986– ; Rsch. Asst., Niels Bohr Lab (Copenhagen) 1963–64; Rsch. Sci., Candn. Ctr. for Inland Waters 1972–73; post-doct. fellow, Physics Dept., Simon Fraser Univ. 1974–75; Rsch. Assoc., Archaeol. Dept. 1975; Asst. Prof. 1975–80; Assoc. Prof. 1981–85; Assoc. Mem., SFU Physics Dept.; author/co-author of approx. 95 sci. papers; recreations: sailing, travel; Home: 1025 Stewart Ave., Coquitlam, B.C.; Office: Burnaby, B.C. V5A 1S6.

**NELSON, James Gordon,** M.A., Ph.D., educator; b. Hamilton, Ont. 3 Apl. 1932; e. McMaster Univ. B.A. 1955; Univ. of Colo. M.A. 1957; Johns Hopkins Univ. Ph.D. 1959; m. 3 children; PROF. OF GEOG. & URBAN & REG. PLAN., UNIV. OF WATERLOO 1983– ; Post Doctoral Fellow Johns Hopkins Univ. 1959–60; Asst. Assoc. and Prof. Univ. of Calgary 1960–71, also served as Head Dept. Geog., Assoc. Dean Planning, Asst. to Vice Pres. Special Projects; Prof. of Geog. Univ. of W. Ont. 1971–75; Dean of Env. Studies, Univ. of Waterloo, 1975–1983; Chrmn., Heritage Resources Centre, Univ. of Waterloo 1986– ; Consultant to Parks Can., Dept. of Environment, Econ. Council of Can.; Dir. Renewable Resources Project, Inuit Tapirisat of Can. 1974–75; mem. non-govt. Candn. Adv. Comte. for Stockholm Conf. on Environment; Alaska Hwy. Pipeline Panel 1976–79; Trustee, Nat. & Prov. Parks Assn. Can. 1968–74 (Past Pres.); Past Pres., Assn. of Cndn. Univ. for Northern Studies; Chrmn. Management Com., Canadn. Northern Studies Trust; rec'd. Kitchener Police Citation 1976; Gilman Fellow; Bissing Post-Doctoral Fellow; Natural Heritage Award, 1978; Candn. Assn. Geog. Award for Scholarly Distinction in Geog., 1983; Social Sci. and Humanities Leave Fellowship 1984–85; Award for Service to Geography in Ont., Ont. Div., Candn. Assoc. of Geographers, 1988; Royal Candn. Geographical Soc. Major Competitive Grant 1992; awarded, Massey Medal, Royal Candn. Geographical Soc. 1993; Fellow, Royal Candn. Geographical Soc. 1993; author 'The Last Refuge' 1973; 'Man's Impact on the Western Canadian Landscape' 1976; Ed. 'Canadian Parks in Perspective' 1971, 'The Scottish and Alaskan Offshore Oil and Gas Experience and the Canadian Beaufort Sea' (With S. Jessen) 1981; 'Planning and Managing Environmentally Significant Areas in the Northwest Territories' 1984; Ed. 'Heritage for Tomorrow' 5 vols. (with R.C. Scace) 1986 and 1987; Ed. 'Arctic Heritage' (with Roger Needham and Linda Norton); Ed. 'Tourism, Monitoring, Planning, Managing' (with Richard Butler and Geoff Wall); various other books and journal articles; Past Pres. Candn. Assn. Geogs.; mem. Am. Assn. Geogs.; Commn. on National Parks and Protected Areas; Internat. Union for the Conservation of Nature and Natural Resources; Sigma Xi; Home: 54 Valley Ridge Cr., Waterloo, Ont. N2T 1J8; Office: University Ave., Waterloo, Ont. N2L 3G1.

**NELSON, Joyce D.,** B.A., M.A.; writer; b. Duluth, Minn. 24 Feb. 1945; d. Richard Charles and Dorothy Irene (Furland) N.; e. Coll. of St. Scholastica B.A. 1967; Arizona State Univ. M.A. 1970; has authored more than 70 mag. articles & essays pub. in Candn. periodicals & 23 hours of radio documentary broadcast by CBC Ideas; public speaker and guest lecturer; author: 'Sign Crimes/Roadkill: From Mediascape to Landscape' 1992; 'Sultans of Sleaze' 1989, 'The Colonized Eye' 1988, 'The Perfect Machine' 1987, 'Battlefronts' (poetry) 1977; co-editor: 'Canadian Film Reader' 1977; Teacher, Creative Writing Dept., Univ. of Victoria 1991–93; West Coast Women & Words Soc. 1989; Dept. of Film Studies, Queen's Univ. 1972–76; cons., Lang. Study Ctr., Toronto Bd. of Edn. 1978–79; fed. Dept. of Communications 1980–81; script cons., Telefilm Canada 1983–85; work included in 'Best Canadian Essays' 1990, 1991; winner, 2nd Prize for Radio Drama, CBC 1983 Lit. Comp.; winner, Oscar & Dorothy Burritt Mem. Award for Film Rsch. 1985; Borestone Mountain Poetry Prize (U.S.) 1977; 'Atlantic Monthly' Creative Writing Award, hon. mention 1966; Neopagan and Leftist Ecofeminist; recreations: collage, tarot, dialectical materialism; clubs: The Women's Glee Club & Terrorist Soc. (Toronto Chap.); Home: #103 - 636 Dallas Rd., Victoria, B.C. V8V 1B5.

**NELSON, Ronald Digby,** C.A., R.I.A.; executive; b. Sunderland, Co. Durham, Eng. 31 Dec 1935; s. Ronald D. Nelson; e. Queen's Univ. C.A. 1964; McMaster Univ. R.I.A. 1967; m. Renée C. d. of A. Sauvageau, Trois Rivieres, Que. 18 Apr. 1963; children: Ronald Digby, Tania Marie; VICE PRES & CHIEF FINANCIAL OFFR., CALGARY OVERSEAS DEVELOPMENT CO., NICOSIA, CYPRUS 1992– and CIBIR OVERSEAS MANAGEMENT LTD., NICOSIA, CYPRUS 1992– ; Treas., Neft Services Ltd. (Calgary, Alta.) 1992– ; Treas., Taroy Corp., Omaha, NE 1991– ; Dir., Pres., Secy. & Treas., Gourmet Popping Corn Co., Omaha, NE; Dir. & Secy., The Scoular Company; Scoular Properties, Inc.; Dir. & Chrmn. of Fin. Ctte., Children's Square, U.S.A.: Trustee and Mem. of Finance Ctte., Boy Scouts of America - Mid America Council; Dir., Pulsar Energy and Resources Inc.; Dir., United Arts of Omaha; Adv. Bd. Mem., Creighton Univ. School of Medicine; Student in Accounts, Butterfield & Steinhoff, Hamilton, Bermuda 1954–60; Acct., Reynolds International Inc. Bermuda 1960–63; Works Acct. Canadian Industries Ltd. Montreal, Shawinigan, Sarnia 1963–67; Gen. Mgr., Aluminum Co. of Canada Toronto, Montreal, Vancouver 1967–70; Vice-Pres. and Controller, Evans Products Co. Ltd. Vancouver 1971–74; Vice Pres. Finance and Administration, Weyerhaeuser Canada Ltd. Vancouver 1974–77; Vice Pres. Project Control and Acct., Foothills Pipelines (Yukon) Ltd., Calgary, Alta. 1978–80; Vice Pres. Finance and Admin., Enron Corp., Calgary, Alta. 1980–84, Gen. Mgr., Finance and Admin., Omaha, Nebraska 1984–86, Gen. Mgr., Project Evaluation, Houston, Texas 1986–87; Dir., Sr. Vice Pres., Chief Financial Offr. & Secy., Scoular Grain Co. 1987–91; Dir., Financial Extve. Inst.; mem., Tax Extve. Inst.; R.I.A. of Alta.,; Candn. Inst. C.A.'s Ont.; Dir. Piccadilly Productions Ltd.; (Past Pres.) Project Management Inst. of Alta. (PMI); Vice Pres. & Dir. Petroleum Accts. Soc. of Western Canada (PASWC); (Past Pres.) and Chrmn. and Dir., Assoc. of Chartered Accountants of Calgary; mem., Ed. Comte., Univ. of Calgary; mem., 1980, '81 and '82 Theme Comm., Calgary Ex. and Stampede; Calgary Professional Club, Y.M.C.A.; Chrmn., Springbank Group Comm., Boy Scout, of Can.; P. Conservative; Anglican; recreations: canoeing, riding, gardening, hiking, skiing; Home: 3030 Signal Hill Dr. S.W., Calgary, Alta.; Office: 1600, 510 5th St. S.W., Calgary, Alta. T2P 3S2.

**NEMETZ, Hon. Nathaniel Theodore,** C.C., Q.C., LL.D.; b. Winnipeg, Man. 8 Sept. 1913; s. late Samuel and late Rebecca (Birch) N.; e. Watrous, Sask. Public Sch.; Cecil Rhodes and Prince of Wales Sch., Vancouver, B.C.; Univ. of B.C., B.A. (1st Class Hons., Hist.) 1934; Vancouver Law Sch., 1937; m. the late Bel Newman, 10 Aug. 1935; one s. Peter Nemetz (Ph.D Harvard); Chief Justice, Supreme Court of B.C. 1973–78; Chief Justice of British Columbia 1979–88; Chancellor, Univ. of B.C. 1972–75; called to Bar of B.C. 1937; cr. K.C. 1950; former Sr. Partner , Nemetz, Austin, Christie and Bruk, former Special Counsel City of Vancouver, City of New Westminster, Mun. of Burnaby, Elec. Assn. of B.C., B.C. Hosps. Assn.; Special Commr. apptd. by Govt of Can. & Prov. of B.C. to inquire into Fishing Industry Dispute, 1954; Special Counsel Pub. Utilities Comn. of B.C. Inquiry into Natural Gas Rates B.C. Electric, 1958 and Inland Natural Gas, 1959; Sr. Counsel, Royal Comn. on Expropriation, 1961; apptd. Judge, Supreme Court of B.C., 1963; Royal Commr. to investigate Election Irregularities, 1965; B.C. Indust. Enquiry Commr. to inquire into dispute of Forest Industry and Internat. Woodworkers, 1966; Special Report to Govt. of B.C. on Swedish Labour Law and Practices, 1967; del., World Assembly of Judges, Geneva, 1967; Free Trade Conf., U.S., Can. and Gt. Brit., N.Y., 1968; Justice Appeal Court of B.C. 1968–75; Publ. 'Judicial Administration and Judicial Independence,' 1976; 'The Jury and the Citizen' 1985; 'The Concept of an Independent Judiciary' 1985; The Factum in Oral Advocacy 1985; The Intermediate Court of Appeal (Stanford) 1986; Alternate Dispute Resolution (Univ. of Br. Columbia Conf. on Internat. Arbitration 1986); 'The Independence of the Judiciary,' Address to Law Sch., Univ. of West. Australia 1987; 'British, American and Canadian Labour Law - A Comparative and Historical Review'; Speaker, 'Alternate Dispute Resolution,' Cambridge Conf., Queens' Coll., Cambridge 1987; 'The Future of Appellate Advocacy in Canada' 1987; 'The Media and the Justice System' Touro College, New York 1987; The Heald Lecture, Univ. of Sask. 1987; The Walter S. Owen Lecture - To Save the Law from Stagnation & Decay 1990; Chrmn. Bd. of Govs., Univ. of B.C., 1965–68 (mem. Senate 1957–66); del. 4th Gen. Conf. Internat. Assn. of Univs., Tokyo, 1965; Commonwealth Univs. Congress, Sydney, 1968; Head, Candn. Educ. Del. to People's Repub. of China 1974; Past Dir., Sick Children's Foundation; Past Chrmn., Univ. Dist. Sch. Bd.; Past Pres., Alumni Association of B.C.; Chrmn., Bd. of Govs. 1965–68, Dir., Candn. Inst. for Advanced Legal Studies (Cambridge); Chrmn. Legal Conf., Stanford Univ. 1986, 1990; First Candn. Del., Judicial Conf. of South Pacific, New Zealand 1987; Hon. Chrmn., Crusade Against Cancer 1988; Co-Chrmn., First Candn.-Australasian Legal Conf., Canberra, Australia 1988; Chrmn., Arbitration Bd. to consider dispute between Japanese Steel Companies and Quintette Coal (B.C.); Gov't. of Canada Appointee to Appeal Tribunal Canada-U.S. Free Trade Agreement 1989; Gov't. of B.C. Commissioner to consider civil servants' severance allowances 1989; Counsel for B.C. Provincial Judges Assoc. (salaries) 1989; Chrmn., Bank of Hong Kong Senior Citizens Selection Award Ctte.; Advisory Ctte., UBC Development Drive; Apptd., Honorary Consul-General for Singapore 1989; Walter Owen Law Professor, UBC 1989; Guest of Honour, Univ. of B.C., the Law Soc., the Candn. Bar B.C. Br. and Vancouver Bar on the occasion of the creation of (1) The Nathan T. Nemetz Chair in Legal History and (2) the Inst. for Alternative Dispute Resolution, 1988; Guest of Honour of Treasurer and Benchers, Gray's Inn, London, Engl. 1988; Guest of Honour, Candn. Judges Conf. of Can., Dinner Ritz Carlton Hotel, Montreal, Que. 1988; Past Pres. Vancouver Lodge B'nai B'rith; Past Pres. Vancouver Inst.; Past Dir., Vancouver Festival; Playhouse Theatre; Vancouver Community Chest; Recipient Human Relations Award, Candn. Council of Christians and Jews, Vancouver 1958, and Beth Emeth Bais Yehuda Brotherhood Award, Toronto, 1968; Univ. of B.C. Students Great Trekker Award, 1969; Hon. Life Mem., Faculty Assn. (U.B.C.) 1972; Certificate of Honour, University Club 1981; Advisor, The Cambridge Canadian Trust; Candn. Judicial Council 1973–88 (el. Vice-Chrmn. 1985–88); mem., Candn. Bar Assn.; Honorary Vice-Pres., Boy Scouts (B.C.); Internat. Law Assn.; Convocation Fndg. mem., Simon Fraser Univ.; Hon. LL.D. Notre Dame of Nelson 1972; Simon Fraser 1975; U.B.C. 1975; Victoria 1976; Univ. of Tel Aviv 1991; Distinction Award U.B.C. Alumni, 1975; Canada Medal 1967; Vancouver East End Bar Award 1974; Silver Jubilee Medal 1977; 125th Canada Medal; Chancellor's Medal, Univ. of B.C. 1988; Blyth Eagles, U.B.C. Alumni Award 1988; Medal, 'Flag of Yugoslavia with Ribbon' 1989; NEGEV Award Dinner 1989; Companion of the Order of Canada 1989; Order of British Columbia 1990; Hon. Fellow, Hebrew Univ., Jerusalem 1976; Special Guest, Amer. Chief Justices Conference, Anchorage, Alaska 1980; Speaker 100th Anniv. Montefiore Club Montreal, 1980; Guest Speaker, American Appellate Judges Conference, Vail, Colorado 1983, Savannah, Georgia 1985; Speaker, Univ. of Western Australia 1987; Freeman of the City of Vancouver 1988; Mem., Am. Arbitration Assoc. 1989; Patron, Laurier Inst.; Patron, Kidney Found. of B.C.; Hon. Chrmn., Vancouver Sun Children's Fund; Hon. Chrmn. CNIB Campaign; Commissioner, Government Inquiry B.C. Ferries Safety Practices 1992; Jewish; recreations: reading; Clubs: University (Past Pres.); Fac. Club, Univ. of B.C.; Vancouver Club, Vancouver; British Columbia; Office: c/o Russell & Dumoulin, 1800 - 1075 W. Georgia St., Vancouver, B.C. V6E 3G2.

**NEMIROFF, Diana Patricia Catherine,** B.F.A., M.A.: curator; b. London, England 1 May 1946; d. William Arthur and Marion Catherine (Conroy) Wilson; e. Ecole des beaux-arts Montreal; Concordia Univ., B.F.A. 1974, M.A. 1985; 1st m. Michael Nemiroff; children: Samantha, Noah; 2nd m. Pierre s. Madeleine and Jules Landry 25 Aug. 1989; CURATOR, NAT. GALLERY OF CANADA 1983– ; Lectr., Concordia Univ. 1979–80, 1982–83; freelance art critic 1978–83; Regional Ed., 'Vanguard' 1982–83; most recently organized exhib.

'Land, Spirit, Power: First Nations at the National Gallery of Canada' 1992 & many other contemporary art exhibs.; Mem., Candn. Mus. Assn.; Native Art Studies Assn.; Pres., Bd. of Dir., Optica Gall. 1980–82; 'B' grant, Can. Counc. 1982–83; author of 1 book chap.; Home: 445 Hartleigh Ave., Ottawa, Ont. K2B 5J3; Office: 380 Sussex Dr., P.O. Box 427, Stn. A., Ottawa, Ont. K1N 9N4.

**NEMNI, Max,** B.A., M.A., C.G.A., Ph.D.; university professor; b. Alexandria, Egypt 13 June 1935; e. C.G.A. 1963; York Univ. B.A. 1968, M.A. 1969, Ph.D. 1976; m. Monique children: Colette, Jacqueline; PROF. OF POLITICAL SCIENCE, LAVAL UNIV. 1977– ; Accountant, Canadian Kodak 1961–67; Teaching Asst., York Univ. 1969–72; Asst. Prof., Laurentian Univ. 1972–77; Prof., Laval Univ. 1988; Assoc. Dean, Fac. of Social Sciences 1986–88; has held several admin. posts; research: Canadian Politics (nationalism, federalism), political theory and history of ideas; extensive participation in symposia; Internat. Pol Sci. Assn.(contbr.: Comparative Federalism Rsch. Ctte.); Mem., Assn. d'écon. pol.; Candn. Pol. Sci. Assn.; Am. Pol. Sci. Assn.; Soc. for Socialist Studies; Certified Gen. Accountants Assn. (Life Member 1986– ); author of scholarly articles; recreations: swimming, skiing, cycling, bridge; Office: Laval Univ., Quebec City, Que. G1K 7P4.

**NERSKA, Andrew F.,** B.A.; executive; b. Tartu, Estonia 27 Nov. 1941; s. Karl and Tuuli N.; e. High Sch. of Montreal; Concordia Univ. B.A. 1968; m. Helen d. Paul and Laura Allen May 1967; two s. Alexander Lloyd, Christopher Andrus; VICE PRES. HUMAN RESOURCES & ADMINISTRATION, PHILLIPS CABLES LTD. 1988– ; joined Bristol-Myers Pharmaceutical Group 1970–80, Dir. and Vice Pres. Personnel; Sonoco Ltd. 1980–88, Dir. Personnel, Vice Pres. Adm. and of Gen. Products Div.; mem. Adv. Bd. Human Resources Mgmt. Assn. Ont.; Communications Ctte. EEMAC; Club: Ontario Racquets; Home: 3100 Ballydown Cr., Mississauga, Ont. L5C 2C8; Office: 200, 300 Consilium Pl., Scarborough, Ont. M1H 3G2.

**NESBIT, Douglas Charles,** B.A., F.A.G.S.; educator; b. London, Eng. 4 Oct. 1926; s. Charles Henry Fletcher and Constance Elspeth (Bruce) N.; e. Crescent Sch. Toronto; Univ. of Toronto Schs.; ex-service Rehabilitation Sch.; Univ. of Toronto B.A. 1949; Ont. Coll. of Educ. 1950; Univ. of W. Ont. postgrad. studies 1962, 1964, 1967; Teacher, Bruce Mines Continuation Sch. 1950–51; Head, GEog. Dept., Banting Mem. High Sch. 1951–84; served with RCAF 1943–44; Pres. of the Bd. of Dirs. Brit. Israel World Fed. (Can.) 1984– , Vice Pres., 1983–84; Dir., 1982–83; Lay Reader, Ang. Ch. 1976–81; Treas. Toronto Br. Friends of Rhodesia Assn. 1971–81; Life mem. Candn. Bible Soc. (Pres. Alliston Br. 1978–90); Pres., South Simcoe Palette Club 1989–91; painter of picture 'If My People ... '; mem. Nat. Council for Geog. Educ.; Ont. Assn. Geog. & Environmental Educ.; Candn. Assn. Geogs.; Assn. Am. Geogs.; Am. Assn. Advanc. Science; Scot. Tartans Soc. (Life); Royal Candn. Legion; Royal Commonwealth Soc.; Monarchist League Can.; recreations: chess, painting, computer science, photography, travel; Club: Empire; Home: P.O. Box 89, Alliston, Ont. L9R 1T9.

**NESBITT, Herbert Hugh John,** Ph.D., D.Sc., F.L.S., F.R.E.S., F.E.S.C., F.E.S.A., F.Z.S.; retired university dean; b. Ottawa, Ont. 7 Feb. 1913; s. Herbert Hugh Wright and Anne Violet (Gould) N.; e. Queen's Univ., B.A. 1937; Univ. of Toronto, M.A. 1939; Ph.D. 1944; Univ. of Leiden, D.Sc. 1951; D.Sc. (hon) Carleton Univ., 1978; m. 1stly, Mary Elizabeth (dec.), d. T. E. Clendinnen, Ottawa, Ont., 24 June 1944; children: Eleanor Anne, Thomas H. D., David A.C., Robert I. M.; 2ndly, Dr. B.E. Wickett; Agric. Scientist, Dept. of Agric., Ottawa, 1939–48; Asst. Prof. of Biol., Carleton Univ., 1948, Assoc. Prof. 1952; Prof. 1956; Prof. Emeritus, 1978; Dean, Faculty of Science 1963–75; Clerk of Senate Carleton Univ., 1975–80; author of over 80 rsch. papers on mites (Acari); Fellow Linnean Soc. of London; Royal Entomol. Soc. London; Fellow, Entomol. Soc. of Can.; Entomological Soc. of America; Zoological Soc. of London; former Chrmn., Bd. of Govs., Algonquin Coll. 1979–85, Ottawa; Pres., Zoological Soc. of Can. 1964–65; United Church; Address: Carleton University, Ottawa, Ont. K1S 5B6.

**NESMITH, Wade Donald,** LL.B.; lawyer; b. Vancouver, B.C. 28 Jan. 1952; s. Melvin Eugene and Adele Patricia (Dunsmore) N.; e. Osgoode Hall York Univ. LL.B. 1977; m. Alison d. Joseph and Arley Molloy 4 Sept. 1982; children: Meghan Jean, Evan Thomas; LANG MICHENER 1993– ; Asst. Crown Atty. Toronto 1979–85; Special Prosecutor Edmonton 1985–87; Dep. Supt. Compliance & Enforcement B.C. Securities Comn. 1987–89; Supt. of Brokers 1989–92; Secy. & Dir., North American Securities Administrators Assn. 1990–92; mem. Law Soc. of Upper Canada; Alta. Law Soc.; Law Soc. of B.C.; Candn. Bar Assn.; Home: 641 Alpine Court, North Vancouver, B.C. V7R 2L7; Office: 2500, 595 Burrard St., Vancouver, B.C. V7X 1L1.

**NETTEN, Edward William,** B.Com., F.C.A., F.C.M.C.; management consultant; b. Corner Brook, Nfld. 17 Oct. 1930; e. McGill Univ., B.Com. (magna cum laude) 1951; C.A. Que. 1953, B.C. 1963, Ont. 1973; m. Barbara 14 May 1988; children: Linda, June, Cynthia, Shirley; with McDonald Currie & Co. as Student and Supvr. Montreal 1951; Cooper Bros. & Co. (Staff exchange) London, Eng. 1955=56; joined Price Waterhouse as Consultant, Montreal 1957, Mgr. 1960, Partner 1965; i.c. Mang. Consulting Services W. Can. Vancouver 1963, Partner i.c. consulting services in mang. controls Montreal 1967, Partner i.c. Montreal office 1968, Partner i.c. client services in mang. planning, information and control 1971; trans. to Toronto 1973; Partner in charge, Toronto Consulting 1974; Mng. Partner for Can., mgmt. consulting services 1981; National Partner 1988–93; mem. Inst. Certified Mang. Consultants Can. (Pres. 1974–76, Past Dir. & Pres.); Pres., Candn. Assoc. of Mang. Consultants 1983–84; author numerous articles on mang. policy, organ., mang. controls, accounting and strategy; Anglican; recreations: tennis, skiing; Clubs: Toronto Club; Ontario Racquet; Home: 1491 Watersedge Rd., Mississauga, Ont. L5J 1A5; Office: 1 First Canadian Place, Box 190, Toronto, Ont. M5K 1H7.

**NEUFELD, Edward Peter,** B.A.(Hons), Ph.D.; economist; b. Nipawin, Sask. 16 Nov. 1927; s. Henry Gerhard and Anna N.; e. Univ. of Sask., B.A.(Hons) 1951; London Sch. of Economics and Pol. Science, Ph.D. 1954 (awarded Hutchinson Silver Medal); m. Arlette, d. Raymond and Andrée Deloge, 28 Dec. 1974 (2nd marriage); children: Dwight, Anna-Marie, Derek, Valery; EXTVE. VICE PRESIDENT, ECONOMIC AND CORPORATE AFFAIRS, ROYAL BANK OF CANADA 1980– ; 1955–72: teacher, then Prof. of Economics at Univ. of Toronto; former Dir., National Life Insurance Co. and Jones Heward Fund Ltd.; Dept. of Finance, Ottawa 1973–79 (Dir. of Internat. Finance, Gen. Dir. of Internat. Trade and Finance, Asst. Dep. Min. of Tax Policy and Legislation Branch; also Dir. of Canada Mortgage and Housing Corp.; Alternate Dir. of Export Devel. Corp.); Hon. Fellow of London Sch. of Economics and Pol. Science; Dir., Atlantic Council of Can.; C.D. Howe Inst. (Policy Analysis Comte.); Le Cercle Canadien de Toronto; Internat. Adv. Bd., Canadian Council for the Americas; author 'Bank of Canada, Operations and Policy' 1958; sect. on financial statistics in 'Historical Statistics for Canada' 1965; 'A Global Corporation' 1969; 'The Financial System of Canada' 1972; numerous articles on economic analysis and stabilization policies and techniques; ed. and contrib. 'Money and Banking in Canada' 1964; religion: United Church of Canada; recreations: tennis, cycling, skiing, curling; Home: 1523 Ballyclare Dr., Mississauga, Ont. L5C 1J4; Office: Royal Bank Plaza, P.O. Box 1, Toronto, Ont. M5J 2J5.

**NEUFELD, Victor R.,** M.D., D.C.M.T., M.A.(Ed.), F.R.C.P.(C); physician; educator; b. Swift Current, Sask. 22 Aug 1935; s. Jacob Albert and Charlotte Marie (Blessin) N.; e. Univ. of Sask. M.D. 1961; Univ. of London (Eng.) D.C.M.T. 1964; Mich. State Univ. M.A. (Ed.) 1971; m. Barbara d. Reuben and Lynn Coleman 19 Dec. 1959; two s. Mark Victor, Reid Alan; DIR., CENTRE FOR INTERNAT. HEALTH, FACULTY OF HEALTH SCIENCES, McMASTER UNIV. 1990– , Prof. of Medicine and Clinical Epidemiology and Biostatistics 1980– ; Physician, Care-Medico Project, Malaysia 1964–66; Clin. Teacher, Univ. of Toronto 1969–70; present Univ. 1971– ; Cons. in Med. Edn. & Health Care various world orgns. and univs.; co-author: 'Assessing Clinical Competence' 1984; co-ed.: 'New Trends in Health Sciences Education, Research and Services' 1982; mem. Am. Coll. Phys.; recreations: running, back-packing; Home: 70 Chedoke Ave., Hamilton, Ont. L8P 4N9; Office: Rm. 3N44B, 1200 Main St. W., Hamilton, Ont. L8N 3Z5.

**NEUFELDT, Victor Alfred,** B.A., Ph.D.; university professor and administrator; b. Yarrow, B.C. 28 Dec. 1933; s. Henry Peter and Margaret (Enns) N.; e. Mennonite Educational Inst. 1953; Mennonite Brethern Bible College, Univ. of B.C. B.A. (Hons.) 1957; UBC Teaching Cert. 1958; Univ. of Washington 1962–63; Univ. of Illinois Ph.D. 1964–69; m. Audrey d. Eva and Jack Beaumont 16 Aug. 1958; children: Geoffrey, Keith, Karin; PROFESSOR, DEPT. OF ENGLISH, UNIV. OF VICTORIA 1968– ; High School Teacher Kitimat, B.C. 1958–62, 1963–64; Dir., First-Year English, Univ. of Victoria 1975–78, 1985–88; Department Chair 1992– ; Edit. Bd., 'English Literary Studies' 1983– , 'Victorian Review' 1987– ; Canada Council Grad. Fellow 1964–68 Phi Kappa Phi 1968; Canada Council/SSHRC Research Grants 1972, 1974–75, 1980–82, 1988–90, 1992–95; Mem., Kitimat Dist. Teachers' Assn. 1958–64 (Pres. 1960–61); Candn. Assn. of Univ. teachers 1968– ; Assn. of Candn. Univ. teachers of English 1968– ; Brontë Soc. (Life Mem.); Victorian Studies Assn. of W. Canada 1972– (Pres. 1984–86); Candn. Assn. of Chairs of English 1992– ; editor: 'The Poems of Charlotte Brontë' 1985, 'The Poems of Patrick Branwell Brontë' 1990, 'A Bibliography of the Mss of Patrick Branwell Brontë' 1993; co-editor: George Eliot's 'Middlemarch Notebooks' 1979; Home: 4290 Parkside Cres., Victoria, B.C. V8N 2C3; Office: Box 3045, Victoria, B.C. V8W 3P4.

**NEVILLE, G. Douglas,** B.Arch., O.A.A., F.R.A.I.C.; architect; b. Toronto, Ont. 7 Apl. 1931; s. George and Isabel (Marr) N.; e. Univ. of Toronto B.Arch. 1957; m. Ann d. Ross and Aileen Walters 27 Dec. 1955; children: Heather, Douglas, Bob, Jane; SR. PARTNER DUNLOP FARROW INC. ARCHS. 1984– ; Grad. Arch. Blackwell & Hagarty 1957–62; Prin. Douglas Neville Arch. 1962–68; Sr. Partner Bregman & Hamann Archs. 1968–84; mem. Ont. Assn. of Archs. (Pres. 1990); Toronto Soc. Archs.; Royal Arch. Inst. Can.; Bd. Trade Metrop. Toronto; United Church (Chrmn. Donminster Un. Ch. 1984–86); recreation: sketching, woodworking, golf; Home: 7 Dumas Court, Don Mills, Ont. M3A 2N1; Office: 450 Front St. W., Toronto, Ont. M5V 1B6.

**NEVILLE, John,** O.B.E.; actor; director; b. London Eng. 2 May 1925; s. Reginald Daniel and Mabel Lillian (Fry) N.; e. Grammar Sch. London, Eng.; Royal Acad. Dramatic Art London; m. Caroline Hooper 9 Dec. 1949; children: Rachel, Emma, Thomas, Sarah, Matthew, Stephen; Artistic Director, Stratford Festival 1985; joined Bristol Old Vic Company 1950–53; played numerous leading parts Old Vic Company, London 1953–61; made first New York appearance Winter Garden Theatre 1956 playing Romeo followed by Richard II, Macduff in 'Macbeth' and Thersites in 'Troilus and Cressida'; after touring US returned to London for 1957–58 season; toured US 1958–59 playing Hamlet and Sir Andrew Aguecheek; directed Henry V 1960; joined Nottingham Playhouse Co. 1961, Assoc. Producer 1961, Jt. Theatre Dir. 1963–67, played various leading roles incl. Macbeth and Sir Thomas More in 'A Man for All Seasons' (appeared in both roles Malta 1961); appeared opening Chichester Festival 1962 as Don Frederick in 'The Chances' and Orgilus in 'The Broken Heart'; toured W. Africa with Co. for Brit. Council 1963; appeared Edinburgh Festival 1970 for Prospect Productions Garrick in 'Boswell's Life of Johnson' and Benedick in 'Much Ado About Nothing'; toured US 1970; films incl.; 'Oscar Wilde' 1960, 'Billy Budd' 1961, 'Topaze' 1961; TV appearances incl.: 'Henry V' 1957, 'Romeo and Juliet' 1957 and 'Hamlet' 1959 both New York; leading role in 'Sherlock Holmes,' Broadway, N.Y. summer 1975; came to Canada, 1972, dir. 'The Rivals' and played Prospero in 'The Tempest,' Ottawa, Judge Brack in 'Hedda Gabler,' Manitoba Theatre Centre, Theatre Dir. at Citadel Theatre, Edmonton, Alta. 1972, dir. 'Romeo & Juliette,' 'The Master Builder.' 'Schweyk in the Second World War,' and 'Antigone,' appeared in several plays; Theatre Dir., Neptune Theatre, Halifax, May 1978, appeared in 'Othello' and 'Staircase,' dir. 'Les Canadiens' and 'The Sea Gull'; played dual roles, Mr. Malcolm & Major Pollock, 'Separate Tables' 1984; Shylock in 'The Merchant of Venice' and Don Armado in 'Love's Labour's Lost' 1984; Artistic Dir., Stratford Festival 1985–89: dir. 'Hamlet' 1986; 'Othello' and 'Mother Courage' 1987; appeared as Anton Chekhov in 'Intimate Admiration' 1987; Henry Higgins in 'My Fair Lady' 1988; Narrator, 'L'Histoire du Soldat,' Edinburgh Festival 1986; Noel Coward in 'An Evening with Noel Coward' (Centre Stage) 1986; narrator in Rick Hansen film 'Heart of the Dragon' 1986; title role in 'Adventures of Baron Munchausen' (film) 1988; served with RN 1942–46; rec'd Alta. Achievement Award; mem. Brit. Actors Equity; Candn. Actors Equity; ACTRA; Anglican; recreations: music, opera, ballet; Club: Savage (London, Eng.); Home: 99 Norman St., Stratford, Ont. N5A 5R8.

**NEVILLE, John,** B.A., M.B.A.; executive; b. Derby, Eng. 7 Jan. 1949; s. Arthur Bray and Audrey Patricia (Snelling) N.; e. Univ. of Victoria (B.C.) B.A. 1969; Stanford Univ., M.B.A. 1975; m. Debby d. Edward and Margaret Sayer 1 Aug. 1981; children: Michael John, Sharon Elizabeth; PRES., JOHN NEVILLE INC., SATELLITE GROUND SYSTEMS DISTRIBUTOR 1988– ; Pres., Island View Investments (VCC) Inc., a venture capital company; Chrmn., Quester Tangent Inc., a marine hydrographics company; Dir., Blackline Reinforced Plastics Ltd. (BRP) a kayak manufacturer; Reefco Manufacturing Corp., a refrigerated container manufacturer; joined Lambert Brothers Shipping London and Tokyo 1971–73; Cons. McKinsey & Co. Inc. Toronto 1975–77; various positions Fednav Ltd. Montréal 1977–83; Vice Pres. & Treas., Spar Aerospace Ltd. 1983, Sr. Vice Pres. 1987–88; recreations: white water kayaking, cross country skiing; Address: 5020 Lockehaven Dr., Victoria, B.C. V8N 4J5.

**NEVILLE, William Franklin Wymark,** M.A.; educator; b. Winnipeg, Man. 15 Sept. 1940; s. William Charles and Audre Isabel (Kaake) N.; e. elem. sch. Winnipeg; high schs. Ottawa, Edmonton and Winnipeg; Univ. of Man. B.A. 1963; Oxford Univ. (Rhodes Scholar, Commonwealth Scholar) B.A. 1966, M.A. 1971; m. Anita d. Harold and Faye Schwartz 20 Sept. 1965; three d. Sarah, Elissa, Jessica; ASSOC. PROF. OF POL. STUDIES, UNIV. OF MAN. 1976– , Asst. to the Pres. 1982– , Dir., Intnl. Develop. Office 1989– ; Lectr., Asst. Prof. and Assoc. Prof. of Politics Trent Univ. 1966–73; Extve. Asst. to Leader of the Opposition Man. Legis. 1973–75; Asst. to Vice Pres. (Acad.) present Univ. 1976–82, Univ. Coordinator of Candn. Studies 1978–82; private cons. and free-lance writing 1970– ; Pub. Affairs Commentator CBC Radio and TV 1978– ; mem., Special Study Fed.-Prov. Relations Man. Task Force on govt. Orgn. & Efficiency 1977–78; Man. Adv. Ctte. Task Force on Candn. Unity 1977–78; mem., Sec. of State's Candn. Studies Writing Awards Ctte. 1983–87; Man. Rhodes Scholarship Selection Ctte. 1974– ; mem. and Chrmn. Winnipeg Pub. Lib. Comn. 1975–78; mem. and Bd. Pres. Winnipeg's Contemporary Dancers 1976–82; mem. Bd. Heritage Winnipeg 1980–82; Dir., Prairie Theatre Exchange 1981–84; Adv. Ctte. Man. Assn. Rights & Liberties 1981–89; mem. Bd., Winnipeg Folk Festival 1985–91; mem. Bd., Royal Winnipeg Ballet 1989–91; mem. Bd. Candn. Paraplegic Assn. 1990– ; Adv. Comm. Social Planning Council of Winnipeg 1991– ; mem. Bd. Winnipeg Housing Rehabilitation Corp. 1983–86; el. to Winnipeg City Council 1979, re-el. 1980, 1983, 1986; Chrmn., Hist. Bldgs. Ctte. 1980–88; Recipient, Heritage Winnipeg's 'Distinguished Service Award' 1989; author various articles and reviews; mem. ed. bd. 'Journal of Canadian Studies' 1970– ; 'Mosaic' 1979–85; 'Arts Manitoba' now 'Border Crossings' 1985– ; 'Inner City Voice' 1993; Urban affairs columnist, 'Winnipeg Free Press' 1989– ; recreations: running, reading, music, philately; Home: 1 – 81 Lenore St., Winnipeg, Man. R3G 2C2; Office: 202 Administration Bldg., Winnipeg, Man. R3T 2N2.

**NEW, C. John;** consultant; b. Prince Albert, Sask. 8 March 1921; s. Charles George and Elizabeth H. (McDowell) N.; m. Una Rae Gillis, 25 Nov. 1944; daughter, Janet Leslie Flora; son, Douglas Charles; Pres., Hiram Walker Marketing Consulting Services, 1983–86; Extve. Vice Pres. & Dir., Hiram Walker, Gooderham & Worts, 1975–83; Pres. and Chief Extve. Offr., Corby Distilleries Ltd., (and subsidiary companies) 1970–76; Pres. & Mgr. Dir., Libby, McNeil & Libby of Canada Ltd., 1966–70, Vice Pres. & Gen. Mgr. 1964–66; Dir., Canada Starch Inc., 1972–92; Dir., London Trust and Savings Corp. 1985–93; Past Gov., Jr. Achievement of Canada; Founder, Jr. Achievement (Chatham, Ont.); Past Dir., Packaging Assoc. of Canada; Candn. Food Processing Assoc.; Assoc. of Candn. Distillers; Chrmn., Assoc. of Candn. Distillers, 1977–80; Benefactor, Royal Ontario Museum, 1971; mem. Candn. Conf. of the Arts; Toronto Bd. of Trade; Clubs: National (Toronto); Granite (Toronto); The Toronto Hunt; Home: 1210, 65 Harbour Sq., Toronto, Ont. M5J 2L4.

**NEW, William H.,** B.Ed., M.A., Ph.D., F.R.S.C.; university professor; b. Vancouver, B.C. 28 Mar. 1938; s. John and Edith Annie (Littlejohn) N.; e. Walter Moberly Sch. 1950; John Oliver H.S. 1956; Univ. of B.C., B.Ed. 1961, M.A. 1963; Univ. of Leeds, Ph.D. 1966; m. Margaret d. Harold and Patricia Ebbs-Canavan 6 July 1967; children: David, Peter; PROF., DEPT. OF ENGLISH, UNIV. OF B.C. 1965– ; Asst. Dean, Fac. of Grad. Studies 1975–77; Ed.: 'Canadian Literature' 1977– ; Mem., Adv. or Ed. Bd., 'Twentieth Century Literature,' Klein Project, C.E.E.C.T. Project, 'WLWE,' 'Commonwealth,' 'Canadian Encyclopedia,' 'Australian & New Zealand Studies in Canada,' 'Short Story,' Smithsonian Series of Studies in Native American Writing; F.R.S.C. 1986; Killam Rsch. Prize 1988; Mem., A.C.U.T.E., A.C.L.A.L.S., A.C.S., A.C.Q.L.; author: 'Malcolm Lowry' 1971, 'Articulating West' 1972, 'Among Worlds' 1975, 'Critical Writings on Commonwealth Literatures' 1975, 'Malcolm Lowry: A Reference Guide' 1978, 'Dreams of Speech and Violence' 1987, 'A History of Canadian Literature' 1989; editor: 'Four Hemispheres' 1971, 'Dramatists in Canada' 1972, 'Modern Canadian Essays' 1976, 'Margaret Laurence' 1977, 'A Political Art' 1978, 'Canadian Writers in 1984' 1984, 'Canadian Short Fiction' 1986, 'Canadian Writers since 1960' 2 vols. 1986, 1987, 'Canadian Writers, 1920–1959' first series 1988, second series 1989; 'Canadian Writers 1890–1920' 1990; 'Canadian Writers Before 1890' 1990; 'Literary History of Canada' vol IV 1990; 'Native Writers and Canadian Writing' 1990; 'Inside the Poem' 1992; co-editor: 'Voice and Vision' 1972, 'Modern Stories in English' 1975, 2nd ed. 1986, 3rd ed. 1991; 'Active Voice' 1980, 2nd ed. 1986, 3rd ed. 1991; 'A 20th Century Anthology' 1984; 'Literature in English' 1993; Office: 1873 East Mall, Vancouver, B.C. V6T 1Z1.

**NEWALL, James Edward Malcolm,** O.C., B.Com.; executive; b. Holden, Alta. 20 Aug. 1935; s. Robert Robertson N.; e. elem. sch. Edmonton, Alta. and Prince Albert, Sask.; Prince Albert Coll. Inst.; Univ. of Sask. B.Com. 1958; m. Margaret Elizabeth Lick; PRES., CHIEF EXECUTIVE OFFR. & DIR., NOVA CORPORATION OF ALBERTA 1991– ; Bd. of Dirs., Alcan Aluminium Ltd.; BCE Inc.; The Molson Companies Ltd.; The Royal Bank of Canada; Chrmn., Business Council on Nat'l Issues; Mem., Advisory Group to the Prime Minister on Executive Compensation in the Public Service; joined Du Pont as internal sales rep. Chem. Dept. Toronto 1957, Series of Assignments in Sales, Marketing and General Management in the Fibres Business 1958–71, Dir. Fibres Group, 1972, Vice Pres. Corporate Devel. 1974, Vice Pres. Marketing 1975, Extve. Vice Pres. 1975, Dir. 1976, Pres. and C.E.O. 1978–89, Chrmn. 1979, Chrmn. & C.E.O. 1979–91; Sr. Vice Pres., E.I. du Pont de Nemours Agricultural Products 1989–91; former Chrmn., Conference Bd. of Canada; Officer, Order of Canada 1994; recreations: golf, reading; Clubs: Forest & Stream; Mount Royal; Rideau (Ottawa); Toronto; Petroleum Club (Calgary); Ranchmens Club (Calgary); Office: 801 – 7th Ave. S.W., Calgary, Alta. T2P 3P7.

**NEWBOLD, Brian T.,** D.Sc., C.Chem., F.R.S.C. (U.K.), F.C.I.C., F.R.S.A.; K.L.J.; educator; b. Manchester, Eng. 21 June 1932; s. John Stanley and Florence (Wray) N.; e. schs. Eng. and Wales; Univ. of Manchester B.Sc. (Chem. & Physiol.) 1953; Laval Univ. D.Sc. (Organic Chem.) 1957, Post-Doctoral Fellow 1957–58; m. Marie Cecile Evelyn, d. late William Patrick LaRoche, 16 Aug. 1958; children: Linda, Trevor; Prof. Chem., Univ. de Moncton 1965– ; Asst. Prof. of Chem. St. Joseph Univ. 1958, Assoc. Prof. 1960, Head Dept. of Chem. 1961; joined present Univ. as Assoc. Prof. and founding Head Dept. of Chem. 1963, Vice-Dean Faculty of Science 1963–69; Dir. of Research, Pres. Research Council (1969–75) and mem. Acad. Senate (1963–75, 1976–77, 1979–85); Bd. of Govs. (1979–85); Vice Pres. Univ. de Moncton 1979–85; Visiting Lectr. in Biochem. Mount Allison Univ. 1962–63; Visiting Prof. Laval Univ. 1975–76; Visiting Prof. Saitama Univ., Japan 1985; Visiting Prof., Université Claude-Bernard Lyon I, France 1986; Visiting Prof., Centre International Francophone pour l'Education en Chimie, Montpellier, France 1986; Visiting Prof., Univ. of São Paulo, Brazil 1987; Pres., 10th Intnl. Conference on Chemical Education 1989; Pres., New Brunswick Science Fair 1991; rec'd Sr. Rsch. Fellowship, Japan Society for Promotion of Science 1985; mem. N.B. Higher Educ. Comn. 1967–74; rec'd 'Plaque de 10 ans' (Univ. Moncton) 1973; mem. and Pres. (1971–72) St. Henri Home & Sch. Assn. Moncton; Candn. nat. repres. Comte. on Teaching Chem., Internat. Union Pure & Applied Chem. 1969–87; Cultural Exchange Comte. Can. Council, 1971–74; co-author 'Chemical Canada' 1970; Editor 'New Trends in chemistry teaching' vol. VI (UNESCO); author or co-author over 120 research publs. incl. book chapters, papers, articles; columnist 'Gliding' Quebec Chronicle Telegraph 1956–58; Sr. mem. Am. Chem. Soc.; Pres., New Brunswick Environ. Council, (1975–79), Pres. 1974–75, Beauséjour Home and Sch. Assn., Moncton; mem. Royal Netherlands Chem. Soc.; Founding Mem., Natural Science & Engn. Research Council of Can. 1978–80; Chem. Inst. Can. (Dir., 1968–71); Candn. Soc. Study Higher Educ. (Extve. Council), 1970–74, 1975–76; Assn. Canadienne française pour l'avancement des sciences (Dir., Prés. Comité des Publs.); Candn. Assn. Univ. Research Adms. (Extve. Council) 1972–74; Hon. Sec. SCITEC 1977–79; Ed. SCITEC Bulletin 1977–79; Founding Ed. Can. Chem. Educ. (1965–75); Rec'd Union Carbide Award for Chem. Educ. 1977; mem. Nat. Council Candn. Fed. of Human Rights, 1980– ; Sr. Univ. Admrs. Course, Univ. of W. Ont. 1980; Consultant to Maritime Provinces Higher Educ. Comn. 1976–80; mem. Comté consultatif, Sci. et tech., Soc. Radio Canada, 1978–85; mem., Comité scientifique, Bulletin du Centre Intnl. Francophone pour l'Education en Chimie 1987– ; mem. Assn. for Educ. of Sci. Teachers, 1979–81; Inst. Candn. des affairs internat., 1979; Liason Officer, Univ.Moncton for C.I.D.A., 1981–85; mem., N.S. Art Gallery (1979–80); Bd. of Govs., Beaverbrook Art Gallery, 1981–88; Consultant to Internat. Devel. Research Centre (1981); Chrmn., Silver Medal Selection Ctte., Atlantic Chapter, Royal Soc. of Arts 1982; mem., Extve. Ctte. (1982–88), and Bd. of Dirs., Council for Candn. Unity 1982– ; mem., Maritime Coliseum-Agrena Comm. 1982–85; N.B. Prov. Chrmn. and mem. Bd. of Dirs., Terry Fox Candn. Youth Centre 1982– ; Hon. Secy., Atlantic Canada Section, Royal Soc. of Arts 1982–91, Pres. 1991– ; mem. Bd. of Dirs., Greater Moncton Chamber of Commerce 1983–85; mem., Moncton Rotary Club 1983–93; Rotary Internat. Paul Harris Fellow 1991; mem. Greater Moncton Pest Control Comn. 1985– ; mem. Comité exécutif, Assn. France-Canada (Moncton) 1986– (Pres. 1989– ); mem. Comité des candidatures (ACFAS); Founding mem., 25-year Club, Univ. de Moncton 1988; mem. Honoraire, Comité consultatif, Sci. et tech., Soc. Radio Canada 1985– ; Commander, Military and Hospitaller Order of Saint Lazarus of Jerusalem 1982–90, Knight 1990– , Commander, Acadia Commandery 1992– ; mem., Assoc. for the Advancement of Sci. in Canada 1983–91; mem., New York Acad. of Sciences 1987–93; Citation Directory of World Researchers (1981); Rec'd Hon. Citizenship and Friendship Medal from Munic. of St. Pierre, French Territory of St. Pierre et Miquelon (1981); Citation in Intnl. Book of Honor, First World Edition (1983); Citation in Five Thousand Personalities of the World, Edition Two (1986); Citation in International Directory of Distinguished Leadership, 2nd Ed. (1987); Citation in Personalities of the Americas, First Commemorative Edition (1987); Cert. of Distinction for Outstanding Contribution (recruiting campaign), Terry Fox Candn. Youth Centre (1983); Citation in Who's Who in The Commonwealth, 2nd Ed. (1983); Cert. of distinction for Outstanding Contribution (invited speaker), Terry Fox Candn. Youth Centre (1983); Chevalier, Ordre français des Palmes Académiques 1991; Anglican; Life mem., Royal Soc. of Arts 1992; Certificate of appreciation, Moncton Amateur Radio Club 1993; Mem., The Chemical Software Soc. of Japan 1993– ; Mem. Editorial Bd., 'Journal of Chemical Software of Japan' 1993– ; recreations: gliding (pilot 1954–58), bridge, hockey, soccer (coach Université de Moncton 1970), reading, philately, numismatics, painting, skating, skiing; Home: 167 Edgett Avenue, Moncton, N.B. E1C 7B4; Office: Dép. de Chimie et Biochimie, Univ. de Moncton, Moncton, N.B. E1A 3E9.

**NEWBORN, Monroe M.,** B.E., M.S., Ph.D.; educator; b. Cleveland, Ohio 21 May 1938; s. Isaac M. and Norma M. (Clapp) N.; e. Rensselaer Polytechnic Inst. B.E. (Elect. Engn.) 1960; Ohio State Univ. M.S. 1962, Ph.D. 1967; m. Barbara S. d. Leo and Eva Moser 29 June. 1975; two d. Amy Leora, Molly Anita; PROF. OF COMPUTER SCIENCE, McGILL UNIV. 1981– ; Instr. in Elect. Engn. Ohio State Univ. 1965–67; Asst. and Assoc. Prof. Columbia Univ. New York 1967–75; Visiting Prof. Israel Inst. of Technol. (The Technion) Haifa, Israel 1973–74; Assoc. Prof. present Univ. 1975, Dir., Sch. of Computer Science 1976–84; author 'Computer Chess' 1975; 'More Chess and Computers' 1981; 'All About Chess and Computers' 1982; 'The Great Theorem Prover' 1989; 'How Computers Play Chess' 1990; mem. Assn. Computing Machinery (Council 1978–81); Internat. Computer Chess Assn. (Vice Pres. 1980–83, Pres. 1983–86); Chrmn. of Extve. Ctte. of Candn. Computer Sci. Chairmen (1983–84); recreation: tennis; Club: Mount Royal Tennis; Home: 4874 Westmount Ave., Westmount, Que. H3Y 1Y1; Office: 3480 University St., Montreal, Que. H3A 2A7.

**NEWBOULD, Francis James Campbell,** Q.C.; lawyer; b. Guelph, Ont. 20 June 1943; s. Francis Henry Samuel and Jean Cameron (Campbell) N.; e. Queen's Univ., B.A. 1964; Univ. of Toronto, LL.B. 1967; m. Irene d. Peter and Sophie Lorenwicz 29 Aug. 1985; children: David F.G., Heather (MacInnes), Peter J.; PARTNER, BORDEN & ELLIOT 1988– ; called to Ont. Bar 1969; Jr. Lawyer, Tilley, Carson & Findlay 1969; Partner, Tilley, Carson & Findlay 1974–88; appt. Q.C. 1981; Mem., The Lawyers Club of Toronto 1969– (Trustee 1977–87, Pres. 1985–86); The Advocates' Soc. 1971– (Dir. 1985–88); Candn. Bar Assoc. (Counc. Mem. 1986–90); Arbitration and Mediation Institute of Ont. (Dir. 1992– ; Chartered Arbitrator); recreations: golf, tennis, skiing; Clubs; Rosedale Golf; Albany; Toronto Cricket, Skating & Curling; Home: 38 Mason Blvd., North York, Ont. M5M 3C7; Office: Ste. 4500, 40 King St. W., Toronto, Ont. M5H 3Y4.

**NEWBOULD, Ian D.C.,** B.A., M.A., Ph.D.; university professor and administrator; b. Guelph, Ont. 20 June 1943; s. Francis H.S. and Jean C. (Campbell) N.; e. Univ. of West. Ont., B.A. 1964; Univ. of Guelph, M.A. 1968;

Univ. of Manchester, Ph.D. 1971; m. Carelia d. Jacobus and Gerritje Vandergrift 25 May 1968; children: Adrian, Sophia, Alexandra; PRES. & VICE CHANCELLOR, MOUNT ALLISON UNIV. 1991– ; Lectr., Baudartius Coll., The Netherlands 1971–73; Asst. Prof., Univ. of Lethbridge 1973–78; Assoc. Prof. 1978–88; Prof. 1988–91; Dean, Fac. of Arts & Sci. 1985–88; Vice-Pres. (Academic) 1988–91; Vis. Fellow, Wolfson Coll., Oxford 1979–80; Hokkaigakven Univ., Sapporo, Japan 1981; Dir., Alta. Rsch. Counc. 1984–91; Candn. Convenor, Internat. Comn. for the History of Parliamentary and Representative Institutions; Anglican; mem., Conf. on Brit. Studies (U.S.); author: 'Whiggery and Reform 1830–1841: The Politics of Government' 1990 and numerous scholarly articles; recreation: golf; Home: Sackville, N.B.; Office: Sackville, N.B. E0A 3C0.

**NEWBOUND, Kenneth B.,** M.Sc., Ph.D.; physicist; educator; b. Winnipeg, Man. 12 March 1919; s. Albert Everard and Bertha Beatrice (Bateman) N.; e. Daniel McIntyre Coll. Inst., Winnipeg, 1935; Univ. of Man., B.Sc. 1940, M.Sc. 1941; Mass. Inst. of Technol., Ph.D. (Physics) 1948; m. 1stly, Lyndell Hilda, d. late Russell St. George Edmonds, 15 July 1947; children: Beatrice Elizabeth, Kenneth Randolph, Lawrence Douglas, Peter Edmonds; m. 2ndly, Carol Vere, d. late Edmund Vere Brown 8 Oct. 1983; PROF. EMERITUS OF PHYSICS, UNIV. OF ALBERTA 1984– , Prof. of Physics 1958–84 and Dean of Science 1976–81; Jr. Research Physicist, Div. of Physics & Elect. Engn., Nat. Research Council, 1941–43; joined present Univ. as Asst. Prof. of Physics 1948, Assoc. Prof. 1953; Asst. to Dean of Arts & Science 1954, Asst. Dean of Arts & Science 1961; Assoc. Dean of Science 1964; Dean of Science 1976–81; Defence Scient. Service Offr., Defence Research Bd., Naval Research Estab., Dartmouth, N.S., 1956–57; served with R.C.N.V.R., Naval Research Estab., Halifax, 1943–45; rank Lt. on discharge; author various papers reporting exper. work from 1940–63; mem., Candn. Assn. Physicists; Anglican; recreations: music, travel, philately; Home: 39 - 303 Twin Brooks Dr., Edmonton, Alta. T6J 6V3

**NEWBURY, Hon. Mary V.M.,** B.A., LL.B., LL.M.; supreme court judge; b. Calgary, Alta.; d. Edward Wm. and Mary Elizabeth (Rogers) N.; e. Univ. of B.C. B.A. (Hons.) 1971, LL.B. 1974; Harvard Univ. LL.M. 1975; JUDGE, SUPREME COURT OF BRITISH COLUMBIA 1991– ; articled student 1975–76; called to Bar of B.C. 1976; Assoc. & Partner, Ladner Downs (Vanc.) 1975–85; Partner, Mawhinney & Kellough 1985–90; Partner, Fraser & Beatty (upon merger with Mawhinney & Kellough) to 1991; Mem., Law Reform Comn. of B.C. 1984–91; Dir., Court House Lib. Soc. of B.C. 1986–90; Chairman 1988–90; author of var. articles; recreations: gardening, music; Office: c/o Court House, 800 Smithe St., Vancouver, B.C. V6Z 2E1.

**NEWCOMBE, Hanna,** B.A., M.A., Ph.D., LL.D.; chemist; author; b. Prague, Czechoslovakia 5 Feb. 1922; d. Arthur and Paula (Seger) Hammerschlag; e. Grimsby H.S. 1941; McMaster Univ. B.A. (Chem.) 1945; Univ. of Toronto M.A. (Chem.) 1946, Ph.D. (Chem.) 1950; m. Alan s. George and Lou Newcombe 8 Sept. 1946; children: Nora Stefanie, A. George, Ian Paul; EDITOR, PEACE RESEARCH ABSTRACTS JOURNAL, PEACE RESEARCH INST. 1962– ; Lab. Analyst, Canada Packers 1943–44; Rsch. Lib. Polymer Corp. 1945; Abstractor, Chem. Abstracts 1945–60; Newcombe Assoc. (transl. firm) 1961–64; Chem. Lab. Supr. McMaster Univ. 1957–58; Instr. Chem. Inst. of Can. 1959–60; Teacher, Ancaster H.S. 1961; Tut. Instr. York Univ. 1977–85, 1987– ; author 'Alternative Approaches to World Government' 1967 (rev. 1974); 'National Patterns in International Organizations' 1975; 'Reform of the U.N. Security Council' 1979; 'Approaches to a Nuclear-Free Future' 1982; 'Design for a Better World' 1983; co-author 'Peace Research around the World' 1969; 'Weighted Voting in International Organizations' 1968; 'Milestone Events' 1975; 'Nations on Record: U.N. General Assembly Rollcall Votes' 1975; 'Alternative Pasts (Weighted Voting)' 1983; Ed. 'World Unification Plans and Analyses' 1980; Ed., 'Hopes and Fears: The Human Future' 1992; mem. Religious Soc. of Friends (Quakers); Sec. Candn. Peace Rsch. and Edn. Assn. 1966–82, Pres. 1991–93; Pres. World Law Found. 1974–85; Pres. World Federalists of Can. 1981–83; Pres. World Federal Authority Ctte. 1980– ; mem. Consortium on Peace Rsch., Edn. and Devel.; International Peace Rsch. Assn. 1981– ; United Nations Assn.; Voice of Women; Hamilton Mundialization Ctte.; Dundas Mundialization Ctte.; Ont. Mundialization Council; Markland Group (Hamilton, Ont.); World Citizens Assembly; Science for Peace; Canadian Pugwash Group; Awards: Hon. LL.D. McMaster Univ. 1982; Lentz Internat. Peace Rsch. Award 1974; World Federalists of Can. Peace Award 1972; Candn. Peace Rsch. and Edn. Assn. Award 1983; Woman of the Year Award (Public Affairs) Hamilton Ont. 1985; Peace Messenger Award, United Nations 1987; First World Citizen of the Year Award, Hamilton Mundialization Ctte. 1988; Address: 25 Dundana Ave., Dundas, Ont. L9H 4E5.

**NEWCOMBE, Howard Borden,** B.Sc., Ph.D., D.Sc., F.R.S.C.; biologist; b. Kentville, N.S. 19 Sept. 1914; s. Edward Borden and Mabel Elsie (Outerbridge) N.; e. Acadia Univ., B.Sc. (Biol.) 1935; McGill Univ., Ph.D. 1939; Imp. Coll. of Tropical Agric., Trinidad, W.I., A.I.C.T.A. 1938; D.Sc. McGill 1966; Acadia 1970; m. Beryl Honor, d. Capt. George W. Callaway, Plymouth, Eng., 14 Feb. 1942; children: Kenneth Donald, Charles Philip, Richard William; 1851 Science Research Scholar, John Innes Hort. Instn., 1939–40; Research Assoc., Carnegie Instn. of Washington, Dept. of Genetics, 1946–47; joined present Co. in 1947; Visiting Prof. of Genetics, Indiana Univ. (spring), 1963; served to Lieut., Brit. R.N.V.R., 1941–46; Head, Population Research Br., Atomic Energy of Canada Ltd, retired 1979; author: numerous scient. papers (mutations in microorganisms; effects of ionizing radiations; methods of study of human population genetics and epidemiology); mem., Internat. Comn. on Radiological Protection, 1965–77; Genetics Soc. Am. (Secy. 1956–58); Am. Soc. Human Genetics (Pres. 1965); Genetics Soc. of Can. (Pres. 1964–65); Home: 67 Hillcrest Ave., P.O. Box 135, Deep River, Ont. K0J 1P0.

**NEWELL, Douglas Wayne;** media buying executive; b. St. John's, Nfld. 20 Oct. 1942; s. Harry Clarence and Emma Evelyn N.; e. West Hill C.I. 1960; m. Manuela d. Josef and Gudrun Beer 23 Dec. 1977; children: Steven, Johanna, Lauren, Michael; PARTNER & SENIOR VICE-PRES., HARRISON, YOUNG, PESONEN & NEWELL INC. 1980– ; Spitzer Mills & Bates 1960–62; Cockfield Brown 1963–65; J. Walter Thompson 1966–68; Gen. Sales Mgr., Nfld. Broadcasting Co. 1969–70; McKim 1971–73; Partner, Major Market Broadcasters 1974–78; Sr. Vice-Pres. & Dir. of Media, Ted Bates 1979; Vice Chair, BBM Bureau of Measurement; Guest Lecturer, Ryerson Broadcast Faculty; recreations: golf, flying; clubs: CedarBrae; Granite; Home: 17 Hawarden Cres., Toronto, Ont.; Office: 1240 Bay St., Toronto, Ont. M5R 2A7.

**NEWELL, Eric P.;** executive; b. Kamloops, B.C. 16 December 1944; s. Mr. and Mrs. A.P. Newell; e. Univ. of B.C. B.A.Sc. (Chem. Engr.) 1967; Univ. of Birmingham, U.K. M.Sc. (Mgmnt. Studies) 1968, Athlone Fellow; m. Kathleen M. Newell 13 November 1971; children: Brian, Colleen, Erin; PRES. & C.E.O., SYNCRUDE CANADA LTD. 1989– ; Computer applications engr., Imperial Oil Ltd. 1969–76; Corporate Planning 1976–79; Product Supply Mgr., 1979–81; Petroleum refinery mngmt. 1981–84; Planning & Develop. Div. Mgr., 1984–86; Vice Pres., Syncrude Canada Ltd. 1986–89; Mem., Assn. of Prof. Engrs. of Ont.; Chrmn., Major Industrial Accidents Council of Canada; Pres., Alberta Chamber of Resources; Dir., Conference Board of Canada; National Council on Education, Conference Bd. of Can.; Keyano Coll. Found.; Dir., Athabasca Univ. Development Institute; Corporate Higher Education Forum; Bd. of Govs., Junior Achievement of Northern Alberta; Chairperson, 1992 Alta. Winter Games; recreations: golf, skiing, bridge, Junior Achievement; Office: Box 4023, 9911 MacDonald Ave., Fort McMurray, Alta. T9H 3H5.

**NEWFELD, Frank;** book designer; publishing consultant; b. Brno, Czechoslovakia 1 May 1928; s. Arnold and Rose (Deutsch) Neufeld; e. Central Sch. of Arts & Crafts, London, Eng. Hons. Dipl. 1952; m. Joan Barrie d. late William Hart 25 Aug. 1958; children: Philip Laurence, David Stefan; Pres., MacPherson Newfeld; Dir. McClelland and Stewart Ltd.; estbd. Frank Newfeld Studio 1954; Teacher, Central Tech. Sch. 1955–56, Ryerson Inst. of Technol. 1956–57, Ont. Coll. of Art 1958–65; joined McClelland and Stewart Ltd. 1963 as Art Dir., Dir. of Design & Production 1964, Creative Dir. 1965, Vice Pres. Publishing 1969, Dir. 1974–82, Consultant 1976–78; joined MacPherson Newfeld Ltd. 1970; Publishing Consultant, Nat. Gallery of Can. 1973–75; Lectr. and mem. Adv. Council, Sheridan Coll.; design and illustration for various publishing firms Can., USA and UK; design for museums and galleries incl. Art Gallery of Ont., Museum of Modern Art N.Y., Nat. Gallery of Can., Nat. Museums of Man, Royal Ont. Museum; design and illustration for various mags.; exhns. of work Can., Czechoslovakia, Germany, Holland, Isreal, Japan, Spain, UK, USA; rec'd numerous awards/certs. since 1955 incl. 6th Annual Book Jacket Competition Scot. 1960, Hans Christian Andersen Awards 1962, 1975, Annual Book Exhn. Leipzig 1963, Internat. Book Exhn. Leipzig Silver & Bronze Medal 1965, Bronze Medal 1977, Printing Industs. Am. 1968, 1971, Soc. of Illustrators 1968, Am. Inst. Graphic Arts 1971, 1972, 1977, 1979, 1984, Look of Books 1970, 1972, 1974, 1976, Ruth Schwartz/CBA Award for Best Children's Book 1978; several awards New York Art Directors Club; Candn. Centennial Medal 1967; Queen's Silver Jubilee Medal 1977; author 'The Princess of Tomboso' 1960; co-author 'Great Canadian Painting' 1965; 'Simon and the Golden Sword' 1976; mem. Royal Candn. Acad. (Council); Am. Inst. Graphic Arts; recreations: horses, theatre; Address: c/o Gage Educational Publishing Co., 164 Commander Blvd., Agincourt, Ont. M1S 3C7.

**NEWHOOK, Cle,** M.A.; b. Norman's Cove, Nfld. 3 June 1943; s. Ernest and Elizabeth (Smith) N.; e. Memorial Univ., Queen's Coll., B.A.(L.Th.) 1965; Keble Coll., Oxford Univ., M.A.(L.Th.) 1967; m. Deborah d. Alan and Betty McOwan 5 Oct. 1968; children: Matthew, Rebecca; PROVINCIAL SECRETARY, NEW DEMOCRATIC PARTY, NFLD. 1989– ; Youth Worker (U.K.) 1965–69; Chaplain, Memorial Univ. of NF 1969–72; Community Worker (U.K.) 1972–82; Extve. Dir., Ocean Ranger Found. 1982–86; Prov. Sec., NDP, Nfld. & Lab. 1986–88; member of various voluntary orgns.; author: 'Mostly in Rodneys,' Cuff Publications 1985; co-author: 'The Tragedy of the Ocean Ranger – Who Cares Now' Breakwater Books 1988; Home: 41 Cornwall Cres., St. John's, Nfld. A1E 1Z6.

**NEWLOVE, John Herbert;** poet; b. Regina, Sask., 13 June 1938; s. Thomas Harold and Mary Constant (Monteith) N.; e. Senior Matriculation, Sask., 1956; m. Susan Mary, d. H. J. Phillips, Vernon, B.C., 9 Aug. 1966; step-children: Jeremy Charles Gilbert, Tamsin Elizabeth Gilbert; author: 'Grave Sirs,' 1962; 'Elephants, Mothers & Others,' 1964; 'Moving In Alone,' 1965, new ed., 1977; 'Notebook Pages,' 1966; 'What They Say,' 1967 and 1968; 'Black Night Window,' 1968; 'The Cave,' 1970; 'Lies' 1972; 'The Fat Man (Selected Poems),' 1977; ed., 'Canadian Poetry: The Modern Era,' 1977; 'Dreams Surround Us' (with John Metcalf), 1977; 'The Green Plain,' 1981 ('La verde piana' translator Carla Comellini, Bologna, 1990); 'The Night The Dog Smiled' 1986; 'Apology for Absence' (selected poems) 1993; other writings inc. works in anthols.; received grants from Canada Council; Governor General's Award, Poetry, 1972; Sask. Writers' Guild Founders' Award 1984; Literary Press Group Award 1986; Poet-in-residence, Loyola Coll. 1974–75; Univ. Western Ont. 1975–76; Univ. of Toronto 1976–77; Regina Public Library, 1979–80; Editor (English), Office of the Commissioner of Official Languages, Ottawa; Address: Box 71041, L'Esplanade Postal Outlet, 181 Bank St., Ottawa, Ont. K2P 1W0.

**NEWMAN, Barry G.,** M.A., Ph.D.; university professor; b. Manchester, Eng. 23 May 1926; s. Frederick Challender and Dorothy Edna (George) N.; e. Manchester Grammar Sch., Eng.; Cambridge Univ., B.A. 1947, M.A. 1951 (Strathcona Open Major Scholar in Math., St. John's Coll.); Sydney Univ., Ph.D. 1952; m. Joan Farmer; one s. Duncan; two d. Joanna, Charlotte; CANADAIR PROF. OF AERODYNAMICS, McGILL UNIV. and CONSULTANT IN APPLIED MECHANICS 1959– ; Secy. Grad. Faculty there 1963–65 and Chrmn., Dept. of Mech. Engn. 1969–72; mem. Senate there, 1979–82; mem. Nat. Research Council Assoc. Comte. on Aerodynamics 1961–64, 1967–69 and 1978–79; and Chrmn. 1968 and 1979; mem., Council Candn. Aero and Space Inst. 1984; Vice Pres., Academy of Science (1985–86) and mem., Counc. Royal Soc. of Can.; mem., Acad. of Sci. 1983 and 1992– ; Dir., Division of Applied Science and Engineering 1992– ; Founding mem., Candn. Acad. of Engr. 1987; Consultant to Canadair Ltd. 1959–70; Pratt & Whitney Canada 1973–91; Pulp & Paper Research Inst. Can. 1979– ; Vice-Chrmn., Aeronautics Advisory Board, Dep't of Transport; Research Student & Jr. Res. Fellow, Sydney Univ., 1947–51; Scient. Offr. Royal Aust. Air Force (Flight Research on Aerodynamic Problems) 1951–53; Research Offr., Nat. Research Council, Ottawa, 1953–55; Univ. Lectr. in Aerodynamics, Cambridge Univ., 1955–58; Canadair Visiting Prof. in Fluid Mech., Laval Univ., 1958–59; Contrib. to: 'Boundary and Flow Control,' 'Scale Effects in Animal Locomotion,' 'Fluid Mechanics of Internal Flow,' 'Progress in Aerospace Sciences, 1987'; Fellow, Candn. Aero. & Space Inst.; Royal Aero Soc. (Rec'd. (with C. Bourque) Edward Busk Mem. Prize 1961); Fellow, Royal Soc. of Canada; Fellow, Candn. Acad. of Engr.; Pres., Faculty Club, McGill Univ. 1993–95; recreation: sailing, music, history; Home: 49 Nelson St., Montreal West, Que. H4X 1G5.

**NEWMAN, Donald Kenneth;** journalist; b. Winnipeg, Man. 28 Oct. 1940; s. Lincoln Rosser and Doris

Angelina (Arnett) N.; e. Highgate School (U.K.); Willingdon Sch.; West Hill H.S.; Kelvin H.S.; United College Winnipeg; m. Audrey-Ann d. William and Alice Taylor 16 May 1964; one s.: Lincoln Taylor (dec.); SENIOR PARLIAMENTARY EDITOR, CBC NATOINAL TV NEWS/NEWSWORLD 1988– ; Legislative Reporter & Columnist, Winnipeg Tribune 1966–67; Political Reporter, Ottawa Bureau, Globe and Mail 1969–71; Washington Correspondent, CTV News 1972–76; CBC TV 1976–79; Sr. Nat. Reporter, 'The National' 1979–81; Editor and Host 'This Week in Parliament' 1981–88; Host, Capital Report, Political File; Public Speaker, Candn. Programming Service; Canspeak; Past PRes., Nat. Press Club; Candn. Parliamentary Press Gallery; Gov., Ashbury College; Anglican; recreations: tennis; clubs: National Press; Home: 2460 Wyndale Cres., Ottawa, Ont. K1H 7A6; Office: Ste. 800, 150 Wellington St., Ottawa, Ont. K1P 5A4.

**NEWMAN, J. Kevin,** B.A.; journalist; b. Toronto, Ont. 2 June 1959; s. George Edmund and Sheila Lorraine N.; e. Erindale S.S. 1978; Univ. of Western Ont. B.A. 1981; m. Catharine d. Gordon and Lois Kearns 15 June 1985; children: Alexander, Erica; HOST, MIDDAY, CBC NATIONAL NETWORK NEWSMAGAZINE 1992– ; Queen's Park Correspondent & General Assignment Reporter, Global TV Network 1981–83; Parl. Correspondent, Global TV News 1983–87; Atlantic Bureau Chief, CTV National News 1987–88; Parl. Corr. 1988–89; Senior Western Corr., CBC National TV News 1989–91; Parliamentary Correspondent, CBC National TV News 1991–92; Ontario Scholar 1978; Dir., CHRW Radio 1979–81; recreations: skiing, canoeing; Office: CBC Broadcasting Center, 25 John St., Toronto, Ont. M5V 3G6.

**NEWMAN, John,** A.O.C.A.; R.C.A.; artist; b. Toronto, Ont. 6 Apr. 1933; s. John William and Pearl (Beatty) N.; e. Ont. Coll. of Art 1952–56; Art Acad. of Cincinnati 1956–57; various European museums 1966, 1971–72, 1976–78; m. Shirley Corrine MacGregor 1 Sept. 1956; three s. John MacGregor, Peter George, Adam Errol; full-time mem. Faculty, Ont. Coll. of Art 1963– , Acting Chrmn. Fine Art Dept. 1977–78; Chrmn. Fine Art Dept. 1979–84; Exhibit Designer Royal Ont. Museum 1958–63; solo exhns.: Victoria Coll. Univ. of Toronto 1963, St. Michael's Coll. 1971, Erindale Coll. 1973, Scarborough Coll. 1974; Rodman Hall Arts Centre St. Catharines 1969; Lefebvre Gallery Edmonton 1971; Althouse Coll. Univ. of W. Ont. 1973; Art Gallery Gander, Nfld. 1973, Corner Brook Arts & Culture Centre and Grand Falls Art & Culture Centre 1974, Mem. Univ. of Nfld. 1974; Galerie de l'Esprit Montreal 1975; Brock Univ. St. Catharines 1976; Art Gallery of Hamilton 1976; Palazzo Strozzi Florence, Italy 1977; Prince Arthur Galleries Toronto 1979 and 1981; Hett Gallery Ltd. Edmonton 1981; Madison Gallery, Toronto 1983; Kinsman, Robinson Galleries, Toronto 1989, 1992, 1994; Centro Culturale Canadese in Roma, Roma, Italy 1992; The Gallery, Stratford 1994; rep. various group exhns. incl. Royal Acad. London 1972, Metrop. Gallery Tokyo, Le Salon 77 Paris, 91 Seoul Watercolours International, Seoul, Korea, Nat. Gallery Can., Montreal Museum of Fine Arts, Art Gallery of Ont., Cincinnati Art Museum; cultural exchange with the People's Republic of China – exhibited, lectured at Sichuan Fine Art Inst.; rep. in perm. and private colls. Can., Eng., Italy, U.S.A.; recipient 1st Prize Internat. Painting Competition Candn. Nat. Exhn. 1956; Art Acad. Grad. Div. Scholarship 1956, Prize for Drawing 1957, Cincinnati; Can. Council Grant 1966; John Alfsen Award for Drawing Candn. Soc. Graphic Art 1973; Candn. Soc. Painters in Watercolour Honour Award 1973, A. E. Ames Purchase Award 1973, Curry Award 1976; Ont. Council for Arts Grant 1976; Sun Oil Canada Ltd. 'On View' Award 1976; Elec. 3 terms, Governing Council of Ont. College of Art; mem. Royal Canadian Academy; Candn. Soc. Painters in Watercolour; recreation: tennis; Address: Ont. Coll. of Art, 100 McCaul St., Toronto, Ont. M5T 1W1.

**NEWMAN, John B.;** investment company executive; b. Waterloo, Ont. 27 June 1934; s. Maitland Fuller and Alice Kilgour (Buckingham) N.; e. Upper Canada College; Univ. of Western Ontario; m. Valerie d. Frederick Johnson 28 Sept. 1962; one d.: Katherine Anne Buckingham; CHAIRMAN, MULTIBANC NT FINANCIAL CORP. 1990– ; Salesman, Money Market Dept., Greenshields Incorporated 1961; estab. Internat. Interest Rate Arbitrage Dept. 1962; estab. Inter-Bank Euro Deposit Dept. 1965; Vice-Pres. & Dir. 1966; estab. N. Am. Div., Tullette Tokyo & Greenshields 1970; Senior Vice-Pres., Dir., Extve. Ctte. 1970; Extve. Vice-Pres., Greenshields Incorporated 1976; Extve. Vice-Pres., Richardson Greenshields 1982; Vice-Chairman 1986; Deputy Chairman, Prudential Bache 1988; Chrmn., AGF Securities Canada Limited; Trustee, AFG Group of Mutual Fund Trust; Canada Trust Income Investment Trust; Dir., Chrmn. & C.E.O., Multibanc NT Finan. Corp.; Dir., Focus Nat. Mortgage Corp.; Multibanc Finan. Corp.; Dir. & Pres., Global Govt. Plus Fund Limited; Dir., Candn. Trinity Life Insur. Co.; Abbey Woods Devel. Ltd.; Twenty/Twenty 1991 Distbn. Ltd.; AGF Group of Mutual Fund Corps.; recreations: outdoor activities, boating; clubs: 48th Highland Officers Assn., The Toronto Club, Toronto Hunt, B & R, India House (N.Y.), Boca Raton (Florida); Home: 178 Forest Hill Rd., Toronto, Ont. M5P 2N3; Office: 610 – 26 Wellington St. E., Toronto, Ont. M5E 1V4.

**NEWMAN, Lloyd M. (Merrill),** B.A.; fashion store executive; b. Detroit, Mich. 29 Sept. 1934; s. Joseph and May (Mercur) N.; e. Detroit P.S. system 1952; Univ. of Mich., B.A. 1956; m. Iris E. d. Norman and Bertha Cappell 28 Aug. 1956; children: Mark H., Shawna G., Amy F.P.; PRES. & C.E.O., NORTELL'S INVESTMENTS & NORTELL REALTY INC. and PRES. & C.E.O. A.M.N. SALES; 1st Lt., U.S. Air Force 1956–59 (Navigator, Electronic Warfare Offr.); Pres. & C.E.O., The Arcade Ladies' Shoppe Ltd. 1960–92; Chrmn., Nova Scotia Film Development Corp.; Life Dir., Neptune Theatre; Past Mem., Canada Council; Past Chrmn., Prince Edward Scholarship Ctte., Prov. of N.S.; Past Pres., Neptune Theatre Found.; Symphony N.S.; Past Gov., Nat. Theatre Sch. of Can.; Past Vice-Pres., P.C. Party of N.S.; Past Nat. Sec., Can.-United Israel Appeal; Pres., Shaar Shalom Synagogue; Dir., Atlantic Jewish Counc.; Past Mem., Halifax Athletic Comn.; recipient, 125th Anniversary of the Confederation of Canada Medal, 1992; recreations: tennis, reading; clubs: South End Tennis, Waegwoltic; Home: 6095 Coburg Rd., #703, Halifax, N.S. B3H 4K1; Office: 3490 Prescott St., Halifax, N.S. B3K 4Y4.

**NEWMAN, Murray Arthur,** C.M., B.Sc., M.A., Ph.D.; retired aquarium director; b. Chicago, Ill. 6 March 1924; s. Paul Jones and Virginia (Murray) N.; e. Univ. of Chicago B.Sc. 1949; Univ. of Hawaii 1950; Univ. of Cal. Berkeley M.A. 1951; Univ. of B.C. Ph.D. 1960; m. Katherine Lloyd Rose d. Godfrey Greene 8 Aug. 1952; one d. Susan; DIRECTOR EMERITUS, VANCOUVER PUBLIC AQUARIUM; Chrmn., Advisory Ctte., National Museum Marine Biology (Aquarium, Taiwan, Republic of China); participated capture first live killer whale 1964; W. Candn. Exhibits and Beluga Pool 1967; New Guinea Expdn. 1969–70; Narwhal Expdn. 1970; Killer Whale Pool 1971; Sea Otter Pool 1973; Seal Pool 1978; Amazon Expdn. 1979; Aquatic Science Centre 1980; Amazon Gallery 1983; Bill Reid Killer Whale Sculpture 1984; Max Bell Marine Mammal Centre 1986; Arctic Canada Pavilion 1990; served with U.S. Navy 1943–46; rec'd Harold J. Merilees Award 1976; Candn. Centennial Medal 1967; Man of Yr. City of Vancouver 1964; Royal Life Saving Soc. Can. Silver Bravery Medal 1992; awarded Commemorative Medal for 125th Anniversary of Candn. Confederation 1992; mem. Candn. Assn. Zool. Parks & Aquariums (Pres. 1978–79); Am. Assn. Zool. Parks & Aquariums (Bd. 1972–75); Internat. Union Dirs. Zool. Gdns.; recreations: boating, fishing, travel; Clubs: Vancouver; Round Table; Home: 4915 Beacon Lane, West Vancouver, B.C. V7W 1K6; Office: (P.O. Box 3232) Vancouver Aquarium, Vancouver, B.C. V6B 3X8.

**NEWMAN, Peter Charles,** C.C. B.A., M.Com., D.Lit. (York), LL.D. (Brock, Wilfrid Laurier, Royal Military Coll. and Queen's), F.R.S.A.; K.C.L.J.; author; editor; b. Vienna, Austria 10 May 1929; s. Oskar Charles and Wanda Maria (Neumann) N.; came to Canada 1940; e. Upper Canada College, Toronto, Ontario; University of Toronto, B.A. 1950; University of Toronto Inst. Business Administration, M.Com. 1954; m. 1. Christina McCall, divorced; 2. Camilla Jane Turner, divorced; two d. Laureen, Ashley; joined the 'Financial Post' as Asst. Editor 1951; apptd. Montreal Ed. 1954 and Production Ed. 1955; resigned 1956 to become Asst. Ed. 'Maclean's Magazine'; appt. Ottawa Ed. 1960, Nat. Affairs Ed. 1963; Ottawa Ed., 'Toronto Daily Star' and syndicated pol. columnist in 29 Candn. newspapers 1964–69; Editor-in-Chief 1969–71; Editor 'Maclean's Magazine' 1971–1982; served as Capt., R.C.N.(R); has written extensively on Candn. business and pol. in many U.S., U.K. and Candn. mags. incl. 'The Times' of London, 'Queen's Quarterly,' 'Public Affairs' and 'The New York Times' 'City and Country Home'; toured Europe for the 'Financial Post' 1954 ; Asia and Middle E. for Maclean's in 1961; author of 'Flame of Power,' intimate profiles of Can.'s greatest businessmen 1959 (became nat. best-seller, reprinted three times); 'Renegade in Power: The Diefenbaker Years' 1963 (became record Candn. pol. best-seller, reprinted seven times); 'The Distemper of Our Times,' pol. hist. of Can. 1963–68, 1968 (Book of Month Club selection); 'Home Country-People, Places and Power Politics' (Lit. Guild Selection) 1973; 'The Canadian Establishment – Vol. 1 The Great Business Dynasties' (all-time Candn. best-seller); 1975 'Bronfman Dynasty' The Rothschilds of the New World' (Book-of-the-Month Club Selection in Canada and U.S. Also published in U.S. as 'King of the Castle'), 1978; 'The Acquisitors: The Canadian Establishment, Volume II' 1981; 'The Establishment Man: A Portrait of Power' 1982 (Literary Guild Feature Selection); 'True North: Not Strong and Free-Defending the Peaceable Kingdom in the Nuclear Age' 1983; Debrett's Illus. Guide to the Candn. Establishment – Gen. Ed., 1983; 'Company of Adventurers: An Unauthorized History of the Hudson's Bay Company,' 'Caesars of the Wilderness' Vol. II 1985, 'Merchant Princes' Vol. III 1991 (all three volumes Nat. #1 Best Sellers and Book of the Month Selections); 'Sometimes A Great Nation: Will Canada Belong to the 21st Century?' 1988; 'Empire of Bay' 1989; '1892: Portrait of a Promised Land'; co-author of 90–minute television documentary awarded CBC's Wilderness Award for best production of year 1967; co-author CBC-TV series 'The Tenth Decade' which won Michener Award for Journalism; author seven-part T.V. series on 'The Canadian Establishment' won four ACTRA awards; awarded Nat. Newspaper Award for Journalism 1971; Univ. of W. Ont. Pres. Medal for Best Mag. Article 1973; Achievement in Life Award by Encyclopedia Brit. Pubs., 1977; Quill Award for Excellence in Candn. Journalism, 1977; Installed Officer Order of Canada April 1979, promoted to Companion Order of Canada 1990; Invested, Knight Commander Order of Saint Lazarus, Apr. 1980; Candn. Authors Assn. Literary Award for Non-Fiction 1986; Invested Kn. of Lippe; North West Territories Royal Life Saving Soc. Medal, Life Saving Soc. of Portugal, Silver Medal Japanese Red Cross Soc.; Depy. Gov. (Can.) Internat. Press Inst. 1969–71; mem. Bd. Govs., Univ. of Toronto 1972–74; Dir., Nat. Youth Orchestra of Can. 1968–72; named Nat. Gov., Shaw Festival 1984; Dir., Saskatchewan Indian Federated Coll. 1984–86; Visiting Prof. of Pol. Science, McMaster Univ. 1969–71; Visiting Prof., Political Sc., York U., 1979–80; Prof., Creative Writing, U. of Victoria 1985–90; Pres., Maritime Defence Assoc. of Can. 1989–91; Dir., St. Paul's Hospital Foundation 1990– ; Dir., Vancouver Internat. Airport Authority 1992– ; recreation: sailing; Clubs: Rideau (Ottawa); Royal Vancouver Yacht Club; Home: 2594 Panorama Dr., Deep Cove, B.C. V7G 1V5; Office: 777 Bay St., Toronto, Ont. M5W 1A7.

**NEWMAN, Stanley I.;** business executive; b. Salisbury, Rhodesia 12 Mar. 1945; s. Leslie Lazarus and Lily N.; e. Prince Edward Sch. Salisbury 1961; m. Beryl d. Raphael and Janie Seider 26 June 1966; children: Michelle Kim, Riette Lesli; PRES., COLOR YOUR WORLD, CORP. 1987– ; Pres. Cost Plus Distribution Inc.; Chrmn. Avinda Electronics; Dir. M.D.F. Packaging; Cons. to Blum Research & Devel., all of Toronto; estbd. mfg. textile and clothing bus. 1966; diversified into plastics 1969 and retail 1970; emmigrated to Eng. 1976; estbd. mfg. furniture components bus. 1978–81; Gen. Mgr. St. Clair Paint & Wallpaper, Toronto 1981 becoming Pres. and Chief Extve. Offr.; cons. 1984–85; Pres. & C.E.O., Avinda Video Inc. 1985–87; recreations: golf, tennis, swimming, riding, skiing; Home: 45 Elgin St., Thornhill, Ont. L3T 1W5; Office: 10 Carson St., Toronto, Ont. M8W 3R5.

**NEWMAN, Sydney,** O.C., F.R.S.A., F.R.T.S.; TV executive and producer; artist & sculptor; b. Toronto, Ont., 1 Apl. 1917; e. Central Tech. Sch., Toronto, in Comm. and Fine Arts Course; m. Margaret Elizabeth McRae (d. 1981); three d. Deirdre, Jennifer, Gillian; PRES., SYDNEY NEWMAN ENTERPRISES, since 1977; Chief Creative Consultant for Canadian Film Devel. Corp., 1978–1984; painter; stage, indust. and interior designer; still and cinema photographer, 1935–41; joined Nat. Film Bd. of Canada, under John Grierson as splicer-boy, 1941; Editor and Dir. of Armed Forces training films and war information shorts, 1942; Producer, 'Canada Carries On,' 1945–52; Extve. Producer in charge of all films for cinemas, incl. short films, newsreels, films for children and travel, 1944–52; over 300 documentaries, incl. U.N. 'Suffer Little Children'; 'It's Fun to Sing' (Venice Award); 'Ski Skill'; 'After Prison, What?' (Canada Award); assigned to NBC in New York to report on TV techniques for Nat. Film Bd. of Can., 1949–50; joined CBC as TV Dir. of Features and Outside Broadcasts, 1952; Supv. of Drama, and Producer, 'Gen. Motors Theatre,' 'On Camera,' 'Ford Theatre,' 'Graphic,' 1954; Producer first plays by Mordecai Richler and Arthur Hailey, incl. 'Flight into Danger,' 'Course for Collision'; Ohio State Award for Religious Drama; Liberty Award Best Drama Series; appt. Supv. of Drama and Producer of 'Armchair Theatre,' ABC TV,

Eng, 1958; comnd. and produced first on-air plays of Alun Owen, Harold Pinter, Angus Wilson, Robert Muller, Hugh Leonard, Peter Luke; also plays by Clive Exton and David Perry; created TV series 'The Avengers' (ABC TV); Head of Drama Group, BBC Television 1963–68, responsible for all drama and opera incl. Benjamin Britten's 'Billy Budd' etc.; 'Z-Cars'; 'The Wednesday Play'; 'The Forsythe Saga'; personally produced 'Stephen D' by Hugh Leonard from James Joyce, 'The Tea Party' by Harold Pinter and 'The Rise and Fall of the City of Mahogany' by Kurt Weill and Bertholt Brecht; created TV series 'Adam Adamant Lives!' and 'Dr. Who' (BBC TV); Extve. Producer, Feature films, Associated British Picture Corp., Elstree, Eng. 1969; Dir. Programmes, C.R.T.C., Ottawa 1970; Dir., CBC, 1972–75; Candn. Film Devel. Corp., 1970–75; Trustee, Nat. Arts Centre, 1970–75; Gov't Film Commr. and Chief Extve., Nat. Film Bd. of Can., 1970–75; Special Adv. on Film to Secy. of State, 1975–77; Gov., Candn. Conf. of the Arts, 1978–82; mem., New Western Film and TV Fdn., 1978–84; gave The Guardian Lecture, Museum of Moving Image, London, Eng. 1988; produced Benjamin Britten's opera 'The Little Sweep' for internat. TV distribution 1989; mem., Brit. Acad. of Film & Television Arts; The Royal Television Soc.; rec'd awards from Soc. of Film and Television Arts, and Writers Guild of Gt. Brit.; Special Recog. Award from Soc. of Motion Pictures and TV Engrs. (U.S.), 1975; Kt. of Mark Twain (U.S.); Hon. Life Mem., Directors Guild of Canada; Fellow Soc. Film & Television Arts (U.K.); Fellow Royal Soc. of Art (U.K.) 1967; Fellow, Royal Television Soc. (U.K.) 1990; Officer, Order of Canada 1981; recreation: reading; Address: 3 Nesbitt Dr., Toronto, Ont. M4W 2G2.

**NEWSON, Wayne Elwood,** B.A.; dairy industry executive; b. Winnipeg, Man. 27 Oct. 1947; s. Lloyd Irving and Elsie Maye (Palmer) N.; e. Univ. of Manitoba B.A. 1969; m. Valerie d. Edwin and Doris Richardson 29 June 1974; children: Mark, Todd; PRESIDENT & CHIEF OPERATING OFFICER, DAIRY DIVISION, BEATRICE FOODS INC. 1992– ; various positions, ending as Corporate Vice-President, Nabisco Brands Limited 1970–87; Vice-Pres., Marketing & International, Tim Horton's Donut Limited 1987–88; Pres., Central Canada Dairies, Ault Foods, John Labatt Limited 1988–92; Dir. & Mem., Extve. Ctte., Nat. Dairy Council; Dir., Internat. Ice Cream Assn.; Quality Checked Dairy Assn.; Dir. & Mem., Extve. Ctte. (Ont.), Grocery Industry Found.; Dir., Tim Horton Children's Found.; recreations: golf, fitness, coaching; clubs: Mississauga Golf & Country, Fitness Inst., Metro Toronto Board of Trade; Office: 295 The West Mall, Ste. 600, Etobicoke, Ont. M9C 4Z4.

**NEWTON, Christopher,** B.A.(Hons.), M.A., LL.D.; actor; director; writer; b. Deal, Kent, Eng. 11 June 1936; s. Albert Edward and Gwladys Maud (Emes) N.; e. Sir Roger Manwood's Sch.; Univ. of Leeds, B.A. (Hons.); Purdue Univ., Univ. of Illinois M.A.; Hon. LL.D., Brock Univ.; Hon. LL.D. Univ. of Guelph; taught at Bucknell Univ., Pennsylvania 1960–61; Visiting teacher at Univ. of Alta., at the National Theatre Sch. and Ryerson; actor with Canadian Players: Cassius in 'Julius Caesar,' Brother Martin in 'Saint Joan'; New Theatre, New York: Tom in 'The Knack'; Stratford Festival: Orsino in 'Twelfth Night,' Aramis in 'The Three Musketeers,' Oberon in 'Midsummer Night's Dream'; Manitoba Theatre Centre: Mick in 'The Caretaker,' Tusenbach in 'The Three Sisters'; Founding Artistic Dir., Theatre Calgary 1968–71, directed: 'The Alchemist,' 'The Three Desks,' 'The Father,' 'Great Expectations,' 'The Entertainer' etc.; Artistic Dir., Vancouver Playhouse 1973–79, directed: 'Julius Caesar,' 'Mr. Scrooge,' 'And Out Goes You,' 'Queer Sights,' 'The Taming of the Shrew,' 'Frankenstein,' 'The Count of Monte Cristo,' 'Camille,' 'MacBeth,' 'Camino Real,' 'Hamlet,' 'The Innocents' etc.; acted Dysart in 'Equus,' Carr in 'Travesties'; Founder with the late Powys Thomas, The Playhouse Acting School 1975; Artistic Dir., Shaw Festival 1979, directed: 'Misalliance,' 'Canuck,' 'Saint Joan,' 'The Singular Life of Albert Nobbs,' 'The Desert Song,' 'Caesar and Cleopatra,' 'Heartbreak House,' 'The Skin of our Teeth,' 'The Lost Letter,' 'On the Rocks,' 'Tom Jones,' 'Major Barbara,' 'You Never Can Tell,' 'Geneva,' 'Man and Superman,' 'Trelawny of the Wells,' 'Millionairess,' 'Lulu,' 'Pygmalion,' 'Point Valaine'; 'The Silver King and Candida'; 1994: 'Sherlock Holmes' & 'Busman's Honeymoon'; co-directed with Marti Maraden 'Tonight We Improvise,' co-directed with Duncan McIntosh 'Roberta,' 'Girl Crazy,' 'Cavalcade'; acted Elyot in 'Private Lives,' Camille in 'A Flea in Her Ear,' Vasili in 'Camille,' Charteris in 'The Philanderer,' Bellerose in 'Cyrano de Bergerac,' Nikolai in 'Breaking the Silence'; Mr. Darling and Captain Hook in 'Peter Pan'; Garry Essendine in 'Present Laughter'; Brasset in 'Charley's Aunt'; Carnaby Leete in 'The Marrying of Ann Leete';

directed for Young Peoples Theatre: 'The Christmas Carol,' 'Dreaming and Duelling' (co-production with Shaw); directed for Pacific Opera: 'Carmen'; directed for the Candn. Opera Co.: 'Die Fledermaus,' 'Madama Butterfly'; 'Patria 1: The Characteristics Man'; directed for Calgary Opera 'Porgy and Bess'; directed for Opera Hamilton 'I Due Foscari'; Vancouver Opera and National Arts Centre, 'The Barber of Seville'; Dora Award 1986, Best Dir. for a musical ('Desert Song'); plays 'Slow Train to Saint Ives' (Man. Theatre Centre); 'You Two Stay Here, the Rest Come with Me' (Theatre Calgary and National Arts Centre), 'The Sound of Distant Thunder' (Vancouver Playhouse), 'The Lost Letter' adapted from the Romanian with Sky Gilbert (Shaw Festival) 1984; recreations: landscape architecture, music; Home: 22 Prideaux St., Niagara-on-the-Lake, Ont. L0S 1J0; Office: The Shaw Festival, Box 774, Niagara-on-the-Lake, Ont. L0S 1J0.

**NEWTON, David Alexander,** F.Inst.D., F.B.I.M.; company director; b. England 6 Oct. 1942; s. Alexander and Hazel (Little) N.; e. Morecambe Grammar Sch., Lancs.; external bus. studies, Manchester; m. Kathleen Mary d. Ernest and Jean Moore 6 March 1965; children: Stewart Alexander, Rebecca; C.E.O. & DIR., HILLSDOWN HOLDINGS PLC 1993– ; Chrmn., Maple Leaf Mills Limited 1987– ; Pres. & C.E.O., Canada Packers Inc. 1990– ; Depy. Chrmn., Maple Leaf Foods Inc. 1992– ; Trainee Mgr., J. Bibby & Sons 1965; Gen. Mgr. & Dir., Anglian Hatcheries 1969; Agric. Dir., Sovereign Chicken 1974; Managing Dir., Ross Poultry Ltd 1980; C.E.O., Buxted Poultry Ltd. 1984; Dir., Hillsdown Holdings PLC 1986; Pres. & C.E.O., Maple Leaf Foods Inc. 1991–92; Chief Oper. Offr., Hillsdown Holdings 1992, C.E.O. 1993; recreation: golf; Home: Falcon House, Mellis, Eye, Suffolk, U.K.

**NEWTON, Elaine Merle Lister,** M.A.; educator; b. Toronto, Ont. 10 March 1935; d. Lou and Faye (Gorvoy) Lister; e. Univ. of Toronto B.A. 1954, M.A. 1956; York Univ. M.A. 1968; m. Alan Wilder; children: Jack, Marla, Lori; ASSOC. PROF., DEPT. OF HUMANITIES, YORK UNIV. 1969– ; former Co-ordinator of Individualized Studies, Dir. Faculty of Arts-Faculty of Educ. Insight Program, Past Sr. Tutor Calumet Coll., mem. Senate; Psychol. YMCA 1954–57; Book Critic Globe & Mail 1954–63; Psychometrist N. York Bd. Educ. 1963–68, Consultant 1971–74; Prof., Humanities, York Univ. 1968– ; Visiting Prof. of Pol. Science Carleton Univ. 1979; Visiting Prof., Univ. of Cape Town 1983 and again in 1984; Victoria Univ., Wellington, New Zealand and Univ. of New Zealand, Aukland Campus 1990–91; papers given Can., U.K., USA, Switzerland, England, Australia and Rep. of South Africa; Ed. 'Mirror of A People'; served Bds. Metrop. Social Planning Council, Nat. Council Jewish Women, Holy Blossom Temple, YM-YWHA; acad. consultant Metrop. Social Services Comte.; planned and conducted Adult Study Groups throughout Toronto; special consultant, Bd. of Philharmonic Centre, Naples, Florida; recipient Prov. Ont. OCUFA Teaching Award 1971; named Toronto's Foremost Prof. by 'Toronto Life' 1981; NDP; Hebrew; recreations: theatre, tennis, music, travel; Club: Mayfair Tennis; Home: 44 Duplex Ave., Toronto, Ont. M5P 2A3; Office: 4700 Keele St., North York, Ont. M3J 1P3.

**NEYSMITH, Brian Ingram,** CFA; financial analyst; b. Montreal, Que. 25 Jan. 1944; s. Arnold W. and Marjory G. (Crabb); e. Sir George Williams Univ., B.Sc. 1966; m. Gloria d. Phillip and Gene Burns 16 July 1966; children: Ronald, Mark, Gary; FOUNDING PRES., CANDN. BOND RATING SERV. 1973– ; Pension Fund Investment Analyst, Northern Telecom 1966–70; Supr., Pension Fund Investments, Bell Canada 1970; Mem., Montreal Soc. of Finan. Analysts; Fellow, Fin. Analyst Fedn.; awarded CFA (Chartered Fin. Analyst), Inst. of Chartered Fin. Analysts; Home: 1117 Cure de Rossi, La Salle, Que. H8N 2M3; Office: 1 Westmount Sq., Westmount, Que. H3Z 2P9.

**NG, Simon S.F.,** B.A.Sc., M.A.Sc., Ph.D.; university professor; b. Canton, China 6 March 1937; e. Univ. of B.C. B.A.Sc. 1962; Univ. of Windsor M.A.Sc. 1964, Ph.D. 1967; m. Daisy Wong 15 May 1965; children: Leslie, Julian; PROFESSOR, DEPT. OF CIVIL ENGINEERING, UNIV. OF OTTAWA 1976– ; Design Engineer, IBM Canada 1966–67; Asst. Prof., Univ. of Ottawa 1967–71; Assoc. Prof. 1971–76; Chair 1979–82; Sec., Fac. of Engineering 1989–93; Office: Ottawa, Ont. K1N 6N5.

**NICHOL, Donald Wingate,** B.A., M.A., Ph.D.; university professor; b. Twillingate, Nfld. 4 Aug. 1952; s. Walter Wingate and Mary Evelyn (Hutton) N.; e. Gordon Graydon Mem. S.S.; Carleton Univ. B.A. (Hons.) 1976, M.A. 1978; Univ. of Edinburgh Ph.D. 1984; m.

Susan Gwyneth d. Robert and Leila Aitken 5 Jan. 1985; children: Leila Evelyn Aitken Nichol, Susannah Marion Aitken Nichol, Robert James Aitken Wingate Nichol; ASSOC. PROF. OF ENGLISH LANGUAGE & LIT., MEMORIAL UNIV. OF NFLD. 1984– ; Tutor, Edinburgh Univ. 1980–84; Open Univ. in Scotland 1983–84; U.K. & Eur. Contbr. Ed., 'Books in Canada' 1982–84; Nfld. Contbr. Ed. 1988– ; freelance writer/literary journalist 1977– (articles & reviews in Candn. & fgn. mags. & newspapers); author: 'Pope's Literary Legacy' 1992; Conference Pres., Candn. Soc. for 18th-Century Studies 1991–92; Pres., Atlantic Soc. for 18th-Century Studies; Extve. Mem., Brit. Soc. for 18th-Century Studies 1993; Mem. Bibliog. Soc. (UK); Oxford Bibliog. Soc.; Edinburgh Bibliog. Soc.; Brit., Candn. & Am. Socs. for 18th-Century Studies; recreation: song-writing, book collecting, carpentry (unplugged), wine making; Home: 13 Hutton Rd., St. John's, Nfld. A1A 2A6; Office: Dept. of English, Memorial Univ., St. John's, Nfld. A1C 5S7.

**NICHOL, Hon. John,** O.C. B.Com., LL.D.; b. Vancouver, B.C. 7 Jan. 1924; s. John M. and Sally (Lang) N.; e. Royal Canadian Naval College 1942–43; University of B.C., B.Com. 1948; m. Elizabeth, d. Kenyon Fellowes, Ottawa, Ont., 1951; three d., Marjorie, Barbara, Sarah; served with R.C.N.V.R. in N. Atlantic and Eng. Channel, 1943–45; Dir., Alcan Aluminium Ltd.; Placer Dome Inc.; mem., Adv. Bd., Royal Trust Co.; New Perspective Fund; mem. Senate of Can. 1966–73; Chrmn., Movement Disorder Institute (Vancouver); Hon. Chrmn., Lester B. Pearson Coll. Pacific; mem., Adv. Bd., Salvation Army; Anglican.

**NICHOL, William James,** B.Sc., P.Eng.; chemical engineer; executive; b. Saskatoon, Sask. 24 Jan. 1920; s. Joseph Irvine and Martha Ann (McKlintock) N.; e. Univ. of Sask. B.Sc. (Chem. Eng.) 1941; m. Edith d. Herbert and Jessie Varley 28 Nov. 1942; children: Irene, Lois, Nancy, William Jr.; Chrmn. & Dir., Columbian Chemicals Canada Ltd. 1985–87; served explosives Candn. govt. World War II; Chief Chem. Gutta Percha Rubber Co. Ltd. Toronto; Chief Chem. and Tech. Mgr. Dunlop Canada Ltd. Ind. Products Div. Toronto 1945–62; Sr. Tech. Mgr. Cities Service Co. (Columbian Carbon Div.) New York 1962, Tech. Coordinator Candn. Co. 1966; Asst. Gen. Mgr. present Co. 1969, Vice Pres. Sales & Adm. 1971; Pres. & Dir. 1974; retired 1985; Chrmn. Ont. Rubber Group 1955; Course Chrmn. Introductory Course to Rubber Technol. Ont. 1958–59 and Advance Course Rubber Technol. 1961; Pres., Hamilton E.-Wentworth Rotary Club 1979–80; mem., Chem. Inst. Can. (dir. 1962); Am. Chem. Soc. (Dir. 1966–69); Assn. Prof. Engs. Prov. Ont.; recreations: golf, fishing, trap shooting; Clubs: Burlington Golf & Country; Home: 1322 Fairway Court, Burlington, Ont. L7P 1M4.

**NICHOLAS, Cindy,** C.M., B.Sc., LL.B.; lawyer; b. Toronto, Ont. 20 Aug. 1957; d. James Paul and Victoria Mary (Dube) N.; e. Univ. of Toronto B.Sc. 1979; Univ. of Windsor LL.B. 1982; m. Raymond s. William and Elizabeth LeGrow 28 March 1987; one d.: Leahanne Nichole LeGrow; called to Bar of Ont. 1984; law practice Alan Eagleson, Q.C.; Sr. Prog. Offr. Donner Candn. Found. and Max Bell Found. 1984–87; el. M.P.P. 1987–90; Law practise in Scarborough 1990– ; marathon swimmer: Lake Ont. 1974, English Channel 19 crossings 1975–82 (2 way crossing 1st for any woman 1977); recipient Scarborough Award of Merit (First) 1974; City of Toronto Award of Merit 1975; named Candn. Woman Athlete of Yr. 1977; Queen of the English Channel (most crossings); Mem. of the Order of Canada 1979; Home: R.R. 5, Claremont, Ont. L1Y 1A2.

**NICHOLL, Christopher Iltyd Hubert,** D.F.C., B.Sc., M.A.Sc., Ph.D., D.C.L.; b. Winnipeg, Man. 22 May 1922; s. Henry Iltyd and Louise Dent (Bell) N.; e. Ridley Coll. St. Catharines, Ont.; Queen's Univ. B.Sc. 1947; Univ. of Toronto M.A.Sc. 1949, Ph.D. 1951; Cambridge Univ. Ph.D. 1960; Bishop's Univ. D.C.L. 1986; m. Margaret Fenwick d. William Duffield Harding, Baltimore, Ont. 19 May 1951; children: John, Katherine, Christina, Sarah, Lucy; Jr. Research Offr. 1947–49, Post doctoral Overseas Fellow 1951; Asst. Research Offr. 1954–56 Div. Mech. Engn. Nat. Research Council, Ottawa; Prof. Agrégé 1956–60, Prof. Titulaire 1960–76 Dépt. Génie Mécanique Univ. Laval, Dir. du Dépt. 1968–71, mem. du Conseil de L'Univ. 1973–76; served with RCAF 1942–45, Pilot att. 514 Sqdrn., R.A.F.; Sch. Commr. Greater Que. Sch. Bd. 1963–65, E. Que. Regional Sch. Bd. 1973–76; Principal and Vice-Chancellor, Bishop's Univ. 1976–86; Pres., Sherbrooke Hospital Foundation; author various research papers in fluid mech.; Fellow, Candn. Aeronautics & Space Inst.; mem. Order Engrs. Que.; Anglican; recreations: walking, sailing; Home: 2000 Ch. Moulton Hill, R.R. #1, Lennoxville, Que. J1M 2A2.

**NICHOLLS, C(harles) G(eoffrey) William,** M.A.; educator; b. Hitchin, Herts., Eng. 10 Oct. 1921; s. late Albert Charles and Kathleen (Thornton) N.; e. St. John's Coll. Cambridge B.A. 1947, M.A. 1949; Wells Theol. Coll. 1951–52; m. Hilary d. late Alexander McCallum 15 July 1950; children: Elizabeth Helen, Paul Charles Alexander, Felicity Kathleen Mary; Prof. 1961–86; and Head of Religious Studies, Univ. of B.C. 1964–83; Travelling Secy. World's Student Christian Fed. 1949–51; Asst. Curate Wendover, Bucks. 1952–54; Chaplain to Ang. Students in Edinburgh 1955–60; Assoc. Prof. of Systematic Theol. St. John's Coll. Univ. of Man. 1960–61; served with Rifle Bgde. 1941–45, rank Capt.; author 'Ecumenism and Catholicity' 1952; 'Systematic and Philosophical Theology' 1969; co-author 'I AMness: The Discovery of the Self Beyond the Ego' 1972; Ed. 'Conflicting Images of Man' 1966; Ed. 'Modernity and Religion' 1987; 'Christian Antisemitism: A History of Hate' 1993; Ed.-in-Chief 'Studies in Religion' 1970–73; numerous articles, book reviews; recipient Norrison Prize in Divinity Cambridge 1950; mem. Candn. Soc. Study Religion (Founding Comte.); recreations: music, photography, running; Home: 7536 Elliott St., Vancouver, B.C. V5S 2N6.

**NICHOLLS, Ralph William,** A.R.C.S., Ph.D., D.Sc., F.R.S.C.; physicist; Univ. professor; b. Richmond, Surrey, Eng. 3 May 1926; s. late William James and late Evelyn Mabel (Jones) N.; e. Co. Sch. for Boys, Hove, Eng. 1943; Imp. Coll. of Science and Technol., Univ. of London, Assoc. Royal Coll. of Science 1945, B.Sc. (Physics) 1946, Ph.D. (Physics) 1951, D.Sc. (Spectroscopy) 1961; m. Doris Margaret, M.D., Ph.D., d. late Frederick McEwen, 28 June 1952; DISTINGUISHED RESEARCH PROF. OF PHYSICS, YORK UNIV. 1983– ; Dir., Atmospheric Physics Laboratory, Inst. for Space & Terrestrial Sci., since 1987; mem., Candn. Network for Space Rsch. 1989– ; Sr. Astrophysics Demonst., Imp. Coll., Univ. of London, 1945–48; joined Univ. of W. Ont. as Instr. 1948, Lectr. 1950, Asst. Prof. 1952, Assoc. Prof. 1956, Prof. 1958, Sr.Prof. of Physics 1963; Prof. 1965–1983 and Chrmn., Dept. of Physics, 1965–69, Walter Gordon Research Fellow 1982–83; Dir., Centre for Research in Earth & Space Science, York Univ. 1965–92; Consultant, Heat Div., US Nat. Bureau of Standards, 1959–60; Visiting Prof. of Aerophysics and Astrophysics, Stanford Univ., 1964, 1968, 1973, 1990; Chrmn., NRC Assoc. Ctte. on Space Research; Chrmn. Science Sub-Cttee. of ICS Space Station Working Group; Chrmn., Candn. Adv. Ctte. on the Scientific Uses of Space Station 1984–89; mem., Solar-Terrestrial Relations Adv. Ctte. of Candn. Space Agency 1989– ; Consultant numerous US and Candn. Aerospace and Govt. Research Labs.; research activities incl. Exper. and Theoretical Lab. Astrophysics, Molecular Spectroscopy, Aeronomy and Atmospheric Physics, Shockwave Phenomena, Rocket Spectroscopy of Aurora, Sun and Moon, Remote Sensing of Earth Resources and Atmospheres; co-author, 'Emission, Absorption and Transfer of Radiation in Heated Atmospheres,' 1972; Ed., 'Canadian Journal of Physics'; Assoc. Ed., 'Journal of Quantitative Spectroscopy and Radiative Transfer'; other writings incl. book chapters and over 270 scient. papers in various prof. journs.; Fellow, Royal Soc. of Canada; Optical Soc. of America; American Physical Soc.; Inst. of Physics; Candn. Aeronautics & Space Inst.; Assoc. Fellow Am. Inst. Aeronautics & Astronautics; mem., Internat. Astron. Union (Pres. Comm 14, 1985–86); Internat. Union Geodesy & Geophysics; Candn. Assn. Physicists and other prof. assns.; Anglican; recreations: writing, music, photography, travel; Home: 9 Pinevale Rd., Thornhill, Ont. L3T 1J5; Office: Dept. of Physics, Room 214, Petrie Bldg., 4700 Keele St., North York, Ont. M3J 1P3.

**NICHOLS, Harold Neil;** management consultant; b. Digby, N.S. 15 June 1937; s. Harold A. and Lillian (Nielsen) N.; e. high sch. grad.; C.M.A. 1970; m. Doris E. Outhouse 2 March 1957; children: Michael, Dale, Sherri, Susan, Lori; CHRMN., PRES. & C.E.O., BATTERY TECHNOLOGIES INC. 1993– ; various financial positions TransCanada Pipelines 1956–90; Extve. Vice Pres. 1988–90; Management Consultant, HNN Services Inc. 1990–93; Dir., Union Bank of Switzerland (Canada); Nova Scotia Resources Ltd.; mem., Financial Executives Inst.; Home: 7 Blackwell Ct., Unionville, Ont. L3R 0C2.

**NICHOLS, Hon. Marcel,** B.A., LL.B.; b. St. Hyacinthe, Que. 16 Dec. 1927; s. J. Ernest and Henriette (Peloquin) N.; e. Univ. of Ottawa, B.A. 1949; Univ. of Montreal, LL.B. 1953; m. Louise Carrier; children (of first marriage): François, Marie, Renée; JUSTICE OF COURT OF APPEAL OF QUE., 1982– ; called to Bar of Que. 1953; Mayor, Drummondville West, 1960–66; Justice, Superior Court of Que. 1968–82; K. of C.; R. Catholic; recreations: fish and game, tennis; Clubs: Club Santiago, Manzanillo, Mexico; Address: 31 Place des Erables, Ste-Julie, Qué. J0L 2S0.

**NICHOLS, (Joanne) Ruth,** M.A., Ph.D.; writer; b. Toronto, Ont. 4 March 1948; d. Edward Morris and Vilas Ruby (Smith) N.; e. Univ. of B.C., B.A. (Religious Studies) 1969; McMaster Univ. M.A. (Religion) 1972, Ph.D. (Theology) 1977; Woodrow Wilson Fellow 1969; Fellow Can. Council 1973; recipient Gold Medal Shankar's Internat. Lit. Competition 1962; Gold Medal Candn. Assn. Children's Librarians 1972; author 'A Walk Out of the World' 1969; 'Ceremony of Innocence' 1969; 'The Marrow of the World' 1972; 'Song of the Pearl' 1976; 'The Left-Handed Spirit' 1978; 'The Burning of the Rose' 1989; 'What Dangers Deep' 1992; Address: c/o McClelland & Stewart, 481 University Ave., Toronto, Ont. M5G 2E9.

**NICHOLSON, Christan Martin,** B.F.A.; artist; b. Saint John, N.B. 29 Dec. 1948; s. William Martin and Beatrice Nellie (Wilson) N.; e. Saint John High Sch. 1967; Univ. of N.B. 1967–69; Mount Allison Univ. B.F.A. 1973; N.S. Coll. of Art & Design M.F.A. program 1974; numerous solo and group exhns. throughout Can.; rep. many univ., govt. and private colls.; awarded numerous official univ., govt. and corporate portrait comns. incl. Dr. S. Skevington, Bath Univ. Eng.; The Hon. J.V. Clyne, former Chancellor Univ. of B.C.; Marion Dewar former Mayor City of Ottawa; Claude Taylor, Chrmn. Air Canada; Edward S. Rogers, Pres. Rogers Communications; William, David & Donald Sobey, for the Sobey Corps., Stellarton, N.S.; I.H. Asper, Chrmn. CanWest-Global, his wife Babs, and children David, Gail & Leonard; currently painting series portraits 34 Candn. authors incl. Mavis Gallant, Irving Layton, Robertson Davies, Antonine Maillet, and Margaret Atwood; recipient Laura Sophia Wood Scholarship 1970; Gairdner Fine Arts Scholarships 1971 and 1972; teaching assistantship N.S.C.A.D.; first prize drawing Atlantic Winter Fair Halifax 1974; purchase awards Univ. of N.B. 1975, City of Saint John 1977, N.B. Art Bank plus many portrait competitions; mem. Soc. Candn. Artists; Print & Drawing Council Can.; United Church; recreatoins: theatre, dance, film, literature; Office: P.O. Box 71052, Ottawa, Ont. K2P 2L9.

**NICHOLSON, John Greer,** Ph.D.; researcher; educator; public speaker; writer; b. Peacehaven, Sussex Eng. 8 May 1929; s. late Arthur and Margaret Maud (Jones) N.; e. Waterloo-with-Seaforth Grammar Sch. 1947; Cambridge Univ. Queens' Coll. B.A. 1952, M.A. 1958; Univ. de Montréal Ph.D. 1963; m. Monique Marguerite Constance Marie d. late Calixte Forthomme 6 Sept. 1952; children: Greer Calixte, Geoffrey William Greer, Giles Timothy Greer; FACULTY ASSOCIATE, CENTRE FOR INTERNAT. RELATIONS, QUEEN'S UNIV. 1993– ; Lectr. in Slavonic Studies, Univ. of London 1952–54; Researcher, Writer and Editor, Am. Comte., Munich 1954–57; Writer, Editor and Head, Russian Sec. CBC Internat. Service, Montreal 1957–61; Asst. Prof. McMaster Univ. 1961–62; Assoc. Prof. McGill Univ. 1962–65, Prof. 1965–79, Chrmn. of Russian & Slavic Studies 1962–71, 1972–78, Chrmn. of French Lang. & Lit. 1973–74; Visiting Prof. of Russian, Oxford Univ. 1972; founding Extve. Dir., Social Sciences and Humanities Rsch. Counc. of Can. 1978–83; Dir., Cambridge Candn. Trust 1983–86, Extve. Dir. 1984; Adjunct Prof., Inst. of Soviet and East European Studies, Carleton Univ. 1986–89; Fulbright Sr. Scholar, Moscow, USSR 1987–88; mem. Acad. Adv. Panel, Canada Counc. 1969–71; mem. Nat. Publ. Comte., Humanities Rsch. Council of Can. 1972–78; mem. Cambridge Soc. of Ottawa 1985–87; mem. Harvard Univ. Club of Ottawa 1985– ; served with military 1947–49; author 'Russian Normative Stress Notation' 1968; numerous articles, research papers and regular newspaper columns on internat. relations; Pres., Candn. Assn. Slavists 1970–71; Montreal Br. Secy., Candn. Inst. Internat. Affairs 1973–75; mem. Candn. Inter-Univ. Council on Academic Exchanges with USSR & Eastern Europe 1975–78, Chrmn. 1976–78; el. mem. Philol. Soc., Gt. Brit. 1971– ; Anglican; recreation: swimming; Home: 595 King St. W., Gananoque, Ont. K7G 2H2.

**NICHOLSON, Martin P.D.,** manufacturer; b. Dodworth, Eng. 30 July 1937; s. Trevor George and Mae Ellis (Hurley) N.; e. Private Schools, Dodworth, Eng.; High Sch. of Comm., Bradston; m. Margaret Lewiss, d. late Henry F. Naylor, 22 May 1962; two s. Peter Roger, Henry Arthur; PRES. AND CHIEF OPERATING OFFR., ROUL LTD. since 1980; Pres., P. D. Lewiss Ltd.; Yawl Containers Ltd.; joined present Co. as Jr. Clerk 1958, Sales Offr. (Can.) 1963, Sales Mgr. 1967; apptd. County Br. Mgr. 1973, Gen. Mgr. 1978 and subsequently Vice-Pres.; Special Rep., Can., Extve. Goods & Service 1965; mem. C.Y.E.A.G.; Freemason; Anglican; recreations: rejuvenation through Yoga, golf, music, sports; Clubs: Harford Mear Golf; Millers Pond Trout; Rotary; Home: 625 Cosburn Ave. Toronto, Ont. M4C 2V1.

**NICKELS, Peter H.;** retired bank executive; b. Rostock, Germany 20 June 1928; s. Hans Theodor and Minne (Prediger) N.; e. Business Sch., Apprenticeship, Textile Engr. Sch., Germany; Concordia Univ., Montreal, B. Comm. 1958; m. Renate d. Joseph Muth 5 May 1957; children: Claudia, Michael, Vivian; Sr. Vice Pres., Marketing & Correspondent Banking Services, Corporate Bank 1986, retired; var. positions, import/export field 1951–56; Extve. Trainee, Candn. Imp. Bank of Comm. 1956; Asst. Eur. Rep., Switzerland 1959; Eur. Rep. 1962; var. managerial positions in Can. & abroad 1966–80; Vice Pres., Eur./Afr./Middle East/London, England & Chrmn., CIBC Ltd. (UK) 1980; Sr. Vice Pres. 1983; Sr. Vice Pres., Can. Int'l Banking & Trade Finance Div., Head Office 1984; recreations: tennis, skiing, swimming; Club: Ontario; Home: 100 Quebec Ave., Toronto, Ont. M6P 4B8.

**NICKERSON, Jerry Edgar Alan,** B.Com.; executive; b. North Sydney, N.S. 28 Apr. 1936; s. Jeremiah Beldon and Jean Frances (Inness) N.; e. Rothesay (N.B.) Coll. Sch. 1953; Dalhousie Univ. B.Com. 1958; m. Jean Frances d. Willoughby Ross Ritcey 20 Sept. 1958; two s. Mark Alan, Jerry Ross; CHAIRMAN H.B. NICKERSON & SONS LTD. and its related companies; Dir. Sydney Steel Corp.; Great West Life Assur. Co.; Halifax-Dartmouth Industries Ltd.; Bank of Montreal; Seaside Cable TV 1984 Ltd.; mem. C.E.O. Organ.; Zeta Psi; Baptist; recreations: golf, tennis; Clubs: Halifax; Home: 59 Meech Ave., North Sydney, N.S.; Office: P.O. Box 130, North Sydney, N.S. B2A 3M2.

**NICKERSON, Mark,** A.B., Sc. M., D.Sc., Ph.D., M.D., F.R.S.C.; educator; physician; b. Montevideo, Minn. 22 Oct. 1916; s. Mark and Ada May (Honey) N.; e. Linfield Coll. (Ore.), A.B. 1939; Brown Univ., Sc.M. 1941; Johns Hopkins Univ., Ph.D. 1944; Univ. of Utah, M.D. 1950; EMERITUS PROF. PHARMACOL. AND THERAPEUTICS, McGILL UNIV., since 1982; Prof. 1975–82; Chrmn. 1967–75; Consultant Royal Victoria Hosp.; Research Biochem., Nat. Defence Research Comte., 1943–44; Instr. in Pharmacol., Univ. of Utah, 1944–47; Asst. Prof. 1947–49; Assoc. Prof. 1949–51; Assoc. Prof., Univ. of Mich., 1951–54; Prof. and Chrmn., Pharmacol. and Therapeutics, Univ.of Man., 1954–67; mem., Josia Macy Jr. Found. Panel on Shock 1951–56; Candn. Drug Adv. Comte., 1960–62; Drug Efficacy Study, U.S. Nat. Acad. of Sciences, 1966–68; mem., Ed. Bds., 'Canadian Journal of Biochemistry and Physiology,' 1956–62; 'Circulation Research,' 1954–59; 'Pharmacologicol Reviews,' 1953–60; 'Proceedings Society for Experimental Biology and Medicine,' 1952–57; 'Annual Review of Pharmacology' 1972–77; 'The Medical Letter' 1976–78; co-author, 'Pharmacological Basis of Therapeutics,' 1955–80; author of over 250 scientific papers published in various professional journs.; discoverer of haloalkylamine adrenergic blocking agents (patents); rec'd John J. Abel Prize for Pharmacol. Research, 1949; Upjohn Award for Pharmacol. Res. in Can. 1978; Fellow, Royal Soc. of Canada 1973; Fellow, Deutsche Akademie der Naturforscher Leopoldina (Halle) 1974; Norman Bethune Professor, People's Republic of China 1975; rec'd Hon. D.Sc. Med. Coll. of Wisc. 1974; Hon. mem., Czechoslovak Med. Soc., 1965; mem., Candn. Physiol. Soc.; Candn. Fed. Biol. Socs. (Chrmn. 1971–72); Nat. Bd. Med. Examiners (Pharmacol. Comte. 1970–74); Pharmacol Soc. Can. (Council 1956–59; Pres. 1960–61); Soc. Exper. Biol. & Med.; Candn. Soc. Clin. Investigation; Am. Chem. Soc.; Am. Physiol. Soc.; Am. Soc. Pharmacol. & Exper. Therapeutics (Council 1969–72, Pres. 1975–76); Brit. Pharmacol. Soc.; Candn. Med. Assn. (Chrmn., Pharm. Comte., 1960–62); Internat. Union Pharmacol. (Council, Treas. 1966–72); Sigma Xi; recreations: bonsai culture, fishing; Home: Wendover, Ont. K0A 3K0; Laboratory: McGill Univ., 3655 Drummond St., Montreal, Que. H3G 1Y6.

**NICKS, Trudy,** B.A., M.A., Ph.D.; museum curator; b. Judah, Alberta 4 Nov. 1942; d. George and May (Ripley) Rumbold; e. Univ. of Alberta B.A. 1966, M.A. 1969, Ph.D. 1980; m. John Stewart s. Stewart and Elizabeth N. 7 Oct. 1967; ASSOCIATE CURATOR-IN-CHARGE, DEPT. OF ETHNOLOGY, ROYAL ONTARIO MUSEUM 1985– ; Curator of Ethnology, Prov. Museum of Alberta 1975–77, 1978–84; Assoc. Curator, Dept. of Ethnology, Royal Ont. Mus. 1984–85; Assoc. Prof. (part-time), Anthropology, McMaster Univ. 1988– ; Rsch. Adv. Ctte., Candn. Mus. of Civilization 1991– ; SSHRCC grants 1978–81, 1991–94; The Getty Grant Program Sr. Rsch. Grant 1991–92; Co-chair, Task Force on Museums and First Peoples sponsored by Assembly of First Nations & Candn. Mus. Assn. 1989–92; Mem., Am. Soc. for Ethnohistory (Councillor 1990–92; Program Chair 1990; Nom. Ctte. 1988); Am. Anthropological Assn.; Council for Mus. Anthropology; Native Am. Art Studies Assn.; Candn. Anthropology Soc.; Rupert's Land Rsch. Centre (Edit. Bd. 1986–94); author: 'The Creative Tradition: Indian Handicrafts and Tourist Art' 1982; co-author: 'Turning the Page: Forging New Partnerships between Museums and First Peoples' 1992; author/co-author of several articles; Home: 85 Jersey Ave., Toronto, Ont. M6G 3A5; Office: 100 Queens Park, Toronto, Ont. M5S 2C6.

**NICOL, Eric P.,** M.A.; writer; b. Kingston, Ont. 28 Dec. 1919; s. William and Amelia Camille (Mannock) N.; e. Lord Byng High Sch., Vancouver, B.C.; Univ. of Brit. Columbia, B.A. 1941, M.A. 1948; Univ. of Paris (Sorbonne) 1949–50 (French Govt. Scholar); m. Myrl Heselton, Sept. 1955 (div.); m. 2ndly Mary Catherine Slinn 1986; Columnist 'Vancouver News-Herald' and 'Vancouver Daily Province'; Radio Writer, C.B.C. (plays); B.B.C. (comedy series and special broadcasts) 1950–51; served in 2nd World War with R.C.A.F., 1942–45; author of 'Sense and Nonsense,' 1947; 'The Roving I,' 1950 (Stephen Leacock Medal for Humour, 1950); 'Twice Over Lightly,' 1953; 'Shall We Join the LadiesD7,' 1955 (awarded Leacock Medal for Humour); 'Girdle Me A Globe,' 1957 (Leacock Medal); 'An Uninhibited History of Canada,' 1960; 'Say, Uncle,' 1961; 'A Herd of Yaks,' 1962; 'Russia, Anyone' 1963, 'Space Age, Go Home'! 1964; 'Like Father, Like Fun' (comedy), 1966; 'A Scar Is Born,' 1968; 'The Fourth Monkey' (stage comedy), 1968; 'Vancouver,' 1970; 'Don't Move!,' 1971; (stage plays-children) 'Beware the Quickly Who,' 1967, 'The Clam Made a Face,' 1968; 'Still A Nicol,' 1972; 'One Man's Media,' 1973; 'Pillar of Sand' (play), 1973; 'Letters To My Son' 1974; 'The Citizens of Calais' (play), 1974; 'There's A Lot of it Going Around,' 1975; 'Canada Cancelled Because of Lack of Interest' (with Peter Whalley illust.), 1977; 'The Joy of Hockey' (with Dave More illust.), 1978; 'Free At Last' (stage comedy) 1979; 'The Joy of Football,' (with Dave More, illust.), 1980; 'Ma' (stage comedy) 1981; 'Golf – The Agony & The Ecstasy' (with Dave More, illust.), 1982; 'Canadide,' 1983; 'Tennis – It Serves You Right' 1984; 'How To...!' (with Graham Pilsworth illust.) 1985; 'The U.S. or US – What's the difference, eh?' (with Dave More illust.) 1986; 'Dickens of the Mounted' 1989; 'Back Talk' (with Graham Pilsworth) 1992; has contrib. articles to 'Macleans,' 'Saturday Night,' etc.; Agnostic; recreations: sports, tennis, badminton; Address: 3993 W. 36th Ave., Vancouver, B.C. V6N 2S7.

**NICOL, Captain Francis Charles;** marine executive; b. Broxburn, Scotland 4 Dec. 1939; s. Francis and Jane Syme (Ross) N.; e. Broxburn H.S.; Leith Nautical Coll. (Edinburgh), Master Cert. 1968; m. Ann c. Thomas and Anne McKechnie 6 Dec. 1969; children: Lee, Kirsty, Murray; PRES. & CHIEF EXTVE. OFFR., THE SHIPPING FEDERATION OF CANADA 1988– ; commenced career at sea with Donaldson Line Ltd. (Glasgow) engaged mainly in North-South Atlantic trades 1956; emigrated to Canada 1968; Marine Supt., Robert Reford Co. 1968–70; Operations Dept., Montreal Shipping Co. Ltd. 1970–73; Mgr., Marine Opns., The Shipping Fed. of Canada 1973–88; Dir., Great Lakes Pilotage Authority; Adv. Counc., Carriage of Hazardous Commodities; Council Mem., Board of Trade of Metropolitan Montreal; Mem., Internat. Cargo Handing Coord. Assn.; Candn. Marine Adv. Ctte.; Pres., Mariners' House of Montreal; Mem., Co. of Master Mariners of Canada (Sec. 1970–73); Chartered Inst. of Transp. (Assoc.); Former Vice-Chrmn., South Shore Protestant Sch. Bd.; School Comnr., St. Lawrence Protestant Sch. Bd. 1980–90; Bd. of Govs., Champlain Regional College; apptd. to Bd. of Govs., Assn. of Maritime Arbitrators of Canada 1991– ; contbg. editor: 'Seaports and the Shipping World' (monthly); editor: 'Maritime Perspective' (quarterly newsletter); recreations: writing, golf, swimming; clubs: United Services, Ports Can. Police Officers' Mess, Ottawa (Hon. Mem.); Home: 1775 Trepanier, Brossard, Que. J4W 2K4; Office: 300 rue St-Sacrement, Ste. 326, Montreal, Que. H2Y 1X4.

**NICOL, Rev. Iain Garden,** M.A., B.D., Ph.D.; educator; b. Cove, Dunbartonshire, Scot. 7 Dec. 1934; s. John Garden and Elizabeth Darroch (Grant) N.; e. Cove and Kilcreggan Primary, Clydebank High Sch.; Univ. of Glasgow M.A. 1959, B.D. 1962, Ph.D. 1971; Univ. of Marburg, W. Germany postgrad. study; m. Ute (dec'd.) d. Emil and Berta Hofmann 25 July 1964; children: Juliet Sonja, Roy Mathias; m. Eleanor Faith d. Kenneth and Mary Rae; Dir. Toronto Sch. of Theology 1980–87; Prof. of Systematic Theol. Knox Coll. Toronto 1975– ; served with Brit. Merchant Navy 1951, RAF Nat. Service 1952–54; held various positions prior to univ. studies 1954–56; Asst. Min. Wellington Ch. Glasgow 1963–65; o. Ch. of Scot. 1964; Asst. becoming Full-time Lectr. in Systematic Theol. Univ. of Glasgow 1965–75; various acad. awards incl. Black Fellowship, Duke of Hamilton Award for Post-Grad. Study Marburg; Princ's Award for Study Oxford; author various articles theol. books and jours.; mem. Am. Acad. Religion; Assn. Theol. Schs. U.S. & Can.; various Cttes. Presb. Ch. in Can.; recreations: tennis, fishing; Home: 55 Stibbard Ave., Toronto, Ont. M4P 2B9; Office: Knox College, 59 St. George St., Toronto, Ont. M5S 2E6.

**NICOLL, John;** real estate executive; b. Windsor, England 2 Apr. 1944; s. John Graham Dalrymple and Kathleen Beatrice (Ogilvy) N.; e. St. Georges, Windsor; Millfield, Somerset; Grenoble Univ., France; m. Alexandra d. Joseph and Anne Steinberg 18 Oct. 1975; children: Tara, Phillip, Mercedes; SR. VICE-PRES., CANADIAN SHOPPING CENTRES, MARATHON REALTY CO. LTD. 1990– ; owner property mngt. co. in England until 1973; joined present firm (Vancouver) 1974 and held var. positions incl. Gen Mgr., B.C. Div.; Vice-Pres., Leasing, Shopping Ctr. Group (Toronto) 1986; Vice-Pres., Operations Bldgs. Group 1989; Mem., Bd. of Trade; Internat. Counc. of Shopping Centres; recreations: skiing, golf; clubs: Kandahar Ski, Capilano, The National, Montreal Racquets; Home: 212 Ranleigh Ave., Toronto, Ont. M4N 1X4.

**NIEDERMAYER, Jack W.,** B.A., D.D.S, FICD; dentist; b. Regina, Sask. 27 Feb. 1938; s. Joseph and Theresa (Felkl) N.; e. Univ. of Sask., B.A. 1960; Univ. of Alta., D.D.S. 1964; m. Nicolette d. Nicolas and Mary Young 15 Aug. 1964; children: Judy, Jill, Jackie, Jan; PRES., CANDN. DENTAL ASSN. 1988–89; Past Pres., Regina & Dist. Dental Soc. 1976; Coll. of Dental Surgeons of Sask. 1977; Mem., Internat. Coll. of Dentists (FICD); Pierre Fauchard Academy; recreatons: golf, curling, hockey, football; clubs: Wascana Golf & Country; Home: 98 Hudson Dr., Regina, Sask. S4S 2W8; Office: 710 – 1805 Rose St., Regina, Sask. S4P 1Z8.

**NIEDERMAYR, Paul,** B.Sc., M.B.A.; distillery executive; b. St-Gallen, Switz. 18 May 1932; e. McGill Univ. B.Sc. 1959, M.B.A. 1966; m. Judith d. Dr. and Mrs. H.A. Peacock; children: Susan, Lisa; Vice-Chairman, United Distillers Canada Inc. 1991–92; Vice-Pres., Opns., Humpty Dumpty Foods Ltd. 1962–75; Pres., La Fromagerie d'Oka Inc. (subs. of Corby) 1975–81; Vice-Pres., Corp. Devel., Corby Distilleries Ltd. 1981–85; Pres. & Chief Extve. Offr., Schenley Canada Inc. 1985–91; recreations: skiing, fishing, hunting, reading, gardening; clubs: Mount-Royal; Home: R.R. #1, Rednersville Rd., Belleville, Ont. K8N 4Z1.

**NIELSEN, Arne Rudolf,** M.Sc.; petroleum executive; b. Standard, Alta. 7 July 1925; s. Aksel Harold and Marie Cathrine N.; e. Univ. of Alta. B.Sc. (Geol.) 1949, M.Sc. (Geol.) 1950; m. 1stly late Evelyn Victoria; 2ndly Valerie Ann Abernethy Thomas Nielsen; children: Allan, Brian, Robin, Gary, Paul, Kent, Dianne, Aksel, Harold; CHRMN., POCO PETROLEUMS LTD. 1993– ; Dir., The Toronto-Dominion Bank; Rockwell International of Canada Ltd.; Aetna Canada; Phillips Cables Ltd.; Coscan Development Corp.; Candn. Petroleum Assoc. (Chrmn. 1970–71, 1984–85); Vaalco Energy Inc.; Candn. Investor Protection Fund; Royal Trust Energy Resources; Fortis Inc.; joined Socony-Vacuum Exploration Co. (now Mobil Oil Can.) as Geol. 1950 serving in Calgary, Edmonton and Regina ultimately becoming Chief Geol.; trans. to U.S. (N.Y., Denver and Houston) 1959 holding sr. exploration and man. positions, rtn'd to Can. as Vice Pres. Exploration Mobil Oil Canada 1966, Pres. 1967; Pres., C.E.O. & Dir., Candn. Superior Oil Ltd. 1978–82; Chrmn., C.E.O. & Dir., Canadian Superior Oil Ltd. (now Mobil Oil Can.) 1982–1986; Chrmn. & C.E.O. Mobil Oil Can. 1986–89; Energy Consultant 1989–90; Pres. & C.E.O., Bowtex Energy (Canada) Corp. 1990–1992; Pres. & C.E.O., Poco Petroleums Ltd. 1992; mem. Assoc. Prof. Engrs. of Alta.; Alta. Soc. Petrol. Geols; Am. Assoc. Petrol. Geols; Am. Inst. Prof. Geols; Houston Geological Soc.; served with Candn. Army 1943–45; Lutheran; Clubs: Petroleum; Ranchmen's; Calgary Golf & Country; Glencoe; Bow Valley; York; Toronto; Office: Bow Valley Sq. IV, 3500, 250 - 6 Ave. S.W., Calgary, Alta. T2P 3H7.

**NIELSEN, Hon. Erik,** P.C. D.F.C., Q.C., LL.B.; barrister; b. Regina, Sask. 24 Feb. 1924; s. Ingvard Evesen and Mabel Elizabeth (Davies) N.; e. Dalhousie Univ., LL.B. 1950; m. late Pamela June, d. Jack Hall, Louth, Lincs., Eng., 3 May 1945; children: Lee Scott, Erik Rolf, Roxanne; PRESIDENT, SOLAR ELECTRIC ENGINEERING, HAWAII, INC. and SOLAR ELECTRIC ENGINEERING DISTRIBUTORS CANADA 1992– ; read law with N.D. Murray, Q.C., Halifax, N.S., and Gordon L.S. Hart, Dartmouth, N.S.; called to the Bar of N.S. 1951 and Yukon 1952; cr. Q.C., 1962; served in 2nd World War with R.C.A.F., Feb. 1942–Oct. 1951; awarded D.F.C.; 1st el. to H. of C. for Yukon in by-el. 16 Dec. 1957; re-el. in subsequent general elections 1958–1984; mem., Candn. Bar Assn.; N.S. Bar Assn.; Minister, Public Works, Canada, June 4, 1979–February 29, 1980; appointed Depy. Opposition House Leader 1980; appointed Opposition House Leader 1981; Leader of the Opposition Feb. 1983 to Sept. 1983; Dep. Prime Minister and Pres. of Queen's Privy Council, 1984–85; Min. of National Defence 1985–86; withdrew from Cabinet, 30 June 1986; tendered resignation as Mem. of Parliament for Yukon 17 Jan. 1987; apptd. Pres., Candn. Trans. Comm., 21 Jan. 1987; apptd. Chrmn., National Transportation Agency 1987; withdrew from public service 1992; mem., Am. Institute of Management; Fellow, Candn. School of Management; author: 'The House is not a Home: An Autobiography' 1989; Progressive Conservative; Anglican; recreations: fishing, hunting, flying; Offices: 75 - 5812 Nani Kailua Pl., Kailua-Kona, Hawaii 96740 U.S.A. and MSPO P.O. Box 31024, Whitehorse, Yukon.

**NIELSEN, James Arthur;** b. Moose Jaw, Sask. 6 Aug. 1938; s. Erling Oscar and Lillian (Douglas) N.; e. Moose Jaw, Sask,; Richmond, B.C.; m. Edith Jean d. Rev. Robert Fred Filer 10 March 1961; children: Robert, Brent, Richard, Darin, Raymond, Christopher, Debra, Julia, Michael; PRES. & C.E.O., CANIMAGING TECHNOLOGIES, INC.; former Min. of Health, B.C.; fed. P. Cons. Cand. for Burnaby-Seymour g.e. 1974; el. M.L.A. for Richmond Prov. g.e. 1975; Min. of Human Resources, B.C. 1986–87; B.C. Social Credit; recreations: reading, writing, trap-shooting, golf; Home: 4271 Waller Dr., Richmond, B.C. V7E 5J4; Office: 1151 - 11871 Horseshoe Way, Richmond, B.C. V7A 5H5.

**NIELSEN, Leslie;** actor; b. Regina, Sask. 11 Feb. 1926; s. Ingvard Evesen and Mabel Elizabeth (Davies) N.; Student, Neighbourhood Playhouse, N.Y.C.; Former announcer, disk jockey Candn. radio; feature films incl. 'The Vagabond King,' 'Forbidden Planet,' 'Ransom!,' 'The Opposite Sex' 1956, 'Hot Summer Night,' 'Tammy and the Bachelor' 1957, 'Night Train to Paris' 1964, 'Harlow,' 'Dark Intruder,' 'Beau Geste' 1965, 'Gunfight in Abilene,' 'The Reluctant Astronaut,' 'Rosie,' 'Counterpoint' 1967, 'Dayton's Devils,' 'How to Commit Marriage,' 'Change of Mind' 1969, 'The Resurrection of Zachary Wheeler' 1971, 'The Poseidon Adventure' 1972, 'Viva Knievel' 1977, 'City of Fire' 1979, 'Airplane!' 1980, 'Wrong to Right' 1982, 'Creepshow,' 'Spaceship' 1983, 'Soul Man,' 'The Patriot' 1986, 'Nuts,' 'Nightstick,' 'Home Is Where the Hart Is' 1987, 'The Naked Gun' 1988, 'Dangerous Curves,' 'The Repossessed,' 'The Naked Gun 21/2' 1991; 'Naked Gun 331/3' 1994; TV films incl. 'Crime Syndicated' 1952, 'Man Behind the Badge' 1954, 'See How They Run' 1964, 'Shadow Over Elveron,' 'Hawaii Five-O,' 'Companions in Nightmare' 1968, 'Trial Run,' 'Deadlock' 1969, 'Night Slaves,' 'The Aquarians,' 'Hauser's Memory' 1970, 'Monty Nash,' 'They Call It Murder,' 'Incident in San Francisco' 1972, 'Searched,' 'The Letters' 1973, 'Can Ellen Be Saved?' 1974, 'Brinks! The Great Robbert' 1976, 'Little Mo' 1978; miniseries incl. 'Back Stairs at the Whitehouse,' 'Institute For Revenge' 1979, 'Ohms,' 'The Night the Bridge Fell Down' 1980, 'Police Squad!,' 'Murder Among Friends' 1982, 'Cave-In' 1983, 'Blade in Hong Kong' 1985; 'The Loner, Fatal Confession: A Father Dowling Mystery; numerous other TV appearances including dramatic series Studio One, Armstrong Circle Theatre, Goodyear Playhouse; TV series incl. 'The New Breed' 1961, 'The Bold Ones' 1963–67, 'Peyton Place' 1965, 'Bracken's World' 1969–70, 'Shaping Up' 1984; author: 'The Naked Truth' 1994; Address: 1622 Viewmont Dr., Los Angeles, CA 90069.

**NIELSEN, Niels Ole,** D.V.M., Ph.D.; educator; veterinary pathologist; b. Edmonton, Alta. 3 Mar. 1930; s. Niels Ludvig and Maren Medom (Hansen) N.; e. Univ. of Alta. 1951; Ont. Veterinary Coll., Univ. of Toronto D.V.M. 1956; Coll. of Vet. Med., Univ. of Minnesota Ph.D. 1963; Amer. Coll. of Vet. Pathology, Diplomate 1963; m. Marilyn Anne, d. Norman Edward Wilson 5 Mar. 1955; children: Margo Lynn; John David; Gordon Ludvig; Dean, Ont. Veterinary Coll., Univ. of Guelph 1985–94; Veterinary Practr. 1956; Instr., Dept. of Vet. Path., Univ. of Minnesota 1957–63; Research Asst., Medical Dept., Brookhaven Nat. Lab., N.Y. 1960–61; Asst. Prof., Dept. of Vet. Path., Univ. of Minnesota 1963–64; Assoc. Prof., Dept. of Vet. Path., Univ. of Sask. 1964; Prof. and Head of Dept. 1968–74; Dean, Western Coll. of Veterinary Medicine, Univ. of Sask. 1974–82; Prof., Dept. Vet. Path., Univ. of Sask. 1982–

84; MRC Visiting Scientist, WHO Escherichia Center, Statens Serum Inst., Copenhagen 1971–72; Visiting scholar, Univ. of California 1982–83; mem. (Bd. of Dirs.) Veterinary Infectious Diseases Org. 1975–83; Candn. Veterinary Medical Assn. (Councillor 1964–68; Pres. 1968–69); Chrmn., Sask. Environmental Adv. Council 1978–82; Bd. of Dirs., Connaught Laboratories Ltd. 1980–86; Bd. of Trustees, Intnl. Laboratory for Rsch. on Animal Diseases 1989– (Chrmn. 1991–94); Bd. of Dirs., Zoological Soc. of Metro Toronto 1992– ; A.V.M.A.; C.V.M.A.; C.V.O.; S.V.M.A.; A.C.V.P.; A.A.A.S.; C.A.V.P.; author articles on diseases of pigs, diseases of the gastrointestinal tract,toxicology, veterinary history and education; Phi Zeta; Protestant; recreations: skiing, canoeing, camping, ceramics; Home: R.R. #6, Guelph, Ont. N1H 6J3.

**NIELSEN, Richard Gordon;** screenwriter/film & TV producer; b. Plaster Rock, N.B. 23 Feb. 1928; s. Hans and Camilla (Mikkelsen) N.; e. Mount Allison Univ. 1947–49; m. Donna Jean d. Harold and Hazel Dunsieth 19 Dec. 1952; children: Camilla, Petrea, Marta; PRES., NORFLICKS PROD. LTD. 1985– ; Fearmans Meat Plant 1944; Dominion Bank 1945; Steel Co. of Can. 1946; Abitibi 1949–50; Bell Tel. 1950; var. posts. incl. BBC assignments in UK 1951–54; Reporter, 'Northern Daily News,' 'Toronto Star' 1954–56; Rsch., Pub. Relns. Dept., Candn. Brotherhood of Railway, Transp. & Gen. Workers 1951–61; Prod./Extve. Prod., CBC, var. prog. incl. 'Public Eye,' 'Document,' 'CBC Weekend' 1961–72; Pres., Intervideo Inc. & Nielsen-Ferns Ltd. 1972–76; Nielsen-Ferns Internat. 1976–86; Chrmn., Primedia Prod. Ltd. 1981–85; Awards: Wendy Michner 1970, Chetwyn 1975, Wilderness 1977, Anik 1985, Gemini 1986; mem., Candn. Film & TV Assn.; ACTRA; author: 'Quebec, Canada 1995' (teleplay) 1983, 'Labour of Love' 1985 (made for TV movie), 'Little Vampire' 1986 (13–pt TV series), 'Comfort Creek' 1989 (feature film); Office: 151 John St., Suite 511, Toronto, Ont. M5V 2T2.

**NIELSSEN, Arild S.,** B.Mech.Eng.; business executive; b. Norway 26 March 1940; e. McGill Univ. B.Mech.Eng. 1963; Stanford Univ. grad. Sch. of Business 1981; m. Doris; PRESIDENT & CHIEF OPERATING OFFICER, CANFOR CORP.; Vice-Pres., Pulp & Paper Mfg., Canfor 1989; Interior Operations 1991; Advisory Bd., Allandale Mutual Insur. Co.; Bd. & Extve. Ctte., Candn. Pulp & Paper Assn.; Adv. Ctte., Univ. of Northern B.C.; club: Vancouver; Home: 740 King Georges Way, West Vancouver, B.C. V7S 1S3; Office: Box 49420, Bentall P.S., Vancouver, B.C. V7X 1B5.

**NIENKAMPER, Klaus H.;** furniture manufacturer; b. Duisburg, W. Germany 22 July 1940; s. Wilhelm H. and Ottilie E. (Emmerich) N.; e. Dusseldorf, W. Germany Merchant's Dip. 1959; m. Beatrix H. d. Heinrich and Gustel Hogenkamp 19 Apr. 1966; children: Rebecca, Ottilie, Klaus; PRESIDENT, NIENKAMPER INC. 1968– ; Pres., Nienkamper Furniture Inc. 1968– ; Chrmn., Nienkamper Inc., USA 1985– ; Sec. Treas. and Partner FR Custom Metal Fabricating Ltd.; estbd. present Co. 1964 mfg. extve. office furniture for maj. corps. and govt. offices; mem. Candn. Business Equipment Mfrs. Assn. (Dir. 1983–84, Chrmn. Office & Contract Furniture Group); recreations: riding, sailing; Home: 619 Avenue Rd., Apt. 401, Toronto, Ont. M4V 2K6.

**NIGHTINGALE, Harvey Michael,** B.A., M.A., M.Ed.; association executive; b. Germany 4 Aug. 1947; s. Jack and Sonia (Cupperberg) N.; e. Univ. of West. Ont. B.A. 1969; York Univ. M.A. 1971; Univ. of Toronto M.Ed. 1978; m. Judith d. Saul and Lily Garden 11 June 1972; children: Steven, Lesley, Jenna; Pres. & C.E.O., Ont. Nursing Home Assn. 1986–92; Sr. Rsch. Offr., O.I.S.E. 1971; Dir., Econ. & Legis. Serv., Ont. Sch. Trustees' Counc. 1973; Extve. Dir., Ont. Nursing Home Assn. 1982; Guest Lectr., Univ. of Toronto; York Univ.; Bd. Mem., Candn. Long Term Care Assn.; Comnr., Edn. Relns. Comn., Coll. Relns. Comn., Govt. of Ont. 1983–85; Mem., Inst. of Assn. Extves.; author of one book chap.; Club: Mayfair; Home: 178 North Meadow Cres., Thornhill, Ont. L4J 3C5.

**NIHMEY, John,** B.A.; corporate president/writer; b. Ottawa, Ont. 22 Sept. 1951; s. Philip and Lily (Monsour) N.; e. Carleton Univ., B.A. (Hons.) 1976; CO-FOUNDER & PRES., NIVA INC. 1979– ; freelance writer 1976–77; journalist/author of syndicated newspaper & mag. column 'Hotels of the World' 1977–80 (Canada's most widely syndicated travel feature); Founder & Pres., NIVA Publishing 1985– ; co-author: 'Time of Their Lives – The Dionne Tragedy' 1986 (Literary Guild alternate selection in Can. & U.S.; pb. & internat. film rights sold); new book forthcoming 1995; recreations: film, travel, music; Office: 800 – 180 Elgin St., Ottawa, Ont. K2P 2K3.

**NIKIFORUK, Peter N.,** Ph.D., D.Sc., F.R.S.A. F.Inst.P., F.I.E.E., F.C.A.E., F.E.I.C., F.C.S.M.E., C.Eng., C.Phy., P.Eng.; educator; b. St. Paul, Alta. 11 Feb. 1930; s. late DeMetro N. and Mary (Dowhaniuk) N.; e. Queen's Univ., B.Sc. (Engn. Physics) 1952; Manchester Univ., Ph.D. (Elect. Engn.) 1955, D.Sc. 1970; m. Eugenie F., d. late William Dyson, 21 Dec. 1957; two d. Elizabeth Mary, Adrienne Eugenie; DEAN OF ENGINEERING, UNIV. OF SASK., since 1973; Chrmn., Bd. of examiners, Assn. of Professional Engs. of Sask.; mem. Bd. of Dir., Sask. Rsch. Council and Chrmn. Finance-Audit Ctte.; mem. Bd. of Dir., C.I.I.T. 1986–91; Chrmn. Sask. Sci. Counc. 1978–83; Mem. Nat. Rsch. Counc. 1973–78; Defence Scient. Offr., Defence Research Bd., Que., 1956–57; Systems Engr., Canadair Ltd., Montreal, 1957–59; joined present Univ. as Asst. Prof., Dept. of Mech. Engn. 1959–61, Assoc. Prof. 1961–65; Prof. since 1965; Head of Dept. 1966–73; Chrmn., Div. of Control Engn., 1964–69; author or co-author of over 250 scient. papers; Fellow, Candn. Acad. Engn.; Candn. Soc. Mech. Engn.; Engn. Inst. Can.; Inst. P.; Inst. Elect. Engrs.; Royal Soc. Arts; mem., Bd. Trade Saskatoon, Sask,; Anglican; Home: 31 Bell Crescent, Saskatoon, Sask. S7J 2W2; Office: Saskatoon, Sask. S7N 0W0.

**NIMMONS, Phillip Rista,** O.C., B.A.; composer; educator; conductor; arranger; clarinetist; b. Kamloops, B.C. 3 June 1923; s. George Rista and Hilda Louise (McCrum) N.; e. Univ. of B.C., B.A. 1944; Scholar, Juilliard Sch. of Music 1945–47; Royal Conserv. Music Toronto 1948–50; m. Noreen Liese Spencer 5 July 1950; children: Holly Jayne, Carey Jocelyn, Phillip Rista Spencer; composer numerous contemporary works incl. piano 'Toccata'; 'Sonatina'; flute/string quartet 'Opus I'; vocal 'Song Cycle' (set to Alexander Pushkin poems); recently 'Duologue' for accordion/clarinet 1984; 'PS42JS' for accordion/clarinet 1985; 'Plateaus: Cariboo Country Tone Poem' for string orchestra/winds 1986; brass quintet 'Celebration' 1980; 'Skyscape: Sleeping Beauty and the Lions' for concert band, world premier EXPO '86, Vancouver, B.C.; 1986; composer, arranger, recording artist 1949– ; appearances and scores incl. film scores, radio, TV, Stage Plays; Theatre Special, Musical Comedy, Variety Shows and own jazz program 1953–XXI, CBC, Toronto Symphony Orchestra, Royal Alexandra Theatre, Crest Theatre, O'Keefe Centre; Expo 67, World Music Week, CMC/IMC of UNESCO, 1975; 'The Trojan Women,' St. Lawrence Centre 1981; over 400 jazz works incl. 'The Atlantic Suite' 1974, 'Transformations' 1975, 'Invocation' world premiere 1976 Olympics; 'Palette à Deux' saxophone/guitar 1979; commissions incl. 'Images Entre Nous' clarinet sonata (prem. James Campbell, Ont. Arts Counc.) 1988; 'The Torch' Candn. Winter Olympics Arts Programme (for opening) 1988; 'Bach in My Own Back Yard' Jazz Octet (Premiere Music at Sharon, Canada Council Commn.) 1988; 'Concerto for Trumpet and Orchestra' (Premiere Dan Warren and Kitchener/Waterloo Symphony, Ont. Arts Council and Laidlaw Found. Commn.) 1988; 'Two-sum' Piano/Vibraphone Due (Premiere 'Pendulum' Jim Hodgkinson and Ted Piltzecker, CBC Commn.) 1989; World premiere by the Esprit Orchestra, 'Of Moods and Contrasts: A Sound Poem' (Laidlaw Foundation Grant) 1994; forthcoming World premiere of (untitled) work for concert band, Fredericton, N.B. (Canada Council Grant) 1994; co-founder Advanced Sch. Contemporary Music 1960, Dir. 1961–66; Touring Artist: Candn. Forces bases (UNEF) with CBC troupe 1965–72, Atlantic Provs. 1974, 1977; Candn., European tours and World tour 1976; Juror: The Canada Council, The Ontario Arts Counc.; The Prison Arts Foundation; Adjudicator: The Kiwanis Music Festival, the Canadian Stage Band Festival (charter mem. 1973, Sr. Adjudicator 1979–84 and past Dir.); Clinician: ISME, the B.C. Teacher's Fed.; Recording Artist: ten albums incl. RCA Victor, Verve, Sackville Recordings, CBC labels; Dir. Jazz Programs; Prof. of Music Univ. of Toronto & Univ. W. Ont. 1970– , Univ. of N.B. summers 1967– , Banff Sch. Fine Arts 1972–81; Courtenay Youth Music Centre & New West Jazz Festival 1979– , Interprov. Music Camp; Univ. W. Ont. 1968– ; Dir., Jazz Program Courtenay Youth Music Centre & New West Jazz Festival; Leader: NIMMONS 'N NINE, NIMMONS 'N NINE PLUS SIX; THE PHIL NIMMONS QUARTET 1953– ; Pres. Nimmons 'N Music Ltd. 1975– ; lectr.: schs., colls. & community groups incl. 'Music In The Classroom' CMC series; awarded Govt. Can. contrib. to Expo 67 1967; BMI (Can.) Cert. Honour 1968; City of Fredericton, N.B. cert. of Recognition Cultural Contrib. 1975; Candn. Soc. Recording Arts & Sciences Juno Award 1976; Gov. of Ont. cert. contrib. Ontario Place 1970–75; PRO Canada, contrib. to music 1980; Toronto Arts Award, excellence in cultural contrib. Canada (music) 1986; Officer, Order of Canada 1994; mem. Adv. Bd. Humber Coll., Banff Sch. Fine Arts; Trustee and Chrmn. York Educ. Clinic 1968–74; mem. Parents Adv. Bd. Thornlea Secondary Sch. 1967–72; past Dir., Faculty Counc., Fac. Music, Univ. of Toronto; Dir. Emeritus, Jazz Faculty, Univ. of Toronto 1991– ; mem. Am. Fed. Musicians of the U.S. and Can.; PRO Can.; Candn. League Composers (Charter); Candn. Music Centre; Candn. Music Counc.; Candn. Acad. of Recording Arts & Sciences; past Dir. Guild of Candn. Film Composers; Address: 114 Babcombe Dr., Thornhill, Ont. L3T 1N1.

**NIND, Thomas Eagleton Westwood,** M.A.; educator; b. London. Eng. 16 June 1926; s. John Warwick and Amy Mary (Greatbatch) N.; e. Windsor Co. Boys' Sch. Eng. 1943; St. Catharine's Coll. Cambridge Univ. B.A. 1946, M.A. 1949; Trent Univ. LL.D. 1991; Royal Sch. of Mines 1950–51; m. Jean Helen d. late Frank F. Marriott 22 May 1954; children: Christopher John Marriott, Sarah Catharine, Andrew Thomas; Pres. and Vice Chancellor, Trent Univ. 1972–79; Prof. of Math.; Dept. Chrmn. 1987–91; Dir. Quaker Oats Co. of Canada Ltd. 1975–80; Asst. Assoc. and Prof. of Geol. Sciences Univ. of Sask. 1958–66; mem. Oil & Gas Conserv. Bd. Sask. 1959–66, mem. Hydrology Subcomte. Nat. Research Council 1964–68; Chrmn. Hydrology Symposium Sask. 1968; Dean of Arts & Science Trent Univ. 1966–71, Vice Pres. (Acad.) 1971–72; Visiting Prof. Universidad Nacional Autonomia de Mexico 1972, Univ. of W. Indies Trinidad 1978; Royal School of Mines, Imperial Coll., London, 1983–84; author 'Principles of Oil Well Production' 1964, 2nd ed. 1981; 'Hydrocarbon Reservoir and Well Performance' 1989; several papers on oil well production and ground water hydrology; Gov. Sir Sandford Fleming Coll. of Applied Arts & Technol. Peterborough 1969–77; Trustee, Peterborough Civic Hosp. 1982–83; Bd. mem., Peterborough Public Lib. 1987– , Bd. Chrmn. 1992– ; mem. Candn. Math. Cong.; Assn. Prof. Engrs. Prov. Ont.; Can. Inst. Mining; Fellow, Cambridge Philos. Soc.; Anglican; recreations: reading, music, gardening, walking; Home: 29 Merino Rd., Peterborough, Ont. K9J 6M8.

**NISKER, Jeffrey A.,** M.D., F.R.C.S.(C), F.S.O.G.C., F.A.C.O.G.; reproductive endocrinologist, medical researcher, university professor; b. Toronto, Ont. 5 Dec. 1949; s. Max and Minnie (Goodman) N.; e. Univ. of Toronto M.D. 1974; Univ. of W. Ont., Residency Training OB/Gyn F.R.C.S.(C) 1978; Univ. of Calif., San Francisco, Fellowship in Repro. Endocrin. 1979; McMaster Univ. 1980; REPRODUCTIVE ENDOCRINOLOGIST, UNIVERSITY HOSPITAL & PROG., UNIV. OF W. ONT.; research: Ethics of Reproductive Technology, influence of hormones in cancer (long-term study showed that endometrial cancer could be prevented with progesterone; also showed the assn. between hormone problems & devel. of endometrial cancer in young women; and demonstrated the importance of aggressive treatment in mngt. of cancer of the cervix in pregnancy); launched 1st Candn. program to address the detection of genetic problems in the pre-embryo; part-time clinical practice of Repro. Endocrin.; Candn. Rep. to Liaison Ctte., Obs./Gyn. 1987–90; Edit. Adv. Ctte., 'Am. J. of Obs. & Gyn. 1987–89; Assoc. Ed., 'ACOG Current J. Rev.' 1988–92; Adv. Bd., 'Int'l J. of Assisted Repro. Tech./Androl.' 1990– ; Extve. Vice-Pres., Soc. of Obs. & Gyn. of Canada 1987–90 (Prog. Chair, annual meetings 1988–90); Chair, Candn. Med. Assn. Council of Affiliate Soc. 1988–92; Candn. Med. Assn. Gen. Council 1987–90; Nucleus Ctte., 1994 World Congress of Obs. & Gyn. 1987–90; Mem., Extve. Reprod. Biol. Ctte., Ont. Med. Assn. 1988– ; Chrmn., SOGC Ethics Ctte. 1993– ; Ont. Ministry of Health Cttes.; 4 journal review cttes.; Mem., Ont. & Candn. Med. Assns.; Soc. of Obs. & Gyn. of Canada (SOGC); Am. College of Obs. & Gynl; Am. & Candn. Fertility Socs.; Am. Inst. of Ultrasound in Med.; Candn. Soc. for Clin. Investigation; Jacob Goldstein Scholar 1974; 1st Prize in Resident Paper Competition (Michigan) 1977; Med. Rsch. Council fellowships 1979, '80; best Rsch. Paper by a Jr. Fellow SOGC 1980; Wyeth Award for Best Paper ISRM 1984; 1st Prize for Scientific Merit 1985; teaching award, UWO; Recognition of Service Award SOGC 1990; Pres., London French Immersion Parents Assn. 1982–83; Bd. of Dir., London Youth Soccer 1987–88; Coach, YMCA Youth Basketball 1986–90; author of over 150 scientific talks & num. sci. articles; co-editor of a book on cancer in pregnancy; recreations: running, music, nordic skiing, kayaking; Office: 339 Windermere Rd., London, Ont. N6A 5A5.

**NIXON, David;** ballet dancer; b. Windsor, Ont.; e. Nat. Ballet Sch.; joined Nat. Ballet of Can. after grad.; first maj. debut as Oberon in 'The Dream' 1979; promoted 2nd Soloist 1980; made debuts 13 ballets 1981–82 season; promoted 1st Soloist 1982; joined Deutsche Oper Berlin Ballet as premier danseur 1985; touring guest artist USA, Italy, Denmark 1982, Australia 1984, 4th and 5th World Ballet Festivals Tokyo 1985 (danced and choreographed 'Lamento') and 1988, Los Angeles, Miami and Chicago 1986; danced title role 'Hamlet' created for him in Berlin 1987 also guest artist Bayerische Staatsoper in Munich dancing first 'Sleeping Beauty'; participated in galas celebrating 750th anniversay of Berlin; invited by Neumeier to dance in Nijinsky Gala, Hamburg 1988; danced in Nureyev's 'Sleeping Beauty' Nat. Ballet Can. and Neumeier's 'Nutcracker' Hamburg 1988; teaching incls. Tokyo Ballet.

**NIXON, Robert Charles Alexander,** B.A.; writer, journalist; b. Winnipeg, Man. 7 May 1956; s. Herbert Evan and Moira Florence (Alexander) N.; e. Univ. of Man., B.A. 1980; News editor, Univ. of Man., 'Manitoban' 1978–79; Reporter, CBC Radio & TV, Toronto, Frobisher Bay, Regina 1980–87; Writing Prof., Chinese People's Univ. for Police Officers, Beijing 1987–88; English Cons., Central China TV, Beijing 1988–89; Sask. Reporters Assn. Best Radio News Story 1985; Candn. Inst. of Mining, Best TV News Story 1987; co-author (with Scott Simmie): 'Tiananmen Square' 1989; recreations: rowing, running, cycling; clubs: Beijing Hash House Harriers, Regina Rowing; Address: c/o Douglas & McIntyre, 1615 Venables St., Vancouver, B.C. V5L 2H1.

**NIXON, Hon. Robert Fletcher,** M.P.P., B.Sc.; farmer; politician; b. St. George, Ont., 17 July 1928; s. Harry Corwin (former Ont. premier, 1943) and Alice Anne (Jackson) N.; e. St. George and Brantford public and high schools; McMaster Univ., B.Sc. (Hons.); Ont. Coll. of Educ.; rec. Hon. LL.D. McMaster Univ. 1976; m. Dorothy Christine, d. T. Owen Loveless, St. George, Ont., 16 Aug. 1952; children: John Corwin, Jane Elizabeth, Harry Owen, Sara Margaret; Agent General, Min. of Economics Develop. and Trade, Ontario House, London, England 1991; el. M.P.P. for Brant-Haldimand (after 1987 redistribution) in by-el., 1962; re-el. 1963, 1967, 1971, 1975, 1977, 1981, 1985, 1987 and 1990; Leader of the Opposition and Ontario Liberal Party 1967–76; Opposition House Leader and Treasury, Revenue and Management Board critic, 1967–76; Senior Cabinet positions including Treasurer of Ontario and Min. of Economics, Min. of Financial Insts., Min. of Revenue, Acting Chrmn. of Management Bd. and Govt. House Leader 1985–87; Deputy Premier as well as serving second term as Treas. & Min. of Economics 1987–90; Leader of the Official Opposition and Leader of the Ontario Liberal Party 1990–91; Pres. of Ont. Liberal Party 1962–63; high school teacher in Sault Ste. Marie and Toronto, 1951 and 1953; head of science dept. North Park Collegiate, Brantford, 1957–61; Liberal; United Church; Home: R.R. 1, St. George, Ont. N0E 1N0.

**NOAKES, David Lloyd George,** B.Sc., M.Sc., Ph.D.; university professor and administrator; b. Hensall, Ont. 3 Aug. 1942; s. Leonard R. and Williamina S. (Sangster) N.; e. Univ. of West. Ont. B.Sc. 1965, M.Sc. 1966; Univ. of Calif., Berkeley PH.D. 1971; m. Patricia d. Olive and Morley Huntley 17 Sept. 1966; one s.: Jeffrey David; DIR., INST. OF ICHTHYOLOGY, UNIV. OF GUELPH 1990– ; Univ. Demonstrator, Dept. of Zool., Edinburgh Univ. 1970–72; Asst., Assoc., Full Prof., Dept. of Zool., present univ. 1972– ; Adjunct Prof., Dép. de sci. biol., Univ. de Montréal; Visiting Prof., Lab. of Ecol., Kyoto Univ. Japan 1988; Mem., Am. Soc. of Ichthyol. & Herpetol.; Am. Fisheries Soc.; Candn. Soc. of Zool.; Internat. Ecol. Cong.; Sigma Xi; Animal Behav. Soc.; Internat. Soc. for Behav. Ecol.; Assoc. Ed. 'Int. J. Envir. Biol. of Fishes' 1975– ; Co-editor: 'The Biol. of Charr and Masu Salmon,' 'Ethol. & Behav. Ecol. of Fishes,' 'Predators and Prey in Fishes'; recreations: photography, gardening; Home: R.R. #1, Hillsburgh, Ont. N0B 1Z0; Office: Guelph, Ont. N1G 2W1.

**NOBES, Robert James,** F.C.A.; chartered accountant; b. Stratford, Ont. 1 Sept. 1941; s. Frederick William and Thelma Viola (Pruss) N.; e. Winston Churchill Collegiage 1961; C.A. 1966; Fellow 1983; m. Frances Erie d. Charlton and Marie McGee 17 Sept. 1966; one d.: Elizabeth Erie; PARTNER, PEAT MARWICK THORNE 1973– ; joined Peat Marwick Mitchell & Co. 1961; Manager 1968; Chrmn., Merchandising Ctte.; Partner in Charge of Profl. Practice, Toronto Office; Mem., Appeals Ctte., Ont. Inst. of C.A.s; F.C.A. 1983; Dir., The Candn. Stage Co. 1992– ; Dir., St. Lawrence Centre for the Arts 1992– ; Gov. & Chrmn., Finance Ctte., Havergal College 1985–92; Dir., Ontario Heart & Stroke Found. 1979–88; Treas. 1979–85; Pres. 1985–86; Dir., Candn. Heart Found. 1985–88; Dir. & Treas., Epilepsy Ont. 1976–80; recreations: cottaging, reading, travel, hiking & birdwatching, golf; clubs: Ontario, Granite; Home: 115 Glengrove Ave. W., Toronto, Ont. M4R 1P1; Office: One Toronto St., Toronto, Ont. M5C 2V5.

**NOBLE, Hon. George Edward,** LL.B.; judge; b. Biggar, Sask. 13 June 1927; s. George Smith and Jessie Chisholm (MacKay) N.; e. Biggar (Sask.) High Sch. 1945; Univ. of Sask. LL.B. 1950; m. Edna Marion d. late Fred S. McKay 15 Aug. 1953; children: Richard D., Janet Lynn, Nancy Ann; JUSTICE, COURT OF QUEEN'S BENCH, SASK. since 1976; read law with E. W. Van Blaricom, Tisdale, Sask.; called to Bar of Sask. 1952; cr. Q.C. 1965; law practice McMillan & Noble, Wadena, Sask. 1953–59; Sallows, Osborn & Noble, Battleford, Sask. 1959–76; Mayor, Town of Wadena, Sask. 1958–59; Chrmn. N. Battleford, Sask. Community Planning Comn. 1962–77; Trustee, N. Battleford Pub. Sch. Bd. 1970–76, Chrmn. 2 yrs.; Lib. Can. for Humboldt-Melfort fed. g.e. 1957; Bencher, Law Soc. Sask. 1974–76, Vice Pres. at time of elevation to Bench; Past Pres., Candn. Judges Conference; Chrmn., Criminal Code Board of Review for Saskatchewan; mem. K-40 Clubs of Can.; Protestant; recreations: golf, curling, skiing, tennis, biking; Home: 226 Trent Place, Saskatoon, Sask. S7H 4S6; Office: Court House, Saskatoon, Sask. S7K 3G7.

**NOBLE, Kimberley Jean,** B.A.; journalist; b. Sudbury, Ont. 30 June 1957; d. Ronald James and Joan Elizabeth (Williams) N.; e. Univ. of Guelph B.A. (Eng. & Fine Art) 1980; Ryerson Polytech. Inst. B.A. (Journalism) 1984; Spouse: Dan s. Anthony and Jeannie Westell; children: Lucy Eliza Westell, Annabel Woodroffe Westell; REPORTER, REPORT ON BUSINESS, THE GLOBE AND MAIL 1984– ; Reporter, Canadian Bureau, Fairchild News Service 1983–84; Adjunct Prof., Univ. of Western Ont. Journalism School 1991–92; Nat. Newspaper Award, Business Reporting 1990, 1991; Mem., Writers to Reform the Libel Law 1992– ; Southern Ont. Newspaper Guild 1984– ; Candn. Assn. of Journalists 1981– ; author: 'Bound and Gagged: Libel Chill and the Right to Publish' 1992; recreations: cycling, gardening, travel; Home: 49 Fern Ave., Toronto, Ont. M6R 1J9; Office: 444 Front St. W., Toronto, Ont. M5V 2S9.

**NOBLE, Stuart Harris,** B.Sc.; newspaper executive; b. Vancouver, B.C. 11 Jan. 1941; s. Stewart Ian and Mina Rebecca (Harris) N.; e. Univ. of B.C. B.Sc.; m. Susan Melnechuk 12 May 1984; children: Kirsten, Kenneth, William, Catherine, Justin; Vice-Pres., Human Resources & Industrial Relations, Pacific Press Limited 1992; various posts ending as Manager, Employee Relations, MacMillan Bloedel Ltd. 1965–77; Dir., Personnel & Industrial Relns., Fording Coal Limited 1977–85; Vice-Pres., Human Resources, Pacific Press Limited 1985; Human Resources & Opns. 1988; Pres. & Chief Op. Offr. 1988; Pres. & C.E.O. 1990–92; Mem., Labor Relations Core Group of Business Counc. of B.C.; Mem., Newspaper Assn. of Am. (Labour Relations Council); Outstanding Service Award, Big Brothers of B.C. 1973; Indus. Relns. Mngt. Assn. Award of Merit 1987–88 (for significant achievement in human resources mngt.); recreations: skiing, tennis, boating, carpentry, gardening; clubs: Terminal City, Arbutus, Vancouver Bd. of Trade; Home: 6700 Whiteoak Dr., Richmond, B.C. V7E 4Z9.

**NODE-LANGLOIS, Patrick,** D. ès Sc.(Econ.); exécutif; né Marseille, France 10 mai 1936; fils Robert et Nelly (Daher) N-L.; é Ecole de Provence (Jésuits) Marseille; Univ. de Paris, Faculté de Droit et de Sc. Econ., Lic. en droit et dipl. de l'Inst. d'adm. des entreprises, D. ès Sc. écon.; ép. Monique, f. Jacques Dalbanne, Neuilly/Seine, France, 11 oct. 1961; enfants: Charles-Eric, Stéphanie, Alexandre, Sonia; VICE-PRES, EXECUTIF, LAFARGE COPPÉE; P.D.G. de Lafarge Fondu International, Directeur Général de Ciments Lafarge - Div. Lafarge Bétons Granulats; Adm. de Lafarge Nouveaux Matériaux, Lafarge Plâtreurope, Générale Sucrière, Compagnie Daher, Compagnie Coppée de Dével. Ind.; anc. Prés. de la Chambre de Commerce Française au Canada et de la Fondation Nationale pour l'Enseignement de la Gestion des Entreprises; Catholique; recreations: natation, ski, golf, montagne; Club: Union Interalliée Cercle du Bois de Boulogne à Paris; résidence: 110 avenue du Roule, 92200 Neuilly-sur-Seine, France; bureaux: 61 rue des Belles Feuilles, 75116 Paris, France.

**NOEL, Albert John,** B.A.(Hons.), M.A., LL.B.; lawyer, public servant; b. Twillingate, Nfld. 17 Jan. 1946; s. William F. and Marion E. (Francis) N.; e. Prince of Wales College 1963; Memorial Univ. B.A. (Hons.) 1968; Carleton Univ. M.A. 1970; Dalhousie Univ. LL.B. 1973; m. Ruth d. Sol and Hilda Gilis Oct. 1974; children: Elliott, Miriam; CLERK, HOUSE OF THE ASSEMBLY (DEP. MIN.) AND LAW CLERK OF THE ASSEMBLY NEWFOUNDLAND 1991– ; admitted to Bar of Nfld. 1974; Solicitor, Dept. of Justice. Govt. of Nfld. & Lab. 1973–77; Legislative Counsel 1977–79; Sr. Legislative Counsel Dept. of Justice and Law Clerk of the House of Assembly 1979–91; appt. Asst. Dep. Min. of Justice 1983–91; Mem., Law Soc. of Nfld.; Soc. of Clerks-at-the-Table in Commonwealth Parliaments; Assn. of Clerks-at-the-Table in Canada; Assn. of Parly. Counsel in Canada; Former Local Sec., Uniform Law Conf. of Can.; Past Vice-Pres., Nfld. Historic Trust; recreations: hiking, nordic skiing, music, gardening; Home: 6 Parsons Pl., St. John's, Nfld. A1A 1Y3; Office: House of Assembly, Confederation Bldg., P.O. Box 8700, St. John's, Nfld. A1B 4J6.

**NOEL, Msgr. Laurent,** B.A., Lic. Phil., D. Théol.; n. St-Just de Bretenières, P.Q., 19 Mars 1920; f. J. Rémi et Albertine (Nadeau) N.; é Coll. de Lévis, B.A. 1940; Grand Sém. de Québec; Faculté de Phil., Univ. Laval, Lic. Phil. 1950; Univ. Angelicum (Rome), D. Théol. 1951; Eveque Auxiliaire, Québec 1963–75; Prof., Faculté de Théol., Univ. Laval, 1951–63; Faculté de Méd., 1952–63; Faculté de Méd., Univ. de Montréal, 1962; et dans plusieurs écoles d'infirmières; Aumonier prov., Assoc. cath. des infirmières, 1957–63; Syndicat professionel des infirmières caths., 1957–63; Administrateur apostolique du diocèse de Hauterine 1974; évêque de Trois-Rivières 1975; Publications: 'De natura gratiae actualis openantis,' 1952; 'Précis de Morale Médicale,' 1962; Collab. à 'La Semaine religieuse de Québec' et 'Le Bulletin des Infirmières catholiques'; Résidence: évêche de Trois-Rivières, 362 Bonaventure, Trois Rivières, Qué. G9A 5J9.

**NOEL, Marc,** B.A., LL.L., LL.B., Q.C.; judge; b. Quebec, Que. 31 Oct. 1948; s. Honourable Camil and Blanche (Belleau) N.; e. Univ. of Ottawa B.A. 1970, LL.L. 1973, LL.B. 1974; m. Louise d. Lucien and Claire Bélair Sept. 1980; children: Catherine, Marie-Louise; JUDGE, FEDERAL COURT OF CANADA 1992– , JUDGE, COURT MARTIAL APPEAL COURT OF CANADA 1993– and MEM., COMPETITION TRIBUNAL 1993– ; Tax Litigation Section, Dept. of Justice (Can.) 1973–74; Partner, Verchere, Noël & Eddy 1975–89; Bennett Jones Verchere 1989–92; Lectr., Que. Bar School 1976–84; McGill Univ. 1977–78; Candn. Inst. of C.A.s 1980–89; Revenue Canada, Taxation 1992; Q.C. 1990; Office: Supreme Court Bldg., Ottawa, Ont. K1A 0H9.

**NOEL, Hon. Nathaniel Stewart,** LL.B.; b. St. John's, Nfld. 29 Nov. 1920; s. Thomas Corbin and Flora May (Winsor) N.; e. Springdale St. Sch. and Bishop Feild Coll., St. John's, Nfld.; Memorial Univ. of Nfld.; Dalhousie Univ., LL.B. 1949; m. Dorothea Olga, d. David R. Thistle, St. John's, Nfld., 26 Apl. 1945; children: Natalie Parsons, Phillip, Carolyn, Neil; JUSTICE, SUPREME COURT OF NFLD. (Supernumerary); called to Bars of N.S. and Nfld. 1949; served with 59th (Nfld.) Heavy Regt. 1940–46; rank Lt.; M.H.A. 1966–71 (Depy. Speaker and Chrmn. of Debates); mem. Royal Candn. Legion; Anglican; recreation: sailing; Office: Supreme Court of Nfld., Duckworth St., St. John's, Nfld. A1C 5V5.

**NOESTHEDEN, John,** M.F.A.; artist, sculptor and assistant professor; b. Netherlands 12 Jan. 1945; s. Johannes G. and Helena C. (Dijkman) N.; e. Windsor Teachers' Coll. 1966; Univ. of Windsor B.F.A. 1973; Tulane Univ. M.F.A. 1975; m. Ruth-Ellen d. Reuben and Nan Rosenberg; children: Jan, Lisa, Matthew; ASST. PROF., UNIV. OF REGINA; collections incl.: Art galleries of Hamilton, Ontario, & Windsor; Can. Counc. Art Bank; Cineplex Odeon Houston; Dept. of External Affairs Ottawa; General Foods Toronto; Guarantee Trust Toronto; Mint Museum Charlotte N.C.; Nickle Arts Mus. Calgary; Skydome C.P. Hotel Toronto; Tom Thomson Art Gall. Owen Sound Ont.; Toronto Archives; T.D. Bank; Toronto Pub. Lib.; Tulane Univ.; Univ. of Windsor; Xerox of Can. Toronto; Zapata Designs Toronto; numerous private collections; several Can. Counc. grants & awards; rep. by Olga Korper Gall. Toronto; recreations: canoeing, cycling; Home: 2251 Wascana St., Regina, Sask. S4T 4K3.

**NOLAN, Ronald,** B.Sc.; engineering executive; b. Calgary, Alta. 18 Apr. 1938; s. Thomas Henry and Lucille Eva (Alexander) N.; e. Univ. of Alta., B.Sc. with distinction 1960; m. Carla-Mae d. Walter and Sylvia Vath 22 Aug. 1958; children: Gregory, Shauna, Joanne; PRES. & CHIEF EXTVE. OFFR., HATCH ASSOC. LTD. 1988– ; admin. of project mngt. & design engr. of major metallurgical facilities incl. steel mills & base metal smelters; joined Trans Alta Power (Calgary) 1960; Domtar (Montreal) 1965; joined Electrical Engr. Group, Hatch Assoc. 1967; Assoc. & Mgr. 1972; Mgr. of Engr. 1978; Vice-Pres. 1980; Evtve. Vice-Pres. 1986; Dir. of a cattle co. engaged in raising & mktg. breeding stock of Simmental beef cattle in Can. & abroad; Dir., Ont. Simmental Assn.; Extve. & Leader, Boy Scout Movement; Coach & co-founder, Black Hawk MTHL minor hockey league; mem., Assn. of Profl. Engrs. of Ont.; Order of Engrs. of Que.; Profl. Engrs. of Alta.; Am. Iron & Steel Inst.; Inst. of Elect. & Elect. Engrs.; co-author of 3 articles; recreations: golf, tennis; clubs: Mississauga Golf, Ontario Racquet, National; Home: 2566 Homeland Dr., Mississauga, Ont. L5K 1H6; Office: 2800 Speakman Dr., Mississauga, Ont. L5K 2R7.

**NOLET, Louis-Paul,** B.Sc.Com., C.A.; executive; b. Montreal, Que. 10 Oct. 1939; s. Oscar and Pauline (Desrosiers) N.; e. Univ. of Montreal (HEC) B.Sc.Com. 1961; m. Henriette d. Dr. Charles Gagnon 27 May 1961; children: Chantal, Bernard; PARTNER, BIRON, LA PIERRE, DUBÉ, NOLET, FALARDEAU, LEBLOND & ASSOCIATE; Dir., Bestar Ltée; Groupe Tremca Inc.; Bastien Inc.; Deca Bois Inc.; F. Pilon Inc.; Forex Inc.; Sogestech Inc.; Regie de l'Assurance Depot du Québec; Auditor, Peat Marwick, Mitchell & Partners 1961–64; Founding Partner, Nolet, Marchand, Martineau & Associates 1964–71; Pres., Avisotech Ltée. 1971–78; Chrmn. of Bd. Mallette, Girouard, Letendre Ltée. 1978–81; Chrmn., Dometal Inc. 1980–89; Vice-Chrmn., The Mallette Financial Corp. 1989; Fellow, Inst. Dirs. (London, Eng.); Chrmn., Fund-raising Campaign, Quebec Cancer Found.; Co-Chief Fund Raiser, Lib. Party of Can. (Que.) 1975–84; Chevalier de l'Ordre Militaire et Hospitalier de St-Lazare de Jérusalem; Commandeur de l'Ordre Nat. 'Honneur et Mérite,' République d'Haïti; author 'L'administrateur de compagnies et le rôle du conseil d'administration' 1981; R. Catholic; Liberal; recreations: golf, skiing, tennis; Clubs: The Mount Royal; Home: 80 rue Berlioz Ile des Soeurs, Verdun, Qué. H3E 1W9; Office: 245, 1253 McGill College, Montreal, Qué. H3B 2Y5.

**NOLIN, Hon. Gaston Jean Claude,** B.A., LL.B.; juge; né Marieville, Qué. 21 août 1923; f. Flavien Gaston et Pauline (Leduc) N.; é. Coll. Mont Saint-Louis 1944; Univ. de Montréal, B.A. 1946, LL.B. 1950; ép. Jacqueline f. J.A. Hector et Germaine Quevillon 8 octobre 1949; enfants: Pierre-Claude, Marie, François, Jacques, Benoît; JUGE DE LA COUR SUPERIEURE DU QUE. 1979– ; stage: Johnson & Tormey, avocats 1946–49; Admis au Barreau du Qué. 1951; membre ou associé des firmes Roux & Verschelden 1951, O'Reilly, Vincent & Nolin 1951–54, Vincent, Nolin & Talbot 1954–68, Nolin, Maranda & Fortier 1968–77, Nolin & Nolin 1977–79; Substitut du Proc. Gén. du Qué. 1955–60; Conseil en loi de la Reine 1968; Juge de la Cour municipale de Ste-Dorothée et de Laval-ouest 1958–60; prés. honoraire du Mouvement Qué.-Can. 1978; Conseil des services sociaux de Montréal 1956–57; Bureau des gouverneurs Coll. Mont Saint-Louis 1965–66; Forces armées canadiennes, Lt. (R) 1949; mem. Assn. Progressiste Conservatrice du Can. (vice prés. Qué. 1950; prés. Région de Montréal 1951; prés. conseil prov. Qué. 1971); Assn. des Anciens M.S.L. (prés. 1957); Conseil du Barreau de Montréal 1961 et 1962; Conseil général Barreau du Qué. 1962; bureau des examinateurs 1963–66; Assn. du Barreau canadien (prés. Comité de droit administratif Qué. 1965 et 1966; Club Bonaventure de Montréal (prés. 1964); Club Saint-Laurent Kiwanis de Montréal (secrétaire 1971–78; membre émérite senior 1979); membre à vie Assn. de bienfaisance des avocats de Montréal 1964; Amis de St-Benoît-du-Lac 1964; Catholique; récreations: pêche, bridge; Adresse: Cartierville, Montréal, Qué. H4J 2C8; Office: ch. 14.71, 1 est, Notre-Dame, Montréal, Qué. H2Y 1B6.

**NOON, Michael,** B.A.; arts and cultural manager; b. Nelson, Lancs., Engl. 20 June 1937; s. Edward Fitzgerald and Ellen (Conway) N.; e. Univ. of Manchester, Engl. B.A. Arch. 1966; St. Mary's Coll., Southampton, Engl. 1954; GENERAL MANAGER ST. LAWRENCE CENTRE FOR THE ARTS 1985– ; Arch. with Raymond Moriyama 1966–68; Campus Planner Ryerson Polytechnical Inst. 1968–70; Dir. of Planning Ont. Coll. of Art 1970–73; Dir. Grants Mgmt. Br., Min. of Culture and Recreation 1973–83; Extve. Dir. Culture Min. of Citizenship and Culture 1983–85; Past Pres., Toronto Theatre Alliance; Pres., Performing Arts Information Services; Bd. Mem., Performing Arts Lodges of Canada, Smile Company; awarded Arch. Registration Counc. of U.K. Scholarship; R. Catholic; recreations: opera, movies, collecting art nouveau; Home: Suite 503, 62 Wellesley St. W., Toronto, Ont. M5S 2X3; Office: 27 Front St. E., Toronto, Ont. M5E 1B4.

**NOONAN, James Stephen,** B.A., B.Th., S.T.L., M.A.; university professor; b. Ottawa, Ont. 26 Aug. 1933; s. James Maurice and Bertha (Gannon) N.; e. St. Patrick's (Ottawa), B.A. 1954; Univ. of Ottawa, B.Th. 1959, S.T.L. 1960; Cambridge Univ., M.A. 1971; m. Norma O'Connor 1991; PROF. OF ENGLISH, CARLETON UNIV. 1967– ; Teacher, St. Patrick's H.S. 1960–64; Prof., St. Patrick's Coll., Carleton Univ. 1967–79; Jules & Gabrielle Léger Fellowship 1986; Former mem., Oblates of Mary Immaculate; strong supporter of Candn. drama & theatre (English & French); author of several articles & reviews; major contbr.: 'The Oxford Companion to Canadian Theatre' 1989, 'The Oxford Companion to Canadian Literature' 1983, 'Supplement to the Oxford Companion to Canadian History and Literature' 1973; editor: 'Biography and Autobiography: Essays on Irish and Canadian History and Literature' 1993; book review editor (English), 'Theatre History in Canada'; book review editor, 'English Studies in Canada'; recreations: music, skiing, swimming, gardening; Home: 32 Lucas Lane, Stittsville, Ont. K2S 1B6; Office: Dept. of English, Carleton Univ., Ottawa, Ont. K1S 5B6.

**NORDAL, Clifford A.,** B.Sc., M.B.A.; hospital executive; b. Gimli, Man. 17 Jan. 1946; s. Jonas and Maria (Thorsteinson) N.; e. Arborg Coll. Inst. 1965; Univ. of N.D., B.Sc. 1969; York Univ., M.B.A. 1976; Candn. Coll. Health Service Execs. Cert. 1984; Fellow 1991; m. Patricia d. Don and Lorraine Fortune 26 June 1974; two d. Kirsten Anne, Lindsey Nicole; PRES. AND CHIEF EXTVE. OFFR., THE QUEEN ELIZABETH HOSP. 1982– ; Systems Analyst, The Wellesley Hosp. 1969–70; Adm. Asst. Addiction Rsch. Found. 1970, Dir. Resources Clin. Inst. 1973–76; joined present Hosp. 1976; Chrmn. H.C.S.O. Foundation Inc. 1983–93; Dir. and Past Chrmn., IST-Healthcomp. Inc. 1983–88; Dir., Candn. Coll. Health Services Execs. 1988– (Chrmn. 1992–93); Governor, Candn. Comprehensive Auditing Found.; Dir., Hospital Council Metro. Toronto 1989–93; Dir., Ont. Hospital Assoc. 1990–92; Past Chrmn. Council of Chronic Hospitals of Ont.; co-author: 'Accountability and Information for Cost-Effectiveness: An Agenda for Action' 1987; 'Reporting on Effectiveness' 1992; recreations: photography, astronomy, woodworking, history; Club: Richmond Hill Country; Home: 72 Centre St. W., Richmond Hill, Ont. L4C 3P7; Office: 550 University Ave., Toronto, Ont. M5G 2A2.

**NORDIN, Ronald H.,** B.A.Sc., C.M.C.; business executive; b. Toronto, Ont. 26 Sept. 1950; s. Henry Randolf and Lois Marguerite (Myrfield) N.; e. Univ. of Waterloo B.A.Sc. 1974; m. Leslie d. Bob and Geraldine Nicholson 24 July 1987; two s.: John Haley, Walker Henry; C.E.O., SOFTWARE QUALITY AUTOMATION 1992– ; Management Consultant, Touche Ross 1974–78; Sales & Marketing Mangement, Cognos 1978–85; Mem., Inst. of Management Consultants of Ont.; recreations: flying, skiing, sailing; Home: 33 York St., Lexington, Mass. 02173; Office: 1 Parka St., Lawrence, Mass. 01843.

**NORDIN, Vidar John,** Ph.D., R.P.F.; educator; consultant; b. Sweden, 28 June 1924; s. John Herman and Beda Catherina (Wahlen) N.; e. Univ. of B.C., B.A. 1946, B.Sc.F. 1947; Univ. of Toronto, Ph.D. 1951; m. Julianne Leona, d. Anton Zerr, 11 Oct. 1947; children: Christopher Eric, M.D., C.C.F.P., Katrin Anne, R.N., M.H.A.; PRESIDENT, V.J. NORDIN AND ASSOCIATES LTD. 1975– ; PROF. EMERITUS, FACULTY OF FORESTRY, UNIV. OF TORONTO, 1986; Dir., Candn. Forestry Accreditation Project 1987–89; Offr. in Charge, Maritimes Forest Pathol. Lab., Fredericton, N.B., 1949–51; Calgary, 1952–57; Assoc. Dir., Forestry Biol. Div., Fed. Agric. Dept., 1958–65; Research Man., Fed. Environment Dept., Ottawa, 1965–71; Dean, Fac. of Forestry, Univ. of Toronto 1971–84; Dean and Prof., Fac. of Forestry and Landscape Architecture, Univ. of Toronto, 1975–78; Extve. Proj. Dir., Canada-Peru Forest Education Proj. 1983–90; Sr. Consultant, China/Canada Univ. Linkage Prog. Aucc. 1987–91; Co-Chrmn., Univ. of Toronto Un. Way Campaign, 1973–74; Bd. Chrmn., Algonquin Forestry Authority Corp. 1974–82; Sr. Consultant, Assoc. of Univs. & Coll. of Canada 1988–93; mem. Prov. Parks Adv. Council 1974–77; Board mem., Forest Engineering Research Institute of Canada; Pres. (1979–80) and mem. Assoc. Univ. Forestry Schools of Canada; Chrmn., (1979) and mem. Nat. Res. Council 1967, Scholarships Selection Ctte. (1977–79); mem., N.R.C. Assoc. Ctte. on Forestry, 1976–79; Ed., 'European Journal of Forest Pathology' 1970–84; Forest Indus. Lectr., Univ. of Alberta 1984; Consolidated-Bathurst Lecturer, Laval Univ. 1985; Hon. Mem., Chinese Soc. of Forestry 1985; Fellow, Can. Institute of Forestry 1992; Invit. Lectures, Southwestern Univ., Kunming, China 1985 and Univ. de Moncton, N.B. 1987; Invitational Paper, Chinese Nat. Forestry Congress, Jiujiang, China 1988; author of over 150 papers and reports in fields of forest protection, mang., educ. and intnl. forestry for various research and trade journs.; consultations in Australia, India, Bangladesh, Brazil, Costa Rica, Peru, Guyana, India, Mexico, Malaysia, Thailand, People's Rep. of China, Venezuela, Soviet Union, Africa, Europe and Canada; Honor al Merito Forestal, Gov't of Peru 1981; Hon. Diploma, Nat. Agrarian Univ. 1987; Hon. mem., Chinese Soc. Forestry 1985; V.J. Nordin Scholarship, Inter. Forestry, Univ. of Toronto; mem., Candn. Inst. Forestry (Pres. 1967–68); mem., C.I.F. Working Group on Intnl. Forestry; mem., S.A.F. Intnl. Working Group; Internat. Union Forestry Research Organs. (Past Subject Group Chrmn.); mem., Tropical Silviculture Group, N. Amer. Forestry Comm. 1982–85; Ont. Forestry Assn. (Dir. 1972–73); Ont. Prof. Foresters Assn. (R.P.F.); Soc. Am. Foresters; Vice-Pres., Canada (1987– ), Treas. and Dir. (1983–86), Intnl. Soc. Tropical Foresters; Rockliffe Flying Club; Candn. Owners and Pilots Assn.; recreations: music, photography, skiing, flying; Office: V.J. Nordin Assocs. Inc., P.O. Box 2368, Stn. D, 340 Laurier Ave. W., Ottawa, Ont. K1P 5W5.

**NORMAN, Maj. Gen. Francis John,** C.D., B.A.; army officer; consultant; b. Montreal, Que. 26 Sept. 1935; s. Hon. Henry Gordon, C.M.G. and Marie Muriel (Hill) N.; e. Trinity Coll. Sch. Port Hope 1952; HMCS Royal Roads 1954; Royal Mil. Coll. B.A. 1956; McGill Univ. B.A. 1957; Royal Mil. Coll. of Sci. UK 1961–62; Candn. Army Staff Coll. 1967–68; Laval Univ. Bicultural Devel. Program 1976–77; Nat. Defence Coll. 1979–80; m. Anne d. Frank and Marion Lemon 10 June 1961; children: LT (N) Mark Arnold Gordon, Peter David; gaz. Lt. Royal Candn. Regt. 1956; Lt. Col. 1968, Directing Staff Candn. Land Forces Command and Staff Coll. 1968–70; Directing Staff Brit. Army Staff Coll. 1970–72; C.O. 1 RCR 1972–73; Col. 1973, Dir. Regional Operations Maritime Command HQ Halifax 1973–76; Chief of Staff Secteur de L'Est Montréal 1977–79; Brig. Gen. 1979; Chrmn. Accomodation Policy Task Force 1980–82; Commandant and Vice Chancellor, Royal Mil. Coll. of Can. 1982–85; Maj. Gen. 1985; Associate Assistant Deputy Minister (Policy) National Defence HQ 1985–86; Commandant, National Defence Coll. 1986–89; PRES., AGWANIS INC.; recipient Cyprus Medal UN Service 1966; Candn. Centennial Medal 1967; Queen's Silver Jubilee Medal 1978; awarded Commemorative Medal for 125th Anniversary of Candn. Confederation 1993; C.D. 1964 and Bar 1974 and 1984; Hon. Lt. Col. Candn. Gren. Gds. 1991– ; Bertrand Stewart Prize Essay Winner 1964, 1968; Sr. Assoc., Conant and Assoc., and Mem., Royaumont Group on the Middle East, Washington, D.C.; Gov., Kingston Gen. Hosp.; Board Mem., Order St. John 1990– ; Gov., Corps. of Commissionaires, Kingston; Mem., Bd. of Mgmnt. and Advisory Council, Centre for Quality in Governance, Toronto; Mem. Bd. of Govs., National Defence College; Assoc. mem. Brit. Inst. Mgmt. 1972; recreations: home repairs, writing, military history; Club: Royal Kingston United Services; Address: 85 Gore St., Kingston, Ont. K7L 2L4.

**NORMAN, Geoffrey Ross,** B.Sc., M.A., Ph.D.; university professor; b. Winnipeg, Man. 10 Nov. 1944; s. Maurice Lester and Ruth (Partridge) N.; e. Univ. of Man., B.Sc. 1965; McMaster Univ., Ph.D. 1971; Michigan State Univ., M.A. 1977; m. Pamela Joy d. William and Edna Renney 25 Jan. 1969; children: Adam Russell, Leigh Sabrina; PROF., CLINICAL EPIDEMIOLOGY & BIOSTATISTICS and FAMILY MEDICINE, MCMASTER UNIV. 1981– ; Rsch. Assoc., Family Med., McMaster Univ. 1970–71; Med. Edn. 1971–76; Asst. Prof., Dept. of Clin. Epidemiol. and Biostats. 1977; Cons. to med. schs. in Holland, England, Germany, Israel, Egypt, Aust. and U.S.; Nat. Health Scholar Award (Health & Welfare Can.) 1977–83; Prov. Health Sci. Award (Ont. Min. of Health) 1984–86; John L. Hubbard Award, Nat. Bd. of Medical Examiners, Philadelphia 1989; co-editor: 'Assessing Clinical Competence' 1984; author: 'PDQ Statistics' 1986; author of numerous scholarly articles; Mem., Assn. of Am. Med. Colls.; Am. Edn. Rsch. Assn.; Am. Psychol. Assn.; Home: 316 MacNab St., Dundas, Ont. L9H 2K9; Office: Health Sciences Centre, 1200 Main St. W., (CE&B), Room 2C15, Hamilton, Ont. L8N 3Z5.

**NORMAND, Robert,** C.A.; business executive; b. Montreal, Que. 9 Jan. 1940; e. Ecole des hautes etudes commerciales; m. Pauline Ross July 1962; children: Patrice, Isabelle; VICE-PRES., FINANCE, GAZ METROPOLITAIN INC.; External Auditor, Richter, Usher & Vineberg 1962–65; Coopers & Lybrand 1966–67; Chief Accountant, Tioxide of Canada 1967–68; Comptroller, Scott-Lasalle Ltd. 1969–71; joined Gaz Métropolitan as Asst. to Vice-Pres. for Finance 1972; promoted to Comptroller, Vice-Pres. Finance & Treasurer and Vice-Pres. Finance & Regulatory Matters; Dir., Daubois Inc.; Le fonds d'investissement Rea Inc. and Trans Quebec & Maritime Pipeline; Financial Executive Institute of Canada (Chairman 1994); Candn. Gas Assn. (Admin. Ctte.);

Home: 177 Grande Côte, Rosemere, Que. J7A 1H5; Office: 1717 du Havre St., Montreal, Que. H2K 2X3.

**NORMAND, Robert,** c.r., LL.L.; b. Montréal, Qué. 24 Sept. 1936; s. Lucien and Éva (Rochon) N.; e. Univ. de Montréal B.A. 1956; Univ. de Sherbrooke LL.L. 1960; Univ. de Paris Dipl. d'études politiques 1962; m. Madeleine d. René and Amabilis Scott 16 Sept. 1961; children: Éric, Yves, Geneviève; VICE PRES., CORPORATE AFFAIRS, UNIMÉDIA INC. 1993– ; Chrmn., La Corporation d'Assurance de personnes La Laurentienne; Dir. Crédit Lyonnais Canada; Invest. Dealers Assn. Can.; Professional Liability Isurance Fund of the Barreau du Québec; Québec Garrisons Club; Swedish General Consul Québec City; mem. Citizen's Forum on Can.'s Future (Spicer Commn.) 1990; Chrmn., Québec Symphony Orch. 1989–92; Vice Pres. Hôpital du St-Sacrement; Vice-Chrmn., Inst. Rsch. Pub. Policy; Legis. Draftsman and Law Clk. Legis. Assembly Québec 1962–71; Dep. Min.: Justice Québec 1971–77, Intergovt'al Affairs 1977–82, Finance 1982–87; Publisher, Le Soleil 1987–93; Sec. Study Ctte. on Expropriation 1968; Vice Pres. Candn. Del. Dip. Conf. travel contracts Brussels 1970; Pres. Candn. Del. Internat. Inst. French Lang. Law Tunis 1974, Paris 1976; Pres. Québec Police Inst. 1974; Chrmn. Ctte. Olympic Security 1974–76; Chrmn. Uniform Law Conf. Can. 1975; Co-Pres. Un. Way Campaign Greater Québec region 1989 and Hon. Chrmn. of region (03) Telethon Cerebral Paralysis 1990; Dir. Caisse de dépôt et placement du Québec 1982–87; recipient Québec Pub. Adm. Award of Excellence 1986; Past Chrmn. Québec Soc. Legal Documentation; mem. Québec Bar; Candn. Bar Assn.; recreations: fishing, hunting; Club: Québec Garnison; Home: 2750, de l'Anse, Ste-Foy, Qué. G1W 2G5; Office: 390 St-Vallier E., Québec, Qué, G1K 7J6.

**NORMANDEAU, André,** Ph.D.; criminologist; educator; b. Verdun, Que. 4 May 1942; s. Gabriel and Laurette (Sauve) N.; e. Univ. de Montréal B.A. 1962, B.Sc. 1964; Univ. of Pa. M.A. (Criminol.) 1965, Ph.D. (Sociol.) 1968; m. Pierrette d. Romeo Lapointe, Montreal, Que. 14 Aug. 1965; children: Alain, Louis, Jean; PROF. OF CRIMINOLOGY, UNIV. DE MONTREAL 1968– , Chrmn. of Criminology 1970–80; Dir., Internat. Centre for Comparative Criminology, Montreal, Que. 1983–88; mem. Rsch. Counc., Min. of Educ., Que. 1970–80; mem. Adv. Comte. Min. of Justice, Ottawa 1975–80; mem. Parole Bd., Min. of Justice, Qué. 1980–88; Policy Advisor, Min. of the Solicitor General, Ottawa 1989–91; author 'Public Opinion and Crime' 1970; 'Deviance and Crime' 1975; 'Armed Robbery in Quebec' 1980; 'Prevention of Crime' 1985; (with Thomas Gabor et al.) 'Armed Robbery: Cops, Robbers and Victims' 1987; 'A Vision of the Future of Policing in Canada' 1990; over 500 articles violence, adm. justice, sociology of law various nat. and internat. publs.; rec'd Lt. Gov. Que. Award 1980; mem. Candn. Criminal Justice Assn. (Dir.); Am. Soc. Criminology (Dir.); Internat. Soc. Criminology (Dir.); R. Catholic; recreations: tennis, cinema, theatre; Home 3150 Kent, Montreal, Que. H3S 1N1; Office: Montreal, Que. H3C 3J7.

**NORRIE, William,** C.M., Q.C., B.A., LL.B., LL.D.; politician; b. St. Boniface, Man. 21 Jan. 1929; s. William and Mary (Rae) N.; e. Principal Sparling Elem. Sch. 1944; Daniel McIntyre Collegiate 1947; United Coll. Univ. of Man. B.A. 1950; Univ. of Man. Law Sch. LL.B. 1955; Queen's Coll., Oxford, Engl. 1953; LL.D. (Hon.) Univ. of Winnipeg 1981; LL.D. (Hon.), Univ. of Man. 1993; m. Helen Isobel d. Jack M. and E. Isobel Scurfield 20 Aug. 1955; children: Duncan Jack William, Fraser Rae, Mark Robertson; CHRMN., SCHOOL DIVISIONS BOUNDARIES REVIEW COMMISSION; Mayor, City of Winnipeg 1979–92, retired; articled with Sir Charles Tupper 1950; joined Tupper Adams & Adams 1955, Partner 1961; Mortgage Investment mgr. Monarch Life Assurance Co. 1963; Partner Richardson, Richardson, Huband, Wright & Norrie 1964; Sr. Partner Richardson & Co.; apptd. Dep. Sec., Law Soc. of Man. 1975; apptd. Queen's Counsel 1977; apptd. Dep. Mayor City of Winnipeg 1977; Trustee Sir William Stephenson Scholarship Trust, Univ. of Winnipeg; former mem. and Chrmn., Winnipeg Sch. Bd.; mem.: Man. Rhodes Scholarship Selection Ctte.; United Ch. of Can.; former mem.: National Comn. on Ch. Union; past Chrmn. Bd. of Regents Univ. of Winnipeg; Dir. and Past Pres. Winnipeg Convention Centre Corp.; Paul Harris Fellow, Rotary Internat.; recipient Legion of Hon. Degree, Candn. Order of Demolay; Life Mem. (and Past Pres.) Man. Assn. of Sch. Trustees; Hon. Mem. Carpenters' Union; Rhodes Scholar Manitoba; Hon. Citizen, City of Setagaya, Japan; Friendship Medal, Republic of Phillipines; Overseas Friendship Medal, Republic of China; Hon. Overseas Legal Representative, City of Chengdu, P.R. China; B'nai B'rith Humanitarian Award; Shevchenko Medal, Ukranian Candn. Ctte.; 1991 Citizen of the Year Award, Winnipeg Chinese Community; recipient, Eagle Feather from Shoal Lake 39 First Nation; Jerusalem, City of Peace Medal 1992; admitted to the Order of Canada 1993; Govt. of Canada, Citation for Citizenship Award; awarded Commemorative Medal for 125th Anniversary of Candn. Confederation; awarded Univ. of Winnipeg Distinguished Alumnus Award 1994; on retirement from the Mayor's Office, estab. by the City of Winnipeg and friends and colleagues of the 'William Norrie International Centre for Environmental Research and Education'; Chrmn., President Jimmy Carter Habitat for Humanity Foundation; Dir., Winnipeg Foundation Board; recreations: swimming, camping; Clubs: Royal Lake of the Woods Yacht; Winnipeg Squash Racquet; Rotary of Fort Garry; Home: 212 Waverley St., Winnipeg, Man. R3M 3L2; Office: Suite W310, 1970 Ness Ave., Winnipeg, Man. R3J 0Y9.

**NORRIS, Alan,** B.A., C.A.; real estate executive; b. Paisley, Scotland 13 Oct. 1956; s. the late George Ernest and Janet (Provan) N.; e. Univ. of Strathclyde B.A.; C.A. Scotland; C.A. Canada; m. Shelly d. the late Glen and Jean Poole 15 Oct. 1983; children: Andrea, Cory, Colin, Kirsten; EXTVE. VICE-PRES. & CHIEF FINAN. OFFR., CONSOLIDATED CARMA CORP. 1988– ; articled with Deloitte Haskins & Sells (Glasgow) 1977–80; Audit Sr./Audit Mgr., Deloitte Haskins & Sells (Calgary) 1980–83; Corp. Controller, present firm 1983–86; Vice-Pres. Finan. 1986–87; recreations: golf; clubs: Bearspaw Golf & Country; Home: 212, Ranch Estates Bay N.W., Calgary, Alta. T3G 2A2; Office: #800, 839 – 5th Ave. S.W., Calgary, Alta. T2P 3C8.

**NORRIS, Geoffrey,** B.A., M.A., Ph.D., F.R.S.C.; university professor; b. Romford, England 6 Aug. 1937; s. Alfred Frederick Henry and Winifred Lucy (Camps) N.; e. Cambridge Univ., B.A. 1959, M.A. 1962, Ph.D. 1964; post-doct. fellow, McMaster Univ. 1964–65; m. Anne d. Lesley and Ida Facer 20 Sept. 1958; children: Grant, Theresa, Brett, Sonia; PROF., DEPT. OF GEOLOGY, UNIV. OF TORONTO 1967– ; Sci. Offr., New Zealand Geol. Survey 1961–64; Rsch. sci., Pan Am. Petroleum Corp. Rsch. Ctr. 1965–67; Asst., Assoc. & Full Prof., Dept. of Geology, Univ. of Toronto 1967– ; Chrmn. 1980–90; Rsch. Assoc., Royal Ont. Mus. 1967– ; Partner, Austin and Cumming Explor.; Alexander von Humboldt Stiftung Fellow 1975–76; Fellow, Royal Soc. of Can. 1984; Secy., Div. of Earth & Space Sciences 1990–92; Dir., Metro Toronto Residents Action Ctte.; Mem., Am. Assn. of Stratigraphic Palynol. (Pres. 1972); Councilor, Geol. Assoc. Can.; Internat. Comn. for Palynol. (Sec.-Treas. 1977–81); Fellow, Geological Soc. of Am.; mem. Candn. Nat. Ctte. of Internat. Union of Geological Sciences 1990– ; Candn. Assn. of Palynol. (Pres. 1982); Pres., White Light Hospice Found.; Club: Faculty; Home: 12 Astley Ave., Toronto, Ont. M4W 3B4; Office: Dept. of Geology, Earth Sciences Centre, Univ. of Toronto, Toronto, Ont. M5S 3B1.

**NORRIS, Harry Stephens,** MBA, P.Eng., CMA; corporate director; financial consultant; b. Bournemouth, England 28 Nov. 1941; s. Harry William Albert and Ada Ruth (Stephens) N.; e. Dynevor Grammar Sch. 1959; Imperial Coll., B.Sc. 1962; Carnegie-Mellon Univ., MBA 1964; m. Barbara d. Setrag and Yevnige Krikorian 11 Sept. 1965; children: Harry, Elizabeth, Mary; PRES., H.S. NORRIS CONSULTANTS LIMITED 1976– ; Corp. Fin. Analyst, Celanese of Can. 1965–67; Div. Controller 1967–70; Dir. & Fin. Controller, Neve Electronic Holdings Limited 1970–72; Mgr., Fin. & Tech. Serv., Export Devel. Corp. 1972–74; Dir., Corp. Planning, Leigh Instruments Limited 1974–76; Dir., Iawah Corp.; Quintel Indus. U.S. Inc.; Dir., First Fruits Found.; Elder, Bridlewood Bible Chapel; Fellow, Inst. of Corp. Dirs.; recreations: fishing, gardening; Club: Rideau; Home: 25 Aleutian Rd., Nepean, Ont. K2H 7C7; Office: 155 Queen St., Suite 900, Ottawa, Ont. K1P 5C9.

**NORRIS, Ken,** M.A., Ph.D.; educator; writer; b. Bronx, N.Y. 3 Apl. 1951; s. Leroy and Theresa (Castellano) N.; e. State Univ. N.Y. Stony Brook B.A. 1972; Concordia Univ. M.A. 1975; McGill Univ. Ph.D. 1980; m. Susan d. Donald and Margaret Hamlett 6 Sept. 1987; two d. Sarah, Zoe; became Candn. Citizen 1985; PROF. OF CANDN. LIT. UNIV. OF MAINE 1985– ; mem. Vehicule Poets 1975–80; ed. bd. Vehicule Press 1975–81; Writer-in-Residence McGill Univ. 1983–84; Visiting Prof. of Candn. Studies W. Wash. Univ. 1987; recipient 3rd Prize Poetry CBC Competition VIII; Lit. papers at McLennan Lib. McGill Univ.; author (poetry) 'Vegetables' 1975; 'The Perfect Accident' 1978; 'Autokinesis' 1980; 'To Sleep, To Love' 1982; 'Whirlwinds' 1983; 'The Better Part of Heaven' 1984; 'Islands' 1986; 'In the Spirit of the Times' 1986; 'Report on the Second Half of the Twentieth Century' 1988; 'In the House of No' 1991; 'Alphabet of Desire' 1991; 'Full Sun: Selected Poems' 1993; maj. critical work 'The Little Magazine in Canada 1925–80' 1984; ed. 'Canadian Poetry Now' 1984; 'Vehicule Days: An Unorthodox History of Montreal's Vehicule Poets' 1993; mem. Writers Union Can.; Assn. Candn. Studies in USA; recreations: baseball, classical music; Office: 304 Neville Hall, Orono, Maine 04469.

**NORRIS, Richard P.,** C.A.; b. Liverpool, U.K. 21 April 1948; s. John Francis Birkett and Eileen Winnifred (Walsh) N.; m. Joyce Clarke 13 Dec. 1969; children: Susan Rachel, Paul James, Michael Timothy; Treasurer, Husky Oil Ltd. 1988–92; Auditor, Revenue Canada Taxation 1970–75; Tax Policy Officer 1975–77; Tax Planning Supvr., Mobil Oil Canada 1977–80; Tax Manager, Aquitaine Co. of Canada 1980–81; Canterra Energy Ltd. 1981–83; Treas. 1983–88; Dir., Commonwealth Geophysical Dev. Co. Ltd.; Gulfview Investments Ltd.; Dir. & Vice-Pres. Finance, Alberta Ballet Co.; Dir. & Treas., Calgary City Ballet 1989–90; taught in-depth tax course on oil & gas at Candn. Inst. of C.A.s; author of one Canadian Tax Foundation paper; recreations: golf, skiing, hiking; clubs: Earl Grey Golf & Country; Home: 24 Bayview Dr. S.W., Calgary, Alta. T2V 3N6.

**NORTH, John Andrew,** B.A., A.L.A.; library consultant/writer; b. St. Albans, Herts., Eng. 13 March 1942; s. Henry Joseph and Eileen (Harvey) N.; e. St. Albans Sch. 1959; North West London Polytechnic A.L.A. 1963; Univ. of Toronto 1976; children: Andrew Peter, Gavin Craig; PRES. & C.E.O., NORCOM ENTERPRISES (Information Consultants) 1989– ; Asst. Lib. Natural Rubber Producers' Research Assn. U.K. 1959–61; Lib., Morgan Bros. (Publishers) Ltd., London, Eng. 1961–64; Mang. Ed., Co-operative Book Centre Toronto 1964–67; Coll. Lib., Centennial Coll. Scarborough 1967–72 and Mount Royal Coll. Calgary 1972–74; Dir., Learning Resources Centre, Ryerson Polytech. Inst. 1974–89; Gov., Ryerson Polytech. Inst. 1978–82; Crime and mystery columnist, Toronto Star; Book reviewer, Quill & Quire; author various articles lib. journs.; short stories in 'Cold Blood II' 1989; 'Cold Blood 3' 1990; 'Cold Blood 4' 1992; Crime Writers of Canada; recreations: crime fiction, gardening, golf; Club: Scarboro' Golf & Country; Home & Business: 46 Hill Cres., Scarborough, Ont. M1M 1J2.

**NORTH, R. Philip M.,** Q.C.; lawyer; b. Deloraine, Man. 11 Nov. 1944; s. Glynn Harris and Hazel Muir (Baxter) N.; e. Brandon Univ., B.Sc. 1966; Univ. Man., LL.B. 1971; m. Freda, d. Frank and Edith Weidenhamer, 19 Aug. 1966; children: Travis Glynn; Susan Elizabeth; Patricia Laura; LAW PARTNER, NORTH & COMPANY since 1976; Pres., Dowtown Rotary Club of Lethbridge; Vice Chrmn., Legal Education Soc. of Alberta; Bencher, Law Soc. of Alta. 1986–92; Chrmn., Alta. Law Found. 1988–92; Past Chrmn., Bd. Govs., Univ. Lethbridge 1978–84; Past Mem. Bus. Adv. Comte., Lethbridge Community Coll.; Past Pres., Lethbridge Bar Assn.; mem. Candn. Bar Assn.; Am. Trial Lawyers Assn.; Alta. Arbitration & Mediation Soc.; Lethbridge Chamber of Commerce (Past Dir. and Vice-Pres.); Office: 600, 220 – 4th St. S., Lethbridge, Alta. T1J 4J7.

**NORTHORP, Supt. Bruce Lionel,** C.M.; retired RCMP officer; b. Vancouver, B.C. 26 March 1927; s. late George Washington and Annie Beatrice (King) N.; e. Sir Alexander McKenzie Pub. and John Oliver High Schs. Vancouver; Candn. Police Coll. Regina 1965; m. Mabel Louisa d. late John Fancy Kerr 26 June 1954; two s. Robert Bruce, Murray Ronald; has served as police offr. over 32 yrs. both uniformed and plainclothes duties; over 23 yrs. service related to plainclothes work involving investig. criminal offences; has directed and participated in many investigs. murders, armed robberies, kidnapping and torture, also activities related to outlaw motorcycle gangs and organized crime; as Police Operations Commdr. and Negotiator has successfully handled many hostage incidents, 2 internat. hijacking incidents and 2 maj. riot/hostage incidents B.C. Penitentiary; final case assignment was the 1981 B.C. investigation into several missing and murdered children which resulted in the arrest and conviction of serial murderer, Clifford Robert Olson; Past Chrmn. ad-hoc Police Comte. dealing with problems that develop during labour dispute/strikes; Past Chrmn. Citizens' Advisory Comte., Vancouver Parole District; served with Candn. Army (RCE) 1945, rec'd war medal; Reserve 1947–49; recipient, RCMP Commr.'s Commendation for Bravery; 2 RCMP C.O.'s Commendations for Outstanding Police Work and letter of recognition from Dir. of FBI; RCMP Long Service Medal with Clasp and Star; Queen's Silver Jubilee Medal; 125th Anniversary of the Confederation of Canada Medal, 1992; Life mem. Kings Co. Hist. Soc. (Sussex Corner, N.B.); Baptist; Home: 4692 Clinton St., Burnaby, B.C. V5J 2K7.

**NORTHOVER, Wallace E.,** M.A., Ph.D.; university professor; b. Trenton, N.J. 1 June 1931; s. Leonard Vernon and Thelma (Rainford) N.; e. Fordham Univ., M.A. (Philos.) 1959; New Sch. for Soc. Rsch., M.A. (Psych.) 1962; York Univ., Ph.D. 1972; m. Elizabeth Ann d. Lenox and Naureen Murray 8 May 1971; one s.: Vincent Alexei; ASSOC. PROF., DEPT. OF PSYCHOLOGY, ATKINSON COLL., YORK UNIV. 1965– ; Lectr., Manhattanville Coll. 1960–62; Univ. of Detroit 1962–65; Assoc. Prof., Dept. of Psychology, York Univ. 1965– ; Master, Atkinson Coll. 1982– ; Vis. Assoc. Prof., McGill Univ. 1976–77; Univ. de Sao Paulo 1980–81; Danforth Found. Teaching Award 1963–64; Mem., A.A.U.P.; C.A.U.T.; Ont. Speech & Hearing Assn.; A.P.A.; C.P.A.; Candn. citizen; recreations: motorcyclist; Home: 40 Windy Golfway, Don Mills, Ont. M3C 3A7; Office: Atkinson College, York Univ., 4700 Keele St., North York, Ont. M3J 1P3.

**NORTHWOOD, Derek Owen,** B.Sc., A.R.S.M., Ph.D., P.Eng., F.I.M., F.A.S.M., F.I.M.M.A., F.I.E.Aust.; professor of engineering materials; b. Hitchin, Herts., England 28 July 1943; s. Owen Samuel and Mary Grace (Flack) N.; e. Letchworth Gr. Sch. 1961; Royal Sch. of Mines, Imperial Coll., B.Sc., A.R.S.M. 1964; Univ. of Surrey, Ph.D. 1968; m. Marilyn Gail d. Paul and Frances Laplante 3 Sept. 1970; children: Melissa Dawn, Layla Devon; PROF. OF ENGR. MATERIALS, DEPT. OF MECH. ENG., UNIV. OF WINDSOR 1989– ; Investig., Brit. Non-Ferrous Metals Rsch. Assn. 1964–65; Grad. Student & Demonstrator, Univ. of Surrey 1965–68; post-doct. fellow/part-time lectr., Univ. of Windsor 1969–71; Metallurgical Engr., Chalk River Nuclear Labs, Atomic Energy of Can. 1971–76; Assoc. Prof., Univ. of Windsor 1976–79; Prof. 1979– ; Assoc. Dean: Rsch./Dir., Office of Rsch. Serv./Pres., Indus. Rsch. Inst. 1980–83; Vis. Prof., Univ. of Queensland 1983–84, May-Aug. 1986; Head, Dept. of Engr. Materials, Univ. of Windsor 1985–89; Visiting Prof., National Univ. of Singapore 1991; Past Mem., Bd. of Dir., Int. Metallographic Soc.; Past Pres., ASM Can. Counc.; Chrmn., Pub. Counc. of ASM Internat.; Fellow, Inst. of Metals (UK); ASM Internat.; Inst. of Metals and Materials Australasia; Inst. Engrs. Australia; Mem., The Metallurgical Soc. of AIME; Microscopical Soc. of Can.; Internat. Assn. for Hydrogen Energy; Internat. Metal. Soc.; Assn. of Profl. Engrs., Prov. of Ont. (P.Eng.); Asian Pacific Materials & Corrosion Assn.; Nat. Assn. Corrosion Engrs.; author/co-author of 136 sci. journal papers & 113 papers in conf. proceedings; editor: 'Corrosion, Microstructure & Metallography' 1985, 'Metallography & Corrosion' 1986; 'Image Analysis and Metallography' 1989; Mem., Ed. Adv. Bd., 'Metallography'; Internat. Ed. Adv. Bd. 'Materials Forum'; recreations: swimming, reading; Home: 133 Ironwood Dr., Amherstburg, Ont. N9V 3V3; Office: Windsor, Ont. N9B 3P4.

**NORTON, David Fate,** B.A., M.A., Ph.D., F.R.S.C.; university professor; b. Hastings, Mich. 7 Feb. 1937; s. Keith S. and Minnie A. (Fate) N.; e. Bethel Coll., B.A. 1959; Grad. study, Univ. of Redlands 1959–61; Claremont Grad. Sch. M.A. 1964; Univ. of Calif., Ph.D. 1966; m. Mary J. d. Ralph O. and Adeline M. Cook 15 June 1957; MACDONALD PROF. OF MORAL PHILOSOPHY, MCGILL UNIV. 1990– ; Visiting Fellow, Rsch. School of the Social Sciences, Inst. for Advanced Study, Australian National Univ. 1990; Lectr., Univ. of Calif. 1965–66; Asst. Prof. 1966–70; Assoc. Prof. 1970–71; Assoc. Prof. McGill Univ. 1971–81; Prof. 1981– ; Mng. Dir., & Editor, McGill-Queen's Univ. Press 1981–85; Fellow, Nat. Endowment for the Humanities 1967–68, 1994; Canada Council Leave 1976–77; Am. Counc. of Learned Soc. 1985; Killam Rsch. 1986, 1987; Royal Society of Canada 1990; Inst. for Adv. Studies in the Humanities, Univ. of Edinburgh 1986; Mem., Inst. for Adv. Study, Princeton 1985–86; Asst. Ed., 'Journal of the History of Philosophy' 1965–71; Bd. of Dir. 1972–83; Assoc. Ed. 1973–75; Extve. Ed. 1975–80; Editor 1980–83; Editorial Ctte. 'Dialogue' 1989– ; Extve. Ctte., The Hume Soc. 1975–76, 1980–84 1986–90 (Chrmn. 1982–84); Adv. Panel, Ctr. for the Study of Candn. Philos. 1980–89; Bd. of Dir., McGill-Queen's Univ. Press 1981–85; Pres. & Acad. Ed., Austin Hill Press 1978–81; Mem., Am. Philos. Assn.; Brit. Soc. for the Hist. of Philos.; Candn. Philos. Assn.; Candn. Soc. for Eighteenth-Cent. Studies; The Hume Soc.; author: 'David Hume: Common-Sense Moralist, Sceptical Metaphysician' 1982 and numerous papers on hist. of modern philos.; editor: 'Cambridge Companion to Hume' 1993; 'McGill Hume Studies' 1979; 'David Hume: Philosophical Historian' 1964; Co-general editor: 'The Philosophical, Political, and Literary Works of David Hume'; Home: 1509 Sherbrooke St. W., Montreal, Que. H3G 1M1.

**NORTON, G. Ron,** M.Sc., Ph.D.; educator; b. Standard, Utah 11 Sept. 1941; s. Glen L. and Irene A. (Salzetti) N.; e. Utah State Univ. M.Sc. 1967, Ph.D. 1971; m. Judith d. Theodore and Lenore Burton 3 June 1967; two s. Marshall, Peter; FULL PROFESSOR, PSYCHOLOGY, UNIV. OF WINNIPEG 1983– ; Chair, Psychology 1986–92; Asst. Prof. of Psychiatry, Univ. of Man. 1986– ; Adjunct Prof. of Psychol., Univ. of Manitoba 1988– ; Cons. Stress & Anxiety Clinic, Clin. Alcoholism Found. Man.; Co-chrmn. Man. Mental Health Rsch. Found.; author 'Parenting' 1977; over 90 articles sci. jours.; co-ed. 'Panic Disorder and Agrophobia' 1991; Fellow, Candn. Psychol. Assn.; Clin. Fellow, Behaviour Rsch. & Therapy Soc.; recreations: reading, golf, weight-lifting; Office: Winnipeg, Man. R2B 2E9.

**NORTON, S. Thomas,** B.A., M.Ed.; association executive; b. Hamilton, Ont. 4 May 1943; s. Stanley Arthur and Martha (Allison) N.; e. Univ. of W. Ont. B.A. 1964; Univ. of Toronto, M.Ed. 1985; continuing student, Univ. of Toronto; m. Mary Carmel; children: Michelle, Christopher; PRES., ASSN. OF CANDN. COMMUNITY COLLEGES 1990– ; Teacher, Humber Coll. of Appl. Arts & Technol. 1969; Staff Training Co-ord. 1971; Chrmn., Admin. 1972; Prin. Lakeshore 1976; Vice Pres., Cont. Learning 1978; Acad. 1980; Cons., Edn. Mngt., Internat.; Futures in Edn., var. Bds. of Edn.; Extve. Dir., Assn. of Candn. Community Colleges 1987–90; Advisor, Federal Policy Develop. (various Ministries incl. Human Resources Development, Industry & Foreign Affairs); author of variety of studies in internat. devel. for ACCC, CIDA, World Bank; recreations: writing, travel in connection with internat. devel.; extensive work in Asia & Africa; designed devel. projects for Canadas Coll. in Kenya, Zambia, Mexico, Philippines, Indonesia, Malaysia, Jordan, India; Office: 1223 Michael St. N., Gloucester, Ont. K1J 7T2.

**NORUP, Henning Magnus,** A.I.I.C.; insurance executive; b. Copenhagen, Denmark 9 Apr. 1944; s. Magnus Valdemar and Gerda Johanne N.; e. Alsgade, Copenhagen, grade 13; Insurance Inst. of Can., A.I.I.C.; children: Shane, Danielle; PRES. & CHIEF EXTVE. OFFR., VEHICLE INFORMATION CTR. OF CAN. 1989– ; Programmer, Data Centralen, Copenhagen 1962–68; Computer Cons., Cover-All Computer Serv. 1968–69; Programming Supvr., Insurance Bureau of Can. 1969–72; Mgr., Opns. 1972–84; Asst. Vice-Pres., Strategic Planning, Mktg., Claims Emergency Co-ord. 1985–89; recreations: sailing, skiing; clubs: Island Yacht; Home: 55 Lake Drive N., Keswick, Ont. L4P 1A5; Office: 175 Commerce Valley Dr. W., Suite 220, Markham, Ont. L3T 7P6.

**NORWICH, Kenneth Howard,** M.D., M.Sc., Ph.D.; educator; physician; b. Toronto, Ont. 8 May 1939; s. Jack and Etta (Salamansky) N.; e. Vaughan Rd. Coll. Inst. 1957; Univ. of Toronto M.D. 1963, B.Sc. 1967, M.Sc. 1968, Ph.D. 1970; m. Barbara d. Philip and Ann Gross 18 June 1963; three d. Marni, Stephanie, Liora; ASSOC. DIR. INST. OF BIOMED. ENG. UNIV. OF TORONTO 1989– , Prof. of Physiol. and of Inst. 1980– , cross-appt. Prof. of Physics 1990– ; Pres. Intercept Press; gen. med. practice; Asst. Prof. of Physiol. and of Applied Sci. & Eng., Inst. of Biomed. Electronics present Univ. 1970, Assoc. Prof. 1975; recipient Starr Medal for Rsch. Faculty of Med. Univ. Toronto 1977; author 'Molecular Dynamics in Biosystems' 1977; 'Classical Theoretical Physiology' 1981; 'Information, Sensation and Perception' 1993; various book chapters; mem. ed. bds. several profl. jours.; mem. Candn. Med. Assn.; Candn. Med. & Biol. Eng. Soc.; Biomed. Eng. Soc.; Soc. Math. Biol.; Internat. Soc. Psychophysics; Alpha Omega Alpha Hon. Med. Soc.; Home: 23 Peveril Hill Rd. S., Toronto, Ont. M6C 3A7; Office: 4 Taddle Creek Rd., Toronto, Ont. M5S 1A4.

**NOURSE, L.W.;** retired manufacturer; b. Grahamsville, Ont. 17 May 1912; s. Rev. Fred Arthur and Nettie May (Underwood) N.; e. Williamson Rd. Pub. Sch. and Malvern Coll. Inst., Toronto; m. Merilyn, d. late Robert Niven, 30 Sept. 1969; one d., Wendie Anne; Clk., Thomson McKinnon, stockbrokers, N.Y., 1933–37; Mgr., Fyfe Oil Filter Ltd. 1937–42; Chrmn. Wix Inc. 1942–84; Chrmn. Eco-Tec-Limited 1970– ; Past Chrmn., Can. Section SAE; recreations: cottage; Clubs: Toronto Hunt; Rotary; Home: 1 Fallingbrook Dr., Scarborough, Ont. M1N 1B3.

**NOVAK, Mark,** B.A., Ph.D.; university professor; b. Jersey City, N.J. 23 Jan. 1948; s. Charles Aaron and Ann Rose (Holzberg) N.; e. Rutgers Univ. B.A. (with distinction) 1969; York Univ. Ph.D. 1973; Harvard Univ., Inst. for the Mngt. of Lifelong Edn. (MLE) 1991; m. Mona d. Phillip and Sylvia Kravis 31 Aug. 1969; children: Christopher, Jonathan, Sean, Daniel; PROFESSOR AND ASSOCIATE DEAN, CONTINUING EDUCATION DIV., UNIV. OF MANITOBA 1989– ; Instructor, Sociology, York Univ. 1972–73; Visiting Prof., Soc. Laurentian Univ. summer 1973; Prof., Soc., Univ. of Wininpeg 1973–89; Visiting Scholar, Med. Psych. Unit, Cambridge Univ. 1979–80; Adjunct Prof., Soc., Univ. of Man. 1989– ; Cons., Continuin Edn. Div., Univ. of Man. 1987–89; SSHRCC leave fellowship 1979–80, 1986–87; Strategic Grant Award 1979–83; Award for Excellence in Edn. Program Design, Candn. Assn. of Univ. Cont. Edn. 1988; Past Mem., Bd. of Dir. for several orgns.; Mem., Adv. Bd., Senior Health Project 1991–93; Mem., Bd. of Dir., Man. Opera Assn. 1992–93; Mem., Winnipeg, C. of C. 1990–93; author: 'Living and Learning in the Free School' 1975, 'Successful Aging' 1985, 'Aging and Society' 2nd ed. 1993 and over 20 articles & chapters in profl. jours. & books; recreations: squash, jogging, hiking, travel; Home: 79 Folkestone Blvd., Winnipeg, Man. R3P 0B4; Office: Rm. 166, Winnipeg, Man. R3T 2N2.

**NOVICK, Louis Jacob,** B.S.S., M.S.W.; hospital administrator; b. N.Y.C. 31 Mar. 1919; s. Max and Anna (Goldfarb) N.; e. Coll. City of N.Y., B.S.S. 1940; Columbia Univ., M.S.W. 1942; m. Miriam, d. Henry and Annie Mishkoff, 26 Mar. 1944; children: Isaac Meir; Shana Razel; Henry Enoch; Extve. Dir., Maimonides Hosp. Geriatric Centre, Montreal 1960–91; Social Worker, Jewish Social Service Bureau (Pittsburgh) 1944; Asst. Extve. Dir., Orthodox Jewish Home for the Aged (Chicago) 1948; Extve. Dir., Milwaukee Jewish Home for the Aged 1953–59; author 21 articles in profl. journals; Fellowship conferred by Candn. Coll. of Health Service Extves. 1985; rec'd. Extendicare Award, Candn. Coll. Health Service Extves. 1982; Queen's Silver Jubilee Medal from Gov. Gen. Can. 1977; Honouree State of Israel Bonds 1977; Outstanding Achievement and Community Leadership Award, Beth Zion Cong. (Montreal) 1967; Consultant, Québec Dept. Social Affairs; Mem. Bd. of Dirs. & Chrmn. of Ethics Ctte., Candn. College of Health Service Extves.; Mem. Item Dev. Sub Ctte., Candn. Coll. of Health Service Execs.; Preceptor, Fac. Admin., Univ. Ottawa; Lectr., Fac. Med., McGill Univ.; Past Pres., Long Term Care Hosp. Div., Quebec Assn. Hosps.; Pres., Miriam Home Found.; Pres., Miriam Home for the Exceptional; Vice Pres. World Conf. of Jewish Communal Service; Columbia Univ. Sch. Social Work Alumni Assn. 1972–75; Pres., Dickanwise Sch. Special Ed. 1969–71; mem., Candn. Coll. Health Service Extves.; Candn. Assn. on Gerontology; Gerontological Soc. (Am.); Comte. on Aging and the Aged, Candn. Jewish Congress (Nat. Chrmn. 1977); mem., Advisory Bd., Long Term Care Monitor; mem., Bd. of Dirs., Federation of Jewish Community Services of Montreal; recreations: Bible study; foreign languages; gardening; Home: 5810 Wolseley Ave., Montreal, Que. H4W 2M1; Office: 8355 rue Mayrand, Montreal, Que. H4P 2E2.

**NOVOTNY, George Milos,** CD, M.D., F.R.C.S.(C), F.A.C.S.; otolaryngologist; educator; b. Prague, Czechoslovakia 7 March 1929; s. late Joseph V. and Maria (Cermak) N.; e. Sr. Matric. Prague X 1948; Charles' Univ. Prague 1st yr. med. 1948–49; Univ. of Toronto M.D. 1958; Queen's Univ. Surg. 1962–63; McGill Univ. Otolaryngol. 1964–67; m. Elfriede Anna d. late Karl Gruber, Austria 20 Dec. 1952; children: Susan Anna, Tina Marie; PROF. OF OTOLARYNGOL., DALHOUSIE UNIV. since 1974, Head 1974–87, Assoc. Prof. Sch. of Human Communication Disorders, Research Assoc. Dept. Psychol. (Grad. Studies), mem. Senate; Dir. N.S. Hearing and Speech Clinic; Sr. Staff, Past Head of Otolaryngol. Halifax Infirmary, Victoria Gen. Hosp.; Sr. Consultant, Candn. Forces Hosp., Halifax; Active Sr. Consultant, The Izaak Walton Killam Hosp. for Children; Consultant, Camp Hill Hosp.; Dartmouth Med. Centre; N.S. Rehabilitation Centre; joined Candn. Forces Med. Service 1957, 'Air' Element, rank Lt. Col. 1972, Consultant in Otolaryngol. since 1967; rec'd CD (Canada Decoration) 1969, Queen's Silver Jubilee Medal 1977; mem. Claims Evaluation Comte. N.S. Med. Services Ins.; Hearing Aid Adv. Bd. N.S. Dept. Consumer Affairs; author or co-author various publs. and papers; mem. Candn. Forces Med. Service Offrs. Assn.; Am. Council Otolaryngol.; Candn. Otolaryngol. Soc. (Educ. Comte. & Council) Pres., 1983–84; N.S. Soc. Ophthalmol. & Otolaryngol.; Dartmouth Med. Soc.; Candn. Soc. Aviation Med.; Soc. Acad. Chrmn. Otolaryngol.; Royal Soc. Med.; Candn. Med. Assn.; N.S. Med. Soc.; Halifax Med. Soc.; E. Can. Otolaryngol. Soc. (Secy.-Treas. 1976–78, Pres. 1978–79); the Coordinating Counc. on Deafness of N.S. 1985; Am. Auditory Soc. 1985; Fellow in Otolaryngol. Dalhousie Univ. 1967, Lectr. 1970, Asst. Prof. 1972, Acting Head 1973; recreations: skiing, sailing, gardening, painting, art; Clubs: Ashburn Golf; Wentworth Valley Ski; Home: 40 Clayton Park Dr., Halifax, N.S. B3M 1L6; Office: Halifax Infirmary, Halifax, N.S. B3J 2H6.

**NOWLAN, David Michael,** M.A., Ph.D.; educator; economist; b. Toronto, Ont. 25 Dec. 1936; s. James Parker and Bernice (Nance) N.; e. N. Toronto Coll. Inst. 1954; Queen's Univ. B.Sc. 1958; Oxford Univ. (Rhodes Scholar) B.A. 1960; Univ. of Toronto M.A. 1963, Ph.D. 1965; m. Nadine d. Victor and Marguerite Murray 1960; one s. Peter James; PROF. OF ECONOMICS, UNIV. OF TORONTO 1973– ; Economist Govt. of Can. 1960–62; joined present Univ. 1965; on leave as Sr. Transp. Econ. Govt. of Tanzania 1966–67; Dir. present Univ.'s planning project in Tanzania 1968–73, Vice Dean Sch. Grad. Studies 1978–81, Vice Pres. (Research and Planning) and Registrar 1981–83, Vice Pres., Research 1983–88; Provostial Advisor on Environmental Studies 1994– ; Extve. mem. Metrop. Toronto Planning Bd. 1972–74; mem. Metro Plan Adv. Ctte. Metrop. Toronto 1975–78; Commnwealth Econ. Mission to Uganda 1979; Vice Chrmn. UNCTAD Group Experts Landlocked Developing Countries 1984; mem. Jamaican Govt.'s Univ. of W. Indies Mona Campus Review Comn. 1984; Dir. Innovations Found. Univ. of Toronto 1984–88; Dir., Information Tech. Rsch. Centre 1987–88; econ. cons. United Nations and various fed., prov. and mun. govts.; recipient D.S. Ellis Meml. Trophy Queen's Univ. 1958; Can. Counc. Fellowships 1963, 1966, 1974; author numerous articles and monographs devel. planning, urban econ., pub. policy and univ. financing; Vice Pres. Candn. Econ. Assn. 1974–76; Home: 149 Admiral Rd., Toronto, Ont. M5R 2L7; Office: 150 St. George St., Toronto, Ont. M5S 1A1.

**NOWLAN, Michael O'Keeffe,** C.D., B.A., B.Ed., M.Ed.; educator; writer; b. Chatham, N.B. 1 Sept. 1937; s. Harold Benedict and Margaret Mary (O'Keeffe) N.; e. St. Thomas Univ., B.A. 1959; Univ. of N.B., B.Ed. 1964, M.Ed. 1986; m. Gertrude d. Leo and Celeste Gallant 17 Aug. 1964; children: Gregory, Mary, Theresa, James, Peter; ACTING ASST. DIR., PROGRAM DEVELOP. & IMPLEMENTATION BRANCH, DEPT. OF EDUC., FREDERICTON, N.B. 1989– ; H.S. Teacher, Loggieville, N.B. 1961–62; Chatham, N.B. 1962–64; Oromocto H.S. 1964–88; Head, English Dept. 1973–78; Vice-Principal, Oromocto H.S. 1978–88; Consultant in English Language Arts, Dept. of Educ., Fredericton, N.B. 1988–89; Past Pres., Dist. 25, N.B. Teachers' Assn.; N.B. Counc. of Teachers of English; has served on several N.B.T.A. cttes.; honoured for service record; Charter Mem., Candn. Counc. of Teachers of English (Pres. 1984–86); Msgr. Boyd Counc. No. 6774, Knights of Columbus; Mem., N.B. Writers' Fed. (Interim Pres. 1982–83); public speaker & conf. participant; Silver Medal, Am. Philatelic Soc. for philatelic writing 1993; Volunteer Serv. Award, Oromocto 1985; Candn. Forces decoration 1971; author: 'Without Introductions' 1989, 'So Still Houses' 1985, 'Godes Rice: A Poem Sequence' 1988 (poetry); 'Yellow Boots for Bobby' 1984, 'Absolutely Absalom' 1981 (child fiction); 'The Last Bell' 1992 (fiction and poetry); co-author: 'The Newfoundland Fish Boxes' 1982 (documentary); editor: 'A Land, A People' 1986, 'Stubborn Strength' 1983, 'Canadian Myths and Legends' 1976, 'The Maritime Experience' 1975 (anthologies), 'Michael Whelan: Folk Poet of Renous River' 1990; co-editor 'Choice Atlantic' 1990; recreations: bridge, stamp collecting; Home: 514 Gardiner St., Oromocto, N.B. E2V 1G3; Office: Dept. of Education, P.O. Box 6000, Fredericton, N.B. E3B 5H1.

**NRIAGU, Jerome Okon,** M.S., Ph.D., D.Sc.; environmental scientist; geochemist; b. Oreri Town, Nigeria 24 Oct. 1942; s. Martin Anadi and Helena (Anaekwe) N.; e. Univ. of Ibadan B.Sc. (Geol.) 1965; Univ. of Wis. M.S. (Geochem.) 1967; Univ. of Toronto Ph.D. 1970; Univ. of Ibadan D.Sc. 1987; m. Martina Oby d. Onwubiko Ifediotu; children: Delbert, Vivianne, Osita; RESEARCH SCIENT.; ENVIRONMENT CAN., CAN. CENTRE FOR INLAND WATERS 1970– ; Adjunct Prof. Dept. of Earth Sciences, Univ. of Waterloo, 1985– ; Adjunct Prof., Dept. of Environmental and Industrial Health, School of Public Health, Univ. of Michigan, Ann Arbor 1992– ; author 'Lead and Lead Poisoning in Antiquity' 1983; ed. 'Advances in Environmental Science and Technology' 1981– ; Edited 22 books including 'Environmental Biogeochemistry' 1976; 'Biogeochemistry of Lead in the Environment' 2 vols. 1978; 'Sulfur in the Environment' 2 vols. 1978; 'Copper in the Environment' 2 vols. 1979; 'Biogeochemistry of Mercury in the Environment' 1979; 'Zinc in the Environment' 2 vols. 1980; 'Nickel in the Environment' 1980; 'Cadmium in the Environment' 2 vols. 1980; 'Phosphate Minerals' 1983; 'Aquatic Toxicology' 1983; Ed. of 'Science of the Total Environment' and on the Editorial Boards of several journals; contrib. numerous papers prof. journs.; mem. Geochem. Soc.; Am. Assn. Advanc. Science; recipient Frank Rigler Memorial Award, Candn. Soc. Limnology 1988; Candn. Nat. Comte. for SCOPE (1980–86); Elected Fellow, Royal Society of Canada 1992; recreations: reading, photography; Home: 187 Seymour Dr., Ancaster, Ont. L9G 4N5; Office: Dept. of Environmental & Industrial Health, School of Public Health, Univ. of Michigan, Ann Arbor, MI 48109, USA.

**NUDDS, Thomas D.,** M.Sc., Ph.D.; educator; wild-life scientist; b. Windsor, Ont. 11 Aug. 1952; s. David Arthur and Charleene Hope (Naylor) N.; e. John McCrae Pub. Sch. 1964; Edith Cavell Sr. Pub. Sch. 1966; Riverside Secondary Sch. 1971; Univ. of Windsor, B.Sc. 1974, M.Sc. 1976; Univ. of W. Ont., Ph.D. 1980; m. Emanuella d. Joseph and Mary Falzon 25 May 1974; children: Benjamin, Erin, Shannon; ASSOC. PROF. OF ZOOL. UNIV. OF GUELPH 1986– ; conducted rsch. evolutionary ecology ungulates (particularly white-tailed deer in Ont.) 1974–76; evolutionary ecology N. Am. waterfowl 1976–80; DOE/NSERC Visiting Fellow Govt. Labs. Prairie Migratory Bird Rsch. Centre, Candn. Wildlife Service, Saskatoon, rsch. prairie waterfowl 1980–81; Asst. Prof. present Univ. 1981–86; Visiting Scientist, Swedish Agricultural Univ., Umeå 1988; recipient Candn. Wildlife Service, Natural Sci's & Eng. Rsch. Council Can. Scholarships 1976–80; Conservation Award McIlwraith Field Naturalists 1979; Detwiler Award Meritorious Grad. Work 1980; Best Sci. Paper Award Wilson Ornithol. Soc. 1982; el. Mem., Am. Ornithols. Union; Councillor, Candn. Soc. Zools. Wildlife Biols. Sect. 1983–85; Assoc. Ed., Jour. Wildl. Manage. 1990– ; cons. to Fed. Govts., Prov. Govts., NGOs resource mgmt.; author or co-author book chapters, over 40 articles sci. jours.; mem., Am. Ornithols. Union; Wildlife Soc.; Am. Soc. Naturalists; Ecol. Soc. Am.; Soc. Cons. Biol.; recreations: camping, carpentry; Home: R.R. 4, Fergus, Ont. N1M 2W5; Office: Guelph, Ont. N1G 2W1.

**NUDELMAN, Harold M.,** B.Sc., F.S.A., F.C.I.A., M.A.A.A.; consulting actuary; b. Toronto, Ont. 17 Sept. 1944; s. Jacob and Sophie (Orfus) N.; e. Bathurst Heights S.S. 1962; Univ. of Toronto B.Sc. 1966; m. Merle d. Kalman and Lola Sokolowski 10 June 1969; children: David, Michael; MANAGING DIRECTOR, WILLIAM M. MERCER CO. INC. 1990– ; Principal, William M. Mercer Ltd. 1980; Fellow, Soc. of Actuaries 1971; Candn. Inst. of Actuaries 1971; Office: P.O. Box 501, BCE Place, Toronto, Ont. M5J 2S5.

**NUFFIELD, Edward Wilfrid,** B.A., Ph.D., F.R.S.C., F.M.S.A.; professor emeritus; b. Gretna, Man. 13 Apr. 1914; s. Jacob and Maria (Loeppky) N.; e. Univ. of B.C. B.A. 1940; Univ. of Toronto Ph.D. 1944; m. Islay d. William and Helen Sturdy 25 Feb. 1939; children: Leslie Helen, Joan Edith, James Edward; Teaching Fellow in Mineral. Stanford Univ. 1940–41; Lectr., Univ. of Toronto 1943 becoming Prof. of Geol. 1962, Assoc. Dean of Arts & Sci. 1962–64, Chrmn. of Geol. 1964–72, Prof. Emeritus of Geol. 1979– ; Hon. Rsch. Assoc. in Chem. Univ. Coll. London 1962–63; Chief, Geol. Field Mapping Party Ont. Dept. Mines 1949–51; Cons. in Mineralogy and Extractive Metall. 1946–79; recipient Sr. Award Royal Soc. Can. 1962; Univ. of Toronto Sesquicentennial Honour Service Award 1977; Queen's Silver Jubilee Medal 1977; Mineral. Assn. Can. Leonard G. Berry Medal 1988; Pres., Mineral Assn. Can. 1956–57; mem., Council Mineral. Soc. Am. 1959–61; mem. Am. Crystallographic Assn.; author 'X-ray Diffraction Methods' 1966; 'With the West in Her Eyes' 1987; 'The Pacific Northwest' 1990; Home: 1835 Morton Ave., Apt. 1603, Vancouver, B.C. V6G 1V3.

**NUGENT, David Alan John;** Family Crest: Baselix; Motto: Decrevi; business man; b. Eng. 1 Nov. 1938; s. John Michael and Evelyn Marjory (Briggs) N.; e. Middlesex Co. Grammar Sch. 1954; MONS Offr. Cadet Sch. 1956; London Bus. Sch. 1962; m. Catherine Ann d. Robert and Margaret Mackenzie 24 June 1987; children: Maxine Lorraine Karen, Justin David St. John (by previous marriage); Margot Elizabeth, Jacqueline Nancy Leggett (wife's children by previous marriage), Johnathon Michael David; PARTNER, PRES. & C.E.O., INSIGNIA GROUP 1973– ; comnd. Parachute Regt. 1956, served 3 yr. tour with S.A.S. Suez, Malaya, Cyprus and other Middle E. areas, GSM and Mentioned in Despatches; joined Revlon Inc. 1960, Gen. Mgr. 1965, various positions Eur. and New York 1966–73; Independent Bus. Cons. in Mktg. 1965; Qualified Ski Instr. Austrian Ski Sch.; Qualified Instr. Brit. Scuba Soc.; author various mktg. papers; mem. IAADFS; CCTFA; Mem. & Dir., Fragrance Foundation U.S.A. & Royal Candn. Military Institute, Chaîne des Rôtisseurs, Brigata del Buongustao; Bd. Trade Metrop. Toronto; Anglican; recreations: skiing, sailing, piano, arts; Club: Bluffers Park Yacht; Home: 110 Glen Rd., Toronto, Ont. M4W 2V9; Office: 150 Duncan Mill Rd., Don Mills, Ont. M3B 3M4.

**NUGENT, Terence James,** B.A., LL.B.; b. Taber, Alta. 9 Dec. 1920; s. late Patrick Bernard abd Bridget (Duke) N.; e. Univ. of Alberta (1946–51), B.A., LL.B.; m. Irene Glugowski, 7 Aug. 1946; one s., Rory Michael; read law with Wm. J. Haddad; called to the Bar of Alta., 1952; served in 2nd World War; enlisted February 1942 with R.C.O.C.; Overseas, Dec. 1942–Feb. 1946; discharged with rank of Cpl.; def. cand. to H. of C. for Edmonton-Strathcona, g.e. 1957; el. for same constit. in g.e. 1958 till def. 1968; Alderman, City of Edmonton 1968–71; member, Alberta Law Society; Conservative; Unitarian; recreation: golf; Home: 9715 – 72 Ave., Edmonton, Alta. T6E 0Y9; Office: 10536 - 106 St., Edmonton, Alta. T5H 2X6.

**NUNN, The Hon. Mr. Justice D. Merlin,** B.A., B.Ed., LL.B., LL.M.; judge; b. Sydney, N.S. 19 Nov. 1930; s. C. Bruce and Florence Mary (Merlin) N.; e. Sydney Acad. H.S.; St. Francis Xavier, B.A. 1950, B.Ed. 1952; Dalhousie Univ. Law Sch. LL.B. 1957; Harvard Univ. LL.M. 1958; m. Joan d. George and Florence Gildersleeve 9 Aug. 1958; children: Mary, Caroline, Bruce, Douglas; JUDGE, TRIAL DIVISION, SUPREME COURT OF N.S. 1982– ; taught school in Halifax and Manitoba, 1951–54; Asst. Prof. of Law, Dalhousie Univ. Law Sch. 1958–59; Asst. to Vice-Pres. of Industrial Relations, Algoma Steel 1959–60; private law practice in Halifax, N.S. 1960–82, ultimately becoming Sr. Partner Cox, Downie, Nunn & Goodfellow; part-time Lectr., Dalhousie Law Sch. 1960–74; Chrmn., Nova Scotia Government Employees Labour Relations Bd.; Dir., Home of the Guardian Angel Adoption Agency; Senior Citizens Housing Comn.; Chrmn. Parish Counc., Candn. Martyrs; mem. Candn. Bar Soc.; Candn. Inst. for Admin. of Justice; Pres., Candn. Judges Conference 1989–90; Former Pres., Halifax-Dartmouth Liberal Assn.; recreation: tennis; Clubs: Waegwoltic; Burnside Tennis; Office: P.O. Box 2314, Halifax, N.S. B3J 3C8.

**NUNN, Mary M.;** artist, teacher, workshop leader; b. Toronto (Hogg's Hollow), Ont. 2 Jan. 1947; d. Alexander Robert and Helen Marie (Alderson) Hogg; e. Carleton Univ. Art History; Ottawa Sch. of Art, Algonquin Coll.; m. George Ian s. Robert and Nancy Nunn 17 May 1968; children: Danielle, Richard Damien; one-woman shows: Atrium Gallery Nepean 1992, Macdonald Club 1986, Greenbank Gallery 1984; purchases of work by govt. & univ. depts., embassies, businesses (doctors & lawyers, etc.) in many countries; Exbn. Co-ord., The Watercolour Soc.; Teacher, Ottawa Bd. of Edn., Buckhorn School of Fine Art, St. Lawrence Coll., Nepean Visual Arts, Memorial Univ. Art Ctr.; watercolour workshops around country; juror, a number of art shows, offered critiques; participant in many local, reg., nat. & internat. shows; believer in the 'Creative Life'; holds a 'Masters Degree in Mistakes'; Fellow, Ottawa Watercolour Soc. (award winner); orgn. memberships: several; recreation: swimming; Address: 2056 Black Friars Rd., Ottawa, Ont. K2A 3K8.

**NUNZIATA, John,** M.P., B.A., LL.B.; politician; lawyer; b. Revelstoke, B.C. 4 Jan. 1955; s. Domenic and Immacolata (Ammirati) N.; e. Runnymede Collegiate Toronto; York Univ. B.A. Pol. Sci. 1977; Osgoode Hall Law Sch. LL.B. 1980; m. Caroline Brett 2 Sept. 1989; one s. Patrick Domenic; MEMBER OF PARLIAMENT; el. to H. of C. for York South-Weston 1984, 1988, 1993; Opposition Critic, Employment 1990–92; mem. Employment & Immigration Ctte. 1990–92; Alderman Borough of York 1978–82; mem. Elections & Privileges Ctte. 1984–85; Justice & Solicitor Gen. Ctte. 1984–90; Opposition Critic, Solicitor Gen. of Can. 1984–92; Advr. Beech Hall Housing Co-op. 1981–82; mem. Borough of York Library Bd. 1982; Borough of York Negotiating Ctte. 1982; Chrmn., York Task Force on Day Care 1981–82; rec'd W.E.H. Cross Trophy 1974; Borough of York Civic Merit Award 1977; Citizen of the Year (George Syme & Harwood Ratepayers Assn.) 1980; R. Catholic; Home: 18 Kings Lynn Rd., Toronto, Ont.; Offices: Rm 366, West Block, House of Commons, Ottawa, Ont. K1A 0A6 and 2687 Eglinton Ave. W., Toronto, Ont. M8M 1T8.

**NURGITZ, Hon. Nathan,** Q.C.; judge; former senator; b. Winnipeg, Man. 22 June 1934; s. Hymie and Dora (Ludwig) N.; e. Machray Sch.; Luxton Sch.; St. John's Tech.; grad. High Sch. 1949; Univ. Man. Arts 1952–54; Law Sch., LL.B. 1958; children: Marshall Lewis; Roben Cheryl; JUSTICE OF THE COURT OF THE QUEEN'S BENCH; Alderman, City West Kildonan

1963–69; Nat. Vice-Pres., Prog. Conservative Party 1970; cr. Q.C. 1977; Bencher, Law Soc. Man. 1978, 1980; Mem., Senate of Canada 1979–93; Candn. Chrmn., Interparliamentary Union; Chrmn., Senate Comte. Legal and Constitutional Affairs; co-author 'Strong and Free' 1970; co-author (with Hugh Segal) 'No Small Measure' 1983; Nat. Pres., Prog. Cons. Party, 1970–71; Nat. Chrmn., Robt. and Mary Stanfield Foundation; Past Pres., Red River Exhn. (Winnipeg); Past Pres. Candn. Club of Winnipeg; Clubs: Carleton; Albany (Toronto); recreation: squash; Home: 11 Blackburn Lane, Winnipeg, Man. R3P 2C1; Office: Law Courts Complex, 408 York Ave., Winnipeg, Man. R3C 0P9.

**NUTARALUK AULATJUT, Elizabeth;** sculptor; b. Ennadai Lake, N.W.T. 1914; 48 group exbns. incl. most recent: 'Three Women of Arviat: Sculpture by Elizabeth Nutaraluk, Lucy Tasseor and Joy Halluk' The Isaacs/Inuit Gall. Toronto 1992; 'Women of the North: An Exhibition of Art by Inuit Women of the Canadian Arctic' Marion Scott Gall. Vancouver 1992; Galerie Saint Merri France 1992; l'Iglou Art Esquimau, Douai (toured 20 cities) France & Belgium; 'Inuit Masterworks' Inuit Gall. of Vancouver 1990; 'The Stone Sculpture of Arviat' McMichael Candn. Art Coll. 1989–90; 'Baffin Images' Orca Aart Chicago, Ill. 1989; collections: Eskimo Museum, Churchill, Man.; Klamer Family Collection & Sarick Collection, Art Gall. of Ont. Toronto; Swinton Collection and Twomey Collection, Winnipeg Art Gall.; Winnipeg Art Gall., Winnipeg, Man.; attended opening 'Sculpture/Inuit: Masterworks of the Canadian Arctic' Philadelphia, Pa. 1973; subject of several articles and catalogues; Home: Arviat, N.W.T.; Office: c/o Candn. Arctic Producers, 1645 Inkster Blvd., Winnipeg, Man. R2X 2W7.

**NUTH, Robert Edgar,** B.Com.; association executive; b. Ottawa, Ont. 19 Sept. 1927; s. George and Jane Cowel (Peters) N.; e. Carleton Univ. B.Com. 1949; m. Lois 31 May 1958; children: Catherine, Janet, Peter; Econ./Stat. Statistics Can., Ottawa 1949–51; Asst. to Mgr. Candn. Construction Assn. Ottawa 1951–57, Gen. Mgr. Montreal Construction Assn. 1957–79, Pres. & C.E.O., Candn. Construction Assn. 1980–90; Past Dir., Le Conseil du Patronat; mem., Inst. Assn. Execs. (Past Chrmn. Montreal); Intnl. Builders' Exchange Execs. (Past Pres. Mgmt. Award); Am. Soc. Assn. Execs.; Associates Carleton Univ. 1982– , Pres. Alumni Assn. 1955–56; mem. Construction Industry Develop. Counc. 1985– ; Clubs: Royal Montreal Golf; Ottawa Hunt Golf; Address: 89 Country Club Dr., Ottawa, Ont. K1V 9W1.

**NUTT, Jim Sutcliffe,** Q.C., B.A., LL.B.; retired diplomat; b. Calgary, Alta. 20 June 1919; s. Fred and Jennie (Sutcliffe) N.; e. Crescent Heights High Sch., Calgary, 1937; Mount Royal Coll., Calgary, 1938; Trinity Coll., Univ. of Toronto, B.A. 1946; Osgoode Hall Law Sch. LL.B. 1949; m. Grace Ethelwyn, d. late Clarence Niddery, 7 Sept. 1940; children: Carol, Ronald; called to Bar of Ont. 1949; joined Dept. of External Affairs 1947 serving in Rio de Janeiro, Washington, San Francisco (Consul General), New York (Consul Gen.), Bermuda (Commr.), Los Angeles (Consul Gen.); served in Ottawa as Head of Legal Div., Head of Defence Liaison Div., Secy. of the Canada/U.S.A. Permanent Joint Board on Defence and subsequently External Affairs Mem., Dir.-Gen., Western Hemisphere Affairs and Depy. Under-Secy. for Admin.; retired 1984; served with RCAF 1939–45; mem., Law Soc. Upper Can.; Can. Bar Association; California-Canada Soc.; Retired Heads of Mission Assn.; Candn. Institute Internat. Affairs; recreation: fishing, photography; Clubs: Chimo; White Pine; Address: Apt. LGB, 300 Queen Elizabeth Dr., Ottawa, Ont. K1S 3M6.

**NUTT, Kenneth Eric (aka Eric Beddows);** artist (Ken Nutt); illustrator (Eric Beddows); b. Woodstock, Ont. 29 Nov. 1951; s. Clarence William and Dorothy (Beddows) N.; e. Huron Park S.S. 1970; York Univ. 1970–72; 1st exhibition 1976; 26 group exhibs., 15 one-man shows (most recent at Evelyn Aimis Fine Art, Toronto 1991), works in 6 public collections incl. Can. Counc. Art Bank, Nat. Lib. of Can.; Teacher, Sr. Graphics, Univ. of Waterloo and Sheridan Coll. 1984; Rsch. Drawing 1983; Life Drawing 1984; Lectr., Hist. of Illus. & Design 1985, 1986; Canada Counc. 'B' Grant 1988; Ont. Arts Counc. Writers Grant 1985, 1986; Artists Grant 1979; Finalist, 1st Ezra Keats Meml. Award 1986; Amelia Frances Howard-Gibbon Award for Best Childrens Book 1983, 1985; Ruth Schwartz Award for Excellence in Childrens Lit. 1984; named to the 1988 International Board on Books for Youth (IBBY) Honour list for 'The Emperor's Panda'; 1988 Toronto Chapter I.O.D.E. Award for 'Night Cars'; The 1989 Elizabeth Mrazk-Cleaver Canadian Picture Book Award for 'Night Cars'; illustrator: 'Zoom At Sea' 1983, 'I Am Phoenix' 1985, 'Zoom Away' 1985, 'The Emperor's Panda' 1986, 'The Cave of Snores' 1987; 'Joyful Noise' 1988; 'Night Cars' 1988; 'Shadow Play' 1990; 'Who Shrank My Godmother's House?' 1992; 'Zoom Upstream' 1992, artwork exhibited at Art Gall. of Ont., the Gallery Stratford and The Art Institute of Chicago; ; Home: 34 Argyle St., Stratford, Ont. N5A 2H5.

**NUTTALL, Grant,** B.Sc.; retired oil executive; b. Toronto, Ont. 20 Nov. 1932; s. Norman and Alcie (Eady) N.; e. Michigan Tech. Univ. B.Sc. (Phi Kappa Phi) 1959; m. Maureen d. Nora and Harry Christie 20 Feb. 1981; children: Wayne Norman, Jacqueline Ann, Virginia Marie; VICE-PRES., EXTVE. DEVEL. & ORGN., IMPERIAL OIL LIMITED 1988–92; Indus. Sales Rep., Imperial Oil Limited 1959; Area Sales Mgr., Retail 1962; held a variety of sales positions in consumer, retail & automotive areas in Ont., Atlantic & Western regions; Auto. Div. Mgr. 1975; Mgr., Extve. Devel. 1981; formerly mem., Adv. Ctte. Univ. of Toronto School of Continuing Studies; Chrmn., Human Resource Advisory Group, Conf. Bd. of Canada; Bd. Mem. Nominating Ctte. and Chrmn. Fundraising Ctte., Kinark Child & Family Services; Chrmn., Fed. Govt. Extve. Exchange Organizing Ctte.; Advisory Bd. Mem., Institute for Management Studies; Mem., University of Toronto Faculty of Management 'Women in Management Task Force' 1992– ; currently business consultant and community representative, Kinark child & family services; Club: Granite; Home: 53 Gustav Cres., Willowdale, Ont. M2M 4G9.

**NUTTALL, Richard N.,** M.D., F.A.C.P.M.; government official; b. Hamilton, Ont. 7 Feb. 1940; s. James William and Margaret Gay (Walsh) N.; e. Univ. of Toronto, B.S.A. 1961; Harvard Univ., M.P.A. 1964; London Univ., M.B. 1974; m. Jane d. George and Patricia Pickering 9 July 1977; children; Andrew Richard, John Patrick; MEDICAL HEALTH OFFICER, REGINA HEALTH DISTRICT 1993– ; var. positions, Fed. Dept. of Fin. 1961–63; Fed. Dept. of External Affairs 1964–68; Fed. Dept. of Nat. Health & Welfare 1977–80; Pres., Rutland Cons. Group Ltd 1981–82 and 1985–87; Pres., Comprehensive Care Corp. (Canada) Ltd. 1982–85; Pres., Richmond Assocs. 1987–90; Pres., Pacific Life Sciences Inc. 1988–90; Medical Health Offr., Govt. of the Northwest Territories 1990–93; Bd. Cert., Am. Bd. of Preventive Med.; Fellow, Am. Coll. of Preventive Med.; Fellow, Am. Coll. of Healthcare Extves.; Certified Mgmt. Consultant; Home: 3371 Westminster Rd., Regina, Sask. S4V 1A7; Office: 1910 McIntyre St., Regina, Sask. S4P 2R3.

**NYBERG, Everett Wayne Morgan,** B.A.; writer; b. Port Arthur, Ont. 16 March 1944; s. Carl Gunnar and Frida Kristin (Bolin) N.; e. Univ. of B.C., B.A. 1966, profl. teacher's cert. 1978; children: Lawrence, Carl; studied poetry writing under Earle Birney; general labourer; Teacher, Douglas Coll. 1974–75; Vanc. Sch. Dist. (substitute teacher) 1978–83; Vanc. Comm. Coll. 1982–84, 1986–87; Am. Sch. of Quito, Ecuador 1984–86; Univ. of B.C. summer 1988; Univ. of Aveiro, Portugal 1989– ; lived in Guatemala 1980; South Korea 1981; author: 'The Crazy Horse Suite' 1979 (verse play), 'Galahad Schwartz and the Cockroach Army' 1987 (children's novel); (Gov. Gen. Award for Lit. 1987); 2nd prize, CBC Lit. Comp. for 'Mark, A Memoir' 1979; Address: Rua 36, No. 764-1$^{0}$ Esq, 4500 Espinho, Portugal.

**NYBURG, Stanley Cecil,** B.Sc., Ph.D., D.Sc.; professor; b. London, Eng. 15 Dec. 1924; s. Cecil Charles and Nina Belle (Dellow) N.; e. King's Coll., London Univ., B.Sc. 1945; D.Sc. 1973; Leeds Univ., Ph.D. 1949; m. Josephine Melville Tuke, 20 Aug. 1949; two d. Anna, Elizabeth Helen; HON. SEN. RES. FELLOW (DEPT. OF CHEMISTRY), KING'S COLL., UNIV. OF LONDON, ENGLAND 1987– ; Prof. Emeritus of Chemistry, Univ. of Toronto 1987 (retired); prev. Sr. Lectr. in Chem., Univ. of Keele, Eng., Pubs.: 'X Ray Analysis of Organic Structures,' 1961; numerous scient. papers; mem. Am. Crystallographic Assn.; Inst. of Physics; recreations: all the arts, piano; Office: Dept. of Chem., King's Coll., Univ. of London, England.

**NYGÅRD, Peter John,** B.Sc., B.A.; apparel executive; b. Helsinki, Finland; s. Eli and Hilkka N.; e. Glenlawn Coll. Inst.; Univ. of N.D. B.Sc., B.A. (Bus. Admin.); CHRMN. NYGÅRD INTERNATIONAL LTD. 1984– ; former Tri-Prov. Supr. Home Furnishings Eaton's Winnipeg; Pres. and Chief Extve. Offr. Tan Jay International 1967–74, Chrmn. & Chief Extve. Offr. 1974–84; Founder and Extve. mem. Man. Fashion Inst. 1968; Extve. mem. Candn. Apparel Mfrs. Inst. 1983–88; Co-Chrmn. Task Force to recommend Long Term. Ind. Strategies Can.'s Textile & Clothing Inds. to Fed. Govt. 1984; Chrmn. Sectoral Adv. Group Internat. Trade Apparel & Fur 1986–89; Pres. Candn. Ladies Fashion Inst. 1986; sponsored fashion show and draw to support Juvenile Diabetes Found. 1988–90; Chrmn. Candn. Helsinki Group; estab. the Nygård Endowment Fund for the Univ. of North Dakota Foundation 1989; set up fundraising program for the Winnipeg Scandinavian Cultural Centre 1990; donated to the Finnish American Heritage Centre's 'Mission of Hope' campaign in Hancock, Mich & named the Centre's theatre lobby in honour of his parents 50th Wedding Anniversary; noted speaker incl. Keynote Speaker 15th Internat. Small Bus. Cong. Helsinki and Entrepreneurial Conf. Toronto; N.Am. Yachting Champion 1976; mem. Candn. Olympic Yachting Team 1976; recipient Sioux Award, Univ. of N.D. Alumni Assn. 1978; Outstanding Candn. Distinction Winnipeg C. of C. 1981; City of Winnipeg's Community Service Award; Govt. House Seal 1986; Delta Signa Pi (Pres.); recreations: sailing, scuba diving, skiing, horseback riding, tennis, architecture; Home: P.O. N7776 Box 203, Nassau, Bahamas; Office: 1 Niagara St., Toronto, Ont. M5V 1C2.

**NYMARK, Alan B.,** B.A., M.A.; public servant; b. Ottawa, Ont. 24 July 1948; s. Harold C. and Eva A. (Irwin) N.; e. Queen's Univ., B.A. 1969, M.A. 1971; London Sch. of Econ., postgraduate work 1971–72; m. Christine d. Richard and Margaret Hodges 17 Nov. 1990; children: Jessica, Whitney, Wellsley; ASST. DEPUTY MINISTER, INDUSTRY AND SCIENCE POLICY, DEPT. OF INDUSTRY, GOVT. OF CANADA 1993– ; Group Leader, Dept. of Finance, Govt. of Can. 1972–74; Tech. Asst. to Extve. Dir., Internat. Monetary Fund 1974–76; Privy Counc. Offr. 1976–79; Spec. Advr., Royal Bank of Can. 1979–81; Dep. Sec. to Cabinet, Fed.-Prov. Relns. Office, Govt. of Can. 1981–83; Policy Dir., Royal Comn. on the Econ. Union & Devel. Prospects for Can. (Macdonald Comn.) 1983–85; Asst. Chief Negotiator, Can.-U.S. Free Trade Agreement, Govt. of Can. 1985–89; Extve. Vice Pres., Investment Canada, Govt. of Can. 1989–93 and Asst. Chief Negotiator, North American Free Trade Agreement, Govt. of Canada 1990–93; Can. Counc. doct. fellowship 1971–72; Protestant; recreations: skiing, sailing; Home: 393 Third Ave., Ottawa, Ont. K1S 2K6; Office: 235 Queen St., Ottawa, Ont. K1A 0H5.

**NYSETVOLD, Wayne Edward,** B.Sc., M.Sc., P.Eng.; executive; b. Edgerton, Alta. 12 Oct. 1940; s. Emil O. and Emmy M. (Johnson) N.; e. Univ. of Alberta, B.Sc. 1962, M.Sc. 1964; m. Ione M. d. Joe and Violet Prete 7 Oct. 1961; children: Trevor, Bruce, Dale, Lisa; DIRECTOR, ENERGY INDUSTRY SERVICES, ANDERSEN CONSULTING; Consultant 1992– ; Technical, Marketing Sales, Management, IBM Canada Ltd. 1964–81; Gen. Mgr., Computer Services, Nova Corporation of Alberta 1981–88, Vice Pres., Computer Information Services, Nova Corp. of Alberta 1988–92; Active Mem., Church of Jesus Christ of Latter-Day Saints (Mormon); recreations: skiing, golfing, hiking, computers, coaching minor sports; Home: 8 Varal Place N.W., Calgary, Alta. T3A 0A7.

**NYSTROM, Lorne Edmund,** P.C., M.P., B.A.; politician; b. Wynyard, Sask. 26 Apr. 1946; s. Andrew Bernard and Elsie N.; e. Wynyard High Sch.; Univ. of Sask., B.A. (Pol. Sci.) 1968; m. Gayle d. Frederick and Helen Morris 14 June 1969; children: Jason François, Natasha Stéphanie; Dep. House Leader, House of Commons 1988; Pres. Sask. NDP Youth 1967–68, Fed. Vice Pres. 1967–69; Leader Regina Campus Univ. NDP 1967; el. to H. of C. g.e. 1968, re-el. since; Observer Nigeria-Biafra War 1968; UN Observer 1969; served as NDP Critic for Youth, Energy, Agric. & Food, Constitution, Trade & Foreign Invests., Regional Expansion, Finance, Revenue, and currently Employment, Constitution and Intergovernmental Affairs; Vice Pres. Fed. NDP 1981–87; Apptd., Privy Council of Canada 1993.

# O

**OAKS, B. Ann,** Ph.D., F.R.S.C.; university professor; b. Winnipeg, Man. 4 June 1929; d. Harold Anthony and Bernice (Farlinger) O.; e. Univ. of Toronto, B.A. 1951; Univ. of Sask., M.A. 1954, Ph.D. 1958; PROF., DEPT. OF BOTANY, UNIV. OF GUELPH 1989– ; Asst. Prof., Biology, McMaster Univ. 1965–68; Assoc. Prof. 1968–74; Prof. 1974–89; Vis. Prof., Univ. of Nancy, France 1980; CHIBA Univ., Japan 1984; Affil. Sci., Plant Biotech. Inst., NRC Lab., Saskatoon, Sask. 1988–92; rsch. has dealt with regulation of nitrogen assimilation during early seedling growth: physiological & molecular aspects; recently initiated a project dealing with soil microorganism/plant interactions which may have great significance in reducing pollution from fertilizers; Mem., Candn. & Am. Societies of Plant Physiol.; Internat. & Candn. Societies of Plant Molecular Biol.; FRSC 1986; Gold Medal, Candn. Soc. of Plant Physiol. 1988; Citation Classic for a review in 'Annual Reviews of Plant Physiology' 1970; Ed. Bd., 'J. of Plant Physiol.,' 'Plant & Cell Physiol.'; author of 88 sci. journal articles, 15 papers in conf. proceedings & 84 abstracts; recreations: reading, politics, skiing, hiking, biking, canoeing, swimming, exploring the Arctic & other parts of the world; Mem., Stratford Fest.; Friends of Algonquin Park; Fed. of Ont. Naturalists; Bruce Trail Hiking Club; Home: P.O. Box 20006, Guelph, Ont. N1H 8H6; Office: Dept. of Botany, Univ. of Guelph, Guelph, Ont. N1G 2W1.

**OANCIA, David;** writer, teacher and editor; b. Stonehenge, Sask. 6 Dec. 1929; e. Twelve Mile Lake Sch., Stonehenge; Central Coll., Moose Jaw; Sir George Williams Univ.; m. Maria Asuncion Prieto-Cereceda, 1963; two s. David Stephen, Patrick John; began journalism with Moose Jaw Times Herald, 1952; subsequently joined The Leader-Post then while with Canadian Press worked in most parts of Can.; on 3 yr. tour in London reported extensively from Europe, N. Africa and Middle East; opened Montreal bureau for Globe & Mail, Toronto, 1963; posted to China, 1965, where main task was reporting on Great Proletarian Cultural Revolution; left China 1968; with Montreal Star 1971–74; Dir. Journalism Program, Sir George Williams Campus, Concordia Univ. 1974–78; Dir. Schl Journalism, Univ. of King's College, Halifax 1978–79; Dir. Television News, C.B.C. 1979; Dir. Informat., Univ. of N.B. 1982–84; mem. Ed. Bd., N.B. Publishing 1984–89; lang. teacher and adviser, Nanjing Aeronautical Inst., Nanjing, China 1990–92; rec'd. Nat. Newspaper Award, 1967; Southam Fellow, Univ. of Toronto 1974–75; Jiangsu (China) Educ. Commission Award for Teaching Excellence 1991; recreations: fishing, camping, travel; Address: 398 Woodstock Rd., Fredericton, N.B. E3B 2J1.

**OBERDORF, Charles Donnell,** B.F.A.; writer / editor; b. Sunbury, Pa. 25 Feb. 1941; s. Charles Donnell and Helen Margaret (Potteiger) O.; e. Carnegie Inst. of Tech., B.F.A. (Theatre) 1963; m. Mechtild d. Bruno and Wilma Hoppenrath 25 Oct. 1977; one d.: Anya; PARTNER, THE OBERDORF PARTNERSHIP 1966– ; Broadcast journalist, WCAU-TV (Philadelphia), CBC AM/FM/TV, CTV, OECA, etc. 1963–74; Restaurant reviewer, Toronto Star 1968–72; Cons., Nat. Film Bd. Still Photo Div. 1969–75; Travel Ed., Saturday Night 1974–77; Assoc. Ed., Weekend Magazine 1977–78; Travel columnist, The Financial Post Magazine 1978–83; Sr. Mng. Extve. Ed., City & Country Home 1983–92; Ed., Stature 1989; freelance magazine writer, editor, photographer 1966–83; Dir., Nat. Mag. Awards. Found. 1990– ; mem., City of Toronto Urban Design Awards Ctte. 1989–92; La Pluma de Plata de Mexico 1977, 1984; Nat. Mag. Awards 1979, 1980, 1984, 1988, 1992; SATW-Univ. of Missouri-Lowell Thomas Award, best guidebook pub. in N. Am. 1988; Mem., Soc. of Am. Travel Writers; Toronto Soc. of Architects; Assoc. Ed. 'Between Friends/Entre Amis' 1976; co-author: 'Fodor's Toronto' 1984, 'First-Class Canada' 1987; recreations: gardening, travel; Office: 93 Duplex Ave., Toronto, Ont. M5P 2A6.

**OBERLE, The Hon. Frank,** P.C.; former politician; b. Forchheim, Germany 24 Mar. 1932; s. Adolf and Rosa (Leibold) O.; e. Germany and Poland; m. Joan Kistner 31 May 1953; children: Ursula, Isabell, Frank, Peter; Min. of Forestry, Govt. of Canada 1989–93; Past Pres., Chetwynd Motors Ltd.; Past Partner, Chetwynd Forest Ind. Ltd.; Ald. Village of Chetwynd 1962–64, Mayor 1968–72; el. to H. of C. for Prince George-Peace River g.e. 1972, re-el. six consecutive elections that followed; served on numerous Standing and Special Cttes., pursuing his special interests in Regional Economic Development, the Natural Resources Sectors and Indian Affairs and Northern Development; P. Conservative Spokesman Min. of State (Mines) 1983–84; Parlty. Secy. to Min. of State (Mines) 1984–85; Mem., Privy Council 1985; Commnr. for the Renovation of Indian Treaties 1985; Min. of State for Science and Technology 1985–89; published major reports on national issues including: 'The Green Ghetto,' 'Equity and Fairness,' 'Human Resources Paradox,' and 'Reviving the Canadian Dream'; Charter Pres., Chetwynd Chamber of Commerce; Chrmn. of the Bd., Chetwynd & Dist. Hosp. 1966–72; R. Catholic; recreations: animal husbandry, ranching.

**OBERSTE BERGHAUS, Gerhard,** B.A., Diplom-Engineer; engineering executive; b. Berlin 23 April 1939; e. Evangelisches Gym. zum Grauen Kloster (Berlin) B.A. 1958; practical training Linnenbrügger & Co., Herne 1958; Tech. Univ. of Karlsruhe for Process Engr., Diplom-Engineer degree 1963; married; two children; PRESIDENT & CHIEF EXECUTIVE OFFICER, KLOCKNER STADLER HURTER 1987– ; Project Engr., Power Plant Dept., Borsig AG Berlin 1963–64; Process Engr., Process Dept., Davy McKee AG 1964–67; Sales Dept. 1967–68; Head, Fertilizer & Anorganic Acid Div. 1968–74; Dir. of Project Mngt. & Engr., Siempelkamp KG Krefeld 1975–77; Dir., Chem. Plant Div., Klöckner Industrie-Anlagen GmbH Duisburg, F.R.G. 1977–87; Mem., Candn. Pulp & Paper Assn.; Candn. German Ch. of Industry and Commerce Inc.; Office: 1400 du Fort Street, Suite 900, Montreal, Que. H3H 2T1.

**OBOMSAWIN, Alanis,** O.C.; producer, director, singer; b. Lebanon, New Hampshire; profl. singing debut, Town Hall, New York City 1960; has toured extensively in Canada, the U.S. and Europe; frequently performs in schools, univs., museums, prisons, art centres, folk festivals & for humanitarian causes; several guest appearances on 'Sesame Street'; worked on first film with Nat. Film Board of Canada 1967; has directed and produced num. filmstrips, two multimedia packages ('Manowan' and 'L'ilawat'), two vignettes, six films, and ten documentaries incl. most recent: a documentary about the events that took place at Oka-Kanesatake (summer 1990) 1992; 'Le Patro Le Prévost, 80 ans après' 1992, 'Walker' 1992, 'No Address' (1988)/'Sans adresse' 1989, 'A Way of Learning' 1988, 'Poundmaker's Lodge: A Healing Place' 1987, 'Richard Cardinal: le Cri d'un enfant métis' 1987; released an album 'Bush Lady' 1988; Order of Canada 1983; Chair, Bd. of Dir., Native Women's Shelter of Montreal; Bd. Mem., Canada Council's Native Advisory Ctte.; dedicated to the well-being of her people and the preservation of the First Nations cultural heritage; Office: c/o National Film Board, Box 6100, Stn. A, Montreal, Que. H3C 3H5.

**O'BRIAN, Peter Beatty,** B.A.; film producer and executive; b. Toronto, Ont. 9 Jan. 1947; s. Peter Geoffrey St. George and Edith Jean (Beatty) O'B.; e. New Park Sch. St. Andrews, Scot.; Gstaad Internat. Sch. Switzerland; Gayhurst Sch. Gerrard's Cross, Bucks., Eng. 1959; Trinity Coll. Sch. Port Hope 1964; Univ. of Toronto Trinity Coll.; Emerson Coll. Boston B.A. 1970; m. Carolyn d. John and Eunice Bennett 19 May 1979; two s. Jack, Ben; Extve. Dir., Canadian Film Centre 1988–91; Pres. Independent Pictures Inc. 1977– ; freelance prodn. staff feature films and TV series 1970–77; feature films (Producer, Co-Producer or Assoc. Producer) incl. 'Me' 1974, 'Love at First Sight' 1975, 'Outrageous' 1976, 'Blood and Guts' 1977, 'Fast Company' 1978, 'The Grey Fox' 1980, 'My American Cousin' 1984, 'One Magic Christmas' 1985, 'John and the Missus' 1986, 'Milk and Honey' 1987, 'The Yellow Dog' 1993; films have won 18 Genies incl. Best Motion Picture 'The Grey Fox' 1983 (also nominated Best Foreign Film of 1983 by Hollywood Foreign Press Assn., The Golden Globe Awards) and 'My American Cousin' 1985; Dir. Nat. Screen Inst. 1987–88; Dir., Festival of Festivals 1988– ; Dir., Candn. Centre for Advanced Film Studies 1991– ; Dir., Screenwriters Forum Inc. 1990– ; recipient CFTA and BCFIA Special Awards for contribution to feature films 1986; chapter co-author 'Making It: The Business of Film and Television Production in Canada' 1987; Vice Pres. Candn. Film & TV Assn. 1985; Home: 64 Duncannon Dr., Toronto, Ont. M5P 2M2; Office: 18 Gloucester St., 4th Floor, Toronto, Ont. M4Y 1L5.

**O'BRIEN, Allan R.B.,** LL.B., M.B.A.; barrister; b. Windsor, N.S. 10 Apl. 1932; s. late Robert Bell and Josephine Marie (Bremner) O'B.; e. King's Coll. Sch., Windsor, N.S.; Univ. of King's Coll.; Dalhousie Univ. Law Sch., LL.B.; Univ. of W. Ont., M.B.A.; m. Helen Mary Louise (d.), d. late Harold Roscoe, 4 Aug. 1957; children: Timothy Harold DeB., Katherine Louise, Robert Andrew; PARTNER, GOWLING, STRATHY & HENDERSON; read law with Burchill, Smith & Co., Halifax, N.S.; called to Bar of N.S. 1960, Bar of Alta. 1961 and Bar of Ont. 1970; Solr., Interprovincial Pipe Line Co., 1960–64; Asst. to Gen. Counsel, 1964–66; former Nat. Organizer, Liberal Party of Can.; mem., Law Soc. of Upper Canada and Candn. Bar Assn.; Phi Kappa Pi; Liberal; Anglican; recreations: skiing, fishing; Clubs: Rideau; Rockcliffe Tennis; Bequia Sailing; Home: 426 Cloverdale, Rockcliffe Park, Ottawa, Ont. K1N 0Y4; Office: 160 Elgin St., Ottawa, Ont. K1N 8S3.

**O'BRIEN, Daniel William,** B.Comm., M.S.W., Adv.Dip. S.W., D.S.W.; university president; b. Halifax, N.S. 11 Jan. 1939; s. James Edward and Ellen Martina (Downey) O.; e. St. Mary's Univ. B.Comm. 1960; St. Mayr's Univ. & Dalhousie Univ. M.S.W. 1962; Univ. of Toronto, doctoral study 1966–8; Univ. of Pennsylvania Av.Dip.S.W. 1975, D.S.W. 1976; m. Valerie d. Bruce and Pauline Hart 28 Aug. 1965; children: Peter, Craig; PRESIDENT, ST. THOMAS UNIV. 1990– ; Psych. Social Worker, Psych. Out-Patient Clinic, Victoria Gen. Hosp. 1962–65; Program Coord., Candn. Mental Health Assn. 1962–66; Lectr., Sch. of Social Work, Dalhousie Univ. 1965–66; Teaching Fellow, Univ. of Toronto 1967–68; Staff Devel. Cons., Prov. of Ont., Dept. of Social & Family Serv. 1968–69; Prof., Assoc. Dean of Faculty of Health Professions & Dir. of School of Social Work, Dalhousie Univ. 1969–90; private social planning & research consultant 1969–90; recipient of many edn. scholarships & fellowships incl.: Univ. of Toronto Grad. Scholarship; Nat. Welfare Post-Grad Scholarship; Laidlaw Found. Fellowship; Killam Fellowship; Hon. Life Mem., N.S. Assn. of Social Workers; Extve. Mem. of gov. councils of num. regional & nat. profl., educational & learned socs. & assns.; author of more than 30 research monographs, scholarly articles, teaching manuals, book chaps. & rsch. papers; had presented more than 65 papers at reg., nat. & internat. acad. & profl. confs.; recreations: tennis, skiing, boating, reading; club: Waegwoltic; Home: 52 Kensington Court, Fredericton, N.B. E3B 1Z7; Office: Box 4569, Fredericton, N.B. E3B 5G3.

**O'BRIEN, David P.,** B.A., LL.B.; energy executive; b. Montreal, Que. 9 Sept. 1941; s. John L. and Ethel (Cox) O.; e. Loyola Coll., B.A. (Hons. Economics) 1962; McGill Univ., LL.B. 1965; m. Gail Corneil 1 June 1968; children: Tara, Matthew, Shaun; CHRMN. OF THE BOARD, PRES. & C.E.O., PANCANADIAN PETROLEUM LTD. 1990– ; Partner, Ogilvy, Renault 1967–77; apptd. Q.C. 1980; Gen. Counsel, Petro-Can. Inc. 1977–80; Sr. Vice-Pres. 1981–84; Extve. Vice-Pres. 1985–88; Pres. & C.E.O., Noverco Inc. 1989– ; Bd. of Dirs., United Westburne Inc.; Mem., Business Council on National Issues; recreations: tennis, golf; Home: 906 Riverdale Ave. S.W., Calgary, Alta. T2S 0Y6; Office: PanCanadian Plaza, 150 - 9th Ave. S.W., Calgary, Alta. T2P 2S5.

**O'BRIEN, Vice-Admiral John Charles,** O.C. (1970), C.D.; b. Hove Sussex, England 16 Dec. 1918; e. Royal Mil. Coll. of Can., 1937; joined Royal Can. Navy 1937; joined destroyer Saguenay for N. Atlantic escort duties, 1940; served for 2 yrs. as Flotilla Signals Offr., 4th Destroyer Flotilla, 1942, followed by signal duties in Can.; served on R. N. Signal Book Comte., 1946 then took command destroyer Crescent; later became Offr.-in-Charge, Communications Sch., Halifax; served for yr. on staff of Supreme Allied Commdr. Atlantic, Norfolk, Va.; became Extve. Offr., HMCS Stadacona, Halifax, 1953; later Extve. Offr. of Aircraft Carrier Magnificent; apptd. Dir., Naval Training, Naval H.Q., 1955 and Dir., Naval Communications there 1957; Co-ordinator, Personnel Structure Comte., 1958–59; took command Bonaventure, 1959; Naval mem., Candn. Joint Staff, Washington, 1961; apptd. Sr. Candn. Offr. afloat Atlantic, 1964; Commdr., Maritime Command 1966–70; Commandant NATO Defence College 1970–73; apptd. Dir. Gen., Revenue Dir., Organizing Comte. for XXIst Olympiade Nov. 1974; awarded Grande Ufficiale del ordine al Merito della Rep. (Italy) 1973; rec'd. Hon. D. Sc. Mil., Roy. Mil. Coll. 1974; Address: 10 - 130 Rideau Terrace, Ottawa, Ont. K1M 0Z2.

**O'BRIEN, John Wilfrid,** M.A., Ph.D., D.C.L., LL.D; univ. past pres.; b. Toronto, Ont. 4 Aug. 1931; s. Wilfred Edmond and Audrey (Swain) O.; e. Owen Sound Coll. & Voc. Inst.; McGill Univ. B.A., 1953; Inst. of Pol. Studies, Paris, France 1954; McGill Univ. M.A. 1955, Ph.D. 1962, LL.D. 1976; Bishop's Univ. D.C.L. 1976; m. Joyce Helen d. Joseph Bennett, 4 Aug. 1956; children: Margaret Anne, Catherine Audrey; RECTOR EMERITUS, CONCORDIA UNIVERSITY 1984– ; joined Sir George Williams Univ. as Lect. in Econ., 1954–57, Asst. Prof., 1957–61; Assoc. Prof. 1961–65; Asst. Dean of Univ. 1961–63; Prof. since 1965; Dean of Arts 1963–68, Vice Princ., Academic 1968–69; Princ. Vice Chancellor & Pres. 1969–74; Rector, Vice Chancellor & Pres., Concordia Univ. 1974–84; mem. Prov. Educ. TV Comte., Dept. Educ. Que., 1962–66 (Depy. Chrmn. 1965–66), mem. Teacher Training Planning Comte. 1964–66; mem. Gauthier Ad Hoc Comte., Univ. Operating Budgets, 1965–68; mem. Council of Univs. (Que.) 1969–76; Pres., Conf. of Rectors & Prins. of Que. Univs. 1974–77; Council of Assn. of Commonwealth Univ., 1975–78; Bd. of Dirs., Assn. of Univs. & Colls., Can., 1977–79; Conseil consultatif sur L'Immigration, Govt. of Que., 1977–79; Hon. mem., Corporate Higher Education Forum 1984– (mem. 1983–84); Bd. of Dir. Montreal YMCA 1969–89; Vanier Coll. 1975–79; Fraser-Hickson Inst. (Pres. 1989–92) 1975– ; Secy.-Treas., Cinematheque Canada 1988– ; Secy.-Treas., World Film Festival Found. 1988– ; mem. Bd. of Dir. World Film Festival Montreal 1985– ; Que. Div., Candn. Mental Health

Assn. 1977–79; Hon. Vice Pres., Que. Prov. Council, Boy Scouts of Can. 1974–90; Hon. Councillor, Montreal Mus. Fine Arts, 1969– ; mem. Extve. Ctte., Alliance Que. 1989– (Chrmn., Bd. of Dirs., 1990–91, 1992– ); author 'Canadian Money and Banking,' 1964 (2nd ed. with G. Lermer 1969); Home: 38 Holton Ave., Westmount, Que. H3Y 2E8.

**O'BRIEN, Hon. Joseph W.,** B.A., LL.B.; judge; b. Edmonton, Alta. 22 Oct. 1933; s. Joseph Wesley and Edna Merle (Eubank) O'B.; e. Queen's Univ. B.A. 1955; Dalhousie Univ. LL.B. 1958; m. Helen d. Wilfred and Lilas Parmelee, Ottawa, Ont. 12 May 1979; children: Carol Anne, David, Steven; JUDGE, SUPREME COURT OF ONT. HIGH COURT 1981– ; called to Bar of Ont. 1960; cr. Q.C. 1974; Past Partner, Cassels, Brock, Toronto 1970–81; Head of Civil Procedure II Bar Admission Course; Lectr. in Continuing Legal Educ. Series, Osgoode Hall Law Sch.; Past Pres., Advocates' Soc.; Past Pres., Ins. Subsection Candn. Bar Assn.; Past mem., Council Toronto Medico-Legal Soc.; recreations: skiing, jogging, golf, scuba diving; Clubs: Bd. of Trade; Boulevard Club; Home: 10 Ravendale Gate, Kleinburg, Ont. L0J 1C0; Office: Osgoode Hall, 130 Queen St. W., Toronto, Ont. M5H 2N5.

**O'BRIEN, Lawrence Robert;** business executive; b. Ottawa, Ont. 19 July 1949; s. Gordon and Doris (Bannerman) O'B.; e. Sch. of Technol., Algonquin Coll. 1971; m. Debbie d. Don and Shirley Green 23 Sept. 1984; children: Michael, Matthew; FOUNDER & C.E.O., CALIAN TECHNOL. LTD. 1982– ; worked as electronics technol. 1971–79; Gen. Mgr., Reltek Inc. 1979–82; purchased Miller Communications 1988; purchased SED Systems of Saskatoon 1990– ; acquired Sky Wave Electronics Ltd. Sept. 1993; Chrmn., Saint-Vincent Hosp. Found. 1990– ; Dir., Candn. Advanced Technology Assn. (CATA) 1991– ; Dir., Inmarsat Users Assn.; Dir., CompAS (Computer Assembly Systems Ltd.); recreations: golden retrievers, squash, golf; Club: Rideau; Home: 77 Loch Isle Rd., Nepean, Ont. K2H 8G7; Office: 300 Legget Dr., Kanata, Ont. K2K 1Y5.

**O'BRIEN, Lynn Denise,** B.A., LL.B.; lawyer, trust company executive; b. Toronto, Ont.; d. Desmond Lorraine and Yvonne Rolande (Proulx) O.; e. Univ. of B.C., B.A. 1977, LL.B. 1982; BANK OF MONTREAL; Office: 1st Canadian Place, Toronto, Ont. M5J 2M4.

**O'BRIEN, Mern,** B.F.A.; arts administrator; b. Syracuse, N.Y. 28 Feb. 1954; e. Syracuse Univ., Sch. of Fine Arts 1972–75; Nova Scotia College of Art & Design B.F.A. 1976; Dalhousie Univ., Sch. of Public Admin. 1988– ; DIRECTOR, DALHOUSIE ART GALLERY 1985– ; Exhibitions Offr., Mt. St. Vincent Univ. Art Gallery 1977–78; Acting Curator, Dalhousie Art Gallery 1978–79; Asst. to Dir., Registrar, Preparator 1979–83; Acting Dir. 1984–85; Candn. citizen 1986; Mem., Candn. Art Museum Directors Orgn.; Atlantic Provinces Art Gallery Assn.; Canada Council Visiting Artists Ctte.; Candn. Museums Assn.; author of exhibition catalogues & brochures; Office: 6101 University Ave., Halifax, N.S. B3H 3J5.

**O'BRIEN, Michael John,** M.A., Ph.D.; educator; b. New York City, N.Y. 27 Apl. 1930; s. Michael J. and Mary E. (Collins) O'B.; e. Regis High Sch. New York 1947; Fordham Univ. B.A. 1951; Princeton Univ. M.A. 1953, Ph.D. 1956; m. Anne Jordan d. Dr. Joseph P. Webb, Kalamazoo, Mich. 25 July 1959; children: David, Emily; PROF. OF CLASSICS, UNIV. OF TORONTO 1969– ; Instr. in Classics Wesleyan Univ., Conn. 1955–56; Instr. to Assoc. Prof. of Classics Yale Univ. 1956–66; Assoc. Prof. of Classics present Univ. 1966–69, Chrmn. of Classics 1973–75, 1975–81; Morse Research Fellow 1963–64; Guggenheim Research Fellow 1972–73; author 'The Socratic Paradoxes and the Greek Mind' 1967; Ed. 'Twentieth-Century Interpretations of Oedipus Rex' (essays) 1968; various articles Greek philos. and tragedy; mem. Classical Assn. Can.; Ont. Classical Assn.; Am. Philol. Assn.; Classical Assn. (Brit.); Soc. Ancient Greek Philos.; R. Catholic; Home: 67 Paperbirch Dr., Don Mills, Ont. M3C 2E6; Office: University College, Toronto, Ont. M5S 1A1.

**O'BRIEN, Michael Wilfrid Peter,** B.A., M.B.A.; oil industry executive; b. Toronto, Ont. 29 Dec. 1944; s. Wilfrid Leo and Claire (Morin) O.; e. Univ. of Toronto B.A. 1967; York Univ. M.B.A. 1975; m. Mary Catherine d. Gerrard and Margaret Lee 1 Oct. 1966; children: Kathleen, Erin, Matthew, Michael; EXECUTIVE VICE-PRES. SUNOCO GROUP, SUNCOR INC. 1992– ; var. mktg. positions, Shell Canada 1967–72; Petroleum Div., Canadian Tire Corp. 1973–75; joined Suncor Inc. 1975; Vice-Pres., Mktg., Sunoco Group 1982–83; Vice-Pres., Mining & Extraction, Oil Sands Group 1984–86; Vice-Pres., Mktg. & Business Devel., Resources Group 1986–89; Vice-Pres., Corp. Devel. 1989–90; Sr. Vice-Pres., Finance & Planning 1991; Sr. Vice-Pres. & Chief Financial Offr. 1991–92; Mem., Catholic Childrens' Aid (Toronto) Planning Bd. 1982–83; Campaign Chrmn., Ft. McMurray United Way 1984–85; Mem., Toronto Bd. of Trade; Candn. Petroleum Institute; Conference Bd. of Can.; recreations: golf, skiing; clubs: Donalda Club, Peterborough Golf & Country; Home: 335 Inglewood Dr., Toronto, Ont.; Office: 36 York Mills Rd., North York, Ont. M2P 2C5.

**O'BRIEN, Peter John,** B.Sc., M.Sc., Ph.D.; university professor; b. London, U.K. 6 July 1937; s. John and Anne Margaret (Russell) O'Brien; e. University College B.Sc. 1959; Birmingham Univ. M.Sc. 1960, Ph.D. 1963; m. Cindy d. Cyril and Lyma Adams 10 Oct. 1975; children: William Mark, Sara Anne; GRADUATE CHAIRMAN & PROF. OF PHARMACY (TOXICOLOGY), UNIV. OF TORONTO 1986– ; Rsch. Fellow, Birmingham Univ. 1962–64; Sr. Rsch. Assoc. 1964–67; Assoc. Prof. of Biochem., Memorial Univ. of Nfld. 1967–74; Prof. 1974–88; Visiting Prof., Johns Hopkins Sch. of Med., Univ. of Texas; Univ. of Mich. 1974–75; Visiting Scientist (Tox.), Karolinska Inst., Univ. of Stockholm 1984–85; Assoc. Dean of Rsch., Faculty of Pharmacy, Univ. of Toronto 1987–91; Drug Safety Rsch. Group, Univ. of Toronto 1992– ; Mem., Grants Ctte., NSERC 1973–76; Nat. Cancer Inst. 1978–82; Assoc. Ed., 'Can. J. of Biochem.' 1974–79, 'Xenobiotica' 1982– , 'Drug Metab. & Drug Interacns.' 1988– , 'J. of Biopharmaceut. Sci.' 1989– , 'Chem. Biol. Interacns.' 1993– ; active in symposia orgn.; active researcher; recipient of sci. grants; Med. Rsch. Council Devel. Grant 1986–96; Mem., Ont. Univ. Ctte. on Health Rsch. 1987– ; Mem., Am. Soc. for Biochem.; The Biochem. Soc.; Am. Assn. for Cancer Rsch.; Soc. of Toxicology; Internat. Soc. for Free Radical Rsch.; editor: 'Microsomes, Drug Oxidations and Chemical Carcinogenesis' 2 vols 1980; co-author: 'Biological Reactive Intermediates' IV 1991, 'Handbook of Free Radicals and Antioxidants in Biomedicine' 1989 and six other books; author: over 190 scientific papers and book chapters; recreations: piano playing, music, cycling, gardening, pets; Home: 49 Van Stassen Blvd., Toronto, Ont. M6S 2N2; Office: 19 Russell St., Toronto, Ont. M5S 1A1.

**O'BRIEN, Robert Neville,** M.A.Sc., Ph.D., F.R.S.A., F.C.I.C.; educator; technology executive; b. Nanaimo, B.C. 14 June 1921; s. Robert Emmette and Mary-Ann (Crossan) O'B.; e. Univ. of B.C. B.A.Sc. (Chem. Engn.) 1951, M.A.Sc. (Metall. Engn.) 1952; Manchester Univ. Ph.D. 1955; m. Helen T. Bryan 28 June 1952; children: Daniel Bryan, Martha Elizabeth Clancie, Robert Douglas Young, Timothy Ian Hal, William Patrick Thomas; Prof. Emeritus of Chemistry 1986– ; Adjunct Prof. 1987– ; Prof. of Chem., Univ. of Victoria 1968–86; Pres., O.E.L. Oxygen Engineering; Secy. and Pres., H & R Electromines Ltd.; served with RCA 1942–43; RCAF 1943–46 (Pilot and Captain), Burma; co-author 'A Laboratory Manual of Modern Chemistry' 1964; author over 120 articles prof. journs., book chapters; Fellow, Chem. Inst. of Can.; mem. Am. Chem. Soc.; Electrochem. Soc.; recreations: flying, boating, canoeing, squash, badminton, gardening; Home: 2614 Queenswood Dr., Victoria, B.C. V8N 1X5; Office: P.O. Box 3055, Victoria, B.C. V8W 3P6.

**O'BRIEN-BELL, John,** M.B.B.S., L.M.C.C., D.R.C.O.G.; physician; b. Birmingham, England 23 June 1929; s. Louis and Greta (O'Brien) O.; e. Blackrock Coll. (Ireland); Sacred Heart Coll. (England); children: Catharine Mary, Andrew John; Far East Land Forces, Malaya, British Army 1948–49; Westminster Med. Sch., London & Rotunda Hosp., Dublin 1949–56; Westminster & St. James Hosps. 1956–58; family practitioner, Letchworth, England 1958–66; Surrey, B.C. 1966– ; Pres., Candn. Med. Assn. 1988–89; past mem., extve. cttes., task forces & councs.; Pres., B.C. Med. Assn.; 1986–87; Chrmn., Gen. Assembly 1984–85; Chrmn., Boundary Bd. of Health 1974–76; Co-ordinator, Citizens Forum (Spicer Commission) 1991; Chair, Surrey Mayors Advisory Ctte. on Violence 1993; former Chrmn. & mem., var. cttes.; New Westminster Kinsman; past mem., Kinsmen; Alderman, Mun. of Surrey, B.C. 1974–76; Founding Ed., 'BCMA News' 1971–78; Ed., Western Med. News 1978–81; author of med. articles; Office: Suite 202, 10216 – 128th St., Surrey, B.C. V3T 2Z3.

**O'CALLAGHAN, Jeremiah Patrick;** journalist; publisher; professor of journalism; b. Mallow, County Cork, Ireland 8 Oct. 1925; came to Can. 1959; s. Michael Joseph and Marguerita (Hayes) O'C.; e. Christian Brothers Sch., Limerick, Ireland; St. Joseph's Elem. Sch., Malvern, Worcestershire, Eng.; Worcester Jr. Commercial Sch.; Cotton Coll., N. Staffordshire; m. E. Joan Abeles d. Paul and Rita Abeles 14 Feb. 1989; children (of previous marriage): Patrick, Michael, Sean, Brendan, Fiona; Reporter, Malvern Gazette, Worcestershire, Eng., 1941–43; Sub-ed., The Northern Echo, Darlington, 1947; Sub-ed., Yorkshire Evening Press, York, 1947–48; Sports Sub-ed., Yorkshire Evening Post, 1948–53; Sub-ed., Liverpool Daily Post and Asst. Ed. Liverpool Echo, 1953–59; Man. Ed., Asst. Publ., Red Deer Advocate, Alta. 1959–68; Asst. to Publ., Edmonton Journal, 1968–69; Extve. Ed., Southam News Service, Ottawa, 1969–71; Extve. Asst. Southam Press, 1971–72; Publ., Windsor Star, 1972–76; Publisher, Edmonton Journal, 1976–82; Publisher, Calgary Herald 1982–89; Co-chair, Federal Task Force on Magazine Industry 1993–94; served with RAF, 1943–47, wireless operator/air gunner; former Chrmn., Candn. Sect., Intl. Press Inst.; Past Pres. Candn. Daily Newspaper Publishers' Assn.; Past Chrmn., The Candn. Press; mem., Commonwealth Press Union; former Bd. Mem., Michener Awards Found.; non-partisan; R. Catholic; recreations: writing, reading; Home: R.R. 4, Picton, Ont. K0K 2T0.

**OCKENDEN, A/V/M/ Gordon Frederick,** D.F.C., C.D.; retired air force officer; b. Vermilion, Alta. 20 July 1923; s. Frederick Clarence and Ruby Elizabeth (Cooper) O.; e. Oliver Pub. and Eastwood High Schs., Edmonton, 1941; 8 Service Flying Training Sch., Moncton, N.B., grad. Fighter Pilot; U.S.N. Ground Controlled Intercept Course, Glenview, Ill. 1948; RCAF Staff Coll. 1959–60; Nat. Defence Coll. 1966–67; m. Mary Patricia, d. R. Slessor, Edmonton Alta. 2 June 1948; 5 sons, Timothy, Gary, Monty, James, Edward; PRESIDENT, TRIMAN CONSULTANTS INC., Kelowna, B.C. 1988– ; joined RCAF 1941; served in Nfld. and N.S. before joining 443 Fighter Sqdn. in Europe; left service 1945 and rejoined as a transport pilot, Edmonton 1946; C.O., 1 Aircraft Control & Warning Unit, St. Hubert, Que.; Chief Controller, 1 Air Defence Group HQ, 1951; served on exchange duties with USAF, Stewart Air Force Base, N.Y., 1953–55; trans. to 61 Aircraft Control & Warning Sqdn., Metz, France as Chief Operations Offr., 1955 becoming C.O. of Sqdn. 1957; Direction Center Chief, Detroit NORAD Sector, 1960; Depy. Dir. of Operations 1962; C.O., RCAF Stn. St. Margarets, N.B. 1964; promoted Col. and apptd. C.O., RCAF Stn. Centralia, 1965; Commdr., Candn. Forces Base, Borden, 1967; Command Dir., NORAD's Command Post, Cheyenne Mt. 1970; promoted Brig. Gen. and apptd. Depy. Asst. Depy. Chief of Staff for Combat Operations, NORAD Command, HQ, Colo. Springs, 1971; awarded USAF Air Weapons Controller Wing 1978; Dir. Gen. Mang. Information Services, NDHQ, Ottawa, 1975; promoted Major General, 1976; Candn. Def. Attaché and Commander, Candn. Def. Liasion Staff, Washington, D.C., 1976–78; retired RCAF and CF, 1978; Dir. & Special Advisor, Internat. Marketing, Defence Products, Bristol Aerspace Ltd., Ottawa, Ont. 1978; consultant for Bristol, 1982–88; Ockenden Pl., Ogilvie, Sub-Division, Edmonton named in his honour, 1982; Nat. Pres., RCAF Assn. 1988–90, Immed. Past Nat. Pres. 1990–92; apptd. Hon. Colonel (DND) of 443 (HS) Squadron, Patricia Bay, BC effective 1 Sept. 1993 (the squadron flys Sea-King helicopters as part of Maritime Pacific Command); elected Area 'H' Dir., Regional District of Central Okanagan 1993–96; Anglican; recreations: volunteer work, golf, skiing; Home: 1665 Pritchard Dr., Westbank, B.C. V4T 1X5.

**O'CONNOR, Arthur J.,** B.Sc. Eng., DSC (Hon.); energy co. executive; b. Harvey, N.B. 26 Oct. 1924; s. Frederick James and Mary (Long) O'C.; e. Univ. of N.B., B.Sc. Eng. (Elect.) 1945; m. Mary Kathleen, d. late John Whalen, 19 Sept. 1950; six s. and two d.; PRES., ENERGY STRATEGIES LTD. 1989– and DEPY. COORDINATOR (NORTH AMERICA) W.E.C. Energy Study; Past Vice-Chrmn., Atlantic Provs. Economic Counc.; Past Chrmn., Can. Major Projects Assoc.; joined N.B. Electric Power Comn. as Engr. (Distribution) 1949; also served as Resident Engr., System Operating Engr., Asst. Chief Engr., Mgr. of Engn., Asst. Gen. Mgr. and Chief Engr., Gen. Mgr., 1967–86, Pres. 1986–89; recip. Ian F. McRae Award; mem. Candn. Nuclear Assn. (Pres. 1973–74); Candn. Elect. Assn. (Past-Pres.); Assn. Prof. Engrs. N.B.; Dir. and Past Pres. and Hon. Mem. Energy Council of Canada; Gov., St Thomas Univ.; Past mem. Science Council of Canada 1977–1983; Fellow of The Canadian Academy of Engineering; K. of C.; R. Catholic; recreations: golf, jogging, tennis, skiing; Home: 467 Squire St., Fredericton, N.B. E3B 3V3.

**O'CONNOR, John P.,** B.Comm., LL.B.; lawyer; b. Ottawa, Ont. 20 Aug. 1942; s. Louis John and Edna (Lalonde) O.; e. St. Patrick's Coll., B.Comm. 1963; Univ. of Ottawa LL.B. 1966; called to Bar, Prov. of Ont. 1968;

m. Debbie d. Doris and Roy Carmody 16 May 1981; children: Kerry, Amy, Julie; CONSULTANT; Pres., Tartan Group of Companies 1980– ; Partner, Nicol, O'Connor & Lazier 1968; Chrmn., Ottawa Gen. Hosp. Found.; Trustee, Ottawa Gen. Hosp.; Dir., Ottawa Sooners; Mem., Fin. Ctte., St. Joseph's Ch.; Chrmn., Treas. Ctte., Fed. Lib. Party for E. Ont.; recreations: tennis, racquetball, golf; Clubs: Laurier, Laurentian Club, Royal Ottawa Golf & Country; Office: 451 Metcalfe St., Ottawa, Ont. K2P 1T1.

**O'DEA, Hon. Fabian,** Q.C., LL.D.; b. St. John's, Nfld. 20 Jan 1918; s. Hon. John V., K.S.G. and May (Coady), M.B.E., O'Dea; e. St. Bonaventure's Coll., 1923–34; Memorial Univ. of Nfld., 1934–36; St. Michael's Coll., Univ. of Toronto, B.A. 1939; Dalhousie Univ., 1939–40; Christ Church, Oxford Univ., B.C.L. 1948; LL.D. Memorial Univ. 1969; m. Constance Margaret, d. Edgar G. Ewing, St. John's, 9 Aug. 1951; children: Deborah, Victoria, Stephen, Jane; Partner, O'Dea, Greene, retired 1990; Lt.-Gov., Nfld. 1963–69; called to Bar of Eng. at the Inner Temple, 1948, Nfld. 1949; cr. Q.C. 1963; practised law in London, Eng., 1948 and in St. John's, Nfld. 1949–1990, until retirement; Rhodes Scholar for Nfld. 1939; Hon. A.D.C. to Gov.-Gen. of Can., 1949–52; Hon. A.D.C. to Lieut.-Govs. of Nfld., 1949–61; Consular Agent for France in Nfld., 1957–62; Hon. Solicitor for Nfld. Prov. Command of Roy. Candn. Legion, 1950–63; Hon. Life mem. of Nfld. Prov. Command of Roy. Candn. Legion 1963; Dir., NewTel Enterprises Ltd. from formation until 1989; Nfld. Telephone Co. Ltd. 1962–89; Browning Harvey Ltd. 1960–93; mem., Bd. of Regents, Memorial Univ. of Newfoundland, 1959–63; Vice-Pres. for Nfld. of Candn. Bar Assn., 1961–63; Secy. Rhodes Scholar Selection Comte. for Nfld. 1951–62, Chrmn. 1963–69; Chrmn., Royal Commission on Nfld. Liquor Commission Leasing 1972; Kt., Order of St. John of Jerusalem (1963); Kt. of Malta 1988; Hon. Coloner, Royal Nfld. Regiment 1994; served in 2nd World War with R.C.N.V.R., 1940–45; on loan to Roy. Navy, 1943–44; C.O., H.M.C.S. Cabot, 1952–55; Commander, R.C.N.R. (retired); Roman Catholic; Residence: 12 Winter Place, St. John's, Nfld. A1B 1J6.

**O'DEA, Francis Donald;** business executive; b. Montreal, Que. 14 June 1945; s. Francis Michael and Andree (Porcheron) O'D.; e. Marymount High Sch. Montreal 1964; Univ. of So. Dakota, Rapid City 1967; FOUNDER, PRES. & DIR., KILRUSH CORP. 1985– ; Pres. and Dir., Proshred Holdings Ltd.; founded The Second Cup Ltd. 1975–85; estbd. Franchise Div. Retail Council Can. 1983; Dir. Samaritan Air Services Ltd.; Dir., Horatio Mgmt. Inc.; Dir. Orthopaedic & Arthritic Hospital; Dir., Commemorative Services of Ont.; Pres. and Dir. Renascent Foundation Inc.; Dir. Renascent Fellowship; Dir., Candn. Found. for AIDS Rsch.; Chrmn., Street Kids Internat.; Candn. Olympic Assn., Standing Ctte. on Ethics; recipient, Canada Volunteer Award 1992; recreations: flying, skiing, tennis; Club: Ontario; Home: 1 Benvenuto Pl., Toronto, Ont. M4V 2L1; Office: 2200 Lakeshore Blvd. W., Suite 102, Toronto, Ont. M8V 1A4.

**O'DEA, Shane,** B.A., M.A.; university professor; b. St. John's, Nfld. 6 July 1945; s. Francis Laurence and Raymonde (Judd) O.; e. Winterton School; St. Bonaventure's College; Beaumont College, Old Windsor; Memorial Univ. B.A. 1966, M.A. 1974; m. Maire d. Helena and Dr. G.A. Frecker 22 Nov. 1968; children: Conor, Niall, Alain; PROFESSOR OF ENGLISH, MEMORIAL UNIV. OF NFLD. & CO-DIRECTOR, CENTRE FOR MATERIAL CULTURE STUDIES 1989– ; College Trades, St. John's Instr. 1969–70; Lectr., Memorial Univ. 1970; Asst. Prof. 1975; Assoc. Prof. 1980; Co-editor (Acting), 'Newfoundland Studies' 1987–88 (Chair, Edit. Bd. 1992– ); Co-Dir., Centre for Material Culture Studies 1988– ; Deputy Public Orator 1992– ; Acting Head, English Dept. 1992–93; Life Mem., Nfld. Historic Trust 1973 (Pres. 1973–75); Southcott Award 1988; Heritage Can. Comm. Serv. Award 1978; Lt.-Gov. Award 1990; Mem., Univ. Distinguished Teaching Award 1988; Council for Adv. & Support of Edn. Candn. Prof. of the Year 1988; Canada 125 Medal 1992; Vice Chair, St. John's Heritage Adv. Ctte. 1977–91; CPAC (Nfld.) Ch. 1977–79; Vice-Pres., Soc. for the Study of Arch. in Can. 1982–83; Mem., Hist. Sites & Monuments Bd. of Can. 1985–92; Chair, Heritage Found. of Nfld. & Lab. 1989–92; author: 'The Domestic Architecture of Old St. John's' 1974; co-author: 'A Gift of Heritage' 1975, 'Ten Historic Towns' (co-ed.) 1978; co-editor: 'Dimensions in Canadian Architecture' 1983; author: num. articles; Home: Retreat Cottage, Kenna's Hill, St. John's, Nfld. A1A 1H9; Office: Ctr. for Material Culture Studies, St. John's, Nfld. A1C 5S7.

**O'DELL, Peter Sidney John;** business executive; b. Bedford, England 19 Jan. 1934; s. Harvey and Ivy Katherine (Vought) O.; e. Luton & S. Bedfordshire Coll., higher nat. cert. 1959; m. Molly d. Ted and Lillian Fisher 29 June 1956; children: Todd, Scott; GENERAL MGR., NORTH AMERICA, ADHESIVES & RESINS, BORDEN PACKAGING AND INDUSTRIAL PRODUCTS 1990– ; Chrmn. & C.E.O., The Borden Company Ltd. (Canada) 1987– ; Works Chem., Brookhirst Igranic 1954–60; Chem., Rsch. Counc. of Alta. 1960; Control Chem. (Edmonton), Borden Chem. Can. 1960–63; Devel. Chem. (Vanc.) 1963–71; Mgr., Rsch. & Devel. 1971–79; Gen. Mgr., West Opns. 1979–86; Pres., Borden Packaging & Industrial Products (Canada) 1987–90; recreations: golf, skiing; Home: 1825 W. Mercer Way, Mercer Island Washington 98040 U.S.A.; Office: 520 - 112th Ave. N.E., Bellevue, WA 98004 U.S.A.

**ODETTE, Edmond George;** B.Sc., Ph.D.; contractor; b. Tilbury, Ont. 1 Jan. 1926; s. Louis L. and E. (Ritter) O.; e. St. Michael's Coll. High Sch. Toronto; Univ. of Toronto B.Sc. 1948; Univ. of Assumption Ph.D. 1970; m. Gloria A. d. Frederick McEwan, Windsor, Ont. 8 Sept. 1951; children: Edmond George, Curtis M., Mary, Anne, Andrea; PRES. & C.E.O., EASTERN CONSTRUCTION CO. LTD. 1951– ; Pres. Sun Construction Co. Ltd.; Associated Leaseholds Ltd.; Dir. Continental Bank; mem. Assn. Prof. Engrs. Prov. Ont.; R. Catholic; recreations: golf, tennis; Clubs: Rosedale Golf; Granite; Lost Tree; Jupiter Hills Golf; Essex Golf; The York; The Badminton and Racquet Club; Home: 21 High Point Rd., Don Mills, Ont. M3B 2A3; Office: 4120 Yonge St., Suite 410, North York, Ont. M2P 2C8.

**O'DETTE, John Herbert,** C.M., M.Sc., P. Eng.; metallurgical engineer; conservationist; b. Brockville, Ont. 17 Feb. 1920; s. Charles Herbert and Gertrude (Brady) O'D.; e. St. Francis Separate Sch. and Brockville Coll. Inst. 1939; Queen's Univ. B.Sc. 1944, M.Sc. 1946; m. Irene Pearl d. late Ross Paul, Napanee, Ont. 14 Sept. 1946; children: Cheri (Mrs. S. Lipin), Leanne (Mrs. M. O'Sullivan), Brian, Craig; retired Sr. Research Engineer, Kingston Research & Development Centre, Aluminum Co. of Canada; mem. Research Div. Consolidated Mining & Smelting Co. (Cominco) Trail, B.C., also postgrad. teaching Queen's Univ. 1944–46; Alcan Research & Devel. Kingston, Ont. 1946–82; Kingston City appointee to Cataraqui Region Conserv. Authority 1970–75, 1978–85; mem. Adv. Comte. to Min. of Lands & Forests Ont. 1968–72; Dir., Ont. Fed. Anglers & Hunters 1952–93 (Past Pres. & Life Mem.); Dir., Candn. Wildlife Fed. 1965–85 (Past Pres. & Life Mem.); Dir., Sportsmen's Conserv. Workshops in Ont. 1960–88; rec'd Carling Conservation Award 1960; White Owl Conservation Award 1974; Winchester Outdoorsman of Yr. 1978; Am. Motors Conservation Award 1979; Carling Conservation Award 1984; Roland Michener Conservation Award 1992; 125th Anniversary of the Confederation of Canada Medal, 1992; served with C.O.T.C. Queen's Univ., also Special Weapons Training Offr., rank Capt.; author numerous articles fish and wildlife, resource mang.; lectr.; Columnist 'Ontario Angler and Hunter'; prepared many briefs resource mang. Ont. and Fed. Govts.; mem. Soc. Explosives Engrs.; R. Catholic; recreations: hunting, fishing, golf, tennis, target shooting, oil painting; photography; Clubs: Kingston & Dist. Rod & Gun (Past Pres. and Dir. & Life Mem.); Frontenac Rifle and Pistol (Pres. & Dir. 1956–90); Home: 377 Bath Rd., Kingston, Ont. K7M 2Y1.

**ODJIG, Daphne;** artist; muralist; b. Wikwemikong (Manitoulin Island), Ont. 11 Sept. 1919; mem. Odawa Tribe; d. Dominic and Joyce Emily (Peachey) O.; m. Chester s. Eric and Myrna Beavon 31 Aug. 1963; children: Stanley, David; step-children: Daniel, Edward, Rebecca; solo exhbns.: 1967: Lakehead Art Centre, Port Arthur, Ont.; 1968: Brandon (Man.) Univ.; 1969: Viscount Gorte, Winnipeg; 1970: Internat. Peace Gardens; 1974: Warehouse Gall. of Native Art, Winnipeg; 1966: Bashford & Schwarz Gall., Calgary; 1977: Wah-Sa Gall., Winnipeg; (and 1978) Images for a Canadian Heritage, Vancouver; Lefebvre Gall., Edmonton; 1979: Pollock Gall., Toronto; Griffin Galleries, Vancouver; 1980: (and 1982) Robertson Galleries, Ottawa; (and 1982) Assiniboia Gall., Regina; 1981: Children of the Raven Gall., Vancouver; The Shayne Gall., Montreal; 1982: Gold Design Fine Arts, Calgary; Retrospective Exhbn. (1946–85) organized by the Thunder Bay National Exhbn. Centre and Centre for Indian art; numerous group shows incl.: 1970: Minot State Univ., N. Dakota, Candn. Guild of Crafts, Place Bonaventure, Montreal; 1971: L'Agence de Cooperation Culturelle et Tech., Canada, France & Belgium; 1972: 'Treaty Numbers' Winnipeg Art Gall.; 1973: Gall. Anthropos, London, Engl.; 'Contemporary Native Art of Ontario,' Centennial Gall. Oakville; 1974: Royal Ont. Mus., Toronto; Janet Ian Cameron Gall., Univ. of Man.; Oakville (Ont.) Exhbn. of Native Art; 1975: Winnipeg Art Gall.; Native Arts Festival, Niagara-on-the-Lake, Ont.; Dominion Gall., Montreal; Wallack Gall., Ottawa; Art Emporium, Vancouver; Woodland Indian Cultural Educl. Centre, Brantford, Ont.; 1976: Agnes Etheington Art Centre, Queens Univ., Kingston, Ont.; 'From Women's Eyes: Women Painters in Canada,' Laurentian Univ., Sudbury, Ont.; Etobicoke (Ont.) Civic Centre; Janet Ian Cameron Gall., Univ. of Man.; Woodland Indian Cultural Educl. Centre, Brantford, Ont.; Contemporary Native Art of Can., Can. House Gall., London, Eng.; 1977: Kinsmen Centre, Calgary; (Brazil) Cultural Found. of Brazilia, Sao Paulo Mus. of Art, Cultural Found. of Bahia Museums of Modern Art, Rio de Janeiro Museum of Modern Art; 'Exhibition of Modern Native Canadian Art' Hart House Art Gall., Univ. of Toronto; 1978: '100 Yrs. of Native American Painting' Oklahoma Mus. of Art; 1982: 'The Indian Individualist Show' joint proj. of Assiniboia Gall., World Assembly of First Nations and Sask. Indian Federated Coll.; comns. incl.: 'Earthmother' for Candn. Pavilion Expo 1970, Osaka, Japan; Centennial Comn., Winnipeg for mural depicting Indian legend 'Creation of the World,' Mus. of Man. 1972; 'From Mother Earth Flows the River of Life' for Cultural Devel. Div., Min. of Indian and Northern Affairs 1974; 'The Indian in Transition' for Nat. Mus. of Man., Ottawa 1978; El Al (Israeli airline) to visit Jerusalem and interpret it visually; incl. in collections of: Winnipeg Art Gall.; Indian & Northern Affairs, Winnipeg; National Museum of Man; Manitoba Indian Brotherhood; Can. Counc. Art Bank; McMichael Candn. Coll., Kleinberg, Ont.; Tom Thompson Gall.; Sir Wilfrid Laurier Univ.; Govt. of Israel, Jerusalem; Nova Corp., Calgary; Petro Canada, Calgary; Ameco Canada Petroleum Ltd., Calgary, and others; recipient Arts Grant for tour and exhbn. of paintings, Smotra Folklore Festival, Yugoslavia 1971; author and illustrator 'Nanabush Indian Legends for Children' (10 books) 1971; resource person: National Native Indian Artists Symposium, Hazelton, B.C. 1983; Soc. of Candn. Artists of Native Ancestry, Ottawa 1985; founding mem. Profl. Native Indian Artists Assn. Inc. 1973; donations: painting for ltd. ed. Serigraph, CKFM Children's Fund Campaign, Hosp. for Sick Children 1981; recipient Swedish Brucebo Found. Scholarship, Visby Island of Gotland, Sweden 1973; Man. Arts Counc. Bursary 1973; Candn. Silver Jubilee Medal 1977; presented with Eagle Feather by Chief Wakageshig, Wikwemikong Reserve in recognition of artistic accomplishments 1978 (an hon. previously reserved for men to acknowledge prowess in hunt or war); Nat. Film Bd. T.V. documentary 'Colours of Pride' 1973; subject CBC-TV documentary 1981; Tokyo Television: 'Window on Canada' Daphne Odjig/Painter 1989; LL.D. (hon. causa) Laurentian Univ. 1982; Univ. of Toronto 1985; Member, Order of Canada 1987; R.C.A. (Royal Candn. Acad. of Art) 1989; Address: P.O. Box 111, Anglemont, B.C. V0E 1A0.

**O'DONNELL, James Francis,** B.A.; bank official; b. Toronto, Ont.; e. De La Salle College; York Univ. B.A. 1959; m. Anne Marie White; four children; SENIOR VICE-PRESIDENT, THE BANK OF NOVA SCOTIA 1985– ; Pres., Commercial Credit Business Services 1972; Pres. 1974; Commercial Credit Corp. Ltd. 1974–79; Gen. Mgr., The Bank of N.S. 1979–85; Dir., Equifax Canada Ltd.; Candn. Transportation Inst. (Bd. Chair); Orthapaedic & Arthritic Hospital (O&A); Metro Bd. of Trade; Bayview Golf & Country; recreations: golf, reading, various sports activities; Office: 181 University Ave., 12th fl., Toronto, Ont. M5R 3K7.

**O'DONNELL, John Hugh,** B.A.Sc., O.L.S., Q.L.S.; professional land surveyor; b. Montréal, Qué. 26 Jan. 1941; s. late John Gerard and late Evarista Mary (McCauley) O'D.; e. Univ. of Laval B.A. Sc. 1969; m. Rachel Faith d. Roger and late Elizabeth Boone 4 Sept. 1965; children: Sean Hugh, Evarista Elizabeth Alana; ASST. DEPY. MIN., SURVEYS MAPPING AND REMOTE SENSING SECTOR, NATURAL RESOURCES CANADA 1987– ; Dir. Trillium Data Group Limited 1985–87; Adjunct Prof. Univ. of Toronto; Project Surveyor Survair Ltd. Ottawa 1969–70; various positions Energy, Mines & Resources Can. 1970–79, Asst. Dir. Topographical Survey 1976–79; Dir. of Operations, Surveying & Mapping, Marshall Macklin Monaghan Limited 1979–82; Dir. of Surveys & Mapping Ont. Govt. 1982–85, Surveyor Gen. of Ont. 1983–85; Vice Pres. and Dir. Marshall Macklin Monaghan Limited 1985–87; Pres. and Dir., MMM Surveys and Consultants Limited 1985–87; Marshall Macklin Monaghan Ontario Limited 1985–87; Dir., Royal Candn. Geograph. Soc.; 1989– ; Global Change Program, Royal Soc. of Can. 1989– ; Secy. Gen., Internat. Union of Surveying and Mapping 1989– ; Dir., Recreation Assn. of the Public Service of Can. 1993– ; mem. Assn. Ont.

Land Surveyors 1975– ; Order Que. Land Surveyors; Candn. Inst. Surveying (Pres. 1978–79); Candn. Assn. Aerial Surveyors (Dir.) 1980–82, 1985–87; Am. Soc. Photogrammetry; R. Catholic; recreations: cross-country skiing, tennis; Home: 119 Margaret Anne Dr., R.R. #3, Carp, Ont. K0A 1L0; Office: 580 Booth St., Rm. 1014, Ottawa, Ont. K1A 0E4.

**O'DONNELL, Patrick Joseph,** Ph.D.; physicist; educator; b. Port Glasgow, Scot. 16 Oct. 1938; s. Daniel and Mary (Blaney) O'D.; e. Univ. of Glasgow B.Sc. 1960, Ph.D. 1963; m. Mary Agnes d. George Reynolds, Baillieston, Scot. Aug. 1964; three s. Daniel Paul, George Ciaran, Quentin Patrick; PROF. OF PHYSICS, UNIV. OF TORONTO 1977– ; Research Asst. Univ. of Durham 1963–65; Acting Chrmn. Div. Physical Science, Scarborough Coll. present Univ; Asst. Prof. of Physics present Univ. 1966–70, Assoc. Prof. 1970–77; SRC (UK) Sr. Research Fellow, Southampton Univ. 1976; Sr. Research Fellow Univ. of Glasgow 1979; Lady Davis Prof., Technion, Haifa 1985; Scientific Assoc., CERN, Geneva 1986; author numerous articles particle physics prof. journs.; mem. Candn. Assn. Physicists (Chrmn. Div. Theoretical Physics 1983–84); Am. Phys. Soc.; Dir., Yukon Advanced Study Inst. 1984; Inst. Particle Physics (Can., Council mem.); recreations: skiing, squash; Club: Skyloft Ski (Candn. Ski Patrol); Office: 60 St. George St., Rm. 1120, Toronto, Ont. M5S 1A7.

**O'DONOGHUE, John Joseph,** B.A., LL.B.; lawyer; b. Peterborough, Ont. 2 Aug. 1941; s. John Francis and Josephine Mary (Killoran) O'D.; e. St. Peters Elem. and High Sch. Peterborough 1958; St. Michael's Coll. Univ. of Toronto B.A. 1962; Osgoode Hall Law Sch. LL.B. 1965; called to Bar of Ont. 1967; m. Elaine d. Metro and Irene Drobot 30 Apl. 1966; one s. Sean Ryan; PARTNER, CHUSID, FRIEDMAN 1985; Partner Macaulay, Lipson, Joseph & O'Donoghue, 1983; Partner, Barlow, Peck & O'Donoghue 1969–83; Jr. Solr. Parkinson, Gardiner, Roberts, 1967–69; contrib. author: 'Shopping Centre Leases, Additions or Expansions to the Centre' 1976; 'Professional Office Practice Management for Medical/Dental Profession' 1984; Executive Guide to Canadian Management, 1985; speaker at various conferences sponsored by Candn. Franchise Assoc., Richard De Boo Ltd., Insight, Inst. for Internat. Rsch., Laventhol & Horwath, Nursing Home Assoc. Ont., Ont. Long Term Residential Care Assoc.; mem. Candn. Bar Assn.; Candn. Franchise Assoc.; Candn. Fed. Independent Business; recreation: badminton; Home: 63 Clifton Rd., Toronto, Ont. M4T 2E8; Office: 30 St. Clair Ave. W., Suite 900, Toronto, Ont. M4V 3A1.

**O'DONOGHUE, Paul Henry,** B.A., B.Th.; insurance broker; b. Toronto, Ont. 24 May 1931; s. Henry Dillon and Stella Mary (Lynch) O'Donoghue; e. St. Michael's Coll., Univ. of Toronto, B.A. 1952, B.Th. 1955; m. Denyse Mercier, 29 March 1969; CHRMN., C.E.O. & DIR., MARSH & McLENNAN LTD.; mem. Mgmt. Comte. and Managing Dir., Marsh & McLennan Inc.; Chrmn. of the Bd., Slough Estates Canada Ltd.; Dir., Pratte-Morrissette Inc.; Banque Nationale de Paris (Canada); Mem., President's Counc., Univ. St. Michael's Coll.; mem. Business Counc. on Nat. Issues; mem., Advisory Bd. of the Royal LePage Commercial Real Estate Fund; mem., Sovereign & Military Order of Malta (Candn. Assoc.); Dir. and Past Pres., Ont. Sect., French Chamber of Commerce; Past Dir., National Ballet of Canada; Candn. Opera Co.; former mem., Extve. Counc., Candn. Chamber of Commerce; Past Chrmn., Ont. Regional Ctte.; Catholic; recreations: tennis, skiing; Clubs: Rosedale Golf; Toronto; Mount Royal; University; Badminton and Racquet; Toronto Bd. of Trade; Caledon Ski (Past Dir.); Home: 109 Warren Rd., Toronto, Ont. M4V 2S3; Office: Canada Trust Tower, BCE Place, 161 Bay St., P.O. Box 502, Toronto, Ont. M5J 2S4.

**O'DONOHUE, Melville J.B.,** Q.C., B.Com., LL.B., F.A.C.T.E.C.; b. Toronto, Ont. 3 Jan. 1923; s. Eugene Joseph and Mary Josephine (Sweeney) O'D.; e. De La Salle College, Oaklands; Univ. of Toronto, B.Com. 1946; Osgoode Hall LL.B. 1951; read law with late Hon. Frank Hughes, Q.C., 1949–51; called to the Bar of Ont., 1951; cr. Q.C. 1963; Fellow Amer. College of Trust & Estate Counsel 1982; m. Gloria, d. of late Albert Knox, K.C. and Olga Knox; children: Mary-Jo, Stephen, Gregory, and Melanie; PARTNER, O'DONOHUE & O'DONOHUE; estb. law firm as sole practitioner 1951 now expanded to O'Donohue & O'Donohue; Dir., Ainsworth Electric Co. Ltd.; A.P. Green Refractories (Canada) Ltd.; Burns Internat. Security Systems Inc.; Federal Security Systems Ltd.; Jamger Investments Ltd.; Ohio Nut and Bolt (Canada) Ltd.; Wells Fargo Armcar Inc.; Wells Fargo Alarm Services of Can. Ltd.; mem. Law Soc. of Upper Canada; Candn. Tax Foundation; Candn. Bar Assn.; Co. of York Law Assn.; Thomas More Lawyers' Guild; Liberal; Roman Catholic; recreations: hunting, farming; Clubs: Granite; Faculty, Univ. of Toronto; National; Toronto Lawyers; Home: 35 St. Edmunds Dr., Toronto, Ont. M4N 2P7; Office: Suite 1600, 390 Bay St., Toronto, Ont. M5H 2Y2.

**O'DONOVAN, Michael Valentine,** P.Eng.; technological executive; b. Clonakilty, Co. Cork, Ireland 14 Feb. 1936; s. Patrick Joseph and Margaret Imelda (O'Donnell) Donovan; e. Boys S.S. 1953; Cambridge Coll. of Arts & Technology; P.Eng. 1959; m. Sheila d. Denis and Constance Leonard 4 Oct. 1960; children: Simon, Christopher, Stephen, Caroline: CHRMN., C.E.O. & FOUNDING MEM., COM DEV LTD. 1990– ; Engr. Pye Telecomm. Ltd. 1959–63; emigrated 1963; Microwave Engr., RCA Ltd. 1963–70; Mgr. Comm. Satellite Transponder Dept. 1970–74; Pres. & Founding Mem., Com Dev Ltd. 1974–90; Can. Award for Excellence for the innovative use of Technology awarded to Com Dev 1984; Dir., Opimian Calif. Vineyard Corp.; Dir., Radarsat Internat. Inc.; Mem., Assn. of Profl. Engrs. of Ont.; Am. Inst. of Aeronautics; Inst. of Elect. & Elect. Engrs.; co-author: 'Microwave Filters for Communications Systems' 1971; recreations: swimming, reading, wine; Office: 155 Sheldon Dr., Cambridge, Ont.

**O'DRISCOLL, Hon. John Gerald Joseph,** B.A., LL.B.; judge; b. Sault Ste. Marie, Ont. 3 March 1931; s. Michael Joseph and Gertrude (Mulligan) O'D.; e. Sacred Heart Sch., Sault Ste. Marie, Ont., Sault Coll. Inst. St. Michael's Coll. Sch., and St. Michael's Coll., Univ. of Toronto, B.A. 1951; Osgoode Hall Law Sch. LL.B. 1954; m. Patricia Marie, d. H. J. Slattery, Toronto, Ont., 17 May 1958; three s. John Joseph, Michael Sean, Patrick Francis (dec.); JUSTICE, SUPREME COURT OF ONT. since 1971; read law with Arthur Maloney, Q.C.; called to Bar of Ont. 1955; cr. Q.C. 1967; R. Catholic; Home: Toronto, Ont.; Office: 130 Queen St. W., Toronto, Ont. M5H 2N5.

**O'DRISCOLL, Robert,** M.A., Ph.D.; university professor; author; b. Conception Harbour, Nfld. 3 May 1938; s. William Joseph and Annie May (Connors) O'D.; e. Conception Harbour (Nfld.) and St. Bonaventure's Coll. St. John's, Nfld. 1954; Memorial Univ. of Nfld. B.A. (Educ.) 1958, B.A. 1959, M.A. 1960; Univ. of London Ph.D. 1963; children: Brian William Butler, Michael Robert, Declan Patrick, Emer Anne; PROF. ST. MICHAEL'S COLL. UNIV. OF TORONTO since 1975; Research Fellow Univ. of Reading 1963–64; Visiting Prof. Univ. Coll. Dublin 1964–66; joined Univ. of Toronto as Asst. Prof. 1966, Assoc. Prof. 1969; Prof. 1975; service with RCN (Reserve), rank Capt.; author: 'Intruder: A Poem' 1972; 'Symbolism and Some Implications of the Symbolic Approach: W.B. Yeats During the Eighteen-Nineties' 1975; 'An Ascendancy of the Heart: Ferguson and the Beginnings of Modern Irish Literature in English' 1976; Ed.-in-Chief (with Lorna Reynolds) 'Yeats Studies' series (five volumes published): 'Yeats during the 1890's' (1971), 'Jack Yeats and John Synge' (1972), 'Yeats and the Theatre' (1975), 'Yeats and the Occult' (1975), 'The Speckled Bird' (1977); Ed. 'Theatre and Nationalism in 20th Century Ireland' 1971; 'A Quest Through Europe, or, The Long Way Round to the Edinburgh Festival' 1980; 'The Celtic Consciousness' (named by the Am. Library Assn. Outstanding Acad. Book of 1982 in U.S.) 1981; 'Dream Chamber: Joyce and Dada' 1982; 'The Untold Story: The Irish in Canada' 1988; 'Nato and the Warsaw Pact Are One' 1990; 'Atlantis Again: The Story of A Family' 1993; 'Triad: Armageddon One' 1993; 'The New World Order and the Throne of the antiChrist' 1993, 'The New World Order in North America: Mechanism in Place for a Police State' 1993; 'New World Order Corruption in Canada' 1994; author various articles; Founder and first Chrmn. Candn. Assn. for Irish Studies 1968–72; Founder and Artistic Dir. Irish Theatre Soc. and Irish Arts Can. 1967–74; Artistic Dir., Celtic Arts (1977–90); Founder, Candn. Celtic Arts Assn.; Extve. Comte. Internat. Assn. Studies Anglo-Irish Lit. since 1969; mem. Nat. Lib. of Ireland Comte.; recreations: book writing and collecting, theatre, talk; Home: Alexander Fraser House, Arthur, Ont. N0G 1A0; Office: 81 St. Mary St., Toronto, Ont. M5S 1J4.

**OESTERLE, Leonhard F.,** R.C.A.; sculptor; b. Bietigheim, Germany 3 March 1915; s. Wilhelm and Sophie (Seher) O.; e. elem. sch. Bietigheim, Germany; Tech. Sch. Stuttgart-Feuerbach, apprenticeship as Fine Mech.; Art Coll. Zurich 1 yr.; studies with Fritz Wotruba, Zug and with Otto Müller, Zurich; INSTR. AND PAST HEAD OF SCULPTURE, ONT. COLL. OF ART; rep. various exhns. Can., USA and Europe incl. retrospective exhn. sarnia 1980, exhn. in Paris 1984, Centre Culturel, Univ. of Paris 1986, 2 retrospective exhbs. in Germany 1991; sculpture work subject of 2 CBC-sponsored films; some sculptures rep. in three feature films: 'Three Men and a Baby,' 'Amerika,' and 'Deadly Business'; commissioned work in public places: Group of Four Bronze Figures at Col. McLaughlin Collegiate in Oshawa, Ont.; Religious Statuary at St. Augustine College chapel in Scarborough, Ont.; 2 Metal Sculptures, one indoor, one outdoors at Central Lab., Govt. of Ont., Toronto, Ont.; Religious Bronzework for Temple Sinai in Toronto, Ont.; Large Sculpture for park in Sarnia, Ont.; Playground sculpture in Berlin-Steglitz-Germany; Large Crucifix for St. Christopher's Church, Mississauga, Ont. 1986; pol. prisoner Germany 8 yrs.; came to Can. 1956; Past Vice Pres. Sculptors' Soc. Can.; mem. Royal Can. Academy of Arts; Ont. Soc. Artists; Lutheran; Home: 27 Alcina Ave., Toronto, Ont. M6G 2E7.

**OFFENBERGER, Allan Anthony,** B.A.Sc., M.A.Sc., Ph.D.; university professor; b. Wadena, Sask. 11 Aug. 1938; s. Mike (dec.) and Ivy Viola (Hagglund) O.; e. Penticton Sr. H.A. 1957; Univ. of B.C. B.A.Sc. 1962, M.A.Sc. 1963; Mass. Inst. of Technology Ph.D. 1968; m. Margaret Patterson 12 April 1963; children: Brian Philip, Gary Allan; PROF. OF ELECTRICAL ENGINEERING, UNIVERSITY OF ALBERTA 1975– ; Asst. Prof. of E.E., Univ. of Alberta 1968; Assoc. Prof. 1970; Visiting Prof., U.K. Atomic Energy Authy. 1975–76; Distinguished Visiting Prof., Oxford Univ. 1992; Past Pres. (& Mem. of Extve.), Candn. Assn. of Physicists 1987–91; Mem., Adv. or Selection Cttes. for Research (NRC, NSERC, AECL, Sci. Council of Canada) 1977–; given 100 invited talks at internat. confs. & insts.; supervised 17 grad. theses & 16 postdoctoral fellows or visiting scientists; Scientific Consultant for industry, univ. & govt. orgns.; Killam Research Fellow Canada Council 1980–82; Dir., Laser Fusion Project 1984–91; Mem., Bd. of Dir., Ont. Laser & Lightwave Rsch. Ctr., Univ. of Toronto 1988–92; Mem., Edit. Bd., Laser and Particle Beams 1987– ; Mem., Candn. Assn. of Physicists, Sigma Chi, Am. Physical Soc.; author/co-author of over 100 pubns. on high power lasers, laser/matter interaction, laser fusion energy rsch., instrumentation techniques; Home: 412 Lessard Dr., Edmonton, Alta. T6M 1A7; Office: Edmonton, Alta. T6G 2G7.

**O'FLAHERTY, Patrick Augustine,** M.A., Ph.D.; educator and writer; b. Long Beach, Conception Bay, Nfld. 6 Oct. 1939; s. Augustus and Jane (Howell) O'F.; e. Mem. Univ. of Nfld. B.A. 1959, M.A. 1960; Univ. Coll. Univ. of London Ph.D. 1963; children: James Keir Coaker, Peter Augustine, Padraic William; PROF. OF ENGLISH, MEM. UNIV. OF NFLD.; Lectr. in Eng. Univ. of Man. 1963, Asst. Prof. 1964–65; Asst. Prof. of Eng. present Univ. 1965, Assoc. Prof. 1968, Prof. 1974; Head 1982–87; freelance broadcaster CBC 1975–78, 1982– ; Cand. for St. John's W. Lib. Party Can. 1979 and for Harbour Grace Lib. Party Nfld. & Labrador 1979; author 'The Rock Observed: Studies in the Literature of Newfoundland' 1979; 'Summer of the Greater Yellowlegs' 1987; 'A Small Place in the Sun' (1989); 'Priest of God' (1989); 'Come Near At Your Peril' 1992; 'Benny's Island' 1994; co-ed. 'By Great Waters: A Newfoundland and Labrador Anthology' 1974; co-author 'Part of the Main: An Illustrated History of Newfoundland and Labrador' 1983; weekly columnist 'As I See It' in 'The Daily News' St. John's 1977–78, 1980–81; contbg. ed., St. John's 'Evening Telegram' 1988–90; weekly columnist 'Patrick's Pen' in 'Newfoundland Herald' 1993–94; various articles scholarly journs.; mem. Can. Council 1981–84; Atlantic Press Council 1983–84; National Library Adv. Bd. 1983–84; Inst. of Research on Public Policy 1985–86; Can. Commonwealth Scholarship & Fellowship Ctte. 1985–87; recreations: walking, reading, fishing; Home: P.O. Box 2676, St. John's, Nfld. A1C 6K1; Office: St. John's, Nfld. A1C 5S7.

**O'FLAHERTY, Thomas Gordon,** B.E., M.Sc.; software executive; b. Halifax, N.S. 15 March 1942; s. Gordon Roy and Frances Gertrude (Holmes) O'F.; e. Dalhousie Univ. B.Sc. 1963; Tech. Univ. of N.S. B.Eng. (Mech.) 1965; Birmingham Univ. M.Sc. 1968; m. Janette d. Brian and Ann Chudleigh-Sutch 7 May 1988; one s. Alexander Thomas; VICE PRES. MARKETING, MODATECH SYSTEMS INC. 1993– ; Co-founder Operational Rsch. Div. N.S. Rsch. Found. 1968, div. Dir. 1970; joined Xerox Canada Inc. 1972–83; Co-founder and Mktg. Partner Bedford Software Ltd. 1983; Founder, Richmond Technologies & Software Inc. 1989; mem. B.C. Technology Industries Assn. (BCTIA); Assn. Profl. Engs. N.S.; Home: 5171 Ranger Ave., North Vancouver, B.C. V7R 3M5; Office: 1681 Chestnut St., Suite 500, Vancouver, B.C. V6J 4M6.

**O'FLYNN, John D.,** Q.C., B.A., LL.B.; judge; b. Belleville, Ont. 26 May 1930; s. John Dale and Mabel Winnifred (Cox) O.; e. Univ. of Toronto B.A. 1952; Osgoode Hall 1956; York Univ. LL.B. 1991; m. Mary d. Willis P. and Elizabeth Freyseng 4 Oct. 1958; children: Dale, Katherine, Pamela; DEPUTY JUDGE OF THE SUPREME COURT OF THE NORTHWEST TERRITORIES 1992– ; practised law Belleville, Ont. 1956–76; Judge, County Court, Co. of Prince Edward 1976; District Court of Ont. 1985; Ontario Court of Justice (Gen. Div.) 1990– ; Trustee, Bridge St. Un. Ch. of Can.; Mem., United Empire Loyalists Assn. of Can.; recreation: golf; clubs: National, Bay of Quinte Country; Home: R.R. #1, Belleville, Ont. K8N 4Z1; Office: Court House, 44 Union St., P.O. Box 680, Picton, Ont. K0K 2T0.

**OGDEN, John David,** B.A., M.B.A., C.L.U., R.H.U., LLIF; insurance executive; b. England 26 June 1936; s. Edwin Stanley and Jane Dorothy (Harris) O.; e. Univ. of Toronto B.A. 1959, M.B.A. 1962; children: David Stanley, Jill Louise; Pres. & C.E.O., Commercial Union Life Assurance Co. 1990; Extve. Dir., Marketing, Imperial Life Assur. Co. 1960–84; Chief Extve. Offr., Candn. Operations, Alico Canada 1985–90; Prov. of Ontario Achievement Award for Distinguished Performance in the Field of Amateur Sport (sailing) 1984; recreations: sailing, skiing, jogging, curling; Clubs: National; Royal Candn. Yacht; Scarborough Golf & Country; Toronto Board of Trade; Boulevard Club; Home: 80 Front St. E., Apt. 325, Toronto, Ont. M5E 1T4.

**OGILVIE, Kelvin Kenneth,** C.M., D.Sc., Ph.D., F.C.I.C.; university administrator and professor/consultant; b. Nova Scotia 6 Nov. 1942; s. Carl Melbourn and Mabel Adelia (Wile) O.; e. Acadia Univ., B.Sc. 1963, B.Sc. (Honours) 1964, D.Sc. (Hon.) 1984; Northwestern Univ., Ph.D. 1968; Univ. of New Brunswick D.Sc. (Hon.) 1991; m. Roleen d. Roland and Mabel Lockhart 7 May 1964; children: Kristine Sheryl, Kevin Alexander; PRESIDENT, ACADIA UNIV. 1993– ; Vice-Pres., Acad., & Prof. of Chem., Acadia Univ. 1987–93; Mem., Dupont of Can. Spec. Summer Practice Group 1964; Asst. Prof., Dept. of Chem., Univ. of Man. 1968–72 (tenure 1971); Assoc. Prof. 1972–74; McGill Univ. 1974–78 (tenure 1978); Fac. Lectr., Dept. of Biochem. 1978; Prof., Dept. of Chem. 1978–88; Dir., Off. of Biotechnol. 1984–87; Bd. of Dir., ens Bio Logicals Inc. 1980–84 (Sci. Adv. Bd. 1979–84; Cons. 1979–89); Nova Biotechnol. Inc. 1986–87; Cons., The Upjohn Co. 1974–78, Candn. Pacific 1986–87; fellowships: E.W.R. Steacie Mem. 1982–84; Chem. Inst. of Can. 1977; Knight of Malta, Order of Merit, Sov. Military Order of St. John of Jerusalem 1985; Candn. Pacific Prof. of Biotechnol. 1984–87; Buck-Whitney Medal, E. N.Y. Section, Am. Chem. Soc. 1983; 1988 McLean's Honor Roll of Canadians Who Made a Difference; Mystery Guest, Front Page Challenge 1989; Mem., Order of Canada 1991; listed NSERC Publication; Great Candn. Success Stories 1991; Manning Principal Award 1992; Invited Lectr. on Biotechnology, Tianjin, China 1985; Fisher Scientific Biotechnology Council 1989–92; Nova Scotia Council on Appld. Sci. & Tech. (CAST), 1989–93; Nova Scotia Voluntary Planning Group 1989– ; Bd. of Dir., Nova Scotia Rsch. Found. Corp. 1990–91; Snider Lectr., Univ. of Toronto 1991; Gwen Leslie Memorial Lectr., CHEAC 1991; Ed. Bd., 'Nucleosides and Nucleotides,' 1981–92; Bd. of Gov., Plant Biotechnol. Inst., Sask. 1987–90; Mem., NSERC Targeted Rsch. Ctte. 1988–91; Chair, Adv. Bd., NRC Institute for Marine Biosciences 1990–93; Scientific Adv. Bd., Allelix Bio-pharmaceuticals 1991–93; Ordre des Chim. du Qué. 1980– ; Am. Assn. for the Adv. of Sci. 1982– ; Chem. Inst. of Can. 1961– ; Assn. Can.-Fran. pour l'Avancement des Sci. 1978– ; mem., National Adv. Ctte. on Biotech. 1989– ; author of 150 journal articles, 91 conf. papers, 12 patents, 200 public lectures; Inventor of BIOLF-62 = Ganciclovir, anti CMV drug marketed worldwide; recreations: curling, fishing, boating, stamp collecting, winter camping, dog sledding; Home: P.O. Box 307, Canning, N.S. B0P 1H0; Office: Wolfville, N.S. B0P 1X0.

**OGILVIE, Margaret Helen,** B.A., LL.B., M.A., D.Phil., F.R.S.C.; barrister and solicitor; educator; b. Falkirk, Scotland 25 Sept. 1948; d. James and Henrietta Susan (Walker) Ogilvie; e. Trinity Coll., Univ. of Toronto B.A. 1971; St. Hilda's Coll., Oxford Univ. D.Phil. 1974, B.A. 1976, M.A. 1976; Dalhousie Univ. LL.B. 1977; m. Dr. David Lindsay Thurburn Conn 21 Apr. 1975; PROFESSOR OF LAW, CARLETON UNIVERSITY 1986– ; articled with Daley, Black and Moreira, Halifax, N.S. 1977–78; called to Bar of Nova Scotia 1978; articled with Osler, Hoskin and Harcourt, Toronto, Ont. 1984; called to Bar of Ontario 1984; elected Fellow, Royal Soc. of Canada 1993; Asst. Prof. of Law, Carleton Univ 1978–81; Assoc. Prof. 1981–86; Lctr. in Law, Faculty of Law (Common Law Section) Univ. of Ottawa 1982–83, 1985–86; Visiting Prof., Faculties of Law and Divinity, Univ. of Edinburgh 1989; Visiting Scholar, Faculty of Law, Univ. of Toronto 1992–93; Sr. Visiting Fellow, Massey College, Univ. of Toronto 1992–93; Visiting Fellow, St. Hilda's College, Oxford Univ. 1993; Dir. of Rsch., Fasken & Calvin 1986–88; Scholar in Residence, Law Dept., Royal Bank of Canada 1992–93; Legal Editor, Carleton Library Series 1979–85; Dir., Carleton Univ. Press 1982–85; Ed. Adv. Bd., Carleton Univ. Press 1988–93; Provost, Carleton Debating Society 1985–86; Contributing Editor, Ottawa L. Rev. 1985–89; Mem., Ed. Bd., Banking and Finance Law Review; Mem., Ed. Bd., Canadian Business Law Journal; Candn. Contributing Ed., Journal of Business Law; Mem. Temporal Comm. St. Andrews Ch., Ottawa 1981–84; Mem. Comm. on Church Doctrine, Presbyterian Ch. in Canada 1984–90; Mem., Senate, Presbyterian College, Montreal 1990–96; Mem., Ctte. on Theological Education, Presbyterian Church in Canada 1993–96; Dir., Am. Friends of St. Hilda's Coll., Oxford 1988–90; author: 'Historical Introduction to Legal Studies' 1982; 'Banking. The Law in Canada' 1985; 'Consumer Law: Cases and Materials' 1989, 2nd ed. 1993; 'Banking Law Cases' 1990; 'Canadian Banking Law' 1991; numerous articles, comments and reviews; Mem. Canadian Bar Assn.; N.S. Barr. Soc.; Law Soc. Upper Can.; Canadian Assn. Law Teachers; Osgoode Soc.; Selden Soc.; Stair Soc.; Canadian Law & Soc. Assn.; Am. Soc. for Legal Hist.; Presbyterian; Home: 12 Ossington Ave., Ottawa, Ont. K1S 3B4; Office: Dept. of Law, Carleton Univ., Ottawa, Ont. K1S 5B6.

**OGILVIE, Richard Ian,** M.D., F.R.C.P.(C.), F.A.C.P.; professor of medicine and pharmacology; b. Sudbury, Ont. 9 Oct. 1936; s. Patrick Ian and Gena Hilda (Olson) O.; e. Univ. of Toronto M.D. 1960, F.R.C.P.(C). 1966; m. Ernestine d. Heinrich and Elisabeth Tahedl 9 Oct. 1965; children: Degen Elisabeth, Lars Ian; PROFESSOR OF MEDICINE AND PHARMACOLOGY, UNIV. OF TORONTO 1983– ; Intern, Toronto Gen. Hosp. 1960–61; Res., Montreal Gen. & Univ. (Alta.) Hosps. 1962–66; Fellow, Clinical pharmacol., McGill Univ. 1966–68; Asst. Prof. 1968–73; Assoc. 1973–78; Prof. 1978–83; Chair, Pharmacol. & Therapeutics 1978–83; Clin. Pharmacol., Montreal Gen. Hosp. 1968–83; Dir., Div. of Clin. Pharmacol. 1976–83; Dir., Div. of Cardiology and Clin. Pharmacol., Toronto Western Hosp. 1983–88; Visiting Prof. at 7 univs. most recent: Univ. of Calgary 1992, Nat. Training Centers for Clin. Pharmacol., Peoples Rep. of China 1986; Mem., Pharmacol. Grants Ctte., MRC 1977–82 (Chair 1980–82); Med. Adv. Ctte., Que. Heart Found. 1976, '82 (Chair 1980–82; Bd. of Dir., PMAC Health Care Found. 1986–92; Hon. Sec.-Treas., Banting Rsch. Found. 1984–87 (Chair, Grant Review Ctte.) 1985–86; Mem., Can. Soc. for Clin. Invest. (Council 1977–80); Can. Hypertension Soc. (Dir. 1979–81, 1989– ; Pres. 1992–93); Candn. Soc. for Clin. Pharmacol. (Pres. 1979–82); Internat. Union of Pharmacol. (Council Mem. 1981–84; Chair 1984–87); Pharmacol. Soc. of Can.; Candn. Cardiovascular Soc.; Am. Soc. of Pharmacol. & Exp. Therapeutics; Am. Soc. Clin. Pharmacol.; Toronto Hypertension Soc. (Pres. 1988– ); Jury, Prix Galien 1993– ; Jury, PMAC Gold Medal of Honour 1989; Chair, Knights of Malta Prize in Med. Ethics 1988– ; Fellow, Candn. Found. for the Advancement of Therapeutics 1967–69; Decorated Knight of Malta Sovereign Military Order of Saint John of Jerusalem; Knight Commander 1987; Knight Grand Cross 1990; Senior Investigator Award, Candn. Soc. for Clin. Pharmacol. 1993; awarded grants from Candn. Kidney Found.; J.C. Edwards Found.; MRC; Que. Heart Found.; Candn. Found. for the Adv. of Therapeutics; Conseil de la rech. en santé du Qué.; editor: 'Hypertension Canada' 1989– ; former edit. bd. mem. of 4 journals; Home: 79 Collard Dr., R.R. #1, King City, Ont. L7B 1E4; Office: 399 Bathurst St., Toronto, Ont. M5T 2S8.

**OGILVIE, Robert D.,** Ph.D.; university professor; b. Ottawa, Ont. 9 Apr. 1941; s. Shirley George and Hilda Muriel (Landon) O.; e. Carleton Univ., B.A. 1962; Hollins Coll., M.A. 1964; Univ. of Cambridge, Ph.D. 1985; m. Margaret F. d. Findlay and Nancy Barnes 11 July 1964; children: Shirley-Anne, Jennifer, Jonathan; PROF., DEPT. OF PSYCHOLOGY, BROCK UNIV.; Chrmn., Dept. of Psychology 1988–91; Sleep Researcher, studying the Psychophysiology of Sleep & Wakefulness; examining the transition into sleep; studying dream psychophysiology; recreations: running, swimming; Home: 50 Bridge St. W., Port Robinson, Ont. L0S 1K0; Office: 500 Glenridge Ave., St. Catharines, Ont. L2S 3A1.

**OGILVIE, Robert Murray,** B.Com., C.A.; executive; b. Ottawa, Ont. 29 May 1945; s. Robert Denzil and Margaret Claire (Murray) O.; e. Mount Allison Univ. B.Com. 1967; McGill Univ. C.A. 1969; m. Robin d. Robert and Elizabeth Thompson 11 Sept. 1980; one s. Robert Anthes; CHRMN., PRES. & C.E.O., TOROMONT INDUSTRIES LTD. 1987– ; Chrmn., Enerflex Systems Ltd.; Dir. Lewis Refrigeration Co.; Aero Tech Mfg. Inc.; Kimmel-Motz Refrigeration Corp.; ScottPolar Corp.; AGF Management Ltd.; Pres. and Chief Extve. Offr. Sentrol Systems Ltd. 1977–82; Pres. Canadian Corporate Funding Ltd. 1983–85; Pres. present Co. 1985; recreations: tennis, skiing; clubs: Cambridge, Toronto Cricket Skating & Curling; Home: 10 Plymbridge Rd., Toronto, Ont. M4N 2H5; Office: P.O. Box 20011, Concord, Ont. L4K 4T1.

**OGLE, Father Robert Joseph,** O.C., B.A., J.C.D., D.D.; priest; b. Rosetown, Sask. 24 Dec. 1928; s. Henry Bernard and Annie Mary (Brennan) O.; e. Univ. of W. Ont. B.A. 1949; Univ. of Ottawa J.C.D. 1957; Univ. of Sask. D.D. 1989; St. Pauls Univ. Ottawa D.D. 1989; FOUNDER, BROADCASTING FOR INTERNAT. UNDERSTANDING 1985– ; o. 1953; various Pastoral Activities Saskatoon diocese; Missy. N.E. Brazil 6 yrs.; recipient Assoc. Award Rsch. Internat. Devel. Rsch. Centre Ottawa 1976; el. to H. of C. for Saskatoon-East (NDP) 1979–84; O.C. 1989; author 'Faculties of Military Chaplains' 1957; 'When the Snake Bites the Sun' 1977; 'North-South Calling' 1986; 'A Man of Letters' 1990; former Pres. W. Conf. Priests; Officer, Order of Canada; rec'd., Honorary LL.D., Univ. of St. Francis Xavier, Antigonish 1992; mem. K. of C.; R. Catholic; recreation: friends; Home: 220, 2902 Louise St., Saskatoon, Sask. S7J 3M2; Office: 249 Main St., Ottawa, Ont. K1S 1C5.

**OGLOFF, James Robert Powell,** B.A., M.A., J.D., Ph.D.; university professor; b. Calgary, Alta. 20 July 1962; s. Alec and Patricia Ruth (Powell) O.; e. Crescent Heights H.S. Calgary 1980; Univ. of Calgary B.A. 1984; Univ. of Saskatchewan M.A. 1986; Univ. of Nebraska College of Law, J.D. (with distinction) 1989, Ph.D. 1990; m. Kathleen Mary d. D.M. Picken 2 June 1984; one d. Aleksandra; ASSOC. PROF. & ASSOCIATE CHAIR OF PSYCHOLOGY, SIMON FRASER UNIV. 1990– ; Assoc. Mem. of Criminolgy, Simon Fraser Univ. 1992– ; Mem., Mental Health, Law and Policy Inst.; Chair Review Panel, Mental Health Act, Ministry of Health B.C. 1992–95; Mem., Am. Psych. Assn.; Candn. Psych. Assn.; Candn. Bar Assn.; Am. Psych. Law Soc.; editor: 'Law and Psychology: The Broadening of the Discipline' 1992; Home: 29, 2662 Morningstar Cres., Vancouver, B.C. V5S 4P4; Office: Burnaby, B.C. V5S 1A6.

**O'HARA, Catherine;** actress, comedienne; b. Toronto, Ont. 4 Mar. 1954; m. Bo Welch 1992; Actress, writer with Second City Toronto 1974; Co-founder of SCTV 1976 (Emmy Award); films incl. 'After Hours' 1985, 'Heartburn' 1986, 'Beetlejuice' 1988, 'Dick Tracy' 1990, 'Betsy's Wedding' 1990, 'Home Alone' 1990, 'Home Alone II' 1993, Little Vegas, Pay Dirt; TV, SCTV, Comic Relief, 'Dream On' (Dir.); Co-writer, SCTV, Cinemax, 1984, Really Weird Tales, HBO 1896; Office: c/o ICM, 8899 Beverly Blvd., Los Angeles, Ca. 90048.

**O'HARA, Jane,** B.A.; journalist; b. Toronto, Ont. 24 July 1951; d. John Gerard and Margaret Elizabeth Charleton O.; e. Univ. of Toronto B.A. 1975; SOUTHAM FELLOW, MASSEY COLLEGE, UNIV. OF TORONTO 1993; Reporter, Toronto Sun 1975; European Bureau, FP News Service 1978 (based in London); Sr. Writer, National Editor, N.Y. & Vanc. Bureau Chief, Maclean's 1979–88; Sports Editor & Columnist, Ottawa Sun 1989; Southam Fellowship Award 1993; Dunlop Award Winner 1990, '92; author: 'Marjorie Nichols: A Very Political Reporter' 1992, 'Union Jack: Labour Leader Jack Munro' 1988, 'Bryan Adams' 1989, 'British Columbia, The Lampoon' 1986; recreations: tennis (Candn. Champion 1975; played on Canada's nat. tennis team in internat. comp. 1968–75); Office: 63 Arundel Ave., Toronto, Ont. M4K 3A3.

**O'HARA, Pat,** B.F.A.; artist; b. Burns Lake, B.C. 19 Apr. 1936; d. Richard C. and Daisy M. (Shaw) O.; e. Univ. of B.C.; Emily Carr Coll. of Art & Design B.F.A. (Honors Painting & Merit Award); m. Richard s. Jake and Anne Schneider 25 June 1965; children: David, Jason; artist at Bau Xi Gall. Vanc. & Toronto; 34 solo or group exhibitions 1969–91; painting in acrylic and multi-media collage on paper & canvas 10' x 5' to 6" x 8"; Teacher, Vancouver Sch. Bd. 13 years; 1 year England; currently teaching Arts Umbrella (Granville Island) children's art sch.; Home: 4613 West 6th Ave., Vancouver, B.C. V6R 1V6.; Studio: 901 Main St., 4th floor, Vancouver, B.C.

**OKA, Takeshi,** Ph.D., F.R.S.C., F.R.S.; physicist; chemist; astronomer; b. Tokyo, Japan 10 June 1932; s. Shumpei and Chiyoko (Ozaki) O.; e. Univ. of Tokyo B.Sc. 1955, M.Sc. 1957, Ph.D. 1960; m. Keiko d. Kozo Nukui, Saitama, Japan 24 Oct. 1960; children: Ritsuko, Noriko, Kentaro, Yujiro; PROFESSOR, UNIVERSITY OF CHICAGO, Dept. of Chem., Astronomy and Astrophysics since 1981; Robert A. Millikan Distinguished Service Professor 1989; Sr. Research Offr., Herzberg Inst. of Astrophysics, Nat. Research Council 1971–81; Asst., Univ. of Tokyo 1960–63; Postdoctorate Fellow, Nat. Research Council 1963, Asst. Research Offr. 1965, Assoc. Research Offr. 1968–71; rec'd Steacie Prize 1972; Earl K. Plyler Prize 1982; mem.; Am. Phys. Soc.; Internat. Astron. Union; Am. Astron. Soc.; Optical Soc. of America; Am. Acad. of Sci. and Arts; recreation: running; Home: 1463 East Park Place, Chicago, IL 60637; Office: 5735 South Ellis Ave., Chicago, IL 60637.

**OKE, Timothy Richard,** B.Sc., M.A., Ph.D., FRSC; university professor; b. Devon, U.K. 22 Nov. 1941; s. Leslie and Annie Kathleen (Smerdon) O.; e. Lord Wandsworth College Basingstoke 1960; Univ. of Bristol B.Sc. (Hons.) 1963; McMaster Univ. M.A. 1964, Ph.D. 1967; m. Margaret d. George and Ethel Lowe 21 July 1967; children: Nicholas James, Kathleen Mary; PROFESSOR, DEPT. OF GEOGRAPHY, UNIV. OF B.C. 1978– ; Asst. Prof., McGill Univ. 1967–70; Univ. of B.C. 1970–71; Assoc. Prof. 1971–78; Head, Dept. of Geography 1991– ; Dir., Thermal Mapping Internat. (Canada) Inc.; Consultant, World Meteorological Orgn.; CMOS Accredited Consulting Meteorologist; President's Prize, Candn. Meteorol. Soc. 1972; Candn. Assn. Geog. Award for Scholarly Distinction 1986; Killam Research Prize 1988; Guggenheim Fellow 1990; Symons Lecture (Royal Meteorol. Soc.); Hooker Visiting Prof. (McMaster); Visiting Fellow, Keble College Oxford; Resident Scholar (Rockefeller Found.); Fellow, Royal Soc. of Canada; Royal Geographical Soc.; Editor, 'Atmosphere-Ocean'; Ed. Bd. Mem., 'Int. J. Climatology,' 'Boundary-Layer Meteorology,' 'Progress in Physical Geography,' 'Atmospheric Environment'; Mem., Am. Assn. of Geographers; Am. Geophys. Union; Am. Meteorol. Soc.; Can. Assn. Geographers; Candn. Meteorol. & Ocean Soc.; Royal Can. Geog. Soc.; Royal Meteorol. Soc.; Royal Soc. Canada; author: 'Boundary Layer Climates' 1978, 1987; co-author: 'The Climate of Vancouver' 1975; co-editor: 'Vancouver and its Region' 1992; author/co-author of 99 scientific jour. articles; supervisor of 9 M.Sc. & 8 Ph.D. theses; recreations: golf, walking; Home: 3776 West 39th Ave., Vancouver, B.C. V6N 3A7; Office 1984 West Mall, Vancouver, B.C. V6T 1Z2.

**OKHAI, Adam Jafaar,** LL.B., C.A., M.B.A., C.M.C.; educational executive; b. Zomba, Zimbabwe 27 Jan. 1955; s. Abu Suleiman and Mariym (Mussa) O.; e. Kings College School 1968; Oxford Univ. LL.B. (Hons.) 1970; Inst. of C.A.s in England & Wales C.A. 1973; Harvard Univ. M.B.A. 1978; single; PRESIDENT & GROUP CHIEF EXECUTIVE OFFICER, MOYER'S INC., KIDS ARE WORTH IT!, LATTA'S INC., MORGAN'S EDUCATIONAL SUPPLIES and many affiliated corps. in Europe & Africa 1989– (selected by 'Financial Post' as best managed corporation); Principal, Authur Young Mngt. Cons. 1980; started an educational co. to develop products for learning disabled children & children with special needs 1983; Pres., Moyer Vico Corp. 1984; director of var. major corps. incl. Comet Internat. Inc.; Fabian Trust; Founder, Pres. & Dir. of Mngt. Diagnostis Inc.; C.E.O., Okhai Electronics Corp.; Mem., Young Pres. Orgn.; Inst. of C.A.s of Ont. 1975– ; Inst. of Management Consultants 1981– ; has served on var. assn. cttes. incl. National School Supply Assn.; recipient of var. awards incl. Retail Council's Award, Am. Retailer Award; Officer, Inst. for the Prevention of Abuse Towards children; active in Institute to Find Missing Children and in assisting, to a modest extent, children in war-torn countries; founder of a community centre in North York to assist young children; co-author: 'Towards 2000'; author: 'Cry Freedom ... A Human Rights Treatise' and var. papers in profl. journals; recreations: biking, swimming; clubs: Young Pres. Orgn. and others; Home: 287 Wycliffe Avenue, Woodbridge, Ont. L4L 3N7; Office: 25 Milvan Dr., Weston, Ont. M9L 1Z1.

**OKO, Andrew Jan,** B.A., M.A.; arts executive; b. London, England 7 Sept. 1946; s. Jan Kazimierz and Julia Helena (Suska) O.; e. Univ. of Calgary B.A. 1968; Univ. of Toronto M.A. 1972; m. Helen Marie Blanc 21 Dec. 1972; children: Sonya Celeste, Michelle Kathleen; DIRECTOR, MACKENZIE ART GALLERY 1986– ; Preparator, Glenbow Mus. 1972–73; Curatorial Asst. 1973–74; Asst. Curator 1974–77; Curator, Art Gallery of Hamilton 1977–86; Past Pres., Sask. Arts Alliance (Pres. 1991–93); author: 'Country Pleasures: The Angling Art of Jack Cowin' 1984; co-author: 'Art Gallery Handbook' 1982; curator/author of numerous exbn. catalogues; Mem., Candn. Museum Assn.; Candn. Art Mus. Dirs. Orgn.; Rotary Club of Regina; recreations: flyfishing, swimming, music; Home: 3388 Westminster Rd., Regina, Sask. S4V 1C2; Office: 3475 Albert St., Regina, Sask. S4S 6X6.

**OKULITCH, Vladimir Joseph,** M.A.Sc., Ph.D., F.R.S.C., F.G.S.A., D.Sc. (Hon.) U.B.C. 1972; dean emeritus; b. St. Petersburg, Russia, 18 June 1906; e. Peabody Grammar Sch., Cambridge, Mass.; Russo-Serbian Lyceum, Belgrade, Yugoslavia; Univ. of Brit. Columbia, M.A.Sc. (Geol. Engn.) 1932; McGill Univ., Ph.D. (Geol.) 1934; Harvard Univ., Research Fellow 1934–36; m. Suzanne, d. Peter V. Kouhar, 19 Jan. 1934; children: Andrew, Peter; DEAN EMERITUS, FAC. OF SCIENCE; Mine Geol., Atlin Silver-Lead Mines, 1930–32; Lectr. and Asst. Prof., Univ. of Toronto, 1936–44; Assoc. Prof. of Geol., Univ. of B.C., 1944–49; subsequently Prof. of Palaeontol. and Stratigraphy and Head Dept. of Geol. there; retired as Dean Emeritus of Science Sept. 1971; Fellow, Palaeontol. Soc.; Geol. Society of America; Royal Astron. Society of Canada; Royal Society of Canada; author of 'North American Pleospongia' (monograph on Cambrian organisms) 1943; has contributed over sixty scientific papers to technical journals; Greek Orthodox; recreations: photography, astronomy, camping, mountain climbing; Club: University; Home: 4504 - 49 St. N.W., Calgary, Alta. T3A 1X4.

**OLAND, Bruce S.C.;** masterbrewer; b. Guildford, Eng. 31 March 1918; s. Col. Sidney Culverwell and Herlinda (deBedia) O.; e. King's Coll. Sch., Windsor, N.S.; Beaumont Coll., Old Windsor, Eng.; Un. Brewers' Acad., U.S.A.; m. Ruth, d. James Edward Hurley, Westfield, N.J., 17 Nov. 1956; children: Richard Hurley, Deborah Ruth; Pres. Culverwell Holdings Ltd.; Lindwood Holdings Ltd.; Oland Investments Ltd.; Dir. Maritime Paper Ltd.; Ben's Ltd.; The Bill Lynch Memorial Fund; Hon. Consul Gen. of Japan at Halifax; served with 1st Halifax Coast Regt., R.C.A., 1939–45; rank Maj. on discharge; Reserve Army 1946–51; joined R.C.N. Reserve 1951; Sr. Reserve Naval Advisor to Depy. Gen. Reserves; rank Commodore; Dir., R.C.N. Benevolent Fund; Past Chrmn. of Bd., Hon. Govs., N.S. Div., Candn. Assn. Mentally Retarded; Dir. and Past Pres., Halifax Sch. for Blind; Dir., Un. Services Inst.; mem., Naval Offrs.' Assn; Nat. Council, Duke of Edinburgh's Award in Can.; Gov. Candn. Corps of Commissionaires, N.S. Div.; R. Catholic; recreations: squash, sailing, numismatics, philately; Home: 'The Anchor,' Marlborough Woods, Halifax, N.S. B3H 1H9; Office: 1475 Hollis St., Halifax, N.S. B3J 1V1.

**OLAND, Derek;** brewery executive; b. Saint John, N.B. 29 Sept. 1939; s. Philip Warburton and Mary Walker (Frink) O.; e. Rothesay Coll. Sch. 1957; Univ. of N.B., B.B.A. 1962; m. Jacqueline Iris d. William and Marjorie Evans 25 June 1965; children; Andrew, Patrick, Matthew, Giles; PRES. & CHIEF OPERATING OFFR., MOOSEHEAD BREWERIES LTD. 1983– ; Dir., Halifax-Dartmouth Ind. Ltd.; L.E. Shaw Ltd.; Maritime Telegraph & Telephone Co. Ltd.; Nova Scotia Power; Pratt & Whitney Canada Inc.; Royal Ins. Can.; joined Moosehead Breweries 1962; Mktg. Mrg. 1964; Gen. Mgr., N.S. Opn. 1968; Dir. & Vice Pres. 1970; Extve. Vice Pres. 1976–83; mem., Bus. Adv. Bd., Dalhousie Sch. of Bus. Admin.; Bd. of Gov., Rothesay Coll. Sch.; Past Pres., United Way of Halifax-Dartmouth; Dartmouth YM-YWCA; Dir., Brewers Assn. of Can.; recreations: skiing, tennis, fishing, sailing; Clubs: Halifax; Royal Nova Scotia Yacht Squadron; Home: 1454 Birchdale Ave., Halifax, N.S. B3H 4E3; Office: 656 Windmill Rd., Dartmouth, N.S. B3B 1B8.

**OLAND, Erik,** B.Mus.; classical singer; b. Saint John, N.B.; s. Geoffrey Charles Lannen and Nancy Alyere (Aucoin) O.; e. Saint John H.S. 1976; Mount Allison Univ. B.Mus. 1981; involved in leading capacity in the premieres of important Canadian works: David Willson in 'Serinette' by Harry Somers, Benjamin in 'The Five of Hearts' by James Fusco, Sidney Herbert in 'Florence' by Timothy Sullivan (operas); 'Prime Time' by John Weinzweig, 'Hymne pour une equinoxe' by Yuri Laniuk (chamber music); performed in Great Britain with Aldeburgh Connection; in France, Spain & Portugal with L'Opera de Montréal; versatile performer (at home in opera & concert repertoire), e.g. Bach: St. John Passion, Mozart: The Magic Flute, Puccini: Madame Butterfly, Faure: Requiem, Vaughan-Williams: Mystical Songs; Voice Teacher, Concordia Univ.; Prize Winner, L'Orch. Symph. de Montréal Competition; s'Hertoganbosch Singing Competition (Holland); 3 Canada Council grants; Roman Catholic; Mem., Union des Artistes; ACTRA; Candn. Authors Equity; compact disc recordings: 'Le Canada Romantique,' 'Les Cantates de Rameau'; recreations: avid swimmer and cyclist; Home: P.O. Box 228, Rothesay, N.B. E0G 2W0; Office: c/o Hart Murdock Artists Management, 204A St. George St., Toronto, Ont. M5R 2N6.

**OLAND, Philip W.,** O.C. (1970), C.D., B.Sc., LL.D., D.Litt.; brewery executive; b. Halifax, N.S. 1910; m. Mary H. Frink, Rothesay, N.B., 1936; children: Derek, Richard, Jane (Mrs. Jane Toward); CHRMN. AND C.E.O., MOOSEHEAD BREWERIES LTD.; Dir. Emeritus, Candn. Imperial Bank of Commerce; Chrmn., Coastal Transport Ltd., Saint John, N.B.; Gov., Confederation Centre of the Arts; Hon. Vice-Pres., New Brunswick Rifle Assoc.; Patron of the Lester B. Pearson College of the Pacific; served with Candn. Army in N.W. Europe; Commdr., 6 Militia Group until 1961; rank Brigadier; Hon. Pres. N.B. Youth Orch.; N.B. Army Cadet League, Inc.; Chrmn. Saint John Foundation Inc.; Office: P.O. Box 3100, Stn B, Saint John, N.B. E2M 3H2.

**OLDHAM, Dennis M.,** B.Com., C.M.A.; insurance executive; b. Montréal, Qué. 20 Apr. 1942; s. Clifford Steven and Eileen (Bausmer) O.; e. Montréal West High Sch. 1958; Sir George Williams Univ. B.Com. 1968; C.M.A. 1971; m. Judy d. Emile and Eugenie Schirmer 22 Sept. 1979; children: Laura, Ryan; SR. VICE PRES. & CHIEF FINANCIAL OFFR., WILLIS CORROON MELLING INC. 1973– ; Mgr. Acctg. JWI Ltd. 1966–73; Dir. Mackay Center for Deaf & Crippled Children; Clubs: Summerlea Golf & Country; Montréal West Curling; Home: 256 Hollis Rd., Beaconsfield, Qué. H9W 2M7; Office: 1500, 1130 Sherbrooke St. W., Montréal, Qué. H3A 2M8.

**O'LEARY, Hon. Dennis F.,** B.A.; judge; b. Downeyville, Ont. 7 Nov. 1926; s. Dennis Michael and Kathleen (O'Brien) O'L.; e. St. Michael's Coll., Univ. of Toronto, B.A. 1949; Osgoode Hall Law Sch.; children: Dennis, Lisanne, Bridget, Sean; JUSTICE, SUPREME COURT OF ONT. since 1973; called to Bar of Ont. 1953; cr. Q.C. 1966; law practice in Hamilton, Ont. 1953–73; former Council mem., Candn. Bar Assn.; Past Pres., St. Thomas More Lawyer's Guild; R. Catholic; recreations: skiing, tennis; Club: Hamilton Lawyers' Club (Past Pres.); Office: Osgoode Hall, Toronto, Ont. M5H 2N5.

**O'LEARY, Hon. Willis Edward,** B.B.A., LL.M.; judge; b. Vulcan, Alta. 6 Sept. 1931; s. Cecil Patrick and Helen D. (Maloney) O'L.; e. Univ. of Denver B.B.A. 1953; Univ. of B.C. LL.B. 1962; Harvard Law Sch. LL.M. 1963; m. Betty Eileen d. Joseph and Elizabeth Barrett 25 May 1962; children: John Willis, Thomas Patrick, Shannon Elizabeth; JUDGE, COURT OF QUEEN'S BENCH, ALTA. 1984– ; Club: Glencoe; Office: 611 – 4th St. S.W., Calgary, Alta. T2P 1T5.

**OLIPHANT, Betty,** C.C. (1985), LL.D. (hon.) Queen's Univ. and Brock Univ. 1978, Univ. of Toronto, 1980; York Univ. D.Litt. (hon.) 1992; b. London, Eng. 5 Aug. 1918; d. Stuart and Yvonne (Mansfield) O.; e. Queen's Coll. Sch. and St. Mary's Coll. Sch., London, Eng.; rec'd. classical ballet training from Tamara Karsavina and Laurent Novikoff; two d.; FOUNDER, THE NATIONAL BALLET SCHOOL; estbd. own sch. for prof. dancers in London, Eng. and created and directed dance sequences in W. End theatres prior to coming to Can. in 1947; estbd. Betty Oliphant School of Ballet 1948–59; Ballet Mistress, Nat. Ballet of Can., 1951–62; Founding Dir., The National Ballet School 1959–79; Artistic Dir. & Ballet Principal 1979–89; Founder & Artistic Advisor 1989–91; Founder 1991– ; Assoc. Artistic Dir., Nat. Ballet of Can. 1969–75; as lectr., examiner and auditioner has travelled across Can., U.S., and abroad; 1967 reorganized the Royal Swedish Opera Ballet Sch.; 1978 reorganized Ballet Sch. of the Royal Danish Theatre; and has visited Moscow and Leningrad as guest of Bolshoi and Kirov Ballet Schs.; attended First Internat. Ballet Competition in Moscow as a guest of honour of Soviet Union, 1969; mem. of jury, Third International Ballet Competition, Moscow, 1977, and Fourth Competition, 1981; mem. of jury, Prix de Lausanne, Switzerland 1991; rec'd. Centennial Medal 1967; Diplôme d'honneur, Candn. Conference of the Arts 1982; created Officer, Order of Can. 1973; Companion, Order of Can. 1985; Molson Prize, 1978; Fellow, The Ont. Inst. for Studies in Educ. 1985; mem. of jury, Third Internat. Ballet Competition, Jackson, Mississippi 1986; Lifetime Achievement Award, Toronto Arts Awards Foundation, 1989; Order of Napoleon, France 1990; Rotary Internat. Paul Harris Fellow 1992; recipient, 125th Anniversary of the Confederation of Canada Medal, 1992; Fellow and Examiner, Imp. Soc. Teachers Dancing; Charter mem. and a Past Pres., Candn. Dance Teachers Assn.; Founding mem., Can. Assn. of Professional Dance Organizations; recreations: reading, swimming, theatre, concerts, music; Club: McGill; Home: 137 Amelia Street, Toronto, Ont. M4X 1E6.

**OLIPHANT, Hon. Jeffrey James,** LL.B.; judge; b. Dauphin, Man. 10 Feb. 1944; s. James Swan and Wilhelmina Opal (Taylor) O.; e. Univ. of Man., LL.B. 1967; m. Irene d. Joseph and Annette Jeannotte 12 July 1969; children: Joel Jeffrey, Renae Jane; ASSOC. CHIEF JUSTICE, COURT OF QUEEN'S BENCH MAN. 1990– ; Assoc. law firm Johnston, Johnston & Johnston (later Johnston, Oliphant, Van Buekenhout & Deans), Dauphin, Man. 1969, Partner 1971–85; cr. Q.C. 1980; Dir. Legal Aid Man. 1973–78; Vice Chrmn. Man. Police Comn. 1978–81, Chrmn. 1981–85; Judge, Court of Queen's Bench Man. 1985–90; Roman Catholic; recreations: flying, golf, hunting; Office: 408 York Ave., Winnipeg, Man. R3C 0P9.

**OLIPHANT, Laurence E. (Larry) III,** B.A.; auto industry executive; b. Evanston, Ill. 27 Aug. 1938; s. Laurence E. (Jr) and Adele Grace (Stern) O.; e. Northwestern Univ. B.A.; m. Denise M. d. Raymond and Nancy McDonald 27 Dec. 1965; children: Laurence IV, David, Nancy, Peter, Elizabeth; PRES. & CHIEF EXTVE. OFFR., VOLVO GM CANADA HEAVY TRUCK 1989– ; Vice-Pres., Great Lakes Reg., White Motor Corp. Chicago 1972–79; Worldwide Truck Parts, Internat. Harvester Chicago 1979–82; Vice-Pres. & Gen. Mgr., Autocar Div., Volvo White Truck Corp. Ogden, Utah 1982–83; Vice-Pres., Sales & Mktg., Volvo GM Heavy Truck Corp., Greensboro, N.C. 1983–89; recreations: family, golf, music; Office: 855 Steeles Ave. E., P.O. Box 1011, Milton, Ont. L9T 4B6.

**OLIVE, David Michael,** B.A.A.; writer; b. Toronto, Ont. 9 Nov. 1957; s. Harold Leslie and Alison Linton (Black) O.; e. Sir Wilfrid Laurier Coll. Inst. Scarborough; Ryerson Polytech. Inst. B.A.A. (Jour.) 1979; m. Margaret Anne O'Reilly d. Michael and Mary Jane O'Reilly 13 Feb. 1982, div. 1992; EDITOR, REPORT ON BUSINESS MAGAZINE, THE GLOBE AND MAIL 1991– ; Ed. Asst., Asst. Ed., Copy Ed., Toronto Life mag. 1979–81; Asst. Ed., Assoc. Ed., Sr. Writer, Canadian Business mag. 1981–84; Sr. Writer, Report on Business Magazine 1984–87; Sr. Writer, Toronto Life 1988–90; Editorial Writer, The Globe and Mail 1990–91; Current Affairs columnist, Globe and Mail 1991–92; Co-editor, 'Body & Soul Magazine' Globe & Mail 1993– ; Book Reviewer, Globe and Mail, Toronto Star, Quill & Quire 1982– ; contbg. ed. 'Canadian Business' 1988–90; 'Guts, Greed and Glory: A Visual History of Modern Canadian Business' (book); 'Corporate Ethics Monitor' 1989– ; ed. 'Management Ethics' 1988–91; business panelist, CBC Radio program 'Later That Same Day' 1989; adjudicator, Applied Ethics Ctte., Social Sciences and Humanities Rsch. Council of Canada 1990; author: 'Just Rewards: The Case for Ethical Reform in Business' 1987; 'White Knights and Poison Pills: A Cynic's Dictionary of Business Jargon' 1990; 'Political Babble: The 1,000 Dumbest Things Ever Said By Politicians' 1992; 'Canadian Political Babble: A Cynic's Dictionary of Political Jargon' 1993; 'Gender Babble: The Dumbest Things Men Ever Said About Women' 1993; lectr., Banff Publishing Workshop (1986–90), Ryerson (1988–90), Toronto Publishing Workshop (1989–90); Dir., Nat. Mag. Awards Found. 1987–90, Pres. 1988–90; Dir. Candn. Centre for Ethics & Corporate Policy 1988–91; Housing Develop. Resource Centre 1990–91; Stop 103 Inc. 1990–91; mem., Candn. Soc. of Magazine Editors 1991– ; recipient Nat. Mag. Awards: Silver 1987, Gold (Pres. Medal) 1988, Hon. Mention 1983, 1985, 1987, 1989; Nat. Bus. Writing Awards 1983, 1985, Hon. Mention 1986; Nat. Jour. Award 1983; Office: 444 Front St. W., Toronto, Ont. M5V 2S9.

**OLIVER, Bobbie;** painter; b. Windsor, Ont. 17 June 1947; d. Ronald Alexander Oliver and Betty Jean (Blair) O.; e. Art Sch. for the Soc. of Arts & Crafts Detroit; St. Alban's Sch. of Art Herts., England; solo exhibitions: Wolff Gallery N.Y. 1985; Freidus/Ordover Gallery N.Y. 1984; R. McLaughlin Gallery Oshawa 1978; Olga Korper Gallery Toronto 1986, '87, '89, '91, '94; group exhibitions: Art Gallery of Ont. (2-person) 1978; Asst. Prof., Rhode Island Sch. of Design 1980– ; Acting Head, Ptg. Dept. 1982–83; Banff Sch. of Fine Art 1981; Head, Summer Prog., Ptg. 1985; Princeton Univ. 1981; Visiting Artist Anderson Ranch Colorado 1989; Can. Counc. Arts Grants (B); Ontario Arts Council; N.Y. State Counc. for the Arts grant; Edward Albee Found. Fellowship; Pollock-Krasner grant; Home: 140 West Broadway, New York, NY 10013.

**OLIVER, Donald H.,** Q.C., B.A.(Hon.), LL.B.; b. Wolfville, N.S. 16 Nov. 1938; s. Clifford H. and Helena I. (White) O.; e. Acadia Univ., B.A. (Hons.) History 1960; Dalhousie Univ., LL.B. 1964; m. M. Linda d. Duncan and Mildred MacLellan 29 Aug. 1981; one d.: Carolynn Marie; SENATOR, THE SENATE OF CANADA 1990; Chrmn., Senate Standing Ctte. on Transport and Communications; Member of the Senate Standing Ctte. on Energy, the Environment and Natural Resources; Past Member of the Senate Standing Ctte. on National Finance; Past Member of the Senate Standing Ctte. on Banking, Trade and Commerce; Past Member of the Special Joint Ctte. on a Renewed Canada; Past Member of the Special Joint Ctte. on Conflicts of Interests; Barrister-at-Law and Legal Counsel, Hennigar, Wells, Lamey & Baker, Barristers and Solicitors, Chester, (1992– ), Stewart, McKelvey, Stirling Scales, Halifax, Barristers & Solicitors, civil litigation (1965–90); Former Dir., P.C. Canada Fund; Mem., Royal Commission Inquiry on Electoral Reform & Party Financing 1990; Lectr., Technical Univ. of N.S.; Saint Mary's Univ.; Dalhousie Law Sch.; Pres., Glen Moir Holdings Ltd.; Former Dir., SOM Holdings Inc.; Can. Counc. Investment Ctte.; Chrmn., Metro Volunteer Resource Ctr.; Nat. Vice-Pres., P.C. Assn. of Can. 1983, 1986; author of a cookbook on French cuisine; recreations: alpine skiing, gardening, operates a Xmas tree plantation; clubs: Halifax, Saraguay; Office: The Senate of Canada, Ottawa, Ont. K1A 0A4.

**OLIVER, The Hon. Herbert Arnold Dimitri;** judge; b. 11 June 1921; s. David and Edith (Wutow) O.; e. Dean Close Sch. Cheltenham, Eng.; London Sch. of Econ. & Pol. Science; Law Soc.'s Sch. of Law London, Eng; m. Jeanne Hilda d. late Maj. H.R. King 10 Jan. 1959; children: David Richard Benedict, Mark Justin Dominic, Alexandra Edith Amelia; JUSTICE SUPREME COURT OF BRITISH COLUMBIA 1990– ; admitted Solicitor (Eng.) 1949 called to Bar, B.C. 1952, Alta. 1973; cr. Q.C. 1982; Bencher of Law Soc. of B.C. 1983–88; law practice London, Eng. 1949–52; Sr. Partner, Oliver Waldock 1952–88; Judge, Co. Court of Vancouver 1988–90; lectr. in advocacy and forensic med. bar assns., law schs., med. schs., forensic soc.'s Can., U.S.A. and Europe; Consul-Gen. of Liberia 1954–88; Secy.-Gen. Vancouver Consular Corps 1957–82; mem. Judicial Council B.C. 1975–81; Vice-Chairman Forensic Psychiatric Services Comn. B.C. 1980–88; Associate Editor, Western Weekly Law Reports 1983–90; served with Royal Norfolk Regt. 1939–46, Control Comn. for Germany; named Kt. Grand Cross Order African Redemption (Liberia); Offr. Fed. Order Merit (W. Germany); Kt. Grace Order St. John Jerusalem (Denmark); Chevalier de l'Ordre National du Mérite (France); Croix de Guerre (France); Freeman of City of London; mem. Internat. Wine & Food Soc. (Founding Pres. Vancouver Chapter); Commandeur de la Chaine des Rotisseurs; Alliance Française de Vancouver (Past Pres.); Vancouver Art Gallery Assn. (Past Vice Pres.); Eng. Speaking Union Commonwealth (Past Dir.); Fellow, Internat. Acad. Trial Lawyers; Fellow, Foundation Legal Research Can.; Gov., Law Found. of B.C. 1983–88; Fellow, Inst. Arbitrators (London); Fellow, Royal Commonwealth Soc.; mem. Law Soc. Eng.; Candn. Bar Assn. (past Chrmn. Criminal Justice Sec.); Vancouver Bar Assn.; Internat. Comn. Jurists; Internat. Bar Assn.; Soc. for the Reform of the Criminal Law; Am. Judges' Assn.; Judicial Mem., Assn. Trial Lawyers Am. (Gov. 1973–82); Trial Lawyers Assn. B.C. Distinguished Service Award; Vancouver East End Bar Award; Brit. Acad. Forensic Sciences; Anglican; recreation: yachting; Clubs: Vancouver; Union (Victoria); East India (London, Eng.); Office: Law Courts, 800 Smithe St., Vancouver, B.C. V6Z 2E1.

**OLIVER, John,** B.Mus., M.Mus., D.Mus.; composer, performer; b. Vancouver, B.C. 21 Sept. 1959; s. Edward and Thelma Isabel (Cameron) O.; e. San Francisco Conservatory of Music; Univ. of B.C. B.Mus. 1982; McGill Univ. M.Mus. 1984, D.Mus. 1992; established in Montreal from 1982–89 with num. performances & comns. by L'Orch. des Jeunes du Qué. & La Soc. de musique contemporaine du Qué.; conductor, guitarist & composer with GEMS; Composer-in-residence, Candn. Opera Co. 1989–91 where 1st opera 'Guacamayo's Old Song and Dance' was comnd & prod. Feb. 1991; Leighton Artist Colony 1989, '91; Camargo Found. 1990; moved to Vanc. 1990 where he continues to write & perform; Composer-in-residence, Vancouver Opera 1993– ; Music in the Morning 1993– ; Co-founder & Co-Dir., Group of the Electronic Music Studio (GEMS), Montreal 1983–87; Mem., MORE (an electroacoustic music ensemble in Vanc.) 1991–93; Assoc. Composer, Candn. Music Centre; Mem., Candn. League of Composers; Candn. Electroacoustic Community; Am. Fed. of Musicians; 1st Prize for Electronic Music & the Canada Council's Grand Prize, 8th CBC Nat. Radio Young Composers' Competition 1988; Dir., La fête colombienne des enfants 1990–91; Home: 9641 Townline Diversion, Surrey, B.C. V3V 2T1.

**OLIVER, Joseph J.,** B.A., B.C.L., M.B.A.; securities regulator; b. Montreal, Que. 20 May 1940; s. Ethel Oliver; e. McGill Univ. B.A. 1961, B.C.L. 1964; Harvard Univ. M.B.A. 1970; children: David, Jeffrey; VICE PRESIDENT, CORPORATE FINANCE, FIRST MARATHON SECURITIES; Vice-Pres. & Dir., Underwriting Div., Merrill Lynch Royal Securities Ltd. 1970–82; Sr. Vice-Pres. & Dir., Nesbitt Thomson Deacon Inc. 1982–91; Extve. Dir., Ontario Securities Commission 1991–94; Mem., Investment Dealers' Assn. (Extve. Ctte. 1985–86); Toronto Stock Exchange (Stock List Ctte. 1988–91); Bd. of Dir. & Extve. Ctte., Mount Sinai Hospital 1985–86; clubs: Cambridge, Island Yacht, Georgian Peaks Ski; Home: 88 Wychwood Park, Toronto, Ont. M6G 2V5; Office: 2 First Canadian Pl., Suite 3100, Toronto, Ont. M5X 1J9.

**OLIVER, Michael Kelway,** M.A., Ph.D., LL.D., D.U.; educator; b.; b. North Bay, Ont. 2 Feb. 1925; s. Canon Gilbert Salt and late Winifred Maud (Kelway) O.; e. Westmount (Que.) High Sch.; McGill Univ., B.A. 1948, M.A. 1950, Ph.D. 1957; Inst. d'Etudes Politiques (Paris), 1949; m. Joan Alexander, d. late Warren D. Nelson and Muriel W. Garrow 18 Dec. 1948; children: David N., James K., Victoria J., Geoffrey M., Cynthia J.; VISITING PROFESSOR, BISHOP'S UNIVERSITY 1993– ; National Pres., United Nations Assn. in Canada 1993– ; Adjunct Prof., Faculty of Social Sciences, Carleton Univ. 1989–93; Prof., Dept. of Political and Admin. Studies, Univ. of Papua New Guinea 1984–88; Dir., Intnl. Dev. Office, Assn. of Universities & Colls. of Canada 1979–83; Pres., Carleton University, 1972–78; Vice Princ. (Acad.) 1967–72, and Prof. Dept. of Pol. Science, McGill Univ.; sometime Research Dir., Royal Comn. on Biling & Bicult.; Past Pres., (Fed.) New Democratic Party; served in 2nd World War, 1943–45; Can. Brit. and N. Europe with 18th Batty., 2nd Candn. Anti-Tank Regt., R.C.A.; discharged with rank of Bombardier; mem., Candn. Pol. Science Assn.; Internat. Pol. Science Assn.; Anglican Church; recreation: golf; Address: 2027 St. Jean, R.R. 3, Magog, Qué. J1X 3W4.

**OLIVER, Paul,** B.Sc., M.A.; food industry executive; b. Cobourg, Ont. 3 Jan. 1951; e. Univ. of Waterloo, B.Sc. 1971, M.A. Econ. 1979; Pres., Green Giant Canada / Fraser Valley Foods, Div. of Pillsbury Canada 1987; Mktg. Product Mgr., Campbell Soup 1977–78; Plant Mgr., Canned Food 1978–81; Gen. Mgr., Frozen Food Div. 1981–82; Vice-Pres. Operations, Pillsbury Canada 1982–87; Pres., Fraser Valley Foods, Div. of Pillsbury Canada 1987–90; Pres., Cdn. Frozen Food Assn. 1986–87; Chrmn., Vegetable Commodity Group, Cdn. Food Processors Assn. 1983–86; Dir., Manitoba Research Counc. 1980–81.

**OLIVER, Peter C.H.,** B.Com.; restaurant executive; b. Cape Town, S. Africa 30 July 1948; s. Guy Howard and Joan Diana (Roberts) O.; e. St. Andrews Coll. S.Africa; McGill Univ. B.Com. 1971; m. Maureen d. Daniel and Eliane Murphy 6 Apl. 1974; children: Vanessa, Jessica, Andrew, Marc; FOUNDER AND OWNER OLIVER'S RESTAURANTS 1978– ; Dir. ATI Corp.; stockbroker Greenshields 1973–74; Partner, Realco Property Ltd. 1974–78; Vice Pres. Juvenile Diabetes Found. Toronto; Home: 9 Salonica Rd., Don Mills, Ont. M3C 2L6; Office: 2433 Yonge St., Toronto, Ont. M4P 2H4.

**OLIVER, Robert Edward;** communications consultant; b. Brough, Eng. 1 Oct. 1913; s. Harry Ernest and Lilian (Vincent) O.; e. high sch., tech. & comm. schs., teachers' coll. Ottawa, Ont.; Queen's Univ. completed 2nd yr. B.Com.; LL.D. (h.c.) Memorial Univ., Nfld. 1986; m. H. Winnifred d. William Henry and Augusta Celia Colton 17 Apr. 1943; children: Douglas Robert, Margaret Ellen Donaldson; Pres. Robert E. Oliver & Assoc. Ltd. 1966–86, retired; Prin. BearBrook Continuation Sch. 1936–39; Sec. Head Govt. of Can. Ottawa 1939–43; Advt. Mgr. R.L. Crain Ltd. Ottawa 1943–46; Asst. Pub. Relations Mgr. Bank of Montreal (Qué.) 1946–48; Rsch. Mgr. Pub. Relations Office Ford Motor Co. of Canada, Windsor 1948–50, Asst. Dir. of Office 1950–56; Supr. Pub. Relations & Advt. Bank of Nova Scotia Toronto 1956–65; Pres. Candn. Advt. Adv. Bd. 1966–81; Interim Pres. Candn. Advt. Found. Toronto 1982–85; Pres., Advt. Standards Counc. 1981–87; Vice Pres. Ont. Welfare Council 1960–63; Dir. Candn. Mental Health League 1964–66; Past Chrmn. Comn. on Continuous Learning; Chrmn. Children's Broadcast Inst. 1982–84; recipient Gold Medal Award Assn. Candn. Advertisers 1974; named Advt. Person of Yr. Candn. Advt. & Sales Assn. 1976; recipient Robert A. McAlear Award, Assn. Candn. Advertisers 1986; author: 'A Canadian Christmas Carol' 1967; 'Money

Matters' 1974; co-author: 'Shopping Sense' 1976; 'Advertising at Work in the Modern Marketplace' 1976; Address: 206, 75 Wynford Hts. Cres., Don Mills, Ont. M3C 3H9.

**OLIVER, William Murray,** R.C.A.; interior designer; b. Aurora, Ont. 16 June 1929; s. Thomas Howard and Leta Pearl (Sproxton) O.; e. Ont. Coll. of Art A.O.C.A. 1952; Ecole de Beaux-Arts Fontainebleau, France; m. Barbara Grace d. Charles Alexander Sharp 30 Aug. 1956; three s. Christopher David, Jeremy Andrew, Charles Adrian; PROP., W. MURRAY OLIVER LTD. 1978– ; Part-time Instr. Ont. Coll. of Art 1963–70, 1974–86; Interior Designer T. Eaton Co. Ltd. Studio of Interior Design 1952–64, Design Dir. Eaton Design Group 1964–73; Design Dir./Design Consultant Skyline Hotels Ltd. 1973–78; rec'd William Blair Bruce Foundation Grant 1966; Fellow, Ontario College of Art 1992; mem. Assoc. of Registered Interior Designers Ont.; Interior Designers Can.; United Church; Club: Arts & Letters; Address: 19 Edgewood Cres., Toronto, Ont. M4W 3A8.

**OLIVIER, Hon. Jacques,** c.p.; executive; b. Hull, Qué. 14 Apr. 1944; s. Alphonse and Fleur Ange (Stafford) O.; e. Univ. Laval courses Ind. Relations 1967; Univ. de Montréal courses Hosp. Adm. 1968; m. Cecile Lachance 11 Apr. 1966; children: Elizabeth, Jacques Jr.; OWNER & PRES. JACQUES OLIVIER FORD INC., St-Hubert, Qué. 1985– ; Special Asst. to Prime Min., Labour Relations 1971–72; el. to H. of C. for Longueuil g.e. 1972, re-el. 1974, 1979, 1980, 1981; Parlty. Asst. to Min. of Labour 1976, Official Opposition Labour Critic and Jt. Chrmn. Employment & Labour Ctte. 1979, Pres. Lib. Caucus 1981–82; nominated Min. of Fitness and Amateur Sport for Can. 1984; former mem. standing Ctte. on Justice & Legal Affairs, on Labour, Manpower & Immigration, on Procedure & Orgn. on Transport; mem. Ctte. Port Mgmt.; Dir. Charles Lemoyne Found.; Vice Pres. Young Libs Assn. Frontenac 1966–67; Vice Pres. Jr. C. of C.; former mem. Candn. World Federalist Parlty. Assn.; Internat. Assn. French Speaking Parliamentarians; Candn. Group Inter-Parlty. Union; Can. U.S. Inter-Parlty. Assn.; Commonwealth Parlty. Assn.; recreation: golf: Club: Montréal Country; Home: 1392 Grande-Allée, Carignan, Qué. J3L 3P9; Office: 4405 Chemin Chambly, St-Hubert, Qué. J3Y 3M7.

**OLIVIER, Suzanne;** artist; b. Montreal, Que. 26 Apr. 1943; d. Jacques and Cecile (Dansereau) O.; e. Ecole des Beaux-Arts de Montreal; several solo and group exhibitions in Toronto and Montreal since 1977; represented by Marianne Friedland Gallery Toronto; La/Folie des Arts Montreal; M.F. Gallery Naples, Florida USA; lives in France to pursue career; Address: 3835 Montée Cooper, St. Anicet, Que. J0S 1M0.

**OLIVIERI, Nancy Fern,** B.Sc., M.D., FRCP(C); haematologist and university professor; b. Hamilton, Ont. 1 June 1954; d. Fernando Anthony and Victoria Frances (Parniak) O.; e. Univ. of Toronto B.Sc. 1975; McMaster Univ. M.D. 1978; Am. Bd. Internal Med. 1981; FRCP(C) Internal Med. 1982; FRCP(C) Haematology 1983; Am. Bd. of Haematology 1984; STAFF SCIENTIST RESEARCH INST., DIV. OF HAEMATOLOGY & ONCOLOGY, THE HOSPITAL FOR SICK CHILDREN 1992– ; Research Fellow, Haem., Harvard Univ. 1984–86; Asst. Prof., Pediatrics, Univ. of Toronto 1986–92; Assoc. Prof. 1992– ; Staff Haem., The Hospital for Sick Children 1986– ; The Toronto Gen. Hosp. 1986– ; Dir., Sickle Cell Disease Prog., Hosp. for Sick Chldren 1986– ; Dir. Thalassemia Prog. 1988– ; Mem., Am. Soc. of Haem.; Am. Soc. of Pediatric Hem./Oncol.; Ont. Med. Assn.; Soc. Pediatric Rsch.; author of articles in medical journals and abstracts; research interests: thalassemia, sickle cell disease, iron chelation, malaria; recreations: tennis, travel; Home: 15 Ellsworth Ave., Toronto, Ont. M5G 2K4; Office: Room 6324, Toronto, Ont. M5G 1X8.

**OLLEY, Robert Edward,** B.A., M.A., Ph.D.; university professor; b. Verdun, Que. 16 April 1933; s. Edwin Henry and Elizabeth (Reed) O.; e. Carleton Univ., B.A. 1960; Queen's Univ., M.A. 1961, Ph.D. 1969; m. Shirley Ann d. George and Edith Dahl 19 Jan. 1957; children: Elizabeth Anne, George Steven, Susan Catherine, Maureen Carolyn; PROFESSOR EMERITUS, UNIV. OF SASK. 1993– ; Vis. Asst. Prof., Queen's Univ. 1964, 1967–68; Asst. Prof., Univ. of Sask. 1963–67, 1968–69; Dir. of Rsch., Alta., Man. & Sask., Royal Comn. on Consumer Problems & Inflation, 1967–68; Sr. Econ. Adv., Bell Canada 1971–73, 1978–79; Assoc. Prof., Univ. of Sask. 1969–71, 1973–74; Prof. of Econ., Univ. of Sask. 1974–78, 1979–93; econ. adv. and cons. to numerous N. Am. cos.; Vice-Pres., Consumers' Assoc. of Canada Found. 1989– ; Mem. Bd. of Dirs. (Sask.), Candn. Council for Native Business 1989–93; Chrmn., Candn. Advisory Ctte. on Consumer Standards, Standards Council of Canada; Mem. Bd. of Dirs., Candn. Communications Research Centre 1992– ; Member, Federal Prairie Task Force on Telecommunications Regulation 1991–92; Chrmn., Consumers' Assn. of Can. 1975–77; Candn. Standards Assn. 1987–89; H.M. the Queen's Silver Jubilee Medal 1977; Consumers' Assn. of Can. Award of Special Merit 1979; mem. Candn. Govt. Specifications Bd. 1978–81; Dir., Candn. Found. for Econom. Edn. 1975–82; Mem. Bd. of Dirs., Internat. Telecommunications Soc. 1985– ; mem. Candn. Econ. Assn.; Am. Econ. Assn.; Royal Econ. Soc.; Econ. Hist. Soc.; Econ. Hist. Assn.; co-author: 'Total Factor Productivity of Canadian Telecommunications Carriers' 1984; co-ed.: 'Consumer Credit in Canada' 1966; ed. of var. conf. proc.; recreations: walking, philately; Address: P.O. Box 1040, 374 Queen St., Niagara-on-the-Lake, Ont. L0S 1J0.

**OLSBERG, Nicholas,** B.A., M.A., Ph.D.; archivist, curator; b. Cheshire, U.K. 3 April 1943; s. Harold and Rosalind Mary (Dexter) O.; e. Oxford Univ. B.A. 1965; Univ. of South Carolina M.A. 1967; Oxford Univ. M.A. 1969; Univ. of South Carolina Ph.D. 1972; CHIEF CURATOR, CENTRE CANADIEN D'ARCHITECTURE 1989– ; Archivist of the Commonwealth, Massachusetts State Archives 1976–79; Coord., Master's Prog. in Hist. & Arch. Methods, Univ. of Mass. 1978–84; Head, Archives of the History of Art, Getty Ctr. for History of Art & Humanities 1984–89; Director, Institue de recherche en histoire de l'architecture 1993– ; Chair, Roundtable on Arch. Records, Soc. of Am. Archivists 1992– ; Chair, Steering Ctte., Found. for Documents of Arch. 1989– ; U.S. Comn. on Preservation & Access Task Force 1989– ; Ch. of St. John the Evangelist, Montreal; author of articles and book chapters; Home: 3539 Lorne Ave., Apt. 2, Montreal, Que. H2X 2A4; Office: 1920 Baille St., Montreal, Que. H3H 2S6.

**OLSEN, Brian L.;** telecommunications executive; b. Kirkland Lake, Ont. 2 June 1946; s. Ole E. and Jean M. O.; e. Northern Coll. (Kirkland Lake), electronic technol. 1968; Univ. of Western Ont., Extve. Mngt. Prog. 1987; m. Diane S. Amant 19 April 1969; children: Sheryl, Christopher; PRESIDENT, OLSEN ENTERPRISES 1993– ; Engr., Planning & Econ. Analysis functions, Bell Canada 1968–75; Engr. Planning, Rate & Tariffs Internat. Consulting, Telesat 1975–81; Mktg. Mgr., Broadcast & Voice & Data Serv. 1981–84; Dir., Brodcast Serv. 1984–88; Business Planning 1988–91; Pres. & Chief Operating Offr., Telesat Enterprises (subs. of Telesat Canada) 1991–93; Dir., Cresset Ventures Inc.; Dir. & Pres., Gloucester Arts Council; recreations: golf, canoeing, camping; Home: 529 Rivershore Cres., Gloucester, Ont. K1J 7Y8.

**OLSON, Allan S.,** B.Sc., M.B.A.; business executive; b. Edmonton, Alta. 16 Oct. 1941; e. Ross Shepard Comp. High; Univ. of Alta., B.Sc. 1963; Univ. of West. Ont., M.B.A. 1965; m. Frances; 3 children; Pres. & C.E.O., Banister Inc. 1990; Chrmn., Stuart Olson Constr. Ltd. and Depy. Chrmn., The Churchill Corp.; Dir., BCE Devel. Corp.; The Churchill Corp.; GWIL Indus. Inc.; IPSCO Steel Limited; APEGGA, P.Eng.; Mem., Young Pres. Orgn.; recreations: golf, skiing, collecting art; Office: 208 Denton Centre, 14925 11 Ave., Edmonton, Alta. T5M 2P6.

**OLSON, Arthur H.;** executive; b. Torquay, Sask. 8 Sept. 1920; s. Gust and Signa (Hultgren) O.; e. Banff Sch. Advanced Mgmt.; Queen's Univ. Bus. Mgmt.; m. Betty d. Russell and Eva Ferguson 28 Feb. 1953; three d. Janet, Susan, Catherine; PRES. THE OLSON GROUP INC. 1979– ; Vice Pres. Anderson/Olson Associates Inc. 1955–59; Nat. Sales Mgr. Selkirk Metalbestos Ltd. 1959–68; Pres. Kaminos Ltd. 1968–77; Pres.: Fireplace Inst. Chicago 1975–77; Candn. Wood Energy Inst. 1976–79 (Chrmn. Past Pres.' Club); Hon. Dir. Candn. Fireplace Inst. since 1980; mem. Standards Ctte.: Candn. Gas Assn.; Underwriters' Labs. Inc.; Office: 69 Dennett Dr., Agincourt, Ont. M1S 2E9.

**OLSON, Brian Franklin,** B.A.; corporation executive; b. Calgary, Alta. 21 Nov. 1951; s. Albert W. and Marjorie E. O. e. Univ. of Calgary, B.A. 1972; m. Pamela 19 May 1973; one s.: David; SENIOR VICE-PRES. HUMAN RESOURCES, NOVA CORPORATION OF ALBERTA 1984– ; various mngt. positions in NOVA 1977–84; Dir., MSERD (on extve. interchange with Fed. Govt.) 1982–84; Dir., Candn. Special Olympics; Extve. Ctte., Council of Human Resources Executives, Conference Board of Canada; Bd. Mem., Calgary Educational Partnerships Foundation; recreations: ranching; Home: De Winton, Alta. T0L 0X0; Office: P.O. Box 2535, Postal Stn. M., Calgary, Alta. T2P 2N6.

**OLSON, David R.,** Ph.D.; professor, registered psychologist; b. Saskatchewan 16 June 1935; e. Univ. of Sask., B.Ed. 1962; Univ. of Alta., M.Ed. 1962; Univ. of Alta., Ph.D. 1963; m. Frances; PROF. OF APPLIED PSYCH., ONT. INST. FOR STUDIES IN EDUCATION, UNIV. OF TORONTO 1966– ; Fellow, Ctr. for Cognitive Studies, Harvard Univ. 1965–66; Netherlands Inst. for Adv. Study in Behav. Sci., Stanford, Calif. 1983–84; Past Dir., McLuhan Prog. in Culture & Technol., Univ. of Toronto 1981–89; FFellow, Candn. Psych. Assn. 1980 (Pres. 1988–89); Fellow, Cognitive Development Unit, MRC, London 1990–91; Mem., Rsch. Bd. of Advr., Am. Biographical Inst.; Ed. Bd.: 'J. of Communication,' 'Interchange,' 'Developmental Review,' 'Language,' 'J. of Educ. Psych.,' 'Research in the Teaching of English,' 'Infancia aprendizaje,' 'Cognitive Development,' 'Visible Language,' 'Behav. and Brain Sciences'; author: 'Cognitive Development: The Child's Acquisition of Diagonality' 1970; 'The World on Paper' 1994; co-author: 'Spatial Cognition' 1983; co-editor: 'Literacy, Language and Learning' 1985, 'Developing Theories of Mind' 1988; 'Literacy and Orality' 1991; Home: 12 Beachview Cres., Toronto, Ont.; Office: 252 Bloor St. W., Toronto, Ont. M5S 1V6.

**OLSON, Hon. Horace Andrew (Bud),** P.C.; farmer; merchant; b. Iddlesleigh, Alta. 6 Oct. 1925; s. Carl M. and Alta I. (Perry) O.; e. Iddesleigh and Medicine Hat; m. Marion Lucille, d. John W. McLachlan, 26 Jan. 1947; children: Sharon Lee, Andrea Lucille, Juanita Carol, Horace Andrew; M.P. for Medicine Hat 1957–58, 1962, 1963, 1965, 1968; Min. of Agriculture, Can. 1968–72; Chrmn., Sub-Comte. for revising rules of procedure H. of C. 1963–64; Citation for Distinguished Citizenship, Medicine Hat College 1968; mem., Econ. Council of Can. 1975–79; Candn. Parlty. delegation to U.S.S.R. and Czechoslovakia 1965; Commonwealth Parlty. delegation to Nigeria 1962; Inter-Parlty. Union delegation to Bulgaria 1977; attended U.N. Gen. Assembly October-November 1966; Chrmn., Alta. Liberal Caucus 1973–74; apptd. to Senate 1977; Chrmn., Special Comte. of the Senate on the Northern Pipeline 1978; Min. of State for Economic Development 1980–82; Min. resp. for Northern Pipeline Agency 1980–84 and Govt. Leader in Senate 1982–84; Inter-Parlty. Union delegation to Nairobi 1984; Can./U.S. Inter-Parlty. Group to Tucson, Arizona 1986; Centennial Medal 1967; Queen's Silver Jubilee Medal 1977; Hon. Col. South Alta. Light Horse Regt. 1970–87; Liberal; Lutheran; recreations: hunting, fishing; Home: Iddlesleigh, Alta. T0J 1T0; Office: The Senate, Ottawa, Ont. K1A 0A4.

**OLSSON, Philip J.,** B.A., M.B.A.; investment banker; b. Cleveland, Tenn. 9 June 1949; s. Nels Arthur and Tommie Dialthe (McCulley) O.; e. Vanderbilt Univ. Nashville, B.A. 1970, M.B.A. 1972; Univ. de Dijon Dip. 1975; London Sch. of Econ. postgrad. rsch. monetary econ. 1975–76; m. G. Gayle d. E.C. Cryer, Jr. and Theresa Payne 1 Aug. 1970; two s. Arthur Erik, Julian Randolf; VICE PRES., DIR. & HEAD OF GLOBAL INVESTMENT BANKING, RBC DOMINION SECURITIES INC. 1992– ; Vice Pres. and Dir. RBC Dominion Securities Inc. and predecessor corps. 1983– , Dir. Mergers & Acquisitions Group (Toronto) 1986–87; Pres., RBC Dominion Securities (Alberta) Inc. 1987–92; Partner, SRG Management Consultants, Nashville 1972–75; Project Finance Offr. Bank of Montreal, Montréal and Toronto 1976–79; joined Pitfield Mackay Ross Ltd. Toronto 1979, trans. Calgary 1980; author publs. energy financing, mergers & acquisitions; Anglican; recreations: fishing, skiing, swimming; Clubs: Calgary Golf & Country; Ranchmen's; National; RCYC; Office: P.O. Box 21, Commerce Court South, Toronto, Ont. M5L 1A7.

**OLTMAN, John R.,** B.Sc., M.B.A.; business executive; b. Litchfield, Ill. 4 March 1945; s. Ervin H. and Ida (Dankles) O.; e. Univ. of Illinois B.Sc.; Northwestern Univ. M.B.A.; CHAIRMAN & CHIEF EXTVE. OFFR., SHL SYSTEMHOUSE INC. 1991– ; various positions ending as Worldwide Managing Partner, Integration Services, Arthur Andersen Worldwide Orgn. 1970–91; Former Mem., Bd. of Partners and Former Chair, Strategic Planning, Arthur Andersen; recreations: skiing, tennis; Address: 50 O'Connor St., Ste. 1616, Ottawa, Ont. K1P 6L2.

**O'MALLEY, Terrence J.;** advertising executive; b. St. Catharines, Ont. 16 Dec. 1936; s. John Dominic and Catherine (McPherson) O'M.; e. St. Catharines (Ont.) Coll. Inst.; Harvard Univ. (Hons. Eng.) 1958; Univ. of Toronto grad. studies; m. Mary Jane d. Mary and John Palmer Nov. 1964; divorced 1985; children: Lauren Paige Kirsten, Teig Palmer John; PRES. AND EXTVE. CREATIVE DIR. VICKERS & BENSON COMPANIES LTD. 1975– ; Dir. Key Publishers Co. Ltd.; Family

Trust Corp.; Vickers & Benson/FKQ Advertising, Buffalo, N.Y.; Copywriter, MacLaren Advertising 1960–61, Young & Rubicam Advertising 1962; Sr. Writer, Creative Group Head, Foster Advertising 1963–64; Creative Group Head Vickers & Benson Advertising 1964, Assoc. Creative Dir. 1968, Creative Dir. 1970, Extve. Vice Pres. & Creative Dir. 1972; recipient Fritz Speiss Award 1982; Carl Dair Award 1983; over 200 nat. and internat. awards for creativity; comm. in Clio Hall of Fame; Dir. Candn. Hearing Soc.; Extve. Ctte. Central YMCA; Council Mem., Sport Marketing Counc.; mem. World Trade Centre; recreations: fitness, running, hockey; Home: 121 Glen Rd., Toronto, Ont. M4W 2W1; Office: 1133 Yonge St., Toronto, Ont. M4T 2Z3.

**O'MARA, Most Rev. John A.,** D.D., J.C.L.; bishop (R. Cath.); b. Buffalo, N.Y. 17 Nov. 1924; s. John Aloysius and Anna Theresa (Schenck) O.; e. St. Augustine's Seminary, Toronto 1944–51; St. Thomas Univ. (Angelicum) Rome 1951–53; BISHOP OF ST. CATHARINES 1994– ; Chancellor Archdiocese of Toronto 1968–69; Sec. to Cardinal McGuigan 1954–69; Rector/Pres. St. Augustine's Seminary 1969–75; Bishop of Thunder Bay 1976–94l o. Bishop by Most Rev. Philip F. Pocock, St. Michael's Cathedral, Toronto 29 June 1976; Pres., Ont. Conf. of Catholic Bishops 1986–92; Dir. Ont. Hosp. Assn. 1961–65; mem. Ont. Hosp. Services Comn. 1964–69; Mem. Pontifical Counc. Cor Unum 1977–89; Address: St. Catharines, Ont.

**O'MEARA, Gary David,** A.B.; headmaster; b. Quebec City, Que. 13 Feb. 1955; s. David Basil and Margaret (Laurie) O.; e. Loyola H.S. 1972; Princeton Univ., A.B. (Hist.) 1976; Univ. de Paris-Sorbonne 1993; m. Suzanne Tevlin d. Barbara and the late E. Murray Tevlin 16 June 1979; HEADMASTER, LYCEE CANADIEN EN FRANCE 1993– ; Teacher, Wasatch Acad., Mt. Pleasant, Utah 1976–77; St. Andrew's Coll., Aurora 1977–78; St. George's Coll., Toronto 1978–88; Head, Econ. 1981–88; Dir. of Studies 1983–85; Head, Upper Sch. 1985–88; Founding Headmaster, Lycee Cambridge 1988–92; Dir. and Partner, O'Meara & Tevlin Associates (Paris) 1992–93; Chrmn., Princeton Alumni Schs. Ctte. (Ont.) 1984–88; Mem., Vis. Ctte. of Candn. Edn. Standards Inst. 1986; Cons., Coll. Bd. 1988; Dir., Cambridge Summer Programmes for Peel Bd. of Educ. & Lycee Cambridge 1990; Dir., Enrichment in Oxford Summer Programme 1993– ; lectr. on numerous occasions for Candn. Found. for Econ. Edn.; developed community serv. prog. for St. George's Coll.; appeared on a TV Ont. series; Sec., Bd. of Dir., Lycee Cambridge 1988–92; Mem. & Sec. of Bd. of Gov., St. George's Coll. 1985–88; Mem., Candn. Found. for Econ. Edn. 1980– ; Chrmn., Princeton Alumni Schs. Ctte. (U.K.) 1989–92; Mem., Extve. Ctte., Princeton Alumni Assn. of Can. 1984–88; Can.-U.K. C. of C. 1988–92; Brit. Assoc. for Candn. Studies 1988– ; Mem., Alliance Française de Cambridge 1991–93; Société des Amis du Louvre; British Council; Musée D'Orsay; author of new sr. div. econ. guidelines, Ont. Min. of Edn. 1987; author, 'Beyond the Courts and Constitution: John A. Macdonald and Early Canadian Federalism' 1976; European Dir., 'Global Vision: Canada's International Competitive Advantage,' a program jointly funded by the Fed. Govt. and private sector Candn. Corps. for the top high school students in Canada 1991; presented paper 'Some Suggestions for Improving Education in Canada: Historical Perspectives and Lessons From Abroad' BACS Conference, King's College, Cambridge, England March 1993; Vice-Pres., Princeton Club of Great Britain 1990–92; recreations: reading, music, theatre, tennis, skiing, travel; Clubs: Royal Overseas League; Canada Club; Home (Canada): 261 Albany Ave., Toronto, Ont. M5R 3C7; Home (France): Casa Rosa, 06230 St-Jean-Cap-Ferrat, France; Office: Place du Centenaire, 06230 St-Jean-Cap-Ferrat, France.

**OMMER, Rosemary Elizabeth,** M.A., Ph.D.; university professor and administrator; b. Glasgow, Scotland 1 May 1943; s. Otto Paul and Rose Martha (McNulty) O.; e. Notre Dame H.S.; Glasgow Univ. M.A. 1964; Notre Dame College of Edn. Teaching Cert. 1965; Memorial Univ. of Nfld. M.A. 1974; McGill Univ. Ph.D. 1979; divorced; children: Andrew, Catriona, Keith, Kenneth; PROFESSOR, DEPT. OF HISTORY, MEMORIAL UNIV. OF NFLD. 1991– ; High School Teacher & Head, Geog. Dept. Scotland 1965–66; emigrated to Canada 1967; McConnell Fellow, McGill Univ. 1974; Asst. Rsch. Prof., Memorial Univ. of Nfld. 1978; Econ. Historian, History Dept. 1983; promoted & granted tenure 1985; Managing Ed., Royal Comn. on Employment & Unemployment - Nfld. 1986; Review Ed., 'Newfoundland Studies' 1985–89; Research Dir., Inst. of Social & Econ. Rsch., M.U.N. 1991; sits on cttes. for nat. funding bodies as well as univ. cttes.; Mem., Edit. Adv. Bd., 'Can. Hist. R.' 1986–89; Examining Bd., Rhodes Scholarships 1985–89; Background Researcher, Maritime Boundary Arbitration between Can. & France 1989–90; Mem., Bd. of Dir., Gorsebrook Rsch. Inst., Saint Mary's Univ.; Chair, Prog. Ctte. & Vice-Pres., Vanier Inst. of the Family; Mem., Candn. Hist. Assn.; editor & contbr.: 'Merchant Credit and Labour Strategies in HIstorical Perspective' 1990; co-editor: 'Volumes Not Values' 1979, 'Working Men Who Got Wet' 1980; author: 'From Outpost to Outport' 1991; recreations: piano playing, choir directing; Home: 17 Allandale Rd., St. John's, Nfld. A1B 2Z3; Office: I.S.E.R., St. John's, Nfld. A1C 5S7.

**ONDAATJE, Michael;** writer; film maker; b. Colombo, Ceylon 12 Sept. 1943; s. Philip Mervyn and Enid Doris (Gratiaen) O.; e. St. Thomas Coll., Colombo, Ceylon; Dulwich Coll., London, Eng.; Bishop's Univ. 1962–64; Univ. Coll., Univ. of Toronto, B.A. 1965; Queen's Univ., M.A. 1967; children: Zillah Quintin, Philip Christopher Griffin; films made incl. 'Sons of Captain Poetry,' 'Great Canadian Hounds,' 'The Clinton Special' (a film about Theatre Passe Muraille's 'The Farm Show'); author: 'The Dainty Monsters' (poetry) 1967; 'The Man with Seven Toes' (poetry) 1968; 'Leonard Cohen' (criticism) 1968; 'The Collected Works of Billy the Kid' (poetry and prose) 1970; 'In the Skin of a Lion' 1987 (winner, Trillium Award); 'The Cinnamon Peeler' 1991; 'Elimination Dance/La Dance Eliminatoire' (Lemire Tostevin, Lola (tr.)) 1991; 'The English Patient' (winner, 1992 Governor-General's Literary Award for Fiction, English language; 1992 Booker Prize; winner, 6th annual Trillium Award); editor: 'The Broken Ark' 1971; 'How To Train A Bassett' 1971; 'Rat Jelly' 1973; 'Coming Through Slaughter' (prose) 1976; 'The Long Poem Anthology' (ed.) 1979; 'There's a Trick with a Knife I'm learning to Do' (poetry) 1979; 'Running in the Family' (fiction) 1982; 'Secular Love' (poetry) 1984; 'From Ink Lake: an anthology of Canadian stories' 1990; stage adaptation of 'The Collected Works of Billy the Kid' performed at the Stratford Festival and Toronto Free Theatre and in theatres in Canada and the U.S.; recipient, Gov.-Gen.'s Award 1970, 1980, 1992; Books in Canada First Novel Award 1977; First Annual Trillium Award (best book published in Ontario in past year) 1987; Booker Prize 1992; Sixth Annual Trillium Award 1992; has developed and bred new strain of spaniel 'The Sydenham Spaniel,' Candn. Kennel Club 1970, with Livingstone Animal Foundation Kennels; mem. staff, Eng. Dept., Glendon Coll., York Univ.; recreations: tennis, films; Office: 2275 Bayview Ave., Toronto, Ont. M4N 3M6.

**ONDAATJE, Philip Christopher;** investment banker; b. Kandy, Ceylon 22 Feb. 1933; s. Philip Mervyn and Enid Doris O.; e. Blundell's Sch. Eng.; London Sch. of Econ.; m. Valda d. Karl Bulins 19 Jan. 1959; children: David, Sarah, Janet; Pres., The Ondaatje Corp. Ltd. 1970; Trainee, National and Grindlays Bank (U.K.) 1951–55; Burns Bros., and Denton Ltd. Toronto 1955–57; Extve., Maclean-Hunter Publishing Montreal 1957–60; The Financial Post Toronto 1961–64; Pitfield, Mackay, Ross & Co. Ltd. Toronto 1965–69; Gov., Lakefield Coll. Sch.; mem. Candn. Olympic Bob-sled Team 1964; author 'The Prime Ministers of Canada: 1867–1967' (1967); 'Olympic Victory, 1964' (1968); 'Leopard in the Afternoon' 1989; P. Conservative; Anglican; recreations: tennis, sailing; Clubs: Badminton & Racquet; Tadenac; Chester (N.S.) Yacht; Royal Bermuda Yacht; Mid Ocean Golf (Bermuda); Coral Beach & Tennis (Bermuda); Queen's Club (England); Somerset County Cricket (England); Home: Glenthorne, Nr. Lynton, N. Devon, England.

**O'NEIL, Mt. Rev. Alexander Henry,** B.D., M.A., D.C.L., LL.D., D.D. (Ang.); archbishop (retired); b. McGillivray Twp., Clandeboye, Ont. 23 July 1907; s. Alexander and Anna (Henry) O.; e. Univ. of W. Ont., B.A. 1928, B.D. 1936, M.A. 1943, D.D. 1945; Huron Coll., L.Th. 1929; Wycliffe Coll., Toronto, D.D. 1954; King's College, Halifax, D.D., 1958; LL.D. Western Ont. 1962; St. Thomas Univ. 1970; m. Marguerite Isabelle, d. John A. Roe, Atwood, Ont., 16 July 1931; one s. Terence; Life mem., Huron Coll. Corp. 1971; Hon. Life Gov., Brit. & Foreign Bible Soc. in Eng., since 1947; Rector of Atwood, 1929–35; Gorrie, 1935–39; Clinton 1939–41; Principal and Prof. of Divinity, Huron Coll., London, Ont., 1941–52; Prof. of Hebrew, Univ. of W. Ont., 1944–52; Gen. Secy., Brit. & Foreign Bible Soc. in Can., 1952–56; Bishop of Fredericton, 1957–63 and Archbishop there 1963–71; Secy., Bd. of Examiners for Divinity Degrees of Ch. of Eng. in Can., 1946–52; mem. of Senate, Univ. of W. Ont., 1941–52; Del. to Gen. Synod of Ch. of Eng. in Can., 1943–52; Dom. Chaplain, Ang. Young People's Assn., 1940–42; D.C.L. Bishop's Univ. 1964; Canada Medal 1967; Home: 1 Grosvenor St., Apt. 807, London, Ont. N6A 1Y2.

**O'NEIL, E.C.,** B.A.Sc., P.Eng.; executive; b. Windsor, Ont. Aug. 1937; s. Charles Edward and Evelyn Mary (Delaney) O'N.; e. Univ of Windsor B.A.Sc. 1961; m. Dorinda (dec.) d. Bob and Mary Cochran 1 Apr. 1968; m. 2ndly, Donna d. Alex and Phyllis Cockell 1987; children (from first marriage): Tim, Rory, Brendan; EXTVE. VICE PRES. & CHIEF OPERATING OFFR., EASTERN CONSTRUCTION CO. LTD. 1985– ; joined present co. 1961, Vice Pres. and Gen. Mgr. Sun Construction co. (subsidiary), Alta. 1978; Chrmn., Gen. Contractors Sect., Toronto Construction Assoc.; Past Pres.; Calgary Gen. Contractors Assn.; Calgary Constrn. Assn.; recreations: skiing, golf, squash; Clubs: Thornhill Golf & Country; Beaver Valley Ski; Home: 58 Julia St., Thornhill, Ont. L3T 4R9.

**O'NEIL, Hugh Patrick,** M.P.P., F.R.I.; politician; b. Belleville, Ont. 10 July 1936; s. John Harold and Lena Elizabeth; e. St. Peter's Separate Sch.; St. Michael's Acad.; Peterborough Teachers' Coll.; m. Donna Grace d. Gertrude and Henry McColl; children: David, Catherine; elected to legis. 1975; re-elected 1977, 1981, 1985, 1987, 1990; Min. of Industry & Technology 1985–87; Min. of Tourism and Recreation 1987–89; Min. of Mines 1989–90; Min. of Culture and Communications 1990; Roman Catholic; Liberal; Clubs: Kiwanis Club; Knights of Columbus; Home: Trenton, Ont.; Office: Queen's Park, Toronto, Ont. M7A 1A2.

**O'NEIL, Maureen,** B.A.; executive; b. 14 Sept. 1943; e. Carleton Univ. B.A. 1964; PRESIDENT NORTH-SOUTH INST. 1989– ; Chief, Social Progs., Social Policy Br. Min. of Communications 1973–74; Dir. Policy Rsch. & Strategic Planning Health and Welfare Can. 1974–78; Dep. Head (co-ord.) Status of Women Can. 1978–86; Sec. Gen. Candn. Human Rights Comn. 1986–87; Dep. Min. of Citizenship Ont. 1987–89; mem. Bd. UN Rsch. Inst. Social Develop. 1989– ; mem. UN Ctte. Devel. Planning 1990–93; Trustee, Inst. for Rsch. Pub. Policy 1977–84; Chair, Bd. of Govs. Carleton Univ. 1993– (Mem. Bd. Govs. 1989–93); mem. ed. adv. bd. Perception Mag., Candn. Council Social Devel. 1977–84; mem. Program Adv. Ctte., Australian Foundation for Internat. Cooperation 1990– ; mem. Program Adv. Ctte. Overseas Develop. Council, Wash. 1989– ; mem. United Nations Status of Women Commission 1981–86; Maureen O'Neil Award in Women's Studies estbd. by Hadassah-Wezo 1985; recipient A.D. Dunton Alumni Award Carleton Univ. 1986; Home: 121 Iona St., Ottawa, Ont. K1Y 3M1; Office: 200, 55 Murray St., Ottawa, Ont. K1N 5M3.

**O'NEIL, William Andrew,** B.A.Sc.; executive; b. Ottawa, Ont. 6 June 1927; s. Thomas Wilson and Margaret (Swan) O'N.; e. Ottawa Tech. High Sch. 1945; Carleton Univ. 1945–46; Univ. of Toronto B.A.Sc. (Civil Engn.) 1949; m. Dorothy d. Ivan Adrian Muir 21 Apr. 1950; children: Janice, Kathy, Jeffrey; SECY.-GEN., INTERNATIONAL MARITIME ORGANIZATION (London, England) 1990– ; Chancellor, World Maritime Univ. (Malmö, Sweden) 1991– ; joined Dept. Transport Ottawa 1949 serving in engn. capacity Lachine and Welland Canals, Resident Engr. with Special Projects Br. 1954; Div. Engr. Welland Canal, St. Lawrence Seaway Authority 1955, Dir. of W. Region 1960, Dir. of Constr. 1964–71; Depy. Adm. Marine Services, Candn. Marine Transport. Adm. 1971–75; Commr. Candn. Coast Guard and Depy. Adm. Marine Transport Adm., CMTA 1975–80; Pres., The St. Lawrence Seaway Authority 1980–90; Dir., Canarctic Shipping Co. 1980–90; Pres., Seaway Internat. Bridge Corp.; Mem. Bd., Thousand Islands Bridge Authority 1980–90; el. Chrmn. Council International Maritime Organ. 1979, re-el. 1981, 1983, 1985 and 1987; apptd. Hon. Commodore Candn. Coast Guard 1981; Mem. of Bd., International Maritime Bureau 1991– ; apptd. Bd. of Govs., World Maritime Univ., Malmö, Sweden 1983–90; rec'd Engn. Medal Assn. Prof. Engrs. Prov. Ont. 1972; Distinguished Pub. Service Award U.S. Dept. of Transport. 1980; Hon. Mem., Candn. Maritime Law Assn. 1989; Hon. Mem., Honourable Company of Master Mariners (U.K.) 1990; Hon. Diploma, Candn. Coast Guard College 1990; Hon. Mem., Internat. Maritime Pilots' Assn. 1991; Hon. mem., Internat. Federation of Shipmasters' Assn. 1993; Doctor of Laws (honoris causa) Univ. of Malta 1993; Hon. mem., Internat. Assn. of Lighthouse Authorities 1994; mem. Assn. Prof. Engrs. Prov. Ont.; Am. Soc. Civil Engrs.; Home: 15 Ropers Orchard, London England SW3 5AX; Office: 4 Albert Embankment, London SE1 7SR England.

**O'NEILL, John,** M.A., Ph.D., F.R.S.C.; educator; b. London, Eng. 17 July 1933; s. John and Catherine (Hayburn) O'N.; e. Finchley Cath. Grammar Sch. 1952; London Sch. of Econ. & Pol. Sci. B.Sc. 1955; Univ. of Notre Dame M.A. 1956; Stanford Univ. Ph.D. 1962; DISTIN-

GUISHED RSCH. PROF. OF SOCIOL. YORK UNIV. 1983– ; External Associate, Centre for Comparative Lit. Sch. of Grad. Studies Univ. of Toronto; Sr. Instr. of French, Greek and Latin Woodside Priory Sch. Cal. 1958–63; Asst. Prof. of Philos. & Humanities San Jose State Coll. 1963–64; Acting Instr. of Econ. Stanford Univ. 1963–64; Asst. Prof. of Sociol. present Univ. 1964, Chrmn. of Sociol. 1969–71; Visiting Prof. Grad. Faculty New Sch. for Social Rsch. N.Y. 1969–70; 1983 Univ. Distinguished Visiting Prof. Ohio State Univ.; Dir. Graduate Programme in Sociology 1993–94; Sr. Scholar, Laidlaw Found., Children at Risk Programme 1992– ; recipient numerous Can. Council and External Affairs awards; author 'Perception, Expression and History' 1970; 'Sociology As A Skin Trade' 1972; 'Making Sense Together' 1974; 'Essaying Montaigne' 1982; 'For Marx Against Althusser' 1982; 'Five Bodies' 1985; 'The Communicative Body' 1989; 'Plato's Cave' 1991; 'Critical Conventions' 1992; ed. 'Modes of Individualism and Collectivism' 1973; 'On Critical Theory' 1976; transl. Maurice Merleau-Ponty 'Humanism and Terror' 1970, 'The Prose of the World' 1973; ed. Intnl. Lib. of Phenomenol. & Moral Sci's.; co-ed. 'Philosophy of the Social Sciences'; frequent lectr. univs. N. Am., W. Europe, Latin Am. and Israel; mem., Intnl. Assn. French-Speaking Sociols.; Société des Amis de Montaigne; Renaissance Soc. Am.; Candn. Sociol. & Anthrop. Assn.; Am. Sociol. Assn.; Soc. Phenomenol. & Existential Philos.; Toronto Psychoanalytic Assoc.; Pres., Toronto Semiotic Circle 1990–91; R. Catholic; recreations: soccer, swimming, walking; Home: 18 Burlington Cres., Toronto, Ont. M6H 2L4 Office: 225 Founders Coll., Downsview, Ont. M3J 1P3.

**O'NEILL, Timothy J.,** B.A., M.A., Ph.D.; economics executive; b. Sydney, N.S. 4 Aug. 1947; s. Bernard Harold and Mary Euphemia (McLean) O.; e. St. Francis Xavier Univ. B.A. 1969; Univ. of B.C. M.A. 1970; Duke Univ. Ph.D. 1979; m. Lois E. d. William and Alice MacPherson 26 June 1969; children: Kiley, Andrew; SENIOR VICE-PRES. & DEPUTY CHIEF ECONOMIST, BANK OF MONTREAL; Lectr., Economics, Univ. of P.E.I. 1970–74; Rsch. Asst. to Prof. Craufurd Goodwin, Duke Univ. 1975; Spec. Asst. to Pres., Cape Breton Devel. Corp. 1976; Academic Visitor, London School of Economics 1985–86; Assoc. Prof., Economics, St. Mary's Univ. 1976–88; Pres., Atlantic Provinces Economic Council 1988; Dir., Candn. Assn. for Business Economics; Candn. Found. for Economic Education; Mem., Candn. Economics Assn.; Atlantic Econ. Assn.; Candn. Reg. Science Assn.; Regional Studies Assn.; Inst. of Public Affairs of Canada; Nat. Statistics Council; Elder & Lay Teacher, Woodlawn United Church; author of numerous research articles, book chapters, conf. papers and studies; recreations: photography; Office: First Canadian Place, Toronto, Ont. M5X 1A1.

**O'NEILL, W. Paul,** B.A., C.A.; executive; b. Toronto 1938; e. Univ. of Toronto B.A. 1960; C.A. (Ont.) 1964; m. Marilyn; children: Michael, Lori; SELF-EMPLOYED; Corp. Extve. Vice Pres. & Chief Financial Officer, Atomic Energy of Canada Ltd. 1982–84; Pres., Radiochemical Co., Atomic Energy of Canada Ltd. 1985–88; Pres. & C.E.O., Nordion Internat. Inc. 1988–92; Home: P.O. Box 546, Merrickville, Ont. K0G 1N0.

**ONLEY, Toni,** R.C.A.; artist; b. Douglas, Isle of Man. 20 Nov. 1928; s. James Anthony and Florence (Lord) O.; e. St. Mary's Primary Sch. and Ingleby Secondary Sch. Isle of Man; Douglas Sch. of Fine Arts 1942–46; Doon Sch. of Fine Art 1951; Inst. Allende Mexico 1957 (scholarship); London, Eng. 1963; m. lstly Mary Burrows (d.) 1950; two d. Jennifer (dec'd.), Lynn; m. 2ndly Gloria Knight 1961; one s. James Anthony; m. 3rdly Yukiko Kageyama 23 Aug. 1979; Prof., Dept. of Fine Arts Univ. of B.C. 1967–76; solo exhns. incl.: Coste House Gallery Alta. 1958; Vancouver Art Gallery 1958; New Design Gallery Vancouver 1959, 1961–62, 1964–66, 1968; Dorothy Cameron Gallery Toronto 1960–62, 1964–65; Blue Barn Gallery Ottawa 1961, 1966; Point Gallery Victoria 1961; Otto Seligman Gallery Seattle 1962; Galerie Camille Hébert Montréal 1963; Commonwealth Inst., London, Eng. 1965; Galeria Agnes Lefort, Montreal 1965, 1967; Pandora's Box Gallery Victoria 1966; N.W. Craft Centre Gall, Seattle 1967; Topham Brown Art Gallery Vernon 1967; W. Circuit B.C. & Alta. 1966–67; Douglas Gallery Vancouver 1967; Owens Gallery Sackville 1967, 1978; Dalhousie Univ. 1967; Confed. Centre Art Gallery Charlottetown 1968; Agnes Etherington Art Centre Kingston 1968; Albert White Gallery Toronto 1968; Gallery Pascal Toronto 1968, 1970, 1972, 1975, 1979; Richard Demarco Gallery, Edinburgh, Scotland 1968; Art Gallery Greater Victoria 1968, 1983, 1989; Griffith Galleries Vancouver 1968; The Print Gall., Victoria 1968; Burnaby Art Gallery 1969; Bau-Xi Gallery Vancouver 1968–69, 1971–80; Simon Fraser Univ. (10 yr. Retro Tour, 9 Centres 1967–69) 1969; Fleet Gallery Winnipeg 1969, 1971; Graphics Gallery San Francisco 1969; Allied Art Centre Brandon 1970; Alta. Coll. Art 1971; Godart-Lefort Galerie Montréal 1971; Univ. of Alta. Edmonton 1971; Univ. of Lethbridge 1971; 1640 Gallery Montreal 1972; Gallery 4, Alexandria Virginia 1975; Hank Baum Gallery, San Francisco, Los Angeles 1975; Waddington Gallery, Montreal 1976; Westend Gallery, Edmonton 1976, 1979–83; Uttley's Gallery, Victoria 1976; Thomas Gallery, Winnipeg 1976, 1978–82; Presentation House, N. Vancouver 1977; S. Alta. Art Gallery, Lethbridge 1978; Nat. Museum of History, Repub. of China 1978; Vancouver Art Gallery retrospective 1978; Candn. Art Gallery, Calgary 1979–80; Kesik Gallery, Regina 1979; Kyles Gallery, Victoria 1979; Memorial Univ. Art Gallery, St. John's 1978; Art Gallery of Nova Scotia, Halifax 1978; Kenneth G. Heffel Fine Arts Inc., Vancouver 1981–89; Hett Gallery Ltd., Edmonton 1981–83; Gallery Aoki, Matsuyama, Japan 1982; Gallery One, Toronto 1983; Galerie Mihalis, Montreal 1985–87; Robertson Galleries, Ottawa 1982–87; Assiniboia Gall., Regina 1987; Heffel Gall., Vancouver 1988–89; Galerie Franklin Silverstone, Montreal, P.Q. 1988; Art Gall. of the South Okanagan, Penticton, B.C. 1988; Chinese Cultural Centre, Vancouver (after painting trip to China) 1988; Vancouver Art Gallery, Etchings 1989; designed set for Tennessee Williams' 'Notebook of Trigorin,' Vancouver Playhouse Theatre 1986; designed costumes and set for 'Gloria,' for choreographer Judith Marcuse, performed at Q.E. Theatre, Vancouver 1986; rep. in numerous maj. nat. and internat. group shows; rep. in various pub. and private colls. incl. Art Gallery Ont., Montreal Museum of Fine Arts Musée d'Art Contemporain Montréal, Vancouver Art Gallery, Seattle Museum of Fine Arts, Museum of Modern Art N.Y., Tate Gallery London, Eng.; Leeds Arts Gallery, Eng.; Victoria & Albert Museum, London, Eng.; The Canada Council Artbank; books: 'Toni Onley, A Silent Thunder' by Roger Boulet (Cerebrus/Prentice Hall) 1981; 'Walls of India' by George Woodcock (paintings by Toni Onley) Lester & Orpen Dennys 1986; 'Voyage en Arctique' (diaries and paintings by Toni Onley; poetry and journey account by Claude Peloquin); 'Onley's Arctic' by Toni Onley, paintings & diaries (Depratto, Onley, Parisien, Peloquin) 1989; 'Onley's Arctic' (diaries and paintings of the High Arctic, Toni Onley) Douglas & McIntyre 1989; CTV 'Only Onley' (30 min. profile documentary) Nov. 1989 & Dec. 1989; recipient Can. Council Grant 1961, 1963; Jessie Dow Award 1960; Spring Purchase Award Montreal Museum Fine Arts 1962; Sam & Ayola Zacks Award 1963 (Polar #1); Can. Council Sr. Fellowship 1964; rep. in Paris Biennial 1961; Candn. Biennials 1959, 1961, 1963, 1965, 1968; Trustee, Emily Carr Coll. of Art Vancouver 1983–84; Vice Chrmn., Canada India Village Aid; cited numerous bibliogs.; recreation: flying (since 1968 has used his own aircraft to search out his subjects from Mexico to Baffin Island; crashed 7 Sept. 1984 on Cheakamus Glacier, Garibaldi Park: both he and passenger, photographer John Reeves, survived); Address: 4279 Yuculta Cres., Vancouver, B.C. V6N 4A9.

**ONYSZCHUK, Mario,** M.Sc., Ph.D., F.C.I.C., C.Chem.; retired educator; b. Wolkow, Poland 21 July 1930; s. Andrew Onyszchuk; e. High Sch. of Montreal 1948; McGill Univ. B.Sc. 1951, Ph.D. 1954; Univ. of W. Ont. M.Sc. 1952; Cambridge Univ. Ph.D. 1956; m. Anastasia Anna Kushnir 27 June 1959; three s. Ivan Matthew, Gregory Andrew, Timothy Stephen; Associate Dean, Faculty of Graduate Studies and Research 1988–92, and Prof. of Chem., McGill Univ. 1968–93 (Retired); Lectr. in Chem. 1956, Asst. Prof. 1957, Assoc. Prof. 1963, Prof. 1968, Chrmn. 1979–85; Visiting Prof., Univ. of Southampton 1968–69, Univ. of Sussex 1977–78; Univ. Paul Sabatier 1985–86 and 1992–93; author or co-author various research articles; mem. Am. Chem. Soc.; Sigma Xi; Protestant; recreations: photography, philately, swimming, tennis, cross-country skiing, skating; Home: 60 Balfour Ave., Town of Mount Royal, Que. H3P 1L6.

**ORCHARD, David H.;** farmer; b. Saskatoon, Sask. 28 June 1950; s. John Ralph and Margaret Anne; e. Halcyonia P.S.; Borden H.S. 1968; Univ. of Saskatchewan Arts & Sciences 1968–70, College of Law 1970–71; Univ. Laval; worked, travelled: Australia, New Zealand, U.S.A., Fiji 1970–71; Europe, North Africa 1972–73; logging industry in B.C. 1974; Longshoreman, B.C. (Vancouver, New Westminster) 1974–75; took over operation of family farm 1975; CHAIRMAN & CO-FOUNDER, CITIZENS CONCERNED ABOUT FREE TRADE (CCAFT) 1985– ; author: 'The Fight for Canada: four centuries of resistance to U.S. Expansionism' Stoddart 1993, 'Free Trade: The Full Story' 1988 and numerous articles; frequent speaker across Canada in public meetings, debates, & interviews on the history & content of the Canada-USA Free Trade Agreement and NAFTA warning Canadians about their implications 1985– ; CCAFT mobilized a massive & successful public campaign in 1988 to have Senate block passage of the Free Trade Agreement & force a general election on its contents; opposed the Meech Lake and Charlottetown Constitutional Accords and calls for cancellation of both the FTA and NAFTA; Farm: Box 206, Borden, Sask. S0K 0N0; Home: 16 – 303 Queen St., Saskatoon, Sask. S7K 0M1; Office: Box 8052, Saskatoon, Sask. S7K 4R7.

**ORCHARD, Hon. Donald Warder,** B.S.A., M.L.A.; politician; b. Miami, Man. 11 Apr. 1946; s. Warder Franklin John and Muriel Bernice (King) O.; e. Miami Elem. Sch.; Midland Coll. Inst. Miami; Univ. of Man. B.S.A. (Agriculture Econ.) 1969; m. Janie Eden d. James A. Simpson, Winnipeg, Man. 19 July 1969; children: Eric Donald, Arlene Eden, Onalee Jill; MINISTER OF ENERGY AND MINES and MINISTER RESPONSIBLE FOR THE MANITOBA HYDRO ACT 1993– ; DEPUTY HOUSE LEADER, PROVINCE OF MANITOBA 1993– ; joined Simplot Chemicals, Regina and Edmonton 1969–73; Agriculture Consultant, Farm Management Instructor and Trustee on several agricultural boards, Miami, Manitoba 1973–77; el. M.L.A. for Pembina prov. g.e. 1977; Progressive Conservative Critic for Health, Communications, Manitoba Telephone System and Manitoba Data Services; Deputy Leader of the Progressive Conservative Party; Deputy Critic for Consumer and Corporate Affairs and Legislative Asst. to the Min. of Education; named Min. of Highways & Transportation 1979; apptd. Min. of Health 1988; Chair of the 1991 Provincial-Territorial Conference of Ministers of Health; P. Conservative; United Church; Office: Legislative Bldg., Room 302, Winnipeg, Man. R3C 0V8.

**O'REGAN, Joseph Mark,** C.A.; chartered accountant; b. St. John, N.B. 21 June 1945; s. Joseph Matthew and Mary Josephine (McCluskey) O.; e. Michael Power H.S. 1962; St. Francis Xavier Univ., B.Com. 1965; m. Heather d. Jack and Olive Renouf 24 Aug. 1968; children: Luke, Matthew, Jake, Paul; TORONTO OFFICE MANAGING PARTNER, ERNST & YOUNG 1993– ; joined Clarkson Gordon 1965; obtained CA 1969; Chrmn., St. Joseph's Health Ctr.; Chrmn., Emmanuel Convalescent Found. 1985–88; Managing Partner, Financial Services Group, Ernst & Young 1988–93; Pres., Humber Valley Hockey Assn. 1985–87; Dir., Ont. C. of C. 1986–90; Dir., The Canadian Club; recreations: golf, tennis, sailing, skiing; club: The Boulevard Club; Home: 99 The Kingsway, Toronto, Ont. M8X 2T6; Office: P.O. Box 251, Ernst & Young Tower, Toronto-Dominion Centre, Toronto, Ont. M5K 1J7.

**O'REGAN, R. Brian,** CD, APR; b. Ottawa, Ont. 29 Sept. 1924; s. Otto Gregory and Kathaleen (Fay) O.; e. Univ. of Wisconsin; U.S. Armed Forces Public Info. Sch.; m. Jean d. Arthur and Agnes Higginson 16 Jan. 1945; children: James A.M., Philip M.; Chrmn., TOT Communications Inc. 1988– ; Offr., Candn. Army 1951–65; Sr. Extve. Offr., Govt. of Canada 1966–74; Public Affairs Dir., Northern Telecom Ltd. 1974–76; Asst. Vice Pres. 1976–82; Vice-Pres. 1982–87; Candn. Forces Decoration; Lamp of Service, Sr. Award of Candn. Public Reln. Soc. 1973; Pres., Candn. War Correspondents Assn.; Mem., Rideau Club; Nat. Press. Club (Former Dir.); Candn. Public Reln. Soc. (Former Vice Pres.); recreations: swimming, genealogy, writing; Home: 2608 - 500 Laurier Ave. W., Ottawa, Ont. L1R 5E1.

**O'REILLY, Gillian Ann;** editor; b. Montreal, Que. 23 June 1956; d. James Meredith and Louisa Laurie (Gill) O'R; e. Univ. of Toronto, B.A. 1978; m. Anthony s. Peter Joseph and Dorothy (Silver) Usher 18 June 1988; children: Alan Peter, Ian James; FREELANCE JOURNALIST AND EDITOR 1989– ; freelance ed., Children's Book News 1989, 1990–91; The Braille Courier 1984–85; Ed., The Candn. Bookseller 1984–89; Chair, Freedom of Expression Ctte., Book & Periodical Devel. Counc. 1986–87; Freelance Eds. Assn. of Can.; North York Heritage Ctte. 1990–93; Address: 63 Deloraine Ave., Toronto, Ont. M5M 2A8.

**O'REILLY, I. Rossa,** M.A., C.F.A., F.C.S.I.; financial executive; b. Dublin, Ireland 22 Dec. 1947; s. E. Kevin I. and Lucyna I. (Piskozub) O.; e. The Peak School Hong Kong; St. Conleth's College Dublin; Trinity College, Univ. of Dublin M.A. 1971; Inst. of Chartered Financial Analysts (Charlottesville, Va.) C.F.A. 1977; Fellow, Candn. Securities Inst. F.C.S.I. 1977; m. Linda Gillette d. A. Towy and Margaret G. Channing 1 July 1971; children: Miranda, Melissa; VICE-PRES. & DIR., WOOD GUNDY INC. 1984– ; Vice-Pres., Dominion Securities 1971–84; Pres., Toronto Soc. of Financial

Analysts 1985–86; Trustee, Inst. of Chartered Financial Analysts 1986– ; Gov., Assn. of Investment Management and Research 1986– ; Chair, Inst. of Chartered Financial Analysts 1992–93; clubs: Royal Canadian Yacht; Home: 99 Hazelton Ave., Toronto, Ont. M5R 2E4; Office: BCE Place, P.O. Box 500, Toronto, Ont. M5J 2S8.

**O'REILLY, James Meredith,** B.Com., C.A.; business consultant; b. Winnipeg, Man. 8 Feb. 1926; s. James and Marion (Meredith) O'R.; e. Upper Can. Coll. Toronto 1943; McGill Univ. B.Com. 1947; C.A. 1950; m. Louisa Laurie d. Evan W. T. Gill 23 July 1955; children: Gillian Ann, James, Sheila Margaret, Diana Catherine; Student-in-Accounts and C.A., McDonald Currie & Co. Montreal 1947–51; Secy.-Treas., Controller, Dir., Rolph-Clark Stone-Benallack Ltd. Montreal 1951–60; Budget Dir., Rolph-Clark-Stone Ltd. Toronto 1960–63; Dir.-Finance, Dominion Forge Co. Windsor, Ont. 1963–68; Controller-Liquifuels Div., Canadian Fuel Marketers Ltd. Toronto 1969–73; Controller, Canada Development Corp. 1973–75; Vice-Pres. & Treas., Canada Dev. Corp., 1976–83; Vice Pres., Bennecon Ltd. 1983–91; served with RCA 1944–45, Reserve 1951–57, rank Lt.; mem. Inst. C.A.'s Ont.; Financial Extves. Inst.; University Club of Toronto; R. Catholic; Home: 90 Willowbank Blvd., Toronto, Ont. M5N 1G6.

**O'REILLY, Robert Richard,** Ph.D.; university professor; b. Montreal, Que. 30 Nov. 1938; s. Alfred Richard and Dolores Eva (Girard) O.; e. Loyola of Montreal, B.A. 1959; Univ. of Montreal, B.Ed. 1960; St. Michael's, Vermont, M.Ed. 1963; Univ. of Alta., Ph.D. 1967; m. Jane d. Sydney and Margaret LeGros 11 Apr. 1961; children: Andrew Robert, Janet Evelyn; HEAD, DEPT. OF EDUCATIONAL POLICY & ADMIN. STUDIES, UNIV. OF CALGARY 1989– ; Teacher, Montreal & N.W.T. 1960–65; Secondary Sch. Vice-Principal, Montreal 1968–69; Asst. Prof., Univ. of Montreal 1967–68; Assoc. Prof., Univ. of Ottawa 1969–80; Extve. Dir., Nat. Legal Aid Rsch. Ctr. 1980–84; Prof., Univ. of Ottawa 1984–88; Dir. of Edn. Studies 1988–89; Trustee, Royal Ottawa Health Care Group 1980–89; Mem., Candn. Edn. Assn.; Candn. Soc. for Studies in Edn.; Am. Edn. Rsch. Assn.; recreations: skiing, swimming, camping; Home: 319 Valencia Pl. N.W., Calgary, Alta. T3A 2C1; Office: Calgary, Alta. T2N 1N4.

**OREOPOULOS, Dimitrios G.,** M.D., Ph.D., F.A.C.P., F.R.C.P. & S.(C); physician; educator; b. 24 May 1936; s. George and Antigoni (Antoniadou) O.; e. Evangeliki School, L Petroyannopoulos, Athens, Greece 1954; Univ. of Athens M.D. 1960; Queen's Univ. Belfast Ph.D. 1969; m. Nancy C. I. d. late Edwin R.K. Hooker 19 Sept. 1971; children: George, Philip, Antigoni, John; DIR., PERITONEAL DIALYSIS UNIT AND KIDNEY STONE CLINIC, TORONTO HOSP. and mem. of Staff Div. of Nephrology there since 1970; Prof. of Med. Univ. of Toronto 1979– , Charles Mickle Fellow 1981; Gardiner award, Metro Toronto Citizen of the Year 1989; Distinguished Physician of the Year, Hellenic Medical Soc., New York 1993; National Torchbearer Award, Am. Kidney Fund 1994; Intern, Resident, Sr. Resident and mem. Staff Dept. Med. Hippokratean Hosp. Greece 1960–64; Specialist in Internal Med. Greece 1963; Sr. Registrar Dept. of Med. Queen's Univ. Belfast 1966–69; served with Greek Army Med. Corps 1960–62; Assoc. Mem., Center for Bioethics, Univ. of Toronto, Coresponding Mem., Academy of Athens; co-author 'Strategy In Renal Failure' 1978; 'An Introduction to Continous Ambulatory Peritoneal Dialysis' 1980; 'Peritoneal Dialysis' 1981; 'Geriatric Nephrology' 1985; 'The Essentials of Peritoneal Dialysis' 1993; 'Nephrology and Urology in the Aged Patient' 1993; Found. and Ed. 'Peritoneal Dialysis Bulletin' now 'Peritoneal Dialysis International'; Found. and Ed. in Chief 'Humane Medicine Journal'; Ed., 'Geriatric Nephrology and Urology Journal'; Co-ed. and Publ.: 'Advances in Continuous Ambulatory Peritoneal Dialysis' 1986; Founder and first Pres., Hippocrates (Greek-Canadian Med. Assoc. of Ont.) 1984–87; Pres., Hellenic Home for the Aged; Mem., Task Force on Access to Professions and Trades in Ont.; Pres. elect, Internat. Soc. for Peritoneal Dialysis 1992– ; First Pres., Internat. Soc. of Nephrology and Urology 1994–97; mem. Greek Soc. Nephrol.; Candn. Soc. Nephrol.; Am. Soc. Nephrol.; Greek Orthodox; Home: 10 Ladywood Dr., Etobicoke, Ont. M9V 1K9; Office: 399 Bathurst St., Toronto, Ont. M5T 2S8.

**ORLOWSKI, Stanislaw Tadeusz,** M.Sc.(Arch.), F.R.A.I.C., R.I.B.A.; architect; b. Skarzysko, Poland 24 Sept. 1920; s. Tadeusz and Irena (Malawczyk) S.; e. Copernicus H.S. Wlodzimierz, Poland; Leicester (Eng.) Univ. read Econ. 1945–46; Leicester Sch. of Arch., Dip. Arch. 1951; Univ. of London M.Sc. (Arch.) 1954; m. Krystyna J. d. Jan and Helena Przyborowski 23 July 1949; three d. Alexandra Maria Izabela, Irena Krystyna, Helena Victoria; Chief Archit., Min. of Education Ont. 1985–86; Assoc. Chief Archit., Min. of Education, Ont. 1980–85, Chief Archit. Min. of Colls. and Univs. 1973–80; Chief Rsch. Archit. 1967–73; came to Can. 1952; held sr. positions Toronto archit. firms Page & Steele, Arthur Heeney, Allward and Gouinlock; Area Archit. S.W. and Central Ont. Dept. Pub. Works Can.; co-ordinated physical facilities planning and devel. 22 Colls. Applied Arts & Technol. 1967–80; cons. edn. and design Candn. and foreign edn. authorities; studied edn. facilities Europe 1968; participated 'Project School to School' Ont. Ctte. to provide edn. and teaching assistance W. Indies 1970–72; Candn. Rep. Internat. Union Archit. Sch. Planning Conf. Berlin 1974; Visiting Prof. of Archit. Europe 1975 & 1977; Candn. Rep. Internat. Union Archit. Edn. Facilities Group 1975–80; Lectr. various colls., univs. and instns. Can. and abroad; mem. Ont. Assn. Archs. Registration Bd. 1976–78; Dir. Ont. Univs. Capital Aid Corp. 1973–82; Chrmn. 14 confs. Sch., Coll. and Univ. Planning Ont.; Co-Chrmn. Pan-Am. Edn. Facilities conf. Morella, Mexico; mem. Adv. Ctte. Dept. Archit. Technol. Ryerson Polytech. Inst. 1976–87; Adv. Ctte. Energy Systems Eng. Technol. Mohawk Coll. Applied Arts & Technol. 1976–83; Adv. Ctte. Interior Design Humber Coll. Appl. Arts & Technol. 1981–87; Counc. Ednl. Facility Planners Internat. Energy Ctte. 1979–86; mem. Scouting movement since 1931, Vice Pres. Polish Boy Scouts & Girl Guides Assn. World 1970–88; mem. Polish Inst. Arts & Sci.'s Can. 1970– ; Pres. Polish Candn. Cong. 1986–90; Chrmn., World Polonia Coord. Counc. 1986–93; author numerous articles various jours.; dir. rsch. publ. over 38 studies edn. facilities 1967–80; Elected Hon. Mem., Ont. Assn. of Architects (for signal and valuable service to the profession) 1992; Awarded a Citation of Service, Council of Educational Facility Planners, International 1991; released from Pechora-lag USSR 1941 (arrested by Russians (NKWD) May 8th, 1940; sentenced to 20 yrs. of hard labour in distant regions of the Soviet Union for Boy Scout activities; held in 6 prisons and in concentration camp 'Piechorlag'; released under Stalin-Sikorski agreement Sept. 1941); joined Polish Army serving with 2nd Polish Corps 8th Brit. Army Middle E., N. Africa, Italy (Captain); recipient Polish and Brit. decorations; Field Marshall Alexander's Scholarship Study in Brit.; mem. Royal Candn. Legion Fort York Br.; Royal Archit. Inst. of Can.; Ont. Assn. Archits. (served various cttes.); Royal Inst. Brit. Archits.; Assn. Polish Engrs. Can. (Pres. 1967–70); Am. Inst. Archits. Ed. Ctte.; R. Catholic; recreations: tennis, skiing, painting, contemporary history; Clubs: Royal Candn. Mil. Inst.; Empire; Home: 42 Braeside Rd., Toronto, Ont. M4N 1X7.

**ORMAN, Hon. Richard Dale,** M.L.A., B.A.; politician; b. Calgary, Alta. 9 June 1948; s. John Charles and Frances Doreen (Cumming) O.; e. Crescent Hts. High Sch. 1967; Univ. of Calgary 1969; E. Washington Univ. B.A. 1971; children: Sean, Riley, Cayley; Min. of Energy Alta. 1989; Chrmn. and Dir. Eventsport International Inc.; Dir. Corpsport Canada Marketing Inc.; Petrol. Landman, Red River Oils 1972; Extve. Assst. Min. Mines & Minerals (Energy) Alta. 1972–75; Special Asst. Min. of Energy Alta. 1976; Pres.: Orman & Benini Land Services Ltd. 1976–79; PLM Resources Ltd. 1979–84; Dir., Corpsport International 1984; Pres., Nexus Resources Ltd. 1985–86; el. M.L.A. for Calgary-Montrose 1986 and apptd. Min. of Career Devel. & Employment 1986–88; Min. of Labour 1988–89; Chrmn. various Cabinet cttes. and mem. Treasury Bd.; Dir. Citizen Advocacy; Candn. Assn. Petrol. Landmen 1976; Chrmn. Special Features, Calgary Exhn. & Stampede; Small Bus. Ctte., Calgary C. of C. 1980; recreations: golf, squash, jogging; Clubs: Glencoe; Canyon Meadows Golf & Country; Home: 508, 300 Meredith Rd. N.E., Calgary, Alta. T2E 7A8 (P.O. Box 6967, Stn. D, Calgary, Alta. T2P 2G2).

**ORMROD, Douglas Padraic,** B.S.A., Ph.D.; university professor and administrator; b. Fort Langley, B.C. 27 May 1934; s. John F. and Ruby E. (Christianson) O.; e. Univ. of B.C. B.S.A. 1956; Univ. of California Ph.D. 1959; m. Esther d. Frank and Dora Marrion 15 June 1957; children: Robert, John, Jacqueline; DEAN, FACULTY OF GRADUATE STUDIES, UNIV. OF GUELPH 1986– ; Instr., Asst. Prof., Univ. of Calif. at Davis 1958–60; Asst. Prof., Assoc. Prof., Prof., Univ. of B.C. 1960–69; Prof. & Chair, Horticultural Sci., Univ. of Guelph 1969–74; Prof. 1974– ; Consulting in Environmental Science: Douglas P. Ormrod, P.Ag. Ltd.; Sigma Xi Distinguished Researcher Award 1978; Ont. Agric. Coll. Distinguished Researcher Award 1985; Mem., Ag. Inst. of Can.; Ont. Inst. of Agrologists; Candn. Soc. of Plant Physiol.; Candn. Soc. for Hort. Sci.; author: 'Pollution in Horticulture' 1977; co-editor: 'Effects of Gaseous Air Pollution in Agriculture and Horticulture' 1982; Home: 145 Niska Rd., Guelph, Ont. N1H 6J3; Office: Guelph, Ont. N1G 2W1.

**ORMSBY, Anthony John,** F.C.A.; retired chartered accountant; b. Toronto, Ont. 25 March 1927; s. Gerald Yeadon and Helen Marion (Macdonell) O.; e. Upper Canada Coll.; C.A. 1951; m. Julia d. Brefney Higgins 20 Dec. 1982; children: Anthony Robert, Timothy John; C.A., Ormsby & Ormsby 1951–61; Offr. & later Pres., Dover Corp. 1961–72; Dir. 1972– ; Partner, and later Chrmn., Spicer MacGillivray 1972–85; Fellow, Inst. of C.A.s 1982; Past Chrmn., Toronto Harbour Comm.; Bd. of Govs., Upper Canada Coll.; Anglican; Conservative; recreation: travel; Clubs: Toronto; York; Home: Kilrie House, Kirkcaldy, Fife, Scotland KY25UW; Office: Ste. 1100, North Tower, Royal Bank Plaza, Toronto, Ont. M5J 2P9.

**ORMSBY, Margaret Anchoretta,** M.A., Ph.D., LL.D., D.Lit., F.R.S.C., O.B.C.; b. Quesnel, B.C. 7 June 1909; d. George Lewis and Margaret Turner (McArthur) O.; e. Univ. of B.C. B.A. 1929, M.A. 1931, D.Lit. 1974; Bryn Mawr Coll. Ph.D. 1937; Univ. of Man. LL.D. 1964; Univ. of Notre Dame Nelson, B.C. LL.D. 1968; Simon Fraser Univ. LL.D. 1971; Univ. of Victoria LL.D. 1976; Head of Hist. Sarah Dix Hamlin Sch. San Francisco 1937–40; Special Lectr. in Hist. McMaster Univ. 1940–43; Lectr. in Hist. Univ. of B.C. 1943, Asst. Prof. 1946, Assoc. Prof. 1949, Prof. 1955, Head of Hist. 1965–74, Visiting Prof. of Hist. 1974–75; Visiting Prof., Univ. of W. Ont. 1977; Univ. of Toronto 1978; recipient Am. State & Local Hist. Soc. Award of Merit 1959, 1975; Candn. Hist. Assn. Regional Hist. Award 1983; Centennial Medal 1967; awarded Commemorative Medal for 125th Anniversary of Candn. Confederation 1992; Annual Ormsby Lecture in B.C. History, Friends of Royal B.C. Museum, Victoria 1991– ; mem., B.C. Heritage Adv. Bd. 1971–83; Bd. Govs. Okanagan Coll. 1980–85; named Freeman City of Vernon 1959; Order of British Columbia 1990; mem., Hist. Sites & Monuments Bd. Can. 1960–68; Sir John A. Macdonald Prize Ctte. in Candn. Hist. 1977–79; author 'British Columbia: A History' 1958, rev. ed. 1971; 'A Pioneer Gentlewoman in British Columbia: The Recollections of Susan Allison' 1976, rev. ed. 1991; introduction 'Fort Victoria Letters 1846–51,' HBRS. xxxii, 1979; 'Coldstream - nulli secundus' 1990; contrib. 'Dictionary of Canadian Biography' vols. IX, X, XI, XII; Life mem., Candn. Hist. Assn. (Pres. 1965–66); Life mem., B.C. Hist. Assn. (Pres. 1949–50); Okanagan Hist. Soc.; Anglican; recreation: fruit growing; Address: 'Garafine' 12407 Coldstream Creek Rd., Vernon, B.C. V1B 1G2.

**OROBETZ, Christina Lydia Clementina,** B.A.; business executive; b. Toronto, Ont. 13 Apr. 1955; d. Roman George and Olga Sonja O.; e. St. Mildred's-Lightbourne Sch.; Univ. of Toronto, B.A. (Hons.) 1976; Sotheby's Works of Art Course 1977–78; Victorian Paintings Dept., Sotheby's Belgravia (U.K.) 1978–80; Dir., European Art Dept. (Can.) 1980–85; Mng. Dir., Sotheby's (Can.) Inc. 1985–86; PRESIDENT, SOTHEBY'S (CAN.) INC. 1986– ; frequent lectr.; Alpha Omicron Pi; Mem., Scholarship Fund Ctte., Nat. Ballet Sch.; recreations: riding, swimming, badminton, canoeing; Clubs: Royal Candn. Yacht; Albany; Home: One Benvenuto Place, Toronto, Ont. M4V 2L1; Office: 9 Hazelton Ave., Toronto, Ont. M5R 2E1.

**ORR, James Cameron,** B.Sc., Ph.D.; educator; b. Paisley, Scot. 10 Aug. 1930; s. James and Jean Stark (Ketchen) O.; e. Paisley Grammar Sch. 1935; Shawlands Acad. 1944; Cheshunt Grammar Sch. Herts. 1947; Royal Coll. of Science (Imp. Coll.) A.R.C.S., B.Sc. 1954; Birkbeck Coll. London; Glasgow Univ. Ph.D. 1960; Iowa State Univ. (Rockefeller Foundation Fellowship); m. Robin Denise Moore 22 Nov. 1958; children: Andrew Cameron, Fiona Kathleen; PROF. OF BIOCHEM. AND CHEMISTRY, MEM. UNIV. OF NFLD. since 1976; Assoc. Dean, Basic Medical Sciences, Univ. of Nfld., 1976–80; Visiting Scholar, Sydney Univ., Australia, 1982–83; Research Chem. Syntex S.A., Mexico City, 1959–63; Research Assoc. to Assoc. Prof. Harvard Med. Sch. 1963–75; mem. Med. Research Council Biochem. Comte., 1978–82, Fellowship Ctte. 1983–86, Centennial Scholarship Ctte. 1992– ; mem. Editorial Bd. of 'Steroids' 1989– ; served with RAF 1949–51, Leading Aircraftsman, Air Sea Rescue; contributing author 'Biochemical Mass Spectrometry' 1972; research and publishing on organic and enzymic reaction mechanisms; mem. of Senate, Memorial Univ.; mem. Am. Chem. Soc.; Am. Soc. Biochemistry and Molecular Biology; Candn. Biochem. Soc.; Endocrine Soc.; Sigma Xi; Royal Scot. Country Dance Soc. Teachers' Assn. Can.; Independent; recreations: sailing, dancing, swimming, chemistry, glass blowing; Home: 360 Hamilton Ave.,

St. John's, Nfld. A1C 1K2; Office: Memorial University Medical School, Prince Philip Dr., St. John's, Nfld. A1B 3V6.

**ORR, Robert (Bobby) Gordon;** hockey player (retired), business executive; b. Parry Sound, Ont. 20 Mar. 1948; m. Peggy; children: Darren Brent; shortstop MacTier, Ont. provincial champion jr. baseball team 1963; from hometown minor hockey ranks to Oshawa Generals OHA junior A club at 14; led team to OHA title 1966; with help of Alan Eagleson signed reported $70,000 pro contract Boston Bruins Sept. 1966; deal considered cornerstone for NHL Players' Assn.; 1966–76 played 651 regular season games scoring 268 goals, 643 assists for 911 points, 949 penalty minutes, plus 74 playoff games, 26 goals, 66 assists for 92 points, 107 penalty minutes; NHL regular season assist record of 102 in 1970–71; record point total for defenceman of 139 same season; playoff assist record with 19, 1971–72; playoff point record for defenceman same season with 24; regular season goals record for defenceman with 46, 1974–75; helped Bruins win two Stanley Cups; played out option, signed by Chicago Black Hawks 1976; six knee operations made future play impossible; assistant coach Chicago 1976–77; recipient Calder Memorial Trophy as NHL rookie of year 1967; Art Ross scoring title 1970, 1975; Hart MVP Trophy 1970, 1971, 1972; Conn Smythe Trophy twice; James Norris Memorial Trophy eight times 1968–75; MVP Canada Cup 1976; Lou Marsh Trophy 1970; Canadian CP poll Male Athlete of Year 1970; Sports Magazine, Sports Illustrated Athlete of Year awards; Office: c/o Hockey Hall of Fame, BCE Place, 30 Yonge St., Toronto, Ont. M5E 1X8.

**ORRELL, John Overton,** M.A., Ph.D., F.R.S.C.; educator; b. Maidstone, Eng. 31 Dec. 1934; s. William Ramsden and Mabel (Hallam) O.; e. Maidstone Grammar Sch. 1953; Univ. Coll. Oxford, B.A. 1958, M.A. 1964; Univ. of Toronto, M.A. 1959, Ph.D. 1964; m. Wendy d. Allan and Winnifred Phillips 23 June 1956; children: Katherine, David John; UNIV. PROF. OF ENGLISH, UNIV. OF ALTA. 1990– ; Asst. Prof. 1961, Assoc. Prof. 1967, Prof. 1974– ; McCalla Rsch. Prof. 1984–85; Kaplan Rsch. Prize 1989; mem. Adv. Council Shakespeare Globe Centre (Chrmn. Arch. Ctte.); author 'Fallen Empires: The Lost Theatres of Edmonton, 1881–1914' 1982; 'The Quest for Shakespeare's Globe' 1983; 'The Theatres of Inigo Jones and John Webb' 1985; 'The Human Stage: English Theatre Design 1567–1640' 1988; co-author, with Andrew Gurr, 'Rebuilding Shakespeare's Globe' 1989; ed. 'Studies of Major Works in English' 1968; 'Western Canadian Dictionary and Phrase Book' 1977; Anglican; recreation: painting houses; Home: 8520 – 104 St. Edmonton, Alta. T6E 4G4; Office: Edmonton, Alta. T6G 2E5.

**ORSER, Brian Ernest,** CM, OC, O.Ont.; professional athlete; b. Belleville, Ont. 18 Dec. 1961; s. Harl Edward and Mary Josephine-Anne (Crouchman) O.; e. Penetanguishene S.S.; eight-time Canadian Mens Champion; two-time Olympic Silver Medalist 1984, '88; 1987 World Champion; World Free Skating Champion 1984, '86, '87, '88; Canadian Mem. to Order of Canada 1984; Officer 1988; Primetime Emmy Award Winner for outstanding performance in classical music / dance programming 1989–90; currently touring in figure skating tour 'Stars on Ice' in US & Canada; Ontario Athlete of the Year 1988; Mem., Canada's Sports Hall of Fame; Co-Chair, 'Skate the Dream' (a tribute to Rob McCall which raised over $500,00 for AIDS rsch. for the Toronto Hospital Found.); author: 'Orser: A Skater's Life' 1988 (bestseller, over 70,000 copies sold); recreations: skiing (winter & water), travelling, swimming, sky diving; clubs: Toronto Cricket, Skating & Curling; Home: 35 McKenzie Ave., Toronto, Ont. M4W 1K1.

**ORSER, Earl Herbert,** B.Com., F.C.A., LL.D.; executive; b. Toronto, Ont. 5 July 1928; s. late Frank Herbert and late Ethel Marjorie (Cox) O.; e. Danforth Tech. High Sch., Toronto, Ont.; Univ. of Toronto, B.Com. 1950; Chart. Acct. 1953; m. Marion Queenie 4 Aug. 1951; children: Darlene, Barbara, Beverley, Nancy; CHRMN., LONDON LIFE INS. CO.; Dir., Trilon Financial Corp.; Chrmn., London Insurance Group; Chrmn., Toronto College Street Centre Ltd; former Pres. & C.E.O., The T. Eaton Co. Ltd. 1975–77; Dir. London Life Ins. Co.; Chrmn., Spar Aerospace Ltd.; Interprovincial Pipe Line Inc.; DMR Group Inc.; Past Chrmn., Bd. of Gov., Univ. of W. Ont.; mem. Univ. College Ctte., Univ. of Toronto; Past Chrmn., Candn. Life and Health Ins. Assn.; Inst. Chart. Accts. Ont.; Financial Extves. Inst.; British-North American Ctte.; Geneva Assn.; United Church; recreations: skiing, tennis; Clubs: National (Toronto); Rosedale; Toronto; St. James's; Granite; London; London Hunt; Office: London Life Ins. Co., 255 Dufferin Ave., London, Ont. N6A 4K1.

**ORSINO, Philip S.,** B.A., C.A.; business executive; b. Toronto, Ont. 21 June 1954; s. Joseph R. and Grace B. (Cisterna) O.; e. Univ. of Toronto, B.A. 1976; m. Helen d. William and Sophie Winkels 4 June 1976; one s.: Joseph William; PRES., PREMDOR INC. 1989– (largest mfr. of doors & mouldings in North Am.; produces over 50,000 doors per day in 18 plants in Canada, U.S. & Europe); Partner, Hilborn Ellis Grant, CA's 1980–84; Pres., Century Wood Door Limited 1984–89 (merged with Premdor Inc. Oct. 1989); Dir., Premdor Inc.; Crown Door Corp. (U.S.); Fraser Valley Forest Products Ltd.; C.A. 1979; Mem. Finance, Audit Cttes., The Toronto Hospital; Dir., Humber Memorial Hosp.; recreations: skiing; club: Beaver Valley Ski; Home: 26 Wimbleton Road, Toronto, Ont. M9A 3R8; Office: Yonge Corporate Centre, 4120 Yonge St., 4th Floor, Suite 402, Toronto, Ont. M2P 2B8.

**ORTIZ-PATIÑO, Jaime;** company executive; b. Paris, France 20 June 1930; s. Jorge Ortiz-Linares and Graziella Patiño; m. Uta Krebber 12 June 1937; children: Carlos, Felipe (by previous marriage); Pres. and C.E.O. Patino Properties Ltd.; Patino Investments S.A.; Valderrama Investments S.A.; Sotoproperties S.A.; Hon. Dir., John Labatt Ltd.; Advisor to the Bolivian Government for European Affairs; Pres. Emeritus World Bridge Fed.; Pres., Valderrama Golf Club, Sotogrande, Spain; Trustee, Fondation S. I. Patiño, Geneva; Lahey Clinic Found., Burlington, Mass.; recreations: bridge, golf, tennis; Home: 47 Grosvenor Square, London W1X 9DE, United Kingdom.

**ORVIG, Svenn,** M.Sc., Ph.D., F.R.S.C.; educator; b. Bergen, Norway 4 Aug. 1920; s. Erik and Laura (Meidell) O.; e. Oslo Univ. cand. mag. 1948; McGill Univ. M.Sc. 1951, Ph.D. 1954; m. Anne d. Ross and Dora Whitehead 16 June 1951; two s. Christopher, Robert; EMERITUS PROF. OF METEOROLOGY, MCGILL UNIV. 1986; PROF. 1965–86 (and Dean of Science 1976–85); Asst. Dir. and Dir., Arctic Inst. of N. Am. 1951–56; Assoc. Prof. present Univ. 1957; Secy., Candn.-Scandinavian Found. 1952–66; Internat. Comm. on Polar Meteorol. 1963–75; Chrmn., Arctic Inst. N.Am. 1971; Gov., McGill Univ. 1968–70, 1981–85; mem. Counc., Royal Soc. Can. 1982–84; served with Royal Norwegian Air Force (with R.A.F.) 1941–45, Pilot, rank Flight Lt.; Norwegian War Medal; author or co-author over 61 publs.; ed. 'Climates of the Polar Regions' 1970; recipient Pres's Prize Candn' Br. Royal Meteorol. Soc. 1964; Andrew Thomson Prize Candn. Meteorol. Soc. 1977; rec'vd. Patterson Medal, Candn. Atmospheric Environ. Service 1982; recreations: skiing, swimming, sailing; Home: 47 Copperfield Dr., Kingston, Ont. K7M 1M3; Office: Dept. of Atmospheric & Oceanic Science, 805 Sherbrooke St. W., Montreal, Que. H3A 2K6.

**ORVIK, Nils,** M.A., Ph.D.; educator; b. Kragero, Norway 3 Jan. 1918; s. Karl August and Lydia Elvira (Larsen) O.; served with Norwegian Army World War II; e. Univ. of Oslo B.A. 1946, M.A. 1948; Univ. of Wis. Ph.D. (Internat. Hist.) 1950; Brit. Council Fellow, London Sch. of Econ. & Pol. Science 1953–54; Internat. Fellow, Harvard Univ. 1962–63; Research Fellow, Univ. of Cal. Berkeley 1968; Columbia Univ. 1969; m. Karen Joy d. Lloyd and Julia Erickson 30 July 1964; children: Tone, Kirsti, Karl, Kari-Lou; PROF. EMERITUS, DEPT OF POLITICAL STUDIES, QUEEN'S UNIV. 1985– ; Norwegian Ministry of Defence Oslo 1951–62, Civil Rep. Directing Staff Norwegian Nat. Defence Coll. 1951–62; Dir. Social Science Sec. Norwegian Defence Research Estab. Oslo 1962–63; Assoc. Prof. of Pol. Science Univ. of Oslo 1963–71, Dir. of Internat. Studies and of Research Group for Internat. Politics 1963–71; Prof. of Pol. Studies 1971–83; Dir. of Centre for Internat. Relations, Queen's Univ. 1975–85; Author: 'Fears and Expectations: Norwegian Attitudes Toward Integration' 1972; 'Sicherheit auf Finnisch, 1972'; 'Departmental Decision-Making' 1972; 'Kampen om Arbeiderpartiet' 1977; 'Christians for Political Action' 1988; 'Norge ved korsveien' 1989; Editor: 'NATO Priorities' 1981; 'Canada and NATO' 1982; Northern Development: Northern Security,' 1983; 'Semialignment and Western Security' 1986; recreations: outdoor activities, hunting, fishing; Home: 665 Willis St., Kingston, Ont. K7M 6J5; Office: Dept. of Political Studies, Queen's Univ., Kingston, Ont. K7L 3N6.

**ORYSCHUK, Roman,** B.Comm., M.B.A.; business executive; b. Montréal, Qué. 16 Aug. 1953; e. McGill Univ. B.Comm. 1976, M.B.A. 1983; m. Diane d. Gaston and Thérèse Dumont 27 May 1978; children: Alexandra, Patrick, Vanessa; PRES. & CHIEF EXTVE. OFFR., GE CAPITAL CANADA EQUIPMENT FINANCING 1993– ; Mktg. Analyst, Gulf Oil Corp. 1976; Sr. Budget Offr. City of Montréal 1976–79; various sr. mgmt. positions The Royal Bank of Canada 1979–87; Vice Pres. Finance, National Bank of Leasing Inc. 1987, Pres. & C.E.O. 1988–93 and Vice-Pres., National Bank of Canada 1989–93; Fellow, Inst. Candn. Bankers; V.P. Equipment Lessors Assn. Can. (Dir.); Montréal C. of C.; Assn. des MBA du Qué.; recreations: tennis, skiing, running, cycling; Home: 165 Mozart, Dollard des Ormeaux, Qué. H9G 2Z5; Office: 600 rue de La Gauchetière ouest, Suite 2760, Montréal, Qué. H3B 4L8.

**OSBALDESTON, Gordon Francis Joseph,** P.C., O.C., B.Com., M.B.A., LL.D.; civil servant; b. Hamilton, Ont. 29 Apr. 1930; s. John Edward and Margaret (Hanley) O.; e. St. Jerome's Coll., Kitchener, Ont. 1947; Univ. of Toronto, B.Com. 1952; Univ. of W. Ont. M.B.A. 1953; Hon. degrees: LL.D. Univ. of W. Ont. 1984; York Univ. 1984; Dalhousie Univ. 1985; Carleton Univ. 1987; m. Geraldine, d. Eugene Keller, Kitchener, Ont., 3 Oct. 1953; children: Stephen, David, Robert, Catherine; SR. FELLOW, SCHOOL OF BUSINESS ADMIN., UNIV. OF WESTERN ONT. 1986– ; joined Dept. Trade & Comm., as Foreign Service Offr., Trade Commr. Service 1953; Vice Consul & Asst. Trade Commr., Sao Paulo, Brazil 1954 & Chicago, Ill., 1957; Consul and Trade Commr., Los Angeles, Cal., 1960; apptd. Asst. Dir., Personnel, Trade Commr. Service, 1964 and Asst. Dir., Operations, 1966; Extve. Dir. 1967; Asst. Depy. Min. Consumer Affairs, Dept. of Consumer & Corp. Affairs 1968; Depy. Secy. of the Treasury Bd. 1970; Depy. Min. Dept. Consumer & Corp. Affairs Can. 1972; Secy. of Treasury Bd. 1973; Depy. Min. Dept. Industry, Trade & Comm. 1976; Secy. Ministry of State for Economic Dev. 1978; appt. Under-Secy. of State for External Affairs, Jan. 1982; Clerk of the Privy Counc. and Secy. to the Cabinet, 1982–85; Hon. Dir., Niagara Inst.; appt. Bd. of Dir., Molson Cos. Ltd. 1986; DuPont of Canada Ltd. 1987; Rockwell Internat. of Canada 1988; National Bank of Canada 1988; Bell Canada 1988; Bow Valley Industries Ltd. 1991; Ellis-Don Construction Ltd. 1991; appt. Officer of The Order of Canada, 1981; rec'd Outstanding Achievement Award of the Public Service, 1981; appt. Queen's Privy Counc. of Can. 1986; recip., Vanier Medal of the Inst. of Public Admin. of Canada 1990; author: 'Keeping Deputy Ministers Accountable' 1989; 'Organizing to Govern' 1992; Psi Upsilon; Roman Catholic; Home: 1353 Corley Dr., London, Ont. N6G 4L4; Office: Sch. of Bus. Admin., Univ. of Western Ont., London, Ont. N6A 3K7.

**OSBORNE, John Lawrence,** B.A., M.A., Ph.D.; university professor; b. Montreal, Que. 4 Sept. 1951; s. Robert Ernest and Beverley Kathleen (Lawrence) O.; e. Univ. of Toronto Schools; Carleton Univ. B.A. 1973; Univ. of Toronto M.A. 1974; Univ. of London Ph.D. 1979; m. Colette d. Angela and John Stubbs 18 May 1974; children: Sarah, Nicholas, Geoffrey; PROFESSOR, DEPT. OF HISTORY IN ART, UNIV. OF VICTORIA 1989– ; Asst. Prof., Univ. of Victoria 1979–85; Assoc. Prof. 1985–89; Chair, Dept. of History in Art 1986–91; Dir., Medieval Studies Programme 1993– ; Visiting Fellow, Corpus Christi College, Cambridge; Dumbarton Oaks Center for Byzantine Studies; Mem., Universities Art Assn. of Canada (Vice-Prs. 1982–85; Pres. 1985–87); Soc. of Canadian Medievalists; Medieval Academy of America; author: 'Early Medieval Wall Paintings in the Lower Church of San Clemente, Rome' 1984, 'Master Gregorius: The Marvels of Rome' 1987; recreations: duplicate bridge, travel; Home: 3531 Plymouth Rd., Victoria, B.C. V8P 4X7; Office: Victoria, B.C. V8W 2Y2.

**OSBORNE, Judith Anne,** M.A., LL.B., LL.M.; university professor; b. Sheffield, England 18 May 1955; d. Charles and Agnes Murray Hogg (Gray) O.; e. Boroughmuir H.S. (Edinburgh); Univ. of Edinburgh, LL.B. 1977; Univ. of Toronto, M.A. 1978; Univ. of B.C., LL.M. 1989; ASSOC. VICE PRES., ACADEMIC, SIMON FRASER UNIV. 1986– ; teaching & rsch., Ctr. of Crim. & Woodsworth Coll., Univ. of Toronto 1978–81; Asst. Prof., Sch. of Crim., S.F.U. 1981– ; Rsch. Cons., Commonwealth Sec. 1978–80; reviewer, 'Canadian Journal of Education' 1987; Treas., L.I.F.E. Resource Ctr. 1986; author: 'Delay in the Administration of Criminal Justice' 1980 plus several other articles; Home: 104 Laval St., Coquitlam, B.C. V3K 6N2; Office: Burnaby, B.C. V5A 1S6.

**OSBORNE, Kenneth William,** B.A., B.Ed., M.A.; university professor; b. Coventry, England 23 Nov. 1936; s. Thomas William and Florence (Lucas) O.; e. Oxford Univ., B.A. (Hons.) 1960; Univ. of Man., B.Ed. 1965, M.A. 1972; m. Janet d. Norman and Maud Keill 18 July 1959; children: Andrew, Richard; PROF., FAC.

OF EDN., UNIV. OF MAN. 1972– ; Royal Air Force 1955–57; Teacher, Winnipeg Sch. Div. 1961–72; Cons./Dir., edn. proj. for Can. Studies Found.; Prov. of Man.; Horizon Can.; Canada's Visual Hist.; Ed., 'The History and Social Science Teacher' 1983–85; Univ. of Man. awards: Stanton Award for Excellence in Teaching 1982; RH Inst. Award for O.S. Contbr. to Interdisciplinary Studies 1983; Dr & Mrs R. Campbell Award for Outreach Activities 1987; Mem., Candn. Hist. Assn.; Candn. Soc. for the Study of Edn.; Author of books, articles and monographs on educational subjects, especially related to citizenship, history teaching, and related matters; recreations: jazz, reading; Home: 740 Townsend Ave., Winnipeg, Man. R3T 2V4; Office: Winnipeg, Man. R3T 2N2.

**OSBORNE, Ronald W.,** F.C.A., B.A.; communications executive; b. Worthing, England 11 May 1946; s. Frederick Charles and Annie Armistice (Mitchell) O.; e. Collyers Sch., Horsham, England 1964; Pembroke Coll., Cambridge, B.A. 1968; C.A., Ont. 1972; F.C.A., Ont. 1988; m. Grace d. Tom and Idalene Snead 15 Mar. 1969; children: David, Charlotte, James; PRES. & CHIEF EXTVE. OFFR., MACLEAN HUNTER LIMITED 1986– ; Clarkson, Gordon, Toronto 1968–76; Partner 1979–81; Partner, Arthur Young, Clarkson Gordon, Rio de Janeiro 1976–79; Chief Finan. Offr., present firm 1981; Pres. & Chief Operating Offr. 1984–86; Dir., Royal Bank of Canada; CTV TV Network; Toronto Sun Pub. Corp.; Finan. Post Co.; Sun Life Assur. Co. of Can.; Dir., Roy Thomson Hall; mem., Business Bd., University of Toronto; Business Counc. on Nat. Issues; Young Pres. Orgn.; Internat. Trade Adv. Ctte.; Chrmn., Sectoral Adv. Group on Internat. Trade for Arts & Cultural Indus.; recreations: cottage, travel; clubs: Toronto; United Oxford/Cambridge (UK); Home: 294 Oriole Parkway, Toronto, Ont. M5P 2H5; Office: 777 Bay St., Toronto, Ont. M5W 1A7.

**O'SHAUGHNESSY, Robert Fyfe,** B.A.Sc., P.Eng.; b. Nanaimo, B.C. 23 June 1933; s. William Thomas and Marguarita Evelyn (Fyfe) O'S.; e. Nanaimo High Sch. 1951; Univ. of B.C. B.A.Sc. (Mech. Eng.) 1956; m. Anne d. Ferris Neave 9 Sept. 1955; children: Patricia Anne, Lynda Ellen, Robert Neave; CHRMN., PRES. & C.E.O., CHRMN. EXEC. CTTE. AND DIR., PACIFIC NORTHERN GAS LTD. 1981– ; Eng. in Training Hawaiian Sugar Planters Assn. 1956–57; Eng., B.C. Electric, Vancouver 1957–61; Prof. Eng., Planning Eng., Mgr. Gas Sales, Westcoast Energy Inc. Vancouver 1962–73; joined present Co. 1973, Vice Pres. and Gen. Mgr.; Pres., Centra Gas British Columbia Inc. 1990–91; Dir., Canadian Gas Assoc.; Dir., Burnaby Hospital Foundation; mem., Assoc. of Prof. Engrs., B.C.; recreations: music, sports; Clubs: SPEBSQSA; Terminal City; UBC Faculty; Home: 7182 Camano St., Vancouver, B.C. V5S 4B9; Office: 1185 W. Georgia St., Suite 1400, Vancouver, B.C. V6E 4E6.

**OSLER, Britton Bath,** Q.C.; b. Ottawa, Ont. 17 Dec. 1904; s. Glyn and Florence K. (Scarth) O.; e. Crescent Sch., Toronto, 1913–15; The Grove, Lakefield, Ont., 1915–16; Ridley Coll., St. Catharines, Ont., 1916–21; Roy. Mil. Coll., Grad. 1925; Osgoode Hall, Toronto, 1929; m. Barbara E., d. Godfrey B. Greene, Ottawa, Ont., 23 Apl. 1930; children: Glyn W., Derek B., Pamela G., G. Featherston; PARTNER EMERITUS, BLAKE, CASSELS & GRAYDON, (Partner 1933); read law with Blake, Lash, Anglin and Cassels (now Blake, Cassels & Graydon) 1926–29; called to the Bar of Ontario, 1929; joined Blake, Lash, Anglin and Cassels 1929; now retired; served with Canadian Mil., as Lieut., Gov.-Gen. Bodyguard, 1926–29; served in World War, 1939–46, with Reserve Army, R.C.A., 1940–42, and as C.O., 10 Light A.A. Regt., R.C.A., C.A.(A.), in Can., 1942–43; at Candn. Mil. Hdqrs., London, 1943–44; C.O., 32 Field Regt., R.C.A. (Reserve), 1945–46; Zeta Psi; Anglican; recreations: fishing, duck-shooting, golf; Clubs: Toronto; Toronto Golf; York; Home: 62A Glen Rd., Toronto, Ont. M4W 2V4; Office: Box 25, Commerce Court West, Toronto, Ont. M5L 1A9.

**OSLER, Campbell Revere,** C.D., Q.C., D.Cn.L., LL.B.; b. Toronto, Ont. 21 June 1918; s. Britton and Marion (Gwyn) O.; e. Upper Canada Coll., Toronto, Ont.; Trinity Coll. School, Port Hope, Ont.; Trinity Coll., Univ. of Toronto; Osgoode Hall Law Sch., Toronto, Ont.; m. Dorothy, d. Lawton Ridout 12 Jan. 1940; children: Elizabeth Victoria, Lawton Britton Campbell, Richard Ridout, Campbell Charles William; Partner, Osler, Hoskin & Harcourt 1950–84; retired; read law with Osler Hoskin & Harcourt, Toronto, Ont., 1945–48 joining the firm as an Assoc., 1948; called to Bar of Ont., 1948; cr. Q.C. 1961; Doctor of Canon Law 1980; Chancellor Emeritus Diocese of The Artic; served with Royal Candn. Artillery in Eng., Italy and France during 2nd World War, 1939–45; discharged to Reserve with rank of Major; Reserve to 1950, retired with rank of Lt. Col.; mem., Candn. Bar Assn.; Co. York Law Assn.; Law Soc. Upper Canada; Phi Kappa Pi; Anglican; recreations: golf, fishing, cruising, shooting; Clubs: The Toronto; Toronto Golf; York; Goodwood; Home: 350 Lonsdale Rd., Toronto, Ont. M5P 1R6; Office: Box 50, First Canadian Place, Toronto, Ont. M5X 1B8.

**OSLER, Gordon Peter;** executive; b. Winnipeg, Man. 19 June 1922; s. Hugh Farquarson and Kathleen (Harty) O.; e. Ravenscourt Sch. Winnipeg; Queen's Univ.; m. Nancy Adina d. Conrad S. Riley 20 Aug. 1948; children: Sanford L., Susan H. (Mrs. R. B. Matthews), Gillian G. (Mrs. Michel Fortier); Chrmn. & Dir., North American Life Assurance Co.; Dir., Household Internat. Inc.; Co-Steel Inc.; joined Osler, Hammond & Nanton Ltd. Winnipeg becoming Pres. and Chief Extve. Offr. 1952; Dir., Toronto-Dominion Bank 1952–93; Dir., Transcanada Pipelines Ltd. 1954–93 (Chrmn. 1983–89); Dir., IPSCO Inc. 1957–93; Chrmn., Pres. and C.E.O. UNAS Investments, Toronto 1964–72; Chrmn. Slater Steel Industries Ltd. 1972–86; Vice Chrmn. and C.E.O. British Steel (Canada) Ltd. 1972–86; Dir., Maclean-Hunter Ltd. 1976–93; served with Royal Candn. Armoured Corps 1942–46, rank Lt.; recreation: golf; Clubs: Toronto; Toronto Golf; York; Everglades Fla.; Home: 112 Dunvegan Rd., Toronto, Ont. M4V 2R1; Office: 55 Yonge St., 8th Flr., Toronto, Ont. M5E 1J4.

**OSLER, Hon. John Harty,** B.A.; retired judge; executive; b. Winnipeg, Man. 28 Feb. 1915; s. Hugh F. and Kathleen (Harty) O.; e. Appleby Coll., Oakville, Ont.; Trinity Coll., Univ. of Toronto, B.A. 1937; Osgoode Hall Law Sch., Toronto, Ont.; m. Elizabeth, d. J.S.H. Guest, Oakville, Ont., 5 June 1937; children: Ann Harty (Malcolmson), Janet Kathleen (McDonald), Hugh John; ALTERNATIVE DISPUTE RESOLUTION practice 1992– ; read law with Cassels, Brock & Kelley, Toronto, Ont.; called to the Bar of Ont., June 1940; cr. Q.C. 1954; engaged in the practice of law since grad. except for war service, limiting practice mainly to labour relations and trade union law; Partner, Jolliffe, Lewis and Osler prior to appointment in 1968; Justice, Supreme Court of Ont. 1968–90; Dir., Special Investigations Unit 1990–92; mem., Candn. Bar Assn. (Vice-Pres. for Ont. 1961–62, Nat. Extve. 1963–64); served in 2nd World War; Lieut. R.C.N.V.R., 1942–45; Phi Kappa Pi (Pres. 1936); recreation: sailing; Clubs: University; Home: 1904, 61 St. Clair W., Toronto, Ont. M4V 2Y8.

**OSMAN, Mohamed O.M.,** B.Sc., Dr.Sc.Tech; university professor and administrator; b. Egypt 10 Aug. 1936; s. Osman Mohamed and Eisha (Abdel-Khader) O.; e. Cairo Univ. B.Sc. 1957; Swiss Federal Inst. of Tech. Dr.Sc.Tech. 1964; m. Silvia d. John 6 Sept. 1966; children: Mona, Karim; PROFESSOR & CHAIR, MECH. ENG., CONCORDIA UNIV. 1987– ; Consultant, Dominion Engineering Works 1968–69; Post-Doctoral Fellow E.T.H. Zurich, Switz. 1964–66; Instructor, Ryerson Polytech. Inst. 1966–67; Asst. Prof. of Engr., Sir George Williams Univ. 1967–70; Assoc. Prof. with tenure 1970–73; Prof. with tenure 1973– ; Consulant, Geb Heller, Bremen, W. Germany 1973–74; Govt. of Egypt Scholarship for Doctoral Study 1958–65; Gov., Bd. of Gov., Concordia Univ.; Mem., ASME, SME, CSME, JSPE, IEEE, IFFToMM; author: 'Machine Tools' 1988, '91, 'Steam Hammer' 1990, 'Carborundum' 1989, 'Drill, Types of Drilling Tools ...' 1984 (World Book Encyclopedia), 'Bolts and Bolted Joints' 1985 (Mech. Design and Systems Handbook) and more than 80 journal articles; over 100 presentations in conferences; Home: 686 Fisher Rd., Hemmingford, Que. J0L 1H0; Office: 1455 de Maisonneuve Blvd. W., H-549, Montreal, Que. H3G 1M8.

**OSMOND, Dennis Gordon,** F.R.S.C, M.B., Ch.B., D.Sc.; medical educator; b. New York, N.Y. 31 Jan. 1930; s. Ernest Gordon and Marjorie Bertha (Milton) O.; e. City of Bath (Eng.) Boys' Sch.; The Grammar Sch. Chipping Sodbury, Eng.; Univ. of Bristol B.Sc. 1951, M.B., Ch.B. 1954, D.Sc. 1975; m. Anne Welsh 30 July 1955; three s. Roger Gordon, Martin Henry, David Richard; CHRMN. DEPT. OF ANATOMY AND CELL BIOLOGY (1985– ) & ROBERT REFORD PROF. OF ANATOMY (1974– ), McGILL UNIV.; Assoc. Prof. of Anatomy 1965–67, Prof. of Anatomy 1967–74; House Surg. Royal Gwent Hosp. Newport, Eng. 1954; House Phys. Bristol Royal Infirmary, Eng. 1955; Demonst. in Anatomy Univ. of Bristol 1957, Lectr. 1959–64; Instr. in Anat. Univ. of Wash. 1960–61; Med. Research Council Visiting Scient. Walter & Eliza Hall Inst. Med. Research Melbourne, Australia 1972–73; Visiting Hon. Research Fellow Univ. of Birmingham 1979; Visiting Scient. Basel Inst. for Immunology, Switzerland 1980; served with R.A.M.C. Eng. 1955–57, rank Capt.; co-ed. 'Stem Cells of Renewing Cell Populations' 1976; numerous articles cellular immunology & haematology prof. journs.; mem. Candn. Assn. Anats. (Pres. 1983–85); Am. Assn. Anats. (Extve. Comte. 1978–82); Anat. Assn. Gt. Brit. & Ireland (Overseas Council mem. 1975–78); Brit. Assn. Clin. Anats.; Internat. Soc. Exper. Hematol. (Bd. Dirs. 1976–79); Candn. Soc. Immunology; Am. Assn. Immunols.; Reticuloendothelial Soc.; Fellow Roy. Soc. of Can. 1984; recreations: travel, theatre, reading, skiing, domestic hobbies; Home: 116 rue de Touraine, St. Lambert, Que. J4S 1H4; Office: 3640 University St., Montreal, Que. H3A 2B2.

**OSTER, Walter;** food service executive; b. Toronto, Ont. 17 May 1939; s. Michael and Pauline Ostapchuk; e. Pacific Western Univ. Los Angeles Hon. Doctor of Comm. Sci. 1988; m. Mary Elizabeth Bobyk 30 Sept. 1961; children: James Stephen, Mitchell Gregory; Pres., The Whaler's Group Inc.; Osta Management Services Ltd.; Marina 4; Lockport Construction; Pres., Hidden Lake Golf & Country Club; mem. Adv. Bd. Foodservices & Hospitality Mag.; Chrmn., Toronto Seaquarium Corp.; Founder, The Whaler's Charities for Children Found.; Dir. Metrop. Toronto Convention Centre; Past Chrmn. Metrop. Toronto Convention & Visitors Assn.; Past Chrmn., Candn. Restaurant & Foodservices Assn.; Council of Metrop. Toronto Bd. of Trade; Chrmn. & Pres., Candn. National Sportsman Show; Chrmn., Candn. National Sportsman Show Fund; Publisher, Outdoor Canada Magazine; Dir. Candn. Hospitality Found.; Dir., National Restaurant Assn., U.S.A.; Variety Club; recipient numerous awards and honours; recreations: boating, fishing, hunting, golf, car racing, antique cars, collecting wines & antiques; Clubs: Hidden Lake Golf & Country (Pres.); Quail Creek Golf & Country (Naples, Fla.); Home: PH1 Admiralty Point, 251 Queen's Quay W., Toronto, Ont. M5J 2N6; Office: 249 Queen's Quay W., Toronto, Ont. M5J 2N5.

**OSTERMAN, The Hon. Constantine E.;** politician; b. Acme, Alta. 23 June 1936; d. Louis Theodore and Pauline (Miller) Oel; m. Joe s. Fritz and Anna O. 30 Oct. 1954; children: Theo, Kurt, Kim, Kelly, Joe Jr.; Mem., Agricultural Rural Economy Cabinet/Caucus Ctte., Environment, Agriculture & Rural Affairs, and Economic Affairs Caucus Cttes. Comnr. & Charter Mem., Alta. Human Rights Comn. 1973–78; Pres., Candn. Assn. of Statutory Human Rights Agencies; elected M.L.A. for Three Hills constituency 1979; Party Whip 1979; Min. of Consumer & Corp. Affairs 1982; Min. of Social Services and Community Health 1986; Min. of Alberta Social Services 1986–89; Min. of Career Development & Employment 1989; Address: 21 Sorrel Cres., St. Albert, Alta. T8N 0K4.

**OSTFIELD, Eric A.,** C.A.; financial executive; b. Winnipeg, Man. 12 March 1944; s. Reuben Charles and Rose (Isaacs) Ostfield; Inst. of C.A.s of Man. C.A. 1966; Inst. of C.A.s of Ont. C.A. 1968; m. Elaine d. Myer and Hannah Katz 7 Aug. 1972; children: Michael Kent, Laurel Susan, Robert James; SENIOR TAX PARTNER, ERNST & YOUNG; on loan to Revenue Canada 1971–72; Partner, Clarkson Gordon (now Ernst & Young) 1974 to date; Office Dir. of Tax, Toronto Office, Ernst & Young 1988–92; speaker and writer on a variety of income tax subjects; Co-Chair, Profl. Adv. Ctte., United Jewish Welfare Fund; Vice-Chair, Audit Ctte., Beth Tzedec Synagogue; Mem., Finance & Budget Ctte., Beth Tzedec Synagogue; recreations: tennis,squash; clubs: Fitness Inst., Mayfair Tennis, Forest Hill Tennis; Home: 577 St. Clements Ave., Toronto, Ont. M5N 1M5; Office: P.O. Box 251, Toronto-Dominion Centre, Ernst & Young Tower, Toronto, Ont. M5K 1J7.

**OSTIGUY, Jean Paul Wilson,** O.C. (1978), LL.D.; investment dealer; b. Montreal, Que., 4 March 1922; s. Paul E. and Marguerite (Wilson) O.; e. Coll. Jean de Brebeuf; Ecole des Hautes Etudes Comm. (Faculty of Comm., Univ. of Montreal); Royal Mil. Coll. of Can., Kingston, Grad. 1942, LL.D. (Hon.) 1978; m. Michelle, d. Achille Bienvenu, 5 Oct. 1946; children: Marc, Claude, Danielle, Denyse, Suzanne; DIR. RICHARDSON GREENSHIELDS OF CANADA LTD. 1982– ; Dir. The General Accident Assurance Co. of Canada; Sintra Ltd.; Kerr Addison Mines Ltd. (Extve. Comte.); Ford Motor Co. of Canada Ltd.; Ciba-Geigy Can. Ltd.; Marmon Group of Canada, Ltd.; Minnova Inc.; Mirabaud Canada Inc.; Dir. Emeritus Canadian Imperial Bank of Commerce; with Stevenson & Kellogg Ltd. 1945–47; Vice-Pres. and Dir. Casgrain & Co. Ltd. 1948–56; Founded Morgan, Ostiguy & Hudon Inc. 1956–72; Pres. & C.E.O. Crang & Ostiguy Inc. 1972–77; Chrmn. Greenshields Inc. 1977–82; Hon. Chrmn. Richardson Greenshields of Canada Ltd. 1982; National Pres., Invest. Dealers' Assn. of Can., 1965–66; Pres., Montreal Chamber Comm. 1966–67; Pres., La Maison des Etudiants Canadiens à Paris; President, Royal Mil. College Club of Canada, 1967–68; Chrmn., Bd. of Trustees for Nat. Museums of Can., 1968–73; Kt. of Magistral Order of Malta; Order of St. Lazarus; served overseas during 2nd World War with 4th Princess Louise Dragoon Guards; wounded 1 Sept. 1944 in Italy and discharged with rank of Capt. Oct. 1945; Roman Catholic; Clubs: Mount Royal; Toronto; Home: 318 Geneva Cres., Town of Mount Royal, Que. H3R 2A9; Office: 4 Place Ville Marie, Montreal, Que. H3B 2E8.

**OSTIGUY, Jean René,** B.A.; art critic and historian; Canadian public service; b. Marieville, Que. 14 Aug. 1925; s. Joseph and Jeanne (Dussault) O.; e. Séminaire de Valleyfield; Univ. of Montreal, B.A. 1947; Ecole des Beaux-Arts de Montréal, 1947–50; Sch. of Art & Design, 1950–52 (Dipl.); m. Denise Aurella, d. Joseph Coté, Valleyfield, Que., 8 July 1953; children: Monique, Christine, David; Research curator, National Gallery of Canada, Ottawa 1967–85; Curator, National Bank of Canada 1986–90; Art Critic for (newspaper) 'Le Devoir,' Montreal, Que.; Lectr. in Hist. of Candn. Art, Univ. of Ottawa 1966–71; Prof. in Basic Design and Hist. of Art, Ecole des Beaux-Arts, Montreal, 1952–55; Prof. of Art Appreciation at Semy. de Valleyfield, Que., and at Valleyfield Sch. Comm., 1952–55; author; 'Un siècle de peinture canadienne (1870–1970),' 1971; 'Adrien Hébert (Premier interprète de la modernité québécoise)' 1986; Roman Catholic; recreations: painting, canoeing; Home: 21 Rue Thibault, Hull, Qué. J9A 1H4.

**OSTRY, Bernard,** O.C., B.A.; consultant; former Canadian public servant; b. Wadena, Sask. 10 June 1927; s. Abraham and Tobie (Goldman) O.; e. Primary Schs., Flin Flon, and Winnipeg, Man.; Pub. Schs., St. John's Coll. and St. John's Tech. High Sch., Winnipeg, Man.; Univ. of Manitoba 1943–48; post-grad. work in field of International Hist. at Univ. of London (L.S.E.) under the late Sir Charles K. Webster and Prof. W. N. Medicott 1948–52; m. Dr. Sylvia; two s., Adam, Jonathan David; Chrmn. & C.E.O., Ont. Educational Communications Authority (TVOntario) 1985–92; Research Assoc., Faculty of Social Sciences, University of Birmingham, England, 1951–55; Special Assist. and Advisor to Leader of Indian Delegation to United Nations, 1951–52; David Davies Fellow in International Hist., University of London, London School of Economics & Political Science, 1956–58; Executive Secretary-Treasurer, Commonwealth Inst. of Social Research, 1959–61; Secretary-Treasurer, Social Science and Humanities Rsch. Councils of Can. 1961–63; Moderator, Nightline, Canadian Broadcasting Corporation, 1960–63; Supervisor, Department of Public Affairs (Radio & T.V.) CBC, 1963–68; (winner of several awards for public affairs broadcasting, including the Ohio State Award and Special Wilderness Award); Chief Consultant to the Canadian Radio Television Commission, 1968–69; Commissioner, Prime Minister's Task Force on Government Information, 1968–70; Assistant Under Secretary of State (Citizenship) 1970–73; Secy.-Gen. and Depy. Min. National Museums of Can. 1974–78; Depy. Min. Communications 1978–80; Spec. Advr. (Culture and Communications Technology), Secy. of State and Min. of Communications, Candn. Embassy, Paris, France 1980–81; Depy. Min. of Industry and Tourism, Ont. 1981–82; Depy. Min. of Industry and Trade, Ont. 1982–84; Depy. Min. of Citizenship & Culture, Ont. 1984–85; Life Member, Candn. Historical Assoc.; Vice Pres., Assoc. of Candn. Television and Radio Artists 1963; Honorary Patron of the Wedge Entomological Research Foundation, McClellandville, South Carolina, U.S.A. 1975–80; Patron, Bicentennial North American Indian Art Exhibit, Art Council of Great Britain, London England 1975–76; Mem., Bd. of Govs., Candn. Conference of the Arts 1977–82, 1986–91; Mem., Administrative Council of the Internat. Fund for the Promotion of Culture, U.N.E.S.C.O., Paris 1975–80; Mem. Bd. of Govs. Heritage Canada 1975–80; Mem. Adv. Ctte. on Cultural Policy, Govt. of Can. 1979–80; Mem. Bd. of Dirs., Festival of Festivals 1982–84; Mem., Candn. Museums Assoc. 1975–80; Dir., Assn. for Tele-Education in Canada (ATEC) 1985–91 (Pres. 1990); Candn. Writers Foundation Inc.; Candn. ORT Organization; National Advisory Council of Candn. Friends of Tel Aviv Univ., Inc.; Trustee, Internat. Inst. of Communications (IIC) 1978–86; Chrmn., Bd. Nominating Ctte., 1986–89; Hon. Trustee 1992– ; Founding mem., Candn. Chapter of IIC, Ottawa 1980; Mem., Candn. Videotex Adv. Ctte.; Mem., Bd. of Govs., Univ. of Guelph 1986– ; Shaw Festival 1986– ; Chrmn., Shaw Festival Bd. 1991–93; Vice-Chrmn., Bd. of Dirs., Agency for Instructional Television 1985–88; Bd. of Dir., Writers' Development Trust 1985– ; Candn. Mediterranean Inst. 1986– ; The Children's Broadcast Inst. 1987–91; Mem., Inst. of Public Admin. of Canada 1987– ; Mem. Adv. Council, The Elgin and Winter Garden Project 1988– ; Mem., Bd. of Adv., Festival of Music of Canada 1988– ; Mem., Bd. of Dirs., Candn. Native Arts Foundation 1990– ; Bd. of Dirs., National Ballet Sch. 1990– ; Mem., Bd. of Dirs., Marshall McLuhan Centre on Global Communications 1990– ; author 'Research in the Humanities and in the Social Sciences of Canada' 1962; 'The Cultural Connection' 1978; 'The Electronic Connection' 1993; articles on Canadian labour and international hist. and politics in 'Canadian Historical Review,' 'Canadian Journal of Economics and Political Science,' & other learned journs., newspapers, mags., etc.; co-author 'The Age of Mackenzie King: The Rise of the Leader' 1955 (re-issued 1976); 'To Know and Be Known' 1969; regular moderator and commentator on CBC, private radio and TV Pub. Affairs Programs; Appointed an Officer of the Order of Canada by the Governor General 1988; awarded Commemorative Medal for 125th Anniversary of Candn. Confederation 1993; recreations: reading, travelling; Address: Suite 4112, Manulife Centre, 44 Charles St. W., Toronto, Ont. M4Y 1R8.

**OSTRY, Sylvia (Mrs. Bernard),** C.C., B.A., M.A., Ph.D., F.R.S.C.; academic; economist; b. Winnipeg, Man.; e. McGill Univ., B.A. (Econ.) 1948, M.A. 1950, Ph.D. 1954; Cambridge Univ. Ph.D. 1954; m. Bernard Ostry; 2 sons; CHRMN., CENTRE FOR INTERNAT. STUDIES, UNIV. OF TORONTO 1990– ; CHANCELLOR, UNIV. OF WATERLOO 1992– ; Chrmn., The National Council of the Candn. Inst. for Internat. Affairs 1990–94; Western Co-Chrmn., The Blue Ribbon Commission for Hungary's Economic Recovery 1990– ; Appointments: McGill Univ., Univ. of Montreal, Univ. of Oxford 1954–64; Statistics Canada, Economic Council of Canada 1964–72; Chief Statistician of Canada 1972–75; Deputy Minister, Consumer and Corporate Affairs, Canada 1975–78; Chrmn., Economic Counc. of Can. 1978–79; Head, Dept. of Economics & Statistics, OECD, Paris 1979–83; Deputy Minister, International Trade, and Coordinator, International Economic Relations 1984–85; Ambassador for Multilateral Trade Negotiations and the Prime Minister's Personal Representative for the Economic Summit 1985; Volvo Distinguished Visiting Fellow, Counc. on Foreign Relations, New York; Sr. Rsch. Fellow, Univ. of Toronto 1989–90; Dir., Power Financial Corp.; Dir., Kellogg Canada Inc.; Chrmn., Internat. Advisory Bd., Bank of Montreal; Advisory Ctte., InterAmerican Development Bank / Economic Commission for Latin America and the Caribbean Project; Bd. Mem., United Nations University/World Institute for Development Economics Research, Helsinki; Expert Adviser, Commission on Transnational Corporations, United Nations, New York; Internat. Advisory Council, Centre for European Policy Studies, Brussels; Advisory Bd., Institute of Internat. Economics, Washington; Mem., Group of Thirty, Washington; Most recent publications include: 'International Economic Policy Coordination,' a Chatham House paper (with Michael Artis) 1986; 'Interdependence: Vulnerability and Opportunity' Per Jacobssen Lecture, 1987; 'Regional Trading Blocs: Pragmatic or Problematic Policy?' (with Michael Aho) 1989 in 'The Global Economy: America's Role in the Decade Ahead' American Assembly, New York 1990; 'Governments and Corporations in a Shrinking World: The Search for Stability,' Council on Foreign Relations N.Y. 1990; 'Uruguay Round: Unfinished Symphony' Finance and Development, Internat. Monetary Fund and World Bank 1991; 'Authority and Academic Scribblers: The Role of Research in East Asian Policy Reform' Institute for Contemporary Studies Press (editor) 1991; 'The Domestic Domain: The New International Policy Arena' Transnational Corps., Vol. 1, No. 1 Feb. 1992; 'The Threat of Managed Trade to Transforming Economies' Occasional Papers No. 41, Group of Thirty, Washington 1993; over 80 publs. on empirical and policy-analytic subjects; Memberships incl.: American Statistical Assoc. (Fellow); American and Canadian Economic Assocs.; Royal Economic Soc.; Advisory Bd., Centre for European Policy Studies, Brussels (Founding Mem.); Institute of Internat. Economic, Washington; Group of Thirty, Washington; Honours incl.: 17 honorary degrees from universities in Canada and abroad; Officer of the Order of Canada 1978; Companion of the Order of Canada 1990; Govt. of Canada Outstanding Achievement Award and Per Jacobsson Foundation Lecture, 1987; Honouree, 1991 Public Policy Forum Testimonial Dinner; Fellow, Royal Society of Canada 1991; Honorary Associate Award, Conference Bd. of Canada 1992; recreations: films, theatre, contemporary reading; Address: 170 Bloor St. W., 5th Floor, Toronto, Ont. M5S 1T9.

**O'SULLIVAN, Donald S.,** B.S.B.A.; business executive; b. Lethbridge, Alta. 1939; ed. Univ. of Denver B.S.B.A. 1962; m. Kathryn; three children; PRESIDENT, O'SULLIVAN RESOURCES LTD.; Vice-Pres., Secretary & Dir., B & B Distributors, Inc.; Dir., Finning Ltd.; The National Life Assurance Co. of Canada; Southgate Pontiac Buick GMC Ltd.; Westin Hotel, Edmonton; Office: 2121 Esso Tower, Scotia Place, 10060 Jasper Ave., Edmonton, Alta. T5J 3R8.

**OSWELL, Kenneth Rupert,** F.C.A., F.C.M.C.; b. Toronto, Ont. 18 May 1922; s. late Rupert Stanley and late Beatrice (Humphreys) O.; e. Eastern High Sch. of Comm.; children: Kenneth Randall, Susan Kathleen (Mrs. D.G. Cornish); admit. Inst. of Chart. Accts. of Ont. 1947; Fellow 1965; Jr. Acct., Chas. Greer & Co., Toronto, 1939–42; joined P.S. Ross & Sons 1945, admit. to Partnership 1953; Partner, Touche Ross (now Deloitte & Touche) Toronto 1953–84; Partner, Touche Ross Mgmt. Consultants (now Deloitte & Touche Mgmt. Consultants) 1958–84; mem. Adv. Counc. Min. of Industry, Trade & Comm. 1970–72; Dir. Internat. Mgmt. Consulting, Touche Ross Internat. 1971–72; Regional Partner, Mediterranean, Middle East and Africa, Touche Ross Internat. 1974–78; Dir. of Marketing, Toronto 1979–81; Nat. Dir. Client Services & Devel. Touche Ross 1982–84; served during 2nd World War in R.C.N.V.R., discharged as Lt.; Campaign Chrmn., Toronto Humane Soc. 1981; Past Pres. North York Br. Metrop. Toronto Y.M.C.A.; Past Pres., Candn. Assn. Mgmt. Consultants; Charter mem. and Past Pres., Inst. of Cert. Mgmt. Consultants of Ontario Fellow 1970; mem., Inst. of Corporate Directors; Society for Advanc. Mgmt.; Inst. Management Consultants Inc. New York; former mem. Council, Inst. Mgmt. Consultants Can.; Fellow, British Inst. of Mgmt.; Pres., K.R. Oswell Consultants Inc. 1993– ; Chrmn., Ontario Share and Deposit Insurance Corp. 1985–91; Dir., Godfrey Hirst Carpets of Canada Ltd. 1992– ; Telesystems SLW Inc. 1987–91; Victorian Order of Nurses Metropolitan Toronto 1987–91; Toronto Transit Consultants Ltd. 1985–91; Freemason; Gov., The Candn. Club of New York 1989–91; Trustee, St. Michael's College Found. 1992– ; mem., President's Council, Candn. Opera Co.; Curators' Circle, Art Gallery of Ontario; Canadian Society of N.Y.; Travellers' Century, Los Angeles; Anglican; recreation: travel, photography; Clubs: Ontario; Granite; Bd. of Trade; Metropolitan (N.Y.); Home: Granite Place, Ste. 1204, 63 St. Clair Ave. W., Toronto, Ont. M4V 2Y9 Office: Box 40, Sun Life Tower, 150 King St. W., Toronto, Ont. M5H 1J9.

**OTIS, Benjamin;** clothing manufacturer; b. Toronto, Ont. 10 Sept. 1918; s. Louis and Rose (Shustik) O.; e. Western Commerce; m. Felicia d. Josef and Sala Ramet 15 May 1945; children: Annette M., Jeffrey L.; CHRMN. & C.E.O., GRAND NATIONAL APPAREL INC. 1990– ; Founding Pres., Mens Wear Traveller Assn. of Can. 1955–56; Founding Mem., Former Vice Pres., Don Valley East Conservative Assn.; Past Pres., Bayview Vill. Assn. 1966–67; rec'd Distinguished Service Award from N.A.M.B.C. 1964, for orgn. 1st mens wear apparel market in Can.; served in European theatre R.C.A.F. 1941–46; rec'd P.C. Recognition Award 1981; mem., Temple Sinai Congregation; Mem., Reform Party; Club: Bayview Country; Home: 44 Forest Grove Dr., Willowdale, Ont. M2K 1Z3; Office: 100 Marmora, Weston, Ont. M9M 2X5.

**OTIS, Jeffrey L.,** B.A., M.B.A.; manufacturer; b. Toronto, Ont. 27 July 1951; s. Benjamin B. and Felicia (Ramet) O.; e. York Univ. B.A. 1973, M.B.A. 1975; m. Sandra d. Harold and Ruth Baker 16 Aug. 1983; two s. Daniel Shawn, Joshua Robert; PRES. & CHIEF OPERATING OFFR. GRAND NATIONAL APPAREL INC. 1975– ; Mgr. Youth & Children's Activities Candn. Nat. Exhn. 1970–74; mem. Adv. Ctte. Men's & Boys' Clothing Ind. Ont. Min. Labour; Adv. Ctte. Fashion Sir Sandford Fleming Coll. Peterborough; mem. Adv. Ctte. Fashion, Seneca College; mem. Candn. Apparel Mfrs. Inst. (Dir.); Apparel Mfrs. Assn. Ont. (Dir.); Founder Candn. Open Frisbee Championship 1972; recreations: boating, fishing, travel; Home: 17 Belinda Court, Richmond Hill, Ont. L4C 8R7; Office: 100 Marmora St., Weston, Ont. M9M 2X5.

**OTLEY, G. Roger,** B.Sc.; executive; b. Huddersfield, Yorks. 22 May 1934; s. late Gerald William and Phillis Mary (Greenwood) O.; e. Bryanston Sch. Dorset, Eng. 1951; McGill Univ. B.Sc. (Agric. Econ.) 1959; m. Carolyn Anne d. late Carl Reeves, Mulgrave, N.S., 8 June 1957; children: Gerald, Kathryn, Tony, John; MANAGING PARTNER, GLOBAL SECURITY SERVICES; Extve. Dir., Canada-Japan Business Ctte.; joined present Co. as Invest. Analyst 1959, Mgr. Invest. Research 1966, Mgr. Invests. 1968, Gen. Supvr. Invest. Research 1969, Asst. Vice-Pres. Pension Trust Services, 1971, Vice-Pres. Pensions 1973; Extve. Vice-Pres., and C.O.O., Computel Systems Ltd., Ottawa, 1974; Group Vice-Pres., Investments, The Royal Trust Company,

1975; Group Vice-Pres., Investments and Trust Services, Royal Trust Corporation of Canada, 1979; Exec. Vice-Pres., Functional Operations, Royal Trust Corp. of Canada, 1982; Sr. Vice Pres., Trust and Investments, Royal Trustco Ltd. 1983–84; Sr. Vice Pres., Corp. Financial Services, Royal Trustco Ltd. 1984–85; Sr. Vice Pres. & Chief Representative Offr., Tokyo 1985–92; Pres., Candn. C. of C. in Japan 1989–91; Advisor to the Chrmn., Royal Trust (Toronto) 1992; Chrmn., YMCA Foreign Support Group, Tokyo 1989; Town Councillor Baie d'Urfe, Que. 1974; Anglican; recreations: tennis, golf; Clubs: The Oakville; Oakville Golf; City Club of Tokyo; Home: 25 Chisholm St., Oakville, Ont. L6K 3W2.

**O'TOOLE, Lawrence J.,** B.A., M.B.A.; public servant; b. Peterborough, Ont. 14 Nov. 1930; s. Thomas Vincent and Mary Loretto (Lynch) O.; e. St. Peter's H.S. 1948; St. Michael's Coll., Univ. of Toronto B.A. 1951; Univ. of Western Ont. M.B.A. 1966; m. Jean d. Thomas and May McCadden 6 July 1957; children: David, Catherine, John, Christopher; COUNSELLOR (EXPENDITURE MANAGEMENT) TO CENTRAL AND EAST EUROPEAN GOVERNMENTS, ORGANISATION FOR ECONOMIC COOPERATION AND DEVELOPMENT (Paris, France) 1993– ; Branch Mngt., Industrial Acceptance Corp. 1952–64; Mktg. Cons., Woods, Gordon & Co. 1966–68; Asst. Undersecretary, Dept. of External Affairs 1968–77; Asst. Sec., Treasury Bd. 1977–82; Federal Economic Development Coord., Toronto 1982–85; Deputy Head, Crown Corp. Privatization Program, Ottawa 1985–86; Extve. Dir., Bureau of Real Property Mngt., Treasury Bd. 1986–90; Deputy Minister, Dept. of Public Works, Ottawa 1990–93; Chrmn. & Chief Extve. Offr., Can. Museums Construction Corp. (Inc.) and Pres., Canada Lands Co. Limited 1990–93; Office: OECD / SIGMA, 38 Boulevard Suchet, Paris 75016, France.

**OTT, Carlos A.,** M.Arch. & U.D., M.R.A.I.C., I.F.A., S.A.U., O.A.A., T.S.A.; architect; b. Montevideo, Uruguay 16 Oct. 1946; s. Carlos and Walkyria O.; e. Univ. of Uruguay, Sch. of Archit. 1971; Fulbright Scholar, Univ. of Hawaii, Honolulu 1971; Washington Univ. Sch. of Archit., St. Louis, Missouri Master Archit. & Urban Design 1972; children: Cecilia, Josephine; CONSULTANT, NORR PARTNERSHIP LIMITED, ARCHIT. ENGRS. 1983– ; Designer Baldwin & Cheshire, Atlanta, Ga.; Assoc. Moffatt & Kinoshita, Archits. 1974–79; Mgr. Archit. Design and Devel. Cadillac Fairview Corp. Ltd. 1979–83; mem. Inst. Français de l'Archit., Paris 1983; Royal Archit. Inst. of Can., Ottawa 1977; Toronto Soc. of Archits. 1977; Assn. de Arquitectos, Uruguay 1971; recipient Urban Studies Grant, Spanish Culture Inst., Madrid 1973; Fulbright-Hays Fellowship, U.S. State Dept. Grant to outstanding foreign students for post-grad. studies 1971; Chevalier de l'Ordre des Arts et Lettres, Paris 1985; Distinguished Alumni Award, Washington Univ. 1986; Gold Medal, Univ. of Uruguay 1986; Chevalier, Legion d'Honneur, Paris 1988; Officier de l'Ordre des Arts et des Lettres, Paris 1991; chosen by Pres. of France as Archit. of Opera Bastille to commemorate 200th anniv. of storming of Bastille in internat. competition of 744 competition entries; Offices: 350 Bloor St. E., Toronto, Ont. M4W 3S6 and 42 Blvd. d'Italie, Montecarlo, Principaute de Monaco.

**OTTENHEIMER, Hon. Gerald,** M.H.A., M.A.; politician; b. St. John's, Nfld. 4 June 1934; s. Frederick and Marguerite (Ryan) O.; e. St. Bonaventure's Coll.; Fordham Univ. N.Y.; Mem. Univ. of Nfld.; Univ. of Paris; Univ. of Rome; Univ. of Ottawa; Cambridge Univ.; m. Alma d. John Cullimore, Trinity, Nfld. 20 Aug. 1957; children: Geraldine, Susanne, Bernadette, Annmarie; APPTD. TO THE SENATE OF CANADA 1987– ; Min. of Justice & Atty. Gen., Nfld. 1979–83; educator, former Leader of the Opposition and Leader of Nfld. P. Cons. Party 3 yrs.; Cand. Fed. g.e. 1965, def.; el. M.H.A. for Waterford-Kenmount prov. g.e. 1966, resigned 1970, re-el. since prov. g.e. 1971; Min. of Intergovernmental Affairs 1972; Min. of Educ. 1972; Speaker 1975; P. Conservative; R. Catholic; Home: 126 Waterford Bridge Rd., St. Johns, Nfld. A1E 1C9; Office: Rm. 367-E - Centre Block, The Senate, Ottawa, Ont. K1A 0A4.

**OTTENSMEYER, Peter,** B.A.Sc., M.A., Ph.D.; university professor, scientist; b. Essen, Germany 23 July 1939; e. Univ. of Toronto B.A.Sc. 1962, M.A. 1963, Ph.D. 1967; m. Erika; children: Mark, Susan, Andrea; PROF., MEDICAL BIOPHYSICS 1977– & SENIOR SCIENTIST, ONT. CANCER INST. 1968– ; Postdoctoral Fellow, Toulouse, France 1967; Asst. Prof., Dept. of Medical Biophysics, Univ. of Toronto 1968; Assoc. Prof. 1974; Chair 197– ; Thomas Eadie Medal, Royal Soc. of Canada 1990; 2T5 Engineering Alumni Award 1987; Citation of Merit, Candn. Cancer Soc. 1985; Venturer Advisor, Scouts Canada 1976–91; author/co-author of more than 70 pubns. on electron microscopy, electron energy loss analysis, & macromolecular imaging; editor: 'Electron Microscopy' vol. 1 & 2 1978, 'Image and Digital Processing in Electron Microscopy' 1988; recreations: music, outdoors, whitewater canoeing; clubs: Scouts; Office: 500 Sherbourne St., Toronto, Ont. M4X 1K9.

**OTTEVANGERS, Nel Vader;** artist, floral designer; b. Dordrecht, The Netherlands 1 June 1931; d. André and Sara Cornelia (Salomé) Vader; e. Seneca Coll. Floral Design (Hons.) 1983; m. Jan H. s. D.C. and S.M.A. (deBoer) O. 11 May 1956; children: Dirk C. and Joyce A., Andrew J. and Angela F.; Home Economics Dept. in Netherlands Hosp. 1953–55 while taking art courses at night; Graphic Artist in commercial art office 1955–56; emigrated to Canada 1956; Commercial Artist, W. Gerry Kavanaugh 1956–57; mothered 2 sets of twins while taking F.A.S. correspondence courses in commercial art 1957–67; grad., art courses in drawing, watercolour, painting 1964, 1967–78; yearly art & craft show at home 1974–80; Teacher, Etobicoke Bd. of Edn. Cont. Edn. Prog. 1983– ; freelance specialty: fresh wedding flowers; Mem., Arts Etobicoke, Art Rental Prog.; devel. painting on cotton, quilted 1980; exbns: Valhalla Inn shows 1980–83 and other galleries & group shows; Gallery on the Lake Buckhorn 1986– ; paintings inspired by beauty of colourful Candn. landscape; Mem., Christian Reformed Church (designs & makes banners for church and designs colour-coord. flower arrangements); recreations: travel, cottage, watersports, enjoying nature; Address: 14 Carsbrooke Rd., Etobicoke, Ont. M9C 3C1.

**OTTO, Carl H.,** LL.B., Ph.D., C.F.A.; investment counsel; b. St. Gallen, Switzerland 14 March 1931; s. Heinrich Hermann and Erika Antonie (Franck) O.; e. Univ. of Freiburg, W. Germany LL.B. 1955, Ph.D. 1959; Inst. Chart. Financial Analysts Va. C.F.A. 1968; m. Michaela d. Walter Jacob 20 Feb. 1961; children: Christina, Valerie, Caroline; MANAGING DIR., AMI PARTNERS INC. 1978– ; Dir., Metropolitan Life Holdings Ltd.; Fleming Canada Partners Inc.; prior coming to Can. 1961 served as Mgr. Foreign Dept., Prince Fugger Bank, Augsburg, W. Germany; joined Invest. Rsch. Dept., Montreal Trust; co-founder, Montreal Investment Management 1968; Past Chrmn., Montreal Children's Hosp. Found.; Dir. McGill Univ./Montreal Children's Hosp. Rsch. Inst.; Past Pres., Montreal Soc. Financial Analysts; Past Founding Dir. Le Cercle Finance et Placement; mem. Inst. Chart. Financial Analysts; Clubs: University; Mount Royal; Home: 9 Hudson Ave., Westmount, Qué. H3Y 1Y6; Office: 900 – 1130 Sherbrooke St. W., Montréal, Qué. H3A 2S7.

**OTTO, Fred D.,** B.Sc., M.Sc., Ph.D., P.Eng.; university professor; b. Hardisty, Alta. 12 Jan. 1935; s. Douglas Frederick and Mable Florence (Teasdale) O.; e. Univ. of Alta. B.Sc. 1957, M.Sc. 1959; Univ. of Michigan Ph.D. 1963; m. Helen d. Clyde and Myrtle Brown 19 Aug. 1960; children: David, Joanne, Catherine; PROF., CHEMICAL ENGINEERING, UNIV. OF ALBERTA 1972– ; Asst. Prof. 1962; Assoc. Prof. 1964; Chair, Dept. of Chem. Engineering 1975–85; Dean, Faculty of Engineering 1985– ; Dir., D.B. Robinson & Assoc.; Telecommunications Research Laboratories; The Laser Inst.; Alberta Microelectronics Centre; Petroleum Recovery Inst.; Candn. Inst. for Petroleum Indus. Devel.; Mem., Candn. Acad. of Engineering; Nat. Research Council 1991– ; Can. Soc. for Chem. Engineering (Pres. 1986–87); APEGGA, AICHE, ASEE; Home: 12319 – 52 Avenue, Edmonton, Alta. T6H 0P5; Office: 5-1 Mechanical Engin. Bldg., Edmonton, Alta. T6G 2G8.

**OUELLET, L'Hon. André,** C.P.(1972), C.R., M.P., B.ès A.; avocat; né à St. Pascal, Qué. 6 avril 1939; f. Albert et Rita (Turgeon) O.; é. Univ. d'Ottawa, B.A. 1960; Univ. de Sherbrooke, LL.L. 1963; Membre Qué. Barreau 1964; ép. Édith, fille de Jean-Marie Pagé et Fernande Carmichaël, 17 juillet 1965; enfants: Sonia, Jean, Olga, Pierre; MINISTRE DES AFFAIRES ÉTRANGÈRES 1993– ; Député, Papineau-St-Michel; élu lors d'une élection partielle en 1967; réélu en 1968, 1972, 1974, 1979, 1980, 1984, 1988 (à chaque élection générale); président du caucus de l'aile québécoise du parti 1968–70; secrétaire parlementaire du ministre des Affaires Extérieures 1970; sec. parl. du min. de la Santé et du Bien-être social 1971; entre 1972 et 1984,successivement occupé les ministères suivants: des Postes; de la Consommation et des Corporations; d'État aux Affaires urbaines; des Travaux publics; du Travail; d'État au Développement économique régional; au 4 sept. 1984, aussi Président du Conseil privé et Leader du gouvernement à la Chambre des communes; porte-parole officiel des Transports 1985; des Affaires extérieures 1988; pour les relations féd.-prov. sept. 1990; membre Commission Bélanger/Campeau, mars 1990; Commission Beaudoin/Edwards, juin 1991; Commission Beaudoin/Dobbie, février 1992; mem.: Barreau de la Prov. de Qué.; Libéral; Catholique; intérêts: tennis, ski, lecture, théâtre; Domicile: 17 Chase Court, Ottawa, Ont. K1V 9Y6; Bureaux: (dans la circonscription) 2348 Jean-Talon Est, Ste. 200, Montréal, Qué. H2E 1V7; (parlementaire) 314, Édifice de l'Ouest, Chambres des communes, Ottawa, Ont. K1A 0A6.

**OUELLET, Fernand,** O.C., D.ès L.; professeur; né Lac-Bouchette, Qué 6 nov. 1926; f. Étienne et Berthe (Fortin) O.; é Univ. Laval B.A. 1948, L.ès L. 1950, D.ès L. 1965; ép. Thérèse f. Romulus et Brigitte Roy 27 dec. 1956; enfants: Françoise, Michèle, Andrée; PROFESSEUR D'HISTOIRE, YORK UNIV. 1986– ; Asst.-archiviste prov. Qué. 1956–61; Professeur d'histoire Univ. Laval 1961–65, Carleton Univ. 1965–75, Univ. d'Ottawa 1975–85, York Univ. 1986– ; Gouverneur du Royal Ont. Museum 1971–74; invité à donner des cours ou des conférences dans une trentaine d'universités canadiennes et américaines; Grand prix littéraire de la ville de Montréal 1967; Lauréat des concours littéraires de la province de Qué. 1967; Prix David 1967; Médaille Tyrrell de la société royale du Can. 1969; titulaire de la chaire Robarts en études canadiennes, York Univ. 1985; Prix du gouverneur général du Can. 1977; Prix Sir. J. Macdonald 1977; officier de l'ordre du Can. 1979; Médaille du centenaire du Can. 1967; Médaille du jubilée de la Reine 1977; auteur d'une dizaine de livres dont 'Histoire économique et sociale du Québec (1760–1850),' 1966 et 'Le Bas-Canada (1971–1840),' 1976, et une cinquantaine d'articles de revues; Directeur de la revue 'Histoire sociale/Social History' 1971–88; membre de la société royale du Can. (Secrétaire honoraire 1977–80); Prés. de la société historique du Can. 1970; Adresse: 92A Alcorn Ave., Toronto, Ont. M4V 1E4; Bureau: 4700 Keele St., North York, Ont. M3J 1P3.

**OUELLET, Gary Q.,** Q.C., B.A., LL.L.; lawyer; consultant; b. Quebec, Que. 9 Jan. 1945; s. Jack and Jo (Quart) O.; e. Loyola Univ., B.A. 1964; Laval Univ., LL.L 1967; m. Renée d. Paul and Gaby (Délage) Frénette 13 Sept. 1973; children: Marie, Jamie, Christopher Ryan; CHRMN. OF THE BD. & C.E.O., GOVT. CONS. INTERNAT. INC. 1985– ; lawyer, Lazarovitz & Assoc. 1967–68; Desrivières, Choquette, Paquet & Ouellet 1968–69; Sr. Partner, DeGoumois, L'Heureux Ouellet 1969–73; Levasseur, Ouellet 1973–85; Couns., The Royal Comn. of Inquiry on Aviation Safety 1979–81; Guest Lectr., Laval Univ.; Dir., The Camirand Acad. of Magic; Mem., C.A.P.A.C.; Que. SPCA; Q.C. 1984; author: 'Manuel Pratique de preuve civile' 1976; contbr.: 'Canadian Lawyer Magazine' 1976–80; recreations: ski, scuba, music, conjuring; Club: Que. Garrison; Home: 1262 Lemoine, Sillery, Que. G1S 1A2; Office: 50 O'Connor St., Ottawa, Ont. K1P 6L2.

**OUELLET, Jean-Pierre E.,** LL.L., B.C.L.; lawyer; b. Montréal, Qué. 17 Jan. 1948; s. Gaston L. and Georgette (Archambeault) O.; e. Univ. de Montréal B.A., LL.L.; Oxford Univ. B.C.L. (Rhodes Scholar Qué. 1971); m. Francine d. Albert Vallée 7 July 1972; children: Charles Etienne, Marc Olivier; LAWYER, STIKEMAN, ELLIOTT 1976– ; Dir. Crédit Commerical de France (Canada); Hartco Enterprises Inc.; Benetton Holdings (Canada) Inc.; called to Bar of Qué. 1971; Exec. Asst. to Premier of Qué. 1973–75; recreations: golf, skiing, running; Clubs: The Mount Royal; Mount Bruno Country; Royal Montréal Golf; Office: 1155 Réné Levesque Blvd. W., Ste. 3900, Montréal, Qué. H3B 3V2.

**OUELLETTE, Roger,** B.Sc.Soc., M.A., D.E.A., Ph.D., E.N.A.; university professor; b. Saint-Basile, N.B. 9 May 1954; s. Alyre and Rita (Beaulieu) O.; e. Univ. Moncton B.Sc.Soc. 1976; Univ. Ottawa M.A. 1978; Sorbonne D.E.A. 1979, Ph.D. 1981; French Natl. Sch. of Pub. Admin. E.N.A. 1986; ASSOC. PROF., UNIV. DE MONCTON 1988– ; Reporter, Radio-Canada's Moncton and Ottawa News Services; Asst. Prof., Univ. de Moncton 1981–83; Advisor for Intergovt. Affairs, Cabinet Sec., Prov. of N.B. 1986–87; Acting Dir. 1987–88; Cross of Merit, Sovereign Military Order of Malta; Pres., Soc. Nat. de l'Acadie; Mem., Candn. Public Admin. Inst.; Candn. Assn. of Pol. Sci.; Soc. Québécoise de sci. pol.; Assn. of Candn. Studies; Deputy Chairman, Commission on Federal Electoral Boundaries for the Prov. of N.B. 1993; author: 'Le Parti Acadien' 1992; co-author: 'Le système politique canadien et ses institutions' 1990; Home: 299 Cameron St., Moncton, N.B. E1C 5Z5; Office: Moncton, N.B. E1A 3E9.

**OUGHTON, Elisabeth (Libby) Ann,** B.A., M.A.; book publisher; b. Toronto, Ont. 13 Feb. 1938; d. John

George and Phyllis Mary (Smalley) O.; e. Guelph C.V.I. 1956; Queen's Univ., B.A. 1959; Cornell Univ. & Rutgers Univ., M.A. 1964; m. Gordon Barclay s. Ruth & Barclay Robinson May 1958, divorced 1965; children: Gillian Constance, David Andrew Barclay; MANAGING EDITOR, THE AYURVEDIC PRESS (Albuquerque, New Mexico) 1993– ; Lab. Tech., Cornell Univ. 1960–63; Mng. Ed., 'This Magazine is about Schools' 1965–67; Researcher & Writer, McClelland & Stewart, 'Natural History of Canada'; Prod., Coach House Press 1970–73; Info. Offr., Assn. of Candn. Pubs. 1973–75; Asst. Dir. 1977–80; Counc. mem. 1981–86; Rights Mgr., Books Canada (U.K.) 1975–77; Partner, Ragweed Press 1980–81; Pres. & Owner, Ragweed Press & Gynergy Books 1981–89; freelance journalist, CBC radio 1984–87; Mem., Atlantic Pub. Assn. (Extve. 1981–82, Pres. 1982–85, Past Pres. & Extve. Mem. 1985–87); Literary Press Group (Extve. 1982–84, Chairperson 1984–85, Extve. 1985–87); Bd. Mem., Great George St. Gallery 1982–83 (Chairperson 1983–84); Secy./Treas., P.E.I. Voice of Women 1987–88; Mem., The Writers' Union of Can.; National Council member, TWUC 1991–92; The League of Candn. Poets; Secy./Treas., Printmakers Council of P.E.I. 1991–92; Extve. Counc., P.E.N.; Past Bd. Mem., Candn. Learning Materials Ctr., Nat. Book Fest.; Atlantic Prov. Book Review and others; rec'd Annual Alumni Achievement Award, Queen's Univ. 1987; Milton Acorn Award (Poetry) 1987; semi-finalist, Alumni of the Year Award, Counc. for the Advancement & Support of Educ. 1988; Carl Sentner Award (Fiction) 1988; Outstanding Contribution to the Literary Arts 1992; author: 'getting the housework done for the dance' (poetry) 1988; co-editor: 'Island Women' 1982; NDP; recreations: wood and clay sculpture, woodblock prints, herbology, the Greek Island of Lesvos; Home: Guernsey Cove, RR. #1, Murray Harbour, P.E.I. C0A 1V0.

**OUGHTON, John Parker,** B.A., M.A.; college professor, writer; b. Guelph, Ont. 11 Dec. 1948; s. John George and Phyllis Mary (Smalley) O.; e. York Univ. B.A. (Hons.) 1972, M.A. 1979; m. Pamela d. Lois and Robert Patterson 22 June 1985; one child: Erin; PROFESSOR OF ENGLISH, FACULTY OF SCIENCE & TECHNOLOGY, SHERIDAN COLLEGE 1988– ; Editor, Communications Dept., York Univ. 1977–79; Editor, Communications & Marketing, Deloitte, Haskins & Sells 1979–80; Vice-Pres., Research, Audvicon Assoc. 1983–86; Lectr., English, Sheridan Coll. 1986–88; Lectr., Business, Acadia Univ. 1987–88; Mem., League of Canadian Poets; recipient, Tom Gallo Award, W.J. Blackhall Colour Award 1987; author: 'Taking Tree Trains' 1973, 'Gearing of Love' 1984, 'Mata Hari's Lost Words' 1988 (poetry) and over 150 articles, reviews and interviews for Canadian periodicals; recreations: writing, skiing, photography; Home: 491 Palmerston Blvd., Toronto, Ont. M6G 2P2; Office: P.O. Box 7500, Brampton, Ont. L6V 1G6.

**OUIMET, Gilles P.,** M.B.A., C.M.A.; financial executive; b. Montreal, Que. 5 Sept. 1944; e. Royal Military Coll. of Can., engr. physics 1967; Queen's Univ. M.B.A. 1972; cert. mngt. acct. 1976; m. Jocelyne Caron; children: Lucie, Christine, Jean-François; EXTVE. VICE-PRES. & DIR., PRATT & WHITNEY CANADA 1991– ; Engr., Candn. Armed Forces 1967–70; var. posts incl. Division Controller & Mgr., Lachine Works Plant, Northern Telecom 1973–77; Controller, present firm 1977; Vice-Pres., Finan. 1980; Opns. 1984; Sr. Vice-Pres., Opns. 1985; Mktg. & Customer Support 1988; Extve. Vice Pres. 1989–91; Mem., Assn. of Profl. Engrs. of Ont.; Profl. Corp. of C.M.A.s fo Que.; Nouveau Performant award 1987; CMA Elite Award 1990; recreations: tennis, skiing, flying, farming; Office: 1000 Marie Victorin, Longueil, Que. J4G 1A1.

**OUIMET, J. Robert,** M.Com., M.Pol. & Soc. Science, M.B.A.; industrialist; b. Montreal, Que.; s. J-René and Thérèse (Drouin) O.; e. Ecole des Hautes Etudes Commerciales, Montreal, M.Com.; Internat. Univ. of Fribourg, M. Pol. & Soc. Science (Magna Cum Laude); Columbia Univ., M.B.A. (Magna Cum Laude); m. Myriam, d. Lionel Maes, Belgium; children: Joanne, Marie-Diane, J. René II, J. Robert II; PRESIDENT, CHIEF EXTVE. OFFR. AND DIR., OUIMET-CORDON BLEU INC.; Cordon Bleu International Ltd.; Clark Foods; Paris Pâté Inc.; Dir., National Bank of Canada; Alliance Industrial Financial Co.; Corporate Foods Ltd.; Fondation de l'Hôpital Notre-Dame; Mem., Extve. Ctte., Conseil du Patronat; Mem., Bd. of Dirs. & Bd. of Govs. du Conseil du Patronat du Québec; mem., Extve. Ctte., Société québécoise d'initiative agro-alimentaire (SOQUIA); Government of Canada Federal Commission on Prosperity, Steering Group; mem. Knights of Malta; Knight of the National Order of Qué.; Knight of le Mont de Sion; Clubs: Saint-Denis; Mount Royal; Hermitage (Magog); Coral Beach & Tennis (Bermuda); Surf (Bal Harbour Fla.); Toronto (Toronto); Metropolitan (New York); Princeton (New York); Office: 8383 J.-René Ouimet, Anjou, Que. H1J 2P8.

**OUIMET, Hon. Roger,** LL.D.; judge (retired); b. Montreal 1908; s. Paul Gédéon and Marguerite (Desmarteau) O.; e. University of Ottawa, B.A., Ph.L. 1926; Laval University, 1928–30; LL.D. (honoris causa) University New Brunswick 1971; m. Odette, d. Right Hon. Ernest Lapointe, 25 Sept. 1937; children: Hugues, Elisabeth (Mrs. Ross Goodwin), André (d. 1976); eight grandchildren; read law with the Rt. Hon. Louis St. Laurent, P.C.; called to the Bar of Que., 1930; cr. K.C. 1944; Crown Attorney, Dist. of Montreal, 1940–44; Fed. Prosecutor and Counsel, in criminal and civil cases; general law practice before trial and appeal courts; Justice, Superior Court of Quebec, 1955–82; Cand. for Action Libérale Nationale in Prov. gen. el., 1935 (Verchères); official cand. for Liberal Party, Prov. el. 1948 (Montréal-St. Jacques); served in Reserve Army, Les Fusiliers Mont-Royal, 1942–45 with rank of Lieut.; Chrmn., Canadian Comte. on Corrections, Ottawa 1965–69; Roman Catholic; recreations: reading, enjoying the many blessings of retirement; Home: 3 Westmount Sq., Westmount, Que. H3Z 2S5.

**OUTERBRIDGE, William Robert,** B.A., M.S.W., M.Crim.; criminologist; Canadian public service; b. Kobe, Japan 10 Aug. 1926; s. Howard Wilkinson and Edna Muriel (Baker) O.; e. McMaster Univ. B.A. 1948; Univ. of Toronto B.S.W. 1950, M.S.W. 1961; Univ. of Cal. (Berkeley), M.Crim. 1966; m. Frances Amelia d. Bertram and Fannie Wardle 7 Aug. 1953; children: Margo J., A. Ross, Howard W., W. Geoffrey; Consultant in Criminology; Musician; Former Chrmn., Nat. Parole Bd.; served in various positions as family counsellor, probation offr., supervising probation offr., criminal courts Toronto and juvenile court Judge 1951–60; Dir. of Staff Devel. Ont. Probation Services 1960–68; mem., Nat. Parole Bd. Ottawa 1969–71; Assoc. Prof., Grad. Sch. of Criminology, Univ. of Ottawa 1971, Prof. of Criminology 1972–74; Adjunct Research Prof. Carleton Univ. 1983–92; recipient, Queen's Silver Jubilee Medal 1977; Internat. Award, Assoc. of Paroling Authorities International 1986; recipient, Canada 125 Medal 1993; Chrmn. Fed. Task Force on Community-Based Residential Centres 1972; author various reports, numerous articles prof. journs.; Founding Extve. Mem., Sex Information and Education Council of Canada (S.I.E.C.(Can.)) 1966–69; Founding Pres., Candn. Assn. Paroling Authorities; mem., Candn. Assn. Prevention Crime (Dir., 1972–73); Am. Corrections Assn. (Exec. 1972–86); Assn. Paroling Authorities Internat. (Exec. 1974–87); Am. Soc. Criminol.; mem., Soc. for the Reform of the Criminal Law 1988– ; mem., Advisory Ctte., Internat. Centre for Criminal Law Reform and Criminal Justice Policy 1991– ; recreations: sports, music (flugelhorn and violin); Address: Home: 534 Golden Ave., Ottawa, Ont. K2A 2E7.

**OUVRARD, Pierre C.M.,** R.C.A.; bookbinder; b. Québec City, Qué. 8 Feb. 1929; s. Jean de la Salle and Bernadette (Boily) O.; e. Coll. Jean de Brébeuf and Ecole des Beaux-Arts, Montréal; Ecole des Arts Graphiques Dipl. in Graphics specialization Art Bookbinding; m. Marie-Thérèse d. Joseph Xavier Guitard 27 Nov. 1973; 4 children (2 by previous marriage); PROP., PIERRE OUVRARD, RELIEUR: Teacher in Hist. of Art and Bookbinding, Cegep Ahuntsic 11 yrs.; Dir. Papeterie St-Gilles (hand-made paper) 1974–82; rep. in numerous exhns. nat. and internat.; author 'La Reliure' 1974; mem. Chambre Syndicale Nationale de la Reliure Dorure (France); Hand Bookbinders of Calif.; Graphic Arts Internat. Union; R. Catholic; Address: 335, rue Principale, St-Paul-de-L'Ile-Aux-Noix, Qué. J0J 1G0.

**OVERALL, Christine Dorothy,** M.A., Ph.D.; educator; b. Toronto, Ont. 25 May 1949; d. Alexander Kenzie and Dorothy Edith Kathleen (Bayes) O.; e. Univ. of Toronto B.A. 1971, M.A. 1972, Ph.D. 1980; m. Edward (Ted) Neil s. Arthur and Catherine Worth 23 March 1973; children: Devon and Narnia Worth; PROF. OF PHILOSOPHY, QUEEN'S UNIV. 1992– ; Prof. of Philos. & Humanities, Marianopolis Coll. Montréal 1975–84; Webster Fellow in Humanities and Asst. Prof. of Philos. present Univ. 1984–86, Queen's Nat. Scholar and Asst. Prof. 1986–87, Assoc. Prof. 1987–92; recipient Can. Council Doctoral Fellowship 1972–75; Ont. Arts Council Writers Reserve Grant 1987; Social Sci's & Humanities Rsch. Council Can. Rsch. Grant 1988; author: 'Ethics and Human Reproduction: A Feminist Analysis' 1987; 'Human Reproduction: Principles, Practices, Policies' 1993; co-ed.: 'Feminist Perspectives: Philosophical Essays on Method and Morals' 1988; 'Perspectives on AIDS: Ethical and Social Issues' 1991; ed.: 'The Future of Human Reproduction' 1989; mem. Candn. Philos. Assn.; Candn. Rsch. Inst. Advanc. Women; Candn. Women's Studies Assn.; Candn. Soc. Women in Philos.; Ont. Philos. Soc.; Office: Kingston, Ont. K7L 3N6.

**OVEREND, Jennifer Mary Catherine,** B.A. B.C.L., LL.B.; barrister and solicitor, petroleum industry executive; b. London, Ont. 13 Dec. 1953; d. George Bruce and Ruth Marion (Janney) O.; e. Neuchatel Jr. Coll., Switz. 1969; Univ. of Toronto, Trinity Coll. B.A. 1975; McGill Univ. B.C.L. 1978, LL.B. 1979; m. Brian s. Stella and Edward Marcil 5 May 1990; SECRETARY & ASSOCIATE GENERAL COUNSEL, ULTRAMAR CANADA INC. 1987– ; Sec. & Corp. Counsel, Majestic Contractors Limited 1981–84; Legal Counsel & Asst. Sec., Ultramar Canada Inc. 1984–86; Dir., Legal Affairs & Public Admin., Monsanto Canada Inc. 1986–87; Dir., Ultramar Capital Corp. 1989–92; specialist cert. in French & German; Candn. Securities Level 1, Hon. Cert.; recreations: sports, travel; clubs: Granite, Muskoka Lakes Assn., Montreal Amateur Athletic Assn., Mount Royal Tennis; Home: 417 Victoria Ave., Westmount, Que. H3Y 2R3; Office: 2200 McGill College Ave., Montreal, Que. H3A 3L3.

**OVEREND, Ralph Phillips,** Ph.D., M.Sc., F.C.I.C.; chemist; b. United Kingdom 7 Apr. 1944; s. Arthur Lewthwaite and Mary (Jones) O.; e. Royal Inst. of Chem., grad. 1966; Univ. of Salford, UK, M.Sc. 1968; Univ. of Dundee, Ph.D. 1972; m. Eileen d. Hilda and Jack Nicholson 21 Aug. 1965; PRINCIPAL RSCH. SCIENTIST, ALTERNATIVE FUELS DIVISION, NATIONAL RENEWABLE ENERGY LABORATORY formerly the SOLAR ENERGY RSCH. INST. 1990– ; Lab. Asst./Exper. Offr., UKAEA (UK) 1960–64; Reactor Chem. 1966–68; Asst. Rsch. Offr., Div. of Chem., NRCC 1974–77; Biomass Policy Advr., Energy, Mines & Resources 1977–79; Task Coord. Renewable Energy R&D, Div. of Engery, NRCC 1979–83; Bioenergy Prog. Mgr. 1983–86; Sr. Rsch. Offr., Inst. Env. Chem., Nat. Research Counc. of Can. 1986–90; Prof. assoc., fac. des sci. appl., Dep. de genie chim., Univ. de Sherbrooke 1983– ; NRCC postdoct. Fellow, 1972–77; UKAEA Under Grad. Bursary 1964–66; Fellow, Chem. Inst. of Can.; Royal Soc. of Chem. (UK); Tech. Section, CPPA; Pres., Candn. Soc. for Peat and Peat Lands 1989–91; author/co-author of more than 100 sci. papers & reviews; Editor, 'Journal of Biomass & Bioenergy' 1991– ; co-editor: 'Fundamentals of Thermochemical Biomass Conversion' 1985, 'Biomass: Regenerable Energy' 1987; recreations: travel, music, nordic skiing; Home: 433 Wright St., #203, Lakewood, CO 80228-1134 USA; Office: 1617 Cole Blvd., Golden, CO 80401-3393 USA.

**OVERMYER, Daniel L.,** B.A., B.D., M.A., Ph.D., F.R.S.C.; university professor; b. Columbus, Ohio 20 Aug. 1935; s. Elmer Earl and Bernice Alma (Hesselbart) O.; e. Westmar Coll., B.A. 1957; Evangelical Theol. Sem., B.D. 1960; Univ. of Chicago, M.A. 1966, Ph.D. 1971; m. Estella d. José and Sara Velázquez 19 June 1965; children: Rebecca Lynn, Mark Edward; Lab. Tech., Proctor & Gamble Corp. 1957; Pastor, Evangelical Un. Brethren Ch. 1960–64; Instr., Dept. of Religion, Oberlin Coll. 1970–71; Asst. Prof. 1971–73; Asst. Prof., Dept. of Asian Studies Univ. of B.C. 1973; Assoc. Prof. 1976; Prof. 1984; Acting Head, Dept. of Rel. Studies 1984–85; Head, Dept. of Asian Studies, 1986–91; Sec.-Treas., Soc. for the Study of Chinese Religions 1975–78, 1982–85; Pres. 1985–88; Richard Stewart Lectr. & Sr. Fellow in the Counc. of Humanities, Princeton Univ. 1983; UBC Killam Faculty Rsch. Prize 1986; FRSC 1988; Mem., Assn. for Asian Studies (China & Inner Asia Counc. 1990–93); Am. Soc. for the Study of Rel.; Candn. Asian Studies Assn.; author: 'Folk Buddhist Religion' 1976, 'Religions of China' 1986; co-author: 'The Flying Phoenix' 1986; recreations: swimming, jogging, hiking, gardening, reading; Home: 3393 West 26th Ave., Vancouver, B.C. V6S 1N4; Office: Dept. of Asian Studies, Univ. of B.C., 1871 West Mall, Vancouver, B.C. V6T 1Z2.

**OWEN, Rev. Derwyn Randulph Grier,** L.Th., M.A., Ph.D., D.D., D.C.L.; (Ang.); retired university professor; b. Toronto, Ont. 16 May 1914; s. the late Mt. Rev. Derwyn Trevor and Nora Grier (Jellett) O.; e. Ridley Coll.; Trinity Coll., Univ. of Toronto, B.A. 1936 and L.Th 1940; Corpus Christi Coll., Oxford, B.A. 1938; M.A. 1942; Union Theol. Semy., 1940–41; Univ. of Toronto Ph.D. 1942; D.D., Wycliffe; St. John's Coll.; King's Coll., Emmanuel Coll., Saskatoon; D.C.L., Bishop's Univ.; m. Anne Kathleen (dec'd) d. late Dr. R. G. Armour, Toronto, 30 May 1942; children: Laura (dec.), David, Timothy; Asst. at St. Cuthbert's Ch., Leaside, Ont., 1941–57 Lect., Dept. of Ethics and Philos., Trinity Coll., 1941–42; Assoc. Prof. in Ethics & Philos.

of Religion, 1946–54; subsequently Prof. of Religious Knowledge 1954–57, Provost and Vice Chancellor 1957–72; Professor of Religious Studies 1972–79; served in World War 1942–46, with Candn. Chaplain Services; Hon. Capt., No. 2 District Depot, Toronto, 1942–43; Westminster Regt., 5th Candn. Armoured Divn. in Eng., Italy, N.W. Europe, 1943–45; Khaki Univ. of Can. Eng., 1945; Publications: 'Scientism, Man and Religion' 1952; 'Body and Soul' 1956; Alpha Delta Phi; Home: 350 Lonsdale Rd., #512, Toronto, Ont. M5P 1R6.

**OWEN, Hon. George Robert Whitley,** M.A., B.C.L.; judge; b. Malta 29 Apr. 1912; s. Frank Whitley and Annie (Birchall) O.; came to Can. 1913; e. McGill Univ. B.A. 1933, M.A. 1934, B.C.L. 1937; Ecole Libre des Sciences Politiques and Sorbonne, Paris; m. Jean Christy d. late James Penrose Anglin 22 May 1940; two d. Jane Christy (Aikman), M. Sherrill (Edwards); Judge, Que. Court of Appeal 1955–87; called to Bar of Que. 1937; cr. Q.C. 1952; law practice Meredith Holden Heward & Holden 1937–55; Lectr. in Law McGill Univ. 1942–69; Anglican; recreations: golf, law; Clubs: Royal Montreal Golf; Kanawaki Golf; Mid Ocean (Bermuda); Hon. Co. of Edinburgh Golfers; R. & A.G.C. St. Andrews; Home: 973 Dunsmuir Rd., Montreal, Que. H3R 3A1.

**OWEN, John,** B.A., M.A.; journalist; b. Indianapolis, Indiana 11 Jan. 1942; s. Herbert T. and Mary Ellen (Yarling) O.; e. Huntington H.S.; Depauw Univ. B.A. 1964; Indiana Univ. M.A. 1972; m. Sheila d. Alec and Elizabeth MacVicar; children: Tess Alexandra, Seth (prev. marriage); CHIEF OF FOREIGN BUREAUX, CBC TV NEWS & CURRENT AFFAIRS; joined CBC 1976; Foreign Editor, CBC TV News; Senior Producer; Extve. Producer; Chief News Editor; Sigma Delta Chi Journalism; Mem., U.K. Foreign Press Assn.; Home: 2 Pilgrims Lane, London NW3, England; Office 43/51 Great Titchfield St., London W1, England.

**OWEN, Michael David,** B.Sc., Ph.D.; university professor; b. Tunbridge Wells, U.K. 5 Sept. 1940; e. Sir Joseph Williamson's Math. Sch.; Univ. of Wales, B.Sc. (Hons.) 1964; Imperial Coll., London; Monash Univ., Ph.D. 1969; post-doct. fellow, Harvard Univ. 1969–70; ASST. then ASSOC. PROF., UNIV. OF WESTERN ONT. 1970– ; research on insect venoms & insect neurochem.; Mem., Candn. Soc. of Zool.; A.A.A.S.; Internat. Soc. of Toxinol.; author/co-author of num. sci. papers; recreations: scuba diving, rugby, squash racquets; Office: Dept. of Zoology, Univ. of Western Ont., London, Ont. N6A 5B7.

**OWEN, Sidney C.,** P.M.D.; b. 1930; e. Harvard Bus. Sch. P.M.D. 1971; Inst. of Bankers, U.K., Fellow; SR. VICE-PRESIDENT, CREDIT DIVISION, THE TORONTO-DOMINION BANK 1983– ; var. branch positions Toronto-Dominion Bank 1957–61; Credit Officer, TD Centre Br., Toronto 1961–63; Asst. Mgr. 1963–67; Sr. Asst. Mgr. 1967–69; District Supvr., S. Etobicoke Dist. 1969–72; Supt. Alta. Div. 1972–74; Mgr., Jasper & 100th St. Br., Edmonton 1974–75; Mgr., Centre Br., Edmmonton 1975–77; Sr. Vice-Pres. & Gen. Mgr., Alta N. Div. 1977–83; Office: Toronto Dominion Ctr., Toronto, Ont. M5K 1A2.

**OWEN, Stephen Douglas,** LL.B., LL.M., M.B.A.; lawyer; b. Vancouver, B.C. 8 Sept. 1948; s. David Milton and Marion Margaret (Reid) O.; e. Shawnigan Lake Sch.; Univ. of B.C., LL.B. 1972; called to B.C. Bar 1973; Univ. of London, LL.M. 1974; I.M.I., Univ. of Geneva, M.B.A. 1986; m. Diane d. John and Eileen Koerner 22 May 1971; children: Taylor Reid, Jason Michael; COMMISSIONER OF RESOURCES & ENVIRONMENT FOR B.C. 1992– ; articled student & assoc., Owen, Bird 1972–75; Teacher, Candn. Univ. Serv. Overseas (Nigeria) 1975–77; Legal Serv. Soc. of B.C. 1977–86, Extve. Dir. 1982–86; Ombudsman of B.C. 1986–92; Criminology Instr., Simon Fraser Univ. 1982; Mem., Atty. Gen.'s Task Force on Public Legal Serv. 1984–85; C.B.A. Nat. Legal Aid Ctte. 1985–86; Legal Advisor, Amnesty Internat. (U.S.A., Gibraltar, Yugoslavia, South Africa) 1983– ; mem. Prov. Counc., Candn. Bar Assn. 1986–92; mem. B.C. Advisory Ctte. on Ethical Issues in Health Care 1987–88; mem. Candn. NGO Election Monitoring Team, Nicaragua 1990; Dir., Institute for Dispute Resolution, Univ. of Victoria 1991– ; Pres., Internat. Ombudsman Inst. 1988–92; Commissioner, Discretion to Prosecute Inquiry 1990; Lieutenant Gov.'s Medal for Leadership in Public Admin. 1992; Dir., Fraser River Mgmnt. Bd. 1992– ; Special Advisor, Bd. of Inquiry into Actions of Candn. Airborne Regiment, Somalia 1993; Adjunct Law Prof., Univ. of B.C. 1993; Consultant, Candn. Internat. Devel. Agency to Thai Parliamentary Ctte. on Justice 1993; Office: 7th Floor, 1802 Douglas St., Victoria, B.C. V8V 1X4.

**OWEN, Thomas Howard,** B.A., M.A., M.Phil., Ph.D.; b. Oshawa, Ont. 31 Oct. 1944; s. Earl Howard and Margaret (Sandilands) O.; e. Univ. of W. Ont. B.A. 1967; Syracuse Univ. M.A. 1968, M.Phil. 1976, Ph.D. 1977; m. Sheila d. George and Olive Smith 21 Sept. 1974; children: Emily Alexandra, Kathryn Elizabeth; SENIOR ENVIRONMENTAL ADVISOR, HARVARD INSTITUTE FOR INTERNAT. DEVELOPMENT, GOVT. OF SLOVAKIA; Lectr. Master of Pub. Adm. prog. Univ. of Man.; Assoc. Inst. of Environmental Studies, Univ. of Toronto; Lectr. Syracuse Univ. 1967–69; Policy Planning Cons. Govt. Can. 1970–71; Project Dir. Peat Marwick & Partners 1971–74; Pres. The Owen Consulting Group Ltd. 1974–83; Dep. Min. of Environment & Workplace Safety & Health, Man. 1983–88; Chair, Dep. Mins. Mgmt. Ctte. Candn. Council Resource & Environment Mins. 1987–88; Ont. Soc. Environmental Mgmt. 1979–83; Associate, Intergroup Consultants Ltd. 1988–94; mem. Inst. Pub. Adms. Can.; Am. Soc. Pub. Adm.; author: 'Community Economic Development in Rural Canada: Handbook for Practitioners' 1981; recreations: thoroughbred owner, standardbred owner/breeder, golf; Home: 84 McCaul St., Brampton, Ont. L6V 1J3; Office: One Eliot St., Cambridge, MA 02138 USA.

**OWEN, Warwick Jack Burgoyne,** M.A., Ph.D., D.Litt., F.R.S.C.; educator; b. Auckland, N.Z. 12 May 1916; s. Walter Graham and Elizabeth Frances (Williams) O.; e. Auckland Grammar Sch. 1933; Univ. of Auckland B.A. 1937, M.A. 1938; St. Catherine's Coll. Oxford B.A. 1941, M.A. 1946; Univ. of Wales Ph.D. 1955; Fellow, Royal Soc. of Canada 1975; McMaster Univ. D.Litt. (hon. causa) 1988; m. Betty Isabel d. James Drummond 20 Dec. 1945; children: Lynette Isabel, Graham Warwick; PROF. EMERITUS OF ENGLISH, McMASTER UNIV. 1981– ; Asst. Lectr. in Eng. Univ. of Auckland 1938–39; Asst. Lectr., Lectr., Sr. Lectr. in Eng. Univ. Coll. of North Wales 1946–65; Prof. of Eng. McMaster Univ. 1965–81; Assoc. Trustee, Dove Cottage Trust, Grasmere, Eng.; Ed. Adviser 'The Wordsworth Circle'; author 'Wordsworth as Critic' 1969; ed., 'Wordsworth's Preface to Lyrical Ballads' 1957; 'Wordsworth & Coleridge, Lyrical Ballads 1798' 1967; 'Wordsworth's Literary Criticism' 1974; 'William Wordsworth, The Fourteen-Book Prelude' 1985; co-ed. 'The Prose Works of William Wordsworth' 1974; numerous articles and notes on William Wordsworth and Edmund Spenser; Can. Council Leave Fellow and Fellow, Inst. Advanced Studies in Humanities Univ. of Edinburgh 1973–74; SSHRCC Leave Fellow and John Simon Guggenheim Mem. Fellow 1980–81; Secy., Academy II, Royal Soc. of Canada 1983–87; served with Brit. Army 1942–46, U.K., N. Africa, Italy, rank Capt.; mem. ACCUTE; MLA; MHRA; Internat. Assn. Univ. Profs. Eng.; Victorian Studies Assn.; recreation: music; Home: 340 Elizabeth Place, Ancaster, Ont. L9G 3G3; Office: Hamilton, Ont. L8S 4L9.

**OWEN-FLOOD, The Honourable Dermod Dimitri;** judge; b. Dublin, Ireland 17 Sept. 1931; s. Joseph Henry and Sheila Patricia (Douglas) O-F.; e. Stonyhurst Coll.; Trinity Coll., Dublin, B.A. (Mod.) M.A., LL.B.; King's Inn, Dublin (Barrister at Law); German Foreign Office Post-Graduate scholarship in International Law at Munich Univ.; m. Pamela d. Michael and Glwadys McCabe 26 Dec. 1957; children: Roderic, Marc, Deirdre; JUSTICE, SUPREME COURT OF BRITISH COLUMBIA 1990– ; admitted to Alberta Bar 1957; Counsel, Dept. Attorney General, Alta. 1956–58; law practice Banff, Alta. 1958–64; admitted to British Columbia Bar 1964; private practice Victoria, B.C. 1964–87; created Q.C. 1983; Judge, County Court of Vancouver Island 1987–90; Former mem., Candn. National Bar Counsel; mem. Attorney General's Task Force on Legal Aid in B.C.; sometime Chrmn. of Bd., Camosun College, Victoria, B.C.; sometime Hon. Treasurer, Banff Mineral Springs Hospital; sometime mem., Institute of Chartered Arbitrators and American Arbitrators Assn.; sometime mem., Earl of Longford's Theatre Company; Captain, Supplementary Reserve, Judge Advocate General; recreations: sailing, skiing; Clubs: Union; Royal Cork Yacht; Office: 850 Burdett Ave., Victoria, B.C. V8W 1B4.

**OWENS, Hugh George,** F.I.I.C.; insurance executive; b. Manitoba 5 Dec. 1935; s. Stanley George and Bertha (Ryzner) O.; e. Insurance Inst. of Canada; Western Business School Management Training Course 1976; m. Marguerite d. Jack and Pearl Gorai 20 June 1959; children: Cameron, Randy; PRESIDENT, PORTAGE LA PRAIRIE MUTUAL INSURANCE CO.; joined present firm 1954; Mem., Portage Hosp. Found. Bd.; recreations: curling, golf; clubs: Portage Curling, Portage Golf; Home: 48 Meighen Ave., Portage La Prairie, Man. R1N 3G4; Office: 749 Saskatchewan Ave. E., Portage La Prairie, Man. R1N 3B8.

**OWENS, John Neal,** B.S., M.Sc., Ph.D., F.R.S.C.; university professor; b. Portland, Oregon 18 April 1936; s. Victor Clarence and Lucille (Davie) O.; e. Portland State Coll. B.S. 1959; Oregon State Univ. M.Sc. 1961, Ph.D. 1963; m. Marje d. Linda and Voldemar Molder 6 Aug. 1977; children: Jeffrey, Cathleen, Brent, Sean; PROFESSOR AND DIRECTOR OF FOREST BIOLOGY, UNIV. OF VICTORIA 1963– ; Instructor, Portland State College 1959–60; Advisor, CIDA, ASEAN-Canada Forest Tree Seed Centre, Thailand Forestry Consultant; Fellow, Royal Soc. of Canada; Sigma Xi, Phi Kappa Phi; Office: Victoria, B.C. V8W 2Y2.

**OWENS, Rev. Joseph,** C.Ss.R., M.S.D., F.R.S.C., (R.C.); b. Saint John, N.B. 17 Apr. 1908; s. Louis Michael and Josephine (Quinn) O.; e. St. Peter's Sch., Saint John, N.B., 1914–22; St. Mary's Coll., Brockville, Ont., 1922–27; St. Anne's, Montreal, Que., 1928–30; St. Alphonsus Semy., Woodstock, Ont., 1930–34; Pontifical Inst. of Mediaeval Studies, Toronto, Ont., 1944–48, M.S.D. (Mediaeval Studies) 1951; PROF. SCH. OF GRAD. STUDIES, UNIV. OF TORONTO since 1961; Staff mem., Pontifical Inst. of Mediaeval Studies, Toronto, since 1954; Mem., Edit. Bd. of 'The Monist'; Parish Asst., St. Joseph's, Moose Jaw, Sask., 1934–35; St. Patrick's, Toronto, Ont., 1935–36; Lect. in Philos., St. Alphonsus Semy., Woodstock, Ont., 1936–40, 1948–51, 1953; Missionary, Dawson Creek, B.C., 1940–44; Lect., Accademia Alfonsiana, Rome, Italy, 1952–53; Visiting Lect., Assumption Univ., Windsor, Jan.-June, 1954; Asst. Prof., Univ. of Toronto, Assoc. Prof. 1954–61; Publications: 'The Doctrine of Being in the Aristotelian Metaphysics,' 3rd ed. 1978; 'St. Thomas and the Future of Metaphysics,' 1957; 'A History of Ancient Western Philosophy,' 1959; 'An Elementary Christian Metaphysics,' 1963; 'An Interpretation of Existence,' 1968; 'The Wisdom and Ideas of St. Thomas Aquinas' (with E. Freeman), 1968; 'The Philosophical Tradition of St. Michael's College, Toronto,' 1979; 'St. Thomas Aquinas on the Existence of God' 1980; 'Human Destiny' 1985; 'Towards a Christian Philosophy' 1990; 'Cognition' 1992; critical reviews in various learned journs.; mem., Metaphys. Soc. of Am. (Pres. 1971–72); Am. Cath. Philos. Assn. (Pres. 1965–66); Candn. Philos. Assn. (Pres. 1981–82); Soc. for Ancient Greek Philos (Pres. 1971–73); Am. Philos. Assn.; rec'd. Hon. D.Litt. Mt. Allison 1975; D.Hum.Litt., Cath. U. 1984; Hon. LL.D., St. Francis Xavier 1988; recreation: swimming; Address: St. Patrick's Rectory, 141 McCaul St., Toronto, Ont. M5T 1W3.

**OWENS, Owen Ernest,** M.Sc., Ph.D.; retired mining executive; b. Montreal, Que. 30 March 1925; s. O.N.H. and E.W. (Whittall) O.; e. McGill Univ. B.Sc. 1948, M.Sc. 1951, Ph.D. 1955; m. Alison Mary Ramsay 1952; children: David Norrey, Jane Meredith, Nancy Margaret; Vice-Pres. Exploration, Cominco Ltd. 1976–93, retired; Dir., Cominco Resources International Ltd.; Globe Stone Corp.; Rio Amarillo Mining Ltd.; Geologist, Inspiration Mining & Development Co. Ltd. 1953–57; joined present firm 1957, Exploration Supt. East. Div. 1963; Cominco International 1965; Mgr. Internat. Exploration 1969; Asst. Dir. Exploration 1970; Vice-Pres. and Managing Dir., Vestgron Mines Ltd. 1971, Pres. 1974–86; Managing Dir. Cominco Europe 1974; Dir. Exploration, Cominco Ltd. 1975; mem. Candn. Inst. of Mining and Mettallurgy; Geological Assn. of Can.; recreations: skiing, tennis.

**OXNER, Her Hon. Sandra Ellen,** B.A., LL.B.; judge; b. Halifax, N.S. 3 Oct. 1941; d. Garnet F. and Catherine Mabel (MacCalder) O.; e. Univ. of King's Coll. B.A. 1961; Dalhousie Univ. LL.B. 1965; m. Donald Percy Keddy 26 Dec. 1985; JUDGE, PROV. COURT (CRIMINAL) OF N.S. 1971– ; Governor, Commonwealth Trust 1989–91; Chrmn., Atlantic Adv. Ctte. to Solr. Gen. on Maximum Security Penitentiaries 1974–75; mem., Nat. Adv. Ctte. on the Female Offender; mem., Nat. Adv. Ctte. on Utilization & Preservation of Human Sperm; Lectr. Sch. of Journalism Univ. of King's Coll. 1980–89; called to Bar of N.S. 1965; Legal Dept. City of Halifax 1965–71; Criminal Law Consultant Law Reform Comn. Can. 1976–77; Pres., Candn. Inst. Adm. Justice 1980–82 (Bd. mem. 1977–85); Gov. Candn. Inst. Advanced Legal Studies 1978–83; Dir., Intnl. Educ. Centre; Nat. Council mem. Candn. Human Rights Assn.; Atlantic Council Christians & Jews 1977–82; Dir., N.S. John Howard Soc. 1968–71; N.S. Heritage Trust Assn. 1972–74; holder Mohr/Cullis lecture-fellowship 1982; Nat. Returning Offr. Nat. Council Women; Assoc. Fellow, Univ. of King's Coll. 1982–90; author 'Discipline and Removal From Office of Provincial Court Judges' 1978; ed. 'The Trial Process' 1981; 'Criminal Justice' 1982;

'Law in a Colonial Society' 1982; Mem., Internat. Wild Waterfowl Assoc., Inc.; Life mem., Royal N.S. Hist. Assn.; N.S. Royal Commonwealth Soc. (Vice Pres. 1983; Pres. 1984–87); Nat. Pres., Royal Commonwealth Soc. of Can.; Hon. Life President, Royal Commonwealth Soc.; Pres., Candn. Assn. Prov. Court Judges 1977, Vice Pres. 1974–76; Exec. Council mem., Commonwealth Magistrates' and Judges' Assn. 1978–85, Vice Pres. 1985–91, Pres. 1991– ; Dir. Atlantic Inst. of Criminology; Vice-Pres., Royal Commonwealth Soc.; Recipient of the Freedom of the City of London, U.K. 1988; Commonwealth Found. Fellow for 1988; United Church; Clubs: Saraguay (Hon. Secy. 1981–84); Zonta Intnl.; Tech. Univ. of N.S. Faculty; Homes: 1354 Robie St., Halifax, N.S. B3H 3E2 and 'Windsong House,' Harrietsfield, Halifax Co. N.S. B3L 4P4; Office: Provincial Court House, 5250 Spring Garden Rd., Halifax, N.S. B3J 1E7.

**OZMON, Kenneth Lawrence,** B.A., M.A., Ph.D.; educator; b. Portsmouth, Va. 4 Sept. 1931; s. Howard Augustine and Annie Josephine (Lynch) O.; e. St. Joseph's High Sch. (Portsmouth, Va.); St. Bernard Coll. (Ala.) B.A. 1955; Cath. Univ. of Am. M.A. 1963; Univ. of Me. Ph.D. 1968; m. Elizabeth Ann d. Raymond Morrison, Bangor, Me. 6 July 1968; two d. Angela Francene, Kendi Elizabeth; PRESIDENT, SAINT MARY'S UNIVERSITY, HALIFAX, since 1979; Dean of Arts, University of P.E.I. Assoc. Prof. and Chrmn. Dept. of Psychol. there since 1969; Teacher St. Bernard High Sch. 1955–57; Instr. St. Bernard Coll. 1960–62; Visiting Lectr. Marianopolis Coll. 1963–65; Lectr. St. Joseph's Teachers Coll. 1964–65; Discussion Leader Thomas More Inst. 1963–65; Asst. Prof. Cal. State Univ. Chico 1968–69; Gov. Univ. of P.E.I. 1974–76; Dir. Atlantic Inst. of Educ. 1976–79; Atlantic Research Centre on Mental Retardation 1977–79; mem. Nat. Council Candn. Human Rights Foundation; United Way of Halifax – Dartmouth (Bd. of Dirs.) 1980–83; United Way Community Volunteer Steering Comte. (Chrmn.) 1981–83; AAU/MPHEC Finance Comte. 1980–83; N.S. Educational Computer Network (Chrmn.) 1979–84; Council of N.S. Univ. Presidents (Chrmn. 1982–85); Assn. of Atlantic Universities (Chrmn. 1985–87); Consortium on Occupational Health and Safety (Dir.); Assoc. of Universities and Colleges of Canada (Vice-Chrmn. 1990–91 & Chrmn. 1991–93) (Chrmn. Audit Ctte. 1991– ; Chrmn. Nominating Ctte. 1991); Assoc. of Commonwealth Univ., (Counc. Mem. 1988–91); Chrmn., Metro Halifax Univ. Presidents Ctte.; Co-Chrmn., Nat. Coord. Ctte., for Nat. Univs. Week 1987; Chrmn., Nova Scotia Human Right Commission 1990– ; Mem. Adv. Bd., Technical Univ. of N.S. 1985– ; Bd. of Dirs., Halifax Bd. of Trade 1988–91; Mem. Bd. of Dirs., Interuniversity Services Inc. 1987– ; Mem. Halifax Bd. of Trade, Internat. Trade Comn. 1985–91; Mem. Advisory Council of the Order of Canada 1991–93; Mem., The Found. for Irish and Candn. Studies 1993; Mem. Bd. of Dirs., Friends of the Nova Scotia Museum of Industry Soc. 1993; recipient, Governor Gen. of Canada Award 1993; author various articles prof. journs. and other publs.; mem. Candn. Assn. Mentally Retarded (Dir.) 1976–79; Candn. Psychol. Assn.; Candn. Assn. Deans Arts & Science (Secy.-Treas. 1973–76); Licenced psychologist (N.S.); Hon. Prof., Univ. of Internat. Bus. & Econ. (Beijing, China); recreations: fishing, golf, running; Home: 5895 Gorsebrook Ave., Halifax, N.S., B3H 1G3.

# P

**PACHECO-RANSANZ, Arsenio,** Dr. en Fil. y Let., F.R.S.C.; educator; b. Barcelona, Spain 8 Feb. 1932; s. Arsenio and Jacoba (Ransanz) Pacheco; e. Univ. of Barcelona Lic. 1954, Dr. en Fil. y Let. 1958; m. Mercedes d. Celestino and Carmen Olivella-Sole 1 Sept. 1956; two s. Arsenio-Andrew, David-George; PROF. OF SPANISH, UNIV. OF B.C. 1980– ; Instr., Univ. of Barcelona, Tutor Colegio Mayor Fray Junípero Serra, Barcelona 1954–56; Lectr., Hochschule fur Wirtschaft und Sozialwissenschaften, Nurnberg, Germany summer 1956; Asst. Lectr., Univ. of Glasgow 1957–59; Univ. of St. Andrews 1959–61, Lectr. 1961–70; Visiting Prof., Univ. of Pittsburgh summer 1966; Assoc. Prof. present Univ. 1970; editor: 'Obres de Francesc de la Via' 1964–68; 'Historia de Xacob Xalabin' 1964; 'Testament de Bernat Serradell' 1971; 'Varia fortuna del Soldado Pindaro' 1975; Mem., Bd. of Dirs., Candn. Federation for the Humanities 1981–85; Pres., Candn. Assn. of Hispanists 1978–81; Pres., North Am. Catalan Soc. 1987–90; Home: 4027 West 37th Ave., Vancouver, B.C. V6N 2W6; Office: Dept. of Hispanic & Italian, Univ. of B.C., Vancouver, B.C. V6T 1Z1.

**PACKER, Katherine H.,** B.A., A.M.L.S., Ph.D.; university professor; b. Toronto, Ont. 20 Mar. 1918; d. Cleve Alexander and Rosa Ruel (Dibblee) Smith; e. Univ. Toronto, B.A. 1941; Univ. Michigan, A.M.L.S. 1953; Univ. of Maryland, Ph.D. 1975; m. William A. Packer, 27 Sept. 1941; child: Marianne Katherine; PROFESSOR EMERITUS, FACULTY LIBRARY AND INFORMATION SCIENCE, UNIV. TORONTO 1984– ; Cataloguer, Wm. L. Clements Library, Univ. Michigan 1953–55; Univ. Man. Library 1956–59; Univ. Toronto Library 1959–63; Head Cataloguer, York Univ. Library 1963–64; Chief Librarian, Ont. Coll. Education 1964–67; joined present Faculty as Asst. Prof. 1967; Assoc. Prof. 1975; Prof. and Dean 1979–84; rec'd Distinguished Alumnus Award, Univ. Michigan 1981; Howard V. Phalin-World Book Graduate Scholarship in Library Science Award 1972; Home: 53 Gormley Ave., Toronto, Ont. M4V 1Y9; Office: 140 St. George St., Toronto, Ont. M5S 1A1.

**PACKHAM, Marian Aitchison,** B.A., Ph.D., FRS(C); university professor; b. Toronto, Ont. 13 Dec. 1927; d. James and Clara Louise (Campbell) Aitchison; e. Weston C. & V. Sch. 1945; Univ. of Toronto B.A. 1949, Ph.D. 1954; m. James Lennox s. Murray and Irene P. 25 June 1949; children: Neil Lennox, Janet Melissa; PROF., DEPT. OF BIOCHEMISTRY, UNIV. OF TORONTO 1975– ; Sr. Fellow and then Lectr. (part-time), Biochem., Univ. of Toronto 1954–63; Rsch. Assoc. (part-time), Physiol. Sciences, Ont. Veterinary Coll. 1963–65; Blood & Cardiovascular Disease Rsch. Unit, Dept. of Medicine, Univ. of Toronto 1965–66; joined present dept. as Lecturer 1966; Visiting Prof., Dept. of Pathology, McMaster Univ.; research interests: biochem. & physiol. of blood platelets in relation to their role in hemostasis & thrombosis; Lt. Gov.'s Silver Medal, Victoria Coll. 1949; Co-recipient, J. Allyn Taylor Internat. Prize in Med. 1988; Mem., Internat. Ctte. on Thrombosis & Haemostasis (Sec. 1984–86) 1979– ; Past Mem. of several extve. cttes. most recent: Blood Diseases & Resources Adv. Ctte., Nat. Heart, Lung & Blood Inst., Nat. Institutes of Health, USA 1986–90; Mem., Candn. Biochem. Soc.; Am. & Can. Socs. of Hematology; Am. Assn. of Pathologists; Candn. Soc. for Clin. Investigation; Council on Thrombosis of Am. Heart Assn.; Internat. Soc. on Thrombosis & Haemostasis; Candn. Atherosclerosis Soc.; author/co-author of over 240 pub. articles; one of the world's most frequently cited scientists; Candn. Ed., 'Thrombosis Res.' 1974–79, 'Platelets' 1990– ; Ed. Bd., 'Atherosclerosis' 1978–89; Ed. Bd. Mem., 'Blood' 1980–85, 'Thrombosis and Haemostasis' 1981– , 'Exper. & Molecular Path.' 1987– ; recreations: skiing; club: Beaver Valley Ski; Home: 65 Glengowan Rd., Toronto, Ont. M4N 1G3; Office: Toronto, Ont. M5S 1A8.

**PACZKOWSKI, Taisia.** See Taisia.

**PADDON, Hon. William Anthony,** O.C., M.D., Dip.P.H., D.Sc.; b. Indian Harbour, Labrador 10 July 1914; s. Harry L., M.D. and Mina (Gilchrist) P.; e. The Lenox (Mass.) Sch.; Trinity Coll. Hartford, Conn. B.Sc. 1936, D.Sc. 1975; N.Y. State Med. Sch. (Downstate) M.D.; Univ. of London Dip.P.H. 1957; D.Sc. (Hon.) Trinity College (Hartford); Memorial Univ. Hon. Degree D.Sc. 1977; m. Sheila Mary d. Frank Fortescue, Essex, Eng. 20 Sept. 1952; children: Elizabeth M., David F., Michael A. C., Thomas F.; Lieutenant Governor of Nfld. and Labrador 1981–86; Dir., Northern Medical Services, Internat. Grenfell Assn., 1960–78, internship St. Luke's Hosp. N.Y. City 1940–42; Resident Med. and Surg., Internat. Grenfell Assn. St. Anthony, Nfld. 1945; Med. Offr. in Charge, North West River, Labrador, Nfld. 1945–60; served on various sch. bds. as mem. or chrmn. 32 yrs.; mem. Bd. Regents, Mem. Univ. Nfld. 1972–74; co-winner Royal Bank of Can. Award 1977; Member, Order of Canada 1978; Officer, Order of Canada 1988; served with R.C.N. 1942–45, Surg. Lt. becoming Surg. Lt. Commdr.; author various prof. articles, papers; Knight of Grace, Most Venerable Order of the Hospital of St. John of Jerusalem; mem. Candn. Med. Assn.; Nfld. Med. Assn.; Coll. of Family Practice; Anglican; Home: North West River, Labrador, Nfld.

**PADY, David W.,** B.A., C.A.; business executive; b. Toronto, Ont. 23 Oct. 1943; e. Upper Canada College 1962; Wilfrid Laurier Univ. B.A. (Hons.) 1966; C.A. 1969; m. Sandra d. George and Jeanne Kennedy 26 Aug. 1967; children: Mitchell William, Adrienne Jeanne; PRESIDENT & OWNER, CHARDONNAY CONSULTANTS LIMITED 1974– ; Price Waterhouse 1966–71; Controller, Vickers & Benson Ltd. 1971–74; Chair & Dir., Willow Pond Assoc. Ltd. 1981– ; Network Video Inc.; Major Games Inc.; Willow Pond Securities Inc.; Schulz Productions Inc. 1979–85; Trans Global Films Inc. 1979–83; Managing Partner, APS Partnership; Ability for Windows Partnership; Director, Canadian Arctic Beverage Corp.; Chair, Bd. of Gov., Wilfrid Laurier Univ.; Dir., Guelph Spring Festival; Former Chair, Moorelands-Kawagama Camp; Treas., The Donkey Sanctuary of Canada; Mem., Niagara Diocese of the Anglican Church (Investment Ctte.); co-author: 'It's Your Money' 1979; recreations: running, golf, hiking; clubs: Cutten; Home: Walnut Ridge Farm, R.R. 6, Guelph, Ont. N1H 6J3; Office: 8199 Yonge St., Suite 300, Thornhill, Ont. L3T 2C6.

**PAGANI, Catherine Mary,** B.Sc., M.M.St.; research associate; b. Guelph, Ont. 14 Dec. 1960; d. Richard Dario and E. Yvonne (Hammar) P.; e. Univ. of Western Ont. B.Sc. 1984; Univ. of Toronto, M.M.St. 1986, Ph.D. 1993; ASST. PROF., DEPARTMENT OF ART, UNIV. OF ALABAMA 1993– ; Asst. to the Costume Designer, Sch. of Dramatic Arts, Univ. of Windsor 1983–84; Museum Intern, Nat. Mus. of History Taipei, Taiwan 1985; Lecturer, Dept. of Art History, State Univ. of N.Y. at Buffalo 1988–92; Chinese Art History, Sch. of Contg. Studies, Univ. of Toronto 1989–93; Research Assoc., Far Eastern Dept., Royal Ontario Museum 1989; SSHRCC fellowship; Ont. Grad. scholarship; Mem., Candn. Museum Assn.; Candn. Asian Studies Assn.; Assn. for Asian Studies (US); College Art Assn.; co-author: 'The First Emperor of China' 1989; author of various articles; recreations: gardening, needlework, swimming; Home: 404 - 19th Ave., Tuscaloosa, Alabama 35401; Office: Dept. of Art, Univ. of Alabama, Box 870270, Tuscaloosa, Alabama 35487-0270.

**PAGE, Austin P.,** B.A.; business executive; b. Sherbrooke, Que. 18 March 1936; s. Charles and Florence (Swift) P.; e. Sherbrooke High Sch. 1953; Queen's Univ. ACBA 1956; N.S. Inst. of Technol. Ind. Eng. Cert. 1963; Sir George Williams Univ. B.A. 1966; m. Suzanne d. Jean Paul and Margot Blouin 8 July 1988; children: Chris, Curtis, Kimberly, Cynthia; EXTVE. VICE PRES. AND CHIEF FINANCIAL OFFR. TRIDEL ENTERPRISES INC. 1982– ; Pres. and C.E.O.: Aluma Systems Corp; The Burke Co.; UMACS Canada Inc. 1992– ; Delbancor Industries Ltd. 1984– ; Magic Foods Inc. 1986– ; Tridel Equities Ltd. 1989– ; Dir., Tridel Enterprises Inc.; Banca Commerciale Italiana of Canada; Aluma Systems Corp.; joined The Canadian Bank of Commerce 1953–62; Allied Chemical of Canada 1962–64; Cooper Lybrands, Nat. Partner 1964–73; Mng. Dir. 1976 Olympic Revenue Progs. Govt. Can. 1973–76; Pres. Paramount Management International, N.Y. 1976–80; Vice Pres. Corporate Devel. VS Services Ltd. 1980–82; mem. Inst. Mgmt. Cons.; recreations: skiing, tennis, squash, sailing, farming; Club: Trident Yacht (Gananoque; Past Gov.); Office: 4800 Dufferin St., Downsview, Ont. M3H 5S9.

**PAGE, Donald Herman,** F.C.G.A., F.C.S.I.; professional accountant; b. St. Thomas, Ont. 2 May 1933; s. late James Herman and Gertrude Georgina (Campbell) P.; e. Tyrconnell Pub. Sch., W. Elgin High Sch., County of Elgin 1951; Westervelt Business Col., 1952; C.G.A. 1962; Univ. of W. Ont. Mang. Training Course, 1972; m. Marion Gertrude, d. late John Clarence MacLean Patterson and Jeanetta Elizabeth (Bobier), 22 Nov. 1952; children: Donald James, Gerald Richard, Paul Douglas, Andrew Patterson, Marion Elaine; VICE-PRES., FINANCE AND ADMIN., TORONTO STOCK EXCHANGE 1993– ; joined Midland Securities Corp. Ltd., London, Ont. 1952; apptd. Comptroller (on merger) 1963, Asst. Secy. 1965, Dir. 1969, Vice Pres. Finance and Admin., Compliance Offr. and Secy. 1971; merger of Midland Doherty Ltd. 1974; Extve. Vice Pres. & C.F.O. 1980–89; Dir. & C.F.O. Midland Doherty Financial Corp. 1983–89, Financial Services Consultant 1989–91; Chief of Compliance, Ontario Securities Commission 1991–92; mem. Boy Scout Assn. 1961–67; Treas., Kiwanis Music Festival Metrop. Toronto, 1966–67; N. York Baseball Assn. 1968–69 (Pres. 1970); Chrmn., Parkwoods Un. Ch. Central Bd., 1972; Toronto Stock Exchange Mem. Seat Holder 1985; elected Bd. of Dir., Candn. Depository for Securities Ltd. 1981–84; elected to Bd. of Gov., Toronto Stock Exchange, 1981, Vice Chairman 1984, Chrmn., Bd. of Gov./TSE 1985–87; joined Panel of Sr. Advisors, Auditor General's office Sept. 1985; mem., Cert. Gen. Acct's Assn. (Bd. of Govs. Ont. 1970; Ont. mem. Nat. Educ. Council 1971–74 and Pres. 1976); Nat. Pres., Candn. Cert. Gen. Acct's 1979–80 (Life mem. 1976); Invest. Dealers' Assn. Can. (Financial Adm. Sec. 1966, Chrmn. 1971–72, Bd. of Dirs., 1985–87; Queen's Jubilee Medal 1978; Freemason; P. Conservative; United Church; recreations: curling, farming; Clubs: Donalda; Empire; Home: 26 Beveridge Dr., Don Mills, Ont. M3A 1N9; Office: The Exchange Tower, 10th Floor, 2 First Canadian Place, Toronto, Ont. M5X 1J2.

**PAGE, Garnet Thomas,** O.C., C.O.N. du M.(Fr), K.C.P.R., K.C.M., K.L.J., B.A., F.C.I.C.; consultant, b. Halifax, N.S. 28 Oct. 1920; s. William Thomas and Mabel Lauretta (Coolin) P.; e. Univ. of Sask., B.A. (Chem.) 1940; CONSULTANT since 1982; Pres., Garnet T. Page Consulting Ltd.; Dir., The Bank of Tokyo, Canada; The Bank of Tokyo Canada Leasing Corp.; part-time Instr., Chem. Dept., Univ. of Sask., 1938–40; Instr. at N.P.A.M. Camps in Chem. Warfare (summers) 1937–40; served in 2nd World War with Candn. Army Active Force, 1940–46; retired with rank of Lieut.-Col.; Gen. Mgr. and Secy., The Chem. Inst. of Canada, 1946–56; Gen. Secy., Engn. Inst. Can., 1956–66; Visiting Prof., Hist. of Science, Univ. of Ottawa, 1954–56; Candn. Del. to UNESCO General Confs., 1946, '48, '49, '50, '52, '54, '56, '85; mem., Candn. Comte. on Brussels World Fair (1958), since 1955; mem., Advisory Council on Prof. Manpower, Dept. of Labour, since 1956; Chrmn., Nat. Adv. Comte. on Technol. Educ. 1961–65; Chrmn., Nat. Tech. & Vocational Training Adv. Council, 1965; Consultant to OECD 1964–65; named Dir., Pilot Projects Br., Dept. Manpower, Can. 1966; Dir. Gen. Tech. Services & Special Projects Div., Dept. Regional Econ. Expansion, Can. 1968–73; Federal Admin., Fed.-Prov. Employment Loans Prog. 1969–73; Pres., Coal Assn. of Canada, 1974–82; Hon. Life Mem., Intern. Comte. for Coal Research; Hon. Life mem., Coal Assoc. of Can.; Can.-Japan Business Cooperation Comte.; Canada-Korea Business Council; Chrmn., Candn. Comte. for UNESCO 'Man and the Biosphere' project 1983–86; Chrmn., Science Advisory Panel & Vice Pres. I.C.C./MAB 1984–86; Publications: numerous papers, reports on U.N. and UNESCO affairs, chem. indust., educ., etc.; mem., Am. Soc. of Civil Engrs.; Am. Soc. of Mech. Engrs.; Candn. Council for Reconstr. through UNESCO (Treas. 1948–52); Candn. Educ. Assn.; Candn. Film Inst. (Dir., 1954–55; mem. of Council since 1946); mem., Inst. for Research in Public Policy; Chancelier National, la Confrerie de la chaine des Rotisseurs, Maitre, la Commanderie de Bordeaux; awarded Silver Medal, Univ. of Turin, 1950; Coronation Medal, King George VI, 1937; Medal from Pope Pius XII 1950; Medal of Greek Red Cross, 1941, Queen Elizabeth II Coronation medal 1953; Queen Elizabeth II 25th Anniv. Medal 1978; Pasteur Medal Inst. Pasteur, Paris, 1948; Officer Order of Can. 1983; Hon. mem., The Candn. Fed. of Chefs de Cuisine; Hon. Dir., The Alberta Restaurant and Foodservices Assoc.; mem., Alberta Office of Coal Res. & Technol.; Alberta Coal Develop. Advisor; Chrmn., Intergovernmental Secretariat to the Action Ctte. on Western Low Sulphur Coal 1987–94; Hon. Consul of France in Calgary 1976–86; recreations: travel, people; Clubs: The Ranchmen's, Calgary, Calgary Polo; Office: Suite 1201, 105 - 26th Ave. S.W., Calgary, Alta. T2S 0M3.

**PAGE, Jack Stewart,** B.A., M.A., Ph.D., C.Psych.; university professor; b. London, Ont. 11 Jan. 1943; s. Jack Hayes and Norma Violet (Rosser) P.; e. Univ. of West. Ont. B.A. 1965, M.A. 1966; Univ. of Toronto Ph.D. 1970; m. Susan d. Michael and Arleen Furgala 27 May 1972; children: Laura, Rosamonde, Lindsay; PROFESSOR, PSYCHOLOGY, UNIV. OF WINDSOR 1986– ; Rsch. Psychologist, Lakeshore Psych. Hosp. 1970; Dir. of Research 1976; Chief Psychologist, Brockville Psych. Hosp. 1979; Assoc. Prof., Psychol., Univ. of Windsor 1981; Acting Head 1992–93; Visiting Prof., Dalhousie Univ. 1987–88; Lectr., Univ. of Toronto 1969–79; Instr., St. Lawrence College 1980–81; Mem., Bd. of Gov., Ont. Psychol. Assn. 1972–74; registered as profl. psychologist in Ont. by Ont. Bd. of Examiners in Psychol. 1971– ; Mem., Ont. Psychol. Assn.; Candn. Psychol. Assn. 1970–81; author: 'Mental Patients and the Law' 1974 and approx. 200 academic articles and paper presentations; recreations: sports, family, computer applications; Home: 1271 Chilver Rd., Windsor, Ont. N8Y 2L2; Office: Windsor, Ont. N9B 3P4.

**PAGE, James E.,** M.A.; federal civil servant; b. Woodstock, Ont. 3 Aug. 1942; s. James Ernest and Simone Alberta Marie (Raymond) P.; e. Queen's Univ. B.A. 1967, M.A. 1968; m. Darlene d. Regina and Peter Gombola 22 July 1967; one s. Graham Peter James; DIR. GEN., EDUCATION SUPPORT, HUMAN RESOURCES AND DEVELOPMENT CANADA (formerly Secretary of State) 1989– ; Adjunct Research Prof., Institute for Canadian Studies, Carleton Univ. 1991– ; formerly Dir., Candn. Studies, Sec. of State Can. 1984–89; worked extensively abroad on devel. edn., adult edn. and Candn. Studies in Eur., Africa, India, Australia and Far E.; mem. Mgmt. Bd. Internat. Council Adult Edn. 1977–86; mem. Comn. Candn. Studies 1973–86; Cons. to Sci. Council Can., Nat. Film Bd., Ont. Edn. Communications Authority, Ont. Inst. Studies in Edn.; Founding Pres. Internat. Council for Candn. Studies 1981–83; Founding Dir. Candn. Studies & Internat. Bureaus, Assn. Candn. Community Colls.; Pres. Assn. Candn. Studies 1977–82; author 'Canadian Studies on Community Colleges' 1973; 'Seeing Ourselves' 1979; 'A Canadian Context for Science Education' 1979; 'Seeing Canada' 1980; 'Reflections on the Symons' Report: The State of Canadian Studies in 1980' 1981; co-author 'Some Questions of Balance: Human Resources, Higher Education and Canadian Studies' 1984; contbr. 'To Know Ourselves: The Report of the Commission on Canadian Studies' 1976; numerous articles, reviews; mem. ed. bd. Jour. Candn. Studies 1979–93; mem. Candn. Assn. Curriculum Studies; Champlain Soc.; Australian & N.Z. Assn. Candn. Studies; Brit. Assn. Candn. Studies; Gesellschaft für Kanada-Studien; Assn. française d'études canadiennes; recreations: golf, tennis; Home: 468 Piccadilly Ave., Ottawa, Ont. K1Y 0H6; Office: Ottawa, Ont. K1A 0M5.

**PAGÉ, Michel,** Ph.D.; educator; biochemist; b. Québec City, Qué. 18 Feb. 1940; s. Hector and Alma (Dussault) P.; e. Laval Univ. B.A. 1960; Ottawa Univ. B.Sc. 1965, Ph.D. (Biochem.) 1969; m. Marthe d. Robert Boudreau 17 Dec. 1966; children: Brigitte, Marie, Charles, Madeleine; PROF. OF BIOCHEM., LAVAL UNIV. 1974– ; Clin. Biochem. Hôtel-Dieu de Québec 1971–81, (Prof. 1982); Asst. Prof. of Biochem. Laval Univ. 1974, Assoc. Prof. 1978, Prof. 1982– ; Pres., Assn. Biochems. Hôpitaux du Qué. 1976; Grant Comte.; Scholar, Nat. Cancer Inst. Can. 1975–81; author over 100 articles, three books ; mem. Am. Assn. Advanc. Science; Am. Soc. Cell Biol.; Am. Assn. Cancer Res.; Internat. Soc. Immunopharmacol.; Internat. Soc. Preventive Oncology; N.Y. Acad. Sciences; Sigma Xi; R. Catholic; Home: 9175 Place Lavallière, Charlesbourg, Qué. G1G 3J9; Office: Dept. de Biochem., Faculté de médecine, Université Laval, Ste-Foy, Qué. G1K 7P4.

**PAGE, Norman,** M.A., Ph.D., F.R.S.C.; educator and author; b. Kettering, UK 8 May 1930; s. Frederick Arthur and Theresa Ann (Price) P.; e. Kettering Grammar Sch.; Emmanuel Coll. Cambridge B.A. 1951, M.A. 1955; Univ. of Leeds PH.D. 1968; m. Jean d. Arthur and Kathleen Hampton 29 March 1958; children: Camilla, Benjamin, Barnaby, Matthew; EMERITUS PROFESSOR, UNIV. OF NOTTINGHAM 1993– ; Head of Dept. of English Studies 1987–90; Prin. Lectr. and Head of English Ripon Coll. UK 1960–69; Asst. Prof. of Eng. Univ. of Alta. 1969; Assoc. Prof. 1970–75; Prof. 1975–85; Emeritus Prof. 1985– ; Prof. of Modern English Literature, Univ. of Nottingham, UK 1985–93; McCalla Rsch. Prof. 1983–84; Guggenheim Fellow 1979–80; Visiting Rsch. Fellow Victorian Studies Centre Univ. of Leicester 1979–80, 1982; recipient Univ. Alta. Rsch. Prize 1983; author 'The Language of Jane Austen' 1972; 'Speech in the English Novel' 1973; 'Thomas Hardy' 1977; 'A.E. Housman: A Critical Biography' 1983; 'A Dickens Companion' 1983; 'A Kipling Companion' 1984; 'E.M. Forster' 1987; 'Muriel Spark' 1990; 'Tennyson: An Illustrated Life' 1992; ed. vols. on Hardy, D.H. Lawrence, Tennyson, Henry James, Nabokov, etc.; ed. 'Thomas Hardy Annual'; 'Thomas Hardy Journal'; frequent lectr. UK, Germany, Spain, Norway, Sweden, Jordan, India, Japan, N.Z.; Pres., Victorian Studies Assn. W. Can. 1975–76; Trustee, Dickens Soc.; Jane Austen Soc. N.Am.; Chrmn., Publications Board, Tennyson Soc.; Vice-Pres., Thomas Hardy Soc.; recreations: travel, music; Home: 23 Braunston Rd., Oakham, Rutland, LE15 6LD, U.K.

**PAGE, Patricia Kathleen (Mrs. William Arthur Irwin);** writer, painter; b. Eng. 23 Nov. 1916; d. late Maj. Gen. Lionel F. and Rose Laura (Whitehouse) P.; came to Can. 1919; e. St. Hilda's Sch. for Girls, Calgary, Alta.; m. Wm. Arthur Irwin, 1950; author of 'The Sun and the Moon' 1944; 'As Ten As Twenty' 1946; 'The Metal and the Flower' 1954; 'Cry Ararat! – Poems New and Selected' 1967; 'The Sun and the Moon and Other Fictions' 1973; 'Poems-Selected and New' 1974; ed. 'To Say the Least' (anthology of short poems) 1979; 'Evening Dance of the Grey Flies' (poems and short story), 1981; Text for 'The Travelling Musicians' music by Murray Adaskin 1984; 'The Glass Air' (Poems, essays, drawings) 1985; Brazilian Journal (prose) 1987; 'A Flask of Sea Water' (fairy tale) 1989; 'The Glass Air - Poems Selected & New' 1991; 'The Travelling Musicians' (children) 1991; 'The Goat That Flew' (sequel to 'A Flask of Sea Water' 1994; also poems, short stories, art criticism, drawings in various magazines and anthologies; winner of Oscar Blumenthal Award (Poetry: Chicago) 1944; Governor-General's Award for Poetry, 1954; National Magazines Award (Gold) for a group of poems 1985; Candn. Authors' Assn. Literary Award for Poetry 1986; B.C. Book Awards Hubert Evens Prize (for 'Brazilian Journal') 1988; Banff Centre Nat. Award 1989; as P. K. Irwin has held one-woman shows in Mexico and Canada, been represented in various group shows and has work in the National Gallery of Canada, the Art Gallery of Ontario and many others; Offr. Order of Can., 1977; D. Litt., Univ. of Victoria 1985; Doctor of Laws (honoris causa) Univ. of Calgary 1989; Doctor of Letters (honoris causa), Univ. of Guelph 1990; Doctor of Laws (honoris causa), Simon Fraser Univ. 1990; Address: 3260 Exeter Road, Victoria, B.C. V8R 6H6.

**PAGE, Robert J.D.,** B.A., M.A., D.Phil.; university professor and administrator; b. Toronto, Ont. 11 Sept. 1940; s. Robert Henry Constant and Louise Stirling (Perrott) P.; e. Bathurst Heights Collegiate; Queen's Univ. B.A. 1963, M.A. 1964; Oxford Univ. D.Phil. 1971; m. Jocelyne d. Grace and Geoff Daw 20 Aug. 1977; children: Douglas, Kate; DEAN, FACULTY OF ENVIRONMENTAL DESIGN & PROF. OF ENVIRONMENTAL SCIENCE, THE UNIV. OF CALGARY 1990– ; Prof. of History & Environ. Studies, Trent Univ. 1967–90; Chair, Environ. & Resource Studies Prog. 1977–81; Dir., Frost Centre 1985–86; Host & Prod., 'The Editorial Page' (TV series) 1972–85; consultant on energy & the environ. to indus. & govt. 1974– ; consultant on trade & the environ. 1991– ; Canada Council Research Award 1977–78; SSHRC Award 1985–86; Bd. of Gov., Trent Univ. 1979–81; Nat. Chair, Ctte. for an Independent Canada 1974–75; Chair, Candn. Environ. Adv. Council 1987–92; Mem., Nat. Round Table on Environ. & Economy 1992– ; Internat. Trade Adv. Ctte. 1991– ; Candn. Delegate to the World Conf. on Changing Atmospheric Environ. 1988; Mem., Environ. Futures Task Force, Govt. of Alta. 1993– ; Bd. Mem., Candn. Univ. Consortium to Asian Inst. of Technology Bangkok Thailand 1990– ; Anglican; author: 'Northern Development: The Canadian Dilemma' 1986 (latest book); recreations: mountain hiking, canoeing, hockey, jogging, cottage; Home: 501 Salem Ave. S.W., Calgary, Alta. T3C 2K7; Office: Calgary, Alta. T2N 1N4.

**PAGEAU-GOYETTE, Nycol,** B.A.; entrepreneur; b. Montreal, Que. 31 Oct. 1943; d. Henri André and Suzanne (Longval) Pageau; e. Univ. of Montreal B.A. 1972; m. Charles s. Juliette and Albert Bourgeois; children: Marc and Philippe Goyette; FOUNDER & PRES., PAGEAU GOYETTE ET ASSOC. 1977– ; Technical Translator, Hydro-Québec 1961–67; freelance technical translator 1967–74; Deputy Dir., Internat. Yough Camp, Corp. des Jeux Olympiques 1975–77; Dir., Soc. de dével. industriel du Qué.; Fonds de solidarité des travailleurs du Que.; Asia Pacific Found.; Hydro-Québec; Conseil can. de la productivité and others; Pres., Metro. Montreal C. of C. 1990–91; Chrmn. 1991–92; Dir., Soc. du Palais de la Civilisation de Montréal; Ecole des technol. supérieures; Bd. Mem., Candn. C. of C.; Mem., Soc. of Translators; C. de C. du Qué.; author: 'International Dictionary of Nuclear Energy' 1965; recreations: swimming; Home: 100 Berlioz, Suite 1703, Ile des Soeurs, Que. H3E 1N4; Office: 407 St.-Laurent Blvd., Suite 500, Montreal, Que. H2Y 2Y5.

**PAGEOT, Jean-Claude,** Ph.D.; university professor; b. Qué. 1 May 1940; s. Jean Marie and Marcelle (Clark) P.; e. Univ. Laval, B.E.P. 1964; Univ. of S. Calif., Ph.D. 1972; m. Jacqueline d. Jules E. Dorion 1 Aug. 1964; children: Marie, Hélène; CHRMN., DEPT. OF LEISURE STUDIES, UNIV. OF OTTAWA 1980– ; Prof., Phys. Ed., C.S.R.M. 1964–65; Dir., Phys. Ed. Dept., C.S. Charlesbourg 1965–67; Cons., Conseil Regional des Loisirs de Qué. 1967–69; Dir., Univ. Rec. Assn., L.A. 1969–72; Prof. Univ. du Qué. à Trois-Rivières 1972–73; Dir., Rec. Dept., Qué. City 1973–80; Extve. Ctte., Fac. of Soc. Sci., Univ. of Ottawa; private cons. in recreation; Dir., Fond. en Adapt. Motrice, F.A.M.; Président, Bd. of Dirs., Centre des aînés francophones d'Ottawa-Carleton (CAFOA); Past Pres., Internat. Fed. of Adapted Physical Activity; Treasurer, Bd. of Dirs., Candn. Bureau on Active Living; Past Pres., Candn. Parks & Rec. Assn.; Home: 1034 Avignon Court, Orleans, Ont. K1C 2R2; Office: Ottawa, Ont. K1N 6N5.

**PAGTAKHAN, Reynaldo Reis,** B.A.(Hons.); student, university executive; b. Winnipeg, Man. 9 Nov. 1969; s. Reynaldo Daluz and Gloria (Visarra) P.; e. Univ. of Manitoba B.A. (Hons.) 1991, LL.B. forthcoming 1994; MEMBER, UNIV. OF MANITOBA BOARD OF GOVERNORS 1992– ; articling student with law firm of Aikins, MacAulay & Thorvaldson 1994– ; Mem., Univ. of Man. Bd. of Gov. Extve. Ctte. 1993– ; Univ. of Man. Senate 1990–91, 1992– ; Mem., Young Liberals of Man. Extve. Ctte. 1989–90; Nat. Council of Candn. Filipino Assns. Youth Action Ctte. (Man.) 1992–93; Mem., Univ. of Manitoba Students' Union Council 1990–91, 1992– ; Home: 6 Sandee Bay, Winnipeg, Man. R2M 1Z1; Office: 30th Floor, 360 Main St., Winnipeg, Man. R3C 4G1.

**PAHL, Milton George,** B.A., M.B.A.; businessman; b. Hanna, Alta. 30 Oct. 1943; s. Packey E. and Rose A (Hardinges) P.; e. Univ. of Alta., B.A. 1966, M.B.A. 1971; m. Rosemary (Schauf); children: John, Jennifer; PRESIDENT & C.E.O., NATIVE VENTURE CAPITAL CO. LTD. 1986; Dir., Fort Chipewyan Lodge Corp.; Aboriginal Logging Ltd.; Neegan Development Corp.; Peigan Craft Ltd.; Richdale Resources Ltd.; varied oil ind. exper. Canada & U.S. 1961–69; Pres., Management Systems Limited 1971–82; Principal, Engineering-Consulting firm 1977–82; Mem., Legislative Assembly, P.C. Party Edmonton Mill Woods 1979–86; Min. Resp. for Native Affairs, Prov. of Alta. 1982–86; Dir., Alberta Oil Sand Tech. & Rsch. Authority 1981–82; Junior Boxing champion of Canada 1957; Golden Boy winner 1959; U.S. Jr. Welterweight Champion 1964; Mem., Edmonton C. of C. Coun. 1978; Chrmn., Energy Conservation Ctte., 1979; Dir., Candn. Energy Res. Inst. 1980–82; Dir., Old Strathcona Found. 1976; Assn. of Profl. Economists of B.C. 1974; Home: 10317 Villa Ave., Edmonton, Alta. T5N 3T8.

**PAÏDOUSSIS, Michael P.,** B.E., Ph.D., F.R.S.C.; educator; b. Nicosia, Cyprus 20 Aug. 1935; s. Pandelis Aristeidou and Parthenope (Leptou) P.; e. Abet Greek Gymnasium Cairo 1953; McGill Univ. B.E. 1958; Cambridge Univ. Ph.D. 1963; m. Vrisseïs d. Anargyros Mavros; THOMAS WORKMAN PROF. OF MECH. ENG. McGILL UNIV. 1986– , Prof. of Mech. Eng. 1976– ; Fellow in Nuclear Eng. General Electric Co. Erith, Kent, Eng. 1958–60; Rsch. Offr. Applied Phys. Div. Atomic Energy of Canada Ltd. Chalk River 1963–67; Asst. Prof. of Mech. Eng. present Univ. 1967, Assoc. Prof. 1970, Chrmn. of Dept. 1977–86; Visiting Sci. in Theoretical & Applied Mechanics Cornell Univ. 1987–88; Cons. Fluidelasticity, Battelle North-West, Richmond, Va. 1968–71; Cons. Flow-Induced Vibrations Atomic Energy of Can. CRNL Chalk River and WNRE Whiteshell, Man. 1971–81; Cons. Commissariat à L'Énergie Atomique, CEN-Saclay, France 1988; Editor, Journal of Fluids and Structures; recipient Brit. Assn. Medal for High Distinction in Mech. Eng. 1958; Inst. Mech. Eng. George Stephenson Prize 1976; awarded Commemorative Medal for 125th Anniversary of Candn. Confederation 1993; Hon. Consul of Cyprus in Montreal; author over 100 papers profl. jours., over 70 papers conf. proceedings; Fellow: Instn. Mech. Engs. (UK), Am. Soc. Mech. Engs., Candn. Soc. Mech. Eng., Royal Soc. of Canada, Am. Acad. Mechanics; Member, Order Engs. Que.; Internat. Assn. Hydraulic Rsch. (Chrmn. Div. III 1981–87); recreations: reading, writing, wind-surfing; Home: PH2, 2930 Edouard Montpetit, Montreal, Que. H3T 1J7; Office: 817 Sherbrooke St. W., Montreal, Que. H3A 2K6.

**PAIKEDAY, Thomas M.,** M.A., L.Ph.; lexicographer; b. Kerala, India 11 Oct. 1926; s. Manuel T. and Anna (Poovelickal) P.; e. St. Joseph's Eng. High Sch. and Univ. Coll. Trivandrum, India; Coll. of the Jesuits, Shembaganur, L.Ph. 1955; Madras Christian Coll. B.A. (1st class hons. in English) 1958; Univ. of Madras, M.A. 1960; Boston (Mass.) Coll. 1962–63; Univ. of Mich. 1963–64; m. Mary d. Kurien and Rosa Kizhakethottam 4 Jan. 1967; children: Anthony, Anne-Marie; CHIEF LEXICOGRAPHER, PAIKEDAY PUBLISHING INC. 1973– ; Lectr. in Eng. St. Joseph's Coll. Tiruchirapalli, India 1958–59, Univ. of Delhi 1960–61; Copy Ed. 'The Statesman' New Delhi 1961–62; 'The Patriot Ledger,' Quincy, Mass. 1963; Asst. Lexicographer, W.J. Gage Ltd. Toronto 1964–66; Ed. Ont. Min. of Edn. 1966–67; Head, Lexicography Div. Holt Rinehart & Winston, Toronto 1967–73; Dictionary Cons. Collier-Macmillan Canada, Toronto 1980–81; Candn. Dictionary Adv. Collins Publishers, Glasgow, UK 1981–82; Chief Ed. 'The Winston Dictionary of Canadian English – Intermediate Edition' 1969, '... Elementary Edition' 1975; 'The Compact Dictionary of Canadian English' 1970; 'The New York Times Everyday Dictionary' 1982; 'The Penguin Canadian Dictionary' 1990; author 'The Native Speaker is Dead!' 1985; numerous articles profl. jours., papers; recipient Jubilee Medal Univ. Madras 1958; Scholarship Boston Coll. 1962–63; mem. Am. Dialect Soc.; Am. Name Soc.; Assn. Computing & Humanities; Assn. Lit. & Linguistic Computing; Authors Guild (N.Y.); Candn. Council Teachers Eng.; Dictionary Soc. N. Am. (Publs. Ctte. 1983–90); Eur. Assn. Lexicography; Modern Lang. Assn. Am.; Teachers Eng. to Speakers Other Langs.; Assoc. Applied Linguistics Rsch. Working Group, York Univ. 1984– ; Syrian Catholic; recreations: tennis, swimming; Address: 1776 Chalkdene Grove, Mississauga, Ont. L4W 2C3.

**PAIKIN, Marnie Marina Suzanne,** B.A., LL.D.; b. Toronto, Ont. 13 Apl. 1936; d. Jack George and Shirley Ruth (Sutin) Sibulash; e. John R. Wilcox Pub. Sch. and Vaughan Rd. Coll. Inst. Toronto 1954; Univ. of W. Ont. B.A. 1958; Univ. of Toronto LL.D. 1981; Univ. of W. Ont., LL.D. 1988; McMaster Univ. LL.D. 1993; m. Lawrence Sidney Paikin, Hamilton, Ont. 18 Dec. 1956; children: Steven Hillel, Jeffrey Shalom; Dir. Southam Inc.; Dir., Westcoast Energy Inc.; Public Governor, Canadian Institute of Chartered Accountants; Dir. Atomic Energy of Canada Ltd. 1985– , Acting Chrmn. 1989–90 and 1992–93; Chrmn., Ont. Aids Adv. Ctte. 1989–91; Bd. of Regents, Mount Allison Univ. 1985–90; Bd. of Govs., McMaster Univ. 1987– ; Candn. Educational Standards Inst. 1987–90; Dir., Canadian Council of Christians and Jews 1983– , Pres. 1988–90; Chedoke-McMaster Hosp. Bd. 1988– ; Ont. Council on University Affairs 1981–87, Chrmn. 1983–87; Candn. Friends of Univ. of Haifa, Bd. 1984–88; Theatre 55 Found. 1983–90; Comptree Inc.; Bd. of Trustees, Toronto General Hospital 1980–87; mem., Inflation Restraint Bd. 1982–86; Ont. Council of Health 1980–83; Governing Council Univ. of Toronto 1972–80 (Chrmn. 1976–80); Trustee, Royal Ont. Museum 1976–80; McMaster Univ. Med. Centre 1970–78; Dir. Hamilton Foundation (Vice-Pres. 1979–80, Pres. 1980–81); McMaster Univ. Med. Centre Foundation 1976–78; Hamilton Performing Arts Corp. 1972–77, (Chrmn. 1973–75); Temple Anshe Sholom 1970–74; Ont. Fed. Symphony Orchestras 1972–75; Lynwood Hall 1969–73; Hamilton & Region Arts Council 1971–73; Hamilton Philharmonic Orchestra Soc. 1968–73, (Pres. 1969–71); Chrmn. Un. Jewish Welfare Fund Hamilton, Women's Div. 1976; Vice Chrmn. Hospitality Comte. Grey Cup Festival 1972; Pres. Deborah Sisterhood Temple Anshe Sholom 1970–72; Secy. Philharmonic Children Hamilton 1967; Social Chrmn. Hillfield Strathallan Parents' Assn. 1967; Life mem. Hamilton Hadassah Organ.; mem. Steering Comte. Hamilton-Wentworth Dist. Health Council 1977–78; Celebrations Comte. City of Hamilton 1972–76 (125 Anniversary Comte. 1971); Mgr. Training Dept. Simpson's London Ltd. 1958–59; rec'd 'Outstanding Woman' Award Prov. Ont. 1975; Queen's Silver Jubilee Medal 1978; 'Excellence in the Arts' Award 1980; Jewish Nat. Fund Negev Dinner, Hamilton Citizen of the Year 1980; Human Relations Award, Candn. Counc. of Christians and Jews 1985; Jewish; recreations: tennis, music, sports; Home: 67 Caroline St. S., P.H. #1, Hamilton, Ont. L8P 3K6.

**PAINTER, Robert Hilton,** B.Sc., Ph.D., C.Chem., F.R.S.C.(U.K.); professor; b. England 27 Nov. 1932; s. Charles Theodore and May (McKenna) P.; e. Holt H.S. 1950; Univ. of Liverpool, B.Sc. (Hons.) 1953, Ph.D. 1956; m. Dorothea d. Albert and Mary Alice (Bell) Weaver 6 Aug. 1955; children: Charles Robert, Catherine Anne; PROVOST & VICE CHANCELLOR, TRINITY COLL., UNIV. OF TORONTO 1986– ; Biochem., Lister Inst. of Preventive Med. 1956–57; Rsch. Assoc., Connaught Med. Rsch. Labs., Univ. of Toronto 1957–68; Assoc Prof., Dept. of Biochem., Univ. of Toronto 1968–74; Prof. 1974– ; Asst. Dean, Sch. of Grad. Studies 1975–79, Acting Dean 1979; Prof., Dept. of Immunology 1974– ; Asst. Dir., Div. of Teaching Labs., Fac. of Med. 1968–75; France-Can. Exchange Sci., MRC, INSERM, CENG, Grenoble, France 1980; mem., Rsch. & Devel. Adv. Subctte., Candn. Red Cross Blood Transfusion Serv. 1982– , Chrmn., 1985–90; Fellow, Royal Soc. of Chem. (U.K.) 1976; recipient, Member of The Order of The Red Cross 1991; Commemorative Medal for 125th Anniversary of Candn. Confederation 1993; Mem., Am. Soc. of Immunology; Am. Soc. of Hematology; Candn. Biochem. Soc.; Candn. Soc. for Immunology; author of more than 70 papers in sci. jours.; recreations: sailing, squash, music; Club: York; Home: Provost's Lodge, Trinity Coll., 6 Hoskin Ave., Univ. of Toronto, Toronto, Ont. M5S 1H8; Office: Dept. of Biochem., Med. Sci. Bldg., Univ. of Toronto, Toronto, Ont. M5S 1A8.

**PAISLEY, Hugh Stewart Douglas,** B.A., LL.B., Q.C.; lawyer / provincial negotiator; b. Windsor, Ont. 9 Nov. 1940; s. James Ross and Catherine Alexandra (Douglas) P.; e. Trinity Coll. Sch. 1959; Trinity Coll., Univ. of Toronto, B.A. 1962; Osgoode Hall Law Sch., LL.B. 1967; m. Joan Elizabeth d. Drs. Elizabeth and Garnet Dixon 11 Sept. 1971; children: Geoffrey, Douglas, Alixe; CHIEF PROVINCIAL NEGOTIATOR, UNSOLD SURRENDERED LANDS 1993– ; called to Ont. Bar March 1969; private practice in litigation; Smiley Allingham & Brown 1970–72; Blaney Pasternak 1972–79; Dep. Dir., Crown Law Office, Civil Min. of the Attorney Gen., Govt. of Ont. 1979–87; Public Trustee, Prov. of Ontario 1987–93; Q.C. 1983; recreations: skiing, tennis, music; clubs: Badminton & Racquet Club of Toronto, Caledon Ski; Home: 43 Glenallan Rd., Toronto, Ont. M4N 1G9; Office: 145 Queen St. W., Toronto, Ont. M5H 2N8.

**PAIVIO, Allan Urho,** M.Sc., Ph.D., F.R.S.C.; educator; b. Thunder Bay, Ont. 29 March 1925; s. Aku and Ida (Hanninen) P.; e. McGill Univ. B.Sc. 1949, M.Sc. 1957, Ph.D. 1959; m. Kathleen d. Norman and Clara Austin 9 Jan. 1946; children: Sandra, Anna Lee, Heather, Eric, Karina; PROF. OF PSYCHOL. UNIV. OF W. ONT. 1967– ; Lectr. Sir George Williams Coll. summer 1957; Rsch. Psychol. Cornell Univ. 1958–59; Asst. Prof. Univ. of N.B. 1959–62; joined present Univ. 1962; recipient Queen's Silver Jubilee Medal 1977; recipient Candn. Psychol. Assn. Award for Distinguished Contribution to Psychol. as a Science 1982; author 'Imagery and Verbal Processes' 1971, reprinted 1979; 'Mental Representations: A Dual Coding Approach' 1986; 'Images in Mind: The Evolution of a Theory' 1991; co-author 'The Psychology of Language' 1981; over 150 articles sc. jours., book chapters; Fellow, Candn. Psychol. Assn. (Pres. 1974–75); Am. Psychol. Assn.; Royal Soc. of Canada; Home: 919 Waterloo St., London, Ont. N6A 3X2; Office: Social Science Center, London, Ont. N6A 5C2.

**PAL, Leslie A.,** Ph.D.; university professor; b. Montreal, Que. 9 Feb. 1954; s. Leslie and Rosa (Petermichl) P.; e. Mount Allison Univ., B.A. (Hons.) 1975; Queen's Univ., M.A. 1976, Ph.D. 1981; m. Mary d. Royd and Marian Beamish 22 May 1976; two s.: Matthew, Michael; PROF. OF PUBLIC ADMINISTRATION, CARLETON UNIV. 1992– ; Asst. Prof. of Pol. Sci., Univ. of Waterloo 1980–82; Asst. Prof., Univ. of Calgary 1982; Assoc. Prof., 1982–89; Prof. 1989–92; Visiting Fellow, Carleton Univ. 1988–89; Freie Universität Berlin 1989; consultant to fed. & prov. agencies; Queen Elizabeth II Scholarship 1980; Assn. of Candn. Studies Writing Award 1988; Extve. Bd. Mem., Inst. of Public Admin. of Can. (Reg. Chap. 1986–88; Nat. 1988–89); Candn. Pol. Sci. Assn. 1989–91; Ed. Bd., 'Canadian Public Administration'; author: 'Interests of State' 1993; 'Public Policy Analysis' 1987, 2nd ed. 1992, 'State, Class, and Bureaucracy' 1988; co-editor: 'Prime Ministers and Premiers' 1988; 'Continental Integration vs. the Nation-State' 1991; co-author: 'The Real Worlds of Canadian Politics' 1989, 2nd ed. 1991, 3rd ed. 1994; Home: 144 Broadway Ave., Ottawa, Ont. K1S 2V8; Office: Ottawa, Ont.

**PALDA, Kristian S.,** B.Comm., M.B.A., Ph.D., JUDr.; university professor; b. Prague, Czech. 21 July 1928; s. Jaroslav and Marie (Velflik) P.; e. Queen's Univ. B.Comm. 1956; Univ. of Chicago M.B.A. 1958, Ph.D. 1963; Charles Univ. Prague JUDr. 1990; m. Isabel d. Oswald and Emilie Cooper 28 Feb. 1959; children: Kristian Filip, Valerie Anne; PROF. OF BUS. ECON., SCH. OF BUS., QUEEN'S UNIV. 1970– ; arrived in Can. 1951; worked at DuPont Can., Montreal between studies; Asst. Prof., Univ. de Montréal 1959–60, 1961–62; Assoc. Prof., SUNY Buffalo 1962–65; Prof., Claremont Grad. Sch., Calif. 1965–70; Partner with wife, Selma Park Antiques, Kingston; Ford Found. doct. dissertation prize 1963; Queen's prize for excellence in rsch. 1987; Mem., John Deutsch Inst., Queen's Univ.; Roman Catholic; Mem., The Fraser Inst.; Am. Econ. Assn.; Am. Mktg. Assn.; Assn. of Admin. Sci. of Can.; author: 'The Measurement of Cumulative Advertising Effects' 1964, 'Economic Analysis for Marketing Decisions' 1969, 'Pricing Decisions' 1969, 'The Science Council's Weakest Link' 1979, 'Industrial Innovation: Its Place in the Public Policy Agenda' 1984, 'The Role of Advertising Agencies in Canada's Service Sector' 1988; 'Innovation Policy and Canada's Competitiveness' 1993; recreations: travel, mushroom picking; Home: Box 1564, Kingston, Ont. K7L 5C8; Office: Kingston, Ont. K7L 3N6.

**PALDUS, Josef,** M.Sc., Ph.D., F.R.S.C.; educator; b. Bzí, Czech Republic 25 Nov. 1935; s. Josef and Ludmila (Daníčková) P.; e. Charles Univ. Prague, M.Sc. 1958; Czechoslovak Acad. of Sci's Prague, Ph.D. 1961; m. Eva Z. d. Franz and Zdena Bajer 26 Jan. 1961; one d. Barbara Alice; PROF. OF APPLIED MATH. AND OF CHEM., UNIV. OF WATERLOO 1975– ; Postdoctoral Fellow Nat. Rsch. Council Can. Ottawa 1962–64, Visiting Sci. 1966, 1968; Jr. Sci. Offr. Inst. of Phys. Chem. Czechoslovak Acad. Sci's Prague 1964–66, Sr. Sci. Offr. and Acting Head Quantum Chem. Div. 1966–68; Visiting Assoc. Prof. of Applied Math. present Univ. 1968–69, Assoc. Prof. 1969–75 and of Chem. 1973–75; Adjunct Prof., Chem. Dept., Univ. of Florida, Gainesville, Fla. 1984– ; Visiting Prof. Univ. de Reims 1973; Univ. Louis Pasteur, Strasbourg 1975–76, 1982–83; Katholieke Universiteit Nijmegen 1981; Technion, Haifa 1983; Inst. for Advanced Study Berlin 1986–87; author or co-author over 190 sci. papers, letters and reviews various sci. jours.; awarded Killam Fellowship 1987–89; J. Heyrovský Gold Medal of Czechoslovak Academy of Sciences 1992; mem. Adv. Ed. Bd. Internat. Jour. of Quantum Chem. 1977–88, Theoretica Chimica Acta 1988–92 and J. Math Chem. 1989– ; mem. Ed. Bd., Comtex Scientific Corp. 1981–83; Jour. of Chem. Phys. 1987–89; Adv. Quantum Chem. 1987– ; Candn.

J. Chem. 1994– ; mem. Bd. of Dirs., Internat. Soc. for Theoretical Chem. Physics; Assoc. Dir., Fields Institute 1992– (Mem. Bd. of Dirs. 1991– ); mem. Internat. Acad. Quantum Molecular Sci.; N.Y. Acad. Sci.; Candn. Applied Math. Soc.; Candn. Chem. Soc.; Am. Inst. Physics; Corr. mem. Académie Européenne des Sciences des Arts et des Lettres; recreation: music; Home: 350 Coleridge Pl., Waterloo, Ont. N2L 2V8; Office: Waterloo, Ont. N2L 3G1.

**PALIARE, Chris G.,** LL.B., LL.M.; lawyer; b. Toronto, Ont. 19 Nov. 1944; s. Norman and Hope (Mladen) P.; e. Osgoode Hall Law Sch. LL.B. 1970; Univ. of Texas LL.M. 1971; m. Eva E. d. Peter and Zofia Marszewski 29 June 1984; children: Alexandra Zoë Marszewski Paliare, Julia Sophia Marszewski Paliare; PARTNER, GOWLING, STRATHY & HENDERSON 1983– ; called to Bar of Ont. with Hons. 1973; Partner, Cameron, Brewin & Scott; merged with Gowling & Henderson 1983; Dir., Candn. Macedonian Place; Candn. Macedonian Fed.; Gov., Metro. Toronto YMCA; Dir., Advocates' Soc. (1989–92); Candn. Bar Assn. (Pres. 1973; Chrmn., Labour Law Subsection 1981–84); author of several articles; recreations: skiing, classical music, cooking; Home: 19 Chestnut Park Rd., Toronto, Ont. M4W 1W4; Office: Suite 4900, Commerce Court West, Toronto, Ont. M5L 1J3.

**PALLISTER, A.E.,** O.C., B.Sc., D.Sc. (Hon.), LL.D. (Hon.), P.Geoph.; geophysicist; b. Edmonton, Alta. 28 Oct. 1927; s. Ernest Henry and Beatrice Amelia (Shore) P.; e. Univ. of Alta., B.Sc. 1948; m. LaVonne Eunice, d. late Maynard S. Larsen, 29 Sept. 1953; children: Jeffrey, Cynthia, Kent; PRES., PALLISTER RESOURCE MGMT. LTD. since 1973; Assoc., Devonian Gp. of Charitable Foundations, Calgary since 1974; Founding Chrmn., Veterinary Infectious Disease Organ., Univ. Sask., Saskatoon; Founding Chrmn., Centre for Cold Ocean Resources Engn., Memorial Univ., St. John's, Nfld.; Founding Chrmn., Centre for Frontier Engineering Res., Univ. of Alta. Edmonton; Past Mem. Bd. of Dirs., NOVA an Alta. Corp. (formerly Alta. Gas Trunk Line Co. Ltd.); Vice-Chrmn., Inuvialuit Arbitration Bd.; Past Mem. Bd. of Dirs., Novacorp International Consulting Ltd.; Past mem. Bd. of Dirs., Husky Oil Ltd.; Past Mem. Bd. of Govs., Science Inst. of the Northwest Territories; Past Dir., Banff Sch. for Advanced Management; Past Chrmn. The Arctic Inst. of N. America; with United Geophysical Co., Calif. in Persian Gulf 1948; Party Chief, Century Geophysical Corp., Canada 1950; Party Chief, Sub-Surface Exploration Ltd. 1952; Asst. Chief Geophysicist, Canadian Seaboard Oil Co. 1954; Tech. Operations Mgr., Accurate Exploration Ltd. 1958; Pres., A. E. Pallister Consultants Ltd.; served in R.C.N.(R), Sub-Lt.; mem. (past Vice-Chrmn.) Science Council of Can.; Alta. Soc. Petroleum Geols. (Past Pres.); Am. Assn. Petroleum Geols., Assn. Prof. Engrs., Geols. and Geophysicists Alta.; Candn. Soc. Exploration Geophysicists; European Assn. Exploration Geophysicists; Naval Offrs. Assn.; Past Dir., Univ. of Calgary Alumni Assn.; Officer of the Order of Canada 1989; D.Sc. (honoris causa) Memorial Univ. of Nfld. 1980; LL.D. (hon. causa) Univ. of Alta., Edmonton 1987; Sr. Vice-Chrmn. Campaign Co-ordinator, United Fund 1971 Campaign; named 'Oilman of the Year' by Oilweek Mag. 1970; has organized multi-disclipline 'Quest' mineral and petroleum exploration programs in Candn. Arctic; author and co-author of numerous scient. papers; Anglican; recreations: tennis, sailing; Clubs: Calgary Petroleum; Glencoe; Toastmasters International (Past Internat. Dir.); Home: 4407 Britannia Dr., S.W., Calgary, Alta. T2S 1J4; Office: Suite 640, 300 Fifth Ave. S.W., Calgary, Alta. T2P 3C4.

**PALLOPSON, Priit,** M.D.; physician; b. Estonia 25 Nov. 1941; s. Jaan and Olga Johanna (Haiba) P.; e. Univ. of Toronto, M.D. 1967; Cert. Family Med. 1975; m. Sharon d. Clarke and Jean Daly 1969; children: Chad, Blair; Pres. Med. Staff, Orillia Soldiers Meml. Hosp. 1984–86, Trustee 1983–86; family med. practice Scarborough, Ont. 1968–70, Orillia, Ont. 1970–77, 1980– ; Asst. Prof. of Family Practice, Univ. of B.C. Med. Sch. 1977–80; mem. Candn. Med. Assn.; Ont. Med. Assn.; Coll. Family Practice Can.; recreations: skiing, basketball, tennis; Home: Wilson Point Rd., R.R. 3, Orillia, Ont. L3V 6H3; Office: 100 Colborne St. W., Orillia, Ont. L3V 2Y9.

**PALM, William Nixon,** B.A.Sc.; business executive; b. Montreal, Que. 23 May 1938; e. Univ. of Toronto B.A.Sc. 1961; former Senior Vice-President, Canadian Airlines International; Sr. management positions, IBM Canada Limited; Dir., Gemini Partners Ltd.; Office: 4676 Bellevue Dr., Vancouver, B.C. V6R 1E6.

**PALMER, James Simpson,** Q.C.; solicitor; b. Charlottetown, P.E.I. 29 Aug. 1928; s. Harold Leonard and Dorothy Campbell P.; e. King Coll.; Prince of Wales Coll.; McGill Univ., B.A. 1948; Dalhousie Univ., LL.B. 1952, LL.D. 1988; Univ. of Calgary LL.D. 1993; m. Barbara d. Emma and Roy Quigley 29 Dec. 1952; children: Valerie, Noelle, Fraley Jane, Sarah; PARTNER, BURNET, DUCKWORTH & PALMER 1956– ; Dir., Amerada Hess Canada Ltd.; Crown Life Ins. Co.; Hillcrest Resources Ltd.; Peters & Co. Ltd.; Sceptre Resources Ltd.; Tombill Mines Ltd.; Wainoco Oil Corp.; Westcoast Energy Corp.; Remington Energy Ltd.; Winfield Energy Ltd.; Chancellor, Energy Resources Inc.; Former Dir., Bank of Canada; Chancellor Emeritus, Univ. of Calgary; Past Chrmn., Candn. Tax Found.; Mem., Candn. Bar Assn.; Law Soc. of Alta.; Former Pres., Calgary Philharmonic Soc.; recreations: tennis, skiing, golf, hiking; Clubs: Calgary Golf & Country; Ranchmen's, Calgary Petroleum; Toronto; Pennask Lake Fishing; Glencoe; Sunningdale Golf; Home: 2726 Montcalm Cres., Calgary, Alta.; Office: 1400, 350 - 7 Avenue S.W., Calgary, Alta. T2P 3N9.

**PALMER, John P.,** B.A., Ph.D.; educator; b. Muskegon, Mich. 20 Oct. 1943; s. John Preston and Eva Helen (Potts) P.; e. Carleton Coll. Northfield, Minn. B.A. 1965; Chicago Theol. Semy. 1965–67; Iowa State Univ. Ph.D. 1971; m. Carolle M. d. Frank and Mary Trembley 6 Aug. 1982; children: Matthew, Rachael, Jacob; DIR. CENTRE FOR ECON. ANALYSIS OF PROPERTY RIGHTS, UNIV. OF W. ONT. 1981– , Dir. Econ. Inst. for Journalists 1984– , Assoc. Prof. of Econ. 1978– ; Instr. in Econ. Iowa State Univ. 1967–71; Asst. Prof. of Econ. present Univ. 1971–78; Visiting Prof. of Econ. Univ. of Guelph 1984, Univ. of Hawaii 1986; Emory Univ. Law Inst. for Econ. 1981; author: 'Ground Transportation in Canada' 1988; co-author: 'Regulation By Municipal Licensing' 1984; ed.: 'The Economics of Patents and Copyrights' 1986; mem. Am. Econ. Assn.; Home: 690 Springbank Dr., London, Ont. N6K 1A1; Office: London, Ont. N6A 5C2.

**PALMER, John R.V.,** B.A., F.C.A.; chartered accountant; b. Halifax, N.S. 29 Aug. 1943; s. Hugh and Jacqueline (Vernon) P.; e. Univ. of B.C., B.A. 1965; m. Adelaide d. Charles and Beatrice Price 10 Aug. 1968; children: Jeremy Nicholas, Megan Elisabeth, Edward Llewellyn; NATIONAL DIRECTOR, FEDERAL AND PROVINCIAL PUBLIC SECTOR PRACTICE, KPMG PEAT MARWICK THORNE 1993– ; Trainee, CIBC 1960–61; Trust Admin., Royal Trust Co. 1965–66; articled student, Thorne Gunn Helliwell & Christenson 1966; C.A. 1969 (Gold Medal for 1st place standing B.C.); Staff C.A. affiliated internat. firm, London England 1970–71; Tax Specialist, Thorne Gunn Vancouver 1971–72; Spec. Asst. to Min. of Nat. Revenue 1972–74; Tax Mgr., Thorne Riddell Vanc. 1974–75; Tax Partner 1975–78; Office Mng. Partner 1978–83; Extve. Partner, Thorne Riddell Toronto 1983–86; Nat. Extve. Partner, Thorne Ernst & Whinney 1986–89; Depy. Chrmn. & Mng. Partner 1989–93; Fellow, Inst. of Chartered Accountants of Ont. 1988; Fellow, Inst. of Chartered Accountants of B.C. 1990; several other past and present community extve. posts; clubs: Toronto, Vancouver; Home: 36 Edgar Ave., Toronto, Ont. M4W 2A9; Office: Suite 1200, KPMG Peat Marwick Thorne Bldg., One Toronto St., Toronto, Ont. M5C 2V5.

**PALMER, Ronald Joseph Frederick,** M.Sc., P.Eng.; b. Southey, Sask. 6 Jan. 1952; s. Joe T. and Julia P. (Flaman) P.; e. Southey Elem. and High Schs. 1970; Univ. of Sask. B.Sc. 1974; Univ. of Man. M.Sc. 1979; m. Laurie d. Phil and Jean Gossard 31 July 1983; two d. Rebecca, Kathryn; PROF. OF ELECTRONIC INFO. SYSTEMS, DEPT. OF ENGINEERING, UNIV. OF REGINA; Founder and Pres. Accutrak Systems Ltd. 1984– ; worked family farm until 1971; Design Eng. BNR Labs Ottawa 1974–76; Standards Eng. Sask-Tel 1977–82; named Eng. of Yr. Regina Eng. Soc. 1985; holds several patents; author or co-author numerous publs., papers navig. & agric.; Sr. mem. Inst. Elec. & Electronic Engs.; mem. Assn. Profl. Engs. Sask.; Regina Eng. Soc.; Am. Soc. Agric. Engs.; Inst. Navig.; recreation: pilot; Club: Regina Flying; Home: 51 Houston Rd., Regina, Sask. S4V 0G3; Office: 3737 Wascana Parkway, Regina, Sask. S4S 0A2.

**PALMER, Valerie,** B.F.A. (Hon.); artist; b. Toronto, Ont. 1950; solo exhibitions: Nancy Poole's Studio 1987, '89, '92; Art Gall. of Algoma Sault Ste. Marie (catalogue) 1985; group exhibitions: Nancy Poole's Studio 'About Faces' 1988, 'Invitational '89' 1989, 'Invitational '88' 1988; Laurentian Univ. Mus. & Arts Ctr. Queen's Park Toronto (Premier's Office) 1988; 'Personal Vision in Landscape,' Cambridge Pub. Gall. 1987; 'Aspects of Contemporary Realism' McIntosh Pub. Gall. 1987; Rodman Hall juried shows 1984, '84; McDonald Gall. Toronto 1983; Nor Art juried show Laurentian Univ. 1980, '83; Ontario North Now, Ontario Place Toronto 1980; 2-man show, McCready Gall. Toronto 1979; Janet Ian Cameron Gall. Univ. of Manitoba 1973; Gall. III, Univ. of Man. 1973; collections: Imperial Oil Co.; General Electric Canada Inc.; Art Gall. of Algoma; Crown Life Insur. Co.; E. York Bd. of Edn.; awards: Ont. Arts Counc. Grant 1989; Canada Counc. Arts Grant 'B' 1988; Canada Counc. Grant (project) 1986; 'Best in Show' Rodman Hall juried show 1984; Audience Award, Rodman Hall juried show 1983; Jurors Award, Nor Art juried show 1982; subject of 'Canadian Geographic' article 1986/87; cover painting for Alice Munro's 'Lives of Girls and Women' (pub. Penguin Books) 1990; Office: c/o Nancy Poole's Studio, 16 Hazelton Ave., Toronto, Ont. M5R 2E2.

**PALMER, Walter James,** B.Sc., LL.B.; lawyer; b. Brampton, Ont. 16 Apl. 1948; s. Frank William and Elma Mae (Hendry) P.; e. Queen's Univ. B.Sc. (Elect. Eng.) 1970, LL.B. 1973; m. Kathryn Ann d. John F. and Helen McRae 1 March 1975; children: Kaitlin Elma, Juliana Helen, Alan James, Michael John William; PARTNER, FASKEN CAMPBELL GODFREY 1980– ; called to Bar of Ont. 1975; joined Campbell, Godfrey & Lewtas (now present firm) 1973; mem. Candn. Bar Assn.; Home: 161 Coldstream Ave., Toronto, Ont. M5N 1X7; Office: P.O. Box 20, Toronto-Dominion Centre, Toronto, Ont. M5K 1N6.

**PALMETER, The Hon. Ian Harold Morton,** B.A., LL.B., Q.C.; associate chief justice; b. Halifax, N.S. 8 July 1929; s. Harold Stirling and Gladys Heys Osborne (Lang) P.; e. Queen Elizabeth H.S.; Dalhousie Univ., B.A. 1950, LL.B. 1953; m. Diane E. d. Carl and Helen Bethune 28 Oct. 1961; children: Geoffrey, Ross, Brian; ASSOCIATE CHIEF JUSTICE, SUPREME COURT OF NOVA SCOTIA 1993– ; admitted to N.S. Bar 1954; gen. prac. 1954–85; Partner, Hart, Cox, Donahoe, Palmeter, Rogers & MacKinnon 1954–59; Cox, Palmeter & Rogers 1959–63; Palmeter & Rogers 1963–68; Blois, Nickerson, Palmeter & Bryson 1968–85; Judge, Co. Court Dist. No. 1 1985; Chief County Court Judge of Nova Scotia 1985–93; Chrmn., Expropriation Compensation Bd., Prov. of N.S. 1979–85; Q.C. 1970; Past Pres., Dalhousie Alumni Assn.; Bd. of Govs., Dalhousie Univ.; Elder, Presbyterian Ch. of St. David (active ch. involvement 40 years); Mem., Masonic Order, 33rd deg. Scottish Rite; Royal Order of Scotland; Former Vice-Pres. & Extve. Mem., Boy Scouts of Can. (N.S.); Commodore, St. Margarets Sailing Club 1975–77; Home & Sch. Assn. Children with Learning Disabilities; recreations: golf, curling; Clubs: Halifax Curling; Ashburn Golf; Home: 1720 Bloomingdale Terrace, Halifax, N.S. B3H 4E5; Office: 1815 Upper Water St., Halifax, N.S. B3J 1S7.

**PALYS, Theodore (Ted) Stephen,** B.A., M.A., Ph.D.; university professor/social scientist/author/filmmaker; b. Winnipeg, Man. 2 Aug. 1951; s. the late Walter Joseph and Jean Victoria (Lozanski) P.; e. Univ. of Man., B.A. 1972, M.A. 1974; Carleton Univ., Ph.D. 1979; Partner in life: Anne-Marie Lascelles; one s.: Tadz Baker; ASSOC. PROF., SCH. OF CRIMINOL., SIMON FRASER UNIV. 1986– ; self employed 1979–80; Vis. Asst. Prof., Univ. of B.C., Dept. of Psychology 1980–81; Asst., Prof., Sch. of Crim., Simon Fraser Univ. 1981–86 (tenure 1985); occasional rsch. cons., Fed. Depts. of Justice, Communications, Solicitor Gen. Can.; independent filmmaker; Extve. Prod., 'Sentencing Dilemma' (Award of Excellence, Assn. for Media & Technol. in Edn. in Can., for best edn. film prod. in Can. in 1985); Mem., B.C. Civil Liberties Assn.; Am. Soc. of Crim.; author of supplement to Fraser Ctte. Report 1984 and num. profl. articles; author: 'Research Decisions: Qualitative and Quantitative Perspectives' 1992; co-editor: 'Regulating Sex: An Anthology of Commentaries on the Finding and Recommendations of the Badgley and Fraser Reports' 1986, 'Transcarceration: Essays in the Sociology of Social Control' 1987; recreations: watching films, photography, skiing, biking, travel, being with my son; Home: 2150 East 13th Ave., Vancouver, B.C. V5N 2C4; Office: Burnaby, B.C. V5A 1S6.

**PAMENTER, David William,** B.A., LL.B.; lawyer; b. Toronto, Ont. 5 Oct. 1947; s. Charles Malin and Bessie C.C. (Benham) P.; e. Wilfrid Laurier Univ. B.A. 1968; York Univ. LL.B. 1971; m. Terri d. Charles and Daisy Faulkner 17 June 1972; children: Susan, Matthew, Jeffrey; LAWYER, LANG MICHENER 1973– ; called to the Ontario Bar 1973; Dir. & Officer of various client companies; Counsel to Scouts Canada, Greater Toronto Region; Mem., Bd. of Trustees, Scarborough Gen. Hosp.; Mem., Candn. Bar Assn.; Mediation and Arbitration Inst. of Ont.; recreations: sailing, running, tennis;

Home: 40 Beaufort Rd., Toronto, Ont. M5J 1M7; Office: 181 Bay St., Ste. 2500, Toronto, Ont. M5J 2T7.

**PANABAKER, John Harry,** C.M., M.A., LL.D.; retired insurance executive; b. Preston, Ont. 31 July 1928; s. John Russel and Violet (Steel) P.; e. High Sch., Preston, Ont.; McMaster Univ., B.A. 1950, M.A. 1954, LL.D. 1981; Wilfrid Laurier Univ., LL.D. 1990; Univ. of Waterloo, LL.D. 1991; m. Janet Mary, d. late David G. Dickson, 24 April 1954; children: David, James, Leslie, Debra, Ian; Dir., Bell Canada, Montreal; Dir., BCE Mobile Commun. Inc., Montreal; Dir., Economical Mutual Ins. Co., Kitchener; Dir., Missisquoi Ins. Co., Frelighsburg, Que.; joined Securities Dept. of Mutual Life of Canada 1950; apptd. Asst. Treas. 1954, Extve. Asst. 1960, Asst. to Pres. 1962, Treas. Jan 1964, Vice-Pres. and Treas. Dec. 1964, Vice-Pres. Investments and Corp. Services 1968, Executive Vice President, 1969, Dir. 1971–89, Pres & C.E.O. 1973, Chrmn. and C.E.O. 1982–84; Chrmn. 1985–89; Hon. Chrmn., 1989–92; Chancellor, McMaster Univ., Hamilton 1986–92; Chancellor Emeritus, McMaster Univ. 1992– ; Pres., K-W Community Foundation 1991–93; Chrmn., Canadian Life & Health Insurance Assn., Toronto 1983–84; Life Office Mgmt. Assn., Atlanta 1977–78; McMaster Univ. 1978–80; Counc. of Bd. Chrmn. of Ont. Univs. 1980; Corporate-Higher Education Forum, Montreal 1986–88; Member of the Order of Canada; recipient, 125th Anniversary of the Confederation of Canada Medal, 1992; Presbyterian; Clubs: National (Toronto); University (Waterloo); Office: 227 King St. S., Waterloo, Ont. N2J 4C5.

**PANARELLA, Emilio;** scientist; b. Ferrandina, Italy 3 Jan. 1933; s. Pietro and Grazia (Petraglia) P.; e. Univ. of Naples Doctorate in Navig. Sci's 1956; m. Maria d. Giovanni and Maria Rambaldi 21 Sept. 1963; children: Lorenzo, Riccardo, Silvia; PRIN. SCIENTIST, ADVANCED LASER AND FUSION TECHNOLOGY INC. 1987– and RESEARCH PROF., DEPT. OF ELEC. & COMPUTER ENGR., UNIV. OF TENNESSEE 1989– ; served as Geophysicist with Air Forces 1958–60, rank Lt.; Teacher, Tech. Inst. of Savona, Italy 1960–61; NATO Postdoctoral Fellow, Polytechnic Inst. of Brooklyn 1961–62; Adjunct Rsch. Offr. Microwave Inst. Nat. Rsch. Council of Italy 1962–64; Rsch. Offr. Nat. Rsch. Council Can. 1964–87; author over 100 sci. publs.; ed. internat. jour. 'Physics Essays'; co-ed. Proceedings NATO Advanced Rsch. Workshop 'Quantum Uncertainties: Recent and Future Experiments and Interpretations' 1987; Fellow, N.Y. Acad. Sci's; Sr. mem. Inst. Elect. & Electronic Engs. Inc.; mem. Am. Physical Soc.; Eur. Physical Soc.; Italian Physical Soc.; recreation: philately; Home: 2012 Woodglen Cres., Ottawa, Ont. K1J 6G4; Office: c/o NRC, Ottawa, Ont. K1A 0R6.

**PANCER, Michael Philip,** B.B.A., C.M.A., C.A.; financial executive; b. Toronto, Ont. 27 Apr. 1957; s. Stanley J. and Evelyn H. (Strauss) P.; e. York Univ. B.B.A. 1980; CHIEF FINAN. OFFR., FAIRWEATHER & SR. VICE-PRES., DYLEX 1991– ; apprenticed with Arthur Andersen & Co. C.A.s; joined George Weston Limited as MIS Mgr. 1983 to automate financial areas; Corporate Controller, Weston Foods Limited 1986; Vice-Pres. & Chief Financial Offr., Holt Renfrew & Co. Ltd. 1988–91; Home: 281 Churchill Ave., R.R. 2, Kettleby, Ont. L0G 1J0; Office: 637 Lakeshore Blvd. W., Toronto, Ont. M5V 1A8.

**PANET, Antoine de Lotbinière,** Q.C., B.Comm., M.Comm., M.Acc., C.A., LL.B.; lawyer; b. Ottawa, Ont. 29 May 1940; s. Antoine de Lotbinière and Mary Louise P.; e. Univ. of Ottawa; Laval Univ. B.Comm., M.Comm., M.Acc., C.A., LL.B.; called to Bar of Ont. 1965; m. Jane Hilton d. William Robert Wilson 24 June 1967; children: Philip de Lotbinière, Erica de Lotbinière; PARTNER, PERLEY-ROBERTSON, PANET, HILL & MCDOUGALL (est. 1971); Special Asst. to Min. of Ind. and Defence Prodn., Can. 1968; Special Asst. to Min. of Ind., Trade and Comm., Can. 1968–69; Lt. (Reserve) Royal Candn. Navy; Ed.-in-Chief, 'National Trade and Tariff Service'; former Ed.-in-Chief, 'Canadian Customs and Excise Reports'; mem.: Candn. Inst. of C.A.s; Candn. Bar Assn.; Internat. Bar Assn.; Candn. Tax Foundation; Past Chrmn. Comm. and Ind. Devel. Corp. of Ottawa-Carleton; Lectr., Faculty of Law, Univ. of Ottawa; author of articles in trade and professional journals; Mem., Bd. of Trustees & Treasurer, Sisters of Charity of Ottawa Health Service; Mem., Advisory Council, Faculty of Admin., Univ. of Ottawa; Mem., Ottawa-Carleton Task Force on Economic Development; Dir. & Secy., Ottawa-Carleton Rsch. Institute; Dir., Boys & Girls Clubs of Canada; Past Vice-Chrmn., Ont. Arts Council; Past Pres., Boys and Girls Club of Ottawa-Carleton; Trustee, Elizabeth Bruyère Health Care Centre; recreations: skiing, sailing, tennis; Clubs: Britannia Yacht; Rideau; Home: 389 Roxborough Ave., Rockcliffe Park, Ont. K1M 0R7; Office: Suite 830, 99 Bank St., Ottawa, Ont. K1P 6C1.

**PANET-RAYMOND, Robert,** B.A.Sc., M.B.A.; b. Montréal, Qué. 27 Oct. 1942; s. Guy and Andrée (Ostiguy) P.; e. Univ. de Montréal, B.A.Sc. 1965; Harvard Univ., M.B.A. 1967; m. Francine d. Louis A. and Aline Martel 26 Aug. 1967; children: Eric, Carl; Pres. & C.E.O., St-Hubert Bar-B-Q Ltd. 1985–1991; Sr. Lectr., Dept. of Indus. Relns., Univ. of Montréal 1967–68; Vice Pres. & Partner, DDA Mngt. Cons. Ltd. 1968–75; Vice Pres., Art Lab. Furniture Ltd. & Ebena Lasalle, Div. of Am. Seating Co. 1975–77; Extve. Vice Pres., Credit Foncier 1977–85; Mem., Extve. Ctte. & Bd. of Dir., St-Hubert Bar-B-Q; Mem. Bd. of Dir., Greater Montreal Convention & Tourism Bureau; Vice-Chrmn., Candn. Restaurant & Food Service Assoc.; Extve. Ctte., Montréal Symphony Orch.; Gen. Vice Pres., 1989 Centraide Montréal Campaign; Mem., Ed. Adv. Bd., Food Service & Hospitality; Chrmn., Adv. Ctte., MacDonald Coll., McGill Univ.; Ord. of Engr. of Qué.; Montréal C. of C.; Nat. Restaurant Assn.; Assn. des Restaurateurs du Qué.; recreations: cycling, tennis, cross-crountry skiing; Club: St-Denis.

**PANG, Peter K.T.,** B.Sc., M.Sc., Ph.D., D.Sc.; university professor/administrator; b. Hong Kong 14 Oct. 1941; s. Kui Ching and Siu Ching (Chan) P.; e. Univ. of Hong Kong, B.Sc. (Gen.) 1963, (Spec.) 1964, D.Sc. 1980; Yale Univ. M.Sc. 1968, Ph.D. 1970; m. Rosemary d. Raymond and Emma Keeley 12 July 1969; children: Naomi, Aidan, Marianna; PROF. & CHRMN., DEPT. OF PHYSIOL. & DIR., TRAD. MED. RSCH. PROG., UNIV. OF ALTA. 1986– ; Yale Univ.: Instr. of Biol. 1970–71; Coll. of Phys. & Surgs., Columbia Univ.: postdoct. fellow in Pharm. 1971–72, Instr. 1972–73, Assoc. 1973–74, Asst. Prof. 1974, Vis. Prof. in Pharmacology 1975–78 (summers), Adjunct Assoc. Prof. of Pharm. 1978–81; Adjunct Prof. 1982– ; Brooklyn Coll., City Univ. of N.Y.: Assoc. Prof. of Biol. 1974–76; Univ. of Chile: Vis. Prof. in Physiol. & Biophys. 1976–78; Texas Tech. Univ. Health Sci. Ctr.: Assoc. Prof. of Pharm. & Therapeut. 1976–80, Prof. of Pharm. 1981–85; Hon. Prof., Jinan Univ. Med. Coll. (Guangzhou, China) 1985– ; Hon. Prof., Peking Union Medical College (Beijing, China) 1989– ; mem. of num. sci. soc.; author, co-author, editor of over 200 sci. pubns.; Home: 205 Carriage Lane, 52225 Range Rd. 232, Sherwood Park, Alta.; Office: Dept. of Physiol., Rm. 7-34A, Medical Sciences Bldg., Univ. of Alta., Edmonton, Alta. T6G 2E1.

**PANGLE, Thomas Lee,** Ph.D.; university professor; b. Gouverneur, N.Y. 29 Nov. 1944; s. James Lee and Helen Louise (Carey) P.; e. Cornell Univ., B.A. 1966; Univ. of Chicago, Ph.D. 1972; m. Lorraine d. Darwin and Jo-Ann Smith June 1984; PROF., DEPT. OF POL. SCI., UNIV. OF TORONTO 1983– ; Lectr., Asst. Prof., then Assoc. Prof., Yale Univ. 1971–79; Assoc. Prof., Univ. of Toronto 1979–83; Fellowships: Nat. Sci. Found. 1966–67, 1970–71, Nat. Endowment for the Humanities, Sr. 1975–76 and 1993–94, Constitutional 1985–86, Connaught 1993–94; Res., Silliman Coll., Yale Univ. 1976–79, Victoria Coll. 1979–84, Guggenheim 1981–82, St. Michael's Coll. 1985– ; Exxon Distinguished Lectr., Univ. of Chicago 1987; Extve. Counc., New Eng. Pol. Sci. Assn. 1979–80; Vis. Prof., Dartmouth Coll. 1982; Univ. of Chicago 1984; Ecole des Hautes Etudes en Sci. Soc. 1987; Media Adv. Panel & Panel on State Progs., N.E.H. 1983–84; Ed. Bd., 'Polis'; 'La Pensée Politique'; Phi Beta Kappa; winner, Benton Bowl, Yale Univ. 1980; Scholar in Res., Rockefeller Found. Study & Conf. Ctr., Italy 1985; Robert Foster Cherry Award for Great Teachers of the World 1992; author: 'Montesquieu's Philosophy of Liberalism' 1973, 'The Spirit of Modern Republicanism' 1988, 'The Ennobling of Democracy' 1992; editor: 'The Roots of Political Philosophy' 1987; co-author: (with wife Lorraine) 'The Learning of Liberty' 1993; transl. & comm.: 'The Laws of Plato' 1980; Home: 200 Concord Ave., Toronto, Ont. M6H 2P3; Office: 100 St. George St., Toronto, Ont. M5S 1A1.

**PANITCH, Leo Victor,** M.Sc., Ph.D.; educator; b. Winnipeg, Man. 3 May 1945; s. Max and Sarah (Hoffman) P.; e. St. John's High Sch. Winnipeg 1962 (Valedictorian); Univ. of Man. B.A. (Hons.) 1967; London Sch. of Econ. & Pol. Science M.Sc. (Econ.) 1968, Ph.D. (Govt.) 1974; m. Melanie Risë d. David and Sylvia Pollock, Winnipeg, Man. 24 Aug. 1967; children: Maxim Serge, Vida Mira; PROFESSOR OF POLITICAL SCIENCE, YORK UNIV. 1984– ; Lectr. Carleton Univ. 1972, Asst. Prof. 1974, Assoc Prof. 1977, Prof. 1982–84; Chrmn., Dept. of Pol. Science, York Univ. 1988–94; Gen. Co-Ed. 'State and Economic Life' series (Univ. of Toronto Press); Co-Founder and Bd. mem. 'Studies in Political Economy'; co-ed. 'The Socialist Register' (Annual, London, Eng.); author 'Social Democracy and Industrial Militancy' 1976; 'Working Class Politics in Crisis' 1986; ed. and co-author 'The Canadian State' 1977; ed. and co-author 'A Different Kind of State?' 1993; co-author 'The Assault on Trade Union Freedoms' 1988, 2nd Rev. ed. 1993; various articles pol. science; mem. Movement for an Independent & Socialist Can. 1973–75; mem. Extve. Ottawa Comte. for Labour Action 1975–84; mem. Candn. Pol. Science Assn.; Comte. on Socialist Studies; The Marxist Inst.; Home: 527 Palmerston Blvd., Toronto, Ont. M6G 2P4; Office: 4700 Keele St., North York, Ont. M3S 1P3.

**PANYCH, Morris Stephen,** B.F.A.; writer, director, actor; b. Calgary, Alta. 30 June 1952; s. Peter D. and Rosemary Adele (Lyons) P.; e. N.A.I.T. Edmonton, radio & TV arts 1971–73; Univ. of B.C. B.F.A. 1977; actor with major roles in over 50 stage plays; plays produced incl. 'Last Call' 1982, 'Contagious' 1984, 'Cheap Sentiment' 1985, 'Simple Folk' 1986, '7 Stories' 1989, 'Necessary Steps' 1990, 'Cost of Living' 1991, 'Nocturne' 1989; published scripts: 'Last Call' Harbour Pub. 1983, '7 Stories' Talonbooks 1990; six-time Jessie Award winner (Vancouver Theatre); director of numerous stage plays; minor roles in film & TV; Artistic Dir., Tamahnous Theatre 1984–86; Office: c/o Harbour Publishing, Box 219, Madeira Park, B.C. V0N 2H0.

**PAPACHRISTIDIS, Niky;** shipping executive; b. Montréal, Qué. 10 Apr. 1941; d. Phrixos Basil and Mariette (Vachon) P.; e. Coll. Marie de France; m. Pierre s. Paul Bove 23 May 1964; children: Alexandre & Frederick Papachristidis-Bove; PRES., PAPACHRISTIDIS (CAN.) LIMITED 1981– ; Sec.-Treas., Papachristidis Maritime Inc. & Papachristidis Tankers Ltd. 1975–80; Vice Pres., Papachristidis Maritime Inc. 1980–81; Chrmn., Probulk (Canada) Limited 1987–89; Dir., Papachristidis (Canada) Limited; Papachristidis (UK) Limited; Bd. Mem., Ballets-Jazz de Montréal; Candn. Mediterranean Inst.; McGill Chamber Orch.; Young Virtuosi; Dir., Eveil Musical de Montréal, Palais de la Civilisation; Mem., Bd. of Trade of Montréal; C. of C. de Montréal; Clubs: St. James, St. Denis, Mount Royal, Mount Stephen, Canadian Club of New York; Home: 2 Westmount Sq., Westmount, Qué.; Office: 1 Westmount Sq., Suite 933, Westmount, Qué. H3Z 2P9.

**PAPAGEORGIOU, Apostolos Nicolas,** M.D., FRCP(C), FAAP; professor of pediatrics, obstetrics & gynecology; b. Volos, Greece 24 Oct. 1937; s. Nicolas Apostolos and Helen (Gouriotis) P.; e. Sorbonne M.D. 1966; Univ. of Montreal & McGill Univ., Ped. 1966–73; McGill Univ., Clinical Rsch. Fellow 1971–73, Chief Med. Res. in Ped. 1972–73; DIRECTOR, NEONATAL/PERINATAL PROGRAM, MCGILL UNIV. 1982– ; Dir., Neonatology, Jewish Gen. Hosp. 1974– ; Chief of Ped., St. Mary's Hospital Centre 1982– ; Chief of Ped., SMBD-Jewish Gen. Hosp. 1986– ; Prof. of Ped., Obstetrics & Gyn., McGill Univ. 1988– ; Dipl. in Neonatal/Perinatal Med., Am. Acad. of Ped. 1975; Cert. Spec., RCPSC 1974, Prov. of Que. 1973, Am. Bd. of Ped. 1973; Pres., Assn. of Neonat. (Que.) 1992; Pres. Elect, Section of Neonat./Perinat. Med., Candn. Pediatric Soc. 1992; Mem., Nucleus Ctte., Royal College of Canada; External Cons., Min. of Health; Osler Award for Outstanding Teacher 1987, Kaplan Award for Best Clin. Teacher 1988 (both McGill Univ.); 1st rec., Hellenic Ladies Benevolent Soc. Award for Outstanding Mem., Montreal Greek Community 1991; Mem. & Vice-Pres., Extve. Ctte., Hellenic Comm. of Montreal Social Serv.; Mem., Group de travail en Neonat. (Que.); Que. Perinatal Mortality Ctte.; Am. & Eur. societies for Ped. Rsch.; Am. Academy of Ped.; Candn. Soc. of Ped.; FRCP(C); Candn. Med. Assn.; Hellenic Ped. Soc.; author/co-author of over 140 pubs. recreations: tennis, skiing, swimming, music; clubs: Hillside Tennis, McGill Faculty; Home: 584 Cote St. Antoine Rd., Westmount, Que. H3Y 2K6; Office: SMBD-Jewish Gen. Hosp., 3755 Cote St. Catherine Rd., Room B-551, Neonatology, Montreal, Que. H3T 1E2.

**PAPE, Gordon Kendrew,** B.A.; author; broadcaster; financial consultant; b. San Francisco, Cal. 16 March 1936; s. late Clifford Baume and late Lethe Mary (Chenevert) P.; came to Can. 1950; e. Three Rivers High Scho., Trois Rivieres, Que. 1954; Carleton Univ. B.A. 1959; Univ. of Toulouse 1960–61 (Rotary Foundation Fellowship); m. Shirley Ann d. late Joseph Peter Cloutier and late Florence (Kean) 5 May 1962; children: Kimberley Anne, Kendrew Gordon, Deborah Margaret; Pres., Gordon Pape Enterprises; Educ. Writer 'The Gazette' Montreal 1961–63, Que. Bureau Chief 1963–66, Partly. Corr. Ottawa 1966–70, Assoc. Ed. Montreal 1973–74; Bureau Chief, Southam News Service, London, Eng. 1970–73; Asst. to Publisher, 'Financial Times of Canada' 1974–76; Publisher, 'The Canadian' mag.

1976–79; Publisher, 'Canadian Weekend' Magazine 1979–80; President and Publisher, 'Today Magazine' 1980–82; Publisher Hume Publishing Co. 1984–87; Host CBC Radio 'Capital Report' 1968–70; Personal finance editor, CBC Radio 'Business World' 1986–88; Financial commentator, TVOntario 'Money$Worth' 1987–90; Sr. editor 'The MoneyLetter' 1988– ; rec'd Heritage Can. Communications Award 1976; Candn. Wine Taster Yr. 1975 Opimian Soc.; author 'Building Wealth' 1988; 'Low-Risk Investing' 1989; 'Retiring Wealthy' 1991; 'Building Wealth in the 90s' 1992; 'The $50,000 Stove Handle' 1993; 'Guide to RRSPs' (published annually); 'Guide to Mutual Funds' (published annually); co-author 'Montreal at the Crossroads' 1975; 'Chain Reaction' 1978; 'The Scorpion Sanction' 1980; 'The Music Wars' 1982; numerous newspaper and mag. articles business and financial topics; CBC Radio broadcaster, Personal Finance and Investing; Past Chrmn. Mag. Assn. Can.; Past Pres. Nat. Mag Awards Foundation; mem. ACTRA; Protestant; recreations: fishing, golf, reading, oenology; Clubs: Donalda; Franklin; Wig & Pen (London); Home: 372 Woodsworth Rd., Willowdale, Ont. M2L 2T6.

**PAPIALUK, Josie Pamiutu;** artist; b. near Issuksiuvit Lake, N.W.T. 1918; medium: drawings, prints, sculptures; 74 group exbns. incl. most recent: l'Iglou Art Esquimau, Douai (toured 22 cities) France & Belgium 1988–92, Albers Gallery of Inuit Art 1992, Galerie du Trait-Carre Charlesbourg, Que. 1991, Artistic Artistry, Hastings-on-Hudson, N.Y. 1990, Candn. Mus. of Civilization Hull, Que. 1990; solo exbns.: The Guild Shop Toronto 1985, Houston North Gallery Lunenburg, N.S. 1984, Marion Scott Gallery Vancouver 1983, Inuit Gallery of Vancouver 1980; works in 15 collections incl. art galleries of N.S. and Winnipeg, Avataq Cult. Inst. Montreal, Candn. Mus. of Civilization, Dennos Mus. Ctr. N.W. Michigan Coll. Traverse City, Mich., Glenbow Mus., Musée du Québec Qué., Qué., Nat. Gallery of Canada, Saputik Mus. Povungnituk, Que.; attended opening of 'Original Drawings' The Guild Shop 1985; subject of articles and catalogues; Home: Povungnituk, Qué.; Office: c/o La Fédération des Coopératives du Nouveau-Québec, 19950 Clark Graham, Baie d'Urfé, Qué. H9X 3R8.

**PAPILLON, Guy,** B.Comm.; investment dealer and restructuration consultant; b. Ste-Foy, Que. 27 Jan. 1954; s. Gustave and Louisette (Tremblay) P.; e. Laval Univ. B.Comm. 1975; m. Marie d. Georgette and Paul Lacroix 27 May 1987; children: Sarah, Eve, Amelie; PRES., GESTION GUY PAPILLON INC. 1982– ; Manager, Human Relations (140 employees), Ciment Québec inc. 1976–77; Mgr., Expansion Project 1978–81; Pres., Cogeneuf Inc. 1982–88; Vice-Pres. & Gen. Mgr., Ciment Québec inc. 1983–88; Pres. & Gen. Mgr. 1985–90; Chrmn. of the Bd., Baie des Chaleurs Aquaculture (1993) inc.; Groupe Cadoret inc.; Les Transports Aéro 2000 inc.; recreations: aviation, skiing, scuba diving; club: Lions; Address: 1639 de la Carrière, Ste-Foy, Que. G1W 3J2.

**PAPINEAU-COUTURE, Jean,** C.C., B.A., B.Mus.; musician; b. Outremont, Que. 12 Nov. 1916; (grandson of Guillaume C., one of the first Candn. composers and conductors); s. Armand and Marie-Anne (Dostaler) P-C.; e. Coll. St. Ignace; Coll. Jean de Brébeuf, B.A. 1938; New England Conservatory of Music, B.Mus. 1941; m. the late Isabelle, d. Dr. Joseph Baudouin, 15 June 1944; children: Nadia, Ghilaine, Francois; Prof. of Theoretical Subjects at Conservatoire de Musique d'Art Dramatique de la P.Q., 1946–64; Prof., Faculty of Music, Univ. of Montreal 1953–85, Dean of the Faculty of Music, 1968–73; mem. of Bd. of Dirs., and Past Pres. of the Canadian Music Center and of The Candn. Music Council; Past Pres., Montreal Br. of Les Jeunesses Musicales du Canada; Candn. League of Composers; Pres. Humanities Research Council, 1977–78; Officer, Order of Canada 1968; Prix Calixa-Lavallée 1962; Canadian Music Council Medal 1973; Prix Denise-Pelletier 1981; Diplôme d'honneur, Candn Conf. of the Arts 1986; Grand Officier de l'Ordre du Québec 1988; 'La mémoire postmodern. Essai sur l'art canadien contemporain' winner of Governor General's Award for Translation 1992; since 1942 has written and publ. many musical works; Roman Catholic; Home: 4694 Lacombe, Montreal, Que. H3W 1R3.

**PAQUET, Gilles,** CM, B. Phil., M.A., F.R.S.C., F.R.S.A.; economist; b. Québec City, Qué. 19 July 1936; s. Charles Noel and Rosette (Marois) P.; e. Laval Univ. B.A. 1956, B. Phil. 1956, M.A. 1960; Queen's Univ. Doctoral studies 1960–62; m. Muriel Moisan 21 Oct. 1958; children: Pascale, Valérie; Dean, Fac. of Admin., Univ. of Ottawa 1981–88; Dean of Grad. Studies and Research, Carleton Univ. 1973–79; Chrmn. of Econ. Carleton Univ. 1969–72; Research Dir. Special Senate Comte. on Science Policy 1968–70; Chrmn. Consumer Research Council 1974–75; Consultant to O.E.C.D. 1974–76; Sec.-Treas., Cdn. Econ. Assoc. 1967–81; Chrmn., Candn. Fed. of Deans of Manag. & Admin. Studies 1984–86; Pres., Assoc. Can-Franc. pour l'Avancement des Sciences 1986–87; Secy./Treas., Royal Soc. of Canada 1983–88; Pres., Assoc. des Economistes Québécois 1989–90; rec'd O.C.U.F.A. Teaching Award 1973; rec'd the Jacques Rousseau medal 1982; rec'd Esdras Minville Medal 1989; co-author 'Patronage et pouvoir dans le Bas Canada au tournant du XIX siècle' 1973; 'La Pensée Économique au Québec Français' 1989; Ed. 'The Multinational Firm and the Nation State' 1972; co-ed. 'Urban Studies: A Canadian Perspective' 1968; 'Canadian Perspectives in Economics' 1974; 'Administration: Unity and Diversity' 1986; 'Education Canada?' 1987; 'Edging Toward the Year 2000' 1989; 'Management en Crise' 1991; author various articles regional devel., econ. hist., regulation of socio-econ. systems; recreations: reading, biking, hiking; Club: Cercle Universitaire d'Ottawa; Home: 18 Woodlawn Ave., Ottawa, Ont. K1S 2S9; Office: 275 Nicholas St., Ottawa, Ont. K1N 6N5.

**PAQUET-SÉVIGNY, Thérèse,** M.A.; sociologist, communications executive; b. Sherbrooke, Que. 3 Feb. 1934; d. René and Marie-Reine (Cloutier) Paquet; e. Undergraduate Programme in Sociology, Sorbonne-Paris Univ. 1966–67; Univ. of Montreal M.A. 1971, Ph.D. programme 1972–74; m. Robert s. Aimé and Maria Sévigny 26 May 1956; children: Eric and Odile Sévigny; PROF., DEPT. OF COMMUNICATIONS, UNIV. DU QUÉBEC IN MONTRÉAL (UQAM) 1993– , DIR., UNESCO CHAIR IN COMMUNICATION AND INTERNAT. DEVELOPMENT and INTERNATIONAL CONSULTANT 1993– ; Pres., BCP Publicité Limitée 1981; Vice-Pres., Communications, C.B.C. 1983–87; Mem., Univ. of Long Island Adv. Bd. 1989; Conseil d'admin. à l'Inst. de recherches politiques 1984–87; Under-Secretary-General for Public Information, United Nations 1987–92; l'Exécutif du Prix Michener 1984–87; Prix Liberté, ALCAN, Le Cercle des femmes journalistes Canada 1990; Doctorate, Honoris Causa, Univ. d'Ottawa 1992; Univ. de Sherbrooke 1991; Bishop's Univ. 1991; Mem. Bd. of Govs., Bishops Univ. 1993– ; Mem., Candn. Assn. of Sociologists & Anthropologists; Internat. Assn. of Sociologists; Internat. Assn. of Communications; author: 'L'Entreprise de l'An 2000, Les Communications dans l'entreprise de l'an 2000' 1981, 'Le Québec et sa culture' 1983, 'The Future of the United Nations: In Search of New Support, Medicine and War' 1989; recreations: reading, films, walking, friends; Home: 1509 Sherbrooke St. W., Apt. 29, Montréal, Qué. H3G 1M1.

**PARADI, Joseph Charles,** M.A.Sc., Ph.D., P.Eng.; executive; b. Budapest, Hungary 18 Jan. 1941; e. Univ. of Toronto B.A.Sc. (Chem. Eng.) 1965, M.A.Sc. 1966, Ph.D. 1975; m. Monika Letzin 1965; two s. Joseph Alexander, David Richard; CHRMN. & PRES., PARCORP LTD. 1980– ; Partner, PMP Assoc.; Prof. of Applied Sci. & Eng. Univ. of Toronto; Cons. in Computer Software National Computing Services Co. 1966–68; Founder, Dir. and Vice Pres., Dataline Inc. 1968, Pres. and Dir., 1970–89; mem., Information Technology Assn. of Canada (Dir. and Past Chrmn. 1972, 1982–83); Assn. Prof. Engs. Prov. Ont.; Information Industry Assoc. Financial Infor. Services Div.; Assoc. of Univ. Tech. Managers; Licensing Execs. Soc.; recreations: golf, hockey, tennis, skiing; Clubs: Mississauga Golf & Country; The National; The Beacon Hall Golf & Country; The Faculty Club; Palm Beach Polo; Home: 670 Meadow Wood Rd., Mississauga, Ont. L5J 2S6; Office: 4 Taddle Creek Rd., Toronto, Ont. M5S 1A4.

**PARADIS, Lieut.-Gen. Jean-Jacques,** C.M.M., O.St.J., C.D., B.A.; army officer (retired); b. Montreal, Que. 7 Nov. 1928; s. Louis A. and Marie Anne (Déry) P.; e. Private Sch. Val-Dombre, Chambly Canton, Que.; Coll. de Montréal; Coll. Jean de Brebeuf, B.A. 1948; m. Margaret, d. Albert Gosselin 26 May 1956; children: Dominique, Marguerite; Dir., Internat. Marketing, Les Industries Valcartier Inc.; retired 1987; Offr. Cadet 1948, enrolling as Lieut. in Vandoos (R22eR) 1950; posted 2nd Bn R22eR Aug. 1950, Korea 1951–52; Winter Warfare and Airborne Training 1952; Staff Capt. A&Q Valcartier 1953; Airborne 2 Bn R22eR 1956; Staff Capt. HQ 4 Candn. Inf. Brigade Germany 1957; Second in Command Co. 3 Bn R22eR, Europe 1958–59; Capt. Adj. 3 Bn 1960; Maj. Co. Commdr. 2 Bn R22eR 1961; Staff Coll. Kingston, Ont. 1963–65; apptd. Brigade Maj. HQ 3rd Candn. Inf. Brigade Gp Gagetown, N.B. 1965; Lieut.-Col. C.O. 3 Bn R22eR 1966–68; Directing Staff and Depy. Commandant Staff Coll. and promoted Col. 1969–70; Imp. Defence Coll., U.K. 1971; promoted Brig.-Gen. and apptd. Commdr. 5 Combat Group Valcartier 1972; promoted Maj.-Gen. and apptd. Depy. Commdr. Mobile Command 1973–75; Chief Personnel Devel. NDHQ 1975–77; apptd. Commdr. Mobile Command and promoted Lieut.-Gen., 1977; Relinquished Command, 1981; R. Catholic; recreations: golf, music, reading; Home: 39 boul. Boilard, Fossambault-sur-le-Lac, Qué. G0A 3M0.

**PARADIS, Hon. Pierre (Joseph-Jacques),** LL.L; M.N.A.; né à Bedford, Québec 16 juillet 1950; f. Louison et Jeannette (Lussier) P.; ét. Coll. Saint-Jean-sur-Richelieu 1970; Univ. d'Ottawa, LL.L. 1973, Cours de maîtrise en lettres de change et en droit des affaires 1974; ép. Anne Chalifour 15 novembre 1979; enfants: François, Hélène; MINISTRE DE L'ENVIRONNEMENT ET DE LA FAUNE 1994– et LEADER PARLEMENTAIRE DU GOUVERNEMENT, QUÉBEC 1992– ; admis. au Barreau du Québec en 1975; avocat fondateur du bureau Paradis, Paradis & associés 1975; élu, lors d'une partielle, député libéral de la circonscription électorale de Brome-Missisquoi 1980; réélu en 1981, 1985, 1989; critique du Parti libéral du Québec à l'Assemblée nationale dans les domaines suivants: engagements financiers et travail; candidat dans le cadre de la course à la direction du PLQ 1983; critique de son parti en matière d'affaires sociales; ministre du Travail, de la Main-d'oeuvre et de la Sécurité du revenue du Québec 1985–88; ministre des Affaires municipales du Québec, responsable de l'Habitation 1988–89; ministre de l'Environnement 1989– ; nommé Leader Parlementaire du Gouvernement, Qué. 1992, nommé à nouveau 1994; catholique; adresse: C.P. 860, 19 Main St., Bedford, Qué. J0J 1A0; bureau: 3900, rue de Marly, 6e étage, Sainte-Foy, Qué. G1X 4E4.

**PARDY, Henry Garfield (Gar),** M.A.; diplomat; b. Bishops Falls, Nfld. 10 Nov. 1939; s. James Conrad and Rosa Blanche (Dean) P.; e. Hunt Meml. Acad. Gander, Nfld.; Acadia Univ. B.A. 1966; McMaster Univ. M.A. 1968; m. Laurel d. Harry and Edith Balsor 3 Sept. 1963; two s. Michael Conrad, Julian Harry; Ambassador to Costa Rica, El Salvador, Honduras, Nicaragua and Panama 1989; joined Meteorol. Service Can. 1956–62, Gander and Goose Bay, Nfld., Frobisher Bay, N.W.T.; joined External Affairs 1967 serving New Delhi 1969–72, Nairobi 1975–78, Washington, D.C. 1978–82; Dir. U.S. Progs. Div. 1983–85 and Asia Pacific S. Relations Div. 1985–89; Candn. Resident Rep. to Inter-Am. Inst. Agric. Sci's; Chrmn. Bds. Dirs. and Govs. Internat. Sch. Kenya 1975–78; Club: Union (San Jose).

**PARÉ, Jean;** publishing executive; author; b. Irma, Alta. 7 Dec. 1927; d. Edward Lindsay and Ruby Edna (Locke) Elford; e. Irma, Alta. grad. Grade XII; m. Hilaire (Larry) s. Donat and Genevive Paré 11 July 1968; children: Lyall, Brian, Grant and Gail Lovig; CO-FOUNDER, COMPANY'S COMING PUBLISHING LIMITED 1981– ; began catering bus. Vermilion, Alta. 1963; Dir. COMAC Food Group Inc.; author Company's Coming cookbook series incl. '150 Delicious Squares' 1981, 'Casseroles' 1982, 'Muffins and More' 1983, 'Salads' 1984, 'Appetizers' 1985, 'Desserts' 1986, 'Soups and Sandwiches' 1987, 'Holiday Entertaining' 1987, 'Jean Paré's Favorites' Vol. One 1988; 'Cookies' 1988, 'Vegetables' 1989, 'Main Courses' 1989; 'Pasta' 1990; 'Cakes' 1990; 'Barbecues' 1991; 'Dinners of the World' 1991; 'Lunches' 1992; 'Pies' 1992; 'Light Recipes' 1993; 'Microwave Cooking' 1993; 'Preserves' 1994; Pint Size Books series, incl. 'Finger Food' 1993; 'Buffets' 1993; 'Party Planning' 1993; recipient, Alberta Opportunity Company 'Entrepreneur of the Year' award 1990–91; Pinnacle Award, Northern Alberta 1992; recreations: travel, reading, cooking, theatre; Home: P.O. Box 441, Vermilion, Alta. T0B 4M0; Office: P.O. Box 8037, Station F, Edmonton, Alta. T6H 4N9.

**PARE, Most Rev. Marius;** bishop (R.C.); b. Montmagny, Que., 22 May 1903; s. Joseph and Lucie (Boulet) P.; Bishop of Chicoutimi, 1961–79; o. Priest 3 July 1927; el. Titulary Bishop d'Ege and Auxiliary to Bishop of Chicoutimi 7 Feb. 1956 (consecrated 1 May 1956); nominated Coadjutor to the See of Chicoutimi, 6 Feb. 1960; Consultor Sacred Congregation for Catholic Teaching, Roma, May 1968–May 1978; Bishop-del. to Nat. Centre of Vocations, Conf. of Bishops of Can. 1961–67 and to Episcopal Comn. of Clergy Seminaries and Vocations (Pres. 1967–74); mem., Extve. (1972–76), Comité du Clergé (1956–79; Pres. 1965–74), Assemblée des Evêques du Qué.; Kt. Grand Cross, Order E. St. Sepulcre; Knight of Columbus, 4th degree; retired 5 Apr. 1979; Publication: 'L'Eglise au Diocèse de Chicoutimi' 1987, 3 Vol.; Address: 927 Jacques-Cartier East, Chicoutimi Que. G7H 2A3.

**PARÉ, Richard,** B.A., B.L.S., NDC.; librarian; b. Quebec City, P.Q. 29 Mar. 1938; s. Rosario and Jeanne (Verreault) P.; e. Le Petit Séminaire (Quebec City); Laval Univ., B.A.; Univ. Ottawa, B.L.S.; National Defence College, NDC; m. Renée, d. René Blanchet, 23 June 1961; children: Michel; Valérie; Nicolas; ASSOC. PARLIAMENTARY LIBRARIAN, LIBRARY OF PARLIAMENT since 1980; Clerk and Library Tech., Laval Univ. Lib., 1957–64; Asst. Lib. Dir.; Coll. des Jésuites (Quebec City) 1964; Chief, Lib. Public Services, CEGEP F.X. Garneau (Quebec City) 1970; Coordinator for Coll. Libs., Quebec Dept. Ed. 1971; Dir. Admin. Lib., Dept. Communications 1973; Dir. Documentation Branch, 1976; Asst. Dir. Legis. Lib., Quebec Nat. Assembly 1979; author 'Le Service du Prêt,' (2nd ed.) 1972; mem., Candn. Lib. Assn.; ASTED, Candn. Study of Parliament Group; Secy./Treas., APLIC/ABPAC (Assn. of Parliamentary Librarians in Canada); Co-Chrmn., Ottawa Valley Book Festival; recreations: tennis; golf; Office: Library of Parliament, Ottawa, Ont. K1A 0A9.

**PARENT, Omer,** O.C. (1971); peintre, éducateur; né Québec, P.Q. 7 avril, 1907; f. Omer et Rachel (Gauvin) P.; é. Ecole des beaux-arts de Qué.; Ecole nat. des arts décoratifs de Paris; ép. Evangeline; f. Charles Bélanger, Qué., le 5 août, 1943; prof., Ecole des beaux-arts de Qué., 1936–70, Dir. des études 1949–54; Prés., Comité des Arts et de l'Educ., Exposition prov., 1951–68; Dir.-fondateur, Ecole des Arts visuels. Univ. Laval 1970–72; 1972 peinture, enseignement temps partiel, Univ. Laval; depuis 1974 peinture et artivités connexes; Professeur émérite de l'Université Laval, 1975; secretaire de la Conf. candn. des arts, 1958; murales, peintures dans de nombreuses collections; Catholique; résidence: 1227, ave. des Pins, Sillery, Que. G1S 4J3.

**PARENT, Hon. (Joseph Albert) Oswald,** B.Com., C.A.; né Hull, Qué. 30 Sept. 1925; f. Alfred et Hélène (Massé) P.; é. Ecole supérieure de Hull; Queen's Univ. B.Com.; ép. Claudette Jean; enfants: quatre; CONSEIL: SAMSON BELAIR/DELOITTE & TOUCHE comptables agréés; Prés. Conseillers Professionnels (Hull) Inc.; Prés. Immeubles Carmen Inc.; Trésorier, Parti Libéral du Qué. 1955–57; elu membre de l'Assemblée Législative du Qué. pour la circonscription électorale de Hull 1956, réélu 1960, 1962, 1966, 1970, 1973; Adjoint parlementaire du ministre du Tourisme, de la Chasse et de la Pêche 1960–66; Ministre d'Etat au ministère des Finances 1970–76; Ministre d'etat au ministère des Affaires Intergouvernementales et responsable des négociations avec la Comn. de la Capitale Nationale 1970–76; Vice-prés. Conseil du Trésor 1971–76; Ministre d'Etat au ministère de la Fonction publique 1972–73; Ministre de la Fonction publique et ministre responsable des négociations collectives avec les employés des secteurs publics et parapublics de Qué. 1973–76; Prés. Fédération des Jeunes Chambres de Comm. du Qué. 1952–53; Vice Prés. Jeune Chambre de Comm. du Can. 1953–55; Sénateur, le Sénat J.C.I. du Can. 1953– ; Prés. régional, La Chambre de Comm. de l'Ouest du Qué. 1955–57; mem. Institut canadien des comptables agréés; Institut des comptables agréés de l'Ont.; Pub. Accts. Council Prov. Ont.; Ordre des comptables agréés du Qué.; corp. professionnelle des administrateurs agréés du Qué; Catholique; récréations: golf, natation, voyages; Clubs: Rivermead Golf; La Gorce Country; Residence: 110 Chemin du Château, app. 2301, Hull, Qué. J9A 1T4; Bureau: 450 - 25 rue Laurier, Hull, Qué. J8X 4C8.

**PARENT, Simon G.,** Q.C. (1959), B.A., LL.M., LL.D.; b. Quebec, Que. 16 Aug. 1913; s. Hon. Senator George, K.C. and Kathleen (Grenier) P.; e. Quebec Semy.; St. Dunstan's Univ.; Laval Univ., B.A. 1934, LL.M. 1937, Docteur en Droit, 1951; m. Louise, d. Hon. Mr. Justice Noel Belleau, 2 March 1943; children: Georges N., Louis B.; Director and Officer of several corporations; Pres., Enterprises Parent-Boisandré Inc.; Counsel, McNicoll & Parent, Advocates 1980–86; Hon. Consul of Italy, 1965–69; Ambassador Extraordinary and Plenipotentiary to Haiti of Sov. Mil. Hosp., Order of St. John of Jerusalem, Rhodes, and Malta, 1976–80; Pres., Assn. of Cdn. Knights of the Sovereign Military Order of Malta, 1981–1982; author of 'Le Nom Patronymique dans le Droit québecois' (1951), 'The Quebec Garrison Club, 1879–1979,' and of articles in French legal periodicals; Gov., Vice-Pres., St. Dunstan's Univ. Alumni Assn., 1952–55; Kt. of Grace of Sovereign Order of Malta (1955), Kt. Grand Cross (1961); read law with Taschereau, Parent, Taschereau & Cannon; called to the Bar of Que. 1938; Prof. (ret.) of Engn. Law, Laval Univ.; served World War, 1939–45; proceeded Overseas 1940; served in field with Royal 22nd Regt. till 1941; trans. to Candn. Mil. Hdqrs., London, in Judge Advocate's Br.; Co. Commdr., Les Voltigeurs de Québec (Motor) 1946–49; O.C. Laval Univ. Contingent, C.O.T.C., rank of Lt. Col. 1949–53; life mem., Heraldry Soc. of Can. (Hon'y Fellow); Royal Candn. Legion, (Ex-Chrmn. of Que. City & Dist. Council); United Services Inst. of Que. (Past Pres.); Life mem., Soc. Généalogique C.-France (1956); Pres., L'Amicale du 22c Inc. (1955–56); Vice-Pres., Candn. Assn., S.M. Order of Malta 1968–69; Roman Catholic; recreations: swimming, skiing; Clubs: Quebec Garrison (Pres., 1964–65); Home: 1144 Turnbull Ave., Quebec, Que. G1R 2X8.

**PARENTEAU, Roland,** B.A., L.Sc. Com.; éducateur; né Montréal, Qué. 13 decembre 1921; f. Arsène et Emerentienne (Bureau) P.; é. Coll. André-Grasset, Univ. de Montréal B.A. 1942; École des Hautes Etudes commerciales L.Sc.Com. 1945; Faculté de Droit. Univ. de Paris; Institut d'Études politiques Paris, Dipl. 1949; ép. Jeanne d'Arc (décédée) f. Léandre Julien (décédé) 28 juin 1947; enfants: Danielle, Michel, Claude, Jean-Luc, Dominique, Eric, PROFESSEUR ÉMÉRITE, ÉCOLE NATIONALE D'ADM. PUBLIQUE; professeur, École des Hautes Etudes Commerciales 1949–64, 1978–85; directeur, Conseil d'Orientation économique du Qué. 1964–68; Office de Planification du Qué. 1968; École Nationale d'Adm. Publique 1969–74, professeur 1974–78, 1983–91; mem. Conseil Supérieur du Travail 1963–65; agent de recherches à la Comn. royale d'Enquête sur les écarts de prix des denrées alimentaires 1958; mem. Exécutif, Inst. Canadien d'Éduc. des Adultes 1961–63; Conseil d'adm. de la Caisse des Dépôts et Placements 1966–69; Conseil scientifique de l'École internationale de Bordeaux 1970–72, 1974–78; missions d'évaluation pour l'ACDI en Algérie 1976–78, au Rwanda 1977, 79, au Bénin 1978, au Sénégal 1981, 1983, au Cameroun 1990, au Niger 1990; auteur: chaps. dans 'Developpement Urbain et Analyse Economique' 1968; 'Le Canada Français d'Aujourd'hui' 1970; 'Regional Economic Development' 1974; 'L'analyse des politiques gouvernementales' 1983; 'Gestion 2001' 1983; éditeur: 'Le management public' 1992; articles nombreux; mem. Assn. canadienne des Économistes (Prés. 1961–62); Société royale du Can.; Académie des Sciences morales et politiques; Conseil de Recherches en Sciences Humaines du Can. 1976–82; Comm. de l'Enseignement supérieur du Conseil Supérieur de l'Éducation du Québec 1981–87; Titulaire de la médaille Vanier, l'Inst. d'Admin. Publique du Can. 1986; catholique; Adresse: 165 Côte Sainte-Catherine, Apt. 1408, Outremont, Que. H2V 2A7.

**PARIS, Alain,** B.A., M.B.Sc., M.Acctg., F.C.A.; chartered accountant; b. Quebec, Que. 9 Sept. 1943; s. Richard and Mélanie (Ferlatte) P.; e. Ecole des hautes études commerciales M.B.Sc. 1969, M.Acctg. 1970; m. Rachelle d. Eugène and Jeanne Cyr 28 Sept. 1968; children: Mireille, Maxime; VICE-PRESIDENT, POISSANT THIBAULT-PEAT MARWICK THORNE 1991– ; Office Managing Partner, Poissant Thibault-Peat Marwick Thorne Laval Office until 1991; frequent guest speaker and author of several specialized courses in tax and financial planning; Dir., Grad. Diploma in Taxation, Ecole des hautes études comm.; Special Independent Advisor, Task Force on Revenue Canada Activities 1984; Vice-Chair, Ctte. on Que. Priorities & Policies 1984; Mem., Bd. of Dir., Assn. de plan. fiscale et finan. du Qué. 1987–89; Gov., Candn. Tax Found. 1988–82; Dir., Candn. Broadcasting Corp.; Oratoire Saint-Joseph du Mont-Royal; Opéra de Montréal; Candn. Cancer Soc.; Pres., Ordre des compt. agréés du Qué. 1991–92;
Home: 132 Thornton Ave., Town of Mount-Royal, Que. H3P 1H6; Office: 2000 McGill College Ave., Ste. 1900, Montreal, Que. H3A 3H8.

**PARIS, Erna,** B.A.; author; journalist; b. Toronto, Ont. 6 May 1938; d. Jules and Christine (Lipkin) Newman; e. Univ. of Toronto, B.A. (Hons.) 1960; Univ. of Paris, dipl. supérieur 1961; m. Thomas More s. Alban Bainbridge and Emily Evangeline (Tolmie) Robinson 26 Apr. 1981; children: Michelle Anne Paris, Roland Charles Paris; feature writing awards, Media Club of Canada 1969, 1974; radio documentary awards, Media Club of Can. 1973, 1974; Nat. Mag. Award, gold medal 1983; The White Award, bronze medal, (Canada & U.S.) 1991; author: 'Jews: An Account of their Experience in Canada' 1980, 'Stepfamilies: Making Them Work' 1984, 'Unhealed Wounds: France & the Klaus Barbie Affair' 1985, 'The Garden and the Gun: A Journey Inside Israel' 1988; co-author: 'Her Own Woman: Profiles of Canadian Women' 1975; anthologized in: 'The Toronto Book' 1976; 'Shaping Canadian Identities' 1978; 'The Spice Box' 1981; 'Best Canadian Essays' 1990; book reviews, radio documentaries, columns; contbr. to var. mags.; Mem., Writers Union of Can.; Internat. PEN (Can.) (past extve. offr. of both); founding Bd. mem., Candn. Reprography Collective (Cancopy); Founding Mem. & Past Pres., Periodical Writers Assn. of Can.; literary agent: Lucinda Vardey, 297 Seaton St., Toronto, Ont. M5A 2T6; Home: 126 Felstead Ave., Toronto Ont. M4J 1G4.

**PARIZEAU, Jacques,** Ph.D.; né à Montréal, P.Q. 9 août 1930; f. Gérard et Germaine (Biron) P.; é. Collège Stanislas, Montréal; licencié École des Hautes Études Commerciales, Montréal; diplôme, Faculté de Droit et Institut d'Études Politiques (Paris); London School of Economics (Londres) Ph.D. (Econ.); ép. feue Alicja Poznanska, 2 avril 1956; enfants: Bernard, Isabelle; remarié à Lisette Lapointe 12 décembre 1992; PRÉSIDENT DU PARTI QUÉBÉCOIS 1988– ; Ministre des Finances, du Revenu et des Institutions financières, président du Conseil du Trésor de la prov. de Québec 1976–84; membre du conseil, Univ. Montréal 1969–74; Directeur de l'Actualité Économique 1955–61; Directeur de l'Institut d'économie appliquée 1973–75; consultant gouvernement du Québec 1961–65; conseiller écon. & financier du Conseil des Ministres du Québec 1965–67; membre des conseils d'adm., Société générale de financement, Caisse de dépôt et placement, Société québecoise d'exploration minière et régie de l'assurdépôts du Québec jusqu'en 1969; chargé de recherche, Comm. royale d'enquête sur le Système bancaire et financier 1963; Prés. du Comité d'études sur l'institutions financières 1966–69; adhésion au Parti Québécois novembre 1969; prés. du Conseil exécutif du Parti Québécois 1970–73; élu député aux élections de novembre 1976, circonscription de l'Assomption; Prés. de la Comm. d'études sur les municipalités 1985–86; Catholique R.; récréations: lecture, musique, horticulture; Club: Cercle de la garnison de Québec; Résidence: 40 avenue Robert, Outremont, Que. H3S 2P2.

**PARIZEAU, Robert,** L.Sc.Comm.; insurance executive; b. Montréal, Qué. 7 Nov. 1935; s. Gérard and Germaine (Biron) P.; e. Coll. Stanislas B.A. 1953; Ecole des Hautes Etudes Commerciales L.Sc.Comm. 1957; m. Monique d. Ernest and Simonne (Bourgeois) Chabot 22 Nov. 1958; children: Marie-Hélène, Eric, Dominique, Jean-Michel; PRESIDENT AND C.E.O., SODARCAN INC. 1978– ; Dir., Dale Parizeau Inc.; MLH + A Inc.; BEP Internat. Inc.; The National Reinsurance Co. of Can.; Dir. and mem. Extve. Ctte., National Bank of Canada; Gaz Métropolitain Inc.; Dir., Power Corp. of Canada; Lévesque Beaubien Geoffrion Inc.; The Canam Manac Group Inc.; Clinical Rsch. Institute of Montreal; Associated Govs., Univ. de Montréal; Société Pro Musica; Jeune Chambre de Commerce de Montréal; recreations: skiing, tennis; Clubs: St-Denis; Mount-Royal; Home: 3556 Grey Ave., Montréal, Qué. H4A 3N6; Office: 1140, boul. de Maisonneuve Ouest, bureau 701, Montréal, Qué. H3A 1M8.

**PARK, Donald Mackenzie,** B.Sc., P.Eng.; engineering executive; b. Montreal, Que. 24 Jan. 1938; s. Duncan Rowan and Mary Elizabeth P.; e. Sir George William Univ., B.Sc. 1962, B.Comm.; m. Barbara d. Jack and Claire Lowery 19 May 1984; children: Keith, Tara, Colin; PRES. & C.E.O., SNC LAVALIN - EUROPE; Supt. Metallurgy, then Steelmaking, then Major Project Mgr., Stelco 1956–74; Asst. Project Mgr., Candn. Arctic Gas/Williams Bros. Eng. Co. 1975–78; Dir. of Engineering, then Gen. Mgr., Assoc. Pullman Kellogg 1978–80; Vice-Pres. & Gen. Mgr., Techman Engr. 1980–83; joined Partec Lavalin Inc. 1984 (Vice-Pres., Soviet Projects, then Vice-Pres. & Gen. Mgr., then Pres.); Owner-Cons., Delta West Devel. Ltd.; Lectr., Northern Alta. Inst. Tech. & L'Ecole Polytechnique; Past Chrmn., Am. Soc. for Metals; Past Dir., Am. Soc. for Statistics; Fac. of Engineering, Univ. of Alta.; Mem., Assn. of Profl. Engrs. of Alta.; Nfld.; Am. Inst. of Mining & Metallurgical Engrs.; Nat. Assn. of Corrosion Engrs.; Fellow, The Canadian Academy of Engineering 1991; recreations: skiing, mountaineering, flying, golf; clubs: Ranchmen's, Petroleum, Glencoe Golf & Country; Home: 44 Ave. L'Horizon, 1150 Brussels, Belgium; Office: Ave. Louise 251, Boite 16, 1050 Brussels, Belgium.

**PARK, Paul Benjamin,** B.A., M.Ed.; educator; b. New York, N.Y. 6 Jan. 1937; s. Benjamin M. and Lorna Lester (MacGillivray) P.; e. Univ. of W. Ont. B.A. 1969; Univ. of Toronto M.Ed. 1974; m. Barbara d. George and Doris Wickham 25 June 1960; children: Margaret, Michael, Catherine; DEAN OF EDUCATION, QUEEN'S UNIV. 1987– ; teacher London Bd. of Educ. 1957–64, Consultant (Gifted Children) 1964–66, Trustee of Bd. 1976–78; Science Program Consultant Ont. Inst. for Studies in Educ. 1966–68; Asst. Prof. of Educ. present Univ. 1969, Asst. Dean of Educ. 1977–79; Dean of Educ., Univ. of W. Ont. 1979–87, Prof. of Educ. 1984; consultant/teacher Brit. Nuffield Foundation, U.S. Office of Educ., UNESCO, IUCN (Switzerland); recipient Award for Outstanding Univ. Teaching Ont. Confed. Univ. Faculty Assns. 1977; Trustee, Can. Council 1972–76; Social Science & Humanities Research Council Can.

1977–82; author 'Curriculum Resources, Primary-Junior Science' 1983; co-author 'Stone Age Man' 1974; 'Metric Measure' 1976; 'Curriculum Implementation, A Resource Booklet' 1982; mem. Candn. Soc. Studies in Educ.; Candn. Assn. Deans Educ. (Chrmn. 1982– ); recreations: billiards, collecting malt whiskey; Home: 61 Kensington Ave., Kingston, Ont K7L 4B4; Office: McArthur Coll., Queen's Univ., Kingston, Ont. K7L 3N6.

**PARKER, Anne Elizabeth,** B.A., LL.B.; lawyer; b. Regina, Sask. 12 Aug. 1959; d. Douglas Morton and Mary Jean (McLean) P.; e. Univ. of Sask. B.A. 1982, LL.B. 1985; DIRECTOR OF CORPORATE COMMUNICATIONS (1989– ) and LEGAL COUNSEL (1987– ) IPSCO INC.; McDougall Ready, Barristers & Solicitors 1985–87; Regina Globe Theatre; Senate, Univ. of Regina; Mem., Candn. Bar Assn.; Mem., Internat. Assn. of Business Communicators; clubs: YWCA, Assiniboia; Home: 2278 Montague St., Regina, Sask. S4T 3K3; Office: P.O. Box 1670, Armour Rd., Regina, Sask. S4P 3C7.

**PARKER, Dale G.,** banker; b. N.S. 16 April 1936; e. Harvard AMP; m. Joan Mary 1962; children: 1 s. Shane; PRESIDENT, WHITE SPOT LTD. and EXECUTIVE VICE PRES., SHATO HOLDINGS LTD. 1992– ; Chrmn., B.C. Financial Institutions Commission 1989– ; Chrmn., Georgia Equity Group, Inc. 1988–89; Chrmn., Pres. & C.E.O., B.C. Bancorp (formerly Bank of B.C.) 1986–89; Pres. & C.E.O., Bank of B.C. 1985–86; Pres., Candn. Banking Operations, Bank of B.C. 1984–85; Extve. Vice-Pres. & Group Extve. Canadian Commercial Banking, Bank of Montreal 1983–84; Extve. Vice-Pres. and Gen. Mgr. Domestic Banking, 1982; Sen. Vice-Pres. B.C. Div., Vancouver 1980; Sen. Vice-Pres. and Asst. Gen. Mgr. Domestic Banking, Toronto 1978; Chrmn., Privatization Adv. Ctte. (B.C. Hydro); Dir., Talisman Energy Inc.; BC Bancorp; Dir., Vancouver Bd. of Trade; Dir. Extve. Ctte., Cancer Found.; Vice Pres. Bd. of Trustees, BC Cancer Agency; Office: Suite 300, 4088 Cambie St., Vancouver, B.C. V5Z 2X8.

**PARKER, Jack Horace,** M.A., Ph.D., F.R.S.C.; educator; b. Parkersville, Ont. 4 Apl. 1914; s. Ernest Frank and Jessie Blanche (Bain) P.; e. Bracebridge (Ont.) High Sch. 1931; Univ. of Toronto B.A. 1935, M.A. 1936, Ph.D. 1941; m. Marjorie Beatrice (d.) d. late William H. Minnes 11 June 1946; children: John Geoffrey Minnes, Ceciley Margaret; PROFESSOR EMERITUS, UNIV. OF TORONTO 1979– , Instr. in Spanish 1936–41, Asst. Prof. of Spanish & Portuguese 1946–53, Assoc. Prof. 1953–57, Prof. 1957–79, Chrmn. of Italian & Hispanic Studies 1966–69, Assoc. Dean (Div. I Humanities) Sch. Grad. Studies 1969–73; Special Lectr. in Spanish 1979–83; Instr. in Spanish Columbia Univ. 1941–42, Ind. Univ. 1942–43; Asst. Prof. of Spanish Univ. of B.C. 1945–46; served as Research Offr. Nat. Research Council Ottawa 1943–45; named Kt. Order Civil Merit Spain 1977; Corresponding mem., Hispanic Soc. of Am. 1990; recipient, Homage of Am. Assn. Teachers Spanish & Portuguese for unique contributions to Hispanism 1993; author 'Breve historia del teatro español' 1957; 'Gil Vicente' 1967; 'Juan Pérez de Montalván' 1975; articles Spanish & Portuguese drama of 16th and 17th centuries; Life mem. Ont. Modern Lang. Teachers Assn.; mem. Candn. Assn. Hispanists (Pres. 1968–70); Am. Assn. Teachers Spanish & Portuguese (Pres. 1975); Modern Lang. Assn. Am.; Internat. Assn. Hispanists; Liberal; Protestant; recreations: gardening, walking, travel; Home: 76 Belmont St., Toronto, Ont. M5R 1P8; Office: Toronto, Ont. M5S 1A1.

**PARKER, James William,** B.Sc.; company executive; b. St. John's Nfld., 22 May 1923; s. John Joseph and Flora (Frew) P.; e. Ampleforth Coll., Yorkshire, Eng., 1933–39; Loyola Coll., Montreal, P.Q., 1940–41; Macdonald Coll. (McGill Univ.), B.Sc. (Agric.) 1947; m. Geraldine Mary, d. Dr. E. Leo Sharpe, St. John's, Nfld., 20 June 1951; children: James Francis, Joan, Janet, Brenda, Barbara, Elizabeth, Louise; PRESIDENT, PARKER & MONROE LTD.; Past mem. Nfld. Adv. Bd., Royal Trust Co.; Pres., Nfld. Bd. Trade 1970–71, 1981–86; mem. Adv. Comte., Real Property of the Nat. Capital Comm.; joined the present firm in Sept. 1947; served in 2nd World War with R.C.A.F., 1943–45, Pilot Offr. (Air Bomber); Roman Catholic; recreation: golf; working on and enjoying country property which includes a nine hole, par 3 golf course at Manuels, Nfld.; enjoys reading 'The Spectator' magazine; Clubs: Rotary (Past Pres.); Home: 39 Topsail Road, St. John's, Nfld. A1E 2A6; Office: Water St., St. John's, Nfld.

**PARKER, Lloyd E.G.,** B.Sc., M.A.Sc.; research executive; b. Armstrong, Ont. 17 Sept. 1937; s. George T.M. and Bertha Vera (Hapko) P.; e. Scollard Hall, North Bay, Ont.; Queen's Univ., B.Sc. 1958; Univ. of B.C., M.A.Sc. 1963; m. Wendy d. Florence and Roger Stewart 4 May 1974; children: Brad, Greg, Sharon, Tracey, Tammie; SENIOR OR/MIS CONSULTANT, PRES., TEE CONSULTING SERVICES 1989– ; Telecom Offr., RCAF 1958–61; Systems Engr. IBM 1963–69; Dist. Mgr., SDL 1969–73; Mgr. of Cons., CSG 1975–77; Pres. & Founder, TEE Cons. Serv. 1977– ; Dir., Ont. Ctr. for Large Scale Computation, Univ. of Toronto 1986–89; mem., NSERC Grant Selection Ctte. (Industrial Engineering) 1993–95; IBM Systems Rsch. Inst. 1966; Mem., Candn. Operational Rsch. Soc. (Nat. Treas. 5 yrs.; Nat. Pres. 1984–85; recipient, Nat. Serv. Award 1986); Inst. of Mngt. Sci.; APEO; CIPS; recreation: private pilot; Office: TEE, 65 Cameo St., Oakville, Ont. L6J 5X9.

**PARKER, Richard D.,** B.Comm., M.A.; b. Calgary, Alta. 20 Aug. 1944; s. Clayton D. and Beatrice M. (Rogers) P.; e. Royal Military College B.Comm. (Hons.) 1966; Univ. of Western Ont. M.A. 1967; m. Mary Ellen d. Gabriel and Josephine Murray 31 Dec. 1984; TAX PRINCIPAL, ARTHUR ANDERSEN & CO. 1990– ; Captain, Canadian Armed Forces 1968–72; various research & planning positions, Revenue Canada, Excise, Ottawa 1972–79; District Manager, Saskatoon 1979–80; Regional Chief, Tax Interpretations, Toronto 1980–87; Tax Manager, Arthur Andersen & Co. 1987–90; in current position resp. for GST, PST & other fed. & prov. taxes, internat. trade & customs matters; recreations: alpine skiing, cycling; clubs: The Fitness Inst., The RMC Club of Canada; Home: 43 Soho Square, Toronto, Ont. M5T 2Z2; Office: 1200 - 45 St. Clair Ave. W., Toronto, Ont. M4V 3A7.

**PARKER, Robert Ross, Jr.;** government relations consultant; b. Acton, Ont. 18 Jan. 1943; s. Robert Ross and Mary Frances (Shelburne) P.; e. St. Andrews Coll., Aurora, Ont. 1960; m. Theresa Marie d. James and Irene Keleher 16 Jan. 1988; two s. Robert Ross, Jonathan Cook; PRINCIPAL, PARKER NORQUAY; previously journalist, writer and broadcaster pol. and econ. coverage; el. to H. of C. for Eglinton 1978–79; Special Adv. Min. of Finance Can. 1979–80; Special Adv., Min. of Finance Can. 1979–80; Vice Pres. and Chief Adv. Govt. Affairs, Royal Bank of Canada 1981–92; Gov. Atwater Inst.; Clubs: Rideau; Royal Ottawa Golf; National Press; National; Home: 28 Belvedere Cres., Ottawa, Ont. K1M 2G4; Office: 701, 99 Bank St., Ottawa, Ont. K1P 6B9.

**PARKER, Hon. William Dickens;** b. Hamilton, Ont. 25 Aug. 1914; s. Robert and Minnie (Dickens) P.; e. Hamilton (Ont.) Central Collegiate; Osgoode Hall Law Sch., Toronto, Ont. (1939); m. the late Inez Eleanor, d. George Hill, Hamilton, Ont., 28 Aug. 1938; children: Deborah, Patricia, John; retired, Chief Justice of the High Court of Justice for Ont.; called to the Bar of Ont., 1939; cr. Q.C. 1953; served in 2nd World War with Candn. Army, 1942–45; Capt., Royal Hamilton Light Inf.; Past mem. of Council, Candn. Bar Assn.; Past Pres., Hamilton Lawyers Club; Phi Delta Phi; Anglican Church; recreation: golf.

**PARKHILL, Douglas Freeman,** B.A.Sc.; D.Eng.; professional engineer; b. Toronto, Ont. 19 Dec. 1923; s. Clarence Freeman and Catharine Beverley (Murphy) P.; e. Univ. of Toronto, B.A.Sc. (Elect. Engn.) 1949; D.Eng. Univ. of Ottawa 1971; m. Gudbjorg Unnur Kristjansson, 29 Jan. 1955; children: Douglas Fridrik, Patricia Bjorg; Engr., Canadian Comstock Frequency Standardization Div., St. Catharines, Ont., 1949–51; Head, Systems Planning Dept., Computing Devices of Canada Ltd., Ottawa, 1951–55; Supvr. of Engn., Crosley Defence and Electronics Div., AVCO of Canada, Weston, Ont., 1955–56; Depy. Mgr. Computer and Electronics Systems Dept., AVCO R & D Div., Wilmington, Mass., 1956–58; Chief Engr., Advanced Devel. Dept., General Dynamics Information Technol. Div., Rochester, N.Y., 1958–61; Head, Communications Satellite Systems Dept., Mitre Corp., Bedford, Mass., 1961–69; Asst. Depy. Min. (Planning), Dept. of Communications 1969–74; Asst. Depy. Min. (Research), Dept. of Communications 1974–84; served with RCAF 1942–45; author, 'Challenge of the Computer Utility,' 1966; Co-ed., 'Gutenberg II,' 1979; co-ed., 'So This Is 1984' 1984; author 'The Beginning of a Beginning' 1987; winner McKinsey Award for 'Distinguished Contribution to Management Literature,' 1966; Alexander Graham Bell Lecture 1980; Winner Conestoga Shield, 1982; Winner Outstanding Achievement Award of Government of Canada, 1982; Awarded ICCC Founders Award 1992; Chrmn., OECD Panel on Computer Comm. Policy 1971–75; Pres. Internat. Council for Computer Commun. 1981–84 term; mem., Assn. Prof. Engrs. Ont.; Inst. Elect. & Electronic Engrs.; Scient. Research Soc. Am.; Unitarian; recreations: swimming, writing; Home: 2000 Islington Ave., Apt. 1510, Etobicoke, Ont. M9P 3S7.

**PARKIN, Alan Cresswell,** B.A., M.D., F.R.C.Psych.; psychiatrist; psychoanalyst; educator; b. England (of Candn. parentage) 9 Nov. 1923; s. Thomas Cresswell II, F.C.A. and Marie Louise P.; e. Univ. of Manitoba B.A. (Gold medal) 1945; Univ. of Toronto M.D. 1949; F.R.C.Psych. (UK); m. Elizabeth d. Dr. Arthur and Ethel McGanity 24 June 1950; children: Carol Cresswell, Patricia Cresswell, Thomas Cresswell III; PSYCHIATRIST IN PRIVATE PRACTICE; Registrar Bethlem Royal and Maudsley Hosps. and National Hosp. for Nervous Diseases, London, Eng. 1950–53; Sr. Registrar King's Coll. Hosp. Med. Sch., London, Eng. 1953–54; author 'A History of Psychoanalysis in Canada'; numerous papers in profl. jours. Can., U.S., and U.K.; has given numerous scholarly addresses in Can., U.S. and U.K.; former mem. Ed. Bd. Internat. Jour. of Psycho-Analysis, Internat. Review of Psycho-Analysis, Psychiatric Jour. of Univ. of Ottawa; Assoc. mem. (1954) and mem. (1959– ) Brit. Psycho-Analytical Soc.; mem. Internat. Psycho-Analytical Assn. 1954; founding mem. 1957, Vice-Pres. 1959–60 and Pres. 1961–63, Candn. Psychoanalytic Soc.; founding mem. 1961 and Chrmn. 1973–77 Candn. Inst. of Psychoanalysis; mem. Candn. Psychiatric Assn. 1955– ; Ont. Psychiatric Assn. 1957– (founding mem. and first Chrmn. 1960–63 Section on Psychotherapy); founding mem. and first Chrmn. 1969–73 Toronto Inst. of Psychoanalysis; Founding Fellow Royal Coll. of Psychiatrists U.K. 1971; Sr. Cons. in Psychotherapy Clarke Inst. of Psychiatry, Toronto 1975– ; founder and first Dir. Centre for Psychotherapy, Clarke Inst. of Psychiatry 1979; Visiting Prof. or Lecturer: Vanderbilt Univ. 1954, Univ. of Manitoba 1973, Univ. of Western Ont. 1977 and 1985, Univ. of Alberta 1980; recreations: rare book collecting, skiing, mountain hiking; Clubs: Zeta Psi Frat. of N. Am.; Aesculapian, Toronto; Home: 23 Tudor Gate, Willowdale, Ont. M2L 1N3.

**PARKIN, Andrew Terence Leonard,** M.A., Ph.D.; university professor; b. Birmingham, England 30 June 1937; s. Francis Stanley and Mary Phyllis Maud (Stansfield) P.; e. Handsworth G.S. 1948–56; Pembroke Coll. Cambridge University, B.A. 1961, M.A. 1965; Bristol Univ., Ph.D. 1969; m. Christine Patricia d. Edward and Helen George 14 June 1959; one s.: Benedict Stephen; divorced; 2nd m. Françoise Alice Marguerite d. Frédéric and Alice Lentsch 28 Apr. 1990; PROF., DEPT. OF ENGLISH, CHINESE UNIV. OF HONG KONG 1991– ; R.A.F. 1956–58; Teacher, Cambridgeshire H.S. for Boys 1961–63; St. George's Sch. 1963–67; Prof., Univ. of B.C. 1970–90; Open Exhibitioner in English, Pembroke Coll. Cambridge Univ. 1958; Winner of Salmon Arm Sonnet Competition 1985; Human Rsch. Ctr. Fellowship, Australian Nat. Univ. 1987; Visiting Scholar, English Dept., A.N.U. 1988–89; named Distinguished Retiring Editor of a Journal 1989 (by Council of Editors of Learned Journals); Hon. Life Mem., Candn. Assn. for Irish Studies; Hon. Life Mem., Candn. Celtic Assoc.; Mem., Internat. Assn. for the Study of Anglo-Irish Lit.; Mem., Writers' Union of Canada; Mem., Internat. Assn. of Univ. Professors of English; Mem., Advisory Bd., Institute for Rsch. into Literatures in English (Graz, Austria); author: 'The Dramatic Imagination of W.B. Yeats' 1978; 'Caesar and Cleopatra' 1980; 'Dancers in a Web' (Poems) 1987; 'Yokohama Days, Kyoto Nights' (poems) 1992; 'File On Nichols' 1993; editor: 'Stage One' 1973; 'The Canadian Journal of Irish Studies' 1975–88; 'Dion Boucicault' 1987; W.B. Yeats's 'The Herne's Egg' 1991; recreations: books, travel, theatre, tennis; Office: Dept. of English, Chinese Univ. of Hong Kong, Shatin, New Territories, Hong Kong.

**PARKIN, Margaret Lillian,** B.A., B.L.S.; librarian; b. Toronto, Ont. 31 Mar. 1921; d. John Hamilton and Margaret Gertrude (Locke) P.; e. Elmwood Girls Sch., Rockcliffe Pk., Ont., Sr. Matric., 1938; Univ. of Toronto B.A. 1942; Ottawa Univ. B.L.S. 1960; FREELANCE LIBRARIAN/INDEXER 1984– ; with Nat. Research Council of Can., 1946–50, Head Report Sec., Div. Mech. Engn.; Dept. of Labour, Econ. and Research Br., Library, 1961–62; Unemployment Ins. Comn., Library, 1962–63; Carleton Univ., Catalogue Dept., 1963–64; Librarian, Candn. Nurses' Assn., 1964–79; Indexer, Canadian Periodical Index 1979–84; served in 2nd World War as Flight Offr., RCAF (WD) 1942–46; Flight Lieut., RCAF, 1951–58; former mem., Bd. of Dirs., VON Ottawa-Carleton; Anglican; recreations: handicrafts; Clubs: Women's Canadian; Canadian (Ottawa); Home: Apt. 1005, 60 McLeod St., Ottawa, Ont. K2P 2G1.

**PARKINSON, Dale Awyn George,** F.C.A. (1980); executive; b. Rochdale, Eng. 2 Sept. 1941; s. George Ernest and Alicia (Nicholls) P.; e. Univ. of Man. C.A. 1967; m. Shanley d. Peter and Muriel Ross 14 Sept. 1963; children: Jane, Janet, Brett; EXTVE. VICE PRES., FINANCE & ADMINISTRATION, INVESTORS GROUP INC. 1987– ; and CHRMN. OF THE BD., INVESTORS GROUP TRUST CO. LTD.; Chrmn. and Dir., Investors Group Trustco Inc.; Investors Syndicate Property Corp.; Pres. & Dir., I.G. Resources Inc.; Chrmn. & Dir., Investors Group Trust Co. Ltd.; Dir., I.G. International Management Ltd.; I.G. Investment Management Ltd.; Investors Syndicate Limited; I.G. Tax Services Inc.; joined Dunwoody & Co. 1959–60; Coopers & Lybrand 1960–66; Supr. Pension Adm. Investors Group Trust 1966, Mgr. Pension Adm. 1968, Treas. 1970, Gen. Mgr. 1973, Vice Pres. and Gen. Mgr. 1974, Pres. and Dir. 1978; Bd. Chrmn. 1986; mem. Council Inst. C.A.'s Man. 1970–73; Fellow, Inst. of C.A.'s 1980; Dir. & Treas., Internat. Scholarship Foundation; Dir., Scholarship Consultants of North America Ltd.; Club: Manitoba; St. Charles Country; Home: 1 Paradise Bay, Winnipeg, Man. R3R 1L2; Office: One Canada Centre, 447 Portage Ave., Winnipeg, Man. R3C 3B6.

**PARKINSON, Edythe A. (Dee),** B.Sc., M.B.A.; oil industry executive; b. Dartmouth, N.S. 4 July 1948; e. Queen's Univ. B.Sc. 1970, M.B.A. (Hons.) 1976; married; EXECUTIVE VICE PRES., OIL SANDS GROUP, SUNCOR INC. 1991– ; Imperial Oil 1976–83; Petro Canada 1983–90; Ontario Hydro 1990–91; author: 'Capital Cost Estimating in the Mineral Processing Industry'; recreations: photography, sports; Office: P.O. Box 4001, Fort McMurray, Alta. T9H 3E3.

**PARKS, Malcolm Gordon,** M.A., Ph.D.; university professor; b. Petite Riviere, Lunenburg Co., N.S. 7 Apr. 1924; s. William Drew and Mildred Maude (Reinhardt) P.; e. Dalhousie Univ. B.A. 1950, M.A. 1951; Univ. of Toronto, Ph.D. 1963; m. Doris Louise d. Lloyd McKnight and Louise Winslow Johnstone 2 Sept. 1950; children: Drew Alexander, Charlotte Martha, Catherine Louise, Eleanor Mary Johnstone; Asst. Prof., Dalhousie Univ. 1956–62; Assoc. Prof. 1962–68; Prof., Dept. of English 1968–89; Chrmn., Dept. of English 1969–72; Asst. Dean, Fac. of Grad. Studies 1977–89; Acting Dean 1981; undergrad. & grad. teaching fields: Renaissance poetry & prose, Candn. lit.; Assoc. Ed.: 'Dalhousie Review' 1957–68; editor: 'Western and Eastern Rambles: Travel Sketches of Nova Scotia' (Howe) 1973, 'The Old Judge' (Haliburton) 1979, 'My Dear Susan Ann: Letters of Joseph Howe to His Wife, 1829–1836' 1985, 'A Strange Manuscript Found in a Copper Cylinder' (De Mille) 1986, 'Acadia' (Howe) 1988; author of articles on Howe, De Mille & Candn. lit.; recreations: music, sports; Club: Dalhousie Fac.; retired 1989; Home: Petite Riviere, Lunenburg Co., N.S. B0J 2P0.

**PARNAS, David Lorge,** B.S., M.S., Ph.D., Dr.h.c., F.R.S.C.; computer engineering professor; b. Plattsburgh, N.Y. 10 Feb. 1941; s. Jacob M. and Hildegarde Marienne (Lorge) P.; e. Carnegie Inst. of Technol., B.S. 1961, M.S. 1964, Ph.D. 1965; m. Lillian Lai Ngan Chik d. S.F. Chik and Y.C. Chan 7 Nov. 1979; children: Henrietta, Jacob; PROF., DEPT. OF ELECTRICAL AND COMPUTER ENGINEERING, McMASTER UNIV. 1991– ; Prof., Carnegie Mellon Univ.; Univ. of N. Carolina; Univ. of Victoria; Prof., Dept. of Computer Inform. & Sci., Queen's 1986–91; Advr., Philips-Electrologica U.S. Naval Rsch. Lab.; IBM; TRW; Bell Labs.; Past Pres., Sci. for Peace; Past Depy. Chrmn., Candn. Pugwash; Mem., Computing Profls. for Soc. Responsibility; Hon. Doctor of Tech. Sci., Swiss Federal Inst. of Technol. (ETH), Zürich 1986; recipient, Norbert Wiener Award 1987; Fellow, Royal Soc. of Can. 1992; author of more than 150 papers & reports; recreation: bicycling; Office: Communications Rsch. Lab., McMaster Univ., Hamilton, Ont. L8S 4K1.

**PARNES, Penny H.,** B.Sc., D.S.P.A.; speech pathologist; b. Toronto, Ont. 8 Feb. 1947; d. Morris L. (dec.) and Anne (Pomotov) Rosner; e. Univ. of Toronto, B.Sc. 1969, D.S.P.A. 1972; m. Richard s. Earl and Esther Parnes 3 Sept. 1969; children: Sarah, Samantha; VICE PRES., HUGH MACMILLAN REHABILITATION CENTRE 1990– ; DIR., AUGMENTATIVE COMMUNICATION SERV., HUGH MACMILLAN MED. CTR. 1980– ; Speech/Lang. Pathol., var. hosps. & clinics 1969–75; Cons. & Founding Mem., Blissymbolics Commun. Inst. 1973– ; Co-Dir., Microcomputer Applications Prog., Hugh MacMillan Med. Ctr. 1982– ; Cons., Ont. Min. of Health 1985–86; Student Rsch. Advr., Univ. of Toronto 1984–88, 1990–91; Bd. of Dir. & Founding Mem., Internat. Soc. for Augmentative & Alternative Commun. 1983– (served extve. positions & cttes. & presently Past Pres.); Mem., Adv. Bd., Trace Centre (U.S.) 1984, 1985; mem., Adv. Ctte., Ont. March of Dimes; Bd. Mem. & Chair, Internat. Centre for the Advancement of Community Based Rehabilitation (a CIDA Centre of Excellence); Asst. Prof., Program in Applied Health Sciences, Univ. of Western Ont.; Asst. Prof., Communication Disorders, Univ. of Toronto 1990– ; Asst. Prof., School of Rehabilitation Therapy, Queen's Univ.; Holy Blossom Temple; Candn. Jewish Forum; Ont. and Candn. Speech & Hearing Assns.; Rehab. Engr. Soc. of N. Am.; Commun. Awareness & Action Group; author of numerous articles & presentations (nat. & internat.); Cons. Ed.: 'Augmentative and Alternative Communication,' 'Encyclopedia of Medical Devices'; Ed. Bd. 'Rehabilitation Technology'; awarded: Editor's Award 1987; Prentke-Romich AAC Award; recreations: sports, travel, reading; Club: Jewish Community Ctr.; Home: 17 Croydon Rd., Toronto, Ont. M6C 1S6; Office: 350 Rumsey Rd., Toronto, Ont. M4G 1R8.

**PARR, James Gordon,** Ph.D., F.R.S.C., P.Eng.; b. Peterborough, England 26 May 1927; s. Reuben Scotney and Edith Grace (Rollings) P.; e. Deacon's School, Peterborough, England; Univ. of Leeds, B.Sc. (Metall.) 1947; Univ. of Liverpool, Ph.D. 1953; m. Carole Elizabeth Vaughan d. Edgar and Joan Vaughan Dec. 1975; children: Mark Anthony, Katharine Elizabeth, Daniel John; WRITER; formerly: Dir. Gen., Ontario Science Centre 1985–88; Chrmn. & C.E.O., TVOntario 1979–85; Depy. Min. Colls. & Univs. Govt. Ont. 1973–79; Professor and Dean, Faculty of Applied Science, University of Windsor 1964–73 and President, Indust. Research Inst. there; Assoc. Prof. and then Prof., Univ. of Alberta 1955–64; Lectr., Univ. of B.C. 1953–55; Lectr., Univ. of Liverpool 1948–53; author: 'Man, Metals and Modern Magic,' 1958; co-author; 'The Engineer's Guide to Steel,' 1965; co-author: 'An Introduction to Stainless Steel,' 1965; 'Any Other Business: How To Be A Good Committee Person,' 1977; 'Is There Anybody There?,' 1979; 'Megafart' 1990; 'Essays' 1991; other writings incl. tech. publs. and articles in prof. and popular press; also frequent contrib. to CBC radio; awarded Centennial Medal; Jubilee Medal; Citizenship Award, Assoc. of Prof. Engrs. of Ont., 1983; Hon. LL.D., Univ. of Windsor 1984; Fellow, Am. Soc. for Metals; Ryerson Polytech Inst.; Ont. Inst. for Studies in Educ.; recreation: photography, music; Club: Arts & Letters, Toronto (Pres. 1982, 1983); Home: 10 Governor's Rd., Toronto, Ont. M4W 2G1.

**PARR, Joy,** B.A., M.Phil., Ph.D., F.R.S.C.; educator; b. Toronto, Ont. 1 Jan. 1949; d. Gordon Minto and Isobel (Mitchell) P.; e. McGill Univ. B.A. 1971; Yale Univ. M.Phil. 1973, Ph.D. 1977; m. Gregory James s. Charles and Dorothy Levine 14 Sept. 1984; FARLEY PROF. OF HISTORY, SIMON FRASER UNIV. 1992– ; previous acad. posts Queen's Univ., Univ. of B.C. and Yale Univ.; Distinguished Visitor State Univ. of N.Y. 1982; Assoc. Prof. Queen's Univ. 1982–88, Prof. 1988–92, Co-ord. Women's Studies 1989–90; Chair Status of Women Ctte. Ont. Confedn. Univ. Faculty Assns. 1987–89; recipient McGill Univ. Fellowship 1968–70; Can. Council Fellowship 1973–76; Woodrow Wilson Fellowship 1971–72; Commonwealth Fellowship 1972; CHR Prize 1987; Hilda Neatby Prize 1987; Riddell Award 1988; Berkshire Prize 1988; Sir John A. Macdonald Prize 1991; Fred Landon Award 1991; Laura Jamieson Prize 1992; Harold Adams Innis Prize 1992; author 'Labouring Children' 1980; 'Childhood and Family in Canadian History' 1982; 'Canadian Women on the Move' 1983; 'Still Running' 1987; 'Gender of Breadwinners' 1990; ed. (Candn.) 'Histoire Sociale' 1984–85; 'Gender and History' 1992–97; mem. various ed. bds.; mem. Candn. Hist. Assn. (Council 1979–81); Home: 218 - 4th St., New Westminster, B.C. V3L 2V1; Office: Burnaby, B.C. V5A 1S6.

**PARRETT, William Glen,** B.A., LL.B., Q.C.; judge of the Supreme Court of British Columbia; b. Victoria, B.C. 16 Oct. 1946; s. Roy Vernon and Maude Rosina (Kirton) P.; e. Mt. View H.S. 1964; Univ. of Victoria B.A. 1968; Univ. of B.C. LL.B. 1972; m. Dianne Frances d. William and Florence Birch 3 July 1971; children: Matthew William, David Neil, Colleen Diana Nicole, Steven Andrew Kyle; JUDGE OF THE SUPREME COURT OF BRITISH COLUMBIA 16 Feb. 1990– ; called to Bar, Prov. of B.C. 14 May 1973; articled with Hope Heinrich & Hansen (Prince George, B.C.); Assoc. & Partner 1973–90; Q.C. 1987; Dir., Legal Aid Soc. of B.C. 1978–79; Gov., Law Found. of B.C. 1980–83; Non-Bencher Mem., Competency Ctte., Law Soc. of B.C. 1983–84; Discipline Ctte. 1985–89; Mem., Justice Reform Ctte. of B.C. 1987–8;; Supreme Court Rules Ctte. 1989–90; recreations: outdoors, canoeing, photography, computers, hockey; Home: 4661 Hunter Place, Prince George, B.C. V2M 6Z7; Office: 1600 Third Ave., Prince George, B.C. V2L 3G6.

**PARRISH, William Bruce;** grain merchant; b. Winnipeg, Manitoba 8 May 1926; s. Frederick William and Vera E. (Cadle) P.; e. Public Schs. and Kelvin Tech. High Sch.; Univ. of Manitoba; m. Donna Marie, d. Dr. J. S. McInnes, Winipeg, Man., 14 July 1954; children: William S., David L., Elizabeth D.; PRES. AND DIR., PARRISH & HEIMBECKER LTD.; Pres. and Dir., Great Lakes Elevator Co. Ltd.; Dir., New Life Mills; Martin Feed Mill Limited; mem., Winnipeg Commodity Exchange (Chrmn. 1967); Chrmn. of the Bd., Grain Insurance & Guarantee Co. Ltd.; Chrmn., The Winnipeg Found.; Past Chrmn., Winnipeg Health Sciences Centre; Past Pres., Candn. Cancer Soc.; Freemason (Scot. Rite); United Church; Club: Manitoba; Home; 4701 Roblin Blvd., Winnipeg, Man. R3R 0G2; Office: 700 - 360 Main Street., Winnipeg, Man. R3C 3Z3.

**PARR-JOHNSTON, Elizabeth,** M.A., Ph.D.; university president; b. New York N.Y. 15 Aug. 1939; d. F. Van Siclen and Helene Elizabeth (Ham) Parr; e. Wellesley Coll. B.A. 1961 (Phi Beta Kappa); Yale Univ. M.A. 1962 (Woodrow Wilson Fellow), Ph.D. 1973; m. Archibald F. s. late Frederick W. and late C. Annie Johnston 6 March 1982; children (by previous marriage): Peter Van S. Bond, Kristina A. Bond; PRES., MOUNT SAINT VINCENT UNIV. 1991– ; Instr. in Econ. Univ. of W. Ont. 1963–67, Univ. of B.C. 1967–70; Visiting Prof of Econ. Wesleyan Univ. Conn. 1970–71; Acad. Assoc. Carleton Univ. 1971–72; Statistics Can. 1972; Regional Econ. Expansion, Dir. Econ. Devel. Analysis 1973–75; Dir. Gov. Affairs Inco Ltd. 1975–79; Sr. Policy Adv. and Chief of Staff to Fed. Min. of Employment & Immigration 1979–80; Mgr. Social & Govt. Trends, Shell Canada Ltd. 1980, Mgr. Macro Environment, Corp. Strategies 1981–84, Mgr. Bus. Environment 1984–85, Mgr. Computer Services 1985–86, Mgr. Information & Computing Operations 1986–87, Mgr. Information & Computing Technology 1987–88, Mgr. Products Strategic Systems, 1988–90; Dir., Bank of Nova Scotia; Nova Scotia Power Inc.; Dir., Investment Dealers Assn.; Dir., Mutual Life Assurance Co. of Canada 1990–93; Calgary Centre for Learning Disabilities 1989–91; mem., National Innovations Adv. Ctte. to the Min. of Human Resource Development; Dir., North/South Institute; Dir., Council for Candn. Unity; Board, Voluntary Planning (Nova Scotia); mem. Infoport Task Force, Calgary Econ. Develop. 1990–91; mem. Ont. Econ. Council 1980–84; Dir. Ont. Centre for Micro Electronics 1983–84; mem. C.D. Howe Policy Adv. Council 1981–85; Dir. Dellcrest Home 1980–83; John Howard Soc. 1981–84; Chair, Council of Nova Scotia Univ. Presidents; Vice-Chair, Atlantic Assn. of Universities; author various govt. studies regional devel., mag. articles pub. policy; Anglican; recreations: skiing, golf, sailing; Clubs: Albany (Toronto); Halifax; Ashburn Golf (Halifax); Chester Golf; Home: The Meadows, Mount Saint Vincent University, Halifax, N.S. B3M 2J6; Office: Mount Saint Vincent University, Halifax, N.S. B3M 2J6.

**PARROTT, Hon. Harry,** D.D.S.; orthodontist; politician; b. Mitchell, Ont. 30 Nov. 1925; s. William C. and Laura Ethel (Horn) P.; e. Mitchell, Ont.; Univ. of Toronto D.D.S. 1947, Dipl. in Orthodontics 1965; m. Isobel Walker, d. John Walker Mitchell Sept. 1947; children: Craig, Nancy, Lori; Past Chrmn., Bd. of Trustees, Ont. Science Centre 1983–85; Lectr. Univ. of Toronto Grad. Clinic and Studies 1965–69; Lectr. Univ. of W. Ont. 1969–71; el. M.P.P. 1971, re-el. until he resigned seat prior to 1981 election; Min. of Colleges and Universities, Ont. 1975–78; Min. of The Environment 1978–81; served Woodstock Bd. of Educ. 1954–56; Woodstock City Council 1961–63, 1966–67; Woodstock Pub. Utilities Comn. 1968–71; Past Pres. Oxford Co. Red Cross; Past Campaign Chrmn. Woodstock Un. Appeal; Chrmn., Fund Raising Ctte. of Woodstock Gen. Hosp. 1987; P. Conservative; Protestant; recreations: standardbred horse farming; Home: R.R. #5, Woodstock, Ont. N4S 7V9; Office: 22 Wellington St. N., Woodstock, Ont. N4S 6P2.

**PARRY, Caroline Balderston,** B.A.; freelance performer, writer, teacher; b. Philadelphia, Pa. 5 June 1945; d. William Gibbons and Mary Evalyn (Kirk) Balderston; e. Westtown Friends Sch. Pa. 1962; Radcliffe Coll. Harvard Univ. B.A. (cum laude) 1966; Hull Coll. of Edn. Yorks. Eng. Grad. Cert. of Edn. 1971; m. David M. s. Richard and Sheila Parry 1 May 1968; children: Evalyn Shanti MacKenzie, Richard Reed Balderston; primary sch. teaching India and England 1967–72; La Leche League Can. 1975–80; Poculi Ludique Societas theatrical adm. Univ. of Toronto 1975–78; nursery sch. teacher 1980–83; freelance performer libs. and schs. since 1976; mem. Mariposa-in-the-Schs. 1981– ; Multi Cultural Arts for Schools & Communities (Ottawa) 1992– ; Inner City Angels (Toronto) 1984–92; recipient Briggs

Travelling Fellowship Radcliffe 1966; Hull Coll. Book Prize for Distinguished Essay 1971; Ont. Min. Citizenship & Culture Volunteer Award 1983; IODE Book Prize Toronto 1987; author: 'Let's Celebrate! Canada's Special Days' 1987; 'Eleanora's Diary, The Journals of a Canadian Pioneer Girl' 1994; editor: 'Zoomerang A Boomerang' 1991 (alt. title 'A Rhyme for Me'); mem. Religious Soc. Friends; CANSCAIP; Candn. & Eng. Folk Music & Dance Soc's.; recreation: morris & country dancing; Home: 135 Britannia Rd., Ottawa, Ont. K2B 5X1.

**PARSON, (George) David;** advertising executive; b. Elmhurst, Ill. 23 Apl. 1938; s. William Ridley and Marjorie Joy (White) P.; e. H.B. Beal Tech. & Comm. High Sch. 1956; m. Joan Elizabeth d. Arthur and Edith Thorneycroft 12 Oct. 1963; children: Christopher Robert, Sara Elizabeth, Katherine Joy; PRES. AND CREATIVE DIR., DAVID PARSON ASSOCIATES LTD. 1970– ; recipient various awards from Mktg. and The Art Dirs. Club Toronto for Stratford Festival, Gallery Stratford, Toronto Symphony; recreations: tennis, woodworking, travel, pilot; Home: 63 James St., Stratford, Ont. N5A 5H9; Office: 342 Erie St., Suite 106, Stratford, Ont. N5A 2N4.

**PARSONS, Arthur Hedley,** B.Sc., M.D.; physician; b. St. John's, Nfld. 9 June 1943; s. Maxwell and Marjorie Florence (Mills) P.; e. Prince of Wales Coll. St. John's 1960; Dalhousie Univ. B.Sc. 1964, M.D. 1969; m. Patricia d. Maj. (Ret'd) William and Gwendolyn Houlihan 10 Oct. 1987; children: Arthur Bradley, Amanda Suzanne (from previous marriage); Ian Patrick (1989); PHYSICIAN, FAMILY PRACTICE ASSOCIATES 1969– ; Occupational Med. Atlantic Offshore Med. Assn. Halifax 1982– ; Dept. Family Med. Dalhousie Univ.; Gov. Dalhousie Univ. 1979–80, Dir. Alumni 1979–81; Dir. Halifax/Dartmouth Un. Way 1983–87; author: 'Health Care Ethics' 1992; 'When Older is Wiser' 1994; Consultant, Biomedical Communications Enterprises; mem. Candn. Med. Assn. (Chrmn. Ctte. on Ethics 1977–87); Founding Dir., The Candn. Soc. of Medical Bioethics; Halifax Med. Soc. (Pres. 1975–76); Candn. Assn. Med. Clinics (Pres. 1979–81); Chrmn., Extve. Ctte., Med. Soc. of N.S. 1987–88; Mem., Voluntary Planning Province N.S.; Am. Medical Writers Assn.; Alpha Omega Alpha, Phi Chi Med. Frat.; recreations: music (professional musician), sailing, scuba diving; Club: Saraguay (Chrmn. Bd. Govs. 1983–84); Home: 4 St. Laurent Place, Halifax, N.S. B3M 4B6; Office: 6155 North St., Halifax, N.S. B3K 5R3.

**PARSONS, James Bryan,** B.A., M.Ed., Ph.D.; university professor / writer; b. Port Allegany, PA 13 Jan. 1948; s. James B. and Patricia J. (Bryan) P.; e. Univ. of Kentucky, B.Ed. 1970, M.Ed. 1971; Univ. of Texas at Austin, Ph.D. 1976; children: Kerry, Jim, Casey; PROF., DEPT. OF SECONDARY EDUCATION, UNIV. OF ALTA. 1976– ; Junior High Sch. Teacher (Soc. Studies & Language Arts), Louisville, KY 1970–73; Teaching Asst. (& Ph.D. student), Dept. of Curriculum & Instruction, Univ. of Texas 1973–76; teaches both grad. & undergrad. levels; public speaker; numerous extve. positions in edn. & charitable orgns. including positions of Vice-Pres., Northern Alta. Ronald McDonald House & Sec., Extve., Baptist Gen. Conf. of Alta.; author/editor of more than 30 books (including texts for secondary social studies & language arts as well as univ.-level texts) & over 100 edn. articles – most recent include 'A Canadian Social Studies' 3rd ed. 1987, 'Japan: Its People and Culture' 1988, 'Roads: The Politics of Decision-Making' 1987, 'Canadians: Responding to Change' 1989, 'Stories of Teaching' 1991; 'A Changing World' 1991; 'What Works' 1992; 'Teaching From The Inside Out' 1992; 'Greece: Discovering The Past' 1993; 'Playing With Language' 1994; Home: Sherwood Park, Alta.; Office: 338 Education South, Edmonton, Alta. T6G 2G5.

**PARSONS, Timothy Richard,** B.Sc., Ph.D., F.R.S.C.; professor emeritus; b. Colombo, Ceylon 1 Nov. 1932; s. Ernest Gordon (C.) and Bridget Mary (Kingdon) Parsons; e. Christ's Hosp.; McGill Univ., B.Sc. 1953, M.Sc. 1955, Ph.D. 1958; m. Doris Hodge 1958, divorced 1978; m. Carol Lalli 1978; children: Stephanie Anne (dec.), Allison Mary, Peter Gordon; PROFESSOR EMERITUS, OCEANOGRAPHY, UNIV. OF B.C. 1971– ; Rsch. Sci., Fisheries Rsch. Bd. of Can. 1958–62, 1964–71; Prog. Spec., Unesco (Paris) 1962–64; Pres., Internat. Assn. of Biol. Oceanography 1976–82; Prize/Medalist, Oceanographic Soc. of Japan 1988; J.P. Tully Medal, Can. Soc. Ocean. Met. 1990; Hutchinson Medal, Am. Soc. Limnol. Oceanogr. 1993; Hon. Fellow, Nat. Bureau of Oceanography of the Peoples Rep. of China 1985; Com. de Perfectionement de l'Inst. Oceanographique (Paris) 1970–78; F.R.S.C. 1970; Mem., Oceanographic Soc. of Japan; Am. Soc. of Limnol. & Oceanography (Pres. 1969); Editor-in-Chief, 'Fisheries Oceanography'; Sigma Xi; Challenger Soc.; La Société franco-japonaise d'oceanographie; author of approx. 125 sci. papers; co-author: 'A Manual of Chemical and Biological Methods for Seawater Analysis' 1985, 'Biological Oceanographic Processes' 1983; 'Biological Oceanography: An Introduction' 1993; recreations: tennis, skiing, hiking; Home: 2851 Alma St., Vancouver, B.C. V6R 3S5; Office: Oceanography, Univ. of B.C., Vancouver, B.C. V6T 1Z4.

**PARTINGTON, Frederick,** B.B.A., C.A.; chartered accountant; b. Toronto, Ont. 18 July 1949; s. Eric and Elsie (Morley) P.; e. Ridley College 1967; Bishop's Univ. B.B.A. 1971; m. Janet d. Ray and Virginia Samson 4 Aug. 1974; children: Bryan, Vanessa; PARTNER, COOPERS & LYBRAND 1981– ; articled with Pollock Little & Co. C.A.s St. Catharines Ont. 1971–74; C.A. 1974; Tax Specialist, Winspear Higgins Stevenson & Co. Edmonton 1975–78; Willetts MacMahon & Co. 1978–81; Willetts MacMahon & Co. merged with Coopers & Lybrand 1980; assigned to Coopers & Lybrand N.Y. Office 1986–87; Council Mem., Inst. of C.A.s of Alta. 1988–91; Mem., Adv. Ctte. to Min. of Consumer & Corp. Affairs (Alta.) on Regulation of Financial Planners 1990; Governing Council Mem., Athabasca Univ.; author of one article and one conference paper; recreations: snow and water skiing, sailing; club: Centre; Home: 13804 – 84 Ave., Edmonton, Alta.; Office: 2700, 10235 – 101 St., Edmonton, Alta. T5J 3N5.

**PARTRIDGE, David Gerry,** B.A., R.C.A., F.R.S.A.; artist; b. Akron, Ohio 5 Oct. 1919; s. Albert Gerry and Edith (Harpham) P.; e. Mostyn House Sch. and Radley Coll., Eng. 1935; Trinity Coll. Sch. Port Hope, Ont. 1938; Trinity Coll. Univ. of Toronto B.A. 1941; Art Students League New York 1948; Slade Sch. London, Eng. 1950–51; Atelier 17 Paris 1958; m. Helen Rosemary d. Capt. John S. Annesley, R.N., 14 June 1943; children: Katharine Annesley, John David Harpham; Art Teacher, Appleby Coll. 1946; Ridley Coll. 1946–50, 1951–56; St. Catharines Coll. Inst. 1952–56; Queen's Univ. Summer Sch. 1958–60; Curator, St. Catharines Pub. Lib. & Art Gallery 1954–56; Teacher, Ottawa Civic Art Centre 1958–61; Trustee, Art Gallery of Ont. 1977–82; nail sculptures incl. Tate Gallery London, Eng.; Nat. Gallery Can.; Art Gallery Ont.; Westminster Cathedral, London, Eng.; Montreal Museum Fine Arts; Gallery New S. Wales Sidney, Australia; Lib. of Cong.; Victoria & Albert Museum (graphics latter 2 colls.); maj. comns. York Univ. Toronto; Toronto City Hall mural; Windsor Art Gallery mural; Bell Trinity-Toronto mural; Canada's Capital Congress Centre, Ottawa, mural; rep. in numerous pub., univ. and private colls.; Centennial Sculpture, St. Martin-in-the-Fields Church, Toronto 1990; rep. Moore Gallery, Hamilton; rec'd Brit. Council Scholarship 1950–51; Sculpture Prize Montreal Museum Fine Arts 1962; R.C.A. Sculpture Competition 1977; served with RCAF 1941, Flying Instr., rank Flight Lt.; mem. London (Eng.) Group of Painters; recreations: cryptic crosswords, tennis, carpentry; Home: 77 Seaton St., Toronto, Ont. M5A 2T2.

**PASCAL, Charles E.,** M.A., Ph.D.; educator; civil servant; b. Chicago, Ill. 21 Apl. 1944; s. Samuel A. and Harriet E. (Hartman) P.; e. Univ. of Mich. B.A. 1966, M.A. 1969, Ph.D. 1969; DEPUTY MINISTER OF EDUCATION AND TRAINING 1993– ; Deputy Minister, Premier's Council on Health, Well-Being & Social Justice 1991– ; Clin. Psychol. since 1968; Lectr. in Psychol. McGill Univ. Centre for Learning & Devel. 1969; Chrmn. Edn. Ctte., mem. Extve. Ctte. and Bd. Govs. McKay Centre for Deaf & Crippled Children Montreal 1970–75; Cons. Day Treatment Centre Montreal Children's Hosp. 1970–77; Visiting Fellow Australian Nat. Univ. 1975–76; Head of Higher Edn. Group Univ. of Toronto and Dir. Ont. Univs. Prog. for Instructional Devel. 1977; Extve. Head Grad. Studies OISE 1981; mem. Gov. Council Univ. Toronto 1981; Pres. Sir Sandford Fleming Coll. of Applied Arts & Technol. 1982; mem. Bd. Govs. Trent Univ. 1982–87; Chrmn. Greater Peterborough Econ. Council 1986; Coll. Rep. to Ctte. Nat. Forum Post-Secondary Edn. 1987; Educator-in-Residence Pacific Mgmt. Devel. Inst. W. Coast Coll. Adms. 1987; Chair, Ont. Council of Regents for Colls. Applied Arts & Technol. 1987–91; Deputy Min., Community & Social Services 1991–93; currently part-time lectr. in governance & acad. leadership OISE; Consulting Dir. Dept. Continuing Edn. Saidye Bronfman Centre 1973–74; Bd. of Dir. McKay Centre 1977; mem. Adv. Bd. Que. Soc. Austic Children 1975–77; Dir. Que. Soc. Emotionally Disturbed Children 1974–77; Extve. Bd. Candn. Soc. Study Higher Edn. 1976–79; Dir. Un. Way; Big Brothers & Sisters; Kawartha Lung Assn.; Arbor Theatre; Artspace; Lindsay Gallery; author numerous publs.; mem. Assn. Candn. Community Colls.; Candn. Psychol. Assn.; Candn. Soc. Study Higher Edn.; Am. Ednl. Rsch. Assn.; Nat. Soc. Performance & Instrn.; Council for Exceptional Children; Am. Assn. Higher Edn.; recreations: books, travel, baseball, tennis, squash; Home: 201 Withrow Ave., Toronto, Ont. M4K 1E2; Office: 6th Floor, Hepburn Block, 80 Grosvenor St., Toronto, Ont. M7A 1E9.

**PASCOE, John Frederick Richard;** company director; b. Reading, U.K. 4 Feb. 1940; s. Sir John and Lady Margaret Pascoe-Scott P.; e. Eton College; Grenoble Univ.; m. Veronica d. David and Elizabeth McQueen 1969; children: Julian John, Louise Margaret Elizabeth; DIR., FINNING LTD.; experience gained in electronics, computer industry, Eastern Europe 1962– ; Chairman, Active Investments Ltd. (a property and trading company); Hampshire Company Plc.; Council Mem., Foundation of Science & Technology London; author (originator): 'Future Imperfect' (science fiction and fact); clubs: Turf Club London; Home: Burgess Farm, Hamstead, Marshall, Newbury, Berks, U.K.; Office: 555 Great Northern Way, Vancouver, B.C. V5T 1E2.

**PASHBY, Thomas Joseph,** C.M., M.D.; physician; b. Toronto, Ont. 23 Mar. 1915; s. Norman Walter and Florence (Barnes) P.; e. Frankland Pub. Sch. and Riverdale Coll. Inst. Toronto 1934; Univ. of Toronto M.D. 1940; m. Helen d. John and Velva Christie 10 June 1941; children: William Thomas, Robert Christie, Jane Elizabeth; staff mem. Hosp. for Sick Children Toronto; Toronto Western Hosp.; Scarborough Centenary Hosp.; Dept. of Ophthalmol. Univ. of Toronto; RCAF 1941–46; Member of the Order of Canada 1981; recipient of numerous awards: CSA Award of Merit 1979; COS Eye Safety Award 1979; OHA Distinguished Service Award 1980; Civic Award of Merit, City of Toronto 1992; CAHA Gordon Juckes Award 1983; Borough of E. York Bulldog Award 1983; Sport Citation, Prov. of Ont. 1986; Canadian Commemorative Award 1867–1992; Jean P. Carriere Award, Standard Counc. of Can. 1988; Canada Sports Safety Award 1989; C.S.A. John Jenkins Award 1989; American Acad. of Ophthalmology Honor Award 1989; Hockey Develop. Centre of Ont. Recognition Award; Candn. Acad. of Sports Medicine Recognition Award; Metro Toronto Hockey League Chamandy Award; Hockey News Man of the Year Award; 'Doctor Tom Pashby Sports Safety Fund' was estab. 1990 - Reg. No. 0852525-11; Candn. Delegate, Internat. Standards Organization (ISO) Tech. Ctte. for Hockey Equipment; Dir., The Institute for Preventative Sports Medicine (Ann Arbor, MI, USA); Mem., Candn. Standards Assn. Sports Cttes. (2); Sr. mem. Candn. Med. Assn.; mem. Candn. Ophthalmol. Soc.; Am. Acad. Ophthalmol.; Club: Royal Candn. Mil. Inst.; Royal Canadian Institute; Home: 24 Donlea Dr., Toronto, Ont. M4G 2M2.

**PASTERNAC, André,** M.D.; cardiologist; b. Toulouse, France 22 July 1937; s. Jacques and Régine (Modry) P.; e. Math. Sup., Lycée Henri IV, Paris 1956; Univ. of Toulouse, Fac. of Sci. 1956–57, M.D. 1963, Univ. of Toulouse, Fac. of Law, Polit. Sci. degree, 1963; Cert. in Biochem. 1964; Harvard Med. Sch. Fulbright Rsch. Scholar in Cardiology 1968–71; Am. Field Serv. Scholarship, Ore. 1954–55; CLINICAL PROF. OF MEDICINE, MONTREAL HEART INST. AND UNIV. OF MONTREAL 1994– ; Fellow in Cardiology, Peter Bent Brigham Hosp. 1968–69; Children's Hosp. Med. Ctr. 1969–71; Toronto Gen. Hosp. and Hosp. for Sick Children 1971–72; Asst. Prof. of Medicine Montreal Heart Inst. and Univ. of Montreal 1972–77; Assoc. Prof. of Med. 1978–94; Visiting Assoc. Prof. of Med. Royal Victoria Hosp. and McGill Univ. 1975–76; Pres. & Extve. Dir., Heart-Brain Rsch. Found.; author articles in profl. jours on various cardiovascular and medical subjects; Home: 3465 Redpath St., Apt. 906, Montreal, Que. H3G 2G8; Office: 5000 Belanger E., Montreal, Que. H1T 1C8.

**PASTERNAK, Eugenia;** C.M.; institution administrator; b. Halychyna, Ukraine 8 Jan. 1919; d. Mychail and Maria (Okonsky) Nowakiwsky; e. Dipl. Tchr Inst. Lviv 1938; Courses in fine art with Kurylas, Monastyrska and O. Novakiwsky; Sch. of singing and piano with Mother Superior Yelena and Yanovich-Kopachynski; Ballet Sch. Suchowersky and Maria Pasternakowa; Teacher's Training Coll. Dipl. 1942; Goethe Univ. Frankfurt A/M, Germany studies in philos. 1945–47; Shaw Business Coll. Toronto 1954–55; Courses in fine arts, Toronto Techn. Sch., Griffith 1951–52; Ont. Coll. of Art, Pepper, White, Griffith; Toronto Art Gallery, Williams 1959, '61, '62; McMaster Univ. Dipl. in Adm. of Homes for Aged 1971; m. Eugene Pasternak (P.Eng.) 19 July 1944; DIR. AND ADM., IVAN FRANKO HOME 1964– ; Pres., Ukrainian Home for Aged, Toronto 1961– ; Princ., Montessori Kindergarten, Ukraine 1938–39; teacher various schs. Halychyna becoming Dir. of Social Services and Educator in Pidlassia; volunteer, 'Man in Trust' for prisoners in German POW camps; Red Cross; after emigration to Can. joined Multiblitz Photography; Legal Acct., Humeniuk and Romanko; recipient Dipl. for her dance group Internat. Festival, Hanow, Germany 1947; several awards for painting; Medal & Scroll Ukrainian Candn. Comte. 1962; Cross & Scroll Free Cossacks of Ukraine 1977; mem. Candn. Assn. Gerontol.; Gerontol. Soc. U.S.A.; Ont. Assn. of Gerontology; Candn. Coll. of Health Services, Ottawa; Ukrainian Pensioner's Club (Pres.); Internat. Platform Assn.; Internat. Biog. Assn. (Life Fellow & Life Patron); Hon. Offr. Free Cossacks of Ukraine; Hon. Chrmn., St. Joseph's Building Fund 1984; citation and medal, Union for Freedom of Ukraine in Australia; recipient of the Bicentennial Medal 1984; apptd. Member of the Order of Canada 1984; recipient of 'First Five Hundred' diploma & silver medal from Internat. Biographical Centre 1985; Governor, Am. Biographical Inst. 1986; Silver Medal of honor, Am. Biographical Inst. 1986; Cultural Doctorate (hon. causa), World Univ. U.S.A. 1986; Ph.D. (hon. causa) in Gerontology, Marquis Giuseppe Scicluna 1987; Laureate and medal of V. Wynnychenko (Kiev, Ukraine) for charitable work (this is the highest recognition in the Ukraine) 1991; Hon. Award, Writer's Assn. of Ukraine for the creation of the Ulas Samchuk Museum 1992; Cert. of Recognition from Brian Mulroney, Prime Minister of Canada, and Don Mazankowski, Depy. Minister of Canada 1992; 125th Anniversary of the Confederation of Canada Medal, 1992; Diploma of Honour, World Federation of Ukrainian Women's Organizations 1992; Grand Ambassador of Achievement Internat., Am. Biograph. Inst., Inc. 1986; Depy. Dir. Gen., Internat. Biographical Centre, Cambridge Eng. 1987; Curator, Ulas Samchuk's Museum and Ivan Franko Home Art Museum 1988; Bonafide Fellow of United Writer's Assn., Madras 1991; P. Conservative; recreations: painting, gardening, bee-keeping, organizing art exhibits, lecturing; writing; Home: 3058 Winston Churchill Blvd., Apt. C209, Mississauga, Ont. L5L 3J1; Office: 767 Royal York Rd., Toronto, Ont. M8Y 2T3.

**PATAVA, M. Jerry,** B.A., M.B.A.; business executive; b. Toronto, Ont. 16 Sept. 1953; e. Univ. of Toronto B.A. 1976; York Univ. M.B.A. 1978; m. Marylou; children: James, Lauren; VICE-PRES. & TREAS., CANADIAN PACIFIC LIMITED 1990– ; Dir., Pres. & Chief Extve. Officer, Canadian Pacific Securities Limited; Asst. Treas., Hiram Walker Resources Ltd. 1978–86; Vice-Pres. & Dir., RBC Dominion Securities Inc. 1986–90; Home: 1164 Greyowl Point, Mississauga, Ont. L4Y 2W4; Office: Suite 1400, Citibank Place, 123 Front St. W., Toronto, Ont. M5J 2M8.

**PATEL, Mahendra,** M.Sc.; b. Dantali, India 1 Feb. 1946; s. Ashabhai Ranehhodbhai and Funaben Ashabhai P.; e. Worcester Tech. M.Sc. 1972; m. Sarla d. Hirabhai P. Patel 14 Dec. 1969; children: Vishal, Viraj; VICE-PRESIDENT, ENGINEERING, PURCHASING & SITE SERVICES, TEMBEC INC.; Designer, E.H. Lambert Consulting Engineer 1973; Imperial Oil Refinery 1973; joined Tembec Inc. as Design Engineer 1974; progressed through positions as project Engr., Sr. Project Engr., Supt. of Engr., Mgr. of Engr. & Purch.; Dir., Envirotem; Tembec Construction Co.; Enertem; Hindu; Mem., Order of Engrs. of Que.; Assn. of Profl. Engrs. of Ont.; Candn. Pulp & Paper Assn.; Home: 90 Veronica Dr., North Bay, Ont.; Office: Temiscaming, Que. J0Z 3R0.

**PATEL, Zav,** B.Sc.; petroleum industry executive; b. Bombay, India 24 Oct. 1950; s. Gustad Meherwan and Freny Gustad (Engineer) P.; e. Loyola College B.Sc. 1972 (magna cum laude); m. Quinee d. Dosu and Behram Daruwala 24 March 1973; children: Kaye Shanaya, Ross Rustom; VICE-PRESIDENT, SUPPLY AND SHIPPING, ULTRAMAR CANADA INC.; Computer Audit Specialist, Clarkson Gordon 1972–78; various positions in Internal Audit Ultramar 1978–84; Dir. (and var. other positions in Supply) 1984– ; Mem., Extve. Ctte. 1991; Gold Medal Loyal Graduating Class 1972; Dir., Zoroastrian Assn. of Quebec 1988–89; club: Beaconsfield Golf; Home: 10 East Gables Cres., Beaconsfield, Que. H9W 4H1; Office: 2200 McGill College Ave., Montreal, Que. H3A 3L3.

**PATERSON, A.K.,** O.C., Q.C., O.Q., B.A., B.C.L., D.C.L.; b. Montreal, Que. 7 March 1932; s. Hartland MacDougall and Jean (Kennedy) P.; e. Trinity Coll. Sch. Port Hope, Ont. 1948; Bishop's Univ. B.A. 1952, D.C.L.; McGill Univ. B.C.L. 1956; m. Joan d. Philip Robb 3 Sept. 1955; children: Robb, Timothy, Angela, Alex; PARTNER, McMASTER, MEIGHEN & ASSOCIATES since 1969; read law with Heward, Holden & Associates; called to Bar of Que. 1957, Bar of Alta. 1971; cr. Q.C. 1973; joined Heward Holden Hutchison Cliff McMaster Meighen 1957; Asst. Prof. of Med. Jurisprudence McGill Univ. 1973; Commr. for Sch. Disputes; Co-Chrmn. Positive Action Comte.; Dir. The Laurentian Bank of Canada; The Laurentian Trust of Canada; Dir., Apu Crepaco Inc.; Chrmn., Alliance-Quebec; Chrmn., Quebec Inst. for Res. and Educ.; Pres. Bishop's Univ.; Pres., MacKay Centre for Deaf and Crippled Children; Gov. and Mem. Extve. Ctte. of McGill Univ. 1986– ; Chrmn., McGill Univ. 1990– ; Dir., Montreal Neurological Inst.; Counc., Montreal Bd. of Trade 1985–88; Chrmn., Stanstead Journal 1987; Brome Lake Theatre; mem. Candn. Bar Assn.; Candn. Medical-Bar Assn. Comte. (Chrmn. 1976); Candn. Bar Council; Vice Pres., Que.-Can. Pre-referendum Comte.; Liberal; Anglican; recreations: golf, tennis, squash, skiing; Clubs: University; Knowlton Golf; Home: 225 Olivier Ave., Westmount, Que.; Office: 630 René-Lévesque Blvd. W., Montreal, Que. H3B 4H7.

**PATERSON, Allen P.,** M.Hort. (RHS), M.Ed., F.L.S.; botanist; writer; b. Haverhill, Eng. 14 Sept. 1933; s. Harry Poole and Edith Olive (Wiseman) P.; e. Price's Sch. Fareham, Hants.; Cambridge Univ. Bot. Gdn. Cert. 1955; Royal Botanic Gardens, Kew Cert. 1958, M. Hort. (RHS) 1958; Univ. of Bristol Cert. Edn. 1959; Univ. of Reading, M.Ed. 1973; m. Penelope d. John and Sylvia Worthington 5 Apl. 1969; children: Mark Christopher John, Eve Louise Flora; Master in charge Rural Studies, Portchester Sch., Hants., Eng. 1959–62; Lectr. in Rural Studies, Culham Coll. of Edn. Abingdon, Oxford, Eng. 1962–68, Sr. Lectr. Profl. Studies 1968–73; Curator, Chelsea Physic Garden, London 1973–81; Lectr. Oxford Poly Inst. 1964–66, Univ. of London Extramural Dept. 1974–81, Inchbald Sch. Design London 1974–81, Dir. Garden course 1979–81; Dir., Royal Botanical Gardens 1981–93; Prof. (part-time) Dept. of Biology, McMaster Univ.; author: 'World of a Tree' (children) 1971; 'Growing Plants' (children) 1972; 'Gardens of Southern England' 1978; 'Book of Garden Ideas' 1979; 'Plants for Shade' 1980; 'History of the Rose' 1983; 'Herbs in the Garden' 1985; 'Plants for Shade and Woodland' 1987; 'Designing a Garden' 1992; co-author: (with Gerard Brender à Brandis) 'To Catch The Light - Images of Royal Botanical Gardens' 1992; also author of several book chapters; cons. ed. 'Creative Gardening' 1984; Fellow, Linnean Soc. of London; mem. Garden Hist. Soc. (Chrmn. 1980–81); Distinguished Adv., Brooklyn Botanic Garden, N.Y.; mem. Advisory Ctte., Garden Conservancy; mem. Master Gardeners Internat. Corp. Advisory Ctte.; recreations: gardening, fly fishing, architecture; Home: Grovehill House, Thornhill, Dumfriesshire, Scotland.

**PATERSON, Christopher Blaikie,** C.A.; b. London, Eng. 11 Nov. 1927; s. Donald Hugh and Dorothy Reed (Blaikie) P.; e. Trinity Coll. Sch. Port Hope, Ont. 1943; Harrow Sch. London, Eng. 1946; McGill Univ. 1946–47; m. Lorraine d. Abraham Gotlib, Toronto, Ont. 19 Apl. 1975; children (by first marriage): Susan, Douglas, Claire; Secretary and Director of Finance, The Canadian Institute for Advanced Rsch. 1989–94; Partner, Price Waterhouse 1967–89; joined Price Waterhouse Vancouver 1947, C.A. 1953, trans. Toronto 1955; mem. Candn. Red Cross Soc. (Pres. Toronto Br. 1971–72, Pres. Ont. Div. 1978–80, Chrmn. Nat. Budget Ctte. 1984–92; Past Dir. Candn. Yachting Assn.; Past Treas. Ont. Sailing Assn.; Past Pres. Candn. Albacore Assn.; Past Dir. Sport Ont.; author various articles; Anglican; recreations: golf, skiing, sailing; Clubs: Toronto Golf; R.C.Y.C.; Caledon Mountain Trout; Home: 51 Rosedale Rd., Toronto, Ont. M4W 2P5.

**PATERSON, Donald Savigny,** D.F.C., B.A.; company executive; b. Fort William, Ont. 22 Apr. 1918; s. Senator Norman McLeod and Eleanor Margaret (Macdonald) P.; e. Ashbury CoLl., Ottawa. Ont.; Bishop's Univ., B.A.; McGill Univ.; m. Jane Bernadette d. John Lynch, Galway, Ireland, 2 Aug. 1947; children: Norman Macdonald, Charles Lynch, John James, Andrew Bartholomew, Ellen Margaret; PRES. AND DIR., N.M. PATERSON & SONS LTD.; Pres. and Dir., Stall Lake Mines Ltd.; Dir., Voyager Explorations Ltd.; served with R.C.A.F. in Can. and Eng. 1940–45; retired with rank Flt. Lt.; Freemason; Zeta Psi; Presbyterian; recreations: golf, fishing, sailing, flying, hunting; Clubs: St. Charles Golf & Country; Royal Lake of the Woods Yacht; Manitoba; Ontario Club; Home: 131 Ridgedale Cr., Winnipeg, Man. R3R 0B4; Office: 609 – 167 Lombard Ave., Winnipeg, Man. R3B 0V5.

**PATERSON, Janet M.,** B.A., M.A., Ph.D.; university professor; b. Berne, Switzerland 21 Jan. 1944; d. Joseph and Magdalena (Danihel) Kirschbaum; e. Univ. of Toronto B.A. 1964, M.A. 1975, Ph.D. 1981; m. John A. s. John and Eleanor P. 10 Oct. 1964; children: John, Neil, Danielle; CHAIR FOR GRADUATE STUDIES, DEPT. OF FRENCH, UNIV. OF TORONTO 1991– ; Language Teacher, Reform School for Girls, Toronto 1965–70; Instructor, French Lang. & Lit., Saint Michael's Coll., Univ. of Toronto 1970–74; Prof., Dept. of French, Univ. of Toronto 1981– ; apptd. to Graduate Faculty, Centre for Comparative Lit. 1988; Mem., research group, Edition critique de l'oeuvre d'Hubert Aquin, UQAM; Gabrielle Roy Prize 1990 for best French language critical work of the year; Vice-Pres., Assn. for Canadian and Quebec Literature 1982–84; Treas. & Sec., Assn. for Canadian Studies 1987–91; author: 'Anne Hébert: architexture romanesque' 1985, 2nd ed. 1990 and 'Moments postmodernes dans le roman québécois' 1990, 2nd ed. 1993 (literary criticism); co-editor: (with John Lennox) 'Challenges, Projects, Texts: Canadian Editing' 1993; (with Marilyn Randall) 'Hubert Aquin: Trou de mémoire' (critical edition) 1993; recreations: cycling, skiing; Home: 30 Wychwood Park, Toronto, Ont. M6G 2V5; Office: 7 King's College Circle, Toronto, Ont. M5S 1A1.

**PATERSON, John Gilbert,** A.M., Ed.D.; educator; psychologist; b. Lethbridge, Alta. 16 March 1933; s. Gilbert Currie and Anne Isabel (Denoon) P.; e. Univ. of Alta., B.Ed. 1956, B.A. 1957; Leland Stanford Jr. Univ., A.M. 1958; Univ. of Wash., Ed.D. 1964; m. Barbara Anne d. William and Louise Wilson 10 Aug. 1957; children: David, Jamie, Duncan; COORDINATOR OF CLIN. SERVICES, FACULTY OF EDUCATION, UNIV. OF ALTA. 1978– , Prof. of Ednl. Psychol. 1970– , Assoc. Dean, Faculty of Education 1991– and Assoc. Chrmn. of Dept. 1987–90; Pres. Psycom Psychological and Counseling Services; Psychol. Cons. Edmonton Gen. Hosp. and Westfield Diagnostic & Treatment Centre; sch. teacher, prin., Dir. of Counselling field of Pub. Edn. during 1950's; joined present Univ. 1967; former Pres. Candn. Ednl. & Psychol. Cons.; guest instr. or prof. nat. and internat. univs. incl. Massey Univ. N.Z., Pontificia Universidade Catolica do Rio de Janeiro, Univ. of Reading, N.E. London Polytechnic, McGill Univ., Univ. of B.C., Univ. of Wash., Univ. of Berne; served as Chrmn. Min.'s Adv. Ctte. Univ. Affairs Alta. and Chrmn. Private Colls. Accreditation Bd. Alta.; Hon. Life mem. Alta. Guidance Council; recipient Gold Ribbon Award for top public affairs radio program in Can. 'That's Living' 1985; Prov. Alta. Achievement Award 1976; Distinguished Service Award Psychols. Assn. Alta. 1983; Pres. Edmonton Downtown Rotary; Hon. Life mem. Edmonton Kennel Club; Dir. Dandie Dinmont Club Can.; author or co-author over 100 articles profl. jours., book chapters; ed. Internat. Jour. Advanc. Counselling 1976–85; co-author 'That's Living' 1988; 'That's Living Too' 1989; 'When You Stand Alone' 1991; 'Masterminding Your Success' 1993; mem. over 20 profl. assns. incl. Candn. Guidance & Counselling Assn. (Hon. Life mem.), Psychols. Assn. Alta. (Extve. Council, Chrmn. Bd. Examiners); Phi Delta Kappa; Delta Upsilon; Fellow, Western Psychological Assn.; recreations: dog showing, curling; Home: 12435 Lansdowne Dr., Edmonton, Alta. T6H 4L4; Office: 1 – 135 Education North, Edmonton, Alta. T6G 2G5.

**PATERSON, Norman Reed,** M.A.Sc., Ph.D., F.R.S.C., P.Eng.; consulting geophysicist; b. London, Eng. 5 Feb. 1926; s. Dr. Donald Hugh and Dorothy Reed (Blaikie) P.; e. Trinity Coll. Sch. Port Hope 1943; Oxford Univ. Special Diploma 1944; Univ. of Toronto B.A.Sc. (Eng. Physics) 1950, Ph.D. (Geophysics) 1955; Univ. of B.C. M.A.Sc. (Geol. & Geophysics) 1952; m. Sally d. John and Helen Broughall 8 Sept. 1950; children: Catherine Osler, John, Michael, Norman; PRESIDENT, PATERSON, GRANT & WATSON LTD. 1973– ; Vice-Pres., Geosoft Inc.; Geophys. Imperial Oil Ltd. and Dominion Gulf Co. 1950–56; Chief Geophys. 1956–63 and Dir. Hunting Survey Corp. Toronto 1960–63; Pres. Huntec Ltd. Toronto 1963–69; private consulting practice becoming Pres. Norman Paterson & Assoc. 1969–73; served with Royal Signals 1943–46, rank Lt.; Adjunct Prof. Queens Univ. 1978–81; Gov. Trinity Coll. Sch. 1975–81; Mem., Univ. Rsch. Incent. Fund (URIF) Selection Ctte. 1989– ; Past Chrmn. Ont. Geosci. Rsch. Fund Review Ctte.; Past mem. Ont. Exploration Technol. Devel. Fund Review Ctte.; cons. UNDP mineral exploration devel. prog. India 1975–85; CIDA mineral exploration progs. Africa 1974–89; Asian Develop. Bank, Indonesia 1987–89; CIDA Thailand 1988–94; invited lectr. Rio de Janeiro 1973, Hyderabad 1977, 1979, 1981, Sydney, Australia 1972, Adelaide, Australia 1988; numerous lectureships Can., U.S.A., U.K. and Europe; Past Dir., Confed. Ch. & Business People; Dir. and Past Pres., St. Thomas' Houses; Past Ch. Warden St. Thomas' Ang. Ch. Toronto; Past Chrmn. Pub. & Social Responsibility Ctte. Ang. Diocese Toronto; holds one patent; author numerous papers, book chapters; Reporter 'Canadian Geophysical Bulletin' 1977–86; Fellow, Geol. Assn. Can.; Royal Society of Canada 1977; mem.,

Soc. Exploration Geophys. (Past Chrmn. Mining Ctte.); Candn. Inst. Mining & metall. (Past Chrmn. Geophys. Ctte. Geol. Div.); Candn. Geophys. Union; Candn. Soc. Exploration Geophys. (Past Pres.); Assn. prof. Engs. Prov. Ont. and B.C.; Dir., Prospectors & Devel. Assn. 1979–81; mem. and contrib. author, Assn. Geosci's. for Intnl. Devel.; Life mem., Oxford Union Soc.; recreations: sailing, tennis, cross-country skiing; swimming; Clubs: RCYC; Engineers; Home: #403, 360 Bloor St. E., Toronto, Ont. M4W 3M3; Office: 5th Flr., 204 Richmond St. W., Toronto, Ont. M5V 1V6; Farm: RR 4, Meaford, Ont. N0H 1Y0.

**PATKAU, John Robert,** B.A., B.E.S., M.Arch., M.A.I.B.C., O.A.A., F.R.A.I.C.; architect; b. Winnipeg, Man. 18 Aug. 1947; s. Abe John and Bertha (Klassen) P.; e. Univ. of Manitoba B.A. 1969, B.E.S. 1969, M.Arch. 1972; m. Patricia d. John and Aileen Gargett 10 Aug. 1974; FOUNDER, PAKTKAU ARCHITECTS 1978– ; general practise in architecture; Progressive Arch. Award for Galleria Condominium 1981, for Barnes House 1993; Canadian Architect Award of Excellence for Blue Quill School 1983, for Pyrch Residence 1984, for Research Office, Alberta Research Council 1984, for Appleton Residence 1986, for Kustin Residence 1987, for Seabird Island School 1989, Canadian Clay and Glass Gallery 1990, for Barnes House 1992; Canadian Wood Council for McGregor Residence 1984, for Seabird Island School; Governor General's Medal for Pyrch Residence 1986, for Seabird Island School 1992, for Appleton Residence 1990; Winning Submission, Canadian Clay and Glass Gallery Competition 1986; Lieutenant Governor's Medal for Seabird Island School 1992; Architectural Inst. of B.C. Honour Award for Pyrch Residence 1988; Governor General's Award for Porter/Vandenbosch Residence 1990; Home: 1875 28 St., W. Vancouver, B.C. V7V 4L9; Office: L110 – 560 Beatty St., Vancouver, B.C. V6B 2L3.

**PATKAU, Karen Anne,** B.F.A., M.V.A.; illustrator; graphic designer; b. Winnipeg, Man. 7 Dec. 1951; d. Abe John and Bertha Louise (Klassen) P.; e. Univ. of Man. B.F.A. 1975; Univ. of Alta. M.V.A. 1980; freelance illustrator and graphic designer since 1981; part-time Design Instr. Communications Dept. Centennial Coll. Applied Arts & Technol. 1985–90; sessional Lectr. in Art & Design Univ. of Alta. 1980–81 and in Visual Arts York Univ. 1981–82; recipient Can. Council Explorations Grant 1983; Ont. Arts Council Grants 1984, 1987, 1988, 1989; Ezra Jack Keats Medal UNICEF 1986; Internat. Graphics Inc. Bronze and Merit Awards 1986; various group exhns. art & graphic design; ilustrator children's books 'Don't Eat Spiders' 1985; 'One Watermelon Seed' 1986; 'Seal is Lost' 1988; co-author and illustrator 'Ringtail' 1987; author and illustrator 'In the Sea' 1990; mem. Candn. Assn. Photogs. & Illus. in Communication; Candn. Soc. Children's Authors, Illus. & Performers; recreations: scuba diving; Address: 203, 980 Broadview Ave., Toronto, Ont. M4K 3Y1.

**PATKAU, Patricia Frances,** B.I.D., M.Arch., M.A.I.B.C., F.R.A.I.C.; architect, university professor; b. Winnipeg, Man. 25 Feb. 1950; d. John Frederick and Aileen Constance (Emmett) Gargett; e. Univ. of Man. B.I.D. 1973; Yale Univ. M.Arch. 1978; m. John Robert s. Abe and Bertha Patkau 10 Aug. 1974; PRINCIPAL, PATKAU ARCHITECTS 1982– ; Asst. Prof., School of Architecture, Univ. of Calif. at Los Angeles 1988–90; Assoc. Prof., Sch. of Architecture, Univ. of B.C. 1991– ; Visiting Prof., Grad. Sch. of Design, Harvard Univ. spring 1993; Progressive Architecture Citation 1981; Canadian Architect Awards of Excellence for Built Work 1983, '84, '86, '87, '89, 90, 92; Canadian Wood Council First Award for McGregor Residence 1984, Honour Award 1992; Governor General's Medal for Pyrch Residence 1986; Winning Submission, Canadian Clay & Glass Gallery Competition 1986; Honour Award, Arch. Inst. of B.C. 1988; Governor General's Award for Porter/Vandenbosch Residence 1990; Governor General's Medal for Appleton Residence 1990, for Seabird Island School 1992; Lieutenant Governor's Medal for Seabird Island School 1992; Progressive Architecture Award for Barnes House 1993; Home: 1875 28th St., W. Vancouver, B.C. V7V 4L9; Office: L110 – 560 Beatty St., Vancouver, B.C. V6B 2L3.

**PATON, A. Mills;** executive; b. Fort William, Ont. 10 Sept. 1932; s. late James Martin and late Edythe L. P.; e. Ryerson Polytech. Inst. Sr. Engr. Tech. 1954; m. Catherine Anne d. the late Malcolm and Margaret Graham 7 May 1955; children: Graham M., Patricia A.; PRES., SEABELL INC. 1989– ; Past Chrmn. and Dir. Seabell Inc.; The Northern Eng. & Supply Co. Ltd. (Pres. 1965–89); Eng. Draughtsman 1954, Sheet Metal & Heating Estimator 1956, Mgr. Sheet Metal Div. 1959, Asst. Gen. Mgr. 1960; recreations: hockey, tennis; Home: 481 Brookmill Rd., Oakville, Ont. L6J 5K6; Office: 10 - 294 Walker Dr., Brampton, Ont. L6T 4Z2.

**PATON, William John Ross,** B.Sc., LL.D.; industrialist; b. Fort William, Ont. 17 July 1915; s. James Martin and Mary A. (Ross) P.; e. Central Sch. Coll. Inst., Fort William, Ont.; Business Coll., Ft. William, Ont.; Tri-State Coll., Angola, Ind., B.Sc. (Mech. Engn.) 1940 m. Margaret, d. Wilmington A. Cross, 1940; children: William, Mary, Anne, Susan; Chrmn. and Chief Extve. Offr., Northern Engineering and Supply Co. Ltd.; Life Gov., Montreal Gen. Hosp.; began with Northern Engineering & Supply Co. Ltd., Fort William, Ont., 1932–37; Canadian Car & Foundry Co. Ltd., Aircraft Div., Fort William, Ont., 1939–40; Dept. of Munitions & Supply, Ammunition Production Div., Toronto, Ont., 1940–41; The Weatherhead Co. of Can., St. Thomas, Ont., 1942–49; joined Robin Hood Flour Mills Limited 1949, became Vice-President; joined Atlantic Sugar Refineries Company Limited as Executive Vice-President and General Manager, 1957, President and Chief Executive Officer 1961–73; Chrmn., Jannock Ltd. 1973–75; Freemason; Protestant; Club: St. Andrews, Delray Beach, Fla.; Everglades, Palm Beach Fla.; Home: 114 Miles St., Thunder Bay, Ont. P7C 1J4.

**PATRICK, Arthur Raymond,** B.Com., C.G.A.; cosmetic company executive; b. Saint John, N.B. 22 June 1943; s. Raymond Redverse and Nora Maude (Stilwell) P.; e. Bedford (Qué.) High Sch. 1961; Sir George Williams Univ., B.Com. 1965, C.G.A. 1968; m. Margaret Anne d. George and Anne Benton 18 March 1967; children: Sherrie Dawn, David Raymond, Julie Ann, Scott George Gregory; PRESIDENT, THE AMERICAS MARY KAY COSMETICS, INC. 1993– ; joined Sun Life Assurance Co. of Canada 1964–70; Avon Products (Canada) Inc. 1970–80; Dir. of Operations, Mary Kay Cosmetics Ltd. 1980, Vice Pres. Operations 1983, Vice Pres. 1985, Pres. 1986–93; mem. Candn. Cosmetic, Toiletry & Fragrance Assn. (Dir. and Chrmn.); Mississauga Bd. Trade; Direct Sellers Assn.; Pres.' Assn.; Treas. Kirkland (Qué.) Hockey Assn. 1973–77; recreations: golf, skiing, water skiing, squash; Club: Empire; Home: 3704 Twin Lakes Way, Plano TX 75093, USA; Office: 8787 Stemmons Freeway, Dallas, TX 75247, USA.

**PATRIQUIN, Douglas,** B.A., M.A., Ph.D.; executive; b. Sherbrooke, Que. 4 Oct. 1946; s. Graham and Jessa P.; e. Queen's Univ. B.A. 1968; Univ. of Toronto M.A. 1969; London Sch. of Econ. Ph.D. 1979; Harvard Business School's Advanced Mngt. Prog. 1988; m. Norah d. Herbert and Ruth Hopps; children: Laura, Michael, Sarah; EXECUTIVE VICE-PRES. & CHIEF OPERATING OFFICER, CANADIAN COMMERCIAL CORP. 1993– and SPECIAL ADVISOR TO THE DEPUTY MINISTER, GOVERNMENT SERVICES CANADA; Asst. Sec. to the Treas. Bd. 1988–93; Fellow, C.D. Howe Inst. 1989; Sec. Gen. of Energy Options 1987–88; Gen. Dir. Energy, Mines & Resources Canada 1986; Asst. Dept. Min. Sask. Dept. of Energy & Mines 1982–86; Dep. Sec. Planning Bur. of the Extve. Council Govt. of Sask. 1979–82; Chief & Asst. Dir., Dept. of Econ. Devel. & Tourism, Govt. of N.W.T. 1974–79; Planning and Policy Officer, Candn. Internat. Devel. Agency Ottawa 1969–72; Home: 74 Gwynne Ave., Ottawa, Ont. K1Y 1X3; Office: 50 O'Connor St., Ottawa, Ont. K1A 0S6.

**PATRY, Marcel,** M.A., Ph.D., D.PH., o.m.i. (R.C.); educator; b. Beaumont, Qué. 31 Jan. 1923; s. Armand and Yvonne (Marcoux) P.; e. Univ. of Ottawa, B.A.-B.P.H. 1945, M.A.(PH) 1947, Ph.D. (PH) 1949, D.PH. 1955; Dir., Inst. of Social Communications, St. Paul's Univ., 1980–85; Prof. in Communication Studies, St. Paul's Univ., 1978–87; Pres. and Rector, St. Paul's Univ., 1968–77; Prof. of Philos., Univ. of Ottawa 1950–68; mem. Assn. Candn. Française pour l'avancement des sciences; Assn. Candn. de Philos.; Assn. Candn. de Communication; author of 'Delienatio Cursus Logicae' 1955; 'L'Object et les Limites de la Logique' 1955; 'Reflexions sur les lois de l'intelligence' 1965; also various briefs and articles in numerous learned and prof. journs.; recreations: canoeing, fishing; Home: 305 Nelson, Ottawa, Ont. K1N 7S5.

**PATTEE, R.P. (Val),** C.D., B.A., M.Sc., M.Gen.; public servant; b. Montreal, Que. 9 Dec. 1934; s. Richard Percival and Mary Elizabeth (Schnebly) P.; e. Lachute H.S. 1953; Sir George Williams Univ. B.A. 1967; Troy State Univ. M.Sc. 1979; m. Joan d. George and Margaret Ross 26 Oct. 1957; children: Richard Percival, Anthony Ross; PUBLIC SERVANT, PROV. OF B.C.; career officer in Canadian Armed Forces (fighter pilot, chief of air force training, etc.); in later years Chief of Intelligence for NATO's Allied Command (Europe) working with a dozen nations and Chief of Intelligence & Security in Canada; on retirement switched to present post, Emergency Health Care, Prov. of B.C.; recreations: skiing; clubs: Union; Home: 2920 Mt. Baker View, Victoria, B.C. V8N 1Z5; Office: Victoria, B.C. V8V 1X4.

**PATTEN, Richard Andrew,** B.A.; former politician; b. Montreal, Que. 13 May 1942; s. William and Claire (Morrissette) P.; e. Sir George Williams Univ. B.A. 1966; m. Penelope d. Irwin and Emma Flemming 2 July 1966; children: Timothy, Chantelle; PRES. & C.E.O., CHILDREN'S HOSP. OF EASTERN ONT. FOUND. 1991– ; Community Dir., Northmount YMCA 1966–68, Extve. Dir. 1968–69; Trainer-Consultant, Nat. Counc. of YMCAs of Guyana 1969–71; Dir., Internat. Progs., Metrop. YMCA, Montreal 1971–76; Extve. Dir., Downtown YMCA, Montreal 1976–79; Dir., Govt. Relations, Nat. Counc. of YMCAs 1981–87; el. to Ont. Leg. for Ottawa Centre 1987; Min. of Govt. Services, Prov. of Ont. 1987–89; Min. of Correctional Services, Prov. of Ont. 1989–90; former mem. NGO Adv. Ctte., World Bank; Pres., Candn. Counc. for Internat. Cooperation 1984–86; Pres., Nat. Adv. Counc. on Urea Formaldehyde Foam Insulation; Unitarian; Liberal; Bd. mem., Ottawa YM-YWCA; Ottawa-Carleton Bd. of Trade; U.N. Assn. in Can.; Pres., Candn. Tulip Festival 1993–94; Bd. Mem., UNIFEM National Bd. 1993–94; recreations: painting, wind surfing, skiing; Office: 415 Smyth Rd., Ottawa, Ont. K1H 8M8.

**PATTERSON, Clyde Rodier,** B.A., M.Div.; b. Portage la Prairie, Man., 14 June 1918; s. the late Margaret S. (Rodier) and the late Walter P.; e. Calgary Pub. Schs.; Univ. of Alta., B.A. 1940, High Sch. Teaching Cert. 1941; Laval Univ., Bicultural-Bilingual Devel. Program, 1967; Cert. in Visual Arts, Ottawa Univ. 1974; Queen's Theological College M.Div. 1987; m. Frances Lillian, d. (late) Samuel Hunter Adams, Q.C., Ganges, B.C., 25 Dec. 1941; children: Sydney Margaret, Douglas Ross; PARISH PRIEST, ST. JOHN THE EVANGELIST CHURCH (ANGLICAN), WHONNOCK, B.C.; High Sch. Vice-Princ. and Princ., 1940–42; Occupational Counsellor, Dept. of Veterans Affairs, 1945–46; Regional Dir., Civil Service Comn. of Can. (Edmonton), 1946–52; Asst. Dir., Personnel Selection, Ottawa, 1952–58, Dir., 1958–62, Dir., Operations 1962–65; Nat. Coordinator, Civil Emergency Measures 1965–76; Volunteer Consultant (Performance Measurement) with Candn. Extve. Svce. Overseas to Treasury of Malaysia 1978–79; Reg'd. Consultant, E.A.C. Amy & Sons, Ottawa 1979–83; Rector, Anglican Parish of Lansdowne Rear; co-author (with wife): 'Harvests Past' 1989; served with R.C.A.C. in Can. and U.K.; retired as Lieut. 1944; Inst. Civil Defence (Fellow honoris causa); Anglican; recreations: photography, local history, gardening, painting, primitive hand tools; writing; Home: 33154 Whidden Ave., Mission, B.C. V2V 2T2.

**PATTERSON, The Hon. Dennis Glen,** B.A., LL.B.; former politician; lawyer; b. Vancouver, B.C. 30 Dec. 1948; e. Univ. of Alta., B.A. 1969 (with distinction); Dalhousie Univ., LL.B. 1972 (Sir. James Dunn Scholar 1969–71); co-vivant Marie Uviluq; children: Bruce Qasigiaq, George Qupaaq, Jessica Tujaqtugaq, Alexander Natsiq; Min. of Health 1992 and Min. of Social Services, Govt. of N.W.T. 1992; Min. Resp. for Workers' Compensation 1991; called to Bar of N.S. 1972, Bar. of B.C. 1974; first Dir., Maliiganik Tukisiinakvik Soc. Iqaluit 1975–81; el. M.L.A. for Iqaluit, N.W.T. 1979–93; Min. of Edn. 1981–87; Assoc. Min., then Min. of Aboriginal Rts. & Constitutional Devel. 1981–87; Min. Resp. for Dept. of Info. 1983; Min. Resp. for Status of Women 1985; Govt. Leader, N.W.T. 1987–92; Min. of Justice 1991–92; Min. of Municipal Affairs 1991–92; Min. of Safety and Public Service 1991–92; recreations: hunting, playing piano; Home: Box 262, Iqaluit, N.W.T. X0A 0H0.

**PATTERSON, Freeman Wilford,** C.M., B.A., M.Div., D.Litt., D.C.L., R.C.A.; photographer; writer; educator; b. Long Reach, N.B. 25 Sept. 1937; s. G. Gordon and Ethel Winifred (Crawford) P.; e. Greys Mills (N.B.) Sch. 1944; Long Reach (N.B.) Sch. 1951; Macdonald Consolidated Sch. Kingston, N.B. grad. 1955; Acadia Univ. B.A. 1959; Union Theol. Semy. New York M.Div. 1962; Univ. of N.B. D.Litt. 1980; Acadia Univ. D.C.L. 1989; Dean of Religious Educ. Albert Coll. Edmonton 1962–65; Photographer Stills Div. Berkeley Studios, Un. Ch. of Can. Toronto 1965–66; freelance photographer 1966– ; Co-Partner Summer Photography Sch., N.B. 1973– ; seminar lectr. across Can., USA and abroad 1972– ; judge nat. and internat. salons; photographs incl. many books incl. 'Canada, A Year of the Land'; 'Canada'; 'Between Friends - Entre Amis' and ' Day in the Life of Canada'; 'The Last Wilderness: Images of the Canadian Wild'; rep. in over 1000 competitive internat. exhns.; colour prints many exhns. incl. Metrop. Museum New York; Nat. Film Bd.'s Can., A Yr. of the

Land, Can.'s Colour Photographers, The Magic World of Childhood, Freeman Patterson Monograph, One Planet: One Man (1993); recipient Nat. Film Bd. Can. Gold Medal 1967; author: 'Photography For the Joy of It' 1977; 'Photography And The Art Of Seeing' 1979; 'Photography of Natural Things' 1982; 'Namaqualand, Garden of the Gods' 1984; 'Portraits of Earth' 1987; photographic author 'In A Canadian Garden' 1989; photographic editor, co-author 'The Last Wilderness: Images of the Canadian Wild' 1990; various articles; Ed. 'Foto Flash' 1964–68; 'Camera Canada' 1968–78; Vice Pres. and Dir., Masterfile 1984–92; Trustee, Nature Conservancy of Canada; Trustee, N.B. School District #19 (1973–89); Hon. EFIAP, Fed. Internationale de l'Art Photographique, Berne; Fellow, Photographic Soc. Am.; Hon. Fellow, Photographic Soc. S. Africa; Hon. Life mem. Toronto Guild for Colour Photography (Dir., Vice Pres., Pres.); Hon. Life Mem. Nat. Assn. Photographic Art (Pres.); N.B. Fed. Naturalists; Candn. Nature Fed. (Comte.); Audubon Soc.; Elected, 1975, Royal Candn. Academy of Art; Gold Medal from Nat. Assn. for Photographic Art 1985; Member, Order of Canada 1985; Photographic Society of Am. Progress Medal (highest award) 1990; Address: Shampers Bluff, Clifton Royal, N.B. E0G 1N0.

**PATTERSON, Jeff W.,** B.A., M.B.A., C.A.; general management executive; b. Orangeville, Ont. 15 Feb. 1952; s. W. Arnold and Viola C. (Pawley) P.; e. Univ. of Western Ont. B.A. 1974; Univ. of Toronto M.B.A. 1990; m. Sandra d. Allen and Donna McKee 21 March 1987; one s.: Taylor Jeffrey Arnold; PRESIDENT, LIVINGSTON INTERNATIONAL INC. 1991– ; Ernst & Young, C.A. 1978; Dir., Canada-U.S. Business Assn. (CUSBA); Mem., Candn. Soc. of Customs Brokers (Chair, Pol. Action Ctte.); Candn. & Ont. Insts. of C.A.s; Internat. Soc. of Strategic Management and Planning; Nat. Customs Brokers & Forwarders Assn. of Am.; Home: R.R. 1, Palgrave, Ont. L0N 1P0; Office: 405 The West Mall, Ste. 400, Toronto, Ont. M9C 5K7.

**PATTERSON, John Breden,** B.A., F.S.A., F.C.I.A.; actuary; b. Windsor, Ont. 9 Sept. 1927; e. Univ. of Toronto B.A. 1949; m. Beryl Norma 1951; children: Kimberly, Chris; PRESIDENT, ACTUARIAL CONSULTANTS OF CANADA LTD.; Asst. Actuary Crown Life Insurance Co. 1949–57; Vice Pres. and Actuary Gerling Global Life Insurance Co. 1957–65; Freemason; Club: Donalda; Home: 54 Beveridge Dr., Don Mills, Ont. M3A 1P3; Office: (P.O. Box 38) 1505, 401 Bay St., Toronto, Ont. M5H 2Y4.

**PATTERSON, Nicholas John,** B.A.; business executive; b. Montreal, Que. 24 Sept. 1940; s. Elmer Goodwin and Helen Catherine (Quain) P.; e. Loyola College; McGill Univ. B.A. 1962; EXECUTIVE DIRECTOR, CANADIAN DEVELOPMENT INSTITUTE 1978– ; Bank of Canada 1962–64; Mercantile Bank & First Nat. City Bank (N.Y.) 1964–66; Toronto Dominion Bank 1966–68; Mills Spence (now Burns Fry) 1968–70; investment consultant (Toronto) 1970–73; Export Devel. Corp. 1973–78; Dir., Larrimac Golf Club 1978–80; author: 'Rent Control in Ontario' and several pub. research papers; clubs: Alpha Delta Phi, Laurentian, Cascades Squash (Founding Dir. 1978); Home: Riverside Dr., Wakefield Village, Que.; Office: Box 66, Stn. B, Ottawa, Ont. K1P 6C3.

**PATTERSON, Peter,** B.Sc., F.S.A.; insurance executive; b. 12 May 1945; e. Univ. of Toronto B.Sc. 1968; post-grad. studies 1969; m. Barbara Ethel 12 July 1969; children: Paul, Andrew; Pres., Chief Extve. Offr. & Dir., The Mercantile & Gen. Reinsur. Co. of America; The Mercantile & Gen. Life Reassur. Co. of America; The Mercantile & Gen. Life Reassur. Co. of Can.; The Mercantile & Gen. Reinsur. Co. of Can.; The Mercantile & Gen. Reinsur. Co. plc (N.A. Life Branch); Home: 7 Ivy Lea Crescent, Toronto, Ont. M8Y 2R3; Office: Ste. 3000, 161 Bay St., BCE Place, Canada Trust Tower, Toronto, Ont. M5J 2T6.

**PATTILLO, James Alexander,** H.B.A.; business executive; b. Toronto, Ont. 13 Aug. 1949; s. Arthur Sydney (DST) and Doris Armitage (Mair) P.; e. Upper Canada Coll. 1969; Univ. of Western Ont. H.B.A. 1973; m. Susan Fleming 3 Oct. 1980; children: Christopher B. Kent, Andrea Jane, Stuart Arthur, Duncan Andrew, Alexander Fleming; PRES., CHIEF EXTVE. OFFR. & DIR., XL FOODS LTD. (CALGARY); Dir., Okanagan Skeena Holdings; Money Market Trader & Corp. Finance Offr., A.E. Ames & Co. 1973–81 (Vanc. 1975, N.Y. 1978, Montreal 1980, Toronto); Vice-Pres., Corp. & Finance, Dominion Securities 1981–83; Vice-Pres., Wood Gundy Ltd. 1983–85; Pres., Pattillo Corp. & Capital Management (Vanc.) 1985– ; clubs: Toronto, Toronto Golf, Vancouver Lawn & Tennis, Glencoe Cal-

gary, North Hatley Boat; Home: 2905 Wolfe St. S.W., Calgary, Alta. T2T 3S1; Office: 250, 1209 – 59th St. S.E., Calgary, Alta. T2H 2P6.

**PATTISON, James A.;** executive; b. Sask. 1 Oct. 1928; s. Chandos P.; e. John Oliver High Sch., Vancouver; Univ. of B.C.; m. Mary Ella, d. George Hudson, Moose Jaw, Sask. 30 June 1951; children: James Allen Jr., Mary Ann, Cynthia; CHAIRMAN, PRES. AND CHIEF EXTVE., THE JIM PATTISON GROUP; Great Pacific Industries Ltd.; estbd. own automobile dealership 1961 and acquired radio stns. in Vancouver and Winnipeg in addition to Muzak franchise for B.C.; purchased control of Neon Products Ltd. 1967; Dir., Innopac Inc.; Paramount Communications; Toronto-Dominion Bank; CP Ltd.; mem. General Motors Pres.'s Adv. Council, 1965–66; Alpha Tau Omega; Office: 1055 W. Hastings St., Vancouver, B.C. V6E 2H2.

**PATTISON, John Charles,** B.A., M.A., Ph.D.; banker; b. Ottawa, Ont. 25 Oct. 1945; s. William Alan and Catherine Ewing (McComb) P.; e. Huron Coll. B.A. 1966; Univ. of West. Ont. M.A. 1968; London Sch. of Econ. Ph.D. 1972; m. Gwen Griffith d. Pauline and Alec Patterson 18 Apr. 1970; children: Jennifer Nicole, Derek Stewart; SR. VICE-PRES., CANDN. IMPERIAL BANK OF COMMERCE 1988– ; Admin., OECD, Paris, France 1972–74; Sr. Rsch. Offr., Ont. Econ. Counc. 1974–77; Asst. Prof., Sch. of Bus. Admin., Univ. of West. Ont. 1977–80; Vice-Pres., Finan., Candn. Imperial Bank of Comm. 1980–83; Mng. Dir., CIBC Limited, London England 1983–86; Huron Coll. Gold Medal 1966; mem., Ch. of St. Leonard's; Kappa Alpha Soc.; author of num. books & articles; recreations: collecting old maps, prints; Club: Ontario; Office: Head Office, Commerce Court, Toronto, Ont. M5L 1A2.

**PATTISON, William Brien,** B.Sc., M.B.A.; executive; b. Vancouver, B.C. 28 Apl. 1932; s. John William and Kathryn (Tonkin) P.; e. Vancouver Coll.; Cornell Univ. B.Sc. 1954; Harvard Univ. M.B.A. 1958; m. Marilyn Smith; children: Brien, Sarah; PRESIDENT, PATTISON INFORMATION INC. and FOUNDER, DELTA HOTELS LTD. (est. 1962), operation and management of hotels; Dir., Canlan Investments Ltd.; Mem. Bd. Govs., Univ. of Guelph, Ont.; Immed. Past Chrmn., Bd. Govs., Ryerson Polytech. Inst., Toronto, Ont.; Chrmn. Tourism Sector, Canada Japan Businessmen's Cooperation Ctte.; Past Chrmn., Tourism Industry Assn. of Canada (TIAC); Dir., British Columbia Paraplegic Foundation; Gov., Washington Athletic Club, Seattle; Aldermanic Candidate, City of Vancouver 1972; named 'Marketing Extve. of the Year' by Sales and Marketing Extves., Vancouver 1975; Alpha Tau Omega; Anglican; recreations: golf, tennis, fishing, gardening; Clubs: Pennask Lake Fishing and Game (Vancouver); Shaunessey Golf & Country (Vancouver); The Vancouver Club; Granite (Toronto); Loxahatchee Club (Jupiter, Fla.); Office: 83 Montclair Ave., Toronto, Ont. M5P 1P5.

**PATTON, Harold P.;** artist; art consultant; restorer; b. Calgary, Alta. 9 Nov. 1929; s. William Lawrence and Ida Wilhelmena (Mackie) P.; e. Vancouver Sch. of Art, 5 yrs.; King Edward H.S.; Banff Sch. of Fine Arts 1946–49; m. Eleanor I. d. Melville and Mary Robertson Ross Cheape Smith (Treacher) 25 Sept. 1953; children: Fiona Mary Margaret, Isabelle Carol Ann(e); Asst. Dir., Allied Arts Ctr. then Dir. of Fine Arts, Sears Vincent Price Fine Arts Gall. 1966–69; Dir., London Arts 1971–72; Co-creator (with Eleanor Patton), fine arts collection, K Mart Internat. 1972–73; plus several colls. incl. Ford Motor, IBM, City Nat. Bank, Detroit Nat. Bank collections; fine artist (3 murals); theatre designer, several Candn. Cos.; completed three major murals in oil for Canneto Soc.; apptd. Restorer and Consultant in Residence to Mt. Sinai Hosp.; Arts & Entertainment Ed., Wright Media Publications; completing for publication 1992 'Conversations With Artists'; Cons., Art Gall. of Victoria, Victoria, P.C.; Johnson Office Furniture, Toronto; K Mart Corp. World H.Q.; Tall Ships, Toronto; W.C. Woolley; Woolley, Dale & Dingwall; Chris Yaneff Internat.; A.G.O.; McDowell Gall.; McMaster Univ.; Haverford Coll.; Artist in residence, Wooley, Dale & Dingwall; Creator, Arts Mngt. & Self Mngt. courses Banff; Candn. Mozart Soc.; Hon. Citizen (with Mrs. Patton), Davenport & Quad cities for creating Gall. of Primitive Art; Metro. Mags. Assn. of Am. Award for articles in music 1969–70; Lectr., Univ. of Windsor, Univ. of Toronto, York Univ., Penn. State Univ., Haverford Coll., & seminars; mem., Alta. Soc. of Artists; Internat. Speakers & Platform Assn. (elected to Pres. Counc. of the Arts 1970–75); Canneto Soc., Downsview; author: 'Catalogue raisonné of Nicholas Hornyansky' forthcoming; Appt'd. Restorer & Conservetor in Res.; Music Ed., 'Chicago Land Magazine' 1966–70, 'Toronto Arts' 1980–84; Music Critic, 'Bir-

mingham Eccentric' 1970–74; Ed., 'People on the Arts' 1985–87; contbr. to several mags.; Fellow, Cambridge Univ., London, England; recreations: collecting books, fine art, rare classical recordings.

**PATY, Donald Winston,** M.D., F.R.C.P.(C); neurologist; educator; b. Peking, China 25 Sept. 1936; s. Robert Morris and Katherine (Behenna) P.; e. Emory Univ. Atlanta, Ga. B.A. 1958, M.D. 1962; m. Jo Anne d. Joe and Grace Haymore 28 Dec. 1958; children: Morris Britten, Beverley Behenna, Breay Winston, Donald Blake; PROF. AND HEAD OF NEUROLOGY, UNIV. OF B.C. 1980– ; Intern., Duke Univ. Med. Center 1962–63; U.S. Pub. Health Service, Peace Corps Kuching, Malaysia 1963–65; Med. Resident, Emory Univ., Grady Hosp. Atlanta 1965–67, Resident in Neurol. 1967–70; Research Fellow, MRC Demyelinating Disease Unit, Newcastle-Upon-Tyne, Eng., Immunology of Multiple Sclerosis; Asst. Prof., Assoc. Prof., Prof. of Clin. Neurol. Sciences Univ. of W. Ont. 1972–80; recipient numerous research grants Med. Research Council Can., Multiple Sclerosis Soc. Can. and Vancouver foundations; Dir. London (Ont.) Symphony Orchestra 1978–80; Advisor to Multiple Sclerosis Soc. Can. London, Ont. 1972–80; Bd. of Dir. MS Soc.; B.C. Div. Vancouver 1980–86; author, co-author and ed. numerous publs. Multiple Sclerosis; mem. Am. Acad. Neurol.; Am. Neurol. Assn.; Candn. Neurol. Soc. (Pres. 1989–90); Alpha Omega Alpha; N. Pacific Soc. Neurol. & Psychiatry; Med. Adv. Bd., MS Society of Canada, Chrmn. Grants Review Ctte. (1986–90) and Internat. Fed. Multiple Sclerosis Soc's; Extve. Ctte., Medical Adv. Bd., Chrmn. of the Medical Mngmt. Ctte.; mem. of several standing committees of the Nat. M.S. Society, U.S.A.; Neuroimmunol. Research Group World Fed. Neurol.; Multiple Sclerosis Res. Group World Fed. Neurol.; Sect. Gen., World Congress of Neurology 1993, Vancouver; recreation: music; Home: 3657 West 24th Ave., Vancouver, B.C. V6S 1L7; Office: Vancouver General Hospital, 222, 2775 Heather St., Vancouver, B.C. V5Z 3J5.

**PAUK, Alexander Peter,** B.Mus., B.Ed.; composer; conductor; b. Toronto, Ont. 4 Oct. 1945; e. OAC student conductors' workshop under Karel Ančerl, Ernesto Barbini, Victor Felbrill, and Boyd Neel 1970–72; Toho Gakuen School of Music Tokyo 1972–73; m. Alexina Diane d. Alexander and Pansy Louie; children: Jasmine Sonia Ariana Alix and Jade Desirée; FOUNDING DIR. & CONDUCTOR, ESPRIT ORCH. 1983– ; Founder, Array West 1973–74; Founder, Music Dir. & Conductor, Days Months and Years to Come 1974–79; Teacher, Courtenay Youth Music Centre 1973–75; Vancouver Community College 1974–78; Conductor, Vancouver Youth Orch. 1974–78; Co-Chair, ISCM World Music Days (Toronto & Montreal) 1984; Music Dir. & Conductor, Satori Festival 1986; has conducted CBC Vancouver Orch., Hamilton Philharmonic, Vancouver Symphony Orch., Vancouver New Music Soc. & NMC; has written over 30 concert works, most of them on commission, in addition to film & TV scores; commissions incl. James Campbell, the CBC, Courtenay Youth Music Centre, Esprit Orch., Joseph Macerollo, NYO, Quebec SO, Vancouver New Music Soc., York Winds; Vancouver's Musician of the Year 1975; Canada Council grant to study in Europe 1978–79; Mem., Candn. League of Composers; Assoc. Mem., Candn. Music Centre; subject of several articles; Home: 323 Synnyside Ave., Toronto, Ont. M6R 2R5.

**PAUL, Derek Alexander Lever,** M.A., Ph.D.; educator; b. Brussels, Belgium 1 Oct. 1929; s. Russell and Kathleen Mary Garston (Wrathall) P.; e. Heronwater Sch. 1943; Marlborough Coll. 1947; Clare Coll. (Open Scholarship) Cambridge, B.A. 1950, M.A. 1954; Queen's Univ., Ph.D. 1958; m.(1) Normelia d. Norman and Emelia Falls; m.(2) Hanna d. Arthur and Georgina Little; children: Antonia, Julian, Lara, John Mark; PROF. OF PHYSICS, UNIV. OF TORONTO 1975– ; joined British United Shoe Machinery Co. UK 1950–53; Lectr. Assoc. Prof. Royal Mil. Coll. Kingston 1953–63; Assoc. Prof. present Univ. 1964; Visiting Prof. Washington Univ. St. Louis, Mo. 1959–60; Univ. of Kaiserslautern 1974; Univ. Catholique de Louvain 1990–91; Cons. House of Markham; Dir. Sci. for Peace 1981–89, Publications Dir. 1988–90; participant internat. Pugwash Movement; author or co-author over 50 papers physics, internat. security; co-ed. 'Defending Europe, Options for Security' 1986; editor: 'Canadian Papers in Peace Studies' 1988–90; Assoc. Inst. Elect. & Electronic Engs.; mem. Candn. Assn. Physicists; Am. Phys. Soc.; UN Assn.; Project Ploughshares; Group of 78; Internat. Peace Rsch. Assn.; recreations: music, writing, postal history; Clubs: Toronto Chamber Soc.; BNAPS; Home: 392½ Markham St., Toronto, Ont. M6G 2K9; Office: Toronto, Ont. M5S 1A7.

**PAUL, Norman P.,** B.S.P.; business executive; b. Winnipeg, Man. 17 March 1944; s. Louis and Sophie P.; e. Univ. of B.C., B.S.P.; m. Marsha d. I. Aaron 16 Aug. 1967; children: Tova, Neri; Chrmn. & Owner, Harbourfront Antique Mkt.; Acura Sherway; Sherway Nissan; Pres. & Owner, Perry Trading; former Pres., Chief Extve. Offr. & Partner, Collegiate Arlington; Robinson-Ogilvy; Pres. (owner), Meditrust Pharmacy Inc.; recreations: jogging, music, 'eating out'; Home: 109 Glenayr, Toronto, Ont. M5P 3C1.

**PAUL, Hon. Réjean F.,** Q.C., B.A., LL.L.; juge; né Chicoutimi, Qué. 27 avril 1943; f. Adrien Robert Paul et Marie-Anna (L'Ecuyer) P.; é. Coll. St-Alexandre Laval B.A. 1963; Univ. d'Ottawa LL.L. 1966; ép. Nicole f. Théophile et Cécile Houle 16 juillet 1966; enfants: Manon, Martin; JUDGE, SUPERIOR COURT OF QUEBEC 1983– ; DEPY. JUDGE, SUPREME COURT OF THE NORTHWEST TERRITORIES 1983– ; apptd. Chrmn., Cree-Naskapi Federal Comn. 6 Feb. 1986; Admis au Barreau 1967; Q.C. (Fédéral) 1979; Avocat, Ministère Fédéral de la Justice (Montréal) 1967–75, Directeur du contentieux criminel 1972–75; Procureur-Chef Comm. d'Enquête sur le Crime Organisé (Qué.) 1975–76; Directeur pour le Qué. Ministère Fédéral de la Justice 1976–81; Commissaire Comm. de Réforme du Droit du Canada 1981–82; Vice Pres., Comm. de Reforme du Droit du Canada 1982–83; Chargé de cours Procédure Criminelle et Preuve 3ème année de Droit Ottawa Univ. 1972–77; Responsable du Droit Pénal, Ecole de Formation Professionnelle du Barreau du Qué. (4ème année de Droit) 1974–80; récréations: chasse, pêche, golf; Club: Kanawaki Golf; Gatineau Rod & Gun; Résidence: 16 Place Berlioz, Candiac, Que. J5R 3Z4; Bureau: boul. 1111 Jacques Cartier est, Bur. R-162, Longueuil, Que. J4M 2J6.

**PAVEY, Michael A.,** B.A.Sc., M.B.A.; electric utility executive; b. Montreal, Que. 6 May 1947; s. Arnold W. and Mary E. (Farnum) P.; e. Univ. of Waterloo B.A.Sc. 1971; McGill Univ. M.B.A. 1973; m. Mary Linda McCaskill 26 June 1971; children: Shannon, Matthew, Mark, Michael Ian; SENIOR VICE-PRESIDENT AND CHIEF FINANCIAL OFFR., TRANSALTA CORPORATION 1993– ; Owner, M.A. Pavey Consulting Services (corp. regulatory & finan. consulting serv. to regulated utility sector) 1986–91; various positions ending as Vice-Pres., Utility Management, Monenco Consulting Serv. 1973–86; Vice-Pres., Corp. Planning, Nfld. Light & Power Co. Limited 1982–86; Vice-Pres., Corp. Planning & Dir., Maritime Electric Co. Limited 1982–91; Dir., Ottawa Valley Power Co. 1982–83; Vice-Pres., Regulatory Services, TransAlta Utilities 1991–93; Home: 1228 Kerwood Cres. S.W., Calgary, Alta. T2V 2N6; Office: Box 1900, 110 – 12 Avenue S.W., Calgary, Alta. T2P 2M1.

**PAVILANIS, Alan Vytautas,** A.B., M.D., C.M., C.C.F.P., F.C.F.P.; physician; b. Neuilly-Sur-Seine, France 23 June 1948; s. Vytautas and Irene (Stencelis) P.; e. Lower Canada Coll., McGill, sr. matric. 1966; Princeton, Univ., A.B. (cum laude) 1969; McGill Univ., M.D. 1973; m. Rasa Vaidila 1991; ACADEMIC STAFF, HÔPITAL NOTRE DAME 1990– ; Intern, Royal Columbian Hosp. 1974; cert, C.F.P.C. 1979, Fellow 1992; family med. prac., B.C. 1974–75; Que. 1975–82; Dir., Adolescent & Youth Med. Serv., Montreal Children's Hosp. 1982–89; Chief, Dept. of Gen. Med., Maisonneuve-Rosemont Hosp. 1989–90; Clin. Rsch., U.K. 1979; Mem., Health & Safety At Work Prog. 1980–81; Nat. Cert. Exam. Ctte., C.F.P.C. 1980–83; Bd. of Dir., Quebec Chapter, C.F.P.C. 1985– (Treas. 1988–89; Pres. elect. 1989–90; Pres. 1990–91; Chrmn. 1991–92); Bd. of Dir., C.F.P.C. 1985–92; Ed. Bd., Can. Fam. Phys. 1986–90; Mem., Public Communications Ctte., CFPC 1986– (Chrmn. 1989– ); Chrmn., Internat. Aid Ctte., Quebec Chapter, CFPC; Teaching staff, Sir Mortimer Davis Jewish Gen. Hosp. 1984– ; Part-time Lectr., McGill Univ. 1978–82; Charge de Clin., Univ. of Montreal 1981–82; Asst. Prof., McGill Univ. 1982– ; Asst. Prof., Univ. of Montreal 1989– ; Bd. of Dir., Dist. of Bedford Assn. for Mentally Retarded 1979–85; Bd. of Dir., Shawbridge Youth Ctrs. 1984–90; Gov., Grad. Soc., McGill Univ. 1983–85; Gov., McGill Soc., Montreal 1986–89; Bd. of Dirs., CLSC J-OCTAVE ROUSSIN 1989–92; Farmer; Mem., Union des Prod. Agric. du Que. 1977– ; Valedictorian, McGill Univ. Med. Class 1973; France-Que. Exchange Scholarship 1971; Univ. of Vilnius (Lithuania) Clin. Scholarship 1972; Mem., Fraternitas Lithuanica; Fedn. of Gen. Practitioners of Que.; Coll. of Family Physicians of Can.; Soc. for Adolescent Med. (Pres., Eastern Candn. Chapter); Candn. Soc. of Bioethics; Internat. Assoc. for Adolescent Health; Alumni Schs. Ctte. of Montreal for Princeton Univ.; Lithuanian Am. Med. Assn.; Amnesty Internat.; Candn. Wildlife Assn.; Health Profls. for Soc. Resp.; Candn Inst. of Internat. Affairs; Townshippers; The Montreal Museum of Fine Arts; The Visual Arts Centre; Heritage Montreal; Bd. Chrmn., Pigeon Park Project; recreations: travel, skiing, squash, sailing, windsurfing, hiking, bicycling, running; Club: Brome Lake Boating; Home: 'Raudonė' Farm, R.R. #4, Sutton W., Que. J0E 2K0; Office: Notre Dame Hospital, 2025 Plessis St., Montreal, Que. H2L 2Y4.

**PAVILANIS, Vytautas,** M.D., F.R.C.P.(c); b. Kaunas, Lithuania 7 June 1920; s. Kazys and Antonina (Eimontas) P.; e. Univ. of Kaunas M.D. 1942; Institut Pasteur, Paris Dipl. in Microbiol. 1947; Dipl. in Serology & Hematol. 1948; m. Irene, Ph.D. d. late Col. Bruno Stencelis 8 March 1947; children: Alain, Christine, Marina Branigan, Ingrid; PROF. EMERITUS, INSTITUT ARMAND-FRAPPIER 1991– ; Assoc. Prof. Univ. de Montréal since 1956, Asst. Prof. 1948–56; Prof. Univ. du Qué. since 1974; Asst. Prof. of Pathol. Univ. of Kaunas 1942–44; Resident Physician in Siegbourg, Germany 1944–45; Asst. Institut Pasteur, Paris 1945–48; Head of Virus Dept. Institut Armand-Frappier 1948–75, Scient. Dir. 1970–75, Research Coordinator 1975–78, Teaching Coordinator 1977; Asst. Dir., Institut Armand-Frappier 1978–83, Consultant 1984– ; Elected Fellow of the Royal Soc. of Canada 1973; recipient Queen's Jubilee Medal 1977; Candn. Soc. of Microbiology award 1984; Hon. doctorate, Inst. Armand Frappier, Univ. of Quebec 1988; co-author 'Manuel de techniques virologiques' 1978; over 137 publs. virol. mem. Coll. of Phys.; Candn. Soc. Microbiol. (2nd Vice Pres. 1966); Candn. Pub. Health Assn. (Chrmn. Lab. Sec. 1969); Virology Club Montreal (Pres. 1969); Candn. Med. Assn.; Candn. Assn. Med. Microbiol.; R. Catholic; recreations: skiing, riding; Home: 4742 The Boulevard, Westmount, Que. H3Y 1V3; Office: (P.O. Box 100) Laval-des-Rapides, Que. H7N 4Z3.

**PAVLICH, Dennis John,** B.A., LL.B., LL.M.; university professor of law; b. Bulawayo, Zimbabwe 24 Dec. 1945; s. Charles Frank and Thelma Silvia (Bushney) P.; e. St. George's College, Harare, Zimbabwe 1963; Witwatersrand Univ. B.A. 1967, LL.B. 1969; Yale Univ. LL.M. 1975; m. Suzanne d. Reuben and Gladys Kahanovitz 13 April 1972; children: Alexis, Nicholas, Jonathan; PROFESSOR, FACULTY OF LAW, UNIV. OF BRITISH COLUMBIA 1984– ; Clerk, Werksmans (Johannesburg); Attorney, Supreme Court of S. Africa 1972; Lecturer, Law Faculty, Univ. of the Witwatersrand 1973–74; Asst. Prof., Univ. of B.C. 1975; Assoc. Prof. 1978; Bd. of Gov., Univ. of B.C.; Bd. of Dir., U.B.C. Real Estate Corp.; American Graduate Scholar 1974; Rotary Scholar 1975; Pres., Condominium Home Owners Assn. 1978; Pres., The Vancouver Inst. 1990– ; author: 'Condominium Law in British Columbia' 1984; co-editor: 'CCH Real Estate Law Guide'; recreations: music, travel; clubs: Faculty; Home: 4492 Crown St., Vancouver, B.C. V6S 2K5; Office: 1822 East Mall, Vancouver, B.C. V6T 1Z1

**PAVLIN, Charles Joseph,** M.D., F.R.C.S.(C); physician; b. Dauphin, Man. 4 Feb. 1944; s. Charles and Emilie (Sahulka) P.; e. Univ. of Manitoba M.D. 1967; Univ. of Toronto F.R.C.S.(C) 1974; m. Margaret d. Rose and Patrick Tighe 22 Dec. 1973; children: Michael, Jessica; PRIVATE PRACTICE IN OPHTHALMOLOGY, TORONTO 1975– ; Captain, Candn. Air Force 1969–71; Cert. Aviation Med., Inst. of Aviation Med., Toronto 1969; Base Surgeon CFB Moosejaw 1969–70; Internal Med. Residency, Nat. Defence Med. Ctr., Ottawa 1970–71; Ophthal. Residency, Toronto 1971–74; Ultrasound Studies, Cornell Univ., N.Y. 1981; estab. ultrasound facilities at Princess Margaret Hosp. & Toronto Gen. Hosp. 1982; Lectr., Univ. of Toronto 1983; Asst. Prof. 1987; Consultant, Princess Margaret Hosp. 1983– (spec. interest in ultrasound applied to ocular tumor imaging); Cert. Ultrasonographer for Collaborative Ocular Melanoma Study; devel. ultrasonic method for determining radioactive plaque position in treating ocular melanomas; major contbn. to opthth. field: Co-developer, Ultrasound Biomicroscope – the first method of producing in-depth images of the living eye at microscopic resolution; on-going rsch. into clin. use of ultrasound biomicroscopy; author of num. papers; speaker at num. internat. meetings incl. Internat. Soc. of Ophthalmic Ultrasound Vienna 1990; World Cong. of Ultrasound Copenhagen 1991; Ophthalmic Surgical Laser Soc. of N.Y. 1991; Am. & European Glaucoma Soc., Reykjavic 1993; Diplomate, Am. Bd. of Ophthal. 1979; Fellow, Am. Acad. of Ophthal. 1980; Secy., Am. Soc. of Opthal. Ultrasound; Mem., Candn. Med. Assn.; Candn. Ophthal. Soc.; Toronto Acad. of Med.; Am. Acad. of Ophthal.; Internat. Soc. of Ophthal. Ultrasound; Assn. for Rsch. in Vision & Ophthal.; Am. Inst. of Ultrasound in Med.; co-author: (with F. Stuart Foster) 'Ultrasound Biomicroscopy of the Eye' 1994; author of many articles; recreations: windsurfing, snowboarding, tennis; clubs: Balmy Beach, Mayfair Lakeshore Tennis; Home: 84 Balsam Ave., Toronto, Ont. M4E 3B7; Office: #212, 597 Parliament St., Toronto, Ont. M4X 1W3.

**PAWLEY, Hon. Howard Russell,** P.C., Q.C., B.A., LL.B., LL.D.; b. Brampton, Ont. 21 Nov. 1934; s. Russell and Velma Leone (Medill); e. Brampton High Sch., Man Teachers Coll., United Coll., University of Winnipeg, Man. Law Sch.; m. Adele, d. Joseph Schreyer 26 Nov. 1960; children: Christopher Scott, Charysse; ASSOC. PROF. (TENURED) POLITICAL SCIENCE DEPT. & THE LAW SCHOOL, UNIV. OF WINDSOR; Assoc. Prof., Political Sci. Dept. 1990–91; Apptd. the Paul Martin Professor 1993; LL.D. (honoris causa) 1993; Premier of Manitoba 1981–88; el. Man. Leg. g.e. 1969; re-el. 1973, 1977, 1981 and 1986; Min. of Public Works (Min. of Government Services) 1969–71; Min. of Municipal Affairs 1969–76; Attorney Gen. and Keeper of the Great Seal 1973–77; Min. responsible for the Liquor Control Act 1976; Min. responsible for the Man. Public Insur. Corp.; and Man. Housing and Renewal Corp.; Chosen Leader of Man. N.D.P. 13 Jan. 1979; el. Premier of Manitoba, Nov. 1981; re-el. 1986; Address: 304 - 75 Riverside Dr. E., Windsor, Ont. N9A 2S4.

**PAWLING, John D.,** B.A.Sc.; management consultant; b. Toronto, Ont. 23 Oct. 1924; s. Charles Roy and Lottie Belle (Hildreth) P.; e. Bloor Coll. Inst., Toronto; Univ. of Toronto, B.A.Sc. 1948; m. Mary Eileen, d. late William B. Clare; two d., Barbara Joan (Hejduk), Kathleen Anne; PARTNER, THE BEDFORD CONSULTING GROUP; Pres., J.D. Pawling and Assoc., Consultants since 1980; Pres. & C.E.O., Mohawk Ind., 1979–80; Pres. & C.E.O., CCM 1981–83; Partner, Haskins and Sells Associates, 1974–79; Vice President Dir., Tecumseh Metal Products Ltd.; Steel Master Tool Co. Ltd.; Dir. Mfg. Services, Price Waterhouse & Co., 1957–59; from 1959–65 variously Mgr. Mfg. Services, Hinde & Dauch (Canada) Ltd., subsequently integrated with Domtar Ltd.; Gen. Mgr. Carton Specialties Div., Domtar Packaging Ltd., Toronto; Asst. to Vice Pres., Domtar Pulp & Paper Ltd.; Dir., Simpson Riddell Stead & Assoc., 1965; Extve. Vice Pres. and Dir., Samson Belair Riddell Stead Inc., Montreal, 1968–72; Pres. and Dir., Riddell Stead & Assocs. Ltd. 1972–74; served as Candn. Offr. on loan to Brit Army 1943–45; N.W. Europe with 1st Bn., Border Regt., 1st Airborne Div.; rank Lt.; recipient Touche Ross Award for his article 'The Crisis of Corporate Boards: Accountability vs. Misplaced Loyalty' 1987; Pres. (1973), Candn. Assn. Mang. Consultants (Dir. since 1969); Mem., Inst. of Corp. Dirs. in Can.; recreation: tennis; Home: 60 High Park Ave., Toronto, Ont. M6P 2R9.

**PAWLIW, Randy W.,** B.Sc.; professional engineer; b. Theodore, Sask. 11 June 1950; s. William and Olga P.; e. Univ. of Sask., B.Sc. 1972; m. Donna; children: five; PRES., CIMARRON PETROLEUM LTD.; Home: Box 74, Priddis, Alta. T0L 1W0; Office: 800, 400 – 3rd Ave. S.W., Calgary, Alta. T2P 4H2.

**PAYETTE, Julie,** B.A., B.Eng., M.A.; Canadian astronaut; b. Montreal, Que. 20 Oct. 1963; e. United World Internat. College of the Atlantic, South Wales, UK Internat. B.A. 1982 (one of 6 Candn. scholarships 1980); McGill Univ. B.Eng. (with distinction) 1986; Univ. of Toronto M.A. 1990; m. François Brissette; CANADIAN ASTRONAUT; Technical Adviser, IBM Canada 1986–88; Visiting Scientist, Communications & Computer Sicence Dept., IBM Research Lab. Zurich, Switz. 1991–92; Speech Research Group, Bell-Northern Research 1992; selected for Canadian Astronaut Program 1992; preparing for Mission Specialist Training, NASA; Greville-Smith Scholarship, McGill Univ. 1982–86; Faculty Scholar, Fac. of Engr. 1983, '84, '85; University Scholar 1986; Top Honours,Basic Systems Training Class, IBM Canada 1987; 2 recognition prizes, IBM Canada; other academic awards incl.: FCAR Que. Grad. Scholarship, Massey Coll. Fellowship, NSERC Candn. Grad. Scholarship 1988–90; Mem., l'Ordre des Ingénieurs du Qué.; Candn. Aeronautics & Space Inst.; Women in Science and Engr. Corp.; 99s (internat. women pilot's assn.); Singer, Montreal Symphony Orchestra Chamber Choir, Orpheus Singers, Tafelmusik Baroque Orchestra Choir; Former Chair, Lionel Massey Fund, Massey College; spokesperson, 1990 Women in Engr. Campaign, Univ. of Toronto; active in varous community activities and has an ongoing commitment to volunteer work; recreations: trained pianist, soprano soloist and chorister, competes in triathlons, enjoys skiing, racquet sports and scuba diving; licensed pilot; fluent in French, English & Italian; conversational in Spanish & German; Office: 6767, Route de l'aéroport, Saint-Hubert, Que. J3Y 8Y9.

**PAYNE, Julien David,** Q.C., LL.D., F.R.S.C.; barrister; educator; author; b. Nottingham, Eng. 4 Feb. 1934; s. Frederick and Kathleen Mary (Maltby) P.; e. Univ. of London, King's Coll. LL.B. (1st) 1955, LL.D. 1980; m. Marilyn d. Leonard and Norma Jodoin 27 Sept. 1985; children: Glanville, Catherine, Simon, Andrew, Rebecca; PROF. OF LAW UNIV. OF OTTAWA 1975– , Prof. Sch. Grad. Studies 1981– ; Pres. Danreb Inc. 1987– ; called to Bar of Ont. 1965; c.r. Q.C. 1981; Asst. Lectr. in Law Queen's Univ. Belfast 1956–60; Asst. Prof. of Law Univ. of Sask. 1960–63; Asst. Prof. of Law Univ. of W. Ont. 1963, Assoc. Prof. 1964, Prof. 1967–70; Prof. of Law Univ. of Alta. 1970–72; Dir. Family Law Project Law Reform Comn. Can. 1972–75; Sessional Prof. of Law Carleton Univ. 1979–81; Visiting Prof. of Law Univ. of Santa Clara Cal. 1978; Simon Sr. Rsch. Fellow Univ. of Manchester 1968–69; Lansdowne Fellow Univ. of Victoria, B.C. 1988; Fellow, Royal Soc. of Canada 1990; Counsel, Kealey, Harris and Blaney 1977–82, Leonard Levencrown 1983–84; Consultant, Dept. of Justice Canada, Child Support Guidelines 1990–91; Consultant, Alberta Law Reform Institute, 'Domestic Relations Act' 1991–92; cons. to various federal and provincial comns. and govt. depts.; cons. and Bd. mem. Inst. Law Rsch. & Reform (Alta.) 1971–72; Hon. Life Fellow, Candn. Inst. Conflict Resolution 1990; Hon. Bd. Mem., Ontario Assn. Family Mediation 1991; Dir. Family & Children's Services London, Ont. 1966–68; mem. Adv. Council Family Mediation Can. 1984–86; Cons. MacDonald Comn. Econ. Union & Devel. Prospects for Canada 1983–84; pioneer unified family courts and no fault divorce in Can.; author or co-author numerous books and articles on Canadian family law and divorce; mem. Internat. Soc. Family Law (Extve. Council 1973–77); Family Mediation, Canada; Ont. Assn. Family Mediation (Pres. Ottawa Chapter 1987–88); recreations: bridge, swimming, reading; Home: 1188 Morrison Dr., Ottawa, Ont. K2H 7L3; Office: 57 Louis Pasteur, Ottawa, Ont. K1N 6N5.

**PAYNE, Lawrence Harold,** B.A., M.A.; oil executive; b. Portage La Prairie, Man. 25 June 1942; s. Harold William and Gladys Goldie (Reimer) P.; e. Lindsay Thurber Comp. H.S.; Univ. of Alta., B.A. 1964; Univ. of Miami 1968; Columbia Univ. M.A. 1970; divorced; children: Lawrence H. Jr., Cindy Lynn, Suzanne Madeleine, Brendan Patrick; PRES. & CHIEF EXTVE. OFFR., ATLANTIS RESOURCES LTD. 1978– ; Landman, PanAm. Petrol. Corp. 1964–67; Explor. Geol., Kerr-McGee Corp. 1970–71; Mgr., Candn. Opns., Sunningdale Oils Limited 1971–72; Vice-Pres., Candn. Opns. 1972–75; Pres. 1975–76; Pres., Sceptre Resources Ltd. 1976–78; Dir., First Interstate Bank of Can.; Dir. & Chrmn., Atlantis Resources Ltd.; Mem., Candn. Soc. of Petrol. Geol.; Am. Assn. of Petrol. Geol.; Candn. Assn. of Petrol. Landmen; recreations: golfing, skiing, motorcycling; clubs: Calgary Petroleum, Calgary Golf & Country; Home: 415 Cliffe Ave. S.W., Calgary, Alta. T2S 0Z3; Office: #900, 202 – 6th Ave. SW, Calgary, Alta. T2P 2R9.

**PAYNE, R. Gordon;** executive; b. Seer Green, Eng. 25 Oct. 1940; s. Gordon Reginald and Sarah Francis (Wild) P.; e. Arethusa Training Ship 1954–56; King Edward VII Nautical Coll. 1957; m. Patricia d. Michael and Victoria Chodachek 27 June 1964; two s. David, Kenneth; PRES., R.G. PAYNE & ASSOCIATES (Int. Port Consultants) 1990– ; Pres. & C.E.O., Internat. Stevedoring Services Ltd. 1989–90; Deck Offr. Brit. Merchant Navy, Furness Withy & Co. Ltd. 1958–62; came to Can. 1962; joined Empire Stevedoring Co. Ltd. 1963–88, Mgr. Centennial Pier Terminal 1970–75, Gen Mgr. Vanterm Container Terminal & Empire Traffic Services 1975–85, Pres. & C.E.O. 1985–88; Founder & Pres., Meridian Stevedoring Co. Ltd. 1988–89; recreations: tennis, golf; Clubs: Hazelemere Golf & Tennis; Terminal City; Home: 1669 – 133A St., S. Surrey, B.C. V4A 6H5.

**PAYNE, Robert Walter,** B.A., Ph.D.; university professor; b. Calgary, Alta. 5 Nov. 1925; s. Reginald Wm. and Nora Winnifred (Cowdery) P.; e. Central Coll. Inst., Calgary 1943; Univ. of Alberta B.A. 1949; Univ. of London Ph.D. 1954; children: Raymond Wm., Barbara Joan, Margaret June, George Reginald Alexander, Robin Charles; PROF. EMERITUS, PSYCHOLOGY DEPT., UNIV. OF VICTORIA since 1991; Consultant psychol. (part-time) W. Park Hosp. for Nervous and Mental Diseases, Surrey, Eng., 1950–52; Lectr. Psychol., Inst. of Psychiatry (Maudsley Hosp.) Univ. of London, 1952–59; Assoc. Prof., Prof. of Psychol., Queen's Univ. (Kingston, Ont.) 1959–65; Temple Univ. Sch. of Med., Phil, Pa., Prof. of Psychol. and Chrmn. Dept. of Behavioural Science, 1965–73, Prof. Psychiatry, 1973–78; Sr. Med. Research Scientist, East. Penna. Psychiatric Inst., Phil, Pa., 1965–78; Dean, Faculty of Human and Social Devel., Univ. of Victoria 1978–83; Prof. of Psychology, Univ. of Victoria 1978–91; served with Can. Army (active) 1943–45; Candn. volunteer medal (with clasp); war medal 1939–45; author of 'Cognitive Abnormalities,' 1973; 'Cognitive Defects in Schizophrenia: Overinclusive Thinking,' 1971; 'Disorders of Thinking,' 1970; 'The Measurement and Significance of Overinclusive Thinking and Retardation in Schizophrenia,' 1966; 'Thought Disorder in Psychotic Patients,' 1960; also chpts. in textbooks and articles in prof. jnls.; rec'd Stratton Research Award in Psychiatry, 1964; Fellow, Br. Psychol. Soc.,; Fellow, Am. Psychol. Assoc.; Fellow, Candn. Psychol. Assoc.; Fellow, Am. Psychopathological Assn.; Club: Univ. of Victoria Faculty; recreations: tennis, reading; Home: 2513 Sinclair Rd., Victoria, B.C. V8N 1B5; Office: P.O. Box 3050, Victoria, B.C. V8W 3P5.

**PAYNE, S. Stewart,** B.A., L.Th., B.D., D.D.; archbishop; b. Fogo 6 June 1932; s. Albert and Hilda Mae P.; e. Meml. Univ. of Nfld, B.A. 1958; Queen's Coll., L.Th. 1958; B.D. by correspondence, Gen. Synod 1968; D.D. honorary from King's Coll. 1981; m. Selma Carlson d. Clement and Myra Penney 11 Oct. 1962; children: Carla Ann, Christopher Stewart, Robert Clement, Angela Marie Louise; ARCHBISHOP OF THE DIOCESE OF WESTERN NEWFOUNDLAND AND METROPOLITAN OF THE ECCLESIASTICAL PROVINCE OF CANADA 1990– ; School teacher 1949, 1950, 1951; Parish Priest, Happy Valley, Labrador 1957–65; Bay Roberts, Nfld. 1965–70; St. Anthony, Nfld. 1970–78; Bishop of the Diocese of Western Nfld. 1978–90; mem., num. cttes. at Nat., Prov. & Diocesan level; recreations: cross country skiing, gardening, walking, reading; Home: 13 Cobb Lane, Corner Brook, Nfld. A2H 2V3; Office: Anglican Diocesan Centre, 25 Main St., Corner Brook, Nfld. A2H 1C2.

**PAYNE, Thomas Charles,** A.B., M.Arch.; architect; b. Chatham, Ont. 9 Dec. 1949; s. Lloyd George and Dorothy Elizabeth (Webster) P.; e. Princeton Univ. A.B. 1971; Ecole des Beaux Arts Paris 1971–72; Yale Sch. of Arch. M.Arch. 1974; m. Irma d. Bohdan and Tanya Osadsa 21 Sept. 1974; children: Natalia Sophia, Nicholas Alexander; PARTNER, KUWABARA PAYNE McKENNA BLUMBERG ARCHS. 1987– ; recent projects incl. Art Gallery Ont. Stage III; Woodsworth Coll. Univ. of Toronto; Trinity Coll. Master Plan; Stratford Festival Master Plan; Stauffer Library, Queen's Univ.; The Fields Institute, Univ. of Toronto; joined Barton Myers Associates 1979–87; projects incl. Portland (Ore.) Centre for Performing Arts, Open Air Theatre Earl Bales Park N. York, Ont.; Adjunct Asst. Prof. of Arch. Univ. of Toronto 1986–89; Guest Critic Sch. of Arch. U of T, Harvard Grad. Sch. Design, Univ. of Waterloo; Pres., Princeton Alumni Assn. Can. 1991– ; Hon. Fellow, Woodsworth College, Univ. of Toronto; mem. Royal Arch. Inst. Can.; Ont. Arch. Assn.; Am. Inst. Arch.; Home: 200 Glen Rd., Toronto, Ont. M4W 2X1; Office: 322 King St. W., Toronto, Ont. M5V 1J2.

**PAYNTER, John Lawrence,** B.A., M.A.; diplomat; b. Victoria, B.C. 11 Apr. 1941; s. Lawrence Newman and Margaret Eleanor (Cranston) P.; e. Fettes Coll. (Scotland) 1959; Univ. of British Columbia, B.A. 1962; Fletcher Sch. of Law & Diplomacy, M.A. 1963; Oxford Univ., M.A. 1965; m. Ingeborg d. Frithjov and Inger Jaeger 13 Apr. 1966; children: Katherine, Jonathan, Sarah; HIGH COMMISSIONER TO INDIA AND AMBASSADOR TO NEPAL 1990– ; Reporter, Toronto Star 1965; Prod., CBC 1966; joined Dept. of External Affairs 1966; Third Sec., Candn. Embassy, Moscow 1967; Asst. Trade Comnr., Hong Kong 1969; First Sec., Candn. Embassy, Peking 1971; Head, China Desk, Dept. of External Affairs 1973; Personnel Div. 1975; Trade & Devel. Couns., Candn. Mission to U.N., Geneva 1977; Dir., Gen. Econ. Relns, Finance & Investment, Dept. of External Affairs 1980; Ctte. Chrmn., U.N. Conf. on Common Fund for Commodities, Geneva 1979–80; Chrmn., North-South Group, Orgn. for Econ. Co-op. and Devel., Paris 1981–82; Candn. Ambassador to Thailand, Vietnam and Laos, 1983–87; Director-Gen., Economic Policy Bureau, Dept. of External Affairs 1987; Asst. Depy. Min., Economic and Trade Policy, Dept. of External Affairs and Internat. Trade Canada 1988–90; recreations: reading, film, swimming; Office: Candn. High Commission, 7/8 Shantipath, Chanakyapuri, New Delhi 110021, India.

**PAYTON, Thomas William;** real estate financial advisor; b. Toronto, Ont. 7 Sept. 1946; s. Alfred and May P.; m. Delaine d. Ernie and Geraldine Bold 24 Apl. 1976; PRESIDENT, DELLYN ADVISORS INC. 1993– ; began career with Canadian Imperial Bank of Commerce; Dir. Bramalea Ltd. 1981–82, Vice Pres. Corporate Finance 1982–88, Sr. Vice Pres. Corporate Finance 1988–90, Sr. Vice Pres. Corporate Finance & Treasurer 1991–93; Office: 8 King St. E., Suite 810, Toronto, Ont. M5C 1B5.

**PEACH, Michael Edwin;** M.A. Ph.D., F.C.I.C.; university professor; b. Nottingham, Eng. 7 May 1937; s. Stanley Morris and Christine Mary (French) P.; e. Rugby Sch. (Eng.) 1951–55; Jesus Coll., Univ. Cambridge, B.A. 1959; Ph.D. 1962; M.A., 1964; m. Angelika, d. Alfred and Else Weisskirchen, 30 Oct. 1964; children: Stephanie Joy; Mary Alexandra; HEAD, CHEMISTRY DEPARTMENT 1991– and PROF., 1976– ACADIA UNIV.; postdoctoral studies Inst. Inorganic Chem., Tech. Univ. Graz (Austria) 1962–63; Inst. Inorganic Chem., Univ. Goettingen (Germany), 1963–65; Asst. Prof., Dalhousie Univ., 1965; Lectr., Loughborough Univ. Tech. (Eng.) 1966; joined present university as Asst. Prof. 1967; Assoc. Prof. 1971; Dir., Grad. Studies & Rsch. 1976–90; Visiting Prof., Inst. Inorganic Chem., Univ. Wuerzburg (Germany), 1974–5 & 1980–81 and Ruhr Univ., Bochum (Germany) 1991; author 83 papers in chemical lit.; NATO Postdoctoral Fellowship 1962–64; Fellowship Alexander von Humboldt Foundation (Bonn) 1974–75 & 1980–81; Fellow, Chem. Inst. Can. 1973 (Chrmn. Inorganic Div. 1973–74, Sec'y.-Treas. Atlantic Sect. 1972–3); mem. Royal Philatelic Soc. Can.; recreations: gardening; skiing; philately; Home: P.O. Box 884, Wolfville, N.S. B0P 1X0; Office: Acadia Univ., Wolfville, N.S. B0P 1X0.

**PEACH, Milton,** B.Ed., B.A.; politician; b. Small Point, Conc. Bay, Nfld. 5 Dec. 1943; s. Gordon and Elizabeth P.; e. Mem. Univ. of Nfld. B.Ed. 1972, B.A. 1981; m. Joan d. Reuben and Susie Noel 11 Sept. 1962; children: Michelle, Sheri; FUNERAL DIR., NOEL'S FUNERAL HOMES LTD. (CARBONEAR, NFLD.) 1991– ; Teacher, Corner Brook 1961–62; Victoria 1964–71; Carbonear 1971–82; employee, Hickman Motors 1966; first elected, M.H.A., Carbonear 1982; re-elected 1985; Parl. Sec., Chrmn., Solicy Policy Ctte. of Cabinet 1985; Min. resp. for Newfoundland and Labrador Housing Corp. & M.H.A, Carbonear 1988–89; apptd. Min. of Fisheries March 1989; defeated M.H.A., for Carbonear April 1989; Chief of Staff to the Leader of the P.C. Opposition in Nfld. 1989–91; Mem., Social Policy Ctte. of Cabinet; Treas. Bd.; Spec. Ctte. of Cabinet; Counc., Town of Carbonear and twice elected Mayor 1977, 1981; Chrmn., Joint Mayors Ctte., Conception Bay N. 1980–82; Mem., Standing Orders Ctte. on Rules & Proc. of the House of Assembly 1987; Vice-Chrmn., Select Ctte. on Food Prices 1983; Hon. Mem., Royal Candn. Legion, Br. 23; Kinsmen Club of Carbonear 1985– ; Mem., Masonic Lodge 1043 (Right Worshipful Master 1982–83); Carbonear Volunteer Fire Dept. 1978– ; Bethany Un. Ch. Men's Serv. Club; Carbonear Kiwanis Club; Past Pres., Conception Bay N. Minor Hockey Assn.; Carbonear Minor Hockey Assn.; 10 yrs. coach of Carbonear Minor Hockey; Level IV Coaching cert.; cert. level 1 referee N.A.H.A.; Carbonear Citizen of the year 1979; Home: P.O. Box 492, Water St., Carbonear, Nfld. A0A 1T0.

**PEACOCK, J. Patrick,** Q.C., B.A., LL.B.; lawyer; b. Calgary, Alta. 2 July 1943; s. N. Ralph and Margaret A. (Rhodes) P.; e. Univ. of Alta. B.A. 1964, LL.B. 1967; m. Virginia Engel; children: Michele, Sandra, Michael, Christopher; PARTNER, PEACOCK LINDER & HALT, BARRISTERS AND SOLRS.; Head of Civil Procedure Course and Instr. Law Soc. Alta. Bar Admission Course 1969–89, Chrmn. Loss Prevention Prog. 1985; mem. Adv. Ctte. Dean of Law Univ. of Calgary 1976–84; Instr. in Comm. Law Inst. C.A.'s Alta. 1969–73; mem. S. Alta. Regional Legal Aid Ctte. 1971–74; Vice Chrmn. Candn. Football League Bd. Govs. 1985; Pres. Calgary Stampeder Football Club 1985–86, Dir. 1979–86; Partner, Macleod Dixon, Barristers & Solicitors 1987; Pres. Calgary Jr. Football Assn. 1975–79, 1982–83; Vice-Chrmn., Bd. of Govs., Mount Royal Community Coll. Calgary 1988; mem. Candn. Bar Assn. (Nat. Pres. 1988–89 and other Extve. positions); Calgary Bar Assn. (Pres. 1978); Law Soc. Alta.; Candn. Inst. Adm. Justice; Internat. Comn. Jurists (Candn. Sect.); Hon. Life Mem., Law Soc. of Sask.; Fellow, American College of Trial Lawyers; Club: Calgary Golf & Country; Home: 122, 3437 – 42nd St. N.W., Calgary, Alta. T3A 2M7; Office: 3700, 400 – 3rd Ave. S.W., Calgary, Alta. T2P 4H2.

**PEACOCK, John J.,** B.Comm., F.C.A.; financial executive; b. Quebec City, Que. 11 May 1943; s. John Robert and Constance Elizabeth (McKeown) P.; e. St. Francis Xavier Univ. B.Comm. 1963; admitted to the Order of C.A.s of Quebec 1966; m. Adrienne d. Florence and the late Thomas McDonald 4 Sept. 1965; children: Mark, Kevin; VICE-PRESIDENT, FINANCE, FEDNAV LIMITED 1979– ; Partner, Clarkson Gordon 1972–79; Dir., Royal Victoria Hosp. Centre and Foundation; The McGill Assoc.; Gov., The Foundation of Quebec Univ. Athletics; clubs: Mount Bruno; University Club of

Montreal; Montreal Badminton & Squash; Home: 53 Belvedere Circle, Westmount, Que. H3Y 1G7; Office: Suite 3500, 1000 de la Gauchetière W., Montreal, Que. H3B 4W5.

**PEACOCK, Kent Alan,** B.A., M.A., Ph.D.; educator; b. Toronto, Ont. 30 July 1952; s. Donald Knight and Barbara Joan (Whatmough) P.; e. Univ. of Toronto B.A. 1976, M.A. 1987, Ph.D. 1991; m. Sharon d. Herbert and Doreen Simmers 28 June 1986; children: Bertrand Lewis Donald, Robert Evan Osborn; ASST. PROF., UNIV. OF WESTERN ONT.; worked for several years in a variety of labouring jobs (carpenter, truck driver) and as an architectural draughtsman in late father's firm 1980–83; Teacher, Dept. of Philosophy, Univ. of Toronto 1990–91; occasional consulting work, Ont. Centre for Large Scale Computation; Univ. of Toronto Open Fellowships 1987–88, 1988–89; SSRHCC Doctoral Fellowships 1989–90, 1990–91; SSHRCC Postdoctoral Fellowship 1991–93 (taken up with Univ. of Western Ontario); Publication: 'A New Look at Simultaneity' Proceedings of Philosophy of Science Assn. 1992 (Vol. I); Sustaining Mem., Leschetizky Assn.; Mem., Candn. Soc. for History & Philosophy of Science; Philosophy of Science Assn.; Am. Philosophical Assn.; Office: Talbot College, Univ. of Western Ont., London, Ont. N6A 3K7.

**PEAKE, Rev. Frank Alexander,** M.A., D.D., D.S.Litt., F.R.Hist.S.; b. Watford, Herts., UK 16 Apl. 1913; s. Alexander Tod and Amy Grace (Clennett) P.; e. Mundella Sch. and Univ. Coll., Cert. in Textiles 1935, Nottingham; Emmanuel Coll., Saskatoon, L.Th. 1943; Univ. of Sask., B.A. 1947; Ch. Divinity Sch. of the Pacific, Berkeley, B.D. 1949; Univ. of Alta., M.A. 1952; Huron Coll., Univ. of W. Ont., D.D. 1965; Thorneloe Univ., D.S. Litt. (Jure Dignitatis), 1974; m. Constance Helen Tyndale, d. late Thomas Kilshaw, 28 Aug. 1945; children: John Maurice Clennett, Kenneth Richard Tyndale, Marjorie Grace (Mrs. Whalen); Associate Professor of History, Laurentian University, Sudbury, Ont. 1966–78, Prof. 1978–80; o. Deacon 1941, Priest 1942; Curate-in-charge of Clandonald, Alberta 1941; Vicar of Onoway 1943, Ponoka 1946; Rural Dean of Wetaskiwin 1947–48; W. Field Secretary, Gen. Bd. of Religious Education 1948–53; Prof. of Ch. Hist., Ang. Theol. Coll., Vancouver 1953–59; Hon. Lectr. in Hist., Univ. of B.C. 1955–59; Examining Chaplain to the Bishop of Kootenay 1955–60; Dir. of Religious Educ., Diocese of Huron, 1959–66; Hon. Associate Priest, Church of the Epiphany, Sudbury, 1966–87; Pastoral Chaplain, Diocese of Algoma 1984–87; Priest-in-charge, St. John the Baptist, Kars, Ont. 1989–94; Pres. and Vice Chancellor, Thorneloe Univ. 1970–74 and 1981–82; mem., Thorneloe Univ., Bd. of Govs. 1974–87 (Life mem. 1987– ); author, 'Seeing and Believing' 1950; 'Towards a Living Faith' 1955; 'The Anglican Church in British Columbia' 1959; 'The Story of British Columbia' 1966; 'The Bishop Who Ate His Boots' 1966; 'The Religious Tradition in Sudbury' (with R.P. Horne), 1983; 'From the Red River to the Arctic' 1989; also numerous hist. articles; contributor, 'Dictionary of Canadian Biography'; 'The Canadian Encyclopedia'; Life mem., Candn. Hist. Assn.; Mem., Candn. Soc. of Church History; Candn. Church Historical Soc. (Life mem. & Hon. Pres.); Anglican; Home: 310 Dalehurst Dr., Nepean, Ont. K2G 4H4.

**PEARCE, John Richard,** M.A.; editor; b. Shrewsbury, Eng. 9 March 1947; s. Richard Evan and Doris Irene (Potter) P.; e. Priory Sch. for Boys Shrewsbury 1965; Pembroke Coll. Cambridge M.A. 1969; m. Gail d. David and Barbara Smart 15 May 1976; ED.-IN-CHIEF, DOUBLEDAY CANADA LTD. 1987– and SEAL BOOKS 1992– ; Ed. Victor Gollancz Ltd. London, Eng. 1969–76; Ed. Clarke, Irwin & Co. Ltd. Toronto 1976, Ed. Dir. 1978–83; Ed. Dir., Irwin Publishing Inc. 1983–87; classical music critic Maclean's mag. 1978–89; author articles on music various mags.; ed. 'The Musical Companion' 1977; co-author 'Author and Editor: A Working Guide' 1983; conducted workshops and seminars Alta. Culture, Book Publishers Profl. Assn., Freelance Editors Assn. Can.; mem. Cambridge Soc. Toronto; Crime Writers Can.; recreations: music, travel, hiking, skiing; Office: 105 Bond St., Toronto, Ont. M5B 1Y3.

**PEARL, Paul Roy,** B.Sc., Ph.D.; computer executive; b. Melbourne, Australia 16 Aug. 1943; s. Aron and Janina (Grosglik) P.; e. Melbourne H.S. 1960; Monash Univ., B.Sc. 1964, Ph.D. 1968; Post-doctoral Fellow, Atomic Energy Comm., France 1968–70; London Univ. 1970–72; m. Frances d. Herman and Genia Cukierman 26 Jan. 1965; children: Davina, Judith; PRESIDENT, DIPIX TECHNOLOGIES INC. 1992– ; Lectr., London Univ., 1972–74;; Sr. Engr., Computing Devices Co. 1974–78; Pres., Dipix Systems Limited 1978–87; Pres., Satmap Inc. 1987–92; Dir., Can.-China Trade Counc.; recreations: sailing, skiing, squash; Home: 13 Winslow Crt., Ottawa, Ont. K2B 8H8.

**PEARSE, Peter Hector,** C.M., B.S.F., M.A., Ph.D., R.P.F., F.R.S.A.; educator; b. Vernon, B.C. 26 Nov. 1932; s. Frederick Robert and Eleanor Jane (Lea) P.; e. Vernon (B.C.) Elem. Sch. 1946; Kamloops (B.C.) High Sch. 1951; Univ. of B.C. B.S.F. 1956; Edinburgh Univ. M.A. 1959, Ph.D. 1962; m. Penelope Ann d. Richard B. Wilson, Victoria, B.C. 28 Apl. 1973; children: Peter Grant, Jane Elizabeth, Sarah Wilson Lea; PROF. OF ECON. & FORESTRY, UNIV. OF B.C. since 1962; Dir., Alcan Aluminium Ltd. 1989– ; Forester-in Training, B.C. Forest Products Ltd. 1956–57; Asst. Lectr. in Econ. Univ. of Edinburgh 1959–61; Econ., Organ. for Econ. Co-op. & Devel. Paris 1961–62; Commr., Royal Comm. on Forest Resources for B.C. 1975–76; Commr., Royal Comm. on Pacific Fisheries Policy 1981–82; Chrmn., Inquiry on Fed. Water Policy 1984–85; Chrmn., Inquiry on Canada's Freshwater Fisheries 1986–88; Proj. Leader & Chrmn., Forest Economics and Policy Analysis Rsch. Unit 1983–88; rec'd Gold Medal Univ. B.C. 1956; various scholarships and research awards; Candn. Forestry Achievement Award 1977; Distinguished Forester Award 1980; Member of the Order of Canada 1988; Fellow of the Royal Society for the Arts 1989; author (as sole Commissoner) 'Timber Rights and Forest Policy in British Columbia' 2 vols. 1976; and (as sole Comnr.) 'Turning the Tide: A New Policy for Canada's Pacific Fisheries' 1982; Co-author (as Inquiry Chrmn.) 'Currents of Change: Final Report of the Inquiry on Federal Water Policy' 1985; 'Rising to the Challenge: A New Policy for Canada's Freshwater Fisheries' 1988; numerous articles and government reports on econ. problems in devel. and mang. natural resources; mem. Candn. Consumer Council 1970–72; Econ. Council Can. 1978–81; Canada West Foundation 1980–82; FAO United Nations Adv. Ctte. on Marine Resources Res. 1981–88; Chrmn. OECD working Group on Natural Resources Mgmt. 1986; Forest Res. Council of B.C. 1982–84; Forestry Res. Adv. Council of Can. 1983–87; Bd. of Dirs., Western Centre for Econ. Research since 1986; Dir., B.C. Forest Foundation 1979–86; Bd. Govs. Univ. B.C. 1978–84; mem. Candn. Ctte. for UNESCO's Man and the Biosphere Program 1990– ; Bd. of Dirs., Vancouver Board of Trade 1991– ; mem. Council of Ecotrust 1991–93; Extve. Bd., Law of the Sea Institute 1991– ; Bd. of Dirs., World Wildlife Fund Canada 1992– ; Assn. B.C. Reg'd Foresters; Candn. Inst. Forestry; Past Pres. and Vice Pres. Univ. B.C. Faculty Assn.; Liberal; recreations: skiing, fishing; Club: Vancouver; Home: 6450 Elm St., Vancouver, B.C. V6N 1B3; Office: Faculty of Forestry, Univ. of B.C., Vancouver, B.C. V6T 1W5.

**PEARSON, Alan Thomas,** B.Com. (Hons.); corporate planning consultant; b. Birmingham, Engl. 27 Apr. 1939; s. Thomas Joseph and Jessie (Wright) P.; e. King Edward VI Sch., Birmingham 1956; Univ. of Birmingham B.Com. (Hons.) 1959; m. Chaviva Milada Hošek d. Emil & Hedy (Weiss) H. 24 May 1991; child: Graham Calvin; PRESIDENT, ALAN PEARSON ASSOCIATES INC. 1982– ; Lieut. Royal Warwickshire Regiment (U.K.) seconded to Ghana Army 1959–62; Sr. Rsch. Cons. The Economist Intelligence Unit Ltd., London, Engl. 1962–66; Fed. Pub. Servant Ottawa: Rural Devel Prog. 1966–68; Statistics Can. 1969–70; Dept. of Ind., Trade and Comm. 1970–72; Min. of State for Urban Affairs 1972–73; Dir. Studies and Rsch. Group, Privy Counc. Office and Fed.-Prov. Relations Office 1973–80; Sr. Assoc., Bus. Counc. on National Issues, Toronto 1980–81; author 'The Western Constitutional Forum Workbook' (citizen's guide to Candn. govt. arrangements) 1984; Pres. Couchiching Inst. on Pub. Affairs 1984–86, Dir. 1981– ; Pres. The Planning Forum (Toronto Chapter) 1986–87, Dir. 1980–88; Founding Pres. Kaypro Computer Users (Toronto) 1983–84; Pres. The Stafford Beer Found. 1986– , Dir. 1985– ; Mem., Extve. Counc., Inst. for Political Involvement 1987–91, Dir. 1986–91; Mem., Institute of Corporate Directors 1992– ; recreations: travel, fitness, microcomputing; Clubs: Royal Candn. Military Inst., Toronto; Bd. of Trade, Metro. Toronto; The Fitness Inst., Toronto; Home: 152 Cambridge Ave., Toronto, Ont. M4K 2L8.

**PEARSON, Arthur MacDonald,** M.Sc., Ph.D.; Canadian public service; b. Brandon, Man. 26 Feb. 1938; s. Arthur Cartwright and Norma Agnes (MacDonald) P.; e. High Sch. Brandon, Man.; Univ. of B.C. B.Sc. 1958, M.Sc. 1960; Univ. of Helsinki Ph.D. 1962; m. Sandra Jean d. Charles Mooney, Prince Albert, Sask. 26 Oct. 1959; children: David Warren Lars, Cynthia Rae, Howard Brent; PRES., WHITEHORSE BEVERAGES LTD. since 1986; PRES. RAMPART DEVELOPMENT CORP. since 1979; Pres., 210446 Holdings Ltd. since 1978; Dyea Developments Ltd. since 1971; Biol. and Research Scientist, Candn. Wildlife Service, Whitehorse 1962–71, Research Scientist Edmonton 1972–74, Acting Head Co-op. Research Program 1975–76; Commr. of Yukon Territory, Whitehorse 1976–8; mem. Whitehorse Bd. of Health 1970–71; Dir. Yukon Social Service Soc. 1967–71 (Pres. 1969–70); Dir. and Charter mem. Univ. of Can. N. 1970–71; Dir. Yukon Research & Devel. Inst. 1968–71; Instr. in Ecology Arctic Summer Sch. Univ. of Alta. 1972–75; Dir. Candn. Soc. Fisheries & Wildlife Biols. 1967–71; Arctic Internat. Wildlife Range Soc. 1970–76; mem. Council Bear Biol. Assn. (Internat.) 1977; Pres., Arctic Division Am. Assoc. for Advancement of Science 1982–83, 1992–93; Pres., Yukon Science Inst. since 1985; Dir., Arctic Inst. of N. Am. (Can.) 1990– ; Dir., Arctic Inst. of N. Am. (U.S.) 1986– ; Pres., Whitehorse Chamb. of Comm. 1987–88; Dir., Candn. Chamb. of Comm. 1988– ; Protestant; recreations: hockey, golf, skiing, hunting, fishing, philately, numismatics; Home: 124 Alsek Rd., Whitehorse, Yukon Y1A 3K6; Office: 6208 – 6th Ave, Whitehorse, Yukon Y1A 1P2.

**PEARSON, Arthur R.,** B.Sc., F.C.A.; chartered accountant; b. Winnipeg, Man. 10 Oct. 1948; s. Arnold A. and Frances L. (Crawford) P.; e. Univ. of Man., B.Sc. 1969, C.A., Man. 1972; m. Allison; children: Sean, Cheryl; C.A. TAX PARTNER, PEAT MARWICK THORNE, WINNIPEG 1979– ; articling C.A. student, Price Waterhouse, Winnipeg 1969–72; C.A. tax spec., Toronto 1972–74; Ernst & Whinney, Winnipeg 1974–75; C.A. Tax Mgr., Peat Marwick 1975–79; part-time lectr., Univ. of Man. 1976–83; Chrmn., Pub. Fin. & Tax Ctte., Winnipeg C. of C. 1977–80; Treas. 1981–85; Bd. of Dir., Royal Winnipeg Ballet 1984–94; Treas., Bd. of Gov., Manitoba Museum of Man & Nature; Candn. Tax Found.; Inst. of C.A.'s of Man. (Chrmn., Tax Ctte. 1979–80; Mem. of Council 1989–92) & Ont.; author of num. profl. articles; co-author: 'Records Retention for Tax and Other Purposes' 1975; recreations: squash, hockey; Club: Manitoba; Home: 6 Woodington Bay, Winnipeg, Man. R3P 1M5; Office: 800 – 200 Graham Ave., Winnipeg, Man. R3C 4M1.

**PEARSON, C. Emmett,** C.A.; health care executive; b. Montreal, Que. 21 March 1946; s. Charles Arnold and Hilda Mary (Thompson) P.; e. McGill Univ. C.A. 1968; m. Judy d. Lawerence E. and Carrie Fiset 21 Sept. 1968; children: Trina, Wendy; EXECUTIVE VICE-PRES., CONTINENTAL PHARMA CRYOSAN INC. 1992– ; Acctg., S. Schwartz & Co. (Schwartz Levitsky Fieldman) 1963–69; Asst.-Treas., J. Pascal Inc. 1969; left as Mem., Extve. Ctte., Bd. of Dir. & Vice-Pres. Finance 1989; Sr. Vice-Pres. Finance & Dir., Continental Pharma Cryosan Inc. 1989–92; Mem., Financial Extve. Inst.; Order of C.A.s of Que.; Montreal Bd. of Trade; recreations: running, tennis; clubs: Sporting Club le Sanctuaire; Home: 121 Northcliff, Beaconsfield, Que. H9W 5Z2; Office: 1625 Sherbrooke St. W., Montreal, Que. H3H 1E2.

**PEARSON, Geoffrey Arthur Holland,** M.A.; b. Toronto, Ont. 25 Dec. 1927; s. Lester Bowles and Maryon Elspeth (Moody) P.; e. Trinity coll. Sch. Port Hope 1945; Univ. of Toronto B.A. 1950; Oxford Univ. M.A. 1952; m. Landon d. Hugh and Alice Mackenzie 26 Dec. 1951; children: Hilary, Katharine, Anne, Michael, Patricia; joined Dept. of External Affairs 1952, Third Secy. Paris 1953–57, First Secy. Mexico 1961–64, Counsellor India 1969–72; Foreign Service Visitor Univ. of B.C. 1972–73; Dir.-Gen. Bureau of UN Affairs Ottawa 1975–78, Adv. on Arms Control and Disarmament Ottawa 1978–80; Ambassador to USSR 1980–83; Extve. Dir., Candn. Inst. for Internat. Peace & Security 1984–88; mem., Patron, L.B. Pearson Coll. of the Pacific; author: 'Seize the Day: Lester B. Pearson and Crisis Diplomacy' 1993; Home: 199 Daly Ave., Ottawa, Ont. K1N 6G1.

**PEARSON, H. William,** P.Eng.; b. Windsor, Ont. 23 Aug. 1940; e. Univ. of Detroit P.Eng. 1964; m. Judith; children: Kathryn, Heather; PRESIDENT, AGRA ENGINEERING GROUP and VICE-PRESIDENT, AGRA INDUSTRIES LIMITED 1990– ; Chesapeake & Ohio Railway 1961–63; Student Eng., Douglas W. Barr Consulting 1965; Sr. Hydraulic Engr., Acres Consulting Serv. Ltd. 1966–70; Vice-Pres. Power, The SNC Group & Pres., SNC Hydro Inc. 1970–89; Sr. Vice-Pres., Power, Telecomm 1985–89; Sr. Vice-Pres., Corp. Devel. 1987–89; Pres., SNC Internat. & Sr. Vice-Pres., Corp. Devel. 1989–92; Mem., Order of Engrs. of Que.; Assn. of Profl. Engrs., provinces of Nfld., N.S. & Ont.; Am. Geophysical Union; Canada-India Business Council; Canada-Arab Business Council; Candn. Power Systems Export Promotion; Am. Mngt. Assn.; Conference Bd. of Can.; Assn. of Consulting Engrs. of Can.; Mississauga Bd. of Trade; co-author: 'Some Aspects of Field Investigations for Accelerated Hydroelectric Development' 1981 and three other pubns.; recreations: scuba diving, skiing, squash; Office: 2233 Argentia Rd., Suite 400, Mississauga, Ont. L5N 2X7.

**PEARSON, Hugh John Sanders,** C.M.; company chairman; b. Edmonton, Alberta 9 Sept. 1921; s. late Hugh Edward and Constance Jukes (Sanders) P.; e. Trinity Coll. Sch., Port Hope, Ont. (1940); Royal Mil. Coll., Kingston, Ont. (1942); m. Kathleen Primrose, d. late William Hastie, 7 Dec. 1945; children: Kathleen Margaret, Ronald Hastie, Ian Sanders; CHRMN., CENTURY SALES & SERVICE LIMITED; Mem., The Bishops Men, Edmonton; Dir., Northam Estates Ltd.; Dir. Prudential Steel Ltd.; Dir. & Gov., Council for Cdn. Unity; Chrmn., Edmonton Adv. Bd., Salvation Army; joined the Taylor Pearson & Carson organization in 1946 and was employed in various capacities, became Manager of Taylor, Pearson & Carson (B.C.) Ltd., in 1956; el. Dir. of the Co., 1957, Pres. 1959; served in 2nd World War with The Calgary Highlanders, overseas 1942–45, rank Capt.; Mentioned in Despatches; Hon. LL.D. 1993; Mem., Order of Canada 1994; Anglican; recreations: shooting, fishing, golf; Clubs: Edmonton; Mayfair Golf and Country; York; Office: 4810 - 92 Avenue, (P.O. Box 1218), Edmonton, Alta. T5J 2M6.

**PEARSON, John Bruce,** B.Comm., M.B.A.; business executive; b. Montreal, Que. 28 July 1931; s. Harold C. and Evelyn G. (Wilkinson) P.; e. McGill Univ. B.Comm. 1954; Univ. of Western Ont. M.B.A. 1958; m. Jocelyn d. Helen and Norman Teare 25 Aug. 1956; children: Thomas Allen, Hugh Ross, Brian John; CHRMN. & CHIEF EXECUTIVE OFFR., BLACKBURN GROUP INC. 1987– ; Lectr., Northwestern Univ. Chicago 1960–62; Asst. Prof., Sch. of Bus. Admin., U.W.O. 1962–65; Partner, May, Pearson & Assoc. (mngt. cons.) 1965–87; Dir., Lewiscraft Limited; Blackburn/Polk Mktg. Serv. Inc.; Blackburn Mktg. Serv. (U.S.) Inc., Fairfax, VA; London Free Press Printing Company Ltd.; Blackburn Radio Inc.; Compusearch Market & Social Research Limited; Netmar Inc.; Urban Decision Systems, Inc. (Los Angeles); recreations: tennis, nordic skiing; clubs: The York; The London Club; London Hunt & Country; Home: 279 Heath St. E., Toronto, Ont. M4T 1T3; Office: Suite 901, 1 St. Clair Ave. E., Toronto, Ont. M4T 2V7.

**PEARSON, Kathleen Margaret (Kit),** M.L.S., M.A.; writer; b. Edmonton, Alta. 30 Apr. 1947; d. Hugh John Sanders and Kathleen Primrose (Hastie) P.; e. Crofton House Sch. Vancouver 1965; Univ. of Alta. B.A. 1969; Univ. of B.C. M.L.S. 1976; Simmons Coll. Center Study Children's Lit. Boston M.A. 1982; Children's Lib. St. Catharines (Ont.) Pub. Lib 1976–77; North York Pub. Lib. 1977–81; Burnaby (B.C.) Pub. Lib. 1982–86, Reference Lib. (part-time) 1986–90; occasional teacher of children's literature and writing for children, Langara Coll., Capilano Coll., U.B.C. and S.F.U. 1983–93; sometime reviewer and critic of children's lit.; author children's novels: 'The Daring Game' 1986; 'A Handful of Time' 1987 (winner Candn. Lib. Assn. Book of Yr. Children's Award 1988); 'The Sky is Falling' 1989 (winner Candn. Lib. Assn. Book of Yr. Children's Award 1990, Mr. Christie's Book Award 1990 and Geoffrey Bilson Award for Historial Fiction for Young People 1990); 'Looking at the Moon' 1991; 'When the Lights Go On Again' 1993; folktale: 'The Singing Basket' 1990; mem. Writers Union Can.; IBBY Can. (Councillor 1987–88); CANSCAIP; Children's Book Centre; Vancouver, Children's Lit. Roundtable CWILL B.C.; recreations: walking, birdwatching, travel; Home: 3888 West 15th Ave., Vancouver, B.C. V6R 2Z9.

**PEARSON, (Lucy) Landon Carter,** B.A., M.Ed.; writer, social activist; b. Toronto, Ont. 16 Nov. 1930; d. Hugh Alexander and Alice Beirne (Sawtelle) Mackenzie; e. Univ. of Toronto, Trinity College B.A. 1951; Univ. of Ottawa M.Ed. 1978; m. Geoffrey s. Lester Bowles and Maryon Elspeth P. 26 Dec. 1951; children: Hilary, Katharine, Anne, Michael, Patricia; CHAIRPERSON, CANADIAN COALITION FOR THE RIGHTS OF CHILDREN; actively involved with childen & children's issues over 40 years; as foreign service spouse raised 5 children in 5 countries: France, Mexico, India, the former Soviet Union and Canada; Co-Founder & Current Chair, 'Children Learning for Living' 1975; Vice Chair, Candn. Comn. for the Internat. Year of the Child 1979; Pres., then Chair, Candn. Council for Children & Youth 1985–90; Vice-Pres., Policy Research Centre on Children, Youth and Families 1989–92; author of num. articles on child devel. & policy issues; Rep., NGO community on Candn. Delegation to World Summit on Children 29–30 Sept. 1990; Canada Volunteer Award 1990; author: 'Children of Glasnost' 1990, '91; editor: 'For Canada's Children' 1979; Home: 199 Daly Ave., Ottawa, Ont. K1N 6G1; Office: 180 Argyle Ave., Rm. 327, Ottawa, Ont. K2P 1B7.

**PEARSON, Peter;** film & television producer & director; b. Toronto, Ont. 13 March 1938; s. Charles Todd and Dorothy (Robb) P.; e. Univ. of Toronto Schs. 1957; Univ. of Toronto, Pol. Sci. 1961; Ryerson Polytech. Inst. Toronto Advanced TV Prodn. 1962; L'Università italiana per Stranieri, Perugia, Italy, Advanced Italian 1963; Centro Sperimentale di cinematografia, Rome, Film Dir. 1964; Alliance Française, Paris, Advanced French 1974; m. Suzanne d. Louis and Jeannette Vachon 15 June 1974; one s. Louis-Charles De Beauce; PRODUCER & DIRECTOR, KEN DRYDEN'S HOMEGAME (6h mini series for television) 1990– ; Pres.: Milne-Pearson Productions 1968–72; Oro Films Ltd. (founded 1970); Dirs.' Guild of Can. 1972–75; Extve. Dir., Telefilm Canada 1985–87; Founding Chrmn. Council Candn. Filmmakers, 1973; Mem. Task Force on the Candn. Film Industry 1985; mem. Govt. Can Film Del. to Russia 1982; Nat. Strategy Conf. Banff 1982; The GAMMA Group 1976–80; Adv. Bd. to Candn. Film Devel. Corp. 1973–75; Toronto Arts Council 1972–74; Film Dir.: 'Bananas From Sunny Quebec' (TV movie) 1993; 'Urban Angel' (2 episodes, TV series) CBC-CBS 1992; 'Snowbird' 1981; 'The Unexpected' 1981; 'The Tar Sands' 1977; 'Kathy Karuks Is A Grizzly Bear' 1977 (nominee ANIK Award Best TV drama); 'Insurance Man From Ingersoll' 1976 (winner 2 CFA Awards, nominated Best TV Drama 1976); 'Only God Knows' 1974; 'Paperback Hero' 1973 (winner 3 CFA Awards, nominee Best Feature Film 1973); 'The Dowry' 1969; 'The Best Damn Fiddler From Calabogie To Kaladar' 1969 (winner CFA Best Film of the Year, several internat. awards, 8 CFA Awards 1969); Producer-Dir. 'The Journal' 1982; Dir.-Writer; CTV 'National Crime Test' 1982; 'Saul Alinsky Went to War' 1969 NFB (winner several Candn. and Internat. Awards); 'Mastroianni' CBC 1965; Producer-Dir.-Writer: 'The Chairman: A Profile of Paul Desmarais' 1981 (nominated Best Documentary Narration ACTRA Awards 1982); 'If I Don't Agree, Must I Go Away' PBS-CBC 1970; 'This Blooming Business of Bilingualism' CBC 1970; 'Whatever Happened To Them All?' CBC 1966; Story ed.-Producer 'This Hour Has Seven Days' CBC 1964–66; Story ed. 'Toronto File' CBC 1962–63; Dir./Producer/Writer various comm. and sponsored films; Dir., 'L'Or et le papier' (6h mini-series) Radio-Canada 1992; Film Screenplays: 'Snowbird' 1981; 'Heaven on Earth' with Margaret Atwood 1986; 'One Man' 1976 (winner Best Original screenplay ACTRA Awards 1977 and CFA Award 1978); 'Tar Sands' 1977; 'Insurance Man From Ingersoll' 1976; 'The Dowry' 1969; Writer, 'Mario, Mike and Mr. Greatness' 1988; author various articles, pub. lecture, conf. papers; Assoc. Prof. of Film Studies Queen's Univ. 1982–83; Concordia 1987–88; guest speaker, various univs. and colls.; weekly columnist, Montreal Gazette 1990– ; Mem. Bd. of Dirs., FUND; Chrmn. of Jury, Banff Television Festival 1991; Home: 417 ave. Mt. Pleasent, Westmount Qué. H3Y 3G9.

**PEARSON, Richard Joseph,** Ph.D., F.R.S.C. II; university professor; b. Kitchener, Ont. 2 May 1938; s. John Cecil and Henrietta Anne (Wallwin) P.; e. Univ. of Toronto, B.A. (Hon.) 1960; Univ. of Hawaii 1961; Yale Univ., Ph.D. 1966; m. Kazue d. Ichisada Miyazaki 12 Dec. 1964; one d. Sarina Riye; PROF., DEPT. OF ANTHROPOLOGY/SOCIOLOGY, UNIV. OF B.C. 1974– ; Asst., Assoc. Prof., Dept. of Anthropol., Univ. of Hawaii 1966–71; Assoc. Prof., present univ. 1971–74; Vis. Prof., Keio Univ. summer 1974; Univ. of Kyoto 1975–76; Yale Univ. 1983; Cur. of Archaeology, U.B.C. Mus. of Anthrop. 1976–79; Co-ed. pro tem 'Current Anthropology' 1980–81; Bd. of Dir., Assn. for Asian Studies 1976–70; Curator, exhibs. of Japanese arch., Japan Soc. N.Y. 1990; Sackler Gall., Smithsonian Inst. 1992; J.S. Guggenheim Fellowship 1979 (deferred to 1980); U.B.C. Killam Rsch. Prize 1986; Mem., Assn. for Asian Studies; Am. Anthrop. Assn.; Soc. for Am. Arch.; editor: 'Archaeology at Lapakahi, Hawaii' 1969, 'Traditional Culture and Society of Korea' vol. 3 1975, 'Windows on the Japanese Past' 1986; author: 'The Archaeology of the Ryukyu Islands' 1969, 'Image and Life' 1978, 'The Ancient Society of East Asia, and Archaeology' (in Japanese) 1984, 'Ancient Japan' 1992; author of numerous jour. articles; recreations: horticulture; Home: 1890 West 17th Ave., Vancouver, B.C. V6J 2M9; Office: 6303 Northwest Marine Dr., Vancouver, B.C. V6T 1Z1.

**PEART, Arthur Francis Whittaker,** M.B.E., M.D., C.M., D.P.H., F.R.S.H., F.R.C.P. (C); b. Freeman, Ont., 9 Feb. 1915; s. Grant Somerville and Bessie Pearl (Whittaker) P.; e. Ont. Agric. Coll., 1933–35; Queen's Univ., M.D., C.M. 1940; Univ. of Toronto, D.P.H. 1943; Harvard Sch. of Pub. Health, 1949–50; Roy. Coll. Phys. & Surgs. Can., Cert. in Pub. Health F.R.C.P.(C) 1953, Fellow in 1972; m. Gwendolyn, 20 Mar. 1943; children: Nancy, Frances, William, James; served in 2nd World War with R.C.A.M.C., 1940–46; held appointments on Staff, Lab. and Field Hygiene Section; awarded M.B.E.; M.O.H., Health Region No. 1, Swift Current, Sask., 1946; in gen. practice, 1947; apptd. Chief, Div. of Epidemiol., Dept. of Nat Health & Welfare, Ottawa, 1948–54; apptd. Asst. Secy., Candn. Med. Assn., 1954, Depy. Gen. Secy., 1960, and Gen. Secy. 1966–70; apptd. Med. Dir., Traffic Injury Research Foundation 1970–75; Chrmn. of Bd. of Dirs., Medifacts Limited 1970–86; Pres., World Med. Assn. 1971; mem. Candn. Med. Assn.; Ont. Med. Assn.; Roy. Coll. of Phys. & Surgs. of Can.; Hon. mem., Am. Med. Assn. 1967; author of articles and reports in med. and pub. health journs.; awarded Queen's Jubilee Medal 1977; Freemason; Anglican; Clubs: Royal Ottawa Golf; recreations: golf, skiing, carpentry; Home: 128 Noel St., Ottawa, Ont. K1M 2A5.

**PEART, Robert (Bob) W.,** B.Sc.(Agr.), M.A.; biologist/consultant; b. St. Thomas, Ont. 14 Dec. 1948; s. James Arthur and Marjorie Alice (Crimes) P.; e. Univ. of Guelph, B.Sc.(Agr) 1972; Univ. of Victoria, M.A. 1982; Nat. Mus. of Can. Fellowship, 1981; m. Mary (Martin) d. Ruth Martin 6 Aug. 1971; MINISTERIAL ASST. TO MIN. OF ENVIRONMENT, LANDS & PARKS, GOVT. OF B.C. 1992– ; Naturalist, Parks Canada 1972–74; Biologist, Candn. Wildlife Serv., Ottawa 1974–76; Swift Current, Sask. 1976–80; Sr. Cons. & Pres., I.L.E. Consulting Service 1981–92; Asst. Dir., Royal B.C. Mus. 1985–88; Extve. Dir., Outdoor Recreation Council of B.C. 1988–91; Mem., B.C. Round Table on the Environment and Economy 1990–92; Mem., B.C. Third Party Advisory Ctte. on Native Land Claims 1990–92; Instr., Univ. of Victoria; Candn. Parks & Wilderness Soc. (Extve. 1979–91, Pres. 1985–87); Mem., B.C. Mus. Assn.; Interpretation Can. (Extve. 1974–78); Heritage Can.; Candn. Nature Fed., etc.; author: 'Tourism' 1982, 'Rivers to Roads' 1985 and other papers; Home: 36 Government St., Victoria, B.C. V8V 2K3.

**PECHET, Howard Erwin,** B.A., M.A.; business executive; b. Edmonton, Alta. 25 Sept. 1948; s. Eugene and Rose (Simkin) P.; e. Univ. of Alta. B.A. 1970; Wash. State Univ. M.A. 1973; m. Henriette d. Cor and Bella Rozenhart 30 Jan. 1971; children: Jason, David; PRES. MAYFIELD INVESTMENTS LTD. 1978– ; Pres., Stagewest Hotel; Mayfield Travel; Medicine Hat Lodge; Extve. Producer Stage West Theatre Restaurants 1974– ; Dir. Canadian Western Bank 1984– ; Dir. Chalmers Investment Corp. Ltd.; Dixieline Productions Ltd.; Fort Nelson Hotel (Alberta) Ltd.; Chris Page & Associates; Effort Soc. (Past Pres. 1987– ); Downtown Businessman's Assoc.; Mem. Young Pres. Orgn.; recreations: hockey, skiing; Office: c/o Mayfield Investments Ltd., 10141 – 122 St., Edmonton, Alta. T5N 1L7.

**PECK, Brig.-Gen. Charles Arnold,** O.B.E., C.D., B.Sc.; retired association executive; b. Hillsboro, N.B. 18 Jan. 1912; s. Charles Allison and Mary Romaine (Beatty) P.; e. Univ. of N.B., B.Sc. (EE) 1932; British Army Staff Coll., Surrey, Eng., grad. 1947; Candn. Nat. Defence Coll., 1961–62; m. Jean Doris, d. J. Stuart Grant, Rockcliffe Park, Ottawa, 18 November 1939; two d. Judith Doris, Susan Jean; PRES., MACHINERY AND EQUIPMENT MFRS. ASSN. OF CAN. 1968–78; served overseas in 2nd World War with Candn. Army in U.K., Italy, N.W. Europe, 1941–45; Army Hdqrs., 1946–50; C.O., Roy. Candn. Sch. of Signals, 1950–55; Dir. of Signals, Army Hdqrs., 1955–58; Depy. Army Mem., Candn. Jt. Staff, London, Eng., 1958–61; Sr. Mil. Adv., Candn. Del. to Internat. Supy. & Control Comn., Indo China, 1962–63; Depy. Adj.-Gen., 1963–64; apptd. Dir.-Gen. of Centennial Planning, Dec. 1964; retired from Candn. armed forces Jan. 1968; mem., Assn. Prof. Engrs., Ont.; Anglican; recreations: golf, skiing; Clubs: Royal Ottawa Golf (Past Pres.); Home: 300 Driveway, Ottawa, Ont. K1S 3M6.

**PECK, Edward Richard Urquhart,** B.Com.; labour relations executive; b. Victoria, B.C. 20 Nov. 1924; s. the late Cyrus Wesley V.C. and Kate Elizabeth (Chapman) P.; e. Univ. of B.C., B.Com. 1949; m. Barbara d. Ronald and Jean Venables 24 Aug. 1964; children: Richard, Timothy, Cy, Cheryl; Chief of Personnel Services, B.C. Power Comn. 1955–61; Staff/Services Mgr., B.C. Hydro 1962–65; Gen. Mgr., Peace Power & Columbia Hydro Constructors 1965–69; Mgr., Labour Relations, B.C. Hydro 1969–71; Pres., Towboat Ind. Relations 1971–73; Vice Chrmn. & Chief Admin. Offr., Labour Relations Bd. of B.C. 1973–79; arbitrator/mediator, private practice 1979–82; Comnr., Compensation Stabilization (wage control) Program of B.C. 1982–87; Special Adviser to Min. of Labour 1987; Comnr., Ind. Relations Council of B.C. 1987–92; Dir., Pacific Vocational Inst. 1980–82; author, 'Report to Minister of Labour on

Multi Employer Bargaining' 1979, 'Conciliation Commissioner's Report – B.C. Telephone Co. and Telephone Workers Union' 1980, 'Classification System Award-Health Labour Relations & Hospital Employees Union' 1982 and many other awards decisions and publications; B.C. Lions Football Club 1985–87; served 1st Btn. Cdn. Scottish Regt., Cdn. Army overseas, World War II, 1943–46; United Church; recreations: tennis, golf, fishing; Club: Hollyburn Country; Home: 5380 Keith Rd., West Vancouver, B.C. V7W 2Y7.

**PECK, George Kelday,** D.V.M.; veterinarian; ornithologist; photographer; writer; b. Toronto, Ont. 13 Dec. 1925; s. John Douglas and Mabel Ethel (Kelday) P.; e. Univ. of Toronto Schs. 1945; Univ. of Toronto Ont. Vet. Coll. D.V.M. 1950; m. Sheila Wilson 14 Nov. 1953; children: Leslie, Mark, Cameron, Erin; m. Diane Schwarz 18 May 1988; clin. small animal practice Vet. Med. 1950–83; affiliated with Royal Ont. Museum as organizer Ont. Nest Records Scheme since 1966, Rsch. Assoc. Dept. Ornithol. 1976; environmental cons. Ont. Hydro, Grey-Sauble Conserv. Authority, Candn. Wildlife Service; mem. Extve. Long Point Bird Observatory; mem. Ont. Ornithol. Records Ctte.; Corn. Lab. Ornithol.; Am. Museum Natural Hist.; Nat. Audubon Soc.; Soc. Candn. Ornithol.; Brodie Club; Toronto Ornithol. Club; recipient Fedn. Ont. Naturalists Conserv. Achievement Award 1988; elective mem. Am. Ornithols. Union 1991; Two Auks Photography estab. with son, representing their natural science photog. collection 1985; author: 'Nature's Children: Squirrels' 1985; 'Le Monde Merveilleux des Animaux: L'ecureuil' 1986; co-author 'Breeding Birds of Ontario: Nidiology and Distribution' vol. 1 1983 (currently under revision), vol. 2 1987; 'Atlas of Breeding Birds of Ontario' (wrote 8 species accounts) 1987; 'Ornithology in Ontario' (wrote chapter & biography) 1994; bird and natural sci. photog. over 30 yrs., rep. in 45 books and annually various mags.; Address: 85 Bruce St., Thornbury, Ont. N0H 2P0.

**PECK, Mary Biggar,** M.A.; historian; writer; b. Montreal, Que. 29 Apl. 1920; d. H. Harris and Grace C. (Lingley) Biggar; e. McGill Univ. B.A. 1941; Carleton Univ. M.A. 1969; m. George W. s. Stanley and Lena Peck 20 Aug. 1942; children: Brenda, Barbara, John, Alexander; rsch. and reports 1964–82: Louisbourg Restoration Project, Ottawa; Candn. Inventory Hist. Bldgs., Quebec City; Hist. Resources Adm., Maritime Aboriginal Rights & Land Claims, Fredericton; Co-ord., Supr. and Writer Exhn. on Hist. of Rideau Canal, Nat. Archives Ottawa; prepared and presented series TV progs. hist. photos & subjects; frequent lectr.; papers delivered various learned socs. and Budapest Conf. Hist. Hosps. Can.; author: 'From War to Winterlude' (150 yrs. Rideau Canal) 1982; 'The Bitter with the Sweet' (N.B. 1604–1984) 1983; 'A New Brunswick Album' 1987, 'A Nova Scotia Album' 1989 (Glimpses of the Way We Were); 'Red Moon Over Spain' (Candn. Media Reaction to the Spanish Civil War 1936–39) 1988; editor: 'A Full House and Fine Singing' (Diaries and Letters of Sadie Harper Allen) 1992; articles various mags.; recreations: travel, reading, gardening; Address (Summer): Lambertville, Deer Island, N.B. E0G 2J0; (Winter): 1, 163 MacKay St., Ottawa, Ont. K1M 2B5.

**PECKFORD, Hon. Alfred Brian,** P.C., M.H.A., B.A. (Ed.), LL.D.; retired P.C. politician; b. Whitbourne, Nfld. 27 Aug. 1942; s. Ewart and Allison (Young) P.; e. Lewisporte High Sch.; Mem. Univ. of Nfld. B.A., B.A. (Ed.) 1966; m. Carol Ellsworth; child: Justin three d. (previous marriage) SueAnn, Carolyn, Stephanie; PRES., PECKFORD CONSULTING LTD. 1989– ; Teacher, Lewisporte 1962–63; High Sch. Teacher, Grant Coll. Inst. Springdale 1966–72, Head of Eng. 1971; el. Pres. Green Bay Dist. P. Cons. Assn. 1971; el. M.H.A. for Green Bay Dist. Prov. g.e. 1972, re-el. since; Special Asst. to Premier 1973; Min. of Mun. Affairs & Housing 1974; Min. of Mines & Energy 1976 as well as Min. of Rural Devel. 1978; el. Leader P. Cons. Party Nfld. & Labrador 1979; sworn in as Premier 26 March 1979, re-el. Premier prov. g.e. June 1979, Apr. 1982, Apr. 1985; Premier of Nfld. and Labrador and Leader of the P. Cons. Party of Nfld. & Labrador 1979–89; rec'd Vanier Award as an outstanding young Candn. 1980; Sworn to the Privy Counc. 1982; LL.D. (hon. causa), Memorial Univ. of Nfld. 1986; recreations: reading, sports, swimming & skiing; Address: 1206 Sunrise Dr., Qualicum Beach, B.C. V9K 2B9.

**PECKNOLD, John C.,** B.Sc., M.D.C.M., D.P.M., F.R.C.P.C.; psychiatrist; b. Montreal, Que. 29 May 1941; s. Alfred A. and Maria (Rondon) P.; e. Univ. of Montreal B.Sc. 1962; McGill Univ. M.D.C.M. 1966; m. Lynn d. Ashley and Margaret Wheeler 27 Aug. 1966; children: Maureen, Sean, Erin; PROGRAM DIR., COMMUNITY PSYCHIATRY CENTRE, DOUGLAS HOSP. 1993– ; Flight Surgeon, Candn. Armed Forces 1967–69; Internal Med. Residency, NDMC 1969–70; Psychiatric Res., McGill Univ. 1970–73; Staff, St. Mary's Hosp. (Psychopharm.) 1973–87; Psychiatrist-in-Chief, St. Mary's Hosp. 1983–87; Dir. of Anxiety Clinic, Douglas Hosp. 1987– ; Assoc. Prof. of Psych., McGill Univ.; author of approx. 100 articles and book chapters; recreations: singing, dancing, gardening; Home: 323 Grosvenor, Westmount, Que. H3Z 2M3; Office: Montreal, Que. H3Z 2M3.

**PEDDIE, Richard A.,** B.Com.; executive; b. Windsor, Ont. 31 Jan 1947; s. Lawrence Edward and June (Martin) P.; e. Univ. of Windsor B.Com. 1970; m. Trudy d. Mr. and Mrs. Harold Eagan 28 Jan. 1977; PRES. AND CHIEF EXTVE. OFFR. STADIUM CORP. OF ONT. LTD. (SKY DOME) 1989– ; Vice Pres. and Gen. Mgr. Cold Beverages & Cereals, General Foods 1978; Pres. Hostess Food Products 1983; Pres. & C.E.O., Pillsbury Canada Ltd. 1985–89; Dir. Liquid Carbonic Inc.; Janes Family Foods Ltd.; CFCF Inc.; Young Pres. Orgn. Ont. Chapter; mem. Bd. of Govs., Univ. of Windsor; recreation: distance running; Home: 52 Chestnut Park Rd., Toronto, Ont.; Office: 1 Blue Jays Way, Suite 3000, Toronto, Ont. M5V 1J3.

**PEDDLE, Ambrose H.;** parliamentary commissioner; b. Corner Brook, Nfld. 8 Oct. 1927; s. James E. and Grace G. (McCarthy) P.; e. St. Henry's Sch.; St. Bernard's Acad.; m. Bessie d. Jacob and Lulu Legge; one s.: David A.; Parliamentary Comnr. (Ombudsman) for Newfoundland 1975–90; pre-Confederation: Nfld. Govt. Railway 1945–47; Customs & Excise 1947–49; post-Confederation: Unemployment Insur. Comn., Govt. of Can. 1949–51; Sales Mgr., Retail Furniture & Appliances 1951–63; Owner/Operator, Small Business Enterprises 1963–75; Mayor, Town of Windsor, Nfld. 1961–66; M.L.A. for Grand Falls 1962–66; M.P. for Grand Falls-White Bay-Labrador 1968–72; Home: 20 Lawton Cres., St. John's, Nfld. A1A 4R5.

**PEDEN, David Murray,** Q.C., D.F.C., B.A., LL.B.; barrister/public servant; b. Winnipeg, Man. 19 Oct. 1923; s. William and Elsie Pearl (Baldwin) P.; e. Portage C.I./Gordon Bell H.S.; United Coll./Univ. of Man., B.A. 1948; Univ. of Man. Law Sch., LL.B. 1952; m. Jean d. Rev. Philip and Margaret Barker 29 Apr. 1949; children: John David, Roderick William, Laura Margaret; Chrmn., Man. Securities Comn. 1968–88; heavy bomber pilot, R.C.A.F. 1941–45; Crown Attorney, Prov. of Man. 1952–55; private practice 1955–57; Gen. Couns., Greater Winnipeg Transit Comn. 1957–60; Corp. Couns., Metro. Corp. of Greater Winnipeg 1960–61; Asst. Dep. Min., Mun. Affairs 1961–64; Dep. Min., Public Utilities 1964–68; Distinguished Flying Cross 1944; Spec. Commendation, C-in-C R.A.F. Bomber Cmd. 1944; Mention in Despatches 1945; Lt. Gov. Gold Medal 1945–46; Gov.-Gen. Medal 1946, 47, 48; Univ. Gold Medal, Fac. of Arts & Sci. 1948; Law Soc. Prize, Hon. A. Morris Exhib. for highest standing in 4 yrs. of law, Univ. Gold Medal in Law 1952; 6 Univ. of Man. Isbister Scholarship 1945–52; invited lectr., Smithsonian 1985; Dir., Atlantic Counc. of Can. 1981–90; Gov., Man. Br. Candn. Corps of Comnrs. 1985–86; Mem. & former Dir., Wartime Pilots & Observers Assn.; Life Mem., Winnipeg Trap & Skeet Club; Mem., Stirling Aircraft Assn.; Commonwealth Air Training Plan Mus.; author: 'Fall of an Arrow' 1978, 'A Thousand Shall Fall' 1979, 'Hearken to the Evidence' 1983 and num. profl. articles pub. worldwide; recreations: hunting, fishing, writing, music, military history; Home: 46 Aldershot Blvd., Winnipeg, Man. R3P 0C8.

**PEDERSEN, Eigil Dalsgaard,** M.A., Ed.D.; educator; b. Montreal, Que. 2 Nov. 1929; s. Arne Dalsgaard and Gudrun (Jorgensen ) P.; e. Macdonald Coll., Montreal, Teaching Cert.; Sir George Williams Univ., B.A. 1956; McGill Univ., M.A. (Educ.) 1961; Harvard Univ., Ed.D. (Sociol.) 1966; Concordia Univ. LL.D. (honoris causa) 1992; m. Madge, d. George Abbott, 28 June 1952; children: John, Philip, David, Gordon, Thomas, Susan; Vice-Princ. (Acad.) McGill University 1972–81; Assoc., Harvard Grad. Sch. of Educ. 1981–82; Visiting Scholar, Centre for Multicultural Educ., Univ. of London Inst. of Educ. 1982; and Professor of Educ.; began as Teacher, Public Schs., Montreal 1952; Lectr. in Educ., McGill Univ. 1958–63; Research Assoc., Harvard Univ. 1965–66; Prof. of Education, McGill University 1958–63, 1966–90; Emeritus Prof. 1990– ; Stanley Knowles Distinguished Visiting Professor, Brandon Univ. 1992; former mem. Canadian Association Professors of Education (Pres. 1971–72); Candn. Educ. Researchers Assn.; Candn. Soc. for Study of Educ. (Vice-Pres. 1972–73); Phi Delta Kappa; recreation: music; Office: 3700 McTavish St., Montreal, Que. H3A 1Y2.

**PEDERSEN, Harold V.,** B.Comm.; petroleum executive; b. Kerrobert, Sask. 15 Dec. 1945; s. Ejnar and Myrtle R. P.; e. Univ. of Saskatchewan B.Comm. 1968; m. Merla J. d. Warner and Luella Keebaugh June 1968; children: Kurt H., Karla J.; PRES., JORDAN PETROLEUM LTD. 1986– ; Exec. Vice-Pres., Inverness Petroleum Ltd. 1980–81; Pres., Inverness Petroleum Ltd. 1981–86; Manager & Vice-Pres., Forest Oil Corp. 1973–80; Dir., Jordan Petroleum Ltd.; Petrolantic Ltd.; Granger Energy Corp.; recreations: boating, skiing; clubs: Calgary Petroleum Club, Calgary Winter Club; Home: 51 Schiller Cres., Calgary, Alta. T3L 1W7; Office: 850, 225 – 5th Ave. S.W., Calgary, Alta. T2P 3G6.

**PEDERSEN, K. George,** O.C., B.A., M.A., Ph.D., F.C.C.T., F.R.S.A.; educator; b. Three Creeks, Alta. 13 June 1931; s. Hjalmar Nielsen and Anna Marie (Jensen) P.; e. Chilliwack (B.C.) Jr. and Sr. High Sch. 1949; Vancouver Prov. Normal Sch. Teaching Dipl. 1952; Univ. of B.C., B.A. (Hist. and Geog.) 1959; Univ. of Washington M.A. (Geog. and Educ.) 1964; Univ. of Chicago, Ph.D. (Educ. and Econ.) 1969; m. Joan Elaine (dec.), d. James Earl Vanderwarker, 15 Aug. 1953; m. secondly, Dr. Penny Ann Pedersen d. Cyril Peter Jones and Eleanor Grey (Macpherson), 31 Dec. 1988; children (of first marriage): Gregory George, Lisa Marie; President, The Univ. of Western Ontario 1985–94; began teaching in Elem. and Secondary Schs., N. Vancouver, B.C. 1952; Past Pres., N. Vancouver Teachers' Assn., N. Vancouver Principals' and Vice Principals' Assn.;Staff Assoc., Midwest Adm. Center, Univ. of Chicago 1965, Teaching Intern there 1966, Research Assoc. (Asst. Prof.) 1966; Lectr. and Asst. Prof., Univ. of Toronto 1968; Asst. Prof. Dept. of Educ., Univ. of Chicago and Assoc. Dir., Midwest Adm. Center, Grad. Sch. of Educ. there 1970; Dean, Fac. of Ed., Univ. of Victoria 1972; Vice-President (Academic), University of Victoria 1975; Pres. & Vice-Chancellor, Simon Fraser Univ. 1979–83; Pres. & Vice-Chancellor, Univ. Of British Columbia 1983–85; Am. Educ. Research Assn.; Past Secy. Treas. of the Canadian Assn. of Deans and Directors of Education; Candn. Educ. Assn.; Candn. Educ. Researchers' Assn; Candn. Soc. for Study of Educ.; Internat. Council on Educ. for Teaching; Comparative & Internat. Educ. Soc.; Candn. Foundation for Econ. Education; National Society for the Study of Education; Candn. Tax Foundation; Cdn. Bureau for Internat. Educ.; Bd. Mem., Commonwealth Assn. of Universities; Vice-Pres., Inter-American Organization of Higher Education 1991–93; Inst. of Public Admin. of Can.; Past Member of Board of Trustees of Discovery Foundation (B.C.); Past Member of Board of Directors of Public Employers Council of B.C.; Past Chrmn., Assn. of Universities and Coll. of Can.; Past mem., Bd. of Gov., Arts. Sciences & Technology Centre, Vancouver; mem., Past Pres. & Bd. of Dir., Canadian Club of Vancouver; mem., Bd. of Dir., Education Network for Older Adults; mem., of Council of Trustees, Inst. for Research on Public Policy; Past mem., Bd. of Dirs.: Vancouver Bd. of Trade; MacMillan Bloedel Ltd., Vancouver; Pulp & Paper Rsch. Inst. of Canada; Past Chrmn. Council of Ont. Universities; Past Chrmn., Ont. Comm. on Interuniversity Athletics; author of 'The Itinerant Schoolmaster: A Socio-Economic Analysis of Teacher Turnover' 1973; also book chapters, articles, reviews, critiques and research papers in numerous prof. journs.; Phi Delta Kappa; Protestant; recreations: skiing, golf, fishing.

**PEDERSEN, Paul Richard,** B.A., M.Mus., Ph.D.; educator; composer; university professor; b. Camrose, Alta. 28 Aug. 1935; s. Einer Richard and Anna (Rasmussen) P.; e. Camrose Lutheran Coll. 1953; Univ. of Sask. B.A. 1957; Univ. of Toronto M.Mus. (Composition) 1961, Ph.D. (Musicology) 1970; m. Jean Frances d. Albert Stollery, Armena, Alta. 6 Aug. 1956; children: Rebecca, David, Katherine, Andrew; DEAN, FACULTY OF MUSIC, UNIV. OF TORONTO 1990– ; Music Dir. Camrose Lutheran Coll. 1962–64; Chair, Theory, Fac. of Music & Dir. Electronic Music Studio, McGill Univ. 1970–74; Assoc. Dean of Music 1974–76, Dean of Music 1976–86, Prof. of Music 1966–90; Dir. McGill Univ. Records 1986–90; consultant to NRC of Canada on polyphonic synthesizer design; Music Editor & Light Programmer, Spectraphonia Pavilion, 'Man and His World' 1970; Mem., Bd. of Regents, Luther College Regina; author various articles psychol. of music; over 40 music compositions various media; mem. Candn. League Composers; Candn. Univ. Music Soc.; Soc. of Composers, Authors and Music Publishers of Can.; Lutheran; recreations: photography, woodworking; Home: 70 Indian Grove, Toronto, Ont. M6R 2Y4; Office: Toronto, Ont. M5S 1A1.

**PEEL, Alexander Leonard,** B.Com., M.B.A.; provincial public servant; b. Quesnel, B.C. 26 June 1935; e. Univ. of B.C., B.Com. 1959; Univ. of Cal. Berkeley

M.B.A. 1967; m. Marilyn; three d. Laurie, Julie, Ellen; joined CNR Montreal as Econ., R and D Dept. 1959; Supt. of Budgets & Cost Control U.S. trucking firm Oakland, Cal. 1962; apptd. to Ministry of Transport, Ottawa 1965; Depy. Min. of Economic Development, B.C. 1974–87; Depy. Min. of Education, B.C. 1987–89; also served as Acting Depy. Min., Dept. of Mines & Petroleum Resources, B.C. & Depy. Min. of Tourism, B.C.; Chrmn., British Columbia Forest Resources Commission, B.C. 1989; mem., Assn. Prof. Econ. B.C.; B.C. Rsch. Counc.; Home: 4464 Sunnywood Pl., Victoria, B.C. V8X 4N4.

**PEEL, Bruce Braden,** M.A., B.L.S.; librarian (retired); b. Ferland, Sask., 11 Nov. 1916; s. late Alice Annie (Switzer) and William John P.; e. Normal Sch., Moose Jaw, Sask.; Univ. of Sask., B.A. 1944, M.A. 1946; Univ. of Toronto Lib. Sch., B.L.S. 1946; Univ. of Alta. LL.D. 1991; m. Margaret Christina, d. James Fullerton, Regina, Sask., 28 July 1950; children: Brian David, Alison Mary; Chief Librarian, Univ. of Alberta, 1955–82; began teaching pub. sch. in Sask. for four yrs.; Canadiana Lib. in charge of Adam Shortt Collection, Univ. of Sask. Lib., 1946–51; Chief Cataloguer Univ. of Alta. Lib., 1951–54; Asst. Chief Librarian, 1954–55; mem. of study team on Resources of Canadian Academic Libraries, 1966–67; Publications: 'The Saskatoon Story, 1882–1952' (with Eric Knowles), 1952; 'A Bibliography of the Prairie Provinces to 1953,' 1956; second enlarged ed., 1973; 'Supplement,' 1963; 'Steamboats on the Saskatchewan,' 1972; Editor, 'Librarianship in Canada, 1946 to 1967,' 1968; 'Early Printing in Red River Settlement' 1974; 'The Rossville Mission Press' 1974; various articles on bibliography and regional history; Tremaine Medal for outstanding service to bibliog. in Can., Bibliog. Soc. of Can. 1975; outstanding service to librarianship award, Can. Library Assn., 1982; Golden Cross of Merit, Polish Government in Exile, 1983; mem. various library assns.; United Church; Home: 11047 – 83 Ave., Edmonton, Alta. T6G 0T8.

**PEEL, Donald Naylor,** B.A., L.Th., B.D., M.A., Ph.D.; educator; author; b. Halifax, Yorks., Eng. 8 Sept. 1923; s. Horace and Sarah (Radcliffe) P.; e. E.York Coll. Inst. 1942; Univ. of Toronto, Univ. Coll. B.A. 1946, Wycliffe Coll. L.Th. 1949, B.D. 1951; Ind. Univ. M.A. 1965, Ph.D. 1967; m. Alice d. Harold and Margaret Sanders 3 May 1947; children: Margaret, Mary, Joy, Lois, Sara; served with Candn. Army Pacific Corps WWII, rank Lt.; Parish of Macklin Diocese of Saskatoon 1949–52; Diocese of Amritsar 1952–69; Interim Prin. Landaur Lang. Sch.; Bd. Govs.: Batala Union Christian Coll. Punjab 1956–69; Woodstock Sch. Landaur 1958–69; Landaur Community Hosp. 1963–69; Founder Continuous Adult Learning & Leadership Movement in Church of North India; Dir. Christian Edn. Huron Diocese 1970–73; Co-ord. Chaplain N.York Gen. Hosp. Toronto 1973–80; Assoc. Prof. of Christian Edn. and Dean of Students, Wycliffe Coll. 1980–88; mem. College Council; Warden of Ch. Army Can. 1987–90; lectr. and seminar leader in lay mins., healing min., evangelism; Proprietor, Donald Peel Pastoral Seminars; Assoc. Evangelist 'Invitation to Live Ministries' 1982– ; Chrmn. Leprosy Mission Can. 1989–92 (Bd. 1975–92); Bd. Scripture Gift Mission Can. 1975–89; Diocese of Toronto Cands. Ctte. and Bishop's Examining Chaplain 1980–88; Council mem. Centre for Christian Studies 1975–80; Grand Prelate, Hospitaller Order St. John Jerusalem (Kts. Hospitaller) 1984– ; Pastor, Asian Christian Fellowship, London, Ont. 1989– ; Hon. Assistant, St. Stephen's Memorial Church, London, Ont. 1988– ; author: 'The Ministry of Listening' 1980; 'O Come Let Us Worship' 1990; 'The Ministry of the Laity' 1990; 'The Ministry of Evangelism' 1992; co-author: 'Care For The Dying And The Bereaved' 1982; 'An Encyclopedia of Christian Ethics' 1987; Anglican; recreations: music, reading, gardening, houseplants, writing, walking; Address: 208 Chesham Place, London, Ont. N6G 3T7.

**PEERS, Frank Wayne,** Ph.D.; educator; b. Alsask, Sask. 18 Jan. 1918; s. Warren Fountain and L. M. (McKim) P.; e. Mount Royal Coll. Calgary; Univ. of Alta. B.A. 1936, B.Ed. 1943; Univ. of Toronto M.A. 1948, Ph.D. 1966; PROF. EMERITUS, POL. SCIENCE, UNIV. OF TORONTO; Asst. Dir. of Extension Univ. of Alta. 1943–47; Asst. Dir. Banff Sch. of Fine Arts 1945–47; Asst. Supvr. and Supvr. of CBC Pub. Affairs Toronto 1948–60, Dir. of Information Programming 1960–63; author 'The Politics of Canadian Broadcasting 1920–51'; 'The Public Eye: Television and the Politics of Canadian Broadcasting 1952–68'; articles various publs.; contrib. to radio and TV programs; former Ed., 'Canadian Journal of Political Science'; mem. Candn. Pol. Science Assn.; Extve. Ctte., Friends of Canadian Broadcasting; recreations: travel, theatre; Office: 100 St. George St., Toronto, Ont. M5S 1A1.

**PEERS, The Most Rev. Michael Geoffrey,** B.A., L.Th., D.D.; clergyman; b. Vancouver, B.C. 31 July 1934; s. Geoffrey Hugh and Dorothy Enid (Mantle) P.; e. Univ. of B.C., B.A. (Hons.) 1956; Universitat Heidelberg Interpreter's Cert. 1955; Trinity Coll., Univ. of Toronto L.Th. 1959; Hon. D.D.: Trinity Coll., Univ. of Toronto 1977; St. John's Coll., Winnipeg 1981; Wycliffe Coll., Toronto 1987; Univ. of Kent at Canterbury, Eng. 1988; Montreal Diocesan Coll. 1989; Coll. of Emmanuel and St. Chad, Saskatoon 1990; Thorneloe Univ. 1991; Bishop's University 1993; m. Dorothy Elizabeth d. The Venerable and Mrs. W.H. Bradley 1963; children: Valerie, Richard, Geoffrey; PRIMATE OF THE ANGLICAN CHURCH OF CANADA 1986– ; o. Deacon 1959 and Priest 1960; Asst. Curate, St. Thomas' Church, Ottawa 1959–61; Diocesan Chaplain, Univ. of Ottawa 1961–66; Instr., Ottawa Teachers' Coll. 1962–66; Rector, St. Bede's Ch. Winnipeg 1966–72; Instr., St. Paul's High Sch., Winnipeg 1967–69; Archdeacon of Winnipeg 1969–74; Incumbent of St. Martin's Winnipeg, St. Paul's, Middlechurch and Priest Supr. River N. Ang. Parishes 1972; Rector, St. Paul's Cath. Regina and Dean, Diocese of Qu'Appelle 1974–77; Bishop of Qu'Appelle 1977–82; Archbishop of Qu'Appelle (Metropolitan of Rupert's Land) 1982–86; former Pres. of Council, Coll. of Emmanuel and St. Chad, Saskatoon; mem. Vancouver Assembly World Council of Chs. 1983 and Canberra Assembly 1991; Co-leader Ecumenical Easter visit to Chs. in Soviet Union 1985; Chrmn. Ecumenical Sect. 1988 Lambeth Conf.; mem., Central Ctte., World Council of Churches 1991– ; Home: 195 Westminster Ave., Toronto, Ont. M6R 1N9; Office: 600 Jarvis St., Toronto, Ont. M4Y 2J6.

**PEETOOM, Adrian,** B.A., M.A.; author; editor; b. The Netherlands 18 Aug. 1934; s. Albert and Gerhardina (Zwarteveen) P.; e. McMaster Univ., B.A. 1958; Univ. of Toronto, M.A. 1983; m. Johanna P. d. Bastian and Margaretha Smouter 30 Aug. 1958; children: Margaret, Albert, Geraldine, Laura, Emily, Jenny; DIR., EDUCATIONAL R & D, SCHOLASTIC CANADA LTD. 1989– ; Indus. Instr., Canada Packers 1958–60; Salesman, R.L. Crain Ltd. 1960–62; pub. speaker & lectr.; Dir., Ctte. for Pub. Justice 1968–71; Ont. Alliance of Christian Schs. 1970–72; Dir., Can. Council Teachers of Eng. 1977–81; Chief Ed. & Mgr., Pub. Div., Scholastic Canada Ltd. 1982–89; author of more than 50 articles; author: 'Safe Risks With Whole Books' 1987; 'Professional Reflections and Connections' 1991; 'ConneXions' 1993; co-author: 'The Workshop Organizer's Little Red Book' 1976; 'Three I's' 1982; 'Professional Manual' 1985; 'Literacy-Based Learning' 1988; 'Reflexions' 1992; transl.: 'Siberian Miracle' 1991; co-transl.: 'Portraits' 1986; Home: 107 Parkwood Dr., Chatham, Ont. N7M 2B1; Office: 123 Newkirk Rd., Richmond Hill, Ont. L4C 3G5.

**PEITCHINIS, Stephen Gabriel;** M.A., Ph.D.; educator; b. Macedonia, Greece, 12 Oct. 1925; s. Gabriel K. and Afrodita (Sarbinoff) P.; e. (primary) Greece; (secondary) Bulgaria 1945; Univ. of Sofia, Bulgaria 1945–49; Univ. of W. Ont., B.A. 1954, M.A. 1955; London Sch. of Econ., Ph.D. 1960; m. Jacquelyn A., Prof., Dept. of Econ., Head, Dept. of Econ. 1985–91 Univ. of Calgary; PROFESSOR EMERITUS, UNIV. OF CALGARY 1992; Instr. in Econ. and Pol. Science, Univ. of W. Ont. 1955–58, Asst. Prof. 1960, Assoc. Prof. 1963; joined present Univ. as Prof. 1968, Dean and Prof., Faculty of Business 1973–76; Research Assoc., Task Force on Labour Relations, Ottawa, 1968; Assoc. Dir., Human Resources Research Council of Alta., 1969–71; Chrmn. and Dir. of Research, Comm. Inquiry into Financing Post-Secondary Educ. in Can. 1970–71; Killam Resident Research Fellow, Univ. of Cal., 1982; author, 'Employment and Wages in Canada,' 1965; 'Canadian Labour Economics,' 1970; 'Labour-Management Relations in the Railway Industry,' 1971; 'Financing Post-Secondary Education in Canada'; 1971; 'The Employability of Welfare Recipients,' 1972; 'The Canadian Labour Market,' 1975; 'The Implications of Technological Change for Employment and Skills,' 1977; 'The Attitudes of Trade Unions Towards Technological changes, 1980'; 'The Employment Implications of Computers and Telecommunications Technology,' 1981; 'Computer Technology and Employment' 1983; 'Issues in Management-Labour Relations in the 1990s,' 1985; 'Women at Work: Discrimination and Response,' 1989; and a number of other studies in the general area of Technology and Employment; also articles in various prof. journs.; mem., Bd. of Gov., Cdn. Council on Social Development; Candn. Econ. Assn.; Am. Econ. Assn.; Indust. Relations Research Assn.; London Sch. Econ. Soc.; recreation: golf; Home: #13, 1901 Varsity Estates Dr. N.W., Calary, Alta. T3B 4T7.

**PEKARSKY, Daniel U.,** LL.B.; executive; b. Edmonton, Alta. 24 Sept. 1937; s. Leo and Minnie (Dlin) P.; e. Univ. of Alta. B.A. 1959, LL.B. 1960; m. Trudy d. late Henry Singer, Edmonton, Alta. 5 March 1963; children: Lise, Josh, Adam; Dir., Intensity Resources Ltd.; Mr. Jax Fashions Inc.; Westcoast Energy Inc.; Pegasus Gold Inc.; Dir. and Offr. numerous private Candn. corps.; called to Bar of Alta. 1961; practiced law Edmonton 1961–79; Pres., The Corporate Advisory Group Inc.; mem. Law Soc. Alta.; Candn. Bar Assn.; Home: 1598 Angus Dr., Vancouver, B.C. V6J 4H3; Office: #1780 – 999 W. Hastings St., Vancouver, B.C. V6C 2W2.

**PELADEAU, Erik;** printing executive; b. Montreal, Que.; s. Pierre and Raymonde (Chopin) P.; e. Collège Bourget (Rigaud); Ecole Hautes Etudes Commerciales, admin.; s. Marie-Josée Poupart; children: Daphné Gabrielle, Didier; SENIOR VICE-PRES. & ASST. TO THE PRESIDENT, QUEBECOR PRINTING INC. 1992– ; acquired Les Etiquettes Lelys 1984; Asst. Vice-Pres., Quebecor Printing 1988; Vice-Pres., Purchasing, Sales & Mktg. 1989; Mem., Extve. Ctte. & Bd. of Dir., Quebecor, Quebecor Printing, Donohue; Mem, Bd. of Dir., Le Groupe PJC Inc.; Owner, Pres. & Bd. of Dir., Le Group Lelys; Bd. of Dir., Ste. Justine Hosp.; clubs: St-Denis, Rosemère Golf; Office: 612 St. Jacques, Montreal, Que. H3C 4M8.

**PÉLADEAU, Pierre,** L.Ph., M.A., B.C.L.; editor; publisher; b. Montreal, Que. 11 Apr. 1925; s. Henri and Elmire (Fortier) P.; e. Académie Querbes; Coll. Jean-de-Brébeuf; Coll. Ste-Marie; Univ. de Montréal L.Ph., M.A.; Univ. McGill B.C.L.; children: Eric, Isabelle, Pierre-Karl, Anne-Marie, Esther, Pierre Jr., Jean; PRESIDENT AND C.E.O., QUEBECOR INC.; Dir. Sodarcan Inc.; Member, Order of Canada 1987; Officier de l'Ordre National du Québec 1989; First Chancellor, Ste-Anne Univ., Nova Scotia 1988– ; Hon. Doctorate, Univ. du Québec; Club: St-Denis; Home: 1373 Chemin Ste-Marguerite, Ste-Marguerite Station, Qué. J0T 2K0; Office: 612 St-James St., Montréal, Qué. H3C 4M8.

**PELCHAT, Jocelyne,** B.A., LL.B.; b. Montréal, Que. 12 Feb. 1942; d. Vic and Thérèse (Darveau) Pelchat; e. Univ. of Montréal B.A., Licence en Droit 1963–66; Univ. of London, Engl. Internat. Law; grad. London Inst. of World Affairs 1968; EXTVE. DIR., SPACE CAMP CANADA 1994– and SR. PARTNER, PELCHAT MORIN & ASSOC. 1991– ; National Film Bd. of Can. 1975–77, Chief of Info. and Promotion 1977–78, Chief of Internat. Mkt. 1978–79, Comnr.'s Office 1979–80; Dir. Distribution and Mktg., Telefilm Canada 1980–82; V.P. Corporate Affairs, Astral Film Enterprises (Astral Bellevue Pathe Inc.) 1982–85; Vice Pres. Dailies, Quebecor Inc. 1985–88; Publisher, Le Journal de Montréal 1987–89; Pres. & C.O.O., Provost/Ronalds-Reynolds Inc. 1989–90; mem. Bds. of Admin., Petro Canada 1985–91; Maritime Life Assurance Co. 1987– ; Université du Québec à Montréal 1990– ; Internat. Trade Adv. Ctte. 1988–91; The Counc. for Candn. Unity 1986– ; Chamber of Commerce of Metrop. Montreal 1987– ; The Candn. Chamber of Commerce 1989–91; Pres. of Audit Ctte. Petro-Canada 1988–91; Petro-Canada Limited 1991– ; Le Devoir Inc. 1993– ; Office: 168 Beverley Ave., Mount Royal, Que. H3P 1K7.

**PELLER, John E.,** LL.B.; business executive; b. Hamilton, Ont. 10 March 1957; s. Joseph A. and Shirley Constance (Martin) P.; e. Univ. of West. Ont. LL.B. 1980; Osgoode Hall Bar Admission Course 1982; L'institut de Touraine 1984; m. Diane d. Mildred and Jack Seymour 1 July 1989; children: John, Jordan, Grayden; PRES. & CHIEF OPERATING OFFICER, ANDRES WINES LTD. 1993– ; Lawyer, Evans, Husband 1980; Sales Rep., Andrés Wines Ltd. 1983; Mgr., Corp. Planning & Devel., Nabisco Brands Inc. 1985; Regional Mktg. Mgr., Grocery Products Div. 1987; Vice-Pres., Sales & Mktg. Planning, Andrés Wines 1989; Bd. of Dir. 1990; Extve. Vice-Pres., Sales & Mktg. 1991; Dir., the Ont. C. of C. (Mem., Sr. Corp. Advisory Group); Mem, Law Soc. of U.C.; Hamilton Law Assn.; Hamilton Med. Legal Soc.; clubs: Hamilton, Hamilton Golf & Country; Home: 1609 Brookbridge, Burlington, Ont. L7P 4S9; Office: P.O. Box 10550, Winona, Ont. L8E 5S4.

**PELLER, Joseph A.,** M.D., M.R.C.P.(E), F.R.C.P.(C); business executive; b. Gara, Hungary 18 Mar. 1926; s. Andrew and Magdalena (Borits) P.; e. Lawrence Park Collegiate, Toronto; Univ. of Toronto M.D. 1948; m. Constance Shirley d. Angus and Mabel Martin 2 Aug. 1952; children: Joseph Jr., Angus, John, James, Jeffrey, Lori; CHAIRMAN, C.E.O. AND DIR., ANDRES WINES LTD. 1966– ; Dir./Trustee, RoyFund Group; Chief of Med. and Dir. Radio-Isotope Lab., Hamilton Civic Hosp. 1960–65; recreations: sailing, swimming, farming; Clubs: Hamilton Golf & Country; Hamilton

Yacht; The Hamilton Club; The Tamahaac (Ancaster, Ont.); Home: 376 Filman Rd., R.R. #1, Ancaster, Ont. L9G 3K9; Office: P.O. Box 10550, Winona, Ont. L8E 5S4.

**PELLETIER, Andrée,** B.A.; actress, sculptor and artist; b. Montreal, Qué. 24 Aug. 1951; d. Gérard and Alexandrine (Leduc) P.; e. Maternelle Leveillée, Montreal 1955; Ecole Ste. Catherine Sienne 1959; Coll. Marie de France 1963; Acad. Michèle Provost 1967; Coll. Ste. Marie 1968; Univ. du Québec, B.A. (Hons.) 1971; exhns. incl. Galerie Gadbois 1962; Pavillon Lafontaine (graphics and sculptures) 1968; Pavillon St Joseph (graphics) 1970; Galerie Luducu (graphics and sculptures) 1972; studied drama under Ghislain Fillion 1966–67; appeared in 'Les Parascos Du Saint-Marie' 1968–69; 'Le Chien Show' Univ. du Qué. 1970; 'Le Show de la Mort' Pavillon St-Joseph 1971; 'An Italian Straw Hat' Stratford, Ont. 1971; 'Ni Professeur Ni Gorille ' La Quenouille Bleue Que. Tour 1972; has appeared in TV, radio and film incl. 'Le Sel De La Semaine' 1969; 'A La Seconds' 1970; 'Pierre, Jean, Jacques' 1970–71 (all TV); 'Le Festin Des Morts' (Nat. Film Bd.) 1965; 'Les Males' (feature film) 1970; 'A Moving Experience' (Nat. Film Bd.) 1973; 'The Man Who Ran Away' (CBC 'To See Ourselves' Series) 1973; 'The Execution of Private Slovik' 1974; 'The Apprenticeship of Duddy Kravitz' 1974 (both feature films); author of 'Manifeste de la Quenouille Bleue' 1972; 'La vie magique de Java le Pou' (illustrator) 1974; recreations: dancing, tennis; Address: 147 rue Abbott, Westmount, Que. H3Z 2K1.

**PELLETIER, Hon. Gérard,** C.C., P.C., B.A.; former politician; b. Victoriaville, Que. 21 June 1919; s. Achille and Leda (Dufresne) P.; e. Nicolet Semy.; Mont-Laurier Coll.; Univ. of Montreal, B.A.; m. Alexandrine, d. Joseph Leduc, Montreal, Que., 27 Feb. 1943; children: Anne-Marie, Louise, Jean, Andrée; Chrmn. of Bd., National Museums Canada 1984–87; Secretary-Gen. Jeunesse étudiante catholique, 1939–43; Field Secy., World Student Relief, Geneva, 1945–47; Reporter, 'Le Devoir' 1947–50; Dir., 'Le Travail' (trade union organ) 1950–61; Editor of 'La Presse,' 1961–65; a Broadcaster and Columnist since 1950; 1st el. to H. of C. for Hochelaga in g.e. 1965; re-el. g.e. June 1968; apptd. Parlty. Asst. to Secy. of State for External Affairs, 20 Apl. 1967; Minister without Portfolio, 20 Apl. 1968; Secy. of State July 1968; Min. of Communications, Trudeau cabinet, 1972–75; Can. Ambassador to France 1975–81; Permanent Rep. to U.N. (New York) 1981–84; Apptd. Companion of the Order of Canada 1978; author 'La Crise d'Octobre' 1971; 'Les années d'impatience' 1983; 'Le temps des choix' 1986; Roman Catholic.

**PELLETIER, Jean;** C.M.; b. Chicoutimi, Qué. 21 Feb. 1935; s. Burroughs and Marie (Desautels) P.; e. Séminaire de Trois-Rivières; Coll. des Jésuites de Québec; Univ. Laval Law and Social Sciences; m. Hélène d. Wilbrod Bhêrer 3 June 1961; children: Jean, Marie; CHIEF OF STAFF TO THE PRIME MINISTER OF CANADA 1993– ; Journalist CFCM-TV Québec 1957; Corr. Radio-Canada Québec 1958–59; Press Secy. Premier of Qué. 1959; Extve. Secy. Comn. des monuments historiques du Québec 1960–62; Technical Advisor to the Secretary of the Province of Québec 1963–64; Broker, Levesque & Beaubien, Québec 1964–70; Vice Prés. Dumont Express, Québec 1970–73; L'Action Sociale Ltée 1973–77; Mayor, Québec City 1977–89; Dir. Festival d'art dramatique du Can. 1961–65; Adm.; Théâtre populaire du Qué. 1966–74; Théâtre du Trident 1970–76; Nat. Pres. Assn. des Scouts du Can. 1969–72; Extve. Dir., Centraide Qué. 1973–77; Prés. Carnaval de Québec 1973; Past Prés., Féd. Candn. Muns. 1982–83; Past Prés. L'Union des Municipalities du Qué. 1986–88; Vice Prés., Assoc. Int. des Maires des Capitales francophones (A.I.M.F.) 1979–89; Pres. Expert Group on old age people policies 1990–91; Chief of Staff to the Leader of the Opposition 1991–93; mem. Extve. Qué. Urban Community 1977–89; Mem. Québec-Ontario task force on the rapid train project in the Québec-Windsor corridor 1989–91; Offr., Ordre de la pléiade of the International Assembly of French parliamentarians; Member of the Order of Canada, 1985; Offr. of the Legion of Honor (France) 1988; recreations: skiing, swimming; Clubs: Cercle de la Garnison; Home: 920 ave des Braves, Québec City, Qué. G1S 1C6.

**PELLETIER, Marcel R.,** Q.C., B.A., B.Ph., LL.L., D.E.S.D.; laywer; b. Palmarolle, Que. 2 Sept. 1936; s. Robert A. and Berthilda (Ayotte) P.; e. Univ. of Ottawa, B.A., B.Ph., LL.L., D.E.S.D.; The Hague Acad. of Internat. Law; McGill Law Fac.; CONSULTANT, SASKATCHEWAN LEGISLATIVE ASSEMBLY 1992– ; Fgn. Serv. Offr., Dept. of External Affairs, Third Sec. & Vice Consul, Candn. Mission to the UN in Geneva, Switz. 1964–66; Rsch. Offr., Lib. of Parliament 1966–69; Clerk Asst. (Legal), House of Commons 1969–83; Law Clerk & Parliamentary Counsel, House of Commons 1983–91; Sec., Candn. Br., Internat. Assn. of French Speaking Parliamentarians & Canada-France Interparlty. Assn. 1968–70; Lectr., Parlty. Law, Univ. of Ottawa 1973– ; Lectr. Pol. Sci., Univ. of Ottawa 1990– ; Guest Lectr., Univ. of Michigan 1986– ; Q.C. 1981; Chevalier de l'Ordre de la Pléiade 1984; Parlty. Dir., Candn. Parlty. Internships Prog. 1970–91; Trustee, Found. for Study of Process of Govt.; Mem., Candn. Assn. of Parlty. Couns. 1983–91; Mem., Assn. of Clerks-at-the-Table-in-Canada (Pres. 1982–83) 1969–91; Candn. Assn. of Law Profs.; recreations: skiing, skating, music; Home: P.O. Box 135, R.R. 1 Lac du Cardinal, Poltimore, Que. J0X 2S0.

**PELLETIER, Pierre Raphaël,** B.A., B.P.H., M.A.; writer, poet, critic, painter, sculptor; b. Hull, Que. 13 Dec. 1946; s. Jacques Yvon and Hughette (Tremblay) P.; e. Saint Paul Univ. and Univ. of Ottawa B.A.(PH) 1968; Univ. of Ottawa, B.P.H. 1970, M.A. 1976; m. Colette d. Denis and Yvette Latrémouille 6 June 1975; children: Isabelle, Gabriel, François; DIRECTOR, CONTINUING EDUCATION, UNIV. OF OTTAWA 1982– ; Visual Art Critic, Radio Canada 1977–80; 'Le Droit' 1976–77, 1968–69; Prof., Philosophy of Art, of Leisure, Univ. of Ottawa 1985–86; School Trustee, Prescott-Russell Public System 1976–82; art consultant; Pres., L'Assn. des auteurs de l'Ont.; L'Alliance culturelle de l'Ont.; Porte-parole Nat. pur le financement des arts au Canada; Artistic Vice-Pres. of cultural fed. (French-Candn.); Pres., Francophone Distance Edn. Network; Edit. Bd. Mem., 'Liaison'; Senate Mem., Univ. of Ottawa; num. solo & group shows (paintings, sculptures, drawing) Que. & Ont.; frequent speaker-lecturer; Mem., Candn. Assn. for Univ. Continuing Edn.; Ont. Council for Univ. Cont. Edn.; Candn. Assn. of Distance Edn.; author: 'Le premier instant' 1992, 'Sur les profondeurs de l'île' 1990, 'Zinc or' 1986, 'Victor Blanc' 1981, 'Temps de vies' 1978 and num. articles on culture, arts; recreations: swimming; Home: 23 rue Castlebeau, C.P. 515, Embrun, Ont. K0A 1W0; Office: 139 Louis Pasteur, Ottawa, Ont. K1N 6N5.

**PELLEY, Marvin Hugh,** B.Sc., B.Eng., P.Eng.; mining executive; b. St. Anthony, NF 24 Nov. 1947; s. Hugh Albert and Alma Josie (Harnett) P.; e. Memorial Univ. of NF, B.Sc. 1969; Tech. Univ. of N.S., B.Eng. with distinction 1973; m. Velma D. d. Mable and Malcolm Gillard 5 Nov. 1965; one d. Rhonda Mary-Jane; VICE-PRES., GROUP VICE-PRES., EXTVE. VICE-PRES., CORP. DEVELOP. & ENGR., PRES., PROJECTS AND COAL, PRES. CORP. DEVELOPMENT & PROJECTS and DIR. CURRAGH RESOURCES INC. 1986– ; mining contractor under contract with Whissel Mining Ltd. 1969–71; Gen. Foreman of Opns., Chief Mining Engr., Iron Ore Co. of Can. 1973–78; Extve. Vice-Pres. & Partner, Baumgartl and Assoc., Ltd. 1978–81; Mgr., Tech. Serv., Dennison Mines Limited, for Quintette Coal Project 1981–86; Extve. Vice-Pres., Westray Mining Corp.; Pres., Frame Mining Corp.; Pres. & Dir., Stronsay Corp.; invited speaker at various profl. assn. meetings; Founding Mem., Springdale Men's Club; mem., Assn. of Profl. Engr. of the Prov. of NF; of B.C.; of the Yukon; United Ch. of Can.; Past mem., Lion's Club; Springdale Men's Club; TUNS Alumni Assn., MUN Alumni Assn.; author of published articles & presentations on mining & related activites; recreations: reading, outdoor activities, canoeing, deepsea fishing, salmon & fly fishing, golf & Lynden Sports Club Alaska (private); Home: 1527 Manorbrook Ct., Mississauga, Ont. L5M 4A9; Office: 95 Wellington St. W., Toronto, Ont. M5J 2N7.

**PELTIER, W. Richard,** B.Sc., M.Sc., Ph.D., F.R.S.C.; professor of physics; b. Vancouver, B.C. 31 Dec. 1943; s. Ernest Lucien and Frances Elaine (Reeves) P.; e. Vancouver Tech. Sch. 1962; Univ. of B.C., B.Sc. 1967; Univ. of Toronto, M.Sc. 1969, Ph.D. 1971; m. Claude-Françoise Marchand 10 May 1979; UNIVERSITY PROF., DEPT. OF PHYSICS, UNIV. OF TORONTO 1979– ; Asst. Prof., present univ. 1973–77; Alfred P. Sloan Found. Fellow 1976–78; E.W.R. Steacie Fellow 1978; Kirk Bryan Award of the Geological Soc. of Am. 1979; Assoc. Prof. 1977–79; Full Prof. 1979–93; Killam Sr. Rsch. Fellow 1980–82; Fellow, Am. Geophysical Union 1986– ; F.R.S.C. 1986; John Simon Guggenheim Found. Fellow 1986–88; Sr. Fellow, Massey Coll. 1989– ; Fellow, Am. Meteorological Soc. 1991– ; recipient, Patterson Medal, Federal Dept. of the Environment 1992; Mem., Candn. Assn. of Physicists; Candn. Meterol. & Oceanographic Soc.; Cand. Geophys. Union; Am. Meterol. Soc.; Am. Geophys. Union; author of 185 sci. articles, book chapters & books; Home: 55 Prince Arthur Ave., #902, Toronto, Ont. M5R 1B3; Office: Toronto, Ont. M5S 1A7.

**PELTON, John S.,** B.Comm., C.A.; business executive; b. Windsor, Ont. 10 May 1946; s. Stafford Baker and Gertrude Lillian P.; e. Univ. of Toronto B.Comm. 1969; Clarkson Gordon C.A. 1972; m. Darlene d. Anthony Couch and Ethelwyn Woolcock 24 May 1969; children: Sarah, Rebecca, Charles, Elizabeth; PRES. & CHIEF EXECUTIVE OFFICER, FEDERAL INDUSTRIES LTD. 1992– ; Dir., Federal Industries Ltd.; Morgan Finan. Corp.; Regal Greetings & Gifts Inc.; Westbury Candn. Life; Chief Finan. Offr., Canavest House Limited 1973–74; Dir. of Finance, Federal Industries Ltd. 1974–76; Treas. & Chief Finan. Offr. 1976–79; Vice-Pres., Finance 1979–86; Sr. Vice-Pres., Corp. Devel. 1986–87; Sr. Vice-Pres. & Dir./Head, Mergers & Acquisitions, Merrill Lynch Canada Inc. 1987–88; Pres. & Chief Op. Offr. & Dir. (& Dir., principal operating subs.), Financial Trustco Capital Ltd. (now FT Capital Ltd.) 1988–90; Morgan Finan. Corp. 1988–91; Pres., Chief Op. Offr. & Managing Partner, Greystone Partners Inc. 1989–91; Pres. & Chief Op. Offr., Federal Industries Ltd. 1991–92; Mem., Candn. Inst. of C.A.s; Inst. of C.A.s of Ont.; of Man.; Home: 2186 Courrier Lane, Mississauga, Ont. L5C 1V2; Office: Suite 400, 180 Attwell Dr., Etobicoke, Ont. M9W 6A9.

**PEMBER, Ian D.,** B.Comm., C.A.; banking executive; b. Toronto, Ont. 31 May 1956; s. William F. and Kathleen M. (Dales) P.; e. Univ. of Toronto B.Comm. 1978; m. Susan B.E. d. John and Barbara Cook 14 May 1983; children: Colin Glenn, Faith Elizabeth, Clare Hope; GENERAL MANAGER, CANADIAN IMPERIAL BANK OF COMMERCE 1991– ; Peat Marwick Thorne 1978–82; C.A. 1980; Vice-Pres., Citibank Canada 1982–91; Office: 700 Lawrence Ave. W., 4th Floor, Toronto, Ont. M5L 1A2.

**PENALIGON, John Jefferson,** B.A., D.H.A., C.H.E.; health executive; b. Toronto, Ont. 3 Sept. 1949; s. Clifford (JHC) and Florence (Stevens) P.; e. Univ. of Toronto, B.A. 1970, D.H.A. 1972; m. Sharon d. James and Margaret McMahon 14 Aug. 1970; children: Sarah, Jonathan; PRES., QUEENSWAY GEN. HOSP. 1986– ; Sr. Cons., Toronto Gen. Hosp. 1972–75; Dir., Spec. Serv., Victoria Hosp. Corp. 1975–79; Asst. Admin., Peel Meml. Hosp. 1979–84; Vice-Pres., Corp. Planning & Devel., Bestview Health Care 1984–85; Pres., Penaligon & Assoc. Health Care Cons. 1985–86; Preceptor & Status only Faculty, Univ. of Toronto Masters in Health Admin. Program; Active Mem., Soc. of Grads. in Health Admin.; CHE mem., Candn. Coll. of Health Services Extves.; Internat. Hosp. Fed.; Mem. at Large, Am. Hosp. Assn.; Vice Chrmn., Bd. of Dirs., Dorothy Ley Hospice; recreations: tennis, motorcycling, squash, boating; Clubs: PCYC; Boulevard; Home: 302 Trafalgar Rd., Oakville, Ont. L6J 3H2; Office: 150 Sherway Dr., Etobicoke, Ont. M9C 1A5.

**PENALUNA, David Reginald,** B.A., M.Ed.; educational administrator; b. Callington, Cornwall, England 25 Dec. 1943; s. Alfred Reginald and Muriel May (Treloar) P.; e. Sutton H.S. 1985 (scholarship); St. Luke's Coll., Exeter Univ., cert. ed. 1967; Univ. of Winnipeg, B.A. 1969; Univ. of Man., B.Ed. 1971, M.Ed. 1980; Univ. of Victoria, pre-Ph.D. 1983; m. Molly d. Thomas and Zena Givens 8 July 1967; children: Mark, Jason; HEADMASTER, ST. MICHAEL'S UNIV. SCHOOL 1988– ; Teacher of Eng. & Housemaster, St. John's Ravenscourt Sch. 1967–74; Teacher of Eng., Southway Comprehensive Sch. England 1974–75; A.A. Leach Sch. Winnipeg 1975–77; Head of Eng., St. John's Ravenscourt Sch. 1977–78; present sch. 1978–84; Principal (jr. sch.) 1984–87; (middle sch.) & Dep. Headmaster 1987–88; Mem., Man. English Curriculum Ctte.; Guest Lectr., Univ. of Man.; Univ. of Victoria; principal actor 'Ups and Downs' (Quest Films feature movie) 1981; 1st ever dir. of musical 'Osmosis'; Bd. of Dir., United Way of Victoria; Victoria's Commonwealth Games Orgn. 1989–94; Greater Victoria's Schools Sports Assn.; Mem., B.C. Coll. of Teachers; Candn. Assn. of Independent Schools; Independent Schools Assn. of B.C.; Pres., 'Incogs' Cricket Club; author of one article; recreations: jogging, reading, writing, languages; clubs: Union Club of Victoria; Address: Reynolds House, 3400 Richmond Rd., Victoria, B.C. V8P 4P5.

**PENCE, Alan R.,** B.A., M.Sc., Ph.D.; university professor; b. Bend, Oregon 28 Oct. 1948; s. Don P. and Evelyn Hughes P.; e. Portland State Univ. B.A. 1970, M.S. 1972; Univ. of Oregon Ph.D. 1980; m.Miriam d. Nathan and Ruth Durbach; children: Leah, Eliot; PROF., SCHOOL OF CHILD & YOUTH CARE, UNIV. OF VICTORIA; front-line worker, program dir. & child care educator 1971–81; joined Univ. of Victoria 1981; Principal, Child Care Consulting; Co-ordinator, Unit for Child Care Research, Univ. of Victoria; co-recipient, RWB Jackson Award, Candn. edn. Rsch. assn. for best

Candn. edn. article 1985; Mem., Soc. for Rsch. in Child Devel.; Internat. Soc. for the Study of Behav. Devel.; Am. Psychological Soc.; Learned Societies of Can.; Am. Sociological Assn.; Candn. Child Care Fed.; author of over 70 articles, chapters & reports; editor: 'Ecological Research with Children & Families' 1988, 'Canadian Child Care in Context' 1992; co-editor: 'Professional Child & Youth Care' 1987, 'Perspectives in Professional Child and Youth Care' 1990, 'Family Day Care' 1992, 'Valuing Quality' 1994; recreations: gardening, skiing, his children's activities; Home: 1955 Waterloo Rd., Victoria, B.C. V8P 1J4; Office: Victoria, B.C. V8W 2Y2.

**PENCER, Gerald Norman;** financial executive; b. Montreal, Que. 26 April 1945; s. Harry and Clara (Bookman) P.; e. Sir George Williams Univ.; m. Nancy d. Irving and Claire (Bidner) Halperin 19 March 1967; children: Stacey, Holly, Clarke; CHAIRMAN & CHIEF EXECUTIVE OFFICER, COTT CORPORATION 1988– ; Associated Student Ventures while at univ.; C.J. Food Services Inc. 1970; Turner Valley Holdings 1980; Financial Trustco Capital 1981; Dir., Onex Corp.; Mount Sinai Hosp.; The Clarke Inst.; Mem., Holy Blossom Congregation; recreations: travelling, fishing; Office: 6525 Viscount Rd., Mississauga, Ont. L4V 1H6.

**PENDERGAST, James F.,** E.M., C.D., D.Sc., U.E.L.; retired regular army officer and civil servant; archaeologist; b. Cornwall, Ont. 26 May 1921; s. Harold James and Mary Evelyn (Thompson) P.; e. St. Columbans Sch.; Cornwall (Ont.) Coll. Inst.; Arty. Staff Course 1950; Candn. Army Staff Coll. 1953; m. Mary Margaret d. late John Strong Denton, 21 Oct. 1944; children: James Denton, Mary Margaret Isobel, Elizabeth Anne, Harold John; Asst. Dir. Operations, Nat. Museum of Man, Nat. Museums of Can. 1972–78; enlisted Stormont Dundas and Glengarry Highlanders NPAM 1936, CASF 1940; served UK Theatre 1941–43, seconded US Army Intelligence 1945, enrolled Candn. Regular Army (Intelligence) 1946, trans. RCA 1949, retired Lt. Col. 1973; Aide-de-Camp Lt. Gov. Sask. 1955–56; United Nations Observer Group in Lebanon 1958; Extve. Officer Land Operations Allied Forces Central Europe 1968–71; largely responsible for archaeological definition of St. Lawrence Iroquoian tribe; co-author: 'Cartier's Hochelaga and the Dawson Site' 1972; author: 'The Massawomeck: Raiders and Traders into the Chesapeake Bay in the Seventeenth Century' Am. Philosophical Soc. 1991; author various articles, books, and papers in archaeol. (since 1962), ethnohistory, history and mil. fields in Canada & U.S.A.; Vice Pres. Candn. Archaeol. Assn. 1971–72; Past Pres., Merrickville Hist. Soc. 1978–79; mem. Champlain Soc.; Ont. Archaeol. Soc. Ottawa Chapter; Pa. Archaeol. Soc.; N.Y. State Archaeol. Assn.; American Soc. for Ethnohistory; Soc. for American Archaeology; Candn. Inst. of Strategic Studies; Past Regional Chrmn., Eastern Ont., Western Que., Heritage Can. 1979–81; Royal Candn. Arty. Assn.; Extve. Central Region, 150th Anniversary Rideau Canal, 1979–82; Charter Trustee, Merrickville Heritage Found. 1983–92; Charter Mem. and Vice Pres., Ont. Counc. of Archaeology 1986–90; rec'd. McGill Univ. D.Sc. (Hon. c.) 1976; U.S. Army Commendation 1947; awarded Queen Elizabeth II Jubilee Medal, 1978; Ontario Volunteer Service Award 1988; Grenville County Historical Soc. Award of Merit 1988; Ont. Archaeological Soc. 25 Year Award 1988; Soc. for Am. Archaeology Crabtree Award for 1991; Fellow N.Y. State Archaeological Assn. 1991; recreations: skiing, philately, history; Home: 'Applegate,' R.R. 4, Merrickville, Ont. K0G 1N0.

**PENELHUM, Terence Michael,** M.A., B.Phil., D.Hu., D.Litt., F.R.S.C.; educator; b. Bradford-on-Avon, Eng. 26 Apl. 1929; s. Charles Arnold and Dorothy Eva (Mustoe) P.; e. Weymouth Grammar Sch.; Univ. of Edinburgh M.A. 1950; Oriel Coll. Oxford (Campbell Fraser Scholar) B.Phil. 1952; Yale Univ. (Eng.-Speaking Union Fellow) 1952–53; Univ. of Lethbridge D.Hu. 1982; Lakehead Univ. D. Litt. 1982; Univ. Waterloo D.Litt. 1990; Univ. Calgary LL.D. 1991; m. Edith d. William and Lucy Andrews 8 July 1950; children: Rosemary Claire, Andrew Giles (d.); PROF. EMERITUS OF RELIGIOUS STUDIES, UNIV. OF CALGARY 1988– , Prof. 1978–88; Lectr. to Assoc. Prof. of Philos. Univ. of Alta. 1953–63; Prof. of Philos. present Univ. 1963–78, Head of Philos. 1963–70, Dean of Arts & Science 1964–67, mem. Bd. Govs. 1967–70; Visiting Prof., Berkeley 1958, Colo. 1959, Mich. 1961, Wash., Seattle 1964 and 1968, Univ. B.C. 1963, Waterloo 1973–74; Dir. Calgary Inst. for Humanities 1976–79; mem. Adv. Acad. Panel Can. Council 1971–75, Chrmn. 1973–74, Chrmn. Negotiated Grants Comte. 1974–78; author 'Survival and Disembodied Existence' 1970; 'Religion and Rationality' 1971; 'Problems of Religious Knowledge' 1971; 'Hume' 1975; 'God and Skepticism' 1983; 'Butler' 1985; 'David Hume: an Introduction to his Philosophical System' 1992; ed. 'Immortality' 1973; 'Faith' 1989; co-ed. 'The First Critique' 1969; awarded, Canada Council Molson Prize in Humanities, 1988; Anglican; Club: Royal Commonwealth; Office: Dept. Religious Studies, University of Calgary, Calgary, Alta. T2N 1N4.

**PENIKETT, Hon. Antony;** politician; writer; b. 14 Nov. 1945; s. Erik John Keith and Sarah Ann (Colwell) P.; m. Lula d. Mary Johns 1974; children: John Tahmoh, Sarah Lahlil, Stephanie Yahsan; LEADER, YUKON NDP 1981– ; Chief Steward Un. Steelworkers Clinton, Creek Yukon 1969–70; Extve. Asst. to Nat. Leader, NDP 1975–76; Mun. Councillor, City of Whitehorse 1977–79; el. to Yukon Legis. Assembly 1978– ; Opposition Leader 1981–85; Premier of the Yukon 1985–92; Nat. Pres. NDP 1981–85; Fed. Councillor NDP 1973– ; Office: P.O. Box 2703, Whitehorse, Yukon Y1A 2C6.

**PENN, Ian M.,** B.A., M.B., B.S., FRAC(P), FRCP(C).; cardiologist; b. Sydney, Aust. 13 Sept. 1952; s. Leon and Lola P.; e. Newington College; Univ. of Sydney B.A. 1977, M.B.B.S. (Hons), 1980 (Archie Cunningham Prize, 1st in final year med.); m. Sandy d. Micky and Frank Whitehouse 24 Nov. 1979; children: Asher, Elisa-Rose, Daniel, Isaac; CARDIOLOGIST & DIRECTOR OF INTERVENTION CARDIOLOGY, VANCOUVER GENERAL HOSP. & CLIN. ASSOC. PROF. OF MED., UNIV. OF B.C. 1993– ; training in internal med. & cardiology, St. George Hosp. & Prince of Wales (Sydney) 1986–88; Fellow in coronary angioplasty (Heritage Rsch. Fellow) Calgary, Alta.; Assoc. Dir. of Rsch. & Edn., Arizona Heart Inst. 1989; Asst. Prof., Med., Univ. of W. Ont. & Dir., Interventional Cardiology, Victoria Hosp. 1990–93; research interest: role of new devices in treating arterosclerotic coronary disease; Instigator & Principal Investigator, TASC II 1989; End Stress 1990; Coinvestigator, Empar Restenosis Trial 1989; Mem., Cardial Soc. of Australia; Candn. Cardiovas. Soc.; Assoc. Mem., Am. Coll. of Cardiol.; Fellow, Australasian Coll. of Physicians & Surgeons; Royal Candn. Coll. of Physicians & Surgeons; author: 'Intravascular Stents: Evolution from Prototype to Clinical Trial' 1992 and over 40 articles; recreations: skiing, windsurfing, hiking, sea kayaking; Office: 865 West 10th Ave., Vancouver, B.C. V5Z 1L7.

**PENNEFATHER, Joan;** government film commissioner; cultural agency executive; b. Montreal, Que. 7 May 1943; d. John and Marjorie (Smeaton-Murphy); e. Marianopolis Coll.; McGill Univ.; Concordia (Loyola) Univ.; Oxford Univ., Eng., B.A. (Hons. History) 1965, B.A. (Comm. Arts) 1975; M.A. (Qual.); B.Phil (incomplete); children: John Fox, Kristian Roberts; GOVERNMENT FILM COMMISSIONER AND CHAIRPERSON, NATIONAL FILM BOARD OF CANADA 1989– ; Audience Co-ordinator and then Asst. to the Dir. of Publicity and Promotion, CFCF-TV 1975–76; Administrator, Candn. Cultural Centre (Paris, France) 1976–77; Sponsored Program Offr., Nat. Film Board of Canada 1977–81; Extve. Asst. to the Depy. Film Commissioner 1981–83; Planning Co-ordinator 1983–86; Secy. Bd. of Trustees 1983– ; Vice Film Commissioner and Dir. of Corp. Affairs 1986–88; Candn. Govt. Film Commissioner by interim 1988–89; Mem. Bd. of Dirs., Telefilm Canada; National Arts Centre; Cinematheque Canada; Academy of Candn. Cinema and Television; l'Institut national de l'image et du son (INIS); Candn. Women in Radio and Television; Banff Television Foundation; Femmes du cinéma, de la télévision et de la vidéo de Montréal; Institut Internat. des Communications; Bd. of Govs., University of Montreal; was the moving force behind a roundtable 'Women, Film and Television – Sharing Worldwide Strategies for Change,' which brought together over 50 women from five continents and served as a pre-conference to the 23rd Annual Conference of the International Institute of Communications (IIC) 1992; recreations: skiing, swimming, canoeing, music; Home: 84 Belmont Ave., Ottawa, Ont K1S 0V3; Office: P.O. Box 6100, Stn. A, Montreal Que. H3C 3H5.

**PENNEFATHER, Sarah J.;** training company executive; b. Montreal, Que. 7 March 1951; d. John Barker and Marjorie Louise P.; e. Concordia Univ.; Ryerson Polytech.; Univ. de Lausanne, Suisse; m. Wayne Robert s. Robert and Marilyn Burns 23 Nov. 1984; one d.: Caitlin Pennefather Burns; PRES. & CO-FOUNDER, EXEGETICS INC.; Asst. Office Mgr., Readers Digest of Canada; Careers Advertising Mgr., Financial Times of Canada; Marketing/Conferences Asst. Mgr., Trigen/Emerald City; Dir., Electronic Desktop Publishing Assn.; Adv. Bd. Mem., Info Canada; Mem., Assn. of System Managers; recreations: skiing, swimming, bridge; Home: 16 First Ave., Toronto, Ont. M4M 1W8; Office: 275 Richmond W., Toronto, Ont. M5V 1X1.

**PENNER, Fredrick Ralph Cornelius,** B.A.; children's entertainer; television performer; b. Winnipeg, Man. 6 Nov. 1946; s. Edward William and Lydia Agathe (Winter) P.; e. J.B. Mitchell Elem. and Kelvin High Sch. Winnipeg 1965; Univ. of Winnipeg B.A. 1970; m. Odette d. Victor and Gianna Heyn 23 Aug. 1981; four children; HOST 'FRED PENNER'S PLACE' CBC Nat. TV 1984– , Nickelodeon MTV U.S. Nat. TV 1989–93; Pres., Cornelius Music Corp.; Vice Pres. Oak Street Music (music publishing and recording label); served Knowles Sch. for Boys Winnipeg residential treatment centres & Children's Home of Winnipeg 1969–72; toured Can. with Kornstock (a musical-comedy troupe) 1973–77; children's performer touring N.Am. since 1978; with choreographer wife Odette, estab. Sundance Childrens Dance Theatre 1978–80; recipient Juno Award Best Children's Album 1988; has released 8 records, 7 nominated for Junos, 3 rec'd 'Parents' Choice Award' and 3 videos 'The Cat Came Back,' 'A Circle of Songs' and 'What A Day'; author 'The Bump' 1984; 'Ebeenezer Sneezer' 1985; 'Rollerskating' 1987; (with Sheldon Oberman) 'The Polka Dot Pony' 1988; 'Sing Along Play Along' 1990; Hon. Chrmn. Rainbow Soc.; Fund Raising Spokesperson Prairie Theatre Exchange; Judicator, Christie Biscuit Book Awards; Hon. Chrmn. Sunshine Fund; Hon. Chrmn. Candn. UNICEF Halloween Campaign 1991–92; Hon. Chrmn., Candn. Down Syndrome Soc.; recipient Order of Canada 1992; Home: Winnipeg, Man.; Office: 1067 Sherwin Rd., Winnipeg, Man. R3H 0T8.

**PENNER, Hon. John,** B.A., B.Ed., M.L.A.; politician; b. Swift Current, Sask. 12 Dec. 1931; s. Cornelius C. and Helena P.; e. Univ. of Sask. B.A. 1965, B.Ed. 1959; m. Josephine d. Abram and Anna Brown 11 July 1953; children: Maxine, Sheila; MINISTER OF CROWN INVESTMENTS CORPORATION & ASSOCIATE MINISTER OF FINANCE 1993– ; Teacher, Sask. schools for 31 years; vice-principal & principal, Swift Current Comprehensive H.S.; was an active member of Sask. Teachers' Fed., serving on many cttes.; conducted teacher training programs in Uganda and Gambia for 2 summers (Project Overseas); co-owner of a business in Swift Current since 1982; Dir., Western Credit Union 16 yrs. (12 yrs. as Pres. of the Bd.); Past Alderman, Swift Current; 1st elected M.L.A. Swift Current g.e. 1991; Min. of Saskatchewan Energy & Mines 1991–93; clubs: Rotary; Home: 345 Powell Cres., Swift Current, Sask. S9H 4L7; Office: Room 346, Legis. Bldg., Regina, Sask. S4S 0B3.

**PENNER, Roland,** Q.C., B.A., LL.B.; b. Winnipeg, Man. 30 July 1924; s. Jacob and Rose (Shapak) P.; e. Univ. of Manitoba B.A. 1949, LL.B. 1961; m. 2ndly Janet Kay d. George and Irene Baldwin 11 Dec. 1982; children: (1st m.) Daniel Michael, Kathleen Anne, Paul Randall; (2nd m.) Anna Rose Baldwin, Laura Margaret Baldwin; DEAN, FACULTY OF LAW, UNIV. OF MANITOBA, 1989– ; Prof., Fac. of Law, Univ. of Man. 1968– ; practiced law with Zuken & Penner 1961–69; Couns. to Zuken, Penner & Assoc. 1969–81; Attorney-Gen., Prov. of Manitoba 1981–87; Min. responsible for the Liquor Control Act, Prov. of Manitoba 1981–87; Min. of Consumer and Corporate Affairs 1983–86; Min. of Education and Min. Responsible for Constitutional Affairs, Prov. of Manitoba 1987–88; author various articles on legal aid, aspects of privacy, police and the law, legal aspects of drug abuse, community legal services, collective bargaining, etc.; appearances in various symposia incl.: 'Values and Morals in Modern Life' Univ. of Man. Centennial symposium 1978; 'Making Law in a Cynical Society' Internat. Conf. on Law and Pub. Opinion, Fac. of Law Univ. of Man. 1981; 'Constraints on the Political Will' Access to Justice Lectr., Fac. of Law, Univ. of Windsor 1983; 'Courts and the Media: An Uneasy Relationship,' Candn. Inst. for Advanced Legal Studies, Cambridge Lectures 1985; 'The Social Context of Criminal Law Reform: Myths and Reality about Criminality and Crime' Reform of the Criminal Law at Inns of Court, London 1987; 'Bridging the Constitutional Gap' (Aboriginal Issues), Candn. Bar Assn. Symposium, Winnipeg Man. 1991; 'Delgamuuku and the Aboriginal Land Question,' Univ. of Victoria Symposium 1991; 'Professionalism in Legal Practice,' Candn. Federation of Law Socs., Calgary; Pres., Candn. Assn. of Univ. Teachers 1979–80 (Chrmn. Collective Bargaining Ctte. 1975–78); Chrmn. Legal Aid Services Soc. of Man. 1972–78; Hon. Couns. Univ. of Man. Fac. Assn.; mem. Admin. Ctte. National Legal Aid Rsch. Centre; Candn. Counc. on Social Devel. (Gov. 1975–76; mem. Extve. Ctte. 1976); Manitoba Assn. of Rights and Liberties; Candn. Civil Liberties Assn.; N.D.P.; Home: 261 Harvard Ave., Winnipeg, Man. R3M 0K1; Office: Winnipeg, Man. R3T 2N2.

**PENNEY, Mt. Rev. Alphonsus Liguori,** LL.D.; archbishop; b. St. John's, Nfld. 17 Sept. 1924; s. Alphonsus Liguori and Catherine (Mullaly) P.; e. St. Bonaventure's Coll. St. John's, Nfld.; St. Paul's Seminary and University of Ottawa, L.PH and L.TH; L.LD, 1980, from Memorial University of Nfld.; ARCHBISHOP OF ST. JOHN'S, NFLD. 1979– ; o. 1949; Asst. Priest becoming Parish Priest 1957–72; named Vicar Forane 1960; Vicar. Gen. 1971; Prelate of Honour 1971; Bishop of Grand Falls, Nfld. 1973–79; Cath. Educ. Comte. 1979– ; served with RCAF 1952–57; Address: P.O. Box 37, St. John's, Nfld. A1C 5H5.

**PENNEY, William Campbell (Bill);** jewellery executive; b. Toronto, Ont. 27 July 1950; s. Dr. Robert Haig and Joan (Campbell) P.; e. Univ. of Waterloo BES 1972; Pa. State Univ. 1986; m. Susan Alicia d. Laurent Regimbald 2 Sept. 1982; children: Justin, Jonathan; Pres., Seiko Canada Inc. 1989; Sales Rep. Timex Canada Ltd. Toronto 1973, Dist. Mgr. Atlantic Provs. 1974, Regional Mgr. 1977, Nat. Sales Mgr. 1978, Dir. Sales & Mktg. 1979; Vice-Pres. Sales Candn. importer/distributor Casio Watches 1980; Vice-Pres. Sales & Mktg. Lorus Div. SC Time Inc. 1982, Vice-Pres. Sales & Mktg. SC Time 1986, Pres., 1988–89; mem. Bd. of Trade Metrop. Toronto; Candn. Jewellers Assn.; Jewellers Vigilance Can. Inc.; recreations: golf, skiing, windsurfing, squash; Clubs: York Downs Golf; Georgian Peaks; Home: 8 Bellside Dr., Unionville, Ont. L3P 7B8.

**PENNINGTON, Sheila,** M.Ed., Ph.D.; psychotherapist; advocate of self healing; b. Toronto, Ont. 8 Apl. 1932; d. Charles Edward and Marion (Haddow) Catto; e. Lawrence Park Coll. Inst. 1951; Univ. of Toronto Victoria Coll., B.A. 1955; Toronto Teachers' College Primary Edn. Specialist Cert. 1956, Ont. Inst. for Studies in Edn. M.Ed. 1966, Ph.D. 1982; m. Ben s. Joe and Anita Harrison June 1975; children: Ann, Alexander, Michael, Timothy; PRES. CENTRE FOR THE HEALING ARTS INC.; Profl. Dancer CBC and mem. 'Canadettes' CNE Grandstand 1949–55; Varsity Cheerleader 1951–54; Primary Specialist Cert. 1956; Miss Toronto Teachers Coll. 1956; N. York Bd. Edn. 1956–59; Rsch. Dept. Toronto Bd. Edn. 1962–65; Psychotherapist, Scarborough Gen. Hosp. 1970–71; private practice (specialty self-healing) 1971–1992; extensive radio and TV interviews; guest speaker workshops Can., US and Europe; recipient Ont. Psychol. Assn. Presidential Award thesis scientific excellence 1981; author: 'Healing Yourself: Understanding How Your Mind Can Heal Your Body' 1988; mem. Assn. Am. Humanistic Psychols.; Candn. Centre for Arms Control & Disarmament; Candn. Peace Alliances; World Federalists of Can.; Amnesty Internat.; Greenpeace; Candn. Civil Liberties Assn.; Clin. mem. Am. & Ont. Assns. Marriage & Family Therapists; recreations: swimming, ballet, symphony music, pets, nature, Native Indian studies, walking, reading; Club: McGill; Address: 14 Thurloe Ave., Toronto, Ont. M4S 2K2.

**PENNYCOOK, Rod,** B.A., M.B.A.; banker; b. Winnipeg, Man. 26 June 1952; s. Rod B. and Eileen Margaret (Murphy) P.; e. Univ. of Manitoba B.A. 1973; Queen's Univ. M.B.A. 1976; m. Francine Marsan 8 Oct. 1983; children: Jacqueline; SR. VICE-PRES., PERSONAL FINANCIAL SERVICES, ROYAL BANK OF CANADA 1993– ; Pres., C.E.O. & Dir., Royal Bank Mortgage Corp.; Dir., Royal Bank Investor Trading; joined Accelerated Mngt. Devel. Prog., Royal Bank of Canada 1976; Asst. Mgr., Main Branch, London, Ont. 1977; Asst. Inspector, Corp. Lending Montreal 1979; Mgr., Credit Policy & Asst. to Vice-Chair 1981; Asst. Mgr., Special Loans Group 1982; Manager, Special Loans Calgary 1984; Sr. Acct. Mgr., Commercial Banking, Commercial Banking Ctr. 1985; Mgr., Oil & Gas Banking 1986; Vice-Pres., Corp. Planning Montreal 1989; Vice-Pres., Residential Mortgages 1991; Sr. Vice Pres., Independent Business & Agriculture 1992; recreations: golfing, curling; clubs: Club Summerlea, Pointe Claire Curling Club; Home: 213 Antoine Villeray, Beaconsfield, Que. H9W 6E8; Office: 1 Place Ville Marie, P.O. Box 6001, Montreal, Que. H3C 3A9.

**PENROSE, Gordon William Gavin,** M.Ed.; writer; b. Hamilton, Ont. 24 July 1925; s. Thomas William and Marian Gertrude (Middleton) P.; e. Univ. of W. Ont., B.A. 1956; Univ. of Toronto, B.Ed. 1958, M.Ed. 1964; m. Marion d. Percy and Cora Seymour 20 Aug. 1948; three d. Lynda, Donna, Sandra; elem. Sch. teacher Hamilton, Ont. 1948–60; Teaching Master, Toronto Teachers' Coll. 1960–69; Master Teacher, York Region Bd. 1969–81; joined Young Naturalist Found. 1977 becoming 'Dr. Zed' in Owl mag. and subsequently 'Dr. Zed' Owl TV and in Chickadee mag.; author 'Dr. Zed's Brilliant Book of Science Experiments' 1977, reprinted 1978, 1980; 'Dr. Zed's Dazzling Book of Science Activities' 1982, reprinted 1985, 1987, 1988, 1989; 'Magic Mud and Other Great Experiments' 1987, reprinted 1988; 'Science Surprises' 1989; 'Dr. Zed's Sensational Science Activities' 1990; 'More Science Surprises' 1992; Fellow, Ont. Inst. Studies in Edn.; CANSCAIP; Writers Union; recreations: photography, lapidary, curling, bowling; Address: 14 Abbeville Rd., Scarborough, Ont. M1H 1Y3.

**PENSA, Claude Marius Victor,** Q.C., B.A., LL.B.; lawyer; b. London, Ont. 14 Dec. 1929; s. Philip and Henrietta (Gianotti) P.; e. Univ. of W. Ont. B.A. 1952; Osgoode Hall Law Sch. LL.B. 1956; m. Elaine d. Louis and Muriel Wettlaufer 4 Oct. 1958; children: Christine Ann, Victoria Marie, Marc Anthony, Jonathan Pierre; SR. PARTNER PENSA & ASSOCIATES 1982– ; Past Dir. Union Gas Ltd.; associated with law firm Mitchell, Hockin and Dawson, London 1956–61; served as special prosecutor under Narcotics Control Act 1966–73; practice in Supreme Court of Ont., Ont. Court of Appeal and Supreme Court of Can.; Counsel Bd. of Edn. City of London, Past Trustee; Founding mem. Fair Action Ins. Reform; Past Trustee Middlesex Law Assn.; Past Chrmn. Bd. Dirs. Regina Mundi Coll.; Mem. Bd., Research Park Corp.; Past Chrmn. Bd. of Govs., Univ. of W. Ont.; mem. Advocates' Soc. (Dir.); Candn. Bar Assn. (Past mem. Ont. Council); Law Soc. Upper Can. (Counsel); Dir., John Robarts Rsch. Institute; R. Catholic; Liberal; recreations: golf, travel; Clubs: London; St. Thomas Golf; Office: Suite 1000, 130 Dufferin Ave., London, Ont. N6A 5R2.

**PENTLAND, Barbara (Lally),** C.M., O.B.C., LL.D.; composer; b. Winnipeg, Man. 2 Jan. 1912; d. Charles Frederick and Constance Christine Lally (Howell) P.; e. Rupert's Land College, Winnipeg; Miss Edgar's and Miss Cramp's School, Montreal; Bertaux School, Paris & composition studies with Cécile Gauthier (continued by correspondence in Winnipeg 1930); organ lessons with Hugh Bancroft; piano with Eva Clare; Fellowship, Juilliard Graduate School, N.Y., instruction in composition, etc. for 3 years (grad. 1939); m. John s. Bronislav Huberman 1958; composed, performed & taught in Winnipeg 1939–42; study with Aaron Copland, Berkshire Music Center, summers '41 & '42; moved to Toronto 1942 and taught at Royal Conservatory, etc.; apptd. Instructor, 3rd & 4th Year Theory & Composition, Univ. of B.C. 1949; resigned 1963 to have more time for creative work; LL.D. (Hon.), Univ. of Manitoba & Simon Fraser Univ.; Diplôme d'Honneur, Candn. Conf. of the Arts; Mem., Order of Canada; recipient, 125th Anniversary of the Confederation of Canada Medal, 1992; Mem., Order of British Columbia; composer: 40 works for piano; 5 pieces for string orchestra; 17 works for orchestra incl. 4 symphonies; 28 instrumental ensembles incl. 5 string quartets; 7 solos for instruments; 8 pieces for solo voice, 4 for choir; 2 stage works: 'Beauty and the Beast' (ballet – pantomime), 'The Lake' (chamber opera; libretto by Dorothy Livesay); Home: 4765 West 6th Ave., Vancouver, B.C. V6T 1C4.

**PENTON, Marvin James,** B.A., M.A., Ph.D.; university professor; b. Clarkbridge, Sask. 27 Apr. 1932; s. Lévis Bosworth and Ida Emily (Hanson) P.; e. Univ. of Arizona, B.A. 1956; Univ. of Iowa, M.A. 1958, Ph.D. 1965; m. Marilyn d. Raymond and Myrtle Kling 28 Apr. 1951; children: David James, John Mark, Anne Marie; PROF. EMERITUS, UNIV. OF LETHBRIDGE 1990– ; Asst. Prof., Univ. of Puerto Rico 1959–60; Northern Mich. Univ. 1960–63; Univ. of Wisconsin 1964–65; Univ. of Calgary 1965–67; joined Univ. of Lethbridge as Asst. Prof. 1967; Prof. of History, 1976–89; Past Chrmn., Dept. of History; Past Pres., Univ. Fac. Assn.; Free Bible Student; Founder and Vice-Pres., Christian Renewal Ministries; mem., National Party; mem. and Past Pres., Candn. Soc. of Church Hist.; Vice Pres., Métis Nation of Alta. (Constitutional Advisor 1991–92); mem. Candn. Catholic Hist. Assn.; Candn. Hist. Assn.; Council of Canadians; Amnesty Internat.; author: 'Jehovah's Witnesses in Canada' 1976; 'Apocalypse Delayed: The Story of Jehovah's Witnesses' 1985; ed. Eng. Edition 'The Gentile Times Reconsidered' 1983; ed. The Bible Examiner 1982–84; The Christian Quest 1986–91; recreations: travel, geneal. rsch.; Home: 58 Coachwood Point West, Lethbridge, Alta. T1K 6A9; Office: Calgary, Alta. T2A 6J4.

**PENTZ, Donald Robert,** M.F.A., R.C.A.; artist; b. Bridgewater, N.S. 18 Sept. 1940; s. Cyril Robert and Marjorie Ione (Frank) P.; e. Davis Mem. High Sch. Bridgewater Sr. Matric. 1959; N.S. Coll. of Art one yr.; Mount Allison Univ. B.F.A. 1966; Univ. of Regina M.F.A. 1979; Banff Sch. of Fine Arts summer 1979; m. Mary Ann Louise d. John Edward Rudolph, Truro, N.S. 31 Aug. 1974; one s. Benjamin Christopher; Asst. Curator, Confed. Centre Art Gallery Charlottetown 1966; Zool. Illustrator Nat. Museum of Natural Science Ottawa 1968–70; instr. various painting workshops 1970–80; Teaching Asst. Visual Arts Univ. of Regina 1977–79; yearly solo exhns. paintings and drawings Halifax, Ottawa, Toronto; Regina, Calgary since 1967; rep. in various group exhns. incl. Expo '67, Montreal Olympics 1976, N.S. Art Bank 1980; rep. in pub., corporate and private colls. incl. Can. Council Art Bank, Art Gallery N.S.; awards rec'd N.S. Govt., N.S. Talent Trust, Sask. Arts Bd.; Centennial Award Best Painting 1967 (Maritime Art Assn.); Twining Scholarship Banff Sch. Fine Arts 1979; Can. Council Award 1980; author/illustrator 'Risser's Beach Salt Marsh' 1975; 'Some Common Shore and Ocean Birds of Nova Scotia' 1975; 'Risser's Beach-Some Common Beach Finds' 1975; weekly columnist ('The Packbasket') 'Bridgewater Bulletin'; mem. Soc. Candn. Artists; recreations: canoeing, ornithology, outdoor sketching, photography, hiking, writing, archery; Address: R.R. 1, Pleasantville, N.S. B0R 1G0.

**PEPER, Dirk,** B.A.; b. Zandvoort, Holland, 6 Jan. 1928; s. H. J. and H. C. (Driehuyzen) P.; e. Huygens Lyceum, Amsterdam, 1940–46; Queensland Univ., B.A. 1957; m. Rose Marie Patten 12 Sept. 1952; children: Tiia, Derek, Heli; PRES., FINCOR MANAGEMENT LTD.; Sr. Vice Pres., Central Capital Management Corp.; Pres. Central Capital Corp.; Asst. Acct., Commonwealth Pub. Service of Australasia, Dept. of Works, Port Moresby, New Guinea, 1951–57; Acct., Canada Metal Co. Ltd., Toronto, 1957–58; Div. Office Mgr., Canada Dry Ltd., Toronto/ Montreal, 1958–61; Comptroller and Dir., Klein Manufacturing Co., 1961–62; Assistant to Comptroller, United Shoe Machinery Corp.; Montreal, 1962–64; Consultant, Mang. Services, Peat, Marwick, Mitchell & Co., Montreal, 1964–68; Comptroller and Depy Min. of Finance, Gov't of Nfld. and Labrador 1968–74; Treasurer and Commissioner of Finance, Municipality of Peel 1974–78; Treas., Ont. Hydro 1978–88; served with Dutch Army Royal Blue Hussars in Indonesia, 1947–51; Home: 1 Clarendon Ave., Apt. 602, Toronto, Ont. M4V 1H8.

**PEPIN, The Right Hon. Jean-Luc,** C.C., P.C., B.A., L.Ph., LL.L., D.E.S.D. (Diploma in Higher Studies of Law); b. Drummondville, Que. 1 Nov. 1924; s. Victor & Antoinette P.; e. Drummondville (Primary); St. Hyacinthe Semy.; Univ. of Ottawa; Univ. of Paris; m. Mary, d. Harding Brock-Smith, Winnipeg, Man., 12 Apl. 1952; two children; former Pol. Science Prof. at Univ. Ottawa; rep. of Nat. Film Bd. in London, 1956–58; first el. to H. of C. for Drummond-Arthabaska, g.e. 1963; appt. Min. without Portfolio, July 1965; Min. of Mines & Tech. Surveys, Dec. 1965, Energy, Mines & Resources, 1966; Min. of Industry, Trade & Comm. 1968 till def. in g.e. 1972; Pres., Interimco Ltd., 1973–75; Chrmn. of the Anti-Inflation Bd., 1975–1977; Co-chrmn., Task Force on Candn. Unity, 1977–79; re-el. to H. of C. for Ottawa-Carleton, g.e. 1979 and 1980; Min. of Transport 1980–83; Min. of State for External Relations, 1983–84; mem. Extve. Comte. Trilateral Comm. until 1975; doctorates from Univs. of Sherbrooke, Laval, Ottawa, Bishop and Carleton; Liberal; Catholic; Home: 16 Rothwell Dr., Gloucester, Ont. K1J 7G4.

**PEPIN, John David,** M.A.; social service and health care executive; b. Ottawa, Ont. 16 March 1944; s. Gerald H. and late Margaret P. (Day) P.; e. St. Patrick's Coll. Ottawa B.A. 1969; Carleton Univ. M.A. 1972; m. Elizabeth Hathaway Siegfried d. DeFois Hathaway Siegfried and Carolyn Gale (White); EXTVE. DIR., ST. JOHN AMBULANCE, ONT. COUNCIL 1988– ; Cons. to corporations and government; Extve. Dir. Family Day Care Services 1978–88; Rsch. Asst. Carleton Univ. Dept. Sociol. 1970; Cons. Dept. Criminol. Univ. of Ottawa 1972; Guidance Dir. Ottawa Boys Club 1967–69; Teacher, Ryerson Polytech. Inst. Toronto 1971–72; Prog. Dir. Youth Services Bureau 1972–78; Chairperson, Custody Review Board, Province of Ontario 1991–93; Chairperson Metro Toronto Day Care Adv. Ctte. 1988 (Ctte. mem. 1985–88); mem. The Rotary Club of Toronto; Family Services Can. 1982–88; Jt. Adv. Ctte. Multi-Service Centres Ottawa 1972–78; Bd. mem., Treas. Big Sister Orgn. Ottawa-Carleton 1973–76; Bd. mem.: Vandalism Alert Toronto 1978–80; Social Planning Council Metrop. Toronto 1979–83; Jessie's Centre for Teenagers Inc. 1981–84; mem. Municipality Metrop. Toronto Task Force on Day Care Planning 1979–81 and 1985–86; City of Toronto Task Force on Work-Related Day Care 1986–87; mem. Ont. Assn. Family Service Agencies 1980–88; Private Home Day Care Assn. Ont. (Pres. 1982–87) 1982–88; mem. Adv. Ctte., Wellesley Hosp. 1987–88; Home: 198 Howland Ave., Toronto, Ont. M5R 3B6; Office: 46 Wellesley St. E., Toronto, Ont. M4Y 1G5.

**PÉPIN, Lucie;** b. St-Jean d'Iberville, Que. 7 Sept. 1936; d. Jean and Thérèse (Bessette) P.; e. St-Jean d'Iberville Hospital, Qué. R.N. 1959; post-grad. studies Notre-Dame Hosp., Montreal 1959–60; Univ. of Montreal 1965; Montreal Sch. of Fine Arts 1966; McGill Univ. 1975; Univ. of Montreal 1977; children: Nathalie, Sophie Ferron; Extve. Dir., Canadian Hemophilia Society 1992; Pioneer in Birth Control Family Planning Clinic, Fac. of Med., Univ. of Montreal 1966–70; Candn. Rep., World Health Org. 1972–79; Nat. Coordinator, Candn. Ctte. for Fertility Rsch. 1972–79; Nat. Coordinator, Commission on the Application of the Abortion Law, Badgley Report, Justice Canada 1975–77; Coordinator, Internat. Conference for Rockerfeller, and Ford Foundation 1978–79; Coordinator, Nat. Symposium, Candn. Fertility Soc. 1977–79; Mem., Commission on Violence Against Children and Youth, Badgley Report, Health and Welfare Canada 1980–83; Vice Pres., Candn. Adv. Council on the Status of Women (Pres. 1981–84); M.P. for Outremont 1984–88; el. Sept. 4, 1984; Member, Parliamentary Task Force on Child Care, Health and Welfare Canada 1986–87; Commissioner, Royal Commission on Electoral Reform and Party Financing 1989–92; Mem., Chamber of Comm., Que.; Assn. des femmes diplômées des universités; Candn. Fed. of Univ. Women; C.D. Howe Inst.; Path Canada.

**PEPINO, Nicholas Jane,** Q.C., LL.B., LL.M.; lawyer; b. London, Ont. 13 Apr. 1947; d. Dr. Lyle Frederick and Margaret Gwendolyn (Rodger) P.; e. Univ. of Toronto Victoria Coll. 1967; Osgoode Hall Law Sch. LL.B. 1970; Univ. of Texas, Austin LL.M. 1971; Law Soc. of Upper Can. Bar Admission 1973; m. James David, s. Reginald and Eileen Pearson 11 Oct. 1974; children: Andrew Walker Rodger, Allison Blaine, Victoria Jane; PARTNER, AIRD & BERLIS 1984– ; articled with Thomson, Rogers 1971–72; founding Partner Jarvis, Blott, Fejer, Pepino practising municipal law and land devel. law 1973–82; joined present firm 1982; cr. Q.C. 1985; Lectr. Law Soc. and Candn. Bar Assn.; Pres. and Dir. Metro Action Ctte. on Pub. Violence against Women and Children 1984; Dir., Candn. Counc. of Christians & Jews 1982–87 (mem. Nat. Extve. 1983–86); mem. Advocates' Soc.; County of York Law Assn.; Candn. Bar Assn.; Rosedale United Ch.; Ont. Human Rights Comn. 1980–82 (Race Relations Div. 1981–82); first woman apptd. to Metrop. Toronto Bd. of Comnrs. of Police 1982–87; Past Dir., Festival of Festivals; Women's Coll. Hosp. Found.; Mem., Univ. of Toronto Acad. Tribunal; Dir., Nat. Life of Canada 1986–88; Candn. Adv. Counc. on the Status of Women 1985–91, Extve. Mem. 1986–91; Home: 147 Roxborough St. E., Toronto, Ont. M4W 1V9; Office: 181 Bay St., Ste. 1800, Toronto, Ont. M5J 2T9.

**PEPPER, Douglas John,** B.A.; editor; b. Toronto, Ont. 20 Feb. 1962; s. Elliott R. and Phyllis T. (Kaplan) P.; e. Forest Hill C.I. 1981 (Ontario Scholar); Univ. of Toronto B.A. (Hons.) 1985; Radcliffe Publishing Procedures Course, Harvard Univ. 1985; single; EXECUTIVE EDITOR, RANDOM HOUSE OF CANADA 1991– ; Executive Asst. to the President, Somerville House Books Limited 1985; Asst. Editor, Random House of Canada 1987 (helped launch Candn. publishing program); Editor 1988; Senior Editor 1989; often speaks to creative writing classes at Univ. of Toronto, York Univ., Humber College, and Ryerson about the editorial & acquisition process; Mem., The University Club of Toronto; Home: 30 Edith Dr., #606, Toronto, Ont. M4R 1Y8; Office: 33 Yonge St., Toronto, Ont. M5E 1G4.

**PEPPER, John J.,** Q.C., B.A., B.C.L.; advocates barristers & solicitors; b. Montreal, Que. 17 Feb. 1928; s. late William and Blanche (Frigon) P.; e. Westmount (Que.) High Sch. 1945; Loyola Coll., B.A. 1949; McGill Univ., B.C.L. 1952; m. Anita Claire, d. Edward J. Turcotte, 19 Sept. 1953; children: John T., David T., Timothy T., Anthony T., Andrew T.; SR. PARTNER, JOHN J. PEPPER, Q.C. AND ASSOCIATES, BARRISTERS & SOLICITORS; Pres. and Dir., Soges Canada Inc.; O.A. Travel Inc.; Dir., CIBC Trust Corp.; read law with Hon. F. Philippe Brais, Q.C., M.L.C. and A. J. Campbell, Q.C. 1949–53; called to Bar of Que. 1953; apptd. Q.C. 1969; assoc. with law firm of Brais & Campbell 1953 and successor firms, now under present name; Dir., St. Mary's Hospital Foundation; Mem. Bd. of Govs., St. Mary's Hosp. Centre; Dir., Corp. of St. Mary's Hospital; Loyola of Montreal (Pres. Alumni and mem. Bd. Govs. 1968–69); mem. Bd. Govs., Concordia Univ.; Past Chrmn. & Pres., Montreal Board of Trade; Pres., Montreal Board of Trade Heritage Found.; mem. Montreal Children's Hosp. Foundation; Fellow Am. Coll. Trial Lawyers; mem. Bar of Que. (mem. Board Discipline 1968–79, General Council & Extve. 1977–79); Pub. Information Bureau, Bar of Que. (1971–79); Bar of Montreal (Dir. Legal Aid Bureau 1962–63, Secy. 1963–65, Batonnier 1978–79); Canadian Bar Assn. (Chrmn. Nat. Membership Comte. & mem. Nat Extve. 1975–1977); Mem. of Council, Secy. (1963) and President (1965) Insurance Section, Quebec Branch); Special Fed. Crown Prosecutor 1954–57; Mem. of Extve. and Bd. of Dirs., Candn. Chamber of Commerce; Kt of Magistral Grace, Sovereign and Mil. Order of Malta; Kt. of Mil. & Hospitaller Order of St. Lazarus of Jerusalem; R. Catholic; recreations: fishing, golf, skiing; Clubs: Mount Royal; St. James's; Forest and Stream; Montreal Badminton & Squash; Quebec Garrison (Quebec); Pres., Delta Upsilon, McGill Inc.; Mount Bruno Golf & Country; Canadian; Home: Le Chateau, 1321 Sherbrooke St. W., Montreal, PQ H3G 1J4; Country residence: Le Boisé, Lac Supérieur, Mont Tremblant, Co. Laurentides-Labelle, Que. J0T 1P0; Office: 1155 Boul. René Lévesque Ouest, Bureau 2500, Montreal, Que. H3B 2K4.

**PEPPER, Kathleen Daly,** R.C.A., O.S.A., A.O.C.A.; artist (landscape & portrait painter and draughtsman); b. Napanee, Ont. 28 May 1898; d. Denis Henry Aldworth and Mary (Bennett) Daly; a descendant of ancient Irish family of Aldworth and Anglo-Norman house of St. Leger; e. Havergal Coll. Toronto; Univ. of Toronto 1920; grad. from Ont. Coll. of Art 1924; studied under Arthur Lismer, J.E.H. MacDonald & J.W. Beatty; l'Academie de la Grande Chaumière Paris 1924–25; Parsons Sch. of Design Paris; wood engraving with René Pottier; post-grad work in etching 1926; early sketching trips to Italy, France and the Basque country; m. George Pepper, artist, 30 Sept. 1929; for seventeen years lived and painted in historic Studio Bldg., Severn St., Toronto; 1931 built log summer studio St. Urbain, Charlevoix, Que. where early French-Candn. life, and Montagnais and Cree Indians of Lac-St.-Jean district were painted, returning each March for winter landscape painting; mem. Ont. Soc. of Artists; Candn. Group of Painters; Royal Candn. Acad. of Arts; Accademia Italia; has contributed regularly to annual exhns. of these socs.; rep. in important travelling exhbns. abroad organized by Nat. Gallery of Can., including: The Group of Seven (1931, 1932, 1936, 1937); British Empire Exhbn., Tate Gallery, London, Eng. 1936; N.Y. World's Fair 1939; Coronation, Royal Inst. Galleries, London, Eng.; Southern Dominions 1936; Buenos Aires 1930; Rio de Janeiro 1944–46; Canadian Women Painters, Riverside Museum, N.Y. 1947; represented in permanent collections of major galleries across Canada including: National Gall. of Can., Ottawa; Art Gall. of Ont., Toronto; Emmanuel Coll. (U. of T.); McMichael Candn. Collection, Kleinburg; Dept. of Northern Affairs, Ottawa; Candn. Embassy, Copenhagen; Candn. Medical Assn. Headquarters, Ottawa; Whyte Museum of the Candn. Rockies; Beaverbrook Museum, N.B.; Legislative Bldgs., Edmonton; Edmonton Gallery; London Art Museum; Glenbow Museum, Calgary; Sarnia Gallery; Ont. Heritage Foundation, Ottawa; portrait commissions include: Hon. Herbert Greenfield (Premier of Alta.) 1946; Dr. Thomas S. Cullen, Surgeon, Baltimore, Md. 1941; Abdessalam El Hadj, Tetuan (Baja de Morocco) 1956; co-illustrator 'Kingdom of Saguenay' by Marius Barbeau, 1936; author 'Morrice' (preface by A. Y. Jackson) 1966; feature article in 'North' (Mar.-Apr. 1962 pub. Dept. Northern Affairs) with reproductions made on Eastern Arctic trip to Grise Fiord, N.W.T.); co-author 'Research on Eskimo Art,' for Dept. of Northern Affairs, Ottawa 1960; awards: an Academic of Italy with Gold Medal 1981; recipient Gold Medal of Merit, International Parliament, U.S.A. 1983; Diploma 'Master of Painting' (Hon. causa), Internat. Seminar of Modern & Contemporary Art 1982; Diploma of Merit, Universitata delle Arti, Salsomaggiore, Italy 1982; Accademia Europea – Premio – European Banner of the Arts 1985; Accademia Italia – Premio – Oscar d'Italia 1986; imp. reproductions include: Portrait of 'Fr-Canadian Boy, Rene' (selected for praise) on cover page of Coronation number of The 'Listener,' (London, England, BBC, May 1937; Portrait 'Alphonse L'Abbe' full page reproduction Coronation number of 'Studio' 'Artists of the Empire,' Aug. 1937 London, Eng.; 'Simeone Tuglavina' reprod. in 'Canadian Prints and Drawings' by Paul du Val; 'Eskimo children Labrador' rep. in 'Passionate Spirits' (100th Ann. R.C.A.); 'Haircut' reprod. on cover 'Canadian Forum' 1940; Bibliographic: 'Dictionary of Canadian Artists' (Colin MacDonald, 1967–69); 'Dictionary of International Biography' 1974; 'Canadian Who's Who' 1982–90; 'Four Decades' (Paul Du Val, 1972); 'Who's Who in American Art'; International Dictionary of the Arts Catalog Premio Centauro d'Oro, Accademia Italia, Salsomaggiore; Catalogue 'Images de Charlevoix' 1784–1950; Painting trips led to most parts of Canada from Atlantic to Pacific; 1960 three months' voyage to eastern Arctic by Govt. hospital ship 'C.D. Howe' to Ellesmere Island, N.W.T.; to the coastal villages of Newfoundland courtesy of Job Bros.; unique trip to the Grand Banks by trawler 'Blue Foam' sketching fishing operations; to Northern Labrador by R.C.M.P. minesweeper; early 1930's to north shore Lake Superior, Lower St. Lawrence, the forest regions of Canton Rousseau Abitibi 1932, Alaska and White Horse 1927; on frequent trips to the Canadian Rockies portrayed the Stony Indians and coal miners of Alberta, the lakes and glaciers in Banff area; Exhibition 'Canmore Workings,' White Museum 1987– ; during year in Spain painted Andulasian villages and in Morocco painted portraits at the palace of the Caliph Tetuan; met Picasso at Vallauris; solo exhns. incl. Vancouver Art Gallery 1945, 1986; Hart House Univ. Toronto 1953; Whyte Museum of the Candn. Rockies 1958; Canmore Museum, Alta. 1989; Banff Sch. Fine Arts (Princess Margaret's visit) 1958; La Jolla, California 1959; Univ. Women's Club, Toronto; group shows include: 5 Women Painters, Hart House, U. of T. 1934; 'Faces of Canada,' Stratford Festival 1964; 'Images de Charlevoix,' Montreal Museum of Fine Arts 1981; two-man exhbns. with George Pepper incl.: Hart House U. of T.; Pratt Library, Baltimore Md.; Arctic paintings, London Gallery; Sarnia Gallery; Arts & Letters Club, Toronto; Heliconian Club; recreations: skiing, cycling, camping; travel; sketching; Clubs: Alpha Gamma Delta Fraternity; Granite; Heliconian; Zonta Toronto; United; Address: 561 Avenue Rd., Apt. 1101, Toronto, Ont. M4V 2J8.

**PEPPER, Thomas Peter,** M.A., Ph.D.; research executive; b. London, Eng. 26 Jan. 1918; s. Charles William and Ellen (Morley) P.; e. Univ. of B.C. B.A. 1939, M.A. (Physics) 1941; McGill Univ. Ph.D. 1948; m. Elizabeth d. James and Kate Purdie 9 May 1953; children: Katherine, Daniel, Penelope; Retired; served with Nat. Research Council Can. 1941–45; radar, war work; Atomic Energy of Canada Ltd. 1947–52, nuclear physics; Isotope Products Ltd., Oakville, Ont. 1952–58, Pres. Isotope Products Inc. Buffalo, N.Y. 1954–58; Head, Physics Div. Sask. Research Council 1958–72, Asst. Dir., 1968–72, Dir. 1972–83; Pres., April-Oct 1983; Past Pres. Prov. Research Organs. (PRO); recreation: jogging (1st Sask. Senior Citizen to run the marathon, Oct. 83); Club: Saskatoon Road Runners; Home: Site J1, C37, R.R. 2, Nanaimo, B.C. V9R 5K2.

**PEPPLER, Mark Steven,** D.Phil.; medical microbiologist; educator; b. Milwaukee, Wis. 10 Feb. 1951; s. Henry James and Genevieve Augusta (Lindert) P.; e. Whitefish Bay (Wis.) H.S. 1969; Univ. of Mont. B.A. 1973; Oxford Univ. (Rhodes Scholar) D.Phil. 1977; m. Ronnene A. d. Howard and Clarene Anderson 3 Aug. 1974; two s. Matthew, Neil; ASSOC. PROF. OF MEDICAL MICROBIOLOGY AND INFECTIOUS DISEASES, UNIV. OF ALTA. 1983– ; Jr. Staff Fellow U.S. Food and Drug Adm. Bureau of Biologics, Bethesda, Md. 1977–79; Expert in Microbiol. U.S. Nat. Insts. of Health, Nat. Inst. Allergy & Infectious Diseases, Rocky Mountain Labs., Lab. of Microbial Structure & Function, Hamilton, Mont. 1979–83; mem. Am. Soc. Microbiol.; Am. Chem. Soc.; Candn. Biochem. Soc.; Candn. Microbiol. Soc.; Episcopalian; Home: 8738 117th St., Edmonton, Alta. T6G 1R5; Office: Edmonton, Alta. T6G 2H7.

**PERCY, Herbert Roland (Bill),** C.D.; author; b. Burham, Kent, Eng. 6 Aug. 1920; s. Herbert George Percy; e. Royal Naval Artificers' Training Estab. Chatham, Eng. 1936–40; RCN Prep. Sch. Esquimalt, B.C. 1954–55; RN Engn. Coll. Manadon, Devon 1955; m. Mary Davina d. late Arthur James 28 March 1942; children: Arthur Jonathan, Roger James, Pauline Elizabeth; author 'The Timeless Island and Other Stories' 1960; 'Joseph Howe' 1976; 'Thomas Chandler Haliburton' 1980; 'Flotsam' novel 1978; 'Painted Ladies' novel 1983; 'A Model Lover' short story coll. 1986; 'Tranter's Tree' novel 1987; 'An Innocent Bystander' novel 1989; 'The Mother Tongue,' essay coll. 1992; short stories various periodicals; rep. Candn., U.S. and U.K. anthols.; Ed. 'The Canadian Author and Bookman' 1963–65; contrib. weekly column 'A Critic at Large' Ottawa Journal 1963–65; N.S. Cultural Life Award 1992; joined Royal Navy 1936 as Engine Room Artificer Apprentice, Engine Room Artificer and Chief 1940–52, served in HM Ships King George V, Hawkins, Belfast and others; Chief Engine Room Artificer RCN 1952–54, Engn. Offr. 1955–71, served in HMC Ships Cape Breton, Quebec, Sioux, Swansea and CFHQ Ottawa, rank Lt. Cdr.; Fellow, Inst. Marine Engrs. (London); mem. Writers' Union Can.; Writers' Fed. N.S. (Founding Chrmn.); Internat. P.E.N.; Amnesty Internat.; Candn. Authors Assn.; N.S. Naval Offrs. Assn.; recreations: tennis, gardening, wood turning, walking; Address: P.O. Box 47, Granville Ferry, N.S. B0S 1K0.

**PERCY, John Rees;** astronomer; educator; university professor and administrator; b. Windsor, U.K. 10 July 1941; s. George Francis and Christine (Holland) P.; e. Univ. of Toronto, B.Sc. 1962, M.A. 1963, Ph.D. 1968;

Ont. Coll. of Edn., secondary sch. teaching cert.; m. Maire d. Orval and Maire Robertson 16 June 1962; one d.: Carol Elaine; PROF., DEPT. OF ASTRONOMY, 1978– , ASSOC. DEAN (SCIENCES) AND VICE-PRINCIPAL (RSCH. & GRAD. STUDIES) ERINDALE COLL., UNIV. OF TORONTO 1989– ; Teacher, Bloor C.I. 1964–65; Lectr., Dept. of Astronomy, Erindale Coll., Univ. of Toronto 1967–68; Asst. Prof. 1968–73; Assoc. Prof. 1973–78; Asst. Chrmn., 1986–89; Leverhulme Fellow, Cambridge Univ. 1972–73; Royal Jubilee Medal 1977; serv. Award, Royal Astron. Soc. of Can 1977; Hon. Pres., Science Teachers' Assoc. of Ont. 1988–91; Vice-Chair, Bd. of Trustees, Ontario Science Centre; Mem., Internat. Astron. Union (Pres., Comn. on Variable Stars; Vice-Pres., Comn. on Teaching of Astron.); Am. Assn. of Variable Star Observers (Pres. 1989–91); Am. Astron. Soc.; Astron. Soc. Pacific (Bd. of Dirs. 1993– ); Royal Candn. Inst. (Pres. 1985–86); Royal Astron. Soc. of Can. (Pres. 1978–80); Candn. Astron. Soc.; and several others; author of numerous papers; co-author: 'Science 10: An Introductory Study' 1988; editor: 'Observer's Handbook' 1970–80; 'The Study of Variable Stars using Small Telescopes' 1986; 'The Teaching of Astronomy' 1990; 'Variable Star Research: An International Perspective' 1991; recreation: travel; Home: 381 Prince Edward Dr., Toronto, Ont. M8X 2L6; Office: Div. of Sciences, Erindale Campus, Univ. of Toronto, Mississauga, Ont. L5L 1C6.

**PERCY, Michael Barrett,** M.A., Ph.D.; educator; b. Banff, Alta. 16 Apl. 1948; s. Richard Barrett and Marguerite (Rice) P.; e. Univ. of Victoria, B.C., B.A. 1971; Queen's Univ., M.A. 1974, Ph.D. 1977; m. Doreen d. Rhodes and Doris Warren 24 June 1989; children: Karen, Kristine, S. Glyn; PROF. OF ECONOMICS, UNIV. OF ALTA. 1979– , Assoc. Chrmn. of Econ. 1985–89, Chrmn. 1990–91, Assoc. Dean (Planning) 1991–93; Asst. Prof. Univ. of B.C. 1976–79; Rsch. Fellow Univ. of Tasmania 1985; Rsch. Dir. Western Centre in Economic Research 1986–88; Cons. to Govts. Alta. & N.W.T., Econ. Council Can., Restrictive Trade Practices Comn., Royal Comn. Candn. Econ. Union, Govt. State of Tasmania FAO; MLA Edmonton Whitemud 15 June 1993; Finance Critic, Liberal Opposition; author or co-author various jour. articles Candn. econ. devel., regional & forest econ.; several monographs; mem. Candn. Econ. Assn.; Am. Econ. Assn.; Cliometrics Soc.; Alta. Forestry Soc.; recreations: hiking, climbing, cross-country skiing; Club: Alpine; Home: 263 Brookside Terr., Edmonton, Alta. T6H 4J6; Office: Edmonton, Alta. T6G 2H4.

**PERCY, Richard Charles William,** M.A.; retired museum curator; b. Bradford, Yorkshire, England 22 Sept. 1927; s. William Henry and Jessie Ada (Kitson) P.; e. King Edward H.S.; Simon Fraser Univ., M.A. 1975; m. Ruth d. Josef and Ellen Olson 30 Dec. 1956; Curator, Mus. of Archaeology & Ethnology, Simon Fraser Univ. 1972–90, retired; Mem., Bd. of Dir., Port Moody Station Museum; Anglican; recreations: antique and classic automobile enthusiast; clubs: Vintage Car Club of Canada, Horseless Carriage Club of Am., Antique Automobile Club of Am.; Home: 663 Colinet St., Coquitlam, B.C. V3J 4X3.

**PEREHUDOFF, Catherine Anne,** B.A.; artist; b. Saskatoon, Sask. 17 Sept. 1958; d. William William and Dorothy Elsie (Knowles) P.; e. Voss Folkschool (Norway), cert. in arts & crafts 1977; Univ. of Sask. B.A. 1981; Univ. of Alta., teacher cert. 1985; numerous artists' workshops in N. Am.; main genre is landscape painting in acrylic & watercolour; has painted since 1977 (1st show 1979); solo exhibitions: Assiniboia Gall. Regina 1979, '81, 83, '85, '87, '90, '93; Art Placement Saskatoon 1982, '88, '91; Front Gall. Edmonton 1987, '90; Elca London Gall. Montreal 1988, '91; Klonaridis Inc. Toronto 1984, '87, '90; Gilman/Gruen Gall. Chicago 1988; Ctr. of Art, Baie St. Paul Que. 1989; Whyte Museum Banff 1990; Grand Forks Gallery 1992; Newzones Gallery, Calgary 1993; group exhibitions incl.: 'Watercolour Painting in Saskatchewan,' Mendel Art Gall. 1980; 'Alberta Artists' Drawings,' Edmonton Art Gall. 1989; 'Femmeuses 90, Expo Femmes Peintres,' Pratt & Whitney Can. 1990; 'Landscape Painting,' Gilman/Gruen Gall. Chicago 1990; work incl. in nat. & internat. collections incl. The Lord Archbishop of Canterbury, Mrs. Andre Gromyko, Royal Bank in Nassau (Geneva, Isle of Man), Candn. Embassies in Tokyo & Buenos Aires; museum collections: Centre D'Art, Baie St. Paul; Canada Council Art Bank; Edmonton Art Gall.; Mendel Art Gall. Saskatoon; Oshawa Art Gall.; Whyte Museum, Banff; watercolour presented to Her Majesty the Queen Mother 1985 by Sask. Govt.; Address: P.O. Box 221, Station Main, Saskatoon, Sask. S7K 3K4.

**PÉREZ, Edgardo L.,** M.D., M.P.H., D.Psych., C.H.E., F.R.C.P.C., D.A.B.P.N.; psychiatrist; university professor; administrator; b. Arecibo, P.R. 21 Mar. 1951; s. Julio R. and Blanca D. (Sotomayor) P.; e. Cornell Univ., B.A. 1971; State Univ. of N.Y., M.D. 1976; Harvard Univ., M.P.H. 1976; Univ. of Ottawa, D.Pysch. 1979; m. Ann d. Joseph and Nora Scullion; CLINICAL PROF., DEPT. OF EPID. & COMMUN. MED. and PSYCHIATRY, UNIV. OF OTTAWA 1990– and PROF., DEPT. OF PSYCHIATRY, UNIV. OF TORONTO; EXTVE. VICE PRES. & CHIEF OF MEDICAL STAFF, HOMEWOOD HEALTH CENTRE 1993– ; Lectr., Univ. of Ottawa Med. Sch. 1980–82; Asst. Prof. 1982–85; Assoc. Prof. 1985–90, Prof. 1990– ; Dir., Day Hosp., Ottawa Civic Hosp. 1980– ; Co-ord., Postgrad. Edn. 1981–85; Dir., Ambulatory Serv. 1982–85; Chief, Dept. of Psychiatry, Ottawa Civiv Hosp. 1985–93; Vice Chrmn., Dept. of Psychiatry, Univ. of Ottawa Med. School 1989–93; Dir., Stress Mgmt. Clinic; Mem., Mental Health Bd., Ottawa Carleton Dist. Health Counc. 1980–86; Ottawa Rev. Bd. (Mental Health Act); Surveyor, Candn. Counc. on Health Facilities; Past Pres., Ont. Assn. of Gen. Hosp. Psych.; author/co-author 33 sci. papers; Home: 60 Hilldale Cres., Guelph, Ont. N1G 4B9; Office: 150 Delhi St., Guelph, Ont. N1E 6K9.

**PÉREZ-GÓMEZ, Alberto,** M.A., Ph.D.; educator; author; b. Mexico City, Mexico 24 Dec. 1949; s. Jorge and Angela (Gomez) Perez y Bouras; e. Escuela Superior de Ingenieria y Arquitectura Mexico City Dip.Arch.Eng. 1971; Cornell Univ. Sch. of Arch.; Univ. of Essex Sch. of Comparative Studies M.A. 1975, Ph.D. 1979; one d. Alejandra; SAIDYE ROSNER BRONFMAN PROF. OF ARCH. HIST., McGILL UNIV. 1987– ; Dir., Institut de recherche en histoire de l'architecture 1990– ; acad. career Mexico 1971–73, Gt. Brit. 1975–77, U.S.A. 1979–82 and Can. 1977–79, 1982– ; Dir. Sch. of Arch. Carleton Univ. 1983–86; Visiting Prof., External Examiner and Adv. Candn. Univs. and Intnl. Insts. incl. Nat. Univ. Mexico City, Va. State Univ., Univ. of Houston, Cranbrook Acad. of Art (U.S.A.), Cambridge Univ.; invited lectr. numerous insts. Europe and N.Am.; author 'Eclosion' poetry 1967; 'Iber' prose poem 1968; 'La Teoria de la Arquitectura' essay 1969; 'La Genesis y Superacion del Funcionalismo en Arquitectura' 1980; 'Architecture and the Crisis of Modern Science' 1983; 'Polyphilo or the Dark Forest Revisited' 1992; Fellow, Mexican Acad. Arch.; Home: 157 St. Paul Ouest, Apt. 31, Montreal, Que. H2Y 1Z5; Office: Sch. of Arch., McGill Univ., MacDonald-Harrington Bldg., 815 Sherbrooke St. W., Montreal, Que. H3A 2K6.

**PERIGOE, Ross Alton Edward,** M.Sc.; university professor of broadcast journalism; b. London, Ont. 30 Sept. 1949; s. John Rae and Elsie Jean (Alton) P.; e. Agincourt C.I. 1969; Ryerson Polytechnical Inst., dipl. 1972; Syracuse Univ. M.Sc. 1976; m. Christina d. Angelo and Fannie Barris 10 Aug. 1975; children: John Evan, Christopher Clarke; ASSISTANT PROF. & DIR., GRADUATE DIPLOMA PROGRAMME, CONCORDIA UNIV. 1985– ; Producer, 'Speaking Out,' TV Ontario 1976–77; Network Publicist, CBC TV 1977–79; Prod., 'Eyewitness News,' WFSB Hartford, CT 1979–80; 'Quebec Report,' CBMT Montreal 1980–81; 'As It Is,' CFCF TV Montreal 1980–81; Program Dir., CBOT TV Ottawa 1981–83; Special Asst., Vice-Pres., Regional Broadcasting, C.B.C. H.Q. 1984; Consultant, CTV Nat. News Toronto 1985; Prod., provincial election, CFCF TV 1981, 1985; Teacher, Seneca College 1976–77; current research: newsgathering habits of Canadians in Florida; T.V. Publicist of the Year Award 1977, CBC TV Toronto; United Ch. of Canada; author of several articles in mags. such as 'Content Magazine,' 'The Eyeopener' & 'Broadcaster Magazine'; co-author of 1 book chapter; recreations: running; club: Montreal West Horticultural Society; Home: 3510 Connaught Ave., Montreal, Que. H4B 1X3; Office: 7141 Sherbrooke St. W., BR 305, Montreal, Que. H4B 1R6.

**PERIN, Roberto,** B.A., M.A., Ph.D.; university professor; b. Montreal, Que. 3 Apr. 1948; s. Valentino and Maria (Lucertini) P.; e. Univ. de Montreal, B.A. (Hons.) 1968; Carleton Univ., M.A. 1970; Univ. of Ottawa, Ph.D. 1975; m. Yvonne d. Jacobus and Maria Kaspers 9 May 1970; children: Pier-Paolo, Dominique, Alexis; Lectr., Ctr. of Candn. Studies, Univ. of Edinburgh 1975–77; Asst. Prof., History, present univ. 1977–81; Assoc. Prof. & Mem., Grad. Fac. 1981– ; Dir., Candn. Acad. Ctr. in Italy 1983–85; Vice-Chair, French Language Adv. Ctte., Toronto Bd. of Edn. 1987; Mem., French Language Adv. Ctte. 1980–82, 1985–88; Chair, History Dept., Atkinson Coll., York Univ. 1989–90; Mem., Candn. Hist. Assn.; Inst. d'histoire de l'Amérique française; Candn. Studies Assn.; Candn. Mediterranean Inst.; author: 'Rome in Canada: The Vatican and Canadian Affairs in the Late Victorian Age' 1990; co-editor: 'Arrangiarsi: The Italian Immigration Experience in Canada' 1989; 'Negotiating With a Sovereign Quebec' 1992; Home: 440 Gladstone Ave., Toronto, Ont. M6H 3H9; Office: 4700 Keele St., North York, Ont. M3J 1P3.

**PERINBAM, Lewis;** world development executive; b. Johore, Bahru, Malaysia 11 May 1925; s. Joseph Devadas and Mary (Heynes) P.; e. Bukit Zahrah Sch.; Hillhead H.S.; Univ. of Glasgow, Scotland; m. Nancy d. Steven Garrett 31 Dec. 1976; SPECIAL ADVISER TO THE PRESIDENT, THE COMMONWEALTH OF LEARNING, VANCOUVER 1991– ; var. positions in Scotland, Malaysia, Britain to 1953; Extve. Dir., World Univ. Serv. of Can. 1953–59; 1st Sec. Gen., Candn. Comn. for UNESCO 1959–64; Co-founder & 1st Extve. Dir., Candn. Univ. Serv. Overseas 1961–62; Rep., World Bank at United Nations & its spec. agencies 1964–69; Spec. Advr. to Pres., Candn. Internat. Devel. Agency 1969; Vice-Pres., Candn. Internat. Development Agency 1974–91; Doctorates in law (Hon. Causa), Univ. of Calgary, York Univ., l'Université du Québec; recipient, Internat. Coop. Year medal 1964; Queen's Silver Jubilee Medal 1977; 1st Internat. Devel. Award for Distinguished Serv. 1983; Spec. Award of the World Assembly of the Internat. Counc. for Adult Edn. 1985; Vis. Scholar, Cambridge Univ. 1986; el. Fellow, Manitoba Inst. of Mgmt. 1987; recipient, APEX Leadership Award for Outstanding Professional Leadership in the Public Service of Canada and to the Community 1991; Mem. Bd. of Trustees, Lester Pearson College of the Pacific; Mem. Advisory Council of CESO; Advisory Bd., Candn. Bureau for Internat. Education; Dir., Internat. Management Inst., New Delhi (India); Mem. Advisory Bd. AIESEC; Mem. Bd. of Dirs., Obor Foundation, NY; Mem., Internat. Advisory Bd., Counterpart, Washington, DC; author: 'North and South' 1983 and foreword to 'Women, Religion and Development in the Third World' 1983; contbr.: 'One World, One Future' 1985; Home: 3955 West Broadway St., Vancouver, B.C. V6R 2C2; Office: The Commonwealth of Learning, 1700 - 777 Dunsmuir St., Vancouver, B.C. V7Y 1K4.

**PERINGER, Christine M.,** B.A., LL.B.; public policy advocate, peace activist; b. Windsor, Ont. 21 April 1960; d. Raymond and Marylyn (Salter) P.; e. St. Clement's Day School 1978; Univ. of Western Ont. B.A. 1980; York Univ., Osgoode Hall Law Sch. LL.B. 1985; m. Randall L. s. Merrill S. and late Muriel Weekes 24 Dec. 1991; one child: Gabriel Kasuba; Coordinator, Centre for Days of Peace 1989–92; Intern, Legislature of Ont. 1982–83; U.N. Graduate Student Intern, Dept. for Disarmament Affairs 1985; Co-dir., Peace Research Inst. (Dundas) 1985–88; Nat. Coord., Election Priorities 1988; the Centre for Days of Peace is a non-profit orgn. promoting the holding of humanitarian ceasefires in armed conflicts; 1986 Peace Rsch. Inst., Dundas was awarded the U.N. Sec.-Gen.'s Peace Messenger Award 1986; Dir., Peacefund Canada 1987–92; Mem., Consultative Group to Canada's Ambassador for Disarmament 1988–92; World Federalists of Canada (Mem., Nat. Bd. of Dir. 1986–89; Co-chair Policy Ctte.; Chair, Women & World Order Ctte.); Candn. Peace Alliance (Steering Ctte. 1987–89); Lawyers for Social Responsibility (Mem., Nat. Bd. of Dir. 1988–89; Osgoode Hall Law School Pres. 1984–85); Internat. Law Soc. (Osgoode Hall Law Sch. Pres. 1983–84; Project Ploughshares, Voice of Women, U.N. Assn.; Group of 78; author: 'How We Work for Peace: Canadian Community Activities' 1987 and various articles, manuals & information bulletins; Mem., La Leche League; Mem., Mothers are Women; recreations: reading, dancing, canoeing, camping; Home: R.R. #4, Lanark, Ont. K0G 1K0.

**PERKIN, Hazel W.;** b. Eng. 12 Apr. 1932; d. Frederick James and Dorothy Alice (Coates) P.; e. Univ. of London Teaching Cert. 1952; Teaching Cert. Qué. 1964, Ont. 1972; Sir George Williams Univ. B.A. 1967 (Lt. Gov.'s Silver Medal for Hist.); McGill Univ. M.A. 1971; PRES., 'GOOD ENGLISH' EDITING SERVICE; Teacher in Eng. 1952–60; Teacher, The Study Sch. Westmount, Qué. 1960–67, Head of Jr. Sch. 1968–70; Principal, St. Clement's Sch. 1970–91, retired; author 'The Shaw Pocket Bible Handbook (Culture of Bible Times)' 1984; various articles prof. jours.; co-ed. Candn. Independent Sch. Jour. 1979–84; contbr. 'Dictionary of Biblical Archaeology' 1983; 'The International Standard Bible Encyclopaedia' Vol. II 1982, Vol. III 1985; 'The Evangelical Dictionary of Theology' 1984; 'The New International Dictionary of the Bible' 1987; Ch. Warden, Ch. of the Transfiguration 1979–83, lay mem. of Synod 1975–78, 1984–89; mem. Candn. Assn. Princs. Independent Schs. for Girls (Pres. 1974–75, Sec. 1971–72); Candn. Assn. Independent Schs. (Pres. 1988–89); Conf. Independent Schs. (Vice-Pres. 1989–90); Nat. Assn. Independent Schs. (US); Nat. Assn. Princs. Independent Schs. for

Girls (US); Club: Zonta (Pres. Toronto 1985–86, Sec. 1982–83, Corr. Sec. 1975–76); Home: 30 Greenfield Ave., Suite 208, Willowdale, Ont. M2n 3C8 and 3 St. Margaret's Court, 38 George St., Ryde, Isle of Wight, England PO33 2EN.

**PERKIN, James Russell Conway,** M.A., D.Phil., D.D.; retired academic administrator; b. Northamptonshire, Eng. 19 Aug. 1928; came to Can. 1965; s. Wm. and Lily Maud (Drage) P.; e. gram. sch. Northamptonshire; Oxford Univ. (Eng.) B.A. 1952; M.A. 1955; D.Phil. 1955; Strasbourg Univ., France 1954–55; m. Dorothy Joan Louise d. John Ingraham Bentley 7 April 1953; children: James Russell, John Conway, Anne Louise; Pres. and Vice Chancellor, Acadia Univ. 1982–93, Retired; Min. of Altrincham Bapt. Ch., Cheshire, Eng. 1956–62; Lectr. New Test. Greek, New Coll., Edinburgh, 1963–65; Assoc. Prof. New Test. Interp., McMaster Divinity Coll, Hamilton, Ont. 1965–69; joined Acadia Univ. as Prof. Religious Studies and Dept. Head, 1969–77; Dean of Arts, 1977–80; Vice Pres. (Academic), 1980–82; served with RAF, 1946–49; author of fourteen books incl. 'Handbook for Biblical Studies,' 1973; 'In Season,' 1978; 'With Mind and Heart,' 1979; 'Seedtime and Harvest,' 1982; 'Reflections and Insights' 1993; several articles on biblical, theological, and linguistic subj. in more than 20 jnls.; mem., Soc. for New Test. Studies; Candn. Soc. for the Study of Religion; Candn. Soc. for Biblical Studies; recreations: reading, gardening, sailing, squash; Home: Box 355, Wolfville, N.S. B0P 1X0.

**PERKINS, Harold Jackson,** B.A., M.Sc., Ph.D.; university administrator; biochemist; educational and management consultant; microcomputer consultant; b. London, Ont. 6 July 1930; s. Harold Campbell and Rita (Jackson) P.; e. Univ. of B.C., B.A. (hons.) 1951, M.Sc. 1953; Iowa State Univ. Ph.D. 1957; m. Mary Louise d. late George Kreutziger 21 Aug. 1954; children: Campbell Jackson, Barry Nelson, David Harris, Stephanie Grace; PRES., EDUSERV MANAGEMENT & CONSULTING, INC. 1985– ; Dir., Prairie Public Television (Manitoba) Inc. 1986– ; Dir., Manitoba Hydroelectric Bd. 1988– ; President and Vice Chancellor, Brandon Univ. 1977–83, and Prof. of Chem. 1977– ; Post-doctoral Fellow Nat. Research Council Ottawa 1957–58; Research Biochem. Can. Agric. Research Stn. Lethbridge, Alta. 1958–63; Assoc. Prof. of Chem. State Univ. of N.Y. Plattsburgh 1963–64, Prof. of Chem. and Dean Faculty of Science & Math. 1964–75, Prof. of Chem. and Dean Grad. Studies & Research 1975–77; Dir., Jeux Can. Winter Games (Brandon) 1979; Brandon Gen. Hosp. 1979–83; Prairie Pub. TV (N.D.) 1981–87; Brandon Chamber Comm. 1977–83; Brandon Univ. Foundation 1980–89; Man. Health Research Council 1980–82; Chrmn. of Bd. Am. Friends Brandon Univ.; author numerous scient. papers biochem. journs.; current research studies: Indian education, quality of education, local control of education by Indian Bands; microcomputer applications; mem. Am. Assn. Advanc. Science; Tissue Culture Assn. (mem. Extve. Council 1975–80); Candn. Soc. Plant Physiols. (W. Dir. 1962–63); Aircraft Owners' & Pilots' Assn.; Candn. Owners & Pilots' Assn.; recipient Award Exceptional Merit State Univ. of N.Y. 1977; Sigma Xi; Anglican; recreations: flying, flight instruction, wilderness canoeing, fly fishing; Home: P.O. Box 21058, Brandon, Man. R7B 3W8.

**PERLEY, E. Michael,** M.A.; health and environmental advocate; b. Ottawa, Ont. 28 Nov. 1946; s. Ernest Clint and Verna Leola (Voll) P.; e. St. Andrew's Coll. Aurora, Ont. 1965; Glendon Coll. York Univ. B.A. 1970; Univ. of Toronto M.A. 1971; DIRECTOR, ONTARIO CAMPAIGN FOR ACTION ON TOBACCO; Asst. to M.L.A. for York Centre Ont. 1971–73; Freelance Rsch. Cons. in Environmental Policy Rsch. and Pol. Campaign Orgn. 1973–78, also rep. Brit. publ. firm in W. Africa during this period; Extve. Dir. Candn. Environmental Law Rsch. Found. 1978–81; Extve. Co-ord., Candn. Coalition on Acid Rain 1981–90; Principal, Perley & Hurley Ltd. 1990–93; recipient Conserv. Achievement Cert., Fedn. Ont. Naturalists 1984; recipient 1989 Ontario Lieutenant-Governor's Award for Conservation; co-recipient, William W.H. Gunn Award, Fedn. Ont. Naturalists 1990; awarded Commemorative Medal for 125th Anniversary of Candn. Confederation 1993; co-author 'Acid Rain: The North American Forecast' 1981 (co-recipient Gov. Gen.'s Award for Conservation, Tourism Industry Assoc. of Can. Award 1981); 'Poisoned Skies' 1991; recreations: philately, writing, canoeing, golf, weight training, tennis; Home: 157A Winchester St., Toronto, Ont. M4X 1B5.

**PERLIN, Arthur Saul,** M.Sc., Ph.D., F.R.S.C.; educator; b. Sydney, N.S. 7 July 1923; s. Benjamin I. and Eva (Gaum) P.; e. McGill Univ. B.Sc. 1944, M.Sc. 1946, Ph.D. 1949; m. Ruth Laurel d. William Freedman, Ottawa, Ont. 18 Nov. 1950; children: Anna, Louise, Deborah, Myra, David; EMERITUS PROFESSOR OF CHEMISTRY, McGILL UNIV. 1991– ; Assoc., Pulp & Paper Rsch. Inst. Can.; Rsch. Offr. Nat. Rsch. Council Can. 1948–67; E.B. Eddy Prof. of Chemistry, McGill Univ. 1967–91; Merck Lectr. Chem. Inst. Can. 1962; C.S. Hudson Award Am. Chem. Soc. 1979; served with COTC 1942–44; mem. Chem. Inst. Can.; Am. Chem. Soc.; Jewish; recreations: music, sports; Home: 3445 Drummond St., Montréal, Qué. H3G 1X9; Office: 3420 University St., Montréal, Qué. H3A 2A7.

**PERLIN, John Crosbie,** C.V.O.; publishing executive; b. St. John's, Nfld. 2 March 1934; s. Albert B., O.C., D.Litt. and Vera (Crosbie), O.C., LL.D. Perlin; e. Holloway Sch. and Bishop Field Coll. St. John's; Appleby Coll. Oakville, Ont.; joined family bus. 1952 and currently PRES. NEWFOUNDLAND PUBLISHING SERVICES LTD.; Dir. WHIN Publications Ltd.; Pres., Perlin Family Charitable Trust; Co-ord., Nfld., Citizens Forum on Canada's Future (Spicer Comn.) 1991; Dir.-Gen. Nfld.'s Arts & Culture Centres 1967–89; Dir. Cultural Affairs for Prov. 1971–89; Councillor Town of Hogan's Pond 1986–90; mem. Fed. Cultural Policy Export Review Bd. 1988– ; Chrmn. Nfld. Govt.'s Perm. Anniversaries & Celebrations Ctte. 1981–90; maj. involvement in chairing, organizing and planning all Royal and Candn. Vice Regal Visits to Nfld. since 1974; apptd. Sr. Hon. Aide-de-Camp to Lt. Gov. of Nfld. 1986 (reapptd. 1991) and Acting Private Sec. 1987; apptd. Candn. Secretary to H.M. The Queen for 1990 Visit to Canada; apptd. by the Queen as Lt., Royal Victorian Order (L.V.O.), New Year's Honours List 1989; Commander, Royal Victorian Order (C.V.O.), July 1990; St. John's Citizen of the Year 1988; Apptd. Hon. Chrmn., 40th Anniversary Ctte. to Commemorate the Founding of the Vera Perlin Soc. for Mentally Handicapped Children; Hon. Life Mem., The Vera Perlin Soc.; Nfld. Drama Society; Hon. Life Mem. & Past Pres., St. John's Regatta Ctte.; The Nfld. Soc. for the Disabled; mem. Adv. Bd. Meml. Univ. Art Gallery 1984–89; Bd. mem. Nfld. and Labrador Arts Council 1980–89; Govt. of Nfld. Art Procurement Ctte. 1985–89; Founding mem. Candn. Assn. Presentors; Past Chrmn. Assembly Arts Adms.; Adv. Bd. Nat. Touring Office Can. Council 1973–77; Nat. Pres. Duke of Edinburgh's Award in Can. since Jan. 1989, Nat. Vice Pres. 1986–89, Pres. Nfld. Council 1982–90; Chrmn. Quidi Vidi-Rennies River Devel. Found. since 1984; Hon. Mem. and Past Chrmn. St. John's Library Bd.; Governor, National Theatre Sch. of Canada 1968–92; apptd. to Bd. of Dirs., Rising Tide Theatre 1992; Bd. of Dirs., Wildlife Habitat Canada 1993; Mem., Grenfell Centennial Ctte. 1992; Extve. Mem. of the Bd., NCC Canadiana Fund; Bd. Mem. Nat. Ballet of Can. 1974–90; Mem., St. John's Internat. Mozart Chamber Music Comp. Ctte. 1991; Founding Mem. & Pres., Nfld. and Labrador Services Council 1990–93; Adv. Council Memramcook Sch. Performing Arts since 1987; Hon. Patron Nat. Screen Inst. Can.; St. John's Salvation Army Adv. Bd.; Adv. Bd. mem. and Past Pres. St. John's Boys & Girls Club; Bd. mem. St. John's Heritage Found.; Chrmn. Atlantic Place Visual Arts Ctte. 1974, Ceremonies & Protocol Ctte. 1977; Jeux Can. Games; Chrmn. Nat. Theatre Festivals Nfld. 1967, 1974, 1977; Past Pres. Nfld. Historic Trust; Past Councilllor Nfld. Bd. Trade; K.C.L.J.; recipient, Royal Candn. Acad. Medal for Contribution to Visual Arts 1978; 125th Anniversary of the Confederation of Canada Medal, 1992; granted 'Distinguished Membership' in all RCMP Messes by RCMP Commnr. Inkster 1992; Consultant, freelance journalist and columnist for the St. John's Evening Telegram; United Church (Bd. Chrmn., Cochrane St. Un. Ch.1991); recreations: tennis, golf, cycling; Clubs: Rotary; Kinsmen (Past Pres. St. John's) 1955–67; Address: 56 Bonaventure Ave., St. John's, Nfld. A1C 3Z6.

**PERLMUTTER, David Martin,** B.Com., C.A.; executive; b. Toronto, Ont. 22 Sept. 1934; e. Univ. of Toronto B.Com. 1956; C.A. 1959; m. Renee 29 June 1961; children: Stacey, Dean; CHRMN., VELVET STAR PRODUCTIONS INC.; Founder 1971, Quadrant Group of Companies (including National Film Finance Corp.; Compass Film Sales Ltd. & several others); Vice Pres. Duncan Mill Group; formerly Partner, Perlmutter Orenstein Giddens, Newman & Kofman, C.A.'s; retired 1968 to form Claranton Management Ltd.; President, Jewish Community Centre Toronto; Club: York Racquets; Home: 47 Elgin Ave., Toronto, Ont. M5P 2R8; Office: 129 Yorkville, Toronto, Ont. M5H 1C4.

**PERRAKIS, Stylianos,** Dpl. Eng., M.S., Ph.D.; university professor; b. Piraeus, Greece 6 March 1938; s. Evangelos and Mary (Melissinos) P.; e. Natl. Tech. Univ. Dpl. Eng. 1960; Univ. of California at Berkeley Ph.D. 1970 (Ford Found. Fellow 1967–70); m. Phyllis d. Louis and Kate Sternberg 10 Aug. 1969; children: Evan-Evangelos, Daniel-Dimitrios; PROF., FAC. OF ADMINISTRATION & DEPT. OF ECONOMICS, UNIV. OF OTTAWA 1980– ; Asst. Prof., Admin., Univ. of Ottawa 1970–73; Assoc. Prof. 1973–80; Visiting Assoc. Prof., Univ. of Calif. at Santa Barbara; Visiting Prof., ESCAE Reims France 1983–84; People's Univ. Beijing China 1990; Univ. de Genève 1990–91; NIDA Thailand 1992; Consultant, The World Bank 1989–90; Dept. of Communications (Can.) 1978–82; Inst. of Candn. Bankers 1987–90; Project Dir., External Affairs & Int. Trade Canada 1992–93; Pres., The Parnassos Cultural Soc. 1988–90; author: 'Canadian Industrial Organization' 1990; co-author: 'Investment' 1993; author/co-author of several journal articles; recreations: literature, movies, sports; Home: 81 Glen Ave., Ottawa, Ont. K1S 2Z8; Office: 136 Jean-Jacques Lussier, C.P. 450, Succ. A., Ottawa, Ont. K1N 6N5.

**PERRAULT, Claude;** business executive; b. Montreal, Que. 30 May 1939; s. Léopold and Emilienne (Girard) P.; e. Univ. of Chicago; Univ. of Sherbrooke; Cornell Univ.; Univ. of Western Ont.; m. Colette d. Armand and Marie-Ange Baron 20 April 1963; one d.: Caroline; President & C.E.O., Provigo Distribution Inc. 1992; Sales Rep., Wilsil Ltd. 1955–61; Advtg., Sales & Mktg. Mgr., Denault Ltd. 1961–75; Operations Mgr. & Gen. Mgr., Provi-Soir 1975–86; Extve. Vice-Pres. & Chief Operating Officer, C Corp. Inc. 1986–89; Pres. & Chief Operating Officer, Provigo Distribution Inc. 1989–92; Dir., Centre des dirigeants d'entreprise 1980–83; Les Prés restaurants 1984–85; Horne & Pitfield 1987–90; C Corp Inc. 1987–93; Loeb Inc. 1992–93; selected as 'Nouveau Performant' (New Performer) by PERFORM & COMMERCE magazine (program aimed at identifying new business leaders); Pres., Co-Chair, Hon. Sponsor of different charitable orgns. (Coupe Excellence to aid amateur sport, United Way and Aliment Aide); active supporter of La Cité de la santé de Laval ; Mem., Candn. Council of Grocery Distributors; Retail Council of Canada; the Greater Montreal C. of C.; recreations: tennis, swimming; Home: 2485 de Lotbinière, Duvernay, Laval, Que. H7E 5B5.

**PERRAULT, Guy,** M.Sc.A., Ph.D., F.R.S.C.; b. Amos, 25 Sept. 1927; s. C. R. and Laurenza (Maurice) P.; e. Ecole Polytech., B.Sc.A. 1949; Univ. of Toronto M.Sc.A., 1951; Ph.D., 1955; m. Hélène d. Pascal Lachapelle of Montreal, 24 June 1957; children: Marie, Sylvie, Isabelle; Retired Professor of Mineral Engn., Ecole Polytechnique; Party Chief, Geol. Mapping, iron ranges, Labrador and New Québec, Iron Ore Company of Canada (summers) 1949–52; Mapping and Prospecting, Norancon Exploration Company Ltd., 1953; apptd. Field Engr., Diamond Drilling Programs, Moneta Porcupine Mines Ltd., 1954–56; Asst. Prof. of Mineralogy, Ecole Polytech., 1956; Assoc. Prof. of Mineralogy and Crystallography, 1957; Prof. of Crystallography, 1965; Emeritus Prof. 1989; Chrmn., dépt. de génie géologique, Ecole Polytechnique, 1966–72; Chrmn., dépt.de génie minéral, École Polytechnique, 1974–75; Vice Pres., Research and Foreign Projects, SOQUEM 1975–77; Man. Dir., Mineral Exploration Research Inst. 1981–83; Hon. Pres., Montreal Gem & Mineral Club; Hon. mem., Walker Mineral. Club; Mérite honorofique, Assn. Etudiants l'Ecole Polytechnic; Fellow, Mineralogical Soc. of Am.; author of numerous scient. papers; mem., Mineral. Assn. Can. (Pres. 1967–68); Geol. Assn. Can.; Ordre des Ingénieurs de la P.Q.; Fellow, Mineral. Soc. Am.; Geol. Soc. of Am.; Soc. of Economic Geologists; Can. Institute of Mining and Metallurgy; awarded Prix Scientifique du Québec (1971); Fellow, Royal Soc. of Can. 1973; Queen's Jubilee Medal 1977; Leonard G. Berry Medal 1989; Prix Scientifique Archambault, LACFAS 1991; Catholic; Home: 11811 Jean Massé, Montreal, Qué. H4J 1S2.

**PERRAULT, Hon. Raymond,** P.C., B.A.; senator; b. Vancouver, B.C., 6 Feb. 1926; s. Ernest Alphonse and Florence (Riebel) P.; e. Sir Guy Carleton Elem. and John Oliver Secondary Schs. Vancouver; Univ. of B.C. B.A. 1947; m. Barbara Joan d. late Albert Edward Walker, 10 Aug. 1963; children: Yvonne Marie, Mark Raymond, Robert Ernest Albert; MEM. OF SENATE OF CANADA 1973– ; el. Leader of Lib. Party in B.C. 1959; el. to B.C. Leg. 1960, 1963, 1966; el. to H. of C. g.e. 1968; Parlty. Secy. to Min. of Labour 1970, Manpower & Immigration 1971; Candn. Sessional Del. and Spokesman to Special Comte. UN, N.Y. 1969; mem. first Candn. govt. del. to Peoples Repub. of China 1971; Candn. rep. and govt. spokesman Internat. Labour Organ. Geneva 1972; mem. Candn. Parlty. del. to Soviet Union 1975; Candn. Cabinet rep. Coronation of King Juan Carlos of Spain 1975; Leader, Can. Del. to U.N. Water Conf., Mar del Plata, Argentina, 1977; summoned to Senate 1973 and Leader of Govt. in Senate 1974–79; Leader of Opposition in the Senate, 1979–80; Government Leader in Senate 1980–82; Min. of State (Fitness & Amateur Sport), Mem., Fisheries Ctte., 1982–83; Mem., Senate Ctte., Banking Trade and Commerce; Dir., Citizens Trust; Dir., Vancouver Canucks, N.H.L.; (Northwest Sports) Hon. Chrm., Vanc. Canadians Baseball Team (Pacific Coast League); Hon. Mem., Kiwanis Internat.; Liberal; R. Catholic; recreations: photography, gardening, swimming; Club: Vancouver; Home: 437 Somerset St., North Vancouver, B.C. V7N 1G4; Office: The Senate of Canada, Rm 471-S, Centre Block, Ottawa, Ont. K1A 0A4.

**PERRAULT, Roger A.,** B.A., B.Ph., M.D., Ph.D., F.R.C.P.(C); medical director; b. Amos, Qué. 24 Sept. 1936; e. Univ. of Ottawa, B.A., B.Ph. 1956, M.D. 1963; Blood Centre, Univ. of Uppsala, Ph.D. 1972; m.; 2 children; Deputy-Secy. General (Operations) Candn. Red Cross Soc. 1986; internship and residency Ottawa Gen. Hosp., Nat. Defence Med. Centre 1964–69, responsible for 1st bank of Frozen Blood in Can. 1965–67; served with RCN 1964–68, rank Surgeon Lt.; Med. Dir. Candn. Red Cross Blood Transfusion Service Ottawa Centre and Asst. Prof. of Med. Univ. of Ottawa 1972–74; Nat. Dir., Blood Transfusion Service, Candn. Red Cross Soc. 1974–86; Adjunct Prof. of Med., Ottawa Univ. 1988– ; recipient Med. Rsch. Council Fellowship 1969–72; Queen's Jubilee Medal 1977; author or co-author numerous prof. publs., abstracts and conf. papers; mem. Internat. Soc. Blood Transfusion (Pres. Internat. Cong. 1980; Vice Pres. 1982–86); Candn. Med. Assn.; Candn. Soc. Hematol.; Chrmn., League Red Cross Soc's Group Blood Transfusion Experts; Home: 628 Pleasant Park Rd., Ottawa, Ont. K1H 5N5.

**PERRELLA, Guido,** D.Eng.; mechanical consulting engineer; b. Italy, 1921 (naturalized Candn. Citizen); e. Univ. of Genoa, D.Eng. (Mech.) 1946; m. Christine, d. Sabino Gallo; s. Italo; PRESIDENT, DBM INDUSTRIES LTD. 1968– ; has been engaged in engn. work in various mfg. plants in Italy, Brazil before coming to Canada as Consultant and Technical Manager respectively to several plants; developed new technologies in several fields presently used around the industrialized world; holder several patents for machines and products; Publ: a tech. book on Cost Calculation (3rd ed.); speaks and writes fluently in five lang.; mem., Corp. Engrs. Que.; Royal Astron. Soc. Can.; Soc. Diecasting Engrs.; Candn. Owners & Pilots Assn.; Internat. Aerobatic Club; Candn. Fighter Pilots Assn.; Roman Catholic; hobbies: astronomy, aerobatic flying; Home: 9 Belvedere Rd., Westmount, Que. H3Y 1P3; Office: 10320 Côte de Liesse, Lachine, Que. H8T 1A3.

**PERRIN, Robert Maitland,** B.A., LL.B., M.B.A.; business executive, lawyer; b. Calgary, Alta. 19 Aug. 1950; s. Albert Maitland and Elizabeth Winifred (Chalmers) P.; e. Univ. of Calgary B.A. 1972; Univ. of Alberta LL.B. 1973; Univ. of Calgary M.B.A. 1988; m. Denise d. William and Catherine Richardson 23 Aug. 1975; VICE-PRESIDENT & GENERAL COUNSEL, HOME OIL COMPANY LIMITED 1991– ; Solicitor, McLaws & Co. 1975; Solicitor / Sr. Solicitor / Dir., Internat. Taxes, Hudson's Bay Oil & Gas Co. Ltd. 1975–82; Sr. Solicitor / Counsel, Home Oil Co. 1982–87; Corp. Sec., Interprovincial Pipe Line Ltd. / Interhome Energy Inc. 1987–91; recreations: squash, hiking, cycling; clubs: Elks, Alpine Club of Canada; Home: 179 Country Hills Close N.W., Calgary, Alta. T3K 3Z4; Office: 3200, 324 – 8th Ave. S.W., Calgary, Alta. T2P 2Z5.

**PERRON, Normand;** executive; b. LaSarre, Que. 10 May 1928; s. Henri and Lucinda (Vandal) P.; e. LaSarre Primary Sch.; Montreal Coll. St. Laurent; Mont St. Louis Coll. comm. grad. 1948; m. Thérèse d. Antonio and Alice Huart 14 Apr. 1952; children: Louise French, Monique Vallée, Pierre, Stéphane; BD. CHRMN. AND CHIEF EXTVE. OFFR. DUSTBANE ENTERPRISES LTD. 1982– ; recreations: travel, reading; Club: Cercle Universitaire d'Ottawa; Home: 402 - 31 Durham Private, Ottawa, Ont. K1M 2J1; Office: P.O. Box 8381, Ottawa, Ont. K1G 3K1.

**PERRON, Paul Joseph,** B.A., Ph.D.; university professor; b. Steinbach, Man. 20 April 1940; s. Georges Eugene and Jane Lydia (McAdams) P.; e. Univ. of B.C. B.A. 1961; Univ of Bordeaux Ph.D. 1965; m. Jacqueline Emilienne d. Georges and Elisabeth Maurin 29 Aug. 1967; PROF., DEPT. OF FRENCH, UNIV. OF TORONTO 1981– ; English Teacher, Lycée Michel Montaigne (France) 1961–64; Prof. of English, La Brede, France 1962–65; Lectr. in French, Royal Military Coll. 1965–66; Asst. Prof. of French 1966–67; Victoria Coll., Univ. of Toronto (tenure granted) 1967–71; Assoc. Prof. 1971–81; various cross-appointments & admin. positions (Comparative Literature, School of Graduate Studies, etc.) 1978– ; currently Chair, Dept. of French 1990– ; Visiting Prof., Queen's Univ. 1966–67; Univ. of Montpellier France 1993; Co-Dir., Univ. of Toronto Balzac Prog. 1976– ; Chevalier de l'Ordre des Palmes Académiques France 1993; Fellow, Camargo Found. (Cassis France) 1994; Pres. & Extve Dir., Toronto Semiotic Circle 1989– ; Acad. Coord., Internat. Summer Inst. for Semiotic and Structural Studies 1990; author/co-author and editor/co-editor of num. journal articles and journals incl. co-ed., '3L Series' (Didier) 1979– , 'Theory/Culture' 1990, 'Semiotics' 1992 and ed., 'A.J. Greimas & J. Fontanille' and 'The Semiotics of Passions' 1993, 'A.J. Greimas and Narrative Cognition' 1993; recreations: fly fishing, squash; Home: 590 Huron St., Toronto, Ont. M5R 2R7; Office: 7 King's College Circle, Toronto, Ont. M5S 1A1.

**PERRON, Pierre O.,** B.A., B.Sc.A., Ph.D.; public servant; b. Louiseville, Que. 19 Aug. 1939; s. René and Germaine (Hardy) P.; e. Laval Univ. B.A. 1959, B.Sc.A. 1963; Univ. of Strathclyde, Glasgow, Scot. Ph.D. Metallurgy 1966; PRES., NATIONAL RSCH. COUNCIL OF CANADA 1989– ; Rsch. Offr. Chalk River Nuclear Lab., Atomic Energy of Canada Ltd. 1966–68; Mgr. Radiation Protection, Hydro-Québec/Gentilly 1968–71; Dir. Materials Sciences Dept., Centre de rech. ind. du Qué. 1971–75, Dir. R. & D. there 1975–82; Assoc. Depy. Min. (Mines), Min. of Energy and Resources, Que. 1982–85; Assoc. Depy. Min., Energy, Mines & Resources Canada 1985–89; Home: 152 Primrose St., Ottawa, Ont. K1R 6M5.

**PERRY, David B.,** B.A.; public finance economist; b. Markham, Ont. 9 Aug. 1939; s. Alfred James and Doris (Millard) P.; e. Pickering Dist. H.S. 1957; Univ. of Toronto B.A. (Hons.) 1961; m. Delia d. Thora and Dennis Harris 21 March 1980; one s.: D. Adam; SENIOR RESEARCH ASSOCIATE, CANADIAN TAX FOUNDATION 1968– ; Economist, Prov. of Ont., Treas. Dept. 1961–66; Research Planner, York County Planning Office 1966–68; commentator on matters of tax and public finance; author: Candn. Tax Journal feature 'Fiscal Figures' 1968– ; Author & Supervisor, 'The National Finances' and 'Provincial and Municipal Finances' annual 1968– ; co-author: 'Financing Canadian Federation' 1994; Candn. section, 'International Aspects of Tax Expenditures' 1985; recreation: woodcarving; clubs: Canadian Racing Drivers Assn.; Home: 8 Gatehead Rd., Willowdale, Ont. M2J 2P5; Office: Suite 1800, 1 Queen St. E., Toronto, Ont. M5C 2Y2.

**PERRY, Frank,** B.A., R.C.A.; sculptor; b. Vancouver, B.C. 15 Jan. 1923; s. Frank and Martha (Mack) P.; e. Univ. of B.C. B.A. 1949; Regent St. Polytechnic London, Eng. Art Sch. 1953–55; Central Sch. Arts & Crafts London, Eng. 1954–55; m. Doris Olson, Dec. 1957 (dec'd. Dec. 1972); remarried Dec. 1977, divorced 1992; exhns. Galleria Numero Florence, Italy 1958; Gimpel Fils Gallery London, Eng. 1959; Laing Gallery Toronto 1959–60; New Design Gallery Vancouver numerous shows 1958–67; Burnaby Art Gallery 1977, 1980; Vancouver Art Gallery 1977; Mira Godard Gallery Toronto 1978; Gallery Move 1979; outdoor sculpture exhns.: Univ. of B.C. 1956, 1958; B.C. Centennial Outdoor Show 1958; Que. Outdoor Nat. Sculpture Show 1960; Vancouver Outdoor Centennial Sculpture Show 1967; rep. in various pub. and private colls. Can. and Europe; recipient Jessie Dow Award Montreal Museum Spring Show 1958; First Prize Sculpture, Burnaby Centennial Outdoor Sculpture Show 1958; First Prize Centennial Outdoor Sculpture Show Vancouver 1967; Can. Council Fellowship 1958; mem. Adv. Design Panel Dist. N. Vancouver 1969–73; served overseas with Royal Candn. Engrs. 1943–46; mem. Sculpture Soc. B.C.; Sculpture Soc. Can.; recreation: fishing; Home: 3526 Everglade Pl., North Vancouver, B.C. V7N 3T9.

**PERRY, Harold Robert;** management consultant; b. Port Arthur, Ont. 11 July 1947; s. Harold Clement and Margaret (Taylor) Peerenboom; e. Purdue, White Oaks Secondary; m. Robin d. Robert and Laurie Brauns 24 Nov. 1973; children: Robert, Lindsay, Gregg; PRES. & SOLE PROPRIETOR, MANDRAKE MGMT. CONSULTANTS LTD. 1970– ; Dir. & Shareholder, Crestwood Schools; recreations: tennis, skiing; Club: Craigleith Ski; Home: 174 Warren Rd., Toronto, Ont. M4V 2S5; Office: 15 Bedford Rd., Toronto, Ont. M5R 2J7.

**PERRY, Kathleen,** B.A., M.L.S.; university administrator; b. Niagara Falls, N.Y. 27 June 1953; d. Clinton and Ellen Gwendoline (Richardson) P.; e. Stratford Central S.S. 1972; Victoria Coll., Univ. of Toronto B.A. 1976; Univ. of W. Ont. M.L.S. 1978; EMPLOYMENT EQUITY COORDINATOR & ACTING ADVISOR TO THE RECTOR ON THE STATUS OF WOMEN 1987– ; Slide Librarian, Concordia Univ. 1978–87; Chair, Univ. Community Div. 1992–94; Co-chair, Joint Pay Equity Ctte. for Women Faculty 1990–91; Social Ctte., Candn. Library Assn.; Annual Conf. Ctte., Treas. & Mem., Negotiation Ctte., Faculty Assn.; Bd. of Dir., YWCA Montreal 1987–92; author of 2 diagnostic reports; Office: K-120, 1455 de Maisonneuve Blvd. W., Montreal, Que. H3G 1M8.

**PERRY, Malcolm Blythe,** B.Sc., Ph.D., D.Sc., F.R.I.C., F.R.S.C.; scientist; b. Birkenhead, U.K. 26 Apl. 1930; s. Cyril Alexander and Hilda (Blythe) P.; e. Univ. of Bristol B.Sc. 1952, Ph.D. 1955, D.Sc. 1969; post-grad. studies Cambridge Univ., Queen's Univ., Univ. de Paris XI; m. Eileen Shaw 10 Aug. 1956; two d. Sara Jane, Judith Anne; PRIN. RSCH. OFFR. AND HEAD OF MICROBIOL. AND IMMUNOCHEM. NAT. RSCH. COUNCIL CAN. 1981– ; Prof. of Microbiol. Univ. of Ottawa; Banting Rsch. Fellow Queen's Univ. 1955, Asst. Prof. Faculty of Med. 1956, R.S. McLaughlin Rsch. Prof. 1960; Rsch. Offr. present Council 1962, Sr. Rsch. Offr. 1971; Sci., Med. Rsch. Council Lab. Mol. Biol. Cambridge Univ. 1969; Sci., Institut de Biochemie Univ. de Paris 1979; recipient 1991 Award of Can. Soc. Microbiol.; 1993 Travelling Lectureship Award of Can. Soc. Microbiol; author over 200 sci. publs. microbiol. and chem.; mem., Royal Society of Can.; Am. Soc. Microbiol.; Candn. Soc. Microbiol.; Home: 769 Hemlock Rd., Ottawa, Ont. K1K 0K6; Office: N.R.C., Ottawa, Ont. K1A 0R6.

**PERRY, (Gordon) Neil,** B.A., M.P.A., A.M., Ph.D., LL.D.; educator; b. Victoria, B.C., 22 Nov., 1909; s. late John Oswald and late Agnes Mary (McLorie) P.; e. Victoria (B.C.) High Sch., 1923–26; Victoria Coll., 1929–31; Univ. of B.C., B.A. (Econ.) 1933, LL.D. 1966; Harvard Univ., M.P.A. 1943; A.M. and Ph.D. (Econ.) 1952; m. Helen McGregor Hunter, 29 June 1940; two d.: Margaret Elaine, Donna Louise; Member, Universities Council of B.C. 1978–87; during depression apptd. Secretary to Econ. Council of B.C.; served Prov. of B.C. in various capacities until 1947 (1st Dir. of Bureau of Econ. and Stat.; Econ. Adviser, Dom. Prov. Relations, 1947); became Asst. Dir., Internat. Econ. Relations Div., Dept. of Finance, Ottawa, 1947; also served as Candn. Alternate Extve. Dir. on Bds. of Internat. Monetary Fund and Internat. Bank for Reconstr. and Devel. (World Bank) and as Financial Counsellor to Candn. Embassy, Washington; invited to Ethiopia as Econ. Adviser to Min. of Finance, 1954, and subsequently Gov. State Bank of Ethiopia; returned to World Bank as Asst. Dir. of Operations in S. Asia and Middle East, 1956; Asst. Dir. of Bank's operation in W. Hemisphere, 1958; appt. Dean of Comm., Univ. of B.C., 1960, 1st Vice-Pres., 1963; loaned to U.N. as Econ. Adviser of E. African Common Services Organ., Apl.-Aug. 1963; Depy. Min. of Educ., B.C. 1965–70; Asst. Depy. Min. Manpower & Immigration, Can. 1970–73; Prof. and Dir., School of Public Admin., Univ of Victoria 1973–77: Prof. Emeritus; Nat. Pres., Inst. of Public Admin. 1976–77; Consultant, Univ. of Sierra Leone 1977–78; Consultant, OECD Manpower and Social Affairs, 1976–78; has served as an Indust. Inquiry Commr. in difficult labour-man. disputes; Mem. of Senate, Simon Fraser Univ. 1965–70; Chrmn., Adv. Council, B.C. Inst. of Tech.; awarded Order of Star of Ethiopia, 1956; Centennial Medal, 1967; author: 'Report of the Advisory Committee on Inter-University Relations' (The Perry Report) 1972; 'The Human Factor in a Transforming World' 1992; also numerous articles for learned and prof. publs.; mem., Candn. Econ. Assn.; Am. Econ. Assn.; Inst. Pub. Adm.; apptd. Chrmn. of Comte. on Inter-Univ. Relations by Min. of Educ., B.C. 1968; United Church; Vancouver Club (life); recreation: golf; Club: Victoria; Home: Apt. 903, 630 Montreal St., Victoria, B.C. V8V 4Y2.

**PERRY, Thomas Ivor;** business executive; b. Lisburn, N. Ireland 18 April 1946; s. Thomas S. and Ruth (McCrea) P.; e. Belfast College for Advanced Technology; Univ. of S. Africa Business Management 1984; m. Linda d. Iris and Albert Hanna 10 Dec. 1971; children: Daryl, Colleen; CO-OWNER, PRESIDENT & GENERAL MANAGER, DIMATEC INCORPORATED; Design Dept., aircraft mfr. co. N. Ireland 1967–72; Mfg. Control Engineer for an internat. abrasives co. in Africa 1972–78; Director of Producton for a diamond drilling supply co. 1978–86; emigrated to Canada 1987; joined Delro Industries as Manager of Business Development; Pres., Darcol Enterprises; Registered Engineer, The Engineering Council (U.K.); Mem., Inst. of Engr. Designers (U.K.); Fellow Corp. Mem., Production Management INst. of S. Africa; Registered Profl. Technologist; Dir., Candn. Diamond Drilling Assn. 1988–91; Mem., Diamond Core Drill Mfrs. Assn. (U.S.A.); recreations: tennis, running, photography; clubs: Kinsmen Reh-Fit

Centre; Home: 49 Kerslake Dr., Winnipeg, Man. R3P 2C8; Office: 180 Cree Cres., Winnipeg, Man. R3J 3W1.

**PERRYMAN, Eric Charles William,** M.A., F.R.S.C.; metallurgist; b. Stanwell, Eng. 7 Feb. 1922; s. Frederick and Violet (Plow) P.; e. Cambridge Univ. M.A. 1943; M. Gladys Winifred Field d. late Ewart Taylor 21 May 1945; children: Gavin, Marcia, Anthony, Roger; Gen. Mgr., Commercial Operations, Atomic Energy of Canada Ltd. 1979–86; retired; joined Metall. Dept. Royal Aircraft Estab. Eng. 1943–46; Brit. Non-Ferrous Metals Research Assn. Eng. 1946–51; Aluminum Laboratories Ltd. Kingston, Ont. 1951–54; on attachment to Atomic Energy of Canada Ltd. 1954–57, joined AECL 1957 becoming Asst. Dir. Chem. & Metall. Div. 1958–60, 1963–65, Dir. of Div. 1965–67, Dir. Fuels & Materials Div. 1967–70, Dir. Applied Research & Devel. 1970–78; Depy. Head of Reactor Materials Lab. UKAEA, Culcheth, Eng. 1960–63; Amnesty Intnl. SERVAS host; author over 45 tech. publs.; Saganaska (Kiwanis) Belleville; Amnesty Internat.; Anglican; recreations: tennis, sailing, gardening, bridge; Club: Loyalist Tennis; Home: R.R. 1 Corbyville, Ont. K0K 1V0.

**PERSAD, Emmanuel,** M.B., B.S., F.R.C.P.&S.(C); psychiatrist; b. Trinidad, W.I. 25 Dec. 1935; s. Kali and Christiana (Baboolal) P.; Nariva Govt. Sch., Progressive Educ. Inst. Trinidad; Durham Univ. M.B., B.S. 1964; Univ. of Toronto Dipl. in Psychiatry 1969 (Gold Medal); L.M.C.C. 1972; m. Decima d. James W. Mignon 1967; children: Sheldon, Natalie; DIR. OF EDUCATION and CONSULTANT to the MOOD DISORDER PROGRAM, LONDON PSYCHIATRIC HOSP. 1989– ; Dir., Postgrad. Education and Assoc. Prof., Dept. of Psychiatry, Univ. of Western Ont.; Staff Psychiatrist, Clarke Inst. of Psychiatry (held several positions incl. Chief of Service, Dir. of Education, Chief of the Affective Disorders - Research Unit, Rsch. Dir., Head of Clinical Rsch. Div., and Chief of the Clinical Psychopharmacology Unit) 1971–89; mem. Ont. Council of Health Task Force on Mental Health Services 1977–79; Adv. Bd., Ont. Manic Depressive Assn.; reviewer several psychiatric journals; Ed. Bd. of two journals; mem., Management Bd., Candn. Brain Bank; mem., Council of Educational and Professional Liaison, Candn. Psychiatric Assn.; co-author one book; co-editor one book; Examiner, Royal College Certification in Psychiatry (oral); Office: 850 Highbury Ave., London, Ont. N5Y 5B8.

**PERSAUD, Trivedi Vidhya Nandan,** M.D., Ph.D., D.Sc., F.R.C. Path.(Lond.), F.F.Path. (R.C.P.I.); educator; b. Port Mourant, Guyana 19 Feb. 1940; s. Ram. Nandan and Deen (Raggy) P.; e. Rostock Univ. Germany M.D. 1965 (Brit. Guiana Scholar 1960–65), Outstanding Student of the Yr. Award 1964, Distinguished Young Scient. Award 1965, D.Sc. 1974; Univ. of the W. Indies Ph.D. (Anat.) 1970; m. Gisela Gerda Zehden; children: Indrani Uta, Sunita Heidi, Rainer Narendra; PROF. OF ANATOMY, UNIV. OF MAN. since 1977; Assoc. Prof. of Obstetrics, Gynecology and Reproductive Sciences 1979– ; Prof. of Pediatrics & Child Health 1989– ; Consultant in Pathology and Teratology, Children's Centre, Winnipeg since 1973; Scient. Staff (Lab. Services) Health Sciences Centre Winnipeg since 1973; Intern, Kleinmachnow Hosp. Potsdam, Germany 1965–66; Govt. Med. Offr. Guyana 1966–67; Lectr. in Anat. Univ. of the W. Indies 1967–70, Sr. Lectr. 1970–72; Assoc. Prof. of Anatomy, Univ. of Man. 1972–75, Prof. of Anatomy and Dir. Teratology Research Lab. 1975–77, Head, Dept. of Anatomy 1977–93; named Hon. Citizen of New Orleans 1972; rec'd Carveth Jr. Scient. Award Candn. Assn. Pathols. 1974; Distinguished Services Award Pan Am. Assn. Anat. 1975; Rh-Inst. Award (Health Sciences) Univ. Man. 1975; Albert Einstein Centennial Medal, Academy of Sciences, Germany 1981; Dr. and Mrs. H.H. Saunderson Award for Excellence in Teaching, Univ. of Manitoba 1985; Andreas Vesalius Medal, Univ. of Pisa, Italy 1986; Visiting Fellow, Wolfson College, Cambridge, England 1988; Hon. Mem., Anatomical Soc. of Germany 1989; Raymond C. Truex Distinguished Lectureship Award, Hahnemann Univ., Philadelphia 1990; J.C.B. Grant Award, Candn. Assn. of Anatomists 1991; author: 'Study Guide and Review Manual of Human Anatomy' W.B. Saunders Co., Philadelphia, 1976 (Revised Ed. 1980); 'Problems of Birth Defects' Univ. Park Press, Baltimore, 1977; 'Prenatal Pathology: Fetal Medicine' Charles C. Thomas, Springfield, 1978; 'Teratogenesis: Experimental Aspects and Clinical Implications' Gustav Fischer Verlag, Jena, 1978; 'Advances in the Study of Birth Defects': Vol. 1. Teratogenic Mechanisms; Vol. 2. Teratological Testing; Vol. 3. Abnormal Embryogenesis: Cellular and Molecular Aspects; Vol. 4. Neural and Behavioral Teratology 1979; Vol. 5. Genetic Disorders, Syndromology and Prenatal Diagnosis; Vol. 6. Cardiovascular, Respiratory, Gastrointestinal and Genitourinary Malformations; Vol. 7. Central Nervous System and Craniofacial Malformations 1982; 'Early History of Human Anatomy' Charles C. Thomas, Springfield, 1984; 'Key Facts in Gross Anatomy' Churchill Livingstone, New York, 1985; 'Basic Concepts in Teratology' Allan Liss Inc., New York, 1985; 'Environmental Causes of Human Birth Defects' Charles C. Thomas, Springfield, 1990; 'Teratologie' Gustav Fischer Verlag, 1992; (with K.L. Moore) 'The Developing Human' W.B. Saunders Co., Philadelphia 1993; (with K.L. Moore) 'Before We are Born' W.B. Saunders Co., Philadelphia 1993; (with K.L. Moore) 'Study Guide and Review Manual of Human Embryology' W.B. Saunders Co., Philadelphia 1993; mem. Royal Coll. Pathols. London; Candn. Assn. Pathols.; Am. Assn. Anats.; Faculty of Pathology, Royal Coll. of Physicians, Ireland; Candn. Assn. Anats. (Vice-Pres. 1979–81; Pres. 1981–83); Midwest Anats. Assn. (Pres. 1979–80); Board of Directors, Canadian Federation of Biological Societies (1981–83); Anatomische Gesellschaft; Teratology Soc.; European Soc. Teratology; Ed. 'West Indian Medical Journal' 1970–73; mem. ed. bds. several med. journs.; Home: 70 Folkestone Blvd., Winnipeg, Man. R3P 0S3; Office: 730 William Ave., Winnipeg, Man. R3E OW3.

**PERSINGER, Michael A.,** B.A., M.A., Ph.D.; university professor; b. Jacksonville, Florida 26 June 1945; s. Milo Alfred and Violet Mae (Knight) P.; e. Univ. of Wisconsin, B.A. 1967; Univ. of Tennessee, M.A. 1969; Univ. of Man., Ph.D. 1971; m. Ghislaine d. Albert and Germaine Lafreniere 1983; one d.: Viger; PROF., LAURENTIAN UNIVERSITY 1979– ; developer of tectonic strain hypothesis to explain luminous phenomena and temporal lobe continuum hypothesis which states occurrence of mystical experiences & related reports are present in different degrees in the normal population; expert, electromagnetic field effects on living systems, neuropsychology; Mem., Adm. Assn. for the Advancement of Sci.; Parapsychol. Assn.; Internat. Soc. of Biometeorol.; Internat. Neurochem. Soc.; author: 'ELF and VLF Electromagnetic Field Effects' 1974, 'The Paranormal' parts 1 & 2 1974, 'Space-Time Transients and Unusual Events' 1977, 'TM and Cultmania' 1980, 'The Weather Matrix and Human Behaviour' 1980, 'Neuropsychological Bases of the God Experience' 1987; over 200 tech. articles on biometerol., psychol., neuropsychol., parapsychol. & geo physics; recreations: martial arts, primarily Chinese forms; Home: 261 Wilson St., Sudbury, Ont. P3E 2S3; Office: Behavioural Neurosci. Lab., Laurentian Univ., Sudbury, Ont. P3E 2C6.

**PERSOFSKY, Renah Alissa;** marketing executive; b. Kitchener, Ont. 2 July 1958; d. Ely and Judith (Friedman) Matlow; m. Abraham s. Jack P. 2 July 1978; one s.: Jonathan; SENIOR VICE PRESIDENT, BRYKER DATA SYSTEMS; Rep., AES Sales; Sales Rep., Lanier Canada; Sales Supvr., Harris Lanier; Nat. Govt. Sales Coordinator; Govt. Sales Rep., MSA; Nat. Sales Mgr., Digital Business Unit, Dun & Bradstreet Software; Past Pres., York Centre Liberal Riding Assn.; Advisory Bd., Stratus Computer Inc.; Home: 6 Steeplechase Ave., Aurora, Ont. L4G 6W5; Office: 120 Commerce Valley Dr. E., Thornhill, Ont. L3T 7R2.

**PESANDO, James Edward,** B.A., M.A., Ph.D.; university professor; b. Toronto, Ont. 25 Oct. 1946; s. Mario Armand and Dorothy (Hall) P.; e. Harvard Univ. B.A. 1967; Univ. of California M.A. 1968; Univ. of Toronto Ph.D. 1971; PROF. OF ECONOMICS, UNIV. OF TORONTO 1979– ; Asst. Prof. of Econ., Univ. of Toronto 1971–75; Assoc. Prof. 1975–79; Dir., Inst. for Policy Analysis, Univ. of Toronto 1985– ; Assoc. Ed. 'J. of Finance' 1977–83; Rsch. Assoc., Nat. Bur. of Econ. Research (Harvard); Mem., Pension Research Council, Wharton Sch., Univ. of Penn.; author: 'The Impact of Inflation on Financial Markets in Canada' 1977 and many papers in profl. journals of econ.; co-author: 'Public and Private Pensions in Canda' 1977, 'Government in Canadian Capital Market' 1978; recreations: running; collecting art and antiques; Home: 88 Bedford Rd., Toronto, Ont. M5R 2K2; Office: 140 St. George St., Toronto, Ont. M5S 1A1.

**PESONEN, Jori Eino,** M.Sc.; retired; b. Tampere 21 Aug. 1925; s. Niilo Kustaa and Hilma Maria (Uusivirta) P.; e. Helsinki Univ. of Tech. Forest Products Dept. M.Sc. 1951; m. Riitta Kyllikki d. Walter and Astrid Marttinen 18 Apr. 1957; children: J. Walter, Jussi Heikki, Eeva Maria Elina; Pres., C.E.O. and Bd. Mem., Valmet Paper Machinery Inc., Helsinki, Finland 1987–90; mem. Bd. Valmet Corp., Helsinki, Finland; Rotomec S.p.A, Casale, Italy; OY Tamfelt Ab, Tampere, Finland; Ateliers de Constructions Allimand, Rives, France; Rsch. Engr. Hallsta Pappersbruk, Sweden 1951; Rsch. Engr. Anglo-Newfoundland Devel. Co. and Anglo-Candn. Pulp and Paper Mills, Can. 1953; Mfg. Engr. United Paper Mills Ltd., Kaipola, Finland 1954; Tech. Mgr. Cartiere del Timavo S.P.A., Italy 1958, Tech. Mgr. Kajaani Oy, Finland 1960, Mill Mgr. 1970; Gen. Mgr. Rautpohja Works 1975, Corp. Vice Pres. & C.E.O. Paper Machinery Group, Valmet Corp. 1980; Club: Rotary; Home: Pietarinkatu 3 A 10, 00140 Helsinki, Finland.

**PETCH, Howard E.,** M.Sc., Ph.D., D. Sc., LL.D., F.R.S.C., O.B.C.; retired physicist; b. Agincourt, Ont., 12 May 1925; s. Thomas Earle and Edith May (Painter) P.; e. Sarnia (Ont.) Coll. Inst. & Tech. Sch.; Norwich (Ont.) High Sch.; McMaster Univ., B.Sc. (Hon. Chem. and Phys.) 1949, M.Sc. (Physics) 1950; Univ. of B.C., Ph.D. (Physics) 1952; McMaster Univ., D. Sc.; Univ. of Waterloo, LL.D.; Univ. of Victoria LL.D. (h.c.); m. late Rosalind June, d. late Alfred E. Hulet, 1949; children: Stephen, Patricia; rem. Linda Schlechte, 1976; one s., Jeremy; PRESIDENT EMERITUS, UNIVERSITY OF VICTORIA; Postdoctorate Fellow, McMaster University, 1952–53; Rutherford Mem. Fellow, Cavendish Lab., Cambridge Univ., 1953–54; Asst. Prof. of Physics, McMaster Univ., 1954–57: Assoc. Prof., 1957–60; Prof. of Metall. and Metall. Engn., 1960–67; Principal, Hamilton Coll., McMaster Univ., 1963–67; Dir. of Research there 1961–67 and Chrmn. Interdisciplinary Materials Research Unit 1964–67; Prof. of Physics, Univ. of Waterloo 1967–74; Pres. (acting) 1969–70; Vice-President Acad., 1967–68, 1970–75; Pres. & Vice Chancellor, Univ. of Victoria and Prof. of Physics 1975–90; served with R.C.A.F. 1943–45; awarded Ont. Research Foundation Schols. 1949–52; Convocation Founder of Simon Fraser Univ. 1965; Chrmn., Seniors Adv. Council of B.C.; mem. Bd. Govs., McMaster Univ.; mem, Candn. Assn. Physicists (Pres. 1967–68); Am. Phys. Soc.; Internat. Union of Crystallography 1954; Am. Crystallographic Assn.; Candn. Research Mang. Assn.; and Inst. of Mining & Metall., Comte. for Research; rec'd. Centennial Medal; Hon. LL.D., Simon Fraser Univ. 1990; Hon. Sc.D., Univ. of B.C. 1990; Order of British Columbia 1990; Miracle Award, Tourism Victoria 1990; Alpha Sigma Mu; recreation: bird watching, gardening, fishing; Home: 3050 Baynes Rd., Victoria, B.C. V8N 1Y7.

**PETCH, John Frank,** Q.C., LL.M., B.A.; lawyer; b. Kitchener, Ont. 25 June 1938; s. the late Lorne Franklin and Margaret Mary (Dietrich) P.; e. Univ. of W. Ont. B.A. 1960; Univ. of Toronto LL.B. 1963, Osgoode Hall LL.M. 1980; m. Eleanor Ruth d. Norman and Marguerite Crawford 6 Sept. 1980; children: Andrea Lauren, Alisa Carolyn, John Britton, Erin Courtney; PARTNER, OSLER, HOSKIN & HARCOURT 1975– ; read law with Osler, Hoskin & Harcourt 1963–65; called to Bar of Ont. 1965; Q.C. 1982; Lectr., Univ. of Toronto Law Sch., Law Soc. of U.C.; Univ. of W. Ont. Law School, Middlesex Law Assn., Queen's Univ. Sch. of Bus., Insight Educational Serv., Candn. Profl. Confs., Fed. Dept. of Finance, Property Forum '92; Mem., Candn. Bar Assn.; County of York Law Assn.; Am. Bar Assn.; Dir., Swire Tech. Serv. Limited; John Swire & Sons (Canada) Ltd.; Corp. Sec., OMERS Realty Corp.; Trustee, var. family trusts; Univ. of Toronto Arbor Award 1990; Treas. Gold Medal, Law Soc. First Prize, Lawyers Club First Prize, Commercial Law & Co. Prize, Criminal Procedure Prize, Bar of Ont. 1965, Univ. of Toronto Law Sch. Gold Medal 1963; Dir., St. Michael's Hosp.; Mem., Univ. of Toronto Electoral Coll. (Extve. Ctte.) 1991– ; Toronto Bd. of Trade Corp. Legis. Ctte. 1991–93; Pres., Univ. of Toronto Law Sch. Alumni Council 1994– (Past Treas.); several other past memberships, directorships & extve. positions; Roman Catholic; recreations: tennis, golf, skiing, hiking; clubs: Toronto Lawn Tenis, Fitnes Inst., Windermere Golf & Country, Caledon Ski; Home: 186 St. Leonards Ave., Toronto, Ont. M4N 1K7; Office: P.O. Box 50,1 First Canadian Place, Toronto, Ont. M5X 1B8.

**PETER, Friedrich,** R.C.A.; graphic designer; calligrapher; educator; visual artist; b. Dresden, Germany 23 Feb. 1933; s. Karl and Lena (Brueckner) P.; e. apprenticeship in graphic design, 1947–50, Dresden; Hochschule für bildende Künste, Berlin, 1950–1956, grad. in lettering and graphic design; Meisterschüler dipl. 1957; m. Christine d. Gotthold Rossbach, Germany, 1 June 1957; children: Jan, Martin, Andrea; INSTR., EMILY CARR COLL. OF ART AND DESIGN 1979– ; came to Canada 1957; Instr. Vancouver Sch. of Art 1958–79; Designer Postage stamps: 'O Canada' 2 postage stamps commemorating Candn. Nat. Anthem 1980; Terry Fox – Marathon of Hope 1982; Candn. Constitution Patriation 1982; Multiculturalism 1990; Calligrapher: 'Im Aufwind' 1977, 4th printing 1981; 'Searching for You' 1978; 'Into your light' 1979; 12 llustrations 'Der Turm' 1979; Book illus. 'Wenn

Mauern fallen' (When Walls Fall) Kreuzverlag, Germany 1989; Murals: 90 feet mural, World Council of Churches Sixth Assembly, Vancouver, B.C., 1983; 30-foot Mural for Lutheran Church in Canada Bi-annual Convention at Centennial Auditorium, Saskatoon, Sask. 1989; Participant in 1980 internat. exhbn. 'Calligraphy Today' sponsored by Internat. Typeface Corp. N.Y., also shown in Israel and Germany 1982; Exhibited at Royal Cdn. Acad. of Arts Centenniary Exhibition, Toronto 1981; Candn. Postage Stamp designers display, Internat. Philatelic Exhibition, Vienna, Austria, 1982; Paintings exhibited in Montreal, Ottawa, Toronto, Halifax and Vancouver galleries since 1986; Display of philatelic design, graphic design and fine art work at Posthouse, Vancouver, B.C. 1987; Exhib. of 'Lettering Paintings' at Regent College, Univ. of B.C. 1989; Contbr. to internat., invitational calligraphy for book publication and internat. traveling exhib.; "3:16" 'Bible Texts Illuminated' by Donald Knuth, Stanford Univ., USA 1990; two simultaneous one-man-shows of drawings inspired by The Middle East Conflict 1991, at Lookout Gallery, Regent College, and Gallery Alpha, March 1991; Awards: Winner of Internat. Typeface Design Competitions, by Internat. Typeface Corp., New York ('Vivaldi' 1966); Letraset Internat. ('Magnificat' 1973); Morisawa & Co. Ltd., Osaka, Japan, in Latin category; Second Internat. Competition ('Sanbika' 1987), First Prize; Third Internat. Competition ('Shinko' 1990), Dorfsman Prize; Fourth Internat. Competition ('Peter Roman' 1993), Bronze Prize; Competition winner for design of XV Olympic Winter Games, Calgary 1988, $100 Gold Coin, Royal Candn. Mint 1987; Competition winner for design of XV Olympic Winter Games, Calgary 1988, Official Sports Medal/gold, silver, bronze, 1987; Candn. Mint/Price Awards: Silver Dollar, City of Regina Centenary, 1981; $100 Gold Coin, Candn. Constitution, 1982; $20 Silver coin for Speed Skating Events of Calgary 1988 Olympic Winter Games, 1985; One dollar coin, special issue 'Celebration of the Arts' by The Royal Candn. Mint 1992; CBC Television Interview, Sunday Arts Entertainment: Coin and Medal Designers 1990; original designs represented in 'The Art of the Coin' exhib. by The Royal Candn. Mint, Toronto 1992 and Vancouver 1993; Since 1989 studies of lettering as art; 1990 Sabbatical trip to see Arabic Calligraphy in Turkey; Author of articles graphic design educ.; Mem. Graphic Designers Can. (Founding mem. B.C. Chapter 1974; Regional Rep. Dist. of B.C.); Membership appointment, Candn. Postage Stamp Adv. Comte., 1982–85; Evangelical (charismatic) Christian; recreations: hiking, painting, drawing; Home: 193 E. St. James Rd., North Vancouver, B.C. V7N 1L1; Office: ECCAD, 1399 Johnston St., Vancouver, B.C. V6H 3R9.

**PETER, Richard Ector,** B.Sc., Ph.D.; university professor; b. Medicine Hat, Alta. 7 Mar. 1943; s. Arthur Ector and Josephine (Wrobleski) P.; e. Univ. of Calgary, B.Sc. (Hons.) 1965; Univ. of Washington, Ph.D. 1969; m. Leona d. Bud and Vivian Booth 27 Dec. 1965; children: Jason Ector, Matthew Thomas Booth; DEAN OF SCIENCE, UNIV. OF ALTA. 1992– ; Post-doct. fellow, Dept. of Pharm., Univ. of Bristol 1969–70; Asst. Prof., Dept. of Zool., Univ. of Alta. 1971–74; Assoc. Prof. 1974–79; Prof. 1979– ; Chrmn., 1984–89, 1990–92; Extve. Mem., Acad. of Sci., Royal Soc. of Can. 1986–88; Pres., Candn. Counc. of Univ. Biol. Chrmn. 1986–87 (Vice-Pres. 1985–86); Bd. of Dir., 'General and Comparative Endocrinology' 1985– ; Assoc. Ed., 'Canadian Journal of Zoology' 1983–86; Mem., Internat. Ctte. on Comp. Endocrin. 1982–89; Pres., Candn. Soc. of Zoologists 1991–1992; Pres., Internat. Fed. of Comparative Endocrinological Socs. 1989–93; Fellow, Royal Soc. of Can.; Fellow, Am. Assn. for the Adv. of Sci.; Pickford Medal 1985; NSERC Steacie Fellowship 1980–82; Mem., Candn. Physiological Soc.; Am. Soc. of Zool.; Endocrine Soc.; Soc. for the Study of Reproduction; Internat. Soc. of Neuroendocrin.; author/co-author of over 240 pub. sci papers & reviews; Home: 14319 – 48 Ave., Edmonton, Alta. T6H 5A3; Office: Dept. of Zoology, Univ. of Alta., Edmonton, Alta. T6G 2E9.

**PETERMAN, Michael A.,** M.A., Ph.D.; educator; b. Toronto, Ont. 18 Dec. 1942; s. Alan William B. and Violet Isabel (Cottingham) P.; e. Univ. of Toronto Schs. 1962; Princeton Univ. A.B. 1966; Univ. of Toronto M.A. 1970, Ph.D. 1977; m. Caroline d. Ross and Althea Willmott 28 Dec. 1967; children: Robert Charles Willmott, Jessica Leigh; PROF. OF ENG. TRENT UNIV. 1986– ; Master, Bishop's Coll. Sch. 1967–70; Part-time Lectr. Bishop's Univ. 1968–70; Part-time Master Crescent Sch. 1970–72; Lectr. present Univ. 1972, Asst. Prof. 1975, Assoc. Prof. 1980, Sr. Tutor, Lady Eaton Coll. 1981–88, mem. Bd. Govs. 1987–88, Assoc. Dean of Rsch. & Grad. Studies 1988–90; Pres. Peterborough Hist. Soc.; Friends of Bata Lib.; Kawartha Jazz Soc.; Peterborough Arts Council; author 'Susanna Moodie' 1983; 'Robertson Davies' 1986; co-ed. 'Susanna Moodie: Letters of a Lifetime' 1985; 'Susanna and John Moodie: Letters of Love and Duty' 1993; Assoc. Ed. Jour. of Candn. Studies 1979–83, Ed. 1983–88, Co-ed. 1988–90, Editor 1990– ; Editorial Bd., Bibliographical Society of Canada; mem. Massey College Assn. Candn. Teachers Eng.; Assn. Candn. Studies; W. Lit. Assn.; Bibliog. Soc. Can.; Anglican; recreations: tennis, hockey, skiing, squash; Home: 520 Homewood Ave., Peterborough, Ont. K9H 2N3; Office: Peterborough, Ont. K9J 7B8.

**PETERS, Douglas Dennison,** B.Com., Ph.D.; economist; banker; b. Brandon, Man. 3 March 1930; s. Dr. Wilfrid Seymour and Mary Gladys (Dennison) P.; e. Brandon (Man.) Coll. Inst.; Queen's Univ., B.Com. 1963 (Medal in Comm.); Wharton Sch. of Finance & Comm., Univ. of Pa., Ph.D. 1969 (Ford Foundation Fellowship 1966); m. Audrey Catherine, d. F. E. Clark, Carnduff, Sask., 26 June 1954; children: David Wilfrid, Catherine Elaine; SECRETARY OF STATE (international financial institutions) 1993– ; Senior Vice Pres. & Chief Econ., Toronto-Dominion Bank 1981–92; Retired from T.D. Bank June 1992 to seek the nomination as the Liberal candidate in the federal riding of Scarborough East; First appointee to the new post of Clifford Clark Visiting Economist, Dept. of Finance Canada, 1983–85; joined Bank of Montreal 1950; held various appts. mainly in Winnipeg (1 Yr. Swift Current, Sask.) 1950–60; joined Toronto-Dominion Bank as Chief Econ. and Head, Econ. Research Dept. 1966, Vice-Pres., 1972; co-author 'The Monetarist Counterrevolution: A Critical Review of Post-1975 Monetary Policy in Canada' 1979; Chrmn. of Min. of Finance's 'Task Force on Alcohol and Tobacco Tax Indexation' Report 1984; mem., Toronto Assn. Business Econ's. (Founding mem. and 1st Pres. 1970–71); Candn. Econ. Assn. (Extve. Council 1969–72); Candn. Assn. for Bus. Econ. (Dir. 1988–92); Am. Econ. Assn.; Nat. Assn. Business Econ's; Am. Finance Assn.; Royal Econ. Soc.; Past Chrmn., Candn. Comte., Pacific Basin Econ. Council, 1980–82; Mem. Bd. of Dir., Workers' Compensation Bd. of Ont. 1985–88; recreation: tennis; Home: Apt. 102, 151 Bay St., Ottawa, Ont. K1R 7T2; Office: 21st Floor, 140 O'Connor St., Ottawa, Ont. K1A 0G5.

**PETERS, Erik,** C.A.; financial executive; b. Berlin, Germany s. Wolfgang and Inge P.; e. C.A. Alberta 1965; m. Patricia d. Joseph and Frieda Carrigan 28 May 1964; children: Jennifer, Thomas; PROVINCIAL AUDITOR OF ONTARIO 1993– ; Price Waterhouse Calgary, Montreal, London (England), Montreal, Ottawa 1960–76; Deputy Dir. General of Computer & Information Systems Study, Office of the Auditor General of Canada (executive interchange) 1976–78; Principal, Office of the Auditor General of Canada 1978; Asst. Auditor General of Canada 1980; Regional Controller, Europe, Africa and Middle East, Alcan Aluminium (Europe) S.A. Geneva, Switz. 1981–83; Vice-Pres., Internal Audit, Candn. Broadcasting Corp. 1983–92; Mem., Canadian Inst. of C.A.s (Rep., Quebec Order of C.A.'s) Bd. of Examiners 1974–80; Chair, Annual Conf. 1986; Public Sector Accounting & Auditing Ctte. 1991–92; Mem., Planning Ctte., Inst. of C.A.s of Ont.; Mem., Bd. of Dir., Queensway-Carleton Hosp. Nepean 1989–92; Pres., Briargreen Community Assn. 1980; recreations: travel, reading; Office: Box 105, 15th Floor, 20 Dundas St. W., Toronto, Ont. M5G 2C2.

**PETERS, Ernest,** B.A.Sc., M.A.Sc., Ph.D., P.Eng., F.R.S.C., F.C.I.M., F.T.M.S.; university professor; b. Steinbach, Man. 27 Jan. 1926; s. Franz Isaac and Margaretha (Klassen) P.; e. Univ. of B.C., B.A.Sc. 1949, M.A.Sc. 1951, Ph.D. 1956; m. Gwynneth d. Rueben John Walker 21 Sept. 1949; children: Charlotte Ann, Gwynneth Elizabeth; PROF. EMERITUS, DEPT. OF METALS & MATERIALS ENGR., UNIV. OF B.C. 1967– ; Royal Candn. Air Force 1943–45; Metallurgist, Geneva Steel Co. 1949–50; Rsch. Engr., Cominco Ltd. 1951–53; Union Carbide 1956–58; Instr., present univ. 1955–56; Asst. Prof. 1958–64; Assoc. Prof. 1964–67; Prof. 1967–91; Vis. Prof., U. of Calif. at Berkeley, 1971, 1983, Monash Univ. 1976; Cons. to many indus. 1958– incl. Cominco Ltd.; Kennecott Copper; Bacon, Donaldson & Assoc.; Westmin Resources Ltd.; Candn. Counc. Killam Scholar 1983–85; Holder of Indus. Rsch. Chair in Hydrometallurgy supported by 11 Candn. companies 1988–92; FRSC; Fellow, Candn. Inst. M. & M.; Metallurgial Soc. (U.S.); James Douglas Gold Medal; Alcan Award; Ernest Peters Internat. Symposium (CIMM, AIME, IIMM, AIMM, IMM) 1992; AIME Mineral Sciences Education Award 1993; Candn. Metal Chemistry Award 1993; Mem., Evangelical Fellowship of Canada; Baptist Ch.; author of over 80 sci. papers & short course notes and 6 patents; recreations: skiing, windsurfing; Home: 2708 W. 33rd Ave., Vancouver, B.C. V6N 2G1; Office: 309 – 6350 Stores Rd., Vancouver, B.C. V6T 1W5.

**PETERS, John Raymond,** C.M; broadcaster; b. Vancouver, B.C. 14 DEc. 1926; s. Walter James and Lucy (Hine) P.; m. Heidi Freya d. Paul and Frieda Sohnel 3 Sept. 1966; three s. Martin, Richard, Lawrence; PRESIDENT EMERITUS, WIC WESTERN INTERNATIONAL COMMUNICATIONS LTD. 1989– ; Pres. & Dir., Peters Management Ltd. 1977– and Communications and Management Consultant 1989– ; Dir., Royal-Sweet Internat. Technologies Inc. 1993– ; Promotion Mgr., London Records Montreal 1949–50; studied TV production New York 1951; Radio/TV Dir., Harold F. Stanfield Advertising Montreal 1952–53; Comm. Mgr. CHCH-TV Hamilton, Ont. 1954–60; Commercial Mgr. CHAN-TV Vancouver 1960; Managing Dir. 1961; Pres., CHAN-TV (Vancouver) and CHEK-TV (Victoria) 1963–81; Pres. & Dir., British Columbia Television Broadcasting System Ltd. 1963–81 and Chrmn. of the Bd. and Dir. 1981–89; Pres., C.E.O. and Dir., WIC Western International Communications Ltd. 1977–89; Chrmn. of the Bd. & Dir., Canadian Satellite Communications Inc. (CANCOM) 1984–89; Mem., Arts and Cultural Industries, SAGIT Ctte., Trade Advisory Cttees. Secretariat, Dept. of External Affairs, Ottawa 1988–91; Co-Chrmn., Task Force on the Economic Status of Canadian Television, Dept. of Communications, Ottawa 1990–91; B.C. Regional Advisor, Federal Provincial Relations Office, Dept. of Communications, Ottawa 1992; Past Chrmn. & Dir., Westcom Radio Group Ltd.; Past Chrmn. & Dir., CHEK-TV Ltd.; Past Dir., Mem. Audit Ctte., Northwest Drug Co. Ltd.; Past Dir., CTV Network; Northwest Sports Enterprises Ltd. (Vancouver Canucks); Okanagan Valley Television Co. Ltd.; Past Vice Pres., Central Can. Assn. Broadcasters; Past Pres. B.C. Assn. Broadcasters; Past Pres., Can. Assn. Broadcasters (mem. Quarter Century Club and Half Century Club); mem., Young Presidents' Organization Alumni; World Presidents' Organization (B.C. Chapter); Founder, Elderstatesman and Patron Member Variety Club Vancouver; Chrmn., Vancouver Symphony Soc. 1988–90 (Dir. 1988–91); Dir., Music 91/British Columbia Year of Music Society 1990–91; Dir., The Council for Business & The Arts in Canada 1992– ; recipient, The Canadian Centennial Medal 1967; Broadcaster of the Year, B.C. Assn. of Broadcasters 1978; awarded Member of the Order of Canada 1984; Variety Clubs Internat. Presidential Citation, London, England 1987; Businessman of the Year, 1989 Awards of Excellence, The Vancouver Junior Board of Trade, Jaycees; Broadcast Citizen of the Year, B.C. Assn. of Broadcasters 1989; CAB Broadcast Hall of Fame Award, Candn. Assn. of Broadcasters 1989; 125th Anniversary of the Confederation of Canada Medal, 1992; recreations: sailing, fishing, golf; Clubs: Vancouver; Royal Vancouver Yacht; West Vancouver Yacht; Capilano Golf; Home: 6020 Eagleride Dr., West Vancouver, B.C. V7W 1W8.

**PETERS, Randolph,** B.Sc., M.Mus.; composer; b. Winnipeg, Man. 28 Dec. 1959; s. Peter Henry and Margaret Alice (Klassen) P.; e. Univ. of Winnipeg B.Sc. 1980; Indiana Univ. M.Mus. (High Distinction) 1986, D.Mus. cand.; m. Cheryl d. Erwin and Leona Janzen 21 Aug. 1988; one son: Joshua; Composer-in-Residence, Canadian Opera Company 1991–93; Assoc. Instr. of Composition & Music Theory, Indiana Univ. 1982–85; Visiting Lectr. in Music Theory & History, Univ. of Waterloo 1986; composer, performer, conductor & producer of concert music & music for film, TV, radio & theatre 1978– ; Vice-Pres., Manitoba Composers Assn. 1988–91; Mem., Candn. League of Composers; Soc. of Composers, Authors & Music Publishers of Can.; Am. Fed. of Musicians; Finalist, CBC Young Composer's Comp.; Winner, Procan Young Composers Comp. (Orch. Music) 1988; Interalia Composers Competition 1989; Composer of the Year, Winnipeg Free Press 1990; Winner, du Maurier New Music Festival Audience Award 1993; composer: 'Nosferatu' (full length opera commissioned by Candn. Opera Co.), 'Dreaming-Tracks' 1991, 'Free Fall' 1987 (orchestral scores), Compact Disc featuring 'Three quarks for Muster Mark! 1990 (chamber music) & 'Tango' (string quartet) 1991; and over 40 film scores (most recent: 'Lost in the Barrens' 'Tramp at the Door' 'Curse of the Viking Grave' & 'The Diviners') & num. concert works; Home: 54 Noble Ave., Winnipeg, Man. R2L 0J4.

**PETERS, Robert David,** B.Comm., B.A., M.A.; public servant; b. Springdale, Nfld. 22 Sept. 1940; s. Cecil George and Edna Beatrice (Sexton) P.; e. Mem. Univ. of Nfld., B.Comm., B.A. (Hons.) 1962, M.A. 1965; m. Media d. late Elliott and Ursula Clarke 4 June 1966; children: David, Geoffrey; DEPUTY MIN., DEPT OF FORESTRY AND AGRICULTURE, GOVT. OF NFLD. & LABRADOR 1985– ; various posts., Govt. of Can.

Indus., Trade & Comm. & Dept. of Reg. Econ. Expansion 1965–76; Asst. Sec. to Cabinet (Planning & Resource Policy), Govt. of Nfld. & Lab. 1976–85; Office: Box 8700, St. John's, Nfld. A1B 4J6.

**PETERSEN, Charles Forrester,** B.A.; financial executive; b. Toronto, Ont. 28 March 1945; s. Niels Forrester and Margaret Bettina (Bauckham) P.; e. Upper Canada College; Univ. of Western Ont. B.A. 1968; m. Riki d. Lou Turofsky 7 June 1987; children: Charles Corbett, Niels Ashton, James Christian; PRES., INVENTURES CAPITAL CORP.; Office: 500, 95 King St. E., Toronto, Ont. M5C 1G4.

**PETERSEN, Holger Martin;** music industry executive, broadcaster; b. Pellworm Island, Germany 23 Nov. 1949; s. George Fredrick and Henny Caroline JoAnne (Liermann) P.; e. Bonnie Doon H.S. 1969; Northern Alta. Inst. of Tech. 2-yr. radio & TV arts course grad. 1971; one s.: Matthew Martin Petersen Hawkeye; OWNER & CHIEF EXTVE. OFFICER, STONY PLAIN RECORDS 1976– and BROADCASTER, BLUES RADIO SHOWS 1970– ; musician & record producer 1971–76; Stony Plain Records is Canada's number one 'Roots & Country Music' label; only prairie label with multi-nat. distbn.; promotes Candn. music internationally; operates 5 music publishing cos.; involved in artist management; has worked with num. Candn. artists incl. Ian Tyson, Long John Baldry, Prairie Oyster, Spirit of the West, Amos Garrett, Neville Bros., John Prine, etc.; over 200 releases; Host/Prod., Natch'l Blues, ACCESS Network 1970– ; Host, Saturday Night Blues, CBC AM Network 1988– ; Founder & Vice-Pres., Edmonton Folk Music Fest. 1979–85; Founder & Vice-Pres., Summerfest 1980–84; Alberta Recording Indus. Assn. 1982–84; mem., various Canada Council music juries 1984– ; Bd. Mem., SOCAN, CIRPA, CARAS (Regional Rep.); Stony Plain has won 5 JUNO Awards and many Candn. Country Music Assn. Awards incl. Publishing Co. of the Year 1992, Record Label of the Year 1991 and several Alberta Recording Indus. Assn. Awards; personal awards incl. Music Industry Person of the Year 1989 & 'Blues With A Feeling' Award, Toronto Blues Soc. 1986; inducted into City of Edmonton 'Cultural Hall of Fame' 1992; recreations: enjoys most sports & outdoor activities; clubs: City Media Club; Home: 9959 – 83 St., Edmonton, Alta. T6A 3N3; Office: 9963 – 83 St., Edmonton, Alta. T6A 3N3.

**PETERSEN, Reginald Lyle,** C.M.A.; b. Red Deer, Alta. 20 Feb. 1942; s. Amil Edward and Emily Etta P.; e. McMaster Univ. C.M.A.; m. Carol d. Bernard and Clara Tatton 19 Aug. 1961; children: Mark, Michael, Shari, Amy, Melissa; CHAIRMAN & CHIEF EXECUTIVE OFFICER, VERSA CARE LTD. 1990– ; Accountant, Canada Packers Ltd. 1959–65; J & A Fleming Ltd. 1965–67; Sec.-Treas., Galt Malleable Iron Ltd. 1967–71; Vice-Pres., Versa Care Ltd. 1971–79; Pres. 1979–90; Bd. of Dir., Trinity Western Univ.; Home: 10 Barberry Place, Cambridge, Ont.; Office: 73 Water St. N., Suite 500, Cambridge, Ont. N1R 7L6.

**PETERSEN, Hon. Sherwin Holger;** politician; b. Rose Valley, Sask. 12 May 1953; s. Orla Holger and Noreen Wilma (Johnson) P.; e. Rose Valley High Sch. 1971; Kelsey Inst. Applied Arts & Sci's Saskatoon grad. Farm Machinery Mechanics 1973; m. Sharon d. Gordon and Emily Wheeler 14 July 1973; children: Shauna, Sheridan; joined J.I. Case as heavy/duty mechanic 1973–75; farming Rose Valley 1975; el. M.L.A. 1982, re-el. 1986; Min. of Highways and Transportation, Saskatchewan 1989–91; Freemason; P. Conservative; Lutheran.

**PETERSON, Aubrey Lynn,** B.Sc.; petroleum executive; b. Moose Jaw, Sask. 3 Mar. 1930; s. Frank Ralph Lynn and Marguerite Juletta (Brandon) P.; e. Moose Jaw Cent. C.I. 1948; Univ. of Sask., B.Sc. 1952; m. Shirley J. d. David and Hulda Lyons 27 Oct. 1956; children: David, Glenn, Nancy; Vice-Pres., Gen. Serv., Imperial Oil Ltd. 1986; Proc. Engr., Imperial Oil Limited 1952; Mktg. Field Dist. Sup. 1962; Co-ord. of Mktg. Planning & Econ. 1963; Building Prod. of Can. Ltd. (Imperial subs.) 1966–69; Planning Co-ord., Planning Serv. Dept., Imperial Oil 1970; Opns. Mgr., Pipeline Div. & Mgr., Dist. Opns. & Co-ord. Div. 1971; Corp. Purch. Mgr. 1976; Mgr., Materials & Serv. Dept. 1983; Chrmn., Purch. Extves. Roundtable 1978–84; Chrmn., Candn. Market Opportunities Prog. 1983–86; Chrmn., Arthritis Soc. Corporate Campaign 1991; recreations: golf, curling, boating; Club: Donalda (Dir. since 1986, Pres. 1990–91); Home: 76 Denlow Blvd., Don Mills, Ont. M3B 1P9.

**PETERSON, David L.E.,** B.P.E., LL.B.; lawyer / clerk of the legislative assembly; b. Fredericton, N.B. 23 Sept. 1942; s. Barbara Winnifred (Hughey) P.; e. N.B. Teachers Coll. 1961; Univ. of N.B., B.P.E. 1965, LL.B. 1969; widower; children: David, Kersta, Bradley; Clerk of the Legislative Assembly of New Brunswick 1979–93; practised law 1969–82; Mem., N.B. Barristers Soc.; Candn. Bar Assn.; Commonwealth Assn. of Clerks-at-the-Table; Assn. of Clerks-at-the-Table in Canada; recreations: sports; Home: 595 Montgomery St., Fredericton, N.B. E3B 2X6.

**PETERSON, The Hon. David Robert,** P.C., Q.C., C.St.J., D.U., LL.D.; b. Toronto, Ont. 28 Dec. 1943; s. Clarence and Laura Marie (Scott) P.; e. Univ. of W. Ont. B.A. 1964; Univ. of Toronto, LL.B. 1967; Univ. of Caen, France; Osgoode Hall Law School; m. Shelley d. Donald Matthews 16 Jan. 1974; children: Benjamin David, Chlöe Matthews, Adam Drake Scott; SR. PARTNER, CASSELS BROCK & BLACKWELL and CHRMN., CASSELS, POULIOT, DOUGLAS, NORIEGA (a national affiliation of Toronto, Montreal & Vancouver law firms & international affiliation with Mexico law firm); Chrmn., Professional Basketball Franchise (Canada) Inc.; Dir., Rogers Communications Ltd.; Cantel Mobile Communications; National Life Assurance Co.; Industrielle-Alliance Life Assurance Co.; National Trust; Banque Nationale de Paris (Canada); Cascades Paperboard Internat. Inc.; Systemhouse Inc.; Speedy Muffler King Inc.; called to Bar in Ontario 1969; apptd. Queen's Counsel 1980; summoned by Her Majesty to Privy Council 1992; Chrmn. & Pres., C.M. Peterson Co. Ltd. and Cambridge Acceptance Corp. 1969–75; first el. M.P.P. for London Centre, 1975; re-el. 1977, 1981, 1985, 1987; Leader of the Ont. Lib. Party 1982 (resigned 1990); Leader of the Official Opposition 1982–85; Premier of Ontario 1985–90; Advisor, Czech. and French Govts. and Chrmn., Commonwealth Team observing 1992 elections in Guyana; Adjunct Prof., York Univ.; Dir., Centre for the Great Lakes; Canadian Club; Cercle Canadien; Confederation Center of the Arts; Council for Candn. Unity; Young Presidents' Organization; Soc. for Educational Visits & Exchanges in Canada; mem., London Chamber of Commerce; Law Soc. of U.C.; United Church; recreations: theatre, riding, jogging, skiing, tennis, reading, gardening; Office: Suite 2100, 40 King St. W., Toronto, Ont. M5H 3C2.

**PETERSON, Jim,** M.P., B.A., LL.B., LL.M., D.C.L.; politician; b. Ottawa 30 Jul. 1941; s. Clarence and Marie P.; e. Univ. of Western Ont. B.A. 1963, LL.B. 1964; Columbia Univ. LL.M. 1967; McGill Univ. D.C.L. 1970; married; MEMBER OF PARLIAMENT, WILLOWDALE 1988– ; Internat. Tax and Business Law 1970–80; United Nations Ind. Develop. Organization 1969–74; Special lectr., Faculty of Law, Univ. of Toronto 1974–79; el. to H. of C. for Willowdale 1980–84, 1988, 1993; Chrmn., Cambridge Acceptance Corp. Ltd. 1984–87; Liberal; recreations: music, reading, theatre, ballet, skiing, golf; Home: 67 Hillholm Rd., Toronto, Ont.; Offices: Rm 426-N, Centre Block, House of Commons, Ottawa, Ont. K1A 0A6 and 5799 Yonge St., Suite 806, Willowdale, Ont. M2M 3V3.

**PETERSON, Kevin Bruce,** B.A.; newspaper executive; b. Kitchener, Ont. 11 Feb. 1948; s. Bruce Russell and Marguerite Elizabeth (Hammond) P.; e. Univ. of Calgary, B.A. 1968; m. Sheila O'Brien 9 Jan. 1981; PUBLISHER, CALGARY HERALD 1989– ; Part-owner Maltese Stables; Edmonton Bureau Chief present newspaper 1972, City Ed. 1976, News Ed. 1977, Bus. Ed. 1978, Mng. Ed. 1978, Ed. and Asst. Publisher 1986, Gen. Mgr., 1987–89, Publisher 1989; Dir., Candn. Mng. Ed.'s Cong. 1983–87; Harry Brittain Meml. Fellow, Commonwealth Press Union, London, Eng. 1979; Chrmn.-Elect, Candn. Daily Newspaper Assn.; Dir., New Directions for News 1992– ; mem. Horsemen's Benevolent & Protective Assn.; Am. Soc. Newspaper Eds.; recreations: thoroughbred horse racing, art collecting; Clubs: Calgary Petroleum; Ranchmen's; Executive Breakfast; Home: 4616 Britannia Dr. S.W., Calgary, Alta.; Office: P.O. Box 2400, Station M, Calgary, Alta. T2P 0W8.

**PETERSON, Hon. Leslie Raymond,** Q.C., O.B.C., C.St.J., K.C.L.J., LL.D., Ed.D., LL.B., F.R.S.A.; b. Viking, Alta. 6 Oct. 1923; s. Herman S. and Margaret (Karen) P.; e. Vikinq High School, Alta.; Camrose Lutheran College, Alberta; McGill Univ.; London University (Eng.); Univ. of Brit. Columbia, LL.B. 1949; Simon Fraser Univ., LL.D. 1965; Notre Dame Univ. of Nelson, Ed.D. 1966; Univ. of BC LL.D. 1993; m. Agnes Rose, d. Harold Hine, Regina, Sask., 24 June 1950; children: Raymond Erik, Karen Isabelle; Chancellor, Univ. of B.C. 1987–93; read law with late Howard C. Coulter; called to the Bar of British Columbia 1949; cr. Q.C. 1960; self-employed barrister, Vancouver, 1949–52; amalg. Peterson & Anderson, 1952, and later Boughton & Co., now Boughton Peterson Yang Anderson; el. to B.C. Leg. for Vancouver Centre Jan. 1956; re-el. 1956, 1960, 1963; el. for Vancouver-Little Mountain 1966; Min. of Educ. 1956–68; Min. of Labour 1960–71; Atty.-Gen. 1968–72; served in 2nd World War; joined Candn. Army (R.C.A.) and served in Eng. and Continent, 1942–46; Past Dir., Westn. Soc. of Rehab.; Past Dir., Y.M.C.A., Victoria, B.C.; Past Pres., Twenty Club; Hon. mem., Vancouver Junior Chamber Comm.; former Vice-Pres., Normanna Old People's Home; mem., Vancouver Bar Assn.; Law Soc. of B.C.; Int. Bar Assn.; Asia Pacific Lawyers Assn.; Founding mem. of Convocation, Simon Fraser Univ. and Univ. of Victoria; Pres. (1964–65), Internat. Assn. of Govt. Labour Officials Chrmn., Standing Comte., Candn. Mins. of Educ, 1965–66; Hon. Deputy, French National Assembly, Paris, France; Hon. Commr. of Labor, State of Okla.; Knight Commander Order of St. Lazarus; Inst. of Corp. Dirs. in Canada; Dir., Tordiam Inc.; Pacific Institute of Deep Sea Tech.; Candn. Foundation for Economic Education; Dir., Shriners Hosp. for Crippled Children, Portland Unit; Dir., The West Vancouver Found.; Chrmn., The Univ. of B.C. Found.; Chrmn., Bd. of Governors, Univ. of B.C., 1979–83; Chrmn., Wesbrook Society, Alumni, UBC 1987; Bd. of Govs., Downtown Vancouver Assoc.; Past Pres., Terminal City Club; Freemason (A.A.O.N.M.S.) Gizeh Temple Shrine (Potentate 1988); recreations: skiing, golf, fishing, hunting; Clubs: Scandinavian Business Men's (Past Pres.); Hazelemere Golf & Tennis (Dir.); Union (Victoria); Terminal City (Vancouver); Home: 814 Highland, W. Vancouver, B.C. V7S 2G5; Office: 2500 - 1055 Dunsmuir St., Vancouver, B.C. V7X 1S8.

**PETERSON, Oscar E.,** C.C. (1984); concert pianist; b. Montreal, Que. 15 Aug. 1925; s. Daniel William and Kathleen Olivia (John) P.; e. Royal Arthur Sch., Montreal; Montreal High Sch.; Montreal Conserv. Music; LL.D., Queen's Univ. 1976; m. Sandra Cythia, d. H. A. King, 23 April 1966; children (by previous m.); Lynn Cheryl, Sharon Vivian, Gay Carol, Oscar Emanuel Jr., Norman Raymond; made a remarkable debut in Carnegie Hall in 1949; has made world wide concert appearances since 1950; has recorded over 80 albums under his own name in the US and Germany and as many as accompanist to Lester Young, Louis Armstrong, Coleman Hawkins and others; has been host for TV series in London (BBC), Vancouver (CTV), and Toronto (CBC); became Officer in the Order of Canada in 1972, Companion 1984; Offr., Order of Arts and Letters (France) 1989; Chevalier, Ordre national du Québec; Oscar Peterson Music Scholarship named in his honour, York Univ. 1986; Pres., Regal Recordings Ltd.; Hon. Pres., Toronto Jazz Club; awards incl. Edison Award (Europe) for best jazz LP of year; Down Beat Award (12 times winner) for year's best jazz pianist; Playboy Award (12 times silver medallist) for best musician's musician; Gold Rose Award, Montreux Jazz Festival 1968; Golden Disc Award (Japan); Achievement Award, Lakeshore Lions Club, Toronto 1966; Award of Appreciation, B'Nai Brith E. Regional Council, Montreal 1969; Toronto 1969; Toronto Civic Medal 1971; Testimony of Gratitude from public of Mexico 1969; Oscar Peterson Trio, award for best jazz combo of the year; nominated 5 times for recording best album of the year, Nat. Acad. Recording Arts and Sciences; inducted into Juno Awards Hall of Fame 1978; Lifetime Achievement Award, Toronto Arts Awards 1991; Freemason; Anglican; recreations: photography, fishing.

**PETERSON, Robert Byron,** B.Sc., M.Sc.; petroleum executive; b. Regina, Sask.; e. Queen's Univ. Chem. Engn. 1961; m. Yvonne Corbin; children: Daniel H., Thomas G.; PRESIDENT AND CHIEF OPERATING OFFICER & DIR., IMPERIAL OIL LTD. 1988– ; Chrmn. Esso Resources Canada Ltd., Calgary 1985– ; Dir., Royal Bank of Canada 1992– ; joined Imperial Oil Ltd., Calgary 1960; held various prodn. related positions 1978; Vice-Pres. and Gen. Mgr. Heavy Oil, Esso Resources 1978; Extve. Vice-Pres. Esso Resources 1979; Depy. Mgr. Producing Dept. Exxon Corp., N.Y. 1980; Pres. and C.E.O. Esso Resources, Calgary 1982; Extve. Vice Pres., C.O.O. & Dir., present co. 1985–88; Chrmn., Conference Bd. of Can. 1993– ; Dir., C.D. Howe Rsch. Institute; mem. Advisory Bd., Salvation Army Metro Toronto; Gov., Junior Achievement of Can.; mem. Assn. of Profl. Engr., Geologists and Geophysicists of Alta.; Home: Toronto, Ont.; Office: 111 St. Clair Ave. W., Toronto, Ont. M4V 1N5.

**PETERSON, Robert Lawrence,** B.Ed., M.Sc., Ph.D., F.R.S.C.; educator; b. Alta. 20 Jan. 1939; s. Robert Louis and Hazel Florence Paula (Wegener) P.; e. Univ. of Alta. B.Ed. 1962, M.Sc. 1964; Univ. of Calif. Ph.D. 1968; two s. Ryan Louis, Christopher Alan; PROF. OF BOTANY UNIV. OF GUELPH 1981– ; Asst. Prof present Univ. 1968, Assoc. Prof. 1972, Prof. 1981; Chair of Botany

1993; recipient Coll. Biol. Sci. Award of Excellence in Teaching 1986; Sigma Xi Career Award for Excellence in Rsch. 1988; Fellow, Royal Society of Canada 1988; George Lawson Medal for career contrib. to Botany 1993; mem. Candn. Bot. Assn./L'Assn. Botanique du Can. (Pres. 1988–89); Sigma Xi; recreations: skiing, curling, bridge; Home: 8 Mollison Court, Guelph, Ont. N1C 1A7; Office: Guelph, Ont. N1G 2W1.

**PETERSON, Roy Eric;** editorial cartoonist; b. Winnipeg, Man. 14 Sept. 1936; s. Lawrence and Ethel (Badger) P.; e. Kitsilano H.S. 1954; m. Margaret d. David and Susan Brand 12 April 1958; children: Lawrence, Gillian, Lisa, Karen, Geoffrey; freelance cartoonist for every major Candn. mag. & internat. mags. & papers incl. The New York Times, Washington Post, Look, TV Guide (US), Spectator, Punch (UK), and var. ad. agencies; started with The Province 1962, Vancouver Sun 1962– ; Maclean's mag. feature 'Peterson on the Prowl' 1964–70; illus., Maclean's, Allan Fotheringham's back-page col. 1978– ; worked for CBC, B.C. schools, edn. TV & promo film for Habitat (UN Conf. on Housing); Mem., Assn. of Am. Edit. Cartoonists 1966– (2nd Vice-Pres. 1979–80; Dir. 1980–81; Vice-Pres. 1981–82; Pres. 1982–83); Assn. of Candn. Edit. Cartoonists 1986– (Pres. 1989–90); Art Dir. Club of Vanc. Award 1963; Graphica '65 Award; Ed. & Pub. N. Am. Award 1966; Nat. Newspapers Awards 1968, 1975, 1984, 1990; three individual prizes, incl. Grand Prize 1973, Internat. Salon of Caricature; 1 gold, 3 silver, 2 bronze Creative Club awards; GraphEx '80 Award of Recognition; Assn. of Am. Edit. Cartoonists Ink Bottle Award 1988; Quill Award 1990; author: 'The Canadian ABC Book' (& illus.) 1977, 'Drawn & Quartered' 1984; co-author: 'The World According to Roy Peterson' 1979 and 6 others.

**PETERSON, William (Bill) Robert;** daily newspaper publisher; b. Saskatoon, Sask. 25 May 1954; s. Robert Oscar and Dorothy P.; e. Univ. of Toronto 1984, Southam Journalism Fellowship; Univ. of Saskatchewan, Bus. Admin. Cert. 1986; Commonwealth Press Union Fellowship, London; single; PUBLISHER, THE STAR PHOENIX 1993– ; Reporter, The Star-Phoenix 1972–79; Communications Dir., Sask. Mining Devel. Corp. 1979–81; Editorial Bd., The Star-Phoenix 1981–83; City Editor 1984–87; Pres., Perk Holdings Canada Ltd. 1987–88; Editor, The Star Phoenix 1988–93; Chrmn., Bd. of Gov., Nat. Newspaper Awards; Mem., Adv. Bd., Univ. of Regina, Sch. of Journalism; Dir., Perk Holdings Inc.; recreations: skiing, golfing; clubs: Big Brothers; Home: 1660 – 424 Spadina Cres., Saskatoon, Sask. S7K 6X7; Office: 204 – 5th Ave. North, Saskatoon, Sask. S7K 2P1.

**PETHERBRIDGE, Stephen;** newspaper editor; b. Bournemouth, England 3 Oct. 1942; s. Henry George and Dorothy Mary (Gwyther) P.; e. Bideford Grammar Sch. 1958; m. Heather Linda d. Sushil and Laura (Donachie) Mallick June 7 1990; children: Samantha Olivia, Victoria Melinda; EDITOR, GLOBE & MAIL CLASSROOM EDITION, GLOBE INFORMATION SERVICES 1992– ; Reporter, Bideford Gazette 1958–61; Harmsworth Newspapers 1961–65; Sub-Editor, Melbourne Herald 1965–68; Asst. Features Ed., Melbourne Age 1968–69; Sr. Ed., Newsday (Melbourne) 1969–70; Sub-Ed., London Sun 1970–71; Sr. Ed., London Evening News 1972–76; Saturday Ed., Toronto Star 1977–78; Depy. Mng. Ed., 1978–80; Mng. Ed. 1980–82; Journalism Prof., Ryerson Polytech. Inst. 1982–87; Extve. Ed., Financial Post 1988–91; recreations: gardening, reading, cooking; Home: 63 Southwood Dr., Toronto, Ont. M4E 2T8; Office: 444 Front St. W., Toronto, Ont. M5V 2S9.

**PETIT, Michel W.,** B.A.; financial executive; b. Montreal, Que. 7 Mar. 1943; e. Sir George Williams Univ. B.A. (Econ.); McGill Univ., Extve. Devel. course; PRESIDENT & CHIEF EXECUTIVE OFFICER, GENERAL TRUST OF CANADA AND SHERBROOKE TRUST COMPANY; Dir., General Trust of Canada; Sherbrooke Trust Company; Home: 3520, Bienvenue, Brossard, Que. J4Z 2Y1; Office: 1100 University St., Montreal, Que., H3B 2G7.

**PETRIE, Daniel,** B.A., M.F.A.; film and television director; b. Glace Bay, N.S.; s. William Mark and Mary (Campbell) P.; e. St. Francis Xavier Univ. B.A. 1942; Columbia Univ. M.A. 1945; Northwestern Univ. 1947–49; m. Dorothea d. June and Walter Grundy 27 October 1946; children: Daniel Jr., Donald, Mary, June; films: 'Cocoon II, The Return,' 'Rocket Gibraltar,' 'Square Dance,' 'The Bay Boy,' 'Six Pack,' 'Fort Apache, The Bronx,' 'Resurrection,' 'The Betsy,' 'Lifeguard,' 'Buster & Billy,' 'A Raisin in the Sun,' 'Lassie'; television: 'The Execution of Raymond Graham' (Emmy nom.), 'The Dollmaker' (Dir. Guild of Am. Award), 'Eleanor and Franklin' (Emmy; Dir. Guild of Am. Award), 'Eleanor and Franklin: The White House Years' (Emmy), 'Sybil' (Emmy & Peabody awards), 'Harry Truman, Plain Speaking' (Emmy nomination), 'The Man and the City,' 'Silent Night, Lonely Night,' 'My Name is Bill W.' (Emmy nomination), 'A Town Torn Apart' (Emmy nomination), 'Mark Twain and Me' (Emmy award); Chrmn., Center for Adv. Film Studies; Am. Film Inst.; Bd. Mem., Candn. Film Inst.; Mem., Acad. of Motion Picture Arts & Sci.; Acad. of TV Arts & Sci.; Guest Lectr., UCLA, USC, New York Univ.; author: 'The Bay Boy' screenplay (Genie award winner for best picture, best screenplay 1985); Home: 13201 Haney Place, Los Angeles, CA 90049.

**PETRIE, Franklin R.,** B.Comm.; retired public servant and association executive; b. Corner Brook, Nfld. 9 Dec. 1929; s. Roy D. and Hilda (Harris) P.; e. Dalhousie Univ. B.Comm. 1951; m. Margaret d. William and Dorothy Roberts of Sydney, Australia 2 Jan. 1953; children: Janine, Julie, Jennifer; BD. DIR., FEDERAL CANDN. COMMERCIAL CORP. and STOTHERT INC. OF VANCOUVER; worked in econ. devel. of Australian external territories 1952–53; served with Candn. Govt. 1954–84; on loan to GATT Secretariat in Geneva 1959–62 and to Privy Counc. Office 1964–66; Candn. Rep to GATT and UN Economic Organizations in Geneva 1967–70; Chrmn. CATT Cttes. incl. GATT Balance of Payments Ctte. 1968–70; Gen. Dir. Pacific, Asia and Africa Bur., Dept. of Ind., Trade and Comm., Ottawa 1970–74; Gen. Dir. Internat. Fin. Br., Dept. Ind., Trade and Comm. 1975; Dir. Gen. Office of Overseas Projects 1977; apptd. Dir. Gen. Bur. of Pacific, Asian, African and Middle Eastern Affairs 1981; Asst. Under-Sec. of State for External Affairs, Bur. of Pacific, Asian, African and Middle Eastern Affairs (Trade Devel.) 1982; apptd. Cons. Gen. of Can., Sydney, Australia 1982; Pres., Canadian Exporters' Association 1984–88, retired; Home: 656 Portage Ave., Ottawa, Ont. K1G 1T4.

**PETRIE, William,** B.A., A.M., Ph.D., F.R.S.C.; physicist; b. Victoria, B.C. 30 Dec. 1912; s. James and Amelia (Robertson) P.; e. Victoria High Sch. 1928; Univ. of B.C. B.A. 1938; Harvard Univ. A.M., Ph.D. 1942; Mass. Inst. of Technol.; m. Isabelle d. Henri and Victorrine Chodat 8 May 1944; children: Heather Louise, Douglas Bruce; wartime rsch. U.S.A. 1940–42; Lectr. in Physics Univ. of B.C. 1942–45; Asst. Prof. Univ. of Man. 1945–46; Assoc. Prof. Univ. of Sask. 1946–51; Defence Rsch. Bd. 1951–71, Depy. Chrmn. 1966–68, Chief Candn. Defense Rsch. Staff London, Eng. 1968–71; recipient Centennial Medal 1967; author 'Keoeeit – The Story of the Aurora Borealis' 1963; 'Orchids of North America' 1981; approx. 45 scientific papers and many classified reports on defence matters; recent publ.: 'The ABC's of Nuclear Strategic Problems,' Candn. Inst. of Internat. Affairs 1984; 'Military Activity in Space – Is There a Choice?' Candn. Defence Quarterly, winter 1985–86; 'A Rocky Road to Reduction of Strategic Nuclear Weapons' Candn. Defence Quarterly, autumn 1987; 'Deterrance - What Lies Ahead?' Candn. Defence Quarterly, winter 1988; recreations: gardening, fishing; Address: 52 – 1255 Wain Rd., R.R. 4, Sidney, B.C. V8L 4R4.

**PETRILLO, Leonard Philip,** B.Sc., LL.B.; corporate executive, general counsel; b. Toronto, Ont. 20 June 1941; s. Philip Ralph and Bernice (Kowalski) P.; e. Univ. of Toronto, B.Sc. 1964; Osgoode Hall Law Sch., LL.B. 1967; Osgoode Hall Bar Admission 1968; Bar of Ont. 1969; children: Larissa, Matthew; VICE-PRES., CORP. AFFAIRS, GENERAL COUNSEL & SEC., THE TORONTO STOCK EXCHANGE 1988– ; Partner, Robinson & Petrillo, Toronto 1969–78; Corp. Counsel, Seel Enterprises Ltd. 1979–81; Gen. Counsel, present firm 1981; Corp. Sec. 1984; Vice-Pres. 1985; Sec. to Bd. of Gov., Toronto Stock Exhange; Mem., Law Soc. of U.C.; Candn. Bar Assn.; The Candn. Corporate Counsel Assn.; Co. of York Law Assn.; Bd. of Trade of Metro Toronto; recreations: travel, cinema, tennis; Office: 2 First Canadian Place, The Exchange Tower, Toronto, Ont. M5X 1J2.

**PETT, Lionel Bradley,** M.D., B.Sc.A., M.A., Ph.D., b. Winnipeg, Man., 13 Nov. 1909; s. Lionel Henry and Sadie Bradley (Saunders) P.; e. Ont. Agric. Coll., B.Sc.A. 1930; Univ. of Toronto, M.A. 1932; Ph.D. 1934; 1851 Exhn. Scholar. (Eng.); Univ. of Stockholm, 1934–35; Cambridge Univ., 1936; Univ. of Alta., M.D. 1942; m. Lois Eileen, d. H. M. McAfee, Edmonton, Alta., 9 May 1941; children: Hugh, Robert; Sr. Fellow in Biochem., Univ. of Toronto, 1933–34; Lect. in Biochem., Univ. of Alta., 1936–40; apptd. Chief, Nutrition Div., by Dom. Govt., 1941; served as Nutritional Adviser to Bermuda Govt. 1942, India 1960, Jamaica 1962, and to UNRRA and Candn. dels. at several internat. conf. on health, food, agric., etc.; has contrib. about one hundred scient. papers to various technical journs.; Protestant; recreations: photography, woodworking; Home: 615 - 2370 Carling Ave., Ottawa, Ont. K2B 8G9.

**PETTEN, Hon. William John (Bonavista);** senator; b. St. John's Nfld. 28 Jan. 1923; s. Hon. Ray and Marjorie (Udle) P.; e. Bishop's Field Coll., St. John's, Nfld.; m. Elsie Bernice, d. Chesley and Elsie Bowden, Aug. 1963; children: Sharon Dawn; Robin Chesley; Raylene Bernice; William John; apptd. to Senate 1968; apptd. Government Whip 1974–79; Opposition Whip 1979–80; Govt. Whip 1980–84; Opposition Whip 1984; Opposition Whip 1984–91; served as Chrmn. on Ctte. of Selection; as Whip on Mass Media Ctte.; Special Ctte. on the Constitution of Can., Internal Econ. Budgets and Admin., Legal and Constit. Affairs, Fisheries, Agriculture, Transport, Standing Rules and Orders Cttes.; Broker 1946–68; Dir. Security Trust; Liberal; Anglican; Office: Senate of Canada, Ottawa, Ont. K1A 0A4.

**PETTER, Andrew J.,** LL.B., LL.M.; university professor; b. Victoria, B.C. 2 Sept. 1953; s. E. Gordon and Elizabeth K. (Abelis) P.; e. Univ. of Victoria, LL.B. 1981; Cambridge Univ., LL.M. 1982; MIN. OF FORESTS, GOVT. OF B.C. 1993– ; Assoc. Prof., Fac. of Law, Univ. of Victoria 1988– ; Solicitor, Const. Law Br., Sask. Dept. of Justice 1983–84; Asst. Prof., Osgoode Hall Law Sch., York Univ. 1984–86; Asst. Prof., Fac. of Law, present univ. 1986–88; Min. of Aboriginal Affairs, Govt. of B.C. 1991–93; Law Soc. of B.C. Gold Medalist 1981; Commonwealth Scholar 1981–82; author of num. articles; Home: 1471 Jamaica Rd., Victoria, B.C.; Office: P.O. Box 2400, Victoria, B.C. V8W 3H7.

**PETTERSON, Andre;** artist, musician, composer; b. Rotterdam Holland 4 Apr. 1950; s. Andre and Johanna (Schuurbiers) P.; annual solo exhibitions at Bau-Xi Gallery Vancouver 1974–92; Gal. l'autre Equivoque 1990, 1992; Kelowna Public Gallery 1989; Gal. Franklin Silverstone 1988; performance, installation, Vancouver East Cultural Ctr. 1986; Kamloops Public Art Gallery 1986; Jackson St. Gallery (Seattle) 1984; 34 group or two-person exhibitions 1975– ; 36 reviews in newspapers & magazines; 16 catalogues (4 solo); numerous public & private collections; 16mm film 'Statutes' 1987 (directed, edited sets, music); numerous music compositions for dance; professional drummer, vocalist 1962– ; numerous benefits (donations of art) 1975– ; National Film Board (Pacific) award 1986; Canada Council (Explorations) 1986; Presentation House (Vanc.) 1977; self-taught artist/musician; Home: 7937 Edson Ave., Burnaby, B.C. V5J 3W8.

**PETTICK, Joseph,** FRAIC; architect; b. Nyirparasznya, Hungary, 8 Oct. 1924; s. Leslie Petuk and Julian (Szepovitch) P.; e. pub. and high schs. Regina, Sask.; became Reg'd Arch. through Apprenticeship Program 1946–54; Univ. of Okla. Sch. of Arch. special student Aesthetic Design, Structure & Town Planning 1955; divorced May 1986; m. 2ndly, Janet Susan Humphries 8 Feb. 1988; estbd. private practice Joseph Pettick, Architect, Regina 1956; projects incl. H.O. Bldg. for Sask. Power Corp. (Regina), new Regina City Hall H.O. Bldg. for Sask. Gov't Ins., Bank of Montreal Bldg. (Regina) and comm. residential inst. indust. and sports bldgs.; served with RCNVR during WW II; Chrmn. Regina Local Housing Authority 1960–64; Rep. RAIC to Internat. Union of Archs.; headed Candn. dels. to World Congs. London, Havana, Paris, Mexico City, Prague; Chrmn. Civic Comte. Regina Chamber Comm. 1961–65; mem. Structural Adv. Group Nat. Research Council formulating 1965 Nat. Bldg. Code; rec'd Massey Medal for Arch. 1961 (Moose Jaw Civic Centre); Life mem. Regina Humane Soc.; Sask. Assn. Archs. (Pres. 1965); past mem. Council RAIC; mem. Illuminating Engn. Soc.; Solar Energy Soc. Can.; Unitarian; Home: 2500 Garnet St., Regina, Sask. S4T 3A4; Office: 2022 Cornwall St., Regina, Sask. S4P 2K5.

**PETTIGREW, Pierre Stewart,** B.A., M.Phil.; international affairs expert; b. Quebec City, Que. 18 Apr. 1951; s. Louis and Charlotte (Grenier) P.; e. Coll. des Jésuites; Univ. of Qué. à Trois-Rivières, B.A. 1972; Laval Univ.; Balliol Coll., Oxford Univ., M.Phil. 1976; VICE-PRES., SAMSON BELAIR DELOITTE & TOUCHE INTERNAT. INC. (MONTREAL) 1984– ; Dir., Politcal Ctte., Nato Assembly, Brussels 1976–78; Extve. Asst. to Que. liberal leader & Pres., Federalist Forces during the referendum on Sovereignty Assn. 1978–81; Fgn. Policy Advr. to the Prime Minister of Can., Privy Council Office 1981–84; received, first Prisme award as Manager of the Year 1989 in the Que. economy from the Ctr. des dirigeants d'entreprises; regular commentator for major written & electronic media in Canada on matters concerning internat. trade federalism & public affairs; Home: 1062 Bernard W., Apt. 22, Outremont, Que. H2V 1V2 and 6 rue a. Bruant, Paris 75018 France; Office: 1 Place Ville-Marie, Suite 3000, Montreal, Que. H3B 4T9.

**PETTIT, Dale Alexander,** B.A., C.A.; business executive; b. Brantford, Ont. 28 Aug. 1940; s. Don LeRoy and Ada Elizabeth (Morrison) P.; e. Univ. of Western Ont. B.A. 1963; Candn. Inst. of C.A.s; m. Pat d. Lloyd and Amy Barker 15 Aug. 1964; children: Erin, Andrew, Michael; VICE-PRES., CHIEF FINANCIAL OFFR. & TREASURER, SILCORP LIMITED 1984– ; Audit Mgr., Clarkson Gordon, Public Accounting 1970–75; Controller, Silcorp Limited 1975–80; Treasurer 1980–84; Pres. & Dir., Silcorp Employee Holdings Limited; Sec. Treas., Execsil Corp.; Treas., Frafin Corp.; Home: 60 Hampton Cres., London, Ont. N6H 2N9.

**PETTY, George S.,** B.Com.; pulp and paper executive; b. Montreal, Que. 1 Aug. 1933; s. George Anson and Laura (White) P.; e. McGill Univ. B.Com. 1954; m. Virginia Heaton 1972; children: Geoffrey, Laura Jean, George Michael; CHRMN. AND CHIEF EXTVE. OFFR., REPAP ENTERPRISES INC.; Repap Wisconsin Inc.; Midtec Paper Corp.; Miramichi Pulp & Paper Inc.; Skeena Cellulose Inc.; Repap Manitoba Inc.; Repap Technologies Inc.; Repap Ferrostaal; Founder, Tembec Inc. 1973; Founder, Penntech Papers Inc. 1969; served with RCAF-ROTC 1951–53; Papermaker of the Year, Paper Trade Journal 1976; Ken Johnson Papermaker Award, Paperage Magazine 1988; Man of the Year, Paper Industry Mgmt. Assoc. 1988; Hon. Doctorate of Philosophy, Bishop's Univ. 1988; Gov., McGill Univ.; recreations: skiing, golf, tennis, sailing; Clubs: Mount Royal; Royal Montreal Golf; Union League; Home: 775 Lexington Ave., Westmount, Que. H3Y 1K9; Office: 1250 Rene-Levesque W., Ste. 3800, Montreal, Que. H3B 4W8.

**PHARAND, Donat,** Q.C.; S.J.D., F.R.S.C.; educator; b. Hanmer, Ont. 7 Dec. 1922; s. Alphonse and Georgiana (Henri) P.; e. Dalhousie Univ., LL.B. 1952, LL.M. 1953; Univ. de Paris LL.D. 1956; Univ. of Mich. S.J.D. 1972; children: Michel, Bernard, Gisèle; PROF. OF LAW EMERITUS, UNIV. OF OTTAWA 1988– , Prof. of Law 1959–88; gen. law practice 1956–59; joined Faculty of Law present Univ. 1959; Acad.-in-Residence Dept. of External Affairs Ottawa 1977–78; Lectr. The Hague Acad. of Intnl. Law summer 1979; Visiting Prof. of Law Dalhousie Univ. 1983; Staff Rsch. Lectureship Award, Univ. of Ottawa 1974; Staff Teaching Award, Univ. of Ottawa 1988; author 'The Law of the Sea of the Arctic' 1973; 'The Northwest Passage' 1984; 'Canada's Arctic Waters in International Law' 1988; mem. various ed. bds.; Pres., Que. Law Teachers Assn. 1979–80; mem., Royal Soc. Can.; Candn. Council Intnl. Law (Pres. 1976–78); Am. Soc. Intnl. Law; Intnl. Law Assn.; Home: 85 Marlborough Ave., Ottawa, Ont. K1N 8E8.

**PHARAND, Gilles,** LL.L.; lawyer; business executive; b. Montreal, Que. 25 May 1944; s. Leopold and Denise (Gougeon) P.; e. Univ. of Montreal LL.L. 1968; m. Lise d. Paul-André and Madeleine Paradis 29 July 1967; children: Patrick, Geneviève; VICE-PRES. ADMIN., SECRETARY & GENERAL COUNSEL, DOMTAR INC. 1987– ; private practice, Bastien & Gervais 1969–70; various positions with Domtar Inc. since 1970; Mem., Quebec Bar; Inst. of C.S.s & Public Administrators; Assn. of Canadian General Counsel; recreations: tennis, skiing; clubs: Club St-Denis; Home: 292 Notre Dame de Fatima, Laval, Que.; Office: 395 de Maisonneuve W., Montreal, Que. H3A 1L6.

**PHEASEY, Frederick W.,** B.Sc., P.Eng.; business executive; b. Victoria, B.C. 3 Aug. 1942; e. Univ. of Alberta B.Sc.Mech.Eng. 1965; CHAIRMAN, DRECO ENERGY SERVICES LTD. 1972– ; Barber Industries 1965–72; Chairman, Hitec Dreco A.S. (Stavanger, Norway); Pres., Global Dewatering Ltd.; Office: 3716 - 93 St., Edmonton, Alta. T6E 5N3.

**PHELAN, John Patrick,** FIIC, ARM; reinsurance executive; b. Kilkenny, Ireland 4 Feb. 1947; s. Michael and Bridie P.; e. Patrician Coll. 1964; Insur. Inst. of Am., Assoc. in Risk Mngt. 1974; Insur. Inst. of Can., Fellowship 1974; m. Laurena d. Anthony and Doreen Bucci 1 Aug. 1970; children: Anthony, Geoffrey, Melinda; PRES. & DIR., MUNICH REINSUR. CO. OF CAN. 1986– ; Legal & Gen. Assce. Soc. 1965–67; Guardian Insur. Co. of Can. 1967; Lukis Stewart Price Forbes 1967–73; Munich Reinsur. Co. of Can. 1973– ; Chief Agent in Can. (Non-Life), Munich Reinsur. Co.; Pres. & Dir., Munich-Can. Mngt. Corp. Ltd.; Pres. & Dir., Munich Holdings Ltd.; Dir., Munich-Life Mngmt. Co.; Munich Am. Serv. Corp.; Munich Am. Cons. Corp.; Munich Am. Intermediary Corp.; The Great Lakes Reinsur. Co.; Chrmn., Reinsur. Rsch. Counc. 1989–91; Chrmn., Bd. of Govs., The Insur. Inst. of Can. 1987–88; recreations: swimming, reading; Club: National; Office: 390 Bay St., Suite 2200, Toronto, Ont. M5H 2Y2.

**PHELIPS, Anthony Pierre Mackenzie Lawrence;** advertising executive; b. Southampton, England 13 Nov. 1954; s. David Edward and Claudie (Cambier) P.; e. Repton Sch., Ealing Hotel Sch.; m. Michelle d. Gisèla and Manfred Pfeiffer 13 Dec. 1983; PRES., INTERESTING PROJECTS INC. 1989– ; Dir., Brahma Kumaris World Spiritual Organisation (Ontario); Extve. Vice Pres. & Mng. Dir., Young and Rubicam Ltd. 1986–89; Mng. Dir., Medicus Intercon Can. 1981; Home: 173 Kenilworth Ave., Toronto, Ont. M4L 3S7.

**PHELPS, Jim,** M.A.; correctional services executive; b. Manitoba 18 May 1942; s. Ernest Arthur and Clara P.; e. Univ. of Manitoba, B.A., 1964, M.A. (Psych.) 1967; m. Pat d. Arthur and Audrey Baldwin 17 Dec. 1983; children: Ezekiel Riordan, Tara Nicole, Arthur James, Karen Ann; CHRMN., REVIEW OF MANAGEMENT INFORMATION SYSTEMS, CORRECTIONAL SERVICE OF CANADA, GOVT. OF CANADA 1993– ; Dist. Dir., Kingston, Nat. Parole Serv. 1970; Warden, Kingston Penitentiary 1971; Warden, Matsqui Inst. 1972–73; Dir. of Policy, Secretariat of Solicitor Gen. of Can. 1974–75; Dep. Comnr., Prairie Region 1976–86; Ont. Region 1987; Deputy Comnr., Correctional Programs & Opns., Correctional Service of Canada 1988–90; Special Advisor to Assoc. Depy. Minister, Ministere de la Securité Publique, Govt. of Qué. 1990–93; Mem., Bd. of Dir., Candn. Criminal Justice Assn.; Office: 340 Laurier Ave. W., 7th Floor, Ottawa, Ont. K1A 0P9.

**PHELPS, Michael E.J.,** LL.M.; executive; b. Montreal, Que. 27 June 1947; s. Arthur A. and Hendrina P. (Von De Roer) P.; e. Univ. of Man. B.A. 1967, LL.B. 1970; London Sch. of Econ. LL.M. 1971; m. Joy d. Donald and Jessie Slimmon 8 Aug. 1970; children: Erica, Julia, Lindsay; PRESIDENT, CHIEF EXECUTIVE OFFICER & DIR., WESTCOAST ENERGY INC. 1988– ; Bd. Chrmn. & Dir.: Westcoast Petroleum Ltd.; Canadian Roxy Petroleum Ltd.; Bd. Vice Chrmn. & Dir., Foothills Pipe Lines Ltd.; Dir., Pacific Northern Gas Ltd.; Mem. Bd. of Govs., Business Counc. of B.C.; Adv. Counc., Fac. of Commerce and Bus. Admin., Univ. of B.C.; Bd. of Dirs.: Canfor Corp.; Interstate Natural Gas Assoc. of America; Candn. Imperial Bank of Commerce; Conference Bd. of Canada; Crown Atty. Prov. Man. 1971–73; Lawyer & Partner, Christie, Degraves, Winnipeg 1973–76; Counsel, Dept. of Justice, Ottawa 1976–78; Extve. Asst. to Min. of Justice 1978–79 and to Min. of Energy, Mines & Resources 1980–82; Sessional Lectr. Carleton Univ. 1977–79; Lectr. Man. Bar Admission Course 1972–75; mem. Law Soc. Man.; Clubs: Vancouver; Hollyburn Country; Office: 1333 W. Georgia St., Vancouver, B.C. V6E 3K9.

**PHILCOX, Brian Anthony;** marketing executive; b. Toronto, Ont. 16 May 1937; s. James Warren and Mary Edith (Rose) P.; m. Bonnie d. Earl and Dorothy Buxton 12 Feb. 1971; children: Cleo Alexandra, Colette Lee; DIR., MKTG. COMMUNICATION, CONSUMERS' GAS CO. 1978– ; previously marketing executive with various advertising agencies, national advertisers, the Federal Government and Loyola Coll.; Past Chrmn., Assn. of Candn. Advtrs. (mem., Advisory Ctte., A.C.A.); Chrmn. & Dir., Candn. Advertising Found. (C.A.F.); Dir., Institute for the Prevention of Child Abuse; Dir., Philippines Canada Business Assn.; Mem.: Communication Ctte., Candn. Gas Assn.; Communication Ctte., Ont. Natural Gas Assoc.; Advertising Ctte., Am. Gas Assoc.; Internat. Assoc. of Business Communicators (IABC); Candn. Direct Marketing Assoc. (CDMA); Guest lectr., Carleton Univ.; N.S. Coll. of Art & Design; Mng. Dir., Waxwing Prodns. Ltd.; Past Chrmn., Corp. United Way Campaign; recreations: photography, woodworking, birding, baking; Home: 139 Scarborough Rd., Toronto, Ont. M4E 3M4; Office: 2235 Sheppard Ave. E., Toronto, Ont. M2J 5B5.

**PHILIP, David Stewart,** B.D.S.; dentist; b. Dundee, Scotland 2 Feb. 1933; s. David and Willamina Kinnoch (Smart) P.; e. Harris Academy; Dundee Tech. Coll.; St. Andrews Univ. B.D.S. 1957; m. Christina d. Christina and Bernard Reilly 9 Aug. 1957; children: David Stewart, Blair Macdonald; private dental practice; Pres., Brit. Dental Students Assn. 1956–57; Victoria Dental Soc. 1971–72; Vice-Pres., Am. N.W. Acad. of Group Dental Practice 1972–74; Chair, Oak Bay Parks & Rec. Comn. 1975–81; Pres., Victoria Cricket Assn. 1974–77; Mem., Am. Acad. of Cosmetic Dentistry 1990– ; Acreditation AACD 1993; Part-time Instructor, Dental Faculty, U.B.C. 1985–87; Accreditation Cons., Am. Acad. of Cosmetic Dentistry 1993; Univ. of Victoria French Language Dipl. 1980; Pres, B.C. Assn. of Colleges 1988–90; Mem., Bd. of Gov., Camosun Coll. 1983–90, Chair 1989–90; Univ. of Victoria 1991– (Chair 1993); recreations: golf, photography; clubs: Victoria Golf, Oak Bay Rotary; Home: No. 3, 1027 Belmont Ave., Victoria, B.C. V8S 3T4; Office: 2015 Oak Bay Ave., Victoria, B.C. V8R 1E5.

**PHILIP, Hon. Edward Thomas,** B.A., M.Ed., M.P.P.; politician; b. Montreal, Que. 11 March 1940; s. Fergus Frederick Philip and Beatrice (Crannery) P.; e. Thomas D'Arcy McGee H.S. Montreal; St. Joseph's Teachers' College; Univ. of Ottawa B.A., M.Ed.; Ont. Inst. for Studies in Education; MINISTER OF MUNICIPAL AFFAIRS and OFFICE OF THE GREATER TORONTO AREA 1993– ; 1st elected to Ont. legis. for Etobicoke-Rexdale g.e. 1975; re-elected g.e. 1977, 1981, 1985, 1987, 1990; Min. of Transportation 1990–91; Min. of Industry, Trade and Technology 1991–93; Co-ord., Leadership Training, Ont. Fed. of Agriculture; Mem., Ont. Assn. for Continuing Education; N.D.P.; R.C.; Home: 65 Riverhead Dr., Rexdale, ON M9W 4G3; Legislative Office: 17th Floor, 777 Bay St., Toronto, Ont. M5G 2E5; Constituency: 1123 Albion Rd., #201, Rexdale, Ont. M9V 1A9.

**PHILIP, Marlene Nourbese,** B.Sc., M.A., LL.B.; writer; lawyer; b. Tobago 3 Feb. 1947; d. Parkinson Bansfield and Undine Altruda (Bowles) Philip-Yeates; e. Univ. of W. Indies B.Sc. 1968; Univ. of W. Ont. M.A. 1970, LL.B. 1973; m. Paul s. Alan and Wyn Chamberlain 1978; children Bruce King, Hardie and Hesper Philip-Chamberlain; articled Parkdale Community Legal Services; law practice 7 yrs. as Staff Lawyer, Parkdale Community Legal Services; Partner, Jemmott and Philip and as sole practitioner to 1983; Vice Chair Workers' Compensation Appeals Tribunal 1986–87; sessional lectr. in Creative Writing York Univ.; cons. and workshop leader Bds. of Edn.; recipient Casa de las Americas Prize for Poetry 1988; Finalist Canadian Library Assn. Prize for Children's Literature 1989; Max and Greta Abel Award for Multicultural Literature (1990) and the Toronto Book Awards 1990 for fiction 'Harriet's Daughter'; Tradewinds Prize for Poetry and Short Story 1988; Guggenheim Fellow in Poetry 1990; McDowell Fellow 1991; author: 'Thorns' poetry 1980; 'Salmon Courage' poetry 1983; 'Harriet's Daughter' fiction 1988; 'She Tries Her Tongue' poetry 1989; 'Her Silence Softly Breaks' poetry 1989; 'Looking for Livingstone: An Odyssey of Silence' fiction 1991; 'Frontiers: Essays and Writings on Racism and Culture' non-fiction 1992; 'Showing Grit: Showboating North of the 44th Parallel' non-fiction 1993; Founding mem. Vision 21; recreations: shortwave, walking, embroidery; Address: c/o Women's Press, 517 College St., Ste. 233, Toronto, Ont. M6G 4A2.

**PHILLIPS, Anthony George,** M.A., Ph.D., F.R.S.C.; educator; scientist; b. Barrow-in-Furness, Eng. 30 Jan. 1943; s. George William and Mabel Lilian (Wood) P.; e. Univ. of W. Ont. B.A. 1966, M.A. 1967, Ph.D. 1970; m. Margo Palmer 1982; PROF. OF PSYCHOL. UNIV. OF B.C. 1980– ; Founder and Dir. Quadra Logic Technologies Inc.; Asst. Prof. of Psychol. present Univ. 1970, Assoc. Prof. 1975; Chrmn. Behavioral Sci's Ctte. Med. Rsch. Council Can. 1982–87; E.W.R. Steacie Fellow (NSERC) 1979–80; Killam Sr. Scholar 1977–78; Univ. B.C. Killam Rsch. Prize 1986; Dir. Can.-India Village Aid Soc.; Tibetan Refugee Aid Soc.; mem. Internat. Brain Rsch. Orgn.; Candn. Assn. Neurosci.; Soc. for Neurosci.; Candn. Coll. Neuropsychopharmacol.; author over 170 sci. articles and book chapters; recreations: travel, hiking; Office: 2136 West Mall, Vancouver, B.C. V6T 1Y7.

**PHILLIPS, David Wayne,** B.A., M.A.; climatologist, weather historian, author; b. Windsor, Ont. 8 Sept. 1944; s. Donald Arthur (dec.) and Jean Elizabeth (Jackson) P.; e. Univ. of Windsor B.A. 1966; Univ. of Toronto M.A. 1971; m. Darlene d. John Clifford and Edna Dudley 8 June 1968; children: Kelley, Jennifer; SENIOR CLIMATOLOGIST, ENVIRONMENT CANADA 1990– ; Physical Scientist, Atmospheric Envir. Serv., Envir. Canada 1967–76; Supt., Candn. Climate Centre 1977–84; Visiting Prof., Univ. of Windsor 1972; McGill Univ. 1976; Secretariat, World Conf. on the Changing Atmosphere: Implications for Global Security, Envir. Canada 1987–89; Public Service Merit Award, Govt. of Canada 1986, '92; Andrew Thompson Prize in Applied Meteorology, Candn. Met. & Ocean. Soc. 1991; Camsell Award for outstanding service to the Society, Royal Candn. Geog. Soc. 1993; Mem., Bd. of Dir., Royal Candn. Geog. Soc. 1987–93; Winter Cities Assn. 1990– ; Mem., Fellow & Patron, Royal Candn. Geog. Soc.; Mem., Candn. Met. & Ocean. Soc.; Candn. Assn. of Geog.; Assoc. Ed., 'Climatological Bulletin' 1990– , 'Chinook' mag. 1989; Columnist, 'Weatherwise' mag. 1972–84, 'Can. Geographic' 1988– ; originator & author, Candn. Weather Trivia Calendar 1985–91; author: 'The Day Niagara Falls Ran Dry! Canadian Weather Facts and Trivia' 1993, 'The Climates of Canada' 1990, 'The Climate of the Great Lakes Basin' 1972, 'Handbook on Climatological Data Sources' 1979, '83, '88, 'The Canadian Climate in Review' 1980, 'Climate Severity Index for Canadians' 1984, 'A Bibliography of Canadian Climate 1977–1981' 1983; co-author: 'Average Annual Water Surplus In Canada' 1967, 'Synthesized Winds and Wave Heights for the Great Lakes' 1970; also author of several book chapters, sci. articles, tech. reports, conf. proceedings (ed.), commentaries, essays & biographies; frequent appearances on nat. radio & TV; regular 60-second question & answer 'Ask The Expert' weather segment on The Weather Network 1992– ; internationally involved with UN World Meteorological Orgn. in various capacities; Chair, nat. celebrations to commemorate 150th anniversary of weather observing in Canada 1991; recreations: acting, photography, gardening; Home: 4 Cranberry Lane, Aurora, Ont. L4G 5X8; Office: 4905 Dufferin St., Downsview, Ont. M3H 5T4.

**PHILLIPS, Donald John,** B.Sc.; mining executive; b. Ebbw Vale, Wales 8 Jan. 1930; s. Archie Thomas Phillips; e. Univ. of Wales B.Sc. 1951; m. Susan Elizabeth Haire 28 Feb. 1986; children: Janet Katherine, Simon Hugh; Chrmn. & C.E.O., Inco Limited 1991; Dir. Toronto-Dominion Bank; Council for Candn. Unity; Mem. Hospitals of Ont. Investments Ctte.; Tech. Offr. Inco Europe Ltd. 1956–67, Sales Dir. 1967–69, Gen. Marketing Mgr. 1969–70, Asst. Mang. Dir. 1970–71, Mang. Dir. 1971–72, Chrmn. and Chief Offr. 1972–77; Pres., Inco Metals Co., 1977; Pres. and Chief Executive Offr. Inco Metals Co. 1979–80; Chrmn., Pres. & C.E.O., Inco Limited 1987–91; served with RAF 1952–54, rank Flying Offr.; Companion, Brit. Inst. Mang.; Fellow, Inst. of Mining and Metallurgy; mem., Business Counc. on National Issues; Ont. Business Adv. Bd.; Candn. Inst. of Mining & Metallurgy; Bd. Trade Metrop. Toronto; recreations: golf, tennis, squash; Clubs: Toronto; National; Home: 65 Harbour Sq., Apt. 401, Toronto, Ont. M5J 2L4.

**PHILLIPS, Edward O.,** M.A.; writer; b. Montréal, Qué. 26 Nov. 1931; s. Archibald Lovell and Dorothy (Skaife) P.; e. McGill Univ., B.A. 1953; Univ. de Montréal, Ll.L. 1956; Harvard Univ., A.M.T. 1957; Boston Univ., M.A. 1962; Montréal Museum Sch. of Art Design Dip. 1968; taught Eng. Boston and Montréal 1957–65; solo exhns. Montréal 1969–73 inclusive; group exhns. Toronto 1972, 1973; taught Drawing Visual Arts Centre Montréal 1974; author (novels) 'Sunday's Child' 1981; 'Where There's A Will...' 1984; 'Buried on Sunday' 1986 (Arthur Ellis Award 1986); 'Hope Springs Eternal' 1988; 'Sunday Best' 1990; 'The Landlady's Niece' 1992; (anthol.) '83: Best Canadian Stories' 1983; 'Fatal Recurrences' 1985; 'Canadian Mystery Stories' 1991; 'Criminal Shorts' 1992; mem. Writers Union Can.; Amnesty Internat.; Union des Ecrivains Québécois; International P.E.N. Crime Writers of Canada; Address: 425 Wood Ave., Westmount, Que. H3Y 3J3.

**PHILLIPS, Edwin C.;** executive; b. Saskatoon, Sask. 19 Oct. 1917; s. Dr. Charles Henry and Beatrice Grace (Johnson) P.; m. Elizabeth Winnifred, d. Edward Westwood Johnston, 27 June 1942; children: Diane, Carol, Glen, Earl, Jane, Sue; CHRMN. OF THE BD., CHENI GOLD MINES INC.; Dir., Balaclava Enterprises Ltd.; Cheni Gold Mines Inc.; Emco Limited; Weiser Inc.; Asst. Buyer, Loblaw Groceterias Co., Toronto, 1938; Advertising Mgr., Canada & Dominion Sugar Co., Chatham, 1945; Asst. to Gen. Mgr., Consumers' Gas Co., Toronto, 1947; Asst. Gen. Mgr., Trane Co. of Canada, Toronto, 1952; Vice Pres. and Gen. Mgr. 1957; Extve. Vice Pres. and Gen. Mgr. 1964; Pres. 1966; joined Westcoast Transmission Co. Ltd. as Vice Pres., 1968; Group Vice Pres. 1969; Vice Pres.-Adm. and Dir. 1970; Extve. Vice Pres. 1971; Pres. 1972; Pres. & C.E.O. 1976–80; Chrmn., 1982–83; Dir. Emeritus, Westcoast Energy Inc. 1989; served with RCAF as Flying Instr. during World War II; Life mem., Candn. Inst. of Plumbing & Heating; Candn. Gas Assn.; Conservative; recreation: riding; Home: 4458 W. 2nd Ave., Vancouver, B.C. V6R 1K5.

**PHILLIPS, G. Randal,** F.S.A., F.C.I.A.; actuary; b. Port-of-Spain, Trinidad 25 May 1955; s. George Christie and Dorothy Isabel (Ferreira) P.; e. Univ. of Waterloo, B.Math 1977; m. Harriet May d. Tony and Monica May 14 Sept. 1985; Extve. VICE PRES. AND ACTUARY, W.F. MORNEAU & ASSOCIATES LTD. 1986– ; Dir. Group Underwriting, The Dominion Life Assurance Co. 1977–85; Dir. Group Operations, The Manufacturers Life Assurance Co. 1986; recreation: swimming; Home: 170 Wheelihan Way, Campbellville, Ont. L0P 1B0; Office: 1500 Don Mills Rd., Toronto, Ont. M3B 3K4.

**PHILLIPS, James Bruce Ross;** journalist; b. Fort William, Ont. 6 June 1930; s. Alexander and Lillian (Foxton) P.; m. Elizabeth d. John and Mary Pellow 20 March 1953; children: Kelly, Allison; PRIVACY COMMISSIONER OF CANADA 1991– ; Journalist, Canadian Press, Calgary Herald, Southam News Services (Ottawa & Washington 1957–69) 1949–84; Ottawa Bureau Chief, CTV Television Network 1969–84; Minister of Public Affairs, Embassy of Canada, Washington D.C. 1985–87; Director of Communications, Office of the Prime Minister 1987–90; Asst. Privacy Commissioner of Canada 1990–91; Winner, National Newspaper Awards of Canada (1962, staff corresponding); Bowater Award for Journalism (1963, economics & business); Mem., Royal Ottawa Golf (Pres. 1980); National Press Club of Canada (Pres. 1962, '63, '68); Former Pres., Parliamentary Press Gallery of Canada 1977; Office: 112 Kent St., Ottawa, Ont. K1A 1H3.

**PHILLIPS, John Edward,** M.Sc., Ph.D., F.R.S.C.; educator; b. Montreal, Que. 20 Dec. 1934; s. William Charles and Violet Mildred (Lewis) P.; e. Colchester Co. Acad. Truro, N.S. 1952; Dalhousie Univ. B.Sc. 1956 (Univ. Medal). M.Sc. 1957; Cambridge Univ. Ph.D. 1961 (Nat. Research Council Overseas Grad. Studentship 1957–60); m. Eleanor Mae d. Marston Richardson, Halifax, N.S. 8 Sept. 1956; children: Heather Anne, Jayne Elizabeth, Jonathan David, Catherine Melinda, Wendy Susannah; HEAD OF ZOOLOGY 1991– and PROF. OF ZOOLOGY, UNIV. OF B.C. 1971– ; Asst. Prof. Dalhousie Univ. 1960–64; Assoc. Prof. Univ. of B.C. 1964–71; Visiting Researcher Dept. Zool. Cambridge Univ. 1972, 1976, 1980–81; Chrmn. Grant Selection Comte. on Animal Biol. Nat. Research Council of Can. 1969–71; Natural Sciences and Engineering Rsch. Council of Can., Council mem. 1983–87; Killam Research Prize, Univ. of B.C. 1989–90; Grant Selection Ctte., Candn. Cystic Fibrosis Found. 1989–91; author over 135 articles in scient. journs. on membrane transport processes, their control, and regulation of blood composition in Arthropods; mem. Candn. Soc. Zool. (Secy. 5 yrs., Vice Pres. 2 yrs., Pres. 1978–79); Am. Physiol. Soc. (Ed. Bd.); Am. Soc. Zools. (Chrmn., Comparative Physiology Section 1984–85); J. Exp. Biol. (Ed. Bd.); Soc. Exper. Biol. UK; Mem. of Senate, Univ. of B.C.; Vancouver Bach Choir; recreation: music; Home: 12908 – 22B Ave., White Rock, B.C. V4A 6Z3.

**PHILLIPS, Mary Jane,** B.A.Sc., M.A., Ph.D., F.C.I.C., P.Eng.; university professor; b. Toronto, Ont. 15 Sept. 1931; d. William Robert and Sara Elizabeth (Wilkins) P.; e. Univ. of Toronto B.A.Sc. 1953; Bryn Mawr College M.A. 1954; Johns Hopkins Univ. Ph.D. 1960; PROF., DEPT. OF CHEMICAL ENGINEERING, UNIV. OF TORONTO 1989– ; E.I. duPont de Nemours & Co. 1954–56; postdoct. studies, NRC Mines Br. 1960–61; Queen's Univ. of Belfast 1961–62; Lectr., Chem. Engr., Univ. of Toronto 1964–72; Asst. Prof. 1972–77; Assoc. Prof. 1977–89; Assoc. Chair 1990–81; Assoc. Dean (Div. III), Sch. of Grad. Studies 1991–94; Dir., Chem. Engr. Rsch. Cons. Limited; Pres., Profl. Engr. Ont. 1993–94 (Pres. Elect 1992–93; Vice-Pres. 1991–92; LGA Councillor 1986–91); Mem., Sigma Xi; Candn. Soc. for Chem. Engr.; A.A.A.S.; author of engineering papers; co-editor: 'Proceedings 9th Internat. Congress on Catalysis' 1988; clubs: Toronto Ladies', Toronto Lawn Tennis, Royal Overseas League; Office: Wallberg Bldg., Toronto, Ont. M5S 1A4.

**PHILLIPS, Michael Burke,** B.A., LL.B., Q.C.; foreign service officer; b. Saskatoon, Sask. 29 Sept. 1939; s. Eugene Edward and Kathleen Mary Frances (Burke) P.; e. St. Paul's H.S., Univ. of Sask., B.A. 1962, LL.B. 1964; m. Oonagh d. Jack and Agnes McGinley May 1975; children: Ciara, Conor Patrick; CANADIAN AMBASSADOR TO SWEDEN, LATVIA, LITHUANIA, ESTONIA 1991– ; Addis Ababa 1966–69; Dublin 1972–74; Nairobi 1977–80; served Ottawa External Aid Office, African & Middle East Div., Legal Opns. Div.; Sr. Dept. Asst. to Sec. of State for External Affairs 1980–83; Min. (Pol. & Public Affairs), Candn. High Comn., London, U.K. 1983–88; Asst. Depy. Min., United States Relations, Dept. of External Affairs, Ottawa 1989–91; admitted to Sask. Bar 1965; Club: Reform Club London; Office: Canadian Embassy, Stockholm, Sweden.

**PHILLIPS, Neil F.,** Q.C., B.A., LL.B., B.C.L.; b. Montreal, Que., 1 Nov. 1924; s. Lazarus, Q.C., and Rosalie (Idelson) P.; e. Westmount (Que.) High Sch.; Williams Coll.; B.A., Yale Univ. Law Sch., LL.B.; McGill Univ., B.C.L.; m. Sharon Whitely, d. James W. Greer, Southern Pines, N.C., 24 Sept. 1957; children: Greer Laurence, Melissa Rosemarie; RESIDENT SENIOR COUNSEL, GOODMAN, PHILLIPS & VINEBERG New York 1984– ; Royal Bank of Canada; The Seagram Co. Ltd.; Yale Alumni Assn. of Canada; read law with Phillips, Bloomfield, Vineberg & Goodman; called to the Bar of Quebec 1950 and the Bar of New York 1985; subsequently Partner and Resident Senior Counsel, Goodman, Phillips & Vineberg; author of 'United States Taxation of Foreign Entities' 1952; served in 2nd World War, R.C.N.V.R. (Lieut.) 1942–45; Phi Alpha Delta; Club: Mount Royal (Montreal); Metropolitan (New York); Home: 15 West 53rd St., New York, N.Y. 10019; Office: 430 Park Avenue, 10th Floor, New York, N.Y. 10022.

**PHILLIPS, Hon. Orville Howard,** D.D.S.; senator; dental surgeon; b. O'Leary, P.E.I., 5 April 1924; s. J. S. and Maude (MacArthur) P.; e. Prince of Wales Coll., Charlottetown, P.E.I.; Dalhousie Univ., D.D.S. 1952; m. Marguerite, d. Robert Woodside, 21 Aug. 1945; children: Brian, Betty, Robert, Patricia; mem. H. of C. for Prince in 1957–62; MEMBER, SENATE OF CANADA 1963– ; served in 2nd World War with R.C.A.F. 1942–45 in Can. and Overseas; mem., P.E.I. Dental Assn.; Royal Candn. Legion; Air Force Assn.; P. Conservative; United Church; recreations: curling, hunting; Homes: Box 155, Alberton, P.E.I. C0B 1B0 (summer) and 2317 Whitehaven Crescent, Ottawa, Ont. K2B 5H2; Office: Rm. 574-S, Centre Block, The Senate of Canada, Ottawa, Ont. K1A 0A4.

**PHILLIPS, Paul Arthur,** B.A., M.A., Ph.D.; university professor; b. Hong Kong 3 Nov. 1938; s. Richard Gaundry and Mary Dyson (Ricketts) P.; e. Victoria College; Univ. of Saskatchewan B.A. (Hons.) 1961, M.A. 1963; London School of Economics Ph.D. 1967; m. Donna d. Don and Ellen Speers 13 Sept. 1958; children: Erin, Nicole; PROFESSOR, ECONOMICS, UNIV. OF MANITOBA 1969– ; Instructor and Research Assoc., Economics, Univ. of B.C. 1964–65; Asst. Prof., Econ., Univ. of Victoria 1965–66; Research Dir., B.C. Fed. of Labour 1966–68; Visiting Asst. Prof., Econ., Simon Fraser Univ. 1968–69; Asst., Assoc., Full Prof., Econ., Univ. of Man. 1969– ; Research Dir. & Extve. Sec., Manitoba Econ. Devel. Adv. Bd. 1974–75 (on leave from univ.); Chair, Manitoba Milk Control Bd. 1975–80; Manitoba Milk Prices Review Comn. 1984–88; Industrial Adjustment Service Cttes. (7); Dir., Slovenian Labour Market Adjustment Study 1988; Labour Arbitrator, Industrial Relns. Consulting; Research Dir., Manitoba Labour-Mngt. Review Ctte. 1973–74; Mem., Soc. for Socialist Studies; Univ. of Man. Faculty Assn.; Candn. Assn. of Univ. Teachers; Man. Opera Assn. Bd. Mem. 1980–86 (Vice-Pres. 1982–84); author: 'Regional Disparities' 1978, rev. ed. 1983, 'No Power Greater' 1967, 'Canadian Political Economy' 1990; co-author: 'Macro-Economic Theory and the Canadian Economy' 1972, 2nd ed. 1983; 'Micro Economic Theory and the Canadian Economy' 1972, 2nd ed. 1983; 'Women and Work' 1983, 2nd ed. 1993; 'The Rise and Fall of the Third Way: Yugoslavia 1945–1991' 1993; editor: 'Incentives Location and Regional Development' 1975, 'Manpower Issues in Manitoba' 1975, 'Labour and Capital in Canada: 1640–1860'); recreations: polo, sailing, opera, skiing; clubs: Springfield Polo (Captain 1983–84), Manitoba Opera Assn. Chorus; Home: 126 Machray Ave., Winnipeg, Man. R2W 0Z3; Office: Univ. of Manitoba, Winnipeg, Man. R3T 2M8.

**PHILLIPS, Paul C.,** B.A., M.B.A., D.M.S., DipM., M.C.I.M.; business executive; b. England 23 Sept. 1953; s. Arnold and Audrey P.; e. City of Birmingham Polytechnic B.A. 1973; Staffordshire Univ. DipM. 1989, D.M.S. 1989, M.B.A. 1992; m. Susan d. Pamela and Duncan Bottomley 16 Feb. 1990; children: Carolyn Louise, Emma Kate; PRESIDENT & CHIEF EXECUTIVE OFFICER, ROYAL DOULTON CANADA LTD. 1992– ; joined Royal Doulton 1977; headed Hotel & Airline Div. (U.S.) until 1988; Chief Executive, Hotel & Airline Div. (U.K.) 1988–90; C.E.O., External Sales Div. 1990–92; Home: 139 Regent St., Richmond Hill, Ont. L4C 9P1; Office: 850 Progress Dr., Scarborough, Ont. M1H 3C4.

**PHILLIPS, Robert A.,** Ph.D.; research scientist; b. St. Louis, MO 2 July 1937; s. Allan Blackmore and Mildred Irene (Fandrich) P.; e. Carlton Coll., Northfield, Minn., B.A. 1959; Washington Univ., St. Louis, Ph.D. 1965; m. Corley d. Raymond and Frances Hamill 12 June 1959; children: Kristin, Michael, Scott; HEAD, DIV. OF IMMUNOLOGY AND CANCER RSCH., HOSP. FOR SICK CHILDREN & PROF., DEPT. OF PEDIATRICS, UNIV. OF TORONTO 1986– ; post-doct. fellow, Ont. Cancer Inst. 1965–67; Sr. Scientist, Ont. Cancer Inst. 1967–86; Asst. Prof., Dept. of Med. Biophys., Univ. of Toronto 1967–71; Assoc. Prof. 1971–76; Prof. 1976– ;

Dept. Chrmn. 1981–86; Office: 555 University Ave., Toronto, Ont. M5G 1X8.

**PHILLIPS, Robert Arthur John,** C.M., B.A.; writer; b. Toronto 19 Apr. 1922; s. Charles and Margaret (Waugh) P.; e. Univ. of Toronto, B.A. 1942; m. Mary Anne (dec'd) d. Charles N. Cochrane, 15 June 1946; three d., Margaret W., Brigid A., Jennifer N.; joined Department of External Affairs 1945; Secy., Candn. Embassy, Moscow, 1947–49; Nat. Defence Coll., Kingston 1949–50; Candn. Secy., Permanent Jt. Bd. on Defence; Privy Council Office, 1952–54; joined Dept. Northern Affairs 1954; Dir., Northern Adm. Br., 1964–65; Asst. Secy. of the Cabinet, Privy Council Office 1965–69; Depy. Director Gen. Information Canada 1970–72; Extve. Dir., Heritage Canada 1973–1978; Pres., Scriptactics (estab. 1983); Co-Pres., SP Publications (estab. 1991); co-publisher, with S.V. Stevenson, of West–Quebec Post & Bulletin and Aylmer Bulletin d'Aylmer (1991); apptd. Member of the Order of Canada 1987; served overseas in 2nd World War with Candn. Army in Can. and N.W. Europe; Anglican: Home: 80 chemin Summer, Cantley, Que. J8V 3J3.

**PHILLIPS, Robert Quaife,** P.Ag., B.S.A.; executive; b. Sarnia, Ont. 10 July 1925; s. William Edward and Emily (Homer) P.; e. Ont. Agric. Coll. Guelph B.S.A. 1947; m. Lorna Jean d. Torge Torgeson 16 Nov. 1949; children: Robert Quaife, Robin Lee Patterson, Kathleen Anne Goodwin, Laurie Jean; Sales Rep. C-I-L Toronto 1947, Winnipeg 1948, Belleville 1949; Advt. and Sales Promotion Mgr. Chipman Chemicals, Hamilton 1955, Sales Mgr. Montréal 1957; Mgr. Agricultural Chemicals Ltd. Toronto 1960, Pres. and Chief Extve. Offr. 1966; Regional Gen. Mgr. Agrico Chemical Co. Div. of Continental Oil Co. Memphis, Tenn. 1968; Nat. Acct. Extve. Agrico International Tampa, Fla. 1970; Dir. of Mktg. Phosphate Rock Export Assn. Tampa 1972, Vice Pres. Mktg. 1977; Pres. & C.E.O. Cansulex Ltd. 1978–90; Chrmn., Robert Q. Phillips Corp. (Canafric Comm. & Cons. Services Divs.) 1991– ; Pres. Can.-China Trade Council; Dir. & chrmn., Pers. Comm. Ducks Unltd. (Can.); Trustee The Soong Ching Ling (Madame Sun Yat-Sen) Children's Fund; Bd. of Gov., Regent Coll. (UBC); Dir. Vancouver Community Coll.; Chrmn. Int. Bus. Prog. & Corp. Fund Campaign; mem. of SAGIT, Sectoral Adv. Ctte. on Internat. Trade (Fed. Govt.); former Candn. rep. to Fertilizer Ind Adv. Ctte. FAO, UN; mem. Agric. Inst. Can.; B.C. Inst. Agrols.; Ret. Mem. Finance Ctte., Int'l. Fert. Ind. Assn.; Candn. Exporters Assn.; Ret. Dir., Found. for Agronomic Rsch. (Dir.); Past Chrmn. Tampa World Trade Council, Gter Tampa C. of C.; mem. Hon. Order Ky. Cols.; Mem., Order of St. John; mem. Vancouver Bd. Trade; Argyll & Sutherland Highlanders Can. Mess; Seaforth Highlanders of Can. Mess; Clubs: Vancouver; Royal Vancouver Yacht; Shaughnessy Golf & Country; Calgary Petroleum; recreations: boating, hunting, shooting; Anglican; Office and Home: 122 - 6505 3rd Ave., Delta, B.C. V4L 2N1.

**PHILLIPS, Robin;** director, actor; b. Haslemere, Surrey Eng. 28 Feb. 1942; s. James William and Ellen Ann (Barfoot) P.; e. Midhurst Grammar Sch., Sussex; trained for stage under Duncan Ross, Bristol Old Vic Theatre Sch.; unm.; came to Canada 1973; first prof. appearance Mr. Puff in 'The Critic' 1959; Assoc. Dir., Bristol Old Vic 1960; acted in Sir Laurence Olivier's first Chichester season 1962; with Oxford Playhouse co. in 'Six Characters in Search of an Author' 1964; Asst. Dir., Royal Shakespeare Co., Stratford-upon-Avon 1965; directed 'The Ballad of the False Barman' Hampstead 1966; Assoc. Dir., Northcott Theatre 1967–68; directed: 'The Seagull,' Thorndike, Leatherhead 1969; 'Tiny Alice' for Royal Shakespeare Co., Aldwych 1970; 'Abelard and Heloise' London and Broadway, N.Y. 1970; 'Two Gentlemen of Verona' for R.S.C., Stratford (Eng.); 'Sing A Rude Song' Greenwich and West End; 'Caesar and Cleopatra' starring Sir John Gielgud and 'Dear Antoine' starring Dame Edith Evans, Chichester 1971; 'Miss Julie' for Royal Shakespeare Co. 1971; 'The Lady's Not for Burning' starring Richard Chamberlin, 'The Doctor's Dilemma' and 'The Beggar's Opera' 1972; instrumental in forming 'Company Theatre'; apptd. Artistic Dir., Greenwich Theatre 1973; directed: 'Rosmersholm,' 'Three Sisters,' 'The House of Bernarda Alba,' 'Not Drowning But Waving,' 'Zorba,' 'Catsplay,' Greenwich 1973; apptd. Artistic Dir. Stratford Festival Theatre (Can.) 1974–80; directed Stratford (Can.) Festival Theatre on nat. tour 'Two Gentlemen of Verona' and 'The Comedy of Errors'; and for festival season 'Measure for Measure,' 'Trumpets and Drums,' 'The Importance of Being Earnest' 1975; Dir. 'Antony and Cleopatra,' 'A Midsummer Night's Dream,' 'The Way of The World' 1976; Co-dir. 'Hamlet' and 'The Tempest,' restaged 'Measure for Measure,' 'The Importance of Being Earnest' 1976; Dir. 'Richard III,' 'The Guardsman,' 'A Midsummer Nights Dream,' 'As You Like It,' 'Hay Fever' 1977; Dir. 'As You Like It,' 'The Devils,' 'Judgement,' 'Macbeth,' 'The Winter's Tale,' 'Uncle Vanya,' 'Private Lives' 1978; Dir. 'King Lear,' 'Importance of Being Earnest,' 'Love's Labour's Lost' 1979; Dir. 'Twelfth Night,' 'Virginia,' 'Much Ado About Nothing,' 'King Lear,' 'Long Day's Journey Into Night,' 'The Seagull,' 'Foxfire,' 'The Beggar's Opera' 1980; 'A' films incl. 'The Wars' (Dir.); 'Miss Julie' (Dir.); 'Decline and Fall' (actor); 'David Copperfield' (title role); 'Tales from the Crypt'; Dir., 'Virginia,' Haymarket Theatre, London, England 1980–81; Dir., World Première of 'Farther West,' Calgary, 1982; Dir., 'The Jeweller's Shop,' Westminster Theatre, London, England 1982; Apptd. Artistic Dir., Grand Theatre Co., London, Ont. Sept. 1982; Dir., for Grand Theatre Co. 'Timon of Athens,' 'Waiting For the Parade,' 'The Doctor's Dilemma,' 'Dear Antoine,' 'The Club,' 'Arsenic and Old Lace,' 'The Prisoner of Zenda,' for CentreStage Co., Toronto; 'Tonight at 8:30,' for National Arts Centre, Ottawa 1983–84; 'New World' 1984; for CentreStage Co., Toronto, 'New World' 1985; Apptd. Dir., Young Company, Stratford Festival Theatre (Can.) 1986; directed: 'Cymbeline,' 'As You Like It,' 'Romeo and Juliet,' 'Journey's End,' Stratford 1987; 'Twelfth Night,' 'King Lear,' 'Oedipus,' 'The Critic,' Stratford 1988; 'A Midsummer Night's Dream,' 'The Crucible,' Edmonton 1989; 'The Philadelphia Story,' London, Ont. and Edmonton 1990; 'Richard III' New York Shakespeare Festival 1990; Apptd. Dir. General, Citadel Theatre, Edmonton 1990; 'Never The Sinner' and 'The Mousetrap,' Edmonton 1991; 'Aspects of Love,' Edmonton and Toronto 1991 and National Tour U.S.A. 1992; 'Romeo and Juliet' and 'Democracy,' Edmonton 1991; 'Lend Me A Tenor,' 'Fallen Angels,' 'Oedipus,' 'Black Comedy,' 'Invisible Friends,' 'The Royal Hunt of the Sun,' 'Hamlet,' 'As You Like It' (Edmonton 1992), 'Man of La Mancha' (Edmonton 1992 and Toronto 1993); 'La Bete,' 'The Two of Us,' 'She Stoops to Conquer,' 'Saint Joan' (Edmonton 1993); 'King John' (Stratford Festival 1993); 'The Marriage of Figaro' (Candn. Opera Co., Toronto 1993); 'Oliver!' Edmonton 1993; 'Cyrano de Bergerac,' 'Macbeth' Edmonton 1994; 'Hay Fever' Winnipeg and Edmonton 1994; recreation: painting; Office: The Citadel Theatre, 9828 - 101A Avenue, Edmonton, Alta. T5J 3C6.

**PHILLIPS, Roderick Goler,** B.A., M.A., D.Phil.; university professor; b. Auckland, N.Z. 14 July 1947; s. Athol Goler and Joanna Emma (Baillie) P.; e. Westlake Boys H.S.; Trent Univ. B.A. 1971; Otago Univ. N.Z. M.A. 1971; Oxford Univ. D.Phil. 1975; divorced; one d.: Zoë Alexandra Quinn-Phillips; PROF., DEPT. OF HISTORY, CARLETON UNIV. 1989– ; N.Z. Post-Grad. Scholar to Oxford 1973–75; Sr. Lecturer, Univ. of Auckland 1976–83; Asst. Prof., Queen's Univ. 1983–86; Assoc. Prof., Brock Univ. 1987–89; Swedish Inst. Fellow, Uppsala Univ. 1983; Rsch. Achievement Award, Carleton Univ. 1992–93; Hon. Mention, Wallace K. Ferguson Prize 1989; Walter Prescott Webb Memorial Lecturer, Univ. of Texas at Arlington 1990; Fellow, Cambridge Group for the History of Population and Social Structure, Univ. of Cambridge 1994; Visiting Fellow, Univ. of New South Wales, Australia 1995; recipient of var. univ., institutional, govt. & SSHRCC rsch. & travel grants to Australia 1984, '90, 92, France 1981, '84, '85, '89, England 1987, Norway 1982, N.Z. 1986, Taiwan 1992, SSHRCC strategic research grant 1993–96; Fellow, Newberry Library Chicago 1988; Fellow, Cambridge Group for the History of Population and Social Structure, Cambridge Univ. 1994; Mem., Candn. Historical Assn.; Western Soc. for French Hist.; Soc. for French Hist. Studies; author: 'Family Breakdown in Late Eighteenth-Century France' 1980; 'Divorce in New Zealand' 1981; 'Putting Asunder: A History of Divorce in Western Society' 1988; 'Untying the Knot' 1991 (various foreign language editions) and var. pamphlets, articles & reviews; editor: 'Marriage and the Family in History' 1994; Home: 278 Holmwood Ave., Ottawa, Ont. K1S 2R3; Office: Ottawa, Ont. K1S 5B6.

**PHILLIPS, Roger,** B.Sc.; executive; b. Ottawa, Ont. 17 Dec. 1939; s. Norman W. F. and Florence Elizabeth (Marshall) P.; e. McGill Univ. B.Sc. 1960; m. Katherine Ann, d. George Wilson, June 1962; one d. Andrée Claire; PRES. AND C.E.O., IPSCO INC. 1982– ; Dir., IPSCO Inc.; The Toronto-Dominion Bank; joined Aluminum Co. of Canada 1960, Asst. to Treas. 1965, Gen. Mgr., Sheet and Plate 1967; Vice Pres., Mill Products, Alcan Canada Products Ltd. 1970, el. a Dir. 1972, Extve. Vice Pres. 1974; Vice Pres., Research, Engineering, and Technology, Alcan Aluminum Ltd. 1980–81; Pres., Alcan International Ltd. 1980–81; Co-Chrmn., Candn. Steel Trade and Employment Congress; Past Chrmn., Council for Candn. Unity; Pres. and Dir., Mel Williamson Foundation; Dir., Inst. for Saskatchewan Enterprise; Public Policy Forum; Candn. Steel Producers Assoc.; Dir., Candn. Labour Market and Productivity Centre; Sask. Chamber of Commerce; Sr. Mem., Conference Bd. Inc. (New York); Mem., Business Council on National Issues; Candn. Assoc. of Physicists; Canada-U.S. Relations Ctte. of Candn. and U.S. Chambers of Commerce; Canada-France Business Relations Club; Nat. Bd. of Adv., AISEC Canada Inc.; Adv. Bd., Western Centre for Economic Rsch.; Club: University; St. Denis; Assiniboia; Home: 3220 Albert, Regina, Sask. S4S 3N9; Office: P.O. Box 1670, Regina, Sask. S4P 3C7.

**PHILLIPS, Ross F.,** F.C.A.; corporate consultant; b. Winnipeg, Man. 21 Oct. 1926; s. Albert Sidney and Olive Ford (Hawkin) P.; e. Daniel McIntyre Coll. Inst., Winnipeg; Univ. of Man.; m. Mary Robinson, d. John Langan King, 28 July 1956; children: David Ferguson, Janet King; Dir., Halifax Ins. Co.; Western Union Insurance Co.; IWG Canada; Trans Alta Utilities Corp.; Trans Alta Corp.; Deutsche Bank (Canada); NN Life Ins. Co. of Canada; Student in Accountants, Millar Macdonald & Co., Winnipeg, 1943; Internal Auditor, Traders Finance Corporation, Toronto, 1949; joined Home Oil Co. as Chief Acct. 1953, Comptroller 1959, Vice Pres.-Adm. 1966, Sr. Vice Pres. Finance 1971, Pres. and Dir. 1973, Pres. and Chief Extve. Offr. Oct. 1973–80 (ret.); Hon. Dir., Calgary Exhibition and Stampede Ltd; mem. Insts. C.A.'s Man. (Fellow mem. 1977) & Alta. (Fellow mem. 1988); Clubs: Glencoe; Earl Grey Golf; Ranchman's; Calgary Petroleum; recreations: golf, swimming; Home: 6925 Lefroy Court S.W., Calgary, Alta. T3E 6H1; Office: Suite 1510, Bow Valley Square II, 205 5th Ave. S.W., Calgary, Alta. T2P 2V7.

**PHILLIPS, Roy A.,** C.M., B.A.Sc., P.Eng.; business executive; b. Vancouver, B.C. 18 May 1918; s. Arthur and Jane Patricia (Little) P; e. Univ. of B.C., B.A.Sc. 1939; m. Barbara Lee, d. Cecil Everett Avis, 24 May 1941; children: Robert N., Gordon A., Catherine L., Nancy L.; PRES., ROY PHILLIPS ADVISORY SERVICES INC.; Engr., Switchgear Dept., Canadian General Electric Co., Peterborough, 1939–49; Chief Engr., Montreal Works, 1949–52; Mgr. Product Planning, Maj. Appliance Dept., 1952–57; Mgr. Marketing, Appliance Div., 1957–64; Pres., Taylor Pearson Carson Ltd. and Taylor Pearson Carson (BC) Ltd., 1964–66; Dir., Prairie Pacific Distributors Ltd., 1964 and Vice-Pres. and Dir., 1965–66; Pres., Prairie Pacific Distributors Western Ltd., Edmonton, 1965–66; Pres., Motor Car Supply Co. of Canada Ltd., Calgary, 1965–66; Vice-Pres., RCA Ltd. 1967–75; Dir. 1968–75; mem. Extve. Comte. of Bd. of Dirs. 1969–75; Corp. Planning 1967; Gen. Mgr. Consumer Electronics & Appliance Div. 1968–74; Consumer Relations 1975; Pres. and Extve. Dir., Candn. Manufacturers' Assn. 1975–84; served with 4th Field Batty. (Reserve) and 4th H.A.A. Batty. (Reserve) during 2nd World War; rank Maj.; Pres., Electronics Industs. Assn. Can. 1968–69, Chrmn. 1969–70; Pres., Intnl. Organization for Standardization 1989–91; mem., Adv. Comte. on Inmate Employment, Correctional Service of Can.; Dir., West End Creche, Toronto; Corp. for Internat. Settlements (Can.) Ltd.; The Candn. Nat. Exhibition Assn.; Mem., Adv. Bd., The Retirement Strategies Group; Mem., Minister's Advisory Council, Candn. General Standards Board; recipient, Member, The Order of Canada; Queen's Jubilee 1975; 125th Anniversary of the Confederation of Canada Medal, 1992; Paul Harris Fellow, Rotary Internat.; Hon. Life Fellow, Standards Engineering Soc.; Life Mem. The Candn. Manufacturers' Assn.; mem., Standards Counc. of Can.; Engn. Inst. Can. (Vice-Pres. 1963–64; mem. Council 1960–64); Corp. Engrs. Que. (Vice-Pres. 1956; mem. Council 1952–56); United Church; Clubs: Forest & Stream; National; Rotary Club of Toronto (Pres. 1987–88); Home: 2180 Marine Dr., Suite 2002, Oakville, Ont. L6L 5V2; Office: Box 466, Oakville, Ont. L6J 5C5.

**PHILLIPS, Stephen Henry;** hotelier; b. Perth, Australia 10 Jan. 1949; s. Evernden Hugh Noel and Barbara Ann (Forster) P.; e. Milton Coll. Bulawayo, S.Rhodesia C.O.P. 1965; A.H. & M.A. Ednl. Inst. East Lansing, Mich. C.H.A.; m. T. Siobhan d. Stephen and Theresa Rigby 26 Aug. 1988; children: Alexis, Simon (by previous marriage), Cailin, Meaghan, Brighid; PRES. HOWARD JOHNSON HOTELS CANADA 1989– ; joined Westin Hotels Vancouver 1965–73; Hyatt Internat. Hotels 1973–78; Delta Hotels 1978–88, Gen. Mgr. and subsequently Vice Pres.; Carlton Internat. Hotels 1988–89, Pres.; mem. Bd. Trade Metrop. Toronto; Hotel Assn. Metrop. Toronto (Dir.); recreations: skiing, golf, tennis, squash; Clubs: Skal; Variety; Home: R.R. 2, Bradford, Ont. L3Z 2A5; Office: 40 Progress Court, Scarborough, Ont. M1G 3T5.

**PHILLIPS, Timothy Adair;** artist; b. Toronto, Ont., 12 March 1929; s. William Eric and Doris Delano (Smith) P.; e. Upper Can. Coll., Toronto, Ont. (Sr. Matric. 1945), pre-med. course, Univ. Academy Simi, Italy and Academy Julien, Paris; also studied with Pietro Annigoni in Italy and Salvador Dali in Spain; m. Helen Gertrude, d. Clarence Lockwood, 11 June 1966; children: Melissa, Melinda; awarded prize, O'Keefe's Young Can. Competition, Art, 1950; one-man show, Upper Grosvenor Gallery, London, Eng., 1963 and then at Galerie Ror Volmar, Paris, 1964; Hon. Mention in the Paris Salon, 1963 and 67; one-man shows at Collectors' Gallery, London, Eng., 1964; Harrovian Gallery, London, Eng., 1974; Flair Gallery, Palm Beach, Fla., 1973, 1977; Ontario Place, Toronto, Ont.; R. M. Gallery, Toronto, 1972, 1973, 1974, 1975, 1976; KAR Gallery, 1978; TAPPA Gallery, Toronto, 1982; Dir., Ont. Inst. of Painters; Conservative; New Apostolic; recreation: swimming; Studio: 476 Richmond St. W., Toronto, Ont. M5V 1Y2.

**PHILLIPS, William James Arthur,** B.A., M.Ed.; consultant; education association executive (retired); b. Collingwood, Ont. 26 Sept. 1936; s. William Vincent and Hazel Vera (Thomas) Phillips; e. Riverdale Coll. Inst. 1954; Toronto Teachers' Coll., teaching cert. 1955; Univ. of Toronto, B.A. 1960; Ont. Inst. for Studies in Edn., M.Ed. 1969; m. the late Joan d. Alexander and Jessie McAllister 20 Aug. 1960; children: Suzanne, Laura; m. Sophia d. William and Eva Zahumeny 19 Sept. 1992; Consultant, Second Career Program Ltd. 1991–92; Teacher, Toronto Bd. of Edn. 1955–67; Master, Ont. Teacher Edn. Coll. 1967–79; Admin. Dir., York Univ. Fac. of Edn. 1979–80; Extve. Staff Mem., Ont. Pub. School Trustees' Assn. 1981–88 (Extve. Dir. 1985–88); Mem., E. York Bd. of Edn. 1972–85 (Chrmn., 1976, 1979, 1983–85; Vice-Chrmn. 1975, 1977); Metro. Toronto Sch. Bd. 1975–76, 1979, 1983–85; Extve. Dir., Ont. Pub. Sch. Trustees' Assn. 1986–88; Associate Extve. Dir., Ontario Public School Board's Assn. 1989–90; Pres., Ont. Teacher Edn. Coll. Fac. Assn. 1978–79; Toronto Elementary Sch. Sci. Assn. 1965–66; Extve. Mem., Sci. Teachers' Assn. of Ont. 1965–70; Candn. Paraplegic Assn. Merit Award 1981; OSSTF Diamond Jubilee Award 1979; Chair, Confederation of Resident and Ratepayer Assocs., Toronto 1994– (Vice-Chair 1989–93); Secy.-Treas., Harbourfront Residents Assn. 1990–92 (Vice-Pres. 1988–90); Secy., Harbourfront Community Centre 1994– (Treas. 1991–93); Treas., Windward Co-op. Homes 1987–89, 1991–92, Pres. 1987, Dir. 1985–89; Chrmn., Metro. Toronto United Way Allocations Sub-Ctte. 1975; E. York Spec. Edn. Adv. Ctte. 1981–85; E. York Community Serv. Bd. 1973; E. York Soc. Planning Counc. 1972; Chapel in the Park Un. Ch. Bd. of Elders 1965–66, 1967–79, 1973; Dir., Thorncliffe Pk. Comm. Orgn. 1969–85; author: Viewpoint Column, Thorncliffe Pk. Bulletin 1972–82; Sci. Sect., Candn. Teacher Mag. 1966–79; editor, Ontario Education Mag. 1986–88; recreations: skiing, gardening, walking; Home: 21 Dale Ave., Suite 621, Toronto, Ont. M4W 1K3.

**PHILLIS, John Whitfield,** D.V.Sc., Ph.D., D.Sc.; educator; b. Trinidad, W.I. 1 Apr. 1936; s. Ernest and Sarah Ann (Glover) P.; e. Kings Sch. Canterbury, Eng. 1951; Canberra High Sch. Australia 1952; Univ. of Sydney B.V.Sc. 1957, D.V.Sc. 1976; Australian Nat. Univ. Ph.D. 1961; Monash Univ. Melbourne D.Sc. 1970; m. Shane Beverly d. Frederick Wright, Bedford, Eng. 24 Jan. 1969; PROF. AND CHRMN. OF PHYSIOL. WAYNE STATE UNIV. since 1981; Lectr. and Sr. Lectr. Monash Univ. 1963–69; Visiting Prof. Ind. Univ. 1969; Assoc. Prof. and Prof. Univ. of Man. 1970–73, Assoc. Dean of Med. Univ. of Man. 1971–73; Prof. and Head of Physiology, Univ. of Sask., 1973–81; Asst. Dean Univ. of Sask. (Med.) 1973–75; Wellcome Visiting Prof., Tulane Univ. 1986; author 'The Pharmacology of Synapses' 1970; Ed. 'Veterinary Physiology' 1976; Ed. 'Adenosine and Adenine Nucleotides as Regulators of Cellular Function' 1991; 'The Regulation of Cerebral Blood Flow' 1993; Co-Ed. 'Physiology and Pharmacology of Adenosine Derivatives' 1983; Ed. 'Progress in Neurobiology'; mem. Ed. Bd. 'General Pharmacology'; mem. Med. Research Council Scholarship Comte. 1973–74, Neurological Science Comte. 1974–79; mem., Scientific Adv. Bds.; Dystonia Medical Research Foundation (1980–84); World Soc. for the Protection of Animals (1981– ); Am. Heart Assn. of Michigan Rsch. Peer Review Ctte. 1985–89, Rsch. Ctte. 1991–93, Rsch. Forum Ctte. 1992– ; served with Australian Nat. Service and Citizens Mil. Forces, rank Lt. 1955; mem. Candn. Physiol. Soc. (Pres. 1978–79); Brit. Physiol. & Pharmacol. Socs.; Soc. for Neuroscience; Internat. Brain Research Organ.; Am. Physiol. Soc.; Anglican; recreations: squash, cycling, fishing, reading, riding; Office: Wayne State Univ., School of Medicine, Detroit, Michigan, USA 48201.

**PHILOGÈNE, Bernard Jean Ruffier,** B.Sc., M.Sc., Ph.D., FESC; university educator and administrator; b. Mauritius 4 May 1940; s. Pierre Raymond and Marie Simone (Ruffier) P.; e. St. Andrew's Sch., Mauritius 1959; Univ. de Montréal, B.Sc. 1964; McGill Univ., M.Sc. 1966; Univ. of Wisconsin, Ph.D. 1970; m. Hélène d. Maxime and Suzanne Lebreux 7 July 1964; children: Simone, Catherine; VICE-RECTOR (ACAD.), UNIV OF OTTAWA 1990– ; Rsch. Offr., Candn. Forestry Serv. 1966–69; Rsch. Sci. 1970–71; Asst. Prof., Dept. of Plant Sci., Univ. of B.C. 1971–74; Asst. Prof., Biology, Univ. of Ottawa 1974–77; Assoc. Prof. 1977–83; Prof. 1983– ; Vice-Dean, Sci. & Eng. 1982–85; Acting Dean 1985–86; Dean, Fac. of Sci. 1986–90; Cons., Internat. Devel. Rsch. Ctr., Candn. Internat. Devel. Agency; U.N. Environ. Program; Orgn. of Am. States; Agence de Coop. Culturelle et Tech.; Radio-Can.; Vis. Prof., Univ. de Sherbrooke 1980; Louisana State Univ. 1981; Vis. Sci., Can.-France NRC Program 1981; Can. Czechoslovakia NSERC program 1984; Mem., Ont. Pesticides Adv. Ctte. 1987–91; Mem., Extve. Ctte., Council of Ont. Univs. 1989–91; Pres., National Consortium of Scientific Socs. 1992–94; Roman Catholic; Mem., Entomol. Soc. of Can. (Fellow 1980); of Ont.; Candn. Pest Mngt. Soc.; Entomol. Soc. of Am.; Am. Inst. of Biol. Sci.; Assn. Can.-Française pour l'avancement des Sci.; Officier, Ordre des Palmes Académiques; Home: 648 Gaines Dr., Gloucester, Ont. K1J 7W6; Office: Univ. of Ottawa, P.O. Box 450, Stn. A, Ottawa, Ont. K1N 6N5.

**PHILPOTT, David G.;** real estate executive; author; b. White Plains, N.Y. 10 Aug. 1927; s. Wilbur Morgan and Ruth (Goodwin) P.; came to Canada, 1931; e. Jarvis Coll. Inst., Toronto, Ont.; Univ. of Toronto; m. Dorothy Joanne Strong, d. Dr. Warren O. Stoddart, Toronto, Ont., 30 May, 1984; children (previous marriage): Stephen Ross, Wendy Ruth; Dir. & Pres., D.G. Philpott & Assoc. Ltd.; Dir., MD Realty Fund (Chrmn.); Scotia Synfuels Ltd.; The Caledon Ski Club (Pres.); The Ballet Opera House Corp. (President); mem. The Writers' Union of Canada; Metro Toronto Bd. of Trade; Began as Draftsman with Molesworth, Secord & Savage, Architects, Toronto, Ont., 1947; Construction staff, Colborne Construction Ltd. of Toronto, 1951; Principal Investments Ltd. 1952; Vice-Pres., Webb & Knapp (Canada) Ltd., 1957; Pres., Trizec Equities Ltd. (formerly Triton Centres Ltd.) 1963; Extve. Vice-Pres., The Cadillac Fairview Corp., 1981; Pres. & C.E.O. Mascan Corp. Ltd., 1984; author 'Dangerous Waters' 1985; recreations: sailing, cycling, skiing, tennis; Clubs; R.C.Y.C.; Caledon Ski; Home: 6 Moore Ave., Toronto, Ont. M4T 1V3.

**PHINNEY, R. Wendell;** b. Kentville, N.S. 16 Feb. 1926; s. Lewis Wendell and Lillian May (Andrews) P.; e. Kings Co. Acad., 1943; Mount Allison Univ., Business Adm. Dipl. 1944; children: Bruce Wendell, Joan Meredith; PRES. PHINNEY HOLDINGS LTD.; Mayor, Town of Kentville 1973–88; served with RCNVR 1944–45; Dir., N.S. Mun. Finance Corp.; Musical Dir. S.P.E.B.S.Q.S.A.; P. Conservative; United Church; Clubs: Lions (Past Pres.); Glooscap Curling (Past Pres.); Home: 7 MacDonald Pk. Rd., Kentville, N.S. B4N 1P2; Office: P.O. Box 931, Kentville, N.S. B4N 4H8.

**PHIPPARD, (John) Gary Thomas,** B.Math; executive, innovator, marketing strategist, catalyst; b. Toronto, Ont. 26 Feb. 1954; s. Robert Lancelot and Jessie Marie (Stevenson) P.; e. ECVI, Oshawa (Hons.) 1972 (Dist. Serv. Award) (Ont. Scholar); Univ. of Waterloo, B.Math (Hons. Comp. Sci. & Bus. Admin.) 1977; Royal Candn. Legion Scholarship; plus 5000 hours research & education 1978– ; m. Karan d. Richard and Jean Williams 1977; one d. Trisha Marie; PRES. & CHRMN., PHIPPARD AND ASSOC. 1983– and GM ADVERTISING SERVICES DIV. 1988–92 & GM A.S.H. TECHNOLOGY MARKETING 1990– ; Showroom Sales, Oshawa Wood Prod. 1968–72; Programmer/Analyst, General Motors Canada, Data Proc. H.Q. 1973–75; Tech. Analyst, SDI Assoc. 1976–77; Sr. Prog./Analyst, Sr. Systems Analyst, Cons., Sr. Proj. Mgr., Client Serv. Mgr., Recruiting Dir., Mgr. Bus. Devel., Br. Mgr. & Dir., Systemhouse Ltd. 1977–83; Vice Pres., Mktg., SNI Systems Network Inc. 1985–86; Mem., VISPAC 1981–82; CVCC 1981–83; VIA 1982–83; CIPS 1985–87; CIDC 1986–87; Ottawa Carleton Bd. of Trade 1986– ; OCEDCO 1993– ; Kanata Economic Development Task Force 1992– ; Vice Pres. & Dir., Kancar Community Daycares Inc. 1990– ; Dir., Rideau Valley Landowner Resource Center 1993– ; Chrmn., IRIS Cons. Ctte. 1982–83; Founding Extve. Dir., CVIA 1982; Royal Candn. Legion Scholarship; Mem., Spec. Adv. Ctte., Univ. of Waterloo 1982; Loyalist Coll. Curriculum Adv. Ctte. 1984–86; Mem., Univ. of Waterloo Alumni Assn. 1978– (Extve. 1987–89); Vol. Fundraiser, Kidney Found. 1984– ; Ctte. Mem., Barrhaven Community Assn. 1983–87; Bridlewood Community Assn. 1988– ; author & ed. cons.; conference speaker, educator and guest speaker (various) 1981– ; Roman Catholic; recreations: yachting, cottage, skiing, painting, woodworking, outdoors.

**PICARD, Alyre Joseph,** B.A., M.D., F.R.C.P.(C), F.I.B.A.; physician; b. Drummond, N.B. 7 Oct. 1942; s. Edmond Joseph and Arthimise (Laforest) P.; e. Univ. Moncton, B.A. 1962; Univ. Laval, M.D. 1967; m. Lucille, d. Georges Eugene Bédard, 29 June 1968; children: Lucie, Judith, Anne, Pierre, Agathe, François; DERMATOLOGIST; Interne, Jeffrey Hale's Hosp. (Quebec) 1967; Resident, Hôtel-Dieu de Québec 1968; C.S.P.Q./F.R.C.P.(C) 1972; began practice dermatology Hôtel-Dieu d'Alma (Alma, P.Q.) 1972; mem. Corp Proff. des médecins du Quebec; Candn. Med. Assn.; Candn. Derm. Assn.; Assn. des Méds. de Langue Française; Assn. Derm. P.Q.; Candn. Derm. Foundation; Univ. Laval Foundation; Am. Acad. Derm.; Internat. Soc. Trop. Derm.; Roman Catholic; recreations: fishing, hunting; Club: Onatchiway; Home: 322 Pente Douce, Alma, Que. G8B 1G8; Office: 725 chemin du Pont Taché Nord, Alma, Lac St-Jean, Que. G8B 5B7.

**PICARD, Ellen Irene,** B.Ed., LL.B., LL.M., LL.D.; b. Blairmore, Alta. 2 Feb. 1941; d. Norman Francis William and Irene Marie (Wells) P.; e. Univ. of Alta. B.Ed. 1963, LL.B. 1967, LL.M. 1980, LL.D. 1992; one s., Andrew; JUSTICE, COURT OF QUEEN'S BENCH (ALTA.) and DEPUTY JUDGE, SUPREME COURT OF THE NORTHWEST TERRITORIES; Asst. Prof. of Law, Univ. of Alta. 1972, Assoc. Prof. 1975–78, Assoc. Dean Fac. of Law 1974–75 and 1980–81, McCalla Prof. 1982–83; Hon. Prof. of Medicine; Hon. Prof. of Law; Barrister & Solicitor Matheson & Co. 1968–72; Examiner, Prof. Examination Bd. of Law 1975; Dir. Univ. of Alta. Health Law Project 1977–86; Cons. to Law Reform Comn. of Can., Alta. Med. Assn., Alta. Nurses Assn., Access Alta. (TV) 1977; mem. Law Soc. of Alta.; Candn. Bar Assn.; Edmonton Bar Assn.; Edmonton Medico-Legal Soc.; Liaison Ctte., Candn. Bar Assn. and Candn. Med. Assn. 1977; Chrmn. Candn. Assn. of Law Teachers, Section on Law and Med. 1976–79; Dir. and mem. Extve. Alta. Inst. of Law Rsch. and Reform 1975–79; mem. Ed. Bd. Health Law in Canada 1979; Vice-Pres., Law Reform Commission of Canada 1991–92; author: 'Legal Liability of Doctors and Hospitals in Canada' 2nd ed. 1984; 'The Doctor-Patient Relationship and the Law' in 'Doctors, Patients and Society' 1980; 'The Tempest of Informed Consent' in 'Studies in Canadian Tort Law' 1977; 'Dental Jurisprudence' 1976; winner Rotary Scholarship, First Class Standing Prize, Univ. of Alta.; Home Econ. Award; Assn. of Jewish Women Prize; Anglican; recreations: skiing, tennis, sailing; Home: 603 Romaniuk Rd., Edmonton, Alta. T6R 1A3; Office: Law Courts, Edmonton, Alta. T5J 0R2.

**PICARD, Laurent A.,** C.C. (1976), B.A., B.A.Sc., D.B.A.; b. Quebec City, Quebec 27 Oct. 1927; s. late Edouard and Alice (Gingras) P.; e. Laval Univ., B.A. and B.Phil. 1947, B.A.Sc. (Physics) 1954; Harvard Univ., D.B.A. 1964; m. Thérèse Germain, Oct. 1954; 4 sons; PROF., FAC. OF MANAGEMENT, McGILL UNIV., 1980– ; Chrmn. Bd., Le Devoir; Bd. of Dirs., Canagex Placements; Videotron; Tele-Metropole; Lombard-Odier Trust; Groupe Jean Coutu; Prof., Faculty of Comm., Laval Univ., 1955–59; Research Assoc. and Asst., Harvard Business Sch., 1960–62; Prof. and Assoc. Dir., l'Ecole des Hautes Etudes Commerciales, Univ. of Montreal, 1962–68; Extve. Vice-Pres. C.B.C. 1968–72, Pres. & C.E.O., 1972–75; joined Marine Industries Ltd. in sr. extve. capacity 1975; Dean, Faculty of Management McGill Univ., 1978–86; first Pres. of Commonwealth Broadcasting Assn.; mem. Comte. for Higher Educ., Superior Council of Educ. Que.; Past Pres., Research Comn. on Shoe Industry of Prov. of Que.; former Commr., Indust. Inquiry Comn. on St. Lawrence Ports; has provided research and consultative services for several industs. incl. aluminum, printing, electronics, chem., rlwy., paper and wood products; mem. Royal Commission on Concentration in the Newspaper Industry; mem. Royal Commission on the Economic Union & Dev. Prospects; Chrmn., Consultative Ctte. (created by the Prime Min.) on the Development of the Montreal Region; Companion of the Order of Canada; Club: Mount Bruno Golf Club; Home: 5602 Wilderton Ave., Montreal, Que. H3T 1R9; Office: Faculty of Management, McGill University, 1001 Sherbrooke St. W., Montreal, Que. H3A 1G5.

**PICHÉ, Marcel,** O.C. (1969), Q.C., B.A., LL.L.; b. Les Éboulements, Co. of Charlevoix, Qué. 16 Feb. 1914; s. Odilon and Antonia (Cousineau) P.; e. St. Louis de Gonzaque, Qué.; Semy. of Qué.; Univ. of Ottawa, B.A. 1935; Laval Univ., LL.L. 1938; Superior Sch. of Comm., Québec, Qué. (Accounting); m. Béatrice, d. Arthur Foster, Québec, Qué., 28 Sept. 1940; one d. Hélène; Counsel, Pouliot, Mercure; Vice-Chrmn. and Dir., Trust

Général Du Canada; Dir., Dieter Hugo Stinnes, Inc.; La Presse; ITT Industries of Can.; ITT Canada Ltd.; Chancellor and mem. Extve. Comte., Univ. of Montréal 1967–77, hon. member since 1978; Clerk-in-Law, Chauveau, Rivard & Blais, Québec, Qué., 1935; Jr. Partner 1938; called to the Bar of Qué. 1938; cr. K.C. 1949; Enforcement Counsel, W.P.T.B., Qué., 1941–44; practised law in firm of Piché & Flynn, Montréal, Qué., 1944; Dir., Jr. Bar Assn., Québec, 1943–44; Prof., Practical Works in Comm. Law, Univ. of Montréal 1952–58; winner of Médaille de Vermeille of French Govt., 1935; Gold Medal for Pub. Debating, Univ. of Ottawa 1935; Prés., Théatre Comn. of Student Assn., Laval Univ., 1937; awarded Order of Canada Medal, 1969; Doctorat Honoris Causa (Law) Univ. of Montréal, 1981; Emeritus Chrmn. of the Bd., Clinical Research Institute of Montreal; mem., Qué. Bar Assn.; Candn. Bar Assn.; Roman Catholic; recreations: reading, golf; Clubs: Mt. Bruno Country; St. Denis; Home: 6000 Deacon Rd., Ph C-7, Montréal, Qué. H3S 2T9.

**PICHETTTE, Claude,** B.A., M.Sc.Soc., D.ès Sc.Eco.; university executive; b. Sherbrooke, Qué. 13 June 1936; s. Donat and Juliette (Morin) P.; e. Univ. de Sherbrooke B.A. 1956; Laval Univ. M.Sc.Soc. 1960; Univ. Aix-Marseille France D.ès Sc.Eco. 1970; m. Renée d. Roger and Priscille Provencher 5 Sept. 1959; children: Anne-Marie, Martin, Philippe; CHIEF EXTVE. OFFR., INSTITUT ARMAND-FRAPPIER 1991– ; mem. Bd. Shermag Inc.; mem. Bd. RONA-DISMAT Inc.; Prof. Univ. de Sherbrooke 1960–70; Dir. Services des Affaires Financières, Ministère de l'Éducation Gouvernement du Qué. 1970–75; Vice Recteur Adm. & Finance Univ. du Qué. à Montréal 1975, Recteur 1977–86; Chief Extve. Offr.: La Société d'Entraide Économique 1986–87; La Financière Coopérants 1987–90; author 'Analyse Micro-Économique et Coopératives' 1972; Prés. Assn. des Économistes Québécois 1977–78; Club: St-Denis; Home: 745 Hartland, Outremont, Qué. H2V 2X5; Office: 531 boulevard des Prairies, P.O. Box 100, Laval, Qué. H7N 4Z3.

**PICK, Martin C.;** seed company executive; b. Hamilton, Ont. 31 Aug. 1939; s. Otto Walter and Marie Elisa (Jakesova) P.; e. Richmond Hill H.S. 1958; m. Denise d. Yvan and Madelienne Ouellet 18 Sept. 1965; children: Charles Thomas, George Anthony; CO-OWNER, PICKSEED CANADA INC. 1959– ; joined father's firm, Otto Pick Agricultural Services 1958 and assumed 50% ownership with lifelong partner (brother) Thomas Pick upon death of Otto Pick 1959; estab. W. Candn. Opn. in Manitoba 1960; estab. Am. affiliate with Thomas & Partner W. Kent Wiley in Oregon 1970; company estab. first Candn. indus. operated forage rsch. 1976; Mem., Candn. Seed Trade Assn. (served on all Cttes., Bd. & Pres. 1991–92); involved with num. govt. & industry cttes.; Volunteer Fundraiser, York Central Hosp.; Past Pres., Richmond Hill Squash Club; recreations: upland game hunting, photography; Home: R.R. 2, Cavan, Ont. L0A 1C0; Office: Box 304, Lindsay, Ont. K9V 4S9.

**PICKARD, Franklin George Thomas,** B.A., P.Eng.; mining executive; b. Sudbury, Ont. 10 Sept. 1933; s. Chester William (dec.) and Margaret Christine P.; e. Queen's Univ. B.A. 1957; m. Audrey Elaine Bull 29 Apr. 1967; two d. Barbara Elaine, Beverly Joan; PRES. AND C.E.O., FALCONBRIDGE LTD. 1991– ; Dir. Falconbridge Ltd.; Falconbridge Dominicana; Falconbridge Nikkelverk; Falconbridge Gold Corp.; Kidd Creek Mines Ltd.; Nickel Development Inst.; Mining Assn. of Canada; joined present Co. 1957, Strathcona Project Metall. Engr. 1964, Strathcona Mill Supt. 1967, Sr. Asst. Smelter Supt. 1974, Chief Metall. Engr. 1975–80; Dir., Metall. & Engn. 1980–82; Vice Pres., Metall. & Engn. 1982–89; Sr. Vice Pres., Metall. Opns. & Tech. 1989–90; mem. Assn. Prof. Engrs. Prov. Ont.; Candn. Inst. Mining & Metall. Engrs.; Am. Inst. Mining & Metall. Engrs.; P. Conservative; Presbyterian; recreation: golf; Club: Ontario; Keowee Key Golf & Country; Spring Lakes Golf; Home: 57 Weeping Willow Lane, Thornhill, Ont. L3T 3R9; Office: Suite 1200, 95 Wellington St. W., Toronto, Ont. M5J 2V4.

**PICKARD, George Lawson,** M.B.E., M.A., D.Phil., D.M.S. (Hon.), F.R.S.C.; educator; b. Cardiff, Wales 5 July 1913; s. Harry Lawson and Phoebe (Crosier) P.; e. Manchester Grammar Sch. Eng. 1932; Hertford Coll. Oxford Univ. B.A. 1935, M.A. 1947, Clarendon Lab. D.Phil. 1937; m. Lilian May d. late Ernest Perry 26 Apl. 1938; 2 children; DIR. INST. OF OCEANOGRAPHY, UNIV. OF B.C. 1958–79; Prof. of Physics since 1954; Emeritus Professor since 1979; Scient. Offr. Royal Aircraft Estab. 1937–42; Scient. Offr. Operational Research Sec. Coastal Command R.A.F. 1942–47, Sr. Scient. Offr. 1944, Princ. Scient. Offr. 1947; Assoc. Prof. of Physics Univ. of B.C. 1947–54; mem. Nat. Research Council Comte. Geodesy & Geophys. 1955–67; Bd. Mang. B.C. Research Council 1960–67; Fisheries Research Bd. of Can. 1963–72; Vice Chrmn. Internat. Coord. Group for Tsunami Warning System for Pacific 1968–75; Visiting Scient. Sec. d'Océanographie, Orstom, Nouméa 1967, 1970, 1975–76; Australian Inst. Marine Science 1976, 1981–86; served on numerous curriculum comtes. for schs. and univs.; served with R.A.F.V.R. 1944–47, Hon. Sqdn. Leader; rec'd Candn. Centennial Medal 1967; Queen's Silver Jubilee Medal 1977; J.P. Tully Medal, Candn. Meteorolog. & Oceanograph. Soc. 1987; author 'Descriptive Physical Oceanography' 1964, 2nd ed. 1974, 3rd ed. 1979, 4th ed. 1981, 5th ed. 1990; co-author 'Introductory Dynamical Oceanography' 1978, 2nd ed. 1983; numerous papers oceanography of fjord estuaries, equatorial oceanography, coral reef studies; Fellow, Am. Assn. Advanc. Science; mem. Am. Geophys. Union; Am. Soc. Limnology & Oceanography (Vice Pres. 1962–63); B.C. Acad. Science (Pres. 1956); Candn. Oceanographic & Meteorol. Soc.; recreations: flying, scuba diving; Home: 4546 W. Fifth Ave., Vancouver, B.C. V6R 1S7.

**PICKERING, Maj.-Gen. Alan,** C.M.M., C.D., B.Sc.; Canadian armed forces (retired); b. Wimbledon, Eng. 18 July 1929; s. late Robert Lawrence and Ethel (Hodgson) P.; came to Can. 1930; e. Sarnia (Ont.) Coll. Inst. & Tech. Sch. 1948; Royal Mil. Coll. Kingston 1953; Queen's Univ. B.Sc. (Mech. Engn.) 1954; R.C.A.F. Staff Coll. 1965–66; U.S. Navy War Coll. 1973–74; m. Margaret Anne d. late Thurlow Ward and Helen (Gill) Campaigne 12 Sept. 1953; children: Brian, Catharine, Lynda, Ellen; DIRECTOR GENERAL INFOSEC, COMMUNICATIONS SECURITY ESTABLISHMENT 1985; Air Cadet Sarnia (Optimist) Sqdn. 1943–48; R.C.A.F. (Supplementary Reserve) 1949–52. (Regular) 1952–68, Candn. Forces 1968–85; Pilot, 435 (Transport) Sqdn. Edmonton 1954–56, 115 Air Transport Unit, UN Emergency Force, Naples 1956–57; Instr., 4 (Transport) Operational Training Unit, Trenton 1957–61, 437 (Transport) Sqdn. 1961–62; Chief, Engn. Div., Gemini Target Vehicle, U.S. Air Force Space Systems Div. Los Angeles 1962–65; Dir. of Cadets & Mil. Training, Royal Mil. Coll. Kingston 1966–69; C.O., 404 Maritime Patrol Sqdn. Greenwood, N.S. 1969–72, Base Operations Offr. 1972–73, Base Commdr. 1974–76; Commdr., Aurora Program Detachment, Burbank, Cal. 1976–79; Commdr., Maritime Air Group, Halifax, N.S. 1979–82; Chief Intelligence and Security, National Defence Headquarters 1982–85; mem. Engn. Inst. Can.; R.C.A.F. Assn.; Armed Forces Communications Electronic Assn. (AFCEA); Candn. Intelligence and Security Assn.; United Church; recreations: golf, sailing, cross-country skiing; Home: 11 Sandringham Court, Nepean, Ont. K2J 2H9; Office: Ottawa, Ont.

**PICKERING, Edward Abram,** C.M., B.A.; b. Windsor, Ont. 20 June 1907; s. Abram James and Oliva (Charbonneau) P.; e. Windsor (Ont.) Coll. Inst.; McMaster Univ. B.A. 1928; m. late Miriam Margaret Drew 20 Oct. 1938 (d. 9 Mar. 1985); children: Janet Elizabeth Formanek, Alan Drew; Asst. Private Secy. to Prime Min. Mackenzie King 1929–38; Asst. to Gen. Mgr. C.B.C. 1938; joined the Simpsons organ. as Circulation Mgr. Mail Order Div., Toronto 1939; Gen. Mgr. Robert Simpson Western Ltd. Regina 1941; Gen. Supt. Employee & Public Relations, Robert Simpson Co. Ltd. Toronto 1950–52; Gen. Personnel Mgr. Simpsons-Sears 1953, Vice-Pres. Personnel 1958, Vice-Pres. Catalogue Order 1966–72; Chrmn. Council of Profit Sharing Industries 1958–66; Pres. Toronto Symphony 1964–67; Project Dir. Special Study Ont. Med. Assn. 1972–73; Chrmn. Ont. Health Disciplines Bd. 1974–82; Pres. Massey Hall 1972–88, and Roy Thomson Hall 1982–88; Club: Rosedale Golf; Home: 80 Highland Cres., Willowdale, Ont. M2L 1G9.

**PICKERSGILL, Right Hon. John W.,** P.C. (1953), C.C. (1970), M.A., M.Litt., LL.D., D.C.L.; b. Wyecombe, Ont. 23 June 1905; s. Frank Allan and Sara C. (Smith) P.; e. University of Manitoba, B.A. 1926 and M.A. 1927; Oxford University, 1927–29 (History); post-graduate studies at Oxford and Paris, summers, 1930–33, 1935 and 1937; m. Beatrice Landon (died 17 Jan. 1938), d. Dr. F.A. Young, Winnipeg, Man., 3 July 1936; 2ndly, M. Margaret, d. J.T. Beattie, Winnipeg, Man., 23 June 1939; children: Jane, Peter, Alan, Ruth; Lecturer in Hist., Wesley College, University of Manitoba, 1929–37; joined Dept. of External Affairs as Third Secy., 1937; served in various capacities in the Prime Minister's office, 1937 till appt. as Clerk of the Privy Council and Secy. to the Cabinet, June 1952–June 1953; sworn of the P.C. and appt. Secy. of State, June 1953; mem. H. of C. for Bonavista-Twillingate, 1953–67; Min. of Citzenship & Immigration, 1954–57; Secy. of State, Apl. 1963–Feb. 1964; Min. of Transport, Feb. 1964–Sept. 1967 when resigned as M.P.; Pres., Canadian Transport Comn. 1967 till retired 1972; author 'The Mackenzie King Record 1939–44' Vol. I 1960; Vols. II, III, and IV (with D.F. Forster) 1968–70; 'The Liberal Party of Canada' 1962; 'Le Parti Liberal' 1963; 'My Years with Louis St. Laurent' 1975; 'Louis St. Laurent' 1981; 'The Road Back, by a Liberal in Opposition' 1986; 'Memoirs' (Fitzhenry & Whiteside) forthcoming 1994; United Church; Home: 550 Maple Lane E., Rockcliffe Park, Ottawa, Ont. K1M 0N6.

**PICOT, Jules Jean Charles,** B.E., M.Sc., Ph.D.; educator; b. Edmundston, N.B. 23 July 1932; s. Joseph Ernest and late Marie Blanche (Lebel) P.; e. St. Francis Xavier Univ. Eng. Cert. 1953; Tech. Univ. of N.S., B.E. (Hons.) 1955; Mass. Inst. of Technol. M.Sc. 1957; Ecole Nationale Supér. de Mecanique et d'Aérotechnique, Poitiers, France 1958–59; Univ. of Minn. Ph.D. (Chem. Engn.) 1966; m. Mary Carol d. late John Adams Creaghan 25 Aug. 1956; children: Mary Nicole, Joseph Andre; PROF. OF CHEM. ENGN. UNIV. OF N.B., Chrmn. of Chem. Engn. 1969–76 and 1990–93; mem. Natural Sciences & Engn. Research Council Grants Comtes. (Chrmn., Chem. & Metall. Engn. Comte. 1974, 1967 Science Scholarship Comte. 1979); various Candn. Council Prof. Engrs. Accreditation Comtes.; various articles transport phenomena in polymers, technol. of aerial spraying insecticides; Owner, Effective Particle Technologies Ltd.; Fellow, Candn. Soc. Chem. Engn. (Past Dir.); mem. Assn. Prof. Engrs. N.B.; Am. Inst. Chem. Engn.; R. Catholic; recreations: cross-country skiing, golf; Home: 29 Simcoe Ct., Fredericton, N.B. E3B 2W9; Office: Fredericton, N.B. E3B 5A3.

**PIDDLESDEN, Derek,** B.Sc., C.A.; financial executive; b. England 17 Jan. 1952; s. Norman John and Dorothy Frances (Hogben) P.; e. Dover Grammar Sch. for Boys (Dover, Eng.) 1970; Univ. of Surrey, B.Sc. (1st class hons.) 1974; Inst. of C.A.s: England & Wales 1977, Alberta 1978, B.C. 1983; VICE PRES. & CHIEF FINANCIAL OFFR., PEOPLES TRUST COMPANY 1993– ; articled with Arthur Andersen & Co., London, Eng. 1974–78; emigrated to Edmonton, Alta. 1978; various acctg. & cons. roles primarily Controller with a finan. group in real estate finan. 1978–82; Depy. Chief Acct., Bank of B.C. 1982–84; Controller & Chief Finan. Offr., CanWest Trust 1984–87; Chief Finan. Offr., Confederation Trust 1988–89; Extve. Vice-Pres. & C.O.O. 1989–91; Pres., D. Piddlesden Consulting 1992–93; Fellow, Inst. of C.A.s England & Wales; H.S. Rugby Captn. & Basketball Capt.; Past Treas., Vancouver Cricket Club 1985–88; Mem., Alta. Inst. Conf. Ctte. 1981; recreations: squash, sailing, cricket; clubs: Terminal City, Vancouver Cricket, Vancouver Rowing; Home: 11250 Paterson Rd., Delta, B.C. V4E 2H2; Office: 14th Floor, 888 Dunsmuir St., Vancouver, B.C. V6C 3K4.

**PIELOU, Evelyn C.,** B.Sc., Ph.D., D.Sc.; biologist and writer; b. Bognor Regis, Eng. 20 Feb. 1924; came to Can. 1947; d. J.B. Hancock and Dorothy Holmes; e. Royal Naval Sch., Twickenham, Eng.; Univ. of London B.Sc. 1951, Ph.D. 1962, D.Sc. 1975; m. D.P. Pielou 22 June 1944; children: Ruth (Shapka), Richard, Frank; Research Scientist Candn. Dept. of Forestry, 1963–64; Research Scientist Candn. Dept. Agric., 1964–67; Visiting Prof., North Carolina State Univ., 1967; Visiting Prof. Yale Univ., 1968; Prof. of Biology, Queen's Univ., Kingston, 1968–71; Killam Research Prof., Dalhousie Univ., Halifax, 1971–74; Visiting Prof. Univ. of Sydney, Australia, 1974; Prof. of Biology, Dalhousie Univ., 1974–81; Oil Sands Environmental Research Prof., Univ. of Lethbridge 1981–86; author of 'Introduction to Mathematical Ecology,' 1969; 'Population and Community Ecology,' 1974; 'Ecological Diversity,' 1975; 'Mathematical Ecology,' 1977; 'Biogeography,' 1979; 'Interpretation of Ecological Data' 1984; 'The World of Northern Evergreens' 1988; 'After the Ice Age' 1991; other writings incl. over eighty research papers, review articles, book reviews, encyclopedia articles on mathematical ecology and evolutionary biogeography; Fellow of the Royal Soc. of Arts; awarded George Lawson medal of the Candn. Botanical Assn. 1984; Eminent Ecologist Award of Ecolog. Soc. of Am. 1986; Distinguished Statistical Ecologist Award of the Internat. Congress of Ecology 1990; Hon. LL.D. (Dalhousie) 1993; Hon. Life Mem., British Ecological Soc. 1993; recreations: hiking, canoeing, skiing, natural hist., gardening; Address: S130/C17, R.R.#1, Denman Island, B.C. V0R 1T0.

**PIEPENBURG, Willard Warren,** M.S., Ph.D.; educator; b. Reedsville, Wis. 6 Oct. 1922; s. Reynold A. and Esther (Otto) P.; e. Univ. of Wis., B.S. 1947, M.S. 1948; King's Coll., Cambridge Univ., Ph.D. (Hist.) 1951; UNIVERSITY PROFESSOR OF HISTORY, YORK UNIV. 1987, Prof. of History 1964–88, Emeritus and Senior

Scholar of the Univ. 1988– ; mem. Dept. of Hist., Univ. of Toronto, 1952–64; Assoc. Dean, Faculty of Arts at present Univ. 1964–71; Dir. Grad Programme in History 1971–80; Nuffield Fellow, U.K., 1961–62; Fullbright Fellow, Cambridge Univ., 1949–51; author, 'Twin Heritages,' 1967; also various articles and reviews in prof. journs.; Anglican; recreations: reading, travel; Home: 50 Quebec Ave., Toronto, Ont. M6P 4B4; Office: 4700 Keele St., North York, Ont. M3J 1P3.

**PIER, Jerome Roland,** B.S., P.Eng.; railway supply executive; b. Mt. Jewett, Pa. 25 June 1926; s. Jerome Warner and Gladys LeJune (Eshbaugh) P.; e. Pa. State Univ. B.S. (Mech. Engn.) 1950; m. Betty d. Clifford and Dorothy Simpson 7 Nov. 1953; children: Bruce, Donald, Clifford, LeJune; PRES., J.R. PIER & ASSOCIATES 1987– ; Dir., Cobra Canada Inc.; Extve. Vice Pres. Benn Iron Foundry Ltd.; Engr., WABCO, Wilmerding, Pa. 1950–64, Mass Transit Engn. Mgr. 1964–69, Propulsion Systems Sales Mgr. 1969–73; Mgr. Special Projects, Rohr Industries, Chula Vista, Cal. 1973, Program Mgr. Turboliner Div. 1974–76, Engn. Mgr. Rail Div. 1976–77; Mgr. Passenger/Transit Marketing, Westinghouse Air Brake, Wilmerding 1977–79, Mgr. Business & Product Planning 1979–80; Vice Pres. and Gen. Mgr., Wabco 1980–86 (Div. of Wabco Standard Inc.); Freemason; Shriner; Dir. Hamilton & Dist. Chamber Comm. (Chrmn., Transport. Comte.); Am. Soc. Mech. Engrs.; Am. Pub. Transit Assn.; Presbyterian; recreations: woodworking; Clubs: Toronto Railway (Dir.); Home: 238 Glen Afton Dr., Burlington, Ont. L7L 1G9.

**PIERCE, Max,** B.A., M.A.; financial executive; b. South Porcupine, Ont. 19 July 1940; Louis and Caroline (Urbanc) P.; e. Univ. of Windsor B.Comm.; Univ. of West. Ont. M.A. 1971; m. Maruta d. Janis and Alma Andzans 15 May 1965; children: Kristin Mara, Matthew Jon; SR. VICE-PRES., FINANCE, FARM CREDIT CORP. 1988– ; var. positions ending as Assistant Dir., Dept. of Finance, Govt. of Canada 1971–88; Mem., Financial Executives Inst.; recreations: sailboarding, skiing; Home: Regina, Sask.; Office: 1800 Hamilton St., Regina, Sask. S4P 4K7.

**PIERCE, Walter Stanley,** C.A.; real estate executive; b. Montréal, Qué. 20 Mar. 1933; s. Stanley and Emily Beatrice (Turner-Nash) P.; e. Verdun H.S. 1951; McGill Univ., pre-req. study for C.A.; C.A. 1960; m. Barbara Joan d. Thomas and Elsie Anthony 25 June 1955; children: Susan, Sherri, Lianne; PRES., BCE DEVEL. CORP. 1986– ; McDonald Currie & Co. (now Coopers Lybrand) 1951–59; Webb & Knapp Can. Limited 1959–64; ACI Prop. Corp. 1964–67; Vice-Pres. & Dir., Robert Morse Corp. Ltd. 1967–72; Pres., Vanmor Holdings Ltd. 1972–82; Sr. Vice-Pres., The Bentall Group 1982–86; Clubs: Vancouver; Terminal; Royal Montréal Curling; Home: 3067 Spencer Court, Vancouver, B.C. V7V 3C5.

**PIERCEY, George Charles,** C.M.M., E.D., C.D., Q.C.; b. Halifax, Nova Scotia 22 February 1919; s. William Drysdale and Annie Margaret (Forbes) P.; e. Dalhousie Univ., B.Com. 1938, B.A. 1939, LL.B. 1941; m. Geraldine May, d. Walter K. Peart, 11 May 1946; children: William, Catherine, Randall, Charles; Pres. & Mang. Dir., Piercey Investors Ltd.; Dir., Nova Scotia Savings & Loan Co. 1956–87, Pres. 1968–75, Pres. & C.E.O. 1975–79; Dir., Maritime Tel & Tel Co. 1968–89; Past Chrmn. Bd. of Govs. Dalhousie Univ.; called to Bar of N.S. 1941; cr. Q.C. 1967; served with RCA and Candn. Intelligence Corps in U.K., Italy and N.W. Europe, 1941–46; rank Capt.; served with Candn. Army Mil. 1948–72; Commdr., Mil. Area Atlantic 1970–72; rank Brig.-Gen.; Hon. A.D.C. to Gov. Gen. Can. 1965–73; Hon. Colonel 33 (Halifax) Service Bn. 1974–91; Dir., World Vision Canada 1977–90; Past Pres. Halifax Youth Foundation; Halifax Jr. Chamber Comm.; John Howard Soc. of N.S.; Royal United Services Inst. of N.S.; North British Soc. of Halifax; Hon. Pres., N.S. Army Cadet League; mem., Adv. Comm. to Director of Sr. Citizens Secretariat; Chrmn., N.S. Adv. Counc. on Heritage Property; Dir., The Army Museum, Halifax Citadel; mem., N.S. Barristers Soc.; Candn. Bar Assn.; Scot. Rite; P. Conservative; United Church; recreations: tennis, skiing, golf; Clubs: Saraguay; Ashburn Golf; Bd. of Trade; Home: 1470 Summer St., Apt. 602, Halifax, N.S. B3H 3A3; Office: 3100 Dutch Village Rd., Halifax, N.S. B3L 4G1.

**PIERS, Rear Admiral Desmond William,** D.S.C., C.M., C.D., D.Sc. Mil., K.C.L.J. retired naval officer; b. Halifax, N.S. 12 June 1913; s. late William Harrington and late Dr. Florence Maud (O'Donnell) P., M.D.; e. Halifax Co. Acad.; Royal Mil. Coll. 1930–32; Royal Naval Staff Coll. 1949; Nat. Defence Coll. 1951–52; m. Janet Macneill, d. late Dr. Murray Macneill, LL.D., M.A., Halifax, N.S., 2 Sept. 1941; one step d., Mrs. Conyers Baker (Caroline Anne Christine Aitken); joined R.C.N. as Cadet 1932; C.O., HMC Destroyer Restigouche and Escort Group Commander Fourth Candn. Escort Group on N. Atlantic convoy routes 1941–43; awarded D.S.C. 1943; C.O., HMC Destroyer Algonguin with Brit. Home Fleet, Scapa Flow, and participated in invasion of Normandy and convoys to N. Russia, 1944–45; (Commdr.), 1945; Extve. Offr. HMC Aircraft Carrier Magnificent 1947–48; Dir., Naval Plans and Operations, Naval Hdqds., Ottawa (Capt.) 1949–50; Asst. Chief of Staff (Personnel and Adm.) to Supreme Allied Commdr. Atlantic, 1952–53; Naval Dir., Nat. Defence Coll. (Commodore) 1953–55; C.O., HMC Cruiser Quebec, 1955–56; Sr. Candn. Offr. Afloat (Atlantic) 1956–57; Commandant, Royal Mil. Coll. Can., and Hon. ADC to His Excellency the Governor General 1957–60; Asst. Chief of Naval Staff (Plans, Operations & Intelligence) Naval Hdqrs., 1960–62; Chrmn. Candn. Defence Liaison Staff, Washington, D.C., and Candn. Rep. on N.A.T.O. Mil. Comte., (Rear Admiral) 1962–66; retired 1967; Agent-Gen. of N.S. in U.K. and Europe 1977–79; Freeman of the City of London, 1978; Hon. Doctor of Mil. Science, Royal Mil. Coll. of Can., 1978; Mem., Order of Canada, 1982; Knight Commander, Order of Saint Lazarus of Jerusalem; Chrmn., Candn. Corps of Commissionaires, N.S. Div. 1988; Mem. of Task Force on Military History Museum Collections 1990; mem. Bd., South Shore Community Service Assn.; Order St. Lazarus of Jerusalem; mem. Bd., 1969 Canada Games, VII Pan Am. Wheelchair Games; Last Post Fund; Fellow, Roy. Commonwealth Soc.; mem., Roy. Candn. Legion; Candn. Civil Liberties Assn.; Roy. United Services Inst. N.S.; Heritage Can.; Heritage N.S.; N.S. Naval Offrs. Assn.; Royal Candn. Naval Assn.; R.M.C. Club of Can.; Writers' Fed. of N.S.; Hon Troop Scouter, Fourth Halifax Scout Troup; Hon. Life Mem., Nat. Trust for Scotland; United Church; recreations: golf, tennis, figure skating, photography; Clubs: Halifax; Halifax Golf and Country; Maritime Seniors' Golf Assn.; Internat. Senior's Golf Inc.; Chester Golf, Curling, Tennis, Figure Skating; Home: The Quarter Deck, Chester, N.S. B0J 1J0.

**PIETROPAOLO, Domenico,** B.Sc., M.A., Ph.D.; university professor; b. Maierato, Italy 11 March 1949; s. Paolo and Maria Carmela (Spano) P.; e. Univ. of Toronto B.Sc. 1971, M.A. 1973, Ph.D. 1980; m. Laura d. Lino and Pia Springolo 12 Aug. 1972; one d.: Mariapia; ASSOC. PROF. OF ITALIAN AND DRAMA & ACADEMIC CO-ORD., GRAD. CENTRE FOR STUDY OF DRAMA, UNIV. OF TORONTO 1992– ; Mem., Assoc. Grad. Faculty, Ctr. for Comp. Lit.; Undergrad Co-ord., Dept. of Italian Studies 1984–87; Grad. Co-ord. 1988–89; Select Panel, Ont. Grad. Scholarship Prog.; Bd. of Dir., Soc. for Mediterranean Studies; Dante Soc. of Toronto (Past Pres.); Excellence in Teaching Award, Sch. of Cont. Studies, U. of T.; Edit. Bd. 'Biblioteca di quaderni d'italianistica'; Bd. of Edit. Advisors, 'Carleton Renaissance Plays in Translation' series; Candn. Ed., 'Studies in Medievalism,' 'Allegoria'; Assoc. Ed., 'Scripta Mediterranea'; author: 'Dante Studies in the Age of Vico' 1988 and num. papers in profl. journals; editor: 'The Science of Buffoonery' 1988; co-editor: 'The Enlightenment in a Western Mediterranean Context' 1984, 'Pirandello and Modern Theatre' 1992; Office: 214 College St., Toronto, Ont. M5T 2Z9.

**PIETRZAK, Ted,** B.A.; arts executive; b. Kitchener, Ont. 18 Sept. 1952; s. Walter S. and Jadwiga (Adamski) P.; e. Univ. of Guelph B.A. 1972; m. Marlene Longdon; one d.: Christina; DIRECTOR, ART GALLERY OF HAMILTON & BURLINGTON CULTURAL CENTRE; has worked in public gallery sectors since 1970; Pres., Ont. Assn. of Art Galleries 1983; Teacher, Humber College, Arts Admin. Prog. 1990, '91; active in boards, commissions and arts councils 1979– ; Office: 123 King St. W., Hamilton, Ont. L8P 4S8.

**PIETRZYKOWSKI, Tomasz,** Ph.D.; educator; b. Lodz, Poland 13 Sept. 1934; s. Henryk and Anna P.; e. Univ. of Warsaw M.A. 1954; Ph.D. 1960 Polish Acad. of Sci.; m. Glenys Allan, d. Gwen and James A. Rennie 26 Nov. 1979; children: Agnieszka Knox, Tara Kamala Slone, Tashi Alexandra; PROFESSOR, SCH. OF COMPUTER SCI., TECHNICAL UNIV. OF N.S. 1984– ; Chrmn. Prograph International Ltd.; Research Asst., Univ. of Warsaw 1953; Research Assoc., Inst. of Mathematical Machines, Polish Acad. of Sci. 1955; Head, Computer Applications Dept., Research Assoc. and Prof. 1960; Depy. Dir. 1962; Prof., Dept. of Computer Sci., Univ. of Waterloo 1968; Prof., Sch. of Computer Sci., Acadia Univ. 1980–84; author various conference papers and articles in profl. journals; Office: P.O. Box 1000, Halifax, N.S. B3J 2X4.

**PIGOTT, Jean;** executive; b. Ottawa, Ont. 20 May 1924; d. George Cecil and Margaret Jane Kelly (Cotter) Morrison; e. Ottawa Ladies Coll.; Albert Coll.; m. Arthur Campbell Pigott 8 Oct. 1955; children: John, David, Mary Jane; CHRMN., CONGRESS CENTRE 1993– ; Pres. & C.E.O., Morrison Lamothe Foods, 1967–76; former Dir. & mem. Audit Comte., Ont. Hydro, to 1976; Dir. of Candn. Devel. Corp. & mem. Audit Comte., to 1976; Dir. Candn. Council of Christians & Jews to 1976; former Chrmn. MacDonald Cartier Library; Chairperson, Ottawa Regional Hosp. Planning Council 1973–76; former Vice Pres. Local Council of Woman (Ottawa); el. by-election Oct. 1976 to House of Commons; Sr. Adv., to Prime Minister Joe Clark on Human Resource 1979; Chrmn. of Bd., Morrison Lamothe Inc. 1980–84; mem., Rt. Hon. Brian Mulroney's governmental transition team Sept. 1984–85; mem. Candn. Assn. of the Club of Rome; Publications: 'Feeding the Nation and the World' (working papr, Policy Committee, Leader of the Opposition) 1979; 'Special Interest Advocacy – a Right, a Necessity or a Danger?'; Bd. of Dir., Bens Bakery; Canadian Tire Corp.; Chrmn., Ottawa General Hospital Foundation; Trustee, Ottawa Gen. Hosp.; Gov. Carleton Univ.; Dir., Trillium Corp.; Centennial Medal (for work for Expo) 1967; Distinguished Service to the Business Community Award, Ottawa Bd. of Trade 1975; Award by Assn. des Détaillants en Alimentation, 1975; Queen's Jubilee Medal 1977; Kiwanis Club of Ottawa Citation as Outstanding Citizen of Ottawa & the Prov. of Ont. (Internat. Women's Year); Knight of the Golden Pencil Award 1978; B'Nai Brith Award of Merit 1987; Hon. Doctorate, Univ. of Ottawa 1988; Hon. Fellow, Royal Architectural Institute of Canada 1990; P. Conservative; Protestant; Clubs: Cercle Universitaire; Rideau (first woman mem.); Albany; Home: 29–255 Botanica Lane, Ottawa, Ont. K1Y 4P8; Country residence: Willow Creek, Gracefield, Que.; Office: 55 Colonel By Drive., Ottawa, Ont. K1N 9J2.

**PIGOTT, Paul Rex;** construction executive; b. Hamilton, Ont. 7 Apl. 1932; PRESIDENT, PIGOTT CONTRACTORS INC. 1982– ; Home: 615 Old York Rd., R.R #1, Waterdown, Ont. L0R 2H0; Office: #609 – 304 The East Mall, Islington, Ont. M9B 6E2.

**PIHL, Robert O.,** M.A., Ph.D.; educator; clinical psychologist; b. Milwaukee, Wis. 2 Feb. 1939; s. Howard Oscar and Evelyn Lorraine (Olander) P.; e. Lawrence Univ. Appleton, Wis. B.A. 1961; Ariz. State Univ., M.A. 1965, Ph.D. 1966; m. Sandra d. Rudoph and Marina Woticky 10 Oct. 1973; children: Christian, Eric; PROF. OF PSYCHIATRY, FACULTY OF MED. McGILL UNIV. 1983– , Prof. of Psychol. 1979– ; Dir. of Psychol. Lakeshore Gen. Hosp. Pointe Claire, Qué.; Co-Dir. Alcohol Studies Group, Douglas Hosp. – McGill Univ.; co-author: 'The Inherited Predisposition to Alcoholism: Characteristics of Sons of Male Alcoholics' 1990; 'Acute Alcohol Intoxication and Neuropsychological Functioning' 1990; 'The Etiology of Drug Abuse'; 'Alcohol and Aggression'; 'Prevention of Substance Abuse with Disruptive Children'; ed. 'Introduction to Abnormal Psychology' 1988; 'Selected Readings in Abnormal Psychology' 1990; Fellow, Am. & Candn. Psychol. Assn.; Home: 225 Bedbrook Ave., Montréal West, Qué. H4X 1S2; Office: 1205 Docteur Penfield Ave., Montréal, Qué. H3A 1B1.

**PIKE, Charles Ronald,** B.A.Sc.; transportation executive; b. Regina, Sask. 9 Dec. 1926; s. John Charles and Eleanor May (Robinson) P.; e. Univ. of B.C., B.A.Sc. 1950; Univ of W. Ont. Mgmt. Training Course 1967; m. Constance d. William and Colina Scobie 29 Sept. 1952; children: Catherine Mary, Susan Leah, Terence James; Sr. Mangmt. Consultant, CP Rail 1987–92, retired; Dir. Public Markets Ltd. 1982–87; The New Harding Group Ltd.; Continuous Colour Coat Ltd. 1983–89; The Industrial Applications of Microelectronics Centre Inc. 1983–89; Joined CP Rail, Eng. 1946, Supt. Toronto Div. 1969, Asst. Chief Eng. Montréal 1972, Dir. of Eng. Corporate Services Canadian Pacific Ltd. 1973, Chief Mech. Offr. CP Rail 1976, Vice Pres. Operation & Maintenance 1979; Vice Pres., Prairie Region CP Rail 1982–87; Dir. Can. Grains Council 1982–87; Bd. of Gov. and Extve. Ctte., Winnipeg Art Gallery (Pres. 1989–90) 1986–90; Councillor Winnipeg C. of C. 1984–85; mem. Transportation Council 1987–90; mem., Sr. Grain Transp. Ctte. 1982–87; Commdr. Order St. John; inducted into Saskatchewan Transportation Hall of Fame 1991; recreation: golf; Clubs: Royal Montreal Golf; St. Charles Country (Governor 1988–93); Peterborough Golf and Country Club; Home: Unit 7 - 689 Whitaker St., Peterborough, Ont. K9H 7K3.

**PIKE, Robert Marden,** B.Sc., M.Sc., Ph.D.; educator; b. Petersfield, Eng. 7 July 1937; s. Dennis John and Mary (Thompson) P.; e. Harvey Grammar Sch. Folkestone, Eng. 1956; London Sch. of Econ. Univ. of London B.Sc. 1959, M.Sc. 1961; Australian Nat. Univ.

Canberra Ph.D. 1965; m. Faye d. Ernest and Ferne Cumber 9 Dec. 1967; children: Eleanor Christina, Christopher John; PROF. OF SOCIOL., QUEEN'S UNIV. and Head of Sociol. 1978–89; Asst. Prof. of Sociol. Univ. of Alta. 1965–69; Rsch. Assoc. Assn. Univs. & Colls. Can. 1967–69; Assoc. Prof. of Sociol. present Univ. 1969; mem. Extve. Ctte. Candn. Soc. for Study Higher Edn. 1987–89, 1990–92; Queen's Academic Colleague to the Council of Ontario Universities 1992–94; author: 'Who Doesn't Get to University and Why' 1970; 'Part-Time Undergraduate Studies in Ontario' 1978; co-ed.: 'Socialization and Values in Canadian Society' 1975; var. articles on Education and on Mass Communications; United Church; recreations: walking, swimming; Home: 96 Richardson Dr., Kingston, Ont. K7M 2T1; Office: Dept. of Sociology, Queen's Univ., Kingston, Ont. K7L 3N6.

**PIKET, Diane Elizabeth,** B.A., LL.B.; lawyer; b. Winnipeg, Man. 6 July 1944; d. Alexander and Alma Amelia (Schmidt) Faulds; e. Univ. of B.C. B.A. 1967, LL.B. 1979; Simon Fraser Univ. Teaching Cert. 1968; LAWYER, MORAN & CO. 1979– ; Dir. Castlegar & Dist. Devel. Bd. 1986–93, Vice Chrmn. 1987–93; apptd. to Columbia River Adv. Ctte. 1989, Chrmn. 1990; Dir. B.C. Hydro & Power Authority 1989–92; Prov. Adv. Council Pub. Legal Edn. Soc. 1987; Dir., Selkirk College 1992– ; awarded Commemorative Medal for 125th Anniversary of Candn. Confederation 1993; Home: 815 5th Ave., Castlegar, B.C. V1N 1W9; Office: P.O. Box 3008, 1233 3rd Street, Castlegar, B.C. V1N 3H4.

**PILKINGTON, Marilyn L.,** B.A.(Hons.), LL.B., Hon. LL.D.; university professor and administrator, lawyer; b. Edmonton, Alta. 13 Nov. 1947; d. Wilfrid and Jean Smith (Currie) P.; e. Strathcona C.H.S.; Univ. of Alta. B.A. (Hons.) 1968; Univ. of Toronto LL.B. 1975; admitted to Bar of Ont. 1977; Law Soc. of U.C., Hon. LL.D. 1994; m. Wayne E. s. Gardiner and Jeanne Shaw 7 March 1970; children: Meredith Sarah, Robert Edward Pilkington Shaw; DEAN, OSGOODE HALL LAW SCHOOL OF YORK UNIV. 1993– ; Law Clerk to The Hon. Mr. Justice Judson, Supreme Court of Canada 1975–76; Litigation Assoc., Tory, Tory, DesLauriers & Binnington 1976–80; Assoc. Prof., Osgoode Hall Law School 1980– ; Mem., Candn. Human Rights Tribunal 1989– ; Chair, Bd. of Inquiry, Ont. Human Rights Code 1987–91; Special Adviser, Standing Ctte. on Fgn. Relns., Senate of Canada (constitutional issues relating to Free Trade Agreement) 1988; Consultant, Law Soc. of U.C. 1990–93; Mem., Cert. of Specialists Bd., Law Soc. of U.C. 1988– ; Research Team, Project on Public Inquiries, Ont. Law Reform Comn. 1991; Dir., Inst. for Rsch. on Public Policy 1972–78; Trustee 1978–88; Dir., Abbeyfild Houses Soc. of Can. 1988–90; Mem., Ont. Council on Univ. Affairs 1978–83; Ctte. on the Future Role of Univs. in Ont. (Fisher Ctte.) 1980–81; Candn. Assn. of Law Teachers Executive 1983–84; Athabasca Univ. (Founding Governing Authority) 1970–71; Pres., The Student's Union, Univ. of Alta. 1968–69; co-author: 'Canadian Business Corporations' 1975; author of articles on constitutional litigation topics; Home: 260 Douglas Dr., Toronto, Ont. M4W 2C1; Office: 4700 Keele St., North York, Ont. M3J 1P3.

**PILON, Jean-Guy,** B.A., LL.L. M.S.R.C. (1968), O.C. (1987); O.Q. (1987); auteur; né St-Polycarpe, 12 nov. 1930; fils Arthur et Alida (Besner) P.; é. Univ. Montréal, B.A. 1951; Univ. Montréal, LL.L. 1954; épouse: Denise Viens; enfants: François, Daniel; Revue Liberté (co-fondateur); Publications (poèmes): 'La Fiancée du Matin,' 1953; 'Les Cloîtres de l'Eté'; 1955; 'L'Homme et le Jour,' 1957; 'La Mouette et le Large,' 1960; 'Recours au pays,' 1961; 'Pour saluer une ville,' 1963; 'Comme eau retenue,' 1969; 'Saisons pour la Continuelle,' 1969 (Prix van Lerberghe); 'Silences pour une souveraine' 1972; 'Comme eau retenue' réédition augmentée 1986; Prix: David (poésie, 1957); Louise-Labé (1969); France-Canada (1969); Gouverneur Général du Canada (mai 1970); Prix Athanase-David (1984); Officier de l'Ordre du Canada (1987); Chevalier de l'Ordre national du Québec (1987); membre Soc. Royale du Canada; Officier dans l'Ordre des Arts et Lettres (France) 1992; Président de l'Académie des lettres du Québec; Président de la 'Rencontre québécoise internationale des écrivains'; Directeur des 'Ecrits du Canada français'; Résidence: 5724 Côte St-Antoine, Montréal, Qué. H4A 1R9.

**PIMLOTT, Norman Arthur,** C.L.U.; federal agency head, retired; b. Victoria, B.C. 4 July 1925; s. James William and Louisa (Rushby) P.; e. Victoria Elem. and High Schs.; Univ. of Toronto C.L.U. 1976; m. Ruth Kathline d. Alexander and Sarah Henderson 5 July 1947; children: R.W. Philip, Colleen R., Susan K.; served with RCNVR convoy N. Atlantic World War II; retail merchant; life ins. mgr.; estate planner; Alderman, Mun. of Oak Bay Victoria, B.C. 1969–79; Past Pres. Kiwanis of Oak Bay; mem. Pension Review Bd. 1979–87; Depy. Chrmn., Veterans Appeal Bd. 1987–90, Chrmn. 1990–91; Home: 1356 St. Patrick St., Victoria, B.C. V8S 4Y4.

**PINARD, Bernard,** M.N.A.; barrister; b. Drummondville, Que. 24 March 1923; s. Arthur and Yvonne (Lupien) P.; e. St. Frederic's Acad.; arts at Nicolet and Joliette Seminaries; Ottawa Univ. and Univ. of Montreal (law); special courses at the Internat. Univ. of Santander, Spain; Hon. Dr.'s degree, Faculty of Law, Sherbrooke Univ., 1966; called to the Bar of Que. 1950; m. Jacqueline, d. Leonidas Lamothe, Drummondville, Que., 18 Sept. 1954; children: Dominique, Elizabeth, Philippe; el. Pres., Young Liberals Assn. of Co. of Drummondville in 1951; el. to Que. Leg. for Drummond, 1952, def. 1956, re-el. 1960, 1962, 1966, 1970; Min. of Roads, Que., 1960–66 and Min. of Public Works and Transport 1970–73; apptd. Judge of Prov. Ct., 1973, Retired 1993; formerly Pres. of Tribunal of Trans. 1973–82; mem., Candn. Bar Assn.; membre, Conférence des Juges du Qué.; Association canadienne des Juges de Cours provinciales; Association québéçoise pour l'étude comparative du droit; formerly mem., Soc. of Concerts, Jeunesses, Musicales; Drummondville Chamber Comm.; hon. mem., Roy. Candn. Legion; former mem. Am. Right of Way Assn. and Commonwealth Parlty. Assn. (Que. Br.); Gov., Drummondville Recreation Centre; K. of C.; Clubs: former mem. Richelieu; des Francs; mem. Garrison (Quebec); Home: 2201 Ch.St-Louis, #403, Sillery, Qué. G1T 1P9.

**PINARD, Gilbert,** B.A., M.D., F.R.C.P.(C); psychiatrist; educator; b. Montreal, Que. 19 July 1940; s. Roland, Q.C. and Gaby (Laurendeau) P.; e. Loyola Coll. Montreal B.A. 1961; Univ. of Montreal M.D. 1965, Dipl. in Studies of Psychiatry 1970; m. Andrée d. Pierre Pouliot 17 Aug. 1963; children: Eric. Marc; PROF. AND CHRMN., DEPT. OF PSYCHIATRY, MCGILL UNIV. since 1986; Psychiatrist, Hôpital Louis-H. Lafontaine, Montreal 1970–76; mem. du Comité de Direction, Institut Nat. de Recherche Scientifique, Montreal 1974–76; Visiting Prof., Southwestern Medical School, University of Texas, 1982–83; Assoc. Dean, Education, Univ. of Sherbrooke 1983–85; mem. Planning Ctte., Fonds de la recherche en santé du Québec, 1987–89; mem., Evaluation Ctte., Royal College of Physicians & Surgeons of Canada 1988– ; author numerous publs. Scient. Research (Psychopharmacol.-Psycholinguistics); mem. Assn. des Psychiatres du Can./Candn.; Candn. Coll. Neuropsychopharmacol.; Assn. Profs. of Psychiatry; Orientation Ctte. Am. Assn. of Profs. of Psychiatry; Sci. Program Comm., Can. Psych. Assn.; Fellow, Am. Psychiatric Assn.; R. Catholic; recreations: sailing, skiing, tennis; Home: 3430 Peel St., Apt. 11-C, Montreal, Que. H3A 3K8; Office: 1033 Pine Ave. W., Montreal, Que. H3A 1A1.

**PINARD, Maurice,** LL.L. M.A., Ph.D.; sociologist; educator; b. Drummondville, Que. 25 Apl. 1929; s. J.-Ernest and Aline (Masson) P.; e. Univ. of Montreal B.A. 195l, LL.L. 1954, M.A. (Law) 1955; Johns Hopkins Univ. Ph.D. (Sociol.) 1967; m. Minola Saragea 10 June 1967; one s. Pierre; PROF. OF SOCIOL. McGILL UNIV.; author 'The Rise of A Third Party: A Study In Crisis Politics' 1971, enlarged ed. 1975; mem. Royal Soc. Can.; R.Catholic: Home: 3467 Vendome Ave., Montreal, Que. H4A 3M6; Office: 855 Sherbrooke St. W., Montreal, Que. H3A 2T7.

**PINARD, Raymond R.,** B.A., B.E.; consultant; b. Trois-Rivières, Qué. 13 May 1930; s. Albert and Mariette (Dufresne) P.; e. Laval Univ. B.A. 1951; McGill Univ. B.E. 1955; m. Estelle d. Antonio Fréchette; children: Andrée, Robert; PRES., R. PINARD CONSULTANT INC.; Gen. Mgr. Kraft Paper & Bd. Div. Domtar 1970, Gen. Mgr. and Vice Pres. Pulp Div. 1973 and Newsprint Div. 1975, Extve. Vice Pres. Pulp & Paper Products Group 1978; Pres., Pulp and Paper Products Group, 1979; Dir., Extve. Vice-Pres. & C.O.O. Domtar Inc. 1981–90; Mtl. Adv. Bd., National Trust; Dir. & Chrmn., Centre Canadien de Fusion Magnétique (CCFM); mem. Tech. Sec., Candn. Pulp & Paper Assn.; TAPPI; Engn. Inst. Can.; Dir. & mem. Extve. Bd., Klöckner Stadler Hurter (K.S.H.); SIDBEC; UAP; South Shore Industries Ltd.; E.F. Walter Ltd.; Past Chrmn. of the Bd., PPRIC; C.P.P.A.; Past Chrmn., C.M.A.; recreations: tennis, skiing, sailing, hunting, fishing, golf; Office: 1250 Blvd. René Lévesque Ouest, 45th Floor, Montréal, Qué. H3B 4W8.

**PINARD, Hon. Yvon,** P.C., B.A., LL.L.; federal court judge; b. Drummondville, Que. 10 Oct. 1940; s. Jean-Jacques and Cécile (Chassé) P.; e. Univ. of Sherbrooke, LL.L.; m. Renée d. Marcel and Juliette Chaput, Richmond, Que. 19 Dec. 1964; two d. Hélène, Andrée; JUDGE OF THE FEDERAL COURT OF CAN., TRIAL DIV. & MEM., EX OFFICIO, FED. COURT OF APPEAL 1984– ; sworn to Privy Counc. & apptd. Pres. of Privy Council and Govt. House Leader 1980–84; Pres., Sherbrooke Univ. Law Faculty 1963; called to Bar of Que. 1964; Pres. and Founder, Drummond Caisse d'Entraide Economique; mem. Adm. Council Centre Communautaire d'Aide juridique Maurice-Bois-Francs region; Gov., Hockey Can.; mem. Commonwealth Parlty. Assn.; Candn. Del. Interparlty. Union; el. to H. of C. for Drummond g.e. 1974, re-el. until 1980 (did not run 1984); Parliamentary Secy. to Pres. of Privy Council 1977; Address: Federal Court of Canada, Ottawa, Ont. K1A 0H9.

**PINDER, George Francis,** B.Sc., Ph.D.; educator; b. Windsor, Ont. 6 Feb. 1942; s. Percy Samuel and Stella Marie (Abbott) P.; e. Univ. of W. Ont. B.Sc. 1965; Univ. of Ill. Ph.D. 1968; m. Phyllis Marie d. Ivan Eugene Charlton, Aylmer, Ont. 14 Sept. 1963; children: Wendy Marie, Justin George; DEAN OF ENGINEERING AND MATHEMATICS, UNIV. OF VERMONT 1989– ; Prof. of Civil Engr., Princeton Univ. 1977– , Chrmn. of Civil Eng. 1980–89; RCA Prof. of Energy Resources 1975– ; joined N.S. Dept. Mines 1968; Rsch. Hydrologist, U.S. Geol. Survey, Water Resources Div. Atlantic Coast Region Arlington, Va. 1968–72; Assoc. Prof. of Civil Eng. Princeton Univ. 1972–77, Dir. Water Resources Prog. 1972–80; cons. various govt. and business orgns.; recipient Horton Award Am. Geophys. Union 1969; O.E. Meinzer Award Geol. Soc. Am. 1975; WUC Medal 1992; Fellow, Am. Geophysical Union 1993; selected Univ. of Vermont Scholar 1993; co-author 'The Finite Element Method in the Simulation of Surface and Subsurface Hydrology' 1977; 'Numerical Solution of Partial Differential Equations in Science and Engineering' 1982; 'Fundamental Concepts in the Numerical Solution of Differential Equations' 1983; 'Computational Methods in Subsurface Flow' 1983; 'Groundwater Contamination from Hazardous Wastes' 1984; 'Numerical Modelling in Science and Engineering' 1988; author or co-author numerous papers, articles, book chapters, reports; co-ed. 'Finite Elements in Water Resources' I 1977, II 1978, III 1980, IV 1982, V 1984; ed. 'Flow Through Porous Media' 1983; mem. various ed. Bds.; mem. Am. Soc. Civil Engs.; Soc. Petrol. Engs.; Am. Geophys. Union; Internat. Soc. Computational Methods in Eng.; Sigma Xi; Phi Kappa Phi Siam; Anglican; recreation: woodworking; Office: College of Engineering and Mathematics, Univ. of Vermont, Burlington, VT 05405.

**PINDER, Herbert Charles,** B.A., M.B.A.; merchant; b. Saskatoon, Sask., 26 April 1923; s. late Mary Helen Charlotte (Rose) and the late Robert Mitford P.; e. City Park Coll. Inst., Saskatoon, Sask.; Univ. of Sask., B.A. 1942; Harvard Grad. Sch. of Business Adm., M.B.A. 1947; m. Shirley Jean, d. late Allan P. Hughes, Regina, Sask., 25 Jan. 1946; children: Herbert C., Jr., Gerald, Richard, Thomas, Patricia; PRES., SASKATOON TRADING CO. LTD. since 1947 (operating Pinder's Drug Stores, Prairieland Drug Wholesale Ltd., Dir., The Royal Bank of Canada; John Labatt Ltd.; TransCanada PipeLines Limited; Western Shopping Centres Limited; Holnam Inc.; Lieutenant-Commander (retired), RCNVR; apptd. Min. of Industry & Econ. Devel. Sask. 1964; active in land and shopping centre devel. since 1956; Past Gov. and Bd. Chrmn., Univ. of Sask.; United Church; recreations: golf, hunting; Club: Kinsmen (Past Nat. Pres. 1953–54); Home: 1001 – 415 Heritage Cres., Saskatoon, Sask. S7H 5N1; Office: 102 Melville St. (Box 1648), Saskatoon, Sask. S7K 3R9.

**PINDER, Leslie Hall,** B.A., LL.B.; writer, lawyer; b. Elrose, Sask. 21 Sept. 1948; d. Raymond Leslie and Margaret Shirley (Rathwell) Hall; e. Univ. of Sask. B.A. 1968; Univ. of B.C. LL.B. 1976; PARTNER, MANDELL PINDER 1982– ; Lectr., Faculty of Arts, Univ. of British Columbia 1992–94; called to the Bar 1977; joined Ladner Downs (Vanc. law firm) 1976; worked as in-house legal council with Union of B.C. Indian Chiefs 1978–82; specializes in land claims; has been involved in major land claims litigation in Canada; Dir., Westwater Research, UBC; Bd. of Dir., View the Performing Arts Soc.; The Writers' Union; author: 'Under the House' Canada 1986, U.K. 1987, U.S. 1988, 'On Double Tracks' (Governor-General's Award Fiction nominee 1990) Canada & U.K. 1990 (novels); 'Isabel Rathbone' 1990, 'Emma Storrow' 1991 (dramatic monologues); short stories; currently comnd. to write Libretto for an opera, 'The World is as Sharp as a Knife' (with music composed by Bruce Ruddell); Home: 3672 West 15th Ave., Vancouver, B.C. V6R 2Z5; Office: 300 – 111 Water St., Vancouver, B.C. V6B 1A7.

**PINK, Darrel I.,** B.A., LL.B., LL.M.; association executive, lawyer; b. Yarmouth, N.S. 8 July 1953; s. Irving C. and Ruth M. (Goodman) Pink, Q.C.; e. Acadia Univ., B.A. 1975; Dalhousie Univ. LL.B. 1978; Univ. of London/London Sch. of Econ. LL.M. 1979; m. Elizabeth d. Anne and Jarad Mullaly 8 Dec. 1985; children: Kristen Glenister, Emma Pink, Nathan Pink; EXTVE. DIR., N.S. BARRISTERS' SOC. 1990– ; called to Bar 1979; practiced with Patterson Kitz Halifax 1979–90; Lectr., Dalhouse Law Sch. 1983– ; Mem. Bd. of Dirs., Metro United Way 1994– ; Pres., Children's Aid Soc. of Halifax 1986–88; Mem., Minister's Task Force on Family & Children's Serv. 1987–88; Extve. Mem., Candn. Jewish Congress (Former Vice-Chair, Law & Social Action Ctte.) 1982–92 and Mem. Constitution & Charter Review Ctte.; Home: 1169 South Park St., Halifax, N.S. B3H 2W9; Office: 1101 - 1645 Granville St., Halifax, N.S. B3J 1X3.

**PINK, Irving C.,** Q.C.; b. Yarmouth, N.S., 10 May 1913; s. Joseph and Rose (Safier) P.; e. Dalhousie Univ. (Arts 1934, Law 1936); L.L.D. (St. Anne's), 1977; m. Ruth Marilyn, d. Solomon and Jeanette Goodman, 19 Oct. 1938; children: Steven, Joel, Ronald, Darrel; SR. PARTNER, PINK, MACDONALD, HARDING; called to Bar of N.S. 1936; cr. Q.C. 1958; former Chrmn. Bd. Trustees Yarmouth Reg. Hosp.; former Pres., N.S. Union of Municipalities; N.S. Education Assoc.; former Vice Pres., N.S. Highway Safety Council; former Mem. Bd. Y.M.C.A. (now on endowment ctte.); N.S. Bar Soc.; Candn. Bar Soc.; Liberal; Hebrew; Club: Rotary; Home: 9 Seminary St., Yarmouth, N.S. B5A 2B3; Office: 379 Main, Yarmouth, N.S. B5A 4B3.

**PINKERTON, Peter Harvey,** M.D., Ch.B., FRCPath, FRCPE, FRCPG, FRCPC; university professor; b. Glasgow, Scotland 14 Feb. 1934; s. Herbert Harvey and Jean Watson (Kerr) P.; e. H.S. of Glasgow 1952; Univ. of Glasgow M.B.Ch.B. 1958; M.D. (Hons.) 1969; m. Mariane d. John and Mary Barbieri 29 July 1966; children: Toni Sinclair, Sandra Jennifer; HEAD, DEPT. OF LABORATORY HAEMATOLOGY, SUNNYBROOK HEALTH SCIENCE CENTRE 1967– ; Lecturer in Haematology, Univ. of Glasgow 1963–65 Visiting Asst. Rsch. Prof., Dept. of Med., State Univ. of N.Y. at Buffalo 1965–67; Asst., Assoc. & Full Prof., Depts. of Pathology & Med., Univ. of Toronto 1967– ; Chair, Mngt. Ctte., Laboratory Proficiency Testing Program, Ont. Med. Assn. 1985–92; Consultant, Ont. Cancer Treatment & Research Found. 1987– ; Bd. of Trustees, Sunnybrook Health Science Centre 1972–74, 1979–81, 1992– ; Mem., Internat., Am., Brit. & Candn. societies of Haematology; Bd. Mem., Internat. Council on Standardization in Haematology 1968–92; Mem., Scientific Advisory Bd., Candn. Blood Agency 1992– ; author/co-author of over 90 peer-reviewed or invited articles on var. aspects of disorders of the blood; recreations: golf, swimming, antiques & objets d'art; clubs: Royal & Ancient Golf, York Downs Golf & Country; Office: Room B204, 2075 Bayview Ave., Toronto, Ont. M4N 3M5.

**PINNELL, Owen Clifford,** P.Eng.; business executive; b. New Zealand 6 Jan. 1947; s. William Thomas and Darcie Agnes P.; e. Auckland Technical Inst. 1972; New Zealand Cert. in Engineering (Mech.); Profl. Engineer, Alta. 1980, B.C. 1992; m. Sal d. Nick and Hilda Spisic 15 Aug. 1981; children: Nicole, Michael; PRESIDENT & CHIEF EXECUTIVE OFFICER, ANADIME CORP. 1992– ; Project Engineer, Anglo American Corp. Zambia 1973–74; Design Engineer, Technip, Paris 1975–77; Sr. Engr. (var. positions & projects), Dome Petroleum Calgary 1978–82; Pres. & C.E.O., Newalta Corp. 1982–92; Dir., Coachlight Resources Ltd.; Anadime Corp.; New Zealand Bobsleigh & Skeleton Assn. 1989–91; Calgary Canadian Irish Athletic Club 1985–86; recreations: bobsled, skiing, golf; Home: 1705 Spyglass Cres., Tsawwassen, Vancouver, B.C. V4M 4E3.

**PINSENT, Gordon Edward,** O.C., LL.D.; actor; writer; director; b. Grand Falls, Nfld., 12 July 1930; s. late Stephen Arthur and Flossie (Cooper) P.; e. Grand Falls (Nfld.) Acad.; LL.D. University P.E.I. 1975; Hon. doctorate: Queen's Univ. 1988; Memorial Univ. of Nfld. 1988; m. Charmion, d. Charles W. King, Toronto, Ontario, 2 November 1962; one child, Leah King; stage experience includes Winnipeg Repertory Theatre, Man. Theatre Centre 1954–60 and in Toronto, Straw-hat Players, New Play Soc., Crest Theatre 1960–69; Stratford (Ont.) Shakespearean Festival 1962, 75; Nat. Arts Centre, Ottawa, Vancouver; other performances incl. radio, TV anthologies and series in Winnipeg, Toronto, Montreal, Los Angeles and N.Y.; Features in Canada; Hollywood and Greece; played role of Quentin Durgens, M.P., CBC TV for 3 yrs.; Wrote and performed, 'Gift to Last,' CBC series TV, 1976–79; performed as Ambassador Ken Taylor, 'Escape from Iran: The Canadian Caper' CTV-CBS, 1981; served with Royal Candn. Regt. 1948–51; author of screenplays & novels, 'John and the Missus' 1974 (also film), 'The Rowdyman' (also film) 1971; 'Easy Down Easy' (stageplay) 1987; 'By the Way' (memoirs) 1993; 'Brass Rubbings' (stageplay) 1989; Officer, Order of Canada, 1978; Winner of three Candn. Film Awards 1972, '80, '87 and two ACTRA Awards 1973, '79; Anglican; recreations: painting, hiking, swimming; Address: 130 Carlton St., PH 8, Toronto, Ont. M5A 2K1.

**PINSKY, Carl,** Ph.D.; university professor; b. Montreal, Que. 15 May 1928; s. Nathan and Dora (Yompolsky) P.; e. Baron Byng H.S. 1945; Sir George Williams Univ., B.Sc. 1954; McGill Univ., M.Sc. 1957, Ph.D. 1961; m. Shirley d. Sam and Edith Firth 18 June 1955; children: David Nathan, Ruth Rheva; PROF., DEPT. OF PHARMACOL. & THERAPEUTICS, UNIV. OF MANITOBA 1978– ; Asst. Prof., Dept. of Physiol., McGill Univ. 1961–62; Dept. of Pharmacol. & Therapeutics, Univ. of Man. 1962–67; Assoc. Prof. 1967–78; Mem., Applied Rsch. Group, Accelerator Ctr., Univ. of Man. 1980– ; Chair, Biomed. Rsch. Review Ctte. of NMUD Health & Welfare Can./Med. Rsch. Counc. Joint Ctte. on Rsch. on Drug Abuse 1976–78; Ctte. Mem., Med. Rsch. Counc. of Can., Ctte. on Toxicol. & Pharmacol. 1980–82, 1985–87; Mem., Strategic Grants Panel on Envir. Quality, NSERC 1989–91; Mem., Expert Advisory Panel, Candn. Network of Toxicology Centres 1992– ; Med. Rsch. Counc. Scholar (Canada) 1963–67; Founding Pres., Montreal Chapter on Biomedical Instrumentation of IEEE 1960; Founding Fellow, Candn. College of Neuropsychopharmacology; mem.: Internat. Narcotics Rsch. Conference (by invitation); Pharmacological Soc. of Can.; Chem. Inst. of Can.; Am. Soc. for Pharmacol. & Experimental Therapeutics; Ctte. mem.: Med. Rsch. Council (Canada) Ctte. on Toxicology & Pharmacol. 1980–82, 1985–87; Manitoba Health Rsch. Council Grant Review Ctte. 1985–86; Rsch. Review Ctte. of Non-Medical Use of Drugs (NMUD) Directorate joint Health and Welfare Canada/MRC program of Rsch. on Drug Abuse (RODA) 1973–76; Manitoba Health Products Adv. Ctte. of Manitoba Rsch. Council 1975–79; Biotechnology Council of Manitoba Rsch. Council 1976–79; Grants Review Ctte., Health Sciences Rsch. Found., Winnipeg 1984; Upjohn Award Ctte., Pharmacological Soc. of Can. 1983–84; Selection Ctte., RODA Summer Scholarship Program 1974; Rsch. on Drug Abuse (RODA) Summer Scholarship Program, Health & Welfare Can. 1972–73; Past Hon. Treas., Manitoba Mental Health Rsch. Found.; Founding Mem. & Past Secy. to Gov. Bd. of the Manitoba Environmental Rsch. Ctte.; mem., Faculty Extve. Council, Faculty of Med., Univ. of Manitoba; Dir. of Graduate Students, Dept. of Pharmacol. & Therapeutics, Univ. of Man. 1990– ; Ext. Reviewer: Alcoholism Found. of Man., Man. Health Rsch. Council, Alta. Mental Health Adv. Council, B.C. Health Care Rsch. Found., Ont. Mental Health Found., Health Sciences Centre Rsch. Found. (Winnipeg); numerous rsch. grants; numerous Job Training/Creation programs (Canada/Manitoba); radio & TV interviewee; numerous local and nat. showings of laboratory activities & scientific commentaries; mem., Chavurat Tefilah Synagogue (Halachic); Past Pres., Herzlia-Adas Yeshurun Synagogue; Past Sci. Cons., Lubavitch Chabad Mikveh; author of 97 pubns. in 43 different peer-reviewed journals covering a wide range of scientific areas (Arch Intern Med, Biochem Biophys Res Commun, Brain Research (4), Brain Res Bull, Br J Pharmacol (2), Can Anaesth Soc J (2), Can Dis Wkly Rpt (2), Can Nucl Soc, Cancer Detection and Prevention, Comp Gen Pharmac, Current Contents, Drug Dependence and Alcholism, EEG Clin Neurophysiol, Epilepsia Europ J Pharmacol (3), Exptl Neurol (2), J Appl Physiol, J Develop Physiol, J Environmental Science and Health (2), J Pharmacol Exptl Ther, J Neurochem, J Neurophysiol, Lancet, Life Sciences (7), Molec and Cell Biochem, Nature (6), Neurochem Res, Neuropeptides, Neurosci and Biobehav Rev, Neurosci Letters (2), NIDA Research Monographs, Nucl Instruments and Methods and Physics Res, Pharmacology Communications, Pharmacol Biochem Behav (2), Proc West Pharmacol Soc (3), Prog Clin Biol Res, Prog Neurophyschopharmacol Biol Psychiatr (4), Psychopharmacol, Res Comm Chem Pathol Pharmacol, Res Comm Psychol Psychiatr Behav (3), Scanning Microscopy, Toxicology Letters, Trends in Pharmacol Sci), 97 abstracts, 8 invited addresses to internat. symposia; recreations: mandolin (performance); clubs: Man. Table Tennis Assn. (Past Sr. Mem.); Home: 663 Jefferson Ave., Apt. 103, Winnipeg, Man. R2V 0P5; Office: 770 Bannatyne Ave., Winnipeg, Man. R3E 0W3.

**PINTAR, M. Mik,** M.Sc., Ph.D.; educator; b. Celje, Slovenia 17 Jan. 1934; s. Rihard and Milena (Kovac) P.; e. High Sch. Ljubljana, Slovenia; Univ. of Ljubljana Dipl. in Engn. Physics 1959, M.Sc. (Physics) 1964, Ph.D. (Solid State Physics) 1966; came to Can. 1966; m. Sandra Dawn d. James A. Burt, Port Carling, Ont. 1974; children: Richard, Katarina, Andrej; PROF. OF PHYSICS, UNIV. OF WATERLOO 1975– ; Dir., Waterloo NMR Center 1985– ; Research Fellow, Inst. J. Stefan, Univ. of Ljubljana 1957–66; Postdoctoral Fellow, McMaster Univ. 1966–67; Asst. Prof. 1967–69, Assoc. Prof. 1969–75; Convenor, Waterloo NMR Summer Inst. 1969–90 and 1st Candn. NMR Summer Institute 1993; Ed. and Co-author 'Introductory Essays-NMR Basic Principles and Progress' 1976; mem. Ed. Bd. 'Bulletin of Magnetic Resonance' 1981– ; author 160 research papers; mem. Candn. Assn. Physicists; Am. Phys. Soc.; Internat. Soc. Magnetic Resonance, (Counc. Mem., Secy. Gen. 1979–83); Ampère Soc.; recreations: skiing, canoeing; Home: R.R. #1, St. Agatha, Ont. N0B 2L0; Office: Univ. of Waterloo, Physics Dept., Waterloo, Ont. N2L 3G1.

**PIPE, Andrew Lawrence,** B.A., M.D.; physician; b. Nottingham, England 28 Feb. 1949; s. Donald William and Josephine (Frost) P.; e. Osnabruck Dist. H.S. 1967; Queen's Univ. B.A. 1970, M.D. 1974; m. Mary Gordon one s. Joshua Gordon; ASST. PROF., UNIV. OF OTTAWA HEART INST., OTTAWA CIVIC HOSP. 1980– ; Internship, Ottawa Civic Hosp. 1974–75; gen. practice, Levack, Ont. 1975–77; internat. travel 1977–79; Team Physician Nat. Basketball Team 1978– ; Nat. Alpine Ski Team 1980– ; Medical columnist, The Globe & Mail 1989–90; Mem., Premier's Counc. on Health Strategy, Prov. of Ont. 1987–91; Mem., Premier's Council on Health, Well-Being and Social Justice 1991– ; Mem., Sub Commission of the I.O.C. Medical Commission: Out-Of-Competition Drug Testing; Pres., Canadian Academy of Sport Medicine 1991–92; Mem., University Council, Queen's Univ.; Vice-Chrmn., Min. Adv. Group on Health Promotion 1985–87; Past Chrmn., Physicians for a Smoke-Free Can.; Chrmn., Nat. Adv. Ctte. on Drug Abuse in Amateur Sport 1987–91; Past Pres, Candn. Acad. of Sport Med.; Dir., Candn. Acad. of Sport Med. (Chrmn., Credentials Ctte.) 1983–93; Chrmn., Public Issues Ctte., Ont. Div., Candn. Cancer Soc. 1991–92; Chrmn., Candn. Centre for Drug Free Sport 1991– ; Mem., Nat. Public Issues Ctte., Candn. Cancer Soc. 1987–92; Fair Play commission 1986–92; Mem., Education Commn., Internat. Federation of Sports Medicine; Chief Med. Offr., Candn. Pan Am. Games Team 1987; Chief Medical Offr., Candn. Summer Olympic Team 1992; recipient Internat. Olympic Ctte. Award for Sport Medicine 1990; recipient, Canada 125 Medal; J.B. McReary Lectr., Univ. of B.C. 1991; J.B. Wolffe Lectr., Am. College of Sport Medicine 1992; Mem., Ont. (Past Chrmn., Section of Sport Med.) & Candn. Med. Assn.; College of Family Physicians of Canada; Candn. Assn. of Sports Sci.; Candn. Cardiovascular Soc.; Acad. of Sports Med.; Am. Coll. of Sports Med.; N.Y. Acad. of Sci.; F.I.B.A. Med. Ctte.; Ottawa-Carleton Med. Legal Soc.; Australian Coll. of Sports Physicians; Editorial Bd., 'The Physician and Sports Medicine'; Internat. Editorial Bd., 'Clinical Journal of Sport Medicine'; author/co-author of several articles; recreations: skiing, reading; Home: 513 Highland Ave., Ottawa, Ont. K2A 2J8; Office: 1053 Carling Ave., Ottawa, Ont. K1Y 4E9.

**PIPPERT, Ralph Reinhard,** B.A., M.S., Ph.D.; retired educator; b. Sheboygan, Wis. 23 March 1922; s. George Frederick and Louise Heartha (Berndt) P.; e. Mission House Coll., B.A. 1944; Univ. of Wis., M.S. 1950, Ph.D. 1959; m. Theresa Ann, d. Frank Fydenkevez, Hadley, Mass., 24 June 1967; children: Mark, Rolf, Eric, Dianne, Christine; Teacher, pub. sch. Wis. 1944; Prof. of Educ., Lakeland Coll., Wis., 1954; Prof. and Asst. Dean, Univ. of Mass., 1959; Prof. and Head Educ. Psychol., Univ. of Man., 1967; Chrmn., Counsellor Educ. Dept., S. Ill. Univ., 1970–71; Dean, Faculty of Education, Brandon Univ., 1972–77; Prof., Faculty of Education, Brandon Univ. 1977–88; author of various articles in prof. journs.; mem., Am. Psychol. Assn.; Candn. Personnel & Guidance Assn.; United Church; recreation: woodcarving; Home: 7 Grant Blvd., Brandon, Man. R7B 2L4.

**PIQTOUKUN, David Ruben;** artist; b. Paulatuk, N.W.T. 10 May 1950; medium: sculpture, drawings, prints, paintings; 24 group exbns. incl. most recent: Surrey Art Gall. B.C. 1992, Art Space Gall. Philadelphia, Pa. 1991, Vancouver Inuit Art Soc. 1991, York Quay Gall. & Leo Kamen Gall. (Earth Spirit Fest.) Toronto 1991, Candn. Mus. of Civilization Hull, Que. 1990; solo exbns.: Expo 1986, N.W.T. Pavilion Vancouver 1986, Family Hall Inuvik, N.W.T. 1983, Gall. of B.C. Arts Vancouver 1974, Arctic Arts Ltd. Edmonton, Alta. 1973; works in 9 collections incl. art galleries of Ontario (Klamer Family Coll.) and Winnipeg, Candn. Mus. of Civilization, Inuit Cultural Inst. Rankin Inlet, N.W.T., Staatliche Museum fur Volkerkunde Munich, Germany; cultural grant 1975; guest speaker, Third Eskimo Art Conf. Ottawa 1980; Mem., Candn. Eskimo Arts Council 1980–83; travelled to Abidjan, Ivory Coast at invitation of Dept. of External Affairs to participate in Canada week; Can. Council Exploration Grant 1984; carved an Inukshuk to commemorate 1st Native Business Summit 1986; painting given as gift to UNESCO 1988; Teacher, 3rd Experimental Stone Workshop 1988; one of eleven artists chosen to participate 3rd Biennial Native Am. Fine Arts Invitational Phoenix, Az. 1987–88; Mem., UNESCO's Candn. Ctte., World Decade of Cultural Devel. 1989; attended opening 'Masters of the Arctic' N.Y. 1989; attended artists-in-residence program, Altos de Chavon Arts Ctr., Dominican Republic 1989; comnd. to create sculpture for Telefilm Can. H.Q. 1989; participant, 'Partnership Workshops,' Inst. of Cultural Affairs, Oaxtepec, Morelos, Mexico; subject of several articles and catalogues; Home: Toronto, Ont.; Office: c/o Paulatuk Fine Art, 132 Lytton Blvd., Toronto, Ont. M4R 1L4.

**PITBLADO, James B.,** B. Comm., M.B.A.; investment dealer; b. Winnipeg, Man. 27 May 1932; s. Edward Bruce and Esther (Johnson) P.; e. Univ. of Manitoba B.Comm. 1953; Wharton Sch. of Fin. & Comm., Univ. of Pa. M.B.A. 1956; m. Sandra d. Owen and Emma Ellinthorpe 10 May 1958; children: Wendy, Diane, David, Jamie, John; HONORARY CHRMN., RBC DOMINION SECURITIES INC. 1992– ; Investment Dept. Great West Life Assurance Co. 1953–54; Research Anal., Merrill Lynch Pierce Fenner & Smith, N.Y. and Toronto 1956–59; Inst'l. Equity Dept., Harris & Partners 1959–73; Extve. Vice-Pres. & Dir., Dominion Securities Ames 1973–81; Chrmn., RBC Dominion Securities 1981–92; Past Chrmn., Investment Dealers Assn. of Can. 1978–79; Past Mem. Bd. of Gov., Toronto Stock Exchange 1968–71; Chrmn. Bd. of Trustees, Hosp. for Sick Children; Dir. Household Financial Corp. Ltd.; Chrmn., National Ballet of Canada; Past Pres. Canadian Club of Toronto; Clubs: Toronto; Mount Royal (Mtl.); recreations: running, skiing, tennis; Address: 4 Cluny Dr., Toronto, Ont. M4W 2P7.

**PITCHER, Comnr. Arthur Ralph;** retired Salvation Army; b. Winterton, Nfld. 30 Oct. 1917; s. Jacob and Clara P.; e. Salvation Army High Sch. St. John's; Meml. Univ. Coll. St. John's; Sch. for Offrs. Training St. John's; m. Elizabeth d. Charles and Jessie Evans 26 Aug. 1942; children: David, Eleanor, Donald; teacher Nfld.; Prov. Youth Secy., Salvation Army, Nfld. 1945–49, C.O., Windsor, Chatham, Edmonton, Vancouver, Youth Secy. S. Ont. 1961–62, Prov. Secy. Nfld. 1962–64, Div. Comdr. Que. & E. Ont. 1964–68, Prov. Comdr. Nfld. 1968–72, Chief Secy. S. Africa 1972–76, Territorial Comdr. Caribbean 1976–79, S. U.S.A. 1979–82, Chrmn. Governing Council Can., mem., Adv. Council to Gen. 1981–84, Territorial Comdr. Can. and Bermuda 1982–84; author 'Memoirs of Peter' 1981; 'Memoirs of Paul' 1984; 'Christmas Remembered' 1985; 'Holiness in the Traffic' 1986; 'People of My Pilgrimage' 1989; 'The Set of the Sails' 1990; Home: 295 Cassandra Blvd., #715, North York, Ont. M3A 1V7.

**PITCHER, Charles G.,** B.A.Sc., P.Eng.; mining executive; b. 21 Oct. 1943; married; children: Mark, Christopher, Jonathan; EXTVE. VICE-PRES. & CHIEF OPERATING OFFR., HILLSBOROUGH RESOURCES LIMITED 1991– ; Miner, Iron Ore Co. of Canada / Brittania Cooper / Eldorado Uranium / Kilembe Copper / Craigmont Copper / Gulf Mt. Taylor 1962–74; Mining Engr., Bechtel Internat. (Australia, Chile, Canada, N. Africa) 1976–80; Teacher & Cons., Sir Sanford Fleming College 1980–83; Partner, Derry, Michener, Booth & Wahl 1983–90; Mem., Order of Engineers of Que.; Cons. Engr. of Ont.; Assn. of Profl. Engrs. of Ont.; Dir., Engineers Club of Toronto; Office: 120 Railroad St., Brampton, Ont. L6X 1G8.

**PITCHER, Patricia Cherie,** B.A., Ph.D.; university professor; b. Tillsonburg, Ont. 20 March 1950; d. William and Rosemary (McInerney) P.; e. Trent Univ. B.A. (Hons.) 1973; McGill Univ. Ph.D. 1992; m. Jean-Jacques s. Hervé and Jeanne Bourque 9 Oct. 1992; MANAGEMENT CONSULTANT AND PROFESSOR OF BUSINESS, ECOLE DES HAUTES ETUDES COMMERCIALES 1984– ; Rsch. Assoc., Ont. N.D.P. 1973–78; Dir. of Econ. & Public Affairs, Toronto Stock Exchange 1978–79; Sr. Vice-Pres., Candn. Fed. of Independent Business 1980–84; Past Dir., Artopex Internat. Inc.; Cambior Inc.; Imperial Life; Laurentian Gen.; Laurentian Group corp.; Gestion Laurentienne Inc.; C.D. Howe Inst.; Candn. Found. for Econ. Edn.; Candn. Fed. of Independent Business; author of numerous articles; recreations: tennis, snowshoeing; Home: Montreal, Que.; Office: 5255 Decelles Ave., Montreal, Que. H3T 1V6.

**PITERNICK, Anne Brearley,** B.A., F.L.A.; retired; librarian; educator; b. Blackburn, Eng.; d. Walter and Ellen (Harris) Clayton; e. Manchester Univ. B.A.; came to Can. 1956; m. George Piternick 6 May 1971; Prof. of Library & Info. Studies, Univ. of B.C. 1978–91; joined Univ. of B.C. Lib. 1956, Head, Science Div. 1960–61, Social Sciences Div. 1964–66, Asst. Prof. 1966–73, Assoc. Prof. 1973–78, Prof. 1978– , Assoc. Dean, Faculty of Arts 1985–90, mem. Senate 1969–72, Senate Lib. Comte. 1969–90, Secy. Faculty Assn. 1967–69; mem. Ctte. on Bibliog. and Information Services for the Social Sciences and Humanities, 1975–84, Chrmn. 1979–84; Nat. Lib. Adv. Bd. 1978–84; Social Sciences and Humanities Research Council of Can., Adv. Academic Panel, 1981–84; Nat. Adv. Cttee. on Culture Statistics, 1985–90 ; Visiting Professor, Graduate School of Library & Information Science, UCLA, Jan.-Mar. 1984; rec'd Queen's Silver Jubilee Medal 1977; Award for Special Librarianship in Canada, Candn. Assoc. for Special Libraries and Information Services 1987; UBC 75th Anniversary Medal 1990; Commemorative Medal for 125th Anniversary of Candn. Confederation 1993; Fellow, Council on Lib. Resources 1979–80; Pres., Candn. Library Assn. 1976–77; Research & Publications in information systems and services; Canadian bibliography; scholarly communication; recreations: music, cuisine; Home: 1849 W. 63rd Ave., Vancouver, B.C. V6P 2H9.

**PITFIELD, Hon. Peter Michael,** P.C., C.V.O., Q.C. (Fed.), B.A.Sc., B.C.L., D.E.S.D., D. Litt. (Hon.); SENATOR; b. Montreal, 18 June 1937; s. Ward Chipman and Grace Edith (MacDougall) P.; e. Lower Can. Coll., Montreal and Sedbergh Sch., Montebello, 1951; St. Lawrence Univ., B.A.Sc. 1955, D. Litt. (Hon.) 1979; McGill Univ., B.C.L. 1958; Univ. of Ottawa, D.E.S.D. 1961; m. Nancy Snow, Toronto 1971; children: Caroline, Thomas, Kate; MEMBER OF THE SENATE OF CANADA, 1982– ; Chrmn., Senate Ctte. on Security & Intelligence 1983–84; Clerk of Privy Council and Secy. to Cabinet 1975–79; 1980–82; read law with Mathewson, Lafleur & Brown, Montreal; called to the Bar of Quebec 1962; cr. Q.C. (Fed.) 1972; C.V.O. 1983; mem. of the Queen's Privy Council for Canada 1984; assoc. with Mathewson, Lafleur & Brown, Montreal, 1956–59; Adm. Asst. to Min. of Justice and Atty. Gen. of Can., Ottawa, 1959–61; Secy. and Extve. Dir., Royal Comn. on Publs., Ottawa, 1961–62; Attache to Gov. Gen. of Can. 1962–65; Secy. and Research Supvr. of Royal Comn. on Taxation 1963–66; joined Privy Council Office and Cabinet Secretariat Govt. of Can. 1965; Asst. Secy. to Cabinet 1967; Deputy Secretary to Cabinet (Plans) and Deputy Clerk of Privy Council 1969; Deputy Minister Consumer and Corporate Affairs 1973–74; Fellow Harvard Univ., 1974; MacKenzie King Professor of Can. Studies, Harvard Univ., 1979–80; Candn. Repr., UNGA New York 1983–84; Lieutenant, R.C.N.R. ret'd; Trustee, Twentieth Century Fund, New York; Dir., Power Financial Corp. 1984; Montreal La Presse, Journaux Trans-Canada Ltée 1985; Great West Life Assurance Co. 1986; Investors Group Ltd. 1986; Dir. & Vice Chrmn., Power Corp. 1984; mem. of Counc., Internat. Inst. of Strategic Studies (London, Eng.); mem., Canadian, Quebec and Montreal Bar Assns.; Candn. Institute of Public Adm.; Candn. Hist. Assn.; Candn. Pol. Science Assn.; Internat. Comn. Jurists; Am. Soc. Pol. & Social Science; Beta Theta Pi; Anglican; recreations: squash, skiing, reading; Clubs: University; Mount Royal (Montreal); Home: 54 Belvedere Cres., Ottawa, Ont. K1M 2G4; Office: The Senate of Canada, Rm. 604, Victoria Bldg., Ottawa, Ont. K1A 0A4.

**PITFIELD, Ward Chipman,** B.Comm.; b. Montreal, Que. 6 Sept. 1925; s. Ward Chipman and Grace (MacDougall) P.; e. Bishops Coll. Sch., Lennoxville, Que.; McGill Univ., B.Comm. 1948; m. Diana, d. William Sutherland, 26 Sept. 1953; children: Chipman, Elizabeth, John, David, Sally; SPECIAL ADVISOR & VICE PRESIDENT, CANADA DEVELOPMENT INVESTMENT CORPORATION; Chrmn. & Dir., Ginn & Co.; Pres. & Dir., Cartierville Financial Corp. Inc.; Chrmn. & Dir., Theatronics International Ltd.; Pres. & Dir., Canada Eldor Inc.; Fletcher Challenge Canada Ltd.; CAE Industries Limited; Trustee, Ontario Jockey Club; Former Chrmn. & Chief Extve. Offr., Pitfield Mackay Ross Ltd.; Former Chrmn., Dominion Securities Pitfield Ltd.; Career: joined Pitfield Mackay Ross Ltd. 1948; Chrmn. Investment Dealers' Assn. 1976–77; Retired Pres. & Dir., Candn. General Investments; Third Candn. General Investments; Candn. General Capital; community involvement: Retired Mem. President's Investment Advisory Ctte., Univ. of Toronto; after 25 yrs of service, Retired as Chrmn., Hosp. for Sick Children Foundation; Founding Mem., Metropolitan Convention Centre; Retired Dir., Candn. National Exhibition; The Young Naturalists Found.; Owl TV; served with the R.A.F. Transport Command 1942–44; Alpha Delta Phi; Anglican; recreations: fishing, shooting, golf, horse-racing and riding; Home: 32 Rose Park Crescent, Toronto, Ont. M4T 1P9; Office: Scotia Plaza, Suite 2703, P.O. Box 320, Toronto, Ont. M5H 3Y2.

**PITMAN, Walter George,** M.A.; educator; journalist; administrator; b. Toronto, Ont. 18 May 1929; s. late Ernest George and late Elsie (Kendrick) P.; e. Univ. of Toronto, B.A. 1952, M.A. 1954; m. Florence Ida, d. late Frank Collinge, 4 Sept. 1952; children: Wade George, Cynthia Lynn, Mark Donald, Anne Lorraine; Dir., Ont. Inst. for Studies in Education 1987–91; Chrmn., Task Force on Advanced Training, Min. of Colleges and Univs. 1991–92; Chrmn., Bd. of the Interim Waste Authority, Greater Toronto Region, Govt. of Ont. 1992–94; Head, Hist. Dept., Kenner Collegiate Inst., Peterborough, Ont., 1956–60; Assoc. Registrar, Assoc. Prof. of History and Dir. Part-Time Studies, Trent Univ., 1965–67; M.P. for Peterborough 1960–62; M.P.P. for Peterborough 1967–71; Weekly Columnist, Toronto Star 1971–74; Dean, Arts & Science, Trent University 1972–75; Pres., Ryerson Polytech. Institute 1975–80; Extve. Dir. Ont. Arts Council 1980–86; Officer, Order of Canada 1992; Order of Ontario 1991; rec'd McGill Univ., Doctor of Law (honoris causa) 1981; York Univ., Doctor of Law (honoris causa) 1989; Trent Univ., Doctor of Law (honoris causa) 1993; Brock Univ., Doctor of Law (honoris causa) 1993; Certificate of Merit, Ont. Psychological Foundation 1989; Centennial Medal 1967; Centennial Medal of O.R.T. 1980; Greer Award (OEA) 1980; Fellow, OISE 1976; Fellow, Ryerson Polytech. Inst. 1984; Fellow, Ont. College of Art 1991; Paul Harris Fellow 1991; Past Pres., Ont. Educ. Assoc.; Chairman, Metro Toronto Comte. on Hum. Rel's, 1977; Past Pres., Candn. Assoc. for Adult Educ., 1978–82; Past Pres., Candn. Civil Liberties Assoc., 1981–85; Bd. Chrmn., Elderhostel Can. 1986–91; Bd. Chrmn., Energy Probe 1986– ; Adv. on Coll. Gov. to Ont. Min of Coll. & Univ. 1986; Mem., Bd. of National Ballet of Canada 1991– ; Extve. Mem., Bd. of Toronto Mendelssohn Choir 1986; Chair, Toronto Mendelssohn Youth Choir 1987–91; NDP; United Church; recreations: choral music, sailing, canoeing, running, cross-country skiing; Home: 1023 Mount Pleasant Ave., Toronto, Ont. M4P 2L9.

**PITSIULAK, Lipa;** artist; b. 21 April 1943; medium: sculpture, drawings, prints; 73 group exbns. incl. most recent: l'Iglou Art Esquimau, Douai (toured 20 cities) France 1988–92, Vancouver Inuit Art Soc. 1991, Arctic Inuit Art Richmond, Va. 1991, The Upstairs Gallery Winnipeg 1991, Virginia Mus. of Fine Arts Richmond, Va. 1990–91; solo exbns.: Gallery Indigena Stratford, Ont. 1991, Gallery Phillip Don Mills, Ont. 1983, The Upstairs Gallery Winnipeg 1979; works in 12 collections incl. art galleries of Ontario (Sarick Coll.) and Winnipeg, Amway Environ. Found. Coll., Candn. Mus. of Civilization Hull, Que.; Inuit Cultural Inst. Rankin Inlet, N.W.T., McMichael Candn. Art Coll. Kleinburg, Ont., Nat. Gallery of Canada; 'Disguised Archer' reproduced as twelve-cent stamp issued 18 Nov. 1977; Explorations Grant, Canada Council 1984; subject of NFB film 1988; subject of articles and catalogues; Home: Pangnirtung, N.W.T.; Office: c/o Inuit Art Section, Indian and Northern Affairs Canada, Les Terrasses de la Chaudière, Ottawa, Ont. K1A 0H4.

**PITSULA, James Michael,** B.A., M.A., Ph.D.; university professor; b. Benito, Manitoba 13 Sept. 1950; s. Michael and Lucille (Picton) P.; e. Campbell Collegiate 1968; Univ. of Sask. B.A. (Hons.) 1972; York Univ. M.A. 1973, Ph.D. 1979; ASSOC. PROF., DEPT. OF HISTORY, UNIV. OF REGINA 1984– ; Lectr., Candn. History, Univ. of Winnipeg 1977–78; Lectr., Univ. of Regina 1978–79; Asst. Prof. 1979–84; Roman Catholic; author: 'Let the Family Flourish: History of the Regina Family Service Bureau 1913–1982' 1982, 'An Act of Faith: The Early Years of Regina College' 1988; co-author: 'Privatizing a Province: The New Right in Saskatchewan' 1990; Office: Regina, Sask. S4S 0A2.

**PITT, David George,** M.A., Ph.D., LL.D.; author; retired university professor; b. Musgravetown, Nfld., 12 Dec. 1921; s. Rev. Thomas J., D.D. and Edith Florrie (Way) P.; e. Pub. and High Schs. in Nfld.; Memorial Univ. Coll.; Mount Allison Univ., B.A. 1946 (magna cum laude), LL.D. (honoris causa) 1989; Univ. of Toronto, M.A. 1948, Ph.D. 1960; m. Una Marion, d. Rev. Wilfred J. and Ethel Woolfrey, 5 June 1946; children: Ruth Marion; Robert David; PROF. EMERITUS OF ENGLISH, MEMORIAL UNIV. OF NFLD. 1982– , Prof. of Eng. at present Univ. 1961–82 and Head of Dept. 1970–82; apptd. Assoc. Prof. of Eng. at present Univ. 1949; Nfld. Senior Jubilee Scholarship 1944; Humanities Rsch. Council Fellowship 1956; Can. Council

Senior Fellowship 1969; Univ. of B.C. Medal for Can. Biography 1985; City of Toronto Book Award Finalist 1985; Nfld. and Labrador Arts Council Artist of the Year Award 1989; ed. 'Here the Tides Flow' by E.J. Pratt 1962; 'Critical Views on Candn. Writers: E.J. Pratt' 1969; no. of sch. and univ. texts incl. Shakespeare and other Eng. classics; author 'Elements of Literacy' 1965; 'Windows of Agates' 1966, 2nd ed., rev. & enlarged 1990; 'E.J. Pratt: The Truant Years 1882–1927' 1984; 'Goodly Heritage' (with Marion Pitt) 1984; 'E.J. Pratt: The Master Years 1927–1964' 1987; 'Towards the First Spike: The Evolution of a Poet' 1987; 'Tales from the Outer Fringe: Five Stories and a Novella' 1990; numerous contrib. to 'The Encyclopedia of Nfld. and Labrador,' 'The Canadian Encyclopedia,' 'The Dictionary of Nfld. and Labrador Biography,' 'Encyclopedia of Post-Colonial Literatures in English,' other books and journals; mem., Humanities Assn. Can.; Assn. Univ. Teachers Eng.; United Church; Home: 7 Chestnut Pl., St. John's, Nfld. A1B 2T1.

**PITTMAN, Ronald Bruce;** film director; writer; b. Toronto, Ont. 4 Feb. 1950; s. Arthur Maurice and Edythe (Newell) P.; e. Royal York Coll.; Kipling Coll.; twenty five yrs. experience in film & tv prodn.; most recent films incl. 'Where the Spirit Lives' 1990 (winner of 25 internat. awards incl. Gemini Award Best TV Movie); last five years various episodes of 'E.N.G.,' 'Adderly' for CBS; 'Neon Rider,' 'Twilight Zone' for MGM; 'Road to Avonlea' for Disney; 'Beyond Reality,' 'Catwalk' for USA Network among others; 'The Painted Door,' 1985 (nom. for Acad. Award and winner of Best Drama Candn. Film & TV Assn. plus num. internat. awards); 'David' and 'Olden Days Coat' (C.F.T.A. Best Dramas 1982, 1981 respectively); 'Screaming Woman' 1986 and 'Let's Play Poison' 1991 (scripts by Ray Bradbury); other films have won many internat. awards; Mem., Directors Guild of Can.; Home: Toronto, Ont.

**PITTS, John W.,** B.Eng., M.B.A.; High Technology executive; b. Victoria, B.C., 13 Oct. 1926; s. Clarence H. and Doris L. (Wilson) P.; e. Brentwood Coll.; McGill Univ., B.Eng. 1949; Harvard Univ., M.B.A. 1951; m. Margaret B., d. K. E. Brunsdale, Minneapolis, 8 June 1951; children: Jennifer B., Cynthia M., Charles K.; PRESIDENT AND CHIEF EXTVE. OFFR., MacDONALD DETTWILER & ASSOCIATES LTD., since 1982; Dir., British Columbia Telephone Co.; Paccar Inc.; British Columbia Sugar Refining Co.; Canada Trust; joined Vancouver Iron & Engineering Works 1951–55; self-employed in own mfg. businesses: Spruce Specialties Ltd., Transco Mfg. Ltd. and S & V Manufacturing Ltd. 1955–70; Chrmn., Pres. & C.E.O., Okanagan Helicopters Ltd., 1970–1982; served with Candn. Army 1945; Alpha Delta Phi; Anglican; recreations: tennis, skiing, sailing, shooting; Clubs: Vancouver; Shaughnessy Golf and Country; Vancouver Lawn Tennis & Badminton; Home: 1742 W. 40th Ave., Vancouver, B.C. V6M 1W2; Office: 13800 Commerce Parkway, Richmond, B.C. V6V 2J3.

**PITTS, Thomas Douglas,** B.A., F.S.A., F.C.I.A.; insurance executive; b. Meaford, Ont. 7 July 1942; s. Beier and Olive P.; e. Univ. of Western Ont. B.A. 1964; Soc. of Actuaries F.S.A. 1971; m. Jeanne Sharon 27 July 1968; children: James Beier, David Thomas; SENIOR VICE-PRES., CANADIAN OPERATIONS, CONFEDERATION LIFE 1990– ; various positions, Confederation Life 1964–71; Mgr., Group Underwriting 1971; Consulting Actuary, Hansen Consultants 1974; Assoc. Treas., Excelsior Life 1977; Cons. Actuary, Tillinghast, Nelson & Warren 1980; Admin. Vice-Pres., Individual Insur., Confederation Life 1984; Vice-Pres., Group Pensions 1985–90; Canadian Operations 1990; Past Dir., Assn. of Candn. Pension Mngt.; Retirement Ctte., Royal Ontario Museum; Mem., Candn. Inst. of Actuaries 1971; Candn. Cancer Soc.; recreations: squash, golf, skiing, bridge; clubs: Wyldewood Golf & Country, Mount Pleasant Club; Home: 53 Lakeshore Dr., Etobicoke, Ont. M9V 1Z5; Office: 1 Mount Pleasant Rd., Toronto, Ont. M4Y 2Y5.

**PIVKO, Ivan B.,** Dipl.Eng., P.Eng., M.A.; business executive; b. L. Mikulas, Slovakia 24 Sept. 1941; s. Branislav Martin and Paula Maria (Roth) P.; e. Slovak Tech. Univ. Dipl.Eng. 1964; Univ. of Toronto M.A. 1972; m. Eva d. Zbynek and Zdenka Karas 4 June 1964; one d.: Ivana; PRES. & CHIEF EXECUTIVE OFFICER, MERFIN HYGIENIC PRODUCTS LTD. 1991– ; military service 1964–65; research engineer 1965–66; Teacher, Univ. of Toronto 1970–74; Engr., Rsch. & Mngt. positions, CPFP Tissue Operations 1974–90; Dir. of Sales & Chief Op. Offr., Merfin Hygienic Products Ltd. 1990–91; Dir., Merfin Canada Tissue Ltd.; Merfin Converted Products Ltd. and subsidiaries; Home: 2852 W. 1st Ave., Vancouver, B.C. V6K 1H4; Office: 7979 Vantage Way, Delta, B.C. V4G 1A6.

**PIZALE, John Joseph,** B.Sc., LL.B.; executive; lawyer; b. St. Catharines, Ont. 19 Aug. 1946; s. the late John Peter and Lucy Ann (Matej) P.; e. St. Michael's Coll. Univ. of Toronto B.Sc. 1967; Osgoode Hall Law Sch. LL.B. 1970; m. Jane d. Alexander G. and late Norah M. Rankin 20 Aug. 1977; children: J. Alexander, Ryan J., Jamie R., J. Whitney, Alexis N.; DIR. FAMOUS PLAYERS DEVELOPMENT CORP. LTD. 1984– ; Pres., Bedford House Limited; Chrmn., Web Offset Publications Ltd.; Dir., Data Networking Services Ltd.; Bedford House Publishing Ltd.; Bedford House International Limited; Simcoe Disposal and Recycling Inc.; called to Bar of Ont. 1972; lawyer and Mng. Partner Aird & Berlis 1972–84; former Instr. Real Property Sect. Bar Admission Course; former mem. Univ. of Toronto Blues, York Univ. Yeomen and Osgoode Hall Owls inter-coll. basketball teams; mem. Art Gall. Ont.; Candn. Bar Assn.; Medico-Legal Soc. of Toronto; Harbourfront Art Gallery; Sigma Chi; recreations: reading, travel, tennis; Club: Mississaugua Golf & Country; Office: Bedford House, 10 Carlson Court, Suite 600, Etobicoke, Ont. M9W 6L2.

**PLAA, Gabriel Leon,** M.Sc., Ph.D.; educator; b. San Francisco, Cal. 15 May 1930; s. Jean and Lucienne (Chalopin) P.; e. Univ. of Cal. Berkeley B.Sc. 1952, San Francisco M.Sc. 1956, Ph.D. 1958; m. Colleen Neva d. Harold Brasefield, Oakland, Cal. 19 May 1951; children: Ernest (d.), Steven, Kenneth, Gregory, Andrew, John, Denise, David; Prof. de Pharmacologie, Univ. de Montréal since 1968, Chrmn., Dépt de Pharmacologie 1968–80, Vice-Dean, Fac. des Études Supérieures 1979–82, and Vice-Dean, Fac. de Médecine 1982–89, Dir., Centre Interuniversitaire de Recherche en Toxicologie since 1990; Asst. Prof. of Pharmacol. Tulane Univ. Med. Sch. New Orleans 1958–61; Assoc. Prof. of Pharmacol. Univ. of Iowa 1961–68; served with US Army Reserve 1952–60, active duty Korea 1953, rank Lt.; rec'd Achievement Award Soc. Toxicol. 1967; Claude Bernard Medal Univ. de Montréal 1971; Thienes Mem. Award Am. Acad. Clin. Toxicol. 1977; Lehman Award Soc. Toxicol. 1980; Education Award Soc. Toxicol. 1987; Ambassador Award Soc. Toxicol. 1987; author or co-author numerous articles and abstracts; Ed. 'Toxicology and Applied Pharmacology'; mem. Ed. Bd. various scient. journs.; mem. Pharmacol. Soc. Can. (Past Pres.); Am. Soc. Pharmacol. & Exper. Therapeutics; Soc. Toxicol. (Past Pres.); Soc. Toxicol. Can. (Past Pres.); Soc. Exper. Biol. & Med. (Councillor); Bd. of Dirs., Candn. Network of Toxicology Centres; Am Acad. Forensic Sciences (Fellow); American Bd of Toxicology (Diplomate); Academy of Toxicological Sciences (Diplomate); Phi Kappa Tau (Vice Pres., Secy.); R. Catholic; Home. 236 Meredith St., Dorval, Que. H9S 2Y7; Office: (C.P. 6128) Montréal, Qué. H3C 3J7.

**PLAMONDON, Jean,** M.A., M.B.A.; consultant; b. Québec City, Qué. 5 Nov. 1944; s. Marcel and Alice (Rinfret) P.; e. Laval Univ. B.A. 1964; Univ. du Qué. Trois-Rivières M.A. 1968; McGill Univ. grad. studies Pol. Sci.; Univ. of W. Ont. M.B.A. 1973; adopted children: Thanh Tu, The Minh Tu, Nguon Cam Dam, Khanh Dieu Tu, Nhut Nguon Dam, Thai Quoc Trinh; PRINCIPAL CONSULTANT, COOPERS & LYBRAND 1990– ; Acct. Offr. Internat. Banking, Bank of Montreal, Montréal 1973–75; Br. Head Mercantile Bank of Canada Québec City 1975–80, Vice Pres. Corporate Planning Montréal 1980–83, Vice Pres. Treasury 1983–85; Pres. and Chief Extve. Offr. Credit Industriel Desjardins Montréal 1985–87; Extve. Vice Pres., Laurentian Bank of Canada 1987–89; Clubs: St-Denis; Home: 47 Melbourne, Town of Mount Royal, Qué. H3P 1E9.

**PLAMONDON, Robert,** B.Com., C.A.; educator; b. Cornwall, Ont. 8 Dec. 1957; s. Joseph Gordon and Jeanette Marie (Lalonde) P.; e. St. Thomas High Sch. Pointe Claire, Qué. 1973; John Abbott Coll. Ste-Anne de Bellevue, Qué.; Carleton Univ. B.Com. 1980, Master Mgmt. Studies 1993; Ont. C.A. 1983 (Ottawa Award Second Highest Standing); m. Karen d. Lorne and Ainslie Walpert 8 Aug. 1981– ; children: Nathaniel Newton Robert, Charlotte Marie Jeanette; PRES., PLAMONDON & ASSOCIATES INC. 1986– ; Faculty Mem., Queen's Univ., Extve. Master of Business Admin. 1991– ; Auditor, Peat, Marwick, Mitchell & Co. 1981–82; Audit Supr. Ward Mallette 1982–83; Controller, McNeely Engineering Ltd. 1983–86; Asst. Prof. of Acctg., Univ. of Ottawa 1987–90; Special Advisor, Goods and Services Tax, Dept. of Finance, Govt. of Canada 1989–91; sometimes lectr. Sch. of Accountancy Ont. Inst. C.A.s, Carleton Univ. and Univ. of Ottawa 1984–87; P. Cons. Cand. for Ottawa Centre g.e. 1988; Chrmn. Cdn. Diabetes Assoc. Sweepstakes Campaign - Ottawa 1989; Volunteer Ctte., P.C. National Convention Aug. 1989; Dir. Cdn. Diabetes Assoc. - Ottawa Branch; Treas. & Dir. Ottawa Carleton Centre for Community Owned Businesses 1989–90; Pres. P. Cons. Assn. Ottawa Centre (Federal) 1986–88, Treas. 1985–86; mem. Big Sisters Assn. Ottawa 1986– ; author 'A Study of Tax Compliance' 1993; 'GST Compliance Costs For Small Business in Canada' 1992; 'Debts, Deficits and Dangerous Complacency' 1988; recreations: golf, skiing, curling; clubs: Royal Ottawa Golf, Rideau Curling, Oyster Reef Golf Club, Hilton Head Is. S.C.; Address: 143 Sherwood Dr., Ottawa, Ont. K1Y 3V3.

**PLANT, B. John,** Ph.D.; educator; b. Smiths Falls, Ont. 2 Aug 1933; s. Bertrand Francis and Evelyn (MacBain) P.; e. R.M.C. of Can. 1953–55; Royal Naval Engineering Coll. 1957–60; M.I.T. Ph.D. 1965; m. Kay d. William and Alice Lawrie 21 Apr. 1956; children: Michael, Lawrie, John, Kirsten; PRINCIPAL, ROYAL MILITARY COLL. 1984– ; Engineering Offr., R.C.N. 1955–70; Naval Reserve 1975–83, rank Capt. (N); Lecturer, R.M.C. 1965–66, Asst. Prof. 1966–67, Prof. & Head E.E. Dept. 1967–72; Dean, Candn. Forces Military Coll. R.M.C. 1973–74; Dean, Grad. Studies & Research, Royal Military Coll. 1972–84; Principal and Dir. of Studies 1984– ; Natnl. Defence Coll. 1970–71; Research Visitor, Div. Systèmes Electroniques, Thomson C.S.F. à Bagnieux (France); Wachtmeister Visiting Eminent Scholar, Chair in Electrical Eng., Virginia Military Inst., Lexington, Va. 1982; Pres., Candn. Soc. of Electrical & Computer Eng. 1989–92; IEEE Centennial Medal (Inst. of Electrical and Electronics Engineers), 1984; The Ont. Prof. Engr. Citizenship Award 1986; awarded Commemorative Medal for 125th Anniversary of Candn. Confederation 1993; author 'Some Iterative Solutions in Optimal Control,' 1967; co-author 'Microcomputers in Measurement, Signal Processing and Control,' 1983; Honorary Aide-de-Camp to Gov. General 1976–84; Officer of the Order of Military Merit, 1984; Fellow, Engineering Inst. of Canada 1989; Fellow, Institute of Electrical and Electronics Engineering 1993; recreations: squash, badminton, gardening; Home: RMC Grounds, Kingston, Ont. K7K 5L0; Office: Principal, Royal Military College, Kingston, Ont. K7K 5L0.

**PLANTE, Normand,** B.A.Sc., M.B.A.; business executive; b. Shawinigan, Que. 13 Oct. 1933; s. Oscar and Lea (Chamberland) P.; e. Laval Univ., B.A.Sc. 1956; Internat. Mngt. Inst., Geneva, Switz., M.B.A. 1957; m. Huguette d. Rolland and Lucille Comtois 1959; one d.: Stéphane; PRES., N. PLANTE & ASSOCIATES 1992– ; Sr. Metallurgist, Alcan 1957–60; Project Engr., Air Liquide 1960–62; Quality Control Mgr. & Chief Metallurgist, Atlas Steel Co. Ltd. 1962–65; Sr. Econ. Advr. to the Délég. gén. du Qué. à Paris, Que. Dept. of Indus. & Commerce 1969–73; Gen. Mgr., Ulmic Inc. 1973–75; Gen. Dir., Conf. des Maires de la Banlieue de Montréal 1975–79; Extve. Dir., Montreal Urban Community 1979–80; Extve. Vice-Pres., BTM Internat. 1980–82; Fed. Econ. Devel. Coord. (Que.), DRIE 1982–88; Pres. & Chief Extve. Offr., Candn. Patents & Devel. Limited 1988–92; Dir. & Mem., Extve. Ctte., Ecole nat. d'Admin. publique 1979–83; Dir., Romeo Vachon Found.; Mem., l'Ordre des Ingén. du Qué.; Inst. of Public Admin. of Can.; Former Mem., CITEC 1984–88; Montreal World Trade Ctr. 1984–87; recreations: golf, travel, music; Home: 1575 Laird, Town Mount-Royal, Que. H3P 2T7.

**PLASKETT, Joseph Francis,** B.A.; artist, painter; b. New Westminster, B.C. 12 July 1918; s. Frank and Mary (Draper) P.; e. Univ. of B.C. B.A. 1938; Vancouver Sch. of Art, evening classes 1940–43; Banff Sch. of Fine Arts 1945; Calif. Sch. of Art 1946–47; Hans Hofmann Sch. 1947–49; Principal, Winnipeg Sch. of Art 1947–49; Teacher (summer), Banff Sch. of Fine Arts 1949; sailed to Eur. 1949; settled in Paris; returned to Canada periodically to teach & exhibit; exhibitions: Vancouver Art Gall. 1942, '44, '52, '54; New Design Gall. Vancouver, Waddington Gall. Montreal & Picture Loan Soc. Toronto 1956–67, Univ. of B.C. 1961; Nat. Gall. travelling show 1971; for the most part paints in Eur./exhibits in Canada; Eur. exhibs.: Musée Gall. Paris, Canadian cultural ctrs. in Paris, Brussels & London 1978 & smaller shows in Paris, London, Marburg & Troyes; Brussels World Fair; San Paulo Biennale; currently exhibits at Klinkhoff Gall. Montreal, Wallack Ottawa, Bau Xi Vancouver & Toronto, Gallery 78 Fredericton; Canada Council fellowship 1967–68; author of several critical essays; recreations: writing memoirs, letters, light verse, playing piano, gardening; club: Royal Overseas League (London); Homes: 2 rue Pecquay, 75004 Paris, France and The Cedars, Bromeswell, Woodbridge, Suffolk LP12 2PN; Office: c/o Bau Xi Gallery, 3045 Granville St., Vancouver, B.C. V6H 3J9.

**PLAUT, W. Gunther,** O.C., J.S.D., D.D., LL.D., D.Hum.Litt.; rabbi; author; lecturer; b. Münster, Germany 1 Nov. 1912; s. Jonas and Selma (Gumprich) P.; e. Univ. of Heidelberg; Univ. of Berlin LL.B. 1933, J.S.D., 1934; Hebrew Union Coll. Cincinnati Rabbi, M.H.L. 1939; D.D. 1964; Univ. of Toronto LL.D. 1978; Cleveland Coll. of Jewish Studies D.Hum.Litt. 1979; York Univ. LL.D. 1987; m. Elizabeth d. Harry and Therese Strauss 10 Nov. 1938; children: Rabbi Dr. Jonathan Victor, Judith, M.A.; pulpits: Chicago, Ill. 1939–48; St. Paul, Minn. 1948–61; Toronto, Ont. 1961–77; Senior Scholar, Holy Blossom Temple, Toronto 1978– ; Adjunct Prof., York Univ. 1991– ; served with U.S. Army as Chaplain 1943–46, rec'd Bronze Star; Chrmn., Gov's. Comn. on Ethics in Govt. (Minn.) 1958–61; Pres., St. Paul Gallery & Sch. of Art 1953–59; World Federalists Can. 1966–68; Chrmn., Un. Jewish Appeal Campaign Toronto 1970; Co-Chrmn. Can.-Israel Comte. 1975–77; Nat. Pres. Candn. Jewish Cong. 1977–80; Vice Chrmn. Ont. Human Rights Comn. 1978–85; Federal appointee, one-person commission to redesign Candian refugee determination 1984–85; Gov. Bd., World Union Progressive Judaism; Pres. Central Conf. Am. Rabbis 1983–85; Adjudicator, Human Rights Court 1987– ; Lectr. Haifa Univ., Ben Gurion Univ., Israel; Adj. Prof., York Univ. Toronto; contrib. various newspapers, mags.; editor Affirmation (human rights quarterly) 1979–87; frequent TV and radio appearances; Negev Dinner Honouree; rec'd Candn. Council Christians & Jews Humanitarian Award; Sadowski Medal Civic Service; Officer, Order of Canada 1978; Order of Ontario 1993; Ed. & principal author 'The Torah' (commentary) 1981; 'Unfinished Business' (autobiog.) 1981; 'Hanging Threads' (short stories) 1978, in U.S.A. 'The Man in the Blue Vest' 1980; 'Time to Think' 1977; 'The Letter' (novel) 1986; 'The Man Who Would Be Messiah' (novel) 1988; 'The Magen David – How the Six-pointed Star Became an Emblem for the Jewish People' 1990, and others; recreations: tennis, golf, chess; Clubs: York Racquets; Oakdale Golf & Country; Primrose; Office: Holy Blossom Temple, 1950 Bathurst St., Toronto, Ont. M5P 3K9.

**PLAXTON, Charles G.,** B.A.Sc., P.Eng.; management consultant; b. Ottawa, Ont. 13 Sept. 1923; s. Hon. Charles Percy and Gabrielle Eva (Faribault) P.; e. Univ. of Toronto Schs. 1942; Univ. of Toronto B.A.Sc. 1949; m. Elizabeth d. Russell and Edith Billings 23 June 1950; children: Nancy, Robert, William; MANAGEMENT CONSULTANT; Managing Dir., Executives Inc. 1989– ; Dir. Greening Donald Co. Ltd. 1984–92 (Past Pres. & C.E.O., retired 1989); Past Chrmn., Greening Donald Inc. (N.J.); Chief Test Eng., Candn. Comstock Co. Ltd. St. Catharines, Ont. 1949–53; Sales Mgr., Reliance Electric & Engineering (Canada) Ltd. Toronto 1953–62; Chief Eng., Reynolds Aluminum Co. of Canada Ltd. Cap-De-La-Madeleine, Que. 1962–64; Trade Promotion Official Dept. Industry, Trade & Commerce Ottawa 1964–70; Mktg. & Export Sales Mgr., Reliance Electric Ltd. Toronto 1970–77; Dir. of Mktg. and Eng. present Co., 1978, Vice Pres. Mktg. and Eng. 1982, Vice Pres. and Gen. Mgr. 1983; served Royal Candn. Navy, North Atlantic Service 1942–45; Assn. Prof. Engs. Prov. Ont.; Candn. Power Sqdn.; Candn. Yachting Assn.; Lake Ont. Racing Council; recreations: sailing; Club: Royal Canadian Yacht; Home: Apt. 2005, 39 Old Mill Rd., Toronto, Ont. M8X 1G6.

**PLAYDON, Kathy (Katherine Carol),** B.Sc.; purebred sheep breeder; b. Dryden, Ont. 22 March 1955; d. David E. and Viola Anna (Jensson) Wall; e. Univ. of Alberta B.Sc. 1976; m. Ralph s. June and Les P. June 1974; CHAIRMAN, ALBERTA SHEEP & WOOL COMMISSION 1991– ; has raised sheep since 1975; began raising registered Finnsheep 1981; Animal Nutritionist, Norwest Labs 1976–84; Instructor, Applied Equine Nutrition, Grant McEwan Community College 1980–82; Mem., Alta. Inst. of Agrologists 1978–84; North Central Sheep Breeders Assn. 1989– ; Canadian Finnsheep Breeders Assn. 1982– ; Alta. Sheep Breeders Assn. 1985– ; Life Mem., American Finnsheep Breeders Assn. 1985– ; Dir., Alta. Combined Training Assn. 1984–86; Northwest Sheep Producers Assn. 1991– ; Shareholder, Edmonton Northlands 1989– ; Canadian Cooperative Woolgrowers 1980– ; Ctte. Mem., Alta. Agriculture Rsch. Inst. 1990, '91; recreations: Equestrian – Level II coach – National talent ID rider; club: Pony Club Instructor; Office: #212, 6715 8th St. NE, Calgary, Alta. T2E 7H7.

**PLESSIS-BÉLAIR, Michel,** M.B.A., F.C.A.; business executive; b. Montréal, Qué. 26 Mar. 1942; s. Lucien P. and Marguerite (Goyette) B.; e. Jean-de-Brébeuf, B.A. 1962; Columbia Univ., M.B.A. 1967; H.E.C., M.Comm. 1965; m. Monique d. Albert and Patricia Lemieux 11 Oct. 1969; children: Stéphanie, Martine; EXTVE. VICE-PRES. & CHIEF FINANCIAL OFFICER, POWER CORP. OF CAN. AND SR. VICE-PRES. FIN. & ADMIN., POWER FINANCIAL CORP. 1986– ; Auditor, Samson Bélair 1967–68; Vice-Pres., Groupe S.M.A.-E.T.D. 1968–74; Vice-Pres., Devel., Dir. of Fin. & Treas., Soc. gén. de fin. du Qué. 1975–79; Sr. Vice-Pres., Marine Indus. Ltd. 1979–81; Extve. V.P. Soc. gén. de fin. du Qué. 1981–86; Dir., Great-West Lifeco Inc. (Audit Ctte.); The Great-West Life Assur. Co. (Audit Ctte.); Great-West Life & Annuity (Audit Ctte.) (U.S.A.); Groupe Bruxelles Lambert S.A. (Belgium); Investors Group Inc. (Audit Ctte. & Investment Ctte.); Power Broadcasting Inc.; Power Corp of Can.; Power Financial Corp. (Extve. Ctte.); Southam Inc. (Audit & Pension Ctte.); Hydro-Québec (Extve. Ctte. & Rsch. & Tech. Ctte.); Sidbec (Extve. & Remuneration Cttes.); École des Hec (Audit Ctte.); Lallemand Inc.; (Hon.), Domtar Inc.; Ordre des comptables agrées du Qué.; recreation: skiing; Club: St.-Denis; Office: 751 Victoria Square, Montréal, Qué. H2Y 2J3.

**PLETCHER, James Henry,** B.A.Sc.; oil company executive; b. Cranbrook, B.C., 4 Aug. 1931; s. Henry and Grace P.; e. Pub. and High Schs., South Burnaby, B.C.; Univ. of B.C., B.A.Sc. (Chem. Engn.); m. Engelina Catherina, d. Gerritt Grootenboer, 1955; children: Allan James, Gary Edward, Grace Margaret, Carolin Jo-Ann; Vice Pres., Special Projects, Numac Oil & Gas Ltd. 1982–93; Engr., Oil & Gas Conserv. Bd., Alberta, 1955; Evaluation & Gas Engr., Canadian Industrial Gas & Oil Ltd., Calgary, 1963; joined Canadian Western Natural Gas Co. & Northwestern Utilities Ltd., as Gas Supply Engr., 1966; Vice Pres. Gas Supply, 1968; Senior Vice. Pres 1973–82; mem., Assn. Prof. Engrs., Alta.; Conservative; United Church; recreations: golf, hunting, fishing, skiing; Clubs: Earl Grey Golf; Royal Glenora; Home: 14108 – 47 Ave., Edmonton, Alta. T6H 0B7.

**PLEWMAN, Veronica Ann,** B.A.; painter; b. Vancouver, B.C. 15 Apr. 1948; s. Lewis Arthur and Joan Irene (Lippitt) P.; e. Mount Elizabeth S.S. 1966; Simon Fraser Univ. 1966–69; Univ. of B.C. B.A. (Fine Arts) 1971; Art Ed. Dept. 1975–76; Wardrobe Asst., CBC-TV 'Beachcombers' 1977; travel, Eur. N. Africa, Can. 1974; first group show 1978; first 2-person show (with Jan Wade) Sechelt, B.C. 1980; first solo show, Community Arts Council Gall. Vanc. 1981; assorted group shows (B.C. & Toronto) 1982–90; solos: 1984 (Sechelt), 1985, '88, '91 (Vancouver), 1988 & '91 at Bau-Xi Gallery; currently rep. by Bau-Xi Gallery; winner, Alcan Scholarship 1966; recreations: swimming, reading, walking; Home: P.O. Box 5051, MPO, Vancouver, B.C. V6B 4A9; Office: c/o Bau-Xi Gallery, 3045 Granville St., Vancouver, B.C. V6H 3J9.

**PLODER, George Leo,** C.A.; business executive; b. Toronto, Ont. 10 April 1940; Queen's Univ. C.A. 1965; m. Anne; 3 children; PRESIDENT, BRACKNELL CORP. 1987– and C.E.O. 1992– ; Manager, Peat Marwick Thorne 1960–66; Asst. Treas. / Corp. Controller / Pres., Jannock Tube, Jannock Corp. 1966–78; Vice-Pres. & Chief Financial Officer, Cavendish Investing Ltd. 1978–86; Pres. 1986–91; Dir., Bracknell Corp.; Patheon, Inc.; Webex Resources; clubs: Ontario Racquet, Mississauga Golf & Country; Office: 150 York St., Suite 1506, Toronto, Ont. M5H 3S5.

**PLOURDE, Gerard,** O.C., B.A., M.Com.; business administrator; b. Joliette Que. 12 Feb. 1916; s. Louis-Georges and Rose deLima (Jolicoeur) P.; e. Jean-de-Brebeuf Coll., Montreal, B.A. 1936; Univ. of Montreal, M.Com. 1939; m. Jeannine, d. R. Martineau, Outremont, Que., 1943; three children; Bd. Vice Chrmn. Cambior Inc.; Hon. Dir., The Molson Cos., U.A.P. Inc.; Northern Telecom Ltd.; Pres. U.A.P. Inc. 1951–70, Chrmn. 1970–86; Roman Catholic; recreation: golf; Clubs: St-Denis; Laval-sur-le-Lac; Mont Bruno Country; Honoris Causa Doctorate, Univ. of Montreal; Home: 6065 de Vimy, Montreal, Que. H3S 2R2; Office: 1010 Sherbrooke West, Suite 2012, Montreal, Que. H3A 2R7.

**PLOURDE, Most Rev. Joseph Aurèle,** D.D., K.H.S.; archbishop (R.C.); b. St. François. Madawaska Co., N.B., 12 Jan. 1915; s. Antoine and Suzanne (Albert) P.; e. Bathurst (N.B.) Coll.; Bourget Coll., Rigaud, Que.; St. Joseph Univ., B.A.; Holy Heart Semy., Halifax; Univ. of Ottawa, Lic. in Social Studies; Gregorian Univ., Rome; Univ. of Moncton, Ph.D. (Hon.) in Educ.; ARCHBISHOP EMERITUS OF OTTAWA; Past Pres., Candn. Cath. Conf.; Chancellor, St. Paul's Univ., Ottawa; author of numerous publications and articles in ecclesiology, spirituality and Catholic education; Kt. of Malta; Address: 1247 Kilborn Place, Ottawa, Ont. K1H 6K9.

**PLUG, Bryan Edward,** C.G.A.; business executive; b. Sarnia, Ont. 2 May 1954; s. Hendrick Cornelius and Greta (Kuindersma) P.; e. Univ. of W. Ont.; C.G.A.; m. Mary Ann Kraak 18 Sept. 1976; children: Danielle Marie, Emily Christine, Trevor James; PRESIDENT, SAP CANADA INC. 1992– ; Cost Accountant, Standard Tube Canada Inc. 1979; Cost Analyst, Agric. Products, C-I-L Inc. 1981; Accounting & Systems Supvr. 1983; Mgr. of Finan. & Mngt. Acctg., Forest Products 1985; Business Analyst & Project Mgr., Information Resources 1987; Mgr. of Professional Services, SAP Canada Inc. 1989; Vice-Pres. & Mng. Dir. 1991; Mem., Information Technology Assn. of Canada; Cert. Gen. Accountants Assn. of Ont. (Founding Pres. Restigouche N.B. Chapter); Bd. of Trade of Metro Toronto; Dir., SAP Canada; Extve. Ctte. Mem., SAP N. Am.; author of numerous articles in var. pubns.; recreations: skiing; Home: 608 Haines Rd., Newmarket, Ont. L3Y 6V5; Office: 4120 Yonge St., Suite 600, North York, Ont. M2P 2B8.

**PLUMMER, Christopher,** C.C. (1968); actor; b. Toronto, Ont., of parents native of Montreal, 13 Dec. 1929; e. Montreal High Sch.; m. 1stly Tammy Lee Grimes (actress), 19 Aug. 1956; one d. Amanda Michael (marriage dissolved); 2ndly, Patricia Audrey Lewis (journalist), 4 May 1962, (marriage dissolved); spent most of his early youth in Senneville, Que.; began training for the stage under Doreen Lewis of the Montreal Repertory Theatre, and Rosanna Seaborn Todd of the Open Air Theatre Company; first professional appearance made at age 17 at Ottawa, Ont., and thereafter for the next two yrs. played in over 75 productions, incl. Shakespeare, Moliere and Shaw plays; also engaged in some radio work; made first Broadway appearance in 'The Starcross Story,' followed by 'Home Is the Hero' and 'The Dark Is Light Enough,' and as 'Jason' in 'Medea' at the International Festival in Paris, later winning considerable applause for his role in 'The Lark' (1955); played Mark Antony opposite Raymond Massey's Brutus in Stratford, Conn. Shakespearean Festival; first played Stratford (Ont.) Shakespearean Festival in 'Henry V,' 1956, proceeding with it to the Edinburgh Festival; played Shakespeare Festival, Stratford, Ont., July 1957, title part in 'Hamlet' and Sir Andrew Aguecheek in 'Twelfth Night'; June 1958, played Benedick in 'Much Ado About Nothing,' Leontes in 'The Winter's Tale' and Bardolph in 'Henry IV' Part 1; A.N.T.A., N.Y., Dec. 1958; played Nickles in 1960, played The Bastard in 'King John,' Mercutio in 'Romeo and Juliet'; made his debut at Shakespeare Mem. Theatre, Stratford-on-Avon in title role of 'Richard III' and Benedick in 'Much Ado About Nothing'; played Henry II in London production of 'Becket' at Aldwych Theatre and later starred same role in West End; summer of 1962, returned to Stratford, Ont., to appear as Cyrano in 'Cyrano de Bergerac,' 11 Nov. 1963; starred on Broadway in title role of 'Artruro Ui' by Brecht, Nov. 1963; last appeared on New York Stage in the role of 'Pizzarro' in 'The Royal Hunt of the Sun' in 1965; made first film appearance 1957; starred in 'Fall of The Roman Empire,' 'The Sound of Music' and 'Inside Daisy Clover'; more film engagements were 'The Man Who Would Be King,' 1975; 'Return of the Pink Panther,' 1975; 'Conduct Unbecoming,' 1975; 'The Silent Partner, 1979'; 'Night of the Generals' – 'Triple Cross' – 'Oedipus Rex' (filmed in Greece) – 'Nobody Runs Forever' 'Lock Up Your Daughters' – 'Battle of Britain' and 'The Royal Hunt of the Sun'; made first T.V. appearance in 1953; has been starred in 'Oedipus Rex'; 'The Lady's not for Burning,' 'The Doll's House,' 'The Prince and the Pauper,' 'Little Moon of Alba,' 'Captain Brassbound's Conversion,' 'Cyrano de Bergerac,' 'Prisoner of Zenda,' 'Time Remembered.' 'Macbeth' (Telstar) and 'Hamlet'; recreations: skiing, piano, tennis; Club: Player's (N.Y.).; Office: 111 W. 40th St., 20th Floor, New York, NY 10018 U.S.A.

**PLUMPTRE, Beryl Alyce (Mrs. Arthur Fitzwalter Wynne),** B.Com, D.C.L., LL.D. (Hon.); retired economist; b. Melbourne, Australia, 27 Dec. 1908; d. Edward Charles and Alyce Maud (Hughes) Rouch; e. Presb. Ladies' Coll., Melbourne; Univ. of Melbourne, B.Com. 1931; Cambridge Univ., post-grad. work; m. 21 May 1938; children: Mrs. Alexander Gillan Wedderspoon, Timothy Wynne; Chairman, Food Prices Review Board 1973–75; Vice Chrmn. A.I.B. 1975–76; Pres., Vanier Institute of the Family, 1968–73; mem., Econ. Council of Can.; Ont. Econ. Council; Candn. Consumer Council; Research Offr., W.P.T.B., 1946–47; Econ. Consultant, Tariff Bd., 1954–55; Econ. Consultant, Royal Comn. on Coasting Trade; mem., Toronto Bd., Children's Aid Soc., 1947–48 and Ottawa Bd., 1950–51; Dir., Consumers' Assn. of Can. (Nat. Pres. 1961–66); mem. Bd, Family Service Agency, Ottawa, 1962–64; Dir., Candn. Welfare Council; Mayor, Village of Rockcliffe Park 1978–85; Chrmn. Nat. Extve., Candn. Inst. of Internat. Affairs, (C.I.I.A.) 1983–87; Trustee, Ottawa General

Hosp. 1983–93; recreations: reading, gardening; Address: 85 Lakeway Dr., Rockcliffe Park, Ottawa, Ont. K1L 5A9.

**PLUNKETT, Lorne Charles,** B.A.; management consultant; b. Ottawa, Ont. 16 Oct. 1941; s. Charles Robert and Marguerite (Glen) P.; e. Sir George Williams Univ., B.A. 1962; m. K. Diane d. E. Glyn and Margaret P. Morley 29 Aug. 1964; one d. Fiona Stacey; PRES. LORNE PLUNKETT & ASSOCIATES LTD. 1974– ; Dir., Henley Training Systems, Henley-on-Thames, Eng.; mem. Ont. Soc. Training & Devel.; Soc. Intercultural Edn., Training & Rsch.; Pres. Candn. Inst. Training & Devel. 1974–76; author: 'Participative Management' 1991; co-author: 'The Proactive Manager' 1983; recreations: golf, antique autos, wine collecting; Clubs: Antique Car (Ottawa); Opimian Soc.; Alvis Owner's; Home: R.R. 7, Nepean, Ont. K2H 7V2.

**PLUNKETT, Tom J.,** M.A.; educator; b. N. Ireland 14 July 1921; s. late Andrew and Emily Florence (Hunter) P.; e. Sir George williams Univ B.A. 1950; McGill Univ. M.A. 1955; m. 1stly Mary Margart McMurchie 1947 (dec. 1965); one d. Linda Ann (dec. 1982); m. 2ndly Edith (Hodge) Latter 14 Apr. 1968; step-children: Susan Travers, John, David, Maria; EMERITUS PROF. OF PUB. ADM., QUEEN'S UNIV. 1987; Rsch. Dir. Fedn. Candn. Municipalities 1951–55; City Mgr. City of Beaconsfield, Qué. 1955–59; Pres. T. J. Plunkett Associates Ltd. 1960–72; Dir. Inst. Local Govt. present univ. 1972–77, Prof. of Pub. Adm. 1977–87 and Dir. Sch. of Pub. Adm. 1977–85; Chrmn. Ctte. Schs. & Progs. in Pub. Adm. Inst. Pub. Adm. Can. 1979–84; cons. Royal Comn. on Govt. Orgn. (Glassco Comn.) 1961–62; Royal Comn. Metrop. Toronto (Goldenberg 1964 and Robarts 1977); headed Candn. team cons. under Columbo Plan to advise State of Singapore 1960; maj. cons. assignments incl. studies numerous Candn. cities, provincial & federal govts.; Adjunct lectr. in urban govt. McGill and Sir George Williams Universities, Univ. de Montréal, Univ. of Calgary; served with RCAF 1940–45, Mentioned in Despatches; recipient Vanier Medal 1983 Inst Pub. Adm. Can.; author 'Muncicipal Organization in Canada' 1955; 'Urban Canada and its Government' 1968; 'City Management in Canada: The Role of the Chief Administrative Officer' 1992; numerous articles Candn. and U.S. jours. and periodicals; co-author: 'The Management of Canadian Urban Government' 1979; 'Metropolitan Winnipeg: Politics and Reform of Local Government' 1983; mem. Inst. Pub. Adm. Can.; recreations: golf, swimming; Home: 30 Collingwood St., Kingston, Ont. K7L 3X4; Office: Kingston, Ont. K7L 3N6.

**POCKLINGTON, Peter H.;** executive; b. Regina, Sask. 18 Nov. 1941; s. Basil B. and Eileen (Dempsey) P.; e. Medway High Sch. London, Ont.; m. Eva d. Jack McAvoy 2 June 1974; two s., two d.; CHRMN., POCKLINGTON FINANCIAL CORP. LTD.; Pres., Westown Ford, Tilbury, Ont. 1967–69; Chatham, Ont. 1969–71; Edmonton, Alta. 1971–82; Acquired Edmonton Oiler Hockey Club 1976, Edmonton Trapper Triple A Baseball Club 1981, Edmonton Brickmen Soccer Club 1987, Gainers (Meat Packing) in 1977, and Swifts Canada in 1980; formed Cromwell Resources Ltd. 1984; formed Hartford Properties Inc. 1985 in Edmonton and purchased Kretschmar Brands Inc. of St. Louis, Mo. in 1985; purchased East Bay Packing Co. of Oakland, Calif. in 1986; Kretschmar Inc. of Toronto 1987; Palm Dairies Ltd. 1987; Canbra Foods Ltd. 1988; Green Acre Farms, Sebastool, Miss. 1988; Green Acre Foods Inc., Nacodoches, Texas 1988; Christian; recreations: golf, skiing; Clubs: Mayfair Golf & Country (Edmonton); Edmonton Golf & Country; Office: 2500 Sun Life Place, 10123 - 99 Street, Edmonton, Alta. T5J 3H1.

**POCOCK, Philip Jackson,** B.F.A.; photographer; artist; b. Ottawa, Ont. 18 Dec. 1954; s. Philip John and Jasmine Dorothea (Jackson) P.; e. Univ. of Waterloo, Systems Design Engr. 1972–75; Ecole Sup. d'Ingen. de Marseille France 1975–76; New York Univ. Film Sch., B.F.A. 1979; d.: Antonia; Instr. of Photography, Internat. Ctr. of Photography NY 1982–87; 12 one person exhibitions incl.: USA: Albany Museum of Art, Geogia 1989; Piezo Electric Gallery, NY 1983, 85, 86, Los Angeles 1987; Greathouse Gallery, NY 1984; The Cooper Union, NY 1981; Canada: London Reg. Art Gall. 1983; Art Gall. of Ont. 1981; Cologne: Galerie Burgis Geismann, 1989; Berlin: Berlinische Galerie 1986; 28 group exhibitions incl.: 'The Spectacle of Chaos,' Chicago 1989; Tamuro Gallery, Tokyo 1987; Mori Gallery, Australia 1985; Indianapolis Mus. of Art 1984; 49th Parallel, NY 1984; author/photographer: 'The Obvious Illusion: Murals from the Lower East Side' 1981; co-publisher and editor, 'The Journal of Contemporary Art' founded 1988; subject of num. mag. & newspaper articles & books; Studio: 330 East 19th St., New York, NY 10003.

**PODBORSKI, Stephen Gregory,** O.C.; alpine skier; b. Toronto, Ont. 25 July 1957; s. Michael Stanley and Jacqueline Louise (Morris) P.; e. Don Mills Collegiate Inst.; m. Kathryn Grace Rooney 13 Aug. 1988; children: Benjamin Marshall Ross, Madelaine Isabel Louise; SKIER, CANDN. ALPINE SKI TEAM since 1973; began skiing at 21/2; racing at 10, Nancy Greene Ski League 1967; named to Nat. Alpine Ski Team 1973–74 season (age 16); World Cup Team 1974–75; 1st top 10 place, World Cup 1975–76; knee surgery 1976, 1980; again in 1983; Candn. Slalom Champion 1977; 7th, World Championships Downhill Garmisch-Partenkirchen W. Ger. 1978; 1st, World Cup Downhill, Morzine France 1980; Bronze Medal, Olympic Games, Lake Placid, N.Y. 1980 (1st Downhill medal for North Am.); 1st, World Cup Downhill: St. Moritz, Switz.; Kitzbühel, Austria; Garmisch-Partenkirchen, W. Ger.; 2nd, World Cup Downhill Overall 1980–81; 1st, World Cup Downhill: Crans-Montana, Switz.; Kitzbühel, Austria; Garmisch-Partenkirchen, W. Ger.; 1st World Cup Overall 1981–82 1st Non-European; 1st Garmisch-Partenkirchen, W. Germany 1983–84; Candn. D.H. Champion 1983 and 1984; co-author 'Ski the Canadian Way,' 1979; 'Podborski!' 1987; 'The Skier's Source Book' 1988; winner Candn. Sports Fed. Athlete of the Year 1981 and 1982; Ont. Athlete of the Year two years; Level III Candn. Ski Instructor Assn.; Level III Candn. Ski Coach Fed. (C.S.C.F.); Level II Examiner C.S.C.F.; Officer, Order of Can.; Candn. Amateur Sports Hall of Fame 1986; Canada Sports Hall of Fame 1987; Candn. Ski Museum Honor Roll 1988; Clubs: Craigleith Ski; Queen City Bicycle; Weston Golf and Country; Bruderschaft-St. Christoph; Olympic Club Canada; recreations: skiing; bicycling; windsurfing, golf; Office: Pod Enterprises Ltd., 6404 Easy St., Whistler, B.C. V0N 1B6.

**PODBREY, Maurice,** C.M., B.A. (Hons.), LL.D. (Hons.); artistic director; b. Durban, S. Africa 25 Apl. 1934; s. Boris and Helen (Garber) P.; e. Durban High Sch.; Univ. of Witwatersrand, B.A. (Hons.) 1955; Johannesburg Coll. of Edn. Teachers Dip. 1956; Rose Bruford Coll. of Speech & Drama (Eng.) 1959; m. Elsa; d. Jack and Gladys Bolam 1 June 1969; children: Nicholas, Alison; ARTISTIC DIR. CENTAUR THEATRE CO. 1969– ; freelance actor/dir. UK 1959–66; Artistic Dir. Chester Playhouse 1964; Asst. Dir. Eng. Theatre Sect. Nat. Theatre Sch. of Can. 1966–69; recipient Centaur Theatre Co. Vantage Arts Acad. Award 1983; Chrmn. Profl. Assn. Candn. Theatres 1979–83; Order of Canada 1991; Honorary Doctorate, Concordia Univ. 1992; Jewish; Home: 11 Lorraine, Westmount, Qué. H3Y 2M8; Office: 453 St. Francois Xavier, Montréal, Qué. H2Y 2T1.

**PODDAR, Satya Narain,** M.A.; economist, tax advisor; b. Kanwat Town, India 13 Feb. 1947; s. Sualal and Prakash (Poddar); e. Delhi School of Economics M.A. 1968; McMaster Univ. M.A. 1969; Univ. of Western Ont. post-grad. studies 1969–71; m. Shaku d. Rampratap Goyal; children: Bipin, Seema, Rishi; TAX PARTNER, ERNST & YOUNG TORONTO 1990– ; Dir., Tax Analysis & Commodity Tax Div., Dept. of Finance Ottawa 1979–87; Sr. Tax Policy Officer / Fiscal Policy Officer 1971–79; Tax Advisor, Ernst & Young Toronto 1987–90; Comnr., Ont. Fair Tax Comn. 1990– ; regular participation in Harvard Univ. & Internat. Monetary Fund tax advisory projects in devel. countries; author/co-author of several published papers; recreations: volunteer services, skiing, swimming, cycling; Home: 7 Claywood Rd., Toronto, Ont. M2N 2R1; Office: Box 251, Ernst & Young Tower, Toronto, Ont. M5K 1J7.

**PODGORSAK, Ervin B.,** M.Sc., Ph.D.; university professor and administrator; b. Vienna, Austria 28 Sept. 1943; s. Franc and Gabriella (Cukale) P.; d. Univ. of Ljubljana, Slovenia Dipl. Ing. (Physics) 1968; Univ. of Wisconsin M.Sc. (Physics) 1970, Ph.D. (Physics) 1973; m. Ana d. Rudolf and Antonia Ambrozic 23 Oct. 1965; children: Matthew, Gregor; PROFESSOR, DEPT. OF RADIATION ONCOLOGY, MCGILL UNIV. 1985– ; Postdoctoral Fellow, Univ. of Toronto (Ont. Cancer Institute) 1973–74; Asst. Prof., Dept. of Rad. Oncol., McGill Univ. 1975–79; Assoc. Prof. 1979–85; Dir., Dept. Med. Phys., Montreal General Hosp. 1979– ; Dir., Medical Physics Unit, McGill Univ. 1991– ; Fellowship, Candn. Coll. of Phys. in Medicine 1980; Certification, Am. Bd. of Med. Physics 1989; Bd. of Dir., Candn. Coll. of Phys. in Medicine 1981–89; Medical Physics Journal 1987– ; Am. Assn. of Phys. in Med. 1989–92; Internat. Stereotactic Radiosurgery Soc. 1992– ; Pres., Candn. Coll. of Phys. in Med. 1987–89; author/co-author of 120 sci. articles on solid state dosimetry, rad. oncol. physics, radiosurgery; Home: 1540 Seville Cres., Brossard, Qué. J4X 1J4; Office: Dept. of Med. Physics, Montreal Gen. Hosp., 1650 ave. Cedar, Montréal, Qué. H3G 1A4.

**PODGORSKI, Andrew Stan,** M.A.Sc., Ph.D.; scientist; b. Warsaw, Poland 5 May 1942; s. Franciszek and Helena (Borowiec) P.; e. Warsaw Tech. Univ. B.A.Sc. 1969; Univ. of Waterloo, M.A.Sc. 1975, Ph.D. 1980; m. Elizabeth Maria d. Ian and Boleslawa Pielaszek Kowalski 31 Oct. 1970; one s. Piotr Franciszek; HEAD, ELECTROMAGNETIC FIELD GROUP, NAT. RSCH. COUNCIL OF CAN. 1987– ; joined Siemens, Vienna 1969–73; present Council 1981; Dir., Friends of Cath. Univ. Poland; author numerous sci. papers; mem. Candn. Standards Assn. (various cttes.); Special Ctte. Radio Interference Candn. Standards Council of Internat. Electrotech. Comn.; Dir., Electromagnetic Compatibility Soc.; Inst. Elect. & Electronic Engs.; R. Catholic; recreation: skiing; Home: 332 Crestview Rd., Ottawa, Ont. K1A 5G6.

**PODILCHAK, Walter,** B.P.E., M.Sc., Ph.D.; university professor; b. Kandyty, Poland 10 Sept. 1953; s. John and Julia (Rutz) P.; e. Univ. of Toronto 1972–75; Univ. of Alta. B.P.E. 1975–77; Dalhousie Univ. M.Sc. 1978–80; Univ. of Calgary Ph.D. 1980–86; one d.: Meagan Jane; PROF., UNIV. OF TORONTO 1990– ; career primarily focuses on interpersonal relationships, humour, organizations; Teacher, Sociol. course, Univ. of Calgary; Red Deer Coll., Univ. of Winnipeg; Cons., YMCA and other community assn.; Dalhousie Grad. Fellowship; Mem., Candn. Assn. for Sociology & Anthropology; Candn. Assn. for Leisure Studies; WLRA International Centre of Excellence; author of scholarly articles; recreations: playing with daughter, dance, aerobics; Office: Erindale Campus, Mississauga, Ont. L5L 1C6.

**PODILUK, Walter,** B.A., B.Ed., LL.D.; provincial civil servant; b. Blaine Lake, Sask. 4 March 1927; s. Alec E. and Anne (Hunchak) P.; e. Blaine High Sch.; Univ. of Sask. B.Ed. 1955, B.A. 1963, LL.D. 1987; m. Sonia d. Kiprian and Mary Trotzuk 12 Aug. 1947; children: Janice, Douglas, Margot, Laurine, Ronald, Joseph; PRES. & C.E.O., ST. PAUL'S HOSPITAL (GREY NUNS) OF SASKATOON; mem. Turtleford Sch. Unit 1947–51; Dept. Health Weyburn 1951–55; Prin. St. Mary's Sch. Saskatoon 1955–63; Asst. Supt. Saskatoon Cath. Schs. 1963–67; Dir. of Edn. Saskatoon Cath. Sch. Bd. 1967–82; Dep. Min. of Social Services Sask. 1982–84 and of Health 1984–88; Extve. Depy. Chrmn., Saskatchewan Commn. on Directions in Health Care 1988–90; Chrmn., Medical Laboratories Licensing Bd. 1990–91; Gov. St. Thomas More Coll. Univ. of Sask. 1973–82; Pres. & C.E.O., St. Paul's Hosp. (Grey Nuns) Saskatoon 1991– (Mem. Bd. Mgmt. 1980–82); Dir. SaskMedia 1981–82; Sask Tel 1982; Century Saskatoon 1977–82; recipient Distinguished Service Award Candn. Assn. Sch. Adms. 1984; City of Saskatoon Leadership Award 1982; Founders Award Coll. of Edn. 1984; Pro Ecclesia Pontifical Medal 1976; Life mem. Candn. Edn. Assn. (Dir. 1976–82); K. of C.; Honorary Life Mem., Saskatchewan Nurses' Assn. 1991; Past Pres. Ukrainian Cath. Council of Canada; recreations: reading, outdoors; Home: 6 – 455 Pinehouse Dr., Saskatoon, Sask. S7K 5X1; Office: 1702 – 20th Street West, Saskatoon, Sask. S7M 0Z9.

**PODLECKI, Anthony Joseph,** M.A., Ph.D.; educator; b. Buffalo, N.Y. 25 Jan. 1936; s. Anthony Joseph and Eugenia Evelyn (Jendrasiak) P.; e. Canisius High Sch. Buffalo 1953; Coll. of Holy Cross Worcester, Mass. B.A. 1957; Lincoln Coll. Oxford Univ. B.A. 1960, M.A. 1962; Univ. of Toronto M.A. 1961, Ph.D. 1963; m. Jennifer Julia d. Prof. G.M.A. Grube, Toronto, Ont. 28 July 1962; children: Christopher, Julia, Antonia; PROF. OF CLASSICS, UNIV. OF B.C. 1975– and Head of Dept. 1975–86; Visiting Prof., Colby Coll., Maine 1987–88; Part-time Instr. in Classics Trinity Coll. Univ. of Toronto 1961–62; Instr. and Asst. Prof. of Classics Northwestern Univ. 1963–66; Assoc. Prof. and Head of Classics Pa. State Univ. 1966, Prof. and Head of Classics 1970–75; Visiting Fellow, Wolfson Coll. Oxford 1970; Visiting Fellow, Clare Hall, Cambridge 1991; author 'The Political Background of Aeschylean Tragedy' 1966; 'Aeschylus' 'The Persians'' verse transl. with commentary 1970, revised 1991; 'The Life of Themistocles' 1975; 'Age of Glory: Imperial Athens in the Age of Pericles' 1975; 'The Early Greek Poets and their Times' 1984; 'Plutarch, Life of Pericles: a Companion to the Penguin translation with Introduction and Commentary' 1987; Ed. 'Ancient Ships' 1964; Aeschylus 'The Eumenides' text, translation and commentary 1989; Euripides' 'Medea' translated with introduction & notes 1991; co-ed. 'Panathenaia: Studies in Athenian Life and Thought in the Classical Age' 1979; various articles

Classical Greek hist. and lit.; mem. Am. Philol. Assn.; Classical Assn. Can.; Archaeol. Inst. Am.; Cambridge Philol. Assn.; Classical Assn. Gt. Brit.; Jt. Assn. Classics Teachers; Classical Assn. Pacific Northwest (Pres. 1977–78); Classical Assn. Candn. W.; NDP; R. Catholic; recreation: choral singing; Home: 4024 W. 18th Ave., Vancouver, B.C. V6S 1B8; Office: C272–1866 Main Mall, Vancouver, B.C. V6T 1W5.

**PODREBARAC, George R.,** B.A., M.Ed., D.Ed.; consultant; b. Welland, Ont. 17 May 1936; s. Rudolph and Esther (Guido) P.; e. McMaster Univ. B.A. 1961; State Univ. of N.Y. at Buffalo M.Ed. 1965; Univ. of Toronto D.Ed. 1982; m. Louise d. Gordon and Vera Misener 8 July 1961; children: Gary, Craig, Scott; MANAGING CONSULTANT, HUMAN RESOURCES AT THE MANAGEMENT SYSTEMS UNIT IN MALTA 1991– ; Teacher/Principal, var. elementary schools 1956–65; Teaching Master, Peterborough Teacher's Coll., Min. of Edn. 1965; Prin., Ont. Teacher Edn. Coll., Hamilton; served in Curriculum Devel. & Special Edn. Branches prior to becoming Asst. Dep. Min. of Edn. Prog.; Dep. Min., Min. of Correctional Serv. 1983; Min. of Edn. & Min. of Coll. & Univ. 1984; Dep. Min., Ont. Human Resources Secretariat 1986; Comnr., Pay Equity Comn., Govt. of Ont. 1987–91; directorships or similar positions, consulting, teaching, etc.; Phi Delta Kappa, Univ. of Toronto Chap.; Hon. Life Mem., Candn. Edn. Assn.; recreations: golf, baseball, gardening; Home: 46 Ravensbourne Cres., Islington, Ont. M9A 2A8.

**PODSIADLO, Richard John M.;** business executive; b. Toronto, Ont. 29 Aug. 1943; s. Andrew and Helen M. (Dyll) P.; e. Univ. of West. Ont. 1963–65; Univ. of Toronto, Dipl.Bus.Admin. 1981; m. Angela d. Handel and Audrey Johnson 5 Oct. 1968; children: Alison, David, Michael; GEN. MGR., PRES. & DIR., NOVO NORDISK CANADA INC. and CONNAUGHT NOVO NORDISK INC. 1990– ; Policy Serv. Supr., State Farm Ins. Cos. 1965–69; var. positions ending as Mktg. & Sales Mgr., Ames Div., Miles Labs. Ltd. 1969–85; Gen. Mgr., Pres. & Dir., Nordisk Can. 1985–90; Mem., Pharm. Mktg. Club of Ont.; Am. Marketing Assn.; Can. Mgmt. Assn.; recreations: tennis, cycling, overseas travel; Home: 261 Beechfield Rd., Oakville, Ont. L6J 5H9; Office: 2700 Matheson Blvd. E., 3rd Floor, West Tower, Mississauga, Ont. L4W 4V9.

**POERSCH, Lorane;** entrepreneur; b. 16 May 1955; e. St. John's-Ravenscourt School 1972; PRESIDENT, DESERT ROSE PRODUCTIONS INC. 1990– ; Manager, Plummer's Arctic Lodges, N.W.T. 1973–88; established Desert Rose Productions (mfr. of natural fibre travel accessories) 1984; current co. develops & distributes envir. educ. materials based on its Eddy the Eco-Dog® character for children; Chairperson, Desert Rose Student Advisory Board; author: 'Beyond Recycling' 1993; recreations: in-line skating, swimming, public speaking; Office: 1775 Corydon Ave., Winnipeg, Man. R3N 2A6.

**POFF, Deborah Charmaine,** B.A., M.A., Ph.D.; university professor and administrator; b. Toronto, Ont. 12 June 1950; d. Gordon James and Marjorie Winnifred (Giles) P.; e. Univ. of Guelph B.A. (Hons.) 1974; Queen's Univ. B.A. (Hons.) 1977; Carleton Univ. M.A. 1979; Univ. of Guelph Ph.D. 1987; m. Alex s. Charles and Josephine Michalos 11 Jan. 1985; DEAN OF ARTS AND SCIENCES, UNIV. OF NORTHERN B.C. 1993– ; Teacher, Philosophy Dept., Univ. of Alta.; Assoc. Prof., Women's Studies & Philosophy, Mt. St. Vincent Univ. 1984–93; Dir., Institute for the Study of Women, Mount St. Vincent Univ. 1990–93; small, private practice as feminist therapist, independent management consultant; Canada delegate, HRH The Duke of Edinburgh Commonwealth Study Tour; Mem., Sex Information Education Council of Canada (Nat. Adv. Ctte. Mem., 1988–90, 1990–92); Candn. Women's Studies Assn. (Pres. 1985–86; Sec.-Treas. 1986–88; Treas. 1988–89); Nat. Action Ctte. on the Status of Women, Maritime Reg. Rep. on the Extve. Council 1986–87; Social Science Fed. of Canada (Bd. of Dir. 1985–88); Candn. Philosophical Assn. (Bd. of Dirs. 1985–87); editor: 'Journal of Business Ethics' 1981– , 'Atlantis: A Women's Studies Journal' 1984– ; co-editor: 'Business Ethics in Canada' 1987, 2nd ed. 1991; author of num. articles on justice, ethics & feminism; Home: 3110 Seton Rd., Prince George, B.C. V2K 4T7; Office: P.O. Bag 1950, Prince George, B.C. V2L 5P2.

**POIRIER, Thelma Rose,** B.Ed.; writer; b. Macworth, Sask. 9 Aug. 1940; d. Leonard Elvin and Mary Aquina (Price) Anderson; e. Univ. of Regina B.Ed. 1987; m. Emile s. Alphonse and Laurette Poirier 10 Oct. 1959; children: Perri, Gary, Robin; author 'Wood Mountain: 1875' play 1985; 'Grasslands: The Private Hearing' 1990; co-author 'Double Visions' poetry 1984; ed. 'Beyond the Range: A History of the Saskatchewan Stock Growers' hist. 1988; recreations: history, weaving; Address: P.O. Box 70, Fir Mountain, Sask. S0H 1P0.

**POIRIER, Yves M.,** B.A., M.Ed., Ph.D.; education; b. Valleyfield, Que. 19 Sept. 1939; s. Jean Marc and Almea G. (Robidoux) P.; e. Univ. of Ottawa B.A. 1963, M.Ed. 1967, Ph.D. 1971; m. Andrée d. Wilfrid and Josée Laroc-que 20 Aug. 1962; one s. Alain; Dean of Education, Univ. of Ottawa 1977–88; Adjunct Prof., Univ. of Manitoba 1985–88; Dir. of Studies Outaouais Regional Sch. Bd. Hull 1965–68; Prof. of Educ. present Univ. 1968–70, Secy. and Acting Dean of Educ. 1970–74; former Vice Pres. CEGEP Hull, Que.; Vice Pres., Revue des Sciences de l'éducation Montreal (Pres. 1982–85); Vice Pres., Association canadienne de l'éducation de langue française; mem., Conseil de l'éducation franco-ontarienne 1984–90; Commission scientifique de l'INRS (Univ. du Québec) 1982–86; Décorations: Compagnie des Cent-Associés francophones; Ordre des Francophones d'Amérique; Auteur de 'Fondements conceptuels de l'administration et de l'organisation'; Co-auteur de 'Fondements conceptuels des phénomènes de l'autorité et du leadership'; Home: 4, 310 Cathcart, Ottawa, Ont. K1N 5C4; Office: Ottawa, Ont. K1N 6N5.

**POISSANT, Charles Albert,** F.C.A.; b. Montréal, Qué. 13 Sept. 1925; s. Adrien and Antoinette (Courchesne) P.; e. L'École des Hautes Études Commerciales, aff. Univ. Montréal, Diplomé; m. Florence d. Georges Drouin, 23 June 1951; children: Louise, Marc André, Hélène, Isabelle; CHRMN. OF THE BD., DONOHUE INC.; mem. Bd. Dirs. & Extve. Ctte., Quebecor Inc.; Premier Choix: TVEC Inc.; Orchestre Métropolitain; l'Association des Manufacturiers du Québec; mem. Bd. Dirs., Banque Nationale du Canada; Candn. Pulp and Paper Assn.; Hôpital du Sacré-Coeur de Montréal; Parc technologique du Québec Métro; Fondation de l'Université de Québec à Montréal; previously Pres. of Poissant Thibault Peat Marwick Thorne, Que. region, & Vice-Pres. & mem. Extve. Ctte.; Past mem. Extve. Ctte. and 1st Vice Pres., Internat. Fiscal Assn. and Past Pres., (Candn. Branch); Past Pres. de l'Ordre des comptables agréés du Qué.; mem., Candn. Tax Found.; mem., C.D. Howe Institute; mem., Business Council on National Issues; Ex-Commissioner, Bélanger-Campeau Commission on the political and constitutional future of Quebec; Conf. Bd. of Can.; Roman Catholic; recreation: golf; Clubs: St. Denis; Laval-sur-le-Lac; Beaver; United Services; Home: 333 Somerville, Montréal, Qué. H3L 1A4; Office: 612 St-James St. W., 12th Flr., Montréal, Qué. H3C 4M8.

**POISSONNET, Michel;** mining executive; b. Andilly France 7 Feb. 1948; e. Mining Engr., Mining School of Nancy France; m. Monique Jacquot; one d.: Sandrine; PRES., COGEMA RESOURCES INC. 1989– ; Dir., Uranium Saskatchewan; Candn. Nuclear Assn.; Rsch. Engr., CEA France 1972–76; Project Explor. Mgr. Niger Africa 1977–78; Opns. Mgr. of a group of uranium mines (Vendée area & Limousin France) 1979–84; Gen. Mgr. for Drilling & Mining Serv. France & overseas 1985–89; Dir., Candn. Nuclear Assn.; Home: 801 – 505, 12th St. E., Saskatoon, Sask. S7N 4H3; Office: 817 – 825, 45th St. W., P.O. Box 9204, Saskatoon, Sask. S7K 3X5.

**POITRAS, Hon. Lawrence A.,** B.A., LL.L.; Chief Justice; b. Montreal, Que. 3 Apl. 1931; s. late Harold Edward and Anne-Marie (Gendron) P.; e. Loyola High Sch. 1948; Loyola Coll. 1951; McGill Univ. B.A. 1953; Univ. de Montréal LL.L 1957; m. Marie-Thérèse, d. Arsène Boivin 10 May 1958; children: Thomas Harold, Anne-Marie, Marie-Claire; JUSTICE OF SUPERIOR COURT QUE. since 1975; appt'd. Associate Chief Justice in 1983, Chief Justice 1992– ; a mem. of the Court Martial Appeal Tribunal since 1979; read law with Duquet, MacKay, Weldon & Tetrault; called to Bar of Que., 1957; cr. Q.C. 1972; part-time newspaperman The Montreal Star 1948–57; mem. law firm Duquet, MacKay, Weldon & Tetrault 1957–70; Partner, Laing, Weldon, Courtois, Clarkson, Parsons, Gonthier & Tetrault 1970–75; Lectr. in Commercial. Law McGill Univ. 1964; Dir. Royal Edward Laurentian Foundation; mem. Extve. Comte. Que. Dir. & Vice Pres. Candn. Red Cross Soc. (1975–84); Gov. Hôpital Marie-Enfant 1976–81; Dir. (1975–83) and Past Vice-Pres., Montreal Chest Hospital; Counc. Mem., Boy Scout of Can. 1984– ; rec'd Distinguished Service Award Town of Dollard des Ormeaux 1975; mem. Candn. Bar Assn. (served in various capacities incl. mem. Que. Council 1972–76 and Nat. Council 1973–76); mem., Qué. S.C. Judges General Comte. since 1977; Dir., Vice-Chrmn. (1979–81), and Chrmn. (1981–83), Candn. Judges Conference; Gov. and mem. of extve. comte. of Candn. Inst. for Advanced Legal Studies; mem., Candn. Judicial Council 1983– ; mem. Royal Comn. on the Donald Marshall, Jr., Prosecution 1986–90; Mem. Bd. of Govs., The Portage Program for Drug Dependencies Inc. 1989– ; Hon. mem., The Internat. Academy of Trial Judges 1992– ; Co-Chrmn., Judicial Conf. on Sect. 15, Candn. Charter, Hull 1985; Les Journées Strasbourgeoises, Strasbourg, France, 1984, 1988 and 1992 and Les Journées Louisionaises, New Orleans, U.S.A. 1991; R. Catholic; recreations: tennis, squash, skiing, golf; Clubs: mem. St. James's Club (1971–76); Montreal Badminton & Squash (Dir. 1975–78); Shawbridge Golf & Country (Dir. 1976–81); Home: 46 Glamis St., Dollard des Ormeaux, Que. H9A 1M5; Office: Montreal Court House, 1 Notre Dame St. E., Montreal, Que. H2Y 1B6.

**POLANYI, John Charles,** C.C., Ph.D., D.Sc., LL.D., F.R.S., F.R.S.C.; educator; b. Berlin, Germany, 23 Jan. 1929; e. Manchester Grammar Sch. Eng; Manchester Univ. B.Sc. 1949, M.Sc. 1950, Ph.D. 1952, D.Sc. 1964; Hon. D.Sc.: Univ. Waterloo 1970, Memorial Univ. Nfld. 1976, McMaster Univ. 1977, Carleton Univ. 1981, Harvard Univ. 1982, Rensselaer Polytech. Inst. 1984, Brock Univ. 1984, Lethbridge 1987, Victoria 1987, Ottawa 1987, Sherbrooke 1987, Laval 1987; D.Sc. Univ. of Manchester 1988; York Univ. 1988; Univ. of Montreal 1989; Acadia Univ. 1989; Weizmann Inst. 1989; Hon. LL.D. Trent Univ. 1977, Dalhousie Univ. 1983, St. Francis Xavier Univ. 1984; m. Anne Ferrar Davidson 1958; children: Margaret, Michael; UNIV. PROF., UNIV. OF TORONTO since 1974 and Prof. of Chem. since 1962; Postdoctoral Fellow, Nat. Research Council Can. 1952–54; Research Assoc. Princeton Univ. 1954–56; Lectr. Univ. of Toronto 1956, Asst. Prof. 1957, Assoc. Prof. 1960; awards and lectureships: Sloan Foundation Fellow 1959–63; Marlow Medal Faraday Soc. 1962; Centenary Medal and Lectureship Chem. Soc. Gt. Brit. 1965; Steacie Prize Natural Science (co-recipient) 1965; Fellow, Royal Soc. of Can. 1966; Noranda Award & Lectureship Chem. Inst. Can. 1967; Mack Award & Lectureship Ohio State Univ. 1969; William D. Harkins Lectr. Univ. Chicago 1970; Reilly Lectr. Univ. Notre Dame 1970; Purves Lectr. McGill Univ. 1971; Fellow, Royal Soc. of London 1971; Brit. Chem. Soc. Award 1971; F. J. Toole Lectr. Univ. N.B. 1974; Philips Lectr. Haverford Coll. 1974; Kistiakowsky Lectr. Harvard Univ. 1975; Camille & Henry Dreyfus Lectr. Univ. Kansas 1975; J. W. T. Spinks Lectr. Univ. Sask. 1976; Laird Lectr. Univ. W. Ont. 1976; Chem. Inst. Can. Medal 1976; Hon. Foreign mem. Am. Acad. Arts & Science 1976; Henry Marshall Tory Medal Royal Soc. Can. 1977; CIL Distinguished Lectr. Simon Fraser Univ. 1977; Gucker Lectr. Ind. Univ. 1977; Remsen Award & Lectureship Am. Chem. Soc. 1978; Jacob Bronowski Memorial Lectr., Univ. of Toronto 1978; Hutchison Lectr., Univ. of Rochester 1979; Companion, Order of Can. 1979; Guggenheim Memorial Fellow 1979–80; Foreign Assoc. Nat. Acad. Sciences USA 1978; Priestly Lectr., Penn State Univ., 1980; Sherman Fairchild Distinguished Scholar, California Institute of Technology, 1982; Barré Lectr., Univ. of Montréal, 1982; Chute Lectr., Dalhousie Univ., 1983; Redman Lectr., McMaster Univ., 1983; Wiegand Lectr., Univ. of Toronto 1984; Condon. Lectr., Univ. of Colorado 1984; Willard Lectr., Univ. of Wisconsin 1984; John A. Allan Lectr., Univ. of Alberta 1984; Owen Holmes Lectr., Univ. of Lethbridge 1985; Walker-Ames Prof., Univ. of Washington 1986; John W. Cowper Distinguished Visiting Lectr., Univ. of Buffalo, SUNY 1986; Visiting Prof. of Chem., Texas A & M. Univ. 1986; Distinguished Visiting Speaker, Univ. of Calgary 1987; Morino Lectr., Japan 1987; J.T. Wilson Lectr., Ontario Sci. Centre 1987; Welsh Lectr., Univ. of Toronto 1987; Spiers Memorial Lecture, Faraday Div'n. Royal Soc. Chem. 1987; Polanyi Lecture, Internat. Union Pure & Appl. Chem. 1988; W.B. Lewis Lecture, Atomic Energy of Can. Ltd. 1988; Consolidated Bathurst Visiting Lectr., Concordia Univ. 1988; Priestman Lectr., Univ. of New Brunswick 1988; Killam Lectr., Univ. of Windsor 1988; Herzberg Lectr., Carleton Univ. 1988; Falconbridge Lectr., Laurentian Univ. 1988; Dupont Lectr., Indiana Univ. 1989; C.R. Mueller Lectr., Purdue Univ. 1989; Scientific Advisory Board, Max Planck Institute for Quantum Optics, Garching, Germany, 1982 to present; Wolf Foundation Prize (co-recipient) 1982; Mem., Pontifical Acad. of Sciences, Rome 1986; NOBEL PRIZE FOR CHEMISTRY (co-recipient) 1986; Isaac Walton Killam Mem. Prize 1988; Royal Medal, Royal Soc. of London 1989; Fellow, Royal Soc. of Edinburgh (FRSE) 1988; Hon. Consultant, Inst. of Molecular Sci., Okazaki, Japan 1989–91; Mem., Nat. Adv. Bd. on Science & Technology 1987– ; publications: over 180 papers scient. journs., articles on science policy and control of armaments various journs., newspapers, mags.; film: 'Concepts in Reaction Dynamics' 1970; co-ed. 'The Dangers of Nuclear War' 1979; Founding Mem., Candn. Pugwash Ctte. 1960; Candn. Ctte. of Scientists and Scholars; Royal Soc. of Can. Ctte.

on Scholarly Freedom; Mem., Am. Acad. of Arts and Sci. Ctte. on Internat. Security Studies; Bd. mem., Candn. Centre for Arms Control and Disarmament; Home: 142 Collier St. Toronto, Ont. M4W 1M3; Office: Dept. of Chemistry, 80 St. George St., Toronto, Ont. M5S 1A1.

**POLE, Charles Douglas;** shipping executive; b. Aberdeen, Scot. 7 Oct. 1928; s. William Alexander and Robina Jane (Blance) P.; e. Robert Gordons Coll., Aberdeen 1939–44; HMS Conway Schoolship, Bangor, N. Wales grad. 1946; Roberts Gordon Sch. of Navigation, Aberdeen 1949, 1952; m. Pamela d. Grace and Cecil Ivison 21 Apr. 1967; children: Anthony, Wendy; VICE-PRES. FLEET DEVELOPMENT, ULS INTERNATIONAL INC./UPPER LAKES SHIPPING LTD. 1984– ; Pres. Provmar Fuels Inc.; served as Navigation Cadet, Clan-Line Steamers of Glasgow 1946–49; employed as 2nd and 3rd Offr., Christian Salvesen of Leith on Antarctic Voyages 1950–53; employed as 1st Mate and Master, Cadwell Marine of Niagara Falls 1954–64; formed Norlake Steamship Co. Ltd. 1964; sailed as Master 1965–68; Supr. of Operations, Canada Steamship Lines 1968–74, Gen. Mgr. 1974–78; Gen. Mgr. Upper Lakes Shipping Ltd. 1978–83; Dir. Great Lakes Pilotage Authority 1980–88; Vice Pres. Fleet Development, ULS Internat. Inc. 1983– ; invented and holds patents on methods of ice breaking and also bulk materials handling; recreations: camping, fishing, skiing; Club: Marine; Home: 32 Pineway Blvd., Willowdale, Ont. M2H 1A1; Office: 49 Jackes Ave., Toronto, Ont. M4T 1E2.

**POLIVY, Janet,** B.S., M.A., Ph.D.; university professor; b. New York, N.Y. 9 Feb. 1951; d. Calvin and Bernice Isabel (Malat) P.; e. Lawrence H.S. 1968; Tufts Univ. B.S. 1971; Northwestern Univ. M.A. 1973, Ph.D. 1975; m. C. Peter s. Ruby and Murray Herman 3 Aug. 1975; children: Lisa, Eric, Saretta; PROFESSOR, DEPT. OF PSYCHOLOGY, ERINDALE COLLEGE, UNIV. OF TORONTO; Asst. Prof., Psych., Loyola Univ. of Chicago 1974–76; Visiting Asst. Prof., Psych., Univ. of Toronto 1976–77; Rsch. Assoc., Clarke Inst. of Psych. 1977–83; current cross-appointments: Prof., Psychiatry, Univ. of Toronto and Rsch. Assoc., Toronto Gen. Hosp., Dept. of Psych.; Pres. & Chair, Stop Dieting, Inc.; Mem., U.S. Nat. Inst. of Health Panel on Obesity (Behav. Ctte.) 1982; Obesity Treatment Adv. Panel, Health & Welfare Can. 1983–87 (Extve. Ctte. 1990); SSHRC Grant Ctte. 1987–88; Assn. for Adv. of Behavior Therapy (Nom. & Elections Ctte. Chair 1982–85); Candn. Reg. of Health Serv. Providers in Psych.; Fellow, Am. Psych. Soc.; Fellow, Candn. Psych. Assn.; recipient of several research awards; Consulting Ed., 'J. of Abnormal Psych.' 1979– , 'Int. J. of Eating Disorders' 1988– , 'J. of Cons. & Clin. Psych.' 1985–86; Assoc. Ed., 'J. of Personality' 1981–86 (Edit. Bd. Mem. 1979–85); Ad hoc reviewer for num. journals; co-author: 'Breaking the Diet Habit' 1983 (APA Media Award runner up 1984), 'Psychology' 3rd ed. 1991; author/co-author of numerous journal & magazine articles, book chapters, conf. presentations and more than 25 invited addresses; co-editor: 'Advances in the Study of Communication and Affect' Vol. 6 1980, Vol. 7 1982; Office: Mississauga, Ont. L5L 1C6.

**POLLACK, Isidore Constantine,** B.A., LL.L., CM, CR; lawyer; b. Quebec City, Qué. 30 Oct. 1913; s. Maurice and Rebecca (Tourantour) P.; e. Comnrs. High Sch., Que.; McGill Univ., B.A.; Laval Univ., LL.L.; m. Roselee d. late Edward A. Hart, Hartford, Conn., 24 July 1950; children: Adelle-Laudrey, Jon Hart; MEM., LETORNEAU AND ASSOCS.; Dir., Trizec Corporation Limited; Dir. and mem. Executive Committee, Trust Général du Canada; Chairman, Quebec Port Authority; Can. Employment and Immigration Advisory Council; practised law with Angers, Caisse & Pollack, Montreal, 1938–39; Department of External Affairs, Ottawa, 1947–51; Secy. Gen. Candn. Del. to U.N., 1950; Pres. and Mang. Dir. M. Pollack Ltée 1951–69; served as Lieut., R.C.N., 1939–46; retired with rank of Commdr.; Past Pres., Chamber Comm. & Indust. Metrop. Que.; Vice Pres., Can.-Israel Chamber Comm. & Indust.; mem., Senate & Conseil, Univ. Laval; Can. Manpower & Immigration Council; Extve. Comte. & Bd. Govs., Candn. Council on Social Devel.; Bd. Govs., Weizmann Inst. Science; Dir., Nat. Youth Orchestra; World Wildlife Fund (Can.); recreations: fishing, tennis, farming; Home: 18300 S.E. Loxahatchee River Rd., Jupiter, Fla. 33458.

**POLLAK, Michael,** M.D., FRCPC; physician, researcher, university professor; b. Montreal, Que. 8 Aug. 1952; s. Bernard and Catherine (Neiger) P.; e. McGill Univ. M.D. 1977; FRCPC (Internal Med.) 1982, (Oncology) 1987; m. Toby d. Moses and Charlotte Shainbaum 30 Oct. 1983; children: Noah, Rebecca; PROF., DEPT. OF MEDICINE & ONCOLOGY, MCGILL UNIV., THE JEWISH GENERAL HOSP. & THE LADY DAVIS INST. FOR MEDICAL RSCH. 1985– ; combines clinical practice as a consultant in oncology with activities in basic & applied research; research involved hormonal treatments for cancer; chair of clinical rsch. projects which revealed important effects of tamoxifen, a drug taken by millions of women worldwide, on the somatomedin family of growth factors; involved in clin. trials of novel, non-toxic cancer therapies; Mem., Am. Soc. for Clin. Oncology; Ont. Med. Assn.; Que. Med. Assn.; Royal College of Physicians of Canada & num. other profl. societies; Cons., IBM Canada (med. software devel.) 1980; N.S.A.B.P., N.C.I.C., C.A.L.G.B. clinical trials groups; Orgn. Ctte., World Somatostatin meeting, Monte Carlo 1991; Chrmn., McGill-Sandoz Canada Breast Cancer Study 1990; awarded Terry Fox Cancer Research Fellowship, Ontario Cancer Inst. 1985, '86; Research grants, Nat. Cancer Inst. of Canada, Cancer Rsch. Soc. of Montreal, Sandoz Canada and others; author of numerous book chapters & scientific reports; Home: 4895 Mira Rd., Montreal, Que. H3W 2B7; Office: 3755 Cote St. Catherine, Montreal, Que. H3T 1E2.

**POLLARD, Andrew,** B.A.Sc., D.I.C., Ph.D., P.Eng.; university professor; b. Harrogate, England 9 July 1948; s. Reginald and Barbara Mary (Wiggins) P.; e. Ryerson Polytech. Inst., Dipl. Mech. Eng. 1970; Univ. of Waterloo, B.A.Sc. 1975; Imperial Coll. of Sci. & Technol, D.I.C. 1978; Univ. of London Ph.D. 1978; m. Elizabeth (Betty) d. John and Martha Longston 15 Aug. 1970; children: Richard, Michael; PROF., DEPT. OF MECHANICAL ENGINEERING, QUEEN'S UNIV. 1990– ; Rsch. Engr. in Training, GSW Rsch. & Devel. 1973–75; Rsch. Engr., Univ. of Waterloo 1975; Rsch. Asst., Imperial Coll. of Sci. & Technol. 1975–78; Asst. Prof., Univ. of Calgary 1978–81; Asst. Prof., Queen's Univ. 1981–83, Assoc. Prof. 1983–90, Prof. 1990– ; Vis. Rsch. Fellow, Univ. Erlangen 1986–87; Alexander von Humboldt Rsch. Fellow 1986–87; Dir., Rsch. Associe, CNRS, CEAT, Poitiers, France 1993–94; Visiting Prof., Univ. de Poitiers, France 1993–94; Founding mem. & Assoc. Dir., Centre for Advanced Gas Combustion Technology 1992– ; Founding mem. & 1st Pres., Computational Fluid Dynamics Soc. of Canada 1992; Mem., ASME; APS; APEO; Sigma-Xi; Assoc. Ed., 'Internat. J. Physico-Chem. Hydrodynamics' 1983–87; Mem. Adv. Bd., Internat. Journal of Computational Fluid Dynamics 1992– , Computational Fluid Dynamics Journal (Japan) 1992– , Applied Scientific Rsch. 1992– ; author/co-author of approx. 90 sci. pubs. incl. 1 book chap.; co-editor: 'Numerical Prediction of Flow, Heat Transfer, Turbulence and Combustion' 1983; recreations: stamp collecting; Home: 232 Avenue Rd., Kingston, Ont.; Office: Dept. of Mechanical Engineering, Queen's Univ., Kingston, Ont. K7L 3N6.

**POLLEY, Kenneth R.;** insurance adjustor; b. Toronto, Ont. 15 June 1941; s. Hugh MacArthur and Elsa Velma (Adams) P.; e. Runnymede Pub. Sch.; Humberside Coll. Inst.; Meisterschaft Coll.; Ryerson Inst. Bus. Adm.; Univ. of Toronto; Ins. Inst. Can.; Am. Mgmt. Assn.; m. Sonia Joy d. Hayward and Susan Clarke 21 Aug. 1981; children: Craig, Stephanie, Derek, Cheryl; PRES. AND CHIEF EXTVE. OFFR. MORDEN & HELWIG GROUP INC. 1983– ; Chrmn., Lindsey Morden Claim Services, Inc. (U.S.); Vale National Training Centers Inc.; Lindsey Morden Claim Services (UK); Pres., Lindsey Morden Claim Services, Ltd. (Canada); Dir., Centapp Services Inc.; FCA International; Hamkin Holdings Ltd. (UK); Fairfax Financial Holdings; previously served Stelco, Continental Insurance Co., Underwriters Adjustment Bureau, The Candle Shop; named Adjustor of Yr. 1990 by CIAA; 2nd Vice-Pres., Candn. Independent Adjusters' Assn.; Dir., Insurance Institute of Canada; Candn. Insurance Adjusters Assn.; Presidents Assn.; Candn. Owners & Pilots Assn.; Pilots Internat.; Am. Owners & Pilots Assn.; recreations: flying, travel, golf, boating, reading; Clubs: Albany; Credit Valley Golf & Country; Willowbrook Golf & Country; Office: 155 University Ave., Toronto, Ont. M5H 3N5.

**POLLOCK, David H.,** B.A., M.B.A.; educator; writer; b. Prince Albert, Sask. 14 June 1922; s. Norman and Bertha (Karner) P.; e. Kinistino High Sch. 1939; Univ. of Sask. B.A. 1946; Univ. of Chicago M.B.A. 1948; Univ. of Chicago postgrad. studies 1949; Toronto Conserv. of Music Sr. Dip.; m. Sheila d. Samuel and Pearl Lepofsky 5 Nov. 1951; children: Michael B., Barry F., Steven J.; ADJUNCT PROF. OF INTERNAT. AFFAIRS CARLETON UNIV. 1987; UN Econ. Affairs Offr. 1951–63 serving in Washington, D.C., Santiago and Mexico City; Special Asst. to Sec. Gen. UNCTAD Geneva 1963–67; Sr. Adv. to Dir. Gen. ILPES and Dir. UN ECLAC Washington 1968–80; Paterson Prof. Norman Paterson Sch. Internat. Affairs Carleton Univ. 1980–87; Visiting Prof. or Guest Lectr. Johns Hopkins Univ., American Univ., York Univ., El Colegio de Mexico; cons. to UN, Inter-American Development Bank, Candn. Senate, CIDA; served with RCAF WWII, Eng. & N.W. Eur., rank Flying Offr.; author 'The USA and Latin American Development' 1978; 'Energy and Development' 1981; 'Global Development During the 1980's' 1980; 'Human Values and Development' 1984; 'The Mulroney Doctrine' 1985; 'The Latin American Debt Crisis' 1986; 'Debt, Development and Democracy' 1988; 'Raul Prebisch Versus the U.S. Government' 1988; co-editor 'Latin American Prospects During the 1980's' 1983; 'Latin America to the Year 2000' 1992; mem. Extve. Cttes. Soc. Internat. Devel.; Candn. Assn. Latin Am. Studies; Centre Econ. Rsch. Latin Am. & Caribbean; UN Assn. Can.; Candn. Assn. Study Internat. Devel.; Candn. Inst. of Internat. Affairs; Inter-Am. Council; recreations: piano, walking, reading; Club: Rideau Valley; Home: 1891 Rideau Garden Dr., Ottawa, Ont. K1S 1G5.

**POLLOCK, Elaine Louise,** A.R.A.D.; ballet teacher / repetiteur / choreographer; b. Vancouver, B.C. 5 Jan. 1964; d. Ronald Walter and Mary Elaine (Tuft) P.; e. Canterbury H.S., OSSHGD 1982; George Brown Coll. Sch. of Dance, dipl. (hons.) 1984 (Lois Smith, art dir.); Mary E. Tuft, A.R.A.D. 1971–82; TEACHER, PIA BOUMAN SCHOOL FOR BALLET & CREATIVE MOVEMENT and THE THORNHILL SCHOOL OF DANCE; teacher, Ballet Acad., Canterbury Community Assn. 1981–82; guest teacher 1988; former teacher, The Oakville School of Dancing, The Dance Dactory and The O'Brien Dance Centre; performed with Dancesmiths, George Brown Coll. (roles incl. 'Swanhilda,' cygnet & principal roles in 'Lyric Dances,' 'L'Esprit de Dance' & 'Chansons du Printemps') 1982–86; with Banff Fest. in 'Facade,' 'Hangman's Reel,' 'Sacra Conversazione' 1984; with Atlantic Ballet Co. in 'Ballet Suite,' 'Collage,' 'Carnival of Animals' 1984; with Ont. Ballet Theatre in 'Aladdin and His Wonderful Lamp' 1985–86; Ballet Mistress, Dancesmiths, George Brown Coll., Sch. of Dance 1986–88; Youth Ensemble 1988; Sub. Teacher 1987–88; Ballet Mistress, Calgary City Ballet 1988; choreography: 'Rêverie' 1987, 'Sajé' 1987, 'Down Peacock Alley' 1988 (George Brown Coll.); co-choreography: 'Pirates of Penzance' (Savoy Soc. of Ottawa) 1985; Address: 1884 Carrere Court, Mississauga, Ont. L5J 4R5.

**POLLOCK, Graham J.;** international telecommunications executive; b. Saskatoon, Sask. 5 Mar. 1928; e. Western Can. H.S.; ICS Engr., 2 yrs.; Banff Sch. of Adv. Mngt., var. courses; m. Margaret Doris d. Wm. and Grace Bell 27 Oct. 1950; children: Bill, Terry, Jim; PRES., ALTA TELECOM INTERNAT. LTD. & ALTA. TELECOM, INC. 1986– ; joined Mannix Group 1948, positions included Vice-Pres., Opns., Loram Ltd. 1964 and Pres., Mannix Co. Ltd.; Pres., MHG Internat. Ltd. (Monenco subs.) 1973; Extve. Vice-Pres., Foothills Pipelines Ltd. 1977; Chrmn. & Chief Extve. Offr., MHG Internat. Ltd. 1980; Pres. & Chief Extve. Offr., Monenco Engr. & Constr. 1983; Dir., Monenco Ltd.; Mem., Candn. Constr. Assn.; Candn. Petrol. Assn.; Banff Sch. of Adv. Mngt. Alumni; Candn. Nuclear Assn.; Candn. Nat. Gas Proc. Supply Men's Assn.; Candn. Gas Assn.; Pipe Line Contr. Assn. of Can. (Past Pres.); Alta. Redi-Mix Concrete Assn. (Past Pres.); Clubs: Calgary Petroleum, Calgary Rotary, Calgary Glencoe, Pinebrook Golf & Country (Past Pres.); Office: 3626 13th St. S.W., Calgary, Alta. T2T 3R1.

**POLLOCK, John Albon,** B.A.Sc., M.B.A.; executive; b. Kitchener, Ont. 18 Jan. 1936; s. Carl Arthur and Helen Isabel (Chestnut) P.; e. Univ. of Toronto B.A.Sc. 1959; Harvard Univ. M.B.A. 1962; m. Joyce d. Chester Smethurst 13 Apl. 1963; children: Kimberlee S., Kristen A., Nichola C., Graham J.A.; CHRMN., ELECTROHOME LTD. 1982; Dir. CAP Communications Ltd.; Canadian General Tower Ltd.; Budd Canada Inc.; S.C. Johnson and Son; Canstar Sports Inc.; Waterloo Scientific Inc.; joined present Co. 1962, Vice Pres., Gen. Mgr. Electronics Div. 1969–71, Extve. Vice Pres. Operations 1971, Pres. 1971–80, Chrmn. of Bd. 1980–82; Past Chrmn. Bd. Govs. St. John's Sch. (Elora); Past Mem. Bd. of Gov., Univ. of Waterloo; Past Mem., The Science Council of Canada; Past Chrmn. Adv. Bd. Centre for Internat. Business Studies, Univ. of W. Ont.; mem. Young Pres.' Organ.; Past Pres., K-W Art Gallery; mem. Bd. Grand Valley Conservation Foundation and of The Freeport Hospital; Dir. The Trillium Found.; Dir. Candn. Clary and Glass Gallery; recreations: sailing, skiing; Clubs: Muskoka Golf & Country; University (Toronto); Rotary; Gyro; Home: R.R. 33, Cambridge, Ont. N3H 4R8; Office: 809 Wellington St. N., Kitchener, Ont. N2G 4J6.

**POLLOCK, Larry;** banker; e. Sask. Inst. of Applied Arts & Science, Bus. Admin. grad.; m. Joanne; children: Stacey, Jeff; PRESIDENT & CHIEF EXECUTIVE OFFICER, CANADIAN WESTERN BANK 1990– ; IAC Ltd. (Moose Jaw, Calgary, Medicine Hat, Edmonton) 1968–79; Asst. Gen. Mgr. & Br. Mgr., Continental Bank of Canada (Edmonton main br.) 1979–85; Reg. Gen. Mgr., Lloyds Bank Can. (Metro. Toronto & Ont.) 1985–87; Vice-Pres., W. Can. (Calgary) 1987–90; Dir., YMCA; Canada West Insur.; recreations: golf; Office: 2300, 10303 Jasper Ave., Edmonton, Alta. T5J 3X6.

**POLLOCK, Robert William,** B.Com.; executive; b. Winnipeg, Man. 20 Oct. 1928; s. Nicholas and Martha (Patterson) P.; e. Kelvin High Sch. Winnipeg. Univ. of Man. B.Com. 1949; CHRMN. DRAKE INTERNATIONAL; Dir. Competitive Systems Inc. (operating fast food for Kentucky Fried Chicken and Burger King in Australia); commenced with Burroughs Corp. Winnipeg. established Office Overload for Winnipeg businesses 1951; commenced Drake Personnel 1959, Industrial Overload 1961, Technical Overload 1962, Medox 1970; expanded operations to USA, UK, Switzerland, S. Africa, Australia, New Zealand, Singapore & Hong Kong; established Drake Computer Systems, Drake Productivity Centres 1983; acquired Computer-PREP Inc., 1986; acquired Market Power Inc. 1990; mem. chief Execs. Orgn.; World Bus. Council; Young Pres. Orgn. (Past Dir. and Sr. Internat. Vice Pres.); recreation: squash; Club: Monte Carlo Squash; Address: Europa Residence, Place des Moulins, Monte-Carlo, Monaco.

**POLLOCK, Samuel,** O.C.; executive; b. Montreal, Que. 15 Dec. 1925; s. Samuel and Maud (Yetman) P.; e. Westmount High Sch.; m. Mary Mimi d. J.B. Kinsella 27 Dec. 1962; children: Mary, Sam, Rachel; CHRMN., JOHN LABATT LTD. and CHRMN. CARENA BANCORP EQUITIES LTD.; Dir. Carena Developments Limited; John Labatt Ltd.; Trizec Corp.; Toronto Blue Jays Baseball Club; Hockey Can.; joined Club de Hockey Canadien Inc. 1947–78; mem. Candn. Sports Hall of Fame; Hockey Hall of Fame; elected to Great Montrealers 1978; Officer of the Order of Canada 1985; Chrmn. Internat. and Olympic Ctte. Hockey Can. 1982–88; Corporate Chrmn. Candn. Cerebal Palsy 1989; Co-Chrmn. Miss Edgars and Miss Cramps Bldg. Campaign 1987–89; Office: Labatt House, BCE Place, 181 Bay St., Suite 200, P.O. Box 811, Toronto, Ont. M5J 2T3.

**POLSKY, Leonard H.,** B.A., LL.B., LL.M.; lawyer (franchising); b. Brandon, Man. 27 June 1944; s. Charles William and Bertha (Schwarzfeld) P.; e. Univ. of B.C. B.A. 1966, LL.B. 1969; London Sch. of Econ. & Political Science LL.M. 1970; m. Carol d. Leonard and Lily Alvarez 17 Sept. 1970; children: Jesse, Sarah; PARTNER & HEAD OF FRANCHISING & INTELLECTUAL PROPERTY PRACTICE GROUP, FERGUSON GIFFORD VANCOUVER (MEM., GOODMAN LAPOINTE FERGUSON) 1990– ; called to Bar in B.C. 1971; Registered Candn. Trade-mark Agent 1972; Partner, Ray Connell to 1990; Lectr. U.B.C. / Course Co-ord. / Instr., Cont. Legal Edn. Soc. of B.C.; Speaker, Legal Edn. Soc. of Alta.; Law Soc. of U.C.; Candn. & Internat. Franchise Assns.; Candn., Wash. St., Am. & Internat. Bar Assns.; Vancouver Bd. of Trade; Industry, Trade & Commerce Canda; Industry & Small Bus. Dev. B.C.; B.C. Trade Dev. Corp.; Fed. Bus. Dev. Bank; Candn. Chamber of Commerce in Japan; Internat. Council of Shopping Centers; Pacific Corridor Enterprise Council; Mem., Spec. Ctte. on Indus. & Intellectual Property, Candn. Bar Assn. 1980–83; Pubs. Sub-Ctte., Cont. Legal Edn. Soc. of B.C. 1981–82; Affil. Rep. to Bd. of Dir. and mem. of Extve. Ctte. 1990–91 and mem. Legal & Leg. Affairs Ctte. 1991– , Candn. Franchise Assn.; Dir., Big Brothers of B.C. & Affiliated Big Sisters; Big Brothers of Canada; World Festival of Photography Soc.; Vancouver Inuit Art Soc.; Mem., Candn., B.C., Am. & Internat. Bar Assns.; Law Soc. of B.C.; Patent & Trademark Assn. of B.C.; Candn. Franchise Assn.; Pacific Franchise Assn.; Alta. Franchisors Inst.; Assoc. Mem., Patent & Trademark Inst. of Canada; Franchise Suppliers Council Mem., Internat. Franchise Assn.; Mem., Advisory Editorial Bd., Journal of Internat. Franchising & Distribution Law, London, England; author/co-author of several articles, reports & papers; recreations: fitness, photography, book collector; club: Arbutus; Home: 1947 W. 19th Ave., Vancouver, B.C. V6J 2P2; Office: #500 – 666 Burrard St., Vancouver, B.C. V6C 3H3.

**POLUBIEC, Mark J.,** H.B.A., M.B.A.; investment banker; b. Toronto, Ont. 24 Oct. 1953; s. George and Elzbieta (Kantypowicz) P.; e. Univ. of W. Ont. H.B.A. 1976; Wharton Sch. Univ. of Pa. M.B.A. 1980; m. Mary Jane Siebens 19 Aug. 1978; three s. Jonathan, Michael, Maxwell; PRESIDENT & CHIEF EXTVE. OFFR., MARPOL INVESTMENTS INC., investment and merchant banking concern since 1993; Burns Fry Limited 1981–93, apptd. Dir. 1986, Mng. Mergers & Acquisitions 1988–90, mem. Planning Ctte. since 1988, Pres. & C.E.O., Security Pacific Burns Fry (and successor corps.) 1990–92; served 5 yrs. financial mgmt. Canadian Pacific Enterprises Ltd. 1974–81; Clubs: Jonathan (Los Angeles); Granite; Georgian Peaks; Mad River Golf; Home: 40 Rosedale Rd., Toronto, Ont. M4W 2P6.

**POLUNIN, Nicholas,** M.A., M.S., D.Phil., D.Sc., C.B.E., F.R.G.S., F.R.Hort.S., F.L.S.; enviromentalist (formerly university professor and scientific explorer); author; editor; foundation executive; b. Checkendon, Oxfordshire, Eng.; s. late Vladimir and Elizabeth Violet (Hart) P. (both noted artists); e. The Hall Sch., Weybridge, Surrey; Latymer Upper Sch., London, Eng.; Oxford Univ. (Christ Church, Open Scholar), B.A. (1st Class Hons., Bot. & Ecol.) 1932; Yale Univ. (Pierson Coll., Henry Fellow, now Assoc. Fellow), M.S. 1934; Oxford Univ. (New Coll.), Sr. Research Scholar 1934–36; Oxford Univ., M.A. 1935, D.Phil. 1935, D.Sc. 1942; Harvard Univ. (Research Assoc.) 1936–37; m. Helen Eugenie d. late Douglas Argyle Campbell, Toronto, Ont. & Montreal, Que., and g.d. of Senator Hon. Archibald Campbell, Toronto, Ont., 3 Jan. 1948; children: April Xenia P. (Ven. Moujin), Dr. Nicholas Vladimir Campbell P., Douglas Harold Hart P.; Secy.-Gen. & Editor, Internat. Confs. on Environmental Future 1971–92; Founding ed., Biological Conservation 1968–74, Environmental Conservation since 1974; Pres. Foundation for Environmental Conservation since 1975; Convener & Gen. Ed., Environmental Monographs & Symposia, since 1979; Chrmn. Editorial Board of Cambridge Studies in Environ. Policy 1984– ; Pres., World Council For The Biosphere 1984– ; Member, Oxford Univ. Lapland Expdn. 1930; Hudson Strait (Labrador and Akpatok Island) Expdn 1931; explored Corsican Mountains 1932; conducted pte expdns. across Lapland, winter and spring 1933, and across Spitsbergen (summer 1933); Fla and Rocky Mts (1934); Candn E. Arctic patrols around Hudson Bay and Strait and to Southampton, Baffin, Devon, and Ellsmere Islands, 1934 and 1936; higher Alps 1935; own expdns. (sponsored by the British Museum) to S.W. Greenland in 1937 (where discovered plants introduced by Vikings from Am.) and N.W. Iceland in 1938 (where failed to detect any such Am. plants); Candn. E. Arctic Airborne Expdn. 1946 (confirmed Spicer Islands in Foxe Basin, & to east discovered last large islands which were confirmed by R.C.A.F. in 1948 and in 1949 named Prince Charles Is. & Air Force Is. & finally put on world map); Candn. W. Arctic 1947, incl. north magnetic pole; visited Alaska and made flight over geog. north pole Sept. 1948 making first recorded observation of microbial life in atmosphere there, also winter flight over north pole Mar. 1949, making various scient. observations; field work in Candn E. Sub-Arctic and Arctic northwards to Cornwallis Island (summer) 1949; arctic plant collections in National Museum of Natural Sciences, Ottawa, U.S. Nat. Herbarium, Washington, D.C., Gray Herbarium of Harvard Univ., Br. Museum (Nat. Hist.) etc.; Fielding Curator and Keeper of the Univ. Herbaria, Univ. Demonst. and Lect. in Bot., Oxford Univ., 1939–47; Lect. of New Coll., Oxford from 1942, and subsequently also Sr Research Fellow there; Visiting Prof. of Bot., McGill Univ. 1946–47; Macdonald Prof. of Botany, McGill Univ., 1947–52; Haley Lecturer at Acadia Univ. 1950; Lecturer in Plant Geography at Yale Univ. and in Biology at Brandeis Univ. 1953–55, while Adviser there and Director of U.S. Air Force Botanical Research Project on Ice-island T-3; Professor of Plant Ecology and Taxonomy, Dir. of Univ. Herbarium, etc., and Head of Dept of Botany, Univ. College of Arts and Science, Baghdad, Iraq, 1956–59, while advising on establ. of Univ. of Baghdad; Guest Prof., Univ. of Geneva, 1959–61 & 1975–76; Prof. of Botany and Head of Dept. 1962–66 and Founding Dean of Faculty of Science, Univ. of Ife, Ibadan and Ile-Ife, Nigeria, where also Dir. of Biol. Garden & took lead in planning main campus; Expdn. to Cameroon where climbed Mt. Cameroon alone; Ed. of 'International Industry,' 1943–46; Founding Ed. of World Crops Books 1954–74 and of Plant Science Monographs 1954–78; Founding Ed. of 'Biological Conservation' 1967–74; Founding Ed. of 'Enviromental Conservation' 1974– ; awarded Goldsmith's Sr. Studentship at Christ Ch., Oxford, 1932–33; Henry Fellowship, Yale University 1933–34; Department of Scient. & Indust. Research (London), Sr. Research Award, 1935–38; Foreign Research Assoc., Harvard Univ., 1938; Rolleston Mem. Prize 1938; Leverhulme Research Award, 1941; Arctic Inst. of N. Am. Research Fellowship, 1946–47; Guggenheim Fellowship, 1950–52; Research Fellowship of Harvard Univ., 1950–53; Ford Foundation Award in Scandinavia and U.S.S.R., 1966–67; Medaille Marie-Victorin for services to Canadian Botany; U.S. Order of Polaris (twice); decorated Comndr. Br. Empire; Indian Ramdeo Medal for Environmental Sciences; International Sasakawa Environment Prize 1987 and UN Secy. General's illuminated and signed certificate 'awarded to Nicholas Polunin in recognition of his most outstanding contribution in the Field of Environment'; subsequently recipient of medals etc. from various countries incl. China, USSR, South Korea, Hungary, The Netherlands, Order of the Golden Ark (Officer); UNEP Global 500 roll of Honour, etc.; served during 2nd World War as vol. mem. of Home Guard from its beginning (Intelligence Offr. i/c East and Central Oxford), 1942–45; author of 'Russian Waters,' 1931; 'The Isle of Auks,' 1932; 'Arctic Unfolding,' 1949; 'Circumpolar Arctic Flora,' 1959; 'Introduction to Plant Geography,' 1960; 'Eléments de Géographie Botanique,' 1967; reports and bulls. for Dept. of Mines & Resources, Ottawa; 3 Vols. on 'Botany of the Canadian Eastern Arctic,' 1940, 1947, 1948; 'The Environmental Future' (Ed.), 1972; 'Growth without Ecodisasters?' (Ed.) 1980; 'Ecosystem Theory and Application' (Ed.) 1986; 'Maintenance of the Biosphere' (Ed. with Sir John Burnett) 1990; 'Surviving With The Biosphere' (Ed. with Sir John Burnett) 1993; 'Environmental Challenges' (Ed. with Mohammad Nazim) 1993; numerous research and review articles contrib. to various Brit., Candn., U.S., Scandinavian & Swiss journs., chiefly on arctic plant taxonomy, phytogeog. and ecology, also on aerobiology and, latterly, conservation and environmental problems; Fellow of A.A.A.S., Arctic Inst. of N.Am.; INSONA (Internat. Soc. of Naturalists, now Vice-Pres.); first Hon. mem., Biological Soc. of Iraq; mem., Brit. Ecological Soc.; collaborator with the World Conservation Union (IUCN), Internat. Soc. of Naturalists (INSONA, now Vice-Pres.), Vernadsky Internat. Centre for Biosphere Studies (Pushchino near Moscow), and other bodies; Bot. Soc. Am. (Life mem.); Bot. Soc. Br. Isles (Life mem.); Brit. Assn. Advanc. Science (Life mem.); Am. Fern Soc. (Life mem.); Asian Soc. for Environmental Protection (Life mem.); North Am. Assn. for Environ. Educ. (Life mem.); International Soc. for Environmental Educ. (Life mem.); Sigma Xi; Christian upbringing; recreations: travel, walking, international stock markets; Clubs: Life mem. Harvard (N.Y.C.); Life mem. Torrey Botanical; Life mem. Field-Naturalists' (Ottawa); Life mem. Reform (London); Sr. Common Rooms of Christ Church and New College (Oxford); Initiator of 'Biosphere Day' 21 Sept. 1991; Address: Environmental Conservation, 7 Chemin Taverney, 1218 Grand-Saconnex, Geneva, Switzerland.

**POLZLER, Frank Julian;** real estate executive; b. Graz, Austria 18 April 1933; s. Franz and Theresa (Tandel) P.; e. Graz H.S.; Ont. Real Estate Brokers lic. 1959; m. Brigitte d. Richard and Erica Kanter 17 April 1983; children: Pamela Theresa, Michael Frank; CHRMN., CO-FOUNDER, REG. DIR., CHIEF EXTVE. OFFR., RE/MAX ONT.-ATLANTIC CAN. 1980– ; Chief Extve. Offr., Polzler Real Estate 1967–80; Dir., Integra Enterprises Inc. (Delaware); Re/Max of New England 1985; Re/Max North Central 1986; RE/Max of Indiana 1987; Dir., Renown Properties Inc., Florida; Pres. & Chief Extve. Offr., Fireball Holdings Corp. Ltd.; three time winner, Re/Max Internat. Reg. Dir. of the Year Award; Re/Max Distinguished Service Award; Office: 7101 Syntex Dr., Mississauga, Ont. L5N 6H5.

**POMER, Bella;** literary agent; b. Toronto, Ont. 30 Aug. 1926; d. Moses and Rachel (Kupferblum) Lieberman; e. Parkdale Pub. Sch.; Parkdale Coll. Inst. 1943; Univ. Coll. Univ. of Toronto 11/2 yrs.; m. Harold Pomer (dec. 1980) 25 Dec. 1945; children: Reva Anne, Janice Elizabeth; Owner, Bella Pomer Agency Inc. 1978– ; Rights Cons., Toronto Pub. Lib. 1979– ; Foreign Rights Rep. Univ. of Toronto Press 1982–88; Subsidiary Rights Mgr. MacMillan of Canada 1971–78; recreations: jazz, opera, chamber music, baroque music, theatre, films, walking, reading; Address: Ph2, 22 Shallmar Blvd. Toronto, Ont. M5N 2Z8.

**POMERANZ, Bruce,** B.Sc., M.D., C.M., Ph.D., D.Sc. (hon.); university professor; b. Montreal, Que. 24 July 1937; s. Abe and Goldie (Heinish) P.; e. McGill Univ. B.Sc. 1957, M.D., C.M. 1961; Harvard Univ. Ph.D. 1967; m. Miriam Varadi d. Solomon Pollack 22 Dec. 1991; one d.: Elyse Buchbinder; PROF., DEPT. OF ZOOLOGY, UNIV. OF TORONTO 1979– and PROF., DEPT. OF PHYSIOL., UNIV. OF TORONTO 1982– ; Internship, Montreal Gen. Hosp. 1961–62; Post-doct. fellow, Harvard Univ. 1962–66; Asst. Prof., Biol., M.I.T. 1966–68; Dept. of Zool., Univ. of Toronto 1968–73; Assoc. Prof. 1973–79; Pres. Amer. Soc. Acupuncture 1991–93; Parker Scholarship (ranking 1st at Harvard) 1962; Dag Hammarsjold Award for Sci. 1986; Weigand Lecture 'Alternative Medicine' 1991; Seirin Prize for Acupuncture 1992; Ed. Bd., Acupuncture: The Scientific

International Journal; Journal of Chinese Medicine; Complementary Therapies in Medicine; Subtle Energies Internat. Journal; Am. Journal of Chinese Medicine; Adv. Bd., Nat. Inst. Electromed.; World Fed. of Chinese Med.; Mem., Soc. for Neurosci.; Internat. Assn. for Study of Pain; Ont. Coll. of Phys. & Surg.; Acupuncture Found. of Can.; co-author: 'Textbook of Acupuncture' 1987, 'Basics of Acupuncture' 1988 and 80 papers; editor: 'Scientific Bases of Acupuncture' 1989; Home: 2 Silvergrove Rd., Willowdale, Ont. M2L 2N6; Office: 25 Harbord St., Toronto, Ont. M5S 1A1.

**POMERLEAU, Jeanne,** Bacc.ès Arts, c.c.l; author; b. Saint-Séverin, Beauce, Qué. 21 Nov. 1937; d. Alfred et Albertine (Vachon) P.; e. Univ. de Moncton B.A.ès Arts 1972; Univ. Laval, cert. in Creative Literature 1986; m. Jean-Claude Dupont 7 Sept. 1963; children: Luc and Marie Dupont; author: 'Les Grandes Corvées beauceronnes' 1987 (novel), 'Le Montreur d'ours' 1988 (novelette; short history), 'Métiers ambulants d'autrefois' 1990 (historical essay); 'Arts et métiers de nos ancêtres 1650-1950' 1994 (historical essay); major interest in French-Canadian culture; conference participant; interviewed by CBC (French); Mem., Cercle d'écriture des étudiant(e)s de l'Univ. Laval; Union des écrivains québécois; Univ. Laval Alumni Assn.; Univ. of Moncton Alumni Assn.; recreations: reading, travel; Home: 2700 rue Mont-Joli, Sainte-Foy, Que. G1V 1C8.

**POMEROY, Fred W.;** labour executive; b. Moose Jaw, Sask. 23 Apl. 1939; s. Alvin Baker and Mabel (Robb) P.; e. Moosomin High Sch. 1957; Labour Coll. of Can. 1969; EXTVE. VICE-PRESIDENT, COMMUNICATIONS, ENERGY AND PAPERWORKERS UNION OF CANADA (CEP) 1992– ; mem. Ont. Premier's Adv. Council; Ont. Labour-Mgmt. Adv. Ctte.; Bd. Dirs. and Extve. Ctte. Candn. Labour Market & Productivity Centre; NDP; recreations: sailing, tennis, cross-country skiing, cycling; Home: 505, 221 Lyon St. N., Ottawa, Ont. K1R 7X5; Office: 350 Albert St., Suite 1900, Ottawa, Ont. K1R 1A4.

**PONTE, Vincent de Pasciuto,** M.A.; city planning consultant; b. Boston, Mass., 27 Oct. 1929; s. Salvatore Raffaele and Marie (Mitrano) P.; e. Harvard Univ., B.A. 1943, M.A. (City Planning) 1949; Univ. of Rome (Fullbright Scholar) 1953–54; came to Can. 1967; HHFA-FHA Site Planning, Washington, D.C., 1950; N.Y. City Planning Dept., Asst. Planner in Transport., 1951–52; Webb & Knapp Inc., Urban Redevel. Dir., N.Y., 1956–58; I. M. Pei & Assocs., N.Y. 1959–63; established Vincent Ponte Town Planning Inc., Montreal, 1964; specialist in problems of downtown areas planning research for large-scale pub. and private projects in N. Am., European and Australian cities; proponent of 'Multi-Level city'; master planning of underground pedestrian systems in Montreal, Place Ville Marie, Place Bonaventure, McGill College Avenue, Quebec and Dallas, Texas, office and retail projects across Canada; Consultant to Nat. Capital Comn.; Guest Lectr., Univs. of Montreal, Wash., State, Houston, York Univ. (Eng.), Rice Univ., Columbia Univ.; author or co-author: 'The American Civil Engineering Practice,' 1957; 'To Everything There Is A Season,' 1967; 'Institute of Planning and Zoning,' 1968; other writings incl. various articles related to arch.; mem., Candn. Inst. Planners; La Corp. Prof. des Urbanistes Que.; Am. Inst. Certified Planners; Roman Catholic; recreation: books (history); Home: 3450 Drummond St., #1119, Montreal, Que. H3G 1Y3.

**POOL, Ian Duncan;** live theatre production; b. Vancouver, B.C. 19 Nov. 1949; s. Arthur Donovan and Joyce Catherine (Elder) P.; e. Banff Sch. of Fine Arts 1967; Univ. of Victoria 1968; children: Jamie Mortenson, David Gallagher; PROD. DIR., THE LIVE ENTERTAINMENT CORP. OF CANADA 1989– ; Tech. Dir., Nat. Arts Ctr. Theatre Dept. 1978–82; Prod. Dir. 1983–87; Tech. Dir., Opening & Closing Ceremonies, XV Olympic Winter Games, Calgary 1987–88; Prod. Dir., Cineplex Odeon Corp., Live Entertainment Div. & Prod. Mgr. 'The Phantom of the Opera' (opened in Toronto 20 Sept. 1989) 1988–89; Theatre Prod. Cons., Univ. of Ottawa, Dept. of Drama 1987; Alta. Achievement Award 1988; Theatre Prog. Scholarship, The Univ. of Victoria 1968; Mem., U.S. Inst. of Theatre Technol.; Internat. Alliance of Theatrical Stage Employees & Moving Picture Machine Operators of the U.S. & Can., Local 398 (Victoria, B.C.); Candn. Actors' Equity Assn.; recreations: off-shore sailing, alpine skiing; Office: 1792 Rockland Ave., Suite 10, Victoria, B.C. V8S 1X2.

**POOL, Léa;** cinéaste; née Geneve, Suisse 8 septembre 1950; f. Jacques et Sylvia (Pool) Mohr; é. Coll. et Gymnase Suisse Bac Litteraire 1969, Bac en Pédogogie 1971; Univ. du Qué. à Montréal Bac en Communication 1978; émigré Qué. 1975; Après avoir réalisé plusieurs vidéos, quelques courts métrages (notamment à l'UQAM) ainsi que des émissions de TV, elle scénarise, tourne et produit, en 1979, un premier long métrage de fiction 'Strass Café' 1980; De 1978–83, parallèlement à ses activités de cinéaste, elle donne des cours sur le cinéma et la vidéo à l'UQAM et travaille au Festival des Films du Monde de Montréal; De 1980–83, elle réalise pour Radio-Québec dix émissions sur les minorités culturelles; En 1984, elle scénarise et réalise un deuxième film de fiction 'L femme de l'hôtel' (sept prix dont le prix de la presse internat. au FFM, prix L.-E.-Ouimet-Molson, Génie de la meilleure actrice, prix du public pour la fiction, à Créteil, France (competition officielle, Berlin 1986); 'Anne Trister' 1986 constitue le dernier volet du triptyque; En 1988, elle signe 'A Corps Perdu', une adaption d'un roman d'Yves Navarre, Kurwenal (competition officielle Venise 1988); Le film est coproduit avec la Suisse; En 1988, elle prépare un documentaire sur les médias comme dernier décor de l'Amérique dans la série 'Parlez d'Amérique'.

**POOLE, James Winfield,** B.A., B.Ed., M.A., S.T.D.; educator; b. St. Stephen, N.B. 16 July 1926; s. Victor Bliss and Florence Agnes (Osborne) P.; e. Milltown (N.B.) High Sch. 1943; St. Joseph's Univ. Memramcook, N.B. 1943–45; Univ. de Montréal B.A. 1947, S.T.B. 1950, S.T.L. 1951, S.T.D. 1952; St. Thomas Univ. B.Ed. 1953; Fordham Univ. M.A. 1962; Univ. of Toledo 1968–69; Univ. of Maryland 1980–81, 1987–88; PROF. OF MATH., ST. THOMAS UNIV. 1954– , Vice Pres. (Acad.) 1977–82, Acting Vice Pres. (Acad.) 1975–77, 1989–90, Pres. Faculty Assn. 1972–73; Pres. Fed. N.B. Faculty Assns. 1973–74; mem. Candn. Math. Soc.; Math. Assn. Am.; Humanities Assn. Can.; Candn. Inst. Internat. Affairs; Candn. Profs. for Peace in Middle E. (Secy.-Treas. Fredericton Chapter 1976–77); Candn. Mental Health Assn.; Sigma Xi; Science for Peace; R. Catholic; recreations: theatre, classical music, travel; Address: St. Thomas Univ., Fredericton, N.B. E3B 5G3.

**POOLE, Nancy Geddes,** B.A., LL.D. (Hon.); art gallery director; b. London, Ont. 10 May 1930; d. John Hardy and Kathleen Edwards (Robinson) Geddes; e. Branksome Hall, Toronto; MacDonald Coll., Univ. of W. Ont., B.A. 1955; Univ. of W. Ont. LL.D. (hon. degree) 1990; m. William Robert s. John and Mary Poole 15 Aug. 1952; one d. Andrea Mary; DIR. LONDON REGIONAL ART AND HISTORICAL MUSEUMS 1985– ; served in areas of community service and edn. as volunteer over 30 yrs.; became Chrmn. Governing Council, Ont. Coll. of Art 1972, mem. of Council, Search Ctte. for Pres. 1975, named Fellow; mem. Bd. Govs. Univ. of W. Ont. 1974–85, chaired Property & Finance Ctte. 1982–85, Audit Ctte. 1979–81, Health Services Ctte. 1977–79, Campus Affairs Ctte. 1981–85; Vice-Chrmn., London Social Planning Council; founded Nancy Poole Galleries, London, Ont. 1969, Toronto 1971; Interim Dir. present Gallery 1981; served as prof., art curator and historian; wrote and produced TV prog. London, (Ont.) artists 1950's; frequent lectr.; recipient first 'Women of Distinction Award' for community service, London YM-YWCA 1984; Dir. Un. Appeal, May Court Club, Hardy Geddes House, Univ. Hosp., Jack Chambers Found.; Founding mem. London Art Gallery Women's Ctte. 1956; mem. Women's Ctte. London Symphony 1956–66; W. Art League 1956–66; author 'The Art of London: A History of Art in London (Ont.) 1830–1980' 1984; ed. and pub. 'Jack Chambers' 1978; Home: 420 Fanshawe Park Rd., London, Ont. N5X 2S9; Office: 421 Ridout St. N., London, Ont. N6A 5H4.

**POOLE, William Robert,** Q.C.; b. Neepawa, Man., 16 May 1918; s. John Silas and Mary Elizabeth (McFadden) P.; e. Univ. of Man. B.A. 1939; McGill Univ., Post Grad. Eng., 1945–46; Osgoode Hall Law Sch., 1946–49; m. Nancy Helen, d. late John Hardy Geddes, 15 Aug. 1952; one d. Andrea Mary; PARTNER, POOLE, BELL & PORTER; Prof., Criminal Law, Univ. of Western Ont.; mem., Ont. Law Reform Comn.; Atty. Gen. Comte. on the Admin. of Justice for Ont.; called to Bar of Ont., 1949; cr. Q.C., 1959; served during 2nd World War with R.C.N., 1939–45; retired with rank of Lt. Commdr.; Chrmn. (1967–68) London Public Lib.; mem., Candn. Bar. Assn.; Middlesex Law Assn.; Zeta Psi; recreations: reading, gardening; Clubs: London; London Hunt; Rideau (Ottawa); York (Toronto); University (Toronto); Canadian (Past Pres.); Office: 100 Fullerton St., London, Ont. N6A 1K1.

**POOTOOGOOK, Kananginak,** R.C.A.; artist; b. 1 Jan. 1935; medium: prints, printmaking, sculpture, jewellery; 121 group exbns. incl. most recent: Nat. Gall. of Canada Ottawa 1992, Westdale Gall. Hamilton 1992, McMichael Candn. Coll. Kleinburg 1991–92; l'Iglou Art Esquimau, Douai (toured 7 cities) France 1991, Inuit Gall. of Vanc. 1991, Albers Gall. San Francisco, Ca. 1991, Feheley Fine Arts Toronto 1991, Bunkamura Art Gall. Tokyo, Japan 1991; solo exbns.: Gall. Indigena Stratford 1989, The Guild Shop Toronto 1988, Candn. Guild of Crafts Que. Montreal 1987, Eskimo Graphics Kitchener 1986, U.N. Conf. on Human Settlements & Dept. of Indian Affairs & Northern Devel. Ottawa (tour) 1976–77, Robertson Galleries Ottawa 1975; works in 31 collections incl. art galleries of Hamilton, London Region, Ontario (Klamer Family & Sarick colls.), Windsor, Winnipeg (Swinton & Twomey Colls.), Canada Council Art Bank Ottawa, Candn. Mus. of Civilization Hull, Que., National Gallery of Can. Ottawa, Inuit Cultural Inst. Rankin Inlet, N.W.T., Metro. Mus. of Art N.Y.; rep. Cape Dorset on good-will tour to Greenland 1958; rep. Cape Dorset artists Stratford exhbn. 1965; comnd. to make four limited ed. prints, World Wildlife portfolio (attended preview Toronto) 1977; attended printmakers' conf. Ottawa 1978; comnd. to make two etchings for 1979 Nat. Museums gift catalogue; R.C.A. 1980; attended openings: 'Kananginak' The Guild Shop 1988, 'Cape Dorset Printmaking 1959–1989' McMichael Candn. Coll. 1989; speaker & panelist, Inuit Art Conf. McMichael Candn. Coll. 1992; subject of several articles and catalogues; Home: Cape Dorset, N.W.T.; Office: c/o Dorset Fine Arts, 33 Belmont St., Toronto, Ont. M5R 1P9.

**POPE, Hon. Alan William,** Q.C.; M.P.P., B.A., LL.B.; lawyer; b. Ayr, Scot. 2 Aug. 1945; s. Reginald Harry P.; e. Timmins High Sch.; Waterloo Lutheran Univ.; Osgoode Hall Law Sch.; m. Linda Marie d. Tony Fillion, Mattice, Ont. 18 Dec. 1976; s. David Alan; LAWYER (private practice); Ald. City of Timmins 1973–74; Nat. Pres. P. Cons. Youth Fed., 1969–71; Cand. prov. g.e. 1975, def.; el. M.P.P. for Cochrane South prov. g.e. 1977; re-el. 1981, 1985, 1987; Parlty. Asst. to Min. of Culture & Recreation 1978 and to Min. of Consumer & Comm. Relations 1978–79; Min. without Portfolio 1979–81; Min. of Natural Resources, Ont. 1981–85; Min. of Health 1985 Attorney Gen., Min. Resp. for French Language Services and Justice Secy. for Justice May-June 1985; P. Conservative; Anglican; Home: 294 Toke St., Timmins, Ont. P4N 6V5; Office: 101 Cedar St. S., Suite 202, Timmins, Ont. P4N 2G7.

**POPE, John A.,** B.Sc., P.Eng.; engineer; b. Red Deer, Alta. 6 Sept. 1942; s. Arthur and Gwen (Saxby) P.; e. Univ. of Alberta B.Sc. 1965; m. Sandra d. Eric A.D. McCuaig, Q.C. 15 May 1965; children: Jill, Nancy, Alison, Jenifer; PRESIDENT, DOMINION EXPLORERS INC. 1991–present; Engr. Manager, Mesa Petroleum Co. 1971–74; Partner, Argwen Ranch 1974–78; Pres., Rutherford Oil & Gas Ltd. 1978–84; Vice-Pres. & Pres., Skywest Resources Corp. 1984–87; Pres., Tygas Resource Corp. 1987–91; Keg River Resources Ltd. 1991; Mem., Assn. of Profl. Engineers, Geologists & Geophysicists of Alta.; recreations: game bird shooting, camping, fishing, travel, golf; club: Calgary Petroleum; Office: 1250 Bow Valley Sq. III, 255 – 5th Avenue S.W., Calgary, Alta. T2P 3G6.

**POPE, (John) Joseph,** D.Litt., F.C.B.A., F.I.C.B.; investment banker; b. Gistoux, Belgium 27 July 1921; s. Lt. Gen. Maurice Arthur, C.B., M.C. and Countess Simonne Marie du Monceau (de Bergendal) P.; e. Ecole St-Dominique, Que. 1928–30; Blackfriars Sch. Laxton, Eng. 1931–33, 1935–37; Model Sch. Ottawa 1933–35; Lisgar Coll. Inst. 1937–39; Univ. of Ottawa 1939; D.Litt. (Medieval Studies) Pontifical Institute of Medieval Studies 1993; m. Claudine d. Louis and Elizabeth de Lannoy 8 June 1953; children: Sybil, Francis, Allan, Lois, Nora, Julian, Michael; PARTNER, POPE & COMPANY 1962– ; Mng. Partner, Scrooge & Marley (real estate holdings); Pres. and Dir. Chaumont Securities Ltd.; Kamm, Garland & Co. Ltd.; Duncan Park Holdings Corp.; Scarley Realty Ltd.; joined Bank of Montreal, Ottawa 1940, Hull 1941–47, Montreal 1947–54; Burns Bros. & Denton Ltd. Toronto, Dir. 1954–62; served in 2nd W.W. with R.C.A. as Regt. Offr. 1942–46; Dir., Mediaeval Studies Found.; Dir. Quebec Central Railway Co.; mem. Invest. Dealers Assn. Can.; Toronto Bond Traders Assn.; Toronto Stock Exchange; Michaelmas Conf.; R. Catholic; Liberal; recreations: collecting mediaeval manuscripts, flying; Clubs: National; Badminton & Racquet; Home: 61 Cluny Dr., Toronto, Ont. M4W 2R1; Office: 15 Duncan St., Toronto, Ont. M5H 3P9.

**POPE, Peter Edward,** A.B., M.Litt., M.A., Ph.D.; university professor, consultant; b. Montreal, Que. 15 Sept. 1946; s. Herbert Edward and Eleanor Margaret (Ham) P.; e. Univ. of Toronto Schools 1964; Princeton Univ. A.B. 1968; Oxford Univ. M.Litt. 1973; Memorial Univ. of Nfld. M.A. 1986, Ph.D. 1992; children: Molly, Laura; ASSISTANT PROFESSOR OF HISTORY, MEMORIAL UNIV. OF NFLD. 1991– ; Prof., CBC Radio &

TV 1966–70; Rsch., Cabinet Office, Queen's Park 1973; Cabinetmaker 1974–78; Managing Dir., Affinities Ltd. 1978–84; Rsch. Asst., Memorial Univ. of Nfld. Archaeology Unit 1984–86; Lecturer in History, MUN & Sea Edn. Assn. 1987– ; Consultancy, Past Present Historic Resources; exbn. of cabinet work MUN Art Gall. 1976; SSHRCC and J.W. Pickersgill doctoral fellowships 1987–90; Fellow, Sch. of Grad. Studies, MUN 1992; Bullen Prize, C.H.A. 1993; Environ. Ctte., Flatrock Nfld.; Dir., Resource Ctr. for the Arts 1980–82; Maritime Studies Rsch. Unit (MUN); C.A.A.; C.N.E.H.A.; S.H.A.; S.P.M.A.; author: 'Popular Follies' 1972 (fiction); 'The Shape of St. John's Through Time' 1988 (exbn. catalogue); 'Finding Information for Newfoundland Documents (F.I.N.D.)' 1989; 'St. John's Harbour Area Archaeological Potential' 1991; recreations: boatbuilding, sailing; Home: 27 Power's Lane, Flatrock, Nfld. A1K 1C6; Office: St. John's, Nfld. A1C 5S7.

**POPOVIC, B. Dejan,** M.S., Ph.D.; educator; b. Belgrade, Yugoslavia 2 Apl. 1950; s. Bozidar and Jelena (Todorovic) P.; e. Univ. of Belgrade B.S. 1974, M.S. 1977, Ph.D. 1981; m. Mirjana d. Bogoljub and Koviljka Josifovic 28 Sept. 1975; children: Ana, Masa; PROF. OF ELECT. ENG. UNIV. OF BELGRADE 1991– ; Assoc. Prof. of Elect. Eng. Univ. of Belgrade 1985– ; Visiting Prof., Univ. of Miami 1991– ; Visiting Prof. Univ. Alta. 1987–88, Adjunct Prof. of Physiol. 1988– ; Asst. Prof. 1982; Cons.: Rehab. Center Dr. Miroslav Zotovic Belgrade 1982– ; Glenrose Hosp. Edmonton 1988– ; author over 100 sci. papers biomed. eng.; 7 lecture books mechanics and biomed. eng.; ed. series 'Advances in External Control of Human Extremeties' vols. VII, VIII, IX, X; ed. 'Automatika' Belgrade; mem. IEEE; Internat. Soc. Prosthetics & Orthotics; Internat. Soc. Biomed. Eng.; Yugoslav Soc. Biomed. Eng. (Pres.); recreations: tennis, swimming, skiing; Address: 506 HMRB, Univ. of Alta., Edmonton, Alta. T6G 2S2 and 11000 Belgrade, Yugoslavia, Ruzveltova 44.

**POPPENK, Nicholas John,** B.Ap.Sc., LL.B.; organizational development executive; b. Swift Current, Sask. 19 Sept. 1949; s. William Gerald and Joan Mabel (Jordan) P.; e. Univ. of Toronto, B.Ap.Sc. 1971, LL.B. 1975; m. Janis d. Alan and Evelyn Galbraith 7 Nov. 1974; one s.: Jordan Lindsay; PRINCIPAL, THE NEW SERVICE ALLIANCE INC. 1989– ; Pres., Podemos Performance 1992– ; Principal, V/NS Education Video Inc. 1991–93; Principal, The Service Conspiracy 1989– ; Corp./Comm. Lawyer, McCarthy & McCarthy 1975–80; Wilson Learning Ltd. 1980–86 (Pres. 1983–86); Chrmn. & Chief Extve. Offr., Impco Health Serv. Ltd. 1986–88; McCarthy Prize in Income Taxation, Bar Adm. Course 1977; recreation: running; Home: 31 Glendonwynne Rd., Toronto, Ont. M6P 3E5; Office: 31 Glendonwynne Rd., Toronto, Ont. M6P 3E5.

**PÓR, John Thomas,** Ph.D., P.Eng.; management consultant; b. Budapest, Hungary 17 March 1947; s. Imre Ø and Livia Ø (Ehrenwald) P.; e. Budapest Tech. Univ., M.Eng. 1970; Veszprém Tech. Univ., Ph.D. 1973; McGill Univ., Mgmt. Dipl. 1984; m. Agnes d. Jenö and Margit Somfai 8 May 1971; children: Daniel R., Andrew M.; MANAGING DIRECTOR, CORTEX APPLIED RESEARCH INC. 1991– ; Theoretical work in heat & mass transfer 1970–73; Internat. Sales Engr. 1973–75; immigrated to Can. 1976; Project Mgr., Combustion Engr. Ltd. 1976–80; Strategic Planner & Internatl. Mktg. Specialist, General Electric Canada 1980–81; Mgmt. Cons't. with Ernst & Whinney, National Partner, William M. Mercer Ltd. 1981; Lectr., York Univ. 1991– ; Mem., Assn. of Profl. Engrs. of Ont.; Planning Forum; Strategic Mgmt. Soc.; author of article and book chapter; recreations: tennis, swimming, classical music, (former mem., Hungarian Jr. Nat. Waterpolo Team); Home: 88 Duplex Ave., Toronto, Ont. M5P 2A4; Office: 45 St. Clair W., Suite 200, Toronto, Ont. M4V 1K6.

**PORELLE, Francis,** B.A.; retired broadcast engineer; b. Cap-Pelé, N.B. 13 Aug. 1928; s. George and Judith P.; e. St. Joseph's Univ. B.A. 1950; m. Eliette d. Yvon Leger 14 July 1951; children: Lucie, René, Louis, Donald, Claire, Frances; Aircraft Controller, R.C.A.F. (rank: Flying Officer) 5 years; Electronic Techician, then Production Manager (12 years), Canadian Broadcasting Corp. 1960–88; Dir. & Chair, Bd. of Dir., Coop Atlantic; Bd. Chair, Conseil Acadien de la Coopeartion; Roman Catholic; recreation: ham radio activities; clubs: Moncton Area Amateur Radio; Address: P.O. Box 89, Grande Digue, N.B. E0A 1S0.

**PORTEOUS, Cameron John;** designer; b. Rosetown, Sask. 2 Feb. 1937; s. John and Eunice H. P.; e. King Edward High Sch. Vancouver 1954; Wimbledon (Eng.) Sch. of Art Dip. Art & Design (Theatre) 1967; div.; children: Sharon, Mark, Ian; HEAD OF DESIGN SHAW FESTIVAL 1979– , Assoc. Dir. Shaw Festival Theatre; Head of Design Vancouver Playhouse 1969–79; designed for most theatres in Can.; exhibited designs Vancouver, Toronto, Prague, Lenningrad (1990); designed for 6 feature films, TV films, videos, operas CBC, CTV; over 180 theatrical designs; served Can. Council Adv. Panel; recipient Candn. Centennial Scholarship London, Eng. 1968; Can. Council Project Grant (devel. lighting simulators) 1974; Queen's Silver Jubilee Medal 1977; Citizen of Yr. Award Vancouver 1978; Dora Mavor Moore Award 1982; Best Costume Design Award Citadel Theatre 1982; author 'Twenty-five Years Retrospective of the Shaw Festival Designs' 1986; co-author 'The Inquiry into Theatre Training in Canada' 1976; Lutheran; recreations: skiing, swimming, cooking; Home: 56 Queenston St., Queenston, Ont. L0S 1L0; Office: P.O. Box 774, Niagara-on-the-Lake, Ont. L0S 1J0.

**PORTEOUS, Hugh A.,** M.A., D.Phil.; administrator; b. Saskatoon, Sask. 25 May 1951; s. George and D. Kathleen (Allingham) P.; e. Univ. of Sask. B.A. 1972; Oxford Univ. Balliol Coll. (Rhodes Scholar, Beit Rsch. Scholar, Can. Counc. Doctoral Fellowship) M.A. 1974, D.Phil. 1978; m. Maria Lucia Borges Loureiro 10 Oct. 1987; children: Miguel Hugo Borges-Porteous; EXECUTIVE ASSISTANT TO THE PRESIDENT & CHIEF EXECUTIVE OFFR., VIA RAIL CANADA INC. 1992– ; Sessional Lectr. in Hist. Univ. of Victoria B.C. 1978–79; Teacher of Hist., Eng. and Drama Shawnigan Lake (B.C.) Sch. 1979–80; Rsch. Asst. Royal Comn. Newspapers, Privy Counc., Ottawa 1980–81; various posts, Labour Can. Ottawa 1981–84; various posts, Via Rail Canada Inc. 1984– ; Secretary-Treasurer, Candn. Rhodes Scholars Found. 1992– ; mem. Bd. of Dirs., Candn. Assn. Rhodes Scholars 1983– ; Anglican; Home: 170, 1250 Pine Ave. W., Montreal, Que. H3G 2P5.

**PORTER, Agnes Helen Fogwill;** writer; b. St. John's, Nfld. 8 May 1930; d. Robert Wright and Amy Evelyn (Horwood) Fogwill; e. Holloway Sch.; Prince of Wales Coll. 1947; m. John Knight (dec'd) s. Heber and Susanna P. 2 July 1953; children: Kathryn Victoria, Margaret Anne, John Robert, Stephen Francis; professional writer since 1962; received awards for fiction, poetry and drama, Nfld. Govt.; shortlisted, Nfld. Govt. Arts Award 1987; for W.H. Smith/Books in Canada First Novel Award 1989; winner, Candn. Library Assn. Young Adult Can. Book Award 1989; winner, Newfoundland and Labrador Arts Council Lifetime Achievement Award 1993; Mem., N.D.P. (Nfld. Pres. 1985); Writers' Union of Can.; Internat. P.E.N.; Nfld. Status of Women Counc.; Ploughshares; author: 'Below the Bridge' 1980 (memoir); 'January, February, June or July' 1988 (novel); 'A Long and Lonely Ride' 1991 (short stories) & short stories, articles, poems, reviews & plays; editor: 'His Promises are Sure' 1988 (church history); co-editor: 'From This Place' 1977 (anthology); recreations: reading, music, theatre, travelling, walking, movies; club: The Longside; Home: 51 Franklyn Ave., St. John's, Nfld. A1C 4L2.

**PORTER, Anna Maria,** O.C., M.A.; publisher; b. Budapest, Hungary; d. Steven and Maria (Racz) Szigethy; e. Univ. of Canterbury, Christchurch, N.Z., B.A. 1964, M.A. 1965; m. Julian s. Dana and Dorothy Porter 8 Jan. 1971; two d. Catherine, Julia; PUBLISHER, PRESIDENT AND DIR., KEY PORTER BOOKS 1982– ; Chrmn., Lester Publishing Ltd. 1991– ; Pres. and Dir., McClelland-Bantam Inc. (Seal Books) 1987–92; Chrmn., Doubleday Canada 1986–91; Dir., Hollinger Inc.; Laurentian Financial; Key Publishers; Alliance Communications Corp.; Dir. & Mem. Extve. Ctte., The World Wildlife Fund Canada; Mem. of Bd., Assn. for Export of Candn. Books; UNICEF (advisory); York Univ. Business School, Advisory; Motovun (Switzerland); Mem. of Council, Assn. of Canadian Publishers; joined Cassell and Co. London, Eng.; Collier Macmillan Ltd. London, Eng. 1967–69; Collier Macmillan Canada Ltd. Toronto 1970; served as Vice Pres. and Ed.-in-Chief McClelland and Stewart Ltd. until 1979; Pres. and Publisher McClelland-Bantam Ltd. (Seal Books) until 1982; Office: 70 The Esplanade, Toronto, Ont. M5E 1R2.

**PORTER, Arthur,** O.C. (1983), M.Sc., Ph.D., F.I.E.E., F.R.S.A., F.C.A.E. (1987) F.R.S.C. (1970); university prof.; b. Ulverston, Lancs., England, 8 Dec. 1910; s. late Mary Anne (Harris) and John William P.; e. Univ. of Manchester, B.Sc. (1st Class Hons. Physics) 1933; M.Sc. 1934, Ph.D. 1936; Mass. Inst. Tech. (1937–39); m. Phyllis Patricia, d. late V. G. Dixon, London Eng., 26 July 1941; one s. John Arthur Harris; PROF. EMERITUS OF INDUSTRIAL ENGINEERING, UNIV. OF TORONTO since 1975; Asst. Lectr., Univ. of Manchester, 1936–37; Commonwealth Fund Fellow, M.I.T., 1937–39; Scient. Offr., Admiralty, London, 1939–45; Princ. Scient. Offr., Nat. Physical Lab., 1946; Prof. of Instrument Tech., Royal Mil. Coll. of Science, 1946–49; Head of Research Div., Ferranti Electric Ltd., Toronto, Ont., 1949–55; Prof. of Light Elect. Engn., Imp. Coll. of Science & Tech., Univ. of London, 1955–58; Dean of Engn., Univ. of Sask., 1958–61; Acting Dir., Centre for Culture & Technol., Univ. Toronto 1967–68; Chrmn. Adv. Comte. for Science and Med., Cdn. World Exhn. Corp. (Montreal, 1967); Acad. Commr., The Univ. of W. Ont. 1969–71; Chrmn. Candn. Environmental Adv. Council 1972–75; Chrmn. Ont. Royal Commission on Electric Power Planning 1975–80; Chrmn. of Bd., Scientists and Engrs. for Energy and Environmental Security Inc. 1981–82; Mem., U.S. Congressional Adv. Panel on 'Future of Nuclear Energy in the United States' 1982–83; Mem., Ministerial Task Force on 'The process of low-level radioactive waste site selection' 1986–87; Centenary Lecturer, Institution of Electrical Engrs., London, Eng. 1971; Professor and Chrmn., Dept. of Industrial Engineering, Univ. of Toronto 1961–76; Pres., Arthur Porter Assoc. Ltd., Ontario; Publications: 'Introduction to Servomechanisms,' 1950; 'Cybernetics Simplified,' 1969; 'Towards a Community University,' 1971; and various scient. research articles in learned journs.; Fellow. Inst. of Elect. Engrs. (London); mem., Soc. of Instrument Tech. (London); Assn. Prof. Engrs., Ont.; Operations Research Soc. Can.; Anglican; recreations: music, tennis, travel; Clubs: Athenaeum (London); Wyndemere C.C. (Naples, Fla.); Home: 3399 Gulf Shore Blvd. N., Apt. 603, Naples Florida 33940, USA.

**PORTER, Bruce T.,** M.B.A., M.P.A., C.A., C.M.C., P.Admin.; b. Toronto, Ont. 12 Nov. 1943; s. Walter Alvin and Doris Ellen (Jarvis) P.; e. York Univ. B.A. 1968, M.B.A. 1969, M.P.A. 1974; C.A. 1972; m. Mary Catherine d. Paul Graham 7 Aug. 1970; two sons: David Bruce, Brian Andrew; joined Clarkson Gordon & Co. 1969–73; Woods Gordon & Co. 1973–78; manager, The Clarkson Co. Ltd. 1978–82; Dir. of Finance, Sterling Trust Corp. 1982; SENIOR VICE PRESIDENT, SECRETARY-TREASURER, ORTECH (formerly Ortech Internat.) 1993– ; Ortech Internat. (formerly Ontario Rsch. Foundation) 1984–94; Teaching Master Seneca Coll.; Chrmn. of Accounting, Finance Adv. Comte. to the Bd. of Govs., Seneca Coll., 1980–82; mem. Found. Bd., Mississauga General Hosp.; mem. Inst. Pub. Adm.; Inst. C.A.'s Ont.; Candn. Inst. C.A.'s; Ont. Inst. of Management Consultants; Financial Extves. Inst.; Chartered Inst. of Secretaries; P. Conservative; Anglican; recreations: flying, scuba diving, curling, golf; Clubs: Bayview Country; Emerald Hills Golf & Country; Prestwick Golf & Country; Home: 16 Paultiel Dr., Willowdale, Ont., M2M 3P3; Office: Sheridan Park Rsch. Community, Mississauga, Ont. L5K 1B3.

**PORTER, Rear-Admiral Henry Timothy,** CMM, CD; retired naval officer; b. Kingston, Ont. 11 Feb. 1938; s. Henry William and Muriel Florence (Dailey) P.; e. St. Lawrence H.S., Cornwall 1955; HMCS Venture 1958; Canadian Forces College 1971; children: Jocelyn Marie, Christopher Timothy; Commanding Offr., HMCS Restigouche (Commander) 1977; HMCS Sask. 1978–80; Commander, Training Group Pacific, Maritime Forces Pacific (Capt(N)) 1983–85; Chief of Staff (Personnel) Maritime Command (Commodore) 1986; Chief of Staff Maritime Command (RAdm) 1987; Chief Personnel Services, Nat. Defence HQ 1989–90; Chief Personnel Careers and Development, National Defence Headquarters (Rear Admiral) 1990–93; Grade of Commander, Order of Military Merit, Canadian Forces Decoration; Special Serivce Medal (NATO); Extve. Dir., Ottawa and District Assn. for the Mentally Retarded; Mem., Woodroofe United Ch.; Home: 1887 Summerfields Cres., Gloucester, Ont. K1C 7B6.

**PORTER, John McKenzie,** M.C., F.R.S.A.; journalist and author; b. Accrington, Lancs., Eng. 21 Oct. 1911; s. the late John McKenzie and the late Amy Muriel (Smith) P.; e. Bolton Sch. Lancs., Eng. 1926; Baine's Grammar Sch. Poulton-le-Fylde, Eng. 1928; m. the late Kathleen d. the late William Gathercole, Bury, Lancs. 5 Sept. 1936; one s. Timothy McKenzie; Radio and TV Commentator; Contrib. Candn., Amer. and British Magazines; Reporter, Manchester Evening Chronicle 1929–31; Feature Writer, Daily Express 1931–36; News Ed. Daily Mirror 1936–38; Film Critic, Evening Standard 1938–39; Night Ed. Daily Sketch 1939; Paris Corr. Kemsley Newspapers 1946–48; Writer, Maclean's Magazine 1948–62; Columnist, Toronto Telegram 1962–71; Columnist and Drama Critic, Toronto Sun 1971–90; served as Rifleman, London Irish Rifles 1939–41; Commissioned The Cameronians (Scot. Rifles) 1941–46, action in Egypt, Syria, Sicily, Italy 1942–44; wounded Battle for Cassino 1944, seconded to Pol. Warfare Extve. Rome, Athens, Vienna 1944–46, rank Maj.;

Trustee Lib. Bd. East Gwillimbury, Ont. 1976–78; author 'Overture to Victoria' a biography of Prince Edward, Duke of Kent 1962; 26 short stories under pseudonym William Bennett 1932–48; The President's Medal, Univ. of W. Ont. 1960 for best gen. article of the year (biogr. of Frederick Varley); City of Rome Gold Medal for best article by a foreigner on subj. of Italy, 1960; el. Fellow, Royal Soc. of Arts, 1971; mem., Imperial Officers' Assoc.; Fort York Br., Royal Candn. Legion; Royal Candn. Military Inst.; P. Conservative; Anglican; recreation: travel; Home: Apt. 302, 95 Prince Arthur Ave., Toronto, Ont. M5R 3P6.

**PORTER, John Robert,** L.èsL., M.A., Ph.D.; university professor, curator, writer; b. Lévis, Que. 28 April 1949; s. John William and Irène (Bernier); e. Laval Univ. L.èsL. 1971, M.A. 1972; Univ. of Montreal Ph.D. 1982; m. Martine Tremblay 26 July 1975; children: Isabelle, Jean-Olivier; DIRECTOR, MUSÉE DU QUÉBEC 1993– ; leading specialist in the field of early Quebec art and has made a significant impact on the museological milieu of the prov. of Que.; Chief Curator, Montreal Museum of Fine Arts 1990–93; Asst. Curator of Canadian Art, Nat. Gallery of Canada 1972–78; Prof. of Art History, Laval Univ.; mem., num. programming & acquisition cttes. for museums across Que.; author of a number of books, catalogues & articles on the history of early painting, sculpture & furniture prodn. in the prov. of Que.; Office: Musée du Québec, Parc des Champs de Bataille, Québec, Qué. G1R 5H3.

**PORTER, Julian,** B.A., Q.C.; b. Toronto, Ont. 4 Dec. 1936; s. Dana Harris and Dorothy Ramsay (Parker) P.; e. Upper Can. Coll.; Univ. of Toronto Schs.; Univ. of Toronto B.A.; Osgoode Hall Law Sch.; m. Anna Marie Szigethy 8 Jan. 1972; children: Susanna, Jessica (from previous marriage), Catherine, Julia; PARTNER, PORTER, POSLUNS & HARRIS; called to Bar of Ont. 1964; cr. Q.C. 1975 mem. Candn. Del. to UNESCO Copyright Convention concerning U.C.C. and Berne Convention, Paris 1971; Past Pres., Candn. Nat. Exhn.; Past Chrmn., Toronto Transit Comn.; mem. Bd. of Govs. The Stratford Shakespearean Festival Foundation of Can.; Key Publishers Ltd.; mem. Advocates Soc.; Delta Kappa Epsilon; P. Conservative (def. cand., 1985 Ont. prov. election); Fellow, Am. College of Trial Lawyers 1993; Protestant; recreations: reading, tennis; Clubs: University; Albany; Badminton & Racquet; Coral Beach & Tennis; The Queen's Club; Home: 16 Rose Park Cres., Toronto, Ont. M4T 1P9; Office: 1201, 100 Yonge St., Toronto, Ont. M5C 2W1.

**PORTER, Wesley Robin;** horticultural consultant; b. Emsworth, Eng. 7 Aug. 1943; s. Charles John and Joan Sadie (Read) Beresford-Porter; e. Sparsholt Coll. Winchester, Eng. 1962; m. Jane Anne d. Henry and Jean Gobbett 22 Feb. 1973; one s. Marcus Beresford; PRIN. WESLEY R. PORTER CONSULTING 1983– ; Horticulturalist, Slack's Carnations, Waterloo, Qué. 1962, Sheridan Nurseries Etobicoke, Ont. 1971; Chief Horticulturalist Whimsy Inc. Toronto 1975, White Rose Nurseries Unionville, Ont. 1975; Wesley R. Porter Consulting Toronto 1978; Sr. Lectr. in Horticulture, Niger State Coll. of Edn. Minna, Nigeria 1981; Instr. Seneca Coll. 1978, George Brown Coll. 1983, Adult Edn. Toronto Sch. Bd. 1985; numerous TV appearances; former garden expert weekly CBC 'Morning' TV prog.; garden expert CFTO 'Eye on Toronto'; TVO 'Green Earth Club' TV prog.; newspaper columnist; frequent contbr. prov. & nat. trade mags.; co-originator 'Gartoons' practical gardening tips; introduced edn. TV progs. Nigeria with frequent appearances; author 'Green Side Up' 1986; 'The Garden Book and Green House' 1989; Hortic. mem. Landscape Ont. Trade Assn.; recreations: fishing, wine tasting; Address: 714, 255 Main St., Toronto, Ont. M4C 4X2.

**PORTER, William Lorne,** B.Comm., C.A.; financial executive; b. Vancouver, B.C. 18 June 1941; s. Clarence William and May Nellie (Thompson) P.; e. Univ. of Toronto B.Comm. 1964; m. Barbara d. Morse and Joan Robinson 27 Oct. 1985; children; David, Thomas, Shannon; Vice President, Finance, The Blackburn Group Inc. 1982–93; Ernst & Young 1964–69; various positions ending as Controller, Bristol Myers Canada Limited 1969–73; Vice Pres. & Sec. Treas., Guthrie Canadian Investments Limited 1973–82; Bd. of Dir., United Way of Canada; Past Chair, United Way of Greater London; Home: 1072 The Parkway, London, Ont. N6A 2W9.

**PORTNER, Christopher,** B.Sc., B.C.L.; lawyer; b. Nairobi, Kenya 17 July 1945; s. Walter and Ilse (Von Rothe) P.; e. McGill Univ. B.Sc. 1967, B.C.L. 1971; m. Susan E. d. Harold and Marjorie Banks 4 Oct. 1975; children: Angela, Matthew; PARTNER, OSLER HOSKIN & HARCOURT 1980– , Mem. Extve. Ctte.; Chair, Commercial Transactions Dept.; called to Bar of Que. 1971 and Ont. 1980; mem. Ogilvy Renault Montreal 1972–78; Vice Pres. and Gen. Counsel Trizec Corp. Ltd. 1978–80; Lectr. McGill Univ. (mem. Bd. Govs. 1970–72) and Loyola Coll. 1976–78; Dir., Daiwa Bank Canada; Trustee, Hosp. for Sick Children Toronto; recipient Queen's Silver Jubilee Medal 1977; mem. Am., Internat. and Candn. Bar Assns.; recreations: tennis, skiing; Clubs: The Toronto; Toronto Lawn Tennis; Granite; Caledon Ski; Home: 271 Inglewood Dr., Toronto, Ont. M4T 1J2; Office: P.O. Box 50, First Canadian Place, Toronto, Ont. M5X 1B8.

**POSER, Ernest George,** M.A., Ph.D.; educator; b. Vienna, Austria 2 March 1921; s. Paul and Blanche (Furst) P.; e. Queen's Univ. B.A. 1946, M.A. (Psychol.) 1949; Univ. of London (Maudsley Hosp.) Ph.D. 1952; m. Maria Jutta d. late Heinz Cahn 3 July 1953; children: Yvonne Melanie, Carol Ann, Michael Paul; ADJUNCT PROF., DEPT. OF PSYCHOLOGY, UNIV. OF B.C. 1984– ; Dir. Behavior Therapy Unit, Douglas Hosp. Centre 1966–83; Asst. Prof. of Psychol. Univ. of N.B. 1946–48; Asst. Prof. of Psychol. McGill Univ. 1954, Assoc. Prof. 1957–69, Prof. 1969–83, Assoc. Prof. of Psychiatry 1963–83; Sr. Psychol. Mental Health Div. Dept. Health N.B. 1952–54; Chief Psychol. Montreal Rehabilitation Centre 1955–57; Dir. of Psychol. Dept. Douglas Hosp. Center 1957–66; Consultant Forensic Psychiatry Unit McGill Univ. 1966–67; Hon. Fellow, Middlesex Hosp. Med. Sch. London, Eng. 1964–65; mem. Que. Govt. Comte. Mental Health Services 1971–72; Visiting Prof. Univ. of Berne 1972–73; recipient numerous Candn. and U.S. research grants; author 'Behavior Therapy in Clinical Practice: Decision-Making, Procedure and Outcome' 1977; co-author 'Behavior Modification with Children' 1973; author numerous articles prof. journs.; Fellow, Candn. psychol. Assn. (Dir. 1960–63); Fellow, Am. Psychol. Assn.; Que. Corp. Psychols. (Dir. 1967–68); Pres., Psychol. Assn. Prov. Que. 1961; recreations: tennis, skiing, swimming; Address: 4517 West 4th Ave., Vancouver, B.C. V6R 1R4.

**POSLUNS, Lynn,** B.Com., M.B.A.; fashion executive; b. Toronto, Ont. 29 May 1958; d. Wilfred and Joyce P.; e. Univ. of Toronto B.Com. 1981, M.B.A. 1983; m. Ken s. Sam and Shirley Crystal 20 June 1982; three s. Bradley, Daniel, Eric; PRES. FAIRWEATHER (DIV. OF DYLEX LTD.) 1989– ; Regional Mktg. Co-ord. Tip Top (Div. of Dylex Ltd.) 1983; Mktg. Liaison, Club International (U.S. Div. of Tip Top) 1985; Co-Merchandise Control Mgr. Fairweather 1986, Co-Gen. Merchandise Mgr. 1987; Office: 637 Lake Shore Blvd. W., Toronto, Ont. M5V 1A8.

**POSNER, Barry Innis,** M.D., F.R.C.P.(C), F.R.S.C.; physician; scientist; b. Winnipeg, Man. 7 Nov. 1937; s. Solomon Dalton and Rebecca (Markovitz) P.; e. Univ. of Man. M.D. 1961; m. Beatrice d. Henry and Florence Melmed 17 June 1962; children: Aaron Zvi, Rebecca Leah, Daniel Seth; DIR. DIV. OF ENDOCRINOLOGY, ROYAL VICTORIA HOSP. 1981– , mem. Extve. Ctte. 1979–82; Chrmn., Extve. Ctte., Rsch. Inst., RVH; Dir., Training Prog. in Endocrinology McGill Univ. 1981– ; Dir., Polypeptide Hormone Rsch. Lab. 1977– ; Asst. Prof. of Med. McGill Univ. 1970, Assoc. Prof. 1975, Prof. 1979; mem., Med. Sci. Adv. Comm. Intnl. Juvenile Diabetes Foundation; mem., N.I.H. Endocrine Study Section 1986–89; Med. Rsch. Council Scholar 1971–76; Chercheur-Boursier de Qué. 1976–86; France-Qué. Exchange Prog. 1976–82; author or co-author over 214 sci. manuscripts; ed. 'Polypeptide Hormone Receptors' 1985; mem. ed. bd. 'Diabetes'; mem. Assoc. of Am. Physicians; Am. Soc. Clin. Investig.; Candn. Soc. Clin. Investig.; Candn. Soc. Endocrinol. & Metabolism; Am. Soc. Biol. Chems.; Am. Soc. Cell Biol.; Am. Endocrine Soc.; Am. Diabetes Assn.; recipient, Distinguished Scientist Award, Candn. Soc. of Clinical Investig., Toronto 1990; Banting and Best Memorial Lecture, 14th Internat. Diabetes Fed., Washington, D.C. 1991; Election to Peripatetic Club 1991; Fellow, Royal Society of Canada: Academy of Sciences 1991; recreations: singing, dancing, reading, bicycling; Home: 360 Wood Ave., Westmount, Que. H3Z 1Z2; Office: Dept. of Medicine, RVH, 687 Pine Ave. W., Room M9.05, Montreal, Que. H3A 1A1.

**POSPIELOVSKY, Dimitry Vladimirovich,** B.A., M.A., M.Phil.; university professor/author; b. Rovno, USSR 13 Jan. 1935; s. Vladimir Konstantinovich and Mariamna Konstantinovna (Ushinsky) P.; e. Eur. 1941–49; H.S. of Montreal 1953; Sir George Williams Coll., B.A. 1957; Univ. of London, M.A. 1961; London Sch. of Econ., M.Phil. 1967; m. Mirjana d. Marija and Petar Dobrovich 24 July 1960; children: Dariya, Andrew, Bogdan; PROF. OF RUSSIAN & MODERN EUROPEAN HISTORY, UNIV. OF WESTERN ONT. 1981– ; Prog. Asst./Broadcaster, BBC, Russ. Serv. 1959–65; Rsch., Comm./Broadcaster, BBC Central Rsch. Unit 1965–67; Rsch. Assoc./Writer, Hoover Institution Stanford Univ. 1967–69; Rsch. Analyst/Section Dir., Radio Liberty Ctte. (W. Germany) 1969–72; Asst. Prof., Univ. of West. Ont. 1972–75; Assoc. Prof. 1975–81; Vis. Fellow 1978–79, 1986–87, Harvard Univ. Russ. Rsch. Ctr.; Keston Coll.; London Sch. of Econ.; Sch. of Slavonic Stud., Univ. of London; Teacher, Russ. Hist., Oklahoma, Carleton & Wilfred Laurier Univs., Colorado Coll., Moscow & Leningrad Theological Schs.; Cons., Radio Liberty; Contbr., radio scripts, Radio Can.; mem., Orthodox Ch.; Am. Assn. for Adv. of Slavic Stud.; Candn. Assn. of Slavists; author: 'Russian Police Trade Unionism' 1971, 'Russian Church under the Soviet Regime' (2 vols) 1984, 'A History of Soviet Atheism in Theory and Practice, and the Believer' (3 vols) 1987 (Vol. I & II), 1988 (Vol. III), 'Na putiakh k rabochemu pravu' 1987; Contbr., 7 books, most recent 'Histoire de l'Église russe' Paris 1989; num. sch. articles & rsch. papers; Home: 431 Fox Ave., London, Ont. N6G 1H7; Office: Social Science Centre, London, Ont. N6A 5C2.

**POST, George;** policy consultant; b. Stirling, Ont. 28 June 1934; s. R. Elmer and Florence (Bailey) P.; e. Stirling (Ont.) High Sch. 1952; Queen's Univ. 1952–56; Northwestern Univ. 1956–59; m. Shirley, d. Luther Alyea, Belleville, Ont. 15 June 1957; children: Ellen, Christine, Richard; ORGANISING SECRETARY, COMMONWEALTH ASSOCIATION FOR PUBLIC ADMINISTRATION AND MANAGEMENT 1993– ; Lectr. Queens' Univ. 1959–62; Research Dept. Bank of Canada 1962, Chief Dept. Banking & Financial Analysis 1970–71; Asst. Secy. to Cabinet, Privy Council Office, Ottawa 1972–74; Vice Chrmn., Economic Council of Canada, 1975–78; Depy. Min. of Consumer and Corp. Affairs 1978–85; Depy. Clerk of the Privy Council Office 1985–86; Federal Econ. Devel. Coordinator (Ont.) 1986–91; Secretary, Indian Specific Claims Commission 1991–92; Extve. Dir., Commonwealth Assn. for Public Administration and Management 1992–93; mem. Inst. of Public Admin. of Canada; United Church; Office: 121 Buell St., #33, Ottawa, Ont. K1Z 7E7.

**POST, Shirley,** S.S.St.J., B.Sc.N.Ed., M.H.A.; health administrator; b. Carrying Place, Ont. 20 Jan. 1935; d. Luther B. and Illa Evelyn (Calnan) Alyea; e. Atkinson Sch. of Nursing, R.N. 1955; Univ. of Ottawa, B.Sc.N.Ed. 1967, M.H.A. 1972; m. George s. Elmer Post 15 June 1957; children: Ellen, Christine, Richard; Vice-Pres., Hosp. for Sick Children Found. 1988; Clinical Instr., Sch. of Nursing, Univ. of Ottawa 1968–70; Dir. of Nursing, Children's Hosp. of Eastern Ont. 1974–76; Extve. Dir., Candn. Inst. of Child Health 1977–87; Serving Sister, Order of St. John; Cons., Candn. Inst. of Child Health 1987–90; Mem., Working Group, Goal IV, Premiers Counc. on Health (Ont.) 1989–90; Mem., Assn. for the Care of Children's Health (Pres. 1981–83); Bd., Candn. Standards Assn. 1987–94; Home: 62 Wellesley St. W., Apt. 705, Toronto, Ont. M5S 2X3.

**POST, Victor Ian,** C.P.A., R.P.S.; photographer; b. Port Colbourne, Ont. 12 May 1953; s. John Edward and Lena T. P.; e. Univ. of Alberta 1969–72; m. Kathryn B.J. d. Harry and June Brown 17 May 1981; FOUNDER, VICTOR POST PHOTOGRAPHY 1972– ; one of the most successful profl. photograph firms in Western Canada (a full service lab and studio); Dir., Nat. Gallery of Canada (Bd. of Trustees); Ctte., Profl. Photographers of Alta.; Mem., Candn. Museum of Contemporary Photography C.M.C.P.; National Science Award & scholarships for research work in lasers and holography (age 16); apptd. to Royal Photographic Soc. by Royal Assent after being chosen as official photographer for every royal visit to Alta. since 1973; Dir., Public Affairs Northern Alta. Radio Club; recreations: ham radio, photography; Home: 90 Beaverbrook Cr., St. Albert, Alta. T8N 2L2; Office: 8 Perron St., St. Albert, Alta. T8N 1E2.

**POTTER, Lianne I.W.,** B.A., LL.B.; lawyer; b. Hamilton, Ont. 24 Nov. 1957; d. Calvin Cuthbert and Winifred Irene (Nelson) P.; e. McGill Univ. B.A. 1979; Oxford Univ. B.A. (Jurisprudence) 1981; Dalhousie Univ. LL.B. 1982; PARTNER, BROCK & POTTER since 1993; called to Bar of B.C. 1983; Partner, Ladner Downs 1989–93; Home: 3536 W. 28th Ave., Vancouver, B.C. V6S 1S2; Office: 401 - 815 Hornby St., Vancouver, B.C. V6Z 2E6.

**POTTER, Norris Franklin,** FICB; banker; b. Tillsonburg, Ont. 20 July 1936; m. Mary Jean Borden 1961; e. RMCS, Queen's Univ.; Comm Lieut regular army, service in Cda. UK and Germany 1954–62; mgt. training CIBC, served in Cda, UK and Switzerland 1962–70; Vice Pres., Internat. banking Toronto Dominion Bank,

London; Pres., Toronto Dominion Bank (Middle East) Beirut 1970–78; Sr. Vice Pres., Internat. Banking, Bank of Montreal 1978–85; Dir., Cdn. Dominion Leasing, Bank of Montreal (Bahamas), Bank of Montreal Internat.; Gov., Canadian Opera Company, Havergal Foundation; Extve. Dir., The World Bank, Internat. Finance Corp.; Multilateral Inv Gtee Agency, Washington 1985–93; Advisor, Dept. of Finance, Ottawa; clubs: Queen's, Toronto, York; Home: 20 McKenzie Ave., Toronto, Ont. M4W 1J9; Office: 1 Front St. W., Toronto, Ont. M5J 1A4.

**POTTER, Richard Bain,** Q.C., B.A., LL.B.; barrister and solicitor; b. Ottawa, Ont. 25 June 1940; s. Frank Arthur and Helen Geraldine (Bain) P.; e. Univ. of Toronto, B.A. 1962; LL.B. 1965; m. Anne d. Dr. William and Margaret Baldwin 18 July 1964; children: David Anderson, Carolyn Suzanne; LAWYER, FASKEN MARTINEAU 1967– ; internat. business lawyer with emphasis on trade & investment, computers, technol. transfer, joint ventures & dispute resolution; public speaker worldwide; Q.C. 1982; Dir., Hiram Walker-Gooderham & Worts Ltd.; Canada/U.K. Chamber of Commerce; Arbor Award, U. of T. 1989; Meredith Mem. Lectr., McGill Univ. 1982; Law Soc. of Upper Can., Spec. Lectr. 1984; Candn. Institute for Advanced Legal Studies, Cambridge 1991; Candn., Am. & Internat. Bar Assns.; Computer Law Assn.; Founding Ed., 'Business Law Reports' 1977–91; recreations: music, cycling, skiing; Clubs: University Club of Toronto; East India Club; Home: 17 Clarendon St., London, England SW1V 2EN.

**POTTIE, Roswell Francis,** B.Sc., Ph.D.; public servant; b. St. Peter's, N.S. 28 Oct. 1933; s. John Henry and Margaret Mary (Landry) P.; e. St. Francis Xavier, B.Sc. 1954; Notre Dame Univ., Ph.D. 1958; m. Huguette d. Emilien and Marie-Mance Lacoste 18 Aug. 1989; children (from previous marriage): Michael, Gregory, Lisa, David; PRIVATE CONSULTANT 1991– ; post-doct., Notre Dame Univ. 1957–58; NRC 1958–60; Rsch. Chem., Dupont (U.S.) 1960–64; Rsch. Offr., NRC 1964–74; Program Offr., MOSST (secondment) 1974–75; Program Analyst, Treas. Bd. 1975–76 (secondment); Asst. to Sr. Vice-Pres., NRC 1976–80; Dir. Atlantic Reg. Office 1980–83; Vice-Pres., Regional Labs. 1983–84; Physical Sci. & Engr. 1984–86; Sr. Vice-Pres. (Labs.) 1986–87; Extve. Vice Pres. 1987–91; Gov. General's Medal 1954; degree with Hon. summa cum laude St. Francis Xavier Univ. 1954; Notre Dame Univ. Grad. Assistantship 1954–57; Bd. of Gov., Ctr. for COLD Ocean Resources Engr.; Counc. Mem., N.B. Rsch. & Productivity Counc.; Mem., Sigma XI Soc.; Candn. Rsch. Mngt. Assn.; author of 35 scientific articles; recreations: swimming, badminton, carpentry, ancient history; Home: R.R. 1, Head of Jeddore, N.S. B0J 1P0.

**POTTLE, Herbert Lench,** M.A., Ph.D., LL.D.; retired public servant; direct descendant of Thomas Pottle, lay preacher who, under Rev. Lawrence Coughlan (sent to Nfld. by John Wesley), helped to establish the Meth. Ch. in early 19th century at Harbour Grace, once Nfld. capital, Carbonear and neighbouring settlements; b. Flatrock, Carbonear District, Nfld. 16 Feb. 1907; s. William Thomas and Patience Susannah (Evely) P.; e. Mount Allison Univ., B.A. 1932, (Gold Medalist); Univ. of Toronto, M.A. 1934, Ph.D. 1937; m. Muriel Ethel, d. Benjamin F. Moran, Trenton, Ont. 2 Aug. 1937; children: Helen Louise, Kathryn Elaine, Herbert Franklin; served on staff, Dept. of Psychol., University of Toronto, 1934–37; Clinical Psychol., Infants Home, Toronto, 1937–38; Executive Officer United Church Schs., Newfoundland, 1938–44; Director of Child Welfare, and Judge of the Juvenile Court, St. John's, Newfoundland, 1944–47; appointed Commissioner for Home Affairs and Educ. in the Nfld. Comn. of Govt. until Confed., 1947–49; 1st el. to H. of A. for Dist. of Carbonear-Bay de Verde, in g.e. 1949 and re-el. g.e. 1951; Minister of Public Welfare, Nfld., 1949–55 when resigned; Secy., Bd. of Information & Stewardship, Un. Ch. of Can., 1955–63; Social Welfare Adviser, Govt. of the (then) United Kingdom of Libya, under the auspices of the United Nations (Headquarters: capital city of Tripoli) 1961–62; Principal Research Offr. (Welfare), Dept. of Nat. Health & Welfare, 1963–68 (Internat. Welfare and Special Projects) 1968–72; former mem. of Board of Govs., Memorial Univ. Coll., St. John's, Nfld.; former Regent of Mount Allison Univ.; U.N. Social Welfare Adv. to Govt. of Libya (on leave) 1961–62; Rapporteur, Interregional Expert Meeting, U.N. on Social Welfare Organ. & Adm., Geneva 1967; Hon. Life mem., U.N. Assoc. in Canada; rec'd. Charles Frederick Allison Award, Mt. Allison Univ. 1984; Doctor of Laws (honoris causa), Mount Allison Univ. 1992; author of 'Dawn Without Light: Politics, Power and the People in the Smallwood Era'; 'Fun on the Rock: toward a Theory of Newfoundland Humour'; 'From the Nart Shore: out of my Childhood and Beyond'; 'The Intern. Quality of Educ. in Canada'; United Church; Home: Sterling Place, 2716 Richmond Rd., Apt. 311, Ottawa, Ont. K2B 8M3.

**POTTOW, Geoffrey William John,** B.Sc., M.S., Ph.D.; executive; b. Windsor, Eng. 21 Jan. 1933; s. Victor John and Nellie Victoria (Tull) P.; e. Univ. of London B.Sc. 1955; The Case Inst. (Fulbright Scholar) M.S. 1957; Univ. of Toronto (Open Fellowship) Ph.D. (Eng.) 1965; m. Constance d. Frank and Matilda Bazos 9 Nov. 1960; children: Victor Frank, Geoffrey James, Jonathan Edwards, Victoria Matilda; PRES. THE BECKER MILK CO. LTD. 1984– ; designed Gas Turbine testing facility Case Inst. of Tech.; designed automatic letter sorting system for Washington Post Office & Pitney Bowes, Conn.; Rsch. & Devel. Eng. Polymer Corp., Canada; lectr. Univ. of Toronto; joined present co. 1965 as head Corporate Devel. & Expansion; Senior Fellow, Massey Coll. Univ. of Toronto; Vice Chrmn. and Dir. Ont. Dairy Council; author 'On Vibration of a Rotating Shaft' 1965; recreation: squash, tennis, skiing; Clubs: Royal Household Bowling; Granite; Craigleith Ski; Toronto Racquet (Life mem.); Muskoka Lakes Golf & Country; Home: 31 The Bridle Path, Willowdale, Ont. M2L 1C9; Office: 671 Warden Ave., Scarborough, Ont. M1L 3Z7.

**POTTS, J(oseph) Lyman,** C.M.; broadcasting and recording consultant; b. Regina, Sask. 11 Nov. 1916; s. William Joseph and Eva dePearl (Warren) P.; e. Central Coll. Inst. Regina, Sask.; m. Michele d. Albert C. Bole, Regina, Sask. 3 Oct. 1940; one s. Joel Lyman Albert; PRES., J. LYMAN POTTS AND ASSOC.; Announcer, Writer, Producer, Program Dir. Radio Stn. CKCK Regina 1935; Program Mgr., Asst. Mgr. Radio Stn. CKOC Hamilton, Ont. 1940; Gen. Mgr. Radio CKSL London, Ont. 1956; Production Mgr. Radio Stn. CJAD Montreal 1959; Gen. Mgr. Radio Stn. CJFM-FM Montreal 1962; transferred to Toronto in 1963 serving as Asst. to Pres., Standard Broadcasting Corp. and Mgr. FM Div., Pres. and Mgr. Dir. Stand. Broadcast Prod. Ltd. (incl Candn. Talent Lib., Standard Broadcast News, Deer Park Music, Conestoga Music, Syndication Serv.) 1965–81 (incl. Mgr. Dir. Standard Brdcst. Corp. (U.K.) Ltd. 1970–74); Vice-Pres., Standard Broadcasting Corp. 1972–81; Protestant; Home: 2160 New St., Burlington, Ont. L7R 1H8.

**POTTS, The Hon. Mr. Justice Joseph Henry,** SBStJ, CD, KLJ, B.A., M.A., LL.M.; judge; b. Saskatoon, Sask. 17 July 1925; s. Maj. Gen. A. E. and Mary (Stewart) P.; e. Public and High Schs. Saskatoon, Sask.; Univ. of Brit. Columbia 1944, 2nd yr. Applied Sci.; Univ. Coll., Univ. of Toronto. 1946–49, B.A. (Hons. Pol. Sc. & Econ.); Trinity Coll., Cambridge Univ. 1949–52, B.A., M.A., LL.M.; m. Dawn, d. Colin and Hilda (Young) Rober, 3 March 1954; children: Joseph, Roberta (Tevlin), Arthur, Richard, Diana, Gordon, Bruce; JUDGE OF THE ONTARIO COURT OF JUSTICE (GENERAL DIV.) 1990– ; Judge of the Supreme Court and mem. of the High Court of Justice for Ont. 1981–90; Depy. Judge of the Supreme Court of the Northwest Territories, 1982; Judge, Court Martial Appeal Court of Canada, 1984; called to Eng. Bar, Gray's Inn 1952, to Bar of Ont. 1953; with firm of Slaght McMurtry & Co. 1953–56; Partner, McTaggart, Potts, Stone, Winters & Herridge (and predecessor firms) 1956–81; cr. Q.C. 1969; served in 2nd World War, R.C.I.C. 1943–46; active service in Holland with Sask. Light Infy. (M.G.), Private; in Can. with Princess Patricia's Candn. Light Infy., Lt.; Univ. of Toronto Contingent C.O.T.C. 1946–49, Capt. & Adj.; 48th Highlanders of Can. 1953–60, Maj.; Past Dir., and mem. Extve. Comte., Bank of Canada; Past Dir., C.S.T. Foundation; Past Pres., Central Neighbourhood House; Past Chrmn. Organ. Comte., Cathedral Dist. Boy Scouts; Past Chrmn., Nat. Membership Comte., Candn. Bar Assn.; Past Chrmn., Public Relations, Membership and Law Day Comtes., and Past Pres., (Ont. Br.) Candn. Bar Assn.; Gov., Can. Inst. for Advanced Legal Studies; mem. of Counc., Internat. Comn. of Jurists (Cdn. Section); Dir., The Cambridge Canadian Trust; Past Warden St. Paul's Anglican Church; Past Dir. and mem. Extve. Council, Inst. for Political Involvement; Past Chrmn., Univ. College Committee; Permanent Pres., University Coll. class of '49; Past Vice-Pres., Univ. of Toronto Alumni Assn.; Past Chrmn. College of Electors, Univ. of Toronto; Anglican; recreations: camping, swimming; Clubs: Empire (Past Pres.); Lawyers (Past Pres.); Royal Commonwealth Soc., Toronto Branch (Past Vice-Chrmn.); Univ. of Toronto Contingent COTC, Past Officers' Mess (Secy.-Treas.); Canadian; Arts and Letters; York County Law Assn.; Candn. Inst. for the Administration of Justice; The Medico-Legal Soc. of Toronto; Can. Inst. of International Affairs; Couchiching Institute of Public Affairs; St. Andrew's Society; St. George's Society; Royal Candn. Mil. Inst.; Fort York Br., Royal Can. Legion; Imperial Officers' Assn. of Canada; Home: 40 Nanton Ave., Toronto, Ont. M4W 2Y9; Office: Osgoode Hall, 130 Queen St. W., Toronto, Ont. M5H 2N6.

**POTTS, Nadia;** ballerina; b. Eng. 1949; came to Can. 1953; e. Nat. Ballet Sch. Toronto; DIRECTOR OF DANCE PROGRAM, RYERSON POLYTECHNIC UNIV. 1989– ; chosen to dance in 'Bayaderka' during 1st season with Nat. Ballet Co. 1966; during 2nd season danced leading roles in 'The Nutcracker' and 'Cinderella'; promoted soloist 1968 and princ. 1969; with Clinton Rothwell won prize for best pas de deux, Internat. Ballet Competition, Varna 1970 and rec'd Bronze Medal for Solo Dance; danced with Baryshnikov 1975 and as Giselle with Nureyev 1976; Address: 43 Benlamond Ave., Toronto, Ont. M4E 1Y8.

**POTVIN, Pierre,** B.A., M.D., L.M.C.C., Ph.D., F.R.C.P.(C); university professor; b. Quebec 5 Jan. 1932; s. Rosario and Eva (Montreuil) P.; e. Univ. Laval B.A. 1950, M.D. 1955; Univ. of Toronto PH.D. 1962; m. Louise d. Ernest and Luce Dube 31 Aug. 1963; children: Aline, Bernard; DEAN, FACULTY OF MEDICINE, UNIVERSITE LAVAL 1986–94; Asst. Prof., Fac. of Med., Univ. Laval 1956; Assoc. Prof., Dept. of Physiology; Prof.; Sec. of Faculty 1974–86; Associate Dean (Executive) 1976–86; Commandeur, Ordre Nat. des Palmes Academiques, Gouv. Français; Chevalier, Ordre National Du Lion, Rep. du Senegal; Honorary Professor, Norman Bethune of Medical Siences, Changhun, China; Office: Quebec, Que. G1K 7P4.

**POTVIN, Thomas Raymond,** O.P., B.Ph., M.Th., D.Th.; prior, university professor and administrator; b. Worcester Mass. 22 Sept. 1934; s. Edgar Joseph and Germaine Betta (Coiteux) P.; e. Univ. of Montreal B.Ph. 1954; Univ. of Ottawa M.Th. 1964; Fribourg, Suisse D.Th. 1975; PROVINCIAL PRIOR, DOMINICANS OR FRIARS PREACHERS OF CANADA 1993– ; Full Professor, Collège Dominicain de Philosophie et de Théologie 1974; Titular Professor 1984; Dean, Fac. of Theology June 1993; Sec.-Treas. 1969–88; Prior, St-Jean-Baptiste Priory 1987–93; Mem., Soc. can. de Théologie; Candn. Soc. of Theology; Catholic Theol. Soc. of Am.; Religious Education Assn.; author: 'The Theology of the Primacy of Christ According to St. Thomas and its Scriptural Foundations' 1973; co-author: 'L'expérience comme lieu théologie' 1983, 'Questions actuelles sur la foi' 1984; Home: 5375 avenue Notre-Dame-de-Grâce, Montréal, Qué. H4A 1L2; Office: 5353, avenue Notre-Dame-de-Grâce, Montréal, Qué. H4A 1L2.

**POULIN, Bernard Aimé;** portrait artist; b. Windsor, Ont. 4 Jan. 1945; s. Aimé Joseph and Marie-Jeanne Thérèse (Lauzière) P.; e. Ecole Normale Ottawa Teaching Cert. 1964; Ont. Dept. Edn. Specialist Cert. in Special Edn. 1969; m. Marie-Paule d. Alphonse and Lucille Charette 21 May 1977; two d. Elaine, Valérie; Bernard A. Poulin Scholarships created for art students: Cambrian Coll., Sudbury, Ont. and Neri Bloomfield School of Art & Design, Haifa, Israel; solo art exhns. incl: Ottawa 1967–90, Toronto 1984, Sudbury 1980–87, Bermuda 1984–91, North Bay 1985; group exhns. incl. Univ. of Ottawa 1967, 1976, 1977, Bermuda Soc. Arts, Laurentian Univ. 1979, Contact Toronto 1979, Visages de Mon Pays Touring Exhibit (Can.) 1980–81, Can. Summer Games Thunder Bay 1981, Sights of Hist. Exhibit (touring) 1981; comnd. portraits incl. the late Gov. Gen. Jules Léger, Mme. Gabrielle Léger, Cardinal Paul-Emile Léger; Senator Rhéal Belisle; rep. in private and corp. art colls. Can., USA, Bermuda, Europe, Australia, Africa, China (Beijing); subject of CBC film 'Hope is a Good Word' (documentary) 1966; author: 'Io E Firenze' (travelogue) 1975; 'Mig' (cartoons) 1980; 'Zap' (children's play) 1983; 'Colored Pencil Techniques' Book: 1, Book: 2, Book: 3, Book: 4; 'Complete Colored Pencil Book' 1992; composer: 'Ron-Ron' (children's song) 1982; 'Just Give Me Time' (song) 1985; author various articles newspapers and jours.; recipient Distinguished Citizens Club Award Ottawa 1968; American Biographical Inst. Award for 'Excellence in Portraiture'; also incl. in '5000 Personalities of the World' 1987; Dir. Children's Aid Soc. Ottawa 1972–76; Sudbury Algoma Hosp. 1980–83; Big Brothers Assn. Sudbury 1979–83 and Ottawa 1983–85; Trustee Children's Hosp. of E. Ont. Ottawa 1984– ; mem. Bermuda Soc. Arts; Am. Soc. of Portrait Painters; Bd. of Dirs., Colored Pencil Soc. of Am.; recreations: sailing, reading; Address: Windjammer Gallery, P.O. Box 2115, 87 Reid St., Hamilton, Bermuda; J. Hall, Agent, Winnipeg, Man.; S. Blake, Agent, Sudbury, Ont.

**POULIN, Gabrielle,** B.A., L. ès L., D.E.S., D. ès L.; écrivain; née Saint-Prosper, Qué. 21 juin 1929; f. Charles-Édouard et Estelle (Champagne) P.; é. Univ. de

Montréal, B.A. 1962, L. ès L. 1967, D.E.S. (études françaises) 1968; Univ. de Sherbrooke D. ès L. 1974; Cambridge Univ. (études de littérature anglaise); ép. René f. Ferréol et Marie-Anne Dionne 1970; Enseignement (écoles, colls, univ.) 1949–75; Critique littéraire Relations 1969–80; Univ. of Toronto Quarterly 1974–76; Lettres québécoises 1976–86; Le Droit 1976–86; Radio MF de Radio-Canada 1976–86; Prix de l'Ambassade suisse 1967; Prix littéraires: Champlain 1979, 'La Presse' 1979; Ottawa-Carleton 1993; Boursière du Conseil des arts du Can., du Gouvernement français, du Conseil des arts de l'Ont.; auteur (essai) 'Les Miroirs d'un poète: image et reflets de Paul Éluard' 1969; (roman) 'Cogne la caboche' 1979, 1990 (transl. 'All the Way Home' 1984); 'Un cri trop grand' 1980; 'Les Mensonges d'Isabelle' 1983, 1990; 'La Couronne d'oubli' 1990; 'Le Livre de déraison' 1994; (poésie) 'Petites Fugues pour une saison sèche' 1991; 'Nocturnes de l'oeil' 1993; (critique) 'Romans du pays 1968–79' 1980; co-auteur (anthologie) 'L'Age de l'interrogation 1937–1952' 1980; éd. 'Rendez-vous, place de l'Horloge' 1993; écrivain en résidence: Bibliothèques publiques d'Ottawa (1988), Cumberland (1991), Gloucester (1992); mem. Union des écrivains québécois; Société des écrivains canadiens; récréations: voyages, films, musique, lecture; Adresse: 1997 Quincy Ave., Ottawa, Ont. K1J 6B4.

**POULIN, Marie-P.,** B.A., M.S.W.; sr. public servant; b. Sudbury, Ont. 21 June 1945; d. Alphonse-Emile and Lucille (Ménard) Charette; e. Acad. Ste-Marie Haileybury, Ont. (Ont. Scholar); Laurentian Univ. B.A. 1966; Univ. of Montreal M.S.W. 1969; m. Bernard A. s. Aimé and Marie-Jeanne Poulin 21 May 1977; two d. Elaine, Valérie; DEPUTY SECRETARY TO THE CABINET (COMMUNICATION AND CONSULTATION) 1992– ; Lectr. Univ. of Montreal 1969–70; Researcher Le Centre des Services sociaux and Lectr. Cegep de l'Outaouais 1971–73; Researcher and Interviewer Radio Can. Ottawa 1973–74; Radio Producer French Services CBC Ottawa 1974–78; Founder-Dir. French Services of CBC N.E. and N.W. Ont. 1978–83, Extve. Dir. Regional Radio & TV Prog. CBC 1983–84, Assoc. Vice Pres. Regional Broadcasting CBC 1984–88; Secy. Gen. of Candn. Broadcasting Corp. and Bd. of Dirs., 1988–90; Vice-Pres., Human Resources, CBC 1990–92; recipient Prix Marcel Blouin best morning show Can. 1983; Le conseil de la vie française en Amérique Medal 1987; voted 'Professional Woman of the Year; 1991 by Réseau des femmes d'affair et professionnelles; Coll.'Cité Collégiale' 1989–92; Laurentian Hosp. 1980–83; Univ. of Sudbury 1979–83; Cambrian Coll. Found. 1980–88; Comnr. for French Lang. Services 1986–89; Arts Court (Vice Pres. 1987–90); RGA (Pres. 1991– ); Club Canadien (mem. Extve. since 1985); Assn. des diplômées de l'Univ. de Montréal; recreations: reading, running; Home: 100 Pretoria Ave., Ottawa, Ont. K1S 1W9.

**POULIN, Roland L.;** sculptor; né. St. Thomas, Ont. 17 avril 1940; s. Louis R. and Gertrude (Leblanc) P.; é. Ecole des Beaux-Arts of Montreal 1969; Atelier Mario Mérola, travail d'assistant 1969–70; Univ. Laval Equivalence de doctorat 1980; experience d'enseignement, Commission des écoles catholiques de Montréal 1969–72; Cours de sculpture, Univ. du Qué. à Montréal 1971–72; Collège du Vieux-Montréal 1972–74; Univ. Laval 1973–81; Collège de Brébeuf 1975–76; Univ. Concordia 1982–83; Univ. d'Ottawa 1987; experience en graphisme: Illus. et maquettiste, Art House Inc. 1960–63; Peelcraft Inc. 1963–64; Concepteur de la revue Parachute 1975–76; Designer à la pige d'affiches d'expositions et de spectacles 1970–80; principales expositions individuelles, entre autres: P.S. 1 New York, N.Y. 1978; Galerie France Morin, Montréal 1982; Agnes Etherington Art Centre, Queen's Univ., Kingston, Ont. 1984; 49th Parallel, Centre for Contemporary Candn. Art, New York 1986; Espace Parachute, Montréal 1986; Museum Van Hedendaagse, Gand, Belgique 1987; Centre culturel canadian, Paris 1989; 23ième foire internat. de Cologne 1989; Galerie Chantal Boulanger, Montréal 1990; Olga Korper Gallery, Toronto 1990; Canada House, Londres, Angleterre 1990; MacDonald Stewart Art Centre, Guelph, Ont. 1990; principales expositions collectives, entre autres: 'Electric Museum' Musée d'art contemporain, Montréal 1974; 'Directions, Montréal' Véhicule Art, Montréal 1976; Bologne Art Fair, Italie 1977; 'Pluralities/ Pluralités' National Gallery of Canada 1981; 'Claude Mongrain/ Roland Poulin' Art Gallery of Greater Victoria, B.C. 1981; 'Lumières, les Cent jours d'art contemporain' Centre internat. d'art contemporain, Montréal 1986; 'The Historical Ruse/ La ruse Historique' The Power Plant, Toronto 1988; Exposition inaugurale, Musée des Beaux-Arts du Canada, Ottawa 1988; Galerie Chantal Boulanger, Montréal 1990; collections: Musée des Beaux-Arts du Canada (Ottawa), de l'Ontario (Toronto), de Montréal; Musée du Québec; Musée d'art contemporain, Montréal; Banque d'oeuvres d'art du Canada (Ottawa); Prêt d'oeuvres d'art, musée du Qué.; Agnès Etherington Art Centre (Kingston, Ont.); Univ. Concordia; Lavalin inc.; Toronto Dominion Bank; recipient of grants, Canada Art Council; Min. des affaires culturelles; Mem., Véhicule Art 1975; Founding Mem., 'Parachute' art magazine 1975–76; publications, entre autres: 'Roland Poulin, sculptures et dessins,' texte de Fernande St-Martin 1983; 'Roland Poulin,' texte de Johanne Lamoureux 1986; 'Roland Poulin,' entrevue avec Chantal Pontbriand (Parachute no. 53, 1988–89); Mem., Commission consultative du Conseil des Arts du Canada 1985; Mem., Comité d'acquisition du Musée d'Art Contemporain de Montréal 1985; Home: 33 chemin du Vide, C.P. 207, Ste-Angele de Monnoir, Que. J0L 1P9.

**POULIOT, Adrien D.,** LL.L.; communications executive; b. Etobicoke, Ont. 27 Feb. 1957; s. Jean A. and Rachel (Lebel) P.; e. Univ. de Sherbrooke LL.L. 1978; m. Hélène Floch 16 June 1985; two s. Simon, Francis; PRES. AND CHIEF OPERATING OFFR. CFCF INC. 1987– ; Chrmn. and Chief Extve. Offr. CF Cable TV Inc.; Vice Chrmn. and Chief Extve. Offr. Télévision Quatre Saisons; Dir. CTV Television Network; read law, law practice Ogilvy Renault Montreal 1979–84; called to Bar of Que. 1979; Asst. to Pres. CFCF Inc. Montreal 1984–87; Vice Pres. and Gen. Mgr. CFCF-TV (CFCF Inc.) 1985–87; Dir.: Montreal Children's Hosp.; Montreal Heart Inst. Rsch. Fund; Dir.: Candn. Entertainment Investors Mgmt. Inc.; Assoc. Gov., Univ. of Montreal; recreations: TV; skiing; Club: Canadian (Dir.); Home: 345 Woodlea Ave., Montreal, Que. H3P 1R4; Office: 405 Ogilvy Ave., Montreal, Que. H3N 1M4.

**POULIOT, François P.;** diplomat and public servant; b. Quebec, Que. 12 Oct. 1940; s. J. Lucien and Cecile (Giguere) P.; e. Univ. Laval, B.A. 1964; m. Jocelyne Pelletier; ASSOC. DEPY. MIN., HUMAN RESOURCES DEVELOPMENT & VICE-CHAIRPERSON, COMMISSION OF EMPLOYMENT AND IMMIGRATION OF CANADA 1993– ; Vol., CUSO Chana 1964–66; Dir. Afr. de l'Est, Uganda 1966–69; UNESCO, Paris 1969–71; 1st Sec., Ambassade de Can., Niger 1971–73; Dir., ACDI Ottawa 1973–79; Min. Aff. Exterieures 1979–81; Vice Pres., ACDI 1981–85; Ambassadeur du Canada, Algeria 1985–87; Vice Pres., Policy, CIDA, Ottawa 1987–88; Sr. Asst. Depy. Min., Corporate and Regulatory Mgmt., Fisheries & Oceans 1988–91; Sr. Asst. Depy. Min., National Health & Welfare Dept. 1991–93; recreations: voice, opera; Office: Jeanne Mance Bldg., Tunney's Pasture, Ottawa, Ont. K1A 0K9.

**POULIOT, Hon. Gilles,** M.P.P.; politician; b. Montreal, Que. 25 May 1942; s. Gilles and Alma (Dupéré) P.; e. Queen's Univ.; Lakehead Univ.; m. Suzanne Benoit 3 July 1971; MINISTER OF TRANSPORTATION, GOVT. OF ONTARIO 1991– and MINISTER RESPONSIBLE FOR FRANCOPHONE AFFAIRS 1990– ; 1st elected to Ont. Leg. g.e. 1985 as member for Lake Nipigon; re-elected g.e. 1987, 1990; served as Min. of Mines & Min. resp. for Francophone Affairs 1990–91; served as N.D.P. critic for Mines, Native Affairs, Northern Transp. & Northern Devel.; Reeve, Twp. of Manitouwadge 6 years (following 2-year term as Councillor) & Extve. Mem., Thunder Bay Municipal League; Dir., Northwestern Ont. Municipal League (3 terms); Trustee, Improvement Dist. of Manitouwadge; Tradesman (flotation operator), Geco, Div. of Noranda Mines; Office: 77 Wellesley St. W., 3rd Floor, Toronto, Ont. M7A 1Z8.

**POULIOT, Jean A.,** O.C., B.A., B.A.Sc.; television executive; Quebec, Que. 6 June 1923; s. of Adrien and Laure (Clark) P.; e. Séminaire de Québec; Laval Univ., Science Faculty; m. Rachel, daughter of Flavius Lebel; children: Jean, Vincent, Louis, Adrien, Martin; CHRMN. OF THE BD. AND CHIEF EXTVE. OFFR. of CFCF INC. and of its wholly-owned subsidiaries, CF Cable TV Inc. and Four Seasons Television Network Inc.; Pres. & C.E.O., Télé-Capitale Ltée. 1971–78; Alexander, Pearson & Dawson Inc.; Past Pres., Broadcast News Ltd.; Television Bureau of Advertising of Can. Inc.; Electronic Research Engineer, Canadian Army, Ottawa 1945–49; Superintendent Canadian Navy Laboratories, Ottawa, 1949–52; Executive Engineer, Television Department, Famous Players Company, Toronto 1952–57; Gen. Mgr. Télévision de Qué. (Canada) Ltd. 1957–62; Man. Dir. of this enterprise 1962–71; Pres. (1965–67), Canadian Assn. of Broadcasters; mem. Assn. Prof. Engrs.; Officer, Order of Canada; recreations: golf; chess; computers; Clubs: The Garrison; Mount Royal; Royal Montreal Golf; Home: 9 Gordon Cres., Westmount, Montreal, Que. H3Y 1N1; Office: 405 Ogilvy Ave., Montreal, Que. H3N 1M4.

**POUND, Richard William Duncan,** O.C., O.Q., Q.C., C.A., B.Com., B.A., B.C.L., PhD. (honoris causa) U.S. Sports Acad.; lawyer; b. St. Catharines, Ont. 22 March 1942; s. William Thomas and Jessie Edith Duncan (Thom) P.; e. McGill Univ. B.Com. 1962, Licentiate in Accounting 1964, B.C.L. 1967; Sir George Williams (now Concordia) Univ. B.A. 1963; m. Julie Houghton d. Donald Kennedy Keith and Annette Jean Bauer 4 Nov. 1977; children: William Trevor Whitley, Duncan Robert Fraser, Megan Christy; step-children: Keith Charles Flavell, Christina Houghton Flavell; MEMBER, STIKEMAN, ELLIOTT (law firm with offices in Montreal, Toronto, Ottawa, Vancouver, Calgary, New York, London, Hong Kong, Washington, Paris, Budapest, Prague and Taipei) 1972– ; Hon. Consul General of Norway; called to Bar of Que. 1968, Bar of Ont. 1980; C.A. Quebec 1964, Ont. 1980; joined Chisholm, Smith, Davis, Anglin, Laing, Weldon & Courtois (now McCarthy, Tétrault) 1965–71; Sessional Lectr. McGill Faculty of Law (Taxation) 1977–80; Lectr. McGill Center for Continuing Educ. 1968–76; Lectr. Que. Real Estate Assn. 1972–78; Adjunct Asst. Prof., Concordia Univ. 1991– ; Secy., Candn. Olympic Assn. 1968–76, Pres. 1977–82; mem. Internat. Olympic Comte. 1978– ; Extve. Bd. 1983–91, 1992– ; Vice Pres. 1987–91; Extve. Comte., Pan Amer. Sports Organization 1979–88; Dir. and mem. Extve. Comte., Organizing Comte. of XV Olympic Winter Games, Calgary 1988; Gov., Olympic Trust of Canada; Gov., Found. for Quebec Univ. Athletics; Dir. and Secy. Candn. Squash Racquets Assn. 1972–77; Double Olympic Finalist (swimming) Rome 1960; recipient 1 gold, 2 silver, 1 bronze medals Commonwealth Games (swimming) Perth, Australia 1962; Candn. Champion Freestyle 1958, 1960, 1961, 1962, Butterfly 1961; mem. Candn. Swimming Hall of Fame; Candn. Amateur Athletic Hall of Fame; Trustee, Martlet Foundation; Pres. Grad. Soc. McGill Univ. 1981–82; Bd. of Govs. McGill Univ. 1986– ; Chrmn. McGill Fund Council; Chrmn. McGill Athletics Bd.; Dir., Allegra Found.; Coaching Assn. of Can. 1976–82; mem. Red Cross Water Safety Comte. Royal Life Saving Soc.; Gen. Ed. 'Doing Business in Canada' 1979–89, Ed.-in-Chief 1989– ; mem. ed. bd. 'Canada Tax Service' 1972–80; Ed., 'Tax Case Notes'; Ed. 'Canada Tax Cases'; 'Stikeman Income Tax Act'; Legal Notes Ed., CGA Magazine; author 'The Olympic Boycott 1980,' 'A Book of Five Rings' in preparation; various book chapters, articles; mem. Candn. Bar Assn.; Candn. Tax Foundation; Internat. Fiscal Assn.; Internat. Assn. of Practising Lawyers; Assn. Québecoise de Planification Fiscale et Successorale; founding mem. and Vice-Pres. Assn. québecoise des juristes en droit sportif; Barreau du Que.; Ont. Bar; Que. Order C.A.'s; Ont. Inst. C.A.'s; Kappa Alpha Society; Protestant; recreations: squash, tennis, swimming, golf; Clubs: Montreal Badminton & Squash; M.A.A.A. (Past Pres.); Hillside Tennis; Mt. Bruno Country; Jesters; Home: 87 Arlington Ave., Westmount, Que. H3Y 2W5; Office: 3900, 1155 René Levesque Blvd. W., Montreal, Que. H3B 3V2.

**POUNDER, Elton R.,** A.F.C., Ph.D., F.R.S.C.; educator; b. Montreal, Que. 10 Jan. 1916; s. Rev. Roy M. and Norval (McLeese) P.; e. McGill Univ., B.Sc. 1934, Ph.D. 1937; m. Marion Crane, d. George S. Wry, 15 Feb. 1941; EMERITUS PROF. OF PHYSICS, McGILL UNIV., 1982, MacDonald Prof. there 1976–82, Prof. of Physics since 1958; Dir., Ice Research Project, since 1955; with Bell Telephone Co. as Engr., 1937–39; apptd. Asst. Prof. of Physics, McGill Univ., 1945, Assoc. Prof., 1948; served in 2nd World War 1939–45; Wing Commdr., R.C.A.F.; awarded Air Force Cross; Fellow Royal Soc. of Can. 1974; mem., Candn. Assn. of Physicists (Pres., 1961–62); Am. Physical Soc.; Am. Geophysical Union; Internat. Glaciological Soc.; recreations: music, skiing; Home: 3468 Drummond St., Montreal, Que. H3G 1Y4.

**POUNSETT, Frank Henry Ralph,** B.A.Sc., P.Eng.; professional engineer; b. London, England 12 Sept. 1904; s. Frank Herbert and Ellen Maria (Dunton) P.; e. Univ. of Toronto B.A.Sc. 1928; m. Margaret d. Donald and Anna MacLean 17 Sept. 1931; children: Donald, Alan; Radio Engineer, DeForest Radio Corp. 1928–34; Chief Engr., Radio Div., Stewart Warner Alemit Corp. 1934–40; Research Enterprises Ltd. 1940–45; Chief Engr. & Mgr. of Manufacturing, Stromberg Carlson Co. Ltd. 1945–52; Chief Engr. & Mgr. of Mfg., Radio & TV Div., Philips Electronics Industries Ltd. 1952–69; Vice-Pres., Radio & TV Div. 1959–69; Dean, Engineering Technology Division, Centennial College of Applied Arts & Technology 1967–71; Mem. & Chrmn. of several technical standards cttes. on radio & TV incl. Pres., Candn. Radio Technical Planning Board 1958–62; Fellow, I.E.E.E. (formerly I.R.E.); Dir. 1949–50; Mem., Hall of Distinction, Univ. of Toronto Engineering Alumni Assn. 1990; recreations: golf, curling, bowling; clubs:

Granite, Donalda; Home: 23 Parkhurst Blvd., Toronto, Ont. M4G 2C7.

**POWE, B.W.,** M.A.; writer, teacher; b. Ottawa, Ont. 23 March 1955; s. Bruce Allen and Alys Maude (Brady) P.; e. Lawrence Park Coll. Inst. Toronto; York Univ. B.A. 1977; Univ. of Toronto, M.A. 1981; m. Robin Leslie d. Milton and Sandra Mackenzie 7 Sept. 1991; children: Katharine Mackenzie, Thomas Cole; author: 'A Climate Charged' 1984, 2nd ed. 1985; 'The Solitary Outlaw' 1987, 2nd ed. 1987; 'Noise of Time' (text for the Glenn Gould Profile), Banff Centre, Maclean-Hunter, Yyiats, 1990; 'A Tremendous Canada of Light' 1993; 'Outage: A Journey into Electric City' 1994; articles, reviews, essays, stories in jours., mags. and newspapers in U.S. and Canada; Professor of Humanities, York Univ. 1989– ; Communications consultant, McLuhan & Davies Communications, Toronto 1984–92; guest speaker and lecturer University Club, University of Toronto Writers' Series, Arts and Cities Conference, Internat. Laserdisc Conf., Calgary, Glendon Coll., the Univ. of Calgary, John Abbott College, Jazz Festival Performances, Banff, Chairman Mills, the Arts & Letters Club, Glenn Gould Found., 21st Century Agenda Conf. 1982– ; recipient Faculty of Arts Book Prize York Univ. 1977; Can. Council Special Rsch. Scholarship Univ. of Toronto 1978–81; Maclean-Hunter Fellowship 1989; Ontario Arts Council Grants 1989, 1990, 1992; recreation: walking, music.

**POWELL, Brian,** M.A.; b. Montreal, Que., 25 May 1934; s. Clifford Baden and Doris Kathleen (Sharples) P.; e. St. George's Sch., Vancouver, B.C., 1942–46; Lower Can. Coll., Montreal, Que., grad. 1952; McGill Univ., B.A. 1956; M.A. 1967; Univ. of London, Dipl. in Business Adm. 1957; Oxford Univ., Dipl. in Educ. 1963; Consultant in English, Prot. Sch. Bd. of Montreal, since 1969; Dir., Powell Foods Ltd.; Teacher of Eng., Lower Can. Coll., Montreal, 1956–66; Asst. Headmaster 1964–66; Lectr., Sydney Univ. and Cranbrook Sch., Sydney, Australia, 1966–67; Instr. in Eng., Phillips Exeter (U.S.A.) Acad., 1967–68; Headmaster, Shawnigan Lake Sch., Quebec 1968–69; teaching and lecturing experience in Eng., Russia and S. Am.; mem., Candn. Nat. Ski Team 1958–64; Winner, Roberts of Kandahar Downhill Ski Race 1957; mem., Que Willingdon Cup Interprov. Golf Team, 1962–63; E. Candn. Six-Mile Road Running Champion 1966; author of 'English Through Poetry Writing,' 1967; 'Making Poetry' 1969; 'Their Own Special Shape' 1974; Ed. 'Jackrabbit: His First Hundred Years,' 1975; mem., Bd. of Mgrs., St. Andrew's Un. Ch., Westmount; Kappa Alpha; P. Conservative; United Church; recreations: travel, sports, reading, writing; Clubs: Mount Bruno Golf: Cascade Golf & Tennis (Dir.); Montreal Badminton & Squash; Address: 38 Church Hill, Montreal, Que. H3Y 2Z9.

**POWELL, Bruce Edward,** B.A., F.I.I.C., C.R.M.; reinsurance executive; b. Toronto, Ont. 7 Oct. 1956; s. Bruce Haslam and June Hazel (Palmer) P.; e. Univ. of West. Ont., B.A. 1978; m. Linda d. Esther and Walter Sontag 13 Aug. 1985; children: Ashleigh Elizabeth Sontag, Elise Victoria Sontag, David Andrew Sontag; PRES., G.J. SULLIVAN CO. LTD. 1991– ; Vice Pres., G.J. Sullivan Co. Reinsurance; with Allstate Ins. 1977–79; Munich Reinsurance 1979–81; Universal Reinsurance Intermediaries / Sterling Universal Ltd. 1981–87; Pres. & C.E.O., Kinimonth Lambert & Co. Ltd. 1987–91; Fellow Ins. Inst. of Can.; recreations: golf, squash, skiing; Clubs: Donalda Club, Toronto Racquet Club; Fitness Inst.; Port Carling Golf & Country Club; Craigleith Ski Club; Home: 235 Bessborough Dr., Toronto, Ont.

**POWELL, David Evan,** B.Sc., D.I.C., F.G.S.; oil company executive; b. Merthyr Tydfil, Wales 6 Apr. 1933; s. David William and Doris Irene (Howells) P.; e. Univ. of Wales, B.Sc. (Hons.) 1959; Royal Sch. of Mines, Imperial Coll., D.I.C. 1960; m. Mabel Victoria d. Lawrence and Dora Chatburn 26 May 1976; children: Roxanne, Gary; PRES. & CHIEF EXTVE. OFFR., HOME OIL CO. LTD. 1991– ; Chief Devel. Geol. Ecuador/Chief Geol. Australia/Group Mgr. Geol., Burmah Oil Co. Ltd. (U.K.) 1959–78; Vice-Pres., Fgn. Exploration, Hudson's Bay Oil & Gas Co. Ltd. 1978–82; Dome Petroleum Ltd. 1982–83; Sr. Vice-Pres., Exploration, Home Oil Co. Ltd. 1983–87, Extve. Vice-Pres. & C.O.O. 1987–91; Extve. Vice Pres., Interhome Energy Inc. 1988–91; Dir., Home Oil Co. Ltd.; Panarctic Oils Ltd.; Minerals Ltd.; Fed. Pipe Lines Ltd.; Minora Resources NL (Australia); Interprovincial Pipe Line System Inc.; Mem., Geol. Soc. of London; Advisory Bd. of Institute of Ocean Sciences; author/co-author num. pubs.; recreations: golf, reading, music, cooking; Clubs: Silver Springs Golf & Country; Calgary Golf and Country Club; Calgary Petroleum; Calgary Ranchmen's; Home: 105, 1815 Varsity Estates Dr. N.W., Calgary, Alta. T3B 3Y7; Office: 1600 Home Oil Tower, 324 – 8 Ave. S.W., Calgary, Alta. T2P 2Z5.

**POWELL, John A.,** B.Sc.; travel executive; b. Calgary, Alta. 21 Aug. 1933; s. Roscoe George and Myrta Edna (Armstrong) P.; e. Univ. of Montana, B.Sc.; m. Gail d. W.B. Smith 3 Jan. 1959; children: Ross, Mike, Lori; PRES., P. LAWSON TRAVEL 1957– ; Board Mem., Global Travel Computer Systems; recreation: golf; Clubs: Lambton; Briars; Home: 39 Old Mill Rd., Suite 2202, Etobicoke, Ont. M8X 1G6; Office: 3300 Bloor St. W., Phase 2, Suite 1200, Toronto, Ont. M8X 2Y2.

**POWELL, Trevor John David,** M.A.; archivist; b. Hamilton, Ont. 3 Feb. 1948; s. David Albert and Morvydd Ann May (Williams) P.; e. Univ. of Sask. Regina B.A. 1971; Univ. of Regina M.A. 1980; m. Marian Jean d. Charles and Jean McKillop 1 May 1976; PROV. ARCHIVIST, SASK. ARCHIVES BD. UNIV. OF REGINA 1988– ; Staff Archivist present Bd. 1973, Dir. Records & Tech. Services 1980, Acting Prov. Archivist 1986–87; Archivist, Diocese of Qu'Appelle 1971– , Registrar 1979– ; mem. Adv. Council Sask. Order of Merit 1988– ; Archivist, Ecclesiastical Prov. of Rupert's Land 1988– ; co-author 'Living Faith: A Pictorial History of the Diocese of Qu'Appelle 1884–1984' 1984; various articles and reviews Sask. hist. and Ang. Ch. hist.; mem. Assn. Candn. Archivists (Dir. without Portfolio 1979–81); Sask. Council of Archives (Sec. 1987–88, 1990–92) ; Soc. Am. Archivists; Candn. Hist. Assn.; Commonwealth Archivists' Assn.; Institute of Public Admin. of Can.; Anglican; recreations: reading, music, walking; Home: 241 Orchard Cres., Regina, Sask. S4S 5B9; Office: Regina, Sask. S4S 0A2.

**POWER, James Patrick,** B.Sc.; executive; b. Yarmouth, N.S. 25 Oct. 1935; s. James Edward and Elsie Mary P.; e. Univ. of N.B., B.Sc. (Civil Engn.) 1957; m. Renee d. Fernand and Fernande Mailhot 24 Oct. 1964; children: Patrick, Stephanie; PRESIDENT, POWER MARKETING GROUP INC. 1983– , exports Candn. resource products to world markets; Joined JOHNS-MANVILLE CANADA INC. 1961 after service with Royal Candn. Engrs. and one yr. with chem. firm; appt'd. Vice Pres. 1977; Pres., Chief Extve. Offr. and Chrmn. of Bd., 1981–83; Former Dir., Kingsey Falls Paper Inc.; Cobra Canada Inc.; Polymer International (NS) Ltd.; Mining Assn. of Can.; Asbestos Information Centre; Extve. Ctte. Asbestos Intnl. Assn. London, Eng.; Institut de Recherche et de Developpment sur l'Amiante; recreation: skiing; Home: 5991 S. Akron Way, Englewood, CO 80111; Office: 6416 South Quebec St., Suite 41, Englewood, CO 80111.

**POWER, Noble Edward Charles,** M.A.; diplomat and public servant; b. Montreal, Que., 17 Sept. 1931; s. Richard Michael Hugh, M.D. and K. M. (Phelan) P.; e. Univ. of Montreal, B.A. 1953; Columbia Univ., New York, Latin Am. Studies, M.I.A. 1955; grad. studies Universidad de Mexico and Sorbonne, Paris, France 1955 and 1956; Oxford (Sr. Assoc. Mem., St. Antony's Coll. 1991–1992–1993); Fellow, Univ. West Indies, Inst. of Social and Econ. Rsch.; m. Janet Bradshaw Morrison; children: Christopher Noble, Susannah Morgan, Alexandra Kay; MEM. OF THE BD. OF DIRS., EXPORT DEVELOPMENT CORP., OTTAWA 1990– ; Mem., Bd. of Dirs., Royal Commonwealth Society; Mem., Bd. of Dirs., CODE; Mem. Bd. of Mgmt., Codrington H.S., Barbados; Mem. Bd. of Gov., I.F.A.D., Rome, Italy 1988–90; Min.'s Staff, Dept. of Nat. Defence, Ottawa, 1956–62; External Aid Office, Ottawa, 1962–66; Dir., Commonwealth Africa Aid Programme, CIDA, Ottawa, 1966–70; served as Head, Candn. Del. to IMF and IBRD meetings and other aid groups, 1966–82; High Commissioner to Barbados and the Eastern Caribbean 1983–87; Vice Pres. (Asst. Depy. Min. External Relations), Canadian Internat. Development Agency 1987–90; ICER Task Force (Interdepartmental Comte. on External Relations), Ottawa, 1970–71; Temp. Duty, Candn. High Comn. Lagos, Nigeria 1971; High Commr. to Ghana and Ambassador accredited to Lomé and Cotonou 1971–74; Dir.-Gen. (Asia) Canadian International Development Agency (C.I.D.A.) 1974–1977; Vice-Pres,, C.I.D.A., 1977–83; Del. to Colombo Plan Conf., Singapore 1974 Washington 1977, Tokyo 1982 and Head Candn. Del. various IBRD and Arab/OPEC Conferences Paris and Vienna 1974–83; Alt. Dir., Bd. of Dir., Export Devel. Corp., Ottawa, 1977–83; Mem., Bd. of Gov., Elmwood, Ottawa, 1977–80; served with the 2nd Btln. Black Watch (RHC) of Can. 1950–54; rank Lieut.; recreations: riding, hunting, skiing, tennis; Clubs: Rideau; Ottawa Valley Hunt (Pres. 1967–70); Barbados Turf; Rockliffe Lawn Tennis; Address: 39 Bittern Crt., Rockcliffe Park, Ont. K1L 8K9 and Richmond, St. Joseph, Barbados, West Indies.

**POWER, Hon. Peter Charles Garneau,** B.Com., LL.B.; b. Montreal, Que. 16 Apr. 1930; s. Francis Xavier Power; e. Dalhousie Univ. B.Com. 1953, LL.B. 1956; m. Jacqueline; 4 children and 4 stepchildren; JUSTICE, ALBERTA COURT OF QUEEN'S BENCH and DEPUTY JUDGE OF THE YUKON TERRITORY and DEPUTY JUDGE OF THE NORTHWEST TERRITORY; called to Bar of Alta. 1957; cr. Q.C. 1976; Ald., City of Red Deer, Alta. 1961–66; Pub. Sch. Trustee Red Deer Sch. Bd. 1971–79; mem. Law Soc. Alta.; Candn. Bar Assn.; R. Catholic; recreations: golf, skiing, sailing; Home: 616 Stratton Terrace, S.W., Calgary, Alta. T3H 1M6; Office: 611 - 4th St. S.W., Calgary, Alta. T2P 1T5.

**POWER, Most Rev. William E.,** D.D., B.A. (R.C.); bishop; b. Montreal, Que. 27 Sept. 1915; s. Nicholas Walter and Bridget Elizabeth (Callaghan) P.; e. St. Patrick's Sch., Montreal, Que.; Montreal Coll., B.A. 1937; Grand Semy., 1937–41; St. Francis Xavier Univ. Hon. LL.D. 1989; Bishop of Antigonish, Bishop 1960–87 (named 12 May, consecrated 20 July, installed 10 Aug. 1960, retired 1987); Chancellor, St. Francis Xavier Univ. since 1960; o. 7 June 1941; Asst. Priest, St. Thomas Aquinas, 1941–42; St. Willibrod's, 1942–47; Vice Chancellor, Diocese of Montreal, 1947–50; Diocesan Chaplain to Young Christian Workers, 1950–59, and Nat. Chaplain, 1955–59; mem. of Extve. of Internat. Young Christian Workers rep. North Am., 1957–59; Parish Priest, St. Barbara's Parish, Lasalle, Que. Apr. 1959–May 1960; served with R.C.N.(R) 1947–51, and inactive force, 1951–60; Pres. (1971–73), Candn. Conf. of Catholic Bishops, mem., Administrative Bd. of C.C.C.B.; Address: St. Francis Xavier Univ., U.P.O. 5000, Antigonish, N.S. B2G 2W5.

**POWIS, Alfred,** O.C. (1984), B.Com.; natural resources executive; b. Montreal, Que. 16 Sept. 1930; s. Alfred and Sarah Champe (McCulloch) P.; e. Westmount (Que.) High Sch., 1947; McGill Univ., B.Com. 1951; m. Louise Margaret Finlayson, 1977; CHRMN., NORANDA INC. 1990– ; Dir., Brascan Ltd.; Canadian Imperial Bank of Commerce; Dal-Tile Group Inc.; Falconbridge Ltd.; Ford Motor Co. of Can. Ltd.; Gulf Canada Resources Ltd.; MacMillan Bloedel Ltd.; Noranda Forest Inc.; Norcen Energy Resources Ltd.; Kerr Addison Mines Ltd.; Sun Life Assurance Co. of Canada; Sears Canada Ltd.; also no. of subsidiaries of Noranda; Invest. Dept., Sun Life Assurance Co. of Can., 1951–55; joined present firm 1956; Asst. Treas. 1958; Asst. to Pres. 1962; Extve. Asst. to Pres. 1961; Dir. 1964; Vice Pres. 1966; Extve. Vice Pres. 1967; Pres. and C.E.O. 1968; Chrmn. & C.E.O. 1977–90; Chrmn. 1990– ; Mem., Policy Ctte., Business Counc. on Nat. Issues (BCNI); Dir., Mining Assn. of Can.; Candn. Inst. of Internat. Affairs; Mem., British North Am. Ctte.; Ont. Business Adv. Council; Vice Chrmn., Bd. of Trustees, Toronto Hosp.; Officer Order of Can. 1984; Anglican; Clubs: York; Toronto; Mount Royal (Montreal); Home: 70 Woodlawn Ave., W. Toronto, Ont. M4V 1G7; Office: P.O. Box 755, BCE Place, Suite 4100, Toronto, Ont. M5J 2T3.

**POWRIE, Thomas Lawrence,** B.S.A., M.A., B.Phil., D.Phil.; educator; b. Assiniboia, Sask. 30 Mar. 1933; s. Oliver and Ethel M. (Lawrence) P.; e. Univ. of Saskatchewan B.S.A. 1954, M.A. 1955; Oxford Univ. B.Phil. 1957, D.Phil. 1962; Rhodes Scholar (Sask.) 1955; m. Gailene d. Edward and Sheelagh Lonergan 25 June 1957; children: Sheelagh, Douglas, Raymond, Robert; PROF. OF ECONOMICS, UNIV. OF ALBERTA 1959– (and Chrmn. Dept. of Economics there 1969–72, Acting Dean of Arts 1988, elected member Bd. of Govs. 1992–94); Office: Edmonton, Alta. T6G 2H4.

**POYNTZ, G.A. Ross,** B.A.; real estate executive; b. Toronto, Ont. 28 Jan. 1944; s. A. Ross and Katherine J. (Wood) P.; e. Univ. of Western Ont. B.A. 1968; children: Michael, Jeremy; VICE-PRES., OPERATIONS, BUILDINGS GROUP, MARATHON REALTY CO. LTD. 1991– ; Regional Vice-Pres. (Edmonton), Morguard Properties Limited 1976–85; Vice-Pres. & Gen. Mgr., Toronto Eaton Centre, Cadillac Fairview Corp. Limited 1985–91; Dir., Muskoka Lakes Assn.; Rotary Club of Toronto; recreations: golf, swimming; clubs: Rosedale Golf, Muskoka Lakes Golf & Country; Home: 601, 345 Lonsdale Rd., Toronto, Ont.; Office: 400, 200 Wellington St. W., Toronto, Ont. M5P 1R5.

**POZNAN, Zoltan J.,** M.D.; physician; b. Ozd., Hungary 15 Dec. 1929; s. Barna and Elizabeth (Ginczinger) P.; e. Med. Sch. of Budapest M.D. 1956; divorced; children: Cheryl Ann (wife of Michael Sereny), Mark John; Resident, Royal Victoria Hosp.; Westminster Hosp.; War Memorial Children Hosp.; Res. & Fellow in Pediatrics & Ped. Cardiology, Cook Co. Hosp.; pediatric practice since 1964; Bd. Mem. & Med. Dir. of After Care

Dept. Emanuel Convalescens Found.; Dr. Daphne DaCosta Memorial Found.; Mem., Candn. Med. Assn.; Ont. Med. Assn. (Chrmn., Edn., Alcohol & Drug Related Problems); Am. Med. Assn. on Alcoholism; Profl. Adv. Ctte., Parents Without Partners Inc.; Co-editor & contrib.: 'Vita Sana Health Mag.'; recreations: boating, skiing, cooking, photography; Home: 30 Castle Frank Rd., Toronto, Ont. M4W 2Z6; Office: 1017 Wilson Ave., Ste. 401, Downsview, Ont. M3K 1Z1.

**PRADES, Prof. Dr. José A.,** M.A., Ph.D.; university professor; b. Valencia, Spain 1 Nov. 1929; s. José and Asuncion (Sierra) P.; e. Seminary Valencia Ph.B. 1949, M.A. (Theology) 1953; Louvain Univ. M.A. (Economics) 1957, M.A. (Pol. Sci.) 1963, Ph.D. (Sociology) 1966; Madrid Univ. M.A. (Pol. Sci.) 1965; Bonn Univ. Post doc., ethics 1967; m. Nicole d. Jules and Elisabeth Carlens 30 June 1971; PROF., UNIV. OF QUEBEC IN MONTREAL 1971– ; Prof., Social School, Valencia 1957–61; Research Worker, Louvain Univ. 1961–63; Asst. Prof. 1965–70; Research Worker, Bonn Univ. 1965–67; Visiting Prof., Madrid Univ. 1968–69; Prof., Institut Catholique de Paris 1969–71; Visiting Prof., La Sorbonne, Paris 1988; Dir., Groupe de Rech. en Ethique Environ., Dept. of Religious Studies, UQAM 1978–80; Ed. Adv. Bd., 'Etudes durkheimiennes / Durkhaim Studies,' 'Religious Studies / Sciences religieuses,' 'Société,' 'Ethica,' 'Medium'; Alexander Von Humboldt Stiftung Scholarship 1965–67; Winner, Internat. Prize in Ethno-anthrop. Studies, Palermo Univ. 1988; Mem. Internat. Soc. for the Sociol. of Religion; Consejo Sup. de investigaciones cientificas (Madrid); Assn. can.-fran. pour l'avancement des sci.; Internat. Assn. of Sociol.; Assn. internat. de sociol. de langue fran.; Internat. Soc. for Environ. Ethics; author: 'Durkheim' 1990, 'Persistance et métamorphose du Sacré' 1987, 'La sociologie de la religion chez Max Weber' 1969; co-author: 'Le sacré' 1991; 'Gestion de l'environnement, éthique et sociéte' 1992; editor: 'Environnement et développement' 1991, 'Durkheim, société et sacré' 1990; translator: 'Fuerza y flaqueza de la religion' 1958; Home: 161 Bas L'Assomption Sud, L'Assomption, Que. J0K 1G0; Office: Box 8888, Stn. A., Montreal, Que. H3C 3P8.

**PRATLEY, Gerald,** C.M., LL.D.; writer; broadcaster; teacher; b. London, Eng. 3 Sept. 1923; s. Arthur and Agnes (Norwood) P.; e. various Schs. and Colls. in Eng.; m. Margaret, d. John Kennedy, 26 April 1948; separated; children: Orize, Denise, Jocelyn; partner-in-life: Risa Shuman; Film Critic and commentator for CBC, CTV, CFRB 1948–75; Dir., Ont. Film Inst. 1968–90; Candn. Film Institute; Stratford Film Festival; Canadian Film Awards; Film Consultant, Centennial Ctte. 1960–75; author 'John Frankenheimer' 1970; 'Cinema of Otto Preminger' 1972; 'Cinema of David Lean' 1973; 'Cinema of John Huston' 1975; 'Torn Sprockets: The Uncertain Projection of the Canadian Film' 1984; film teacher, Univ. Toronto, York Univ., Seneca Coll., McMaster Univ.; Ryerson Polytechnic; Award of Merit, Min. of Culture, Poland 1981; CFTA Award 1990; Member Order of Can. 1984; LL.D. (honoris causa), York Univ. 1991; Life Achievement Award, Calgary Film Celebration 1992; LL.D. (honoris causa) Univ. of Waterloo 1993; LL.D. (honoris causa) Bowling Green State Univ., Ohio 1994; Life Patron, Toronto Film Soc.; Life Mem., Ont. Film Assn.; mem., Arts & Letters Club; Film Studies Assn. of Canada; Royal Commonwealth Soc.; St. George's Soc.; Churchill Soc.; Acad. of Candn. Cinema; Candn. Motion Picture Pioneers: Toronto Press Club; P.E.N.; ACTRA (Life); Writers Guild of Can.; mem. Internat. Juries, Cracow, Chicago, Montreal (and other) Film Festivals; Arts Columnist, Toronto Sun 1981–83; Toronto Star; Can. Correspondent Int. Film Guide, London; mem., Classification Bd., Ont. Theatres Branch; Adult Programming Adv. Bd., TVOntario; Adv. Ctte. to the Film Studies Program, Ryerson Polytechnic Inst. 1980–90; Protestant; Office: 5460 Yonge St., Ste. 1007, North York, Ont. M2N 6K7.

**PRATT, Christopher,** O.C.(1973), C.C. (1983), B.F.A., D.Litt., LL.D., R.C.A.; artist and printmaker; b. St. John's, Nfld.; e. Prince of Wales Coll., St. John s Nfld. 1952; Glasgow (Scot.) Sch. of Art; Mt. Allison Univ. B.F.A. 1961; has exhibited throughout Can., the U.S. and in the U.K.; colls. incl. Nat. Gallery of Can.; served on Canada Council, 1976–82; Club: Past Commadore, Royal Nfld. Yacht; Address: P.O. Box 87, Mount Carmel, St. Mary's Bay, Nfld. A0B 2M0.

**PRATT, Ewart Arthur,** B.Sc.; company executive; b. St. John's, Nfld. 20 March 1919; s. late Hon. Sen. Calvert Coates and late Agnes Green (Horwood) P.; e. Holloway Sch. and Prince of Wales Coll., St. John's Nfld., Phillips Exeter Acad., Exeter, N.H., 1935–38; Univ. of Pennsylvania, B.Sc. (Econ.) 1942; m. Yvonne, d. late James Rorke, Carbonear, Nfld., 30 Oct. 1943; children: Kathleen Agnes, James Rorke; CHAIRMAN, STEERS LTD. (Merchants, estbd. 1924); Pres., Pratt Representatives (Nfld.) Ltd.; Pres., Colonial Business Properties Ltd.; Dir., Standard Manufacturing Co. Ltd. 1957–92; Newfoundland Light & Power Co. Ltd. 1964–90; Pratt Investment Co. Ltd.; Dir., Candn. Imperial Bank of Commerce 1978–90; Dir., T and M Winter Ltd. 1985–91; C.N. Marine Corp. 1972–84; Terra Nova Telecommunications Co. Ltd. 1972–84; Dir. Canadian National Railways 1972–84; mem., former St. John's Adv. Bd., Canada Permanent Trust Co.; Bd Govs., Coll. of Fisheries, St. John's, Nfld., 1960–80; served in 2nd World War as Offr., R.C.N., 1942–45; Hon. Colonel 36 (Nfld.) Services Battalion; mem., Nfld. Bd. Trade (Councillor, 1950–52, 1964–65; Pres. 1967); Extve. Council, Candn. Chamber Comm. (Dir. 1967, Nat. Dir. 1968–69, Vice Pres. for Nfld. 1971–72); Candn. Council, Internat. Chamber Comm. (Dir. 1960–83); Candn. Mental Health Assn., Nfld. Div. (Pres. 1970–71); Un. Church; recreation: boating; Clubs: Rotary (Pres. 1974–75); Bally Haly Golf; R.N.S.Y.S.; Royal Newfoundland Yacht; Granite (Toronto); Mount Royal (Montreal); University (Montreal); Canadian (N.Y.); Metropolitan (N.Y.); Pass-a-Grille Yacht; Office: P.O. Box 8517, St. John's, Nfld. A1B 3N9.

**PRATT, J. Ronald,** B.Ap.Sc., M.B.A.; business executive; b. Vancouver, B.C. 31 March 1941; s. Fredrick H. and Isabel M. (MacMillan) P.; e. Univ. of B.C. B.Ap.Sc. 1964; Univ. of Western Ont. M.B.A. 1968; m. Joanne d. Pearl and Oliver Holmes 1971; children: Shannon, Stephen; VICE-PRESIDENT AND GENERAL MANAGER, OFFICE DOCUMENT SYSTEMS, XEROX CANADA; Process Engineer / New Business Ventures / Engineering Manager, DuPont Canada 1964–70; Partner, Plandex Ltd. 1971–72; variety of staff & field assignments leading to present position, Xerox Canada 1973– ; Extve. Mem., Inst. for Market Driven Quality, Univ. of Toronto; recreations: tennis; clubs: Toronto Cricket, Skating & Curling; Home: 32 Saunders St., Toronto, Ont. M5M 3S4; Office: 5650 Yonge St., North York, Ont. M2M 4G7.

**PRATT, Mary Frances,** B.F.A., R.C.A.; artist; b. Fredericton, N.B. 15 March 1935; d. William John and Katherine Eleanore (McMurray) West; e. Mt. Allison Univ. B.F.A. 1961; m. Christopher 12 Sept. 1957; principle dealers Mira Godard, Toronto; Equinox, Vancouver; book: 'Mary Pratt' by Sandra Gwyn & Gerda Moray 1989; Hon. doc. letters from Mem. Univ. of Nfld.; Dalhousie Univ.; St. Thomas Univ. 1989; Univ. of Toronto 1990; Mt. Allison Univ. 1992; Mem. Bd. of Regents, Mt. Allison Univ. 1983–91; Fed. Cult. Policy Review Comn. (Applebaum-Hébert Comn.) 1980–81; Can. Counc. 1987–93 and others; Mem., Royal Candn. Acad. Assn.; co-author: 'Across the Table' 1985; Home: Box 87, Mt. Carmel, Nfld. A0B 2M0.

**PRATT, R. John,** B.Arch.; b. London, Eng. 28 Feb. 1907; s. John and Norah (Kelly) P.; e. Private Tuition in Eng; McGill Univ., B.Arch. 1933; m. Dorothy Nesbitt, d. Fleetwood Ward, Montreal, Que., 19 Aug. 1935; two s. John Stuart, Robin Alan; 2ndly, Louise, d. Dr. A. Giguere, Montreal, Que., 23 Dec. 1958; mem., Bd. of Govs., Nat. Theatre Sch. of Can.; Bd. of Dirs., Lakeshore Gen. Hosp., Montreal; McGill Chamber Orchestra; Montreal Repertory Theatre; General Contractor, 1933–35; Owner-Builder, residential property, and Operator of Residential Realty, since 1935; pioneered in Candn. Motion Pictures, 1936–48; Theatrical production in Can. and U.S., 1948–59; pioneered in Candn. TV Films, 1950–52; engaged in Civic pol. and radio-TV, films 1952–57 and in Civic and Fed. pol. since 1957; 1st Vice-Chrmn. of Metrop. Council of Arts of Greater Montreal; mem., Master Planning Comte., Metrop. Corp. of Montreal; served in McGill C.O.T.C. 1928–36; Commnd. in 6th Duke of Connaught's Royal Candn. Hussars in 1936; resigned rank of Major to join Navy in 1942; toured with Navy Show, 1943–46; Alderman of Dorval, 1952–55, and Mayor there 1955–64; el. to H. of C. for Jacques Cartier-La Salle, g.e. June 1957 and re-el. g.e. March 1958; def. g.e. Apl. 1963; apptd. Depy. Dir. of Operations and Producer of Entertainment Expo '67; mem., Order Archs. Que.; Royal Arch. Institute of Can.; Actors Equity; Am. Guild of Variety Artists; Assn. of Candn. Radio & Television Artists; Gov., Candn. Jr. Chamber Comm.; Pres., Bldg. Owners & Mgrs. Assn.; Destination Habitat Corp.; Pres., St. Patrick's Development Corp.; St. Patrick's Soc. Montreal; Les Ballets Jazz du Can.; The Montreal Museum of Fine Arts; The Canadian Club of Montreal; The Candn. Inst. of External Affairs; The Roy. Candn. Hussars Inst.; Naval Offrs. Assn. of Can.; Hon. Life Mem., Bldg. Owners and Managers Assn. of Montreal; Conservative; recreation: theatre; Clubs: Naval Officers; Bonaventure; Royal St. Lawrence Yacht; Home: 66 Allan Point, Dorval, Que. H9S 2Z2.

**PRATT, Robert Cranford,** B.A., M.Phil., F.R.S.C.; educator; b. Montreal, Que. 8 Oct. 1926; s. Robert Goodwin and Henrietta (Freeman) P.; e. West Hill High Sch. Montreal 1943; McGill Univ. B.A. 1947; Inst. d'Etudes Politiques, Paris; Balliol Coll. Oxford Univ. (Rhodes Scholar) M.Phil. 1952; m. Renate d. Dr. Gerhard and Heidi Hecht, Germany 15 July 1956; children: Gerhard, Marcus, Anna; PROF. EMERITUS OF POL. SCIENCE, UNIV. OF TORONTO 1993– ; Prof. of Pol. Science, Univ. of Toronto 1966–93; Dir., Rsch. Project, Candn. Development Assistance Policies 1991– ; Dir., Rsch. Project, Western Middle Powers and Global Poverty 1984–88; Acting Dir., Development Studies Prog. 1983–84; Dir. Internat. Studies Programme 1967–72; Lectr. Makerere Univ. Coll. Uganda 1954–56; Asst. Prof. McGill Univ. 1952–54 and 1956–58; Research Offr. Inst. Commonwealth Studies, Oxford 1958–60; Princ., Univ. Coll., Dar-es-Salaam, Tanzania 1961–65; Consultant, Candn. Internat. Dev. Agency, Ford Foundation, Office of the Pres. Tanzania, United Nations Univ., Gov't Tanzania, World Bank; rec'd Killam Award 1969; Research Fellowship, Internat. Devel. Research Centre 1978–79; Commonwealth Visiting Prof., Univ. of London, Eng. 1979–80; Visiting Rsch. Fellow, Development Centre, OECD, Paris 1987; mem. Ecumenical Forum of Can., Chrmn. 1980–83; Chrmn. Ed. Bd. Perspectives on Development Series, Camb. Univ. Press. 1971–77; Ed. Bd., The Political Economy of World Poverty Series, Univ. of Toronto Press 1981–85; mem. Ed. Bd., Political Economy of Development, Cambridge Univ. Press 1986– ; author: 'The Critical Phase in Tanzania 1945–68: Nyerere and the Emergence of a Socialist Strategy' 1976; co-author: 'Buganda and British Overrule' 1960; editor: 'Canadian International Development Assistance Policies: An Appraisal' 1994; 'Middle Power Internationalism: The North South Dimension' 1990; 'Internationalism Under Strain: The North-South Policies of Canada, the Netherlands, Norway and Sweden' 1989; co-editor: 'Christian Faith and Economic Justice: Towards a Canadian Perspective' 1989; 'Human Rights in Canadian Foreign Policy' 1988; 'Towards Socialism in Tanzania' 1979; 'A New Deal in Central Africa' 1960; acad. articles on African politics, devel. issues and Candn. foreign policy; mem. Candn. Assn. African Studies (Pres. 1976–77); Candn. Pol. Science Assn.; Candn. Assn. Study Internat. Dev. (Extve. Ctte. 1992– ); NDP; United Church; Home: 205 Cottingham St., Toronto, Ont. M4V 1C4; Office: Dept. of Political Science, Univ. of Toronto, Toronto, Ont. M5S 1A1.

**PRATTE, Claude,** Q.C.; b. Quebec City, Que. 11 Jan. 1925; s. Gaston and late Jeannette (Verge) P.; e. Univ. of Montreal; Laval Univ.; B.A., LL.L.; m. France, d. His Excellency the late Hon. Onésime Gagnon, Quebec City 15 June 1957; Pres., Les Immeubles des Braves Ltée; Sopra Investments Ltd.; Vice Pres., Radio Saguenay Ltée; Inter-Québec Publicité Inc.; Dir., Candn. Pacific Ltd.; Canadian Pacific Hotels; Canadian Pacific Hotels Holdings Inc.; Canadian Pacific Forest Products Ltd.; General Am. Life Reinsurance Co. of Canada; Compagnie Luxembourgeoise de Télédiffusion SA; SA OUI FM Pradeur Inc.; mem., Bar Que.; Candn. Bar Assn.; Fellow, Royal Soc. of Arts; R. Catholic; recreations: fishing, hunting; Clubs: The Mount Royal; Mount Stephen; Canadian (Montreal); Home: 720 Chemin St. Louis, Quebec, Que. G1S 1C2; Office: 1150 Claire-Fontaine St., Quebec, Que. G1R 5G4.

**PRATTE, France Gagnon,** B.A., M.A.; architectural historian; b. Quebec 7 February 1929; d. Onesime and Cécile (Desaultels) G.; e. Laval Univ. B.A.(Phil.) 1952; Univ. of Toronto B.A. studies; Laval Univ. B.A.(History of Art) 1978, M.A.(Hist. of Arch.) 1980; m. Claude s. Gaston Pratte 15 June 1957; children: Cécile-Nathalie, Caroline-Anita; PRESIDENT & CHAIRMAN, COUNCIL OF MONUMENTS & SITES FOR QUEBEC; private consultant; architectural historian since 1980; Vice-Pres., Continuité Press; Vice Chair, Maxwell Project, McGill Univ.; Spokesman, Coalition for Safeguarding the old Port of Quebec; Advisory Ctte. on Old Que. 1986–92; Adv. Group, Heritage Policy Cultural Affairs 1987–88; Mem., Bd. of Dir., Heritage Montreal; C.D. Howe Mem. Found.; Canadiana Fund, Nat. Capital Comn.; Candn. Mediterranean Inst.; Jeffrey Hale Hosp. Found.; Mem., Quebec City C. of C.; Heritage Canada Found.; Assn. for Preservation Techniques; Nat. Trust for Hist. Preservation (US); Internat. Council of Monuments & Sites; PARIS; Nat. Geographic Soc. (US); author: 'L'Architecture et la nature à Québec aux XIXe siècle: les villas' 1980, 'Maison de campagne des Montréalais, l'architecture de Edward et W.S. Maxwell' 1989, 'Country Houses for Montrealers, the Architecture of Edward and W.S. Maxwell' 1989; co-author:

'Chateau Frontenac: Hundred Years in a Castle' 1993, 'The Architecture of Edward & William Maxwell' 1991; recreations: reading, swimming, photography, travelling; Home: 720 chemin St.-Louis, Quebec, Que. G1S 1C2; Office: 82 Grande-Allée W., Quebec, Que. G1R 2G6.

**PRATTE, Josette;** écrivain; née Qué. 23 août 1951; f. Yves et Marie (Bender) P.; é. Couvent des Ursulines, Qué.; Coll. Jean de Brébeuf, Montréal; ép. Bernard Clavel 22 juillet 1982; auteur: 'Et je pleure' 1981, 'Les Persiennes' 1985 (romans); résidence: Prieuré Sainte-Anne, 33550 Capian, France.

**PRATTE, Hon. Louis,** B.A., LL.L.; judge; b. Québec City, Qué. 29 Nov. 1926; s. Garon and Georgine (Rivard) P.; e. Laval Univ., B.A. 1947, LL.L. 1950; Univ. de Paris Faculté de droit et des sciences économiques, diplôme d'études supérieures en droit privé 1960; m. Charlotte d. Judge Thomas and Marie (Dupuis) Tremblay 2 July 1953; children: Marie, François; JUDGE, FED. COURT OF CAN. (APPEAL DIV.) 1973– ; called to Bar of Qué. 1950; law practice St-Laurent & Associates 1950–53; Zellers Ltd. 1953; Pratte, Tremblay & Associates 1954–60; Prof. of Civil Law, Laval Univ. 1963–71; Judge Trial Div. present Court 1971–73; Home: 1105, 175 Laurier St., Hull, Que. J8X 4G3; Office: Supreme Court Building, Ottawa, Ont. K1A 0H9.

**PRATTIS, James Ian,** B.A., B.Litt., Ph.D.; university professor; b. Corby, Eng. 16 Oct. 1942; s. Thomas Anderson and Miriam Elsie (Ovens) P.; e. Univ. Coll., London, B.A. 1965; Balliol Coll., Oxford, B.Litt. 1967; Univ. of B.C. Ph.D. 1970; m. 1stly Gaisma Vera d. Stefan and Ausma Kadegis 1966; divorced 1991; children: Iain, Andrew, Catriona, Alexander, Michael, Sean; m. 2ndly Stacey Lynn 27 July 1991; PROF. OF ANTHROP., CARLETON UNIV. 1985– ; Community Devel. Offr., Sarawak 1960–62; Dir. of Irrigation Proj., Greece 1964; Lectr., Vancouver City Coll. 1969; Sessional Lectr., Univ. of B.C. 1970; joined Carleton Univ. as Asst. Prof. 1970; Candn. Mus. Contract, Que. Hebridean Proj. 1976; North Sea Oil Impact Study 1977–78; carpenter, lobster fisherman 1981; committed to world peace & global transformation through personal responsibility and example; devel. and edn. cons.; Dir., T.A.D.A.C. Rsch. Group, Carleton Univ.; Rsch. Assoc., Ethnic Studies Inst., Carleton Univ.; author: 'New Directions in Economic Anthropology' 1973; 'Economic Structures in the Highlands of Scotland' 1977; 'Reflections – The Anthropological Muse' 1985; about 100 scholarly articles; recreations: tai chi, skiing; Address: Dept. of Anthropology, Carleton Univ., Ottawa, Ont. K1S 5B6.

**PRAZNIK, Darren Thomas,** B.A., LL.B., M.L.A.; barrister & solicitor; b. Selkirk, Man. 19 May 1961; s. Bernard James and Marjorie Helen P.; e. Lord Selkirk Reg. School 1979; Univ. of Winnipeg B.A. 1982; Univ. of Manitoba LL.B. 1985; m. Shelly Dale d. John and Diane Coupland; children: Katlin Rose, Jessica Elizabeth; MINISTER OF LABOUR AND NORTHERN AFFAIRS, PROV. OF MANITOBA 1993– ; articled with Darcy & Deacon; called to Bar of Man. 1986; Special Asst. to Hon. Jake Epp, Min. of Nat. Health & Welfare 1986–88; 1st elected M.L.A. for Lac du Bonnet g.e. 1988; re-elected 1990; Min. of Labour & Min. Resp. for Civil Service Act 1991; Min. Resp. for Workers Compensation Act 1991; Minister of Northern & Native Affairs 1993; Office: Room 156, Legislative Bldg., Winnipeg, Man. R3C 0V8.

**PREFONTAINE, Daniel Charles,** Q.C., LL.M.; Canadian public servant; b. Prince Albert, Sask. 5 Aug. 1940; e. Rockhurst Univ. Kansas City, Mo. B.A. 1961; Univ. of Sask. LL.B. 1964; Univ. of Mo. LL.M. 1978; m. Marguerite Charlebois 24 Aug. 1963; children: Nicole, Lise, Rachelle; CHIEF POLICY COUNSEL, COMPLIANCE, ABORIGINAL JUSTICE AND INTERNATIONAL CRIMINAL LAW, DEPT. OF JUSTICE 1992– and PRES. & C.E.O., THE INTERNAT. CENTRE FOR CRIMINAL LAW REFORM AND CRIMINAL JUSTICE POLICY (Vancouver, B.C.) 1994– ; cr. Q.C. 1982; private law practice 1964–70; Crown Prosecutor 1967–70; Counsel Dept. of Justice, Can. 1971; Asst. Supt. of Bankruptcy (Legal) 1972–73; Dir. of Policy Solr. Gen. of Can. 1973–76; Dir. of Leg. Candn. Bar Assn. 1976–77; Teaching Fellow, Univ. of Mo. 1977–78; Dir. of Policy Dept. Justice Can. 1978–81, Gen. Counsel 1981–83; Asst. Depy. Min., Policy Programs & Research 1983–92; mem. Law Soc. Upper Can.; Candn. Bar Assn.; L'assn. des avocats d'expression Française d'Ontario; Candn. Inst. Adm. Justice: Home: 8 Port Royal, Aylmer, Qué. J9J 1C6; Office: 801 – Varette Bldg. – 130 Albert St., Ottawa, Ont. K1A 0H8.

**PREGER, George Andrew,** Fil.kand., M.Sc., C.M.C.; management consultant; b. Vienna, Austria 16 Apr. 1936; s. Paul and Hertha (Leitner) P.; e. St. Edward's Sch., Oxford 1955; Goteborg Univ., Fil.Kand. 1963; Calif. Am. Univ., M.Sc. 1983; Inst. of Mngt. Cons. of Ont., C.M.C. 1980; m. Kersti d. Gustaf and Brita Eriksson 12 Sept. 1967; children: David, Eva; Sweden: Trainee, Svenska Unilever; Prod. Mgr., Henkel (Sverige) AB; Sr. Prod. Mgr., Husqvarna AB; Canada: Proj. Extve., N.B. Devel. Corp.; Asst. Gen. Mgr., Optyl (Can.) Ltd.; Extve. Cons., Stevenson & Kellogg 1974–79; Internat. Partner, Urquhart, Preger & Stern Extve. Recruiters 1979–86; specializes in assisting transnational companies; Extve. Vice Pres., later Pres., Boyden Assocs., an internat. Executive Search firm, 1986–89; Pres., George Preger & Associates Inc., a Human Resources Consulting firm; speaks English, Swedish, German, Hungarian; Sess. Lectr., Sir Wilfrid Laurier Univ.; Hon. Alumnus, Technion-Israel Inst. of Technol.; Trustee, Riverdale Hosp. 1986; Hon. Dir., Swedish Candn. C. of C. (Chrmn. of Bd. 1983–86); Fellow Institute of Directors in Canada; Dir.-at-large, Junior Achievement of Canada; recreations: tennis, skiing, walking; Office: 41 MacPherson Ave., Toronto, Ont. M5R 1W7.

**PRENGER, J. Harry,** B.Comm., M.B.A.; banker; b. Holland 22 June 1941; s. John Hendrick and Sjeersche (Berger) P.; e. Carleton Univ. B.Comm. 1970; York University M.B.A. 1980; one d.: Jill Anne; VICE-PRES. & MGR., BUSINESS BANKING CENTRE, ROYAL BANK OF CANDA 1993– ; joined Royal Bank Hamilton 1957; Asst. Gen. Mgr., Area H.Q., London, Eng. 1970; subsequent positions incl. Vice-Pres., Multi-Nat. Corp. U.K., Ireland & Nordic countries, Vice-Pres., Govt. Bus. & Finan. Inst. Toronto, Vice-Pres., Mktg., Metro Toronto & Area H.Q., Vice-Pres., Mktg., H.O. Corp. Banking Toronto; Dir. & Vice-Chair, Jr. Achievement (Metro Toronto & York Region); 1 of 3 Founding Mem., Leacock Found. for Children; Mem., Rotary Club of Kitchener; Adv. Ctte. Mem., Carleton Univ.; clubs: Lambton Golf & Country, Fitness Institute; Home: 15 Ellen St. W., Kitchener, Ont. N2H 4K1; Office: 30 Duke St. W., 8th fl., Kitchener, Ont. N2H 3W5.

**PRENT, Mark George,** B.F.A.; sculptor; b. Montreal, Que 23 Dec. 1947; e. Sir George Williams Univ. B.F.A. 1970; solo exhns. incl. Sir George Williams Art Galleries Montreal 1971, 1978–79; The Isaacs Gallery Toronto 1972, 1974, 1978, 1981, 1984, 1986, 1990; Warren Benedek Gallery N.Y. 1972; York Univ. Toronto 1974; Akademie der Kunste Berlin 1975–76; Kunsthalle Nurnberg, W. Germany 1976; Stedelijk Museum Amsterdam 1978; Musée d'art contemporain Montreal 1979; Art Space Peterborough, Ont. 1979; Saw Gallery Ottawa 1979; Salle Tremblé, Alma, P.Q. 1982; Gall. Fucito, Montreal 1984; Forest City Gallery London, Ont. 1985; Galerie Esperanza, Montreal 1986, 1988, 1990, 1991; The Power Plant, Toronto 1987; Centre D'Exposition Circa, Montreal 1993; Galerie de la Tour, Basel, Switzerland 1993; rep. in various group exhns. incl. Survey '70 Montreal Museum of Fine Arts; R.C.A. Travel Exhn. 1971; 8e Biennale de Paris, Musée nat. d'art moderne, Musée d'art moderne de la ville de Paris 1973; 9 out of 10 travel exhn. Ont. 1974–75; Candn. Contemporary Sculpture, Centre Saidye Bronfman Montreal 1978; Birmingham (Ala.) Festival of the Arts 1979; 11th Internat. Sculpture Conf. Dupont Centre, Washington, D.C. 1980; Que. Sculpture 1970–80, Musée d'art contemporain Montreal and Chicoutimi 1980; Maison de la Culture Rennes, France 1980–81; 'Sculpture 1980,' Maryland Inst., Coll. of Art, Baltimore, Md.; 'Prince, Prent, Whiten,' The Agnes Etherington Art Centre, Kingston, Ont., 1981; Univ. of Hawaii and Manoa, Hawaii, 1980; 'Art Against Repression' Art Space, Peterborough, Ont. 1982 (travelling exhn.); 'East-West Encounter' Exhn. & Symposium, Bombay, India 1985; Le Botanique, Centre Culturelle Wallonie-Bruxelles, Brussels, Belgium 1986 (travelling exhn.); 'Miniatuur-Museum' Reflex Modern Art Gallery, Amsterdam, Holland 1992; rep. various pub. colls. incl. Art Bank Can., Art Gallery of Ont., Sir George Williams Art Galleries, Musée d'art contemporain, Musée du Québec; Collaborative tour with Butoh dancers 'Tetsuro Fukuhara and Bodhi Sattva with sculptures by Mark Prent' travelling in Quebec, Ontario (incl. The National Gallery of Canada), Vermont and New York City 1991; Art Gallery of Vancouver, BC; Reflex Modern Art Museum, Amsterdam, Holland; documentary films; 'If Brains Were Dynamite, You Wouldn't Have Enough to Blow Your Nose' 1976; 'Mark Prent: Overmood' 1980; recipient Can. Council Arts Awards 1971, 1972, 1973, 1975, 1978; Sr. Arts Grants 1979, 1980, 1981, 1985, 1987, 1991; Guggenheim Mem. Foundation Fellowship 1977; Victor M. Lynch-Staunton Award 1978; Guest of Deutsches Akademischer Austauschdienst Artist in Berlin Program 1975; Ludwig Vogelstein Foundation Fellowship 1985; Art Matters 1988, 1989; Address: 35 Bank St., St. Albans, VT 05478.

**PRENTICE, Barry Everett,** B.A., M.Sc., Ph.D., P.Ag., M.C.I.T.; university professor; b. Port Perry, Ont. 10 May 1950; s. Everett Robert and Christina Elizabeth (Brekkee) P.; e. Univ. of West. Ont. B.A. 1974; Univ. of Guelph M.Sc. 1979; Univ. of Manitoba Ph.D. 1986; m. Mary d. George and Helen Baldock 17 April 1976; children: Ross, Ian, Carla; PROFESSIONAL ASSOC., TRANSPORT INST. & ASSOC. PROF., AGRICULTURAL ECON. & FARM MGNT., UNIV. OF MANITOBA 1992– ; Rsch. Assoc. & Lectr., Univ. of Guelph 1979–82; Lectr. & Ph.D. Cand. 1983–85; Professional Assoc. & Asst. Prof. 1986–89; Acting Dir., Transport Inst. 1991–92; Mem., Market Devel. Ctte., Flax Council of Canada 1986–93; Bd. Mem., Candn. Assoc. for Prod. & Inventory Control Winnipeg Chap. 1986– (Vice-Pres., Edn. 1986–91); Councillor, Candn. Transp. Rsch. Forum 1991–93; Mem., Expert Ctte. on Agric. Mktg. & Trade 1991–93; CTRF Paper Comp. Awards 1988, 1991 (3rd), 1989 (1st); Internat. Cargo Handling Ass. Award 1991; Candn. Wheat Bd. Fellowship 1984–85; Ont. Grad. Scholarship 1977–78; Candn. Agric. Econ. Soc. M.Sc. thesis 1979 (2nd); co-author: 'The Effects of the Canada-US Trade Agreement on Transborder Trucking' 1992, 'A Comparative Analysis of Economic Impacts at Canadian Airports' 1992, 'Transport-Related Opportunities ...' 1992, 'The Transborder Competetiveness of Canadian Trucking' 1992; editor: 'Transportation to Mexico' 1993; recreation: baseball coach; club: Richmond Reds (Mosquitos); Home: 91 Purdue Bay, Winnipeg, Man. R3T 3C6; Office: Winnipeg, Man. R3T 2N2.

**PRESCOTT, Michael Peter,** B.Comm., M.B.A.; investment executive; b. Windsor, Ont. 7 Sept. 1936; e. Univ. of Detroit B.Comm. 1959, M.B.A. 1960; m. Betty Paton; children: Nancy Jane, Jonathan Peter Michael; PRESIDENT, ZURICH CANADA INVESTMENT MANAGEMENT LIMITED and SENIOR VICE PRESIDENT, INVESTMENTS, ZURICH CANADA 1988– ; Prudential Insur. Co. of Am. 1960–65; Sun Life Assur. Co. of Can. 1966–81; Midland Doherty Limited 1981–85; Travelers Canada 1985–88; Dir., Zurich Canada Investment Management Limited; Royal Canadian Military Inst.; recreations: Russian billiards, landscape gardening; clubs: Royal Canadian Military Institute; Home: 11 Cortleigh Cres., Toronto, Ont. M4R 2C6; Office: 400 University Ave., Toronto, Ont. M5G 1S7.

**PRESHING, William A.,** B.A., B.Ed., M.B.A., Ph.D.; professor emeritus; b. Edmonton, Alta. 24 April 1929; s. John and Teresa (Steiner) P.; e. Univ. of Alberta B.Ed. 1952, B.A. 1957; Univ. of Western Ont. M.B.A. 1956; Univ. of Illinois Ph.D. 1965; m. Lillian d. Allaster and Marion Linnell 27 June 1959; children: William David, Susan Marion, Carolyn Jane; PROFESSOR EMERITUS, FACULTY OF BUSINESS, UNIV. OF ALBERTA 1991– ; Asst. Prof., Univ. of Alberta 1957–62; Assoc. Prof., Univ. of Calgary & Assoc. Dir., Mngt. Studies, Banff Ctr. for Cont. Edn. 1965–69; Univ. of Alberta, Dir., Institutional Rsch. & Planning 1969–77; Dir., Community Relations 1978–81; Prof., Fac. of Extension & Adjunct Prof., Business 1982–89; Associate Dean (Undergrad. Prog.), Business 1989–90; Dir., Office of Community Relations 1991; Mem., Am. Mktg. Assn.; Sales & Mktg. Extve.; Edmonton Econ. Devl. Authority; Shippers Supply Ltd.; Russell Ultra Sound Ltd.; Point of Call Ltd. Airlines; Inst. of Public Admin. of Canada; World Trade Ctr. Edmonton; Pres., William A. Preshing and Assoc. Ltd.; Dir., Edmonton Northlands; Alberta Art Found.; Alta. Found. for the Performing Arts; Alta. Found. for the Arts; Edmonton Symphony; Chair, Mktg. Ctte., Universiade 1981–83; Mem., Senate of Newman Theol. College 1981–86; Co-Chair, Municipal Anniversary Ctte., City of Edmonton 1979–80; author: 'Cases for Managerial Decision' 1964; 'Business Management in Canada: An Introduction' 1974, '79 and over 300 articles on mktg. & mngt.; co-author: 'Concepts and Canadian Cases in Marketing' 1973; recreations: jogging, reading; clubs: Univ. of Alberta Faculty Club; Home: 13908 – 86 Ave., Edmonton, Alta. T5R 4A9; Office: Room 2-28C Bus. Bldg., Univ. of Alberta, Edmonton, Alta. T6G 2R6.

**PRESSEY, Alexander William,** B.A., M.A., Ph.D.; educator; author; b. Ethelbert, Man. 8 Feb. 1939; s. William and Anna (Kunka) Prysiazniuk; e. Univ. of Manitoba B.A. 1959, M.A. 1961; Univ. of Alta. Ph.D. 1965; m. Joyce d. Hermon and Bertha Hedison 16 May 1959; children: Cindy Dawn, Heather Lynn, Christopher Alexander; PROFESSOR OF PSYCHOLOGY, UNIVERSITY OF MANITOBA 1973– ; Capt. (Ret.) Candn. Army (M), Armour PSO 1958–65; Instr. Univ. of Man. 1960–61; Rsch. Psychologist, Moose Jaw, Sask. 1961–

63; Asst. Prof. of Psych. present Univ. 1965–68, Assoc. Prof. 1968–73; author: integrative field theory of visual distortion; 50 scientific articles on perception; contribs. to popular media on Western Candn. issues; ed. 'Readings in General Psychology: Canadian Contributions' 1970; Fellow Candn. Psychological Assn. 1973; Visiting Scholar Univ. of Cambridge 1972, Milan 1978, Georgia 1978, Vanderbilt 1978, Kansas State 1983, Frankfurt 1983, 1986; Max Planck Inst. 1986; Univ. of New South Wales 1993; Visiting Scientist Am. Psychological Assn. 1975; recipient Natural Sciences and Engineering Rsch. Counc. grants 1965–84; Can. Counc. gratn 1978; mentioned in 'Who's Who in the Midwest' 1976; mem. Psychonomic Soc.; Pres. Man. Psychological Soc.; Chrmn. Candn. Psychological Assn. Convention 1970; mem. Counc., St. John's Coll. 1982, 1993; recreations: curling, golf; Club: Granite Curling; Home: 917 Wicklow Place, Winnipeg, Man. R3T 0J1; Office: St. John's Coll., Univ. of Man., Winnipeg, Man. R3T 2N2.

**PRESSMAN, Irwin S.,** B.Sc., M.B.A., Ph.D.; educator; b. Thunder Bay, Ont. 17 Aug. 1939; s. Ben and Fanny (Sternberg) P.; e. Univ. of Man. B.Sc. 1960; Cornell Univ. Ph.D. 1965; Univ. of Toronto M.B.A. 1984; m. Elaine d. David and Ann Steingarten 10 Oct. 1966; divorced 1992; children: Ari, Amy, Sarah; ASSOC. PROF. OF MATH. AND STATS. CARLETON UNIV. 1971– , Chrmn. Integrated Sci. Studies 1987–91; Pres. Pressman and Associates; Forschungsassistant E.T.H. Zurich 1965–67; Asst. Prof. Ohio State Univ. 1967–71; NSERC Sr. Ind. Fellow Bell Northern Research 1984–85; Visiting Assoc. Prof. of Computer Sci. Univ. of Toronto 1982–84; Research Scholar, IBM Canada 1991–92; Woodrow Wilson Fellow 1960–62; mem. Candn. Operational Rsch. Soc. (Pres. Ottawa Chapter 1989–90); Candn. Math. Soc.; recreations: skiing, swimming; Home: 30 Glendenning Dr., Nepean, Ont. K2H 7Y9; Office: Carleton Univ., Ottawa, Ont. K1S 5B6.

**PREST, Victor Kent,** M.Sc., Ph.D., F.R.S.C.; geologist; b. Edmonton, Alta. 2 Apr. 1913; e. pub. schs. Edmonton, Toronto and London; high schs. London and Winnipeg; Univ. of Man. B.Sc. 1935, M.Sc. 1936; Univ. of Toronto Ph.D. 1941; m. E. S. Patricia Horder, 24 Oct. 1942; children: Sherron Gail (Mrs. G. C. T. Armstrong), Wayne H. Prest; Party Chief, Ont. Dept. Mines 1937–40; Research Lab. International Nickel Co., Copper Cliff 1941; Perm. Staff Ont. Dept. Mines 1945–50 and Geol. Survey of Can. 1950–77; Consultant, Ont. Geol. Survey, Toronto 1978–81; self-employed glacial geologist and Pres. Veekay Consultants Ltd. 1979–90; served with RCNVR 1942–45, rank Lt.; author book chapters geol. of soils in Can., conserv. geol. features in Can., and Quaternary geol. of Can.; numerous prof. reports, papers and maps on bedrock and surficial (glacial) geol. incl. 'Canadas Heritage of Glacial Features'; Fellow, Roy. Soc. Can.; mem. Geol. Assn. Can.; Candn. Quaternary Assn. (awarded 1st W.A. Johnston Medal 1987); Assn. Québecois pour l'Etude du Quaternaire (Hon. mem.); Internat. Union Quaternary Rsch. (Hon. mem. 1987); Am. Quaternary Assn.; Christian Scientist; recreation: curling; Clubs: City View Curling (Pres. 1958); Hon. Gov. Gen.'s Curling (Pres. 1972); Candn. Br., Royal Caledonia Curling Club (Council of Mang. 1974–79; Hon. Life Mem., 1986); Home: Apt. 405, 1465 Baseline Rd., Ottawa, Ont. K2C 3L9.

**PRESTON, Mr. Justice Bruce McLean,** B.Comm., M.A., LL.B.; supreme court judge; b. Edmonton, Alta. 13 May 1939; s. Lawrence William and Anne Melissa (McLean) P.; e. Univ. of B.C., LL.B. 1971; divorced; one d.: Meredith Anne; JUDGE, SUPREME COURT OF BRITISH COLUMBIA 1990– ; articled with Wilson, King & Co., Prince George, B.C.; called to Bar of B.C. 1972; practised with Preston & Chamberlist, Prince George 1975–78; with Boyle & Company, Penticton 1979–87; Judge, County Court of Cariboo 1987–90; Home: 301 – 1675 Hornby St., Vancouver, B.C. V6Z 2M3; Office: Begbie Square, 651 Carnarvon St., New Westminster, B.C. V3M 1C9.

**PRESTON, James Carstairs,** B.A., C.A.; manufacturer; b. Stratford, Ont. 17 Apr. 1951; s. William Jeffrey and Isabel (Carstairs) P.; e. Univ. of W. Ont. B.A. 1974; m. Brenda G. d. Alvin and Angeline MacKay 1 Sept. 1973; children: James Jeffrey, Christopher David, Andrew McKay, Kathryn Lindsay; PRESIDENT, PRESTONIA OFFICE PRODUCTS LTD. 1976– ; Acct., Peat Marwick Mitchell & Co. 1974–76; Past Pres. Stratford General Hosp.; Vice Pres., Stratford Shakespearean Festival; Home: 21 Centre St., Stratford, Ont. N5A 1E4; Office: 163 King St., Stratford, Ont. N5A 6T1.

**PRESTON, Melvin Alexander,** C.D., M.A., Ph.D., D.Sc., F.A.A.A.S. (1980), F.R.S.C. (1961); educator; b. Toronto, Ont. 28 May 1921; s. Gardener Alexander and Libbie Hazel (Melvin) P.; e. Earl Haig Coll. Inst., Willowdale, Ont.; Univ. of Toronto, B.A. 1942, M.A. 1946; Univ. of Birmingham, Ph.D. 1949; McMaster Univ. D.Sc. 1983; m. Dorothy Mary Knowles, d. Randal Whittaker, Birmingham, Eng., 16 Aug., 1947; two s. Jonathan Melvin, Richard Franklyn; 2ndly. Eugene, d. F. Shearer, Simcoe, Ont., 25 June 1966; Asst. Lectr. in Math. Physics, Birmingham Univ., 1947–49; Asst. Prof. Physics, Univ. of Toronto, 1949–53; McMaster Univ. appointments 1953–77: Assoc. Prof. and Prof. of Physics, Prof. of Applied Mathematics, Chrmn. of Applied Mathematics, 1962–65 and 1975–77, Dean of Graduate Studies 1965–71; Emeritus Prof. 1986– ; Extve. Vice Chrmn. of Adv. Comte. on Acad. Planning Council of Ont. Univs. 1971–75; Prof. of Physics (1977–86) and Vice Pres. (Academic) (1977–82), Univ. of Saskatchewan; Nuffield Travel Grant for Research 1957; National Research Council Senior Fellow, Copenhagen, 1963–64; Distinguished Visiting Prof., Univ. of Texas ( Austin) 1965 and Texas Tech. Univ. 1975; recipient Gold Medal, Putnam Intercollegiate Mathematical Competition 1942; Canada Centennial Medal; research interests are theoretical and nuclear physics; Publication: 'Physics of the Nucleus,' 1962; 'Structure of the Nucleus,' 1975, and papers in physics; retired R.C.A. major; served in 2nd World War in Can. and U.K.; Trustee, Dundas Twp. Sch. Area Bd., 1954–57 (Chrmn. 1957–59); mem., Bd. of Govs., Hillfield-Strathallan Coll. 1966–71, 1987–90; Pres. (1971) Candn. Assn. of Graduate Schs.; Chrmn. (1970–71) Ont. Council on Grad. Studies; mem., Bd. of Governors McMaster Univ. 1966–68, 1976–77; Fellow, Am. Physical Society; mem., Candn. Assn. Physicists (Councillor 1951–52, 1983–5, Treas. 1952–58); Pres., Saskatchewan Sailing Assoc. (1980–83); Vice-Pres., Canadian Yachting Association 1981–86; Anglican; recreation: sailing; Clubs: Royal Hamilton Yacht, Rotary, Royal Hamilton Military Inst.; Address: Physics Dept., McMaster Univ., Hamilton, Ont. L8S 4M1.

**PRESTON, W. Jeffrey;** manufacturer; b. Montreal, Que. 18 April 1916; s. James and Flroence (Campbell) P.; e. Public Sch. and Stratford (Ont.) Coll. Inst.; m. Isabel, d. Alexander Carstairs, 27 Jan. 1945; children: Jane, James, William; Chrmn., Prestonia Stationery Limited; MacMillan Office Appliances Ltd.; Coordr., Stratford General Hosp. Bldg. Fund 1984–87; Pres. (1965) Stratford United Appeal; Chrmn., Stratford YM-YWCA Foundation; mem., Stratford Bd. Educ.; Past Chrmn. Stratford Parks Bd., Past Pres., Candn. Furniture Mfrs. Assn.; Past Pres., Candn. Office Products Assoc.; Past Pres., Stratford Rotary Club; Paul Harris Fellow, Rotary Club; Comte. of Stewards of St. Johns Ch.; served in 2nd World War, 1940–1945, Major, Cameron Highlanders of Ottawa; served in Britain, France; Mentioned in Despatches; Vice Pres., Stratford General Hospital Found.; mem., Candn. Office Products Assn. (Past Pres.); United Church; recreations: golf, curling; Club: Stratford Country & Curling; Home: 12 Diana Court, Stratford, Ontario N5A 5B1 Office: 163 King St., Stratford, Ont. N5A 4S2.

**PRETTY, David Walter,** M.B.A.; retired insurance executive; b. Toronto, Ont. 23 Aug. 1925; s. Joseph Melville and Olive Francis (Page) P.; e. Blythwood Pub. Sch., 1938 and Earl Haig Coll. Inst., 1943; Univ. of Toronto, B.Com. 1947, M.B.A. 1955; unm.; PRES. PRETTY CONSULTANTS INC., 1980– ; Chrmn., Ontario Share & Deposit Insurance Corp.; Chrmn., General Accident Assurance Co. of Can.; Dir., Ontario Blue Cross; Colonial Life Ins. Co.; Realfund; Associate Investors Ltd.; joined North Am. Life, 1947; apptd. Mgr., Securities Dept., 1950; Asst. Treas. 1955; Assoc. Treas. 1959; Treasurer 1965; Vice President and Treasurer 1966; Vice-Pres., Finance 1968; Extve. Vice-Pres. 1971; Pres., 1972–80; rec'd. Centennial Medal; Gov., Ont. Br. and former Nat. Vice Pres., Royal Life Saving Soc. Can.; Past Chrmn., Div. of Finance & Investment Comte., United Church of Canada; Past Pres., Bd. of Govs., The Queen Elizabeth Hosp.; Past Chrmn. of the Bd. of Regents, Victoria Univ.; Past Pres., The Boy Scouts Assn. of Metro Toronto; Past Chrmn. Metro Toronto Adv. Bd. of the Candn. Nat. Inst. for the Blind; Vice-Chrmn., North York Gen. Hosp. Found.; Liberal; Un. Church; recreation: gardening; Clubs: Toronto; Granite; Bd. of Trade Metrop. Toronto; Office: 45 Carlton St., Suite 905, Toronto, Ont. M5B 2H9.

**PRÉVOST, (Joseph Gaston Charles) André;** composer; educator; b. Hawkesbury, Ont. 30 July 1934; e. St-Jérôme, Qué.; Séminaire de St-Thérèse; Coll. de St-Laurent; studied harmony and counterpoint, composition CMM (Premier prix harmony, composition 1960); rec'd Sarah Fischer Concerts composition prize 1959; Chamber Music Award Amis de l'art foundation 1959; studied analysis with Olivier Messiaen, Paris Conserv. and worked with Henry Dutilleux, Ecole normale 1961 (Can. Council and Que. Govt. grants); studied electronic music with Michel Phillipot at ORTF, Paris 1964; teacher at Séminaire de Joliette and Coll. des Eudistes, Rosemont 1962; joined Faculty of Music, Univ. of Montreal 1965; attended Berkshire Music Center Tanglewood 1965; rec'd Prix d'Europe for composition 1963; symphonic work 'Fantasmes' rec'd Amis de l'art foundation prize 1963 and Montreal Symphony Orchestra prize 1964; U.S.A. premiere Carnegie Hall 1977; rec'd comn. for musical work on 'Man and His World' Expo 67; recording of his 'Sonato' for violin and piano rec'd Festival du disque Prize, Montreal; 'Suite for String Quartet' comnd. by Ten Centuries Concerts Toronto in collaboration with Candn. Music Centre and Candn. Confed. Centennial Comn. 1966, premiered by Orford String Quartet 1968; 'Terre des Hommes' for large orchestra, 3 choirs and 2 narrators premiered Place des Arts 1967 at inauguration Expo 67 World Festival; by late 1970's had rec'd and completed over 20 comns. from orchestras and other organs. incl. 'Paraphrase' for string quartet and orchestra premiered by Toronto Symphony Orchestra (also comnd. by TSO) and Orford String Quartet 1980; 'Cantate pour cordes' premiered at Guelph Spring Festival 1987; 'Menuhin-Prévost, a Creative Adventure' CBC broadcast 1990; named Dir. Candn. Music Centre 1971; Pres. Groupe Nouvelle-Aire 1973; rec'd Candn. Music Council Medal 1977; St-Jérôme auditorium named after him; mem. Candn. League Composers; affiliate PRO Canada; Assoc., Candn. Music Centre; Address: 227 ave Querbes, Outremont, Montreal, Que. H2V 3W1.

**PRÉVOST, Ed,** B.A., M.B.A., C.A.A.P.; executive; b. Baie Comeau, Qué. 26 May 1941; s. Omer and Jeanne (Ouellet) P.; e Loyola Coll. Montréal B.A. (Hons. Hist.) 1962; Sch. of Bus. Admin., Univ. of W. Ont. M.B.A. 1964; L'Institut de la Publicité canadienne, C.A.A.P. 1964–65; m. Anna-Marie d. Charles Murphy 20 June 1964; children: Marc, Eric, Luc, Louise; PRES. AND CHIEF EXTVE. OFFR. PARA INC. 1991– ; 1983; Sr. Vice Pres., Carling O'Keefe Breweries of Canada Ltd 1983–89; Acct. Extve. J. Walter Thompson Co. Ltd. Montréal 1964–66; Cockfield Brown & Co. Ltd. Montréal 1966–67; Acct. Supr. 1967, Group Mgr. & Vice Pres. 1968; Gen. Mgr. CJRP radio stn. Québec 1969–71; Extve. Vice Pres. & C.E.O., Radiodiffusion Mutuelle Ltée, Montréal 1971, Pres. & C.O.O. 1973; Extve. Vice Pres. Civitas Corp. Ltd. 1973, Pres., C.E.O. and Bd. Chrmn. of the operating cos. 1974–82; Pres. & C.E.O., La Brasserie Molson O'Keefe Ltée. 1983–89; Pres. & C.E.O., Sico Inc. 1989–91; Bd. Chrmn., Stephens and Towndrow Co. Ltd., Toronto 1973–74; Chrmn. of Bd. Radiomutuel, Montréal 1976; mem. Internat. Broadcast Inst. London, Eng.; mem. Extve. Ctte. Montréal Heart Inst. Rsch. Fund 1981; Chrmn. 1979–81; Founding Pres. Western Bus. Sch. Club Montréal 1972 and mem. Adv. Ctte. 1978; Gov., Candn. Advertising Found. 1982; Chrmn., Telefilm Canada 1983–86; Bd. Chrmn., L'Assoc. des Brasseurs du Québec 1984–86; N.C.M.R.D., Univ. of Western Ont. 1986; Vice Pres., Bd. of Dirs., Loyola High Sch. Found., Concordia 1987; Dir.: Bureau of Measurement 1971–78; La Chambre de Comm. de Montréal; Co-Pres. Cinématographic Ctte. 1980–81; Chrmn. Assn. des M.B.A. du Qué (AMBAQ) 1985–86; La Jeune Chambre de Comm. de Montréal 1977; Sec. and former Treas. Inter-Am. Assn. Montevideo; Past Pres. Am. Mktg. Assn. Qué. mem. Montréal Bd. Trade; YPO Que. Chapt. Chrmn. 1987; Candn. Assn. Broadcasters (Dir. 1975, Vice Chrmn. 1976–77, Chrmn. 1978–79, Extve. Ctte. 1980–81); R. Catholic; recreations: skiing, tennis, hockey, travel, reading; Clubs: St-Denis; Royal Montreal Golf; Home: 2301 Bennington Gate, Oakville, Ont. L6J 5Z4.

**PRICE, Arthur R.,** P.Eng.; oil company executive; b. Calgary, Alta. 22 Oct. 1951; e. Univ. of Alta., B.Sc. 1973; married; three children; PRES. & C.E.O., HUSKY OIL LTD. & HUSKY OIL OPNS. LTD. 1984– ; supv. & mngt. of design & construction of capital projects, nat. gas & petrochem. related fields, NOVA 1973–79; Vice-Pres., Husky Oil Ltd. & Extve. Vice-Pres. Husky Oil Opns. Ltd. 1979–84; Dir., IPSCO, Inc.; Mem., A.P.E.G.G.A.; Office: P.O. Box 6525, Stn. D, Calgary, Alta. T2P 3G7.

**PRICE, Derek Graham,** B.A.; computer services executive; b. Shanghai, China 5 Nov. 1934; s. Graham and Catherine (Morgan) P.; e. Westcliff High Sch.; Cambridge Univ. B.A. 1957; m. Annette d. Charles and Dorothy Young 26 March 1960; children: Natalie, Annabel, Adam; Pres., Comshare Ltd. 1970; Dir., Comshare U.K.; Comshare B.V.; Dialog Intnl.; Sales Extve. De La Rue Bull Ltd. 1959–64; Sales Dir., G.E.I.S. 1964–68; Gen. Mgr. G.E. (Germany) 1968–70; Dir., Dialog

Ltd. (U.K.) 1970; Pres., Cadapso 1976–77, Dir. 1976–83 and 1986–88; mem., Bd. Trade Metrop. Toronto; Anglican; recreations: golf, skiing, scuba diving; Clubs: Ontario Racquets; Mississauga Golf & Country; Royal Woodbine Golf; Home: 1490 Watersedge Rd., Mississauga, Ont. L5J 1A4.

**PRICE, Ralph Morton,** B.A., M.D.; physician; b. Montreal, Que. 25 Nov. 1939; s. Clarence Cecil and Laurene Beatrice (Walker) P.; e. elem. sch. St. Lambert, Que.; high sch. Barrie, Ont.; McMaster Univ. B.A. 1961; Univ. of Toronto M.D. 1965; m. Patricia d. John and Blanche Hoare 31 Jan. 1962; children: Kimberley, Matthew, Taylor; ASSOCIATE, MEDICAL ASSOCIATES OF PORT PERRY 1969– ; med. staff Oshawa Gen. Hosp. 1966– ; Community Mem. Hosp. Port Perry 1969– ; Jr. Intern Toronto Western Hosp. 1965–66; Assoc., Brooklin (Ont.) Med. Centre 1966–68; Dir., Grumble Hill Ltd. Port Perry 1969– ; Dir. Robert McLaughlin Gallery Oshawa 1976–79; antiquarian; folk art authority; participant Stanley House Conf. Vernacular Art 1978; N.Y. State Hist. Soc. Colloquium on Am. Folk Art, Cooperstown 1983; Charter Mem., Friends of Historic Deerfield, Deerfield, Mass.; Charter Mem., Friends of the Candn. Museum of Civilisation; sculptor: (one man shows) Mira Godard Gallery, Toronto Sept. 1991; Port Perry Library, May 1992; author ''Twas Ever Thus' (selection E. Candn. folk art) 1979; foreword 'Ontario Decoys' 1982; mem., Royal Ont. Museum; Art Gallery of Ont.; Robert McLaughlin Gallery, Oshawa; P. Conservative; Anglican; recreations: tennis, nordic skiing, collecting art & antiques, books; Clubs: Port Perry Tennis; Oshawa Racquets; Home: 1320 King St., R.R.4, Port Perry, Ont. L9L 1B5; Office: General Delivery, Port Perry, Ont. L9L 1L9.

**PRICE, Raymond Alexander,** B.Sc., M.A., Ph.D., D.Sc., P.Eng., F.G.S.A., F.R.S.C.; b. Winnipeg, Man. 25 March 1933; s. Alexander Fredrick and Edith Olga (Arlt) P.; e. Univ. of Man. B.Sc. 1955; Princeton Univ. M.A. 1957, Ph.D. 1958; D.Sc. (hon. causa), Carleton Univ. 1987; D.Sc. (hon. causa) Mem. Univ. of Nfld. 1989; m. Wilhelmina Sofia d. Theodore John Geurds 15 Sept. 1956; children: Paul Raymond, Patricia Ann, Linda Marie; PROF. OF GEOLOGICAL SCIENCES, QUEEN'S UNIV. 1990– ; Geol. and Research Scient. Geol. Survey of Can. Dept. Energy Mines & Resources Can. 1958–68; Dir.-General 1982–87; Asst. Depy. Min. 1987–88; Sr. Rsch. Scientist, Geol. Survey of Canada, Dept. of Energy, Mines and Resources Can. 1988–90; Assoc. Prof. Queen's Univ. 1968–70, Prof. of Geol. Sciences, 1970–81, Head of Geol. Sciences 1972–77, Visiting Prof. 1988–90; Fellow, Royal Soc. of Can.; Foreign Assoc., U.S.A. National Acad. of Sciences; Honorary Foreign Fellow, European Union of Geosciences; Fellow, Geol. Soc. America; Fellow, Geol. Assn. Can; mem. Assn. Prof. Engrs. Prov. Ont; Pres. Internat. Council of Scientific Unions Interunion Comm. on the Lithosphere (1980–85); Pres., The Geological Soc. of Am. 1989–90; Ed. 'Tectonics' 1987–90; R. Catholic; Home: 28 Riverside Dr., R.R. #1, Kingston, Ont. K7L 4V1; Office: Dept. of Geological Sciences, Queen's Univ., Kingston, Ont. K7L 3N6.

**PRICE, T. Derek,** B.Math., C.A.; financial executive; b. Paisley, Scotland 28 Nov. 1951; s. Thomas and Sarah (Brentnall) P.; e. Univ. of Waterloo B.Math. 1974; Vice-Pres., Finance, Granges Inc. 1989; Staff Accountant, Pannell Kerr Forster 1975–79; Supervisor, Internal Audit / Coord., Cash Mngt. & Foreign Exchange / Asst. Controller, Cominco Fertilizers / Vice-Pres. Finance, Western Canada Steel Limited subs., Cominco Ltd. 1979–89; Mem., Inst. of C.A.s of B.C.; Financial Executives Inst.; Treas. Mngt. Assn. of B.C. (Pres. 1985); recreations: skiing, squash; clubs: Vancouver Bd. of Trade; Home: Box 27075, Collingwood P.O., Vancouver, B.C. V5R 6A8.

**PRICE, Timothy R.,** B.A., C.A.; chartered accountant; b. Reigate, England 26 Jan. 1943; e. Univ. of Victoria B.A. 1964; C.A. 1969; m. Frances Baird; children: Robert, Rosamond, Louise, Matthew; MANAGING PARTNER & CHAIRMAN, HEES INTERNAT. BANCORP INC. 1988– ; Chartered Accountant, Touche, Ross & Co. (Montreal) 1965–69; Pres. & Chief Op. Offr., Mico Enterprises Limited 1970–80; Pres. & Chief Extve. Offr., Hees Internat. Bancorp Inc. 1980–88; Dir., Astral Comminucations Inc.; Hees Internat. Bancorp Inc.; Noranda Forest Inc.; Candn. Psychiatric Research Fdn.; St. Michael's Hosp. Fdn.; York Univ. Fac. of Admin. Studies, Dean's Adv. Ctte.; Office: Suite 4500, BCE Place, 181 Bay St., Toronto, Ont. M5J 2T3.

**PRICE, William Robert,** C.A.; executive; b. Montréal, Qué. 3 July 1939; s. William H. and Mary H. (Ridell) P.; e. McGill Univ. C.A. 1963; m. Nancy (dec'd) d. Leslie and Anna Louise Palmer 9 Sept. 1961; children: William Leslie, Mary Louise; SENIOR VICE PRES., INNOTECH AVIATION LIMITED 1971– ; joined Campbell Sharp 1955–69 becoming Gen. Partner; Extve. Vice Pres. Bouchard & Co. Ltd. 1969–71; mem. Qué Inst C.A.'s; R. Catholic; Club: Forest & Stream; Home: 21 Lakeshore #513, Pointe Claire, Que. H9S 5N3; Office: 595 Stuart Graham Blvd., Dorval, Que. H4Y 1E3.

**PRICHARD, John Robert Stobo,** M.B.A., LL.M.; educator; b. London, Eng. 17 Jan. 1949; s. John Stobo and Joan Suzanne (Webber) P.; e. Upper Can. Coll. Toronto 1967; Swarthmore Coll. 1970; Univ. of Chicago M.B.A. 1971; Univ. of Toronto LL.B. 1975; Yale Univ. LL.M. 1976; m. Ann Elizabeth d. William and Margaret Wilson 19 Dec. 1975; three s. Wilson Robert Stobo, Kenneth David Stobo, John William Stobo; PRES., UNIV. OF TORONTO 1990– ; Prof. of Law 1988– , Assoc. Prof. of Law 1982–88, Asst. Prof. of Law 1976–81; Fellow, Trinity Coll. 1989– ; Fellow, Massey Coll. 1990– ; Assoc., Centre for Industrial Relations 1979– ; Assoc., Inst. for Policy Analysis 1978– ; Visiting Assoc. Prof. of Law, Yale Law Sch. 1982–83; Visiting Prof. of Law, Harvard Law Sch. 1983–84; Dean of Law, Univ. of Toronto 1984–90; Mem., Ont. Law Reform Comn. 1986–90; Chrmn., Ctte. of Ont. Law Deans 1987–89; Chrmn., Council of Candn. Law Deans 1988–89; Chrmn., Fed./Prov./Territorial Review of Liability and Compensation Issues in Health Care 1987–90; Dir. of Rsch. Alaska Hwy. Pipeline Inquiry 1977; labour arbitrator and mediator; Vice Chrmn., Ont. Crown Employees Grievance Settlement Bd. 1977–86; Trustee, Royal Ont. Museum; recipient Angus MacMurchy Gold Medal 1975; Viscount Bennett Fellowship 1975–76; author 'Public Ownership: The Calculus of Instrument Choice' 1983; co-author 'Canadian Business Corporations' 1977; 'Canadian Competition Policy: Essays in Law and Economics' 1979; 'Federalism and the Canadian Economic Union' 1983; mem. Law Soc. Upper Can.; Candn. Assn. Univ. Teachers; Candn. Assn Law Teachers; recreations: children, fishing, tennis; Home: 93 Highland Ave., Toronto, Ont. M4W 2A4; Office: 27 King's College, Toronto, Ont. M5S 1A1.

**PRIDDLE, Roland,** M.A.; public servant; b. Govan, Scot. 19 Dec. 1933; s. Alfred Edouard and Hanna (Steiner) P.; e. Cambridge Univ., M.A. (Geog.) 1955; Univ. of Cal. (Berkeley) and Univ. of Ottawa, M.A. (Econ.) 1976; m. Valerie d. Albert and Edith Levy 26 March 1960; children: Stephen, Mark, Philip, Timothy, Ruth, Lois; CHRMN. NAT. ENERGY BD. 1986– ; Econ., Shell International Petroleum Co. Ltd. London, Eng. 1956–61; Sr. Analyst, Bataafse Internationale Pet. Maatschappij, The Hague 1961–65; Chief, Special Projects, Nat. Energy Bd. (NEB) 1965–66; Dir. Oil Policy Br., NEB 1966–74; Sr. Adv. Can./US Oil and Gas, Energy Mines & Resources (EMR) 1974–76, Sr. Adv. Petroleum Utilization, EMR 1976–77; Chrmn. Energy Supplies Allocation Bd. 1976; Chrmn. Petroleum Compensation Bd. 1977; Dir. Gen. Petroleum, EMR 1977–79; Asst. Dep. Min. Petroleum, EMR 1979–86; Office: 311 – 6th Avenue S.W., Calgary, Alta. T2P 3H2.

**PRIEST, Margaret Diane,** M.A., R.C.A.; artist, educator; b. Tyringham, Buckinghamshire, England 15 Feb. 1944; d. Arthur Edmund and Gertrude (Tommason) P.; e. Dagenham Co. H.S. 1963; S.W. Essex Tech. Coll. & Sch. of Art 1964; Maidstone Coll. of Art, Dip. in Art & Design 1967; Royal Coll. of Art M.A. 1970 (silver medalist); m. Tony s. Donna (Creed) and Paul Scherman 1 Sept. 1972; children: Leo, Georgia, Claudia; ASSOCIATE PROFESSOR, DEPT. OF FINE ART, UNIV. OF GUELPH 1983– ; Lecturer, Harrow Sch. of Art 1970–74; St. Martin's Sch. of Art 1972–76; Univ. of Waterloo, Sch. of Architecture 1982–83; Univ. of Toronto 1983– ; Visiting Critic to schools of art & arch. in England, Canada & U.S.A.; mixed & solo exhibs. in Canada, England, U.S. & abroad 1970– ; works in numerous public & private collections in Can. & abroad; artist with winning team for The Bay/Adelaide Park Comp. 1990; Designer of the Bay/Adelaide 'Monument to Construction Worker's' installed 1993; Arts Counc. of Gr. Brit. award 1969; John Minton scholarship 1970; Ont. Arts Counc. Drawing Award 1981; Bd., Gershon Iskowitz Found. 1988– ; Mem., University Art Assn. of Can.; Home: 38 Dunvegan Rd., Toronto, Ont. M4V 2P6; Office: Dept. of Fine Art, Univ. of Guelph, Guelph, Ont. N1G 2W1.

**PRIEST, Robert;** writer; singer; b. Walton-on-Thames, England 10 July 1951; s. Edward and Beatrice P.; e. Fairmont Pub., Galloway Pub. and West Hill High Schs.; Univ. of Waterloo studies in Math.; m. Marsha Kirzner; one s. Eli Kirzner-Priest; author: 'The Visible Man' 1978; 'Sadness of Spacemen' 1980; 'The Man Who Broke Out Of The Letter X' 1984; 'The Short Hockey Career of Amazing Jany' 1986 (NFB animation forthcoming); 'The Ruby Hat and other poems' 1987; 'The Mad Hand' 1988; 'Ten Big Babies' 1989; 'Scream Blue Living: New and Selected Poems' 1992; 'Day Songs, Night Songs' 1993; 'Knights of the Endless Day' 1993; Recordings incl. 'The Robert Priest E.P. (rock) 1982; 'Summerlong' (The Boinks) 1984; 'Congo Toronto' video and single 1986; resident topical song writer CBC 'Is Anybody Home' 2 seasons; Address: c/o Penguin Books Canada Ltd., Suite 300, 10 Alcorn Ave., Toronto, Ont. M4V 3B2.

**PRIESTNER, Edward Bernard;** business executive; b. Hamilton, Ont. 4 June 1936; s. William Joseph and Helen Gladys (Osbaldeston) P.; e. Univ. of W. Ont., B.A. 1958; m. Marianne d. Albert and Velma Baker 23 May 1959; children: Lorraine, Patricia, Nancy; Chrmn. of the Board, Westinghouse Canada Inc. 1991–93; Supr., Prudential Ins. Co. 1958–61; Treas. Asst., Westinghouse Canada Inc. 1961–64; Asst. Treas. 1964–71; Treas. 1971–75; Vice Pres. & Treas. 1975–78; Vice Pres. Fin. 1978–81; Vice Pres., Opns. 1981–84; Extve. Vice Pres., Opns. 1984–85; Dir. 1984; Pres. & C.E.O. 1985–91; Chrmn. of the Bd. 1991–93; Vice Pres., Westinghouse Electric Corp. 1985–91; Dir., Allendale Ins.; Mem., Ont. Business Adv. Counc.; Chair of Bd. of Govs., McMaster Univ.; Bd of Gov., Junior Achievement of Hamilton-Wentworth; Steering Ctte., United Way of Burlington, Hamilton-Wentworth; Dir., Alzheimer Foundation Inc. of Halton-Wentworth; recreations: sailing, golfing; Clubs: Hamilton, Hamilton Golf & Country, C. of C.; Home: 616 Northshore Blvd. E., Burlington, Ont. L7T 1X2; Office: 120 King St. W., P.O. Box 2510, Hamilton, Ont. L8N 3K2.

**PRINCE, Alan T.,** M.A., Ph.D.; retired scientist; civil servant; b. 15 Feb. 1915; e. Univ. of Toronto, B.A. 1937, M.A. 1938; Univ. of Chicago, Ph.D. 1941; m. Virginia Lea 1942; children: Mary Kaschub, Linda Anderson; Pres., Atomic Energy Control Board, 1975–78; Junior Research Chemist, Division of Chem., Nat. Research Council, 1940–43; Research Chem. and Petrographer, Canadian Refractories Ltd., Kilmar, Que., 1943–45; Lectr., Univ. of Man., 1945–46; joined Dept. of Mines & Tech. Surveys as Head, Ceramic Sec., Mines Br., Ottawa, 1946–50; Head, Phys. and Crystal Chem. Sec., 1950–55; Sr. Research Off., Mineral Dressing and Process Metall. Div., 1955–59; Chief, Mineral Sciences Div., 1959–65; Dir., Water Research Br., Dept. Energy Mines & Resources 1965–67; Dir. Gen., Inland Waters Br., Dept. Environment 1967–73; Asst. Depy. Min. (Planning & Evaluation) Dept. Energy, Mines & Resources 1973–75; Pres., Atomic Energy Control Bd., 1975; published articles and patents; Candn. Chrmn. (four Adv. Bds.). Internat. Jt. Comn., Great Lakes Water Quality Bd.; Fraser River Flood Control Bd.; Sask.-Nelson Basin Bd.; Okanagan Basin Bd.; Fellow Chem. Inst. Can.; Mineral. Soc. Am.; mem., Candn. Inst Mining & Metall.; Mineral Assn. Can.; Assn. Prof. Engrs. Ont.; Home: 5445 Riverside Drive (P.O. Box 106), Manotick, Ont. K4M 1A2.

**PRINCE, Elizabeth Hilary;** artist; b. Johannesburg, S. Africa 7 Aug. 1945; d. Louis Jack and Hilda Charlwood (Frye) P.; e. Roedean Sch.; Johannesburg Art Sch. 1965; St. Martin's Sch. of Art 1966; m. Peter s. Gordon and Clarice Hide 14 July 1967; children: Rebecca (dec.), Sarah, Michael; emigrated from S. Africa to Brit. 1966; resided in Edmonton, Alta. since 1978; moved from abstact painting to landscape painting in 1980; paints in watercolour, oil & acrylic; first solo exhib., Front Gall. Edmonton 1986; currently exhibiting works with Front Gall. Edmonton & Virginia Christopher Gall. Calgary; attended 1st Leighton Found. Landscape Workshop 1989; selected group exhibs. incl.: 'Spaces & Places,' Alta. Art Found. travelling exhib. 1986–87 (to Japan 1990); 'Living Nature,' Nat. Mus. of Natural Sci. Ottawa 1987; 'Mountains in the EAG Collection,' Edmonton Art Gall. 1986; 'The Works,' Edmonton Art Gall. 1989; selected public collections: Edmonton Art Gall., Alta. Art Found., Univ. of Alta., Texaco, Coca Cola, Esso Resources Canada, B.P. Canada, Univ. of Alta. Hosp., AGT, Athabasca Univ., Grant MacEwan Coll. Edmonton; Home: 11620 – 49th Ave., Edmonton, Alta. T6H 0H1.

**PRINCE, Michael J.,** B.A., M.P.A., Ph.D.; university professor; b. Toronto, Ont. 7 April 1952; s. Albert George and Ilva Hermione (Campbell) P.; e. Carleton Univ. B.A. (Hons.) 1975; Queen's Univ. M.P.A. 1976; Exeter Univ. Ph.D. 1979; m. Karen d. Donald and Maxine Wallace 7 Aug. 1976; children: Jessica, Kathleen; LANSDOWNE PROF. OF SOCIAL POLICY, FAC. OF HUMAN & SOCIAL DEVEL., UNIV. OF VICTORIA 1987– ; Teacher, Sch. of Public Admin., Carleton Univ. 1978–87; Radio Commentator, CBO Morning, CBC Radio Ottawa 1982–84; Trustee, Juan de Fuca Hospitals Soc.; Dir., Juan de Fuca Hospitals Found.; Mem., Inst. of Public Admin. of Canada; Candn. Council on Social Development; author: 'Policy Advice and Organizational Survival' 1983; co-author: 'Federal and Provincial Budgeting' 1986, 'Public Budgeting in Canada' 1988, 'Aid for Small Business Exporting Firms' 1990; editor: 'How Ottawa Spends: Tracking the Tories' 1986, 'How Ottawa Spends: Restraining the State' 1987; Home: 1525 Prospect Place, Victoria, B.C. V8R 5X7; Office: Box 1700, Victoria, B.C. V8W 2Y2.

**PRINCE, Richard Edmund,** B.A., R.C.A.; artist; educator; b. Comox, B.C. 6 Apr. 1949; s. Charles Robert and Patricia Rosalene (Stubbs) P.; e. Univ. of B.C. B.A. 1971, grad. studies 1972–73; Assoc. Prof. of Art Univ. of B.C. 1978– ; Pres. Bd. Dirs. Green Thumb Theatre for Young People 1979–82; Instr. in Sculpture Vancouver Sch. of Art (Night) 1973–74; Vancouver Community Coll. Langara 1974–75; Artist in Residence Queen Charlotte Island, Nat. Museums of Can. 1975; Juror City of Vancouver Art Purchase Award Program 1976; Bd. of Dirs., Vancouver Art Gallery 1977–80; solo exhns. incl. N.S. Coll. Art & Design 1974; Burnaby Art Gallery 1979, Isaacs Gallery Toronto 1976, 1978, 1982; Equinox Gallery Vancouver 1977, 1982, 1988, 1992; Hamilton Art Gallery 1984; Charles H. Scott Gallery Vancouver 1985; Candn. Cultural Centre, Rome, Italy 1987; Forty-Ninth Parallel, N.Y. 1989; rep. in numerous group exhns. since 1970; rep. in pub., corporate and private colls. incl. Nat. Gallery Can., Can. Council Art Bank, Vancouver Art Gallery; rec'd Can. Council Arts Bursary 1972–73, Arts Grants 1974–75, 1977–78; Art Vancouver '74 Purchase Award 1973–74; cited various bibliogs.; Univs. Art Assn. Can. (B.C. Rep. to Bd. Dirs. 1981–84); Elec. to Royal Candn. Academy, 1978; Address: 285 W. 18th Ave., Vancouver, B.C. V5Y 2A8.

**PRINCIPE, Walter H.,** c.s.b., M.A., dipl.E.H.E., M.S.D., F.R.S.C., D.H.L.; university professor; priest; b. Rochester, N.Y. 15 Oct. 1922; s. Arthur S. and Louise (Masnaghetti) P.; e. Univ. of Toronto, B.A. 1946, M.A. 1951; Pont. Inst. of Med. Studies, M.S.L. 1951, M.S.D. 1963; Sorbonne, Univ. de Paris, dipl. de l'École Prat. des Hautes Études 1954; Saint John Fisher Coll., D.H.L. (hon. causa) 1988; FELLOW EMERITUS, PONT. INST. OF MED. STUDIES, 1992– (Inst. Professor 1989–92, Sr. Fellow, 1964–89, Jr. Fellow 1962–64); Ordained 1949; Prof., Univ. of Toronto 1964–92; Prof., Fac. of Theol., Univ. of St. Michael's Coll. 1953–92 (first Dean 1955–62); fellowships: Guggenheim 1967; Can. Counc. 1975; SSHRCC 1982–83; Assn. of Theol. Sch. Scholar 1978; SSHRCC 1992–95; Mem., Internat. Theol. Comn. 1980–85; F.R.S.C. 1984– ; Hon. Mem., Candn. Theological Soc. 1987; rec'd John Courtney Murray Award, Catholic Theol. Soc. of Am. 1987; Extve. Bd. Mem., Candn. Fedn. for the Humanities 1976–78 (Chair 1976–77); Ed. Bd. Mem.: 'Theological Studies'; Former Ed. Bd. Mem.: 'Mediaeval Studies' (Chair of Ed. Ctte. 1988–89), 'Studies and Texts,' 'Studies in Christianity and Judaism,' 'Toronto Journal of Theol.' (hon.); Cons., Candn. Conf. of Cath. Bishops; Guest Lectr., var. univs. incl. Chinese Acad. of Soc. Sci. 1983; Catholic; Mem., Congreg. of St. Basil; Royal Soc. of Can.; Assn. Internat. d'Études Patrist.; Candn. Patrist. Soc.; Candn. Theol. Soc.; Cath. Theol. Soc. of Am. (el. Pres. 1990–91; Past Pres. 1991–92); Catholic Commn. on Intellectual and Cultural Affairs; La Soc. Can. de Théol.; Society for the Study of Christian Spirituality; has held num. extve. positions in above orgns. & others; author: 'Introduction to Patristic and Medieval Theology' 2nd ed., 1982; 'Theology of the Hypostatic Union in the Early Thirteenth Century,' 4 vols. (1963–75); 'Faith, History and Cultures: Stability and Change in Church Teachings' 1991 and num. articles; recreation: music (amat. clarinetist); Address: 59 Queen's Park Crescent East, Toronto, Ont. M5S 2C4.

**PRINGLE, Heather A.,** B.A., M.A.; journalist; b. Edmonton, Alta. 8 Dec. 1952; d. Alexander Leitch and Gretta Isabel (Cooney) P.; e. Univ. of Alberta B.A. 1973; Univ. of B.C. M.A. 1976; m. Geoffrey s. Molly and George Lakeman 11 March 1978; FREELANCE JOURNALIST 1993– ; Fiction & Poetry Editor, Branching Out magazine 1977–79; Asst. Ed., Hurtig Publishers 1978–79; freelance journalist 1980–89; Contbg. Ed., National Geographic Traveler Magazine 1989– ; Assoc. Ed., Equinox Magazine 1989–90; Senior Editor, Equinox Magazine 1990–93; Nat. Magazine Award 1988; Author's Award 1992; Bd. of Dir., Branching Out Magazine. 1979–80; recreations: running, reading, gardening; Home: 104, 1868 East 11th Ave., Vancouver, B.C. V5N 1Z1.

**PRINGLE, John Alexander,** E.D., C.D., B.Acc., P.Mgr.; university administrator; b. Treherne, Man. 6 Aug. 1915; s. Eva Maude and Ernest Hamilton P.; e. Elem. Schs. Winnipeg, Man. 1922 and Craik, Sask. 1928; High Sch. Craik, Sask. 1930 and Harris, Sask. 1932; Univ. of Sask., B.Acc. 1938; m. Marion Ethel, d. late Henry Thompson 29 April 1942; children: Robert John, Donald Alexander, Harry William; ret. Vice-Pres., Adm. (Emeritus), Univ. of Saskatchewan 1975–82; joined Sask. Govt., Prov. Auditor's Dept. 1939; Asst. Bursar, Univ. of Sask. 1947, Business Mgr. 1956, Controller and Treas. 1957; COTC Univ. of Sask. 1936; 2nd Lt.-Maj. 8Fd Regt R.C.A. 1939–45, Italy and N.W. Europe; Mil.-Maj. O/C 18 Batty RCA, and subsequently Lt. Col. and C.O. 17 LAA Regt. R.C.A., 10 Med. Regt. R.C.A. and Brig-Gen. Commdr. 21 Mil. Group 1946–63; Trustee, Army Benevolent Fund 1962–79; Chrmn. Saskatoon Poppy Fund 1963–91; Chrmn. Bd. Govs. Corps. Commissionaires Saskatoon 1982–87; mem. Nat. Bd. of Gov. 1984–87, Adv. Bd. for Mil Colls. 1973–76; Chrmn. North Sask. Bd. CNIB, 1982–87; mem. Nat. Council CNIB 1981–87; Community Mem., Nat. Parole Bd. 1985–89; Extve. Dir., Saskatoon Found. 1982–90; Financial Extves. Inst.; Candn. Assn. Univ. Business Offrs. (Past Pres. and Hon. Life mem.); Past mem. Batten Comn. on Public Accounting 1966–67; recipient, Commemorative Medal for 125th Anniversary of Candn. Confederation 1992; Un. Church; Clubs: Faculty; Saskatoon; Joel; Rotary; Home: 1124 Main St., Saskatoon, Sask. S7H 0K9.

**PRINGLE, Robert W.,** O.B.E. (1967), B.Sc., Ph.D., C. Phys., F.Inst.P., F.R.S.E. (1964), F.R.S.C. (1955); physicist; b. Edinburgh, Scot. 2 May 1920; s. late Robert and late Lillias Dalgleish (Hair) P.; e. George Heriot's Sch., Edin.; Univ. of Edinburgh, B.Sc. (1st Class Hons. in Physics) and Ph.D.; m. Jean Clunas, d. late John Foster Stokes, Tweed, Ont 21 Sept. 1948; children: Vivien Claire, Robert Shaun, David Moray, Andrew Roderick John; Lectr. in Physics., Edin. Univ., 1945–48; Assoc. Prof. of Physics, Univ. of Man., 1948–50; Prof. 1950–56; Chrmn. of Physics Dept., 1953–56; from 1949–56 was responsible for the devel. of a research group in nuclear physics at Univ. of Man., specializing in nuclear spectroscopy, and in the devel. of the 'scintillation counter'; Managing Director, Nuclear Enterprises Ltd., Edinburgh 1956–76; Pres., Nuclear Enterprises Ltd., Winnipeg, Man. since 1950; mem., Astron., Space, and Radio Bd. of Science Research Council of U.K. 1970–72; mem., Science Research Council of U.K. (and Nuclear Physics Bd. there) 1972–76; Scottish Econ. Council 1971–74; mem. of Court of Edinburgh Univ. 1967–75; Trustee, Scottish Hospitals Endowments Research Trust 1976–88; Hon. Fellow, Royal Scottish Soc. Arts 1972; Fellow, Amer. Physical Soc. 1950; Mem. of the Athenaeum, London; Home: 27 Avenue Princess Grace, Monaco; Office: Nuclear Enterprises Ltd., 61 Cordova St., Winnipeg, Man.

**PRIOR, John Ernest Charles,** FCMC; management consultant; b. Harpenden, Herts, England 16 Nov. 1938; s. Horace Charles and Evelyn Lois (Carter) P.; e. Berkhamsted School 1949–57; articled with firm of C.A.s; m. Ulla d. Edwin and Elsa Salmi 17 Oct. 1964; children: Natasha, Andrew; PRES., J.P. CONSULTANCY INC. 1981– ; England & Wales Inst. C.A. 1963; joined Price Waterhouse 1964; Financial Auditor in Scandinavia 1964–65; Systems Analyst and Consultant, London, England 1966–69; Sr. Cons. & Mgr., Price Waterhouse Assoc. Toronto 1969–78; Staff of Corp. Controller, Esso Europe, Exxon 1979–80; Former Pres. & Bd. Mem., Inst. of Cert. Management Consultants of Ont.; Fellow, Inst. of Cert. Mngt. Cons. of Ont.; Fellow, Inst. of C.A.s in England & Wales; Mem., Canadian Friends of Finland (Former Bd. Mem.); Old Berkhamstedians' Assn.; recreations: tennis, nordic skiing, travel; Home: 117 Meadowcliffe Dr., Scarborough, Ont. M1M 2Y1.

**PRITCHARD, Huw Owen,** Ph.D., D.Sc., F.R.S.C.; educator; b. Bangor, N.Wales 23 July 1928; s. Owen and Lilian Venetia (McMurray) P.; e. Altrincham Grammar Sch. 1945; Univ. of Manchester B.Sc. 1948, M.Sc. 1949, Ph.D. 1951, D.Sc. 1964; m. Margaret d. Thomas and Margaret Ramsden 3 Nov. 1956; children: Karen, David; PROF. OF CHEM., YORK UNIV. 1965– ; Distinguished Rsch. Prof. of Chem. 1983; Asst. Lectr. in Chem. Manchester Univ. 1951–54, Lectr. in Chem. 1954–65; author 'Quantum Theory of Unimolecular Reactions' 1984; co-author 'Statistical Mechanics and Spectroscopy' 1974; author or co-author over 200 tech. papers phys. and theoretical chem.; recreations: cricket, soccer, chess, bridge; Home: R.R. 1, Bolton, Ont. L7E 5R7; Office: Dept. of Chemistry, York Univ., 4700 Keele St., Downsview, Ont. M3J 1P3.

**PROCTOR, Diane Nyland;** director; choreographer; actress; b. Kitchener, Ont. 20 Jan. 1944; d. Lloyd Gofton and Frieda Martha (Tschoeltsch) Nyland; e. Elizabeth Ziegler Elem. Sch.; Kitchener-Waterloo Coll. Inst.; m. Frank s. Charles and Kathleen Proctor 30 Jan. 1970; children: Kelly, Toby; performed in over 50 Candn. stage, TV and film prodns. incl. Nat. Ballet Co. of Can. (dancer) 1961–62, nat. tours 'Spring Thaw' 1964–65, 1967–68, Josie Pye role 'Anne of Green Gables' Charlottetown Festival 1965–69 and Belinda in 'Johnny Belinda' 1968–69, Tracy in CTV Series 'The Trouble with Tracy' 130 episodes 1970–71; dir. and choreographer over 50 Candn. prodns. incl. 'Nunsense' 1986–87, 'Rose is a Rose' Candn. Opera Co. 1987; Artistic Dir. Press Theatre 1982–85; Interim Artistic Dir., Kawartha Summer Theatre (Lindsay, Ont.) 1993; Artistic Dir., Kawartha Summer Theatre 1994; Past mem. Adv. Ctte. Niagara Coll. Theatre Centre; recipient Dora Mavor Moore Award Choreography 'Nunsense' 1986; Dora Nominee Best Dir. and Best Choreographer 'Funny Girl/ 1984; mem. Cabaret & Musical Theatre Alliance (Ctte.); Candn. Actors Equity Assn. (Past mem. Extve.); Alliance Candn. Cinema, TV & Radio Artists; recreation: golf; Office: Talent House, 186 Dupont St., Toronto, Ont. M5R 2E8.

**PROCYK, Donald Richard;** corporation executive; b. Cardinal, Ont. 20 April 1946; s. Frank and Eva Marie Antionette (Pontbriand) P.; e. S. Grenville Dist. H.S. 1964; Queen's Univ. B.Comm. (Hons.) 1969; Univ. of Toronto M.B.A. 1970; m. Margaret d. Mary and Douglas Major Pearson 2 Aug. 1969; children: Jason Frank, Kenneth Douglas; PRESIDENT, JIM PATTISON SIGN GROUP 1992– (world's largest electrical sign co.); Financial Manager, Huntec (70) Ltd. 1970; Acctg./Purch. Mgr., Huyck Canada Ltd. 1972; Finan./Opns. Planning Mgr. 1976; Finan. Mgr., T.P.S. Industries Ltd. 1981; Part Owner & Vice-Pres., Chase Manufacturing Ltd. 1984; Gen. Mgr., Ont. Region & Extve. Vice-Pres., Jim Pattison Sign Group 1986; Moffatt scholarship 1964–69; Corn Products International; Pres., Arnprior Minor Hockey Assn. 1978–80; Pres., Sign Assn. of Canada 1991–93; Dir. 1987–91; recreations: cottage, reading, golf, hunting, home improvement; Home: 91 Carrington Dr., Richmond Hill, Ont.; Office: 555 Ellesmere Rd., Scarborough, Ont. M1R 4E8.

**PROLL, Douglas A.,** B.Comm., C.A.; financial executive; b. Saskatchewan 26 Sept. 1950; s. Arthur E. and Winnifred V. (Grey) P.; e. Naicam H.S.; Univ. of Saskatchewan B.Comm 1973; m. Gloria J. Zentner 6 May 1972; children: Josh D., Sarah J., Nathan B.; VICE-PRES., FINANCE, TREASURER & ASSISTANT SECRETARY, RENAISSANCE ENERGY LTD. 1988– ; Price Waterhouse 1973–83; Sulpetro Limited 1983–87; Mem., Candn. Petroleum Tax Soc. (Past Dir.); Financial Extves. Inst.; Office: 3000, 425 First St. S.W., Calgary, Alta. T2P 3L8.

**PROSSER, David John,** M.A.; journalist; b. Aberdeen, Scotland 16 March 1953; s. Douglas and Isobel (Alsop) P.; e. Aberdeen Univ., M.A. 1975; Queen's Univ., M.A. 1977; m. Barbara d. Cecil and Martha Dunn 20 May 1978; Editorial Page Editor, Kingston Whig-Standard 1990–91; announcer, Grampian Television, Scotland 1975; actor & admin. asst., Theatre 5, Kingston 1978; joined Whig-Standard as arts reporter and Book Review Ed. 1978; Asst. Ed., Whig-Standard Mag. 1980; Entertainment Ed., Kingston Whig-Standard 1981–90; part-time lectr., Queen's Univ. 1985–86; Nathan Cohen Award for Excellence in Theatre Criticism 1985, 1986, 1987; Centre for Investigative Journalism Award 1987; National Newspaper Award for Criticism 1988 and 1989; National Newspaper Award for Editorial Writing 1991; Awarded Southam Fellowship for Study, Univ. of Toronto 1991–92; Pres., Candn. Theatre Critics Assn. 1988–91; mem. Centre for Investigative Journalism; Internat. Assn. of Theatre Critics; author: 'Out of Afghanistan' 1987; recreations: sailboarding, bicycling, amateur theatre; Home: 427 Tanglewood Dr., Kingston, Ont. K7M 7V8; Office: 306 King St. E., Kingston, Ont. K7L 4Z7.

**PROTO, Frank William,** B.A.; executive; b. Moose Jaw, Sask. 9 Apr. 1942; e. Univ. of Sask. B.A. 1963; m. Jean I. McArthur 21 Aug. 1966; children: Michael, Karen; PRESIDENT, AEC PIPELINES 1982– ; Sr. Vice Pres. Alberta Energy Co. Ltd. 1980– ; joined latter Co. 1975; Dir., Edmonton Telephones; Pacific Coast Energy; Liberal; recreation: collecting antique fountain pens; Office: 1200, 10707 – 100 Ave., Edmonton, Alta. T5J 3M1.

**PROTTI, Raymond Joseph,** M.A.; federal civil servant; b. Edmonton, Alta. 7 Dec. 1945; s. Louis Henry and Therése Marie (Gagnon) P.; e. Univ. of Alta. B.A. (Hons.) 1968, M.A. 1970; London Sch. of Econ. & Pol. Sci. postgrad. studies 1972–74; m. Sheila d. Jack and Josephine Dobson 12 Sept. 1970; two s. Michel, Nicholas; DIR., CANADIAN SECURITY INTELLIGENCE

SERVICE 1991– ; Econ. Adv. Govt. Can. 1968–71, Dept. of Finance 1974–76, Treasury Bd. 1976–77, Privy Council Office 1977–80; Special Adv. Min. of Finance Govt. B.C. 1980–81; Dir. Policy & Planning Min. State Social Devel. Can. 1981–83; Asst. Dep. Min. Dept. Labour Can. 1983–85; Dep. Sec. (Social Devel.) Privy Council Office 1985–87; Dep. Sec. (Operations) Privy Council Office 1987–90; Depy. Min., Labour Canada 1990–91; recipient Duncan Alexander McGibbon Gold Medal in Econ.; Office: P.O. Box 9732, Station T, Ottawa, Ont. K1A 0A6.

**PROUDFOOT, The Honourable Madam Justice Patricia M.,** B.A., LL.B., LL.D.; justice; b. Kronau, Sask. 13 Mar. 1928; d. Joseph Edmond and Elizabeth Ophelia (Bast) Fahlman; e. Rutland H.S. 1945; Kelowna Sr. H.S. 1946; Univ. of B.C., B.A. 1949, LL.B. 1952; m. Arthur s. George and Elizabeth P. 3 Apr. 1959; JUDGE OF THE SUPREME COURT OF THE NORTHWEST TERRITORIES 1991– ; called to Bar as barrister & solicitor in B.C. 1953; general law practice 1953–71; appointed to Provincial Court of B.C. 1971; County Court of Vancouver 1974; Supreme Court of B.C. 1977; Supreme Court of Yukon 1982; Court of Appeal B.C. & Yukon 1989; Royal Commission on Incarceration of Female Offenders 1978; Mem., Fed. Ctte. to Investigate Sexual Offences against Children 1980; Hon. LL.D., Simon Fraser Univ. 1975; 1st woman appointed to County Court & Supreme Court in B.C.; 1st woman appointed to Criminal Div. of Prov. Court; Hon. Mem., Big Sisters of B.C. Lower Mainland; club: Shaughnessy Golf (social mem.); Home: 2296 McBain Ave., Vancouver, B.C. V6L 3B1; Office: 800 Smithe St., Vancouver, B.C. V6Z 2E1.

**PROUDMAN, Colin Leslie John,** B.D., M.Th., D.D.; Anglican priest; b. Grimsby, England 2 Sept. 1934; s. Byron John and Edith Kathleen (Sandford) P.; e. Royal Naval College, Dartmouth 1952; Univ. of London B.D. 1960, M.Th. 1963; m. Sylvia d. Adrian and Marjorie Bell 27 Dec. 1961; children: Mark Francis, Clare Louise; Royal Navy 1950–55; ordained 1961–62; Diocese of St. Alban's 1961–64; Chaplain & Lectr., Queen's College & Memorial Univ. Newfoundland 1964–67; Nat. Staff, Anglican Ch. 1967–73; Principal, College of Emmanuel, & St. Chad, Sask. 1973–78; Dir., Post Ordination Training, Toronto 1978–90; Dean of Divinity, Trinity College, Univ. of Toronto 1990–92; Canon, St. James' Cathedral, Toronto; Prov. of Ont. & City of North York Awards re: North Yorkers for Disabled Persons; Founder & Dir., North Yorkers for Disabled Persons 1981–87; Dir., Home Again Found. 1984–87; recreations: sailing, music; clubs: Royal Naval Sailing Assn., Bluffers Park Yacht Club; Home: 38 Red Maple Court, Willowdale, Ont. M2K 2T3.

**PROULX, Pierre-Paul,** B.Comm., M.A.; university professor, consultant; b. Timmins, Ont. 6 Aug. 1938; s. Rosario Joseph and Béatrice (Phillion) P.; e. Univ. of Ottawa B.Comm. 1960; Univ. of Toronto M.A. 1961; Princeton Univ. M.A. 1964, Ph.D. studies; children: Pierre, Jean-François, Rachel, Maya; PROF., DEPT. OF ECONOMICS, UNIV. OF MONTREAL 1966; Prof., McGill Univ. 1964–66; consultant to the private and public sectors domestically & abroad; Asst. Dep. Min., DRIE, Ottawa; Pres. & Vice-Pres. of internat. & local-regional non-profit organizations; Vice Pres., North Am. Cities Internat.; author of over 75 articles on internat. trade, industrial & regional devel., internat. cities & econ. devel. strategy; recreations: reading, travel; Home: 3145 Linton, Montreal, Que. H3S 1S5; Office: P.O. Box 6128, Station A, Montreal, Que. H3C 3J7.

**PROVAN, John Lloyd,** B.Sc., M.B., M.S., FRCS, FRCS(C), FACS.; professor of surgery; b. Newport, U.K. 9 Aug. 1931; s. Andrew Lloyd and Gwyneth Mary (Evans) P.; e. Univ. College, London B.Sc. 1953; Univ. College Med. Sch. M.B., B.S. 1956, M.S. 1968; m. Judith d. Harry and Lillian Joynt 28 Dec. 1974; children: Joanna, Frances, Richard, David, Jennifer; PROFESSOR OF SURGERY, UNIV. OF TORONTO 1983– ; Sr. Lectr. in Surgery & Hon. Cons. Surgeon, Univ. College Hosp. Med. Sch., Univ. of London (UK) 1967–9; Staff Surgeon, The Wellesley Hosp. 1969–91; Chief Div. of Vascular Surgery 1975–92; Surgeon-in-Chief 1983–88; Assoc. Dean Postgrad. Med. Edn., Fac. of Med., Univ. of Toronto 1988– ; Pres., Candn. Soc. of Vascular Surgery 1983; Am. Assn. for Surg. Edn. 1988; Mem., Bd. of Gov., Am. Coll. of Surgeons; various appts., Royal Coll. of Phys. & Surg. of Can. 1990–92; author of more than 100 articles or book chapters; recreations: sailing, music, gardening; club: Royal Canadian Yacht; Home: 27 Macpherson Ave., Toronto, Ont. M5R 1W7; Office: 620 University Ave., Suite 802, Toronto, Ont. M5G 2C1.

**PROVENZANO, Diana,** B.Comm., C.A.; business executive; b. Toronto, Ont. 8 Jan. 1958; d. Elio and Lucia (Trevisiol) Dalla Nora; e. McMaster Univ. B.Comm. 1980; C.A. 1982; m. Luigi s. Alfredo P. 25 June 1983; one s.: Nicholas; DIRECTOR OF FINANCE & ADMIN. & COMPANY SECRETARY, CANADIAN OXYGEN LIMITED 1988– ; various positions, Coopers & Lybrand 1980–84; Sec.-Treas., Candn. Oxygen Limited 1984–88; Dir., Candn. Oxygen Limited 1992– ; Mem., Ont. Assn. of C.A.s; Candn. Diabetes Assn.; Balmoral Home Assn.; Catholic Women's League; Treas., Camp Huronda; recreations: cycling, hiking; Home: 78 Bowring Walk, Downsview, Ont. M3H 5Z6; Office: 89 The Queensway W., Mississauga, Ont. L5B 2V2.

**PROVENZANO, Hon. Michelangelo,** LL.B.; judge; b. Cranbrook, B.C. 25 Sept. 1922; s. Francesco and Lucia (De Luca) P.; e. Cranbrook High Sch. 1940; Univ. of B.C. LL.B. 1949; m. Charlotte d. Harry and Marion Wilks 20 May 1948; two s. Michael Frank, Philip John; JUDGE, SUPREME COURT OF B.C. 1990– ; read law with Colin D. McQuarrie New Westminster, B.C. 1949–50; Partner Graham Provenzano & Graham, Cranbrook 1950–63; Judge Co. Court of Kootenay, Cranbrook 1963–90; served with RCAF 1943–45; mem. Candn. Bar Assn.; Candn. Judges Conf.; Candn. Inst. Adm. Justice; recreations: golf, skiing, boating, swimming; Clubs: Gyro Cranbrook; Cranbrook Golf; Home: 412 – 14th Ave. S., Cranbrook, B.C. V1C 2X6; Office: 102 – 11th Ave. S., Cranbrook, B.C. V1C 2P3.

**PROVOST, Hon. Jean Antoine,** B.A., LL.B.; judge; b. Quebec, Que. 10 Dec. 1927; s. Antoine and Louise Hélène (Lécuyer) P.; e. Coll. Stanislas, B.A. 1946; Royal Candn. Naval Coll. 1946–48; Univ. de Montreal, LL.B. 1951; m. Denyse d. L. Eugène and Juliette Potvin 6 Sept. 1952; children: François, Claude, Marie, Martin, René; SUPERIOR COURT JUDGE, MONTREAL, QUE. 1978– ; admitted to Bar 1952; specialized civil, torts & insur. law; appointed Q.C. 1971; Mem., Candn. Bar Assn.; Candn. Conf. of Judges; Candn. Inst. for the Admin of Justice; Club: Austin Fish & Game; Home: 79 Place Elmwood, Outremont, Que. H2V 2E6; Office; 1 Notre-Dame Est, #16.51, Montreal, Que. H2Y 1B6.

**PROZES, Andrew,** B.M., M.B.A.; business executive; b. Geislingen, Germany 21 Jan. 1946; s. Karl and Salme (Lember) P.; e. Univ. of Waterloo B.M. (Hons.) 1969; York Univ. M.B.A. 1975; m. Elizabeth d. Dick and Betty Hogerwerf 15 Aug. 1969; children: Kevin, Darin; PRESIDENT, SOUTHAM INFORMATION & TECHNOLOGY GROUP, SOUTHAM INC. 1991– ; Vice-Pres., Financial Serv. Group and Vice-Chair & Chief Extve. Offr., MFS Ltd. 1979–88; Sr. Vice-Pres., Information Tech. Mktg., Southam Bus. Communications Inc. 1989–91; Dir. & Extve. Ctte., Information Indus. Assn. (US); Information Tech. Assn. of Can.; Dir., Candn. Advanced Tech. Assn.; Vision 2000; recreations: golf, skiing, tennis, squash; clubs: Mississauga Golf & Country (Past Pres.), Fitness Inst., National; Home: 2059 Beaverbrook Way, Mississauga, Ont. L5H 4C2; Office: 1450 Don Mills Rd., Don Mills, Ont. M3B 2Z7.

**PRUESSEN, Ronald W.,** B.A., M.A., Ph.D.; university professor; b. New York, N.Y. 10 July 1944; s. Ernest and Lena (DeFries-Dion) P.; e. Queen's Coll., City Univ., B.A. 1965; Univ. of Pennsylvania, M.A. 1966, Ph.D. 1968; m. Alice J. d. Charles and Adelaide Simon 28 Aug. 1965; children: Linda, Michael, Caroline; PROF., DEPT. OF HISTORY, UNIV. OF TORONTO 1975– ; Fac. Mem., Temple Univ. 1968–75; United Ch. of Can. (Chs. & Internat. Affairs Ctte.); author: 'John Foster Dulles: The Road to Power' 1982 (Pulitzer Prize nominee in biography); co-editor; 'Reflections on the Cold War' 1974; Office: Dept of History, Univ. of Toronto, Toronto, Ont. M5S 1A1.

**PRUETER, William Robert,** B.A., LL.B., LL.M.; financial services executive, general counsel; b. Oakville, Ont. 7 Sept. 1946; s. Dr. Kenneth Frederick and Marian Isabel (Archibald) P.; e. Victoria Univ., Univ. of Toronto B.A. (Hons.) 1969; Osgoode Hall Law Sch., York Univ. LL.B. (Hons.) 1972, LL.M. (Hons.) 1984 m. Janet A. d. Gordon and Jean Haugh 17 Oct. 1970; children: Barrett Thomas, Timothy Sheldon; VICE-PRES., CORP. STRATEGIC SERVICES, COUNSEL & CORP. SEC., METROPOLITAN LIFE INSUR. CO. 1991– ; Assoc., McCarthy & McCarthy 1974–76; Sr. Solicitor, Gulf Canada Limited 1977–82; Assoc. Gen. Counsel, Gulf Canada Limited 1983–86; Vice-Pres. & Assoc. Gen. Counsel, MetLife 1986–87; Vice-Pres., Counsel & Corp. Sec. 1987–91; Dir., Asset Management Internat. Inc.; Metropolitan Insur. Co.; Metropolitan Life Holdings LImited; Metropolitan Life Insur. Co. of Can.; Metropolitan Trustco Limited; Morguard Investments Limited; Morguard Mortgage Investment Co. of Can.; Bronze Medal, Osgoode Hall Law Sch. 1972; Matthew Wilson Memorial Scholarship; Dir., Salvation Army of Can. Ottawa; Jr. Achievement of Metro. Toronto; Mem., Law Soc. of U.C.; Law Soc. of Alta.; Candn. Bar Assn.; County of York Law Assn.; Ottawa-Carleton Bd. of Trade; Candn. Club of Ottawa; author: 'Non-Resident Perspectives on New Directions for the Financial Sector' 1987, 'Guide to Combines Compliance: A Backgrounder' 2 vols. 1985, 'Canadian Merger Law: A Critique' 1985, and one journal article; recreations: music, arts, theatre, writing, skiing, fitness, travel; clubs: Rideau Club of Ottawa; Home: 39 Ryeburn Dr., Gloucester, Ont. K1G 3N3; Office: 99 Bank St., 13th Fl., Ottawa, Ont. K1P 5A3.

**PRUITT, William O.,** B.Sc., M.A., Ph.D., D.Sc. (hon. causa); educator; biologist; b. Easton, Md. 1 Sept. 1922 (Candn. Citizen 1970); s. William Obadiah and Janye (Garlington) P.; e. Univ. of Md. B.Sc. 1947; Univ. of Mich. M.A. 1948, Ph.D. 1952; Univ. of Alaska D.Sc. (honoris causa) 1993; m. Erna d. Jacob and Emma Nauert 5 Feb. 1951; children: Cheryl Ann, Charles Robert; PROF. OF ZOOL. UNIV. OF MAN. 1970– ; joined Arctic Aeromedical Lab. Fairbanks 1953–56; Candn. Wildlife Service, Co-op. Caribou Investig. 1957–58; Assoc. Prof. of Biol. Univ. of Alaska 1959–62, Meml. Univ. of Nfld. 1965–69; Visiting Prof. Univ. of Okla. 1963–65; Assoc. Prof. of Zool. present Univ. 1969–70; Founder Taiga Biol. Stn. 1973; recipient Distinguished Naturalist Award (Seton Medal) Man. Nat. Soc. 1984; Govt. Can. N. Sci. Award (Centenary Medal) 1989; Vilhjalmur Stefansson Award Univ. Man. 1989; author 'Wild Harmony: Animals of the North' 3rd ed. 1988; 'Boreal Ecology' 1978; various sci. papers, articles; films incl. 'Caribou Year: The Life History of the Barren Ground Caribou' 50 mins., colour 1959; 'The Barren Ground Caribou of Northern Canada' (co-author) Nat. Film Bd. 17 mins., colour 1970; 'Techniques in Boreal Ecology' Part A 'Environmental Analysis', Part B 'Animal Populations and Activity'. 16 mm teaching films 1973; Fellow, Arctic Inst. N. Am.; Fellow, Explorers Club; Office: Winnipeg, Man. R3T 2N2.

**PRUPAS, Melvern Irving;** video consultant; b. Montreal, Que. 16 Dec. 1926; s. Harry Archie and Esther (Braunstein) P.; World War II, W.O.I, Precision Squad Kiwanis Air Cadet Squadron Royal Candn. Air Force and C.O. Major William Dawson Candn. Army Cadet Battalion 1940–45; e. Sir George Williams Univ.; Montreal Technical Institute; N.Y. State Coll. of Agric.; Mt. Allison Univ.; Cornell Univ.; Univ. Guelph; m. Sheila d. Israel Ditkofsky 21 Mar. 1948 (div. Jan. 1981); m. Myrtle d. Sydney Levine 17 Sept. 1981; children: Michael, Lorne, Norman, David, Dianne; PRES., MEL PRUPAS ASSOCS. 1990– ; Pres., MPA Envirolaser 1991– ; Pres., MPA Investment Properties Inc. 1986– ; Pres., Prupas Studio Consultants 1986– ; Pres. & Dir., Dadnaram Ltd. of Montreal 1972–93; Pres. & Dir., Ambassador Food Sales Ltd. 1981–91; Salesman, Crescent Cheese Co. 1947, Sales Mgr. 1951, Vice Pres. and Dir. 1956, Vice Pres. and Dir., Secy. 1972–77; Secy.-Treas. and Dir. Les Produits Laitiers Marieville Ltée 1956–72, Vice Pres., Secy. and Dir. 1972–77; Vice Pres. and Dir. Maycrest Co. Ltd. 1960–77; Founder En Ville Newspaper 1962; Secy.-Treas., Founder, Dir., Proops Press Inc. 1967–70; Dir. Planning International Cinema Corp. Montreal and Los Angeles 1980–81; Pres. MPA Video Distributors 1981–85; Chrmn., MPA Video Inc. 1985–86; Chrmn., Regional Video Distrib. Inc. of Halifax 1985–86; recipient Scouters Warrent Boy Scouts Can. 1963; Chevalier Medal Chaine des Rotisseurs 1964; Ida Steinberg Mem. Trophy Combined Jewish Appeal 1969; Lord Strathcona Medal For General Efficiency 1942; Lord Strathcona Medal for Marksmanship 1942; Golden Gloves Heavyweight Boxing Champion 1942; mem. Candn. Olympic Basketball Team 1948; YM-YWHA Sports Hall of Fame 1993; Boy Scouts of Can., Cubmaster 1957–68; Dir. Prov. Que. Food Brokers Assn. 1968–70; mem., Mount Royal Property Owners Assn. 1960–71 (Dir. 1968–70); Cong. Beth El 1957– , Vice Pres. 1964–65, 1971–73, Secy. 1969–70, Pres. 1973–75; Chrmn. Food Div. Combined Jewish Appeal 1961–63, Trade Co-ordinator 1964–65, Vice Chrmn. Trades 1969–70 and Spec. Names 1972–73; Dir. Jewish Nat. Fund 1970–72; YM-YWHA of Montreal 1941– , Mem. Bd. of Dirs. 1954–72, Governor-Benefactor 1956–77, 1988– , Membership Campaign Chrmn. 1966; Vice Pres. Algonquin Home & Sch. Assn. 1971–72; mem. Candn. Restaurant Assn.; Chaine des Rotisseurs; Confrerie des Vignerons de St. Vincent; Guilde Fromagers Confrerie de St-Uguson; Montreal Anglers & Hunters Assn.; Montreal Bd. Trade; Nat. Assoc. of Video Distributors; Candn. Chamber Comm.; Comm. Travellers Assn. Can.; Video Software Dealers Assn. of America; Candn. Assn. of Video Distributors (Vice-Pres. 1983–85); Food Brokers Assn. Can.; Food Services Executives Assn.; Candn. Importers Assn.; Can.-Israel Chamber Comm.; Candn. Council Christians & Jews; Jewish

Theol. Semy. Am.; Am. Museum Natural Hist.; Playrights Workshop; B'nai Brith; Y.M.-Y.W.H.A.; Life Mem., Candn. Professional Sales Assn.; recreations: photography, architectural drafting, stamp collecting, handgun & rifle target shooting, golf, swimming, fishing; Clubs: Montreal Anglers & Hunters; Amici (Pres. 1950–51, 1965–66); Home: 5350 MacDonald Ave., Suite 1706, Montreal, Que. H3X 3V2; Office: 970 Montee de Liesse, Suite 209, Montreal, Que. H4T 1W7.

**PRUS, Victor Marius,** M.Arch., R.C.A., F.R.A.I.C., C.I.P., R.I.B.A., Hon. F.A.I.A.; architect; b. Poland 19 Apl. 1917; e. Chelmno 1930–35; Warsaw Tech. Univ. Dipl. Arch. 1939; Univ. of Liverpool 1945–47 Inq. Arch. (M. Arch.), m. Maria Fisz 22 Sept. 1948; came to Can. 1952; PRINC., VICTOR PRUS & ASSOCIATES, ARCHITECTS AND URBANISTS; Arch.: Montreal Convention Centre; New Internat. Airport, Barbados; Observatory Mauna Kea, Hawaii; Grand Théâtre de Québec; Conserv. of Music, Que.; Montreal Metro Stns.: Bonaventure, Mt. Royal, Langelier; Brudenell River Resort, P.E.I.; Place Longueuil Commercial Centre; Rockland Shopping Centre; Centaur Theatres, Montreal; Expo '67 Stadium; James Lyng Sch., Montreal; recipient Massey Medal for Arch.; Candn Arch. Award; 1st Prize Que, Performing Arts Centre; 1st Prize RCAF Mem.; 1st Prize Montreal Congres Centre; visit. prof. McGill Univ., 1953, 1966, 1972; prof. Ecole d'arch. Quebec 1959; visit. prof. Washington Univ. St. Louis, Mo., 1978; served with 305 (P) Sqdn. RAF World War II, rank Flying Offr.; rec'd Polish Cross of Valour (twice); Fellow, Royal Arch. Inst. of Can.; Academician, Royal Can. Academy of Arts; Hon. Fellow, Am. Inst. Archs.; mem. Royal Inst. Brit. Archs.; Candn. Inst. Planners; Home: 108 Senneville Rd., Senneville, Que. H9X 1B9; Office: 224 Place d'Youville, Montreal, Que. H2Y 2B4.

**PRUZANSKI, Waldemar,** M.D., F.R.C.P.(C), F.A.C.P., F.A.C.R.; physician; scientist; educator; b. Warsaw, Poland 23 Oct. 1928; s. Adam and Sonia (Wojniunski) P.; e. Hebrew Univ. Hadassah Med. Sch. Jerusalem M.D. 1956; m. Vera d. Edmund and Henrietta Hochfelsen 1963; children: Mark, Corinne; HEAD, DIV. OF IMMUNOLOGY, THE WELLESLEY HOSP. 1973– , Sr. Phys. 1968; Prof. of Med. Univ. of Toronto 1977– , Dir. Immunol. Diagnostic & Rsch. Centre 1973– , Dir. Inflammation Rsch. Group 1988– ; Rsch. Fellow Dept. Immunochem. Weizmann Inst. of Sci. Israel 1964; Dep. Chief of Med. Asaf Harofe Hosp. Tel-Aviv Univ. 1964–65; Rsch. Assoc. Columbia Univ. Inst. Cancer Rsch. N.Y. 1965–66; Asst. Prof. of Med. present Univ. 1968, Assoc. Prof. 1972, mem. Inst. Immunol. 1975–85; author or co-author over 340 publs., 22 book chapters; author and ed. 2 books; assoc. ed. Jour. Rheumatology; Fellow, Candn. Arthritis & Rheumatism Soc.; Am. Coll. Rheumatol.; mem. Candn. Soc. Clin. Investig.; Candn. Soc. Immunol.; Candn. Med. Assn.; Am. Fedn. Clin. Rsch.; Am. Assn. Immunols.; N.Y. Acad. Sci.'s; Office: 160 Wellesley St., Toronto, Ont. M4Y 1J3.

**PRYCHIDNY, Walter,** B.Comm., C.A., C.B.V.; business executive; b. Deep River, Ont. 3 April 1951; s. John and Nadine (Stoneda) P.; e. Univ. of Toronto B.Comm. 1974; m. Deborah d. Winfield and Phyllis Cornell 13 May 1972; children: Aaron Winfield, Adam Jon; CHIEF EXECUTIVE OFFICER, COMMONWEALTH HOSPITALITY LTD.; articled with Price Waterhouse Toronto C.A. 1976; acted as C.F.O. of several private-held companies in real estate, construction & hospitality industries; Chartered Bus. Valuator (CVA) 1980 (highest marks in entrance examination); Dir., Transamerica Inc.; Dir. & Pres., Ramada Canada Franchise Ltd.; Mem., Inst. of C.A.s of Ont.; Candn. Inst. of C.B.V.s; recreations: skiing, golf, squash; Home: P.O. Box 098, Puslinch, Ont. N0B 2T0; Office: 31 Fasken Dr., Etobicoke, Ont. M9W 1K8.

**PRYSTAWSKI, Walter;** violinist; concertmaster; b. Toronto, Ont. 12 Feb. 1933; s. Justyn and Mary P.; e. Parkdale Coll. Inst. 1950; Univ. of Toronto Arts Dip. 1953; Wolfgang Schneiderhan Lucerne, Switzerland Masterclasses; m. Victoria d. Charles and Alice MacMillan 19 May 1956; children: Linda, Laurence; Concertmaster, Nat. Arts Centre Orch. 1969; Prof. of Violin: Univ. of Ottawa; Conservatoire de Musique du Québec, Hull; Lucerne Conserv. 1960–69; Violinist: Pierrot Ensemble 1988– ; Toronto Symphony 1953–59; CBC Symphony Toronto 1956–69; Lucerne Trio Switzerland 1965–69; Violinist & Concertmaster Lucerne Festival Strings 1960–69; Violin Soloist, Lucerne Festival Strings, Nat. Arts Centre Orch. and Orquestra Ciutat de Barcelona; various recordings; recreations: reading, computers; Home: 50 Parkland Cres., Nepean, Ont. K2H 7W5.

**PSUTKA, Dennis Anthony,** B.A., M.D.; university professor; b. Hamilton, Ont. 1 June 1939; s. Joseph and Helen (Patzalek) P.; e. Univ. of Toronto, St. Michael's Coll. B.A. 1959, Med. Sch. M.D. 1963; m. Rose Marie d. John and Marion Delaney; one s.: Paul; ASSOC. PROF., FAMILY MED., MCMASTER UNIV. 1988– ; Family Med. Grimsby Ont. 1964–74; Dir., Emergency Serv., McMaster Univ. Med. Ctr. & Asst. Prof. Fam. Med. 1974–79; Hamilton Civic Hosp. & Assoc. Prof. 1979–81; seconded to Ont. Min. of Health 1981–87; Dir., Emergency Health Serv. 1981–83; Asst. Dept. Min. 1984–87; Dir. & Head of Section Emergency Services, Chedoke McMaster Hospitals 1988–93; Consultant, Agnew Peckham; Drug Quality & Therapeutics Ctte. Ont.; Drug Reform Secretariat Ont. Min. of Health; Peat Marwick; Hay Management Consultants; Chair, Emergency Health Serv., Hamilton-Wentworth; Chair, Emergency Health Services Delivery Alternatives and Utilization Review Ctte., Ont. Min. of Health; Chair, Emergency Cardiac Care Coalition of Ont., Heart and Stroke Found.; recreations: sailing; clubs: Fifty Point Yacht; Home: 25 McNab Dr., Grimsby, Ont. L3M 2Y7; Office: HSC-2R1, 1200 Main St. W., Hamilton, Ont. L8N 3Z5.

**PUDDEPHATT, Richard John,** B.Sc., Ph.D., FRSC; university professor; b. Aylesbury, U.K. 12 Oct. 1943; s. Harry and Ena (Bowler) P.; e. University College B.Sc. 1965, Ph.D. 1968; m. Alice d. Walter and Ruth Poulton 14 June 1969; children: Susan Clare, Antony James; PROF., UNIV. OF WESTERN ONTARIO 1978– ; Teaching Postdoct. Fellow, Univ. of W. Ont. 1968–70; Lectr., Univ. of Liverpool 1970–77; Sr. Lectr. 1977–78; Fellow, Royal Society of Canada; author: 'The Periodic Table of the Elements' 1986, 'The Chemistry of Gold' 1978; Home: 199 Carriage Hill Dr., London, Ont. N5X 3N4; Office: London, Ont. N6A 5B7.

**PUDDESTER, Harold 'James' Pratt;** provincial supreme court justice; b. St. John's, NF 18 May 1946; s. Harold G. and J. Gwenyth (Pratt) P.; e. Prince of Wales Coll. 1963; Memorial Univ. of NF, B.A. 1968; Dalhousie Univ., LL.B. 1971; m. Margaret J. d. J. Carson and Florence B. Hudson 25 Feb. 1967; children: Leigh James Harold, Kathleen Claire; JUSTICE, SUPREME COURT OF NFLD., TRIAL DIV. 1989– ; admitted to practice of law Dec. 1971; Assoc. & Partner, O'Dea, Greene 1971–80; Sr. Partner, Puddester/Orsborn 1980–89; Q.C. 1984; part-time lectr., Meml. Univ. of NF 1970s; Law Soc. of NF: Founding Chrmn., Bar Admission Prog. Ctte., 1974–80; Bencher, 1978–80; Chrmn., Legis. Ctte. 1987–89; Candn. Bar Assn.: Nat. Chairperson Young Lawyers Section 1976; Nat. Extve. 1978–80; Chrmn., St. John's & E. Residential Tenancies Bds. 1981–86; Driver's Licence Supension Review Bd. 1980–89; Mem., Un. Ch.; Candn. Bar Assoc.; Candn. Judges Conference; Candn. Inst. for the Admin. of Justice; recreations: automobiles (old & new), reading; Home: 129 Waterford Bridge Rd., St. John's, Nfld. A1E 1C7; Office: P.O. Box 937, St. John's, Nfld. A1C 5M3.

**PUDDINGTON, Ira Edwin;** M.Sc., Ph.D., D.Sc., F.R.S.C., F.C.I.C., F.A.I.C.; retired from Canadian public service; b. Clifton, Royal, N.B. 8 Jan. 1911; s. Charles E. and Elizabeth (Currie) P.; e. Prov. Normal Sch., Fredericton, N.B.; Mount Allison Univ., B.Sc. 1933; McGill Univ., M.Sc. 1936 and Ph.D. 1938; D.Sc.: Mount Allison Univ. 1967; Carleton Univ. 1975; Memorial Univ. 1977; m. Hazel Jean, d. James Duncan, Upper Blackville, N.B., 27 Aug. 1936; one s. James; Consultant and Researcher Emeritus, National Research Council; former Dir., Div. of Chem., National Research Council, 1952–1974; Lectr., McGill Univ., 1936–37; Sir George Williams Coll., Montreal, Que., 1937–38; mem., N.R.C., Colloid Sec., Chem. Div., 1938–74; Pres., Chem. Inst. Can. 1967–68; recreation: gardening; Home: 2324 Alta Vista Drive, Ottawa, Ont. K1H 7M7; Office: N.R.C., Montreal Road, Ottawa, Ont. K1A 0R9.

**PUDDINGTON, John C.,** B.A., M.B.A.; investment executive; b. Montreal, Que. 23 Jan. 1943; e. Sir George Williams Univ. B.A. 1968; McMaster Univ. M.B.A. 1971; m. Doris Kulessa 1983; PRES. TRILWOOD INVESTMENTS LTD. 1989– ; Dir. National Trustco; National Trust Company; Premier Trust Company; Fairfax Financial Services Ltd.; Office: P.O. Box 523, Suite 4320, Canada Trust Tower, BCE Place, 161 Bay St., Toronto, Ont. M5J 2S1.

**PUGH, Anthony Roy,** M.A., Ph.D., F.R.S.C.; university professor of French; b. Liverpool, England 16 Aug. 1931; s. Walter and Mary Dilys (Jones) P.; e. Liverpool Inst. H.S.; Pembroke Coll., Cambridge Univ., B.A. (Hons.) 1953, M.A. 1956, Ph.D. 1959; m. Mary d. Wilfrid and Dilys Hooton 29 Dec. 1962; children: Elizabeth, David, Margaret; PROF., DEPT. OF FRENCH, UNIV. OF N.B. 1969– ; Asst. Lectr., King's Coll. (London) 1956–59; Lectr., Queen's Univ. (Belfast) 1959–69; author: 'From Montaigne to Chateaubriand' 1964, 'Beaumarchais: "Le Mariage de Figaro"' 1968, 'Balzac's Recurring Characters' 1974, 'The Composition of Pascal's Apologia' 1984; 'The Birth of "A la recherche du temps perdu"' 1987; presently working on the chronology of Proust's mss.; recreation: music; Home: 47 Simcoe Court, Fredericton, N.B. E3B 2W9; Office: Dept. of French, Univ. of N.B., P.O. Box 4400, Fredericton, N.B. E3B 5A3.

**PUGH, Paul M.,** B.Sc., M.B.A., F.L.M.I., CFA; investment executive; b. Montreal, Que. 18 Oct. 1946; s. Lewis and Margaret Pearl (D'Aubin) P.; e. McGill Univ. B.Sc. 1967, M.B.A. 1971; C.F.A. 1978; Fellow, Life Mngt. Inst. 1984, 1993; PRESIDENT & DIRECTOR, PPM FUND MANAGERS (CANADA) LIMITED and PPM REAL ESTATE MANAGERS (CANADA) LIMITED; var. positions, Sun Life Assur. Co. of Canada 1971–85; Vice-Pres., Dominion of Canada Gen. Insur. Co. and Sr. Vice-Pres., Empire Life of Canada 1985–88; Vice-Pres. & Partner, Hodgson Roberton Laing Limited 1988–91; Sr. Vice-Pres., Investments, Prudential Assur. Co. of Canada 1991–93; Dir. & Past Pres., Toronto Soc. of Finan. Analysts; recreations: photography, travel, sports; clubs: Toronto Racquet; Home: 19 Fulton Ave., Toronto, Ont. M4K 1X6; Office: 141 Adelaide St., Suite 300, Toronto, Ont. M5H 3L9.

**PUGLIESE, Olga,** B.A., M.A., Ph.D.; university professor; b. Toronto, Ont. 4 Nov. 1941; d. Giosuè and Anna (Cressatti) Zorzi; e. Northview Heights C.I. 1959; Univ. of Toronto B.A. 1963, M.A. 1964, Ph.D. 1969; m. Guido s. Emilio and Rosina P. 9 Aug. 1969; FACULTY MEMBER, DEPT. OF ITALIAN, UNIV. OF TORONTO 1967– ; Fellow, Victoria College, Univ. of Toronto 1978– ; Undergraduate Sec., Dept. of Italian 1973–74; Co-ord., Renaissance Studies Programme, Victoria College 1983–85; Graduate Co-ord., Dept. of Italian 1984–88; Sec.-Treas., Candn. Soc. for Renaissance Studies 1976–78; Rep. for Italian Lit., Renaissance Soc. of Am. 1982–84; Chair, Toronto Renaissance & Reformation Colloquium 1985–86; translator: 'The Profession of the Religious' and 'Principal Arguments from "The Falsely Believed and Forged Donation of Constantine"' by Lorenzo Valla 1985; co-editor: 'Ficino and Renaissance Neoplatonism' 1986; author of 27 articles in European & N. Am. journals, etc.; Home: 32 Northmount Ave., Downsview, Ont. M3H 1N4; Office: Toronto, Ont. M5S 1A1.

**PULFER, James K.,** D.Sc., P.Eng.; retired; b. Rosser, Man. 4 May 1932; s. Charles Elmer and Marion Elanor (James) P.; e. Univ. of Man. B.Sc. 1953, M.Sc. 1954, D.Sc. 1984; m. Rolande Hotte 14 Nov. 1959; children: Suzanne Elisabeth, Charles Edouard, James Robert; Extve. Vice Pres., Assn. of Provl. Rsch. Orgns. 1990–92, Retired; joined Nat. Rsch. Council Can. Rsch. & Devel. in Electronics, Space Technol., Computing 1954–71, Dir. Computation Centre 1971–72, Dir. Div. Elect. Eng. 1975–80, Vice Pres. Labs. 1981–84, Vice Pres. Finance 1984–86, Comptroller 1986–90; Prog. Analyst Fed. Treasury Bd. 1973–75; Co-Chrmn. Candn. Info. Processing Soc. Cert. Council 1987–92; mem. CIPS; QCWA; Assn. Prof. Engs. Prov. Ont.; Home: 1756 Laxton Cres., Ottawa, Ont. K2C 2N3.

**PULLAN, Christopher Bruce,** B.A., M.A., Dip.Ed.; conductor, academy executive; b. Goole, Eng. 21 Aug. 1943; s. Robert Bratby and Alice (Holmes) P.; e. Tiffin School England 1961; King's Coll. Cambridge B.A. 1964, M.A. 1967; New Coll. Oxford Dip.Ed. 1965; m. Lynda d. Roderick and Gladys Clark 25 Aug. 1969; children: Sarah Elizabeth, Alison Clare, Miranda Kate; PRESIDENT, VANCOUVER ACADEMY OF MUSIC 1993– ; Director of Choral Music, Tiffin School 1965–74; Music Dir., Nonsuch Opera 1971–74; Asst. Music Dir., Gemini Opera 1969–74; Dir. of Music, St. George's School (Vancouver) 1974–75; Assoc. Prof. of Music, Western Washington Univ. 1975–85; Prof. 1985–93; Chairman, Dept. of Music. 1985–91; co-author: 'The Management of Voice Disorders' 1994; several recordings as Conductor, Vancouver Bach Choir; singer 'Night' Eliot Weisgarber with the Vancouver Chamber Choir; recreation: golf; Home: 2567 York Ave., Vancouver, B.C. V6K 1E4; Office: 1270 Chestnut St., Vancouver, B.C. V6J 4R9.

**PULLEYBLANK, Edwin George,** Ph.D., F.R.S.C.; educator; b. Calgary, Alta. 7 Aug. 1922; s. late William George Edwin and Ruth Elizabeth (Willoughby) P.; e. Central High Sch. Calgary 1939; Univ. of Alta. B.A. 1942; Univ. of London Ph.D. (Chinese) 1951; m. Winona Ruth (d. 1978), d. late Douglas McCrum Relyea, Prescott, Ont. 17 July 1945; children: David Edwin, Barbara Jill, Marcia Ruth; PROF. EMERITUS, UNIV. OF

B.C. 1988– , Prof. of Asian Studies 1966–87, Head of Asian Studies 1968–75; joined Nat. Research Council Ottawa 1943–46; Lectr. Sch. of Oriental and African Studies Univ. of London 1948–53; Prof. of Chinese Univ. of Cambridge 1953–66, Fellow of Downing Coll. 1954–66; author 'The Background of the Rebellion of An Lu-shan' 1955; 'Chinese History and World History' (inaugural lecture) 1955; 'Middle Chinese' 1984; 'Lexicon of Reconstructed Pronunciation in Chinese'; co-ed. 'Historians of China and Japan' 1961; numerous articles and reviews learned journs. and coll. publs. Chinese and Central Asian Hist., linguistics; mem. Philol. Soc.; Am. Oriental Soc.; Linguistic Assn. Am.; Candn. Soc. Asian Studies (now Candn. Asian Studies Assn.), Pres. 1971–74; Candn. Linguistic Assn.; Home: 2708 West 3rd Ave., Vancouver, B.C. V6K 1M5.

**PULLMAN, Anthony John,** B.A., C.A.; financial executive; b. Jerusalem 22 Aug. 1945; s. John Hartley and Ada Jean (Lusted) P.; e. Bradfield Coll. Berks. UK 1963; Keble Coll. Oxford B.A. 1966; m. Claire d. Geoffrey Sowels 17 Aug. 1974; children: Sarah, James, Emma, Edward; VICE-PRESIDENT, FINANCE AND ADMINISTRATION, CN POWER INTERNAT. 1993– ; joined Touche Ross & Co. London, UK, Montréal, Calgary 1967–80; Vice Pres. and Controller Alberta Power Ltd. Edmonton 1980–85; Vice Pres., Planning & Budgeting, Atco Ltd. 1985–93; Dir. Calgary Pub. Lib. Bd. 1979–80; Dir. Edmonton Convention Centre Assn. 1984–85; Dir. Calgary District Hosp. Group 1985–91, Vice Chrmn. 1987–89, Chrmn. 1989–91; 2nd Vice-Chrmn., Calgary Police Commission 1992–93; mem. Inst. C.A.'s Eng. & Wales 1970, Alta. 1979; Dir., Protection Mutual Insurance Cdn. Adv. Bd. 1985– ; Dir., Alta. Blue Cross 1989– (Vice Chrmn. 1993– ); recreations: philately, tennis; Home: 429 Ronning St., Edmonton, Alta. T6R 1Z2; Office: 10035 - 105 St., Edmonton, Alta. T5J 2V6.

**PUNNETT, Robert D.,** B.A., LL.B.; barrister & solicitor; b. Vancouver, B.C. 23 July 1952; s. Ronald L. and Barbara W. P.; e. Simon Fraser Univ. B.A.; Univ. of B.C. LL.B.; m. Christine d. Peter and Renate Mueller 2 June 1984; children: Benjamin James William, Katherine Elizabeth Taneisha, Alexander Thomas Sebastian; PARTNER, PUNNETT & JOHNSTON 1978– (general practice); Former Mem., Prov. Couns., Candn. Bar Assn.; Dir., Museum of Northern B.C.; Home: 2055 Seal Cove Circle, Prince Rupert, B.C. V8J 2G4; Office: #7, 222 – 3rd Ave. W., Prince Rupert, B.C. V8J 1L1.

**PURCELL, Rev. Canon Borden Conrad,** B.A., S.T.B.; priest; b. Athens, Ont. 8 Nov. 1928; s. George A. and Beatrice A. (Trotter) P.; e. Athens H.S.; Bishop's Univ., B.A. 1951; Trinity Coll., S.T.B. 1954; m. Carter d. Frederic and Mildred Dorwart 22 June 1955; children: Mary Kathleen, Michael Frederic, John Patrick; IMMIGRATION AND REFUGEE BD. OF CANADA (Convention Refugee Determination Div.) 1988– ; Curate, Grace Ch. (Hamilton) 1954–55; Rector, Christ Ch. (St. Catharines) 1955–59; St. Hilda's (Oakville) 1959–63; St. John's (Thorold) 1963–69; St. John's (Ottawa) 1969–81; Canon, Christ Ch. Cathedral (Ottawa) 1972– ; Chrmn., Anglican Book Soc. & Canterbury Book Stores 1969–78; Mem., Counc. of Assoc. Parishes 1958– ; Cons. Ctte. on Human Rights, Candn. Counc. of Chs. 1982; Chrmn., Ont. Human Rights Comn. 1982–88; Nat. Counc. of the Candn. Human Rights Found. 1985; Corp. of Trinity Coll. 1986; Founding Mem., Toronto Inter-Faith Counc. on Soviet Jewry 1985; Pres., Candn. Assn. of Statutory Human Rights Agencies 1986; Delegate, Internat. Cons. on Human Rights (Ireland) 1978 and Candn. Rep. for other worldwide seminars & conventions; P.C.; author of several papers & articles; recreations: gardening, water sports, skiing, travel; Home: Charleston Lake, R.R. #1, Athens, Ont. K0E 1B0; Office: 222 Nepean St., Ottawa, Ont. K2P 0B8.

**PURDON, John Sefton,** B.A.; retired provincial civil servant; b. England 5 June 1934; s. Frederick Field and Hilda Florence (Oberg) P.; e. St. Columba's College, St. Albans, England; Univ. of Toronto B.A. (Hons.) 1968; m. Diana Susan d. Richard Meek 10 Sept. 1959; children: Jennifer Susan, Jonathan Andrew, Michael William Frederick, Nicholas Timothy Richard Marcus; former Asst. Deputy Min., Min. of Finance, Govt. of Ont.; British Army 1952–54; Sales (U.K.) 1954–57; insurance 1957–64; Ontario Civil Service 1968– ; recreations: reading, carpentry, boating, gardening; clubs: Madawaska; Home: 30 Kimbolton Court, West Hill, Ont. M1C 3G2.

**PURDUE, Shaun W.,** B.A., C.A.; broadcasting executive; b. Newmarket, Ont. 29 Jan. 1952; e. Univ. of Western Ont., Richard Ivy Sch. of Business Admin. B.A. (Hons.) 1975; C.A. 1977; m. Violet Burke; PRES., CFCN COMMUNICATIONS LIMITED 1986– ; Auditor, Deloitte Haskins & Sells (Calgary & Toronto) 1975–77; Audit Senior, Touche Ross & Co. (Calgary) 1977–78; Chief Accountant, CFCN Communications Limited 1978–80; Controller 1980–82; Vice-Pres., Finance, Sec.-Treas. & Dir. 1982–86; Dir., Banff TV Festival; Western Assn. of Broadcasters; Alta. Broadcasters' Assn.; Milner Fenerty Found.; recreations: skiing, golf, running; Office: Box 7060, Station E, Calgary, Alta. T3C 3L9.

**PURDY, Alfred;** writer; b. Wooler, Ont. 30 Dec. 1918; s. Alfred and Eleanor Louise P.; e. Dufferin Pub. Sch., Trenton, Ont.; Albert Coll., Belleville, Ont.; Trenton (Ont.) Coll. Inst.; rec'd. Can Council Fellowships 1960 and 1965; m. Eurithe Mary Jane, d. James Parkhurst, Belleville, Ont., 1 Nov. 1941; one s. Alfred; served with RCAF during 2nd World War; Books published: 'The Enchanted Echo' 1944; 'Pressed on Sand' 1955; 'Emu, Remember' 1957; 'The Crafte So Longe To Lerne' 1956; 'Poems for All The Annettes' 1962; 'The Blur In Between' 1963; 'The Cariboo Horses' 1965; 'North of Summer' 1967 'Wild Grape Wine' 1968; 'The New Romans' (anthol.) editor 1968; 'Love in a Burning Building' 1970; 'Storm Warning' 1971; 'Selected Poems' 1972; 'Hiroshima Poems' 1972; 'On the Bearpaw Sea' 1973; 'Sex and Death' 1973; 'In Search of Owen Roblin' 1974; 'Sundance at Dusk' 1976; 'The Poems of Al Purdy' 1976; 'Storm Warning 2' 1976; 'At Marsport Drugstore' 1977; 'No Other Country' 1977; 'A Handful of Earth' 1977; 'No Second Spring' 1978; 'Moths in the Iron Curtain' 1978; 'Being Alive, Poems 1958–78' 1978; 'The Stone Bird' 1981; 'Bursting into Song': An Al Purdy Omnibus' 1982; 'Morning and It's Summer' (autobiog.) 1982; 'Birdwatching at the Equator' 1983; 'The Bukowski/Purdy Letters 1964–1974' 1983; 'Piling Blood' 1984; 'Selected Poems' (Russian transl.) 1986; 'Collected Poems' 1986 (Gov. General's Award 1987 and Candn. Author's Assn. Award 1987); 'The Woman on the Shore' 1990; 'A Splinter in the Heart' (novel) 1990; 'Margaret Laurence-Al Purdy - A Friendship in Letters' 1993; 'Cougar Hunter' (limited to 200 copies) 1993; 'Reaching for the Beaufort Sea (autobiography) 1993; ed. & introduced Andrew Suknaski's 'Wood & Mountain Poems' 1976; ed. & introd. Milton Acorn's 'I've Tasted My Blood' 1969; has written radio and television plays, short stories, articles; recipient, Governor Gen. Literary Award for Poetry, 1966; President's Medal of the Univ. of W. Ont. for best poem by a Candn. publ. in a mag., 1963; A.J.M. Smith Award, 1973; Acad. of Can. Writers 1977; Jubilee Medal 1978; Officer of the Order of Canada, 1982; Order of Ontario 1987; Canada Council Grant 1986; Milton Acorn People's Poet Award 1991; 125th Anniversary of the Confederation of Canada Medal, 1992; Can. Council Fellowship, Greece, Italy, Eng. 1968–69; Hiroshima, Japan 1971; Can. Council awards to South Africa 1973, Peru 1975, Galapagos Islands 1980; former Writer-in-Res. Loyola (Mtl.) 1973–74; Univ. of Man. 1975–76; Univ. of W. Ont. 1977–78; N.D.P.; recreation: travelling; Address: 9310 Lochside Dr., Sidney, B.C. V8L 1N6.

**PURDY, Gary Rush,** P.Eng., B.Sc., M.Sc., Ph.D., F.R.S.C.; university dean; b. Edmonton, Alta. 8 Oct. 1936; s. Kent Edward and Bertha (McNaught) P.; e. Univ of Alberta B.Sc. 1957, M.Sc. 1959; McMaster Univ. Ph.D. 1962; m. Ruby Elinore d. Florita and Arden Smith 3 June 1961; children: Anne, Ruth, Jonathan, Daniel; DEAN, FAC. OF ENGINEERING, MCMASTER UNIV. 1989– ; Rsch. Assoc., Univ of Alta. 1959–60; Postdoct. Fellow, McMaster Univ. 1962–63; Assoc. Dean, Sch. of Grad. Studies 1971–74; Asst. Prof., Engineering 1963–67; Assoc. 1967–71; Acting Dean 1986–87; Chair, Materials Sci. & Engr. 1978–81, 1984–86; Visiting Prof., Central Electricity Rsch. Labs. (UK) 1969–70; Royal Inst. of Technology (Stockholm) 1976–77; Inst. Nat. Polytech.de Grenoble 1983–84; Fellow, Royal Soc. of Can. 1991; Candn. Metal Physics Medal 1990; Hon. Prof., Univ. of Sci. & Tech., Beijing, P.R.C. 1983; C.D. Howe Mem. Fellowshp 1969; Mem., Council of Ont. Deans of Engr. (Chair 1993–94); Assn. of Profl. Engrs. of Ont.; Candn. Inst. of Mining & Metallurgy; Am. Soc. for Metals; Materials Rsch. Soc.; author of over 100 refereed journal papers, 25 refereed conf. proceedings; editor: 'Fundamentals and Applications of Ternary Diffusion' 1990, 'Advances in Phase Transitions' 1988, 'Solute-Defect Interactions, Theory and Experiment' 1986; recreations: choral music, woodworking; Home: 144 Flatt Ave., Hamilton, Ont. L8P 4N3; Office: Hamilton, Ont. L8S 4L8.

**PURDY, Henry Carl,** R.C.A.; F.R.S.A., A.N.S.C.A.; artist; educator; b. Wolfville, N.S. 6 Nov. 1937; s. Carl Augustus and Florence Margaret (Langille) P.; e. elem. and jr. high schs. Wolfville; Armdale (N.S.) High Sch. 1954; N.S. Coll. of Art Assoc. 1958 (Lt. Gov.'s Medal); N.B. Inst. of Technol. Vocational Teachers Cert. 1963; m. Gertrude Ann d. Herbert Hill, Halifax, N.S. 19 Apl. 1959; children: Henry Scott, Daniel Blair, Sharon Mary; Graphic Artist, CFCY-TV Charlottetown 1958–63; designed, instituted and taught comm. art course Prov. Vocational Inst. 1963–69; designed and taught comm. design program Holland Coll. 1969–77, Chrmn. Applied Arts Div., designed formation Sch. Visual Arts 1977; Former Dir., Centre of Creative Arts, Holland Coll. (mem. Bd. Govs. 1969–73); comns. incl. 22 ft. sculpture Confed. Centre Charlottetown 1973; 12 ft. metal fountain Parkdale, P.E.I.; murals, 11 ft. sculpture Univ. P.E.I.; solo exhns. incl. N.B. Museum & Theatre N.B. 1974; St. Dunstans Univ. 1968; Isle St. Jean Gallery Charlottetown 1974; Gallery On Demand 1976; Confed. Centre 10 yr. retrospective 1978; Rothman Gallery Moncton 1980; four one man shows in 1981: Truro, N.S.; Moncton, N.B.; Summerside, P.E.I.; Sydney, N.S.; Sunbury Shores, N.B.; two two-man shows in 1981: Charlottetown, P.E.I.; St. Andrews, N.B.; rep. in various group shows, nat. and internat. pub. and private colls.; 3 Murals at the Candn. Coast Guard College, Sydney, N.S.; one-man exhibition, City Hall Gallery, St. John, N.B. 1983; published drawings in work 'Icons' 1981, 'Francis' 1983, 'I Am My Own Seasons' 1984, 'Epigrammatically Yours' 1988; comm. issue 1983 Sand Patterns features drawings & poems; silscreen prints comnd. by Nfld. Parks & Hist. Sites & P.E.I. Parks and People; designed stained glass windows in Assumption & Our Lady of the People churches; painting in the collection of P.E.I. Art Bank 1983; 1983 workshops given in Toronto, Ont.; Souris, P.E.I.; Ch'town, P.E.I.; Alberton, P.E.I.; Summerside, P.E.I.; Halifax, N.S.; Chrmn. Design Comte. P.E.I. Centennial 1973 and 1981; Mem., Senate Univ. of P.E.I. 1970–74; Founding Mem. P.E.I. Council of Arts 1974, past Chrmn.; Mem., Extve. P.E.I. Handcraft Council 1989–93; P.E.I. Extve. Comte. Task Force on Candn. Unity; Bd. Atlantic Inst.; CAR (P.E.I.) Artists Union 1990– ; P.E.I. Festival of the Arts Committee 1990; Artists for Amnesty; Bd., Memmramcook Inst.; Chrmn., Visual Arts for Canada Winter Games to be held in P.E.I. 1991; rec'd Painting and Sculpture Awards P.E.I. 1967; 4 published works drawings and poetry; pub., 'Prince Edward Island Sketchbook' (a book of 113 drawings); Gold Medal Art P.E.I. 1973; Elected to Royal Canadian Academy of Art 1978 (P.E.I. Vice-Pres. 1989– ); received Royal Soc. of Arts (Manufacturers of Commerce) Atlantic Region Silver Medal for contribution to the Fine Arts in Atlantic Canada, 1981; Made Fellow of the Royal Soc. of Arts 1982; apptd. to Task Force on Training in the Candn. Cultural Sector 1990; elected to the Council RCA 1990 Extve.; mem. Town of Parkdale Planning Review Ctte. 1990; Maritime Art Assn. (P.E.I. Vice Pres.); Sand Patterns Publ. Assn.; Assn. Candn. Studies; Candn. Vocational Assn.; Assn. Candn. Community Colls.; Chamber Comm. Greater Charlottetown; Friends Confed. Centres; Bd. of Govs., Candn. Conference of the Arts, 1983; Apptd. to Extve. and Bd. of the Fathers of Confederation Centre of the Arts Trust 1983; Vice Pres., (Atlantic Region) RCA 1983; served on Canada Council 1984–90; mem. of Bd. for Dance Montage; mem., Candn. Soc. of Educ. through Art 1983; Great George St. Gallery 1990; Candn. Soc. of Color 1983; Candn. Artists Representation (P.E.I.) 1983; Apptd. special Chrmn. of Policies & Priorities Ctte. for P.E.I. Council of the Arts; Anglican; recreations: sports, cross-country skiing, reading, music, teaching night art classes & giving workshops; Home: 6 St. Peters Rd., Parkdale, P.E.I. C1A 5N2; Office: Burns Ave., West Royalty, P.E.I. C1A 7N9.

**PURDY, J. Lawrence (Larry);** retired insurance executive; b. St. Boniface, Man. 28 May 1927; e. Angus Business Sch.; Univ. of Toronto Extension Dept.; m. Betty Boland 7 June 1952; children: Diane, Jared; Pres. & C.E.O., The CUMIS Group 1990–92; Asst. Accountant, Blue Cross 1947; Asst. Mgr., Credit Union League of Man. 1950; Special Rep., Manitoba, Sask. & N. Ont., CUNA Mutual Insur. Soc. (now CUMIS Life Ins. Co.); District Mgr. 1964; Regional Mgr. 1966; Dir. of Agencies for Canada 1968; Eastern Region Mgr. 1970; Vice-Pres., EAstern Reg. 1972; Field Operations 1973; Field Operations & Mktg. 1975; Sr. Vice-Pres. 1980; Chief Operation Offr. & Sr. Vice-Pres., CUMIS Gen. Insur. Co. 1984; Extve. Vice-Pres., The CUMIS Group 1988; Dir., The CUMIS Group Limited (also Pres. & C.E.O.); CUMIS Life Insur. Co. 1990–92; CUMIS Gen. Insur. Co. 1990–1992; Candn. Northern Shield Insur. Co. 1990–92; Candn. Co-op. Credit Soc.; Co-op. Trust Co. of Canada; Candn. Co-op. Assn.; ex officio dir., CUNA Mutual Insur. Group 1990–92; Head Office: Box 5065, 151 North Service Rd., Burlington, Ont. L7R 4C2.

**PURITT, Paul,** M.A., Ph.D.; national trade union representative; b. Montreal, Que. 28 July 1938; s. Nathan and Ethel (Marder) P.; step-mother: Jean (Schacter) Puritt; e. Univ. of Toronto B.A. 1959, M.A. 1961; Univ. of Illinois Ph.D. 1970; m. Sheila d. Maurice and Diane (Tilly) Swerling 6 March 1960; divorced; children: Edan, Jeffrey; NATIONAL REPRESENTATIVE INTERNAT. AFFAIRS DEPT., CANDN. LABOUR CONGRESS, S. AFRICA 1992–94; Ph.D. Rsch., Mount Meru, Tanzania 1964–66; Sr. Lectr., Univ. of Dar es Salaam 1966–70; Asst. Prof., Univ. of Calgary 1970–71; San Jose State Univ. 1971–73; Visiting Prof., Univ. of Toronto 1973–74; Trent Univ. 1973–75; Regional Dir., OXFAM Ont. 1975–78; Program Devel. Offr. for S. Africa, OXFAM Canada 1978–84; Coord., Ctr. d'Information et de documentation sur le Mozambique et l'Afrique Australe, CIDMAA Montreal 1982–84; Internat. Affairs Dept., Candn. Labour Congress Ottawa 1984–90; Extve. Dir., Southern Africa Education Trust Fund 1990–92, Trustee 1992– ; Fellow, Royal Anthropological Inst.; Chrmn., TCLSAC 1975–78; Vice-Pres., CIDMAA 1984– ; recreations: reading, TV, nordic skiing; Address: 213 Summerhill, Sally's Alley, Kentview 2196, Johannesburg, South Africa.

**PURVIS, A. Blaikie,** B.A., M.B.A.; executive; b. New York, N.Y. 20 Nov. 1924 (came to Can. Dec. 1924); s. Rt. Hon. Arthur Blaikie, P.C., and Margaret (Jones) P.; e. Eton Coll., Eng., 1938–43; Bishop's Coll. Sch., Lennoxville, Que., 1940–41; McGill Univ., B.A. 1949; Harvard Business Sch., M.B.A. 1951; m. Andrea Vaillancourt 15 Dec. 1990; children from previous marriage: Michael, Christopher, Lois Mary, Andrew; joined Calvin Bullock, Ltd., Montreal in 1951; Pres. & Managing Dir. 1972–84; Vice-Chrmn. until retiring in 1987; Sr. Officer, Canadian Investment Fund, Ltd. for 30 years, Pres. and Dir. 1984 until retiring in 1987; served with Brit. Army 1943–46; commd. Lt. in Scots Guards 1944; served in N.W. Europe and occupation of Germany; served on various Montreal area Sch., Ch. and Club Bds. and Comtes.; Past Chrmn., Investment Funds Inst. of Canada; Former Regent Candn. Inst. of Financial Planning; Anglican; recreations: skiing, sailing, racquets; Clubs: University; Montreal Racket; Home: Le Chateau, Apt. E50, 1321 Sherbrooke St. W., Montreal, Que. H3G 1J4.

**PUTNAM, Rev. Max,** D.D. (Presb.); minister; b. Smiths Falls, Ont. 12 Jan. 1920; s. Hope Chiles and Lucy Olivia (Robinson) P.; e. Smiths Falls (Ont.) Secondary Schs.; McGill Conservatory (vocal); Univ. of W. Ont.; Knox Theol. Coll., Hon. D.D.; Moderator, Presb. Church in Can. 1972–73; served in World War II, five years, R.C.E.M.E. in Can., Eng., N.W. Europe; P. Conservative; Address: Christian Retreat Renfrew, RR 6, Renfrew, Ont. K7V 3Z9.

**PUTNAM, Robert Garth,** B.A., B.Ed., M.A.; educator; author; b. Toronto, Ont. 7 March 1937; s. Donald Fulton and Jean Lucille (Wiles P.; e. Oakville Trafalgar High Sch. 1955; Univ of Toronto B.A. 1959, B.Ed. 1973; Univ of Ga. M.A. 1961; m. Barbara Jane d. Robert and Inez Cruise 8 July 1961; children: Lori Christine, Donald Robert; PRINCIPAL, WESTERN TECHNICAL COMMERCIAL SCH. 1988– ; Lectr. in Geog. Univ. of Waterloo 1961; Teacher and Head of Geog. Oakwood Coll. Inst. Toronto 1962–72; Vice Prin. Northern Secondary Sch. Toronto 1972–78, Bickford Park High Sch. 1979–80; Principal, Parkdale Coll. Inst. 1980–88; Lectr. in Geog. Univ. of Toronto 1964–87; Bd. Dirs. Ont. Secondary Sch. Prin.'s Council 1979–87, Chairperson 1985–86; Mem., OSSTF Rsch. Ctte., 1987–93 (Chairperson 1989–92); co-author: 'A Geography of Urban Places' 1970; 'Pollution: the Effluence of Affluence' 1971; 'Canada: A Regional Analysis' 1970, metric ed. 1979; 'The Industrial Geography of Canada' 1984; Trustee, Central Un. Ch. Weston; Home: 134 King St., Weston, Ont. M9N 1L5; Office: 125 Evelyn Cres., Toronto, Ont. M6P 3E3.

**PUTNAM, Robert Wayne,** B.A., M.D.; b. Truro, N.S. 7 Feb. 1944; s. Robert Edmund and Phyllis (Barnhill) P.; e. Truro elem. and high schs. 1961; Mount Allison Univ. B.A. 1964; Dalhousie Univ. M.D. 1969; M. Joan Joyce Ervin 26 Dec. 1968; children: Kimberley, Lorian, Stefan; ASSOC. DEAN FOR ADMISSIONS AND STUDENT AFFAIRS 1989– ; Asst. Dean and Dir. Continuing Med. Educ., Dalhousie Univ. 1977–89; private practice Fredericton, N.B. 1969–75; Asst. Dir. Div. Continuing Med. Educ. Dalhousie 1975, Acting Dir. 1977; mem. Med. Soc. N.S.; Coll. Family Phys. Can.; Standing Comte. on Admissions and Student Affairs, Assn. Candn. Med. Colls.; Soc. of Medical Coll. Dir. of Continuing Med. Educ.; United Church; recreations: music, skiing; Home: 6429 Norwood St., Halifax, N.S. B3H 2L4; Office: Rm C-23, CRC Bldg., Dalhousie Univ., Halifax N.S. B3H 4H7.

**PUTTOCK, Nigel W.,** M.A., P.Eng.; manufacturer; b. Horsham, Eng. 27 Jan. 1927; s. late Eric C. and Mary W. P.; e. Oundle Sch., Northamptonshire, Eng.; Clare Coll., Cambridge Univ., M.A.; m. Barbara Ann, d. late A. J. C. Arley Bugler, Horsham, Eng., 1949; children: Roger Nigel Arley, Shirley Mary, Pamela Jane, Carol Ann; CHRMN., BYTEX INTERNAT. SERVICES LTD.; Dir., Candn. Assn. of Home Builders; Salesman, Transparent Paper Ltd., Eng., 1948; Gen. Mgr., Tubular Case & Carton Co. Ltd., 1949; Gen. Mgr., Flexible Packaging Ltd., 1950; Gen. Mgr., Flexible Packaging Div., Metal Box Co. Ltd., Eng., 1954; Production Mgr., Ont. Plant, Transparent Paper Products Ltd., Toronto, 1957; Extve. Vice Pres., Montreal, 1957; Gen. Mgr., Interstate Building Products Ltd., Hamilton, 1958; Asst. to Pres., Western Gypsum Products Ltd., Winnipeg, 1959; Extve. Vice Pres. 1960; Pres., Western Gypsum Products Ltd., Toronto, 1963; Pres., Westroc Ind. Ltd.; Chrmn. and Pres., Barringham Plastics Ltd.; Blue Diamond Transport Rentals Ltd.; Perlite Ind. Ltd.; Wesco Paints Ltd.; Western Gypsum Ltd.; Westroc Building Components Ltd.; served with RAF and RAF Vol. Reserve 1946–54; Fellow, Inst. Dirs. (U.K.); mem., Assn. Prof. Engrs. Ont.; recreations: sailing, tennis, music; Clubs: Oakville; Devonshire (London, Eng.); Home: 70 Navy St., Oakville, Ont. L6J 2Y9.

**PUXLEY, Rev. Canon Herbert Lavallin,** M.A., L.Th., D.D., D.C.L., D.Litt. (Ang.); retired univ. president b. Goring-on-Thames, England, 6 Nov. 1907; s. Herbert and Kate P.; e. Eton Coll. (Capt. of Oppidans, Chairman of Eton Soc., etc.); Brasenose Coll., Oxford (Heath Harrison Exhibitioner, Bible Clerk, etc.), B.A. (Hons.) 1929, M.A. 1934; Commonwealth Fund Fellow, Yale Univ. (1929–32), M.A. 1931; Trinity Coll., Toronto, Ont., L.Th. 1948, Hon. D.D. 1955; D.C.L. Acadia 1962; D.D. King's 1963; Wycliffe 1966; D.Litt St. Mary's (Halifax) 1965; m. Mary Robertson, d. Mr. Justice Geo. H. Sedgewick, Toronto, Ont., 22 June 1932 (Diamond Wedding Anniversary 22 June 1992); children: Mary, Peter, David; Canon, All Saints Cath., Halifax, N.S.; o. Deacon, Dec. 1947, and Priest, May 1948; Prof. of Econ., St. John's Coll., Agra, India, 1932–40; incumbent of Roches Point, Ont., 1947–49; Gen. Secy., Student Christian Movement of Can., 1949–53; Asst. Secy., Candn. Council of Churches (Dept. of Overseas Missions & Evangelism), 1953–4; Pres., Univ. of King's College, 1954–63; Dir., Canadian School of Missions and Ecumenical Institute 1963–73; retired 1973; Chairman Ecumenical Study Commission on Religion in Public Education; served in 2nd World War; Comnd. in Indian Army, Nov. 1940; retired as Lieut.-Col., 1946; Publications: 'Critique of the Gold Standard' 1933; 'Agricultural Marketing in Agra District' 1935; 'Christian Land Settlements' 1941; numerous articles in 'Indian Economic Journal,' 'Asia,' etc.; Chaplain, Order of St. Lazarus of Jerusalem 1967; Knight Commander, 1970; Religion in Public Education 1969–73; Home: 45 Dahlia St., Dartmouth, N.S. B3A 2S1.

**PYATT, Alan,** B.Sc.; executive; b. Somerset, Eng. 1 Apr. 1942; s. Edward Alan and Ada Emily (Reddecliffe) P.; e. King's Coll. Durham B.Sc. (Chem. Eng.) 1964; m. Gwendoline d. Joseph and Elsie Bunney 17 May 1965; two s. David, Andrew; PRES., CHIEF EXTVE. OFFR. AND DIR., SANDWELL INC. 1986– ; Asst. Div. Eng. Bowater Paper Corp. Eng. 1964–65; Plant Metall. Anglo-American Corp. Kitwe, Zambia 1965–69; Dept. Supt. Canadian Electrolytic Zinc Ltd. Qué. 1969–72; Prodn. Mgr. Michelin Tire Corp. Clermont-Ferrand, France 1972–73; Vice Pres. Mining & Metall. The SNC Group Montréal 1973–81, Vice Pres. Eng. 1983–86; Sr. Vice Pres. Operations, Hudson Bay Mining and Smelting Co. Ltd. Toronto 1981–83; mem. Candn. Inst. Mining & Metall.; Inst. Mining & Metall. UK; Candn. Pulp & Paper Assn.; Inst. Corporate Dirs. Can.; recreations: photography, cabinetry, boating; Club: Vancouver (B.C.); Ontario (Toronto); Home: 4666 West 2nd Ave., Vancouver, B.C. V6R 1L1; Office: Corporate Park Place, 666 Burrard St., Vancouver, B.C. V6C 2X8.

**PYLE, Alan J.,** B.A., M.B.A.; financial executive; b. Toronto, Ont. 27 Aug. 1946; s. Donald Graham and Mary Christine (Shaughnessy) P.; e. Stanford Bus. Sch. M.B.A.; University of Toronto B.A. (Hons.); children: Ryan, Colin; EXTVE. VICE-PRES., NORTH AMERICAN TRUST 1986– ; Dir., First City Realty Investments Ltd.; First City Realty Investment Corp.; Portland Lakes Devel.; Systems Analyst, IBM Canada 1970–71; Finan. Analyst, Traders Group 1972–73; various positions, the last being Sr. Vice-Pres., Real Estate Div., Mercantile Bank of Can. 1973–86; Rep. Canada in 1967, 1971 Pan-American games & 1972 Olympics in Water Polo; Past Dir., Candn. Water Polo Assn.; recreations: triathlons, squash, swimming; clubs: Cambridge, Granite; Home: 91 Walmsley Blvd., Toronto, Ont. M4V 1X7; Office: 151 Yonge St., Toronto, Ont. M5C 2W7.

**PYNN, Garfield Allan,** B.Com., M.B.A.; educator; b. Grand Falls, Nfld. 11 Dec. 1940; s. Stephen and Clara P.; e. Grand Falls Acad. 1957; Meml. Univ. of Nfld. B.Com. 1965; Univ. of W. Ont. M.B.A. 1969; m. Margaret d. James and Marie Keough 12 June 1981; children: Robert, Stephen; Full Professor, Memorial Univ. of Nfld. 1978–91; Chrmn. of Bd., Newfoundland Hardwoods Ltd.; joined Bank of Montreal 1957–68 becoming Br. Mgr.; Dupont of Canada Ltd. Montreal 1968; Asst. Prof. Sch. of Business present Univ. 1969, Assoc. Prof. and Dir. 1974–78, Acting Dean 1982–83; served as Edn. Dir., St. John's Bd. Trade; mem., Prov. Govt. Fishing Ind. Adv. Bd.; Mem. Bd. of Dirs., National Entrepreneurship Develop. Inst.; Dir., Atlantic Entrepreneurial Inst.; Mem. Bd. of Dirs., St. John's Home Care; mem., Bd. of Women's Enterprise Bureau; mem., Consultative Group Social Sci. & Humanities Rsch. Council on Rsch. in Candn. Business Schs.; Chrmn., Grad. Scholarship Ctte. Assn. Univ. & Colls. Can. 4 Yrs.; Founding Dir., Intnl. Council for Small Business-Can., Pres.; mem., Royal Comn. Health Care Costs; Chrmn., Study Renumeration Levels Mems. House of Assembly Nfld. 1980 and 1989; recreations: woodworking, barbershop harmony, sports; Home: 43 Pine Bud Ave., St. John's Nfld. A1B 1M6; Office: Elizabeth Ave., St. John's, Nfld. A1C 5S7.

# Q

**QADEER, Mohammad A.,** Ph.D.; educator; b. Lahore, Pakistan 24 Feb. 1935; s. Shamas ud din and Maqbool Begum; e. Univ. of Punjab B.Sc. 1953, M.A. 1959, M.S. 1963; Univ. of R.I. M.C.P. 1966; Columbia Univ. Ph.D. 1971; m. Susan d. Harry Silver 18 March 1970; children: Nadra, Ahmer, Ali; PROF. SCH. URBAN AND REGIONAL PLANNING QUEEN'S UNIV. 1978– , Assoc. Prof. 1971–77, Dir. of Sch. 1986; Exec. Sec. Family Planning Assn. Pakistan 1959; taught sociol. Univ. of Punjab and later mem. founding faculty Dept. of Town Planning, Engineering Univ. Lahore; came to Canada 1971; cons. numerous local, provl. and fed. agencies; served UN panels and undertaken UNDP consultancy misssions; Visiting Scholar/Lectr. Cambridge and Sheffield Univs.; recipient Fulbright Travel Fellowship 1964–65; William Kinney Fellowship Columbia 1969; Peter Nash Award achievements internat. planning 1988; author 'Urban Development in the Third World' 1983; 'The Evolving Urban Land Tenure System in Canada' 1985; 'Canadian Towns and Villages: An Economic Profile 1981' 1986; co-author 'Towns and Villages in Canada' 1983; assoc. ed. 'Plan Canada' 1976–81; Home: 800 Johnson St., Kingston, Ont. K7L 2B5; Office: Kingston, Ont. K7L 3N6.

**QIATSUK, Lukta;** artist; b. 14 March 1928; s. Kiakshuk (a well-known sculptor); m. Pudloo; son: Pootogook; medium: sculpture, drawings, prints, printmaking; 33 group exbns. incl. most recent: The McMichael Candn. Art Coll. Kleinburg, Ont. 1991–92, Inuit Gall. of Vancouver 1990, Feheley Fine Arts Toronto 1990, Candn. Mus. of Civilization Hull, Que. 1990, Orca Aart Chicago, Ill. 1989; works in 18 collections incl. art galleries of London Region, Ontario (Klamer Family & Sarick colls.), Winnipeg (Lindsay & Swartz and Swinton colls.), Canada Council Art Bank, Candn. Mus. of Civilization, GE Canada, Inuit Cultural Inst. Rankin Inlet, N.W.T., Nat. Gallery of Can., Royal Ontario Museum, Smith College Mus. of Art, Northampton, Ma.; assisted in making the mace of the N.W.T. 1955; attended opening of 'Cape Dorset Printmaking 1959–1989' McMichael Candn. Coll. 1989; subject of several articles and catalogues; Home: Cape Dorset, N.W.T.; Office: c/o Dorset Fine Arts, 33 Belmont St., Toronto, Ont. M5R 1P9.

**QUAIFE, Darlene Barry,** M.A.; writer; b. Calgary, Alta. 1 Sept. 1948; d. Clifford Nelson and Elsie Violet (Cole) Barry; e. Univ. of Calgary B.A. (honours) 1975; Univ. of Alta. M.A. 1986; m. Ron s. Thomas and Flora Quaife 12 Sept. 1970; Instr. in Creative Writing, Journalism and Lit. Univ. of Calgary 1977– ; Instr. in Creative Writing, Lit. and Composition Mount Royal Coll. Calgary 1978– ; novelist, poet, short story and freelance writer periodicals, newspapers, media, pub. relations; freelance ed.; author: 'Bone Bird' (novel) 1989; recipient, The Commonwealth Writers Prize (Best first book in the Canada/Caribbean region) 1989; author: 'Days & Nights on the Amazon' (novel) 1994; mem. Writers' Union of Can.; Internat. P.E.N.; Glenbow Museum; BraggArts Theatre Soc.; Writers Guild Alta.

(Exec. Bd. 1989–90); recreations: hiking, mountain climbing, running, kayaking, skiing; Address: c/o Turnstone Press, 607 - 100 Arthur St., Winnipeg, Man. R3B 1H3.

**QUALTER, Terence Hall,** Ph.D.; educator; b. Eltham, N.Z. 15 Apl. 1925; s. Michael Frederick and Kathleen Mary (Hall) Q.; e. Univ. of N.Z. B.A. 1951; London Sch. of Econ., Univ. of London Ph.D. 1956; m. Shirley Anne d. late John Alfred Card, Masterton, N.Z. 19 May 1951; children: Karen Anne, Matthew John, Paul Michael, Adam James; Prof. of Pol. Science, Univ. of Waterloo 1967; Lectr. Un. Coll. Winnipeg 1957–58; Special Lectr. Univ. of Sask. 1958–60; Lectr. in Pol. Science present Univ. 1960, Asst. Prof. 1961, Assoc. Prof. 1964, Chrmn. of Pol. Science 1965–67, 1970–73; author 'Propaganda and Psychological Warfare' 1962; 'The Election Process in Canada' 1970; 'Graham Wallas and the Great Society' 1980; 'Opinion Control in the Democracies' 1985; 'Conflicting Political Ideas in Liberal Democracies' 1986; 'Advertising and Democracy in the Mass Age' 1991; numerous articles pol. science; served with Royal N.Z. Air Force 1944–46; R. Catholic; recreation: travel; Home: 249 Stoneybrook Dr., Kitchener, Ont. N2M 4M1; Office: Dept. of Political Science, Univ. of Waterloo, Waterloo, Ont. N2L 3G1.

**QUARRINGTON, Glenn Austin,** C.H.R.P.; human resources executive; b. Toronto, Ont. 15 Nov. 1949; s. Austin Noel and Dorothy Florence (Ceauette) Q.; e. Vincent Massey C.I.; Trent Univ.; Sr. Vice-Pres., Human Resources, EnRoute Card Internat. Inc. 1991; Personnel Mgr., Montreal Trust Co. 1972–74; var. positions ending as Corp. Personnel Mgr., Dylex Ltd. 1974–78; Dir. of Employee Relations, McDonald's Restaurants of Canada Ltd. 1978–81; Vice-Pres., Human Resources, Royal LePage Limited 1981–91; Pres. & Bd. Chairperson, Human Resources Professionals Assn. of Ont.; Mem., Human Resources Mngt. Adv. Ctte., Ryerson Sch. of Business Management; Mem., General Arts & Sci. Advisory Ctte., George Brown Coll.; recreations: audiophile, squash; Home: 3430 Peel St., Suite 12A, Montreal, Que. H3A 2K8.

**QUARRINGTON, Paul Lewis;** writer; b. Toronto, Ont. 22 July 1953; s. Bruce Joseph and Mary Ormiston (Lewis) Q.; e. Victoria Park Secondary Sch. 1971; Univ. of Toronto 1972–73; author (novels) 'The Service' 1978; 'Home Game' 1983; 'The Life of Hope' 1985; (play) 'The Second' 1981 (performed 25th St. Theatre, Saskatoon 1982); 'King Leary' 1987; 'Hometown Heroes' 1988; 'Whale Music' 1989 (Winner of Governor General's Award for Fiction, 1990); (play) 'The Invention of Poetry' (performed Candn. Stage, Toronto; Citadel Theatre, Edmonton) 1989; (play) 'The Invention of Poetry' published 1990; 'Logan In Overtime' (novel) 1990; 'Camilla' (screenplay) 1993; co-author: (with Eugene Lipinski) 'Perfectly Normal' 1990; (with Gregory Dummett) 'Giant Steps' (screenplay) 1992; (with Richard Jay Lewis) 'Home Game' (screenplay) 1993; co-produced & recorded LP 'Quarrington/Worthy' 1978; performed (bass) on LP's and live engagements with Rock Band 'Joe Hall and the Continental Drift'; named one of Can.'s top 10 writers under forty-five 1986; Periodical Distrib. of Canada Authors Award (Canada's Most Promising New Writer) 1986; Winner, Stephen Leacock Award for Humour 1987; recipient Genie Award, Best Original Screenplay for 'Perfectly Normal' 1991; National Magazine Award for Humour 1993; mem. Scarborough Fly & Bait Casting Assn.; Trout Unlimited; recreations: fishing, swimming, running; Home: 150 First Ave., Toronto, Ont. M4M 1X1.

**QUART, Robert D.,** B.Com.; credit union executive; b. Quebec City, Que. 4 Feb. 1942; s. Harry D. and Therese D. (Dagneau) Q.; e. St. Patrick's High Sch. Quebec City; Univ. of Ottawa B.Com. 1965; m. Louise d. Alexandre Coulombe 25 Sept. 1965; two d. Valerie, Jennifer; CHIEF EXEC. OFFR. VANCOUVER CITY SAVINGS CREDIT UNION 1988– ; Chrmn. & Dir., Citizens' Trust Company; Vice-Chrmn. & Dir., Ethical Funds Inc.; Dir., VanCity Insurance Services; Group Supr. Group Ins. London Life Insurance Co. 1965–67; Pension Trust Offr. Montreal Trust 1967, Dir. of Funds 1973, Mgr. Vancouver Br. 1976, Regional Vice Pres. W. Region 1980, Vice Pres. Br. Operations H.O. 1981–82; Pres. Wicklow West Holdings 1982–85; Vice Pres. Trust, Vancouver City Savings Credit Union 1985–88; Dir. St. Vincent's Health Care Society; Dir., Candn. Club of Vancouver; mem. Bd. Trade Vancouver; Clubs: Vancouver; Arbutus; Home: 72 – 5531 Cornwall Dr., Richmond, B.C. V7C 5N7; Office: 515 West 10th Ave., Vancouver, B.C. V5Z 4A8.

**QUIGLEY, Maureen A.,** B.A., M.Sc.; planning & policy consultant; b. Hamilton, Ont. 8 May 1950; d. Dr.

Gerard John and Florence Mary (Murphy) Q.; e. Univ. of Toronto, St. Michael's Coll. B.A. 1972; London Sch. of Econ. M.Sc. 1974; m. T. Patrick s. John M. & Ena M. R.; children: Aislinn Elizabeth, Kyla Patricia; PRES., MAUREEN QUIGLEY & ASSOC. 1986– ; Policy Analyst, Prov. Secretariat for Soc. Devel., Govt. of Ont. 1974–78; Dir., Policy & Planning, Metro. Toronto Dept. of Community Serv. 1978–84; Policy Advisor to Chrmn., Mun. of Metro. Toronto 1984–86; consultant to both private & public sector clients spec. in faciliation of strategic planning & project mngt.; Nat. Inst. of Nutrition; Public Policy Adv. Ctte.; Lectr., Fac. of Med., Univ. of Toronto; Mem., Inst. of Public Admin. of Can.; Inst. of Health Serv. Mngt. (U.K.); Pres. Comn. on Future of Health Care, Univ. of Toronto 1990; Trustee, Hosp. for Sick Children 1988– ; Mem. Bd. of Dirs., Regional Geriatric Program of Metro Toronto 1993– (Chair 1994); Dir., Sr. People's Resources in N. Toronto 1984–92 (Pres. 1989–90); Dir., Sancta Maria House 1984–88; Mem., Inst. of Public Admin. of Can.; author: 'Citizen Participation in Development in the City of Toronto' 1971; recreations: skiing, walking; club: Royal Candn. Yacht; Home: 19 Colin Ave., Toronto, Ont. M5P 2B6; Office: 1881 Yonge St., Suite 600, Toronto, Ont. M4S 1Y6.

**QUILICO, Gino,** O.C.; baritone; b. New York City, N.Y. 29 Apr. 1955; s. Louis and Carolina (Pizzolongo) Q.; e. Univ. of Toronto Dip. in Operatic Performance 1978; m. Kathryn d. Hugh and Judith Stephenson 3 May 1980; children: Enrico, Sofia; Candn. opera debut 'The Medium' (Mr. Gobineau) Toronto 1978; Am. debut 'The Magic Flute' (Papageno) Milwaukee 1978; joined The Paris Opera 1980–83 playing various operatic roles; Covent Garden debut 1983 'Faust,' 'Elisir d'Amore,' 'Barber of Seville,' 'Boheme,' 'Carmen'; twice toured S. Korea and Japan; also performed in Vienna, Venice, Rome, Florence, Bologna, Geneva, Lyon, Nice, Toulouse, Philadelphia, Washington, San Francisco, Dallas, Montréal, Toronto, Bonn, Munich, Cologne, Berlin, Hamburg, Buenos Aires, Edinburgh Festival, Aix-en-Province Festival; Salzburg Festival; Metropolitan Opera debut 'Manon' (Lescant) 1987, that same year he sang with his father, Louis Quilico (Manon) making history at the Met as the first father and son to ever appear together; performed World Premiere 'Montsegur' 1985; performed World Premiere 'Ghosts of Versailles' at Metropolitan Opera 1991; 'Orfeo' (Orfeo) feature film; 'Boheme' (Marcello) feature film; sixteen recordings with EMI, DGB, ERATO etc.; also twelve operatic videos; named 'Artist of the Year' by Candn. Music Council 1988; Canada's first Goodwill Ambassador to the U.N.H.C.R. 1990; Officer, Order of Canada 1993; recreations: wood carving, oil painting, tennis.

**QUILICO, Louis,** C.C. (1975); opera singer; b. Montreal, Que. 14 Jan. 1929; s. Louis and Geanne (Gravel) Q.; e. Mannes Coll. of Music, New York City; Conservatoire de Musique du Québec à Montréal; Conservatorio di Musica 'Santa Cecilia' Rome, Italy; m. 1stly: the late Carolina Pizzolongo 29 Oct. 1949; 2 children: Donna Maria, Gino; m. 2ndly: Christina Petrowska 30 Nov. 1993; PRINCIPAL BARITONE AND STAR OF THE METROPOLITAN OPERA CO. New York City; Prof. of Music Univ. of Toronto; mem. Paris Opera Co. Paris, France; Covent Garden, London, Eng.; Candn. Opera Co., Toronto, Ont.; Bolshoi Opera, Moscow; Rome Opera, Italy; Colon Opera, Buenos Aires; Mexico Opera; New York City Opera; rec'd Centennial Medal 1967; R. Catholic; recreations: photography, model building; Address: 31 Claver Ave., Toronto, Ont. M6B 2V7.

**QUINN, Frank,** B.A., M.A., Ph.D.; federal public servant; b. Toronto, Ont. 1 Sept. 1939; s. Oliver A. and Marie G. (Haddow) Q.; e. St. Michael's Coll., Univ. of Toronto B.A. 1962; Univ. of Washington M.A. 1965, Ph.D. 1970; m. Deede d. Theodore and Dorothy Murnane 1967; children: Timothy, Dorothy; WATER POLICY ADVISOR, ENVIRONMENT CANADA 1986– ; Water Planner, Energy Mines & Resources 1968–71; Project Mgr., Nat. Water Needs Study 1972–73; Head, Social Impacts, Water Mngt. Branch, Envir. Canada 1974–83; Dir. of Rsch., Inquiry on Federal Water Policy 1984–85; Reg. Dir., Am. Water Resources Assn. 1978–80; Ont. V.P., Candn. Water Resources Assn. 1982; Assoc. Ed., 'Can. Water Resources Journal' 1976–85; Candn. Rep., Natural Resources Mngt. Group, OECD 1987–89; Instructor, Univ. of Arizona 1965–66; Sessional Lecturer in Geog., Univ. of W. Ont. Fall 1973; Univ. of Ottawa Winter 1987, '90; Univ. of Victoria summer 1987, '94; Adjunct Prof., Nat. Resources Mngt., Simon Fraser Univ. 1989–93; co-author: 'Water Diversion and Export: Learning from Canadian Experience' 1992; author of 35 papers & reports on water

mngt. & policy; recreations: sports, travel, classical & jazz music; Home: 4 Leacock Dr., Kanata, Ont. K2K 1R8; Office: Ottawa, Ont. K1A 0H3.

**QUINN, Gordon James,** B.A.; business executive; b. Estevan, Sask. 14 Nov. 1934; s. James Gordon and Myrtle (Paul) Q.; e. Notre Dame Coll. Wilcox, Sask.; Univ. of Ottawa B.A. 1957; m. Bea Osborne 17 Aug. 1990; children: Traci, Leslie, Doug; FOUNDER, PRES. AND CHIEF EXEC. OFFR. QUINN'S OILFIELD SUPPLY LTD. 1965– ; Pres. Q-Bar Equipment Ltd.; Can West Oil Tool Ltd.; Pembina Pump Ltd.; Dir. Parkland Industries; Drummond Brewing Ltd.; joined Continental Emsco Co. Ltd. 1957–65; named Small Bus. Person of Yr. 1984; Gov. Red Deer Coll. 1977–80; Pres. Red Deer C. of C. 1977–78; recreation: golf; Club: Red Deer Golf & Country (Pres. 1975, 1990); Address: P.O. Box 846, Red Deer, Alta. T4N 5H2.

**QUINN, Terry J.,** B.Comm.; business executive; b. Quebec City, Que. 7 Feb. 1942; s. Sarsfield Patrick and Nora (Lyons) Q.; e. St Patrick's H.S. 1960; St Francis Xavier Univ., B.Comm. 1964; m. Micheline d. Paul Godbout 22 Aug. 1964; children: Michael, Paul, Nathalie; PRES. & CHIEF OPERATING OFFR., NSK-RHP CANADA INC. 1994– ; Sales, Prod. & Mktg. positions, CIL 1964–74; Dir., Sales & Mktg., Fulmen Inc. 1974–81; Vice-Pres., Imperial Mfg. 1981–82; Gen. Mgr., Groupe IPA 1982–88; Pres. & Dir., RHP Can. Inc. 1988–93; Pres. & Dir., Albion Bearing Co. Ltd.; Pres. & Dir., Candn. Soccer Assn.; Dir., British Candn. Trade Assoc.; Mem., Auto. Indus. Assn. of Can. (Chrmn. of Bd. 1984–85; Dir. 1981–86); Br. Candn. Trade Assn.; Bearing Specialists Assn.; Power Transmission Distrib. Assn.; recreations: sports; club: Mount Stephen; Home: Trelawny Circle, Mississauga, Ont.; Office: 5585 McAdam Rd., Mississauga, Ont. L4Z 1N4.

**QUINTIN, Clark Gil,** B.Comm.; marketing executive; b. Calgary, Alta. 6 Nov. 1953; s. Ronald and Blanche (Reid) Q.; e. Univ. of Calgary B.Comm. 1975; m. Joan d. Dr. Bruce Hunter 5 July 1975; one d.: Megan; VICE-PRES. & GENERAL MANAGER, WESTERN CANADA, IBM CANADA LTD. 1990– ; Systems Engr., IBM Canada 1975; held marketing positions in data processing div.; marketing mngt. positions in Vancouver, Toronto & Calgary incl. Branch Mgr., IBM's Calgary Br. 1984–86; participant in company's mngt. acceleration program N.Y. 1987; Admin. Asst. to Chairman & Chief Extve. Offr., IBM Corp. 1987–88; Marketing Operations Mgr., IBM Central/Atlantic Region 1988; Mem. Extve. Ctte., Bd. of Gov., Business Council of B.C.; The Fraser Inst.; Vancouver Bd. of Trade; Jr. Achievement; Simon Fraser Univ. President's Club; Dir., ISM Information Systems Management (B.C.) Corp. and ISM Information Systems Management (Alberta) Corp.; recreations: skiing, sailing, reading; Home: 5333 Westhaven Wynd, West Vancouver, B.C. V7W 3E8; Office: 701 West Georgia St., Vancouver, B.C. V7Y 1G1.

# R

**RAAPHORST, G. Peter,** B.Sc., M.Sc., Ph.D., F.C.C.P.M.; medical physicist; university professor; b. Holland 8 Sept. 1946; s. B.C. and G.A. (Lekkerkerker) R.; e. Univ. of Waterloo, B.Sc. 1972, M.Sc. 1974, Ph.D. 1976; m. Ginette Bourque; children: Marc, Philip; HEAD, MED. PHYSICS DEPT., OTTAWA REG. CANCER CTR., PROF. OF PHYSICS, CARLETON UNIV. & PROF. OF RADIOL., UNIV. OF OTTAWA 1985– ; involved in clin. radiotherapy, physics & rsch.; Principal Investigator, Radiobiol. Rsch. Prog., Ottawa Reg. Cancer Ctr.; Allied Sci. Staff, Dept. of Radiol., Ottawa Civic Hosp. and Ottawa Gen. Hosp.; Office: Med. Physics Dept., Ottawa Reg. Cancer Ctr., 190 Melrose Ave., Ottawa, Ont. K1Y 4K7.

**RABEAU, Yves,** B.A., M.Com., Ph.D.; educator; economist; b. Montréal, Qué. 15 Aug. 1941; s. Yvon and Fernande (Fauvel) R.; e. Coll. André Grasset B.A. 1962; Ecole des Hautes Etudes Commerciales M.Com. 1965 (Médaille du lieutenant-gouverneur du Qué. 1965); Mass. Inst. of Technol. Ph.D. 1970; m. Suzanne d. Dr. Jean Grenier 1966; children: Marie-Claude, Pascale; PROF. OF ADM. SCI'S UNIV. DU QUÉ. à MONTRÉAL 1989– ; Pres. Econobec Inc.; Asst. and Assoc. Prof. Ecole des Hautes Etudes Commerciales 1969–74; Assoc. and full Prof. of Econ. Univ. de Montréal 1975–89; Cons. various Royal Comns.: incl. Wage & Prices 1976, Kent 1981, McDonald 1984–85, govt. depts., private enterprise, various orgns. author various books, reports, jour. articles; mem. Qué. C. of C. (Econ. Adv.);

Qué. Forecasting Group; Candn. Econ. Assn.; Am. Econ. Assn.; recreations: skiing, tennis, hiking, cycling; Home: 1437 Boul. Mont-Royal, Outremont, Qué. H2V 2J5; Office: P.O. Box 6192 Succ. A, Montréal, Qué. H3C 4R2.

**RABIN, Cedric,** B.Sc.; investment counsellor; b. London, U.K. 9 Jan. 1937; s. David and Fanny (Mindel) R.; e. Univ. of S. Carolina, B.Sc. 1958; Georgetown Univ. 1958–59; State Univ. of N.Y. 1961–63; m. Judith A. d. William and Lila Faux 16 Dec. 1967; children: M. Jeffrey, Adrienne D.; VICE-PRES. & DIR., ALTAMIRA MANAGEMENT LTD. 1988– ; Lectr., Econ. Laurentian Univ. 1959–60; Portfolio Mgr., Royal Trust Co. 1964–71; Vice-Pres., Equities, Internat. Trust Co. 1971–74; Cominco, Vancouver 1974–76; Treas., Am. Internat. Group 1976–77; Extve. Vice-Pres. & Dir., E.J. McConnell & Assoc. 1977–85; Partner, Rabin, Budden Partners (Investments) 1985–88; Clubs: Albany; Royal Canadian Military Inst.; Home: 245 Rosedale Heights Dr., Toronto, Ont. M4T 1C7 and 4651 Gulfshore Blvd. N., Naples, FL 33940.

**RABINOVITCH, Robert,** B.Comm., M.A., Ph.D.; b. Montreal, Que. 1 Mar. 1943; s. Samuel and Esther R.; e. McGill Univ. B.Comm. Econ. 1964; Univ. of Pa., Wharton Sch. of Fin. M.A. 1965; Univ. of Pa. Ph.D. Econ. and Fin. 1971; m. Cecil Ainslie d. John and Jessie Eileen Nelson 8 Aug. 1971; children: Rebecca, Jonathan; EXTVE. VICE PRES. & C.O.O., CLARIDGE INC., Montreal 1990– ; Bd. of Dirs., Cineplex Odeon Inc.; CBCI Telecom Inc.; Prime Restaurants Group; Instr. Econ. and Fin., Univ. of Pa. 1966–68; Econ. Dept. of Fin. Canada 1968; Special Asst. Dept. of Secy. of State 1968–71; Offr. Privy Counc. Office 1971–74; Dir. Gen. Social Policy and Prog., Dept. of Communications 1974–76; Asst. Secy. to the Cabinet (Social Policy, Priorities and Planning) Privy Counc. Office 1976–79; Sr. Asst. Secy. to Inner Cabinet, Privy Counc. Office 1979; Sr. Asst. Secy. to Cabinet (Priorities and Planning) 1979; Depy. Secy. to the Cabinet (Plans), Privy Counc. Office 1979–82; Depy. Min. of Communications 1982–85; mem. Adv. Ctte. Order of Canada 1985–86; Under Secy. of State, Secretary of State Dept. 1985–86; Sr. Vice Pres., Claridge Inc., Montreal 1987–90; recreations: cultural events, skiing, squash; Club: M.A.A.A.; Home: 596 Victoria Ave., Westmount, Que. H3Y 2R9; Office: 1170 Peel St., Montreal, Que. H3B 4P2.

**RABINOWITCH, David George,** B.A., R.C.A.; b. Toronto, Ont. 6 March 1943; s. Joseph and Ruthe Calverley R.; e. Richmond Hill (Ont.) Pub. and High Schs., 1963; Univ. of W. Ont., B.A. (Eng.) 1966; one-man shows incl. Pollock Gallery, Toronto, 1968; 20/20 Gallery, London, Ont., 1968; Carmen Lamanna Gallery, Toronto 1969–84; Joseph Helman Gallery, St. Louis 1971; Gallery Rolf Ricke, Cologne 1971–74; Bykert Gallery, N.Y. 1973, 1975; Ronald Greenberg Gallery, St. Louis 1974, 1990; Diane Stimson Gallery, Vancouver 1973; Galleriaforma, Genoa, 1974, 1975; Daniel Weinberg Gallery, San Francisco 1974, 1978; Franco Toselli, Milan 1975; Museum Wiesbaden, 1975; Clocktower, N.Y., 1976; Hetzler-Keller, Stuttgart, 1975–78; Texas Gallery, Houston 1975, 1978; Galleria la Polena, Genoa, 1977; Haus Lange Museum, Krefeld, 1978; Galerie M, Bochum, 1977–90; Annemarie Verna, Zurich, 1977–93; Richard Bellamy Gallery (Oil and Steel) N.Y. 1978–93; Museum voor Hedendaagse Kunst, Gent, Belgium 1978; Galerie Mailhot, Montreal, 1979; Haus Ester Museum, Krefeld, 1987; Kunsthalle Tübingen, 1987; Kunsthalle Bielefeld, 1988; Kunstmuseum Düsseldorf, 1988; Flynn Gall., N.Y. 1989–93; Galerie nächst St. Stephan, Vienna 1990; Galerie Renos Xippas, Paris 1991–93; Kunsthalle Baden-Baden 1992; Galerie Nationale du Jeu de Paume, Paris 1993; Peter Blum, N.Y. 1993; Group shows include: 20/20 Gallery, London, 1967, 1970; Can. Trust Show with David Mirvish Gallery, Toronto 1968; Pollock Gallery, Toronto 1968; Nat. Gallery of Can. 1968, 1984, 1987; Art Gallery of Ont. 1968, 1969, 1970, 1971, 1973–74, 1978–80, 1985; Carmen Lamanna Gallery, Toronto 1969–83; La Jolla Museum of Contemporary Art, La Jolla, 1971; Ringling Museum of Art, Sarasota, 1971; Joseph Helman, St. Louis 1972–73; Yale Univ. Art Museum, 1973, 1976; Hetzler Keller, Stuttgart 1975–78; Richard Bellamy Gallery (Oil and Steel), N.Y. 1978, 1981–87; Staatsgalerie, Stuttgart 1974; Kunsthalle, Cologne 1974; Wallraf-Richartz Museum, Cologne 1974; Staedtisches Museum, Leverkusen 1975; Bykert Gallery, N.Y. 1975–76; 'PS1,' N.Y. 1976, 1978; Museum of Fine Arts, Montreal 1976, 1984, 1986, 1991; Kunstverein Stuttgart, 1976; 'Forum Metall' Linz, Austria 1977; 'Documenta' VI, VII and VIII, Kassel 1977, 1982, 1987; Westfaelisches Landesmuseum, Muenster 1977; Museum of Modern Art, Paris 1970, 1972, 1977, 1982, 1991; Museum of Modern Art, N.Y. 1977, 1979; Cologne Art Fair 1977, 1986, 1988–89; Bologna Art Fair 1977; 'Z.B. Skulptur,' Kunstinstitut Frankfurt, 1978; Harbourfront Art Gallery, 1979, 1981; 'Intnl. Sculpture of the 20th Century' Basel 1980; Haus Lange Museum, Krefeld 1980, 1985, 1989; Arte Verso, Genoa 1980; Margo Leavin, Los Angeles 1981; 'Construction in Process' and Museum Sztuki, Lodz, Poland 1981; Galerie m, Bochum 1980–92; Flow-Ace Gallery, Los Angeles 1983, 1989; Museum Wiesbaden 1984; Musée d'art Contemporain de Montreal 1985, 1986, 1989; Werkstatt Kollerschlag, Austria 1985–90; Kunsthalle Bremen 1985; Skulpturenmuseum, Marl 1986; Museum Ludwig, Cologne 1986; 49th Parallel, N.Y. 1987; Zeitlos, W. Berlin 1988; Kröller-Müller Museum, Otterlo 1988; Kunstverein, Braunschweig 1989; Museum Haus Esters, Krefeld 1989; '256 Colors & Basics on Form,' Kunstmuseum, Zürich 1989; 'Einleuchten,' Deichtorhallen, Hamburg 1989–90; Galerie Ricke, Kunstverein Cologne 1989; Galerie nächst St. Stephan, Vienna 1989, 1990; 'Situation Kunst,' Haus-Weitmar, Bochum 1990; Muzeum Historii Miasta, Lodz 1990; Staatsgalerie Moderner Kunst, Munich 1990; Kunstmuseum Düsseldorf; Galerie Pierre Huber, Geneva 1991; 'Détente: Czechoslovakian and International Art' Dum Kmeni, Brno; Art-Centre Zacheta, Warsaw 1991–93; 'Schwerpunkt Skulptur' Kaiser-Wilhelm Museum, Krefeld 1992; Kunstmuseum Winterthur; Knoll Gallery, Budapest; Guggenheim Fellow 1975; Lynch-Staunton Award of Distinction, Canada Council 1977; National Endowment for the Arts 1986–87; mem. Faculty, Yale Univ. 1974–75; Prof. of Sculpture, Staatliche Kunstakademie Düsseldorf 1984– ; Artist's statements published in: 'Heart of London' Art Gallery of Ont., 1968; 'Project '74' Kunsthalle, Cologne, 1974; 'Skira Art International' 1979; 'Structures for Behaviour' (Art Gall. Ont.) 1978; 'Ten Canadian Artists' (Art Gall. Ont.) 1980; 'International Sculpture of the 20th Century' catalogue (Basel) 1980; 'David Rabinowitch, Skulpturen' (Museum Haus Lange, Krefeld) 1978; 'Documenta VII & VIII Catalogs' 1982, 1987; 'David Rabinowitch: The Ottonian Construction of Vision Drawings' Kaiser Wilhelm Museum, Krefeld 1987; 'David Rabinowitch, Sculptures, 1963–70' Karl Kerber Verlag, Bielefeld, 1987; 'David Rabinowitch' Kunsthalle Tübingen, 1987; 'David Rabinowitch: Sculpture for Max Imdahl,' Flynn and Oil & Steel, New York 1990; 'Rolf Ricke,' Walther König, Cologne 1990; 'David Rabinowitch: The Gravitational Vehicles,' Galerie Nächst St. Stephan, Vienna and Galerie Renos Xippas, Paris 1991; 'Parkett,' Zürich 1991; 'Arts Magazine' 1991; 'Artforum,' New York 1991; 'Blast,' New York 1991; 'Das Kunstwerk,' Stuttgart 1991; 'Détente,' Brno, Warsaw, Vienna 1991; 'Alberto Giacometti,' Musée d'Art Moderne de la Ville de Paris 1991; 'David Rabinowitch: Werke 1967–76' Staatliche Kunsthalle Baden-Baden 1992; 'David Rabinowitch: Drawings of a Tree, 1972–79' Richter 1993; 'David Rabinowitch: The Collinasca Cycle' Peter Blum 1993; 'Kunst und Kirche' Darmstadt 1993; Studio: 49 East 1st St., New York, N.Y. 10003.

**RABINOWITCH, Royden L.;** sculptor; b. Toronto, Ont. 6 Mar. 1943; s. Joseph and Ruthe Elizabeth (Calverley) R.; e. Univ. of W. Ont. Coll. of Mus.; Royal Conservatory of Mus., Toronto; m. Elizabeth d. Anne and Edgar Ewart 25 Sept. 1973; recent solo exhns.: The Clocktower, N.Y.C.; John Weber Gall., N.Y.C.; David Bellman Gall., Toronto; Museum van Hedendaagse Kunst, Gent, Belgium; Städtisches Museum Abteiberg Mönchengladbach, West Germany; Oliver Dowling Gall., Dublin; Fabian Carlsson Gall., London, Engl.; Orchard Gall., Londonderry, N. Ireland; Furkapasshöhe, The Alps, Switzerland; Krzysztofory Museum, Krakow, Poland; Muzeum Akademii Sztuk Pieknych, Warsaw, Poland (with Joseph Beuys); Galerie Media, Neuchatel, Switzerland; Foksal Gallery, Warsaw, Poland; Peter Pakesch Gallery, Vienna, Austria; Museum Sztuki, Lodz, Poland; Atelier del Sur, La Gomera, Canary Islands; Kuntsmuseum Bern, Switzerland; Wiener Secession, Vienna, Austria; Haags Gemeentemuseum, The Hague, Netherlands; Haus für konstructive und konkrete Kunst, Zürich, Switzerland; Neue Galerie, Kassel, Germany (with Per Kirkeby); recent group shows: 'American Drawing in Black & White 1970–80,' Brooklyn Mus., N.Y.C.; 'New York Drawing' The Aldrich Museum of Contemporary Art, Ridgefield, CT, USA; 'Richard Long, Royden Rabinowitch, Lawrence Weiner,' David Bellman Gall., Toronto; 'Drawings for Sculptures,' Seagram Bldg., N.Y.C., Montreal Mus. of Fine Art, Vancouver Art Gall.; 'Peace Gifts: Joseph Beuys/Richard Long/Royden Rabinowitch/Lawrence Weiner,' Clare Coll., Cambridge Univ., U.K.; 'Works in European Collections,' Gulbenkian Museum, Lisbon, Portugal; 'Spuren, Skulpturen und Monumente ihrer präzisen Reise,' Kunsthaus Zürich, Switzerland; 'Eye Level,' Stedelijk van Abbemuseum, Eindhoven, Netherlands; 'De Sculptura' Wiener Festwochen, Vienna, Austria; 'Chambre d'Amis' Museum van Hedendaagse Kunst, Gent, Belgium; 'Bodenskulptur,' Kunsthalle Bremen, West Germany; 'Skulptur Sein' Städtische Kunsthalle Düsseldorf, W. Germany; 'Idea of North,' 49th Parallel Gall., N.Y.C.; 'Joseph Beuys & Royden Rabinowitch: Works in the Museum Sztuki w Lodzi Collection'; 'Zeitlos,' Berlin, W. Germany; 'Poesis,' Kunstmuseum Bern, Switzerland; 'Open Mind,' Musuem van Hedendaagse Kunst, Gent, Belgium; 'Einleuchten' Deichtorhallen, Hamburg, Germany; '60th Anniversary Exhibition of ther Muzeum Sztuki, Lodz' Muzeum Sztuki, Lodz, Poland; 'Platz Verführung – Klassische Beispiele' Stuttgart and Environs, Germany; 'Documenta 9' Kassel, Germany; 'Maximal/Minimal,' Museum van Hedendaagse Kunst, Gent, Belgium; 'Lyon-Lodz,' Musée d'Art Contemporain de Lyon, France; 'Het Koninklijk Paleis,' Kunsthal Rotterdam, Netherlands; 'GAS' Bordeaux, France; 'Acquisitions 1987–1992,' Museum van Hedendaagse Kunst, Gent, Belgium; 1$^{ere}$ Triennale des Ameriques-Présence en Europe 1945/92' Maubeuge, France; 'De la main à la tête, l'object theorique' Domaine de Kerquehennec, Centre d'Art Contemporain, Lochminé, France; selected collections: National Gall. of Can., Ottawa; Museé d'Art Contemporain, Montreal; Montreal Mus. of Fine Art, Montreal; Art Gall. of Ont., Toronto; London Regional Art Gall., London, Ont.; Australian National Gall., Canberra; Aldrich Museum of Contemporary Art, Ridgefield, CT; Joseph Seagrams and Sons Inc., N.Y.C.; Ludwig Museum, Köln, W. Germany; Museum Sztuki, Lodz, Poland; Museum van Hedendaagse Kunst, Gent, Belgium; Städtisches Museum Abteiberg Mönchengladbach, W. Germay; Panza di Biumo Coll., Varese, Italy; Rozelle Museum, Ayr, Scotland; Sarabhai Family, Ahmedabad, India; Muzeum Akademii Sztuk Pieknych, Warsaw, Poland; Ulster Mus., Belfast, N. Ireland; Kunsthaus Zürich, Switzerland; Municipal Gall. of Modern Art, Dublin, Ireland; Toronto Convention Centr, Toronto; Canada Council, Ottawa; Collection Furkapasshöhe, Switzerland; Fitzwilliam Mus., Cambridge, U.K.; Stedelijk van Abbemuseum, Eindhoven, Netherlands; Nationalgalerie Berlin, W. Germany; Haags Gemeentemuseum, The Hague, Netherlands; Kunstmuseum Bern, Switzerland; Sammlung Friedrichshof, Austria; FRAC, Lille, France; Wiener Secession, Vienna, Austria; Foksal Gallery, Warsaw, Poland; Neue Galerie, Kassel, Germany; Kornwestheim Museum, Germany; Museum of Calais, France; Stedelijk Museum, Amsterdam; commissions: 'Rotation and Translation of the Top' 1983, Sarabhai Family, Ahmedabad, India; 'Eloges de Fontenelle' 1984 Toronto Convention Centre; 'Faith in Whole Bodies – Bell in Name Only' 1986, Museum van Hedendaagse Kunst, Gent, Belgium (under construction); 'Three Rolled Conic Surfaces Applied to a Region of Curved Space Maintaining Local and Somatic Descriptions' 1987, Furkapasshöhe, The Alps, Switzerland; 'Tomb of Dr. Josef Hoet' 1987, Gent, Belgium; 'Handed Surfaces Appled to Two Lily Ponds,' Haags Gemeentemuseum, Netherlands (under construction); Kornwestheim Train Station, Germany; recent publs. on sculpture: 'Development of the Early Sculptures Leading to the Most Recent Sculptures' 1983; 'Barrel Constructions of Royden Rabinowitch' (by David Bellman) 1983; 'Drawings by Sculptors: Two Decades of Non-Objective Art in the Seagram Collection' (by David Bellman) 1983; 'Royden Rabinowitch – Sculptures and Drawings in the Collection' (by Jan Hoet, Museum of Hedendaagse Kunst, Gent, Belgium) 1983; 'Royden Rabinowitch' (by Dr. Johannes Cladders, Städtisches Museum Abteiberg Mönchengladbach, W. Germany) 1984; 'Exhibition - Dialogue' Modern Art Centre, Calouste Gulbenkian Found., Lisbon, Portugal (text: Jan Hoet) 1985; 'Spuren, Skulpturen und Monumente ihrer prazisen Reise' Kunsthaus, Zurich, Switzerland (by Harald Szeemann) 1985; 'Eye Level' Stedelijk van Abbemuseum, Eindhoven, Netherlands (by R.H. Fuchs) 1986; 'De Sculptura' Wiener Festwochen, Vienna (by Harald Szeemann) 1986; 'Bodenskulptur' Kunsthalle Bremen, Germany (by Siegfried Salzmann) 1986; 'Chambres d'Amis' Museum van Hededaagse Kunst, Gent, Belgium (by Jan Hoet) 1986; 'Skulptur Sein' Städtische Kunsthalle Düsseldorf, Germany (by Harald Szeemann) 1986; 'Die Sammlung Ludwig' Museum Ludwig, Köln, Germany (by Karl Ruhrberg) 1986; 'Royden Rabinowitch, Sculpture – Body' Galerie Krzysztofory, Krakow, Poland (by Jaromir Jedlinski) 1987; 'Royden Rabinowitch – Works in Polish Collections' Muzeum Sztuki, Lodz, Poland (by Jaromir Jedlinski) 1987; 'Lesson of Emanuel Feuermann III, 1986 – 7 Manifolds in 10 Locations with Varied Handed Additions, 1987' Galerie Krzysztofory, Krakow, Poland (by Jaromir Jedlinski) 1987; 'Joseph Beuys & Royden Rabinowitch – Works in the Collection of the Muzeum Sztuki, Lodz' Museum Akademii Sztuki Pieknych, Warsaw, Poland (by Jaromir Jedlinski) 1988; 'Zeitlos' Hamburger Bahnhof, Berlin, Germany (by Harald Szeemann) 1988; 'Royden Rabinowitch' Galerie Foksal,

Warsaw, Poland (by Wieslaw Borowski) 1988; 'Open Mind' Museum van Hedendaagse Kunst, Gent, Belgium (by Jan Hoet) 1989; 'Einleuchten' Deichtorhallen, Hamburg, Germany (by Harald Szeemann) 1989; 'Royden Rabinowitch – Skulpturen 1990' Kuntsmuseum Bern, Switzerland (by Hans Christoph von Tavel) 1990; 'Who Ordered This?' Atelier del Sur, La Gomera, Canary Islands (by Jan Hoet) 1990; 'Royden Rabinowitch – Wiener Secession' Vienna, Austria (by Adolf Krischanitz) 1991; 'Platz Verfuhrung – Klassische Beispiele' Stuttgart, Germany (by R.H. Fuchs) 1992; 'Documenta 9' Kassel, Germany (by Jan Hoet) 1992; 'Lyon-Lodz,' Musée d'Art Contemporain de Lyon, France (by Jaromir Jedlinski) 1992; 'Royden Rabinowitch, Sculpture 1962–1992' Haags Gemeentemuseum, The Hague, Netherlands (by Rudi Fuchs) 1992; 'GAS' Bordeaux, France (by Harald Szeemann) 1993; 'Royden Rabinowitch, Sculpture and Drawing 1992/1993' Haus für konstruktive und konkrete Kunst, Zurich, Switzerland (by Elisabeth Grossman and Rudi Fuchs) 1993; Chrmn. of Fine Art, Ont. Coll. of Art, Toronto 1973–74; Lectr., Yale Univ.; Royal Coll. of Art, London, U.K.; St. Andrew's Univ., Scotland; Cambridge Univ., U.K.; el. Visiting Assoc. 1983–84 and Visiting Fellow 1984–85 and Life Mem. 1986 of Clare Hall, Cambridge Univ., U.K.; awarded five consecutive Can. Counc. Arts Grants; seven consecutive Can. Counc. Sr. Arts Grants; 'Lynch-Stanton' Can. Counc. Award for very distinguished artists 1986; recreation: history and philosophy of science; Address: Jan Verspeyenstraat 15, B-9000 Gent, Belgium.

**RABOY, Marc,** Ph.D.; journalist; educator; b. Baltimore, Md. 17 Feb. 1948; s. Samuel and Alice (Baum) R.; e. McGill Univ. B.Sc. 1968, M.A. 1981, Ph.D. 1986; m. Sheilagh d.Ernest and Marjorie Hodgins 17 Dec. 1983; one s. Sean Michael; PROF. OF COMMUNICATION, UNIV. OF MONTREAL 1993– ; profl. journalist 1969–77, journalist in alternative media since 1969; Lectr. in French Can. Studies McGill Univ. 1981–83; Lectr. in Journalism Concordia Univ. 1980–86; Assoc. Prof. of Journalism and Pub. Communication, Laval Univ. 1986–93; contract rsch. NHK (Japan Broadcasting Corp.), Broadcasting Culture Rsch. Inst. and L'institut québécois de recherche sur la culture; recipient rsch. grants Social Sci's & Humanities Rsch. Council Can.; Co-organizer internat. conf. 'Media and Crisis' Quebec 1990; author 'Libérer la communication: Médias et mouvements sociaux au Québec 1960–1980' 1982; 'Movements and Messages: Media and Radical Politics in Quebec' 1984; 'Missed Opportunities: The Story of Canada's Broadcasting Policy' 1990; 'Les médias québécois: presse, radio, télévision, câblodistribution' 1992; ed. 'Old Passions New Visions: Social Movements and Political Activism in Quebec' 1986; co-ed. 'Communication For and Against Democracy' 1989; 'Media, Crisis and Democracy: Mass Communication and the Disruption of Social Order' 1992; ed. bd. Candn. Jour. Communication; mem. Internat. Assn. for Mass Communication Rsch.; Union for Democratic Communication; Institut canadien d'éducation des adultes; Candn. Communication Assn. (Bd. mem. 1988–90); Assn. Candn. Journalists; Fédn. professionnelle des journalistes du Qué.; Home: 749 Antonine-Maillet, Outremont, Qué. H2V 2Y4; Office: Box 6128, Station A, Montreal, Qué. H3C 3J7.

**RABY, Gyllian,** M.A.; artistic director; playwright; b. Shropshire, Wales 7 March 1959; d. Edward Keith and Dorothy (Eastwood) R.; e. Malvern Girls' Coll.; Hanley Castle High Sch.; Manchester Univ. B.A. 1980; Univ. of Calgary M.A. 1982; m. Nigel s. Gerald and Beryl Scott 1983; children: Xavier, Nellie-Zoë; Artistic Dir., Northern Light Theatre 1988; Founding Artistic Dir. One Yellow Rabbit Performance Theatre 1982, Co-Artistic Dir. 1984; Asst. Prof. of Eng./Drama Univ. of Man. 1983–84; freelance dir. and sessional instr. Univ. of Calgary 1985–87; mem. Theatre Working Ctte. Calgary Winter Olympics 1988; mem. Alta. Coalition Against Pornography; E.M. Media, Video Art Gallery; Alta. Conf. for Theatre 1987–88; recreation: hiking, reading; Home: 10192 – 87 St., Edmonton, Alta. T5H 1N5.

**RACE, David Humphrey,** B.Eng., P.Eng.; electronics executive; b. Darlington, England 22 Mar. 1929; e. Queen Elizabeth I G.S.; McGill Univ., B. Eng. 1957; m. Janet Struthers 15 Sept. 1953; one s.: David Andrew; CHRMN. & CHRMN. OF THE EXTVE. CTTE., CAE INC. 1993– ; Engr. Mgr., Candn. Aviation Electronics Ltd. 1957–65; Mgr., Missiles & Space Systems Engr., Canadair Ltd. 1965–69; Pres., CAE Aircraft Ltd. 1969–77; Vice Pres., Opns., CAE Indus. Ltd. 1977–84; Extve. Vice-Pres., CAE Industries Ltd. 1984–85; Pres. & Chief Extve. Offr., CAE Inc. 1985–93; Dir., CAE Inc.; Dir., The Bank of Nova Scotia; Dir., Genstar Capital Corp.; Trustee, The Fraser Inst.; recreations: sailing; Clubs: National, Manitoba; Home: 47 Valecrest Dr., Islington, Ont.; Office: Commerce Court West, Suite 5300, P.O. Box 85, Toronto, Ont. M5L 1B9.

**RACHLIS, Michael,** M.D., M.Sc., FRCP(C); community medicine physician, private health policy consultant; b. Winnipeg, Man. 4 Oct. 1951; s. Harry Lion and Ruth R.; e. Univ. of Manitoba M.D. 1975; McMaster Univ. M.Sc. 1988; Staff Physician, South Riverdale Community Health Ctr. 1976–84; Res. in Community Med., McMaster Univ. 1984–88; Asst. Prof., McMaster Univ. (part-time) 1988– ; Staff Physician, Hassle Free Clinic (part-time) 1988– ; private consultant in health policy; Mem., Edit. Bd. 'Iatrogenics'; Mem., Consultative Ctte. on Chronic Disease Control, Health & Welfare Can.; co-author: 'Second Opinion: What's Wrong with Canada's Health Care System and How to Fix It' 1989; Fellow, Royal Coll. of Phys. & Surg. 1988; Address: 13 Langley Ave., Toronto, Ont. M4K 1B4.

**RACICOT, Pierre,** B.A., B.Sc.; b. Montréal, Qué. 17 Aug. 1939; s. Georges and Beatrice (Vezina) R.; e. Coll. St-Viateur, B.A. 1959; Univ. de Montréal, B.Sc. (Hons.) 1962; m. Elizabeth d. Frances and Reginald Wallace 21 Sept. 1968; one child: Ling Jie; VICE-PRES., AMERICAS BRANCH, CANADIAN INTERNATIONAL DEVELOPMENT AGENCY 1993– ; Prof. of Math., Coll. St-Viateur 1962–65; Tunisia 1965–67; Proj. Offr., External Aid Office 1967–69; First Sec. (Devel.), Candn. Embassy, Dakar 1969–72; Prog. Admin., CIDA 1972–74; Analyst, Treas. Bd. 1974; Dep. Dir., Spec. Prog., Manpower & Immigration 1975; Couns. (Devel.), Candn. Embassy, Abidjan 1976–77; Beijing 1984, 1985; Vice-Pres., Francophone Africa Branch, Candn. Int. Devel. Agency, 1985–89, Vice-Pres., Anglophone Africa Branch 1989–91, Vice-Pres., Africa and Middle-East Branch 1991–93; Reg. Dir., CIDA 1978–80; Dir., Off. of V.P., Bilateral Prog. 1980–82; Dir. Gen., Policy Coord. 1983–84; recreations: golf, sailing; Home: 109 chemin des Capucines, Hull; Office: 200 Promenade du Portage, Hull, Qué. K1A 0G4.

**RACINE, André,** B.A., F.C.A.S., F.I.C.A., A.S.A.; actuary, insurance executive; b. Rimouski, Que. 20 May 1954; s. Lucien and Lucile (Bertin) R.; e. Univ. Laval B.A.; m. Diane d. Alexandre and Monique Landry 6 Sept. 1980; children: Pierre-Luc, Benoît; PRESIDENT AND CHIEF OPERATING OFFICER, THE NATIONAL REINSURANCE CO. OF CANADA 1992– ; Actuarial Analyst, Sobeco Consulting Group 1974–79; Insurer's Advisory Orgn. 1979–80; Actuarial Mgr., Le Groupe Desjardins Assur. Gén. 1980–84; Insur. Vice-Pres. 1984–88; Consultant, Tillinghast (opened Montreal office of multinat. actuarial cons. firm) 1988–90; Extve. Vice-Pres., The Nat. Reinsur. Co. of Can. 1990–91; Dir. & Pres., Reinsurance Mngt. Co. of Can. Inc.; Gestas Inc.; Office: 1140 de Maisonneuve Blvd. W., Montreal, Que. H3A 1M8.

**RACINE, Jacques,** B.A., L.Th., B.Sc.Soc.; educator; b. Québec, Qué. 17 Dec. 1941; s. Henri and Thérèse (Pelletier) R.; e. Univ. Laval B.A. 1961, L.Th. 1965, B.Sc.Soc. 1969; VICE-RECTEUR EXÉCUTIF DE L'UNIVERSITÉ LAVAL 1989– ; Prof. present Univ. 1970–72, 1977– , Vice Dean of Theol. 1979–82, Dean of Theol. 1982–89; mem. Bd. Govs.; Superior, Grand Séminaire de Qué. 1972–77; mem. Ministry Ctte., Assemblée des évêques du Québec; membre du Conseil supérieur de l'éducation du Québec; Prés. de la Commission de l'enseignement supérieur du Conseil supérieur de l'éducation du Qué.; author 'Idéologies au Canada français 1938–39' 1978; 'Situation du catholicisme québécois' 1982; recreation: tennis; Home: 161, rue Aberdeen, Québec, Qué. G1R 2C9; Office: Bureau 1634, Pavillon des sciences de l'éducation, Université Laval, Québec, Qué. G1K 7P4.

**RACINE, Yolande,** B.A., M.F.A.; curator and art historian; b. Montréal, Qué. 29 Feb. 1948; d. Jacques and Simonne (Legault) R.; e. Coll. Jean-de-Brébeuf Montréal, B.A. 1969; Univ. de Montréal, B.F.A. (Hist. Art) 1972, M.F.A. 1980; children: Marianne, Simon; HEAD OF MULTI-MEDIA CREATIONS, MUSÉE D'ART CONTEMPORAIN DE MONTRÉAL 1993– ; Researcher, Musée Ferme Saint-Gabriel, Montréal 1971; Pre-archivist art hist. documentation Cegep Vieux-Montréal 1972, Pedagogical cons. Fine Arts Dept. 1978; Head of Edn., Animation & Communications Dept. Musée d'art contemporain de Montréal, 1973–74, Curator 1978–82; Curator of Contemporary Art, Montreal Museum of Fine Arts 1982–92; Teacher, Faculty of Fine Arts and Faculty of History of Art, Concordia Univ. 1992–94; Curator, Musée d'Art Contemporain de Montréal 1993; Freelance Researcher, 1975–76; study trip Asia, Middle E. and N. Africa 1977; mem. Jury, Can. Council Ottawa, Ministère des Affaires culturelles Qué. and others; author 'Avant-scène de l'imaginaire/Theatre of the Imagination' 1984; 'Betty Goodwin: oeuvres de 1971 à 1987/Works from 1971–1987' 1987; co-author 'L'Architecture traditionnelle,' 'Le mobilier traditionnel,' 'L'orfèvrerie traditionnelle,' 'Les instruments d'artisanat' 1973; 'Albert Dumouchel, rétrospective de l'oeuvre gravé' 1974; 'Tendances actuelles au Québec' 1980; 'Le monde selon Graff' 1987; Contributor to 'The Dictionary of Art' London, Eng. 1988; for the Betty Goodwin exhbn.: Award of Excellence 1988, presentation category, Candn. Museums Assoc., Special Mention 1988, Société des musées québécois; for the Betty Goodwin catalogue: Award of Excellence 1988, Am. Federation of Arts; mem. Société des musées québécois; Candn. Museums Assoc.; Internat. Council Museums; Home: 4193 Ave West Hill, Montréal, Qué. H4B 2S8; Office: 185 rue Sainte-Catherine Ouest, Montréal, Qué. H2X 1Z8.

**RACKUS, George Keistutis;** painter; print-maker; muralist; b. Kalvarija, Lithuania 29 May 1927; s. George and Anna (Kildušytė) Račkauskas; e. Wayne State Univ. 1948–50; Ont. Coll. of Art 1951–52; Ecole des beaux arts (France) 1953–56; Acad. de Andre L'Hote (France) 1953–56; m. Denise d. Denis and Kathleen Moritz 21 July 1962; children: David Keistutis, Philip Claudejus; 1st major Candn. exhib., Galerie Agnes Lefort Montreal 1960, followed by Picture Loan Soc. Toronto 1960, Gallery Moos 1962, Commonwealth Inst. Art Gall., London, U.K. 1970, New Brunswick Museum, N.B. 1973, Atlantic Provinces Art Circuit 1972–73, Grimsby Art Gall. Ont. 1986, Vilnius Fine Arts Museum, Lithuania 1988, Lithuanian Art Circuit 1988–89 (50 one-man exhibs. to date in Eur. & N. Am.); group exhibs. incl. Can. Painter-Etcher & Engravers Soc., Can. Graphic Soc., Ont. Soc. of Artists, Colour & Form Soc., Can. National Art Gall. Australian tour 1967–68 and more recently, 5 Can. Artists Exhib. Warsaw & Pultusk, Poland 1989 on tour 1989–90, Internat. Exhibs. Vilnius Fine Arts Museum 1990 (toured Lithuania through 1990); Kariya, Japan 1990; major & public collections incl.: Nat. Gall. of Can., Art Gall. of Ontario, Ciurlionis Galerija Chicago, Victoria & Albert Museum London, Vilnius Fine Arts Museum, and many others; developed the anodizing of aluminum as an art form; conducted a Candn. Art Workshop Group & Exhibit, Academia Das Artes, Azores 1990; producer of video & film documentaries; author: 'CFS' documentary 1992; art teaching includes Dundas Valley School of Art, Six Nations Indian Reserve Brantford, McMaster Univ. Hamilton, Brock Univ. St. Catharines; listed in Ont. Index of Can. Artists; Who's Who in American Art; mem., Ont. Soc. of Artists; Colour and Form Soc. (administrator); Mississauga Arts Council; Art Gall. of Ont. (artist life mem.); recreations: scuba diving, sailing; Studio: 1998 Lakeshore Rd. W., Mississuaga, Ont. L5J 1J8.

**RADCHUCK, Robert Paul,** B.Sc., P.Eng., F.C.A.; chartered accountant; b. Stewiacke, N.S. 1 May 1941; e. Dalhousie Univ. B.Sc. 1962; Technical Univ. of N.S. P.Eng. 1964; C.A. Quebec 1967; C.A. N.S. 1975; m. Irene Szuler 10 Feb. 1979; children: Paul, Katherine; MANAGING PARTNER, ATLANTIC REGION, KPMG MANAGEMENT CONSULTING 1993– ; C.A. Student & C.A., Clarkson Gordon 1964–73; Financial Officer, Brascan Internat. Trading Ltd. 1973–75; Management Consultant, KPMG Management Consulting (then Thorne Riddell Assoc.) 1975–79; joined Peat Marwick Thorne (then Thorne Riddell) 1979; Partner 1979; Financial Cons., Union of N.S. Municipalities; Partner-in-Charge, Adv. Serv., Halifax; Managing Partner, Halifax, Peat Marwick Thorne 1982–93; elected Fellow of Inst. 1991; Chair, Voluntary Planning & Past Chair, Bd. of Gov., Art Gallery of N.S.; Past Chair, Bd. of Advisors, AIESEC Dalhousie Univ.; Past Pres., Halifax Bd. of Trade; Mem., N.S. Roundtable on the Environ. & the Econ.; Mem., Inst. of C.A.s of N.S. & Que.; Inst. of Public Admin. of Canada; Assn. of Profl. Engrs. of N.S.; Candn. Owners & Pilots Assn.; author/co-author/editor of num. articles for business & profl. pubns.; recreations: skiing, golf, flying; clubs: Halifax, Halifax Bd. of Trade, Waegwoltic, Saraguay; Home: 6661 South St., Halifax, N.S. B3H 1V4; Office: Suite 1600, 1959 Upper Water St., Halifax, N.S. B3J 3N2.

**RADDALL, Thomas Head,** O.C. (1970), LL.D., D.Litt., D.C.L., F.R.S.C.; author; b. Hythe, Kent, Eng. 13 Nov. 1903; s. Lt.-Col. Thomas Head, Sr., D.S.O. (Winnipeg Rifles, killed in action 1918) and Ellen (Gifford) R.; e. St. Leonard's Sch., Hythe, Eng.; Chebucto Sch., Halifax, N.S.; Halifax Acad.; Dalhousie Univ., LL.D. 1949; m. Edith Margaret, d. Frederick Freeman, Milton, N.S., 9 June 1927; children: Thomas, Frances; served as Bookkeeper for a N.S. pulp mill, 1923–27; Clerk, constr. co., 1928; Acct., newsprint paper mill, 1929–38; served as Wireless Offr. on various R.N. transport vessels and later Candn. Merchant Marine and E. Coast wireless stns., 1918–22; Lieut., Reserve Army, 1942–43; winner of Gov.-Gen's. Award for Candn. Lit., 1944, 48 and 57; awarded Lorne Pierce Medal by Roy. Soc. Can. for outstanding contrib. to Candn. Lit., 1956; Fellowship, Haliburton Soc., King's Coll., N.S., 1945; author 'Pied Piper of Dipper Creek' 1939; 'His Majesty's Yankees' 1942; 'Roger Sudden' 1944; 'Tambour' 1945; 'Pride's Fancy' 1946; 'The Wedding Gift and Other Stories' 1947; 'History of West Nova Scotia Regiment' 1948; 'Halifax, Warden of the North' 1948; 'The Nymph and The Lamp' 1950; 'Tidefall' 1953; 'A Muster of Arms' 1954; 'The Wings of Night' 1956; 'The Path of Destiny' 1957; 'The Rover' 1958; 'The Governor's Lady' 1959; 'Hangman's Beach' 1966; 'Footsteps On Old Floors' 1968; 'In My Time' (autobiog.) 1976; 'The Mersey Story' 1979; 'The Dreamers' 1986; mem., Queens Co. Hist. Soc.; N.S. Hist. Soc.; Candn. Hist. Assn.; Royal Candn. Legion (Past Pres. Queen's Br.); Officer, Order of Canada 1970; Canadian Literature Medal, Univ. of Alberta 1977; Award of Merit for Literary Excellence, City of Halifax; Honorary Degrees: St. Mary's Univ. D.Litt. 1969; Univ. of Kings College D.C.L. 1972; St. Francis Xavier Univ. D.Litt. 1973; United Church; Home: 44 Park St., Liverpool, N.S. B0T 1K0.

**RADFORTH, Norman William,** M.A., Ph.D., F.R.S.C. (1959); palaeobotanist; organic terrain consultant; b. Barrow-in-Furness, Lancs., Eng., 22 Sept. 1912; s. Walter Joseph and Kate Emma (Langley) R.; e. Primary Schs., Eng. and Can.; Univ. of Toronto, B.A. 1936, M.A. 1937; Glasgow Univ., Ph.D. 1939; m. Isobel, d. Dr. Milton H. Limbert, Parry Sound, Ont., 30 June 1939; children: John Robert, Janice Langley; CONSULTANT, RADFORTH & ASSOC., since 1977 and Hon. Research Assoc., Univ of N.B.; Prof. and Head, Dept. of Botany, McMaster Univ. 1946–51, Chrmn. Dept. Biology, 1960–66; Chrmn. Organic and Associated Terrain Research Unit there 1963–68; Prof. and Head Dept. of Biol. and Dir., Muskeg Research Inst., Univ. of N.B. 1968–77; Chrmn. Subcomte. on Muskeg, Assoc. Comte. on Geotech. Research, Nat. Research Council, 1948–75; Dir., Roy. Bot. Gardens, Hamilton, Ont., 1946–53; Demonst., Glasgow Univ., 1937–39; Roy. Soc. of Can. Research Fellow, 1938–39; Special Lect., McMaster Univ. 1939–40; Lect. Univ. of Toronto, 1940–41; Prof. and Dir. Muskeg Research Inst., Univ. of N.B., 1970–77; Hon. Ed., Journal of Terramechanics; Past Pres., Internat. Soc. for Terrain Vehicle Systems; has written prof. papers on bot. and palaeobot. topics and on terrain interpretation (muskeg); Protestant; recreation: oil painting; Address: Parry Sound, Ont. P2A 2W9.

**RADLER, Franklin David,** B.Com., M.B.A.; publisher; b. Montreal, Que. 3 June 1942; e. Queen's Univ. M.B.A. 1967; m. Rona Beverley Lassner 26 March 1972; children: Melanie, Melissa; PRES. CHIEF OPERATING OFFR. & DIR., HOLLINGER INC.; The Ravelston Corp. Ltd.; Dominion Malting Ltd.; Chrmn., American Publishing Co.; Slumber Lodge Development Corp. Ltd.; Valley Cable TV; Fort Langley Legacy Found.; Pres., Argcen Inc.; Sterling Newspapers Ltd.; Extve. Vice Pres. and Dir., Argus Corp. Ltd.; Dir., La Société UniMedia (1980) Inc.; The Daily Telegraph plc; Insurance Corp. of British Columbia; Century 21 Real Estate Canada Ltd.; Guy F. Atkinson Holdings Ltd.; The Canadian Press; Sugra Ltd.; Saturday Night Magazine Inc.; Cayman Free Press Ltd.; mem. Candn. Press; Candn. Daily Newspaper Publishers Assn.; Young Pres. Organ.; Adv. Bd., Fac. of Business, Memorial Univ. of Nfld.; Home: 2146 S.W. Marine Drive, Vancouver, B.C.; Office: 1827 West 5th Ave., Vancouver, B.C. V6J 1P5.

**RADU, (Robert) Kenneth,** B.A., M.A.; college teacher; b. Windsor, Ont. 4 Jan. 1945; s. John and Anna (Corches) R.; e. Runnymede C.I. 1964; Victoria Coll., Univ. of Toronto, B.A. (Hons.) 1970; Univ. of Waterloo, M.A. 1973; Dalhousie Univ., doctoral student 1973–75; m. Diane d. Roy and Edna Hibbard 21 June 1968; children: Joshua, Eryn, Tristan; TEACHER (PROFESSEUR), DEPT. OF ENGLISH, JOHN ABBOTT COLLEGE 1975– ; part-time lectr. in English, Loyola Coll. 1975–76; Concordia Univ.1977–79; Ed., 'Matrix'; Dir.-Gen., 'Matrix' Pubs. Soc.; Prov. of Ont. Grad. Fellowships 1970–72; Izaak Walton Killam Grad. Scholarship 1974, 1975; author: 'Distant Relations' 1989 (novel; winner, 1989 QSpell Prize for Fiction; nominated for the 1990 Books in Canada/W.H. Smith First Novel Award); 'The Cost of Living' 1987 (short stories; nom. for 1988 Gov.-Gen.'s Award for Fiction); 'Letter to a Distant Father' 1987 (poetry collection); 'A Private Performance' 1990 (short stories; winner of 1991 QSPELL Prize for Fiction); 'Treading Water' 1992 (poetry); 'Home Fires' 1992 (novel); recreations: swimming, gardening, biking, reading, piano; Home: 206 Ch-Sen-neville, Senneville, Que. H9X 3L2; Office: John Abbott College, C.P. 2000, Ste-Anne de Bellevue, Que. H9X 3L9.

**RADULOVICH, Mary-Lou Fox,** B.A.; arts executive; b. Whitefish Lake Reserve, Ont. 1935; e. Espanola H.S.; Laurentian Univ. B.A.; Fac. of Education, Fed. Indian College Sask. working on M.Ed.; m. Steven R.; one s.: Steven; CO-FOUNDER & DIRECTOR, OJIBWE CULTURAL FOUNDATION 1974– ; Teacher, Espanola, Sault Ste Marie, Wikwemikong Reserve, Elliot Lake (primary school); Ont. Training School for Girls, Galt; Manitoulin Island H.S. (initiated and taught Native studies); counsellor to Native students; Founding Mem., Manitoulin Indisn Studies Ctte. (founded to develop Native curriculum material for primary schools on 5 Island reserves); Indian Edn. Cons., DIAND, Manitowaning, Manitoulin Island; Eagle Feather from Cree elders; apptd. to Nat. Ctte. on the Status of Women 1982; Outstanding Adventurer Award, Zonta Club One, Toronto 1982; Order of Ont. 1991; Hon. Doctorate, Laurentian Univ. 1992; author: 'Why the Bees Have Stingers'; 'Ko-Ko-Ko the Owl'; 'The Way It Is'; Office: West Bay Reserve, Box 278, Manitoulin Island, Ont. P0P 1G0.

**RADWANSKI, George,** B.A., B.C.L.; journalist; b. Baden-Baden, W. Germany 28 Feb. 1947; s. Pierre Arthur and Isabella (Latoszynska) R.; e. Loyola H.S., Montreal 1964; McGill Univ. B.A. 1968, B.C.L. 1971; m. Julie d. Steven and Margaret Szasz 8 Aug. 1970; one s., Adam Pierre; GEORGE RADWANSKI AND ASSOCIATES; Staff Reporter, promoted to Sr. Staff Writer, The Montreal Gazette 1965–72, Assoc. Ed. 1972–74, Assoc. Ed. and Nat. Affairs Columnist (Ottawa based) 1974–75; Ottawa Ed. and Nat. Affairs Columnist Financial Times of Canada 1975–79; Editorial Page Editor, The Toronto Star 1974–81; Editor-in-Chief 1981; author: 'Trudeau' (political biog.) 1978; co-author 'No Mandate But Terror' (about Que. F.L.Q. crisis) 1971; recipient National Newspaper Award 1980, 1981; Club: Granite; Home: 62 Cheritan Ave., Toronto, Ont. M4R 1S6; Office: 1200 Bay St., Suite 300, Toronto, Ont. M5R 2A5.

**RAE, Alan James;** business executive; b. Toronto, Ont. 15 June 1925; s. Alexander and Mildred Irene (McCrimmon) R.; e. Univ. of W. Ont., B.A.; m. Nora d. Maxwell and Marjory Bowman 27 Jan. 1979; children: John, Robert, Bruce, Douglas; MANAGING DIR., EXEC. INC.; PRES., MARKETERS INC.; Product Mgr., Sales & Mktg., Procter & Gamble Co. of Can. 1950–57; Client Mgmt., Cockfield Brown 1957–58; Mktg. & Gen. Mgmt., Unilever Canada 1958–85; Pres., Lever Brothers Ltd. 1969–85; Pres., Candn. Advertising Found. 1985–89; Club: Rosedale Golf; Home: 337 Keewatin Ave., Toronto, Ont. M4P 2A4.

**RAE, Barbara Joyce,** C.M., M.B.A.; administrator; b. Prince George, B.C. 17 May 1931; d. Alfred and Lottie Kathleen Davis Holmwood; e. Victoria High Sch. (Edmonton); Simon Fraser Univ. M.B.A. 1975; m. George Suart; sons: Jamie, Glenn, John; CHAIRMAN, ADIA CANADA LTD. 1974– ; Dir., B.C. Telephone Co.; B.C. Telecom; Candn. Imperial Bank of Commerce; Grosvenor Internat. Holdings Ltd.; Seaboard Life Insurance Co.; Xerox Canada Ltd.; Chancellor Emeritus, Simon Fraser Univ. 1986–93; Niagara Institute; National Advisory Ctte. on Science & Technology, B.C.; KCTS 9 Seattle Public Television; Dir., Salvation Army, B.C. Branch; Dir., Imagine; Dir., Candn. Centre for Philanthropy; recipient: Mem., Order of Canada 1993; Canadian Woman Entrepreneur 1992 (BC 1st Place Winner); Order of B.C. 1991; Canada Volunteer Award 1990; 1987 Entrepreneur of the Year Award, B.C.; 1987 West Vancouver Achievers Award; 1986 Business Woman of the Year, YWCA Vancouver; 1985 Simon Fraser Univ. Outstanding Alumnae Award; Premier's Econ. Adv. Ctte., B.C. 1988–91, Judicial Appointments Ctte. 1988–90; Gen. Chrmn., United Way of the Lower Mainland, Vancouver 1987; Chrmn., Salvation Army Red Shield Vancouver Campaign 1986; Vice-Chrmn., B.C. Inst. of Technology 1976–80; Pres., Junior Achievement of B.C. 1984; past Dir., Candn. Assn. of Temporary Services; Dir., Vancouver Bd. of Trade 1972–76; recreations: skiing; tennis; Home: 2206 Folkestone Way, West Vancouver, B.C.; Office: (P.O. Box 49292), Ste. 734 – 1055 Dunsmuir St., Bentall Centre, Vancouver, B.C. V7X 1P5.

**RAE, Robert Keith,** B.A., B.Phil., LL.B.; politician; b. Ottawa, Ont. 2 Aug. 1948; s. Saul Forbes and Lois Esther (George) R.; e. pub. schs. Ottawa and Washington, D.C.; Internat. Sch. of Geneva 1966; Univ. of Toronto, Univ. Coll. B.A. 1969, LL.B. 1977; Oxford Univ. Balliol Coll. (Rhodes Scholar) B.Phil. 1971; m. Arlene d. Al Perly and Hannah (Florence), Toronto, Ont. 23 Feb. 1980; children: Judith Florence, Lisa Ruth, Eleanor Grace; PREMIER and MINISTER OF INTERGOVERNMENTAL AFFAIRS, PROVINCE OF ONTARIO 1990– ; Leader, NDP, Ont. 1982– ; called to Bar of Ont. 1980; el. M.P. for Broadview-Greenwood by-el. 1978, re-el. 1979, 80; Financial Spokesman for NDP in H. of C. 1979–82; resigned federal seat, March 1982; el. to provincial legislature of Ont. as mem. for York South, Nov. 1982; re-el. May 1985; re-el. Sept. 1987; Leader of the Official Opposition 1987–90; re-el. Sept. 1990; Premier of Ontario, October 1, 1990; mem. Comn. on Univ. Govt. Univ. of Toronto 1968–69; community worker London, Eng. 1973–74; extensive legal aid and community work Toronto since 1974; Asst. to Candn. Gen. Counsel, Un. Steelworkers of Am. 1975–77; Special Lectr. in Indust. Relations Univ. of Toronto 1976–77; author various articles on pol. theory, Candn. politics, indust. relations, constitutional and labour law; Vice Chrmn. Can.-U.S. Interparlty. Group 1979–82. NDP; recreations: tennis, golf, skiing, fishing, music, reading; Office: Queen's Park, Toronto, Ont. M7A 1A2.

**RAGAN, Edward John,** M.D.; physician; b. Toronto, Ont. 21 May 1938; s. John Louis and Anna Maria (Andruskevicete) Ragauskas; e. Univ. of W. Ont. B.A. 1960, M.D. 1965; Johns Hopkins Univ. M.P.H. 1974; m. Judith d. Peter and Gertrude Romyn 31 Dec. 1960; children: Elizabeth, Mitchell; DIR., CANADA'S INTERNATIONAL IMMUNIZATION PROGRAM, CANADIAN PUBLIC HEALTH ASSOCIATION 1987– ; Med. Offr. Dept. of Aborigines Gombak Aborigine Hosp., Gombak, Malaysia 1966–68; Med. Dir. Candn. Univ. Service Overseas 1968–73; Coordinator Fed.-Prov. Comte. on Health Services for Elderly Ottawa 1974–76; Head of Health Services, Bank of Canada 1975–87; Sr. Med. Adviser Can. Health Survey Ottawa 1976–78; mem. Justice Berger Royal Comn. Inquiry Indian & Inuit Health Participation 1979–80; Emergency Physician, Riverside Hosp. Ottawa 1970–82; Del. WHO/UNICEF Conf. on Primary Health Care 1978; recipient Fellowship Internat. Devel. Research Centre; Chairperson Candn. Public Health Assn. Adv. Comte. Sudan & Egypt internat. health projects 1981–87; mem. Candn. Public Health Assn. Internat. Health Secretariat; author various articles, papers; mem. Candn. Med. Assn.; Candn. Pub. Health Assn.; Candn. Soc. for Internat. Health; Ont. Med. Assn.; Am. Pub. Health Assn.; Am. Occupational Health Assn.; Royal Soc. Tropical Med.; Soc. Internat. Devel.; Home: 150 Billings Ave., Ottawa, Ont. K1H 5K9; Office: 1565 Carling Ave., Ottawa, Ont. K1Z 8R1.

**RAGINSKY, Nina,** B.A., R.C.A., O.C.; artist; b. Montreal, Que. 14 Apr. 1941; d. Bernard Boris and Helen Thérèsa R.; e. Rutgers Univ. B.A. 1962; one d. Sofie Katrina; studied painting with Roy Lichtenstein; studied sculpture with George Segal; studied Art History with Allan Kaprow, Rutgers Univ.; Teacher & Lectr. in field 1963–79; Freelance photographer Nat. Film Bd. of Can. 1963–81; Instr. in Metaphysics, Emily Carr Coll. Art 1973–81; Painter, Salt Spring Island, B.C. 1989– ; Sr. artist, jury Can. Council; selected Can. rep. in Sweden for Sweden Now Mag. 1979; solo exhns. incl. Vancouver Art Gallery; Victoria Art Gallery; Edmonton Art Gallery; Art Gallery of Ont.; San Francisco Mus. of Art; Acadia Univ.; Nancy Hoffman Gallery, N.Y.C.; Meml. Univ. Nfld. Art Gallery; group exhns. incl.: Rutgers Univ. 1962; Montreal Mus. Fine Arts 1963; Nat. Film Bd. of Can. 1964, '65, '67, '70, '71, '76, '77; Internat. Salon Photography, Bordeaux, France 1968; Nat. Gallery Ottawa 1968; Eastman House, Rochester, N.Y. 1969, Vancouver Art Gallery 1973, '80; Mural for Conference Centre, Ottawa 1973; Field Mus., Chicago 1976; Edmonton Art Gallery 1978, '79; Walter Philips Gallery 1979; Glenbow Mus. Gallery 1979; Harbourfront Community Gallery 1980; Hamilton Art Gallery 1980; Musée Maisil de St. Lambert 1981; Mendel Art Gallery 1981; Dunlop Art Gallery, Regina 1981; Pegasus Gallery, Salt Spring Island 1994; represented in permanent collections: Nat. Film Bd., Stills Div., Ottawa; Banff Sch. Fine Arts; Nat. Gallery, Ottawa; George Eastman House; Wadsworth Atheneum; Edmonton Art Gallery; various private collections; photographs incl. various books such as 'Call Them Canadians,' 'Canada Year of the Land,' 'Between Friends-Entre Amis' 'BANFF Purchase,' and other Nat. Film Bd. publs., Aperture #88; work incl. various nat. and internat. mags.; Bd. of Dirs., Island Watch, Salt Spring Island, B.C. 1993– ; Mem., Royal Can. Acad. Arts; apptd. Officer of the Order of Canada 1985; recreations: walking, rowing, gardening; Home & Office: R.R.# 2, Beddis Rd., Comp. #7, Ganges, B.C. V0S 1E0.

**RAGSDALE, Ronald G.,** B.S., Ph.D.; retired professor; b. La Crosse, Wisconsin 23 Feb. 1936; s. Edward

Eugene and Carol Bernice (Erickson) R.; e. Univ. of Wisconsin B.S. (Hons.) 1961, Ph.D. 1965; m. Charlotte d. Abner and Adala Anton 9 June 1962; one d.: Heidi Sue; Weapons Control Systems Mechanic, U.S. Air Force 1955–59; Rsch. Assoc. & Asst. Prof., Univ. of Pittsburgh 1964–66; Ast. Prof., Ont. Inst. for Studies in Edn. 1966–67; Assoc. Prof. 1967–88; Prof., Dept. of Measurement, Evaluation, and Computer Applications 1988–93; Visiting Fellow, Univ. of Essex 1973; Visiting Prof., Univ. of London 1973; half-time with OISE N.W. Field Centre (Thunder Bay, Ont.) 1979–80; seconded to Computer in Edn. Centre, Ont. Min. of Edn. 1984; Editor-in-Chief, 'Can. J. of Education/Revue can. de l'education' 1975–78; Edit. Bd. Mem., 'Education and Computing'; Nat. Defense Edn. Act Title IV, Fellow in Experimental Design, Dept. of Edn. Psych., Univ. of Wisconsin 1961–64; Mem., Bd. of Dir., The Church Army in Canada; Mem., Am. Edn. Rsch. Assn.; Assn. for Computing Machinery; Candn. Soc. for the Study of Edn.; Am. Evaluation Assn.; Candn. Edn. Rsch. Assn.; Edn. Computing Orgn. of Ont.; author: 'Programming Projects across the Curriculum' 1977, 'Computer in the Schools' 1982, 'Evaluation of Microcomputer Courseware' 1983, 'Datamaskiner i skolen' 1983, 'Permissible Computing in Education' 1988; co-author: 'A Comparative Analysis of CHOICES and SGIS' 1980; recreations: hiking; Home: 6 Oswald Cres., Toronto, Ont. M4S 2H6; Office: 252 Bloor St. W., Toronto, Ont. M5S 1V6.

**RAHILLY, Thomas Francis Jr.,** B.Sc., P.Eng.; retired industrialist; b. Sault Ste. Marie, Ont. 8 Apr. 1916; s. Thomas Francis and Violet Regina (Kennedy) R.; e. Pub. and High Schs., Sault Ste. Marie; Queen's Univ., B.Sc. 1939; m. Evelyn, d. Richard A. Brown, 4 July 1942; two s.: Thomas Francis, Richard James (deceased); Anglican, Clubs: Hamilton; Hamilton Golf & Country; Home: 713 Courtland Pl., Burlington, Ont. L7R 2M7.

**RAIKEN, Steven Arthur,** B.A., M.S.W., C.S.W., C.H.E.; health and social services executive; b. Buffalo, N.Y. 18 April 1949; s. Morris and Ruthann (Goldstein) R.; e. Amherst Central H.S. 1967 (highest ranking boy in class of 417); State Univ. of N.Y. at Buffalo, B.A. 1971 (magna cum laude, Phi Beta Kappa); Univ. of Toronto, M.S.W. 1977 (ranked 3rd in class of 117); m. Pamela d. Charles and Robina Thompson 8 May 1977; children: Jonathan Peter, David Alexander; SENIOR PRINCIPAL, NATIONAL CONSULTING GROUP, ERNST & YOUNG 1994– ; Profl. musician (guitar & vocals) in folk group (perf. U.S. & Can.) 1971–73; Psych. Asst., Clarke Inst. of Psych. 1973–75; Policy Devel. Offr., Community Serv. Dept., Mun. of Metro. Toronto 1977–80; Dir., Evaluation & Planning, Children's Aid Soc. of Metro. Toronto 1980–85; Cons./Sr. Cons./Mgr., Peat Marwick Cons. Group 1985–88; Extve. Dir., Metro. Toronto Dist. Health Counc. 1988–89; Principal, Peat Marwick Stevenson & Kellogg 1989–90; Principal, Ernst & Young 1990–93; extensive public speaker; Mem., Ont. Assn. of Profl. Soc. Workers (Treasurer 1991–93); Ont. Coll. of Cert. Social Workers; Candn. Coll. of Health Serv. Extves.; Institute of Certified Management Consultants of Ont. (Prospective Mem.); Health and Welfare Ctte., The Candn. Chamber of Commerce; principal consultant for various governmental policy studies; contbr./co-author of several articles; recreations: reading, music, jogging; Office: Ernst & Young Tower, 24th Floor, Toronto-Dominion Centre, P.O. Box 251, Toronto, Ont. M5K 1J7.

**RAINBOTH, Peter L.,** B.A.; retired public servant; b. Thetford Mines, Qué. 2 July 1933; s. Leonard Edward and Blanche Ruth (Payette) R.; e. Loyola Coll.; Carleton Univ., B.A. 1955; Laval Univ.; m. Mary Ellen d. John and Dorothy Lamb 5 Sept. 1956; children: Lynn, Ann, Thomas; Deputy Comnr. of Official Languages, Govt. of Canada 1986–92; Personnel Admin., Shell Oil Co. 1955–58; Sr. Personnel Offr., Nat. Film Bd. of Can. 1958–62; Dir. of personnel 1962–68; Group Chief, Staff Relns. Div., Treasury Bd. Sec. 1969–73; Dir., Policy & Prog. 1974–79; Dir.-Gen., Personnel, Dept. of Indus., Trade & Comm. 1979–83; Dir., Sr. Personnel Sec., Privy Council Office 1983–85; Lectr., Public Admin., Carleton Univ.; recreations: sailing, skiing, historical writings; Home: 2502 – 1081 Ambleside Dr., Ottawa, Ont. K2B 8C8; Office: 110 O'Connor St., Ottawa, Ont. K1A 0T8.

**RAJAGOPAL, Indhu,** M.A., M.Litt., Ph.D.; educator; b. Madras, India 28 Jan. 1938; d. Kandasami and Meenambal (Ellapa) Perumal; e. Univ. of Madras B.A. 1956, M.A. 1958, M.Litt. 1965; Univ. of Toronto Ph.D. 1979; one child: Sudhashree; ASSOC. PROF. OF SOCIAL SCI. YORK UNIV. 1992– ; Asst. Prof. of Pol. Sci. & Pub. Adm. Univ. of Madras 1958, Assoc. Prof. 1966; came to Can. as Ont. Grad. Fellow 1967; part-time faculty, Faculty of Arts and Atkinson Coll. present Univ. 1970–85; Asst. Prof. of Social Sci. 1985–92; mem. Exec. Ctte. Towards 2000 Indo-Candn. Community Conf. 1989; Dir. Elizabeth Fry Soc. 1984– , Vice Pres. 1987; Founder and Chairperson Flight 182 Relief Prog. Toronto 1985; recipient Madras Univ. undergrad. merit awards; Ont. Grad. Fellowship 1967; Ont. Govt. Rsch. Grant Indian Immigrant Aid Rsch.; author 'The Tyranny of Caste' 1985; Principal Investigator, SSHRC funded ($109,000), National Survey of Part-time Faculty in Canadian Higher Education; Co-ord., Multimedia Courseware Development; Dir. Candn. Asian Studies Assn. 1979–80 (mem. S. Asia Council Exec. 1987–88); Trustee Vedanta Soc. 1979–82, ed. 10th anniversary jour. 1979; mem. Shastri Indo-Candn. Inst.; Women's Adv. Ctte. COSTI Italian Immigrant Aid Assn.; recreations: S. Indian classical veena music, aerobics; Home: 8 Yewfield Cres., Don Mills, Ont. M3B 2Y5; Office: 4700 Keele St., North York, Ont. M3J 1P3.

**RAJAN, Balachandra,** M.A., Ph.D., F.R.S.C.; educator; b. Toungoo, Burma 24 March 1920; s. Arunachala and Visalam Tyagarajan; e. Cambridge Univ. B.A. 1941, M.A. 1944, Ph.D. 1946; m. Chandra d. G.K. Seshadri Sarma 29 Aug. 1946; one d. Tilottama; PROFESSOR EMERITUS, UNIV. OF WESTERN ONT. 1985– ; Dir. of Studies in Eng. Trinity Coll. Cambridge 1945–48; mem., Indian Foreign Service 1948–61; Chrmn. Exec. Bd., UNICEF 1955–57; Resident Rep. of India to Intnl. Atomic Energy Agency 1957–59; Prof. of Eng., Delhi Univ. 1961–64, Dean of Arts 1963–64; Visiting Prof. Inst. for Rsch. in Humanities, Univ. of Wis. 1964–65; Sr. Prof., Univ. of W. Ont. 1966–85; Fellow, Trinity Coll. Cambridge 1944–48; Honoured Scholar Milton Soc. Am. 1979; Chauveau Medallist Royal Soc. Can. 1983; author 'Paradise Lost and the Seventeenth Century Reader' 1947; 'The Dark Dancer' (novel) 1958 (Book Soc. Choice, transl. German, Swedish and Yugoslavian); 'Too Long in the West' (novel) 1961; 'W.B. Yeats: A Critical Introduction' 1965; 'The Lofty Rhyme: A Study of Milton's Major Poetry' 1970; 'The Overwhelming Question: A Study of the Poetry of T.S. Eliot' 1976; 'The Form of the Unfinished: English Poetics from Spenser to Pound' 1985; ed. 3 colls. essays on Milton; Founder and Ed. 'Focus'; Pres., Milton Soc. Am. 1971–72; Home: 478 Regent St., London, Ont. N5Y 4H4; Office: Dept. of English, London, Ont. N6A 3K7.

**RAJAN, Tilottama,** B.A., M.A., Ph.D.; university professor; b. New York, N.Y. 1 Feb. 1951; d. Balachandra and Chandra (Sarma) R.; e. Central S.S. (London, Ont.) 1968; Trinity Coll., Univ. of Toronto B.A. (Hons.) 1972; Univ. of Toronto M.A. 1973, Ph.D. 1977; PROF., DEPT. OF ENGLISH & CENTRE FOR THE STUDY OF THEORY, UNIV. OF WESTERN ONTARIO 1990– ; Asst. Prof., Huron Coll., Univ. of West. Ont. 1977–80; Asst. & Assoc. Prof. of English, Queen's Univ. 1980–85; Visiting Prof., Univ. of Calif. (San Diego) 1984; Internat. Inst. for Semiotic & Structural Studies, Univ. of B.C. 1988; Prof., Univ. of Wisconsin-Madison 1985–90; H.I. Romnes Prof., Univ. of Wisconsin 1987–90; Adv. Bd., 'PMLA'; Wordsworth Circle, European Romantic Review; Extve. Ctte. NASSR; A.C.L.S. Grant-in-Aid 1986–87; SSHRCC Leave Fellowship 1984–85; Guggenheim Fellowship 1987–88; SSHRCC Rsch. Fellowship 1991–94; Mem., M.L.A., A.C.L.A., C.C.L.A., Soc. for the Study of Narrative Lit.; Internat. Assn. of Philos. & Lit.; Keats-Shelley Assn.; Wordsworth-Coleridge Assn.; author: 'Myth in a Metal Mirror' 1967 (poems); 'Dark Interpreter: The Discourse of Romanticism' 1980, 'The Supplement of Reading: Figures of Understanding in Romantic Theory and Practice' 1990 (scholarly books); recreations: feeding and observing squirrels; Home: 870 Wellington St., London, Ont. N6A 3S7; Office: Dept. of English, Univ. of Western Ont., London, Ont. N6A 3K7.

**RAJHATHY, Tibor,** D.Sc., F.R.S.C.; retired research director; b. Pozsony, Hungary 27 March 1920; e. Royal Hungarian Univ. of Tech. Sciences Budapest B.Sc. 1942, M.Sc. 1943; Univ. of Agric. Sciences Budapest D.Sc. 1948; m. Judith d. Antal and Judith Weninger 13 Aug. 1949; children: Gabor, Judith; Rsch. Asst. Genetics Inst. Budapest 1941–43; Asst. Prof., Univ. of Agric. Sciences Budapest 1947–50; Head, Genetics Dept. Agric. Rsch. Inst. Hungarian Acad. Sciences Martonvasar 1950–56; Cytogeneticist 1956–67, Head Cytogenetics Sect. 1967–76 Ottawa Rsch. Stn.; Dir., Ottawa Rsch. Stn., Research Branch, Agric. Canada 1976–84; Hon. Doctorate (Dr.h.c.) Univ. of Horticulture and Food Industry, Budapest 1990; Hon. Life Mem., Hung. Plt. Breeders Assoc., Budapest 1990; recipient Distinguished Service to Oat Improvement Award Am. Oat Workers Conf. 1982; co-author 'Genetics' 1948; 'Wheat and Wheat Breeding' 1955; 'Cytogenetics of Oats' 1972; over 92 rsch. papers 1948–80; Candn. Ed. 'Journal of Plant Breeding' W. Germany 1972–85; mem., Genetics Soc. Can. (Treas. and Dir. 1965–68); recreations: literature, music, gardening; Home: 42 Farlane Blvd., Nepean, Ont. K2E 5H5.

**RAJIC, Negovan;** writer; b. Belgrade, Yugoslavia 24 June 1923; s. Vladimir and Zagorka (Vuletic) R.; e. Gymnasium of Belgrad Leaving Cert. 1941; Univ. of Belgrad eng. studies 1945; Dip. in Etudes Techniques Supérieures Paris 1963; Dip. in Elect. Eng. CNAM Paris 1968; m. Mirjana d. Sava and Angelina Knezevic 28 March 1970; children: Anna, Nicolas; Fought in the Resistance during the Second World War; escaped Yugoslovia 1946 arriving France 1947 resuming studies in eng. 1950 (Ctte. for Free Eur. Scholarship); rsch. eng. physics lab. École Polytechnique de Paris 1956–63; teacher in electronics France 1963–69; came to Can. 1969 becoming Prof. of Math. Cegep Trois-Rivières to 1987; author'Les Hommes-Taupes' 1978, Eng. transl. 'The Mole Men' 1980; 'Propos d'un vieux radoteur' 1982, Eng. transl. 'The Master of Srappado' 1984; 'Sept roses pour une boulangère' 1987, Eng. transl. 'Seven Roses for a Baker' 1988; 'Service pénitentiaire' 1988, Eng. transl. 'The Shady Business' 1989; numerous articles, short stories; 'Le Puits ou histoire sans queue ni tête' play; recipient Prix Esso du Cercle du Livre de France 1978; Prix Air Canada best short story 1980; Prix Slobodan Yovanovitch, Assn. des écrivains et artistes serbes en éxil 1984; Prix littéraire de Trois-Rivières 1988; mem. PEN Internat.; Assn. Writers Qué.; Hon. mem. Assn. Serbian Writers, Belgrade; Greek Orthodox; recreation: skiing; Address: 300 Dunant, Trois-Rivières, Qué. G8Y 2W9.

**RAKOCY, John Gerard,** B.A., M.B.A.; leasing executive; b. Detroit 6 Nov. 1959; s. Leonard and Mary Jane (Krausman) R.; e. Michigan State Univ. B.A. 1981; Loyola Univ. M.B.A. 1986; m. Diane d. Mike and Annette Entinger 30 Aug. 1986; one s.: Robert; PRESIDENT, GE CAPITAL AUTO LEASE, GENERAL ELECTRIC CAPITAL CANADA INC. 1990– ; Finance, General Electric Company 1981–83; Sales 1983–85; Sales Mngt. 1985–87; Marketing 1988; Corporate Finance 1989; recreations: tennis; Office: 9 Ezes Dr., Suite 190, Marlton, New Jersey 08053.

**RAKOFF, Vivian Morris,** M.A., M.B., B.S., F.R.C.P.(C), F.A.P.A., F.A.C.P., F.R.C.Psych.; university professor; psychiatrist; b. Capetown, S. Africa 28 Apr. 1928; s. David and Bertha Lillian R.; e. Univ. of Capetown, B.A. 1947, M.A. 1949; Univ. of London, M.B., B.S. 1956; McGill Univ., Dipl. Psychol. Med. 1964; London, Eng., M.R.C.S., L.R.C.P. 1956; Canada, F.R.C.P.(C) 1964; m. Gina d. Betty and Simon Shochat 27 Nov. 1959; children: Simon, Ruth, David; Prof. & Chrmn., Dept. of Psych., Univ. of Toronto; Dir. & Psych.-in-Chief, Clarke Inst. 1980–90; Surg. Intern, St. Charles Hosp. 1957; Med. Intern, Victoria Hosp. 1958; Sr. Intern, Groote Schuur Hosp. 1958; Psych. Resident 1959–61; Resident, McGill Univ. 1961–63; Staff Psych., Jewish Gen. Hosp. 1963; Lectr., McGill Univ. 1964; Asst. Dir., Rsch., Jewish Gen. Hosp. 1965; Asst. Prof., McGill Univ. 1966; Dir., Rsch., Jewish Gen. Hosp. 1967; Assoc. Prof. & Dir. Postgrad Edn., Dept. of Psych., Univ. of Toronto 1968–74 (apptd. Prof. 1971); Prof. of Psych. Edn. 1974; Co-ord., Edn., Clarke Inst. 1977; Psych.-in-Chief, Sunnybrook Med. Ctr. 1978; author: 'Nonquasi' CBC Radio Play 1967; 'Mandelstam's Witness' CBC TV Play 1975; co-author: 'Beaverbrook' CBC TV Play 1967; co-editor: 'Psychiatric Diagnosis' 1977, 'Guidelines for the Use of Psychotropic Drugs' 1984, 'Handbook on the Use of Drugs in Psychiatry' 1984, 'A Method of Psychiatry' 2nd ed. 1985; Jewish; recreations: gardening, travel; Home: 21 Dale Ave., Terrace E, Toronto, Ont. M4W 1K3.

**RAKOWSKA-HARMSTONE, Teresa,** B.A., A.M., Ph.D.; university professor; b. Poznan, Poland 12 Aug. 1927; d. Tadeusz Jan and Jadwiga Wanda (Kopczynska) Rakowski; e. McGill Univ. B.A. (Hons.) 1950; Radcliffe Coll. & Harvard Univ. A.M. 1952; Harvard Univ. Ph.D. 1966; divorced; one s.: Andrew Thaddeus Harmstone; PROF., DEPT. OF POLITICAL SCIENCE, CARLETON UNIV. 1974– ; Instr., Rutgers Univ. 1960–66; Asst. Prof., Carleton Univ. 1966–68; Assoc. Prof. 1968–74; Dir., Inst. of Soviet & East Eur. Studies 1973–75; Chair, Dept. of Pol. Sci. 1986–89; Visiting Prof., McGill Univ. 1966–67, 1969–70; George Washington Univ. 1971–72; Wellesley Coll. (Kathryn W. Davis Prof. of Slavic Studies) 1983; U.S. Naval Acad. (Sec. of the Navy Fellow) 1989–90; Research Fellow & Visiting Scholar, Inst. of Sino-Soviet Studies, George Washington Univ.; Inst. of Internat. Pol. & Econ. (Yugoslavia); The Hoover Inst. (Calif.); The Russian Rsch. Ctr., Harvard Univ.; Stiftung Wissenschaft und Politik (Germany); Univ. of Warsaw & Inst. for the Study of Politics, Polish Acad. of Sciences (Poland); Extve. Dir., League of Women Voters of the U.S. & League of Women Voters Edn. Fund (Washington, D.C.) 1970–72; mem., profl. assns. in pol. sci. & Slavic Studies; author: 'Russia and Nationalism in Central Asia: The Case of Tadzhikistan' 1970; num. contbns. to edited volumes & profl. journals & govt. reports; co-author, editor or co-editor: 'Communist States in Disarray' 1972, 'Perspectives for Change in Communist Societies' 1979, 'Communism in Eastern Europe' 1979, 1984 (rev. & enlarged); recreations: swimming, bicycling, tennis; Home: 433 Pleasant Park Rd., Ottawa, Ont. K1H 5M9; Office: Ottawa, Ont. K1S 5B6.

**RAKOWSKY, Allan A.,** B.A., LL.B.; Barrister and Solicitor; b. Toronto, Ont. 20 Apr. 1947; s. Stanley and Ida (Kerkofsky) R.; e. York Univ., B.A. 1970; Univ. of West. Ont., LL.B. 1973; Law Soc. of Upper Can., Call to Bar (Hons.) 1975; m. Dayle d. Julius and Pearl Caplan 10 Aug. 1969; children: Andrew, Jeremy, Dylan; PARTNER, ROSE, PERSIKO, RAKOWSKY 1984– ; Assoc. Solicitor, Zaldin and Fine 1975–77; Partner, Chusid, Rakowsky, Polson & Shapero 1977–83; Mem., Candn. Bar Assn.; Toronto Homebuilders Assn.; Home: 2671 Bathurst St., Toronto, Ont. M6B 2Z9; Office: Suite 700, 55 University Ave., Toronto, Ont. M5J 2K4.

**RALLS, Stephen James,** M.A., L.R.A.M.; piano accompanist, university teacher; b. Hertford, England 1 July 1944; s. Edgar Frederick William and Ida Joyce (Keeble) R.; e. Harrow Weald Co. Grammar Sch. 1955–63; Merton College, Oxford B.A. 1966, M.A. 1979; Royal Academy of Music L.R.A.M. 1969; MUSIC STAFF, OPERA DIVISION, FACULTY OF MUSIC, UNIV. OF TORONTO 1978– ; Répétiteur, Welsh Nat. Opera 1969–70; English Opera Group 1972–75; English Music Theatre Co. 1976–78; recital accompanist: appearances at Bath, Aldeburgh, City of London, Edinburgh, Guelph, Banff, Shaw, Elora festivals, Music at Sharon, Festival of the Sound; also London, Toronto, Ottawa, N.Y., Chicago, Winnipeg, etc.; num. broadcasts on BBC & CBC radios (esp. as pianist with Aldeburgh Connection); recordings: 'Music of Percy Grainger,' 'Death in Venice' (Britten), 'Songs of Oskar Morawetz,' 'The Lyrical Art of Mark Pedrotti'; creation of over 40 programs on musical & lit. themes for Aldeburgh Connection; coach, Britten-Pears Sch. for Adv. Musical Studies, Aldeburgh England 1974– ; Coach/Répétiteur, Candn. Opera Co., Nat. Arts Centre, Toronto Symphony, Banff Sch. 1978– ; Co-Artistic Dir. & Founder, Aldeburgh Connection Concert Soc. 1982– ; Mem., Merton Soc.; Home: 74 Follis Ave., Toronto, Ont. M6G 1S6; Office: Toronto, Ont. M5S 1A1.

**RAMAN, Kolluru Venkata,** B.Sc., M.L., LL.M., J.S.D.; professor of law; b. Yellamanchili, A.P., India 15 July 1932; s. Kolluru Mahadeva Rao and Kolluru Satyavathi O. (Anivilla Satyavathi); e. Maharajha's Coll., B.Sc. 1953; Andhra Univ., B.L. 1955, M.L. 1958; Stanford Univ., LL.M. 1963; The Hague, NL, dipl. de droit int. de la Haye 1963; Yale Univ., J.S.D. 1967; m. Vijaya (Voleti) d. Sitarama and Rajeswari Murty 28 Sept. 1960; children: Gita, Madhav; PROF., QUEEN'S UNIV. 1978– ; Lectr., Marathwada Univ. 1958; Univ. Grants Comn. Rsch. Fellow, Osmania Univ. 1958–60; Reader 1960–63; Rsch. Fellow, Yale Law Sch. 1969; Vis. Assoc. Law Prof., Queen's Univ. 1970; Sr. Fellow in Internat. Peace & Security Studies, UNITAR, United Nations 1970–78; Vis. Lectr., Temple Univ. 1976; Vis. Prof., Seton Hall Univ. 1977; McGill Univ. 1986; Lectr., Law of Torts, Native Law Prog., Univ. of Sask. 1991–92; participant UNITAR/CEESTEM Proj. on New Internat. Econ. Order; Cons., Internat. Peace Acad.; Ctr. on Transnat. Corpns.; U.N. proj. on Formulation of a Code of Conduct gov. Transnat. Corpns.; The Ambrose Gherini Prize (Yale) 1967; Mem., Candn. Counc. of Internat. Law; Am. Soc. of Internat. Law; Former Comm. Ed. Bd. Mem.; 'Whig Standard'; author: 'The Ways of the Peace Maker' 1977; editor: 'Conflict Management Through the United Nations' 1978, co-author: 'The Objectives of the New International Economic Order' 1979; recreations: music, photography; Home: 35 Dickens Dr., Kingston, Ont. K7M 2M5; Office: Fac. of Law, Queen's Univ., Kingston, Ont. K7L 3N6.

**RAMINSH, Imant,** B.Mus., A.R.C.T.; composer, conductor, teacher; b. Ventspils, Latvia 18 Sept. 1943; s. Alfred Wilhelm and Alma (Ploss) R.; e. Jarvis C.I. 1961; Royal Conservatory of Toronto A.R.C.T. 1962; Univ. of Toronto B.Mus. 1966; Akademie Mozarteum, Salzburg 1966–68; Univ. of B.C. 1968–69; Univ. of Victoria 1975–77; m. Becky Benita d. Orville and Merva Strube 21 June 1975; one d.: Lisa Alexandra Soleil; estab. Music Dept., College of New Caledonia, Prince George, B.C. 1969–71; Founding Conductor, New Caledonia Chamber Orch. 1970–75 (now Prince George Symph.); Choral Dir., Okanagan Symph. Choir 1978–82; Founding Conductor, Aura Chamber Choir 1979– ; Nova Children's Choir 1983–86; Youth Symph. of the Okanagan 1989– ; recipient of many comns. for musical compositions from Vanc. Chamber Choir, Vanc. Bach Choir, B.C. Choral Fed., C.B.C., Okanagan Music Fest. for Composers, Richard Eaton Singers & many others; 1990 recipient, Nat. Choral Award, Assn. of Candn. Choral Conductors for composition 'Magnificat'; 1992 winner of Melodious Accord Choral Literature Search; works have been performed in Canada, U.S., Britain, Eur., U.S.S.R. & Australia by Vanc. Chamber Choir, Vanc. Bach Choir, Elmer Iseler Singers, Toronto Mendelssohn Choir, Stockholm Chamber Choir, Toronto Children's Chorus, Glen Ellyn Children's Chorus, Ave Sol (Riga Chamber Choir), Purcell String Quartet, Masterpiece Trio, CBC Van. Orch., Vancouver Symph., Symph. N.S., Okanagan Symph. & many others; Assoc. Composer, Candn. Music Centre; Mem., Candn. League of Composers; Assn. of Candn. Choral Conductors; B.C. Choral Fed.; Soc. of Composers, Authors & Music Pubs. of Canada; author of many choral and chamber music pubns. incl. 'Magnificat,' 'Songs of the Lights,' 'Northwest Trilogy,' & 'Ave Verum Corpus'; major choral works recorded on 1992 CD 'Songs of the Lights' (CBC SM5000 series) by Vancouver Chamber Choir and CBC Vancouver Orchestra; Parks Naturalist & Interpreter, B.C. Parks, summers since 1976; as an employee of Bufo, Inc. (W. Vanc.) since 1984; recreations: natural history, photography, canoeing, hiking; Home: 11600 Upper Summit Dr., Vernon, B.C. V1B 2B4.

**RAMPHAL, The Honourable Sir Shridath Surendranath,** LL.M., O.E., O.M., O.C.C., G.C.M.G., Q.C.; international consultant; b. Berbice, Guyana 3 Oct. 1928; s. James Isaac and Grace (Abdool) R.; e. Queen's Coll.; King's Coll. LL.M. 1952; Harvard Law Sch. 1962; m. Lois Winifred King 16 Aug. 1951; children: Ian, Mark, Susan, Amanda; BOARD OF GOVERNORS, INTERNATIONAL DEVELOPMENT RESEARCH CENTRE; various positions, governments of Guyana and Fed. of the West Indies 1953–75; Secretary-General of the Commonwealth 1975–90; 1990 onwards: Pres., World Conservation Union; Co-Chair, Comn. on Global Governance; Council Mem., Internat. Negotiating Network (Atlanta); Extve. Chair, Internat. Steering Ctte., Rockefeller Found. Prog. for Leadership in Envir. & Devel.; Chancellor, Univ. of the West Indies; Univ. of Guyana; Univ. of Warwick; former affiliations: Mem., Brandt Comn. on Internat. Devel. 1977–90; Palme Comn. on Disarmament & Security Issues 1980–89; Brundtland Comn. on Envir. & Devel. 1984–87; Independent Comn. on Internat. Humanitarian Issues 1983–87; South Comn. 1988–90; Chair, UN Ctte. for Devel. Planning 1984–87; The West Indian Comn. 1990–92; Special Adviser, Sec.-Gen. UNCED 1991; The Albert Medal 1988; The Rene Dubos Human Envir. Award 1993; Fellow, Royal Soc. of the Arts; author: 'One World to Share' 1980, 'Inseparable Humanity' 1988, 'An End to Otherness' 1990, 'Our Country, the Planet' 1992; recreations: photography, cooking; club: The Athenaeum; Home: 31 St. Matthew's Lodge, 50 Oakley Sq., London, U.K. NW1 1NB; Office: Flat 1, 188 Sutherland Ave., London, U.K. W9 1HR.

**RAMSAY, Donald A.,** M.A., Ph.D., Sc.D., Fil. Hed. Dr., F.R.S., F.R.S.C., F.A.P.S., F.C.I.C.; research scientist; b. London, Eng. 11 July 1922; s. Norman and Thirza Elizabeth (Beckley) R.; e. Latymer Upper Sch., London, Eng., 1933–40; St. Catharine's Coll., Cambridge Univ., B.A. 1943, M.A. 1947 Ph.D. 1947; Sc.D. 1976; Doctoris honoris causa, Univ. de Reims, France 1969; m. Nancy d. Frederick and Mary Beatrice (Garside) Brayshaw 8 June 1946; children: Shirley Margaret, Wendy Kathleen, Catharine Jean, Linda Mary; Principal Research Offr., Nat. Research Counc. 1968–87; joined Council as Jr. Research Offr., 1947–49; apptd. Asst. Research Offr., 1949–54; Assoc. Research Offr., 1954–61; Sr. Research Offr., 1961–68; mem., Candn. Assn. Physicists; Chem. Inst. Can.; Vice Pres. Acad. of Sci. Royal Soc. of Can. 1975–76; Hon. Treas. Royal Soc. of Canada 1976–79, 1988–91; recipient, Centennial Medal 1982; Queen Elizabeth II Silver Jubilee Medal 1977; awarded Commemorative Medal for 125th Anniversary of Candn. Confederation 1992; CIC Medal (Chem. Inst. of Can.) 1992; Alexander von Humboldt Rsch. Award 1993; Publications: Numerous articles on molecular spectroscopy and molecular structure, esp. free radicals; Un. Church; recreations: organ playing, rowing, fishing; Club: Leander; Home: 1578 Drake Ave., Ottawa, Ont. K1G 0L8; Office: 100 Sussex Dr., Ottawa, Ont. K1A 0R6.

**RAMSAY, Malcolm A.,** B.Sc., M.Sc., Ph.D.; university professor; b. St. Boniface, Man. 29 Apr. 1949; s. Alexander and Irene (Wood) R.; e. Simon Fraser Univ., B.Sc. (Hons.) 1978, M.Sc. 1980; Univ. of Alta., Ph.D. 1986; m. Susan Elizabeth d. Peter and Loretta Posthuma 12 Sept. 1986; one s.: Nicholas Hearne; ASSOC. PROF., DEPT. OF BIOLOGY, UNIV. OF SASKATCHEWAN 1989– ; postdoct. fellow, Candn. Dept. Fisheries & Oceans 1986–87; Asst. Prof., present univ. 1987–89; Fellow, Linnean Soc. London; Mem., Am. Physiol. Soc.; Candn. & Am. Socs. of Zoolog.; and other nat. & fgn. socs.; Dir., Science Institute of the Northwest Territories; Mem., Candn. Global Change Program, The Royal Soc. of Can.; author of over 30 pubs. in evolutionary ecol.; recreations: music, mountain walking; club: University (Sask.); Home: 1238 Elliott St., Saskatoon, Sask. S7N 0V6; Office: Saskatoon, Sask. S7N 0W0.

**RAMSAY, Russell H.,** C.M.; former politician; b. Sault Ste. Marie, Ont. 5 Aug. 1928; s. Russell Aylmer and Ailene (Marshall) R.; e. Sault Coll. Inst; Queen's Univ. Summer School; m. Margaret A. d. Arthur and Elizabeth Nichols 11 Aug. 1951; children: Russell David, Ronald Arthur, Karen Elizabeth, Kathryn Lee, Roderick Paul; Min. of Labour, Ont. 1982–85; def. Ont. Prov. election, May 1985; Pres., and Gen Mgr., Hyland Radio TV Ltd., and Lake Superior Cablevision Ltd. until Aug. 1976; Vice-Pres. and Gen Mgr., Huron Broadcasting Ltd., 1976–79; Mem., Business Advisory Council, Utilities Division, Great Lakes Power Corp. Ltd., 1979–80; first elected M.P.P. Sault Ste. Marie, by-el. 1978; Parl. Asst., Min. of Labour 1980–81; Prov. Secy., Resources Devel. 1981–82; appt. Chrmn. Ont. Health Disciplines Bd. 1986; apptd. Pres. Sault Ste. Marie Economic Corp. 1986; apptd. Extve. Vice Pres. and Gen. Mgr., Industrial Accident Prevention Assn. 1987– ; Dir., Pelmorex Communications Inc. 1990– ; Hon. mem., Assoc. Commercial Travellers; past mem., Athletic Bd. of Control, Lake Superior State Coll., Sault Ste. Marie, Mich.; Past Secy., Art Gallery of Algoma; Past Affiliations: Mem. Bd. of Governors, Algoma School of Nursing; Pres. YMCA, 1972–73, 1973–74; Dir., The Canadian Association of Broadcasters, 1969–74; Chrmn. United Appeal Campaign, 1962; Chrmn. United Appeal Services, 1964 and 1965; Pres., Sault Ste. Marie Rotary Club, 1959–60; District Governor, Rotary International, 1968–69; Chrmn. Rotary Sports Celebrities' Hockey Game Dinner, 1952 through 1969; Chrmn. Rotary Club Oldtimers' Hockey Game, 1962 through 1969; Elder, Central United Church, 1962 through 1965; Dir. Sault Ste. Marie Chamber of Commerce, 1962–63; Interim Pres., Sault Ste. Marie Association for the Mentally Retarded, 1966; Pres., Central Canada Broadcasters' Association, 1968; City Council, January 1975–June 1975; Chrmn. Radio/TV Advisory Committee, Canadore College, North Bay, Ont., 1967–77; Chrmn. 75th Anniversary, Sault Collegiate Institute, 1977; Mem. Algoma Health Unit, 1975–77; Pres., Bd. of Directors, Plummer Memorial Public Hospital, 1976–78; Mem. Joint Hospitals' Adv. Committee, 1972–76, 1978–79; Citizen of the Year, B'Nai B'rith Soc. 1967; Centennial Medal 1967; Rotary Club, Man of the Year 1969; 2nd recipient, Howard Caine Memorial Award from Can. Broadcasters Assn. 1970; Sault Ste. Marie Hockey Hall of Fame 1975; Medal of Merit from Municipality of Sault Ste. Marie 1978; 125th Anniversary of the Confederation of Canada Medal, 1992; Distinguished Citizen Award, Lake Superior State Univ. 1993; Order of Canada 1993; Home: 23 ParkShore Dr., Sault Ste. Marie, Ont. P6A 6B1.

**RAMSBOTTOM, Brig.-Gen. Robert Murray,** C.D., B.Sc.; military officer; aerospace engineer; b. Perth, Ont. 18 Apr. 1939; s. Robert Harris and Blanche Irene (Lashley) R.; e. Almonte H.S. 1956; Royal Military Coll. of Can., B.Sc. 1960; RCAF Aylmer, aerospace engr. training, summers 1957, 1958; m. Jacqueline d. A.L. and B.E. Evans 15 Apr. 1963; one d.: Tara Leigh; DIRECTOR GENERAL, AEROSPACE ENGINEERING AND MAINTENANCE, DEPT. OF NAT. DEFENCE 1987– ; assigned to RCAF Uplands 1960; served 11 Tech. Serv. Unit Montreal, RCAF St. Hubert, RCAF Bagotville; promoted Squadron Leader 1967; attended Royal Air Force Staff Coll. (U.K.) 1970; assigned to 1 Candn. Air Group Baden-Soellingen Germany 1971–72; promoted Lt. Col. 1972; served HQ 4th Allied Tactical Air Force Ramstein, Germany 1972–74; posted Directorate, Aerospace Prog. Mgmt. NDHQ, Ottawa 1974–77; Dir 1977; promoted Col. 1977; assigned to CF Training System HQ Trenton 1977–80; attended National Defence Coll. 1980–81; Dep. Project Mgr., CF-18 Fighter Acquisition Project 1981; promoted Brigadier General 1984; Project Mgr., CF-18 Project 1984–87; Candn. Forces Decoration; United Ch. of Can.; recreations: sports, gardening, music; Address: 2315 Evelyn Heights, Victoria, B.C. V9E 1C4.

**RANCE, Derek Clive,** P.Eng., M.B.A., B.Sc.; mining executive; b. Durban, S. Africa 27 Sept. 1936; s. Peter Colin and Mary R.; e. Glenwood H.S. 1954; Univ. of the

Witwatersrand, B.Sc. 1959; Univ. of West. Ont., M.B.A. 1963; m. Cynthia d. John and Marie Sanders 31 Aug. 1963; children: Keith John Colin, Hugh Mill Colin; PRES. & C.O.O., IRON ORE CO. OF CANADA 1989– ; Chief Mine Engr., Brynnor Mines Ltd. 1963–65; Mine Mgr. & Dir., Dickenson Mines Ltd. 1965–75; Gen. Mgr., Carol Proj., Iron Ore Co. of Can. 1975–81; Vice-Pres. & Gen. Mgr., Quintette Coal Ltd. 1981–83; Mining Cons., Phillips Barratt Kaiser Engr. 1983–85; Pres. & C.E.O., Cape Breton Devel. Corp. 1985–87; Pres., Rance Assocs. 1987–89; Candn. Inst. of Mining & Metal., Past Presidents Medal 1980; Mem., Am. Inst. of Mining Engrs.; Assn. of Profl. Engrs. of Ont.; Candn. Inst. of Mining & Metal. (past extve. mem.); recreations: skiing, sailing, golf, tennis; Address: 905 Arnaud Cres., Sept-Iles, Que. G4R 3C6.

**RAND, Calvin G.,** M.A., LL.D.; arts and education consultant; b. Buffalo, N.Y. 15 May 1929; s. George Franklin and Isabel (Williams) R.; e. Nichols Sch. Buffalo 1947; Princeton Univ. B.A. 1951; Columbia Univ. M.A. 1954; York Univ. LL.D. 1984; m. Patricia d. Ronald and Gertrude Andrew 18 Aug. 1951; children: Robin, Melissa, Jennifer, Lucinda, Elizabeth; CHRMN. OF COUNCIL OF FINE ARTS CENTRE, STATE UNIV. OF NY AT BUFFALO 1988– ; Prin. Calvin Rand Consultancy 1985– ; Gov. Shaw Festival Theatre Found.; Dir. Niagara Inst., Founder and first Pres. 1971–79; Founding Chrmn. and Dir. Shaw Festival 1965–79; Head of Hist. Riverdale Country Sch. New York 1955–61; Lectr. in Humanities and Philos. State Univ. of N.Y. Buffalo 1961–68, Acting and Assoc. Dir. Cultural Affairs 1968–71, Adjunct Prof. of Theatre; Pres. Am. Acad. Rome, N.Y. and Rome, Italy 1980–84; Dir. Rand Capital Corp. Buffalo; Fellow, Vanier Coll. York Univ., Chrmn. World Encyclopedia of Contemporary Theatre; mem. N.Y. State Council on Arts 1978–82; Dir. Albright-Knox Art Gallery 1972–76, 1978–82, 1984–88, 1992– ; Gov. Nat. Theatre Sch. Can. 1968–74; Dir., Burchfield Art Center Buffalo 1992– ; named 'Man of the Year' Buffalo Council World Affairs 1976; rec'd Special Citation for Devel. Shaw Festival, Ont. Arts Council 1976; named Arts Patron of the Year 1990, Western NY Arts Council & Buffalo Chamber of Commerce; Vice Chair, Irish Classical Theatre, Buffalo, NY 1993; author various scholarly articles, theatre and book reviews; recreations: tennis, skiing, hiking; clubs: Players (New York), Saturn (Buffalo), Princeton (New York); Home: 160 John St., Niagara-on-the-Lake, Ont. and 61 Oakland Pl., Buffalo, N.Y. 14222; Office: Box 855, Niagara-on-the-Lake, Ont. L0S 1J0.

**RAND, Duncan Dawson,** B.A., B.L.S.; librarian; b. Biggar, Sask. 28 Oct. 1940; s. Dawson Ellis and Elizabeth Edna (Gabie) R.; e. Univ. of Sask. B.A. 1965; McGill Univ. B.L.S. 1964; m. Nancy Jean Daugherty 7 Sept. 1963; children: Duncan, Thomas, Jennifer, John; CHIEF LIBRARIAN, LETHBRIDGE PUBLIC LIBRARY 1974– ; Lib. Coordinator Regina Separate Sch. Bd. 1966–69; Asst. Chief Lib. Regina Pub. Lib. 1969–71; Depy. Dir. London (Ont.) Pub. Lib. and Art Museum 1971–73, Acting Dir. 1973–74; Pres., Lethbridge Council Candn. Parents for French 1981; Pres., Lethbridge Lifelong Learning Assn. 1976; Trustee, S. Alta. Art Gallery Assn. 1975–77; recipient Regina Pub. Lib. Honeyman Scholarship 1963; co-author 'Prairie Conference on Library Standards for Canadian Schools' 1968; various book chapters, articles; mem. Sask. Genealogical Soc. (Pres. 1970–71); Lib. Assn. Alta. (Pres. 1986–87); Candn. Assn. Pub. Libs. (Pres. 1976–77); Candn. Lib. Assn. (Dir. 1976–77); Pres., Assoc. Prof. Librarians of Lethbridge 1983–84; Lethbridge Chamber Comm. (Dir. 1975–76); Dir. Lethbridge Musical Theatre 1990; Ipallosh 1976– ; recreations: golf, hiking, running, reading, musical theatre; Office: 810 – 5th Ave. S., Lethbridge, Alta. T1J 4C4.

**RANDALL, David,** B.Sc., Ph.D., F.R.S.C.; university professor; b. London, U.K. 15 Sept. 1938; s. Albert William and Rhoda Elizabeth (Gibson) R.; e. Univ. of Southampton, B.Sc. 1960, Ph.D. 1963; m. Hilary d. Thomas and Florence Gadd 12 Sept. 1961; separated 1986; divorced 1992; m. Xiang Hong 1993; children: Juliet, Nicholas, Marion, Elizabeth, Anna; PROF., ZOOLOGY DEPT., UNIV. OF B.C. 1963– and CONCURRENT PROF., NANJING UNIV., PEOPLES REPUBLIC OF CHINA 1993– ; External examiner, Zoology National Univ. of Singapore 1989–91; NATO Visiting Scholar, Univ. of Milan, Italy 1991; Vis. Sci., People's Republic of China 1982, 1986, 1988, 1992; Max Planck Inst. for Exper. Med. 1967; Mem., EPA group visiting Russia re joint US-USSR agreement on Co-op. in environ. protection 1983–84; Sci. Collaborator, Bamfield Marine Station 1980, 1988; Alpha Helix Expedition, Palau 1979, Amazon River 1976; Univ. of Texas Port Arkansas Marine Station 1978; and several other projects; Vis. Prof., Univ. Nairobi, Kenya 1988; Vis. Prof., George Washington Univ., Washington DC 1988/89; Killam/University Fellow, Flinders Univ. 1981–82; F.R.S.C. 1981; Guggenheim Fellow & Vis. Lectr., Bristol Univ. 1968–69; Pres., Candn. Soc. of Zool. 1984; Mem., World Health Orgn. Ctte. 1985; NSERC Strategic Grants Ctte. 1985; Mem., Review Board for Biology for Swedish Natural Science Rsch. Council 1993–94; worldwide lectr.; Ed. Adv. Bd., 'Journal of Comparative Physiology' 1978– ; 'Fish Physiology & Biochemistry' 1985; 'Journal of Experimental Biology' 1981–84; Assoc. Ed.: 'Marine Behaviour and Physiology' 1980; co-author: 'The Evolution of Air Breathing Vertebrates' 1980, 'Animal Physiology' 1977, 1982, 1989; co-editor: Fish Physiology series (12 vols.); ed.: Zoophysiology series (Springer-Verlag) 1982; author of numerous scholarly articles; serves on several review cttes.; Home: #308 – 5450 University Boulevard, Vancouver, B.C. V6T 1K4; Office: 6270 Univ. Blvd., Vancouver, B.C. V6T 1K4.

**RANDALL, Joan Walwyn,** B.A.; company director; b. Toronto, Ont., 27 Feb. 1928; d. Arthur G. and Ruth (Harris) Walwyn; e. St. Clement's Sch. 1945; Univ. of Toronto, B.A. (Modern History) 1949; Invest. Dealers' Assn., Candn. Securities Course 1970; m. the late William O. Randall; children: Joanne Williams, William Walwyn R., Janet Gould; DIR. & MEM., AUDIT CTTE. and CONDUCT REVIEW CTTE., NN LIFE INSURANCE CO. OF CANADA 1977– ; Trustee, National Gallery of Canada, Ottawa, mem. Acquisition Ctte. 1989–93, Marketing and Programme Ctte. 1990–93; Mem., Appeal Ctte. Institute of Chartered Accountants of Ont. 1991– ; Mem., National Board, Junior Achievement of Can. 1991– ; Chrmn., Gov. Counc., Univ. of Toronto 1988–89, Vice-Chrmn. 1985–88; mem. of Council 1980–89; mem. Extve. Ctte. 1983–89 and var. other cttes. 1980–89; Mem., Admissions Ctte., Faculty of Medicine 1989– ; Mem., Dean's Advisory Council, Faculty of Mngmt. 1989– ; Mem. Bd. of Trustees, Sunnybrook Hosp. 1988–89; Banting Rsch. Foundation 1982–84; Hosp. Univ. Bd., Univ. of Toronto 1985–89; Mem. Bd. of Trustees, Royal Ont. Museum 1972–77, 1988–89; Extve. Ctte. 1972–77, Vice-Chrmn. 1976–77; mem., Finance and Investment Ctte. 1972–91; Curatorial Planning Ctte. 1985– ; Levy Acquisition Ctte. 1990– ; Institute of Contemporary Culture 1993– ; Hon. Trustee, ROM; Chrmn., Hon. Trustees' Co-ordinating Ctte. 1985–87; Founder Chrmn., Mems. Vol. Ctte. 1958; ROM delegate to World Fed. Friends of Museums, Paris 1984; to ICOM conf. Buenos Aires 1986; Founder Sec., Can. Fed. Friends of Museums, and member, 1977– ; Mem., Bd. of Trustees, National Museums of Canada, Consultative Ctte., National Museum of Natural Science, National Gallery of Canada 1987–90; Gov., Ridley College, St. Catharines, Ont. 1977–91; Dir., Toronto Arts Prodns. (now Candn. Stage Co.) 1978–82; Founding Pres., Rosedale Br., Arthritis Society; Dir., Eye Rsch. Institute of Ont. 1983–88; Celebration Ctte., Toronto Internat. Festival 1982–84; Am. Assn. Mus. (Trustee Section); Metrop. Mus. of Art, N.Y.; Life Mem., Art Gall. of Ont.; Benefactor mem., R.O.M.; Timothy Eaton Memorial Ch. Toronto; First Annual Outstanding Achievement Award for Volunteerism, Min. of Citizenship & Culture, Ont. 1986; Arbor Award, Univ. of Toronto 1990; awarded Commemorative Medal for 125th Anniversary of Candn. Confederation; Clubs: Badminton & Racquet (Dir. 1991– ); Muskoka Lakes Golf & Country Club; Residence: 39 South Dr., Toronto, Ont. M4W 1R2.

**RANDALL, Stephen James,** B.A., M.A., Ph.D.; professor of history; b. Toronto, Ont. 9 Sept. 1944; s. John James and Dorothy Evelyn (Rook) R.; e. Univ. of West. Ont., B.A. 1966; Univ. of Toronto, M.A. 1967, Ph.D. 1972; m. Diane d. Anne and Sidney Fitt Aug. 1966; children: Alexandra Elizabeth, Matthew Stephen; IMPERIAL OIL-LINCOLN MCKAY CHAIR IN AMERICAN STUDIES, FAC. OF SOC. SCIENCES, UNIV. OF CALGARY 1989– and DEAN, FACULTY OF SOCIAL SCIENCES 1994– ; Lectr. in English, Univ. nacional, Bogotá 1967; Lectr. to Asst. Prof., History, Univ. of Toronto 1971–74; McGill Univ. 1974–89 (Dept. Chrmn. 1975–78, 1983–87; 2 terms, Senate); 1 term, Acad. Adv. Panel, SSHRCC; Mem., Candn. Assn. of Am. Studies (Extve. Sec. 1989– ); Candn. Hist. Assn.; Orgn. of Am. Historians; Soc. of Historians of Am. Fgn. Relns.; Petroleum Hist. Soc.; author: 'The Diplomacy of Modernization' 1977 (finalist ms, Frederick Jackson Turner comp. of Orgn. of Am. Hist. & Ferguson Prize, Candn. Hist. Assn.), 'United States Foreign Oil Policy' 1985 (selected by 'Choice' as 1 of outstanding books of year on N. Am. hist.); 'The United States and Colombia: Hegemony and Interdependence' 1992; 'Ambivalent Allies: The United States and Canada' (with J.H. Thompson) 1994; editor: 'North America Without Borders' 1992; co-editor: 'The Study of United States History in Canada' 1985; journal editor: 'International Journal,' Candn. Institute of Internat. Affairs; 'Canadian Review of American Studies,' Canadian Assn. for Am. Studies; recreations: tennis, music; Office: Calgary, Alta. T2N 1N4.

**RANGANATHAN, Subramanian,** ndc, B.Sc., M.Sc., M.Tech., Ph.D.; university professor; b. Madras, India 12 April 1941; s. Chandrasekar and Lakshmi (Venkatesan) Subramanian; e. Delhi Univ. B.Sc. (Hons.) 1960, M.Sc. 1962; Indian Inst. of Technology M.Tech. 1963; Cornell Univ. Ph.D. 1967; m. Lakshmi d. Anantharaman and Rugmani Kalyanakrishnan 2 Sept. 1970; one child: Shoba; PROFESSOR, MATHEMATICS & COMPUTER SCIENCE, ROYAL MILITARY COLLEGE OF CANADA 1984– ; Rsch. Assoc., Cornell Univ. 1967–68; Rsch. Assoc., Royal Military College of Canada 1968–69; Asst. Prof. 1969–79; Assoc. Prof. 1979–84; Head, Dept. of Math. & Comp. Sci. 1985– ; Visiting Scientist, MIT 1978; AERE, Harwell, U.K. 1981–82; Visiting Assoc., CALTECH 1979; on exchange to Royal Military Coll. of Science, Shrivenham, U.K. 1981–82; Visiting Prof., Univ. of B.C. 1986; Visiting Fellow, Australian Nat. Univ. 1992; selected to attend Nat. Defence College 1990–91; defence research board grants continuously since 1975; Mem., Candn. Assn. of Physicists; Am. Physical Soc.; Candn. Inst. of Neutron Scattering; author/co-author of over 50 sci. papers in profl. journals; recreations: tennis, golf, squash, bridge; Home: 795 Marwood Place, Kingston, Ont. K7P 2C2; Office: Kingston, Ont. K7K 5L0.

**RANGER, Keith Brian,** B.Sc., Ph.D., F.R.S.C.; educator; b. Salisbury, Eng. 11 Aug. 1935; s. Eric John and ivy Edna (Sawyer) R.; e. Aylesbury Grammar Sch. 1953; Univ. Coll. London B.Sc. 1956, Ph.D. 1959; children: Stephen Keith Thomas, Sara Anne; PROF. OF MATH, UNIV. OF TORONTO 1970– ; Asst. Lectr. Bedford Coll. Univ. of London 1958–61; Lectr. present Univ. 1961, Asst. Prof. 1963, Assoc. Prof. 1966; recipient State Scholarship with Distinction in Pure Math., Applied Math. and Physics 1953; author or co-author over 70 papers prof. jours.; mem., Candn. Math. Soc.; recreations: music, golf; Home: 78 Petman Ave., Toronto, Ont. M4S 2S8; Office: Toronto, Ont. M5S 1A1.

**RANGER, Pierre,** B.A.Sc., P.Eng.; b. Hawkesbury, Ont. 14 Oct. 1941; s. Aurele and Isabelle (Lanthier) R.; e. Univ. of Montreal B.A.Sc., P.Eng. 1966; m. Louise 8 July 1967; children: Eric, Louis-Philippe, Jean-Pierre; PRESIDENT & CHIEF EXECUTIVE OFFICER, CEGELEC ENTERPRISES LIMITED (formerly BG Checo Internat. Limited); LAVALIN 1966–86; Gen. Mgr., Grande-Baie Aluminum Smelter Project 1977–81; Project Mgr., Construction Projects, Algiers (Govt. of Algeria) 1981–83; Project Dir., Bécancour Aluminum Smelter Project; UTDC Inc. 1986–91; Vice-Pres., Operations then President; Mem., Order of Engineers of Quebec; Montreal C. of C.; Engineering Inst. of Canada; Home: 3 Blvd. Simard, Apt. 406, St. Lambert, Que. J4S 1Y8; Office: 7151 Jean-Talon St. E., Suite 1000, Place Carillon, Anjou, Que. H1M 3R4.

**RANKIN, John James,** B.Sc., M.B.A.; college president; b. Hamilton, Ont. 3 Oct. 1943; s. James and Marion Jean (MacFarlane) R.; e. McMaster Univ. B.Sc. 1966, M.B.A. 1971; m. Wilma Anne d. Dorothy (Cliffe) and Henry Johns 28 July 1967; children: Michael James, Sara Elizabeth; PRES., THE GEORGE BROWN COLL. OF APPLIED ARTS & TECHNOL. 1991– ; Mngt. Cons., Peat Marwick Stevenson and Kellogg 1976–79; Vice-Pres., Human Resources, Northern Telecom 1979–88; Sr. Vice-Pres., Mitel Corp. 1989–91; Home: 20 - 2103 Berwick Dr., Burlington, Ont. L7M 4B7; Office: 500 MacPherson Ave., Toronto, Ont. M5R 1X1.

**RANKIN, Linda M.,** B.A.; communications executive; b. Foam Lake, Sask. 16 June 1946; e. Univ. of Sask. B.A. 1968; Vice-Pres., Business Development, Telesat Canada & Chief Extve. Offr., Telesat Enterprises Inc. 1988; var. positions in Human Resources Mngt., Policy Devel. & Sales, Bell Canada 1972–81; Human Resources Mgr., Telesat 1981; Dir., Personnel & Public Affairs 1982; Vice-Pres., Admin. 1983; Telecommunication Services 1984; Chrmn., Advanced Broadcasting Systems of Canada 1990– ; Bd. Mem., Banff TV Festival Foundation 1989–91, 1992– ; Past Chrmn., DVS Communications; Past Chrmn., Téléport de Montréal Limitée.

**RANKINE, Peter Frederick,** B.Sc., M.B.A., P.Eng.; executive; b. Newcastle, N.B. 21 May 1945; s. Frederick William and Elva Jean (MacKenzie) R.; e. Univ. of N.B. B.Sc.(EE) 1967; York Univ. M.B.A. 1982; m. Mary Lou d. Lyle and Louise Jex 22 Aug. 1970; children: Craig, Megan; VICE PRES. HONEYWELL LTD. 1988– ; Eng.

Canadian General Electric 1967–70; joined present Co. 1970 serving various positions incl. Dir. of Strategic Planning, Div. Mgr., Group Dir.; Dir. EEMAC (Sec. 1989–90, Treas. 1990, Vice Chrmn. 1991, 1993); Dir., CABA (Chrmn. 1988–91); mem. Assn. Profl. Engs. Prov. Ont.; Bd. Trade Metrop. Toronto; United Church; recreations: skiing, boating; Club: Granite; Home: 27 Dunlace Dr., Willowdale, Ont. M2L 2R8; Office: 740 Ellesmere Rd., Scarborough, Ont. M1P 2V9.

**RANSEN, Mort;** film producer, director, writer; b. Montreal, Que.; m. Ellen Garvie; children: Chaya, Yoshi, Joshua, Hannah; OWNER, RANFILM PRODUCTIONS INC. 1988– ; has been making films since 1961; director/writer, Nat. Film Bd. 1961–84; made 26 films; has written, directed 14 dramas, 5 of these feature length since 1984; participant, cultural exchange: worked in Sweden & made several award-winning films for Swedish TV 1969; winner of 15 internat. awards as dir. & writer; 1st feature from Ranfilm Prodns. 'Falling Over Backwards' is now in distribution; Home: 837 Isabella Pt. Rd., R.R. 1, Fulford Harbour, B.C. V0S 1C0; Office: P.O. Box 411, Ganges, B.C. V0S 1E0.

**RANSOM, Jeremy;** ballet dancer; b. St. Catharines, Ont.; s. Ross Ernest and Barbara Lane (Reynolds) R.; e. Memorial P.S. St. Catharines; National Ballet School Toronto; PRINCIPAL DANCER, THE NATIONAL BALLET OF CANADA 1980– ; made his debut with National Ballet as Gennaro in 'Napoli' 1982; other roles incl. The Prince in 'Nutcracker,' Espada in 'Don Quixote,' Colas in 'La Fille Mal Gardée,' Franz in 'Coppélia,' Lensky in 'Onegin' (a signature role), Oberon in 'The Dream,' poet in 'Les Sylphides,' The Mad Hatter in 'Alice' (world premiere 1986), the husband in 'La Ronde' 1987, Anubis in 'Sphinx' 1991, Pan in 'Daphnis and Chlöe' 1991; has also created roles in 'Have Steps Will Travel' 1988, 'Time Out with Lola' 1991, 'The Need' 1990, 'the second detail' 1991 and numerous others; recent leading roles incl. 'Dream Dances' 1989, 'Etudes' 1990, 'Concerto for Flute and Harp' 1990, 'Song of the Earth' 1991; James Kudelka's specially commissioned 'The Miraculous Mandarin' 1993; John Neumeier's world premiere 'Now and Then' 1993; performed as soloist with Zurich Ballet 1986–87; toured throughout Italy as guest artist with 'Stars and Soloists of Canadian Ballet' 1985; performed with Australian Ballet 1989 as James in 'La Sylphide'; with Ballet Met (Ohio) as Franz in 'Coppélia' 1990; with 'St. Petersburg Renaissance' telethon in St. Petersburg, Russia as Lensky in 'Onegin' 1991; film work incl. role of Lensky in 'Onegin' and the Mad Hatter in 'Alice' (CBC-TV Primedia prodns.); first appearance as the Prince in 'Swan Lake' Lewiston, N.Y. 1991; Peter Dwyer Scholarship, Nat. Ballet Sch.; Canada Council Grant; Bronze Medal, Sr. Men's Div., 3rd U.S. Internat. Ballet Competition (Jackson, Miss.) 1986; recreations: travel, photography, food, movies, writing; Office: 157 King St. E., Toronto, Ont. M5C 1G9.

**RAOUL, Valerie Anne,** B.A., M.A., Ph.D.; educator; b. Eng. 15 Sept. 1941; d. George Frederick and Mabel Florence (Reid) Underwood; e. Cambridge Univ. B.A. 1963; London Sch. of Econ. Dip. Soc. Adm. 1964; Bristol Univ. Cert. Ed. 1965–66; McMaster Univ. M.A. 1971; Univ. of Toronto Ph.D. 1978; m. Yvon s. Alain and Hortense Raoul 3 June 1972; children: Alain, Stephanie, Melanie; PROF. OF FRENCH UNIV. OF B.C. 1979– ; Head of French Dept. 1991– ; taught Eng. as second lang. in Thailand and France and French at high sch. level in Eng. prior to arrival Can. 1970; grad. work and part-time teaching McMaster Univ. and Univ. of Toronto 1970–79; joined present univ. 1979, Coordinator Women's Studies 1988–90; recipient SSHRC Leave Fellowship 1984–85, Rsch. Time Stipend 1988–89; Rsch. grant 1991–95; author 'The French Fictional Journal. Fictional Narcissism/Narcissistic Fiction' 1980; 'Distinctly Narcissistic Diary Fiction in Québec' 1993; co-ed. 'The Anatomy of Genders' 1992; various articles lit. mags. and jours.; mem. Assn. Candn. & Que. Lits. (Vice Pres. 1986–88); Assn. des Professeurs de français des Univs. canadiennes (W. Rep. 1986–90); Candn. Women's Studies Assn.; Candn. Comp. Lit. Assn.; Home: 4443 W. 13th Ave., Vancouver, B.C. V6R 2V2; Office: Vancouver, B.C. V6T 1Z1.

**RAPHAEL, Andrew J.,** B.A., M.A.; international market and business development specialist; b. Vancouver, B.C. 4 May 1954; s. Leslie Allan and Anita Nicky R.; e. Brentwood College 1972; Univ. of Toronto B.A. 1976; Univ. of B.C. M.A. 1981; m. Louisa d. Yvonne and Kam Tong Leung 4 Sept. 1988; DIRECTOR, CORP. BUSINESS DEVEL., CANADA MALTING GROUP 1992– ; Econ. Devel. Specialist (Malaysia/Thailand), World Bank 1977–79; Trade Devel. Offr., Govt. of B.C. 1981–83; Assoc. Trade Dir., Govt. of Alta. 1983–85; Vice-

Pres. Asia Pacific, MRI Internat. Inc. 1985–88; Dir., Internat. Programs, Govt. of Canada 1988–90; Extve. Dir., Canada Beef Export Fed. 1990–92; Advisor, Canada Beef Export Fed.; Advisor/Lectr., Asia Pacific Management Cooperative Program; Dir., Agri-Food Competitiveness Council; Mem., Assn. of Strategic Planners; author: 'Regional Development in Industrialising Nations' 1981; 'Overview of Export Markets' 1991; recreations: reading, music, bicycling, travel; Office: 10 – 4 Seasons Place, #600, Toronto, Ont. M9B 6H7.

**RAPOPORT, Anatol,** S.M., Ph.D., D.Hum.Litt., LL.D.; F.A.A.S.; b. Lozovaya, Russia 22 May 1911; s. Boris and Adel R.; e. Vienna Hochschule fur Musik Dipls. in Piano, Composition, conducting 1934; Univ. of Chicago S.B. 1938, S.M. 1940, Ph.D. (Math.) 1941; Univ. of W. Mich. D.Hum. Litt. (Hon.) 1971; Univ. of Toronto LL.D (hon.) 1986; m. Gwen Goodrich 29 Jan. 1949; children: Anya, Alexander, Charles Anthony; PROFESSOR OF PEACE STUDIES, UNIV. OF TORONTO 1984– ; Instr. Math. Ill. Inst. Technol. 1946–47; Research Assoc., Asst. Prof. Comte. Math. Biol. Univ. of Chicago 1947–54; Fellow, Center Advanced Study Behavioral Sciences, Stanford, Calif. 1954–55; Prof. of Math. Biol. and Sr. Research Math., Mental Health Research Inst. Univ. of Mich. 1955–70; Prof. of Psychol. and Math. Univ. of Toronto 1970–80; Prof. Emeritus 1980– ; Guest Prof., Univ. of Warsaw 1961–62; Vienna Inst. Advanced Studies 1968, 1976, 1977; Tech. Univ. of Denmark 1968–69; Wissenschaftszentrum Berlin 1978; Univ. of Hiroshima 1978; Univ. of Louisville 1979; Dir., Vienna Inst. For Advanced Studies 1980–83; Ludwig-Maximilian Univ. Munich 1989; served with U.S. Air Force 1942–46, rank Capt.; author 'Science and the Goals of Man' 1950; 'Operational Philosophy' 1953; 'Fights, Games and Debates' 1960; 'Strategy and Conscience' 1964; 'Two-Person Game Theory' 1966; 'N-Person Game Theory' 1970; 'The Big Two' 1971; 'Conflict in Man-Made Environment' 1974; 'Game Theory as a Theory of Conflict Resolution' 1974; 'Semantics' 1975; 'Mathematische Methoden in den Sozial Wissenschaften' 1980; 'Mathematical Models in the Social and Behavioural Sciences' 1983; 'General Systems Theory' 1986; 'The Origins of Violence' 1989; 'Decision Theory and Decision Behaviour' 1989; 'Peace An Idea Whose Time Has Come' 1992; co-author 'Prisoner's Dilemma' 1965; 'The 2X2 Game' 1976; 'Canada and the World' 1992; Ed. 'General Systems' 1956–77; Assoc. Ed. 'Journal of Conflict Resolution'; 'Behavioral Science'; over 300 articles; recipient Lenz Internat. Peace Research Prize 1976; Harold D. Lasswell Award Pol. Psychol.; Fellow Am. Acad. of Arts and Sci's; mem. Am. Math. Soc.; Candn. Math. Council; Soc. Math. Biol.; Internat. Soc. Gen. Semantics (Pres. 1953–55); Soc. Gen. Systems Research (Pres. 1965–66); Candn. Peace Research & Educ. Assn. (Pres. 1972–75); Science for Peace (Pres. 1984–86); Home: 38 Wychwood Park, Toronto, Ont. M6G 2V5; Office: Univ. College, Univ. of Toronto, Toronto, Ont. M5S 1A1.

**RAPOPORT, Janis,** B.A.; writer; editor; b. Toronto, Ont. 22 June 1946; d. Maxwell Lewis and the late Roslyn (Cohen) R.; e. Univ. of Toronto, B.A. 1967; 2nd m. Douglas s. Douglas and Lucille Donegani 20 May 1980; children: Jeremy, Sara, Julia (Seager), Renata (Donegani); Editor, 'Ethos' Magazine 1983–87; Ed. & Rsch., 'Which?' & Paul Hamlyn Ltd. 1968–70; Assoc. Ed., 'Tamarack Review' 1970–82; num. workshops, readings & talks 1973– ; Asst. Ed., Bellhaven House 1971–73; Story Ed., CBC TV Drama 1973–74; Playwright-in-res., Tarragon Theatre 1974–75; Banff Centre (summer) 1976; freelance writer, ed. & lit. cons. 1975– ; Assoc. Co-ord., 'Words Alive' 1980–84 and 1988; part-time Instr., Sheridan Coll. 1984–86; Writer-in-Residence, St. Thomas Public Lib. 1987; Writer-in-Residence, Beeton Public Library 1988; Writer-in-Residence, Dundas Public Library 1990; Writer-in-Residence, North York Public Library 1991; Instr., Sch. of Continuing Studies, Univ. of Toronto 1988– ; Can. Counc. Arts Award 1981–82; N.Y. Art Dirs. Club Award of Merit ('Imaginings') 1983 and ('poem' on Univ. of Guelph poster) 1983; A.I.G.A. Cert. of Excellence ('Imaginings') 1983; Outstanding Achievement Award, Am. Poetry Assn. 1986; Toronto Arts Council Rsch. and Develop. Award 1990, 1992; Dir., Ethos Cult. Devel. Found. 1981– ; Mem., Writers' Union of Can., Playwrights' Union of Can.; The League of Candn. Poets; Writers' Guild of Can.; author: 'Upon Her Fluent Route' 1991; 'Winter Flowers' 1979; 'Jeremy's Dream' 1974; 'Within the Whirling Moment' 1967 (poetry); 'Dreamgirls' 1979 (drama); co-author: 'Imaginings' 1982 (lim. ed. fine-art portfolio); co-editor: 'Landscape' 1977 (poetry); work has appeared in mags., anthols., newspapers & radio; Prod.: 'Dreamgirls' 1979 and subsequently (and in 1987 in French), 'And She Could Eat No Lean' 1975; 'Gilgamesh' 1976; profiled on

TV Ont.'s 'Canadian Literature Series'; recreations: aerobics, cycling, baseball; Address: c/o The Writers Union of Canada, 24 Ryerson Ave., Toronto, Ont. M5T 2P3.

**RAPSON, W(illiam) Howard,** M.A.Sc., Ph.D., D.Eng., D.Sc., F.R.S.C. (1971), F.C.I.C. (1942), H.F.C.I.C. (1981), F.C.A.E. (1987), C.Chem. (1984), P.Eng. (1953); Chemical Engineer; b. Toronto, Ont., 15 Sept. 1912; s. Alfred Ernest and Lillian Jane (Cannicott) R.; e. Riverdale Coll. Inst., Toronto, Ont., University of Toronto, B.A.Sc. 1934, M.A.Sc. 1935, Ph.D. 1941; D.Eng. (Hon. c.) Univ. of Waterloo, 1976; D.Sc. (Hon. c.) McGill Univ., 1980; D.Sc. (Hon. c.) Univ. of Guelph 1990; m. Mary Margaret, d. late Martin Livingstone Campbell, 29 Jan. 1937; children: Margaret Lillian, Lorna Jean, Linda Mary, William Howard, Jr.; UNIVERSITY PROFESSOR EMERITUS, UNIV. OF TORONTO 1981– ; Prof. of Chemical Engn., Univ. of Toronto 1953–81, Univ. Prof. 1976–81; Bd. Chrmn., W.H. Rapson Ltd. 1977 (Pres. 1964–77); Pres., Chem. Engn. Research Consultants Ltd. 1970–81 (Vice Pres. 1963–70); Consulting Chem. Engr., since 1953; Demonst. in Chem. Engn., Univ. Toronto, 1934–40 and Instr. 1940; Research Chemist, Candn. Internat. Paper Co., Hawkesbury, Ont., 1940–48; i/c of Pioneering Research, Indust. Cellulose Research Ltd., Hawkesbury, Ont., 1948–53; inventor of Candn. and foreign patents on chem. processes; Trustee, Hawkesbury Pub. Sch. Bd., 1947–53 (Chrmn. 1949–53); served in 2nd Bn. (Reserve) Stormont, Dundas & Glengary Highlanders 1942–45; mem., Tech. Section, Candn. Pulp & Paper Assn. (Weldon Gold Medal, 1954; Chrmn. 1969–71; Hon. Life mem. 1973; John S. Bates Memorial Gold Medal 1993); Fellow, Chem. Inst. Can. (Palladium Medal 1980, Hon. Fellow 1981, President 1985–86); mem., Assn. Prof. Engrs. Ont. (Gold Medal, 1977); Tech. Assn. of Pulp & Paper Industry (U.S.A.) (Dir. 1973–76, TAPPI Gold Medal, Hon. Life mem. 1977); Candn. Soc. for Chem. Engn. (Dir. 1967–68; R. S. Jane Award 1966); mem. Bd. Govs. Ont. Inst. for Studies in Educ. 1970–77; mem., Am. Inst. of Chem. Engrs., (Forest Prod. Div. Award, 1977); Anselme Payen Award, Am. Chem. Soc. 1978; Foreign mem., Swedish Roy. Acad. of Engn. Sciences, 1978; Shalimar Gold Medal, Indian Pulp & Paper Assn., 1975; Medal of the Brazilian Pulp & Paper Tech. Assn., 1974; McCharles Prize, Bd. of Govs., Univ. of Toronto, 1966; Royal Society of Canada, James W. Eadie Medal 1981; Canada Council, Killam Memorial Prize 1986; United Church; recreation: photography; water skiing; Home: 110 Bloor St. W., Suite 1001, Toronto, Ont. M5S 2W7.

**RAPTIS, Leda Helen,** M.Sc., Ph.D.; university professor; b. Athens, Greece 30 Dec. 1950; d. Napoleon and Elli (Papandreou) R.; e. Univ. of Athens M.Sc. 1973; McGill Univ. M.Sc. 1975; Univ. of Sherbrooke Ph.D. 1979; m. Kevin s. Keith and Shirley Firth 5 Oct. 1988; children: Andromahi, Leif; ASSOCIATE PROF., QUEEN'S UNIV. 1993– ; Research Assoc., Nat. Research Council 1984–85; Asst. Prof., Queen's Univ. 1986–93; Damon-Runyon, Walter Winchell Cancer Rsch. Postdoctoral Fellowship (US) 1981; King George V Silver Jubilee Cancer Rsch. Postdoct. Fellowship (Nat. Cancer Inst.) 1981; Medical Rsch. Council Centennial Fellowship 1981; author/co-author of several research papers; recreations: skin diving; Home: 487 Victoria St., Kingston, Ont. K7L 3Z8; Office Kingston, Ont. K7L 3N6.

**RASKY, Harry,** B.A., LL.D.; film and TV producer, director, writer; b. Toronto, Ont. 9 May 1928; s. Louis and Pearl (Krazner) R.; e. Regal Rd. Pub. and Oakwood Coll. Inst. Toronto; Univ. of Toronto, B.A. 1949, LL.D. 1982; m. Ruth Arlene Werkhoven, 21 March 1965; children: Holly Laura, Adam Louis; Reporter no. of daily Newspapers Kirkland Lake, Ont., 1949; News editor-producer, CHUM, Toronto, 1950; News editor-producer CKEY, Toronto, 1951–52; co-founder news-documentary dept., CBC, 1952–55; Assoc. editor, Saturday Night, 1955; producer-dir.-writer, N.Y.C. 1960–61; Pres. Harry Rasky Productions Inc. since 1967; received world-wide acclaim for documentaries on Marc Chagall, Tennessee Williams, Arthur Miller and George Bernard Shaw; has produced, directed and written programs for maj. TV networks in Can., U.S. and Eng.; world leaders interviewed incl. Pres. and Mrs. Johnson, Mrs. Roosevelt, Fidel Castro, David Ben Gurion, King of Sweden, Martin Luther King, Emperor Haile Selassie, Queen Elizabeth, foreign ministers of most major nations, Lester Pearson; performers directed incl. Orson Welles, Sir Ralph Richardson, Dame Edith Evans, Dirk Bogarde, James Mason, Emlyn Williams, Lynn Redgrave, Siobhan McKenna, Bob Hope, Jack Benny, Benny Goodman, Mahalia Jackson, Christopher Plummer, Geneviève Bujold, John Colicos; stage dir. in Eng.

and Can.; Lectr., New Sch. for Social Research, Columbia Univ., Iowa State Univ.; over 200 Internat. awards incl. Venice Film Festival 1970 ('Upon This Rock'); Emmy and Internat. Golden Eagle Awards ('Hall of Kings'); San Francisco Film Festival Participation Prize; Peabody Award, TV Guide Award; Sylvania Award; Freedom Foundation; Sch. Bell Award; Ohio State; Overseas Press Club; Am. Council for Better Broadcasts Award; Candn. Radio Award; awarded Commemorative Medal for 125th Anniversary of Candn. Confederation; books incl. 'Lower than the Angels'; 'Tales of Acapulco Ladies'; 'Tennessee Williams': A Portrait in Laughter & Lamentation'; 'Stratas, an affectionate tribute' 1988; memoirs, 'Nobody Swings on Sunday' 1980; 'TV Bitch'; play, 'No Big Deal'; recent films incl. 'Stratasphere'; 'Being Different'; 'The Spies Who Never Were'; 'Raymond Massey: Actor of the Century' 1984; 'The Mystery of Henry Moore' 1985; 'Karsh: The Searching Eye' 1986 (Emmy nomination); 'To Mend the World' 1987; 'Degas' 1988; 'Northrop Frye - The Great Teacher' 1990; 'The Magic Season of Robertson Davies' 1990; 'The Dispossessed: The War Against the Indians' 1992 (recipient, 12 Internat. prizes for excellence of achievement); honored with retrospective by CBC 'Rasky's Gallery: Poets, Painters, Singers, Saints' 1988; honored by the Film-makers Union at the Moscow Film Festival 1991 for 'outstanding contribution to the culture of the 20th Century,' with a retrospective of his work; contrib. to various newspapers and mags.; mem., Dirs. Guild Am.; Writers Guild Am. (Offr); Acad. TV Arts & Sciences (judge); winner Cert. of Special Merit, Motion Picture Academy, L.A. 1984; EMMY 1986; Director's Guild of America best non-fiction director 1986; first filmmaker to be given Hon. degree by Univ. of Toronto 1982; recreation: swimming; Office: c/o CBC, Box 500, Stn. A., Toronto, Ont. M5W 1E6.

**RASMINSKY, Louis,** C.C. (1968), C.B.E., B.A., D.C.L., LL.D., D.H.L., economist; banker; b. Montreal, Que. 1908; s. late David and Etta (R); e. Pub. Schs., Toronto, Ont. and Harbord Coll. Inst. there (winner of three scholarships); Univ. of Toronto, B.A. (Hons. Econ.) 1928, LL.D., 1953; Hon. Fellow London Sch. of Economics 1959; D.H.L. Hebrew Union Coll. 1963; LL.D. Queen's 1967; D.C.L. Bishop's 1968; LL.D. McMaster 1969; Hon. Doctorate, Yeshiva University 1970; LL.D. Univ. of B.C. 1971; Trent 1972, Concordia 1975; Univ. of W. Ont., 1978; Carleton Univ. 1987; m. Lyla, d. late Harry Rotenberg of Toronto, Ont.; children: Michael, Lola; GOV. BANK OF CANADA 1961–1973; joined staff of Econ. and Financial Sec. of League of Nations, 1930; joined staff of Bank of Canada, 1940; organ. Res. & Stat. Sec., Foreign Exchange Control Bd., 1940; Asst. to Chrmn., 1941; Chairman (Alternate), 1942; Extve. Asst. to Govs. Bank of Canada 1943–54; Depy. Gov., 1955–61; Extve. Dir., Internat. Monetary Fund, 1946–62; Internat. Bank for Reconstruction & Devel., 1950–62; Alternate Gov. for Can., Internat. Monetary Fund; Chrmn., Bd. Govs., Internat. Devel. Research Centre, 1973–78; rec'd 'Outstanding Public Service Award' 1968; Vanier Medal, Inst.-Public Adm. 1974; recreations: golf, fishing, Clubs: Cercle Universitaire (Ottawa); Rideau; Five Lakes (Wakefield, Que.); Home: 1006 – 20 The Driveway, Ottawa, Ont. K2P 1C8.

**RASMUSSEN, Theodore,** M.D., M.S., F.R.C.P. & S(C.); b. Provo, Utah, 28 April 1910; s. Andrew Theodore and Gertrude (Brown) R.; e. Univ. of Minn., 1927–30; Univ. of Minn. Med. Sch., 1930–34; Mayo Foundation, Rochester, Minn., 1936–39; Montreal Neurol. Inst. of McGill Univ., 1939–42; B.S. and M.B. 1934, M.D. 1935, M.S. 1939; M.D. (Hons.) Univ. of Edinburgh, 1980; Hon. Dr. of Med., Univ. of Umea, Sweden 1988; m. Catherine Cora, d. R.McG. Archibald, 18 Dec. 1947; children: Donald, Ruth, Mary, Linda; PROF. OF NEUROL. & NEURO-SURG., McGILL UNIV., since 1954; Sr. Neurol. consultant, Montreal Neurol. Inst., since 1972; Lectr. and Res. Fellow, McGill Univ., 1946–47; Prof. of Neurol. Surg., Univ. of Chicago, 1947–54; Depy. Dir. and Neurosurgeon, Montreal Neurol. Inst. 1954–60; Dir., 1961–72; Neurol. & Neurosurgeon-in-chief, Royal Victoria Hosp. 1961–72; served in 2nd World War; active duty U.S. Army Medical Corp, October 1942 (First Lt.) to March 1946 (Lt. Col.); Chief of Neurosurgical Section, 14th Evacuation Hosp., China-Burma-India Theatre; rec'd. 'Outstanding Achievement-Award' Univ. Minn. (1958), Univ. of Chicago (1963); Ambassador Award, Epilepsy Internat. 1979; Emeritus Prof. Award, McGill Univ., 1980; Penfield Award, Candn. League Against Epilepsy 1982; Lennox Award, American Epilepsy Soc. 1986; Distinguished Service Award, The Soc. of Neurological Surgeons 1988; Publications: 'Cerebral Cortex of Man' (with Wilder Penfield), 1950; 'Functional Neurosurgery' (with Raul Marino Jr.) 1979; over 165 contrib. to prof. journs. textbooks and monographs; Alpha Omega Alpha; Sigma Xi, etc.; Christian; Club: Canadian; Home: 29 Surrey Drive, Montreal, Que. H3P 1B2; Office: 3801 University St., Montreal, Que. H3A 2B4.

**RASTORP, Robert Harry,** B.A.; executive; b. Matheson, Ontario, 1 Sept. 1932; s. Robert C. Rastorp and Florence (Child); e. Univ. of Toronto B.A.; m. Gertrude Elizabeth Walsh, 30 May 1964; children: Rob Alex Neil. PRES. & C.E.O., FIRST BRANDS (CANADA) CORP. 1986– ; Dir., OMMRI II: Corporations in Support of Recycling; Former Sr. Vice Pres., Union Carbide Canada Ltd.; Former Dir., Grocery Products Mfrs. Can.; Dir., Electronic Data Interchange Council; Dir., Soc. of the Plastics Ind.; Gov., YMCA of Metro Toronto; mem. Bd. Trade Metrop. Toronto; Automotive Industries Assn.; Candn. Mfrs. Assn.; recreations: Member of the Magic Circle, London, Eng.; International Brotherhood of Magicians, fishing, gardening, art; Office: 100 Consilium Place, 5th Flr., Scarborough, Ont. M1H 3E3.

**RATCLIFFE, Edward Bevan,** B.A.Sc., P.Eng.; executive; b. Hamilton, Ont. 1 July 1919; s. Edward Bevan and Lydia (Ward) R.; e. Bartonville Sch. 1932; Delta Coll. Inst. Hamilton 1937; Univ. of Toronto B.A.Sc. 1941; m. Elinor d. Burnham and Mary Gill 8 Oct. 1978; children: Linda, Janis, Bevan, Starr; FOUNDER, ARRISCRAFT CORP. 1983– ; Supr. Dupont of Canada Nylon Div. 1941–46; Founder, Ratcliffe Engineering 1946; Abbotsford Homes Ltd. 1949; Angelstone Ltd. 1949; Adair Marble Quarries 1968; Dir., Devel. Services Intnl. of Canada 1977– ; Unitarian Universalist Assn. 1959–62; Pres., Candn. Abortion Rights Action League 1975–76; Unitarian; recreations: boating, tennis, swimming; Address: (P.O. Box 3190) Cambridge, Ont. N3H 4S8.

**RATH, Ulrich E.G.,** B.Sc., M.Sc.; mining executive; b. Weiden, W. Germany 7 July 1946; s. Ulrich and Veronica (Redlin) R.; e. Concordia Univ. B.Sc. (Hons.) 1967; Univ. of Alta. M.Sc. 1969; m. Carol d. George and Katherine Elliott 25 April 1967; children: Chris, Jeffrey, Matthew; VICE-PRESIDENT BUSINESS DEVELOPMENT, RIO ALGOM LIMITED 1992– ; Senior Field Geol. & Project Mgr. 1966–72; Asst. to Hon. R.L. Stanfield 1972–74; Policy Analyst, Min. of Natural Resources 1974–75; Extve. Officer, The Mining Assn. of Canada 1976–79; Dir., Corp. Affairs, Hudson Bay Mining & Smelting 1979–83; Pres. & Sr. Partner, FOCUS 1983–87; Vice-Pres. & Mgr., acquisitions, WestGold 1988–92; Pres. & Dir., Shamrock Resources 1989–91; Dir., Coastech Rsch. 1988–91; NRC Scholarship 1969–72 Fulbright Scholarship 1973; Yale Lecture Series 1975; Guest Lecturer, Univ. of Toronto 1974–75; Co-Chair, Northern Mineral Adv. Sub-Ctte. 1979; Mem., P.C. Party 1972– (has held var. nat. & regional offices & positions); recreations: archeology and origins of early man to N. Am. incl. field research, collecting artifacts; Home: 99 Alcorn Ave., Toronto, Ont. M4V 1E5; Office: 120 Adelaide St. W., Suite 2600, Toronto, Ont. M5H 1W5.

**RATHGEB, Charles I.;** private investments; s. Charles C.R.; m. Rosemary, d. Desmond Clarke, Montreal, Que.; Dir., Rathgeb Foundation Inc.; Olympic Trust of Can.; Rathgeb Holdings; Home: 180 Teddington Park, Toronto, Ont. M4N 2C8; Office: North York City Centre, Suite 700, 5160 Yonge St., North York, Ont. M2N 6L9.

**RATTRAY, David William Thomas,** B.Comm., F.C.G.A., C.I.A., C.F.E.; public servant; b. Sherbrooke, Que. 1 Sept. 1947; s. Leslie Charles and Eileen Doris (Gleason) R.; e. Concordia Univ. B.Comm. 1968; Cert. Gen. Accountants Assn. of Can. C.G.A. 1974; Inst. of Internal Auditors C.I.A. 1978; Assn. of Certified Fraud Examiners 1993; m. Marion d. Harold and Eva Robinson 31 May 1969; children: Scott David Robinson and Kevin Robinson; ASSISTANT AUDITOR GENERAL, GOVT. OF CANADA 1988– ; Comptroller, Sherelco (Sherbrooke, Que.) 1971–73; joined Office of the Auditor General of Canada 1973; Fellow Award, The Cert. Gen. Accountants Assn. of Can.; Life Mem., Cert. Gen. Accts. Assn. of Ont.; awarded Commemorative Medal for 125th Anniversary of Candn. Confederation; Chair, Finance Ctte., Scouts Canada 1988–92; Treas. 1991–92; Vice-President 1992– ; Mem., Financial Mngt. Inst. of Canada; Mem., Cert. Gen. Accts. Assn.; Inst. of Internal Auditors; Conf. Bd. of Canada-TQM Forum 1991– ; Council of Logistics Mngt. 1991– ; Assn. of Certified Fraud Examiners 1993– ; Mem., Internat. Federation of Accountants 1993– ; recreations: ice hockey, golf, dancing; clubs: Carleton Golf & Yacht, Kanata Towne Squares; Home: 26 Barrhaven Cres., Nepean, Ont. K2J 1E8; Office: 10th Floor W., 240 Sparks St., Ottawa, Ont. K1A 0G6

**RATTRAY, R. Keith,** B.Comm.; financial executive; b. St-Jean sur Richelieu, Que. 29 April 1936; s. Gordon Stewart and Doris (Knight) R.; e. Chambly Co. H.S. 1953; Sir George Williams Univ. B.Comm. 1960; m. Heather d. Helen and Ralph Mumby 21 May 1982; children: Graham, Wendy; EXECUTIVE VICE-PRES., CHIEF FINANCIAL OFFICER & DIR., GOODFELLOW INC. 1972– ; Clerk, Auditor Freight & Receipts Dept., Candn. Pacific Railways 1954–55; Production Control & Expediting Clerk, Pirelli Cables 1955–56; General & Cost Acctg. Clerk (summer student) 1957–60; Auditor, Price Waterhouse 1960–65; joined Goodfellow Inc. 1965– ; Vice-Pres., Montreal Area Square Dance Assn. 1988–89; recreations: golf, square dancing; Home: 135 Bathurst Ave., Pointe-Claire, Que. H9S 5A2; Office: 225, rue Goodfellow, Delson, Que. J0L 1G0.

**RATUSHNY, Edward Joseph,** C.M., Q.C., B.A., LL.M., S.J.D.; educator; b. Kamsack, Sask 18 May 1942; s. Dmitro and Tillie R.; e. Univ. of Sask. B.A. 1964, LL.B. 1965; Univ. of London LL.M. 1968; Univ. of Mich. LL.M. 1972, S.J.D. 1979; m. Lynn d. Calvin and Marjorie Allen 30 Apr. 1966; children: Kimberly Anne, Daniel Paul John, Gregory Allen; PROF. OF LAW, UNIV. OF OTTAWA 1976– ; Dir. Human Rights Rsch. & Edn. Centre Ottawa 1983–86; called to Bar of Sask. 1965, Ont. 1972; law practice Makaroff & Co. Saskatoon 1965–67; Exec. Asst. to Fed. Cabinet Min. 1968–70; Assoc Prof. of Law Univ. of Windsor 1970–73; Special Adv. to Mins. of Justice, Ottawa 1973–76; Cons.: Ont. Law Reform Comn., Can. Law Reform Comn., Ont. Publ Complaints Comnr., Fed. Depts. of Justice, Solr. Gen., Transport, Nat. Revenue, Can. Counc., C.B.C., R.C.M.P.; Candn. Judicial Council, Bureau of Competition Policy; Chrmn. numerous Bds. of Inquiry pursuant to Ont. Human Rights Code; Vice Chrmn., Ont. Crown Employees Grievance Settlement Bd.; Counsel, Cohen Bd. of Review Environmental Contaminants 1980; mem. Min.'s Task Force on Immigration 1980; Chief Counsel and Staff Dir. Nat. Inquiry into Illegal Migrants in Can. 1983; Special Counsel to Min. of Transport on Transp. Disabled Persons 1984; Special Adv. to Refugee Status Adv. Ctte.; Constitutional Counsel, Zuber Public Inquiry into Ontario Courts 1986; General Counsel: Bd. of Comnrs., Chief and Police Force, Colter Public Inquiry into Niagara Regional Police Force 1988; Asst. Counsel, McEachern Inquiry into N.S. Judges 1990; Cmnr., Royal Commission on Systemic Discrimination in Criminal Justice System in Ontario; Registered Agent, NHL Players' Assn.; author: 'Self-Incrimination in the Canadian Criminal Process' 1979; 'A New Refugee Determination Process for Canada' 1983; 'Accessibility Standards for Disabled and Elderly Persons' 1984; 'Independence of Federal Administrative Tribunals and Agencies' 1990; numerous articles legal jours.; mem. Candn. Bar Assn.; Inst. Pub. Adm. Can.; Council of Can. Admin. Tribs.; Candn. Inst. Adm. Justice; Candn. Civil Liberties Assn. (Dir.); Nat. Council Crime & Delinquency; Internat. Comn. Jurists; Internat. Third World Legal Studies Assn.; Amnesty Internat.; Member of the Order of Canada 1992; mem. St. John's Ukrainian Cath. Ch.; recreations: ice hockey, swimming, playing saxophone, coaching minor hockey; Club: Le Cercle Universitaire; Home: 23 Lacewood Court, Ottawa, Ont. K2E 7E2; Office: 118 Fauteux Hall, Ottawa, Ont. K1N 6N5.

**RAUF, Tariq,** B.A., B.Sc., M.A.; nuclear arms control specialist; b. New Delhi, India 19 Oct. 1949; s. Mohammad and Vidya (Ram Gopal) R.; e. Univ. of Panjab B.A. 1970; London Sch. of Econ., B.Sc. 1973; Univ. of London M.A. 1977; Oxford Univ., post-grad. studies 1977–78; Univ. of Toronto, doctoral studies & rsch. 1980–86; SR. RSCH. ASSOC., CANDN. CENTRE FOR GLOBAL SECURITY (formerly Canadian Centre for Arms Control and Disarmament) 1987– ; Coord., Nuclear Non-Proliferation Proj. 1987– ; Member Academic Council on the United Nations System 1992–93; Advisor with Canada's arms control delegations to Geneva (1990) and New York (1991 and 1993); Member, Special Panel of Experts to the Sub-Committee of the House of Commons Standing Committee on External Affairs and Internat. Trade (1990); Lectr., Quaid-i-Azam Univ., Pakistan 1973–76; Vis. Lectr., Nat. Defence Coll., Pakistan 1973–76; Rsch. Assoc., Pakistan Inst. of Strategic Studies 1973–80; Teaching Asst., Univ. of Toronto 1980–85; joined Candn. Centre for Arms Control & Disarmament as Rsch. Assoc. 1986–87; Ed., 'Barometer' 1989–92; 'Arms Control Chronicle' 1986–89; Ford Found. Fellow in Dual Expertise (Internat. Security/Arms Control and Soviet/East Europ. Studies), Univ. of Toronto 1981; mem. Arms Control Assn.; U.S. Naval Inst.; author: 'Regional Approaches to Nuclear Non-Proliferation' 1993; 'Naval Arms Control in the Arctic' 1992; 'Nuclear Deterrence and Non-Proliferation' 1991; num. articles on arms control; co-author: 'Opening Pandora's Box: Nuclear-Powered Submarines and the Spread of Nuclear Weapons' 1988; 'Security Co-operation in the Arctic: A Canadian Response to Murmansk' 1989; recreations: music, drama, reading, travel; Home: 704 – 153 Nepean St., Ottawa, Ont. K2P 0B5; Office: 710 – 151 Slater St., Ottawa, Ont. K1P 5H3.

**RAUHALA, Ann Elaine,** B.A., B.A.A.; journalist; b. Sudbury, Ont. 7 Dec. 1954; d. Esko Alexander and Iona Anna (Tormala) R.; e. Loellen Park S.S. Sudbury 1973; Univ. of Toronto B.A. 1977; Ryerson Polytech. Inst. B.A.A.(Applied Arts, Jour.) 1979; m. Lorne s. Lazer and Mary Slotnick 27 Feb. 1990; one son: Sam Aleksander Nathan; COLUMNIST, FOREIGN ED. THE GLOBE AND MAIL 1989– ; Asst. to Foreign Ed. present newspaper 1983, Reporter Women's Issues 1986; recipient Robertine Barry Award in Jour. Candn. Rsch. Inst. Advanc. Women 1988; Exec., S. Ont. Newspaper Guild 1988, 1989; Home: 441 Grace St., Toronto, Ont. M6G 3A8; Office: 444 Front St. W., Toronto, Ont. M5V 2S9.

**RAUTER, Rose Marie,** B.Sc.F., M.Sc.F.; forest industry executive; b. Toronto, Ont.; e. Jarvis C.I. 1961; Univ. of Toronto B.Sc.F. 1965, M.Sc.F. 1968; Univ. of Calif. at Berkeley invited post-doctoral student 1983; PRESIDENT, ONT. FOREST INDUSTRIES ASSN. 1992– ; Research scientist in forest genetics, Ont. Min. of Nat. Resources 1965–66, 1968–79; Supvr. of several forestry programs 1979–88; Mgr., Ont. Forest Indus. Assn. 1988–92; participated & chaired many nat. & internat. groups incl. 2 5-year terms as Chair, Working Group for Internat. Union of Forest Rsch. Orgns. rep. 122 countries; current boards & cttes. incl. Adv. Ctte., Fac. of Forestry, Univ. of B.C.; Bd. of Dir., Wildlife Habitat Canada; Forestry Adv. Ctte., Nat. Roundtable on the Environment and the Economy; external interests range from relaxing in a canoe, to growing flowers, to woodworking to cheering for the Blue Jays; Office: 130 Adelaide St. W., Ste. 1700, Toronto, Ont. M5H 3P5.

**RAVACLEY, Michel A.,** B.Sc., P.Eng., M.B.C., C.M.C.; management consultant; b. Montreal, Que. 16 April 1953; s. Andre and Irène (Venne) R.; e. Univ. of Montreal B.Sc. 1977; McGill Univ. M.B.A. 1982; m. Francine d. Laurent and Liliane Chauret 2 Oct. 1976; children: Sophie, Jessica; PARTNER, PEAT MARWICK STEVENSON & KELLOGG 1987– ; Industrial Engineer, Société de Transport Montreal 1976–77; Director of Operations Planning, Regional Manager Operations Planning, Manager Maintenance Operations & Industrial Engineer, CN 1978–83; Dir. of Logistics, Plant Mgr. & Corp. Mgr. Operations Analysis, Canada Post 1983–87; Mem., Canadian Assn. of Logistics Management (Dir. Que. 1988–91); Candn. Soc. for Industrial Engineering (Pres. 1982; Gov. 1990– ); Home: 489 Cr. Boyer, Ile Bizard, Que. H9C 2S3; Office: 3400 de Maisonneuve W., Westmount, Que. H3Z 3B8.

**RAWI, Ousama;** film director; b. Baghdad, Iraq 1939; s. Najib and Fazilah (Daghestani) R.; e. Edinburgh Acad. Scot.; m. Rita d. John and Enid Tushingham 1981; PRESIDENT, RAWIFILM INC. 1980– ; Pres. Triumph Entertainment Corp.; joined film ind. London, Eng. 1964; newsreel cameraman 1965; freeland dir. of photog. 1967– ; filmed numerous TV commercials and feature films; came to Can. 1980 and co-founded Aisha Film Co. Ltd., subsequently amalgamated to form Rawifilm Inc.; opened London, England office Rawi Macartney Ltd. 1989– ; recipient numerous internat. awards in cinematog. and directing; Chrmn. Candn. Ind. Comm. Producers Assn.; mem. IATSE Local 667; BECTU Eng.; Dirs. Guild USA; Brit. Acad. Film; Brit. Soc. of Cinematographers; Acad. Candn. Cinema; Office: P.O. Box 1256, Station K, Toronto, Ont. M4P 3E5.

**RAWLENCE, David James,** B.Sc.(Hons.), M.Sc., Ph.D.; university professor and administrator; b. Christchurch, N.Z. 21 Sept. 1942; s. William George and Nina Turnbull Millar (Smith) R.; e. Christchurch Boys H.S. 1960; Univ. of Canterbury (N.Z.) B.S. 1965, M.Sc. (Hons.) 1967; Univ. of N.B. Ph.D. 1970; m. Anne Margaret Muriel d. Margaret and Ralph Creighton 8 Sept. 1984; children: David James II, Michael Stuart, Madeleine Rachel Louise, Sara Jane Margaret; VICE-PRESIDENT, ACADEMIC, ATHABASCA UNIVERSITY 1993– ; Lecturer in Biology, Univ. of N.B. 1966–71; Scientist, Dept. of Sci. & Indus. Rsch., Lower Hutt, N.Z. 1971–74; Lecturer, Continuing Edn., Univ. of Canterbury 1974–78; Asst. Prof. of Biology, Univ. of N.B. 1978; Assoc. Prof. of Biology & Chair, Div. of Sciences 1980; reappointed Chair 1983, '85; Prof. of Biology 1986– ; Dean of Science, Athabasca Univ. 1993; Shell Oil (N.Z.) Ltd. Scholarships 1961, '62, '63; Merit Award, Univ. of N.B. 1988; George Frederick Matthew Fellowship, N.B. Mus. 1989; Mem., Phycological Soc. of Am.; Internat. Phycological Soc.; Am. Quaternary Assn.; author: 'A Guide to the Phytoplankton of the St. Croix Estuary New Brunswick' 1987, one book chapter & numerous publications in refereed journals; co-author: 'Lake Ellesmere: A Review of the Lake and its Catchment' 1974; Home: Box 2063, Athabasca, Alta. T0G 0B0; Office: Box 10,000, Athabasca, Alta. T0G 0B0.

**RAWLYK, George Alexander,** Ph.D.; educator; b. Thorold, Ont. 19 May 1935; s. Sam and Mary (Kautesk) R.; e. McMaster Univ. B.A. 1957; Rhodes Scholar 1957; Univ. of Rochester M.A. 1962, Ph.D. 1965; m. Mary d. Howard and Florence Pike 19 Aug. 1959; children: Anna, Miriam; PROF. OF HISTORY, QUEEN'S UNIV. 1969– (and Chrmn. of Dept. 1976–85); Lectr. Hist. Dept. Mt. Allison Univ. 1959–61; Asst. Prof. Dalhousie Univ. 1963–66; Assoc. Prof. present Univ. 1966–69; Assoc. Dir. McGill-Queen's Univ. Press 1979–84; Scholar in Residence, Harvard Univ. 1981–82; 1985–86; Hayward Lectr., Acadia Univ. 1983; W.S. MacNutt Lectr., Univ. of N.B. 1986; Winthrop P. Bell Chair of Maritime Studies at Mount Allison Univ. 1987–88; named 'Planter Scholar,' Acadia Univ. 1990; Scholar-in-Residence, Cushwa Center, Notre Dame Univ. Fall Term 1992; Baptist; N.D.P.; mem. Counc., Champlain Soc. 1973–91; author: 'Yankees at Louisbourg' 1967; 'Nova Scotia's Massachusetts: A Study of Massachusetts-Nova Scotia Relations 1630–1784' 1973; 'Streets of Gold' (for children) 1980; 'Ravished by the Spirit: Revivals, Maritime Baptists and Henry Alline' 1984; 'Wrapped Up in God: A Study of Several Canadian Revivals and Revivalists' 1988; 'Champions of Truth' 1990; co-author: (with Ruth Hafter) 'Acadian Education in Nova Scotia' 1970; (with Gordon Stewart) 'A People Highly Favoured of God' 1972; (with Kevin Quinn) 'The Redeemed of the Lord Say So' 1980; (with Mary-Alice Downie) 'A Proper Acadian' 1980; editor: 'Historical Essays on the Atlantic Provinces' 1967; 'Revolution Rejected' 1967; 'Joseph Howe' 1967; 'The Atlantic Provinces and the Problems of Confederation' 1979; 'New Light Letters and Songs' 1983; 'The Sermons of Henry Alline' 1986; 'Henry Alline' 1987; 'Canadian Baptists and Christian Higher Education' 1988; co-editor (with R. Bowles and B. Hodgins): 'Protest, Violence and Social Change' 1972; 'Canada and the U.S.' 1973; 'Canadiens, Canadians and Québecois' 1974; 'The Indian' 1975; 'The Canadian North' 1977; 'Regionalism in Canada' 1979; (with P.G.A. Griffin-Allwood and J.K. Zeman) 'Baptists in Canada 1760–1990' 1989; 'The Canadian Protestant Experience 1760–1990' 1990; Home: 596 Earl St., Kingston, Ont. K7L 2K7; Office: History Dept., Queen's Univ., Kingston, Ont. K7L 3S9.

**RAY, Ajit Kumar,** D.Sc., F.R.Ae.S., F.A.A.A.S.; b. Calcutta, India 1 Feb. 1925; s. late Dr. Jyotish Chandra and late Kiron Moyee R.; e. Calcutta Univ. B.Sc. (Hon. Math./Asutosh Mem. Scholar) 1944, M.Sc. (Applied Math./Gold Medal & Univ. Prizeman) 1947; Göttingen Univ. W. Germany D.Sc. (Math.) 1955 (Humboldt Scholar); children: Arindam (Bob), Leena (Indrani); Consultant & Advisor, Fundamental Research Inst., Can.; Prof. of Applied Math. Asutosh Coll. Calcutta Univ. 1948–56; Reader, Indian Institute of Sci., Bangalore 1956–60; Research Offr. Nat. Research Council Can. 1960–64; Rsch. Scientist, (Mathematical Advisor), Transport Ministry, Canada 1964–65; Prof. of Math. Clarkson Coll. of Technol. Potsdam, N.Y. 1965–66; Prof. of Math. and Dir. of Research Univ. of Ottawa 1966–82 (retired); Visiting Res. Prof., Centre of advanced study in Applied Math., Calcutta Univ., India (1970, 1976); participant at numerous nat./internat. seminars, symposia and conferences; recipient Cert. of Merit Distinguished and Outstanding Reviewer Applied Mechanics Reviews, USA 1980, 1982; Certificate of Merit (1984) by M/s: Am. Inst. of Aeronautics & Astronautics for distinguished contributions to the advancement of Aeronautice & Astronautics during the past twenty five years; Nat. Research Grant 1967; Special Foreign Scholar Calcutta Univ. 1954; Holder of President's Gold Medal and prizes in school at Calcutta, 1940; Nominee (1983) Pearson Peace Prize (Canada); cons., Candn. Parliamentary task forces (incl. Proceeding of Senate, Candn. Parliament Transport and Communication Comms. 1984); Royal Comm. on the Ec. Union and Development Prospects for Canada 1984), prov. legislators, and others; solicited briefs to Royal Soc. of Can. 1984–85 and others; Consultant, Internat. Centre for Genetic Engineering & Biotechnology, Trieste, Italy 1988; Judge, Junior Scientists' Competition, Indian Science Congress, GOA 1993; participant, Candn. Learned Societies Conference, Ottawa (June '93); World Congress of Religions, Chicago (August '93); Internat. Nuclear Congress, Toronto (October '93); contributor & participant, Internat. Symposium on AIR-SEA Interface, Marseille, France (June '93); 2nd Gauss Symposium, Internat. Conference on Medical Mathematics and Physics, Münich, Germany (August '93); author over 60 research publs. nat. and internat. scient. journs.; Fields of expertise: Mathematics and its applications to Non-linear partial differential equations in light of his two-layer theory in Fluid dynamics, Aerodynamics, Heat-transfer, Bio-mathematics, Geophysics, Nuclear Physics, Meteorological, Oceanographical Sciences; Classical Numerical, Functional, Discrete Mathematics, Education and Science Policy; Fellow Inst. of Mathematics and its Implications (U.K.); Fellow, mem. AFAIAA (U.S.A.); MSCITEC (Can.); GAMM (Emeritus mem.) (Germany); Life mem. Indian Science Cong.; Calcutta Math. Soc.; MSIAM; Hindoo; recreations: music, photography, golf; Address: 318 A Innes Park, 2767 Innes Rd., Gloucester, Ont. K1B 4L4.

**RAY, Arthur Joseph,** M.Sc., Ph.D.; educator; b. Chicago, Ill. 20 Oct. 1941; s. Arthur Joseph and Jean Constance (Dunn) R.; e. Univ. of Wis., B.S. 1963, M.S. 1965, Ph.D. 1971; m. Dr. Dianne Newell children: Jeannine, Richard; PROF. OF HIST. UNIV. OF B.C. 1981– ; Asst. Prof. of Geog. York Univ. 1970, Assoc. Prof. 1974–80; author: 'Indians in Fur Trade' 1974; co-author: 'Give Us Good Measure' 1978; 'Early Fur Trades of Canada' 1976; 'Illustrated History of Canada' 1987; co-ed.: 'Old Trails and New Directions' 1980; 'Canadian Fur Trade in the Industrial Age' 1990; mem. ed. bds. Rupert's Land Hist. Soc., Native Studies Review; recreation: swimming; Office: Vancouver, B.C. V6T 1W5.

**RAY, Bryan H.;** business executive; b. Toronto, Ont. 17 July 1945; s. Howard Ritter and Carol Marie (Janis) R.; e. Ryerson Polytech. Inst. 1967; m. Lynn d. Bruce and Ethel Ramsay 30 Aug. 1969; children: TerriLynn, Regan; PRESIDENT, CHIEF EXTVE. OFFR. & DIR., HERO INDUSTRIES LTD. 1990–present; Vice-Pres., Marketing, Gilson Bros. 1977–79; Vice-Pres., Mktg., Noma Outdoor Products then Pres., Noma Leisure Produts 1979–90; recreations: hockey, boating; Home: 5467 Westhaven Wynd, West Vancouver, B.C.; 2719 Lake City Way, Burnaby, B.C. V5A 2Z6.

**RAYMOND, Bruce Alan,** B.A.; television and film producer, distributor and marketing consultant; b. London, Eng. 20 May 1925; s. Francis Howard Bruce and Sarah (Abbott) R.; e. Woodland Sch. and Verdun (Qué.) High Sch.; Sir George Williams Coll. Montréal; McGill Univ. B.A. 1949; m. Rita d. Henri and Janet Roy 3 Sept. 1955; one s.: Donovan; PRES. AND FOUNDER, GROUP OF RAYMOND COMPANIES 1969– ; Bus. Mgr., Actor Candn. Repertory Theatre Ottawa 1949–52; freelance writer and actor 1952–57 writing some 200 TV progs., films & radio progs.; Mgr. Montreal Repertory Theatre, Mountain Playhouse, Candn. Players, Montreal Ballet Theatre; Theatre Critic CBM Radio; joined CBC 1957–69, founded Nat. Talent Relations Office, Toronto French radio service, FM Radio Network, Prog. Dir. Eng. Radio Networks and Eng. TV Network; produced first theatrical film 'Blue City Slammers' Cineplex Odeon 1987; guest lectr. McGill Univ., Univ. of Syracuse, Ryerson Polytech. Inst., Conestoga Community Coll.; Dir., Roman Hollywood Pictures of Delaware; Chair Adv. Ctte. Film & TV Prodn. Prog. Humber Coll.; frequent award juror; Life patron and President, Variety Club; named Outstanding mem. Assn. Candn. Radio & TV Artists 1950; recipient Christopher Award and Houston Internat. Film Festival Silver Award for prodn. 'Special People'; author: 'History of Canadian Radio' 1962; Pres., Variety Club of Ont.; Dir., Mount Sinai Hospital, Toronto; Trustee, Hugh MacMillan Rehabilitation Centre, Toronto; Bd. Mem., Variety Equestrian Centre of Ont.; mem. Candn. Film & TV Production Assn.; Acad. Candn. Cinema/TV; Acad. TV Arts & Sci. USA; Assoc. Nat. Assn. TV Prog. Execs.; recreations: theatre, reading; Club: Albany; Home: 353 St. Clair Ave. E., Toronto, Ont. M4T 1P3; Office: 238 Davenport Rd., Toronto, Ont. M5R 1J6.

**RAYMOND, Yvonne R.,** B.A., M.S.W.; social worker; b. Sherbrooke, Qué. 18 Oct. 1924; d. Joseph Georges and Joséphine (Codère) Roy; e. Mont-Notre-Dame High Sch. Sherbrooke; Univ. de Montréal B.A. 1945, M.S.W. 1948; m. Antoine, D.D.S. s. Alphonse Raymond; children: Yves, Christiane, Elisabeth, Geneviève, Pierre; Consultant, Royal Comn. Status Women 1968–70; Social Worker, Que. Assn. Mental Retardation 1969; Candn. Mental Health Assn. 1970; Extve. Dir. Fédération des Oeuvres de Charité Canadiennes-Françaises Montréal 1970–75; Dir. of Planning, Centraide, Montréal 1975–76; Chief, Clients' Services, Candn. Nat. Inst. Blind Que. Div. 1977–81, Asst. Extve. Dir. 1981–82; Regional Dir., Conseil de l'Age d'Or, Mtl.-Lac St-Louis 1983–84; Conseillère Relations humaines, Manoir l'Age d'Or, Mtl. 1984–91; Chrmn., Nat. Welfare Council 1982–85, mem. 1978–85; Secy., Corp.

de Société Service Social aux Familles 1969–70; mem. Conseil d'Adm. de Boscoville 1967–70; Pres., Assn. des femmes diplômes des Univ. de Montréal 1964–65; Vice Chrmn. Conseil de Politique Scientifique Qué. 1974–77; mem. Med. Research Council 1977–82; Co-Chrmn. Nat. Comte. Internat. Yr. of Disabled 1980–81; mem. Nat. Adv. Bd. Bilingual Dists. 1972–75; co-author 'Women University Graduates in Continuing Education and Employment' 1966; Home: 355 Ellerton, Montréal, Qué. H3P 1E1.

**RAYNAULD, André,** O.C., S.R.C.; économiste; n. La Pocatière, Que. 20 Oct. 1927; f. Ernest-Léopold et Blanche (Gauthier) R.; e. Univ. de Montréal, B.A. 1948, M.A. 1951; Univ. de Paris, Dr. de l'UN. (Science économique) 1954; m. Michelle f. Gaston Nolin, Outremont, 15 Oct. 1951; enfants: Françoy, Olivier, Dominique, Isabelle; Asst.-Prof., Science Economique, 1954–58; Prof. agrégé 1958, et dir., Dept., Science Economique, 1958–63 et 1965–67; Prof. titulaire 1966; Dir. et fondateur, Centre de recherche en développement Economique, Univ. de Montreal 1970–72; Prés. du Conseil Econom. du Can. 1972–76; élu M.N.A. (Qué.) 1976–80; Prof. titulaire Univ. de Montréal 1980–92; Sr. Fellow, The Institute for Rsch. on Public Policy 1992– ; Publications: 'Croissance et structure économiques de la Province de Québec' 1960; 'Institutions economiques canadiennes' 1964; 'The Canadian Economic System,' 1967; 'Le développement économique' 1967; 'Les orientations du développement économique régional dans la Province de Québec' 1971; 'Le financement des caisses de retraite' 1970; 'La propriété des entreprises au Québec' 1974; 'Le financement des exportations' 1979; 'L'Aide Publique au Financement des Exportations/Government Assistance to Export Financing,' Conseil Economique du Canada 1983, 'The External Financing of Tunisia's Imports,' OECD, Paris 1988, 'Financing Exports to Developing Countries,' Development Centre of the OECD, Paris 1992; Co-editor: (with Gilles Bertin) 'Economic Integration in Europe and North America/L'intégration économique en Europe et en Amérique du Nord,' éditions Clément Juglar, Paris 1992; et nombreux autres travaux et articles; Mem. Am. Econ. Assn.; Société Canadienne de Sc. economiques (Prés. 1967–68); mem. Conseil Econ. du Can. 1966–69; Conseiller, Econ. du Sous-Ministre des Finances, 1967–68; mem., Soc. Royale du Canada 1968– ; Can. Economics Assn. (Prés., 1983–84); Président, Inst. Canadien des affaires publiques 1961–62; Chef de mission, Haute-Volta, pour l'UNESCO, 1961; mem., Soc. Radio-Canada; 1964–67; Aviseur, Etudes Economiques, Commission Royale sur le Bilinguisme et le Biculturalisme 1964–70; mem. Advisory Group, INTERFUTURS, OECD, Paris, 1976–1979; mem. Economic Advisory Panel Minister of Finance, 1982–84; head of An Economic Strategy Group in Tunisia, 1982–86; Rsch. Fellow, OECD, Paris 1986; mem. Adv. Group, Public Mngmt. Service OECD 1990–92; apptd. Officer of the Order of Canada 1986; Prix de carrière du Conseil du patronat du Québec 1986; Invited Professor, Coll. de France in Paris 1987; designated Distinguished Associate of the Atlantic Economic Society 1989; Emeritus Prof., Univ. of Montreal; Missions à l'étranger, Burkina Faso, Niger, Côte D'Ivoire, Zaire, Cameroun, Japon, Srilanka, Guatemala, Brésil, Mexique, Tunisie; D.Sc.Econ. hon., Univ. de Sherbrooke 1976; Univ. d'Ottawa 1976; Catholique; Résidence: 4820 rue Roslyn, Montréal, Qué. H3W 2L2; Bureau: I.R.P.P., 1470 rue Peel bu. 200, Montréal, Qué. H3A 1T1.

**RAYNER, Gerald Theodore,** M.B.A., M.P.A.; former Canadian public servant; b. Montreal, Que. 19 March 1929; s. late William Eric and Dorothy Anne (Addyman) R.; e. Montreal High Sch. for Boys; Bishop's Univ. B.A. 1951; Harvard Univ. M.B.A. 1953, M.P.A. 1973; m. Barbara Marion d. late Austin Ralph Chadwick 26 Sept. 1970; one s. Michael Edward Chadwick; PRES., RAYNER, CHADWICK MANAGEMENT SERVICES 1990– ; Member of Faculty, Can. Centre for Management Development 1985–90; Sr. Asst. Under Secy. of State 1977–84; Contracts Mgr., Comm. Mgr., Co. Secy., Rolls-Royce of Canada Ltd., Montreal 1953–64, Dir. Rolls-Royce Inc., New York 1962–64; Depy. Dir., Dir. Aerospace Br. Dept. of Industry Ottawa 1964–68; Treasury Bd. Secretariat 1968–72; Asst. Under Secy. of State-Corporate Mang. Dept. Secy. of State 1973–77; mem., Human Rights Tribunal Panel; mem., Organization Ctte., General Synod; Dir., Bishop Hamilton Sch.; mem., Heritage Canada Found.; Historical Soc. of Ottawa; Anglican; recreations: skiing, sailing, Canadiana; Clubs: Rideau; Royal St. Lawrence Yacht (Montreal); Canadian Club of Ottawa; Address: 190 Dufferin Rd., Ottawa, Ont. K1M 2A6.

**RAYNER, Gordon;** artist; b. Toronto 1935; Instr., various art schools in Canada; percussionist, Artists' Jazz Band; has travelled throughout Europe, Asia, Central & S. America; one man exhibs. incl.: The Isaacs Gall. 1969, '61, '64, '66, '68, '71, '73, '75, '77, '79, '81, '82, '84, '86, '88, '89 (Mexican drawings), '90; Concordia Art Gall. Montreal 1987; Moore Gall. Hamilton 1985; Max Hutchinson Gall. N.Y. 1984; Equinox Gall. Vancouver 1981; 'Gordon Rayner Retrospective' (travelling throughout Can.) 1979–80; Sir George Williams Univ. 1971; The Blue Barn Gall. Ottawa 1965; group exhibs. incl.: Mississauga Civic Ctr. Art Gall. 1987; Galerie Esperanza Montreal 1986; Diane Farris Art Gall. Vanc. 1985; Concordia Art Gall. Montreal 1984; Art Gall. of Ont. 1984 and travelling exhib. 1983–84; Hart House, Univ. of Toronto 1984; Winnipeg Art Gall. 1983; Anchorage, Fairbanks, Juneau Alaska 1982; Art Gall. at Harbourfront Toronto 1982 and several others; major comns. incl.: Cineplex Complex Toronto 1985; Toronto Dance Theatre 1983; Cedar Ridge Gall. Scarborough 1983, etc.; recipient of several grants; collections incl.: Agnes Etherington Art Ctr. Kingston; Art Gall. of Brant; of Ontario; of Windsor; Canada Council Art Bank; City Trust Vanc.; Confed. Art Gall. P.E.I.; Crown Life Toronto; Dept. of External Affiars; Friends of Confederation Trust P.E.I.; Hart House Art Gall.; Hirshhorn Coll. Washington and many others; Office: 1493 Dupont St., Toronto, Ont. M6P 3S2.

**RAYNER, Michael H.,** C.St.J., B.A., F.C.A.; Canadian chartered accountant; b. Halifax, N.S., Nov. 18 1943; s. late V./Adm. Herbert S. and Betty (Snook) R.; e. Carleton Univ. B.A. 1965; C.A. 1969; F.C.A. 1982; m. Susan E. Crawley 1966; children; Jonathan, David, Michael, Sylvia; PRESIDENT, CANDN. INSTITUTE OF CHARTERED ACCOUNTANTS 1992– ; Touche Ross & Co. 1965–70; Educ. Co-ordinator, Audit Services Bureau, Dept. Supply & Services, Ottawa 1970–72; Sr. Project Offr. Treasury Bd. Secretariat, Ottawa 1972–75; Extve. Secy. Independent Review Comte. on the Office of Auditor Gen. Can. 1974–75; various positions including Depy. Auditor Gen. Planning/Reports/Standards Br. and Acting Auditor Gen. Can., Office of Auditor Gen. Can. 1975–81; Partner, Price Waterhouse 1982–85; Comptroller General of Canada 1985–88; Partner, Deloitte & Touche 1988–92; mem., Candn. Inst. C.A.'s (CICA) & Ont Inst. C.A.'s; mem., Extve. Comte., Ottawa C.A. Assoc. 1971–75; mem., Prof. Dev. Policy Comte. 1976–77 & Ed. Adv. Bd. 1980–82, CICA; Chrmn., CICA Study Group on Federal Crown Corporations Legislation 1983–84; mem., CICA Comn. to Study the Public's Expectations of Audits (Macdonald Comn.) 1986–88; Candn. rep., Public Sector Comte., Internat. Fedn. of Accountants 1987–90; mem., Auditor General's Independent Adv. Comte. on Govt. Accounting and Auditing Standards 1982–85; mem., Internat. Adv. Comte., Canada – U.S. Fed. Govt. Reporting Study 1985–86; Gov., Candn. Comprehensive Auditing Foundation (CCAF) 1980–89; mem., CCAF Independent Panel on Effectiveness Reporting & Auditing in the Public Sector 1986–87; Treas., 1976–80 & Registrar 1982–92, St. John Ambulance Priory Can.; Bd. mem., Ont. Arts Council 1990–93; Anglican; Clubs: Rideau; Royal Ottawa Golf; The Country Club, Aylmer, Qué.; Home: 67 Chatsworth Dr., Toronto, Ont. M4R 1R8; Office; 277 Wellington St. W., Toronto, Ont. M5V 3H2.

**RAYNER, Robert M.,** B.Sc., M.B.A.; financial executive; b. London, England 21 Sept. 1946; s. Henry John and Kathleen Mary (Edwards) R.; e. Bristol Univ. B.Sc. 1968; London Business Sch. M.B.A. 1976; m. Mindy S. d. George and Faye Miller 28 May 1979; SENIOR VICE-PRESIDENT & CHIEF FINANCIAL OFFICER, ESSROC CANADA INC. 1988– ; Senior Engineer, Sir William Halcrow & Partners (U.K.) 1968–74; var. financial positions incl. Director, Finance, Pepsico Inc. (N.Y.) 1976–88; Dir., ESSROC Materials Inc.; San Juan Cement; Mem., Inst. of Civil Engineers (U.K.); Financial Executives Inst. (U.S.); recreations: running, golf, theatre, music; Office: 949 Wilson Ave., Downsview, Ont. M3K 1G2.

**REA, Samuel Arthur, Jr.,** Ph.D.; university professor; b. Indianapolis, Ind. 10 Nov. 1944; s. Samuel Arthur and Eleanor Carey (Appel) R.; e. Harvard Univ. A.B. 1966, Ph.D. 1972; m. Wendy d. Peter and Dawn Thompson 27 June 1981; one d.: Sarah Dawn; PROF., DEPT. OF ECON. & FAC. OF LAW, UNIV. OF TORONTO 1981– ; Asst. Prof., Dept. of Econ., Univ. of Toronto 1971–76; Assoc. Prof. 1976–81; Fellow, Yale Law Sch. 1982–83; Pres., Jurecon Limited; Dir., Emkay Inc.; author: 'Disability Insurance and Public Policy' 1981; co-author: 'Public and Private Pensions in Canada' 1977; recreations: sailing, skiing; Club: Royal Candn. Yacht; Home: 213 Balmoral Ave., Toronto, Ont. M4V 1K1; Office: 150 St. George St., Toronto, Ont. M5S 1A1.

**READ, Rt. Rev. Allan Alexander,** B.A., D.D. S.T.D. b. Toronto, Ont., 19 Sept. 1923; s. Alec P. and Lillice (Matthews) R.; e. Whitney School, Forest Hill Village Schs., Toronto; Univ. of Toronto, B.A., L.Th.; Trinity Coll., D.D.; Wycliffe Coll., D.D.; Thornloe Univ. S.T.D.; m. Mary Beverly Sophia d. Frank E. and Edna (Martin) Roberts, 28 Sept. 1949; children: John, Elizabeth, Peter Michael, Martha; Bishop of Ontario, Kingston 1981–91; Parish of Mono with seven churches, Diocese of Toronto 1947–54; Trinity Ch. and Rector of Barrie 1954–71; Founder, Barrie East End Mission (Parish of St. Giles) 1954; Dir., Diocese of Toronto Student and Clergy Rural Training Sch. 1949–75; Chrmn., Diocesan Town and Country Church Ctte. 1952–62; Mem., Barrie School Bd. 1954–63; Canon, St. James Cathedral, Toronto 1957; Archdeacon of Simcoe 1961; Chrmn., Provincial Synod Rural Church Ctte. 1953–63; Mem., General Synod Rural Church Unit 1955–65; Chaplain, Simcoe County Gaol 1955–71; Suffragan Bishop of Toronto 1972–81; St. Patrick's Cathedral, Trim, Diocese of Meath and Kildare, Ireland 1992; St. George's Dunster Benefice, Somerset, Diocese of Bath and Wells 1993; Christ Church Vespers; Mem. General Synod, The Anglican Church of Can. 1959–89; Mem. Provincial Synod 1955–91; Mem. Anglican World Wide Lambeth Conference 1978, 1988; Publications: 'Unto the Hills'; 'Shepherds in Green Pastures'; Memberships: Rural Workers Fellowship, North Am.; Albany Club (Toronto 1972–81; Awards & Honours: Rural Workers Fellowship of Am., Rural Ministry Award 1953; Hon. Pres., Rural Workers Fellowship 1981– ; Citizen of the Year, City of Barrie 1966; Honorary Reeve, Black Creek Village, Toronto and Metropolitan Region Conservation Authority 1977; Hon. Life Mem. 1979; Govt. of Ont. Citizenship Awards; recreations: music, hymnology, reading, gardening, stamps; Home: 39 Riverside Dr., R.R. 1, Kingston, Ont. K7L 4V1.

**READ, Donna Vera;** film maker; b. Toronto, Ont. 22 Dec. 1938; d. Howard Richard and Iris Emily (Clark) Cooper; e. York Coll. Inst. 1957; Ryerson Inst. of Technol. Radio & TV Arts 1960; m. Nash s. Nicholas and Elizabeth (Butters) Read 17 Jan. 1981; children: Dawn, Jeffry, Nicholas, Jesse, Ben; film maker Great Atlantic & Pacific Film Co.; Asst. ed. 'Act of the Heart' 1968; ed. Nat. film Bd. 1970–84; Dir. 'Kripalu'; Nat. Film Bd. 'Too Dirty for a Woman' 1983; 'Adam's World' 1985; 'Goddess Remembered' 1989; 'Burning Times' 1990; 'Full Circle' (co-production between Great Atlantic & Pacific Film Co. and The National Film Bd.) 1992; Address: 36 Horseshoe Rd., Box 433, Morin Heights, Que. J0R 1H0.

**READ, Elfreida;** writer; b. Vladivostok, Russia 2 Oct. 1920; d. Albert and Maria (Yacub) Ennock; e. Shanghai Pub. Sch. for Girls Sr. Cambridge Sch. Cert. 1936; m. George Jeffery s. Walter Stanley and Kate Winnifred Read; children: Jeani, Philip; author (juvenile): 'The Dragon and the Jadestone' 1958, 1971; 'The Magic of Light' 1963; 'The Enchanted Egg' 1963, 1965; 'The Spell of Chuchuchan' 1966, 1967; 'Magic for Granny' 1967; 'Twin Rivers' 1968; 'No One Need Ever Know' 1971; 'Brothers By Choice' 1974, 1986 (also TV mini series and movie 1986); 'The Message of the Mask' 1981; 'Kirstine and the Villains' 1982; 'Race Against the Dark' 1983; (play): 'Plays for Special Days' 1993; (prose poems): 'Growing Up In China' 1985; (autobiog.): 'A Time of Cicadas', 'Guns and Magnolias' 1989, 'Congee and Peanut Butter' 1990; 'Fresh Lettuce and New Faces' 1992 (4 vols.); recipient awards children's stories, poetry, play-writing; mem. Writers' Union Can.; Address: 2686 W. King Edward Ave., Vancouver, B.C. V6L 1T6.

**READ, John F.,** B.Sc., Ph.D., F.C.I.C.; educator; b. Reading, Eng. 11 Apl. 1940; s. Frederick William and Marjorie Francis (Adams) R.; e. Nottingham Univ. B.Sc. 1961, Ph.D. 1964; m. Lesley d. John and Olga Lambert 27 July 1963; three d. Christine Lynn, Suzanne Lynne, Julie Lesley; PROF. OF CHEMISTRY, MOUNT ALLISON UNIV. 1979– ; Post-doctoral Fellow Northwestern Univ. 1964–65; Teaching Fellow, Hope Coll. Holland, Mich. 1965–66; Asst. Dean of Arts & Sci. present Univ. 1970–73, Assoc. Dean 1974–75, Dean 1975–78, Acting Head of Math. & Computer Sci. 1976–77, Acting Head of Psychol. 1976–77, Dean of Science 1981–91, Head of Commerce 1987–90; Visiting Scholar, Univ. of Leeds 1992; Visiting Adjunct Prof., New Mexico State Univ. 1993; Past Chrmn., Atlantic Prov. Council Sci's.; Past mem., Exec. Atlantic Div. Chem. Inst. Can.; Past mem., N.B. Health Services Adv. Ctte. and N.B. Distance Education Ctte.; Citizen Adv. Ctte. Westmorland Inst.; Past Chrmn., Atlantic Assn. Deans Arts & Sci.; Past Secy.-Treas., Candn. Assn. Deans Arts & Sci.; contbr., 'Advances in Catalysis' 1969; sr. author 17 refereed publs. sci. jours.; recreation: stained glass;

Home: 15 Woodlane Dr., Sackville, N.B. E0A 3C0; Office: Sackville, N.B. E0A 3C0.

**READ, Kenneth (Ken) John,** B.A.; sports broadcaster/marketing executive; b. Ann Arbor, Mich. 6 Nov. 1955; s. John Hamilton and Dorothy (Dee) Anne (Burden) R.; e. Univ. of Calgary; Univ. of West. Ont. B.A. 1984; m. Lynda d. Jack and Gerri Robbins 7 July 1984; children: Erik, Kevyn; PRES., READ & COMPANY 1983– ; Mem., Candn. Nat. Ski Team 1973–83; Candn. Olympic 1976 (Innsbruck), 1980 (Lake Placid), 1984 (Barcelona); first Candn./N. Am. male to win World Cup Downhill (Val d'Isere 1975); winner of 5 world cup titles & 11 Nat. Championship titles; currently Skiing colour analyst and Olympic commentator, CBC TV Sports and host of 'The Read Report'; columnist, 'Ski Canada Magazine'; 'The Financial Post'; contributor, 'Skiing Magazine'; 'Sport Switzerland'; Event mktg. clients include: AGFA Canada Ltd.; Banff Caribou Lodge; Bollé Canada Inc.; Candn. Airlines Internationtal; Coca-Cola Ltd./Coca-Cola Bottling Ltd.; Deloitte & Touche; Delta Hotels & Resorts; Descente Ltd.; Lotus Development Canada Ltd.; Paris Glove; Salomon; SunLife of Canada; Swix Sport USA Ltd.; Toshiba of Canada Ltd.; Awards and Honours: Candn. Athlete of the Year 1978 (Lou Marsh Award); Candn. Amateur Male Athlete of the Year 1979 (Norton Crowe Award); Mem., Order of Canada; Canada's Sports Hall of Fame; Candn. Olympic Hall of Fame; Honour Roll of Candn. Skiing; Alberta Sports Hall of Fame; co-carrier of Olympic Torch on final leg into McMahon Stadium 1988 Olympics; Candn. Olympic Assn.: Mem. 1981– , Vice-Pres. 1985–93, Founding Chrmn. Candn. Athletes Adv. Counc. 1981–85, Mem. Olympic Team Selection Ctte. 1983–93, Chrmn. Olympic Club Canada 1986–90, Chrmn. Olympic Legacy Coaching Fund 1989– , Chrmn. Olympic Torch Scholarship Ctte. 1989– , Chrmn. Candn. Amateur Sports Hall of Fame Selection Ctte. 1990–93, Chef de Mission 1992 Candn. Olympic Team (Barcelona); XV Olympic Winter Games: Advisory Bd., 1988 Olympic Bid Ctte. 1979–81, Safety Expert Alpine Skiing Venue 1985–88, Founding Chrmn. OCO'88 Olympians Ctte. 1985–88; Internat. Ski Federation: Safety Expert 1986– , Technical Delegate 1988– , Mem., Alpine Ctte. Extve. Bd. 1988– ; Calgary Olympic Development Assn. (CODA): Mem. Board 1986–90, Executive 1988–90, Training Centre Ctte., Education Ctte., Sport Ctte.; Patron, Josh Byrne Soc. (Fundraising for brain injury rsch. and rehab.); Mem., Alberta Alpine Foundation; Honorary Dir., Calgary Special Olympics; Calgary Chapter Juvenile Diabetes Foundation; Gardiner Foundation Breakfast for Scouts Canada; mem. Western Candn. Ski Foundation; Chrmn., Delta Sport Foundation; author: 'White Circus' 1987; 'Ski the Canadian Way' 1979; recreations: golf, hiking, backpacking, orienteering, cycling, running (road); clubs: Lake Louise Ski, Foothills Wanderers Orienteering, Osler Bluff Ski Club; Glencoe Golf & Country; Home: 3806 Fifth St. S.W., Calgary, Alta. T2S 2C8; Office: 1842 - 14th Street S.W., Calgary, Alta. T2T 3S9.

**READ, Wallace Stanley,** P.Eng., D.Eng. (Hon. Causa); association president; b. Corner Brook, Nfld., 18 Apl. 1930; s. James Alexander and Olive May (Rafuse) R.; e. Corner Brook Pub. Sch., 1946; Mt. Allison Univ., Engn. Cert. 1949; Tech. Univ. of N.S., B.Eng. (Elect.) 1951, D.Eng. (Hon. Causa) 1992; m. Ida Marjorie Laura, d. late Arthur Wellon, Deer Lake, Nfld., 15 Jan. 1960; four s., Wallace Arthur James, David Alexander, Christian William, Gregory Allister Frederick; PRESIDENT, CANADIAN ELECTRICAL ASSOCIATION since 1985; Dir., Elect. Engr. on Capital Expansion, Bowater's Newfoundland Pulp and Paper Mills Ltd. Corner Brook, 1951; Chief Engr., Bowater Power Co. Ltd. Deer Lake, 1955, Plant Supt. 1959, Asst. Gen. Mgr. 1962; joined Newfoundland and Labrador Power Comn. as Chief Engr. 1964, Depy. Chrmn. 1968, Chrmn. 1974, Pres. 1975; named Sr. Vice-Pres., Newfoundland and Labrador Hydro and Pres., Churchill Falls (Labrador) Corp. 1975; Pres., C.E.O. and Dir., Lower Churchill Development Corp. and Exec. Vice-Pres., Newfoundland and Labrador Hydro 1979; awarded A.G.L. McNaughton Gold Medal, Inst. of Electrical and Electronics Engrs. 1980; mem. Assn. Prof. Engrs. Nfld.; Fellow, Institute Electrical and Electronic Engrs.; Fellow, Engineering Inst. of Can.; Freemason (P.M.); Anglican; recreations: hunting, fishing; Home: 44 Thorburn Rd., St. John's, Nfld. A1B 3L9; Office: 1 Westmount Square, Montreal, Que. H3Z 2P9.

**REANEY, James,** M.A., O.C., F.R.S.C.; poet; playwright; university teacher; b. nr. Stratford, Ont., 1 Sept. 1926; s. James Nesbitt and Elizabeth (Crerar) R.; e. University of Toronto (Univ. Coll.), B.A. 1948, M.A. 1949, Ph.D. 1958; m. Colleen Thibaudeau, 29 Dec. 1951; two children; author of 'The Red Heart' (poetry), 1949; 'A Suit of Nettles,' 1959, rec'd. Gov. General's Award for Poetry, 1949, 1959 and 1962; 'The Killdeer,' 1959, winner of award for best Candn. play performed at Dom. Drama Festival, Vancouver 1960; 'The Boy with an R in his hand' (hist. fiction), 1965; in 1967 John Hirsch produced 'Colours in the Dark' at Stratford Festival; recent plays incl. 'Listen to the Wind,' 'Name & Nicknames,' 'The Easter Egg'; 'The Donnellys: Sticks & Stones, St. Nicholas Hotel, Handcuffs' (trilogy); with the composer John Beckwith, two operas: 'Night Bloming Cereus' and 'The Shivaree'; 'Baldoon,' 'The Dismissal,' 'Wacousta,' 'King Whistle,' 'Fourteen Barrels from Sea to Sea,' 'Antler River,' 'Cloud Shadows,' 'Stereoscope,' 'I, The Parade,' 'The Canadian Brothers'; opera 'Serinette' with Harry Somers, musical play on the Brontës with John Beckwith, also with latter a detective opera 'Crazy to Kill'; 'Sleigh Without Bells: A Donnelly Ghost Story' 1991; wrote and publ. with Alphabet Press 'The Dance of Death at London, Ontario'; with Porcupine's Quill 'Take the Big Picture' (for children) 1986; edited and published a literary review 'Alphabet 1960–70'; contributor of various short stories published in Candn. mags.; Cong.; works in progress: 'Taptoo' opera libretto for the 1994 Toronto tercentenary, a book on the Brontës; adaptation of Carroll's 'Alice Through the Looking Glass' for Stratford Shakespeare Festival 1994; recreation: piano, painting; Address: English Dept., University of Western Ontario, London, Ont. N6A 3K7.

**REAY, Lt.-Gen. Gordon Michael,** B.A., CMM, MBE, CD; Canadian Forces officer; b. Yorkshire, England 30 May 1943; e. Royal Military College of Canada B.A. 1965; m. Lesley d. Peter and Barbara (Macrae) Kertland; one s.: Brendan; COMMANDER, LAND FORCE COMMAND, CANADIAN FORCES 1993– ; joined 2nd Battalion, Princess Patricia's Canadian Light Infantry (2 PPCLI) 1965 (var. appointments); Staff, Mobile Command H.Q. Saint-Hubert, Que.1969; attended Candn. Land Forces Command & Staff College Kingston 1971; returned to 2 PPCLI as Operations Officer & Company Commander 1971–75 (operation tour U.N. force Cyprus); Operations Officer, 1 British Corps H.Q. Bielefeld Germany 1975–77; Sr. Staff Officer, Operations, 1st Candn. Brigade Group H.Q. 1977–79; Commander, 1st Battalion, PPCLI 1979–81; Dir. of Military Manpower Distbn. 1981–83; Special Policy Asst. to Asst. Dep. Min. (Personnel), NDHQ 1983–85; Brigadier-General, Nat. Defence College 1985; seconded to Fgn. & Defence Policy Secretariat, Privy Council Office 1986–87; Commander, 1 Candn. Brigade Group 1987–89; Major-Gen. 1989; Chief Land Doctrine & Operations Ottawa 1989–91; Deputy Commander of Land Force Command, Saint-Hubert 1991–93; Commander of the Order of Military Merit 1991; Member of the Order of the British Empire 1975; Commander of the Legion of Merit (US); Special Service Medal; UN Medal (Cyprus); Canada 125 Medal; Candn. Decoration with second clasp; recreations: golf, military history, oenology; Office: St. Hubert, Que. J3Y 5T5.

**REBICK, Judy,** B.Sc.; advocate; b. Reno, Nevada 15 Aug. 1945; d. Jack and Ruth (Schutter) R.; e. Mount Royal H.S. 1964; McGill Univ. B.Sc. 1967; single; VISITING PROFESSOR, DEPT. OF POLITICAL SCIENCE, UNIV. OF REGINA 1993– ; Dir., Special Projects, The Candn. Hearing Soc. (currently Dir. of Mngt. Training Program for deaf & hard of hearing on part-time basis) 1980– ; Bd. Mem., National Action Ctte. (NAC); Chairperson, (NAC) Reproductive Choice & Employment Equity Cttes. 1988–90; Pres., (NAC) on the Status of Women 1990–93; Founder of Nat. Employment Equity Network, Co-Chair Disabled People for Employment Equity 1987–89; Spokesperson, Ont. Coalition for Abortion Clinics 1981–87; Bd. of Dir., Intercede 1988–89; Lay Mem., Ont. Judicial Council; Mem., Ont. Fed. of Labour Women's Ctte. 1986–89; Pres., Ont. N.D.P. Women's Ctte. 1986–88; recipient, Deaf Community Service Award May 1990; Office: Regina, Sask. S4S 0A2.

**RECTOR, Maurice;** retired company executive; b. Sodus Mich. 12 Jan. 1908; s. Samuel James and Florence Etta (Griffith) R.; e. Pub. and High Sch., Dowagiac, Mich.; Univ. of Miami (two yrs.); American Sch. of Baking; m. Audrey Catherine, d. David Evans, Peterborough, Ont., 5 Oct. 1934; children: Alan David, Robert Maurice, Catherine Florence; Vice Chairman, the Griffith Laboratories Ltd., 1946–77 (ret.); joined the Griffith Laboratories, Incorporated in Chicago, Illinois in 1929; Freemason; Protestant; recreations: golf, photography, fishing; Club: Rotary (Toronto-Leaside) Past Pres., Past Dist. Gov., Rotary Internat.: Home: 4 Willow St., Apt. 802, Waterloo, Ont. N2J 4S2.

**REDELMEIER, Flavia Elliott,** B.A., M.A.; volunteer professional; b. Toronto, Ont. 9 March 1926; d. Leighton Henry and Catherine Flavia (Canfield) Elliott; e. Branksome Hall (Girls') School 1943; Univ. of Toronto B.A. 1948, M.A. 1951; m. Ernest Julius Hugo s. Willy and Iska R.; 29 Dec. 1950; children: David Hugh, William Leighton; BOARD MEMBER, CANADIAN MUSEUM OF NATURE 1990– ; Curatorial Assistant, Royal Ont. Museum 1948–50; Volunteer (Docent, Curatorial, Decorating, Chairman 1973–74); Board Mem. 1968–73 (incl. Chair, Collections Ctte.); Chair, Compensation & Personnel Ctte., Candn. Mus. of Nature; Pres., York Central Hospital Assn. & rep. to Hospital Bd. 1964–66; Girl Guides of Canada: Brown Owl Trainer; Candn. Extve. Ctte.; Camping Comnr. for Canada, etc.; Mem., Anglican Ch. of Canada (St. Mary's Richmond Hill Choir Mem. 35 years); Garden Club of Toronto (Past Pres.; accredited flower show judge, etc.); Herb Soc. of Am. 1978– ; Chair, Civic Garden Centre 1975–77; author/co-author of gardening articles & lectures esp. herb-related or museum topics; recreations: gardening, photography, travel, colour slide talks on museum & gardening topics; clubs: Toronto Ladies; Home: Southbrook Farms, Box 147, Richmond Hill, Ont. L4C 4X9 and (in Toronto): 4 Cluny Ave., Toronto, Ont. M4W 1S5.

**REDFERN, John D.,** B.Sc., P.Eng.; executive; b. Ottawa, Ont., 9 May 1935; s. Harry Clare and Mary Margaret Evelyn (MacLaurin) R; e. Carleton Univ. D.Eng. (honoris causa) 1992; Queen's Univ., B.Sc. (Civil Engn.) 1958; m. Ann Findlay, d. Alexander Watson, Ottawa, Ont. 29 June 1957; children: John Stephen, Bruce Douglas, David Scott, Christine Evelyn; CHRMN. LAFARGE CANADA INC. since 1985; Vice-Chrmn., Lafarge Corp. Reston, Virginia; Project Mgr., Ont. Dept. of Highways, Kingston, Ont. 1958; Tech. Sales Engr., Canada Cement Co. Ltd., Ottawa 1958; Sales Mgr., Maritime Cement, Moncton, N.B. 1962; Dist. Sales Mgr., Canada Cement Ottawa 1965 and Toronto 1966, Vice Pres. Halifax 1969; Vice Pres. & Gen. Mgr. W. Region 1971; Vice-Pres. Operations 1974; Extve. Vice-Pres. and Gen. Mgr. 1976; Pres. & C.E.O. 1977–83; Pres. & C.E.O., Lafarge Corp. 1983–85; Chrmn. & C.E.O., Lafarge Canada Inc. 1983–85; Dir., CTL (Construction Tech. Labs., Inc.), Skokie, IL; Dir. Lafarge Canada Inc.; Lafarge Corp.; Chrmn., The Corporate-Higher Education Forum; Dir., Montreal Trust; Dir., Montreal General Hospital Foundation; Chrmn., The Coalition to Renew Canada's Infrastructure 1992; Member Candn. Portland Cement Assn.; Past Chrmn., Portland Cement Assn.; served with RCN, Sub. Lt. (Ret.); member Assn. Prof. Engineers. Ont.; Candn. Mfrs. Assn.; Candn. Chamber Comm.; Candn. Constr. Assn.; Bd. of Gov., Le Conseil du Patronat du Qué.; United Church; recreations: skiing, golf, squash, swimming; Club: M.A.A.A.; Mount Royal; St. James; Royal Montreal Golf; The Forest and Stream Club; Glencoe (Calgary); Home: 319 Pinetree Cres., Beaconsfield, Que. H9W 5E2; Offices: 606 Cathcart St., Montreal, Que. H3B 1L7; Lafarge Corporation, 11130 Sunrise Valley Dr., Reston, Va. 22091–4332.

**REDFORD, Donald Bruce,** M.A., Ph.D., F.R.S.C.; egyptologist; educator; b. Toronto, Ont. 2 Sept. 1934; s. Cyril and Kathleen (Coe) R.; e. Univ. of Toronto B.A. 1957, M.A. 1958, Ph.D. 1965; Brown Univ. 1959–62; m. Susan d. Frank Pirritano, Scranton, Pa. 30 Jan. 1982; children by previous marriage: Philip, Christopher; and 2 sons: Alexander, Aksel; PROF. OF NEAR EASTERN STUDIES, UNIV. OF TORONTO 1969– , Lectr. 1961, Asst. Prof. 1965, Assoc. Prof. 1967; Consultant Akhenaten Temple Project, Univ. Museum, Univ. of Pa. in Cairo 1971, Dir. 1972– ; Dir., The Mendes Expedition to Lower Egypt 1990– ; Research Assoc. Univ. Museum Univ. of Pa. 1972– ; Royal Ont. Museum 1973– ; Assoc. Trustee, Am. Schs. Oriental Research 1977– ; co-organizer Internat. Cong. on Egyptology, Cairo 1975; guest lectr. and keynote speaker many univs. and museums; participated First Cong. on Hist. & Archaeol. of Jordan, Oxford 1980; recipient Reuben Wells Leonard Scholarship; Lyle Silver Medal for Hebrew; W. R. Taylor Mem. Scholarship; 2 Univ. of Toronto Open Fellowships; Teaching Fellowship Brown Univ.; 5 major S.S.H.R.C.C. Research Grants; 5 Can. Council Grants; 4 Killam Program Fellowships; 5 Smithsonian FCP Grants; Am. Research Center in Egypt; Editor, Journal of The Society of the Study of Egyptian Antiquities; Vice-Pres., The Canadn. Institute in Egypt; author 'Akhenaten, The Heretic King,' 'Egypt, Canaan and Israel in Ancient Times' and numerous publs.; Anglican; Home: 22 Nesbitt Dr., Toronto, Ont. M4W 2G3; Office: 4 Bancroft Ave., Dept. of Near Eastern Studies, Univ. of Toronto, Toronto, Ont. M5S 1A1.

**REDHEAD, Carl Joseph;** radio broadcasting executive; b. San Fernando, Trinidad & Tobago 15 Sept. 1936; e. Presentation College (Trinidad); m. Lenore d.

Garneth and Yvonne Philbert 25 June 1960; children: Clint, Sean; VICE-PRES. & ASST. GEN. MGR., CHIN AM/FM 1981– ; Career in Trinidad: Asst. Elementary Sch. Teacher 1955–59; Class A Operator, FCL Chemicals 1959–62; Radio Announcer, Radio 610 1962–65; Chief Announcer & Special Events Commentator 1965–69; freelance News Anchor, T&T TV 1966–68; Career in Canada: Copy/Continuity Chief, CHIN Radio 1969; Operations Mgr. 1969–73; Vice-Pres., Opns. 1973–81; Dir. (and designer of the programming format), Milestone Communications Limited (a 'Black Urban Contemporary' radio format for Toronto which received extensive media coverage and public protest when bid for licence was turned down by CRTC); Mem., Humber College Radio Course Adv. Bd.; Served on 1983 CRTC Consultative Ctte. on Music & FM Radio; 1986 Census Advisory Panel (Toronto), Stats Canada; Chrmn., Subctte. on Meteorology, Fed. Govt. Metrication Program 1982–84; Former panel Mem., Multiculturalism & the Media forum (Ont. Adv. Concl. on Multiculturalism & Citizenship); presented paper on Ethnic Radio Broadcasting's Archival Past to 1991 Toronto Conference; former Studio Prodn. Instr., Nat. Inst. of Broadcasting; guest lectr. on ethnic broadcasting issues, Ryerson & other institutions; public speaker; student of metaphysics – Unarius curriculum; recreations: electronics, table tennis; Home: 4 Hart St., Richmond Hill, Ont. L4C 7T7; Office: 622 College St., 4th Floor, Toronto, Ont. M6G 1B6.

**REDHEAD, Paul Aveling,** B.A., M.A., Ph.D., F.A.P.S., F.I.E.E.E., F.R.S.C., F.A.V.S.; physicist; b. Brighton, Eng. 25 May 1924; s. Daniel Albert and Gwedoline (Aveling) R.; e. Taunton Sch. 1942; Cambridge Univ. B.A. 1944, M.A. 1948, Ph.D. 1969; m. Doris Beatrice d. late A. J. Packman 1948; children: Mrs. Janet Anne Randall, Mrs. Patricia Joan Redhead; RESEARCHER EMERITUS, INST. OF MICROSTRUCTURAL SCIENCES, NAT. RESEARCH COUNCIL OF CAN.; Scientific Offr., Dept. Naval Ordnance 1944–45, Scientific Offr., Services Electronics Research Lab. (Brit. Admiralty) 1945–47; Research Offr. Nat. Research Council Can. 1947–54, Head of Electron Physics Sec. 1954–70, Head Program Planning and Analysis Group 1970–71, Dir. Gen. (Planning) 1972–73, Group Dir. Phys./Chem. Science Labs. 1974–83, Dir. Div. of Physics 1973–86, Chrmn., Adv. Bd. on TRIUMF 1975–90, Chrmn., Committee of Directors 1981–86, Secy., Science & Technology Policy Ctte. 1986–89; Chrmn., History Ctte., American Vacuum Society 1987–93; Dir., Ont. Centre for Materials Rsch. 1989–91; Chrmn., Scientific and Industry Advisory Ctte., Ont. Centre for Materials Rsch. 1990– ; rec'd Medard W. Welch Award, Am. Vacuum Soc. 1975; rec'd Queen Elizabeth Jubilee Medal 1977; rec'd Medal for Achievement in Physics, Candn. Assoc. of Physicists 1989; Pres., Am. Vacuum Soc. 1967; Pres. Ottawa Chapter, Ont. Heart Foundation 1973–77; author 'The Physical Basis of Ultra-High Vacuum' 1968; over 70 scient. papers electron, vacuum and surface physics; Ed., Journal of Vacuum Science & Technology 1970–74; Asst. Ed.-in-Chief, Candn. Journals of Research 1974–87; Fellow, Inst. of Electronic and Electrical Engrs. (IEEE) 1958; Fellow, Royal Soc. of Can. 1968; Fellow, Am. Physical Soc. 1970; Fellow and Hon. Mem., Am. Vacuum Soc. 1970; mem. Candn. Assn. Physicists; Home: 1958 Norway Cres., Ottawa, Ont. K1H 5N7; Office: Inst. of Microstructural Sciences, National Rsch. Council, Ottawa, Ont. K1A 0R6.

**REDHILL, Michael H.;** poet/playwright; b. Baltimore, Md. 12 June 1966; s. Marshall Leo and Linda Ruth (Strasberg) R.; e. York Mills C.I.; Indiana Univ.; York Univ.; Univ. of Toronto B.A. 1992; Banff Sch. of Fine Arts writing program 1986, 1987, 1988; Co-founder & Editor-in-Chief, Yak Magazine 1986; Keisler Poetry Prize 1985; League of Candn. Poets Nat. Poetry Contest, 1st prize 1988; Leighton Artists Colony 1990; Norma Epstein Award for Poetry 1990; E.J. Pratt Prize for Poetry 1991; mem., Tarragon Theatre/Chalmers Playwrighting Unit 1992; mem., Coach House Press Editorial Bd. 1993– ; Jewish; author: 'Music for Silence' (poetry) 1985; 'Impromptu Feats of Balance' (poetry) 1990; 'Lake Nora Arms' (poetry) 1993; 'Be Frank' (play) at Toronto Fringe Festival 1991, 'Hanging Gardens of Willowdale' (play) at Tarragon Spring Arts Fair 1992; 'Heretics' (play) at Alumni Theatre 1992; 'The Monkey Cage' (play) at The Under the Umbrella Festival 1993; Home: 23 Harrison Rd., Willowdale, Ont. M2L 1V3.

**REDMOND, Donald Aitcheson,** B.Sc., B.L.S., M.S.; librarian; b. Owosso, Mich., 19 May 1922; s. Athol Aitcheson and Hilton Edna (Rhind) R.; e. Mount Allison Univ., B.Sc. 1942; McGill Univ., B.L.S. 1947; Univ. of Ill., M.S. (Lib. Science) 1950; m. Ruth Marian, d. late Frank Clinton White 1948; children: Christopher, Derek, Margaret; Librarian, Candn. Book Center, Halifax, 1948–49; N.S. Tech. Coll., Halifax, 1949–60; Science and Engn. Librarian, Asst. Dir. of Libs. (Reader Services) Univ. of Kans., 1961–65; Tech. Lib. Advisor, Ceylon Inst. of Scient. and Indust. Research, Colombo, 1957–58; Dir. of Lib., Middle E. Tech. Univ., Ankara, 1959–60; Chief Librarian, Queen's Univ., 1966–77; Principal Librarian, Queen's Univ. 1977–87; author, 'Sherlock Homes among the Pirates' 1990; 'Sherlock Holmes, a Study in Sources' 1982; 'BSJ 1946–69' (a cumulated index to Baker St. Journ.), 1970; edit. checklist and index of Conan Doyle Coll., Metro. Toronto Central Library, 1972, 1974; also articles in prof. lib. and other journals; mem., Baker St. Irregulars; Sherlock Holmes Soc. of London; United Church; recreations: Sherlock Holmes, Meccano, model railways; Home: 9 St. Catherine St., Kingston, Ont. K7K 3R9.

**REDPATH, James Stockton,** P.Eng.; b. Montréal, Qué. 24 Sept. 1936; s. James Botterell and Margaret Isobel (Stockton) R.; e. Percival H.S.; Bishop's Coll. Sch. 1954; McGill Univ., P.Eng. (Hons.) 1958; Works of Art Program, Sotheby's 1987; D.Litt. (hon. causa), Nipissing Univ. 1988; m. Roberta d. Raymond Gushue 31 Jan. 1976; children: Carolyn Jeffers, Lorraine Margaret, John Philip, Sarah Anne; CHRMN., J.S. REDPATH LTD. 1986– , Founding Pres. 1962–86; Pres., RME Capital Corp. 1968– ; Gen. Mgr., North Bay Arts Centre 1988–90; Chrmn., Northern Ont. Relocation Program, Art Selection Ctte. 1990–92; Dir., Skega Canada Ltd. 1988– ; Adv. Bd. Chrmn., Candn. Tunneling Assn. 1972–78; Dir., Jarvis Clark Co. 1968–80; Campbell Red Lake Gold Mines Ltd. 1978–82; Mines Accident Prev. Assn. of Ont. 1982–86; Dir., Pegasus Gold Inc. 1990– ; Dir., Mid-Canada Communications (Canada) Corp. 1993– ; Dir., Bishop's College School 1993– ; Dir., Redpath Gallery 1994– ; Prov. of Ont. Assn. of Profl. Engrs. Engr. Medal 1975; Candn. Inst. of Mining & Metallurgy Past Pres. Medal 1981; author: 'Collaring a Shaft in Deep Overburden at Chimo Gold Mines Ltd.' 1963, 'Creighton No. 9 Shaft 7, 137 Feet Sunk in One Lift' 1970, 'Mining Contractors – A Necessary Evil or an Increasingly Valuable Service to the Industry' 1971; co-author: 'Securing Maximum Effectiveness from Mining Contractors' 1976, and other pubns.; recreations: hunting, fishing; Club: Caughnawana Fishing & Hunting; Home: R.R. 3, Regal Rd., North Bay, Ont. P1B 8G4.

**REDWAY, Hon. Alan,** P.C., Q.C., B.Com., LL.B.; b. Toronto, Ont. 11 March 1935; s. Alan Edwin Sydney and Phyllis May (Turner) R.; e. Univ. of Toronto; Osgoode Law Sch.; m. Mary Louise Harvey, 1962; children: Kimberley, Andrea; Minister of State (Housing) 1989–91; Mayor, East York, Toronto 1977–82; Alderman, 1972–76; Metro Toronto Exec. Comm. 1977–82; East York Hydro Comm. 1977–82; el. House of Commons g.e. 1984; re-el. 1988; Sworn to the Privy Council 1989.

**REED, Alice Mary,** B.F.A.; artist; b. Toronto, Ont. 27 May 1957; d. Percy Arthur and Enid Agnes (Gilson) R.; e. Mount Allison Univ. B.F.A. 1980; full-time profl. artist since 1980; mem. and Atlantic Regional Director for Candn. Soc. of Painters in Water Colour; solo exhns. incl. Meml. Univ. of Nfld. (toured Nfld. & Labrador) 1981; N.B. Museum Saint John 1983; Confedn. Centre Art Gallery Charlottetown 1983; Justina M. Barnicke Gallery Hart House Univ. of Toronto 1984; Libby's of Toronto (2 person 1984), 1987, 1989, 1990, 1992; Art Gallery of N.S. (toured 4 Atlantic Provs.) 1985–87; Houston North Gallery Lunenburg 7 exhns. 1982–90, Halifax 1993; Windrush Galleries Ltd. Saint John 1982, 1984, 1986, 1988; Kitchener/Waterloo Art Gallery, Ont. 1988; Duke of Argyle Gallery, Halifax, N.S. 1989, 1991; teacher of watercolour painting in classes and workshops at universities and colleges in Atlantic Canada; rec'd. grant from Nova Scotia Dept. of Culture; rec'd. 2 grants from Elizabeth Greenshields Foundation; Scholarships: Mount Allison Univ., Lavinia Estabrooks, and Graphic Arts Internat. Union; rep. various corporate and pub. colls.; cited various mags. and art jours.; mem. Candn. Nature Fedn.; World Wildlife Can.; Ecology Action Centre; recreations: swimming, hiking, reading, music; Address: Halifax, N.S.

**REED, Hon. Barbara Joan,** B.A., LL.B., LL.M.; judge; b. St. Catherines, Ont. 25 Mar. 1937; d. Joseph Cornwall and Marjorie (Grainge) Savage; e. Univ. of Toronto B.A. 1960; Dalhousie Univ. LL.B. 1968, LL.M. 1970; m. Robert Barry s. Clifford and Grace Reed 3 Sept. 1960; children: Christopher, Bruce, Thea; JUDGE, TRIAL DIVISION, FEDERAL COURT OF CANADA 1983– ; Chrmn., Competition Tribunal, 1986–92; Asst. Prof. Univ. of Ottawa Common Law Sect. 1971–73; Legal Offr. Dept. of Justice Ottawa 1973–74; Constitutional Adv. to Privy Counc. Office and Fed. Prov. Relations Office 1974–80; Dir. Legal Services Fed. Prov. Relations Office 1980–82; Legal Couns. Privy Counc. Office 1982–83; called to Bar of Ont. 1971; Q.C. 1982; Dir. Civil Service Co-op. 1980–83; mem. Law Soc. of Upper Can.; Candn. Assn. for the Admin. of Justice; various ch. offices; recreation: cross-country skiing; Home: 160 Clearview, Ottawa, Ont. K1Z 6S5; Office: Supreme Court Bldg., Ottawa, Ont. K1A 0H9.

**REED, Greg Arthur,** B.Sc., M.B.A.; management consultant; b. Hamilton, Ont. 28 May 1954; s. Arthur Ernest and Donna Marie Eva (Willrich) R.; e. Univ. of Toronto B.Sc. 1977; Harvard Univ., Grad. Sch. of Bus. M.B.A. 1983; m. Heather Anne d. Haldane and Shirley Howe 1 Sept. 1984; children: Arthur Erik, Katherine Heather; PRINCIPAL, McKINSEY & COMPANY 1990– ; Mktg. Rep., IBM Canada 1977–81; Assoc., present firm, London, England, New York, Toronto 1983–90; Dir., National Ballet of Canada 1992– ; Chrmn., Advocacy Task Force, Arthritis Soc. (Ont. Div.) 1991–93; Mem., Royal Astronomical Soc. of Canada; Un. Ch. of Can.; recreations: running, classical music, photography; club: Harvard Bus. Sch. (Toronto); Office: 175 Bloor St. E., 12th floor, Toronto, Ont. M4W 3R8.

**REED, R. Alex,** B.A.; university administrator; b. Toronto, Ont. 11 April 1955; s. Robert William and Olga Elizabeth (Hoare) R.; e. Trent Univ. B.A. (Hons.) 1979; m. Shirley E. d. Douglas Quinney 31 Oct. 1975; children: Joscelyn, Adam, Eric, Joshua, Jared; REGISTRAR, ATHABASCA UNIV. 1992– ; Sr. Admissions-Liaison Officer, Trent Univ. 1978–82; Asst. Registrar-Admissions & Grad. Studies, Brock Univ. 1982–85; Asst. Registrar-Admissions, Athabasca Univ. 1985–88; Assoc. Registrar 1988–91; Acting Registrar 1991–92; extensive committee work; frequent lecturer, guest speaker, workshop presentor; Mem., Extve., Nat. Assn. of Registrars of the Univs. of Canada 1994; Hon. Chair, Athabasca Univ. Student Assn. 1993; Ctte. Mem. for organizing Gov. Gen. Candn. Studies tour in Alta 1993; re-elected Chair, Athabasca Reg. Econ. Devel. Council 1993; Mem., Assn. of Registrars of Univs. & Colleges of Can.; Western Assn. of Registrars of the Univs. & Coll. of Can.; Am. & Pacific assns. of Coll. Registrars & Admissions Officers; Assn. of Reords Mgrs. of Am.; Candn. Soc. for the Study of Higher Edn.; Internat. Customer Serv. Assn.; Home: Box 3122, Athabasca, Alta. T0G 0B0; Office: Box 10,000, Athabasca, Alta. T0G 2R0.

**REEKIE, Charles Douglas,** C.A.; industrialist; b. Montreal, Que. 20 Aug. 1924; e. Elizabeth Ballantyne Pub. Sch., Montreal W.; Montreal W. High Sch.; McGill Univ.; Chart. Acct., 1948; m. Lorna Elsie Bridge, Montreal; children: Jennifer Ann Howard, John Douglas; VICE CHRMN., BD. OF DIRS., CAE INDUSTRIES LTD. since 1985; Dir., Can. Pacific Ltd.; Colonia Life Ins. Co.; United Dominion Industries Ltd.; Marathon Realty Co. Ltd.; PanCanadian Petroleum Ltd.; The Boiler Inspection and Ins. Co. of Can.; Candn. Pacific Securities Ltd.; with Sharp Milne & Co., Chart. Accts., Montreal 1941–47; Riddell Stead Graham & Hutchison, Chart. Accts. 1947–49; Secy.-Treas., Canadian Baker Perkins Ltd. 1950–55; joined present Co. (then Candn. Aviation Electronics Ltd.) 1955, Pres. Northwest Industries Ltd. (a subsidiary) Edmonton, Alta. 1963–67; Pres. & C.E.O., CAE Industries Ltd. Toronto, Ont. 1967–85; mem., Order of Chart. Accts. Ont. recreations: golf, reading; Clubs: Lyford Cay; Lambton Golf & Country; Home: 18 Taylorwood Dr., Islington, Ont. M9Y 4R7.

**REEVES, Beatrice;** retired farmer/association executive; b. Toronto, Ont. 12 Mar. 1921; d. David and Beatrice Maude (Barrett) Ross; e. Verdun H.S.; Sir George Williams Univ.; m. Malcolm F., P.Eng.; s. Frank & Alene R. 7 Nov. 1942; children: David M., Ronald F., Mary E., Susan Jane; PRES., FED. WOMEN'S INST. OF CAN. 1985–88; managed 50–acre fruit farm; Pres., real estate co.; Pres., Fed. Women's Inst. of P.E.I. 1973–75 (Life Mem. 1975– ); Chrmn., Fin. Ctte., World Conf. of Assoc. Country Women of the World (Vanc. 1983) 1981; Pres.-Elect, Fed. Women's Inst. of Can. 1982; F.W.I.C.; Rep., U.N. meeting of non-govt. orgns., Nairobi, Kenya 1985; Chair, Adv. Counc. on Status of Women for P.E.I.; Bd. Mem., P.E.I. Addiction Found.; Bd. Mem., Candn. Addiction Found. 1979–82; recipient, Order of Canada Medal 1992; Health & Welfare Can. cert. of merit; Red Cross, cert. of merit for water safety serv. 1963; Jubilee Medal 1977; Pres., P.E.I. Presbyn. Un. Ch. Women 1972–74; school trustee; sponsor: 'Challenge from a Changing Lifestyle: Adolescent Parenthood in P.E.I.' 1980; Home: Box 1574, Charlottetown, P.E.I. C1A 7N3.

**REEVES, Hubert,** O.C., B.A., B.Sc., M.Sc., Ph.D.; physicist; b. Montreal, Que. 13 July 1932; e. Univ. of Montreal B.A. 1950, B.Sc. 1953; McGill Univ. M.Sc. 1955; Cornell Univ. Ph.D. 1960; m. Camille Scoffier 2 Feb. 1987; children: Gilles, Nicolas, Benoit, Evelyne; DIRECTEUR DE RECHERCHES, CENTRE NATIONALE DE LA RECHERCHE SCIENTIFIQUE, PARIS & CONSEILLER SCIENTIFIQUE, COMMISSARIAT A L'ENERGIE ATOMIQUE, SACLAY FRANCE 1965– ; Asst. Prof., Univ. of Montreal 1960–64; Consultant, Inst. for Space Studies, NASA, N.Y. & Teacher, Columbia Univ. 1960–64; Visiting Prof., Univ. Libre de Bruxelles, Belgium 1964–65; Astronomy Dept., Berkeley Univ. 1981 (½-year sabbatical); Assoc. Prof., Dept. of Physics, Univ. of Montreal 1989– ; Prof., Univ. Paris VII 1986– ; research: thermonuclear reactions in stellar cores: fusion of carbon & oxygen; spectrum of solar neutrinos; R & S processes in stars; origin of light atoms, lithium, beryllum, & boron; abundance of deuterium & helium in solar system & universe; baryonic densities of the universe; quark-hadron transition in cosmology; origin & devel. of free energy in the universe; origin of the solar system; Hon. Doct.: Univ. of Montreal 1983, Univ. of Berne 1989, Univ. of Moncton, N.B. 1991; Chevalier de l'Ordre du Mérite, Rep. Française 1976; Chevalier de la Légion d'Honneur (France) 1986; Mem., Acad. Canadienne-française 1988; Grand Prix de la Francophonie décerné par l'Acad. Française 1989; Officier, l'Ordre du Canada; Membre de la Societé Royale du Canada; Officier de l'ordre National du Québec 1993; author (scientific): 'Stellar Evolution and Nucleosynthesis' 1968, 'Nuclear Reactions in Stellar Surfaces' 1972; (popular science): 'Patience dans l'azur' (Prix de la Fond. de France 1982; Prix de la Soc. fran. de Physique 1985; transl. in 11 languages) 1982, 'Poussières d'étoiles' 1984, 'L'heure de s'enivrer' (Prix Blaise Pascal de la ville de Clermont-Ferrant; transl. in 6 languages) 1988; 'Malicorne' 1990; 'Compagnons de Voyage' 1992; sci. films: 'Les étoiles naissant aussi,' 'Le Soleil, notre étoile,' 'La vie dans l'univers,' 'Un soir, une étoile,' 'cosmologie'; and approx. 100 sci, articles; Office: Batiment 28, 91191 Gif-sur-Yvette, France.

**REEVES, Jacques D.,** B.Arch., F.R.A.I.C.; architect; b. Ottawa Ont. & Nov. 1930; e. McGill Univ. B. Arch. 1957 (Design Award Anglin Norcross, Candn. Pittsburgh Industries Ltd. Scholarship); PRINCIPAL, LES ARCHITECTES REEVES ET ASSOCIÉS 1992– ; collab. with various offices Montréal on Ottawa City Hall, Windsor Hotel restoration 1957–60; Partner, Jean-Claude La Haye and Jean Ouellet, Town Planners and Archs. 1961–84; maj. projects 1980–84 incl. Hôtel Méridien Complexe Desjardins Montréal, Candn. Embassy Bldg. Belgrade, Yugoslavia; Arch. Adv. to Min. of Edn. Qué. 1966–72; O.A.Q. Chrmn. Task Force Prof. Liability Ins.; Chrmn. Burwell Coon Travelling Award RAIC 1984; Chrmn., Town of Mount-Royal Architectural Ctte. 1981–91; Regional Rep. Centraide 1982–84; mem. various juries community arch. achievements 1984–85; McGill Alma Mater Fund Class 1957 Rep. 1957– ; mem. Adm. Ctte. Héritage Montréal 1985–86; recipient Massey Medal Habitations les Ilots St-Martin and Garage Louis Colin Univ. de Montréal 1976; Design Award elem. sch. Qué. 1964; Design awards for Candn. Wood Construction 66' Institut Coopératif Desjardins; Candn. Design Concrete Awards Program 1971 for Garage Louis Colin Univ. Montreal; mem. Ordre des architectes du Qué. (Vice Prés. 1979–84, Prés. 1985–86–87); Council mem., Royal Architectural Inst. of Can. 1988–91; Candn. Delegate to L'Union Internat. des Architectes 1989–93; Les Architectes Reeves Auger Boisvert 1989–91; Chrmn., Design Ctte. of the Nat. Capital Commn. 1990–91; Registrar College of Fellows RAIC and Senior Advisory Ctte. 1990–92; Assn. des architectes en pratique privée du Qué.; Prés. Inst. de la maçonnerie du Que. 1986–87; mem. Quebec Chaptre of the Candn. Construction Rsch. Bd.; mem., Standing Ctte. on Fire Protection NRC; R. Catholic; recreations: golf, skiing, sailing, tennis; Home: 1451 Argyle, Montréal, Qué. H3G 1V5; Office: 8000 Saint Denis St., Montréal, Qué. H2R 2G1.

**REEVES, John;** athlete, author, broadcaster, composer; b. Merritt, B.C. 1 Dec. 1926; s. Rev. A.G . and D. H. (Swinburn) R.; e. St. John's Coll., Cambridge Univ., B.A. (Classics) 1948; m. Cathryn Kester 1986; athletic achievements include former holder Candn. veteran records for half-mile, mile, two miles, three miles, six miles, ten miles; founder Hart House Marathon; joined CBC as Radio Producer (Music and Drama) 1952; pioneered stereophonic broadcasts in Canada 1954; authored world's first quadriphonic radio play in 1970; introduced Kunstkopf recording N. Amer. 1975; received Italia Prize for Radio Drama 1959; John Drainie Award for Distinguished Contribution to Broadcasting 1977; Gabriel Prize for Religious Broadcasting 1978; served with Brit. Intelligence Corp. 1948–49; author: 'A Beach of Strangers' 1960; 'Triptych' 1972; 'The Arithmetic of Love' 1976; 'Murder by Microphone' 1978; 'Murder before Matins' 1984; 'Murder with Muskets' 1985; 'Death in Prague' 1988; numerous radio plays, features and documentaries, and TV films; also a body of verse some of which issued in 1954 by Hallmark Recordings; composer, chamber and choral pieces; principal works include: 'Hallelujah Psalms'; 'For the Feast of All Hallows'; 'Two Fifteenth Century Lyrics': 'Canons for String Orchestra'; 'The Deploration of Rachel'; 'Missa Brevis'; 'Compline Cantata'; 'Ecumenical Evening Service'; 'Twelve Haikuku'; 'Aphorisms'; 'Antiphons'; 'Commemorations'; 'Advent Cantata'; 'Four Songs for Voice and Violin'; 'Salvator Mundi'; 'Threnody for the People of Poland'; 'Veni Creator Spiritus'; 'Rossetti Prelude and Fugue'; 'Requiem Mass'; 'Death and Resurrection'; 'Seven Last Words'; In Memoriam Primo Levi'; 'Death and Resurrection'; avocation: Czechoslovak politics; rec'd Masaryk Award 1989 for 'a significant contribution to the cause of free Czechoslovakia'; Clubs: Univ. Toronto Track; Home: 85 Duggan Ave., Toronto, Ont. M4V 1Y1.

**REEVES, John Alexander,** R.C.A.; photojournalist; b. Burlington, Ont. 24 Apl. 1938; s Walter James and Jean (McCrimmon) R.; e. Burlington Central High Sch. 1956; Sir George Williams Art Sch. 1957; Ont. Coll. of Art A.O.C.A. Dipl. 1961; prof. gen. features photographer for maj. mags. Can. and USA; many assignments Nat. Film Bd. Still Photo Div.; served as Consultant to Nat. Film Bd. in production of 'Between Friends-Entre Amis' 1976; contrib. to numerous N.F.B. books and exhns. incl. 'Call Them Canadians' (book & exhn.) 1967; 'Image 5' (book and exhn.) 1968; 'Many Happy Returns' N.W.T. Centennial (exhn.) 1969; coll. 'Fifty Portraits of Canadian Women' exhibited as a monograph Nat. Conf. Centre Ottawa 1975; coll. 'Thirty Portraits of Women' Deja Vue Gallery Toronto 1977; 'The Magic Word,' Nat. Photog. Collection of Public Archives, 1981; 'Photojournalism,' NFC Gallery, Ottawa, 1981; 'Inuit Art World,' The Canadian Centre of Photography, 1982 (one-man show); began writing for mags. 1972 preparing several feature articles for 'Toronto Life'; produced photographic and written essay on Jean Vanier's work with mentally handicapped in France for 'Maclean's' 1973; contrib. ed., Canadian Art Magazine 1984; has produced word-and-picture packages on interesting people for maj. mags.; comns. rec'd from various business enterprises involving annual reports, recruiting and promotional material; co-author 'John Fillion – Thoughts About My Sculpture' 1968 (selected for exhn. Am. Inst. Graphic Arts Book Show 1969); photog., 'Debretts Illustrated Guide to the Canadian Establishment,' Methuen, Canada; 'Authors' (3 man show), Harbour Front Gallery, Aug. 1983; John Reeves One Man Show, The Jane Corkin Gallery, Dec. 83 and Jan. 84; recipient various Graphic Arts Awards incl. acceptance Le Fed. Internationale de l'Art Photographique Exhn. 1968, 1969; rec'd Internat. Assn. Printing House Craftsmen Award 1977; Graphica Club Montreal and Toronto Art Dirs. Club Awards; Cdn. Nat. Magazine Award for Photo-journalism, 1980; R.C.A. Council 1985–87; commenced radio and TV broadcasting activities 1968 becoming Host of 'Toronto in Review' CBC radio; many appearances on radio and TV shows; cited various bibliogs.; Council mem. Royal Candn. Acad. 1980–81; 1984–85; Anglican; recreation: sailing; Address: c/o Jane Corkin Gallery, 179 John St., Toronto, Ont. M5T 1X4.

**REEVES, Leonard Wallace,** Ph.D., D.Sc., F.C.I.C., F.R.S.C.; educator; b. Bristol, Eng. 8 Feb. 1930; s. Wallace Edward and Violet Edith (Smith) R.; e. Univ. of Bristol B.Sc. 1951, Ph.D. 1954, D.Sc. 1965; PROF. OF CHEM. AND PHYSICS UNIV. OF WATERLOO 1969– ; Post-doctoral Fellow Univ. of Cal. Berkeley 1954–56, Nat. Rsch. Council Can. Ottawa 1957–59; Asst. to Full Prof. Univ. of B.C. 1958–69; Visiting Prof. Univ. of Sao Paulo 1967–81, founded rsch. lab.; Noranda Lectr. Chem. Inst. Can. 1969; author over 160 rsch. publs. various jours.; Foreign mem. Nat. Acad. Sci's Brazil; Fellow of Royal Society of Canada (1979); United Church; Address: P.O. Box 521, Paisley, Ont. N0G 2N0.

**REEVES, Hon. Paul G.;** judge; b. Ottawa, Ont. 27 June 1928; s. late J. Oscar and Marie-Jeanne (Lemieux) R.; e. Coll. de Saint-Laurent (Que.), B.A. 1948; Univ. de Montréal, LL.L. 1952; Goethe Inst., Montreal, degree in German lang. 1973; m. Agnès G., d. C.E. Millet, Longueuil, Que. 23 May 1955; children; Hélène, Jean Isabelle, Marie-Agnès; JUSTICE, SUPERIOR COURT, QUE., since 1973; read law with Marcel Piché; called to Bar of Que. 1952; cr. Q.C. 1967; Prof. of Eng., Coll. de St. Laurent 1952; Part-time Prof. of Law 1953–62; Legal Advisor, Claims Dept., United Provinces Insurance Co. 1953; Jr. Partner, Pagé Beauregard Duchesne Renaud & Reeves 1957; Partner, Lalande Brière Reeves Paquette & Longtin 1963–67; Crown Atty. 1962–64; Mun. Judge, Ville Le Moyne 1962–73; Legal Advisor and Dir., Reeves Security Agency Ltd. 1955–73; Sr. Partner, Reeves Longtin Cantin & Villeneuve 1968–73; has served on various bar comtes.; responsible for post-grad. teaching ins. law, Prof. Law Sch. of Que. Bar 1970–71; author various articles in legal journs.; mem. Candn. Bar Assn.; R. Catholic; recreations: skiing, travel, photography, theatre, concerts; Home: 630 Victoria Ave., Longueuil, Que.; Office: Court House, Longueuil, Que. J4M 2J6.

**REEVES-STEVENS, Francis Garfield;** writer; b. Oakville, Ont. 21 April 1953; s. Donald Hill and Mary Louise (Freeman) Stevens; e. Book Pub. Prog., Centennial Coll. 1971–74; m. Judith d. Arthur and Evelyn Reeves 7 Oct. 1977; Ed. Asst., Holt, Rinehart & Winston of Can. Ltd. 1974; Promotion Asst., Collier-Macmillan Can. Ltd. 1974–75; Mathematics Prod. Ed. 1975–77; Partner, First Image Design Studio 1977–80; Instr., Book Prod. & Design, Centennial Coll. 1978–79; Co-owner, Reeves-Stevens Inc.; author: 'Bloodshift' 1981; The Ultimate Trivia Game Book series (TV) 1984; 'Dreamland' 1986; 'Phoenix: The Final Cure' (screenplay) 1986; 'Children of the Shroud' 1987; 'Fast Food' (screenplay) 1987; 'Canadian all 8: Portraits of Our People' 1988; 'Nighteyes' 1989; 'Dark Matter' 1991; co-author: (with Paul Till): The Ultimate Trivia Game Book series (pop. music) 1984; (with C. Kingsburgh & S. Heaslip): 'Kid's Stuff' 1984; (with Judith Reeves-Stevens): 'For Women's Eyes Only' 1984, 'Science Around Me' (45–title primary sci. textbook series) 1987, 'Unicorn Story Disks 1, 2, and 3' and 'Unicorn Story Baker' (edn. software) 1986, 'Star Trek: Memory Prime' (novel) 1988; co-writer (with J. Reeves-Stevens): 'Corporate Squad' TV series – shared credit: 'Story Editors'; Address: c/o Seal Books, 105 Bond St., Toronto, Ont. M5B 1Y3.

**REFORD, Alexander Robert,** B.A., M.A.; university administrator; b. Ottawa, Ont. 15 Oct. 1962; s. Michael Stephen and Aurora Frances (Tewksbury) R.; e. Philemon Wright H.S.; CEGEP de l'Outaouais; Univ. of Toronto, St. Michael's Coll. B.A. (Phil.) 1984; New Coll., Oxford Univ. B.A. (Mod. Hist.) 1986, M.A. 1993; Univ. of Toronto M.A. (Hist.) 1988; DEAN OF COLLEGE, UNIV. OF TORONTO, ST. MICHAEL'S COLL., 1988– ; Asst. Dean 1986–87; Dean of Men 1987– ; Jr. Fellow, Massey Coll. 1987–89; Moss Scholar, Univ. of Toronto 1984; New Coll. 1st VIII, Head of the River, Oxford 1986; Anglican; recreations: rowing, Candn. hist.; Club: Leander (England); Home: 81 St Mary St., Toronto, Ont. M5S 1J4 & Moylinny Farm, 1303 Mountain Rd., Aylmer, Que. J9H 5E1.

**REFORD, Lewis Alexis Meighen,** B.A.; business executive; b. Montreal, Que. 15 June 1934; s. Lewis Eric and Katharina Nickolaievna (Pletschikoff) R.; e. Selwyn House Sch.; Trinity Coll. Sch.; Univ. of Bishop's Coll., Sorbonne; New Coll., Oxford Univ.; Univ. of Barcelona; m. the late Manon d. Jean A. de Watteville 13 Jan. 1962; children: Nikola, Geoffrey; PRES., MMRM INC. 1975– ; Pres., Robert Reford Inc. 1971– ; Treas., Montreal Bd. of Trade 1985–86; Chrmn., Shipping Fed. of Can. 1986–88; Dir., Multiport Ship Agencies Network (Rotterdam); Chartered & Internat. Shipbrokers P & I Club Ltd. (London); Gov., Montreal Diocesan Theol. Coll. 1981–87; Mem., Ch. of St. James the Apostle (Anglican); Club: University Club of Montreal; Home: 3200 Trafalgar Ave., Montreal, Que. H3Y 1H7; Office: 221 St. Sacrement St., Montreal, Que. H2Y 1X2.

**REFORD, Robert W.;** b. London, Eng. 1 May 1921; s. Robert Bruce Stephen and Evelyn Margaret Robinson (MacInnes) R.; came to Canada 1946; e. Winchester Coll., Eng. 1934–39; New Coll. Oxford Univ. 1940; m. Stephanie Lee McCandless 26 Nov. 1972; children: Lisa E., Sharon V. (by previous marriage); step-children: James A. and Nancy B. Hudson; MEMBER, IMMIGRATION & REFUGEE BD. 1988– ; with British United Press 1946–52; Ottawa Liaison Offr., CBC Internat. Service 1953–65; Edit. Writer, Ottawa Citizen 1965–67; U.N. Correspondent 1968; Special Asst. to Dir. of Research, U.N. Inst. for Training & Research 1970; Extve. Dir., Candn. Inst. of Internat. Affairs, 1971–78; Pres., Reford-McCandless Internat. Consultants Corp.; Reford-McCandless Internat Inst. 1978–88; Pres., U.N. Assn. in Canada 1985–87; mem., Immigration & Refugee Bd.; served in 2nd World War, Irish Guards 1940–46; active service in N.W. Europe and Malaya; author: 'Canada and Three Crises' 1968; 'UNSSOD II and Canada' 1981; 'The Other Road to Security' 1982; 'Tracking Ambiguity' 1985; 'New Discoveries:

Canada's National Security Interests in the North Pacific' 1989; co-ed., 'Canada Challenged: The Viability of Confederation' 1979; recreations: golf, skiing; Clubs: Rideau; Royal Ottawa Golf; Toronto Golf; Home: R.R. 1, Crescent Beach, La Have, N.S. B0R 1C0.

**REGAN, David,** B.Sc., A.R.C.S., M.Sc., Ph.D., D.Sc., F.R.S.C.; educator; researcher; b. Scarborough, England 5 May 1935; s. Randolph and Muriel Frances R.; e. Scarborough H.S. 1953; Imperial Coll., London Univ. 1957, B.Sc., A.R.C.S. 1958, M.Sc., D.I.C. 1964, Ph.D. King's Coll., London Univ., 1959, P.G.C.E.; m. Marian d. Frederick and Alice Marsh 15 Aug. 1959; children: Douglas Lawrence, Howard Michael; NSERC/CAE INDUSTRIAL RESEARCH CHAIR IN VISION IN AVIATION 1993– ; CO-DIRECTOR HUMAN PERFORMANCE IN SPACE LAB 1989– ; Prof. of Ophthalmol., Univ. of Toronto & Prof. of Psychol., York Univ. 1987– ; Lectr. in Physics, London Univ. 1960–65; Reader, Univ. of Keele 1965–75; Prof. of Psych., Dalhousie Univ. 1976–80; of Physiol. 1980–84; of Otolaryngol. 1980–84; of Med. 1984–87; of Ophthalmol. 1980–87; Dir., Ctr. for Rsch. in Vision & Hearing 1978–87; State of New Jersey Prof. of Electr. Engr., Rutgers Univ. 1985–86; Vis. Prof., Dept. of Med. Phys., Amsterdam 1985–86; Playfair Clinician Scientist 1989; Staff Sci., Toronto Western Hosp. 1988; Cons. inventor, Wilkinson-Graviner Group U.K.; Cons., Westinghouse Inc. 1971–75; visual factors in highway & other accidents 1978–81; Mem., NRC (USA) Steering Ctee. on visual simulation in flight training 1988– ; Nat. Inst. of Health (USA) Multi Ctr. Amblyopia Assessment Sensory & Motor Disorders Panels, 1988– ; Prentice Medal, Am. Acad. Optometry 1990; F.R.S.C.; D.Sc. (Lond.); Distinguished Rsch. Prof., York Univ. 1991– ; F.O.S.A.; F.A.A.O.; I.W. Killam Rsch. Fellow 1991–93; I.W. Killam Rsch. Prof. 1978–82; Max Foreman Prize for Med. Rsch.; mem., Optical Soc. of Am.; Assn. for Rsch. in Vision & Ophthal.; Experimental Psychol. Soc.; Colour Vision Group; author: 'Evoked Potentials in Psychology, Sensory Physiology and Clinical Medicine' 1972, 'Human Brain Electrophysiology' 1989; editor: 'Spatial Vision' 'Binocular Vision' 1989; co-editor: 'Systems Approaches in Vision' 1985; Ed. Bd. 'Vision Research,' 'Spatial Vision,' 'Clinical Vision Research'; author of over 200 sci. articles & 200 abstracts of talks & book reviews; 8 patents on med. instrumentation; recreations: cricket, walking; Home: 785 Cummer Ave., North York, Ont. M2H 1E8; Office: York Univ., 4700 Keele St., North York, Ont. M3J 1P3.

**REGAN, Francis Vincent,** Q.C., B.Com., LL.B.; b. Toronto, Ont. 13 Dec. 1922; s. James D. and Irene (Duggan) R.; e. Univ. of Toronto; Osgoode Hall Law Sch., Toronto, Ont.; m. Barbara Jane, d. John Callahan, Q.C., 26 April 1947; children: Paul, Michael, John, Rosemary, Deborah, MaryAnne; read law with Reid, Allen, Hunter and Campbell, Toronto, Ont.; called to the Bar of Ont. 1949; cr. Q.C. 1964; mem., York Co. Law Assn.; Pres., Candn. Assn. of the Sovereign Military Order of Malta; R. Catholic; Club: Ontario; Office: 65 Queen St. W., Suite 1507, Toronto, Ont. M5H 2M5.

**REGAN, (Helen) Gail,** Ph.D., M.B.A.; b. Toronto, Ont. 5 July 1944; d. Paul James and Helen Doris (Gardiner) Phelan; e. Univ. of Toronto B.A. 1965, Ph.D. 1973, M.B.A. 1978; m. 8 June 1963; children: Sean, Tim, Ellen, Honor; Vice-Chrmn., Cara Operations Ltd.; Pres., Cara Holdings Ltd; Bd. mem., Cara Operations; Cara Holdings; Langar; T.J.R. Holdings; Women's Coll. Hosp.; Gardiner Found.; Probe Found.; Recovery Publications; Women's College Hospital Foundation; author various articles; recreations: sailing, skiing, tennis; Clubs: Badminton & Racquet; R.C.Y.C.; Ojibway; Osler; Toronto Lawn Tennis; Home: 1 May Sq., Toronto, Ont. M4W 1S8; Office: 230 Bloor St. W., Toronto, Ont.

**REGAN, Hon. Gerald A.,** P.C., Q.C.; lawyer, politician; b. Windsor, N.S. 13 Feb. 1928; s. late Walter Edward and Rose M. (Greene) R.; e. Windsor (N.S.) Acad. 1946; St. Mary's Univ.; Dalhousie Univ.; Dalhousie Law Sch. LL.B. 1952; m. A. Carole, d. John H. and Margaret Harrison, 17 Nov. 1956; children: Gerald, Geoffrey, Miriam, Nancy, David, Laura; called to the Bar of N.S. 1954; cr. Q.C. 1970; Counsel, Patterson Kitz 1988–90; Lib. cand. in prov. g.e. 1956 and 1960 and in fed. g.e. 1962; el. to H. of C. in g.e. 1963; 1st Candn. to be named Chrmn. of Extve. Comte. of Commonwealth Parlty. Assn., served 1973–76; el. Leader, Lib. Party in N.S., 1965; el. M.L.A. in prov. g.e. 1967 for Halifax Needham; re-el. g.e. 1970; Premier of N.S. 1970–78; Chrmn., N.S. Power Corp 1970–76; el. to H. of C. in g.e. 1980 in Halifax; Secretary of State & Minister of Labour and Min. responsible for Fitness and Amateur Sport 1980–82; Minister of International Trade 1982–84; def. candidate, Gen. Election, 1984; Dir., Sceptre Resources Ltd.; Roman Corp.; Provigo Inc.; United Finan. Mngt. Ltd.; Candn. Surety; Air Atlantic; Tennis Canada; Chrmn., Candn. Exporters Assn.; Trenton Works Inc.; Gov., Olympic Trust of Can.; Hon. LL.D. St. Mary's Univ. 1982; Univ. Ste. Anne 1991; mem., N.S. Barristers Soc.; Liberal; R. Catholic; recreations: tennis, skiing; Club: Halifax; Office: P.O. Box 828, Stn. B., Ottawa, Ont. K1P 5P9.

**REGEHR, Rev. John,** B.Ed., M.A., Th.D. (Mennonite); educator; minister; b. Mexico 29 Dec. 1925; s. Henry and Katherine (Siemens) R.; came to Canada 1926; e. Mennonite Coll. Inst., Gretna, Man. 1947; Univ. of Manitoba, B.A., B.Ed. 1950; Winona Lake Sch. of Theol. (summers) M.A.; Mennonite Brethren Bible Coll. 1950 (part-time 1960–65) B.D.; N. Am. Baptist Semy. (part-time) 1957–59; S. Baptist Theol. Semy., Th.D. 1970; m. Mary, d. late Jacob H. Unger, 27 Aug. 1949; children: Reynold John, Sharon Lenore, James Mark, Jenny Marie; Instr., Mennonite Brethren Bible Coll., Winnipeg, Man. 1968–91 and Acting Pres. there 1972–1974; Recovery of Hope counselling service 1990– ; o. 1957; began teaching in Jr. and Sr. High Sch., West Kildonan, Winnipeg 1950; Princ., H.C. Avery Elem. Sch., Winnipeg 1956; Pastor, Silver Lake Mennonite Brethren Ch., Marion, S. Dak. 1957; Instr., Mennonite Brethren Coll. Inst. 1959–66; Asst Pastor, Elmwood Mennonite Brethren Ch. 1962–66; Pastor, Georgetown (In.) E.U.B. Ch. 1966–68; mem. Bd. Interfaith Pastoral Ins. 1972–74; articles and sermons published in numerous theological magazines and journs.; Home: 275 Bredin Drive, Winnipeg, Man. R2K 1N7.

**REGENSTREIF, S. Peter,** Ph.D.; university professor; political consultant; b. Montreal, Que., 9 Sept. 1936; s. Albert Benjamin and Miriam Lillian (Issenman) R.; e. Strathcona Acad., Montreal, 1949–53; McGill Univ., B.A. (Pol. Science & Econ., 1st Class Hons.) 1957; Cornell Univ., Ph.D. (Govt.) 1963; children: Anne Erica, Mitchell Chester, Jeffrey Gershon, Gail Aviva; PROF. EMERITUS OF POL. SCIENCE AND CANDN. STUDIES, UNIV. OF ROCHESTER, since 1992; Research Assoc. there, 1961–63; Asst. Prof. 1964–66, Assoc. Prof. 1966–70, Prof. 1970–92; Pol. Columnist, Toronto Star 1963–82, (Montreal Star 1962 and 1963); Editorial Consultant, Chicago Sun-Times 1988–90; Pres., Policy Concepts Inc., Toronto; political Consultant, Bunting Warburg 1973–90; Loewen, Ondaatje, McCutcheon 1991– ; Commentator, Broadcaster, CKO Radio 1984–89; Visiting Prof., Univ. of Montreal, 1965, Glendon Coll., 1968–69; with McGill COTC 1954–57; rank Lt. Suppl. Reserve; Consultant Royal Comn. on Bilingualism and Biculturalism; a Pol. broadcaster for C.B.C., C.T.V., and CKO Radio; author of 'The Diefenbaker Interlude: Parties and Voting in Canada' 1965; numerous articles in various learned journs.; mem., Am. Assn. for the Advancement of Science; Candn. Pol. Science Assn.; Am. Pol. Science Assn.; Assn. of Candn. Studies in the U.S.; Phi Beta Kappa; Hebrew; recreation: music (pianist); Home: 30 Glen Ellyn Way, Rochester, NY 14618, USA.

**REGER, Paul H.,** F.L.M.I.; insurance executive; b. Elmira, Ont. 17 Oct. 1942; s. Harvey Walter and Salome (Snyder) R.; e. Elmira Dist. H.S. 1961; m. Josephine d. Cliff and Vera Marsh 27 June 1969; children: Sarah Rachael, Ashley Meaghan; INVESTMENT VICE-PRES., MARKETABLE BONDS, MUTUAL LIFE OF CANADA 1991– ; joined acctg. dept., present firm 1961; Securities Dept. Acctg. 1963; Computer System Devel. 1966; Bond Dept. 1971; Mgr., Marketable Bonds 1979; Asst. Vice-Pres. 1988; Fellow, Life Management Inst.; Investment Subctte., Nat. Cancer Inst.; Investment Subctte., K-W Community Foundation; recreations: gardening, fishing, photography; Home: R.R. 4, Elmira, Ont. N3B 2Z3; Office: 227 King St. S., Waterloo, Ont. N2J 4C5.

**REGESTER, Michael Paul Stearn Dinsmore,** M.B.A., C.A.; insurance executive; b. Ipswich, U.K. 2 Feb. 1942; s. Paul John Dinsmore and Barbara Shorten (Stearn) R.; e. Oundle Sch. (U.K.); Simon Fraser Univ. M.B.A. 1972; m. Susan Beth d. Charles A. and Roslyn Sachs April 1978; children: Lauren Ashley, Emily Robyn; EXTVE. VICE-PRES. (TORONTO), CONFEDERATION LIFE INSUR. CO. (EST. 1871) 1990– ; Chrmn. & C.E.O., Confederation Trust Co. (est. 1987) 1992– ; Accountant, Turquand Youngs & Co. (U.K.) 1961–65; C.A., Clarkson Gordon & Co. (Toronto) 1965–67; Asst. Supt. of Agencies, U.S. 1972–73; Marketing Vice-Pres., Individual Insur., U.S. (Toronto/Atlanta) 1979–84; Vice-Pres., Individual Insur., U.S. (Atlanta) 1984–89; Sr. Vice-Pres., Candn. Opns. (Toronto) 1989–90; Dir., Confed. Investment Counselling Limited; Confed. Treas. Serv. Limited; Confederation Financial Services (Canada) Ltd.; Mem., Inst. of C.A.s (U.K.) 1965– ; Candn. Inst. of C.A.s 1967– ; Georgia Soc. of Cert. Public Accountaints 1982– ; Anglican; Recreations: tennis, squash, golf; clubs: Donalda, Toronto Cricket, Curling & Skating, Dunwoody (Atlanta), East India and Sports (U.K.); Home: 61 Alexandra Blvd., Toronto, Ont. M4R 1M1; Office: 321 Bloor St. E., Toronto, Ont. M4R 1H1.

**REGIER, Henry Abraham,** B.A., M.Sc., Ph.D.; educator; b. Brainerd, Alta. 5 March 1930; s. Abraham Peter and Margareta Davidovna (Kroeger) R.; e. Queen's Univ. B.A. 1954; Cornell Univ. M.Sc. 1959, Ph.D. 1961; m. Lynn d. Henry and Katharine Dyck 6 July 1956; three d. M. Christine R. Betts, Andrea L.R. McClure, Susan H.; PROF. OF ZOOLOGY, UNIV. OF TORONTO 1966– ; Dir., Inst. Environ. Studies, Univ. of Toronto 1989– ; Secondary Sch. Teacher Niagara Falls, Ont. 1955–57; Rsch. Sci. Lake Erie fisheries Ont. Govt. 1961–63; mem. faculty Cornell Univ. 1963–66; joined present univ. 1966; Chief, Fisheries Br. FAO Rome 1970–71; Candn. Comnr. Great Lakes Fishery Comn. 1980–89; Chrmn. various internat. cttes. FAO Rome, UNESCO Paris; author or co-author numerous scholarly and sci. papers fisheries, aquatic ecol. and renewable resource mgmt.; mem. Am. Fisheries Soc. (Pres. 1978–79); Internat. Ecol. Assn.; Internat. Assn. Gt. Lakes Rsch.; Royal Soc. of Can. Centenary Medal 1986; recreation: scholarly rumination; Home: 21 Hollybrook Cres., Willowdale, Ont. M2J 2H5; Office: Ramsay-Wright Labs., Toronto, Ont. M5S 1A1.

**REGNIER, Marc Charles,** B.A., LL.B.; executive; b. Rockland, Ont. 24 Apl. 1939; s. Lucien and Josephine (Mattar) R.; e. Univ. of Ottawa B.A. 1960, LL.B. 1964; m. Claudette Picard; one s. Mathieu; SENIOR VICE PRES. AND GEN. COUNSEL, AVENOR INC. 1986– ; Dir., NBIP Forest Products Inc.; Pacific Forest Products Ltd.; special asst. and solr. Legal Sec. Combines Br. 1960–66; solr. and Secy. Celanese Canada Ltd. 1966–72; Secy. and legal counsel Microsystems International Ltd. 1972–75, Sr. Group Counsel, Northern Telecom Ltd. 1974–75; Vice Pres. and Gen. Counsel CIP Inc. 1976; Dir. Montreal Internat. Music Competition; Montreal Symphony Orchestra; Fondation de l'Hôpital St-Luc; Vie des Arts; Festival de Théâtre des Amériques; mem. Law Soc. Upper Can.; Que. Bar; Assn. Candn. Gen. Counsel (Past Pres.); Candn. Bar Assn. (Past Nat. Chrmn. Corporate Counsel Sec. 1979–80); Licensing Extves. Soc.; recreations: music, travel, fishing; Club: St-Denis; Home: 632 Dunlop Ave., Outremont, Qué. H2V 2V9.

**REHAK, Peter Stephen,** B.A.; journalist; b. Bratislava, Czech. 9 June 1936; s. the late Richard and Helen (Gross) R.; e. McGill Univ. B.A. 1959; m. Louise d. Samuel (dec'd) and Elizabeth Rouse 30 June 1962; children: Anna, Ellen; EXTVE. PRODUCER, CTV TELEVISION 1981– ; newspaper reporter 1959–62; Foreign Corresp., Foreign Sub-Ed., Bureau Chief (Bonn, Prague, Vienna), Assoc. Press 1962–72; Parlty. Corresp., Montreal Star 1972–73; Bureau Chief (Toronto, Ottawa), Time Mag. 1973–76; Sr. Producer, Foreign Ed., CBC Television News 1976–81; Producer, 'W5,' CTV Television 1981– ; rec'd Overseas Press Club of Am.'s George Polk Mem. Award for best reporting requiring exceptional courage & enterprise and Annual Award for best newspaper or wire service reporting from abroad 1968; Assoc. Press Managing Eds. Award for best reporting 1968; co-author (with Leonard Mitchell): 'Undercover Agent' 1988; Office: 250 Yonge St., Toronto, Ont. M5B 2L7.

**REICHENBACH, Olivier;** artistic director; b. Hammamet, Tunisia 20 Dec. 1942; s. Claude and Andrée (Messager) R.; e. Baccalauréat (French) in Philos. Paris, France; one s. Emmanuel; Artistic Dir., Theatre du Nouveau Monde 1982; cameraman TV and films 1962–65; Stage Mgr. Paris, Eur., N.Africa, USA, Can. tours 1965–67; Stage Mgr. and Tech. Dir. present Théâtre 1967–71; Dir. 1971–89, over 85 prodns. staged incl. musicals and operas maj. theatre co's Qué., NAC Ottawa, Opera de Montréal, Festival Ottawa, Banff Festival; taught acting, stage mng. and set designing maj. theatre schs. Qué.; Co-founder and mem. Bd. Le Conseil Québécois du Théâtre 1983–86; Artistic Dir. Théâtre du Trident (Qué.) 1973–75; recipient Felix Award ADISQ for best staging rock-opera 'Starmania' 1981; recreations: sailing, golf, fishing.

**REICHERT, Donald Karl,** B.F.A., R.C.A.; artist; b. Libau, Man. 11 Jan. 1932; s. George and Theresa (Riehl) R.; e. Libau, Man. 1947; St. John's Coll. Sch. and St. Paul's Coll. Winnipeg 1951; Univ. of Man. B.F.A. 1956; Instituto Allende Mexico 1957–58; m. Mary d. Ernest Thorpe 17 June 1957; children: Karl, Lisa, Jacob, Ernest; PROF. EMERITUS OF ART, UNIV. OF MAN. SCH.

OF ART, Acting Dir. of Sch. 1973–74; solo exhns. incl. Winnipeg Art Gallery 1960, 1969, 1975, 1982, 1993; Brian Melnychenko Gallery, Winnipeg 1983– ; Yellow Door Gallery Winnipeg 1965; rep. in numerous group shows incl. Mexico City 1958; St. Ives Cornwall 1963; Travelling Exhns. W. Painting '67, Nat. Gallery 1968; Candn. Canvas Time/Life 1975–76; 150 Yrs. of Art in Man. 1970; W. Candn. Painting Bronfman Centre Montreal 1974; Montreal Olympics '76; Artist-in-Residence Univ. of N.B. 1961–62; joined Univ. of Man. Sch. of Art 1964; Teacher, Banff Sch. of Fine Arts summer 1974, Visiting Artist 1979; Visiting Artist Mt. Allison Univ. 1975; Instr. in Painting Emily Carr Coll. of Art 1979; rep. in Can. Council Art Bank and many pub. and private colls.; Bd. mem., Border Crossings Magazine 1983–93; RCA Council 1984; Manitoba Arts Council Project 1988; Visual Arts Grant 1989; rec'd Can. Council Art Awards Jr. 1962–63, Sr. 1968–69, 1975–76; recreations: painting, drawing, canoeing, cyclng, autocross, photography, reading; Home: 228 Glenwood Cres., Winnipeg, Man. R2L 1J9; Office: Winnipeg, Man.

**REICHMANN, Michael H.,** B.A.; executive; b. London, Eng. 25 June 1944; s. Jack and Flora (Mednikoff) R.; e. Stanstead Coll. Qué. 1961; Sir George Williams Univ., B.A. 1964; m. Wendie d. Seymour and Dorothy Flaster 18 Sept. 1976; one s. Joshua Michael; EXTVE. VICE-PRESIDENT, CO-FOUNDER & DIRECTOR, ALPHANET TELECOM INC. 1987– ; began career as profl. photographer CBC-TV, several photographic books incl. Nat. Film Bd. Can. perm. coll.; held various mktg. positions several firms incl. Panasonic Canada and Rutherfords 1974–80; Dir. of Mktg. TV Ont. 1980–82; Vice Pres. Sales & Mktg. Candn. Press News Agency 1982–84; Co-inventor and holder of 5 granted Canadian, US and international patents in the field of telecommunications; author over 75 mag. articles various aspects consumer electronics ind.; Home: 137 Blantyre Ave., Scarborough, Ont. M1N 2R6.

**REICKER, James Allen,** B.A.; retail bookstore owner/manager; b. St. John, N.B. 7 Oct. 1943; s. Otty Montesque and Catherine Jane B. (Wolfe) R.; e. Northlea P.S., Leaside H.S., Queen's Univ. 1969; Univ. of Toronto 1970–71; m. S. Elizabeth d. Valentine and William Roy Richmond 27 Nov. 1971; one s.: James Edmund Alexander; OWNER/MGR., PRIME CRIME BOOKS 1985– ; Naval Reserve Serv. 1965–77 (ret'd as Lt., HMCS Carleton); progressive promotions with var. depts. of fed. govt. ending as Sr. Finan. Planning Analyst, Employment & Immigration 1971–84; Co-winner, Derrick Murdoch Award 1987 (awarded 1988); Regl. Co-ord., Jane Austen Soc. of N. Am.; Extve. mem., Ottawa Regl. Booksellers Assn. 1986–92; Hon. mem., Capital Crime Writers (Ottawa); mem., Anglican Church of Can.; editor: 'On the Grapevine' newsletter 1984–85; amateur radio operator (VE3 PWQ); private pilot licence; recreation: wine appreciation; clubs: Crime Writers of Can. PEN Internat. ('Friend'); Home: 176 Begonia Ave., Ottawa, Ont. K1H 6E4; Office: 891 Bank St., Ottawa, Ont. K1S 3W4.

**REID, Alexander Darrell Gordon (Tony);** investment dealer; journalist; mining executive; b. Vancouver, B.C. 8 July 1937; s. late Alexander K. Gordon and Margaret Lillie (McLaren) R.; e. Prince of Wales Coll. Vancouver; children: Alexander Richard, Michael Bruce, Susan Margaret; VICE PRES. & DIR., THOMSON KERNAGHAN & CO. LTD. 1986– ; Chrmn. & Dir., Morgain Minerals Inc.; Dir., Orcana Resources; joined invest. firm Osler, Hammond & Nanton, Vancouver 1957–58; The Western City Co. Vancouver 1958–60; Greenshields Inc. Montreal and Toronto 1961–63; Resident Dir. D.D. Creighton & Co. Ltd. 1963–66; Vice Pres. Brawley Cathers Ltd. 1966–70, 1977–81; F.H. Deacon & Co. Ltd. 1970–74; Dir. MBA Securities Ltd. 1974–76; Vice Pres. & Tech. Analyst, Walwyn Stodgell Cochran Murray Ltd. 1981–86; weekly columnist (business) Toronto Sun 1978–93; regular contrib. The Financial Post 1962– ; Columnist The Investors Digest 1977–91; Ed. The Financial Post Investors Handbook 1976; Wrote Technical Analysis Course for Hume Publishing 1983; contrib. to The Financial Times, Saturday Night, The Globe and Mail; mem. Toronto Soc. Financial Analysts; Candn. Soc. of Technical Analysts; recreations: skiing, golf, snorkeling, travel, art, photography; Clubs: Caledon Ski; Devils Pulpit Golf Assoc.; Cambridge; Royal Candn. Military Institute; Shaughnessy Golf (Vancouver); Home: R.R. #1, Palgrave, Ont. L0N 1P0; Office: 200, 365 Bay St., Toronto, Ont. M5H 2V2.

**REID, Angus Edward,** M.A., Ph.D.; executive; sociologist; b. Regina, Sask. 17 Dec. 1947; s. Earnest Angus and Lorna Marie (Hogan) R.; e. Univ. of Man. B.A. 1969, M.A. 1971; Carleton Univ. Ph.D. 1974; m. Margaret d. Edward and Mary Balcaen July 1969; children: Jennifer, Andrew; FOUNDER, CHRMN. AND CHIEF EXTVE. OFFR. ANGUS REID GROUP 1979– ; prior to present appt. served as Assoc. Prof. Univ. of Man.; cons. various corps., govt. agencies, assns. and special interest groups; recipient acad. honours and awards incl. Can. Council Doctoral Fellowship and Nat. Rsch. Scholar Award; author numerous columns Candn. newspapers and mags. incl. Angus Reid Poll carried by 18 daily newspapers; mem. Bd. various corps. and philanthropic orgns. incl. Nestle Enterprises and Vancouver Playhouse Theatre; Home: 3840 Bayridge Ave., West Vancouver, B.C. V7V 3J2; Office: 1199 West Hastings Ave., 11th Floor, Vancouver, B.C. V6E 3T5.

**REID, Barbara Jane;** illustrator; b. Toronto, Ont. 16 Nov. 1957; d. Robert and Dora R.; e. Lawrence Park Coll. Inst.; Ont. Coll. of Art 1980; m. Ian Robert s. Ralph and Irma Crysler 24 Oct. 1981; freelance illus. since 1980; illus. (children's books) 'The New Baby Calf' 1984; 'Have You Seen Birds' 1986; The 'Zoe' Series 1991; 'Two By Two' 1992; IODE Illus. Award 1986; Can. Council Prize 1986; Ruth Schwartz Award Children's Lit. 1986; Elizabeth Cleaver Award 1987 and 1993; Ezra Jack Keats Award 1988; Mr. Christie Book Award 1991; mem. CANSCAIP; Children's Book Centre; Address: 37 Strathmore Blvd., Toronto, Ont. M4J 1P1.

**REID, Bruce Hunter,** B.A.Sc., M.B.A., P.Eng.; executive; b. Hamilton, Ont. 23 Aug. 1939; s. Hunter Thomas and Helen Dorothy (Tatro) R.; e. Oakville Trafalgar High Sch. Ont. 1958; Univ. of Toronto B.A.Sc. (Civil Engn.) 1962; Univ. of W. Ont. M.B.A. 1964; m. Samantha d. Ilmar and Christine Jogi 14 Oct. 1967; children: Daniel, Scott, Marc, Kristoffer; PRESIDENT AND CHIEF EXTVE. OFFR., THE BRICK WAREHOUSE CORP. 1991– ; Chrmn., Pres. & C.E.O., W.H. Smith Canada Ltd. 1982–90; Chrmn. & C.E.O., W.H. Smith Inc. U.S.A. 1989–90; Pres. & C.O.O., W.H. Smith Canada Ltd. 1981; Dir., W.H. Smith Canada Ltd. 1981–90; Dir., W.H. Smith Inc. U.S.A. 1985–90; Vice Pres., International Paints Canada Ltd. Montreal 1976, Extve. Vice Pres. 1976–81; Dir. of Marketing 1972; Vice Pres. Operations, Packaging Systems Group, Ex-Cell-O Corp. Detroit 1972–76; Other: Xerox Corp. Toronto, Canadian International Paper Co., Montreal; Chrmn., Retail Council of Canada 1988–90, Dir. 1981–90, 1993– ; Advisory Bd., Univ. of Western Ontario Business School 1992– ; Advisory Bd., CIRASS, Univ. of Alberta Business School 1992– ; Dir., The Toronto Symphony 1988–91, The Renascent Treatment Centres 1986–91, V.O.N. (Peel) 1985–91, Credit Valley Hosp. 1988–91, Tul Safety Equipment Ltd. 1981–91; Clubs: Toronto Club; York; Credit Valley Golf; Home: 1411 Dundas Cres. N., Mississauga, Ont. L5C 1E8; Office: 16930 - 114 Ave., Edmonton, Alta. T5M 3S2.

**REID, Carolyn M.;** retired executive; b. St. Catharines, Ont. 23 May 1938; d. Daniel G. and Cecilia M. (Lynch) Leo; e. St. Joseph's H.S. 1955; continuing edn. courses: Niagara College, Brock Univ., Bell Inst. for Profl. Development; m. John Blair s. James Reid 9 May 1960; children: Gregory James, Barry Daniel; Clerk, Bell Canada 1955; Manager 1958; resigned 1960; re-engaged 1962; various management positions in Niagara Falls, St. Catharines & Toronto; retired as Niagara Regional Manager 1993; Dir., Ont. Housing Corp. 1990– ; Former Comnr., Niagara Parks Comn. 1987–89; Canada 125 Medal; Chair, Bd. of Trustees, Brock Univ. 1993– ; Pres., United Way of St. Catharines 1984; Dir., St. Catharines C. of C. 1986–88; clubs: St. Catharines, Beechwood Golf; Home: 113 Rose Ave., Thorold Ave., Thorold, Ont. L2V 3E2.

**REID, David E.,** B.Sc., M.A.Sc., P.Eng.; pipeline executive; b. St. Thomas, Ont. 10 Jan. 1943; s. Murray and Betty (Evans) R.; e. Queen's Univ. B.Sc. (Hons.) 1965; Univ. of Toronto M.A.Sc. 1967; m. Nancy d. Harry and Sally Blake 6 Dec. 1969; children: Graeme, Lindsay; VICE-PRES., ENGINEERING, TRANSCANADA PIPELINES 1990– ; joined TransCanada Pipelines 1967; held positions of increasing resp. in head office & field orgn.; Vice-Pres., Operations 1989–90; recreations: golf, skiing, amateur radio; clubs: Glencoe Golf & Country, Glencoe; Home: 2715 Cartier St. S.W., Calgary, Alta. T2T 3J5; Office: P.O. Box 1000, Stn. M, Calgary, Alta. T2P 4K5.

**REID, Dennis Richard,** M.A.; curator; art historian; b. Hamilton, Ont. 3 Jan. 1943; s. Walter Alexander and Letitia Ethel (Johnson) R.; e. Univ. of Toronto, B.A. 1966, M.A. 1967; m. Alison Sheila, d. R. G. D. Anderson, Toronto, Ont., 1966; two d., Jessica Alison, Naomi Gloria; CURATOR OF CANADIAN ART, ART GALLERY OF ONTARIO since 1979 and PROFESSOR, GRADUATE DEPT. HISTORY OF ART, UNIV. OF TORONTO since 1987; Assoc. Prof. since 1979; joined National Gallery of Can. as Asst. Curator 1967; Curator of Post-Confed. Art 1970; has organized numerous exhns. with accompanying catalogues, written books, and lectured; author, 'The MacCallum-Jackman Bequest,' 1969; 'The Group of Seven,' 1970; 'A Bibliography of the Group of Seven,' 1971; 'Bertram Brooker,' 1973, revised and enlarged 1979; 'A Concise History of Canadian Painting,' 1973, second edition 1988; 'The Jack Pine,' 1975; 'Edwin Holgate,' 1976; 'Our Own Country Canada,' 1979; the Canadian entries for 'The Oxford Companion to Twentieth Century Art,' 1981; 'Twentieth Century Canadian Painting, 1900–1965' Tokyo, 1981; 'Alberta Rhythm: The Later Work of A. Y. Jackson,' 1982; 'Historische Maleiri Kanadas,' in 'O Kanada,' 1983; 'From the Four Quarters, Native and European Art in Ontario 5000 BC to 1867 AD,' 1984; 'Canadian Jungle: The Later Work of Arthur Lismer,' 1985; 'Atma Buddhi Manas: The Later Work of Lawren S. Harris,' 1985; 'Collector's Canada: Selections from a Toronto Private Collection,' 1988; 'The Group of Seven, Selected Watercolours, Drawings, and Prints from the Collection of the Art Gallery of Ontario,' 1989; 'Lucius R. O'Brien, Visions of Victorian Canada,' 1990; 'Impressionism in Canada' in 'World Impressionism: The International Movement, 1860–1920,' 1990; 'Exploring Plane and Contour: The Drawing, Painting, Collage, Foldage, Photo-Work, Sculpture and Film of Michael Snow from 1951 to 1967,' in '1951-1993, Visual Art, The Michael Snow Project' 1994; also various articles for art journs.; Home: 79 Borden St., Toronto, Ont. M5S 2M8.

**REID, Donald Grant,** B.Sc., M.Sc.; wildlife ecologist; b. Nairobi, Kenya 20 May 1954; s. Ian Christie and Barbara Joan (Herian) R.; e. Dundas (Ont.) Dist. High Sch. 1972; Univ. of Guelph B.Sc. 1977; Univ. of Calgary M.Sc. 1984; MEM., DEPT. OF ZOOLOGY, UNIV. OF B.C. 1989– ; Rsch. Biol. World Wildlife Fund and Rsch. Assoc. in Biol. Sci's Univ. of Calgary 1985–88 (rsch. ecology giant & red pandas and Asiatic black bears Sichuan, China); mem. Dept. Biol. Univ. Calgary and Rsch. Assoc. Arctic Inst. N.Am. 1979–85 (rsch. ecology river otters and beavers Alta.); Rsch. Tech. Candn. Wildlife Service (ecology arctic colonial seabirds Coburg & Baffin Islands) 1979–81 summer; Rsch. Tech. grizzly bear habitat quality Alta. (Bios Environmental Consultants), biophys. inventory (Gulf Canada Ltd.), white-tailed deer habitat requirements (Univ. Guelph); author or co-author numerous papers wildlife mgmt.; recipient Prov. Alta. Grad. Fellowship 1979–80; Candn. Wildlife Service Wildlife Biol. Scholarship 1980–81; mem. Candn. Soc. Environmental Biols. (1985 Rep. Environment Council Alta.); Candn. Nature Fedn.; Arctic Inst. N. Am.; Candn. Parks & Wilderness Soc.; recreations: climbing, canoeing, photography; Office: 6270 University Blvd., Vancouver, B.C. V6T 1Z4.

**REID, Donald Walter,** B.A.; film producer, writer, composer; b. Barrie, Ont. 23 May 1929; s. Walter Anderson and Norine Jennie (Webb) R.; e. Univ. of W. Ont. B.A. 1952; Osgoode Hall Law Sch. 1958; m. Ruth Boyle 24 May 1952; children: Lora J.J. Maroney, Marc R.E., Nina R.; PRES. REID ENTERTAINMENT CORP.; Pres. and Dir. Calgroup Graphics Corp. Ltd.; Reid Chartwell Productions Inc.; Reid Chartwell Animation Inc.; D.W. Reid Film Corp.; Dir. Bare Creek Investments Ltd.; Reid Dunblane Corp.; Extve. Gulf Oil Corp. 1952–54; private law practice 1958–68; musician, film and TV producer, writer 1968– ; over 300 film and TV prodns. completed for internat. mkts.; 200 TV scripts 'The Adventures of Snelgrove Snail'; feature films incl.: 'Bachelor Noneymoon,' 'A Cinderella Story of Stocks and Blondes,' 'Christopher's Snowman,' 'Prince of Plums,' 'Wynken, Blyken and Nod in Noom'; Fellow, Acad. Med. Toronto; mem. ACTRA; SOCAN; Variety Clubs Internat.; Arabian Horse Assn.; Zeta Psi; Phi Delta Phi; Elder, Presb. Ch. of Can.; recreations: music, swimming, reading; Home: R.R. 7, Thamesville, Ont. N0P 2K0.

**REID, E.A. Stewart,** M.D., C.M., F.R.C.P.C., F.A.C.P.; retired cardiologist; b. Montreal, Que., 29 June 1917; s. Rev. Dr. William D. and Daisy F. (Stanford) R.; e. Westmount (Que.) High Sch., 1934; McGill Univ., B.A. 1938; M.D.C.M. 1942; Dipl. Internal Med. 1952; m. Barbara M., d. late Hugh Pibus, Magog, Que., 1952; children: Jane B., Dr. Stewart E., Dugald A. S.; former Director of Cardiology, Montreal Gen. Hospital; Assoc. Prof. Med., McGill Univ.; Consultant in Cardiology, Ormstown Hosp.; Huntingdon Co. Hosp.; Cowansville Hospital; Medical Resident, Montreal Gen. Hosp., 1942–43, 1946–47, 1949–50; Mass. Gen. Hosp., Cardiology, 1947–48; Hammersmith Hosp., London, Eng., 1948–49; served with R.C.A.M.C. 1942–46 in U.K. (1943), Italy (1943–44), N.W. Europe (1945); awarded

Snyder (Econ.) 1937–38, Caverhill (Cardiology) 1947–49 and Life Assn., 1949–52, fellowships; has written sundry med. articles for prof. journs.; Fellow, Am. Coll. Physicians; Fellow, Royal Coll. of Physicians (Can.); Sr. Mem., Candn. Med. Assn.; Certified Specialist, P.Q.: Fellow, Am. Coll. Cardiology (Gov. Quebec Br. 1967); Am. Coll. Chest Phys.; Past Pres., Montreal Soc. Cardiol.; Fellow, Am. Heart Assn.; member Candn. Cardiovascular Assn.; Presbyterian; recreations: gardening, skiing; Home: 36 Conference Hill, Knowlton, Que. J0E 1V0.

**REID, Escott Meredith,** C.C. (1971), M.A.; b. Campbellford, Ont., 21 Jan. 1905; s. Rev. Alfred John and Morna (Meredith) R.; e. Trinity Coll., Toronto, B.A. (1st Class Hons. in Pol. Science) 1927; Rhodes Schol., Ont., 1927; Jr. George Webb Medley Schol. in Econ. (Oxford) 1928; Gladstone Mem. Exhn. Schol. (Christ Ch.) 1929; Rockefeller Fellow, Soc. Sciences, 1930–32; Oxford Univ. (Christ Ch.) B.A. (1st Class Hons. in Modern Greats) 1929, M.A. 1935; (Hon.) Doctor of Laws, Mount Alison, York, Carleton Univs.; m. Ruth Murray, d. William Herriot, Winnipeg, Man., 30 Aug. 1930; children: Patrick Murray, Morna Meredith, Timothy Escott Herriot (see below); Skelton-Clark Fellow, Queen's Univ., 1972–73; Clk., Audit Department, Government of Ont., Toronto 1921–23; National Secy., Candn. Inst. Internat. Affairs 1932–38; Acting Prof., Govt. and Pol. Science, Dalhousie Univ. 1937–38; 2nd Secy., Candn. Leg. at Wash., D.C., 1939–41; Dept. of External Affairs 1941–44; 1st Secy., Wash., D.C. 1944–45; Counsellor, London 1945–46; Counsellor, Ottawa, 1946–47; Asst. Under-Secy. of State for External Affairs 1947–48; Acting Under-Secy., Depy. Under-Secy. 1948–52; High Comnr. for Canada to India, 1952–57; Ambassador to Germany, 1958–62; Dir. of Operations for S. Asia and Middle East, Internat. Bank for Reconstruction & Devel., 1962–65; First Principal, Glendon Coll., York Univ. 1965–69; Consultant to Pres., Candn. Internat. Devel. Agency 1970–72; attended the following unofficial international conferences 1933–38; Institute of Pacific Relations, Banff, 1933, and Yosemite 1936; British Commonwealth Relations, Toronto 1933; Internat. Studies, London, 1935; attended foll. official internat. confs. as Adviser or Alternate Rep. on Candn. del.: Internat. Civil Aviation, Chicago 1944; San Francisco 1945; Extve. Comte. of the Prep. Comn. of the U.N. and Prep. Comn., London 1945; 1st session of the Gen. Assembly, U.N., London and N.Y. 1946; 2nd session, N.Y. 1947; Commonwealth Foreign Ministers, Colombo, 1950; Chrmn., Gen. Assembly's Comte. on Procedures and Organ. 1947; 12th Session of the Gen. Assembly, 1957; Publications: 'The Future of the World Bank' 1965; 'Strengthening the World Bank' 1973; 'Time of Fear and Hope: The Making of the North Atlantic Treaty 1947–49,' 1977; 'Envoy to Nehru,' 1981; 'On Duty: A Canadian at the making of the United Nations, 1945–46,' 1983; 'Hungary and Suez 1956: A View From New Delhi' 1987; 'Radical Mandarin: The Memoirs of Escott Reid' 1989; Anglican; Home: R.R. 2, Ste. Cécile de Masham, Qué. J0X 2W0.

**REID, Fiona,** B.A.; actor; b. Whitstable, Kent, England 24 July 1951; d. Grainger Wilson and Ruth Hilda (Becky) (Sharpe) R.; e. Lawrence Park C.I. 1969 (Ont. scholar); McGill Univ. B.A. (with distinction) 1972; Banff Sch. of Fine Arts 1970, 1971; m. McCowan Thomas s. William and Elizabeth Thomas 14 Aug. 1977; children: Alec Reid Thomas, Julia Elizabeth Becky Thomas; performed in major theatres across Can., also London, England, in feature film, radio & tv.; performed as Cathy King in 'King of Kensington' for 3 seasons; mem., Stratford Fest., 2 seasons; Shaw Fest. 1983–85 and 1989–92 in various roles incl. Amanda in 'Private Lives,' Jane in 'Calvacade,' Lady Utterword in 'Heartbreak House'; title role 'Hedda Gabler'; 'Point Valaine'; past mem., Bd. of Dir., Toronto Arts Awards Found.; mem. Bd. of Dir., Candn. Stage Co.; honoured by McGill Alumnae Assn.; ACTRA Radio Award for best performance by an actress 1986; Office: c/o Oscars and Abrams Associates, 59 Berkeley St., Toronto, Ont. M5A 2W5.

**REID, Frank Joseph,** B.A., M.Sc., Ph.D.; university professor; b. Edmonton, Alta. 25 Nov. 1947; s. Frank Elvin Roscoe and Mabel Viola (Fadden) Reid; e. Univ. of B.C. B.A. 1970; London Sch. of Economics M.Sc. 1971; Queen's Univ. Ph.D. 1975; m. Billie d. Avtar and Surinder Sandhu 2 Sept. 1989; PROF., CENTRE FOR INDUS. RELATIONS & DEPT. OF ECON., UNIV. OF TORONTO 1989– ; Instr., Econ., Queen's Univ. 1973–74; Lectr., Pol. Econ., Univ. of Toronto 1974–75; Asst. Prof. 1975–79; Assoc. Prof. 1979–89; Acting Dir., Ctr. for Indus. Relns., Univ. of Toronto 1991–93; consultant to various agencies incl. Govt. of Australia, Govt. of New South Wales, ILO, Govt. of Canada (Labour, Employment & Immigration), Ont. Govt. (Labour, Human Resource Secretariat), Metro Toronto, OPSEU, Alta. Human Rights Comn., AIB, Macdonald Comn.; Women's Bureau; Comn. of Inquiry into Part-Time Work; co-author: 'Sharing the Work: An Analysis of the Issues in Worksharing and Jobsharing' 1981, 'Wage and Price Behavour in Canadian Manufacturing: An Econometric Analysis' 1979; recreations: sailing, tennis, squash; Home: 21 Cheritan Ave., Toronto, Ont. M4R 1S3; Office: Toronto, Ont. M5S 1A1.

**REID, Ian Angus Ross,** B.A.; politician; b. St. John's, Nfld. 31 July 1952; s. Ian Job and Margot Grant (Ross) R.; e. Univ. of Western Ont. B.A. 1974; Extve. Asst. to John C. Crosbie then Min. of Fisheries, Min. of Mines & Energy, & Dep. Premier of Nfld. 1975–76; Extve. Asst. to Mr. Crosbie as M.P. of St. John's W. & Chief of Staff during Mr. Crosbie's enture as Min. of Finance 1979; Managing Dir., Atlantic Prov., Public Affairs Internat. 1980–83; Sr. Cons., Public Affairs Resource Group 1984–86; Special Advisor to Finance Min. Michael Wilson 1987; Special Asst. to Prime Min. Brian Mulroney 1987–88; 1st elected Mem. of Parl. for St. John's E. 1989; Parly. Sec. to Min. of Fisheries and Oceans 1989–91; to Min. of Indian Affairs 1991–93; Min. of Fisheries & Oceans 1993; Dir. & Vice-Pres., St. John's Bd. of Trade; Dir., St. John's Boys & Girls Club; Address: 138A Percy St., Ottawa, Ont. K1R 6E1.

**REID, James Allan 'Stuart,'** B.Sc.; university administrator; b. Toronto, Ont. 9 March 1955; s. John Robert and Dorothy (Colhoun) R.; e. McMaster Univ. B.Sc. 1978; m. Vicki d. Robert (deceased) and Lois Wood 28 May 1983; children: Jamie, Victoria; EXECUTIVE DIRECTOR, EXTERNAL RELATIONS, THE UNIVERSITY OF CALGARY; served McMaster Univ. in a variety of positions incl. high school liaison, coordinator of staff training and development, personnel officer for Univ. library system, Dir. of Development, Special Gifts in McMaster's Alumni & Devel. Office; Pres., McMaster Students' Union 1977 and Extve. Ctte. Mem., Nat. Union of Students; Sec., Univ. of Calgary Found.; Mem., Council for the Advancement and Support of Edn.; Treas., Candn. Council for the Advancement of Edn.; United Way Calgary Campaign Cabinet 1992, '93; Bd. Mem., Calgary Police Service Museum Soc.; has served on a variety of prov. & nat. cttes. and has spoken extensively at confs. & workshops related to mngt. & performance appraisal systems & fundraising; Mem., Alta. C. of C.; Calgary C. of C.; recreations: golf, sailing; Home: 3644 Utah Drive N.W., Calgary, Alta. T2N 4A7; Office: 248 Scurfield Hall, 2500 Univ. Drive N.W., Calgary, Alta. T2N 1N4.

**REID, Hon. John M.,** M.A.; b. Fort Frances, Ont. 8 Feb. 1937; s. John M. and Marie Ena (Harrington) R.; e. Univ. of Man. B.A. 1959, M.A. (Hist.) 1961; Univ. of Toronto (Hist.) 1961–65; m. Marie Ellen, d. Edward O. Balcaen, 19 Feb. 1966; children: Katherine, John, Arianne, George; PRES., CANDN. NUCLEAR ASSN. 1990– ; Chrmn., John Reid Consulting; Founding Chrmn. Assoc. of Former Members of Parliament 1987–90; Mem., H. of C. 1965–84; Chrmn. H. of C. Standing Comte. on Broadcasting, Film and Assistance to the Arts 1969–72; Parlty. Secy. to Pres. of Privy Council 1972–75; Min. Federal-Provincial Relations 1978–79; Chrmn. H. of C. Comte on Procedure and Organization 1978; Extve. Dir., Forum for Young Canadians 1985–90; Liberal; R. Catholic; Home: 33 Bedford Cr., Ottawa, Ont. K1K 0E6; Office: 725, 144 Front St. W., Toronto, Ont. M5J 2L7.

**REID, John S.,** B.A., M.A.; association executive; b. London, Ont. 28 Sept. 1949; s. Jack William and Geraldine Louise (Miller) R.; e. Univ. of North Carolina, B.A. (Hons.) 1972; Carleton Univ. M.A. 1973; L'Univ. d'Aix Marseille, dipl. in French Lang. & Lit. 1977; PRES., CANDN. ADVANCED TECHNOL. ASSN. 1991– ; stock broker; Commerce Offr., Fed. Dept. of Indus., Trade & Comm. & Energy, Mines & Resources, Can. 1976–79; Dir., Legislative Activities, Mining Assn. of Can. 1979–86; Vice Pres. & Gen. Mgr., Candn. Advanced Technol. Assn. 1986–91; Epstein Scholarship 1973–74; Mem., Candn. Inst. of Mining & Metallurgy (Past Chrmn.); Mem., National Rsch. Council Advisory Bd. 1993– ; Vice-Chrmn., Minister's Adv. Counc. to Can. Employment & Immigration; author of numerous articles & reviews; Home: 97 Hopewell Ave., Ottawa, Ont. K1S 2Y9.

**REID, Joseph Boutelle,** M.Sc., F.Inst.P.; retired; b. Danville, Que. 17 Dec. 1913; s. Andrew Dunn and Mary Winifred (Boutelle) R.; e. Sydney Academy 1930; Univ. of Manitoba B.Sc. 1935; Oxford Univ. B.A. 1937, M.Sc. 1939; Rhodes Scholar (Manitoba) 1935; Univ. of Man. Gold Medal in Hon. Sci. Course 1935; Fellow Inst. of Physics 1944; m. Marjorie d. George and Winifred Young 30 Sept. 1939; children: Mary Charlotte, Helen Elizabeth, Jane Louisa, Eva Margaret; Research Physicist, Kodak Ltd. (U.K.) 1938–42; Sr. Scientific Offr., Royal Aircraft Establishment 1942–45; Sr. Control Offr., Control Comn. for Germany 1945–46; Prog. Specialist, UNESCO (Paris) 1947–51; Tech. Assistance Team Head (New Delhi) 1952–54; Tech. Dir. Adalia Computations Ltd. 1955–57; Mgr. Electronic Data Proc., Trans-Canada Air Lines 1957–61; Mgr. Prog. Methods, Aluminum Co. of Canada 1961–69; Cons. en Communications, Univ. du Qué. 1970–78; Cons. St. Lawrence Seaway Authority 1972–74; Belgian Govt. 1974; Govt. of Que. 1974–76; Counsellor, Federal Business Devel. Bank Counselling Assistance to Small Enterprises (CASE) 1982–92; Pres. Refugee Aid Soc. 1962–66; Lakeshore Unitarian Ch. 1965–67; Candn. Information Processing Soc. 1975–76; Candn. Metric Assn. 1979–89; Address: 379 Sackville St., Toronto, Ont. M5A 3G5.

**REID, Margot Grant,** R.N.; housewife; b. St. John's, Nfld. 9 Oct. 1927; d. George William and Olive V. (Atlee) Ross; e. Dalhousie Univ. 1945–47; Royal Victoria Hosp., Montreal, grad. 1950; m. Ian Job s. W. Angus and Gladys Job Reid 30 June 1951; children: Ross, Douglas, Jane, Tim, Sarah; Dir., Fed. Bus. Devel. Bank 1976–82; mem., Labatt Nfld. Adv. Bd. 1976–88; Nfld. Medical Bd. 1976–85; Bd. mem. Janeway Childrens Hospital 1966–75; mem. Nat. Adv. Bd., Imagine; Bd. mem. Reid, Newfoundland Co.; Life mem., Candn. Cancer Soc.; Dir. General Hospital Health Found. 1985–88; Trustee, Forum for Young Canadians; Past Pres., Nfld. Div. Candn. Cancer Soc.; Dir., Natl. Cancer Inst. 1982–86; mem., Natl. Bd. of Dir., Candn. Cancer Soc. 1979–85; recipient, 125th Anniversary of the Confederation of Canada Medal, 1992; Mem. Sr. Advisory Bd., Lakecrest School; recreations: tennis, gardening, crafts, skiing; Home: 125 Rennie's Mill Rd., St. John's, Nfld. A1B 2P2.

**REID, Hon. Marion Loretta,** M.L.A.; former politician; former educator; b. North Rustico, P.E.I. 4 Jan. 1929; d. the late Michael Joseph and the late Loretta Josephine (Whelan) Doyle; e. North Rustico Elem.; Stella Maris Elem.; Prince of Wales Coll.; Univ. of P.E.I.; S.D.U.; Certificate 5 Teacher's Licence; Winner of John H. Bell debate and Lord Strathcona prizes 1945; Awarded sabbatical leave study 1972–73; Awarded scholarship for Academic Excellence 1973; m. Lea P. Reid 1949; children: Maureen, Colleen, Kevin, Bethany, Mary Lea, David, Andrew, Tracy; LIEUTENANT GOVERNOR OF P.E.I. 1990– ; 21 yrs. teaching career, last four years as Principal, St. Ann's Elem. Sch.; Mem. Bd. of Govs., and Secy. P.E.I. Teachers' Fedn. 1970–77; Mem. Teacher Recruitment Team, Curriculum Comm., Negotiating Strategy Comm., and Status of Women Comm.; Past-Pres., Sterling Women's Inst.; St. Ann's C.W.L.; Past-Leader, Stanley Bridge 4–H Club; Founding Mem., Q.E.H. Found.; Mem., Charlottetown Zonta Club; Hon. Patron, Laubach Literacy of Canada; Prov. Chapter IODE; el. to P.E.I. Legislature 1979; re-el. g.e. 1982, 1986; Apptd., Depy. Speaker 1979; Mem. Standing Ctte.: Education, Health and Welfare, Agriculture, Tourism and Parks; Sworn in as Speaker of the P.E.I. Legislature 1983; Del.: CPA Conf., Westminster 1984; CPA Conf., Kenya 1983; CPA Conf., Isle of Man 1984; CPA Conf., Victoria, Toronto, Quebec City, Ottawa, Fredericton and Halifax; Opposition House Leader 1986–89; Sworn in as Lieutenant Governor of P.E.I. 1990; Invested as Dame of Grace in the Order of St. John 1990; Address: Government House, P.O. Box 846, Charlottetown, P.E.I. C1A 7L9.

**REID, The Honourable Milton Reginald,** B.A., B.S.W., LL.B.; provincial court judge; b. Norris Point, Nfld. 18 Jan. 1943; s. Augustus Douglas and Margaret Elsie (McKenzie) Reid; e. Norris Point Mem. H.S.; Mem. Univ. of Nfld., B.A. 1970, B.S.W. 1971; Dalhousie Law School, LL.B. 1983; continuing adult edn., French language training; m. Marina d. Augustus and Martha Ford 17 Apr. 1965; one d.: Elaine Martha; JUDGE, PROVINCIAL COURT OF NFLD., 1983– ; Teacher 1960–63; Social Worker 1965–72; Parole Offr. 1972–75; apptd. Magistrate, Provincial Court of Nfld. 1975; served throughout Nfld. & lab. incl. N. Lab. working in native and Metis communities; admitted to Nfld. Bar 1983; duties incl. Youth Court Judge, Civil Court Judge & Criminal Court Judge; apptd. Co-ordinating Judge, St. John's Provincial Court 1990– ; apptd. Notary Public 1976; Comnr. of Supreme Court of Nfld. 1977; Founding Mem., Nfld. Assn. of Social Workers; Past mem., Nfld. Teachers Assn.; Lions Club; Atlantic Prov. Corrections & Crim. Assn.; Past Dir., YMCA; Mem., Nfld. Prov. Judges Assn. (Vice-Pres. 1979–80; Pres. 1983–85); Candn. Assn. Prov. Court Judges (Prov. Rep. for Nfld. 1983–87); Candn. Bar Assn.; St. Mark's

Anglican Ch.; Editor-in-Chief 'Provincial Judges Journal / Des Juges Provinciaux 1987–92; author: 'A Handbook for Justices of the Peace in Newfoundland & Labrador' 1994; recreations: reading, hiking, fishing, amateur photography, curling; Home: 41 Baker St., St. John's, Nfld. A1A 5G3; Office: Box 68, Atlantic Place, 215 Water St., St. John's, Nfld. A1C 6C9.

**REID, (William Adrain) Patrick Lockhart,** O.C., M.C., C.D.; corporation executive, retired diplomat; b. Belfast, N. Ireland 14 Nov. 1924; s. William James and Kathleen Hamilton (Lockhart) R.; e. Methodist College Belfast; Queen's Univ. Belfast; Royal Military Academy Sandhurst (Belt of Honour); Canadian Army Staff Coll. (P.S.C.); m. Alison d. Neville and Lady Jean (Lennard) Cumming; children: Amanda Kathleen, Michael Cameron Lockhart; Dir., Aerospatiale Canada; Toda Internat. Resorts of Canada; Internat. Maritime Centre; British Regular Army 1942–54 (Major); Troop Leader, North Irish Horse (Italy 1944–45); Comdr., Military Police Singapore 1945–46; Adjutant 14th/20th King's Hussars 1948; Staff Officer, N.A.T.O. 1952; emigrated to Canada 1954; worked in film, TV & advtg.; Dir., Candn. Govt. Exhib. Comn. 1962–68; Dir. Gen., Public Affairs, External Affairs 1972–78; Min., Canada House London 1978–81; Pres., Internat. Bureau of Expositions Paris 1978–82; Consul Gen. of Canada, San Francisco 1986–88; Comnr. Gen. of Canada at six world exhbns.; Ambassador & Comnr. Gen., 1986 World Exposition Vancouver 1982–86; Chrmn., Airshow Canada; Globe '92; former Chrmn., Vancouver Port Corp.; Officer, Order of Canada 1987; Military Cross; Candn. Decoration; Centennial Medal; Great Cross of Order of Merit of Peru; Order of Chrysanthemum of Japan; Sales & Mktg. Extve. of B.C. 1984; Internat. Sales Extve. 1986; 1st Distinguished Leadership Award, Simon Fraser Univ. 1986; Downtown Vanc. Assn. Award 1986; Outstanding Citizen of Year, Kiwanis Founs. 1989; Community Leadership Award, Bd. of Trade (with wife Alison) 1990; Dir., Man-in-Motion Society; B.C. Paraplegic Found.; Vancouver Symphony Soc.; Anglican; Mem., Commonwealth Soc.; Internat. Dragon Boat Festival; Pres. Club, Simon Fraser Univ.; World Trade Centre; Bd. of Trade Vanc.; recreations: riding, yachting; clubs: Cavalry and Guards; Home: 5692 Elm St., Vancouver, B.C. V6N 1A4.

**REID, Pierre,** B.Sc., D.Sc.; informaticien, professeur, administrateur; né à Jonquière le 16 août 1948; études classiques et collégiales; études de premier cycle à l'Univ. Laval B.Sc. 1970; bourses d'excellence des gouvernements du Québec et de la France; études de doctorat en sciences à l'Univ. de Paris XI (Orsay) D.Sc. 1974; deux enfants: Marie-Claire, Catherine; RECTEUR DE L'UNIVERSITE DE SHERBROOKE 1993– ; conseiller en informatique, IBM Canada 1973–76; professeur à l'Univ. du Qué. à Chicoutimi 1976–78; à l'Univ. de Sherbrooke 1978– ; vice-doyen, Fac. d'admin. 1986–87; dir. du prog.MBA 1987–89; vice-recteur à l'admin. 1989–91; expérience du milieu des affaires en tant que gestionnaire et conseiller en gestion; admin. du Théâtre du Sang Neuf et de Musica Nova; loisirs: vélo, musique; domicile: 1555, rue Simard, Sherbrooke, Qué. J1J 3Z7; bureau: Sherbrooke, Qué. J1K 2R1.

**REID, Robert (Bob) Thomas Franklin,** B.Ed.; b. Melville, Sask. 25 Sept. 1948; s. Robert George and Doreen Emily (Parker) R.; e. Univ. of Sask. B.Ed. 1971; m. Paulette d. Noel and Blanche Chabot 10 July 1970; children: Jason David, Sean Thomas; PRESIDENT, FOOTHILLS PIPELINES LTD. 1993– ; Dir., Petroleum Industry Training Service 1988– ; Cameco Corp. 1992– ; Foothills Pipelines Ltd. 1993– ; various teaching/edn. admin. postings in Sask. 1970–80; Analyst/Sr. Analyst, Sask. Finance 1980–82; Asst. Dep. Min., Sask. Energy & Mines 1982; Sask. Health 1983; Dep. Min., Sask. Energy & Mines 1983–87; Extve. Dir., Independent Petroleum Assn. of Can. 1987–89; Vice Pres., Corp. Develop. & Planning, Sceptre Resources Ltd. 1989–91; Vice Pres., Corp. and Business Develop., Pan-Alberta Gas Ltd. 1991–93; Roman Catholic; Mem., Candn. Inst. of Mining & Metallurgy; Calgary C. of C.; recreations: golf, skiing; Club: Calgary Petroleum; Home: 40 Scenic Ridge Cres. N.W., Calgary, Alta. T3L 1V2.

**REID, Hon. Robert Franklin,** Q.C., B.A., LL.B.; lawyer; b. Stratford, Ont. 21 June 1923; s. Robert Alexander and Edith (Robens) R.; e. Univ. of W. Ont. B.A. 1945; Osgoode Hall Law Sch. LL.B. 1949; m. Elisabeth Denise Hall, d. the late Maj. A. Denison Pearce, 3 Sept. 1949; children: John Denison, Deborah Robens, Elisabeth Jane Rivers (Mrs. André Calla); COUNSEL, TEPLITSKY, COLSON BARRISTERS 1990– ; Apptd. Justice, Supreme Court of Ontario 1974, resigned to return to the bar 1990; read law with Hon. Leopold Macaulay, Q.C. and W.B. Common, Q.C.; called to Bar of Ont. 1949; cr. Q.C. 1961; practised law as General Counsel in Toronto; Lectr. in Adm. Law Osgoode Hall Law Sch. 1951–60; mem. Jt. Comte. on Legal Aid (report basis for present Ont. Legal Aid Plan); lectr. and mem. various confs. on adm. law and law relating to addictions Can. Mexico and USA; served as Pilot RCAF (Winner, Madore trophy); Depy. Secy. Law Soc. Upper Can. 1955–58; Trustee, Co. York Law Assn., 1957–61; has also served as mem. of Bd., Edward Johnston Music Foundation; Mem. of Council, Candn. Bar Assn.; Pres. Festival Singers; Pres. Save the Children Fund (Toronto); Pres. Advocate's Soc.; Consultant to Ont. Ctte. on Taxation (The Smith Report, 1967); Consultant to Task Force on Admin. of Workmen's Compensation Bd., 1973; Counsel to Commission on Government of Univ. of Toronto 1969; author 'Administrative Law and Practice' 1971 and numerous papers on legal topics; co-author 'Advocacy: Views from the Bench' 1983; Editor, 'Reid's Administrative Law' (Carswell); Co-Chrmn., Hearing Ctte., Toronto Stock Exchange; Co-Chrmn., Hearing Ctte., Investment Dealers Assn.; Mem. (occasional), Ontario Municipal Board; Legal Consultant, Ontario Human Rights Review Task Force 1992; Legal and Mediation Advisor, Royal Commission on Indian Claims (Canada); Dir., Candn. Society for the Advancement of Legal Technology; Mem., Council of Candn. Administrative Tribunals; Dir., National Institute for Administrative Tribunals; Mem., Arbitration & Mediation Institute (Ont.); Delta Upsilon; Anglican; Club: Royal Candn. Military Inst.; Office: 70 Bond St., Toronto, Ont. M5B 1X3.

**REID, Robert J.,** M.A.Sc., P.Eng.; natural gas pipeline executive; b. Regina, Sask. 22 March 1942; s. Robert Douglas and M. Eleanor (Young) R.; e. Univ. of Sask. B.A.Sc. 1964; Univ. of Waterloo M.A.Sc. 1975; m. Arlene R. Jennings 7 Oct. 1967; one d. Sandra Joanne; PRES. IROQUOIS GAS TRANSMISSION SYSTEM 1987– ; Eng. Westinghouse Ltd. 1964–67; Eng. TransCanada PipeLines Ltd. 1967, Sr. Eng. positions 1968–74, W. Area Mgr. 1977, Vice Pres. Eng. & Operations 1981, Vice Pres. Sales & Rates 1984–87; mem. Assn. Profl. Engs. Prov. Ont. and Prov. Man.; Pres. Oakville (Ont.) Curling Club 1976–77; recreations: curling, windsurfing; clubs: Mississauga (Ont.) Golf & Country; Darien (Conn.) Country; Home: 60 Teller, Rd., Trumbull, Conn. 06611; Office: One Corporate Dr., Suite 606, Shelton, Conn. 06484.

**REID, Scott Jeffrey,** B.A., M.A.; writer; b. Hull, Que. 25 Jan. 1964; s. G. Gordon and Leatrice (Sibales) R.; e. Carleton Univ. B.A. 1985, M.A. 1990; m. Song Poh Lan 22 June 1989; recreations: skiing, reading philosophy, sandlot baseball; author and journalist 1990– ; contributing editor, 'Liberty' magazine; author: 'Canada Remapped: How the Partition of Quebec Will Reshape the Nation' 1992, 'Lament for a Notion: The Life & Death of Canada's Bilingual Dream' 1993; Address: 171 Cowley Ave., Ottawa, Ont. K1Y 0G8.

**REID, Sheryll;** communications consultant; b. Calgary, Alta. 3 Jan. 1947; d. Frederick Arnold and Margaret Dean (Maclean) Brewster; e. Univ. of Toronto; m. Gary Frederick s. Ross and Beryl Reid 29 Aug. 1969; two s. Daniel Frederick Cavan, Brandon Geoffrey; PRES. AND CHIEF EXTVE. OFFR., SHERYLL REID COMMUNICATIONS (formerly Argyle Communications Inc.) 1987– ; joined Tisdall Clark & Partner 1977–79, Cons. 1978; Vice Pres. Client Services present Co. 1980, Pres. 1985; Dir. Music Toronto; Candn. Children's Dance Theatre; recipient Candn. Pub. Relations Soc. Award of Excellence 1986; mem. Candn. Pub. Relations Soc.; Internat. Assn. Bus. Communications; recreations: reading, music, theatre; Home: 54 Beech Ave., Toronto, Ont. M4E 3H4; Office: 64B Shuter St., Suite 201, Toronto, Ont. M5B 1B1.

**REID, Stephen Douglas;** writer; b. Massey, Ont. 13 March 1950; s. George Douglas and Sylvia Jean (Shiels) R.; m. Susan d. Edward and Judy Musgrave 12 Oct. 1986; two d. Charlotte, Sophie Alexandra; author: 'Jackrabbit Parole' (fiction) 1986; also short fiction, poems, reviews in various mags. and newspapers; profiled CBC TV 'Fifth Estate' 1986; CTV 'Lifetime' 1987, 1988; BCTV, CBC News; recipient First Prize Nat. Prison Arts Writing Competition 1986–87; Can. Council B Grant 1988–89; B.C. Film Screenwriting Fellowship 1989; Dir., Prison Arts; mem. Writers Union Can.; B.C. Fedn. Writers; Address: P.O. Box 2421, Sidney, B.C. V8L 3Y3.

**REID, Thomas Edward;** public, government, investor relations and management consultant; b. Hamilton, Ont. 4 Jan. 1939; s. Francis Edward and Marion Daisy (Evans) R.; e. Chatham (Ont.) Coll. Inst.; Coll. d'enseignement général et professionel Jonquière, Qué.; Hons., Candn. Securities Inst.; Sheridan Coll. Oakville, Ont. cert. French; La Sorbonne, Univ. de Paris, France cert. French; Univ. of Toronto studies pol. sci., Candn. hist.; m. Susan Maureen Elizabeth Murphy; children: Tommie Jo, Bobbie Jo, Katharine; Pres., Reid Mgmt. Ltd. 1973; pub. relations cons. 1968– ; radio and TV commentator 1971– ; reporter, columnist Chatham Daily News 1960–62; radio news and prog. dir. 1962–68; Mgr. Pub. Affairs Canadian General Electric 1971–73; cons. to maj. Candn. and Am. corps., prof. firms and assns.; regular contbr. columns pub. relations Marketing Magazine and marketing and law firm management Law Times; Past Chrm.: Accreditation Ctte. Candn. Pub. Relations Soc.; Pub. Relations Ctte. Candn. Mfrs. Assn.; Dir. Better Business Bureau 1973; mem. Pub. Relations Soc. Am.; Assn. Candn. TV & Radio Artists; recreation: tennis; Clubs: Oakville, Toronto Athletic, Toronto Press; Home: 317 Gloucester Ave., Oakville, Ont. L6J 3W8.

**REID, Thomas Patrick,** B.A.; association executive; b. Fort Frances 2 Jan. 1943; s. John Mercer and Ena Marie (Harrington) R.; e. Atikokan Elem. and H.S.; Univ. of Manitoba B.A., two yrs. grad. studies in Econ.; m. Maureen d. Dr. Gerard and Florence Quigley 9 June 1979; children: Aislinn Elizabeth, Kyla Patricia; Pres. & C.E.O., Ontario Mining Assn.; mem. provincial parliament Ont. 1967–84; Pres. Ontario Liberal Party 1976; Pres. Candn. Counc. of Publ. Accounts; co-owner Internat. Travel Services 1968–71; Cons. Candn. Comprehensive Auditing Found. 1977–78; co-owner Lake of the Woods Houseboats 1977–80; co-owner Coldstream Holiday Properties 1972– ; mem., CIMM, PDA; former Chrmn., Quetico Found.; mem., Provincial Auditor's Adv. Ctte.; Secy./Treas. MRD, Mining Research Directorate Inc.; Clubs: Royal Candn. Yacht; Toronto Bd. of Trade; Home: 110 Yonge St., Suite 1501, Toronto, Ont. M5C 1T4.

**REID, Timothy Escott Herriot,** B.A., M.A., M.Litt., A.M.P.; executive; economist; management consultant; educator; public servant; b. Toronto, Ont. 21 Feb. 1936; s. Escott Meredith and the late Ruth (Herriot) R.; e. Lisgar Coll. Inst. 1952; Ridley Coll. 1954; Univ. of Toronto Hons. B.A. 1959; Yale Univ. M.A. 1960; Oxford Univ. (Rhodes Scholar Ont. 1960) M.Litt. 1965; Harvard Bus. Sch. A.M.P. 1983; m. Julyan Fancott 8 Oct. 1962; children: Dylan, Vanessa; PRES., CANDN. CHAMBER OF COMMERCE 1989– ; Halfback Hamilton Tigercat Football Club 1962; Extve. Sec. Candn. Inst. of Pub. Affairs 1962–63; Asst. to Pres., Asst. Prof. of Economics, Sec., Fac. of Grad. Studies, Rsch. Assoc. for Public Policy, York Univ. 1963–72; defeated candidate federal general election 1965; Nat. Educ. Ctee. Candn. Inst. of Internat. Affairs 1965–67; mem. Provisional Counc., Company of Young Canadians 1966–69; Bd. of Dir. Ridley Coll. 1966–67; project director, Task Force on the Structure of Canadian Industry, Govt. of Can. 1967; mem. Bd. of Dir., Metro Toronto Social Planning Counc. 1968–69; Nat. Ctte., Rhodes Scholarship Trust 1967–69; Research Cons., Special Ctte. on Poverty, Senate of Canada 1970; M.P.P. Scarborough E. Ont. 1967–71 and Official Opposition Spokesman for Education, Univ. Affairs; Bd. of Gov. Scarborough Centenary Hospital 1968–71; Prin. Admin., Economist, Manpower and Social Affairs, Orgn. for Economic Co-operation and Devel. (OECD), Paris 1972–74; joined Public Service of Can. 1974–85; Dir., Effectiveness Evaluation Div., Asst. Sec. of Effectiveness Evaluation, Acting Depy. Secy., Planning Branch Treasury Bd.; Dep. Sec. Treas. Bd., Office of Comptroller Gen. of Can.; Asst. Dep. Min., Planning and Coordination, Dept. of Regional Economic Expansion; Extve. Dir., Regional and Industrial Program Affairs, Dept. of Regional Industrial Expansion; Asst. Depty. Min., responsible for Tourism Canada, 1984–85; Cons., U.S. Nat. Sci. Found. 1979–82; Dir. and Extve. mem., Canada Mortgage and Housing Corp. 1980–82; Chrmn. Working Party on Regional Devel., OECD 1982–84; organized 1st internat. conf. of OECD Mins. responsible for Regional Development Policies, Stockholm 1982; headed 18 Nation OECD Study visit to Japan on 'High Tech and Regional Econ. Dev.' 1984; Dean, Fac. of Business and Prof. of Business Mngmt., Ryerson Polytechnical Inst. 1985–89; Comnr., Ont. Securities Comn. 1987–89; Chrmn. Rsch. Ctte. and Mem. Extve. Bd., Inst. of Public Admin. of Can. 1985–87; Tourism consultant China, Trinadad & Tobago 1986–87; mem. Steering Ctte. to establish the Ont. Inst. for Skills Training 1986–87; mem. Bd. of Dir., Candn. Paraplegic Assoc. (Ont. Br.) 1988–91; Depy. Head, Business Mission to Taiwan 1991; Business Co-Chair of the Bd. of Dirs., Candn. Labour Market and Productivity Centre (CLMPC) 1993– ; mem., Internat. Trade Advisory Ctte. (ITAC), Govt. of Canada 1991– ;

mem. Bd. of Dir., Candn. Extve. Service Organization (CESO) 1991– ; Chair, Steering Ctte., Forum for International Trade Training (FITT) 1992–94; editor and contbr. 'Contemporary Canada' 1969; author various articles; 'Beaver' Cup, Hamilton Tigercats 1962; played in Grey Cup 'Fog Bowl' 1962; inducted to the Univ. of Toronto Sports Hall of Fame 1993; Outstanding Young Man of the Year, Toronto Jr. C. of C. 1969; recreations: skiing, tennis, skating, swimming, jogging; Club: Rideau (Ottawa).

**REID, Vincent P.,** Q.C., B.A., LL.B.; business executive; b. Wilkes-Barre, Pa. 14 Oct. 1929; e. Univ. of Toronto B.A. 1950; Osgoode Hall Law School LL.B. 1954; m. Joan d. Larkin and Anne Maloney 23 June 1951; 7 children; DIRECTOR AND VICE-PRES., MOSS, LAWSON & CO. LTD. 1990– ; Lawyer, Osler Hoskin & Harcourt 1954–69; retired from partnership 1969; Dir. & Vice-Pres., Cochran Murray Ltd. (now Midland Walwyn Ltd.) 1970–90; Dir., H. Paulin & Co. Ltd. 1974– ; clubs: Rosedale Golf & Country, Craigleith Ski, Atlantis Golf (Florida); Home: 619 Avenue Rd., Apt. 303, Toronto, Ont. M4V 2K6; Office: One Toronto St., Ste. 410, Toronto, Ont. M5C 2W3.

**REID, William J.,** B.Com.; industrial executive; b. Montreal, Que. 8 June 1925; s. George Orion and Janet Reid (Bell) R.; e. Strathcona Acad., Montreal, 1939–43; McGill Univ., B.Com. 1947; Centre d'Etudes Industrielles Geneva Cert. in Internat. Business Adm. 1949; m. Joan Patricia, d. Donald Lloyd Witter, Montreal, Que., 14 June 1952; children: Andrea Janet, Heather Anne, Suzanne Patricia; summer student, Alcan Aluminium Ltd. Arvida and Shawinigan Falls 1944–46; with Aluminum Securities Ltd. 1947–48 and 1949 becoming Vice President 1961–65; Assistant Treasurer, Southeast Asia Bauxites Ltd., 1955 (Director and Treasurer 1963–64); Chief Financial Officer in Brazil, 1955–61 (Secretary-Treasurer, Alumino do Brazil S.A., Sao Paulo; Treas., Alumino Minas Gerais, S.A., Minas Gerais); Vice Pres. Finance, Treas. and Dir., Aluminum Co. of Canada Ltd. 1966–73; Vice Pres. Finance and Dir., Alcan Internat. Ltd. 1973–77; Vice-Pres. Finance, Vice-Pres. Treas., and Sr. Vice Pres. Finance, Air Canada 1977–85; Sr. Vice Pres., Finance, Air Canada 1984–86; Sr. Vice Pres., Pension Fund Mgmt. 1986–87; Sr. Vice-Pres., Corp. Finance, Air Canada 1987–88; Extve. Vice Pres. & Chief Finan. Offr., Air Canada 1988–90 (retired); Sigma Chi; Protestant; recreations: golf, photography, skiing; Club: Royal Montreal Golf; Home: 430 Laird Blvd., Town of Mount Royal, Que. H3R 1Y2.

**REID, Rev. William Stanford,** M.A., Th.M., Ph.D., F.R.S.A., F.R.Hist.S. (Presb.); professor b. Montreal, Que. 13 Sept. 1913; s. late Rev. William Dunn and Daisy Fanny (Stanford) R.; e. McGill Univ., B.A. 1934 (Eng. and Hist.) and M.A. 1935 (Hist.); Westminster Theol. Semy., Phila., Pa. (1935–38), Th.B., Th.M.; Univ. of Penna. (Leib Harrison Grad. Fellow), Ph.D. (Hist.) 1941; Hon. L.H.D., Wheaton Coll., Ill. 1975; Hon. D.D., Presbyterian Theological Coll., Montreal 1979; m. Priscilla, d. late Henry Stewart Lee, 24 Aug. 1940; PROF. EMERITUS UNIV. OF GUELPH 1980; Trustee, Westminster Theol. Semy 1948–83; mem., Bd. of Mang. of Presby. Theol. Coll. of Montreal, 1943–45; Min., Fairmount Taylor Presb. Ch., Montreal 1941–45; Founder and Min. of the Presb. Church of the Town of Mount Royal, Que. 1945–51; mem., Dept. of History, McGill Univ. 1941–65, Warden of Douglas Hall, there 1952–65; Univ. Marshal 1950–65, Dir. of Men's Residences 1952–65; founder and first chrmn., Dept. of Hist., Univ. of Guelph, 1965–70; rec'd. grants from Candn. Social Science Research Council (1944), and Am. Philos. Soc., Phila. (1947 and 1949); Candn. grant for research in Candn. Hist. and Am. grant for study in Scot. and European hist.; Special Lectr., Free Univ. of Amsterdam 1955, Oxford Univ., 1959, Univ. of the West Indies, 1962–64, Westminster Theological Seminary, Philadelphia, 1972, 75, 78, Fuller Theological Seminary, Auburn Univ. 1978; Trinity Evangelical School, Deerfield Ill. 1979; Ont. Theological Seminary 1979, Knox College, Toronto 1979; Union Theological Seminary, Tokyo, Japan; Reformed Theological Seminary, Kobe, Japan; Hop Tong Theological Seminary, Seoul, Korea; Presbyterian Church Conferences, Melbourne, Sydney & Brisbane, Australia; Knox College, Dunedin, N.Z., 1980; Presbyterian Theological Hall, Melbourne, Australia, 1982–84; author of 'The Church of Scotland in Lower Canada,' 1936; 'Economic History of Great Britain,' 1954; 'The Scottish Reformation,' 1960; 'Skipper from Leith: The Life of Robert Barton of Over Barnton,' 1962; 'Christianity and Scholarship' 1966; 'The Protestant Reformation: Revival or Revolution',' 1968; 'Trumpeter of God: A Biography of John Knox' 1974; 'A Century and a Half of Witness 1828–1978: The Story of St. Andrews Presbyterian Church, Guelph, Ontario,' 1980; ed. and contributor, 'Called to Witness; Profiles of Canadian Presbyterians'; 'The Scottish Tradition in Canada,' 1976; 'John Calvin: His Influence in the Western World' 1982; various articles on Scot. & Candn. hist. and on theol. in learned journs.; mem., Royal Hist. Soc.; Scottish Church History Soc.; Economic and Social History Soc. of Scotland; Medieval Acad. of Am.; Hist. Soc. of Montreal (Hon. Pres.); Am. Soc. of Ch. Hist. (Council); Pres., Conf. on Scottish Studies 1970–72; former mem., Candn. Hist. Assn.; Scot. Hist. Soc.; rec'd. Grant from Inst. for Advanc. Christian Studies 1970; Canada Council 1969, 1967, 1970, 1976, for research in Scot. hist. and 1973, for sabbatical; Gov't. of France 1966, 1968; Retired 1978; Independent Liberal; recreations: painting, camping, travel, photography, Club: Faculty (Univ. Guelph); Guelph-Wellington Men's Club; Address: Apt. 906, 19 Woodlawn Rd. E., Guelph Ont. N1H 7B1.

**REIFEL, George Conrad,** B.Comm., M.B.A.; real estate executive; b. Calgary, Alta. 29 Dec. 1950; s. George Henry and Norma Eileen (Williams) R.; e. Delta S.S. 1968; Univ. of B.C. B.Comm. 1974; Univ. of West. Ont. M.B.A. 1976; m. Wendy H. d. Kit and Fred Newton 25 Sept. 1976; MANAGING PARTNER, REIFEL COOKE GROUP OF COMPANIES 1986– ; Vice-Pres., Finance, Daon Development Corp. 1976–86; Dir., Granville Savings & Mortgage Corp.; Invan Mortgage Corp.; Dir., B.C. Waterfowl Soc.; Ducks Unlimited Canada; The Nature Trust of B.C.; The Vancouver Club; Hernando Island Holdings Limited; Past Dir., Candn. Cancer Soc.; United Way; Mem., Ridley Coll. Alumni Assn.; Delta Kappa Epsilon Alumni Assn.; recreations: fishing, hunting, wildlife viewing; Clubs: The Vancouver, Royal Vancouver Yacht, Vancouver Lawn Tennis & Badminton, Tyee, Pennask Lake Fishing and Game, Steelhead Society of B.C., Kirkland Island Waterfowl Society; Home: 2883 Point Grey Rd., Vancouver, B.C. V6K 1A7; Office: 1055 W. Hastings St., Guinness Tower, Ste. 440, Vancouver, B.C. V6E 2E9.

**REIFFENSTEIN, Rhoderic John,** B.Sc., Ph.D.; educator; b. Montreal, Que. 1 Nov. 1938; s. George Eric and Grace Edna (Mingie) R.; e. Montreal West H.S. 1955; McGill Univ. B.Sc. 1959; Univ. of Man. Ph.D. 1965; m. Joan M. d. Thompson and Dorothy Cooper 1 July 1961; children: Margaret, Andrew, Sarah, Michael; PROF. OF PHARMACOL. UNIV. OF ALTA. 1983– ; Teaching Fellow in Pharmacol. Univ. of Man. 1959–64; Asst. Prof. of Pharmacol. present Univ. 1964, Assoc. Prof. 1972; Rsch. Assoc. Anesthesia Rsch. McGill Univ. 1968, Visiting Prof. of Physiol. 1979–80; Visiting Sci. Sch. of Pharm. Univ. of London, UK 1971–72; co-ed. Proceedings Internat. Conf. Hydrogen Sulphide Toxicity, Banff 1989; mem. Pharmacol. Soc. Can. (Treas. 1987–94); Brit. Pharmacol. Soc.; Soc. for Neurosci.; Soc. Toxicol. Can.; Am. Assn. for the Advancement of Science; Candn. Assn. for Neuroscience; European Soc. for Neurochemistry; The New York Academy of Sciences; Western Pharmacology Soc.; Office: 9 – 70 Medical Sciences Building, Edmonton, Alta. T6G 2H7.

**REILLY, Bruce,** A.R.P.S.; photographer; b. Toronto, Ont. 10 Nov. 1933; s. Thomas Smith and Jean Garnet R.; e. Vaughan Rd. Coll.; N.Y. Inst. of Photography, grad. 1959; m. Carole d. James A. and Jessie B. Curtis 1 Aug. 1968; children: Jeffery, Linda; PRES., THE PIPER STUDIO LIMITED (WEDDING CTR.) 1960– ; served 10 yrs. overseas with Royal Candn. Air Force as photographer; Piper has been largest wedding photography studio in Can. since 1966; currently also largest complete wedding centre; Pres., Wedding Council of Ont.; Piper Studios Sch. of Photography; winner of 20 ribbons through Profl. Photographers of Ont.; Dir., Bluffers Park Yacht Club (4 yrs.); Un. Ch.; Life mem., York Central Hospital Assoc.; Mem., Heritage Circle, North York General Hosp.; Mem., Royal Photographic Soc.; Profl. Photographers of Ont. and of Can.; Zion Wexford Masonic Temple 1964– ; Toronto Lodge of Perfection 1991; Toronto Sovereign of Rose Croix 1991; Moore Sovereign of Scottish Rite 1991; Rameses Shrine Temple 1991; recreations: sailing, golf; Clubs: El Shamaly; Bayview Golf; Whitby Yacht; Home: 391 Woodland Acres Cr., R.R. 2, Maple, Ont. L6A 1G2; Office: 431 Wilson Ave., Toronto, Ont. M3H 1T5.

**REIM, William M.;** corporate executive; b. Montreal, Que. 11 June 1942; s. Louis and Thelma (Baranoff) R.; e. McGill Univ., B.A. 1965, M.B.A. 1968; m. Marilyn d. Harry and Geraldine Friedlander 12 May 1963; children: Max, Douglas, Scott; PRES. & C.E.O., M-CORP INC. 1983– ; Sr. Devel. Extve., Cadillac Fairview Corp. 1972–77; Sr. Vice Pres., Credit Foncier 1978–83; Club: Montefiore; Hillsdale Golf & Country; Home: 61 Granville Rd., Hampstead, Que. H3X 3B7; Office: 8250 Decarie Blvd., Suite 310, Montreal, Que. H4P 2P5.

**REIMER, Donald S.;** b. Steinbach, Manitoba, 22 Jan. 1933; m. 25 June 1953; three sons; DIR., REIMER EXPRESS ENTERPRISES LTD; Office: 1400 Inkster Blvd., Winnipeg, Man. R2X 1R1.

**REIMER, H.,** B.A.Sc.; consultant; b. Waterloo, Ont. 23 July 1926; s. David and Anna (Wiens) R.; e. Univ. of Toronto B.Sc. 1948; m. Beverley d. Gordon and Stella Harrison 1 Oct. 1949; children: Aynslie, Heidi, Karl; Consultant, Lowen Ondaatje McCutcheon 1988–92; Exploration Geologist, Dominion Gulf Co. 1948–53; Mining Analyst, Richardson Securities 1953–70; Sr. Mining Analyst & Dir., Loewen Ondaatje McCutcheon 1970–88; Dir., Morrison Petroleums Ltd.; Orvana Minerals Corp.; Golden Star Resources; Office: 460 Chartwell Rd., Oakville, Ont. L6J 4A5.

**REINBLATT, Gary,** B.Comm.; advertising executive; b. Montreal, Que. 9 May 1945; s. Sam and Sonia (Bruker) R.; e. Sir George Williams Univ. B.Comm. 1967; m. Sandra d. Russell & Lillian Way 15 Oct. 1973; children: B.J., George; SR. VICE-PRES., MARKETING, MCDONALD'S RESTAURANTS OF CANADA LTD. 1971– ; with Needham, Harper & Steers 1969–71; mem. Exec. Ctte. Bureau of Broadcast Measurement; Lawrence Park Athletic Assn.; Metro Toronto Convention and Visitors Bureau; recreations: skiing, tennis, reading; Clubs: Alpine Ski; Toronto Cricket; Balsam Lake Sailing; Mac's Video; Trans Canada Matchcover; Admiral's; Home: 153 St. Leonard's Ave., Toronto, Ont. M4N 1K6; Office: McDonald's Place, Toronto, Ont. M5C 3L4.

**REINERTSON, Lawrence C. (Lawrie);** mining executive; b. Kamloops, B.C. 23 Apl. 1945; s. Chester Walter and Isabel Laura R.; e. B.C. Inst. of Technol. Mining 1970; MNG. DIR. PLACER PACIFIC LTD. 1990– ; Mng. Dir.: Kidston Gold Mines Ltd., Australia; Misima Mines Ltd. (PNG); joined Noranda Inc. 1965–87; Sr. Vice Pres. Placer Dome Inc. 1987–90; Home: 98 Gloucester St., Sydney, N.S.W., Australia; Office: GPO Box 4315, Sydney, N.S.W., Australia 2001.

**REINSCH, Anthony Ernest,** B.A., M.A., M.Sc.; economist; b. Lanigan, Sask. 3 June 1954; s. Gustav Walter and Edna Alma (Rode) R.; e. Univ. of Calgary B.A. 1976, M.A. 1977; London Sch. of Econ. M.Sc. 1978; Univ. of Western Ont. Ph.D. 1981; VICE-PRESIDENT, WORLD OIL & INTRNAT. ENERGY STUDIES, CANADIAN ENERGY RESEARCH INST. 1989– ; Senior Economist, Ont. Hydro 1980–82; Intergovt. Finance, Alta. Treas. 1982–84; Senior Economist, Indus. & Commodities, Bank of Montreal 1984–86; Mgr., Rsch., Candn. Energy Research Inst. 1986–89; Lecturer, Mount Royal College 1974–77, 1988–89; Univ. of Calgary 1976–77, 1987–92; U.W.O. 1978–80; York Univ. 1980–82; Univ. of Alta. 1983–84; Dipl. in Devel. Econ., Inter-Univ. Ctr. for Post-grad. Studies, Dubrovnik, Yugoslavia 1977; Pres., Econ. Soc. of Calgary 1987–88; Extve. Mem. 1986–90; Reg. Dir., Candn. Assn. for Bus. Econ. 1988–90; Extve. Ctte. Mem., Calgary Chap., Internat. Assn. for Energy Econ.; author: 'Containing Iraq' 1993, 'Oil in the Former Soviet Union' 1992, 'Challenging OPEC' 1992, 'After the Crisis' 1991, 'Canadian Crude Oil Supply-Demand Balances' 1989; Editor: 'World Oil Market Analysis'; Dep. Ed., 'Geopolitics of Energy'; Edit. Bd. Mem., 'Energy Policy,' 'Energy Studies Rev.' Mem., Rsch. Ctte., Candn. Global Change Program, Royal Soc. of Can.; frequent speaker at nat. & internat. seminars & confs.; regular media contbr.; recreations: squash, climbing, curling; Home: 23 Point McKay Ct. N.W., Calgary, Alta T3B 5B7; Office: 3512 – 33 St. N.W., Ste. 150, Calgary, Alta. T2L 2A6.

**REINTAMM, Norman Illis,** B.A.; conductor; b. Hamilton, Ont. 10 Aug. 1958; s. Artur and Endla (Viilup) R.; e. Hillfield-Strathallan Coll. Hamilton; Univ. of Toronto; McMaster Univ. B.A. 1981; Royal Coll. of Music London, Eng.; Conductor, Toronto Pops Orch. 1985; Apprentice Conductor Vancouver Chamber Choir; former Organist Christ's Ch. Cath. Hamilton, Ont. and orch. affiliations with McMaster Univ. Symphony Orch., Cath. Chamber Orch., Hamilton Philharmonic Orch.; guest conducting incls. Windsor Symphony Orch., Kitchener-Waterloo Symphony Orch., Eastman Sch. of Music Rochester, N.Y., Stadt Solingen Symphony Orch. W. Germany, Prague Radio Symphony Orch., Symphony Nova Scotia, Young London (Eng.) Ballet Co. Orch., Royal Coll. of Music Sinfonia London, Opera Hamilton (repetiteur), Ensemble Sir Ernest MacMillan, Cath. Chamber Symphony Orch. Vancouver, Philharmonia Orch. Toronto; recipient Hon. Mention Leslie Bell Conducting Scholarship 1979, Aspen Music Festival Conducting Scholarship 1979, Aspen Music Festival Conducting Scholarhip 1979 (USA), Els-

Kaljot Vaarman Conducting Scholarship 1981 (Sweden), Cobbett-Hurlestone Prize 1982 (Royal Coll. Music), Theodore Stier Conducting Award 1982 (Royal College of Music); Kawai Can. Music Ltd. Artist 1986; composer ballet 'Rupert Bear' premiere London, Eng. 1982, choir & organ 'Jubilate Deo,' 'Miss Brevis,' 'Out of the Deep' premiers Hamilton, Ont. 1983–84, 'Four Songs' solo voice & piano Simcoe, Ont. 1985; recreations: private pilot, sailing, amateur radio; Home: 455 Aberdeen Ave., Hamilton, Ont. L8P 2S4.

**REISMAN, Sol Simon,** O.C. (1978) M.A.; financial executive; b. Montreal, Que., 19 June 1919; s. Kolman and Manya R.; e. McGill University, B.A. (Hons. Econ. and Pol. Science) 1941, M.A. (summa cum laude) 1942; London Sch. of Econs. (1945); m. Constance Augusta, d. W.N. Carin, Montreal, Que., 17 Oct. 1942; children: John Joseph, Anna Lisa, Harriet Frances; PRES., TRADE & INVESTMENT ADVISORY GROUP; Chrmn. of the Bd., Ranger Oil Ltd.; Dir. & Chrmn. of the Audit Ctte., Geo. Weston Ltd.; Dir., Ballard Power Systems Inc.; Ballard Battery Systems Corp.; TRIUMF-KAON Ventures Office Advisory Bd.; Hughes Aircraft of Canada Ltd.; Faxon Canada Ltd.; Ambassador (Trade Negotiations) and Chief Negotiator for Canada of Canada-U.S. Free Trade Agreement; joined Civil Service of Can. Dept. Labour 1946, trans. Dept. Finance same yr.; Dir. Internat. Econ. Relations Div., Dept. Finance 1954–57; Gen. Dir. of Econo. and Internat. Affairs, Dept. of Finance 1957–61; Assistant Deputy Minister, Dept. Finance 1961–64; Depy. Min. Industry 1964–68; Secy. of Treas. Bd. 1968–70; Depy. Min. Finance 1970–75; Royal Commissioner to investigate Candn. Auto Ind. 1978; Chief Negotiator for Canada on the Aboriginal Land Claims in the Western Arctic 1983; Canadian Delegation to Geneva Trade and Tariff Conf., 1947; World Conf. on Trade and Employment, Havana, 1947–48; 1st Session, Gen. Agreement on Tariffs & Trade; all sessions of GATT, 1948–54; Econ. & Social Council, U.N., Geneva (1952) and N.Y. (1953); Commonwealth Finance Ministers Conf., London, 1950 and Mont Tremblant 1957; Commonwealth Trade & Econ. Conf., Montreal 1958; participated in negotiation of numerous trade agreements during this period; served as Asst. Director of Research on Royal Comn. on Canada's Econ. Prospects, 1955–57 (author of book prepared for the Comn. 'Canada-United States Economic Relations,' 1957, and two books entitled 'Canada's Export Trade' and 'Canadian Commercial Policy'); served in 2nd World War with R.C.A. as Regt. Offr. 1942–46; Overseas Nov. 1942–Jan. 1946 with 11th, 15th and 17th Field Arty. (Troop Commander); Outstanding Public Service Award Can. 1974; Bd. Govs. Carleton Univ.; member, Ottawa Chapter, Economical and Political Science Association (Director); Am. Econ. Assn.; Candn. Econ. Pol. Science Assn.; Hebrew; recreations: golf, skiing, fishing, reading; Clubs: Five Lakes Fishing; Rideau; Rideau View Golf & Country; Home: 146 Roger Road, Ottawa, Ont. K1H 5C8; Office: Metropolitan Centre, 50 O'Connor St., Suite 1611, Ottawa, Ont. K1P 6L2.

**REISS, Timothy James,** F.R.S.C., B.A., M.A., Ph.D.; university professor, author; b. London, England 14 May 1942; s. James Martin and Margaret Joan (Ping) R.; e. Hardye's Sch. 1953–59; Manchester Univ., B.A. (Hons.) 1964; Univ. of Illinois, M.A. 1965, Ph.D. 1968; 2nd m. Patricia Jane Penn Hilden Aug. 1988; children: Matthew James, Suzanna Jean, Justin Timothy; PROF. & CHAIR, COMP. LIT., NEW YORK UNIV. 1987– ; Instr./Asst. Prof., Yale Univ. 1968–73; Assoc. Prof. to Full Prof., Univ. of Montreal 1973–83; Dir., Comp. Lit. 1976–81; Prof., Emory Univ. 1983–86; Vis. Prof., Univ. of Toronto 1976–77; Univ. of B.C. 1979; N.Y. Univ. 1982; Univ. of Montreal 1984–87; CUNY 1985; SUNY Binghamton 1990; Samuel Candler Dobbs Prof., Emory Univ. 1986–87; Vis. seminar series: Georgia Tech. 1986, 1987; Portland State Univ. 1988; SUNY Binghamton 1989; Cons., Univ. of West. Ont., Univ. of Toronto & others 1979; extensive lecturer; Morse Fellowship, Paris 1971–72; Sr. Fellow, Oxford (Can. Counc.) 1977–78, (SSHRCC) 1983–84; ACLS Fellow 1986–87; Guggenheim Fellow, Cambridge 1990–91; FRSC 1983; Fellow, Acad. of Lit. Studies 1986– ; author: 'Toward Dramatic Illusion' 1971, 'Tragedy and Truth' 1980, 'The Discourse of Modernism' 1982, 1985, 'The Uncertainty of Analysis' 1988; 'The Meaning of Literature' 1992 (selected 'Best Academic Book of 1992' by Choice magazine and winner 1992 Morris D. Forkosch prize for 'Best Book in Intellectual History'); editor: 'Science, Language and the Perspective Mind' 1973; co-editor: 'De l'ouverture des disciplines' 1982, 'Tragique et tragédie dans la tradition occidentale' 1983; approx. 100 essays & book chaps.; Home: 1 Washington Square Village, PH-H, New York, N.Y. 10012; Office: 19 University Pl., 4th Fl., New York, N.Y. 10003.

**REITMAN, Ivan,** B.Mus.; motion picture producer/director; b. Czechoslovakia 27 Oct. 1946; s. Leslie and Klara R.; emigrated to Can. 1950; e. Hamilton Univ. B.Mus.; m. Genevieve Robert 9 Dec. 1975; children: Jason, Catherine; Dir., 'Meatballs,' 'Stripes,' 'Ghostbusters,' 'Legal Eagles,' 'Twins,' 'Ghostbusters II'; Prod., 'National Lampoon's Animal House,' 'Heavy Metal' and 'Greed' (live TV variety); Extve. Prod., 'Casual Sex?,' 'Feds'; stage productions: 'Spellbound' (Toronto), 'Magic Show' (Broadway), 'Merlin' (Broadway; Tony award nom.); his production company, Ivan Reitman Productions is overseeing TV animated series 'The Real Ghostbusters' & 'The Slimer Show'; Mem., Directors Guild of Am.

**REITZ, Jeffrey Gould,** B.Sc., Ph.D.; university professor; b. St. Paul, Minn. 20 Sept. 1944; s. Frank Bryan and Marjorie Elizabeth R.; e. Columbia Univ. B.Sc. 1965, Ph.D. 1972; one d.: Jennifer Joweyne Petersen; PROF. OF SOCIOLOGY, UNIV. OF TORONTO 1970– ; Department Chair 1980–85; Rsch. Associate, Centre for Industrial Relations, Univ. of Toronto 1983– ; author: 'The Survival of Ethnic Groups' 1980 and num. articles & book chapters; co-author: 'An Introduction of Applied Sociology' 1975, 'Non-Official Languages' 1976, 'Cultural Boundaries and the Cohesion of Canada' 1980, 'Ethnic Identity and Equality' 1990; Visiting Scholar, Univ. of Calif. at Los Angeles 1990–91; Univ. of Sydney 1991; Univ. of London 1985; Univ. of Bristol 1983; Visiting Prof., Univ. of Tsukuba 1982–83; Cons., Sec. of State for Multiculturalism; Ont. Anti-Racist Secretariat, Ont. Min. of Culture & Citizenship; Social Planning Council of Metro Toronto; Child Abuse Prog., Ont. Min. of Community & Social Serv.; Children's Aid Soc. of Metro Toronto Found.; Candn. House of Commons Standing Ctte. on Labour, Employment & Immigration; Mem., Toronto Mayor's Ctte. on Community & Race Relns. 1990–92; Rsch. Bd., Child Youth and Family Policy Rsch. Inst. 1988–90; SSHRCC Leave Fellowship 1977, '82; Mem., Am. Sociological Assn. (Chair, Soc. Practice Ctte. 1989–90); Home: 8 Ferrier Ave., Toronto, Ont. M4K 3H4; Office: 203 College St., Toronto, Ont. M5T 1P9.

**REKAI, Catherine (Kati),** C.M.; writer; b. Budapest, Hungary 20 Oct. 1921; d. Desider Elek and Ilona (Hajdu) E.; e. Budapest, Hungary; m. Dr. John s. Victor and Grete Rekai 15 Aug. 1941; children: Julie, Judyth; author series of travel books for children 'The Adventures of Mickey, Taggy, Puppo and Cica and How They Discover ...' ('... Toronto'; 'Ottawa'; 'Montreal'; 'Budapest'; 'Vienna'; 'The Netherlands'; 'Switzerland'; 'Brockville, Kingston'; 'The Thousand Islands'; 'France'; 'The George R. Gardiner Museum of Ceramic Art'; 'Italy'; Toronto 200;) many publ. in French and Braille; stage shows incl.: 'The Great Totem Pole Caper'; 'The Boy Who Forgot'; 'The Tale of Tutenkhamen'; videocassette 'The Great Totem Pole Caper'; columnist for Hungarian Life/Magyar Elet, Toronto; The Spark Magazine; Regular contributor to CHIN-Radio Hungarian Broadcast on Candn. Cultural Events; Cons., Public Relations, Central Hosp., Toronto; Dir., Canadian Scene (News Service for Canada's Ethnic Media); Performing Arts Magazine; Vice-Pres., Museum of Childhood; former mem. Multicultural Adv. Ctte., Toronto Hist. Bd.; Former Mem., Metro. Toronto District Adv. Bd.; Crest Theatre Women's Ctte.; former Co-Chrmn. Publ. Relations, Guild of St. Lawrence Centre for the Arts; past mem. Exec. Toronto Welcoming Ctte.; mem. Writer's Union of Can.; Chair, External Affairs Ctte., Canscaip/Assn. of Children's Writers and Illustrators; P.E.N. Internat.; George R. Gardiner Mus.; Stratford Festival; Candn. Opera Company; Ethnic Journalists and Writers Club; awarded Prix Saint-Exupéry Francophonie, Paris, 1988; Certificate of Honour for Contribution to Canadian Unity; Award of Merit Am. Biographical Inst.; Knighthood St. Laszlo of Hungary 1980; Rakoczi Award 1991; Cross of Merit (for contribution to Candn.-Hungarian Cultural Development, Republic of Hungary 1993; Mem., Order of Canada 1993; included in Dictionary of International Biography; recreations: swimming, reading, walking, travelling, opera, theatre; Address: 21 Dale Ave., #623, Toronto, Ont. M4W 1K3.

**RELPH, Edward,** B.A., M.Phil., Ph.D.; university professor; b. Wales 18 May 1944; s. Bernard and Joan Margaret (Roberts) R.; e. Univ. of London B.A. 1965; London Sch. of Economics M.Phil. 1967; Univ. of Toronto Ph.D. 1973; m. Irene d. Borys and Molly Kovaleski 3 Oct. 1970; children: Alexandra, Gwyneth; CHAIR, DIVISION OF SOCIAL SCIENCES, SCARBOROUGH COLLEGE, UNIV. OF TORONTO 1991– ; apptd. to faculty, Geography, Univ. of Toronto 1973; Prof. 1988; Visiting Prof., Univ. of Minnesota 1976; Mem., Candn. Assn. of Geographers; Environmental Design Rsch. Assn.; author: 'Place and Placelessness' 1976 (Japanese trans 1992), 'Rational Landscapes' 1982, 'The Modern Urban Landscape' 1987 (Portuguese trans 1990), 'The Toronto Guide: The City, Metro, the Region' 1990; author of numerous papers; extensive keynote speaker; Home: 100 Melrose Ave., Toronto, Ont. M5M 1Y7; Office: Scarborough, Ont. M1C 1A4.

**RÉMILLARD, Hon. Gil,** B.A., B.Ph., LL.L., D.LL.; b. Hull, Qué. 25 Nov. 1944; s. Carmel and Jeannine (Desjardins) R.; e. Univ. of Ottawa, B.A. 1964, Ph.B. 1965, B.Pol.Sc. and LL.L. 1968; Univ. of Nice, Degree in advanced studies in Public Law 1970, D.LL. (cum laude) (Doctorat d'État - highest grade of doctorate in France) 1972; called to Bar of Qué. 1969; m. Marie Dupont; one s. Nicholas Philippe; BYERS CASGRAIN; Host-Researcher, Public Affairs, CBC (Radio-Can.) 1965–68; Prof. of Law, Laval Univ. 1972–85; Lawyer, Chouinard, Rémillard, Robinson and Bussières 1976–77; Guest Prof. in many Canadian, European and American Universities; Adviser, Fed. Min. of Communications 1983–84; Special observer, U.N.O. 40th Anniv. Session 1985; Adv. constitutional matters to Prime Min., Can. 1985; el. M.N.A. for Jean-Talon 1985; Min. of Internat. Relations 1985–88; Min. responsible for Candn. Intergovernmental Affairs of Quebec 1985–93; Min. of Public Security 1988–89; Min. of Justice, Attorney Gen. 1988–93; Chrmn. of the Legislative Ctte. 1988–93; author of many works, essays, leading articles and commentaries including in particular: 'Le Fédéralisme canadien (Candn. Federalism), constitutional elements of formation and development, Québec-Amérique, Montréal 1980; 'Le Fédéralisme canadien, Volume I, Constitution Act, 1867, Québec-Amérique, Montréal, 1983; Volume II, 'Patriation of the Constitution' 1985; many works, essays, leading articles and commentaries; Honours: Scholarship from the Department of Education, Canada Rsch. Council (Humanities); Doctor of Law (honoris causa) Univ. Aix-Marseille III, (France) 1990; Office: 1 Place Ville Marie, Bureau 3900, Montreal, Que. H2B 4M7.

**REMPEL, Garry Llewellyn,** B.Sc., Ph.D., F.R.S.C., F.C.I.C.; university professor and administrator; b. Regina, Sask. 20 Aug. 1944; s. Henry J. and Grace V. (Pullman) R.; e. Univ. of B.C. B.Sc. 1965, Ph.D. 1968; m. Flora Ng 20 Sept. 1975; PROFESSOR, CHEMICAL ENGINEERING, UNIV. OF WATERLOO 1980– ; NRC postdoctoral fellow, Imperial Coll. of Sci. & Tech. (U.K.) 1968–69; Asst. Prof., Chem. Engr., Univ. of Waterloo 1969–73; Assoc. Prof. 1973–79; Assoc. Chair, Grad. Studies, Chem. Engr. 1983–86; Chair, Chem. Eng. 1988– ; Mem., Co-ord. Ctte., Univ. of Waterloo-Tech. Transfer & Licensing Office 1990– ; Polymers & Plastics Prog. Mngt. Ctte.; Academic Leader, Ont. Centre for Materials Rsch. 1992– ; Bd. of Dir., Waterloo Ctr. for Process Devel., Univ. of Waterloo 1988–90; Consultant, Polysar Rubber Corp., Ortho McNeil Inc., Inst. for Polymer Rsch., Univ. of Waterloo; Thomas W. Eadie Medal, Royal Soc. of Can. 1993; Gold Award for Bus. Excellence (Invention Category), Govt. of Canada (awarded to Polysar Ltd.) 1987; Fellow, Royal Soc. of Can.; Chem. Inst. of Can.; Mem., Candn. Soc. of Chem. Engr.; Am. Inst. of Chem. Engr.; Am. Chem. Soc.; Soc. of Chem. Industry; author of over 100 scientific pubns.; 13 patents granted; Home: 532 Sandbrooke Ct., Waterloo, Ont. N2T 2H4; Office: Dept. of Chem. Eng., Univ. of Waterloo, Waterloo, Ont. N2L 3G1.

**RENAUD, J.F.A. Marc,** B.A., M.Sc., Ph.D.; university professor; b. Montreal, Que. 19 Feb. 1946; s. Andre and Fleurette (Laporte) R.; e. Collège St-Viateur B.A. 1966; Univ. of Montreal M.Sc. 1969; Univ. of Wisconsin Ph.D. 1975; m. Christine d. Paul and Yvonne Colin May 1982; children: Nicolas, Marie; PROFESSOR OF SOCIOLOGY, UNIV. OF MONTREAL 1975– ; Dir., Groupe de rech. sur les aspects sociaux de la prévention, Univ. of Montreal 1984–91; Vice-Pres., Candn. Inst. of Advanced Research 1991– ; Pres., Conseil Québécois de la Rech. Sociale, Gouv. du Qué. 1991– ; Invited Researcher, Ecole Polytechnique, Paris 1982–83; Scientific Advisor, Comn. d'enquête sur les serv. de santé et les serv. sociaux, Gouv. du Qué. 1985–87; participation in various cttes. incl. CRSH, FCAR, FRSQ, Ont. Workers' Comp. Inst., etc.; Mem., Am. Sociological Assn.; Assn. Can. des Sociologues et Anthropologues de Langue Française; author: 'Les solutions des Québécois aux problèmes de santé' 1988; 'Le droit de refus: une révolution tranquille' 1989; editor: 'La gestion de la santé' 1977, 'Médecine et Société: les années '80' 1981, 'Travail, Santé, Prévention' 1987; recreations: skiing, bicycling; Home: 40 Hazelwood, Outremont, Que. H3T 1R3; Office: GRASP, Univ. of Montreal, Box 6128, Montreal, Que. H3C 3J7.

**RENAUD, Richard J.,** B.Comm., C.A.; financial executive; b. 1946; e. Loyola Coll. (Concordia Univ.)

B.Comm. 1969; McGill Univ. C.A. 1971; m. Carolyn Edith Hayes; children: Philip, Marc, Andrea, Paul; VICE CHAIRMAN, BENVEST CAPITAL INC. 1991– ; Indenture at Ernst & Whinney 1969–72; Indepedent Business Consultant, Concordia Univ. 1975–86; Founder, CMP Mineral and Oil and Gas Partnerships 1981; Chrmn., CS Resources Limited; Pres. & Dir., Northbrock Capital Inc.; Dir., Dundee Bancorp Inc.; Immedia Infomatic Inc.; Benvest Capital Inc.; Marleau, Lemire Inc.; Philanderer Inc.; Radiomutuel Inc.; Weider Health & Fitness; Yorbeau Resources Inc.; Canstar Sports Inc.; Pres. & Dir., La Fond. des Bien Cuits/The Roasters' Found.; Bd. of Gov. & Dir., St. Mary's Hosp.; Dir., Toujours Ensemble Inc.; Bd. of Trustees, Coll. Stanstead; Bd. of Gov., Concordia Univ.; Mem., Concordia Univ. Alumni Assn.; Internat. Wine & Food Soc.; Loyola H.S. Alumni Assn.; Order des Comptables Agréés du Qué.; Shahwandahgooze Fishing & Hunting Club; University Club; Home: 49 Brock North, Montreal W., Que. H4X 2G1; Office: 1155 René-Lévesque Blvd. W., Suite 2205, Montreal, Que. H3B 4T3.

**RENAUD, Robert A.,** M.A.; automobile industry executive; b. Windsor, Ont. 5 Sept. 1947; s. Urgele A. and Florence (Pinsonnealt) R.; e. Univ. of Windsor M.A. 1972; Univ. of Western Ont., Western Extve. Prog. 1990; m. Christine d. Frank and Isabel Farrell 13 June 1970; children: Jeffrey, Matthew; VICE-PRESIDENT, PARTS, SERVICE & TECHNICAL PROGRAMS, CHRYSLER CANADA LTD. 1991– ; Human Resources Serv. & Vehicle Sales responsibilities, Chrysler Canada for Canada & U.S. 1972–84; Regional Mgr., Alta. 1984–87; Dir., Renault Opns. (U.S.) 1988–89; Mgr., Marketing Opns. & Planning 1989–90; Dir., Chrysler Canada Ltd.; Candn. Automotive Inst.; Past Dir., United Way of Windsor; recreations: coaching assistant for minor baseball and hockey; Home: 605 Primrose Place, Tecumseh, Ont. N8N 4C7; Office: 2450 Chrysler Centre, Windsor, Ont. N8W 3X7.

**RENAULT, Suzanne,** B.C.L.; lawyer, business executive; b. Montreal, Que. 22 May 1954; d. Paul Fernand and Louise (Morin) R.; e. McGill Univ. B.C.L. 1976; Quebec Bar School 1977; VICE-PRESIDENT, LEGAL AFFAIRS & SECRETARY, LE GROUPE VIDÉOTRON LTÉE. 1988– ; private practice with Ogilvy Renault 1977–85; Dir. of Legal Affairs, Vidéotron 1985–88; Mem., Candn. Bar Assn.; Candn. Assn. of Corporate Counsel; Assn. des secrétaires et chefs de Contentieux du Québec; recreations: sports, gardening; Home: 10590 Verville, Montreal, Que. H3L 3E8; Office: 2000 Berri St., Montreal, Que. H2L 4V7.

**RENDALL, James Allen,** LL.M.; educator; b. Clarksburg, Ont. 6 Aug. 1933; s. William Allen and Vera Bernice (Henning) R.; e. Univ. of Toronto Victoria Coll. B.A. 1955; Osgoode Hall Law Sch. LL.B. 1962; Univ. of Mich. LL.M. 1965; m. Katharine d. Alan and Wanda Boyce 4 Aug. 1956; three s. Alan, Edward, Andrew; PROF. OF LAW, UNIV. OF CALGARY 1978– ; called to Bar of Ont. 1964; Asst. Prof., Assoc. Prof. and Prof. of Law, Univ. of W. Ont. 1965–73; Visiting Prof. Dalhousie Univ. 1972–73 (Can. Council Leave Fellowship), Prof. of Law 1973–78; Acting Dean of Law present Univ. 1980–81, Assoc. Dean 1981–83; Visiting Prof. Victoria Univ. of Wellington 1983–84; co-ed. 'Canadian Cases on the Law of Insurance' 1983; 'Canadian Taxation Law' 1981; author various articles, book chapters; mem., Bd. Legal Edn. Soc. Alta. 1981–83; Bd. Candn. Inst. Resources Law 1980–83; Bd. Law Inst. Pacific Rim 1982– ; mem. Exec., Candn. Assn. Law Teachers 1981–83, Chrmn. Tax Sect. 1972–74, 1976–78; Home: 3615 Parkhill St. S.W., Calgary, Alta. T2S 2Z5; Office: Calgary, Alta. T2N 1N4.

**RENFREW, Robert Morrison,** B.A.Sc., P.Eng.; transportation research executive; b. Glasgow, Scot. 11 March 1938; s. Robert Morrison and Elizabeth Christina R.; e. Univ. of Toronto B.A.Sc. 1960; m. Hilary d. Philip and Una Tate 14 May 1960; children: Scott, Steven, Leslie Ann, Robert; DIVISIONAL DIRECTOR, RAILWAYS AND SYSTEMS ENGINEERING, ACER CONSULTANTS LTD. 1992– ; various ind. positions elec., electronics and plastics industries 1960–75; product devel. prog. mgr. 1975–79; Sr. Vice Pres. and subsequently Exec. Vice Pres. UTDC Ltd., Chief Operating Offr. UTDC R&D Ltd. 1979–83; Exec. Dir. Candn. Inst. of Guided Ground Transport, Queen's Univ. 1983–86; Sr. Vice Pres. Engineering and Business Development, UTDC-Lavalin 1986–92; mem., Assn. Prof. Engs. Prov. Ont.; Home: 3 Teconia Close, Headley Down, Hants. England GV35 8EY England; Office: 24 Medawar Rd., Guildford, Surrey GV2 5AR, England.

**RENISON, George Everett,** D.S.O., E.D., U.E.; b. Hamilton, Ont. 25 Aug. 1918; s. Mt. Rev. Robert John, D.D., and Elizabeth Maud (Bristol) R.; e. Trinity Coll. Sch., Port Hope, Ont.; Trinity Coll., Univ. of Toronto; m. Nancy E. d. John T. Stirrett, 15 Dec. 1945; children: Carol Ann, Katharine, Michael Barrie; served in 2nd World War with 48th Highlanders of Canada; commanded Hastings & Prince Edward Regiment and First Canadian Infantry Brigade; D.S.O.; Mentioned in Despatches; Staff College, Camberley (p.s.c. and Dagger); subsequently Honorary Colonel of the Hastings & Prince Edward Regiment; Chancellor of Renison College, Univ. of Waterloo; Chrmn., Communications Inc.; Chrmn., Candn. Artists & Artisans; Pres., Inter-Canadian Hotels Ltd.; Fellow of the Institute of Directors; formerly Chairman and Chief Executive Officer W.H. Smith Canada Ltd.; Harvey Woods Ltd.; Granfel PLC and subsidiaries; formerly Dir., Barclays Bank of Can.; Longwoods Internat. Inc.; Continental Golin/Harris Communications Inc.; Granada Canada Ltd.; The Retail Council of Canada; Chrmn., Convocation, Trinity College, Univ. of Toronto; Governor of St. George's College; Candn. Booksellers Assoc.; Zeta Psi; Conservative; Anglican; recreation: golf; Clubs: Toronto, Badminton & Racquet; East Sussex National; Toronto Hunt; York; Home: 532 Blythwood Rd., Toronto, Ont. M4N 1B3.

**RENLUND, Richard C.,** B.Sc., D.V.M., M.Sc.; university administrator; b. Port Arthur, Ont. 27 Sept. 1952; s. Karl Viktor and Else Sofia (Mårtens) R.; e. Univ. of Guelph, B.Sc. (Hons.) 1975; Ont. Vet. Coll., Guelph, D.V.M. 1979; Univ. of Toronto, M.Sc. 1980; Rsch. Fellow, Dept. of Labs., Mt. Sinai Hosp. 1979–80; DIR., DIVISION OF COMPARATIVE MED., FAC. OF MED., UNIV. OF TORONTO 1988– ; Vet. Pathol., Fac. of Med., present univ. 1980–83; Pathologist, Warner Lambert/Parke-Davis Rsch. Inst. 1983–86; Head, current dept. & univ. 1986–88; Assoc. Prof., Dept. of Pathol. and Dept. of Physiol., Fac. of Med., Univ. of Toronto; Assoc. Scientist, Mt. Sinai Hosp. Rsch. Inst.; Cons. Veterinarian, Ont. Cancer Inst., Mt. Sinai Hosp. Rsch. Inst.; Cons. Vet. Pathol., Dept. of Labs., Mt. Sinai Hosp.; mem., Royal Coll. of Vet. Surg.; US & Candn. Acad. of Pathol.; Candn. Assn. of Vet. Pathol.; College of Veterinarians of Ont.; Candn. Assn. of Lab. Animal Med.; Am. Assn. for Lab. Animal Science; recreations: fitness, Canadian art; club: YMCA; Home: 61 St. Clair Ave. W., #1906, Toronto, Ont. M4V 2Y8; Office: Rm. 1236, Med. Sci. Bldg., University of Toronto, Toronto, Ont. M5S 1A1.

**RENNER, Theodore H.,** B.Sc., M.B.A.; petroleum executive; b. Postlin, Germany 4 May 1945; e. Univ. of Man., B.Sc. 1968; Univ. of W. Ont., M.B.A. 1974; m. Lois; children: Mark, Meaghan; PRESIDENT AND DIR., KIORA RESOURCES INC. 1984– ; various pos., Hudson's Bay Oil & Gas Limited 1968–72; Evaluation Engr., Sproule & Assocs. 1972–74; Mgr. Corp. Planning, Norcen Energy Resources Ltd. 1974–77; Mgr. Oil & Gas Div., Luscar Ltd. 1977–79; Dir., Precambrian Shield Resources Ltd. 1979–87; Extve. Vice Pres. & C.E.O. 1979–80; Pres. & C.E.O. 1980–86; Pres., C.E.O. & Dir., Mark Resources Inc. (formerly Precambrian Shield Resources Ltd.) 1986–87; Pres., Chief Extve. Offr. & Dir., Saskatchewan Oil & Gas Corp. 1987–93; Past Pres., Dir., Private Energy Research Assoc.; Dir. & Past Chrmn., CERI Ltd.; Past Dir., Candn. Assn. of Petroleum Producers; mem., Alta. Assn. of Prof. Engrs.; Sask. Assn. of Prof. Engrs.; Energy, Chemicals, and Petrochemicals Sectoral Advisory Group on Internat. Trade; mem., Advisory Ctte.; Trustee, The Nature Conservancy of Canada; Clubs; Assiniboia; Wascana Country; Glencoe; Home: 3630 Selinger Cres., Regina, Sask. S4V 2H2.

**RENNIE, Donald A.,** C.M., B.S.A., Ph.D.; university professor; b. Medicine Hat, Alta., 21 Apl. 1922; s. Edward MacKenzie and Leila Nellie (Andrews) R.; e. High Sch., Gull Lake, Sask.; Univ. of Sask., B.S.A. 1949; Univ. of Wisconsin, Ph.D. 1952; m. Margaret June, d. late W. J. S. Hooper, 28 Aug. 1948; children: Robert John (B.S.A., M.Sc., Ph.D.), Wendy Diane (B.S.N., M.Sc.), Joan Darlene (B.A.); DEAN EMERITUS, COLLEGE OF AGRICULTURE, UNIV. OF SASKATCHEWAN 1989– ; served with Bank of Nova Scotia, Swift Current, Sask., as Bank Clk., 1940–42; joined present Univ. as Asst. Prof., Dept. of Soil Science, 1952–57; Assoc. Prof. 1957–64; Prof. & Hd. 1964–81; Prof. 1981–84; Dean, College of Agriculture 1984–89; Pres., Soil Conservation Canada 1989–90; Dir., Sask. Inst. of Pedology, 1965–81; served as Head, Soils, Irrigation and Crop Production Section, Internat. Atomic Energy, Vienna, Austria, 1968–70; served as Pilot, 407 Coastal Command Sqdn., Eng., 1942–45; rec'd Am. Chem. Soc. Award 1967; Centennial Medal 1967; author of 92 research papers for scient. journs.; Fellow, (1978) Agric. Inst. Can. (Dir. 1958–60, Vice Pres., 1959–60); Fellow (1971) Candn. Soc. Soil Science (Secy.-Treas. 1957–59, Pres. 1976–77); Fellow, Am. Soc. Agron. 1972; Fellow, Soil Science Soc. Am. 1976; Fellow, Crop Science Soc. Amer. 1985; recipient, West Can. Agron. Award 1979; Inducted into the Sask. Agric. Hall of Fame 1983; SIA Distinguished Agrologist Award 1989; L.B. Thompson, Conservation Award 1990; awarded Hon. Life Mem., Sask. Agr. Grads Assoc. 1991; Hon. mem., Seager Wheeler Farm Historic Soc. 1992; Western Canada Fertilizer Assn. 'Award of Merit' 1992; Member of Order of Canada 1992; awarded, 125th Anniversary of the Confederation of Canada Medal, 1992; mem., Internat. Soc. Soil Science; Candn. Assn. Univ. Teachers; apptd. to the Board of Trustees, The National Museum of Science and Technology 1991– ; Past Master, Lodge Progress No. 92; Past Patron, Regal Chapter No. 132, O.E.S.; Past Principle, Royal Arch Chapter #4, and Past District Deputy Grand Master, G.L.S.; Grand Master, The Grand Lodge of Sask. 1990–91; awarded Distinguished Service (Science) gold medal, Royal Arch Masons Internat. 1987; United Church; recreations: golf, curling; Home: 134 Highbury Pl., Saskatoon, Sask. S7H 4X7.

**RENNIE, Graham S.,** B.A., M.B.A.; investment manager; b. Hong Kong 12 May 1953; s. the late George Sutherland and Adelaide McNeil R.; e. H.S. Billings HLC; Univ. of Western Ont. B.A. 1974; McMaster Univ. M.B.A. 1979; m. D. Christine d. James and Dorothy Smith; children: Garrett, Evan, Colleen; PRESIDENT & MANAGING PARTNER, INTEGRA CAPITAL MNGT. CORP. 1987– ; Prudential Assurance 1980–82; Vice-Pres., Manuvest 1982–84; Vice-Pres., Dixon Krogseth Investment Counsel 1984–85; Senior Vice-Pres. & Dir., Trafalgar Capital Mgmt. 1985–86; recreations: skiing, tennis, golf; clubs: Fitness Inst., Ont. Racquet, Caledon Ski; Office: 55 University Ave., Suite 1100, Toronto, Ont. M5J 2H7.

**RENNIE, Janice G.,** B.Comm., C.A.; real estate executive; b. Edmonton, Alta. 29 June 1957; d. Graham G. and Gwendolyn A. (Allen) M.; e. McNally Comp. H.S. (Hons.) 1974; Univ. of Alta. B.Comm. (with distinction) 1979; C.A. 1981; m. Bruce W. s. William and Evelyn R. 19 April 1980; two s.: Daniel Allen, Spencer William; PRESIDENT, PRAIRIES & NWT REGION, PRINCETON DEVELOPMENTS LTD. 1991– ; joined Clarkson Gordon 1979; Audit Mgr. 1983; Comptroller, Princeton Developments Ltd. 1985–86; Vice-Pres. & Comptroller 1986–87; Treas. 1987–90; Pres. & Managing Dir., Princeton Devel. (Sask.) Ltd. 1989– ; Pres., Bellanca Devel. Ltd. 1990– ; Dir., NOVA Corp.; Audit Ctte. Mem. and Public Policy Risk Environment Ctte. Mem., NOVA Corp.; Candn. Inst. of C.A.s Silver Medal & Founder's Prize 1980; Inst. of C.A.s of Alta. Gold Medal 1980; Dean's List, Univ. of Alta. 1975–79; Marsh & McLennan Ltd. Centennial Scholarship; Bd. of Gov. Prize (twice); Pacific Petroleums Ltd. Scholarship; Lennie M. McNeill Memorial Prize (twice); Fruehauf Trailer Co. of Canada Limited Bursary; Touche Ross & Co. Scholarship; The Commerce Cup (awarded by peers in Fac. of Commerce) 1978; Dir. & Mem., Investment Ctte., Edmonton Community Fdn.; Dir., N.W.T. Legislative Assembly Bldg. Soc.; Dir. & Mem., Extve. Ctte., YMCA Edmonton 1989–90; Dir., Treas. & Extve. Ctte. Edmonton C. of C. 1987–90; Deputy Chrmn., Trade & Finance Div. & Cabinet Mem., Edmonton & Area United Way 1989–90; Dir., Sec. & Treas., Accounting Education Fdn. of Alta. 1983–86; Office: #1400, 9945 – 108 St., Edmonton, Alta. T5K 2G6.

**RENOUF, Harold Augustus,** O.C., B.Com., C.M.A., F.C.A., L.L.D.; business consultant; b. Sandy Point, Nfld. 15 June 1917; s. late Capt. John Robert and late Louisa Maud (LeRoux) R.; e. elem. and high schs. Halifax, N.S.; Dalhousie Univ. B.Com. 1938; C.A. 1942; C.M.A. 1950; m. Janet Dorothy d. late John T. Munro, Halifax 16 June 1942; children: Janet Dorothy, Ann Louise (Mrs. Evan Petley-Jones), John Robert, Susan Elizabeth (Mrs. Scott Thompson); Pres., Fundy Industries Ltd. Halifax, N.S.; Dir. The Nova Scotia Municipal Finance Corp.; joined H. R. Doane and Co. 1938, Partner 1942, Partner-in-charge New Glasgow, N.S. 1947–62, Partner-in-charge Mang. Services Halifax 1963–67, Chrmn. of Partnership 1967–75; mem. Bd. Dirs. Associated Accounting Firms International, New York 1967–75; Commr., Anti-Inflation Bd., Atlantic Region 1975, Chrmn. of Bd. 1977–79; Chrmn., Petroleum Monitoring Agency, 1980–82; Chrmn., VIA Rail Canada Inc. 1982–85; Consultant to N.S. Prov. Mun. Fact-Finding Comte. 1967–70; former Dir. Cape Breton Development Corp.; Canadian National Railways; Laurentian Financial Group PLC, London, Eng.; Laurentian Life plc, Gloucester, Eng.; The Imperial Life Assurance Co.; Past Chrmn. Budget Comte. Pictou Co. Un. Appeal; Trustee St. Andrew's Un. Ch. Halifax; Chrmn., Adv. Bd., Dalhousie Sch. Business Adm. 1978–86; former Dir.,

Candn. Inst. Child Health; Hon. Chrmn., Dalhousie Univ. Alumni Assoc. 1987–89; author Royal Comn. Reports Milk Industry Inquiry Comte. 1966–67, Price Structure of Gasoline & Diesel Oil in N.S. 1968; rec'd Queen's Silver Jubilee Medal 1977; invested as Officer of the Order of Canada, 1979; awarded Commemorative Medal for 125th Anniversary of Candn. Confederation 1992; received honorary LL.D Dalhousie, 1981; mem. Inst. C.A.'s N.S. (Pres. 1948); Candn. Inst. C.A.'s (Pres. 1974–75); Soc. Mang. Accts. N.S.; Candn. Tax Foundation (Gov. 1969–71); Freemason; Liberal; United Church; recreations: boating, fishing; Clubs: Halifax; Saraguay (Treas. 1972–75); Waegwaltic; Home: 6369 Coburg Rd., Apt. 1605, Halifax, N.S. B3H 4J7.

**RENOUF, Miriam Alleyne Priscilla,** B.A., M.A., Ph.D.; university professor; b. St. John's, Nfld. 8 Aug. 1953; d. Henry Thomas and Miriam Alleyne (Suckling) R.; e. Memorial Univ. of Newfoundland B.A. 1974, M.A. 1976; Univ. of Cambridge Ph.D. 1982; ASSOC. PROF., ARCHAEOLOGY UNIT, DEPT. OF ANTHROPOLOGY, MEMORIAL UNIV. OF NEWFOUNDLAND 1989– ; Asst. Prof., present univ. 1981–89; Dir., Port au Choix Archaeology Project 1984– ; Social Sciences Editor, 'Studies in Polar Research' series, Cambridge Univ. Press 1988–92; Bd. of Trustees, Candn. Museum of Civilization (Mem., Extve. Ctte.; Chair, Strategic Planning Ctte.) 1990– ; Editorial Bd., Journal of Nfld. Studies 1992– ; Canada Council Special M.A. Scholarship 1974–75; Rothermere Fellowship 1977–80; SSHRCC Doctoral Fellowship 1979–80; recipient, President's Award for Outstanding Rsch. (M.U.N.) 1992; author: 'Prehistoric Hunter-Fishers of Varangerfjord, Northeastern Norway' 1989; also author of a variety of academic papers; Office: Archaeology Unit, Memorial Univ. of Nfld., St. John's, Nfld. A1C 5S7.

**RENZONI, Louis S.,** M.Sc., D.Sc.; chemical engineer, b. Copper Cliff, Ont., 7 Feb. 1913; s. Secondo and Emma (Furlani) R.; e. St. Michael's Coll. Sch., Toronto, Ont. (Grad. 1931); Queen's Univ., B.Sc. 1935, M.Sc. 1936, D.Sc. 1969; m. Germaine, d. late Adelard DeGuire, 27 Dec. 1937; children: Carl L., Joanne R. Tomlinson, Peter D., Louis T.; Past Pres., Chem. Inst. of Canada, Chemist, G. F. Sterne & Sons, Brantford, Ontario, 1936; Research Chemist. Inco, Port Colborne, Ontario, and Superintendent of Research there, 1944; Mgr. of Process Research (Canada), Toronto, Ont. 1960; apptd. Asst. Vice Pres., Toronto, 1964; Vice-Pres., Inco 1967–77; consultant to Inco, 1977–81; Dir., McIntyre Research Fdn., Toronto; mem., Am. Inst. of Mining Metall. & Petroleum Engrs.; Am. Chem. Soc.; Candn. Inst. Mining & Metall.; Fellow, Chem. Inst. of Can. (Past Pres.); Past Chrmn., Cdn. Nat. Comm., Internat Union of Pure and applied Chemistry; Fellow, Am. Assn. For Advanc. Science; Publications: many papers and articles on Metallurgy; holds patents on Extractive Processes in Nickel Metall.; rec'd. Gold Medal Award, Extractive Metall. Div. of Am. Inst. of Mining, Metall. & Petroleum Engrs., 1960 and 1963; H. T. Airey Mem. Lecture Award, Metall. Div., Candn. Inst. of Mining & Metall.; R. S. Jane Mem. Award, Chem. Inst. of Can., 1968; Roman Catholic; Clubs: Engineers; Home: 44 Charles St. W., Apt. 4711, Toronto, Ont. M4Y 1R8.

**REUBER, Grant L.,** O.C., B.A., A.M., Ph.D., LL.D., F.R.S.C.; executive; b. Mildmay, Ont., 23 Nov. 1927; s. Jacob Daniel and Gertrude Catherine (Wahl) R.; e. Walkerton (Ont.) High Sch.; Univ. of Western Ont., B.A. (Hons. Econ.) 1950; Harvard Univ., A.M. (Econ.) 1954, Ph.D. (Econ.) 1957; research student Sidney Sussex Coll., Cambridge Univ., 1954–55; LL.D., Wilfrid Laurier Univ. 1983, Simon Fraser Univ. 1985, Univ. of Western Ont. 1985; m. Margaret Louise Julia, d. Clifford J. Summerhayes, Springfield, Ont., 21 Oct. 1951; children: Allison Rebecca, Barbara Susanne, Mary Margaret; CHRMN., CANADA DEPOSIT INSURANCE CORP. 1993– ; Chancellor Emeritus, Univ. of W. Ont.; Economic Adviser, Govt. of Lithuania 1991–92; with Bank of Canada Research Dept., 1950–52; Dept. Finance (Econ. & Internat. Relations Div.) Ottawa, 1955–57; Univ. of W. Ont., Asst. Prof. Econ. 1957–59, Assoc. Prof. 1959–62, Prof. and Head of Dept. 1963–69; Dean Faculty of Social Science 1969–74; Vice-Pres. (Acad.) and Provost, mem. Bd. of Gov. 1974–78; Sr. Vice Pres. and Chief Economist, Bank of Montreal 1978–79; Depy. Min. for Finance, Ottawa, 1979–80; Extve. Vice Pres., Bank of Montreal 1980–81; Depy. Chrmn. Bank of Montreal, 1981–83; Pres. and Chief Operating Offr. 1983–87; Depy. Chrmn., 1987–89; Lecturer, School of Business, Univ. of Chicago 1991–93; mem., Institute for Economic Research, Queen's Univ. 1961; staff mem., Royal Comm. on Banking and Finance, 1962–63; Consultant on Internat. Trade, Nat. Council of Applied Econ. Research, New Delhi, 1964; Consultant, OECD Paris 1969–72; Chrmn., Ont. Econ. Council, 1973–78; numerous contrib. in econ., univ. and banking publs.; Past Pres., Candn. Econ. Assn., 1967–68; Pres., Canadian Ditchley Foundation; Dir., Genstar Capital Corp.; Opinac Energy Ltd.; C.D. Howe Inst. (Chrmn. 1983–88); mem., Adv. Comte., School of Bus. Univ. of W. Ont.; Fellow, Royal Soc. of Can.; Officer of the Order of Canada; Anglican; recreation: tennis; Home: 90 Glen Edyth Dr., Toronto, Ont. M4V 2V9; Office: Suite 1200, 79 Wellington St. W., P.O. Box 156, Toronto Dominion Centre, Toronto, Ont. M5K 1H1.

**REUCASSEL, William Ross;** b. Toronto, Ont. 14 Jan. 1937; s. William and Dora (Kear) R.; e. William Burgess, Danforth Park and Selwyn St. Clair Sec. Schs., Toronto, Ont.; St. Andrew's Coll., Aurora, Ont.; Waterloo (Ont.) Coll.; Univ. of W. Ontario; m. Pamela Elizabeth; children: Kenneth William, Catherine Helen, John Ross; CHRMN. AND C.E.O. INTERNATIONAL GROUP; Chrmn. & C.E.O., IGI Boler Inc., U.S.A.; IGI Intnl. Waxes Canada; IGI Baychem Inc. U.S.A; Trustee, St. Andrew's Coll.; mem., Packaging Assn. Can.; Adhesives Manufacturers Assn. USA; Rubber Div., Am. Chem. Soc.; Young President's Organization, Inc.; The Board of Trade of Metro Toronto; The Conference Board of Canada; Dir., Nat. Community Bank of New Jersey; United Church; recreations: tennis, golf, swimming; Clubs: Donalda; Granite; Scarborough Golf & Country; Office: 50 Salome Dr., Agincourt, Ont. M1S 2A8.

**REVELL, Ernest John,** M.A., Ph.D.; educator; botanical artist; b. Bangalore, India 15 Apl. 1934; s. Alfred John and Edith Mary Peckham (Sheppard) R.; e. The Dragon Sch. Oxford, Eng. 1946; Ridley Coll. St. Catharines, Ont. 1952; Univ. of Toronto, Trinity Coll. B.A. 1956, Ph.D. 1962; St. John's Coll. Cambridge B.A. 1958, M.A. 1962; m. Ann Margaret d. John Stuart Morgan, Philadelphia, Pa. 6 June 1959; children: Alfred John, Bridget Margaret; PROF. OF NEAR EASTERN STUDIES, VICTORIA COLL., UNIV. OF TORONTO; illustrator 'And Some Brought Flowers' 1980; botanical art exhns. various galleries Ontario; The Hunt Inst., Pittsburg 1983; Fedn. of British Artists, The Mall Galleries, London (Eng.) 1984, 1987; Grenfell Silver Medal for Art Display, Royal Horticultural Soc. 1987; Fellow, Soc. of Botanical Artists 1986; author various books and articles biblical Hebrew grammar and hist. of biblical text; Fellow, Royal Soc. of Can. 1986; Fellow, Inst. for Advanced Study, The Hebrew Univ., Jerusalem 1983–84; Fellow, Inst. for Advanced Studies in the Humanities, Edinburgh Univ. 1986–87; mem. Am. Oriental Soc.; Assn. Jewish Studies; Soc. Old Testament Study; Brit. Sch. Archaeol. in Jerusalem; Royal Hortic. Soc.; Champlain Soc.; Anglican; recreation: gardening; Home: 151 Blythwood Rd., Toronto, Ont. M4N 1A5; Office: Dept. of N.E.S., Univ. of Toronto, Toronto, Ont. M5S 1A1.

**REVILLE, David Ralph,** b. Brantford, Ont. 19 Apr. 1943; s. Richard W. and Kathleen M. (Bolt) R.; m. Catharine d. E.O. and D.E. Jones 15 Dec. 1986; one d.: Jane; one grand-daughter: Marley; SPECIAL ADVISOR TO THE PREMIER OF ONTARIO 1990– ; Mem., Ont. Legislature for Riverdale Riding 1985–90; Owner, Alternative Plumbing 1972–84; Alderman, Ward 7, City of Toronto 1980–85; first el. M.P.P. for Riverdale 1985; re-el. 1987; Candn. Mental Health Assn. (Metro Br.) Public Distinction 1981, 1990; N.D.P. 1987–90; Caucus Whip; Chair, Neighbourhood Legal Serv. 1972–74; Winchester Community Counc. 1974–76; author: 'There come a knocking on my head' 1968 (poetry); 'Don't spyhole Me' in 'Shrink Resistant' 1988 (autobiog.); co-author: 'User Involvement in Mental Health Services in Canada' 1989; 'Do the Right Thing Right' 1990; Home: 71 Millbrook Cr., Toronto, Ont. M4K 1H5.

**REVUSKY, Samuel H.,** Ph.D.; educator; b. Tel-Aviv, Israel 2 Aug. 1933; s. Abraham Samuel and Hannah Faige (Starkstein) R.; e. Columbia Univ. A.B. 1956; Ind. Univ. Ph.D. 1961; m. Bow Tong d. Joe and Pek Har Lett 26 Dec. 1963; one s. Jonathan Abraham; PROF. OF PSYCHOL. MEML. UNIV. OF NFLD. 1971– ; Rsch. Assoc. US Veterans Adm. 1961–64; Rsch. Psychol. US Army 1964–68; Assoc. Prof. Northern Ill. Univ. 1968–71; author or co-author numerous profl. publs.; Fellow, Am. Psychol. Assn.; mem. Candn. Psychol. Assn.; Home: 102 Newtown Rd., St. John's, Nfld. A1B 3A5; Offfice: St. John's, Nfld. A1C 5S7.

**REYKDAL, Gordon J.;** business executive; b. Calgary, Alta. 9 Feb. 1957; s. Walter and Margaret G. (Johnson) R.; m. Carrie L. Withrow 22 Jan. 1977; children: Barret, Brandi; CHAIRMAN, PRESIDENT & CHIEF EXTVE. OFFR., RTO ENTERPRISES INC. 1991– ; Chairman, President & Chief Executive Officer, Rentown Enterprises Inc. 1987–91; Dir., Juvenille Diabetes; Home: 36 Castle Keep, Edmonton, Alta. T5X 5K6; Office: 15501 Stony Plain Rd., Edmonton, Alta. T5P 3Z1.

**REYNOLDS, David Edward Holden,** P.Eng., C.Eng., M.Sc., F.I.StructE.; engineer; b. Scunthorpe, Eng. 10 July 1935; s. Edward Alleyne and Gladys Fanny (Holden) R.; e. Worksop Coll.; N. Lindsey Tech. Coll., M.Struct.E., C.Eng. 1960; Cranfield Coll. of Aeronautics, M.Sc. 1962; Univ. of Calgary, dipl.Bus. Adm. 1969; m. Mary d. Sophie and William Seamer 26 Nov. 1960; children: Louise, Amanda; PRES., CANDN. WELDING BUREAU 1987– ; Struc. Design Engr., United Steels Struct. Co. 1954–64; Br. Welding & Struc. Engr., Dominion Bridge Co. 1964– ; Br. Ch. Engr. 1970; Mgr., Tech. Serv., Corp. Engr. Group 1971–80; Dir., Rsch. & Technol. AMCA Internat. (formerly Dominion Bridge) 1980–87; Mem., Welding Inst., U.K.; Can.; CSA, AWS, IIW and ISO Tech. Cttes.; APEO, OIQ, Inst. of Struc. Engrs.; Lincolnshire Ironmasters Prize 1964; Fellow, Inst. of Struc. Engrs. 1970– ; Vuchnich Award 1986; Mem., Soc. of Indus. Archeol.; recreations: music, theatre, indus. archeol., sailing; Home: 3925 Renfrew Cres., Mississauga, Ont. L5L 4J5; Office: 7250 West Credit Ave., Mississauga, Ont. L5N 5N1.

**REYNOLDS, Hon. John;** businessman; b. Toronto, Ont. 19 Jan. 1942; s. Thomas Douglas (dec'd) and Helen Alberta (Martindale) R.; m. Yvonne d. Elvina and Roger Heath 4 Dec. 1983; children: Paul, Mike, Rob, Kelly, Katie, Neil, Christopher; PARTNER, SCOTTSDALE CORPORATE MANAGEMENT GROUP (Arizona) and VICE CHRMN. HYGEIA PHARMACEUTICALS INC. (San Diego, CA); Min. of the Environment 1989–91; elected M.P. for Burnaby-Richmond-Delta 1972–74; re-elected 1974–77; elected M.L.A. for W. Vancouver-Howe Sound 1983, 1986; Social Credit Party leadership cand. 1986; Speaker of the Legislative Assembly of B.C. 1986–89; Past Chrmn., Bd. of Internal Economy, B.C. Legislature; Past Chrmn., Agric. Ctte.; Public Accts. Ctte.; Parl. Sec., Min. of Health; Pres., B.C. Br., Commonwealth Parl. Assn.; Vice Chrmn., Commonwealth Parliamentary Assn. Exec. Ctte.; Founding Mem. and Chrmn., Gordie Howe Found. for Disabled Athletes; Mem., Internat. Churchill Soc.; Bd. of Govs., 1994 Commonwealth Games; recreations: tennis, fishing; club: Hollyburn Country; Home: 1650 – 1185 West Georgia St., Vancouver, B.C. V6E 4E6; Office: Scottsdale Corp. Mgmnt. Group, 310 - 14555 N., Scottsdale, Arizona 85260.

**REYNOLDS, John Lawrence,** B.A.; writer; b. Hamilton, Ont. 5 Nov. 1939; s. John Henry and Mable Irene (Winegarden) R.; e. Westdale H.S., Hamilton; McMaster Univ., B.A. 1974; m. Judith Suzanne Soucie 1993; children: Jeffrey David, Courtney Lee; Creative Dir., R.T. Kelley Inc.; periodical feature writing in major mags. incl. Quest, Toronto Life, Candian Living; travel & sports photography; commercial & documentary film directing; radio announcing; instrumental music (toured Eur. with jazz band 1961); Cert. Advtg. Agency Practioner, Inst. of Candn. Advtg. 1964; Pres., Crime Writers of Canada 1993–94; author: 'The Man Who Murdered God' 1989 (winner, Arthur Ellis Award for Best First Crime Novel); 'And Leave Her Lay Dying' 1990 (novel); 'Whisper Death' 1991; 'Gypsy Sins' 1993; 'Solitary Dancer' 1994; Address: 873 Falcon Blvd., Burlington, Ont. L7T 3B5.

**REYNOLDS, Katherine Louise;** writer; b. Kinross, P.E.I. 9 Oct. 1919; d. John Donald and Katherine May (Bruce) MacLeod; e. Sir Andrew MacPhail Scholarship to Prince of Wales College, grad. 1938; m. the late Ralph s. Hattie and Edward R. 19 July 1941; children: Rennie, Carol, Gary, Jackie; Teacher, Valleyfield East Sch. P.E.I. 1938–39; Civil Servant, Dependent's Allowance Bd. Ottawa 1941; Researcher, CBC Radio 1960; Program Researcher, CJOH Ottawa 1961–62; Prodn. Asst. 1967–71; as wife of a Foreign Serv. Offr. lived in Czechoslovakia, Switzerland, Denmark, England, Ethiopia, Costa Rica; Edn. & Social Dir., Volunteer's Assn., Queensway-Carleton Hosp. 1989–92; Mem., Liberal Party of Canada; author: 'Agnes: The Biography of Lady Macdonald' 1979, four papers on the role of women in the Dept. of External Affairs 1980–82 & one scholarly article 1974; recreations: hiking, gardening; clubs: Country Club, Aylmer, Que. (Bd. of Dir. 1991–92); Home: 2302 – 1171 Ambleside Dr., Ottawa, Ont. K2B 8E1.

**REYNOLDS, Ralph Edward,** B.A.; diplomat; b. Sarnia, Ont., 27 March 1920; s. Joshua Edward and Hattie May (Hack) R.; e. Lisgar Coll. Inst. Ottawa 1939; Queen's Univ. B.A. 1949, post-grad. studies Hist. 1949–50 (Sir James Aikens Fellow in Canadian history); m. Katherine Louise (author 'Agnes: The Biography of

Lady MacDonald'); d. late John D. MacLeod, Kinross, P.E.I., 19 July 1941; children: Rennie, Carol (Mrs. Derek Godsmark), Gary, Jackie (Mrs. Jim Mercer); Tutor in Hist. Royal Mil. Coll. Kingston 1948–50; Jr. Research Offr. Nat. Research Council of Can. Ottawa 1950; joined Dept. of External Affairs 1950, served in Commonwealth, Econ., Consular and European Divs., Second Secy. Prague 1953, Advisor Candn. Perm. Del. to UN Geneva 1954, Second Secy. Copenhagen 1956 (First Secy. 1958), Econ. Div. Ottawa 1959, Counsellor London (Eng.) 1962, Chargé d'Affaires a.i. Warsaw 1967, Dir. Transport, Communications and Energy Div. 1967 (Ottawa), Ambassador to Ethiopia with concurrent accreditation to Madagascar and Somalia 1971, Ambassador to Costa Rica with concurrent accreditation to Honduras, Nicaragua, Panama and El Salvador 1975; Special Adv. to Extv. Dir., Immigration & Demographic Policy, C.E.I.C. 1978; Co-ordinator, Internat. Appointments, Dept. of External Affairs, 1980; retired March 1985; headed Candn. Dels. to Internat. Confs. 1969–74 (INTELSAT Conf. Washington, Container Conf. and Code of Conduct for Liners Confs. Geneva); served with RCAF 1940–45, Territorial Patrol Pilot, rank Flight Lt.; mem. Retired Heads of Mission Assoc. (RHOMA); Army of the Cussewago (Am. Civil War Buffs Group); Candn. Inst. of Internat. Affairs (CIIA); Anglican; recreations: riding, hiking, paddling, golf; Club: Country Club, Aylmer, Que.

**REYNOLDS, Richard G.,** B.Eng., M.B.A.; transportation executive; b. Sherbrooke, Que. 21 June 1946; s. Wesley and Alice (Turner) R.; e. McMaster Univ. B.Eng. 1968, M.B.A. 1973; m. Ursula d. Rudi and Lisa Wirth 10 Aug. 1968; children: Travis, Darcy; VICE-PRES., MARKETING, TRIMAC TRANSPORTATION SYSTEM 1990– ; Captain, Signal Corp, Candn. ARmed Forces 1968–71; Consultant, Trimac Consulting Serv. LTd. 1974–76; Branch Mgr. (Vanc.), Rentway Canada Ltd. (Trimac subs.) 1977–79; Vice-Pres., Western Reg. 1979–83; Mgr., Services, Bantrel Engineering (Trimac subs.) 1983–85; Region Mgr., Trimac Transp. System 1985–90; Pres., Northern Resource Trucking Ltd. (Trimac subs.) 1986– ; recreations: jogging, skiing, sailing, kayaking; clubs: 400; Home: R.R. #2, Cochrane, Alta. T0L 0W0; Office: P.O. Box 3500, Calgary, Alta. T2P 2P9.

**REYNOLDS, Ross B.,** B.S., M.B.A; entertainment executive; b. Philadelphia, Pa. 28 April 1939; s. Alexander Hardcastle and Gladys Campbell (Baker) R.; e. Yale Univ. B.S. 1961; Stanford Univ. M.B.A. 1966; m. Jane d. Edward and Mildred Carney 20 March 1967; children: Scott, Steven; PRESIDENT, MCA RECORDS CANADA 1983– ; Manager, Procter & Gamble 1961–64; consultant, Kates Peat Marwick 1966–68; Pres., GRT of Canada 1968–78; Extve. Vice-Pres., WEA Music of Canada 1978–89; Vice-Pres., Candn. Recording Industry Assn.; Past Dir., Candn. Assn. of Recording Arts & Sciences; recreations: tennis, squash, skiing; club: Toronto Lawn Tennis; Office: 2450 Victoria Park Ave., Willowdale, Ont. M2J 4A2.

**REYNOLDS, William Derek,** B.A.; freelance artist, photographer; b. Toronto, Ont. 19 Nov. 1947; s. Eric and Gladys Marion (Young) R.; e. Wilfrid Laurier Univ. B.A. 1974; m. Margaret d. Lyle and Bernice Fleming 17 May 1975; one-man exhn 'Recent Graphics' Wells Gallery Ottawa 1977; paintings and/or drawings various nat. and internat. corporate, private and univ. colls.; photographs published by 'The New York Times', 'Landmarks' mag. Toronto, 'Nature Canada', 'Reader's Digest', 'The Friends of Algonquin'; author 'Point Pelee' 1981; 'Algonquin' 1983; 'Wildflowers of Canada' 1987; 'Seasons of Light: Images of Ontario' 1988; 'Algonquin' 1993; mem. Fedn. Ont. Naturalists; recreations: golf, canoeing, snowshoeing; Address: P.O. Box 331, Kingston, Ont. K7L 4W2.

**RHIND, John A.,** M.Com., M.B.A.; life insurance executive; b. Toronto, Ont. 1 May 1920; s. John E. and Sybil (Gayford) R.; e. Univ. of Toronto Schs., 1933–38 (Matric.); Univ. of Toronto, B.Com. 1942 and M.Com. 1953; m. Katharine Elizabeth, d. G. E. D. Greene, Agincourt, Ont., 24 Sept. 1948; children: Susan, Ian, Alexander; CHRMN., MIDLAND WALWYN INC.; Dir., Confederation Life Insurance Co.; Economic Investment Trust Ltd.; Candn. Occidental Petroleum Ltd.; Confederation Trust Co.; Hon. Trustee, Royal Ontario Museum; Past chrmn. Toronto Western Hosp. and honorary mem. Bd. of Trustees; with Invest. Dept. of Nat. Life Assnce. Co. of Can., 1945–47; Econ. & Statistician, Mills, Spence & Co., Stockbkrs., Toronto, Ont. 1947–48; Treas., Nat. Life Assnce. Co. of Can. 1948–55; apptd. Vice-Pres., 1955; Gen. Mgr., 1957; Pres. 1966; Confederation Life, Pres. & C.E.O. 1976–81; Chrmn. & CEO, 1982–85; Chrmn. 1985–90; Chrmn. Extve. Ctte. 1990–93; served in 2nd World War; Comnd. in 1942; served in Italy and N.W. Europe with RCA, 11th Field Regt.; Past Pres., Candn. Life Ins. Assn.; Anglican; recreations: golf, fishing; tennis; Clubs: Toronto Golf; Badminton & Racquet; Osler Bluff Ski; University; York; Queens; Home: 38 Edgar Ave., Toronto, Ont. M4W 2A9; Office: One Mount Pleasant, Toronto, Ont. M4Y 2Y5.

**RHIND, John Christopher,** F.I.I.C., C.A.E.; insurance executive; b. Birmingham, Eng. 19 Feb. 1934; s. John James and Helen Florence (Walker) R.; e. Salesian Coll., Oxford, Eng.; York Univ. Mang. Educ. Program 1972–75; Certified Association Executive 1980; m. Rita D. d. John Evans, Broadstairs, Eng. 21 June 1958; children: Catherine, Michael John, Christopher James, Sarah Caroline; PRES. AND CEO. THE INSURANCE INST. OF CAN. 1974– ; joined Car & General Insurance Co. U.K. prior 1958; Pearl Assurance Co. Toronto 1958–59; Guardian Insurance Co. of Canada 1959–74; Asst. Gen. Mgr., The Ins. Inst. Can. 1975, Gen. Mgr. 1977, Pres. & C.E.O. 1978– ; served with Royal Army Service Corps 1952–54, rank Sgt.; mem. Adv. Council, Sch. of Contin. Studies, Univ. of Toronto; mem., Insurance Advisory Ctte., Univ. of Calgary; Past Chrmn., Business Adv. Comte. George Brown Coll.; Past Chrmn., Certification Council I.A.E.; author or co-author various book chapters, ins. articles; Gen. Mgr., Ins. Inst. Ont.; mem. Candn. Soc. of Assoc. Extves.; Soc. of Insurance Rsch.; Internat. Insurance Soc.; Albany Club; P. Conservative; R. Catholic; Club: Beverly Golf & Country, Copetown; recreations: golf, writing; Home: 1011 Red Pine Cres., Mississauga, Ont. L5H 4E4; Office: 18 King St. East, Toronto, Ont. M5C 1C4.

**RHODES, Andrew James,** M.D., F.R.C.P.(C). F.R.C.P. (Edin.), F.F.P.H.M., F.R.S.C.; medical microbiologist; b. Inverness, Scotland, 19 Sept. 1911; s. William Thomas and Maud (Innes) R.; e. Wellington Coll., Berkshire, Eng., 1924–29; Univ. of Edinburgh (1929–34) M.B., Ch.B. (Hons.), M.D. 1941, F.R.C.P. (Edin.) 1941; Chrmn. Rabies Adv. Comte., Ont. Ministry of Nat. Resources, 1979–87; Med. Dir., Public Health Labs., Ont., Min. of Health, Toronto, 1970–76; Lecturer in Bacteriology, University of Edinburgh, 1934–41; Pathologist Roy. Infirmary, Shrewsbury, England, 1941–45; Lecturer in Bacteriology, London (England) School of Hygiene and Tropical Medicine, 1945–47; Prof. Emeritus, Dep't. of Microbiology, Univ. of Toronto, 1977; Research Assoc., Connaught Medical Research Labs., Univ. of Toronto, 1947–53; Dir., Sch. of Hygiene, Univ. of Toronto and Head, Dept. Microbiol. there 1956–70; Head, Grad. Dept. Hygiene 1956–70; Prof., Univ. of Toronto since 1947; Consultant in Virology, The Hosp. for Sick Children, Toronto, since 1951 (Dir., The Research Inst., 1953–56); Anglican; Home: 79 Rochester Ave., Toronto, Ont. M4N 1N7.

**RIBENBOIM, Paulo,** B.Sc., Ph.D., F.R.S.C.; educator; b. Recife, Brazil 13 March 1928; s. Moysés and Anna (Drechsler) R.; e. Colegio Anglo Americano and Colegio Andrews, Rio de Janeiro, 1945; Univ. do Brasil, B.Sc. 1948; Univ. de São Paulo, Ph.D. 1957; m. Huguette, d. Henri and Charlotte Demangelle, 19 Dec. 1951; two s.: Serge Charles, Eric Leonard; PROF. OF MATHEMATICS, QUEEN'S UNIV.; visiting lectr. univs. in Can., U.S.A., S.Am., Mexico, Europe, Africa and Japan; author, 'Théorie des Groupes Ordonnés,' 1963' 'Functions, Limits and Continuity,' 1964; 'Théorie des Valuations' 1964; 'Rings and Modules,' 1969; 'Algebraic Numbers,' 1972; 'L'Arithmétique des Corps,' 1972; '13 Lectures on Fermat's Last Theorem,' 1979; 'The Book of Prime Number Records,' 1988; 'The Little Book of Big Primes,' 1991; 'Catalan's Conjecture' 1994; also over 120 research papers and articles; Ed., 'Queen's Papers in Pure and Applied Mathematics'; 'Mathematical Reports of the Acad. of Sciences, Roy. Soc. of Can.'; Assoc. Ed., 'Expositiones Mathematicae' from Mannheim; Assoc. Ed. 'Portugaliae Mathematica'; Fulbright Fellow, Univ. Illinois, Urbana, IL 1959–62; rec'd. hon. degree from Univ. de Caen, France 1979; Prize for Excellence in Research, Queen's Univ., 1983; former Assoc. Ed., Candn. Journal of Mathematics; mem. Am. Math. Soc.; Candn. Math. Soc.; Soc. Mathématique de France; Soc. Mathématique Suisse; Soc. Brasileira Mat.; Home: 4 Watts, Cres., Kingston, Ont. K7M 2P3; Office: Kingston, Ont. K7L 3N6.

**RIBNER, Herbert Spencer,** M.S., Ph.D., F.R.S.C. (1976); physicist; b. Seattle, Wash., 9 Apr. 1913; s. Herman Joseph and Rose Esther (Goldberg) R.; e. Cal. Inst. Tech., B.S. 1935; Wash. Univ., St. Louis, M.S. 1937, Ph.D. 1939; m. Lelia Carolyn, d. Harvey R. Byrd, 29 Oct. 1949; children: Carol, David; DISTINGUISHED RESEARCH ASSOCIATE, N.A.S.A. LANGLEY RESEARCH CENTRE 1978– and PROF. EMERITUS, INST. FOR AEROSPACE STUDIES, UNIV. OF TORONTO 1986– ; Prof., Inst. for Aerospace Studies, Univ. of Toronto 1959–86; with Brown Geophysical Co., Houston, 1939–40; Langley Lab N.A.C.A., 1940–49; Lewis Flight Propulsion Lab., Cleveland, N.A.C.A., Division Consultant, later Section Head, 1949–54; Research Assoc., later Asst. and Assoc. Prof. of Aerophysics, Inst. of Aerophysics, Univ. of Toronto, 1955–59; Consultant to De Havilland Aircraft of Canada Ltd., Min. Transport, General Electric & others; Visiting Prof., Department of Aeronautics, University of Southampton, 1960–61; Staff Scientist, NASA Langley Res. Ctr. 1975–76; Publications: over 100 scient. papers and articles; Chrmn. Sonic Boom Panel, Internat. Civil Aviation Organ. 1969–70; mem. Candn. Acoustical Assn. (Chrmn. 1966–68); Fellow, Acoustical Soc. Am. (former mem., Noise Comte., Fellow Comte.); Am. Physical Soc.; Candn. Aero. & Space Inst. (Chrmn. Astronautics Sec. 1958–59; Turnbull Lectr. 1968); Am. Institute Aero. & Astronautics (mem., Aero-Acoustics Comte. 1970–73, Aero-Acoustics Award 1976, Dryden Lecture, 1981); Adv. Comte. Hearing, Bioacoustics & Biomechanics, U.S. Nat. Acad. Sciences, 1972–74; Home: 60 Inverlochy Blvd., Apt. 608, Thornhill, Ont. L3T 4T7.

**RICARD, André,** B.Péd., L.ès.L.; auteur; né. Sainte-Anne-de-Beaupré 18 oct. 1938; f. Côme and Marie (Gariépy) R.; é. Univ. Laval B.Péd. 1959, L.ès.L. 1962; Conservatoire d'Art dramatique du Qué. 1965; ép. Mary Eleanor f. J. Wilfrid et Eleanor C. (Metzler) Brennan 18 mai 1972; auteur de huit pièces de théâtre, toutes rep. et publiées, de plusieurs pièces radiophoniques et télévisuelles, de deux suites poétiques, et de nouvelles, André Ricard a également signé trois traductions de dramaturges anglais et américains et collaboré à des long métrages de fiction; prix Court métrage de la comm. radiophonique des prog. de langue française 1978; prix de création dramatique, Place des Arts (Montréal) 1988; Cofond. et dir. artistique, Théâtre de l'Estoc 1957–68; A contribué, comme scripteur ou réalisateur à quelques séries radiophoiques et, comme concepteur, scénariste et réalisateur à des films, documentaires destinés à Radio-Canada; mem., SARDEC, CEAD, AQAD, UNEQ, P.E.N. internat.; Comité de dir. de la Rencontre québécoise internat. des écrivains 1986–90; président du Centre des Auteurs dramatiques; auteur: 'La Vie exemplaire d'Alcide 1$^{er}$ le pharamineux et de sa proche descendance' 1973, 'La Gloire des filles à Magloire' 1975, 'Le Casino voleur' 1978, 'La Longue Marche dans les avents' 1984, 'Le Tir à blanc' 1983, 'Le Déversoir des larmes' 1988; toutes oeuvres pour le théâtre et publiées à Montréal; 'L'Immortelle Entrecôte' in '20 ans' 1986; 'Les Baigneurs de Tadoussac' 1993 (poésie); résidence: 841, ave. de Bienville, Québec, Qué. G1S 3B9.

**RICCI, Nino Pio,** M.A.; writer; b. Leamington, Ont. 23 Aug. 1959; s. Virginio and Amelia (Ingratta) R.; e. York Univ. B.A. 1981; Concordia Univ. M.A. 1987; Univ. of Florence; teacher Eng. lang. and lit. secondary sch. Ogun State, Nigeria 1981–83; teacher creative writing and Candn. lit. Concordia Univ. Montreal 1987–88; author: 'Lives of the Saints' novel 1990; 'In a Glass House' novel 1993; recipient, F.G. Bressani Prize for Fiction 1990; Gov. General's Award for Fiction 1990; W.H. Smith/Books in Canada First Novel Award 1990; Short List, QSPELL Award for Fiction 1990; Betty Trask Award 1991; Winifred Holtby Prize for Best Regional Novel 1991; Short List, Los Angeles Book Prize 1991; Dir. Candn. Centre Internat. PEN 1990–94; mem. Amnesty Internat.

**RICE, Marnie E.,** B.A., M.A., Ph.D., C.Psych.; research psychologist; b. Hamilton, Ont. 11 Feb. 1948; d. David Jack and Marion Ruth (Cook) McKee; e. Aldershot H.S.; Univ. of Western Ont.; McMaster Univ. B.A. (Hons.) 1970; Univ. of Toronto M.A. 1971; York Univ. Ph.D. 1975; m. Gregory Allan s. Frank and Irene R. 15 Oct. 1971; children: Andrea Kathryn, Austin David; Director of Research, Penetanguishene Mental Health Centre 1988– ; Assoc. Prof. of Psychology (Adjunct) Queen's Univ. 1991– ; Assoc. Prof. of Psychiatry (part-time) McMaster Univ. 1992– ; Clinical Psychologist, Oak Ridge Div., Mental Health Ctr., Penetanguishene 1975–80; Research Psychologist, Rsch. Dept. Penetanguishene 1980–88; Acting Dir. of Research 1984–86; research interests incl. assessment & treatment of sex offenders, arsonists, & other dangerous psych. patients; the prediction of dangerousness; & other issues related to psych. patients, esp. mentally disordered offenders; Ed. Bd., 'Journal of Interpersonal Violence'; Ontario Scholar 1966; Univ. of W. Ont. Admission Scholarship 1966–67; Dean's Hon. List, UWO 1967; McMaster Univ. 1968–70; 1970 Woodrow Wilson Alternate; Nat. Rsch. Council Scholarship 1970–71; Canada Council Doct.

Fellowship 1972–75; author of over 50 articles in schol. journals; co-author: 'Violence in Institutions: Understanding, prevention and control' 1989; recreations: swimming, jogging, photography; Home: 675 Hugel Ave., Midland, Ont. L4R 4N6; Office: Box 5000, Penetanguishene, Ont. L0K 1P0.

**RICE, Hon. Robert C.,** B.A., B.C.L.; judge; b. St. Jacques, N.B. 3 June 1930; s. Edward F. and Maud (Berube) R.; e. St Thomas Coll. B.A. 1952; Univ. of N.B., B.C.L. 1956; m. Colette d. Roland and Lina Michaud 16 July 1983; children; Diane, Charles, Patty, James, Louise (by previous marriage); JUDGE, COURT OF APPEAL, N.B. 1985– ; called to Bar of N.B. 1957; cr. Q.C. 1972; private law practice 1957–85; Pres./Founder Mont Farlagne Ski Centre Edmundston; Pub. Intervenor, N.B. Tel Rate Applications 1976–85; mem council, Madawaska Barristers' Soc. 1965–79, Pres. 1975–76; Vice Pres., Founder, N.B. Barristers' Soc. 1977–79, Pres. 1979–81; Pres. N.B. Trial Lawyers' Assn. 1984–85; recreations: skiing, tennis; Home: 34 Foley Court, Fredericton, N.B. E3B 2R8; Office: P.O. Box 6000, Fredericton, N.B. E3B 5H1.

**RICH, Colwyn George;** executive; b. Cardiff, Wales 12 Nov. 1927; s. Robert George Rich; e. Manchester Coll. of Technol. Assoc. 1950; m. Jean d. Charles McRae; children: Peter John, Jane Elizabeth, David Michael; PRES. AND DIR.: CHAMPLAIN INDUSTRIES LIMITED; RICHOLCO HOLDINGS INC.; Chrmn. & Dir.: Champlain Industries Inc., U.S.A.; Champlain Protex Ltd. U.K.; Dir., Champlain Industries Educational Foundation; Grand Valley Conservation Foundation; Trustee, The Nature Conservancy of Canada; came to Can. 1967; Office: 7200 West Credit Ave., Mississauga, Ont.

**RICHARD, Gilles,** M.Sc.; administrator; b. Québec, Qué. 5 Sept. 1934; s. Maurice and Gabrielle (Rémillard) R.; e. Laval Univ., M.Sc. 1959; m. Andrée d. Roland and Anita Beaudin 5 Sept. 1959; children: Philippe, Nathalie; PRES., RICHARD & CIE LTÉE. 1960– ; Carnaval de Qué. 1969– ; Office du Tour. & Congres du Qué. Métro 1974–75; Soc. Inter-port de Qué. 1974–79; C. de C. & de l'Indus. du Qué. Métro 1976; Incorp. of Les Immeubles Lavoisier 1977; Incorp. of Plani Design Inc. 1980; Incorp. of Gilco Investments 1991; Dir., Sidbec Dosco; Home: 520 Laurier Ave., Québec, Qué. G1R 2L2; Office: 2150 Lavoisier, Ste-Foy, Qué. G1N 4B1.

**RICHARD, Hon. Guy A.,** B.A., B.C.L., LL.D.; judge; b. Sainte-Anne de Kent, N.B. 5 June 1932; s. André Richard and Rose (Caissie) R.; e. High Sch. Saint Joseph Coll. 1946; Saint Joseph Coll. (now Univ. of Moncton) B.A. 1953; Univ. of N.B., B.C.L. 1958; Univ. of Moncton LL.D. 1987; m. Germaine d. Edmour and Céline (Turbide) Thériault 27 Dec. 1956; children: André, Jolène, Denis, Martine, Carole; CHIEF JUSTICE, COURT OF QUEEN'S BENCH, N.B. 1982– ; law practice Bouctouche, N.B. 1958–71; nominated to Co. Court of N.B. 1971; Chrmn. Judges Assn. for Dist. & Co. Courts Atlantic Provs. 1973–76; nominated to Supreme Court of N.B. 1976 and to Court of Appeal N.B. 1978; Vice Chrmn. Candn. Judicial Council 1988; Dir. Stella-Maris Hosp. 1963–71; Dir. and Chrmn. George-Dumont Hosp. 1967–70; mem. and Chrmn. Univ. Moncton Devel. Ctte. 1975–76; Dir. Theatre N.B. 1980–84; Nat. Theatre Sch. Can. 1982–85; Chrmn. and Dir. Kent Homes Ltd., Kent Investments Ltd. and Dir. Laurentide Chemicals, Atlantic Div. Ltd. 1963–71; Sec.-Treas. Kent & Westmorland Lib. Assn. 1958–71; recreation: tennis; Home: 6 – 211 Bromley Ave., Moncton, N.B. E1C 5V5; Office: 770 Main St., P.O. Box 5001, Moncton, N.B. E1C 8R3.

**RICHARD, The Hon. Mr. Justice J. Edward,** B.Sc., LL.B.; supreme court judge; b. Charlottetown, P.E.I. 14 Aug. 1946; s. John N. and Mary O. (Cormier) R.; e. St. Dunstan's Univ., B.Sc. 1967; Dalhousie Law Sch., LL.B. 1973; m. Mary Lou d. Ben and Ruth Callaghan 27 May 1967; children: Chantal, James, Douglas; JUDGE, SUPREME COURT OF THE NORTHWEST TERRITORIES 1988– ; Offr., Candn. Armed Forces 1963–70; law practice, Yellowknife, N.W.T. 1973–88; Q.C. 1986; Former Pres., Law Soc. of N.W.T.; N.W.T. Br., Candn. Bar Assn.; Arctic Winter Games Corp.; M.L.A., N.W.T. 1984–88; Home: 5701 – 51A Ave., Yellowknife, N.W.T. X1A 1G6; Office: Box 188, Yellowknife, N.W.T. X1A 2N2.

**RICHARD, The Hon. Jean,** B.A., LL.L.; superior court judge; b. 8 Dec. 1935; s. Alexandre and Jeanne (Pouliot) R.; e. Univ. Laval, B.A. 1957; Univ. de Sherbrooke, LL.L. 1961; Univ. of London, postgrad. acad. dipl. in law 1967; children: Marie-Eve, Jean-Sébastien; JUDGE, SUPERIOR COURT OF QUÉBEC 1981– ; admitted to Qué. Bar 1961; Asst. Sec. to Cabinet, Ottawa 1970–71; Asst. Gen. Sec. to Cabinet, Québec 1973–75; Office: 300 Jean Lesage Blvd., #R-352, Québec, Qué. G1K 8K6.

**RICHARD, Jean L.,** B.Eng., M.B.A.; executive; e. Coll. Militaire Royal de St-Jean; Royal Mil. Coll. of Can. B.Eng. (Civil) 1962; Univ. of W. Ont. M.B.A. 1969; SR. VICE PRES., ASSET MANAGEMENT, TRIZEC PROPERTIES LIMITED; served as offr. RCN; Canada Cement Co. Ltd. Montreal and Toronto 1965–67; Research & Econ. Dept. Greenshields Inc. Montreal 1969–70, Institutional Sales London, Eng. 1970–73, Corporate & Project Financing Montreal 1973–77, Corporate Finance Partner Alta. 1977–80; Bank of Montreal, Sr. Vice-Pres., Corporate & Government Banking, Calgary, Montreal and Toronto 1980–86; mem., Assn. Prof. Engrs. Prov. Ont.; Dir., Royal Victoria Hosp., Montreal; Dir., Urban Development Institute of Canada (U.D.I.); Pres., Quebec Urban Development Institute; Clubs: The Mount-Royal, The Royal Montreal Golf, Montreal; Office: 5 Place Ville Marie #1615, Montreal, Que. H3B 4M9.

**RICHARD, Hon. Kenneth Peter,** B. Com., LL.B.; judge; b. Dartmouth, N.S. 31 Jan. 1932; s. Harry Bernard and Jean Grace (Tobin) R.; e. St. Thomas Aquinas Sch. and Queen Elizabeth High Sch. Halifax 1948; St. Francis Xavier Univ. B.Com. 1952; Dalhousie Univ. LL.B. 1967; m. Elizabeth Bernadette d. David Fraser Sears 15 Aug. 1953; children: Debra Marie, Kenneth Peter, Stephen David, Gary Andrew, Michael Tobin; JUDGE, TRIAL DIV., SUPREME COURT OF N.S. 1978– ; called to Bar of N.S. 1967; part-time lectr. in Business Law, St. Francis Xavier Univ. 1970–76; Seminar Leader, Candn. Hosp. Assn. 1975–77; Vice Chrmn. N.S. Environmental Control Council 1973–76; Dir. Atlantic Trust Co. 1974–76; mem. Adv. Bd. Montreal Trust Co. 1970–74; Ald. City of Halifax 1963–66; Lib. Cand. Halifax Chebucto prov. g.e. 1967; Past Pres., Atlantic Provs. Chamber Comm.; St. Martha's Hosp. Antigonish; mem. Council, N.S. Barristers Soc. 1969, Candn. Bar Assn. 1972–74; mem. Candn. Judges Conf.; Am. Assn. Law & Medicine; R. Catholic; recreations: running, boating, fishing; Home: 110 Hazelholme Dr., Halifax, N.S. B3M 1N5; Office: (P.O. Box 2314) The Law Courts, Halifax, N.S. B3J 1S7.

**RICHARD, Lili,** B.F.A.; artist; b. St. Lazare, Cte. Bellechase, Que. 10 Nov. 1938; d. Napoléon and Rose (Dumas) Bilodeau; e. Univ. of Laval, medical technician degree 1958; Univ. of Que. in Montreal B.F.A. 1983; m. Claude s. Henriette and Edouard R. 13 Oct. 1962; children: Julie, Simon, Rémi; exhibitions incl.: Galerie L'autre Equivoque Ottawa 1986, '89; Galerie 22 Mars Montreal 1986; 'Femmes Forces' Mus. of Que. 1987; Galerie Madeleine Lacerte Que. City 1988, '91; Galerie Daniel Montreal 1988, '90; Biennale de dessin, de l'estampe et du papier Alma, Que. 1989; 'Entrée libre à l'art contemporain' (internat. art fair) 1989; Galerie Lavalin Montreal 1989; Hotel de Ville de 4e arrondisement Paris, France 1990; 'Dans dix ans l'an 2000' Montreal 1990; Galeria Op-era Geneva, Switz. 1991; Galerie, London Montréal 1992; 1st prize, Symposium, Baie St. Paul 1987; collections incl.: Loto-Qué.; SNC Inc.; Prov. Que. Contemporary Art Museum Mtl.; Royal Bank of Can.; Musée du Qué.; Musée Marsil St-Lambert; United Westburne; Bell Canada; Min. of Revenue of Qué.; Corp. of the City of Ottawa; Teleglobe Canada; Art Bank of Can.; Min. of Tourism, Fish & Game of Qué.; Mem., Conseil de la peinture du Qué.; Home: 3545 Berne, Brossard, Qué. J4Z 2P1; Office: 10 Ontario St. W., #705, Montréal, Qué.

**RICHARDS, Darrell,** B.Sc.; transport consultant; b. Weyburn, Sask. 19 Jan. 1954; s. James Ewan and Marjorie Doris (Wilke) R.; e. Univ. of Sask. B.Sc. 1976; m. Jennifer d. Craig and Margaret McKay 17 May 1986; children: Simon, Lauren; RESEARCH DIR., TRANSPORT CONCEPTS 1991– ; Rsch. Asst. H. of C. 1976–83; Financial Offr. La Pause Velo Ltée 1983–90; Pres., Transport 2000 1989–90; Eastern Vice Pres. 1990–91; Home: 201 Somerset St. E., Ottawa, Ont. K1N 6V1.

**RICHARDS, Earle Gordon,** B.A., C.A.; financial planner; b. Toronto, Ont. 12 Jan. 1949; s. Earle Blake and Anne Bowes (Taylor) R.; e. Univ. of West. Ont. B.A. (Hons.) 1972; EXECUTIVE VICE-PRESIDENT, T.E. FINANCIAL CONSULTANTS 1991– ; obtained C.A. Clarkson Gordon 1974; Senior Tax Manager 1981; joined T.E. Financial Consultants Ltd. 1985; shareholder & Dir. 1986; Office: 141 Adelaide St. W., Toronto, Ont. M5H 3L5.

**RICHARDS, Elizabeth Anne,** B.Sc., M.S., PHEc.; university professor; b. Edmonton, Alta. 23 Feb. 1945; s. Allin Williams and Elizabeth Annie (Cogswell) Frost; e. Univ. of Alberta B.Sc. 1966; Utah State Univ. M.S. 1968; m. 15 Aug. 1968; children: William Nairn, David Cogswell, John Welbourne; PROF., FAC. OF HOME ECONOMICS, UNIV. OF ALBERTA 1987– ; Lecturer, Univ. of Alta. 1968–70; Asst. Prof. 1970–78; Assoc. Prof. 1978–87; Acting Assoc. Dean 1982–83; Honorary Visiting Scholar, Manchester Inst. of Sci. & Tech. 1972; Visiting Textile Conservator, Provincial Mus. of Alta. 1982; Consultnt, KCR Textile Consultants Ltd. 1971– ; Interim Chair, Environ. Choice Prog., Candn. Dept. of the Environ. 1992–93 (Bd. Mem. 1992– ); Dir., KCR Textile Consultants Ltd.; Mary A. Clark Memorial Scholarship, Candn. Home Economics Assn. 1993–94; Life Mem., Candn. Home Econ. Assn.; Am. Assn. of Textile Chem. & Colorists; Mem., Internat. Geosystethics Soc.; Am. Quilt Study Group; Candn. Quilt Study Group; Candn. Quilters Assn.; author: 'Consumer Textile Laboratory Manual' 1991; co-author: 'Geotextile and Geomembrane International Information Source' 1984; recreations: skiing, cycling, quilting; Home: 9031 Saskatchewan Dr., Edmonton, Alta.; Office: Office: 301 Printing Services Bldg., Edmonton, Alta. T6G 2N1.

**RICHARDS, George R.,** B.S.F.; business executive; b. Golden, B.C. 1 June 1932; s. George R. and Johanna P. (Van Hoepen) R.; e. Univ. of B.C. B.S.F. 1959; m. Selma-Jo d. Tom and Lil Dixon 24 April 1957; children: Christian, Timothy; EXECUTIVE VICE-PRES., SOLID WOOD, B.C., ALTA. & ONT., WELDWOOD OF CANADA LTD.; Operations Forester, Celgar 1959–63; Operation Forester then Chief Forester, P. George Northwood 1964–69 Gen. Mgr., Vice-Pres. Forestry & Mfg. Lumber, Peace Wood Products 1970–73; Gen. Mgr. of 2 Operations, Weldwood of Canada then Vice-Pres. of Interior Operations 1974 until assuming present position; Dir., Weldwood of Canada; Dir. & Pres., Burns Lake Specialty Wood; Babine & Houston Forest Products; Dir., Canwel (distbn. co. for Canfor & Weldwood); Forintek; Council of Forest Industries (Past Chair); Mem., Variety Club; Science World; Registered Profl. Foresters; Candn. Inst. of Foresters; recreations: gardening, fishing, boating; clubs: Terminal City, Royal Vancouver Yacht; Home: 4680 Piccadilly N., Vancouver, B.C. V7N 1E2; Office: P.O. Box 2179, Vancouver, B.C. V6B 3V8.

**RICHARDS, Henry (Harry) Hamilton,** F.I.I.C.; insurance executive; b. Kingston, Jamaica 4 Feb. 1941; s. Edward Karl and Joyce (Robertson) R.; e. Wolmers H.S. (Kingston Jamaica) 1959; m. Beverly Grace d. Neil and Jenny Cameron 29 Dec. 1960; children: Janet Travor, Scott; EXECUTIVE VICE-PRES., MARSH & MCLENNAN LTD. 1992– ; joined Marsh & McLennan Limited 1960; held various positions within company; Head, Vancouver Office 1983–92; Fellow, Insur. Inst. of Can. (F.I.I.C.); Pres., Neurological Centre Vancouver; recreations: fishing; clubs: Vancouver, Terminal City; Home: 2845 West 31st Ave., Vancouver, B.C. V6L 2A3; Office: 1300, 510 Burrard St., Vancouver, B.C. V6C 3J2.

**RICHARDS, James Paul,** B.A.Sc., M.B.A.; executive; b. Toronto, Ont. 15 July 1934; s. late James Stanley and Margaret Ellen (Newall) R.; e. Forest Hill Coll. Inst. 1952; Univ. of Toronto B.A.Sc. (Indust. Engn.) 1956, M.B.A. 1962; m. Marjorie Joyce Garson, Ph.D. June 1978; children: James Timothy, Jennia Penelope, Jordan Chandler, Sara Gwyn Fairly, Matthew Thomas Beam; PRESIDENT, GLASS PACK LTD. 1969– ; Pres., Sci-Can Scientific Ltd. 1972– ; Pres., Proscience Inc. 1992– ; Foreign Service Offr. and Trade Commr. Govt. Can. 1962–66, Rio de Janeiro 1963–66; Pres., Johns Scientific Inc. 1979–92; Pres., Tay River Stove Co. Ltd. 1981–91; Dir, Ont. Worker's Compensation Bd. 1987–91; Pres., Candn. Red Cross (Ont. Div.) 1980–81 (Vice Pres. 1976–80); Trustee, United Way of Metro. Toronto 1983–91; Trustee, Metro. Toronto Community Found. 1989– ; mem. Assn. Prof. Engrs. Prov. Ont.; Art Gallery of Ont.; recreations; hiking, skiing, tennis, music, theatre; Clubs: Granite; Craigleith Ski; Home: 1 Heathbridge Park Dr., Toronto, Ont. M4G 2Y6; Office: 175 Hanson St., Toronto, Ont. M4C 1A7.

**RICHARDS, John Guyon,** Ph.D.; university professor; b. Exeter, Devon, England 19 Aug. 1944; s. Arthur Guyon and Elizabeth Mary (Mitchell) R.; e. Univ. of Sask., B.A. 1964; Cambridge Univ., B.A. 1966; Washington Univ., Ph.D. 1982; m. Christiane d. Raoul and Marcelle Marcesse 21 Sept. 1966; children: Anna-Catherine; PROF., FAC. OF BUSINESS, SIMON FRASER UNIV. 1978– ; Vis. Asst. Prof., Univ. of Sask. 1970–71; Legis. Sec., Min. of Health & mem. of govt. (NDP) caucus, Prov. of Sask. 1971–73; independent mem. 1973–75; MLA 1971–75; co-author: 'Prairie Capitalism' 1979; 'Delivering the Goods' 1992; co-editor: 'Canada, What's Left?' 1986, 'Resource Rents and Public Policy in Western Canada' 1987; 'Social Democracy Without Illusions' 1991; 'Inroads' (a journal of opinion); recreations: cycling, Russian novels; Home: 1 - 1570 East 22nd Ave., Vancouver, B.C. V5N 2P1; Office: Burnaby, B.C. V5A 1S6.

**RICHARDS, Larry Wayne,** M.Arch.; architect, critic and educator; b. Marion, Ind. 24 Nov. 1944; s. Lowell Byron and Virginia June (Wright) R.; e. Miami Univ. B.Arch. 1967; Yale Univ. M.Arch. 1975; PROF. OF ARCH., UNIV. OF WATERLOO 1988– ; Assoc. Prof. and Dir. Sch. of Arch. 1982–87; joined the Arch.'s Collaborative, Cambridge, Mass. 1967; following 9 months study and work in Florence, Italy became Asst. Prof. in Arch., Ball State Univ., Muncie, Ind. 1972; Asst. Prof. of Arch. Tech. Univ. of N.S., Halifax 1975–80, estbd. N.S. Tech's Campus Design Studio, apptd. Campus Design Coordinator; Mem., NETWORKS LTD. Halifax; Asst. Prof., Univ. of Toronto 1980–81; exhns. of work incl. Power Plant Toronto, SESC Fabrica de Pompeia Sao Paulo, Cooper-Hewitt Museum New York, Akademie der Kunste West Berlin; author 'Larry Richards: Works 1977–80' 1980; Founding mem., Candn. Arch. Mag. Soc. and 'Trace'; mem., ed. bd. ACSA 'Journal of Arch. Ed.' 1985–87; apptd. to Fine Arts Adjudication Ctte. S.S.H.R.C.C. 1985–87; Guest Curator and Editor, Candn. Centre for Architecture 1987–89, editor 'CCA: Building and Gardens' 1989; Depy. Commissioner for Canada and CCA for 1991 Venice Architecture Biennale; co-editor, 'Toronto Places' 1992; Arch. Heritage Advisor to Trent Univ. 1992– ; articles various mags.; mem./assoc.: Am. Inst. Archs.; Royal Arch. Inst. Can.; Ont. Assoc. Arch.; Home and Studio: 501, 2645 Bloor St. W., Etobicoke, Ont. M8X 1A3; Office: Univ. of Waterloo, Waterloo, Ont. N2L 3G1.

**RICHARDS, Leonard,** M.A., M.S.W., Phil.M., Ph.D.; educator; social worker; consultant; b. Aberdare, Wales 2 Nov. 1921; s. Abraham and Martha (Price) R.; e. King's Coll. Cambridge; Univ. of London, Sch. of Econ. & Pol. Science, Sch. of Oriental & African Studies; McGill Univ.; Univ. of Toronto; m. Geneviève d. Auguste and Juliette Ceppe Jan. 1949; children: Alan, Christine; Professor Emeritus of Social Work 1985– ; Consultant, Social Administration; Served with Royal Army Med. Corps 1936–42; Indian Army Frontier Force Regt. and Frontier Corps 1942–47; Adm. Offr. and Magistrate Overseas Civil Service 1948–59; social worker and educator 1959–84; Prof. and Dean of Faculty of Social Work, Univ. of Calgary (ret. 1984); Home: 2, 7001 Eden Drive, Sardis, B.C. V2R 1E7.

**RICHARDS, The Honourable Ronald J.,** Q.C., B.A., B.Ed., LL.B.; judge; b. Montreal, Que. 16 Sept. 1946; s. Harry H. and Patricia M. (Crawford) R.; e. Acadia Univ. B.A. 1968, B.Ed. 1969; Univ. of N.B., LL.B. 1972; m. Bonnie d. Marie and Ronald Newhook 16 July 1977; two s.: Michael, Robert; JUDGE, ONTARIO COURT OF JUSTICE, PROVINCIAL DIVISION 1992– ; Crown Attorney, Halifax, N.S. 1974–75; Dir., Student Affairs (Dean of Students), Mt. Allison Univ. 1975–78; Sr. Crown Attorney, Gander 1978–80; St. John's 1980–83; Assoc. Dep. Attorney Gen. & Dir. of Public Prosecutions 1983–85; Dep. Min. of Justice & Dep. Attorney Gen., Govt. of Nfld. & Labrador 1985–90; Dir. of Criminal Law Policy, Ministry of Attorney General of Ont. 1990–92; Mem., Candn. Bar Assn.; Law Soc. of Nfld.; N.S. Barristers' Soc.; Assn. of Trial Lawyers of Am.; Law Soc. of Upper Canada; Chambers: 1191 Eglinton Ave. E., Scarborough, Ont. M1P 4P4.

**RICHARDS, Sheila;** homemaker, community volunteer; b. Shawinigan Falls, Que. 1 Aug. 1927; d. Percy and Lorna (Kerr) Radley (both dec.); e. Notre Dame Secretarial Sch. (Mother House) 1946; m. the late Wendall R. 2 June 1950; children: Robert, Douglas; Bd. Mem., Blyth Festival 1978– (Pres. 1980–82); Bd. Mem., Guelph Spring Festival 1989–93; National Programme Ctte., Girl Guides of Canada 1970–75; Co-Founder, Brussels Citizen's Weekly Newspaper 1987 (Board Mem. 1987– ); Co-Founder, Blyth Festival Singers 1980; Medal of Merit, Girl Guides of Canada; United Church; Home: Box 89, Brussels, Ont. N0G 1H0.

**RICHARDS, Vincent Philip Haslewood,** A.L.A., B.L.S.; library and book industry consultant; b. Sutton Bonington, Notts., Eng. 1 Aug. 1933; s. Philip Haslewood and Alice Hilda (Moore) R.; e. Richmond & East Sheen Grammar Sch. London, Eng. 1949; Kingston Polytechnic Coll., Kingston-Upon-Thames, Surrey 1950; Army Sch. of Educ., Beaconsfield, Bucks., Teaching Cert. 1952; Ealing Coll. (Sch. of Librarianship) London, Eng. A.L.A. 1955; Univ. of Okla. B.L.S. 1966 (Bachelor of Lib. Studies); B.C. Cert. of Prof. Librarianship; m. Ann d. Frank Beardshall, Scarborough, Eng. 3 Apl. 1961; children: Mark, Christopher, Erika; LIBRARY AND BOOK INDUSTRY CONSULTANT 1989– ; Consultant, Manresa Coll. London, Eng., St. Augustine's Abbey Lib., Ramsgate, Eng. and Westminster Abbey Lib., Mission, B.C. 1954–67; joined Brentford & Chiswick Pub. Libs., London, Eng holding various positions incl. Asst. Reference Librarian and Asst. Cataloguer 1949–56; Asst. Librarian, B.C. Pub. Lib. Comn, Peace River Br.; Dawson Creek, B.C. 1956–57; Asst. Dir. Fraser Valley Regional Lib. Abbotsford, B.C. 1957–67; Chief Librarian, Red Deer (Alta.) Coll. 1967–77, Bd of Govs. 1972–73, Pres. Faculty Assn. 1971–72; Dir. Red Deer Educ. TV Authority 1975–77; Dir. of Libraries, Edmonton Pub. Library 1977–89; Pres., Library Assoc. of Alta., 1984–85; Dir., Alta. Foundn. for the Literary Arts 1984–86; Vice Pres. Jeunesses Musicales; Adv. Bd. mem. Sch. Paperback Journ. N.Y. 1962–65; served with E. Surrey Regt. (Cadet Corps) 1948–49, Royal Sussex Regt. 1951, Royal Army Educ. Corps 1952–53 Instr., Middle E. and Egypt 1952–53, R.A. (Territorial Reserve) London 1954–56; contrib. to prof. journs. librarianship in U.K., U.S. and Can.; Dir., Candn. Assn. Coll. & Univ. Libs. 1971–74; mem. Candn. Lib. Assn.: Pacific Northwest Lib. Assn. (Secy. 1958); Third Order of Mt. Carmel; Dir., Reform Party; R. Catholic; recreations: reading, music, photography, travel, camping, cross-country skiing; Home/Office: 184 Devine Dr., Saltspring Island, B.C.

**RICHARDSON, Arthur John Hampson,** B.A.; b. Lennoxville, Que. 31 July 1916; s. Arthur Vernon, M.A., D.C.L. (Vice Princ., Bishop's Univ.), and Margaret Wynona (Thornton) R.; e. Bishop's Coll. Sch. 1924–32; Bishop's Univ., B.A. 1935; McGill Univ., 1936; m. Marie Gertrude, d. David Couture of Ste. Marie (Beauce), Que., in Ottawa, Ont. 20 Dec. 1947; children: Marie Elizabeth Margaret, Peter David Arthur, John Andrew, Marie Suzanne; Chief, Map Div., Public Archives of Can., 1946–54; subsequently Chief, Nat. Hist. Sites Div., Secy. Hist. Sites & Monuments Bd. of Can. and Head, Arch. Hist. Sec., Dept. Indian & Northern Affairs; Historian, Clan MacArthur (Internat.) 1988– ; served in 2nd World War; Lieut. (S.B.), R.C.N.(R), 1942–46; author 'Guide to ... Buildings in the Old City of Quebec' 1970; 'Quebec City: Architects, Artisans and Builders' 1984; many biographies in 'Dictionary of Canadian Biography' and articles in 'Bulletin of the Assn. for Preservation Technology'; Fellow, Assn. for Preservation Technology; Fellow, Soc. of Antiquaries of Scotland; Gabrielle Léger Medal, Candn. Heritage Found. 1987; Anglican; recreations: walking, swimming, reading; Home: Apt. 1908, 400 Stewart St., Ottawa, Ont. K1N 6L2.

**RICHARDSON, Beverley J. Burgess,** M.D., F.R.C.P.(C); physician; educator; b. Montreal, Que. 3 Feb. 1948; d. Frederick Ashton and Helene (Flach) Burgess; e. Univ. of Toronto M.D. 1972; m. Robert s. Horace and Margaret Richardson 21 Aug. 1970; two s. David, Michael; CHIEF MED. STAFF AFFAIRS, WOMEN'S COLL. HOSP. 1990– , Attending Phys. Dept. of Med. 1980– ; Asst. Prof. of Med. Univ. of Toronto; Pres. Med. Staff Assn., Women's Coll. Hosp. 1988–90; Chair, Gender Issues Ctte., Faculty of Medicine, Univ. of Toronto 1992– ; Co-Chair, Ctte. on the Status of Women, City of Toronto 1992– ; Chair, OMA District 11 1993– ; Office: Suite 422, 60 Grosvenor St., Toronto, Ont. M5S 1B6.

**RICHARDSON, Cameron S.,** B.Com.; executive; b. Tuberose, Sask. 1932; e. Univ. of Alta. B.Com. 1953; SR. VICE PRES. FINANCE & DIR., ATCO LTD.; DIR., DEPY CHRMN. & CHIEF FINANCIAL OFFR., CANADIAN UTILITIES LTD.; Assessor, Fed. Dept. Nat. Revenue 1953–59; joined ATCO Industries Ltd. 1959; Chamber Comm.; Home: 2028 Uralta Rd. N.W., Calgary, Alta. T2N 4B4; Office: 1600, 909 – 11 Avenue S.W., Calgary, Alta. T2R 1N6.

**RICHARDSON, David I.,** B.Com., F.C.A.; chartered accountant; b. Toronto, Ont. 11 Oct. 1941; s. George Grainger and Margaret Louise (Everett) R.; e. Upper Can. Coll. Toronto; Univ. of Toronto B.Com. 1963; C.A. 1966; m. Kathryn Moira d. Dr. Frederick and Dorothy Cuddy 14 June 1969; two s. Andrew, Matthew; EXTVE. PARTNER, ERNST & YOUNG; Chrmn., Ernst & Young Inc.; mem. Finance Ctte. St. James Cath. Toronto; mem. Candn. Inst. C.A.'s; Ont. Inst. C.A.'s; Candn. Insolvency Assn.; Bd. Trade Metrop. Toronto (Chrmn. Insolvency & Creditors' Rights Ctte.); Fed. Govt. Bankruptcy and Insolvency Advisory Ctte.; Anglican; recreations: fishing, hiking; Home: 19 Roxborough St. E., Toronto, Ont. M4W 1V5; Office: P.O. Box 251, Toronto-Dominion Centre, Toronto, Ont. M5K 1J7.

**RICHARDSON, George Peter,** B.Arch., B.D., Ph.D.; educator; b. Toronto, Ont. 6 Jan. 1935; s. George Grainger and Margaret Louise (Everett) R.; e. Upper Can. Coll. 1952; Univ. of Toronto B.Arch. 1957, Knox Coll. B.D. 1962; Clare Coll. Cambridge Ph.D. 1965; m. Nancy d. Donald and Jean Cameron 22 Dec. 1959; children: Mary Rebekah, Susan Elizabeth, Jonathan Peter, Ruth Anne; PROF. OF RELIGIOUS STUDIES, UNIV. OF TORONTO 1974– ; Partner, Richardson & Sievenpiper Construction Co. 1954–57; Arch., John B. Parkin Associates 1957–59; Campus Min. (unordained) Knox Presb. Ch. Toronto 1965–69; Asst. and Assoc. Prof. of Theol. Studies Loyola Coll. Montreal 1969–74, Asst. to Dean of Arts 1971–72, Asst. to Acad. Vice Pres. 1972–73, Coordinator Loyola Lacolle Centre Educ. Devel. 1973–74; Chrmn. Div. of Humanities Scarborough Coll. Univ. Toronto 1974–77; Principal, Univ. Coll., Univ. of Toronto 1977–89; mem. Senate Presb. Coll. Montreal 1969–76; author 'Israel in the Apostolic Church' 1969; 'Paul's Ethic of Freedom' 1979; co-author 'The Trial of Jesus' 1970; 'Law in Religious Communities in the Roman Period' 1991; ed. 'From Jesus to Paul' 1984; 'Anti-Judaism in Early Christianity' 1986; 'Studies in Christianity and Judaism/Études sur le christianîsme et le judaïsme'; Managing Ed. 'Studies in Religion/Sciences Religieuses' 1986– ; Associate Editor, Wilfrid Laurier University Press 1991– ; mem. ed. bd. CRUX 1967–78; ARC 1973–74; mem. Studiorum Novi Testamenti Societas; Am. Acad. Religion; Soc. Biblical Lit.; Candn. Soc. Study Religion; Candn. Soc. Biblical Studies (Extve. 1972–82, Extve. Secy. 1978–82; V. Pres., 1983–84; Pres. 1984–85); Inst. for Biblical Research (Secy. 1971–77); Chrmn. Joint Practice Bd. (Engineers & Architects) 1984– ; Vice Pres., Candn. Corp. for Studies in Religion 1991–93; Home: 42 St. Andrew's Gardens, Toronto, Ont. M4W 2E1; Office: Toronto, Ont. M5S 1A1.

**RICHARDSON, George Taylor,** B.Comm., LL.D.; business executive; b. Winnipeg, Man. 22 Sept. 1924; s. late James Armstrong and Muriel (Sprague) R.; e. Grosvenor Sch.; St. John's Ravenscourt Sch.; Univ. of Man., B.Comm. 1946; Univ. of Man., LL.D. (Hon.) 1969; Univ. of Winnipeg LL.D. (Hon.) 1990; m. Tannis Maree Thorlakson 30 Oct. 1948; two sons, one daughter; CHAIRMAN AND MNG. DIR., JAMES RICHARDSON & SONS, LIMITED 1993– ; joined James Richardson & Sons, Limited, Winnipeg 1946; Vice-Pres. 1954; Pres. 1966; Honorary Chrmn. & Dir., Richardson Greenshields of Canada Limited; Chrmn., Richardson Realty Ltd.; Lombard Place Ltd.; Richardson Oil & Gas Limited; Winnipeg Inn Ltd.; Pres., Richardson Stock Farms Ltd.; Dir., Pioneer Grain Company, Limited; Pioneer Grain Terminal Ltd.; Topnotch Nutri Ltd.; Buckerfield's Ltd.; Top-Notch Feeds Ltd.; Green Valley Fertilizer Ltd.; Sorel Elevators Ltd.; Richardson Terminals Ltd.; INCO Ltd.; United Canadian Shares Ltd.; Du Pont Canada Inc.; Goderich Elevators Ltd.; mem. Chicago Bd. of Trade; Bd. of Trade of Kansas City; Winnipeg Commodity Exchange; Hon. Dir., Canada's Aviation Hall of Fame; recreations: hunting, flying (helicopter); Clubs: Manitoba; St Charles; Vancouver; Toronto; Home: Briarmeade, P.O. Box 158, St. Germain, Man. R0G 2A0; Office: Richardson Bldg., One Lombard Place, Winnipeg, Man. R3B 0Y1.

**RICHARDSON, Jr., Howard E.,** M.Sc.; association executive; e. Univ. of Wis. B.Sc. 1961, M.Sc. 1963; PROFESSIONAL SERVICES CONSULTANT, RIGHT ASSOCIATES 1992– ; Exec. Dir. Ont. Div. Candn. Mental Health Assn. 1973–91; former Special Adv. Nat. Dept. Health & Welfare Can.; Asst. Dir. Nat. Inst. on Mental Retardation, York Univ.; Asst. Dir. Regional Rsch. & Training Centre Univ. of Ore.; Cons. Presidential Task Force Health Agencies & Sch. Bds. USA; Nat. and Provl. Health/Edn. Orgns. Can.; lectr. Bar Admission Course Law Soc. Upper Can.; author various publs. USA and Can.; Office: 90 Burnhamthorpe Rd. W., Suite 500, Mississauga, Ont. L5B 3C3.

**RICHARDSON, Hon. James Armstrong,** P.C.; b. Winnipeg, Man. 1922; s. late James Armstrong and Muriel (Sprague) R.; e. St. John's-Ravenscourt Sch.; Queen's Univ., B.A.; m. Shirley Anne, d. John R. Rooper, Shamley Green, Surrey, Eng., 10 Sept. 1949; two s., three d.; Dir. Emeritus, Candn. Imperial Bank of Commerce; Pres. Jarco Ltd.; Chrmn. & Dir., Max Bell Found.; Hon. Pres. Commonwealth Games Assn. of Canada & Dir. Canada's Challenge for America's Cup; with James Richardsons & Sons, Ltd., 1945–68; el. to H. of C. for Winnipeg, S., g.e. June 1968; apptd. Min. without Portfolio, July 1968; Min. Supply & Services 1969–72; re-el. g.e. 1972; apptd. Min. of Nat. Defence 1972; re-el. g.e. 1974; resigned 1976 over constitutional language issue; crossed the floor of H. of C. to sit as Independent, 1978; served with R.C.A.F. as Pilot; Un.

Church; recreations: sailing, golf; Home: 407 Bower Blvd., Winnipeg, Man. R3P 0L6.

**RICHARDSON, John E.,** B.Com., M.B.A., F.C.A.; insurance executive; b. Toronto, Ont. 5 May 1933; s. George Graingerand Margaret Louise (Everett) R.; e. Upper Can. Coll. 1950; Univ. of Toronto, B.Com. 1954; C.A. 1957; Harvard Bus. Sch. M.B.A. 1965; m. Pamela d. John and Muriel Hooper 23 June 1961; children: David, Katharine, Elizabeth, Janet; DEPUTY CHRMN. LONDON INSUR. GROUP, INC. 1986– and VICE CHRMN., GREAT LAKES GROUP INC. 1989– ; Chrmn., Pres. & C.E.O., Wellington Insur. Corp. 1989– ; Chrmn., Meloche-Monnex Inc. 1989– ; Pres., First Property and Casualty Corp. 1987– ; Dir., London Insur. Group Inc.; Wellington Insurance; Great Lakes Group Inc.; Meloche-Monnex Inc.; Allendale Mutual Insurance, Candn. Advisory Bd., 1987; Sr. Partner, Ernst and Young 1965–85; Past Dir. Un. Way Can.; Un. Way Ont.; Chrmn. and Trustee, Queen Elizabeth Hosp.; Past Chrmn. Un. Way Toronto; Past Rector's Warden, Grace Ch. on the Hill (Ang.); recreations: golf, squash, tennis, skiing; Clubs: University (Past Pres.); Rosedale Golf; Badminton & Racquet (Dir.); Craigleith Ski; Office: 38F Royal Trust Tower, Toronto, Ont. M5K 1G8.

**RICHARDSON, Mary Frances,** B.Sc., Ph.D.; university professor; b. Barbourville, Ken. 3 Sept. 1941; d. Leroy Langdon and Mary Patricia (Jones) R.; e. Univ. of Kentucky B.Sc. 1963, Ph.D. 1967; PROFESSOR OF CHEMISTRY, BROCK UNIV. 1981– ; Rsch. Assoc., Wright-Patterson Air Force Base (US) 1967–71; Asst. Prof. of Chem., Brock Univ. 1971–75; Assoc. Prof. 1975–81; Chair, Dept. of Chem. 1979–82; Assoc. Mem., Womens Studies Program 1990– ; Fellow, Candn. Inst. of Chem.; OCUFA Teaching Award 1990; CASE Candn. Prof. of the Year 1992; Mem., Candn. Soc. of Chem.; Am. Chem. Soc.; Am. Crystallographic Assn.; Candn. Womens Studies Assn.; author of more than 60 publications; recreations: hiking, making beer; clubs: University Women's, Canadian Amateur Brewers Assn., American Homebrewers Assn., Bruce Trail Assn., Fedn. of Ontario Naturalists; Home: 1 St. John Lane, St. Catharines, Ont. L2R 7K4; Office: St. Catharines, Ont. L2S 3A1.

**RICHARDSON, Robert Lloyd,** B.A., M.A.; b. Renfrew, Ont. 10 April 1930; e. Queen's Univ. B.A. (Hons.) 1958 (Gold Medal Economics); Univ. of Sydney M.A. 1966; m. Irene Anderson 15 Sept. 1952; children: Garry, David; DIR., AGRA INDUSTRIES 1992– ; Trade Comnr. Serv., Dept. of Indus., Trade & Comm. (ITC) 1958–59; Trade Comnr., Port of Spain 1959–62; Sydney, Aust. 1963–65; Internat. Commodity Trade Policy, ITC 1965–67; Mgr., Career Assignment Prog., Public Serv. Comn. 1968–70; Internat. Econ. Trade Relns., Fin. 1970–71; Group Chief, Indus. & Nat. Resources Div., Treasury Bd. Sec. 1971–72; Dir. 1972–74; Asst. Sec., Programs Branch 1974–77; Dep. Sec. 1977–82; Comnr., Fgn. Invest. Review Agency 1982–85; Dep. Min., Internat. Trade, Dept. of External Affairs 1985–86; Pres. & C.E.O., Export Devel. Corp. 1986–91; Club: Royal Ottawa; Home: 4 Gillespie Cres., Ottawa, Ont. K1V 9X8.

**RICHARDSON, Royden R.,** B.A.; investment banker; b. Winnipeg, Man. 9 Sept. 1953; s. James A. and Shirley A. (Rooper) R.; c. Univ. of Manitoba B.A. 1975; m. Beverley E.G. d. Alan Taylor 3 May 1981; children: R. Ronald, Bryden R., Quinn A.; SENIOR VICE-PRES., RICHARDSON GREENSHIELDS OF CANADA LIMITED and VICE CHAIRMAN, RICHARDSON GREENSHIELDS LIMITED; Dir., Magna International Inc.; Westmead Limited; Jr. Achievement of Canada; recreations: skiing, flying; clubs: Toronto, Granite, St. Charles Country; Office: 130 Adelaide St. W., 12th fl., Toronto, Ont. M5H 1T8.

**RICHARDSON, Thomas Boyce;** writer and filmmaker; b. Wyndham, New Zealand 21 March 1928; s. Robert and Letitia Linda (Boyce) R.; e. Southland Boys' H.S.; Newbattle Abbey Adult Ed. Coll. (Scotland) 1952–53; m. Shirley d. William Roy and Eva Ruth Norton 9 June 1950; children: Ben, Robert, Thom, Belle; FREELANCE WRITER/FILMMAKER, OTTAWA 1977– ; Copyholder, Southland Times (N.Z.) 1946; Reporter, Southland Daily News 1946–48; The Evening Star 1948–50; The Daily Mercury (Australia) 1950; Editor, Kurukshetra Weekly (India) 1951; Factory labourer, waiter, (U.K.) 1951–52; Reporter, The Coventry Standard 1953–54; Northern Daily News (Canada) 1954; Winnipeg Free Press 1955–57; The Montreal Star 1957–71 (London Correspondent 1960–68, assoc. ed. 1968–71); freelance writer, filmmaker, Montreal 1971–75; contract contrib., The Listener (N.Z.) 1975–76; Visiting prof., Univ. of Waterloo, 1976–77 (winter term); co-winner, Nat. Newspaper Award 1961; Robert Flaherty Award, Brit. Acad. of Film and TV Arts 1975; films directed: 'Job's Garden' 1972, 'Our Health is Not for Sale,' 'Who Will I Sentence Now?' 1977, 'For Future Generations' 1985; 'Super-Companies' 1987; 'Blockade! Algonquins Defend the Forest' 1990; 'Flooding Job's Garden' 1991; co-dir., 'Cree Hunters of Mistassini' 1974, 'Our Land is Our Life' 1975, 'North China Commune' 1979, 'North China Factory' 1980, 'China: A Land Transformed' 1980, 'Two Dreams of a Nation' 1981, 'The Great Buffalo Saga' 1985; numerous films written & researched incl. UNICEF's Academy Award nominee 'The Children of Soong Ching Ling' 1985; mem., Alliance of Candn. TV and Radio Artists; author; 'James Bay, The Plot to Drown the North Woods' 1972, 'The Future of Canadian Cities' 1972, 'Strangers Devour the Land' 1976; 'Time to change' 1990; 'People of Terra Nullius' 1993; co-author: 'Life of the Party' 1985; ed. 'Drumbeat' 1989; contrib.: various internat. newspapers & magazines, CBC pub. aff. programs, radio & TV 1955– ; recreations: cricket, tennis, tabletennis, reading, movie-going; Home: 53 Second Ave., Ottawa, Ont. K1S 2H4.

**RICHARDSON MacDONALD, Kate;** editor; b. Toronto, Ont. 6 Dec. 1960; d. William Albert and Joan Elizabeth (Streatfield) Wiseman; e. Lawrence Park C.I.; Ryerson Polytech. Inst., applied arts dipl.; m. Denis F. Macdonald 14 July 1990; EDITOR, IMAGES MAGAZINE 1993– ; Fashion Consultant, The Bay, Hudson's Bay Co. 1982–85; Sales Mgr., Simpsons The Room, Designer Boutiques 1985; Planning Mgr., Central Buyer, Hudson's Bay Corp. (Bay/Simpsons) 1985–87; Assoc. Beauty Ed., FLARE Mag. 1987–88, Fashion & Beauty Dir. 1990–93; Mem. & Extve. posts, Fashion Group Internat. 1985– ; Ctte. Mem., Ryerson Search Ctte. for Sch. of Fashion Chrmn.; Bd. & Extve. Mem., Found. for Canadians Facing Cancer; Home: 30 Whitehall Rd., Toronto, Ont. M4W 2C6; Office: 777 Bay St., Toronto, Ont. M5W 1A7.

**RICHER, Jean H.,** C.M., B.A., B.Eng.; transportation executive; b. Montreal, Que. 24 March 1918; s. Georges and Alice (Blain) R.; e. Jean de Brébeuf Coll., Montreal; Univ. of Montreal, B.A.; McGill Univ., B.Eng.; m. Louise, d. late René Turcot, 1 June 1946; children: Claire, Suzanne, Hélène, Georges, Louis; joined Quebec North Shore Paper Co., Baie Comeau, Que., 1946; with H.O., Montreal Tramways Co., 1946 becoming Extve. Asst. 1947, Supvr. of Timetables 1949 and Asst. Supt. of Transport, 1952; joined Brazilian Traction, Light and Power Co. Ltd., Rio de Janeiro, as Extve. Consultant on mass transport, 1955; apptd. Asst. to the Pres. and Gen. Mgr., Montreal Transport Comn., 1956; Dir. of Transport. Services, 1956; joined Candn. National Railways as Special Asst. to Vice Pres., St. Lawrence Region, 1962; Asst. Mgr., Montreal Area, 1963; Mgr., Champlain Area, 1963–64; Vice Pres., Passenger Sales & Services, 1965–67; Vice-Pres., St. Lawrence Region 1968–72; Extve. Vice Pres. System 1972–76; Sr. Vice-Pres., System 1976–77; Dir., Canac Consultants Ltd.; served with RN and RCN 1943–46; Alderman, City Westmount 1965–72; Pres., Westmount Mun. Assn. 1964; Centraide Montreal 1975–77; Pres., Montreal Symphony 1977–78; Pres., J.H. Richer Associés Ltée.; Mem. Bd. of Dirs., The Guardian Ins. Co. of Canada 1972–88; The Montreal Life Ins. Co. 1974–84; Franki Canada Ltd. 1976–86; Telesat 1972–76; CN France 1968–83; Imasco Ltd. 1974–90; Central Vermont Railway 1966–91; National Sport & Recreation Centre 1972–80; Participaction 1978–84; Les Dauphins Sur-Le-Parc, Société en Co-Proriété 1991– ; mem., Bd. of Govs., McGill Univ.; Montreal Gen. Hosp.; Member of the Order of Canada; R. Catholic; recreations: tennis, skiing, golf, reading, bridge, walking, sailing; Clubs: University; Montreal Indoor Tennis; Mt. Bruno Country; Laurentian Golf and Country; Home: Les Dauphins Sur-le-Parc, 3535 avenue Papineau, App. 2008, Montréal, Qué. H2K 4J9; Country residence: Lac Manitou, Québec.

**RICHER, (François) Yvon,** M.L.S.; consultant; b. Hull, Que. 2 July 1943; s. François and Yvette (Villeneuve) R.; e. Univ. of Ottawa B.A. 1964, B.L.S. 1965; Univ. of Toronto M.L.S. 1971; m. Suzanne d. André Naubert 4 Feb. 1967; one s. François-Yves; CONSULTANT 1993– ; Sr. Cataloguer Laval Univ. Lib. 1965–68, Head Catalogue Dept. 1968–71, Head Processing Div. 1971–75; Asst. Dir. (Systems) Catalogue Br. Nat. Lib. Can. 1975–76; Assoc. Univ. Lib. Univ. of Ottawa 1976–78, Univ. Librarian 1978–88; mem. Candn. Lib. Assn.; ASTED (Pres. 1985); R. Catholic; Home: 1992 Summerfields Cr., Orleans, Ont. K1C 7B4.

**RICHERT, George Edward,** M.Ed., Ph.D.; educator; b. Waldheim, Sask. 27 Jan. 1936; s. Abram and Mathilda (Schultz) R.; e. Univ. of Sask. B.Ed. 1958, M.Ed. 1963; Univ. of Alta. Ph.D. 1968; m. Pearl d. Isaac and Nettie Janzen 28 June 1957; children: Colin Trent, Dean Courtney; PRESIDENT, MENNO SIMONS COLLEGE, UNIV. OF WINNIPEG 1992– ; Special Advisor, Candn. Teachers' Fed., Internat. Assistance Program, 1984–86; Special advisor to Min. of Indian Affairs 1983–84; Vice Pres. Acad. Sask. Indian Federated Coll. 1982–83; teacher rural Sask. sch. 1954–55; Shellbrook High Sch. Sask. 1958–59; Princ. Shellbrook Composite High Sch. 1959–63; Asst. to Depy. Supt. Edmonton Pub. Sch. Bd. 1966–67; Extve. Asst. Candn. Teachers' Fed. 1968–71; Continuing Educ. Centre Univ. of Lagos, Nigeria (CIDA) 1971–73; Assoc. Prof. of Educ. Univ. of Regina 1973–74, Assoc. Dean of Educ. 1974–78, Acting Dean of Educ. 1978–79, Dean of Educ. 1980–83, Prof., Educational Admin. 1983–92; Consultant to Indonesian Ministry of Educ. & Culture in Teaching Educ. 1979–80; Special Advisor, Candn. Teachers' Fedn. Internat. Programs 1983–87; Evaluator, Norwegian Union of Teachers Leadership Training Program in Kenya 1987; Dean, Faculty of Social Work, Univ. of Regina 1988–90; Visiting Prof., Develop. Studies, Menno Simons Coll., Univ. of Winnipeg 1990–91; Dean, Faculty of Education, Univ. of Regina 1991–92; Candn. Dir. of Joint Develop. Projects (Univ. of Regina - Univ. of Yaounde, Cameroon and Univ. of Regina - Educational Inst. of Jilin Province, China); Distinguished Visiting Esau Professor in Development Studies, Menno Simons College, Univ. of Winnipeg 1990; Pres., Menno Simons College, Univ. of Winnipeg 1992– ; evaluator of internat. development programs; author or co-author various research reports, articles; Chair, Mennonite Central Ctte. of Can.; Vice-Chairperson, Conf. of Mennonites in Can. 1986–92; mem., Ed. Bd., Cameroon Journal of Educ.; recreations: woodworking, cross-country skiing; Addresses: Menno Simons College, Univ. of Winnipeg, 515 Portage Ave., Winnipeg, Man. R3B 2E9.

**RICHES, Graham Charles Parley,** B.A., M.A., Dip.S.A.; university professor; b. Eye, Suffolk, U.K. 1 Feb. 1941; s. Charles and Katharine Alice (Parley) R.; e. Christ's Hosp. 1952–60; Cambridge Univ. B.A. 1964, M.A. 1968; London Sch. of Econ., Dip.S.A. 1965; m. Mary d. Grace and George Haywood 25 June 1988; children: Naomi, Rebecca, Stefan and Sarah, Simon Haywood-Anderson; PROF. OF SOCIAL WORK, UNIV. OF REGINA 1974– ; Voluntary Serv. Overseas, Sarawak, S.E. Asia 1960–61; Adult Edn. Offr., Masasi, Tanzania 1963; Orgn. Sec., Assn. of London Housing Estates 1965–68; Lectr., Dept. of Soc. Work, Univ. of Hong Kong 1968–71; Dir., Liverpool Univ. Settlement 1974; Dir., Sask. Comm. Edn. Ctr., Univ. of Regina 1978–80; Asst. Dean 1981–83; Acting Dean 1983–84; Dir., Soc. Admin. Rsch. Unit 1981–83, 1986– ; Nat. Health & Welfare Rsch. Award 1978; Hon. Sec., Brit. Assn. of Settlements 1972–74; Bd. of Regina Food Bank 1985– (currently Pres.); Mem., Sask. & Candn. Assns. of Soc. Workers; Candn. Assn. of Schools of Soc. Work (Bd. 1985–88; Vice-Pres. 1985–86); Internat. Counc. of Soc. Welfare; Internat. Network on Unemployment & Soc. Work; Founder Mem., Soc. Policy & Admin. Network; Regina Child Hunger Coalition; author: 'Food Banks and the Welfare Crisis' 1986 and numerous articles; co-editor: 'Can. R. of Soc. Policy' 1979– ; Ed. Bd. Mem., 'Can. J. of Soc. Work Education' 1978–82, 'Perception' 1982–85; recreations: cross country skiing, oil painting; Club: Old Blues; Home: 2744 Robinson St., Regina, Sask. S4T 2R6.

**RICHLER, Daniel Jonathon;** broadcaster; writer; b. London, Eng. 22 Dec. 1956; s. Mordecai and Florence (Wood) R.; e. St. Paul's Eng.; Coll. Stanislas, Mtl.; CEGEP Marianopolis, Mtl.; McGill Univ. 1977; broadcaster various radio stns. Montreal and Toronto 1979–88; Creative Head Adult Arts Programming, TV Ontario 1989–92; Host, Extve. Producer 'Imprint' (TV Ontario) 1990–93; Host, Producer 'The New Music' City-TV, The Much Music Network; Host, CBC The Journal (Arts Corr.) and TV Ont. (Host 'Full House') during above period.; curated Candn. Music & Art Video Festival 1984, Candn. Consulate, London, Eng.; Bd. of Dir. Toronto Arts Awards; director, 'Mini-Movies' 1988–89; author 'Kicking Tomorrow' 1991; author various articles Candn. publs. incl. Sat. Night; Hon. mem. Big Sisters Assn. Ont.; Mem. New Hegelians Motorcycle Club; Office: P.O. Box 200 Station Q, Toronto, Ont. M4T 2T1.

**RICHLER, Mordecai;** writer; b. Montreal, Que. 27 Jan. 1931; s. Moses Isaac and Lily (Rosenberg) R.; m. Florence Wood, 27 July 1960; children: Daniel, Noah, Emma, Martha, Jacob; Awards and Hons. rec'd.: Can. Council Jr. Arts Fellowship, 1959–60 (renewed, 1960–61); Guggenheim Fellowship, creative writing, 1961–62; President's Medal, Univ. Western Ont. (Best Gen. Article publ. in Can., 1963); Can. Council Sr. Arts Fellowship, 1966–67; Paris Review Humour Prize for excerpt from 'Cocksure,' 1967; Winner, Commonwealth Writers' Prize 1990; Commonwealth Writers Award 1991; author: (novels) 'The Acrobats' 1954; 'Son of a Smaller Hero' 1955; 'Choice of Enemies' 1957; 'The Apprenticeship of Duddy Kravitz' 1959; 'The Incomparable Atuk' 1963; 'Cocksure' 1968; 'Hunting Tigers Under Glass' (essays and reports) 1968; 'The Street Stories' 1969; 'St. Urbain's Horseman' (novel) 1971 (Gov. Gen.'s Lit. Award 1972); 'Jacob Two-Two Meets the Hooded Fang' (Ruth Schwartz children's book award) 1976; 'Joshua Then and Now' (novel) 1980; 'Solomon Gursky was Here' (novel) 1989; 'Home Sweet Home: My Canadian Album' (essays) 1984; 'Jacob Two-Two and the Dinosaur' 1987; 'Oh Canada! Oh Quebec! Lament for a Divided Nation' (non-fiction) 1992; editor: 'New Canadian Writing' 1969; 'Best of Modern Humour' 1983; (anthols.) 'Points of View,' 'Modern Occasions,' 'Best American Short Stories' 1963, 'Great Canadian Writing,' 'Canadian Short Stories,' 'A Book of Canadian Short Stories,' 'Ten for Wednesday Night,' 'The First Five Years,' 'Writers on World War II'; (films) No Love for Johnnie, Life at the Top; Awarded for Screenplay of 'The Apprenticeship of Duddy Kravitz': Amer. Screenwriter' Guild, Best Comedy; ACTRA, best Candn. Screen play; Academy Award Nomination, best comedy screenplay; Paris Review Humor Prize 1968; Gov. Gen.'s Lit. Award 1968 and 1972; Golden Bear Award, Berlin Film Festival 1975; Commonwealth Writer's Award 1992; stories, essays, criticism regularly in English and Am. mags.; was Writer-in-Residence at Sir George Williams Univ., Montreal 1968–69 and apptd. same post at Carleton Univ. 1972–88; Ed. Bd. Book of the Month Club, N.Y. 1977; Address: c/o McClelland & Stewart, 481 University Ave., Toronto, Ont. M5G 2E9.

**RICHMOND, Anthony Henry,** B.Sc., M.A., Ph.D., F.R.S.C.; educator; b. Ilford, Essex, Eng. 8 June 1925; s. late Henry James and late Ellen Bertha (Hankin) R.; e. Co. High Sch. Ilford 1943; London Sch. of Econ. B.Sc. (Econ.) 1949); Univ. of Liverpool M.A. 1951; Univ. of London (external student) Ph.D. 1965; m. Freda d. late Owen John Williams 29 March 1952; child: Glenys Catriona; PROF. EMERITUS, YORK UNIV. and SENIOR SCHOLAR 1989– ; Dir. Inst. for Behavioural Rsch. 1979–82; Rsch. Offr. Univ. of Liverpool 1949–52; Lectr. Univ. of Edinburgh 1952–63; Reader, Bristol Coll. of Science and Technol. 1963–65; came to Can. 1965; Prof. of Sociol., York Univ. 1965–89; Visiting Prof. Univ. of B.C. 1960–61; Univ. of Sussex 1970; Australian Nat. Univ. 1971, 1977; Univ. of Wales 1978; St. Antony's College, Oxford 1984–85; rec'd various Can. Council and SSHRCC Fellowships and Awards; served with Friends Ambulance Unit 1943–46; author 'Colour Prejudice in Britain' 1954, 2nd ed. 1971; 'The Colour Problem' 1955, revised ed. 1961; 'Post-War Immigrants in Canada' 1967, reprinted 1970; 'Migration and Race Relations in an English City' 1973; 'Immigration and Ethnic Conflict' 1988; 'Caribbean Immigrants: A Demo-Economic Analysis' 1989; co-author 'Immigrant Integration and Urban Renewal in Toronto' 1973; 'Factors in the Adjustment of Immigrants and their Descendants,' 1980; ed. with Introduction 'Readings in Race and Ethnic Relations' 1972; co-ed. 'Internal Migration: The New World and the Third World' 1976; author or co-author book chapters, research monographs, papers in refereed journs.; mem. ed. bds. various journs.; mem. Candn. Sociol. & Anthrop. Assn.; Candn. Population Soc.; Society of Friends; recreations: photography, walking, classical music; Home: #710, 7811 Yonge St., Thornhill, Ont. L3T 4S3; Office: 4700 Keele St., Downsview, Ont. M3J 1P3.

**RICHMOND, Brian;** theatre director; b. Vancouver, B.C. 22 Jan. 1947; s. Harry and Edith (Smith) R.; e. Simon Fraser Univ.; m. Janet d. Jack and Ruth Wright 8 June 1970 (div. 1978); children: Celine, Jacob; actor, Holiday Theatre, Vancouver Playhouse, Centaur theatre 1966–71; Founding Artistic Dir., Persephone Theatre 1975–77; Dramaturge, Montreal Playwright's Workshop 1980–82; Artistic Dir., Magnus Theatre 1983–87; Artistic Dir., Theatre Passe Muraille 1988–91; has directed nearly 70 profl. prods. in Can.; guest teacher, National Theatre Sch. of Can., Concordia Univ., McGill Univ., Simon Fraser Univ., N.Y. State Univ., Waterloo Univ., York Univ.; Founding Chrmn., Saskatoon Union of the Arts 1976; China Month Ctte., Vancouver 1978; Pres., Toronto Theatre Alliance 1990–91; 3 time nominee and winner 1989 Dora Mavor Moore Award, Best Director; currently pursuing aims of successful Canada Council Arst Grant A application; recreations: motoring, reading; Home: 53A Langley Ave., Toronto, Ont. M4K 1B4.

**RICHMOND, John Russell,** R.C.A.; artist; writer; b. Toronto, Ont. 25 Oct. 1926; s. John Melville and Sylvia Elizabeth (Newberry) R.; e. Frankland Pub. Sch. Toronto 1939; Fergus (Ont.) High Sch. 1944; Ont. Coll. of Art 1947; mem. Faculty, Ont. Coll. of Art 1975–90; estbd. Upper Canada Scribble Works 1972; Publisher 'Gambit' 1958–63; author 'Tearful Tour of Toronto's Riviera' 1961; 'Around Toronto' 1969; 'Sex Stuff' 1970; 'Discover Ontario' 1974; 'Discover Toronto' 1976; columnist 'Discover Ontario' 1969–79; various articles, reviews mags.; rec'd Can. Council Grant 1966, 1968; Ont. Arts Council Grant 1978, 1980, 1985; Dir. Latcham Gallery, Stouffville, Ont. 1980–81; Publisher, editor 'Bicameral Review' 1984–89; produced world's largest narrative mural (24,800 sq. ft.) for world's largest Food Terminal, Cambridge, Ont. 1991; Exec. Council, Royal Can. Academy 1980–81, 1988–89; recreations: skiing, swimming, farming, building; Address: R.R.4, Uxbridge, Ont. L9P 1R4.

**RICHMOND, Robert Dick,** B.S.E.; aerospace executive; b. Winnipeg, Man. 13 Jan. 1919; s. Robert Hector and Martha Agnes (Queen) R.; e. Robt. H. Smith Sch. Winnipeg; Oakwood Coll. Inst. Toronto; Univ. of Mich. B.S.E. (Aeronautical Engn.) 1942; m. Anne Edgar d. George Gilchrist 26 Sept. 1942; children: Roberta Ann, George Robert; CONSULTANT (AEROSPACE) 1988– ; joined Nat. Research Council Ottawa 1942; Fairchild Aircraft Ltd. Montreal 1942–47; Canadair 1947, Vice Pres. Missiles & Systems Div.; Vice Pres. Operations and Dir. United Technologies Corp., Pratt & Whitney of Canada, Montreal 1960; Pres. and Chief Extve. Offr., Dir. and Corporate Vice Pres., McDonnell Douglas of Canada, Toronto 1970–74; Pres., Chief Operating Offr. and Dir., Spar Aerospace Ltd. Toronto 1974–80; Consultant 1980–81; Extve. Vice Pres. & C.O.O., Canadair Ltd. 1981–87; recipient C.D. Howe Award C.A.S.I. 1979; Fellow, Founding mem. and Past Pres. Candn. Aeronautics & Space Inst.; Assoc. Fellow, Am. Inst. Aerospace Science; mem. Engn. Inst. Can.; Assn. Prof. Engrs. Prov. Ont.; Hon. Life Mem., Air Industries Assn. Can. (Past Chrmn.); Lambda Chi Alpha; Past Chrmn. Candn. Del. NATO Indust. Adv. Group; former mem. various comtes. Science Council Can.; Past Gov. Ont. Research Foundation; Past mem., Dept. of Revenue Advisory Ctte. on Scientific Rsch.; United Church; recreations: fishing, hunting, skiing; Clubs: Royal St. Lawrence Yacht; Granite; Home: 39 Old Mill Rd., Apt. 106, Toronto, Ont. M8X 1G6.

**RICKER, Marvi,** B.Sc., M.Sc.; foundation executive; b. Parnu, Estonia 27 Oct. 1943; d. Oswald Alexander and Ameila (Randma) Heinola; e. Univ. of Toronto B.Sc. 1966, M.Sc. 1967; m. John Carman s. Dr. Carman and Leonara (Stephens) R. 9 Dec. 1978; stepchildren: Catherine Ann, Judith Patricia, Martha Clare; EXTVE. DIRECTOR, THE RICHARD IVEY FOUNDATION 1990– ; Chem. Instr., Scarborough Coll., Univ. of Toronto 1967–71; Asst. to Principal, 1971–75; Extve. Asst. to Vice-Pres., External Affairs, Univ. of Toronto 1975–76; Community Relns. Coord. 1977–84; Dir., Public & Community Relns. 1984–90; Dir., Hungarian Rsch. Inst. of Canada 1986– ; Mem., CIUT-FM 1986–88; Counc., Ont. Univ. Communications & Govt. Relns. Ctte. 1986–89; Univ. Affairs Bd., Gov. Counc., Univ. of Toronto 1989–90; Trustee, Nat. Mus. of Sci. & Technol. 1990– ; Dir., Canadian Scene 1990–91; Quality Assurance Task Force, London Bd. of Education 1992–93; Engineering Science Advisory Council, Univ. of W. Ont. 1993– ; Special Projects Allocations Ctte., United Way 1980, '81; Rakoczi Medal 1990; Candn. Counc. for Advancement of Edn. pubn. award 1986; Estonian Arts & Letters Soc. Cultural Support Award 1981; Counc. for Advancement & Support of Edn. program award 1980; NRC scholarship 1967; Lutheran; author: 'The Public Institution in a Multicultural Society' 1983; club: McGill 1975–86; London Club 1992– ; Home: 47 Doncaster Ave., London, Ont. N6G 2A1; Office: 618 Richmond St., London, Ont. N6A 5J9.

**RICKER, William Edwin,** O.C., M.A., Ph.D., LL.D., D.Sc., F.R.S.C. (1956); biologist; ret. public servant; b. Waterdown, Ont. 11 Aug. 1908; s. Harry Edwin Benson and Rebecca Helena (Rouse) R.; e. Coll. Inst., North Bay, Ont.; Univ. of Toronto, B.A. 1930, M.A. 1931, Ph.D. 1936; D.Sc. Manitoba 1969; LL.D. Dalhousie University 1973; married Marion Torrance, daughter late John Cardwell, 30 March 1935; children: Karl Edwin, John Fraser, Eric William, Angus Clemens; Scient. Assistant, Biol. Bd. of Canada, 1931–37; Junior Scientist, International Pacific Salmon Fisheries Commission, New Westminster, B.C., 1938; Asst. Assoc. and Prof. of Zool., Indiana Univ., 1939–50; Editor, Fisheries Research Bd. of Canada, 1950–62; Acting Chairman, Fisheries Research Bd. of Can. 1963–64; Chief Scientist, 1965–73; received Wildlife Society Award for the 'outstanding publication in aquatic wildlife ecology and management,' 1953–54 and 1959; Baldi Mem. Lectr., International Cong. of Limnology, Helsinki 1956; Publications: (monographs) 'Stoneflies of South-Western British Columbia' 1943; 'Systematic Studies in Plecoptera' 1952; 'Handbook of Computations for Biological Statistics of Fish Populations' 1958; 'Russian-Eng. Dictionary for Students of Fisheries and Aquatic Biology' 1973; 'Computation and Interpretation of Biological Statistics of Fish Populations' 1975; 'Effects of the Fishery and of Obstacles to Migration on the Abundance of Fraser River Sockeye Salmon' 1987; numerous papers contrib. to scient. journs. and bulls.; mem., Am. Assn. Advanc. Science; Am. Fisheries Soc. (Award of Merit 1969); Candn. Soc. of Zool.; Candn. Soc. of Environmental Biol.; Am. Soc. of Limnol. & Oceanography (Pres. 1959); Arctic Inst. N. Am.; Entomol. Soc. of B.C.; Internat. Assn. for Limnol.; Wilson Ornithol. Soc.; awarded Flavelle Medal of Royal Soc. Can. 1969; awarded F.E.J. Fry medal of Candn. Soc. of Zoologists 1983; apptd. Officer, Order of Canada 1986; recipient Eminent Ecologist Award 1990, Ecological Soc. of Am.; recreations: hiking, golf; Club: Explorers (N.Y.); Home: 3052 Hammond Bay Rd., Nanaimo, B.C. V9T 1E2.

**RICKERD, Donald,** C.M., Q.C., B.A., M.A.; foundation executive; b. Smiths Falls, Ont. 8 Nov. 1931; s. Harry and E. Mildred (Sheridan) R.; e. Queen's Univ. B.A. 1953; St. Andrews Univ. Scot. 1951–52; Oxford Univ. B.A., 1955, M.A. 1963; grad. of Osgoode Hall Law Sch. 1959; LL.D., Queen's Univ. 1985; D.C.L., Mount Allison Univ. 1985; LL.D., Trent Univ. 1986; LL.B. York Univ. 1991; m. Julie d. John Rekai 1968; one s. Christopher Robert John; PRESIDENT, MAX BELL FOUNDATION 1989– ; read law with Fasken & Calvin; called to Bar of Ont. 1959; law practice Fasken & Calvin 1959–61; York Univ. 1961–68, Registrar and Secy. of Senate, Master-Winters Coll., Asst. Prof. Faculty of Adm. Studies; Pres., Donner Candn. Foundation 1968–89; Pres. W. H. Donner Foundation Inc., New York 1971–87; mem. Royal Comn. inquiry RCMP 1977–81; former Chrmn., Ont. Coll. of Art; mem. of Bd., Robarts Rsch. Inst., London, Ont.; former Chrmn. Internat. Standing Comte. on Philanthropy; Bd. Chrmn., Dräger Canada Ltd., Toronto; Bd. Chrmn., St. Lawrence Resin Products Ltd.; Mem. Bd. & Vice Chrmn., Central Hosp., Toronto; former mem. of Bd., Upper Canada Coll.; mem. of Bd., Queen's Univ.; mem. of Bd. of Regents, Mt. Allison Univ.; mem. of Bd. George & Helen Vari Found., Toronto; mem of Bd. Elfriede Dräger Meml. Found., New York City; mem. Law Soc. Upper Can.; cr. Q.C. 1977; Member, Order of Can. 1984; recreations: tennis, boating; Clubs: University (Toronto); Home: 21 Elm Ave., Toronto, Ont. M4W 1M9; Office: Suite 3516, P.O. Box 105, Aetna Tower, Toronto-Dominion Centre, Toronto, Ont. M5K 1G8.

**RIDDELL, John Evans,** B.Eng., M.Sc., Ph.D., F.R.S.C., F.G.A.C. F.G.S.A.; retired; b. Montreal, Que. 21 May 1913; s. Clarence Percival and Mary Marguerite (Evans) R.; e. Westmount High Sch. (Sr. Matric. 1931); McGill Univ., B.Eng. (Mining) 1935, M.Sc. (Geol.) 1936, Ph.D. (Geol.) 1953; m. Helen Joan, d. late Dr. Edward Archibald, 8 Feb. 1939; children: John, Joanna, Michael, Edward, Christie; Former Pres., International Geochemical Associates Ltd. (Retired); Chrmn. Coxheath Gold Holdings Ltd. 1985–88; Surveyor, Union Corp., Johannesburg, S.A., 1936–38; Field Engr., Dome Mines Ltd., N.W.T., 1939; Special Lectr., Dept. of Geol., Univ. of Sask., 1947–49; Asst. Prof., Dept. of Geol. Sciences, McGill Univ., 1950–56; Assoc. Prof., 1956–58; Chrmn., Dept. of Geol., Carleton Univ., 1958–61; served in 2nd World War with R.C.A.F. 1940–45; F.O., Navig. Instr., 1940–43; Flight Lieut., Navig., Bomber Command, 1943–45; Mentioned in Despatches (1945); mem., Candn. Inst. Mining & Metall.; Assn. Expl. Geochem; Am. Inst. Min. and Met. Eng. Sigma Xi; Phi Kappa Pi; Anglican; recreations: skiing, sailing; Address: 298 Bedford Highway, Halifax, N.S. B3M 2K8.

**RIDDELL, Norman Harold,** B.A., M.A., Ph.D.; civil servant; b. Moose Jaw, Sask. 26 Dec. 1944; s. Harold Alva and Ruth Margaret (Evans) R.; e. Univ. of Sask., B.A. 1965, M.A. 1967; Univ. of London; Stanford Univ., Ph.D. 1971; m. Claudia d. Jacques et Marguerite Sancandi; children: Morgane Evelyne, Guendalina Constance, Eleanor Olivia; SOUS-MINISTRE, MINISTÈRE DES AFFAIRES INTERNATIONALES, DE L'IMMIGRATION ET DES COMMUNAUTÉS CULTURELLES, GOUVERNEMENT DU QUÉBEC; Instr., Univ. of Sask. 1968; Fgn. Serv. Offr., Dept. of External Affairs (N.Y., Stockholm, Dakar, Jeddah, London, Brasilia) 1971–84; Mem., Fin. Ctte., Commonwealth Secretariat; Bds. of Mngt., Commonwealth Fund for Tech. Coop., Commonwealth Youth Prog., Commonwealth Found. 1977–81; Spec. Asst. for Foreign Affairs, Prime Minister's Office 1974–75; Advr., Parl. Ctte. on Canada's Relations with Developing Countries, House of Commons 1981–82; Assoc. Depy. Min., Extve. Counc., Govt. of Sask. 1984; Depy. Min. to the Premier & Cabinet Sec., Govt. of Sask. 1984–88; Sous-ministre, Ministère des Communautés culturelles et de l'Immigration, Gouvernement du Québec 1988–93; Secrétaire Général Associé, Conseil Exécutif, Gouvernement du Québec 1988; Adv. Counc. Mem., Inst. of Intergovt. Relns.; Dir., Inst. for Rsch. in Public Policy; Public Policy Forum; Mem., Commission concernant les besoins de la relève des gestionnaires pour la Fonction publique quebecoise; Mem., Ch. of England; Inst. of Public Admin. of Can.; recreations: chamber music, painting; Home: 3980, Côte des Neiges, Apt. A14, Montréal, Qué. H3H 1W2.; Office: 360, rue McGill, Suite 4.02, Montréal, Qué. H2Y 2E9.

**RIDDELL, Wayne Kerr,** B.Mus., C.M.; choral conductor; b. Lachute, Que. 10 Sept. 1936; s. Horace Everett and Olive Anita (Kerr) R.; e. McGill Univ. B.Mus. 1960; Founded Tudor Singers of Montreal 1962 (became fully profl. choir 1976; undertook extensive tour of U.K. and Euorpe); Dir. of Music, Erskine & American Ch. 1965; Lectr., Marianopolis Coll., Univ. of Montreal 1965–68; Asst. Prof., Fac. of Music, McGill Univ. & Dir. of Choral Activities of Dept. 1968; Dir. of Music, Ch. of St. Andrew & St. Paul, Montreal 1972; Master Conductor, Annual National Choral Conductors Symposiums 1978–86; Chorus Master, Montreal Symphony Orch. 1980–86; resigned all positions to become a freelance choral conductor 1986; Guest Conductor, Nat. Youth Choir 1988; Festival: Candn. Children's Choirs in Concert (CBC TV documentary) 1989: Festival: Canadian Youth Choirs in Concert 1990; Choral Artist in Residence, Sask. Choral Fed. 1991; Special guest conductor for opening concert of World Symposium of Choral Music, Vancouver 1993; Special guest conductor for the 1993–94 season of the Winnipeg Singers and the Ottawa Pro Musica; 4 concerts in France and Belgium forthcoming Nov. 1994; Tudor Singers won 1st 'Leslie Bell Competition,' CBC 1963; Choir of Ch. of St. Andrew & St. Paul won first 'Healy Willan Award,' Canada Council 1980; awarded 3-month 'study tour' as guest of W. German Govt. 1976; Order of Canada for outstanding contbn. to Candn. choral music 1988; awarded 'Distinguished Service Award,' Assn. of Candn. Choral Conductors 1992; Presbyn.; Mem., Assn. of Candn. Choral Conductors; Am. Choral Dir. Assn.; Royal Candn. Coll. of Organists; recreations: travel, fitness, bridge; Home: No. 1 Wood Ave., Apt. 401, Westmount, Que. H3Z 3C5.

**RIDDELL, William Andrew,** O.C. (1974), M.Sc., Ph.D., L.L.D., F.C.I.C.; b. Hamiota, Man. 6 July 1905; s. Thomas and Jane Taylor (Rankin) R.; e. Univ. of Manitoba, B.A. 1925, B.Sc. 1926; Univ. of Sask., M.Sc. 1928; Research Fellow, Leland Stanford Jr. Univ., Ph.D. 1931; m. late Beryl Evelyn (deceased 1981), d. late Frederick James Oaten, 21 Aug. 1931; two d. Catherine Jane, Mary Margaret; m. 2ndly Doris E. Newson 1983 (deceased 1993); Chrmn., Sask. Arts Bd. 1950–65; mem., Nat. Bd., Candn. Centenary Council; Councillor, Chem. Inst. of Can. (1953); joined staff of Univ. of Sask. as Instr., 1926; Lectr., 1928; Asst. Prof. of Chem., Regina Coll., 1931–36; Research Chemist, Fisheries Research Bd. of Can., 1935–38; Prov. Analyst, Sask., 1938–50; Dir., Divn. of Labs., Sask. Dept. of Pub. Health, 1942–50; Dean and Prof. Chem., Regina Coll., Univ. of Sask., 1950–62; apptd. Principal 1962 Regina Campus, Univ. of Sask. (ret. 1973); Chrmn., Sask. Arts Bd. 1950–65; Chrmn., Bd. of Nursing Educ. 1977–1982; Treas., Wascana Centre Authority, 1961–70; mem., Chrmn. S. Sask. Hosp. Centre Bd. 1971–76; Extve. mem., Sask. Research Council; Mem., Museum Services Ctte., City of Regina 1985–89; Chrmn., Sask. Awards Counc. 1986–90; Fellow, Am. Assn. Advanc. Science; Chrmn., Health Sci. Library Council, Regina 1977–81; United Church; recreations: writing histories of local institutions, music, cabinet work; Club: Gyro (Past Pres.); Address: 303, 1002 Gryphon's Walk, Regina, Sask. S4S 6X1.

**RIDDLE, Peter H.,** M.A., Ph.D.; educator; composer; b. Long Branch, N.J. 29 Dec. 1939; s. C. Kenneth and Evelyn Mae (Hulse) R.; e. Lebanon Valley Coll. Annville, Pa., B.Sc. 1961; Trenton (N.J.) State Coll. M.A. 1972; S. Ill. Univ. Ph.D. 1974; m. Gail M. d. Harold and Gertrude Bull 23 June 1962; children: Kendrick David, Anne Rebecca; DIR. SCH. OF MUSIC, ACADIA UNIV. 1983– , Prof. of Music 1969– ; Dir. of Music, N. Hunterdon Regional High Sch. Annandale, N.J. 1961–67; W. Kings Dist. High Sch. Auburn, N.S. 1967–69; joined present Univ. 1969; recipient N.S. Music Educators' Assn. Comn. New Music for Band 1985; composer many concert band works, several chamber works and jazz ensemble works; over 100 additional works composed and available in manuscript; author of four books on collecting and operating old toy trains including 'Trains from Grandfather's Attic' (1991) and 'Wiring Your Lionel Layout' (1991); mem. Candn. Music Educators Assn.; N.S. Music Educators Assn.; Composers, Authors & Publishers Assn. Can.; Candn. Univ. Music Soc.; Phi Delta Kappa Internat.; recreations: model railroading, photography, cycling; Home: 20 Cortland Cres., Kentville, N.S. B4N 4X3; Office: 227 Denton Hall, Wolfville, N.S. B0P 1X0.

**RIDEOUT, Thomas Gerard;** politician; b. Fleur de Lys, White Bay 25 June 1948; s. Alfred and Francis (Noftall) R.; e. Memorial Univ. of Nfld. & Labrador; m. Jacinta d John and Mary Traverse 12 Apr 1971; children: Terrance, Tina, Margaret, Karilynn; Teacher & Vice-Principal, St. Pius X Central H.S. 1970–75; el. M.L.A. Dist. Baie Verte-White Bay 16 Sept. 1975; re-el. 1979, 82, 85, 89; apptd. Min. of Culture, Recreation & Youth Oct. 1984; Parliamentary Asst. to Premier of Nfld. & Labrador 1982–84; Min., Dept. of Fisheries, Govt. of Nfld. 1985–89; Premier of Nfld. and Labrador 1989; Vice Chrmn., Resource Estimates Ctte. 1979–80; recreations: hunting, fishing; Home: 110 Cowan Ave., St. John's, Nfld. A1E 3P3.

**RIDINGTON, Robin,** B.A., Ph.D.; educator; b. Camden, N.J. 1 Nov. 1939; s. William R. and Edith F. (Farr) R.; e. Swarthmore Coll. B.A. 1962; Harvard Univ. Ph.D. 1968; m. Jillian d. William and Ida Botham 26 Sept. 1976; children: Eric, Amber, Juniper; PROF. OF ANTHROP. UNIV. OF B.C. 1989– , Asst. Prof. 1967, Assoc. Prof. 1979, mem. Exec. Ctte. Faculty Assn.; recipient Hubert Evans Prize for Non-fiction 1989; author 'Trail to Heaven' 1988; 'Little Bit Know Something' 1990; numerous publs.; fieldwork Beaver and Omaha Indians; recreation: sailing; Home: RR 2, Galiano, B.C. V0N 1P0; Office: Vancouver, B.C. V6T 2B2.

**RIDLEY, Una Lynette,** R.N., B.Sc.N., M.A.; educator; b. Jamaica 7 Apl. 1933; d. Thomas and Mabel R.; e. Mannings High Sch. Sr. Matric.; Kingston Pub. Hosp. R.N.; Univ. of Windsor B.Sc.N. 1963; Mich. State Univ. M.A. 1971; DEAN OF NURSING, UNIV. OF LETHBRIDGE 1989– ; Sch. Nurse Knox Coll. Jamaica 1954; Staff Nurse, Univ. of W. Indies 1955–57; Nursing Sister, Eng. 1958–59; Staff Nurse, Windsor, Ont. 1959–60; Teacher, Grace Hosp. Sch. of Nursing Windsor 1960–64; Dir., Sarnia (Ont.) Gen. Hosp. Sch. of Nursing 1964–67; devel. prog. and became first Dir. St. Clair Regional Sch. of Nursing, Sarnia 1967–70; Dir., Sch. of Nursing Kingston (Ont.) Gen. Hosp. 1971–73; Chairperson, Health Services Dept. Kingston Campus St. Lawrence Coll. 1973–76, Acting Prin. Kingston Campus 1976–77, Prin. Brockville Campus 1978–80; Dean of Nursing, Univ. of Sask. 1980–89; mem., Candn. Assn. Univ. Schs. Nursing; Alta. R.N.'s Assn.; CUCHID; SWAAC; recreations: weaving, travel, books, cooking; Home: 214 Sherwood Pl., Lethbridge, Alta. T1K 6E7; Office: Lethbridge, Alta. T1K 3M4.

**RIDOUT, Derek Michael,** B.A.; business executive; b. Toronto, Ont. 25 Feb. 1943; e. Univ. of Western Ont. B.A. (Hons.) 1965; m. Margo J. Giroux d. Victoria (Tory) and Jeffrey (Jeff); PRES. & CHIEF EXECUTIVE OFFICER, SILCORP LIMITED 1992– ; Dir., Sales & Mktg., Warner-Lambert Caribbean then Senior Vice-Pres. & Partner, Currie Leyman Consulting 1965–78; Vice-Pres., Mktg. & Sales, Seven-Up Canada Inc. 1978–83; Dir. of Marketing 1976–78; Pres. 1980–83; Pres. & Chief Extve. Offr., Mac's Convenience Stores 1983– ; Pres. & C.O.O. present firm 1990–92; Pres. & C.E.O. Silcorp Ltd. 1992– ; Dir., Candn. Grocery Found.; Hon. Dir., Muscular Dystrophy Assn. of Canada; Mem., Young President's Orgn.; Past Dir. & Chrmn., Candn. Soft Drink Assn.; Past Dir. & Extve. Ctte. Mem., Grocery Products Mfrs. of Canada; recreations: squash, tennis, golf; clubs: Granite (Dir.), Rosedale Golf, Muskadasa Tennis; Home: 6 Eastview Dr., Toronto, Ont. M5M 2W4; Office: 10 Commander Blvd., Scarborough, Ont. M1S 3T2.

**RIECKHOFF, Klaus Ekkehard,** B.Sc., M.Sc., Ph.D.; scientist; educator; b. Weimar, Germany 8 Feb. 1928; s. Herbert J. and Gertrud (Nagel) R.; e. High Sch., Abitur 1946, Weimar, Germany; Karlsruhe Univ., math. & physics 1947–49; Univ. of B.C., B.Sc. 1958, M.Sc. 1959, Ph.D. (Physics) 1962; m. Marianne Neder, 30 Dec. 1949; children: Bernhard A., Claudia A., Cornelia A.; PROF. EMERITUS OF PHYSICS, SIMON FRASER UNIV. 1993– ; Research Staff mem., IBM-Research Lab., San Jose, Cal. 1962–65 (Research Consultant there 1967–69, Visiting Scientist 1976–77); joined Simon Fraser Univ. as Assoc. Prof. of Physics 1965, Full Prof. 1966–93, Acting Dean of Science 1966–67, Assoc. Dean of Grad. Studies 1973–76; mem. of Senate 1965–93; mem. Bd. of Govs. 1978–84 and 1987–93; Visiting Professor, Inst. of Applied Physics, Karlsruhe Univ., Germany, 1969–70; Visiting Professor, Dept. of Physics, Univ. of Puerto Rico in Mayagüez 1987, 1989; Dept. of Chem., Univ. of Queensland, St. Lucia, Qsld. Australia 1987; Inst. of Physics IV, Univ. of Bayreuth, Bayreuth, Germany 1987, 1990; author or co-author of over 60 research papers in areas of Solid State Physics, Molecular Physics and Nonlinear Optics published in various scient. journs. and conf. proceedings; mem. Candn. Assn. Physicists; Am. Phys. Soc.; Am. Assn. Advanc. Science; W. Spectroscopy Assn. (Extve. 1964–68); Candn. Assn. Univ. Teachers; Aircraft Owners & Pilots Assn. (U.S.A.) Home: 212 Newdale Court, N. Vancouver, B.C. V7N 3H1; Office: Burnaby, B.C. V5A 1S6.

**RIEDEL, Bernard E.,** C.D., B.Sc., M.Sc., Ph.D., D.Sc. (Hon.); retired university dean; b. Provost, Alta. 25 Sept. 1919; s. Martin Ewald and Naomi Edna (Klingaman) R.; e. Fairview (Alta.) Rural High Sch., 1937; Univ. of Alta., B.Sc. (Pharm.) 1943, M.Sc. (Pharm.) 1949, D.Sc. (Hon.) 1990; Univ. of W. Ont., Ph.D. (Biochem.) 1953; Inst. of Nuclear Studies, Tenn., Course in Radioisotope Technol. 1956; m. Julia Constance (dec'd 1992) d. late Dr. William Clare McClurg, 5 March 1944; children: Gail Lynne (Mrs. W. Kinloch), Dwain Edward, Barry Robert; DEAN AND PROF., FACULTY OF PHARM. SCIENCES, UNIV. OF BRIT. COLUMBIA, 1967–84; Coord. of Health Sciences 1977–84; Asst. Prof. of Pharm., Univ. of Alta., 1946–50, Assoc. Prof. 1953–58, Prof. 1959; Extve. Asst. to Vice Pres. 1961–67; Dept. of Health Research Fellow, Atomic Energy of Can. Ltd., Chalk River, summer 1953; summer Research Scientist, Suffield Exper. Stn., Defence Research Bd., 1957; served with RCAF during World War II; Navig.-Bombardier with Coastal Command; rank Flying Offr. on discharge; Univ. of Alta. Sqdn. Support Offr. 1949–50; C.O. Univ. of Alta, Sqdn. with rank Wing Commdr. 1954–67; Med. Research Council 1969–73; Extve. Edmonton Region, Boy Scouts of Can.; Dir., Assn. Univs. and Colls. of Can.; Trustee UBC Health Sciences Centre Hosp.; Trustee Cancer Control Agency of B.C. (Pres. 1984–85); Extve. Mem. & Bd. Mem., B.C. Lung Assn. (Vice Pres. 1989, Pres. 1990–92); Extve. Can. Lung Assn.; Trustee, B.C. Transplant Soc. (Chrmn., 1986–89); mem., Scientific Advisory Ctte., B.C. Health Rsch. Foundation 1991; Pres., Professors Emeriti, UBC 1993– ; rec'd. Gold Medal in Pharm. 1943; Lt. Gov.'s Gold Medal for Proficiency 1943; Candn. Forces Decoration 1960; Centennial Medal 1967; UBC 75th Anniv. Medal 1990; awarded Commemorative Medal for 125th Anniversary of Candn. Confederation 1992; contrib. over 28 articles to scient. journs.; Honorary Life Mem., B.C. Coll. of Pharm. (Councillor); Alta. Pharm. Assn.; Candn. Pharm. Assn.; Assn. Faculties Pharm. Can. (Chrmn. 1959 and 1969); Candn. Biochem. Soc.; Pharmacol. Soc. Can.; Am. Assn. Advanc. Sci.; Assn. Deans Pharm. Can.; Liberal; Protestant; recreations: golf, curling; Clubs: Vancouver Curling; University; Point Grey Golf & Country; Home: 8394 Angus Dr., Vancouver, B.C. V6P 5L2.

**RIEDL, W.R.,** B.Com., M.B.A.; investment consultant; e. Univ. of B.C. B.Com. 1963; York Univ. M.B.A. 1969; Chart. Financial Analyst; PRES. & DIR., CANADIAN OIL SECURITIES INC.; Pres. & Dir., Fairvest Securities Corp. (institutional stock brokerage, mem. of Montreal Exchange); Pres. and Dir., Lighthouse Resources Inc.; Dir., Mannville Oil & Gas Ltd.; Founding Pres. Candn. Assn. Petrol. Invest. Analysts; mem. Nat. Assn. of Petroleum Investment Analysts; Chrmn. of the Bd., Yonge St. Mission; recreations: tennis, squash, skiing; Clubs: Adelaide; Rosedale; Home: 176 Golfdale Rd., Toronto, Ont. M4N 2B9.

**RIEL, Maurice,** C.P., C.R.; sénateur; avocat; n. St-Constant, Co. Laprairie, Que., 3 avril, 1922; f. Ubald et Robertine (Charron) R.; e. école primaire, St-Constant; Coll. Ste-Marie, Montréal, Que.; Coll. St-Jean, St-Jean, Que.; Coll. Ste-Croix, Montréal, B.A. 1940; Univ. de Montréal, LL.B. 1944; ép. Laurence; 3 enfants, 10 petits-enfants; CONSEIL ET ASSOCIE, STIKEMAN, ELLIOTT; mem. du Sénat du Canada en 1973, Prés. du Sénat Dec. 1983 à Oct. 1984; Admis au Barreau du Qué., 1945; nommé C.R. 1958; Admin. Air Liquide du Canada Ltée; Alcatel Cable Canada Inc.; Atlas-Gest Inc.; GEC-Alsthom Internat. Inc.; GEC Alsthom Energie Inc.; Degrémont Infilco Ltée; Dumez North America Inc.; mem. Soc. des Amis de Colette; Chambre de Comm. Française au Can.; Union Internale. des Avocats; Libéral; Catholique; récréations: arts, vie de campagne; Club: Mount Royal; Résidence: 2 Westmount Sq., Apt. 1302, Westmount, Qué.; H3Z 2S4 Bureau: Suite 3900, 1155 René Lévesque Blvd. West, Montréal, Qué. H3B 3V2.

**RIESE, Karl Theodore,** M.D., F.R.C.S.(C); b. Selkirk, Man. 31 Jan. 1930; s. Henry B. and Helene (Schilling) R.; e. Univ. of Man., M.D. 1954, F.R.C.S. 1958; Dipl. Am. Bd. of Surg. 1963; m. Carmel M., d. Marc Regnier; Prof. of Surgery, Univ. Of Manitoba and Consultant Medical Dir., St. Boniface Gen. Hosp.; Office: 409 Tache, Winnipeg, Man. R2H 2A6.

**RIÈSE, Laure E.,** M.A., Ph.D.; university professor emeritus; b. Neuchâtel, Switzerland 28 Feb. 1910; d. Frédéric and Laure (Vuilleumier) R.; e. Secondary Sch., Switzerland; Dipl. d'Etude Sup.; Dipl. de l'Inst. de Phonétique (La Sorbonne); came to Canada, 1928; Univ. of Toronto, B.A. 1933, M.A. 1935, Ph.D. 1946; PROF. OF FRENCH, VICTORIA UNIV.; and Assoc. Ed., Modern Drama and Prof. at the Grad. Centre for Study of Drama; Radio and TV Broadcaster for the French Sch.; Publications: 'L'Ame de la Poésie Canadienne Française' (anthology); 'Les Salons Littéraires féminins du Second Empire à nos jours' (awarded Broquette-Gonin Lit. Prize from L'Acad. Française, 1962); 'Un peu de nouveau'; translated in French of Kati Rekai: Les Aventures de Mickey, Taggy, Puppo et Cica à la découverte de Montréal; Les Aventures de Mickey, Taggy, Puppo et Cica en France; has written many articles and reviews for French Canadian and French American journals, and journals in France; Chrmn., Cdn. Swiss Cultural Assn.; Gov., Fed. of Alliances française of Can.; Hon. Pres., Alliance Française de Toronto; Ont. Modern Language Teacher's Assn.; Founder and Pres., French Salon in Toronto; Vice Pres., Ont. Multicultural Francophone Assn.; Correspondent (newspaper) L'Express de Toronto; mem., La Soc. des Gens de Lettres de France; Arts and Letters Club; Heliconian Club; mem., Internat. Assoc. of Literary Critics; Candn. Ethnic Journalist's Assoc.; Writer's Club of Toronto; Mem. du Conseil des Ecoles Françaises de la Communauté urbaine de Toronto; mem. of Bd., World Council for Global Co-operation; mem. of Bd., D.W.D. (Dying with dignity); Founding mem., Friends of the Royal Academy of Arts; Founding mem., Library Rsch. Foundation of Canada; Press mem., French office of information, cultural - Social; Volunteer mem., Gardiner Museum; Chevalier de la Légion d'Honneur (France) 1971; Offr. d'Instruction Publique; Officier d'Académie 1946, Palmes Académiques (received several medals from France); Officier des Arts et des Lettres, France 1990; Hon. Pres., Alliance Française of Toronto; Life mem., Société Histoire de Toronto; Hon. Vice Pres., English Speaking Union; Officer, Order of Canada; Order of Ont.; Dame of Order of St. Lazarus of Jerusalem; Doctor of Sacred Letters (hon. causa); Chrmn. Archimedes Award Foundation; Hon. Pres. du Regroupement des écrivains de Toronto; Gouverneur de la Fédération des Alliances Française du Canada; Médaille commémorative du 125 anniversaire de la Confédération du Canada 1992; Officer of the Companionate of Merit in the Military and Hospitaller Order of Saint Lazarus of Jerusalem; Life mem., La Société d'Histoire de Toronto; A primary French school in Scarborough has been named Ecole Laure–Rièse; Protestant; recreations: reading, travelling; Home: 103 Avenue Rd., Apt. 912, Toronto, Ont. M5R 2G9.

**RIFAT, David,** D.A.; teacher; communicator; artist; theorist; b. Edinburgh, Scotland 30 Sept. 1934; s. M.A. and Magdalen (Gallaway-Murray) R.; e. Edinburgh Coll. of Art D.A. 1957, post grad. 1958, travelling scholar (Italy & Greece) 1959 (highly commended); m. Sandra d. Walter and Ruth Dobbs 31 Dec. 1985; children: Marka, Jason, Rachel, Matthew; PROF., FAC. OF ARTS AND SCIENCE, UNIV. OF TORONTO 1969– ; Dept. Head, Carlise College of Art 1960; Asst. Prof., Univ. of Calif. at San Diego 1964; has taught at Fac. of Edn. and Scarborough Coll., Univ. of Toronto; has exhibited nationally & internationally; Bd. of Dir., Arts Place Gallery of Brantford; Chair, Hart House Art Ctte.; Assoc. Chair, Dept. of Fine Art; First Prize, Royal Scottish Acad. Award; First Prize, Ont. Arts Council Editions I; Andrew Grant Post Grad. Scholarship; Andrew Grant Travelling Scholarship; Andrew Carnegie Travelling Scholarship; author: 'Aspects de l'Ontario à l'occasion du bicentenaire de l'Ontario: Art in Ontario Today'; recreations: reading, games; clubs: Hart House, Mimico Tennis, Faculty; Home: 5 Lake Shore Dr., Toronto, Ont. M8V 1Y9; Office: Sidney Smith, 100 St. George Street, Toronto, Ont. M5S 1A1.

**RIGAULT, André Albert L.,** L.ès L.; retired university professor; b. Chambourcy, France, 6 June 1922; s. Camille V. and Pierrette J. (Maison) R.; e. Faculty of Letters, Univ. of Paris (1944–49), L.ès L. 1947; Dipl. d'Etudes Supérieures (1948); Dipl. de Phonétique (1949); m. Odette S., d. Jean Bruet, Bandol, France, 1948; children: Elisabeth, Olivier, Geneviève, Véronique, Marie-Clotilde, Antoine; Prof., Gen. Phonetics, Phonology, McGill Univ. (Retired 1985) and Chrmn. Department Linguistics 1966–71; Dir., Phonetics Research Lab. there, since 1963, Lang. Lab., 1961–69; Asst. Prof., Inst. of Phonetics, Sorbonne, Paris, 1948–49; Asst. Prof., Dept. of Romance Lang., McGill Univ., 1949–61, Assoc. Prof. 1961–65, Prof. 1965–85; Dir., McGill French Summer Sch., 1954–61; Research Fellow, Canada Council, 1959–60, 1971–72, 1978–79; Visiting Lectr., Univs. Besançon, Rennes, Rabat, Prague, Bucharest, Michigan; Chevalier, Légion d'honneur; Officier, Ordre des Palmes Académiques (France); mem., Société de Linguistique de Paris; Canadian Linguistic Association (President 1970–72); Secy. Gen., 7th Internat. Cong. Phonetic Scs., Montreal 1972; Linguistic Society of Am.; Pres. Assn. Prof. Français au Can. 1969–75; mem. Hon. Comte., 8th Internat. Cong. Phonetic Scs. Leeds, Eng. 1975; Assn. Phonétique Internationale; Internat. Permanent Council of Phonetic Sciences; Internat. Linguistic Assn.; Hon. mem. Council Phonetic Soc. Japan 1972; Chrmn. Comité-Inter-univ. de Recherches Linguistiques sur le Français au Canada, 1964–69; Hon. Vice-Pres., Internat. Soc. of Phonetic Sci., 1979; engaged in research on the analysis and synthesis of speech, Univ. of Lund (Sweden) and Univ. of Edin., 1959–60; Royal Inst. of Technol. (Stockholm) 1972, 1979; author of seven books and 40 papers on linguistics; R. Catholic; Home: 116 Trenton Ave., Ville Mont-Royal, Qué. H3P 1Z4.

**RIGELHOF, Terrance Frederick,** B.A., B.Th., M.A.; writer; b. Regina, Sask. 24 Apr. 1944; s. Philip and Katherine (Behm) R.; e. Univ. of Sask., B.A. 1965; Univ. of Ottawa, B.Th. 1967; McMaster Univ., M.A. 1968; m. Ann d. Frank William Johnson 11 June 1968; Lectr., St. Mary's Univ. 1969–72; Univ. of P.E.I. 1973; Teacher, Dawson Coll. 1974– ; freelance book reviewer, 'Globe and Mail,' 'Montreal Gazette,' 'Books in Canada'; mem., PEN, Writers' Union of Can.; Qspell (Bd. of Dir. 1989–91); author: 'A Beast with Two Backs' 1981, 'The Education of J.J. Pass' 1983, 'Je t'aime, Cowboy' 1993; Home: 436 Grosvenor Ave., Westmount, Que. H3Y 2S4.

**RIGG, Arthur George,** M.A., D.Phil.; university professor; b. Wigan, England 17 Feb. 1937; s. George William and Alice Rose (Rose) R.; e. Wigan G.S.; Pembroke Coll., Oxford Univ., B.A. 1959, M.A. 1962, D.Phil. 1966; m. Jennifer d. Ronald and Vi Dickie 4 July 1964; PROF., CTR. FOR MEDIEVAL STUDIES, UNIVERSITY OF TORONTO 1976– ; Lectr., Merton Coll. Oxford 1961–66; Vis. Asst. Prof., Stanford Univ. 1966–68; Assoc. Prof., Ctr. for Med. Studies, Univ. of Toronto 1968–76; Acting Dir. 1976–78; Assoc. Dir. 1980–86, 1991–92; Vis. Fellow, Pembroke Coll. 1979–80; Chrmn., Ctte. for Med. Latin Studies 1968–76, 1984– ; Connaught Senior Fellow, 1992–93; Mem., Monarchist League of Can.; Med. Acad. of Am.; P.C. Party (resigned 1986 in protest against party's anti-smoking stance); author: 'Gawain on Marriage' 1986, 'The Poems of Walter of Wimborne' 1978, 'Editing Medieval Texts written in England' 1977, 'The English Language' 1968, 'A Glastonbury Miscellany of the Fifteenth Century' 1968; co-author: 'Piers Plowman: the Z-version' 1983; 'A History of Anglo-Latin Literature 1066–1422' 1992; Gen. Ed.: 'Toronto Medieval Latin Texts' 1970– ; recreations: walking; Home: 8 Petman Ave., Toronto, Ont. M4S 2S8; Office: 39 Queen's Park E., Toronto, Ont. M5S 1A1.

**RIGHTER, Julie,** MD, FRCPC; medical microbiologist; b. Hungary 12 March 1948; d. Nicholas and Violet (Forgacs) R.; e. Fac. of Med., Univ. of Toronto MD 1971; FRCPC 1975; m. Raphael s. Otto and Lora Schick 16 May 1971; children: Ruth, Jonathan; ASST. PROF., DEPT. OF MICROBIOLOGY, FACULTY OF MEDICINE, UNIV. OF TORONTO 1981– ; Head of Microbiology & Infection Control, Toronto East General & Orthopaedic Hospital 1977–92; Extve. Mem., Medical Staff Assn. (Sec.-Treas. 1990; Vice-Pres. 1991); Consultant, Excel Bestview Medical Labs. 1981– ; Psychotherapist 1992– ; Past Cons., Candn. Standards Assn.; Ont. Hosp. Assn.; Ont. Ministries of Environment & Labour on Biomedical Waste Issues; Mem., Ont. Min. of Health Drug Quality & Therapeutics Ctte. 1989–94, Acting Chair 1992–93, Chair 1993–94; Mem., Ont. Medical Assn. (Lab. Proficiency Testing Prog. Bacteriology Ctte. 1992–93); Candn. Assn. of Med. Microbiol. (Council Mem. 1982–83; 1991–93); Assn. of Med. Microbiol. of Ont. (Sec.-Treas. 1985–87; Pres. 1987–89); Am. Soc. for Microbiol; Candn. Infectious Disease Soc.; Infectious Diseases Soc. of Am.; Brit. Soc. for Antimicrobial Chemotherapy; General Practice Psychotherapy Assn.; Ont. Soc. of Clinical Hypnosis; past pursuits: devel. of biomedical waste policies which provide cost-effective worker & environ. protection; rational & cost-effective antibiotic utilization policies in hosps., office practice & Ont. Drug Benefit; author of many medical pubs.; recreations: classical music; Home: 228 Coldstream Ave., Toronto, Ont. M5N 1Y3.

**RIIS, Nelson Andrew,** B.Ed., M.A.; member of parliament; b. High River, Alta. 10 Jan. 1942; s. Hans and Signe (Wieseth) R.; e. Univ. of B.C., B.Ed. 1965, M.A. (Geog.) 1970; m. Irene d. Harry and Muriel Hill 20 Feb. 1966; children: Nils Petter, Jonathon James; DEPUTY LEADER and HOUSE LEADER, NEW DEMOCRATIC PARTY 1991– ; Teacher, Kamloops, B.C. 1965–68; Instructor Soc. Sci. Chrmn., Cariboo Coll. 1970–80; Alderman, City of Kamloops 1973–78; Sch. Trustee 1978–80; elected to Parliament 1980; House Leader, New Democratic Party 1986–93; NDP; Small Business & Finance Critic; Commonwealth Parl. Assoc; Inter-Parl. Union; Canada-China Inter-Parl. Assoc.; Canada-Israel Inter-Parl. Assoc.; Canada-Italy Inter-Parl. Assoc.; Hon. mem., IWA; Dir., Royal Geographic Society; mem., Kamloops Chamber of Commerce; Kamloops Art Gallery; Kamloops Mounted Drill Team; Kamloops Museum Assoc.; Royal Candn. Legion; ANAVETS; Council of Candns; Kamloops Fish & Game Assn.; Hon. mem., Kamloops Labour Council; Friends of Wells Gray Park; Adv. Bd., Kamloops Economic Develop. Corp.; Hon. mem., of Cariboo Univ./Coll. Alumni Assoc.; mem., Loyal Order of Moose; Lutheran; recreations: hiking, riding, painting (watercolours), carving (soapstone); Club: Sons of Norway; Kamloops Fly Fishers; Home: 1 - 219 Victoria St., Kamloops, B.C. V2C 2A1; Office: 437 WB, House of Commons, Ottawa, Ont. K1A 0A6.

**RILEY, Anthony William,** D.Phil., F.R.S.C.; educator; b. Radcliffe on Trent, Eng. 23 July 1929; s. late Cyril Frederick and late Winifred Mary (White) R.; e. West Bridgford Grammar Sch. Notts., Eng. 1947; Univ. of Manchester B.A. 1952; Univ. of Tübingen D.Phil. 1958; m. Maria Theresia d. late Karl Walter, Schwäbisch Gmünd, Germany 16 July 1955; children: Christopher Karl Cyril, Katherine Mary, Angela Theresia; EMERITUS PROF. OF GERMAN LANG. AND LIT., QUEEN'S UNIV.; Lektor, Univ. of Tübingen 1957–59, 1960–62; Asst. Lectr. Queen Mary Coll. Univ. of London 1959–60; Asst. Prof. of German present Univ. 1962, Assoc. Prof. 1965, Prof. 1968–92, Head of German Lang. & Lit. 1967–76; Distinguished Visitor, Univ. of B.C. 1980; Lansdowne Visitor, Univ. of Victoria, B.C. 1981; served with Brit. Army 1947–49; author 'Elisabeth Langgässer Bibliographie mit Nachlassbericht' 1970; co-ed. F.P. Grove's 'The Master Mason's House' 1976; 'Fanny Essler' 1984; general editor 'Alfred Döblins Ausgewählte Werke in Einzelbänden' including 'Der Oberst und der Dichter/Die Pilgerin Aetheria' 1978; 'Der unsterbliche Mensch/Der Kampf mit dem Engel' 1980; 'Jagende Rosse/Der schwarze Vorhang und andere frühe Erzählwerke' 1981; 'Wadzeks Kampf mit der Dampfturbine' 1982; 'Kleine Schriften I (1902–1921)' 1985; 'Kleine Schriften II (1922–24)' 1990; 'Schicksalsreise. Bericht und Bekenntnis' 1993; co-ed. 'Echoes and Influences of German Romanticism: Essays in Honour of Hans Eichner' 1987; numerous articles learned journs.; awarded Prize for Excellence in Research, Queen's Univ. 1983; Hermann Boeschenstein Medal, Candn. Assoc. of Univ. Teachers of German 1987; Konrad Adenauer Rsch. Award of the Federal German Chancellor, Alexander von Humboldt Foundation, Bonn (1989); Secretary, Academy of Humanities and Social Sciences, The Royal Soc. of Canada 1992–95; mem. Candn. Assn. Univ. Teachers German (Vice Pres. 1973–75, Pres. 1975–76); Humanities Assn. Can.; Thomas Mann-Gesellschaft; Deutsche Schillergesellschaft; Internat. Vereinigung für Germanische Sprach- und Literaturwissenschaft; Internat. Alfred Döblin-Gesellschaft (Vice Pres. 1984–95); recreation: gardening; Home: 108 Queen Mary Rd., Kingston, Ont. K7M 2A5; Office: Kingston, Ont. K7L 3N6.

**RILEY, Ginetta (Gina) Lori,** B.Sc.; artistic director, choreographer; b. Windsor, Ont. 6 Jan. 1953; d. Italo and Teresa (Lini) Lori; e. F.J. Brennan H.S. 1971; Univ. of Waterloo B.Sc. (Hons.) 1975; intensive dance classes & studies in Canada, U.S. & England 1980–89; m. Robert Graham s. John and Dorothy R. 2 Aug. 1975; one d.: Jessica Lori; FOUNDER, ARTISTIC DIRECTOR, CHOREOGRAPHER, & DESIGNER, GINA LORI RILEY DANCE ENTERPRISES 1979– ; her dance co. (incorp. in 1981) is S.W. Ontario's only profl. dance co. with a staff of 8 touring throughout Canada incl. the N.W.T.; choreographer of over 30 works produced for stage, TV & film; former dancer with several dance ensembles incl. Judy Jarvis Dance & Theatre Co. 1975–77; Dance Advr. to several bds. of edn.; Mem., W. Ont. Regional Arts Adv. Ctte., Min. of Edn.; Univ. of Windsor Instr., School of Dramatic Art 1982–87; Guest in Resident for num. bds. of edn., colleges & univs. in

Canada & U.S.; Dance Assessor, Ont. Arts Council and part of hand-picked delegation travelling to U.K. to investigate dance & strategies; Winner, num. choreographic grants 1977– ; 1990 Winner, Fabian Lemieux Award for Outstanding Contbn. to Arts Edn.; 1989 Civic Recognition Award; 1971 Female Athlete of the Year Award; Treas., Judy Jarvis Dance Found.; recreations: golf, curling, home economics; clubs: Roseland Golf & Curling, Little River Ladies Golf League (Sec.); Home: 8363 Riverside Dr. E., Windsor, Ont. N8S 1E7.

**RILEY, Hugh Sanford,** B.A., LL.B.; financial executive; b. Montreal, P.Q. 15 Mar. 1951; s. Robert Sanford Riley and Hope Meribeth Cameron (Stobie) Coyne; e. Queen's Univ., B.A. 1971; Osgoode Hall Law Sch., LL.B. 1975; m. Deborah J. d. James N. and Madeline Doyle 7 Sept. 1975; H.S. RILEY INVESTORS GROUP; Assoc. & Partner, Taylor McCaffrey Chapman & Sigurdson 1976–85; Vice-Pres. and later Extve. Vice-Pres. & C.O.O., Great Lakes Group Inc. 1985–89; Extve. Vice-Pres. & Chief Operating Offr., Trilon Financial Corp. 1989; Dir., Trilon Finan. Corp.; Great Lakes Group Inc.; Northgate Explorations Limited; Royal LePage Limited; Comcheq Inc.; Morgan Trust Co.; 20/20 Group Financial Ltd.; Couns., Taylor McCaffrey Chapman & Sigurdson; Dir., Ont. Special Olympics; Candn. Hearing Soc. Found.; mem., Law Soc. of Manitoba; clubs: Royal Candn. Yacht Club; Office: 1 Canada Centre, 447 Portage Ave., Winnipeg, Man. R3C 3B6.

**RILEY, Ronald Thomas,** B.E., M.B.A.; executive; b. Toronto, Ont. 28 Feb. 1935; s. Ronald T. and Margaret M. (Black) R.; e. Bishop's Coll. Sch., Lennoxville, Que.; McGill Univ., B.E. (Mech.) 1956; Univ. of Pa., Wharton Grad. Sch., M.B.A. 1959; m. Jessie M. Fulcher, 27 Sept. 1963; three children; CHRMN., CHATEAU INSURANCE COMPANY; Dir., Canfor Corp.; Hollinger Inc.; St. Laurent Compagnie de Reassurance; Canadian Investment Fund, Ltd.; Bullock American Fund; Bullock Asset Strategy Fund; Bullock Growth Fund Ltd.; joined Canadair Ltd., Montreal, 1956, as Design Engineer; joined Crucible Steel of Canada Ltd., 1959, as Assistant Manager, Production Control; joined Canadian Pacific Limited, Montreal, 1961 as Programmer Analyst; held various positions in rail marketing in Montreal and Toronto, in rail operations in Calgary and Vancouver becoming Gen. Mgr., Operations for Pacific Region; Dir., Corporate Planning, Office of the Chrmn. and Pres., Canadian Pacific Limited, Montreal, 1971; Vice Pres., Transport & Telecommunications, 1972; Vice-Pres. Administration, 1976; Vice-Pres. Corporate, May 1981–Dec. 1985; Pres. & C.E.O. Calvin Bullock, Ltd. 1986–90; Clubs: Hillside Tennis; Mount Bruno Golf; University (of Montreal); Mount Royal; Office: Suite 1000, 1130 Sherbrooke St. W., Montreal, Que. H3A 2M8.

**RIMROTT, Friedrich Paul Johannes,** M.A.Sc., Ph.D., Dr.Ing., D.Eng., P.Eng., C.Eng., F.E.I.C., F.C.S.M.E., F.A.S.M.E., F.I.Mech.E.; engineer; b. Halle, Germany 4 Aug. 1927; s. late Ernst Georg Johannes and Margarete (Hofmeister) R.; came to Canada 1952; e. Martin Luther Univ. Halle 1946; Univ. Karlsruhe, Dipl.Ing. 1951; Univ. of Toronto M.A.Sc. 1955; Penn. State Univ., Ph.D. 1958; Ecole Polytech. Montreal 1960; Tech. Hochschule Darmstadt, Dr.Ing. 1961; Univ. of Victoria, Hon. D.Eng. 1992; m. Elsa Doreen, d. late Robert Henry McConnell 7 April 1955; children: Karla (Mrs. C.R. Honey), Robert, Kira, Elizabeth-Ann; PROFESSOR EMERITUS OF MECH. ENGN., UNIV. OF TORONTO since 1993; Mng. Dir., Deutsche Sprachschulen (Metro Toronto) Inc. 1967–91; Asst. Prof. Penn. State Univ. 1958; Asst. Prof. Univ. of Toronto 1960, Assoc. Prof. 1962, Prof. 1967; Visiting Prof., Wien 1969, 1986, Hannover 1970, Bochum 1971, Wuppertal 1978, Hamburg-Harburg, 1987, 1989, Lanzhou 1989, Magdeburg 1992, 1993; Consultant Univ. de la Habana 1972; Founding Chrmn. Candn. Congs. Applied Mechs.; Candn. Consultative Council on Multiculturalism 1973–78; Candn. Soc. Mech. Engn. (Pres.); Candn. Metric Assn. (Pres.); Verein Deutscher Ingenieure; Gesellschaft für Angewandte Math. und Mech. (Dir.); Am. Acad. Mech.; German-Candn. Hist. Assn. (Vice-Pres.); Pres., XVth Internat. Congress of Theoretical and Applied Mechanics, Toronto 1980; Chrmn., CSME Forum 1990, Toronto; author of over 100 scholarly papers in mech. and mech. engn.; books 'Was du ererbt' (with W. Eichenlaub); 'Mechanics of the Solid State' (with J. Schwaighofer); 'Theoretical and Applied Mechanics' (with B. Tabarrok); 'Introductory Orbit Dynamics'; 'Introductory Attitude Dynamics'; CANCAM Award 1989; Sigma Xi; Lutheran; Home: 6 Thurgate Cres., Thornhill, Ont. L3T 4G3; Office: 5 King's College Rd., Toronto, Ont. M5S 1A4.

**RINALDO, Sandie,** B.A.; broadcast journalist; b. Toronto, Ont. 16 Jan. 1950; d. Morris and Mary (Herman) Bryks; e. York Univ. B.A. (Hons.) 1973; m. Michael s. Allan and Rose Rinaldo 28 Nov. 1971; three d. Amanda, Emma, Margalit; ANCHOR, CTV WEEKEND NEWS 1991– ; joined CTV 1973, Prodn. Co-ord. Researcher W5 moving to Story Producer, CANADA AM 1976, Reporter-at-Large there 1977, Reporter CTV News 1978, Back-up Co-Host 1978, News Anchor 1980, Alternate Anchor CTV NAT. NEWS 1981, Anchor Weekend Edition 1985 and back-up Anchor to Nat. News, Sr. Ed. CFTO-TV and Co-Anchor World Beat News 1989–91; frequent guest speaker corporate, univ. and charity events; recipient Bronze Medal Best News Anchor N.Y. Internat. Film & TV Festival 1989; Silver Medal Houston Internat. Film Festival for analysis single current news story 1990; Silver Medal New York Internat. Film & TV Festival, Coverage Ongoing News Story, Series 1990; co-producer video cassette 'Childbirth From Inside Out' (winner Am. Film & Video Assn. Hon. Mention Best Video 1990); mem. Acad. Candn. Cinema & TV; recreations: theatre, dance, music; Office: CTV Television Network Ltd., P.O. Box 3000, National News, Agincourt Postal Stn., Agincourt, Ont. M1S 3C6.

**RING, William D.,** B.Comm., C.A.; b. Dartmouth, N.S. 2 May 1947; s. Reginald G. and Helen M. (Jackson) R.; e. Dalhousie Univ. B.Comm. 1970; Ont. Inst. of C.A.s C.A. 1972; m. Nancy E. d. Lloyd and Millicent Brimicombe Dec. 1968; children: Elizabeth D., Timothy A.; VICE PRESIDENT, FINANCE, CROSSLEY CARPET MILLS LIMITED 1987– ; Touche Ross & Co. Ottawa 1970–72; Management Consultant, Canadian Motor Industries Dartmouth 1972–74; Controller, Industrial Estates Limited Halifax 1974–79; Vice Pres. Finance 1979–87; Anglican; recreations: skiing; clubs: Halifax; Home: 47 Marigold Dr., Truro, N.S. B2N 6E7; Office: 435 Willow St., Truro, N.S. B2N 5G2.

**RIOPELLE, Jean-Paul,** C.C. (1969); painter; sculptor; b. Montreal, Que. 1923; has been painting in Paris since 1947 where he has established himself as the most internationally acclaimed Canadian painter of the 20th century; his painting 'Toscin' (1953) chosen by Nat. Gallery to be sent abroad representing Candn. work; paintings selected for exhibit at 42nd Pittsburgh Internat. Exhn. (inaugurated by Andrew Carnegie 'to show old masters of tomorrow') 1961; recipient UNESCO award 1962; a 3–week exhn. of 82 paintings at Nat. Gallery, Ottawa 1963; retrospective exhn. Art Gall. of Ont. 1963; 'Ficelles et Outres Yeux' Exhn., Musée d'Art Moderne, Paris 1971; book on Riopelle by Pierre Schneider pub. 1971.

**RIOUX, Hon. Claude,** B.A., LL.L.; judge; b. Sayabec, Que. 20 May 1930; s. Albert and Aline (Mercier) R.; e. Jesuits Coll. Quebec City B.A. 1950; Laval Univ. LL.L. 1953; m. Marie-Jose. Marcel Garneau, Arthabaska, Que. 2 Dec. 1961; one d. Sophie; JUDGE, SUPERIOR COURT OF QUE. since 1979; called to Bar of Que. 1954; cr. Q.C. 1970; practiced law particularly with Camil Noël, Q.C. and Jacques Alleyn, Q.C. 1954–66; Assoc. Depy. Min. of Justice Que. Govt. 1966–70, 1973–75 and Dep. and Assoc. Secy.-Gen. Extve. Council 1975–79; R. Catholic; Home: 403 – 5 Jardins Merici, Quebec City, Que. G1S 4N7; Office: 300 Blvd. Jean-Lesage, R-356, Quebec City, Que. G1K 8K6.

**RIOUX, Diane,** B.A.; éxécutif d'association; née. Montréal, Qué. 30 décembre 1949; f. Roger et Claire (Lanteigne) R.; é. Univ. d'Ottawa B.A. 1972; ép. Gilbert f. Laurent Brunet 15 juillet 1972; enfants: Guillaume, Judith; VICE-PRÉSIDENTE, CONSEIL CONSULTATIF CANADIEN SUR LA SITUATION DE LA FEMME; Adjointe au Sec. gén. du IXe congrès de Sciences politique 1972; Coord. action communautaire CLSC de Hull 1977; Adjointe admin. Journal La Presse 1985; responsable du service de l'Acceuil et des renseignements Assemblée nat. du Qué. 1986; Attachée politique de divers min. du gouv. du Qué. 1988; Professionelle autonome et prop. d'une entreprise de relations publiques 1990; dans le cadre de mon travail je donne des conférences sur des questions qui sont prioritaires aux dossiers féminins tel que la violence faite aux femmes, la santé, femmes en affaires; a été mem. du conseil d'admin. du Centre Le Pont a été Prés. de Soc. Can. du Cancer chap. de Trois Rivières; Vice-Prés. de la Croix-Rouge chap. Trois-Rivières; mem., C. de C. de Trois Rivières; Club Rotary de Trois Rivières; rés.: 4805, des Chenaux, Trois Rivières, Qué.; bureau: 875 – 2021 Union, Montréal, Qué. H3A 2S9.

**RIOUX, Jacques E.,** B.A., M.D., M.P.H.; physician; educator; b. Ste.-Anne des Monts 13 Nov. 1935; s. Joseph Emile and Marie Clémence (Bouchard) R.; e. Univ. of Montreal B.A. 1955; Laval Univ. M.D. 1960; Univ. of Calif. Master of Pub. Health 1976; m. Juanita H. Henry Bongartz 22 Jan. 1966; children: Sébastien, Stéphane, Sophie; PROFESSOR OF OBSTETRICS AND GYNECOLOGY, FACULTY OF MEDICINE, LAVAL UNIVERSITY 1978– ; Residency in Surg. Hôpital de l'Enfant Jésus Que. 1960–61; Basic Sci. in Surg. Grad. Sch. of Med. Univ. of Pa. 1961–62; Residency in Surg. Hahnemann Med. Coll. and Hosp., Pa. 1962–63; Residency in Obstetrics/Gynecology Union Memorial Hosp.; Hosp. for the Women of Maryland; Johns Hopkins Hosp. 1963–67; Residency at La Clinique Gynécologique de la Faculté de Méd. de Paris 1967–68; introduced laparoscopy in Can. 1968; Asst. Prof. Sch. of Med. Laval Univ. 1968–73; orgn. first sperm bank 1972; invented bipolar tubal forcep for female sterilization 1973; Chief of Gynecology Le Centre Hospitalier de l'Univ. Laval 1972–77, 1985– ; Assoc. Prof. Sch. of Med. Laval Univ. 1973–78; sabbatical yr. Sch. of Pub. Health, Univ. of Berkeley 1975–76; began prog. of extra-corporeal fertilization and embryo transfer at C.H.U.L. 1979; Pres. Candn. Fertility Soc. 1973–74; Sec., Vice-Pres. and Pres. Am. Assn. of Gynecological Laparoscopists 1972–78; Vice-Pres. and Trustee Candn. Ctte. for Fertility Rsch. 1976– ; co-author: 'Reproduction: Manuel Pratique/A Practical Manual' 1973; 'A Manual of Laparoscopy' 1974; 'An Atlas of Hysterosalpingography' 1979; 'L'Insémination Artificielle Thérapeutique' 1983; 'Laparoscopy and Hysteroscopy in Gynecological Practice ' 1985; author and co-author of over 100 papers on human reproduction; recreations: scuba diving, tennis, racquetball; Home: 2776 Sasseville, Ste.-Foy, Que. G1W 1A2; Office: C.H.U.L., 2705 Boul. Laurier, Ste.-Foy, Que. G1V 4G2.

**RIPLEY, Robert Trueman,** B.A., B.Ed., M.Ed.; high school teacher; b. Truro, N.S. 5 Sept. 1951; s. Robert Douglas and Edith Rebecca (Seaman) R.; e. Acadia Univ. B.A. 1972, B.Ed. 1973; Dalhousie Univ. M.Ed. 1994; m. Dr. Patricia Nellie d. G. Ernest and Ellen A. Waring 10 July 1982; HISTORY AND POLITICAL SCIENCE TEACHER, WEST KINGS DISTRICT HIGH SCHOOL 1973– ; Social Studies Dept. Head 1986– ; High School Soccer Coach 1980–91; one of several N.S. teachers to introduce pol. sci. to H.S. curriculum 1973; recognized by N.S. Dept. of Edn. 17 July 1984 for 'leadership and service to education in the Prov. of N.S.'; well-known across N.S. for innovative approaches in teaching Candn. politics; currently completing rsch. on the teaching of nat. identity issues in Schools of Edn. at Candn. Univs.; Rep. for Atlantic Canada on Extve. of the Candn. History of Edn. Assn. 1992– ; Mem., Bd. of Gov., Acadia Univ. 1980–93; Bd. of Mngt., Kings Regional Rehab. Centre 1980–92; Mem., United Ch. of Canada; P.C. Party (Prov. Extve., P.C. Party of N.S. 1989–92; Pres., Kings West P.C. Assn. 1980–92); author: 'National Identity' (paper presented to Biennial Conf., Candn. History of Edn. Assn. 1992); recreations: soccer, travel; Home: P.O. Box 1364, Wolfville, N.S. B0P 1X0; Office: P.O. Box 79, Auburn, N.S. B0P 1A0.

**RISK, Michael John,** B.Sc., M.Sc., Ph.D.; university professor; b. Toronto, Ont. 17 Feb. 1940; s. John C. and Kathleen N. (Perdue) R.; e. Univ. of Toronto B.Sc. (Hons.) 1962; Univ. of Western Ont. M.Sc. 1964; Univ. of Southern Calif. Ph.D. 1971; m. Patricia d. W. and R. Stephen 1965; children: Andrea Christine, Meredith Eileen; PROF., DEPT. OF GEOLOGY, MCMASTER UNIV. 1982– ; Asst. Prof., McMaster Univ. 1971; Ssco. Prof. 1976; Visiting Prof., Univ. of Costa Rica 1977; James Cook Univ. (Australia) 1980; Adjunct Prof., Marine Serv., Univ. of Puerto Rico 1989– ; internat. devel. work in Central America, Indian & Pacific Oceans funded by CIDA, IDRC, ICOD & IUCN; research on biogeology funded by GSA, Ont. Govt., NSERC; NSERC scholarships & awards; nominated, McMaster Teaching Award; author of approx. 100 refereed pubns. in geobiology; recreations: skiing, running, woodworking; Home: 1813 Fiddlers Green Rd., R.R. #2, Ancaster, Ont. L9G 3L2; Office: Hamilton, Ont. L8S 4M1.

**RISKE, Barbara Elizabeth,** B.A., A.M.M., A.R.C.T.; musician; b. Winnipeg, Man. 27 Oct. 1946; d. William Albert and Elizabeth Gertrude (Lane) Malcolm; e. Kelvin H.S. 1964; Univ. of Man. B.A. 1967, A.M.M. 1967 (Hons.); Univ. of Toronto A.R.C.T. 1965; m. William Kenneth s. Norman and Janette R. 28 April 1973; children: Elizabeth Nicola, William Norman Malcolm; PRINCIPAL PIANIST, ROYAL WINNIPEG BALLET 1990– and PRINCIPAL KEYBOARD PLAYER, WINNIPEG SYMPHONY ORCHESTRA 1985– ; Pianist, Royal Winnipeg Ballet 1966–69; Eliot Field Ballet (N.Y.) 1969; Am. Ballet Theatre 1969–72; Royal Winnipeg Ballet 1972–76; freelance musician 1976–89; estab. prog. of prep. studies, Sch. of Music, Univ. of Man. 1984; Teacher 1984–89; Isbister Scholarship; 'Best Pianist,' Internat. Ballet Comp. Helsinki 1991; discography incl. 'Spirit Reel' for Blue Ocean Recordings & num. recordings for CBC; Bd. Mem., Man. Conservatory of Music & Arts; Women's Musical Club; Jr. Musical Club; Assoc. Artistic Dir., Chamber Soc. 'Aurora Musicale'; Home: 59 Kingsway Ave., Winnipeg, Man. R3M 0G2; Office: 380 Graham Ave., Winnipeg, Man. R3C 4K2.

**RISKE, William Kenneth;** cultural services consultant; b. Lamont, Alta. 9 May 1949; s. Norman Elmer and Clara Jeanette (Krause) R.; e. Univ. of Alberta 1967-69; m. Barbara d. William and Elizabeth Malcolm 28 April 1973; children: Elizabeth Nicola, William Norman; CULTURAL SERVICES CONSULTANT 1992– ; Stage Manager, Royal Winnipeg Ballet 1971–73; Production Stage Mgr. 1973–76; Production Mgr. 1976–77; Assoc. Gen. Mgr. 1977–79; Gen. Mgr. 1979–92; Mem., Assn. of Cultural Extves.; Candn. Assn. of Profl. Dance Organizations (Pres. 1985–88); Dancevision (Pres. 1990); recreations: curling, skiing; clubs: Winnipeg Winter; Address: 59 Kingsway Ave., Winnipeg, Man. R3M 0G2.

**RISKIN, Mary (Winifred) Walters,** B.Ed.; writer; editor; b. Wainwright, Alta. 25 Nov. 1949; d. Robert Kenneth and Marjorie Alice (Roe) Walters; e. Univ. of Alta. B.Ed. 1970; m. Gerald A. Riskin 23 Feb. 1973, div. 1981; children: Daniel Kenneth, Matthew David; WRITER AND EDITOR 1990– ; jr. high sch. teacher Thorhild, Wetaskiwin and Edmonton, Alta. 1971–75; Exec. Dir. Writers Guild of Alta. 1982–87, Sec. 1980, mem.; Ed.-in-Chief, Lone Pine Publishing 1988–90; Founding mem. Bd. Alta. Found. for Lit. Arts 1984–87; mem. Bd., Treas. Wordworks Soc. Alta. 1985–87; Juror, Can. Council Writing Grants 1987, 1989; Writers' & Publishers' Adv. Ctte. to Min. of Culture, Alta. 1987–89; extensive reading, speaking and teaching engagements incl. readings '88 Olympics Arts Festival and Harbourfront Toronto 1988; recipient Alta. Culture Writing Grant 1982, 1990; Alta. Found. Lit. Arts Grants 1987, 1991; Writers Guild Alta. Award Excellence in Writing (novel cat.) 1987; Alta. Achievement Award 1987; Canada Council Grant 1990; author: 'The Woman Upstairs' novel 1987; short stories various lit. mags.; mem. Rio Terrace Community League (Bd. 1987–88); recreations: culture, sports; Home: 280 Hillcrest Pl., Edmonton, Alta. T5R 5X6.

**RIST, John Michael,** M.A., F.R.S.C. (1976); educator; b. Romford, Eng. 6 July 1936; s. Robert Ward and Phoebe May (Mansfield) R.; e. Brentwood Sch. Eng. 1954; Cambridge Univ. B.A. 1959, M.A. 1963; m. Anna Thérèse d. Sidney Vogler, London, Eng. 30 July 1960; children: Peter, Alice, Thomas, Rebecca; PROF., OF CLASSICS & PHILOSOPHY, UNIV. OF TORONTO 1983– ; Lectr. in Greek Univ. of Toronto 1959, Asst. Prof. 1963, Assoc. Prof. 1965, Prof. 1969–80, 1983– ; Life Mem., Clare Hall, Cambridge 1991– ; cross-apptd. St. Michael's Coll. 1983–90; Chrmn. Grad. Dept. Classical Studies 1971–75; Regius Prof. of Classics Univ. of Aberdeen 1980–1983; former Bd. mem. Oxfam Can.; Canairelief; Past Pres. Coalition for Life; author 'Eros and Psyche' 1964; 'Plotinus, the Road to Reality' 1967; 'Stoic Philosophy' 1969; 'Epicurus: An Introduction' 1972, Italian Transl. 1978; 'On the Independence of Matthew and Mark' 1978; Ed. 'The Stoics' 1978; 'Human Value' 1982; 'Platonism and its Christian Heritage' 1985; 'The Mind of Aristotle' 1989; over 60 articles mainly on ancient philos and patristics.; served with RAF 1954–56; mem. Classics Assn. Can.; recreations: swimming, walking, travel; Office: 16 Hart House Circle, Univ. of Toronto, Toronto, Ont. M5S 1A1.

**RITCHIE, Albert Edgar,** C.C. (1975), LL.D.; diplomat (retired); b. Andover, N.B., 20 Dec. 1916; s. Stanley W. and Beatrice (Walker) R.; e. Mount Allison Univ., B.A. 1938; Oxford Univ. (Rhodes Scholar), B.A. 1940; LL.D. Mt. Allison Univ. 1966; LL.D. St. Thomas Univ. 1968; LL.D. Carleton Univ. 1985; m. Gwendolin, d. late John G. Perdue, Ottawa, Ont., 20 Dec. 1941; children: Gordon, Heather, Donald, Holly; Ambassador to Ireland 1976–80; with Brit. Purchasing Comn., 1941–42; Minstry of Econ. Warfare Mission (Brit. Embassy), Washington, 1942–44; joined Dept. of External Affairs as 3rd Secy., Washington, July 1944; 2nd Secy. 1946; resigned 1946 to become Special Asst. to Asst. Secy.-Gen., Econ. Affairs Dept., U.N., 1946–47; Special Asst. to Extve. Secy. of U.N. Prep. Comte. and Conf. on Trade and Employment, 1947–48; rejoined External Affairs as Foreign Service Offr., 1948; 1st Secy., London, Dec. 1948, Counsellor, 1952; Ottawa, May 1952; Candn. Embassy, Washington, D.C.; Min., 1957; Chargé d'Affaires a.i. 1958–59; Asst. Under-Secy. of State for External Affairs, Ottawa, 1959 and Depy. Under-Secy., 1964; Ambassador to U.S.A. 1966–69; Under-Secy. of State for External Affairs, 1970; Outstanding Achievement Award, Public Service of Canada 1974; Un. Church; recreations: walking, skating, reading, fishing; Home: 336 Frost Ave., Ottawa, Ont. K1H 5J2.

**RITCHIE, Alexander Charles,** M.B., Ch.B., D.Phil., F.R.C.P.(C); b. Auckland, N.Z. 2 Apl. 1921; s. Percy Charles and Olive Muriel (Hodge) R.; e. Univ. of Otago, N.Z., M.B., Ch.B. 1944; Oxford Univ. D.Phil. 1950; m. Susan d. D. Liszauer 10 Oct. 1956; CONSULTANT IN PATHOLOGY, MOUNT SINAI HOSPITAL 1989– ; Prof. of Pathol. Univ. of Toronto 1961–89, Prof. Emeritus 1986– ; Head of Pathol. 1961–74; consultant to various hosps. 1961– ; Brit. Empire Cancer Campaign Oxford 1947–49; Philip Walker Student Oxford Univ. 1950–51; Visiting Fellow Chicago Med. Sch. 1951–52; Mass. Gen. Hosp. 1953–54; Asst. Prof. of Pathol. and Miranda Fraser Assoc. Prof. of Comp. Pathol. McGill Univ. 1954–61; Head Div. Pathol., Toronto Gen. Hosp. 1961–69, Pathol.-in-Chief 1969–74, Sr. Pathol. 1974–86, Consulting Pathol. 1986– ; Pres. World Pathol. Foundation 1980–83; Director, Candn. Liver Foundation 1970–88; Pres. World Assn. Soc.'s Pathol. 1981–84; author various med. papers; recipient Candn. Centennial Medal 1967; Queen's Silver Jubilee Medal 1977; apptd. Admiral, Texas Navy 1977; recipient Gold Headed Cane, World Assn. of Societies of Pathology 1987; Fellow, Royal Coll. Pathol.; Fellow, Royal Coll. Pathol. Australasia; Fellow, Royal Coll. Phys. Surg. Canada; Fellow, College of American Pathologists; Hon. Mem., Sociedad Peruana de Patologia 1978; Societé Française de Biologie Clinique 1979; Candn. Assn. of Pathologists (Pres. 1967–69) 1983; Assn. of Clinical Pathologists (U.K.) 1984; Corresponding Mem., Deutsche Gesellschaft für Laboratoriumsmedizin 1979; Member: Am. Assn. for Cancer Research; Candn. Medical Assn. (Emeritus); Ont. Medical Assn. (Emeritus); Internat. Academy of Pathology (Emeritus); Ont. Assn. of Pathologists; Pluto Club (Am. Assn. of Academic Pathologists); Club: York; Home: 625 Avenue Rd., Toronto, Ont. M4V 2K7; Office: 601a, Mount Sinai Hosp., 600 University Ave., Toronto, Ont. M5G 1X5.

**RITCHIE, Cedric E.,** O.C.; banker; b. Upper Kent, N.B. 22 Aug. 1927; s. E. Thomas and Marion (Henderson) R.; e. Bath (N.B.) High Sch.; CHAIRMAN & DIR., THE BANK OF NOVA SCOTIA since 1974; Chrmn., C.E.O. & Dir., The Bank of Nova Scotia Properties Inc.; Scotia Realty Ltd.; Chrmn. & Dir., Scotia Leasing Ltd.; The Bank of Nova Scotia Trinidad and Tobago Ltd.; The Bank of Nova Scotia Trust Co.; The Bank of Nova Scotia Trust Co. (Caribbean) Ltd.; The Bank of Nova Scotia Trust Co. (Cayman) Ltd.; The Bank of Nova Scotia Channel Islands Ltd.; The Bank of Nova Scotia Asia Ltd.; The Bank of Nova Scotia Trust Co. Channel Islands Ltd.; The Bank of Nova Scotia Trust Co. (Bahamas) Ltd.; Scotiabank (U.K.) Limited; The Bank of Nova Scotia Internat. Ltd.; The Bank of Nova Scotia Trust Co. of Trinidad and Tobago Ltd.; The Bank of Nova Scotia Jamaica Ltd.; The West India Company of Merchant Bankers Ltd.; BNS Internat. (Barbados) Ltd.; BNS Internat. (United Kingdom) Ltd.; Scotiabank (Ireland) Ltd.; Scotia Insurance (Barbados) Ltd.; Scotiabank Jamaica Trust and Merchant Bank Ltd.; Scotia Properties Quebec Inc.; Chrmn. Canadian Business Comte. on Jamaica; Canada-Philippines Council; Pres., Mem. and Trustee, The Spencer Hall Foundation; Dir., Mercedes-Benz Canada Inc.; BNS International (Hong Kong) Ltd.; The Canada Life Assurance Co.; Ingersoll-Rand Co.; Maduro & Curiel's Bank N.V.; Moore Corp. Ltd.; Minorco; The Nova Scotia Corp.; Pacific Basin Economic Council, Candn. Ctte.; Solidbank Corp.; Boracay Ltd.; Banco Sud Americano; Internat. Monetary Conference; Poonpipat Finance & Securities Co. Ltd.; Grupo Financiero Inverlat, S.A.; Multibanco Comermex; NOVA Corp. of Alta.; Scotiatrust (Asia) Ltd.; Dir.-at-Large, Junior Achievement of Can.; Gov.: Olympic Trust of Can.; Member: Dalhousie Univ. Bd. of Govs.; Officer of the Order of Canada 1981; mem. Adv. Comte., Sch. of Business Admin., Univ. of W. Ont.; Adv. Counc., Candn. Exec. Service Orgn.; Internat. Adv. Counc., Centre for Inter-American Relations; Chairman's Council of the Americas Soc.; Hon. Ctte., Candn. Organization for Development through Education; Hon. Dir., SONAR (Save Our Northwest Atlantic Resources); joined present Bank, Bath, N.B. 1945; served at various Maritime brs. and in Montreal; transf. to Inspection Staff; apptd. Asst. Inspector 1954; Accountant, Toronto Branch 1956; Inspector, Credit Dept., Gen. Office 1959; Asst. Mgr., Toronto Br. 1959; Chief Acct. 1960; Asst. Gen. Mgr., Adm. 1963; Jt. Gen. Mgr. 1966; Chief. Gen. Mgr., International 1968; Chief Gen. Mgr. 1970; Dir. 1972; Pres. & C.E.O. 1972; Chrmn., Pres. & C.E.O. 1974; Chrmn. & C.E.O. 1979; Chrmn. of the Bd. and Chrmn. of the Extve. Ctte. 1993; Officer of the Order of Canada 1981; Office: Scotia Plaza, 44 King St. W., Toronto, Ont. M5H 1H1.

**RITCHIE, Charles Stewart Almon,** C.C. (1969), M.A., D.C.L., F.R.S.L.; diplomat; b. Halifax, Nova Scotia 23 Sept. 1906; s. William Bruce Almon Ritchie, K.C., and Lilian Constance Harriette (Stewart) R.; e. Trinity Coll. Sch., Port Hope, Ont.; Univ. of King's Coll., Halifax, N.S.; Oxford Univ., B.A., M.A. 1929; Harvard Univ., M.A. 1930; Ecole Libre des Sciences Politiques, Paris (1931); D.C.L.: Univ. of King's Coll., Trent Univ., McGill Univ., Acadia Univ.; D. Litt.: Mount Allison Univ., St. Mary's Univ., Carleton Univ., York Univ.; m. Sylvia Catherine Beatrice, d. James Smellie, Ottawa, Ont., 16 Jan. 1948; joined Dept. of External Affairs as Third Secy., Aug. 1934; Third Secy., Washington, Oct. 1936; Second Secy., London, Jan. 1939, First Secy. Jan. 1943; First Secy., Ottawa, Jan. 1945; Counsellor, Paris, Jan. 1947; Asst. Under-Secy. of State for External Affairs, Jan. 1950, Deputy Under-Secy., Nov. 1952; Ambassador to Federal Republic of Germany, and Head of Military Mission, Berlin, May 1954; Ambassador and Permanent Rep. to the United Nations, Jan. 1958–62; Ambassador to the United States, 1962–66; Permanent Rep. and Ambassador to the N. Atlantic Council and to the Office of EEC, 1966–67; High Commr. to U.K. 1967; Special Advisor to Privy Council, Ottawa, 1971–73; Author, 'The Siren Years' 1974; 'An Appetite for Life' 1977; 'Diplomatic Passport' 1981; 'Storm Signals' 1983; 'My Grandfather's House' 1987; Fellow, Royal Soc. of Literature; Hon. Fellow, Pembroke Coll., Oxford University, 1963; Anglican Church; Club: Brooks's (London); Rideau (Ottawa); Address: 216 Metcalfe St., Ottawa, Ont. K2P 1R1.

**RITCHIE, Gordon,** M.A.; management consultant; b. Washington, D.C. 21 Feb. 1944; s. Albert Edgar and Gwendolyn Lenore (Perdue) R.; e. Carleton Univ., B.A. 1966; Ecole Nationale d'Adm. Publique, M.A. 1973; Harvard Bus. Sch. AMP 1981; m. Margaret Armstrong 21 May 1966; children: Jillian Heather, Martin Donald; CHRMN. & C.E.O., STRATEGICO INC. 1988– ; Dep. Sec. Min. of State for Econ. Devel. 1978–82; Assoc. Dep. Min. DRIE 1982–85; Fed. Econ. Devel. Coordinator 1985; Ambassador & Dep. Chief Negotiator for Canada 1986–88; Bd. of Dirs., Telemedia Inc.; Laidlaw Inc.; Univ. of Ottawa Heart Institute; L'Observatoire de l'ENAP; National Capital Harvard Business School Alumni Club; mem., C.D. Howe Inst. Policy Analysis Ctte. and Canadian-American Ctte.; recreations: chess, micro computers, swimming, golf, downhill & cross-country skiing; Office: 20th Floor, 45 O'Connor St., Ottawa, Ont. K1P 1A4.

**RITCHIE, James Cunningham,** Ph.D., D.Sc.; educator; b Aberdeen, Scot. 20 July 1929; s. Alfred, O.B.E., Ph.D., F.R.S.E. and Mary Anne (Cunningham) R.; e. Robert Gordon's Coll. Aberdeen 1947; Univ. of Aberdeen B.Sc. 1951, D.Sc. 1961; Sheffield Univ. Ph.D. 1955; m. June d. Benjamin and Sarah Hope 13 Nov. 1981; children: Ian Douglas, Kenneth Grant, Barbara Joyce; EMERITUS PROFESSOR OF BOTANY, UNIV. OF TORONTO 1992– ; Prof. of Botany 1970–92; Sr. Rsch. Scholar Royal Exhn. 1851 Botanical Gdn. Montréal 1954–55; Nat. Rsch. Council Postdoctoral Fellow Univ. of Man. 1955–56, Asst. and Assoc. Prof. 1956–65; Chrmn. of Life Sciences Div., Scarborough Coll., Univ. of Toronto 1970–75; Visiting Prof. and Acting Assoc. Dir. Laboratoire de Palynologie CNRS Montpellier, France 1983, Sr. Sci. Fellowship (NATO) 1980; Visiting Prof. Univ de Montréal 1983; Sr. Killam Rsch. Scholar Can. Council 1977–79; author 'Past and Present Vegetation of the Far Northwest of Canada ' 1984; 'Postglacial Vegetation of Canada' 1987; Founding mem. Candn. Bot. Assn. (Pres. 1968; George Lawson Medal 1985); Brit. Ecol. Soc.; Ecol. Soc. of Am. (W.S. Cooper Award 1990); Am. Quaternary Assn.; L'Assoc. québecoise pour l'étude du quaternaire; Fellow, Royal Soc. of Canada (1989); recreations: music, squash, swimming; Address: 'Pebbledash Cottage', Corfe, Taunton, England, UK TA3 7AJ.

**RITCHIE, James Morgan,** M.B.A., C.A.; business executive; b. Vancouver, B.C. 9 Nov. 1942; s. Harry Alexander and Dorothy Olga (Thacker) R.; e. West Vancouver High Sch. 1959; C.A. 1965; York Univ. M.B.A. 1986; m. Anne d. John and Mary Dewar 17 Sept. 1966; two d. Kathleen Maria, Nicole Anne; VICE PRES. FINANCE AND DIR. THE CANADA METAL CO. LTD. 1984– ; Dir. Canada Metal Investments Ltd.; Jank Investments Ltd.; James M. Ritchie Holdings Ltd.; Environ Metal Recycling Ltd.; Evergreen Manufacturing Corp.; articled with and C.A. Frederick Field & Co. 1960–65; Internal Auditor Northern Construction Co. and J.W. Stewart Ltd. 1965–67; Auditor Price Waterhouse (Venezuela) 1967–68; Finance Mgr. Coca Cola Venezuela 1968–75; Controller: Chubb Security Toronto 1975–81; Vulcan Packaging 1981–84; recreation: tennis; Club: Mayfair Lakeshore; Office: 721 Eastern Ave., Toronto, Ont. M4M 1E6.

**RITCHIE, Judith Anne,** R.N., B.N., M.N., Ph.D., D.Sc. (Hon.); university professor and research administrator; b. Saint John, N.B. 16 June 1943; d. Louis McCoskery and Mary Catherine (Hogan) R.; e. St. Vincent's Girl's H.S. 1961; Univ. of N.B., B.N. 1965; Univ. of Pittsburgh, M.N. 1969, Ph.D. 1975; PROFESSOR OF NURSING, DALHOUSIE UNIV. 1985– and DIR. OF NURSING RESEARCH, IWK CHILDREN'S HOSP. 1986– (rsch. focus on seriously ill children & their families); Staff Nurse, Montreal Children's Hosp. 1965–66; Clin. Nurse Spec., Children's Hosp. of Pittsburgh 1970–72; Lectr., Univ. of N.B. 1966–68; Asst. Prof. 1974–77; Assoc. Prof. 1977–78; Vis. Prof., U. of Calif. 1982–83; Assoc. Prof., present univ. 1978–85; Pres., Candn. Nurses Assn. 1988–90; has served on several nurses assn. cttes. (N.B., N.S. & nat.); consultant; conf. speaker; Candn. Nurses Found. Scholar 1968–69, 1969–70, 1973–74; MRC studentship 1972–74; D.Sc. (honoris causa) Univ. of N.B. 1989; U.S. Dept. of H.E.W. Profl. Nurse Traineeship 1972; Sigma Theta Tau 1970; R.C.; Mem., Assn. for Care of Children's Health (Pres., Atlantic 1979–82); Candn. Nurses Found. (Chair, Rsch. Ctte. 1986–88); Candn. Assn. of Univ. Schools of Nursing; Candn. Assn. of Univ. Teachers; Candn. Nursing Rsch. Group; Candn. Pediatric Nurses Interest Group; Ed. Bd. 'Journal of Pediatric Nursing'; Assoc. Editor, 'Canadian Journal of Nursing Research'; author of several articles & book chaps.; recreations: music, choirs; Home: 55 Meadowlark Cres., #401, Halifax, N.S. B3M 3R2; Office: Sch. of Nursing, Dalhousie Univ., Halifax, N.S. B3H 3J5.

**RITCHIE, Lewis,** B.Comm., C.A.; chartered accountant; b. Canada 19 Dec. 1946; s. David and Lillian (Nemeroff) R.; e. McGill Univ. B.Comm. 1972; m. Aida d. Albert and Yanina Edery 11 July 1976; children: Dana, David, Keren; VICE-PRESIDENT, FINANCE & CHIEF FINANCIAL OFFICER, CINRAM LTD.; Office: 2255 Markham Rd., Scarborough, Ont. M1B 2W3.

**RITCHIE, Marguerite Elizabeth Winnifred,** Q.C., B.A., LL.B., LL.M., LL.D.; b. Edmonton, Alta. 20 May 1919; d. Allan Isaac and Marguerite Blanche (Baxter) R.; e. Univ. of Alta. B.A. 1943, LL.B. 1943, LL.D. 1975; Dalhousie Univ. Exchange Scholarship; McGill Univ. LL.M. 1958; Univ. of Alta. LL.D. (Hon.) 1975; FOUNDER-PRESIDENT, HUMAN RIGHTS INST. OF CAN. 1979– ; read law with Howard T. Emery, Q.C. Edmonton; called to Bar of Alta. 1944; joined Fed. Pub. Service (Combines Investig.) 1944; Fed. Dept. of Justice 1949, Legal Advisor in Constitutional and Intnl. Law, UN, Parlty. procedure, domestic law questions; seconded as Exec. Asst. to Hon. E.D. Fulton and Hon. Lionel Chevrier (Mins. of Justice); apptd. Sr. Adv. Counsel Dept. Justice; Legal Adviser to Candn. Del. to Hague Conference on Air Law 1955; adviser to UN Human Rights Ctte. 1962; cr. Q.C. (Fed.) 1963; mem., Interdept'al Cttes. maj. questions UN, Criminal Law, Intnl. Law, Law of Sea, Conventions and Intnl. Agreements, Status of Women; participated drafting 1968 Fed. Divorce Act; prepared and participated landmark Reference to Supreme Court of Can. re Ownership Offshore Resources B.C. 1967–68; Vice Chairperson Fed. Antidumping Tribunal 1972–79; First Legal Advr. Elizabeth Fry Soc. Ottawa; Lectr. in Constitutional Law Carleton Univ. 1967–68; Visiting Lectr. Treaties and Treaty-making Univ. of Ottawa; Visiting Lectr. Status of Women Trent Univ., McGill Univ.; consultant to various organs., penal reform groups; recipient Centennial Medal 1967; Indian Women's Group Special Award 1973; Prov. of Ont. Outstanding Woman Award 1975; author various articles mags. and journs.; mem., Law Soc. Alta.; Candn. Bar Assn.; Intnl. Law Assn.; Intnl. Comn. Jurists; Intnl. Abolitionist Fed.; Candn. Fed. Univ. Women; recreations: travel, walking, reading, plants; Clubs: University Women's (Pres. 1958–60 Ottawa); Federal Lawyers; Home: 30, 216 Metcalfe St., Ottawa, Ont. K2P 1R1; Office: 303 – 246 Queen St., Ottawa, Ont. K1P 5E4.

**RITCHIE, Robert Jamieson,** B.Sc., M.B.A.; railway executive b. Ormstown, Que. 5 Oct. 1944; s. Ian David and Helen Mary (Jamieson) R.; e. Hudson H.S. 1963; McGill Univ. B.Sc. 1967; Univ. of Western Ont. M.B.A. 1970; m. Tatiana Miloradovitch 2 Feb. 1974; children: Nicolai, Ian; PRESIDENT, CP RAIL SYSTEM 1990– ; Research Analyst, Canadian Pacific Limited 1970; Marketing Rep., CP Rail 1972; Marketing Dir. 1974; Marketing Mgr. 1976; Gen. Mgr., Marketing 1977; Gen. Mgr., Marketing & Sales 1979; Asst. Vice-Pres. Marketing 1981; Vice-Pres., Marketing & Sales 1984; Extve. Vice-Pres. 1987; Chairman of the Board: Incan Superior Limited; Delaware & Hudson Railway Co., Inc.; Dir., Fording Coal Limited; Soo Line Corp.; The Toronto Terminals Railway Co.; The N.B. & Canada Railroad Co.; The Shawinigan Terminal Railway Co.; CP Ships in Bermuda; Shaw Industries Ltd.; Pointe-à-Callière Montreal Museum of Archeology & History Corp.; Canada Maritime Services Limited; Adv. Bd., The Montreal Gen. Hosp. Corp.; Faculty of Science, McGill Univ.; Mem., Chartered Institute of Transport in Canada; National Freight Transportation Assn.; clubs: Montreal Racquet; Montreal Badminton & Squash; Hudson Yacht; Mount Royal; Montreal Traffic; Montreal Railway; Royal Oak Tennis; Office: Room 215, Windsor Station, 910 Peel St., P.O. Box 6042, Station Centre-Ville, Montreal, Que. H3C 3E4.

**RITCHIE, Ronald Stuart,** M.A.; business executive; corporate director; b. Charing Cross, Kent Co., Ont. 4 July 1918; s. Thomas Duncan and Maggie (Sterritt) R.; e. Univ. of W. Ont., B.A. (Gold Medallist in Econ. and Pol. Science) 1938; Queen's Univ., M.A. (Econ.) 1960; m. Phyllis, d. Alfred Ernest and Mary Ann (Eldridge) Plaskett, Toronto, Ont. 4 Feb. 1950; children: Beverly Janet, Barbara Diane, Patricia Ann, Karen Heather, Margot Lynn; CHRMN., FUTURELINE COMMUNICATIONS CO. LTD. 1990– ; Life Underwriter, Standard Life Assurance, London, Ont. 1938–39; Lectr., Econ. Dept., Ont. Agric. Coll., Guelph, Ont. 1940–41; Extve. Asst. to Depy. Chrmn., Wartime Prices & Trade Bd. 1941–44; Mgr., Ottawa Civil Service Recreational Assn. 1944–45; Depy. Chief Prices Div., W.P.T.B. 1945–47; joined Imperial Oil Ltd. and posted to Standard Oil Co. (N.J.) 1947; Head Econ. & Stats. Group. Co-Ordination & Econ. Dept., Toronto 1948–50; Asst. Mgr., Co-ordination & Econ. Dept. 1950–52; Asst. Div. Mgr., Ont. Marketing Div., Toronto 1953–55; Mgr., B.C. Marketing Div., Vancouver, B.C. 1955–58; Asst. Gen. Mgr., Marketing Dept., Toronto 1958; Employee Relations Mgr. 1959–60; Extve. Asst. to the Bd., Special Projects 1962–63; on loan as Extve. Dir., Roy. Comm. on Gov't. Organ. Nov. 1960–Jan. 1962; Dir., Imperial Oil Ltd. 1963–74; Sr. Vice Pres. 1971–74; P. Conservative cand. Algoma, 1974 g.e.; Princ. Asst., Office, Ldr. of Opposition, Ottawa 1974–75; elected M.P., York East 1979; apptd. Parly. Secy. to Min. of Finance 1979; Sr. Policy Advr., Investment Dealers Assn. of Can. 1980–83; Chrmn. & C.E.O., The Candn. Depository for Securities Ltd. 1983–86; Dir., Consolidated NBS Inc. 1990– ; Chrmn., Canadian Ditchley Foundation; Gov., The Ditchley Foundation (U.K.); Dir., Treasr., Past Pres. & mem. National Extve. Comte., Candn. Council of Christians and Jews 1980–87; Dir. North-South Inst. 1975–79; Gov. Found. for Int. Tng. in Third World Countries 1977–82; mem. Bd. of Govs. Univ. of Guelph 1966–71 (Chrmn. 1968–71); mem. Club of Rome; Canada-U.S. Comte., Canadian Chamber of Commerce 1967–73, Chrmn. 1972–73; Gov. The Atlantic Inst., Paris 1965–89; Nat. Extve. Comte. Candn. Inst. Internat. Affairs 1960–75; Dir. and Past Chrmn. Atlantic Counc. of Can 1965–90.; Past Chrmn., Bd. of Dirs., Orthopaedic & Arthritic Hosp., Toronto 1968–90; Founder & Chrmn. Inst. for Research on Public Policy 1972–74; Candn. Del., Commonwealth Conf., Lahore, Pakistan 1954; ILO, Geneva, 1960, and various internat. relations confs.; author of: 'NATO: The Economics of an Alliance' 1956; 'An Institute for Research on Public Policy' 1971; 'Ritchie Report on Canada's Postal Service' 1978; Ed. and Publisher 'The Canadian Conservative'; also various articles on management, econ. policy and internat. affairs; recreations: golf, skiing, swimming, music, reading; Clubs: The Toronto Club (Toronto); Address: 511 – 92 King St. E., Toronto, Ont. M5C 2V8.

**RITTER, Archibald R.M.,** Ph.D.; educator; b. Chesley, Ont. 25 Oct. 1941; s. Archibald C.E. and Anne Cameron (Milne) R.; e. Queen's Univ. B.A. 1964; Univ. of W. Ont. M.A. 1965; Univ. of Texas Ph.D. 1972; m. Joan d. Alistair and Margaret Gamble 18 June 1989; children: Alexandra, Archibald, David, Margaret, Vanessa; FULL PROF. OF ECON. and of SCH. OF INTERNAT. AFFAIRS, CARLETON UNIV. 1992– ; joined present Univ. 1969, Assoc. Prof. of Econ. 1974–92; Econ. UN Econ. Comn. Latin Am. 1973–74; Sr. Econ. (Exec. Interchange) Energy, Mines & Resources Can. 1979–80; Sr. Econ. Long Range Planning Unit Min. of Planning & Nat. Devel., Kenya 1985–88; Cons. Econ. Council Can.; North-South Inst.; Commonwealth Secretariat, London; CIDA; Energy, Mines & Resources Can.; author 'The Economic Development of Revolutionary Cuba' 1974; 'Development Strategy and Structural Adjustment in Chile, 1970–1992: From the Unidad Popular to the Concertación' 1992; co-ed. 'Latin America and the Caribbean to the Year 2000' 1990; Pres. Candn. Assn. Latin Am. & Caribbean Studies 1989–90, Sec. Treas. 1982–86; Home: 65 Ruskin St., Ottawa, Ont. K1Y 4A8; Office: Ottawa, Ont. K1S 5B6.

**RITTER, Erika Elizabeth,** B.A., M.A.; writer and broadcaster; b. Regina, Sask. 26 Apl.; d. Peter M. and Margaret J. (Cody) R.; e. McGill Univ., B.A. 1968; Univ. of Toronto, M.A. 1970; freelance writer in theatre, radio drama, short fiction and humorous essay writing since 1975; freelance on-air broadcast work for CBC radio since 1982 incl. hosting 'Dayshift' 1985–87; 'Aircraft' 1988–90; Can. Counc. grants; ACTRA Award; Chalmers Play Award; Periodical Assn. Award; author: 'A Visitor from Charleston,' 'The Splits,' 'Winter 1671,' 'Automatic Pilot,' 'The Passing Scene,' 'Murder at McQueen' (plays 1975–86); 'Urban Scrawl' (book) 1984; 'Ritter in Residence' (book) 1987; Mem., Playwrights Union of Can.; Writers Union of Can.; ACTRA, Amnesty Internat.; PEN; Internat. Performing Artists for Nuclear Disarmament; recreations: tennis, bicycling; Address: c/o Writers Union of Canada, 24 Ryerson Ave., Toronto, Ont. M5T 2P3.

**RIVARD, Gilles,** LL.B., Q.C.; public servant; e. Laval Univ. LL.B.; called to Bar of Quebec 1958; m. Lucie Rondeau, M.D.; five children; CHAIRMAN, NATIONAL TRANSPORATION AGENCY OF CANADA 1993– ; Former Senior Partner, Rivard, Rivard; has served govt. of Canada in many capacities; Mem., Ctte. on Airports 1985; Nat. Postal Museum Advisory Ctte. 1987; Ctte. for Evoluton of Airports Canada 1987–92; Lawyer, Comn. of Inquiry on the 'Sociéte des Alcools du Québec,' Prov. of Que. & Dir., Québec Industiral Loan Office; Chair, Nat. Transportation Act Review Comn. 1992; Mem., Candn. Bar Assn., C. of C. and others; Founder & Pres., Pavillion of Prevention of Heart Diseases; Pres., Hydro-Pontiac Inc. until 1993; Mem., Bd. of Dir., Ducks Unlimited (Canada) 1980; Council of Candn. Admin. Tribunals 1993; Pres., Qué. Junior Bar Assn. 1966–67; Mem., Gen. Council & Extve. Ctte., Que. Prov. Bar Assn. 1966–68, 1974–76; Batonnier of the Québec Bar 1975–76; Q.C. 1973; clubs: Quebec Garrison, Quebec Rotary (Pres. 1973–74); Office: 344 Slater St., 15th Floor, Ottawa, Ont. K1A 0N9.

**RIVARD, Jean,** Q.C., LL.L.; b. Quebec, Que. 22 Dec. 1926; s. late Antoine and Lucille (Garneau) R.; e. Jesuits' Coll., Quebec, Que.; Laval Univ., LL.L. 1950; m. Janine, d. late Hon. Jean Raymond, 7 Nov. 1954; children: Louise, Michèle, Line, Pierre, Guy; SR. PARTNER, FLYNN RIVARD AND ASSOC.; called to Bar of Que. 1950; cr. Q.C. 1964; R. Catholic; recreations: golf, sailing; Clubs: Quebec Garrison; Royal Quebec Golf; Home: 250 Grande Allée O., Quebec, Que. G1R 2H4; Office: 70 Dalhousie, Quebec, Que. G1K 7A6 and 2020 University, Montreal, Que. H3A 2A5.

**RIVE, Lt. Col. David Edward,** C.D., A.de C.; software company executive; b. Toronto, Ont. 12 Jan. 1951; s. Edward Moore and Inez Norine (Firman) R.; e. Univ. of Toronto Schs.; Univ. of Toronto Scarborough Coll. 1 yr.; m. Denise d. Augustin and Dorothy Marchildon 22 Mar. 1975; Pres. Creative Personnel Systems Inc. 1985– ; Assoc., Creative Planning Insurance Agencies Ltd. 1972–86; Credit Analyst Dun & Bradstreet of Canada 1971–72; served with Candn. Armed Forces Reserve since 1969, past C.O. Queen's York Rangers; Office: 65 Overlea Blvd., Suite 407, Toronto, Ont. M4H 1P1.

**RIVERIN, Bruno,** B.Sc.A., electrical engineering M.B.A.; financial executive; b. Chicoutimi, Que. 29 Mar. 1941; e. Laval Univ. B.Sc.A. 1966; Univ. of Sherbrooke M.B.A. 1970; Univ. of Paris, post-grad studies in internat. finan. 1971; PRES. & CHIEF EXTVE. OFFR., INVESTISSEMENT DESJARDINS 1994– ; Sales Engr., Esso 1966; Gentec 1967; Market Analyst, Air Canada 1968–69; Finan. Analyst, Caisse de dépôt et placement du Québec 1971; Asst. to Sr. Vice-Pres. (Eastern Reg.), Mercantile Bank of Can. 1971; Vice-Pres., Finan. & Admin., Montreal Féd. of the Desjardins Group 1977; Fédération des caisses populaires Desjardins de Montréal et de l'Ouest-du-Québec (Desjardins Group) 1977; Founding Pres., Caisse centrale Desjardins (the Group's banking subsidiary) 1980; Pres. & Chief Extve. Offr., The Montreal Exchange 1987–94; Chrmn., Internat. Finan. Ctrs. Orgn. of Montreal; Dep. Gov., Candn. Investor Protection Fund; Candn. Securities Institute; Rep., La Féd. internat. des Bourses de valeurs; Mem., Ordre des ingénieurs du Qué.; Montreal C. of C.; French C. of C.; C.D. Howe Inst. (Que. Div.); Laval & Sherbrooke Univ. Alumnae Assns.; Dir., Ste-Justine Hosp. Found.; Armand-Frappier Found.; Quebec Aeronautical Training Centre; clubs: Montreal Amateur Athletic Assn., St-Denis, St-James, Richelieu Golf; Office: 2 Complexe Desjardins, Suite 1717, Montreal Que. H5B 1B8.

**RIVERS, Jason Keller,** B.Sc., M.D.; univ. asst. professor; b. Ottawa, Ont. 8 April 1956; s. Albert and Goldie (Schachter) R.; e. Nepean H.S. 1974; Univ. of Toronto B.Sc. (Hons.) 1977; Univ. of Ottawa M.D. (magna cum laude) 1981; m. Helen d. Dr. Ronald and Shiela Heacock 21 Nov. 1987; one s.: Alexander; ASST. PROF., DERMATOLOGY, UNIV. OF B.C. 1990– ; Internship, Dalhousie Univ. 1981–82; Dermatology residency, Ottawa Univ. 1983–85; Overseas Sr. Registrar, St. John's Hosp. London (UK) 1985–86; Fellow in Melanoma, N.Y. Univ., Skin & Cancer Ctr. 1987–88; Sydney Melanoma Unit, Univ. of Sydney (Australia) 1988–90; Nat. Dir., Candn. Dermatology Assn. Skin Cancer Awareness Prog.; Med. Cons., Environment Canada; Mem., Royal College of Physicians of Canada; Am. Academy of Dermatology; Candn. Dermatology Assn. (Chair, Public Relns. 1990– ); W.H.O. Melanoma Group; author/co-author of more than 60 med. pubs.; recreations: scuba, sailing, skiing, wilderness canoeing, horseback riding; Home: 42 West 11th Ave., Vancouver, B.C. V5Y 1S5; Office: 855 West 10th Ave., Vancouver, B.C. V5Z 1L6.

**RIVEST, The Hon. Jean-Claude,** LL.B.; senator; b. L'Assomption, Que. 27 Jan. 1943; s. Victor and Yvette (Lafortune) R.; e. Coll. de l'Assomption 1962; Univ. of Montreal LLB. 1966, grad. dipl. (constitutional law) 1968; called to Bar of Quebec 1966; single; SENATOR, THE SENATE OF CANADA 1993– ; Political Asst. to Jean Lesage, Official Leader of the Opposition, Que. Nat. Assembly 1968–70; Political Adviser to Robert Bourassa, Premier of Que. 1970–76, 1985–93; Senior Political and Parliamentary Adviser to Gérard D. Lévesque, Leader of the Official Opposition, Quebec National Assembly 1976–79; 1st elected MNA for Jean-Talon (Que.) 1979 (Vice-Chair, Parl. Ctte. on Institutions; Sr. Opposition Critic for Fed.-Prov. Relns. & Internat. Relns. 1979–85, Cultural Affairs 1979–81, and Public Serv. 1981–85; actively worked at the college and univ. levels for the 'NO' forces (Canada option) in the 1980 referendum campaign; Official Opposition Critic for Que. City Reg. 1979–85; Office: Room 404, Victoria Bldg., 140 Wellington St., Ottawa, Ont. K1A 0A4.

**RIVEST, Roland,** M.Sc., Ph.D., F.C.I.C., F.A.A.A.S.; educator; b. Rawdon, Que. 19 Apr. 1923; s. Euclide and Regina (Ricard) R.; e. elem. sch. Rawdon, Qué.; Séminaire de Joliette; Univ. de Montréal B.Sc.; M.Sc., Ph.D.; m. Marguerite d. Louis-J. Trottier 4 July 1953; children: Louis-Paul, Marie-Josée, Natalie, Chantal; EMERITUS PROFESSOR, UNIV. DE MONTREAL 1987– , Prof. of Chem. 1964– ; part-time Instr. Univ. of Cal. 1950–51 (Berkeley), part-time Lectr. 1951–52; Asst. Prof. of Chem. present Univ. 1952, Assoc. Prof. 1958, Chrmn. of Chem. 1963–68, Vice Dean Sciences 1968–72, Vice Dean Arts & Sciences 1972–79, Dean of Arts & Sciences 1979–87, Emeritus Professor 1987– ; author over 50 papers scient. journs.; Chrmn. Inorganic Chem. Div. Chem. Inst. Can. 1961, Councillor 1963–68, mem. Bd. and Dir. of Membership 1965–68; mem. adm. council, Assn. Canadienne Française pour l'Avancement des Sciences 1964–67, Chrmn. of Bd. 1965–67; R. Catholic; recreations: swimming, skiing, tennis, golf; Address: 42 Wicksteed, Mont-Royal, Qué. H3P 1P7.

**RIVINGTON, Robert Neville,** B.Sc., M.D., F.R.C.P.(C), F.A.C.P., F.C.C.P.; respirologist; educator; b. Montréal, Qué. 1 May 1949; s. Neville and Ruth (Chatham) R.; e. Queen's Univ. B.Sc.(Hon.) 1971, M.D. 1974; m. Karen d. Stuart and Kathleen McClave 12 Aug. 1972; two d. Katherine Angela, Andrea Laurel; ASSOC. PROF. OF MED., UNIV. OF OTTAWA, OTTAWA CIVIC HOSP. 1984– and HEAD, DIVISION OF RESPIROLOGY, OTTAWA CIVIC HOSP.; Internal Med. Residency Queen's Univ. Affiliated Hosps. 1974–76; Respirol. Residency McGill Univ. Affiliated Hosps. 1976–78, Rsch. Fellow Meakins Christie Lab. 1978–79; Lectr. present Univ. 1979, Asst. Prof. of Med. 1982; Charter mem. Physicians Smoke-Free Can.; author or co-author of over 40 med. articles; presented over 45 abstracts sci. meetings; mem. 10 profl. and acad. socs.; recreations: golf, skiing, travel; Club: Ottawa Hunt & Golf; Home: 86 Country Club Dr., Ottawa, Ont. K1V 9Y7; Office: 1053 Carling Ave., Ottawa, Ont. K1Y 4E9.

**ROACH, B. Jeffrey;** business owner; b. Valleyfield, Que. 15 Oct. 1942; s. Bernard James and Doris Isabelle (Rafter) Roach; e. St. Patrick's Coll., Univ. of Ottawa, B.Sc. 1964; Grad., Mgmt. Training Course, Sch. of Bus., Univ. of Western Ont.; m. Diana d. Sydney and Sheila Wynne-Jones 15 Sept. 1968; children: Emily, Elizabeth, Patricia; PRESIDENT, JEFF ROACH & ASSOCIATES INC. 1993– ; Sr. Vice Pres., Corp. Comm. & Pub. Affrs., CIBC 1986; Retail Opns. Trainee, M. Loeb Ltd. 1964–65; Supr., News & Info., Bell Canada 1966–72; Extve. Asst. to Mayor of Ottawa 1973–74; Pub. Affairs Adv., Imperial Oil Ltd. 1974–77; Sr. Cons., Heal Shaw Walden Ltd. 1978–79; Dir., Corp. Comm., Bell-Northern Rsch., Ottawa 1979–82; Asst. Vice-Pres., Corp. Comm., Northern Telecom Ltd. 1982–85; Vice Pres., Pub. Relns., CIBC 1985–86; Accredited Mem., Candn. Pub. Relns. Soc.; Grad., Sr. Extve. Prog., Queen's Univ. Sch. of Bus.; Grad., Mgmt. Training Course, Univ. of West. Ont.; Bd. mem., Albany Club; Bd. Mem. AMICI; Bd. Mem., International Readings at Harbourfront; Club: Albany; Home: 159 Madison Ave., Toronto, Ont. M5R 2S6.

**ROACH, Charles Conliffe (Charley),** B.A., LL.B.; lawyer; b. Trinidad & Tobago 18 Sept. 1933; s. Caleb Edward and Muriel Adinah R.; e. Belmont Boys' Intermediate Sch. 1948, St. Mary's Coll. Port-of-Spain 1952; Univ. of Sask. B.A. 1958; Univ. of Toronto LL.B. 1961; m. Hetty d. Richard and Agnes Gittens 12 Oct. 1962; children: Sunset, Dawn, Kikelola; FOUNDER AND PARTNER, ROACH, SCHWARTZ & ASSOCS. 1968– ; Candn. resident 1955; called to Bar of Ont. 1963; Asst. Metro. Solr. 1963–68; Founding Chrmn. Caribana 1966; Chrmn., First Internat. Conf. Black Lawyers & Jurists 1985; Founder, Movement Minority Electors; Co-Chrmn. Internat. Ctte. Against Racism 1973–78; named Lawyer of Yr. 1985 Nat. Conf. Black Lawyers USA and Can.; author 'Canada In Us Now' poetry 1976; 'Root For The Ravens' poetry 1977; various papers internat. human rights law; Founder, Candn. Martin Luther King Jr. Day Commemorative Found.; Vice Chair and North American Coordinator, Internat. Pan African Movement; mem., Delos Davis Law Guild; mem., Internat. Assn. Elimination Forms Racial Discrimination; recreations: guitar, keyboards, poetry, painting; Home: 6 Humewood Dr., Toronto, Ont. M6C 2W2; Office: 688 St. Clair Ave., W., Toronto, Ont. M6C 1B1.

**ROACH, Kent William,** B.A., LL.B., LL.M.; educator; b. Montreal, Que. 27 July 1961; s. Howard and Margaret Grace (Lay) R.; e. Univ. of Toronto, Victoria Coll. B.A. 1984 (Gov. Gen.'s Gold Medal), LL.B. 1987 (Dean Cecil A. Wright Key); Yale Univ. LL.M. 1988; m. Janice d. Cecil and Sharon Cox 16 Dec. 1989; daughter: Erin Keara; ASST. PROF. OF LAW UNIV. OF TORONTO 1989– ; Law Clk. for Madam Justice Bertha Wilson Supreme Court of Can. 1988–89; Project Dir. Ont. Law Reform Comn. Project Law of Pub. Inquiries 1990–92; co-author 'Regulating Traffic Safety' 1990; 'Cases and Materials on Criminal Law and Procedure' 6th ed. 1991; 'Civil Litigation' 4th ed. 1991; 'Constitutional Remedies in Canada' 1994; numerous law review articles; ed.-in-chief Univ. of Toronto Faculty of Law Review 1987; mem. Osgoode Soc.; Ontario Bar; recreations: running, bicycling, tennis; Home: 225 Palace St., Whitby, Ont. L1N 5G1; Office: 78 Queen's Park, Toronto, Ont. M5S 1A1.

**ROACHE, Gordon;** artist; b. Halifax, N.S. 26 Dec. 1937; s. John Francis and Mary Anna (Jenkins) R.; e. St. Mary's Univ. 1962–66; m. Jovanna d. Joseph and Hazel Isaac 21 July 1978; one s. René; began painting in 1960; first one-man show 1967; 35 one-man exhibits and many group exhibits across Can.: Halifax, St. John's, Charlottetown, St. John, Edmundston, Moncton, Montreal, Ottawa, Guelph, Aberfoyle, Trenton, Toronto, Hamilton and Calgary 1968–81; annual one-man exhibits, Halifax 1981–94; participated in the Dalhousie Med. Rsch. Art Auctions 1980–84; painting included in corp., govt. and priv. collections in N. Am., Europe and Japan; painting included in N.S. Centennial Collection 1967; Art Gall. of N.S. permanent coll. 1973; N.S. Art Bank 1975; The National Bank 1984; City Hall, Hakadate, Japan 1989; N.S. Teacher's College 1991; rec'd award at Candn. Forces Art Exhibit Ottawa 1966; rec'd First Place Award, Maritime Art Assn. 1978; CBC Film 'Portraits of the Maritimes' 1982; author: 'A Halifax ABC' 1987 (one of the best picture books in Can., Candn. Lib. Assoc. 1987); Choice Book, Candn. Children's Book Centre 1988–89; paintings included in the National book 'Canadian Childhoods' 1989; 30 yr. retrospective Exhib., Art Gallery of N.S. 1990; Exhib., N.S. Teachers College 1991; featured on MITV - Global Network - 6 O'Clock TV News; recreations: swimming, music, art history; Address: 6038 Cedar St., Halifax, N.S. B3H 2J3.

**ROAZEN, Paul,** A.B., Ph.D., F.R.S.C.; professor of social and political science; b. Boston, Mass. 14 Aug. 1936; s. Julius and Anna R.; e. Harvard Coll. A.B. 1958; Harvard Univ. Ph.D. 1965; divorced; children: Jules Heller Roazen, Daniel Heller Roazen; PROFESSOR OF SOCIAL & POLITICAL SCIENCE, YORK UNIV. 1974– ; Instr. & Asst. Prof., Dept. of Govt., Harvard Coll. 1965–71; Assoc. Prof., present univ. 1971–74; author: 'Freud: Political and Social Thought' 1968, 1986, 'Brother Animal: The Story of Freud and Tausk' 1969, 1990, 'Freud and His Followers' 1975, 1992, 'Erik H. Erikson: The Power and Limits of a Vision' 1976, Helene Deutsch: A Psychoanalyst's Life' 1985, 1992, 'Encountering Freud: The Politics and Histories of Psychoanalysis' 1990, 'Meeting Freud's Family' 1993; editor: 'Sigmund Freud' 1973, 1987, 'Lippmann's Public Philosophy' 1989, 'Hartz's The Necessity of Choice' 1990, 'Tausk's Sexuality, War and Schizophrenia' 1991, 'Deutsch's Psychoanalysis of the Sexual Functions of Women' 1991, 'Deutsch's The Therapeutic Process, The Self, and Female Psychology' 1992; Fellow, Royal Soc. of Canada 1993; Home: 31 Whitehall Rd., Toronto, Ont. M4W 2C5; Office: Founders College 315, York Univ., 4700 Keele St., North York, Ont. M3J 1P3.

**ROBART-MORGAN, David J.;** investment executive; b. Bulawayo, Zimbabwe 30 Sept. 1949; s. Peter and Georgina Kathleen Mae (Whitehead) R.; e. Gilbert Rennie H.S. Zambia; St. Stephens Coll., Balla Balla, Zimbabwe; 2nd m. Janet d. Joe and Margaret Revelry 6 May 1989; children: Andrew, Ian, Jason, Joanna, Russell, Katy, Richard; NATIONAL OPERATIONS MANAGER, RICHARDSON GREENSHIELDS OF CANADA LIMITED 1985– ; joined present firm 1969; Mgr., Acctg. Systems 1977; Director & Vice-Pres. 1986; Dir. & Extve. Ctte., Candn. Depository; Mem., FAS; Chrmn., CDS Steering Ctte.; Warden, Lorne Park St. Pauls; Home: 853 Kowal Dr., Mississauga, Ont. L5H 3T3; Office: 130 Adelaide St. W., Toronto, Ont. M5H 1T8.

**ROBB, Christopher John,** B.A.; oil industry executive; b. Montreal, Que. 25 Nov. 1943; s. Dr. James Preston and Mary Grierson (Waller) R.; e. Westmount Sr. H.S. 1961; Univ. of N.B., B.A. (Econ.) 1965; m. Phyllis I. d. Alexander and Patricia Tait 29 July 1967; children: James Alexander, Kathleen Alison; Pres., Canstates Energy 1990; var. posts ending as Western Can. Sales Mgr., Dupont of Can. 1966–73; var. posts incl. Gen. Mgr., Grandview Indus. Ltd. and ending as Extve. Vice-Pres., Noranda Gas Indus., Noranda Mines Ltd. 1974–85; Pres., Canstates Energy 1985–90; Dir., Robco Inc.; Devran Petroleum Ltd.; Terex Resources Inc.; Pres., Pelican Finan. Ltd.; Golden Hind Holding Corp. Ltd.; recreations: ranching, skiing, guitar, squash; clubs: Glencoe, Bow Valley; Home: 3219 7th St. S.W., Calgary, Alta. T2T 2X8.

**ROBB, J. Preston,** M.Sc., M.D., C.M., F.R.C.P.; neurologist; b. Montreal, Que. 4 April 1914; s. Joseph Doig and Janie McLeod (Preston) R.; e. Westmount High Sch.; McGill Univ., B.Sc., M.Sc. (Neurol.), M.D., C.M.; m. Mary Grierson, d. Stephen Waller, 19 Oct. 1940; children: William David, Christopher John, Mary Alison, James Bruce; SR. CONSULTANT, MONTREAL NEUROLOGICAL HOSP.; Hon. consultant: St. Vincent de Paul Hosp., Brockville; Brockville General Hosp.; Children's Hosp. of Eastern Ont.; Emeritus Prof. of Neurology and Neurosurg., McGill Univ.; Consultant, Montreal Children's Hosp.; Chrmn. Emeritus, Robco; served in 2nd World War with R.C.N.V.R., 1941–45, Surg. Lt. Cmdr.; mem., Candn. Med. Assn.; Candn. Neurol. Soc.; Montreal Neurol. Soc.; Fellow Am. Acad. of Neurol.; Am. Neurol. Assn.; United Church; recreations: fishing, farming; Club: University; Address: Box 43, Lyn, Ont. K0E 1M0.

**ROBB, James Alexander,** Q.C., B.A., B.C.L.; lawyer; b. Huntingdon, Que. 3 May 1930; s. late Alexander George and late Irma Mary (Martin) R.; e. Huntingdon Acad.; McGill Univ. B.A. 1951, B.C.L. 1954; Univ. of Montreal postgrad. studies 1961–63; m. Katherine Ann d. late Norman Teare and the late Helen Quayle 25 June 1960; children: Laura, John, Andrew; PARTNER, STIKEMAN, ELLIOTT, MONTREAL; Dir. Robapharm (Canada) Ltd.; C. Itochu (Canada) Ltd.; YKK Canada Inc.; Hitachi (HSC) Canada Inc.; Champlain Industries Ltd.; NGK Spark Plugs Canada Ltd.; Hitachi Credit Canada Inc.; Descente Canada, Inc.; Klöckner, Stadler, Hurter Ltd.; Domtar Inc.; Quebec/Japan Business Forum (Pres. 1993–94); called to Bar of Que. 1955; cr. Q.C. 1971; Pres. Westmount Lib. Assn. 1971–72; Vice Pres. Lib. Party Que. (Prov.) 1976–79; Chrmn. Martlet Foundation Bd. Trustees 1967–69; mem. Adv. Comte. McGill Univ. Centre for Regulated Industries 1981– ; Gov., McGill Univ.; mem. Westmount Sch. Bd. 1972–73; Prot. Sch. Bd. Greater Montreal 1972–74 (Vice Chrmn. Parents' Comte. -1973–74); Pres., The Candn. Club of Montreal 1990–91; Pres. McGill Student Soc. 1953–54; Chrmn. Consumers' Assn. Can. Regulated Industries Bd. 1976–79; mem. Que. Trade Del. to Japan 1974; Coll. Council, Marianopolis Coll. 1978–85; mem. Que. Bar Assn.; Candn. Bar Assn.; Am. Bar Assn.; Am. Arbitration Assn., Commercial Panel; Treas. Jr. Bar Assn. 1964 (Council 1960–64); Phi Kappa Pi (Pres. 1952); served with RCAF (Reserve) 1949–54, rank Flying Offr.; Fondation du Barreau de Montréal; Liberal; Protestant; recreations: politics, skiing; Clubs: Montreal University; Kanawaki Golf, Kanawaki; Royal Montreal Curling; Home: 9 Renfrew Ave., Westmount, Que. H3Y 2X3;

Office: 3800, 1155 Réne-Lévesque Blvd. W., Montreal, Que. H3B 3V2.

**ROBB, Joseph D.,** B.A.; pulp & paper industry executive; b. Hamilton, Ont. 27 Oct. 1944; s. William D. and Frances W. (White) R.; e. Lower Canada College 1963; Mount Allison Univ. B.A. 1968; m. Nancy d. Jack and Jean Grainger 13 Sept. 1969; children: William, Stuart; Senior Vice-Pres., Sales & Marketing, Spruce Falls Power & Paper Co. 1991; Sales & Sales Admin., Anchor Packing Co. 1968–75; Gen. Mgr., Ontario Rubber Co. 1975–78; Robco Inc. 1978–84; Marketing Mgr., Spruce Falls Power & Paper Co. 1984–88; Gen. Sales Mgr. 1988–89; Vice-Pres., Sales & Marketing 1989–91; Dir., Spruce Falls Power & Paper Co. Ltd.; Robco Inc.; Candn. Hearing Soc.; recreations: skiing, squash, swimming; clubs: Toronto Cricket Skating & Curling; Home: 5600 Philip Turcot, Montreal, Que. H4C 1V7.

**ROBB, William D.;** manufacturer, retired; b. Detroit, Mich. 29 July 1911; m. Frances Wilmington White, 11 Sept. 1937; children: Judith (Mrs. Ian Griffin), Joseph Doig, Jennifer (Mrs. Steven Dattels); retired Dir., Robco Inc.; Anchor Packing Co. Ltd.; Albion A.A.P. Inc.; Vice Pres. and Dir., Ontario Rubber Co.; Dir., Solidur Canada Ltd.; Thermofab Ltd.; Pres., Springdale Foundation; Vice Pres., Ont. Deafness Research Foundation; Can. Hearing Soc. Foundation; Dir., Wild Life Preservation Trust; Past Pres., Montreal Boys' Home; Camp Weredale; Gov., Weredale Foundation; Past Dir., Roy. Victoria Hosp.; Chrmn. Bd. of Trustees, St. Andrew's Ch., Westmount; mem. Adv. Bd. Montreal YMCA; Clubs: Mount Royal; Forest & Stream; York; Rosedale (Toronto); Rotary Toronto (Past Dir.); Rotary Montreal; Ojibway (Pointe au Baril, Ont.; Past Pres.); Home: 25 Cedarwood Ave., Willowdale, Ont M2L 2X6; Offices: 5600 Philippe-Turcot St., Montreal, Que. H4C 1V7 and 10 Jutland Rd., Toronto, Ont. M8Z 2G9.

**ROBBIE, Roderick George,** Dipl. Arch, Dip.TP, FRAIC, OAA, RIBA, MCIP, OPPI, RCA; architect and planner; b. Poole, U.K. 15 Sept. 1928; s. William George and Gladys May (Sargeant) R.; e. Arch. & Town Planning Schools (UK) Dip.Arch. (Hons.), Dip.TP 1949–54; m. Enid C. d. Katherine and Walter Wheeler 20 Dec. 1952; children: Karen, Nicola, Caroline, Angus; PRESIDENT, ROBBIE SANE ARCHITECTS INC.; began career with British Rail 1954; worked with Belcourt & Blair and Peter Dickinson Assoc. Arch.; designed the Candn. Pav. at Expo '67 as Partner, Ashworth, Robbie, Vaughan & Williams Archs.; portfolio incl. design of Toronto SkyDome, Guelph & York Univ. Science complexes, concept design for proposed Scarborough Aquatic Ctr., etc.; Tech. Dir. & Co-founder, SEF Project, Metro Toronto Sch. Bd.; has worked with partner Arun Sane for over 20 years; Principal, RAN Internat. Arch. & Engr.; RAN Consortium; Pres., Computecture Inc.; Dir., Arcanco Inc.; Keen Communication Systems Inc.; Special Award for Toronto SkyDome, Inst. of Structural Engrs. (UK) 1990; Quaternario Award (Venice) 1990 for SkyDome; Miss. Urban Design Award, West Credit S.S. 1984; 1st Prize, Low Energy Bldg. Design Award, Public Works Canada/Energy Mines & Resources 1980; nom. Engr. News Record Construction Man of the Year 1967; frequent guest lecturer; Academician, Royal Acad. of Arts 1990; FRAIC 1989 (Mem. 1962– ); RIBA 1951; MCIP 1974; OAA 1957; Mem., Town Planning Inst. of Can. 1961; The Arch. Assn. 1951; several past extve. positions; author: 'Minds' 1983; co-author: SEF series of 7 books for elem. & sec. schools; recreations: watercolour painting; Home: 16 Cornish Rd., Toronto, Ont. M4T 2E2; Office: 11 Soho St., Suite 204, Toronto, Ont. M5T 1Z6.

**ROBBINS, Barry D.,** B.Sc., M.B.A.; business executive; b. San Francisco, Calif. 3 March 1943; e. Boston Univ. B.Sc., M.B.A.; m. Toni; children: Brent, Elise; PRES. & CHIEF EXTVE. OFFR., GOODYEAR CANADA INC.; clubs: St. George's Golf & Country; Home: 1335 Green Eagle Dr., Oakville, Ont. L6M 2N1; Office: 10 Four Seasons Place, Etobicoke, Ont. M9B 6G2.

**ROBBINS, Brian Andrew,** B.A.Sc., P.Eng.; corporate executive; b. Toronto, Ont. 31 Dec. 1946; s. Herbert Henry and Audrey Ethel (Champion) R.; e. Univ. of Waterloo, B.A.Sc. 1970; m. Sheila E. d. George and Jessie McKay 21 Dec. 1968; children: Nicole, Mathew; PRES. & C.E.O., EXCO TECHNOLOGIES LTD. 1978– ; Dir., Tecsyn Internat. Inc.; joined Exco Tech. Ltd. 1970; Founded Unex Enterprises Ltd. 1980 (a real estate holding company); recreations: hunting, fishing; Clubs: Goodwood, Beacon Hall Golf (Director); Timberlane Tennis; The Fitness Institute; Home: Hazelburn, 9 Jarvis Ave., Aurora, Ont.; Office: 60 Spy Ct., Markham, Ont. L3R 5H6.

**ROBBINS, William Miller,** B.Sc., B.A., M.B.A.; hospital executive; b. Hamilton, Ont. 1 May 1940; s. William Wegner and Marjorie Lenore (Miller) R.; e. Westdale S.S. Hamilton 1959; Queen's Univ. B.Sc. 1963; Concordia Univ. B.A. 1965; Queen's Univ. M.B.A. 1968; m. Joyce G.F. d. Philip and Alexandrina Smith 10 July 1965; children: Edward, Elizabeth; EXECUTIVE VICE-PRES., THE WELLESLEY HOSPITAL 1989– ; Systems Manager, IBM 1963–68; Mgr., Peat Marwick & Partners 1968–71; Extve. Dir., Ont. Govt. 1971–79; Pres. & Chief Extve. Offr., Boyd Stott & McDonald Technologies Limited 1979–84; Vice-Pres. Finance & Corp. Devel., Sciex Div., MDS Health Group Limited 1984–89; Mem., Candn. College of Health Service Executives; Assn. of Profl. Engr., Ont.; Queen's Business Club; recreations: skiing, windsurfing, sailing, reading; clubs: The Boulevard, The Toronto Ski; Home: 98 Valecrest Dr., Islington, Ont. M9A 4P6; Office: 160 Wellesley St. E., Toronto, Ont. M4Y 1J3.

**ROBERGE, Fernand A.,** Ing., M.Sc.A., Ph.D.; éducateur, ingénieur biomédical; né Pontbriand, Co. Megantic, Qué. 11 juin 1935; f. Lauréat et Léonilde (Paré) R.; é. Ecole Polytech. (génie), Univ. de Montréal, M.Sc.A., 1960; Univ. McGill, Ph.D., 1964; ép. Gladys, f. Charles Pagé, Montréal, 8 février 1958; enfants: Vivyane, Carolyne, Eric, Nicolas; Institut de Genie Biomed., Ecole Polytechnique et Universite de Montreal (Dir., 1978–88), Chef de Serv. 1973–88, Coord. technol. méd., Hôpital du Sacré Coeur, Montréal; Conseil des Sciences du Can. (1971–74); mem. Conseil de Recherches Sci. Nat. & Génie (1981–88); Fellow, Candn. Med. and Biol. Engn. Soc.; Fellow, Inst. of Elect. and Electronics Engineers; Biomed. Engn. Soc.; Soc. Canadienne de Physiol.; écrit environ 250 articles scient., chapitres de livres, etc.; D. W. Ambridge Award, Univ. McGill, 1964; Prix Rousseau, ACFAS, 1986; Prix Léon-Lortie, Soc. St-Jean Baptiste de Montréal 1987; Catholique; récréations: golf, natation; résidence: 216 Lazard, Ville Mont. Royal, Que. H3R 1N9.

**ROBERGE, Hon. Gabriel,** B.A., B.Ph., LL.L.; retired judge; b. St. Ferdinand d'Halifax, Frontenac, Que. 30 March 1918; s. P. Allyre and Irene (Duchesneau) R.; e. Semy. of Quebec, B.A. 1938; Laval Univ., B.Ph. 1938, LL.L. 1941; m. Denyse, d. Jules E. Lemay, 29 Sept. 1956; one d. Suzanne; Justice, Superior Court of Que. 1963–93, Retired; read law with St.-Laurent, Gagné, Devlin & Taschereau; called to the Bar of Que. 1941; practised law alone 1942–43 and 1946–48; Partner, Talbot & Roberge 1948–56; alone 1956–58; Roberge & Gobeil 1958–63 continuously in Thetford Mines, Que.; served in Candn. Army, Inf. and Law Br. 1943–46, Capt. Supplementary Reserve (retd.); M.P. for Megantic (Liberal) 1958–62; K.C.L.J., C.M.L.J.; R. Catholic; recreations: golf, skiing; Clubs: Cap Rouge Country; Quebec Garrison; Home: 250 W. Grande-Allée, Apt. 1305, Québec, Que. G1R 2H4.

**ROBERGE, Philippe,** LL.L.; notary and legal adviser; b. Inverness, Que. 16 Oct. 1924; s. P. A. and Irène (Duchesneau) R.; e. Univ. of Montreal, B.A. 1945; Univ. of Laval, LL.L. 1948; m. Hélène, d. Louis Morin, 24 Sept. 1949; children: Louis, Paule, Jacques; PARTNER, ROBERGE ET ROBERGE 1991– ; Dir., Laurentian Bank of Canada; Laurentian Trust of Canada Inc.; Montreal Heart Inst. Rsch. Foundation; Centre Hospitalier Côte-des-Neiges Foundation; called to the Bar of Que. 1948; in law practice as Notary, Thetford Mines, Que. 1948–61, specialising in mining and corporate law with experience in mun. affairs; joined McLean, Marler, Common & Tees, Montreal 1962–89; Practised law with Pelletier, Poirier, Leroux & Kimmel 1989–91; Lt., les Voltigeurs de Qué.; City Councillor, Thetford Mines 1955; recreation: golf; Home: 6000, Chemin Deacon, App. L-7, Montreal, Que. H3S 2T9; Office: 507 Place d'Armes, Suite 1200, Montreal, Que. H2Y 2W8.

**ROBERGE, René-Michel,** B.èsA., B.Th., L.Th., D.Th.; professeur de théologie; né Charny, Qué. 8 juillet 1944; f. Henri et Beatrice (Fradet) R.; é. Univ. Laval B.èsA. 1965, B.Th. 1967, L.Th. 1969, D.Th. 1971; ép. Jacinthe f. Bertrand et Mariette Leblanc 12 juillet 1975; enfants: Jean-Michel, Pierre-Étienne; PROFESSEUR DE THÉOLOGIE FONDAMENTALE ET D'HISTOIRE DE LA THÉOLOGIE À L'UNIVERSITÉ LAVAL 1971– ; Prof. titulaire depuis 1983; Vice-doyen de la Fac. de théologie 1988–89; Doyen 1989– ; Prof. invité dans diverses universités canadiennes; Prés. de la Féd. des Assocs. de Prof. d'Univ. du Qué. 1973–74; Vice-Prés. fondateur du Syndicat des prof. de l'Univ. Laval 1974–75; Dir. de la revue 'Laval théologique et philosophique' 1987–92; auteur d'une cinquantaine de pubs et de nom. communications en patristique, en théol. fond. et systém. et en documentation spéc.; mem. de plusieurs assocs. sci: Internat. Assoc. for Patristic Studies, Candn. Soc. of Patristic Studies, N. Am. Patristics Soc., Soc. can. de théologie, etc.; Prés. et mem. de divers conseils d'admin.; consultant pour divers organismes; auteur: 'Abrégé de patrologie' 1976, réed. 1977, eds. revues et augmentées en 1983, '85, '89, 'Guides du documentaliste pour le dépouillement et l'analyse des périodiques, des éditions de textes patristiques, des monographies, etc.' 1979, 'Révélation et théologie' 3e éd. 1993, 'Connaître le Dieu de Jésus-Christ' 1982, 'Histoire de la théologie chrétienne' 1983, éd. revue en 1985, '89; à ces titres s'ajoutent plus d'une trentaine d'articles sci., une centaine de recensions et comptes rendus parus dans diverses revues sci. ainsi que de nom. articles de vulgarisation; domicile: 9505 Marie-Parent, Québec, Qué. G2K 1K4; bureau: Fac. de théologie, Univ. Laval, Québec, Qué. G1K 7P4.

**ROBERT, Jacques P.,** B.E., P.Eng.; b. Arvida, Qué. 16 July 1944; s. Jean Maurice and Gilberte (Trudelle) R.; e. Ecole Polytechnique, Univ. de Montréal, B.E.(Mech.) 1969; m. Liette d. Jean and Denise Hardy 18 July 1970; one s. Jean-François; Dir., Jenkins Canada Inc. 1989– ; Sales Eng. Texaco Canada 1969–72; Canron Inc. 1972–73; Sales Mgr. Treco Inc. 1973–75; Gen. Mgr. Norcom Homes 1975–77; Canrep Inc. 1977–79; Canron Plastics 1979–85; Vice Pres. & Dir., Canron Inc. 1985; Pres., Canron Pipe 1989; Dir., Candn. Inst. Plumbing & Heating; recreations: golf, skiing; Club: Montréal Country; The National; Home: 1700 Edgewood, St-Bruno, Qué. J3V 4R2.

**ROBERT, Jean-Claude,** L.èsL, M.A., Doctorat, F.R.S.C.; university professor, historian; b. Montreal, Que. 27 Mar. 1943; s. Jean-Paul and Jeannette (Riendeau) R.; e. Ecole secondaire Saint-Stanislas 1959; Univ. de Montréal, B.A. 1966, L.èsL 1969, M.A. 1971; Univ. de Paris I, doctorat en histoire 1977; m. Claire d. Gisèle and Georges McNicoll 4 Sept. 1967; PROF. RÉGULIER, DÉP. D'HISTOIRE, UNIV. DU QUÉBEC A MONTRÉAL 1975– ; Acctg. Clerk, Dominion Stores Ltd. 1960–66; Hist. Teacher, Ecole secondaire Mont-de-LaSalle 1967–69; Socio Cultural Serv., CEGEP de Joliette 1969–71; Chargé de cours, Univ. du Qué. à Chicoutimi 1974; Dir., Dép. present univ. 1977–79; Prog. d'études avancées 1985–87; Mem., Comité interministériel sur les archives judiciaires 1987–89; Adv. Bd., Candn. Historical Review 1982–85; Conseil d'Admin., Fonds FCAR 1988–93; Inst. d'hist. de l'Am. française (past extve. positions); Candn. Hist. Assn. (Counc. 1980–83, 1988–92; Vice-Pres. 1988–89; Pres. 1989–90); author: 'Du Canada français au Québec libre' 1975; 'Atlas historique de Montréal' 1994; co-author: 'Histoire du Québec contemporain' 1979, Quebec: A History 1867–1929 (transl.) 1983; 'Le Québec depuis 1930' 1986; 'Quebec Since 1930' (transl.) 1991; author/co-author of 60 articles & contribs.; Home: 3241 Cedar Ave., Westmount, Que. H3Y 1Z6; Office: C.P. 8888, Montreal, Que. H3C 3P8.

**ROBERT, Lucie,** B.A., M.A., Ph.D.; university professor; b. Jonquiere, Que. 22 May 1954; d. Marcel and Julie (Boutet) R.; e. CEGEP de Hull 1973; Laval Univ. B.A. 1976, M.A. 1980, Ph.D. 1987; one s.: Jeremie; PROFESSOR, DEPT. OF LITERARY STUDIES, UNIVERSITY OF QUEBEC AT MONTREAL 1986– (tenure 1989); Research Assoc., Dictionnaire des oeuvres littéraires du Québec (Laval, Que.) 1978–86; Editorial Bd. Mem., 'Voix & Images/Littérature Québécoise' 1982– ; Editor 1988–92; Affiliate Mem., Ctr. de Rech. en Litt. Québécoise, Univ. Laval; Prix Edmond-de-Nevers 1980–91; Candn. Fed. for the Humanities, Best Book in French 1990–91; author: 'Le Manuel de Mgr. Camille Roy' 1982, 'L'Institution du littéraire au Québec' 1989; co-author: 'Dictionnaire des oeuvres littéraires du Qué.' 1978–87, 'La Vie littéraire au Québec, 1764–1914' 5 vols. 1991–97; contbr.: 'Jeu,' 'Poetics Today,' 'Rech. Sociographiques,' 'Etudes françaises,' 'Etudes littéraires,' 'Spirale,' 'Lettres québécoises,' 'Voix & Images/Littérature québécoise'; recreations: swimming, biking; Home: 5125 rue Marquette, Montreal, Que. H2J 3Z4; Office: Box 8888, Station A, Montreal, Que. H3C 3P8.

**ROBERTS, Barbara Ann,** Ph.D.; university professor; b. Riverside, Calif. 22 Sept. 1941; d. Paul Curtis and Charlotte Ruth (Bowman) R.; e. Simon Fraser Univ., B.A. 1972, M.A. 1976; Univ. of Ottawa, Ph.D. 1980; m. F. David s. F. Graham and Mildred Elizabeth (Oldfield) Millar 1979; children: Michael Paul and David Sean Hoffman; PROF. OF WOMEN'S STUDIES, ATHABASCA UNIV. 1992– ; has taught at universities in N.S., Que., Sask., & Man.; involved in various community-based action-rsch. projects 1980–89; Assoc. Prof. present Univ. 1989–92; Co-ord., Peace Tent, UN Decade of Women, NGO Forum, Nairobi 1985; active feminist scholar & author; lecturer, Canada & abroad; Bd. of Dir., Soc. Sci. Fed. of Can. 1989–90; Treas.,

Candn. Women's Studies Assn. 1989–92; Bd. of Dir., Ovum Pacis (Internat. Women's Peace Univ.) 1989–91; mem., Religious Soc. of Friends (Quakers); NDP; Candn. Rsch. Inst. for the Advancement of Women; Voice of Women; author: 'A Reconstructed World: Gertrude Richardson, A Biography' 1994; 'Whence They Came: Deportation from Canada 1900–1935' 1988; and numerous scholarly articles; co-author: 'A Decent Living: Women in the Winnipeg Garment Industry' 1991; recreations: gardening, reading, feminist mysteries & science fiction, walking; Home: 10933 – 73rd Ave., Edmonton, Alta. T6G 0C3; Office: P.O. Box 10,000, Athabasca, Alta. T0G 2R0.

**ROBERTS, Edward Moxon,** Q.C., B.A., LL.B.; lawyer; politician; b. St. John's, Nfld. 1 Sept. 1940; s. Harry Duncan and Mary Katharine (Moxon) R.; e. Holloway Sch. and Prince of Wales Coll., St. John's, Nfld.; St. Andrew's Coll., Aurora, Ont.; Univ. of Toronto B.A. 1960, LL.B. 1964; m. Eve d. Jane Field and the late Jack Hargraft; children: Catherine Elizabeth and Caroline Alexandra; MINISTER OF JUSTICE, ATTORNEY GENERAL FOR NEWFOUNDLAND and GOVERNMENT HOUSE LEADER 1992– ; Assoc. Priv. Sec. to the Hon. J.W. Pickersgill 1963; Exec. Asst. to the Hon. J.R. Smallwood, Premier of Nfld. and Labrador, 1964–66; apptd. to newly-created posn. of Parlty. Asst. to Premier 1966–68; entered Cabinet as Min. of Publ. Welfare 1968–69; Min. of Health 1969–72; el. Leader Lib. Party of Nfld. and Labr. Feb. 1972; re-el. (running against Mr. Smallwood) Oct. 1974, def. Oct. 1977; Leader of the Opposition 1972–77; House Leader of the Opposition during leadership of the Hon. Donald C. Jamieson 1979–80; Chrmn. Pub. Accounts Ctte. 1982–84; el. to House of Assembly for Dist. of White Bay North g.e. 1966, re-el. 1971, 1972; el. to H. of A. g.e. 1975 for newly-created Dist. of Strait of Belle Isle, re-el. 1979, 1982; did not seek re-el. in 1985 general election; Chrmn. of the Ctte. on the Constitution apptd. by Govt. of Newfoundland and Labrador 1991; elected to the House of Assembly for the District of Naskaupi, Labrador in a by-election in 1992, and re-elected in g.e. 1993; represented Nfld. and Labrador at the Multilateral Meetings on the constitution held under the Chairmanship of the Right Honourable Joseph Clark between March and August 1992, culminating in The Charlottetown Accord; apptd. Govt. House Leader 1992; called to Bar of Nfld. 1965; joined Halley, Hickman, Hunt and Adams (now Halley, Hunt), St. John's, Nfld. 1978 becoming Sr. Partner until retirement in 1992; Q.C. 1979; apptd. Master of the Supreme Court of Nfld. 1989; several family-owned and -controlled corps.; Past Dir., Fortis Trust Corporation; Chrmn. of the Bd. of Trustees, Waterford Hosp., St. John's 1990–91; Chrmn. of the Bd. of Trustees, The General Hospital Corporation, St. John's 1991–92; Ed. 'The Varsity' under-grad. newspaper, Univ. of Toronto 1960–61; Pres. Candn. Univ. Liberal Fedn. 1961–62; mem. United Ch. of Can.; various orgns. within Masonic order; Nfld. Game, Fish and Protection Soc. Ltd.; Candn. Bar Assoc.; Candn Maritime Law Assoc.; Life Mem., Brigus Historical Society; Nfld. Historical Soc.; recreations: reading (mostly biography, hist. and current affairs); collecting Newfoundlandia; Home: Pond Head, Hogan's Pond Rd., St. John's, Nfld. A1B 4J9; Office: Dept. of Justice, Confederation Building, P.O. Box 8700, St. John's, Nfld. A1B 4J6.

**ROBERTS, Ernest Albert Kevin,** M.A.; educator; b. Adelaide, Australia 8 March 1940; s. Albert Keith and Audrey (Morris) R.; e. Univ. of Adelaide, B.A. 1961; Simon Fraser Univ., M.A. 1968; Univ. of Exeter, Ph.D. studies 1972; m. Maria d. Roxy and Evangelo Kourakis 15 Aug. 1966; two s. Anthony Kourakis, Jonathan Keith; LECTR. IN ENG. MALASPINA COLL. 1969– ; Teacher, S. Australian high schs. 1962–66; Comm. Salmon Fisherman 1974–78; Writer-in-Residence, Wattle Park Coll. Adelaide 1983; author (poetry): 'Cariboo Fishing Notes' 1972; 'West Country' 1975; 'Deep Line' 1976; 'Stonefish' 1978; 'S'ney'mos' 1977; 'Nanoose Bay Suite' 1982; 'Marshall Lake' 1987; 'Red Centre Journal' 1992; (fiction): 'Flash Harry and the Daughter of Divine Light' 1980; 'Picking the Morning Colour' 1985; 'Tears in a Glass Eye' 1988; (play): 'Black Apples' (poems) 1993; mem. League Candn. Poets; Writers Union Can.; recreations: fishing, hunting, tennis, philately; Home: 8014 Johnston Lane, Lantzville, B.C. V0R 2H0; Office: 900 5th St., Nanaimo, B.C.

**ROBERTS, Eve Hargraft,** Q.C., B.A., LL.B.; lawyer; b. Chatham, Ont. 17 Nov. 1939; d. John S. and Jane (Coate) Hargraft; e. Univ. of Toronto B.A. 1960; Osgoode Hall Law Sch. LL.B. 1963; m. Edward M. s. Harry and Katharine Roberts 28 Apr. 1982; two d. Jessica, Alison; PARTNER, HALLEY, HUNT 1985– ; called to Bar of Alta. 1965, Nfld. 1981; cr. Q.C. 1989; Chair, Nfld. Human Rights Comm. 1989– ; Dir. Inst. Feminist Legal Studies Osgoode Hall Law Sch. 1990; Terra Nova Chamber Players 1985– ; Founding Dir. Women's Legal Edn. & Action Fund 1985–87; mem. St. John's Estate Planning Council; Planned Parenthood; LEAF Nfld. (Chair 1987–88); Women's Network; St. John's YM-YWCA (Dir. 1986–89); Atlantic Ed. Carswell's Practice Cases 1981– ; Ed. Western Weekly Reports 1978–81; Home: Box 23181, Hogan's Pond Rd., St. John's, Nfld. A1B 4J9; Office: Box 610, St. John's, Nfld. A1C 5L3.

**ROBERTS, Frank;** industrial designer; b. Boston, Mass. 23 April 1931; s. Maurice and Doris (Benson) R.; e. Yale Univ.; m. Dominique d. Alfred and Janine Leval 20 Oct. 1991; children: Joy, David, Brian, Samantha, Laurant, Gregory; 11 grandchildren; PRES., OBUS FORME LTD. 1979– ; emigrated to Canada 1959; home builder, designer & land developer 1959–79; 1st patent 1980 for 1st Candn. orthopedic back rest device exported to 26 countries; holds num. patents & trade marks around the world; Pres., Bio-Support Indus. Ltd.; Foam Moulded Prod. Ltd.; Patrington Properties Ltd.; Inventor with Global Indus. Ltd. on the Obus/Global seating; Korean War Veteran; Technol. Exellence Award, Ont. Assn.of Cert. Engrs.; Disting. Donor Award, Governor's Club, Candn. Mem. Chiropractic College 1993 (estab. 1st undergrad. scholarship 1990; 1st copr. mem., Gov. Club); Design Canada Award; estab. Obus Forme Lotta Dempsey Award, Ryerson Univ., sch. of Journalism; Mem., Cystic Fibrosis Found. (65 Roses Club); clubs: Primrose, Turnberry Isle Golf (Florida); Office: 550 Hopewell Ave., Toronto, Ont. M6E 2S6.

**ROBERTS, Gildas Owen,** M.A., B.Ed., Ph.D.; educator; b. Johannesburg, S. Africa 5 Dec. 1932; s. Evan William and Mabel Irene Mary (Beynon) R.; e. Selborne Coll. East London, S. Africa 1948; Univ. of Cape Town B.A. 1951, M.A. 1953, B.Ed. 1955, STC 1975; Ohio State Univ. Ph.D. 1966; m. Patricia d. Charles Frears and Madge Howe 10 June 1963; children: Rachel, Sarah, Evan, Griffith; Prof. of Eng., Memorial Univ. of Nfld. 1977–93; Instr. in Classical Langs & Comp. Lit. Ohio State Univ. 1961–65; Asst. Prof. present Univ. 1965–67, Assoc. Prof. 1971–77, Pres.'s Award Distinguished Teaching 1990–91; Sr. Lectr. in Eng. Univ. of Cape Town 1967–71; author 'Joseph of Exeter: Iliad of Dares Phrygius' 1970; 'Seven Studies in English' 1971; 'Angels of God' novel 1974; 'Chemical Eric' novel 1974; 'Lotus Man' novel 1983; 'Beowulf' verse transl. 1984; 'Gander Snatch' novel 1991; Clk. of Session St. Andrew's Ch. (Presb.) St. John's, Elder since 1968; P.Conservative; recreations: reading, travel; Club: Crow's Nest Officers; Home: 504 The Tiffany, 7 Tiffany Lane, St. John's, Nfld. A1A 4B7.

**ROBERTS, Gordon S.,** Ph.D.; university professor; b. New York, N.Y.; s. the late Lawrence Gordon and Ruth (Berlin) R.; e. Oberlin Coll., B.A. (High Hons.) 1967; Boston Coll., M.A. (with distinction) 1968, Ph.D. 1972; Nat. Defense Edn. Act Fellow 1967–72; children: Jack, Ramona, Rebecca, Sarah; BANK OF MONTREAL PROFESSOR OF FINANCE, DALHOUSIE UNIV. 1988– ; Asst. Prof., Babson Coll. 1972–76; joined present univ. 1976; Vis. Assoc. Prof., Univ. of Victoria 1980; Vis. Rsch. Fellow, Univ. of Zimbabwe 1982; Vis. Prof., Xiamen Univ. 1986; Vis. Scholar, Univ. of Arizona 1988; Visiting Fellow, Univ. of Toronto 1991; teaching & prep. of edn. materials for Inst. of Candn. Bankers, Advanced Mngt. Ctr., Dalhousie Univ.; consulting for New Zealand Treasury 1993; incl. in '100 Most Frequent Contributors to the Finance Literature' Financial Management 1988; Trustee, Investments Ctte. for Pension & Endowment Funds & Retirees' Trust, Dalhousie Univ. 1980–91; Regional Dir., Canada 1992– , Finan. Mngt. Assn. & Admin. Sciences Assn. of Can. (several extve. positions for both); author: 'Financial Management Cases for Zimbabwe' 1984 and over 30 profl. articles; co-author: 'Contemporary Financial Management' 1987; 'Fundamentals of Corporate Finance' First Canadian Edition 1993; Editor, 'Financial Review' 1984–86; Assoc. Ed. 1986–87; Editor: 'Finance' Vol. 2 1981; Area Co-ed.: 'Can. J. of Admin. Studies' 1987–90; Ed. Adv. Bd., 'Can. Investment Review' 1988–91; Assoc. Ed., 'Journal of Financial Research' 1991– ; recreations: running, reading, wine; clubs: University (Dalhousie); Home: 9 Cleveland Cres., Dartmouth, N.S. B3A 2L5; Office: Halifax, N.S. B3H 1Z5.

**ROBERTS, Harry Duncan,** C.M., M.D., F.R.C.S.(C.) L.L.D.; surgeon, retired; b. St. John's Nfld., 21 Nov. 1908; s. Job Henry and Effie Jane (Taylor) R.; e. Meth. Coll.; Mem. Univ.; McGill Univ.; Dalhousie Univ., M.D. 1936; Memorial Univ., LL.D. (Hon.) 1980; m. Mary Katharine, d. Edward Gilmour Moxon, Truro, N.S., 21 June 1938; three s., Edward Moxon, Harry Douglas, Peter Job; Dir., Nfld. Steamships Ltd. 1974–80; Foundation Co. of Canada Ltd. 1968–83; mem. Bd. of Regents, Mem. Univ. 1968–74; Adv. Bd. Canada Permanent Trust Co. 1963–84; mem. Bd. of Finance (Nat.), Un. Ch. 1968–71; Royal Comn. on Econ. State and Prospects of Nfld. and Labrador, 1965–67; Chrmn., Gower St. Ch. Bd. of Stewards 1954–71; mem. Un. Ch. and Prot. Sch. Bds. 1940–68; Chrmn., Prince of Wales Coll. Bd., 1954–62; organ. Sea Cadets in Nfld. 1951; Pres., Guards Athletic Assoc., 1960–62; Nat. Pres., Navy League of Can., 1964–66; rec'd. Centennial Medal 1967; Jubilee medal, 1978; Order of Canada 1979; mem., Nfld. Med. Assn. (Hon. Secy. 1939–47; Pres. 1950; Extve. 1962–65); Candn. Med. Assn. (Pres., 1971–72); Freemason; Liberal; United Church; Clubs: St. John's Fish & Game; Rotary; Home: Apt. 306, 156 Portugal Cove Rd., St. John's, Nfld. A1B 4H9; Office: P.O. Box 13640, St. John's, Nfld. A1B 4G1.

**ROBERTS, J.D.;** television anchor; b. Toronto, Ont. 15 Nov. 1956; s. James Gardiner and Kathleen Burney (Hawkins) R.; e. Erindale S.S. 1974; Univ. of Toronto; m. Michele d. John and Sheila Mosey 7 July 1979; children: Kyle John, Taylor Avery; Anchor, Canada AM, CTV Television; Newscaster & Program Host, CFOS Radio; News & Program Host, CHYM Radio; Disk Jockey, CJBK Radio; CHUM Radio; Host, New Music Program, Entertainment Reporter for City Pulse, Video Jockey, Much Music, News Anchor City Pulse, CITY TV; News Anchor at Network Stn. WCIX-Miami, CBS Television.

**ROBERTS, Jack W.,** B.A., F.S.A., F.C.I.A.; consultant; b. Toronto, Ont. 2 Apr. 1930; s. William and Mary Cecelia (Novak) R.; e. Univ. of Toronto B.A. 1952; m. Norma Gertrude d. George and Gwen Horwood 6 May 1970; children: Linda Gail Beatty, Curtis William Roberts; Consultant; Pres. & C.E.O. Canadian General Life 1983–89; Bd. of Dirs., Westbury Canadian Life 1989– ; joined Crown Life Insurance Co. 1952–82; mem. Soc. of Actuaries; Candn. Inst. of Actuaries; recreations: tennis, bridge, golf, boating; Clubs: Granite; Muskoka Lakes Golf and Country; Home: F19, 288 Mill Rd., Etobicoke, Ont. M9C 4X7.

**ROBERTS, James Russell,** B.A., M.A.; economist; b. Toronto, Ont. 3 Dec. 1956; s. Woodrow Wilson and Elma Mary (Parson) R.; e. Don Mills C.I. 1974; Laval Univ., B.A. 1982, M.A. 1986; Rsch. Assoc., Research Group on Economics of Energy & Natural Resources, Dept. of Econ., Laval Univ. 1986; mem., Am. Econ. Assn.; Home: 10 Christie St., Quebec, Que. G1R 4J5.

**ROBERTS, Hon. John,** P.C., B.A., B.Phil., D.Phil.; politician; b. Hamilton, Ont. 28 Nov. 1933; s. John Cecil and Jean Fitch (Batty) R.; e. Oakwood Coll. Inst. Toronto; Univ. of Toronto; Oxford Univ. Trinity Coll., St. Anthony's Coll.; Ecole Nationale d'adm., Paris; Min. of Science and Technol., Can. and Min. of the Environment 1980–83; Min. of Employment & Immigration, Aug. 1983–84; Sec. of State, 1976–79; Foreign Service Offr. Dept. of External Affairs 1963–66; Extve. Asst. to Min. of Forestry & Rural Devel. 1966–68; el. to H. of C. g.e. 1968; Parlty. Secy. to Min. of Regional & Econ. Expansion; def. g.e. 1972, re-el. 1974, def. 1979, re-el. 1980 (St. Paul's) def. 1984; Sworn of Privy Council 1976; Liberal Leadership Candidate, 1984; author: 'Agenda for Canada: towards a new liberalism' 1986.

**ROBERTS, John Peter Lee,** C.M., M.A.; cultural executive; writer; lecturer; b. Sydney, Australia 21 Oct. 1930; s. Noel Lee and Myrtle Winnifred (Reid) R.; e. State Conservatorium of Music, Sydney, N.S.W., C.M. 1981; Carleton Univ. M.A. 1988; m. Christina d. Christine and August van Oordt 28 July 1962; children: Noel, Christina, Olga; DEAN, FACULTY OF FINE ARTS, UNIV. OF CALGARY 1987– ; Mus. Prod. CBC Radio, Winnipeg 1955–57; Mus. Prog. Orgn. CBC Radio 1957–65; Supr. of Mus. CBC Radio 1965–71; Head of Radio Mus. and Variety 1971–75; Special Adv. Mus. and Arts Devel. 1976–77; Dir. Gen. Candn. Mus. Centre 1977–81; Special Adv. to Chrmn. Candn. Radio Television Telecommunications Comn. 1981–83; Sr. Adv. Cultural Devel. Candn. Broadcasting Corp. 1983–87; author; lecturer on music, media and cultural policy in univs. and institutions and numerous articles on same subjects; Pres. Candn. Mus. Coun. 1968–71, 1975–77; Pres. Les jeunesses musicales du Can. 1980–83; Pres. Internat. Mus. Counc. (UNESCO), Paris 1977–79; Vice-Pres. Internat. Inst. for Audio-Visual Communications and Cultural Devel., Vienna 1976– ; Pres., 1987– ; Chrmn. Internat. Mus. Day 1975–83; Vice-Pres. Musicians Internat. Mutual Aid Fund, Geneva 1978–79; Chrmn. Internat. Vocal Competition, Rio de Janeiro 1979; Pres. Glenn Gould Foundation, Toronto 1984–94; Founding Pres. 1994– ; Chair., Candn. Assoc. of Fine Arts Deans 1989–93; mem. Order of Canada 1981; Cross of Honour for Sci. and the Arts, Austria 1981;

Hon. Doctorate (DFA, Doctor of Fine Arts) Univ. of Victoria 1992; Home: Box 22, Site 33, R.R. 12, Calgary, Alta. T3E 6W3; Office: 2500 University Dr. N.W., Calgary, Alta. T2N 1N4.

**ROBERTS, Kenneth Bryson,** M.B., B.S., M.A., D.Phil.; educator; b. London, Eng. 7 Sept. 1923; s. William Charles Roberts, O.B.E.; e. Emanuel Sch. London; Univ. of London M.B., B.S. 1945; Oxford Univ. M.A., D.Phil. 1952; m. Ruth Mary d. E. St. John Catchpool, C.B.E. Apl. 1945; children: Daniel John, Peter Simon, Alason Clare, Benjamin Hugh; PROF. EMERITUS, MEMORIAL UNIV. OF NFLD. since 1988; Lectr. in Physiol. Exeter Coll. Oxford Univ. 1950–53; Assoc. Prof. of Physiol. Med. Sch. Baghdad 1954–56; Sr. Lectr. in Physiol. Med. Sch. Edinburgh Univ. 1956–61; Reader in Physiol. Univ. of London 1961–68; Prof. of Physiol. present Univ. 1968–78, Assoc. Dean of Med. 1968–75; John Clinch Prof. Hist. of Med. & Physiol. Memorial Univ. of Nfld. 1978–88; co-author 'General Pathology' 1954; 'Introduction to Molecular Biology' 1964; 'Companion to Medical Studies' 1968; 'The Fabric of the Body: European Traditions in Anatomical Illustration' 1992; various papers in scient. journs.; mem. Council, Med. Research Council 1968–73, mem. various comtes. since 1968; Past Chrmn. Scient. Adv. Subcomte. Candn. Heart Foundation; mem. various scient. and med. socs.; NDP; recreations: books, films, gardening; Office: 43 Quidi Vidi Rd., St. John's, Nfld. A1A 1C2.

**ROBERTS, Philip Davies,** M.A., B.Mus., ARCCO; author; musician; b. Sherbrooke, Que. 9 Oct. 1938; s. Geoffrey Davies and Mary (Williams) R.; e. Magog (Que.) H.S.; Inst. Feller Grande-Ligne, Que.; Princess Elizabeth H.S. Magog; Acadia Univ. B.A. 1959; Jesus Coll. Oxford B.A. 1962, M.A. 1966; Univ. of Sydney (Australia) B.Mus. 1980; m. Carol Berney 1978, div. 1984; children: Rachael Ann, Megan Leah; Teacher of English Briam Inst., Univ. of Madrid and Brit. Inst. Madrid 1963; Sub-Ed., Reuters, London, Eng. 1964–66; Pub. Relations Cons. Peters Bishop & Partners, London, Eng. 1966–67; Lectr. in Eng. Univ. of Sydney, Australia 1967–74, Sr. Lectr. in Eng. 1974–80; Founding Ed. Island Press, Sydney 1970–80; freelance writer and musician 1980– ; author 'Plain English: A User's Guide' 1987; 'How Poetry Works' 1986; poetry: 'Just Passing Through' 1969; 'Single Eye' 1971; 'Crux' 1973; 'Will's Dream' 1975; 'Selected Poems' 1978; 'Letters Home' 1990; co-author 'Models of English Style' 1970; ed. 'The Inside Eye: A Study of Oxford College Life' 1961; 'Poet's Choice' 1970–1979; mem. P.E.N. International; founding mem. Australian Poets' Union; mem. Royal Canadian College of Organists; mem. Writers' Union of Canada; mem. Writers' Fedn. N.S.; Candn. Assn. Rhodes Scholars; Councillor, Town of Annapolis Royal; Address: P.O. Box 557, Annapolis Royal, N.S. B0S 1A0.

**ROBERTS, Richard Jack,** B.E.Sc., J.D.; law professor, labour arbitrator; b. London, Ont. 5 July 1942; s. Arthur George and Alice Isobel (Mitchell) R.; e. Univ. of Western Ont. B.E.Sc. 1965; Georgetown Univ. Law Center (Washington, D.C.) J.D. 1970; m. Rochelle d. Alfred and Mariette Roy 10 Sept. 1965; children: Jeannine, Maria-Lise; LAW PROF., FACULTY OF LAW, UNIV. OF WESTERN ONTARIO 1973– ; Law Clerk, Judge Malcolm R. Wilkey, U.S. Court of Appeal, Dist. of Columbia 1970–71; Assoc., Steptoe & Johnson 1971–73; Of Counsel, Peter Steinmetz & Assoc. (Toronto) 1986–88; Labour Arbitrator, Canada & U.S. & Vice-Chair, Ont. Public Serv. Grievance Settlement Board 1976– ; Past Dir., Canada-U.S. Law Inst.; Consultant, Bureau of Competition Policy, Consumer & Corp. Affairs Canada; Bureau of Intellectual Property; Vice-Pres. & Dir., London-Middlesex Liberal Assn. 1987–91; Vice-Pres., London West Liberal Assn. 1985–87; author: 'Anticombines & Antitrust' 1980, 'Competition / Antitrust: Canada & United States' 1991; 'The Private Right of Action: Treble Damage Antitrust & Actions in the United States' 1982; Home: 1058 The Parkway, London, Ont. N6A 2W7; Office: London, Ont. N6A 3K7.

**ROBERTS, Thomas (Tom) Keith,** R.C.A., O.S.A.; artist; b. Toronto, Ont. 22 Dec. 1908; s. Percy and Frieda (Humme) R.; e. N. Toronto (Ont.) Coll. Inst.; Central Tech. Sch., Toronto; Ont. Coll. of Art; m. Mary Regina, d. late James Quigley, 14 Sept. 1940; two d., Jane Grenville, Celia Mary; has exhibited with Royal Candn. Acad. since 1931, Ont. Soc. of Artists since 1929, Montreal Museum of Fine Arts since 1932 and Candn. Nat. Exhn. since 1931; exhibits in many travelling exhns.; a full-time painter, out-of-doors in 4 seasons, paints in Canada from coast to coast, (and in Bermuda) experimentally in studio; solo exhibitions in Halifax, Montreal, Ottawa, Toronto, Winnipeg, Vancouver; rep. in many pub. and private colls. in Can., U.S.A. and Europe; winner of Rolph Clarke Stone Award 1949; served with RCE during World War II; mem. (life), Ont. Soc. of Artists 1944– ; Roy. Candn Acad. of Arts, 1945– ; Liberal; Protestant; recreations: hockey, music, reading, travel; Address: 1312 Stavebank Rd., Mississauga, Ont. L5G 2V2.

**ROBERTS, William Dwight,** B.A., M.A., M.B.A.; broadcast executive; b. Drummondville, Que. 3 Sept. 1952; s. William Henry and Freda Joyce (Crook) R.; e. Bishops Coll. Sch.; Trent Univ., B.A. 1973; Lakehead Univ., Grad. Dip. Bus. Admin.; Loyola College, Grad. Dip. Communic. Arts; St. Mary's Univ., M.B.A. 1976; Sorbonne Nouvelle, M.A. 1977; Univ. de Paris, diplome de langue française 1977; Univ. of Stockholm Internat. Inst.; Carleton Univ. Inst. Candn. Studies; Banff Sch. Fine Arts; Univ. of Notre Dame, Brdcst. Mgmt.; Charles I. Travelli & Swedish Instit. scholar; m. Catherine Allman; children: Kristian, Nora Claire; SENIOR DIRECTOR GENERAL, INTERNATIONAL AFFAIRS, TVONTARIO 1990– ; radio producer CJAD, CFRB 1973; film & TV critic 1973–77; Sessional Lectr. Communications Carleton Univ. 1977–79; Sessional Lectr. Osgoode Hall 1993; Special Adv. Fed. NDP Leader's Office 1978–80; Fed. Council NDP 1980; Rsch. Secretary & Exec. Asst. Socialist Internat., London, UK 1980–81; Constitutional Co-Ordinator Sask. Govt. 1980–82; Sr. Policy Analyst CRTC 1982–86; Sr. Vice Pres. Candn. Assn. of Broadcasters 1986–88; Sr. Managing Director, Ext. Relations, TVOntario 1988–90; ed., TV PLUS 1986–88; Dir., Couchiching Inst. Pub. Aff.; CanWorld Fdn.; Past Dir.: Banff TV Festival 1986–88; Children's Broadcast Inst. 1986–89; Dalhousie Community & Social Services Centre, Ottawa 1985–87; Centretown Parents Daycare Co-op, Ottawa 1985–86; Jurist, Gemini Awards 1986–87; Japan Prize 1989; CanPro 1991; Jury Dir., Prix TVOntario Awards 1992; Jurist, Banff Festival of Mtn. Films 1993; Guest Lectr. Carleton Univ. 1987, McGill Univ. 1987, York Univ. 1988, Univ. of W. Ont. 1988; Dir.: ATEC (Assoc. for Tele-education in Can.); Patron Niagara Inst.; 1990 Cda.-Japan Film/TV Coprod. treaty mission; 1991 7th Cda.-Japan TV Execs. Mtg.; Sec.-Gen. Public Broadcasters Internat. 1991; Organizing Ctte. PBI 1992; Speaker: TV'92 Gemini Awards; Atlantic Film Festival '92; Supporting mem., Art Gallery of Ont.; Candn. Film Centre; mem., Academy of Candn. Cinema & Television; Broadcast Exec. Society (BES); Broadcasting for Internat. Understanding; Group of 78; Assn. for the Study of Candn. Radio and TV; Toronto Film Festival; Motion Picture Foundation of Canada; Museum of Broadcast Comm. (Chicago); Amnesty Internat.; Candn. Inst. of Internat. Affairs; Variety Club; Internat. Inst. of Communications; Founding Mem., Centre for Investigative Journalism; Candn. Assn. of Journalists; CUSO; Frontier College; Outward Bound; Oxfam-Canada; Alpine Club of Canada; Sierra Club; various articles on travel, broadcasting, social policy, constitution, international and public affairs; recreations: karate, scuba, mountain climbing, film, photography, travel, cooking; Home: 446 Arlington Ave., Toronto, Ont. M6C 3A2; Office: 2180 Yonge St., Box 200, Stn. 'Q,' Toronto, Ont. M4T 2T1.

**ROBERTS, William Hardy;** bookseller/consultant; b. Aberdeen, Scotland 8 Sept. 1931; s. William and May Elizabeth (Hardy) R.; e. priv. edn. England; m. Carole d. Diana and Arthur Betts 1975; one child (by previous marriage): William; two step-children (of present marriage): Stephanie, Victoria; Pres., Shirley Leishman Books Ltd. 1961, retired; emigrated to Canada 1954; Candn. citizen; Founding Mem., Book & Periodical Devel. Counc. 1975 (Co-Chrmn., Task Force on Book Distr. 1978–80); Mem., Ont. Arts Counc. Literary Prog. Adv. Ctte. 1985–87; Candn. Booksellers Assn. (Pres. 1978–79, Dir. 1975–80); Candn. Telebook Agy. (Pres. 1983–85, Dir. 1981–85); Can. Counc. Adv. Panel on Promotion & Distr. 1975–78; Sr. Assoc., Peat Marwick & Partners (involved in studies in regard to the book publishing industry) 1985– ; Consultant, Federal Department of Communications in revisions to the Book Publishing Industry Development Program 1985–86; author: 'An Outline of the Canadian Distribution System for Canadian Authored and Imported Titles' 1984, 'Development of Options for Action in Key Sections of Canadian Book Distribution' 1984; Contrib.; 'The Canadian Encyclopedia' 1985; recreations: books, travel, movies; Address: Burritts Rapids, Ont. K0G 1B0.

**ROBERTSON, Angus W.J. (Ron),** M.A., B.C.L.; diplomat; b. Toronto, Ont. 30 May 1930; s. Angus Gerald and Catherine (Waldron) R.; e. Bishop's Univ. B.A. 1950; Oxford Univ. B.A. 1953, M.A. 1956; McGill Univ. B.C.L. 1956; The Hague Acad. of Intnl. Law summer 1966; m. Terhi M.E. Salomaa Apr. 21 1988; children: Miranda C.G., Anthony A.W., N.A. Alexander, Catriona Zöe; MIN. & DEPY. PERMANENT REP., CANDN. PERMANENT MISSION TO THE U.N. AND CANDN. DELEGATION TO THE CONF. ON DISARMAMENT, Geneva; Schoolmaster, Sedbergh Sch. Montebello, Que. 1946–47; Cadet Pilot RAFVR 1951–54; Econ. Analyst, Jones Heward & Co. Montreal 1954; grad. legal training Stikeman & Elliott, Montreal 1956–57; joined Dept. of External Affairs 1959; Third Secy. Colombo 1961, Second Secy. and Acting Trade Comnr. 1962; Legal Div. Ottawa 1964; First Secy. Candn. Perm. Mission to UN New York 1967, Counsellor 1969; Counsellor The Hague 1970; Dir. Legal Adv. Div. 1972; Dir., United Nations Economic and Social Affairs Div. 1975; Co-ordinator Appts. to Intnl. Organs. 1979; Ambassador to Finland 1980; Special Advisor on Maritime Boundaries 1984; Dir., United Nations Affairs Div. 1985; Life mem., Clan Donnachaidh Soc.; Clubs: Rackets (Montreal); Hillside Tennis (Montreal); Rockcliffe Tennis (Ottawa); Khandahar Ski (UK); Home: 28 Ave. Riant Parc, 1209 Geneva, Switzerland; Office: 1 rue du Pré-de-la-Bichette, 1202 Geneva, Switzerland.

**ROBERTSON, Hon. Brenda Mary;** senator; b. Sussex, N.B. 23 May 1929; d. John James and Clara (Rothwell) Tubb; e. Sussex (N.B.) High Sch.; Mount Allison Univ.; m. Wilmont Waldon Robertson, 23 July 1955; children: Douglas John, C. Leslie Rae, Tracy Beth; SENATOR, THE SENATE OF CANADA; 1st el. (& first woman el.) to N.B. Leg. in prof. g.e. 1967; re-el. 1970, 1974, 1978 and 1982; Min. of Youth and Social Serv. 1970–74 (1st woman cabinet min. in N.B.); Min. of Health N.B. 1975–82; Chrmn., Social Program Reform 1982–84; Apptd. to the Senate of Canada Dec. 1984; Past Prov. Pres., N.B. Home Econ. Assn. (1952–53); Past Pres. N.B. Women's P. Cons. Assn.; United Church; Office: Victoria Building, 140 Wellington St., Ottawa, Ont. K1A 0A4.

**ROBERTSON, Catherine Jean,** B.A., B.J.; executive; b. Cut Knife, Sask. 14 Nov. 1945; d. Francis J. and Hazel I. R.; e. Univ. of Sask. B.A. 1967; Carleton Univ. B.J. 1968; m. Alex A. Shorten; PRES., ROBERTSON ROZENHART INC. 1985– ; Pres., Core Group Publishers Inc.; Dir., Aiesec (UBC); Dir., Insurance Corp. of B.C.; former Chrmn. Vancouver City Savings Credit Union; Trustee Vancouver Art Gallery; Office: 270 – 1075 West Georgia St., Vancouver, B.C. V6E 3C9.

**ROBERTSON, David Leroy,** B.Comm.; bank executive; b. Sydney, N.S. 13 Aug. 1941; s. Thomas and Florence (Falconer) R.; e. St. Mary's Univ. B.Comm. 1971; m. Donalda d. Donald and Christine Walker 9 May 1964; children: Lesley, David; SR. VICE-PRES. & GENERAL MANAGER, U.S.A., ROYAL BANK OF CANADA 1991– ; joined Royal Bank (Sydney, NS) 1958; returned to school 1967–71; Asst. Mgr., Toronto (main branch) 1971; Sr. Asst. Agent, San Francisco 1975; Manager, Corp. Finance, Sr. Vice-Pres. & Gen. Mgr.'s office, Toronto 1977; Extve. Dir., Royal Bank of Canada (London) Ltd. (U.K.) 1979; Orion Royal Bank Ltd. 1981; Vice-Pres., Corp. & Gov. Banking, U.K., Ireland & Nordic Countries 1982; Vice-Pres., World Corp. Banking 1984; Vice-Pres., Corp. & Govt. Banking Ont. 1985; Vice-Pres. & Mgr., Toronto Main Branch 1986; Sr. Vice-Pres., Corp. Finance 1987; Corp. Banking 1989; Bd. of Trustees, Inst. of Internat. Bankers 1992; Adv. Bd., Americas Soc. Corp. Prog.; Bd. of Dir., The Candn. Soc. of N.Y.; recreations: fishing, hunting; clubs: Canadian Club of New York, Westchester Country, Goodwood, New York Athletic, Economic Club of New York; Home: 201 E. 62nd St., Apt. 11A, New York, N.Y. 10021; Office: Financial Sq., 24th fl., New York, N.Y. 10005-3531.

**ROBERTSON, David Struan,** Ph.D.; consulting geologist; b. Winnipeg, Man. 3 Mar. 1924; e. Colin Archibald and Maud (Hocken) R.; e. Univ. of Man., B.Sc. (Hons., Phys. Chem. & Geol.), 1946; Columbia Univ., Ph.D. (Geol.), 1949; m. Wanda Lee, d. Lennon Spears, 24 Jan. 1951; children: Jennifer Lynne, Joanna Lee, Julia Merriam; Party Chief, Geol. Survey of Can., 1946–49; Asst. Prof., Univ. of Va., 1949–51; Sr. Research Geol., International Nickel Co., 1951–53; Chief Geol. (Angola), E. J. Longyear Co., 1953–54; Chief Geol. and Vice-Pres., Stancan Uranium Corpn., 1955–58; Vice-Pres. and Dir., Stanrock Uranium Mines Ltd., 1956–67; Pres., GMX Corpn., 1958–60; Consulting Geol., Pres. David S. Robertson & Associates Ltd., Chrmn. David S. Robertson & Associates, Inc., Denver, Colorado 1960–87; Dir., Combustion Engineering - Superheater 1983–86; Partner, Coopers & Lybrand 1981–87; Dir., Placer Dome Inc.; Dakota Mining Corp.; Orvana Minerals Corp.; Chrmn., Ashton Mining of Can. Inc.; Ventures Trident, L.P.; mem., Assn. Prof. Engrs., Ont.; Candn. Inst. Mining & Metall. (Pres. 1993–94); Soc. Econ. Geols.; Geol. Assn. Can.; Geol. Soc. Am.; Delta Upsilon; United Church; recreation: curling; cross country skiing, fishing; Clubs: Granite; Ontario; Home: 10 King

Maple Place, Willowdale, Ont. M2K 1X6; Office: Suite 900, 390 Bay St., Toronto, Ont. M5H 2Y2.

**ROBERTSON, Edward John,** M.A., M.Ed.; provincial civil servant; b. Dundee, Scot. 20 Apl. 1931; s. Thomas Dargie and Annie (McKelvie) R.; e. Lawside Acad. Dundee 1949; Univ. of St. Andrews Queens Coll., M.A. 1953, Un. Coll., M.Ed. 1955 (Clyde-Henderson Scholarships); m. Dilys d. Arthur Ffolliott 6 Sept. 1974; children: Amelia, Thomas, (Anne, Fiona, Jane by previous marriage); BD. MEMBER, ONTARIO ENERGY BOARD 1982– ; Flying Offr. RAF 1955–58; Mktg. Esso Standard (Eastern) Inc. 1958–63, Africa, Middle E.; Lectr. in Philos. Univ. of Strathclyde Glasgow 1963–65; Personnel Dir. Avon Rubber Co. Melksham, Eng. 1965–67; Dir. of Rsch. Eng. Employers Fedn. London, Eng. 1967–73; Dir. Ind. Relations Div. Confedn. Brit. Ind. London 1973–77; Sr. Policy Adv. Industry & Tourism Ont. 1977–79, N. Affairs Ont. 1979–83; Dep. Min. Ind., Trade & Technol. Man. 1983–86; Acting Pres. & C.E.O., Manitoba Telephone System 1986–87; Chrmn., Manitoba Public Utilities Bd. 1988–91; recreation: tennis; Home: 6 Norwood Rd., Toronto, Ont. M4E 2R8; Office: 26th Floor, 2300 Yonge St., Toronto, Ont. M4P 1E4.

**ROBERTSON, Gardner Thomas,** C.D., B.A., F.I.C.B.; b. Toronto, Ont. 25 Apr. 1926; s. Thomas Preston and Sarah (Gardner) R.; e. Univ. of Toronto, Victoria Coll. B.A. 1949, Ont. Coll. of Educ. 1954; Sch. of Tank Technol. U.K., 1951–52; m. Jene Agnes, d. Edward McClung, 15 July 1950; children: Jane, Ian, Kathryn Ann; Vice Pres., Corporate Staffing, Bank of Montreal 1985–92; Retired; Ford Motor Co. of Canada Ltd., Oakville, 1957–66; held various positions incl. Training & Safety Mgr.; joined Bank of Montreal 1966; served as Manpower Planning & Development Manager for four years; apptd. Asst. to President then Vice President (Marketing), 1970; Sr. Vice Pres., Personnel 1975; Vice Pres., Training, 1981–83; Vice Pres., Employee Relations, 1983–85; Vice Pres., Personnel, Falconbridge Nickel Mines, 1978–81; Lecturer, Department of Continuing Education, McGill University, 1967–73; Prof., Sheridan College 1990–94; served with Royal Canadian Armoured Corps and Royal Candn. Dragoons during World War II and post-war; rank Maj.; Fellow, Inst. of Canadian Bankers; mem., Univ. of Toronto Alumni Assn.; Inst. Candn. Bankers Past Chrmn., Bd. of Gov.; Am. Soc. Training & Devel. (Past Pres. Ont, Chapter); Sales & Marketing Extves.-Internat.; Presbyterian and Elder, Knox-Oakville; recreations: reading, woodworking; Clubs: University; Home: 75 Kingsford Place, Oakville, Ont. L6J 6E2.

**ROBERTSON, George Hillyard;** writer, broadcaster; b. Regina, Sask. 4 Nov. 1922; s. Thomas Hillyard and Ida (Voligny) R.; e. Victoria Pub. Sch., Campion Coll. and Central Coll., Regina, 1939; Wesley Un. Coll., Winnipeg, 1944–45; m. Phyllis May, d. Edmund Andrews, Sydney, N.S., 9 Oct. 1954; children: George Gavin, Athol Edmund, Morna Cairine; Announcer, CJRM Regina, 1939–40; Announcer-Actor, CBC Winnipeg, 1940–42, 1944–45; Producer, CBC Internat. Service, 1945–46; Freelance Writer and Broadcaster, Montreal, 1946–49 and Toronto, since 1949; writings incls. over 100 dramas produced by CBC TV and radio, gen. articles for various mags. (Toronto Ed., 'Canadian Art,' 1952–54) and documentary films; 1st radio drama 1943 and 1st TV drama 1952, CBC; wrote 30 episodes 'Moment of Truth' for NBC/CBC-TV; 50 episodes 'Scarlett Hill' CBC/ATV TV; created 'Quentin Durgens, M.P.' and wrote all episodes CBC/TV; created (with Sandy Stewart) 'The Winners' CBC/TV; developed, princ. writer and script ed. 'House of Pride,' all episodes CBC/TV; co-writer and assoc. producer 'Snelgrove Snail' World synd. TV; writer and assoc. producer 'The Law and You' TV synd.; acted in TV and radio drama series incl. 'CBC Stage,' 'Ford Theatre,' 'GM Presents,' 'Show of the Week'; commentary and criticism incl. CBC's 'Critically Speaking,' 'CJBC Views the Shows'; wrote and broadcast 'Worth Knowing' daily 1952–60; narrator National Film Board films; Co-founder Jupiter Theatre 1951; nominated for Canadian Film Awards 'Best Screenplay' ('The Night Nothing Happened'), 1969; nominated for ACTRA Award, Best Radio Drama ('Galileo – The Martyr That Never Was') 1986; Academy of Canadian Cinema & Television Margaret Collier Awards for body of work in TV 1993; feature films include 'The Road to Chaldaea,' 1968; 'Face-Off' 1970; 'Party Games' 1970; co-author (with Scott Young), 'Face-Off,' novel 1971; served as Radar Tech. with RCAF 1942–44; mem., Alliance Candn. TV & Radio Artists (Pres., Montreal Br., 1946–48); Anglican; recreations: bridge, swimming, cooking; Club: Toronto Lawn Tennis; Home: 158 Glen Rd., Toronto, Ont. M4W 2W6.

**ROBERTSON, (Robert) Gordon,** P.C., C.C., LL.D., F.R.S.C., D.C.L.; b. Davidson, Sask. 19 May 1917; s. John Gordon and Lydia Adelia (Paulson) R.; e. Public and High Schs., Regina, Sask.; Univ. of Sask., B.A. 1938, LL.D. 1959; Oxford Univ., B.A. (Juris.) 1940, D.C.L. 1983; Univ. of Toronto, M.A. 1941, LL.D. 1973; LL.D. McGill University, 1963; Dalhousie, 1977; British Columbia, 1982; Carleton, 1990; D.Univ. Laval, 1975; Ottawa, 1982; m. Beatrice Muriel, d. late Rev. Dr. and Mrs. C. B. Lawson, Toronto, Ont., 14 Aug. 1943; children: John Lawson, Karen Martha; PRESIDENT, NETWORK ON THE CONSTITUTION 1990– ; Chancellor, Carleton Univ. 1980–90; Third Secy., Dept. of External Affairs, 1941; Asst. to Under-Secy. of State for External Affairs, 1943–45; Secy. to the Office of the Prime Minister, 1945–49; Member of Cabinet Secretariat (Privy Council Office), 1949–51; Asst. Secy. to the Cabinet, 1951–53; Depy. Min., Dept. of N. Affairs & Nat. Resources, 1953–63; Commr., N.W. Terr., 1953–63; Clerk of the Privy Council and Secy. to Cabinet 1963–75; Secy. to Cabinet for Prov.-Fed. Relations 1975–79 (ret.); Pres., Inst. for Resch. on Public Policy 1980–84, Fellow in Residence 1984–90; awarded Vanier Medal by Inst. Pub. Adm. Can. 1970; Hon. Fellow, Exeter College, Oxford; United Church; recreations: swimming, reading; Clubs: Rideau; Home: 20 Westward Way, Rockcliffe Park, Ottawa, Ont. K1L 5A7.

**ROBERTSON, H. Rocke,** C.C. (1969), B.Sc., M.D., C.M., D.Sc., LL.D., F.R. S. (C.) F.R.C.S.(C), F.A.C.S., F.R.C.S.(E); b. Victoria, B.C., 4 Aug. 1912; e. St. Michael's Sch.; Ecole Nouvelle, Coppet, Switzerland; Brentwood Coll.; McGill Univ., B.Sc. 1932, M.D. 1936; D.C.L. Bishops Univ. 1963; LL.D., Manitoba, Toronto, Victoria, (B.C.) 1964, Glasgow 1965, Michigan, Dartmouth 1967, McGill 1970, Sir George Williams 1971; D.Sc., Brit. Columbia 1964; Memorial 1968; Jefferson 1969; D. de l'Un. Montréal 1968; m. Beatrice Roslyn Arnold, Montreal, Que.; four children; Interne, Montreal General Hospital, 1936–38; Clinical Assistant in Surgery, Royal Infirmary, Edinburgh, 1938–39; Jr. Assistant in Surgery, Montreal General Hospital, 1939–40; Chief of Surg., Vancouver, (B.C.) Mil. Hosp., 1944–45; Head Surg., Shaughnessy Hosp., D.V.A., 1945–59; Prof. of Surg., Univ. B.C., 1950–59; Surgeon-in-Chief (Protem) Peter Bent Brigham Hospital Boston 1956; Visiting Lectr., Harvard Univ. 1956; apptd. temp. Dir., Professorial Unit, St. Bartholomew's Hosp., London Eng. 1958; Surg.-in-Chief, Montreal Gen. Hosp. Chrmn., Dept. of Surg., Faculty of Medicine of McGill Univ., 1959–62; Principal and Vice-Chancellor, McGill Univ. 1962–70; served in second World War with R.C.A.M.C., 1940–45, served overseas with No. 1 C.G.H. and No. 2 F.S.U.; discharged with rank of Lieut.-Col.; author of numerous articles in scient. journs; has lectured extensively in Can. and United States; Bd. of Curators, Osler Library, McGill Univ.; Royal Coll. Physicians and Surgs. Can. (Vice-Pres. 1955); Hon. Archivist 1977–92; Am. Coll. Surg. (Bd. of Regents 1961); Nat. Rsch. Counc., Can. 1962–65; Sci. Council of Can. 1976–82; Founding mem., Conf. Rectors and Principals, Universities of Que. (Pres. 1968–69); Commander of the Order of St. John (1983); Hon. Pres. Mont St-Hilaire Nature Conservation Centre; Past Pres. Traffic Injury Resch. Foundation of Can.; Home: R.R. 2 Mountain, Ont. K0E 1S0.

**ROBERTSON, Heather-jane,** B.A., M.Sc.; educator, writer, researcher; b. Saskatoon, Sask. 9 June 1949; d. Chester Douglas and Constance Barbara (Blewett) R.; e. Univ. of Saskatchewan B.A. 1968; Univ. of Alberta P.G. Dip. in Education 1969; Univ. of Houston M.Sc. Education 1984 (great distinction); m. Dwight A. s. Joseph and Velma Renneberg 8 Aug. 1980; children: Mark Anthony, Caitlin D.; DIRECTOR, PROFESSIONAL DEVELOPMENT SERVICES, CANADIAN TEACHERS FED. 1985– ; Elementary School Teacher, Saskatoon 1969; joined Sask. Teachers' Fed. 1976; research focus: quality of life of girls and women, trends in education; extve. prod., several edn./training videos; consultant to univ. faculty, prov./fed. govt. depts, school divisions & educators, non-govt. orgns.; Mem., Extve. Ctte., Candn. Centre for Policy Alternatives; Nominee, YWCA Woman of the Year 1981; Persons' Award 1993; Outstanding Achievement Award, EdPress America 1983; Senate, Univ. of Sask. 1978–83; Disabled Persons' Community Resource 1989–92; REACH 1991– ; Community Action on Violence against Women, YWCA 1992– ; Mem., Candn. Soc. for the Study of Edn.; Assn. for Supervision & Curriculum Devel.; Nat. Staff Development Council; Candn. Cong. on Learning Opportunities for Women; Candn. Rsch. Inst. for the Advancement of Women; editor: 'The Idea Book' 1988, 'A Capella' 1990; author: 'The Better Idea Book' 1992, 'Progress Revisited' 1993, 'Gender and School Restructuring' 1989, 'Thumbs Down! A Classroom Response to Violence Towards Women' 1990; recreation: tennis; Home: 31 Southpark Dr., Gloucester, Ont. K1B 3B8; Office: 110 Argyle Ave., Ottawa, Ont. K2P 1B4.

**ROBERTSON, Heather Margaret,** M.A.; writer; b. Winnipeg, Man. 19 March 1942; d. Harry and Margaret (Duncan) R.; e. Kelvin High Sch. 1958; Univ. of Man. B.A. 1963; Columbia Univ. M.A. 1964; m. Andrew Kennedy s. Douglas and Helen Marshall 11 July 1975; one s. Aaron; Reporter, Winnipeg Tribune 1964–66; Producer CBC Winnipeg 1969–71; freelance writer 1971– ; recipient Woodrow Wilson Fellowship 1963–64; author non-fiction 'Reservations Are For Indians' 1970; 'Grass Roots' 1973; 'Salt of the Earth' 1974; 'A Terrible Beauty: The Art of Canada at War' 1977; 'The Flying Bandit' 1981; 'More Than A Rose: Prime Ministers, Wives and Other Women' 1991; 'On the Hill: A People's Guide to Canada's Parliament' 1992; fiction 'Willie: A Romance' 1983 (Books in Canada First Novel Award 1983; Canadian Authors' Assn. Fiction Prize 1984); 'Lily, A Rhapsody in Red' 1986; 'Igor, A Novel of Intrigue' 1989; Ed. 'A Gentleman Adventurer: The Arctic Diaries of Richard Bonnycastle' 1984; 'I Fought Riel' by Major Charles Boulton 1985; mem. Writers Union of Canada; ACTRA; Address: 175 Sherwood Ave., Toronto, Ont. M4P 2A9.

**ROBERTSON, Ian Bruce,** B.A., M.B.A.; business executive; b. Montreal, Que. 20 June 1940; s. Harold Rocke and Beatrice Roslyn (Arnold) R.; e. Shawnigan Lake Sch. 1957; McGill Univ. B.A. 1961; Harvard Bus. Sch. M.B.A. 1966; m. Bonnie d. Jim and Georgia Galloway 6 July 1962; children: Wesley, Stuart, Susan; EXTVE. DIR., CANADA-ASEAN CENTRE, SINGAPORE 1990– ; Corp. underwriting, Wood Gundy Limited 1966–68; var. sr. posts, Candn. Internat. Devel. Agency 1968–78, incl. Bd. of Dir., Asian Devel. Bank, Manila 1971–73; Mktg. Extve., H.A. Simons Group 1978–81; Co-founder & Pres., MRI Internat. Inc. 1981–89; Vice Pres., Marketing, British Columbia Trade Develop. Corp. 1989–90; recreations: running, tennis, golf, skiing; Home: 16 Balmoral Park, #03-01, The Balmoral, Singapore 1025; Office: 80 Anson Rd., #15-02, IBM Towers, Singapore 0207.

**ROBERTSON, Ian Ross,** B.A., M.A., Ph.D.; university professor; b. Mermaid, P.E.I. 30 Jan. 1944; s. Major Albert Seymour and Elizabeth Catherine (MacLeod) R.; e. West Kent Sch., Queen Charlotte H.S.; Prince of Wales Coll.; McGill Univ., B.A. 1965, M.A. 1968; Univ. of Toronto, Ph.D. 1974; ASSOC. PROF. OF HIST., SCARBOROUGH COLL., UNIV. OF TORONTO 1979– ; Vis. Lectr., Queen's Univ. 1971–72; Lectr., Univ. of Toronto 1972; Asst. Prof. 1974; delegate, World Univ. Serv. Internat. Seminar in Poland 1962; author of several articles & scholarly papers on aspects of Candn. intellectual hist. & the hist. of P.E.I.; Recipient 1988 Publishing Award of P.E.I., Museum and Heritage Found.; mem., Candn. Hist. Assn.; Candn. Civil Liberties Assn.; Toronto Blues Soc.; Life Mem., P.E.I. Mus. & Heritage Found.; contbr. editor: 'Where to Eat in Canada' 1980; recreations: travel, theatre, film, music, culinary arts, jogging; Office: Div. of Humanities, Scarborough Coll., Univ. of Toronto, Scarborough, Ont. M1C 1A4.

**ROBERTSON, James Hutton;** businessman; b. Edinburgh, Scotland 13 Nov. 1938; s. John and Helen Hutton (Pollock) R.; e. Northkelvinside Sr. Secondary Sch., Glasgow, Scot.; m. Dorothy O'Brien 25 May 1963; children: James Bruce, Ian Brian; CHRMN. OF BD. & C.E.O., NORTHWEST TERRITORIES POWER CORP.; Dir., PWA Corp.; NWT Energy Corp.; apprentice Elec. Tech. Barr and Stroud Ltd., Glasgow 1954–56; Mgr., Dist. Mgr., Northern Stores Dept. Hudson's Bay Co. 1956–69; Mayor Town of Inuvik 1973–78, 1981–84; Past Pres. N.W.T. Assn. of Municipalities; Chrmn. NWT Business Council; Address: P.O. Box 1760, Inuvik, N.W.T.

**ROBERTSON, James McDonald,** D.V.M., Dipl.Int.Med., M.Sc.; university professor; b. Edinburgh, Scotland 27 Feb. 1940; s. Albert and Florence Mary (Lyall) R.; e. Univ. of Toronto, D.V.M. 1961; Univ. of Penn., Dipl.Int.Med. 1963, M.Sc. 1966; m. Judith d. Argel and Ruth Warner 12 Sept. 1976; children: Stacy, Wendy, Theodore, Andra; ASSOC. PROF., DEPT. OF EPIDEMIOL. & BIOSTAT., UNIV. OF WEST. ONT. 1975– ; Asst. Instr., Sch. of Vet. Med., Univ. of Penn. 1961–62; Med. Rsch. Counc. Rsch. Fellow 1962–66; Asst. Prof., Univ. of Sask. 1966–69; Assoc. Prof. 1969–71; Asst. Prof., Univ. of West. Ont. 1971–75; Assoc. Prof. 1975– ; Dir., Occupational Health & Safety Resource Ctr., UWO 1986– ; Cons., Envir. Health Assn. of the Carbon Black Indus. Inc. 1974– ; Consultant, Technical Ctte., Canada Portland Cement

Assoc. 1987– ; rsch.: cancer epidemiol., occupational epid., vitamin E. & cataracts, epid. of Alzheimer's Disease, envir. epid. of adverse reproductive effects; Eleanor Roosevelt Internat. Cancer Fellow 1971–72; Mem., Am. Assn. for the Adv. of Sci.; Am. Coll. of Epid.; Soc. for Epid. Rsch.; Candn. Vet. Med. Assn.; Coll. of Vet. of Ont.; Ont. Vet. Med. Assn.; author/co-author of several sci. papers; recreations: fishing, gardening, philately, reading; Home: 829 Hickory Rd., London, Ont. N6H 2V3; Office: London, Ont. N6A 5C1.

**ROBERTSON, John Archibald Law,** M.A., F.R.S.C.; scientist; b. Dundee, Scot. 4 July 1925; s. John Carr and Ellen (Law) R.; e. Dundee High Sch.; Epsom (Eng.) Coll.; Clare Coll. Cambridge B.A. 1950, M.A. 1953; m. Betty Jean d. Robert and Catherine Moffatt 26 June 1954; children: Ean Stuart, Clare Deborah (Mrs. K. Kortner), Fiona Heather; CONSULTANT; Mem., Atomic Energy Control Board's Advisory Ctte. on Nuclear Safety 1988– ; served with R.E. Brit. and Indian Armies 1943–47, rank Capt.; joined Metall. Div. UK Atomic Energy Authority Harwell 1950–57; Rsch. Offr. Atomic Energy of Can. Ltd. Chalk River 1957–63, Head, Reactor Materials Br. 1963–70, Dir. Fuels & Materials Div. 1970–75, Asst. to Vice Pres. 1975–82; Dir. of Program Planning, Atomic Energy of Can. Ltd. Research Co. 1982–85; author 'Irradiation Effects in Nuclear Fuels' 1969; ed. (Intnl.) 'Journal of Nuclear Materials' 1967–71; rec'd W.B. Lewis Medal, Candn. Nuclear Assoc. 1987; W.J. Kroll Zirconium Medal 1993; recreations: cross-country skiing; Home: 1 Kelvin Cres., P.O. Box 2047, Deep River, Ont. K0J 1P0.

**ROBERTSON, John R.,** F.C.A.; former Canadian civil servant; b. Toronto 29 Aug. 1933; e. C.A. Ont. 1959, Fellow 1976; m. Lillian Margaret, June 21, 1958; children: Melodie Colleen, Robbyn Lyn, Noreen Jacqueline; Pres., Tax-Ex Ltd. & Partner, Robertson McDonald Chartered Accountants 1989; served as auditor Toronto and Calgary Dist. Offices Revenue Can., Taxation; Dir., Audit Review Div. Taxation Operations Br. 1970–73, Asst. Dir. Tech. Interpretations Div. 1973–75, Dir. Tax Avoidance Div. 1975–77; Dir. Gen. Corporate Rulings Directorate 1977–82; Dir. Gen. Audit Directorate, Revenue Canada Taxation, Can. 1982–86; Dir., Gen. Compliance Rsch. and Investigation Directorate, Revenue Canada Taxation, Can. 1986–89; served various community assns.; Home: 1910 Oakdean Cres., Ottawa, Ont. K1J 6H3.

**ROBERTSON, The Honourable Mr. Justice Joseph T.,** B.Comm., LL.B., LL.M.; judge; b. Antigonish, N.S. 24 June 1949; s. H. Theodore and Monica (Gallagher) R.; e. St. Mary's Univ. B.Comm. 1972; Univ. of N.B. LL.B. 1977; London School of Econ. & Pol. Science LL.M. 1978; m. Susan d. Dr. and Mrs. W. Breton Stewart; children: Luke, Monica; JUDGE, FEDERAL COURT OF CANADA (APPEAL DIV.) 1992– and APPTD. TO COURT MARTIAL APPEAL COURT OF CANADA 1992– ; admitted to Bar of N.B. 1977; Lawyer, Goodwin & Ellsworth 1978; Asst. Prof., Univ. of N.B. 1979; Assoc. Prof. 1983; Prof. 1988; Mem., Candn. Bar Assn. (N.B. Br.) 1980– (Council Mem. until 1985; organizer & participant in cont. legal edn. prog.); Legal Counsel, N.B. Task Force on Housing 1988–89; elected Mem., Univ. of N.B. Senate 1989–92; Merit Award, Univ. of N.B. 1983; Morguard Literary Award 1988; publications in various journals; Home: 1859 Fairmeadow Cres., Ottawa, Ont. K1H 7B8; Office: Suite 37, Supreme Court Bldg., Ottawa, Ont. K1A 0H9.

**ROBERTSON, Neville Ashley;** b. Redhill, Surrey, Eng. 24 Sept. 1939; s. Andrew James and Nellie Ethel (West) R.; e. Mid-Essex Tech. Coll. Chelmsford, Essex, Eng. CGE 1955; North-East Essex Tech. Coll. and Sch. of Art Colchester CPE 1960; m. Gwendolyn d. Edward and Elizabeth McGonigal 6 June 1970; children: Benjamin, Samuel, Laura; Pres. and Founder, Ampersand Typographers 1984; Compositing Apprenticeship 1955–61; Royal Army Ordnance Corps, computer transition 1961–63; Graphic Trades internship 1963–75; emigrated to Can. 1975; Prodn. Mgmt. 1975–82; Advtg. Agency Mgmt. 1982–84; installed first profl. Desktop Publishing operation in Can. 1985; named MacUser Desktop Publisher of Yr. 1986; Chrmn. Adv. Bd. Electronic Pub. George Brown Coll. Applied Arts Toronto 1988– ; Founder/Pub./Contbr. Graphic Perspective mag. 1985–88, Electronic Composition and Imaging mag. 1987–90; Founding Dir. Electronic Desktop Pub. Assn. 1986; Pres., Toronto Typographic Assn. 1990–91; Home: 22 Zima Cres., Bradford, Ont. L3Z 1Z7.

**ROBERTSON, Norman W.;** executive; b. Regina, Sask. 19 Feb. 1937; m. Betty Sturgess; children: Brent, Greg, Grant; PRES. AND C.E.O., ATCO ENTERPRISES INC. 1988– ; Dir. Atco Ltd.; Atcor Resources Ltd.; Canadian Utilities Limited; Mutual Life of Canada; Prudential Steel Ltd.; Southam Inc.; joined present Co. 1961; Pres., Calgary Petroleum Club; mem. of Nat. Bd. for Hockey Canada; Home: 6801 Livingstone Dr. S.W., Calgary, Alta. T3E 6J2; Office: 800, 919 - 11th Avenue S.W., Calgary, Alta. T2R 1P4.

**ROBERTSON, Commodore Owen Connor Struan,** O.C. (1970), G.M., R.D., C.D., D.Sc., MIL; master mariner; arctic consultant; b. Victoria, B.C. 16 March 1907; s. Capt. George Edward Livingstone and Mabel Johanna (Connor) R.; e. Univ. Sch., Victoria, B.C., 1915–16; Shawnigan Lake Prep. Sch., B.C., 1917–19; St. Albans Sch., Brockville, Ont., 1920–23; West Hill High Sch., Montreal, 1923–24; obtained Masters (Foreign Going) Cert. of Competency, 1932; RCAF Search and Rescue and Survival Sch., grad.; McGill Univ., D.Sc.; m. Marjorie Sylvia, d. late George Wise, 21 Aug. 1939; two d. Sandra Louise, Michele Straun; began career with Candn. Govt. Merchant Marine (cargo ships); Third Offr. to First Offr., Candn. Nat. Steamships (passenger ships); Sub-Lt., RCN Reserve, 1931; served in RCN in various appts. (Lt. to Capt.) 1938–46; Extve. Offr. and C.O. Sail Training Ship and Auxillary Cruiser; C.O., Minesweeper and as Flotilla Commdr., Offrs. Training Estab., Fleet Estab. and H.M.C. Dockyard, Halifax and as King's Harbour Master; C.O., Fleet Estab., H.M.C. Dockyard, Ships in Reserve and as King's Harbour Master, rank A Capt., 1946–52; also C.O., Destroyer and as Flotilla Commdr.; C.O., H.M.C.S. Niobe; served as Sr. Candn. Naval Offr. with RN; Naval mem., Candn. Jt. Staff (London); Candn. Naval. mem., Mil. Agency for Standardization; Naval. Adv. Comte. of W. Europe Regional Planning Staff; Commdr. (designate) Arctic Patrol and Research Vessel, service with U.S.N. forces in Arctic, 1952–54; Commanding H.M.C.S. Labrador, Arctic Research and Patrol Vessel (circumnavig. of N. Am.), 1954–57; also Commdr., U.S.N. Task Group 6.3; on loan to U.S.N. as Depy. Commdr. for Polar Operations; Mil. Sea Transport Service; Commdg. H.M.C.S. Niagara, Naval mem. Candn. Jt. Staff (Washington), 1957–62; during this period loaned to U.S.N. for various periods on Polar operations; retired from RCN 1962; Depy. Dir., Arctic Inst. of N. Am. (on loan to Expo '67 as Scient. Adviser), 1962; Co-Founder, Northern Associates Reg'd., 1967; conducted Panarctic Sea Lift to Melville Isl., environmental study for S.S. Manhattan, 1968–69; has served as Gov., Arctic Inst. of N. Am.; Hon. Lectr., McGill Univ.; mem., Geotech. Comte., Nat. Research Council; Dir., Last Post Fund; mem., Nat. Comte. on N. & Arctic Scouting; Arbitrator, Maritime Appeals Bd.; Chrmn., Comte. on Shipbldg. in Can.; Consultant; David Sarnoff Research Lab.; U.S. Office of Naval Research; USAF Geophys. Comte.; Comn. on N. Transport.; awarded Back Grant; Massey Medal; Centennial Medal; writings incl. articles for various tech. publs., book chapters, TV and radio documentaries; Fellow, Arctic Inst. N. Am.; mem., Marine Techonol. Soc.; Club: University; Home: 108 King St., Oakville, Ont. L6J 1B1.

**ROBERTSON, Robert Earl,** B.A., LL.B.; lawyer; b. Kingston, Ont. 18 March 1950; s. Earl Hugh and Wilma Pauline (Earl) R.; e. McGill Univ. B.A. 1971; Univ. of Western Ont. LL.B. 1976; m. Susan d. Gerald and Kathleen Taylor 26 July 1980; children: Rachel Mary, Devon Victoria; ASSOCIATE GENERAL COUNSEL, INTERNATIONAL DEVELOPMENT RESEARCH CENTRE 1978– ; called to Bar of Prov. of Ontario 1978; Pres., Amnesty Interntional Canada 1980–81; Pres., South-East Ottawa Community Services; Chrmn. Bd. of Managers and Chrmn., Mission and Outreach Ctte., St. Timothy's Presbyn. Church; Extve. Ctte. Mem., World Alliance for Nutrition and Human Rights; author: 'The Right to Food – Canada's Broken Covenant' 1989; Home: 1819 Florida Ave., Ottawa, Ont. K1H 6Y9; Office: 250 Albert St., Box 8500, Ottawa, Ont. K1G 3H9.

**ROBERTSON, Ronald Neil,** Q.C., M.A., B.C.L., LL.B.; b. Regina, Sask. 14 Oct. 1930; s. Col. John Gordon and Lydia Adelia (Paulson) R.; e. Merchant Taylor's Sch., Engl.; Dalhousie Univ. B.A. 1952; Oxford Univ. Magdalen Coll. B.A. 1954, B.C.L. 1955, M.A. 1983; Osgoode Hall Law Sch., LL.B. 1957; Rhodes Scholar (N.S.) 1952; m. Sheila d. Theodore and Marjorie Graham 23 Nov. 1957; children: David, Neil, Sarah, Colin; PARTNER AND FORMER CHAIR, FASKEN CAMPBELL GODFREY and PARTNER, FASKEN MARTINEAU; articled with Herridge, Tolmie & Fasken, Robertson, Aitchison, Pickup & Calvin; called to Bar of Ont. 1957, Q.C. 1971; Certified Specialist Civil Litigation, Law Society of Upper Canada; Chair, Law Society Bankruptcy and the Insolvency Law Specialty Ctte.; Lectr., professional programmes, York Univ., McGill Univ., Law Soc. of Upper Can., Candn. Bar Assn.; former mem. Minister's Adv. Ctte. on Bankruptcy Act; Dir., Canada Deposit Insurance Corp.; Sec., Oxford Univ. Found. of Can.; mem. United Ch.; Candn. Bar Assn.; Advocates' Soc.; Internat. Bar Assn.; Arbitration & Mediation Inst. of Can.; Contrib. Ed. 'Holmstead and Gale, Rules of Practice'; Clubs: The Toronto; The Ontario; Caledon Riding and Hunt; United Oxford and Cambridge University Club (London); Home: 188 Glencairn Ave., Toronto, Ont. M4R 1N2; Office: Box 20, Toronto-Dominion Centre, Toronto, Ont. M5K 1N6.

**ROBERTSON, Shirley Elizabeth,** MPA; photographer; b. Halifax, N.S. 19 Apr. 1926; d. Fred Browne and Gladys Frances (Greenough) Barnstead; e. Le Marchant St. Sch., Queen Elizabeth H.S. 1945; Master of Photographic Art 1988; m. George B. s. Olive and Burnley R. 6 May 1950; children: Heather Elizabeth, Cynthia Joyce, Judith Marion, Janet Shirley; Civil Servant 1945–50; became a profl. photographer 1975 with interest in pictorial, nature & child photography; Dir., Loblaws Cos. Ltd. 1987– ; Mem., Un. Ch. of Can.; Photographic Guild of N.S.; Maritime Profl. Photographers Assn.; author & pub.: 'Borrowed Light' 1985; recreations: photography, boating, enjoying and photographing nature; Home: 1470 Summer St., Apt. 203, Halifax, N.S. B3H 3A3.

**ROBERTSON, William James;** crown corporation executive; b. Toronto, Ont. 8 Jan. 1946; s. Bruce Alexander and Dorothy Margaret (Hemphill) R.; e. elem. and high schs. Ont.; m. Elizabeth Anne d. late Barry Bertrand Benness 30 Sept. 1978 (divorced); children: Ian Gregory, Lindsay Anne; DIR., SALES SOUTHWEST DISTRICT, GREAT LAKES DIV., CANADA POST CORP. 1993– ; licenced Air Traffic Controller 1967–83; Ont. Regional Dir. CATCA 1973/1975, Nat. Vice Pres. 1975/1979; Pres., Candn. Air Traffic Control Assn. 1979–83; Mgr., Employee Relations, Canada Post Corp. 1983–84; Dir. Labour Relations, Canada Post Corp. 1984–86; Dir., Personnel and Labour Relations, York Div., Canada Post Corp. 1986–87; Dir., Mail Operations Support, York Div. 1987–93; mem. Chamber of Commerce, London; mem. 1994 Campaign Cabinet, London/Middlesex United Way; Lifetime Hon. Mem., Candn. Air Traffic Control Assoc.; mem. Internat. Fed. Air Traffic Controllers Assn. (Regional Vice Pres. N. and Central Am. 1977/1979); Anglican; Home: 504 – 600 Talbot St., London, Ont. N6A 5L9; Office: 300 Wellington St., London, Ont. N6B 3P2.

**ROBICHAUD, Hon. Hédard-J.,** O.C, P.C. (Can.); b. Shippegan, N.B. 2 Nov. 1911; s. John G. and Amanda (Boudreau) R.; e. Acad. Ste. Famille Tracadie; Sacred Heart Univ.; Saint-Joseph Univ.; m. Gertrude, d. Frederick Leger, 25 Oct. 1937; nine children; Lieutenant Governor, N.B., 1971–82; Inspector of Fisheries with Dominion Govt., 1938–46; Dir. of Fisheries for N.B., 1946–52; 1st el. to H. of C. for Gloucester, G.E. 1953; Minister of Fisheries, 22 Apl. 1963–68; summoned to the Senate of Can. July 1968–71; Hon. Director, National Sea Products Limited; mem. Roosevelt Campobello International Park Com. 1970– ; Liberal; Roman Catholic; recreation: fishing, golf; Home: 707 - 85 Range Rd., Ottawa, Ont. K1N 8J6 and 202 Blanchard, Caraquet, N.B. E0B 1K0.

**ROBICHAUD, Hon. Louis J.,** C.C. (1971), P.C. (1967), Q.C., B.A., D.C.L., LL.D., Dr. Pol. Sc.; senator; b. St. Anthony, New Brunswick, 21 October 1925; s. Amédée and Annie (Richard) R., both Acadians; e. Sacred Heart Univ., Bathurst, N.B., B.A. 1947, Dr. Pol. Sc. 1960; Laval Univ., 1946–49; admitted to the Bar of N.B. 1952; LL.D., New Brunswick 1960, Montreal, St. Joseph's, 1961; Ottawa 1962, St. Dunstan's 1964, St. Thomas 1965, McGill, Dalhousie 1969, D.C.L., Mount Allison 1961, Moncton 1973; m. Lorraine (dec'd) d. P. B. Savoie, Neguac, N.B., 9 Aug. 1951; children: Jean-Claude (dec'd), Paul, Louis-René, Monique; first el. to N.B. Leg., g.e. 1952; Leader of Opposition in the Leg., 1958–60; Premier 1960–70 and Attorney General, N.B. 1960–65; Min. of Youth 1968–70; Leader of Opposition 1970; Chrmn. Candn. Sec. Internat. Jt. Comn. 1971; summoned to Senate of Can., 21 Dec. 1973; read and articled in law with Albany Robichaud, Q.C.; cr. Q.C. July 1960; sworn of the Privy Council July 1967; Companion, Order of Canada Oct. 1971; Liberal; Roman Catholic; Home: 7 Pineland Ave., Nepean, Ont. K2G 0E5; Office: Senate of Canada, Ottawa, Ont. K1A 0A4.

**ROBICHAUD, Michel;** couturier; b. Montréal, Qué. 9 June 1939; s. Emile and Charlotte (Laberge) R.; e. Scholar, Chambre Syndicale de la couture parisienne 1960–61; Probationer, Nina Ricci's Workshop, Paris 1962; Designer, Guy Laroche House of Fashion, Paris 1962; m. Lucienne d. Léo Lafrenière, Shawinigan Sud, Qué. 7 March 1963; PROP., MICHEL ROBICHAUD INC.; R. Catholic; Club: Beaver; Commander of 'L'Ordre de Napoléon' 1986; Home: 980 rue Pratt, Montréal, Qué. H2V 2V1; Office: C.P. 190 Outremont, Montréal, Qué. H2V 4M8.

**ROBIDOUX, Leon A.;** retired businessman, writer; b. Saint Constant, P.Q. 18 Aug. 1923; s. Arthur and Simone (Guérin) R.; e. Collège Ste-Marie (Classical) conventum 1942; 8 evening courses & 1 correspondence course; m. the late Yvonne Tremblay; widower; children: Carole, the late Christine; Delivery Boy, 'La Presse' and Grocery Clerk, Buywell Store (while at school); Royal Candn. Air Force 1942–44 (Sergeant, Aerial Gunner); Private, Special Serv. Task Force, U.S. Army Air Corps 1945–46; Freight Acctg. Clerk, Candn. Pacific Railway 1942; Production / Sales Clerk, Minneapolis Honeywell Reg. Co. 1944–45; Public Relations Dept., Am. Overseas Airline 1945–47; Outside Rep. & Investigator, Household Finance Corp. 1947; various positions up to Vice-President with Hugh Russel & Sons Limited 1948–78; Pres., Les Industries D'Acier Laurier Ltd. 1978–87; Commissioner of Oaths; Former Dir., Hugh Russel Sons Ltd.; Master Mechanical Co. Ltd.; Applied Computer Ltd.; Canadian Bearings Ltd.; Central Engineering Ltd.; Summers Limited; author: 'Les Cajeux' 1974, 'Alberic Bourgeois' 1978, 'Les Voyages de Ladelauche autour du monde' 1982, 'Le Vieux Prince' 1988, 'L'Art de Parler en Public' 1989; 'Les Mordus du Golf' Les Publications Proteau 1992; 'À L'Assaut du Féminisme!' 1992; recreations: golf, painting, writing, travel; clubs: Saint-Denis, Pointe Clarie Curling, Laval-sur-le-Lac Golf, Montreal Advertising-Sales, Montreal Bd. of Trade (all former); Home: 175 Fieldcrest, Pointe Claire, Que. H9S 4A5.

**ROBIDOUX, Réjean;** university professor emeritus; b. Sorel, Que., 24 juin 1928; f. René et Marianne (Millette) R.; é. Angelicum (Rome), L.Ph. 1950, L.Th. 1954; Univ. d'Ottawa, B.A. 1955; Univ. Laval, L.ès L. 1957, Dipl. E.S. 1958; Sorbonne (Paris), D. de l'U. 1962; ép. Viviane, f. Lionel et Jeanne Gougeon; 1 f.: Marc; PROFESSEUR DE LITTERATURE FRANÇAISE ET CANADIENNE-FRANCAISE, UNIV. D'OTTAWA, 1957–67, 1974–89; Univ. de Toronto 1967–74; mem. de la Soc. Royale du Canada 1980; auteur: 'Roger Martin du Gard et la religion' (essai) 1964 (Prix du gouverneur général), 'Le roman canadien-francais du XXe siècle' 1966; 'Le traité du Narcisse d'André Gide' 1978; 'La Création de Gérard Bessette' (Essai) 1987; 'Poésies complètes 1896–1941 d'Émile Nelligan' (édition critique) 1991; 'Connaissance de Nelligan' (essai) 1992; boursier Killam 1985; résidence: 211 rue Wurtemburg, #412, Ottawa, Ont. K1N 8R4; bureau: Dép. des lettres françaises, Univ. d'Ottawa, Ottawa, Ont. K1N 6N5.

**ROBILLARD, J.E. Edmond,** o.p.; né Saint-Paul-l'Ermite, Qué. 20 decembre 1917; f. William et Marie Jeannotte (dit Lachapelle) R.; é. Sainte-Paul-l'Ermite 1924–28; Coll. de l'Assomption 1928–36; Coll. dominican d'Ottawa 1937–41; Catholic Univ. Washington, D.C. 1942 et Dominican House of Studies 1942–43 L.en Théol.; Univ. de Montréal Dr.en Théol. 1945; Ecole biblique de Jérusalem 1969; Cambridge Univ. Theol. 1969; Univ. catholique-luthérienne Bonn 1970; Archives newmaniennes Birmingham 1972 (boursier du Conseil des Arts Ottawa); Prof. de philosophie et de théologie Couvent Dominican d'Ottawa 1943–50; Prof. de théologie Institut de Sciences religieuses Univ. de Montréal 1955–67, Prof. titulaire Faculté de Théologie 1967–85; auteur (en liturgie): 'Pour suivre le Christ en ses mystères' 1950–55; 'La messe de tous les dimanches et des principales fêtes de l'année sur des chorals de Jean-Sébastien Bach' 1986; 'Chantons le Jour du Seigneur' 48 textes liturgiques, musique de Lise Paskko, Pero éditeur 1990; (oeuvres personnelles): 'L'Unicorne' tragédie en cinq actes sur le drame d'Abélard et d'Héloise 1967; poèmes: 'Blance et Noir' 1963; 'Le temps d'un peu' 1980; 'Au soleil de ma nuit' 1985, traduction de 'Seeded in Sinai'; 'Sous le signe de Dracula' 1985, traduction d'une oeuvre roumaine; 'La réincarnation: rêve ou réalité' 1981; 'Québec Blues: réflexions chrétiennes sur le suicide' 1983; 'Nos racines chrétiennes, dans l'histoire d'Israel et du monde méditerranéen' 1985; 'Tout ce qu'il vous dira, faites-le' 1987; 'S. Justin (l00–165? ap. J.C.): l'itinéraire philosophique' 1989; 'Qui aime connaft Dieu' 1989; Traductions (en philosophie et théologie): 'De l'analogie et du concept d'être' 1963; 'L'idée d'Université' 1968 et les 'Conférences sur la doctrine de la justification' 1980 sont des traductions de John Henry Newman; 'La sagesse et les 1050 sentences du mime syrien Publilius Lockius' editions du Vermillon, Ottawa 1992; co-auteur ou éditeur livres nombreux; Prés. local (Montréal) et général (Québec-Ottawa), Société des écrivains canadiens 1973–79; mem. l'Académie des Lettres du Québec; Adresse: 2715 Côte Sainte-Catherine, Montréal, Qué. H3T 1B6.

**ROBINS, Sydney Lewis,** B.A., LL.B., LL.M., LL.D.; b. Toronto, Ont. 24 May 1923; s. Samuel and Bessie (Kamarner) R.; e. Univ. of Toronto, B.A. 1944, LL.B. 1947; Osgoode Hall Law Sch., 1947; Harvard Law Sch., LL.M. 1948; LL.D. (hon.): Law Soc. of Upper Can. 1981; Yeshiva Univ. 1988; m. Gloria, d. S. I. Robinson, Winnipeg, Man., 8 Aug. 1951; children: Erica, Gregg, Reid, Blair; JUSTICE, ONT. COURT OF APPEAL, 1981– ; appt. Supreme Court of Ont., 1976; formerly sr. partner Robins & Robins; called to Bar of Ont. 1947; cr. Q.C. 1962; Special Lectr., Osgoode Hall Law Sch., 1948–61; Lectr., Law Soc. Special Lectures, 1960–62, 1976 and 1979; past mem., Senate, York Univ.; Hon. Gov., Baycrest Home for the Aged; Past Dir., New Mount Sinai Hosp.; Past Gov., Beth Tzedec Synagogue; Past Hon. Counsel, United Jewish Welfare Fund of Toronto; Bencher, Law Society of Upper Canada, since 1961 (Treasurer 1971–73; Past Chrmn. Continuing and Legal Educ. Comtes.); mem., Candn. Bar Assn. (Council mem.; Past Chrmn. Civil Justice Sec. & Labour Relations Sec.); Chrmn., Law Foundation Ont. 1974–76; mem., Club: Oakdale Golf & Country (Dir.); Office: Osgoode Hall, Toronto, Ont. M5H 2N5.

**ROBINSON, Ann Elisabeth,** B.Pharm., Ph.D., F.R.S.C. (UK), F.C.I.C., C.Chem. (UK) (Ont.); civil servant; b. Ilford, Essex, UK 9 Apr. 1933; d. Ronald Sidney and Kathleen Muriel (Evershed) R.; e. Queen Anne's Sch. Caversham 1950; Univ of London B. Pharm. 1955, Ph.D. 1958; m. 1stly Dr. Richard George Lingard 1960 (dec.); 2ndly Prof. Francis Edward Camps 1972 (dec.); CONSULTANT; Adjunct Prof. Univ. of Toronto 1979– ; Asst. Lectr. in Pharm. Chem. Chelsea Coll. Univ. of London 1957–59, Lectr. 1959–64; Lectr. in Forensic Med. London Hosp. Med. Coll. 1964–68, Sr. Lectr. 1968–77; Hon. Toxicologist London Hosp. 1977; Chief, Occupational Health Lab. and Cons. in Toxicol. Ont. Ministry of Labour 1978–80; Asst. Dep. Min. of Labour, Ont. (Occupational Health & Safety Div.) 1980–87; Sci. Policy Adviser, Occupational and Environmental Health & Safety, Ont. Min. of Labour 1987–91; Adviser, World Health Organization's International Programme on Chemical Safety 1991–93; Gov. Candn. Centre Occupational Health & Safety 1981–88; Mem., Institute for Risk Rsch., Univ. of Waterloo 1991– ; various cons. assignments forensic med. and toxicol. UK and abroad 1965–77; author numerous publs.; co-ed. 'Gradwohl's Legal Medicine' 3rd ed. 1976; co-author: 'Substance Abuse in the Workforce' 1992; mem. Royal Commonwealth Soc. and many learned socs. UK, Can. and U.S.A.; Clubs: Soroptimist Internat. of Toronto (Pres. 1985–87); Home: 601, 80 Quebec Ave., Toronto, Ont. M6P 4B7.

**ROBINSON, Christopher Michael,** B.Comm., M.B.A., Ph.D., C.A.; university professor; b. North Bay, Ont. 22 Mar. 1950; s. Frederic Cooper and Frances Christina (Bradfield) R.; e. Trinity Coll., Univ. of Toronto B.Comm. 1974; Fac. of Mngt., Univ. of Toronto M.B.A. 1980, Ph.D. (Fin.) 1985; C.A. Ont. 1977; m. Isabelle d. George and Antoinette Mikosza 31 July 1977; one s.: Denys Ivan; ASSOC. PROF., FAC. OF ADMIN. STUDIES, YORK UNIV. 1989– (teaches corporate and personal finance, financial statement analysis, environmental management); Analyst, Shell Can. 1974–75; C.A., Thorne Riddell 1975–78; Asst. Prof. of Fin., Fac. of Admin. Studies, York Univ. 1983–89; freelance bus. writer 1978– ; Nat. Bus. Writing Award 1980; SSHRC doctoral fellow 1980–82; Mem., Pollution Probe; Fed. of Ont. Naturalist; Bruce Trail Assn.; Recycling Council of Ont.; Friends of the Earth; Administrative Sciences Assn. of Canada; Candn. Acad. Acctg. Assn.; Alternative Perspectives on Finance Group; Centre for Ethics and Corporate Policy; co-author: 'Materiality: An Empirical Study of Actual Auditor Decisions' 1985, 'Personal Financial Management' 2nd ed. 1987; recreations: skiing, cycling, hiking; Home: 46 Glenforest Rd., Toronto, Ont. M4N 1Z8; Office: 4700 Keele St., North York, Ont. M3J 1P3.

**ROBINSON, Dennis Jay,** M.Sc., Ed.D.; psychologist; b. Salinus, Cal. 8 Jan. 1944; s. Jay Leo and Sylvia Marie (Anderson) R.; e. Univ. of Utah B.Sc. 1967, M.Sc. 1969; 3275th Tech. Sch. Lackland AFB Cert. Drug Edn. Counselling 1972; Univ. of Ariz. Ed.D. 1979; m. Sherry L. Smith 29 Dec. 1978; part-time private practice Clin. Neuropsychol., Rehabilitation & Hypnosis, Peterborough, Ont. 1982– ; U.S. Air Force Offr., Social Actions and Personnel Measurements Psychol. 1969–73; Neuropsychometrist-Counsellor Psychiatric Services Centre Tucson, Ariz. 1975–80; Neuropsychol., Dept. of Psychol. Neuropsychol. Services, Peterborough Civic Hosp. 1980; Assoc. Faculty (Psychol.) Pima Comm. Coll. Tucson 1977–80; Rehabilitation Psychol. St. Mary's Hosp. Tucson 1979–80; author various papers; mem., Intnl. Neuropsychol. Soc.; Nat. Academy of Neuropsychologists; Am. Psychol. Assn.; Ont. Psychol. Assn.; Am. Assn. Counselling & Devel.; Home: 2099 Fox Farm Rd., Peterborough, Ont. K9K 1P7.

**ROBINSON, H. Basil,** O.C., M.A.; consultant; b. Eastbourne, Sussex, Eng. 3 Mar. 1919; s. late Basil O. and Charlotte Agnes (Graham) R.; e. N. Shore Coll. N. Vancouver, B.C. 1937; Univ. of B.C. B.A. and Rhodes Scholar 1940; Oxford Univ. M.A. 1948; Hon. Fellow, Oriel College, Oxford, 1975; m. Elizabeth Ann d. late G. H. Gooderham 16 Dec. 1950; children: Katharine, David, Ann, Geoffrey; joined Dept. External Affairs 1945, UN Div. 1949, London, Eng. 1951, Paris 1955, Head Middle E. Div. Ottawa 1956, Special Asst. (External Affairs) Office of Prime Min. 1957, Min. Washington 1962, Asst. Under-Secy. of State for External Affairs, Ottawa 1964, Depy. Min. of Indian Affairs and N. Devel. 1970, Under-Secy. of State for External Affairs 1974; Commr., Northern Pipeline 1977; Dept. of External Affairs, Special Advisor to Undersecretary 1979; Principal, Management Studies Program, Public Service Commission, Touraine, Que., 1981; Cdn. Army 1942–45, Can. UK and N.W. Europe; author: 'Diefenbaker's World: A Populist in Foreign Affairs,' 1989; Officer of the Order of Canada 1990; Protestant; Clubs: Rideau; MCC (London, Eng.); Home: 17 Mariposa Ave., Ottawa, Ont. K1M 0T9.

**ROBINSON, J. Lewis,** M.A.; Ph.D.; b. Leamington, Ont. 9 July 1918; s. William John and Emily Laverne (Dunphy) R.; e. Kennedy Coll. Inst., Windsor, Ont.; Univ. of W. Ont., B.A. 1940; Syracuse Univ. M.A. 1942; Clark Univ., Ph.D. 1946; m. Mary Josephine, d. C. Herbert Rowan, Fredericton, N.B., 14 Oct. 1944; children: David Norman, Jo-Anne Marie, Patricia Louise; PROF. EMERITUS, DEPT. of GEOGRAPHY, UNIV. OF B.C.; Geographer, N.W. Terr. Adm., Dept. of Mines & Resources, 1943–46; author of 14 books and more than 100 professional articles, chapters and maps on aspects of the geog. of Can., including 'Resources of the Canadian Shield,' 'British Columbia: 100 Years of Geographical Change'; and 'Concepts and Themes in the Regional Geography of Canada.' Encyclopedia articles on Canada, or parts of Canada published in the following: The Canadian Encyclopedia; Britannica; Funk and Wagnalls; American Peoples; Colliers; Crowell-Colliers; World Book; Groliers Book of Knowledge; Arete; Chambers (England); Universalis (France); Verlag Herder (Germany); Pres., Candn. Assn. of Geographers, 1955–56; awarded Candn. Geog. Soc. Massey Medal 1971; Service to the Profession Award from Candn. Assn. of Geog. 1976; Hon. LL.D. (Univ. of Western Ont.) 1984; Hon. LL.D. (Univ. of B.C.) 1994; Address: Univ. of British Columbia, Vancouver, B.C. V6T 1Z2.

**ROBINSON, Lyman Rand;** lawyer; b. Winnipeg, Man. 12 Nov. 1938; s. Frederick Stratford and Marie Mabel (Hartwell) R.; e. Univ. Saskatchewan, B.A. 1962; LL.B. 1963; Harvard Univ., LL.M. 1968; m. Charlene, d. Stephen and Helen Kitney, 18 May 1963; child: Dake; PROF. OF LAW, FACULTY OF LAW, UNIV. VICTORIA since 1975; articled to and practiced law with Crease & Co. (Victoria) 1963–67, 1985–86; joined Queen's Univ. as member of Faculty of Law 1968; Assoc. Dean Law 1971–75; Acting Dean Law 1973–74; joined present univ. as member of Faculty of Law 1975; Assoc. Dean Law 1979–80; Dean of Law 1980–85; author: 'British Columbia Debtor-Creditor Law and Precedents' 1993; and numerous legal articles; Pres., Candn. Assn. Law Teachers (1975–76); apptd. Q.C. 1984; mem. Law Reform Comn. of B.C.; mem. Candn. Human Rights Tribunal Panel; mem. R.C.M.P. Public Complaints Commn.; Home: 2895 Phyllis St., Victoria, B.C. V8N 1Y8; Office: Faculty of Law, Univ. of Victoria, P.O. Box 2400, Victoria, B.C. V8W 3H7.

**ROBINSON, Michael Playfair,** B.A., Dip. Prehistoric Arch., LL.B.; executive director and adjunct professor; Boston, Mass. 15 Jan. 1951; s. Geoffrey Charles Francis and Frances Mary Playfair (Roberts) R.; e. Univ. of B.C., B.A. 1973; Univ. Coll. Oxford Univ. (Rhodes Scholar 1973) Dip. in Prehistoric Archaeol. 1974; Univ. of B.C., LL.B. 1978; m. Lynn d. Bruce and Joyce Webster 4 June 1977; children: Lancelot William Frederick, Caitlin Playfair Davies; EXTVE. DIR. & ADJUNCT PROF., ARCTIC INST. OF NORTH AMERICA, UNIV. OF CALGARY; Sr. Socio-Economist, Northern Pipeline Agency 1979–80; Special Advr. and Mgr., Socio-Economics (Offshore Exploration, Coal Mine, Tar Sands Development, and Northern Pipelines etc., Petro-Canada 1980–86; past Chrmn. Education and Native Candn. Opportunities Cttes. (and three time recipient Achievement Award) Calgary C. of C.; Dir. Strathcona Found.; Dir., Arctic Inst. of N. Am.; Pres., Friends of the Earth Canada; Sec'y-Treas., Assoc. of Candn. Univs. for Northern Studies; Co-Chrmn., Univ. of Calgary Environmental Initiatives Ctte.; author: 'Sea Otter Chiefs' 1978; numerous academic articles in peer reviewed journals and books; co-author: 'The Monkman Pass and Trail' 1982; 'Coping With the Cash' 1989; recreations: running, ocean kayak touring, wilderness camping; Clubs: Calgary Commerce Club, Strathcona Alumni; Home: 7 Edgehill Cres. N.W., Calgary, Alta. T3A 2X4; Office: 11th Flr., Library Tower, Univ. of Calgary, 2500 University Dr. N.W., Calgary, Alta. T2N 1N4.

**ROBINSON, Paul E.,** M.A.; broadcaster; conductor; author; b. Toronto, Ont. 21 March 1940; s. Denis Owen and Helen Elizabeth (Franklin) R.; e. N. Toronto Coll. Inst. 1958; Univ. of Toronto B.A. 1962, M.A. 1965; double bass with Frederick Zimmerman, New York; Salzburg Mozarteum 1969, conducting with Bruno Maderna and Herbert von Karajan; m. Marita d. Peter and Maria Ensio 17 June 1966; children: Marcus, Marja-Liisa; Artistic Dir., Toronto Philharmonic Orch. 1989– ; Lectr. Univ. of Hong Kong 1966–69; Asst. Prof. State Univ. of N.Y. Fredonia 1970–72; Music Dir., Victoria Chamber Symphony, Hong Kong 1967–69; Music Dir., CJRT-FM 1972–92; Music Dir., CJRT Orchestra 1974–92; Music Dir., Toronto Arts Prodns. St. Lawrence Centre 1980–82; mem. Adv. Bd. Frederick Harris Music Co. 1983–88; Pres. Ont. Fed. Symphony Orchestra 1982–84; mem. Assembly Royal Conservatory of Music 1982–88; Bd. mem. Mozart Soc. (Can.) 1984–92; frequent guest conductor with Candn. and Am. orchestras; Host and Producer numerous CJRT progs. incl. 'Records in Review,' 'The Art of the Conductor,' 'A Night at the Opera'; author 'Art of the Conductor Series' Vol. I 'Herbert von Karajan' 1975, Vol. 2 'Leopold Stokowski' 1977, Vol. 3 'Georg Solti' 1979, Vol. 4 'Leonard Bernstein' 1982; recreations: tennis, golf; Home: 415 Melrose Ave., Toronto, Ont. M5M 1Z6; Office: 376 Benoit Rd., East Hill, Sutton, Que. J0E 2K0.

**ROBINSON, Peter,** B.A., M.A., Ph.D.; writer; b. Castleford, Yorkshire 17 Mar. 1950; s. Clifford and Miriam (Jarvis) R.; e. West Leeds Boys' High; Univ. of Leeds, B.A. 1974; Univ. of Windsor, M.A. 1975; York Univ., Ph.D. 1983; emigrated to Canada in 1974; taught part-time while pursuing post-grad. degrees, then taught at community colleges in Toronto; teaches occasionally incl. 'Mystery Writing' course, George Brown Coll. and Ryerson Polytechnic; Writer-in-Residence, Univ. of Windsor; mem., Crime Writers of Can.; Crime Writers' Assn. (U.K.); Internat. Crime Writers' Orgn.; author: 'Gallows View' 1987 (short-listed for best first novel awards in Can. & U.K.), 'A Dedicated Man' 1988 (short-listed for 1989 Arthur Ellis Award), 'A Necessary End' 1989, 'The Hanging Valley' 1989 (short-listed for the 1990 Arthur Ellis Award); 'Caedmon's Song' 1990 (short-listed for 1991 Arthur Ellis Award); 'Past Reason Hated' (winner of 1992 Arthur Ellis Award for Best Novel) 1991; 'Wednesday's Child' 1992; short story 'Innocence' (winner of 1991 Arthur Ellis Award for Best Short Story); recreations: classical music, reading.

**ROBINSON, Ralph Allan,** B.Sc., M.B.A.; food industry executive; b. Montreal, Que. 30 July 1948; s. James Henry and Katie Sara (Giles) R.; e. McGill Univ. B.Sc. 1970; York Univ. M.B.A. 1972; m. Linda d. Bill and Juanita Malone 14 May 1977; children: Lindsey, Danielle, Katie; PRESIDENT, NEILSON DAIRY; Analyst, Canadian Investment Industry; Finance Executive, Food Industry; Dir., National Dairy Council 1992; Home: 15 Bunker Road, Thornhill, Ont. L4J 1K3; Office: 279 Guelph St., Halton Hills, Ont. L7G 4B3.

**ROBINSON, Robert Reid,** B.A., D.Phil.; educator; b. Westkirby, Eng. 16 Apl. 1936; s. Robert Douglas and Sheena (Shannon) R.; e. Moseley Hall Grammar Sch. Cheadle, Eng.; Balliol Coll. Oxford B.A. 1958, D.Phil. 1962; m. Annabel d. George and Marjorie Cast 1964; children: Heather, Alasdair; ASSOC. VICE PRES. UNIV. OF REGINA 1984– ; Rsch. Assoc. Cornell Univ. 1962–65; Asst. Prof. of Chem. Univ. of Regina 1965; Dean of Arts, 1974–84; Vice Chrmn., S. Sask. Hosp. Bd.; mem., Chem. Inst. Can.; Royal Soc. Chem.; Home: 91 Newton Cres., Regina, Sask.; Office: Regina, Sask. S4S 0A2.

**ROBINSON, Spider;** writer; s. Charles and Evelyn R.; m. Jeanne 19 July 1975; one d. Terri; author (novels) 'Telempath' 1976; 'Mindkiller' 1982; 'Night of Power' 1985; 'Time Pressure' 1987; 'Callahan's Lady' 1988; 'Lady Slings the Booze' 1992; (novelette) 'Copyright Violation' 1990; (collections) 'Callahan's Crosstime Saloon' 1977 (named Best Book for Young Adults Am. Lib. Assn. 1977); 'Antinomy' 1980; 'Time Travelers Strictly Cash' 1981; 'Melancholy Elephants' 1984 (publ. twice in USSR, in a magazine and an anthology 1986); 'Callahan's Secret' 1986; 'Callahan and Company' 1987 (omnibus); 'True Minds' 1990; 'User Friendly' 1991; (anthol.) 'The Best of All Possible Worlds' 1980; co-author 'Stardance' (w. Jeanne Robinson) 1978; 'Starseed' (with Jeanne Robinson) 1991; recipient John W. Campbell Award Best New Writer 1974; semifinalist, Mr. Universe 1975; Locus Awards Best Critic 1976 and Best Novella 1977; Hugo Awards Best Novella 1976, 1977 and Best Short Story 1983; Nebula Award Best Novella 1977; E.E. Smith Meml. Award Speculative Fiction 1977; Pat Terry Meml. Award 1977; Can. Council Grants 1983, 1984, 1986, 1989; N.S. Dept. Culture Project Grants 1986, 1987; Book Review Ed. 'Galaxy' 1974–77; 'Destinies' 1977–79; 'Analog' 1978–80; Chrmn. Exec. Council Writers Fedn. N.S. 1981–83; Founding Chrmn. Dance Advance Assn. 1981–83; Dir. Nova Dance Theatre Assn. 1983–87; Address: c/o Eleanor Wood, Spectrum Agency, 111 8th Ave., Ste. 1501, New York, N.Y. 10011.

**ROBINSON, T. Russell,** B.Comm., M.A., Ph.D.; public service executive; b. Vancouver, B.C. 8 Oct. 1938; s. George Russell and Leona Pearl (Ferris) R.; e. Univ. of B.C. B.Comm. 1961; Yale Univ. M.A. 1962, Ph.D. 1966; m. Louise d. Antoine and Jacqueline Caron 21 Oct. 1972; children: David, Kirk, Adrian, Daniel; DEPUTY SECRETARY TO THE CABINET, PRIVY COUNCIL OFFICE 1993– ; Asst. Prof., Univ. of Western Ont. 1966–69; Visiting Prof., Univ. of B.C. & Univ. of Toronto 1969–70; Dir., Planning Branch, Treas. Bd., Govt. of Can. 1970–73; Asst. Dep. Min., Policy Rsch. & Planning, Health and Welfare Can. 1973–78; Social Affairs Directorate, and Econ. & Statistics Directorate, OECD (Paris) 1978–81; Asst. Dep. Min., Policy Coord., Consumer & Corp. Affairs 1981–86; Asst. Deputy Min., Fed.-Prov. Relations & Social Policy, Dept. of Finance 1986–93; Deputy Secy. to the Cabinet for Federal-Provincial Relations 1993 (three months); Sr. Advisor to the Deputy Min. of Finance on Fiscal Federalism 1993 (five months); Consultant, Royal Comn. on Taxation; Econ. Council of Canada; Nat. Bur. of Econ. Research; Bd. & Extve. Cttes.: Candn. Econ. Assn., Inst. of Public Admin. of Canada, 'Can. Public Policy' journal, Canada Mortgage & Housing Corp.; author/co-author of num. pubs. & articles in areas of fiscal & tax policy, econ. stabilization, social policy & fiscal federalism; recreations: swimming, golf, skiing; Home: 10 Rock Ave., Ottawa, Ont. K1M 1A6; Office: 5th Floor, 155 Queen St., Ottawa, Ont. K1A 0A3.

**ROBINSON, Thomas More,** B.A., B.Litt.; educator; b. Houghton-Le-Spring, U.K. 4 Nov. 1936; s. Alban Bainbridge and Emily Evangeline (Tolmie) R.; m. Erna Paris 26 Apr. 1981; stepch. Michelle Paris, Roland Paris; e. Ushaw Coll. Durham, U.K. 1956; Univ. of Durham B.A. 1961; Oxford Univ. B.Litt. (Greek Philos.) 1965; Sorbonne 1962–63; Dean, Sch. of Graduate Studies & Prof. of Philos. & Classics, Univ. of Toronto 1984–89; Chrmn., Dept. of Philos. there 1979–81; Vice-Dean, School of Graduate Studies, 1981–84; came to Can. 1964; writer and host 'The Greek Legacy' CBC FM Radio 'Ideas' Series 1978; host 'Philosophers at Work,' TVOntario 1981; Ed. 'Phoenix' 1971–76; co-ed. 'The Phoenix Pre-Socratics Series'; author 'Plato's Psychology' 1970; 'Contrasting Arguments: An Edition of the Dissoi Logoi' 1979; 'The Greek Legacy' 1979; 'Heraclitus: Fragments' 1987; various articles and reviews Greek philos.; mem. Candn. Philos. Assn.; Classical Assn. Can. (Council 1969–78); Am. Philol. Assn. (Nominating Comte. 1971–74); Manuscripts Review Comte., Univ. of Toronto Press; Editorial Comte., 'Philosophers in Canada' Monograph Series 1980–84; Adv. Comte. on Academic Planning, OCGS, 1980–81; Ont. Council on Grad. Studies 1979–89 (Chrmn., 1983–84); Pres., Candn. Federation for the Humanities 1988–90 (Vice Pres. 1986–87); Bd. of Dirs., OISE 1990–92; Pres.-elect, Internat. Plato Soc. 1992; Pres., Soc. for Ancient Greek Philosophy 1993; Hon. Pres., Internat. Assn. for Greek Philosophy 1993; Home: 126 Felstead Ave., Toronto, Ont. M4J 1G4; Office: Toronto, Ont. M5S 1A1.

**ROBINSON, Virginia Mary,** B.Sc., M.D., C.C.F.P.; physician; b. Toronto, Ont. 14 July 1953; d. Peter Ryerse and Margaret Amelia (Armour) Griffin; e. Branksome Hall 1971; Carleton Univ. 1972; McGill Univ., B.Sc. 1976; Univ. of Toronto, M.D. 1980; m. Gregor s. MacKenzie and Nora Robinson 1977; children: Alexandra Amelia, Esmée Anne; rotating internship North York Gen. Hosp. 1980–81, Assoc. Staff 1982– ; certificant in the Candn. Coll. of Family Practitioners 1988; gen. family practice 1982– ; Faculty mem. & teacher, Dept. of Family and Community Medicine, Univ. of Toronto; Dir. Lawrence Park Med. Bldg.; recipient Dalhousie Law Alumni Award of Merit for 'outstanding contribution to medicine' 1986; recreations: tennis, skiing, riding; Club: Badminton & Racquet; The Dog; Home: 157 Alexandra Blvd., Toronto, Ont. M4R 1M3; Office: 216, 250 Lawrence Ave. W., Toronto, Ont. M5M 1B2.

**ROBINSON, Col. William George MacKenzie,** O.B.E. (1944), C.A.; b. Port Arthur, Ont. 28 Nov. 1914; s. William (Writer to H.M. Signet) and Jane Thomson (Doctor) R.; e. St. Clements Sch. and Upper Can. Coll., Toronto; C.A. Feb. 1947 (Life mem., Sept. 1986); m. Nora, d. Ernest G. West, Toronto, 9 Feb. 1940; children: Ian MacKenzie, Andrew MacKenzie, Gregor MacKenzie, Sheila West, Phyllis Mary, Nora Blair; Gov., Art Gallery of Hamilton; with Dominion Bank, 1933–35; Clarkson Gordon & Co., 1935–48; with Gordon MacKay & Co. Ltd. Dir. and Vice-Pres., 1951–62; Pigott Group Vice Pres. Finance 1962–79; served in 2nd World War 1939–45; Capt., Toronto Scot. Regt. (M.G.) 1939; Maj. 1941; Lt.-Col. 1945; attended Cdn. War Staff Coll., Kingston, Ont., 1942; G.S.O. II, 1 Cdn. Corps, 1943; Bde. Maj., 3rd Cdn. Inf. Bde., 1944 G.S.O.1, 4th Cdn. Armoured Div., 1945; apptd. Hon. Col. Toronto Scottish Reg't. 1977–1980; awarded O.B.E.; twice Mentioned in Despatches; awarded Golden Aristion Andrias (Greece); Presbyterian; Clubs: Badminton & Racquet (Toronto); The Hamilton; Tamahaac; Home: 51 Markland St., Hamilton, Ont. L8P 2J5.

**ROBLIN, Hon. Duff,** P.C., C.C. (1970), LL.D.; b. Winnipeg, Manitoba 17 June 1917; s. C. D. and Sophia May (Murdoch) R.; grandson of Sir R. P. Roblin, Premier of Manitoba, 1900–15; e. Winnipeg Public Schs.; St. John's Coll. Sch., Winnipeg, Man.; Univ. of Manitoba; Univ. of Chicago; LL.D., McGill 1967; Man. 1967; Winnipeg 1968; m. Mary L. MacKay, 30 Aug. 1958; one s. Stephen Andrew, one d. Jennifer Mary; first el. to Manitoba Leg., g.e. Nov. 1949; re-el. g.e. 1953, 1958, 1959, 1962, and 1966; chosen Leader of P. Conservative Party in Manitoba 18 June 1954; sworn in as Premier and Pres. of the Counc. June 1958; sworn to the Privy Counc. 1967; resigned as Premier of Man. Nov. 1967; resigned as M.L.A. May 1968; Pres. and Dir., Canadian Pacific Investments Ltd. 1970–75; summoned to Senate of Can., 1978; Cabinet Min. & Leader of the Govt. in the Senate, 1984–86; served in 2nd World War; Wing Commdr., R.C.A.F., 1940–46; Anglican; Address: 977 Century Blvd., Winnipeg, Man. R3H 0W4.

**ROBSON, John M.,** M.A., Sc.D., F.R.S.C., F.A.P.S.; physicist; b. London, Eng. 26 March 1920; s. Stanley and Elsie Norah (Forster) R.; e. Clifton Coll., Bristol, Eng.; Kings Coll., Cambridge Univ., B.A. 1942, M.A. 1945, ScD. 1963; m. Helen Phyllis, d. Victor Summerhays, 17 June 1950; children: Michael, Elisabeth, Peter; EMERITUS PROFESSOR, McGILL UNIV.; with Radar Research and Devel. Establishment, Eng., 1942–45; came to Can. 1945; joined Atomic Energy Research Establishment, 1945–50; Atomic Energy of Can. Ltd., 1950–60; Chrmn., Dept. of Physics, Ottawa Univ. 1960–68; Chrmn., Dept. Physics, McGill Univ., 1968–76; Prof., Dept. Physics, McGill Univ. 1968–85; Head, Dept. Physics, Sultan Qaboos Univ., Oman 1986–88; mem., Nat. Research Council 1967–73; Hon. Secy., Royal Soc. Can. 1968–1970; author of over 30 scient. papers; has specialized in radioactivity of the neutron; Pres., Candn. Assn. of Physicists 1966–67; Anglican; recreations: fishing, golf; Address: P.O. Box 381, Lakefield, Ont. K0L 2H0.

**ROBSON, John Mercel,** M.A., Ph.D., F.R.S.C.; university professor; b. Toronto, Ont. 26 May 1927; s. William Renton Mercel and Christina Henderson (Sinclair) R.; e. Swansea Pub. Sch. and Runnymede Coll. Inst., Toronto; Univ. of Toronto, B.A. 1951, M.A. 1953, Ph.D. 1956; m. Ann Provost, d. Dr. Bertie Wilkinson, Toronto, 8 Aug. 1953; children: William, John, Ann Christine; PROFESSOR EMERITUS, MASSEY COLLEGE, UNIV. OF TORONTO; Teaching Fellow, Dept. of Eng., Univ. Coll., Univ. of Toronto, 1952–54; Instr. in Eng., Univ. of B.C., 1956–57; Asst. Prof., Univ. of Alta., 1957–58; joined Victoria College, Univ. of Toronto as Asst. Prof. 1958–63; Assoc. Prof. 1963–67; Prof. of English 1967–92; Principal 1971–76; author: 'The Improvement of Mankind: The Social and Political Thought of John Stuart Mill,' 1968; 'The Hmnnn Retort,' 1970; 'What Did He Say?' 1988; Ed., 'Collected Works of J. S. Mill,' also author of numerous articles and book chapters and ed. of various works; adv. ed., 'Wellesley Index'; Consulting Ed. 'Scholarly Publishing,' 'Utilitas'; Pres., Internat. Society for Utilitarian Studies; mem., Adv. Ed. Bd., Bertrand Russell Papers, McMaster Univ., Bentham Comte., Univ. Coll. London, Eng., Centre for Editing Early Candn. Texts, Carleton Univ., Victorian Periodicals Review; Arts and Letters Club; Brit. Studies Assn.; Rsch. Soc. for Victorian Periodicals; Victorian Studies Assn.; recreation: reading, word-processing, golf; Home: 28 McMaster Ave., Toronto, Ont. M4V 1A9.

**ROBSON, Stuart Thomas,** B.A., D.Phil.; educator; b. Vancouver, B.C. 13 July 1940; s. William Marshall and Ellen (Clark) R.; e. Univ. of B.C., B.A. 1962; Oxford Univ. (Rhodes Scholar for B.C. 1962) D.Phil. 1966; m. Wendy (dec'd) d. Reginald and Myra Moir 28 Aug. 1965; children: Jennifer Margaret, Kathleen Ellen; PROFESSOR OF HISTORY, TRENT UNIVERSITY 1966– ; Home: R.R. #11, Peterborough, Ont. K9J 6Y3; Office: Traill College, Trent Univ., Peterborough, Ont. K9J 7B8.

**ROCCA, Pat;** business executive; b. Sambiase, Italy 4 Aug. 1942; s. Bernardo and Giovanna (Mercuri) R.; e. high sch.; m. Joan Quinlan 26 Sept. 1964; children: Patrick, Cathy, Tanya; PRES., RGL REALTY INC. and URBAN CONSULTANTS (1989) LTD. 1960– ; developed & built 40 shopping ctre. incl. 5 major malls, 2 Howard Johnson hotels, several office complexes & $100 million Market Square downtown development; gen. contr. or project mgr. on over 170 other devel. in Maritimes, incl. 5 regional hosps.; developed properties in excess of $1 billion; Past Pres., Saint John Bd. of Trade; New Brunswick Construction Assn.; Past Vice Pres. New Brunswick Candn. Construction Assoc.; Gov. of Atlantic Prov. Econ. Counc.; Dir., Candn. Public Real Estate Inst.; Bd. of Trustees, YMCA; recreation: running; Home: 1400 Beaufort Dr., Burlington, Ont. and York Point at Market Square, Saint John, N.B.; Offices: 4087 Harvester Rd., Unit 8, Burlington, Ont. L7L 5M3 and 1190 Fairville Blvd., Saint John, N.B.

**ROCH, Ernst,** D.F.A. (hon.), R.C.A., A.G.I.; graphic designer; b. Osijek, Croatia 8 Dec. 1928; s. Hans Roch; e. Staatliche Meisterschule fur angewandte Kunst Graz, Austria, M.F.A. 1953; came to Can. 1953; children: Ursula M.D., Uli, Barbara; PROP. ROCH DESIGN 1978– ; Asst., Prof. Hans Wagula Graz, Austria 1952–53; Designer, Y & M Studio Montreal 1954–59; Design Dir. Montreal Office James Valkus Inc. N.Y. 1960; own office graphic design 1960–65; Princ. and Founding mem. Design Collaborative Ltd. Montreal and Toronto 1965–77; Founding mem. Signum Press Ltd. 1973; mem. Postage Stamp Design Adv. Comte. Can. Post 1975–80; mem. curatorium Internat. Inst. Inform. Design, Vienna 1988– ; maj. projects incl. visual identity program Nat. Arts Centre Ottawa 1965; organization and design of exhibitions 'Munich Olympic Games,' Montreal Museum Fine Arts and Art Gallery Ont. 1972 and 'AGI Posters,' Place Ville Marie, Montreal 1982; official poster Montreal Olympic Games 1976; definitive issue postage stamp Queen Elizabeth II 1963, commemorative postage stamps: Sir Oliver Mowat 1967; Early Candn. Locomotives, 1983, 1984, 1985, 1986; Christmas 1988; Candn. Mushrooms 1989; editor/designer 'Arts of the Eskimo: Prints' 1974; author/designer 'Paper Zoo' 1973; recipient numerous awards and prizes Can., USA and Europe incl. Am. Inst. Graphic Arts, Lahti (Finland) Poster Biennale, Leipzig Internat. Book Fair, Biennale of Graphic Design Brno, Czechosolovakia, Poster Biennale Warsaw; D.F.A. (hon. causa), N.S. Coll. of Art and Design 1988; work represented in permanent collections: Public Archives, Ottawa; Library of Congress, Washington D.C.; Museum of Modern Art, New York; Wilanów Poster Museum, Warsaw; cited numerous bibliogs.; Fellow, Assn. Graphic Designers Can.; mem. Royal Canadian Academy of Arts; Alliance Graphique Internationale; Am. Inst. Graphic Arts; Design Austria; Address: P.O. Box 1056, Station B, Montreal, Que. H3B 3K5.

**ROCHE, Douglas James,** O.C., B.A.; diplomat; professor; b. Montreal, Que. 14 June 1929; s. James Joseph and Agnes (Douglas) R.; e. St. Patrick's High Sch. Ottawa 1947; St. Patrick's Coll. Univ. of Ottawa B.A. 1951; m. Eva Mary d. Michael Nolan. Ottawa, Ont. 26 Sept. 1953; children; Evita, Michaelene, Douglas F., Mary Anne, Patricia; CANADIAN AMBASSADOR FOR DISARMAMENT 1984–89; Leader, Candn. Delegation to the Disarmament Ctte., United Nations, New York; el. Chrmn. of First Ctte. dealing with internat. peace and security issues, 43rd Session of the U.N. General Assembly 1988; Reporter, 'Ottawa Journal' 1949–50; Pol. Reporter, 'Toronto Telegram' 1952–55; Reporter and Columnist, 'Catholic Universe Bulletin; 1956–57, Cleveland; Assoc. Ed., 'Sign Magazine' 1958–65, Union City, N.J. (rec'd Cath. Press Assn. Award Best Mag. Article 1963); Founding Ed., 'Western Catholic Reporter' 1965–72, Edmonton (Paper won 11 nat. awards Cath. Press Assn. and Assoc. Ch. Press, ed. cited for Best Ed. Writing 1971); el. to H. of C. for Edmonton Strathcona 1972, 1974, for Edmonton S. 1979, 1980; P. Cons. Spokesman on External Affairs 1977–79, Cons. to Candn. Delegation to U.N. 2nd Special Session on Disarmament; Chrmn. P. Cons. Caucus Ctte. on External Affairs 1979, Parlty. Secy. to Secy. of State for External Affairs. DN. Del. to 34th Gen. Assembly UN; Secy., Edmonton Council Chs. 1970–71; Pres., Candn. Ch. Press 1971; mem. Nat. Council (Alta.), Candn. Human Rights Foundation 1978–80; Candn. mem., North-South Roundtable & Soc. for Internat. Devel. 1978– ; Vice Chrmn., Parlty. Task Force on North-South Relations 1980; Internat. Pres., Parliamentarians Global Action 1980–84; Pres., U.N. Assoc. in Can. 1984–85; el. Hon. Pres., The World Federation of U.N. Assns., Geneva Switzerland 1985, (1st Candn to receive this honour); Visiting Prof., Univ. of Alberta 1989– ; Distinguished Fellow, Candn. Centre for Global Security; mem., Candn. Pugwash Group; author 'The Catholic Revolution' 1968; 'Man to Man' 1969; 'It's A New World' 1970; 'Justice Not Charity: A New Global Ethic for Canada' 1976; 'The Human Side of Politics' 1976; 'What Development Is All About: China, Indonesia, Bangladesh' 1979; 'Politicians for Peace' 1983; 'United Nations, Divided World' 1984; 'Canada and the Pursuit of Peace' 1985; 'Building Global Security: Agenda for the 1990's' 1989; 'In the Eye of the Catholic Storm' 1992; 'A Bargain for Humanity: Global Security By 2000' 1993; various book chapters, articles; numerous Candn. and foreign lectures and study tours; rec'd., World Peace Award, World Federalists of Canada 1983; Premier's Award 1984 (Alta.); Hon. LL.D., Simon Fraser Univ. 1985; Hon. D.D., St. Stephen's Coll., Edmonton; Hon. LL.D. University of Alberta 1986; rec'd., Thakore Foundation Award in recognition of prolonged and distinguished work towards disarmament, global peace and peace education 1992; named Officer of the Order of Canada 1992; P. Conservative; R. Catholic; recreations: skiing, swimming, reading; Office: 8923 Strathearn Dr., Edmonton, Alta. T6C 4C8.

**ROCHELEAU, Serge,** B.A.; executive; b. Montreal, Que. 24 Apl. 1942; s. Honoré and Gertrude (Cadieux) R.; e. Univ. of Montreal B.A.; children: Katerine, Jean-François, Luc; PRES., C.O.O. AND DIR., PRENOR GROUP LTD.; Chrmn., Pres., C.E.O. & Dir., Prenor Financial Ltd.; Vice-Pres. and Dir., Canaprev Inc.; Dir., Bolton Tremblay Funds Inc.; Bolton Tremblay Inc.; BT Landmark Resource Fund Inc.; Groupe Val Royal Ltée.; Placements Louisbourg Inc.; Prenor Equity Inc.; Groupe Watier Inc.; R. Catholic; Home: 206 Morrison, Ville Mont-Royal, Que. H3R 1K6; Office: Suite 1200, 1100 University St., Montreal, Que. H3B 3A4.

**ROCHER, Guy,** C.C. (1971), Ordre national du Québec (1991), M.A., Ph.D.; professeur; né. Berthierville, Qué. 20 Avril 1924; fils Barthelemy et Jeanne (Magnan) R.; é. Univ. de Montreal, B.A. 1943; Univ. Laval, M.A. (Sociologie) 1950; Harvard Univ., Ph.D. (Sociol.) 1957; enfants: Genevieve, Anne-Marie, Isabelle, Claire, Marié à Claire-Emmanuèle Depocas; PROF. TITULAIRE, UNIV. DE MONTREAL, depuis 1960 et sous-ministre au développement culturel, Gouv. du Qué., 1976–79; depuis 1979 attaché au Centre de recherche en droit public, Faculté de Droit, Univ. de Montréal; Sous-Ministre au Développement Social, Gouvernement du Québec, 1981–83; Pres. du Conseil d'administration de Radio-Quebec 1979–81; (Dir. Dept. Sociol. 1960–65; Vice-Doyen, Faculté des Sciences Sociales 1962–67); Asst. Prof., Univ. Laval. 1952–58. Prof. Agrégé, 1958–60; mem., Comn Royale d'enquête sur l'Enseignement (Québec) 1961–66; Prés. Comn. D'enquête sur la nouvelle Univ. Francaise à Montréal, 1965; Gouv. du Coll. Canadien des Travailleurs, 1963–66; du Bureau de la Radio Diffusion, 1966–68; mem. Comn. Scolaire d'Outrement, du Conseil d'adm. du conseil des Oeuvres de Montréal, 1966–68; Vice-Pres., du Comité sur la recherche universitaire de la Soc. roy. du Can. 1989–90; mem., Conseil de recherche du l'Institut canadien de recherche avance (depuis 1986); mem., conseil d'administration du Centre de droit preventif (depuis 1990); Fellow, de l'Am. Sociol. Assn.; (Prés. 1961–62) de l'Assn. Canadienne de Sociol.; Prés. (1966–67) de l'Assn. Canadienne des Sociologues et Anthropologues de langue Francaise; Trésorier (1958–59) Assn. Internat. des Sociol. de langue Francaise; Prés., Nat. de la Jeunesse Etudiante Catholique, 1945–48; Foreign mem. de l'American Acad. of Arts and Sciences; mem. de la Soc. royale du Can.; Publ. 'Famille et Habitation' (en collab.) 1960; Rapport de la Comn. Royale d'enquête sur l'Enseignement (en collab.) 5 vols. (1963–1966); 'Introduction à la sociologie générale' (3 vols.), 1968; 'Le Québec en mutation,' 1973; 'Talcott Parsons et la sociologie américaine,' 1972; 'Ecole et société au Québec' (en collaboration), 1971; 'Continuité et rupture: Les sciences sociales au Québec' (en collaboration) 1984; 'Entre les rêves et l'histoire' (en collaboration) 1989; 'Le Québec en jeu' (en collaboration) 1992; nombreux articles; Catholique; Résidence: 5610 avenue Decelles, app. 16, Montréal, Qué. H3T 1W5.

**ROCHESTER, Michael Grant,** M.A., Ph.D., F.R.S.C.; university professor; b. Toronto, Ont. 22 Nov. 1932; s. Reginald Baillie and Ruth Ellen (Bonwick) R.; e. Earl Haig C.I. 1950; Univ. of Toronto, B.A. (Hons.) 1954, M.A. 1956; Univ. of Utah, Ph.D. 1959; m. Elizabeth d. Francis and Jessie Manser 9 May 1958; children: Susan Patricia, (Catherine) Fiona, John Rowland; Aerodynamicist, A.V. Roe Can. Ltd. 1954–55; Lectr., Univ. of Toronto 1959–60; Asst. Prof. Phys. 1960–61; Asst. Prof., Univ. of Waterloo 1961–65, Assoc. Prof. 1965–67; Assoc. Prof., Meml. Univ. of Nfld. 1967–70, Prof. Phys. 1970–82, 1986– , Prof. Earth Sci. 1982– , Univ. Rsch. Prof. 1986– ; Vis. Prof., York Univ. 1974–75, 1982–83; Univ. of Queensland 1977; McGill Univ. 1990–91; Mem., Internat. Astron. Union Comn. on the Rotation of the Earth 1973– ; Candn. Nat. Ctte. for Internat. Union of Geodesy & Geophys. 1974–75, 1984–88; Internat. Geodynamics Project 1971–79; NSERC, Earth Sci. Grant Selection Ctte. 1979–82; F.R.S.C. 1983; Royal Soc. of Can., Earth Sciences Section Extve. 1984–90 (Convenor, 1987–89); Bd. of Dirs., Lithoprobe Project, 1986–91; Tuzo Wilson Medal, Candn. Geophys. Union 1986; Baha'i Faith (Dir., Nat. Spiritual Assembly of the Baha'is of Can. 1963–92); Mem., Am. Assn. for the Advancement of Sci.; Am. Geophys. Union; Candn. Applied Mathematics Soc.; Candn. Assn. of Phys., Candn. Geophys. Union; Royal Astron. Soc. of London; Soc. of Sigma Xi; recreations: hiking, swimming, reading; Office: Dept. of Earth Sci., Memorial Univ. of Nfld., St. John's, Nfld. A1B 3X5.

**ROCHETTE, Louis,** M.Com., F.C.A., C.M.A.; b. Quebec City, Que. 19 Feb. 1923; s. Evariste and Blanche (Gaudry) R.; e. St. Dominique, Que.; Coll. St. Charles Garnier, Que.; St. Joseph High Sch., Berthierville, Que.; Laval Univ., M.Com. 1948; m. Nicole, d. E. C. Barbeau, Verdun, Que., 12 Oct. 1968; children: Louise, Anne, Guy; PRESIDENT, GESCONAV INC. 1982– ; Chrmn. & C.E.O. Davie Shipbuilding, Lauzon P.Q. 1976–1982; Vice Chrmn. & Dir., Socanav Inc.; Leader Manufacturing Inc.; Dir., Hawker Siddeley Can. Inc.; Chief Auditor, Retail Sales Tax Service, Province of Quebec, 1953–55; Treas., Davie Shipbuilding Ltd., 1955–65; Financial Dir. and Treas., Sidbec, 1965–66; Extve. Vice Pres. Marine Ind. Ltd. 1966–76; served as Pilot with RCAF 1943–45; Hon. Col., Sixth Field Artillery Reg.; author, 'Le Rêve Séparatiste,' 1969; Fellow, Inst. C.A.'s; Mgmt. Accts.; Past Pres., Candn. Shipbuilding and Ship-repairing Assn.; Gov., & Past Pres., Council for Candn. Unity; Gov., Chamber of Commerce of the Province of Quebec; Gov., Laval Univ. Found.; Quebec Opera Found.; mem., Canada, Lloyds Register of Shipping; recreations: fishing, skiing, sailing; Clubs: Garnison; Ocean Reef; Address: 1080 Des Braves Ave., Quebec, Que. G1S 3C8.

**ROCHON, Gerard Omer,** B.A.; television producer; b. Windsor, Ont. 10 Feb. 1934; s. Gerard Normand and Eulalie Marie (Langis) R.; e. St. Anne's S.S. 1948; Assumption H.S. 1952; Univ. of Detroit, B.A. 1957; m. Eileen d. Edward and Cecile MacNeil 15 June 1957; children: Colette (m. Bradley Sommerville), Michele (m. Daniel McEnery), Elise (m. Werner van Bastalaar); VICE-PRES. & EXTVE. PROD., CFTO-TV 1974– and VICE PRES. & EXTVE. PROD., GLEN-WARREN ENTERTAINMENT 1989– ; TV Dir., Detroit Bd. of Edn. (WTVS) 1956–57; Dir. & Stage Mgr., CKLW-TV 1958–60; Prod./Dir. (Variety & Sports), CFCF-TV 1960–64; CFTO-TV 1965–70; Extve. Prod., 'Separation' (movie), Miss Can. Pageants 1970–74; Vice-Pres. & Extve. Prod., 'Stars on Ice,' 'Circus,' 'Olympic Specials,' 'Quebec in Transition'; Pres. & Vice-Pres., Gerry Rochon Prodn. Ltd., Global TV 1978– ; Prod., CBC, 'Genie Awards' 1980; Vice-Pres. & Extve. Prod., CFTO-TV, 'The Littlest Hobo,' 'Thrill of a Lifetime,' 'The Papal Visit,' 'Frank Mills Christmas Special' 1980–86; apptd., Extve. Prod., Opening and Closing Ceremonies for Host Broadcaster 'Winter Olympics 1988'; 1986; Internat. Film & TV Fest. of N.Y., 1982 Bronze Medal, 1983 Gold, 1984 Silver for 'The Littlest Hobo'; 1985 Silver Medal for 'The Papal Visit'; Vice-Pres. & Extve. Prod., Glen-Warren Prods. Ltd. 1989; Prod., (film feature) 'Divided Loyalties'; 1990 Bronze Medal Houston Film Festival; Mem., Nat. Assn. of TV Prog. Extves.; Candn. Prog. Extves.; recreations: sailing, fitness, tennis, squash; Clubs: The Royal Candn. Yacht (Communications Ctte.); The Fitness Inst.; Home: 556 Merton St., Toronto, Ont. M4S 1B3; Office: CFTO-TV, Box 9, Station O, Toronto, Ont. M4S 1B3.

**ROCHON, Paul L.,** B.Sc., Ph.D., P.Eng.; university professor and administrator; b. Hawkesbury, Ont. 27 May 1949; s. Raymond and Carmel (Chabot) R.; e. Univ.of Ottawa B.Sc. 1972, Ph.D. 1976; m. Karen d. Earl Courtney 25 April 1985; children: Martha, Ike, Nathan; PROFESSOR, PHYSICS, ROYAL MILITARY COLLEGE OF CANADA 1988– ; postdoctoral work, Univ.

of Montreal 1976–77; Asst. Prof., Physics, Royal Military College 1977; Assoc. Prof. 1983; Head of Physics 1991– ; Home: 19 Mack St., Kingston, Ont. K7L 1N7; Office: Kingston, Ont. K7K 5L0.

**ROCK, Hon. Allan Michael,** P.C., B.A., LL.B., Q.C.; lawyer; b. Ottawa, Ont. 30 Aug. 1947; s. James Thomas and Anne Dane R.; e. Univ. of Ottawa B.A. 1968, LL.B. 1971; m. Deborah Kathleen d. Daniel and Margaret Hanscom 24 June 1983; children: Jason, Lauren, Andrew, Stephen; MINISTER OF JUSTICE and ATTORNEY GENERAL, GOVT. OF CANADA 1993– ; first el. to House of Commons (Etobicoke Centre) 1993; sworn to the Privy Council 1993; former Senior Partner, Fasken Campbell Godfrey and Fasken Martineau; elected Bencher of Law Soc. 1983, '87, '91; Treas., Law Soc. of U.C. 1992; Former Chair, Discipline & Legal Edn. Cttes.; Fellow (Elected), Am. College of Trial Lawyers; Certified Specialist in Civil Litigation; Chair, Litigation Dept., Fasken Campbell Godfrey; Office: Dept. of Justice, 239 Wellington St., Ottawa, Ont. K1A 0H8.

**ROCK, Gail Ann,** Ph.D., M.D., FRCP; physician; educator; hematopathologist; b. Winnipeg, Man. 20 Oct. 1940; d. James Clifford and Ann Leween (Walecke) Dolan; e. St. Patrick's Coll. B.Sc. 1962; Univ. of Ottawa Ph.D. 1966, M.D. 1972; m. William s. George Rock 21 May 1966; two d. Christine, Jennifer; ASSOC. PROF. OF MED. UNIV. OF OTTAWA 1986– ; Med. Dir. Ottawa Centre Candn. Red Cross, B.T.S. 1974–88; mem. Bd. Ottawa Carleton Econ. Devel. Corp. 1988; recipient City of Ottawa Civic Award for Outstanding Innovation 1988; author or co-author over 160 sci. articles, 42 book chapters and editor of 4 reference books; editor: 'Quality Assurance in Transfusion Medicine'; Pres. World Assn. Apheresis 1988–90; Am. Soc. Apheresis 1987–88; Chrmn. Candn. Apheresis Study Group 1982–91; ed. Transfusion Sci.; cons.; recreations: swimming, tennis, scuba, skiing; club: Cercle Universitaire; Address: 270 Sandridge Rd., Ottawa, Ont. K1L 5A2.

**ROCKBURN, Kenneth Richard;** journalist; b. Ottawa, Ont. 16 Apr. 1947; s. Alfred and Mary (Esdale) R.; e. Carleton Univ. Sch. of Journalism 1968–70; m. Sheila Bird d. James and Lydia Bird 13 July 1979; children: Lauren Rachel, Ellis Marshall; News Dir., CHEZ-FM, Ottawa 1981; Founding Mem., Living Radio 1970; community activist, Ottawa 1974–77; joined CHEZ-FM 1977; Trainer, Dept. of Indian Affairs 1979–80; Ed., Metro Magazine, Ottawa 1989–90; rec'd two Nat. Radio Awards 1988; rec'd Nat. Radio Award 1989; nominated Nat. Radio Award 1990; Dir., Planned Parenthood Ottawa 1985–88; mem. Radio & Television News Dirs. Assn.; Candn. Assn. of Journalists; Home: 78 Hamilton Ave. N., Ottawa, Ont. K1Y 1B9.

**ROCKETT, Beverley Anne;** fashion director; b. Toronto, Ont. 14 Feb. 1931; d. John and Evelyn Pearl (Bedford) Hamm; e. Bishop Strachan Sch.; Branksome Hall 1949; Ont. Coll. of Art; children: Robin Annabelle, Paul Anthony, Eden Alexandra; Vice-Pres., & Fashion Dir., Theo Dimson Design Inc. 1983; television 1956–75: CBC Tabloid, CBC Living, City TV Sweet City Woman; actress: CBC General Motors Theatre, Ford Theatre; photography: Chatelaine, Maclean's, Saturday Night, Star Weekly, Week-End, The Canadian (magazines); 'Requiem for a Heavyweight,' 'All the Way Home,' 'Equus' (films); T.D.F. Prod., The Nat. Art Ctr., The Nat. Ballet of Can.; TV Prod., Bob Schulz Prod. 1979–80; Fashion & Beauty Ed., City Woman Mag. 1980–83; awards: Women Who Make a Difference 1989; Nat. Mag. Awards (Gold and Silver) 1981–84; Fest. of Candn. Fashion; Art Dir. Club of Toronto, Annual Show; Norma Awards (N.Y.); RAC Awards (Chicago); Bd. Mem., Toronto Workshop Prod.; Mem., Gov. Counc. & Auction Ctte., The Shaw Fest. 1986–89; Bd. of Dirs., The Fashion Group Inc.; Art Dir. Club of Toronto; Home: 184 Gage, Niagara-on-the-Lake, Ont. L0S 1J0.

**RODER, John Carling,** B.A., Ph.D.; immunologist; b. Niagara Falls, Ont. 17 July 1950; s. John and Helen R.; e. Univ. of Western Ont. B.A. 1973, Ph.D. 1977; m. Marylou d. Peter and Corey Van Engelen May 1973; children: Jessica, Nathan; HEAD, DIV. OF MOLECULAR IMMUNOLOGY AND NEUROBIOLOGY, MT. SINAI HOSPITAL 1985– ; Asst. Prof., Queen's Univ. 1979; Assoc. Prof., Queen's Univ. 1982; Assoc. Prof., Univ. of Toronto 1985; Prof., Dept. of Immunology & Dept. of Molecular & Medical Genetics 1987– ; Inst. of Medicl Sci. 1991– ; Collip Medal (UWO) for Outstanding PhD thesis in Med. Sciences; Killam Post-Doct. Rsch. Scholarship 1977–79; Internat. Union Against Cancer ICRETT Award 1977; Swedish Cancer Soc. Guest Researcher Award 1978; Basmajian Award, Queen's Univ. 1983–84; MRC Scientist Award 1988–93; Cynader Award, Candn. Soc. of Immunology 1990; author/co-author of over 188 scientific articles and abstracts in some of the best journals; recreations: squash, hiking, canoeing; Office: 600 University Ave., Toronto, Ont. M5G 1X5.

**RODGER, Ginette Lemire,** B.ScN., M.N.Adm.; executive; nurse; b. Amos, Que. 18 Mar. 1943; d. Joseph and Blanche (Gagnon) Lemire; e. Univ. of Ottawa, Dip. in Nursing 1964, B.ScN. 1966; Univ. of Montreal M.N. Adm. 1971; D.Sc. (h.c.) Univ. of New Brunswick 1985; LL.D. (h.c.) Queen's Univ. 1989; D.Nursing.Sc. (h.c.), Univ. de Sherbrooke 1990; m. William James Rodger; children: Robert, Phillipe, Sabrina; PRESIDENT, LEMIRE RODGER & ASSOCS.; Extve. Dir., Canadian Nurses Assn. 1981–89; gen. duty nurse urban and rural areas 1964–68, 1972–73, 1985; Long Term Planning, Notre-Dame Hospital, Montreal 1968–72, in charge of Nursing Rsch. 1973–74, Dir. of Nursing 1974–81; author: 'Making the Right Decisions or Making the Decision Right: Do Policy Makers Care About Ethics' 1992; 'Advancing Doctoral Preparation for Nurses: Social, Political and Economic Influences and Professional Nursing Association Perspectives' 1990; 'The Influences of Our Successes On Society' 1990; 'Nursing in the 21st Century' 1990; 'The Code of Ethics for Nursing' 1988; 'Nurses: Partners in the Changing Health Science' 1988; 'Access: Is It Just a Question of Dollars?' 1987; 'New Horizons and New Constraints' 1987; 'The Destiny of Nursing: Interaction of the Discipline with Society' 1986; 'La Nature du service infirmier de base' ['The Nature of Basic Nursing Services'] 1980; 'Sur La Corde Raide' ['On the Tightrope'] 1977; 'La Synergie des soins physiques et de l'approache psychologique dans le réduction du stress chez les patients en période postopératoire' ['Synergy of Physical Care and Psychological Approach Towards a Reduction of Stress in Post-Operatory Patients'] Univ. of Montreal 1971; Nat. and Internat. speaker: more than 100 presentations; Past Chrmn. and Surveyor, Candn. Council on Hospital Accreditation 1972–86; Med. Rsch. Council of Can. 1986–88; Nat. Health & Community Services, Candn. Red Cross Soc. 1981–88; Service Adv. Ctte. Victorian Order of Nurses for Can. 1981–89; Nat. Dep. Dir. Health Care St. John Ambulance 1981–88; Ed. Bd. 'Journal of Advanced Nursing' (England); Candn. Coll. of Health Service Extves.; Am. Soc. for Hospital Nursing Service Admin.; Am. Hosp. Assn.; CNA/Candn. Hosp. Assn. Jt. Ctte. for Extension Course in Nursing Mgmt. 1978–89; Sec-Treas. Candn. Nurses Found. 1981–89; First Sec.-Treas., Candn. Nurses Protective Soc. 1987–89; Past Pres., CEGEP Mainsoneuve 1978–81; Past Chrmn., Nursing Ed. Ctte. Quebec Min. of Ed. 1978–80; Essential Services Ctte. Que. Min. of Labour 1978–80; mem. Bd., Candn. Nurses Assn. 1978–80; mem. Bd., Notre Dame Hosp. 1976–79; Ph.D. Laws (hon. causa), Queen's Univ. 1989; Hon. Life Mem. Reg. Nurses Assn. Ont. 1989; Ginette-Lemire Rodger Wing at CNA Headquarters 1988; Ginette Lemire Rodger Scholarship in Nursing by CNA Bd. 1988; Ph.D. Science (hon. causa), Univ. of New Brunswick 1985; Commander, Order of St. John 1985; Hon. mem., Ont. Public Health Assn. 1985; recipient Ryerson Fellowship Award 1984; Vigor Prize 1980; Serving Sister Order of St. John 1979; Office: 9938 – 86th Ave., Edmonton, Alta. T6E 2L7.

**RODGER, Maj.-Gen. Norman Elliot,** C.B.E. (1944), C.D.; Canadian Army (retired); b. Amherst, N.S. 30 Nov. 1907; s. late Norman Clarence and late Hattie Thompson (McLennan) R.; e. Cumberland County Academy; Roy. Mil. Coll. Grad. (Hons.) 1928; McGill Univ., B.Sc. (Civil) 1930; m. Isabel, d. late W. F. Wilson, Ottawa, 8 Sept. 1934; three s. Wilson, Nicholas, Elliot; joined Candn. Army, Royal Candn. Engineers, 1928; District Engn. Officer, Kingston, 1938–39; served in World War, 1940–45; attended War Staff Coll., Camberley, Eng., 1940; Personal Asst. to Gen. A. G. L. McNaughton, 1941–42; Brig. Gen. Staff, Candn. Mil. Hdqrs., London, 1942–43; commanded 10th Candn. Inf. Bgde., 1943–44; Chief of Staff H.Q 2nd Candn. Corps, 1944–45; Commdr., Order of British Empire; Commdr. Legion of Merit (U.S.); Commdr., Order Orange Nassau (Netherlands); Candn. Army Staff, Wash., 1945–1946; Q.M.G., Candn. Army, Ottawa, 1946–50; attended Imp. Defence Coll., 1951; G.O.C. Prairie Command, 1952–55; Vice Chief of the Gen. Staff, 1955; Chrmn., Manitoba Liquor Control Comn., 1959–68; Colonel Commandant of Royal Canadian Army Cadets 1966–69; recipient, Queen Elizabeth II Coronation Medal 1953; Canada Medal 1967; Queen Elizabeth II Silver Jubilee Medal 1977; awarded Commemorative Medal for 125th Anniversary of Candn. Confederation 1992; Service Cross of Royal Life Saving Soc.; Anglican; Club: Royal Ottawa Golf; recreations: canoeing, golf, fishing; Address: 902 – 40 Boteler, St., Ottawa, Ont. K1N 9C8.

**RODGERS, Sanda,** B.A., LL.B., B.C.L., LL.M.; university professor/administrator; b. New York, NY 12 June 1947; s. Dan and Ruth (Steigerwald) R.; e. Case Western Reserve Univ., B.A. 1971; McGill Univ., LL.B. 1974, B.C.L. 1975; Univ. of Montreal, LL.M. 1978; one d.: Shoshana; DEAN, FACULTY OF LAW, UNIV. OF OTTAWA 1994– ; Prof. & Vice-Dean, Faculty of Law 1977–94; Bd. of Dir., Amethyst Womens Addiction Ctr.; Mem., Law Soc. of Upper Canada; Cons., var. govt. orgns. on health law & policy; co-author: 'Mobility Rights' in 'Perspectives on the Canadian Economic Union' (Macdonald Comn. Report) 1986; co-editor: 'Issues in Tort Law' 1983; Home: 10 Broadway Ave., Ottawa, Ont.; Office: 57 Louis-Pasteur St., Ottawa, Ont. K1N 6N5.

**RODNEY, William,** D.F.C., B.A., M.A., Ph.D., F.R.G.S., F.R.Hist.S.; university professor; b. Drumheller, Alta. 5 Jan. 1923; s. Jonathon and Helen Marjorie (Forest) R.; e. Univ. of Alta. B.A. (Hons.) 1950; Univ. of Cambridge, England B.A. 1952; M.A. 1956; Univ. of London, England Ph.D. 1961; m. Helen, d. John and Annabelle McGregor 2 Sept. 1950; children: Helen Catherine; John William McGregor; PROF. EMERITUS, ROYAL ROADS MILITARY COLLEGE 1988– ; served with R.C.A.F. 1941–45; Beaver Club Trust Fellow 1950–52; Strathcona Travel Exhibition 1951–52; Univ. of London Research Grant 1959; Can. Council pre-Doctoral Fellowship 1959–61; Nato Fellowship 1963–64; Soc. Sci. Research Council Grant in Aid of Publication 1967; Can. Council Leave Fellowship 1968–69; Can. Council Research Grant 1972; Dept. of Ext. Affairs Travel Grant 1977; Can. Council Sr. Leave Fellowship 1978–79; Dean of Arts, Royal Roads Military Coll. 1979–88; awarded D.F.C. and Bar, 1944–45; Award of Merit and Distinction, Am. Assn. for State and Local History 1970; Univ. of B.C. Medal for Popular Biography 1970; mem. Am. Assn. for the Advancement of Slavic Studies; Candn. Assn. of Slavists; Candn. Hist. Assn. (Life mem.); Candn. Inst. of Internat. Affairs; Commnr., Candn. Commission of Military History; Johnian Soc.; Royal Commonwealth Soc.; Fellow, Royal Geographical Soc.; Royal Hist. Soc.; Dir., Cambridge Canadian Trust; Art Gallery of Greater Victoria Found.; author, 'Neutralism in the Northern Nato States' 1965; 'Soldiers of the International: A History of the Communist Party of Canada 1919–1929' 1968; 'Kootenai Brown His Life and Times' 1969; 'Joe Boyle King of the Klondike' 1974; numerous articles; recreations: gardening; bird watching, tennis; Home: 308 Denison Rd., Victoria, B.C. V8S 4K3; Office: Royal Roads Military College, FMO Victoria, B.C. V0S 1B0.

**ROE, Gerald L.,** P.Eng.; oil industry executive; b. Cardston, Alta. 28 June 1943; s. Gerald F. and Margaret W. (Brack) R.; e. Montana State Univ., B.Sc. 1965; m. Hazel d. Fred Bloom; children; Rhonda, Lori, Kerri, Charles; Pres., Chief Extve. Offr. & Chrmn., Trilogy Resource Corp. 1984; Sr. Prodn. Engr., Hudson's Bay Oil & Gas Co. 1965–68; Sr. Engr., Texas Pacific Oil Co. 1968–72; Sundance Oil Can. Ltd. 1972–74; Mgr., Candn. Opns. 1974–75; Vice Pres. 1975–77; Sr. Vice Pres. 1977–80; Pres. 1980–81; Vice Pres., Sundance Oil Co. Inc. 1977–80; Pres. 1981; Pres. & Chief Op. Offr., Dir., Acting Chief Extve. Offr. & Acting Chrmn., Trilogy Resource Corp. 1983–84; Dir., DEB Explorations Ltd.; DEB Resources Ltd.; DEB Hydrocarbons Ltd.; DEB Petroleum Internat. Ltd.; Sundance Oil Company Inc. 1975–81; DEB Petroleum (1980) Ltd. 1981–83; Assoc. Dir., Calgary Exhib. & Stampede; Mem., APEGG; Candn. Charolais Assn.; Dir., Alta. Charolais Assn. (Pres. 1978–79); Alta. Cattle Breeders Assn. (Pres. 1983–84); Home: R.R. #1, Airdrie, Alta. T0M 0B0.

**ROEBUCK, Sidney Robert,** B.A., Q.C.; retired judge; b. Toronto, Ont. 23 Apr. 1919; s. Joseph and Ida R.; e. Harbord Coll. 1937; Univ. of Toronto, B.A. 1941; Osgoode Hall Law Sch., grad. 1948; m. Rosie d. Benno and Hana Weisberg 28 Dec. 1948; one d. Helen; active service, Candn. Army 1941–45; law practice, Roebuck & Woolfson 1952–66; Q.C. 1966; Prov. Judge, Prov. of Ont., Criminal Div. 1970–77; Sr. Judge, Judicial District of York (Metro West) 1977–1988; Mem., Adath Israel Cong.; apptd., Life mem. Provincial Criminal Judges Assn.; Dir., Last Post Fund (Ont.).

**ROEDDE, William Adolph,** B.A., B.L.S.; librarian; b. Vancouver, B.C. 10 May 1925; s. William August and Viola Maude (White) R.; e. Univ. of B.C., B.A. 1950; McGill Univ. B.L.S. 1951; children: Mary Gretchen, Stephen August; Librarian Fort William (Ont.) Pub. Lib. 1951–53; Dir. Northwestern Regional Lib. System Thunder Bay, Ont. 1953–58; Asst. Dir. Prov. Lib. Service Govt. Ont. 1958–60, Dir. 1960–80; Dir. Research & Devel. Ont. Pub. Libs. Program Review 1980–81; Museum Archivist, Royal Ont. Museum 1981–85; Can.

Council Fellow 1959; author various lib. and travel articles; served with RCNVR 1944–46, Telegrapher; mem. Candn. Lib. Assn.; Ont. Lib. Assn.; recreations: cycling, canoeing; Home: 16 Oneida Ave., Toronto, Ont. M5J 2E3.

**ROGACKI, Andrew W.,** B.A., M.B.A.; insurance executive; b. Lodz, Poland 21 Sept. 1947; s. Arkadiusz and Helena (Szereszewska) R.; e. Univ. of Calif. at Berkeley B.A. 1971; Univ. of Michigan M.B.A. 1973; m. Pamela d. Nancy and Edwin Dryden 21 Apr. 1973; children: Susan, David; CANDN. DIV. PRES., PROGRESSIVE CASUALTY INSUR. CO. & PRES., PROGRESSIVE CASUALTY INSUR. CO. OF CANADA 1987– ; Sr. Finan. Analyst, General Motors Treasurer's Office N.Y. 1973–74; Sr. Corp. Planner, Pepsico 1975; Mgr., Affiliate Investment Review & Team Leader, Corp. Lending, Mexico, Chase Manhattan Bank 1975–81; Vice-Pres. Corp. Banking Mexico / Latin America / Special Country Unit, Bank of Montreal 1981–87; Home: 39 Danville Dr., Willowdale, Ont. M2P 1J2; Office: 200 Yorkland Blvd., Suite 500, Willowdale, Ont. M2J 5C1.

**ROGAN, R. Eric,** B.Comm., C.A.; business executive; b. Yorkton, Sask. 9 March 1938; e. Univ. of Saskatchewan B.Comm. 1960; EXECUTIVE VICE PRES. & CHIEF FINANCIAL OFFICER, STELCO INC. 1991– ; various managerial positions in acctg. & treas., Stelco Inc. 1964–84; Works Accountant, Hilton Works 1984; General Works Manager, Lake Erie Works 1989; Dir., Extve. Vice-Pres. & Treas., Baycoat; Extve. Ctte. Mem., Jannock Steel Fabricating Co.; Past Bd. Mem., Family Service Agency of the Burlington YMCA and of the Chedoke Hosp.; Mem., Inst. of C.A.s of Ont.; Am. Iron & Steel Inst.; Office: Stelco Tower, 100 King St. W., P.O. Box 2030, Hamilton, Ont. L8N 3T1.

**ROGERS, Benjamin,** B.A., M.Sc. (Econ.); diplomat; b. Vernon, B.C. 3 Aug. 1911; s. Reginald Heber and Anna Elizabeth (Fraser) R.; e. Prince of Wales Coll., Charlottetown, P.E.I. (1927–30); Dalhousie Univ., B.A. 1933; Univ. of London, M.Sc. (Econ.) 1935; m. Frances, d. Dr. M. D. Morrison, Halifax, N.S., 27 Nov. 1939; one s. David M.; prior to joining Dept. External Affairs 1938, employed briefly by Royal Inst. of Internat. Affairs, London, England, and Candn. Inst. of Internat. Affairs (as Acting Nat. Secy. 1937–38); served in Canberra, 1939–43, Washington 1943–44, Rio de Janeiro 1944–48, Ottawa 1948–50; Chargé d'affaires, Prague, 1950–52; Ottawa 1952–55; Ambassador to Peru 1955–58, to Turkey, 1958–60; Deputy High Commr. to Brit., 1960–64; Ambassador to Spain and Morocco, 1964–69; Ambassador to Italy and concurrently High Commr. to Malta 1970–72; apptd. Chief of Protocol, Dept. of External Affairs 1972, retired 1975; co-author (with R. A. MacKay) 'Canada Looks Abroad,' 1938; United Church; recreations: community activities, skiing; Address: 140 Rideau Terrace, Apt. 10, Ottawa, Ont. K1M 0Z2.

**ROGERS, Edward Samuel,** O.C., B.A., LL.B., D.Sc. (Hon.), LL.D. (Hon.); communications executive; b. Toronto, Ont. 27 May 1933; s. Edward Samuel and Velma Melissa (Taylor) R.; e. Upper Can. Coll., Toronto; Univ. of Toronto (Trinity Coll.), B.A. 1956; Osgoode Hall Law Sch., LL.B. 1961; read law with Tory, Tory, DesLauriers & Binnington; called to the Bar Ont. 1962; m. Loretta Anne Robinson, d. Rt. Hon. Lord and Lady Martonmere of Bermuda and Nassau, 25 Sept. 1963; children: Lisa Anne, Edward Samuel, Melinda Mary, Martha Loretta; PRESIDENT AND C.E.O., ROGERS COMMUNICATIONS INC.; Chrmn., Unitel Communications; Vice Chrmn., Rogers Cable T.V. Ltd.; Rogers Cablesystems Ltd.; Rogers Broadcasting Ltd.; Rogers Cantel Inc.; Rogers Cantel Mobile Inc.; Dir., Toronto-Dominion Bank; Canada Publishing Corp.; The Hull Group; Mercedes Benz Canada Inc.; Teleglobe Canada Inc.; Junior Achievement of Canada; Gov., Lyford Cay Club; Sigma Chi; P. Conservative; Anglican; Clubs: Balboa Bay (Calif.); Royal Canadian Yacht; Muskoka Golf & Country; York; Albany; Granite; Rideau (Ottawa); Lyford Cay (Nassau); Canadian Club of New York; Home: 3 Frybrook Rd., Toronto, Ont. M4V 1Y7; Office: P.O. Box 249, Toronto-Dominion Centre, Toronto, Ont. M5K 1J5.

**ROGERS, Harold Allin,** O.C., O.B.E.; Retired; b. London, Ont. 3 Jan. 1899; s. Charles Frederick Arthur and Minnie (Dawe) R.; e. Colborne St. Pub. Sch. and Westervelt Business Sch. London, Ont.; m. Elspeth A. d. Rev. William A. McIlroy 12 Sept. 1925; children: Harold Stewarton, Diane Patricia; former Pres., Canadian Telephones Rentals Ltd.; T. R. Services Ltd.; Beaverton Boatel; former Publisher and Pres., H. A. Rogers & Co. Ltd. (business sold 1970); Chrmn., Telephone Comte., Ont. Hydro Electric Comn. 1953–56; Ont. Telephone Authority (now Comn.) 1956–58; Pres., Ont. Telephone Development Corp. (Crown Co.) 1956–58; Founder, Kinsmen & Kinette Clubs of Canada, Nat. Chrmn. Kinsmen War Services World War II; Pres. Nat. Adv. Council of All Service Clubs of Can. (men and women) after World War II at request Candn. Govt.; Paul Harris Fellow-Rotary Internat.; mem. Bd. Educ. Village of Forest Hill (Chrmn. 1944–51, Vice Chrmn. 1939–43); joined 173rd Argyle & Sutherland Bn. 1916, served in France & Belgium with 54th Kootenay Battalion 1917–18, gassed at Paschendaele, wounded Amiens Front 1918, invalided to Eng., discharged 1919; rec'd Centennial Medal 1967; Queen's Silver Jubilee Medal; Lamp of Learning Secondary Sch. Teachers Ont.; Hon. Citizen of Man. and City of Winnipeg; Freedom of the City given by numerous cities Can.; el. to Hamilton Hall of Distinction 1987; recipient, 125th Anniversary of the Confederation of Canada Medal, 1992; Freemason (Life mem.); United Church; Clubs: Kinsmen & Kinette Clubs of Canada; Address: 7 Overbank Cres., Don Mills, Ont. M3A 1W1.

**ROGERS, Harry G.,** B.A.; Canadian public servant; b. Toronto, Ont. 24 Apr. 1931; s. Lionel Trueman and Ethel Pearl (Gilmour) R. (dec.); e. Univ. of W. Ont. B.A. 1954 (Econ. & Pol. Sci. Gold Medalist); m. Micheline Ouellette 14 Mar. 1987; children: Tanya, Kim; DEPUTY MIN., FEDERAL ECONOMIC DEVELOPMENT (ONT.) 1993– ; joined Ford Motor Co. 1955 served as Sec.-Treas. Malaya, S. Africa, Central Finance Staff Exec. Mich., Gen. Mgr. Ford of Japan, Tokyo; Xerox Corp. 1969–73, Mgr. Internat. Financial Operations Stamford, Conn., Asst. Controller, Operations, Rochester, N.Y.; Vice Pres. Finance/Vice Pres. Mktg., Vice Pres. Operations Xerox Canada Inc. Toronto 1973–78; Comptroller Gen. Treasury Bd. of Can. Ottawa 1978–84; Dep. Min., Taxation Canada, Ottawa 1984–87; Dep. Min., Industry, Science and Technology Canada (Ottawa) 1987–92; Chrmn., Ottawa Gen. Hosp. 1981–89; Dir., Niagara Inst. 1988– ; Dir., Public Policy Forum 1988–91; Home: 88A Glen Rd., Toronto, Ont. M4W 2V6; Office: 1 Front St. W., Toronto, Ont. M5J 1A4.

**ROGERS, Henry Edwin,** B.A., M.Ed., M.A., Ph.D.; university professor; b. Amarillo, Texas 22 May 1940; s. Henry Claibourne and Leta Elena (Spencer) R.; e. Yale Univ. B.A. 1962, M.A. 1965, Ph.D. 1967; Univ. of Toronto M.Ed. 1982; children: David Anthony, Iain Andrew MacEanruig; PROF., DEPT. OF LINGUISTICS, UNIV. OF TORONTO 1967– ; Vice-Pres., Faculty Assn. 1984–89; Pres., Univ. of Toronto Faculty Club 1990–91; author: 'Theoretical and Practical Phonetics' 1991; Office: Toronto, Ont. M5S 1A1.

**ROGERS, James Edward,** B.A., M.B.A., C.H.F.C., C.F.P., R.F.P.; financial advisor; b. Vancouver, B.C. 15 Jan. 1945; s. Lloyd Pryce and Mary Irene R.; e. Univ. of B.C., B.A. 1963; Simon Fraser Univ. M.B.A. 1974; m. Penny d. Bill and Claire Rheinhart 15 Dec. 1973; children: Sandra, Devon, Andrea, Jordan; CHRMN. & CHIEF EXTVE. OFFR., THE JAMES E. ROGERS GROUP LTD. 1974– ; a firm of financial advisors and benefit consultants; Mem., Fraser Inst.; recreations: squash, jogging; Clubs: The Arbutus; Shaughnessy Golf; Home: 4164 Pine Cres., Vancouver, B.C.; Office: 5th Flr., 1770 W. 7 Ave., Vancouver, B.C. V6J 4Y6.

**ROGERS, John A.,** B.Comm., C.A.; health industry executive; b. Toronto, Ont. 4 Oct. 1945; s. the late John A. and Wilma A. (Hazlitt) R.; e. Univ. of Toronto B.Comm. 1968; Clarkson Gordon C.A. 1971; Harvard Univ. Adv. Mngt. Prog. 1984; m. Lynda d. John and the late Pearl Davy 16 Aug. 1968; children: Andrea, Lesley, John; PRESIDENT & CHIEF OPERATING OFFICER, MDS HEALTH GROUP LIMITED 1991– ; Sr. Staff Accountant, Clarkson Gordon 1968–73; Controller, MDS Health Group Limited 1973–76; Sec.-Treas. & C.F.O. 1976–78; Vice-Pres., Finance 1978–85; Pres., MDS Physician Serv. Div. 1985–91; Mem., Young Pres. Orgn.; Bd. of Dir. & Chair, MDS Hudson Valley Labs., Inc.; Ont. Asn. of Medical Labs; Ont. Inst. of C.A.s; Public Accountants Council of Ont.; Lectr., Univ. of Toronto; Auditor, Humber Valley Un. Ch. 1992; Extve. Ctte., Whiting Beach Cottagers' Assn.; recreations: tennis, fitness; clubs: Muskadasa Tennis (Extve. Ctte.; Treas. 1990–92; Pres. 1993– ), Skyline Fitness, Toronto Bd. of Trade, Craigleith Ski; Home: 7 Edenbridge Dr., Etobicoke, Ont. M9A 3E8; Office: 100 International Blvd., Etobicoke, Ont. M9W 6J6.

**ROGERS, John Patrick,** B.A.; executive; b. Montréal, Qué. 14 Feb. 1928; s. James Terence and Alice Quinlan Kavanagh R.; e. McGill Univ. B.A. 1949; m. Maureen S. Loftus 1973; HONORARY DIRECTOR, THE MOLSON COMPANIES LTD.; Dir., Canada Malting Co. Ltd.; Clk. Molson's Brewery Ltd. 1950 becoming Pres. and Chief Exec. Offr., The Molson Companies 1985; Gov. Olympic Trust of Canada; Gov., Montreal General Hospital; Vice Chrmn. YMCA; Patron & Dir., Outward Bound Canada; mem. Adv. Bd. Nat. Assn. Underwater Instrs.; Gov., Royal National Lifeboat Institute (U.K.); recreations: fitness, sports; Address: 40 King St. W., Ste. 3600, Toronto, Ont. M5H 3Z5.

**ROGERS, Lloyd E.,** RRA, RPA, SIOR; realtor; b. Minnedosa, Man. 28 July 1934; s. Gordon Edward and Suzan Eva May (Wheatland) R.; e. Brandon Collegiate; Registered Review Appraiser; Real Property Administrator; Mem., Soc. of Industrial & Office Realtors; m. Mary d. Phil Collins 26 June 1964; children: Clayton, Kimberly, Krista; PRESIDENT, LLOYD REALTY LTD.; Tool Designer, Federal Pioneer 7 years; Real Estate Supvr., Household Finance 5 years; Pres., Lloyd Realty Ltd. 30 years; Rogers Leasing Ltd. 25 years; Lloyd Construction 14 years; Lloyd Interiors Ltd. 9 years; Lloyd Communications 2 years; Lloyd Investments Ltd. 14 years; Nat. Heritage Award 1984; 3rd paper Candn. Construction Congress 1991; Former Chair, Candn. Construction Rsch. Board Sask.; Former Dir., Sask. & Candn. C. of C.; Nat. Chair, Energy Mngt. Task Force (NRCan.); Former Pres., Regina C. of C.; Sask. & Candn. Boma; Former Dir., Boma Int.; Dir., Eastview Rotary 1984; Member 20 years; recreations: hunting, photography, motorsport; clubs: Rotary, Salesmasters; Home: 21 Hogarth Place, Regina, Sask. S4S 4S8; Office: 1779 Albert St., Regina, Sask. S4P 2S7.

**ROGERS, Norman MacLeod,** Q.C., B.A., LL.B., LL.D.; lawyer; b. Halifax, N.S. 20 July 1922; s. Arthur W. MacLeod and Irene Frances (Ganter) R.; e. Upper Can. Coll. Toronto 1938; Westmount High Sch. 1939; Queen's Univ. B.A. (Hons.) 1943 and Hon. LL.D. 1987; Osgoode Hall Law Sch., Barrister-at-law 1948; m. Joan d. Martin and Rita Sowden 22 June 1946; children: Brian MacLeod, Carol Joan, Robert Norman Dean; COUNSEL, BORDEN & ELLIOT 1988– ; called to Bar of Ont. 1948; cr. Q.C. 1961; Assoc. Tilley, Carson & Findlay 1948–88; served with Candn. Army 1943–45; Dir., Augat Electronics Inc.; Past Chrmn., Candn. Scholarship Trust Foundation; Past Chrmn. Bd. Trustees Queen's Univ.; Past Chrmn. Candn. Law Information Council, Ottawa; Chrmn. Law Soc. Foundation, Osgoode Hall; Past Chrmn. Churchill Soc. for Advancement of Parliamentary Democracy; Past National Chrmn., United Nations Assn. in Canada; recipient Centennial Medal 1967; Queen's Silver Jubilee Medal 1977; Life mem. St. Andrew's Soc.; mem., Law Soc. Upper Can., Bencher 1973–79; Candn. Bar Assn. (mem. Council 1962–66); Internat. Bar Assn.; Baptist; Liberal; recreations: tennis, cross-country skiing, fly fishing, tree farming; Clubs: Lawyers' (Pres. 1964); Toronto; Badminton & Racquet; Cuckoo Valley Fishing; Home: 8 Ridgefield Rd., Toronto, Ont. M4N 3H8; Office: 40 King St. W., 42nd Flr., Toronto, Ont. M5H 3Y4.

**ROGERS, Rix Gordon,** C.M., M.Sc.; b. Fort William (Thunder Bay), Ont., 5 June 1931; s. Albert Henry and Evelyn Sadie (Heard) R.; e. Univ. of Toronto, B.A. 1954; Springfied (Mass.) Coll., M.Sc. 1956; YMCA Cert. 1959; m. Barbara Ann, d. Carl Dawes, Franklyn, N.Y., 22 Dec. 1956; children: Mark, Scott, Susan, Deborah, Karin; DIRECTOR EMERITUS, THE INSTITUTE FOR THE PREVENTION OF CHILD ABUSE 1994– ; Chrmn., Finance Ctte., Candn. Found. on Compulsive Gambling 1985– ; Fellowship Student, Counsellor and Group Work Supr. at various YMCA Brs.; Extve. Secy., Lakeshore Br. YMCA 1956–63; Coordinator of Program and Staff Devel., Metrop. Office YMCA, 1963–65; Asst. Gen. Secy., Montreal YMCA, 1965–68; Gen. Secy. 1968–70; Asst. to Pres. 1970–71; Gen. Secy., Nat. Counc. of YMCA of Can. 1971–86; Chrmn., Coalition of Nat. Voluntary Organizations in Canada Apr. 1984 to Nov. 1986; Special Adv. to the Min. of Nat. Health and Welfare on Child Sexual Abuse 1987–90; Interim Dir., Candn. Child Welfare Assn. 1990–91; Chief Extve. Offr., The Institute for the Prevention of Child Abuse 1991–93; Lectr., Dept. of Applied Social Science, Sir George Williams Univ. & mem. Bd. of Govs.; Past Dir., Lakeshore Gen. Hosp. Foundation; mem., Extve. Comte., Montreal Council of Social Agencies; Mem., Economic Council of Canada 1989–92; Bd. mem., Assn. of Leisure Time Services; Past Pres., Pointe Claire Chamber Comm.; Companion, Fellowship of Honour, YMCA Canada 1988; 1st Candn. elected to the YMCA Hall of Fame (Springfield, Mass.) 1988; Member of Order of Canada 1989; recipient, 125th Anniversary of the Confederation of Canada Medal, 1992; Presbyterian; recreations: skiing, golf, boating, camping; Address: 28 Brookfield Rd., Oakville, Ont. L6K 2Y5.

**ROGERS, The Hon. Robert G.;** O.C., O.B.C., K.St.J., LL.D., D.Sc.M., C.D.; b. Montreal, Que. 19 Aug. 1919;

s. George Harold and Eva Rebecca (Gardner) R.; e. Univ. of Toronto Schs.; Univ. of Toronto; m. Elizabeth Jane Hargrave, d. Ralph Henry and Doreen H.; children: R. John, Mrs. Susan Russell, Mrs. R.O. Jackson; CHANCELLOR, UNIV. OF VICTORIA; Lieutenant-Governor of British Columbia, 15 July 1983 to 9 Sept. 1988; former Dir., Candn. Imperial Bank of Commerce; Genstar Corp.; Gulf Can. Ltd.; Canadian Reinsurance Company; Canadian Reassurance Company; Hilton Canada Ltd.; Placer Development Ltd.; RCA Ltd.; Rockwell Intnl. (Canada); Dir., Royal General Insurance Co.; Partner, Norman A. Smith Co., 1945–47; Gen. Mgr., Philip Carey Ltd., Montreal, 1947–50; served in various extve. capacities with Domtar Ltd., 1950–60; joined Crown Zellerbach Can. Ltd. in 1960; el. Dir. and Exec. Vice Pres. 1962; Pres. & C.E.O. 1964–76; Chairman of the Board, 1976–82; Chrmn., Canada Harbour Place Corp., 1982–83; served with Royal Candn. Armoured Corps (1st Hussars) during 2nd World War in U.K. and Europe, including D-Day invasion; Hon. Col., Rocky Mountain Rangers Feb. 1985–90; Former Affiliations: *Business/Professional*: mem., Canada-Asia Pacific Foundation; Canada-Japan Business Cooperation Ctte.; Dir., Intn. Chamber of Commerce (Candn. Council); Trustee, Olympic Trust of Can.; Vice-Chrmn., Pacific Basin Economic Council (Candn. Ctte.); Chrmn., Candn. Pulp & Paper Assoc.; Council of Forest Ind. of B.C.; Forintek Canada Ltd.; Seaboard Lumber Sales Ltd.; Seaboard Shipping Ltd.; *Advisory*: mem., Candn. Business & Ind. Intnl. Advisory Council; Export Trade Development Bd.; B.C.-mem., Univ. of Western Ont. School of Business Admin. Adv. Bd.; Western Business School Club of B.C. Adv. Council; Chrmn., Candn. Extve. Services Overseas (CESO) B.C. Ctte.; Candn. Forestry Adv. Council; *Service*: Hon. Vice Pres., Nat. Council, Boy Scouts of Can.; Bd. of Govs., B.C. Lions; Chrmn., Pacific Region & mem., Nat. Bd. of Govs., Can. Council of Christians & Jews; Dir., Candn. Geriatrics Research Soc.; Council on Candn. Unity; Chrmn., Crofton House School; Vice-Chrmn., Bd. of Govs., Lester B. Pearson College of the Pacific; Chrmn., Bd. of Govs., Victoria Commonwealth Games Soc.; Commissioner, B.C. Forest Resources Commission; mem., Univ. of Victoria Foundation; mem., Rotary Club of Montreal; Convocation Founder, Simon Fraser Univ.; Dir, Intnl. Council, United World Colleges; Resources Ctte., Univ. of B.C.; Council, Vancouver Bd. of Trade; Dir., Nat. Bd., World Wildlife Fund Canada; Mem. Advisory Bd., Military Colleges, Min. of National Defence (Chrmn., Royal Roads Ctte.); Anglican; recreations: golf, fishing; Clubs: Vancouver; Victoria Golf; Union (Victoria); Fairwinds Golf & Country; Address: 701 – 1033 Belmont Ave., Victoria, B.C. V8S 3T4.

**ROGERS, William R.,** B.Ap.Sc., M.B.A., P.Eng.; executive; b. Regina, Sask. 6 July 1940; s. Roy and Grace (Furneaux) R.; e. Davin Sch. Regina; Oak Bay High and Victoria (B.C.) Coll.; Univ. of B.C.B.Ap.Sc. (M.E.) 1963; Stanford Univ. M.B.A. 1968; m. Ann Mary d. D.M. Mackenzie, Trail, B.C. 9 Oct. 1965; children: Janine Grace, Catharine Ann, William Mackenzie; Pres., Prem-Comm Inc. 1989; joined United Aircraft of Canada Ltd. 1963–66 serving as Aerodynamics Engr. and Sales Engr.; American Standard (Div. of Wabco-Standard Ltd.) 1968–76 serving as Asst. to Vice Pres. Finance, Mgr. Systems and Data Processing, Mgr. Engn., Plant Mgr.; joined Canadian Cablesystems Ltd., and Rogers Cablesystems Inc. 1976; Vice Pres., Rogers Cablesystems Inc. 1985–89; Pres., Canadian Cablesystems Ltd. 1985–89; Dir. Cable 10 Mississauga Ltd.; mem. Assn. Prof. Engrs. Prov. Ont.; Assn. Systems Mang.; Bd. Trade Metrop. Toronto; Protestant; recreations: sailing, swimming, curling; Home: 14 Wainwright Dr., Islington, Ont. M9A 2L7.

**ROGERS, William Selby,** M.A.; university professor; b. Toronto, Ont. 6 July 1918; s. William Henry and Lillian Maria Selby (Carter) R.; e. Univ. of Toronto (Trinity Coll.), B.A. (Modern Lang.) 1940; Columbia Univ., M.A. 1941; awarded French Govt. Scholarship for study in France at Sorbonne, 1946–47; m. Marjorie Anne Bryan Sims, 1950 (divorced 1970); children: Patricia Lilian, Cynthia Rae; m. Marjory Peters Seeley 1976; Prof. & Head French Dept., Trinity Coll., Univ. of Toronto, 1949–72; Dean of Arts and Programme Dir. 1973–78; Asst. to the Dean of Arts & Science, Univ. of Toronto (Public Relations) 1984–85; Professor emeritus of French 1984– ; served in 2nd World War, joining R.C.N.V.R. as Sub-Lieut. and serving in Intelligence Div., Naval Service Hdqrs., Ottawa; resigned with rank of Lieut. 1944; joined UNRRA 1944 and served with that organ. overseas till 1946; among other duties assisted in founding UNRRA D.P. Univ. in Munich; Can. Council Sr. Research Fellow in Paris, France, 1961–62 1971–72; Chrmn. of Humanities Research Council of Can., 1964–66; mem. Toronto Mendelssohn Choir 1947–72, Dir. 1950–92; mem., Alliance Française of Toronto (Pres. 1949–52); mem., Candn. Del. to UNESCO Gen. Confs. 1968, 1970; Mem.-at-large, Candn. Nat. Comn. for UNESCO 1970–73; recreations: travel, arts, languages, music; Club: Arts & Letters; Home: 24 Bishop St., Toronto, Ont. M5R 1N2.

**ROHER, Eric Michael,** B.A., M.A., LL.B.; lawyer; b. Toronto, Ont. 4 Aug. 1954; s. Douglas Conrad Roher and Lila (Shiner) Weiss; e. Univ. of Toronto B.A. (Hons.) 1977; Brown Univ. M.A. 1980; McGill Univ. LL.B. 1985; m. Elizabeth Mary d. James and Mary Campbell 22 May 1983; children: Jessica Simone, Rebecca Amy Mirl, Sophie Isabelle Grace; SOLICITOR, BORDEN & ELLIOT 1988– ; called to Bar in Ont. 1987; articled with Tilley, Carson & Findlay 1985–86; Solicitor 1987–88; specializes in labour relations and employment law; particular emphasis on education law, freedom of information and pension issues; also provides advice and advocacy on human rights matters; S.J. Birnbaum, Q.C. Scholarship for Estate Planning, Law Soc. of U.C. 1987; Dir., Candn. Assn. for the Practical Study of Law in Edn.; Pres., St. Andrew-St. Patrick Liberal Riding Assn.; author: 'Labour and Employment Law Reform' 1993, 'Violence in a School Setting' 1993, 'The Social Contract Act and the Municipalities' 1993, 'The Rights of Divorced or Separated Parents to Information Relating to their Child's Education' 1993, 'Sexual Harassment and Municipalities' 1992 and several articles; recreations: canoeing, swimming, cycling, tennis; Home: 92 Wells Hills Ave., Toronto, Ont.; Office: Scotia Plaza, 40 King St. W., Toronto, Ont. M5H 3Y4.

**ROHMER, Richard,** Major-General (retired), C.M.M., O.C., D.F.C., KStJ, C.D., Of.L (Belg.), Q.C., B.A., LL.B., LL.D.; b. Hamilton, Ont. 24 Jan. 1924; s. Ernest and Marion (Wright) R.; e. High Sch. Fort Erie, Ont.; Assumption Coll., Univ. Western Ont., London, Ont., B.A. 1948; Osgoode Hall, Toronto, Ont.; m. Mary-O., d. Walker Whiteside Q.C.; two d.; Catherine, Ann; MEMBER, ROHMER & FENN, Barristers, Toronto; Chancellor Emeritus, U. of Windsor; Chrmn., Royal Comn. on Publishing (Ont.)1970–72; counsel, Royal Comm. on Metro Toronto 1975–77; Chrmn. and Originator, Mid-Canada Devel. Corridor Concept and Conf.; Patron, Metro Toronto St. John Ambulance; called to Bar of Ont. 1951, Bar of Northwest Territories 1970; read law with Phelan, O'Brien and Phelan; cr. Q.C. 1960; served with R.C.A.F. 1942–45 as Fighter Pilot; participated in D-Day invasion of Normandy and with Second Tactical Air Force, France, Belgium and Holland; awarded D.F.C. 1945; flew Vampire jet fighters with R.C.A.F., Toronto, Reserve 1950–53; commanded both 400 Sqdn. (City of Toronto) and 411 Sqdn. (Co. of York) 1952–53; retired 1953, rank Wing Commdr.; apptd. Hon. Lt. Col. and then Col. 411 Co. of York Squadron, Reserve 1971; apptd. Brig. Gen. and Sr. Air Reserve Advisor to chief of Defence Staff and Commander of Air Command, 1975; apptd. Commander of newly formed Air Reserve Group in Air Command 1976; promoted to Major-General & apptd. Chief of Reserves, Can. Armed Forced responsible to Chief of Defence Staff for Militia & Naval, Air and Communications Reserves 1978–81 (ret.); served on Council of Twp. North York 1958–59; served on Bd. Govs. and Secy. North York Gen. Hosp.; former Chrmn., Don Mills Foundation for Senior Citizens Charitable Foundation Inc., operating Thompson House, Home for Aged (138 beds), Don Mills, Ont. and Taylor Place; Bd.; Candn. Bar Assn.; awarded Centennial Medal 1967; Commissioner's Award for Public Service to N. W. Territories 1972; awarded Jubilee Medal 1978; Apptd. Commander of the Order of Military Merit, 1979; Officer of the Order of Leopold (Belgium) 1989; Officer of the Order of Canada 1990; awarded 125th Anniversary of the Confederation of Canada Medal, 1992; LL.D. Univ. of Windsor, 1975; LL.B. York Univ. 1991; author: 'The Green North: Mid-Canada,' 1970; 'The Arctic Imperative' 1973; 'Ultimatum' (novel) 1973; 'Exxoneration' (novel) 1974; 'Exodus/U.K.' (novel) 1975; ' Separation' (novel) 1976; 'E.P. Taylor, 1978' (non-fiction) 'Balls!' (novel) 1979; 'Periscope Red' (novel) 1980; 'Patton's Gap' 1981, (non-fiction); 'Separation II' 1981 (fiction); 'Triad' 1981, (fiction); 'Retaliation' 1982 (fiction); 'How To Write a best seller' (non-fiction) 1984; 'Massacre 747' (non-fiction) 1984; 'Starmageddon' (fiction) 1986; 'Rommel & Patton' (fiction) 1986; 'Red Arctic' (fiction) 1989; Delta Chi; Home: Dundurn Hall, 241 Third St., Collingwood, Ont. L9Y 1L2; Office: Suite 1E, 20 Prince Arthur Ave., Toronto, Ont. M5R 1B1.

**ROHT, Toivo,** M.A.; book publisher; b. Tallinn, Estonia 21 Aug. 1937; s. Juri and Hermilde Pauline (Leibach) R.; e. Coll. Militaire Royal St-Jean, Qué. 1958; Royal Mil. Coll. Kingston B.A. 1960; Queen's Univ. M.A. 1967; m. Sandra d. Edwin and Josephine Goranson 26 Aug. 1960; div. 1985; children: Jeremy, Melissa; m. 2ndly Deborah, d. Howard and Elizabeth Sprague 29 March 1986; PUBLISHER, THOR COMMUNICATIONS 1992– ; Director, Univ. of Ottawa Press 1987–91; served with Candn. Army NATO Forces Europe 1960–63, rank Capt.; Transl. (French to English) Govt. of Qué. 1966–68, Dir. Foreign Lang. Transl. Service 1968–70; Exec. Dir., Candn. Book Publishers' Council 1970–75; Gen. Mgr., McClelland and Stewart Ltd. 1975–78; Dir. of Publ. Nat. Museums of Can. 1978–82; Publisher, Candn. Govt. Publishing Centre 1982–87; Bd. of Dirs., Candn. Book and Periodical Council 1989–91; Assoc. for the Export of Candn. Books 1988–91; Vice Pres., Assoc. québécoise des presses universitaires 1988–91; Mem. Soc. for Scholarly Publishing 1987–91; Bd. Vice Chrmn. & Dir., Ottawa Dance Theatre 1982–87; Montreal Intnl. Book Fair 1972–78; Look of Books Design Competition Corp. 1972–75; contbr. 'Encyclopedia Canadiana' 1974; 'Book Trade of the World' 1975; 'Library Trends' 1978; 'Scholarly Publishing in Canada: Evolving Present, Uncertain Future' 1988; transl. Jean Hamelin 'The Theatre in French Canada 1936–1966' 1967; 'Government of Quebec and the Constitution' 1967 and other publs.; recreations: sailing, photography; Club: Royal Military Coll.; Home: 1658B River Road, R.R. #3, Manotick, Ont. K4M 1B4.

**ROKEBY-THOMAS, Rev. Howard R.,** P.H., E.C.L.J., B.Sc., L.Th., M.A., Ph.D., F.R.G.S., F.R.S.A. (Ang.), F.H.S.C.; b. Eastcombe, Gloucestershire, Eng., 13 June 1907; s. Egbert Ivan and Ethel Ann (Bartlett) T.; e. Inst. Philotech, Bruxelles B.Sc. (Econ. Geog.) 1935; Wycliffe Coll., Toronto, L.Th. 1939; M.A. 1960; Ph.D. (Burton) 1961; m. Anna Elma, R.N., d. Frederick Edwin Roszell, Puslinch, Ont., 10 Aug. 1936; children: Emily (Mrs. Dr. J. W. McLean), David, Derwyn; Rector, Kirkton, Ont. 1969–72; Port Stanley Marina Limited Executive Vice President 1959–62 Director, 1959–71; o. Deacon and Priest, Toronto, 1934; Missy., Cambridge Bay, Victoria Land, 1934–39; 1st Missy. to visit King Wm. Land and Matty Isl., 1936; mem., Univ. of Toronto - Yale Univ. seminar conference on North American Indian 1939; Rector Walter's Falls 1939–41; Port Stanley, 1948–60, Diocese of Huron; Advertising Mgr., 'Canadian Churchman,' 1958–69 and Huron 'Church News,' 1950–67; Hon. Asst., Christ Ch., Scarboro, Ont., 1960–62; Church of The Redeemer, Toronto, 1963–69; served in World War 1941–45 as H. Capt. with Candn. Chaplain Service in Can. and U.K. and with Roy. Candn. Regt. in Italy; Fellow Roy. Commonwealth Soc.; mem., Soc. of Genealogists; Ont. Genealogical Soc.; Hon Soc. of Cymmrodorion; at one time interested in aviation and was one of original mem. of the London Aeroplane Club 1925; has lect. to Roy. Geog. Soc. on S.E. Victoria Island and the Queen Maud Gulf 1944; author: 'Church in the Valley,' 1949; 'Chronicle of the Rooks and Ravens,' 1950; 'The Family of Roszell in Canada' 1986; 'Illumino' 1989; Contbr., 'Encyclopedia Arctica'; articles in learned and popular publ. since 1931; Hospitaller Order of St. John of Jerusalem, Knight 1972, Bailiff Grand Cross 1975, Grand Chancellor 1975–78; Grand Bailiff 1979–80, Prelate 1981 (Grand Priory of Can.); Military and Hospitaller Order of St. Lazarus of Jerusalem, Knight 1974; Ecclesiastical Commander, 1981; Hon. Sr. Fellow, Renison College (Univ. of Waterloo) 1985; Freemason; recreation; travel; Club: Empire; Address: Apt. C-313, Saint Luke's Place, 1624 Franklin Blvd. (H), Cambridge, Ont. N3C 3P4.

**ROLAND, Charles Gordon,** M.D.; educator and historian; b. Winnipeg, Man. 25 Jan. 1933; s. John Sanford and Ethel Leona (McLaughlin) R.; e. Kenora-Keewatin Dist. High Sch. 1951; Oakwood Coll. Inst. Toronto 1952; Univ. of Toronto premed. 1952–54; Univ. of Man. M.D., B.Sc. (Med.) 1958; m. Constance Lynn d. late Dr. Roy W. Rankin, Tillsonburg, Ont. 22 Sept. 1979; JASON A. HANNAH PROF. HISTORY OF MEDICINE, McMASTER UNIV. 1977– , Assoc. mem. Dept. Hist. 1978– ; private med. practice Tillsonburg, Ont. 1959–60, Grimsby, Ont. 1960–64; Sr. Ed. Journal of Am. Med. Assn. Chicago 1964–69; Lectr. Northwestern Univ. 1968–69; Chrmn., Dept. of Biomedical Comm., Mayo Clinic & Mayo Foundation, Rochester, MN, 1969–77; Assoc. Prof. Mayo Med. Sch. Rochester 1969, Prof. 1973–77; Sid Richardson Visiting Professor of Medical Humanities, Univ. of Texas Medical Branch, Galveston 1984; Curator, Osler Lib. McGill Univ.; coeditor 'Sir William Osler: An Annotated Bibiography with Illustrations' 1987; 'Secondary Sources in Canadian Medical History: A Bibliography' 1984; ed., 'Health, Disease and Medicine: Essays in Canadian History' 1983; author: 'Clarence Meredith Hincks: A Biography' 1990; 'Courage Under Seige: Disease, Starvation, and Death in the Warsaw Ghetto' 1992; co-author 'An Annotated Bibliography of Canadian Medical Periodicals 1826–1975' 1979; 'An Annotated Checklist of Osleriana' 1976; Ed. bd., 'Canadian Bulletin of the History of Medicine', 'Journal History of Medicine & Allied Sciences (New Haven) and 'Scientia Canadensis'; numerous scholarly publs. hist. med. Can., hist. med. journalism and hist. World War II; mem. Am. Osler Soc. (Pres.); Candn. Soc. Hist. Med. (Pres. 1993–95); Internat. Soc. for the History of Medicine; Am. Assn. Hist. Med. and other assns.; recreations: mountaineering, scuba diving; Clubs: Literary (Chicago); Osler (London, Eng.); Toronto Med. Hist.; Theta Kappa Psi; Home: Ste. 1106, 1201 North Shore Blvd., Burlington, Ont. L7S 1Z5; Office: 3N10–HSC, Hamilton, Ont. L8N 3Z5.

**ROLFES, Hon. Herman Harold,** B.A., B.Ed., M.Ed.; b. Humboldt, Sask. 13 July 1936; s. Joseph and Josephine (Heckmann) R.; e. St. Peter's Coll. Muenster, Sask.; Teachers' Coll. Saskatoon 1955–56; Univ. of Sask. B.A. 1960, B.Ed. 1964, Masters Degree in Guidance & Counselling 1971; m. Myrna Josephine d. Robert Hopfner, Lake Lenore, Sask. 4 Apl. 1961; children: Debora Lynne, Brian Joseph; former Princ. St. Paul's N. Elem. Sch. Saskatoon, St. Charles Elem. Sch., Bishop Murray Elem. Sch., St. Philip's Elem. Sch.; former Dir. of Guidance, Holy Cross High Sch. Saskatoon; el. M.L.A. for Saskatoon Nutana South 1971, re-el. 1975, 1978, 1986, 1991; Min. of Social Services, 5 Nov. 1975; addit. portfolio of Min. of Continuing Education, 21 Dec. 1978; mem., Treasury Bd.; Min. of Health, Sask. 1979–82; elected Speaker of Sask. Leg. Ass. 1991; Past Pres., Saskatoon Elem. Teachers' Assn.; St. Thomas More Alumni Assn.; K. of C.; NDP; R. Catholic; recreations: tennis, golf, curling; Home: 2802 Calder Ave., Saskatoon, Sask. S7J 1W1.

**ROLLAND, Lucien Gilbert,** O.C., K.C.S.G., D.C.Sc., B.A., B.A.Sc., C.E.; industrialist; b. St. Jerome, Que. 21 Dec. 1916; s. Olivier and Aline (Dorion) R.; e. Jean de Brebeuf Coll. and Loyola Coll., Ecole Polytechnique, Montreal, Que.; Univ. of Montreal, B.A., B.A.Sc., C.E.; m. Marie, d. Louis-Raoul deLorimier, 30 May 1942; children: Nicolas, Natalie, Stanislas, Dominique, Christine, Etienne, David; CHAIRMAN, ROLLAND INC. (Estbd. 1882) Chrmn. & Dir., Rolland Paper Corp.; Select Robinson Inc. formerly C.H. Robinson Paper Co.; Dir., Atlantic Salmon Fedn.(U.S.); Chrmn., & C.E.O., Atlantic Salmon Fedn. (Can.); Hon. Dir., Montreal Symphony Orchestra; Governor, Notre Dame Hospital; Hôpital Marie Enfant; Montreal Children's Hosp.; Montreal Gen. Hosp.; Hon. Vice Pres., Canadian Red Cross Soc.; began as Engr., Rolland Paper Co. Ltd., Mt. Rolland, Que., 1942; Mgr., St. Jerome Mill, 1947; Asst. Gen. Mgr., 1949; Vice-Pres. and Gen. Mgr., 1952; Pres. and Gen. Mgr. 1952; Pres. & C.E.O., 1978; Chrmn., Pres. & C.E.O., 1984; Chrmn. & C.E.O., 1985; Chrmn. 1991; cr. Kt. Commdr. Order of St. Gregory 1958; mem., Candn. Pulp & Paper Assn.; Order Prof. Engrs. Que.; Montreal Bd. of Trade; Candn. Chamber Comm.; Chambre de Comm. de la P.Q.; Engn. Inst. Can.; (Hon.) mem., Univ. of Montréal Bd. of Dirs.; Roman Catholic; recreations: hunting, fishing; Clubs: Forest & Stream; St-Denis; Montreal Indoor Tennis; Mount Royal; Home: 1321 Sherbrooke St. W. Apt. B-60, Montreal, Que. H3G 1J4; Office: Suite 1400, 2000 McGill College Ave., Montreal, Que. H3A 3H3.

**ROLLASON, W. Peter,** B.Comm., C.A.; real estate executive; b. Toronto, Ont. 26 April 1939; s. William and Margaret (Lucas) R.; e. Univ. of Toronto B.Comm. 1962; Price Waterhouse C.A. 1966; m. Suzanne d. Howard and Margery Griffin 17 Sept. 1964; children: Heather, Michael, Leslie; CHIEF FINANCIAL OFFICER, ROYAL LEPAGE LIMITED 1987– ; Price Waterhouse 1963–76; Regional Controller, Royal LePage Limited 1976–82; Controller 1982–87; Mem., Govt. Affairs Ctte., FEI; Adv. Council for Business Sch., Centennial College; Office: 400, 39 Wynford Dr., Toronto, Ont. M3C 3K5.

**ROLLINS, Maurice H.;** contractor/developer; motel executive; b. Tweed, Ont. 25 May 1927; s. Harry Wilmot and Maude Sarah (Houston) R.; e. Belleville C.I. grade XIII; Pharmacist Apprenticeship; m. Marilyn d. Art and Gena MacDermaid 15 Oct. 1971; children: Peter, Mark, Christine, John, Jeff; PRESIDENT AND OWNER, M.H. ROLLINS INVESTMENTS INC., JOURNEY'S END MOTELS INC., JOURNEY'S END U.S.A., JOURNEY'S END DEVEL. LTD. and CONTINENTAL JOURNEY'S END INC. 1980– ; CHRMN. & C.E.O., JOURNEY'S END CORP. 1986– and CHRMN. CHOICE HOTELS CANADA 1993– ; Pres. and Owner: Rollins Construction Ltd. 1955–80; Rollins Lumber Ltd. 1962–80; Rollicare Inc. Property Mgmt. 1968–80; Bay City Constrn., Tackaberry Farms, B.E.P. Constrn., Mapleview Realty Ltd., Almo Developments Ltd., Auden Park Developments Ltd. 1960–80; Fontaberry Homes Residential Constrn. England, France, Switzerland 1965–69; Dir. and Cons. to Rollins Constrn. Ltd. (a subsid. of Standard Trustco) 1980–86; mem. United Ch.; recipient Ont. C. of C. Award for Business Achievement (Journey's End Motels Inc.) 1984; recipient Canada Award for Business Excellence, Entrepreneurship category 1987; recreation: tennis; Club: Belleville Sales and Advertising; Home: R.R. #2, Belleville, Ont. K8N 4Z2; Office: 199 Front St., Ste. 100, Belleville, Ont. K8N 5H5.

**ROMAINE, Henry Simmons,** B.A.; insurance executive; b. New York, N.Y. 30 May 1933; s. Theodore Cole and Cornelia Neilson (Simmons) R.; e. St. Mark's Sch., Southboro, Mass., 1950; Harvard Coll., B.A. 1954; m. Susan Donaldson; children: Henry S. Jr., Hilary H., Kathryn K.; Vice Chrmn. & Chief Investment Offr., American General Corp.; Pres. & Trustee, Mutual of New York 1981–86; joined Mutual of New York as Invest. Analyst 1958; former Chrmn. and Trustee, MONY Real Estate Investors; Former Dir., MONY Life of Can.; Life Insurance Council of N.Y.; Dir., Financial Life Assurance Co. of Canada; mem. Adv. Bd., Chemical Bank; served as U.S. Naval Aviator 1954–57; rank Lt. on discharge; Episcopalian; Clubs: The Links; Harvard; The Houston; Home: 606 West Friar Tuck, Houston, Texas 77024; Office: 2929 Allen Parkway, Houston, Texas 77019.

**ROMAN, Stephen George,** B.A.; business executive; b. Toronto, Ont. 3 Feb. 1953; s. Stephen B. and Betty (Gardon) R.; e. Univ. of Guelph B.A.; m. Janine Paula d. Gino and Silvana Cilio 31 Mar. 1990; children: Abianna, Kristina; PRES., EXALL RESOURCES LIMITED (international mineral exploration and development); worldwide experience with natural resource development; successfully financed & devel. oil & gas and gold projects in W. Africa, Guyana, S. Am. & Alta.; spent several years as under ground and open pit miner progressing through engr. depts. & later devel. projects & mngt.; Vice-Pres. & Dir., Exploration & Devel. Denison Mines Ltd.; Roman Corp.; mem., Candn. Institute of Mining, Metallurgy and Petroleum; Dir., World Wildlife Fund; Yodan Kobujitsu Karate Doh Fed.; commercial pilot; Trustee, Candn. Warplane Heritage Mus.; Mem., Experimental Aircraft Assn.; recreations: flying, scuba diving, tennis; Office: 8 King St. E., Suite 1705, Toronto, Ont. M5C 1B5.

**ROMANCHUK, Judith M.,** B.Sc.; investment executive; b. Edmonton, Alta. 1 Nov. 1946; d. John William and Zenovia Elziene (Sauchuk) R.; e. Univ. of Alta. B.Sc. 1967; Candn. Securities Course; Security Inst. Am. Wharton Sch. of Bus. 1980; SENIOR VICE-PRES. & BRANCH MGR., BBN JAMES CAPEL INC.; Vice Pres. and Dir., Dean Witter Reynolds (Canada) Inc. 1982; Dir. Alberta Television Network Corp.; Export Development Corp. (Audit Ctte. 1990); Hon. Consul Finland, Calgary; mem. SAGIT - Financial Services; invest. dealer since 1970; Dir. Nat. Ballet; Trustee Alta. Blue Cross; MAC - Faculty of Bus. Univ. of Calgary, mem. Exec. Council and Chairperson Govt. Relations Ctte.; recipient, Order of White Rose of Finland, Knight's Cross First Class 1988; Past Pres.: Calgary S. Fed. P. Cons. Assn.; Calgary Egmont P. Cons. Assn.; Past Dir. Calgary C. of C.; Trustee, Cathedral Church of the Redeemer Heritage Bldg. Trust; recreations: skiing, tennis, music, collecting Candn. art; Office: 702, Home Oil Tower, 324 - 8 Ave. S.W., Calgary, Alta. T2P 2Z2.

**ROMANOW, Hon. Roy John,** Q.C., B.A., LL.B.; s. Michael and Tekla R.; e. Bedford Rd. Coll.; Univ. of Sask.; m. Eleanore; PREMIER OF SASKATCHEWAN 1991– ; el. M.L.A. for Saskatoon Riversdale prov. g.e. 1967, re-el. until 1982 then 1991; Prov. Secy. 1971–72; Atty. Gen. 1971–82; Min. of Intergovernmental Affairs, Sask. 1979–82; el. M.L.A. for Saskatoon Riversdale prov. g.e. 1986; el. Leader, Sask. N.D.P., Leader of the Opposition 1987; played major role in the inter-provincial negotiations which led to the patriation of the Canadian Constitution and the formulation of the Canadian Charter of Rights and Freedoms; co-author 'Canada Notwithstanding' 1984; Office: Rm. 226, Sask. Leg. Bldg., Regina, Sask. S4S 0B3.

**ROMANOW, Walter Ivan,** B.A., M.A., Ph.D.; educator; b. Saskatoon, Sask. 29 Apr. 1924; s. Dmytro and Maria (Samson) R.; e. Univ. of Sask. B.A. 1951; Univ. of Windsor M.A. 1964; Wayne State Univ. Ph.D. 1974; m. Yvonna, d. Ivan Schepansky, 1 Jan. 1949; children: Mrs. Oksana Stewart; Martin; Mrs. Lydia Beaudry; Stephen; PROF. EMERITUS; PROF. OF COMMUNICATION STUDIES, UNIVERSITY OF WINDSOR since 1968; Operations and Station Mgr., CFQC-TV, Saskatoon 1953–63; Aide-de-Camp to Lt. Gov. of Sask., 1960–63; Lectr. in English and Dir., Media Centre, Univ. of Windsor, 1964–67; Chrmn., Dept. of Communication Studies, 1968; Dean of Student Affairs 1986–87; Dean, Faculty of Social Science 1981–86; awarded Citation for Outstanding Contribution to University Teaching, Ont. Confederation of Univ. Faculty Assns. 1973; Certificate of Appointment, City of Windsor 1977; Trustee, Windsor Public Library Bd.; mem. bd., John Howard Soc., Windsor and Essex County 1979–81; Dir., Candn. Journal of Communications 1982–87; co-author 'Mass Media and Political Processes in Canada' 1983; 'Media Canada: An Introductory Analysis' 1992; author and co-author numerous articles in journals and periodicals in field of communications; mem. Internat. Press Inst.; Assn. for Education in Journalism; Royal Candn. Legion; Candn. Parachute Battalion Assn.; Candn. Communication Assn. (past Vice-Pres.); served in Royal Candn. Corps of Signals (Reserve) 1940–42; Candn. Army, parachutist with British Sixth Airborne Div. 1942–46; recreations: golf; bicycling; military history; Home: 11135 – 83 Avenue, Suite 2101 College Plaza, Edmonton, Alta. T6G 2C6.

**ROMBOUT, Luke,** C.M., B.F.A., F.R.S.A.; museum executive; b. Amsterdam, Holland 4 May 1933; e. Amsterdam; Mount Allison Univ. B.F.A. 1967; Univ. of Cal. Berkeley Cert. Museum Mgmt. Inst. 1980; EXEC. DIR. McCORD MUSEUM OF CANDN. HIST. 1989– ; came to Can. 1954, Candn. Citizen 1959; Asst. Curator Beaverbrook Art Gallery Fredericton 1960; Lectr. in Candn. Art Hist. Mount Allison Univ. 1968–71, Acting Curator Owens Art Gallery 1965–67, Curator 1967, Dir. 1968–71; Lectr. in Art Hist. N.S. Coll. of Art & Design 1970; Dir. and Asst. Prof. Prog. in Visual Arts York Univ. 1971–72; Lectr. in Candn. Art Hist. Univ. of Ottawa 1974–75; mem. Adv. Panel Can. Council 1969–70, Dir. Art Bank, Canada's Council 1972, Head Visual Arts & Film Sect., Canada's Council 1974; Dir. Vancouver Art Gallery 1975; mem. Bd. Anna Wyman Dance Theatre 1976; Juror 1st Candn. Biennale Prints & Drawings Calgary 1978; mem. Candn. Museums Assn. (Council 1968–71, Chrmn. Profl. Relations Ctte. 1970–71, Vice Pres. 1970–71); Candn. Art Museums Dirs. Orgn.; Am. Assn. Museum Dirs.; Assn. internat. des critiques d'art (Dir. 1982, Pres. Candn. Sect.); Visual Arts Consultant, EXPO '86, Vancouver; Home: Le Cartier, 1115 Sherbrooke St. W., Montreal, Que. H3A 1H3; Office: 690 Sherbrooke St. W., Montreal, Que. H3A 1E9.

**ROMPKEY, Hon. William H.,** M.P., M.A.; politician; b. Belleoram, Nfld. 13 May 1936; s. William Henry and Margaret Lillian Edith (Fudge) R.; e. Bishop Feild Coll. St. John's, Nfld.; Mem. Univ. of Nfld.; Univ. of London; Univ. of Toronto; m. Carolyn Cicely d. Harvey and Dorothy Pike, St. John's, Nfld. 15 Apl. 1963; children: Hilary Nanda, Peter Jonathan; CHRMN., HOUSE OF COMMONS STANDING CTTE. ON NATIONAL DEFENCE AND VETERANS AFFAIRS and CO-CHRMN., SPECIAL JOINT CTTE. ON CANADA'S DEFENCE POLICY 1994– ; Supt. of Educ. Labrador 1968–71; Pres., Labrador N. Chamber Comm. 1968–69; former Lt. RCN (R); el. to H. of C. for Grand Falls-White Bay-Labrador g.e. 1972, re-el. since (riding renamed Labrador for 1988 election); Parlty. Secy. to Min. of Environment 1972 and to Min. of Manpower & Immigration 1974; Appointed Min. of Revenue, 1980; Min. of State (Small Business & Tourism), Canada 1982–83; Min. of State (Mines) Jan. 1984; Min. of State (Transport), June 1984; Opposition Critic, Consumer and Corporate Affairs, Sept. 1984, Defence, Sept. 1985–Jan. 1987; Secy. of State and Mines Jan. 1987–88, Defence 1988–93; Liberal; Anglican; Home: 4 Costello Ave., Ottawa, Ont. K2H 7C4; Office: House of Commons, Ottawa, Ont. K1A 0A6.

**RONALD, Allan Ross,** B.Sc., M.D., F.R.C.P.(C); physician, educator, researcher; b. Portage, Man. 24 Aug. 1938; s. David E. and Muriel M. (MacFarlane) R.; e. Univ. of Manitoba 1955–61 B.Sc. and M.D. (Hons.); Univ. of Maryland 1962–65; Univ. of Washington 1965–68; m. Myrna Jean d. Peter and Mary Marchyshyn Oct. 1962; children: Wendy, Sandra, Vickie; ASSOC. DEAN, UNIV. OF MANITOBA FACULTY OF MEDICINE, RSCH. 1993– and HEAD, SECTION OF INFECTIOUS DISEASES, ST. BONIFACE GEN. HOSP. 1991– ; Head, Infectious Diseases, Univ. of Manitoba/Health Sci. Centre 1968–85; Prof. & Head, Med. Microbiology, Univ. of Man. 1976–85; Distinguished Prof. & Head, Dept. of Internal Med., Univ. of Man. & Physician-in-Chief, Health Sci. Centre 1985–90; Visiting Prof., Univ. of Nairobi 1980–93; Extve. Ctte., Medical Research Council 1990–93; Councillor, Infectious Disease Soc. of Am. 1990–93; Bd. Mem., Candn. Bacterial Diseases Network 1990– ; Univ. of Manitoba Alumni Jubilee Award 1990; Thomas Parran Award, Am. Ven. Disease Assn. 1991; Pres., Christian

Medical Dental Soc. 1977–78; Founding Leader, Assiniboia Charleswood Community Ch.; author of over 200 scientific pubns. and 140 book chapters & reviews; recreations: skiing, water sports; Home: 3232 Assiniboine, Winnipeg, Man. R3K 0B1; Office: 409 Tache Ave., Winnipeg, Man. R2H 2A6.

**RONALD, Thomas Iain,** B.Law, M.B.A., F.C.A.; bank executive; b. Glasgow, Scot. 16 Feb. 1933; s. Newton Armitage and Elizabeth Rae (Crawford) R.; e. Hutchesons' Grammar Sc. Glasgow 1950; Glasgow Univ., B.Law 1956; Inst. of C.A.'s of Scotland, C.A. 1956; Harvard Business Sch., M.B.A. 1963; m. Cristina d. Daniel and Thérèse de Yturralde 30 Aug. 1962; children: Christopher, Isobel; VICE-CHRMN., CIBC 1992– ; Dir., CIBC; Adv. Bd. of Dirs., Amdahl Canada Ltd.; The North West Company Inc.; Loblaw Companies Limited; Wittington Investments, Ltd.; Leon's Furniture Ltd.; Mobil Oil Canada, Ltd.; Chrmn., Commcorp Financial Services Inc.; Articled Clk. Peacock & Henry, Glasgow 1950–55; Sub-Lt. R.N. 1956–58; various Controller positions Alcan Aluminum Ltd 1958–61; Mgr. Peat, Marwick & Mitchell, N.Y. & Paris 1963–65; Vice Pres. Finance, Indal Ltd. 1965–71, Gamble Canada Ltd. 1971–72; Treas. Hudson's Bay Co. 1972–74, Controller Dept. Stores 1974–75, Vice Pres. Finance 1976–81; Pres. and Chief Exec. Offr. Zellers Inc. 1982–85; Exec. Vice Pres., & Dir., Hudson's Bay Co. 1985–87; Pres., Mngmt. Services Group, CIBC 1987–88; Pres., Administrative Bank, CIBC 1988–92; Fellow, Inst. of C.A.'s of Ont. 1982; Dir. Toronto Symphony Orch.; mem. Lawrence Pk. Community Ch.; recreations: tennis, squash, music,; Clubs: Granite; Cambridge; Toronto Hunt; Montreal Badminton & Squash; Toronto; Home: 24 Crescent Rd., Toronto, Ont. M4W 1S9; Office: Commerce Court West, Toronto, Ont. M5L 1A2.

**RONALD, William,** R.C.A.; artist; broadcaster; b. Stratford, Ont. 13 Aug. 1926; s. William Stanley and Lillian May (Plant) Smith; e. Ont. Coll. of Art 1951; m. Helen Marie d. Russell Higgins, 6 Sept. 1952 (div. 1988); two d. Suzanne Marie, Dianna Louise; m. Alana Michelle d. Jack Harris 18 Nov. 1989; Founder, Painters Eleven; One-Man Shows: Hart House Univ. of Toronto 1954; Greenwich Gallery Toronto 1957; Kootz Gallery New York 1957, 1958, 1959, 1960, 1962, 1963; Laing Galleries Toronto 1960; Isaacs Gallery Toronto 1963; Douglas Coll. Rutgers Univ. 1963; David Mirvish Gallery Toronto 1965; Dunkelman Gallery Toronto 1965; Tom Thompson Mem. Gallery Owen Sound 1971: Brandon Univ. 1972; Robert McLaughlin Gallery Oshawa 1975; Morris Gallery Toronto 1975; Musee d'Art Contemporain Montreal 1975; Rodman Hall Arts Centre St. Catharines 1975; Beaverbrook Art Gallery Fredericton 1975; Confederation Centre Art Gallery & Museum Charlottetown 1975; Edmonton Art Gallery 1975; Burnaby Art Gallery 1976; Art Gallery of Windsor 1976; Gustafssen Gallery Brampton 1976; one man shows, Morris Gallery, Toronto 1977–80; Gallery Quan. Toronto 1981 & 1982; Wells Gallery, Ottawa, 1981; Galerie Dresdnere, Toronto 1983; 'William Ronald – The Prime Ministers,' Art Gallery of Ontario, Toronto, Windsor Art Gallery, Manulife Centre, Edmonton 1984; Moore Gallery, Hamilton 1984; Robert Vanderleelie Gallery, Edmonton 1984; Galerie La Belle Epoque, Montreal 1985; Art Gall. of N.S., Halifax, N.S. 1985 and The New Brunswick Museum, St. John, N.B.; La Galerie d'Arts Contemporains, Montreal 1987; 'William Ronald – The Prime Ministers,' The Joliette Museum, Joliette, Que. 1988; rep. in 70 museums and pub. colls. incl.: Art Gallery of Ont., Brooklyn Museum, Carnegie Inst., Solomon R. Guggenheim Museum, Museum of Modern Art N.Y., Nat. Gallery of Can., Montreal Museum of Fine Arts, Phoenix Art Museum, Baltimore Museum of Art, Gallery of Modern Art Washington, Newark Museum, N.J. State Museum; bibliog. 'A Concise History of Canadian Painting,' 'Four Decades,' 'Great Canadian Painting,' 'On the Enjoyment of Modern Art,' 'Contemporary Canadian Painting,' '300 Years of Canadian Art,' 'Catalogue, Toronto Painting 1953–65,' 'Contemporary Canadian Art,' 'Landmarks in Canadian Art,' art journs. and mags. incl. 'Art International,' 'Macleans,' 'New Yorker,' 'Time' and 'Saturday Night'; host CBC TV 'The Umbrella' 1966–67, CBC FM Radio 'Theme & Variations' 1968, CBC Radio 'As it Happens' 1969–72, CITY-TV 'Free For all' 1972–74; rec'd Hallmark Art Award 1952, Nat. Award-Candn. Sec. Internat. Guggenheim Awards 1956, Second Biennial Exhn. Candn. Painting Nat. Gallery Can. 1957; Can. Council Sr. Arts Award 1977.

**RONSON, R. Louis,** B.Sc., B.Ch.E.; corporate executive; b. Toronto, Ont. 21 Feb. 1915; s. Julius and Sarah (Salzman) Rosenblatt; e. Univ. of Toronto and Lawrence Inst. of Technol. B.Ch.E. 1938; m. Hildegarde d. Anne (Streicher) and Otto Kohle 13 Aug. 1947; children: Jeremy, Rhonda; Vice Chrmn., Ont. Human Rights Commission 1985–91; retired Chrmn. Work Wear Corp. of Canada Ltd. 1982–86; Chrmn. Ella Skinner Uniforms Ltd. 1982–86; La Corp. Work Wear du Que. 1982–86; Dir. (and Chrmn. Audit Ctte.) Bank Hapoalim (Canada) 1982– ; Dir. Constitution Insurance Co. of Canada 1962–88; Gen. Mgr. Sunshine Uniform Supply Co. Ltd. 1952–55, Exec. Vice Pres. 1955–69, Pres. and C.E.O. 1969–74; Pres. and C.E.O. Work Wear Corp. of Canada Ltd. 1975–80, Dep. Chrmn. and C.E.O. 1981; Pres. Textile Rental Inst. of Ont. 1976–81, Pres. Emeritus 1982– ; Dir. Textile Rental Serv. Assn. of Am. 1979–82; Pres. Canada-Israel Chamb. of Comm. 1978–80, Hon. Vice Chrmn. 1986–90, Hon. Chrmn. 1990– ; Commnr., Ont. Human Rights Commission Feb. 1985–Aug. 1985 (Vice Chair Aug. 1985–Aug. 1991; Dir., Trustee, Mt. Sinai Hosp. 1974–89, Bd. of Govs. 1973– ; Trustee, Bequest and Endowment Fund, United Jewish Welfare Fund of Toronto; Dir.: Candn. Friends of Haifa Univ.; Candn. Technion Soc. (Vice Pres. 1984–86); Candn. Society for the Weizmann Inst. of Science 1985–87; RP Eye Research Found. 1979–88; Mgmt. Bd. Leah Posluns Theatre; recipient National Human Relations Award Candn. Coun. of Christians and Jews 1979; Hilde and Lou Ronson Found. for Overseas Students, estbd. by Univ. of Haifa in Israel 1984; Mr. & Mrs. Lou Ronson Family Endowment for Perpetual Student Aid, established at the Hebrew Univ. of Jerusalem; R. Lou Ronson Rsch. Inst. on Anti-Semitism estbd. by League for Human Rights of B'nai Brith Canada 1979; listed in Who's Who of World Jewry; Nat. Co-Chrmn. Candn. Counc. of Christians and Jews 1978–86; Vice-Pres. Jewish Comm. Ctr. 1978–81; Hon. Vice-Pres., 1982– (Dir. 1962–82; apptd. Life Dir. 1982); Nat. Exec., Candn. Jewish Congress 1971–83 (Vice-Chrmn. Ont. Region 1974–80); Ont. Reg. Exec. Candn. Jewish Congress 1971–83, 1992–95; Candn. Jewish Congress National Council 1992–95; Chrmn. Joint Community Reln's Ctte. of Candn. Jewish Congress & B'nai Brith (Ont. Reg.) 1977–79; Pres. B'nai Brith Canada 1979–80; (National Chrmn. League for Human Rights 1974–75; National Archives Chrmn. 1983–89); Exec. Ctte., Internat. Counc., B'nai Brith Internat. 1981–86; Nat. Adv. Counc., Anti-Defamation League of B'nai Brith Internat. 1982– , A.D.L. Comnr. 1968–74, 1980–82; Vice Pres., B'nai Brith International 1988–92 (Bd. of Gov. 1978–80, 1986–92; mem. Adv. Counc. 1984– ); Exec. Ctte. Toronto Jewish Congress 1976–82; City of North York Ctte. on Community, Race & Ethnic Relations 1988–91; recipient, Voluntarism Award, Ont. Min. of Citizenship 1993; Mem., Beth Sholom Synagogue; Royal Arch Masons; Pi Lambda Phi Frat.; Royal Ont. Museum; Art Gall. of Ont.; Candn. Jewish Historical Soc.; lifetime coll. of personal papers on file at National Archives of Canada, Ottawa, Ont.; mem., North York Power and Sail Squadron; recreations: golf, skiing, boating; Club: Oakdale Golf and Country (Dir. 1984–88); Home: 65 Spring Garden Ave., Apt. 2311, Willowdale, Ont. M2N 6H9 and Ruperts Landing, Unit 18, R.R. 3, Collingwood, Ont. L9Y 3Z2.

**ROOKE, Constance Merriam,** M.A., Ph.D.; educator; editor; b. New York City, N.Y. 14 Nov. 1942; d. Charles Merriam and Hilary (Fitch) Raymond; e. Smith Coll. B.A. 1964; Tulane Univ. M.A. 1966; Univ. of N. C. Ph.D. 1973; m. Leon s. Jesse and Louise Rooke 25 May 1969; one s. Jonathan Blue; ASSOCIATE VICE-PRES. ACADEMIC, UNIV. OF GUELPH 1994– ; Prof. of Eng. 1988– ; Chair, Dept. of Eng., Univ. of Guelph 1988–93; Ed. The Malahat Review, Univ. of Victoria 1983– , ed. The Carolina Quarterly 1968–69; Lectr. in Eng., Univ. of Victoria 1969, Asst. Prof. 1973, Assoc. Prof. 1981, Chair (first) Women's Studies Prog. 1979, Dir. Learning & Teaching Centre 1981–83; Dir. Kaleidoscope Theatre; mem. Adv. Ctte. Writing & Publ. Can. Council; author: 'Reynolds Price' (lit. criticism) 1983; 'Fear of the Open Heart' (lit. criticism) 1989; editor: 'Night Light: Stories of Aging' (anthol.) 1986; 'Writing Away: The PEN-Canada Travel Anthology' 1994; other publs. incl. 50 critical essays, 13 short stories and over 100 reviews; 3M Teaching Fellow, 1987; mem. Candn. Periodical Publishers Assn. (Dir.); Assn. Candn. Univ. Teachers Eng.; Candn. Rsch. Inst. Advanc. Women; Extve., Candn. Federation of the Humanities; Bd. of Dirs., PEN International, Candn. Centre; Home: Eden Mills, Ont. N0B 1P0; Office: Dept. of English, Univ. of Guelph, Guelph, Ont. N1G 2W1.

**ROOKE, The Honourable John D.,** B.A., LL.B.; justice; b. St. Rose, Man. 20 Jan. 1948; s. Daniel William and Ethel Irene (Evans) R.; e. Univ. of Sask. Regina B.A. 1970, Saskatoon LL.B. 1970; m. Gayle F.A. d. George (dec'd) and Kathleen Jobson 23 Aug. 1969; children: Marcus D., Laura D.; JUSTICE OF THE COURT OF QUEEN'S BENCH OF ALBERTA 1991– ; articled to Burnet Duckworth & Palmer 1970, practised with 1971–91, Partner 1976–91; admitted to Alta. Bar 1971; admitted to NWT Bar 1978; cr. Q.C. 1987; Past Chrmn., Private Vocational Schools Advisory Council, pursuant to the Alberta Private Vocational Schools Act; Past Mem., Arbitration Bd. on Freight Claims, Alta. Trucking Assn.; Previously apptd. Board of Inquiry Pursuant to the Individual's Rights Protection Act of Alta., Alta. Dept. Labour; Former Adjudicator Labour Canada; Past Chrmn., Arbitration Boards pursuant to Canada Labour Code, Alta. Labour Relations Act & Code, and Alta. Public Service Employee Relations Act; Past Mem.: Law Society of Alta.; Law Society of the Northwest Territories; Calgary C. of C.; Accredited Arbitrator, Alta. Arbitration and Mediation Soc. and Chartered Arbitrator (C.Arb.), Arbitration and Mediation Inst. of Canada Inc.; Past Dir. Royal Canadian Mint; Former Leader, Boy Scouts of Canada; Mem., Candn. Bar Assn.; Calgary Bar Assn.; Anglican; Clubs: Bankers Hall (Calgary); Fairmont Hot Springs Mountainside Golf (B.C.); Office: The Court House, 611 – 4 Street S.W., Calgary, Alta. T2P 1T5.

**ROOKE, Leon;** writer; b. Roanoke Rapids, North Carolina 11 Sept. 1934; s. Jesse Lofton and Louise (Grey) R.; e. Univ. of N. Carolina; m. Constance d. Charles and Hilary Raymond 1969; one s.: Jonathan; O. Henry Award 1965; Candn. Fiction Magazine Annual Prize 1974; Epoch Prize 1975; Nat. Endowment for the Arts Fellowship 1978; Can./Aust. Literary Prize 1981; Author's Award, Paperback Novel of the Year 1981; Gov. Gen Award for Fiction 1983; Author's Award, Short Story 1987; Pushcart Prize 1988; Okanagan Fiction Prize 1989; North Carolina Award for Literature 1990; author: 'Last One Home Sleeps in the Yellow Bed' 1968, 'Vault' 1973, 'Krokodile' 1973, 'The Broad Back of the Angel' 1977, 'The Love Parlour' 1977, 'The Magician in Love' 1980, 'Fat Woman' 1980, 'Cry Evil' 1980, 'Death Suite' 1981, 'The Birth Control King of the Upper Volta' 1983, 'Shakespeare's Dog' 1983, 'Sing Me No Love Songs I'll Say You No Prayers, Selected Stories' 1984, 'A Bolt of White Cloth' 1984, 'How I Saved the Province' 1989, 'A Good Baby' 1989, 'The Happiness of Others' 1991, 'Who Do You Love?' 1992 and approx. 250 short stories publ in N. Am. & Eur. journals & anthologies; plays: 'Sword/Play' 1974 (Cubiculo Theatre, N.Y.); 'Ms America' 1974 (Factory Lab Theatre, Toronto); 'Krokodile' 1974 (Playwright's Coop); 'The Good Baby' 1986, 1990 Rev. version (Caravan Stage Co. B.C.); 'Shakespeare's Dog' 1989 (Workshop West Theatre, Edmonton); 'The Coming' 1991 (Caravan Stage Co.); co-editor: 'Best Canadian Stories' 1981, 1982, 'The New Press Anthology #1' 1984, 'The New Press Anthology #2' 1985; 'The MacMillan Anthology #1' 1988; 'The MacMillan Anthology #2' 1989; Dir., Eden Mills Writers' Festival; Home: 209 Main St., Eden Mills, Ont. N0B 1P0; Office: c/o Bukowski Agency, 125 Dupont St., Toronto, Ont. M5R 1V4.

**ROONEY, Paul George,** B.Sc., Ph.D., F.R.S.C. (1966); university professor; b. New York City, N.Y., 14 July 1925; s. Geoffrey Daniel and Doris Elizabeth (Reeve) R.; e. Univ. of Alberta, B.Sc. 1949; Cal. Inst. of Tech., Ph.D. 1952; m. Mary Elizabeth, d. Albert E. Carlisle, June 1950; children: Francis, Elizabeth, Kathleen, John, James; PROF. EMERITUS OF MATHS., UNIV. OF TORONTO, since 1991; Lecturer, University of Alta., 1952–54, Asst. Prof., 1954–55; Asst. Prof., Univ. of Toronto, 1955–60; Assoc. Prof., 1960–62; Prof. 1962–91; served in 2nd World War with Candn. Army, 1944–45; author of various tech. articles in math. journs.; mem., Candn. Math. Soc. (Pres., 1981–83); Am. Math. Soc.; Math. Assn. Am.; Liberal; Anglican; Home: 7 May Street, Toronto, Ont. M4W 2X9.

**ROONEY, Robert James Campbell;** theatre director; b. Romford, Eng. 30 May 1950; s. Pearse Lucas and Brenda Campbell (Kellock) R.; e. St. Ignatius Grammar Sch. Stamford Hill, Eng.; Edmund Campion Grammar Sch. Hornchurch, Eng.; Drama Centre, Chalk Farm, London, Eng. Dip. Drama 1971; m. Brenda d. Carl Eby 29 May 1975; two d. Rebecca Campbell, Caitlin Polly Violet; Artistic Director, Toronto Workship Productions 1986, Resident Dir. 1985–86; came to Can. 1975; Candn. Citizen 1985; Resident Dir. Dept. of Drama & Film Studies Brock Univ. St. Catharines 1979–82; served as a dir. developing new scripts Playwrights' Workshop Banff Centre for the Arts 1984–86; produced and directed Toronto Arts Against Apartheid Festival Gala, Royal Alexandre Theatre May 1986; plays directed incl. 'Tête à Tête' by Ralph Bordman; 'The Lesson' Ionesco; 'The Real Inspector Hound' Stoppard; 'Gone The Burning Sun' by Ken Mitchell (which toured the People's Republic of China); 'Theatre in the Time of Nero and Seneca' by Edward Radzinsky; 'When the Wind Blows' by Raymond Briggs; 'The Jail Diary of Albie Sachs' by

David Edgar; own adaption of 'A Christmas Carol' by Charles Dickens.

**ROOTMAN, Irving,** B.A., M.Phil., Ph.D.; university professor; b. Calgary Alta. 21 Oct. 1941; s. Sidney Abraham and Lillian (Wolman) R.; e. Univ. of Alberta B.A. 1964; Yale Univ. M.Phil. 1967, Ph.D. 1970; m. Barbara d. Gershon and Gertrude Shaffer 30 Dec. 1967; children: David Elliot, Adam Jay (Shaffer Rootman); PROFESSOR, DEPT. OF PREVENTIVE MED. & BIOSTATISTICS & DIR., CENTRE FOR HEALTH PROMOTION, UNIV. OF TORONTO 1990– ; Rsch. Assoc., Univ. of Calgary Med. Sch. 1970–73; Chief, Epid. & Social Rsch., Non-Medical Use of Drugs Directorate, Health & Welfare Can. 1973–78; Health Promotion Studies, Health Promotion Directorate 1978–87; Consultant, World Health Orgn., Geneva 1979–80; Sr. Scientist 1980–81; Dir., Program Resources Div., Health Promotion Directorate, Health & Welfare Can. 1987–80; Mem., World Health Orgn. Expert Panel on Drug Abuse; Co-Dir., North York Community Health Promotion Rsch. Unit; Mem., Heart Health Action Project and Ont. Heart Health Network steering cttes.; Edit. Bd. Mem., 'Health Promotion International'; Bobbs Merrill Award, Yale Univ. 1967; Co-chair, Healthy Communities Metro; Mem., Nat. Social Action Ctte., Candn. Council of Reform Congregations steering ctte.; co-editor/co-author: 'Health Promotion in Canada' 1994; co-editor: 'Drinking and Casualties' 1990, 'Health Promotion Survey Tech. Report' 1989, 'Community Response to Alcohol Problems' 1984, 'Guidelines for Investigating Alcohol Problems & Developing Appropriate Responses' 1984; recreations: swimming; club: Faculty; Home: 190 Lowther Ave., Unit D, Toronto, Ont. M5R 1E8; Office: 100 College St., Suite 207, Toronto, Ont. M5G 1L5.

**ROOTS, Clive George;** zoo and wildlife consultant; b. Coventry, England 14 Aug. 1935; s. George William and Kathleen Elsie (Waters) R.; e. Aberaeron Grammar Sch.; Ardwyn Grammar Sch.; London Polytechnic Inst.; m. Jean d. Stanley and Irene Cox 1 Oct. 1960; children: Helen Lesley, Simon Paul; ZOO AND WILDLIFE PARK CONSULTANT 1992– ; Supt., Emperor Valley Zoo, Trinidad 1960–62; Gen. Curator, Dudley Zoo, England 1962–66; Curator, Winged World, Morecambe, England 1966–70; Dir., Assiniboine Park Zoo, Winnipeg, Man. 1970–92; Design Cons., Zool. Gardens; Can. Counc. Rsch. Grantee 1975; Mem., Internat. Union of Dir. of Zool. Gardens; Candn. and Am. Assns. of Zool. Parks & Aquariums (Candn. Pres. 1977–78); author: 'Wild Harvest' 1970, 'Softbilled Birds' 1970, 'Apes and Monkeys' 1970, 'Tropical Birds' 1971, 'Exotic Birds for Cage & Aviary' 1971, 'Exotic Pets' 1972, 'Animals of the Dark' 1974, 'Animal Invaders' 1976, 'Endangered Species, Canada's Vanishing Animals' 1987, 'The Bamboo Bears' 1989; recreations: travel, photography; Home: 695 Pine Ridge Dr., Cobble Hill, B.C. V0R 1L1.

**ROOTS, James Douglas,** B.A., M.A., D.B.E.D.; association executive; b. Toronto, Ont. 25 Oct. 1955; s. Reginald Arthur and Irene Margaret (Peto) R.; e. Univ. of Toronto, B.A. 1977; Centennial Coll., dipl. in book editing & design 1981; Humber Coll. & Candn. Ctr. for Philanthrop., cert. in fundraising & mngt. 1989; Carleton Univ. M.A. (Political Sci.) 1994; m. Dorothea-Joan d. James and Daisy (Peterson) Sweeney 1 Oct. 1988; son: Emerson James Arthur; EXTVE. DIR., THE CANDN. ASSN. OF THE DEAF 1986– ; freelance writer & editor 1977–86; author: 'Pah!-litics: Deaf and Disabled Political Participation and Activity' 1992; Dir., Candn. Hearing Soc.; Bob Rumball Ctr. for the Deaf; Adv. Counc. Chairperson, Disability Inform. Serv. of Can.; Founding Delegate, Charter Disability Rights Counc.; Vice-Pres., Walter Dinsdale Centre for the Empowerment of Disabled Canadians; Mem., Ont. Advisory Council on Disability Issues; Office: 205 - 2435 Holly Lane, Ottawa, Ont. K1V 7P2.

**ROPCHAN, Donald James,** B.B.A., F.C.S.I.; financial executive; b. Dauphin, Man. 23 April 1944; s. Peter G. and Doris D. (Heth) R.; e. Univ. of Oregon, B.B.A. 1967; Life Insurance Agency Mngt. Assn., Agency Life Insur. 1968; Fellow, Candn. Securities Inst. 1978; m. Susan S. d. Norman and Katherine Barton 5 May 1990; children: Peter D., Timothy J.; PRESIDENT, CITCO FINANCIAL CORPORATION 1983– ; Agency Sec., Dir. of Agency Training, Dir. of Agencies, etc., The N.W. Life Assur. Co. of Canada 1967–73; Jones Cable & Co. 1973; Securities Broker, Kippen & Co. 1974; Account Extve., Paine Webber Jackson Curtis Ltd. 1974–80; Extve. Vice-Pres., Citco Financial Corp. 1980; Sr. Vice-Pres., N.W. Life Assur. Co. 1980–82; Pres., Citizens Trust Co. 1982–87; Pres. (all since 1983): Citco Finan. Corp., Citco Realty Ltd., Citco Leasings Ltd., Citco Investments Ltd., Citco Growth Investments Ltd.; Secretary, Imperial Evergreen Casket Corp. 1988– ; Pres., Channel View Development Inc. 1992– ; recreations: golf, boating, fishing; clubs: Terminal City; Home: 2655 Bellevue Ave., West Vancouver, B.C. V7V 1E5; Office: 6952 Greenwood St., Burnaby, B.C. V5A 1X8.

**ROPER, Henry,** M.A., Ph.D.; university teacher and administrator; b. Halifax, N.S. 9 Feb. 1940; s. Henry Leamon and Mary Caroline (Hawkins) R.; e. Queen Elizabeth H.S. 1957; Dalhousie Univ. B.A. 1961; Univ. of Cambridge (U.K.) B.A. 1964, M.A. 1968, Ph.D. 1972; m. Phoebe d. Huntly and Margaret (Margot) Redpath 1961; DIR., KING'S FOUNDATION YEAR PROGRAMME 1992– ; Lectr. in Hist., Mount Saint Vincent Univ. 1966–68; Asst. Prof. of Hist., Huron Coll. 1970–76; Jr. Fellow, Univ. of King's Coll. 1977–78; Asst. Prof. of Hum. 1978–80; Assoc. Prof. 1980– ; Registrar 1978–87; Vice-Pres. 1983–86; Interim Vice-Pres., 1991–92; Archbishop Owen Mem. Lectr., Anglican Ch. of Can. 1987; Bd. of Gov., Univ. of King's Coll. 1980–86, 1991– (Sec. 1981–83); Dalhousie Univ. 1983–87; Atlantic Sch. of Theology 1983–86, 1993– ; Prov. of N.S. Student Aid Higher Appeal Bd. 1987–89; Bd. of Dirs., The Dr. Helen Creighton Memorial Found. 1990– ; Anglican; Mem., Royal N.S. Hist. Soc. (Papers Chrmn. 1983–84); The Cambridge Soc.; author: 'Administering the Elementary Education Acts, 1870–85' 1976 and articles & reviews in sch. jours.; recreations: gardening, walking, TV; club: Dalhousie; Home: 1648 Larch St., Halifax, N.S. B3H 3X1; Office: Halifax, N.S. B3H 2A1.

**ROSCOE, Elizabeth A.,** B.A.; b. Hamilton, Ont. 24 July 1956; d. Stan Maurice and Joan Marion (Pipe) R.; e. Univ. of Guelph B.A. 1978; m. 27 Aug. 1988; SENIOR VICE PRES., PUBLIC AFFAIRS AND REGULATORY DEVELOPMENT, CANADIAN CABLE TELEVISION ASSOCIATION 1992– ; Pres. & Chief Operating Offr., Advance Planning & Communications Ltd. 1988–92; Managing Dir., Public Affairs, Earnscliffe Strategy Group 1990–92; Extve. Asst. to Hon. Michael Wilson, P.C., M.P. 1980–83; Consultant, Public Affairs International 1983–84; Chief of Staff to Hon. Barbara McDougall, P.C., M.P. 1984–88; Bd. mem., Children's Hosp. of Eastern Ont.; Progressive Conservative; recreations: skiing, tennis, squash; Club: Albany; Home: Larrimac, Québec; Office: 360 Albert St., Suite 1010, Ottawa, Ont. K1R 7X7.

**ROSCOE, Patrick;** writer; b. Formentera, Spain 8 March 1962; e. Tanzania, E. Africa; Reading, Eng.; Victoria, B.C.; Candn. citizen; author (short stories) 'Beneath the Western Slopes' 1987; 'Birthmarks' 1990; 'Love is Starving for Itself' 1993; (novel) 'God's Peculiar Care' 1991; numerous publs. various Candn. mags. and lit. jours.; rep. various anthols.; recipient Western Mag. Award for Fiction 1984; Candn. Fiction Mag. Annual Contbr.'s Prize 1985; Okanagan Fiction Award 1987; First Prize Short Story CBC Lit. Competitions 1989; Second Prize Short Story CBC Lit. Competitions 1992; Mem., Writers' Union of Canada; PEN Internat.; Address: 3867 Tupper St., Vancouver, B.C. V5Z 3B9.

**ROSE, Albert,** Ph.D.; educator; b. Toronto, Ont. 17 Oct. 1917; s. Mark Edward and Frances (Spiegel) R.; e. Riverdale Coll. Inst. Toronto 1935; (Fourth Alumni Scholarship, University Coll. 1935) Univ. of Toronto B.A. 1939 (H.A.C. Breuls gold Medal); Univ. of Ill. M.A. 1940, Ph.D. 1942; m. Thelma Bernice d. Samuel Aaron Harris, Toronto, Ont. 7 June 1942; children: Jeffrey Raymond, Leslie Harris, Janis Margaret; PROF. OF SOCIAL WORK, UNIV. OF TORONTO since 1956; Prof. Emeritus, 1983; Dir. Ont. Housing Corp.1964–79; Ont. Council Health 1973–79; Beacon Hill Lodges Ltd. Winnipeg 1975–87; Jewish Vocational Service; mem., Scientific Adv. Ctte. Gerontology Research Council of Ont. 1980–90; Hon. mem. Inst. Housing Mang. Ont.; Chrmn., Metropolitan Toronto Housing Authority, 1980–86; Asst. Econ. J. D. Woods & Gordon 1942–43; Research Dir. Welfare Council Toronto 1946–48; Asst. Prof. present univ. 1948, Assoc. Prof. 1952, Dir. Sch. of Social Work 1969–72 and Dean Faculty of Social Work 1972–76; Founding Mem., Centre for Urban and Community Studies (1962) and Program in Gerontology (1976), Univ. of Toronto; Visiting Prof. Bar Ilan Univ. Israel Feb. 1982; Hebrew Univ. of Jerusalem, Candn. Studies Prog. Jan-July 1985; awarded Sr. Fellowship, Central Mortgage & Housing Corp. 1962–63; Centennial Medal 1967; served with Candn. Army 1943–46, rank Lt.; author 'Local Housing Conditions and Needs' 1953; 'Regent Park: A Study in Slum Clearance' 1958; 'Governing Metropolitan Toronto' 1973; 'Canadian Housing Policies, 1935–80,' 1980; Ed. 'A People and Its Faith' 1959; various book chapters, studies for govt'al and voluntary organs., numerous articles in prof. journs.; mem. Candn. Inst. Pub. Adm.; Candn. Assn. Social Workers (Pres. 1971–73); Candn. Council Social Devel.; Internat. Fed. for Housing & Planning; Nat. Assn. Social Workers (US); Candn. Assn. Schs. Social Work; Community Planning Assn. Can. (Vice Pres. 1955); Bd. of Dirs., Candn. Urban Institute 1993– ; Bd. of Govs., Univ. of Haifa, Israel 1993– ; recreations: philately, numismatics; Home: 225 Cortleigh Blvd., Toronto, Ont. M5N 1P6; Office: 246 Bloor St. W., Toronto, Ont. M5S 1A1.

**ROSE, Barrie David,** B.Com., M.B.A., F.C.A., C.A.; b. London, England 1 April 1930; s. Harry and Tema (Hyman) R.; e. City of London Sch. (U.K.); London Sch. of Econ. B.Com. 1951; Inst. of C.A.s C.A. (B.C., Ont. & U.K.); Northwestern Univ. M.B.A. 1955; m. the late Amelia Oelbaum 26 Jan. 1957; children: John Adam, Robert Andrew, Paul Anthony; m. Carol Ann Rose 24 Sept. 1991; CHAIRMAN & CHIEF EXTVE. OFFR., ANDROCAN INC. (& affiliates) 1970– ; Peat, Marwick, Mitchell & Co. (London & Vancouver) to 1953; Koehring Co. 1955–56; Coplan Rose & Assoc. 1956–57; Acme Paper Products (Reed Internat.) 1957–70; Dir., Noma Indus. Ltd.; Harris Steel Group Inc.; Autrex Inc.; F.C.A. 1985; Dir., Roy Thomson Hall; Toronto Symphony Orch.; Technion Univ.; Mount Sinai Hosp.; Baycrest Hosp.; Gov., Weizmann Institute of Science; Ben-Gurion Univ.; Vice-Pres., Nat. Ballet of Canada 1970s; Chrmn., United Way Toronto 1975; Mem., Young Presidents' Orgn. 1970–80; World Presidents' Organization; Candn. Assn. of Family Enterprise; recreations: music, theatre, country, travel, reading, and not exercising; club: Ontario; Home: Suite 3108, 99 Harbour Square, Toronto, Ont. M5J 2H2; Office: 50 Bartor Rd., Weston, Ont. M9M 2G5.

**ROSE, Bram,** B.A., M.D., Ph.D., F.R.C.P., F.A.C.P., F.R.S.C.; b. Montréal, Qué. 21 Apl. 1907; s. Isaac and Sara (Kirschberg) R.; e. Argyle Sch., Westmount High Sch. 1924; McGill Univ. B.A. 1929, M.D. 1933, Ph.D. 1938; m. Rosa d. Stanley and Helen Johnson 31 Dec. 1941; children: Peter Douglas, Ian Robert, Barbara Susan; PROF. EMERITUS OF MED., MCGILL UNIV.; Rsch. Asst. McGill Univ. Clinic 1936–39, Rsch. Assoc. 1939–40; Asst. Prof. of Med. McGill Univ. 1950, Assoc. Prof. 1955, Prof. of Experimental Med. 1964–75; First Harry Webster Thorpe Prof. Experimental Medicine; Asst. Physician Royal Victoria Hosp. Montreal 1942, Assoc. Physician 1951, Physician 1961, Allergist-in-Chief 1951–74, Dir. Div. Immuno-chem. & Allergy 1951–74; First Harry Alexander Visiting Prof. Barnes Hosp. Wash. Univ. St. Louis, Miss.; Visiting Prof. Univ. Hosp. Univ. of London (Eng.) 1970; mem. Allergy & Immunology Training Grant Ctte. U.S.P.H. Nat. Inst. Allergy & Infectious Diseases Bethesda, Md. 1960–65; Chrmn. Ctte. on Standardization Allergens NIH Bethesda 1958–60; mem. Grants Ctte. Immunology & Transplantation Candn. Med. Rsch. Council 1968–72, Centennial Fellowships Ctte. 1972–77; Chrmn. Sci. Adv. Ctte. Trudeau Foundation & Rsch. Inst. Saranac Lake, N.Y. 1975, mem. Bd. Trustees 1965– ; served with RCAF 1940–46, Liason Offr. in Aviation Med. Rsch. London, Eng. 1943–45; author or co-author over 180 sci. papers; Sec. Ed. 'Immunological Diseases' 3 eds. 1961, 1971, 1978; rec'd. Candn. Centennial Medal 1967; Fellow, Candn. Soc. Immunology (Pres. 1971–73, Honoured with an Intnl. Symposium Montreal 1972); honoured with a satellite symposium at the 6th Intnl. Congress of Immunology on 'Regulation of IgE Synthesis' 1986; guest of honour, XX Brazilian Congress of Allergy and Immunology, Rio de Janeiro, Brazil 1986; N.Y. Acad. Sci's.; Hon. Life mem. Candn. Thoracic Soc.; Hon. mem. French, Argentine, Iranian, Mexican, Brit., Australian & Brazilian Allergy Soc's.; mem. Candn. Physiol. Soc.; Am. Soc. Clin. Investig.; Assn. Am. Physicians; Am. Assn. Immunols.; Intnl. Assn. Allergy & Clin. Immunol. (Pres. 1960–61); Am. Acad. Allergy (Pres. 1955–57); Candn. Soc. Allergy & Clin. Immunol. (Past Pres.); Sigma Xi; recreations: music, alpine skiing, electronics; Clubs: 70+ Ski; Peripatetic; Hermitage Club; Home: R.R.3, Magog, Que. J1X 3W4; Office: 22 Laurier, Magog, Que. J1X 2K3.

**ROSE, Clyde,** M.A.; publisher; b. Fox Island, Nfld. 7 Aug. 1937; s. Simeon and Christina (Baggs) R.; e. High Sch. Burgeo, Nfld.; Sir George Williams Univ.; Mem. Univ. of Nfld. B.A. 1959, M.A. 1969; m. Jean Ann d. Laura and Cecil Farrell 2 May 1969; children: Jonathan Benjamin, Rebecca Laura Elizabeth; FOUNDER AND PRESIDENT, BREAKWATER BOOKS LTD. 1973– ; Teacher, Corner Brook, Nfld. and Montreal; awarded Can. Council Fellowship to lecture Commonwealth Inst. Brit.; Prof. of Eng. Mem. Univ. of Nfld. 1972; ed. 'Baffles of Wind and Tide' 1973; 'The Blasty Bough' 1974; 'East of Canada' 1975; recipient several publishing awards incl. Best Illustrated Children's Book Published in Can. 1977 and Stephen Leacock Award for Best Book of Humour Published in Can. 1977; Pres., Assoc. of Candn. Publishers 1988–89; recreations: swimming, scuba diving, tennis; Home: St. John's, Nfld.; Office: 100 Water St., St. John's, Nfld. A1C 6E6.

**ROSE, Rev. Ernest John,** C.D., B.A., L.S.T., M.Sc.Ed.; headmaster; b. Sault Ste. Marie, Ont. 25 March 1940; s. Cecil Samuel and Marguerite Virginia (Peplow) R.; e. Bishop's Univ. Lennoxville, Qué., B.A. 1963, L.S.T. 1964; Niagara Univ. Lewiston, N.Y., M.Sc.Ed. 1981; m. Jane d. Anthony and Milicent Hufton 1 Aug. 1964; children: Michael, Shannon, John; HEADMASTER (15th), ALBERT COLLEGE 1990– (MEM. BD. OF GOVS.); o. Deacon 1964; Ang. Priest 1965, Diocese of Algoma; Curate, Ch. of the Epiphany, Sudbury, Ont. 1964–66; Priest-in-Charge, Bala, Ont., the Muskokas 1966–67; Chaplain, RCAF W. Coast 1967–70; Chaplain, Ridley Coll. St. Catharines, Ont. 1970–81, Founding Housemaster for Girls 1978–81, C.O. 162 Cadet Corps 1970–81; Headmaster (Founding) Holy Trinity Sch. 1981–90, mem. Bd. of Dirs., Quinte Dance School; mem. Synod Ang. Diocese Toronto; Mem. (Padre) 418 Wing RCAFA; mem. Senate, Victoria Univ,; Mem., Rotary Club of Belleville; Church Organist; private pilot licence 1957; recreations: hockey, canoe-camping, fishing; Home and Office: Albert College, 160 Dundas St. W., Belleville, Ont. K8P 1A6.

**ROSE, Jeffrey Raymond,** B.A., M.I.R.; public servant; trade unionist; urban planner; b. Toronto, Ont. 23 Sept. 1946; s. Dr. Albert and Thelma (Harris) R.; e. Univ. of Toronto Schs. 1964; Univ. of Toronto B.A. (Honours) Pol. Sci. and Econ. 1968; London Sch. of Econ. Mackenzie King Travelling Fellow 1968–69; Univ. of Toronto Master of Ind. Relations 1983; m. Dr. Sandra d. Dr. Thomas and Harriet Black; one s. Adam; DEPUTY MINISTER, MINISTRY OF INTERGOVERNMENTAL AFFAIRS (ONT.) 1991– ; Planner City of Toronto Planning Dept. 1976–80; Pres. CUPE Local 79, 1980–83; National Pres., Candn. Union of Public Employees 1983–91; mem. Exec. of Ont. Div. of CUPE 1981–83; mem. Exec. Metro Toronto Labour Counc. 1981–83; Exec. mem., Ontario New Democratic Party 1982–91; gen. Vice-Pres. Candn. Labour Congress 1983–91; mem., Bd. of Dirs., Inst. for Rsch. on Public Policy 1988–91; mem., Federal Counc., NDP 1988–91; Home: 55 Sunnydene Cres., Toronto, Ont. M4N 3J5; Office: 6th Floor, Mowat Block, Queen's Park, Toronto, Ont. M7A 1C2.

**ROSE, Lewis Norman,** B.Comm., C.A.; business executive; b. Cape Town, S. Africa 16 Feb. 1959; s. late Boris and Denise Sonia (Rosencrown) R.; e. Sea Point Boys' H.S. (S. Africa) 1976 (Head Prefect & Stephen Hon. 1976); Univ. of Toronto, B.Comm. 1981 (Pres., Comm. Stud. Assn. 1980–81); C.A. 1983; completed var. Can. & US securities courses & exams.; speaker: Insight and Cdn. Institute of Business Valuators seminars; m. Elana Nancy d. Dr. James and Gladys Mayers 6 July 1986; children: Bradley Jason, Samantha Genna; SENIOR VICE-PRES. & CHIEF FIN. OFFR., MAPLE LEAF FOODS INC. (formerly Canada Packers Inc.) 1990– ; Exam. Marker, Inst. of C.A.s of Ont. 1983; Audit Sr., Coopers & Lybrand 1981–84; Asst. Vice-Pres., Treasury & Operations Mngt., Wood Gundy Inc. 1984–86; Mergers & Acquisitions, Wood Gundy Inc. 1986–87; Chief Financial Offr. and Dir., Maple Leaf Mills Ltd. 1987–90; Dir., Maple Leaf Foods Inc.; Corp. Foods Limited; recreations: rugby, squash, soccer, cricket; Club: Forest Hill Tennis; Home: Toronto, Ont.; Office: 30 St. Clair Ave. W., Suite 1500, Toronto, Ont. M4V 3A2.

**ROSE, Michael Robertson,** B.Sc., M.Sc., D.Phil.; university professor; b. Iserlohn, Germany 25 July 1955; s. James Barry Studley and Charlotte Julia (Horsey) R.; e. Queen's Univ., B.Sc. (Hons.) 1975, M.Sc. 1976; Univ. of Sussex, D.Phil. 1979; one s. Darius; PROF. OF EVOLUTIONARY BIOLOGY, UNIV. OF CALIF. 1990– ; NATO Sci. post-doct. Fellow, Univ. of Wisconsin 1979–81; Asst. Biology Prof., Dalhousie Univ. 1981–85, Assoc. Prof. 1985–88; Assoc. Prof., Univ. of Calif. 1987–90; NSERC Univ. Rsch. Fellow 1981–88; Mem., Soc. for the Study of Evolution; Genetics Soc. of Am.; Gerontological Soc. of Am.; Am. Assn. for the Advancement of Science; author: 'Quantitative Ecological Theory' 1987, 'Evolutionary Biology of Aging' 1991; recreations: music, philosophy; Office: Dept. of Ecology & Evol. Biol., Univ. of Calif., Irvine 92717.

**ROSE, Richard Hugh,** B.F.A.; theatre director, film director, playwright, theatre producer; b. Maracaibo, Venezuela 18 Jan. 1955; e. York Univ. B.F.A. 1978; Candn. Ctr. for Advanced Film Studies 1990; FOUNDING ARTISTIC DIR., NECESSARY ANGEL THEATRE 1978– ; Dir., Young Company, Stratford 1994– ; Dir. (Necessary Angel Th.): '3 In the Back, 2 In the Head,' 'King Lear,' 'Glenn,' 'Property,' 'Not Wanted on the Voyage,' 'The Europeans,' 'The Half of It,' 'Coming through Slaughter' (playwrighting nom.) 'Newhouse,' 'The Castle,' 'Mein' (playwrighting award; audience choice award (Belgrade)), 'Tamara (Toronto)'; Stage Dir., Stratford Festival, Manitoba Theatre Ctr., Blyth Fest., Theatre Plus, Centaur Theatre, Tarragon Theatre,; Dir., Tamara (N.Y. & L.A.) (stage directing awards); Opera Dir., Opera Hamilton's Don Giovanni and Ctr. for Contemporary Opera N.Y.C.; Film Dir., 'Giant Steps' for O'B and D Films; 'Love Clinic' for Ctr. for Adv. Film Studies 1990; Guest Dir., Nat. Theatre Sch., York Univ.; Instructor, Univ. of Toronto Graduate Centre for Drama, Equity Showcase, York Univ. Grad. Prog.; Dir. Res., Ctr. for Adv. Film Studies 1990; Assoc. Dir., Stratford Shakespearean Fest. 1991; stage dir. nominations for Glenn 'The Europeans,' 'The Possibilites,' & 'Tamara' (N.Y.C.); co-stage adaptor: 'Not Wanted on the Voyage' & 'Coming through Slaughter'; Co-playwright: 'Newhouse'; Co-conceiver: 'Tamara'; several projects currently in development stage; Office: Suite 201, 490 Adelaide St. W., Toronto, Ont. M5V 1T2.

**ROSEHART, Robert G.,** Ch.E., B.A.Sc., M.A.Sc., P.Eng., Ph.D.; chemical engineer; university administrator; b. Owen Sound, Ont. 29 July 1943; s. Clarence Daniel and Evaline (Sutton) R.; e. Annandale H.S. Tillsonburg, Ont. 1962; Univ. of Waterloo Ch.E., B.A.Sc. 1967, M.A.Sc. 1968, Ph.D. 1970; m. Rita June d. William and Margaret Purvis 26 Aug. 1967; children: Robert Jr., William, Karen Ann.; PRESIDENT, LAKEHEAD UNVERSITY 1984– ; industrial experience with Fiberglas Canada, A.E.C.L., Canadian General Electric; Asst. Prof. present Univ. 1970, Dean. of Univ. Schs. 1977–84, Dir. Resource Centre for Occupational Health & Safety 1978–84; ; Sci. Couns. Porter Royal Comn. on Elec. Power 1975–77; Exec. Interchange Environment Planning EPS, Govt. of Can. 1982; environmental cons. to fed. and prov. govts.; Tech. Cons. to Ont. Select Ctte. of Hydro Affairs 1978–80; recipient many rsch. grants and author many tech. publs.; Dir. Thunder Bay C. of C. 1983–86 Vice Chrmn. Thunder Bay Econ. Devel. Corp. 1984–86; apptd. mem. Ont. Forestry Counc.; mem., Candn. Pulp and Paper Assn.; Chrmn., Ont. Adv. Ctte. on Resource Dependant Communities 1986; Chrmn.: Lake Superior PLUARG Panel 1978–79; CSA Ctte. on Solar Collectors Standards 1977–80; Bd. of Dirs., Boise Cascade Canada Ltd., Ont. Energy Corp. (1993); recreations: curling, skiing, boating; Club: Univ. of Toronto; Home: 588 Riverview Dr., Thunder Bay, Ont. P7C 1R7; Office: Thunder Bay, Ont. P7B 5E1.

**ROSEN, Adrienne E.,** B.A.; business executive; b. Toronto, Ont. 10 April 1954; d. Adrian Alfred and Jane Elizabeth (Manning) Potts; e. York Univ. B.A. 1989, B.A. (Honours) Philosophy 1992; CHIEF EXTVE. OFFR., THE INTERNATIONAL COURIER 1984– ; Vice-Pres., Applause Community Development Corp. 1985–91; Instr. in Philosophy, Dept. of Cont. Edn., Seneca College; Advisory Bd., Bone and Mineral Group, Univ. of Toronto 1990– ; Bd. Mem., Centre for Feminist Rsch., York Univ. 1991– ; Major Scholarship Award for outstanding scholarship in philosophy, Atkinson Coll. 1989, 1991; Home: 884 Palmerston Ave., Toronto, Ont. M6G 2S2; Office: 344 Dupont St., Suite 304, Toronto, Ont. M5R 1V9.

**ROSEN, Keith Michael,** M.A., D.Phil., C.A.; chartered accountant, taxation specialist; b. Carshalton, Surrey, England 15 July 1948; s. Mark and Doris Anne (Cashman) R.; e. Kings Coll. Sch., Wimbledon 1956–65; Nat. Science Demy. 1966–70; Magdalen Coll., Oxford Univ. B.A. (Hons.) 1970, M.A. & D.Phil. 1973; m. Kathleen d. Robert and Marjorie Rickert 1 Nov. 1985; PARTNER, STERN COHEN, CHARTERED ACCOUNTANTS 1982– ; articling student, Clarkson Gordon & Co. 1973–76; C.A. 1976–77; Tax C.A. 1977–78; Partner, Bulmash Weiler Rosen 1978–80; Head, Taxation Serv., Stern Cohen 1980–82; Mem., MENSA; Oxford Soc.; Internat. Wine & Food Soc.; clubs: The St. Clair, The Pont Street; Home: 86 Roslin Ave., Toronto, Ont. M4N 1Z2; Office: Suite 1600, 22 St. Clair Ave. E., Toronto, Ont. M4T 2S3.

**ROSEN, Robert,** B.S., M.A., Ph.D.; educator; b. Brooklyn, N.Y. 27 June 1934; s. Benjamin and Sarah Rebecca (Cooper) R.; e. Brooklyn Coll. B.S. 1955; Columbia Univ. M.A. 1956; Univ. of Chicago Ph.D. 1959; m. Patsy d. Clarence and Agnes Guinand 4 May 1958; children: David Guy, Judith Louise, Jacob Allan; PROF. OF PHYSIOL. AND BIOPHYSICS DALHOUSIE UNIV. 1980– ; Univ. of Chicago 1960–65, Rsch. Assoc., Asst. Prof.; State Univ. of N.Y. Buffalo, Assoc. Prof. of Math. & of Biophys. Sci's 1966–69, Prof. 1969–75, Assoc. Dir. Center for Theoretical Biol. 1970–75; Killam Prof. present Univ. 1975–80; Cons. Clinical Technologies Associates 1986– ; author 'Optimality Principles in Biology' 1967; 'Dynamical System Theory in Biology' 1970; 'Fundamentals of Measurement' 1978; 'Anticipatory Systems' 1985; 'Life Itself' 1991; ed. 'Foundations of Mathematical Biology' 3 vols. 1972; 'Progress in Theoretical Biology' 1972–81; Home: 64 Bedford Highway, Halifax, N.S. B3M 2J2; Office: Halifax, N.S. B3H 4H7.

**ROSEN, Robert W.,** B.A.; business executive; b. Flin Flon, Man. 21 June 1943; s. Jack and Zeta (Schacter) R.; e. Univ. of Alta. B.A. 1968; div.; children: Geoffrey, Elizabeth, Katherine; PRES. AND CHIEF EXEC. OFFR. CITY LUMBER CORP. & LUMBER CITY MILLWORK 1973– ; Pres. & C.E.O., West Edmonton Centre Corp. 1988– ; Chrmn.: Edmonton Econ. Devel. Authority 1989–92; Forestry Task Force 1989– ; N. Alta. Inst. Technol., Forestry Devel. 1989– ; Extve. & Steering Ctte., Economic Development Strategy for Edmonton 1991– ; Co-Chrmn. Japanese Botanic Garden Project Univ. of Alta. 1989– (Dir. 1987–88); Chrmn., Mayor's Lunch for the ARTS 1989, 2nd Annual 1989; Bd. of Govs., The Univ. of Alta. 1991– ; Bd. Dirs. Edmonton Art Gallery, Chrmn. Fund Raising; recipient: Gold Ring Award (leadership) Univ. of Alta.; Past Chrmn., Young Pres.' Orgn. Alta. Chapter (Award for outstanding Education Program for Canada and North West United States Regions); Edmonton Econ. Development Authority; Past Pres., Edmonton and Northern Alta. Retail Lumberman's Assn.; Pres., Edmonton Retail Builders Assn. 1977–78; Past Dir.: Minerva Found.; N. Alta. Children's Hosp. Found.; Jewish Community Council; Alta. Israeli Chamber of Commerce; Chrmn., Cultural Affairs Winter Cities Showcase '88 'A Celebration of Japan'; mem. Candn. Chamber of Commerce; Edmonton Chamber of Commerce; Economic Development Edmonton; Bd. of Gov. & Chair, Finance Ctte., Univ. of Alta.; recreation: squash; Clubs: Centre; Mayfair Golf & Country; Home: 1402, 11826 – 100 Ave., Edmonton, Alta. T5K 0K3; Office: 15711 – 128 Ave., Edmonton, Alta. T5V 1K4.

**ROSENBAUM, Stanford Patrick,** B.A., M.A., Ph.D., F.R.S.C.; university professor, literary historian; b. Vancouver, B.C. 17 March 1929; s. Harry and Dorothy Ella (Reveles) R.; e. Univ. of Colorado B.A. 1951; M.A. Rutgers Univ. M.A. 1955; Pembroke Coll., Oxford 1956; Cornell Univ. Ph.D. 1960; m. Naomi d. Michal and Max Black 1958; children: Susanna, Samuel; PROFESSOR EMERITUS, UNIVERSITY OF TORONTO 1991– ; Instructor, Cornell Univ. 1959–60; Indiana Univ. 1960–62; Asst. Prof. 1962–65; Assoc. Prof., Univ. of Toronto 1965–67; Prof. 1967–91; Visiting Prof., Queen's Univ. 1989; Fulbright Scholarship, Oxford 1956–57; fellowships: Carnegie Found. Interdisciplinary Fellowship in lit. & phil., Brown Univ. 1962–64; Guggenheim 1968–69; Canada Counc. Leave 1974–75; SSHRC Leave 1980–81; Connaught Sr. 1984–85; Killam Rsch. 1989–91; Fellow, Royal Soc. of Canada 1991; editor: 'A Concordance to the Poems of Emily Dickinson' 1964, 'Henry James's The Ambassadors: A Norton Critical Edition' 1964, 1994, 'English Literature and British Philosophy: A Collection of Critical Essays' 1971, 'The Bloomsbury Group: A Collection of Memoirs, Commentary, and Criticism' 1977, 1987; 'Virginia Woolf's Women & Fiction: The Manuscript Versions of A Room of One's Own' 1991; 'A Bloomsbury Group Reader' 1993; author: 'Victorian Bloomsbury: The Early Literary History of the Bloomsbury Group' vol. 1 1987, 'Edwardian Bloomsbury: The Early Literary History of the Bloomsbury Group' vol. 2 1994; Home: 28 Playter Blvd., Toronto, Ont. M4K 2W2.

**ROSENBERG, Alvin B.,** Q.C., B.A.Sc.; lawyer; justice; b. Toronto, Ont. 26 Feb. 1925; s. Henry Samuel, Q.C. and Esther (Smith) R.; e. Univ. of Toronto B.A.Sc. 1946; Osgoode Hall Law Sch. 1949; m. I. Gloria d. Meyer and Lillian Perlman 26 June 1948; children: Ellen; Paul, David, Anne, Joan, Lilli, Betsy; JUSTICE, THE SUPREME COURT OF ONTARIO, TRIAL DIVISION 1983– ; Partner, Rosenberg, Smith (and predecesser firms) 1949–66; called to Bar of Ont. 1949; cr. Q.C. 1960; Sr. Partner, Rosenberg Smith Paton Hyman 1966–83; Guest Lectr., Univ. of Toronto Law Sch.; Consultant to several Fed. Crown Corps. and Prov. Ministries; served with RCAF 1944–45; Founding Dir. Univ. Teaching Hosp. Assn.; Past Chrmn. Mount Sinai Inst.; twice Chrmn., Toronto United Jewish Appeal; former Chrmn. Emeritus Mount Sinai Hosp.; Past Chrmn. Univ. Hosp. Relations Comte. Univ. of Toronto; former Dir. Haifa Univ.; former Hon., Counsel, Toronto Jewish Congress; former Offr. and Dir. of over 100 additional communal organizations, philanthropic organizations and private corporations; author 'Condominium in Canada' 1969; mem. ed. bd. Advocates' Quarterly and Construction Law Letter; various book chapters, articles, etc.; maj. publ. for Appraisal Inst. Can., and author of three chapters of Anger Honsberger's legal text on real property; Commissioner of Investigation for Fed. Transp. Ministry regarding fishing vessel safety and author of report; Lectr., Candn. Bar Assoc. annual meeting; Judge, Osgoode Hall and Univ. of Toronto Moot Court; recreations: tennis, hiking, skiing, windsurfing; Clubs: Primrose; York Racquet (Founder); Wymbolwood Beach (Hon. Counsel); Tennis Club of Palm Beach (Founder); Office: Osgoode Hall, Toronto, Ont. M5H 2N5.

**ROSENBERG, Dufflet (Arlene Judith);** bakery executive; b. Toronto, Ont. 24 Oct. 1954; d. Joseph Simon and Ruth (Kates) R.; e. Glen Rush P.S.; Ledbury Park Jr. High; Alternative & Independent Studies Prog. North York; Univ. of Toronto 1 yr.; common law spouse: Martin Kohn; PRESIDENT, DUFFLET PASTRIES INC.; Dir., Great Cooks; Teacher, Desserts for 'Great Cooks' and other demonstrations; Bd. of Dir., Interval House; Gala Ctte., Candn. Found. for Aids Rsch.; Mem., Knives & Forks Organic Growers Assn.; Bakery Production Club; Candn. Restaurant & Food Assn.; Candn. Fed. of Independent Business; Step Ahead Assn.; Toronto Culinary Guild; recreations: cycling, aerobics, skiing; clubs: The McGill; Home: 1079 Queen St. W., Toronto, Ont. M6J 1H3; Office: 41 Dovercourt Rd., Toronto, Ont. M6J 3C2.

**ROSENBERG, Edmond Simon,** C.A.(S.A.); financial executive; b. Johannesburg, S. Africa 24 May 1929; s. Wilfred and Hilda Esther (Shapiro) R.; e. King Edward VII H.S., Johannesburg; Univ. of the Witwatersrand, Johannesburg, Cert. in Theory of Acctcy.; Transvall (S. Africa) Soc. of Chartered Accts. C.A.; m. Valerie d. Abe and Annyce Blieden 17 Jan. 1960; children: Graham L., Mark S.; Chairman and Pres., Skyview Securities Inc. and Skyview International Financial Corp.; served articles for C.A. degree 1948–53; Dir. Lion Shipping Co. (Pty) Ltd. 1957–62; Chrmn. and Fin. Dir. C.R.P. Ins. Brokers 1962–76; Dir. Credit Info. Services (Pty) Ltd. 1970–75; Chrmn. and Fin. Dir. Trident Steel (Pty) Ltd. 1972–79; Dir. various property cos. 1962–81; past Chrmn. Parent-Teachers' Assn. Crossroads Sch., Johannesburg, S. Africa; recreations: golf, tennis, theatre; Clubs: Banbury Tennis; Mayfair Racquet; Home: 65 Mossgrove Trail, Willowdale, Ont. M2L 2W2.

**ROSENBERG, Philip J.,** B.Sc.Phm.; retail executive; b. Toronto, Ont. 18 Aug. 1936; s. Max and Blanche R.; e. Parkdale Collegiate (Hons.) 1955; Univ. of Toronto B.Sc.Phm. 1959; m. Judy d. Kenneth and Rose Silverstein 4 Sept. 1988; children (from prev. marriage) Susan, Lisa, Beth, David, Jonathan, Jeremy; DIRECTOR & GEN. MGR., A & P DRUG MART LTD. 1985– ; Pharmacy Owner (3 stores) 1959–73; Vice-Pres., Store Planning & Merch., Top Drug Mart Ltd. 1974–78; Retail Cons. 1978–82; Dir. of Opns., Super X Drugs Ltd. 1981–84; Dir., Health & Beauty Aids, A & P Stores (Can.) 1988–91; Past Pres., M.T.P.A.; Past Chancellor, Rho Pi Phi Pharm. Frat.; Past Chrmn. and Member., Convention Ctte., Retail Counc. of Can.; Office: 5559 Dundas St. W., Islington, Ont. M9B 1B9.

**ROSENBLATT, Joe;** poet; editor; b. Toronto, Ont. 26 Dec. 1933; s. Samuel and Bessie (Tee) R.; e. Toronto Central Tech. Sch.; George Brown Coll.; m. Faye, d. Howard Lorne Smith, 13 Oct. 1970; one s. Eliot Howard; author 'Voyage of the Mood' 1960; 'The L.S.D. Leacock' 1963; 'The Winter of the Luna Moth' 1968; 'Greenbaum' (drawings) 1970; 'Bumblebee Dithyramb' 1972; 'Blind Photographer' 1973; 'Dream Craters' 1974; 'Virgins & Vampires' 1975; 'Top Soil' 1976; 'Dr. Anaconda's Solar Fun Club' (drawings) 1978; 'Loosely Tied Hands' 1979; 'Tommy & the Ant Colony' 1979; 'Sleeping Lady' 1980; 'Brides of the Stream' 1984; 'Poetry Hotel' selected poetry 1985; 'Escape From The Glue Factory' 1985; artwork incl. 'Snake Oil' limited edition (100 copies) of portfolio of 30 drawings, 1979; Editor, 'Jewish Dialogue' (fiction, poetry, short stories) since 1969; poems included in numerous anthologies, notably Oxford Book of Canadian Verse (1968), (1982), Poets of the Sixties (Eli Mandel ed.) 1973, Penguin Anthology of Canadian Verse (R. Gustafson ed.) 1976, Poets of Canada (J.R. Colombo ed.) 1978, Literature in Canada (D. Daymond & L. Monkman ed.); contributed to numerous periodicals; appeared on many T.V. and radio networks, incl. readings & interviews; lectures and readings at Artists Workshops, high schools, colleges; Writer-in-Residence, Univ. W. Ont., Sept. 1979–Apr. 1980; Univ. of Victoria (1980–81); Saskatoon Library 1985–86; Univs. of Rome and Bologna 1987; nom. for Gov. Gen.'s Short List, 1974; Gov. Gen.'s. Award for Poetry 1976; Can. Council Sr. Arts Award 1973, 1976, 1980, 1987; Ont. Arts Council Poetry Award 1970; B.C. Book Award for Poetry 1986; N.D.P.; Hebrew; recreations: fishing, boating; cat fancier; Home: 221 Elizabeth Ave., Qualicum Beach, B.C. V9K 1G8.

**ROSENBLUM, Simon,** B.Comm., M.A.; policy advisor; b. Glace Bay, N.S. 10 Feb. 1949; s. Arthur and Fanny (Gorelick) R.; e. St. Mary's Univ. B.Comm. 1970; State Univ. of N.Y. (Binghamton) M.A. 1974; Northeastern Univ. 1985; CHIEF OF STAFF TO THE MINISTER OF FINANCE, ONTARIO, MINISTRY OF FINANCE 1993– ; Lectr., Sociology, Laurentian Univ. 1978–81; Labour Studies, Cambrian Coll. 1982–85; Nat. Political Affairs Co-ord., Project Ploughshares 1985–90; Vice-Pres., Ont. N.D.P. 1985–90; Internat. Affairs Ctte., Fed. N.D.P. 1990–91; Nat. Extve., Candn. Friends of Peace Now 1987–91; Policy Advisor to the Treasurer of Ont., Min. of Treasury & Economics 1991–93; author: 'The Non-Nuclear Way' 1981, 'Misguided Missiles' 1985; co-editor: 'Canada and the Nuclear Arms Race' 1983, 'The Search for Sanity' 1984, 'The Road to Peace' 1988, 'Debating Canada's Future' 1991; recreations: tennis; Home: 47 St. Clair Ave. W., #403, Toronto, Ont. M4V 3A5; Office: Frost Bldg. S., 7th Floor, Queen's Park, Toronto, Ont. M7A 1Y7.

**ROSENBLUTH, Gideon,** Ph.D.; educator; b. Berlin, Germany 23 Jan. 1921; e. London Sch. of Econ. 1938–40; Univ. of Toronto B.A. 1943; Columbia Univ. Ph.D. 1953; m. Annemarie Fischl 1944; two children; Prof. of Econ. Univ. of B.C. 1962–86; Civil Servant, Govt. of Canada 1943–47; Lectr., Princeton Univ. 1949–50; Research Training Fellowship, Social Science Research Council (U.S.) Nat. Bureau of Econ. Research, N.Y. 1950–51, Research Assoc. 1951–52; Asst. Prof of Econ. Stanford Univ. 1952–54; Assoc. Prof. of Econ. Queen's Univ. 1954–62; Visiting Assoc. Prof. Univ. of Wash. 1961; author 'Concentration in Canadian Manufacturing Industries' 1957; 'The Canadian Economy and Disarmament' 1967, new ed. 1978; co-author 'Canadian Anti-Combines Administration 1952–60' 1963; co-editor 'Restraining the Economy' 1986; 'False Promises: The Failure of Conservative Economics' 1992; various publs. prof. journs., book chapters, papers; mem. Candn. Econ. Assn. (Chrmn. Stat. Comte. 1958–60; Mng. Ed., CJE, 1972–76; Pres. 1978–79); Am. Econ. Assn.; Candn. Assn. Univ. Teachers (Pres. 1966–67); Royal Soc. Can.; Home: 4639 Simpson Ave., Vancouver, B.C. V6R 1C2; Office: 2075 Wesbrook Pl., Vancouver, B.C. V6T 1W5.

**ROSENFELD, Jason;** executive; b. Montreal, Que. 27 July 1952; s. Hyman and Rebecca (Bialik) R.; e. McGill Univ.; Concordia Univ.; children: Michael, Sarah; PRESIDENT, CANADIAN FINANCIAL CO. 1979– ; joined Bank of Nova Scotia Montreal 1972–75; Richter, Usher, Vineberg, C.A.'s, Montreal 1975–78; Office: 1100, 400 De Maisonneuve Blvd. W., Montreal, Que. H3A 1L5.

**ROSENTHAL, Howard S.,** B.A., C.A.; chartered accountant; b. Toronto; e. Univ. of Waterloo B.A.; C.A. Ontario; NATIONAL PROFESSIONAL DEVELOPMENT PARTNER, BDO DUNWOODY WARD MALLETTE; Office: Box 32, Royal Bank Plaza, Toronto, Ont. M5J 2J8.

**ROSENTHAL, Joseph (Joe),** R.C.A.; artist; b. Kishinev, Rumania 15 May 1921; s. Samuel Rosenthal; came to Can. 1927; e. Central Tech. Sch. 1940; Ont. Coll. of Art 1946; m. Margaret Joyce d. Walter Louis Dowson 14 Feb. 1948; children: Susan Mary M.D., Ronald Lee; over 25 solo exhns. since 1961 Toronto, Hamilton, Detroit, Winnipeg, Edmonton, San Francisco, Ottawa; rep. in many group exhns. incl. London, Paris, Brussles, Berlin 1988; travelled extensively on study and sketching trips throughout Canada and the North-West Territories, U.S.A., England, Mexico, Cuba, Holland, Italy, France, Spain, Greece Jordan, Israel, Egypt, W. Germany, Switzerland and Turkey; rec'd 1st Prize Art Gallery of Ont. War Poster Competition 1941; Can. Council Grant 1969; author 'Old Markets, New World' 1964; 'Indians, A Sketching Odyssey' 1971; 'As the Artist Sees It' 1971; Exhn. Chrmn. 50th Anniversary Sculptors Soc. Can. 1978; Winner, Nat. Sculpture Competition for Dr. Sun Yat-Sen Monument, 1983; finalist, Internat. Sculpture Comp. for Sir Seretse Khama statue, Republic of Botswana; Television Profile, 30 min. 1993; represented in many public and private collections in Canada, U.S.A., Europe; served with Candn. Forces 1942–45; mem. Royal Canadian Academy; Ont. Soc. Artists; Candn. Artists Representation; recreations: swimming, reading; Address: 49 Belvedere Blvd., Etobicoke, Ont. M8X 1K3.

**ROSENTHAL, Peter,** M.A., Ph.D., LL.B.; mathematician; lawyer; b. New York City, N.Y. 1 June 1941; s. Harold and Esther S. (Posner) R.; e. Queens Coll. City Univ. of N.Y. B.A. 1962; Univ. of Mich. M.A. 1963, Ph.D. 1967; Univ. of Toronto LL.B. 1990; m. Carol d. David and Phyllis Kitai 14 July 1985; children: Alan, Jeffrey, Michael, Daniel, Esther; PROF. OF MATH. UNIV. OF TORONTO 1976– ; joined present Univ. 1967, Asst. Prof. 1967, Assoc. Prof. 1971; parallel career in law; recipient Nat. Rsch. Council Can. Rsch. Grant 1968– ; Sr. Rsch. Fellowship Gt. Brit. 1973; Nat. Sci. Found. Grant U.S. 1974–83; Students Adm. Council Award Best Teaching in Sci's 1986; co-author 'Invariant Subspaces' 1973; numerous rsch. articles math. jours.; several short stories, legal articles; Home: 367 Palmerston Blvd., Toronto, Ont. M6G 2N5; Office: Mathematics Dept., Univ. of Toronto, Toronto, Ont. M5S 1A1.

**ROSINGER, Eva L.J.,** M.Sc., Ph.D., P.Eng.; scientist; engineer; b. Prague, Czech. 21 July 1941; d. Leopold K. and Anna (Simak) Hartl; e. Tech. Univ. Prague M.Sc. Chem. Engn. 1963, Ph.D. Chem. 1968; Univ. of Toronto P.D.F. Chem. Engn. 1970; m. Herbert E. s. Eugene and Theresia R. 27 Nov. 1969; DIRECTOR GENERAL, CANDN. COUNCIL OF MINISTERS OF THE ENVIRONMENT 1990– ; Rsch. Engr. Inst. of Fine Ceramics, Karlsbad, Czech. 1967–68; post-doctoral Fellow, Dept. of Chem. Engn., Univ. of Toronto 1968–70; Tech. Info. Services, Tech. Univ., Aachen, W. Germany 1970–72; with AECL Rsch. Whiteshell Laboratories: Rsch. Scientist 1973–79; Sect. Head. 1979–80; Scientific Asst. to Dir. Waste Mgmt. Div. 1980–84; Mgr., Environ. and Safety Assessment Br., 1984–85; Exec. Asst. to the Pres., AECL Rsch., Ottawa, 1986–87; Dir., Waste Mngmt. Concept Review, AECL Rsch. 1987–90; author over 40 scientific reports and papers on environ. issues, waste mgmt., environ. assessment, polymer science, and chem. processes in nuclear ind.; Vice Pres. Radioactive Waste Mgmt. Ctte. OECD/NEA, Paris 1982–85; Pres., Candn. Nuclear Soc. 1989–90 (mem. of Counc. 1979–91); Bd. of Dirs., Candn. Nuclear Assn. 1989–90; Bd. on Radioactive Waste Mngmt., U.S. National Acad. of Sciences 1989–90; Bd. of Dir., Winnipeg Symphony Orchestra 1990– ; Adv. Ctte., Univ. of Waterloo 1990– ; Adv. Ctte. on Nuclear Safety, Atomic Energy Control Bd. 1991– ; Bd. of Dir., 1989 Candn. Engr. Memorial Found. 1990– ; Elected Council mem., Assn. of Profl. Engrs. of Man.; Bd. of Dir., Emnployment Projects for Women Inc. 1992– ; Adv. Bd., Inst. for Tech. Dev., Univ. of Manitoba 1992– ; Bd. of Dir., Candn. Council for Human Resources in Env. Industry 1993– ; Dir., Candn. Assn. of Nordic Ski Instrs. 1977 (qualified cross-country ski coach, instr. and examiner); recreations: cross-country skiing; orienteering, wilderness trekking, photography; Home: 12 Chopin Blvd., Winnipeg, Man. R2G 2E1; Office: CCME Secretariat, 326 Broadway, Suite 400, Winnipeg, Man. R3C 0S5.

**ROSLAK, The Hon. Mr. Justice Yaroslaw,** B.A., LL.B., Q.C.; justice of queen's bench; b. Chortkiw, Ukraine 18 Aug. 1927; s. Michael and Olena (Pihut) R.; e. Sr. Matric., Innsbruck, Austria 1946; Univ. of Innsbruck, Law Fac. 1946–48; Univ. of Alta., B.A. 1952; LL.B. 1953; m. Maria d. Dmytro and Anna Punak 4 June 1965; children: Larissa, Oleh Michael; JUSTICE OF QUEEN'S BENCH, ALBERTA 1987– ; articled with Messrs Harvie & Yanda (to Mr. D. Yanda) May 1953 to May 1954; admitted Alta. Bar Aug. 1954; Private practice, Bonnyville, Alta. 1954–59; Couns., Alta. Dep. Att. Gen. 1959–70; Asst. Dir., Cr. Justice 1970–75; Dir., Crim. Justice 1975–82; Dir., Appeals 1985–87; appt. Q.C. Jan. 1976; Pres., Edm. Br., Ukrainian Candn. Ctte. 1971–73; Ukr. Prof. & Bus. Club 1976; Alta. Crown Attorneys' Assn. 1971–73; Mem., Univ. of Alta. Senate 1977–83; club: Royal Glenora; Home: 308 O'Connor Close, Edmonton, Alta. T6R 1L6; Office: Law Courts, 1A Sir Winston Churchill Sq., Edmonton, Alta. T5J 0R2.

**ROSS, Alan Gordon,** B.Comm., F.C.A.; former public servant; b. Geraldton, Ont. 21 April 1938; s. Robert Gordon and Isabella McDonald Carter (Finlayson) R.; e. Carleton Univ. B.Comm. 1959; m. Donna d. Jose and Irene Holmes 8 Oct. 1960; children: Andrea, Alexander; Senior Asst. Deputy Minister, Supply & Services Canada 1986–93; Dir., Financial Policy, Comptroller General 1973–78; ADM, Corp. Mngt., Agriculture Canada 1978–86; Pres., Civil Serv. Coop. Credit Soc. 1981–86; Council Mem., Inst. of C.A.s of Ont. 1984–87; F.C.A. 1988; Deputy Reeve, March Township 1972–76; Pres., Financial Management Inst. 1975; Kanta Community Assn. 1971; recreations: skiing, golf, tennis; Home: 28 Carr Cres., Kanata, Ont. K2K 1K4.

**ROSS, Alastair Henry,** B.Sc., M.B.A.; petroleum executive; b. Calgary, Alta. 29 March 1923; e. Univ. of Alta. B.Sc. (Civil Engn.); Harvard Univ., M.B.A.; m.; two s., four d.; PRES. & DIR., ALLARO RESOURCES

LTD. and CHRMN., PETROREP CANADA LTD.; Dir., National Westminster Bank of Canada; Amaulico Fund Ltd.; P. Burns Resources Ltd.; Phillips Petroleum Canada Ltd.; BCE Inc.; Canadian Investment Fund, Ltd.; Bullock Growth Fund Ltd.; Past Pres. Ind Petroleum Assn. of Can.; Past Pres., Western Decalta Petroleum Ltd. Pembina Pipeline Ltd.; Past Pres., Calgary Chamber of Comm.; Past Dir., United Way of Calgary (past gen chrmn.); past mem., Economic Council of Can; Chrmn., Calgary Research and Development Authority; Dir., Cndn Energy Research Inst.; Calgary Airport Authority; recreations: golf, skiing, reading; Club: Calgary Petroleum (Past Pres.); Ranchman's; Calgary Golf and Country; Home: 5503 Elbow Dr., Calgary, Alta. T2V 1H7.

**ROSS, Christopher Arbuthnott,** B.Sc., M.B.A., Ph.D.; university professor and administrator; b. Trinidad, W.I. 14 Aug. 1948; s. Christopher Sills Arbuthnott and Estelle (Salandy) R.; e. Univ. of the West Indies B.Sc. 1972; Univ. of Western Ont. M.B.A. 1974, Ph.D. 1982; m. Carole d. Mariette and Robert Duhaime 10 Oct. 1981; children: Alix, Arielle; DEAN, FACULTY OF COMMERCE & ADMIN., CONCORDIA UNIV. 1992– ; Ast.Prof., Concordia Univ. 1981–83; Assoc. Prof. 1983– ; Assoc. Dean, Grad. Studies & Rsch. 1983–88; Acting Dean, Fac. of Commerce & Admin. 1990–92; Dir., Joint Ph.D. Prog. in Admin. (Concordia, H.E.C., McGill and UQAM) 1985–88; Visiting Prof., Tianjin Univ., PRC 1987, '90; Univ. of the West Indies 1992; Vice-Pres. & Dir., Mathieu Da Costa Business Devel. Corp. Inc. 1993– ; Mem., Internat. Adv. Council, Dept. of Management Studies, Univ. of W.I.; Mem., Am. Mktg. Assn.; Acad. of Mktg. Science; Admin. Sci. Assn. of Can.; author of num. articles; recreations: wine and beer making, home renovation; Home: 204 Cote St. Antoine Rd., Westmount, Que. H3Y 2J3; Office: 1455, de Maisonneuve Blvd. W., Montreal, Que. H3G 1M8.

**ROSS, Colin A.,** M.D., F.R.C.P.(C); psychiatrist; b. Sarnia, Ont. 14 July 1950; s. William King and Evelyn Margaret (Bruneau) R.; e. Univ. of Alta. M.D. 1981; m. Nancy d. William and Marion Keys 8 Feb. 1986; children: Simeon, Dana, Andrew, Keir; DIR. DISSOCIATIVE DISORDERS UNIT, CHARTER HOSPITAL OF DALLAS 1991– ; joined St. Boniface Hospital 1985; Dir., Dissociative Disorders Clinic, Dept. Psychiatry, St. Boniface Hospital 1988–91; Assoc. Prof. of Psychiatry 1988–91; Laughlin Fellow Am. Coll. Psychiatrists 1985 (mem. 1990); Morton Prince Award Sci. Achievement 1989 and President Internat. Soc. Study Multiple Personality & Dissociation 1993–94; recipient provl. and nat. agencies rsch. grants; author 'Northern Studies' 1975; 'Portrait of Norman Wells' 1985; 'Adenocarcinoma and Other Poems' 1989; 'Multiple Personality Disorder: Diagnosis, Clinical Features and Treatment' 1989; co-ed. 'Panic Disorder and Agoraphobia' 1991; 'The Osiris Complex Case Studies in Multiple Personality Disorder' 1994; 'Satanic Ritual Abuse' forthcoming; recreation: running; Office: 6800 Preston Rd., Plano, Texas 75024 U.S.A.

**ROSS, Cyrus Alexander,** B.Sc.; executive; b. Winnipeg, Man. 15 Jan. 1933; s. William Field and Angele Margaret (Boulette) R.; e. Univ. of Manitoba B.Sc. 1953; m. Bernice d. Edward and Eunice McCulloch 5 Nov. 1977; children: Susan, Karen, Colette, Sandra; step-children: Carolyn, Warren, Shannon; PRES. AND GEN. MGR., NORDEX EXPLOSIVES LTD. 1974– ; Pres. and Gen. Mgr. Canalex Resources Ltd.; Geologist, Hudson Bay Mining and Smelting, Exploration 1953–57; Tech.-Serv. Rep., CIL Explosives 1957–60; founding Partner, then Vice-Pres., Delta Explosives Ltd. 1961–70; a Founder Nordex Explosives Ltd. in 1970, Pres. since 1974; cons., geology and blasting, explosives technol.; Chrmn. Harmony House (for recovering alcoholics) 1975–80; mem. C.I.M.M.; inventor: two patents issued to CIL 1960 for noise control and pre-shear techniques; patents issued to Nordex re mixing techniques and novel explosives; recreations: camping, gardening; Clubs: Harmony House; S.T.E.P.S.; Home: 90 Second St., Kirkland Lake, Ont. P2N 1R9; Office: Box 790, Kirkland Lake, Ont. P2N 3K4.

**ROSS, Donald James,** B.Sc.; pipe line executive; b. Brockville, Ont. 1 April 1926; s. Donald Mercer and Margaret Esther (Kerr) R.; e. Brockville C.I. 1946; McGill Univ., B.Sc. 1951; m. Lola d. Thomas and Mary Donahue 1953; children: Lorene Margaret, Sharilyn Ann; Extve. Vice-Pres. & Chief Op. Offr., Interprovincial Pipe Line Co. 1988; Engr. Dept. 1953; Mgr., Oil Movements 1966; Asst. Mgr., West. Div. Opns. 1970; Project Mgr., Sarnia-Montreal Project 1975; Asst. to Pres. 1977; Mgr., Engr. Dept. 1979; Vice-Pres., Engr. 1983; Vice-Pres., Opns. & Engr. 1986; Dir., Interprov. Pipe Line (NW) Ltd.; Lakehead Pipe Co. Inc.; Edmonton Petroleum Club; Mem., Profl. Engrs. of Ont. Assn.; Assn. of Profl. Engrs. of Alta. recreations: hiking, golf, hockey; Home: 13908 Buena Vista Rd., Edmonton, Alta. T5R 5S1.

**ROSS, Graeme D.A.,** B.A., M.B.A., F.B.A.; business executive; b. Montréal, Qué. 6 Dec. 1944; s. Donald and Jean Elizabeth (MacIntyre) R.; e. Bishop's Coll. Sch. Lennoxville, Qué.; McGill Univ. Jr. Matric. (Head Boy; Most Efficient Cadet); Concordia Univ. (S.G.W.U.) First Class Hons., B.A. 1974; C.S. of M., F.B.A. 1986; M.B.A. 1989; CHRMN., PRES. & CHIEF EXTVE. OFFR., IONIZING ENERGY COMPANY OF CANADA LTD. 1983– ; Chrmn. and Chief Exec. Offr. Maritime Applied Science & Technology Ltd. 1983– ; Dir. IEC; MAST; Gamma Technology International Inc., Va.; Sommelier Ltd.; Chrmn., Mgr. Consulting Services, Canatom Inc. 1978–82, Asst. to Pres. 1982; Cons. U.N.'s IAEA Adv. Group on Electron Beam Processing of Flue Gases; Finalist Ernest C. Manning Awards 1982; Certificate of Merit Canada Awards for Business Excellence – Invention 1988; co-author 'Analysis of Project Management Philosophies' 1981; 'Philosophy of Cost Control Management of Mega Projects' 1981; 'Issues and Criteria of Site Selection of an Irradiator' 1982; 'Overview of Irradiation Food Processing' 1983; 'The Evergreen Process: A Solution to Salt Curing' 1987; 'Electron Beam Curing of Stack Gases' 1987; 'Overview of Electron Accelerators' A.M.I. Speech 1992; 'Evergreen Hides for the World's Leather Industry' 1994; Co-developer of U.S. and Candn. Hide Curing Patents using ionizing energy processing; mem. Candn. Assn. Advanc. Sci.; former mem., Academy of Science; Candn. Elect. Assn. (Founder Ctte. Constrn. & Commissioning 1982); mem., Candn. Assn. Physicists; Candn. Nuclear Soc.; Candn. Mgmt. Assn.; BCS Alumni Assoc.; Comnr., Clan Ross Assoc. of Can.; Fredericton Soc. St. Andrew (Dir. 1980); R.H.R. Black Watch Assn.; York Sunbury Hist. Soc.; recreations: salmon fishing, golf; Clubs: Fredericton Garrison (Vice Pres. & Dir.); Centurion; United Services Inst.; Rotary (former mem.); Office: P.O. Box 393, Stn. A., Fredericton, N.B. E3B 4Z9.

**ROSS, Henry Raymond;** govt. relations, business and communication consultant; b. Toronto, Ont. 9 Nov. 1919; s. Joseph and Mary (Rotenburg); e. elem and sec. sch. Toronto; Art College of Ont. 1939; m. Ann Clarfield 5 Nov. 1944; children: Janice Carol, Ellen Louise; PRESIDENT, HENRY R. ROSS CONSULTANTS, INC.; Chrmn., ICA ACA Joint Broadcast Cmte.; Dir., Candn. Advertising Research Found.; Trustee, Am. Fed. of Musicians; Pres., Ross Ferris, Motion Picture Theatres, 1946; Sr. Vice Pres., Dir. F.H. Hayhurst Co., 1957–79; Pres., Contemporary Art Ltd. 1969– ; Pres., H.M.S. Investments 1975– ; Advisor, Fed. and Prov. govts. in development of advertising, business practice laws; author of articles on advertising, communications, govt. relations; Fellow, Inst. of Candn. Advertising; mem., Adv. Bd., Humber Coll.; Gov., Inst. of Occupational Therapists; Internat. Inst. of Communications; Broadcast Exec. Soc.; Conservative; Clubs: Donalda; Art Directors; recreations: golf, bridge; Home: 127 Munro Blvd., Willowdale, Ont. M2P 1C7; Office: 55 Eglinton Ave. E., Ste. 505, Toronto, Ont. M4P 1G9.

**ROSS, J. Nicholas,** B.A., M.A., C.A.; chartered accountant; b. Toronto, Ont. 19 Jan. 1936; s. Donald and Constance Jean (McLaughlin) R.; e. Univ. of Toronto Schools; Upper Canada Coll. 1955 (Head Boy and Gov. Gen. Medalist); Trinity Coll., Univ. of Toronto, B.A. (Hons.) 1959 (Scholarship); Cambridge Univ., M.A. 1961; m. Lynn M. d. Clayton and Rosalind Williams 19 Aug. 1965; children: Nancy R., Timothy N., Cameron J.; PARTNER, ERNST & YOUNG 1970– ; joined Clarkson Gordon, (now Ernst & Young) 1961; Dir., Butterfield & Co. (Bermuda); Enerflex Systems Inc. (Calgary); Mem., Inst. of C.A.s of Ont. (Gold Medalist 1964); Candn. Inst. of C.A.s (Silver Medalist 1964); Mem., C.D. Howe Inst. (Policy Adv. Ctte.) 1986–94; Pres., The Ticker Club 1993–94; Dir., Candn. Assn. of Family Enterprise, Ont. Div. 1992–94; Chrmn., Long-Range Planning Ctte., Upper Canada Coll. 1978–87; Mem., Extve. Ctte., U.C.C. 1978–87, Chrmn. Bldg. Ctte., U.C.C. 1988–92; Treas. then Pres., Anglican Womens' Training Coll. 1962–82; Mem., Grace Church on-the-Hill, Anglican (Rectors Warden 1979); recreations: golf, tennis, squash, skiing, fishing; Clubs: Canadian; Toronto Golf; Mid-Ocean Golf; Mayfair Lakeshore Racquet; Badminton & Racquet; Home: 113 Garfield Ave., Toronto, Ont. M4T 1G2; Office: P.O. Box 251, Toronto-Dominion Ctr., Toronto, Ont. M5K 1J7.

**ROSS, John Ronald;** executive; b. Toronto, Ont. 7 June 1934; s. John and Signe Ellen (Hendrickson) Vellinga; e. Chartered Life Underwriter 1964; m. Tuula d. Esa and Tyne Skytta 25 June 1966; children: Stephen, David, Michael, Julie Anne; PRESIDENT, CORPORATE PLANNING ASSOCIATES 1978– ; Agent Great-West Life Assurance Co. 1956–68, Br. Mgr. 1968–71, Agency Mgr. 1971–78; Past Pres. Candn. Assn. for Corporate Growth; Campaign Chrmn. Candn. Cancer Soc. (former Pres. Toronto Dist.); recreations: golf, squash, tennis, fitness, skiing; Clubs: Albany, Cambridge, Caledon Ski, John's Island Club (Vero Bch., Florida); Lambton Golf, St. George's Golf & Country; Home: 37 Roxborough St. W., Toronto, Ont. M5R 1T9; Office: 36 Toronto St., Suite 800, Toronto, Ont. M5C 2C5.

**ROSS, M.A. Eleanor,** R.N., M.Sc.N.; chief nurse; association executive; b. New Richmond, Qué. 18 Sept. 1941; d. Joseph Francis and Marie Agnes (LeBlanc) Mercier; e. S. Waterloo Meml. Hosp. Galt, Ont. R.N. 1963; Univ. of Toronto B.Sc.N. 1978, M.Sc.N. 1983; m. George Forbes s. Walter and Lucienne Ross 12 Oct. 1963; children: Daryl W., Bradley F., Larah M.; CHIEF OF NURSING PRACTICE, WOMEN'S COLLEGE HOSPITAL 1992– ; Clin. Assoc. in Nursing Univ. of Toronto 1983– ; Head Nurse Chronic Respiratory & Rehab. Unit W. Park Hosp. 1977–80, Rsch. Assoc. 1981–82; Teaching Asst. in Nursing Univ. of Toronto 1981–82; Clin. Nurse Specialist-Respiratory, Sunnybrook Medical Centre 1982–92; Part-time Adm. Coordinator, Queen Elizabeth Hosp. 1984–85; Coordinator and Lectr. Jt. Cont. Edn. & Respiratory Course Univ. Toronto/Victorian Order Nurses 1985–87; mem. Premier's Council Health Strategy 1987–91; mem. Metrop. Toronto Inter-Agency Smoking & Health 1979–84; recipient Candn. Lung Fellowships 1980–81; Sigma Theta Tau; Pres.-Elect, Candn. Nurses Assn. 1992–94; Pres. Reg'd Nurses' Assn. Ont. 1987–89; Candn. Nurses Respiratory Soc. 1983–84; York & Toronto Respiratory Care Soc. 1981–82; mem. Bd. Candn. Lung Assn. 1983–84; mem. Bd. Metrop. Toronto & York Region Lung Assn. 1983–86, Pres., 1990–92; mem. Am. Thoracic Soc.; Candn. Gerontol. Nursing Assn.; Candn. Nursing Rsch. Interest Group; Club: University Women's; Home: 560 Huron St., Toronto, Ont. M5R 2R7; Office: 76 Grenville St., Toronto, Ont. M5S 1B2.

**ROSS, Malcolm,** O.C., M.A., Ph.D., D.Litt., LL.D., D.S.L., F.R.S.C. (1955); university professor; b. Fredericton, N.B. 2 Jan. 1911; s. Charles Duff and Cora Elizabeth (Hewitson) R.; e. Univ. of New Brunswick, B.A., 1933, D.Litt., 1962, LL.D. St. Thomas Univ. 1976 D. Litt., Trent Univ., 1982; D.Litt., Dalhousie, 1983; D. Litt., Univ. of Edinburgh 1986; LL.D., Queen's Univ. 1989; D.Litt. Univ. of Windsor 1989; D.S.L., Trinity College (U. of T.) 1990; D.Litt. Acadia Univ. 1991; Officer of the Order of Canada 1976; Lorne Pierce Medal of R.S.C., 1982; Univ. of Toronto, M.A. 1934; Cornell Univ., Ph.D. 1941; m. Lois Natalie, d. A. V. Hall, Toronto, Ont., 4 June 1938; one d. Julie Martha; THOMAS McCULLOCH PROF., DALHOUSIE UNIVERSITY, since 1973, (Prof. Emeritus 1982); Visiting Prof., Candn. Studies, Univ. of Edinburgh, 1982–83; Editor of 'Queen's Quarterly,' 1953–56; Lecturer, Cornell University, 1939–41; Indiana University, 1941–42, attached to Distribution Div., National Film Board, Ottawa, 1942–45; joined English Dept. of Univ. of Manitoba, 1945, resigning in 1950; Guggenheim Fellow, 1949–50; apptd. Prof. of Eng., Queen's Univ., 1950; Prof. and Head, Dept. of Eng., 1957–60; James Cappon Prof. of Eng., 1960–62; Prof. of Eng. Lit., Trinity Coll., Univ. of Toronto 1962–68 and Dean of Arts there 1965–68; apptd. Prof. of English, Dalhousie University 1968; Visiting Prof., Univ. of Edinburgh, 1982–83; Chrmn., Nuffield Comte. on Humanities and Social Sciences, 1961–62; Publications: 'Milton's Royalism,' 1943; 'Our Sense of Identity,' 1954; 'Poetry and Dogma,' 1954; 'The Arts in Canada,' 1958; Ed. 'Man and his World' (with John Stevens) 1961; 'The Impossible Sum of Our Traditions' 1986; Ed., New Canadian Library 1958–78; various articles in learned journs.; Awarded Diplome d'Honneur, Candn. Conference of the Arts 1990; Apptd. to Adv. Bd. of Nat. Library of Can., 1977; mem. Arts Adv. Panel, Can. Council, 1980–84; mem., Nat. Extve., Humanities Assn. of Can.; Chrmn. of the NCCUC Comte. in Teaching and Research; mem.; Acad. Panel of the Can. Council, 1966–68; Pres. (1970–71) Sec. II, Royal Soc. Can.; Chrmn. (1969–72) Dalhousie Comte. on Cultural Activities; Northern Telecom International Award in Canadian Studies (1985); Anglican; recreations: music, gardening; Home: 1750 Connaught Ave., Halifax, N.S. B3H 4C8.

**ROSS, Michael Crowe,** B.Com., C.A., C.M.C.; management consultant; songwriter; composer; b. Edmonton, Alta. 11 Oct. 1939; s. Sam Gibson and Annis Iola (Crowe) R.; e. Univ. of B.C. 1957–58; Carlton Univ., B.Com. 1961; step children: Marcia, Aleah, James;

PRES., TOTAL MANAGEMENT INC. 1987– ; Staff Acct., Clarkson Gordon & Co. 1961–66; Comptroller, Bros. and Denton Ltd. 1966–70; Vice-Pres. & Treas., Burns Foods Ltd. 1970–75; Pres., Michael Ross Consultants Ltd. 1975– ; Vice-Pres., Fin. & Admin., B.C. Auto. Assn. 1983–85; Supt. of Brokers & Real Estate, Prov. of B.C. 1986–87; 1st prize 1986 Pacific Songwriters Assn. Songwriters Comp.; Mem., B.C. Inst. of C.A.s; B.C. Inst. of Mngt. Cons.; Home: 45 - 3111 Beckman Place, Richmond, B.C. V6X 3R3.

**ROSS, Murray George,** O.C. O.Ont., M.A., Ed.D., D.C.L., D.Litt., D.Un., F.A.S.A., LL.D.; president emeritus; b. Sydney, N.S. 12 April 1910; s. George Robert and Catherine (MacKay) R.; e. Acadia Univ., B.A. (Econ. and Sociol.) 1936; Univ. of Toronto, M.A. (Sociol.), 1938, LL.D. 1971; Univ. of Chicago, post-grad. work (Sociol.) 1939; Columbia Univ., Ed.D. (Sociol Psychol.) 1949; Acadia Univ., D.C.L. 1960; Univ. of Toronto, LL.D. 1970; York Univ., D.Litt. 1971; Laurentian Univ., LL.D. 1976; m. Janet Kennedy, M.D., F.C.F.P. d. Col. W. A. Lang, 10 May 1941; children: Susan Janet, Robert Bruce; Hon. Dir., Nat. Council of YMCA; retired, Chrmn. Bd. of Trustees, Ont. Hist. Studies Series; Research Assoc., Candn. Youth Comn., 1945–47; Extve. Secy., Candn. Inst. of Pub. Affairs, 1945–48; Assoc. of Social Work, Univ. of Toronto, 1951–55; Prof. 1955; Extve. Asst. to Pres., 1956–57; Vice-Pres. 1957–60; Pres., York Univ. 1960–70 and Professor of Social Sc. there 1970–72 since when President emeritus; former member Board of Trustees, George R. Gardiner Museum of Ceramic Art; Fellow, Am. Sociol. Assn.; mem., Am. Acad. of Pol. and Social Science; Former Chrmn., Bd. of Trustees, Ontario Historical Studies Series; Former Mem., Bd. of Trustees, Sunnybrook Hospital & Ontario Hospital Assn., Former Chrmn., Education Adv. Cttee., Sunnybrook Hospital; Former Chrmn., Task Force on Mental Health for Ontario Council of Health; former Pres., Candn. Institute on Public Affairs; Former Mem., Bd. of Dirs., Empire Club of Canada; Former Dir., Candn. Club of Toronto; Former Mem., Ontario Government Commission on the Aims of Education; Publications: 'The New University,' 1961; 'Case Histories in Community Organization,' 1958; 'New Understandings in Leadership' (with C. E. Hendry), 1957; 'Community Organization: Theory and Principles,' 1955; 'The Y.M.C.A. in Canada,' 1951; 'Religious Beliefs of Youth,' 1950; 'Towards Professional Maturity' (Ed.), 1948; 'The Years Ahead: A Study of the Canadian Y.M.C.A.,' 1945 (completed as Dir. of this study); 'New Universities in the Modern World,' 1965; 'The University: The Anatomy of Academe,' 1976; 'Canadian Corporate Directors on the Firing Line,' 1980; 'The Way Must Be Tried: Memoirs of a University Man' 1992; also numerous pamphlets incl. 'Education in the U.S.S.R.,' 1958; UNESCO Report, 'Theory and Principles of Community Development,' 1954; 'Education in Canadian Institutions,' 1952; 'The Way Must Be Tried: Memoirs of a University Man' 1992; many articles in prof. mags. and journs. incl. 'The Ethical Goals of Modern Education,' 1962; 'How to Fight Failure in High School,' 1961; 'Trends in Higher Education,' 1961; Awarded Centennial Medal, 1967; Borden Medal (Book Award), 1976; Silver Jubilee Medal, 1978; Officer, Order of Canada, 1979; Order of Ontario, 1988; 125th Anniversary of the Confederation of Canada Medal, 1992; Protestant; recreations: bridge, tennis, music, reading; Clubs: Arts and Letters; Queen's; Badminton & Racquet; Hillsboro; York; Home: 75 Highland Cres., Willowdale, Ont. M2L 1G7; Office: Glendon College, 2275 Bayview Ave., Toronto, Ont. M4N 3M6.

**ROSS, Norman A.,** B.Com., LL.B.; lawyer; b. Toronto, Ont. 27 Oct. 1943; s. Norman James and Marie Henriette (Fortier) R.; e. Regiopolis Coll. Kingston; St. Francis Xavier Univ. B.Com. 1966; Queen's Univ. LL.B. 1969; m. Catherine d. Albert West and Madeline Lugsdin Lowes 30 Dec. 1983; two s. Norman Patrick, James Bradley; Partner, Fraser & Beatty 1976–93; Dir. New York Life Insurance Co. of Canada; called to Bar of Ont. 1971; Dir. Amici Camping Charity; Past Pres. P. Conserv. Bus. Assn. 1985–87; Theatre Beyond Words 1977–87; mem. Candn. Bar Assn.; Co. Law Assn.; Lawyer's Club; R.Catholic; recreations: fly fishing, skiing, tennis; Clubs: RCYC; Blue Mountain Trout; Osler Bluff Ski; Home: 500, 1 Clarendon Ave., Toronto, Ont. M4V 1H8; Office: Suite 3300, Commerce Court West, Toronto, Ont. M5L 1B2.

**ROSS, Robert Hugh,** B.Comm.; publisher; b. Shawinigan, Que. 19 Feb. 1941; s. Hugh Daniel and Edith M. (Genge) R.; e. Mount Royal H.S. Montreal 1958; Sir. George Williams Univ. B.Comm. 1962; m. Judith d. Robina and Charles Thompson 19 Dec. 1964; children: Noelle, Aimee; PRESIDENT & DIR., D.C. HEATH CANADA LTD. 1972– ; Estate Acct. Dept. Royal Trust Co. Montreal 1962–64; Mktg. Dept. Rep. Holt Rinehart & Winston of Canada Ltd. 1964–66, Mktg. Mgr. 1966–68; Vice-Pres. Mktg. present firm 1968–72; mem. Sch. Group, Candn. Book Publ. Counc. 1974–75 (Pres. Sch. Group 1976; 2nd Vice-Pres Counc. 1977; 1st Vice-Pres. 1978; Pres. Counc. 1979); mem. Muskoka Lakes Assn.; Sir. George Williams Univ. Grad. Soc.; recreations: tennis, skiing, cycling; Club: Toronto Lawn Tennis; Home: 333 St. Clair Ave. E., Toronto, Ont. M4T 1P3; Office: 1600, 100 Adelaide St. W., Toronto, Ont. M5H 1S9.

**ROSS, Robin,** M.B.E., M.A., LL.D. (Hon.); retired university official; b. Tayport, Fife, Scotland 25 Jan. 1917; s. Robert and Marjorie R.; e. Hamilton Acad., Scot.; St. Andrews Univ., M.A. (1st Class Hons. in Classics); Jesus Coll., Oxford; m. Elspeth Madge, d. Franklin Ritchie, Lake Port, Cal., 14 Aug. 1946; one s. Ian; Dist. Magistrate and Collector, Indian Civil Service, 1940–47; Principal, Commonwealth Relations Office, 1947–57; Supervisor of Adm., Central Mortgage & Housing Corp., Ottawa, Ont., 1957–58; apptd. Assistant Registrar, University of Toronto, 1958; Registrar 1959; Vice-Pres. and Registrar 1967; Vice Provost 1972; Vice-Principal and Registrar, Erindale Campus July 1977–82; Special Lecturer In Latin, Erindale College; 1966–67 Coordinator of Federal Govt. Activities in Higher Education in Department of Secretary of State; Publication: 'The Short Road Down' 1984; served in 2nd World War; 2nd Lieutenant, Queen's Own Cameron Highlanders; Presbyterian; recreations: golf, fishing, stamp collecting, writing; Address: 168 Thetis Ave., Qualicum Beach, B.C. V9K 1R7.

**ROSS, Romaine Kay,** Q.C., LL.M.; lawyer, author; b. Wellandport, Ont., 7 Oct. 1903; s. James Alway and Sarah Agnes (Kay) R.; e. Osgoode Hall Law Sch., grad. 1931; Univ. of Toronto, LL.B. 1937, LL.M. 1943; m. Mary Margaret, d. Dr. Stephen F. Millen and Mary Ella (Wilcox), Woodslee, Ont., 31 Oct. 1939; three d. Jane Elizabeth, Mary Kay, Suzen Elaine; called to Bar of Ont., 1931; cr. K.C. 1947; appeared as Counsel before Judicial Comte., H.M. Privy Council in 1951; submitted brief before Special Comte. of Senate of Can. on Human Rights and Fundamental Freedoms; submitted Brief to Senate-House of Commons Special Joint Cttee. on Constitution of Canada in 1980; pol. speaker (P.C.) in Ont. for candidates, 1926–1963; el. to Council, Village of Port Dalhousie, 1946, Reeve then Mayor, 1949; mem., Lincoln County Council, 1948; mem., St. Catharines City Council, 1951–60; def. cand. (Fed.) for Lincoln, 1953, 1963; author of: 'Local Government in Ontario,' 1949, 2nd ed. 1962; 'Regional Government in Ontario' 1970; former mem., Lincoln County Board of Education; Ontario Association Children's Aid Societies (past President); St. Catharines and District, Chamber of Comm. (past Pres.); mem., Canadian Bar Assn. (Past mem. Council); Life mem, Law Soc. of Upper Can; Candn. Authors Assn. (Past mem. Nat. Exec.); P. Conservative; United Church; recreations: travel, reading, athletics; Clubs: St. Catharines Golf; Port Dalhousie Yacht; Home: 18 South Dr., St. Catharines, Ont. L2R 4T8.

**ROSS, Saul,** M.A., Ed.D.; educator; b. Montréal, Qué. 6 May 1934; s. Al and Goldie (Berlin) R.; e. Sir George Williams Univ. B.A. 1956; Western Reserve Univ. Cleveland M.A. 1957; Univ. of Toronto OISE Ed.D. 1986; m. Pamela d. Irving and Leah Small 19 June 1958; children: Karyn Reesa, Dana Ilene; PROF. OF HUMAN KINETICS & PHYSICAL EDN., UNIV. OF OTTAWA 1988– ; Teacher, Dept. Head Outremont High Sch. Montréal 1959–67; Teacher, High Sch. of Comm. Ottawa 1967–69; Asst. Prof. present Univ. 1969, Assoc. Prof. 1981, Prof. 1988; ed. 'Persons, Minds and Bodies' 1988; author over 15 book chapters and over 45 articles profl. jours.; Pres. Jewish Community Centre Ottawa 1980–81; Pres. Assn. Profs. Univ. Ottawa 1979–81; Collective Bargaining Co-op. Candn. Assn. Univ. Teachers 1987–89; Ont. Confederation of Univ. Faculty Assns. 1988–89, Pres. 1992– ; Chrmn. Philos. Sport & Phys. Activity Ctte. and Internat. Relations Ctte. Candn. Assn. Health, Phys. Edn. & Recreation; recreations: racquetball, theatre, ballet; Home: 206 – 205 Somerset St. W., Ottawa, Ont. K2P 0J1; Office: Ottawa, Ont. K1N 6N5.

**ROSS, Shannon M.,** B.Comm., C.A.; chartered accountant; b. Edson, Alta. 3 Nov. 1951; d. James Cecil and Mary Francis (Antoniuk) Ross; e. Univ. of Alberta B.Comm. 1976; TREASURER, CORNUCOPIA RESOURCES LTD. AND VICE-PRES., CORPORATE AFFAIRS, QUARTZ MOUNTAIN GOLD CORP. 1990– ; C.A./Articling Student, MacGillivray & Co. 1975–79; C.A., Public Practice, Davidge & Co. 1979–84; Supvr., Internal Audit & Sr. Internal Auditor, Cominco Ltd. 1985–87; Asst. Dir. of Finance, Corp. of the Dist. of W. Vancouver 1987–88; Controller & Treas., Cornucopia Resources Ltd. 1988–89; Treas., Cornuopia Rescources Ltd. 1991– ; Treas. & Bd. Mem., Edmonton Big Sister Soc. 1979–84; Mem., I.C.A.B.C. 1984– ; I.C.A.A. 1975–85; Office: 355 Burrard St., Ste. 540, Vancouver, B.C. V6C 2G8.

**ROSS, (James) Sinclair;** writer; b. Wild Rose, Sask. 22 Jan. 1908; s. Peter and Catherine Foster Fraser R.; Grade 11 schooling, Wild Rose Sch. District; Joined Royal Bank of Canada in 1924, retired 1968; author 'As For Me and My House' 1941; 'The Well' 1958; 'The Lamp at Noon and Other Stories' (stories) 1968; 'Whir of Gold' 1970; 'Sawbone's Memorial' 1974; 'The Race and Other Stories' 1982.

**ROSS, Thomas McCallum,** B.Sc.Phm., M.B.A.; association executive; b. Hamilton, Ont. 5 May 1931; s. Laverne and Della (McCallum) R.; e. Univ. of Toronto B.Sc.Phm. 1955, M.B.A. 1961; m. Marguerite d. Donald and Hilda Ross 14 Aug. 1954; children: Thomas, Gregory (dec'd), Karyn; EXEC. DIR., CANDN. RETAIL HARDWARE ASSN. 1964– ; Mgr., Sutherland Pharmacy, Hamilton 1955–60; Assoc. Sec., Candn. Pharm. Assn. 1960–63; Rsch. Staff, Royal Comn. on Health Services 1963–64; Founding Fellow, Hardware Mgmt. Inst.; Council Mem., Internat. Assn. of Ironmongers Assns. 1970– ; Chief Admin. Offr., Candn. Wholesale Hardware Assn. 1970–89; mem. Candn. Ch. of Comm.; People for Sunday Assn. (Pres. 1987/88); Pres. & Chrmn., Coalition against Open Sunday Shopping 1988–89; Dir., Russell R. Mueller Rsch. Found. 1984–86; mem. Candn. Soc. of Assn. Execs. (Dir. 1990–92); Am. Soc. of Assn. Execs.; author: 'Pharmacist Manpower in Canada' (Royal Comn. Rept.) 1966; recipient, Pinnacle Award, Candn. Soc. of Assoc. Execs. 1989; recreation: tennis; Home: 59 Walby Dr., Oakville, Ont. L6L 4C6; Office: 6800 Campobello Rd., Mississauga, Ont. L5N 2L8.

**ROSS, Veronica;** writer; b. Hannover, W. Germany 7 Jan. 1946; d. Fred and Estha (Balke) Flechtman; e. Mount Allison Univ., credits; m. Richard s. Frank and Florence O'Brien 7 Nov. 1986; author: 'Goodby Summer' 1980, 'Dark Secrets' 1983, 'Homecoming' 1987, 'Order In the Universe' 1990 (short stories); 'Fisherwoman' 1984, 'Hannah B.' 1991 (novels); num. pubs. in mags.; Assoc. Ed., 'Antigonish Review'; Fiction ed., 'Canadian Author'; Short-term writer-in-res., St. Mary's Univ. 1987, Write-in-res., Thunder Bay Pub. Library 1987–88; London Public Library 1990–91; Candn. Periodical Pub. Awards for 'Whistling' 1980, 'God's Blessings' 1984; Benson-Hedges Mag. Writing Award 1977; Mem., Writers' Union of Can.; Candn. Authors Assn.; Home: 397 Heritage Dr., Kitchener, Ont. N2B 3K9.

**ROSSANT, Janet,** M.A., Ph.D.; research scientist; educator; b. Chatham, UK 13 July 1950; d. Leslie and Doris Christina (Mantel) R.; e. Chatham Grammar Sch. 1969; St. Hugh's Coll. Oxford, B.A. 1972, M.A. 1977; Darwin Coll. Cambridge, Ph.D. 1976; m. Alexander D. s. James and Madeleine Bain June 1977; children: Jennifer Rossant Bain, Robert Andrew Bain; SR. SCI. MOUNT SINAI HOSP. RSCH. INST. 1985– ; Prof., Med. Genetics 1988– ; Assoc. Prof. of Med. Genetics, Univ. of Toronto 1985–88; Rsch. Fellow in Zool. Oxford Univ. 1975–77; Asst. Prof. of Biol. Sci's Brock Univ. 1977–81, Assoc. Prof. 1981–85; recipient Gibb's Prize Zool. Oxford 1972; Beit Meml. Fellowship 1975; E.W.R. Steacie Meml. Fellowship 1983; Nat. Cancer Inst. Can. Rsch. Assoc. 1985; Howard Hughes International Scholar 1991; co-ed. 'Experimental Approaches to Mammalian Embryonic Development' 1986; author or co-author over 100 articles various sci. jours.; Mem. of Council, Am. Soc. Cell Biol.; mem., Brit. Soc. Devel. Biol.; Candn. Soc. Cell Biol.; Sci. for Peace; recreations: running, cooking; Home: 151 Fairview Ave., Toronto, Ont. M6P 3A6; Office: 884, 600 University Ave., Toronto, Ont. M5G 1X5.

**ROSSER, Walter W.,** M.D., C.C.F.P., F.C.F.P., M.R.C.G.P.; university professor and administrator; b. Ottawa, Ont. 9 Dec. 1941; s. Frederick Thomas and Catherine Logan R.; e. Queen's Univ. M.D. 1967; m. Janet d. Harold and May McLung 18 June 1966; children: Thomas, Nancy; CHRMN., FAMILY & COMMUNITY MED., UNIV. OF TORONTO 1991– ; Postgrad. Training, Univ. of Toronto 1967–70; Instr., Univ. of Ottawa, Family & Community Med. & Epid. 1970; Asst. Prof. 1972; Assoc. Prof. 1978; Prof. 1982; Chrmn., Family & Community Med., Univ. of Ottawa 1982; McMaster Univ. 1986; Pres., N. Am. Primary Care Rsch. Group 1991–93; Bd. Mem., Hamilton Community Health Clinic 1987–91; Mem., Task Force on the Use & Provision of Med. Serv. in the Prov. of Ont. 1987–91; Past Mem./Chair, CME Self Exam. Prog. Cttee., Coll. of Family Physicians of Can.; Queen's

Medal, 25th Anniv. Coronation 1987; Lit. Award, CFPC 1970; Rsch. Award, Queen's Univ. 1967; Mem., Candn. Med. Assn.; Ont. Med. Assn.; Coll. of Family Physicians of Can.; Soc. of Teachers; co-author: 'Primary Medical Care of Children and Adolescents' 1987; author of 33 peer reviewed & 47 non-peer reviewed pubns. in internat. journs.; Home: 153 Amberley Blvd., Ancaster, Ont. L9G 3V3; Office: 620 University Ave., Suite 801, Toronto, Ont. M5G 2C1.

**ROSSITER, Eugene P.,** Q.C., B.B.A., LL.B.; barrister and solicitor; b. Morell, P.E.I. 9 Sept. 1952; s. Leo F. and Anna A. (Pierce) R.; e. St. Francis Xavier Univ., B.B.A. 1974; Dalhousie Univ., LL.B. 1978; m. Florence M. d. William Power 15 Aug. 1975; children: Conor J.E., Patrick W.L.; BARRISTER & SOLICITOR, STEWART MCKELVEY STIRLING SCALES 1978– ; admitted to Bar of Prov. of P.E.I. 1978; Queen's Counsel 1991; Mem., P.E.I. Law Soc.; Candn. Bar Assn.; P.E.I. Bench & Bar Council 1984–91; P.E.I. Supreme Court Rules Ctte. 1986– ; P.E.I. Law Soc. Council 1993–94; Chrmn., Bd. of Dir., P.E.I. Sch. of Nursing; Central Sch. of Nursing Assts. 1983–89; Bd. Mem., Queen Elizabeth Hosp. 1981–91; Bd. of Dir., Sport P.E.I. 1991–93; Chrmn. Extve. Ctte., Stewart McKelvey Sterling Scales 1992–94; recreations: general sports; Home: 33 Charlotte Dr., Charlottetown, P.E.I. C1A 2N6; Office: 65 Grafton St., Charlottetown, P.E.I. C1A 8B9.

**ROSSITER, James Randell,** B.Sc., M.Sc., Ph.D.; scientist; businessman; b. London, Ont. 17 Apr. 1947; s. Roger James and Helen Margaret (Randell) R.; e. Neuchatel Jr. Coll., Switz. 1965; Univ. of West. Ont., B.Sc. (Hons.) 1969; Univ. of Toronto, M.Sc. 1971, Ph.D. 1977; m. Amy d. Kenneth and Gene Burdick 4 Sept. 1976; children: Katherine Margaret, Benjamin James; PRES. & CO-FOUNDER, CANPOLAR INC. 1983– ; Adjunct Prof., Ctr. for Earth & Space Sci., York Univ. 1991– ; Grad. Fellow, Lunar Sci. Inst., Houston, Texas 1970–71; Part of Apollo 17 Lunar Surface Electr. Properties Experiment Sci. Team; Ctr. for Cold Ocean Resources Engr., Mem. Univ. of NF: rsch. sci.; leader of ice detection group; Asst. Prof., Dept. of Physics 1976–80; Engr. Mgr., Vice-Pres., Opns. & Vice-Pres., Sales/Mktg., Huntec (70) Limited 1980–83; Dir., Canpolar Inc. 1983– ; Canpolar East Inc. 1989– ; CRTW Capital Corp. 1993– ; Telecommunications Rsch. Inst. of Ont. 1987–93; Instrumar Limited 1983–86; Lectr., Univ. of Alta. & York Univ. 1985–88; Sub-Ctte. on Snow & Ice, NRC 1984–90; Adv. Ctte., Commun. Rsch. Lab., McMaster Univ. 1983–86; NSERC Indus. Rsch. Fellow 1980–85; Gold Medal in Geophysics, Univ. of Western Ont. 1969; mem., Soc. of Explor. Geophys.; Internat. Glaciol. Soc.; author/co-author of over 60 sci. pubns. & tech. reports; editor: 'Proceedings of the Internat. Workshop on the Remote Estimation of Sea Ice Thickness' 1980; Dir., Friends of Walker Avenue School 1985–93; recreations: sailing, skiing, swimming, travel, jogging; club: The Madawaska Club Limited; Home: 58 Valentine Dr., North York, Ont. M3A 3J8; Office: 1450 Lodestar Rd., Downsview, Ont. M3J 3C1.

**ROSSITER-THORNTON, John Francis,** M.B., B.Ch., B.A.O., F.R.C.P.C.; doctor, psychiatrist, professor; b. Dublin, Ireland 4 Oct. 1947; s. Ronald and Johanna Amelia (Blake) Rossiter-Thornton; e. Belvedere Coll. 1966; Univ. Coll. Dublin, M.B., B.Ch., B.A.O. 1972; m. Maria G. d. Patrick and Luiga Manning 6 Sept. 1972; children: Ronald, Lisa, Natalia; CLINICAL DIRECTOR, HAMILTON PROGRAM FOR TRAFFIC INJURY REHABILITATION 1993– ; Dir., Rossiter-Thornton Seminars for personal development 1991– ; Medical internship, St. Vincent's Hosp. 1973; Psych. Training, St. Brendan's Hosp. 1973–74; Univ. of Toronto 1974–78; developed and directs prog. for relatives & friends of schizophrenics which has rec'd internat. recognition (Significant Achievement Award, Am. Psych. Assn. 1981 & Letter of Commendation from Candn. Friends of Schizophrenics 1986 for this prog.) 1977– ; Psych. & Staff, Addiction Rsch. Found. & Clarke Inst. 1978–80; Clin. Coord., Psychotherapy Ctr., Clarke Inst. 1980–82; Head of Prog. for Schizophrenic Patients 1982–88; Service Chief, Div. Treating Longterm Schizophrenia, Clarke Inst. of Psych. 1989–93; Dilectures internationally; program organizer; Asst. Prof., Dept. of Psych., Univ. of Toronto 1981– ; co-author: 'Living & Working with Schizophrenia' 1982, 2nd edition 1991 and many booklets & rsch. articles; co-author & ed.: 'Schizophrenia Simplified' 1991; represented Ireland in 1965 Student Games in Vienna (swimming); swimmer, Irish Internat. Swim Team 1966; emigrated to Can. 1974; Candn. citizen 1977; Home: P.O. Box 1165, P.O. Stn. Q, Toronto, Ont. M4T 2P4.

**ROSTOKER, Gordon,** B.Sc., M.A., Ph.D.; educator; b. Toronto, Ont. 15 July 1940; s. Louis and Fanny R.; e. Univ. of Toronto B.Sc. 1962, M.A. 1963; Univ. of B.C., Ph.D. 1966; m. Gillian d. Herbert and Elsie Farr 29 June 1966; children: Gary David, Susan Birgitta, Daniel Mark; PROFESSOR OF PHYSICS, UNIVERSITY OF ALBERTA 1979– ; NRC Overseas Post-Doctoral Fellowship 1966–68; Asst. Prof. of Physics present Univ. 1968, Assoc. Prof. 1973, Assoc. Chrmn. Physics 1976–79; Dir. Inst. of Earth and Planetary Physics 1985–91; author or co-author 130 publications on solar-terrestrial interactions; mem. Assoc. Ctte. of Geodesy and Geophysics, NRC 1971–74; mem. Grant Selection Ctte. NRC 1973–76 (Chrmn. Ctte. on Space & Astronomy 1976); mem. Ctte. on Internat. Sci. Exchanges NRC 1977–79; mem. Ctte. on Physics and Astronomy NSERC 1979–82; mem. Spec. Ad Hoc Ctte. on Physics and Astronomy NSERC 1987–91; mem. Grant Selection Ctte. for Sci. Publications NSERC 1988–92; mem. Advisory Bd. of Herzberg Astrophys. Inst. NRC 1991– (Chrmn. 1993–94); mem. Steering Ctte., Internat. Magnetospheric Study 1973–79; Chrmn. Div. III, Internat. Assn. of Geomagnetism and Aeronomy 1979–83; Ed. Candn. Jour. of Physics 1980–86; Chrmn., SCOSTEP Sol. Terr. Energy Prog. 1987– ; Assoc. Ed. Jour. of Geophysical Rsch. 1976–79, 1992– ; Assoc. Ed. Jour. of Geomagnetism and Geoelectricity 1993– ; past Sec.-Treas. Candn. Geophysical Union 1973–74; mem. Candn Assn. of Physicists (Chrmn. Div. of Aeronomy and Space Physics 1977–78); Am. Geophysical Union; NRC Exchange Sci. U.S.S.R. 1977; recipient The E.W.R. Steacie Prize 1979; McCalla Rsch. Professorship, Univ. of Alta. 1983–84; Annual Killam Professorship, Univ. of Alta. 1991–92; recreations: bridge, golf; Home: 11626 - 71 Ave., Edmonton, Alta. T6G 0A8; Office: Edmonton, Alta. T6G 2J1.

**ROTENBERG, Ronald Hyman,** Ph.D., M.B.A., B.Com.; university professor; b. Montreal, P.Q. 4 Nov. 1941; s. Philip and Celia (Teman) R.; e. Sir George Williams Univ. (Montreal), B.Com. 1965; McMaster Univ., M.B.A. 1966; Pennsylvania State Univ., Ph.D. 1974; m. Vivien, d. Menhert and Rachel Pollak, 13 June 1965; children: Amy Rosanne; Andrew Stuart; Cara Francine; PROF. BROCK UNIV.; Pres., Rotenberg Research (Marketing Rsch. Consulting); Prof., Concordia Univ. 1966–77; Advertising, Sales, and Sales Promo Mgr., Bernal Labs Ltd. (Montreal) 1961–65; Pres., Ronald Rotenberg & Assocs. Can. Ltd. Marketing Research 1974– ; co-author, 'Cases and Readings in Marketing,' 1974; 'The Benefits and Cost of Evening Shopping to the Canadian Economy, v.1,' 1969; 'Advertising – A Canadian Perspective' 1985; Office: Brock Univ., St. Catharines, Ont. L2S 3A1.

**ROTH, John Andrew,** M.Eng.; engineering executive; b. Calgary, Alta. 6 Oct. 1942; s. Henry and Sophia (Brix) R.; e. McGill Univ. B.E. 1964, M.Eng. 1966; m. Margaret Anne 1968; PRESIDENT, NORTEL NORTH AMERICA (a Division of Northern Telecom); served as Design Eng. RCA Montreal; joined company 1969; trans. to Northern Telecom Ltd. 1974, Div. Gen. Mgr. Stn. Apparatus 1977, Vice Pres. Operations 1978; Extve. Vice Pres. Bell Northern Research Ltd. 1981; Pres., 1982; Extve. Vice Pres., Product Line Management, Northern Telecom Ltd., Mississauga Corporate Offices 1986; Mem., Science Counc. of Can.; Chrmn., McMaster Management of Technology Inst. (MTI); Mem., Nat. Adv. Bd. on Science & Technology; mem. Assn. Prof. Engs. Prov. Ont.; Office: 2920 Matheson Blvd. E., Mississauga, Ont. L4W 4M7.

**ROTH, Millard S.,** B.Mgt. Eng., M.Sc.; private company expansion equity investor; management and financial consultant; b. Toronto, Ont. 28 Oct. 1937; s. Manuel J. and Juanita (Axler) R.; e. Pub. and High Schs., Toronto; Rensselaer Polytechnic Inst., Troy, N.Y., B.Mgt.Eng. 1959; Purdue Univ., M.Sc. (Indust. Mang.) 1960; m. Sonia, d. Max Kaplan, 12 Apr. 1962; children: Andrew, Maxine; PRESIDENT AND DIR., CORPORATE GROWTH ASSISTANCE LTD. since 1967; Pres. and Dir., Candn. Motion Picture Distrubutors Assn.; Copyright Collective of Canada; Dir., Banco Consolitek; Baycrest Centre; Certified Collateral Corp. of Canada Ltd.; Lease-Rite Corp. Inc.; Inst. of Mang. Consultants of Ont.; recreation: golf; Club: Oakdale Golf & Country.

**ROTH, Stephen J.,** B.A., BCL; attorney; film & television producer & executive; b. Montréal, Qué. 20 June 1941; s. Max and Lilian (Marks); e. McGill University, B.A. 1963, BCL 1966; m. Sheila d. Harry and Anne Rosenstein 29 May 1966; children: Dara, Elie, Ava; admitted to Bar, Prov. of Que. 1967; priv. practice, Montréal 1967–77; Film & TV Producer & Extve.; Bd. of Dirs., Western & Pacific Resources Corp. and Hariston Corp.; Pres. & C.E.O., Kelley Resource Recovery Corp.; Chrmn. & C.E.O., Metanetix Marketing Corp.; recreations: horseback riding; Home: 330 Spadina Rd., Suite 2102, Toronto, Ont. M5R 2V9.

**ROTHENBERG, Jack Edward;** financial broker; b. Montréal, Qué. 26 June 1945; s. David and Ella R.; e. Adath Israel, Guy Drummond, Strathcona Acad., Outremont High Sch. (all in Montréal); m. Pearl d. Leizer and Rena Lottner 16 Oct. 1966; children: Robert, Kimberley; PRES. AND FOUNDER, ROTHENBERG & ROTHENBERG ANNUITIES LTD. 1979– ; estbd. Jack Rothenberg and Associates 1964; mutual fund salesman 1967; joined London Life 1970–79; founded Rothenberg & Rothenberg Mortgages Services Ltd. 1983 and Rothenberg Capital Management Inc. 1986; formed Jack Rothenberg Enterprises Inc. 1988; Formed Rothenberg & Rothenberg (Calgary) Ltd. 1992; Founded J.R. Photography Inc. 1992; Jack Rothenberg recognized as Wildlife Photographer winning numerous awards and having exhibitions of his work throughout Canada and the U.S.; Past Chrmn. Invest. Bd. First Fitness Financial Inc.; Chrmn., Invest. Bd. Westbury Investment Group; sometime lectr., McGill Univ., sr. citizens course; guest speaker numerous chs. and synagogues; guest appearances numerous radio and TV talk progs.; held various seminars; Life mem. Million Dollar Round Table; Dir. Fedn. Candn. Independent Deposit Brokers; mem. Annuity & RRIF Brokers Assn. (Past Pres.; mem. Chrmn.); Exec. Chevra Kadisha B'nai Jacob Synagogue; recreation: photography; Club: Montreal Camera (Treas.); Office: 4420 St-Catherine St. W., Montréal, Qué. H3Z 1R2.

**ROTHMAN, Claire,** B.A., B.C.L., M.A.; writer; b. Montreal, Que. 14 Aug. 1958; d. Melvin Leonard and Joan Elizabeth (Presant) R.; e. McGill Univ. B.A. 1981, B.C.L. 1984; Concordia Univ. M.A. 1988; m. Arthur s. Richard and Hélène Holden 6 Sept. 1987; children: Jacob Clement, Samuel Leonard; has worked in law, journalism, translation (French to English) and teaching; primary interest is writing fiction; Mem., Writers' Union of Canada; The Candn. Literary Translators' Assn.; The Barreau du Québec; author: 'Salad Days' 1990 (short stories); translator: 'The Influence of a Book' by Philippe Aubert de Gaspé (fiction) 1993; co-translator: 'In the Eye of the Eagle' 1990; 'The Traitor and the Jew' by Esther Delisle (non-fiction) 1993; Address: 4643 Sherbrooke St. West, Apt. 17, Montreal, Que. H3Z 1G2.

**ROTHMAN, Hon. Melvin L.,** B.A., B.C.L.; judge; b. Montreal, Que. 6 Apl. 1930; s. Charles and Nellie (Rosen) R.; e. Roslyn Sch. and Westmount (Que.) High Sch., 1946; McGill Univ., B.A. 1951, B.C.L. 1954; m. Joan Elizabeth, d. F. W. Presant, Toronto, Ont., 4 Aug. 1954; children: Ann Elizabeth, Claire Presant, Margot Sneyd; JUDGE, QUEBEC COURT OF APPEAL, since 1983; Dir., Cdn. Judges Conf.; called to Bar of Que. 1955; cr. Q.C. 1971; practised law with Phillips Vineberg Goodman Phillips & Rothman until 1971; Justice, Que. Superior Ct. 1971–83; Deputy Judge, Supreme Court of N.W. Territories since 1977; has served as Pres., McGill Students Soc.; Dir., Summerhill Homes Inc.; Dir. and Secy., Inst. Philippe Pinel; Secy., McGill Law Grads. Assn.; Trustee and Gov., Martlet Foundation; Pres., Jr. Bar Assn. Montreal; mem. Council, Bar of Montreal (Dir., Legal Aid Bureau); Jewish; recreations: skiing, sailing, photography; Clubs: Trident Yacht; Laurentian Lodge Ski; Home: 487 Argyle Ave., Westmount, Que.; Office: 10 St Antoine St. E., Montreal, Que. H2Y 1A2.

**ROTHMAN, Mitchell Pierson,** A.B., M.S.; consultant; b. Syracuse, N.Y., U.S.A., 3 May 1942; s. R. Raymond and Arlene (Pierson) R.; e. Phillips Exeter Acad., Exeter, N.H.; Harvard Coll., A.B. 1964; Grad. Sch. of Indust. Admin.; Carnegie-Mellon Univ., M.S. 1970; m. Laurel, d. Alfred and Lilyan Weiss, 15 June 1969; children: Reuven R., Arlene Jessica, Jonathan W.; CONSULTING ECONOMIST, ACRES INTERNATIONAL LTD. 1993– and CHIEF ECONOMIST, LESOTHO HIGHLANDS DEVELOPMENT AUTHORITY 1993– ; Asst. Prof., Fac. of Admin. Studies, York Univ. 1971–74; M.P.R. Assocs., Consulting 1974–76; Can. Imp. Bank of Comm.: econ. 1976–77, mgr., Indust. and Regional Analysis 1977–79, Asst. Sr. Econ. 1979–80, Sr. Econ. 1980–82; Chief Economist, Ontario Hydro 1982–93; Principal, M.P.R. Assocs., Consulting; lectr., York Univ. 1974–78; sessional lectr., Univ. of Toronto 1979–80, 1983; Bd, mem., Kenya/Canada Energy Advisory Project 1989–92; Pres., Can. Chapter, Internat. Assn. of Energy Economists 1983–90; Treasurer, Internat. Assn. for Energy Economics; Dir., Poculi Ludique Societas 1985–87; mem., Am. Econ. Assn., Candn. Assn. of Bus. Economists; author of sev. scholarly articles; religion: Jewish; Pres., Congregation Darchei Noam 1987–89 (Treas. 1980–81); recreations: squash, sailing; Club:

Toronto Athletic; Lakeshore Yacht; Office: Acres Internat. Ltd., 480 University Ave., Toronto, Ont. M5G 1V2.

**ROTHNEY, Gordon Oliver,** M.A., Ph.D., LL.D., F.R.H.S.; historian; b. Town of Richmond, Que. 15 Mar. 1912; s. William Oliver, M.A., B.D., Ph.D. and Agnes Brodie (Linklater) R.; e. Sherbrooke, Que., High Sch.; Univ. of Bishop's Coll., B.A. (1st Class Hons. in Hist.; Gov.-Gen. Medal) 1932; Univ. of London (King's Coll.), M.A. (with "Mark of Distinction") 1934, Ph.D. 1939; Memorial Univ. of Nfld., LL.D. (Hon.) 1987; m. Alice Russell, d. Rev. Alex. R. Ross, 31 July 1943; children: William Oliver, Russell George, late Jean Elizabeth; PROFESSOR OF HISTORY (retired); taught sch. at Shekatika Bay, Que. Labrador Coast, 1932; at Bishop's Coll. Sch., Lennoxville, Que., 1939–41; Social Sciences Div., Sir Geo. Williams College, Montreal, 1941–52 (Prof. of History 1948–52); Prof. and Head, Dept. of Hist., Memorial Univ. of Nfld., 1952–63; first Dean of Arts, Lakehead Univ., Thunder Bay, Ont., 1963–68; Visiting Prof. of Hist., Univ. of W. Ont., 1969–70; Prof. of History, Univ. of Man., 1970–79; summer appts.: Rural Adult Ed. Service, McGill Univ., 1940; Wartime Infor. Bd., Ottawa, 1943; Univ. of Sask., 1946, 1947, 1956, 1962; Laval, 1948; C.F.B., Baden, West Germany, 1978; Que. Govt. European Post-grad Scholarship 1932–34; Can. Council Sr. Research Fellow, New Delhi, India, 1959–60; Geneva, 1968–69; charter-member, Comité (Bureau) de Direction, Institut d'Hist. de l'Amerique française (Montreal), 1947–71; Council, Can. Hist. Assn., 1948–51; Corp., St. John's Coll., Man. 1972–86; rep. of Canada, Gen. Ass., Internat. Congress of Hist. Sciences, Sweden, 1960, Vienna, 1965; Chrmn., Humanities Research Council of Canada, 1963–64; Centennial Medal 1967; Fellow, Royal Hist. Soc., London, Eng., 1969; Fellow, St. John's College, Univ. of Manitoba 1970, Hon. Fellow 1983; author of 'Newfoundland: A History' (Can. Hist. Assn.); 'Canada in One World'; articles and reviews; contested Brome, P.Q. Prov. el., 1944 (Bloc populaire canadien), and Port Arthur, Fed. els., 1965, 1968 (N.D.P.); a Nfld. Dem. Party delegate at N.D.P. founding convention, Ottawa, 1961; rep. CCF at Praja Socialist Party Silver Jubilee, Bombay 1959, and NDP at Congress of Socialist International, Eng., 1969; United Church; Home: 333 Vaughan St., Suite 904, Winnipeg, Man. R3B 3J9.

**ROTHSCHILD, John A.,** B.A., M.B.A., C.A.; business executive; b. Toronto, Ont. 11 July 1949; s. Marvin J. and Sybil (Winters) R.; e. Univ. of Toronto B.A.; Univ. of W. Ont. M.B.A.; m. Susan d. Alan and Helen Frome 6 Nov. 1979; one s.: Adam; PRES., ROTHSCHILD HOLDINGS LTD.; Dir., The Casteel Group Inc.; Akstel Inc.; Luscar Oil & Gas Ltd.; Prime Restaurants; Mem., Candn. Inst. of C.A.s, Que. & Ont.; recreations: golf, skiing; Home: 955 St. Clare Rd., T.M.R., Que. H3R 2M8; Office: 1170 Peel St., Ste. 800, Montreal, Que. H3B 4P2.

**ROTHSCHILD, Maj.-Gen. Robert P.,** M.B.E. (1944), C.D.; retired army officer; b. Cochrane, Ont., 22 Dec. 1914; s. Benjamin and Anne Frances (Silverstone) R.; e. Westmount (Que.) High Sch.; Royal Mil, Coll., Kingston, Ont., Grad. 1936; McGill Univ. B.Sc. (Mining Engn.) 1938; Nat. Defence Coll., 1951; m. Patricia Esmée, d. George Loranger Magann, 17 July 1950; children: Michael Robert, George Emmanuel, Jonathan Andrew, Esmée Ann, Alison Mary; joined Royal Candn. Horse Arty., 1938 as Lieut.; served with Candn. Army during the 2nd World War; Capt. and Adj., R.C.H.A. 1940; Candn. War Staff Course, 1941; Bgde. Major support Group 5 Candn. Armoured Div., 1941–42; Major and Batty. Commdr., 110th Field Batty, R.C.A., 1942–43; Bgde. Major, 2nd Candn. Armoured Bgde., 1943–44; promoted Lieut.-Col. and apptd. G.S.O. 1, H.Q. 2nd Candn. Corps, 1944–45, G.S.O. 1, H.Q. 3 Can. Div. CAOF 1945–46, Dir. Candn. Army Staff Coll. 1946–47; Candn. Mil. Attaché, Athens, Greece, 1947–50; Candn. Army mem. of Dir. Staff, Nat. Defence Coll., Kingston, Ont., 1951–53; Deputy Co-ordinator, Jt. Staff, Nat. Defence Hdqs., 1953–54; Dir. Gen. Ops. and Plans, Army H.Q. 1954–55; Coord. Jt. Staff N.D.H.Q. 1955–57; Dir. Reg. Offr. Trg. Plan N.D.H.Q. 1957–60; Army Mem. Candn. Jt. Staff London, Eng. 1960–62; Q.M.G. Candn. Army, 1962–65; Commdr., Materiel Command 1965–68; Deputy Comptroller-General, Candn. Forces H.Q., 1968 till retirement in 1970; Mentioned in Despatches, 1945; Offr., Order of Orange-Nassau (With Swords); Jewish; recreations: philately, photography; Home: RR 1, McDonald's Corners, Ont. K0G 1M0.

**ROTHSTEIN, Aser,** B.A., Ph.D.; research scientist; b. Vancouver, B.C. 29 Apl. 1918; s. Samuel and Etta (Wiseman) R.; e. King Edward High Sch., Vancouver, 1934; Univ. of B.C., B.A. 1938; Univ. of Cal. (Berkeley), 1940; Univ. of Rochester, Ph.D. 1943; m. Evelyn, d. late Leo Paperny, 18 Aug. 1940; children: Sharon Liptzin, David Michael, Steven Jay; DIR. EMERITUS, RESEARCH INST., THE HOSP. FOR SICK CHILDREN 1972–86 and Prof. Med. Biophysics, Pediatrics, Univ. of Toronto; University Professor, 1981; joined U.S. Atomic Energy Project as Asst. 1943–45; Assoc. 1945–47; Chief, Physiol. Sec., 1948–58; Assoc. Dir. 1961–65; Acting Head, Div. Radiation Chem. and Toxicology, 1963–64; Co-Dir. 1965–72; Instr. in Pharmacol., Univ. of Rochester Sch. of Med. and Dent., 1946; Asst. Prof. 1948; Assoc. Prof. 1953; Assoc. Prof., Radiation Biol., 1958; Prof. 1960; Vice Chrmn., Dept. of Radiation Biol. and Biophys., 1961; Co-Chrmn. 1965–72; author of over 300 tech. articles, reviews, book chapters; Ed., 'Journal of General Physiology'; 'Journal Membrane Biology'; 'Journal of Cellular Physiology'; 'Current Concepts in Membranes and Transport'; recipient: Gairdner Award 1986; Elected Royal Soc. of Canada 1987; mem. Internat. Cell Research Organ. of UNESCO (Council); Biophys. Soc. (Council); Internat. Union Physiol. Sciences (Chrmn. Comte. Cell Physiol.); Internat. Union Pure & Applied Biophysics (Secy. Commission Membrane Biophys.); Society General Physiologists (President); Am. Physiol. Soc.; Am. Assn. Advanc. Science; recreations: concerts, theatre, travel, tennis, squash, skiing; Home: 33 Harbour Sq., Toronto, Ont.; Office: 555 University Ave., Toronto, Ont. M5G 1X8.

**ROTHSTEIN, Samuel,** B.A., M.A., B.L.S., Ph.D., D.Litt.; librarian; educator; b. Moscow, Russia 12 Jan. 1921; s. Louis Israel and Rose (Checov) R.; came to Can. 1922; e. Univ. of B.C., B.A. 1939, M.A. 1940; Univ. of Cal. grad. studies 1941–42, B.L.S. 1947; Univ. of Wash. grad. studies 1942–43; Univ. of Ill. Ph.D. (Lib. Science) 1954; York Univ. D.LITT. 1971; m. Miriam Ruth d. late Max Teitelbaum 26 Aug. 1951; two d. Linda Rose, Sharon Lee; PROF. OF LIBRARIANSHIP. UNIV. OF B.C. 1970– ; PROFESSOR EMERITUS 1986– ; Teaching Fellow Univ. of Wash. 1942–43; Princ. Lib. Asst. Univ. of Cal. Lib. 1946–47; Reference Librarian, Univ. of B.C. Lib. 1947, Head of Acquisitions Dept. 1948, Asst. and Assoc. Univ Librarian 1954, Acting Univ. Librarian and Dir. Sch. of Librarianship 1961, Dir. and Prof. of Librarianship 1961–70; Prof., School of Librarianship, 1970–86; Professor Emeritus 1986– ; Visiting Scholar Univ. of Hawaii 1969; Visiting Prof. Univ. of Toronto 1970, Hebrew Univ. Jerusalem 1973; Consultant, Science Secretariat Can. 1969, various univ. libs. 1970–77; Visiting Librarian Univ. of Toronto 1979; Research Fellow, University of Toronto Centre for Research in Librarianship 1981–82; Dir. Vancouver Jewish Community Centre 1962– ; Past Pres.; served with Candn. Army, Intelligence Corps Can. and Europe 1943–46; rec'd Carnegie Corp. Fellowship 1951–54; Dr. Helen Gordon Stewart Award (BCLA) 1970; Outstanding Service to librarianship award (C.L.A.) 1986; ALISE (Assoc. for Lib. and Inform. Sci. Educ.) Award for Professional Contribution to Library and Information Science Education 1988; Beta Phi Mu Award (Am. Lib. Assn.) 1988; Hon. Life Mem. (B.C.L.A.) 1986; Hon. Life Mem. (C.A.L.S.) 1986; Hon. Life Mem. (P.N.L.A.) 1987; author 'The Development of Reference Services' 1955; 'Training Professional Librarians for Western Canada' 1957; co-author. 'As We Remember It' 1970; 'The University – The Library' 1972; 'Rothstein on Reference' 1989; mem. ed. bds. several journs.; contrib. to several encyclopedias; various articles and reviews; mem. Assn. Am. Lib. Schs. (Past Pres.); Candn. Assn. Univ. Teachers; Canadian Association of Library Schools (President 1982–84); B.C. Lib. Assn. (Past Pres.); Pacific Northwest Lib. Assn. (Past Pres.); Candn. Lib. Assn. (Past Councillor); Am. Lib. Assn. (Past Councillor); Candn. Council of Library Schools (Past Sec'y); Vancouver Public Library Trust (Pres. 1987–88); Bd. of Dirs., Jewish Federation of Greater Vancouver 1993– ; Jewish; recreations: reading, golf, bridge; Home: 1416 W. 40th Ave., Vancouver, B.C. V6M 1V6; Office: 2075 Wesbrook Mall, Vancouver, B.C. V6T 1W5.

**ROTMAN, Joseph L.,** B.A., M.Com.; executive; b. Toronto, Ont. 6 Jan. 1935; s. Manny and Goldie R.; e. Univ. of W. Ont., B.A. 1957; Univ. of Toronto, M.Com. 1960; Columbia Univ., Ph.D. studies 1960–62; m. Sandra d. Saul David Frieberg 23 June 1959; children: Janis, Kenneth; CHRMN., PRES. AND CHIEF EXTVE. OFFR., CLAIRVEST GROUP INC.; Chrmn., Tarragon Oil and Gas Limited; Petro Partners; Dir., American Barrick Resources Corp.; Horsham Corp.; Pres., Art Gallery Ont.; Dir., The Toronto Hosp. Found.; Dir., Bd. Govs. & Co-Chrmn., Research Adv. Ctte., Baycrest Centre Geriatric Care; Dean's Adv. Council, Faculty of Mgmt., Univ. of Toronto; Nat. Counc., Candn. Inst. Internat. Affairs; Past Chrmn. Candn. Friends Israel Museum; recreations: tennis, skiing; Club: York Racquets; Home: 142 Forest Hill Rd., Toronto, Ont. M4V 2L9; Office: 1701, 22 St. Clair Ave. E., Toronto, Ont. M4T 2S3.

**ROTSTEIN, Abraham,** B.A., Ph.D.; educator; b. Montreal, Que. 10 Apl. 1929; s. Hyman and Fanny (Mosenson) R.; e. Bancroft Sch. and Baron Byng High Sch. Montreal 1945; McGill Univ. B.A. 1949 grad. work Univ. of Chicago 1949–50, Columbia Univ. 1950–51; Univ. of Toronto Ph.D. 1967; m. Diane Louise Whitman, Lansing Mich. 18 Feb. 1966; children: Daniel, Eve; Prof. of Econ. Univ. of Toronto, Sr. Fellow Massey Coll.; served as Indust. Econ. 1951–59; Founding mem. Univ. League for Social Reform 1962; Comte. for an Independent Can. 1970; Can. Inst. for Ecomonic Policy, 1979; mem. Fed. Task Force: Foreign Ownership and Structure of Candn. Indust. (Watkins Report) 1967–68; author 'The Precarious Homestead, Essays in Economics, Technology and Nationalism' 1973; 'Rebuilding from Within, Remedies for Canada's Ailing Economy' 1984; co-author 'Dahomey and the Slave Trade' 1966; Mang. Ed. 'The Canadian Forum' 1968–73; Ed. 'The Prospect of Change, Proposals for Canada's Future' 1965; 'Power Corrupted, The October Crisis and the Repression of Quebec' 1971; An Industrial Strategy for Canada' 1972; 'Beyond Industrial Growth' 1976; co-Ed. 'Independence, The Canadian Challenge' 1972; 'Read Canadian, A Book About Canadian Books' 1972; 'Nationalism or Local Control' 1972; 'Getting it Back, A Program for Canadian Independence' 1974; 'Beyond Industrial Growth,' 1976; Jewish; recreation: music; Home: 102 Admiral Rd., Toronto, Ont. M5R 2L6; Office: 100 St. George St., University of Toronto, Toronto, Ont. M5S 1A1.

**ROTSTEIN, Maxwell L.,** B.A., LL.B., F.T.I.; lawyer; b. Canada 19 Aug. 1937; s. Meyer Q.C. and Marjorie (Axler) R.; e. Univ. of Toronto B.A. 1959; Univ. of Toronto Law Sch. LL.B. 1962; m. Nancy-Gay 4 June 1967; children: Marcia-Joy, Stephen, Tracy; CHAIRMAN & CHIEF EXTVE. OFFR., MUNICIPAL FINANCIAL CORP.; called to Bar of Ont. 1964 (with hons.); law practice 1964–70; candidate for York South riding, fed. election 1965; Chrmn. & Chief Extve. Offr., The Municipal Savings & Loan Corp.; The Municipal Trust Co.; MSL Properties Limited; Municipal Fin. Leasing Corp.; Dir., Municipal Bankers Corp. (1931) Limited; Barrie C. of C. spec. achievement award 1977; Capt., Univ. of Toronto Debating Team 1960; Pres., Student's Law Soc., Univ. of Toronto Law Sch. 1962; Dir., The Jewish Home for the Aged 1976–82; Candn. Rep., Counc., Internat. Union of Building Soc. & Savings Assn.; Mem., Simcoe Co. Law Assn.; Dir., Trust Co. Assn. of Can.; Chrmn., Trust Company Assn. of Canada 1993–94; Clubs: Barrie Golf & Country, Cambridge, Masonic Order, Mt. Sinai Lodge, Ramsees Temple; Office: P.O. Box 147, 70 Collier St., Barrie, Ont. L4M 4S9.

**ROULSTON, Keith William,** B.A.; playwright/journalist; b. Wingham, Ont. 23 Jan. 1947; s. Clifford James and Mary Esther (Purves) R.; e. Lucknow Dist. H.S. 1966; Ryerson Polytech. Inst., B.A. 1969; m. Jill Christine d. James and Esme Twiner 21 Dec. 1968; children: Christina, Jennifer, Craig, Erin; author: 'The Shortest Distance Between Two Points' 1977, 'His Own Boss' 1978, 'McGillicuddy's Lost Weekend' 1979, 'Fire on Ice' 1981; co-author: 'Another Season's Promise' 1986; Co-founder, Blyth Summer Festival; Gen. Mgr. 1978–83; Founder, Pub., Ed., 'The Village Squire' 1973–79; 'The Rural Voice' 1975–78, 1992– ; Ed., Pub., 'Teeswater News' 1975–77; 'The Blyth Standard' 1972–77, 'The Citizen' (community owned newspaper) 1985– ; Winner, Jack Sanderson Award for editorial writing, Candn. Community Newspaper Assoc. 1988; 1st Huron Co. Fed. of Agric. Award for outstanding contbr. to agric. 1976; Mem., Candn. Union of Playwrights; Past Pres., Huron Co. Hist. Soc.; Home: R.R. 3, Blyth, Ont. N0M 1H0; Office: North Huron Pub. Co. Inc., Box 429, Blyth, Ont. N0M 1H0.

**ROUNTHWAITE, Her Honour Judge Ann Elizabeth,** B.A., LL.B.; provincial court judge; b. Montreal, Que. 8 July 1950; d. Dr. Francis John and Rachel Alma (Horton) R.; e. Neuchâtel Junior Coll. 1968; Trinity Coll., Univ. of Toronto, B.A. 1971; Osgoode Hall Law Sch., LL.B. 1975; m. Richard V. s. Margaret and Vincent Griffin 11 Aug. 1979; children: Derek Michael, Diana Darrell; PROV. COURT JUDGE, B.C. 1986– ; Vice Pres., Candn. Assoc. of Prov. Court Judges 1993– ; Mem., Extve. and Educ. Ctte., B.C. Prov. Judges' Assoc. 1987–90; Mem., Editorial Ctte., Judges' Handbook 1989– ; Advisory Panel, Laskin Memorial Moot 1988– ; called to B.C. Bar 1976; practiced crim. law as def. counsel & appeared before admin. tribunals; appeared in all levels of B.C. courts & Supreme Court of Can.; Couns., Royal Comns.; Inquiry on the Incarceration of Female Offenders 1978; West Coast Oil Ports

Inquiry 1977–78; Inquiry into Uranium Mining 1979–80; Inquiry into Habitual Criminals 1983; and B.C. Public Utilities Comn. 'Site C' Hearings; Cons., Law Reform Comn. of Can.; Fed. Min. of Labour; B.C. Legal Services Comn.; B.C. Justice Devel. Comn.; City of Vanc. Office of the Mayor; Instr., B.C. Cont. Legal Edn. 1984–86; Lectr., Simon Fraser Univ. 1980–86; Founder & Dir., West Coast Environ. Law Assn. 1975–86; Co-ord., Pollution Probe 1971–72; Dir., Community Planning Assn. of Can., B.C. Br. 1977–78; Candn. Environ. Law Rsch. Found. 1972–75; Sudbury Envir. Law Assn. 1973; writer/broadcaster for radio & TV 1971–77; CBL Toronto, CHNO Sudbury, CFTR Toronto, CHQM, CKLG & CHEK-TV Vancouver; author: 'Pollution Law in Canada' 1975 and book reviews & newspaper columns 1968–76; recreations: reading, skiing, swimming, nature walks; Office: 4465 Clarence Taylor Cres., Delta, B.C. V4K 3W4.

**ROURKE, Glenn Russell,** B.A., B.P.H.E., M.B.A.; banker; b. Quebec City, Que. 3 July 1944; s. Russell James and Violet Electa (Jordan) R.; e. Quebec H.S. 1962; Queen's Univ. B.A., B.P.H.E. 1966; Univ. of West. Ont. M.B.A. 1969; children: Jennifer, Alexandra; MANAGING DIRECTOR, CORPORATE BANKING, MONTREAL I/C PROV. OF QUE. & ATLANTIC PROVINCES, BANK OF MONTREAL 1984– ; joined Bank of Montreal 1970; var. positions in Asia Pacific Div., Internat. Banking incl. postings in Tokyo, Singapore & Hong Kong culminating in resp. for People's Rep. of China & Hong Kong 1970–81; Vice-Pres., World Corp. Banking, Toronto 1981; Past Pres., Que. Ctte., Candn. Bankers' Assn.; Dir., Royal Victoria Hosp.; Montreal YMCA Found.; Past Chrmn., Bd. of Gov., Weston Sch. Inc. Montreal; recreations: squash, golf, hiking; clubs: Royal Montreal Golf, Montreal Amateur Athletic Assn.; Office: Place D'Armes, Montreal, Que. H2Y 3S8.

**ROUSSEAU, Alain P.,** C.M., M.D., F.R.C.S.(C); ophtalmologist; educator; b. Paris, France 10 March 1929; s. Paul and Marguerite (Alain) R.; e. Coll. Ste Anne de la Pocatière 1949; Coll. universitaire Laval B.A. 1951; Univ. Laval M.D. 1956; L.M.C.C. 1956; Ophthalmol. Specialization Harvard Univ. 1958, Univ. of Toronto 1958–61; certified 1963; F.R.C.S. (C) 1963; Retina Fellowship, Retina Foundation, Boston, Mass., 1961–62; m Madeleine d. late Leon Leduc 29 Sept. 1958; children: Denis, Anne, Hélène; PROF. AND HEAD OF OPHTHALMOL., LAVAL UNIV. 1968– ; Dir. of Ophthalmol. C.H.U.L. 1970–89; mem., Examinations Comte. 1981–84, Nucleus Comte. 1980–86, Accreditation Comte. 1984–90, Roy. Coll. Phys. & Surg. Can.; Chrmn., Bd. Examiners in Ophthalmol., Que. Corp. Surgs. and Royal College, 3 terms each; ; Asst. Prof. Laval Univ. 1966, Assoc. Prof. 1968, Prof. 1975; Hôpital de l'Enfant-Jésus 1963–70, Head of Ophthalmol. 1965–70; served with RCAMC (R) 1955–57, rank Capt., Consultant Candn. Armed Forces 1969–72; Visiting Lectr. in France 1971 and 75 and in Italy 1985; Visiting Lectr. Montpellier Fr. 1987, 1990 and 1992; Guest Speaker, Soc. Fr. d'Ophthalmol. 1986; Visiting Prof. McGill Univ. 1976; Member, Order of Canada 1988; Commemorative Medal, 125th Anniversary of Candn. Confedn. 1992; mem. Nat. Defence Research Bd. Vision Sec.; Adv. Comte. Candn. Nat. Inst. Blind; author or co-author numerous articles, papers; mem. Club Jules Gonin; Retina Soc. (Founding mem.; Vice Pres. 1987–89; Pres. 1989–91); mem., Soc. Française d'ophtalmologie (Canadian delegate 1984– ); Pres., Assn. Candn. Un. Prof. Ophtholm. 1988– ; Am. Acad. Ophthalmol.; Pres., Candn. Opthalmological Soc. 1984–85; Soc. Canadienne d' Ophtalmologie (Council); Soc. d'Ophtalmologie de Qué.; Candn. Med. Assn.; Retina Service Alumni, Mass. Eye & Ear Infirmary Boston; Schepens Intern Soc.; R. Catholic; recreations: tennis, skiing, cycling; Home: 2790 Mont Royal, Quebec City, Que. G1W 2E2; Office: 2705 Boul. Laurier, Quebec City, Que. G1V 4G2.

**ROUSSEAU, Jeannine Marie,** B.A., LL.L.; b. Montreal, Que. 29 Aug. 1941; d. Joseph Rodolphe and Mary Sarah (MacIntosh) R.; e. Coll. Jesus-Marie d'Outremont (Univ. of Montreal) B.A. 1961; Univ. of Montreal LL.L. 1965; JUSTICE OF THE SUPERIOR COURT OF QUEBEC; called to Bar of Que. 1966; comm. law practice with various legal firms Montreal 1966–71; Asst. Secy. and Legal Counsel, Janin Foundation Group, Montreal and Toronto 1971–76; Asst. Secy. & Counsel Northern Telecom Ltd. Montreal, 1976–77; Secy. and Gen. Counsel, Asbestos Corp. Ltd., 1977–79; Vice Pres., Secy. and Gen. Counsel 1979–82; Secy. & Legal Counsel, The Montreal Exchange 1982–84; Secy., Telemedia Corp. 1984–87; mem. Candn. Bar Assn.; Candn. Judges Conf.; Candn. Inst. for the Administration of Justice; Office: Palais de Justice, 1 Notre-Dame St. E., Montreal, Que. H2Y 1B6.

**ROUSSEL, Claude;** artist; b. Edmundston, N.B. 6 July 1930; s. Denis and Dorothée (Pelletier) R.; e. Edmundston High Sch.; Ecole des Beaux Arts, Montreal, teaching Dipl. in Art, 1955 Sculpture Dipl., 1956; m. Brigitte (dec.); m. Raymonde Blanchard; children: Denise, Francine, Claire, Suzanne, Huguette, Sylvie; Resident Artist, Professor and Founder of Art Dept. and Art Gallery, Univ. de Moncton, 1963–92, retired; Art Instructor, Edmundston Public Sch., 1956–59; Asst. Curator, Beaverbrook Art Gallery, Fredericton, N.B., 1959–61; completed over 30 sculpture and mural projects in Canada and the United States; rep. in N.B. Museum; Mount Allison Univ.; Dalhousie Univ.; Univ. de Moncton; O'Keefe Centre, Toronto; Smithsonian Inst., Washington; Confed. Art Gallery; recent exhns, incl. Smithsonian Inst.; Terre des Hommes, Montreal; Centre Culturel de Chauvigny, France; Owens Art Gallery; 1 man shows: Univ. de Moncton; Confed. Art Gallery; N.B. Museum, Saint John, 1976; Art Gallery of N.S., Halifax, 1977; Univ. de Moncton, 1977; Galerie Colline, Edmundston 1978; Owens Art Gallery, 1979; Solo Exhibition toured six Quebec galleries from Drummondville to Montréal 1981 and 1982; Acadia Univ. Art Gallery, Wolfville, N.S. 1989; Retrospective Exhib., Galerie D'Art, Univ. de Moncton 1993; granted a Sr. Fellowship by the Can. Council to study arch. decoration, 1961; awarded, Allied Arts Medal by Royal Arch. Inst. Can., 1964 and ten prizes in sculpture and painting in nat. competitions since 1951; First Prize, St. John City Hall Sculpture competition, 1972; winner of a comm. for a sculpture at site of Sailing Olympics, Kingston, Ont., 1976; selected to represent Can. at the Seoul Internat. Sculpture Garden for the 1988 Olympics; awarded first prize at the second Marion McCain Exhibition, Beaverbrook Art Gallery, Fredericton 1989; selected to create a special monument project for Moncton's centennial 1989–90; works presented in film 'Painting a Province' and on television 'Take 30,' 1963; 'Sketches of Our Towns' 1992; subject of book: 'Claude Roussel, Sculptor' 1987; mem. Can. Council, 1972–75; Rep. Candn. Artist Representation 1970–72; Elected to L'ordre de la Pléiade 1982; named Member of the Order of Canada 1984; recipient, 125th Anniversary of the Confederation of Canada Medal, 1992; Catholic; recreations: camping, sculpture garden; Home: 905 Amirault, Dieppe, Moncton, N.B. E1A 1E1.

**ROUTLEDGE, Marie Isabelle,** B.A.; curator; b. Toronto, Ont. 23 Aug. 1951; d. Stewart and Jacqueline Marie (Choiniere) R.; e. Ridgemont High Sch. 1970; Coll. Notre Dame de Bellevue Quebec City 1970–71; Univ. of Toronto B.A. 1975; m. Jeffrey G. Blackstock 16 May 1980; children: Jill Elaine Marie, Scott Douglas; ASSOC. CURATOR INUIT ART, NATIONAL GALLERY OF CANADA 1993– ; Contract Researcher, Curator, Inuit Art Sect. Indian & Northern Affairs Can. 1975–79, Rsch. & Documentation Co-ord. 1981–84; Mgr. Theo Waddington Gallery, N.Y.C. 1979–81; Asst. Curator Candn. Art (Inuit) Nat. Gallery of Can. 1985–93; author (exhn. cat.) 'Inuit Art in the 1970's' Agnes Etherington Art Centre 1979; 'Pudlo: Thirty Years of Drawing' Nat. Gallery Can. 1990; ed. 'Inuit Art and Crafts' mag. 1981–84; Treas. Ottawa Native Art Study Group; Pres. Native Art Studies Assn. Can.; recreation: sailing; Office: P.O. Box 427, Station A, Ottawa, Ont. K1N 9N4.

**ROUTTENBERG, Mark,** B.A., C.A.; business executive; b. Montreal, Que. 25 May 1942; s. Max and Raelene (Baker) R.; e. Concordia Univ., B.A. 1964; McGill Univ., C.A. 1969; m. Frema d. David and Betty Miller 30 Aug. 1964; children: Michael Kennth, Lawrence Jay; PRESIDENT, FREEMARK INVESTMENTS INC.; C.A. in public practice 1964–77; Controller, Ideal Group 1977–82; Chrmn. & C.E.O., Ideal Plumbing Group Inc. 1982; recreations: golf, tennis; club: Elmridge Golf & Country Club; Home: 4175 Ste Catherine Ouest, Westmount, Que. H3Z 1P4; Office: 7077 Park Ave., Suite 503, Montreal, Que. H3N 1X7.

**ROUX, Jean-Louis,** B.A., C.C., R.S.C.; arts executive; actor; writer; stage director; b. Montreal, Que. 18 May 1923; s. Louis and Berthe (Leclerc) R.; e. Coll. Ste Marie; Univ. de Montréal, B.A. (cum Laude) 1943, med. studies 1943–46; Drama scholarship from French Govt. 1947–48; m. Monique d. Odette and Léo Oligny 28 Oct. 1950; one s.: Stéphane; Dir. Gen., The Nat. Theatre Sch. of Can. 1982–87; stage: approx. 100 roles in Can. & abroad incl. 'Higgins' (Pygmalion), 'Maitland' (Temoignage Irrecevable), 'Titus' (Berenice), 'Lear' (Le Roi Lear); radio: numerous roles, Radio-Canada incl. 'Néoptolème' (Philoctète); television: approx. 40 roles in var. dramas & series incl. 'Ovide' (La Famille Plouffe), 'Le Comte' (La Répétition), 'Gregor' (Le Canard sauvage); film: eight roles in flims such as 'Docteur Louise,' 'The Pyx,' 'Two Solitudes'; director: approx. 50 plays incl. 'Le Soulier de Satin,' 'On n'a pas tué Joe Hill,' 'Le Neveu de Rameau'; script writer: many Radio-Can. TV & radio prodns.; author: 'Bois-Brulés' 1967; co-author: 'En Grève' 1963; transl.; 'Julius Caesar' 1972, 'Equus' 1975; adaptation: 'L'Ouvre-Boite' 1974; military training 1942–46; Founder, Le Théatre d'Essai de Montréal 1950; Théatre du Nouveau Monde 1951; Sec. Gen. 1953–63; Artistic Dir. 1966–82; Offr., numerous arts orgns., cttes. & bds.; Hon. Men., Univ. of Montreal Alumni; Life Gov., The National Theatre School of Can.; Centenary of Confederation Medal 1967; Soc. St.-Jean Baptiste Victor-Morin Prize 1969; Kiwanis Cert.; Best Actor, Congrès du Spectacle 1960; Officer (1971) and Companion of the Order of Canada 1987; Molson Prize 1977; Royal Soc. of Can. Mem. 1982; World Theatre Award 1985; Ph.D. (hon.) in Arts, Univ. of Laval 1988; Law Doctorate (hon.) Concordia Univ.; recreations: tennis, chess swimming; Home: 4145 Blueridge Cres., #2, Montreal, Que. H3H 1S7.

**ROVETO, Conie I.,** B.A., B.Ed.; financial services executive; b. Montreal, Que.; e. Univ. of Toronto B.A. 1971, B.Ed. 1973; PRESIDENT, CHIEF EXECUTIVE OFFICER & DIRECTOR, UNITED FINANCIAL MANAGEMENT LTD. 1993– ; Mgr., Orgn. Planning, Canada Permanent Trust 1981–83; Trust Bus. Systems 1983–84; Project Dir., Investments 1985; Asst. Vice-Pres., Fund Serv., Canada Trust Company 1986; Vice-Pres., Mktg., Central Guaranty Trust 1988–89; Central Capital Mngt. Ltd. 1987–89; Extve. Vice-Pres., United Finan. Mngt. Ltd. 1989–93; Pres., C.E.O. & Dir., United Finan. serv. Ltd. 1990–93; Dir., Ont. Film Devel. Corp.; Senate & Academic Planning Ctte., Univ. of St. Michael's College; Office: 200 King St. W., Suite 1202, Toronto, Ont. M5H 3W8.

**ROVINESCU, Olivia Miranda,** B.Ed., M.A.; educational administrator, writer, teacher; b. Romania 16 Nov. 1952; s. Ionel and Adriana (Pollinger) R.; e. McGill Univ. B.Ed. 1976, M.A. 1982, Ph.D. studies 1983–84; m. Clifton s. Mary and Harold Ruggles 15 Aug. 1981; children: Amanda Jennifer, Alexandria Marika; DIRECTOR, LACOLLE CENTRE FOR EDUCATIONAL INNOVATION, CONCORDIA UNIV. 1984– ; Teacher, John Abbott College 1983–84; Sessional Lectr., College Marie Victorin 1985–91; McGill Univ. 1987–93; presenter at 7 international conferences and num. in-service training seminars in critical & creative thinking; organized 2 confs.; keynote speaker, Que. Fed.of Home & School 1993; photographer: work displayed in exbns & pub. in books & mags.; Concordia Univ. Scholarship; McConnell Memorial Fellowship; McGill Univ. Scholarship; Scholarship-Dir. gen. de l'enseignement sup.; Mem., Literacy Partners of Que.; Que. Assn. of Adult Learners; Bd. of Dir., Nomad Scientists 1986– ; Sec. (elected), Education Undergrad. Soc. 1976; co-author: 'Expressions of Montreal's Youth' 1974, 'Exploring the World of Work' 1975, 'Words on Work' 1981; co-editor: 'Dimensions of Literacy in a Multicultural Society' 1993; author/co-author of several articles; recreations: cycling, hiking, photography; Home: 3421 Montclair, Montreal, Que. H4B 2J3; Office: 7141 Sherbrooke St. W., Montreal, Que. H4B 1R6.

**ROWAND, Robert Scott,** B.A., M.H.Sc.; hospital administrator; b. Edmonton, Alta. 9 Jan. 1954; s. James George and Marguerite Evelyn (Johnstone) R.; e. Ross Sheppard Composite High Sch. 1971; Univ. of Alta. B.A. 1974, Master of Health Services Adm. (M.H.Sc.) 1976; PRES., CHIEF EXEC. OFFR. AND DIR. THE WELLESLEY HOSP. 1990– ; Asst. to Pres. Foothills Hosp. Calgary 1976–78; Asst. Exec. Dir. St. Paul's Hosp. (Grey Nuns) Saskatoon 1978–81, Assoc. Exec. Dir. 1981–85; Vice Pres. Corporate Devel., Foothills Hosp. 1985–90; Lectr.; Social & Preventive Med. Univ. of Sask.; Community Health Sci's Univ. of Calgary; Health Adm. Univ. of Toronto; Teaching Hosp. Surveyor Can. Council Health Facilities Accreditiion; recipient Alta. Achievement Award 1988; recreations: skiing, weightlifting; Home: 475 Ontario St., Toronto, Ont. M5X 1M6; Office: 160 Wellesley St. E., Toronto, Ont. M4Y 1S3.

**ROWAT, Donald Cameron,** M.A., Ph.D.; university professor, retired; b. Somerset, Man. 21 Jan. 1921; s. William Andrew and Bertha Elizabeth (Moore) R.; e. Sask. and Ont.; Univ. of Toronto, B.A. 1943; Columbia Univ. M.A. 1946, Ph.D. 1950; m. Frances Louise, d. John E. Coleman, Mart, Texas 1948; children: Linda, Steven; EMERITUS PROF. OF POLITICAL SCIENCE, CARLETON UNIV.; Rsch. Asst., Dept. of Finance, Ottawa 1943–44; Adm. Offr., Dept. Nat. Health & Welfare 1944–45; Lectr. in Pol. Science, N. Texas State

Teachers Coll. 1947; Dir. of Research, Inst. Pub. Affairs and Lectr. in Pol. Science, Dalhousie Univ. 1947–49; Lectr. in Pol. Science, Univ. of Brit. Columbia 1949–50; Asst. Prof. Pol. Sci., Carleton Coll. 1950–53, Assoc. Prof. 1953–58, Prof. 1958–92; U.N. (TAA) Expert on Pub. Adm., Ethiopia 1956–57; Acting Dir., Sch. of Pub. Adm., Carleton Univ. 1957–58; Chrmn., Ctte. on University Government, Candn. Assn. of Univ. Teachers 1959–60; Canada Council Senior Fellow in Western Europe 1960–61, and studying Federal Capitals 1967–68; Chrmn. 1962–65, and Supvr. Graduate Studies 1965–66, Dept. of Pol. Sci.; Co-Dir., Eighth Annual Seminar, Canadian Union of Students 1965; Extve. Ctte., Candn. Assn. of Univ. Teachers 1965–67; member, Editorial Ctte. & Group Chrmn., 32nd American Assembly (on the ombudsman) 1967; Co-Commr., Comn. on Relations between Univs. and Govts. 1968–69; Chrmn. Policy Comte. for Parlty. Internship Program 1971–76; Visiting Prof. Univ. of Calif., Berkeley 1972; Exchange Fellow Univ. Leningrad 1974; Canada Council Leave Fellow, Western Europe 1974–75; Board, Canadian Political Science Assn. 1974–78, President 1975–76; Council & Extve. Ctte., Social Science Rsch. Council of Canada 1974–78, Vice Pres., 1978–79, and Chrmn., Ctte. on the Freedom of Communication of Social Scientists 1980–82; NATO Fellow studying access to info. laws, summer 1977; Appraisals Ctte., Ont. Council Grad. Studies 1977–80, 1983–86; Nat. Archives Advisory Council on Records 1977–87; Carleton Senate 1979–81; SSHRC Leave Fellow to study and lecture on access and ombudsmen in France, India, Japan and Sweden 1981–82; Bd. of Dirs., Can. Civil Lib. Assn. 1981–84; Editorial Bd., Internat. Rev. of Admin. Sciences 1983– ; Chrmn., Academic Advisory Bd. of Ombudsman Forum, Internat. Bar Assn. 1984– ; research and lectures on federal capitals, ombudsmen and access to information in Australia and New Zealand 1990; mem., Ontario Assessment Review Bd. 1993– ; author: 'The Reorganization of Provincial-Municipal Relations in Nova Scotia' 1949; 'Your Local Government' 1955 (2nd ed. 1975); 'The Canadian Municipal System: Essays on the Improvement of Local Government' 1969; 'The Ombudsman Plan: The Worldwide Spread of an Idea' 1973 (shorter rev. ed. 1985, Japanese ed. 1989, Spanish 1990, and Chinese forthcoming); 'Public Access to Government Documents: A Comparative Perspective' 1978; co-author: (with René Hurtubise) 'The University, Society and Government' 1970; editor: 'Basic Issues in Public Administration' 1961; 'The Ombudsman: Citizen's Defender' 1965 (2nd ed. 1968, Spanish ed. 1973); 'The Government of Federal Capitals' 1973; 'The Ombudsman in Finland' (written by Mikael Hidén) 1973; 'Administrative Secrecy in Developed Countries' 1979 (French ed. 1977, Japanese ed. 1982); 'International Handbook on Local Government Reorganization' 1980; 'Public Administration in Developed Democracies' 1988; Co-editor: 'Studies on the University, Society and Government' 1970; 'The Provincial Political Systems' 1976; 'Political Corruption in Canada' 1976; has also edited 15 books of grad. student essays published by Carleton's Dept. of Political Science 1973–92; has written no. of reports, etc. and more than 100 articles on pol., govt. and adm.; rec'd. no. of critical reviews incl. Sunday Times (London), and award from Internat. Ombudsman Institute for outstanding service to the ombudsman institution; Address: Dept. of Political Science, Carleton Univ., Ottawa, Ont. K1S 5B6.

**ROWAT, William A.,** B.A.; senior civil servant; b. Drayton, Ont. 5 June 1946; s. Lloyd and Leone R.; e. Univ. of Waterloo B.A. (Hons.) 1972; ASSOCIATE DEPUTY MINISTER, TRANSPORT CANADA 1993– ; one s.: Jason; various positions with federal government 1973–80; Dir., Atlantic Fisheries Development Branch, Fisheries & Oceans 1980–81; Resource Allocations Atlantic Operations 1982–84; Dir. Gen., Operations Directorate, Atlantic Fisheries Serv. 1984–86; Asst. Dep. Min. Atlantic Fisheries Serv. 1986–88; Asst. Sec. to Cabinet, Govt. Operations & Labour Relns., Privy Council Office 1988–91; Economic and Regional Development 1991–93; recreations: skiing, reading; Home: 239E Argyle Ave., Ottawa, Ont. K2P 1B8; Office: Place de Ville, Tower C, 29th Floor, 330 Sparks St., Ottawa, Ont. K1A 0N5.

**ROWCROFT, John Edward,** B.Sc., M.Sc., Ph.D., F.S.S.; university professor; b. Maidstone, England 20 Jan. 1944; s. Eustace Honour and Joyce Mary (Flint) R.; e. Erith Gr. Sch. 1963; Univ. of Manchester, B.Sc. 1966, M.Sc. 1967; Simon Fraser Univ., Ph.D. 1979; m. Pamela d. Stephen and Mary Jean Ritchie 8 Sept. 1981; PROF., DEPT. OF ECON., UNIV. OF NEW BRUNSWICK; Math. Teacher, Lancashire Co. Counc., Eng. 1968; Hon. Rsch. Fellow, Univ. of Lancaster 1987–89; Lectr., Econ. & Soc. Statistics, Univ. of Kent at Canterbury 1972–73; Prof., Dept. of Econ., Univ. of New Brunswick 1973; Instr., Opns. Mngt., B.C. Inst. of Technol. 1980–81; Dir., Grad. Studies in Econ., Univ. of N.B. 1974–79, 1981–83; Lectr., Econ. & Stat., Soc. of Indus. Accts.; research & presentations for Consumer Rsch. Counc., Stats. Can. & Dept. of Manpower; Can. Counc. Doct. Fellowships 1969–70, 1971–72; elected Fellow, Royal Stat. Soc. 1968; admitted to Mensa 1965; Former Pres., Coll. Hill Credit Union Ltd.; Mem., Candn. Transp. Rsch. Forum; Candn. Econ. Assn.; Am. Econ. Assn.; author: 'Mathematical Economics: An Integrated Approach' 1994; co-author: 'Consumer Co-operation in Atlantic Canada' 1976; author/co-author, rsch. papers in profl. jours.; recreation: alpine skiing, sailing, Calvin and Hobbes; Office: P.O. Box 4400, Fredericton, N.B. E3B 5A3.

**ROWE, David John,** M.A., D.Phil., F.R.S.C.; university professor; b. Totnes England 4 Feb. 1936; s. Herbert Tyack and Marguerite Ella Bertram (Whitehead) R.; e. Kingsbridge Grammar Sch. 1954; Cambridge Univ., B.A. 1959; Oxford Univ., M.A., D.Phil. 1962; m. Una Mary d. Harold and Stella Dawson 4 Oct. 1958; children: Mark Jørgen Dawson, Jacqueline Amanda; PROF. OF PHYSICS, UNIV. OF TORONTO 1974– ; Ford Found. Fellow, Niel's Bohr Inst. Copenhagen 1962–63; U.K. Atomic Energy Authority Fellow, A.E.R.E. Harwell England 1963–66; Res. Assoc., Univ. of Rochester 1966–68; Assoc. Prof., present univ. 1968–74; Chrmn., Theoretical Physics Div., C.A.P. 1970–71; Mem., Ed. Bd., 'Physical Review C' 1983–86; 'Journal of Physics G' 1989– ; Alfred P. Sloan Fellow 1970–72; The Rutherford Meml. Medal & Prize (Royal Soc. of Can.) 1983; F.R.S.C. 1986; Killam Research Fellow 1990–92; Mem., Candn. Assn. of Physicists; Am. Physical Soc.; Royal Soc. of Can.; author: 'Nuclear Collection Motion' 1970; editor: 'Dynamic Properties of Nuclear States' 1972; recreations: music (piano playing), tennis, skiing; clubs: United Oxford & Cambridge Univ. Club; Home: 5 Scarth Rd., Toronto, Ont. M4W 2S5; Office: Toronto, Ont. M5S 1A7.

**ROWE, Kevin S.;** banker; b. Seldom come bye, Nfld. 14 Feb. 1938; e. Curtis Academy, St. John's, Nfld.; m. Valma Jean, R.N. 28 Aug. 1958; children: Todd, Michelle, Natalie, Scott; EXEC. VICE PRES., THE BANK OF NOVA SCOTIA, PACIFIC REGIONAL OFFICE, HONG KONG, 1987– ; Dir., BNS International (Hong Kong) Ltd.; The Bank of Nova Scotia Asia Ltd.; Solidbank Corp., Philippines; Scotiatrust (Asia) Ltd.; Boracay Limited; worked in many of the Bank's branches in Can. 1955–70; Agent present Bank New York 1970–73, Area Mgr. Puerto Rico, Brit. & U.S. Virgin Islands 1973–77; Sr. Vice-Pres. & Gen. Mgr. present Bank Pacific Regional Office 1977–83; Exec. Vice-Pres. & Gen. Mgr., The Bank of Nova Scotia, Toronto 1983–87; Office: Scotia Plaza, 44 King St. W., Toronto, Ont. M5H 1H1.

**ROWE, William John Allan,** M.B.A., Chevalier St. John of Jerusalem; airline/tourism consultant; retired airline executive; b. Portage La Prairie, Man. 15 Sept. 1933; s. George Raymond and Mary Elizabeth R.; e. Central H.S. 1952; Queen's Univ.; Simon Fraser Univ., M.B.A. 1972; m. Elaine L. d. Elsie and John Saunders 30 July 1954; children: David, Jodi, Gregory; AIRLINE/TOURISM CONSULTANT; Passenger Agent, Trans. Can. Airlines 1952–59; Supvr., TCA 1959–65; Sales Rep. 1965–67; Asst. Regl. Sales Mgr. 1967–73; Dir., Passenger Sales & Serv. 1973–75; West. Regl. Sales & Serv. Dir. 1975–77; Gen. Mgr. B.C. 1977–80; Vice-Pres., Atlantic Can. 1980–83; West. Reg. & Pacific 1983–85; Sales & Serv. Canada 1985–86; Sr. Vice Pres., Passenger Canada 1986–88; Sr. Vice-Pres., Passenger Sales & Service, Western Can. & Pacific Rim 1988–91; Sr. Vice Pres., Assoc. Airlines Jan. 1989–Dec. 1989; Dir., Air BC; Dir., Airshow Canada; Reserve Offr., Candn. Army; Centennial Medal 1967; Former Mem., Univ. Counc. of B.C. 1978–79; Former Gov., Atlantic Prov. Econ. Counc. 1981–83; Dir., Pacific Basin Econ. Counc.; Chair, External Board, Simon Fraser Univ., Faculty of Business Admin.; Past Chrmn., Tourism Industry Assn. of Can.; Dir., Pacific Rim Institute of Tourism; Mem., GATT SAGIT, Business and Professional Services, Govt. of Canada; Mem., Jr. C. of C. (Nat. Pres. 1964–65); Chaine des Rotisseurs; Candn.-Japan Soc.; recreations: salmon fishing, boats; Clubs: President's Club (Simon Fraser Univ.); Vancouver Club; Office/Home: 5672 Groveridge Wynd, Delta, B.C. V4L 2C9.

**ROWE, William Neil,** M.A.; lawyer; author; politician; b. Grand Bank, Nfld. 4 June 1942; s. Sen. Frederick William and Laura Edith (Butt) R.; e. Curtis Acad. St. John's, Nfld. 1958; Meml. Univ. of Nfld. B.A. 1962; Univ. of N.B. Law Sch. 1964; Oxford Univ. (Rhodes Scholar) M.A. (Jurisprudence) 1966; m. Penelope d. Lewis and Olga Ayre 25 May 1967; children: Steven, Toby; LAWYER, WILLIAM N. ROWE LAW FIRM 1967– ; el. M.H.A. Nfld. 1966–82, apptd. Min. 1968–72, Opposition House Leader 1972–74, el. Leader Nfld. Lib. Party 1977, Leader of Opposition 1977–79; daily open-line radio host VOCM St. John's; frequent commentator Nfld. and nat. media; Sir James Dunn Scholar in Law 1962; author 'Clapp's Rock' (novel) 1983, serialized CBC radio 'Morningside'; 'The Temptation of Victor Galanti' (novel) 1989; 'Is That Yor Bill? (book of essays) 1989; recreation: squash; Club: Fort William Racquets; Home: 10 Forest Rd., St. John's, Nfld. A1C 2B9; Office: P.O. Box 5007, St. John's, Nfld. A1C 5V3.

**ROWED, David Watson,** B.A., M.D., FRCSC; neurosurgeon; b. London, Ont. 21 July 1941; s. Hubert Edgar and Eva Grace (Boyd) R.; e. St. Mary's Dist. C.I. 1959; Univ. of West. Ont., B.A. 1962, M.D. 1966; m. Maureen d. Kevin and Gabrielle Casey 9 Jan. 1988; children: Laura, James, Sean, Casey; HEAD, DIV. OF NEUROSURGERY, SUNNYBROOK MEDICAL CTR. 1986– ; Assoc. Prof., Dept. of Surgery, Univ. of Toronto; internship & residency, Univ. of Alta. Hosp. 1966–68; residency, Univ. of West. Ont. 1968–69; Univ. of Toronto Jan.–June 1971; Univ. of Chicago July 1971–June 1972; Univ. of W. Ont. July 1972–June 1973; FRCSC 1973; Univ. of Glasgow, Fellow Jan.–June 1974; Staff Surgeon, present hospital 1974–86; mem., Candn. Neurosurg. Soc.; Candn. Stroke Soc.; Cong. of Neurolog. Surgs.; Royal Soc. of Med.; Toronto Acad. of Med.; Clin. Rsch. Soc. of Toronto; Internat. Union of Angiology; recreations: sailing, flying; club: Aesculapian; Home: 21 Palomino Cres., Willowdale, Ont. M2K 1W2; Office: 2075 Bayview Ave., Toronto, Ont. M4N 3M5.

**ROWLAND, Beryl,** M.A., Ph.D., D.Lit., D.Litt.; professor; author; b. Scot.; came to Can. 1952; e. Univ. of Alta., M.A. 1958; Univ. of B.C., Ph.D. 1962; U. of London, D.Lit. 1980; Univ of Mt. St. Vincent, hon. D Litt. 1982; m. Dr. Edward Murray Rowland, 3 Sept. 1947; PROF. OF ENGLISH, YORK UNIV. since 1971; Asst. Prof. 1962; Assoc. Prof. 1968; Distinguished Research Prof., 1983– ; Visiting Scholar, Univ. of Victoria 1987–89; Adjunct Prof., Univ. of Victoria 1989– ; author: 'Blind Beasts: Chaucer's Animal World,' 1971; 'Animals with Human Faces: A Guide to Animal Symbolism,' 1973; 'Birds with Human Souls: A Guide to Bird Symbolism,' 1978; 'Medieval Woman's Guide to Health: The First Gynecological Handbook,' 1981; editor: 'Companion to Chaucer Studies' 1968–rev. ed., 1979; 'Chaucer and Middle English Studies in Honor of Rossell Hope Robbins' 1974; 'Earle Birney: Essays on Chaucerian Irony' 1985; 'Poetry in English: The Middle Ages' 1987; Assoc. ed.: 'The Variorum Chaucer'; 'Florilegium'; 'English Studies in Canada'; 'The Chaucer Review'; 'Bestia'; 'The Spirit of the Court' 1985; 'Cressida in Alberta' (winner of Alberta Golden Jubilee Drama Award 1955); CBC Drama 'Behold a Pale Horse,' 1956; also author of over 100 articles published in the learned journals in Canada, Europe, Japan and the U.S.; Dir., Goward House Society 1990– ; mem., Assn. Candn. Univ. Teachers Eng.; Humanities Assn.; Internat. Assn. Univ. Profs. Eng. (mem., Internat. Consult. Comte, 1974– ); (bibliographer of the 'Bulletin'); Huntington Fellow, 1976; Eng. Assn.; Modern Langs. Assn. (Chrmn. Sec. III 1975, Life mem. 1992– ); Medieval Acad. America; New Chaucer Soc. (internat. Secy. 1978–83), (Pres., 1984–86); Epopée Animale, Fable et Fabliau, Société Internationale (mem., Consult. Comte. 1985– ; Winner, Amer. Univ. Presses Book Award 1974; awarded Commemorative Medal for 125th Anniversary of Candn. Confederation 1993; Club: Victoria Golf; Home: 2203 – 2829 Arbutus Rd., Victoria, B.C. V8N 5X5.

**ROWLAND, David,** Ph.D.; publisher; b. Toronto, Ont. 20 June 1944; s. Willard H. and Viola (Bulmer) R.; e. Univ. of Toronto, B.Comm. 1966; M.B.A. 1967; Donsbach Univ. (Calif.) Ph.D. (Nutrition) 1980; College of Divine Metaphysics (Calif.) D.D. 1992; PRES. CREATIVE NUTRITION CAN. CORP. 1983– ; Pres., Candn. Nutrition Institute 1983–93; Advisor, Healthways Medical Center, Mexico 1993– ; Chrmn., Nutritional Prod. Indus. Task Force 1987–89; Reg. Nutritional Cons. 1986–93; Pres., Nutrit. Cons. Orgn. of Can. 1983–88; Ont. Vice-Pres., National Health Products Assn. 1987–89; Eastern Vice-Pres., Candn. Health Foods Assn. 1989; Dir., Nutrit. Cons. Orgn. of Canada 1983–93; Minister, Church of Divine Metaphysics 1991– ; discoverer, 'Universal Technique' TM (energy balancing method of integrating body, mind, emotions and spirit); Publisher: 'Health Naturally' 1992– ; 'Nutrition News' 1985–89; author: 'Are Your Deficiences Showing?,' 'Who Needs Food Supplements?' 1985; 'Balancing Body Chemistry,' 'Vascular Cleansing: New Hope for Heart Disease' 1986; 'Herbalism Simplified,' 'Homeopathy

Simplified' 1990; 'Digestive & Glandular Rejuvenation' 1991; 'How to Give Nutritional Advice Legally' 1992; 'Say No To Heart Disease' 1992; 'Listen To Your Body' 1993; mem., New York Acad. of Sciences 1993– ; Residence: 98 Caro Mio 1, Sark, Channel Islands, GB GY9 0SE.

**ROWLATT, John Donald,** B.Comm., Ph.D.; university administrator; b. Carman, Man. 10 June 1944; s. Laurence Hague and Janet May (Eagle) R.; e. Univ. of Sask. B.Comm. 1967; Princeton Univ. M.A. 1969, Ph.D. 1971; m. Geri d. Elwood and Evelyn Robinson 3 July 1970; children: Megan, Todd; VICE-PRESIDENT, FINANCE & OPERATIONS, UNIV. OF VICTORIA 1993– ; Asst. Prof. of Econ., Univ. of Sask. 1971–73; Sr. Policy Analyst, various departments, Federal Government 1973–80; Assoc. Dep. Min. of Finance & Dep. Min. of Labour, Govt. of Sask. 1980–85; Vice-Pres. (Admin.), Univ. of Sask. 1985–93; Bd. of Dir. & Extve. Ctte., Veterinary Infectious Disease Orgn. 1985–93; Woodrow Wilson Fellow 1967; University Prize, Most Distinguished Grad., Commerce 1967; Bd. of Dir., Royal Univ. Hospital Sask. 1983–85; author: 'Welfare and the Incentive to Work' 1972 and journal articles & commentaries; recreations: walking, reading; Home: P.O. Box 241, Saanichton, B.C. V0S 1M0; Office: P.O. Box 1700, Victoria, B.C. V8W 2Y2.

**ROWLES, Charles A.,** B.S.A.(Distinction), M.Sc., Ph.D.; university professor; b. Crandal, Man. 8 May 1915; s. Thomas and Gertrude Mary (Williamson) R.; e. Univ. of Sask. B.S.A. with distinction, 1935 (Sask. Research Scholarship) and M.Sc. 1937; Univ. of Minn., Ph.D. 1940; m. Janet M. Doyle, Feb. 13, 1976; children: Charles Garfield, Thomas Gordon; PROFESSOR EMERITUS AND HONORARY PROF., UNIV. OF B.C.; Soil Surveyor, Univ. of Sask., 1935–37 and Lectr., Dept. of Soils there 1940–41; Chief Chemist and Inspecting Offr. (Chem. and Explosives Divn.), Inspection Bd. of U.K. and Can., Winnipeg, 1941–42, Valleyfield, Que., 1942–43, and at Hdqrs. Ottawa, 1943–45; Assoc. Prof. of Soils, Ont. Agric. Coll., 1945–46; apptd. Assoc. Prof., Univ. of B.C., 1946; Prof. of Soil Science, Univ. of B.C., and Chrmn. of the Dept., since 1956–80 (retired); mem. Bd. of Mang. (1956–60) B.C. Research Council; Senate, Univ. of B.C. 1960–63; Tech. Adv. to Govt. of Venezuela, FAO of U.N. 1962–63; Hon. mem., The Big Block Club, Univ. of B.C.; Cert. of Recognition for Outstanding Contrib., B.C. Chapter, Soil and Water Conservation Soc. of Am. 1989; Fellow, Candn. Society of Soil Science 1990; mem., Chem. Inst. Can.; Candn. Soc. of Soil Science; Internat. Soc. of Soil Science; Agric. Inst. of Can.; B.C. Inst. of Agrol.; Pacific Regional Soc. of Soil Science (First Pres. 1982–83); Sigma Xi; Protestant; Home: 4660 W. 10th Ave., Apt. 1404, Vancouver, B.C. V6R 2J6.

**ROWLEY, Graham Westbrook,** M.B.E., C.M., LL.D., M.A.; educator; b. England 31 Oct. 1912; s. Stamford Harry and Emma Mary R.; e. Giggleswick Sch. 1926–31; Clare Coll. Cambridge B.A. 1934, M.A. 1936; Staff Coll. Camberley 1941; Nat. Defence Coll. Kingston 1961–62; m. Diana d. John and Grace Crowfoot Aug. 1944; children: Anne, Susan, Jane; Adjunct Professor, Inst. of Canadian Studies, Carleton University 1984–90; Retired; archeol. excavation and geog. exploration in Hudson Bay, Foxe Basin and Baffin Island 1936–39; served in Candn. Army overseas 1939–46, ret. as Lieut.-Col.; engaged in Arctic rsch. for Defence Rsch. Bd. 1946–51; Sec., Adv. Ctte. on Northern Devel. 1951–67; Visiting Fellow, Clare Hall, Cambridge 1968–69; Scientific Adv., Dept. of Indian Affairs and Northern Devel. 1969–74; author: 'The Circumpolar North' 1978; numerous scientific articles; awarded Massey Medal, Royal Candn. Geog. Soc. for outstanding personal achievement; Coronation Medal; Jubilee Medal; U.S. Arctic and Antarctic Service Award; military service medals; past Chrmn. Arctic Inst. of N. Am.; past Pres. Arctic Circle; mem. Prehistoric Soc.; Glaciological Soc.; recreations: skiing, travel; Club: Rideau; Harvard Travellers; Home: 245 Sylvan Rd., Ottawa, Ont. K1M 0X1.

**ROWLINSON, Elizabeth Maude Hunter,** B.Sc., M.A., Ph.D.; univ. administrator and educator (retired); Anglican deacon; b. Sutton, Surrey, England 22 May 1930; d. Charles and Mary (Maude) Hunter; e. Wallington County Sch. for Girls; St. Hugh's Coll., Oxford, B.A. 1951, M.A. 1955; Lady Margaret Hall, Oxford, B.Sc. 1953; Northwestern Univ.; McGill Univ. Ph.D. 1965; Montreal Diocesan Theological Coll.; ordained 1993; m. Hugh s. Frank Rowlinson and Winifred (Jones) Grimshaw 7 Aug. 1953; children: Matthew, Andrew, Mark; Defence Rsch. Bd. of Can. 1954–56; Asst. Prof., Assoc. Dean of Students, McGill Univ. 1965–78; Dean of St. Hilda's Coll., Dean of Women and Fellow of Trinity Coll., Univ. of Toronto 1978–91; Assoc. Chaplain, McGill Univ. 1993– ; author and editor of mathematical and other publications; recreations: music, mountain walking, travel; Homes: 3415 Hutchison, Montréal, Qué. H2X 2G1 and 43 Eight Mile Point, R.R. 1, Orillia, Ont. L3V 6H1.

**ROWLINSON, Hugh C.,** D.Phil.; science and business executive (retired); b. Handforth, Eng. 24 Feb. 1929; s. Frank and Winifred (Jones) R.; e. Oxford Univ., B.A. 1951, M.A., D.Phil. 1953; m. Elizabeth d. Charles and Mary Hunter 7 Aug. 1953; children: Matthew, Andrew, Mark; Vice Pres., Rsch. & Technol., CIL Inc. 1984–88; Retired; Post-Doctoral Fellow, Northwestern Univ. 1953–54; Nat. Rsch. Counc. 1954–56; joined CIL as Rsch. Chem. 1956; Patent Agent 1958; Rsch. Sect. Mgr. 1962; Corp. Planning Mgr. 1971; Vice Pres. & Gen. Mgr., Plastics 1977; Dir. & Chrmn., Mgmt. Ctte., Inst. for Chem. Sci. & Technol. 1986–88; Gov., Candn. Plastics Inst. 1982–84; Fellow, Chem. Inst. of Can.; Dir., Candn. Soc. Chem. 1991– ; Chrmn., Candn. Nat. Ctte., IUPAC (Internat. Union of Pure & Applied Chem.) 1989– ; Dir., Candn. Chem. and Physics Olympiads 1988–91; Anglican; recreation: sailing; Club: Barrie Yacht; Homes: (winter) 3415 Hutchison, Montréal, Qué. H2X 2G1; (summer) R.R. 1, Orillia, Ont. L3V 6H1.

**ROWNTREE, Jessie-May Anna,** B.A.; university administrator; b. Toronto, Ont. 26 Nov. 1956; d. Ernest Anthony and Barbara June (Graham) R.; e. Sir John A. Macdonald C.I. 1975; York Univ. B.A. (Hons.) Fine Arts 1981, English 1984; m. Gordon s. Pearl and Richard Bontoft 21 Dec. 1979; children: Nicole Elizabeth and Lindsay Michelle Bontoft; DIRECTOR OF COMMUNICATIONS, YORK UNIVERSITY 1989– ; Production Asst., Candn. Inst. for C.A.s 1979; Owner, Rowntree Assoc. (specialized in taking projects from concept to printed product) 1980–83; Gazette Editor, York Univ. 1984; Managing Editor 1985; Asst. Dir., Communications 1987; Mem., Internat. Assn. of Business Communicators; Candn. Council for the Advancement of Education; Council for the Advancement & Support of Education; Chair, Ont. Universities Public Affairs Council 1993–94; recipient, Val Hudson Award for outstanding contbn. to college life, Atkinson College, York Univ.; Ont. Co-ord., Candn. Orgn. for Parttime Univ. Students 1981–82; Pres. 1982–84; Past Pres. 1984–85; editor: 'Modern Canadian Eloquence' 1985; recreations: karate, curling; Home: 1010 Lockwood Circle, Newmarket, Ont. L3X 1M1; Office: 4700 Keele St., North York, Ont. M3J 1P3.

**ROWSELL, Harry Cecil,** O.C., D.V.M., D.V.P.H., Ph.D.; professor (retired); b. Toronto, Ont. 29 May 1921; s. Joseph Bede and Ida May (Woolfrey) R.; e. Ont. Vet. Coll., D.V.M. 1949; Univ. of Toronto, D.V.P.H. 1950; Univ. of Minnesota, Ph.D. 1956; m. Anne d. Ernest Leslie and Mary Elizabeth Bradshaw 14 Sept. 1946; children: Carol, Paul, Craig, John; Extve. Dir., Candn. Council on Animal Care 1968–92; Lt., Royal Candn. Navy, 1941–45; Asst. Prof. Dept. of Bacteriology, Ont. Vet. Coll. 1953–56; Prof. Head, Div. of Pathological Physiology 1958–65; Head, Dept. of Vet. Pathology, West. Coll. of Vet. Med., Univ. of Sask. 1965–58; Prof. Dept. of Pathology, Faculty of Medicine, Univ. of Ottawa 1970–86, Prof. (VPT) 1992– ; Pres., Internat. Council for Lab. Animal Sci. 1979–87; Cons., Am. Assn. for the Accreditation of Lab. Animal Care; Ed. Adv. Bd., Inst for Study of Animal Problems; Mem., Humane Practices Ctte., Candn. Vet. Med. Assn.; Lab. Animal Med. Ctte., Ont. Vet. Assn.; Ctte. on Seals and Sealing; Pres., Animal Air Trans. Assoc. 1987–89; Dir., Scientists Center for Animal Welfare 1983–89; 14 prof. soc.; Ed. Bd., Elsevier Publishing Co., Internat. Whaling Comm; Replica Red Gate, Univ. of Tokyo 1973; Hon. Doctorate of Laws Degree, Univ. of Sask. 1980; Hon. Doctorate of Laws Degree, Univ. of Guelph 1987; Charles River Canada Award, Candn. Assn. for Lab. Animal Sci. 1980; Medal, Acad. of Sci., U.S.S.R. 1983; Hon. Professorship, Peking Union Medical Coll., Beijing PRC 1986; Officer, Order of Canada 1988; recipient, 125th Anniversary of the Confederation of Canada Medal, 1992; Hon. Membership, Chinese Assoc. for Laboratory Animal Sci.; Hon. Associateship, Royal Coll. of Veterinary Surgeons 1987; Hon. Membership, British Laboratory Animal Veterinary Assoc. 1987; Hon. mem., Institute of Animal Tech. 1990; Candn. Veterinary Med. Assoc. Humane Award 'in recognition of compassion for animals and concern for the well-being of the animal kingdom' (1st recipient) 1987; Pres., Candn. Assoc. for Lab. Animal Sci. 1970–71; Assoc. Ed.: 'Canadian Veterinary Journal' 1962–67; Contrib. author: 'The Canadian Encyclopedia' 1985, 'The Contribution of Laboratory Animal Science to the Welfare of Man and Animals' 1985, 'Scientific Perspectives on Animal Welfare' 1982, 'Animals in Education' 1980, 'Worldwide Furbearer Conference Proc.' 1980, 'The Future of Animals, Cells, Models....' 1977, 'CRC Handbook of Lab. Animal Science' 1974; numerous scientific papers & presentations; recreations: swimming, cross-country skiing; Home: 16 Sandwell Cres., Kanata, Ont K2K 1V3.

**ROWZEE, (Edwin) Ralph,** S.M., D.Sc., F.C.I.C.; chemical engineer; b. Washington, D.C. 17 May 1908; s. Edwin Styears and Henrietta (Carpenter) R.; e. Pub. and High Schs., Washington, D.C.; Mass. Inst. of Tech., S.B. (Chem. Engn.), 1930 and S.M. (Chem. Engn.) 1931; Laval Univ., D.Sc. 1955; m. Mary Elizabeth, d. Mrs. S. J. Hudson of Detroit, Mich., 22 Apl. 1935; children: Susan Anne, Mary Elizabeth, Nancy Lee; Hon. Chairman of Board, Polysar Ltd.; Chemical Engineer, Goodyear Tire & Rubber Co., Akron, Ohio, 1931–42; Mgr., Candn. Synthetic Rubber Ltd., 1942–44; Dir. of Research & Devel., Polysar Ltd., 1944–46; subsequently Dir. of Sales, Mgr., Vice-Pres., mem. Bd. of Dir. and apptd. Pres. 1957; Special Temporary Commn. of Lt. Col. Candn. Army 1945; Purvis Mem. Lectr. of Soc. of Chem. Industry, 1949; Eighteenth Foundation Lectr., Inst. of Rubber Industry, England, 1963; Chrmn. of Bd. POLYSAR 1972–78; UTDC (Urban Transport. Devel. Corp.) 1973–83; Dir. UTDC 1983–84; Railtrans Ltd. 1983 to 1986; rec'd R. S. Jane Mem. Lectr. Award of Chem. Inst. Can., 1960; mem., Chem. Inst. of Can. (Pres., 1954–55); Sarnia Chamber of Comm. (Pres., 1949–50; Dir. 1947–55); Candn. Chamber of Comm. (Dir. 1953); Am. Chem. Soc.; Soc. of Chem. Industry U.K. (Pres. 1969–70); Phi Sigma Kappa (Pres., Omicron Chapter, M.I.T., 1929–30); Anglican; Home: 580 Woodrowe Ave., Sarnia, Ont. N7V 2W2.

**ROY, Adolphe J.,** Q.C., B.A., LL.B.; lawyer; business executive; b. Armagh, Bellechasse Co., Que. 6 Aug. 1930; s. J. J. Aimé and Marie-Louise R.; e. Semy. of Qué. B.A.; Laval Univ. LL.B. 1955; Laval Univ. Faculty of Soc. Sciences grad. 1960; Coll. Civil Defence grad. 1962; Coll. Nat. Defence grad. 1974; m. Lucie d. Joseph Dussault, Quebec City, Que. 8 June 1955; children: Marie Elaine, François Allan, Julie June, Marie Shirley; GEN. MGR., A.S.F.E.T.M. since 1984; called to Bar of Que. 1956; cr. Q.C. 1971; legal practice Beaupré, Choquette & Roy 1956–58; Dionne & Roy 1958–60; City Clerk and Legal Adv. City of Charlesbourg 1960–65; City Clerk of Quebec City 1966–69; Special Adv. to Prime Min. of Que. 1969–77; Assoc. Secy. Gen. of Cabinet Que. 1970–75; Depy. Min. of Transport Que. 1971–72; Chrmn. and Gen. Mgr. Que. Deposit Ins. Bd. 1975–77; Counsel law firm Amyot, Lesage, Bernard, Drolet 1977–79; Vice Pres. & Gen. Mgr. Restel Internat. (Que.) 1982–84; Lectr. Laval Univ. Faculty of Comm. & Adm. Sciences 1964–69, Faculty of Law 1965–69; mem. Prof. Corp. of Indust. Rel. Consultants 1989; Hon. mem. Offrs. Mess Royal 22nd Regt. 1968–84; mem., Knight of Malta; former mem. Candn. Progress Club; former Dir., La Société Amour des Jeunes; Prière Secours; Services Myriam Beth'lehem; mem. Bd. Jr. Bar Assn. 1958; mem. Que. Bar Assn.; mem. Bd., Vice Pres. and Regional Pres., Prov. Vice Pres., mem. Nat. Extve., Vice Pres. and Nat. Pres. Inst. Pub. Adm. Can. 1965–73; Anciens de Laval; Am. Soc. of Assn. Exec.'s; CEPAQ; Am. Soc. of Assn. Exec.; Prix Distinction Gérard Dion 1991 Excellence Award; R. Catholic; recreations: jogging, bridge, tennis, swimming; Home: 2525–B Havre des Iles, Apt. 605, Laval, Que. H7W 4C5; Office: 3565 East, Jarry St., Suite 202, Montreal, Que. H1Z 4K6.

**ROY, André,** B.A.Sc., M.B.A., P.Eng.; educator; b. Can. 16 Feb. 1940; s. Eugene and Gertrude (Lussier) R.; e. Univ. Laval B.A.Sc. 1964; Univ. de Sherbrooke M.B.A. 1969; m. Cecile Gosselin 28 Aug. 1981; two s. Martin, François; PROF. OF BUS. SCH. UNIV. DE SHERBROOKE 1970– , Head of Mgmt.; served with RCN 1960–67, rank Lt.; mem. Bd. La Sauvegarde Insurance Co. 1983–90; Dir. Planiservice Estrie inc. 1984–91; Pres. & Chrmn. of Bd. Fedn. des Caisses Desjardins de l'Estrie; Mem. of the Bd., Confédération des caisses populaires d'économie Desjardins du Québec; La Société financière des caisses Desjardins inc.; La Société de services des caisses Desjardins inc.; Caisse centrale Desjardins inc.; Investissement Desjardins inc.; Internat. Comnr. Scouts du Can. 1975–76, Nat. Comnr. 1976–78; Chrmn. Fondation Hôpital d'Youville, Sherbrooke; Dir. Fondation Mgr Jean-Marie Fortier Sherbrooke; author: 'Management, Concepts and Practices' 1988; 'Administration et Developpement Cooperatif' 1976; recreation: farming; Home: 6050 route 143, Waterville, Que. J0B 3HC; Office: Univ. of Sherbrooke, Sherbrooke, Que. J1K 2R1.

**ROY, Bernard A.,** Q.C., B.A., LL.L.; lawyer and Queen's Counsel; b. Quebec City 8 Mar. 1940; s. Joseph Philippe and Kathleen (Coote) R.; e. Seminaire de Que. B.A. 1960; Laval Univ. LL.L. 1963; m. Madeleine d.

René and Françoise Marien 11 July 1975; one s., Philippe; SR. PARTNER, OGILVY RENAULT BARRISTERS AND SOLICITORS 1991– ; Principal Secy., Office of the Prime Min. of Can. 1984–88; Assoc. Ogilvy, Renault Barristers and Solicitors 1966–73, Partner 1973–84; Resumed Partnership at Ogilvy, Renault 1989; mem. Candn. and Que. Bars; Pres. Bd. of Govs., Royal Victoria Hosp. 1978–83; Pres. Bd. of Govs., Royal Victoria Hosp. Corp. and Found. 1982–84; Life Gov., Royal Victoria Hosp.; Gov., Royal Victoria Hosp. Corp.; mem. Bd. of Govs., Université de Montréal; Chrmn., Bd. of Govs., National Theatre Sch. of Canada; Bd. of Trustees, Stanstead College; McCord Museum of Candn. History; Dir., Domtar Inc.; Imasco Ltd.; Métro-Richelieu Inc.; Canadian National; Intrawest Corp.; Trizec Corp. Ltd.; Hon. Dir., Noranda Inc.; Chrmn., Bd. of Trade of Metropolitan Montreal; Montreal Symphony Orchestra; recreations: hockey, tennis, squash; Clubs: Indoor Tennis Club (Montreal); Montreal University Club; Magog Hermitage; Ottawa Rideau; Office: 1981 McGill College Ave., Suite 1100, Montreal, Que. H3A 3C1.

**ROY, Christian,** B.Sc.A., M.Eng., Ph.D.; university professor; b. Montreal, Que. 28 Feb. 1951; s. Jacques and Jacqueline (Paquette) R.; e. Coll. Marie-Victorin, D.E.C. 1970; Univ. de Sherbrooke, B.Sc.A. 1974, Ph.D. 1981; McGill Univ. M.Eng. 1976; 2nd m. Paulyne d. Réal and Lydia Lagacé 1988; children: Xavier, Delphine, Chantal; PROF., DEPT. OF CHEM. ENGR., UNIVERSITE LAVAL 1991– ; Pres., Pyrovac International Inc.; Pyrovac Institute Inc.; inventor, researcher & developer of new process called vacuum pyrolysis for the transformation of industrial wastes to higher value products; Asst. Prof., Univ. de Sherbrooke 1981–85; Asst. Prof., Univ. Laval 1985–87; Assoc. Prof., Univ. Laval 1987–91; Cons., more than 40 firms & 15 agencies worldwide 1978– ; referee, grant cttes. incl. NATO, NSERC, FCAR; NSERC Univ. Rsch. Fellow 1981–90; Noranda fellowship 1978–80; NSERC Postgrad. scholarships 1977–79; Min. of Education of Quebec Scholarships 1975–78; recipient, Soc. of Chem. Indus. Gold Key Award 1975; Candn. Council of Profl. Engrs. Young Engr. Achievement Award 1989; Fellow, Chem. Inst. of Can. 1990; Albright and Wilson Americas Award 1990; Program Chrmn., 45th Candn. Chemical Engineering Conference 1995; First Chrmn., Permanent Ctte. on the Environment of the Order of Engr. of Que.; Chrmn., U. de Sherbrooke kindergarten 1982–84; Mem. Ed. Adv. Bd., Found. for Chem. Engr. Rsch. Develop.; Mem., E.M.R. Nat. Adv. Ctte. on Bioenergy; Mem., Order of Engr. of Que.; Candn. Soc. of Chem. Engr.; Chem. Inst. of Can.; Am. Chem. Soc.; Assoc. Candn.-Fran. pour l'Avancement des Sci.; National Geographic Society; Internat. Editorial Bd., Journal World Resource Review; author/co-author of 60 journ. articles, 76 proceedings articles & several book chapters; owns 16 patents; invited conf. speaker worldwide; recreations: cross-country skiing, fishing, reading, theatre; Home: 1560, avenue du Parc Beauvoir, Sillery, Qué. G1T 2M4; Office: Pavillon Pouliot, Qué. G1K 7P4.

**ROY, Claude C.,** O.C., M.D., FRCP(C); university professor, physician; b. Quebec City 21 Oct. 1928; s. Joseph Phillipe and Kathleen (Coote) R.; e. Laval Univ. B.A. 1949, M.D. 1954; m. Simone d. Hon. Judge Jean and Simone (Décarie) St-Germain 2 June 1962; children: Sophie, Brigitte, Geneviève; PROF. OF PEDIATRICS, UNIV. OF MONTREAL 1970– & HEAD, DEPT. OF PEDIATRICS, SAINTE-JUSTINE HOSPITAL 1990– ; Internship Quebec City; Residency Training, McGill & Harvard univs. 3 years; practiced gen. Pediatrics, Quebec City 5 years; research, Univ. of Colorado Med. Centre 2 years; Asst. Prof., Univ. of Colorado 1966–68; Assoc. Prof. 1968–70; Visiting Prof., Geneva 1975–76; Paris 1988–89; teaching & research career, Sainte-Justine Hospital 1970– ; Chair 1991– ; Head, Research Centre 1977–82; Head, GI Serv. & Research Unit 1982–90; Former Chrmn., Med. Adv. Bd., Candn. Cystic Fibrosis Found.; Med. Adv. Bd., Candn. Found. for Ileitis & Colitis; Chrmn., Rsch. Projects Panel, The Arthritis Soc. of Canada; Mem. of Council, Medical Rsch. Council of Canada; Bd. Mem., Respiratory Disease Network, Ctr. of Excellence; Panel Chair, Arthritis Soc. of Can.; Sci. Council, Lady Davis Inst. Inc.; Mem., Candn. Inst. for Acad. Medicine; Past President, Candn. Soc. for Clin. Investigation; Sass Kortsak Award Candn. Assn. for the Study of Liver; Officer, Order of Canada 1990; First Harry Shwachman Award for outstanding contribution, Am. Gastroenterological Assn. 1987; Mem., Bd. of Trustees, Ctr. Internat. de l'Enfance; co-author: 'Pediatric Clinical Gastroenterology' 1972, '77, '83, '93; recreations: skiing, tennis, cycling, jogging; clubs: Mohawk Tennis; Home: 2150 Cambridge Rd., Mount-Royal, Que. H3R 2Y3; Office: 3175 Ste-Catherine Rd., Montreal, Que. H3T 1C5.

**ROY, Denis,** B.A., B.Sc., P.Eng.; business executive; b. Victoriaville, Que. 18 Aug. 1936; e. Sem. St-Joseph B.A. 1958; Univ. Laval B.Sc. 1962; m. Yvet St-Hilaire; PRESIDENT, ENTREPRISES VIBEC INC. 1978– ; Min. des Transports du Que. 1962–66; has worked in private sector since 1966; Partner, Lemay Construction 1973–78; Mem., Ordre des ingénieurs du Qué.; C.I.M.M.; Candn. Exporters' Assn.; Former Pres., Que. Road builders & Heavy Construction Assn. 1983–84; club: St-Denis; Office: 575 boul. Industriel est, Victoriaville, Que. G6P 6T2.

**ROY, François R.,** B.A., M.B.A.; business executive; b. Quebec, Que. 20 May 1955; s. Jean-B. and Claire (Charland) R.; e. Upper Canada Coll. 1974; Victoria Coll. B.A. 1978; Univ. of Toronto M.B.A. 1980; CHIEF FINANCIAL OFFICER, QUEBECOR INC. 1991– ; joined The Bank of Nova Scotia 1980; posted in Toronto, New York City, Los Angeles & Montreal; Dir. of Finance, Le Groupe SGF 1986; Asst. Vice-Pres., Finance, Quebecor Inc. 1990; Dir., Montreal Mus. of Fine Arts; Montreal Internat. Music Competition; The Internat. Festival of Films on Art; Vie des Arts; recreations: oenology, arts; Home: 2156, rue Sherbrooke o., Apt. 11, Montréal, Que. H3H 1G7; Office: 612, rue Saint-Jacques, Montréal, Que. H3C 4M8.

**ROY, Hedley Edmund Herbert,** B.A.Sc., M.S., Ph.D., P.Eng; consulting engineer; b. Brantford, Ont. 27 Sept. 1932; s. William Jeffers and Violet Emily (Yates) R.; e. Univ. of Toronto B.A.Sc. 1955; Univ. of Ill. M.S. 1960, Ph.D. 1963; PRES. NORR PARTNERSHIP LTD. 1986– ; Registered Professional Engr., Province of Ontario, states of California and Florida; designated Consulting Engineer, Province of Ontario; joined John B. Parkin Associates (now present firm) 1956, Assoc. 1963, Partner 1964; Mng. Partner, Neish Owen Rowland & Roy (successor firm) 1974–86; Dir. The Toronto Symphony 1970–86, Exec. Ctte. 1981–86; Dir. Assn. Cand. Orchs. 1980–88; Pres. 1984–86; mem., Natural Sciences & Engr. Rsch. Council of Can. (NSERC) Civil Engr. Grants & Selection Ctte. 1977–80; Chrmn. 1979–80; mem. NSERC Open Ctte., Strategic Grants Program 1983–85; mem., Univ. of Illinois Coll. of Engineering Adv. Bd. 1987–89; author or co-author numerous articles profl. jours.; Fellow, Am. Concrete Inst.; Fellow, Am. Soc. of Civil Engrs.; Baptist; recreations: skiing, golf, music; Club: York; Home: 1202, 330 Spadina Rd., Toronto, Ont. M5R 2V9; Office: 350 Bloor St. E., Toronto, Ont. M4W 3S6.

**ROY, Henry A.,** B.E., M.B.A.; business executive; b. Ottawa, Ont. 29th July 1947; e. McGill Univ., B.E. (Mech.) 1970; Harvard Sch. of Business, M.B.A. 1976; Internat. Mgmt. Inst. Geneva, Internat. Prog. Sr. Execs. 1982; m. Diane P. Morin Aug. 1969; children: Louis Sébastien, Henri Olivier; EXECUTIVE VICE-PRESIDENT & CHIEF FINANCIAL OFFR., TRIZEC CORP. 1991– ; Dir., Cambior Inc.; Trizec Properties Ltd.; Hahn Company; Central Park Lodges Ltd.; Chief of Staff and Exec. Asst. to Min. of Finance and Pres. of Treasury Bd. Govt. Qué. 1971–74; Sr. Acct. Mgr. Bank of Montreal, Montréal 1976–77; joined Standard Oil Co. Cleveland 1977 (Kennecott), Vice Pres. Finance and Chief Financial Offr. Processed Mineral Sector incl. Carborundum Electro Minerals and Kennecott/QIT Fer et Titane (Montréal) 1980–83, Dir. of Corporate Finance and Investments 1983–85; Exec. Vice Pres., Provigo Inc. 1985–90; Chrmn. & C.E.O., Consumers Distributing, Horne and Pitfield, Medis Pharmaceutical and Provigo Corp. (USA); Group Vice Pres., International Telecom, BCE Inc.; Chrmn. & C.E.O., BCE-Telecom International Inc. 1990–91; mem. Financial Execs. Inst.; Clubs: Petroleum; Mount Royal; Home: Suite 1400, 318 – 26th Ave. S.W., Calgary, Alta. T2S 2T9; Office: 1700 Bankers Hall, 855 Second Street S.W., Calgary, Alta. T2P 4J7.

**ROY, Jacques H.,** CD, BA, MD; physician, administrator; b. Montreal, Que. 9 Feb. 1936; s. Euclide and Germaine (Frenette) R.; e. College Saint-Laurent, Que. 1958; Univ. of Montreal MD; m. Pierrette d. Lorrette and Albert Gauthier 30 Dec. 1960; children: Carolyne, Martin, Isabelle; DIRECTOR GENERAL, HEALTH CARE SERVICES, CORRECTIONAL SERVICE OF CANADA, OTTAWA 1989– ; Royal Canadian Army Medical Corps 1963; Family Physician, Fabre Medical Centre, Laval, Que. 1966; Canadian Forces Medical Services 1976; Diploma in Addiction Medicine, Univ. of Toronto Med. Sch. 1983; Mem., Bd. of Gov. Regional Psychiatric Centre, Abbotsford, B.C.; Chrmn., Bd. of Gov. Regional Psych. Ctr., Saskatoon; Mem., Bd. of Dirs., Candn. Medical Soc. on Alcohol and Other Drugs; Vice-Pres., Internat. Council of Prison Medical Services; Mem., Candn. Medical Assn.; Ont. Medical Assn.; Am. Correctional Health Services Assn.; Health and Welfare Canada Public Health Medical Advisory Board; recreations: hiking, cycling, skiing; Home: 100 Bruyère St., Apt. 201, Ottawa, Ont. K1N 5C6; Office: 340 Laurier Ave. W., Ottawa, Ont. K1A 0P9.

**ROY, Jean Robert;** retired Canadian executive; b. Timmins, Ont. 12 Nov. 1923; s. Joseph Pierre and Anna Marie (Morin) R.; e. Ecole St. Antoine Timmins; Univ. of Ottawa; Queen's Univ.; m. Georgette d. Mathias and Aurore Clément 4 Feb. 1947; children: Jean R. Jr., Louise M.; Pres., Standards Council of Canada 1981–85; co-owner Senator Motor Hotels Timmins and Sudbury 1962–89; Chief Acct., Forest Products firm 1944–45; Owner and Operator, Lumberyard Welland, Ont. 1946–49; various constrn. ind. positions Toronto 1949–52; supervision and quantity surveying large constrn. projects Buffalo, N.Y. 1952–56; co-owner and Gen. Mgr., Roy Construction & Supply Co. Ltd. Timmins 1956–79; el. mem. H. of C. g.e. 1968, 1972, 1974, retired 1979; Chrmn., Nat. Govt. Caucus 1971–74; mem., Nat. Exec. Lib. Party Can.; Comnr. Intnl. Jt. Comn. 1979, Acting Chrmn. 1981; Pres., Standards Counc. of Can. 1981–84; Extve. Consultant, Ont. Lumber Manufacturers Assoc. 1986–87; service Timmins High Sch. Bd.; Children's Aid Soc. Porcupine; St. Mary's Hosp. Bd.; McIntyre Arena Study Ctte.; Mountjoy Planning Bd.; mem., Candn. and Ont. Insts. Quantity Surveyors; Standards Eng. Soc.; Inst. Assn. Execs.; R. Catholic; recreation: golf; Club: Spruce Needles Golf & Country; Home: (P.O. Box 1940) Delnite Rd., Timmins, Ont. P4N 7X1.

**ROY, Jean-Louis,** L.Ph., M.A., Ph.D.; publisher; author; b. Normandin, Qué. 1 Feb. 1941; s. Louis and Rita (Morin) R.; e. Laval Univ. B.A. 1962; Univ. de Montréal L.Ph. 1964, M.A. 1965; McGill Univ. Ph.D. 1972; Univ. Ste-Anne, Doctorat honorifique 1985; children: Stephen, Elizabeth; SECRÉTAIRE-GÉNÉRAL DE LA FRANCOPHONIE (Agence de Coopération culturelle et Technique) ACCT 1989– ; Assoc. Prof. of Hist. French Can. Studies Prog. McGill Univ. 1969–80, Dir. of Prog. 5 yrs.; Comnr. Que. Govt.'s Comn. des droits et libertés de la personne 1980–81; Publisher, Le Devoir 1981–86; Délégué Gén. du Québec à Paris 1986–89; Délegué général du Québec à Paris 1986–89; frequent commentator radio and TV; Pres., Human Rights League 1972–74; Pres., Que. Fed. Assns. Univ. Teachers 1978–81; Prés., Comité internat. sur l'avenir des institutions francophones 1987; author 'Maitres chez nous (Dix années d'action française) 1917–1927' 1978; 'Les programmes électoraux du Québec, Tome I: 1867–1927, Tome II: 1931–1966' 1970; 'Les frontières défuntes' poetry 1972; 'Rameaux du vieil arbre' poetry 1973; 'Edouard-Raymond Fabre, libraire et patriote canadien 1799–1854' history 1974; 'L'Arche dans le regard' poetry 1975; 'La marche des Québécois, le temps des ruptures 1945–1960' 1976; 'La Beauceronne, Marie à Georges à Joseph' novel 1977; 'Le nationalisme québécois' (ed.) Vol. V No. 2 'Revue canadienne des études sur le nationalisme québécois' 1978–79; 'Le Choix d'un pays, le débat constitutionnel Québec-Canada 1960–1976' history 1978; 'Terre féconde' poetry 1979; '1992, l'Europe au XXIième siècle' 1988; 'La Francophone, l'émergence d'une alliance? Montréal, Canada 1989 (HURTUBISE HMH - Diffusion Hatier); Office: 13, Quai André Citroën, 75015 Paris, France.

**ROY, John Reid,** M.B.,Ch.B., F.R.C.P.(Glasgow & Edinburgh), F.R.C.P.(C); psychiatrist; educator; b. Cumbernauld, Glasgow, Scot. 10 Apl. 1926; s. James Millar and Helen Patrick (Reid) R.; e. Lenzie Acad. Scot. 1944; Univ. of Glasgow Med. Sch. M.B.,Ch.B. 1949, training in psych.; Univ. of London Acad. Dip. Psychol. Med. 1958; Med. Council Can. Licentiate 1971; m. Flora d. Duncan and Margaret Boyd March 1954; two s. Nicholas John, Jonathan Reid; PHYS.-IN-CHARGE GERIATRIC PSYCHIATRY O.P. CLINIC CHEDOKE-McMASTER HOSPS. and Asst. Prof. of Psychiatry 1978– ; Prof. of Psychiatry and (inaugural) Head Div. Geriatric Psychiatry McMaster Univ. 1988– ; served with Brit. Royal Army Med. Corps 1950–52, rank Capt.; Med. Offr. King Alfred Sch. Ploen, Schleswig-Holstein one yr.; Cons. Psychiatrist St. Nicholas Hosp. Newcastle-upon-Tyne 1959–69 and Shotley Bridge Gen. Hosp. North-West Durham; devel. Ind. Therapy Rehab. Prog.; planned Geriatric Psychiatry Services; Chrmn. Group Med. Adv. Bd. over 4 yrs.; private psychiatry practice Ont. 1969–79; joined present Univ. 1979; devel. and dir. first clin. Geriatric Psychiatry Service Hamilton-Wentworth Dist. and acad. Div. of Geriatric Psychiatry McMaster Univ.; estbd. speciality clinic diagnosis memory & cognitive disorders in late life; former Chrmn. Aging Unit Sub-group which inaugurated undergrad. geriatric teaching at McMaster; Assoc. mem. Dept. of Eng. McMaster; Cons. Psychiatrist Emergency Team St. Joseph's Hosp. Hamilton; Hamilton Psychiatric Hosp.; recipient Merit Award Newcastle-upon-Tyne Regional Hosp. Bd. 1969; Found.

mem. Royal Coll. Psychiatrists London 1971; co-ed. and contbr. 'Topics in Psychiatry' 1958; contbr. 'Contemporary Themes in Psychiatry: A Tribute to Sir Martin Roth' 1989; author 36 monthly articles ongoing series 'Aging in Mythology'; author or co-author various articles profl. jours.; mem. Am. Psychiatric Assn.; Candn. Med. Assn.; Candn. Acad. Geriatric Group; Home: 111 Chatterson Dr., Ancaster, Ont. L9G 1B6; Office: P.O. Box 2000, Stn. A, Hamilton, Ont. L8N 3Z5.

**ROY, Louise,** M.Sc., Ph.D.; financial services executive; b. Québec 3 Dec. 1947; d. Louis and Henriette (Gagnon) R.; e. Univ. de Montréal B.Sc. 1971; Univ. of Wis. M.Sc. 1972, Ph.D. 1974; SENIOR VICE-PRES., THE LAURENTIAN GROUP CORPORATION 1992– ; Dir. Laurentian Bank of Canada; Videotron Inc.; Provigo Distrib. Inc.; cons. private firms 1974–76; Dept. Planning & Devel. Prov. Qué. 1976–79; Dir. Projects Transport Council Montréal area 1979–81; Adv. to Min. of Transp. Qué. 1981–83, Dir. Studies & Planning 1983–85; Pres. & C.E.O., Montreal Urban Community Transit Corp. 1985–92; Dir., Québec Chamber of Commerce; Chrmn., Qué. Leader Network; mem. Conseil des gouverneurs associés de l'Univ. de Montréal; recipient grants Woodrow Wilson Found., Candn. Arts Council, Ministère de l'Edn. du Qué.; nominated Woman of Yr. adm. category 1986; Faculty of Comm. & Adm. Concordia Univ. Award of Distinction 1988; Chomedey-de Maisonneuve Prize Soc. St-Jean Baptiste 1988; Edouard-Montpetit Prize 1992; Office: 1100 René-Lévesque Blvd. West, Montréal, Qué. H3B 4N4.

**ROY, Pierre L.,** B.Comm., C.G.A.; financial executive; b. Quebec City 7 April 1950; e. Concordia Univ. B.Comm. 1972; McGill Univ., dipl. acctg. 1975; Hautes Etudes Commerciales, C.G.A. 1980; m. Nancy A. Morrison; 4 children; VICE-PRES., FINANCE & CHIEF FINANCIAL OFFICER, DMR GROUP INC. 1988– ; Bd. of Dirs., DMR Group Inc.; Pixart Industries Inc.; Qadrant Internat. Pty. Ltd.; Director, Finance, Bell Canada 1976–83; Vice-Pres. & Treas., Dominion Textile 1983–88; Dir., Finance Extve. Inst.; Centaur Theatre; Mem., Council of Financial Extves., Conference Bd. of Canada; recreations: skiing, tennis; club: University; Office: 2300, 1200 McGill College Ave., Montreal, Que. H3B 4G7.

**ROY, Reginald H.,** C.D., M.A., Ph.D., F.R. Hist.S; educator; b. New Glasgow, N.S. 11 Dec. 1922; s. Charles Henry and Florence Hanna (Potkin) R.; e. Victoria Coll. 1948; Univ. Brit. Columbia, B.A., M.A. 1951; Univ. of Wash. Ph.D. 1963; m. Ardith Joan, d. Franklyn Christie 1945; one d. Franklyn Ann; EMERITUS PROF. OF HISTORY, UNIV. OF VICTORIA 1990– ; Prof. of History, Univ. of Victoria since 1959; Assoc. and Acting Dean of Grad. Studies, 1973–75; with Army Hist. Sec., Candn. Army H.Q. 1951; Dom. Archives 1953; B.C. Prov. Archives 1954; Instr., Royal Roads Mil. Coll. 1958; served in Candn. Army 1939–45, Can. and Overseas; rank Inf. Lt.; apptd., Hon. Lt.-Col., 741 (Victoria) Communication Squad. 1989; mem. and Past Pres., Cdn. Inst. Internat. Affairs (Victoria Br); mem., International Institute of Strategic Studies; mem. and Past Chrmn., Candn. Assn. for Security and Intelligence Studies; author of 10 books and over 35 articles; United Church; recreations: reading, gardening; Club: Union Club of B.C.; Home: 2841 Tudor Ave., Victoria, B.C. V8N 1L6.

**ROY, Robert Michael McGregor,** B.Sc., M.A., Ph.D.; educator; b. Nanaimo, B.C. 10 June 1942; s. Gregor Henderson and Muriel Beryl (Michel) R.; e. Univ. of Toronto B.Sc. 1963, M.A. 1965, Ph.D. 1968; m. Marilyn d. Bert and Angelina Piccini 10 June 1967; one s. Matthew; Assoc. Prof. of Biol. Concordia Univ. 1975– ; joined C.N.E.N. Rome 1968–69; Lectr. Univ. of Toronto 1969–70; Asst. Prof. of Biol. Sir George Williams Univ. 1970–74; Chrmn. of Biol. Concordia Univ. 1978–82; Dean of Div. III Fac. of Arts & Sci., Concordia Univ. 1982–85; Dir., Priory Sch. Inc. Montreal 1981–85; Home: 298 Corot Rive, Nuns' Island, Montreal, Que. H3E 1L6.

**ROY, Roger,** B.A., B.Sc.Pharm., L.Ph.; pharmacist; b. New York 3 Feb. 1936; s. Clermont and Fleurette (Plante) R.; e. Ottawa Univ. B.A. 1959; Laval Univ. B.Sc.Pharm. 1964; divorced; children: Nathalie, Denis, Alexander; independent pharmacy 1965–75; joined Groupe Jean Coutu 1976 (2 pharmacies: Val D'Or, Malartic); Pres., Socroy Inc.; Roymick Inc.; Aldena Inc.; Hospital Bd., Hopital St. Sauveur 1981–81; Corp. Hopital St. Sauveur 1969–91; Council Mem., Medical Research Council of Canada 1991–92; recreations: alpine skiing, golf; clubs: Mount Stephen 1979– ; Home: 1024 boul. Forest, Val D'Or, Que. J9P 2L7; Office: 823 – 3rd Ave., Val D'Or, Que. J9P 1S8.

**ROYTENBERG, Max,** B.S.A., M.S.A., P.Ag.; food industry executive; b. Winnipeg, Man. 10 April 1934; s. George and Susan (Estrin) R.; e. St. John's Tech. 1952; Univ. of Manitoba B.S.A. 1957; Univ. of Toronto M.S.A. 1958; m. Carole d. Edith Gold 18 Sept. 1977; children: David, Deborah, Judith, Daniel; VICE-PRES., MEMBER SERVICES & PUBLIC AFFAIRS, CANADIAN COUNCIL OF GROCERY DISTRIBUTORS 1992– ; Economist, Agric. Can. 1958–63; Extve. Asst., Steinbergs Ltd. 1963–65; Sec., Mngt. Ctte. 1965–67; Manager, Store Opn. 1967–69; Dir. of Marketing 1969–70; Div. Manager 1971–75; Gen. Mgr., Candn. Egg Marketing Ageny 1975–80; Pres., Roygold Marketing 1981–92 (internat. consulting); C.A.E.S. Best Masters Thesis Award 1975; Public Service Management Devel. Award 1961; Lecturer, McGill Univ. 1972–73; numerous memberships; author of several articles; Home: 1870 Barnhart Place, Oshawa, Ont.; Office: 600 – 210 Dundas St. W., Toronto, Ont. M5G 2E8.

**ROZEMA, Patricia,** B.A.; filmmaker; b. Kingston, Ont. 20 Aug. 1958; d. Jan Rozema and Jacoba Berandina (Vos) R.; e. Calvin Coll. B.A. (philos.) 1981; FILMMAKER, VOS PRODUCTIONS LTD. 1983– ; Assoc. Producer CBC TV 'The Journal' 1981–83; Dir., Writer, Ed., Producer 'Passion: A Letter in 16 MM' 30 min. dramatic film; Dir., Writer, Co-producer, Ed. 'I've Heard the Mermaids Singing' feature length film (winner of 10 internat. awards incl. Prix de la Jeunesse Directors Fortnight Cannes 1987); Dir., Writer, Ed., Exec. Producer 'White Room' feature film ( winner of 4 Internat. Awards) 1990; Dir., Writer 'Desperanto' in 'Montréal vu par...' feature film 1991; Office: 20 Borden St., Toronto, Ont. M5S 2M9.

**ROZOVSKY, Lorne,** B.A., LL.B., Q.C.; lawyer; b. Timmins, Ont. 13 Sept. 1942; s. Hyman and Gladys (Freiman) R.; e. Univ. of N.B., B.A. 1963; Univ. of Toronto LL.B. 1966; m. Fay d. Murray and Beatrice Frank 16 Dec. 1979; two s. Joshua Israel, Aaron Abraham; LAWYER, PATTERSON, KITZ, 1984– ; Adjunct Assoc. Prof. of Law & Med., Dalhousie Univ.; Vice-Pres. & Secy., Lefar Health Associates, Inc.; cr. Q.C. 1984; Legal Couns., N.S. Dept. of Health and N.S. Health Services & Ins. Comn. 1967–78; private law practice 1978–84; author: 'Canadian Hospital Law: A Practical Guide' 1974, 2nd ed. 1979; 'The Canadian Patient's Book of Rights' 1980; co-author 'Canadian Manual on Hospital By-Laws' 1976; 'Legal Sex' 1982; 'The Canadian Law of Patient Records' 1984; 'Canadian Health Facilities Law Guide' (with monthly supplements) 1983; 'Canadian Dental Law' 1987; 'The Canadian Law of Consent to Treatment' 1990; 'Canadian Health Information: A Legsal and Risk Management Guide' 2nd ed.; 'AIDS and Canadian Law'; co-editor 'Rozovsky Risk Management Report' (monthly newsletter); over 500 articles health law; Hon. Fellow, Am. Coll. of Legal Medicine; mem. Shaar Shalom Synagogue; Pres., Nova Scotia Medical Legal Soc.; Writers' Federation of Nova Scotia; Mem. Bd. of Dirs., National Ballet of Canada; Home: 5843 MacLeod Dr., Halifax, N.S. B3H 1C6; Office: P.O. Box 247, Halifax, N.S. B3J 2N9.

**RUBBO, Michael Datillo,** B.A., M.A.; film director; b. Melbourne, Aust. 31 Dec. 1938; s. Sydney Datillo and Ellen Christine (Gray) R.; e. Scotch Coll., Sydney Univ., B.A.; Stanford Univ., M.A.; divorced; one s.: Nicolas; m. Ekaterina Korolkevich; one d. Ellen; foster parent of child in Guatemala and Roumania; worked at N.F.B. for 20 yrs, winning approx. 40 prizes for films; teacher, Australian Film Sch. & Harvard Univ.; painter; freelance writer & dir., 1984– ; since leaving NFB has made 3 children's feature films 'Peanut Butter Solution,' 'Tommy Tricker & the Stamp Traveller,' and 'Vincent and Me' (winning numerous prizes including an Emmy 1992); notable documentaries include 'Sad Song of Yellow Skin,' 'The Man Who Can't Stop,' 'Solzhenitsyn's Children,' 'Waiting for Fidel,' 'Margaret Atwood, once in August'; Prof. of Film, Harvard Univ. 1988–89; recreations: tennis, landscape painting; Home: 719 De L'epee, Outremont, Que. H2V 3V1.

**RUBENSTEIN, Hymie,** B.A., M.A., Ph.D.; university professor; b. Toronto, Ont. 31 Jan. 1943; s. David and Lily (Shore) R.; e. Univ. of Toronto B.A. 1966, M.A. 1968, Ph.D. 1976; 4.5 years of anthropological field rsch. St. Vincent, West Indies 1969–93; m. Nopsie d. Cecil Arthur and Matilda Rebecca Chewitt 24 April 1973; one d.: Esther Vincentia; PROFESSOR, ANTHROPOLOGY, UNIV. OF MANITOBA 1989– ; Rsch., Teaching Asst., Univ. of Toronto 1967–69; Lectr. 1968; Visiting Asst. Prof., Univ. of Alta. 1972–73; Lectr., Univ. of Manitoba 1973–76; Asst. Prof. 1976–80; Assoc. Prof. 1980–89; External Examiner, Univ. of the West Indies 1986–93; rsch. interests: Caribbean soc. & culture, anthropology & drugs, internat. migration, and peasants; Research Fellowship, Inst. for the Humanities, Univ. of Man. 1993–94; has been awarded num. fellowships and research & travel grants 1967– ; Mem., Caribbean Studies Assn.; Am. Ethnol. Soc.; Foreign Fellow, Am. Anthropol. Assn.; Assoc., Current Anthropol.; Life Mem., St. Vincent Nat. Trust; author: 'Coping with Poverty' 1987; co-editor: 'Small Farming and Peasant Resources in the Caribbean' 1988; newspaper columnist 'The Vincentian' (St. Vincent, W.I.) of column entitled 'The Drug Dilemma'; recreations: jogging, walking, travelling; Home: 197 Augusta Dr., Winnipeg, Man. R3T 4H3; Office: Winnipeg, Man. R3T 5V5.

**RUBES, Jan.;** opera and concert singer; actor; director; b. Volyne, Czechoslovakia 6 June 1920; s. Jan and Ruzena (Kellnerova) R.; e. Real-Gymnasium, Strakonice, Czechoslovakia, 1938; Med. Sch., Prague Univ.; Prague Conserv. of Music (won scholarship) m. Susan Douglas, 22 Sept. 1950; children: Christopher Jan, Jonathan Mark, Anthony Dean; prior to musical career won several championships in skiing and tennis; became youngest basso at Prague Opera House in 1945 singing over 30 leading operatic bass roles there and at the Opera House of Pilsen; selected to rep. Czechoslovakia at Internat. Music Festival in Geneva, 1948; came to Can. 1948; gained recognition through CBC radio show he authored and starred as singer-narrator 'Songs of my People' 1953–63; TV dramas: 'Charlie Grants' War,' 'Catsplay,' 'The Harvest' (CBC); T.V. Series: 'Crossings' (ABC); 'Kane and Abel' (CBS); 'Little Gloria' (NBC); 'Campbells' (CTV); 'The Day Grandad Died'; appeared as guest in other TV series such as: 'E.N.G.,' 'Street Legal,' 'Fame,' 'Life Goes On,' 'Max Glick' etc.; author and star of 'Guess What,' education T.V. children's program 1975–1983; film roles incl. 'Forbidden Journey,' 'The Incredible Journey'; 'Lions for Breakfast'; 'The Amateur'; 'Witness'; 'One Magic Christmas'; 'Outside Chance of Maximilian Glick'; 'Courage Mountain'; 'Dead of Winter'; 'Class Action'; 'Deceived,' 'Birds II,' 'Coming of Age,' 'Roommates,' 'Mighty Ducks 2,' 'Mesmer' etc.; musical comedy roles incl. 'South Pacific,' 'The Sound of Music,' 'Cabaret,' 'Man of La Mancha'; has sung over 100 leading bass roles in 6 langs. with such co's as Candn. Opera Co., New York City Centre, Pittsburgh, Washington, Chicago, New Orleans, Seattle, and in Mexico and Germany; has toured U.S. and Can. in concert and/or with symphony orchestra; sang operas at Stratford, Ottawa, Montreal, Vancouver Festivals; tought at Royal Conserv. Opera Sch., York Univ., Univ. of Windsor, Artist in Residence at Wilfred Laurier Univ., Waterloo, 1981; Dir. Touring for C.O.C. (Toronto) 1974–76; took part in opening of 'Young People Theatre Centre,' 1977, founded by wife Susan, in a multimedia show known as 'Laterna Magica'; rec'd Centennial Medal 1967; Queen's Jubilee Medal; 1978; named Hon. Citizen of Winnipeg, Saskatoon, Sydney (N.S.); received Doctorate H.C. University of Guelph, June 1983, Canadian Nat. Senior Tennis Champion; Gemini Award Winner 'The Two Men' (Best Supporting Actor) 1990; recipient, Earle Grey Award for Lifetime Work in Candn. Television 1991; Address: 44 Charles St. W., Apt. 2813, Toronto, Ont. M4Y 1R7.

**RUBIN, David Aaron,** C.St.J., Q.C., B.A., LL.B.; lawyer; b. Toronto, Ont. 12 May 1938; s. Irving Morris and Ida Freda (Kapatz) R.; e. Oakwood Coll. Inst.; Univ. of Toronto Univ. Coll. B.A. 1961; Osgoode Hall Law Sch. LL.B. 1964; m. Patricia d. Arthur and Esther Gelber 19 Sept. 1967; two s. Gerald, Noah; PARTNER, GOWLING, STRATHY & HENDERSON 1989– ; Dir. Pentair Canada Inc.; PCA Canada Inc.; GFT Mode Canada Inc.; General DataComm Ltd.; called to Bar of Ont. 1966; Q.C. 1978; private law practice 1978; Cameron, Brewin & Scott 1978–83; Gowling & Henderson 1983–89; Dir. Candn. Intelligence & Security Assn. 1970– , Pres. 1978–80; Dir. Jewish Vocational Service Metrop. Toronto 1968– , Pres. 1985–87; mem. Exec. Ctte. Candn. Jewish Cong. Ont. Region 1983– ; Gov. Mount Sinai Hosp. 1988– ; Exec. Ctte. St. John Ambulance Metrop. Toronto 1984– , Chrmn. 1987–90; Dir. St. John Ambulance Ont. 1987– , Vice Pres. legal 1990– ; Dir. Candn. Soc. for Weizmann Inst. Sci. 1987– ; Dir. The Co-Opera Theatre 1975–83, Pres. 1976–80; service Candn. Forces (R) 1961– , rank Capt.; Aide-De-Camp to Lt. Gov. of Ont. 1972–85; Chrmn. Legal Div. Campaign Easter Seal Soc. Toronto 1982–84, mem. Fundraising Adv. Ctte. 1985–90; mem. Hon. Ctte. Canada Memorial Found.; mem. Can.-Israel Cultural Found.; Empire Club (Dir. 1978–82); recipient Karen Hayesod Fundraising Award 1967; Queen's Silver Jubilee Medal 1978; C.St.J. 1991; awarded Commemorative Medal for 125th Anniversary of Candn. Confederation; Vice-Chrmn., Comm. Law Jour.; Chrmn., Pub. Ctte. 'Scarlet to Green, A History of Intelligence in the Canadian

Army' 1981; author various publs.; mem. Candn. Bar Assn.; Law Soc. Upper Can.; Co. York Law Assn.; Am. Bar Assn.; Comm. Law League Am.; Bd. Trade Metrop. Toronto; recreation: tennis; Clubs: Mayfair Lakeshore Racquet; Home: 303 Russell Hill Rd., Toronto, Ont. M4V 2T7; Office: 4900 Commerce Court West, Toronto, Ont. M5L 1J3.

**RUBIN, Don,** M.A.; educator; theatre critic, editor, publisher; b. Brooklyn, N.Y. 25 Nov. 1942; s. Irving M. and Louise L. (Singer) R.; e. High Sch. of Performing Arts New York grad.; Hofstra Univ. New York B.A. 1960; Univ. of Bridgeport (Conn.) M.A. 1966; m. Patricia d. Gordon and Joan Keeney 20 Dec. 1987; children (by previous marriage to Gretchen Anner): Joshua, Varya, Ilya; PROF. OF THEATRE, YORK UNIV. 1968– , Original Faculty Mem., Faculty of Fine Arts 1969, Chrmn. of Theatre 1979–82; began profl. acting career in New York; began writing theatre criticism 'Show Business Newspaper' N.Y. 1956 and later 'Backstage Magazine'; Theatre Critic 'The New Haven Register' Conn. 1964; 'Toronto Star' 1968; freelance CBC Radio 1968–78; Founder & Ed. 'Canadian Theatre Review' 1974–82; Ed. 'World Encyclopedia of Contemporary Theatre' UNESCO 6 vols. 1982– ; Pres. Candn. Centre Internat. Theatre Inst. 1987–89, mem. Can. ITI Exec. Bd. 1979– ; Co-Founder Toronto Drama Bench (critics) 1971 and Candn. Theatre Critics Assn. 1978; mem. Internat. Exec. Comm. Internat Theatre Inst. Paris 1987–89; Visiting Lectr. in Theatre Univ. of Bordeaux, Nat. Theatre Sch. of the USSR and of Bulgaria, Univ. of Bologna, Univ. of Debrecen (Hungary), universities and theatre schools across China (1991) and other Canada. and US instns.; documentary progs./interviews CBC Radio and TV, CITY-TV; ed. 'Canada on Stage' 8 vols. 1974–82; 'Canada's Playwrights: A Biographical Guide' 1980; critical articles various mags. and newspapers; contbr. many internat. jours. and books; recreations: reading biographies, sports, stamp collecting; Office: 4700 Keele St., North York, Ont. M3J 1P3.

**RUBIN, Jeffrey Gordon,** B.A., M.A.; financial executive; b. Toronto, Ont. 24 Aug. 1954; s. Leon Julius and Shirley (Gordon) R.; e. Univ. of Toronto B.A. (with distinction) 1976; McGill Univ. M.A. 1981; Home: 26 Albemarle Ave., Toronto, Ont. M4K 1H7; CHIEF ECONOMIST, WOOD GUNDY, VICE-PRESIDENT, AND DIRECTOR, WOOD GUNDY INC. 1991– ; Senior Policy Advisor, Ont. Min. of Treas. & Econ. 1981–88; Senior Economist, Wood Gundy 1988; Office: BCE Pl., Box 500, Toronto, Ont. M5J 2S8.

**RUBIN, Norman,** B.Sc., M.A., M.F.A.; environmentalist; b. Boston, Mass. 20 Apl. 1945; s. Morris and Gertrude (Kastan) R.; e. Newton S. (Mass.) High Sch. 1962; Mass. Inst. Technol. B.Sc. 1966; Boston Univ. M.A. 1968; Princeton Univ. M.F.A. 1970; div.; RESEARCH ASSOC., BOREALIS ENERGY RESEARCH ASSN. 1991– ; DIRECTOR, NUCLEAR RSCH. 1985– and SENIOR POLICY ADVISOR, ENERGY PROBE TORONTO 1992– ; Teaching Asst. Princeton Univ. 1970–71, Instr. 1971–74; Visiting Lectr. Univ. of Toronto 1974–76, Lectr. 1976–78; Nuclear Power Researcher Energy Probe Toronto 1978–85; mem. Nat. Bd. Dirs. Sci. for Peace 1986– ; Dir. Ind. Power Producers Soc. Ont. 1989–91; Steering Ctte. Campaign for Nuclear Phaseout 1989– ; Tech. Adv. Ctte. Ont. Nuclear Emergency Plan 1989– ; Greenprint for Can. Working Ctte. 1988– ; Bd. Advs. Waterloo Inst. Risk Rsch. 1987– ; Steering Ctte. Ont. Environment Network 1986–87; Mem., Ont. Round Table on Environment and Economy Task Force on Energy and Minerals 1991; guest host 10 episodes 'Fragile Nature' TV Ont. 1990–91; author or co-author numerous articles, briefs nuclear affairs; mem. Scarborough Men's Volleyball Assn.; recreations: sailing, cycling, volleyball, gardening; Club: North Toronto Sailing; High Park Ski Club; Home: 174 Major St., Toronto, Ont. M5S 2L3; Office: 225 Brunswick Ave., Toronto, Ont. M5S 2M6.

**RUBINOFF, Arnold Sidney,** B.Com., M.A.; business consultant; b. Toronto, Ont., 13 Feb. 1926; s. Meyer Philip and Sally (Spector) R.; e. Givens Pub. Sch. and Central High Sch. of Comm., Toronto, 1944; Univ. of Toronto, B.Com. 1948, M.A. (Econ.) 1949; m. Florence Alma, d. Frederick Pike, R.R. 4, Athens, Ont., 19 May 1954; children: Carolyn Beth, Philip Andrew, David Matthew; joined Nat. Income Div., Dom. Bureau of Statistics, 1950–56; seconded to Econ. Sec., NATO Secretariat, Paris, 1956–59; joined Econ. Analysis and Financial Affairs Div. of Finance Dept., 1959; Dir., Econ. Analysis Div., 1964–70, Dir., Fed.-Prov. Relations Div. 1970–73; Gen.-Dir., Tax Policy & Fed.-Prov. Relations, 1973–76; Asst. Deputy Min., Econ. Programs & Govt. Finance, 1976–1981; Acting Asst. Deputy Minister, Tax Policy, 1980–81; Senior Asst. Deputy Min. Finance 1981–84; Candn. Exec. Dir., Inter-American Development Bank 1984–88; Sr. Assoc., Govt. Rsch. Corp. 1988–89; Consultant, Hill and Knowlton 1989–91; participated in Govt.'s Bilingual and Bicultural Devel. Programme, Quebec City, 1967–68; served as mem. and as Head, Candn. Dels. to various OECD meetings, Paris, 1961–69; mem., Fed. Govt. Del. to Fed.-Prov. meetings of Continuing Comte. of Officials on Econ. and Fiscal Matters, 1964–75; Secy., Fed. Prov. Comte. on Econ. and Fiscal Matters, 1970; served with RCASC (Militia) 1951–56; rank Lt.; Hebrew; recreations: golfing, travel, reading; Club: Bretton Woods Recreation Center; Home: 7811 Whiterim Terrace, Potomac, MD, U.S.A. 20854.

**RUBINOFF, Lionel,** M.A., Ph.D.; educator; consultant; writer; broadcaster; b. Toronto, Ont. 7 Sept. 1930; s. Benjamin and Hilda Ann (Belfer) R.; e. Harbord Coll. Inst. 1949; Acad. of Radio Arts Toronto, 1950; Queen's Univ. B.A. 1956; Univ. of Toronto M.A. 1957, Ph.D. 1964; m. Suzanne d. Ralph and Frances Hagey 18 May 1956; children: Aaron, Ingrid, Daniel, Leah, David; PRINC., JULIAN BLACKBURN COLL. AND VICE DEAN OF ARTS AND SCIENCE, TRENT UNIV. 1980–85; Prof. of Philos. 1971– ; Chrmn., Dept. of Philosophy 1991– ; prof. radio and stage actor CBC Radio and New Play Soc. 1939–50; Instr. in Philos. Univ. of Toronto 1957–59; Prof. of Philos. & Social Science York Univ. 1960–71; elected mem. N. York Bd. Educ. 1970–73; writer, broadcaster, educ. consultant CBC Radio and TV and TV Ont. 1964– ; Co-chrmn. Educ. Council Health and the Environment 1978–81; Dir. Candn. Soc. for Environmental Educ. 1980– ; mem. S. Central Region Adv. Council TV Ont. 1975–81; Dir. Peterborough Un. Community Services 1975–78; Dir., Peterborough Festival of the Arts 1985– ; Extve., Candn. Soc. for the Study of Practical Ethics 1987–89; Extve., Ont. Philosophical Soc. 1989–91; Dir., Kawartha Jazz Society 1989– ; Mem. Bd. of Govs., Trent Univ. 1991–93; author: 'Pornography of Power' 1968, German transl. 1972; 'Collingwood and the Reform of Metaphysics' 1970; ed. 'Faith and Reason: Essays in the Philosophy of Religion' by R.G. Collingwood, 1968; Ed. F.H. Bradley's 'The Presuppositions of Critical History' 1968; Ed., 'Tradition and Revolution' 1971; Ed., 'Objectivity Method and Point of View: Essays in the Philosophy of History' 1991; contrib. to various books and Journals; recipient Medal in Philos. Queen's Univ. 1956; George Paxton Young Mem. Fellowship Univ. Toronto 1957 and George Sidney Brett Mem. Fellowship 1956; Can. Council Fellowships 1959, 1960, 1966, 1967; recreations: cross-country skiing, long distance running, music; Home: R.R. 7, Peterborough, Ont. K9J 6X8; Office: Trent Univ., Peterborough, Ont. K9J 7B8.

**RUBINOFF, Robert A.;** President private investment company; b. Toronto, Ont. 24 March 1939; s. David and Rachel (Rosenberg) R.; e. Masonville Pub. Sch., London, Ont. 1951; Medway High Sch., Arva, Ont. 1956; Univ. of W. Ont. 1956–58; New York Univ. 1958–59; m. Anne Cressy Marcks, 3 July 1970; two s., Daniel, Matthew; Pres. and Dir., Daray Holdings Ltd.; Inglewood Holdings Inc.; Sheffield Inc.; Chrmn., Woodbridge Moulded Prod. Ltd.; Dir., Delta Hotels Ltd.; The Equitable Trust Co.; Mandarin Capital Inc.; National Fibretech Inc.; On-Line Services; Para Inc.; Place Resources Corp.; Softkey Software Products Inc.; Mt. Sinai Hosp.; Managing Partner, The White Oaks Grp.; Pres., Ont. Chamber of Comm. 1981; Chrmn. Minaki Lodge Resort Ltd. 1984–85; joined Leeds Sportswear Ltd. 1959; Pres. 1963; joined Commonwealth Holiday Inns of Can. Ltd., becoming Innkeeper, Holiday Inn, London S. 1966, Dir. of Operations 1967, Vice Pres.-Inn Operations 1967, opened London, Eng. Office as Dir. of European Operations 1968, Vice Pres. 1968, Sr. Vice Pres. 1972, Extve. Vice Pres. and Dir. 1975–79; Dir., Mount Sinai Foundation; Clubs: York Racquets; Caledon Ski; Home: 166 Warren Rd., Toronto, Ont. M4V 2S5; Office: Suite 302, 162 Cumberland St., Toronto, Ont. M5R 1A8.

**RUBINSKY, Holley,** B.A., M.Ed.; writer, educator, practitioner of the Usui System of Natural Healing (Reikei); b. Los Angeles, Calif. 18 May 1943; d. Richard Allen and Ella Elizabeth (Elston) Woolf; e. Univ. of Calif. at L.A., B.A. 1965, M.Ed. 1973; m. Carroll Ballard 3 Oct. 1964; divorced; one d.: Robin Elliot B.; m. Yuri Ivan s. André and Anna (Dawidowicz) R. 30 June 1984; stories published in Redbook, McCall's and Cosmopolitan under Holley Ballard & Kate Elliot 1968–76; stories published in various Candn. literary journals 1986–92; anthol. in 'Redbook's Famous Fiction' 1974, 'The Macmillan Anthol. I' 1988, 'Journey Prize Anthol.' 1989, 'Frictions II: Stories by Women' 1993; Teacher, L.A. 1968–75; Resource Teacher, Kaslo, B.C. 1976–83; Co-ord., Banff Pub. Workshop 1983, 1984; Banff Writing Prog. 1984, 1985; Instr., Banff Writing Prog. 1986, 1987; Instr., Univ. of Toronto Sch. of Cont. Studies 1988–90; M.C.A writing scholarship award (UCLA) 1964; Samuel Goldwyn Writing Award (UCLA) 1965; Finalist, Western Mag. Awards 1988, 1989; Winner, Gold Medal for Fiction, Nat. Mag. Awards 1989; Winner, The McClelland & Stewart Journey Prize 1989; mem., Kootenay Lake Hist. Soc.; author: 'Rapid Transits & Other Stories' 1990; editor: 'The Event Horizon: Essays on Hope, Sexuality, Social Space and Media(tion) in Art' 1987; Mem., Ed. Bd., 'Descant' 1987–89; recreation: fishing; Mem., Writers; Union of Can.; Friends of Kaslo Shipyard; Home: P.O. Box 872, Kaslo, B.C. V0G 1M0; Office: #904 – 50 Prince Arthur Ave., Toronto, Ont. M5R 1B5.

**RUBINSKY, Yuri,** B.A., B.Arch.; author; editor; software architect; b. Tripoli, Lebanon 2 Aug. 1952; s. André Ivan and Anna (Dawidowicz) R.; e. Brock Univ. B.A. 1972; Univ. of Toronto B.Arch. 1979; m. Holley d. Richard and Ella Woolf 30 June 1984; PRES. SOFTQUAD INC. 1985– ; Vice Pres. Consulting present Co. 1984–85; Founding Co-Dir. Banff Publishing Workshop 1980–84, Dir. 1985–86; CHAIRMAN, SGML OPEN CONSORTIUM 1993– ; Chrmn.: Standards and the Desktop Conf. Boston 1988; Standard Generalized Markup Lang. (SGML) Conf. Atlanta 1989, Philadelphia 1990, Providence 1991, Danvers, MA 1992, Boston, MA 1993; mem. Computer-aided Acquisitions & Logistics Support (CALS) Industry Steering Group Standards and Electronic Publishing working groups 1990– ; mem. IGES/PDES Organization (Product Data Exchange using ISO STEP) 1992– ; Chrmn., ISO 10303/TC184/SC4/T14-STEP Technical Publications; mem. Internat. Ctte. for Accessible Document Design (for Print Disabled) 1991– ; recipient Graphic Communications Assn. Award for Achievement in Tech. Documentation Ind. 1989; co-author: 'Christopher Columbus Answers All Charges' 1993; 'A History of the End of the World' 1982; mng. ed. 'Not The Globe and Mail' 1984; co-author and producer 'SGML: The Movie' 1990; editor: 'The SGML Handbook : The Authoritative Reference to International Standard 8879: Standard Generalized Markup Language' 1990; 'The SGML Primer' 1991; mem. Kootenay Lake Hist. Soc.; Friends of Kaslo Shipyard; Home: P.O. Box 872, Kaslo, B.C. V0G 1M0; Office: 810, 56 Aberfoyle Cres., Toronto, Ont. M8X 2W4.

**RUBIO, Mary Henley,** Ph.D.; university professor; b. Mattoon, IL 2 Oct. 1939; d. Thomas Edward and Selma Anna (Eversole) H.; e. DePauw Univ., B.A. (cum laude) 1961; Univ. of Illinois, M.A. 1965; McMaster Univ., Ph.D. 1982; m. Gerald John s. Joseph and Josephine R. 1963; children: Tracy Katherine, Jennifer Joanna; ASSOC. PROF. OF ENGLISH, UNIV. OF GUELPH 1967– ; emigrated to Can. from U.S.A. 1967; Co-founder & current co-editor, 'CCL: Canadian Children's Literature/Littérature canadienne pour la jeunesse' 1975; Co-editor: 'KANATA: An Anthology of Canadian Children's Literature' 1976; Editor: 'The Genesis of Grove's "Adventure of Leonard Broadus": a Text and Commentary' 1983; Co-editor: 'The Selected Journals of L. M. Montgomery' Vol. 1, 1985, Vol. 2, 1987, Vol. 3, 1992; member ISRCL, ACUTE, ACQL, ChLA, Osborne Collection of Early Children's Lit.; Home: R.R. 6, Guelph, Ont. N1H 6J3; Office: U. of Guelph, Ont. N1G 2W1.

**RUBY, Clayton Charles,** LL.M.; barrister; b. Toronto, Ont. 6 Feb. 1942; s. Louis W. and Marie (Bochner) R.; e. Forest Hill Coll. Inst. Toronto; York Univ. B.A. 1963; Univ. of Toronto LL.B. 1967; Univ. of Cal. Berkeley LL.M. 1973; PARTNER, RUBY & EDWARDH; called to Bar of Ont. 1969; author 'Law Law Law' 1973; 'Sentencing' 1974, 3rd ed. 1987; Ed., Canadian Rights Reporter; various legal articles; part-time columnist, The Toronto Star Newspaper; Bencher, Law Soc. Upper Can.; Community Assoc., Social Planning Council of Metropolitan Toronto; Trustee, The Starlight Foundation; mem. Amnesty Internat.; The Writers Union of Canada; Dir., P.E.N. Canada; Mem., South Africa Education Trust Fund (Legal and Constitutional Commissions); Hon. Patron, Native Men's Residence; Home: 3 Rosedale Rd., Toronto, Ont. M4W 2P1; Office: 11 Prince Arthur Ave., Toronto, Ont. M5R 1B2.

**RUDD, D'Alton Stafford (Bill),** B.A., F.C.I.A., F.S.A.; actuary; company executive; b. Montreal, Que., 30 Nov. 1929; s. D'Alton Stafford and Ada Isabelle (LeRiche) R.; e. London (Ont.) Central Coll. Inst. 1942–44; Ridley Coll., St. Catharines, Ont., 1944–47; Univ. of W. Ont., B.A. 1951 (Gold Medal Actuarial Science); m. Ann Elizabeth, d. H. C. Cottrell, Vancouver, B.C., 8 March 1958; children: Sally, John; PRES., D.S. RUDD ASSOC. LTD., since 1982; apptd. to Pension Commission of Ontario 1963–85 and Vice Chrmn. from 1967; Trustee, London Bd. of Educ., 1967–69 (Chrmn. 1968); Pres.,

London P. Cons. Assn., 1969–72; Anglican: recreations: skiing, tennis; Clubs: London (London); London Hunt (London); Granite (Toronto); Albany (Toronto); Home: 149 Victoria St., London, Ont. N6A 2B6; Office: Ste. 620, 200 Queens Ave., London, Ont. N6A 1J3.

**RUDERMAN, Armand Peter,** B.S., M.B.A., M.A., Ph.D.; educator (retired); community service; b. Brooklyn, N.Y. 19 Nov. 1923; s. late Louis M. and Lillian G. (Prigohzy) R.; e. Harvard Univ. B.S. 1943, M.A. 1946, Ph.D. 1947; Univ. of Chicago M.B.A. 1944; m. Alice Helen d. Late Joseph Holton 17 June 1948; children: Ann (Mrs. William Keane), Mary (Mrs. Alan Cooke) William, John; Prof., Health Administration, Dalhousie Univ. 1980–89; Prof. Emeritus, 1989– ; taught econ. various Am. univs. 1946–50; Stat. Internat. Labour Office 1950–59; Stat. and Econ. Adv. Pan American Health Organ. 1960–67; Prof. of Health Adm. Sch. of Hygiene, Univ. of Toronto 1967–75; Founding Dean of Admin. Studies; Dalhousie Univ. 1975–80; Visiting Prof., Social Medicine & Public Health National Univ. of Singapore, 1982–83; served as Chrmn. Pub. Health Research Adv. Comte. Dom. Council Health, 1969–71; Coordinator Ont. Jt. Comte. on Phys's Compensation 1973–75; Chrmn., Soc. & Econ. Working Group of the World Health Org. (WHO) Tropical Disease Research Programme, 1979–83; Mem. Bd. of Dirs., Northwestern General Hospital, Toronto 1991– ; Centennial Hospital Linen Services 1992– ; mem. Etobicoke Bd. of Health 1991– ; mem. Region 3 Extve. Ctte., Ont. Hosp. Assn. 1994– ; consultant on health adm. and econ. to prov. and nat. govts., internat. agencies; author over 60 prof. articles, textbook chapters and monographs; mem. Candn. Pub. Health Assn (Past Chrmn. Med. Care Sec.); recreations: amateur radio, reading, writing, walking; Home: 2 Charleston Rd., Islington, Ont. M9B 4M7.

**RUDGE, Christopher Harry,** B.P.H.E.; printing & publishing industry executive; b. Coventry, England 16 July 1945; s. Harry and Olga (Dreidger) R.; e. Univ. of Toronto, Queen's Univ., hons. grad.. B.P.H.E. 1969; m. Janet d. James and Ruth Nutter 24 Aug. 1985; one s.: Ryan James Christopher; one d. Diane Michelle Olga; VICE-PRES. OPERATIONS, WESTERN CANADA, QUEBECOR PRINTING INC. 1991– ; Nat. Advtg. Sales Mgr., Financial Post 1979–83; Gen. Mgr., Sales & Mktg., Maclean Hunter Printing 1983–86; Pres., Web Offset Publications Ltd. 1986–91; Profl. Athlete & Team Mgr. (Lacrosse), educator; Vice-Chrmn., Candn. Printing Indus. Assn.; Adv. Bd., Ontario Crafts Counc.; recreations: golf, tennis, cooking, gardening; Clubs: Thornhill Golf & Country; University; Bd. of Trade (Toronto); Vancouver Club; Office: 950 Homer St., Vancouver, B.C. V6B 2W7.

**RUDIN, Ronald,** B.A., M.A., Ph.D.; university professor; b. Cleveland, Ohio 31 Aug. 1950; s. Abe and Belle (Weiner) R.; e. Univ. of Pittsburgh B.A. 1972; York Univ. M.A. 1973, Ph.D. 1977; m. Phyllis d. Harold and Florence Woll 17 June 1973; one s.: David; PROFESSOR, CONCORDIA UNIV. 1991– ; Lecturer, Univ. of Toronto 1975–76; Asst. Prof., Concordia Univ. 1976–81; Assoc. Prof. 1981–91; author: 'Banking en français: The French Banks of Quebec' 1985, 'Forgotten Quebecers' 1985, 'In Whose Interest?: Quebec's Caisses Populaires' 1990; Home: 4349 Rosedale, Montreal, Que. H4B 2G8; Office: 7141 Sherbrooke St. W., Montreal, Que. H4B 1R6.

**RUDNER, Martin,** B.A., M.A., M.Litt., Ph.D.; university professor; b. Montréal, Qué. 11 June 1942; s. Moe and the late Esther (Hockenstein) R.; e. Adath Israel Acad. 1955–59; McGill Univ., B.A. 1963, M.A. 1965; Univ. of Oxford, M.Litt. 1969; Hebrew Univ. of Jerusalem, Ph.D. 1974; m. Judith d. Jack and Lena Levine 4 July 1965 (divorced 1992); one d.: Aliza Tamar; PROF. & ASSOC. DIR., NORMAN PATERSON SCH. OF INTERNAT. AFFAIRS, CARLETON UNIV. (Assoc. Prof. 1984–88, Assoc. Dir. 1985–86, 1988–93, Full Prof. 1988– ); Dir., Centre for Internat. Rsch. & Training, Carleton Univ. 1990–93; Rsch. Fellow/Lectr., Hebrew Univ. of Jerusalem 1969–75; Sr. Rsch. Fellow, Rsch. Sch. of Pacific Studies 1975–80; Acad. Asst. to Vice-Chancellor, Australian Nat. Univ. 1980–82; Vis. Fellow, Inst. of S.E. Asian Studies 1971, 1975; Cons., Policy & Asia branches, C.I.D.A. 1982– ; International Practice, Government Consulting Group 1988– ; Vis. Lectr., Tel Aviv Univ.; Sch. of Advanced Internat. Studies; Johns Hopkins Univ.; Australian National Univ.; Ed. Bd. Mem., 'Asian Journal of Public Administration'; Can. Counc. Fellowship 1965–68; Carleton Univ. Scholarly Achievement Award 1986; Chrmn., Prog. Ctte., Can. Malaysia Conf., Ottawa 1986; mem., Agudath Israel Cong.; Temple Israel; mem., Candn. Acad. Assocs., Atlantic Council of Canada, Mission to NATO, SHAPE, Candn. Forces Europe 1989; mem., Jewish War Veterans of Canada; Pres., Candn. Counc. for S.E. Asian Studies 1984–87; Vice-Pres., Candn. Asian Studies Assn. 1984–87; Found. Chrmn., Malaysia Soc., Asian Studies Assn. of Australia 1977–78; mem., Bd. of Dirs., Trade Facilitation Office Canada 1989– ; Candn.-Indonesian Business Council, 1987– ; mem., Independent Review Panel for Asia Pacific Economic Cooperation Human Resource Development Network, Project 1993– ; author: 'Nationalism, Planning and Economic Modernization in Malaysia' 1975; 'Canada and the Philippines: The Dimensions of a Developing Relationship' 1990; 'Telecommunications and Development in ASEAN Countries: Canadian Perspectives on Aid, Trade and Technology Cooperation' 1992; and num. scholarly articles, reports & documents; editor: 'Society and Development in Asia' 1970; 'Canada-Malaysia towards the 1990s' 1988; co-editor: 'Issues in Malaysian Development' 1979; recreations: philatelly, music, oriental carpets; Club: Carleton Univ. Faculty; Ottawa Asia Soc.; Home: 23 Sandhurst Court, Ottawa, Ont. K1V 9W9; Office: Ottawa, Ont. K1S 5B6.

**RUDNYCKYJ, Jaroslav Bohdan,** M.A., Ph.D., F.I.A.A.(Paris); university professor and diplomat; b. Peremyshl-Zasannja 28 Nov. 1910; s. Anthony and Juliana (de Shawala) R.; e. Univ. of Lviv, M.A. 1934, Ph.D. 1937; m. Marina d. Dmytro Antonovych, 1943; two children; Prof. Prague, 1940–45; Heidelberg and Munich, 1945–48; 1949 joined Univ. of Manitoba; founding head, Dept. of Slavic Studies, Univ. of Man.; Prof. Emeritus 1977; visiting lecturer, Universities of Adelaide, Sydney, Melbourne, Monash 1978–79; visiting prof., Univ. of Ottawa, 1979–80; mem., Roy. Comm. on Bilingualism & Biculturalism; numerous learned assns. and insts. incl. Ukrainian Free Acad. of Sciences; Acad. Internat. Sciences et Lettres (Paris); Centre Internat. Sciences Onomastiques (Louvain); Am. Name Soc. (Pres. 1959); Candn. Linguistic Assn. (Pres. 1958–60); Linguistic Circle, Man. & N. Dakota (Pres. 1971–72); Candn. Assn. of Slavists (Pres. 1959); Hist. & Scient. Soc. of Manitoba; Ukrainian Research Inst. of Volyn,' etc.; author, lit. critic and translator; greatly contrib. to Slavic Candn. lit. criticism by his many reviews of poetry, prose, and drama; author of over 280 books incl. 10 vols. of travel diaries; numerous articles in learned journs.; awarded San Remo Medal, 1963, Margaret McWilliams Medal, 1971; Julius Barbeau Medal 1988; Trustee, Institut of Central Europ. Studies, Montreal 1988; founder of 'Onomastica,' since 1951; 'Slavistica,' since 1948: Vice Chrmn., Public Lib. Bd., Winnipeg, Man.; Candn. Hon. Life mem. Internat. Centre of Onomastics, Belgium; mem., Humanities Research Council, Ottawa, 1967–71; Chrmn. Human Rights Comte., Canadian Citizenship Fed. 1975–81; Vice Pres. Canada Press Club (Winnipeg) 1975–76; Dir., Candn. Citizenship Fed., 1977–84; Adv., Library of Congress, 1977–79; Adv. Nat. Library, Ottawa, 1980–81; Pres., Ukrainian World Acad. Comte., 1977–80; hon. mem., Cdn. Bibliographic Soc.; Pres., Ukrainian Mohylo-Mazepian Academy of Arts and Science 1978–92; Chrmn., Comte. Human Rights of Cdn. Citizenship Federation 1989– ; mem., Gov't. (in exile), Ukrainian National Republic, 1978–89; Pres. Intern. Academy of Humanities and Social Sciences of Canada Inc., 1981–87; Officer, Order of Canada 1993; Honorary Citizen, City of Stryi, Ukraine 1993; Hon. Mem., Scientific Institute in Peremyshl, Poland 1993; Prof. Christian; recreation: travel; Clubs: University; Royal Overseas League; Home: 5790 Rembrandt, #404, Montréal-Cote St. Luc, Que. H4W 2V2.

**RUDRUM, Alan William,** B.A., Cert.Ed., Ph.D., Th.A.; author, editor, professor of English literature; b. Great Yarmouth, England 30 Nov. 1932; s. William Arthur and Kathleen Nora (Staff) R.; e. Doncaster Gr. Sch. 1951; Univ. of London, King's Coll., B.A. 1954; Cambridge Univ., Cert.Ed. 1955; Nottingham Univ., Ph.D. 1961; Australian Coll. of Theol., Th.A. 1962; m. 1stly Heather Chambler 1955, div. 1969; 2ndly June d. Alexander and Ellen Sturrock 9 May 1969; children: Helga, Nicolas, Ursula (by first marriage); Catharine, Sarah; PROF. OF ENGLISH LIT., SIMON FRASER UNIV. 1969– ; Lectr., Univ. of Adelaide 1958–64; Queen's Univ. of Belfast 1964–66; Asst. Prof., Univ. of Calif. 1966–68; Prof., Kent State Univ. 1968–69; fellowships: Huntington Library 1968, 1982, Can. Counc. & SSHRC leave 1974–75, 1981–82, Killam Rsch. 1986–88, Clark Library 1988; Member of Senate, Simon Fraser Univ. 1988–90; First J.S. Woodsworth Resident Scholar, Simon Fraser Univ. 1989; Visiting Sr. Rsch. Fellow, Jesus College, Oxford 1989–90; Mem., Candn. Assn. of Univ. Teachers; Assn. of Candn. Univ. Teachers of English; Milton Soc. of Am.; Candn. Soc. for Renaissance Studies; Chrmn., AAUP Enquiry on Mus. & Speech Bldg. Incident, Kent State Univ. (report pub. 1969); ACUTE Ctte. to consider Unemployment & Underemployment of Qualified Univ. Teachers of English in Can. (report pub. 1979); author/editor: 'Johnson' in 'Poems of Johnson and Goldsmith' 1965, 'A Critical Commentary on Paradise Lost' 1966, 'A Critical Commentary on Comus and Shorter Poems' 1967, 'Modern Judgements on Milton' 1968, 'A Critical Commentary on Samson Agonistes' 1969, 'The Complete Poems of Henry Vaughan' 1976, 'Writers of Wales: Henry Vaughan' 1981, 'The Works of Thomas Vaughan' 1984; 'Essential Articles on Henry Vaughan' 1987; numerous articles and reviews, mainly on 17th century English literature; recreations: kayaking, photography, woodwork; Club: Diamond Univ.; Home: 2326 West 35th Ave., Vancouver, B.C. V6M 1J6; Office: English Dept., Simon Fraser Univ., Burnaby, B.C. V5A 1S6.

**RUDSON, Wayne Bernard,** B.Com., C.A., C.B.V., A.S.A.; accountant; b. Toronto, Ont. 6 Sept. 1959; s. Philip Frederick and Dorothy Joy (Rotstein) R.; e. York Mills Coll. Inst. 1978; Univ. of Toronto B.Com. 1982; m. Alison d. George and Sharon Zuckerman 20 May 1986; children: Rebecca Jo, Megan Gabrielle; MNG. PARTNER RICHTER & ASSOCIATES INC. 1990– ; cons. bus. valuation, financial litigation and investig. & forensic acctg.; appeared as expert witness before the courts; author various articles and papers; Chrmn., Candn. Inst. Chart. Bus. Valuators, Toronto Workshop Ctte.; Am. Soc. Appraisers, Toronto Chapter; Can. Kappa Alumni Assn. of Pi Lambda Phi (Dir.); recreations: skiing, golf; Clubs: Oakdale Golf & Country; Office: 90 Eglinton Ave. E., Toronto, Ont. M4P 2Y3.

**RUEDY, John,** M.D.C.M., FRCPC, FACP; university professor and administrator; b. Ottawa, Ont. 12 March 1932; s. Richard and Haneli (Bachmann) R.; e. Queen's Univ. M.D.C.M. 1956; m. Nancy d. Gilbert and Marion Burwash 5 Nov. 1966; children: Christine, Natali, Nicolas, Heidi; DEAN & PROFESSOR OF MEDICINE AND PHARMACOLOGY, DALHOUSIE UNIV. 1992– ; Asst. Instructor in Pathology, Grad. Sch. of Med., Univ. of Penn. 1959–60; Demonstrator, Univ. of Toronto 1960–61; Asst.Prof. of Pharm., Therapeutics & Med., Univ. of Man. 1965–66; Prof. of Med. & Pharm., McGill Univ. 1974–78; Founding Head, Div. of Clin. Pharm., Montreal Gen. Hosp. 1966–78; Head, Pharm. & Therapeutics, McGill Univ. 1975–78; Prof. of Med. & Pharm., Univ. of B.C. 1978–92; Head, Med., St. Paul's Hosp. Vanc. 1978–92; Mem., Bd. of Dir., Bioject Med. Technologies 1988– ; Dir., Candn. HIV Clin. Trial Network 1990–93; co-author: 'On Call: Principles and Protocols' 1989, 2nd ed. 1993; recreations: kayaking, hiking, skiing, gardening; Home: 1210 Cromwell Rd., Halifax, N.S. B3H 4L2; Office: Sir Charles Tupper Bldg., Halifax, N.S. B3H 4H7.

**RUETER, William,** R.C.A., M.G.D.C.; graphic designer; b. Kitchener, Ont. 4 Aug. 1940; s. Gustav and Gladys (Brubacher) R.; e. Bathurst Heights Secondary Sch. North York 1959; City Literary Inst. London, Engl. 1960–61; Ont. Coll. of Art 1962–65; m. Marilyn d. Eric Meister 28 June 1968; two s. Lucas, Simon; SR. DESIGNER, UNIV. OF TORONTO PRESS 1976– ; Prop. The Aliquando Press; Designer, Leslie Smart & Associates Toronto 1965–68; Designer, Univ. of Toronto Press 1969– ; recipient The Look of Books, Toronto 3rd Prize 1974, 1976; Schönste Bücher aus Aller Welt, Leipzig Bronze Medal 1976, hon. diploma 1987; Internat. Buchkunst-Ausstellung, Leipzig Bronze Medal 1977, 1989, Silver Medal 1982; various awards Design Can., Am. Inst. Graphic Arts, Assn. Am. Univ. Presses; rep. in nat. and internat. book and design exhns.; Lectr. Faculty of Fine Arts York Univ. 1973–75; Seneca Coll. North York 1977; Georgian Coll. Barrie 1979; Massey Coll. Toronto 1980; Am. Typecasting Fellowship New Rochelle, N.Y. 1980; Lectr. Sheridan Coll. Oakville, 1981, 1983, 1989; Univ. of Waterloo, 1985; Internat. Rice Rsch. Inst., Philippines 1986, 1987; Univ. of the West Indies 1988; Faculty of Library Science, Univ. of Toronto 1989; Ryerson Polytechnical Inst. 1990–92; Hatcher Library, Univ. of Michigan 1993; rec'd Can. Council Grant 1968; author 'Order Touched with Delight' 1976; numerous articles aspects of printing and reviews; Ed. 'The Devil's Artisan'; mem. Assn. Am. Univ. Presses Book Design & Production Comte. 1975; Juror, The Look of Books, Toronto 1975, mem. Jury Selection Comte. 1976; Ont. Assn. Art Galleries Annual Show 1980; The Art of the Book 1988; Founding mem. Soc. Candn. Book Designers; mem. Royal Candn. Acad. 1976; Soc. Graphic Designers Can.; Assn. Typographique Internationale; Am. Printing Hist. Assn.; Typocrafters; Am. Typecasting Fellowship; Can. Assn. for the Advancement of Netherlandic Studies; Candn. Bookbinders and Book Artists Guild; recreations; private printing, hand binding, music; Home: 236 Major St., Toronto, Ont. M5S 2L6; Office: 47 Willcocks St., Toronto, Ont. M5S 1A1.

**RUFF, Norman John Robert,** B.Sc., M.A., Ph.D.; university professor; b. Barking, England 7 Nov. 1939; s. Alfred James and Hannah Rose (Carter) R.; e. Univ. of Southampton, B.Sc. (Econ.) 1961; McMaster Univ., M.A. 1965; McGill Univ., Ph.D. 1973; divorced; children: Andrew Lawrence, Simonne Frances; ASST. PROF. OF POL. SCI., UNIV. OF VICTORIA 1973– ; Treas. Bd. Staff, Prov. of N.B. 1962–65; Sec., N.B. Royal Comn. on Employer-Employee Relns. in the Public Serv. 1966–67; Comnr., B.C. Royal Comn. on Employer-Employee Relns. in the Public Serv. 1972; Vis. Asst. Prof., U.B.C. 1968–69; Dir., Extve. Devel. Training Prog., present univ. 1974–76; Grad. Studies Extve. Ctte. 1987–89; Lectr. 1969–73; Public Affairs Commentator; Arbitrator; Mem., B.C. Legis. Internship Prog. Ctte. 1982– ; Ed. Bd. 'B.C. Studies' 1989– ; Comnr., Federal Comn. on Electoral Boundaries for BC 1993–94; Mem., Candn. Pol. Sci. Assn. (Dir. 1975–77); Inst. of Public Admin. of Can.; Candn. Tax Found.; Soc. qué. de sci. pol.; co-author: 'Reins of Power, Governing British Columbia' 1983 and various articles & reports; recreations: music, theatre, hiking; Home: 1734 Kisber Ave., Victoria, B.C. V8P 2W7; Office: Dept. of Political Science, Univ. of Victoria, P.O. Box 3050, Victoria, B.C. V8W 3P5.

**RUFFMAN, Alan,** B.Sc., M.Sc.; marine geophysicist; b. Toronto, Ont. 10 July 1940; s. Kenneth Charles and Dorothy Eleanor (Stuart) R.; e. Univ. of Toronto Schools 1959; Univ. of Toronto, Victoria Coll. B.Sc. (Hons.) 1964; Dalhousie Univ. M.Sc. 1966, Ph.D. studies 1966–70; m. Linda P. d. Pearl and Hilbert Christiansen 19 Aug. 1967; PRESIDENT, GEOMARINE ASSOCIATES LTD. 1986– ; worked for Ont. Dept. of Mines, Geol. Survey of Canada and Geologinen Tutkimuslaitos in Finland during univ. studies; Bedford Inst. of Oceanography 1970–71; Pres., Seascope Consultants (private consulting) 1971– ; Co-founder, Pres. & Vice-Pres., Geomarine Assoc. Ltd. 1973–85; identified and named Orphan Knoll (450 km NE of Nfld.) 1970; first Candn. participant on Deep Sea Drilling Project; recognized & named the Weekend Dykes in N.S. 1987; first to find an onshore geol. record of the 1929 tsunami which resulted from a 7.2 earthquake off Nfld. 1993; has run marine geophysical projects in Beaufort Sea, Arctic Islands, Northwest Passage, Baffin Bay, Hudson Bay, Labrador Sea & Shelf, Strait of Belle Isle, Gulf of St. Lawrence, on the Grand Banks and the Scotian Shelf as well as internat. work; Adv. Ctte., Dalhousie Univ. Centre for Marine Geology; Charter Mem., Nat. Marine Council 1988–93; Bd. Mem., Marine Geoscience Div., Geol. Assn. of Canada 1992–94; other past executive positions; organized conf. commemorating the 1917 Explosion in Halifax Harbour; curator of 2 shows on the art of the 1917 Explosion; co-author: 'Pre-confederation Historical Seismicity of Nova Scotia with an Examination of Later Events' 1988; co-editor: 'Proceedings of the Conference on the 1917 Explosion in Halifax Harbour and Its Consequences' 1994; author/co-author of about 100 scientific papers, articles & reports; recreations: nordic skiing, hiking; club: Salter Street Yacht Squadron; Home: 202 Fergusons Cove Rd., Box 136, Site 14, R.R. 5, Armdale, Halifax Co., N.S. B3L 4J5; Office: Box 41, Station M, Halifax, N.S. B3J 2L4.

**RUGGLES, Charles Mervyn,** C.M., B.Sc.; art conservator; b. London, Eng. 25 June 1912; s. late Charles and late Ethel (Langford) R.; e. Lisgar Coll. Inst. Ottawa; St. Patrick's Coll. Univ. of Ottawa B.Sc. 1935; m. Winnifred d. late A. W. Hughes 4 Nov. 1944; children: William Peter, Janet Evelyn, Mary Anne; Chem. Asst., Chem. Lab. Canadian International Paper Co. Gatineau, Que. 1936–40; Art Conservator, Nat. Gallery of Can. 1945–48, Chief Conservator 1948–60, Chief Scient. Research Conservator 1960–70, Head of Restoration & Conserv. Lab. 1970–77; Prof., Master of Art Conserv. Program Sch. of Grad. Studies Queen's Univ. 1977–79; served with RCAF and RAF 1940–45 in Europe, Malta & Middle East rank Flight Lt.; rec'd Queen's Silver Jubilee Medal; study tour maj. art conserv. labs. six European countries 1969, art labs. and museums Japan 1970, conserv. labs. Moscow and Leningrad 1974; by invitation, mem. Official Candn. Del. opening exhn. 'Canadian Landscape Painting' in Peking followed by visits to several restoration labs. China 1975; consultant, Public Archives of Canada 1979–84; bilingual consultant in art. conservation, Montréal Mus. of Fine Arts, 1980–84; consultant and lecturer, Nat. Laboratory for Conservation of Cultural Property, Lucknow, India, 1981; Sr. Consultant and Advisor in Art Conservation, National Gallery of Canada 1983–84; appt'd. Bd. of Dirs., Pomerantz Inst. for the Advancement of the Conservation of Artistic and Historic Works (non-profit organization for educ. and rsch. (Chicago) 1988; recipient, 50th anniversary of the siege of Malta medal 1992; Commemorative Medal for 125th Anniversary of Candn. Confederation 1992; author numerous articles relating to art restoration and conserv. including 'A Resurrected Portrait and its Case History,' 'The Care of Prints and Drawings,' 'A Reynolds Revived,' 'The Interpretation of Double Paintings,' 'A History of Art Conservation in Canada: Developments to the Early 1970's,' 'Practical Application of Deacidification Treatment of Works of Art on Paper,' 'An Exercise in Authentication,' 'Stereomicography Using the Binocular Microscope' and 'An Art Fraud Case'; Fellow, Internat. Inst. for Conserv. Historic & Artistic Works (London, Eng.); Fellow, Am. Inst. Conserv. Historic & Artistic Works (Washington, D.C.); senior mem. Chem. Inst. Can.; Founding mem. and first Chrmn. Candn. Assn. Prof. Art Conservators; First Hon. mem. and Councillor, Internat. Inst. for Conserv. (Candn. Group) 1978; mem. Candn. Owners & Pilots Assn.; Royal Candn. Flying Clubs Assn.; Ottawa Flying Club; Royal Candn. Legion; Anglican; Bilingual (French and English); recreation: flying light aircraft; Home: 15 Letchworth Rd., Ottawa, Ont. K1S 0J3.

**RUGGLES, Clifton Bruce,** B.Ed.; writer, artist, educator; b. Montreal, Que. 20 Nov. 1951; s. Harold and Mary (Eskins) R.; e. McGill Univ. B.Ed. 1977, Cert. in Special Ed. 1981, M.A. in progress; m. Olivia d. Ionel and Adriana Rovinescu 15 Aug. 1981; children: Amanda Jennifer, Alexandria Marika; HIGH SCHOOL TEACHER, PROTESTANT SCHOOL BOARD OF GREATER MONTREAL 1977– ; Regular Columnist, Montreal 'Gazette' 1990– ; exhibited artwork: Leonard & Bina Allen Gall.1993, Black Studies Ctr. 1992, Afro Festival 1991, Mile End Lib. 1985, Gall. Les Giroflees 1983, Internat. Arts Fest. 1980; Part-time fac. mem., Art Edn., Concordia Univ. 199–94; Head Teacher Status, Protestant Sch. Bd. of Greater Montreal 1989–94; Part-time instructor, Techniques of Specialized Edn., Coll. Marie Victorin 1987–89; extensive public speaker incl. media interviews and seminars; presenter at 6 conferences; designer of 3 educational programs; Pres., Ethno-Diffusions 1993; Co-editor, PAPT Sentinel 1989; Pres., Education Undergrad. Soc. 1976; Annette S. Hill Scholarship, McGill Univ. 1970–76; Scarlet Key Award 1976; Canada Council grant 1976; author of num. articles; co-author: 'Expressions of Montreal's Youth' 1974, 'Exploring the World of Work' 1974, 'Words on Work' 1981; recreations: basketball, cycling, jogging; Home: 3421 Montclair, Montreal, Que. H4B 2J3; Office: 6000 Fielding, Montreal, Que.

**RUGGLES, Edgar Lenfest,** B.E.; retired civil engineer; company president; b. Regina, Sask., 12 Aug. 1913; s. late Emma (MacLachlan) and Edgar N. R.; e. Public and High Schools, Regina, Sask.; Univ. of Sask., B.E. (Civil Engn.) 1935; m. Jean F., d. late Robert G. Cooke, Fillmore, Sask., 4 May 1940; children: Donald, Allan, Robert; Past Pres. and Dir Dir., Perolin-Bird Archer Limited (Water treatment chemicals and equipment, and indust. chemicals, Estbd. 1929); with Geol. Survey of Canada, 1935–37; joined the present Co. in 1937 as Field Engineer in Western Canada; District Mgr., 1943–46; Assistant Gen. Mgr., 1946–51; Vice-Pres. and Gen. Mgr., 1951–58; el. a Dir., 1952; Pres. 1958–77; Chrmn. 1977–78; mem., Engn. Inst. Can.; United Church; recreations: music, photography; Club: Rotary (Pres. 1955–56, Gov., Rotary Internat., Dist. 707, 1958–59); Home: 4726 Sunnymead Way, Victoria, B.C. V8Y 3B7.

**RUGGLES, Richard Irwin,** B.A., M.A., Ph.D., FRGS, FRCGS; professor emeritus of geography; b. Toronto, Ont. 27 June 1923; s. Ray Alexander and Ethel Winifred (Hamilton) R.; e. Lawrence Park Coll.; Univ. of Toronto B.A. (Hons.) 1945; Syracuse Univ. M.A. 1947; London Sch. of Econ. & Pol. Sci. Ph.D. 1958; Columbia Univ. Russian Inst. Summer Prog. 1948; m. Mildred Elizabeth d. James and Kate Mary (Savage) Duncan 21 Aug. 1954; children: Myles Alexander, Margaret Arlene; PROFESSOR EMERITUS OF GEOGRAPHY, QUEEN'S UNIV. 1988– ; Lecturer, McMaster Univ. 1947–50; Asst. Prof., Univ. of B.C. 1953–60; Assoc. Prof., Queen's Univ. 1960; Prof. 1962; Founder, Dept. of Geog. 1960; Head of Dept. 1960–69, 1972–73, 1978–79; recipient of several fellowships, grants and awards incl. Cert. of Merit, Candn. Hist. Assn. 1992; Councillor, Vice-Pres. & Pres., Candn. Assn. of Geog 1955–71; career incl. several executive ctte. appointments incl. Comnr., Internat. Cartographic Assn. 1985–89; Mem., Candn. Assn. of Geog.; Assn. of Am. Geog.; Internat. History of Cartography Assn.; Fellow, Royal Geog. Soc.; Royal Candn. Geog. Soc.; Rupert's Land Research Centre; Cartographic Ed., 'Atlas of British Columbia Resources' 1956; Edit. Bd. & Cartographic Design in vols. I and II, 'Historical Atlas of Canada' 1987–92; co-author: 'Historical Atlas of Manitoba' 1970 (gift to H.M. Queen Elizabeth, Man. Centennial); author: 'A Country So Interesting: The Hudson's Bay Company and Two Centuries of Mapping 1670-1870' 1991 and several papers, profl. reports & reviews; recreations: art, lapidary; Home: 1 – 1927 Tzouhalem Rd., R.R. 5, Duncan, B.C. V9L 4T6.

**RUGGLES, Robert T.,** B.Sc., M.B.A.; investor; b. Waterloo, Iowa, U.S.A. 11 Oct. 1931; s. Thomas C. and Georgia B. (Whitmer) R.; e. Centerville H.S. 1949; Centerville Community Coll. 1951; N.Y. Univ. B.Sc. 1954; New York Univ. M.B.A. 1956; m. Francine d. Francois and Emerentienne Paré 31 May 1958; children: Ruth, Anne; OWNER & CHAIRMAN, RUGGLES INVESTMENT SERVICES 1985– ; Economist, Statistician, Planner, var. Candn. & U.S. corps. 1954–66; Vice-Pres. Pension Fund Investments and Mem. of Bd., Imasco Ltd. 1966–80; Chair, Ruggles & Crysdale, Inc. 1980–85; resigned all board memberships 1985–88; originated, organized & established many youth sports teams and leagues 1970–78; estab. Ruggles Family Scholarship, Georgetown Univ.; estab. Ruggles Merit Scholarship Fund, Bates College; estab. Gladwin-Ridings Scholarship Funds, Univ. of Toronto and Georgetown Univ.; Mgr., Que. Jr. Women's Softball Team (winner Nat. Championship & Canada Games Gold Medal 1977); Chair, Georgetown Univ. Medical Ctr. Extve. Ctte.; Mem., Georgetown Univ. Bd. of Regents & Regents Extve. Ctte. 1988–93; Office: 55 Harbour Square, #1711, Toronto, Ont. M5J 2L1.

**RUGMAN, Alan M.,** B.A. Hons., M.Sc., Ph.D.; university professor; b. Bristol, Eng. 9 June 1945; came to Canada 1968, Candn. citizen 1973; s. Kenneth M. and Dorothy Irene R.; e. Dumfries Acad. (Scotland); Univ. Leeds, B.A. Hons. 1966; Univ. London, M.Sc. 1967; Simon Fraser Univ., Ph.D. 1974; m. Helen 1970; child: Andrew M.; PROFESSOR OF INTERNATIONAL BUSINESS, UNIV. OF TORONTO since 1987; Lectr., Dept. Econ., Univ. Winnipeg 1970, Asst. Prof. 1973, Assoc. Prof. 1978; Assoc. Prof. Finance, Concordia Univ. 1979; Dir. & Prof., Centre for Internat. Business Studies, Dalhousie Univ. 1980–87; Visiting Research Fellow, Univ. of Reading 1976–77; Visiting Assoc. Prof., Grad. Sch. Bus., Columbia Univ. 1978–79 and 1982; Visiting Scholar, Harvard Univ., Center for Internat. Affairs, 1984; Visiting Professor, London Bus. Sch. 1985; Univ. of Hawaii 1985, 1987, 1989; Univ. of Alta. 1988; Western Washington Univ. 1992–93; U.C.L.A. Spring 1993; Sloan Sch., M.I.T. Fall 1993; Rsch. Dir., Ont. Centre for Internat. Business 1988–92; author: 'International Diversification and the Multinational Enterprise,' 1979; 'Multinationals in Canada,' 1980; 'Inside the Multinationals,' 1981; 'Outward Bound: Canadian Direct Investment in the United States' 1987; 'Multinationals and Canada - United States Free Trade,' 1990; 'Japanese Direct Investment in Canada' 1990; co-author 'International Business' 1985; 'Megafirms' 1985; 'Administered Protection in America' 1987; 'Global Corporate Strategy and Trade Policy' 1990; editor and contributor 'New Theories of the Multinational Enterprise,' 1982; 'Multinationals and Technology Transfer,' 1983; 'International Business in Canada,' 1989; 'Research in Global Strategic Management' (Annual) 1990–94; 'Foreign Investment and Nafta' 1994; Co-editor and contributor, 'Multinationals and Transfer Pricing,' 1985; 'Business Strategies and Free Trade' 1988; other writings include over 100 papers, in prof. journals and collections; mem. International Trade Adv. Ctte. 1986–88; Sectoral Advisory Group on International Trade 1988–94; Academy of Intnl. Business (Vice Pres. 1989–90) elected a Fellow 1991; N. American Economics and Finance Assoc. (Dir. 1979–90, Secy-Treas., 1980–81; Pres. 1984–85); Am. Economics Assn., and other prof. societies; Sr. Fellow, Massey College; recreations: jogging, sailing, tennis; Office: Faculty of Management, Univ. of Toronto, 246 Bloor St. W., Toronto, Ont. M5S 1V4.

**RUIZ, Thomas,** M.D.; pathologist; b. Cuenca, Spain 24 Aug. 1936; s. Thomas and Maria (Lopez) R.; e. Univ. of Zaragoza, Spain M.D. 1960; Univ. of Madrid Pub. Health Dip. 1962; Pathol. Que. 1970; m. Denise d. Eugene and Rose-Alice Houle 9 Aug. 1979; children: Anik, Marie-Eve; PATHOLOGIST, CHG HOSP., Gatineau, Que. 1988– ; Asst. Prof. of Pathol. Univ. de Montréal 1964–89; Intern Zaragoza Mil. Hosp. 1961–62; Asst. Prof. of Histol. Univ. of Zaragoza 1960–61; Resident in Pathol. Notre-Dame Hosp. 1964–69; Sainte Justine Hosp. 1968; Pathologist, BMP Hosp., Cowansville, Que. 1969–88, Dir. Labs. 1970–75; Pathol. CHG Hosp. Granby, Que. 1978–88; Pres., Med. Council, BMP Hospital Cowansville, Can. 1974–75; served with 20th Regt. Artillery Spanish Army 1961–62; mem., Candn. Assn. Pathols.; Candn. Assn. Cytol.; Intnl. Acad. Pathol.; Que. Assn. Pathols.; N.Y. Acad. of Scis.; Home: 23 De Sanary, Gatineau, Qué. J8T 7R8.

**RULE, Jane Vance,** B.A.; author; b. Plainfield, N.J. 28 March 1931; d. Arthur Richards and Carlotta Jane

(Hink) R.; e. Palo Alto (Cal.) High Sch. 1947; Mills Coll. Oakland, Cal. B.A. 1952; Univ. Coll. London, Eng. 1952–53; Stanford Univ. 1953; Teacher of Eng. Concord (Mass.) Acad. 1954–56; Asst. Dir. Internat. House Univ. of B.C. 1958–59, sometime lectr. in Eng. or Creative Writing 1959–73; rec'd Ardella Mills Award 1951; Can. Council Jr. Arts Scholarship 1969–70, 1970–71; Candn. Authors' Assn. Award Best Novel 1978; Benson & Hedges Award Best Short Stories 1978; Gay Acad. Union (U.S.A.) Lit. Award 1978; The Fund for Human Dignity (USA) Award of Merit, 1983; Candn. Institute for the Blind 'Talking Book of the Year' 1991; author novels 'The Desert of the Heart' 1964; 'This Is Not For You' 1970; 'Against the Season' 1971; 'The Young in One Another's Arms' 1977; 'Contract With the World' 1980; 'Memory Board' 1987; 'After the Fire' 1989; 'Lesbian Images' (Criticism and social comment) 1975; 'Theme for Diverse Instruments' (short story collection) 1975; 'Outlander' (stories & essays) 1981; 'A Hot-Eyed Moderate' (essays) 1985; 'Inland Passage and Other Stories' 1985; numerous short stories mags. and anthols., articles; mem. Writers Union Can.; PEN; Phi Beta Kappa; recreations: swimming, collecting paintings; Address: The Fork Route 1, S19 C17, Galiano, B.C. V0N 1P0.

**RUMBALL, Donald A.,** B.A., F.I.A., F.C.I.A.; writer/consultant; b. Johannesburg, S. Africa 11 May 1941; s. Gordon Eric and Elizabeth Ross R.; e. St. Andrew's Coll. 1958; Witwatersrand Univ., B.A. 1962; Inst. of Actuaries, Fellow 1966; m. Jill d. Tom and Joan Dunphy 3 Mar. 1979; one d.: Natalie; Assoc. Actuary, Group Pensions & Life, Prudential Assur. Co. 1967–71; Assoc. Ed., Business, Financial Post 1972–81; Founding Ed., Small Business Magazine 1981–87; numerous awards for journalism; Mem., Candn. Inst. of Internat. Affairs (Chrmn., Annual Conf. Ctte. 1982; Prog. Ctte. 1979–83); Dir., Candn. Council for Small Business & Entrepreneurship; author: 'State of Small Business – Ontario' 1987, 1989, 1990; 'The Entrepreneurial Edge' 1989; 'State of Small Business and Entrepreneurship, Atlantic Provinces' 1991, 1992, 1993; Extve. Dir., National Entrepreneurship Development Institute 1991–93; recreations: sports, reading, history; Clubs: University Club of Toronto (Past Pres.), York Cricket (Past Pres.); Home: 39 Birchview Cres., Toronto, Ont. M6P 3H9.

**RUMMERY, Terrance E.,** B.Sc., Ph.D., D.Sc., F.C.I.C., F.C.N.S., ndc, P.Eng.; crown corporation executive; b. Brockville, Ont. 1937; s. the late Albert Edward and Evelyn Maud (Hayter) R.; e. Queen's Univ. B.Sc. (Hons.) 1961, Ph.D. 1966, D.Sc. (honoris causa) 1993; m. Margaret Dianne d. Keith Gilbert and Margaret Eileen Walker 27 March 1967; children: Tara, Marcus; PRESIDENT, AECL RESEARCH 1990– ; Engineer, Brockville Chemicals, then Ont. Rsch. Foundation; Research Scientist, Am. Labs. of Airco Speer Carbon and Graphite; joined Research Chem. Br., Whiteshell Labs. in Pinawa, Man., AECL 1971; Branch Leader 1976; Dir., Nuclear Fuel Waste Management Div. 1979; attended Canada's Nat. Defence College 1984–85; Team Leader in reactor sales mktg. activities in Netherlands & Yugoslavia, AECL CANDU 1985; Mgr., AECL nuclear propulsion unit (liaison with fed. govt.) 1988; Special assignment, Corporate Office 1989; Acting Pres., AECL Rsch. June 1989; Acting Pres. & C.E.O., AECL Feb.-June 1993; Mem., Univ. of Toronto Centre for Nuclear Engineering Adv. Bd.; Carleton Univ. Adv. Bd. for the Environmental Engineering Program; conducted research in crystallography while on post-doctoral fellowship at Univ. College, London, England 1966–67; Fellow, Chem. Inst. of Can.; Cdn. Nuclear Soc.; Mem., Assn. of Profl. Engrs. of Ont.; Am. Nuclear Soc.; Past Mem., Queen's Univ. Adv. Council on Engineering; author of approx. 40 pubs. and reports; Office: 344 Slater St., Ottawa, Ont. K1A 0S4.

**RUMSEY, Terry H.,** B.A.; businessman; b. Toronto, Ont. 9 March 1945; s. Herb and Jean R.; e. Univ. of Toronto B.A. 1968; m. Susan d. George and Mary Court 2 March 1967; children: David, Michael, Jennifer; PRESIDENT, CARLSON MARKETING GROUP LTD. 1989– ; General Manager, Merchandising, Wormald Fire Systems 1981–84; Vice-Pres. Sales, Carlson Marketing Group Ltd. 1987; Extve. Vice-Pres. & General Manager 1988–89; Dir., Tourism Industry of Canada (Bd.); Sigma Chi Fraternity; recreations: cottage, hunting, squash; clubs: Boulevard; Office: 3300 Bloor St. W., 14th Floor, Centre Court, Toronto, Ont. M8X 2Y2.

**RUNCIMAN, Alexander McInnes,** O.C., C.D., L.L.D.; b. Invergordon, Ross-shire, Scot. 8 Oct. 1914; s. Alexander and Evelyn (Anderson) R.; e. Pub. & High Schs. in Scot. and Can.; LL.D. Univ. Manitoba 1974; Univ. of Sask. 1977; m. Marjorie Evelyn, d. James Dick, Abernethy, Sask., 8 Oct. 1949; two d. Dorothy E., Catherine J.; Mem., Manitoba Round Table on Environment and Economy 1988–91; lived on farm until emigrated to Canada in his teens and settled on farm nr. Balcarres, Sask.; after mil. service, returned to farm and operated grain and livestock projects 1945–61; Pres., United Grain Growers Ltd. 1961–81; became Secy. of Abernethy United Grain Growers Local Bd., Sask., when it was organized in 1953; el. to Bd. Dirs., 1955; served during 2nd World War with RCOC., Jan. 1940 to July 1945; in Gt. Brit., N. Africa, Sicily and Italy; discharged as W.O.I.; hon. Col., Queen's Own Cameron Highlanders of Can.; active in community affairs as Municipal Councillor, School Secretary, 4–H Club Leader and many other activities; member, Candn. Delegation to Internat. Wheat Agreement Negotiations in Geneva, 1962 and 1978; mem. Candn. Govt. Oilseeds Trade Mission to Japan, 1964; mem. Candn. del. to GATT Cereals negotiations, Geneva, 1967; Del. to Internat. Fed. of Agric. Producers' Conf. (IFAP) in Dublin, Eire, 1963, New Zealand, 1964, England 1966, Austria 1974; mem. econ. Council Can. 1974–80; Chrmn., Bd. of Trustees, Victoria Gen. Hosp. 1986–88; Chrmn. of the Bd. of Govs., The University of Manitoba 1983–88; rec.'d. Centennial Medal; Queen's Silver Jubilee Medal; 125th Anniversary of the Confederation of Canada Medal, 1992; apptd., Officer of the Order of Canada, 1983; Life mem., Canola Council of Can.; Univ. of Man. Alumni Assn.; Hon. Life mem. Candn. Seed Growers' Assn.; Hon. mem. Agric. Inst. Can.; Man. Inst. Agrols.; Candn. Seed Trade Assn.; mem. Candn. Agricultural Hall of Fame; Sask. Agricultural Hall of Fame; St. Andrew's Soc. Winnipeg (Pres. 1966–67); Protestant; recreations: bowling, golf; Clubs: Manitoba; Winnipeg Winter; Home: 404 - 200 Tuxedo Ave., Winnipeg, Man. R3P 0R3.

**RUNNALLS, John David,** B.A., M.I.A.; non-profit organization executive; b. Toronto, Ont. 30 May 1944; s. John Frederick and Ethel Bernice (Beattie) R.; e. Univ. of Toronto, B.A. 1966; Columbia Univ., M.I.A. 1968; m. Esther d. Rolande and Jean Piette 21 Aug. 1976; children: Matthew, Jeremy; SENIOR ADVISOR, INTERNATIONAL DEVELOPMENT RESEARCH CENTRE 1993– and DIR., ENVIRONMENT AND SUSTAINABLE DEVELOPMENT PROGRAMME, INSTIT. FOR RESEARCH IN PUBLIC POLICY 1987– ; Vice-Pres. & Dir., N. Am. Office, Internat. Inst. for Environ. & Devel. 1981–88; Rsch. Dir., Albert Schweitzer Chair, Columbia Univ. 1968–72; Dir. of Rsch., Barbara Ward Book 'Only One Earth' 1971; Fellow, Adlai Stevenson Inst. 1973; Vice-Pres. & Dir., London Office, Internat. Inst. for Environ. & Devel. 1974–81; cons. to U.N. Conf. on the Environ.; U.N. Environ. Prog.; Nat. Film Bd. of Can.; Candn. Habitat Secretariat; World Bank; Asian Devel. Bank; Chrmn., Adv. Bd., Sch. of Resource & Environ. Studies, Dalhousie Univ. 1986– ; Chrmn., Am. Ctte. on Internat. Conservation 1985–87; Mem., Ont. Roundtable on Environment and Economy 1988– ; Council mem., World Resources Inst.; Bd. Mem., 'Ecodécision' magazine; Mem. Counc., World Conservation Union; co-author (with B. Ward, L. D'Anjou) 'The Widening Gap' 1971; recreations: squash, racquetball; Home: 188 Dufferin Rd., Ont. K1M 2A6.

**RUNNALLS, Oliver John Clyve,** B.A.Sc., M.A.Sc., Ph.D., F.R.S.C., P.Eng.; professor emeritus of nuclear engr. & energy studies (Univ. of Toronto); b. Barrie Island, Ont. 26 June 1924; s. John Lawrence and Ethel Mae (Arnold) R.; e. Public and High Schs. North Bay, Ont.; Candn. Army Univ. Course (Univ. of Toronto) 1944; Univ. of Toronto, B.A.Sc. (ceramic engn.) 1948, M.A.Sc. (metall. engn.) 1949, Ph.D. (extractive metall.) 1951; Nat. Defence Coll. 1960; m. Vivian Constance, d. late George Stowe 13 Sept. 1947; children: David John, Catherine Ruth; PRES., O.J.C. RUNNALLS & ASSOCS. LTD. 1989– ; Bd. mem., Ont. Hydro; Uranerz Exploration and Mining Ltd.; Candn. Nuclear Assn.; Candn. mem. of Internat. Adv. Ctte., Concord-Nuexco Internat. Corp., Denver, CO; commenced with Atomic Energy of Canada Ltd. metall. research and devel. Res. Chem. Br., Chalk River, Ont. 1951, Head Fuel Devel. Br. 1956–59, Head Research Metall. Br. 1961–67; Asst. Dir. Chem. and Materials Div. Atomic Energy of Canada Ltd. 1967–69; Chief Liaison Offr. Europe, Paris 1969–71; Sr. Adviser, Uranium and Nuclear Energy, Dept. of Energy, Mines and Resources, Ottawa, 1971–79; Extve. Vice Pres., Uranium Canada Ltd. 1974–79; Prof. of Energy Studies, Faculty of Appl. Sci. and Eng., Univ. of Toronto 1979–89; Chrmn., Centre for Nuclear Engr., Faculty of Appl. Sci. and Eng., Univ. of Toronto 1983–89; mem of Bd., Cdn. Energy Research Inst. Calgary 1975–79; served in 2nd World War R.C.C.S. 1944–45; mem. Assn. Prof. Engrs. Ont.; Candn. Nuclear Assn.; Can. Nuclear Soc; author of some 100 scient. papers and reports primarily on ceramic and metall. research and devel., and on uranium, nuclear and energy policy; awarded Queen's Silver Jubilee Medal 1977; B.T.A. Bell Commemorative Medal 1979; Ian F. McRae Award, Candn. Nuclear Assoc. 1980; Fellow, Royal Soc. of Can. 1983; recreations: skiing, woodworking; Address: 170 Lytton Blvd., Toronto, Ont. M4R 1L4.

**RUNTE, Roseann,** B.A., M.A., Ph.D.; educator; writer; b. Kingston, N.Y. 31 Jan. 1948; d. Robert Benedict and Anna Loretta (Schorkopf) O'Reilly; e. State Univ. of N.Y. B.A. 1968; Univ. of Kans. M.A. 1969, Ph.D. 1974; m. Hans R. s. Johannes and Ilse Runte 1969; PRESIDENT AND VICE-CHANCELLOR, VICTORIA UNIV. 1994– ; Lectr. and Lang. Lab. Dir. Bethany Coll. 1970–71; Lectr. Adult Studies Saint Mary's Univ. 1971–72; Prof. of French Dalhousie Univ. 1972–83, Asst. Dean of Arts & Sci. 1980–82, Chair of French 1980–83; Pres. Univ. Sainte-Anne 1983–88; Principal, Glendon College 1988–94; Hon. Doctorates Acadia Univ. 1989, Meml. Univ. of Nfld. 1990; Prix de Poésie François Coppée Acad. française 1988; Chevalier dans l'Ordre des Palmes Académiques 1985; Pres. Candn. Commission for UNESCO; Past Chair Publs. Ctte. Hannah Inst.; Past Bd. mem. Associated Med. Services; Past Exec. Bd. Candn. Soc. Study Higher Edn.; Treas. Internat. Comparative Lit. Assn.; Past Adv. Ctte. mem. Nat. Lib.; Past Bd. mem. Art Gallery of N.S.; author (poetry) 'Brumes bleues' 1982; 'Faux-soleils' 1984; 'Renga' 1994; (pubs.) 'Birmanie blues' 1993; editor: 'Studies in Eighteenth-Century Culture' Vol VII 1977, Vol VIII 1978, Vol IX 1979; co-ed. 'Man and Nature' Vol. I 1982; 'Le Développement local' 1986, transl. as 'Local Development: The Future of Isolated Cultural Communities and Small Economic Regions' 1987; 'De l'Oralité à l'écriture' 1991; 'Lectures canadiennes' 1993; numerous articles, reviews, essays; lit. review ed. 'French Review'; ed. bd. Dalhousie French Studies; mem. Modern Lang. Assn.; Am. Assn. Teachers of French; Société française d'étude du XVIIIe siècle; Assn. des profs. de français des univ. et colls. canadiens; Candn. Soc. Eighteenth-Century Studies (Past Pres.); Candn. Fedn. Humanities (Past Pres.); Past Pres., ACFAS (Toronto); Dame Commander, Order of Saint John of Malta 1992; recreations: reading, photography, sports; Office: 2275 Bayview Ave., Toronto, Ont. M4N 3M6.

**RUNTZ, Michael William Paul,** B.Sc.(Hons.); author, nature photographer, university lecturer, naturalist; b. Arnprior, Ont. 12 May 1954; s. Weldon Walter and June Donna (Lewis) R.; e. Carleton Univ. B.Sc. (Hons.) 1987; m. Heather d. Ron and Birthe Lang 21 June 1980; two sons: Harrison Gabriel William, Dylan Ronald Paul; N.D.T. Specialist, Noranda Metals 1975–82; Interpretive Naturalist, Point Pelee Nat. Park 1982–84; Ont. Peregrine Falcon Survey, World Wildlife Fund 1985; Interpretive Naturalist, Algonquin Prov. Park 1972–74, 1986– ; Sessional Lectr., Carleton Univ. 1989– ; Ont. Field Naturalists Outstanding Service Award; Ottawa Field Naturalists' Club Anne Hanes Natural History Award; Mem., Ottawa Field Naturalists' Club; Macnamara Field Naturalists' Club (Pres. 1983–86, 1994– ); Former Mem., Ont. Bird Records Ctte.; author: 'Moose Country' 1991, '92, 'Algonquin Seasons' 1992, 'The Explorer's Guide to Algonquin Park' 1993, 'Beauty and the Beasts' 1994; currently working on two books; photography rep. by Geostock; Home: 51 Ottawa St., Arnprior, Ont. K7S 1W9.

**RUPPEL, Robert P.,** F.S.A., F.C.I.A.; consulting actuary; b. Kitchener, Ont. 16 Oct. 1953; s. Rupert P. and Doris A.E. R.; e. Univ. of Waterloo B.Math. 1980; m. Mary L. d. Duncan and Helen Kinahan 7 Aug. 1976; children: Sean, Jennifer, Michael; PRINCIPAL & CONSULTING ACTUARY, TOWERS, PERRIN 1978–81, 1988– ; Actuarial Asst., National Life 1975–78; Principal & Cons. Actuary, William M. Mercer Limited 1982–88; extensive experience in employee benefits consulting & financial analysis; clients are major Canadian employers; Fellow, Candn. Inst. of Actuaries (Chrmn., Younger Actuaries Ctte. 1983); Soc. of Actuaries; recreations: skiing, baseball; Home: Oakville, Ont.; Office: 1501, 175 Bloor St. E., Toronto, Ont. M4W 3T6.

**RUPRECHT, Hon. Tony,** M.P.P., M.A.; politician; b. Konstantinow, Poland 12 Dec. 1942; s. Antoni and Ida (Forgiarini) R.; e. Laurentian Univ. B.A. (Honours) 1969; Wichita State Univ. M.A. 1971; Miami Univ. Ph.D. work (1971–73); OPPOSITION CRITIC, MINISTRY OF CITIZENSHIP AND PROVINCIAL ANTI-DRUG STRATEGY; el. Sr. Ald. Ward 2 Toronto, 1978, re-el. 1980; el. M.P.P. for Parkdale prov. g.e. 1981, Caucus Critic Social Devl., Citizenship, Culture & Multiculturalism, also Metro Toronto Transp.; Minister responsible for Disabled Persons (first apptd.) 1985–87; Minister without Portfolio for Multiculturalism 1986–

88; Parliamentary Asst., Ministry of Community and Social Services 1990; published: 'Toronto's Many Faces' (Whitecap Books Inc.) 1990; Prof. of Pol. Sci., taught at York Univ., Carleton Univ. and Laurentian Univ.; published: 'The Graduate School Game' (Brandon Univ. Press) 1976; Chrmn., Can. at the Crossraods Conf. Laurentian Univ. 1978; special Adv. to Que. Farmers' Assn. to examine impact of Bill 101; Ont. Govt. Co-ordinator: Rick Hanson Man in Motion Tour; Chrmn. and Adv. Parkdale Property Tax Reform Ctte.; author Tax Reform Bill H.R. 4727 for U.S. Cong.; several papers US-Candn. Relations and related topics; Scholar of the Year Award, Laurentian Univ., Huntington Coll. 1969; Knight of Malta, S.M.O.J.J.; Estonian Gold Medal of Honour; Medal of Valour & Merit, Govt. of Portugal; Polish Gold Cross of Merit; Medal of Honour, Philippine-Canada Friendship; Hon. Fellowship, Candn. School of Management; Club: Kiwanis; International Oratorial Trophy Winner (Kiwanis) 1975; Home: 71 Springhurst Avenue, Toronto, Ont. M6K 1B5; Office: Parliament Bldgs., Queen's Park, Toronto, Ont. M7A 1A2.

**RUSE, Michael,** B.A., M.A., Ph.D., F.R.S.C.; university professor; b. Birmingham, England 21 June 1940; s. William Redvers Escott and Margaret (Fentiman) R.; e. Bootham Sch. 1953–59; Univ. of Bristol, B.A. 1962; McMaster Univ., M.A. 1964; Univ. of Bristol, Ph.D. 1970; m. Elizabeth d. John and Patricia Matthews 16 Feb. 1985; children: Nigel, Rebekah, Emily, Oliver, Edward; PROF., DEPTS. OF PHILOSOPHY & ZOOLOGY, UNIV. OF GUELPH 1974– ; Lectr., present univ. 1965–69; Asst. Prof. 1969–71; Assoc. Prof. 1974–74; Vis. Prof., Indiana Univ. 1976; Vis. Scholar, Harvard Univ. 1983–84; Assoc. & Fellow, Wolfson College, Cambridge, England 1985–86; John Simon Guggenheim Fellowship 1983–84; Isaak Walton Killam Fellowship 1985–87; FRSC 1986; author: 'Molecules to Men' 1990, 'The Darwinian Paradigm' 1989, 'Philosophy of Biology Today' 1988, 'But is it Science?' 1988, 'Homosexuality' 1988, 'Taking Darwin Seriously' 1986 (also issued in Spanish, Italian, Portuguese, Polish), 'Darwinism Defended' 1982, 'Is Science Sexist?' 1981, 'The Darwinian Revolution' 1979 (also in Spanish), 'Sociobiology' 1979, 2nd ed. 1984 (also in Span., Port. & Italian), 'The Philosophy of Biology' 1973 (Span., Russian, Italian); editor: 'Philosophy of David Hull' 1988, 'Readings in the Philosophy of Biology' 1988, 'Nature Animated' 1982; recreations: cooking, reading, walking; Home: 44 Edinburgh Rd. N., Guelph, Ont. N1H 5P9; Office: Dept. of Philosophy, Univ. of Guelph, Guelph, Ont. N1G 2W1.

**RUSH, James Cameron,** B.A., M.A., Ph.D.; university professor & administrator; b. Sarnia, Ont. 2 Dec. 1946; s. Ian Cameron and Joan Mary (Thompson) R.; e. The Univ. of Western Ont., B.A. 1968; Univ. of Detroit, M.A. 1971; Univ. of Minnesota, Ph.D. 1981; m. Claudia d. Eugen and Ruth Engel 8 Oct. 1977; children: Heidi, David, Jessica, Justin; Prof., Organizational Behaviour, Univ. of Western Ontario 1992; Personnel Mgr., Nat. Computer Systems 1973; Lectr. Coord., Undergrad., Psych., Univ. of Minn. 1973–75; Rsch. Cons., Control Data Corp. 1975–77; Asst. Prof., present univ. 1977–84; Assoc. Prof. 1984; Dir., MBA Program, Sch. of Administration 1988–92; Pres., Rush Cons. Group; Fellow, Ctr. for Creative Leadership, Greensboro, N.C. 1974; Dir., Goodwill Indus. 1979–80; mem., Acad. of Mngt.; Am. & Candn. Psych. Assn.; co-author: 'Making the Match' 1986, 'Effective Managerial Action' 1988; Home: 42 Pine Ridge Dr., London, Ont. N5X 3G8; Office: London, Ont. N6A 3K7.

**RUSK, James Arthur,** B.Sc.(Agr.), M.Sc.; journalist; b. Belleville, Ont. 16 Sept. 1943; s. Clifford Arthur and Doris Lillian (McKague) R.; e. Univ. of Guelph, B.Sc.(Agr.) 1965, M.Sc. 1970; m. Ronni d. Benjamin and Helen D. 31 May 1970; children: Bruce Arthur, Mark Joseph; REPORTER, QUEEN'S PARK BUREAU, THE GLOBE & MAIL; Candn. Broadcasting Corp. 1966–67, 1970–71; Report on Bus., Globe & Mail 1967–68, 1971–79; Parliamentary Corr. 1979–85; China Correspondent 1985; Spec. Asst., Hon. H.A. Olson, Fed. Ag. Min. 1968–70; Nat. Bus. Writing Award 1976, (hon. mention) 1978; Office: 444 Front St. W., Toronto, Ont. M5V 2S9.

**RUSK, Sue;** artist; b. Montreal, Que. 26 April 1937; d. David and Ethel Selma (Bald) Rubin; e. Macdonald Coll., McGill Univ. 1955; Fine Arts, Concordia Univ.; Montreal Mus. of Fine Arts; Saidye Bronfman Ctr.; Centre Visual Arts Montreal; m. Marvin Bernard s. Harry and Miriam R. 27 June 1957; children: Ilene Naomi, Bonnie Lynn, Peter Mark; Teacher, Elem. Sch. 1956–61; Directed, devel. & taught, Sch. of Creative Arts for Children Montreal 1972–80; Instr. of Painting & Drawing, Saidye Bronfman Ctr. 1984– ; one-woman exhibs.: Winnipeg 1978; Denver 1981; Ottawa 1982; Toronto 1984, '89; Montreal 1985, '88, '90, '94; Quebec City 1989; participant in juried exhibs. in Can., U.S.A., Japan, Spain, France, Taiwan & Brazil; public & corp. collections incl.: Sony Music; Bell Canada; Prat & Whitney; Corvallis Collection, Oregon Univ.; Lavalin Montreal; Prêt d'œuvres d'art, Musée du Qué.; CP Montreal; Bank Leumi Montreal; Cabo Frio Mus. Brazil; Alcan Montreal; Winnifred Denny Burnaby B.C.; Nat. City Bank Cleveland; Bank Tokai du Canada Montreal; Mississauga Lib.; Physical Fitness Instr. 1973– ; currently printmaking at Atelier Graphia Montreal; painting & drawing private studio Montreal; Jewish; Mem., Atelier Graphia (printmaking); Conseil Québecois de L'Estampe; Cons. de la Peinture du Qué.; Print & Drawing Counc. of Can.; Montreal Print Collectors Soc.; Printmaking Atelier Saidye Bronfman Ctr.; Home: 15 Kilburn Cres., Hampstead, Que. H3X 3B8.

**RUSSEL, H. Dunbar,** B.Sc., M.B.A.; business executive; b. Montreal, Que. 8 May 1946; s. Bruce Sutherland and Jane Alexander (Urquhart) R.; e. McGill Univ. B.Sc. 1967; Univ. of West. Ont. M.B.A. 1970; m. Sandra d. Archibald and Mary Nicolson Aug. 1969; children: Jennifer, Jeffrey, Gail; PRESIDENT & CHIEF EXECUTIVE OFFICER, ONTARIO BLUE CROSS 1986– ; Assoc. Systems Engr., IBM Canada Ltd. 1967–68; Consultant, SDI Assoc. Ltd. 1970–73; Comptroller, MONY life Insur. Co. of Canada 1973–77; Vice-Pres., Operations 1977–81; Vice Pres. Finance and Chief Financial Offr. 1981–84; Vice-Pres., Diversification and Finance 1984–86; Dir., Ont. Blue Cross; Blue Cross Life Insur. Co. of Can.; Health Assistance for Travellers; Managed Dental Care of Can.; Candn. Assn. of Blue Cross Plans; 611458 Ont. Ltd.; Past Dir., Big Brothers of Metro Toronto; N. Toronto Hockey Assn.; Lake of Bay's Sailing Club; People's Warden, St. John's Anglican Ch.; recreations: tennis, skiing; Home: 1 Weybourne Cres., Toronto, Ont. M4N 2R2; Office: 150 Ferrand Dr., Toronto, Ont. M3C 1H6.

**RUSSELL, Aubrey Alexander,** Q.C.; lawyer; b. St. Stephen, N.B. 2 Oct. 1929; s. Aubrey Harold and Elva Claire (Doten) R.; e. St. Stephen H.S.; Acadia Univ.; Queen's Univ.; Osgoode Hall Law School; m. Nancy Eleanor d. A. Grahame Stewart 26 Jan. 1957; children: Aubrey Sandford, Jeddie Elva, Grahame Stewart, Charlotte Victoria; COUNSEL, CASSELS BROCK & BLACKWELL 1990– ; read law, Cassels Defries Des-Brisay 1955; called to Bar of Ontario 1956; joined Cassels Brock Kelley 1956; Partner 1960; Q.C. 1971; Trustee, Sunnybrook Med. Ctr. 1966–85 (Vice-Chair 1982–85, Trustee Emeritus 1986– ); Chair, Sunnybrook Found. 1982 (Dir. 1982–91; Hon. Dir. 1991– ); Anglican; Mem., The Candn. Bar Assn.; The County of York Law Assn. (Pres. 1982); recreations: skiing, tennis, squash, hiking; clubs: The University Club of Toronto, Osler Bluff Ski; Home: 37 Ridge Dr., Toronto, Ont. M4T 1B6; Office: Scotia Plaza, 40 King St. W., Suite 2100, Toronto, Ont. M5H 3C2.

**RUSSELL, Dale A.,** Ph.D.; scientist (paleontologist); b. San Francisco, Calif. 27 Dec. 1937; s. Clarence Rush and Marion Carolyn (Lundberg) R.; e. Columbia Univ., Ph.D. 1964; Yale Univ., post-doct. work 1964–65; naturalized Canadian; m. Janice d. Santi and Louise Alberti 18 July 1964; children: Francis, Maria, Elizabeth; CURATOR, FOSSIL VERTEBRATES, RESEARCH DIV., CANDN. MUSEUM OF NATURE 1965– ; spec. interest in dinosaurian taxonomy, evolution & extraterrestrial models for dinosaurian extinction; field work in Can., U.S. (incl. collab. with U.S. Nat. Aeronautical & Space Agency), Mexico, E. Africa, China; elected Phi Beta Kappa upon rec. B.A.; U.S. Nat. Sci. Found. Fellow 1958–61, 1964–65; Roman Catholic; Mem., Soc. of Vertebrate Paleontol.; author: 'A Vanished World' 1977, 'An Odyssey in Time: The Dinosaurs of North America' 1989; num. tech. pubs.; recreation: jogging; Home: 12 Grangemill Ave., Nepean, Ont. K2H 6A6; Office: Ottawa, Ont. K1P 6P4.

**RUSSELL, David Edward;** technological executive; b. Liverpool, U.K. 11 June 1947; s. Edward and Irene (Jennions) R.; e. Maghull Gr. Sch.; m. Julie d. John and Laura Allen 10 Aug. 1968; children: Allen, Colin, Carrie Anne; PRES., DIR. & CHIEF EXTVE. OFFR., RUSSELL TECHNOL. INC. 1972– ; Appren., Non-Destructive Testing, English Electric Co. 1965; emigrated to Can. 1966; Trainee & Jr. Tech. then Mgr. & Sr. Level Tech., Warnock Hersey Int'l. 1966–70; Sr. Level Tech., Hanson Materials Engr. Ltd. 1970–72; founded Russell Ultra-Sound Serv. 1972; Cyberscope Industries Inc. 1984; mem., Candn. Soc. N.D.T.; Am. Soc. N.D.T.; Am. Soc. of Metals; papers presented at Nat. Assn. of Corrosion Engrs., C.S.N.D.T. & Intercan '87; Teacher, N.D.T. at N.A.I.T. 1978–81 (evenings); winner Astech Award, Alberta Science & Tech. (for leadership in technology development) 1993; Hon. Level 3 (Radiography) 1982; recreations: golf, tennis, scuba; Office: 4909, 76 Ave., Edmonton, Alta. T6B 2S3.

**RUSSELL, Dennis C.;** Ph.D., D.Sc.; professor emeritus; b. Southampton, Eng. 4 Sept. 1927; s. Henry Charles and Doris Violet (Render) R.; e. Univ. of Sheffield B.Sc. 1948 (Edgar Allen Scholarship 1945–48); Univ. of London M.Sc. 1952, Ph.D. 1958, D.Sc. 1972 (Rsch. Studentships 1952–54); m. Joyce d. Percy and Charlotte Brown 21 Dec. 1951; two s. Julian, Jeremy; PROF. EMERITUS (MATH.) YORK UNIV. 1989– ; Asst. Lectr. Coll. Advanced Technol. (now City Univ. London) 1949–52; Asst. Lectr. and Lectr. Keele Univ. 1955–60; Assoc. Prof. Mount Allison Univ. Sackville, N.B. 1960–62; Prof. of Math. York Univ. 1962–89, Chrmn. of Dept. 1962–69; Visiting Prof. Tel-Aviv Univ.; recipient Candn. Math. Cong. Summer Rsch. Fellowships 1961, 1963, 1965–67; Nat. Rsch. Council Can. Sr. Rsch. Fellowship 1968; Can. Council Leave Fellowships 1969, 1976–77; German External Acad. Rsch. Grant 1971; Nuffield Found. Rsch. Travel Grant 1973; Natural Sci's & Eng. Rsch. Council Can. Internat. Collaborative Rsch. Grant 1982; Can./USSR Exchange Prog. Rsch. Visit 1989; Natural Sci's & Eng. Rsch. Council/Nat. Rsch. Council Rsch. Operating Grants 1969–91; over 170 rsch. lectures univs. and confs. 17 countries; author or co-author some 56 scholarly articles internat. rsch. jours., over 150 reviews; Fellow, Inst. of Math. & Applications; mem. Math. Assn. Am.; Candn. Math. Soc. (Council 1967–71, 1973–75); London Math. Soc.; Am. Math. Soc.; Home: Dormy, Whitwell Rd., Ventnor, Isle of Wight, Eng.; Office: 4700 Keele St., North York, Ont. M3J 1P3.

**RUSSELL, The Hon. Frederick William,** C.M., K.St.J., LL.D.; b. St. John's Nfld. 10 Sept. 1923; s. late Herbert J., C.B.E. and Jean (Campbell) R.; e. Holloway Sch. and Prince of Wales Coll., St. John's; Dalhousie Univ.; Atlantic Sch. for Advanced Bus. Admin., Halifax; m. Margaret Miriam, d. late Ewart C. and Helen (Cline) Cross, Port Credit, Ont., 14 June 1946; children: Douglas, Janice, James, Peter; LIEUTENANT GOVERNOR OF NEWFOUNDLAND 1991– ; formerly, in St. John's: Pres., General Auto Leasing 1950–80; Terra Nova Motors 1962–79; Gen. Industries 1980–88; Delta Holdings 1980–88; Fremar Investments Ltd. 1980–91; Dir., Atlantic Pilotage Authority, Halifax 1971–75; Candn. Ind. Renewal Bd., Montreal 1983–87; National Sea Products Ltd. (Past Dir. & mem., Extve. Ctte.; Past Chrmn., Audit Ctte.), Halifax 1985–91; Nfld. Employers Labour Relations Counc. 1982–90; Vice-Chrmn., Nfld. Labour-Management Cooperation Ctte., St. John's 1975–88; Atlantic Enterprise Bd., Moncton 1986–88; Adv. Bd., Atlantic Canada Opportunities Agency 1989–91; ACOA Ctte. Project Review Ctte., Moncton 1988–91; past mem., Communications Ctte., ACOA, Moncton; Royal Trust Adv. Ctte., St. John's; Extve. Devel. Ctte., Govt. of Nfld. & Lab.; Nfld. Labour Relations Bd. 1953–88; served with R.C.A.F. as Pilot 1942–45; retired as Wing Commdr., R.C.A.F. (R) 1955; Life Mem., Cdn. Fighter Pilot's Assoc.; Mem., 410 RCAF Squadron Assoc.; 125 RAF (NF) Squadron Assoc.; one of the founders, Royal Cdn. Air Cadets, St. John's 1950; Founding Mem., Hon. Aide-de-Camp (RCAF), Gov. Gen. Massey & Gov. Gen. Vanier, Nfld. 1955–63; Hon. Aide-de-Camp (RCAF), Lt. Gov. of Nfld. 1954–62; Founding Mem., St. James Un. Ch., St. John's 1959; Pres., Nfld. Bd. of Trade 1960; Mem. Exte. Ctte., Candn. Chamber of Comm. 1967–72; Chrmn., Bd. of Regents, Memorial Univ. of Nfld. 1974–82 (mem. Bd. of Regents 1961–82); Chrmn., United Ch. Sch. Bd., St. John's 1974–82; Dir., St. John's Rotary Club 1975; Hon. LL.D., Meml. Univ. of Nfld. 1976; Member of the Order of Canada 1979; Knight of Justice, Order of St. John 1992; Hon. Colonel, 103 Search and Rescue Unit, Gander 1992; United Church; recreations: skiing, fishing; Clubs: Rotary (St. John's); Eagle River Salmon; Officers (Crow's Nest); Home: P.O. Box 5160, St. John's, Nfld. A1C 5V5; Office: Government House, Military Rd., St. John's, Nfld. A1C 5W4.

**RUSSELL, Hilary Anne,** B.A.; writer and researcher; b. Kingston, Jamaica 24 Oct. 1947; d. Vincent H. and Alice Joan (McNeil Smith) McFarlane; e. The Queen's Sch. Kingston, Jamaica; Walt Whitman High Sch. Bethesda, Md. 1964; Carleton Univ. B.A. (Hons.) 1969; m. Richard T. s. Ralph and Christina Russell 8 Aug. 1970; one s. Blake Thomas; STAFF HISTORIAN, NAT. HIST. SITES DIRECTORATE 1970–93; seconded by Candn. Human Rights Commn. 1991–92; seconded by Ont. Heritage Found. to serve as Project Historian, Elgin and Winter Garden Theatres Toronto 1985–89; Co-Dir. Conf. 'Bethune: His Times and His Legacy/son epoque et son message' McGill Univ. 1979; del. special tour

China organized by Chinese People's Assn. for Friendship with Foreign Countries 1980; recipient City of Toronto Book Award 1990; Ed., 'Image' (Sandy Hill newspaper) 1991–93; Dir. Action Sandy Hill, Ottawa 1990–91; Pres. Home & Sch. Assn. Rockcliffe Park Pub. Sch. 1988–89; Chair Rockcliffe Book Fair 1988; mem. Friends Ronald McDonald House, Ottawa 1990; mem. various planning cttes. Ottawa Bd. Edn. Confs., Council Elem. Sch. Parents 1987–88; Exec. mem. Can.-China Friendship Soc. Ottawa 1981–87; author 'All that Glitters: A Memorial to Ottawa's Capitol Theatre and its Predecessors' 1975; 'Double Take: The Story of the Elgin and Winter Garden Theatres' 1989; contbr. various popular and scholarly jours. and 'American National Biography,' 'The Canadian Encylopaedia,' 'The Dictionary of Canadian Biography,' 'Oxford Companion to Theatre History'; mem. YM-YWCA; recreations: running, skiing; Home: 219 Blackburn Ave., Ottawa, Ont. K1N 8A9; Office: F5, 25 Eddy, Hull, Qué. K1A 0H3.

**RUSSELL, James Christopher,** B.Sc., M.Sc., Ph.D.; medical scientist; educator; b. Montreal, Que. 24 Oct. 1938; s. Keith and Elma (Crockett) R.; e. Dalhousie Univ. B.Sc. 1958; Univ. of Saskatchewan M.Sc. 1959, Ph.D. 1962; m. Wendy d. Norman and Winnifred Spencer 2 Dec. 1961; one d., Katrina; PROFESSOR OF SURGERY, UNIV. OF ALBERTA 1981– ; Fellow Gen. Elec. Co. Dept. of Physical Chem. Leeds 1962–64; post-doctoral Fellow Chem. Dept. present Univ. 1964–67, Asst. Prof. Dept. of Surgery 1967–72, Assoc. Prof. 1972–81, Dir. Biochem. Lab. Surgical-Med. Rsch. Inst. 1967–72, mem. Exec. Ctte. Gen. Fac. Counc. 1980–85, Grad. Adv. Dept. of Surgery 1979–92; Scientific and Research Cons., Medical Staff, Univ. of Alberta Hospitals 1979– ; Fellow, Nat. Acad. of Clin. Biochem (USA); Fellow, Candn. Acad. Clin. Biochem; Sec.-Treas. Alta. Soc. of Clinical Chemists 1977, Chrmn. 1978; mem. Counc., Candn. Soc. of Clinical Chemists 1980–81; mem. Counc., Candn. Atherosclerosis Soc. 1987–90; Ed. Bd. Physiological Chem. and Physics and Med.; Chrmn. Energy Policy Ctte. 1978–81; Econ. Policy Ctte. 1981–85; cand. Alta. N.D.P. prov. g.e. 1979, 1982, 1986; recreations: music, flying, skiing, backpacking, gardening; Home: 13619 Buena Vista Rd., Edmonton, Alta. T5R 5R5; Office: 275 Heritage Medical Research Centre, Univ. of Alta., Edmonton, Alta. T6G 2S2.

**RUSSELL, John Stephen,** B.A., M.A., Ph.D.; b. Vancouver, B.C. 19 Apr. 1956; s. James Bernard and Donna Lou Fowler (Lomow) R.; e. Univ. of B.C., B.A. (Hons.) 1978; Cornell Univ. M.A. 1991, Ph.D. 1994; m. Joy Kathleen Russell M.D. (Lucas) d. George and Laura Lucas 17 Aug. 1979; son: Nicholas James; Extve. Dir., B.C. Civil Liberties Assn. 1984–88; Extve. Asst., B.C. Civil Liberties Assn. 1980; public spokesperson & author of briefs & submissions on civil liberties, human rights policy & law reform; appearance before fed. & prov. legisl. rev. cttes.; author & editor of var. BCCLA pubns.; Social Sciences and Humanities Rsch. Council of Can. Post-doctoral Fellow 1993–95 (taken up at Mansfield College, Oxford Univ.); Past Vice Pres., Concerned Citizens Drug Study and Educational Soc.; Vice-Pres., B.C. Civil Liberties Assn.; editor/contbr.: 'Liberties' 1989; recreations: choral singing, violin, viola; Home: 295 West 21st, Vancouver, B.C. V5Y 2E4; Office: Mansfield College, Oxford Univ., Oxford, England OX1 3TF.

**RUSSELL, Loris Shano,** M.A., Ph.D., LL.D., F.R.S.C., F.G.S.A.; palaeontologist; b. Brooklyn, N.Y. 21 Apl. 1904; s. Milan Winslow and Matilda (Shano) R.; e. Pub. and High Schs., Calgary, Alta.; Univ. of Alta., B.Sc. 1927; Princeton Univ., M.A. 1929, Ph.D. 1930; m. Grace Evelyn LeFeuvre, 1938; Curator emeritus, Royal Ontario Museum and Prof. Emeritus, University of Toronto, since 1971; Field Geologist, Research Council of Alberta, 1928–29; Assistant Palaeontologist, Geol. Survey of Canada, Ottawa, 1930–37; Assistant Professor of Palaeontol. (1937–48) and Assoc. Prof., Univ. of Toronto, 1948–50; Ass. Dir. (1938–46) and Dir. (1946–50), Royal Ont. Museum of Palaeontology; Chief of Zoology Sec., Nat. Museum of Can., 1950–56; Dir., Nat. Museum of Canada, 1956–63; Chief Biologist, Royal Ontario Museum, and Prof., Dept. of Geol., Univ. of Toronto, 1963–71; Adjunct Rsch. Scientist, Tyrrell Museum of Palaeontology (Alta.) 1988– ; served in 2nd World War in Candn. Active Army Major, 1942–45; in N.P.A.M. with R.C.C.S. (Reserve) for 3 yrs. after 2nd World War; author of over 100 papers on the geology and vertebrate or invertebrate palaeontol. of W. Can.; three books on 19th C. material culture; Fellow, Paleontol Soc.; Soc. Vertebrate Paleontol.; Geol. Assn. Can.; Candn. Museums Assn.; Hon. mem., Royal Cdn. Inst.; Ottawa Field Naturalists Club; mem., awarded Willet G. Miller Medal by Royal Soc. Can., 1959; Silver Jubilee Medal, 1978; Billings Medal by Geol. Assn. Can. 1984; Romer/Simpson Medal, Soc. of Vertebrate Paleontology 1992; recreations: amateur radio, painting, antiquarian research, a heritage of light, handy things to have around the house, everyday life in colonial Canada; Home: 55 Erskine, Apt. 1702, Toronto, Ont. M4P 1Y7.

**RUSSELL, Nicholas,** B.A., M.A.; university professor; b. Teddington, England 9 Oct. 1938; s. Arthur Wolseley and Marjorie Violet Anne (Pendleton) R.; e. Aldenham Sch. 1956; McGill Univ. B.A. (Hons.) 1964; Univ. of London M.A. (Hons.) 1966; Univ. of Wales, Ph.D. 1994; m. Sharon Elisabeth d. Arthur and Elisabeth Plows 30 May 1964; children: Ian Arthur, Geoffrey David; ASSOC. PROF., SCH. OF JOURNALISM, UNIV. OF REGINA 1983– ; Reporter, S. London Suburban Newspapers Group 1956–59; CFCF-TV, Montreal 1961–62; Ed./Prof., B.B.C., London 1966–67; Writer-ed., Candn. Press., Vanc. 1967–68; Head, Journ. Prog., Vanc. Commun. Coll. 1968–83; writing coach to Candn. newspapers & R/TV stations; Mem., Assn. for Edn. in Journ. & Mass Comm.; Commonwealth Journ. Assn.; Commonwealth Assn. for Edn. in Journ. & Comm.; Candn. Assn. of Journalists; editor: 'The Quarrymen of History' 1987; 'Trials & Tribulations' 1986; author: 'Morals and the Media: Ethics in Canadian Journalism' 1994; recreations: restoring antique furniture; Home: 2528 Retallack St., Regina, Sask. S4T 2L3; Office: Regina, Sask. S4S 0A2.

**RUSSELL, Peter Howard,** O.C., M.A., F.R.S.C., LL.D. (h.c.); educator; b. Toronto, Ont. 16 Nov. 1932; s. Alexander William and Jean Port (Griffin) R.; e. Univ. of Toronto Schs.; Univ. of Toronto B.A. 1955; Oxford Univ. (Rhodes Scholar) M.A. 1957; m. Eleanor Sewell d. late Robert A. Jarvis 16 May 1958; children: Catherine, Mary, Barbara, Alexander; PROF. OF POL. SCIENCE, UNIV. OF TORONTO: Dir. of Research, Royal Comn. of Inquiry RCMP; Chair, Judicial Appointments Adv. Ctte. (Ont.) 1989–92; Pres., Candn. Law & Society Assoc. 1987–89; Pres., Candn. Pol. Science Assn. 1990–91; Visiting Prof. Harvard Univ. 1967; Prof., Makerere Univ. Uganda 1969–71; Princ. of Innis Coll. Univ. of Toronto 1971–76; Dir., Graduate Studies, Dept. of Political Sci., Univ. of Toronto 1987–93; rec'd C. D. Howe Fellowship 1967–68; Officer of the Order of Canada; Fellow, Royal Soc. of Can.; Hon. LL.D: Univ. of Calgary; Law Society of Upper Canada; author 'Nationalism in Canada' 1967; 'Leading Constitutional Decisions' 1983; 'The Supreme Court as A Bilingual and Bicultural Institution' 1969; 'The Administration of Justice in Uganda' 1971; 'The Judiciary in Canada' 1987; 'Constitutional Odyssey: Can Canadians Become a Sovereign People?' 1992; various articles constitutional law, Supreme Court, judicial power, Indian land claims; Anglican; Home: 14 Wychwood Park, Toronto, Ont. M6G 2V5.

**RUSSELL, Richard Doncaster,** M.A., Ph.D., F.R.S.C., P.Geo.; university professor emeritus; b. Toronto, Ont. 27 Feb. 1929; s. late Ada Gwennola (Doncaster) and late Richard Douglas R.; e. N. Toronto Coll. Inst., 1942–47; Univ. of Toronto, B.A. (Physics and Chem.) 1951, M.A. (Physics) 1952, Ph.D. (Geophysics) 1954; post doctorate Univ. of Chicago and Oxford Univ.; m. Virginia Ann Reid, d. late Bernard Clippingdale, 11 Aug. 1951; children: Linda Jean, Morna Ann, Mary Joyce; Assoc. Vice Pres. Academic, Univ. of British Columbia 1983–86; Prof. of Geophysics 1963–91, and Professor Emeritus since 1991; Head of the Dept. of Geophysics & Astronomy 1968–79; Assoc. Dean of Science, 1980–83; mem. of Bd. of Govs. 1978–81; Lectr., Univ. of Toronto, 1954–56; Asst. Prof. of Physics, 1956–58; Prof. of Physics and mem. Inst. Earth Sciences, 1962–63; joined present Univ. as Assoc. Prof. of Physics and mem. Inst. Earth Sciences, 1958; Acting Dir., Inst. of Astronomy & Space Sciences, 1969–70; J. Tuzo Wilson medal of Candn. Geophysical Union 1992; mem. Candn. Geophys. Union; B.C. Geophys. Soc.; Candn. Soc. Expl. Geophys.; Am. Geophysical Union; Home: 226 – 4955 River Rd., Delta, B.C. V4K 4V9.

**RUSSELL, Hon. Ronald S.,** C.D., M.L.A.; politician; b. Auckland, N.Z. 22 July 1926; e. Ryerson Inst. of Technol. grad. in Indust. Math.; Queen's Univ. Psychol.; Candn. Forces Staff Sch. grad.; Sch. of Mang. Engn. grad.; SPEAKER OF THE LEGISLATIVE ASSEMBLY, N.S. 1991– ; served with Royal N.Z. Air Force, Royal Australian Air Force World War II, RCAF 1950–1973 as a pilot; now Hon. Lt. Col. 420 Air Reserve Squadron, Shearwater; mem. Council West Hants Mun. (5 yrs.); West Hants Sch. Bd., Bd. Health and Bd. Hants Co. Sr. Citizens' Home; el. M.L.A. for Hants West prov. g.e. 1978; re-el. since; Speaker H. of A. 1978–80; Min. of Consumer Affairs and Min. Resp. for Admin. Residential Tenancies Act, 1980–81; Chrmn., Management Bd., N.S. and Min. in charge of Admin. of Civil Service Act and Min. in charge of Admin. of Liquor Control Act 1981–85; Min. of Health, N.S., Min. in charge of Admin. of Drug Dependency Act and Registrar General 1985–87; Solicitor General, N.S., Min. in charge of Admin. of Liquor Control Act 1987–89; Apptd. Min. of Labour and Min. in charge of Admin. of the Liquor Control Act 1989–91; P. Conservative; Home: P.O. Box 130, Falmouth, N.S. B0P 1L0; Offices: Province House, P.O. Box 1617, Halifax, N.S. B3J 2Y3 and 1 Government Place, 7th Floor, 1700 Granville St., Box 1617, Halifax, N.S. B3J 2Y3.

**RUSSELL, Sheila MacKay,** R.N.; public health nurse; author; b. Airdrie, Alberta, 10 May 1920; d. William MacKay and Catherine (Reid) R.; e. Central High Sch., Calgary, Alta., Grad. 1937; Calgary Gen. Hosp. (Grad. in Nursing) 1942; Univ. of Alberta (Grad. in Pub. Health Nursing), 1944; m. 7 Mar. 1947; Staff Nurse, Red Deer Mun. Hosp., Alta., 1942–43; Prov. District Nurse, Alta., 1944–45; Asst. Dir. of Pub. Health Nursing and Asst. Dir. of Health Educ., Alta., 1945–47; author of 'A Lamp Is Heavy,' 1950; 'The Living Earth,' 1954; assorted short stories, prof. articles and health manuals; Protestant; Address: 501 – 1845 Robson St., Vancouver, B.C. V6G 1E4.

**RUST, Charles Hammond,** B.A.; business executive; b. Toronto, Ont. 15 Sept. 1934; s. Edward Preston and Mary Valary (Hammond) R.; e. Trinity Coll. Univ. of Toronto B.A. 1957; m. Anne Louise d. W. Herbert and Ruth Moore 4 Nov. 1978; two d. Catherine, Jennifer; PARTNER, RUST ASSOCIATES INC. MARKETING CONSULTANTS; Vice Chrmn., Brenlor Realty Corp.; Dir., Bell Sygma Systems Management; Developing Countries Farm Radio Network; Systems Engineering and Sales Mgmnt. positions IBM Canada 1957–78; Pres. & Gen. Mgr., Dir. StorageTek Canada Inc. 1978–90; recreations: painting, golf; Home: 23 Roxborough St. W., Toronto, Ont. M5R 1T9.

**RUST, Velma Irene,** B.Sc., M.Ed., Ph.D.; educator; economist; b. Edmonton, Alta. 22 May 1914; d. Cecil Johnstone and Lillie Almena (Runions) Miller; e. Univ. of Alta. B.Sc. 1934, Teacher's Dipl. 1935, B.Ed. 1944, M.Ed. 1947; Univ. of Ill. Ph.D. 1959; m. Ronald Stuart (dec.) s. James and Agnes Rust 9 Apl. 1955; teacher Alta. schs. 1936–42, 1943–44; Inspr. Inspection Bd. of UK and Can. in Montreal 1942–43; Secy. to Dean of Educ. Univ. of Alta. 1944–52, Lectr. then Asst. Prof. of Math. Educ. 1952–56, Dir. of Student Teaching 1954–56; Grad. Asst. Univ. of Ill. 1956–59; Researcher in Directorate of Personnel Planning RCAF HQ Ottawa 1960–62; Chief of Staff Training, Inspection Services Dept. of Nat. Defence 1962–65; Stat., Aviation Stat. Dept. Transport Can. 1965–67; Policy Analyst, Health & Welfare Can. 1967–79; Sessional Lectr. in Calculus and Trigonometry Carleton Univ. 1959–62; Kappa Delta Pi; author various articles prof. journs.; mem. Un. Empire Loyalists' Assn.; Am. Contract Bridge League; mem. of Session, Un. Ch. of Can. MacKay Un. Ch., several Genealogical Societies; recreations: genealogical research, duplicate bridge, golf, gardening, travel, badminton, swimming; Club: University Women's; Address: 811 Adams Ave., Ottawa, Ont. K1G 2Y1.

**RUST-D'EYE, George Hastings,** B.A., LL.B., LL.M.; lawyer; b. Toronto, Ont. 19 Jan. 1944; s. George Hastings and Anne Kathleen (Wallace) R.; e. Humberside Coll. Inst. 1961; York Univ. B.A. 1964; Osgoode Hall LL.B. with Hon. 1969, LL.M. 1983; m. Dora d. William and Margaret Dobie 11 July 1969; children: Anne Dioness, Victoria Catherine; PARTNER, WEIR & FOULDS 1991– ; with Bank of Montreal 1964–66; called to Bar of Ont. 1971; Lawyer Lang, Michener, Cranston, Farquharson and Wright 1971–73; Solicitor Metro Toronto Legal Dept. 1973–89 (Couns. Metro Licensing Comn. 1975–82; Couns. Metro Legis. and Planning/Legis. and Licensing 1975–82, 1984–86; Metro. Solicitor 1986–89); Lawyer, Weir & Foulds 1989–91; Mem., Metro. Toronto Emergency Adv. Ctte. 1979–86; author: 'Discretion Not Open to Question: The Power to Refuse a Municipal Licence in Ontario' 1976; 'Morality and Municipal Licensing: The Untouched Constitutional Issues in City of Prince George v. Payne' 1978; 'Municipal Licensing: Enabling Legislation and By-Laws' 1981; 'Cleaning Up Yonge Street: Municipal Regulation of Sexual Morality in Metropolitan Toronto 1971–1983' 1983; 'Saving the Best to Last: The Legislative Framework of Preserving Man-made Heritage' 1987; 'An Unpleasurable Experience: The Power to Dismiss a Municipal Officer' 1988; 'Tiers Are Not Enough: The Exercise of Upper-Tier Planning Responsibilities in the Greater Toronto Area' 1989; 'The Shift Toward Inter-regional Planning: How Will it Affect the Development Industry' 1989; 'Access to Municipal Government: Freedom of Information, Protection of Privacy and the Right to Attend Meetings' 1989; 'Drafting Municipal Legislation: A Weird Science' 1989; 'Heritage Buildings and the Planning Process' 1990; 'The Public's Business' 1990; 'Policy Implications: The Education Development Charges' and 'How to Determine Education Development Charges' (with Marilyn L. Sparrow) 1990; 'Heritage Buildings and the Planning Process' 1990; 'Who's In Charge? - An Update on Inter-Regional Planning in the Greater Toronto Area' 1991; 'Free Municipal Information - How to Take Advantage of the Right of Access to Municipal Records and Information' 1991; 'Water Power - A Summary of Legal Principles Relating to Constitutional Division of Powers, Proprietary Rights and Municipal Jurisdiction Over Land Covered by Water or Ice' 1991; 'Green Machines - The Environmental Responsibilities of Ontario Municipalities' 1991; 'Highest and Best Use: Open Space in the 1990's' 1991; 'Hanging Out to Dry - Personal Liability of Municipal Members of Council, Officers and Employees' 1991; 'Planning for Sustainability - Towards Integrating Environmental Protection into Land-Use Planning' (co-authored) 1991; 'To Serve and Protect - The Duty of Police Officers to Protect Citizens from Acts of Third Parties' 1991; 'Spinning Wheels: Relationships Between Governments in Planning' 1991; 'Where to Next ...? - Recourse from Decisions of Administrative Tribunals' (co-authored) 1991; 'Municipalities as Parties to Legal Proceedings' 1992; 'Nasty Neighbours' Noise and Nuisances' 1992; 'Municipal Powers and Responsibilities for Protecting the Environment' 1992; 'New Planning - New Interests - The Sewell Commission Approach to Implementing Provincial Intent' 1992; 'The OMB - The Handy All-Purpose Board' 1992; 'Municipalities as Parties to Litigation' 1992 14 Adv. Q.91; 'Canada's Constitutional Crisis' (co-authored) 1992; 'Municipal Conflict Law in Transition - The Ontario Experience' 1992; 'Case Comment: Rayside v. Commission on Election Finances the Corporation of the City of Toronto and Betty Disero,' published in Municipal Attorney, September-October 1992; pub. 'Cabbagetown Remembered' 1984; pub. series of articles on subjects of local hist. interest in 7–News 1975–78; Lectr. on hist. and heritage of City of Toronto; mem. Candn. Bar Assn.; Chrmn., Municipal Law Section, Candn. Bar Assn. (Ont.); Vice-Chrmn., Community Issues Ctte., Metrop. Toronto Board of Trade; Fac. Bar Admission Course, Law Soc. of Upper Can. 1982–85; Toronto Hist. Bd. 1975–87 (Chrmn. 1984–86); Pres. Don Vale Assn. of Homeowners and Residents 1973–74; Vice-Pres Toronto Br., Archit. Conservancy of Ont. 1976–79; recipient City of Toronto Service Award 1981; Ont. Volunteer Service Award (10 yrs.) 1985; Chrmn., Museum of Toronto Task Force 1985–88; Home: 376 Sackville St., Toronto, Ont. M4X 1S5; Office: 15th Flr., Exchange Tower, 2 First Canadian Place, Toronto, Ont. M5X 1J5.

**RUSTED, Nigel Francis Scarth,** B.Sc., M.D., C.M., D.Sc. (Hon.), F.R.C.S.(C), F.A.C.S., F.I.C.S.; b. Salvage B.B., Newfoundland 1 July 1907; s. late Rev. Canon Ernest Edward and Faith Amy Margaret (Hollands) R.; e. Bishop Field Coll. (1923–25) and Memorial Coll. (1925–27), St. John's, Nfld.; Dalhousie Univ., B.Sc. 1929 and M.D., C.M. 1933; m. Florence Haig, d. Thomas Anderson, M.D. 21 June 1944; children: Joan Margaret, Elaine E. W., Thomas Nigel; Hon. Surgeon, St. John's Gen. Hosp.; Sr. Consultant, Grace Gen. Hosp.; Hon. Surg., St. Clares Hospital; Janeway Children's Hospital; Clinical Prof. of Surg., Memorial Univ. of Newfoundland; Retired; Anglican; recreations: fishing, philately, amateur radio, photography; Address: 28 Monkstown Rd., St. John's, Nfld. A1C 3T3.

**RUTECK (ORR), Sherry;** transportation executive; b. Calgary, Alta. 13 Oct. 1962; d. John and Ann (Mandryk) R.; e. Univ. of Calgary; m. Gordon s. Lorraine and Robert Orr 14 Sept. 1991; one s.: Mitchell; PRESIDENT & OWNER, TRANS-MUTUAL TRUCK LINES 1983; Bd. of Dir., Alberta Trucking Assn. 1984– (Sec. Treas.); frequent public speaker (univs., confs. & media) 1988– ; Successors Award, Canadian Buisness Magazine 1989; Executive of the Year, Alta. Cert. Management Consultants 1990; One of the Top 100 Entrepreneurs under 30 in N. Am., Assn. of Collegiate Entrepreneurs 1992; Hon. Chair in Business, Grant McEwan Community College Edmonton 1992; Home: 6976 Christie Bria Manor S.W., Calgary, Alta. T3H 2R3; Office: 4427A 72nd Ave. S.E., Calgary, Alta. T2C 2G5.

**RUTHERFORD, The Hon. Douglas James Anderson;** b. Toronto, Ont. 12 Aug. 1941; s. William Samuel and Elizabeth Ann (Anderson) R.; e. Univ. of Toronto Schs. 1960; York Univ. B.A. 1963; Univ. of Toronto LL.B. 1966; m. Anne M. d. Rev. Dr. A.L. and Merelie Griffith 8 Sept. 1972; one d. Jane; one s. Ian; JUDGE, ONTARIO COURT OF JUSTICE (GENERAL DIVISION) 1991– ; Vice Chrmn., Canada Pension Appeals Bd. 1991– ; called to Bar of Ont. 1968; Man. 1974, NWT 1979 and YT 1980; Q.C. 1980; joined Blake, Cassels, Toronto 1968–69; Sr. Prosecutor, Dept. Justice, Toronto 1970–73, Dir. Winnipeg Justice Office 1974–76; Gen. Counsel Dept. Consumer & Corporate Affairs Ottawa 1976–78; Dir. of Criminal Law Ottawa 1978–80; Queen's Counsel 1980; Asst. Depy. Attorney General of Can. 1980–86; Assoc. Depy. Minister of Justice 1986–91; Home: 129 Broadway Ave., Ottawa, Ont. K1S 2V7; Office: Court House, Ottawa, Ont. K2P 2K1.

**RUTHERFORD, Paul Frederic William,** B.A., M.A., Ph.D.; educator; b. Middlesex, England 22 Feb. 1944; s. William and Blanchette May (Herren) R.; e. Carleton Univ. B.A. 1965; Univ. of Toronto M.A. 1966; Ph.D. 1973; children: Jennifer; Stephanie; PROF., DEPT. OF HISTORY, UNIV. OF TORONTO 1982– ; Lectr. 1969; Asst. Prof. 1973; Assoc. Prof. 1975; Prof. 1982– ; Chrmn., Dept. of Hist. 1982–87; author: 'The Making of the Canadian Media' 1978; 'A Victorian Authority: The Daily Press in Late Nineteenth-Century Canada' 1982; 'When Television Was Young: Primetime Canada 1952–1967' 1990; 'The New Icons? The Art of Television Advertising' 1994; ed. 'Saving the Canadian City: The First Phase, 1880–1920' 1974; Address: Dept. of History, Univ. of Toronto, Toronto, Ont. M5S 1A1.

**RUTHERFORD, Col., The Hon. Robert Campbell,** M.B.E., C.D., LL.B.; b. Owen Sound, Ont. 29 Nov., 1922; s. Brig. Gen. Thomas John Rutherford C.B.E. E.D. and Helen (Sibbald); e. Pub. and High Sch.s, Owen Sound; Khaki Coll. of Can. London, Eng. 1946; Osgoode Hall Law Sch. 1950; m. The Late Elizabeth Ann Sutcliffe, Sept. 1949; children: Susan Elizabeth, Robert Sutcliffe; m. Donna Lee d. William Robert Lawrence Richard, Kitchener, Ont. Nov. 1975; JUDGE, THE SUPREME COURT OF ONTARIO and MEM., HIGH COURT OF JUSTICE FOR ONTARIO; read law with Thomas N. Phelan, Q.C. and Brendan O'Brien, Q.C.; called to the Bar of Ont. 1950; cr. Q.C. 1960; specialized as Trial Counsel; Lectr. in Civil Procedure, Bar Admission Course Law Soc. Upper Can. for 17 yrs.; Part-time Lectr. in Trial Procedure Osgoode Hall, York Univ.; enlisted in Grey & Simcoe Foresters, June 1940; served as Tank Commdr. Royal Canadn. Armoured Corps Africa, Italy, N.W. Europe during World War II; C.O. Gov. Gen. Horse Guards 1956–60; (Hon. Lt. Col. G.G.H.C. 1976–80; Hon. Col., Grey & Simcoe Foresters 1980–; Hon. Aide-de-Camp to Gov. Gen. Vincent Massey and Gov. Gen. Georges Vanier; rec'd Queen's Silver Jubilee Medal; 1975; Vice-Chrmn., Criminal Compensations Bd. 1971–76; former Bencher Law Soc. Upper Can. past mem. Council Medico-Legal Soc. Toronto; mem., Candn. Bar Assn.; Advocats Society; Chrmn., Gurkha Welfare Trust (Can.); Hon. Life. Dir., Candn. Equestrian Fed.; Past Gov. Trinity Coll. Sch.; Gov., Corps of Commissionaires of Ont.; Dir., Royal Commonwealth Soc.; mem., St. Andrew's Soc.; Delta Chi; Grand Knight, the Order of Saint Lazarus; Order of Constantine Magni; Order of St. John; United Church; recreation: equestrian activities, golf, gardening; Clubs: Hon. Pres. of Royal Candn. Mil. Inst. (Pres. 1972–77); Tor. North York Hunt Club; Lawyers'; Cavalry & Guards; Club: London, Eng.; Owen Sound. Golf & Country; Home: Ste. 832, 21 Dale Ave., Toronto, Ont. M4W 1K3; Office: Osgoode Hall, 130 Queen St. W., Toronto, Ont. M5H 2N5.

**RUTHERFORD, Robert Thomas,** F.C.A.; chartered accountant; b. Niagara Falls, Ont. 9 Jan. 1939; s. Thomas Robert and Constance (Fisher) R.; e. East York Collegiate O.S.S.H.G.D. 1957; Inst. of C.A.s of Ont. C.A. 1962; m. Arlene Stirton 14 April 1960; children: Geoffrey, Adrienne, Christopher; PROFESSIONAL PRACTICE PARTNER, PEAT MARWICK THORNE 1992– ; joined Thorne, Mulholland, Howson & MacPherson 1957; elected Partner, Thorne Gunn 1973; Dir., Quality Control, Thorne Riddell 1973–88; Nat. Dir., Acctg. & Auditing, Thorne Ernst & Whinney 1989; Partner-in-Charge, Nat. Profl. Standards, Peat Marwick Thorne 1989–92; Mem., Council & Mgt. Ctte., Candn. Insolvency Pract. Assn. 1993–94; Pres., Inst. of C.A.s. of Ont. 1991–92; Vice-Pres., 1989–91; Council 1984–92; Gov., Candn. Inst. of C.As. 1989–90, 1991–92; Chrmn., Joint Steering Ctte. 1985–89; Acctg. Standards Ctte. 1981–82; F.C.A. 1982; Paul Harris Fellow, Rotary Club of Toronto 1990; Bd. Chrmn., Rosseau Lake College 1986–87; recreations: tennis, curling; clubs: Toronto Cricket Skating & Curling Club (Pres. 1982), Ontario Club, Bd. of Trade, Rotary Club of Toronto; Home: 77 Lawton Blvd., Toronto, Ont. M4V 1Z6; Office: Yonge Corporate Centre, 4120 Yonge St., Suite 500, North York, Ont. M2P 2B8.

**RUTHVEN, Douglas Morris,** B.A., M.A., Ph.D., Sc.D., F.R.S.C.; university professor; b. Ernakulum, India 9 Oct. 1938; s. Joseph Morris and Beryl (MacKay) R.; e. Christ's Hosp., Horsham England 1950–7; Univ. of Cambridge, B.A. 1960, M.A. 1963, Ph.D. 1966; m. Patricia d. Harry and Evelyn Goodwin 20 July 1968; one d.: Fiona Beryl; PROF. OF CHEMICAL ENGINEERING, UNIV. OF N.B. 1975– ; Design Engr., Davy Power-Gas Corp. (U.K.) 1961–63; Asst. Prof. of Chem. Engr., present univ. 1966–72; Assoc. Prof. 1973–74; rsch. in fundamentals of adsorption & the devel. of adsorption separation processes.; cons. to various nat. & internat. cos. on process applications of zeolites & other molecular sieve adsorbents; Univ. of Cambridge, Sc.D. 1988; F.R.S.C. 1989; mem., Am. Inst. of Chem. Engrs.; author: 'Principles of Adsorption and Adsorption Processes' 1984; co-author: (with Jörg Kärger) 'Diffusion in Zeolites' 1992; awarded Max Planck Rsch. Prize (jointly with Prof. J. Kärger) 1993; recreations: Scottish country dancing; Home: R.R. 1, Mouth of Keswick, N.B. E0H 1N0; Office: Univ. of New Brunswick, Fredericton, N.B. E3B 5A3.

**RUTLEDGE, Graeme Kent,** F.C.A.; chartered accountant; b. Montreal, Que. 2 Aug. 1941; s. Stanley Graham and Amy Matilda (Thomas) R.; e. McGill Univ. C.A. program; m. Helen d. Jean and Gordon Welsh 16 Aug. 1969; children: James, Stuart, Robert; PARTNER, DELOITTE & TOUCHE 1969– ; Mem., Policy Board, Deloitte & Touche; provides services to financial services industry; Mem., Deloitte Touche Tohmatsu Internat. Banking & Securities Ctte.; Financial Institutions Task Force, Candn. Inst. of C.A.s; Dir. & Mem., Finance Ctte., Montreal Children's Hospital Found.; clubs: Mount Royal, Saint James's, Forest & Stream; Office: 1 Place Ville Marie, Suite 3000, Montreal, Que. H3B 4T9.

**RUTTAN, Hon. John Graham,** M.A., B.C.L., LL.D.; retired judge; b. Winnipeg, Man. 11 Feb. 1913; s. Arthur Charles and Beatrice Wilson (Robertson) R.; e. Monterey Pub. Sch., Coll. Private Sch., Oak Bay High Sch. 1929, Victoria (B.C.) Coll. 1930; Univ. of B.C. B.A. 1933; Oxford Univ. B.A. (Hon. Sch. of Jurisprudence), M.A., B.C.L. 1936; Univ. of Victoria LL.D. (Hon. c.) 1978; m. Mary-Louise d. late Charles E. Harrison, Hamilton, Ont. 8 June 1946; children: Stephen Forsyth, Susan Elizabeth, Robert Graham, Deborah Jane; called to Bar of B.C. 1937; practised law Victoria, B.C. 1937–39, 1946–56; Judge, Supreme Court of B.C. 1956–88; served with RCNVR 1940–45, convoy duty N. Atlantic, anti-submarine specialist R.N., rank Lt. Commdr.; mem. Oak Bay Council 3 yrs.; Past Pres. Family & Children's Service; Hon. Dir. B.C. Automobile Assn.; Anglican; Clubs: Union; Victoria Golf; Arbutus; Home: 2463 Currie Rd., Oak Bay Victoria, B.C. V8S 3B6.

**RUTTER, Nathaniel W.,** B.S., M.S., Ph.D., P.Geol., F.R.S.C.; university professor; b. Omaha, Neb. 22 Nov. 1932; s. John Elliot and Karleen (Ludden) R.; e. Tufts Univ. B.S. 1955; Univ. of Alaska M.S. 1962; Univ. of Alberta Ph.D. 1966; m. Marie d. Carl and Gladys Munson 11 Sept. 1961; children: Todd, Christopher; PROF., GEOLOGY, UNIV.OF ALBERTA 1977– ; Geologist, Venezuelan Atlantic Refining Co. 1955–58; Rsch. Sci., Geol. Survey of Can. 1965–74; Head, Urban Projects 1974; Environ. Advisor, Nat.Energy Bd. 1974–75; Assoc. Prof., Geol., Univ. of Alta. 1975–77; Chair 1980–89; Pres., Westlund Cons. Corp.; Killam Annual Prof.; Fellow, Royal Sco. of Can.; Hon. Visiting Prof., Academia Sinica; Sr. Fellow, Wissenschafskolleg zu Berlin; Mem., Assn. of Profl. Engrs.; geol. & Geophys. of Alta.; Internat. Union Quaternary Rsch. (V.P. 1982–87; Pres. 1987–91); Candn. Quat. Assn. (V.P. 1981–82); Geol. Soc. Am. (Mngt. Bd. Dir. 1982–84); Candn. Nat. Com., Internat. Geol. Correlation Prog., UNESCO 1986– ; Pres., Internat. Union Quat. Rsch. Congress 1981–87; Mem., Internat. Geosphere-Biosphere Prog.; Rsch. Ctte., Can. Global Change Prog. 1992– ; Chair, Global Change Com. INQUA 1991– ; ; Chair, Earth Sci. Grants Ctte., NSERC; author of over 150 journal articles; Assoc. Editor: 'Arctic,' 'Geosci. Can. Quat. Rsch.'; Edit. Bd. Mem., Quat. Sci. Revs.; editor-in-chief: 'Quaternary Internat.'; recreations: boating; clubs: Cosmos, Explorers; Home: Box 45, Site 310, R.R. Stony Plain, Alta. T7Z 1X3; Office: Edmonton, Alta. T6G 2E2.

**RYAN, Aidan F.,** B.Sc., B.E.; public utility executive; b. St. John's, Nfld. 19 Oct. 1934; s. John J. and Amelia F. R.; e. Meml. Univ. of Nfld. B.Sc. 1955; McGill Univ. B.E. 1957; m. Vera d. Jake and Annie Bourne 11 Aug. 1958; children: Stephen, Marie, David; PRES., C.E.O. AND DIR. NEWFOUNDLAND LIGHT AND POWER CO. LTD. 1990– ; Dir. Fortis Inc.; served present Co. and predecessors since 1957; Club: St. John's Rotary; Home: 31 McNeilly St., St. John's, Nfld. A1B 1Y9; Office: 55 Kenmount Rd., St. John's, Nfld. A1B 3P6.

**RYAN, Aylmer Arthur,** M.A., LL.D.; educator; b. Can., 5 Aug. 1912; s. Robert Arthur and Mabel Agnes (Miller) R.; e. Mount Royal Coll., Calgary, Alta.; Univ. of Alta., B.A. 1939, M.A. (Eng.) 1940; Univ. of Cal., Berkeley, 1941–42, 1948–49; Sir George Williams Univ., LL.D. 1972; m. Mona Margaret, d. late James Skead, 10 Nov. 1946; children: Cynthia Kathleen, Philip James, David Arthur; Prof. of Eng., Provost and Extve. Asst. to Pres., Univ. of Alta., now retired; served with COTC 1939; Candn. Army Can., Eng. and Italy, 1942–46; rank Maj.; Candn. Army Active Reserve 1950–60; rank Lt. Col.; mem. Candn. Assn. Univ. Teachers Eng.; Candn. Student Affairs Assn. (Past Pres., rec'd Award of Outstanding Merit 1967); Awarded Candn. Assn. of Coll. and Univ. Student Services Award of Merit, 1977; Univ. of Alberta Alumni Golden Jubilee Award, 1977; Phi Kappa Pi; Protestant; recreation: sports; Home: 11811 - 87 Ave., Edmonton, Alta. T6G 0Y5.

**RYAN, His Hon. Judge Bernard T.,** B.Comm., LL.B.; provincial criminal court judge; b. Pendleton, Ont. 22 Oct. 1935; s. Thomas A. and Ethel (Moore) R.; e. St. Patrick's Coll., B.Comm. 1958; Univ. of Ottawa, LL.B. 1961; admission to Ont. Bar 1962; m. Patricia d. Frank and Florence Billie 1965; children: Terry, Maureen; JUSTICE, ONTARIO COURT OF JUSTICE (PROVINCIAL DIV.); Partner, Moore, Ryan, Tunney 1962–72; formerly Criminal Court Judge, Prov. of Ont. 1972; Special Crown Prosecutor; Dir., Ottawa Hunt & Golf Club; Ottawa Boys & Girls Club; Candn. Nat. Inst. for the Blind; recreations: squash, jogging; Clubs: Ottawa Athletic; Rideay Tennis; Home: 2000 Norway Cres., Ottawa, Ont. K1H 5N7; Office: 161 Elgin St., Ottawa, Ont. K2P 2K1.

**RYAN, Carey Ann,** B.A., B.Ed., M.Ed.; educator; b. Saint John, N.B. 18 Oct. 1948; d. Mr. Justice Henry Edward and Mary Catherine (Boyle) R.; e. St. Vincent's H.S. 1966; Univ. of N.B. B.A. 1970; St. Thomas Univ. B.Ed. 1973; Univ. of N.B. M.Ed. 1979; m. Francis J. s. Clarence and Pearle McHugh 13 April 1984; PRINCIPAL, ST. VINCENT'S HIGH SCHOOL; began teaching career at Holy Trinity School 1970; Economics Teacher, St. Vincent's H.S. 1972; held positions of classroom teacher, Guidance Counsellor, Vice-Principal and currently Principal; active in profl. activities at prov. & local levels as mem. of N.B.T.A. and served on several cttes. estab. by Dept. of Edn. & Bd. of School Trustees, Dist. 8; Bd. of Gov., Univ. of N.B.; Bd. of Dir., Jr. Achievement of Saint John; Candn. Mental Health Assn. (Saint John Br.); Past Chair & Mem. Bd. of Trustees, Saint John School of Nursing; Extve. Dir. & Hon. Pres., St. Vincent's Alumnae Assn.; Founder & Co-chair, Belfast Children's Vacation, Saint John Inc.; Mem., Irish Candn. Cultural Assn. of N.B.; Delta Kappa Gamma Soc. Internat.; N.B. Liberal Assn.; Federal Liberal Party (Saint John riding); Home: 857 Anderson Dr., Saint John, N.B. E2M 4G2; Office: 1 Cliff St., Saint John, N.B. E2L 3A8.

**RYAN, Claude;** journalist; politician; b. Montreal, Que. 26 Jan. 1925; s. Henri-Albert and Blandine (Dorion) R.; e. Collège St-Croix, Montréal, 1937–44; Sch. of Social Service, Univ. of Montreal, 1944–46; Dept. of History, Pontifical Gregorian Univ., Rome, 1951–52; m. Madeleine (dec.), d. Jos.-L. Guay, 21, July 1958; children: Paul, Monique, Thérèse, Patrice, André; MEMBER OF THE NATIONAL ASSEMBLY, MIN. OF MUNICIPAL AFFAIRS, MIN. OF PUBLIC SECURITY AND MIN. RESPONSIBLE FOR THE ADMIN. OF THE FRENCH LANGUAGE CHARTER 1990– ; Gen. Secretary, L'Action Catholique Canadienne, 1945–62; Pres., Inst. canadien d'Educ. Adultes, 1955–61; Pres., Committee on Adult Education, Youth Ministry, Govt. of Quebec. 1962–63; Dir., La Caise populaire St-Louis-de France 1956–68; Editorial Writer, 'Le Devoir' 1962–78; Editor-Publisher, 'Le Devoir' and Gen. Mgr., Imprimerie Populaire Ltée., 1964–78; Leader, Quebec Liberal Party 1978–82; mem., Nat. Assembly of Que. for Argenteuil, 1979–81; re-el. 1981, 1985 and 1989; Leader, The Official Opposition, National Assembly, Que. 1979–82; Chrmn. and Leader of the "NO" campaign in the referendum on Quebec's constitution future, May 1980; resigned as Leader of the Que. Liberal party 1982; Min. of Educ. and Min. of Higher Educ. and Science 1985; Mem. of Nat. Assembly, Min. of Education and Min. of Higher Education and Science 1985–; Min. responsible for the application of the Charter on the French Language 1989; re-elected riding of Argenteuil, 1989; appt'd. Min. of Education, Min. of Higher Educ. & Sci., and Min. responsible for the Admin. of the French Lang. Charter 1989; appt'd. Min. of Municipal Affairs, Min. of Public Security and Min. responsible for the Admin. of the French Language Charter 1990; mem. Bd. of Dir., Canadian Press; Canadian American Committee; mem. Bd. of Trustees, U.N. Inst. for Training and Research (all three bds. 1964–71); author, 'Le Travail en Comité,' 'Le Devoir et la Crise d'Octobre 1970,' 'Un Québec Stable' and numerous articles on Quebec, Canada and related topics in newspapers and periodicals; rec'd Nat. Newspaper Award, 'Editorials' Category 1965; Nat. Press Club Award 1966; Human Relations Award, Candn. Council of Christians & Jews, 1966; Jewish Labour Committee Award for his defence of human rights 1969; 'Quill Award' of the Windsor Press Club for his contribution to Canadian journalism 1971; apptd. to Candn. News Hall of Fame, 1968; Liberal; Roman Catholic; recreations: reading, walking; Home: Montréal, Que.; Office: 20 Chauveau Ave., 3rd Flr., Quebec, Que. G1R 4J3.

**RYAN, Francis J.,** Q.C.; b. St. John's, Nfld., 28 March 1926; s. James V. and Edith (McGrath) R.; e. Holy Cross Sch., Nfld., St. Bonaventure's Coll., Nfld.; m. Sheila Anne, d. Hon. Mr. Justcie C. J. Fox, 21 April 1949; Children: Dennis J., John N., Robert G.; PARTNER, STEWART MCKELVEY STIRLING SCALES; former Dir., Abitibi Price Inc. and a number of other companies; Past Chrmn. Adv. Bd. Montreal Trust Co. in Nfld.; Past Gov., Candn. Tax Foundation; past Commissioner of Conference on Uniformity of Legislation; called to Bar of Nfld. 1947; cr. Q.C. 1963; mem. Law Soc. Nfld.; Past Vice-Pres. for Nfld., Candn. Bar Assn.; R. Catholic; recreation: fishing; Home: 9 Winter Ave., St. John's, Nfld.; Office: Cabot Place, 100 New Gower St., St. John's, Nfld. A1C 5V3.

**RYAN, Jim F.,** M.B.A., B.Sc.; automotive retail executive; b. London, Ont. 21 July 1948; s. Patrick and Helen Ann (Wenechuk) R.; e. Univ. of West. Ont., B.Sc. 1970; York Univ., M.B.A. 1972; m. Dora d. Bill and June Ballan 17 Mar. 1979; children: Carol, Christine; SENIOR VICE PRESIDENT, DEALER RELATIONS, CANADIAN TIRE CORP. 1992– ; various positions ending as Manager, Automotive, Shell Canada 1972–85; Dir., Mktg. Serv., Petro-Canada 1985–86; Pres., Pyne Mngt. 1986–88; Pres., Petroleum, Canadian Tire Corp. 1988–92; Home: 9 Ferndell Circle, Unionville, Ont. L3R 3Y7; Office: 2180 Yonge St., Toronto, Ont. M4P 2V8.

**RYAN, Leo Edward,** B.Sc.; b. Montreal, Que., 24 Oct. 1909; s. Leo George and Mary Bond (Doran) R.; e. McGill Univ. (Grad. Chem. Engn.); m.; has two s. and one d.; joined Mallinckrodt Company (fine chemicals) on leaving univ.; apptd. Vice-Pres. and Dir. of Monsanto Canada Ltd., 1945, Extve. Vice-Pres. in 1949, el. Pres., 1955; Chrmn. of the Bd., 1962, till resignation 31 Dec. 1964; Pres., Candn. Exporters' Assn., 1957–58 (Hon. Pres. for Life); Mem., The New York Academy of Sciences; recreations: fishing, golf, gardening, philately; Clubs: Union; Royal Colwood Golf; Victoria Golf; Home: #401 – 1033 Belmont Ave., Victoria, B.C. V8S 3T4.

**RYAN, Louis Patrick,** B.A.Sc., P.Eng.; b. Toronto, Ont. 31 Dec. 1920; s. William Arthur and Marie Blanche (Rishea) R.; e. Niagara Falls Coll. for Boys 1939; Univ. of Toronto, B.A.Sc. 1949; m. Berniece d. Charles and Grace Hyatt 8 Sept. 1942; children: Michael Hyatt, Kevin Patrick, Ann Marie; Gen. Sec. Assn. Profl. Engs. Ont. 1976–86; served with RCAF 1941–45; joined Ontario Hydro 1949–61, co-designer Queenston Floral Clock, Mgr. Niagara Area; joined present Assn. 1961 serving as Dir. of Communications; Lectr. in Orgn. & Mgmt. McMaster Univ. R.I.A. Extension Course 4 yrs.; Past mem. Eng. Alumni Council Univ. of Toronto; Charter mem. and 3 times Chrmn. Interprofl. Liaison Group; Past Sec. Profl. Engs. Found. for Edn.; Past Dir. Toronto Chapter Inst. Assn. Execs.; Kiwanis St. Catharines; cr. Companion of the Order of the Sons of Martha for service to the engineering profession; 1992 Arbor Award for outstanding voluntary service to Univ. of Toronto; Mng. Ed. and contbr. 'Engineering Dimensions' 1980–86; (formerly 'Ontario Digest,' Past Ed.); recreation: photography; Clubs: Toronto Press; Home: 154 Lloyd Manor Rd., Islington, Ont. M9B 5K3.

**RYAN, Noel,** B.A., M.L.S., M.B.A.; librarian; b. Saint John, N.B. 27 May 1925; s. late Fergus James and late Evelyn Grace (Hayes) R.; e. Cath. High Sch. Montreal 1944; McGill Univ. 1947–49, M.L.S. 1967; Sir George Williams Univ. B.A. 1964; Northland Univ. MBA, 1983; m. Doreen Lillian d. late William Webster and late Gladys L. (founder N. York Lib. System) Allison 19 Dec. 1950; children: Colin Allison, Karen Jennifer; Building Project Mgr., Mississauga Library System 1987–88; Chief Consultant, Hour Management Consulting 1989– ; Vice Pres. Temco Electric Manufacturing Co. Montreal 1949–57; Owner, Local Photo, Montreal 1957–67; Chief Librarian, Dorval, Que. 1967–69, Brampton, Ont. 1969–71; Chief Librarian, Mississauga Library System 1971–87; served with Victoria Rifles of Can. (Reserve) 1942–44, Candn. Inf. Corps 1944, Black Watch of Can. 1945, Cameron Highlanders of Ottawa 1945–46; Candn. Volunteer Service Medal and Clasp; France-Germany Star, War Medal; co-author 'Juxtapoised' 1974; recreations: music, painting, pottery, writing; Home: #35, 55 Falconer Dr., Mississauga, Ont. L5N 1B3.

**RYAN, (Sylvester) Perry,** Q.C., B.A., LL.B., LL.M.; lawyer; b. Toronto, Ontario 12 January 1918; s. Ernest Anthony and Mary Marguerite R.; e. St. Mary's Separate Sch., Barrie, Ont.; Barrie Coll. Inst.; St. Michael's Coll., Univ. of Toronto, B.A., 1939; Osgoode Hall LL.B., 1942; York Univ. LL.M., 1977; Univ. of the Air Grad. 1980; m. Dolores Margaret, d. late Arthur and Georgianna Pothier, Thunder Bay, Ontario, 2 April 1956; children: Anne Marie, Michael Anthony; First Chrmn., Health Services Appeal Bd. of Ontario; Dir., Brompton 80 Inc.; Canmark Services Ltd.; Old Saw Hunt Club Inc.; read law with Briggs, Frost & Birks; called to the Bar of Ontario 1942; served in the 2nd World War with C.O.T.C., Osgoode Hall; def. candidate for Greenwood (Toronto) in g.e. 1949; el. to H. of C. for Spadina (Toronto) in g.e. 1962; re-el. until def. Oct. 1972; Past Chrmn., NATO Parlty. Assn.; Past Vice Chrmn., Standing Comte. on External Affairs and Nat. Defence; Past mem., Standing Comte. NATO/N. Atlantic Assembly; Co-Chrmn. of Spec. Comte on Nat. and Royal Anthems; mem., Law Soc. of Upper Can.; Monarch of Lions'; Past Pres., Anson Hunt Club; Past Pres. Kawartha Soaring Club Inc.; Past Pres. Omemee Gliding and Country Ltd.; Past Pres. Catholic Big Brothers of Toronto; recreations: golf, tennis, hunting, fishing, power flying, gliding, boating; Office: Ryan Island Rd., R.R. #4, Omemee, Ont. K0L 2W0.

**RYBCZYNSKI, Witold Marian,** B.Arch., M.Arch.; writer; university professor; b. Edinburgh, Scotland 1 Mar. 1943; s. Witold Kasimir and Anna Jadwiga (Hoffman) R.; e. Loyola Coll. H.S. 1960; McGill Univ., B.Arch 1966, M.Arch. 1972; m. Shirley d. Cecile and Leonard Hallam 15 Nov. 1974; MEYERSON PROF. OF URBANISM, UNIV. OF PENNSYLVANIA 1994– ; priv. archit. practice 1970–82; Prof. of Archit., McGill Univ. 1974–93; Cons., United Nations; World Bank; Internat. Devel. Rsch. Ctr.; Candn. Internat. Devel. Agency; Royal Archit. Inst. of Can. Medal 1966; QSPELL Prize for Non-Fiction Writing 1988, 1989; Alfred Jurzykowski Foundation Award 1993; Hon. Fellow, Am. Institute of Architects 1993; Mem., Authors Guild; Ed. Bd., 'Open House International'; Contb. ed., 'Saturday Night'; author: 'Paper Heroes' 1980, 'Taming the Tiger' 1983, 'Home' 1986; 'The Most Beautiful House in the World' 1989; 'Waiting for the Weekend' 1991; 'Looking Around' 1992; recreation: rowing; Home: 230 Rex Ave., Philadelphia, PA 19118; Office: 215 Meyerson Hall, Univ. of Pennsylvania, Philadelphia, PA 19104-6311.

**RYLEY, Alan Clair,** B.Comm., F.C.A.; chartered accountant; b. Windsor, Ont. 23 June 1930; s. Edmund Gerald and Beatrice Bertha (Hockin) R.; e. Univ. of Toronto, B.Comm. 1952; m. Jocelyn Campbell 19 June 1954; children: Alan, Jeffrey, Jennifer, Janet; PARTNER, COOPERS & LYBRAND 1960– ; joined Coopers & Lybrand 1952; recreations: golf, skiing; Clubs: Granite; Muskoka Lakes Golf & Country; Craigleith Ski; Home: 98 St. Leonard's Ave., Toronto, Ont. M4N 1K5.

**RYMEK, Edward,** B.A., B.Sc.E.E.; civil servant; b. Mossbank, Sask. 18 Sept. 1939; s. Michael and Janet (Marszall) R.; e. Gravelbourg Coll. B.A. 1960; Univ. of Manitoba B.Sc.E.E. 1965; m. Cecile d. Paul and Germaine Moquin 4 May 1963; children: Michael, Marc; DIR., INFORMATION & TECHNOLOGY EXPLOITATION, CANDN. INTELLECTUAL PROPERTY OFFICE, INDUSTRY CANADA 1990– ; Patent Examiner, Candn. Patent Office 1965–73; Patent Agent, Candn. Patents & Development Limited 1973–83; Mgr., Business Development 1983–90; Roman Catholic; Fellow, Patent & Trademark Inst. of Can.; Mem., Assn. of Profl. Engrs. of Ont.; Candn. Assn. of Univ. Rsch. Administrators; recreations: scuba diving, skiing, camping; clubs: RCMP 'Beavers' Scuba Club; Home: 1860 Elmridge Dr., Gloucester, Ont. K1J 6R7; Office: Industry Canada, Ottawa, Ont. K1A 0C9.

**RYMES, Thomas Kenneth,** Ph.D.; university professor; b. Toronto, Ont. 24 Oct. 1932; s. Henry John and Margery Mildred (Downing) R.; e. Univ. of Man., B.A. (Hons.) 1955, McGill Univ., M.A. 1958, Ph.D. 1968; m. Elizabeth Anne Bull 22 Sept. 1956; children: E. Carolyn, Paul C., John M.; PROF., DEPT. OF ECON., CARLETON UNIV. 1963– ; Economist, Statistics Can. 1958–63; Anglican; Mem., Royal Econ. Soc.; Candn. Econ. Assn.; Internat. Assn. for Rsch. in Income & Wealth;

Conf. for Rsch. in Income and Wealth; author: 'On Concepts of Capital and Technical Change' 1971; 'Keynes's Lectures, 1932–35: Notes of a Representative Student' 1989; co-author: (with Alexandra Cas) 'On Concepts and Measures of Multifactor Productivity in Canada, 1961–80' 1991; recreation: tennis; Home: 1233 Willowdale Ave., Ottawa, Ont. K1H 7S5; Office: Dept. of Econ., Carleton Univ., Ottawa, Ont. K1S 5B6.

**RYSSTAD, (Susan) Jean,** B.A.; writer; b. Goderich, Ont. 5 Oct. 1949; d. William James and Helen Annie (MacDonald) McDonald; e. Goderich Dist. Collegiate; Univ. of Windsor, B.A. 1971; m. Tom s. Maxine and Olav R. 26 jan. 1981; children: Maggie, Dylan; author: 'Travelling In' 1990 (short stories); co-author: 'Coming Attractions' 1989, 'Journey Prize Anthology' 1989, 'Uncommon Waters' 1991 (short fiction); writes for CBC Radio Drama (Morningside), original & adaptations aired 1989, '91; CBC Literary Competition Fiction Category, 3rd Prize; Home: P.O. Box 1080, Prince Rupert, B.C. V8J 4H6.

# S

**SABA, George C.,** B.A., M.A.; economist; b. Lachine, Que. 3 July 1944; s. Chehade E. and Mary (Nemer) S.; e. McGill Univ. B.A. 1965, M.A. 1967; m. Janice d. George and Josephine Nicola 26 June 1977; children: Marie, Joy, Katherine, Thomas; VICE-PRESIDENT & CHIEF ECONOMIST, MONTREAL TRUST 1991– ; Vice-Pres. & Chief Economist, Greenshields Inc. 1970–82; Chief Economist, Montreal Trust 1982–90; Mem., Economic Policy Ctte., Candn. C. of C. (Chrmn. 1985–88); National Dir., Candn. Assn. for Business Economics; Bd. of Trustees, St. George Orthodox Ch. of Montreal (Chrmn. 1985–87); Dir., Cedars Home for the Elderly; clubs: Montreal Amateur Athletic Assn.; Home: 312 London Dr., Beaconsfield, Que. H9W 5X5; Office: Place Montreal Trust, 1800 McGill College Ave., Montreal, Que. H3A 3K9.

**SABIA, Maureen Joanne,** B.A., LL.B.; lawyer; writer; b. Montreal, Que. 14 Apr. 1941; d. Michael Joseph and Laura Louise (Villella) S.; e. McGill Univ., B.A. (Hons.) 1962; Univ. of Toronto, LL.B. 1965; MNGMNT. CONSULTANT, MAUREEN SABIA INTERNAT. 1986– ; Chrmn., Export Development Corp. 1991– ; Dir., Candn. Tire Corp. Limited (Audit Ctte. Mem., Social Responsibility Ctte., Management Resources & Compensation Ctte.); Prospectus Solicitor, Ont Securities Comn. 1967–68; Asst. Couns., Ont. Law Reform Comn. 1968–74; Dir., Rsch. & Policy & Solicitor to the Bd., Ont. Municipal Employees Retirement Bd. 1974; Candn. Pacific Limited 1974–80; Gen. Couns., Redpath Indus. Ltd. 1980–86; Dir., Laurentian Gen. Insurance Co. 1988–91; Mem. Bd. of Trustees, Sunnybrook Med. Centre (Chrmn., Rsch. Ctte.; Mem. Priorities & Planning Ctte.); Chrmn., The Sunnybrook Medical Centre Found.; Chrmn. Adv. Bd., Women in Mngmnt. Rsch. Programme, Univ. of Western Ont.; Bd. of Govs., Univ. of Guelph; Mem., Law Soc. of Upper Can.; recreations: reading, needlepoint; Home: 619 Avenue Rd., Apt. 304, Toronto, Ont. M4V 2K6; Office: One University Ave., Suite 802, Toronto, Ont. M5J 2P1.

**SABINE, John William,** B.A., LL.B.; executive; b. Toronto, Ont. 20 Aug. 1945; s. John Howard and Margret (Reid) S.; e. Univ. of West. Ont. B.A. 1967, LL.B. 1970; m. Susan d. Ruth and Edwin Yelf 9 Aug. 1969; children: Anne, Christopher, Douglas, Alexandra; club: University; PRESIDENT & CHIEF EXECUTIVE OFFICER, ARBOR CAPITAL INC. 1992– ; Mem., Law Soc. of U.C. 1972; Asoc., Campbell Godfrey & Lewtas 1972–77; Partner, Campbell Godfrey & Lewtas and Fasken Campbell Godfrey 1977–92; Dir., Discovery West Corp.; Minera Rayrock Inc.; Dinecorp Inc.; Memorial Gardens Canada Limited; Rectors Warden, St. Brides Anglican Ch. 1979–80; Mem., Securities Adv. Ctte., Ont. Securities Comn. 1991–92; clubs: University; Home: 2430 Deer Run Ave., Oakville, Ont.; Office: 2 Jane St., Toronto, Ont. M6S 4W8.

**SABLATASH, Mike,** M.Sc., Ph.D., P.Eng.; research scientist; b. Bienfait, Sask. 30 Sept. 1935; s. Fred and Katryna (Rawlinko) S.; e. Univ. of Man. B.Sc. (Elect. Engn.) 1957, M.Sc. (Elect. Engn.) 1964; Univ. of Wis. Ph.D. 1968; m. Sophie (d. 1971) d. John and Olena Dmyterko 5 Aug. 1961; children: Tania Deirdre, Loren Dante Michael (d. 1971), Lisa Genevieve; SENIOR RESEARCH SCIENTIST, INDOOR WIRELESS COMMUNICATIONS 1992– ; Scient. Advisor Information Technol., Communications Research Centre, Dept. of Communications, Can. 1981–86, Research Scient., Consultant and Scientific Advs. Communications Sciences, Image Communications & Telidon Program 1978–81; Sr. Research Scientist, Advanced Video Systems 1986–1991; mem. Scient. Staff, Northern Electric Co. R & D Labs. Ottawa 1961–65; Teaching and Research Asst. Univ. of Wis. 1965–68; Asst. Prof. of Elect. Engn. Univ. of Toronto 1968–72; Sr. Analyst and Math., Nat. Energy Bd. 1972–76; Head, Local Data Networks and Research Scient. Computer Communications, Dept. of Communications Ottawa 1976–78; Sessional Lectr. in Network Analysis and Synthesis Univ. of Ottawa 1965; Consultant, Computer-Aided Design of Communication Networks, Aladdin Electronics, Nashville 1967; mem. Consociates Consulting Group Univ. of Toronto 1968–72; Sessional Lectr. Dept. Systems Engn. & Computer Science Carleton Univ. 1979; visiting Prof. in Elect. Engn. Univ. of Man. 1981; author of over 100 technical papers, invited papers and reports; recipient NRC Research Grants 1958–59, 1969–72; Ford Foundation Grants 1965–68; IEEE Broadcast Tech. Soc. 1989 Scott Helt Mem. Award for an outstanding series of papers published in the IEEE Transactions on Broadcasting; presented 2-day workshops on HDTV Systems, their Design Principles and Relationships with Computers and B-ISDN, Commun. Sciences Instit., Univ. of Southern Calif. 1990; Marine Communications Rsch. Centre, St. John's, Nfld. and Dept. of Elect. Eng., Univ. of Toronto 1991; presented 2½-day workshop on ATV Systems, Wavelets and the Uncertainty Principle Applied To ATV, as an invited consultant to Tektronix Corp., Beaverton, Oregon 1991; presented 9 invited seminars on wavelets and their applications and 2 on ATV systems, at four Canadian Universities and 3 Canadian research organizations and published 7 conference papers 1992; Visiting Rsch. Prof., Tokyo Institute of Technology Jan. 10–Apr. 10 1994, doing research and presenting seminars on wavelets and their applications, and on channel coding for all-digital HDTV transmission; Sr. Mem., Inst. Elect. & Electronic Engrs.; mem. Candn. Soc. of Electrical and Computer Engineers; Assn. Prof. Engrs. Prov. Ont.; N.Y. Acad. Sciences; Am. Stat. Assn. Ottawa Chapter; Prof. Inst. Pub. Service Can.; Am. Math. Assn.; Sigma Xi; Ottawa Field Naturalists; recreations: tennis, squash, running, music, skiing, ballroom dancing; Clubs: Sir Robert Borden Tennis; RA Ski; Home: 23A Bertona St., Nepean, Ont. K2G 4G6; Office: P.O. Box 11490, Stn. H, Ottawa, Ont. K2H 8S2.

**SABOURIN, Jean Pierre,** M.B.A.; business executive; b. Ottawa, Ont. 30 July 1949; e. Univ. of Toronto M.B.A. 1990; m. Dale Laurie d. Daniel and Eunice Dunlop; children: Cheryl, Lisa; PRES. & CHIEF EXECUTIVE OFFICER, CANADA DEPOSIT INSURANCE CORP. (a federal Crown corp.) 1990– ; Dir., Christie Lake Camp 1994– ; Hotel Div., Canadian Nat. Railways 1969–76; Chief Accountant, Canada Deposit Insur. Corp. 1976–83; Chief Operating Officer 1983–90; recreations: golf; clubs: Club de Golf Outaouais, Cercle Univ. d'Ottawa, Rideau; Home: 1950 chemin du Clairvaux, Gloucester, Ont. K1C 6A9; Office: 50 O'Connor St., Suite 1700, Ottawa, Ont. K1P 5W5.

**SABOURIN, Louis,** F.R.S.C., Ph.D., LL.L.; educator; b. Quebec, Que. 1 December 1935; s. Rolland P. and Valeda (Caza) S.; e. Univ. of Ottawa, B.A. (Pol. Science), 1956, LL.L. 1961; Sorbonne, Dipl. de Litt, Française Cont. 1957; Inst. Etudes Pol. de Paris, Dipl. Internat. Relations 1958; Quebec Bar 1962; Ph.D. Columbia Univ. 1971; D. Univ. nat. du Dahomey (Africa) 1973; m. Agathe, d. Dr. C. E. Lacerte, St. Eugene, Ont., 18 July 1959; children: Pierre, Nicole, Nathalie; DIR., GROUPE D'ETUDE, DE RECHERCHE ET DE FORMATION INTNL. (GERFI); Prof., Intnl. Economic Organ., Ecole Nationale d'Administration Publique, Univ. Du Quebec and visiting Prof., Paris-Sorbonne; Faculty of Law, Université de Montréal 1989– ; McGill Univ. 1990– ; Legal advisor, Hudon, Gendron, Harris, Thomas (Montréal) 1989– ; Past Pres., OECD Development Center in Paris, France, 1977–82; Founder and Past Dir., Inst. for Internat. Co-op., Univ. of Ottawa, and Prof. of Pol. Science; Past Dean, Faculty Social Sciences; Established programmes for and in several Third World countries; French Govt. Fellow, 1956; Ford Internat. Fellow, Columbia Univ., 1962–63; Can. Council Scholar, Stanford & Harvard Univ., 1963–64; Visiting Sr. Research Fellow, Jesus Coll., Oxford 1974–75; Visiting Prof. several Candn. and foreign univs. incl. Univ. Laval (1965–67), Northwestern Univ., Chicago 1975–77; Guest Scholar, Univ. of Notre Dame and Stanford 1992– ; has written numerous books and articles on Canadian foreign policy and public law, international organizations and development; Quebec Bar; Candn. Council of Internat. Law; Société québécoise de Droit international; mem., Candn. Inst. Internat. Affairs; Past Pres., Can. Assn. African Studies; Past Pres., Soc. Can. De Science Pol.; Past Pres., International Comte. Social Science Research Council Can.; Pres., Scient. Council 'Ecole internat. de Bordeaux'; mem., Inst. Intnl. Jacques Maritain (Rome); elected, Roy. Soc. Can. 1977, to Club of Dakar, 1978; Pontifical Commission Justice & Peace (Vatican) 1984; Assoc. des écrivains de langue française 1986; Founder, Conseil des Relations Internationales de Montreal; Président de la Société de Droit International Economique 1988; Chevalier de l'Ordre de la Pléiade de la francophonie 1988; Chevalier de la légion d'honneur de France 1989; Titular of the "Foi et justice sociale" Chair, St-Paul Univ., Ottawa 1989–90; mem., North South Round Table 1979–89; mem. Bd., Asia Pacific Foundation of Canada 1984–90; elected to Pontifical Academy of Social Sciences 1994; R. Catholic; recreation: travel; skiing; jogging; wine tasting (Grand Officier du Tastevin); Office: GERFI-ENAP, 1001, rue Sherbrooke est, Suite 300, Montréal, Qué. H2L 4Z1.

**SACHSE, Armin Michael,** C.I.M.; financial executive; b. Winnipeg, Man. 24 Aug. 1940; s. Kurt and Jean (Rokyta) S.; c. Univ. of Manitoba C.I.M.; m. Kathryn Kelly-Schulz; children: Brigitte, Christine, Jeffrey; VICE-PRES., MARKETING & TRAINING, GE CAPITAL CANADA (formerly National Bank Leasing Inc.); Acct. Mgr., Industrial Acceptance; Regional Mgr., Avco Delta Winnipeg; Area Mgr., Avco Leasing Vancouver; Mktg. Mgr., Canpac Leasing Montreal; Product Mgr., Royal Bank (1st Finan. Serv. Product Mgr. Toronto); creator of a unique computerized finan. analysis mktg. program which combines mktg., sales, client & account mgr. training in 1 program; recreations: skiing, hiking, travel; Home: 1718 Pengilley Place, Clarkson Village, Mississauga; Office: 300 – 150 York St., Toronto, Ont. M5H 3A9.

**SACKETT, David Lawrence,** F.R.S.C., M.D., M.Sc.Epid., F.R.C.P.C.; academic physician; b. Chicago, Ill. 17 Nov. 1934; s. DeForest and Margaret Helen (Ross) S.; e. Lawrence Coll. 1956; Univ. of Illinois 1960; Harvard 1967; m. Barbara d. Charles and Genevieve Bennett 29 June 1957; children: David Joel, Charles Allan, Andrew Bennett, Robert DeForest; PROF. IN MEDIINE AND CLINICAL EPIDEMIOLOGY & BIOSTATISTICS, MCMASTER UNIV.; Founding Chair, Clinical Epidemiology and Biostatistics, McMaster Univ.; Physician and Chief, Chedoke-McMaster Hosps.; Head, Div. of Gen. Internal Med.; Candn. & Am. Soc. for Clinical Investigation, Assn. of Am. Physicians, J. Allyn Taylor Internat. Prize in Med.; Alpha Omega Alpha Distinguished Teaching Award; Trillium Clinical Scientist Award; Fellow, Royal Soc. of Canada; author: 'Methods of Health Care Evaluation' 1971, 'Compliance with Therapeutic Regimens' 1976, 'Compliance in Health Care' 1979, 'Clinical Epidemiology' 1985, 'Clinical Epidemiology' 1992 (2nd ed.) plus 200 scientific articles; recreations: sailing, hiking, running; Home: R.R. #1, Markdale, Ont. N0C 1H0; Office: Henderson Gen. Div., Room 408, McMaster Univ. Clinic, 711 Concession St., Hamilton, Ont. L8V 1C3.

**SACKS, Stephen L.,** A.B., M.D., F.R.C.P.(C); physician; educator; businessperson; b. Akron, Ohio 4 Apl. 1948; s. the late Leon J. and Anne B. (Marshall) S.; e. Univ. of Pa., A.B. 1969; Univ. of Cincinnati, M.D. 1975; Univ. of Toronto Internal Med. 1978; Stanford Univ. Med. Center Infectious Diseases 1980; m. Marika d. the late Joseph and Krystina Nytko 8 Aug. 1971; children: Adrian Jacob, Rebecca Laura; DIR. HERPES CLINIC, UNIV. OF B.C. 1980– ; Prof. of Med. and teacher Depts. Med. Dentistry, Pharmacol. 1980– ; Pres., Community Clinical Rsch. Centres Intern Inc.; Cons. several pharm. firms; Postdoctoral Fellow Div. Infectious Diseases Stanford Univ. 1978–80; Founder present Clinic 1980; recipient Univ. of Cincinnati Med. Coll. Alumnal Award 1975; The Donald M. Whitelaw Award, Univ. of B.C. 1993; Med. Rsch. Council Fellow 1978–80; various grants MRC, U.S. Nat. Inst. Health, B.C. Health Care Rsch. Found.; author 'The Truth About Herpes. What Everyone Should Know' 1983, French transl. 1983; 'The Truth About Herpes' 1986, 1989, 1994; over 100 sci. publs. herpes rsch. & antiviral treatment; mem. B.C. Med. Assn. (Infectious Dis. Comm. Council on Health Prom.); Candn. Infectious Disease Soc.; Infectious Disease Soc. Am. (Fellow); Candn. Soc. Clin. Rsch.; Am. Fedn. Clin. Rsch.; Am. Soc. Microbiol.; Internat. Soc. for Antiviral Rsch. (Intern Council); Home: 3963 West 23rd Ave., Vancouver, B.C. V6S 1L1; Office: 1124 - 1134 Burrard St., Vancouver, B.C. V6Z 1Y8.

**SADAVOY, Joel,** M.D., D.Psych., FRCP(C); psychiatrist; b. Ottawa, Ont. 5 Feb. 1945; s. Benjamin and Belle (Fogel) S.; e. Lisgar Coll. 1962; Univ. of Ottawa; Univ. of Toronto, M.D. 1968, D.Psych. 1972; m. Sharian d. Max and Helen Smolack 20 Nov. 1977; children: Marion, Andrew, Beth, Daniel; PSYCHIATRIST-IN-

CHIEF, MOUNT SINAI HOSPITAL 1994– ; Dir. of Geriatric Psychiatry Services, Mount Sinai Hosp., Toronto; Fellowship, Psych. 1973; CESO Volunteer St. Lucia BWI 1969; Rotating internship 1969; Chief Res., Mt. Sinai Hosp. 1972; Asst. Prof., Psych., Univ. of Toronto 1977; Assoc. Prof. 1986; Staff Psych., Mt. Sinai Hosp. 1973–80; Bd. of Dir., Am. Assn. of Geriatric Psych. 1988–91; Cons., Am. Psych. Assn., Ctte. on Aging 1989–91; Head, Division of Geriatric Psychiatry, Univ. of Toronto 1991–94; Profl. Adv. Bd., Candn. Psych. Rsch. Found. 1987–90; Ed. Bd. 'J. of Geriatric Psychiatry'; Asst. Ed., Am. J. Geriatric Psychiatry; Cons. (Psych.), Mt. Sinai Hosp. 1980–91; Bd. of Dirs., Jewish Family Child Serv. Toronto 1985–88; Senior Care Toronto 1985–88; Bd. of Advisors, Internat. Newsletter on Elder Abuse; Hon. Mem., Internat. Psychogeriatric Assn.; Founding Pres. 1991–93, Candn. Academy of Geriatric Psychiatry; Mem., Candn. Psych. Assn.; Ont. Psych. Assn. (Extve., Psychotherapy section 1982); Israel Med. Assn.; Am. Assn. for Geriatric Psych.; Internat. Psychogeriatric Assn.; Extve., Ont. Psychogeriatric Assn. 1983–82; editor: 'Treating the Elderly with Psychotherapy' 1987; co-editor: 'Psychiatric Consequences of Brain Disease in the Elderly' 1989, 'Comprehensive Review of Geriatric Psychiatry' 1991; recreations: racquet ball, reading, travel; Home: 212 Glenayr Rd., Toronto, Ont. M5P 3C3; Office: 600 University Ave., Toronto, Ont. M5G 1X5.

**SADDLEMYER, (Eleanor) Ann,** LL.D., D.Litt., M.A., Ph.D., F.R.S.C., F.R.S.A.; educator; author; b. Prince Albert, Sask. 28 Nov. 1932; d. Orrin Angus and Elsie Sarah (Ellis) S.; e. Univ. of Sask. B.A. 1953 (Eng. & Psychol.) 1955 (Eng. Hons.), D.Litt. 1991; Queen's Univ. M.A. 1956, LL.D. 1977; Bedford Coll. Univ. of London Ph.D. 1961; Univ. of Victoria D.Litt. 1989; McGill Univ. D.Litt. 1989; Univ. of Windsor D.Litt. 1990; MASTER OF MASSEY COLL., UNIV. OF TORONTO 1988– ; PROF. OF ENGLISH, VICTORIA COLL., UNIV. OF TORONTO since 1971 and Prof. of Drama, Grad. Centre for Study of Drama; Lectr. Victoria (B.C.) Coll. 1956–57, Instr. 1960, Asst. Prof. 1962, Assoc. Prof. (Univ. of Victoria) 1965, Prof. 1968–71; Lectr. Univ. of Sask. summer 1957; Dir. Grad. Drama Centre, Univ. of Toronto 1972–77, Acting Dir., 1985–86; Visiting Prof. Berg Chair N.Y. Univ. 1975; Sr. Fellow, Massey Coll. 1975–88; mem. Univ. Council Queen's Univ. 1975–80; mem. Chancellor's Council, Victoria Univ. 1984– ; Guggenheim Fellow 1965 and 1977; Univ. of Toronto Connaught Sr. Research Fellow 1986; Distinguished Service Award, Prov. of Ont. 1985; Univ. of Toronto Alumni Award 1990; YWCA Toronto Woman of the Year Award 1994; Vice Pres. Bd. Theatre Plus, 1973–83; mem., Bd. of Dir., Colin Smythe Publishers Ltd.; author 'The World of W. B. Yeats' (with Robin Skelton & others) 1965; 'In Defence of Lady Gregory, Playwright' 1966; 'The Plays of J. M. Synge, Books One and Two' 1968; 'Synge and Modern Comedy' 1968; 'The Plays of Lady Gregory' 4 vols. 1970; 'A Selection of Letters from J. M. Synge to W. B. Yeats and Lady Gregory' 1971; 'Letters to Molly: J. M. Synge to Maire O'Neill' 1971; 'Theatre Business, the correspondence of the first Abbey Theatre directors' 1982; 'The Collected Letters of J. M. Synge' Vol. I 1983, Vol. II 1984; 'Lady Gregory Fifty Years After' (with Colin Smythe and others) 1987; Gen. ed., 'Early Stages: Essays on Theatre in Ontario 1800–1914' 1990; various articles and reviews; co-ed. of journal, 'Theatre History in Canada/Histoire du Théâtre au Canada' 1979–86; mem. Ed. Bds. 'Irish University Review'; 'Canadian Journal of Irish Studies'; 'Themes in Drama'; 'The Shaw Review'; mem. Internat. Assn. Study Anglo-Irish Lit. (Past Chrmn.); Assn. Candn. Theatre Hist. (Founding Pres.); Candn. Assn. Irish Studies; NDP; recreations: acting, book collecting, music, theatre, travel; Home: 100 Lakeshore Rd. E. #803, Oakville, Ont. L6J 6M9.

**SADIQ, Nazneen,** B.A.; writer; b. Spinagar, Kashmir 19 June 1944; d. Anwar and Dilafroze (Sirrajuddin) Shiekh; e. Hinnbird College, Univ. of Punjab B.A.; m. Salim D. s. E.A. S. 26 July 1964; children: Laara, Sheerin, Zorana; author of four published books and book reviews & political commentary for the 'Globe & Mail,' 'Now,' 'Toronto South Asian Review'; taught creative writing workshops at elementary schools & the Young Author's Camp of Canada; recipient of num. Ont. Arts Council & Secretary of State grants; Bd. Mem., P.E.N. Canada; Mem., Writers Union of Canada; recreations: tennis, skiing, squash, riding, a student of flamenco dancing; Home: 49 Castle Harbour Lane, Thornhill, Ont. L3T 3A3.

**SADLEIR, (Charles) David,** B.A.Sc., M.A.Sc., Ph.D., P.Eng.; university administrator; b. Guelph, Ont. 12 Oct. 1940; s. Charles Whitehead and Thelma Rosemary (Ross) S.; e. Sarnia Central C.I. 1960; Univ. of Toronto B.A.Sc. 1964, M.A.Sc. 1965; Lancaster Univ. (U.K.) Ph.D. 1967; m. Gillian ('Jill') d. Joseph and Iris Clark 11 Dec. 1982; children: Jonathan David, Geoffrey Scott, Catherine Mary; VICE-PRES., COMPUTING & COMMUNICATIONS, UNIV. OF TORONTO 1989– ; var. positions, Imperial Oil Limited 1967–73; Vice-Pres., Information Systems, Reed Ltd. 1973–77; Vice-Pres., Devel., B-N Software Research, Inc. 1977–79; var. positions ending as Asst. Vice-Pres., Business Devel. (H.Q. Mktg. & Devel.), Bell Canada 1979–89; Edit. Assoc. 'European J. of O.R.' 1986– ; Chair, Sub-Ctte. on Micro-Electronics, Ont. C. of C. 1983–84; Advisor, Diebold Rsch. Prog. 1980–83; Edit. Advisor, Auerbach Pubs. 1974–78; Spec. part-time Lect., Grad. Sch. of Business & Sch. of Cont. Studies, Univ. of Toronto 1968–71; part-time Lectr., Admin. Studies, Univ. of Alta. 1972–73; part-time Lectr., Ind. Eng., Univ. of Toronto 1992– ; Queen's Scout; Mem., Candn. contingent to Pan-Pacific Jamboree, Australia & Jubilee Jamboree, England; First Candn. Pres., Key Club Internat.; Ontario Scholar; Grad. Fellowship, Univ. of Lancaster; World Telecom Award; Chair, 5th York Mills Scout Group 1976–78; Strategy Bd., Fac. of Math., Univ. of Waterloo 1974–89 (Chair 1979–81); Supercomputer Management Bd., OCLSC 1990–91; Board Mem., Univ. of Toronto Press 1991; Board Mem., Communications Competition Coalition 1990–92; Full Mem., Operational Research Soc. (U.K.); Mem., Candn. Information Processing Soc.; P.Eng., Assn. of Profl. Engrs., Geologists, Geophysicists, Alta.; author of several articles, most recent: 'From Dickens to Digital,' Can. J. of Information Science 1991; recreations: stamp collecting, furniture making, museum quality aircraft models, squash; Home: 10 Hopperton Dr., Willowdale, Ont. M2L 2S6; Office: Simcoe Hall, 27 King's College Circle, Toronto, Ont. M5S 1A1.

**SADLEIR, Richard H.,** B.A., M.A., Litt.D.; b. Toronto, Ont., 23 April 1929; s. Harry Llewellyn and Mary Irene (Hay) E.; e. Univ. of Toronto, Trinity Coll., B.A. 1951; Ont. Coll. of Educ. 1953; Trinity Coll., Cambridge, M.A. 1956; m. Joan Walker, d. John J. Robinette, Toronto, Ont., 19 Dec. 1959; children: Thomas Robinette, Mary Walker, Catherine Hay; Exec. Comm. of Convocation, Trinity Coll., 1952–54; Eng. Master, Upper Canada Coll., 1956–63 also House Master of Scadding's House there; Dean of Men, Trent Univ. 1963 and Master, Peter Robinson Coll. there 1964–69; Vice Pres. and Assoc. Prof. Eng. Trent Univ. 1969–75; Principal, Upper Canada Coll. 1975–88; Headmaster, Lycée canadien, St. Jean Cap Ferrat, France 1988–91; Dir., Peterborough Community Concert Assoc., 1965–71; Chrmn., Peterborough Symphony Orchestra Bd; 1968–71; Ont. Fed. of Symphony Orchestras, 1970–71; Mem., Corp., Trinity Coll., Univ. of Toronto, 1969–80 (Exec. Comm. 1977–80, 1993– ; Vice Chrmn. 1980); Pres. Can. Headmasters Assoc. 1979–80; awarded Centennial Medal 1967; Hon. Degree, D.Litt., Trent Univ. 1989; Home: 21 Clarendon Ave., Toronto, Ont. M4V 1H8.

**SADLER, Douglas Campbell,** B.A., LL.D.; freelance naturalist writer and photographer; b. London, England 6 Aug. 1916; s. Bertram Campbell and Kate Frances Salter (Symes) S.; e. Bec S.S. (U.K.); Peterborough Teachers College 1969; Trent Univ. B.A. 1978; m. Joan d. Frank and Charlotte Reading 8 Aug. 1942; one d.: Heather; served in British Army in World War II 1941–47; active serv. in N.W. Eur. June–Oct. 1944, wounded, POW, Army of Occupation, Germany; Battalion Adjutant then Personnel Selection Offr., S.E. Asia; granted hon. rank of Captain on discharge; farmer, ad man, teacher (Northumberland & Peterborough Co. Bds.), vice-principal; Outdoor Edn. Cons. 1969–76; part-time teacher, Sir Sandford Fleming College 1976–92; Nat. Winner, Kortright Award for Excellence of Writing 1965, '66, '67, '68, '70; City of Peterborough Award of Merit 1966; Hon. Mem. (1975) & Richards Edn. Award (1986), Fed. of Ont. Naturalists; LL.D. (honoris causa) Trent Univ. 1988; Sustainable Devel. Award Peterborough 1990; awarded Commemorative Medal for 125th Anniversary of Candn. Confederation 1993; former Chrmn., Public Liaison Ctte., Peterborough City-Co. Waste Mngt. Study; active with many environ. bodies; Extve., Fed. of Ont. Naturalists 1955–68 (Pres. 1966–68); served at Prov., Reg. & Local Levels, Atlas of Breeding Birds of Ont. Project 1981–86; Nature Tour Leader, Point Pelee, Hudson Bay, Arizona, Yucatan, Cuba, Nfld., etc.; author: 'Studying Insects' 1971, 'Studying Plants' 1972, 'Our Heritage of Birds: Peterborough County in the Kawarthas' 1983, 'Reading Nature's Clues: A Guide to the Wild' 1987 & 2nd ptg., 'Winter: A Natural History' 1990 (all lavishly illus. with own photographs); contbr. to anthologies & mags.; co-author: 'Birds from the Ground: The Record of Archaeology in Ontario' forthcoming; environ. / nature column, 'Peterborough Examiner' 1957– (weekly); widely travelled in North, Middle & S. Am. & S. Africa; Home: R.R. #4, Peterborough, Ont. K9J 6X5.

**SADLER, James Arthur,** B.Eng.; mining executive retired; b. Montreal, P.Q., 26 Mar. 1915; s. James and Lavenia (McCollough) S.; e. Verdun (Que.) High Sch.; Westmount (Que.) High Sch.; McGill Univ., B.Eng. (Mining) 1944; m. Thelma Marion, d. Llewellyn Adams, Verdun, P.Q., 15 June 1940; children: Wayne, Heather, Barry, Sherry; former President, Rio Tinto Canadian Exploration Ltd. (Estbd. 1953); worked in various mines in Canada before and after grad., incl. Siscoe Gold Mines, Hollinger Gold Mines, International Nickel Co. of Can., and Kerr-Addison Gold Mines; in 1946 accepted a post in Tanganyika, E. Africa as Mine Capt. and rose through Mine Supt., Gen. Supt., Asst. Mgr. to Gen. Mgr. of Geita Gold Mining Co. Ltd.; travelled through much of Central Africa incl. 'Copper Belt' of N. Rhodesia; returned to Can., 1955 as Asst. Mgr. of Chibaugamau Explorers Ltd.; Chief Mining Engr., Mines Br., Prov. of Manitoba, 1955–56; joined Rio Algom Ltd. as Asst. Mgr. 1956; retired as Vice Pres. (Exploration) 1977; mem., Candn. Inst. Mining & Metall.; Home: 7 Gwynewth Dr., Carlisle, Ont. L0R 1H2.

**SADLER, S.W.R.,** B.B.A.; company executive; b. Montreal 24 Nov. 1938; s. Albert Corneil and Esther Isabel (Walsh) S.; e. Lower Canada Coll., 1951–57; Univ. of New Brunswick, B.B.A. 1962; children: Grant S. A., Erika V.; PRESIDENT AND GEN. MGR., SADLER INC.; Pres., Montreal Polo Club; Dir., Rotary Club of Montreal; Treas., Optimus Ltd.; Protestant; recreation: flying, sailing, skiing, riding, polo; Office: 1845 William St., Montreal, Que. H3J 1R6.

**SAFARIAN, Albert Edward,** B.A., Ph.D., F.R.S.C.; b. Hamilton, Ont., 19 Apl. 1924; s. Israel and Annie (Simonian) S.; e. Jarvis Coll. Inst., Toronto, 1937–42; Univ. of Toronto, B.A. (Pol. Econ.) 1946; Univ. of Cal. (Berkeley), Ph.D. (Econ.) 1956; m. Joan Elizabeth, d. C. H. Shivvers, Phoenix, Ariz., Jan. 1950; children: Mark, David, Laura, Paul; PROF. OF BUSINESS ECON., UNIV. OF TORONTO, since 1989; Sr. Fellow, Centre for Internat. Studies, Massey Coll., Trinity Coll.; Assoc. Dir., Economic Growth and Policy Program, Candn. Institute for Advanced Research; Dean, Sch. of Grad. Studies 1971–76; Stat., Balance of Payments, Dom. Bureau of Stat., Ottawa, 1950–55; Assoc. Prof., Prof. and Head, Dept. of Econ. and Pol. Science, Univ. of Sask., 1956–66; Professor of Economics, Univ. of Toronto 1966–89; mem., Task Force on Structure of Indust., Ottawa, 1967; author: 'The Canadian Economy in the Great Depression,' 1959; 'Foreign Ownership of Canadian Industry,' 1966; 'Canadian Federalism and Economic Integration,' 1974; 'Governments and Multinationals' 1984; 'Multinational Enterprise and Public Policy' 1993; mem., Candn. Econ. Assn. (Pres. 1976–77); Ont. Econ. Council 1974–81; Cdn.-Amer. Comm. 1972–93; Candn. Nat. Ctte. on Pacific Economic Co-operation 1985–88; Dir., Zoryan Inst. of Can. 1986–90; Pres., Danny Grossman Dance Co. 1982–85; Home: 36 Colin Ave., Toronto, Ont. M5P 2B9.

**SAFDIE, Moshe,** O.C., B.Arch.; architect, urban designer; b. Haifa, Israel 14 July 1938; s. Leon and Rachel (Esses) S.; e. McGill Univ., B.Arch. 1961 (Lt.-Gov.'s Gold Medal); LL.D. (Hon.) McGill Univ., 1982; m. Nina, d. Henry Nusynowicz, 6 Sept. 1959; children: Taal, Oren; re-married Michal Ronnen, 7 June 1981; children: Carmelle, Yasmin; Israeli Army training 1970; arch. of Habitat, Montreal, 1967; Yeshivat Porat Joseph and sephardic Synagogue, Old City of Jerusalem, 1970; Coldspring New Town, Baltimore, Maryland; Keur Farah Pahlavi New Town, Senegal; Ivory Coast Blood Centres; Mamilla Central Business District, Jerusalem; Musée de la Civilisation, Quebec City 1988; Le Musée des Beaux Arts de Montréal, Montréal, Que. 1991; National Gallery of Canada, Ottawa 1988; Ballet Opera House, Toronto, Ont.; e. Robina New Town, Gold Coast, Australia; Columbus Center, New York; Hebrew Union Coll., Jerusalem; Cambridge Center, Cambridge, Mass.; Hebrew Union Coll. Cultural Ctr. for Am. Jewish Life, Los Angeles, Calif.; the Esplanade on the Charles, Cambridge, Mass.; Ottawa City Hall, Ottawa, Ont.; Harvard Business Sch., Boston, Mass.; Harvard-Radcliffe Hillel Hse., Cambridge, Mass.; Library Square, Vancouver, B.C.; author of 'Beyond Habitat,' 1970; 'Beyond Habitat by Twenty Years,' 1987 (2nd ed.); 'For Everyone a Garden,' 1974; 'Form and Purpose,' 1982; 'The Harvard Jerusalem Studio,' 1986; 'Jerusalem: The Future of the Past,' 1989; and various publs. relating to arch. incl. Process Architecture No. 56, special issue; Ian Woodner Studio Professor of Architecture and Urban Design, Harvard Grad. Sch. of Design 1984–89; Officer, Order of Canada; mem., Order of Archs. of Que; Royal Canadian Academy of Arts; Ont. Assn. of Archs.; Am. Inst.

of Archs.; Fellow, Royal Arch. Inst. Can.; Assn. Engrs. & Archs. Israel; Dir., Urban Design Program, Harvard Grad. Sch. of Design 1978–84; Chrmn., Internat. Design Conf. Aspen 1980; awards incl. Le Prix d'excellence in Arch., Que. Order of Archs.; Doctorate in Sciences (Hon.), Laval Univ.; Member of the Order of Canada; Massey Medal for Arch.; D.F.A. (Hon.) Univ. of Victoria; LL.D. (Hon.), McGill Univ.; The Lt.-Gov.'s Medal (Can.); Gold Star Award, Philadelphia Coll. of Art; A.I.R.A. Architect of the Year; Construction Man of the Year, Engineering News-Record: Rechter Prize for Arch. (Israel); Tau Sigma Delta Gold Medal; and numerous design awards, incl. Urban Design Concept Award, U.S. Dept. of Housing and Urban Development 1980, for Coldspring New Town; and the Rechter Prize, from Architects and City Planners of Israel, 1972; Offices: 165 Avenue Rd., Suite 501, Toronto, Ont. M5R 2H7; 3601 University St., Montreal, Que. H3A 2B3; 100 Properzi Way Somerville, MA 02143; 4 Ha'emek St., Jerusalem, Israel 94106.

**SAFFRAN, David,** B.A., M.B.A.; consultant; b. Montreal, Que. 2 Sept. 1951; e. McGill Univ. B.A. 1972; York Univ. M.B.A. 1975; m. Karen E. Rubin; children: Luke, Alexis, Mark; VICE PRESIDENT, DECIMA RESEARCH 1993– ; Canadian Facts, Peat Marwick Stevenson & Kellogg 1975–78; Canada Trust 1979–80; Bank of Montreal 1980–90; Sr. Vice Pres., Commercial Union Assur. Co. of Canada 1990–93; recreations: photography, sailing; Home: 138 Deloraine Ave., Toronto, Ont. M5M 2A9.

**SAFTY, Adel,** B.Ed., M.A., D.E.S.L.A., Ph.D.; university professor; television commentator; b. Cairo, Egypt 15 Dec. 1953; s. Abdel Aziz Bey El Safty and Atiat Ali (Moursy) S.; e. Univ. of Paris III, B.Ed. 1974, M.A. 1975, 1976; Inst. of French Teachers (La Sorbonne) 1976; Univ. of Paris, I, D.E.S.A. 1977, Ph.D. (with mention of distinction) 1980; PROF., UNIV. OF B.C. 1988– ; Univ. of Toronto 1976–77; French Immersion Programs (B.C.) 1978–88; Simon Fraser Univ. 1982–87; keynote speaker, guest lectr. & speaker at prov., nat. & internat. conferences; author of numerous articles on the Middle East, the Arab-Israeli Conflict & on cultural, linguistic & bilingual edn. issues; contbr.: Globe & Mail; guest political analyst, nat. TV; principal author/editor: 'Pour un Enseignement Dynamique et Efficace' (Univ. of Que. Press) 1990; author: 'Camp David to the Gulf: Negotiations, Language and Propaganda, and War' 1992; author/editor: 'L'enseignement efficace: théories et pratique (Univ. of Que.) 1993; Home: 3196 Heather St., Apt. 102, Vancouver, B.C. V5Z 3K3; Office: 2125 Main Mall, Vancouver, B.C. V6T 1Z5.

**SAGER, Eric William,** B.A., Ph.D.; university professor; b. Vancouver, B.C. 11 Feb. 1946; s. Arthur H. and Dorothy (Planche) S.; e. Univ. of B.C. B.A. 1966, Ph.D. 1975; m. Brenda d. Gordon and Verda Clark 1979; children: Catherine, Zoe; PROF., HISTORY DEPT., UNIV. OF VICTORIA 1990– ; Asst. Prof., Univ. of Winnipeg 1975–76; Memorial Univ. of Nfld. 1976–79; Univ. of Toronto 1979–83; Univ. of Victoria 1983–86; Assoc. Prof. 1986–90; Sec., Public History Group, Univ. of Victoria; Mem., Candn. Hist. Assn.; First Vice-Pres., Candn. Nautical Rsch. Soc. 1990–92; author: 'Seafaring Labour: The Merchant Marine of Atlantic Canada 1820–1914' 1989; co-author: 'Maritime Capital: The Shipping Industry in Atlantic Canada 1820–1914' 1990; Home: 4126 Cabot Place, Victoria, B.C. V8N 4V8; Office: Victoria, B.C. V8W 3P4.

**SAGINUR, Raphael,** A.B., M.D.C.M., F.R.C.P.C; physician b. Montreal, Que. 4 Sept. 1948; s. Reuben and Mindel (Chananie) S.; e. Dartmouth Coll., A.B. 1969; McGill Univ., M.D.C.M. 1973; m. Deborah Susan Mitchell 18 May 1975; children: Michael, Madelaine, Alexandra; HEAD, INFECTIOUS DISEASE DIVISION, OTTAWA CIVIC HOSP. 1983– & ASSOC. PROF. OF MED., UNIV. OF OTTAWA 1988– (Asst. Prof. 1983); post-grad. training McGill Univ. & Tufts Univ.; joined Jewish Gen. Hosp. 1980; Lectr., then Asst. Prof., Fac. of Med., McGill Univ. 1980–83; Mem., Candn. Infectious Disease Soc.; Fellow, Infectious Disease Soc. of Am.; Royal Coll. of Phys. of Can., Am. Soc. for Microbiol.; Candn. Public Health Assn.; Candn. Soc. for Internat. Health; Candn. Soc. for Med. Bioethics; Candn. Soc. for Clinical Investigation; Candn. Assoc. for Clinical Microbiology and Infectious Diseases; Internat. Assoc. for Med. Assistance to Travellers; Que. Assn. of Med. Microbiol.; Candn. Med. Protective Assn.; author of var. med. articles; Home: 960 Mooney Ave., Ottawa, Ont. K2A 3A1; Office: Dept. of Med., Ottawa Civic Hosp., 1053 Carling Ave., Ottawa, Ont. K1Y 4E9.

**SAGO, Antonio (Tony) E.W.,** C.M.A.; business executive; b. Toronto, Ont. 15 Sept. 1946; s. Antonio and Mary (Zawacki) S.; e. York Univ., B.B.A. (Hons.) 1975; Soc. of Mngt. Accts., C.M.A.; m. Judy d. Don and Lil Hamilton 29 Nov. 1969; children: Heather, Greg; VICE-PRES., JOSTENS INC. 1990– ; Controller, Beaver Homes 1975–77; Mgr., Finan. Planning, Willson Office Speciality 1977–78; Sr. Controller, Qualico Devel. Ltd. 1978–80; Div. Mgr., Singles Family Housing 1981–85; Vice-Pres., Finan., Jostens Can. Ltd. 1985–89, Pres. & Gen. Mgr., 1989– ; Office: 5501 Norman Center Dr., Minneapolis, Minn. 55437 USA.

**SAHL, Morton Lyon,** B.Sc.; comedien; b. Montreal, Que. 11 May 1927; s. Harry S.; e. Compton Jr. Coll.; Univ. of S. Calif. B.S.; 1st m. Sue Babior 25 June 1955 (div. 1957); 2nd m. China Lee; 1 s.: Morton Jr.; Editor, Poop from the Group; Experimental theatre also writing for little mags., L.A. & San Francisco; entertainer, Hungry I, San Francisco from 1953; other night club engagements incl. Basin St. East and Copacabana N.Y.C., Chez Paree and Mister Kelley's Chicago, Crescendo L.A., Americana Miami Beach, Flamingo Las Vegas; performer: radio and TV incl. appearances radio show ABC Comedy News TV show, Steve Allen Show, Jack Paar Show, Eddie Fisher Show, Nightline; also special shows Acad. Award show, Wide Wide World; summer monologue appearance, Highland Park, Ill., monologues on long-playing records, Verve Records; on Broadway in revue: 'The Next President' 1958; motion pictures incl. 'In Love and War' 1958, 'All the Young Men' 1960, 'Doctor, You've Got to be Kidding' 1967, 'Hungri i Reunion' 1981, 'Nothing Lasts Forever' 1984; talk show host: Station WRC Washington 1978; author: 'Heartland' 1976; appeared in TV film 'Inside the Third Reich' 1982; one-man show Broadway 1987; served to pvt. USAAF, World War II.

**SAILA, Pauta;** artist; b. Kilaparutua, N.W.T. 1916; m. Pitaloosie; medium: sculpture, drawings, prints; 96 group exbns. incl. most recent: The McMichael Candn. Art Coll. Kleinburg, Ont. 1991–92, Albers Gall. San Francisco, Ca. 1991, Inuit Gall. of Vancouver 1991, Vancouver Inuit Art Soc. 1991, Feheley Fine Arts Toronto 1990, 1991, Maison Hamel-Bruneau Ste-Foy, Que. 1990–91, Arctic Artistry Hastings-on-Hudson, N.Y. 1990, l'Iglou Art Esquimau, Douai (toured 6 cities) France 1987–91, Candn. Mus. of Civilization Hull, Que. 1990, Glenbow Museum Calgary 1990; solo exbns.: Gallery One Toronto 1981, Arctic Arts Edmonton 1977; works in 32 collections incl. art galleries of London Region, Ontario (Klamer & Sarick colls.), Windsor, Winnipeg (Bessie Bulman, Swinton & Twomey colls.), Candn. Mus. of Civilization, Nat. Gallery of Can. (Feheley Coll.), Inuit Cultural Inst. Rankin Inlet, N.W.T., Musée des beaux-arts de Montréal, Royal Ontario Museum, Smithsonian Inst.; participant, Internat. Sculpture Symposium Toronto 1967; attended opening of 'In the Shadow of the Sun' Dortmund, Germany 1988, subject of several articles and catalogues; Home: Cape Dorset, N.W.T.; Office: c/o Dorset Fine Arts, 33 Belmont St., Toronto, Ont. M5R 1P9.

**SAILA, Pitaloosie;** artist; b. 11 Aug. 1942; m. Pauta; medium: drawings, prints; 80 group exbns. incl. most recent: Marion Scott Gall. Vancouver 1992, l'Iglou Art Esquimau, Douai (toured 19 cities) France 1989–92, McMichael Candn. Art Coll. Kleinburg, Ont. 1992, Albers Gall. San Francisco, Ca. 1991, Arctic Artistry Hastings-on-Hudson, N.Y. 1990, Candn. Mus. of Civilization Hull, Que. 1990; solo exbns.: Gallery One Toronto 1981, Beckett Gall. Hamilton 1974, Inukshuk Gall. Waterloo 1974; works in 21 collections incl. art galleries of Greater Victoria, London Region, Ontario (Klamer Family Coll.), Winnipeg, Amon Carter Mus. of Western Art Fort Worth, Texas, Canada Council Art Bank, Candn. Mus. of Civilization, Inuit Cultural Inst. Rankin Inlet, N.W.T., Musée des beaux-arts de Montréal, Nat. Gall. of Can. Ottawa; animated short featured in NFB film 'Animation from Cape Dorset' 1972; attended openings: Beckett Gall. Hamilton 1974, 'In the Shadow of the Sun,' Dortmund, Germany 1988; 'Fisherman's Dream' print reproduced on Candn. stamp 1977; etching incl. in limited ed. portfolio containing works of seven Inuit artists; 'Arctic Madonna' chosen for 1983 UNICEF card; subject of several articles and catalogues; Home: Cape Dorset, N.W.T.; Office: c/o Dorset Fine Arts, 33 Belmont St., Toronto, Ont. M5R 1P9.

**ST-AMOUR, André,** B.Sc., Math., F.S.A., F.C.I.A.; insurance executive; b. LaSalle, Que. 21 Feb. 1951; s. Gérard and Lucile (Caussignac) S.; e. Univ. of Montreal, B.Sc.Math 1971; F.S.A. 1981; F.C.I.A. 1981; m. Nicole d. Gaétane and Wallace Lussier 2 June 1973; children: Amélie, Nicolas, Frédéric; PRES. & CHIEF EXECUTIVE OFFR., GENERAL AMERICAN LIFE REINSURANCE CO. OF CANADA 1992– ; Chief Agent for Canada, General American Life Insurance Co. 1993– and Unione Italiana Di Riassicurazione S.P.A. 1993– ; Actuarial Asst., Standard Life 1971–75; Pension Admin., MLH+A Cons. Actuaries 1975–79; Dir. of Techn. Serv., La Laurentienne, Mutuelle d'Assurances 1979–86; Mercer Consulting Actuary in pension/benefits 1986; Sr. Actuary, CN Rail 1986–89; Extve. Vice-Pres., Life Div., The National Reinsurance Co. of Canada 1989–92; Mem., Bd. of Dir., General American Life Reinsurance Co. of Canada; Cdn. Assn. of Familial Hypercholesterolemia; recreations: alpine skiing, golf; Home: 7375 Place Malraux, Brossard, Que. J4Y 1S5; Office: 1140 de Maisonneuve Blvd. West, Suite 802, Montreal, Que. H3A 1M8.

**ST-AMOUR, Denis;** business executive; b. Montreal, Que. 24 Jan. 1947; s. Roland and Kathleen S.; e. economics, psychology; m. Marie Ross 1968; children: Christie, James; PRESIDENT, DRAKE BEAM MORIN (MONTREAL) INC. 1984– ; Pres., Drake Beam Morin-Canada Inc. 1990–92; Mem., Assn. of Que. Professionals in Human Resources; Board of Trade of Metropolitan Montreal; Bd. of Dir., World Vision Canada; Founding Pres., Ballet West of Montreal; Chair, Annual Christian Sports Celebrities Breakfast; Past Mem., Bd. of Dir., Arts Council; Montreal Urban Community; Gemini Gymnastics Club; Big Brothers; clubs: St. James's, Blainville Golf & Country; Home: Montreal, Que.; Office: Suite 600, 999 de Maisonneuve Blvd. W., Montreal, Que. H4A 3L4.

**ST. GEORGE, M. Elyse Yates;** painter, writer; b. Merritton, Ont. 8 Dec. 1929; d. Richard Edward and Marie Philomene (Robertson) Y.; e. St. Catharine's Coll. & Voc. Sch.; Doon Sch.; Coll. of Flyde, U.K.; Univ. of New Hampshire; Univ. of Sask.; m. Leonard Bruce s. Lillian and Claude S. 29 Aug. 1953; sons: Leonard Kerry, Hillary Sean; painting & exhib. in U.S. & Can. since 1960; paintings have been featured on book covers & posters and 'Grain,' 'Arts West,' & 'NeWest Review,' 'ARC'; freelance Visual Art Advr. and Adjudicator, in Sask. 1980's; 1974 Canada Council Grant, printmaking; 1984 Canada Council Explorations Grant, poetry; 1978 Sask. Arts Bd. Grant, (Sr.) 1989; New Hampshire Artists Association's (NHAA); Weston Assoc. Award, Currier Gall. 1970; Sask. Writers Guild Poetry Prize 1989; League of Candn. Poets Poetry Prize; Mem. of Bd., A.K.A. Gallery 1970s; Mem., SWG Writers Artists Colony Ctte. and Bd., Sask. Moving Collective 1980s; Pres., Group 5 Gall. 1980s; Mem., Sask. Writers Guild; The Writers Union of Canada; League of Candn. Poets; author: 'White Lions in the Afternoon' 1987 (poetry, paintings, etchings); 'Heading Out' 1986, 'More Garden Varieties' 1989, 'League of Canadian Poets 25th Anniversary Issue' ARC Magazine 1991, 'Vintage 93' (anthologies); working on new book, and paintings for exhib. at Regina's Susan Whitney Gall. 1992 and Mendel Gall., Saskatoon 1995; recreations: cartooning, music; Address: 711 Preston Ave., Saskatoon, Sask. S7H 2V1.

**ST. GERMAIN, Hon. Gerry,** P.C.; businessman; commercial pilot; b. St. Boniface, Man. 6 Nov. 1937; s. Michel and Mary Kathleen (James) S.; e. St. Francois Xavier, Man.; Winnipeg Comml. Pilot Grad. 1960; Univ. of B.C. Real Estate 1976; m. Margaret d. Herman and Matilda Schilke 25 Nov. 1961; children: Michele, Suzanne, Jay; MIN. OF STATE (TRANSPORT), MIN. OF STATE (FORESTRY) FED. GOVT. 1988; Mem. of Parliament, House of Commons 1983–88; Apptd. to the Senate of Canada 1993– ; joined R.C.A.F. 1956; City of St. Boniface Police Force 1960; commenced bus. ventures focusing on residential constrn. and agric. operations 1965; Chrmn. and Dir. B.C. Poultry Ind.; B.C. Rep. Candn. Broiler Counc.; Chrmn. St. Thomas More Coll. Bd. of Pursuit of Excellence; recreation: golf; Club: Vancouver Golf; Address: 5982 – 243rd St., Langley, B.C. V3A 6H4.

**ST. GERMAIN, Guy,** LL.L., M.A., C.M.; éxécutif; n. St-Hyacinthe, Qué. 8 mars 1933; f. Joseph Lucien et Angéline (Audet) St. G.; e. Coll. Jean-de-Brébeuf B.A. 1953; Univ. de Montréal LL.L. 1956; Barreau du Qué. 1957; Merton Coll. Oxford Univ. M.A. 1960 (Boursier Rhodes 1957); Inst. des Hautes Etudes Politiques Paris 1961; é Denise f. Dr. Rosaire Lauzer 25 juin 1958; enfants: Charles, Claire, Philippe, Antoine; PRÉS., PLACEMENTS LAUGERMA INC.; mem. du conseil d'admin., Banque Nationale du Canada; Provigo Inc.; Candn. Reinsurance Co.; Candn. Reassurance Co.; Dir., Fondation Denise & Guy St-Germain; Corporation Financière Power; Great West Life Assurance Co.; Fondation J. Armand Bombardier; récréations: natation, pêche, tennis; Club: St-Denis; Résidence: 48 Robert, Outremont, Qué. H3S 2P2.

**SAINT-JACQUES, Bernard,** B.A., M.A., M.S., Ph.D., D.èsL.; university professor; b. Montreal, Que. 26 Apr. 1928; s. Albert and Germaine (Lefebvre) S.; e. Univ. of Montreal, B.A. 1949, Licence 1954; Sophia Univ. (Tokyo), M.A. 1962; Georgetown Univ., M.S. 1964; Univ. of Paris, Ph.D. 1966, D.èsL. 1975; m. Marguerite d. Alexandre Fauquenoy 3 Apr. 1967; PROF. OF LINGUISTICS, AICHI SHUKUTOKU UNIV. (JAPAN) 1990– and PROF. EMERITUS, UNIV. OF B.C. 1989– ; Asst. Prof. in French & Linguistics, Sophia Univ. 1966–67; Linguistics, present univ. 1966–67; Assoc. Prof. 1969–78; Prof. of Linguistics 1978–89; Guest lectr. in Candn., French, Am. & Japanese univs.; speaks, reads & writes English, French, & Japanese; mem., Royal Soc. of Can.; Linguistic Soc. of Am.; The Assn. of Teachers of Japanese; The Candn. Soc. for Asian Studies; Founding Mem., B.C. Assn. of Translators & Interpreters; Rsch. Ctte. on Sociolinguistics; author: 'Analyse structurale de la syntaxe du japonais moderne' 1966, 'Structural Analysis of Modern Japanese' 1971, 'Aspects sociolinguistiques du bilinguisme canadien' 1976; editor: 'Language and Ethnic Relations' 1979, 'Japanese Studies in Canada' 1985; co-author: 'Aspects of Bilingualism' 1978, 'The Languages of Immigrants' 1979, 'Atipa revisité' 1989; 'Langue et Identité' 1990; 'Quelques Aspects des emprunts lexicaux du japonais moderne' in 'Mélanges Léon: Phonétique, Phonostylistique, Linguistique et Littérature' 1992; Home: 1226 Seymour Blvd., N. Vancouver, B.C. V7J 2J8; Office: Dept. of Linguistics, UBC, Vancouver, B.C. V6T 1Z1.

**SAINT-JACQUES, Madeleine,** B.A.; advertising executive; b. Montreal, Que. 27 June 1935; d. Henri and Marie-Jeanne (Ostiguy) S.; e. Univ. of Montreal B.A.; PRESIDENT, YOUNG & RUBICAM MONTREAL 1990– ; Sec., Young & Rubicam 1955; became writer, producer and in 1970 the Creative Director; Extve. Vice-Pres. & General Manager 1977; Dir., Télé-Métropole; Ultramar Corporation Inc.; Premier Choix: TVEC Inc.; Gov., Candn. Advtg. Found.; Vice-Pres., La Corp. des célébrations du 350e anniv. de Montréal; honoured in 1975 and 1976 by Assn. of Candn. Advertisers for outstanding service to the community; 1st woman in Canada to receive the Gold Medal Award for the person who made the greatest contbn. to Candn. advertising 1977 (the highest distinction in the Candn. advtg. world); Award of Distinction, Faculty of Commerce and Admin., Concordia Univ. (for outstanding achievement in finance, commerce and service to the community) 1992; Management Achievement Award, Management Undergraduate Soc., McGill Univ. 1993; Dir., 'Terry Fox Humanitarian Award Program'; Canadian Club of Montreal (Pres. 1993–94); recreations: enjoys reading, skiing, playing tennis and golf; Home: 601 Habitat 67, Montreal, Que. H3C 3R6; Office: 1600 René-Lévesque Blvd. W., Montreal, Que. H3H 1P9.

**ST-JACQUES, Robert James,** M.A., M.B.A., C.A.; insurance executive; b. Montréal, Qué. 29 Nov. 1948; s. Jean and Suzanne (Lacroix) St-J.; e. Univ. of Toronto M.A. 1970; York Univ. M.B.A. 1972; Candn. Inst. C.A.'s, C.A. 1974; m. Carol d. George Barrington and Helen Reading 14 June 1969; children: Robert, Marc, Michelle; PRES. AND CHIEF EXEC. OFFR., LAURENTIAN FINANCIAL INC., CHRMN. OF THE BD. & C.E.O., THE IMPERIAL LIFE ASSURANCE CO. OF CANADA and LAURENTIAN LIFE; joined Peat, Marwick, Mitchell 1972, assignment Eur. 1974–76, Partner 1979, Partner-in-Charge Consulting Practice, Montréal 1983; Vice Pres. Strategic Planning Celanese Canada Inc. 1984, Exec. Vice Pres., Dir. and mem. Exec. Ctte. 1985; Vice Pres. and Chief Financial Offr., Laurentian Group Corp. and Chief Exec. Offr. Laurentian Technology 1986–87; Exec. Vice Pres. Laurentian Group Corp. 1988 and Pres. & C.E.O., Candn. Operations, The Imperial Life Assurance Co. of Canada 1988; recreations: golf, swimming, tennis, basketball; Home: 60 Beechwood Ave., Willowdale, Ont. M2L 1J3; Office: 1100 René Lévesque Blvd. W., Montréal, Qué. H3B 4N4.

**ST-JEAN, Denis L.,** C.M.A., C.I.M., P.Mgr.; sheet metal industry executive; b. Montreal, Que. 24 Sept. 1933; s. Alcide and Florence (Duchesne) S.; e. Ecoles des Hautes Etudes Commerciales C.M.A. 1963; Univ. of Toronto & McMaster Univ. (correspondence); McGill Univ.; m. Marielle d. Adélard and Jeanne Lizotte 12 July 1958; children: Manon, Pierre, Luc; VICE-PRES., SEC.-TREAS. & DIR., ROBERT MITCHELL INC. 1974– ; Profl. Mngt. Acctnt., Canadian Arsenals Ltd. 1951–58; Asst. Chief Acctnt., Canadian Bronze Ltd. 1959–60; Budget Supvr., present firm 1960–61; Asst. Sec.-Treas. 1962–63; Sec.-Treas. 1964–74; Mem., Soc. of Mngt. Acctnts.; Candn. Inst. of Mngt.; Finan. Extves. Inst.; Home: 142 Morel St., Repentigny, Que. J6A 3E8; Office: 350 Décarie Blvd., St-Laurent, Qué. H4L 3K5.

**ST. JOHN, Oliver Peter,** M.Sc., Ph.D., Master of Orkney; university professor; b. Victoria, B.C. 27 Feb. 1938; s. Frederick Oliver and Elizabeth (Pierce) St. John; e. Woodbridge Sch. 1955; Univ. of B.C., B.A. 1960; London Sch. of Econ., M.Sc. 1963; Univ. of London, Ph.D. 1972; m. Barbara Albertson Huck d. Dr. D.B. and Eliz. (Jackson) Albertson 3 Apr. 1985; children: Juliet, Nicola, Oliver, Lucy (St. John), Dawn, Cameron, Jane, Erin (Huck); ASSOC. PROF., UNIV. OF MAN. 1972– ; Lectr., Univ. Coll., London 1963–64; Univ. of Man. 1964–66; Asst. Prof. 1966–72; Vis. Prof., Carleton Univ. 1981–82; Candn. Forces Base Lahr, West Germany 1985, 1990, 1991; Dir., Counter Terror Study Ctr.; Adv. Ctte., Acad. Relns., Dept. of External Affairs 1980–90; Cons., Candn. Armed Forces; CBC; CTV; Heir Presumptive to the Earldom of Orkney (U.K.) House of Lords; Anglican; Mem., Royal Inst. of Internat. Affairs 1962; Candn. Inst. of Internat. Affairs 1964– (Pres. Winnipeg Br. 1971–73); Candn. Profs. for Peace in the Middle East 1982– ; Candn. Assn. for the Study of Intelligence & Security 1986– ; United Nations Assn. 1988– ; author: 'Fireproof House to Third Option' 1977, 'Mackenzie King to Philosopher King' 1984; 'Air Piracy, Airport Security and International Terrorism: Winning the War Against Hijackers' 1991; recreations: tennis, squash, swimming, boating, cycling; Home: 200 Dromore Ave., Winnipeg, Man. R3M 0J3; Office: St. John's Coll., Univ. of Man., Dysart Rd., Fort Garry, Man. R3T 2N2.

**ST-PIERRE, Claude J.,** M.B.A.; diplomat; b. Rimouski, Que. 27 Dec. 1932; s. Joseph A. and Lucie (Gagnon) St-P.; e. Laval Univ. B.B.A. 1956; Univ. of Toronto M.B.A. 1971; m. Elaine d. Ted and Irene Stopyra 19 Oct. 1979; one d. Judith; Extve. Dir., Assoc. for the Export of Canadian Books 1987; joined Dept. of External Affairs, Can. 1956 serving in various positions Rome, Paris, Port of Spain, Theran, Boston; Chief Inspr. Foreign Operations, Ottawa 1979–82; Ambassador to Cameroon with accreditation to Gabon Equatorial Guinea, Chad, Central African Republic, Sao Tome and Principe 1982–84; Diplomat in residence York Univ. 1984–85; Dir., Francophone Affairs External Affairs 1985–86; recreations: skiing, golf, reading; Clubs: Rivermead Golf (Ottawa).

**SAINT-PIERRE, Guy,** B.A.Sc., M.Sc., D.I.C.; né Windsor Mills, Qué. 3 août 1934; f. Armand et Alice (Perra) Saint-Pierre; é. Univ. Laval, B.Sc., 1957; Imp. Coll. Science and Technol., D.I.C., 1958; Univ. de Londres, M.Sc., 1957–59; ép. Francine, f. Marcel Garneau et Françoise Champoux; 4 mai 1957; enfants: Marc, Guylaine, Nathalie; PRES. ET CHEF. DE LA DIRECTION, GROUPE SNC INC. 1989– ; Suncor Inc.; SNC; Banque Royale du Canada; General Motor du Canada Ltée; Officier dans le Corps de Génie Royal Candn., Camp Gagetown, N.B., 1959–64; Régistraire, Corp. des Ingénieurs du Qué., 1964–66; Dir. techn., IRNES, 1966–67; Vice Prés., Acres Qué. Ltée, 1967–70; Min. de l'Education du Qué, 1970–72; Min. de l'Industrie et Comm. du Qué. 1972–76; Adjoint au Prés. de John Labatt Ltée., 1977; Prés, & Dir. Gen. Les Minoteries Ogilvie Ltée., 1978–88; Gouverneur, Conseil du Patronat du Québec; Pres., Assoc. des Manufacturiers Canadiens 1985; Membre du Conseil canadien des chefs d'entreprise; Président du conseil, Conference Board du Canada; Chambre de Comm. de Montréal; l'Ordre des Ingénieurs du Qué.; l'Inst. Candn. des Ingénieurs; Ordre Militaire et Hospitalier de St.-Lazare de Jérusalem; Officier de l'Ordre du Canada; Libéral; Catholique; récréations; natation, golf, ski; Clubs: Mount Bruno Golf; St.-Denis; Mount Royal; Forest and Stream; Résidence: 1227 ouest, rue Sherbrooke, app. 64, Montréal, Qué. H3G 1G1; Office: 2 Place Félix-Martin, Montréal, Que. H2Z 1Z3.

**SAINT-PIERRE, Jacques,** M.A., Ph.D.; statistician; b. Trois-Rivières, Qué. 30 Aug. 1920; s. Oscar and Lucie (Landreville) S-P; e. Univ. de Montréal, 1945–51, M.A. (Math.); Univ. of N. Carolina, Ph.D. (Math. Stat.) 1954; m. Marguerite Lachaine, 15 July 1947; children: Marc, Guy, André; Louis, François, Mireille; PROF. EMERITUS, UNIV. DE MONTREAL, 1983– ; Vice Pres., Planning, 1972–82; full professor 1960–83; Vice-Dean and Dir. of Studies, Faculty of Sciences (1961–64); Dir. of Computing Centre (1964–71), of Computer Science Dept. (1966–69); has publ. numerous scient. papers in math. stat. and allied topics; Pres. Candn. Assn. of Univ. Teachers, 1965–66; Home: 4949 Earnscliffe, Montréal, Qué. H3X 2P4; Office: C.P. 6128, Montréal, Qué.

**ST. PIERRE, Leon E.,** Ph.D.; university professor;.b. Edmonton, Alta. 1 Sept. 1924; s. Joseph Leon and Adele St. P.; e. Univ. of Alta., B.Sc. (Hons. Chem.) 1951; Univ. of Notre Dame, Ph.D. (Chem.) 1954; m. Pauline E. A., d. Louis T. Oel, Calgary, Alta., 25 July 1949; children: Denise L.; Jerome P., Noel J., Louis C.; Claire G., Martin G., Michele A.; PROFESSOR EMERITUS, McGILL UNIV. 1990– ; Professor of Polymer Chem. since 1965; Chemist, General Electric Research Laboratory, Schenectady, N.Y., 1954–61; Mgr. Polymer and Interface Studies Sec., 1962–65; Chrmn., Dept. of Chem., McGill Univ. 1972–76; co-author, 'High Polymer Series' Vol. XIII ('Polyethers') 1964; has written over 90 papers and holds four patents; inventor of new family of aluminum lubricants now licensed world-wide by Gen. Electric; served with R.C.A.F. 1944–45 and Candn. Inf. Corp. 1945–46; mem., Chem. Inst. Can.; Am. Chem. Soc.; Faraday Soc.; Soc. Plastics Engrs.; Am. Assn. Advanc. Science; N.Y. Acad. Science; R. Catholic; recreations: skating, music; Home: Frelighsburg, Que. J0J 1C0.

**ST. PIERRE, Paul;** writer; b. Chicago, Ill. 14 Oct. 1923; s. Napoleon and Pearl Clayton (Stanford) St.P.; e. high sch., Dartmouth, ,N.S.; m. Carol Mildred Roycroft 19 Dec. 1950; m. Melanie Anne McCarthy 17 Nov. 1978; children: Paul Robert, Michelle Anne, Suzanne Ellen, Yesica Tapia; reporter, feature writer, ed. and columnist 'Columbian' New Westminster, BC 1945–46; 'News Herald' Vancouver 1946; 'Vancouver Sun' 1947–68, 1972–79; el. to H. of C. for Coast Chilcotin (Liberal) 1968–72 serving as Parlty. Secy. to Secy. of State for External Affairs, Secy. Nat. Govt. Caucus, Rapporteur Scientific Ctte., NATO Parliamentary Group; Official Observer O.A.S.; mem. B.C. Police Comn. 1979–83; Host 'Game Country' TV series; served with RCAF 1941–42; recipient Teleplay Award 'Antoine's Wooden Overcoat' 1965; CBC TV Wilderness Award 'How to Break a Quarter Horse' 1966; Spur Award, W. Writers Am. 'Smith and Other Events: Tales of the Chilcotin' 1985; author: 'Boss of the Namko' juvenile fiction 1965; 'Breaking Smith's Quarter Horse' adult fiction 1966; 'Sister Balonika' play 1969; 'Chilcotin Holiday' columns 1970, revised ed. 1984; 'In The Navel of The Moon' novel 1993; 'British Columbia: Our Land' photographs 1981; 'Chilcotin and Beyond' columns 1989; 'How to Run the Country' stageplay first produced Playhouse Theatre, Vancouver 1967; numerous Teleplays broadcast by CBC TV; scripts 'Cariboo Country'; Home: P.O. Box 964, Fort Langley, B.C. V0X 1J0.

**SALANSKY, Norman,** Ph.D., Doctor of Science; university professor; b. Lithuania, Kaunas 23 May 1936; s. Moses Elyja and Ida (Lipman) S.; e. Krasnoyarsk H.S. 1952; Krasnoyarsk Univ. physics & math dept. 1957; Siberian Branch, USSR Acad. of Sciences Ph.D. 1964, Doctor of Sciences 1968; Business Mngt. School Montreal 1982; one s.: Michael; CHIEF SCIENTIST, INTERNATIONAL MEDICAL MACHINES INC. 1985– ; Scientist, then Dept. Head, Physics Inst., USSR Acad. of Sciences, Siberian Br. 1957–75; Prof., Krasnoyarsk State Univ. 1969–75 (rsch. incl. building 1st magneto-optical high density disk 1968); 220 papers & books pub. & 18 patents obtained; supervised 20 Ph.D.s & 35 Master theses; lost all scientific positions when he applied for Exit Visa from USSR 1975; worked as member of domestic team (Vilnius) & devel. yoga skills while under KGB interrogation 1975–77; permitted to leave USSR after Cyrus Vance (former US Sec. of State) met L. Breznev in Moscow & pleaded on his behalf 1977; Senior Physicist, then Mgr., Corp. R & D, Toronto 3M Canada Inc. 1977–85; Adjunct Prof., Inst. of Aerospace Studies, Univ. of Toronto 1980– ; Univ. of Miami, College of Eng. 1993– ; involved in technology transfer from Eastern Block countries to Canada 1987– (eight trips to USSR concluded in four joint ventures, num. agreements & collaborative efforts); present research on CODETRON (a device for remote control of brain biochem. which controls pain) and Low Energy Laser Therapy for treatment of dermatological & musculoskeletal problems; Technology Transfer Consultant to NRC 1987–89; invited speaker to NRC, IBM, 3M, Applied Magnets, Physics & Elect. Engr. depts. of many univs. (Purdue, Toronto, Waterloo, Western, Miami, etc.); Bd. of Dir., EHM Rehabilitation Technolgies Inc.; IMM Inc.; Sr. Mem., IEEE, APS, OSA, CAP; Mem., ISTS - Ont. Ctr. of Excellence; Internat. Ctte. of Thin Films; Edit. Bd. Am. Jour. IEEE Transactions on Magnetics; Solid State Physics Council; USSR Academy of Sciences; recreations: yoga, swimming, mystery novels; Home: 14 Meadow Heights Court, Thornhill, Ont. L4J 1V6; Office: Inst. of Aerospace Studies, Univ. of Toronto, 4925 Dufferin St., Downsview, Ont. M5R 5T6.

**SALCUDEAN, Martha,** B.Sc., M.Eng., Ph.D.; educator; b. Romania 26 Feb. 1934; d. Edmond and Charlotte (Hirsch) Abel; e. Univ. of Cluj B.Sc. 1956, M.Eng. 1960; Univ. of Bucharest Ph.D. 1968; m. George s. George and Laetitia Salcudean 28 May 1955; one s. Septimio Edmond (Tim); ASSOCIATE VICE-PRESIDENT OF RESEARCH, UNIV. OF B.C. 1993– ; Sr. Rsch. Staff Rsch. Centre for Metall. Bucharest, Heat Transfer Lab. 1963–

75; Prof. Univ. of Ottawa 1977; Prof. and Head of Mech. Eng. present Univ. 1985; mem. various granting cttes. Natural Sci's & Eng. Rsch. Council Can.; Nat. Heat Transfer Can. Ctte.; mem. Governing Council of the National Rsch. Council; mem. National Adv. Panel on Advanced Industrial Materials, Min. of Industry, Science and Technology; recipient, 1991 B.C. Science and Engineering Award in Applied Science and Engineering (Gold Medal); Fellow, The Candn. Acad. of Engineering; awarded Commemorative Medal for 125th Anniversary of Candn. Confederation 1993; author or co-author over 160 papers and one book fluid flow & heat transfer; Office: 2324 Main Mall, Vancouver, B.C. V6T 1W5.

**SALE, Kirkpatrick,** B.A.; writer; b. Ithaca, N.Y. 27 June 1937; s. William M. Jr. and Helen (Stearns) S.; e. Cornell Univ. B.A. 1958; m. Faith d. P.M. and Ruth Apfelbaum 1962; children: Rebekah, Kalista; Journalist, Jersey Journal, New Leader, Chicago Tribune, San Francisco Chronicle, New York Times 1958–65; Editor, New Leader 1959–61; N.Y. Times Magazine 1965–68; Nation 1981–82; Instructor, Univ. of Ghana 1963–65; Bd. of Dir., E.F. Schumacher Soc. (Chair 1992– ); Learning Alliance; PEN Am. Center; Hudson Biogregional Council; Bd. of Advisors, Emergency Civil Liberties Ctte.; Inst. for Reflection on the Second Law; The Center for Sustainable Development; Ecological Soc. Project; N. Am. Bioregional Congress; Contbg. Ed., 'The Nation'; author: 'SDS' 1972, 'Power Shift' 1975, '80, 'Dwellers in the Land: The Bioregional Vision' 1985, 'Conquest of Paradise: Christopher Columbus and the Columbian Legacy' 1990, 'The Green Revolution, American Environmental Movement, 1962–92' 1993; contbr. to nat. magazines and newspapers; Address: c/o Joy Harris, 156 Fifth Ave., New York, N.Y. 10010.

**SALES, Michel,** B.A., F.L.M.I.; insurance executive; b. France, 8 March 1928; s. Clement A. and Agnes A. (Angot) S.; e. High Sch., Paris, France; Univ. of Paris, B.A. 1947; children: Dominique M., Andrée A., Michel J., Anna-Christina; VICE CHRMN. & DIR., NORTH AMERICAN REASSURANCE CO. 1991– ; Chrmn. & C.E.O., Swiss-Am Reassurance Co.; Alpine Life Insurance Co.; Atlantic Internat. Reinsurance Co.; Vice Chrmn. & Dir., Atrium Corp.; Dir., North American Reinsurance Co.; SwissRe Holding (North Am.) Inc.; Swiss Reinsurance Co. (N.A.) Inc.; North Atlantic Internat. Reinsurance Co.; served with French Foreign Service in S.Am. as Asst. to Trade Commr., 1948–49; joined Confederation Life Assn., Toronto, 1950–51; Prudential Insurance Co. of America, Toronto, 1951; North American Reassurance Co., N.Y. City, 1959; helped organize Canadian Reassurance in 1960; apptd. Secy. and Chief Underwriter; Vice-Pres. and Chief Underwriter 1963–66; Extve. Vice-Pres., 1966–68; Pres. and Dir. 1968–86; Pres., Dir. & C.E.O. 1986–91; Depy. Chrmn. & Dir., SwissRe Mang. Ltd. 1976–89; Pres. & C.E.O. Candn. Reinsurance Co. 1977–89; mem., Life Office Mang. Assn.; Candn. Chamber of Comm.; Conservative; R. Catholic; recreations: swimming, sailing; Club: Granite; Home: 362 Russell Hill Rd., Toronto, Ont. M4V 2P9; Office: 237 Park Ave., New York, NY 10017.

**SALHANY, Hon. Roger Elias,** B.A., LL.B.; judge; b. Cornwall, Ont. 21 Oct. 1937; s. Nelson and Sadie S.; e. Bishop's Coll. Sch. Lennoxville, Que. 1954; McGill Univ. B.A. 1958; Osgoode Hall Law Sch. LL.B. 1961; Cambridge Univ. Dipl. Comparative Legal Studies 1962; m. Terri Wilkinson; children: Karen Ruth, Roger Christopher, Alison, David; JUSTICE, ONT. COURT OF JUSTICE; called to Bar of Ont. 1964; cr. Q.C. 1976; served with Victoria Rifles 1956–58, rank 2nd Lt.; Bencher of the Law Soc. of Upper Canada 1975–78; author: 'Canadian Criminal Procedure' 6th ed. 1994; 'The Police Manual of Arrest, Seizure and Interrogation' 5th ed. 1991; 'The Origin of Rights' 1986; 'Cross-Examination – Art of the Advocate' 1988; 'Basic Guide to Evidence in Criminal Cases' (1990) 2nd ed. 1992; 'Criminal Trial Handbook' 1992; co-author 'Studies in Canadian Criminal Evidence' 1972; numerous articles on criminal law; Anglican; recreations: skiing, swimming, tennis, gardening; Home: RR #1, New Dundee, Ont.; Chambers: 20 Weber St., Kitchener, Ont. N2H 1C3.

**SALLOT, Jeffry George,** B.Sc.; journalist; b. Cleveland, Ohio 19 Oct. 1947; s. George Edward and Nancy Therese (St. John) S.; e. Kent State Univ., B.Sc. 1970; m. Rosemarie d. Joseph and Marguerite Boyle 11 Oct. 1975; children: Michael, Kathryn; DIPLOMATIC CORRESPONDENT, THE GLOBE AND MAIL 1991– ; Reporter, Akron Beacon Journal 1969–71; Toronto Star 1971–72; Parliamentary Corr. 1972–74; Reporter, The Globe and Mail 1974–79; Edmonton Bureau Chief 1979–82; Parliamentary Corr. 1982–85; Ottawa Bureau Chief 1985–88; Moscow Bureau Chief 1988–91; Pol. Commentator, CBC radio 'Morningside' 1984–87; Mem., Access to Info. Ctte., Candn. Daily Newspaper Pubs. Assn. 1985–86; Ctr. for Investigative Journalism 1978– ; Parliamentary Press Gallery 1982–88, 1991– ; Extve. Ctte., Toronto Newspaper Guild 1976–78; Pulitzer Prize in Journalism (shared) 1971; Vis. Fellow, Candn. Ctr. for Arms Control & Disarmament 1985; Media Fellow, Asia Pacific Foundation of Canada 1992; author: 'Nobody Said No' 1979 and num. articles; contbr.: 'The Media, the Courts and the Charter' 1986, 'The Canadian Encyclopedia' 1985; recreations: tennis, squash; Club: Nat. Press; Permanent Address: 1704 Laurelwood Pl., Orleans, Ont. K1C 6Y8; Office: 721 Hemlock Rd., Ottawa, Ont. K1K 0K7.

**SALLOUM, Fares F.,** B.Sc.E.E., M.B.A.; utilities executive; b. Ghana 13 Oct. 1948; s. Fouad F. and Marie-Rose (D'Agata) S.; e. Univ. of Alberta B.Sc.E.E. 1973; Univ. of B.C. M.B.A. 1981; m. Diane d. Roy Hamilton 4 Sept. 1971; children: Nicole L., Simone M.; Vice-President, Emerging Business, B.C. Telephone Company 1991–93; joined B.C. Tel 1973; various sr. engineering & marketing positions before becoming Div. Mgr. of Portable Communication Services 1985; Gen. Mgr., B.C. Cellular Limited 1986; Dir. of Developing Business with resp. for B.C. Tel. Mobility Cellular Limited, B.C. Mobile Ltd., Candn. Telephones & Supplies Ltd., B.C. Tel. Support Services Ltd., Pachena Industries Ltd., Microtel Limited and Portable Communications Div. 1988; Dir., Mobility Canada; Microtel Limited; Pachena Industries Ltd.; B.C. Tel. Support Services Ltd.; B.C. Tel. Mobility Cellular Limited; B.C. Mobile Ltd.; Canadian Telephones & Supplies Ltd.; ISM Information Systems Management (BC) Corp.; SRI Strategic Resources Inc.; Vice Chair, Bd. of Gov., Meadow Ridge School; Mem., Vancouver Board of Trade; Terminal City Club; Assn. of Profl. Engineers of B.C.; recreations: golf; Home: 140 Ravine Dr., Port Moody, B.C. V3H 4T2.

**SALMAN, M. Abid,** F.C.A. (UK); chartered accountant; b. Hyderabad, India 6 Apl. 1943; s. Salman A. and Munnan S. Ali; e. Ashbury Coll. Ottawa 1956; King's Coll. Taunton 1958–64; C.A. 1968; m. Riffat d. Abid and Iffat Bilgrami 17 Oct. 1969; children: Zahid, Inji; BUSINESS ADMINISTRATOR, SACRED HEART SCHOOL OF MONTREAL 1993– ; Factory Acct. Pakistan Tobacco Co. Ltd. 1968–72; Supr. Ernst & Whinney C.A.'s UK 1972–74; Sr. Mgr. Peat, Marwick 1974–82; Vice Pres., Treas. and Controller Wabasso Inc. 1981–85; Vice Pres. Finance, Sec. Treas. and Dir., RHP Canada Inc. 1985–92; Dir. RHP Bearings Inc. (USA) 1985–92; Albion Bearing Co. Ltd. 1985–92; Canadian Pollard Bearings Co. Ltd. 1985–92; Clubs: M.A.A.A.; Home: 370 rue Senecal, Ile Bizard, Qué. H9C 2G4.

**SALMON, C. R. B.,** M.C., C.A.; b. England; e. England; served in the 2nd World War with British Army, 1939–46 and discharged with rank of Lieut.-Col.; joined Peat, Marwick, Mitchell & Co., Chart. Accts., London, Eng., following the war; apptd. Secy.-Treas. of the Rank Group of Canadian Co.'s in 1951 and el. a Dir., 1952; retired in 1983; Home: 68 Hawksbury Dr., Willowdale, Ont. M2K 1M5.

**SALOMON, Carole Janice,** B.A., M.B.A.; marketing & sales executive; b. Montreal, Que. 8 April 1948; d. Maurice R. and Fay F. (Goldberg) Applebaum; e. McGill Univ. M.B.A. 1975; m. David s. Irwin S. 26 June 1970; children: Angela Gayle; SR. VICE-PRES., MARKETING, PUROLATOR COURIER LTD. 1989– ; Mktg. Mgr., Montreal Trust 1971–77; Vice-Pres., Mktg., Confectionary Div., Nabisco Brands Ltd. 1977–87; Vice-Pres., Nat. Sales & Mktg., Ronalds Printing (div. of BCE Publitech) 1987–89; Dir., Household Finance Corp.; Household Trust; M.D. Management; Laurier Life; W.H. Smith Can. (1986–89); Am. Family (1985–87); Nat. Advtg. Benevalent Assn. (1987–88); Mem., Bd. of Trade; Elmridge Golf Club; Am. Mktg. Assn.; Candn. Direct Mktg. Assn.; The Founders Club; Home: 293 Forest Hill Rd., Toronto, Ont. M5P 2N7; Office: 5310 Explorer Dr., Mississauga, Ont. L4W 4H6.

**SALSMAN, Dean W.;** company executive; b. Waterville, N.S. 11 July 1923; s. Richard D. Salsman; e. Waterville High Sch.; m. Evelyn M., d. Sidney Stc Jones, 8 Oct. 1948; children: Richard, Alan, Robert, Lyn; PRESIDENT, SALSMAN INVESTMENTS LIMITED; served as Chrmn. and C.E.O. of Industrial Estates Ltd, 1971–1978; Dir., Blue Cross of Atlantic Canada; Maritime Steel & Foundries Limited; mem., Halifax Industrial Comm.; World Business Council; mem. Financial Adv. Ctte., Mount St. Vincent; served with R.C.N. 1942–47; Past Pres. Constr. Assn. of N.S.; Past Pres., Young President, Organization; Halifax Y.M.C.A.; Hon. Consul for the Kingdom of the Netherlands 1982–93; Liberal; United Church; recreations: golf, curling; Clubs: Ashburn Golf; Halifax Curling; The Halifax (past Pres.); Saraguay; Home: 1760 Connaught Ave., Halifax, N.S. B3H 4C8; Office: 6080 Young St., Suite 315, Halifax, N.S. B3K 5L2.

**SALTER, Robert Bruce,** O.C. (1977), O.Ont. (1988), M.D., M.S., F.R.S.C., F.R.C.S.(C), F.A.C.S., F.H.S.C., Hon. Dr.Med., Hon. D.Sc., Hon. LL.D., Hon. D.Litt.S., Hon. F.R.C.S. (Glasg. 1970, Edin. 1973, Eng. 1976, Ire. 1978); Honorary F.C.S. (South Africa 1973), Hon. F.R.A.C.S (1977), Hon. M.C.F.P.C. (1977); b. Stratford, Ont. 15 Dec. 1924; s. Lewis Jack and Katherine G. (Cowie) S.; e. Lawrence Park Coll. Inst., Toronto; Univ. of Toronto, M.D. 1947, M.S. 1959; Post-grad. studies, Toronto and London, Eng.; m. Agnes Robina, d. Hector McGee, 3 July 1948; children: David, Nancy, Jane, Stephen, Luke; PROF. OF ORTHOPAEDIC SURGERY, UNIV. OF TORONTO and Sr. Orthopaedic Surg. and Research Assoc., Hosp. for Sick Children; Bd. of Trustees, Wycliffe Coll., Univ. of Toronto; apptd. to Med. Research Council Can. 1967; Council of Roy. Coll. of Phys. and Surgs. 1967 (Vice Pres. for Surg. 1970–71, Pres. 1976–78); Heraldry Soc. of Can (Pres. 1981–83); Development of innominate osteotomy (Salter Operation) for dislocation of the hip; original research on growth plate injuries; many aspects of joint cartilage pathology; Legg-Perthes' disease; originator of Continuous Passive Motion for diseased and injured joints; Visiting Prof. at 140 Universities in 30 countries; Lister Prize in Surgery 1959; George Armstrong Peters Prize 1959; Royal College Medal in Surgery 1960; Centennial Medal 1967; Gairdner Foundation Internat. Award for Med. Science, 1969; Sims Commonwealth Prof. 1973; Nicholas Andry Award 1974; Charles Mickle Fellowship Award 1975; Candn. Silver Jubilee Medal 1977; Kappa Delta Rsch. Award 1987; Candn. Medec Award of Excellence, 1989; Robert Danis Internat. Surgical Prize 1989; Gold Medal of the Cyril and Metodji Univ. of Skopje, Yugoslavia 1989; Arthur H. Huene Internat. Award 1992; Ross Award 1992; Offr., Order of Canada 1977; Order of Ont. 1988; Offr., Order of St. John 1977; awarded Commemorative Medal for 125th Anniversary of Candn. Confederation; Commander, Order of St. John 1981, Knight 1992; Commander, Order of St. Lazarus 1984, Knight 1992; rec'd hon. degree from Univ. of Uppsala of Sweden (500th Anniv.) 1977; Fellow, Royal Soc. of Can. 1979; appointed Univ. Prof., Univ. of Toronto, 1981; rec'd. hon. degree from Memorial Univ. of Newfoundland, 1983; Dalhousie Univ. 1985; Hon. Prof., Univ. Buenos Aires 1986; rec'd. hon. degree from Wycliffe Coll., Toronto 1988; hon. degree from Univ. of Toronto 1993; author of over 150 scient. articles and two textbooks related to orthopaedic surg.; Anglican; recreations: oil painting, heraldry, Canadiana; Home: 5 North Sherbourne, Toronto, Ont. M4W 2S9; Office: 555 University Ave., Toronto, Ont. M5G 1X8.

**SALTMAN, Judith Michele,** B.L.S., M. Children's Lit.; educator; b. Vancouver, B.C. 11 May 1947; d. Harry Lionel and Ruth (Berezovsky) S.; e. Edith Cavell Elem. and Eric Hamber Secondary Schs. Vancouver; Univ. of B.C. B.A. 1969, B.L.S. 1970; Simmons Coll. Boston M. Children's Lit. 1982; one d. Anne; PROF. OF CHILDREN'S AND YOUNG ADULTS' LIT. AND LIB. SERVICE UNIV. OF B.C. SCH. OF LIB., ARCHIVAL & INFO. STUDIES 1983– ; Children's Lib., Toronto Pub. Lib., W. Vancouver Meml. Lib., Vancouver Pub. Lib. 1970–82; author 'Goldie and the Sea' 1987; 'Modern Canadian Children's Books' 1987; co-author 'The New Republic of Childhood: A Critical Guide to Canadian Children's Literature in English' 3rd ed. 1990; ed. 'The Riverside Anthology of Children's Literature' 6th ed. 1985; mem. Candn. Lib. Assn.; Am. Lib. Assn.; B.C. Lib. Assn.; Children's Lit. Assn.; Candn. Soc. Children's Authors, Illus. & Performers; Internat. Bd., Books for Young People; recreations: artwork, reading, child rearing; Office: 831, 1956 Main Mall, Univ. of B.C., Vancouver, B.C. V6T 1Y3.

**SALUTIN, Rick,** B.A., M.A.; writer; b. Toronto, Ont. 30 Aug. 1942; s. Saul and Freda (Levenson) S.; e. Forest Hill C.I.; Brandeis Univ., B.A. 1964; Columbia Univ., M.A. 1967; New Sch. for Soc. Rsch., N.Y., grad. study 1967–70; author: '1837 A History/A Play' (with Theatre Passe Muraille) 1976, 'Les Canadiens' (Chalmers Award, Best Candn. Play) 1977; 'Joey' (with Rising Tide Theatre of Nfld.) 1981 (plays); 'The Organizer, A Canadian Union Life' 1980, 'Marginal Notes, Challenges to the Mainstream' 1984, 'Waiting for Democracy' 1989, 'Living In A Dark Age' 1991 (non-fiction); 'A Man of Little Faith' (W.H. Smith/Books in Canada First Novel Award) 1988 (fiction); 'Inside from the Outside' 1970–75 (radio); 'Maria' 1977, 'Grierson and Gouzenko' 1986 (television); editor: 'This Magazine' 1973– ; Lectr., Candn. Studies, Univ. of Toronto 1978– ; Maclean Hunter Chair in Communications Ethics, Ryerson Polytechnic Univ. 1993–94; Chrmn., Guild of Candn. Playwrights 1978; contbr. to num. mags.; Nat. Mag. Award for Comment & Criticism 1981, 1983; Toronto Arts Award for Writing & Publishing 1991; Home: 350 Markham St., Toronto, Ont. M6G 2K9.

**SALZMAN, Glen,** B.F.A.; film producer, director, writer; b. Montreal, Que. 16 June 1951; s. Paul and Susanne (Blum) S.; e. Mount Royal High Sch. 1968; Am. Sch. Switzerland 1969; York Univ. B.F.A. 1976; McGill Univ. 1988; m. Rebecca d. Dennis and Patricia Yates 3 Aug. 1980; children: Zoe, Pablo, Pascal; PRODUCER, CINEFLIX INC.; film credits incl. 'Milk and Honey' feature film (Genie Best Original Screenplay 1989); TV dramas 'Reaching Out' 1980; 'Introducing Janet' 1981; 'Jen's Place' 1982; various children's films; currently producing feature film on Oct. Crisis 1970; participant 1987 Sundance Workshop; Founder The Gorge Cinema (repertory cinema) Elora, Ont.; recreation: sports; Offices: Suite 190, 238 Davenport Rd., Toronto, Ont. M5R 1J6 and 5578 Esplanade, Montreal, Que. H2T 3A1.

**SAMJI, Zoolfikar H.H.,** C.A.; insurance executive; b. Dares Salaam, Tanzania 22 July 1948; s. Hussein Habib and Nurbanu (Karsan) S.; e. H.H. Agakhan Boys Sch., Dar-es-Salaam; Inst. of C.A.s in England and Wales C.A. 1973; Inst. of C.A.s of Ont. C.A. 1977; m. Nazma d. Roshanali and Gulbanu Ladha 11 March 1973; children: Hanifa, Yasmeen; PRESIDENT & CHIEF EXECUTIVE OFFR., CONFEDERATION TRUST COMPANY 1991– and VICE-PRESIDENT, RETAIL OPERATIONS, CONFEDERATION LIFE INSURANCE COMPANY 1993– ; Auditor, Price Waterhouse 1974–75; various positions, Confederation Life Insur. Co. Canada 1975–83; Dir. of Information Services & Finance (U.K.) 1983–87; Dir. of Financial Services 1987–90; Mng. Dir., Confederation Bank Ltd. 1989–90; Group Pension Vice Pres., Confederation Life Insur. Co. 1990–93; Home: 36 Crestview Rd., Toronto, Ont. M5N 1H6; Office: 1 Mount Pleasant Rd., Toronto, Ont. M4Y 2Y5.

**SAMPLE, John T.,** M.A., Ph.D.; educator; b. Kerrobert, Sask. 4 May 1927; s. George Frederick and Catherine (Scheidt) S.; e. Univ. of B.C., B.A. 1948, M.A. 1950, Ph.D. 1955; m. Dorothy Gwendolyn Lambe, 2 May 1953; children: Catherine, Frederick, Irene, Michael, Patricia; PROFESSOR EMERITUS OF PHYSICS, UNIV. OF ALBERTA 1987– ; Scientist, TRIUMF 1992– ; Gen. Mgr., Technology Div., Ebco Industries 1988–90; Ebco Technologies Inc. 1990–92; Scient. Offr., Defence Research Bd. of Can., 1955; joined present Univ. as Asst. Prof. 1958, Assoc. Prof. 1960, Prof. 1965, Chrmn. of Dept. 1967–76; Dir., TRIUMF 1976–81; Exec. Dir., B.C. Secretariat on Research 1981–88; Visiting Scientist, Brookhaven Nat. Lab.; mem., Universities Council of B.C., 1982–87; Trustee, Terry Fox Foundation, 1983–90; Dir., Pacific Isotopes and Pharmaceuticals Ltd., 1983–90; Dir., B.C. Space Sciences Society 1991– ; author of numerous research papers in physics journs.; mem., Candn. Assn. Physicists; Am. Phys. Soc.; Am. Inst. Physics; Am. Assn. Physics Teachers; Home: 6625 Balaclava St., Vancouver, B.C. V6N 1M1.

**SAMPLES, Reginald McCartney,** C.M.G., D.S.O., O.B.E., . B.Com.; b. 11 Aug. 1918; s. William and Jessie S.; e. Rhyl Grammar Sch., Wales; Liverpool Univ., B.Com.; m. Elsie Roberts Hide, 1947; two s., 1 step-d.; served with R.N.V.R. (Air Branch) 1940–46; torpedo action with 825 Squadron, Eng. Channel 1942 with Scharnhorst and Gneisenau; wounded; rank Lt. (A); Central Office of Information (Econ. Ed., Overseas Newspapers), 1947–48; Br. Diplomatic Serv. 1948–78; CRO (Brit. Inf. Services, India), 1948; Econ. Information Offr., Bombay, 1948–52; Ed.-in-Chief, BIS, New Delhi, 1952; Depy.-Dir., BIS, New Delhi, 1952–56; Dir., BIS, Pakistan (Karachi), 1956–59; Counsellor (Information) & Dir., BIS, Can. (Ottawa), 1959–65; Counsellor (Information) to Brit. High Commr. India and Dir. BIS India (New Delhi), 1965–68; Ass't Under Secy. of State, Commonwealth Office, 1968; British Consul-General, Toronto 1969–78; Asst. Dir., Royal Ont. Museum, 1978–83; Director, National Ballet of Canada 1970–88 (President, 1978–80); Director, Canadian-Scottish Philharmonic Foundation; Volunteer, recording for the blind, CNIB; recreations: tennis, watching ballet; Clubs: Queens, The Naval (London); Address: 44 Jackes Ave., Apt. 1105, Toronto, Ont. M4T 1E5.

**SAMUEL, Thenganamannil John,** M.A., Ph.D.; demographer, educator; b. Kerala, India; s. Thomas John and Mariamma (Varkey) T.; e. Univ. of Kerala M.A. 1958; Univ. of Toronto Ph.D. 1965; Univ. of Chicago Cert. in Demog. 1965; m. Aleyamma d. Mathai Pulimoottil T. and Saramma Kattappuram 29 Dec. 1960; three s.: John, Mathew, Jacob; SPECIAL ADVISOR, IMMIGRATION POLICY, EMPLOYMENT AND IMMIGRATION CANADA 1992– ; Adjunct Rsch. Prof. of Sociol. Carleton Univ. 1985– ; Asst. Prof. Univ. of Kerala, India 1958–61, 1965–66; Commonwealth Scholar in Can. 1961–65; Sr. Econ., Ont. Govt. 1967–68; Sr. Econ. & Sec. Rsch. Grants Prog. Manpower & Immigration Can. 1969–79; Dir., Race Relations, Secretary of State 1988–89; Chief, Demographic Policy 1985–88 and Immigration & Demographic Analysis 1979–85, Employment and Immigration Canada; Sr. Dir. of Projects 1989–92; Trustee, Ottawa Bd. Edn. 1976–80, Chrmn. Mgmt. Ctte., Special Ednl. Needs Ctte., Task Force Multiculturalism, Multiculturalism Ctte.; Trustee, Riverside Hosp. Bd. 1984–90; recipient Lepper Meml. Gold Medal, M.R.V. Gold Medal, A.V. George Gold Medal, Univ. of Kerala; author: 'The Migration of Canadian Born Between Canada and the United States 1955–69' 1969; co-author: 'Impact of Migration in the Receiving Countries: Canada' 1993; over 50 papers sci. jours.; Founder-Publisher and first Ed. 'The Canadian India Times'; Pres. India-Can. Assn.; Indo-Candn. Community Centre; Canasian Forum; Adv. Ctte. on Visible Minorities, City of Ottawa; mem. Internat. Union Sci. Study Population, The Hague; Population Assn. Am.; Candn. Population Soc.; Internat. Sociol. Assn.; National Advisory Ctte. to RCMP on Multicultural Issues; recreation: badminton, tennis; Home: 2060 Chalmers Rd., Ottawa, Ont. K1H 6K5; Office: Place du Portage, Phase II, Hull, Que. K1A 0M5.

**SAMUEL, William Morris,** Ph.D.; university professor; b. Windber, Pa. 28 July 1940; s. David William and Mary Grace (Hoffman) S.; e. Juniata Coll. (Pa.), B.Sc. 1962; Penn. State Univ., M.Sc. 1965; Univ. of Wisconsin, Ph.D. 1969; children: Beth Lynn, Benjamin Warren; PROFESSOR OF ZOOLOGY, UNIV. OF ALBERTA 1981– ; post-doct. fellow, Univ. of Alta. 1969–70; Asst. Prof. of Zoology 1971–75; Assoc. Prof. of Zool. 1976–80; McCalla Rsch. Prof. 1989–90; Assoc. Dean Rsch. Faculty of Science 1991–92; mem., The Wildlife Soc.; Wildlife Disease Assn.; Am. Soc. of Parasitologists; Entomological Soc. of Am.; Soc. for Conservation Biology; Candn. Soc. of Zool.; editor: 'First International Mountain Goat Symposium' 1978, 'Sixth Biennial Symposium, Northern Wild Sheep and Goat Council' 1988; recreations: nature photography, fishing, camping; Home: 10738 – 85th Ave., Edmonton, Alta. T6E 2K8; Office: Edmonton, Alta. T6G 2E9.

**SAMUELS, Joseph William,** B.A., LL.B., LL.M.; lawyer; labour arbitrator; b. Regina, Sask. 4 Apr. 1942; s. Victor and Clara Aileen (Heirsh) S.; e. Queen's Univ., B.A. (Hons.) 1963, LL.B. 1966; London Sch. of Econ., LL.M. 1967; called to Ont. Bar 1971; m. Pamela d. William and Lisabel Godfrey 13 June 1965; children: Mina Beth, Robin Brian, Noah Z.; OWNER, SAMUELS ARBITRATION SERV. LTD. 1983– ; Law Faculty, Univ. of Alta. 1967–69; Univ. of West. Ont. 1969–86 (Prof. 1969–86); Cons., Dept. of External Affairs; Candn. Red Cross Soc.; U.N. Environment Prog. on Internat. Humanitarian Law & Internat. Control of Weather Modification; Labour Arbitrator, govt. panels & priv. indus. 1975– ; Mem., Extve. Bd., Candn. Counc. on Internat. Law 1984–88; author of over 30 scholarly articles; Editor-in-Chief, 'The Univ. of West. Ont. Law Review' 1984–86; mem., Organizing Ctte., Permanent Conference on Nuclear Weapons and the Law 1985–89; Mem., Bd. of Dir. and Chrmn. of Finance, Orchestra London Canada 1989–91; Vice-Pres. Finance, Congregation Or Shalom London 1988–92; Vice-Pres. & Chrmn. of Fund-raising, Temple Israel, London 1993– ; recreations: photography, music (clarinet), chess, cycling, walking, skiing, canoeing; Address: 281 Commissioners Rd. E., London, Ont. N6C 2T3.

**SANCTON, Andrew Bain,** B.A., B.Phil., D.Phil.; educator; b. Montreal, Que. 17 Jan. 1948; s. John William and Mary Alice (Bain) S.; e. Ormstown H.S. 1964; Bishop's Univ. B.A. 1968; Queen's Coll. Oxford Univ. (Rhodes Scholar Que. 1968) B.Phil. 1970, D.Phil. 1978; m. Pamela d. Clifford and Yvonne Brown 26 July 1969; one d. Rebecca Mary Yvonne; one s. Derek Thomas Richard; DIRECTOR OF THE LOCAL GOVERNMENT PROGRAM, DEPT. OF POLITICAL SCIENCE, UNIV. OF WESTERN ONTARIO 1986–92 and 1993– ; Lectr. Pol. Sci. there 1970–73, 1977–78; Asst. Prof. 1978–83; Assoc. Prof. 1983–93; Prof. 1993– ; Instr. Pol. Sci. and Humanities, Marianopolis Coll., Montreal 1974–77; mem. Federal Electoral Boundaries Comn. for Ont. 1982–86 and 1993– ; Bd. of Dirs., Ont. Municipal Mngmt. Inst. 1988– ; Candn. Pol. Sci. Assn.; Inst. of Public Admin. of Can.; author: 'Governing the Island of Montreal' 1985; various articles in scholarly journs.; co-editor: 'City Politics in Canada' 1983; 'Metropolitan Governance: American-Canadian Intergovernmental Perspectives' 1993; Home: 434 Saint George St., London, Ont. N6A 3B4; Office: London, Ont. N6A 5C2.

**SANDBROOK, Richard (KRJ),** B.A., M.A., D.Phil., F.R.S.C.; university professor; b. Epsom, U.K. 5 Apr. 1943; s. Kenneth James and Betty Margaret (Hanson) S.; e. Carleton Univ., B.A. (Hon.) 1966; Univ. of Toronto, M.A. 1967; Univ. of Sussex, D.Phil 1971; m. Judith d. William and Eleanore Barker 20 July 1968; one d: Samantha Blythe; PROF., DEPT. OF POL. SCI., UNIV. OF TORONTO 1980– ; Asst. Lectr., Univ. of Nairobi 1968; Asst. then Assoc. and Full Prof., Dept. of Pol. Science, Univ. of Toronto 1970–92; Dir., Devel. Studies Prog. 1983–89; F.R.S.C. 1984; author: 'The Politics of Africa's Economic Recovery' 1993; 'The Politics of Africa's Economic Stagnation' 1985; 'The Politics of Basic Needs' 1982, 'Proletarians and African Capitalism' 1975; co-author: 'The Labouring Poor and Urban Class Formation' 1977; co-editor: 'The Development of an African Working Class' 1976; 'Empowering People: The Development of Community, Civil Associations and Legality in Africa' 1993; series editors: 'The Political Economy of World Poverty,' Univ. of Toronto Press, 1982–85, 'Third World Development' Cambridge Univ. Press, 1986– ; Ed. Bd. Mem., 'Canadian Journal of African Studies'; 'Journal of International Development'; Mem., Royal Soc. of Can.; Vice Pres., Candn. Assn. of African Studies; Candn. Civil Liberties Union; Amnesty Internat.; recreations: squash, tennis; Club: Trinity Coll. Tennis; Home: 256 Cottingham St., Toronto, Ont. M4V 1C6; Office: Dept. of Pol. Sci., Univ. of Toronto, Toronto, Ont. M5S 1A1.

**SANDELL, Michael Angus;** investment counsellor; b. El Paso, Texas 4 Oct. 1946; s. Angus and Hazel (McCombs) S.; e. Las Cruces High Sch. N.Mex. 1964; New Mexico State Univ.; m. Heidi d. Barry and Elaine Lind 20 Dec. 1984; children: Virginia Elaine, Elliott Angus; PRINCIPAL, LANCASTER INVESTMENT COUNSEL 1988– ; Vice Pres. Guardian Capital 1984–85; Sr. Vice Pres. Aetna Capital Management 1985–87, Pres. 1987–88; came to Can. 1968; Home: 2015 Elmhurst Ave., Oakville, Ont. L6J 1W9; Office: 1 First Candn. Pl., Suite 5750, Toronto, Ont. M5X 1A9.

**SANDERS, Andrew T.;** writer; b. Budapest, Hungary 23 Apr. 1934; s. Laszlo and Hermine Mimi (Schlesinger) Szekely; e. Budapest Coll. of Chem. Tech. 1954; m. Judith d. Imre and Magda Komlos 18 Apr. 1959; PRES., A.T. SANDERS ASSOC. INC. 1976– ; Rsch. Chem. Connaught Lab. 1960–66; The Manufacturers Life Insurance Co. 1967–75, Data Processing Vice-Pres. 1972–74, Planning Vice-Pres. 1975; Pres. & C.E.O., CAPSCO Software Can. Ltd. 1979–87; author numerous tech. and mgmt. papers pub. in Best's Review, Financial Post, Canadian Datasystems, Life Ins. in Can.; recreations: classical music, bridge, harpsichord building, philosophy, theology; Home: 54 Gilgorm Rd., Toronto, Ont. M5N 2M5.

**SANDERS, Robert Mark,** B.A.; publisher; b. Montréal, Qué. 8 Aug. 1948; s. Robert Lewis and Awdrie W. (Elkington) S.; e. W. Can. High Sch. Calgary 1966; Univ. of Alta. B.A. 1970; children: Mark Duncan Lewis, Carrie Elizabeth; PUBLISHER, GREYSTONE BOOKS ( a div. of Douglas & McIntyre) 1993– and DOUGLAS & McINTYRE LTD. 1987– ; Grad. Teaching Asst. Univ. of Alta. 1971–73; Sales Rep. Holt Rinehart & Winston Ltd. 1973–74; Teacher/Instr. in Eng./Communications Kelsey Inst. Saskatoon 1974–75; Mng. Ed., Dir., Publishing Dir., W. Producer Prairie Books, Saskatoon 1975–87; mem. Candn. Copyright Inst.; Adjudicator/Instr. Banff Publishing Workshop 10 yrs.; mem. Assn. Candn. Publishers (Pres. 1987–88); Faculty, Simon Fraser Univ.; recreations: fly fishing, jazz music, golf.

**SANDERSON, Eric (Sandy);** radio executive; b. Toronto, Ont. 10 Oct. 1948; s. George Douglas and Miriam Wentworth (House) S.; e. Leaside H.S.; Univ. of Toronto; Univ. of Western Ontario; m. Anne d. Robert W. and Sheila Chard 23 May 1970; children: Timothy, Katherine; EXTVE. VICE-PRES. & GEN. MGR., EASTERN RADIO OPERATIONS, ROGERS BROADCASTING LTD. 1990– ; Morning Announcer, Program Dir., CKAR Huntsville 1970–73; Production Dir., CJBK London 1973; Creative Dir., CKGM Montreal 1974–77; Asst. Prog. Dir., WABC N.Y. 1977–80; Program Dir., WLS Chicago 1980–81; Dir. of Programming, ABC Radio Network N.Y. 1982; Program Dir., CFTR Toronto 1983; Vice-Pres., Programming, Rogers Broadcasting Ltd. 1986; Sr. Vice-Pres., Programming 1987; Vice-Pres. & Gen. Mgr., CFTR 1988; Mem. of the Board, F.A.C.T.O.R.; recreations: squash, golf, tennis; clubs: Mayfair Lakeshore, Toronto Athletic; Markham Golf &

Country; Office: 25 Adelaide St. E., Toronto, Ont. M5C 1H3.

**SANDERSON, Robert Owen,** B.A., C.A.; b. Duncan, B.C. 8 July 1947; s. George D. and Louisa Mabel (Owen) S.; e. Simon Fraser Univ. B.A. 1969; C.A. 1972 (B.C.); PRES., KPMG PEAT MARWICK THORNE INC. 1989– ; Trustee in Bankruptcy 1976; Partner Peat Marwick Thorne 1978; mem. Insts. C.A.'s B.C., Y.T. and Ont.; Candn. Insolvency Practitioners Assn.; Ont. Insolvency Assn.; Insolvency Inst. of Canada; Comm. Law League Am.; Clubs: Ontario; Rotary; Office: 3300 Commerce Court West, Toronto, Ont. M5L 1B2.

**SANDERSON, Stanley F.;** financial advisor; b. Vancouver, B.C. 1 June 1933; e. King Edward High Sch. Vancouver 1950; Univ. of Toronto 1957; m. Elizabeth d. Alfred and Elizabeth Ransom 29 Dec. 1954; children: Robert, Barbara, Richard, David; VICE PRES. AND SR. FINANCIAL ADVISOR, EQUION SECURITIES CANADA LIMITED 1991– ; joined American Hospital Supply Corp., Med. Product Sales Vancouver 1951, trans. to Toronto 1954; Candn. Sales, Howmedica Corp. Toronto 1957, trans. to New York, Gen. Sales Mgr. N. Am. New York 1962; Pres. and Founder, Professional Medical Industries Ltd. Toronto 1967 and Professional Medical Supplies Inc. New York 1970; Sr. Cons. and Vice Pres. Professional Economic Consultants Toronto 1980; Pres. and Founder, S.F. Sanderson & Associates Ltd. 1986–90; Pres. Candn. Surgical Trade Assn. 1977–79; Founding Pres. Candn. Assn. Financial Planners 1983–85, Chrmn. Bd. Dirs. 1985–86, R.F.P. 1987; Candn. Inst. Financial Planning C.F.P. 1982; Candn. Securities Institute C.I.M. and F.C.S.I. 1993; recreations: golf, power boating; Clubs: Mississauga Golf & Country; Great Lakes Cruising; Home: 2791 Rosewood Lane, Oakville, Ont. L6J 7M4; Office: 212 King St. W., Toronto, Ont. M5H 1K5.

**SANDHAM, (Herbert) James,** D.D.S., M.Sc., Ph.D.; educator; b. Lethbridge, Alta. 30 Sept. 1932; s. John Robert and Mildred (Fuller) S.; e. Univ. of Alta. D.D.S. 1957; Univ. of Man. M.Sc. 1963, Ph.D. 1967; m. Joyce d. Clarence and Isabel Bowman 8 Oct. 1955; four s. Dennis, Douglas, Graham, Stewart; PROF. OF DENTISTRY, UNIV. OF TORONTO 1976– , cross appts. Prof. of Microbiol. Faculties of Med. and Pharm.; Hon. Prof. of Stomatology, Hubei Medical Coll., Wuhan, China 1987– ; Project Specialist, Chinese Provincial Universities Development Project, Hubei Medical Coll., Wuhan, China 1987; served Candn. Army as Dental Offr. 1957–60, rank Capt.; private dental practice Dryden, Ont. 1960–62; Asst. Prof. of Med. Microbiol. Univ. of Man. 1966–68; Asst. Prof. and Investigator, Univ. of Alabama in Birmingham, Inst. Dental Rsch. 1968–71; Assoc. Prof. of Dentistry present Univ. 1971–76; Med. Rsch. Council Can. visiting Prof. of Dentistry, Univ. of Alta. 1982; Univ. of Sask. Visiting Lectr. 1989; mem. Candn. Assn. Dental Rsch. (mem. Exec. 1976–78, 1982–92, Pres. 1988–90); recreation: dinghy sailing; Home: Apt. 704, 120 Rosedale Valley Rd., Toronto, Ont. M4W 1P8; Office: 124 Edward St., Toronto, Ont. M5G 1G6.

**SANDIFORD, Peter A.,** B.Comm., M.S.; business executive; b. Canada 24 Oct. 1944; s. Peter Johnston and Elsie (Watson) S.; e. McGill Univ. B.Comm. 1967; Univ. of California M.S. 1972; m. Marilyn Pickard 21 Dec. 1968; children: Lauren, Rebecca, Peter, Katharine; VICE CHAIRMAN, SHL SYSTEMHOUSE INC. 1991– ; Senior Consultant, Price Waterhouse 1972–74; Dir., Welfare Systems, Govt. of Canada 1974–75; Vice Pres. & Gen. Mgr., SHL Systemhouse Inc. 1975–84; Pres. & chief Operating Officer 1984–91; Dir., CADAPSO 1986–88; ADAPSO 1988–90; clubs: Rideau; Office: 501, 50 O'Connor St., Ottawa, Ont. K1P 6L2.

**SANDLER, Marilyn Eleanor,** B.A.; marketing research executive; b. Toronto, Ont. 10 Apr. 1941; d. Morris Joseph and Lily (Lehr) Somers; e. Univ. of Toronto B.A. 1961; children: Leslie Anne, Julie Kathryn, Jeremy Michael; CHAIRMAN & C.E.O., CREATIVE RESEARCH INTERNATIONAL INC. 1984– ; Co-Founding Partner and Vice Pres. present firm 1971, Pres. and Chief Oper. Offr. 1982; Past Pres. Profl. Mktg. Rsch. Soc. 1978–79; Past Pres. Candn. Assn. Mktg. Rsch. Orgns. 1986–87; Home: 18 Caldow Rd., Toronto, Ont. M5N 2P7; Office: 700, 100 Sheppard Ave. E., Toronto, Ont. M2N 6N5.

**SANDOR, Anna,** B.A.; screenwriter; b. Budapest, Hungary; d. Paul and Agnes Elizabeth (Laszlo) Sandor; e. Harbord Coll. Inst. Toronto 1968; Univ. of Windsor B.A. 1971; m. William s. Drs. James and Ruby Gough 31 July 1981; one d. Rachel Alice; Screenwriter: 'Amelia Earhart: The Final Flight' TNT 1994; 'The Anissa Ayala Story' NBC 1993; 'A Stranger in the Family' CBS/CTV 1993; 'Miss Rose White' A Hallmark Hall of Fame Presentation, NBC, 1992; 'Stolen: One Husband' CBS 1990; 'Tarzan in Manhattan' CBS 1989; CBC TV movies 'Two Men' 1988; 'Mama's Going to Buy You a Mockingbird' 1987–88; 'The Marriage Bed' 1986, 'Charlie Grant's War' 1985, 'A Population of One' 1980; feature film: 'Martha, Ruth and Edie' (co-writer) 1988; head writer and writer over 30 episodes 'King of Kensington' CBC 1975–80; co-writer 9 episodes 'Seeing Things' CBC TV 1983–85; co-creator series 'Hangin' In' 7 seasons; 'Running Man'; 'High Card' (CBC 'For the Record' anthol. series) 1982–83; 'Danger Bay' 4 episodes 1986–88 CBC/Disney Channel; Lectr. in Writing for TV, Summer Inst. of Film, Ottawa; Contbr. Screenwriting workshops incl. Humanitas Master Writers Workshop 1993; Emmy nomination for 'Miss Rose White' 1992; recipient Humanitas Award 1993; Chris Plaque, Best Script, Columbus Film Fest. 1989; ACTRA Award Best Writer Original TV Drama 1986; Prix Anik 1981, 1985, 1986, and 1989; Co-Chrmn. Crime Writers of Can. 1985–86; mem. Acad. of Television Arts & Sci.; Writers Guild of Am. & Can.; recreations: music, reading, ballet; Address: c/o Steve Weiss, William Morris Agency, 151 El Camino Dr., Beverly Hills, CA 90212.

**SANDOR, Thomas,** Dipl. Chem., Ph.D., F.R.S.C.; biochemist; educator; b. Budapest, Hungary 3 Nov. 1924; s. Miksa and Irén (Förstner) S.; e. Pázmány Péter Univ. Budapest Dipl. Chem. 1948; Univ. of Toronto Ph.D. 1960; m. Vera d. Dr. István and Elizabeth Várkonyi 5 July 1949; one d. Catherine-Susanne; Sr. Research Associate, Laboratoire d'Endocrinologie, Centre de Recherche, Hôpital Notre-Dame, Montréal, Qué. 1959– ; Career Investigator Med. Research Council Can. 1962–91; Consulting Biochem. Hôpital Notre-Dame 1968–92; Rsch. Prof. of Medicine, Univ. de Montréal 1970–92; Attaché de recherche, Institut Alfred-Fournier Paris 1949–50; Research Fellow Hosp. for Sick Children Toronto 1951–56; Research Biochem. Hôtel-Dieu Hosp. Montréal 1956–59; Research Asst. Prof of Med. 1961–67; Research Assoc. Prof. of Med. Univ. de Montréal 1967–1970; Assoc. mem. Div. of Exper. Med., Dept. of Med. McGill School of Med. Montreal 1969– ; Visiting Prof. of Zool. Univ. of Sheffield, U.K. 1970–71, 1979–80; Visiting Prof. of Biochem. Univ. of Buenos Aires, Argentina 1974. Organized one of the first research labs, specializing in comparative endocrinology and comparative steroid biochemistry of nonmammalian vertebrates and invertebrates in Can. Author or co-author of over 140 research publs. Candn. and internat. scient. journs.: various book chapters: invited lectr. univs. Can., U.S., U.K., France, Germany, Spain, India, Hong Kong. Recipient Nuffield Foundation Candn. Travelling Fellowship 1964; Schering Travelling Fellowship 1966; The Endocrine Soc. Travelling Fellowship 1968; Science Research Council (U.K.) Sr. Visiting Research Fellowship 1966, 1970–71, 1979–80. Fellow, Royal Society of Canada (F.R.S.C. 1980); mem. Candn. Biochem. Soc.; Ordre des Chimistes du Québec (Specialist Diploma in Clinical Biochem.); Biochem. Soc. (U.K.); The Endocrine Soc. (U.S.); Soc. for Endrocrinol. (U.K.); European Soc. Comp. Endocrinols. (Founding mem.); Am. Soc. Zools.; Cands. for Health Research (Dir. 1976–79, 1982–85); Corr. Ed. Journ. Steroid Biochem. 1970–79; mem. Bd. Eds. Gen. and Comparative Endocrinol. 1974–81; Gouverneur à vie, Hôpital Notre-Dame; Home: 5194 West Broadway, Montréal, Qué. H4V 2A2; Office: Hôpital Notre-Dame, 1560 Sherbrooke St. E., Montréal, Qué. H2L 4M1.

**SÁNDORFY, Camille,** Ph.D., D.Sc., F.C.I.C., F.R.S.C.; educator; b. Budapest, Hungary 9 Dec. 1920; s. late Dr. Kamill and Paula (Fényes) S.; e. Cistercian Coll. Budapest 1939; Univ. of Szeged, Hungary B.Sc. 1943, Ph.D. 1946; Sorbonne D.Sc. 1949; m. Rolande d. late Etienne Cayla, Paris, France 24 Aug. 1971; PROF. DE CHIMIE, UNIV. DE MONTREAL since 1959; Asst. Tech. Univ. Budapest 1946; Attaché de Recherches, Centre Nat. de la Recherche Scientifique, France 1947–51; Postdoctorate Fellow, Nat. Research Council of Can. 1951–53; joined Univ. de Montréal 1954; Visiting Prof. Univ. of Paris 1968, 1974; rec'd 1er prix de livre scientifique du Qué. 1967; Médaille Pariseau 1974; Killam Mem. Scholarship 1978; Herzberg Award 1980; Prix Marie-Victorin of Quebec, 1982; Chemical Inst. of Canada medal, 1983; H.C. Doctor, Univ. Moncton 1986; Univ. Szeged (Hungary) 1988; Medal of World Assn. of Theoretical Organic Chemists 1990; Compagnon de Lavoisier (Order of Chemists of Quebec) 1992; Gold plaquette J. Heyrovsky of the Czech Academy of Science; author 'Les Spectres Electroniques en Chimie Théorique' 1959; 'Electronic Spectra and Quantum Chemistry' 1964; co-author 'Semi-empirical Wave-Mechanical Calculations on Polyatomic Molecules' 1971; over 240 research publs. in chem; mem. Internat. Acad. Quantum-Molecular Science; European Academy Arts, Science and Literature; Hungarian Academy of Science; Home: 5050 Roslyn, Montréal, Qué. H3W 2L2; Office: Montréal, Qué. H3C 3J7.

**SANDWELL, Bernard Danton,** B.A., LL.D.; retired book publisher; b. Boston, Mass. 24 Jan. 1915; s. Arnold Hugh and Helen (Bower) S.; e. Elem. Schs. in B.C.; Harris Acad., Dundee, Scotland; 2ndary Sch. Que.; Upper Can. Coll. Toronto; Univ. of Toronto, B.A. (Pol. Science & Econ.) 1938; LL.D., Trent Univ., 1980; m. Helen Mary, d. A. R. Kaufman, Kitchener, Ont., 10 June 1939; children: Joan Patricia, Douglas Bernard, Mary Helen; former Chrmn. of Bd. and Pres., Burns & MacEachern Limited; former Vice Pres. and Dir., House of Anansi Press Ltd., Toronto; upon graduation joined Educ. Dept., Macmillan Co. of Can. Ltd., Toronto; apptd. Asst. Mgr., Coll. and Med. Books Dept., 1946, Mgr. 1948; el. Mang. Dir., Collier-Macmillan Can. Ltd. of Galt and Toronto, 1961; during 2nd World War served with the Irish Regt. of Can. in Italy and Holland, rank Capt.; Hon. Bd. mem., Trent Univ. (Chrmn. Bd. Govs. 1971–75); Past Chrmn., Candn. Book Publishers Assn.; Past Trustee, Ont. Waterfowl Research Foundation; Hon. Fellow, Champlain Coll., Trent Univ.; rec'd Centennial medal, 1967; Anglican; recreations: waterfowl research, fly fishing, wilderness travel; Home: Granite Place, 61 St. Clair Ave. W., Suite 1605, Toronto, Ont. M4V 2Y8.

**SANDYS, Judith,** B.A., M.S.W., Ph.D.; university professor and administrator; b. Montreal, Que. 21 Dec. 1943; d. Charles and Ida (Piafsky) Bloome; e. McGill Univ. B.A. 1964; Univ. of Calif. at Berkeley M.S.W. 1966; Univ. of Toronto Ph.D. 1993; m. Howard s. Anne and Bernard S. 7 June 1964; children: Cheryl, Jay, Natasha; DEAN, FACULTY OF COMMUNITY SERVICES, RYERSON POLYTECHNIC UNIV. 1993– ; extensive continuing involvement in social service organizations, developments and education; Extve. Dir., West Island Adaptation Services 1973–77; Community Living (Mississauga) 1978–87; Teacher, Ryerson Polytechnic Univ. 1990– ; consultant on disability issues to orgns. in Canada & Australia; Doctoral Fellowship, SSHRC; Chair, BALANCE; Bd. Mem., Centre for Rsch. & Edn. in Human Serv.; involved in task groups for Toronto Citizen Advocacy; Ont. Assn. for Community Living; Mem., S. Ont. Training Group (providing training in social role valorization theory) Social Role Valorization Devel., Training & Safeguards Council; author: 'Community Living for People with Developmental Handicaps: Implications for Social Work Practice' (manual); Home: 37 Denlow Blvd., Don Mills, Ont. M3B 1P6; Office: 350 Victoria St., Toronto, Ont. M5B 2K3.

**SANDYS-WUNSCH, John William Kervyn,** M.A., D.Phil.; university administrator; clergyman; b. Sault Ste. Marie, Ont. 7 May 1936; s. Theodore Vincent and Jean Eleanor (Rossiter) S.; e. Cowichan H.S., Duncan, B.C. 1952; Univ. of B.C., B.A. 1956; Oxford Univ. (Rhodes Scholar B.C. and Christ Church 1956) B.A. 1958, M.A., D.Phil. 1961; grad. studies Univ. de Strasbourg 1959–60; Universität Tübingen 1960–61; m. Sheila d. George and Elise Harper 8 July 1961; children: Michael, Donald, Helen; Asst. Parish of Sandwick, Courtenay 1961–62; Incumbent, West Coast Mission (Tofino-Ucluelet) 1962–65; Asst. Rector, St. John's Church, Victoria, B.C. 1965–66; Lectr. Queen's Coll., St. John's, Nfld. 1966–68; Asst. Prof. Meml. Univ. 1968, Assoc. Prof. 1973, Prof. 1980; Pres., Thorneloe Univ., Sudbury, Ont. 1982–91; recipient Rotary Found. Scholarship 1960; German Academic Exchange Scholarship 1961; Jaspers Lectureship Ripon Hall Oxford 1973–74; Pres. Candn. Soc. for Biblical Studies 1977–78; mem. Anglican Ch. of Can.; author: various journal articles; papers at conference; Ed., 'Studies in Religion' 1990; recreation: gardening; Office: 825 Alget Rd., Mill Bay, B.C. V0R 2P0.

**SANE, Dean M.,** B.A., M.H.A.; hospital administrator; b. Lampman, Sask. 11 Sept. 1937; s. Lambert and Eleanor (Schnell) S.; e. Univ. of Sask. B.A. 1965; Univ. of Ottawa M.H.A. 1967; m. Olivia d. John Balon 13 Aug. 1960; children: Joette, Margot, Jodie; PRESIDENT, THE CREDIT VALLEY HOSPITAL 1981– ; Asst. Administrator, Victoria Union Hosp. 1967–67; Administrator, North York Gen. Hosp. 1970–81; Preceptor/Lectr., Univ. of Ottawa (Masters in Health Admin.), Univ. of Toronto (Masters in Health Sci. Admin.), Candn. Sch. of Mngt. Toronto, McMaster Univ. (M.B.A. Health Serv. Admin.); Robert Wood Johnson Award, Univ. of Ottawa and Johnson & Johnson Co. 1967; Office: 2200 Eglinton Ave. W., Mississauga, Ont. LM 2N1.

**SANGER, Clyde William,** M.A.; writer; research executive; b. London, Eng. 20 Nov. 1928; s. Gerald Fountaine and Margaret Hope (Munroe) S.; e. Shrewsbury Sch. UK 1947; Brasenose Coll. Oxford M.A. 1956; m. Penelope d. Philip and Ottilie Ketchum 27 June 1959; children: Richard, Matthew, Toby, Daniel; DIR. OF COMMUNICATIONS, NORTH-SOUTH INST. 1989– ; joined 'Evening Sentinel' Staffordshire 1952–54; 'Daily Mail' London 1954–57; 'Central African Examiner' Salisbury, S. Rhodesia 1957–59, Asst. Ed., Ed.; 'The Guardian' Africa, N.Y. 1959–67, Candn. corr. 1967–89; 'The Globe and Mail' Toronto 1970–72, ed. writer; Special Asst. to Pres. CIDA 1970–72; Assoc. Dir. Internat. Devel. Rsch. Centre Ottawa 1972–77; Dir. of Info. Commonwealth Secretariat, London 1977–79 (member of the Commonwealth Observer Group, Kenya and Pakistan elections); mem. Bd. CUSO 1969–72; Candn. Council Internat. Co-op. 1986–88 (mem. Fact Finding Mission Namibia 1989); Found. Internat. Training Toronto 1977–87; Broadcasting for Internat. Understanding Ottawa 1988– ; News Concern Internat.; Unitarian Service Ctte. Can. 1985–89 (Nat. Chrmn. 1988–89); Lectr. in Jour. Carleton Univ. since 1981, Zimbabwe Inst. Mass Communications 1982; Candn. corr. 'The Economist' since 1967; author 'Central African Emergency' 1960; 'Half a Loaf: Canada's Semirole in Developing Countries' 1969; 'Safe and Sound: Disarmament and Development in the Eighties' 1982; 'Lotta and the USC Story' 1986; 'Ordering the Oceans: The Making of the Law of the Sea' 1987; 'Canadians and the United Nations' 1988; co-author 'Stitches in Time: The Commonwealth in World Politics' 1981; recreations: soccer, cycling, chess, poetry; Home: 299 First Ave., Ottawa, Ont. K1S 2G7; Office: 200, 55 Murray St., Ottawa, Ont. K1N 5M3.

**SANGSTER, Brant G.,** B.E.; oil company executive; b. New Glasgow, N.S. 10 July 1946; s. Whitman D. and Lillian Jean S.; e. Dalhousie Univ. B.E. 1968; VICE-PRESIDENT, CENTRAL REGION, PETRO-CANADA PRODUCTS; Imperial Oil 13 years; joined Petro-Canada 1982; worked in Products, Corporate and Resources divisions, latterly as Vice-Pres., Corp. Devel. & Vice-Pres., Business Analysis & Support, Resources; Chair, Regional Management Ctte., CPPI-Ont. Div.; Dir., Petro Partners; Touchcom Inc.; recreations: sailing, golf, computer music arranging; clubs: Port Credit Yacht, Toronto Board of Trade; Home: 38 Blythwood Rd., Toronto, Ont. M4N 1A1; Office: 5140 Yonge St., Ste. 200, North York, Ont. M2N 6L6.

**SANKEY, Charles Alfred,** B.A.Sc., M.Sc., Ph.D., D.Sc. (Hon.), LL.D. (Hon.), F.R.S.A., F.C.I.C., P.Eng.; b. Waskada, Man. 31 July 1905; s. Charles Arthur and Anna Josephine (Ponton) S.; e. Belleville (Ont.) High Sch.; Upper Can. Coll., Toronto; Univ. of Toronto, B.A.Sc. (Chem. Engn.) 1927 (medallist), (Hall of Distinction 1980); McGill Univ., M.Sc. (Chem.) 1928, Ph.D. (Chem.) 1930; Queens Univ., Hon. D. Sc. 1980; Brock Univ., Hon. LL.D. 1983; m. Alice Winifred, d. Archibald E. Wallace, 1 Oct. 1938; children: George H. King, John D., Mrs. P. L. Northcott (Grace W.), Janet E.; Chemist, Research Dept., Price Bros. & Co. Ltd., Quebec, Que., 1930–35; joined The Ontario Paper Co. Ltd. as Research Engr. 1935, Research Dir. 1943, Vice-Pres., Research 1965–70; publications and patents in pulp and paper technol., vanillin and other by-products, lignin and lignosulfonic acids; author of 'PAPRICAN: The First Fifty Years' 1976; Fellow, American Association Advancement Science; mem., American Institute Chemical Engineers; Am. Chem. Soc.; Assn. Prof. Engrs. Ont., (Citizenship Award, 1978); Technical Section, Canadian Pulp and Paper Association (Honorary Life member, Past Councillor; Past Chairman Research Committee; Past Chrmn. Comte. on Phys. & Chem. Standards; Weldon Medallist; F. G. Robinson Service Award); Tech. Assn. Pulp & Paper Indust. (U.S.); Tech. Sec., Australia & New Zealand Pulp & Paper Indust.; Chancellor, Brock Univ. 1969–74; (Hon. Life mem. Faculty Club); St. Catharines, Ont. Citizen of the Year 1973; Freemason; (Past Active mem. Supreme Council, A. & A.S.R.; Vice Pres. Scottish Rite Charitable Found. of Can. (1979–84); P.D.D.G.M.); recreation: music; Home: 46 South Dr., St. Catharines, Ont. L2R 4V2.

**SANTA BARBARA, Joanna,** M.B.B.S., F.R.A.N.Z.C.P., F.R.C.P.(C); child & family psychiatrist; b. Brisbane, Australia 18 July 1943; d. William Jeffrey and Helen Viva (Sherry) Rodwell; e. Univ. of Queensland, grad. med. sci. 1964, med. 1967; N.S.W. Inst. of Psych. 1972; m. Jack s. John and Angela S. 1978; children: Josh, Jonah, Jeffrey; child & family psychiatrist, Prince of Wales Hosp., Sydney, Aust. to 1976; Psychiatrist, Thistletown Reg. Ctr. for Children to 1979; Chedoke Child & Family Ctr. to 1986; presently in private practice; Asst. Prof., Dept. Psych., Univ. of Toronto 1976–79; McMaster Univ. 1979– ; Instr., Introductory Peace Studies 1988–90; Psych. Cons., Wentworth Co. Bd. of Edn.; Psych. Cons., Family Practice Unit, McMaster Univ. 1986–90; Pres., Candn. Physicians for Prevention of Nuclear War 1991–92; Council mem. & lecturer, Centre for Peace Studies, McMaster Univ.; best known for work with and for children in dealing with nuclear threat & promotion of world peace (lectured in Can., U.S. & Aust. on these & other issues); Mem., Group of 78; recreations: time with children, novels; Home: R.R. 2, Lynden, Ont. L0R 1T0; Office: 925 King St. W., Hamilton, Ont. L8S 1K7.

**SANTANGELI, Frank;** mutual fund executive; b. Liverpool, England 20 June 1934; s. Louie and Ellen (Curran) S.; e. St. Francis Xavier's College, Liverpool; Sch. of Slavonic Studies, Cambridge; m. Anne Gauge 21 Dec. 1957; children: David, Peter, Susan; PRES. & CHIEF EXTVE. OFFR., FINSCO SERVICES LIMITED 1984– ; served in British Army Intelligence 1953–54; Salesman, Excelsior Life 1958; Asst. General Mgr., Occidental Life Insurance co. 1960; Marketing Planning Offr., Sun Life of Canada 1970; Corp. Planning Offr. 173; Mngt. Serv. Offr. 1975; Assoc. Comptroller 1976; Corp. Sec. 1979; Vice-Pres., Marketing 1980; Chrmn., Investment Funds Inst. of Canada; holds both Candn. and Am. CLU designations; recreations: golf, tennis; clubs: York Downs Golf & Country; National Club (Toronto); Home: 80 Front St. E., Suite 511, Toronto, Ont. M5E 1T4; Office: 110 Yonge St., Suite 500, Toronto, Ont. M5C 1T4.

**SANTOS, Humberto,** M.B.A., B.Comm., F.I.C.B.; banking executive; b. Portugal 4 Apr. 1944; e. Concordia Univ., B.Comm. 1976, M.B.A. 1979; Harvard Bus. Sch. 1986; PRES. & CHIEF EXECUTIVE OFFR., DESJARDINS LAURENTIAN FINANCIAL CORP. and PRES. & CHIEF EXECUTIVE OFFR., CAISSE CENTRALE DESJARDINS; Chrmn. of the Bd., Laurentian Bank of Canada; Desjardins Federal Savings Bank (Hallandale, Fl.); Mem. Mgmt. Ctte., Desjardins Confederation; Vice-Pres., Data Processing, Nat. Bank of Can. 1976; D.P. Opns. 1979; Leasing 1981; Sr. Vice-Pres., Admin. 1982; Branch Opns. 1984; Extve. Vice-Pres., Branch opns. 1984–87; Extve. Vice-Pres., Corporate Banking 1987–89; Sr. Extve. Vice-Pres., Banking Affairs, National Bank of Canada 1989–90; Dir., Gulf Oil 1975–76; Bank of Montreal 1969–75; Mem. Bd. of Dirs., St. George's Sch. of Montreal; Ctr. Soc. d'Aide aux Immigrants; Mem. Bd. of Govs., Concordia Univ. and Pres. of Business Adv. Bd.; recreations: travel, tennis, skiing; Office: 1 Complexe Desjardins, 40th Floor, P.O. Box 10500, Desjardins Branch, Montréal, Qué. H5B 1J1.

**SANWAL, Bishnu D.,** Ph.D., D.N.Sc., F.R.S.C.; educator; b. Almora, India 25 May 1927; e. Univ. of Delhi Ph.D. 1953; Fed. Inst. Technol. Zurich D.N.Sc. 1956; m. Madhu 1960; children: Anil, Sabra; PROF. OF BIOCHEMISTRY, UNIV. OF W. ONT. 1973– and Chrmn. of Biochemistry 1973–83; Asst. Prof. Univ. of Man. 1959, Assoc. Prof. 1963, Prof. 1965–69; Prof. Univ. of Toronto 1969–73; recipient Outstanding Rsch. Award Candn. Soc. Microbiol. 1968; author or co-author various publs.; Fellow, Royal Society of Canada 1979; mem., Am. Soc. Biol. Chems.; Candn. Biochem. Soc.; Metabolic Regulation Group Intnl. Union of Biochem; Archives Indian Acad. Neurosci's (ed. bd. Enzymol.); Home: 72 Hampton Cres., London, Ont. N6H 2N9; Office: Health Sciences Centre, London, Ont. N6A 5C1.

**SAPERGIA, Barbara,** B.A., M.A.; writer; b. Moose Jaw, Sask. 1943; d. Bill and Rose Davies; e. Univ. of Sask. B.A. (cum laude) 1964; Univ. of Man. M.A. 1966, pre-master's program 1973; m. Geoffrey Ursell 8 July 1967; author: 'Foreigners' 1984 (fiction); 'South Hill Girls' 1992 (fiction); numerous short stories and poetry pub. in anthologies & magazines incl. most recent: 'Eating Avocados' in 'Kitchen Talk' 1993; 7 professional stage productions incl. most recent: 'Roundup' 1990 (pub. 1992); feature film script: 'Matty and Rose' 1992; 9 radio dramas incl. 'The House by the River' 1993, 'Eating Avocados' 1992; subject of interview by Doris Hillis for 'Plainspeaking: Interviews with Saskatchewan Writers' 1988; has participated in several workshops and writing classes incl. May Writers Studio, Banff School of Fine Arts 1989, Banff Screenwriters Workshop 1988; Sask. Writers Guild's Major Award for Drama for 'Roundup' 1989, 'Double Take' 1985; for poetry, short fiction & non-fiction (1st prize in each category) 1976; Sask. Arts Bd., Sr. Artists Award 1986–87; Playwright in Residence, Persephone Theatre 1985–86; Canada Council 'B' grant 1984–85, short-term grant 1992; Dept. of Culture & Youth Awards for Children's Lit. 1982, Screenwriting 1981, Poetry 1978; Founding Mem., Thunder Creek Co-op; Treas., Sask. Writers Guild 1976–77; Pres., Sask. Playwrights Ctr. 1987–88, 1988–89; Western Vice-Chair, Playwrights Union of Can. 1989–91; Mem., Writers Union of Canada, ACTRA, P.E.N., SOCAN.

**SAPONJA, Walter,** B.Sc., P.Eng.; professional engineer; b. Edson, Alta. 17 Oct. 1938; e. Univ. of Alta. B.Sc. 1961; SENIOR VICE-PRES., OPERATIONS, TRANSALTA UTILITIES CORP. 1990– ; joined present firm 1961; various tech. posts 1974; Mgr., Thermal Opns. 1974–78; Dir., Power Production 1978–81; Vice-Pres., Power System Opns. 1981–86; Sr. Vice-Pres., Generation 1986–90; Dir., AEC Power Ltd.; Candn. Electrical Assn.; Electric Utility Planning Council; PowerSmart Inc.; TransAlta Fly Ash Corp.; Mem., Assn. of Profl. Engr., Geol. & Geophysicists of Alta.; Office: 110 – 12th Avenue S.W., Box 1900, Calgary, Alta. T2P 2M1.

**SARAH, Robyn;** writer; b. New York, N.Y. 6 Oct. 1949; d. Leon Lipson (dec.) and Toby (Palker) Belkin; e. McGill Univ. B.A., M.A.; Conservatoire de musique du Québec (Concours, clarinet); author: 'Shadowplay' 1978, 'The Space Between Sleep and Waking' 1981, 'Anyone Skating on that Middle Ground' 1984, 'Becoming Light' 1987 (poetry); 'The Touchstone' 1992 (poetry); 'A Nice Gazebo' 1992 (fiction); Contact: c/o Vehicule Press, P.O. Box 125, Place du Parc Station, Montréal, Qué. H2W 2M9.

**SARGENT, Linda Marie,** B.A., M.B.A., C.H.R.P., F.C.A.M.; business and association executive, educator, consultant; b. Maidenhead, Berkshire, England 18 Jan. 1950; d. Rea Franklin and Mary Elizabeth (Clark) S.; e. Stouffville Dist. S.S. 1968; Trinity Coll., Univ. of Toronto B.A. (Hons.) 1972; Candn. Sch. of Mngt. F.B.A. 1982; Northland Open Univ. M.B.A. 1982; Human Resources Profl. Assn. of Ont. C.H.R.P. 1989; MANAGING DIRECTOR, JUVENILE DIABETES FOUNDATION CANADA (TORONTO CHAPTER) 1989– ; Manager, Market Research, Loblaws Supermarkets Limited & National Grocers Co. Ltd. 1974–80; Manager, Manpower Planning 1980–81; Dir., Training and Development 1981–85; Vice-Pres., Human Resources & Devel. 1985–89; Pres., Linda Sargent Enterprises Inc. 1989– ; Assoc. Prof., Northland Open Univ. 1988– ; Comnd. a Colonel on Staff of Gov. of Kentucky 1993; Vice-Pres. & Dir., Ont. Centre for Mngt. Studies 1993– ; Dir., Candn. Inst. of Cert. Admin. Mgrs. 1989– ; George Brown College: Chair, Retail Adv. Ctte. 1981–90, Mktg. Adv. Ctte. 1993– ; Cornell Univ., Food Indus. Mngt. Adv. Bd. 1988–89; Fellow, Candn. Inst. of Cert. Admin. Mgrs. 1991 (C.A.M. 1986); Fellow (Hon.), Ont. Centre for Mngt. Studies 1993; Past Pres., Candn. Sch. of Mngt. Alumni Assn. 1984–88; Mem., Candn. Soc. of Assn. Extves. 1989– ; co-author: 'Employee Assistance Program' 1989; author of num. articles in business pubs; num. seminars & speeches for businesses & assns.; Home: Willowdale, Ont.; Office: 320 – 49 The Donway West, Don Mills, Ont. M3C 3M9.

**SARLOS, Andrew,** O.C., F.C.A.; b. Budapest, Hungary 24 Nov. 1931; emigrated to Canada 1956; s. Julius and Frederika (Szigeti) S.; e. Pub. Sch., Hungary; Univ. of Budapest, Faculty of Econ., grad. 1956; C.A., Toronto 1962; m. Mary Fennes, Aug. 1958; one s., Peter; CHRMN., ANDREW SARLOS & ASSOCIATES LIMITED (investment counsellors and portfolio managers); Chrmn., Central European Investment Corp.; Founder & Dir., The First Hungary Fund; Dir.: Ontario Hydro (Chrmn. Pension Ctte.); The Horsham Corporation; Alliance Communications; The Live Entertainment Corp. of Can.; The Vigoro Corporation (USA); Mem. Bd. of Govs., Toronto Hospital Foundation and Mem. Toronto Hospital Finance Ctte.; Mem. Bd. of Govs., The Univ. of Waterloo; mem. Nat. Council, Candn. Inst. of Internat. Affairs; Founding Mem., International Management Center, Budapest, Hungary (Chrmn. Advisory Bd.); Founding Mem., Budapest Stock Exchange; Founder & Mem. Adv. Bd., East/West Exchange Program, York Univ.; former Chrmn., Hungary Reborn (exhib. & cultural festival) 1991; former Co-Chair, Welcome Canada/Bienvenue Canada in Budapest, Hungary (largest exhib. of Candn. culture outside of Canada) 1993; recipient: Honorary Doctorate Degree, St. Mary's Univ. 1991; FCA distinction, Ontario Chapter of Chartered Accountants 1991; Order of the Flag of the Hungarian Republic decorated with Laurels from the President of Hungary 1991; Medal for 1956 revolutionary activities from Hungarian Republic 1992; Officer, Order of Canada 1992; Commemorative Medal for 125th Anniversary of Candn. Confederation 1993; author: 'Fireworks: The Investment of a Lifetime' (autobiography) 1993; recreations: sailing; Clubs: Albany; Donalda; Address: P.O. Box 51, Toronto-Dominion Tower, Toronto-Dominion Centre, Toronto, Ont. M5K 1E7.

**SARRAZIN, Christian,** B.A., M.A.; executive; b. Ferme-Neuve, Que. 27 Oct. 1949; s. Oscar and Cécile (Godmer) S.; e. Coll. Jean-de-Brébeuf B.A. 1970; McGill B.A. (Econ.) (Hons.) 1972; Univ. Louvain M.A. (Econ.) 1974; m. Suzanne d. Jean and Aurise Lafleur 9 Sept.

1972; children: François-Xavier, Laurence, Dominique; VICE-PRESIDENT, ASIA PACIFIC, TELEGLOBE CANADA INC. 1993– ; Trade Comnr., Candn. Consulate Gen. San Francisco 1975–78; Attaché, Candn. Comn. Hong Kong 1978–79; 1st Sec., Candn. Embassy Beijing 1979–81; Dir., Govt. Relns., Candn. Exporters Assn. 1981–83; Corp. Mngt., Dept. of External Affairs 1983–85; Dir., Corp. Planning 1985–86; Consul Gen. Shanghai 1986–88; Dir., Press Office, Dept. of External Affairs 1988–89; Vice-Pres., Corp. Affairs, Candn. Commercial Corp. 1989–92; Extve. Vice-Pres. & C.O.O., Candn. Commercial Corp. 1992–93; Home: 2415 Dwight Cres., Ottawa, Ont. K1G 1C7; Office: 50 O'Connor St., Ottawa, Ont. K1A 0S6.

**SARSONS, Kenneth Dixon;** business consultant; b. Ardenode, Alta. 1 Nov. 1926; s. Philomen Ernest and Anna (Hovde) S.; e. Crescent Heights H.S. Calgary; m. Audrey d. Otto and Ella Seversen 12 March 1949; children: Ramona Anne, Alan James, Christopher John; PRES., KEN SARSONS CONSULTING 1989– ; Clerk, C.P.R. 1947–49; var. positions, Robin Hood Flour Mills 1949–67; Dir., Industrial Div., Saskatchewan Wheat Pool 1967–75 (played leading role in merging div. with Co-op Vegetable Oils (Man.) & Agra Industry (Sask.)); Chief Extve. Offr., CSP Foods Ltd. 1975–81; conducted studies for Japan Econ. & Trade Orgn. & Sask. Dept. of Agriculture 1982–84; Chief Extve. Offr., CSP Foods Winnipeg 1984–86; XCAN Grain 1986–88; current and recent mngt. projects for XCAN Grain Ltd., Sask. Wheat Pool & Prov. of Sask.; Dir., SunRype Foods; Dir., Asia Pacific Found. of Canada; Candn. Co-op. Assn. on Indian Project, C.I.D.A.; Comnr., Barber Comn. re privatization of SaskEnergy; leader of successful mission to China for B.C. Tree Fruits Ltd.; Mem., Pacific Basin Econ. Council (Candn. Ctte.); Canada-Japan Bus. Ctte. (Co-Chair, Agric., Forestry & Fisheries); Candn. Nat. Millers Assn.; Canola Council of Canada (Extve. Ctte. Bd. Mem.); Candn. Export Assn.; POS Pilot Plant Corp. (Chrmn. 3 yrs.); Chrmn., Environmental Sector, P.B.E.C. Internat. Meeting Japan; Taiwan; Australia (presentation); keynote speaker, Co-op. Mngt. Forum on Globalization Saskatoon; recreations: gardening, reading, woodworking; Mailing address: 3860 Dryden Rd., R.R. #2, Site 28A, C.8, Peachland, B.C. V0H 1X0.

**SARWER-FONER, Gerald J.,** C.D., M.D., F.R.C.P.&S.(C), F.R.C. Psych. (Gt. Br.); psychiatrist; educator; b. Volkovsk, Poland 6 Dec. 1924; s. Michael and Ronia (Caplan) S-F.; e. Univ. of Montreal B.A. (Loyola Coll.) 1945, M.D. 1951; McGill Univ. D. Psychiatry 1955; Western Reserve Univ. Psychiatry 1952–53; Candn. Inst. of Psychoanalysis 1958–62; m. Ethel d. I. Sheinfeld, Montreal, Que. 28 May 1950; children: Michael, Gladys, Janice, Henry, Brian; PROF. OF PSYCHIATRY, WAYNE STATE UNIV. (Detroit, MI) 1989– ; Prof. of Psychiatry, Univ. of Ottawa 1971– ; Visiting Prof. of Psychiatry Laval Univ. since 1964; Consultant in Psychiatry, Royal Ottawa Hosp.; Nat. Defence Med. Centre Ottawa; Ottawa Gen. Hosp.; Children's Hosp. of E. Ont.; Hôpital Pierre Janet, Hull; Dir., Lafayette Clinic 1989–92; Chrmn. Scient. Program Comte. VI World Cong. of Psychiatry, Honolulu 1977; Chrmn. Comte. on Psychiatry and the Law 1974–77; Chrmn. Task Force on Model Commitment Code Am. Psychiatric Assn. 1975–77; mem. Panel on Psychiatry, Defence Research Bd. of Can. 1958–62; Adv. Comte. on Health City of Westmount, Que. 1969–74; Life Gov. Queen Elizabeth Hosp. Montreal (Dir. of Psychiatry 1966–71); Consultant to Prot. Sch. Bd. Westmount and N.D.G. 1966–71; Ottawa Bd. of Educ.; Consultant in Psychiatry and Dir. Psychiatric Research Queen Mary Veterans' Hosp./McGill Univ. 1955–61; Lectr. in Psychiatry Univ. of Montreal 1953–55; Demonst., Lectr., Asst. and Assoc. Prof. of Psychiatry McGill Univ. 1955–71; Dir., Dept. of Psychiatry Ottawa Gen. Hosp. 1971–87; Prof. and Chrmn. of Psychiatry, Univ. of Ottawa 1974–86; Visiting Prof. of Psychiatry Chicago Med. Sch. 1968–76; Hassan Azima Mem. Lectr. Soc. Biol. Psychiatry; First Samuel Bellet Mem. Lectr. Inst. of Law & Psychiatry Univ. of Pa. 1978; Sandoz Visiting Prof. of Psychiatry of Candn. Med. Schs. 1976–77; Karl Stern Mem. Lecture, U. Ottawa, Fac. Medecin, 1979; Simon Bolivar Lecturer, Am. Psychiatric Assn. Annual Meeting, (New Orleans) 1981; Sigmund Freud Award of the Amer. Assoc. Psychoanal. Physicians 1982; First Dr. Burton J. Conn Meml. Lectr., San Diego Psychiatr. Soc. 1986; Dr. Douglas D. Goldman Mem. Lectr. G.W.A.N. 1987; POCA Award Lecture 1990; Psychiatric Outpatient Centers of America Award & Lecture 1990; W.A. Silverberg Award, Am. Acad. of Psychoanalysis 1990; 15th Zigmond M. Lebensohn Lecturer, Sibley Memorial Hosp., Washington, D.C. 1991; Asst. Psychiatrist and Dir. Psychiatric Clin. Investigation Unit, Jewish Gen. Hosp. Montreal 1955–66, Assoc. Psychiatrist 1961–71; service RCAMC (CA(M), rank Lt. Col.; author 'The Dynamics of Psychiatric Drug Therapy' 1960; 'Research Conference on the Depressive Group of Illnesses' 1965; 'Psychiatric Cross-Roads – The Seventies' 1972; author or co-author over 130 scient. papers, teaching audio and video tapes; Founder and Ed-in-Chief 'The Psychiatric Journal' Univ. of Ottawa 1976–89 (Editor Emeritus 1989– ); Assoc. Ed. 'Bulletin Amer. Acad. Pychiat. Law' 1974–84; Adv. Ed. 'Psychosomatics' 1978–84; mem. various ed. bds.; ed. reviewer and contrib. ed. various prof. journs.; Fellow and mem. Bd. Regents, mem. long range plan. comm., Am. Coll. Psychiatrists; Fellow, mem. of Bd. and Pres., Am. Coll. Psychoanalysts; Foundation Fellow, Royal Coll. Psychiatry (UK); Charter Fellow, Am. Coll. Neuropsychopharmacol.; Fellow, Am. Psychiatric Assn. 1954–87, Life Fellow 1987; Internat. Coll. Psychosomatic Med. (Sec. since 1979–81); Fellow, Am. Assn. Advanc. Science; Am. Orthopsychiatric Assn. 1954–87, Life Fellow 1987; Fellow, Am. Acad. of Psycho Analysis; Fellow, Am. Coll. Mental Health Administration; Fellow, Coll. Internat. Neuropsychopharm; Fellow, World Psychiatric Assn. 1982; Chrmn. Sci. Prog. VI World Congress 1974; Vice-Pres., Sect. on Educ. 1989– ; Mem. Internat. Adv. Com. 9th World Congress, Rio de Janeiro 1993; Diplomate, Am. Bd. Psychiatry and Neurology; Founder, Group-Without-A-Name Psychiatric Research Soc.; mem. Candn. Assn. Profs. Psychiatry (Pres. 1975–76, 1981–86); Que. Psychiatric Assn. (Pres. 1966–68, Treas. 1959–66); Candn. Psychoanalytic Soc. (Pres. Nat. Soc. 1978–82); Michigan Psychoanalytic Soc.; Intern. Psychoanalytic Assn.; Am. Acad. Psychiatry and the Law (Pres. 1975–77); Candn. Psychiatric Assn. (Dir. 1958–62), Soc. for Biol. Psychiatry (U.S.) (Vice-Pres., 1981, Pres.-Elect 1981–82, Pres. 1983–84); Am. Coll. Psycholanalysts (Pres. 1984–85); Am. Assn. for Social Psychiatry (Vice Pres. 1987–90, Pres. Elect. 1990–92, Pres. 1992–94; Chrmn. Scientific Program Ctte. 12th World Congress Soc. Psychiat., Washington, D.C. 1989–90); and mem. various other med. assns.; Knight of Malta of Sovereign Military Order of St. John of Jerusalem 1985; recreations: fishing, swimming, rowing; Clubs: Cosmos (Washington, D.C.); Royal Candn. Military Inst. (Toronto); Home: 3220 Bloomfield Shores Dr., West Bloomfield, MI 48323; Office: 3220 Bloomfield Shores Dr., West Bloomfield, MI 48323 and Room 202, 1453 Prince Rd., Windsor-Western Hospital, Windsor, Ont. N9C 3Z4.

**SATOK, David;** company president; b. Toronto, Ont. 22 Aug. 1931; s. Max and Molly (Silverberg) S.; e. Oakwood Coll. Inst., Toronto; Univ. of Toronto; m. Lyla, d. late Percy Stern, 12 Dec. 1958; children: Paula, Mark, Maxine, Jonathan; Pres., La Scala Construction; Greatok Group Ltd., International Pharmadyne Ltd., Asstock Construction Ltd.; Dir., Jewish Telographic Agency (N.Y.); Morris Pulver Fund, Toronto; Officer, Candn. Jewish Congress, Ont. Region; Pres., Cedarvale Rate Payers Assn. 1968; Toronto Home Builders Assn. 1969; Past Chrmn. Extve. Comte., Ont. Adv. Comte. on Housing; Chrmn. Nat. Exec. Comte., Candn. Jewish Congress; Chrmn. Nat. Budgeting Comte., Chrmn. Candn. Jewish Congress Central Region; Vice Pres., Toronto Jewish Congress; Chrmn., Nat. & Regional Community Relations Comte.; recreations: book collecting, tennis; Home: 400 Walmer Rd., Suite 2425, Toronto, Ont. M5P 2X7.

**SATTLER, Rolf,** Ph.D., F.L.S., F.R.S.C.; botanist; educator; b. Göppingen, Germany 8 March 1936; s. Otto and Emma (Mayer) S.; e. Univ. of Tübingen 1955–56; Univ. of Innsbruck 1956–57; Univ. of Kiel 1957–58; Univ. of Basel 1958–59; Univ. of Munich Ph.D. 1961; m. Liv Hamann 1 May 1963; div. 1986; PROF. OF BIOL., McGILL UNIV. 1977– ; NATO Fellow Univ. of Alta. 1962–63, Univ. of Cal. Davis 1963–64; Asst. Prof. present Univ. 1964, Assoc. Prof. 1969; Visiting Prof. Naropa Inst. Boulder, Colo. 1976; Freie Universität W. Berlin 1979; recipient Candn. Bot. Assn. Lawson Medal 1974; author 'Organogenesis of Flowers. A Photographic Text-Atlas' 1973; 'Biophilosophy: Analytic and Holistic Perspectives' 1986; ed. 'Theoretical Plant Morphology' 1978; 'Axioms and Principles of Plant Construction' 1982; mem., Intnl. Soc. Plant Morphols. until 1992 (N.Am. Sec. 1981–85); Candn. Bot. Assn. (mem. Exec. Ctte. 1972–75, Chrmn. Gen. Sect. 1975–76); Bot. Soc. Am.; Linnean Soc. London; Royal Soc. Can.; Candn. Soc. Study Hist. & Philos. Sci. (Sec. Laurentian Br. 1977– ) until 1992; Candn. Soc. for Theoretical Biology; Internat. Soc. for the Hist., Philos. & Social Studies of Biology; Sigma Xi; The Scientific and Medical Network; Internat. Assn. for New Science; The Center for Process Studies; Office: 1205 Dr. Penfield Ave., Montreal, Que. H3A 1B1.

**SAUCIER, Guylaine,** C.M., F.C.A.; executive; b. Noranda, Qué. 10 June 1946; d. Gérard and Yvette (Thiffault) S.; e. C.A. 1971; Mem. L'Ordre des Comptables Agréés du Québec; former Pres. Chambre de Commerce du Québec; former Pres. Assn. des manufacturiers de Bois de Sciage du Québec; Mem. Boreal Inc.; Mem. Comn. of Inquiry on Unemployment Ins.; Mem. Petro-Canada; Mem. Bell Canada; Mem. Hawker Siddeley; Mem. Sodarcan; Bank of Montreal; Mem. Univ. of Montreal; Mem. Tembec; recreation: tennis; Club: Hillside Tennis: Home: 1321 Sherbrooke St. W., #C-61, Montréal, Qué. H3G 1J4.

**SAUDER, Daniel N.,** B.A., M.A., M.D.; university professor and administrator; b. Hamilton, Ont. 15 April 1949; e. York Univ. B.A. 1971, M.A. 1972; McMaster Univ. M.D. 1975; PROFESSOR AND CHIEF, DIVISION OF DERMATOLOGY, UNIV. OF TORONTO 1990– ; Visiting Prof., Dermatology Br., NIH, Bethesda, Maryland 1982–85 Asst. Prof., Div. of Dermatology, McMaster Univ. 1982–85; Assoc. Prof. 1985–90; Mem., Edit. Bd., 'J. of Investigative Dermatology,' 'Lymphokine Res.,' 'J. of Am. Academy of Dermatology' (Asst. Ed.), 'Regional Immunology,' 'Can. J. of Derm.' (Assoc. Ed.),'Clinical Immunology Review'; Bd. of Dir., Am. Soc. for Clinical Investigation; Candn. Soc. for Derm. Surgery; Medical Dir., Ont. Outward Bound; Regional Medical Assoc. of Hamilton, Ont.; recipient of num. awards incl. election to Am. Soc. of Clin. Investigation 1992; McMaster Distinguished Alumni Gallery; Fellow, Am. Coll. of Physicians & Surgeons; Mem., Ont. Med. Assn. 1974– ; Candn. Med. Assn. 1974– ; Am. Coll. of Phys. 1976– ; Soc. of Investigative Derm. 1977– ; Derm. Found. 1978– ; Royal Coll. of Phys. & Surgeons of Canada 1980– ; Am. Fed. for Clin. Rsch. 1982– ; Am. Derm. Assn. 1988– ; author of 76 peer reviewed articles, 23 book chapters & 77 abstracts; recreations: skiing, aerobics; Home: 96 Munro Blvd., Willowdale, Ont. M2P 1C4; Office: 2075 Bayview Avenue, Toronto, Ont. M4N 3M5.

**SAUL, John Shannon;** university professor/writer/activist; b. Toronto, Ont. 4 May 1938; s. Wilford Montgomery and Dorothy Edith (Shannon) Saul; e. Lawrence Park C.I.; Univs. of Toronto, Princeton, London 1956–65; m. Patricia Chalmers 20 July 1962; children: Nicholas John, Joanne Elizabeth; PROF., DEPT. OF SOC. SCI., ATKINSON COLL. & PROF. OF POL. SCI., GRAD. FAC., YORK UNIV. 1973– ; as Sr. lectr., Univ. of Dar es Salaam, Tanzania 1965–72 estab. close contacts with num. S. African liberation movements incl. volunteer work with the Front for the Liberation of Mozambique (FRELIMO) and visit to liberated areas with FRELIMO guerillas 1972; invited by FRELIMO as Candn. rep., Mozambican independence celebrations 1975; Vis. Prof., Univ. of Eduardo Mondlane and FRELIMO Party Sch. 1981–82; denied visa, illegally entered South Africa to report on developments there 1988; Founding Mem., Toronto Ctte. for the Liberation of S. Africa 1972– ; Mem., Ed. Working Group, 'Southern Africa Report'; Ed. Bd., 'This Magazine' 1973– ; Assoc. Ed., 'Review of African Political Economy' and 'Transformation' (South Africa); Past Assoc. Ed., 'Studies in Political Economy'; author: 'Canada and Mozambique' 1974, 'The State and Revolution in Eastern Africa' 1979, 'O Marxismo-Leninismo no Contexto Mozambicano' 1985, 'Socialist Ideology and the Struggle for Southern Africa' 1990, 'Recolonization and Resistance in Southern Africa' 1992; and over 100 articles, num. papers, lectures, & media appearances on 4 continents; co-author: 'Essays on the Political Economy of Africa' 1973, 'The Crisis in South Africa' 1981, 1986; editor: 'A Difficult Road: The Transition to Socialism in Mozambique' 1985; co-editor: 'Socialism in Tanzania' (2 vols.) 1973, 'Rural Cooperation in Tanzania' 1974; recreations: playing basketball, and piano, record-collecting/listening (esp. jazz/'roots music'); Home: 17 Kendal Ave., Toronto, Ont. M5R 1L5; Office: 4700 Keele St., North York, Ont. M3J 1P3.

**SAUMIER, André,** L.Th., M.A., M.B.A.; financial executive; b. Montreal, Que. 26 Aug. 1933; s. Robert and Georgette (Sansoucy) S.; e. Univ. of Montreal, B.A. (Hons.) 1950; Angelicum Univ., L.TH. (Hons.) 1955; Univ. of Chicago, M.A. 1958; Harvard Univ., M.B.A. 1962; children; Sonia, Geneviève, Vérushka; CHRMN., SAUMIER FRÈRES CONSEIL 1989– ; Rsch. Dir., Battelle Mem. Inst., Columbus (Ohio) 1962–63; Dir. of Rsch., Candn. Council on Urban & Reg. Rsch. 1963–65; Asst. to Pres., Societé Générale de Financement 1965–67; Asst. Dep. Min. (Ottawa) Rural Develop., Regional Econ. Expansion, Urban Affairs 1967–75; Depy. Sec. to Cabinet, Dep. Min. of Natural Resources (Quebec) 1975–79; Sr. Vice Pres. & Dir., Richardson Greenshields of Canada Ltd. 1979–85; Pres. & Chief Extve. Offr., Montreal Exchange 1985–87; Chrmn., Saumier Morrisson & Davidson Partners Inc. 1987–89; Chrmn., Soc. Nat. de l'Amiante; Productions Virage Inc.; Sebentar Holdings Inc.; Vice-Chrmn., Alpha Capital Inc.; Simpa

Inc.; Dir., Unilever Canada Ltd.; Alyvanor Inc.; Vista Strategic Management Inc.; Candn. Golden Investment Fund Inc.; Canada-ASEAN Center; Prix Colin 1950; Offr. of the Nat. Order of Niger; Officer, Military & Hospitalier Order of St. Lazarus of Jerusalem; Gov., Theatre du Nouveau-Monde; Wilfrid Pelletier Found.; Quebec Press Council Found.; mem., Harvard Business School Club; Montreal Foreign Relations Counc.; C.D. Howe Institute; North Am. Institute; Consultant, Harvard Institute of Internat. Development; Ministry of Finance of Indonesia; co-author: 'Une Ville a Vivre,' 'Planning the Canadian Environment,' 'Environnement et Urbanisme,' 'Quebec Inc.'; recreation: scuba diving; Home: 65 S-Paul W., App. 403, Montreal, Que. H2Y 3S5; Office: 5 Place Ville-Marie, Suite 1234, Montreal, Que. H3B 2G2.

**SAUNDERS, Alastair Corston de Cusance Maxwell,** B.A., D.Phil.; senior civil servant; b. Halifax, N.S. 11 Apr. 1949; s. Richard Lorraine de Chasteney Holbourne and Sarah Cameron (Macintyre) S.; e. Gorsebrook Sch. Halifax 1959; Halifax Grammar Sch. 1962; Fettes Coll. Edinburgh, Scot. 1966; McGill Univ. B.A. 1971 (McCaskill Scholar 1967–71, Univ. Scholar 1968–71); Oxford Univ. (Rhodes Scholar) D.Phil. 1979 (Can. Counc. Doctoral Fellow 1974–76); m. Christine Frances Corston 1989; DIRECTOR OF INTERGOVERNMENTAL AFFAIRS, GOVT. OF N.S. 1988– ; Mellon Post-doctoral Teaching Fellow in Hist. Cornell Univ. 1980–82, Adjunct mem. Cornell Soc. Humanities; Rsch. Fellow John Carter Brown Lib. Brown Univ. 1983; Policy Advisor, Cabinet Secretariat 1984–88; Research Adv., Nova Scotia Legislative Select Ctte. on Health 1984; Rsch. Adv., N.S. Royal Comm. on Post-Secondary Education 1984–85; Secy., N.S. Interdepartmental Ctte. on Home Care 1986–87; Research Advisor, N.S. Community Coll. Study Ctte. 1987–88; Chrmn., N.S. Interdepartmental Ctte. on Government Programs for Disabled Persons 1987–88; Secy., Cabinet Ctte. on Social Planning and Development 1988–89; Chrmn., Advisory Ctte. on University Financing 1989; Chief Negotiator, N.S. Delegation, Multilateral Meetings on the Constitution 1992; Alternate Chief Negotiator, N.S. Delegation, Internal Trade Barrier Reduction Negotiations 1993– ; author 'A Social History of Black Slaves and Freedmen in Portugal 1441–1555' 1982; awarded Commemorative Medal for 125th Anniversary of Candn. Confederation; mem. Inst. of Publ. Admin. of Can.; Soc. Authors (U.K.); Anti-Slavery Soc. (U.K.); Heritage Trust of Nova Scotia; North British Society (Halifax); recreations: sailing, walking, photography, reading; Home: 37 Limardo Dr., Dartmouth, N.S. B3A 3X2; Office: P.O. Box 1617, One Government Place, 1700 Granville St., Halifax, N.S. B3J 2Y3.

**SAUNDERS, Doris B.,** M.A., M.Litt., LL.D.; b. Winnipeg, Man. 1901; d. W.J. Saunders; e. Univ. of Man., B.A. and M.A.; Oxford Univ., Diploma in Educ. 1923, and B. Litt. 1936; Univ. of B.C., LL.D. 1957; Prof. Emeritus, Univ. of Man., 1968; M.Litt. Oxford Univ., 1979; formerly Prof. of English and sometime Dean of Jr. Women there; awarded Travelling Scholar., Candn. Fed. of Univ. Women, 1925–26; Winifred Cullis Lecture Fellowship, England, 1966; Hon. Fellow, Univ. Coll., Univ. of Man., 1968; mem., Winnipeg Poetry Soc.; Pres., Univ. Women's Club of Winnipeg, 1943–45; Pres., Women's Br., Candn. Inst. Internat. Affairs, 1951; Pres. Candn. Fed. of Univ. Women, 1955–58; Pres. Winnipeg Br., Humanities Assn., 1967–68; Pres. Women's Candn. Club of Winnipeg, 1976–78; Pres., Twenty Club, 1980–82; awarded Centennial Medal (Canada), 1967 and Commemorative Medal for 125th Anniversary of Candn. Confederation 1992; Delta Delta Delta; Home: 503, 245 Wellington Cres., Winnipeg, Man. R3M 0A1.

**SAUNDERS, Earl Frederick,** M.D., FRCP(C); physician; b. Toronto, Ont. 27 Apr. 1937; s. Irving Marvin and Celia (Landau) S.; e. Univ. of Toronto, M.D. 1961; m. Brenda d. David and Selma Eisen 1959; children: Arthur, Lawrence, Richard; DIR., BONE MARROW TRANSPLANT PROG., THE HOSP. FOR SICK CHILDREN 1981– ; Instr. in Ped., Univ. of Cincinnati, Coll. of Med. 1965–68; Assoc. in Ped., Univ. of Toronto 1968–70; Asst. Prof. 1970–76; Assoc. Prof. 1976– ; Sr. Staff Physician, Hosp. for Sick Children 1968– ; Fellow, Leukemia Soc., N.Y. 1965–67; Royal Coll. of Physicians & Surg. of Can. 1967– (& Mem.); Mem. of Bd. of Trustees, Hospital for Sick Children 1990–94; Pres. Medical Staff, Hosp. for Sick Children 1992–94 (Vice Pres. 1990–92); Med. Dir., Camp Oochigeas for Children with Cancer; mem., Candn. Hemat. Soc.; Am. Soc. of Hemat.; Candn. Soc. for Clin. Investigation; Am. Fed. for Clin. Rsch.; Soc. for Ped. Rsch.; Am. Soc. of Ped. Hemat.-Oncol.; Ont. Med. Assn.; Candn. Med. Assn.; Ont. Coll. of Physicians & Surgeons; Royal Coll. of Physicians & Surgeons of Can.; author & co-author of 8 med. book chapters & 118 sci. papers & abstracts; recreations: skiing, bicycling, music, wine; Office: 555 University Ave., Toronto, Ont. M5G 1X8.

**SAUNDERS, Hon. Mr. Justice Edward,** B.A., LL.B.; judge; b. Toronto, Ont. 17 June 1925; s. Robert Porteous and Annie Maude (West) S.; e. Crescent Sch. 1937 and Upper Can. Coll. 1943 Toronto; Trinity Coll. Univ. of Toronto B.A. (Hon.) 1949; Osgoode Hall Law Sch. 1953; LL.B. 1990; m. Mary Louise d. Ven. Archdeacon Julian Sale and Mary Smedley (White), Port Arthur, Ont. 16 Sept. 1950; children: Elizabeth Anne, Michael James, Catherine Mary (Hicks); JUSTICE, ONT. COURT OF JUSTICE (GEN. DIV.); called to Bar of Ont. 1953; cr. Q.C. 1968; McMaster Montgomery & Co. 1953–54; Osler Hoskin & Harcourt 1954–77, Partner 1959–77; appt. Justice of Supreme Court of Ont. 1977; Warden Christ Ch. Deer Park 1974–76; Dir. Downtown Ch. Workers Assn. 1976–77; Candn. Tax Foundation (Gov. 1966–69); Candn. Bar Assn.; mem. Corp. Trinity Coll. Univ. of Toronto (1983–90); mem. Community Adv. Bd., Queen St. Mental Health Centre (1985–88); Trustee, Wycliffe Coll., Univ. of Toronto 1988– ; mem. Ont. Law Reform Commn. Adv. Bd. 1989– ; Chrmn. of panel assessing Ont. Hydro Demand/Supply Plan 1990–93; served with Candn. Army 1943–46, UK and N.W. Europe 1944–45, Reserve Militia 1947–51; Anglican; recreations: tennis, golf; Clubs: Badminton & Racquet; Toronto Golf; University; Home: Toronto, Ont.; Office: Osgoode Hall, Toronto, Ont. M5H 2N5.

**SAUNDERS, Harry James;** insurance executive; b. Eastleigh, Hampshire., Eng. 8 Sept. 1932; e. Peter Symonds, Winchester; m. Aileen Elizabeth McNamee 2 Aug. 1958; children: Anthony John, Michael Charles, Kathleen Allison; PRES. & C.E.O. (CAN.), ZURICH INSURANCE CO., ZURICH INDEMNITY CO. OF CANADA; Underwriter, Ocean Accident, Southampton, Eng. 1953; Underwriter present co. Toronto 1956, Alta. Br. Mgr. Edmonton 1960, Asst. Mgr. Toronto 1966, Automobile Mgr. Can. 1968, Asst. Mgr. Can. 1973, Mgr. for Can. 1974; served with RAF 1951–52; recreations: golf, sailing, squash, bridge; Clubs: Ontario; Mississauga Golf & Country; Poret Credit Yacht; Ontario; Home: 1048 Roper Ave., Mississauga, Ont. L5H 1B9; Office: 400 University Ave., Toronto, Ont. M5G 1S7.

**SAUNDERS, Peter Paul,** B.Com.; financier; b. Budapest, Hungary 21 July 1928; s. Peter Paul, LL.D., and Elizabeth (Halom) Szende; came to Canada, 1941; e. Vancouver Coll. (1944); Univ. of British Columbia, B.Com. 1948; m. Nancy Louise, d. R. G. McDonald, New Westminster, B.C., 11 Feb. 1956; two d. Mrs. Christine Elizabeth McBride, Paula Marie; PRES., SAUNDERS INVESTMENT LTD. 1987– ; Pres. & Dir., Harlan Fairbanks Co. Ltd.; Dir., Boreal Insurance Inc.; Greene Valley Concessions; Computrol Security Systems Ltd.; Wajax Ltd.; WIC Western Intnl. Comm. Ltd.; Molnar Capital Corp.; Northwest Sports Enterprises Ltd.; mem., Vancouver Adv. Bd., National Trust Co.; Dir., Counc. for Business and the Arts in Can.; Dir., The Arthritis Soc., B.C. & Yukon Division; after grad. from univ., employed by Candn. Pac. Rly. Co. as an Acct. in Vancouver, B.C., remaining with the Rly. for three years during which had several promotions; one of the Founders of Laurentide Financial Corp. Ltd. and its Pres. from inc. in 1950 to 1966; Vice Chrmn., Laurentide Financial Corp. Ltd. 1966–67; Chrmn. & Pres., Coronation Credit Corp. Ltd./Cornat Indus. Ltd. 1968–78; Versatile Corp. 1978–87; recreations: golf, skiing, hunting, boating; Clubs: Vancouver; Roy. Vancouver Yacht; Shaughnessy Golf and Country; Thunderbird Country (Rancho Mirage); Vancouver Lawn Tennis & Badminton; Home: 3620 Alexandra St., Vancouver, B.C. V6J 4B9; Office: P.O. Box 49352 – Bentall Centre, 3144 - 1055 Dunsmuir St., Vancouver, B.C. V7X 1L4.

**SAUNDERS, Richard Lorraine de Chasteney Holbourne,** M.D., F.R.M.S., F.R.S.E.; university professor; b. Grahamstown, S. Africa, 29 May 1908; s. Col. Frederick Anastasius (F.R.C.S.) and Lucy Anderson (Meiklejohn) S.; e. St. Andrews Coll., Grahamstown, S. Africa; Rhodes Univ. there; Edinburgh Univ., M.B., Ch.B., 1932, M.D. 1940; m. Sarah Cameron, M.B., Ch.B., d. Maj. Alexander Cameron Macintyre, M.C., Croix de Guerre 25 Mar. 1936; one s.: Alastair Corston de Cusance Maxwell; Cons. in Microfocal Radiography, Nat. Inst. of Health (N.I.H.) Cerebro-vascular Project, Washington; served as Visiting Phys., Settler's Hosp., S. Africa, 1932–33; House Surg., Bradford Royal Infirmary, Eng., 1933; Lectr. and Demonst. in Anat., Univ. of Edinburgh, 1933–37; came to Can. 1937; Asst. Prof. of Anat., Dalhousie Univ., 1937–42; Assoc. Prof. 1942–48; Prof. of Path. Anat. and Dir., of Med. Museums there, 1948–50; Head of Anatomy Dept. 1950–73 when emeritus; Research Prof. Inst. da Rocha Cabral, Lisbon, 1973–74 and Radcliffe Infirmary, Oxford, Eng. 1974–80; author 'X-ray Microscopy' in Encyc. Microscopy & Microtechnique; co-author 'X-ray Microscopy in Clinical and Experimental Medicine'; author 'Microfocal Radiography of Brain' and numerous articles on microcirculation; mem. Am. Assn. of Anat.; Fellow Am. Assn. Advanc. Sci.; Alpha Eta Chapter of Phi Rho Sigma (Hon. mem.); Alpha Omega Alpha; recreations: sailing, sketching; Home: 'Summerhill,' West Jeddore by Head of Jeddore, Halifax Co., N.S. B0J 1P0.

**SAUNDERS, Richard Merrill,** M.A., Ph.D.; historian; b. Gloucester, Mass., 16 Nov. 1904; s. Lee and Grace Martha (Merrill) S.; e. Quincy High Sch., Mass.; Clark Univ., B.A. 1924, M.A. 1925; Cornell Univ., Ph.D. 1931; m. Anna Blythe, d. Robert Haldane West, 30 June 1929; one d., Sarah Jane; Instr. in Hist., Am. Univ. of Beirut, Lebanon, 1925–28; Teaching Asst. in Ancient Hist., Cornell Univ., 1928–30; Boldt Fellow in Hist. there, 1930–31; Lect. in Hist., Univ. of Toronto, 1931–38, Asst. Prof. 1938–43, Assoc. Prof. 1943–54, Prof. 1954–71; former Assoc. Ed., 'Candn. Hist. Review'; mem., Fed. Ont. Naturalists (Past Dir.); Past Pres., Toronto Field Naturalists' Club; Pres. (1966–67), Candn. Hist. Assn.; Past Chrmn., Toronto Ornithological Club; author of 'French Canada and Britain' (transl. of 'Ton Histoire est une épopée,' by Abbé Arthur Maheux), 1942; 'Education for Tomorrow' (ed.) 1946; 'Flashing Wings,' 1947; 'Carolina Quest,' 1951; co-author of 'Canadian Wildflowers,' 1976 and 'Candn. Wildflowers through the Seasons,' 1982; has contrib. to journs., articles on French Can., the Middle East, on birds and on historiography; United Church; recreations: ornithology, nature photography; Home: 9 McMaster Ave., Toronto, Ont. M4V 1A8.

**SAUTER, William F.,** C.P.O.(C), F.C.B.C.; retired prosthetist; b. Loerrach, W. Germany 21 July 1928; s. August and Bertha (Reinacher) S.; e. J.P. Hebel Sch. 1942; Commerce Coll. 1944 (Loerrach); cert. in prosthetics, Freiburg, W. Germany 1951; Candn. Bd. of Cert., Prosthetics/Orthotics 1968; m. Elisabeth d. Gottfried and Elisabeth Bulling 28 Aug. 1948; children: Ulrich, Friedrich, Thomas; Prosthetic Consultant, Hugh MacMillan Rehab. Centre 1990–93, retired; Prosthetist/Orthotist, Basel Switz. 1953–55; Supr./Fitter, Orthopedic Appliance Res. Toronto 1961–64; Rsch. & Teaching Prosthetist, Ont. Crippled Children's Ctr. 1964–77; Cont. Coord., Powered Prosthetic Prog., Hugh Macmillan Rehab. Ctr. 1977–90; Fellow, Candn. Bd. for Cert. of Prosthetists & Orthotists (Pres. 1975–76); Chrmn., Upper Limb Externally Powered Prosthetic Soc.; Mem., Adv. Counc., George Brown Prosth/Orth Prog.; Cons./Lectr., U.N.B. Bioengr. 1974–81; Vice-Pres., Ont. Assn. of Prosth/Orth 1972–74; recipient Medal for Achievement in Science & Culture, Univ. of Bologna 1990; author of several articles on prosthetics; recreations: bee-keeping, canoeing; Home: 1680 Concession 6, R.R. 4, Uxbridge, Ont. L9P 1R4.

**SAUVAGEAU, Florian,** B.A., LL.L., M.Sc.; educator; journalist; b. Québec, Qué. 6 Feb. 1941; s. Agénor and Bernadette (Savard) S.; e. Univ. Laval, B.A. 1961, LL.L. 1964; Univ. of Ill., M.Sc. (Journalism) 1974; m. Paule d. P.E. Royer 23 Dec. 1976; PROF. OF COMMUNICATIONS, LAVAL UNIV. 1978– ; Co-Chrmn. Task Force on Broadcasting Policy, Dept. Communications, Can. 1985–86; Sec. Comn. des etudes Univ. Laval 1966–67, Professeur Adjoint 1969–72, 1978–82; News Ed. Le Soleil, Québec 1967–69, Mng. Ed. 1972–73; Host and Journalist (Pub. Affairs) CBC Radio Montréal (French Network) 1969–70, Radio-Can. (radio and TV) 1973–84; Chargé de Cours Univ. de Montréal 1974–79, Univ. de Dakar 1978; mem. Candn. Del. UNESCO 22nd Gen. Conf. Paris 1983; co-author 'Si l'Union Nationale m'était contée' 1978; 'Droit et journalisme au Québec' 1981; co-ed. 'Les journalistes' 1980; co-ed. 'Qu'est-ce que la liberté de presse' 1986; co-author several documentary films Nat. Film Bd. Can.; mem. Qué. Bar; Home: 129 Royale, Ste-Pétronille, Qué. G0A 4C0; Office: Québec, Qué. G1K 7P4.

**SAUVAGEAU, Philippe;** né Trois-Rivières, Qué. 11 juin 1940; é. Séminaire St-Joseph Trois-Rivières Baccalauréat ès arts 1961; Univ. de Montréal Baccalauréat en bibliothéconomie et bibliographie 1962; Univ. d'Ottawa études de maîtrise en français et en bibliothéconomie 1967; PRÉS.-DIR. GÉN. BIBLIOTHÈQUE NATIONALE DU QUÉ. 1989– ; Conservateur adjoint, Service régional des bibliothèques de la Mauricie 1962–64; Responsable des services techniques, Bibliothèque municipale Trois-Rivières 1962–64; Administrateur délégué, Bibliothèque régional de Nord de l'Outaouais 1964–70, Bibliothèques centrales de prêt de l'Outaouais et du

Saguenay 1971–75; Dir. Bibliothèque de Québec 1975–80; Dir. gén. Institut canadien de Québec 1980–89; Cons. Assemblée nationale du Québec 1983, Villes de Lévis, Lauzon, Victoriaville et Chicoutimi 1985, 1988, Agence de coopération culturelle et technique 1986, 1988, 1989; Prés. Comn. d'étude sur les bibliothèques publiques du Québec 1987; mem. de Trident, Québec 1976– ; Conférence canadienne des arts 1970– ; Prés. du Secrétariat perm. des peuples francophones, Québec 1979–89; Administrateur du Festival du film de Québec 1986–87; Prix de développement culturel 'La Laurentienne' Conseil de la culture de la région de Québec 1986; Chevalier de l'ordre des arts et des lettres, Ministère de la Culture et de la Communication du gouvernement français 1988; Auteur 'Comment diffuser la culture' 1969, mémoires, manuels, différents articles; mem. du Comité interrégional des bibliothèques publiques 1975–89; mem. de l'ASTED, CBPQ, CLA; Bureau: 125, rue Sherbrooke Ouest, Montréal, Qué. H2X 1X4.

**SAUVÉ, Roger,** B.Soc.Sc., M.A.; futurist and planner; b. Glengarry Co., Ont. 4 June 1944; s. Adelard and Roseabelle (St. Pierre) S.; e. Glengarry Dist. H.S. 1965; Univ. of Ottawa B.Sc. 1968, M.A. 1969; children: Roxanne, Eric; MANAGER, CORPORATE PLANNING, SASKATCHEWAN WHEAT POOL 1987– ; Pres., People Patterns Consulting 1990– ; Economist & Analyst, Imperial Oil 1969–74; Economist, Bank of Commerce 1974–76; Mgr., Econ. Rsch., Eaton's 1976–78; Mgr., Econ. Analysis, Inco Ltd. 1978–81; Dir., Business Analysis, Crown Investment Corp. of Sask. 1982–84; Pres. & Owner, Sask-Trends Monitor 1984–87; Pres., Toronto Assn. of Business Economics 1975–76; Part-time Instr., Univ. of Regina & SIAST 1986; Official Univ. of Ottawa Del. to 'Second Century Week' Edmonton 1967; Pres., Caisse populaire française de Regina 1988–91; Dir., Conseil de la coop. de la Sask. 1988–92; Comnr. of Pubs., Univ. of Ottawa 1966; Mem., World Future Soc.; Candn. Assn. for Business Economics; Nat. Assn. for Business Economics; author: 'Canadian People Patterns' 1990; 'Borderlines: A Comparison of Canadians and Americans' 1994; columnist, 'Saskatoon Star-Phoenix' & 'Regina Leader Post' (weekly) 1985–87; recreations: aerobics, racquetball, reading, writing; Home: 3223 E. Gould Bay, Regina, Sask. S4N 6S4; Office: 2625 Victoria Ave., Regina, Sask. S4T 7T9.

**SAVAGE, Candace Mary,** B.A.; writer; b. Grande Prairie, Alta. 2 Dec. 1949; d. Harry Gordon and Edna Elizabeth (Humphrey) Sherk; e. J.R. Robson H.S. 1967; Univ. of Alta., B.A. (Hons.) 1971; m. the late Arthur D. s. Robert and Louise Savage 22 Aug. 1971; one d.: Diana Cathryn; self-employed writer, book editor & pub. cons. preparing books, articles, radio progs., filmstrips & TV scripts 1975–84; Public Affairs Offr., Govt. of N.W.T. 1984–87; Co-ord., Info./Edn., Sci. Inst. of the N.W.T. 1987–89; Writer-in-Residence, Saskatoon Public Library 1990–91; Mem., Nat. Evaluation Ctte., Sci. Culture Can. 1987–90; National Council, The Writers' Union of Can. 1991–92; Mem. Extve., Sask. Arts Alliance 1993–94; author: 'Aurora: The Mysteries of Near Space' 1994; 'Wild Cats' 1993; 'Peregrine Falcons' 1992; 'Eat Up' 1992; 'Get Growing' 1991; 'Trash Attack' 1990; 'Grizzly Bears' 1990; 'Science Alive' 1988; 'Wolves' 1988; 'Eagles of North America' 1987; 'The Wonder of Canadian Birds' 1985; 'Pelicans' 1985; 'Our Nell' 1979; co-author: 'Wild Mammals of Western Canada' 1979; 'Herstory Calendar' 1976–79; 'A Harvest Yet to Reap' 1976; recreations: skiing, singing, poetry; Home: 302 Albert Ave., Saskatoon, Sask. S7N 1G1.

**SAVAGE, George Alfred,** C.A.; insurance executive; b. Waterford, Ont. 6 Sept. 1914; s. Thomas Charles and Martha Alice (Christie) S.; e. C.A. 1950; m. Dorothy Ruth, d. Dr. A.H. and Hazel (Robertson) Fromow, 3 June 1944; children: Ruth Blair, Margaret Robertson, Stephen Harris, John Burgess; DIR. & CHRMN. OF THE BD., GUARANTEE CO. OF NORTH AMERICA 1983–90; retired; Secretary-Treasurer, Kitchens Ltd., Brantford, 1949–50; Sr. Partner, Waters, Savage, Horne & Ronson (C.A.'s), Brantford and Simcoe, 1950–65; Vice Pres. and Secy.-Treas., Duo-Matic of Canada Ltd., Waterford, 1965–68; Pres. and Mgr. 1968–70; Vice Pres. and Dir., Brant Beverages Ltd., Brantford, 1954–71; Secy.-Treas. and Dir., London Bottling Ltd., London, 1969–71; Pres. and Dir., Duo-Heet Distributors Ltd., Waterford, 1968–70; Dir., Pres. & C.E.O., Guarantee Co. of N. America, 1971–83; Dir., Frank Cowan Co. Ltd., 1975–82; Dir., Princeton Holdings Ltd. 1975–85; Dir., Beth Sar Shalom Mission Inc. (Hamilton) 1973–80; Am. Bd. Mission to the Jews (New York, N.Y.) 1975–80; mem., Indust. Commission Waterford 1965–71; Inst. C.A.'s Ont.; recreation: numismatics; Homes: 1904, One Concorde Pl., Don Mills, Ont. M3C 3K6.

**SAVAGE, Graham,** B.A., M.B.A.; communications executive; b. UK 16 Mar. 1949; s. William Alfred and Jean Dorothy S.; e. Queen's Univ. B.A. 1970, M.B.A. 1972; m. Elise Orenstein; children: G. McKay, Gillian E., Coby O., Caley J.; SR. VICE PRES. & CHIEF FINANCIAL OFFR., ROGERS COMMUNICATIONS INC. 1989– ; Dir. Unitel Communications Holdings Inc.; Rogers Communications Inc.; Rogers Broadcasting Limited; Rogers Cablesystems Ltd.; Rogers Cantel Mobile Communications Inc.; Vitran Corp.; Alias Research Inc.; Toronto NBA Team; Invest. Analyst, National Trust Co. 1972–73, Burns Fry Ltd. 1973–75; Dir. Invest. Planning present Co. 1975, Vice Pres. Invest. Planning 1979–86; Sr. Vice-Pres., Investments 1986–89; recreations: running, tennis, map collecting; Home: 113 Coldstream Ave., Toronto, Ont. M5N 1X7; Office: P.O. Box 249, Toronto-Dominion Centre, Toronto, Ont. M5K 1J5.

**SAVAGE, Howard Gordon,** M.D.; university professor, zoo-archaeologist; b. Oakville, Ont. 28 Dec. 1913; s. Gordon Bennett Jull and Emily Luella S.; e. Univ. of Toronto M.D. 1937; m. Dorothy d. Jack and Florence Dalious 29 March 1941; children: Richard, Kenneth, Nancy; ADJUNCT PROF. OF ANTHROPOLOGY, UNIV. OF TORONTO 1980– ; Resident Staff, Hosp. for Sick Children 1937–41; Med. Officer, Royal Candn. Air Force 1941–45; Attending Staff, Hosp. for Sick Children & priv. paed. practice 1946–69; Rsch. Assoc., Ornithology, Royal Ont. Mus. 1969– ; Anthropology, Univ. of Toronto 1969–80; Pres., Ont. Archaeological Soc. 1972, '73, '76; Chair, Med. Arch. & Anthrop. Section & Mem. of Council, Acad. of Med., Toronto; Recipient, Norman Emerson Medal, Ont. Arch. Soc. 1984; Mem., Candn. Arch. Assn.; Sec., Brodie Club (Nat. Hist.) 1978– ; co-author: 'Avian Osteology' 1981; 'Birds From The Ground' in press; clubs: Brodie, Faculty Club, U of T; Home: 97 Glenview Ave., Toronto, Ont. M4R 1P9; Office: Toronto, Ont. M5S 1A1.

**SAVAGE, Hugh Baldwin,** B.Com., C.A., F.C.I.S.; b. Montreal, P.Q. 10 May 1913; s. Edward Baldwin and Marion Douglas (Creelman) S.; e. High Sch. of Montreal; Trinity Coll. Sch. Port Hope, Ont.; McGill Univ., B.Com., L.I.A. 1936; Order of Chart. Accts., C.A. 1938; m. Margaret Elizabeth, d. John B. How, Bronxville, N.Y.; one s. John Edward Clark; Dir., Malabar Ltd.; Boule Rock Hotel Inc.; H.B. Savage (Quebec) Inc.; Audit Clerk, Peat, Marwick, Mitchell & Co., 1936–38; Div. Acct., Canadian Industries Ltd., 1939; Group Acct., Defence Industries Ltd., 1940–41; Lectr. in Accountancy, McGill Univ. and Sir George Williams Univ., 1946–48; formed own firm of Chart. Accts. presently Hugh B. Savage Chart. Account; served in 2nd World War with R.C.N.V.R., 1941–45; Lt. Commdr., R.C.N.(R); Mun. Councillor, City of Montreal, 1957–60; Dir., City Improvement League; Pres., Jr. Chamber Comm., 1960; Chrmn., Prot. Bd. of Sch. Commrs., City of Montreal; Gov., Trinity College School; Montreal General Hospital; author of 'Tax-Saving'; Life Mem., Order of Chart. Accts. Que.; Chart. Inst. of Secretaries and Administrators; Am. Marketing Assn.; Montreal Advertising & Sales Extves. Assn.; Protestant; Liberal; recreations: swimming, skiing, hunting, fishing; Clubs: Irish Protestant Benevolent Soc.; Cascade Golf Club of Metis; M.A.A.A.; Naval Officers Assn.; Mount Royal Tennis; Home: Suite 812, Le Fort de la Montague, 3577 Atwater, Montreal, P.Q. H3H 2R2; Office: 1310 Greene, Montreal, P.Q. H3Z 2B2.

**SAVAGE, John Lawrence;** former politician; b. Qualicum Beach, B.C. 23 Feb. 1936; s. Harold Roland and Veronica Mary (Wolfe) S.; e. Univ. of B.C., dipl. in Agric. 1956; m. Margaret V. d. Charles Johnson 14 Oct. 1959; children: Kim, Pamela, Lori; Min. of Native Affairs, Govt. of B.C. 1991–92; Alderman, Dist. of Delta 1985; M.L.A. Delta 1986; Min. of Agriculture & Fisheries, Govt. of B.C. 1986–90; Min. of Parks 1990–91; Pres. & Dir., Delta C. of C. 1981–82; Dir., B.C. Fed. of Agric. 1976–86 (Pres. 1983–85); Extve. Dir., Candn. Fed. of Agric. 1978–86 (Comm. Chrmn. 1980–86); Chrmn., Delta Parks & Rec. Comn. 1985; recreations: golf, hunting; Home: 6706 London Dr., Delta, B.C. V4K 3N3.

**SAVAGE, Robert H.,** B.Sc., M.Sc., M.S., D.R.C.; engineering executive; b. Peace River, Alta. 19 May 1938; s. William Douglas and Ella Margaret (Strang) S.; e. Univ. of Alta. B.Sc. 1960; Univ. of Aberdeen M.Sc. 1962; Royal Coll. of Sci. & Technol., Dipl. Environ. Engr. 1963; Northwestern Univ. M.S. 1966; m. Sherrie d. John and Margaret Perkins 3 May 1961; children: Patrick Robert, Carole Margaret; EXECUTIVE VICE PRES., CONSULTING ENGINEERING, UMA GROUP LTD. 1991– ; Athlone Fellow studying in U.K. 1961–63; Project Engr., Underwood McLellan & Assoc. Ltd. 1963–65; Internat. Road Fed. Scholar studying in U.S. 1965–66; Chief Engr., Calgary Opn., Deleuw Cather Canada 1966–70; Transport. Div., Underwood McLellan & Assoc. Ltd. 1970–78; Vice Pres., Edmonton Reg. Mgr., UMA Engineering Ltd. 1978–91; Hon. Life Mem., Assn. of Profl. Engrs., Geol. & Geophysicists of Alta.; Fellow, Inst. of Transp. Engrs.; Mem., Engineering Faculty Adv. Bd., Univ. of Alta.; clubs: St. Albert Curling, Edmonton Petroleum: Home: 23 Glacier Pl., St. Albert, Alta. T8N 1R7; Office: 17007 – 107 Ave., Edmonton, Alta. T5S 1G3.

**SAVAGE, Thomas H.,** CBE; executive; b. Belfast, N. Ireland 21 Nov. 1928; s. Thomas Hixon and Martha Foy (Turkington) S.; e. Belfast H.S.; Indian Army, Officers Training Coll.; Univ. of Toronto Dept. of Ext. (Industrial Mgmt.); m. Evelyn Phyllis d. Harry and Flo Chapman 17 Jan. 1976; CHAIRMAN, NORTH AMERICAN TRUST CO. 1992– ; Dir., Acklands Ltd.; ITT Canada Ltd.; ITT Industries of Canada; North American Trust Co.; Supvr. Industrial Engn., W.J. Gage Ltd. 1954–59; Mgr. Process Engn., Coutts Hallmark Greeting Cards 1959–62; Chief Industrial Engr., Electric Reduction Co. 1962–63; Mgr. Operations Improvement, Distribution Serv., Union Carbide Canada Ltd. 1963–68; Mgr. Mgmt. Serv. and Dir. Staff Operations, CDA, ITT Canada Ltd. 1968–69, Pres. 1970–77; Chrmn., ITT Canada Ltd. 1977–93; Sr. Offr., Canada ITT Corp. 1978–93; Lectr., industrial engineering, plannning and organization, Univ. of Toronto, Extension Dept. (10 yrs.); Chrmn., Adv. Bd. and Life Mem. The Candn. Inst. of Mgmt.; mem. Ont. Business Adv. Counc.; Mem. of the Bd., Candn. Labour Market Productivity Centre; Mem., Am. Inst. of Industrial Engnr.; Dean's Adv. Council of the Faculty of Mngmt., Univ. of Toronto; Chrmn., Bd. of Gov. West Park Hosp.; Dir., National Retinitis Pigmentosa Eye Research Found. of Canada; Chrmn., Adv. Bd., Boys & Girls Clubs of Can.; Commander of the Order of the British Empire 1990; Clubs: Lambton Golf & Country; The Ontario; Office: 151 Yonge St., Toronto, Ont. M5C 2W7.

**SAVARD, Guy,** B.Comm., M.Sc., O.P.M., ADM.A.; exécutif financier; né à Coaticook, Cantons de l'Est, Qué. 17 jan. 1943; f. Emile et Thérèse (Trudeau) S.; é. St. Francis Xavier Univ. 1961–63; Univ. Laval B.Comm. 1964, M.Sc. 1965; Harvard Univ. O.P.M. 1982; ép. Marié à Odette Tessier; enfants: David, Pierre, Anne-Marie, Geneviève; PRÉS. ET CHEF DE L'EXPLOITATION & MEM. DU CONSEIL D'ADMIN., CAISSE DE DÉPÔT ET PLACEMENT DU QUÉBEC; Touche Ross & Cie 1965–67; Assoc., Larochelle Savard Gosselin Gobeil et Assoc. 1968–71; Associé de Samson Bélair 1970–1989, associé dir. et mem. du conseil d'admin. 1981–89; Vice-prés. et mem. du comité exécutif de la Société de développement industriel (S.D.I.) 1985–90; Mem. du conseil d'admin. et du com. exécutif, Raymond, Chabot, Martin, Paré; Vice-prés. national, Raymond, Chabot, Martin, Paré; Président, C.G. Raymond, Chabot, Martin, Paré 1989–90; mem., Ordre des C.A.s du Qué.; Inst. of C.A.s of Ont.; L'Inst. can. des C.A.s; Harvard Business Sch. Assn. of Montreal (ancien prés.); Univ. Laval; St. Francis Xavier Univ.; Mem. fond., Estrie capital 1989; Mem. du conseil d'admin., Inst. nat. de la rech. sci. 1989; Gouv., Fac. de l'Admin., Univ. de Sherbrooke 1986; Clubs: Mont Royal, Hermitage, Montréal; bureau: 1981, avenue McGill College, Montréal, Qué. H3A 3C7.

**SAVARD, Jean-Guy;** éducateur et linguiste; né. St-Alban, Qué. 7 août 1931; f. Alfred et Angélina (Lahaye) S.; e. Univ. Laval B.A. 1955, B.Péd. 1956, L. en Péd. 1963, L.ès L. 1965, Dipl. d'études supérieures en linguistique 1966; ép. Réjeanne Marcotte 25 août 1956; enfants: Jacinthe, Raymond, Yolande, Vincent; Prof. Univ. Laval depuis 1966; Dir. intérimaire du Dépt. de linguistique 1970–71; Dir. du Centre internat. de recherche sur le bilinguisme 1972–78; Prés. de la Comm. de la recherche, Univ. Laval 1978–84; Adjoint au Recteur 1984–87; Secrétaire du Centre francophone de recherche en informatisation des organisations 1987–89; Vice-doyen de la Faculté des arts 1988–93; Secrétaire de la Faculté des arts 1989–93; gratification pour succès dans l'enseignement; Ministère de l'éduc. du Qué. 1961; Bourse d'études du Ministère de l'éduc. du Qué. 1963–66; subventions de recherche du Conseil des arts et du Secrétariat d'Etat (Ottawa) et du Ministère de l'éduc. du Qué.; auteur 'La valence lexicale' 1970; 'Les indices d'utilité du vocabulaire fondamental français' 1970; 'Bibliographie analytique de tests de langue/Analytical Bibliography of Language Tests' 1969 et 1977; co-auteur 'Le vocabulaire disponible du français' 1971, du Test Laval formules A, B, et C et de Minorités linguistiques et interventions: Essai de typologie 1978; mem. Ass. canadienne de linguistique appliquée (prés. 1977–79); Ass. canadienne de linguistique; Ass. des prof. de français des univ. canadiennes; Ass. canadienne-française pour l'avancement des sciences; membre correspondant de la Fédération canadienne des études humaines, 1971–81; prés. du comité des candidatures de l'Ass. canadienne de linguistique appliquée, 1979–85; Dél. de l'Ass. can. de ling. appliq. à la Comm. des tests de l'Ass. internat. de ling. appliq. 1980–84; responsable du Comite des Actes du Ve. congrès internat. de linguistique appliquée; membre du Comité de sélection des bourses Killam 1987–90; résidence: 3334 Radisson, Ste-Foy, Qué. G1X 2K3.

**SAVARD, Marcel R.,** M.Comm., F.C.A.; lottery executive; b. Sherbrooke, Que. 11 Oct. 1926; e. Séminaire de Sherbrooke; Mont-St-Louis College, Univ. of Montreal; Ecole des Hautes Etudes Comm. M.Comm., C.A.; PRESIDENT/DIRECTOR GENERAL, RÉGIES DES LOTERIES DU QUÉBEC 1986– ; Founder, Larochelle, Savard & Assoc. 1950–70; Parter in Charge, Samson Bélair 1970–79; Pres., Extve. Ctte. & Pres. 1979–86; Mem., Candn. Reconstruction Bd. 1982–86; Financial Consultant, Banque mondiale 1973–74; Mem., Conseil de planification et développement du Qué. 1971–75; Fellow, Ordre des comptables agréés du Qué. 1982; Vice-Pres., Bd. of Dir., Hôpital Sacré-Coeur de Montréal 1986– ; Pres., Club Richelieu 1963; Caisse populaire sociale Sherbrooke 1965; Fonds de retraite des empl. de la Ville de Sherbrooke 1964–69; Fond. des maladies du coeur 1971; Assn. de la Santé mentale 1970; Conseiller municipal, Sherbrooke 1956–69; récréations: golf, tennis, voyages; clubs: Laval-sur-le-Lac, Hermitage; Home: 30, Berlioz Rive, Condo 1200, Ile-des-Soeurs, Que.; Office: 2055 Peel, No. 600, Montréal, Que. H3A 2K9.

**SAVARD, Pierre,** M.S.R.C., D.ès L.; historien; professeur; né Québec, Qué. 10 juin 1936; f. Charles E. et Gilberte (Lavallée) S.; é. Petit Séminaire de Qué.; Univ. Laval B.A., B.Ph., L. ès L., Univ. de Lyon D.E.S. (histoire); D. ès L. Univ. Laval (histoire); ép. Susan Blue Warder, Baltimore Md. 6 Juin 1960; enfants: Marie, François, Michel; PROF. TITULAIRE AU DEPARTEMENT D'HISTOIRE, UNIV. D'OTTAWA; Prof. Adjoint puis Agrégé d'Histoire, Univ. Laval 1961–72, Dir. Dép. d'Histoire 1970–71; Prof. Agrégé puis Titulaire d'Histoire, Univ. d'Ottawa depuis 1972; Dir. de recherches associé., Ecole des Hautes Etudes en Sciences Sociales (Paris) 1988; Collab. régulier à l'Université Saint-Paul (Ottawa) 1985– ; Dir. du Centre de Recherche en Civilisation Canadienne-Française 1973–85; Dir. Dép. d'Histoire 1985–88; Prés. du Groupe d'Etude des Arts chez les Franco-Ontariens (rapport 1977); auteur, 'Jules-Paul Tardivel, La France et les Etats-Unis 1851–1905' 1967 (Prix Raymond Casgrain); 'Le Consulat Général de France à Québec et à Montréal 1859–1914' 1970; 'Aspects du catholicisme canadien-français du XIXe siècle,' 1980; directeur de publication de dix volumes; collaborateur à plusieurs ouvrages dont six tomes parus depuis 1987 de 'Textes poétiques du Canada français' et co-directeur du 'Dictionnaire de l'Amérique française' 1988; manuels scolaires; 85 articles de revues savantes et chapitres d'ouvrages sur l'histoire culturelle du Canada français; mem., Soc. Royale du Can.; Soc. des Dix; Soc. historique du Can. (ancien président); Fédération Canadienne des études humaines (ancien président); Inst. canadien de la Méditerranée, ancien vice-prés. (Rome); Conseil intnl. d'études canadiennes (ancien prés.); Société des Professeurs d'histoire du Québec (président-fondateur et membre honoraire); Assoc. italienne d'études canadiennes (membre honoraire); catholique; récréations: marche, voyages; Adresse: 3242 chemin Southgate, Ottawa, Ont. K1V 8W2; Bureau: Département d'histoire, Université d'Ottawa, Ottawa, Ont. K1N 6N5.

**SAVARYN, Peter,** C.M., Q.C., B.A., LL.B., LL.D.; lawyer; b. Zubretz, Ukraine 17 Sept. 1926; s. Michael and Anna (Atamaniuk) S.; e. Univ. of Alta. B.A. 1955, LL.B. 1956; Candn. Securities Course 1968; m. Olga, d. Josyf and Olena Prystajecky 14 July 1951; children: Vera Irene, Michael Joseph, Halia Anne; SR. PARTNER, SAVARYN & SAVARYN (estbd. 1959); emigrated to Can. as farm hand 1949; articled and practiced law with Amerongen & Burger 1957–59; called to Bar of Alta. 1957; cr. Q.C. 1974; Chancellor Univ. of Alta. 1982–86 (Gov. and Senator 1972–78; 1982–86); Pres. World Congress of Free Ukrainians 1983–88; Chrmn. Heritage Trust, Edmonton; Mem., Ukrainian Candn. Centennial Commn.; Mem., Adv. Panel, for Citation for Citizenship Awards (Min. of State); Vice-Pres., Bishop Budka Charitable Soc.; Chrmn., Hon. Ctte., Kurimoto Japanese Garden, Univ. of Alta.; Chrmn., Friends of the Univ. of Alta.; Hon. Pres. Ukrainian Candn. Profl. and Business Federation 1983 (Nat. Extve. 1973–75, 1979–81); Dir. St. Michael's Nursing Home; mem. YMCA; Fort Edmonton Hist. Foundation; Ukrainian Candn. Comte. Edmonton (Past Pres.); Chrmn., Alta. Ukrainian Commemorative Soc.; Ukrainian Prof. & Business Club Edmonton (Past Pres.; Hon. Life mem.); Alta. Cultural Heritage Council (Founding mem.); Past Pres., Alta. P. Cons. Assn.; Edmonton East P.C. Assn.; Past Vice-Pres. National P.C. Party (for Alta.); Official Del. to Prov. and Nat. Leadership Conventions since 1955; Chrmn. numerous P.C. comtes., meetings, seminars; fund raiser; campaign mgr. civic, prov. and nat. cands.; named Hon. Citizen of Winnipeg 1964; Shevchenko Medal Ukrainian Candn. Comte.; LL.D. (hon. causa), Univ. of Alberta 1987; Member, Order of Canada 1987; Outstanding Service Award, Ukrainian Candn. Profl. & Business Fed.; Badge of Eternal Fire in Gold Ukrainian Scouts (Nat.); awarded Commemorative Medal for 125th Anniversary of Candn. Confederation; Citation for Meritorious Service Credit Union Movement Edmonton; Ukrainian Catholic; recreations: history, hiking, political organising; Home: 7507 Rowland Rd., Edmonton, Alta. T6A 3W4; Office: 403, Bank of Montreal Bldg., 10089 Jasper Ave., Edmonton, Alta. T5J 1V2.

**SAVILE, Douglas B(arton) O(sborne),** B.S.A., M.Sc., Ph.D., D.Sc., F.R.S.C.; mycologist; b. Dublin, Ireland 19 July 1909; s. Hugh Osborne and Kathleen E. (Barton) S.; e. Braidlea Sch., Bristol, Eng.; Weymouth Coll., Weymouth, Eng.; McGill Univ., B.S.A. (Macdonald Coll.) 1933, M.Sc. 1934, D.Sc. (Hon.) 1978; Univ. of Mich., Ph.D. 1939; m. Constance Eleanor, d. late Walter B. Cole, 1939; children: Harold A., Elizabeth (Mrs. D. F. Rhodes); Research Assoc. Emeritus, Can. Dept. Agric. (formerly Princ. Mycologist there); has carried out Bot. and Mycological field work in Newfoundland, N.S., N.B., Quebec, Ontario, Manitoba, Alta., B.C., Keewatin and Franklin; worked in Arctic 1950, '58, '59, '60 and '62; served with R.C.A.F. (Aero-Engn. Br.), 1941–43; author of 'Collection and Care of Botanical Specimens,' 'Arctic Adaptations in Plants,' and some 150 research papers; Fellow, American Association Advanc. of Science (mem. Council 1962, '64, '65); Arctic Inst. N.Am.; mem., Am. Ornithols. Union; Am. Soc. Plant Taxonomists; Candn. Bot. Assn. (Lawson Medal 1976); Candn. Phytopathol. Soc.; Internat. Assn. Plant Taxonomists; Mycological Soc. Am. (Distinguished Mycologist Award 1988); Soc. for Study of Evolution (Ed. Bd. 1959–61); recreations: ornithology, gardening, hist. of science; Home: 357 Hinton Ave., Ottawa, Ont. K1Y 1A6; Office: Biosystematics Research Centre, Central Experimental Farm, Ottawa, Ont. K1A 0C6.

**SAVOIE, Donald Joseph,** B.A., B.Sc.Comm., M.A., D.Phil.; university professor; administrator; b. St. Maurice, N.B. 8 Apr. 1947; s. Adelin François and Léa (Collette) S.; e. Univ. de Moncton, B.A. 1968, B.Sc.Comm. 1969; Univ. of New Brunswick, M.A. 1972; Oxford Univ., D.Phil. 1979; m. Linda d. Lloyd and Corena Dempsey 6 May 1972; children: Julien, Margaux; THE CLÉMENT-CORMIER CHAIR IN ECONOMIC DEVELOPMENT, UNIV. DE MONCTON 1990– ; Prog. Analyst, Govt. of N.B. 1971–74; var. positions, Dept. of Reg. Econ. Expansion, Govt. of Can. 1974–82; Dir., Prov. Analysis, Fed.-Prov. Relns. Office 1981–83; Founder & First Extve. Dir., Candn. Institute for Research on Regional Development (CIRRD) 1983–87; Asst. Secy., Corporate and Public Affairs, Treasury Bd., Govt. of Can. 1987–88; Visiting Prof., Sch. of Public Admin., Carleton Univ. 1988–89; Cons. & Advr. for govt. & priv. assns.; Mem., Economic Counc. of Can. 1990–92; Mem., Steering Ctte. of Canada's Prosperity & Competitiveness planning exercise 1991–92; Mem., Canada's International Trade Advisory Ctte. 1991–93; Mem., Adv. Counc., Inst. for Intergovern. Affairs, Queen's Univ. 1983–88; Prof., Univ. of Moncton 1983–90; Rsch. Ctte., Inst. of Pub. Admin. of Can. 1984–87; Nat. Extve. 1985–87; Chrmn., Ctr. for Food Rsch., Univ. de Moncton 1984–88; Honours: Inaugural recipient, Smiley Prize 1990–92; Officer, Order of Canada 1993; Fellow, Royal Soc. of Canada 1992; Doctorate Honoris Causa in Law, Univ. Ste-Anne 1993; author: 'Federal-Provincial Collaboration' 1981, 'Regional Economic Development' 1986; 'The Politics of Public Spending in Canada' 1990; 'Regional Economic Development: Canada's Search for Solutions,' 2nd edition, (U. of T. Press) 1991; 'Revue sur le développement regional' 1992; co-author 'La lutte au développement: Le cas du Nord-est' 1988; 'Regional Policy in a Changing World' 1990; 'Le défi des pêches au Nouveau-Brunswick,' Moncton, Les Editions d'Acadie, 1992; and num. scholarly articles; editor: 'Canadian Journal of Regional Science' 1985–89; 'The Canadian Economy' 1986; co-editor: 'Essais sur le développement régional' 1985, 'Regional Development' 1988; 'Canadians and Regional Development at Home and in the Third World' 1988; 'Le Nouveau-Brunswick en l'an 2000 / New Brunswick in the year 2000' 1989; 'Innovations & Trends in Management Development 1991; 'Equity and Efficiency in Economic Development' 1992; 'The Maritime Provinces: Looking to the Future' 1993; 'Transition: Taking Power' 1993; Ed. Bd. mem., 'Canadian Public Administration' 1985–89; recreations: golf, reading, travelling; Home: 2380 Whitehaven Cres., Ottawa, Ont. K2B 5H5; Office: CIRRD, Univ. de Moncton, Moncton, N.B. E1A 3E9.

**SAVOIE, Hon. Georges,** B.A., LL.L.; judge; b. Roberval, Lake St. John, Qué. 29 Nov. 1927; s. Dr. Louis-Philippe and Thérèse (Bernier) S.; e. Jésuites Coll. St. Charles Garnier, Québec City B.A. 1948; Laval Univ. LL.L. 1951; m. Gisèle d. late Joliette P. Lemieux, Québec City, Qué. 15 Nov. 1952; children: Louis Philippe, Marc, Claire, Pierre; JUDGE, SUPERIOR COURT OF QUE. since 1978; called to Bar of Qué. 1952; C.R. Q.C. 1968; Jr. Partner, Desruisseaux, Fortin & Savoie 1954–58; private law practice Richmond, Qué. 1958–71; Sr. Partner, Leblanc Barnard & Associates 1971, Barnard, Fournier, Savoie 1972, Fournier, Savoie, Demers & Associates 1974–78; Mayor, Town of Richmond 1967–68; Campaign Mgr. and Legal Advisor Lib. cands. prov. and fed. els. 1963–66; Pres. R.C. Sch. Bd. and Commr. 1960–68; Pres., St. Francis Bar 1968, also served as counsellor and Secy.; R. Catholic; recreations: sailing, jogging, skiing; Home: 1570 Longchamp, Sherbrooke, Qué. J1J 1J1; Office: Court House, 375 King St. W., Sherbrooke, Qué. J1H 6B9.

**SAVOIE, Leonard N.,** B.Sc., M.B.A.; transportation executive; b. Manchester, N.H. 8 Aug. 1928; came to Canada 1928; s. Joseph Peter and Angelina (Desmarais) S.; e. Queen's Univ., B.Sc. (Mech. Engn.) 1952; Univ. of Detroit, M.B.A. 1955; m. Elsie Anne, d. Albert Berscht, 9 June 1951; children: Deborah Anne, Judith Lynn, Andrew Peter; VICE-CHRMN., ALGOMA CENTRAL CORPORATION; Pres., Algoma Steamships Ltd.; Algocen Mines Ltd.; Dir., Casualty Co. of Can.; Dominion of Canada General Insurance Co.; E-L Financial Corp. Ltd.; Empire Life Ins. Co.; Great Lakes Power Ltd.; Newaygo Forest Products Ltd.; with Kelsey-Hayes Canada Ltd. as Indust. Engr., Windsor, Ont. 1952; Mang. Consultant, P.S. Ross & Partners, Toronto 1960; Pres. and Gen. Mgr., Kelsey Hayes Canada Ltd. 1964; mem. Bd. Trustees, Plummer Hospital; Dir., Windsor Indust. Comn. 1969–70; mem. Assn. Prof. Engrs. Ont.; Engn. Inst. Can.; Candn. Chamber Comm.; Young Presidents Organ. Inc.; recreations: golf, bridge, fishing, photography; Clubs: Toronto; Algo; Golf & Country; Railway (Toronto); Home: 19 Atlas St., Sault Ste. Marie, Ont. P6A 4Z2; Office: 289 Bay St., Sault Ste. Marie, Ont. P6A 5P6.

**SAVOIE, Paul,** M.A.; writer; b. Saint-Boniface, Man. 11 Jan. 1946; s. Emile and Edith (Bibeau) S.; e. Univ. of Manitoba M.A. 1969; Carleton Univ. M.A. 1974; Lectr. in French & English Lit., Saint-Boniface College 1969–73; freelance translator 1973–80; Program Offr., Explorations Program, Canada Council 1980–86; Writer-in-Residence, Metro Toronto Reference Library 1988; Translator, Royal Ont. Museum 1989; Program Offr., Ontario Arts Council (Franco-Ontarian Office) 1990; Me., League of Canadian Poets; L'UNEQ; author: 'Contes statiques et névrotiques' 1990 (short stories), 'Amour flou' 1993, 'Shadowing' 1993, Translation of the poetry of Louis Riel 1993, 'Bois brûlé' 1989, 'The Meaning of Gardens' 1987, 'Soleil et ripaille' 1987, 'Acrobats' 1982, 'La maison sans murs' 1979, 'Nahanni' 1976, 'Salamandre' 1974 (poetry), 'A la façon d'un charpentier' 1985 (poetic journal); Home: 203 – 22 Tichester Rd., Toronto, Ont. M5P 1P1.

**SAVOIE-ZAJC, Lorraine,** M.Sc., Ph.D.; university professor; b. Trois-Rivières, Qué. 5 Aug. 1948; d. Paul Emile and Rollande (Bareil) Savoie; e. Syracuse Univ. M.Sc. 1971; Indiana Univ. Ph.D. 1987; m. Mladen d. Branko and Danica Zajc 31 Aug. 1969; one d.: Milena; PROFESSOR OF EDUCATION, UNIV. OF QUEBEC IN HULL 1975– ; Teacher of French as a Second Language to Civil Servants, Canada Civil Service 1971–72, 1974–75; Lecturer, Univ. of Montréal 1972; Media Advisor, Min. of Education Que. 1973–74; currently Head of Masters & Ph.D. Programs in Edn. present univ.; Mem., Comm. des études, UQAH 1991– ; involved in 2 internat. devel. projects: teaching to teachers' trainees (Haiti), teaching faculty members involved in UQAH Master of Edn. Prog. (Brazil); Sec.-Treas., Qualitative Research Assn. 1992– ; Vice-Pres. & Pres., Conseil Interinstitutionnel pour le progrès de la tech. éducative 1992–94; author: 'Les Modèles de changement planifié en éducation' 1993, 1 book chapter and articles dealing with qualitative research methodology, school dropouts, planned change in edn., instructional design; recreations: reading, gardening; Home: 5 Lavandou, Gatineau, Qué. J8T 5M3; Office: C.P. 1250, Succ. B., Hull, Qué. J8X 3X7.

**SAVORY, Roger Mervyn,** Ph.D., F.R.S.C.; educator; b. Peterborough, Eng. 27 Jan. 1925; s. late Henry Savory; e. Oxford Univ. B.A. (Oriental Studies) 1950; Univ. of London Ph.D. (Persian Studies) 1958; m. Kathleen Mary d. late Bertram Plummer 27 March 1951; children: Jill Elizabeth Hawken, Julian Roger; PROF. OF MIDDLE EAST AND ISLAMIC STUDIES, UNIV. OF TORONTO 1976–87; Professor Emeritus 1987– ; mem. Gov. Council of Univ. 1982–87; mem., Exec. Ctte. of Governing Council, 1983–87; Lectr. in Persian Sch. Oriental & African Studies Univ. of London 1950–60; Assoc. Prof. of Near E. Studies present Univ. 1960–61, Assoc. Prof. of Islamic Studies 1961–65, Prof. and Assoc. Chrmn. 1965–68, Prof. and Chrmn. 1968–73, Prof. 1973–76 (dept. change to present name); cross-apptd. to Trinity Coll. Middle E. & Islamic Studies, Religious Studies 1976; Ed. Asst. New Ed. 'Encyclopaedia of Islam' 1954–56, Ed. Secy. Eng. Ed. 1956–60; author 'Iran Under the Safavids' 1980 (Persian tr. by Ahmad Sabā 'Īrān-e 'Asr-e Safavī' Tehran 1984); 'Studies on the History of Safavid Iran' 1987; co-author 'Persia in Islamic Times: A Practical Bibliography of Its History, Culture and Language' 1964; Ed. 'Introduction to Islamic Civilisation' 1976; transl. 'The History of Shah ᶜAbbas the Great (Tārīk-e ᶜĀlamārā-ye ᶜAbbāsī)' 2 vols. 1978; co-ed. 'The Persian Gulf States: A General Survey' 1980; Gen. Ed. 'Logos Islamikos: Studia Islamica in honorem Georgii Michaelis Wickens' 1984; Gen. Ed. (one of three) 'Studies in Middle Eastern History' 9 vols. of Oxford series 1985– ; co-editor, 'The Islamic World: From Classical to Modern Times' (Essays in Honor of Bernard Lewis) 1989; numerous book chapters, contribs. to encyclopaedias, articles, reviews; served with Brit. Army and Foreign Service (in Iran 1945–47) 1943–47; Dir. Middle E. Studies Assn. N. Am. 1969–71 (Vice-Pres. 1973–74); 2nd Vice-Pres. Huguenot Soc. of Canada, 1983–85; Pres. Oriental Club of Toronto 1968–69, 1983–84; mem. Extve. Ctte., Prayer Book Soc. of Canada 1986–90; mem. Extve. Ctte., Prayer Book Soc. of Canada (Toronto Branch) 1991– ; Fellow, Trinity College; Anglican; recreation: gardening; Home: 55 Mason Blvd., Toronto, Ont. M5M 3C6; Office: Trinity College, Toronto, Ont. M5S 1H8.

**SAWATSKY, John,** B.A.; journalist; b. Winkler, Man. 8 May 1948; s. Jacob and Katharine (Wiebe) S.; e. Simon Fraser Univ., B.A. (Hon.) 1974; PROF. ADJUNCT, CARLETON UNIV. 1990– ; Reporter, 'Vancouver Sun' 1970–74; Ottawa Corr. 1975–79; Rsch. Co-ord., B.C. Petroleum Corp. 1974–75; Mem., Parl. Press Gall. 1975– ; freelance journalist & book writer 1979– ; Max Bell Prof. of Journalism, Univ. of Regina 1984–85; Sess. Lectr., Carleton Univ. 1985–90; Founding Mem., Ctr. for Investigative Journalism; Michener Award for Public Serv. Journalism 1976; Outstanding Alumni Award for Profl. Achievement, Simon Fraser Univ. 1985; author: 'Men in the Shadows' 1980; 'For Services Rendered' 1982 (Best non-fiction paperback of the year, 1983); 'Gouzenko: The Untold Story' 1984; 'The Insiders' 1987; 'Mulroney: The Politics of Ambition' 1991; recreations: bicycling; Clubs: Ottawa Bicycle, Cyclists Touring; Home: 475 Bay St., Ottawa, Ont. K1R 6A7.

**SAWCHUK, Oryst Hary,** M.Arch.; architect; community planner; b. Winnipeg, Man. 23 Feb. 1928; s. Michael and Sophia (Demkiw) S.; e. Univ. of Man. B.Arch. 1954, M.Arch. 1955; one s.: Sergei Harry; PARTNER, SAWCHUK PEACH ASSOCIATES 1957– ; Planning Adv. Sudbury Planning Ctte. 1955–59; Louis Fabbro Arch. 1955–57; mem. Adv. Bd. Laurentian Univ. Museum & Art Centre; Prov. N. Devel. Council Sudbury 1987–91; Mem. Bd., National Shevchenko Musical Ensemble Guild of Canada; Group exhns. include: Synergos-2, Art by Ukrainian Manitoban Artists, by Manitoba Ukrainian Arts Council, the University of Winnipeg, Manitoba 1991; contemp. visual art of Sudbury, Gallery North, Ontario North Now, Ontario Place 1990; Exhib. of Ukrainian Candian Artists, Artist Union of Ukraine, Kiev 1985; NORART Exhib. of Northern Ont. Art Laurentian Univ. Museum and Art Centre 1982, 1980, 1979; SCA Soc. of Candn. Artists, McDowell Gal. (Toronto) 1978; Gallerie Signal (Montreal) 1977; Danelli Gallery (Toronto) 1976; Scarborough Civic Centre 1975; O.I.S.E. (Toronto) 1975; open juried show Eton's Gallery (Toronto) 1971, 1970; Merton Gallery (Toronto); NOAA Juried shows 1969–73; solo exhibs.: Laurentian Univ., Museum & Arts Centre 1981, 1976, 1972; Danelli Gallery (Toronto) 1976; Evans Gallery (Toronto) 1974; Sudbury Theatre Centre 1973; publications: Art Magazine Vol. 4, No. 12, Fall 1972; recipient CMHC Fellowship in Community Planning 1954; Ont. Profl. Planning Inst. Award for Service 1986; Pres. Sudbury Craft & Arts Found. 1980–81; mem. Royal Arch. Inst. Can.; Ont. Assn. Archs. (Chrmn. N. Ont. Chapter 1970–73); Town Planning Inst. Can. (Chrmn. N. Ont. Chapter 1970–71); Candn. Inst. of Planners; Soc. Candn. Artists; N. Ont. Artists Assn.; Ont. Profl. Planning Inst.; Assn. Cons. Planners; Pres. Sudbury & Dist. C. of C. 1987–88; Dir. Ont. C. of C. 1986–88; Office: 198 Oak St., Sudbury, Ont. P3C 1M7.

**SAWICKI, The Honourable Joan,** B.Ed.; speaker of the legislative assembly; b. Vancouver, B.C. 18 Sept. 1945; d. John and Genowefa Jean (Kopec) S.; e. Skeena Jr. Sr. H.S.; Univ. of Victoria B.Ed. 1968; m. G. Gary s. William and Velma Runka 21 Feb. 1978; SPEAKER OF THE LEGISLATIVE ASSEMBLY, PROV. OF B.C. 1991– ; Scientific Ed., Canada Dept. of Agric. 1970; Secondary Sch. Teacher 1968–69, 1971–72; Land Use Consultant 1973–91; Business Partner, G.G. Runka Land Sense Ltd. 1978–91; Council Mem., City of Burnaby; Mem., Greater Vanc. Reg. Dist. Waste & Environ. Ctte. & Metro. Bd. of Health 1987–90; Dir., Burnaby Family YMCA 1984–87; Burnaby Hosp. Bd. 1987–90; Burnaby Multicultural Soc. 1985–91; recreations: curling, hiking, backpacking; Home: Burnaby, B.C.; Office: Parliament Bldgs., Victoria, B.C. V8V 1X4.

**SAWICKY, Boris,** B.Sc., M.B.A.; energy executive; b. W. Germany 3 Jan. 1947; s. Walter and Helen (Macalap) S.; e. Univ. of Waterloo, B.Sc. 1970; State Univ. of N.Y. at Buffalo, M.B.A. 1977; m. Linda d. Harry and Marion Enns 1 May 1970; children: Craig Steven, Jennifer Christine; Pres., Moli Energy (1990) Limited 1986; various fin. & prod. positions, Union Carbide Canada Ltd./Corp. (Ont./Tennessee) 1970–86; Past Bd. Mem., Welland Co. Hosp. Bd.; Treas./Dir., YMCA; United Way of Welland, Pt. Colborne & Adv. Bd. of J.A. of Niagara Reg.; Home: 12524 – 251st St., Maple Ridge, B.C. V2X 8E4.

**SAWYER, John Arthur,** B.Com., M.A.; Ph.D.; economist; b. Toronto, Ont. 24 Aug. 1924; s. Arthur J. and Bessie S. (Livingstone) S.; e. Oakwood Coll. Inst., Toronto, 1943; Univ. of Toronto, B.Com. 1947, M.A. 1948; University of Chicago, Ph.D. 1966; m. Virginia Kivley, d. late George M. Peterson, 30 Dec. 1952; three s. Peter Douglas, Robert James, Alan Bruce; EMERITUS PROF. OF ECONOMICS, UNIV. OF TORONTO 1990– ; Prof., Faculty of Mngmt. 1965–90; Prof., Dept. Econ. 1969–90; Chrmn., Commerce Programs, Faculty of Arts and Sci. 1983–85; Assoc. Dean (undergraduate), Faculty of Management, 1983–86; Acting Dean, Faculty of Management 1985–86; Dir., Inst. Policy Analysis 1975–80; Associate Dean, School of Graduate Studies 1970–72; Lectr., Dept. of Pol. Econ., Univ. of Alta., 1949–50; Asst. Prof., Dept. of Econ., Royal Mil. Coll. of Can., 1951–53; Econ., Dom. Bureau of Stat., Ottawa, 1953–60; joined present Univ. as Asst. Prof. 1960; apptd. Assoc. Prof. 1961; mem., Candn. Econ. Assn.; Am. Econ. Assn.; mem. Bd. of Dir., Data Clearing House for Soc. Sciences in Canada, 1973–78; Harold Innis Fdn., 1977–80; author: 'Macroeconomics: Theory and Policy in the Canadian Economy' 1975; 'Macroeconomic Theory: Keynesian and Neo-Walrasian Models' 1989; co-author: 'The TRACE Econometric Model of the Canadian Economy' 1972; Editor and Contributor: 'Modelling the International Transmission Mechanism' 1979; recreations: photography, golf; Home: 118 Betty Ann Dr., Willowdale, Ont. M2N 1X4.

**SAXE, Henry,** O.C., R.C.A.; sculptor; b. Montreal, Que. 24 Sept. 1937; s. Joseph Peter and Rachel (Magil) S.; e. Ecole des Beaux-Arts Montreal; m. Jeanne d. Col. James and Margaret Harrison; children: Sophie, Louis; rep. Can. Paris Bienale 1968; Venice Bienale 1978; Internat. Sculpture Middleheim 1971; solo exhns. incl. Nat. Gallery Can. 1968; Olga Korper Toronto; Gilles Gheerbrant Eur.; Esperanza Montreal; retrospective: Musée d'Art Contemporain, Montreal 1994; recipient numerous Can. Council Awards; Lynch Staunton Award 1984; Officer of the Order of Canada 1988; Commemorative Medal, 125th Anniversary of Candn. Confedn. 1992; Address: Tamworth, Ont. K0K 3G0.

**SAXE, Stewart D.,** B.A., LL.B.; lawyer; b. Toronto, Ont. 11 March 1947; s. Percy and Bernice (Cohen) S.; e. Univ. of Waterloo B.A. 1969; Osgoode Hall Law Sch. LL.B. 1973; m. Dianne d. Dr. Morton and Gloria Shulman 10 June 1973; children: Rebecca, David, Shoshanna; INTERNATIONAL PARTNER, BAKER & MCKENZIE 1983– ; Sr. Solicitor, Ontario Labour Relations Bd. 1975–76; Dir. 1976–79; joined Baker & McKenzie 1979; Managing Partner 1988–91; Mem. Policy Ctte. 1989–91, 1993– ; Mem., Global Profl. Devel. Ctte. 1990–94; Dir., Deprenyl Rsch. Limited 1987– ; Deprenyl Animal Health Ltd. 1990– ; taught Industrial Relns., McMaster Univ. 1977–78; Mem., Personnel Assn. of Ont. (awarded desig. of Cert. Human Resources Profl.); author: 'Ontario Employment Law Handbook' 1st ed. 1982, rev. ed. 1986, 2nd ed. 1989, 3rd ed. 1992; co-author: 'Pay Equity Handbook' 1st ed. 1987, rev. ed. 1992, 'Employment Contracts Handbook' 1990; editor: 'On Strike, and How to Prevent Getting There' 1993; Home: 248 Russell Hill Rd., Toronto, Ont. M4V 2T2; Office: 112 Adelaide St. E., Toronto, Ont. M5C 1K9.

**SAXENA, Praveen,** M.Phil, Ph.D.; university professor; b. Meerut, India 16 March 1957; s. Anand Swarup and Sarla S.; e. Delhi Univ. M.Phil. 1979, Ph.D. 1983; Univ. of Sask. postdoctoral rsch. 1984–88; m. Sangeeta d. Mathuresh and Madhuri 2 March 1982; children: Swati, Shivam; PROFESSOR OF HORTICULTURAL BIOTECHNOLOGY, UNIV. OF GUELPH 1989– ; Scientist, Dept. of Vegetable Crops, Univ. of Florida; discovered 'super seed' technology (an economical way to mass propagate plants including new varieties with increased disease resistance & environmental durability); invited chair, several sessions of internat. rsch. meetings; Mem., Internat. Assn. of Plant Tissue Culturists; Am. Soc. of Horticultural Sci.; author of 53 rsch. papers in internat. journals; Home: 3 Christopher Court, Guelph, Ont. N1G 4A1; Office: Univ. of Guelph., Guelph, Ont. N1G 2W1.

**SAYEED, Khalid Bin,** M.A., Ph.D.; educator; b. Bellary, India 20 Nov. 1926; s. Abdul Rahman and Sayeeda S.; e. Univ. of Madras, B.A. 1947, M.A. 1948; London Sch. of Econ. & Pol. Sci., B.Sc. 1951; McGill Univ., Ph.D. 1956; m. Janet d. Holly and Ruth Callender May 1954; children: Adil, Miriam; PROFESSOR EMERITUS, QUEEN'S UNIVERSITY 1993; Lectr. in Pol. Sci. Univ. of Dacca 1951–53; Rsch. Assoc. Inst. Islamic Studies, McGill Univ. 1957–59, Visiting Prof. of Pol. Sci. 1967–69; Asst. Prof. of Pol. Sci., Univ. of N.B. 1959–61; Asst. Prof. Queen's Univ. 1961, Assoc. Prof. 1964, Prof. of Political Studies 1966–93; Visiting Assoc. Prof. of Pol. Sci., Duke Univ. 1965; Visiting Rsch. Prof. Am. Inst. Islamic Affairs, Am. Univ. 1984–85; UN Cons. to Mgmt. Training Centre Govt. Iran 1970–71; UN Pub. Adm. Adv. to Plan Orgn. 1971; author: 'Pakistan the Formative Phase' 1961, 2nd ed. 1968; 'The Political System of Pakistan' 1967; 'Politics in Pakistan: The Nature and Direction of Change' 1980; 'Western Dominance and Political Islam: Challenge and Response' 1994; mem. Coll. of Fellows Internat. Assn. Middle E. Studies; Candn. Pol. Sci. Assn.; Middle E. Studies Assn.; Indian Inst. Pub. Adm.; Assn. Muslim Social Sci's; Muslim; recreation: tennis; Home: 170 Fairway Hills Cres., Kingston, Ont. K7M 2B4; Office: Kingston, Ont. K7L 3N6.

**SAYER, Michael,** B.Sc., Ph.D., P.Eng., FRSC; university professor; b. Newport, U.K. 6 Nov. 1935; s. Charles Claude and Elizabeth Mary (Southcott) S.; e. Univ. of Birmingham B.Sc. 1957; Univ. of Hull Ph.D. 1961; m. Anne d. Reginald and Patricia Rogers 27 Aug. 1960; children: Jane, Suzanne, Andrew, Christopher; PROF. OF PHYSICS, QUEEN'S UNIV. 1962– and PROF. OF MATERIALS & METALLURGICAL ENGINEERING, QUEEN'S UNIV. 1990– ; postdoctoral fellow, U.B.C. 1960–62; Asst., Assoc., Full Prof., Queen's Univ. 1962– ; Head, Physics 1977–82; Assoc. Dean (Rsch.) 1984–87; Visiting Prof., Trent Univ. 1965–66; Visiting Fellow, Sheffield Univ. 1972–73; Dir. of Rsch., Almax Indus. 1986–87; Editor, 'Can. Ceramics Q.' 1986– ; Mem., Candn. Engr. Accreditation Bd. 1987– ; Ministers Nat. Adv. Council, Canmet, Ontario Ctr. for Materials Rsch.; Fellow, Royal Soc. of Can.; Silver Award for Tech. Transfer, Canada Awards for Bus. Exellence 1986; Hon. Mem., Candn. Ceramic Soc.; Roman Catholic; Mem., Candn. Ceramic Soc. (Pres. 1986–87; Editor-in-Chief 1986– ; Fellow 1993); Am. Ceramic Soc.; Materials Rsch. Soc.; author of over 120 journal articles, 40 conf. presentations, 5 patents and 2 book chapters; recreations: walking, sailing; Home: 97 Yonge St., Kingston, Ont. K7M 1E4; Office: Kingston, Ont. K7L 3N6.

**SAYWELL, John Tupper,** M.A., Ph.D.; writer and university professor; b. Weyburn, Sask. 3 Apr. 1929; s. John Ferdinand Tupper and Vera Margaret S.; e. Victoria Coll., Univ. of B.C., B.A., M.A.; Harvard Univ. Ph.D.; children: Elizabeth Lynn, John Stephen Tupper, Graham Anthony Tupper; UNIVERSITY PROFESSOR and Professor of History and Environmental Studies, York University; Lect., Univ. of Toronto 1954, Asst. Prof. 1957, Assoc. Prof. 1962; Prof. and Dean, York Univ. 1963–73; Editor, Candn. Hist. Review 1957–63; Candn. Annual Review 1960–79; author 'The Office of Lieut.-Gov.' 1957, 1986; 'The Canadian Journal of Lady Aberdeen' 1960: 'Lord Minto's Canadian Papers' 1983; 'Making the Law' 1991; 'Just Call Me Mitch' 1991; 'Parliament and Politics' (column) Candn. Annual Review 1960–79; numerous mag. and newspaper articles and book reviews; mem., Candn. Hist. Assn.; Candn. Pol. Sc. Assn.; Home: 158 Fulton Ave., Toronto, Ont. M4K 1Y3; Office: 4700 Keele St., North York, Ont. M3J 1P3.

**SAYWELL, Shelley Jayne,** B.A.; documentary filmaker; writer; b. Ottawa, Ont. 5 July 1955; d. William George and Jane S.; e. Candn. Acad. Kobe, Japan; Univ. of Toronto, Ont. B.A. 1976; began documentary film and TV career 1978; Researcher, 'Vietnam: The Ten Thousand Day War' CBC-Thames TV, Researcher/Assoc. Writer book of same title by Michael Maclear 1981; Producer CBC Series 'Going Great'; Dir., Writer and Co-producer 'Shahira' documentary TVO, Channel 4 and A & E; Dir. & Producer 'The Greenpeace Years' CBC, NFB; Dir., Producer & Writer, 'No Man's Land' CBC 1994; recipient Candn. Council Grant 1983; Candn. Acad. Film & TV Gemini nomination Best Dir. Documentary 1988; Cert. Outstanding Achievement Women in Film Festival L.A. 1988; Red Ribbon Award Am. Film & Video Festival 1989; author 'Women in War: First Hand Accounts from World War II to El Salvador' 1985; contbg. author 'Ourselves Among Others' 1987; Address: #367 – 238 Davenport Rd., Toronto, Ont. M5R 1J6.

**SAYWELL, William George Gabriel,** B.A., M.A., Ph.D.; administrator; b. Regina, Sask. 1 Dec. 1936; s. John Ferdinand Tupper and Vera Marguerite (Sayles) S.; e. Univ. of Toronto B.A. Modern Hist. 1960, M.A. 1961, Ph.D. Chinese Hist. 1968; m. Helen Jane d. Charles and Verna Larmer; children: Shelley Jayne, William James Tupper, Patricia Lynn; PRESIDENT & C.E.O., ASIA PACIFIC FOUNDATION OF CANADA 1993– ; Prof., Dept. of East Asian Studies, Univ. of Toronto; Chrmn. Dept. of East Asian Studies there 1971–76; Dir. Univ. of Toronto/York Univ. Centre on Modern East Asia 1974–75; Principal Innis Coll. Univ. of Toronto 1976–79; Vice-Provost Univ. of Toronto 1979–83; Pres. and Vice-Chancellor, Simon Fraser Univ. 1983–93; Sinologist and First Sec. Candn. Embassy, Beijing 1972–73; author book and articles on Chinese hist. and current Chinese foreign and mil. affairs; Chrmn., Candn. Nat. Ctte. Pacific Economic Co-operation; Bd. of Westcoast Energy Inc.; Spar Aerospace Ltd.; awarded Woodrow Wilson Fellowship 1960–61; Canada Counc. 1961–62, 1968–69; Foreign Area Fellowship, Ford Found. 1967–68; recreation: tennis; Address: 2104 – 738 Broughton St., Vancouver, B.C. V6G 3A7.

**SAZIO, Ralph J.,** B.S., M.A.; business executive; b. South Orange, N.J. 22 July 1922; s. Anthony D. and Margaret (Aurillo) S.; e. United States Air Corp. 1943–46; Coll. of William & Mary, Williamsburg B.S. 1948; Columbia Univ. M.A. 1949; C.L.U. 1952; m. Rose L. d. Virginio and Rose Matthews 28 Dec. 1946; children: Mark, Margaret Giroux; PRESIDENT, RALPH J. SAZIO LTD. 1964– ; Teacher, McKeesport (Pa.) High Sch. 1949–50; Life Underwriter 1950–63; Player and Ass. Coach Hamilton Tiger-Cats 1950–52, Asst. Coach 1953–62, Head Coach 1963–67, Gen. Mgr. 1968–72, Pres. and Gen. Mgr. 1973–81; Pres., Toronto Argonauts Football Club Inc. 1981–90; named Coach of Year Candn. Football League 1964; Hall of Fame (Athletic) William and Mary; Pres. Candn. Football League 1975, Chrmn. of Bd. of Govs. 1983; Candn. Football League Hall of Fame (Builder) 1988; Pres., Cath. Children's Aid Soc. Hamilton; Alcohol Rsch. Found. Hamilton; Social Services Council Hamilton; Dir., Hamilton YMCA; Hamilton CYO (Pres.); Gov., Variety Village; Laidlaw Transp. Ltd.; recreations: tennis, golf; Clubs: Hamilton Golf & Country; Burlington Rackets; Home: 876 Glenwood Ave., Burlington, Ont. L7T 2J9.

**SCACE, Arthur R.A.,** Q.C., B.A., LL.B., LL.D.; lawyer; b. Toronto, Ont. 22 July 1938; s. Arthur L. and Jean (Simmons) S.; e. Univ. of Toronto Schs. 1956; Univ. of Toronto B.A. 1960; Harvard Univ. M.A. 1961; Oxford Univ. B.A. 1963; Osgoode Hall Law Sch. LL.B. 1965; m. Susan M. d. Gordon E. and Kathryn M. Kernohan 15 Aug. 1963; children: Jennifer C., A. Patrick G.; PARTNER, McCARTHY TÉTRAULT 1972– , joined firm in 1967; Dir., The Canada Life Assurance Co.; N.M. Davis Corp. Ltd.; National Westminster Bank of Can.; Pres. and Dir., Henry White Kinnear Foundation; Dir., AWB Charitable Foundation; Ennisteel Corp.; Sceptre Investment Counsel Ltd.; Garbell Holdings Ltd.; Gardiner Group Capital Ltd.; Candn. Sec. Rhodes Trust; Bencher, Law Soc. Upper Can.; author 'Income Tax Law of Canada' 1983, 5th Ed.; Hon. LL.D.: Law Society of Upper Canada 1991, York Univ. 1993; Dir., Canadian Opera Company; Clubs: Toronto; Toronto Golf; Harvard Club of New York; Badminton & Racquet, Tadenac, Toronto; Cambridge; Home: 130 Lawrence Cr., Toronto, Ont. M4N 1N6; Office: Suite 4700, Toronto Dominion Bank Tower, Toronto-Dominion Centre, Toronto, Ont. M5K 1E6.

**SCACE, Robert Chaston,** M.A., Ph.D.; consulting geographer; b. Aberdeen, Scotland 20 Oct. 1942; s. Norman Chaston and Isobel (Robertson) S.; e. Aberdeen Grammar Sch. 1960; Aberdeen Univ., M.A. (Hons.) 1964; Univ. of Calgary, M.A. 1968, Ph.D. 1972; m. Margaret d. Ken and Doris Wright 9 June 1973; one d.: Shauna Ruth; MANAGER OF CALGARY OPERATIONS, SENTAR CONSULTANTS LTD. 1990– ; Associate, Heritage Resources Centre, Univ. of Waterloo 1986– ; President, Scace & Associates Ltd. 1973– , consulting geographers; Principal (Mgr., Resources & Planning) Reid Crowther & Partners Ltd. 1983–86 (joined co. 1978); engaged in broad range of studies incl. dams and reservoirs, heritage, conserv. & recreation areas, mines, power plants, Indian Reserves, river basins, urban areas, etc.; major projects incl. Slave River Hydro Feasibility Study 1980–82, Sarcee Trail Planning Project 1983–85, Canadian Assembly Project 1983–87, Dinosaur World Heritage Site Planning Project 1984– , Peace River Sub-basin Water Management Project 1986–90; key planning roles in several major confs.; Dir. (Alta.) Candn. Environment Industry Assn. 1989–92; Unaffiliated mem., Public Adv. Ctte., Environ. Counc. of Alta. 1976–91; mem., CBC Adv. Ctte. on Sci. & Tech. 1978–82; Nat. & Prov. Parks Assn. of Can., now Candn. Parks and Wilderness Soc. (Bd. of Trustees 1974–79, Vice Pres. 1977–79) 1965– ; J.B. Harkin Conserv. Award Ctte. (Chrmn.) 1977–87; Candn. Assn. of Geographers (Councillor 1983–86) 1964– ; Arctic Inst. of North Am.; Internat. Union for Conserv. of Nature; Can. Water Resources Assn.; Royal Geograph. Soc. (Fellow); author/editor of numerous documents, reports & papers; co-editor & contbr. to numerous books incl. 'Heritage for Tomorrow, The Canadian Assembly Project' 5 vols 1986–1987; Govt. of Can., Nat. Parks Centennial Award 1985; Killam Scholar 1967–68, 1968–69, 1969–70; recreations: canoeing, skiing; Home: 2416 Sandhurst Ave. S.W., Calgary, Alta. T3C 2M6; Office: 1122 4th St. S.W., Suite 200, Calgary, Alta. T2E 1M1.

**SCALES, Alan K.,** Q.C., LL.D.; lawyer; b. Summerside, P.E.I. 16 Oct. 1934; s. Austin Alexander and Lillian (Dobson) S.; e. Univ. of W. Ont. Honours Business Adm. 1958; Dalhousie Univ. LL.B. 1961; m. Patricia K. d. late Dr. Harold Shaw 6 July 1963; children: Brian Geoffrey, Gary Shaw, Carolyn Patricia; SR. PARTNER, STEWART McKELVEY STIRLING SCALES; Dir., The Island Telephone Co. Ltd.; Chrmn., Bd. of Dirs., Marine Atlantic Inc.; called to Bar of P.E.I. 1961; cr. Q.C. 1973; P. Conservative; United Church; recreations: golf, tennis; Home: 41 Queen Elizabeth Dr., Charlottetown, P.E.I. C1A 3A8; Office: 65 Grafton St., Charlottetown, P.E.I. C1A 8B9.

**SCANLON, John Michael,** B.A.; executive; b. Toronto, Ont. 22 May 1953; e. Univ. of Toronto Victoria College B.A. 1975; m. Betti Lou 1983; children: Amanda, Nicholas; joined Pitney Bowes Leasing 1980, Controller 1983, Dir. Finance & Planning 1986, Vice Pres., Finance 1989; mem. Financial Extves. Institute; Board of Trade; recreations: golf, tennis, skiing; Home: R.R. 3, Caledon, Ont. L0N 1C0.

**SCANLON, Kevin Michael;** journalist, writer; b. Cork, Ireland 15 Dec. 1949; s. Michael John Barry and Dorothy (Hall) S.; e. Emery Collegiate 1968; m. Trish Ann d. Joseph and Teresa Worron 1 March 1978; one s.: Kevin Michael, Jr.; SPORTS EDITOR/COLUMNIST, FINANCIAL POST & FIELD CORRESPONDENT, EQUINOX MAGAZINE 1994– ; Reporter, Welland Tribune 1969; Stratford Beacon-Herald 1970–72; Toronto Sun 1973–79; Feature Writer, Toronto Star 1979–85; Assoc. Ed., Maclean's Magazine 1986–88; Deputy Sports Editor/Columnist, Financial Post & Field Correspondent, Equinox Magazine 1989–94; Adv. Bd. (Journalism), Centennial College 1982–90, 1992– ; Mem., Actra (Writer's Guild); Nominee, Gemini Award 1988 (best dramatic writing); Winner, Hugh Smythe Award for Science Writing 1991; Winner, Candn. Science Writers' Assn. Award 1992 (Magazines - Science and Society) and Co-winner (Magazines - Science and Technology); co-author (with Denis Gibson): 'Midnight in Morocco' episode of 'Adderly' TV show broadcast on CBS & Global 1987; recreations: ice hockey, photography; Home: 20 Brockton Ave., Unit 17, Toronto, Ont. M6K 1S5; Office: 333 King St. E., Toronto, Ont. M5A 3X5.

**SCARFE, Alan;** actor; director; writer; b. Harpenden, Eng. 8 June 1946; s. Neville Vincent and Gladys Ellen (Hunt) S.; e. London Acad. Music & Dramatic Art, Eng. 1966; m. Barbara March d. Edward and Irene Maczka 27 Aug. 1979; children: Jonathan, Antonia; Stage Mgr. Barkerville Festival 1962; played Mark Antony 'Julius Caesar' Vancouver Playhouse 1964; Coventry, London, Liverpool 1966–68, began directing 1967; 'Ecstasy of Rita Joe' Nat. Arts Centre Ottawa opening 1969; Shaw Festival 1970; King Lear and Tony Lumpkin, Stratford Festival 1972; Petruchio, Stratford Festival Tour Denmark, Holland, Poland and USSR 1973; Shaw Festival tour Maritimes, 'Devil's Disciple' 1974; Stratford Festival 1976–79: Othello, John Barrymore, Dir. Beckett's 'Not I'; recent films incl. 'Deserters' 1983 (Genie Nomination Best Actor 1983), 'The Wars' 1983, 'The Bay Boy' (Genie Award Best Supporting Actor 1984), 'Joshua Then and Now' 1985; 'Overnight' (Genie Nomination Best Actor 1985); 'Iron Eagle II' 1987; 'Kingsgate' 1988; 'Double Impact' 1990; 'Lethal Weapon 3' 1991; 'The Portrait' 1992; Dir. 'Romeo and Juliet' Neptune Theatre, Halifax 1983; 'The Homecoming' CentreStage, Toronto 1984; numerous radio and TV credits: Duke 'Measure for Measure' Stratford Festival 1985; Musical Debut 'Africanis Instructus' Music Theatre Group New York 1986 and tour to Madrid, Paris, Lille; in New York and Los Angeles: Playwrights Horizons, N.Y. Theatre Workshop, N.Y. Shakespeare Festival; 'Macbeth' on Broadway; Writer, new film work 'The Tenders,' 'Who Killed Kit Marlowe'; 1992 season Stratford, Ontario, Prospero, Uncle Vanya, Eddie 'Entertaining Mr. Sloane'; recipient Queen's Birthday Medal 1977; biographee, Who's Who in America; nominated: Dora Award Best Direction 1981 for 'Last Meeting of the Knights of the White Magnolia'; ACTRA Award 'Certain Practices' CBC 1980, 'Christopher Marlowe' CBC Radio 1972; Assoc. Dir. Stratford Festival 1976–77; mem. Bd. Preston Jones Play Symposium, Houston, Texas; mem. Candn., Brit., and U.S. Actors' Equity Assns.; Alliance Candn. Cinema, TV & Radio Artists; Screen Actors Guild; Am. Fedn. of TV and Radio Artists; Acad. Candn. Cinema; Office: Q.F. Productions Inc., Vancouver, B.C. and Los Angeles; Select Artists Representatives, New York, N.Y.; Judy Schoen and Assoc., L.A.; Hodgson and Co., Vancouver; Address: 21452 Encina Rd., Topanga, CA 90290.

**SCARFE, Brian Leslie,** B.A., B.Phil., D.Phil.; economist; consultant; educator; b. England 2 Feb. 1943; s. Neville Vincent and Gladys Ellen (Hunt) S.; e. Univ. of B.C., B.A. 1963; Oxford Univ. (Rhodes Scholar B.C. 1963) B.Phil. 1965, D.Phil. 1970; children: Andrew Gregory, Adam Christian, Timothy Christopher, Katherine Margaret; PROFESSOR OF ECONOMICS, UNIV. OF REGINA 1988– ; Asst./Assoc. Prof. Univ. of Manitoba 1968–77 (and Acting Head Dept. of Economics 1976–77); Prof. and Chrmn., Dept. of Economics, Univ. of Alta. 1977–87; Assoc. Vice-Pres. (Rsch.), Univ. of Alta. 1987–88; Vice-Pres. (Academic) Univ. of Regina 1988–93; Research Dir., Western Centre for Econ. Rsch. 1987–88; Sr. Rsch. Economist, Prices and Incomes Comn., Ottawa 1970–71; Cons. Bank of Canada 1974; Alta. Personnel Admin. 1984–88; Petroleum Monitoring Agency 1985–88; Instr. Banff Sch. of Advanced Mgmt. 1982– ; Senior Univ. Administrators Course 1991–92; mem. Bd. of Mngmt., TRIUMF 1989–93; Pres., Candn. Assn. of Univ. Rsch. Administrators 1991–92; author: 'Price Determination and the Process of Inflation in Canada' 1972; 'Cycles, Growth and Inflation: A Survey of Contemporary Macrodynamics' 1977; 'Financing Oil and Gas Exploration and Development Activity' 1984; 'The Accommodation, Food and Beverage Industry in Canada' 1987; co-editor: 'The Alberta Heritage Savings Trust Fund' 1980; 'The Collected Economic Papers of C.L. Barber' 1982; numerous jour. articles, scholarly papers, book chapters, book reviews, rsch. monographs on macroeconomics, monetary theory and energy economics; recreations: skiing, climbing, water sports, music; Home: 1078 Quailwood Place, Victoria, B.C. V8X 4P2; Office: c/o President's Office, Univ. of Regina, Regina, Sask. S4S 0A2.

**SCARFE, Jeremy C.,** B.A.; communication services executive; b. London, Eng. 15 May 1936; s. late Helen Cameron (Wallace) S.; e. Trinity Coll. Sch. Port Hope, Ont., Univ. of N.B., B.A. 1960; m. Janet d. John B. (Lt. Gov. of N.B.) and Marion McNair 15 June 1963; children: John-Jeremy, Peter, Julian; PRES., CREATIVE DIRECTION GROUP INC. 1977– ; Advertising Mgr. Scarfe & Co. Ltd. 1960–63; Acct. Exec.: Richard Meltzer Advertising (San Francisco) 1963–65; Bradley-Vale Advertising 1965–67; Vice Pres. Creative Dir. MacLaren Advertising 1967–77; Dir., C.M. Hincks Inst.; Camphill Found.; Candn. Acid Rain Found.; Adv. Bd. Candn. Assoc. of Psychoanalytic Psychotherapists for Children; Muskoka Lakes Assn.; Past Dir.: Toronto Free Theatre; Extend-A-Family; Cedar Highland Ski Club: Home: 93 Lonsdale Rd., Toronto, Ont. M4V 1W4; Office: 99 Atlantic Ave., Suite 415, Toronto, Ont. M6K 3J8.

**SCARGILL, Matthew Harry,** B.A., Ph.D., F.R.S.C.; educator; b. Barnsley, Yorks. Eng. 19 Sept. 1916; s. late Matthew and Emma (Lister) S.; e. Wheelwright Grammar Sch. Eng.; Univ. of Leeds B.A. 1938, Ph.D. 1940; m. Eileen Mildred d. late Harry Tomlin, Summerland, B.C. 1948; Prof. of Linguistics, Univ. of Victoria 1964–81; Dean of Grad. Studies 1968–70; Dir. Lexicographical

Centre since 1964; rec'd Queen's Silver Jubilee Medal 1978; author 'Modern Canadian English Usage' 1974; 'Short History of Canadian English' 1977; 'Dictionary of Canadianisms' 1967; 'An English Handbook,' 1982; Home: 1704 Monteith, Victoria, B.C. V8R 5X3; Office: c/o Sono Nis Press, 1745 Blenshard St., Victoria, B.C. V8W 2J8.

**SCHABAS, Ann H.,** B.A., B.L.S., M.A., A.M., Ph.D.; b. Toronto, Ont. 14 May 1926; d. Barker and Margaret Adele (Keeling) Fairley; e. Univ. of Toronto, B.A. 1948, B.L.S. 1964; Smith College, A.M. 1949; Univ. of London, M.A. 1970, Ph.D. 1979; m. Ezra s. Hyman and Minnie S. 28 Oct. 1949; children: William, Richard, Margaret, Michael, Paul; PROFESSOR EMERITUS, UNIV. OF TORONTO; Dean, Fac. of Library & Inform. Sci., Univ. of Toronto 1984–90; Profl. Librarian 1964–66; Prof., Lib. Sci., Univ. of Toronto 1966–91; Cons., British Library; Communications Can.; TVOntario; Pres., Indexing and Abstracting Soc. of Can. 1984–86; Home: 809 – 61 St. Clair Ave. W., Toronto, Ont. M4V 2Y8.

**SCHABAS, Ezra,** B.S., M.A.; educator; musician; b. New York, N.Y. 24 Apl. 1924; s. Hyman and Minnie (Anker) S.; e. Juilliard Sch. of Music Artist Dipl. (Clarinet) 1943, B.S. 1947; Conservatoire de Nancy, France Dipl. (Theory & Clarinet) 1945; Columbia Univ. M.A. 1948; Am. Conserv. Fontainebleau Dipl. (Theory) 1949; Eastman Sch. of Music; m. Ann d. Barker and Margaret Fairley 29 Oct. 1949; children: William, Richard, Margaret, Michael, Paul; Prof. of Music, Univ. of Toronto 1952–85; Now Prof. Emeritus; Lectr./Prof., Univ. of Mass. 1948–50; W. Reserve Univ. 1950–52; Clarinetist; soloist, chamber player, conductor: CBC, Stratford Festival, Univ. of Toronto; Chrmn. Performance, Opera Dept. Univ. of Toronto 1968–78; Principal, Royal Conservatory of Music 1978–83; Founder and First Pres., Assn. Candn. Orchestras 1972–74; Special Consultant, Ont. Arts Council 1985–89; mem. Canada Council Adv. Arts Panel 1981–84, 1989–93; Consultant, Govt. Trinidad & Tobago 1975–76; Instr., Gen. Dir. Nat. Youth Orchestra Can. 1960–65; author: 'Theodore Thomas: America's Conductor and Builder of Orchestras, 1835–1905' 1989; and papers on musical educ. Teheran 1967; Medellin (Colombia) 1968; Dijon (France) 1968; Rosario (Argentina) 1970; Oxford Univ. 1970; Oslo 1990; Candn. ed. Musical Courier (N.Y.) 1954–62; recipient Candn. Centennial Medal 1967; recreations: tennis, hiking; Address: 809 – 61 St. Clair Ave. W., Toronto, Ont. M4V 2Y8.

**SCHABAS, Richard,** M.D., M.H.Sc., F.R.C.P.(C); medical doctor; b. Cleveland, Ohio 19 Dec. 1951; s. Ezra and Ann Henrietta (Fairley) S.; e. North Toronto C.I. 1969; William Ellis Sch. (U.K.), gen. cert. adv. 1970; Univ. of Toronto M.D. 1976, M.H.Sc. 1982; m. Dr. Patti d. Gerald and Frances Rose 1975; children: Karl, Martha, Gregory, Alice; CHIEF MED. OFFR. OF HEALTH & DIR., PUBLIC HEALTH BRANCH, ONT. MIN. OF HEALTH 1987– ; rotating intern, St. Joseph's Hosp. 1976–77; Gen. Practice, Parry Sound, Ont. 1977–78; Res., Internal Med., Univ. of Toronto 1978–81; Community Med. 1981–83; FRCP(C) in Internal Med. 1982; in Community Med. 1983; Med. Offr. of Health, East York, Ont. 1983–87; Asst. Prof., Fac. of Med., Univ. of Toronto; Milton H. Brown Award 1983; Mem., Ont. Med. Assn.; Home: 256 Lytton Blvd., Toronto, Ont.; Office: 5th fl., 15 Overlea Blvd., Toronto, Ont. M4H 1A9.

**SCHACHAR, Russell James,** M.D., F.R.C.P.(C); physician; b. Brantford, Ont. 17 Sept. 1947; s. Benjamin Victor and Ethyl (Garalich) S.; e. Brantford C.I. 1965; Univ. of Toronto M.D. 1971; McMaster Univ., spec. training in psych. 1975; Inst. of Psych., London, England, post-grad. rsch. 1975–80; m. Sara Katz; children: Annie, Samuel; DIRECTOR FOR PSYCHIATRIC RESEARCH, HOSP. FOR SICK CHILDREN; Dir., Outpatient Dept. of Psychiatry 1985; specializes in clin. & rsch. in children with learning & behavioural problems; Mem., Assn. for Rsch. in Child Psychol. & Psych. (U.K.); Candn. Acad. of Child Psych.; Candn. Psych. Assn.; author of many sci. articles & book chapters; Home: 57 Castlewood Rd., Toronto, Ont. M5N 2L1; Office: 555 University Ave., Toronto, Ont. M5G 1X8.

**SCHACHTER, Albert,** D.Phil.; educator; b. Winnipeg, Man. 22 Aug. 1932; s. Harry and Rebecca (Raskin) S.; e. McGill Univ. B.A. 1955; Oxford Univ. D.Phil. 1968; m. June d. late Charles Hoysager 11 Aug. 1960; PROF. OF CLASSICS, McGILL UNIV. 1972– (Hiram Mills Prof. of Classical Philology, 1983– ), Chrmn. of Classics 1970–74 and 1986–91; Assoc. Dean (Academic), Faculty of Arts 1988–91; Acting Dean, 1989; Commonwealth Study Grant Fellow, Inst. of Classical Studies, London 1965 and 1985; Visiting Fellow, Wolfson Coll. Oxford 1982–83; author 'Cults of Boiotia' Vols. 1 and 4 1981, Vol. 2 1986; co-author 'Ancient Greek: A Structural Programme' 1973; Gen. Ed. 'Teiresias' 1971– ; various articles ancient Boiotia and teaching of ancient Greek; mem. Classical Assn. Can. (Vice Pres. 1987–89); Hellenic Soc.; Am. Philol. Assn.; Archaeol. Inst. Am.; Home: 5559 Borden Ave., Côte St. Luc, Montreal, Que. H4V 2T7; Office: 855 Sherbrooke St. W., Montreal, Que. H3A 2T7.

**SCHACHTER, Jean-Pierre,** B.A., M.A., Ph.D.; university professor; b. Marseilles, France 9 Apr. 1941; s. Benno and Phillipine (Pollack) S.; e. Bronx High Sch. Sci. 1957; City Univ. N.Y., B.A. 1963; M.A. 1964; Syracuse Univ., Ph.D. 1969; m. Judith, G., d. Hyman and Helen Guthwin, 22 Apr. 1971; children: Theodore Benno; Michael Eli; PROF. OF PHILOSOPHY, HURON COLLEGE 1968– ; Dean of Arts and Social Science, 1982–94; Staff, Bucknell Univ. 1967–68; Home: 64 Sherwood Ave., London, Ont. N6A 2E2; Office: Huron College, 1349 Western Rd., London, Ont. N6G 1H3.

**SCHACHTER, Ricky Kanee,** B.A., M.D.; physician; b. Melville, Sask. 23 Dec. 1918; d. Sam and Rose Kanee; e. Univ. of Sask., B.A. 1940; Univ. of Toronto, M.D. 1943; Columbia Univ. Post-Grad. Training, New York Post-Grad. Sch. 1944–45; m. Ben Schachter 1942; children: Bonnie, Gary Daniel; ASSOC. PROF. OF MED., UNIV. OF TORONTO, DIV. OF DERMATOLOGY, WOMEN'S COLL. HOSP. 1945– ; Dir. Psoriasis Edn. & Rsch. Centre, Women's Coll. Hosp. 1976– ; Cons. in Dermatol. Princess Margaret Hosp.; Assoc. Phys. in Med. Toronto Gen. Hosp.; served various cttes. and depts. Women's Coll. Hosp. incl. Chief Div. of Dermatol. to 1985; honoured Tribute Dinner 1985; Lifetime Achievement Award, Toronto Dermatological Soc. 1989; Glen Sawyer Service Award, Ont. Medical Assn. 1989; Ricky Kanee Schachter Dermatology Centre, Women's College Hospital opened 1991 named in honour; author or co-author numerous publs. nat. and internat. dermatol. lectr. since 1955; Pres.: Fedn. Med. Women Ont. Div. 1960–61; Med. Alumnae Univ. of Toronto 1970–71; Candn. Dermatol. Assn. 1978–79; Acad. Med. Dermatol. Sect. 1983–85; Toronto Dermatol. Assn. 1983–85; Adv. Council Rep. Am. Acad. Dermatol. 1983–85, Rep. on Council 1983–86; Rep. on Council Atlantic Dermatol. Soc. 1983–86; Fellow, Royal Coll. Phys. & Surgs. Dermatol.; recreations: travel, reading, music; Office: Women's College Hospital, 76 Grenville, Toronto, Ont. M5S 1B2.

**SCHACTER, Alvin Simon,** C.A.; business executive; b. Montreal, Que. 14 Oct. 1939; s. Jack and Jean (Marcovitch) S.; e. McGill Univ., C.A. 1961; m. Shirley d. Ben and Anne Druker 10 Nov. 1963; children: Kerry, Robert; MANAGING DIR., SLF CONSULTANTS; former Chief Operating Offr., Warrington INc.; former Sr. Offr., Cemp Investments Ltd.; Office: 1980 Sherbrooke St. W., 10th Floor, Montreal, Que. H3H 1E8.

**SCHAEFER, Carl Fellman,** O.C., R.C.A. (1964); artist; b. Hanover, Ont. 30 Apr. 1903; s. John D. S.; e. Pub. and High Schs, Hanover, Ont.; Ont. Coll. of Art, Toronto, Ont., under Arthur Lismer, J.E.H. MacDonald, C.M. Manley, George A. Reid, Robt. Holmes and J.W. Beatty 1921–24; Central Sch. of Arts and Crafts, London, Eng.; Univ. of Waterloo, D. Lett. (Hon.) 1976; m. Lillian Marie Evers, N. Dakota, 17 Mar. 1927; children: Mark, Paul; Instr., Ont. Coll. of Art., Toronto, Ont. 1948; Head, Drawing & Painting Dept. 1956–68; Chrmn. Emeritus, Painting Dept. 1968–70; Free-Lance Artist and Designer until 1931; Instr. of Art, Central Tech. Sch., Toronto, Ont. 1931–47; Instr., Art Centre, Art Gall. of Toronto 1935–37; Dir. of Art, Hart House, Univ. of Toronto 1934–56; Instr. Candn. Recreational Inst., Nat. Council, YMCA, Lake Couchiching Ont. 1934–36; Instr. in Art, Trinity Coll. Sch., Port Hope, Ont. 1936–39, 1946–48; awarded Fellowship in painting by Guggenheim Meml. Found., N.Y. 1940–41; Instr., Sch. Fine Arts (painting div.), Queen's Univ. 1946–51, Doon Sch. of Fine Arts, Doon, Ont. 1952–64; Upper Can. Acad. 1965; Instr. Schneider Sch. F.A., Actinolite 1967–88; Exhns. incl. Group of Seven, 1928 and 1931; 1st Internat. Expn. of Wood Engraving Poland 1933; Century of Cdn. Art, Tate Gall., London 1938; 11th Internat. Exhn. Water Color, Brooklyn Mus. 1941; 20th Int. Chicago Art Inst. 1940–41; New York World's Fair 1939; Nat. Gall., London, Eng. 1944; Mus. of Modern Art, Paris 1946; 50 Years of Painting, Art Gall. of Toronto 1949; first Candn. Exhn. to Asia (India, Ceylon, Pakistan) 1955; Australia 1955–56; first Biennial, Sao Paulo, Brazil 1951–52; Nat. Gallery, Washington 1950; Internat. Exhn., Contemporary Candn. Art, Mexico City 1960; Exhn. of Candn. Paintings to Bermuda 1962; Retrospective Exhn. 1969; 'Candn. Painting in the Thirties' (cross-Can.) 1975; 'Half a Century of Water Colour' AGO 1975; one-man show, Roberts Gall., Toronto, 1963, 70; Commonwealth Arts Festival, Eng. 1965; '300 Years of Canadian Art' Nat. Gallery, Ottawa 1967; Aviation Paintings, Candn. War Museum, Ottawa 1972; Twenty-Seven Wartime Paintings, Jerrold Morris Gall., Toronto 1974; Exposition of Candn. Paintings, China 1975; 'Carl Schaefer: Thirty-Five Years of Painting' 1932–67; McLaughlin Gall., Oshawa touring 1976; Portrait Drawings, Jerrold Morris Gall., Toronto 1976; '100 Yrs., Evol. of the Ont. Coll. of Art' AGO 1976; 'Art Deco Tendencies' Art Gall. of York Univ. 1977; 'Cdn. Paintings in the Univ. of Toronto' AGO 1978; Univ. of Waterloo 1976; 'Carl Schaefer Paintings 1931–67' Tom Thompson Meml. Gall., Owen Sound 1978; '20th Cent. Drawings' The Gall., Stratford 1979; 'Carl Schaefer's Hanover Paintings in the Thirties' Edmonton Art Gall. 1980; Victoria Art Gall., B.C.; Glenbow Mus., Calgary; Saskatoon Art Gall.; Dalhousie Art Gall.; Confederation Ctr. of the Arts 1981; AGO 1981; '100th Anniversary, Royal Candn. Academy of Arts' Roberts Gall. Toronto 1980; 'Candn. Artists of Second World War' Robert McLaughlin Gall., Oshawa, Ont. 1981; 'Canada Packers Collection' AGO 1982; 'Early Watercolours' Downstairs Gall., Edmonton 1981; 'Artists' Choice' Roberts Gall. 1982; 'Heritage & The New Wave Part 1' Rodman Hall Arts Centre, St. Catharines, Ont. 1982; 'A Distant Harmony: Comparative Exhbn. of Painters from Can. & the U.S.' Winnipeg Art Gall. 1982; 'Artists' Choice' Roberts Gall. 1983; 'The Candn. Landscape' Firestone Coll., Canada House, London 1983; Plymouth, Paris, Madrid, 1984; Lisbon, Athens, Milan, Rome, Oldenburg, Dusseldorf, Nat. Gall. Belgrade 1985; 'Images of the Land' Glenbow Museum, Calgary 1985; 'Canadian Block Prints 1919–1945' touring Can. 1985; 'Artists' Choice' Roberts Gall. 1985; 'From the Shadows' City of Toronto Archives, Market Gallery, Toronto; 'The 1940's, A Decade of Painting in Ontario' AGO Touring Ont. 1984–85; 'Kingston Views,' selection from 'Old Fort Henry' series, painting and drawings 1949–55, Agnes Etherington Art Ctr., Queen's Univ., Kingston, Ont. 1985; participated in 12 Centennial Exhns.; held over 16 one-man shows, rep. in several permanent coll. incl. Nat. Gall. (Ottawa); Art Gall. of Ont. (Toronto); Hart House (Univ. of Toronto); Queen's Univ.; Art Gall. of Hamilton; Dalhousie Univ.; Vancouver Art Gall.; Royal Bank of Can.; Va. Museum Fine Arts (Richmond); Art Bank Can.; Univ. of Guelph; Laurentian Univ., Sudbury; Winnipeg Art Gall.; Edmonton Art Gall.; Memorial Univ. of St. John's, Nfld.; Confed. Art Gall. (Charlottetown, P.E.I.); Glenbow Museum (Calgary, Alta.); Univ. Lethbridge; Hopkins Art Gall., Dartmouth Coll., (Hanover, N.H.); Shell Resources (Calgary, Alta.); A.E. Ames and Co. (Toronto); Dartmouth Heritage Museum (Dartmouth, N.H.); Rodman Hall Art Gall. (St. Catharines, Ont.); Sarnia Art Gall.; Windsor Art Gall.; Reed Paper Co.; Metropolitan Life; Sir George Williams Univ. (Montreal); Tom Thomson Meml. Gall. (Owen Sound); Glenhurst Gall. (Brantford); 7 Annil Hill Art Gall. (Burnaby, B.C.); Candn. Imperial Bank of Comm. (Toronto); Bank of Montreal (Montreal); Rothmans Ltd. and private collections in Canada, England and U.S.A.; served in 2nd World War 1943–46; appointed Official War Artist R.C.A.F. 1943; wounded twice 1944; made 129 paintings and drawings now in National War Museum, Ottawa; awarded 1939–45 Star; Candn. Volunteer Medal with Clasp; Defense of Great Britain Medal; War Medal; awarded Coronation Medal 1953; Centennial Medal 1967; Queen's Jubilee Medal 1978; Publications: 'Watercolour as a Painting Medium' Maritime Art Magazine 1943; 'Atlantis on the Artic Circle' Canadian Art Magazine 1946; 'Northward Journal, 24 drawings with diaries, 1926–27'; 'Carl Schaefer, Twelve Northern Drawings 1926–33' 1979; 'Carl Schaefer, Twelve Farm Drawings 1927–32' 1980; 'The Northern Imagination Illustrated by Carl Schaefer' 1983; subject of 'The Prints of Carl Schaefer 1922–45' by Andrew J. Oko, Art Gall. of Hamilton, in Revue d'Art Canadien 1984; 'Noman's Land' by Gwendolyn MacEwen, illus. with drawings by Carl Schaefer, Toronto 1985; 'Carl: Portrait of a Painter, from Reminiscence and Letters' by George Johnston, illus. with drawings and photographs by Carl Schaefer, 1986; cover drawing 'The Wahanipatai' (1926) for 'Who's Who in Canadian Literature 1987–1988'; 'Fields with Evening Sky' painting reprod. for jacket cover of Margaret Laurence's 'The Diviners' 1988; 'Storm over the Fields' and 'Ontario Farm House' paintings reprod. in 'A Concise History of Canadian Painting' by Dennis Reid, 2nd ed. 1988; el. Life Fellow, Internat. Inst. Art & Letters 1958; Fellow, O.C.A., Toronto 1976; Fellow, Roy. Soc. of Arts, London, Eng. 1977; mem., Candn. Group of Painters 1936; Candn. Soc. of Graphic Art 1932 (Hon. mem. 1961); Candn. Soc. of Painters in Watercolour 1933 (Life Hon. mem. 1982); O.C. 1978; Royal Candn.

Acad. of Arts (Assoc. 1949, Academician 1964, Companion 1972); Hon. Life Mem., AGO 1988; Home: 157 St. Clements Ave., Toronto, Ont. M4R 1H1.

**SCHAEFER, Donald Elwood McKee;** investment dealer; b. Fordwich, Ont. 1 Sept. 1923; s. Ira H. and Hazel (Sothern) S.; e. Fordwich (Ont.) Cont. Sch.; m. Elizabeth M., d. late Frank Allin, 5 July 1947; children: Judith Anne, John David; SENIOR VICE PRESIDENT & DIR., NESBITT THOMSON INC. since 1966; joined present firm 1950; Mgr., Kitchener, Ont. Office, 1954–57; Mgr. Institutional Sales, Toronto, 1957–60; Mgr., Prov. of Que., 1960–65; Appointed Dir., 1962; Asst. Sales Manager, Montreal, 1965–66; Senior Vice President 1966; Mgr., Bond Dept. 1966–70; Sr. Vice-Pres., Ont. 1970–79; resident Dir., London 1979–85; Investment Portfolio Adv. 1985; served with the R.C.A.F. during the 2nd World War; Conservative Protestant; recreations: curling, golf, boating; Clubs: National; Thornhill (Ont.) Country; London Hunt; The London; Home: 3 Elmbank Rd., Thornhill, Ont. L4J 2B6; Office: 14th Flr., Exchange Tower, 2 First Canadian Place, Toronto, Ont. M5X 1J4.

**SCHAEFER, H.G.,** B.Com., F.C.A.; b. Calgary, Alta. 18 Oct. 1936; s. Ernest A. S.; e. Univ. of Alta. B.Com. 1957; Alta. C.A. Inst. C.A. 1959; F.C.A. 1990; m. Joanne M., d. Gustav Wiedenroth, Edmonton, Alta. 26 Sept. 1958; children: Katherine, Karen, Robert; CHRMN. OF THE BD., CHIEF FINANCIAL OFFR. AND DIR., TRANSALTA UTILITIES CORP.; Chrmn., C.F.O. and Dir., TransAlta Resources Corp.; Vice Pres. Finance and Dir., AEC Power Ltd.; Dir., TransCanada PipeLines Ltd.; Alberta Microelectronic Centre; Candn. Energy Rsch. Inst.; Keyword Office Tech. Ltd.; Sun Life Trust; Telus Corp.; Protestant; recreations: badminton, squash, tennis; Clubs: Ranchmen's; Winter; Home: 1239 – 18th St. N.W., Calgary, Alta. T2N 2G8; Office: Box 1900, 110 – 12th Ave. S.W., Calgary, Alta. T2P 2M1.

**SCHAEFER, Theodore Peter,** M.Sc., D.Phil., F.C.I.C., F.R.S.C.; educator; b. Gnadenthal, Man. 22 July 1933; s. Paul Jacob and Margareta (Wiebe) S.; e. Mennonite Coll. Inst. Gretna, Man. 1950; Univ. of Man B.Sc. 1954, M.Sc. 1955; Oxford Univ. D.Phil. 1958; m. Nicola Caroline d. late Hugh Sewell, Majorca, Spain 26 Dec. 1960; children: Catherine, Dominic Peter, Benjamin Richard; UNIVERSITY DISTINGUISHED PROF., UNIV. OF MAN.; joined Univ. Man. as Asst. Prof. 1958; Visiting Scient. Nat. Research Council Can. Ottawa 1959, 1962, Argonne Nat. Labs. USA 1967, 1968, Nat. Phys. Lab. UK 1960, 1964, Oxford Univ. 1964, 1971; Extve. Chem. Inst. Can. 1977–79; mem. Nat. Research Council Can. Grants Comtes. 1975–77; mem. Nat. Sci. & Eng. Research Council of Can., 1980–84; rec'd Noranda Award Chem. Inst. Can. 1973; Herzberg Award Spectroscopy Soc. Can. 1975; Teaching Award, Grad. Students Assn., Univ. of Man. 1980; D.Sc. (h.c.) Univ. of Winnipeg 1982; mem. Nat. Sci. & Eng. Research Counc. of Can. Grants Comte. 1988–90; author numerous papers and reviews nuclear magnetic resonance; mem. Candn. Assn. Univ. Teachers; Protestant; recreations: walking, reading, music; Home: 210 Oak St., Winnipeg, Man. R3M 3R4; Office: 330 Parker Bldg., Winnipeg, Man. R3T 2N2.

**SCHAEFFER, Jonathan Herbert,** B.Sc., M.Math., Ph.D.; university professor; b. Toronto, Ont. 4 June 1957; s. Fred and Beverly (Kaplan) S.; e. Univ. of Toronto, B.Sc. 1979; Univ. of Waterloo, M.Math 1980, Ph.D. 1986; Chess master, one of top 50 players in Can.; rsch.: artificial intelligence, parallel and distributed computing; author of chess program 'Phoenix', tied for 1st place in 1986 World Computer Chess Championship (Cologne, W. Germany); co-organizer, 1989 World Computer Chess Championship (Edmonton); co-author Checkers program, 'Chinook', 1989 World Computer Checkers Champion; 2nd in 1990 U.S. National Open, winning right to play Dr. Marion Tinsley for World Checkers Championship (first computer program to earn right to play for a human World Championship); In 1992, Chinook played Dr. Tinsley for the World Checkers Championship. The result was 4 wins for Tinsley, 2 for Chinook and 33 draws. This was the first time in history that a computer had defeated a reigning World Champion (human) in a non-exhibition match (in any game); Mem., ACM; IEEE; AAAI; CIPS; ICCA (Editor); recreations: book collecting, sports, chess, Arctic history; Home: #37, 52148 Range Rd. 231, Sherwood Park, Alta. T8B 1A6; Office: Dept. of Computing Sci., Univ. of Alta., Edmonton, Alta. T6G 2H1.

**SCHAFER, R(aymond) Murray;** composer; author; b. Sarnia, Ont. 18 July 1933; s. Harold J. and Belle (Rose) S.; e. studied piano with Alberto Guerrero, theory and composition with John Weinzweig Royal Conservatory of Music Toronto 1950–55; Royal Coll. and Royal Acad. Music London L.R.S.M. 1954; studied with Peter Racine Fricker, Eng. 1958; m. 1stly Phyllis Mailing 2 Feb. 1960; m. 2ndly Jean C. Reed 18 Sept. 1975; free-lance journalist and broadcaster Europe 1956–60; founder, organizer Ten Centuries Concerts 1961, Pres. 1961–62; Artist-in-Residence Meml. Univ. of Nfld. 1963–65; Resident-in-Music Communications Centre Simon Fraser Univ. 1965–69, Prof. 1970–75; composer various works incl. 'From the Tibetan Book of the Dead' 1968; 'Son of Heldenleben' 1968; 'String Quartet' 1970; 'Music for the Morning of the World' 1972; 'Miniwanka' 1973; comns. from various organs. incl. Fromm Foundation, Serge Koussevitsky Foundation, CBC; author 'British Composers in Interview' 1963; 'The Composer in the Classroom' 1965; 'Ear Cleaning' 1967; 'The New Soundscape' 1969; 'The Book of Noise' 1970; 'When Words Sing' 1970; 'The Rhinoceros in the Classroom' 1974; 'E.T.A. Hoffman and Music' 1975; 'Creative Music Education' 1976; 'The Tuning of the World' 1977; 'On Canadian Music' 1984; 'Dicamus et Labyrinthos' 1985; 'The Thinking Ear' 1986; several books transl. into Spanish, Japanese and Italian; contbr. numerous articles various nat. and intnl. jours.; recipient Can. Council Arts Award 1968–69; Fromm Music Foundation Award 1969; Serge Koussevitzky Music foundation Award 1969; Can. Music Council Medal 1972; Guggenheim Fellow 1976; Leger Prize 1978; Priz Arthur Honegger 1980; Banff Centre School of Fine Arts National Award 1985; mem., Candn. League Composers; Performing Rights Organization of Canada; Candn. Music Council; Phi Mu Alpha Sinfonia; Address: R.R. 2, Indian River, Ont. K0L 2B0.

**SCHAFFTER, Henry John Pemell,** M.A.; headmaster; b. Isfahan, Iran 12 Dec. 1925; s. Dr. Charles Merrill, O.B.E., F.R.C.S. (Edin.) and Grace (Brownrigg) S.; e. Trent Coll. Derbyshire, Eng. 1944; King's Coll. Cambridge Univ. B.A. 1950, M.A. 1955; m. Catherine Anne d. Frederick Joseph Overend 14 July 1952; children: Catherine, Timothy, John; HEADMASTER EMERITUS 1988; joined Upper Can. Coll. Toronto 1950, Head of Hist. and Geog. Dept. Prep. Sch. 1954–68, Asst. to Headmaster Prep. Sch. 1967–69; Headmaster St. Johns Ravenscourt Sch. Winnipeg 1969–77; St. Michaels Univ. Sch. 1977–88; served with RAF 1944–47; Bd. mem. Winnipeg Symphony Orchestra 1975–77; Hon. Fellowship St. John's Coll. Univ. of Man. 1973; co-author 'The Winds of Change' 196l; 'Modern Perspectives' 1969; mem. Candn. Independent Schs. Headmasters' Assn.; Pacific Northwest Independent Schs. Headmasters' Assn.; Lit. Soc. Cambridge; Kings Coll. Cambridge Rugby Football Club; Queen's Jubilee Medal; R. Catholic; recreations: antique firearms, Candn. hist.; Home: 2385 Lyn Cresc., Victoria, B.C. V8S 4Y6.

**SCHAFHEITLIN, Don,** B.Sc., M.Sc.; computer industry executive; b. Niagara Falls, Ont. 18 Aug. 1950; s. Frederick Blake and Mary Ruth (Robinson) S.; e. Queen's Univ. B.Sc. 1973; Univ. of Toronto M.Sc. 1974; m. Suzanne d. Oscar and Ruth Shank 26 Aug. 1972; children: Jesse, Jody; VICE-PRES., CENTRAL AND WESTERN CANADA, DUN & BRADSTREET SOFTWARE SERVICES (CANADA) L.P. 1990– ; Data Administrator, Royal Insurance 1974–82; Mgr., Data Admin. & Decision Support Serv., Northern Telecom Canada 1982–84; Mgr., Presales Consultants, MSA (now Dun & Bradstreet Software Services) 1984–86; Central Region Sales Mgr. 1986–87; Vice Pres., Profl. Services 1988–92; Mem., Database Assn. of Ont. (Pres. 1980–81); Home: 904 Melton Dr., Mississauga, Ont. L4Y 1K8; Office: 10 Bay St., Ste. 400, Toronto, Ont. M5J 2R8.

**SCHECHTER, Martin,** M.D., M.Sc., Ph.D., FRCPC; physician/university professor; b. Toronto, Ont. 16 Dec. 1951; s. Hyman Louis and Leana (Swartz) S.; e. York Univ., B.A. 1973; Univ. of B.C., M.A. 1975; Polytechnic Inst. of NY, Ph.D. 1977; McMaster Univ., M.D. 1981; Univ. of Toronto, M.Sc. 1983; Fellow of the Royal College of Physicians and Surgeons of Canada 1991; m. Janet d. Marilyn and Albert Heavyside 26 Dec. 1984; children: Cynthia, Rachel; PROF., FAC. OF MED., UNIV. OF B.C. 1992– ; Asst. Prof., Swarthmore Coll. 1977–78; Rsch. Fellow, Nat. Cancer Inst., Epidemiol. Unit 1983; Asst. Prof., Fac. of Med., Univ. of B.C. 1983–89, Assoc. Prof. 1989–92; Prin. Investigator, Vancouver Lymphadenopathy-AIDS Study 1985– ; Nat. Health Rsch. Scholar Award, Nat. Health & Welfare 1986–91; Nat. Health Rsch. Scientist Award, Nat. Health & Welfare 1991–98; Mem., B.C. Coll. of Phys. & Surg.; Candn. Soc. for Clin. Invest.; Can. Inst. Acad. Med.; Internat. Epidemiol. Assn.; Am. Fed. for Clin. Rsch.; Soc. for Medical Decision Making; Candn. Pub. Health Assn.; B.C. Aids Secretariat; World Health Organization Steering Group on AIDS Epidemiology; Past Pres., Candn. Assn. for HIV Rsch.; Nat. Director, Candn. Nat. HIV Trials Net.; author of 298 med. articles & abstracts; Home: 3966 W. 31st Ave., Vancouver, B.C.; Office: Mather Bldg., Vancouver, B.C. V6T 1Z3.

**SCHEIBEL, The Hon. Eugene A.,** B.A., LL.B.; court of Queen's bench judge; b. Regina, Sask. 10 Feb. 1938; s. Phillip John and Helene Anne (O'Byrne) S.; e. Univ. of Ottawa, B.A. 1962; Dalhousie Univ., LL.B. 1962; m. Yvette d. David and Rita Toupin 13 June 1964; children: Stephen, Gregory; JUDGE, COURT OF QUEEN'S BENCH FOR SASK. 1981– ; admitted to Sask. Law Soc. 1963; Sr. Partner, Scheibel, Thompson, Rath & Oledzki; Past Dir., of num. cos.; Lectr., Sask. Bar Admission Course; Mem., Queen's Bench Rules Bd.; Sask. Surrogate Bd.; Home: 39 Heritage Pl., Regina, Sask. S4S 2Z7; Office: 2425 Victoria Ave., Regina, Sask. S4P 0S8.

**SCHELEW, Michael Stephen,** B.A., LL.B., LL.M.; lawyer; b. Moncton, N.B. 7 Feb. 1951; s. Irving and Lillian Stephanie (Lackman) S.; e. Mount Allison Univ. 1969–70; Univ. of W. Ont., B.A. 1974; Dalhousie Univ., LL.B. 1975; Columbia Univ., LL.M. 1976; Univ. of Paris doctural studies 1976–77; m. Lom Chanthala 25 Oct. 1981; two d. Marianne, Natalie; DEPUTY CHAIR, IMMIGRATION AND REFUGEE BOARD 1994– ; called to Bar of Ont. 1979; staff lawyer Rexdale Community Info. Directory Toronto 1979–80; Partner, Heifetz, Crozier & Schelew 1980–94; part-time lectr. Innis. Coll. Univ. of Toronto 1977–86; Past Pres. Candn. Counc. for Refugees; Vice Pres. & Pres., Candn. Section, Amnesty Internat. 1982–84 and Chair, Internat. Mandate Review Ctte., Amnesty Internat. 1987–90; mem., Inst. for Internat. Affairs, B'nai Brith Canada; mem. Ethics Ctte., Baycrest Centre for Geriatric Care; mem. Advisory Council, Centre for Refugee Studies of York Univ.; former Bd. Mem., Toronto Chinese Community Services Assoc.; invited to deliver paper on refugee policy by Candn. Institute for Advanced Legal Studies at the Strasbourg Lectures in Strasbourg, France in July 1992; author various articles refugee policy; recreations: tennis, skiing, swimming; Home: 35 Strathearn Blvd., Toronto, Ont. M5P 1S9; Office: 1 Front St. W., 5th Floor, Toronto, Ont. M5J 1A4.

**SCHERMBRUCKER, William Gerald (Bill),** B.A., M.A., Ph.D., P.G.C.E.; fiction writer, community college instructor; b. Eldoret, Kenya 23 July 1938; s. Christopher Frederick and Mavis (Munnik) S.; e. St. Mary's Sch., Nairobi 1953; Kearsney Coll., Natal 1954; Univ. of Cape Town, B.A. 1958; Univ. of London, P.G.C.E. 1960; Univ. of B.C., M.A., Ph.D. 1974; 3rd wife: Sharon d. Abraham and Leona Sawatsky 17 March 1984; children: David, Jeff, Mark (1st marriage); Julia (3rd marriage); INSTR., ENGLISH COORD., HUMANITIES DIV. CHAIR, CAPILANO COLLEGE 1968– ; High Sch. Teacher, Nairobi and Kikuyu 1958–64; Extramural Lectr., Univ. of E. Africa 1964; Bd. Mem., C.P.P.A. 1978–79; Candn. Commonwealth Scholar 1964; U.B.C. MacMillan Fellowship 1967; CBC Lit. Comp. 2nd prize 1980; B.C. Book Prizes Ethel Wilson Fiction Award 1989; Campaign Mgr. for Nathaniel Frothingham, U.S. Senate Dem. Primary, Vermont 1974; Mem., The Writers' Union of Can.; author: 'The Aims and Strategies of Good Writing' 1976, 'Chameleon and Other Stories' 1983 (short stories), 'Mimosa' 1988 (novel), 'Motortherapy' 1993 (short stories); editor: 'The Capilano Reader' 4th ed. 1989, 'The Capilano Review' 1977–82; recreations: nordic skiing; Home: 1226 Kilmer Rd., N. Vancouver, B.C. V7K 1R1; Office: 2055 Purcell Way, N. Vancouver, B.C. V7J 3H5.

**SCHIEDER, Rupert M.,** Ph.D.; lecturer/editor; b. Fort Frances, Ont. 8 Sept. 1915; s. Francis Joseph and Alice Mary (Baylie) S.; e. Univ. of Toronto B.A. 1938, M.A. 1947, Ph.D. 1954; PROF. EMERITUS, DEPT. OF ENGLISH, TRINITY COLL., UNIV. OF TORONTO 1958– ; R.C.A.F. 1942–46; Prof., Head of English, Candn. Serv. Coll., Royal Roads, B.C. 1951–58; Asst., Assoc., Prof., Dept. of English, Trinity Coll., Univ. of Toronto 1958– ; Chrmn., Hart House Music Ctte. 1972– ; Hon. Life Mem., Hart House 1989; Pres., Friends of the Library, Trinity Coll.; Univ. of Toronto Arbor Award 1992; Hon. Fellow, Trinity Coll. 1993; ed. with Intro.: Grainger: 'Woodsmen of the West' (1908) 1964, Grey: 'The Cure of St. Philippe' (1899) 1970, Traill: 'Canadian Crusoes: A Tale of the Rice Lake Plains' (1852) 1986; author: chapters in 'A Literary History of Canada' 1965; Home: 2002 – 278 Bloor St. E., Toronto, Ont. M4W 3M4.

**SCHIEFER, (Hans) Bruno,** D.V.M., Ph.D.; university professor & administrator; b. Cologne, Germany 25 Aug. 1929; s. Wilhelm and Therese (Meyer) S.; e. Veterinarian, Munich 1956; Dr. Med. Vet. (D.V.M.), Munich 1958; Dr. Habil (Ph.D.), Munich 1965; m. Elisabeth d. Dr. Hans and Dr. Anne Hesse 6 Sept. 1957; children: Bernhard, Barbara, Monica, Michael; DIR., TOXICOLOGY RSCH. CTR., UNIV. OF SASK. 1982– ; practising Veterinarian 1956–58; Rsch. Asst., Munich 1958–60; Asst. Prof. 1960–69; Rsch. Assoc., Univ. of Conn. 1966–67; Assoc. Prof., present univ. 1969–71; Prof. of Vet. Pathol. 1971– ; Fulbright Scholarship 1966–67; mem., Soc. of Toxicol. of Can. (Pres. 1983–85); Candn. Fed. of Biol. Soc. (Treas. 1984–86); Candn. Vet. Med. Assn. 1975– ; Candn. Assn. of Vet. Pathol. 1976– ; author of over 240 sci. pubs. incl. 15 books or book chapters; club: Rotary; Home: 69 Harvard Cres., Saskatoon, Sask. S7H 3R2; Office: Saskatoon, Sask. S7N 0W0.

**SCHIFF, Harold I.,** M.A., Ph.D., F.C.I.C., F.R.S.C.; educator, scientist; b. Kitchener, Ont. 24 June 1923; s. Jacob and Lena (Bierstock) S.; e. Univ. of Toronto, B.A. 1945, M.A. 1946, Ph.D. 1948; m. Dorothy Fane Daphne, d. William Line, 30 Dec. 1948; children: Jack Michael, Sherry Lin; Univ. Prof. York Univ.; PRES. UNISEARCH ASSOC. INC.; Dir., Candn. Inst. for Research in Atmospheric Chemistry; Dir., Scintrex Limited; National Research Council Fellow, 1948–50; Asst. Prof., McGill Univ., 1950; Assoc. Prof. 1954; Prof. 1960–65 and Dir., Upper Atmosphere Group; Prof., Chrmn., Dept. of Chem. and Dir., Natural Science, York Univ. 1964; Dean of Science 1965–72; Univ. Prof., 1980– ; Dir., Centre for Atmospheric Chem., York Univ. 1985–89; Extve. Dir., Candn. Inst. for Rsch. in Atmospheric Chem. 1985–89; Pres., Unisearch Associates Inc.; Sr. Fellow, Inst. for Advanced Study, Berlin 1989–90; Consultant, U.S. Dept. of Comm.; Nuffield Fellow, Cambridge, Univ., 1959–60; author (with L. Dotto), 'The Ozone War' 1978; Distinguished Author Award, U.S. Dept. of Comm., 1966; author of over 200 research papers; 50 tech. reports and chapters in four scient. books; two patents; mem. Ed. Bd. 'Planetary & Space Science,' 'Internat. Journ. Photochem'; Journal of Atmospheric Chemistry; Special Adv. Ctte. on the Environment, City of Toronto; Chrmn., Montreal Sec., Chem. Inst. Can. 1953 (Chrmn. Educ. Div. 1962); mem., Internat. Union of Pure and Applied Chemistry, Comm. on Atmospheric Chemistry; mem., Comte. on Stratospheric Pollution, Govt. Canada, Scient. Adv. Council, Candn. Extve. Ctte. Internat. Global Chemistry, Internat. Geosphere-Biosphere Programme; U.S. Acad. of Sci. Comm. on Impact of Stratospheric Change; Chrmn., U.S. Acad. of Sci., Panel on Stratospheric Chemistry; Candn. Assn. Univ. Teachers; Assoc. Comtes. of Nat. Research Council; Fellow, Royal Soc. of Can.; Sigma Xi; Home: 60 Donwoods Dr., Toronto, Ont. M4N 2G5.

**SCHILLER, Peter Wilhelm,** dipl. Chem. ETH, Dr.sc.tech. ETH, F.R.S.C.; biomedical researcher, university professor; b. Frauenfeld, Switz. 9 Feb. 1942; s. Wilhelm Friedrich and Rosa Clara (Haering) S.; e. Thurgauische Kantonsschule Frauenfeld, Matura 1961; Swiss Fed. Inst. of Technol. dipl. Chem. ETH 1966, Dr.sc.tech. 1971; DIR., LAB. OF CHEM. BIOLOGY & PEPTIDE RESEARCH, CLIN. RESEARCH INST. OF MONTREAL 1975– ; Rsch. Assoc., Biology, Johns Hopkins Univ. 1971–73; Rsch. Fellow, Nat. Insts. of Health 1973–75; Adjunct Prof., Exp. Med., McGill Univ. 1978– ; Prof., Med., Univ. of Montreal 1975–92; Pharmacol. 1992– ; Visiting Scholar, Biochem., Univ. of Washington 1969–70; Visiting Prof., ETH Zurich 1979; Mem., Candn. Heart Found. and Nat. Inst. of Health grant cttes.; Internat. Adv. Ctte., Inst. of Drug Rsch. (Berlin); Planning Ctte., Am. Peptide Symp.; Council and Pres. of the Am. Peptide Soc.; Chair, Gordon Rsch. Conf. on Chem. & Biol. of Peptides; various edit. bds.; frequent nat. & internat. guest speaker, lecturer; Cons., BioChem Pharma Inc.; Kern Prize and Silver Medal, ETH Zurich 1971; Max-Bergmann Medal, Max-Bergmann Soc. for the Adv. of Peptide Rsch. 1987; Marcel-Piché Prize, Clin. Rsch. Inst. of Monteal 1987; Fellow, Royal Soc. of Can. 1991; author/co-author of over 180 sci. pubns.; Home: 3475, rue de la Montagne, app. 1212, Montreal, Que. H3G 2A4; Office: 110 ouest, av. des Pins, Montreal, Que. H2W 1R7.

**SCHILLER, Ruth Boswell,** O.C., Assoc.Mus.; clinician, conductor, adjudicator, music educator; b. Victoria, P.E.I. 29 Oct. 1931; s. Robert Keith and Ruth Adeline (McGregor) Boswell; e. Mount Allison Univ. Assoc.Mus. 1954; studied McGill Conservatory of Music; children: Caroline, Leanne, Heidi; music specialist for approx. 30 years; instrumental and Orff specialist; guest conductor, adjudicator & lecturer; Bd. Mem., N.B. Choral Fed., Moncton Community Concert Series; Bd. Mem., Assn. of Candn. Choral Conductors; Mem., Music Curriculum, Dept. of Edn.; Internat. Choral Fed.; Am. Choral Dir. Assn.; Past Sec.-Treas., Nat. Candn.

Music Educators Assn. of Canada; Past Program Chair, N.B. Teachers Assn. Music Council; estab. Hillsborough Girls' Choir 1980 (engaged in internat. competitions; 'N.B.'s Ambassadors of Song'; Leslie Bell Choral Award 1981, '83; Award of Merit for videotape 1983; rep. Canada at XVI Internat. Soc. of Music Edn., Eugene, Oregon; 1st place, 17th Internat. Youth & Music Fest., Vienna, Austria; 2nd video released 1990; rep. Canada at XIX Internat. Soc. of Music Edn., Helsinki, Finland); Order of Canada 1992; recipient, André Thaddée Bourque and Louise Manny Award for Excellence in Music for 1992 (presented by Govt. of N.B. Jan. 1993); Commerative Medal for the 125th Anniv. of the Confederation of Canada in recognition of significant contribution to Compatriots, Community and to Canada 1867–1992; Protestant (Elder, Un. Ch.); Home: 416 MacAllister Ave., Riverview, N.B. E1B 4H7; Office: Caledonia H.S., Hillsborough, N.B. E0A 1X0.

**SCHINDLER, Ludwig O.,** A.R.I.D.O., I.D.C., A.S.I.D.; interior designer; b. Kaiserslautern, Germany 23 Dec. 1932; s. Ludwig Karl and Emma Wilhelmina (Stutzenberger) S.; e. Tech. Engr. Furniture Design & Mgf., Kaiserslautern, Masters 1949; Archit. Studies, Heidelberg 1952; m. Pamela d. Phyllis (Corin) and Walter Henry Born 23 June 1951; children: Brian John, Ronny Karl, Gabriele Elfriede; Dir., L.S. Holding Group; Design Dir., Total Environmental Planning Ltd.; World-Class Power Boat Racer, Outboard Marine Corp. Factory Team; N. Am. & Candn. Champ., Formula I Power Boat Racing; Past Pres., Sports Craft Div., Candn. Boating Fed.; Prof. Mem., Assn. of Reg. Interior Designers of Ont. (mem. Ethics Ctte.); Prof. Mem., Interior Designers of Can.; Am. Soc. of Interior Designers (Bd. Mem. 1993–94; I.F. Bd. Mem. & Chapter Co-Chair); author of various articles; recreations: exercising, skiing, tennis, power boating, travel, photography; Clubs: Fitness Inst.; Office: 65B West Beaver Creek Rd., Richmond Hill, Ont. L4B 1K4.

**SCHIOLER, John Pontoppidan,** M.A.; consultant; b. Winnipeg, Manitoba 8 Jan. 1933; s. Knud and Kirsten (Pontoppidan) S.; e. Univ. of Manitoba, B.A. (Hons.) 1956; Univ. of Rochester, M.A. 1958; Oxford (Rhodes Scholar) B.A. 1959, M.A. 1962; Laval Univ. (French) 1973–74; m. Gail Alexandra Olmsted; one d. Tegan; Permanent Rep. of Can., ICSC, Hanoi 1961–62; Second Secy. Candn. Embassy Rome 1962–64 and to High Comn. Cyprus 1964–65; Extve. Asst. Commonwealth Secy.-Gen., London 1965–66; Counsellor, Candn. High Comn., Lagos 1969–71; Acting Dir. Defence Relations Div., External Affairs 1972 and Dir., Middle East Div. 1972–73; Ambassador to Zaire, Burundi, Rwanda and Congo 1974–76; Dir. Staff Relations and Compensation, Ext. Affs. 1976–78; Policy Adviser, Off. of the Pres. of the Privy Council 1978–80; Dir. Middle East Div. 1980–83; Ambassador to Egypt & Sudan, 1983–85; Acting Director General for Africa, External Affairs 1985–86; Chrmn., Southern Africa Task Force 1986–89; Dir. Gen., Canada Arab Business Council 1990– ; Address: 128 Fourth Ave., Ottawa, Ont. K1S 2L4.

**SCHIPIZKY, Frederick Alexander,** B. Musc., M.MUsc.; professional musician; composer; performer; conductor; b. Calgary, Alta. 20 Dec. 1952; s. Antony and Elisabeth (Fogel) S.; e. Univ. of B.C., B. Musc. 1974; Juilliard Sch., M. Musc., 1978; priv. studies with John Beckwith, H. Freedman, M. Adaskin, E. Levinson, D. Walter, Roger Sessions, David Diamond, Elliot Weisgarber, Jean Coulthard; m. Ruth d. Rachel and Dewey Fagerburg 4 Aug. 1984; children: Anton Nicholas, Paul Alexander; BASSIST, VANCOUVER SYMPHONY ORCH. 1978– ; major compositions: 'Kleine Suite für Streichorchester' 1977, 'Symphonic Sketches' 1982, 'Fanfare for the Royal Visit' 1983, 'Divertimento for String Orch.' 1983, 'Quintet for Oboe, Harp, Violin, Viola and Contrabass' C.B.C. Commn. 1983, 'Symphony No. 1' 1985 (comnd by V.S.O. through Can. Counc. & perf. twice during V.S.O. Japan tour 1985); 'Quiet Eve' (choir & orch.) 1987; 'Symphony #2' 1988 (comnd. by C.B.C. Vancouver Orch. for 50th Anniv.); 'Two Ritual Dances' (vln., vla., fl.) 1988 (comnd by T.S.O.); 'From Under the Overture' 1990 (commn. by V.S.O. perf. eight times during V.S.O. tour of B.C. 1990); 'Aurora Borealis' 1992 (commn. by the Prince George Symphony in celebration of the convocation ceremonies of the new University of Northern British Columbia); recordings: 'Quatrains, Phyllis Mailing,' 'Schipizky, Three Songs for Mezzo-Soprano & Piano,' 'Poems by Tennyson & Browning'; various CBC radio & TV appearances; Former principal bass, Nat. Youth Orch. of Can. and the Juilliard Philharmonia; performed with Montreal Symphony Orch., Victoria Symphony, Esprit Orchestra, as well as Arraymusic and Purcell String Quartet; Assoc. Comp., Candn. Music Ctr.; Mem., Candn. League of Comp.; Fac. Mem., Vancouver

Acad. of Music; Fac. Mem., Douglas College 1989– ; Courtenay Youth Music Centre 1986; Bd. Mem., Vancouver New Music Soc.; Days, Months and Years to Come & Magnetic Band; Jean Coulthard Scholarship 1973; Okanagan Comp. Fest. 1st Prize 1974; various Canada Council Grants; New York State Council of the Arts Grant; Juilliard Scholarship 1976–78; Juilliard Teaching Fellowship in Theory 1977–78; Mem., P.R.O. Can.; recreations: golf, cross-country skiing; Club: McCleery Golf; Home: 5390 Larch St., Vancouver, B.C. V6M 4C8; Office: The Orpheum, 601 Smithe St., Vancouver, B.C. V6B 5G1.

**SCHIPPER, Harvey,** B.A.Sc., MD, FRCP(C); physician, university professor; b. Toronto, Ont. 2 Apr. 1947; s. Frank Leon and Florence Helen (Pearlman) S.; e. Oakwood C.I.; Univ. of Toronto, B.A.Sc. 1968; MD 1972; m. Karen Paula d. Harold and Maxine Minden 27 July 1975; children: Rachel, Elyse; HEAD, ONCOLOGY, ST. BONIFACE HOSP.; DIR., WHO COLLABORATING CTR. FOR QUALITY OF LIFE IN CANCER CARE 1988– ; trained in internal med. in Toronto; subsequent specialty training in cancer med.; current profl. interests are focused on health care delivery & Third World linkages; Assoc. Prof., Univ. of Man.; Dir., Outreach Program; Manitoba Cancer Found. 1978– ; Mem., WHO Expert Group on Quality of Life; Mem., Extve. Ctte., Nat. Surg. Adjuvant Breast Prog.; Clincial Trials Scholar, Nat. Cancer Inst. 1981–85; Bd. of Dir., Candn. Cancer Soc. 1982–92; Chrmn., Joint Internat. Affairs Ctte. 1990–92; Office: St. Boniface Gen. Hosp., 409 Tache Ave., St. Boniface, Man. R2H 2A6.

**SCHLECH, Walter Frederick III,** B.A., M.D., F.A.C.P., F.R.C.P.(C); physician; educator; b. Coronado, Calif. 31 Mar. 1946; s. Walter Frederick and Barbara Ann (Bowser) S.; e. Loretto Sch. Musselburgh, Scot. 1961–63; Williston Acad. Easthampton, Mass. 1963–64; Williams Coll. B.A. 1971; Cornell Univ. M.D. 1975; m. Mary d. Marshall and Anna May Austin 7 June 1975; children: Austin, Walter, Jane, Peter, Michael; PROF. OF MEDICINE, DALHOUSIE UNIV. 1992– ; Fellow, Vanderbilt Univ. Med. Sch. 1978–80; Epidemic Intelligence Service CDC Atlanta, Ga. 1980–82; joined present Univ. 1982; author or co-author numerous sci. articles; Past Pres., Candn. Infectious Disease Soc.; recreations: rugby, fishing, hunting, philately; Club: Waegwoltic; Home: 6035 Cherry St., Halifax, N.S. B3H 2K4; Office: ACC 5014 Victoria General Hospital, Halifax, N.S. B3H 2Y9; Seasonal: Grace Farm, R.R. 6, Bridgewater, N.S.

**SCHLEDERMANN, Peter,** Ph.D.; archaeologist; professor; writer; b. Copenhagen, Denmark 22 March 1941; s. Holger and Hanne (Dindler) S.; e. Univ. of Alaska B.A. 1969; Memorial Univ. of Nfld. M.A. 1971; Univ. of Calgary Ph.D. 1974; SR. RSCH. ASSOC., ARCTIC INST. OF NORTH AM. 1988– ; Chair for Northern Studies, Trent Univ. 1989; field rsch. in Alaska 1965–69, Labrador 1970, Baffin Island 1971–73, High Arctic Canada and Greenland 1974–92; Archaeology Dept., Univ. of Calgary, Asst. and Assoc. Prof. 1975–78, Adjunct Assoc. Prof. 1978– ; Extve. Dir., Arctic Inst. of North Am. 1979–86; Adjunct Assoc. Prof., Univ. of Victoria 1986–90; consultant and advisor to industrial firms, museums, etc.; Founder and mem., Northern Studies Group, Univ. of Victoria 1986–88; Fellow, Arctic Inst. of N. America; mem. of Council, Comité Artique 1980–89; counc. mem., Bd. mem., Assn. of Candn. Univs. for Northern Studies 1978–86; mem. of Alaskan science prize Candidate Review Comte. 1983–86; Assoc. Ed., 'Arctic'; author of several books and numerous articles in learned journals; recreations: books, hiking, sailing, music; Home: 426 – 21st Ave. N.W., Calgary, Alta. T2M 1J5.

**SCHLEEH, Hans,** R.C.A.; sculptor; b. Koenigsfeld, Germany 1928; studied at Lahr under Richard Class; settled in Montreal, Que., 1951; comnd. to do sculptures for several chs. incl. Ste. Anne de Beaupré Basilica; participated in several group exhns. 1953–60; one-man exhns. incl., Dominion Gallery, Montreal, 1960, 65, 66, 68, 69, 70, 74, 76, 79; New Art Centre Gallery, N.Y. 1962; Kunsthalle, Duesseldorf, Germany 1964; group exhns. incl., Salon de la jeune Sculpture, Paris 1966, 67; Stratford, Ont. 1966; Expo, Montreal 1967; Que. Sculptors Assn. 1965–70; Musee d'Art Contemporain, Montreal 1970–71; Musee Rodin, Paris 1970–71; Landesmuseum, Bonn, Germany 1971; IV Exposition Internat. de Sculpture Contemporaine, Paris 1971; Goethe Inst., Toronto 1978; studied in France, Italy, Switzerland and Germany, 1963–64; works in perm. collections in Can., U.S. and Europe incl., Art Gallery of Winnipeg; Vancouver Art Gallery; Sarnia Art Gallery; St. Catharine's and Dist. Arts Council; Univ. of Sherbrooke; Queen's Univ.; Stormking Arts Centre, Mountainville, N.Y.; Christie Manson and Woods, London,

Eng.; Nathan Cummings, Chicago; J. A. MacAulay Collection, Winnipeg; Tel Aviv Museum, Israel; Bloomfield Collection, London, Eng.; Toronto-Dominion Bank, Place des Arts, Montreal Trust Co.; Ciba Co., Upper Trafalgar Place, Plaza Cote des Neiges, Montreal Mus. F.A.; and Musée d'Art Contemporain (Montreal); Chamber of Comm., Duesseldorf, Germany; Address: #604, 20 Edgecliffe Golfway, Don Mills, Ont. M3C 3A4.

**SCHLESINGER, Benjamin,** B.A., M.S.W., Ph.D., F.R.S.C.; university professor; b. Berlin Germany 20 July 1928; s. Abraham and Esther (Trisker) S.; e. Sir George Williams Univ., B.A. 1951; Univ. of Toronto, M.S.W. 1953; Cornell Univ., Ph.D. 1961; m. Rachel d. Hannah and Felix Aber 29 Mar. 1959; children: Avi, Leo, Esther, Michael; PROF., FAC. OF SOCIAL WORK, UNIV. OF TORONTO 1960– ; Social Worker, Jewish Immigrant Aid Soc. (Montreal) 1948–51; Children's Aid (Toronto) 1953–57; Ont. Psychol. Found. Award 1987; Leo La Freniere Memorial Award, Ont. Family Life Educators Assoc. 1988; Mem., Vanier Inst. of the Family; Nat. Counc. on Family Relns.; author of 22 books, most recent: 'Canadian Families in Transition' 1992 (with Rachel Schlesinger); 'Canadian Families: A Resource Guide' 1989 (with Rachel Schlesinger); 'Abuse of the Elderly: Issues and Annotated Bibliography' 1988, (with Rachel Schlesinger); 'Jewish Family Issues' 1987; 'Sexual Abuse of Children in the 1980s' 1986; 'Sexual Abuse of Children: A Resource Guide and Annotated Bibliography' 1982; 'The One-Parent Family in the 1980s' (5th ed.) 1985 (Japanese version 1987); 'What About Poverty in Canada' 1982; 'Families: Canada' 1980; and over 300 profl. papers; editor: 'Social Problems in Canada' and 'Canadian Social Patterns' series; Fellow, Royal Society of Canada 1993; Home: 415 Roselawn Ave., Toronto, Ont. M5N 1J9; Office: 246 Bloor St. W., Toronto, Ont. M5S 1A1.

**SCHLESINGER, Joe;** journalist; author; b. Vienna, Austria 11 May 1928; s. Emmanuel and Lilli (Fischl) S.; e. Univ. of B.C.; m. Myra E. d. G. Alfred and Neola Kemmer 27 Apr. 1963; children: Leah, Ann; CHIEF POLITICAL CORRESPONDENT, CANADIAN BROADCASTING CORP. (TV NEWS) 1991– ; Reporter, Vancouver Prov., Toronto Star and United Press Internat. (London) 1955–62; Asst. Managing Ed. European Edition New York Herald Tribune, Paris 1962–66; Foreign Ed., Toronto Star 1967; Exec. Producer CBC National News, Toronto 1968–69, Head CBC TV News 1969–70; Foreign Correspondent, CBC, Far East 1970–74; Paris 1974–79; Washington 1979–90; Berlin 1990–91; LL.D. (Honoris causa), Univ. of B.C. 1992; Home: 140 Rideau Terrace, Ottawa, Ont. K1M 0Z2; Office: CBC, 150 Wellington St., Ottawa, Ont. K1P 5A4.

**SCHLITT, Dale M.,** S.T.L., O.M.I., Ph.D.; university professor and administrator; b. St. Louis, Mo. 26 April 1942; s. Martin Francis and Adele Rose (Kunz) S.; e. Gregorian Univ. Rome Italy S.T.L. 1970; Claremont Graduate School Calif. Ph.D. 1983; PROFESSOR OF THEOLOGY, SAINT PAUL UNIV. 1983– ; Secretary of the Faculty of Theology, Saint Paul Univ. 1991–93; Vice-Dean and Dir. of Grad. Studies 1993– ; Pastor Danish-Speaking Catholics Denmark 1972–74; Assoc. Pastor, Green Bay, Wi. 1970–71; Academic Consultor, Central U.S. Province of the Missionary Oblates of Mary Immaculate 1980–93; Research Fellow, Inst. for the Advanced Study of Religion, Divinity Sch., Univ. of Chicago 1986–87; ordained Catholic Priest 1969; Mem., Missionary Oblates of Mary Immaculate 1963– ; author: 'Hegel's Trinitarian Claim: A Critical Reflection' 1984, 'Divine Subjectivity: Understanding Hegel's Philosophy of Religion' 1990; recreations: swimming; clubs: Ottawa Athletic; Home: 175 Main St., Ottawa, Ont. K1S 1C3; Office: 223 Main St., Ottawa, Ont. K1S 1C4.

**SCHLOSSER, John Lewis,** C.M., LL.D.; investment executive; b. Indian Head, Sask. 17 May 1928; e. High School, Estevan, Saskatchewan; University of N. Dakota, 1947, 1948, 1951; Univ. of Alta., 1949–50; m. Kathleen Patricia, d. H. A. Scott; children: Walter Scott, Mary Ann (Dixon), Arden Patricia (Narusevicies); PRESIDENT, SCHLOSSER FAMILY HOLDINGS LTD.; Chrmn., Edmonton Telephones Corp.; Pres., Dir., Princeton Developments Ltd.; Northwestern Utilities Ltd.; Pirelli Canada Inc.; Weldwood of Canada Limited; Sunwapta Broadcasting; Equitable Life of Canada; mem. of Alta. Adv. Bd., National Trust Co. Ltd.; Past Chrmn. Bd. Govs., Univ. of Alberta; mem. Clyford E. Lee Foundation; Past Pres., The Edmonton Symphony Soc.; Un. Community Fund of Edmonton; Edmonton Art Gallery; Boy Scouts of Can. (Edmonton & Prov.); served as Pilot, 418 Reserve Sqdn. RCAF; recreations: sailing, skiing, fishing, hunting, reading; Home: 7427 - 119 St., Edmonton, Alta. T6G 1W2; Office: Room 1400, Petroleum Plaza N. Tower, 9945 - 108 St., Edmonton, Alta. T5K 2G6.

**SCHMEISER, Douglas A.,** Q.C., LL.M., S.J.D.; educator; lawyer; b. Bruno, Sask. 22 May 1934; s. Charles A. and Elsie (Hazelwanter) S.; e. Bruno Pub. and High Schs.; Univ. of Sask. B.A. 1954, LL.B. 1956; Univ. of Mich. (Cook Rsch. Fellow) LL.M. 1958, S.J.D. 1963; m. Irene d. Dr. Alex and Maria Ositis 6 Dec. 1980; children: Mary Ellen, Douglas, James, Robert, Gary, Peggy; PROF. OF LAW, UNIV. OF SASK. 1961– ; Constitutional Adv., Govt. of Man. 1979–81, 1988– ; Assessor Discipline Ctte. Coll. Phys. & Surgs. Sask. 1981– ; Pres., Sask. Natural History Soc. 1992– ; cons. constitutional and other matters various govts. and law firms; labour arbitrator; Chrmn., Sask. Comn. on Judges' Salaries and Benefits 1990–91; Chrmn. Law Reform Comn. Sask. 1982–87; read law with Hon. Emmett M. Hall; called to Bar of Sask. 1958; cr. Q.C. 1982; law practice Saskatoon 1958–61; Dir. Grad. Legal Studies present Univ. 1969–74, Dean of Law 1974–77; mem. Bd. Examiners Law Soc. Sask. 1968–74, Chrmn. 1974–77; UNESCO internship Human Rights Div. Paris 1978; Study Adm. Justice Candn. Arctic 1967, 1969 (sponsor Donner Candn. Found.); Constitutional Adv. and Del. Sask. Fed.-Prov. Confs. 1968–71; mem. Adv. Acad. Panel Can. Counc. 1971–74; Rsch. Policy Ctte. Social Sci. Fedn. Can. 1976–79; Del. and Adv. First Mins. Confs. on Constitution 1967–71, 1979–81, 1988–92; Project Dir. Candn. Internat. Devel. Agency re Univ. of Khartoum 1981–93; Visiting Scholar Univ. of Sydney, Australia 1980; Dir. Saskatoon United Way 1962–90, Pres. 1967–69, Campaign Chrmn. 1985; mem. Counc. Candn. Human Rights Found.; Trustee Saskatoon Cath. Sch. Bd. 1964–69; author: 'Civil Liberties in Canada' 1964; 'Canadian Criminal Law' 1966, 1973, 1977, 1981, 1985; 'The Native Offender and the Law' 1974; mem. Candn. Assn. Law Teachers (Dir. 1970–75, Pres. 1973–74); Saskatoon Bar Assn. (Dir. 1964–69, Pres. 1968–69); Candn. Bar Assn.; Law Soc. Sask.; Soc. Pub. Teachers Law; recreations: travel, bridge, nature; Club: Saskatoon; Home: 22 Simpson Cres., Saskatoon, Sask. S7H 3C6; Office: Saskatoon, Sask. S7N 0W0.

**SCHMIDT, Grant Jacob,** M.L.A., LL.B.; lawyer; politician; b. Balcarres, Sask. 21 July 1948; s. George and Helen Regina (Banerd) S.; e. Univ. of Sask. LL.B. 1972; m. Sheron d. William and Olga Stecyk 28 Aug. 1971; children: Kurt, Luke; ASSOCIATE, SCHMIDT & GRAFF LAW OFFICE; articled with Dielschneider & Rathgaber 1972–73; Partner, Rathgaber & Schmidt 1973–85; Partner, Schmidt & Graff 1985–86; M.L.A., Melville, Sask. 1982–91; Min. of Labour, Govt. of Sask. 1985–87; Min. of Social Services 1986–88; Min. Responsible for Workers' Compensation Bd. 1986–90; Min. of Human Resources, Labour & Employment 1987–90; Min. of Consumer & Comm. Affairs 1989–90; Min. of Economic Diversification and Trade 1990–91; Min. of Justice, Attorney General, Provincial Secretary 1991; Vice-Chair, Sask. Government Insurance 1989–91; Founding Vice-Chair, S.G.I. Canada Insurance Group; Mem., St. Paul's Luth. Ch.; Dir., Terry Puhl Found.; Pres., Century Properties Ltd.; Law Soc. of Sask.; Melville Lions Club; P.C. Parties of Can. & Sask.; recreations: golf, curling, boating, cycling; Home: 16 Vanier Dr., Melville, Sask. S0A 2P0; Office: 131 3rd Ave. E., Melville, Sask. S0A 2P0.

**SCHMIDT, Robert Leo;** b. Winnipeg, Man. 17 May 1937; s. Leo and Anne S.; e. Winnipeg, Man.; m. F. Gail d. George and Phoebe Herrod, Lloydminster, Sask. 20 Aug. 1960; three children; Retired Financial Consultant, Quotes Canada Inc.; Mem., Alta. Education Attendance Bd.; Past Asst. Vice-Pres., Regional Manager, Alberta & Manager Calgary Br., Financial Trust Company, Calgary; Past Vice Pres. Crown Trust Co.; Past Reg. Vice-Pres., Guaranty Trust Co.; Past Mgr., Montreal Trust Co., Calgary & Edmonton Branches; Past Dir., Alta. Theatre Projects Fdn.; Past Chrmn. N.B. Sec. Trust Co's Assn. Can.; Past Pres. Saint John N.B. Lions Club; Past Treas. Kiwanis Club Edmonton Downtown; Chrmn. & Dir., United Way, Calgary, 1982; Fellow Trust Co's Inst. (F.T.C.I.); recreations: curling, reading, gardening; Club: Glencoe; Home: 755 Cedarille Way S.W., Calgary, Alta. T2W 2G9.

**SCHNEIDER, Gerd,** B.Sc., M.D., C.C.F.P., F.C.F.P.; family physician; b. New Ulm, Germany 10 Apr. 1944; s. Oscar and Elizabeth (Haegner) S.; e. Univ. of Toronto, B.Sc. 1966, M.D. 1970; C.C.F.P. 1972; F.C.F.P. 1992; m. Faith Joynson 30 Aug. 1969; children: Erika, Monika, Stefan; family medicine since 1973; Med. Dir., Glebe Ctr. 1975– ; active full-time staff, Ottawa Civic Hosp.; part-time Health Services, Carleton Univ. 1974–76; community preceptor for teaching med. students, Univ. of Ottawa & Queen's Univ.; 1987 Research Prize given by 'The Canadian Family Physician' for 11-year study of home births in my practice; Nat. Sec. of Candn. Physicians for the Prevention of Nuclear War (CPPNW) 1986– ; Editor & Prodn. Mgr., 'The CPPNW Quarterly' 1986– ; recreations: boardsailing, skiing, gardening, cycling, reading, music; Home: 30 Broadway Ave., Ottawa, Ont. K1S 2V6; Office: 202 - 474 Holland Ave., Ottawa, Ont. K1Y 0Z5.

**SCHNEIDER, William George,** O.C. (1976), M.Sc., Ph.D., D.Sc., LL.D., F.R.S.C., F.R.S.; research chemist; b. Wolseley, Sask., 1 June 1915; s. Michael and Phillipina (Kraushaar) S.; e. Luther Coll., Regina, Sask.; Univ. of Sask., B.Sc. 1937, M.Sc. 1939; McGill Univ., Ph.D. 1941; Acadia, D.Sc. 1976; Harvard Univ. (post-doctoral research) 1941–43; D.Sc. York 1966, Memorial 1968, Sask., Moncton, McMaster, Laval 1969, New Brunswick, Montréal, McGill 1970, Acadian Univ., 1976, Regina Univ., 1976, Ottawa Univ., 1978; LL.D. Alberta 1968; Laurentian 1968; m. Jean Frances, d. Frank Purves Saskatoon, Sask., 2 Sept. 1940; two d. Judith Ann, Joanne Frances; PRES., INTNL. UNION OF PURE AND APP. CHEM., 1983–85; ret. Pres., Nat. Research Council, 1967–80, (Vice-Pres., Scientific 1965–67); joined N.R.C., Pure Chem. Div., 1946; Research Physicist at Oceanographic Inst., Woods Hole, Mass., under contract with OSRD-NDRC and U.S. Navy, 1943–46; Cert. of Merit, U.S. Navy (1946); Publications: Co-author 'High Resolution Nuclear Magnetic Resonance,' 1959; over 120 publ. papers in physical chem.; Fellow, Chem. Inst. Can. (Dir. 1956–59, Medal 1961, Montreal Medal 1973); Fellow, Royal Soc. of Can. 1951; Fellow, Royal Soc. (London) 1962; mem., Am. Chem. Soc.; Am. Physical Soc.; rec'd. Henry Marshall Tory Medal of Royal Soc. of Can. 1969; recreations: tennis, skiing; Office: 65 Whitemarl Dr., Unit 2, Ottawa, Ont. K1L 8J9.

**SCHNELL, Bruce Robert,** B.S.P., M.B.A., Ph.D., Ph.C., P.E.B.C., F.C.S.H.P.; b. Maymount, Sask. 1 May 1937; s. Leonard William and Nellie (Rankin) S.; e. Univ. of Sask. Coll. of Pharm. B.S.P. 1960; Univ. of Toronto Sch. of Business M.B.A. 1966; Univ. of Wis. Sch. of Pharm. Ph.D. 1971; m. June Gladys d. Everett Johnsson, 9 Oct. 1961; children: Gregory, Sandra; EXTVE. DIRECTOR, THE CANDN. COUNCIL FOR THE ACCREDITATION OF PHARMACY PROGRAMS 1993– ; joined present Univ. as Asst. Prof. 1966, Assoc. Prof. 1971, Prof. 1976, Dean of Pharmacy, 1976–82, Vice-Pres. (Academic) 1982–90, Vice-Pres. (External) 1990–92, International Liaison Offr. 1991–93; Chairman, Edit. Adv. Panel, Compendium of Pharmaceuticals & Specialties; Assoc. Ed. Canadian Journal of Hospital Pharmacy, 1966–82; mem. Pharm. Examining Bd. of Can. (Pres. 1973, Extve. Comte.); Chrmn., Joint Ctte. on Drug Utilization, Sask. Dept of Health 1977–83; Dir., Cdn. Foundation for the Advancement of Pharmacy (Pres., 1982); Bd. of Dirs., Wanuskewin Heritage Park 1989– ; Saskatoon United Way 1990–92; Bd. of Management, St. Paul's Hosp. (Saskatoon) 1991–92; Assn. of Deans of Pharm. of Can. (Vice Pres. 1977, Pres. 1978) 1976–82; Candn. Academy of Hist. of Pharm.; Hon. mem., Candn. Society of Hospital Pharmacists; Hon. Life Mem., Candn. Pharm. Assn.; Hon. Life Mem., Sask. Pharm. Assn.; Medical Research Council Canada 1980–85; MRC Awards Ctte. for Career Investigators 1988–93 (Chrmn. 1991–93); Chrmn., Formulary Ctte., Sask. Prescription Drug Plan; Fellow, Candn. Soc. of Hospital Pharmacists; mem., Bd. of Regents, St. Andrews Coll. 1978–85 (Extve. Ctte. 1978–85); Mem., Rsch. Personnel Career Awards Ctte., Nat. Health Rsch. and Development Program 1985–89; Mem., Saskatoon Rotary Club 1987– (Dir. 1991–92); Address: 123 Thorvaldson Bldg., Univ. of Sask. Campus, Saskatoon, Sask. S7N 0W0.

**SCHNER, Joseph George,** S.J., A.B., M.A., M.Div., Ph.D.; priest, university professor and administrator; b. St. Boniface, Man. 1 Jan. 1942; s. Joseph George and Josephine Frances (Poplick) S.; e. St. Paul's H.S. 1958; Fordham Univ. A.B. 1967; Univ. of Windsor M.A. 1970; St. Mary's Univ. M.Div. 1974; Univ. of Toronto Ph.D. 1978; PRESIDENT, CAMPION COLLEGE, UNIV. OF REGINA 1986– ; entered Soc. of Jesus 1961; ordained presbyter of the Roman Catholic Ch. 1974; High School Teacher & Counsellor, St. Paul's H.S. 1970–71; Psychologist, Toronto Metro Sep. Sch. Bd. 1976–81; Asst. Prof., Campion College 1981–84; Dean & Assoc. Prof. 1984–86; Mem., Bd. of Gov., St. Paul's College Winnipeg 1986– ; Regis College Toronto 1984–91; Mem., Ont. Psych. Assn.; Registered by Ont. Bd. of Examiners in Psych.; Mem., Psych. Assn. of Sask.; Reg. by Sask. Psych. Assn.; Mem., Assn. for Psych. Type; author: 'Failure of the Escape from Intimacy' 1984 and var. journal articles; Office: Regina, Sask. S4S 0A2.

**SCHNOOR, Jeffrey Arnold,** B.A., LL.B., Q.C.; lawyer, administrator; b. Winnipeg, Man. 22 June 1953; s. Toby and Ray S.; e. Univ. of Manitoba B.A. 1974, LL.B. 1977; EXECUTIVE DIRECTOR, MANITOBA LAW REFORM COMMISSION 1986– ; called to Manitoba Bar 1978; Assoc. & Partner, McJannet Weinberg Rich 1978–86; Q.C. 1992; Mem., Governing Council, Manitoba Bar Assn. 1988– ; Lectr., Law Soc. of Man. Bar Admission Course 1981– ; Counsel, Guertin Born 1988–90; Chair, Bus. Law Subsection, Man. Bar Assn. 1985–86; frequent speaker; Mem., Fed. of Law Reform Agencies of Can. 1986– ; Uniform Law Conf. of Can. 1986– ; Univ. Gold Medal 1974 and many other awards for high standing in Arts & Law; United Way of Winnipeg: Mem., Bd. of Trustees & of Extve. Ctte. 1990– , Sr. Vice-Pres. & Pres.-Elect 1993–94, Treas. 1991–92; Home: 104 Harvard Ave., Winnipeg, Man. R3M 0K4; Office: 405 Broadway, 12th fl., Winnipeg, Man. R3C 3L6.

**SCHOCHET, J. Immanuel,** B.A., M.A., M.Phil., D.D., Ph.D., Rabbi; professor, rabbi, author; b. Switz. 27 Aug. 1935; s. Dov Yehudah and Sarah (Musensohn) S.; e. Univ. of Windsor; Univ. of Toronto; McMaster Univ.; Univ. of Waterloo, Ph.D. 1974; Rabbinical Coll. of Lubavich, Brooklyn, NY; m. Jettie d. Abraham and Judith Elzas 5 June 1962; children: Oryah, Yitzchak, Sharonne, Yisroel; PROF. OF PHILOS. & RELIGION, HUMBER COLL. 1971– ; Vis. Prof. of Jewish Phil. & Jewish Mysticism, Maimonides Coll. 1980–86; Rabbi, Kielcer Congreg. 1959– ; frequent lectr. & commentator worldwide on social, ethical & religious issues; Prov. of Ont. Grad. Fellow 1964–66, 1967–69; Can. Counc. Doct. Fellow 1970–72; author: 'Baal Shem Tov' 1961, 'Mystical Concepts in Chassidism' 1968, 'The Great Maggid' 1974, Who is a Jew? 1987, 'The Mystical Dimension' 1990, 'Chassidic Dimensions' 1990, 'Marei Mekomot-Mafteichot Tanya' (2 vols.) 1985–87; editor: 'Keter Shem Tov' 1974, Sifrei Hamaggid' 1974, 'Tzavaat Harivash' 1975; translator: 'Yud-Tet Kislev' 1964 'Igeret Hakodesh' 1968, 'Likkutei Sichot' (5 vols.) 1980–1990 (all partial lists); Home: 55 Charleswood Dr., Downsview, Ont. M3H 1X5.

**SCHOECK, Richard J.,** M.A., Ph.D., F.R.H.S., F.R.S.C. (1967); university professor and scholar; b. New York, N.Y. 10 Oct. 1920; s. Gustav J. and Frances M. (Kuntz) S.; e. McGill Univ., 1937–38; Mil. Service Schs., 1941–45; Princeton Univ., 1946–49, M.A., Ph.D.; m. Reta R., d. late William J. Haberer, June 1945; divorced 1976; children: Eric, Christine, Jennifer; m. 2ndly, Megan S. Lloyd, Feb. 1977; UNIV. PROF. OF ENGLISH AND AMERICAN LIT., UNIVERSITÄT TRIER 1987–90 (Head - Geschäftsführer 1988–89); EMERITUS PROF. OF ENGLISH AND HUMANITIES, UNIV. OF COLORADO; Adjunct Prof., Univ. of Kansas 1990– ; Resident Scholar, Rockefeller Centre at the Villa Serbelloni, Bellagio 1974, 1989; mem. Extve. Comte., Collected Work of Erasmus (First Co-ordinating Ed., Toronto 1969–71); Works of Thomas More; Works of George Buchanan; Am. Journ. Jurisprudence; mem. Ed. Comte., Complete Works of Richard Hooker; mem. Bd. Trustees, Natural Law Forum (Notre Dame); mem. Univ. of Toronto Senate (1964–68); Adv. Bd., Candn.-Am. Inst., Univ. of Windsor; Columbia Univ. Seminar in Legal Hist.; Catholic Comn. on Intellectual & Cultural Affairs (Washington); Gen. Ed., Chicago-Toronto series of Lit. Criticism 'Patterns of Literary Criticism'; Instr., Cornell Univ. 1949–55; Asst. and Assoc. Prof., Univ. of Notre Dame, 1955–61; Prof. of Eng., St. Michael's Coll., Univ. of Toronto 1961–71 and Head of Dept. there 1965–70; Prof. of Vernacular Lit., Pontifical Inst. of Mediaeval Studies, Toronto, 1961–71; Fellow, Yale Univ., 1959–60; Vincent J. Flynn Chair of Letters, College of St. Thomas, Minn. (1960); Visiting Prof. of Eng., Princeton Univ., 1964; Fellow, Fund for Advanc. of Educ., 1951–52; Director Research Activities, Folger Shakespeare Lib. and Dir. Folger Inst. of Renaissance and 18th Century Studies, Washington, D.C. 1970–74; Adjunct Prof. of Eng., Catholic Univ. of Am. 1972, Univ. of Md. 1972–74; Prof. of Eng. and of Medieval and Renaissance Studies, Univ. of Md. 1974–75; Chrmn., Dept. of Integrated Studies, Univ. of Colorado 1976–79; Chrmn., Comparative Literature, 1983–84; Visiting Prof. of Humanities, Univ. of Dallas 1985; Consultant Nat. Endowment for Humanities since 1972; served in 2nd World War in Signal Corps and Parachute Troops, U.S. Army, discharged with rank of 1st Lieutenant; author: 'The Achievement of Thomas More' 1976; 'Intertextuality and Renaissance Texts' 1984; 'Erasmus Grandescens' 1988, and 'A Raging Against Chaos' (poems) 1989; 'The Making of a Renaissance Humanist: Vol. 1 of a Biography of Erasmus' 1990–91, 'The Prince of Humanists' Vol. 2 1993; 'The Knight's Book' (poems) 1993; 'The Eye of a Traveller' (poems); Co-editor: 'Chaucer Criticism' I and II 1960–61; 'Voices of Literature' I and II 1964; Editor: 'Legends of the Saints' 1961; 'Editing Sixteenth-Century Texts' 1966; Ascham's 'Scholemaster' 1966; 'Shakespeare Quarterly' 1972–74; numerous articles in learned journals; ed. contrib. Ed., 'New Catholic Encyclopedia'; former Assoc. Ed. 'Neo-Latin News' 1955–63; Asst. Ed. 'Natural Law Forum' 1958–60; Gen. Ed. 'The Confutation of Tyndale' by Sir Thomas More, 3 Vols. 1973; Special ed. and contrib. to 'Canada' number of 'Review of National Literatures' 1977; Special ed. and contrib. to 'Sir Thomas Browne and The Republic of Letters' English Language Notes 1982 and co-ed. special number on Milton ELN 1982; Gen. ed., 'Renaissance Masters, Binghamton 1991– ; ed. ACTA BONONIENSIS: Proceedings of the Int. Assn. for Neo-Latin Studies, Bologna 1979 (Binghamton, 1985); Co-Ed., ACTA TORONTONENSIS: Proceedings of the Int. Assn. for Neo-Latin Studies, Toronto 1988 (Binghamton 1991); Contributor to numerous internat. congresses; has done research on early hist. of Inns of Court (awarded John Simon Guggenheim Mem. Foundation Fellowship 1967); Sr. Fellow, Canada Council; Rep. Modern Lang. Assn. Am. on Ad Hoc Comte. for Copyright Law Revision 1972–75; mem., Internat. Assn. for Neo-Latin Studies (Pres. 1976–79); mem., Soc. for the History of Rhetoric; Fulbright Rsch. Fellow (France and Holland) Summer 1984; Visiting Fellow, Inst. for Advanced Studies in Humanities (Edinburgh) 1984–85; Resident Scholar, Herzog August Bibliothek, Wolfenbüttel (Fall 1986); Visiting Scholar, Corpus Christi College, Oxford 1994; mem., Renaissance Soc. of Am. (Rep. for legal history on Council); Modern Lang. Assn. of Am.; Internat. Assn. of Univ. Prof. of Eng. (I.A.U.P.E.); recreations: travel, swimming; Club: PEN (N.Y.); Home: 232 Dakota, Lawrence, KS 66046.

**SCHOELER, Paul Jean René,** B. Arch., F.R.A.I.C. R.C.A.; architect; b. Toronto, Ont. 29 Oct. 1923; McGill Univ. B.Arch. 1951, Town Planning 1951–54 (CMHC Scholarship); PARTNER, SCHOELER & HEATON; private arch. practice since 1958; Design Awards incl. Gold Medal 13th Milan Triennale; First Prize Arch. Competition for Juvenile & Family Court Bldg. Ottawa; Hon. Mention Arch. Competition Ottawa Builders Exchange; Candn. Housing Design Council Design Award 1976 (Sr. Citizens Apt. Bldg. Kanata); various annual design awards Ont. Assn. Archs.; RAIC Festival of Arch. Awards (2) of Merit 1979 (J.W.I. Office Bldg. and Charlebois High Sch. Ottawa); Canadian Architect design awards (2) 1981; served with Candn. Army, First Special Service Force Italy; mem. Ont. Assn. Archs.; Order Archs. Quebec.; Royal Arch. Inst. Can.; Royal Canadian Academy; Office: 148 Bank St., Ottawa, Ont. K1P 5N8.

**SCHOEMPERLEN, Diane Mavis,** B.A.; writer; b. Fort William, Ont. 9 July 1954; d. William George and Ida Carolina (Tait) S.; e. Westgate H.S. 1973; Lakehead Univ., B.A. (1st class standing) 1976; single; one s.: Alexander Tait; Instr., Creative Writing, St. Lawrence Coll.; Upper Canada Writers' Workshop; The Kingston Sch. of Writing; Univ. of Toronto Writers' Workshop; Poetry Canada Review Prize 1980; Canadian Author and Bookman Okanagan Award for Short Fiction 1983; Writers' Guild of Alta. Award for Short Fiction 1987; Silver National Magazine Award 1989; grants: Ont. Arts Counc.; Can. Counc.; Alta. Found. for Literary Arts; Mem., The Writers' Union of Can.; P.E.N.; author: 'Double Exposures' 1984; 'Frogs and Other Stories' 1986; 'Hockey Night in Canada' (stories) 1987; 'The Man of My Dreams' (short-listed for Gov. General's Award & Trillium Award) 1990; 'Hockey Night in Canada and Other Stories' 1991; 'In the Language of Love' 1994; fiction pubd. in numerous mags. & anthols. incl.: 'The Fiddlehead'; 'Quarry'; 'Event'; 'The New Quarterly'; 'The Malahat Review'; 'Saturday Night'; 'The Macmillan Anthology 1 and 3'; 'The Rocket, The Flower, The Hammer and Me'; '87 and 90 Best Canadian Stories'; 'The Old Dance'; 'Alberta Bound'; 'Women and Words'; 'Canadian Short Stories: Fifth Series'; 'The New Story Writers'; Home: 32 Dunlop St., Kingston, Ont. K7L 1L2; Office: c/o TWUC, 24 Ryerson Ave., Toronto, Ont. M5T 2P3.

**SCHOENAUER, Norbert,** M.Arch., F.R.A.I.C., R.C.A.; educator; architect; b. Reghin, Romania 2 Jan. 1923; s. Norbert and Ira (Gergelyffy Mischinger) S.; e. Royal Hungarian Tech. Univ. Budapest B.Arch. 1945; Royal Acad. Fine Arts Copenhagen Cert. in Arch. 1950; McGill Univ. M.Arch. 1959; m. Astrid d. Johannes Christiansen; EMERITUS PROF. OF ARCH., McGILL UNIV., Dir. Sch. of Arch. there 1972–75; arch. and planning practice with Maurice Desnoyers 1967–75 (Fermont, new town in Northern Quebec); Extve. Dir. CMHC Nat. Office 1975–77; Candn. Del to UN Econ. Comn. Europe, Budapest 1976, Ottawa 1977; Consultant to Polservice, Poland 1978; recipient several awards and prizes designs in nat. arch. competitions; author: 'Introduction to Contemporary Indigenous Housing' 1973; '6,000 Years of Housing' Vols. 1–3 1981 (Spanish edition 1984 and Japanese ed. 1985); 'History of Housing' 1992; co-author: 'The Court-Garden House' 1962; 'University Housing in Canada' 1966; 'New Households, New Housing' 1989; 'Grassroots Greystones & Glass Towers' 1989; 'World Collective Houses: 200 in the 20th Century' 1990; contributor: 'Canadian Encyclopedia' (1985) and Am. Institute of Architect's 'Encyclopedia of Architecture' (1988); several mag. articles on Housing and Town Planning; Fellow, Royal Arch. Inst. Can.; mem. Royal Academy of Arts; mem. Order Archs. Que.; Corp. Professionnelle des Urbanistes du Qué.; Lutheran; Home: 3220 Ridgewood Ave., Apt. P-2, Montreal, Que. H3V 1B9; Office: 815 Sherbrooke St. W., Montreal, Que. H3A 2A7.

**SCHOENHALS, Paul John,** B.Ed.; businessman; b. Clinton, Ont. 5 Nov. 1941; s. Stewart John and Phyllis Lillian (Elliott) S.; e. Nutana Coll. Inst. Saskatoon 1960; Univ. of Sask. B.Ed. 1964, Post-grad. Dipl. 1970; children: Susan, Ryan, Karyn; PRES., PETROLEUM INDUSTRY TRAINING SERVICE 1989– ; Dir., Potash Corp. of Saskatchewan; Upton Resources; Petroleum Industry Training Service; Min. of Urban Affairs and Min. of Culture and Recreation, Sask. 1982–83; Min. of Energy and Mines July 1983–85; Min. responsible for Saskatchewan Oil and Gas Corp. 1983–85; Min. of Tourism and Small Business, Supply and Services, Science and Technology 1985–86; Min. Responsible for Employment Development Agency 1985–86; Vice Chrmn., Potash Corp., Sask. Jan. 1983–87; Chrmn., Potash Corp. of Sask. 1987–89; former Chrmn. Sask. Water Corp.; former Chrmn. Legislative Review Ctte.; High Sch. Teacher of Hist. and Physical Educ. Saskatoon Pub. Bd. of Educ. 1967–82; Co-ordr. Phys. Ed. Dept., Aden Bowman Coll. Inst. 1981–82; Coach of Saskatoon Hilltops 1975–79 (Candn. Jr. Football Champions 1978); Home: Calgary, Alta. T2T 4T3; Office 13, 2115 - 27th Ave. N.E., Calgary, Alta. T2E 7E4.

**SCHOFIELD, John Alexander,** B.A., M.B.A., M.A., Ph.D.; university professor and administrator; b. Leeds, U.K. 19 July 1940; s. George Eric and Betty (Nesham) Sc.; e. Durham Univ. B.A. (Hons.) 1962; Indiana Univ. M.B.A. 1964; Simon Fraser Univ. M.A. 1968, Ph.D. 1972; m. Josephine d. Robert and Dorothy Benson 1967; ASSOCIATE VICE-PRESIDENT, ACADEMIC, UNIV. OF VICTORIA 1992– ; Economist, British Oxygen Co. Ltd. (U.K.) 1964–66 Consultant Economist, PA Internat. Mngt. Consultants (U.K.) 1971–72; Asst., Assoc., Full Prof., Univ. of Victoria 1972– ; Chair, Dept. of Econ. 1986–91; Acting Dir., Sch. of Business 1989–90; Dir., Pacific N.W. Regional Econ. Conf. Bd. 1980–82; Beta Gamma Sigma; Sigma Iota Epsilon; Mem., Candn. Econ. Assn. (Vice-Pres. 1991); Candn. Regional Sci. Assn. (Pres. 1990–91); author: 'Cost-Benefit Analysis in Urban and Regional Planning' 1987, pbk. 1989; recreations: cricket, golf, reading, swimming, jogging, hiking, cinema, theatre; club: Cowichan Golf & Country; Home: 182 Barkley Terrace, Victoria, B.C. V8S 2J6; Office: P.O. Box 1700, Victoria, B.C. V8W 2Y2.

**SCHOGT, Henry Gilius,** M.A., Ph.D., F.R.S.C.; Retired; b. Amsterdam, Netherlands 24 May 1927; s. Johannes Herman and Ida Jacoba (van Rijn) S.; e. Barlaeus Gymnasium Amsterdam 1945; Univ. of Amsterdam Dept. Romance Langs. B.A. 1947, M.A. 1952, Dept. Slavic Langs. B.A. 1949, M.A. 1951; Univ. of Utrecht Ph.D. 1960; m. Corrie d. Philip Salomon Frenkel 2 Apl. 1955; children: Barbara, Philibert Johannes, Elida; Prof. of French, Univ. of Toronto 1969–92; Univ. of Groningen, Docent 1953–63 (Russian); Univ. of Utrecht, Wetenschappelijk hoofdambtenaar 1954–63 (French); Sorbonne, Univ. of Paris, Maître-assistant 1963–64 (Gen. Linguistics); Princeton Univ. Visiting Lectr. 1964–66 (Russian and French); Assoc. Prof. of French Univ. Toronto 1966, Chrmn. Grad. Dept. French 1972–77; author 'Les Causes de la double issue de e fermé tonique libre en français' 1960; 'De Palm die door het dak breekt' (8 short stories transl. from Russian into Dutch) 1966; 'Le Système verbal du français contemporain' 1968 'Sémantique synchronique: synonymie, homonymie, polysémie' 1976; co-author 'La Phonologie' 1977; 'Linguistics, Literary Analysis, and Literary Translation' 1988; over 50 articles phonology, verbal systems, semantics, diachronic linguistics, various book reviews; recreations: hiking, gardening; Home: 47 Turner Rd., Toronto, Ont. M6G 3H7.

**SCHOLEFIELD, Peter Gordon,** B.Sc., M.Sc., Ph.D., D.Sc.; research executive; b. Newport, Wales 26 June 1925; s. Tom and Margaret (Bithell) S.; e. Newport H.S. 1942; Univ. of Wales, B.Sc. 1944, M.Sc. 1946; McGill

Univ., Ph.D. 1949; Univ. of Wales, D.Sc. 1960; m. Erna d. Gordon and Wilma Cooper 29 Sept. 1951; children: David Andrew, John Gordon, Paul Frederick; DIR. OF GRANTS AND AWARDS, ALBERTA HERITAGE FOUNDATION FOR MEDICAL RSCH. 1992– ; Sr. Rsch. Fellow, McGill-Montreal Gen Hosp. Rsch. Inst. 1949–57; Asst. Prof., Biochemistry, McGill Univ. 1957–60; Assoc. Prof. 1960–65; Prof. & Dir., McGill Univ. Cancer Rsch. Unit 1965–69; Asst. Extve. Dir., National Cancer Inst. of Canada 1969–80, Extve. Dir., 1980–91; Special Adviser to the C.E.O., National Cancer Inst. of Canada 1991–92; recipient, R.M. Taylor Medal 1990; Commemorative Medal for 125th Anniversary of Candn. Confederation 1993; Home: 161 Allanhurst Dr., Islington, Ont. M9A 4K5; Office: 3125 ManuLife Place, 10180 – 101 St., Edmonton, Alta. T5J 3S4.

**SCHOLLAR, Jim Aubry;** food industry executive; b. Winnipeg, Man. 16 June 1921; s. Herbert Malton and Elizabeth Jane (Doran) S.; m. Dorothy Velma d. Wilf and Eleanor Skelding 24 Nov. 1945; children: Patricia, Sharon; CHRMN., THE GRIFFITH LABS. LTD. 1986– ; Vice-Pres., Sales & Mktg. 1963–74; Pres. & Chief Extve. Offr. 1974–86; Dir., Corp. Foods Ltd.; Squadron Navigation Offr., 429 Squadron (awarded D.F.C.); Past Chrmn., Health Counc. of Metro. Toronto; Anglican; Master Mason; recreations: curling, golf; Clubs: Donalda (Past Pres.); Home: 3800 Yonge St., Apt., 707, Toronto, Ont. M4N 2N6; Office: 757 Pharmacy Ave., Scarborough, Ont. M1L 3J8.

**SCHON, Denise,** B.A.; book publisher; b. Woodstock, Ont. 1 Feb. 1956; d. Robert Conrad and Barbara Margaret (Sale) S.; e. Glendon Coll., York Univ. B.A. 1978; Carleton Univ. Sch. of Journalism 1978–79; VICE PRES. & PUBLISHER, MACMILLAN CANADA 1989– ; Editorial Asst., Deneau & Greenberg 1979–81; Literary Agent, Nancy Colbert & Assoc. 1982–83; Sr. Editor, Doubleday Canada 1983–85; Editorial Dir., General & Profl. Books, McGraw-Hill Ryerson 1985–89; Faculty, Ryerson Publishing Program; Pres., Book Publishers Profl. Assn. 1992–93; Bd. of Dir., Trade Group, Candn. Book Publishers' Council; Office: 29 Birch Ave., Toronto, Ont. M4V 1E2.

**SCHOONOVER, Jason Brooke Rivers Morgan,** B.A.; writer; b. Melfort, Sask. 14 Sept. 1946; s. Vernon Lennis and Linda Lena S.; e. elem. and high schs. Sask., Ont.; Univ. of Sask.; Simon Fraser Univ. B.A. 1969; PRES. SCHOONOVER PROPERTIES 1975– ; Announcer, CKOM Radio Saskatoon 1970–71; Announcer, Music Dir., Promotion Mgr., Producer CFQC Radio Saskatoon and freelance stage and CBC broadcaster 1972–77; Columnist Westworld Mag. 1975–77; travel writer since 1978; Pres. Rolling Thunder Sound 1972–77; Windjammer Trading (Bangkok & Saskatoon) 1978–83; Vice Pres. Jeweler's Gallery 1979–82; internat. museologist anthrop. colls. Far East since 1978; writer, dir., producer multi-media staged prodn. John Diefenbaker's 80th birthday Saskatoon 1975; recipient B'nai B'rith Media Human Rights Award on behalf of CFQC Radio 1976; author (novel) 'The Bangkok Collection' 1988; 'Thai Gold' 1989; recreations: travel, outdoors, reading; Clubs: Explorers N.Y. (Fellow); Foreign Corr's Thailand; Home: 720 University Dr., Saskatoon, Sask. S7N 0J4.

**SCHOULS, Peter Arthur,** B.A., M.A., Ph.D.; university professor; b. The Netherlands 1 Dec. 1937; s. Joost Job and Adriana Johanna (Klink) S.; e. Chatham C.I. 1957; Univ. of Toronto B.A. 1960, M.A. 1962, Ph.D. 1967; m. Jeanette d. Jacob and Grace Tamminga 20 Aug. 1960; children: Timothy, Jacquelynn, Michelle; PROFESSOR, DEPT. OF PHILOSOPHY, UNIV. OF ALBERTA 1976– ; Lecturer, Philosophy, Univ. of Toronto 1964–67; Asst. Prof., Phil., Univ. of Alta. 1967–70; Assoc. Prof. 1970–76; Chair 1970–76, 1988–89; Dept. of Religious Studies 1988–90; Dept. of East Asian Languages and Literatures 1992–93; Visiting Prof., Free Univ. of Amsterdam 1977; Hon. Fellow, Inst. for Advanced Studies in the Humanities, Edinburgh Univ. 1983; Faculty of Arts Undergrad. Teaching Award 1989; McCalla Professorship 1982, '87; author: 'The Imposition of Method: A Study of Descartes and Locke' 1980, 'Descartes and the Enlightenment' 1989, 'Reasoned Freedom: Locke and Enlightenment' 1992 plus over 20 articles in learned journals; recreations: music, walking, swimming, sailing, skiing; Home: PH4, 10135 Saskatchewan Dr., Edmonton, Alta.; Office: Edmonton, Alta. T6G 2E5.

**SCHOUTEN, Albert Jacob (Jaap),** M.Arch., M.Sc.; city planner; b. Hilversum, The Netherlands 16 June 1942; s. Jan Karel and Jacoba Christina Hendrina (Den Hartog) S.; e. Technol. Univ. of Delft, M.Arch. 1968; Univ. of Toronto M.Sc. 1972; m. Maria d. Jan and Roelie Hoogenkamp 15 June 1968; children: Eric Jan, Claire Christine; VICE-PRES., NAT. PROGRAMMING, NAT. CAPITAL COMN. 1988– ; private cons., planning & arch., U.S. & Europe 1968; City Planner, City of Edmonton 1969–70; Cons., Transport Can. 1971; various capacities, Nat. Capital Comn. 1972–79; Extve. Dir., Planning 1981–86; Vice Pres., Planning 1987–88; Award of Excellence, Candn. Inst. of Planners 1972; Mem., Candn. Inst. of Planners; recreations: tennis, skiing; Home: 71 Irving Place, Ottawa, Ont. K1Y 2A2; Office: 161 Laurier Ave. W., Ottawa, Ont. K1P 6J6.

**SCHRAMEK, Tomas,** B.F.A.; ballet dancer; b. Bratislava, Czechoslavakia 11 Sept. 1944; s. Hans and Valerie (Neudorfer) S.; e. high sch. Bratislava; Acad. of Musical & Theatrical Arts Bratislava B.F.A. 1968; m. Deborah d. sidney D. and Florence Todd 10 June 1982; one d. Julia-Vally; one s. Milan Julius; PRINCIPAL CHARACTER ARTIST and COMPANY TEACHER, NATIONAL BALLET OF CANADA 1992– ; mem., SLUK, Slovakian Folk Dance Co. 1959–68, Princ. Dancer 1964–68; joined present Co. 1969, Soloist 1971, Principal Dancer 1973; teacher Nat. Ballet Sch., Lois Smith Sch. of Dance, les ballet jazz, Quinte Dance Centre, Studio Dance Theatre; mem. Actors' Equity Assn.; ACTRA; Home: 117 Welland Ave. Toronto, Ont. M4T 2J4; Office: 157 King St. E., Toronto, Ont. M5C 1G9.

**SCHREYER, Right Hon. Edward Richard,** P.C., C.C., C.M.M., C.D., B.A., P.Paed., B.Ed., M.A., LL.D.; b. Beausejour, Man. 21 Dec. 1935; s. John and Elizabeth (Gottfried) S.; e. Beausejour (Man.) Collegiate; United Coll., Winnipeg, Man.; St. John's Coll., Univ. of Man., B.A., B.Paed., B.Ed., M.A.; McGill Univ. LL.D.; Doctorat Science Social Univ. D'Ottawa; m. Lily, d. Jacob Schulz, 30 June 1960; children: Lisa, Karmel, Jason, Toban; Canadian High Commissioner to Australia 1984–88; Companion of the Ord. of Can.; Cmdr. of the Ord. of Military Merit; first el. to Manitoba Legislature 1958 (youngest mem. of Legislature); re-el. 1959 and 1962; Prof. of Pol. Sc. and Internat'l Relations, St. Paul's Coll., Univ. of Man. 1962–65; el. to House of Commons for Springfield 1965, re-el. 1968 as M.P. for Selkirk; el. Leader of Manitoba N.D.P. June 1969; Premier of Man. 1969–77 (Min. of Dom.-Prov. Relations, Min. of Finance 1972–74, Min. of Hydro 1971–77); Gov.-Gen. of Canada and Cmmdr. in Chief of Canada 1979–84; Roy. Candn. Armoured Corps Sch.; mem., Candn. Assn. of Univ. Teachers; Commonwealth Parliamentary Assn.; Inter-Parlty. Union; Governor General Vanier Award as outstanding Young Canadian, 1975; Prof. of Economic & Resource Geog. of the U.S.S.R., Univ. of Winnipeg 1989–90; Simon Fraser Univ. 1991; Candn. Resources & Public Admin., Simon Fraser Univ. 1991; Dist. Fellow, Energy & Resource Economics, Institute of Integrated Energy Systems, Univ. of Victoria 1992– ; Dir., CITIC (Canada) Ltd. 1991– ; Swan-é-set Bay Resort & Country Club 1991– ; Chrmn. Candn. Shield Foundation 1984– ; recreations: golf, wood & stone sculpting; Clubs: Rideau, Ottawa; Office: 250 Wellington Cr., Unit 401, Winnipeg Man. R3M 0B3.

**SCHROEDER, Andreas Peter,** M.A.; author; translator; editor; b. Hoheneggelsen, W. Germany 26 Nov. 1946; s. Ernst and Ruth Annemarie (Bartel) S.; came to Can. 1951; e. John Oliver High Sch. Vancouver 1965; Univ. of B.C., B.A. 1969, M.A. 1972; m. Sharon Elizabeth d. Rev. David Brown; two d. Sabrina Anne, Vanessa Elizabeth; Dir., Canadian Fiction Magazine; 'Grain'; Freelance Broadcaster CBC Radio 1968–74; Lit. Critic/Columnist Vancouver Province newspaper 1968–72; Co-Founder and Ed.-in-Chief, Contemporary Literature in Translation 1968–83; Lectr. in Creative Writing Univ. of Victoria 1974–75, Univ. of B.C. 1985–87, Simon Fraser Univ. 1989–90; Writer-in-Residence, Regina Public Lib. 1980–81, Univ. of Winnipeg 1983–84, Fraser Valley Library (Clearbrook) 1984, Fraser Valley Coll. 1987; author 'The Ozone Minotaur' (poetry) 1969; 'File of Uncertainties' (poetry) 1971; 'UNIverse' (poetry) 1971; 'The Late Man' (short fiction) 1972; 'Shaking It Rough' (non-fiction) 1976; 'Toccata in "D"' (novella) 1984; 'Dust-Ship Glory' (novel) 1986; 'Word for Word – The Business of Writing in Alberta' (non-fiction) 1988; 'The Eleventh Commandment' (short fiction) 1990; 'The Mennonites in Canada: A Photographic History' (non-fiction) 1990; in progress 'The Illegal Smile' (novel); 'Three micro-Novels'; 'Possible Treasures, Interim Mysteries' (poetry); co-ed. 'Stories From Pacific and Arctic Canada' 1974; stories and poems incl. in 58 Candn. and U.S. anthols.; serially published in over 100 lit. mags.; 416 pub. readings of work; over 250 feature-length articles various mags. and newspapers; Chrmn. Public Lending Right Comn. of Canada 1986–88; Vice Chrmn. Writers' Union Can. 1975, Chrmn. 1976; B.C. Rep. League Candn. Poets 1972, 1974; mem. ACTRA; P.E.N. Club; Fed. B.C. Writers; Sask. Writers' Guild; recipient Can. Council Grants 1969, 1971, 1975, 1979, 1986; Nat. Film Bd. Can. scriptwriting prize 1971; Woodward Mem. Prize for Prose 1969; short-list Gov. Gen.'s Award (non-fiction) 1977; finalist, Sealbooks First Novel Award 1983; NDP; defunct Mennonite; recreations: skydiving, motorcycle touring, downhill skiing; Address: c/o Douglas & McIntyre Ltd., 1615 Venables St., Vancouver, B.C. V5L 2H1.

**SCHROEDER, John G.,** B.Comm., C.A.; business executive; b. Winkler, Man. 26 March 1947; e. Univ. of Manitoba B.Comm. 1970; VICE-PRESIDENT, FINANCE, PARKLAND INDUSTRIES LTD.; Dir., Ensign Resource Serv. Group Inc.; Petrostar Petroleums Inc.; Office: 236, 4919 - 59 St., Red Deer, Alta. T4N 6C9.

**SCHROEDER, Thomas Leonard,** A.B., Ph.D.; university professor; b. Akron, Ohio 26 June 1947; s. Charles H. and Marion B. (Buzenberg) S.; e. Princeton Univ. A.B. 1969; Indiana Univ. Ph.D. 1983; m. Susan d. Douglas and Wilma Gutheil 30 May 1976; children: Peter H., David N.; ASSOC. PROF. OF MATHEMATICS EDN., STATE UNIV. OF NEW YORK AT BUFFALO 1993– ; Assoc. Prof., Fac. of Edn., Univ. of Calgary 1980–88; Assoc. Prof, Fac. of Edn., Univ. of B.C. 1988–93; Visiting Assoc. Prof., Edn., Simon Fraser Univ. 1987; Extve. Mem., B.C. Assn. of Mathematics Teaches; Mem., Candn. Math. Edn. Study Group; Internat. Group for the Psych. of Math. Edn.; Nat. Council of Teachers of Math. (Adv. Ctte. on Profl. Devel. 1987–90, Chair 1989–90); Comn. on Profl. Standards for Teaching 1989–91; Co-recipient, Outstanding Profl. Achievement Award 1986, Candn. Assn. for Studies in Edn. Admin.; Dir., Univ. of Calgary Credit Union Ltd. (Pres. 1983–85); Bible Study Fellowship Internat. (Discussion Leader); author/co-author of more than 50 papers, articles, chapters and reports; editor, consultant, contbr. to profl. pubs. such as 'Professional Standards for Teaching Mathematics' 1991; recreations: cycling, hiking, sailing; Home: 114 So. Cayuga Rd., Williamsville, NY 14221-6731 USA; Office: Dept. of Learning & Instruction, Graduate School of Education, State Univ. of New York at Buffalo, Buffala, NY 14260-1000 USA.

**SCHUELE, Alban Wilhelm,** B.Sc.; chemical industry executive; b. Germany 28 April 1944; s. Wilhelm and Emma (Utz) S.; e. Arizona State Univ. B.Sc. 1969; Am. Grad. School of Intern. Management (Thunderbird) 1970; m. Grayce LaGrotta; children: Jason, Kathleen; PRES., HOECHST CANADA INC. – CELANESE CANADA INC. 1991– ; Vice-Pres., Chase Manhattan Bank (N.Y., Milan, Hamburg, & Frankfurt) 1970–80; Asst. Treas., Hoechst Celanese Corporation (Somerville, N.J.) 1980–81; Treasurer 1982–85; Vice-Pres. & Treas. 1985–88; Vice-Pres., Quality & Communications, Hoechst Celanese Corp. 1988–89; Pres., Specialty Products Group 1989–91; Mem., Candn. Advisory Board of Allendale 1991– ; Mem. of the Board, Candn. Chemical Producers' Assn. (CCPA) 1991– ; Soc. of Chem. Industry 1991– ; Mem., Conference Board, Council on Canada/U.S. Economic Relations; Dir., Information and Referral Centre of Greater Montreal 1994– ; recreations: golf, tennis, skiing, music; clubs: Mount Royal, Summerlea Golf (Montreal), Raritan Valley Country (N.J.); Office: 800 Réne-Lévesque Blvd. W., Montreal, Que. H3B 1Z1.

**SCHULICH, Seymour,** B.Sc., M.B.A., C.F.A.; mining executive; b. Montreal, Que. 6 Jan. 1940; e. McGill Univ., B.Sc. 1960, M.B.A. 1965; Univ. of Virginia, Chartered Fin. Analyst, 1969; m. Tanna H. Goldberg 23 Nov. 1969; children: Deborah, Judith; CHRMN. AND CHIEF EXTVE. OFFR., FRANCO-NEVADA MINING CORP. LTD. 1984– and VICE-CHRMN., BEUTEL, GOODMAN & CO. LTD. 1991– ; Treas. Supr., Shell Oil 1961–63; Head of Rsch. & Dir., Eastern Securities Ltd. 1965–68; Pres., Beutel, Goodman & Co. Ltd. 1968–91; Pres., Dynamic Fund of Canada 1975–90; Chrmn., Euro-Nevada Mining Corp. Ltd.; Pres., Nevada Capital Corp. Ltd.; Dir., Highridge Resources Ltd.; Founder, 'Investors Digest of Canada'; Bache Found. Fellowship 1963; Gov., Mount Sinai Hosp.; Dir. & Gov., Jr. Achievement of Can.; recreations: jogging, weight training, tennis, skiing; Home: 25 Junewood Cres., Willowdale, Ont. M2L 2C3.

**SCHULTZ, Erich R.W.,** B.A., B.D., M.Th., B.L.S.; Retired; b. Rankin, Ont. 1 June 1930; s. William H. and Martha (Geelhaar) S.; e. Univ. of W. Ont. B.A. 1951; Waterloo Luth. Semy. B.D. 1957; Univ. of Toronto M.Th. 1958, B.L.S. 1959; Librarian and Archivist, Wilfrid Laurier Univ. (formerly Waterloo Lutheran University) 1960–91; Pastor, St. Paul's Lutheran, Ellice Twp., Ont. 1954–56; Librarian, Waterloo Luth. Semy. 1959–91, Lectr. 1959–70; Archivist, Eastern Synod,

Evangelical Lutheran Church in Canada 1961– ; ed. and bibliogr, 'Ambulatio Fidei: essays in honour of Otto W. Heick' 1965; 'Vita Laudanda: essays in memory of Ulrich S. Leopold' 1975; translator, 'Getting Along with Difficult People' (by Friederich Schmitt) 1970; mem., Ont. Library Assn. (Vice-Pres. 1967–68, Pres. 1968–69); Inst. of Professional Librarians of Ont. (Vice Pres. & Pres. 1969–70); Amer. Theological Library Assn. (Vice Pres. & Pres. 1975–77, Program Ctte., Chrmn. 1982–85); Candn. Libr. Assn. (mem. CLA and CACUL Cmtes., Convenor CLA Outstanding Service Award Cmte. 1978–80); OCUL Ont. Counc. of Univ. Libraries (Chrmn. 1978–80); Assn. of Candn. Archivists; Candn. Lutheran Historical Conference; Waterloo Historical Soc. (Vice Pres. 1980–82, Pres. 1982–84); Kitchener-Waterloo Commy. Concert Assn. (Bd. of Dir., Vice-Pres. 1986–88; Pres. 1988–90); Waterloo Regional Heritage Found. 1990–92; Lutheran; recreations: music, golf; Home: 235 Erb St. E., Waterloo, Ont. N2J 1M9.

**SCHULTZ, Richard John,** B.A., M.A., Ph.D.; university professor; b. South Porcupine, Ont. 2 Oct. 1945; s. Carl Mark and Margaret Jean (Smith) S.; e. York Univ., B.A. 1968; Univ. of Manchester, M.A. 1970; York Univ., Ph.D. 1976; children: Mark, Kate; Prof., Pol. Sci., Glendon Coll., York Univ. 1972–75; Staff Offr., Fed.-Prov. Relns. Office, Govt. of Can. 1975–77; Prof., Pol. Sci., McGill Univ. 1978– ; Dir., Centre for the Study of Regulated Indus., McGill Univ. 1982–90; independent consultant to business & govts.; Assoc. Ed., 'Can. Public Policy' 1980–84; Fellow, Counc. on Econ. Regulation 1985–91; Vis. Rsch. Fellow in Legal Theory, Law, Univ. of Toronto 1984; Program on Infor. Resources Policy, Harvard Univ. 1985; Visiting Prof., Duke Univ. 1994; Mem., Adv. Ctte., Inst. of Intergovt. Relns., Queen's Univ.; Sectoral Adv. Group on Internat. Trade to Min. for Internat. Trade 1986–91; Mem., Candn. Pol. Sci. Assn.; Inst. of Public Admin. of Canada; Internat. Institute of Communications; Am. Political Science Assn.; author: 'Federalism and the Regulatory System' 1979, 'Federalism, Bureaucracy and Public Policy' 1980 and over 20 articles & chaps. in acad. journals & books; co-author of 4 books incl. most recently 'Exploiting the Information Revolution' 1989; co-editor: 'Canadian Political Process' 1970, '73, '79, 'Pipeline Regulation and Inflation' 1983, 'Local Telephone Pricing' 1984; Home: 127 Clandeboye Ave., Westmount, Que. H3Z 1Y9; Office: 855 Sherbrooke St. W., Montreal, Que. H3A 2T7.

**SCHULTZ, Siegfried (Fred) Henry,** B.A.; association executive; b. Ottawa, Ont. 16 Oct. 1936; s. Henry Herman and Marie Emilie (Oelsner) S.; e. Lisgar C.I. 1955; Carleton Univ. B.A. (with distiction) 1966; m. Frances d. Winston and Mae Currie 20 May 1961; children: Paul, Craig, Stephanie; EXECUTIVE DIRECTOR, CANADIAN ASSN. OF CHIEFS OF POLICE 1990– ; Mem., Royal Canadian Mounted Police 1956–90 (retired as Asst. Commr.); general police duties P.E.I. 1956–61; RCMP Security Serv. 1961–84; Commanding Officer, RCMP 'N' Div. Ottawa 1984–88; Dir., Candn. Police College Ottawa 1984–88; Dir. of Corporate Services, RCMP H.Q. Ottawa 1988–90; RCMP Long Service Medal; Mem., Internat. Assn. of Chiefs of Police; Candn. Soc. of Assn. Extves.; recreations: golf, fitness; clubs: Hylands Golf; Home: 3002 Marcel St., Ottawa, Ont. K1V 8H7; Office: 112 Kent St., Suite 1908, Ottawa, Ont. K1P 5P2.

**SCHULTZ, Walter Arthur,** C.A.; consultant; b. Winnipeg, Man. 16 Jan. 1928; s. late Ludwig and late Matilda (Hoffman) S.; e. St. John's High Sch. 1946; Angus Sch. of Comm. Accounting Cert. 1947; Univ. of Man. C.A. 1955; m. Dorothea d. late Conrad and late Marie Brethauer 8 Aug. 1952; children: Laurie Ann, Walter David, Brenda Marie, Mark Douglas; CONSULTING and VOLUNTEER WORK 1993– ; Audit Group Head Taxation Div. Revenue Can. 1955–63; Extve. Secy. Div. Information Services, Candn. Lutheran Council 1963–67, Lutheran Council in Can. 1967–76; Extve. Dir., Lutheran Council in Can. 1976–86; Treas. Can. Sec. Lutheran Ch. in Am. 1963–85; mem. Comn. on World Service Lutheran World Fed. Geneva 1977–86; Asst. Comptroller, Lutheran World Federation 1986–90, Dir. of Finance & Admin. 1990–92 (Retired); Dir. Lutheran Life Ins. Soc. Can. 1972–86; mem. Finance Comte. Candn. Council Chs. 1964–86; recipient Distinguished Service Award Lutheran Brotherhood Ins. Minneapolis 1967; Inst. C.A.'s Man.; recreations: photography, walking; Home: 16 Magellan Bay, Winnipeg, Man. R3K 0P8.

**SCHULZ, Robert,** B.A., B.S.M.E., M.B.A., Ph.D.; educator; consultant; b. Long Branch, N.J. 20 Aug. 1943; s. Robert A. and Anna (Fuga) S.; e. St. Vincent Coll. Latrobe, Pa. B.A. 1965; Univ. of Notre Dame B.S.M.E. 1966 (Dean's List 1966); Univ. of Pittsburgh M.B.A. 1967; Ohio State Univ. Ph.D. 1971 (Pacesetter's Award 1971); PROF., ACAD. DIR. OF PETROLEUM LAND MGMT., and CO-ORDINATOR OF UNIV. TEACHING DEVELOP. OFFICE 1991– , THE UNIV. OF CALGARY 1973– ; Pres. Scenario Management Consultants Ltd. Calgary 1987– ; Asst. to Pres. Kerry-Fab Inc. Pittsburgh 1967; Rsch. Asst. Office. Tech. & Bus. Services Ohio State Univ. 1968, Teaching Asst. Mktg. Dept. 1969; Sr. Cons. Assoc. Management Horizons Inc. Columbus 1969–70, Mngmt. Horizons Data Systems Inc., Computer Conversion Coordinator 1970, Dir. Tech. Edn. 1971, Dir. Edn. 1972–73; Assoc. Prof. of Mgmt. present Univ. 1973–88, Chrmn. Policy & Environment Area 1975–77, Acad. Dir. Petroleum Land Mgmt. 1983– , Prof. 1988– ; recipient Special Appreciation Award Univ. of Technol. Lae, Papua-New Guinea 1985; recipient 6 awards outstanding teaching incl. 1987 3M Teaching Fellowship; Special Service Award Candn. Assn. Petrol. Landmen 1987; 25 Alta. Achievement Awards as coach Calgary's intercoll. bus. competition teams; Dir. Calgary Sponsor & Refugee Soc. 1979–81; Alta. Cath. Sch. Trustees' Assn. Blueprints Ctte. 1981–87; Global Food Bank Assn. 1986–87; Presidential Adv. Ctte. St. Mary's Cath. Coll. Calgary 1986– ; Chrmn., Align to 21st Century Task Force, Calgary Economic Develop. Authority 1989– ; Chrmn., Calgary Catholic Diocesan Synod Coordinating Ctte. 1990– ; author over 30 comnd. reports and acad. papers; facilitator over 800 workshops and seminars primarily time mgmt., manager as coach, learning styles, and corporate planning; Hon. mem. Candn. Assn. Petrol. Landmen; Assoc. mem. Am. Assn. Petrol. Landmen; recreations: golf, basketball, jogging; Club: Silver Springs Golf & Country; Home; 24 Chateaux-on-the-Green, 1815 Varsity Estates Dr. N.W., Calgary, Alta. T3B 3Y7; Office: 438 Scurfield Hall, 2500 University Dr. N.W., Calgary, Alta. T2N 1N4.

**SCHUMACHER, C. John,** LL.B., M.B.A., F.I.C.B., C.F.A.; financial executive; b. Halifax, N.S. 7 June 1955; s. Charles Clement and Barbara Marie (MacIntyre) S.; e. Univ. of Toronto LL.B. 1980; called to the Bar of Law Soc. of U.C. 1982; Univ. of Western Ont. M.B.A. 1984; Fellow, Inst. of Can. Bankers C.B.A. 1985; Inst. of Chartered Fin. Anal. C.F.A. 1990; Vice Chairman, Toronto Dominion Securities Inc. 1991; SENIOR VICE-PRES., GLOBAL CAPITAL & MONEY MARKETS GROUP, TORONTO-DOMINION BANK 1993– ; Mem., Internat. Forex Assn.; Money Market Assn.; Bond Traders Assn.; Dir., TDSI, TDSI (USA); club: St. Georges Golf & Country; Office: Box 1, T-D Centre, Toronto, Ont. M5K 1A2.

**SCHUSTER, Rudolf;** ambassador; b. Košice, Czechoslovakia 4 Jan. 1934; e. Faculty of Construction Engr., Slovak Technical Inst., Bratislava 1959; married; 2 children; Ambassador of the Czech and Slovak Federal Republic to Canada 1990–92; Asst., Hydrology and Hydraulic Inst. of Slovak Academy of Sciences, Bratislava 1960–62; Dir., Energetic Investment Dept. and Tech. Dir., East Slovak Steelworks 1963–74; Depy. Mayor, City of Košice 1975–83, Mayor 1983–86; Chrmn., East Slovak Region National Ctte. 1986–89; Chrmn., Slovak National Council 1989–90; Scientific Diploma, Field of Environmental Protection 1984; Mem., Slovak Writers' Assn.; author of many novels, radio and TV plays; Address: Embassy of the Czech and Slovak Federal Republic, 50 Rideau Terrace, Ottawa, Ont. K1M 2A1.

**SCHWARCZ, Henry Philip,** A.B., M.Sc., Ph.D., F.R.S.C.; university professor; b. Chicago, Ill. 22 July 1933; s. Arthur and Zita Elizabeth (Strauss) S.; e. Univ. of Chicago, A.B. 1952; Calif. Inst. of Technol. M.Sc. 1955, Ph.D. 1960; m. Molly Ann d. David A. Robinson 20 Dec. 1964; one s.: Joshua Arthur; PROF. OF GEOLOGY, MCMASTER UNIV. 1962– ; Bd. of Dirs., Lithoprobe (NSERC) 1991– ; Rsch. Assoc., Enrico Fermi Inst. 1960–62; Vis. Prof., Hebrew Univ. of Jerusalem 1975–76, 1982–83; rsch. in stable isotope geochem., dating of archaeol. sites, environ. geochem.; Fulbright Fellow (Italy) 1968–69; Fellow, Geolog. Soc. of Am.; Royal Soc. of Can.; Visiting Fellow, Clare Hall, Cambridge Univ. 1991–92; Killam Fellow, Canada Council 1993–95; Mem., Geolog. Assn. of Can.; Geochem. Soc.; author of many sci. papers, book chapters, etc.; Assoc. ed.: 'Geochimica et Cosmochimica Acta'; Ed. Bd.: 'Journal of Archaeological Sciences'; Rivista di Anthropologia; Geolog. Soc. of Am. Archaeological Geolog. Div. Award 1991; recreation: violin; Home: 127 Cline Ave. N., Hamilton, Ont. L8S 3Z7; Office: 1280 Main St. W., Hamilton, Ont. L8S 4M1.

**SCHWARTZ, Alan M.,** B.A., B.C.L., LL.B., Q.C.; investment executive; b. Montreal, Que. 9 Feb. 1945; s. Nathan and Molly (Brandes) S.; e. Concordia Univ. B.A. 1967; McGill Univ. B.C.L. 1970, LL.B. 1971; m. Alison d. Cleeve and Patricia Hooper; children: Dana Lauren, Jared Benjamin; PARTNER, GLUSKIN SHEFF & ASSOC. 1989– ; Partner, Fogler, Rubinoff 1973–88; served as counsel to the Ont. Select Cttes. on Hydro Affairs and on Highway Safety; Chair, Ont. Health Prof. Legis. Rev.; Vice-Chair, Ont. Task Force on the Implementation of Midwifery; Dir., Media Reinsur. Corp.; Past Mem., Ont. Econ. Council; Vice-Pres., Bd. of Trustees, Art Gallery of Ont.; Dir., Art Found. of the Profl. Art Dealers Assn.; Arts Found. of Greater Toronto; club: Canadian; Home: 126 Warren Road, Toronto, Ont. M4V 2S1; Office: 20 Queen St. W., Ste. 2014, Toronto, Ont. M5H 3R3.

**SCHWARTZ, Arthur Bert,** B.A.Sc., M.B.A., P.Eng.; executive; b. Toronto, Ont. 27 Oct. 1927; s. Benjamin and Fay (Minster) S.; e. Univ. of Toronto B.A.Sc. (Aeronautical Eng.) 1950; New York Univ. M.B.A. 1961; m. Muriel Henrietta Atkins 28 Apr. 1949; children; Steven Hal, Ruth Ellen, Sandra Lee Mendlowitz, Sidonie Helene; PRES. A.B. SCHWARTZ AND ASSOCIATES INC. 1986– ; Asst. Chief Planning Eng., Group Leader Initial Projects Office, Stress Analyst, Design Eng. Avro Aircraft Ltd. 1950; Acting Adm. Mgr., Prog. Control Supr., Project Eng. Curtiss Wright Corp. Curtiss Div. (USA) 1959; Prog. Mgr. Subcontracts USN X-22A VTOL Aircarft; Mfg. Mgr. NASA Lunar Module Ascent Engine; Mfg. Dir. USAF Minuteman Post Boost Propulsion System; Mgr. Mfg. Prog. Control Bell Aerospace Corp. (USA) 1963; Eng. Mgr. deHavilland Aircraft of Canada Ltd. 1969; Div. Mgr. Helicopter Recovery Systems DAF Indal Ltd. 1978; Vice Pres. Resources Mgmt., Vice Pres, Prog. Mgmt., Vice Pres. Projects Eng. Candu Operations, Atomic Energy of Canada Ltd. 1979; Pres., A.B. Schwartz and Assocs. Inc. 1986; Assoc. Fellow, Candn. Aeronautics & Space Inst.; mem. Assn. Prof. Engs. Prov. Ont.; Candn. Nuclear Soc.; Jewish; recreations: walking, swimming, sailing; Address: 92 Whitehorn Cres., Willowdale, Ont. M2J 3B2.

**SCHWARTZ, Bryan Paul,** LL.B., LL.M., J.S.D.; professor of law; b. Regina, Sask. e. Queen's Univ. LL.B. 1978; Yale Univ. LL.M. 1980, J.S.D. 1986; m. Beverly (Weiss); children: Michael, Eliana; PROFESSOR, FACULTY OF LAW, UNIV. OF MANITOBA 1981– ; articled Minister of Justice, Ottawa 1979–80; Constitutional Cons., Attorney General of Sask. 1981; Constitutional Advr., Attorney General of Man. 1982–88; Chair., Constitutional Law Section, Candn. Bar Assn. 1987–89; Mem., Bars of Ont. & Man.; Arbitrator under Manitoba Labour Relations Act 1991– ; Rh Inst. Award for Outstanding Scholarship in the Humanities 1988; author: 'First Principles' 1986; 'First Principles, Second Thoughts: Aboriginal Peoples, Constitutional Reform and Canadian Statecraft' 1987; 'Fathoming Meech Lake' 1987; 'Opting In: The New Federal Proposals on the Constitution' 1992; 'Still Thinking: A Guide to the 1992 Constitutional Referendum'; author of regular 'Law and Society' column, Globe and Mail and articles in legal jours.; Office: Winnipeg, Man. R3T 2N2.

**SCHWARTZ, Gerald Wilfred,** B.Com., LL.B., M.B.A.; businessman; b. Winnipeg, Man. 24 Nov. 1941; s. Andrew O. and Lillian (Arkin) S.; e. Univ. of Man. B.Comm. 1962, LL.B. 1966; Harvard Univ. M.B.A. 1970; m. Heather Reisman; children; Carey, Jill, Andrea, Anthony; PRES., C.E.O. AND DIR., MEM. EXTVE. COMTE., ONEX CORP.; Chrmn. of Bd., Sky Chefs Inc.; Dir., Automotive Industries Holdings Inc.; ProSource Distribution Services Inc.; Mem. Gov. Counc. and Extve. Ctte., Univ. of Toronto; Council for Business and the Arts in Canada; Dir. & Treasr., Mt. Sinai Hosp.; Mem. Bd. of Associates, Harvard Business School; Dir., Candn. Counc. of Christians & Jews; Dir., Candn. Friends of Tel Aviv Univ.; Dir., Candn. Soc. for the Weizmann Inst. of Science; Dir., Harvard Business School Club of Toronto; called to Bar of Man. 1966; law practice Asper, Freedman & Co. Winnipeg 1966–68; Assoc., Corporate Finance, Estabrook & Co. Inc. N.Y. 1970, Vice Pres. Corporate Finance 1971; Sr. Assoc., Bear, Stearns & Co. 1973, Vice Pres. Corporate Finance 1974; Pres., mem. of the Exec. Ctte. CanWest Capital Corp. 1977–83; Assoc. Prof. (Adj.) N.Y. Univ. Grad. Sch. Business Adm.; recreation: tennis; Office: 161 Bay St., Toronto, Ont. M5J 2S1.

**SCHWARTZ, Leo;** business executive; b. Montreal, Que. 24 Mar. 1924; s. Issac and Polly (Rosen) S.; e. two years high school; m. Laura d. Herman and Celia Galler 21 Oct. 1945; children: Martin, Alan, Jeffrey; PRES. & CHRMN. OF THE BOARD, DOREL INDUSTRIES INC. 1962– ; mfr. of baby products; merged with son's business & became public co. 1987; purchased Cosco Co. (Columbus, IN) 1988; purchased Charleswood Co. (St. Louis, MI) 1990; Dir., Summit Sch.; recreations: boating, stained glass, woodworking; Home: 6950 Côté St.

Luc Rd., #709, Montreal, Que. H4V 2Z9; Office: 4750 des Grandes Prairies, St. Leonard, Que. H1R 1A3.

**SCHWARTZ, Nancy E.,** Ph.D.; nutritionist; b. Moose Jaw, Sask. 1 Oct 1947; d. Maurice and Sally (Fisherman) S.; e. Univ. of B.C., B.H.E. 1968; Ohio State Univ., Ph.D. 1973; m. Glenn R. Williams 11 Oct. 1975; one s. Gregory; DIR., NATIONAL CENTER FOR NUTRITION AND DIETETICS 1990– ; Therapeutic Dietitian & Nutrition Instructor, Queen Elizabeth Hosp., Montreal 1969–70; Asst./Assoc. Prof. & Dir. of Continuing Edn. in Nutrition & Dietetics, Univ. of B.C. 1973–87; Pres., Nat. Inst. of Nutrition 1987–90; W.H.O./P.A.H.O. Cons. 1979 and 1986; rec'd Nestlé Achievement Award 1987; Fellow, Candn. Dietetic Assn. 1989; mem. Candn., Am. Dietetic Assns.; Am. Inst. of Nutrition; Soc. for Nutrition Edn.; Cdn. Soc. for Nutritional Sciences; Sigma Xi; Scientific Rsch. Soc.; author of 2 books and 34 scholarly or profl. jour. articles; recreation: travel; Office: 216 W. Jackson Blvd., Suite 800, Chicago, IL 60606-6995, USA.

**SCHWARZMANN, Maurice,** M.A.; b. Malaga, Spain 21 Dec. 1920; s. Louis and Aurelia (Monterde) s.; Mill-Hill School, London, England; Institut Frilley (Hautes Etudes Commerciales), Paris, France; University of McGill; University of Toronto B.A. (Political Science & Economy), M.A. 1950; m. Patricia D. Finlayson de la Guardia, d. late John Finlayson; October 30, 1975; children: Violet, Robert, Edward, Ronald and Patricia; appt. to Dept. Trade & Commerce, May, 1949; Dir. Intr. Trade Relations Br., 1958; Minister (Econ), Canadian Embassy, Washington D.C. 1959–1964; Assist. Deputy Minister, Trade & Ind. Policy, Ottawa, 1964; participated in Cndn. Ministerial Trade Mission to Latin America, 1953; Trade Agreements with Spain and Portugal, 1954; GATT Review Conf., Geneva, 1954; Commonwealth Finance Ministers Conf., Mt. Tremblant, 1957; Commwth. Trade & Econ. Conf., Montreal, 1958; Canada-U.S., Canada-Japan and other Ministerial Conferences; Chairman Cdn. Delegations to numerous trade & economic negotiations, GATT, OECD, Textiles and Intr. Wheat Agreements; Minister Cdn. Delegation to Kennedy Round Trade Negotiations, Geneva, 1964–1967; Member Ministerial Mission to Latin America, 1968; InterAmerican Development Bank Conf., Quito, Ecuador, 1972; Ambassador to Mexico and concurrently to Guatemala, 1972–75; Ambassador to Venezuela and concurrently Dominican Republic, 1975–77; served in Second World War, 1943–46, with Canadian Army Intelligence Corps, UK and Netherlands, incl. Supreme Headquarters Allied Expeditionary Forces, London, & First Candn. Corps Headquarters, Utrecht; left Govt. Service to enter private activities as Business Consultant in March 1977; Address: 1250 Amherst, Los Angeles, Calif. 90025.

**SCHWASS, Rodger Daniel,** B.A., M.Ed., Ed.D.; educator; b. Port Elgin, Ont. 4 Apl. 1936; s. Daniel and Gladys Winifred (Rodgers) S.; e. Saugeen Dist. High Sch. Port Elgin 1954; Univ. of Toronto B.A. 1961, M.Ed. 1964, Ed.D. 1972; m. Mary Catherine d. Stuart and Marion Byers 18 July 1959; children: Ronald, Richard, Catherine, Marion; PROFESSOR, FAC. OF ENVIRONMENTAL STUDIES, YORK UNIV. 1976– (Dean of Faculty 1976–82, and Dir. Office of Internat. Services, York Univ. 1982–84); Primary Sch. Princ. S.S. #3 East Luther Twp. (Grand Valley) 1954–55: Assoc. Dir. Farm Programs CKNX Radio/TV, Wingham, Ont. 1955–58; Ed./Mgr. Nat. Farm Radio Forum, Toronto 1958–64; Vice Pres. Hedlin Menzies & Associates 1965–69; Vice Pres. Acres Consulting Services 1969–76; Vice Pres. Candn. Internat. Consulting Econs. 1972– ; Gov. Humber Coll. Applied Arts & Technol. 1978–83; Chrmn. Adv. Comte. Resources Mang. Banff Centre; mem. Internat. Assn. Univs. Comte. on Impacts of Technol. Change; Policy Chrmn. Lib. Party of Can. 1984–90; Chrmn., Task Force on Northern Conservation 1983–85; extensive work on development of National Conservation Strategies in Pakistan, Jamaica, Tanzania, Kenya, Indonesia; various reports, policy guidelines, articles; recreations: squash, farming; Home: 71 The Kingsway, Toronto, Ont. M8X 2T3; Office: 4700 Keele St., North York, Ont. M3J 1P3.

**SCHWEINBENZ, Horst,** B.A., F.O.T.F.; teacher, association executive; b. Heidlberg, Germany 23 Oct. 1949; s. Otto and Genevieve (Wilson) S.; e. Cathedral Boys H.S. 1968; McMaster Univ. B.A. 1974; Hamilton Teachers College 1970; m. Carol d. Katleen and Arthur Marshall 3 July 1971; children: Kristie, Amanda; PRESIDENT, ONTARIO TEACHERS FEDERATION 1992–93; Elementary School Teacher; Pres., Hamilton-Wentworth Unit, Ont. English Cath. Teachers Assn. (OECTA) 1978; Chief Negotiator (4 times) 1976–90; Extve. of Provincial 1990; Gov., Ont. Teachers Fed. 1984–93; Chair, Pension Partners Ctte., Ont. Teachers Fed. & Govt. of Ont. 1992–93; Mem., Min. of Edn. & Training Adv. Council on Edn. Finance Reform 1992–93; Annual Award OECTA named in honour of Horst Schweinbenz: 'The Horst Schweinbenz Silver Palate Award'; Mem., St. Margaret Mary Parish; editor: 'Around OECTA' bi-weekly newsletter 1987–90, L.E.A.C. Report (newsletter) 1991–92; recreations: stained glass; Home: 115 Elmhurst Dr., Hamilton, Ont.; Office: 700, 1260 Bay St., Toronto, Ont. M5R 2B5.

**SCHWEITZER, Eugene Howard;** consultant; retired executive; b. Kincardine, Ont. 20 June 1915; s. Edward A. and Jeanette (Ludwig) S.; e. Kincardine High Sch.; Curtiss-Wright Tech. Inst., Los Angeles, Calif., 1940; m. Helen Bernice, d. Charles G. Taillon, Kincardine, Ont., 10 May 1957; Vice-Pres., Commuter Operations, Pratt & Whitney Aircraft Of Canada Ltd. to 1981; mem., Canadian Aero. and Space Inst.; Canadian Aviation Historical Society; Protestant; recreations: gardening, swimming; Home: RR #1, P.O. Box 428, Kincardine, Ont. N2Z 2Y8.

**SCHWITZER, Eric Lincoln,** B.Sc., S.M.; investment banker; b. Montreal, Que. 22 March 1951; s. Douglas Hood and Lillian Maud S.; e. McGill Univ. B.Sc. 1972; M.I.T. S.M. 1975; m. Diane d. J.W. and Ruth Moreland 26 Sept. 1981; children: Kelly, Katie, Thomas; SENIOR VICE-PRESIDENT, SCOTIAMCLEOD INC.; Dir., ScotiaMcLeod Inc.; clubs: Hollyburn Country, Capilano Golf; Office: 609 Granville St., 11th fl., Vancouver, B.C. V7Y 1H6.

**SCIPIO DEL CAMPO, Andrew H.,** B.A.; investment executive; b. Montréal, Qué. 29 Dec. 1952; s. André and Marie (Schretlen) S. del C.; e. Loyola CEGEP 1971; Loyola Coll. B.A. 1973; m. Emily d. Alex and Emily Krajicek Jan. 1990; two s. Andrew, Eric; two stepsons: Karl, Erik; PRES. AND CHIEF EXTVE. OFFR. SCOTIA SECURITIES INC. 1990– ; joined Montreal Trust 1974–83; Vice Pres. 1983; Vice Pres. & Dir., Lafferty, Harwood & Partners Ltd. 1983–86; Vice Pres. & Dir., Scotia Securities Inc. 1987–88; Pres., C.E.O. & Dir., Guardinvest Securities Inc. 1988–90; Vice Chrmn., Dir., Investment Funds Institute of Can. (IFIC) 1993; Chrmn., Retail Distributor, IFIC 1993; Past Pres. Qué. Heart Stroke Found. 1982–83; Dir., Heart & Stroke Found. of Canada (Past Pres. 1990–91); Clubs: Ontario; Oxford; Home: 1227 Lorne Park Rd., Mississauga, Ont. L5H 3A7; Office: 1 Richmond St. W., Suite 700, Toronto, Ont. M5H 3W4.

**SCOBIE, Stephen Arthur Cross,** M.A., Ph.D.; educator; author; b. Carnoustie, Scot. 31 Dec. 1943; s. Arthur Cross S.; e. Univ. of St. Andrews M.A. 1965; Univ. of B.C. Ph.D. 1969; m. Sharon Maureen d. Joseph Melville McHale, Langley, B.C. 6 May 1967; PROF. OF ENGLISH, UNIV. OF VICTORIA 1981– ; joined Univ. of Alta. Dept. Eng. 1969–81, Prof. 1980–81; Guest Prof. of Candn. Studies, Christian-Albrechts-Universität Kiel, Germany 1990; rec'd Gov. Gen.'s Award for Poetry 1980; author (poetry) 'Babylondromat' 1966; 'In the Silence of the Year' 1971, repr. 1973; 'The Birken Tree' 1973; 'Stone Poems' 1974; 'The Rooms We Are' 1975; 'Airloom' 1975; 'les toiles n'ont peur de rien' 1979; 'McAlmon's Chinese Opera' 1980; 'A Grand Memory for Forgetting' 1981; 'Expecting Rain' 1985; 'The Ballad of Isabel Gunn' 1987; 'Dunino' (short-list Gov. Gen. Award 1990) 1988; 'Remains' 1990; 'Ghosts: A Glossary of the Intertext' 1990; co-author 'The Pirates of Pen's Chance' 1981; critical study 'Leonard Cohen' 1978; 'bpNichol: What History Teaches' 1984; 'Signature Event Context' 1989; 'Alias, Bob Dylan' 1991; over 20 critical articles Candn. lit. and experimental poetry various publs.; short stories; poetry readings across Can. and Twelfth Internat. Sound Poetry Festival, New York 1980; co-ed. 'The Maple Laugh Forever: An Anthology of Canadian Comic Poetry' 1981; mem. League of Candn. Poets (Vice Pres. 1972–74, 1986–88); recreations: movies, Bob Dylan, golf; Home: 4278 Parkside Cres., Victoria, B.C. V8N 2C3; Office: Victoria, B.C. V8W 2Y2.

**SCOLLIN, Hon. John Ambrose,** M.A., LL.B.; judge; b. Edinburgh, Scot. 6 Oct. 1927; s. John Benedict and Mary Veronica (McGhee) S.; e. Holy Cross Acad., Edin.; Univ. of Edin., M.A. 1948, LL.B. 1950; m. Rita, d. Charles and Elizabeth McGregor, 21 Oct. 1950; children: John Charles, Lorraine Maria; JUDGE, COURT OF QUEEN'S BENCH FOR MANITOBA 1981– ; admitted Solicitor in Supreme Court 1950; called to Scottish Bar 1954; magistrate, Brit. Colonial Service, E. Africa 1954–57; Court Attorney, Man. 1957–60; partner, Pitblado and Hoskin, Winnipeg 1960–66; Dept. of Justice, Ottawa: Dir. Criminal Law Section, Asst. Dep. Attorney Gen., Chief Gen. Counsel 1966–81; also mem. of Bars of Ont. and Sask.; lectr. in Law of Evidence, Man. Law Sch.; Vans Dunlop Scholarship in Law, Univ. of Edin.; appointed Q.C. (Fed.) 1969, Q.C. (Man.) 1970; author: 'Pre-trial Release: A Commentary on the Bail Reform Act' 1972, 2nd ed. 1977; Home: 30 Birkenhead Ave., Winnipeg, Man. R3P 0P1; Office: Law Courts, Broadway and Kennedy, Winnipeg, Man. R3C 0P9.

**SCOTLAND, Randall Blaine,** B.A., M.A.; magazine editor; b. Calgary, Alta. 22 July 1954; s. John Andrew and Grace Eloise (Pottruff) S.; e. Univ. of Calgary, B.A. 1977; Univ. of Windsor, M.A. 1978; FINANCIAL POST; Asst. Ed., 'Oilweek,' Maclean Hunter (Calgary) 1978; Staff Writer, 'Marketing' 1980; News Editor, 'Marketing' & Editor, 'Creativity' (a quarterly supplement to 'Marketing') 1986; Assoc. Editor, 'Marketing,' Maclean Hunter Ltd. 1988; winner of Kenneth R. Wilson Memorial Award for excellence in business writing 1985; Co-Chrmn., Communications Ctte., Nat. Advtg. Benevolent Soc.; Home: 40 Alexander St., #909, Toronto, Ont. M4Y 1B2; Office: 333 King St. E., Toronto, Ont. M5A 4N2.

**SCOTT, Andrew Edington,** B.Sc., Ph.D., F.C.I.C.; educator (ret.); b. Newport-on-Tay, Scot. 27 Apr. 1919; s. John Colville and Edith (Mathers) S.; e. Madras Coll. St. Andrews, Scot. 1939; Univ. of St. Andrews B.Sc. 1949, Ph.D. 1959; m. Vivien Nelson d. late George Nelson Weekes, London, Ont. 27 July 1946; one d. Vivien Edith Nelson; PROFESSOR EMERITUS, UNIV. OF WESTERN ONT. and Dean, Fac. of Science there 1966–79, and Prof. of Chem. there since 1965; also mem. Bd. of Govs. 1974–78; Research Fellow Ont. Research Foundation Toronto 1950–53, Research Chem. 1956–60; Research Chem. Electric Reduction of Canada Ltd. Toronto 1953–55; Lectr. Bristol Univ. 1960–62; joined present Univ. as Asst. Prof. 1963, Assoc. Prof. 1964, Head Dept. Chem. 1965–66; holds two patents; served with Black Watch 1939–41, RA 1941–46, rank Capt.; author several scient. publs.; Presbyterian; recreation: walking; Home: 451 Westmount Dr., London, Ont. N6K 1X4.

**SCOTT, Angus C.,** M.A.; educator; b. Hamilton, Ont. 19 Aug. 1925; s. S. W. C. and Marie L. (Morris) S.; e. Ridley Coll., St. Catharines, Ont. (1937–43); Univ. of Toronto, B.A. 1949; Cambridge Univ., B.A. 1952, M.A. 1957; Harvard Univ., 1960–61; m. Lorna P., d. J.G. Hungerford, 25 June 1959; children: Peter J.C., Douglas H., Sally P., Angus M.B., Robert Norman Seagram; CONSULTANT, CANADIAN PARKS AND WILDERNESS SOCIETY 1992– ; Exec. Secy., Candn. Assn. of Independent Schools 1992– ; Exec. Secy., Conference of Independent Schools 1984– ; Teacher, Appleby Coll., Oakville, Ont. 1949–50; Teacher, Trinity Coll. Sch. 1952, Housemaster 1955, Asst. Headmaster 1959, Headmaster 1962–83; National Dir., The Duke of Edinburgh's Award in Can. 1984–85; Exec. Vice-Pres., present Society 1986–92; served in R.N.V.R. (Fleet Air Arm) 1944–46; Life Gov., Trinity Coll. Sch.; mem., Bd. of Govs., Kingsway Coll. Sch.; Pres., University Club.; Dir., Empire Club; Kappa Alpha; Anglican; recreations: canoeing, squash, skiing; Clubs: University (Toronto); Badminton and Racquet (Toronto); Address: 82 Walmsley Blvd., Toronto, Ont. M4V 1X6.

**SCOTT, Anthony Dalton,** O.C., B.Com., M.A., Ph.D., LL.D., F.R.S.C. (1969); university professor; economist; b. Vancouver, B.C. 2 Aug. 1923; s. Sydney Dunn and Edith (Dalton) S.; e. Prince of Wales High Sch., Vancouver, 1940; Univ. of B.C., B.Com. 1946, B.A. 1947; Harvard Univ., A.M. 1949; London Sch. of Econ., Ph.D. 1953; Hon. Ll.D., Univ. of Guelph 1980, Univ. of B.C. 1992; m. Barbara Ruth, d. Chief Justice J. O. Wilson, 1953; two children; PROF. EMERITUS OF ECON., UNIV. OF BRIT. COLUMBIA; joined Univ. as Lectr., Summer Session 1949; faculty mem. 1953–55 and 1956–89; Acting Head, Dept. of Econ. and Pol. Science, 1962–63; Head, Econ. Dept., 1965–69; Asst. Lectr., London Sch. of Econ., 1950–53; Research Worker, Dept. of Applied Econ., Cambridge Univ., 1949–50, Visitor 1959–60; Staff, Royal Comn. on Can's Econ. Prospects, 1955–56; served with Candn. Army (Armoured Corps) 1943–45; mem., Nat. Adv. Council on Water Resources Research; Senate, Univ. of B.C., 1964–70; Extve., B.C. Natural Resources Conf., 1963; Can. Council Sr. Research Fellow 1959–60; Lilly Faculty Fellow, Univ. of Chicago, 1964–65; Can. Council Killam Award 1972, 1974, 1986–87; Wm. Lyon Mackenzie King Prof., Harvard Univ. 1983–84; co-author: 'Output, Labour and Capital in the Canadian Economy' 1958; 'Canadian Economic Policy' 1961, rev. ed. 1965; 'Manual of Benefit-Cost Analysis' 1962; 'The Common Wealth in Ocean Fisheries' 1966; 'Efficiency in the Open Economy: Collected Writings on Canadian Economic Problems and Policies' 1969; co-author (with Paul A. Samuelson) 'Economics' Cdn. Edition 1966, 5th ed. 1980; author:

'Natural Resources: The Economics of Conservation' 1954, 1973 and 1983; co-author 'The Brain Drain' 1977; ed. and contrib. 'Natural Resources Revenues: A Test of Federalism' 1976; co-author 'The Economic Constitution of Federal States' 1978; 'The Design of Federations' 1980; Ed. and Contrib. 'Progress in Natural Resource Economics' 1985; 'Economics of Water Exports' 1985; mem. ed. bd. various journals and extve. bds of various professional assns.; Ed., Canadian Public Policy/Analyse de Politiques, 1982–86; Pres., Candn. Pol. Science Assn. 1966–67; Pres., Academy of Humanities and Social Sciences, Roy. Soc. of Can. 1979–80; Commissioner, Cdn. section, Internat. Joint Comm'n. (Can.-U.S. Boundary Waters Treaty) 1968–72; Reserve Bank of Australia Fellow, 1977/8; Anniversary Medal, 1978; Officer, Order of Canada (O.C.) 1982; Innis-Gérin Medal, Royal Soc. of Can. 1987; Gerhardsen Prize 1993; Home: 3906 W 36th Ave., Vancouver, B.C. V6N 2S8.

**SCOTT, Brian;** artistic director; b. Ceylon 8 Dec. 1929; s. Robert and Jessie Margurite (Thompson) S.; e. Internat. Ballet Sch. London, Eng. (scholarship); Rutherford Coll. Newcastle-On-Tyne; Fellow Imp. Soc. Teachers of Dancing Cecchetti Br.; FOUNDING ARTISTIC DIR. QUINTE BALLET SCHOOL 1972– , Prof. school founded 1979; former mem. Original Ballet Russe, Internat. Ballet, London's Festival Ballet, Nat. Ballet Can.; numerous London West End prodns., BBC TV, various musicals USA and Can.; recipient Can. Council Grant 1970–72; City of Belleville Award 1986; Commemorative Medal for 125th Anniversary of Candn. Confederation 1992; N.E. Eng. Amateur Ballroom Champion 1945; recreation: cooking; Office: P.O. Box 534, Belleville, Ont. K8N 5B2.

**SCOTT, Campbell;** artist; educator; b. Milngavie, Scotland 5 Oct. 1930; s. Robert and Catherine (Tulloch) s.; came to Can. Sept. 1951; e. Milngavie H.S., Scotland 1945; Glasgow Sch. of Art; Royal Technical Coll., Glasgow; served five-yr. apprenticeship as woodcarver/joiner 1946–51; carpenter 1951–53; one-man show, Upstairs Gallery, Toronto 1960; student of woodblock printing, Japan 1963; student of graphic design and furniture, Royal Acad. of Art, Copenhagen 1965; student of engraving and etching with S.W. Hayter, Paris 1966; invitation section, First Biennial Internat. Show of Graphics, Krakow, Poland 1966; Internat. Group Show, F.A.A.P. Gravura S'Paulo, Brazil 1968; Internat. Group Show, Norrkoping Museum, Sweden 1968; one-man show, Rodman Hall Art Centre, St. Catharines, Ont. 1968; invitation sect., First British Internat. Print Biennial 1969; selected for travelling exhibition of graphics by Nat. Gallery of Can. 1969; one-man show, Gallery Pascal, Toronto 1969; Fifth Burnaby Print Show, B.C. 1969; Candn. Graphics Show circulated by Gallery of Ont. 1969; Third Internat. Biennial, Krakow 1970; Nat. Exhibition of Amer. colour prints 1970; 4th Amer. Biennial of Engraving, Santiago, Chile 1970; Exhibition of Candn. Graphics, Candn. Embassy, Washington, D.C. 1971; First Internat. Print Exhibition, Gallery Bleu, Philippines 1972; selected for 'Who's Who in American Art' 1979; designed and built house with studio at Niagara-on-the-Lake 1974; represented in the following public collections: Brit. Museum, London; Montreal Mus. of Art (Samuel Bronfman Collection); Hamilton Art Gallery, Hamilton, Ont.; Victoria & Albert Mus., London, England; Bibliotheque National, Paris; Scottish Nat. Gallery of Modern Art; Rodman Hall Art Gallery, St. Catharines, Ont.; Sarnia Art Gallery, Ont.; Art Gallery of Ont., Toronto; London Art Gallery, Ont.; Niagara Falls Public Library (Bronze Sculpture); St. Catharines Public Library (Wood Sculpture); Univ. of Guelph Master Print Collection; mem., Print and Drawing Council of Can.; recreation: sailing; Home: 89 Byron, Niagara-on-the-Lake, Ont. L0S 1J0.

**SCOTT, Charles Wesley Moore,** B.Comm., M.B.A.; communications executive; b London, Ont. 15 Jan. 1947; s. James Ralph Becher and Margaret Isabel (Moore) S.; e. Univ. of Toronto Trinity Coll. B.Comm. 1968; Harvard Sch. of Bus. Adm. M.B.A. 1970; m. Marilyn d. John and Doris Swan 10 May 1975; children: Jeffrey, Heather; PRES. & CHIEF EXTVE. OFFICER, STENTOR RESOURCE CENTRE INC. 1993– ; Dir., Bell Northern Rsch.; Union Bank of Switzerland (Canada); joined Bell Canada in 1970, various positions in Finance and Marketing 1970–84; Vice Pres. Regulatory Matters 1984–85; Vice Pres. Finance 1985–86; Vice Pres. Finance & Corporate Performance 1986; Extve. Vice Pres. (Finance & Admin.) & C.F.O. 1987–89; Extve. Vice-Pres., Corporate, BCE Inc. 1989–90; Pres., Bell Ontario 1990–93; Co-Chair, Bd. of Visitors, Duke Univ. Sch. of Candn. Studies; Trustee, Hospital for Sick Children; mem. Financial Execs. Inst.; Dir., Metro Toronto Learning Partnership; Anglican; recreations: skiing, golf, travel, cuisine; Clubs: Toronto; University (Montreal); Royal Montreal Golf; Donalda (Toronto); Office: Suite 1800, 160 Elgin St., Ottawa, Ont. K2P 2C4.

**SCOTT, Chris,** B.A., M.A.; author; b. Hull, Yorkshire 17 June 1945; e. Hull Univ., B.A. 1966; Manchester Univ., M.A. 1967; State Univ. of Pennsylvania; m. Heather Sherratt; one d.: Kirsten Vega; Teacher, Humanities Dept., York Univ.; Creative Writing, Toronto Three Schools; Writer-in-Residence, Concordia Univ. 1988–89; Cumberland Twsp. Public Library 1989–90; has broadcast as reviewer for The Arts in Review (CBC); reviewed for 'Books in Canada,' 'The Toronto Star,' 'The Globe & Mail,' 'Montreal Gazette,' and 'The Ottawa Citizen'; Fulbright Scholar; Arthur Ellis Award 1988; Former Chrmn., Lavant, Dalhousie & N. Sherbrooke Edn. Trust Fund; Former Trustee, Lanark Union Lib. Bd.; mem., Writers' Union of Can.; author: 'Bartleby' 1971, 'To Catch a Spy' 1978, 'Antichthon' 1982, 'Hitler's Bomb' 1983, 'The Heretic' 1985, 'Jack' 1988 (novels); Home: R.R. #1, McDonald's Corners, Ont. K0G 1M0.

**SCOTT, David George Brian,** B.A.Sc., M.B.A., C.A., P.Eng., C.M.C., C.F.P.I.M.; business executive; b. Toronto, Ont. 11 May 1947; s. Ralph Vernon and Joan Muriel (Smith) S.; e. Univ. of Toronto B.A.Sc. 1973; York Univ. M.B.A. 1977; m. Isabel Duncan 21 Nov. 1970; children: Joanne, Susan; VICE-PRES. FINANCE & ADMIN. AND CHIEF FINANCIAL OFFR., GEAC COMPUTER CORP. LIMITED 1990– ; obtained C.A. designation, Arthur Andersen & Co. 1973–77; Consultant, Arthur Andersen 1978–85; Vice-Pres. Operations, Protective Plastics 1986–88; Vice-Pres. Mfg., AHA Mfg. 1989–90; Mem., Candn. Inst. of Internal Auditors (Chapter Pres. 1981); Candn. Inst. for Industrial Engineering (Chapter Pres. 1979); clubs: Boulevard, Metro Toronto Bd. of Trade; Home: 53 Lambeth Rd., Etobicoke, Ont. M9A 2Y8; Office: 11 Allstate Pkwy., Ste. 300, Markham, Ont. L3R 9T8.

**SCOTT, David Sanborn,** M.Sc., Ph.D.; professor; b. Québec City, Qué. 15 July 1935; s. Gilbert B. and Alberta B. (Sanborn) S.; e. pub. and high schs. Belleville, Ont.; Queen's Univ. B.Sc. 1959, M.Sc. 1963; Northwestern Univ. Ph.D. 1967; m. Dr. Marianne B. Scott; children by previous marriage: Penelope Lee, Susan Elizabeth, Douglas Shaw, Peter David; PROFESSOR OF MECH. ENGINEERING AND DIR., INST. FOR INTEGRATED ENERGY SYSTEMS, UNIV. OF VICTORIA 1989– ; Prof. of Mech. Eng., Univ. of Toronto 1976–89; Shift Foreman Cold Rolling Mill Steel Co. of Canada 1959–60; Supr. Forming Dept. Fiberglas Canada Inc. 1960–62; Asst. Prof. of Mech. Eng Univ. of Toronto 1966, Assoc. Prof. 1969, Prof. and Chrmn. 1976–83; Founding Dir., Inst. for Hydrogen Systems 1983–86; Chrmn., Federal Adv. Group on Hydrogen Opportunities for Canada 1985–86; Visiting Prof. Inst. Sound Vibration Rsch. Univ. of Southampton 1974–75; mem. Assn. Prof. Engs. Prov. Ont.; recreation: sailing, bicycling; Home: 1601 Hollywood Place, Victoria, B.C. V8S 1J6; Office: Inst. for Integrated Energy Systems, P.O. Box 3055, Victoria, B.C. V8W 3P6.

**SCOTT, Donald Clayton,** B.A., F.C.A.; executive; b. Windsor, Ont. 30 July 1927; e. Univ. of W. Ont. B.A. (Business Adm.) 1949; m. Eilleen Isabel 2 Dec. 1950; children: Christine L., Lauren J., Barbara K., Robert D.; Commissioner, Ont. Insurance Commission 1990–93; Chrmn. & C.E.O., Clarkson Gordon (now Ernst & Young) 1979–87; joined Clarkson Gordon 1949, Partner 1956, Mang. Partner-Montreal 1963 and Toronto 1967, Chrmn. Mang. Comte. 1972; played prof. football with Toronto Argonauts 1949–51; Dir. Sunnybrook Found.; Past Pres. Candn. Arthritis Soc.; Adv. Comte. to the School of Business Admin., Univ. of Western Ont.; Fellow, Ont. Inst. C.A.'s; mem. Inst. C.A.'s Ont. (Pres. 1978–79, Extve. Comte. 1974–79, Council 1972–79); Candn. Inst. C.A.'s (Bd. Govs. 1976–79); recreations: golf, standardbred racing; Clubs: Toronto; Granite; Rosedale Golf; Home: 33 Daneswood Rd., Toronto, Ont. M4N 3J7.

**SCOTT, Donald John,** B.A., B.L.S.; librarian; b. Florence, Cape Breton, N.S. 17 July 1940; s. William Lawson and Jessie Elizabeth (Grainger) S.; e. Florence Composite Sch. 1956; Sydney Mines High Sch. 1957; Mount Allison Univ. B.A. 1963; McGill Univ. Lib. Sch. B.L.S. 1964; m. Jeanette Anne d. Herbert Fredrick Poole, New Annan, P.E.I. 16 July 1966; two s. Peter William, Jeffery Michael; DIR., CULTURE & HERITAGE DIVISION, P.E.I. DEPT. OF COMMUNITY AND CULTURAL AFFAIRS; mem. Atlantic Provs. Lib. Assn. (Past Pres.); Mem., Candn. Conference of the Arts; United Church; recreations: outdoor activities, gardening, photography, reading, sailing; Club: Charlottetown Yacht (Past Commodore); Home: Tea Hill Cres., R.R. 1, Charlottetown, P.E.I. C1A 7J6; Office: Box 7500, Enman Cres., Charlottetown, P.E.I. C1A 8T8.

**SCOTT, Donald S.,** M.Sc., Ph.D., F.C.I.C.; P.Eng.; university professor; b. Edmonton, Alta 17 Dec. 1922; s. Robert James and Clara Regina (Allen) S.; e. Univ. of Alta., B.Sc. 1944, M.Sc. 1946; Univ. of Illinois, Ph.D. 1947–49; m. Dorothy Phyllis, d. R. Alexander Hensel, Edmonton, Alta., 17 May 1945; children: Garry Alexander Donald (dec.), Jillian Damaris Clare; PROFESSOR EMERITUS, UNIV. OF WATERLOO; joined Imperial Oil Ltd. N.W.T. 1944; Nat. Research Council of Can., Ottawa, 1946; Asst. and Assoc. Prof. Univ. of Brit. Columbia, 1949; Shell Visiting Prof., Cambridge Univ., 1963; Prof. and Chrmn. Dept. Chem. Engn., Univ. of Waterloo 1964; Acting Dean, Faculty of Engn. 1969; Assoc. Dean, Fac. of Eng. 1980; Visiting Fellow, Royal Sch. of Mines, Imperial Coll. London, England 1971; Res. Consultant to various Co's.; author of over 80 research papers, articles, monographs, books, etc.; N.R.C. Fellowship, 1947; Univ. of Illinois Fellowship, 1948, Plummer Medal, Engn. Inst. of Can., 1962; Best Publication 1966, (Can. Journal of Chem. Engn.); Centennial Medal, 1967; Queen's Jubilee Medal, 1977; R.S. Jane Memorial Award, Candn. Soc. of Chem. Engn. 1988; Mem. Candn. Acad. of Engr. 1990; Ryerson Fellowship, Ryerson Polytechnical Institute 1992; Sr. Research Fellowship, Brit. Research Council 1971; Candn. Soc. for Chem. Engn. (Vice Pres. 1970–71, Pres. 1971–72); Am. Inst. Mining & Metall. Engrs. Am. Inst. of Chem Engrs., Fellow; American Chem. Society; Sigma Xi; Phi Lambda Upsilon; Delta Upsilon; Protestant; recreations: golf, skiing, curling; Home: 382 Arden Place, Waterloo, Ont. N2L 2N7.

**SCOTT, Doug;** trust company executive; VICE-PRESIDENT, SUN LIFE TRUST CO.; Home: 7905 Bayview Ave., Unit 122, Thornhill, Ont. L3P 7N3; Office: 36 Toronto St., Toronto, Ont. M5C 2C5.

**SCOTT, Douglas Schofield,** B.A., LL.B., Q.C.; lawyer; b. Hamilton, Ont. 21 Oct. 1926; s. Silas Warren Cheever and Marie Louise (Morris) S.; e. Hillfield Sch., Hamilton; Univ. of Toronto B.A. 1949; Osgoode Hall Law Sch. LL.B. 1953; LAWYER, PRES. OF THE MARKLAND GROUP 1985– ; law practice in Hamilton with Martin & Martin (mainly commercial law) 1953–85; Queen's Silver Jubilee Medal 1977 for organizing a 'Voters' Assembly' with the Couchiching Inst. for Public Affairs; Pres., Hamilton Br., Candn. Inst. of Internat. Affairs during 1960s & 70s; Pres., Hamilton Philharmonic Orch. Soc. 1965–66; P.C.; Trustee, Hamilton Bd. of Edn. 1960; author: 'The Concept of Treaty-Mandated Compliance Legislation Under the Biological Weapons Convention' 1991; co-author (principal): 'Disarmament's Missing Dimension' 1990; Fellow, Candn. Institute of Internat. Affairs for consultation on disarmament matters; recreations: skiing, bicycling; Address: 201 – 93 Bold St., Hamilton, Ont. L8P 1T8.

**SCOTT, Douglas W.,** B.A.Sc.; consulting engineer; b. Toronto, Ont. 24 January 1940; s. Walter and Rosa (Franklin) S.; e. Univ. of Toronto B.A.Sc. 1962; m. Diane d. Phyllis & David Moncrieff 14 Sept. 1963; children: Kathryn, Jennifer; VICE PRES., PROCTOR & REDFERN LIMITED 1988– ; joined Proctor & Redfern 1962; worked on variety of land devel. & munic. engr. projects in S. Ont.; opened Thunder Bay br. office as Mgr. 1971; Dir. 1981; Vice-Pres., Northern Ont. branches 1985; Chrmn. 1988–91; Chrmn., Housel & Assoc., Tampa, Fla. 1988; Comnr., Kenora Area Local Govt. Study 1981; Chrmn., McKellar Gen. Hosp. Bd. of Gov.; Dir., Alpha Court; Mem., APEO, CSCE; several past extve. posts; recreations: Thunder Bay City & Legion Band, boating; Home: 1423 Ridgeway St., Thunder Bay, Ont.; Office: 200 South Syndicate Ave., Thunder Bay, Ont. P7E 1C9.

**SCOTT, Most Rev. Edward Walter,** C.C., B.A., L.Th., D.D. (Ang.); b. Edmonton, Alta. 30 Apl. 1919; e. Univ. of Brit. Columbia, B.A.; Theol. Col., Vancouver, L.Th., 1942; m. Isabel Florence Brannan, Fort Frances, Ont.; children: Maureen (Mrs. Peter Harris), Patricia Anne (Mrs. Paul Robinson), Douglas, Elizabeth Jean (Mrs. David Bacon): ARCHBISHOP OF THE ANGLICAN CHURCH OF CANADA, since 1971; Rector, St. Peter's, Seal Cove, Prince Rupert, B.C., 1942–45; Gen. Secy., Student Christian Movement, Univ. of Man., 1945–49; also part-time lectr. St. John's Coll.; Rector, Ch. of St. John the Baptist, Fort Garry, 1949–55 and St. Jude's, Winnipeg 1955–60; named Dir. of Social Service and Priest-Dir. of Indian Work for Diocese of Rupert's Land, 1960; helped estbd. first Indian-Metis Friendship Centre; Moderator, Central Ctte., The World Council of Churches 1975–83; Companion of The Order of Canada

1978; joined staff of Ch.'s nat. hdqrs., Toronto, 1964; consecrated Bishop of Kootenay 1966; Primate, Anglican Church of Canada 1971; Address: 29 Hawthorn Ave., Toronto, Ont. M4W 2Z1.

**SCOTT, Eric Duff,** HBA; investment dealer; b. Toronto, Ont. 21 Dec. 1936; s. Eric Duff and Pauline Marie (Graves) S.; e. Upper Canada Coll. 1957; Univ. of West. Ont., HBA 1961; m. Betty Anne d. Roland and Pat Brouseau 23 Sept. 1977; children: Jonathan Booth, Michael Booth; CHRMN., QUADRA LOGIC TECHNOLOGIES INC. 1991– ; Chrmn., Peoples Jewellers Corp. 1993– ; Pres., Multibank NT Financial Corp. 1990– ; Multibanc Financial Corp. 1990– ; Dir., First Australia Prime Income Investment Co. Ltd.; Global Government Plus Fund, Ltd.; Spruce Falls Inc.; First Commonwealth Fund; Alias Research Inc.; OSF Inc.; Bramalea Ltd.; Gentra Inc.; ACC Telenterprises Ltd.; Computer Brokers of Can. Inc.; Advisor, Spencer Stuart Canada Ltd.; Govt. Fin., Greenshields Inc. 1961; Corp. Fin. 1965; Vice-Pres. 1970; Sr. V.P. 1973; Extve. Vice-Pres. 1976; Extve. Vice-Pres., Richardson Greenshields of Can. Limited 1982; Deputy Chrmn., Merrill Lynch Can. Inc. 1984–87; Chrmn., Toronto Stock Exchange 1987–89; Chrmn., Prudential-Bache Securities Can. Ltd. 1987–90; recreations: golf, tennis, skiing; Clubs: Rosedale Golf (Dir.); Cambridge; Craigleith Ski; Home: 8 Sunnydene Cres., Toronto, Ont. M4N 3J6; Office: 70 University Ave., Ste. 400, Toronto, Ont. M5J 2M4.

**SCOTT, Fenton,** B.Sc., M.Sc., P.Eng.; consulting engineer; b. Fredericton, N.B. 22 Oct. 1927; s. James Stanley and Clement Victoria (Fenton) S.; e. Univ. of N.B. B.A.Sc. 1948, M.Sc. 1950; m. Vilma Eileen d. Stanley and Ina MacCallum 30 Aug. 1950; children: Dawn, Sharon, Jill Graeme; Geologist, Noranda Mines 1948–55; Exploration Mgr., Central Manitoba Mines 1955–57; Area Mines 1957–64; Consulting Engr., Geosearch Consultants 1964–69; Chief Geologist, Imperial Oil, Minerals 1969–72; Exploration Mgr., Imperial Oil 1972–75; Vice Pres., Esso Minerals Canada 1975–82; Self-Employed Consulting Engineer 1982–93; Pres., Hollinger North Shore Exploration Inc.; Louvicourt Gold Mines Inc.; La Fosse Platinum Group Inc.; Dir., MVP Capital Ltd.; Dundee-Palliser Resources Ltd.; Fairlady Energy Inc.; Ateba Mines Ltd.; Dir., Prospectors and Developers Assn. of Canada; Mem., Geological Assn. of Canada; Assn. of Exploration Geochemists; Registered Professional Engineer, Ont.; Life Mem., Candn. Inst. of Mining & Metallurgy; author of num. articles on mineral exploration & geology; recreations: golf, skiing; clubs: Donalda, Ontario, Toronto Ski; Home: 17 Malabar Place, Don Mills, Ont. M3B 1A4; Office: 4100 Yonge St., Suite 360, Willowdale, Ont. M2B 2P5.

**SCOTT, Gail,** B.A.; writer; b. Ottawa, Ont.; d. Henry James and Vira (Darlene) S.; e. Queen's Univ. B.A. 1966; L'Univ. de Grenoble, France; divorced; one d. Anna; joined Canadian Press 1967–69; The Gazette 1970–73; freelance writer The Globe and Mail, The Gazette, Maclean's mag.; author: 'Spare Parts' (short stories) 1982; 'Heroine' (novel) 1987; 'Spaces Like Stairs' (essays) 1989; 'Main Brides' (novel) 1993; Co-author: 'La Théorie, un dimanche' 1988; Founding ed. 'Spirale' French language Montréal cultural monthly and 'Tessera' bilingual jour. feminist writing & criticism.

**SCOTT, Gerald William,** M.B., M.S., F.R.C.S.(C); surgeon; educator; b. London, Eng. 12 Jan. 1931; s. Frederick William and Constance Ella (Burgess) S.; e. Univ. Coll. Univ. of London M.B., B.S. 1955; Mayo Clinic and Grad. Sch. of Med. M.S. 1964; m. Beryl d. Arnold and Cecelia Hubbard 14 May 1955; children: Martin, Nigel, Elizabeth, Celia, Ian; SURGEON, LADY MINTO GULF ISLANDS HOSP., SALT SPRING ISLAND, B.C. 1989– ; Teaching Fellow in surgery Univ. of Alta. 1964; Surgeon Holy Cross Hosp. and Calgary Gen. Hosp. 1965; Assoc. Prof. of Surgery Univ. of Calgary 1968; Prof. of Surgery Univ. of Alta. 1973 and chief of Surgery Charles Camsell Hosp. Edmonton; mem., Test Ctte. in Surgery Med. Council of Can.; recipient Fulbright Scholarship 1960; E. Starr Judd Award Mayo Clinic 1964; Visiting Prof., Univ. of Auckland, N.Z. 1978; Sir Peter Freyer Mem. Lectr. Univ. Coll. Galway 1983; author 150 publs. gastrointestinal research; mem., Candn. Assn. Clin. Surgs.; Candn. Assn. Gen. Surgs.; Candn. Assn. Gastroenterol.; Candn. Med. Assn.; B.C. Med. Assn.; Brit. Pharmacol. Soc.; Intnl. Soc. Gastrointestinal Motility; W. (US) Surg. Assn.; recreation: landscape painting; Home: Box 787, Ganges, B.C. V0S 1E0; Office: Lady Minto Gulf Islands Hosp., Box 307, Ganges, B.C. V0S 1E0.

**SCOTT, Graham W.S.,** Q.C., LL.B.; lawyer; b. Halifax, N.S. 13 Nov. 1942; s. Thomas Wilson and Winifred (Shatford) S.; e. Rothesay Coll. Sch. N.B. 1960; Univ. of W. Ont. B.A. 1965, LL.B. 1966; m. Gail d. Claude J. and Dorothy Scott 10 Mar. 1973; two d. Gillian, Genevieve; PARTNER, McMILLAN, BINCH 1984– ; called to Bar of Ont. 1968; cr. Q.C. 1980; law practice Chappell, Walsh & Davidson 1968–70; Exec. Asst. to Leader of Opposition Govt. of Can. 1970–76; Exec. Co-ordinator Planning & Operations Min. of Atty.-Gen. Ont. 1976, Asst. Dep. Atty-Gen. Courts Adm. 1976–78, Assoc. Sec. of Cabinet and Sec. Policy & Priorities Bd. Ont. 1978–79, Dep. Min. of Environment Ont. 1979–81, Dep. Min. of Health Ont. 1981–84; Dir. Connaught Laboratories Ltd.; Past Chrmn., Public Policy Forum, Co-Chrmn., Prime Ministers Advisory Ctte. on Restructuring Govt., Baycrest Centre Geriatric Care; C.D. Howe Institute; Advisory Ctte., Ont. Law Reform Commission; mem., Ont. Health Industries Advisory Ctte.; mem. Candn. Bar Assn.; Law Soc. Upper Can.; American Bar Assn.; Univ. W. Ont. Alumni Assn.; Naval Offrs.' Assn. Can.; P. Conservative; Candn. Inst. Strategic Studies; Clubs: Empire; Albany; Home: 169 Old Forest Hill Rd., Toronto, Ont. M6C 2G7; Office: P.O. Box 38, Royal Bank Plaza, South Tower, Toronto, Ont. M5J 2J7.

**SCOTT, Henry James,** M.D., D.C.L., F.R.C.S.(C), F.A.C.S.; retired surgeon, professor; b. Montreal, Quebec, 16 January 1918; s. Hon. William Bridges and Esther Florence (Aird) S.; e. Selwyn House School 1925–27; Roslyn School 1927–30; Westmount (P.Q.) High Sch. 1930–32; Trinity Coll. Sch. 1932–34; Bishop's Univ. B.A. 1937; McGill Univ. M.D. 1941, Dipl. in Surgery, 1951; F.R.C.S.(C) 1950; m. Audrey MacKenzie; former Dir., Div. of Thoracic & Cardiovascular Surgery, Montreal General Hospital; mem., Am. Assn. for Thoracic Surg.; Central Surg. Assn.; Home: 411 - 1745 Cedar Ave., Montreal, Que. H3G 1A7.

**SCOTT, Ian Barry;** transportation executive; b. Montréal, Qué. 2 Feb. 1930; e. primary and secondary schs. Montréal; McGill Univ.; CHRMN. AND C.E.O., CP RAIL SYSTEM 1990– and EXEC. VICE PRES., CANADIAN PACIFIC LIMITED 1988– ; joined Canadian Pacific Ltd. Montréal 1949, Gen. Mgr. Pub. Relations & Advertising 1973, Vice Pres. Adm. and Pub. Affairs 1981; Chrmn. and C.E.O., CP Rail 1985–89; Chrmn., Pres. and C.E.O. 1989–90; Dir., Assn. of Am. Railroads; Candn. Pacific Ltd.; The Candn. Trust Co.; Montreal Trustco Inc.; Montreal Trust; Soo Line Corp.; United Dominion Industries Inc.; United Dominion Industries Ltd.; Alliance for a Drug Free Canada; Railway Assoc. of Can.; The Royal Victoria Hospital Found.; former Chrmn. & Mem. Emeritus; Past Chrmn. Pub. Affairs Council, Conf. Bd. Can.; mem., National Freight Transportation Assn.; Clubs: Mount Royal; The York; Office: Windsor Station, Montréal, Qué. H3C 3E4.

**SCOTT, J. Michael G.,** B.Comm.; financial executive; b. Toronto, Ont. 9 Sept. 1927; s. William Pearson and Joan Alix (Grierson) S.; e. Upper Can. Coll. and Univ. of Toronto Schs., Toronto; University of Toronto B.Comm. 1950; m. Janet White, d. Douglas W. Ambridge, 21 Oct. 1950; children: Peter Ambridge, Thomas Wentworth, Sarah Barlow, Geoffrey Lawson, Martha Grierson, Mary Linley; VICE-CHRMN. SCOTIAMcLEOD INC. 1985– ; 35 years with Wood Gundy Inc.; Dir., Bombardier Inc.; Weyerhaeuser Canada Ltd.; Chateau Insurance Co.; Past Chrmn., Bd. of Trustees, Sunnybrook Health Sci. Ctr.; Mem., Investment Dealers Assn. of Can.; C.D. Howe Inst.; Club de Relations d'Affaires Canada-France; Anglican; recreations: fishing, hunting, tennis, golf; clubs: Mount Royal; Toronto; Toronto Golf; Ristigouche Salmon; York; Vancouver; Home: 103 Dunloe Rd., Toronto, Ont. M5P 2T7; Office: 32nd Floor, P.O. Box 433, Commercial Union Tower, Toronto, Ont. M5K 1M2.

**SCOTT, Jack H.,** B.Comm.; food industry executive; b. Windsor, Ont. 24 Feb. 1941; e. Univ. of Detroit B.Comm. 1963; m. Fleurette; children: Jason, Andrea; PRESIDENT & GENERAL MANAGER, OSHAWA FOODS 1990– ; sales & management positions 1966–78; Pres., Hostess Food Products 1978–83; Pres. & Chief Extve. Offr., General Foods 1983–89; Pres., Food Service Companies, Oshawa Group 1989–90; Dir., National Life Assur. Co. of Canada; Home: 13 Pine Ridge Lane, Brampton, Ont. L6W 1G6; Office: 6355 Viscount Rd., Mississauga, Ont. L4V 1W2.

**SCOTT, Jacquelyn Thayer,** M.B.A., Ph.D.; university administrator, writer; b. Russell, Kansas 17 Oct. 1945; d. Jack Lloyd Thayer and Orpha (Scott); e. Univ. of Kansas; Univ. of Manitoba M.B.A. 1980; Univ. of Colorado Ph.D. 1992; divorced; children: Jared J., Angela, Meghan (Wolf); PRES., UNIV. COLLEGE OF CAPE BRETON 1993– ; City Editor, The Columbian Newspapers 1968–75; Sr. Editor, Candn. Press Bureau (Vanc.) 1975–76; Pres., Jacke Wolf & Assoc. 1975–76; Dir., Project Manage, Contg. Edn. Div., Univ. of Man. & Winnipeg Found. 1981–84; Asst. Prof. & Head, Management Studies 1984–86; Dir., School of Continuing Studies, Univ. of Toronto 1987–92; Pres., ResourceWorks Inc. (mngt. consulting to voluntary & public sector orgns.) 1990–92; Chair, Council of Ont. Univs. Status of Women Ctte. 1991–93; Pres., Candn. Assn. for Univ. Contg. Edn. 1992–93; Chair, Natl. Education Organizations Ctte. 1993– ; Pres., Ont. Council for Univ. Contg. Edn. 1990–91; Founding Mem., N. Am. Alliance for Contg. Edn. 1991; Mem., Woodsworth, Innis College Council, Univ. of Toronto 1990–92; Copyright Adv. Group, Assn. of Colleges & Univ. of Canada 1991– ; Nat. Newspaper Award (edit. writing) 1970; B.C. Newsperson of the Year (B.C. School Trustees' Assn.) 1972; several program & promotional awards, Candn. Assn. for Univ. Contg. Edn.; Mem., Ass. of Profl. Engrs. of Ont. Task Force on Admissions 1991–93; Mem., Assn. for Rsch. on Nonprofit and Voluntary Assns.; Candn. Soc. for the Study of Higher Edn.; Sr. Women Academic Administrators of Canada; author: 'Facilitating Community and Project Development' 1984, 'Improving Boardsmanship Skills 1983, 'Meeting Management' 1983, 'Financial Management for Small, All-Volunteer Organizations' 1983, 'The Executive Director Search' 1982, 'The Voluntary Crisis: Legal and Fiscal Issues Affecting Voluntarism' 1982; co-author: 'Making a Difference: A Manual for Board Members' 1991; recreations: reading, fishing, music, autoharp; Office: P.O. Box 5300, Sydney, N.S. B1P 6L2.

**SCOTT, John Andrew,** B.A., M.A., Ph.D.; university professor; b. Corner Brook, Nfld. 6 Apr. 1943; s. David J. Frederick and Isobel Ruth (McArthur) S.; e. St. Bonaventure's Coll. 1960; Memorial Univ., B.A. 1964; Cambridge Univ., M.A. 1968; Edinburgh Univ., Ph.D. 1975; m. Jennifer d. Bernard and Margaret Jean Kennedy 16 June 1966; children: Ian, Kirstine, Sarah, Mark; PROF., DEPT. OF PHILOSOPHY, MEMORIAL UNIV. 1971– ; Rothermore Fellow, Cambridge 1964–68; Lectr., Dept. of Greek, Edinburgh Univ. 1969–71; Asst. & Acting Dean, Grad. Studies, present univ. 1980–83; Panel of Arbitrators 1985– ; Head, Dept. of Philos. 1987–93; Comnr., R.C. Enquiry into Sexual Abuse 1989; Vice-Pres., Mediation Devel. Ltd.; co-author: 'The Vexed Question' 1988, 'University Research and the Future of Canada' 1989; 'Winter Commission'; co-author & editor: 'Sharing Intellectual Property' 1986; Home: Box 503, Tolt Rd., St. Phillips, Nfld. A1L 1C1; Office: St. John's, Nfld. A1C 5S7.

**SCOTT, Rev. John Donald,** B.A., candidate M.B.A.; humanitarian executive; b. Edmonton, Alta. 15 Sept. 1938; s. John Herbert and Margaret Ethel (Hominiuk) S.; e. Victoria C.H.S. 1956; Candn. Bible College dipl. 1962; Candn. Mngt. Assn. Mngt. Cert. & Pres. Course Cert. 1992–93; California Coast Univ. concurrent B.A., M.B.A. 1994; m. Nola d. Douglas C. and Lorna D. Hartley 19 May 1958; children: Lorilee Dawn, Heidi Darlene, Jeffrey Donald, Mark Douglas; PRESIDENT, WORLD VISION CANADA 1987– ; Paper Carrier, Edmonton Journal age 10; Branch Manager (55 carriers) age 16; joined Candn. Navy 1956; released for med. reasons 1959; Pastor, Christian & Missionary Alliance, Nipawin, Sask. 1962–64; ordained to Christian Min. 1964; Missionary, Laos 1964–71; Dir. in Laos, World Vision (WV) Internat. 1971–73; Founded World Vision Found. of Thailand 1973; Dir., WV Vietnam 1975–75; Dir., WV Thailand 1975–77; Regional Dir., Latin Am. & the Caribbean 1977–80; developed work for WV in 8 countries in this area; Regional Dir., Asia & S. Pacific 1980–82; Group Dir., Communications & Mktg., WV Can. 1983–87; Vice-Pres., WV Internat.; Mem., Partnership Sr. Mngt. Team; Mem., Chairman's Council, Regent College, Univ. of B.C.; Adv. Bd. Mem., Nat. Native Bible College; frequent world traveller and public speaker; Licensed Clegyman, Christian & Missionary Alliance; Council Mem., Evangelical Fellowship of Can.; author of editorials for 'Childview' WV Canada's official mag.; recreations: golf, skating, walking; Home: 6980 Cordingley Crescent, Mississauga, Ont. L5N 4Z3; Office: 6630 Turner Valley Rd., Mississauga, Ont. L5N 2S4.

**SCOTT, John Douglass,** B.Sc.; executive; b. Port McNicoll, Ont. 29 Apr. 1920; s. Rev. William J. and Helen (Ford) S.; e. Pub. Sch., Owen Sound, Ont.; High Sch., Flesherton and Stirling, Ont.; Queen's Univ., B.Sc. (Mech. Engn.) 1942; m. Jean, d. Dr. R. M. Parker, 18 Aug. 1944; children: Gordon, Brian, Deborah; CHRMN., CROWN CORK & SEAL CAN. INC.; Dir., Crown Cork & Seal Co. Inc.; Crown Cork & Seal West Indies Ltd.; joined present Co. as Jr. Engr., 1945; Vice-Pres. and Dir. 1950; Extve. Vice-Pres. 1967; served with RCN in N. Atlantic 1942–45; rank Lt.; mem., Soc. Soft Drink Techs.; Master Brewers Assn.; Assn. Prof. Engrs.

Ont.; Candn. Mfrs. Assn.; Bd. Trade Metrop. Toronto; United Church; recreations: golf, skiing, boating; Home: 32 HiMount Dr., Willowdale, Ont.; Office: 7900 Keele St., Concord, Ont. L4K 2A3.

**SCOTT, John Wilson,** M.A., M.D.; physician; retired university professor; b. Toronto, Ont., 7 July 1915; s. Dr. Paul Lindsay and Mary Agnes (Wilson) S.; e. Oakwood Coll. Inst., Toronto, Ont.; Univ. of Toronto (Victoria), B.A. 1937, M.A. (Physiol.) 1938, M.D. 1941; Post-grad. study, Toronto Gen. Hosp. (1941 and 1946–47), Atomic Energy Project, Chalk River (1947), Montreal Neurol. Inst. (1948). Nat. Hosp., Queen Sq., London, Eng., Nuffield Fellow (1948–49) m. Grace Winnifred, d. late Russell Workman, North Bay, Ont. 7 June 1941; children: Aleda Mary, James Russell; Assoc. Prof. 1956–60, Prof. of Physiology, Univ. of Toronto 1960–78; Dir. of EEG Lab., Toronto Gen. Hosp.; Consultant to Sunnybrook Hosp., D.V.A., Toronto 1951–62; Consultant in Electroencephal. to R.C.A.F. (1956); served in 2nd World War; Surg. Lieut, R.C.N.V.R., May 1942; apptd. to R.C.N. Med. Research Unit, 1942; promoted Surg. Lieut-Commdr. 1945 for duty with Royal Navy; trans. to inactive service Aug. 1946; Dir., Associated Medical Serv. 1976–91; mem., Acad. Med. Toronto (mem. of Council; Editor of 'Bulletin,' 1949–62; Treas. 1966–69; Pres. 1970–71); Hon. Fellow, 1990; Candn. Neurol. Soc. (Council 1952–55); Eastern Assn. Electroencephal. (Pres., 1960); Am. E.E.G. Soc. (Council 1958–59); Ont. Med. Assn.; Candn. Med. Assn.; Chrmn., R.C.N. Personnel Research Comte. (1954–65), Surg. Gen. Adv. Comte. (1963); Pres. (1960–62), York Pioneer & Hist. Soc.; mem. Toronto Hist. Bd. 1968–1982 (Chrmn. 1977–80); author and jt. author of a no. of articles relating to his special field in scient. journs.; United Church: recreations: gardening, painting, medical and local history; Clubs: Arts and Letters; Home: 15 Braemar Ave., Toronto, Ont. M5P 2L1.

**SCOTT, Kenneth C.,** B.Eng., P.Eng.; crown corporation executive; b. Halifax, N.S. 16 March 1932; s. Charles Vincent and Loretta Anne (Peake) S.; e. St. Mary's Univ. High Sch. 1948; St. Mary's Univ. Dip. in Eng. 1951; Tech. Univ. of N.S. B.Eng. 1953; m. Laraine d. Fred and Mildred Tanner 11 May 1953; children: Paul, Beverly, Richard, Mary, Theresa; GEN. MGR. REGIONAL DEVELOPMENT CORP. 1986– ; joined Canada Mortgage & Housing Corp. 1953–59, various positions Nfld., N.S., N.B. & Ottawa; Gen. Mgr. Atlantic Region-Residential & Comm. Devel. Community Enterprises Ltd. 1959–65; J.W. Lindsay Construction Comm. Devel. Halifax 1965–67; Dir. of Devel. New Brunswick Housing Corp. 1967–70, Pres. 1970–83; Dep. Min. of Supply & Services N.B. 1983–86; Pres. Algonquin Properties 1983–86, Fredericton Hotel Co. 1983–86; mem. Candn. Ctte. Bldg. Rsch. 1983–85; Candn. Constrn. Rsch. Bd. 1985–86; Mil. Compound Bd. Prov. N.B. 1983–88; mem. Assn. Profl. Engs. N.B.; R. Catholic; Office: 377 York St., P.O. Box 428, Fredericton, N.B. E3B 5R4.

**SCOTT, Laura Falk,** B.A., B.C.L.; lawyer; b. Chicago, Ill. 29 May 1947; d. Alfred Bernard and Evelyn Roberta (Keer) Falk; e. Cornell Univ. B.A. (Hons.) 1969; McGill Univ. B.C.L. (Hons.) 1975; m. Michael s. Irving and Thelma Scott 19 July 1970; one d.: Julia Rose Falk Scott; VICE-PRES., LEGAL AFFAIRS, GENERAL COUNSEL & SEC., JOSEPH E. SEAGRAM & SONS, LIMITED 1990– ; Assoc., Rappaport, Whelan, Bessner, Feldman & Ross 1976–81; Gen. Counsel & Asst. Sec., Joseph E. Seagram & Sons Limited 1981–82; Gen. Counsel & Sec. 1982–90; Dir., Joseph E. Seagram & Sons Limited & all other Seagram Candn. affiliates; Dir. & Sec., The Seagram Museum; Editor-in-Chief, 'McGill Law J.' 1974–75 (first female editor); Bd. of Editors 1973–75; I. Ballon Medal for most outstanding contbn. to 'McGill Law J.' 1975; Lazarus Phillips Prize for Corp. Law & Taxation 1975; Carswell Prize for Highest Standing 1975; Univ. Scholarship 1974–75; Mem., Que. Bar Assn.; Candn. Bar Assn.; Candn. Corp. Counsel Assn.; The Lord Reading Law Soc.; Inst. of Chartered Secretaries & Administrators (P.Adm.) (Extve. Council, Que. Div.; Chrmn., Legis. Ctte. 1987–91); Candn. Mfrs. Assn. (Legis. Ctte.); Conference Bd. of Canada (Council of Sr. Legal Extves.); Bd. of Dirs., Theatre Company; Office: 1430 Peel St., Montreal, Que. H3A 1S9.

**SCOTT, Marianne Florence,** B.A., B.L.S., LL.D., D.Litt.; librarian; b. Toronto, Ont. 4 Dec. 1928; d. Merle Redvers Scott and Florence Ethel (Hutton); e. McGill Univ. B.A. 1949, B.L.S. 1952; York Univ. LL.D. (Hon.) 1985; Dalhousie Univ. LL.D. (Hon.) 1989; Laurentian Univ. D.Litt. (Hon.) 1990; NATIONAL LIBRARIAN OF CANADA 1984– ; Asst. Lib., Bank of Montreal 1952–55; Law Lib., McGill Univ. 1955–73, Law Area Lib. 1973–74, Lectr. in Legal Bibliog. 1964–74, Dir. of Libraries 1975–84; recipient Queen's Silver Jubilee Medal 1977; Co-founder and Ed., 'Index to Canadian Legal Periodical Literature' 1963– ; author various articles; mem. Internat. Assn. Law Libraries (mem. of Bd. 1969–71); Am. Assn. Law Libraries (mem. of Comtes. 1973–77); Candn. Assn. Law Libraries (Pres. 1963–69, Extve. Bd. 1973–75), First Hon. mem. 1980– ); Corp. Prof. Librarians Que. (Vice Pres. 1975); Candn. Assn. Research Libs. (Pres. 1978–79, Past Pres. 1979–80, Exec. 1980–81, Secy-Treas. 1983–84); mem. Libs. Sub-Comte., Conf. des Recteurs et des Principaux des Universités du Qué. (Chrmn. 1976–78); UNICAT/TELECAT Mgmt. Comte. (Chrmn. 1975–80) Candn. Library Assn. (First Vice Pres. 1980–81, Pres. 1981–82, Past Pres. 1982–83); Internat. Fedn. of Library Assn. (Hon. Comte., 48th Gen. Conf., Montreal 1982); Centre for Research Libraries (Dir. 1980–86; Program Comte. 1983–88); Chrmn., Conf. of Dirs. of National Libraries 1988–92; Home: 119 Dorothea Dr., Ottawa, Ont. K1V 7C6; Office: 395 Wellington St., Ottawa, Ont. K1A 0N4.

**SCOTT, (Robert James) Munroe,** B.A., M.A.; writer; b. Owen Sound, Ont. 9 Feb. 1927; s. William John and Hellen Douglass (Ford) S.; e. Almonte H.S. 1945; Queen's Univ. B.A. 1948; Cornell Univ. M.A. 1950; m. Hilda d. Joseph and Emma Davison 29 Sept. 1951; children: David Randall, Ian Donald, Robert Munroe; Staff writer, Crawley Films Ltd. 1950–57; freelance writer 1957– ; writer/dir. for CBC-TV series 'The Tenth Decade,' 'First Person Singular (The Pearson Memoirs),' 'One Canadian (The Diefenbaker Memoirs)'; writer: documentary films for NFB, Intertel, CBC-TV, Un. Ch. of Can., Nat. Counc. of Churches, Carillon Films, etc.; drama for 6 CBC-TV series; stage plays premiered at St. Lawrence Ctr., Theatre Aquarius, Kawartha Summer Theatre; writer of the Sound & Light Show for Parliament Hill 1984– ; biographer of Dr. Robert McClure; playwright; columnist; Writer-in-Residence, Univ. of Guelph 1974; Ont. Min. of Culture 'Writer-in-Residence' Lindsay Public Library 1987–88; recipient, Blue Ribbon, Am. Film Fest. 1960, 1967; ACTRA award for Radio Drama 1974; Spec. Jury Award, Candn. Film Awards 1974; OCNA Bell Can. Award (Best Columnist) 1987; Commemorative Medal for 125th Anniversary of Candn. Confederation; Mem., Un. Ch. of Can.; Writers Guild of Canada (ACTRA); Playwrights Union of Can.; author: 'African Manhunt' 1959, 'McClure – Years of Challenge' 1979, 'McClure – The China Years' 1977, 'Waltz for a pagan drum' 1988, 'From Nation to Colony' 1988; plays: 'Wu-feng' 1971, 1982, 'Shylock's Treasure' 1982, 'The Devil's Petition' 1982, 'McClure' 1988; recreations: sailing, cross country skiing; Club: Lindsay 20; Home: R.R. 1, Fenelon Falls, Ont. K0M 1N0.

**SCOTT, Peter Dale,** Ph.D.; university professor / writer; b. Montreal, Que. 11 Jan. 1929; s. the late Francis Reginald and the late Marian Dale S.; e. Westmount H.S. 1945; McGill Univ., B.A. 1949, Ph.D. 1955; Inst. d'Etudes Politiques, Paris 1950; Univ. Coll., Oxford Univ. 1950–52; m. 1stly Mary Elizabeth Marshall 16 June 1956; children: Catherine, Thomas, John; m. 2ndly Ronna d. Norman and Joan Kabatznick 22 June 1993; PROF., UNIV. OF CALIF. AT BERKELEY 1980– ; Lectr., McGill Univ. 1955–56; Candn. Fgn. Serv. (U.N. & Warsaw) 1957–61; Lectr./Asst. Prof., Speech Dept., Univ. of Calif. 1961–66; English Dept., Assoc. Prof. 1968; Sr. Fellow, Internat. Ctr. for Devel. Policy 1987– ; Guggenheim Fellowship 1969–70; Freedom Award, Internat. Ctr. for Devel. Policy 1987; Dir., Polish Arts & Culture Found. 1965–70; Assn. for Responsible Dissent 1988; Writer-in-Residence, Univ. of Toronto 1992; author: 'The War Conspiracy' 1972, 'Crime and Cover-Up' 1977, 'Rumors of No Law' (poems) 1981, 'Coming to Jakarta' (poem) 1988; 'Listening to the Candle' (poem) 1992; 'Deep Politics and the Death of JFK' 1993; 'Murmur of the Stars' (poems) 1994; co-author: 'The Politics of Escalation in Vietnam' 1966; 'The Assassinations' 1967, 'The Iran-Contra Connection' 1987; 'Cocaine Politics' 1991; co-transl.: 'Selected Poems of Zbigniew Herbert' 1968; Candn. citizen; recreations: birdwatching; Office: English Dept., Univ. of Calif., Berkeley, CA 94720.

**SCOTT, Richard Glenn,** C.A.P., F.L.M.I.; treasury executive; b. Winnipeg, Man. 19 April 1949; s. Francis James and Ruby Daisy (Harrison) S.; e. St. James Collegiate 1968; Red River Community College, Computer Analyst-Programmer 1971; Fellow, Life Office Mngt. Assn. 1976; Candn. Securities Course 1979; Officer Dir., Cdn. Sec. Inst. 1987; m. Judith d. Charles and Aileen Fred 11 July 1970; children: Brian Richard, Laura Catherine; ASSISTANT VICE-PRESIDENT, TREASURY, CONFEDERATION TRUST CO. 1989– ; Computer Systems Analyst, Thorne Gunn & Co. 1971–74; Computer Systems Auditor, Great West Life 1974–78; Senior Money Market Trader 1978–82; Senior Bond Trader 1982–84; Regional Treasury Mgr., T.D. Bank 1984–85; Nat. Treasury Sales Mgr., Bank of N.S. 1985–87; Vice-Pres., Money Markets, Pemberton Securities 1987–89; Mem., United Ch. of Canada; Dixie Curling Club; Foster Parents Plan of Canada; Toronto Film Soc.; Coach, Mississauga Football Assn.; recreations: golf, curling, philately, classical guitar; Home: 1863 Pattinson Cres., Mississauga, Ont. L5J 1H6; Office: 321 Bloor St. E., Toronto, Ont. M4W 1H1.

**SCOTT, Stephen Allan,** B.A., B.C.L., D.Phil.; university professor/barrister; b. Montreal, Que. 25 May 1940; s. Irving Harold and Thelma Ada (Vaintrub) S.; e. Westmount (Que.) High Sch. 1957; McGill Univ. B.A. 1961, B.C.L. 1966 (Elizabeth Torrance Gold Medal); Queen's Coll. Oxford, D.Phil. 1969; PROF. OF LAW, MCGILL UNIV. 1977– ; articled law student, Stikeman, Elliott, Tamaki, Mercier & Robb, Montreal 1966–67; called to Bar of Que. 1967; Teaching Staff, Fac. of Law, McGill Univ. 1967– ; Mem., Ctte. on Profl. Training & Bar Examiner, Bar of Que. 1975–84; Couns. public and comm. law matters since 1967– ; appellate litigation courts Que. and Can.; briefs for and witness, various fed. and prov. parlty. cttes.; radio and TV broadcasts & newspaper articles; panelist various confs. legal matters; recipient some 15 grad. and undergrad. prizes, scholarships and fellowships; author various studies Royal Comns. of Inquiry; contbr. to symposia; articles law reviews; Ed.-in-Chief McGill Law Jour. 1965–66; mem. Legal Ctte. Alliance Que. 1983– ; mem. Candn. Bar Assn. (Chrmn. Que. Prov. Sub-Sect., Constitutional & Internat. Law Sect. 1971–73); recreations: swimming, skiing, tennis, films, books, public affairs; Clubs: Monkland Tennis; United Oxford & Cambridge Univ. (London, Eng.); Home: 906, 3033 Sherbrooke St. W., Montreal, Que. H3Z 1A3; Office: 3644 Peel St., Montreal, Que. H3A 1W9.

**SCRAIRE, Jean-Claude;** financial executive; b. Montreal, Que. 25 Aug. 1946; s. Paul and Constance (Beaulac) S.; e. Univ. of Montreal; McGill Univ.; children: Louis-Martin, Jean-François, Valérie; SENIOR VICE-PRESIDENT, CAISSE REAL ESTATE GROUP AND CHAIRMAN OF SUBSIDIARIES 1993– ; private law practice 1970–74; various mngt. positions, govt. of Que. 1974–81; Legal Advisor, Caisse de dépôt et placement du Qué. 1981; Dir. Legal Affairs; Sr. Vice-Pres., Legal & Corp. Affairs 1983; Sr. Vice-Pres. in charge of real estate investments 1986; Chair, Bd. of Dir., Soc. immobilière Trans-Québec; Ivanhoé; Cadim; Mem., Bd. of Trade of Metro Montreal; conseil des relations internat. de Montréal; Internat. Ctr. for Rsch. & Training in Major Projects Mngt.; Forum des gens d'affaires Qué.-Japon; French C. of C. in Canada; Forum internat. des soc. de comm.; Amnesty Internat.; club: Mount Stephen; Home: 23, rue Scraire, Lac Paul, Bellefeuille, Que. J0R 1A0; Office: 1981 McGill College Ave., 8th fl., Montreal, Que. H3A 3C7.

**SCRIVEN, John,** P.Eng.; business executive; b. England 9 May 1935; s. Charles and Mary (Stackhouse) S.; e. Lancaster Royal Grammar Sch. 1953; Stafford Co. Tech. Coll., dipl. 1958; Centre de etudes indus., Geneva 1968–69; m. Jean d. John and Elizabeth Turner 22 Aug. 1959; children: Renata Jayne, Dwayne Alan; PRES. & GEN. MGR., TESHMONT CONSULTANTS INC. 1981– ; Apprentice & Devel. Engr., English Electric Co. 1953–60; Aluminum Co. of Can. Ltd. 1961–72; var. positions incl. Mgr. of Contracts, Chief Electr. Engr., Mgr. of Opns. & Gen. Mgr., Teshmont Engr. Inc. 1972–81; Dir., Man. HVDC Rsch. Ctr.; Dir., I.D. Group Inc.; Mem., Man. C. of C.; Inst. of Electrical & Electronics Engrs.; recreations: hiking, skiing; Clubs: Manitoba; Charleswood Ski; Office: 1190 Waverly St., Winnipeg, Man. R3T 2E2.

**SCRIVENER, Margaret;** m. Richard Harding Scrivener; MEM., MARTIN & MEREDITH LIMITED; el. M.P.P. 1971, re-el. 1975, 1977, 1981; mem. Task Force Housing Policy 1973; Parlty. Asst. to Min. of Housing 1974; Min. of Govt. Services 1975; Min. of Revenue 1977; Chrmn. Ont. Task Force Prov. Rail Policy 1980; Chrmn. Criminal Injuries Compensation Bd. 1985–88; Dir. Prime Mentors Can.; Trustee, Mem. Gov. Council and Extve. Ctte., Wycliffe Coll. Univ. of Toronto; Dame Commander, Order of St. Lazarus; former Owner-Operator Belhaven Farms; Vice Chrmn. and Mem. at Large Metro Toronto Planning Bd. 1960–72; Hon. Life mem. Am. Guernsey Cattle Breeders Assn.; Community Planning Assn. Can.; Hon. Dir., Empire Club of Can.; Hon. mem. St. George - St. David Progressive Conservative Assoc.; Clubs: Albany; Canadian Club of Toronto; Royal Candn. Yacht; Toronto Hunt.

**SCRIVER, Charles Robert,** O.C., M.D.C.M., F.R.S., F.R.S.C.; scientist; educator; b. Montreal, Que. 7 Nov. 1930; s. Walter DeMoulpied and Jessie Marion (Boyd) S.; e. McGill Univ. B.A. 1951, M.D.C.M. 1955; m. Esther d. Carleton and Esther Peirce 8 Sept. 1956; children: Dorothy Ellen, Peter Carleton, Julie Boyd, Paul Peirce; PROF. OF PEDIATRICS, GENETICS & BIOL. McGILL UNIV. 1969– and ALVA PROFESSOR OF HUMAN GENETICS 1994– ; Intern Royal Victoria Hosp. Montreal 1955–56; Resident Royal Victoria Hosp. and Montreal Children's Hosp. 1956–57; Children's Med. Center Boston 1957–58; McLaughlin Travelling Fellow Univ. Coll. London 1958–60; Chief Resident (Pediatrics) Montreal Children's Hosp. 1960–61, Physician 1961– ; Asst. Prof. of Pediatrics present Univ. 1961, Markle Scholar 1961–66, Assoc. Prof. 1965; recipient Wood Gold Medal 1955 McGill; Mead Johnson Award Am. Acad. Ped. 1968, Borden Award 1973; Nutrition Soc. Can. Borden Award 1969; Candn. Soc. Clin. Invest. Malcolm Brown Award 1979; Am. Soc. Human Genetics, William Allan Award 1978; Gairdner Foundation International Award 1979; McLaughlin Medal, Royal Soc. Can. 1981; Candn. Rutherford Lectr. Royal Soc. (London) 1983; Prix Sarrazin, Club Rsch. Clin. Qué. 1988; Ross Award Can. Ped. Soc. 1990; Award of Excellence, Genetics Soc. of Can. 1992; Elected Fellow, Royal Soc. (London) 1991 and Am. Assoc. Adv. Sci. 1992; Annual Lecturer, Royal College of Phys. & Surg. 1992; Prix d'Excellence, Inst. Rsch. Clin. de Montréal 1993; D.Sc. (Hon.) Univ. of Manitoba 1992, Glasgow Univ. 1993, Univ. de Montréal 1993; co-author: 'Amino Acid Metabolism and its Disorders' 1973; 'Garrod's Inborn Factors in Disease' 1989; Sr. editor 'Metabolic Basis of Inherited Disease' 1989– ; author or co-author over 500 sci. articles; mem. Sci. Counc. Can. 1984–90; Genetics Study Sect. Med. Rsch. Council Can. 1976–81, Co-Dir./Dir. MRC Genetics Group McGill 1972– ; Assoc. Dir. Can. Genetic Disease Network (NCE Prog.) 1989– ; mem. Med. Adv. Bd. Howard Hughes Med. Inst. 1981–88; Metabolism Study Sect. NIH Washington, D.C. 1968–72; Pres. Candn. Soc. Clin. Invest. 1974–75; Soc. Pediatric Rsch. 1975–76; Dir., Am. Soc. Human Genetics 1971–74, Pres. 1986; Pres., Soc. Study Inborn Errors Metab. (UK) 1988; Pres. Elect Am. Ped. Soc. 1993– ; Chrmn. Ctte. on Genetics Am. Acad. Pediatrics 1976–83; 2nd Vice Pres. Fonds de Recherche en Santé du Qué. 1977–83; Officer, Order of Canada 1986; Elder, Presbyn. Ch. Montreal W.; recreations: literature, music, photography; Home: 232 Strathearn Ave., Montreal, Que. H4X 1Y2; Office: Montreal Children's Hosp., 2300 Tupper St., Montreal, Que. H3H 1P3.

**SCULLY, Hugh Edwards,** B.A., M.D.,C.M., M.Sc., F.R.S.C.(C), F.A.C.S., FACC; cardiovascular surgeon; b. Windsor, Ont. 16 Oct. 1940; s. Hugh Ballard and Elizabeth Joyce (Edwards) S.; e. high schs. Ottawa, Paris, Geneva (Internat. Sch.); Queen's Univ., B.A. 1963, M.D.,C.M. 1965, M.Sc. 1967; m. Vanessa Harwood (prin. ballerina) d. Peter and Hazel Harwood 14 June 1980; children: Laura, Alexa, Shannon; PROF. OF SURGERY, PROF. OF HEALTH ADMINISTRATION, UNIV. OF TORONTO; CARDIOVASCULAR SURGEON, TORONTO GEN. HOSP. 1974– and SENIOR SURGEON, THE TORONTO HOSPITAL; Dir. Surg. Edn. 1984– ; Chrmn. Med. Adv. Bd. (Chief of Staff) 1984–86, Trustee 1982–86; Dep. Surg.-in-Chief 1988–89; Dep. Head, Cardiovasc. Surg., The Toronto Hosp. 1989– ; Nat. Med. Adv. Candn. Automobile Sport Clubs 1971–90; Med. Dir. Candn. Racing Drivers Assn.; Emergency Co-ordinator Grand Prix of Can.; mem. for Can. Med. Comn. Fedn. Internat. du Sport Automobile; Advisory Bd. of Dirs., Motorsport Rsch. Inst., McGill Univ. 1989– ; Cons. Surg. Nat. Ballet Can., Hon. Gov. 1984–86; Bd. of Dirs., Ottawa Ballet 1989– ; Vice-Chrmn. of the Bd., Toronto Hosp. Found.; author or co-author numerous sci. papers; mem. Ont. Med. Assn. (Bd. mem. 1981– ; Exec. 1983–84; Treas. 1984–85; Bd. Chrmn. 1985–86; Vice Pres. 1986–87; Pres. 1987–88; Chief Negotiator 1983–87); Candn. Med. Assn. (Bd. mem. 1986– ; Extve. Ctte. mem. 1988–89); Mem., National Manpower Ctte.; Chrmn., Council Health Policy and Economics, Candn. Medical Assn. 1989– ; Internat. Soc. Surg.; Ont. Health Rev. Panel 1986–87; Premier's Council on Health Strategy for Ont. 1988–91; Candn. Cardiovascular Soc.; Soc. thoracic Surgs.; Am. Assn. Thoracic Surg.; Am. Assn. Acad. Surg.; Candn. Soc. Cardiovascular & Thoracic Surgs.; Internat. Soc. Heart Transplantation; Medico-Legal Soc. Toronto; York Founders; recreations: skiing, fishing, auto racing; Clubs: Caledon Ski; University; Home: 316 Spadina Rd., Toronto, Ont. M5R 2V6; Office: 226–13EBN, Toronto General Hospital, 200 Elizabeth St., Toronto, Ont. M5G 2C4.

**SCULLY, Robert G.,** B.A., M.A.; journalist, TV & radio host, translator, consultant, producer; b. Ottawa, Ont. 28 Mar. 1950; s. Jean-Louis and Mance (Cossette) S.; c. Saint Piux X H.S. 1966; Goethe Inst., Munich, Mittelstufe 1968; McGill Univ. B.A. 1970, M.A. 1974; engaged to Sylvie d. Claude and Françoise de Lorimier; TV PRODUCER, TELEMISSION INFORMATION (& others) 1990– ; Latin Am. Correspondent, 'Le Devoir' 1969–70; Arts & Lit. Ed. 1970–75; N.Y. Correspondent, 'La Presse' 1975–83; Radio Host, CBC for 'Musique de la Louisiane' (Lafayette/N.Y.) 1975–83; Lit. Agent, Noramtel Internat. (N.Y./Paris) 1975–88; TV Host, CBC for 'Impact,' 'USA,' 'Scully Rencontre,' 'Scully en direct,' 'Démocraties' (co-host), 'Venture' 1983– ; Communications Cons., Scully, de Lorimier Assoc. & others 1981– ; Creative Dir. (with Patrick Watson) for 'Heritage Minutes' 1990– ; Gemini/Gémeaux Awards, Acad. of Candn. Cinema & TV: Best Host 1987, and 1988; Trustee, Starlight Found. of Can.; Roman Catholic; scriptwriter & narrator: 'La America latina del Norte' 1977; editor: 'Morceaux du grand Montréal' 1979; Lit. Transl.: 'Wild to Mild' by Réjean Ducharme 1980; author: 'Les lumières de Manhattan' 1983; fluent & working languages: English, French, German, Spanish; base of opn.: Montreal, N.Y., Paris, Toronto; club: University; Office: Case 98, place du Parc, Montreal, Que. H2W 2M9.

**SEABROOK, Victor Melville,** Q.C.; barrister and solicitor; b. Ottawa, Ont. 25 June 1928; s. Richard Melville and Marjorie Edith (Crawford) S.; e. Univ. of Toronto, B.A. 1951; Osgoode Hall, Toronto, Ont.; children: Richard Melville, Peter Cameron, Timothy Victor; PARTNER, SEABROOK & ASSOCS.; Pres. & Dir., Denver TC, Inc.; Dir. International Oiltex Ltd.; Seamel Inc.; read law with McMillan, Binch, Stuart, Berry, Dunn, Corrigan & Howland, Toronto, Ont.; called to Bar of Ont. 1955; cr. Q.C. 1965; mem., Candn. Bar Assn.; Candn. Tax Found.; County of York Law Assn.; P. Conservative; Anglican; recreations: golf, skiing; Clubs: Albany; Canadian (New York); Toronto Golf; Office: Ste. 1900, P.O. Box 40, Royal Trust Tower, Toronto-Dominion Centre, Toronto, Ont. M5K 1B7.

**SEADEN, George,** B.A., B.Eng., M.Sc., P.Eng.; civil engineer; b. 26 May 1936; s. Simon and Mary S.; e. Fribourg Univ. Switzerland B.A. 1954; McGill Univ. B.Eng. 1958; Harvard Univ. M.Sc. 1968; Northwestern Univ., Sr. Mngmt. Diploma 1992; m. Linda H. Mutch; children: Amy, Maia; DIR. GENERAL, INST. FOR RSCH. IN CONSTRN. NAT. RSCH. COUNCIL CAN. 1984– ; Staff Eng. Gatineau Power 1958–59; Mgr. Warnock Hersey 1959–60; Eng., Ent. Fougerolle, France 1960–62; Assoc. Cartier, Coté, Piette, Montréal 1962–67; Adv. Urban Affairs, Govt. Can. 1969–71; Pres., Archer, Seaden & Assoc. Montréal and Kleinfelt Consultants Toronto 1971–84; Visiting Prof. Univ. of Ottawa 1969–71; invited speaker (Canada, U.S., international) on strategic planning, construction mngmt. and R&D issues; Advisor to World Economic Forum; Ed. bd. mem., Construction Business Review (US); Building Research and Practice (UK); co-author 'Trends in Building Construction Techniques Worldwide'; Pres. Comm. internationale du bâtiment 1989–92; Dir. Candn. Constrn. Rsch. Bd., Constrn. Ind. Devel. Bd.; Past Chrmn. St-Andrew's Sch. Westmount, Qué.; licenced to practice engineering in Ontario and Quebec, chartered engr. (U.K.); recreations: skiing, sailing; Clubs: Mount Royal Tennis; Home: 80 Lyttleton Gdns., Rockcliffe Park, Ont. K1L 5A6; Office: Ottawa, Ont. K1A 0R6.

**SEAGRAM, Norman Meredith,** B.A.Sc., M.Sc.; b. Toronto, Ont., 10 July 1934; s. Norman Oliver and Constance Beatrice (Mills) S.; e. Trinity Coll. Sch., Port Hope, Ont.; Univ. of Toronto, B.A.Sc. 1958; Univ. of Birmingham (U.K.) M.Sc. 1964; m. Joyce Elizabeth, d. Frederick William McMackon, Victoria, B.C., 21 Aug. 1958; children: Susan Elizabeth, Norman Philip, Joseph Frederick, Samantha; CHAIRMAN AND CHIEF EXTVE. OFFICER, CANADIAN LIQUID AIR LTD. 1993– ; Chrmn., Harbourfront Centre; Gov., Olympic Trust of Canada; Trinity Coll. Sch.; mem., International Council - INSEAD; Business Council on National Issues; commenced as Engr., Rootes Ltd., Coventry, U.K. 1958; Consultant, Associated Industrial Consultants Ltd., and Mngmt. Sciences Ltd., United Kingdom, Kenya, Tanzania, Zimbabwe, and Halifax & Toronto, Canada 1960–68; Anthes Imperial Ltd., Toronto 1968–70; Vice Pres., Molson Breweries of Canada Ltd., Montreal 1970–77; Pres., Seaway/Midwest Ltd., Toronto 1978–82; Sr. Vice Pres., Admin., Molson Breweries of Canada Ltd., Montreal 1982–83; Pres., Molson Western Breweries Ltd., Calgary 1983–85; Pres., Molson Ont. Breweries Ltd. 1985–86; Extve. Vice Pres., The Molson Companies Ltd. 1986–92; Chrmn., Molson Breweries of Canada Ltd.; Club de Hockey Canadien, Inc.; Vancouver Canadians Baseball Ltd. 1986–88; mem. Assn. Prof. Engrs. Ont.; Alpha Delta Phi; P. Conservative; Anglican; recreations: tennis, squash, golf, skiing, hockey; Clubs: Toronto Club; Toronto Badminton & Racquet; Mount Royal; Montreal Badminton & Squash; Hillside Tennis; Empire; Home: 47 Chestnut Park Rd., Toronto, Ont. M4W 1W7; Offices: 1155 Sherbrooke St. W., Montreal, Que. H3A 1H8 and 250 Bloor St. E., Main Floor, Toronto, Ont. M4W 1E6.

**SEAGRAM, Norman Oliver,** Q.C., B.A., LL.B.; b. Toronto, Ont. 6 Sept. 1908; s. Norman and Gladys May (Buchanan) S.; e. Trinity Coll. Sch., Port Hope, Ont.; Univ. of Toronto, B.A. 1930; Osgoode Hall, Toronto, Ont. 1933; m. Constance Beatrice Mills, 14 Sept. 1933; children: Norman Meredith, John David, Robert Michael; ASSOCIATE GOWLING, STRATHY AND HENDERSON; called to the Bar of Ontario, 1933; cr. Q.C. 1954; Wing Commander, R.C.A.F. in 2nd World War, 1940–45; mem., Toronto Bd. Trade; Alpha Delta Phi; Conservative; Anglican; recreations: golf, curling, skiing, Clubs; Toronto; Toronto Golf; University; Badminton & Racquet; Toronto Cricket, Skating & Curling; Toronto Lawyers: Royal & Ancient Golf (St. Andrews, Scotland); St. Andrews Golf Club (Scotland); Home: Granite Place, 63 St. Clair Ave. W., Toronto, Ont. M4V 2Y9; Office: Ste. 3800, Commerce Court West, Toronto, Ont. M5L 1J3.

**SEALY, Paul Addis Henry,** B.Comm., C.A., M.B.A.; business executive; b. Lloydtown, Ont. 13 Nov. 1933; s. Ronald John and Ada Blanche (Winter) S.; e. Sir George Williams Univ., B.Comm. 1959; McGill Univ. C.A. 1961; York Univ., M.B.A. 1970; m. E. Diana d. Roberts and Margaret Davis; children: Jocelyn Anne, Jennifer Anne; CHRMN. & TREASURER, BORDEN METAL PRODUCTS (CANADA) LTD. 1990– ; Treasury Dept., Shell Can. Ltd. 1953; Audit Staff, Touche Ross & Co. 1959; Mgr. of Costs & Budgets, Atlas Steels Ltd. 1963; Asst. Div. Comptroller, Mining Div., Rio Algom Mines Ltd. 1965; Sec.-Treas., Borden Metal Prod. (Canada) Ltd. 1970–74, President 1974–90; Dir., Borden Metal Prod. (Can.) Ltd.; Tekmet Limited; Mem., Un. Ch. of Can.; Ordre des Comptables Agréés du Qué. 1961– ; The Inst. of C.A.'s of Ont.; The Candn. Tax Found.; mem., Bd. of Trade of Metro. Toronto; recreations: photography, travel; Home: Ste. 712, The Ports, 1177 Yonge St., Toronto, Ont. M4T 2Y1 and R.R. 4, Tottenham, Ont. L0G 1W0; Office: 50 Dayfoot St., Beeton, Ont. L0G 1A0.

**SEAMAN, Byron J.,** B.Sc.; petroleum executive; b. Sask. 1923; e. Univ. of Sask. B.Sc. (Mech. Engn.) 1945; m. Evelyn Virginia, Sept. 1948; children: Karen Gayle, Ronald James, Deborah Joan, Allan Byron; Dir., Bovar Inc.; Champion Bear Resources Ltd.; Encal Energy Ltd.; Chrmn., Candn Ctte. of Det norske Veritas; former Instr. in Mech. Engn. Univ. of Sask.; Geophysicist, Carter Oil Co.; Liaison Engr. Constr. Dept. Gulf Oil; Seismograph Operator Western Geophysical; joined brother Seaman Engineering and Drilling Co. Ltd. 1949 (which company later became Bow Valley Industries Ltd.), Vice Pres. and Dir. Bow Valley 1960, Sr. Vice Pres. 1968, Extve. Vice Pres. 1975, Vice Chrmn. 1976; Chrmn. & C.E.O., Bow Valley Resource Services Ltd. 1976–87; Chrmn. Bovar Inc. (formerly Bow Valley Resource Services Ltd.) 1988–90; Mem., Premier's Advisory Council on Science & Tech.; Govt. Appointee, Adv. Bd., Alberta Children's Hosp.; Hon. D.Sc. Univ. of Saskatchewan 1992; Home: #11 Bel-Aire Place S.W., Calgary, Alta.

**SEAMAN, Daryl Kenneth,** O.C., B.Sc., LL.D.; petroleum executive; b. Rouleau, Sask. 28 Apr. 1922; s. late Byron L. and Mae (Patton) Seaman; e. publ. and high schs., Rouleau, Sask.; Univ. of Sask., B.Sc. (Mech. Eng.) 1948; m. Lois Maureen de Long (dec.); four children: Robert, Kenneth, Gary, Diane; PRESIDENT & CHAIRMAN, DOX INVESTMENTS INC.; Co-Founder, Bow Valley Industries Ltd. (est. 1962); Dir., Gobi Oil & Gas Ltd.; Renaissance Energy Ltd.; Encal Energy Ltd.; Trimac Ltd.; Potash Corp. of Sask. Inc.; NOVA Corp. of Alta.; Pan-Alberta Gas Ltd.; Lakeside Farm Industries Ltd.; Founding Dir., Vencap Equities Alberta Ltd.; Co-owner & Dir., Calgary Flames Hockey Club; Chrmn., Nat. Advisory Ctte., Banff Sch. of Managment; Honorary Chrmn., The Western Heritage Centre Soc.; Gov., Olympic Trust of Can. and Chrmn., Alta. Div. 1984–88; Co-Chrmn., Team Petroleum Olympics Fund 1987–88; Chrmn., Engn. Expansion Fund Univ. of Sask. 1969–72; Calgary Chrmn., Nat. Corporations Ctte., Univ. of Sask. 1977–81; Ctte. Mem., Geological Sciences Fund, Univ. of Sask. 1984–87; Mem., Calgary Ctte., Engn. Advancement Trust, Univ. of Sask.; Mem., Calgary Sports Adv. Ctte.; Mem., Royal Comn. on the Economic Union and Development Propsects for Canada 1983–85; Hon. Life Mem., Assoc. of Prof. Engr., Geologists and Geophysicists; Frank Spragins Award, A.P.E.G.G. 1984; McGill

Mgmt. Achievement Award 1985; Gov. Hockey Canada Found. 1979; Saskatchewan Oil & Gas Ind. Hall of Fame 1989; Paul Harris Fellowship Award, Rotary Club 1993; Officer, Order of Canada 1993; Hon. LL.D., Univ. of Sask.; Univ. of Calgary 1993; R.C.A.F. Pilot, Flying Offr., 1941–45; operations with 500 Squadron R.A.F. in N. Africa and Italy; awarded Govt. of France Citation, N. Africa 1943; Un. Ch. of Can.; recreations: ranching, golf, hunting, skiing; Clubs: Ranchmen's; Royal Air Force; Earl Grey Golf; Calgary Petroleum; Calgary Golf and Country; University of Calgary Chancellor's; Office: 500, 333 – 5th Ave. S.W., Calgary, Alta. T2P 3B6.

**SEAQUIST, Ernest Raymond,** B.A.Sc., M.A., Ph.D.; university professor; b. Vancouver, B.C. 19 Nov. 1938; s. Egron Emanuel and Sigrid Alice (Back) S.; e. Univ. of B.C., B.A.Sc. 1961; Univ. of Toronto, M.A. 1962, Ph.D. 1966; m. Gloria d. William and Mabel Jenkins 11 June 1966; children: Jonathan William, Carolyn Suzanne; PROF., DEPT. OF ASTRONOMY, UNIV. OF TORONTO 1978– ; Lectr., Univ. of Toronto 1965–66; Asst. Prof. 1966–71; Assoc. Prof. 1972–78; Assoc. Chrmn., Dept. of Astronomy 1973–88, Chrmn. 1988– ; Dir., David Dunlap Observatory 1988– ; rsch. field: radio astronomy; Pres., Candn. Astron. Soc. 1986–88; mem. & chrmn. of numerous cttes.; Mem., Candn. Astron. Soc.; Internat. Astron. Union; Am. Astron. Soc.; Royal Astron. Soc. of Can.; recreation: painting; Home: David Dunlap Observatory, Box 360, Richmond Hill, Ont. L4C 4Y6; Office: Toronto, Ont. M5S 1A1.

**SEARLE, James Elmhurst,** B.Arch., F.R.A.I.C., Hon. F.A.I.A. architect; b. Winnipeg 13 June 1929; s. James Winning and Agnes Elizabeth (Graham) S.; e. Univ. of Manitoba, B. Arch. 1951; m. Judith P. Menzies Mylrea, d. A. Wilfrid Menzies, Toronto, March 1974; children of previous marriage: Lauraine, James, Christine, Michael; MANAGING DIR., SEARLE CONSULTING 1982– ; joined staff of firm headed by Smith and Carter on grad.; Assoc., 1954, Partner 1959, firm merging with John B. Parkin, Toronto, firm 1969; Man. Partner, Searle Wilbee Rowland; Partner, Smith Carter Partners; Pres. S.W.R. Consultants Ltd., all 1969–73; Sr. Vice Pres. Abbey Glen Property Corp. 1973–77; Pres., Genstar Commercial Development Co.; Sr. Vice Pres., Genstar Projects (Middle East) Ltd. 1977–79; Sr. Vice Pres., Genstar Construction Ltd., Internat. Div. 1979–81; Vice Pres., Genstar Corp. 1981–82; F.R.A.I.C. (Pres., 1967–68); Hon. Fellow, Am. Inst. of Archs.; mem., Ont. Assn. Archs; Anglican; Clubs: Winnipeg Squash Racquet (Life mem.); The University Club of Toronto; Home: 3 South Close, Highgate, London N6 5UQ England.

**SEARS, Garry Martin,** M.A.; management consultant; b. Ottawa, Ont. 25 Jan. 1955; s. James Eugene and Dorothy Joan (Martin) S.; e. Carleton Univ. B.A. (Hons.) 1976; Univ. of Toronto M.A. 1979; m. Patricia d. Harold and Lorraine Roe 22 Oct. 1981; children: Caitlin, Patrick; PARTNER, KPMG MANAGEMENT CONSULTING 1991– ; joined present firm (formerly Peat Marwick Stevenson & Kellogg) 1979; specializes in science & technology management, industry competitive analysis & market research; Pres., Candn. Evaluation Soc., Nat. Capital Chap. 1991–92; Mem. Program Ctte., The Planning Forum; recreations: running, piano: Home: 52 Jarlan Terrace, Kanata, Ont. K2L 3L3; Office: World Exchange Plaza, 10th Floor, 45 O'Connor St., Ottawa, Ont. K1P 1A4.

**SEARS, John T.,** B.Com., M.B.A., D.B.A.; educator; b. Antigonish, N.S. 19 Oct. 1931; s. Cyril Francis and Irene G. (MacDonald) S.; e. St. Francis Xavier Univ., B.Com. 1952; Univ. of Detroit, M.B.A. 1954; Harvard Univ., D.B.A. 1966 m. Mary Ann, d. J. C. Hemeon, Liverpool, N.S. 23 May 1955; children: Stephanie (Mrs. Ronald Giammarino), Meaghan (Mrs. Joseph Petruzzella), Mark, (late) Siobhan, Mairi (Mrs. David MacFarlane); Prof. of Business Adm., St. Francis Xavier Univ. 1969– ; Dean of Arts there 1970–81 and Dean of Science 1972–81, Academic Vice-Pres. 1984–87, 1991– ; joined present Univ. as Lectr. in Business Adm. 1954, Asst. Prof. 1956–57, Assoc. Prof. 1960–69, Prof. since 1969; Visiting Prof. of Business Adm., Univ of W. Ont. 1968–69, 1978–79 and 1987, and at Univ. of B.C. 1988; Dir., Industrial Estates Ltd. 1970–75; mem., Regional Adv. Council, Fed. Business Devel. Bank 1978–81; Pres., Bd. of Trustees. St. Martha's Hospital, Antigonish, 1972–85; Gov., Inst. Canadian Bankers 1971–73; mem., Nova Scotia Region Enterprise Devel. Bd. of Dept. of Industry, Trade and Commerce, 1981–83; Dir., Candn. National Railways, Halifax Ind. Ltd., C.N. Hotels 1983–85; author 'Institutional Financing of Small Business in Nova Scotia' 1972; mem., Financial Mgmt. Assn.; Admin. Sciences Assn. of Can. (ASAC); R. Catholic; recreations: skiing, golf, fishing; Home: 52 Hawthorne St., Antigonish, N.S. B2G 1A4; Office: Antigonish, N.S. B2G 1C0.

**SEARS, Malcolm Raymond,** MB, ChB, FRACP, FRCPC; university professor; b. New Plymouth, N.Z. 8 Feb. 1942; s. Raymond Leonard and Elsie Mildred (Warner) S.; e. New Plymouth Boys' H.S. 1959; Univ. of Otago Medical School MB, ChB 1961–65; m. Jan d. Allan and Jessie Ashby 22 Aug. 1964; children: Christopher, Joanna; PROFESSOR OF MEDICINE, MCMASTER UNIV. 1990– ; Medical Internship/Residency, Dunedin, N.Z. 1966–69; Teaching & Rsch. Fellow, Univ. of Otago 1970–71; Sr. Fellow, Univ. of Wash. 1971–73; Sr. Lectr., Univ. of Otago 1974–86; Assoc. Prof. 1987–90; Visiting Prof., McMaster Univ. 1986; Principal Investigator, Asthma Rsch. Study Dunedin 1979– ; Invited Lectr., nat. & internat. respiratory meetings; Mem., Am. Thoracic Soc.; Am. Acad. of Allergy & Immunology; Candn. Thoracic Soc.; Thoracic Soc. of Australia & N.Z.; recognized internat. authority on epidemiology of asthma & relationship between treatment adverse effects & asthma severity; Chair, Med. Adv. Panel, Asthma Found. of N.Z. 1987–90; Med. Rsch. Council of N.Z. Asthma Task Force 1979–90; Christian; author of 8 book chapters, 60 orig. rsch. papers, 35 abstracts of presentations to learned societies; recreations: music, travel; Home: 90 Highland Park Dr., Dundas, Ont. L9H 6G8; Office: FRCAU, St. Joseph's Hosp., 50 Charlton Ave. E., Hamilton, Ont. L8N 4A6.

**SEATON, Hon. Peter D.,** LL.B., LL.D. (Hon.); judge; b. Vernon, B.C. 29 Apr. 1924; s. William Lyle and Margaret P. (Dickson) S.; e. elem. and high schs. Vernon, B.C.; Univ. of B.C. LL.B. 1950; Univ. of Victoria LL.D. (Hon.); m. Doreen M. d. William and Mabel Curry 21 May 1949; JUSTICE OF APPEAL, COURT OF APPEAL B.C. and JUDGE, COURT OF APPEAL Y.T. 1973– ; called to Bar of B.C. 1950; law practice Morrow & Davidson, Vernon, B.C., Partner, Morrow Davidson & Seaton (later Davidson & Seaton); Judge, Supreme Court of B.C. 1966; served with RCAF 1942–46; recreations: sailing, skiing; Home: 580 Knockmaroon Rd., West Vancouver, B.C. V7S 1R6; Office: Law Courts, 800 Smithe St., Vancouver, B.C. V6Z 2E1.

**SEBELIUS, Helen,** M.F.A.; artist; educator; b. Sask. 4 Sept. 1953; d. Everett Vernon and Albina Marie (Gosselin) S.; e. Alta. Coll. of Art Calgary Visual Arts Dip. 1978; N.S. Coll. of Art & Design M.F.A. 1987; one d. Nikko Michelle Snyder; solo exhns. incl. Olga Korper Gallery Toronto 1983, 1985, 1991; Anna Leonowens Gallery Halifax 1987; Virginia Christopher Galleries 'Drawings: Ten Year Survey 1979–89' 1989; rep. numerous group exhns. incl. Alta. Coll. Art Gallery, Nickle Arts Museum, Glenbow Museum Calgary, Edmonton Art Gallery, Le Musée de Saguenay, Clermont Ferrand France, Hobart Tasmania; various pub., corporate and private colls. incl. Alta. Art Found., Can. Council Art Bank, Dept. External Affairs, Glenbow Museum; sessional instr. in drawing, painting and textiles Alta. Coll. of Art and Univ. of Calgary since 1981; recipient Alta. Culture & Multiculturalism Project Grants 1983, 1984, 1990; Can. Council Travel Grant 1985, Project Grant 1983, 1984; Address: 214 9 Ave. N.E., Calgary, Alta. T2E 0V4.

**SECCARECCIA, Mario Sebastiano,** B.A., Ph.D.; university professor; b. Galluccio, Caserta, Italy 1 Jan. 1952; s. Antonio and Maria Luisa (Martucci) S.; e. McGill Univ. B.A. (Hons.) 1974, Ph.D. 1983; m. Giovanna M. d. Domenico and Angela Mazza 31 July 1982; children: Nadia, Antonio, Alessandro; ASSOCIATE PROF., ECONOMICS, UNIV. OF OTTAWA; Lecturer, then Asst. Prof., now Assoc. Prof., Dept. of Econ., Univ. of Ottawa 1978– ; part-time cons. economist for trade unions; Lectr. in Econ., Labour Coll. of Canada 1988, '91, '94; Mem., Edit. Ctte., 'Collection des sciences sociales' 1991– , 'La Collection d'économie politique' 1989–92, Candn. Centre for Policy Alternatives Ottawa 1983–87; Canada Council Doctoral Fellowship 1976–78; Mem., Soc. can. de sci. écon.; Hist. of Econ. Soc.; Assn. for Evolutionary Econ.; Ctte. for Monetary & Econ. Reform; Adv. Bd. Mem., Canadians for Constitutional Money; co-editor: 'Les pièges de l'austérité, dette nationale et prospérité économique' 1993, 'Milton Friedman et son oeuvre' 1993; author of approx. 20 sci. journal articles & 12 book chapters as well as popular pamphlets & tech. reports; recreations: bicycling, swimming, squash; Home: 434 rue François, Gatineau, Que. J8P 5V5; Office: 550 Cumberland St., Ottawa, Ont. K1N 6N5.

**SECORD, Lloyd Calvin,** B.Sc., F. E. I. C., F.C.A.S.I.; consulting engineer; b. St. Thomas, Ont. 28 Aug. 1923; s. late Eleanor Louva (Ward) and late Cortland Lionel S.; e. Queen's Univ., B.Sc. (Hons.) 1945 (Gold Medal for highest standing in Mech. Engn.); m. Lillian Gordon, d. late John Frederick Mutrie, 14 Sept. 1944; one s. Timothy Scott; PRES. & CHIEF EXTVE. OFFR., DENEB INCORPORATED; Chrmn., TC69, Standards Counc. of Can.; Dir. & Past Chrmn., Electric Vehicle Assn. of Can.; mem. Adv. Counc., Ryerson Polytech. Inst., Toronto; Past Chrmn., Space Comm., Aerospace Ind. Assoc.; Past Pres., Candn Nuclear Assn.; mem. Assn. Prof. Engrs. Ont.; Soc. Automotive Engrs.; Candn. Soc. Mech. Engrs.; author of numerous papers and presentations; holds patents in Can., U.S., U.K. and Europe; Protestant; recreations: golf, sailing; Clubs: St. Georges; Home: 413 The Kingsway, Islington, Ont. M9A 3W1.

**SECRETAN, Lance H.K.,** M.A., Ph.D., F.R.S.A., F.I.E.C.; management consultant; writer; public speaker; b. Amersham, UK 1 Aug. 1939; s. Kenyon and Marie-Therese (Haffenden) S.; emigrated to Canada 1959; e. St. Peter's Bournemouth; Univ. of Waterloo; Univ. of S. Cal. M.A. (magna cum laude) 1980; London Sch. of Econ. & Pol. Sci. Ph.D. 1984; two d. Natalie Marie, Sandi Lee McCallum; m. Tricia (nee Sheppard); FOUNDER & PRES. THE THALER CORP. INC. 1972– and THALER RESOURCES LTD. 1981– ; Sales Mgr., J.J. Little and Ives 1959–60; Analyst, Toronto Stock Exchange 1960; Sales Mgr., Office Overload, Toronto 1960–67; Mng. Dir. Manpower Ltd. Group of Co's. (UK, Ireland, Middle E., Africa), London, UK 1967–81; former Prof. of Entrepreneurship McMaster Univ., Visiting Prof. York Univ.; Founder 'The New Values Movement'; frequent lectr., guest speaker; weekly newspaper columnist; Cons. to nat. and internat. corps., govts.; author: 'How To Be An Effective Secretary' 1972; 'From Guns to Butter' 1983; 'Managerial Moxie' 1986, rev. ed. 1993; 'The Masterclass' 1988; 'The Way of the Tiger' 1989; 'The Personal Masterclass' 1992; 'Living the Moment' 1992; mem. MENSA; Royal Soc. of the Arts; Inst. of Employment Consultants; Special Goodwill Ambassador to The Canadian Assn. for the United Nations Environment Program - CANADA - 1990; Club: University; Address: R.R.2, Alton, Ont. L0N 1A0.

**SEDAWIE, Norman William;** television producer-director-writer; b. Vancouver, B.C. 1 Oct. 1928; s. Fred and Jessie Elizabeth (Wood) S.; e. Pub. and High Schs., Vancouver; m. Gayle Ina, d. Jack Gibson and Lola (Pitchford), Port Hope, Ont. 23 June 1956; three s.; Mark, Glen, Grant; Pres., Tel-Pro Entertainment Inc.; writer, ed. Vancouver Sun 1945 and Vancouver Province to 1954; writer, producer, dir., CBC TV, Toronto, 1954–65; numerous TV credits in Hollywood incl. long term contracts with Danny Kaye and Tom Smothers co's; winner of various TV awards; first prize in Montreux, Switzerland TV festival for co-production with Gayle Gibson Sedawie of Rich Little's Christmas Carol (winner of Internat. Emmy, 1979 for same program); Official Video of Candn. Museum of Civilization 1990; mem., Dirs. Guild Am.; Nat. Acad. TV Arts & Sciences; Writers Guild Am.; ACTRA; recreation: reading, gardening; Home: Mississauga, Ont. and Roseburg, Oregon.

**SEDRA, Adel S.,** B.Sc., M.A.Sc., Ph.D., P.Eng., F.I.E.E.E.; university professor, academic administrator; b. Egypt 2 Nov. 1943; s. Chafik and Helene (Monsour) S.; e. Cairo Univ. B.Sc. 1964; Univ. of Toronto M.A.Sc. 1968, Ph.D. 1969; m. Doris d. William and Marjorie Barker 5 May 1973; children: Paul, Mark; VICE-PRESIDENT AND PROVOST, UNIV. OF TORONTO 1993– ; Instructor & Rsch. Engr., Cairo Univ. 1964–66; Grad. Student & Teaching Asst., Univ. of Toronto 1966–69; Asst. Prof. 1969–72; Assoc. Prof. 1972–78; Prof. 1978– ; Chair, Dept. of Elect. Engr. 1986–93; Mem., Electrical Engr. Consociates ltd. 1969– (Pres. 1979–81); Founding Mem. & Dir., Information Technol. Rsch. ctr.; Fellow, Inst. of Elect. & Elect. Engrs. 1984– ; Ryerson Polytech. Inst. 1988; Winner, 1988 Terman Award, Am. Soc. of Engr. Edn.; 1993 ITAC Award; Reg. Profl. Eng. in Ont.; Mem., Am. Soc. of Engr. Edn.; author of over 120 pub. papers and 3 books incl. 'Microelectronic Circuits' 1982, '87, 91 (co-author, K.C. Smith) (trans into Spanish, Hebrew, Korean, Greek); Home: 18 High Park Blvd., Toronto, Ont. M6R 1M4; Office: 27 King's College Circle, Simcoe Hall, Toronto, Ont. M5S 1A1.

**SEEBER, Orville Alexander,** B.A.; geological consultant; mining executive; b. Ottawa, Ont. 17 Nov. 1913; s. Harrie Cooper and Jean (Alexander) S.; e. Ogdensburg, N.Y. Schs.; Queen's Univ., B.A. (Geol. & Minerol.) 1937; former Vice Pres., Explorations, Quebec Sturgeon River Mines Ltd.; Dir., Explorations, Anglo-Candn. Exploration (ACE) Ltd.; Exec. Vice Pres. Anglo-Dominion Gold Exploration Ltd.; Vice Pres. Bachelor Lake Gold

Mines Inc.; Geol., Falconbridge Nickel Mines Ltd., 1938–45; Chief Field Geol. 1945–54; Chief Geol., M. J. Boylen Engineering Offices, 1954–69; Vice-Pres., Exploration, Northgate Exploration Ltd. 1969 till formed own geol. consultant firm 1972; received C A.O. Dufresne Award, 1981; mem., Candn. Inst. Mining & Metall.; Soc. Econ. Geols.; Geol. Assn. Can.; Presbyterian; recreations: fishing, photography; Home: R.R. 1, Elginburg, Ont. K0H 1M0.

**SEEMAN, Philip,** M.Sc., M.D., Ph.D.; educator; b. Winnipeg, Man. 8 Feb. 1934; s. Jacob and Fanny (Wigdor) S.; e. Baron Byng High Sch. Montreal 1950; McGill Univ. B.Sc. 1955, M.Sc. 1956, M.D. 1960; Rockefeller Univ. Ph.D. 1966; m. Mary Violette d. Alexander Szwarc 30 June 1959; children: Marc, Bob, Neil; PROF. OF PHARMACOL. UNIV. OF TORONTO since 1977; Chrmn. of Pharmacol. 1977 to 1987; Interneship, Harper Hosp. Wayne State Univ. Detroit 1960–61; Med. Research Council Can. Fellow, Cambridge Univ. 1966–67; joined present univ. 1967; rec'd 12 awards in neuroscience and psychiatry; Chrmn. Hawthorne Bilingual Sch. Toronto 1976; Ed. 'Frontiers in Neurology and Neuroscience Research' 1974; 'Principles of Medical Pharmacology' 1976; author 350 articles; mem. Soc. Neuroscience; Candn. Pharmacol. Soc.; Am. Coll. Neuropsychopharmacol.; Am. Chem. Soc.; Ont. Coll. Phys. & Surgs.; Fellow, Roy. Soc. (Can.); Home: 32 Parkwood Ave., Toronto, Ont. M4V 2X1; Office: Medical Sciences Bldg., Toronto, Ont. M5S 1A8.

**SEGAL, Brian,** M.S.W., M.Sc., Ph.D.; educator; b. Montreal, Que. 28 Apr. 1943; s. Morris J. and Sadye (Dankner) S.; e. McGill Univ. B.Sc. 1964; Yeshiva Univ. New York M.S.W. 1967; Univ. of Pittsburgh M.Sc. 1969, Ph.D. 1971; m. Bunny d. Maurice and Becky Marcovitch 29 Oct. 1967; children: Jill, Scott, Matthew; PUBLISHER, MACLEAN'S MAGAZINE 1993– ; Bd. of Dirs., IBM Canada Ltd.; Design Exchange, Toronto; Union Gas Ltd.; J.M. Schneider Inc.; Sun Life Trust; Assoc. Prof. of Social Work Carleton Univ. 1973; Sr. Policy Adv. Nat. Museums of Can. Ottawa 1977–78; Consultant, Fed. Dept. Communications (telecommunications policy) 1979; Adv. Ont. Ministries of Correctional Services and Community & Social Services 1975–79; Pres., Ryerson Polytechnical Inst. 1980–88; Pres. & Vice-Chancellor, Univ. of Guelph 1988–93; mem., Extve. Ctte., Council of Ont. Univs.; Chairperson, Nat. Forum on Post-Secondary Education 1987; Ont. Comm. on Interuniv. Athletics; Candn. Advanced Technology Assn.; Chair, Council of Ontario Universities; 1991–93; Chair, AUCC Commission of Inquiry on Candn. Univ. Education 1991; mem. Bd. of Govs. The Inst. of Candn. Bankers; Chairperson, Nat. Innovations Adv. Ctte. (Min. of Employment and Immigration); Communications Ctte., Counc. of Ont. Univs.; Bd. of Dirs., Zoological Society of Metropolitan Toronto; author numerous articles telecommunications, manpower planning, social welfare various journs.; Clubs: R.C.Y.C.; University; Home: 313 Oriole Parkway, Toronto, Ont. M5P 2H6; Office: 777 Bay St., 7th Floor, Toronto, Ont. M5W 1A7.

**SEGAL, Harold J.,** B.Sc., M.S., Ph.D.; university professor; b. Winnipeg, Man. 6 March 1941; e. Univ. of Man., B.Sc. Pharm. 1962; Purdue Univ., M.S. 1966, Ph.D. 1968; DIR. KOFFLER INSTITUTE FOR PHARMACY MNGMT. 1990– and PROF., FAC. OF PHARMACY, UNIV. OF TORONTO 1985– ; Rsch. Assoc., Candn. Pharm. Assn. 1968–70; Asst. Prof., Univ. of Toronto 1970–75; Assoc. Prof. 1976–85; Cons., profession, ind., govt.; Mem., Ont. Pharm. Assn.; co-author: 'Contemporary Marketing in Canada' 1974; and 19 booklets on pharm. mgmt.; Gen.-ed. & contrib., 'Pharmacy Management in Canada' 1989; Ed. Bd. Mem., Journal of Pharmaceutical Marketing and Management; Pharmacy Practice; Office: 569 Spadina Ave., Toronto, Ont. M5S 1A1.

**SEGAL, Hugh D.,** B.A.; executive; b. Montreal, Que. 13 Oct. 1950; s. Morris J. and Sadye Kaufman (Dankner) S.; e. Univ. of Ottawa B.A. 1972; m. Donna Jacqueline d. Donald Fraser Armstrong, Kingston, Ont. 29 May 1976; one d. Jacqueline Sadye Armstrong; Chief of Staff, Office of the Prime Minister 1992–93; Legislative Asst. to Leader of Opposition, H. of C. 1972–75; Princ. Secy. to Premier of Ont. and Campaign Secy. Ont. P. Cons. Party 1975–77; Dir. Corporate Affairs John Labatt Ltd. London, Ont. 1977–79; Assoc. Secy. of Cabinet and Secy. Policy & Priorities Bd. Ont. 1979–82; Past Vice-Chrmn., TACT Inc.; Past Chrmn., Cornerstone Strategic Holdings Ltd.; Past Dir.: Candn. Children's Found.; The Toronto French Sch.; Earnscliffe Strategy Group Inc., Ottawa; Municipal Financial Corp., Barrie, Ont.; Inst. Strategic Studies, Toronto; Past Vice Pres., Atlantic Council of Canada; Skelton Clark Fellow (1990–91) Queen's Univ., Kingston; Past Vice-Chrmn., Inst. of Candn. Advertising; co-author 'No Small Measure' 1982; 'Election' 1989; Jewish; P. Conservative; recreations: boating, tennis; Clubs: Albany, Toronto; Rideau, Ottawa; Cercle Universitaire, Ottawa; Address: 26 Hillcroft Dr., Kingston, Ont. K7L 4E8.

**SEGAL, Seymour;** artist; b. Montreal, Que. 25 May 1939; s. Morris Jack and Saidye (Dankner) S.; e. Baron Byng H.S.; Ecole des Beaux-Arts 1958–59; basically self-taught; m. Marie Josée d. Renée and Jean René Grondin 24 Sept. 1988; children: Eloïse, Sara-Lola, Alice; invited artist & visiting prof. at colleges & univs.; Dawson Coll. 1973, '74; Univ. de Qué. in Montreal 1977–85; Moncton Univ. 1986; Univ. of S.W. Mass. every summer from 1983– ; Co-Creator of 'Drawing from Within' (a specific approach to teaching, painting & seeing); Dir., Atelier Seymour Segal (a summer inst. of intensive workshops) 1989– ; Artistic Dir., Painting & Drawing Dept., Sch. of Fine Arts, Saidye Bronfman Ctr. 1988– ; painting in public and private collections incl. The Montreal Mus. of Fine Art, Le Musée du Qué.; The Art Gallery of Kitchener, Waterloo, Ont.; Lavalin; Reitmans; Cemp Assn. (Montreal); David Hughs Assn. (Toronto); The Canada Council Art Bank; The Claridge Collection, Montreal; co-author (with Hugh Hood): 'Scoring, The Art of Hockey' 1979; Address: 3869 rue Principale, P.O. Box 384, Dunham, Que. J0E 1M0.

**SEGUIN, André,** B.Com.; retired executive; b. Les Cedres, Que. 17 March 1931; s. Elzéard and Germaine (Menard) S.; e. Sir George Williams Univ. B.Com. 1959; m. Joan R. d. Eugene and Edna Feeley 7 Sept. 1957; children: Richard A., Joanne M.; Regional Business Manager, Quebec Atlantic Stanchem Inc. 1989–91; Sales Order Clk. CIL Inc. 1951, Sales Rep. 1955, Sales Supr. 1964, Sales Mgr. and Works Mgr. 1967, Sales Supr. 1972, Mgr. Sales 1974, Personnel Mgr. Que. Region 1978; Exec. Vice Pres. Hanson Inc. 1979–80; Pres., Hanson Inc. 1980–86; Mgr., Urethanes CIL Inc. 1986–89; mem. Soc. Plastic Engs. (Pres. 1964); Metal Finishers Suppliers Assn. (Chrmn. 1982–83); Vice-Chrmn., SPI Polyurethanes 1988; Home: 97 Oakland, Beaconsfield, Que.

**SÉGUIN, Claude,** B.A., B.A.A., M.P.A., Ph.D.; b. Montreal, Que. 27 Feb. 1950; s. André and Thérèse (Francoeur) S.; e. Univ. of Montreal B.A. 1969; Ecoles des Hautes Etudes Commerciales B.A.A. 1972; Syracuse Univ. M.P.A. 1974, Ph.D. 1978; m. Francine d. Joseph Edouard and Françoise Roy 9 Oct. 1972; children: Charles, François; SENIOR VICE-PRESIDENT, FINANCE AND CHIEF FINANCIAL OFFICER, TELEGLOBE INC. (Montréal) 1992– ; Extve. Asst., Min. of Finance, Quebec 1977–80; Treasury Bd.: Asst. Dir., Health Policy 1980–81; Dir. of Planning 1981–83; Asst. Dep. Min. of Finance, Quebec: Treasury, Financial Policies, Crown Corp. 1983–87; Dir. of Corp. Planning and Projects, Noverco 1987; Deputy Minister of Finance, Govt. of Quebec 1988–92; Gov., Montreal Stock Exchange; Dir., Le Devoir Inc.; Fellowship, Arts Council of Canada; Ministry of Education Quebec; recreations: skiing, tennis, biking; Home: 73 Beverley Ave., Mount-Royal, Que. H3P 1K5; Office: 1000, rue de La Gauchetière ouest, Montréal, Que. H3B 4X5.

**SEQUIN, Margaret E. Anderson;** see **ANDERSON, Margaret E. Sequin.**

**SEGUIN, Robert-Lionel,** D.ès L.; ethnologue; auteur; né Rigaud, Qué. 7 mars 1920; é. Univ. de Montréal licencié ès sciences sociales, économiques et politiques 1951; Univ. Laval diplôme d'études supérieures en histoire 1962, docteur ès lettres et histoire 1964; Sorbonne docteur ès lettres et sciences humaines 1972; Univ. Strasbourg docteur ès lettres et ethnologie; ép Huguette Servant; PROFESSEUR, Chercheur invité au CÉLAT, Faculté des Lettres, Univ. Laval; travail périodique au Musée national des arts et traditions populaires de Paris; auteur 'Le mouvement insurrectionnel dans la presqu'île de Vaudreuil 1837–1838' 1955; 'L'équipement de la ferme canadienne aux XVIIe et XVIIIe siècles' 1959; 'Les moules du Québec' 1963; 'Les granges du Québec' 1963; 'La civilisation traditionnelle de l'"habitant" aux 17e et 18e siècles' 1967; 'La victoire de Saint-Denis' 1968; 'Le costume civil en Nouvelle-France' 1968, 'La maison en Nouvelle-France' 1968; 'Les divertissements en Nouvelle-France' 1968; 'Les jouets anciens du Québec' 1971; 'Les ustensiles en Nouvelle-France' 1972; 'La vie libertine en Nouvelle-France au XVIIe siècle' 2 vol. 1972; 'L'esprit révolutionnaire dans l'art québécois' 1973; L'injure en Nouvelle-France' 1976; 'La sorcellerie au Québec du XVIIe au XIXe siècle' 1978; 'L' Equipement aratoire et horticole ancien au Québec' 2 vol. 1981; quelque cent cinquante articles (ethno-historiques) publiés dans des cahiers, bulletins et revues du Québec et de France; tous ces travaux traitent de la civilisation traditionnelle du Québec; prix littéraires: Gouverneur général du Can. 1967; Broquette Gonin (Académie française) 1967; France-Québec 1973; Duvernay (Société Saint-Jean-Baptiste) 1976; mem. Soc. d'ethnologie française (Paris); Soc. des Dix (Qué.); Soc. royale du Can.; Catholique; Adresse: Grand-Ligne, Rigaud, Qué. J0P 1P0.

**SEHON, Alec,** B.Sc., M.Sc., Ph.D., D.Sc., F.R.S.C.; university professor; b. Galati, Romania 18 Dec. 1924; s. Herman and Paula (Koriman) S.; e. Victoria Univ. of Manchester (U.K.), B.Sc. (Hon.) 1948, M.Sc. 1950, Ph.D. 1951, D.Sc. 1965; m. Irene d. May and Fred Parrish 22 July 1950; children: Anthony Alexander Parrish, Caroline Margaret; Prof. & Head, Dept. of Immunol., Fac. of Med., Univ. of Manitoba 1969–93; grad. study, Univ. of Manchester 1948–51; Post-doct. fellow, NRC Labs 1951–52; Rsch. Assoc., Calif. Inst. of Tech. & Inst. of Biochem, Uppsala Sweden 1952–53; Asst. Prof., Exp. Med., McGill Univ. 1953–59; Founding Co-Dir., Div. Immunochem. & Allergy Res. 1955–59; Dir., Lab. for Biophysical- & Immuno-chem., Dept. of Chem. 1959–69; Hon. Lecturer, Dept. of Biochem. 1959–69; Asst. Prof. of Chem., McGill Univ. 1956–61; Assoc. Prof. Chem., 1961–64; Prof. Chem., 1964–69; Dir., MRC Group for Allergy Rsch., Univ. of Man. 1973–93; Sabbaticals: Harvard 1963–64, Walter & Eliza Hall Inst. Melbourne (Aust.) & Univ. College (U.K.) 1973–74, Pasteur Inst. (France) 1984–85; Fellowships: Chem. Inst. Can. 1959; Assoc. Allergy & Immunol. Argentina; Sr. Rsch., NRC (Can.); John Simon Guggenheim Mem. Found. 1963; Am. Coll. of Allergy & Immunol. 1964; Am. Assn. Advance Sci. 1965; Am. Acad. Allergy & Immunol. 1967; Royal Soc. of Can. 1969; Thomas W. Eadie Medal, RSC 1977; Dist. Serv. Award, Am. Acad. Allergy 1982; Dist. Prof., Univ. of Man. 1982– ; St. Boniface Rsch. Found. Internat. Award 1983; Clemens von Pirquet Medal, Austrian Soc. Allergol. & Immunol. 1992; Mem., several Grants & Awards Cttes.; Can. Soc. Clin. Investigations; Am. Assn. of Immunol.; Candn. Soc. of Immunol. (Pres. 1969–71); N.Y. Acad. Sci.; Soc. Franc. d'Immunol.; British Soc. Immunol.; Chrmn., Can. Fed. of Biol. Soc. 1972–73; Pres., Coll. Internat. Allergologicum 1986–90; Founding Chrmn., 1st Gordon Rsch. Conf. of Immunochem. & Immunobiol. 1966; author of over 300 sci. papers & patents; broad rsch. interests: immunoregulation, allergy, transplantation, oncology; recreations: swimming, theatre, music; Club: Winnipeg Winter; Office: 730 William Ave., Winnipeg, Man. R3E 0W3.

**SEIDAH, Nabil G.,** B.Sc., Ph.D., FRSC; research scientist; b. Cairo, Egypt 1 Feb. 1949; s. Georges Alfred and Maggy (Toutounji) S.; e. Cairo Univ. B.Sc. 1969; Georgetown Univ. Ph.D. 1973; m. Dunja d. Nenad and Nada (Anic) Vukadin 21 Sept. 1973; children: Mark, André; DIRECTOR, LAB. BIOCHEM. NEUROENDOCRINOLOGY, CLINICAL RSCH. INST. OF MONTREAL 1983– ; Adjunct Prof., Med., McGill Univ. 1989– ; Rsch. Full Prof., Med., Univ. of Montreal 1990– ; Tenure Full Prof., Biochem. 1992– ; spent sabbatical at Pasteur Inst. (France) 1987–88; The Clarke Inst. of Psychiatry Award 1977; Marcel Piché Award 1983; Fellow, Royal Soc. of Canada 1991; Mem., N.Y. Acad. of Sciences; Protein Soc.; Endocrine Soc.; Soc. de Neuroendocrin. Expérimentale; author of 307 publications as of August 1993; Home: 274 Corot, Nun's Island, Que. H3E 1K7; Office: 110 Pine Ave. W., Montreal, Que. H2W 1R7.

**SEIDELMAN, William Edward,** B.Sc., M.D.; university professor, family physician; b. Vancouver, B.C. 19 March 1941; s. Harry and Esther (Blank) S.; e. Sir Winston Churchill H.S.; Univ. of B.C. B.Sc. 1964, M.D. 1968; m. Racheline d. Abdou and Allegra Dayan 5 Sept. 1967; children: Aviva Michèle, Ayëla Nicole, Rhona Danièle; MEDICAL DIR., HIV AMBULATORY SERVICES, WELLESLEY HOSPITAL 1993– ; Internship, Mt. Sinai Hosp. Serv., City Hosp. Ctr., Elmhurst 1968–69; Cert., College of Family Phys. of Can. 1974; Staff Physician, REACH Clinic Vanc. & Clin. Instr., Ped., Univ. of B.C. 1971–76; joined Dept. of Family Med., McMaster Univ. 1976; Med. Dir. (Founding), N. Hamilton Comm. Health Ctr. 1986–88; Prof. Dept. of Family Medicine 1991– ; Active Staff, Hamilton Civic Hospitals 1977– ; research interest: ethical challenges arising from Med. in Nazi Germany, HIV/AIDS & primary care; Founding Vice-Pres., Assn. of Ont. Health Ctrs. 1981–83; Vice Chair, Task Force on Primary Care, Ont. Min. of Health 1982; Visiting Prof., Ben Gurion Univ. 1983–84; Cons., Negev Project Israel 1983–84; Scholar-in-Res., Lord Immanuel Jakobovitz Ctr. for Jewish Med. Ethics, Ben Gurion Univ. 1991; Bd. of Dir., N. Hamilton Comm. Health Ctr.; Bd. of Dir., Assoc. Med. Services Inc.; Chair, AMS Edn. Adv. Ctte.; Bd. of Gov., Cong.

Beth Jacob (Hamilton); Bd. of Dir., Jewish Fed. of Hamilton-Wentworth; co-author: 'The Politics of Reform in Medical Education and Health Services: The Negev Project' 1992; Office: HIV Programme, 160 Wellesley St. E., Toronto, Ont. M4Y 1J3.

**SEIGEL, Harold O.,** Ph.D., P.Eng.; geophysicist; b. Toronto, Ont. 8 Mar. 1924; s. Max J. and Bessie Miriam (Lerner) S.; e. Lansdowne Pub. Sch. and Harbord Coll. Inst. Toronto 1942; Univ. of Toronto B.A. 1946, M.A. 1947, Ph.D. (Geophys.) 1949; m. Marilyn d. Nathan and Esther (Sherman) Silver 24 Mar. 1968; children: Joel Allan, Laurie Anne, Marcie Beth; CHRMN., SCINTREX LTD. 1991– ; Asst. Mgr. Newmont Exploration Ltd. Jerome, Ariz. 1948–52; Cons. Geophys. Toronto 1952–56; Pres. Seigel Associates Ltd. 1956–64; Pres., Scintrex Ltd. 1964–91; Chrmn., Scintrex Ltd. 1991– ; Distinguished Lectr. Candn. Inst. Mining & Metall. 1981; Gen. Chrmn., Exploration '87 Conf., Toronto; Chrmn., External Adv. Ctte. to the Geological Survey of Can. for Geophysics; recipient of J. Tuzo Wilson Medal in Geophysics awarded by Candn. Geophysical Union 1985; Distinguished Service Award, Prospectors & Developers Assoc. 1987; A.O. Dufresne Award for Mineral Exploration in Can., Candn. Inst. of Mining and Metallurgy 1988; Home: 9 Oxbow Rd., Don Mills, Ont. M3B 1Z9; Office: 222 Snidercroft Rd., Concord, Ont. L4K 1B5.

**SEILER, Joseph H.,** B.Sc., M.Eng., P.Eng.; electronic engineer; b. Bonnyville, Alta. 4 Apr. 1950; s. Henry and Magdalena (Fiedler) S.; e. Univ. of Alta., B.Sc. 1972; Technical Univ. of N.S., M.Eng. 1980; m. Barbara d. John and Norma Senger 6 May 1972; children: Carmen, Cathy, Leslie; PRES. & C.E.O., SEIMAC LIMITED 1986– ; Pres., Oceanroutes Can. Inc. 1992– ; Offr. training, C.A.F. 1972; Royal Naval Engr. coll. 1973; Dept. head, HMCS Ottawa 1975; Defence Rsch. Establishment Atlantic 1979; Opns. Mgr. & Vice-Pres., Seimac Limited 1982; Past Chrmn., Atlantic Section and Sr. Mem. IEEE; Mem., Marine Technol. Soc.; Dartmouth Bd. of Trade; APENS; recreation: jogging; Home: 28 Cunningham Dr., Bedford, N.S. B4A 2B4; Office: 271 Brownlow Ave., Dartmouth, N.S. B3B 1W6.

**SELBY, Ralph Fraser,** F.C.A.; chartered accountant; b. Windsor, Ont. 15 Oct. 1935; s. Alfred Rogers and Lillian L. S.; e. Forest Hill C.I. 1953; Candn. Inst. of C.A.s C.A. 1959; m. Mary Gourlay1959; children: Judith, Debbie, Donald; PARTNER, PRICE WATERHOUSE 1970– ; joined Price Waterhouse 1954; Fellow, Inst. of C.A.s 1973 for distinguished serv. to the profession, specializing in owner-managed business, leasing & finance; Dir., Chair of Acctg. Ctte., Equipment Lessors Assn. of Canada; Past Pres., Downtown Business Council Toronto; Past Mem., City of Toronto, Econ. Devel. Ctte.; author: 'Risk Management' 1984, 'Leasing in Canada: A Business Guide' 1981, 2nd ed. 1992; recreations: golf, badminton, bridge; clubs: Lambton Golf & Country; The Ontario Club; Office: 3300, 1 First Canadian Pl., Toronto, Ont. M5X 1H7.

**SELBY, William Ernest,** B.Sc., FCIS, P.Admin.; university executive; b. Calgary, Alta. 16 Oct. 1929; s. Ernest Raymond and Sarah Laura (McQueen) S.; e. Univ. of Alta., B.Sc. 1953; m. Mary d. Harry and Vera Whittaker 10 Aug. 1968; children: William John, Gillian Mary, Jennifer Elizabeth; SPECIAL ADVISOR, DONOR RELATIONS, THE UNIV. OF CALGARY 1991– ; Jr. Landman then var. positions, Hudson's Bay Oil & Gas Co. Ltd. 1955–66; Corp. Sec. & Asst. to Pres. 1966 (and later Chrmn., Bd. of Dirs.); Offr., Dome Petroleum Ltd. 1982; Dir., Community Relns., Univ. of Calgary 1984–91; Special Advisor to the President, The Univ. of Calgary 1991–92; Dir., Alberta Achievement Award; Nickle Arts Mus.; Can-Aide Found; Past Pres., Jr. Achievement of S. Alta. (Calgary); Calgary Zool. Soc.; Trustee, Calgary Zoological Foundation; Trustee, P. & C. Whyte Found.; Mem., Bd. of Gov. & Chrmn., Candn. Auto. Assn.; Gov. & Past Chrmn., Alta. Motor Assn.; Adv., Calgary Inst. for Hum.; mem., City of Calgary Visual Arts Bd.; Anglican; Progressive Conservative; Mem. & Past Chrmn., Alta. Br., Inst. of Chartered Sec. & Admin.; recreations: golf, skiing, hiking, swimming; Clubs: Calgary Golf & Country; Glencoe; Commerce; Home: 2714 Montcalm Cres. S.W., Calgary, Alta. T2T 3M6; Office: 2500 University Dr. N.W., Calgary, Alta. T2N 1N4.

**SELF, Hazel,** R.N.; community services coordinator; b. Bath, U.K. 28 March 1948; d. Peter Barnard and Beryl York (Wood) S.; e. St. George's Hospital R.N. 1969; COMMUNITY SERVICES COORDINATOR, THE GAGE TRANSITIONAL LIVING CENTRE, WEST PARK HOSP. 1989– ; R.N. in U.K. 1968–70; Princess Margaret Hosp. Toronto 1970–74; The Toronto Doctors' Hosp. 1974–78; sustained spinal cord injury resulting in quadriplegia 1978; numerous volunteer activites recognized by the Office for Disabled Persons' Community Action Award & Min. of Community & Social Serv. (Community Service Award) 1981–89; Mem., Lyndhurst Spinal Cord Centre Advisory Ctte.; Board Trustee, Hugh McMillan Rehabilitation Centre; co-author: 'Attendant Services: Options for Consumers in Ontario' 1989; recreation: watercolours; Home: 483-49 Henry Lane Terr., Toronto, Ont. M5A 4B5; Office: 82 Buttonwood Ave., Toronto, Ont. M6M 2J5.

**SELINGER, Stanley Lyon,** B.A., B.C.L., Dip.D.C.; lawyer; b. Montréal, Qué. 27 Dec. 1939; s. Julius Max and Edith (Balacan) S.; e. Sir George Williams Univ. 1961; Osgoode Hall Law 1962; McGill Univ. 1965; Faculté Internationale pour l'Enseignement du Droit Comparé Coimbra, Portugal 1966; m. Andrea C.S. Lockhart 2 July 1985; children: Tamara, Benjamin, Gabriel; SR. PARTNER, SELINGER, KAZANDJIAN 1982– ; Intnl. Assoc. (first) Am. Bar Assn.; mem., Montreal, Que. and Candn. Bar Assns; Clubs: Montefoire, Montreal; Metropolitan (New York); residence: 680 Hartland, Outremont, Que. H2V 2X4; Office: 210, 1980 Sherbrooke St. W., Montréal, Que. H3H 1E8.

**SELLO, Allen Ralph,** B.Comm., M.B.A.; oil company executive; b. Winnipeg, Man. 22 June 1939; e. Univ. of Manitoba B.Comm. (Hons.) 1963; Univ. of Toronto M.B.A. 1964; m. Mary Lou Riordon 3 June 1972; children: Clint, Monique, Daren; VICE-PRES. FINANCE & CHIEF FINAN. OFFR., GULF CANADA RESOURCES LTD. 1988– ; Mgr., Mktg. Analysis, Ford Motor Co. of Can. 1972–75; Mgr., Product Plans 1975–78; Asst. Treas. 1978–79; Dir., Acctg., Gulf Canada Ltd. Toronto 1979–81; Dir., Finan. Planning 1981–82; Controller 1982–85; Vice-Pes. & Controller, Gulf Can. Corp. Calgary 1985–86; Vice-Pres. Finan. 1986–88; recreations: squash, skiing, tennis, golf; clubs: Glencoe, Glencoe Golf & Country, Calgary Petroleum; Home: 1203 Baldwin Cres. S.W., Calgary, Alta. T2V 2B6; Office: 401 – 9th Avenue S.W., Calgary, Alta. T2P 2H7.

**SELLS, Bruce Howard,** B.Sc., M.A., Ph.D., FRS(C); educator; b. Ottawa, Ont. 15 Aug. 1930; e. Carleton Univ. B.Sc. 1952; Queen's Univ. M.A. 1954; McGill Univ. Ph.D. 1957; PROFESSOR OF MOLECULAR BIOLOGY, UNIV. OF GUELPH 1983– ; Demonst. Chem. Labs. McGill Univ. 1954–57; Damon Runyon Research Fellow, Lab. of Animal Morphology, Free Univ. of Brussels 1957–59, Statens Seruminstitut, Copenhagen 1959–60; Cancer Research Scient. Roswell park Mem. Inst. Buffalo 1960–61; Research Assoc. Columbia Univ. 1961–62; Asst. Prof. of Biochem. St. Jude Children's Research Hosp. and Univ. of Tenn. 1962–64, Assoc. Prof. 1964–68, mem. of Hosp. and Assoc. Prof. of Univ. 1968–72; Prof. and Dir. of Molecular Biology, Memorial Univ. 1972–79; Assoc. Dean, Div. of Basic Medical Sciences, Faculty of Medicine Memorial Univ. of Nfld. 1979–83; Dean, College of Biological Science, Univ. of Guelph 1983–94; Visiting Research Scient. Inst. Animal Genetics, Univ. of Edinburgh 1969–70; Killam Sr. Research Fellow 1978–79, Inst. Research in Molecular Biol. Paris, France; MRC Visiting Scientist, Institut Pasteur, Paris, France 1989; Elect. Fell. of the Royal. Soc. (Canada), 1982; Mem. of Candn. Comte of the Intl. Union of Biochemistry, 1982–85; Assoc. Ed. Candn. Journal of Biochemistry 1974–82; mem. Biochem. Grants Panel, M.R.C. 1973–78; mem. Counc., Medical Research Council of Can. 1980–83; Manpower Ctte., Candn. Arthritis Society 1983–86; NRC Subctte. on Biological Phenomena 1983–86; Centennial Fellowship Panel, M.R.C. 1980–84; Pres., Candn. Biochem. Soc. 1981–82; Scientific Officer, Nat. Cancer Inst., 1979–81; Mem., Selection Panel for the Steacie Prize 1986, 1987; Mem., Life Sciences Division Fellowship Review Ctte., Academy of Science, The Royal Soc. of Canada 1990–92; Mem., MRC Standing Ctte., Candn. Genetic Disease Network (CGDN) 1991–93; Chair Standing Ctte. (CGDN) 1993– ; Ayerst Award Selection Ctte., Candn. Biochemistry Soc. 1990; Ontario Health Rsch. Council Adv. Ctte. 1992; Med. Research Council Can. Visiting Scient. Award; Centre Nat. Recherche Scientifique, Exchange Scient. Award; Home: R.R. 6, Guelph, Ont. N1H 6J3.

**SELLS, David Victor,** B.Sc., M.B.A.; executive; b. Stoughton, Wis. 23 July 1945; s. Oliver John and Ruth Pauline (Olson) S.; e. Univ. of Wis., B.Sc. 1968; York Univ., M.B.A. 1977; m. Diana d. Homer and Lillian Montague 22 June 1968; children: Jeremy, Joanna; PRES. D.V. SELLS & ASSOCS. 1990– ; Pres., Anglers Petroleum Ltd. 1985– ; Anglers Petroleum Internat. 1993– ; Pres., Northcor Group of Companies 1984–89; Home: 128 Strathbury Circle S.W., Calgary, Alta. T3H 1P9; Office: 1605 - 8th Ave. S.W., Calgary, Alta. T2P 3R5.

**SELTZER, Gareth Sean;** investment counsellor; b. Toronto, Ont. 1962; s. John and Rae Dorene S.; e. Univ. of Western Ont. 1984; VICE-PRESIDENT, PRIVATE BANKING, GUARDIAN CAPITAL ADVISORS, GUARDIAN CAPITAL GROUP LIMITED 1992– ; Group Benefit Analyst, GBB Buck Cons. Limited 1984–86; Pension Specialist 1986–88; Benefit Cons. 1988–89; Vice-Pres., Deferred Compensation Serv., The Hull Group 1989–90; Dir., The Duke of Edinburgh's Award 1993– ; Candn. Hearing Soc. Found. 1991– ; Empire Club of Can. 1990– ; Mem., Assn. of Candn. Pension Management (Former Chair; confs. on pension reform; speaker to Inst. of C.A.s of Ont.); Internat. Benefits Information Service Chicago (Candn. Correspondent 1986–90); Personnel Assn. of Ont. (Former Mem., Employee Benefits Ctte.); Bd. Mem., Young Extve. Ctte., Toronto Festival of Festivals 1989–91; author of journal articles; recreations: music (collector & composer), prestidigitation, scuba diving, skiing, film; clubs: Ontario, Founders Club (Skydome), Hot Stove, Reel Club (Candn. Ctr. for Advanced Film Studies) 1992– ; Home: 69 Boultbee Ave., Toronto, Ont. M5J 1B2; Office: 110 Yonge St., 19th fl., Toronto, Ont. M5C 1T4.

**SENIOR, Elinor Laurie Kyte,** M.A., Ph.D.; writer; historian; b. Sydney, N.S. 30 Dec. 1926; d. Frederick Laurence and Suzannah Whymouthe (Roberts) Kyte; e. Louisburg (N.S.) Pub. Sch. 1943; McGill Univ., B.A. 1952, Ph.D. 1976; Memorial Univ. of Nfld., M.A. 1959; m. Hereward s. Roy and Evelyn Senior 22 Sept. 1954; children: Hereward, John, Jean, Harvey; Reporter 'Sydney Post Record' 1946–48; Women's Ed. 'Montreal Star' 1953–55; Pub. Lectr., Writer and Assoc. Prof. McGill Univ. and Marianopolis Coll. Montréal 1973–85; Acadia Univ., Wolfville, N.S. 1986–87; St. Francis Xavier Univ., Antigonish, N.S. 1987–88; Visiting Prof. of Military and Strategic Studies, Acadia Univ. 1988–89; author 'British Regulars in Montreal: An Imperial Garrison 1832–1854' 1981; 'Roots of the Canadian Army in the Montreal District 1846–1870' 1981; 'From Royal Township to Industrial City: Cornwall 1784–1984' 1983; 'Redcoats and Patriotes: The Rebellions in Lower Canada 1837–38' 1985; ed. 'The Cannon's Mouth' (newsletter Candn. Mil. Hist. Group); mem. Candn. Comn. Mil. Hist. 1986–89; Council, Soc. Army Hist. Rsch. London, Eng. 1982–87; mem. Un. Empire Loyalists Heritage Br. (Hist. Cons.); Monarchist League Can. Montréal Br.; Mil. Soc. Ireland; Montréal Pro-Life; Anglican; recreations: fencing, swimming; Club: Montréal Fencing; Home: 2043 Vendome Ave., Montréal, Qué. H4A 3M4.

**SENIOR, Hereward,** M.A., Ph.D.; educator; b. Brooklyn, N.Y. 22 Dec. 1918; s. Roy and Evelyn (de Courcy-White) S.; e. Oceanside High Sch. 1939; McGill Univ., B.A. 1948, M.A. 1951, Ph.D. 1959; m. Elinor d. Frederick and Suzannah Kyte 22 Sept. 1954; children: Hereward, John, Jean, Harvey; PROF. OF HISTORY, McGILL UNIV. 1971– ; served with Candn. Army 1943–46, Can. & NW Eur.; schoolmaster, Bishop's Coll. Sch. Lennoxville, Qué. 1955–57; Asst. Prof. Meml. Univ. of Nfld. 1957–59, Candn. Service Coll. Royal Roads 1959–61; Lectr. Univ. of Toronto 1961–63; Asst. Prof. of Hist. present Univ. 1963, Assoc. Prof. 1966–71, Prof. of History 1971– ; author 'Orangeism in Ireland and Britain 1795–1836' 1966; 'Orangeism: The Canadian Phase' 1972; 'The Fenians and Canada' 1978; co-author 'Victorious in Defeat: the Loyalists in Canada' 1984; 'The Last Invasion of Canada: The Fenian Raids 1866–70' 1991; numerous hist. articles scholarly and popular jours. incl. 'The Genesis of Canadian Orangeism' (awarded Cruikshank Medal 1968); columnist 'Monarchy Canada'; Chrmn. Montréal Br. Monarchist League Can. 1970– , Ed. Dir. 1988– ; Hon. Vice Pres., United Empire Loyalist; mem. Candn. Inst. Internat. Affairs; Royal Commonwealth Soc.; St. Patrick's Soc.; Anglican; recreations: fencing, jogging, swimming; Club: Montréal Fencing; Home: 2043 Vendome Ave., Montréal, Qué. H4A 3M4; Office: Montréal, Qué. H3A 2T5.

**SENKIW, Roman I.,** Ph.D.; trust company executive; b. Austria 26 Aug. 1945; s. Michael and Maria (Ciesielski) S.; e. McGill Univ., B.A. 1966; Carleton Univ.; Univ. of Virginia, Ph.D. 1974; m. Erica d. Commander Michael and Carrol Tomkinson 25 Oct. 1969; children: Christina, Alex, Andrea; DIR. & SECY.-TREAS., COMMUNITY TRUST COMPANY LTD. 1990– ; Dir. & Vice-Pres., Tomkinson Senkiw Assoc. Inc. 1987– ; Dir., Rallye Footwear Inc. 1990– ; Economist, Internat. Monetary Fund 1972–74; Sr. Econ., Internat., Royal Bank of Can. 1974–76; Chief Adviser, Internat. Affairs, Bank of Montreal 1977–86; Extve. Vice-Pres. & Chief of

Staff, Deak Internat. 1987; Pres. & Chief Extve. Offr., Maple Leaf Shoe Co. Ltd. 1987–88; Extve. Vice Pres. & C.O.O., Countrywide Ontario Inc. 1989–90; Senior Policy Adviser, Ont. Min. of Industry, Trade and Technology 1990–93; Former Dir., Candn. Commercial Corp. 1987–89; Pres. & Dir., Assn. of Political Risk Analysts 1985–86; Dir., Caisse Populaire Desjardins Ukrainienne 1977; author of five articles in banking journals; Home: 4066 Sawmill Valley Dr., Mississauga, Ont. L5L 2Y6.

**SENST, Graham D.,** M.B.A.; trust company executive; e. Univ. of Western Ont. M.B.A.; VICE-PRESIDENT, SPECIAL LOANS GROUP, CANADA TRUST; Dir., CB Commercial Real Estate Group Canada Inc.; Office: 161 Bay St., Toronto, Ont. M5J 2T2.

**SEPHTON, Peter Stanley Jr.,** B.A., M.A., Ph.D.; educator; b. Chicago, Ill. 24 June 1957; s. Peter Stanley and Baribel Lovelace (MacLean) S.; e. Hillfield-Strathallan Coll.; McMaster Univ. B.A. 1980; Queen's Univ. M.A. 1981, Ph.D. 1984; m. Susan Elizabeth d. Freeman G. and F. Elizabeth Pettet 25 June 1983; children: Peter William, Jennifer Lynn; PROF. OF ECON. UNIV. OF N.B. 1986– ; Researcher, Bank of Canada 1978 and Ont. Min. of Treasury & Econ. 1979; Econ., Federal Business Development Bank 1980; Prof. Univ. of Regina 1984–86; recipient MacKenzie Meml. Prize in Devel. Econ. 1980; various articles profl. jours. and newspapers; mem. Am. Finance Assn.; Candn. Econ. Assn.; Atlantic Can. Econ. Assn.; recreations: jogging, swimming; Home: 279 Woodlawn Lane, Fredericton, N.B. E3C 1J4; Office: Fredericton, N.B. E3B 5A3.

**SERENY, John Thomas;** building products executive; b. 21 Feb. 1927; s. Farkas and Elisabeth (Weinberger); children: Michael Peter, David Gordon; PRES. & CHIEF EXTVE. OFFR., GREEN FOREST LUMBER CORPORATION; recreations: tennis, skiing, flying; Club: York Racquet; Home: 27 Alderwood Dr., Don Mills, Ont. M3B 1E3; Office: 194 Merton St., Toronto, Ont. M4S 3B5.

**SERRUYA, Aaron;** retail executive; b. Toronto, Ont. 26 Jan. 1966; s. Sam and Clara (Bensimon) S.; e. Thornlea S.S.; m. Shauna d. Claude and Gail Halpin 18 Dec. 1987; children: Racheal, Sammy; CO-FOUNDER, YOGEN FRÜZ INTERNATIONAL LTD. 1986– , VICE-PRES., YOGURTY'S YOGURT DISCOVERY and PRES., PRËTZLZ INC. (Founded 1992); over 350 frozen yogurt franchises worldwide, over 197 in Can., 52 in USA, 2 in England, 12 in Spain, 19 in France, 7 in Belgium, 10 in Italy, 17 in Israel, 5 in Panama, 4 in Costa Rica, 5 in Portugal, 3 in Morocco, 6 in Guatemala, 12 in Venezuela, 11 in Mexico, 5 in Thailand, 5 in Taiwan, 15 in Indonesia, 2 in Singapore, 2 in Hong Kong, 4 in China, 4 in Columbia, 3 in Ecuador, 5 in Chile, 4 in Switzerland, 2 in Egypt, 3 in Dominican Republic; recipient, #3 of the world renown ACE Top 10 North American entrepreneurs under 30 years of age; #1 Franchise in our category in North America acknowledged by Entrepreneur Magazine 1993 and Top 40 under 40 years of age acknowledged by Entrepreneur Magazine 1992; recreations: golf, tennis, skiing; Home: 37 Robinwood Trail, Thornhill, Ont. L4J 6K6; Office 7500 Woodbine Ave., Markham, Ont. L3R 1A8.

**SERRUYA, Michael;** retail executive; b. Morrocco, Tangier 24 June 1964; s. Sam and Clara (Bensimon) S.; e. Ryerson Polytech. Inst.; PRES., YOGURTY'S YOGURT DISCOVERY, PRES. & CO-FOUNDER, YOGEN FRÜZ INTERNATIONAL LTD. 1986– and CO-FOUNDER, PRËTZLZ INC. (Founded 1992) 2 locations in Canada; over 350 frozen yogurt franchises worldwide, over 197 in Can., 52 in USA, 2 in England, 12 in Spain, 19 in France, 7 in Belgium, 10 in Italy, 17 in Israel, 5 in Panama, 4 in Costa Rica, 5 in Portugal, 3 in Morocco, 6 in Guatemala, 12 in Venezuela, 11 in Mexico, 5 in Thailand, 5 in Taiwan, 15 in Indonesia, 2 in Singapore, 2 in Hong Kong, 4 in China, 4 in Colombia, 3 in Ecuador, 5 in Chile, 4 in Switzerland, 2 in Egypt, 3 in Dominican Republic; recipient, #3 of the world renown ACE Top 10 North American entrepreneurs under 30 years of age; #1 Franchise in our category in North America acknowledged by Entrepreneur Magazine 1993 and Top 40 under 40 years of age acknowledged by Entrepreneur Magazine 1992; recreations: squash, tennis; Home: 54 Markwood Lane, Thornhill, Ont.; Office: 7500 Woodbine Ave., Markham, Ont. L3R 1A8.

**SERSON, R. Scott,** B.A.; civil servant; b. Ottawa, Ont. 6 March 1948; s. William Bower and Ada May (Robinson) S.; e. Carleton Univ. B.A. 1970; m. Katharine Anne Miller 9 May 1970; children: Joel, Matthew; ASSOCIATE DEPUTY MINISTER, HEALTH CANADA 1993– ; Health and Welfare 1975; Min. of State for Social Devel. 1980; Asst. Sec. to the Cabinet, Office of Aboriginal Constitutional Affairs, Fed.-Prov. Relations Office (FPRO) 1984; Gen. Dir., Fed.-Prov. Relations & Social Policy, Dept. of Finance 1987; Fiscal Policy and Economic Analysis 1989; Dep. Sec. to the Cabinet, Intergovt. and Aboriginal Affairs, FPRO 1989; Home: Orleans, Ont.; Office: Room 2140, Jeanne Mance Bldg., Tunney's Pasture, Ottawa, Ont. K1A 0K9.

**SERVANT, J. Arthur,** B.Sc.A., P.Eng.; transportation executive; b. St-Félicien, Que. 25 Sept. 1939; s. Arthur and Gabrielle (Lepage) S.; e. Laval Univ. B.Sc.A. 1964; m. Sylvaine d. Jos and Orpha Lapointe 18 Dec. 1965; children: Guy, Marc, Paul; PRESIDENT & CHIEF OPERATING OFFICER, CABANO TRANSPORTATION GROUP INC. 1987– ; Engineering Consultant 1964–70; Vice-Pres. & Chief Executive Officer, Hamel Transport Inc. 1970–80; Vice-Pres. & Chief Operating Officer, Expeditex Ind. 1980–87; Pres., Quebec Trucking Assn.; Past Pres., Quebec Trucking Assn.; Past Dir., Candn. Trucking Assn.; Quebec Transportation Man of the Year 1991; Home: 2077 Pierre Beaubien, Vimont, Laval, Que.; Office: 6600, chemin St-François, St-Laurent, Que. H4S 1B7.

**SERVICE, Pat (Patricia Olive),** B.A.; artist; b. Alberni, B.C. 4 Feb. 1941; d. Andrew Gray and Agnes Greer (Wallace) S.; e. Victoria H.S. 1959; Univ. of B.C. B.A. 1963; m. David Grant s. Linda Marie and David Herbert Nelson 16 May 1964; children: David Cameron, Greer Louisa; many solo exhibs. 1979– incl.: Gallery One, Toronto 1991; Miriam Shiell Fine Art Toronto 1990, Buschlen-Mowatt Gallery, Vancouver 1983, '90, '91, '92; Wade Gall. Los Angeles 1988, '89; Wade Gall. Vancouver 1985, '86, '88, Waddington & Shiell Gall. Toronto 1986, '87, The Gallery/Art Placement Sask. 1985, '87; Candn. Art Galleries Calgary 1987, '91; also represented by Kathleen Laverty Gall. Edmonton; group exhibs. incl.: 1993 Tresors D'Art, Singapore; 1992 Tokyo Internat. Art Fair, Tokyo; 'Still Life' Transamerica Gall. Los Angeles 1990, 'North of the Border' Whatcom Museum (WA) 1990, 'Chicago Internat. Art Expo.' 1987, '90, 'Zoo Zone' Grand Forks Art Gall. B.C. 1988, 'Contemporary Canadian Art' Edmonton Art Gall. 1983; paintings included in num. priv. & corp. collections; comn. of 40 monoprints for Extve. Life Insur. Co. Los Angeles 1989; attended profl. workshops for artists Univ. of Sask. 1980–86; participant, Triangle Artists' Workshop (N.Y.) 1983 & 1993; Publication: 'Drawn To The Edge: The Paintings of Pat Service' (introductory essay by Robert Christie. Commentary by Charles Killam) Vancouver: Buschlen-Mowatt 1992; awarded Commemorative Medal for 125th Anniversary of Candn. Confederation; Home: 6009 Elm St., Vancouver, B.C. V6N 1A8.

**SESHADRI, Rangaswamy,** Ph.D., P.Eng.; educator; b. Madras, India 27 Aug. 1945; s. Rajendram Seshadri and Shantha (Krishnamachari) Rangaswamy; e. Univ. of Jabalpur, India B.E. (Hons.) 1967; Indian Inst. Technol. Madras M.Tech. 1969; Univ. of Calgary M.Sc., Ph.D. 1974; m. Sherry d. Barry and Audrey Middleton 19 June 1975; children: Jagan Nathan, Jana Kaye; DEAN OF ENGINEERING AND APPLIED SCIENCE, MEMORIAL UNIV. OF NFLD. 1993– ; Pres. and Tech. Dir. Dynatek Engineering Corp. Regina; Project Eng. EBA Engineering Consultants Edmonton 1974; Intermediate Eng. Associated Engineering Service Ltd. Edmonton 1977; Sr. Eng. Syncrude Canada Ltd. Edmonton/Fort McMurray, Eng. Assoc. Fort McMurray 1978; Assoc. Prof. of Engineering, Univ. of Regina 1987–88, Prof. of Engineering 1988– , Dean of Engineering 1989–93; co-author 'Group Invariance in Engineering Boundary Value Problems' 1985; mem. Assn. Profl. Engs. Sask.; Candn. Soc. Mech. Engs.; Am. Soc. Mech. Engs.; Home: 43 Wilkie Rd., Regina, Sask. S4S 5Y3; Office: Regina, Sask. S4S 0A2.

**SESSLE, Barry John,** B.D.S., M.D.S., B.Sc., Ph.D.; professor and dean; b. Sydney, Aust. 28 May 1941; s. Frederick George and Sadie Isobel (Lawson) S.; e. Sydney Univ. B.D.S. 1963, M.D.S. 1965, B.Sc. 1965; Univ. of New South Wales Ph.D. 1969; m. Mary d. Marshall and Helen Baldwin; children: Erica Jane, Claire Marie; PROF., DENTISTRY, UNIV. OF TORONTO 1976– ; Scholar Dental Found. Sydney Univ. 1963–64; Teaching Fellow, Univ. of N.S.W. 1965–68; Vis. Asso., U.S. Nat. Inst. Dental Rsch. 1968–70; Assoc. Prof., Dental School, Univ. of Toronto 1971–76; Chair, Di. Biol. Scis. 1978–84; Assoc. Dean Rsch. 1985–90; Dean 1990– ; Mem., Dental Sci. Grants Ctte., Candn. Med. Rsch. Council 1979–82; Cons., Mem. or Chair, NIH grants or site review ctte. 1976– ; Mem., Edit. Adv. Bd., 'Arch. Oral Biol. J.' 1988– ; Edit. Bd., 'Pain J.' 1989– ; 'Dysphagia J.' 1990– ; Internat. Assn. Dental Rsch. Oral Sci. Award 1976; Teacher Award, Candn. Fund for Dental Edn. 1977; Candn./France Sci. & Tech. Co-op. Program Award 1988; Grantee, Candn. Med. Rsch. Council 1971– ; NIH 1974– ; Mem., Internat. Assn. Dental Rsch. (Pres., Candn. Div. 1977–78; Sec.-Treas. Neurosci. Group 1976–79; Pres. Neurosci. Group 1985–86; Vice-Pres. 1992–93; Pres. elect 1993–94); Mem., Internat. Assn. Study Pain (Sec. Candn. Ch. 1982–88; Council Mem. 1993– ); Internat. Union Physiol. Sci. (Sec. Oral Physiol. Comn. 1983–92); Soc. Neurosci. (Pres. S. Ont. Ch. 1982–83); co-author: 'The Neural Basis of Oral & Facial Function 1978; co-editor: 'Mastication and Swallowing' 1976, 'Orofacial Pain and Neuromuscular Dysfunction' 1985, 'Effects of Injury on Trigeminal and Spinal Somatosensory Systems' 1987, 'Trigeminal Neuralgia' 1992 and 143 sci. papers; recreations: reading, tennis, travel; Office: 124 Edward St., Toronto, Ont. M5G 1G6.

**SETTERFIELD, George Ambrose,** Ph.D., F.R.S.C.; biologist; educator; b. Halifax, N.S. 29 Aug. 1929; s. late Ambrose Charles and Ethyl Violet Setterfield; e. Univ. of B.C. B.A. (Hons.) 1951; Univ. of Wis. Ph.D. 1954; m. Diana Evelyn d. late Hugh Charter 19 May 1951; children: Thomas Neal, David George, Jennifer Ann, Christopher, Wayne; retired Prof. of Biol. Carleton Univ. since 1984; Instr. in Biol. Univ. of B.C. 1954–56; Asst. Research Offr. Nat. Research Council Ottawa 1956–58, Assoc. Research Offr. 1958–62; Assoc. Prof. of Biol. Carleton Univ. 1962–64; Prof. 1964–84; Chrmn. of Biol. 1963–68; Sabbatical Leave, Dept. de Biologie, Laval Univ. 1968–69; Nat. Research Council Saskatoon 1977–78; co-ed. 'Biochemistry and Physiology of Plant Growth Substances' 1968; author some 70 papers on original research in cell biology in scient. journs.; rec'd Queen's Silver Jubilee Medal; Hon. Life mem. Candn. Soc. Cell Biol. (Pres. 1974–75); Hon. Vice Pres., 4th Int. Congress Cell Biology 1988; recreations: bicycling, wilderness hiking, canoeing and kayaking, photography; Home: 1063 Glen Forest Way, R.R.#1, Victoria, B.C. V9B 5T7.

**SEVER, Peter Joseph,** B.A., M.B.A.; impresario; b. Prague, Czechoslovakia 6 May 1946; s. John Hanus and Susan Eve (Firt) S.; e. York Univ., B.A. 1968, Hons. B.A. 1971, M.B.A. 1972; m. Sharon d. Joseph and Edith Prater 20 March 1984; Dir. & Consultant, Malartic Hygrade Gold Mines (Canada) Ltd. 1987; CUSO Teacher in Ghana, W. Africa 1968–70; joined mgmt. Nat. Ballet of Can. 1972–76; self-employed mgmt. cons. various arts orgns. incl. Can. Council 1976; travelled Africa researching & writing indigenous culture 1976–77; Pres. and Founder, General Arts Management Inc. 1977–87; opened New York office 1984, also Los Angeles office; represents various artists & orgns. incl. Nat. Ballet of Can., Stratford Shakespearean Festival, Jon Vickers, Orford Quartet, Anton Kuerti, Royal Candn. Air Farce, Moe Koffman, Dizzy Gillespie, Vancouver Symphony Orch.; helped prog. opening season Roy Thompson Hall, Toronto; frequent speaker and panelist performing arts confs., meetings, govt. panels Can. and USA; lectr. M.B.A. courses York Univ.; Dir. Toronto Arts Awards; recipient several univ. scholarships; Dean's Honours List M.B.A.; Queen's Scout; mem. Amnesty Internat.; People for Am. Way; recreations: performing arts, fitness, wilderness, travel; Address: 651A Queen St. E., Toronto, Ont. M4M 1G4 and 5720 Mosholu Ave., New York, N.Y. 10471.

**SEVERANCE, Christopher Churchill,** B.A., B.Ed., M.A.; museum administrator; b. Sydney, N.S. 12 Aug. 1943; s. Glenwood and Freda (Bray) S.; e. Univ. of King's Coll. B.A. 1965; Dalhousie B.Ed. 1966; St. Mary's M.A. 1973; EXECUTIVE DIRECTOR, P.E.I. MUSEUM 1991– ; Teacher, King's College Sch. 1966–71; Dir., Miners Museum 1972–74; Curator, London Historical Museums 1974–87; General Manager, London Regional Art & Historical Museum 1988–91; Dir., Charlottetown YMCA Bd.; Mem., Rotary Club; Candn. Mus. Assn.; Home: 145 Bunbury Rd., Charlottetown, P.E.I. C1A 9E5; Office: 2 Kent St., Charlottetown, P.E.I. C1A 1M6.

**SEVIER, Gerald Leslie,** R.C.A.; artist; b. Hamilton, Ont. 25 Jan. 1934; s. Frank Leslie Sevier; e. Brantford (Ont.) Coll. & Vocational Sch. 1952; Ont. Coll. of Art 1956 (Comm. Advertising Medal); m. Jean Eleanor d. Jack Wratten, Brantford, Ont. 21 Sept. 1956; children: Shawn, Jason, Tim, Theo; PROP., SEVIER & ASSOC./ARTISTS LTD. (comm. design & illustration); Teacher, Ont. Coll. of Art; solo exhns. incl. Sobot Gallery Toronto 1963, 1964, 1967; Shaw-Rimmington Gallery Toronto 1968; Merton Gallery Toronto 1970, 1973, 1975, 1979, 1980, 1981, 1984, 1985; Art Gallery of Brantford (retrospect) 1975; Kensington Gallery, Calgary 1981, 1986, 1988; exhns. Glenhyrst Gardens Brantford 1961, 1968; one man retrospect – Arts & Letters Club, Toronto, 1982, 1993; one man show, Gustafsson Gallery, Toronto, 1983; one man show, Quan Schieder Gallery, Toronto 1987, 1989, 1990; rep. in many group exhns. since 1961; rep. in various pub., corporate and private colls.; awards incl. Art Dirs. Club Toronto and New York, USA Illustrator Club, Graphics mag. Europe; Club: Arts & Letters; Home: 137 Glengrove Ave. W., Toronto, Ont. M4R 1P1.

**SEVIGNY, Col. the Hon. Pierre,** P.C. (Can. 1959), E.D., B.A., B.Com.; b. Quebec City, 12 Sept. 1917; s. Hon. Albert, P.C. and Jeanne (Lavery) S.; e. Loyola Coll., Montreal, Que.; Laval Univ., B.Com.; Quebec Semy., B.A.; m. Corinne, d. late R. P. Kernan, 22 June 1946; children: Pierrette, Albert, Robert; Extve.-in-Residence and PROF. OF FINANCE – FACULTY OF COMMERCE, CONCORDIA UNIV., Montreal, P.Q.; Gov., Montreal Gen. Hosp.; Pres. Horizon Investments Co.; Vice Pres. Horizon Realities Inc.; Dir. The Savoy Found. for Epileptics; 1st el. to H. of C. for Longueuil in g.e. 1958; re-el. g.e. June 1962; el. Depy. Speaker of H. of C., 1958; apptd. Assoc. Min. of Nat. Defence in Diefenbaker Govt., 1959; resigned his portfolio 9 Feb. 1963; def. g.e. Apr. 1963; served in 2nd World War; enlisted 1939; retired 1946; service in Eng. and W. Front; Polish Virtuti Militari; French Croix de Guerre; Belgian Croix de Guerre; Past Pres., Candn. Club of Montreal; Kt. Grand Cross of Order of Lazarus of Jerusalem (Chancellor for Can.); author: 'This Game of Politics' 1965; P. Conservative; Roman Catholic; recreations: bridge, golf, chess; Clubs: M.A.A.A.; Montreal; Home: 1101 - 3495 rue de la Montagne, Montreal, Que. H3G 2A5.

**SEVIGNY, The Honourable Pierrette,** B.A., B.Ed., B.C.L., Q.C., J.S.C.; superior court judge; b. Montreal, Que. 3 June 1947; d. Colonel The Honourable Pierre, P.C. and Corinne (Kernan) S.; e. Convent of the Sacred Heart; Loyola College B.A. 1967; McGill Univ. B.Ed. 1968, B.C.L. 1973; admitted to Bar of Prov. of Que. 1975; m. Richard s. John and Anne McConomy 22 June 1968; one d.: Elisabeth McConomy; JUDGE AT THE SUPERIOR COURT OF THE PROVINCE OF QUEBEC 1992– ; articled Ogilvy, Cope, Porteous, Montgomery, Renault, Clarke & Kirkpatrick 1974; Reg. Law Dept., CNR, St. Lawrence Region 1974–75; Attorney 1975–81; Partner, McConomy, De Wolfe, MacDougall 1981–92; Prof., LaSalle College 1981; concordia Univ. 1983–89; Q.C. 1989; Mem., Que. Bar Assn. 1975–92; Montreal Bar Assn. 1975–92 (Pres., Cté. de la formation permanente 1990–91); Candn. Bar Assn. (Extve., Que. Section 1990–92); Delegate, Nat. Conf., Report on the Status of Women, Ottawa 1978; Conf., Les Femmes et la Constitution, Ottawa 1989; Seminar Leader, Couchiching Conf. 1991; Founder & Former Pres., Residence Project Chance Inc.; Founder & Dir., Montreal Catholic Counselling 1983–88; Trustee & Dir., Pillars Trust Fund Inc. 1981–87; Montreal Bd. of Trade Rep. to Conseil Cons. des Aéroports de Montréal 1985–86 (Extve. Mem. & Vice-Pres. 1985–86); Dir., S.P.C.A. Montreal; Dir., Candn. Council of Christians & Jews 1991–92; Dir. Montreal Assn. for the Blind 1990–92 (Hon. Treas. & Dir. 1991–92); recreations: skiing, golf, reading; clubs: Montreal Thistle Curling; Home: 370 Wood Ave., Westmount, Que. H3Z 1Z2; Office: 1 Notre Dame St. E., Room 6.28, Montreal, Que. H2Y 1B6.

**SEWELL, Edward John Charles,** B.A., LL.B.; b. Toronto, Ont. 8 Dec. 1940; s. William S. and Helen (Sanderson) S.; e. Univ. of Toronto B.A. 1961 (Victoria Coll.), LL.B. 1964; one s. Nicholas; City Columnist, The Globe and Mail 1984–86; Mayor, City of Toronto 1978–80; el. Ald. mun. el. 1969, re-el. until 1980; re-el. again 1981; called to Bar of Ont. 1967; author 'Sense of Time and Place' 1972; 'Up Against City Hall' 1972; 'The Shape of the City: Toronto Struggles with Modern Planning' 1993; various articles mun. matters newspapers and mags.; mem. Law Soc. Upper Can.; Address: 122 Riverdale Ave., Toronto, Ont. M4K 1C3.

**SEXTON, John Edgar,** Q.C., LL.B., B.Sc., P.Eng.; lawyer; b. Ottawa, Ont 28 Oct. 1936; s. the late George Beaumont, M.D. and Irene (Griffith) S.; e. pub. and high schs. London, Ont.; Queen's Univ. B.Sc. 1959; Univ. of W. Ont. LL.B 1962; m. Rosemary Robinson Black, M.A., LL.B., d. Judge and Mrs. John B. Robinson, Haileybury, Ont. 9 May 1979; children: Timothy Edgar, John Christopher, Jennifer Ann; stepchildren: Stephanie Ann and John Beverley Robinson Black; CHRMN. & SR. PARTNER, OSLER, HOSKIN & HARCOURT, Barristers and Solicitors 1977– ; Dir. Brunswick Mining & Smelting Corp.; Irving Oil Limited; Gov.: The Advocates Soc. Inst.; Past Dir., Soc. for Educational Visits and Exchanges in Canada; called to Bar of Ont. 1964, N.B. 1979, Alta. 1985; cr. Q.C. 1978; Instr. in Civil Procedure I, Bar Admission Course 1967–73; Special Lectr. for Law Soc. of Upper Can. 1974, 1979; Guest Instr. Osgoode Hall Law Sch. Intensive Trial Advocacy Workshop 1980; Chrmn., Conf. on Corporate Litigation 1981; Faculty Mem., 150th Anniversary Advocacy Program, Osgoode Hall 1984; Guest Lectr., Meredith Lectures, McGill Univ. 1984; Special Counsel, Fed. Govt., in anti-trust prosecutions; Bank Inquiry 1985; Counsel: Inquiry into the Petroleum Industry; Inquiry into the Post Office; recipient Professional Achievement Award, Univ. of Western Ont. Law Assn.; Fellow, Am. Coll. Trial Lawyers; Past Chrmn., Municipal Law Sect., Candn. Bar Assn.; former Dir. Advocates' Soc.; mem. Internat. Bar Assn.; Am. Bar Assn.; Assn. Prof. Engs. Prov. Ont.; Bd. Trade Metrop. Toronto; Antique & Classic Boat Soc.; recreations: antique boats, travel, racquetball, sailing; Club: Toronto; Home: 60 Castle Frank Rd., Toronto, Ont. M4W 2Z8 and Fisher Island, Charleston Lake; Office: P.O. Box 50, First Canadian Place, Toronto, Ont. M5X 1B8.

**SEXTON, Rosemary,** B.A., M.A., LL.B.; writer; b. Haileybury, Ont. 20 Dec. 1946; d. his honour Judge John Beverley and Julia Mary (Bridger) Robinson; e. Haileybury public & high schools; Havergal College; Laurentian Univ. B.A. 1968; College of Edn. interim h.s. assistant cert. Type B 1969; specialist guidance cert. 1973; Univ. of Toronto B.A. (Hons.) 1973; York Univ. M.A. 1976; Osgoode Hall Law School LL.B. 1976; m. J. Edgar s. Dr. G. Beaumont and Irene (Griffith) S. 9 May 1979; children: Stephanie Anne, John Beverley Robinson Black; stepchildren: Timothy Edgar, John Christopher and Jennifer Ann Sexton; English & Latin Teacher, New Liskeard S.S. 1968–69; West Hill S.S. 1969–72; articled with law firm Holden Murdoch Finlay Robinson 1976–77; called to bar of Ontario 1977; Tax Editor, CCH (Canada) Ltd. 1977–78; Society Columnist, The Globe and Mail 1988–93; author: 'The Glitter Girls' 1993; Mem., Ont. Censor Bd. 1978–81; served on boards of following orgns. 1982–87: Family Day Care Services of Metro Toronto, Toronto Symphony Women's Ctte., Toronto Pops Orchestra, Candn. Psychiatric Awareness Ctte., Arthritis Soc. (Rosedale branch), Wellesley Hosp. Auxiliary, Soc. for Edn. Visits & Exchanges in Canada, St. George-St. David PC Riding Assn., Laurentian Univ.; recreations: reading, travel; Home: 60 Castle Frank Road, Toronto, Ont. M4W 2Z8; Fisher Island, Charleston Lake, Ont. K0E 1B0; Thornton Cliff, 275 King St. E., Brockville, Ont. K6V 1E3.

**SEYMOUR, Harry Taylor,** B.S.A., B.A.Sc., M.B.A., P.Eng., F.F.A.F.; investment executive; b. Hamilton, Ont. 19 May 1936; s. Harry Irvine and Isabella Gourlay (Black) S.; e. public and high schs., Ottawa; Univ. of Toronto, (Ont. Agricultural Coll.) B.S.A. 1961, B.A.Sc. 1962; Univ. of West. Ont., M.B.A. 1966; m. Lillian Jeanette, B.A., M.L.S., d. George and Violet Stanley 24 Apr. 1964; children: Sasha, Jeanette; Managing Partner, Waterston Group of Companies 1988– ; Pres., C.E.O. & Dir., Pathfinder Learning Systems Corp.; Pres. & Dir., Bay Port Midland Holdings Ltd.; Prod. Engr., John Deere Limited 1961–64; Timberjack Limited 1965; Analyst, Pitfield Mackay Ross Limited 1966–68; Asst. to Pres. 1968–69; Mgr., Vancouver Br. 1969–70; Dir. & Mgr., Rsch. 1970–72; Mktg. 1972–74; Vice-Pres. & Dir., Rsch. 1974–76; Institutional Sales-Québec 1976–78; Rsch. 1978–81; Inst. Sales-Rsch. & Corp. Fin. Co-ord. 1981–84; Vice-Pres. & Dir., Dominion Securities Inc. (successor company of Pitfield Mackay Ross Ltd.) 1974–88; Pres. & Dir., Dominion Securities Investment Management Inc. 1984–88; Sec. & Dir., Dominion Securities Found. 1980–88; Fellow, Fin. Analyst Fed. 1974– ; Pres., The Empire Club of Can. 1985–86; Dir., The Empire Club Foundation 1988– ; Vice-Chrmn., Treas. & Dir., Youth Employment Skills (YES) Can. Inc. 1986– ; Trustee, Art Gallery of Ont. Found. 1987–93 (Chrmn. 1991–93); Dir., City of Toronto Economic Development Corp. 1992– ; Mem., Assn. of Profl. Engrs. of Ont.; Toronto Soc. of Fin. Analysts; Univ. of West. Ont. Bus. Sch. Club; author: 'Royal Commission on Corporate Concentration – Argus Corporation' report 1976; United Church; recreations: tennis, skiing, golf; Clubs: Badminton & Racquet; York; Queen's; Eastbourne Golf; Caledon Ski; Address: 181 Roxborough Dr., Suite 200, Toronto, Ont. M4W 1X7.

**SEYMOUR, Lynn (Mrs. Colin Edward Jones);** C.B.E.(1976); ballet dancer; b. Wainwright, Alberta, 8 March 1939; d. Edward Victor and Marjorie Isabelle (McIvor) Springbett; e. Public Schs. and Kitsilano High Sch., Vancouver, B.C.; Royal Ballet Sch., London, Eng.; m. 16 July 1963; Ballet teachers in Can.: Jean Jepson, Nicholai Svetlanoff; principal teachers in Eng.: Winnifred Edwards, Barbara Fewster, Pamela May, Erling Sunde, and in U.S.A. Valentina Peryaslanec; created rôles for The Royal Ballet: Adolescent Girl in 'The Burrow' (MacMillan), The Bride in 'Le Baiser de la Fee' (MacMillan), The Girl in 'The Invitation' (MacMillan), Gourouli in 'Les Deux Pigeons (Ashton), Principal Figure in 'Symphony' (MacMillan), 2 Sonnets in 'Images of Love' (MacMillan), Juliet in 'Romeo & Juliet' (MacMillan); other principal rôles for Royal Ballet incl.: Odette-Odile in 'Swan Lake' (Petipa), Giselle in 'Giselle' (Perrot-Coralli), Princess Aurora in 'Sleeping Beauty' (Petipa), Cinderella in 'Cinderelle' (Ashton), Ophelia in 'Hamlet' (Helpmman), The Bride in 'Le Féte Etrange' (Howard), The Girl in 'Solitaire' (MacMillan), Principal Girl in 'Danses Concertante' (MacMillan); Guest artist with Stuttgart Ballet and Nat. Ballet of Canada; left Can. in Sept. 1953 to join Royal Ballet Sch.; joined Royal Ballet in 1956, first created rôle, 1956, first principal rôle 1957, since when has preferred created and modern works to classics; third generation Candn. on both sides of her family; recreation: cinema.

**SHAA, Aqjangajuk;** artist; b. 17 March 1937; medium: sculpture, drawings, prints; 62 group exbns. incl. most recent: Winnipeg Art Gall. 1992, l'Igloo Art Esquimau, Douai (toured 9 cities) France 1988–92, Inuit Gall. of Vancouver 1990, Feheley Fine Arts Toronto 1990, Arctic Artistry Hastings-on-Hudson, N.Y. 1990; solo exbns.: Cottage Craft Gifts & Fine Arts Ltd. Calgary 1984, Inuit Galerie Mannheim, Germany 1982, Robertson Gall. Ottawa 1981, Franz Bader Gall. Washington, D.C. 1980, Waddington Galleries Montreal 1979, Toronto 1978, The Innuit Gall. of Eskimo Art Toronto 1970, 1974; works in 15 collections incl. art galleries of Ontario (Klamer Family & Sarick colls.), Windsor, Winnipeg (Hudson's Bay Co. & Twomey colls.), Canada Council Art Bank, Candn. Mus. of Civilization Hull, Que., Inuit Cultural Inst. Rankin Inlet, N.W.T., Metro. Mus. of Art N.Y., Musée des beaux-arts de Montréal, National Gall. of Canada; subject of several articles and catalogues; Home: Cape Dorset, N.W.T.; Office: c/o Dorset Fine Arts, 33 Belmont St., Toronto, Ont. M5R 1P9.

**SHADBOLT, Douglas,** B.Arch., D.Eng. (hon.), M.A.I.B.C., F.R.A.I.C.; architect; educator; b. Victoria, B.C. 18 Apr. 1925; s. Edmund and Alice Mary Maud (Healy) S.; e. Univ. of B.C.; McGill Univ.; Univ. of Ore. B.Arch. 1957; N.S. Tech. Coll. D.Eng. (hon.) 1969; Carleton Univ., D.Eng. (hon.) 1982; m. Sidney Osborne Craig; children: Catherine Shand Craig, James Osborne Craig; PROFESSOR EMERITUS, SCHOOL OF ARCHITECTURE, UNIV. OF B.C. 1990– ; Dir., School of Architecture, Univ. of B.C. 1979–90; ACSA Distinguished Professor 1987; Asst., then Assoc. Prof. of Arch. McGill Univ. 1958–61; Prof. and Founding Dir. Sch. Arch. N.S. Tech. Coll. Halifax 1961–68; Prof. and Founding Dir. Sch. Arch. Carleton Univ. Ottawa 1968–79 and Founder Sch. Indust. Design 1973; Home/Office: 4525 Gothard St., Vancouver, B.C. V5R 3K8.

**SHADBOLT, Jack,** O.C. (1972), LL.D.; artist; b. Shoeburyness, Eng. 4 Feb. 1909; s. late Edmond and Alice Mary Maude S.; e. Victoria (B.C.) High Sch. 1925; Victoria Coll. 1927; Victoria (B.C.) Normal Sch. 1928; André L'Hote Sch. of Art, Paris 1937; Euston Rd. Art Sch., London, Eng. 1937; Art Students League, N.Y.C. 1948; LL.D., Univ. of Victoria 1973, Simon Fraser 1978, Univ. of B.C. 1978, Bishops Univ. 1988; m. Doris Kathleen, d. late Rufus Meisel, 20 Sept. 1945; Former Head, Drawing & Painting Sec., Vancouver Sch. of Art and sometime juror. lectr. and writer; incl. in exhns.: Venice Biennial; Carnegie Internat.; Pittsburgh; Sao Paulo; Tate Gallery, London, Eng.; World Fairs Brussels and Seattle; Warsaw; Toulouse; Mexico City; Chicago; Sydney; one-man shows incl. New York, San Francisco, Seattle, Portland, Montreal, Toronto, Vancouver; Restrospectives, Thirty Yrs. Nat. Gallery, Ottawa and travelling; Ten Yrs. Retrospective, Vancouver Art Gallery 1975; Early watercolours Victoria Art Gallery 1980; Multiple-panelled works, Vancouver Art Gallery retrospective 1984; Cross-cultural works retrospective; Peterborough Art Gallery 1984: Jack Shadbolt and the Coastal Indian Image – retrospective; Univ. of B.C. Museum of Anthropology 1986; 60 yr. Retrospective, Glenbow Museum 1991; Collections (public): Brooklyn, Cleveland, Portland, Seattle and all major Candn. galleries; in many private and corp. collections; Mural Comns. incl. Edmonton Internat. Airport; CBC Bldg., Vancouver; McMillan Bloedel Bldg.; Odeon Cineplex Bldg.; Confederation Centre, Charlottetown, P.E.I.; Nat. Arts Centre, Ottawa; rec'd Candn. Guggenheim Internat. Award 1957; Candn. Govt. Overseas Fellowship (France, Italy and Greece); Univ. of Alta. Nat. Painting Award 1969; received Order of Canada 1972; Molson Prize 1978; O.S.A. Award 1981; Gershon Iskowitz Award 1990; received Order of British Columbia 1990; served in 2nd World War; Freeman, City of Vancouver 1989; Acting Adm. Offr., Candn. War Artists; author 'In Search of Form' 1968; 'Mind's I' (poems) 1973; 'Act of Art' 1981; also numerous articles concerning art in various journs.;

Address: 5121 Harborview Rd., N. Burnaby, B.C. V5B 1C9.

**SHADWICK, Martin William,** B.A., M.A.; educator, writer; b. Sudbury, Ont. 11 Dec. 1953; s. Vernon Richard and Betty Margaret (Puckett) S.; e. A.Y. Jackson S.S. 1972; York Univ. B.A. 1976, M.A. 1978; doctoral studies; RESEARCH ASSOC., CENTRE FOR INTERNAT. & STRATEGIC STUDIES, YORK UNIV. 1984–88, 1990– ; Lectr., Dept. of Pol. Sci., Glendon Coll. 1981–82; Trent Univ. 1981–82; York Univ. 1982–85, 1990–91; McLaughlin Coll. 1986– ; Contbg. Ed., 'Aviation & Aerospace' 1990– ; 'The Wednesday Report' 1987–88; 'Aerospace Can./Aerospace Can. Internat.' 1985–87; 'Canadian Defence Quarterly' 1992– ; Editor, 'The Wednesday Report' 1988–89; Dept. of Nat. Defence Scholarship 1979–81; Anglican; Mem., Assn. for Candn. Studies; Candn. Aviation Hist. Soc.; Candn. Inst. of Internat. Affairs; Candn. Inst. of Strategic Studies; Candn. Ctr. for Global Security; Inst. of Public Admin. of Can.; commentator; guest lectr.; resource person/cons. for internat. relns. seminars; author/co-author of 135 articles, monographs, conf. papers, book chapters & submissions to parl cttes.; recreations: world band radio; Office: 4700 Keele St., North York, Ont. M3J 1P3.

**SHAFFER, Beverly Victoria,** B.A., M.Sc.; film maker; b. Montréal, Qué.; d. Phillip and Anne (Simack) S.; e. McGill Univ. B.A. 1966; Boston Univ. M.Sc. 1971; FILM DIR. & PRODUCER, NAT. FILM BD. OF CAN. 1976– ; High Sch. Teacher, Malcolm Campbell High Sch. Montréal 1967–69; Assoc. Producer WGBH TV Boston 1971–75; Dir. 'Children of Canada' film series Nat. Film Bd., Dir./Producer 'To A Safer Place'; recipient Academy Award Hollywood 1978 ('I'll Find A Way'); over 20 internat. film awards; Office: National Film Board, P.O. Box 6100, Montréal, Qué. H3C 3H5.

**SHAFFER, Edward H.,** Ph.D.; university professor; b. Pittsburgh, Pa. 26 Jan. 1923; s. Meyer J. and Sylvia (Bubligoff) S.; e. Univ. of Michigan B.A. (Hons.) 1948, M.A. 1949; Columbia Univ. Ph.D. 1966; m. Florence d. Max and Martha Schill 28 Feb. 1959; children: Martha, Paul; PROF. EMERITUS, DEPT. OF ECON., UNIV. OF ALTA. 1988– ; Asst. Prof., Western Wash. State Coll. 1965–68; Occidental Coll. 1968–70; Prof., Dept. of Econ., Univ. of Alta. 1970–88; Presidents Fellow, Columbia Univ. 1964; frequent commentator in media on econ. events; Mem., Candn. Econ. Assn.; Am. Econ. Assn.; West. Econ. Assn.; Assn. for Evolutionary Econ.; Vice-Pres., Lower Mainland Chapter, Veterans against Nuclear Arms 1988– ; author: 'The Oil Import Program of the United States' 1968, 'The United States and the Control of World Oil' 1983, 'Canada's Oil and the American Empire' 1983; recreations: bicycling, photography; Home: PH6 – 522 Moberley Rd., Vancouver, B.C. V5Z 4G4.

**SHAFFER, Paul;** musician, bandleader; b. Thunder Bay, Ont. 28 Nov. 1949; m. Cathy Vasapoli; Band Mem., Fabulous Fugitive Thunder Bay 1964–68; keyboardist, Howard Shore Band & actor NBC's Saturday Night Live 1975–80; Mem., Blues Bros. Band 1978–79; Leader & Keyboardist, The World's Most Dangerous Band NBC's Late Night with David Letterman 1982– ; Mus Dir., Godspell (Toronto) 1972; Musician, The Magic Show (N.Y.C.) 1974; (Gilda Radner's music revue) Live in New York 1979; (off-Broadway prodn.) Leader of the Pack 1984; recording artist; keyboardist; Briefcase Full of Blues (Blues Bros.) 1978; Made in America 1980; The Honey Drippers (Honey Drippers) 1985; Karate Kid II (film soundtrack) 1986; regular cast mem. (TV series) 'A Year at the Top' 1977; film appearances incl. 'This Is Spinal Tap' 1984; solo album 'Coast to Coast' 1989 (2 Grammy noms.).

**SHAFRAN, Grace Brenda,** LL.B.; broadcasting executive; b. Toronto, Ont. 11 Sept. 1956; e. Univ. of Windsor LL.B. 1980; m. Edward John Shafran; VICE-PRES. & GENERAL COUNSEL, BATON BROADCASTING INCORPORATED & SUBSIDIARIES 1989– ; Legal Couns., Baton Broadcasting Inc. & Subs. 1986–89; Assoc., Isenberg & Assoc. 1982–85; Mem. Extve. Ctte., Business & Profl. Women's Div., United Jewish Appeal; recreations: travel, skiing, fitness; Office: Box 9, Station O, Toronto, Ont. M4A 2M9.

**SHAMSIE, Jalal,** B.Sc., M.B.B.S., F.R.C.Psych., F.R.C.P.(C); university professor; b. Delhi, India 29 Jan. 1930; s. Nasseer and Nasri S.; e. Univ. of Punjab B.Sc. 1947, M.B.B.S. 1953; F.R.C.P.(C) 1962; F.R.C.Psych. 1982; m. Aline d. Alfred Delest 19 Dec. 1959; children: Yasmine, Amina; PROF., UNIV. OF TORONTO 1980– ; started 1st Adolescent Unit in Canada, Douglas Hosp. Montreal 1963; started a Court Clinic Montreal 1965; Dir., Child & Adolescent Serv., Douglas Hosp. 1968; Reg. Dir., Children Serv., Royal Ottawa Hosp. 1971; Clinical Dir., Thistletown Reg. Ctr. Toronto 1972; founded Inst. for the Study of Antisocial Behav. in Youth 1987; Editor & Founder, Youth Update newsletter 1983; Dir., Rsch. & Edn., Thistletown Reg. Ctr.; Consultant, Clarke Inst. of Psych.; Hon. Cons., Peel Memorial Hosp.; Mem., Candn. Psych. Assn.; Ont. Med. Assn.; Candn. Med. Assn.; Candn. Academy of Child Psych.; fellowships: Royal Coll. of Physicians & Surgeons of Can. 1973; Royal Coll. of Psych. of G.B. 1982; author of over 20 articles in profl. jours.; editor of 6 books incl. most recent: 'Youth With Conduct Disorder: What Is To Be Done?' 1991; recreations: golf, films, music; clubs: Bd. of Trade; Home: 32 Grovetree Rd., Etobicoke, Ont. M9V 2Y2; Office: 51 Panorama Court, Etobicoke, Ont. M9V 4L8.

**SHAND, John (Jack) F.;** association executive; b. Toronto, Ont. 8 June 1956; s. Frederick Page and Frances Jean MacKenzie (Robertson) S.; e. Univ. of Toronto, B.A. 1978; Certified Assoc. Executive (CAE) 1987; PRES., CANADIAN SOCIETY OF ASSOCIATION EXECUTIVES 1986– ; employed in hotel indus. 1978–79; Gen Mgr., Candn. Shoe Retailers' Assn. Inc. 1979; Pres. Candn. Shoe Retailers' Assn. 1984–86; Co-Founder, Foundation for Assn. Rsch. and Education; Extve. Ed., 'Association Management Handbook' 1988; 'The Role of Volunteers in Non-Profit Organizations' 1990; Dir., Amyotrophic Lateral Sclerosis Soc. of Can. 1989–91; Chrmn., Lou Gehrig Ironman Week, Toronto 1990–92; Extve. Education Ctte. of the Business Advisory Council, Michael C. DeGroote Sch. of Business, McMaster Univ.; Mem., Cdn. Soc. of Assoc. Extves.; Am. Soc. of Assoc. Extves.; Metro Toronto Bd. of Trade; Life Mem., ALS Soc. of Cda.; Home: 1120 Queen's Ave., Oakville, Ont. L6H 2B5; Office: 40 University Ave., Suite 1104, Toronto, Ont. M5J 1T1.

**SHANLY, Coote Nisbitt Patrick,** B.Com.; retired financial and manufacturing executive; b. Quebec City, Que. 24 Oct. 1925; s. late Coote Nisbitt and Berys Alleyn Rolt (Sharples) S.; e. St. George's Sch. Quebec; St. Alban's Sch. Brockville; Lower Can. Coll. Montreal; Queen's Univ. B.Com. 1949; m. Nonie Mary d. Arthur Fitzpatrick, Que City 24 June 1950; three s. Walter Patrick Francis, Charles Coote Nisbitt (deceased), John James Arthur (deceased); Pres. and Dir., J.S.W. Holdings Ltd. 1973–85; Pres. and Dir. Crane Carrier (Canada) Ltd. 1973–78; Vice-Pres. and Gen. Mgr. Teledyne Canada Tsp. Group 1974–77; Pres., Dir., & C.E.O., Dynatel Inc., 1978–81; Chrmn., Gormanston Holdings Ltd. 1986– ; Chrmn., Gormanston Waste Systems Inc. 1987– ; Vice Pres. and Dir., Queensway Tank Lines Ltd.; Roads Resurfacing Co. Ltd.; Dir., Tandem Mgt. Ltd.; Carefree Travel Ltd.; Kaps Transport Ltd.; Mackenzie Air Ltd.; Bolster Transport Ltd.; R. R. Dales Const. Co. Ltd.; Power Motive Products Inc.; Norcan Parts and Equip't. Ltd., 1975–79; Sunnybrook Stables Ltd. 1978– ; joined Royal Bank of Canada 1944; Industrial Acceptance Corp. Ltd. 1951–73 serving in various positions incl. Vice Pres. and Gen. Mgr. Indust. Financing & Leasing Operations; Reserve Offrs. Training Course; P. Conservative; Anglican; recreation: antique and classic cars; Clubs: Granite; RCYC; Mount Royal (Montreal); Homes: Suite 305, Highgate, 3 Concorde Place, Don Mills, Ont. M3C 3K7; 'Le Caprice,' Point-au-Pic, Co. Charlevois, Que. G0T 1M0; Mailing Address: Box 310, Station R, Toronto, Ont. M4G 4C3.

**SHANNON, Deborah Lynn,** P.D.P., B.A., A.P.M.R.; pharmaceutical-health care executive; b. Squamish, B.C. 6 Oct. 1956; d. Albert Thomas and Jean Alexandra (Perigo) S.; e. Simon Fraser Univ. P.D.P. 1979, B.A. 1984; PROFESSIONAL AREA MANAGER, PHARMACEUTICAL PRODUCTS DIV., ABBOTT LABORATORIES LTD. 1991–present; Aerobics Instructor (part-time) Gold's Gym 1984–89; admin. positions, BC Rail Ltd. 1981–87; Sales Rep., Cellular Telephone Div., Cantel Inc. 1987–90; Branch Mgr., Downtown Vanc. Operations, ADIA Canada Ltd. 1990–91; Alumni Rep., Bd. of Gov., Simon Fraser Univ. 1991–94, 1994–96; Alumni Rep., Convocation Senator 1988–93; Pres., Alumni Assn. 1988–89; Vice-Pres. 1987–88; Bd. Mem 1984–90; chaired several cttes incl. 25th Anniversary Homecoming; 1st Place, Masters Women, SFU Alumni Fun Run 1993; 2nd Place 1992; Charter Mem., SFU Swimming Alumni Assn.; Pres., Constituency Assn., Vancouver Little Mountain Social Credit Party; Mem., Vancouver A.M. Tourist Services Assn.; recreations: running, swimming, classical piano; Address: 19 – 877 West 7th Ave., Vancouver, B.C. V5Z 1C2.

**SHANNON, Gerald Edward,** B.J.; diplomat; b. Ottawa, Ont. 8 June 1935; s. Gerald Edmund and Kathleen (Burke) S.; e. Nepean High Sch. Ottawa; Carleton Univ. B.J. 1957; m. Mrs. Anne Park Shannon; children: Michael Thomas, Steven Patrick; AMBASSADOR FOR MULTILATERAL TRADE NEGOTIATIONS AND CHIEF NEGOTIATOR, PERMANENT REPRESENTATIVE AND AMBASSADOR TO THE UNITED NATIONS IN GENEVA AND TO THE CONFERENCE ON DISARMAMENT IN GENEVA 1990– and concurrently, AMBASSADOR TO GATT 1991– ; Depy. Min. for Internat. Trade and Assoc. Under-Secy. of State for External Affairs 1986 and in addition named as the Northern Pipeline Comnr. 1988; joined Dept. of External Affairs Ottawa 1963, Third Secy. Washington 1964, First Secy. Belgrade 1969, Depy. Dir. Comm. Policy Div. Ottawa 1972 and Dir. 1974, Ambassador to Korea 1977, Min. (Econ.) Washington 1978; Depy. Head of Mission, 1981; Asst. Depy. Min., Tax Policy, Internat. Trade and Finance, Dept. of Finance 1983; Sr. Asst. Depy. Min., Internat. Trade and Finance & Econ. Development 1984; served with COTC 1954–57, Pilot Offr.; Anglican; recreations: outdoor sports; Office: Office of the Permanent Rep. of Canada to the Office of the U.N., 1, rue Pré-de-la-Bichette, CH-1202 Geneva, Switzerland.

**SHANNON, Joy Marianne,** b. Toronto, Ont.; d. Charles and Jessica (Lennard) Sedgwick; e. Univ. of Toronto; McGill Univ., Concordia, B.A., B.F.A., FCCHSE; widow of James Grant Shannon MD FRCS(C); children: Patricia Ellen, James David; Dir. Gen., Montreal Neurological Hosp.; and Montreal Neurol. Institute; Gov., McGill Univ.; Fellow, Canadian College of Health Executives; elected Quebec representative to Bd. of Dirs., Canadian College of Health Service Extves.; Vice Pres., Professional Services Ctte., CCHSE; recreations: music, golf; Clubs: North Hatley Golf & Tennis; University (Montreal); Home: Box 138, North Hatley, Que. J0B 2C0.

**SHANNON, Hon. Melvin Earl,** B.A., LL.B.; judge; b. Near Harris, Sask. 22 March 1927; s. Robert Andrew and Beatrice May (Lakey) S.; e. Delisle, Sask.; Univ. of Sask. B.A. (distinction) 1947, LL.B. (distinction) 1949 (Carswell Prize); m. Suzanne Sarah d. late Ernest Arlington McCullough 24 June 1952; children: Sarah Ann, Mel Andrew, Daniel Howard, Kathleen, Stephen Michael, Ann; JUSTICE, COURT OF QUEEN's BENCH OF ALTA. since 1973; read law with R.L. Fenerty, Q.C.; called to Bar of Alta. 1950; cr. Q.C. 1968; Counsel, Mclaws & Co. 1950–53; estbd. Shannon & Cook 1954, Sr. Partner; Ald. City of Calgary 1953–54; def. Lib. Cand. for Calgary S. fed. g.e. 1958; Trustee Patrons Fund Candn. Lawn Tennis Assn.; Past Pres. Kts. Round Table; formerly mem. Law Soc. Alta. (Bencher 1968–73, Pres. 1973); Candn. Bar Assn.; recreations: tennis, squash, golf, french lang., reading; Clubs: Glencoe (Dir. 1961–71, Pres. 1969–71); L'Alliance Française; Home: 4108 Crestview Rd., Calgary, Alta. T2T 2L4; Office: Court House 611 – 4th St. S.W., Calgary, Alta. T2P 1T5.

**SHAPIRO, Harold Tafler,** Ph.D.; economist/university president; b. Montreal, Que. 8 June 1935; s. Maxwell and Mary (Tafler) S.; e. McGill Univ., B.Comm. 1956 (Lt. Gov. Medal in Commerce); Princeton Univ., Ph.D. 1964 (Harold Helm Fellow, Harold Dodds Sr. Fellow); m. Vivian Bernice Rapoport 19 May 1957; children: Anne, Marilyn, Janet, Karen; PRES., & PROF. OF ECON. & PUB. AFFAIRS, PRINCETON UNIV. 1988– ; Asst. Prof., Dept. of Econ., Univ. of Michigan 1964–67; Assoc. Prof. 1967–70; Prof. 1970–76; Chrmn. 1974–77; Prof. Econ. & Pub. Policy 1977–87; Vice-Pres., Acad. Affairs 1977–79; Pres. 1980–87; Rsch. Adv., Bank of Can. 1965–72; Cons. forecasting, U.S. Treas. 1965–68; Dir., Dow Chem.; Mem., President's Council of Advisors on Science and Technology (PCAST) 1990– ; Mem., New Jersey Commn. Sci. & Tech. 1988–91; Trustee, Alfred P. Sloan Found. 1980– ; Interlochen Center for the Arts 1988– ; Chrmn., Spec. Pres. Ctte., The Rsch. Libraries Group 1980–91; Mem., Gov. High Tech. Task Force, Mich. 1980–87; Comn. on Jobs & Econ. Devel. 1983–87; Carnegie Comn. on Coll. Retirement 1984–86; Bd. Adv. Am. Bd. 'Internal Medicine' 1985–88; Mem. Extve. Ctte., Assn. Am. Univ. 1985–90; Mid-Decade Rec. Com. Prog. in Edn. & Culture, The Ford Found.; Mem. Bd. of Dirs., The American Council on Education 1989–92; Mem., Inst. of Medicine; Mem., Am. Philosophical Soc.; Fellow, Am. Academy of Arts and Sciences; Fellow, Mich. Soc. Fellows (Sr.); Office: Princeton, NJ 08544.

**SHAPIRO, Irving,** B.A., LL.L.; lawyer; b. Montréal, Qué. 19 July 1936; s. Isaac and Rose (Yampolsky) S.; e. Strathcona Acad.; McGill Univ. B.A. 1958; Univ. de Montréal LL.L. 1961; m. Barbara d. S.W. Weber, Q.C. 24 Dec. 1961; children: Davina, Jeffrey, Elliot; PARTNER, PHILLIPS, FRIEDMAN, KOTLER 1984– ; called to Bar of Qué. 1962; Home: 636 Kindersley Ave., Town of Mount Royal, Qué. H3R 1S5; Office: 900, Place du Canada, Montréal, Qué. H3B 2P8.

**SHAPIRO, Jerry,** B.Sc., M.D., C.M., FRCP(C); dermatologist, clinical professor; b. Montreal, Que. 3 June 1954; s. Philip and Brajna S.; e. McGill Univ. B.Sc. 1976, M.D., C.M. 1981; Univ. of B.C. FRCP(C) 1985; DIRECTOR & FOUNDER, UNIVERSITY OF BRITISH COLUMBIA HAIR CLINIC 1986– ; the UBC hair clinic is a research, treatment and transplant centre serving clients from all of N. Am.; Clinical Asst. Prof., Div. of Dermatology, Fac. of Med., Univ. of B.C.; author of numerous sci. articles on hair loss/alopecia areata in the dermatologic literature; Office: 855 W. 10th Ave., Vancouver, B.C. V5Z 1L7.

**SHAPIRO, Stanley Jack,** A.B., M.B.A., Ph.D.; university professor and administrator; b. Boston, Mass. 15 Jan. 1934; s. Samuel Myer and Esther Jenny (Trombly) S.; e. Harvard College A.B. (cum laude) 1955; Wharton School of Finance & Commerce M.B.A. 1959; Univ. of Pennsylvania Ph.D. 1961; m. Roberta d. Aaron and Sophie Kosofsky 4 June 1960; DEAN, FACULTY OF BUSINESS ADMINISTRATION, SIMON FRASER UNIV. 1987– and Prof. of Marketing 1981– ; Asst. Prof., Wharton School 1961–64; Vice-Pres., MRC Ltd. (a marketing research firm) 1965–67; Assoc. Prof. & Prof. of Marketing, McGill Univ. 1967–81; Dean, McGill Fac. of Management 1973–78; Chrmn., Candn. Fed. of Deans of Management & Admin. Sciences 1987–89; Senior Fellow, Academy of Marketing Science; School Trustee, Burnaby, B.C. 1987–90, 1990–93; elected Gov., Academy of Marketing Science 1986–94; Mem., Am. Marketing Assn.; Liberal Party of Canada; co-author: 'Basic Marketing' (Candn. ed), 7 eds. of this vol. & three of an abridged version pub. 1975–94; author/editor of sixty articles on marketing; recreations: municipal politics; Home: 201 – 1675 Augusta Ave., Burnaby, B.C. V5A 2V6; Office: Burnaby, B.C. V5A 1S6.

**SHARKEY, Robert John,** B.A., M.Sc., M.A., Ph.D., F.C.I.A., F.S.A.; actuary, insurance executive; b. Ottawa, Ont. 17 Nov. 1948; s. William Robert and Mary Gavina (Miller) S.; e. Carleton Univ. B.A. (Hons.) 1970; McGill Univ. M.Sc. 1972, M.A. 1974, Ph.D. 1982; m. Charlotte d. William and Marion Mould 23 June 1973; children: Charlotte Alicia, Emma Louise, William Daniel; VICE-PRESIDENT, INVESTMENTS, SUN LIFE ASSURANCE CO. OF CANADA 1993– ; joined Sun Life 1978; worked in corp. actuarial 1978–82; in pensions 1982–88; in investments 1988– ; Officer 1985; Dir., Pension Systems 1986; Vice-Pres., Asset Mngt. 1990; Woodrow Wilson Fellowship; F.C.I.A. and F.S.A. 1985; Office: 150 King St. W., Toronto, Ont. M5H 1J9.

**SHARMA, Arjun D.,** B.Sc., M.D., FRCPC, FACC, FACP; physician; executive; b. Bombay, India 2 June 1953; s. Hari D. and Gudrun C. S.; e. Univ. of Waterloo, B.Sc. 1972; Univ. of Toronto, M.D. 1976; m. Carolyn d. Marguerite Burleigh 9 May 1981; children: Allira, Eric, Harrison; DIR., INTERVENTIONAL ELECTROPHYSIOLOGY, SUTTER MEMORIAL HOSP. 1990– ; Partner, Diagnostic and Interventional Cardiology Consultants; Rsch. Assoc., Washington Univ. 1981–83; Asst. Prof. of Med. 1983–88, Hon. Lectr., Pharm. & Toxicol., Univ. of West. Ont. 1985–87; Assoc. Prof. of Med., Univ. of West. Ont., Univ. Hosp. 1988–89; Asst. Prof., Pharm. & Toxicol., Univ. of West Ont. 1988–89; Clinical Assoc. Prof., Univ. of California, Davis 1990– ; Cons., Medtronic Inc.; Sutter Community Hosp. Rsch. Ctte. 1991– ; recipient: John Melady Award 1972; Dr. C.S. Wainwright Scholarship 1973–75; Toronto General Hosp. Prize for Rsch., 1st prize 1980, 2nd prize 1981; Ont. Min. of Health Career Scientist Award 1983–89; Rsch. grants from Medical Rsch. Council and Candn. Heart Foundn. 1983–89; Fellow, Am. College of Physicians 1990; Internal Grants Reviewer, Candn. Heart Foundn. 1988; Session Chrmn., Am. Heart Assn. Scientific session 1989; Annual Scientific Sessions Faculty NASPE 1990, 1991, 1992, 1993; Faculty Am. College of Chest Physicians Annual Sessions 1991; Program Coordinator, 'Electrophysiology: Outlook for the 90's' Sacramento 1991; Mem., Sacramento - Eldorado Medical Soc. 1989– ; California Medical Assn. 1989– ; Extve. Ctte., Sutter Heart Institute 1991– ; Mem., Ont. Med. Assn.; N.Y. Acad. of Sci.; Am. Fed. for Clin. Rsch.; Am. Coll. of Physicians; Royal Coll. of Physicians & Surg.; Am. Coll. of Cardiol.; NASPE; author, 220 scientific publications; reviewer, scientific publications; Office: 3941 J St., Suite 260, Sacramento, Ca 95819.

**SHARMAN, Rodney William,** B.Mus., Reifediplom, Ph.D.; composer; b. Biggar, Sask. 24 May 1958; s. John Clifford and Irene Evelyn Iva (Stockman) S.; e. Victoria Conservatory of Music; Univ. of Victoria School of Music B.Mus. 1980; Staatliche Hochschule für Musik, Reifediplom 1985; State Univ. of N.Y. at Buffalo Ph.D. 1991; num. performances in Canada, U.S., Eur., S. Am., Australia & Hong Kong incl. the Almeida Fest. U.K. 1990, Huddersfield Fest. U.K. 1987, '89, '93, Bang on a Can N.Y. 1991, '93, Confrontaties (portrait concert) Rotterdam 1991, Complexity? Netherlands 1990, Holland Fest. 1985, '93, Bourges France 1987, Gaudeamus Netherlands 1984, Darmstadt Summer Courses for New Music Germany 1986, '88, '90, '92; performers incl. Montreal, Vanc. & Victoria Symph. Orchs., CBC Van. Orch., Netherlands Ballet Orch., Arraymusic, Ensemble SMCQ, Het Nieuw Ensemble, Arditti String Quartet; many soloists incl. Erica Goodman, harp; Yvar Mikhashoff, Anthony de Mare, James Clapperton, piano; Colin Tilney, harpischord; Asst. Prof., Simon Fraser Univ. 1992–93, Sessional Lectr. 1993– ; Sessional Lectr., UBC 1991–92; Wilfrid Laurier Univ. 1990–91; Guest Composer, Inst. of Sonology, Utrecht, Netherlands 1983–84; Guest Lectr., Darmstadt 1986, '88, '90, '92, Rotterdam Conservatory, McGill etc.; Flutist, Stadttheaterorchester, Freiburg im Breigau, Germany 1981–83; 1990 Kranichsteiner Music Prize; 1986 Tuition Prize Darmstadt; 1st Prize, 1984 CBC Nat. Radio Comp. for Young Composers, etc.; Council, Candn. League of Composers 1988– ; Sec. 1989– , Pres. 1993– ; Pres., Internat. Soc. for Contemp. Music, Candn. Section 1991– ; Voting Mem., Candn. Music Centre; Mem., SOCAN; selected works: 'Echo and Narcissus' 1990–91, 'Phantom Screen' 1991, 'In Deepening Light' 1989, 'Opera Transcriptions: Turandot' 1989, 'Madama Butterfly' 1990, 'La Rondine' 1991, 'The Proximity of Mars' 1988, 'Dark Glasses' 1988, 'Erstarrung' 1984, 'Chiaroscuro' 1982; discography: 'Cordes Vides,' 'Companion Piece,' 'Dark Glasses,' 'The Proximity of Mars', 'Erstarrung'; recreations: swimming, weight training, languages; clubs: YMCA; Home: #804 – 1025 Gilford St., Vancouver, B.C. V6G 2P2; Office: School for the Contemporary Arts, Simon Fraser Univ., Burnaby, B.C. V5A 1S6.

**SHARP, Alfred Edward,** P.Eng.; energy consultant; b. Winnipeg, Man. 25 June 1925; s. Alfred and Elizabeth (Duff) S.; e. McGill Univ. Chem. Engr. 1951; children: Valerie, George, Stephen, David; m. Wendy Jane d. John L. Neilans 25 Aug. 1984; PRES., A.E. SHARP AND ASSOCIATES LTD. 1987– ; PRES., A.E. SHARP LIMITED 1987– ; PRES., A.E. SHARP CONSULTANTS LTD. 1980– ; Engr., North American Cyanamid Ltd. 1951–55; Vice Pres. Operations, Greater Winnipeg Gas Co. 1955–67; Vice Pres. Utility Operations Northern and Central Gas Corp. Ltd. 1967; Pres. and Dir. Gaz Metropolitain, Inc. 1967–76; Pres., C.E.O. & Dir., H. Zinder and Associates Canada Ltd., and Dir. Zinder Companies Inc. (Washington, D.C.) 1976–80; mem. Assn. Profl. Engrs. Ont.; Assn. Profl. Engrs. Que.; Candn. Gas Assoc.; Ont. Natural Gas Assn.; Anglican; recreations: music, woodwork, reading; Home: 276 Hounslow Ave., Willowdale, Ont. M2N 2B8; Office: 903, 2 Sheppard Ave. E., Willowdale, Ont. M2N 5Y7.

**SHARP, Isadore;** hotel executive; b. Toronto, Ont. 8 Oct. 1931; s. Max and Lena (Godfrey) S.; e. Forest Hill Coll. Inst., Toronto; Ryerson Inst. (Honours in Arch. 1952 and Silver Medal for Outstanding Academic Achievement and Extra-Curricular Activity); m. Rosalie, d. Joseph Wise, 6 Sept. 1955; four s. Jordon, Gregory, Anthony, Christopher (dec.); CHAIRMAN, PRESIDENT & C.E.O., FOUR SEASONS HOTELS INC. and its principal operating co., Four Seasons Hotels Ltd.; entered hotel industry 1960, opened first Four Seasons Hotel in downtown Toronto 1961; Four seasons currently owns or operates 28 properties in the U.S., Canada, Japan, Indonesia, Italy, Mexico, Singapore and the Caribbean; and 11 Regent hotels in Asia, Australia, New Zealand, the South Pacific, the United Kingdom, and the U.S.; Dir., Terry Fox Humanitarian Award Program; Dir., Council for Candn. Unity; Dir., Bank of Nova Scotia; Dir., Bank of Nova Scotia Trust Co.; Dir., Clairvest Group Inc.; Dir. Adv. Bd., The Financial Post; Mem. of Bd., Mt. Sinai Hospital; Mem. of Bd., Governors' Council of North York Gen. Hospital; Apptd. Premier's Advisory Ctte. on Extve. Resources, Province of Ont.; Officer, Order of Canada 1993; recreations: tennis, skiing; Clubs: Devil's Glen Ski; York Racquets; Office: 1165 Leslie St., Don Mills, Ont. M3C 2K8.

**SHARP, Hon. Mitchell W.,** P.C., O.C., B.A., D.Sc., LL.D.; b. Winnipeg, Man. 11 May 1911; s. Thomas and Elizabeth S.; e. Univ. of Manitoba, B.A. 1934, LL.D. 1965; London Sch. of Economics 1937; Univ. of Ottawa D.Sc. 1970; Univ. W. Ont. LL.D. 1977; Officer, Order of Can. 1983; m. Daisy Boyd (dec'd), 23 April 1938; one s. Noel; m. Jeannette Dugal, 14 April 1976; PERSONAL ADVISER TO PRIME MINISTER OF CANADA 1993– ; Commr., Northern Pipeline Agency 1978–88; concurrently Co-Chrmn. of Task Force on Conflict of Interest July 1983–May 1984; Appts. incl. Offr., Dept. of Finance, Ottawa 1942–51; Dir. of Economic Policy Div. 1947–51; Assoc. Depy. Min. of Trade and Commerce 1951–57; Depy. Min. 1957–58; Min. of Trade & Comm. 1963–65; Min. of Finance 1965–68; Secy. of State for External Affairs 1968–74; Pres. Privy Council and Leader of Govt., H. of C. 1974–76; (resigned from Cabinet 1976); resigned from Parlt. 1 May 1978; Liberal; United Church; Home: 33 Monkland Ave., Ottawa, Ont. K1S 1Y8.

**SHARPE, C. Richard,** B.A.; executive; b. St. Catharines, Ont. 11 Feb. 1925; e. St. Catharines, Ont.; Univ. of W. Ont. B.A. (hons.) (Business Adm.); m. Peggy Pepler; one s., three d.; CHRMN. & DIR. SEARS CANADA INC. 1989– ; Chrmn. Sears Acceptance Co. Inc.; Vice Chair & Dir., Liquor Control Bd. of Ont.; Dir. Bell Canada; B.C.E. Inc.; Canadian Imperial Bank of Commerce; Mediacom Inc.; Noranda Forest Inc.; Omers Realty Corp.; Wellesley Hosp.; Mem. Toronto Commercial Advisory Council, Royal LePage Limited; joined Simpsons Ltd. Toronto 1950 continuing with Simpsons-Sears Ltd. upon formation 1953; held various positions incl. Buyer, Merchandise Mgr., Gen. Merchandise Mgr.; apptd. Vice Pres. Merchandising 1970; apptd. Chrmn. & C.E.O. 1979; Served overseas as pilot with RCAF 1943–46; Jet Flying Reserve 1950–55; Past Chrmn. and Dir., Retail Council Can.; Past Nat. Chrmn. and Dir., Jr. Achievement of Can.; Chrmn. of Bd. of Govs., Sir Edmund Hillary Foundation; Gov., Jr. Achievement of Peel Region; Member, Advisory Council, School of Business Admin., University of Western Ontario; Adv. Bd., Boys' and Girls' Clubs of Can.; Gov., Olympic Trust of Can.; recipient, National Retail Merchants Assn. (NRMA) Internat. Award 1987; Fellow, Ryerson Polytechnical Inst. 1988; recipient, Retail Council of Canada's Distinguished Candn. Retailer Award 1990; Hon. Colonel, 436 Transport Squadron 1992; awarded Commemorative Medal for 125th Anniversary of Candn. Confederation; recreations: golf, fishing, skiing; Clubs: Toronto; York; Toronto Golf; University; Home: 759 Cardinal Pl., Mississauga, Ont. L5J 2R8; Office: 222 Jarvis St., Toronto, Ont. M5B 2B8.

**SHARPE, Gilbert Stanley,** LL.M.; provincial civil servant; lawyer; b. Toronto, Ont. 2 Apl. 1944; s. David (Shopsowitz) and Laura (Petegorsky) S.; e. Univ. of Toronto B.A. 1966; York Univ. and Univ. of Texas Clin. Psychol. 1966–69; Osgoode Hall Law Sch. LL.B. 1972, LL.M. 1973; DIR. OF LEGAL SERVICES, MIN. OF HEALTH ONT. 1987– ; Part-time Prof. of Health Sci's McMaster Univ. 1986– , Chrmn. Health Sect. Postgrad. Acad. Studies, Part-time Assoc. Prof. 1976–86; Visiting Prof., Faculties of Law, Medicine, Dentistry, Health Professions and Health Administration, Dalhousie Univ. 1993; Visiting Prof., Institute for Health Law, Loyola Univ., Chicago 1994; Asst. Prof. of Law Univ. of Ottawa and Visiting Prof. of Med. 1973–75; Legal Counsel present Min. 1975–87; Chief Mental Disorder Project Criminal Law Review Dept. of Justice 1981–87; mem. Clin. Ethics Ctte. Chedoke-McMaster Hosps.; cons. World Health Orgn. and other nat. and internat. orgns.; author: Ont. Mental Health Act, Independent Health Facilities Act, Consent to Treatment Act, Mental Disorder Amendments to the Criminal Code; 'The Law and Medicine in Canada' 1987; 'HIV Seroprevalence Studies Report' 1991; co-author 'Doctors and the Law' 1977; ed.-in-chief Health Law in Can. 1976– ; mem. Candn. Inst. Law & Med. (Pres.); Internat. Acad. Law & Mental Health (Dir.); Law Soc. Upper Can.; Variety Club; Am. Coll. Legal Med.; Am. Soc. Law & Med.; Co. of York Law Assn.; recreations: golf, tennis, scouts; Club: National; Home: 34 Vesta Dr., Toronto, Ont. M5P 2Z5; Office: 10F Hepburn Block, 80 Grosvenor St., Toronto, Ont. M7A 1S2.

**SHARPE, Marjorie Mary Alice Johnston,** B.A., M.S.; foundation executive; b. Toronto, Ont. 5 June 1931; d. Charles Franklin and Dorice Phoebe (Brown) J.; e. Forest Hill Village Schools 1948; Univ. of Toronto, B.A. 1951; Nat. Coll. of Education (Evanston, Ill.) M.S. 1984; m. Alexander Beatty s. Alexander and Emma S. 27 July 1968; one s.: Gordon Franklin Cheesbrough; two stepsons: Alexander Beatty Sharpe III, Stephen Roberts Sharpe; Pres. & Chief Extve. Offr., Community Foundation for Greater Toronto 1985– ; Teacher, North York Bd. of Edn. 1959–68; Nat. Bd. Mem. & 1st Vice-Pres., Assn. of Jr. Leagues (N.Y.) 1974–77 (served several task forces); Extve. Dir., Am. Dental Hygienists' Assn. (Chicago) 1981–84; Pres., Sharpe & Assoc. 1977–81, 1984–85; Am. Soc. of Allied Health Professions, Inc., Visiting Nurse Assn. of Chicago, Inc., Taylor Inst., Inc. 1984–85; Pres. Ctte. for Employment of the Handicapped, Women's Ctte. 1984–85; Bd. Mem., Candn. Paraplegic Assn. Ont. 1990–94; Chair., Found. Ctte.,

Candn. Ctr. for Philanthropy 1987–94; Bd. mem., Community Foundations of Can. 1992–94; mem., Council of Foundations' Ctte. on Community Foundations, Washington, D.C. 1991–94; recreations: golf, tennis, swimming; clubs: Badminton & Racquet, Toronto Cricket Skating & Curling; Home: 7 North Sherbourne, Toronto, Ont. M4W 2S9.

**SHARPE, Robert James,** B.A., LL.B., D.Phil.; lawyer; b. Brantford, Ont. 4 Dec. 1945; s. Ira Sutherland and Eleanor Jane (Cooper) S.; e. Univ. of W. Ont., B.A. 1966; Univ. of Caen, France, Certificat Pratique de Langue Française 1968; Univ. of Toronto, LL.B. 1970; Oxford Univ., D.Phil. 1974; m. Geraldine d. Alice and Frederick Bull 14 Sept. 1968; children: Anne, Claire, Stephen; DEAN, FACULTY OF LAW, UNIV. OF TORONTO 1990– ; called to Bar of Ont. 1974; Assoc. MacKinnon, McTaggart subsequently McTaggart, Potts, Stone & Herridge 1974–76; joined present Univ. 1976, Prof. of Law 1983– ; Dir. Constitutional Litigation Prog. 1985–87; Extve. Legal Officer, Supreme Court of Canada 1988–90; author 'The Law of Habeas Corpus' 1976 (2nd ed. 1989); 'Interprovincial Product Liability Litigation' 1982; 'Injunctions and Specific Performance' 1983 (2nd ed. 1992); 'Charter Litigation' 1987; 'The Last Day, The Last Hour: The Currie Libel Trial' 1988; numerous periodical articles; Home: 103 Glenview Ave., Toronto, Ont. M4R 1R1; Office: Faculty of Law, 78 Queen's Pk., Toronto, Ont. M5S 2C5.

**SHARWOOD, Gordon Robertson,** B.A., M.A.; investment banker and financier; b. Montreal, Que. 26 Feb. 1932; s. late Robert W. and Joan M. H. Sharwood; e. Selwyn House Sch., Montreal; Bishop's Coll. Sch., Lennoxville, Que.; McGill Univ.; Oxford Univ.; Harvard Univ.; two s., one d.; PRES., SHARWOOD AND COMPANY, investment bankers and finan. consults.; Dir., Candn. Pacific Express and Transport; Dover Industries; Nu-Tech Precision Metals Inc.; Family Trust Corp.; Go Vacations Inc.; Founder & Hon. Chrmn., Candn. Assoc. of Family Enterprise; joined The Canadian Bank of Commerce, Montreal, 1956; Assistant Manager, Hamilton, Ont., 1957; Assistant Manager, Vancouver, B.C., 1958; Manager, Economics Department, Toronto, 1959; Agent, New York, 1960; Asst. Gen. Mgr., Canadian Imperial Bank of Commerce, Toronto 1962; Regional Gen. Mgr., Toronto, 1963; Depy. Chief Gen. Mgr., H.O., 1966; Chief Gen. Mgr. 1968–69; Chrmn. Extve. Comte., Traders Group Ltd., Toronto 1970; Vice Chrmn. and Vice Pres., Guaranty Trust Co. of Can. 1971; el. Pres. 1972 and Chrmn. 1975; founded Sharwood and Co., 1976; Dir., C.D. Howe Inst.-HIPAC (Exec.), The Nat. Youth Orchestra; Hon. Dir., Public Policy Forum (Ottawa); Clubs: Toronto; Toronto Golf; Badminton & Racquet; Alpine Ski; Office: 8 King St. E., #300, Toronto, Ont. M5C 1B5.

**SHATNER, William,** B.A.; actor; b. Montreal, Que. 22 March 1931; s. Joseph and Anne Shatner; e. McGill Univ. B.A. 1952; m. 1stly Gloria Rand 12 Aug. 1956 (divorced 1969); m. 2ndly Marcy Lafferty 20 Oct. 1973; 3 d.; stage debut 1952; appeared Montreal Playhouse summers 1952, 1953; juvenile roles Candn. Repertory Theatre Ottawa 1952–53, 1953–54; appeared Stratford (Ont.) Festival 1954–56; Broadway appearances incl. 'Tamburlaine the Great' 1956; 'The World of Suzie Wong' 1958; 'A Shot in the Dark' 1961; films incl. 'The Brothers Karamazov' 1958; 'The Explosive Generation' 1961; 'Judgement at Nuremburg' 1961; 'The Instruder' 1962; 'The Outrage' 1964; 'Dead of Night' 1974; 'The Devil's Rain' 1975; 'Star Trek' 1979; 'Star Trek II: The Wrath of Kahn' 1981; 'Star Trek III: Search for Spock' 1983; 'Star Trek IV: The Voyage Home' 1985; 'Star Trek V: The Final Journey' 1989; 'Star Trek VI: The Undiscovered Country' 1991; 'Loaded Weapon' 1992; TV movies and appearances incl. 'Omnibus,' 'Studio One,' 'U.S. Steel Hour,' 'Alfred Hitchcock Presents,' 'Naked City,' 'Alcoa Premiere,' 'Twilight Zone,' 'Bob Hope Chrysler Theatre,' 'Name of the Game,' 'Mission Impossible,' 'Testimony of Two Men,' 'The Tenth Level,' 'The Andersonville Trial'; star TV Series 'Star Trek' 1966–69, animated series 1973–75; 'Barbaray Coast' 1975–76; 'The Bastard' 1978; 'Disaster on the Coastliner' 1979; 'T.J. Hooker' 1981–86; 'TekWar' 1994; rec'd Tyrone Guthrie Award 1956; Theatre World Award 1958; mem. Actors Equity Assn.; A.F.T.R.A.; Screen Actors Guild; A.C.T.A.; Address: c/o Larry Thompson Orgn., 1440 S. Sepulueda Blvd., Suite 118, Los Angeles, CA 90025.

**SHATTNER, Jerome,** B.Eng.; computer industry executive; b. Montreal, Que. 9 Sept. 1945; s. Moe Elliot and Florence (Shindler) S.; e. Outremont H.S. 1962; McGill Univ., B.Eng. 1968; m. Carol d. Walter and Violet Palac 20 Dec. 1969; children: Michael, Andrea; PRES., HITACHI DATA SYSTEMS 1987– ; management, marketing & technical positions, IBM Canada 1968–79; Principal & Co-founder, LGS Data Processing Con. 1979–83; Co-founder, Sand Technology Systems Internat. Inc. 1983– ; Office: Ste. 7000, 380 Saint-Antoine St. W., Montreal, Que. H2Y 3X7.

**SHAUL, Sandra Marcia,** B.A., Maître-ès-Lettres; editor; b. Buffalo, N.Y. 18 Apl. 1950; d. David Lloyd and Shirley (Rapp) S.; e. Bathurst Hts. Secondary Sch. Toronto 1968; York Univ. B.A. 1972; Univ. de Paris X Maître-ès-Lettres 1973; m. Christopher John s. Peter and Elizabeth Watt Varley 18 Apl. 1986; EXEC. ED. ROTUNDA MAG. ROYAL ONT. MUSEUM 1985– , Head, Publications and Print Services, ROM 1991– ; contbg. ed. 'Artmagazine' 1973–76, assoc. ed. special issue on sculpture 1977–78; part-time course dir. Fine Arts Atkinson Coll. York Univ. 1975–79; helped to organize fundraising body and curator Habourfront Art Gallery Toronto 1978–79; Supr. Publs./Assoc. Curator The Edmonton Art Gallery 1979–82; Prodn. Mgr. Key Porter Books 1982–85; recipient Doctoral Scholarship Govt. of France 1973–76; author 'A Popular Guide to Canada's Museums and Art Galleries' forthcoming; numerous catalogues, articles, reviews; mem. Candn. Magazine Publishers' Assn. Publicity Ctte.; mem. Candn. Reprography Collective; Candn. Soc. of Magazine Editors (Treas.); Jewish; recreations: cooking, hiking, reading, running; Club: Bruce Trail; Home: 6 Kendal Ave., Toronto, Ont. M5R lL6; Office: 100 Queen's Park, Toronto, Ont. M5S 2C6.

**SHAVER, Alan Garnet,** B.Sc., Ph.D.; university professor; b. Brockville, Ont. 17 Dec. 1946; s. Garnet John William and Edna Jane (Bowen) S.; e. Carleton Univ. B.Sc. 1969; M.I.T. Ph.D. 1972; PROFESSOR, DEPT. OF CHEMISTRY, MCGILL UNIV. 1989– ; Postdoct. Fellow, Univ. of W. Ont. 1972–74; Teaching Postdoct. Fellow 1974–75; Asst. Prof., McGill Univ. 1975–79; Assoc. Prof. 1979–89; Chair 1991– ; Mem., Chem. Inst. of Can.; Am. Chem. Soc.; Assn. of the Chem. Profession of Ont.; author of over 100 peer-reviewed articles and papers; Office: Montreal, Que. H3A 2K6.

**SHAVER, Donald McQ.,** O.C., D.Sc.; executive; b. Galt, Ont. 12 Aug. 1920; s. James Earl and Betsy Duncan S.; e. McGill Univ. Honorary D.Sc. 1983; children: Donald Jr., Jill, Wendy, Jonathon; FOUNDER AND CHIEF EXEC. OFFR. D. McQ. SHAVER BEEF BREEDING FARMS (INT'L) LTD. 1985– ; Chrmn. and Chief Exec. Offr. Deemcque Investments Ltd.; Dir.: Gore Mutual Insurance Co.; Canada Development Investment Corp.; Founder and Chief Exec. Offr. Shaver Poultry Breeding Farms Ltd. until 1985; mem. Candn. Agric. Hall of Fame; Am. Poultry Hall of Fame; Charter mem. World's Poultry Sci. Hall of Fame; Entrepreneur-in-Residence Univ. of Guelph 1985; Trustee, Univ. of Guelph Heritage Fund; Pres.'s Council; Dir. Cambridge Meml. Hosp. 1986; mem. Pres's Council Univ. of Waterloo; Hon. Col. The Highland Fusiliers Can. 1988; Life mem. Am. Poultry Hist. Soc.; Hon. Life mem. Ont. Profl. Agrols.; Home: R.R.6, Cambridge, Ont. N1R 5S7; Office: Box 817, Cambridge, Ont. N1R 5W6.

**SHAW, Allan Cameron,** B.Sc., M.B.A.; manufacturer; b. Halifax, N.S. 23 Nov. 1942; s. Ronald Harry S.; e. Queen Elizabeth High Sch. Halifax 1960; Dalhousie Univ. B.Sc. 1964; Harvard Business Sch. M.B.A. 1971; m. Leslie Ann d. Frederick Alexander Baldwin, Halifax, N.S. 30 July 1965; children: Lisa Gabrielle, Sarah Naomi; PRES., GEN. MGR. & DIR., THE SHAW GROUP LTD. (formerly L.E. Shaw Ltd.) since 1979; Pres. and Dir. L.E. Shaw Transport Ltd.; Nova Scotia Sand & Gravel Ltd.; Suburban Industries Ltd.; Dir. Clayton Developments Ltd.; held various positions Pyramid Structural Concrete Div. of present co. incl. Mgr. 1964–69, Vice Pres. Mfg. 1971–74; mem. Voluntary Planning Bd. Prov. of N.S., Dir. and Chrmn. Mfg. Sector; Am. Concrete Pipe Assn. (Dir. 1970–73, Chrmn. Candn. Region 1973); Nat. Concrete Producers Assn. (Dir. 1971–77, Pres. 1975); Clay Brick Assn. Can. (Dir. 1972, Pres. 1976–77); Constr. Mang. Labor Bureau Ltd. (Dir. 1975, Chrm. 1978); Unitarian; recreation: tennis; Clubs: Waegwoltic; Burnside Tennis; Halifax; Home: 6463 Coburg Rd., Halifax, N.S. B3H 2A6; Office: P.O. Box 996, Halifax, N.S. B3J 2X1.

**SHAW, Denis Martin,** M.A., Ph.D., F.R.S.C. (1961); geochemist; university professor emeritus; b. St. Annes, Lancs., England, 20 Aug. 1923; s. Norman Wade and Alice Jane Sylvia (Shackleton) S.; e. Emmanuel Coll., Cambridge, B.A. 1943, M.A. 1948; Univ. of Chicago (Salisbury Fellow), Ph.D. 1951; m. Doris Pauline, d. late Dr. C. A. Mitchell, Ottawa, Ont., 6 April 1946; divorced; children: Geoffrey, Gillian, Peter; m. 2ndly, Susan Louise Evans, d. Dr. E.L. Evans, Port Credit, Ont. 9 April 1976; EMERITUS PROF., McMASTER UNIV. 1989; mem. of the Faculty, McMaster Univ. since 1949; Chrmn., Dept. of Geol. 1953–59, 1962–66; Dean of Grad. Studies 1979–84; part-time Geol. Offr. with Ont. Dept. of Mines 1949, 1950, 1958 and with Que. Dept. of Mines 1954–56; Visiting Prof. at Ecole Nat. Supérieur de Géol., Univ. de Nancy, 1959–60, Inst. de Minéralogie, Univ. de Genève, 1966–67; served in 2nd World War with R.A.F. Transport Command, Signals Offr., 1943–46; Publications: about 100 articles in scient. journs.; former Ed. 'Geochimica et Cosmochimica Acta'; mem. Geochem. Soc.; Mineral. Soc. Can.; Willet G. Miller Medal of Roy. Soc. of Can., 1981; Past Presidents' Medal: Mineral. Soc. Can., 1985; Chrmn. Awards Ctte., Roy. Soc. Can., 1982–93; Home: 1801 – 130 St. Joseph's Dr., Hamilton, Ont. L8N 2E8.

**SHAW, Donald Reginald,** P.Adm., F.C.I.S.; b. Toronto, Ont. 14 Oct. 1928; s. William Reginald and Lillian (McBride) S.; e. Oriole Park P.S.; N. Toronto Coll. Inst. 1948; Shaw Colls. 1950; m. Patricia Mae d. LeRoy and Mabel Drew 28 Apl. 1952; 4 d. Jo-Anne Derry, Cynthia Jean Aldred, Donna Lorraine McKenna, Penelope Lillian DePiero; CONSULTANT FOR BUSINESS EDUCATION (associated with Shaw Colleges) 1990– ; joined Shaw Colleges 1950 (Pres. Shaw Colleges Ltd. 1976–90); Pres., The Fashion Inst. of Canada 1973–90; Past Dir., Assn. Candn. Career Colls. (Pres. 1966–67); mem. Guild Ind., Comm. & Instl. Accts.; Bd. Trade Metrop. Toronto; Business Education Relations Ctte.; Past Pres., Private Career Edn. Council Ont. 1982–83; Inst. of Chartered Secretaries and Administrators in Canada; Founding mem. Candn. Fedn. Independent Bus.; National Comnr., National Accreditation Comm.; Past Pres., Kiwanis Club of Toronto Found.; Past Pres., Kiwanis Club of Toronto; 32 degree Mason (P.M. Harmony Lodge) Shriner; recreations: cottaging, boating, curling; Clubs: Granite; Thornhill Country; Home: 126 Cambridge Cres., Richmond Hill, Ont. L4C 6G3.

**SHAW, Donna Mary,** B.Sc.Pharm.; association executive; b. Brandon, Man. 30 May 1935; s. James Jordan and Mary Fleming (Gilmour) Jones; e. Oakwood H.S.; Brandon College; Univ. of Manitoba B.Sc.Pharm. 1959; divorced; EXECUTIVE DIRECTOR, CANDN. FOUNDATION FOR PHARMACY 1987– ; Staff Pharmacist, St. Boniface Gen. Hosp. 1957–62; Dir. of Pharm. 1962–67; Sessional Lectr., Univ. of Manitoba 1959–67; Staff Pharm., St. Michael's Hosp. 1969–74; Extve. Dir., Candn. Soc. of Hosp. Pharm. (CSHP) 1967–87; Bus. Mgr., 'Can. J. of Hospital Pharm.' 1982–87; Vice-Pres., CSHP 1965–66; Pres. 1966–67; Dir., Candn. Found. for Pharm. 1979–87; Sec.-Treas., Candn. Hosp. Pharm. Residency Bd. 1977–87; CSHP Bd. of Fellows 1968–87; Pres., Candn. Bd. of Specialties in Pharm. 1989–90; CSHP, Ortho Distinguished Service 1985; CPhA Meritorious Serv. 1988; Hon. Mem., Am. Soc. Hosp Pharm. 1983; Zeta Tau Alph Fraternity, Cert. of Merit 1979, Honor Ring 1966; Pres., ZTA, Toronto Alumnae Chapt. 1979–82, 1989–92; ZTA, Dist. Pres. 1982–89; Pres., Toronto Chapter, Candn. Soc. of Assn. Extves. 1981–82; CSAE Nat. Chrmn. 1984–85; Chrmn., Past Chief Elected Offrs. Roundtable 1988– ; Hon. Life Mem., CSAE 1992; Mem. & Chrmn. of num. cttes.; recreations: curling, riding, walking, fitness, reading, theatre, music; clubs: Lambton Golf & Country; Home 1810 – 55 Maitland St., Toronto, Ont. M4Y 1C9; Office: 603 – 123 Edward St., Toronto, Ont. M5G 1E2.

**SHAW, The Hon. Mr. Justice Duncan Weld,** B.A., LL.B.; supreme court judge; b. Vancouver, B.C. 21 Nov. 1932; s. Duncan Keith and Gladys Noyes (Weld) S.; e. Prince of Wales H.S. 1950; Univ. of B.C., B.A. 1955, LL.B. 1956; m. Patricia d. Albert and Elizabeth Gardner 1 Apr. 1961; children: Madeleine G., R. Keith; JUDGE OF THE SUPREME COURT OF B.C. 1987– ; Barrister & Solicitor, Davis & Co. 1958–87; Queen's Counsel 1982; Fellow, Am. Coll. of Trial Lawyers 1982; Dir., Univ. Hospital Foundation; Past Chrmn., Legal Serv. Soc. of B.C.; Home: 1389 Matthews Ave., Vancouver, B.C. V6H 1W7; Office: 800 Smithe St., Vancouver, B.C. V6Z 2E1.

**SHAW, Edgar Albert George,** B.Sc., Ph.D., F.R.S.C.; physicist; b. Teddington, Middlesex, Eng. 10 July 1921; s. Albert and Lily Florence (Hill) S.; e. Harrow Co. Sch. Eng. 1937; Acton Tech. Coll. London 1938–40; Imp. Coll. Univ. of London 1946–50, B.Sc., Ph.D.; m. Millicent Selina d. late Arthur Chandler, New York City, N.Y. and Baltimore, Md. 6 Oct. 1945; children: Jennifer, Kenneth; RESEARCHER EMERITUS, INST. FOR MICROSTRUCTURAL SCIENCES, NATIONAL RESEARCH COUNCIL OF CAN. since 1986; Lectr. Univ. of Ottawa 1958–75; Tech. Offr. Ministry of Aircraft Production (London) and Brit. Air Comn. (Washington) 1940–46; Asst. Research Offr. Div. of Physics, Nat. Research Council of Can. 1950–53, Assoc. Research Offr. 1953–60, Sr. Research Offr. 1960–74; Principal Research Offr. 1975–86, Head, Acoustics Sect. 1975–85, inventions incl. Hearing Protector (high-spring constant liquid filled cushion), Improved Earphone (variable effective coupling vol.), Probe Microphone with Horn Coupling; mem. Internat. Comn. on Acoustics 1972–78, Chrmn. 1975–78, Assoc. mem. 1985–87; Comte. on Hearing, Bioacoustics & Biomechanics, U.S. Nat. Acad. of Science, mem. since 1965, Extve. council 1973–75; Candn. Liaison Ctte., Internat. Union of Pure and Applied Physics, Secy. 1978–84, Chrmn. 1984–87; Co-Chrmn., Internat. Comn. on the Biological Effects of Noise 1988–93, Member-at-large 1993– ; author over 50 research papers, book chapters; acoustical waves & vibrations, hearing measurements, hearing protection, physiol. acoustics, urban noise, electroacoustics; Fellow, Royal Soc. of Can.; Fellow, Acoustical Soc. Am. (Vice Pres. 1968–70, Pres. 1973–74); Fellow, Inst. of Acoustics (Brit.); rec'd Rayleigh Medal awarded by Institute of Acoustics (Brit.), 1979; mem. Candn. Assn. Physicists; Inst. of Physics (Brit.); Presbyterian; recreations: walking, cross country skiing, gardening, reading; Home: 1391 Wesmar Dr., Ottawa, Ont. K1H 7T4; Office: Ottawa, Ont. K1A 0R6.

**SHAW, Gary Bruce,** CLU; insurance executive; b. Peterborough, Ont. 28 Sept. 1948; s. George and Helena S.; e. Tottenham Grammar Sch. (U.K.); Printer's College, City & Guilds of London Inst. Dipl. (U.K.); m. Marian d. Allen and Joan Dennis 12 Oct. 1968; one d.: Kirstin Ann Adkins; SENIOR VICE-PRES., DISTRICT SALES DIV., LONDON LIFE INSUR. CO. 1991– ; Sales Rep. Peterborough, Ont., London Life 1978; Staff Manager 1980; Regional Manager 1985; transferred to London as Reg. Mgr. 1987; Reg. Vice-Pres. S.W. Ont. 1988; Vice-Pres., District Sales Div. 1990; recreations: golf, baseball, walking; clubs: Westhaven Golf & Country; Home: 423 Viscount Rd., London, Ont. N6K 1H9; Office: 255 Dufferin Ave., London, Ont. N6A 4K1.

**SHAW, Hon. James Keith,** LL.B.; judge; b. Vancouver, B.C. 10 Jan. 1930; s. Duncan Keith and Gladys Noyes (Weld) S.; e. King Edward High Sch. Vancouver 1947; Univ. of B.C. LL.B. 1955; m. Daphne d. Howell and Lu Harris 11 July 1953; children: Catherine, Susan, Duncan, Jamie, Allison; JUDGE, PROV. COURT NORTH VANCOUVER 1984– ; read law with Guild, Yule & Co. Vancouver 1955–57; called to Bar of B.C. 1956; law practice Prince Rupert, B.C. 1957–68; Magistrate, Coquitlam, Port Coquitlam and Port Moody 3 yrs., Burnaby 3 yrs. 1968–74; Magistrate, Cayman Islands, B.W.I. 1975–77; Judge, Prov. Court New Westminster, B.C. 1977–79; Administrative Judge Coast Dist. 1979–81; Assoc. Chief Judge 1981–84; Home: Mt. Gardner Rd., Bowen Island, B.C. V0N 1G0; Office: 200 E. 23rd St., N. Vancouver, B.C. V7L 4R4.

**SHAW, James M.;** manufacturer; b. Maryland, U.S.A. 4 Sept. 1920; s. James Marvin and Emma (Kiehne) S.; came to Canada 1932; e. Public Sch. and North Toronto Collegiate; McGill Univ.; m. Helena, d. late W. H. A. Verweij, Nijmegen, Netherlands; children: Alexandra Nicole, James Nicholas; PRESIDENT, NOXZEMA CANADA LTD. 1954–78; Hon. Chrmn. 1978; Dir. Noxell Inc. 1966–78; Dir. C.G. Jung Foundation N.Y. 1960–66; Co-founder and Dir., Analytical Psy. Soc. of Ont. 1970, Pres. 1978; co-founder and Pres., West End Productions and West End Studios Ltd. 1974–78; served in 2nd World War Overseas with R.C.A.F., as Pilot; on operations as Flying Offr. with R.A.F. Bomber Sqdn. No. 77 (shot down in Holland, 1944, P.O.W. till 1945); recreations: psychology, history, tennis, sailing, flying; Clubs: R.C.Y.C.; Granite; The Queens (Chart. mem.); Home: 13 Riverside Cres., Toronto, Ont. M6S 1B5.

**SHAW, James Robert,** B.A.; executive; b. Brigden, Ont. 14 Aug. 1934; s. Francis Earl and Lottie Myrtle (Gaw) S.; e. Mich. State Univ. B.A. 1958; m. Carol d. Gordon and Abigail Bulman 21 July 1956; children: James Jr., Heather, Julie, Bradley; PRES., CHRMN. & DIR., SHAW CABLESYSTEMS LTD. 1966– ; Dir. Shaw Industries 1968– ; Pres. Shaw Family Found.; Dir. Mannville Oil & Gas Ltd.; CANCOM; joined Shaw Industries group of companies 1958 serving in various capacities incl. Pres. Western group of co.'s Regina, Edmonton, Vancouver, Calgary; Rotarian; Protestant; recreations: skiing, golf; Club: Mayfair Golf & Country; Edmonton Petroleum; Centre; Home: 52129 – Highway 14, Sherwood Park, Alta. T8B 1E2; Office: 7605 – 50 St., Edmonton, Alta. T6B 2W9.

**SHAW, Michael,** M.Sc., Ph.D., D.Sc., F.R.S.C.; scientist; b. Barbados, W.I. 11 Feb. 1924; s. Anthony and Myra (Perkins) S.; e. Lodge Sch., Barbados, W.I. (1935–43); McGill Univ., B.Sc. (1st Class Hons. Botany), 1946, M.Sc. 1947, Ph.D. 1949; Post doctoral Fellow Bot. Sch., Cambridge, Eng. (1949–50); Ph.D. ad eund. Univ. Sask. 1971; D.Sc. (Honoris causa) McGill Univ. 1975; m. Jean Norah, d. late N.W. Berkinshaw, 16 Oct. 1948; children: Christopher Anthony, Rosemary Ellen, Nicholas Richard, Andrew Lawrence; UNIVERSITY PROFESSOR EMERITUS, UNIVERSITY OF B.C. 1989– ; Univ. Prof. 1983–89; Prof. Agric. Botany, 1967–83; Dean, Faculty Agric. Sciences 1967–75; Vice Pres. (Acad.) 1975–81; Vice Pres. (Acad.) and Provost Univ. B.C., 1981–83; Associate Professor of Biol., University of Saskatchewan, 1950–54; Professor 1954–67 and Head of Dept. 1961–67; Fellow Royal Soc. of Can., 1962; mem. Biol. Council of Can. (Pres. 1972 and 1987–89); Am. Soc. Plant Physiols; Am. Phytopath Soc.; Candn. Soc. Plant Physiols. (Pres. 1963); Candn. Phytopath. Soc.; Candn. Bot. Assn. (Pres. 1980); N.Y. Acad. of Sciences; Science Council Study Group on Agric., 1966–67; Research Ctte., Candn. Agric. Svces. Co-ord. Comte., Candn. Dept. of Agric., 1967–75; Adv. Council, Western Coll. of Vet. Med., Univ. of Sask., 1967–75; Sci. Council of Can., 1976–82; Nat. Scis. and Engn. Res. Council of Can. 1978–80; rec'd. Gold Medal, Candn. Soc. Plant Physiols. 1971; Fellow, Am. Phytopath. Soc. 1973; Flavelle Medal, Roy. Soc. of Can. 1976; Queen's Jubilee Medal 1977; Gold Medal, Biol. Council of Canada, 1983; Fellow, N.Y. Acad. of Sciences, 1983; Fellow, Candn. Phytopath Soc. 1986; Editor, 'Canadian Journal of Botany,' 1964–79; Ed. Bd., 'Physiological Plant Pathology,' 1971–81; author of over 95 papers in sci. journals; recreations: reading, writing verse, walking, swimming; Home: 1792 Western Parkway, Vancouver, B.C. V6T 1V3.

**SHAW, Neil M.;** company executive; b. Montreal, Que. 31 May 1929; s. Harold LeRoy and Fabiola Marie (McGowan) S.; e. Knowlton (Que.) High Sch. 1946; m. Frances Audrey, d. R.H. Robinson, Knowlton, Que. 7 June 1952; children: David, Michael, Cynthia, Andrea, Sonia; m. 2ndly Elizabeth (Pixie) Mudge Massey 15 Sept. 1985; VICE-CHRMN. REDPATH INDUSTRIES LTD. since 1981 and Dir. since 1972; CHRMN. & C.E., TATE & LYLE PLC, London Eng. 1986–92, Executive Chrmn. Tate & Lyle PLC 1992– ; Chrmn. and Dir., Tate & Lyle Industries Ltd., 1981; Tate and Lyle Holdings Ltd., 1981; Dir.: A.E. Staley Manufacturing Co., Decatur, Illinois, U.S.A.; Tunnel Refineries London, England 1981; United Biscuits (Holdings) PLC; Candn. Imperial Bank of Commerce, Toronto; World Sugar Rsch. Org.; Americare Corp.; Alcantara (Portugal); G.R. Amylum n.v. (Brussels, Belgium); Clerk, Royal Bank of Canada, 1946; Trust Officer, Crown Trust Company, 1947; joined present Co. as Executive Assistant 1954; Merchandising Mgr. 1958; Export Sales Mgr., Tate & Lyle Ltd., London, Eng., 1963; Vice Pres. & Gen. Mgr., Canada & Dominion Sugar Co. Ltd. 1967; Pres., Daymond Ltd. 1969; Pres., Redpath Industries 1972; Companion, British Institute of Management 1981; Chrmn. of Business in the Community 1991; Chrmn. Anglo-Candn. Support Group Care; mem. Counc. of Advisors to the Premier of Que.; mem. Listed Companies Advisory Ctte. 1991; British North American Ctte. 1991; Dir., M & G Inverstment Income Trust 1991; Chrmn., Assn. of Lloyds Members 1991; Partners of the World 1990; mem. Food Assn.; mem. Prince's Youth Business Trust; Adv. Council. Mem., Candn. Universities Soc. of Great Britain (C.U.S.); Candn. Memorial Found.; Youth Enterprise Council; London Enterprise Agency; Gov., Reddy Memorial Hospital; Montreal Memorial Hospital; Fellow, Inst. of Grocery Distrib.; Anglican; recreations: skiing, golf, sailing; Clubs: Toronto Golf; Toronto; Brooks' (London); Office: Tate & Lyle, PLC, Sugar Quay, Lower Thames St., London, Eng.

**SHAW, Robert Fletcher,** C.C. (1967), D.Eng., D.Sc.; consulting engineer; b. Montreal, P.Q. 16 February 1910; s. John Fletcher and Edna Mary Baker (Anglin) S.; e. Pub. Schs. in Montreal, Lethbridge, Calgary, Edmonton and Grad., in Revelstoke, B.C., with Gov. Gen's. Medal in 1925; Revelstoke High Sch., 1928; McGill Univ., B.Eng. (Civil) 1933; D.Sc. (Hon. causa) McMaster 1967; D.Eng. (Hon. causa) Technical Univ. of Nova Scotia; 1967; D.Sc. (Hon. causa) McGill 1985; D.Sc. (hon. causa) Univ. N.B. 1986; m. Johann Alexandra, d. John MacInnes, Toronto, Ont. 24 Dec. 1935; Consultant to Monenco Consultants Limited, 1975–92; Consultant to Dept. of Ind. Devel., Gov't of Nfld. and Labrador, 1979–80; Chrmn. Research Policy Advisory Comte., Centre for Cold Ocean Resources Eng. (C. Core), Memorial Univ. of Nfld., 1981–82; began learning construction business as Labourer in 1933 serving with the Foundation Co. and its subsidiaries, and with Dominion Bridge Co. Ltd., A. Janin & Co. Ltd., Duranceau & Duranceau and Anglin-Norcross Corp. Ltd., in various capacities; apptd. Asst. to Vice-Pres. of Foundation Co. of Can. Ltd. i/c constr. June 1940; subsequently apptd. Asst. to Pres., i/c Design Dept., 1941, 1942; Mgr., Pictou (N.S.) Shipyard Foundation Maritime Ltd., 1943–45; Asst. to Pres. (Engn.) 1946; Mgr., Engn. Dept., 1949; on loan to Dept. of Defence Production, Ottawa, May 1951–Dec. 1952 as Vice-Pres. and Chief Engr. Defence Construction (1951) Ltd., and as Candn. Rep. on N.A.T.O. Engn. Team on Airfield Constr.; Vice-Pres., The Foundation Co. of Can. Ltd., 1950–58; Extve. Vice Pres., 1958–62, Pres., 1962–63; Depy. Commr.-Gen., Vice Pres. and Dir., Candn. Corp. for the 1967 World Exhibition, (Expo'67) 1963–68; Commr. Gen. and Pres., 1968; Vice Principal, McGill Univ. 1968–71; Chrmn. Bd. and Dir., Foundation of Canada Engineering Corp. Ltd. 1969–71; Depy. Min. Dept. of the Environment, 1971–74; Gov., Univ. N.B. 1975–86, Chrmn., 1978–80; Pres., Moneco Pipeline Consultants 1975–78; President, Canadian Assn. for Retarded Children, 1962–65; Mem. Bd. of Dir., Concours International de Musique de Montreal 1966–88; Pres., Grad. Soc. McGill Univ., 1964–65, Gold Medal 1968; Pres., Order of Engrs. Que., 1953; Pres., Engn. Inst. Can. 1975–76, Fellow 1975; Julian C. Smith Medal 1967; Keefer Medal 1979; mem. Assn. of Prof. Engrs. Ont., Gold Medal 1968; Gold Medal, Cdn. Council of P. Eng. 1979; Hon. Chrmn., Engineering Centennial Bd. 1987; Fellow, Candn. Acad. of Eng. 1987; Sigma Chi; Protestant; recreations: swimming, golf, Clubs: Royal Montreal Golf; Montreal Amateur Athletic Assn.; Home: C29, 3980 Cote des Neiges Rd., Montreal, Que. H3H 1W2.

**SHAW, Timothy Milton,** M.A., Ph.D.; educator; b. Surrey, Eng. 27 Jan. 1945; s. Arnold James and Margaret Eleanor S.; e. Windsor Grammar Sch. 1963; Univ. of Sussex B.A. 1967; Univ. of E. Africa M.A. 1970; Princeton Univ. M.A. 1971, Ph.D. 1975; m. Jane L. Parpart d. Elbert and Barbara Little 2 Sept. 1983; children: Benjamin, Amanda; PROF. OF POL. SCI. AND INTERNAT. DEVEL. STUDIES, DALHOUSIE UNIV. 1982– ; Teaching Fellow Makerere Univ. Uganda 1968–70; Asst. Prof. present Univ. 1971–77, Assoc. Prof. 1977–82, Dir. Pearson Inst. Internat. Devel. 1985–87, Internat. Devel. Studies 1985–89, Centre for African Studies 1983–89 & Centre for Foreign Policy Studies 1993– ; Lectr. Univ. of Zambia 1973–74; Visiting Assoc. Prof. Carleton Univ. 1978–79; Visiting Sr. Lectr. Ife (now Obafemi Awolowo) Univ. Nigeria 1979–80; Visiting Prof. Univ. of Zimbabwe 1989; Visiting Prof., Rhodes Univ. South Africa 1993; cons. various nat. and internat. agencies; Hallsworth Rsch. Fellow Univ. of Manchester 1991; recipient various grants since 1981; author: 'Towards A Political Economy For Africa' 1985; 'Reformism & Revisionism in Africa's Political Economy' 1993; co-author: 'Nigeria: Illusions of Power' 1995; co-ed.'Africa Projected' 1985; 'Economic Crisis in Africa' 1985; 'Coping With Africa's Food Crisis' 1989; 'Corporatism in Africa' 1990; 'Africa in World Politics' 1990; 'Peace, Development and Security in the Caribbean' 1990; 'Studies in the Economic History of Southern Africa' 2 vols. 1990 & 1991; 'Prospects for Development & Peace in Southern Africa in the 1990s' 1992; 'Beyond Structural Adjustment in Africa' 1992; 'The Political Economy of the Foreign Policy of ECOWAS States' 1994; 'The South at the End of the Twentieth Century' 1994; gen. ed.: Macmillan Press Series on Internat. Pol. Economy 1984– ; mem. Adv. Bd. Univ. Press of Am. 1978– ; Editorial Bd., 'Third World Quarterly' 1992– ; Pres. Candn. Assn. African Studies 1984–85; Pres., Candn. Assn. Studies Internat. Devel. 1993–94 & Board, WUSC 1989– ; recreations: jogging, swimming, tennis; Club: Waegwoltic; Home: 1143 Studley Ave., Halifax, N.S. B3H 3R8; Office: Halifax, N.S. B3H 4H6.

**SHAW, W. David,** A.M., Ph.D., F.R.S.C.; university professor; b. Ottawa, Ont. 2 July 1937; s. William Edward and Helen Mabel (Graburn) S.; e. Glebe C.I. 1955; Univ. of Toronto, B.A. 1959; Harvard Univ., A.M. 1960, Ph.D. 1963; m. Carol Ann d. Rush Robinson 20 Sept. 1969; children: Catherine Ann, Jennifer Ellen, Margaret Elaine, Carolyn Alyssa, Jeffrey David; PROF. OF ENGLISH, VICTORIA COLL., UNIV. OF TORONTO 1975– ; Asst. Prof., Cornell Univ. 1963–69; Vis. Assoc. Prof., Univ. of Calif. 1968–69; Assoc. Prof., Victoria Coll., Univ. of Toronto 1969–75; Prof. 1975– ; Sr. Killam Rsch. Fellow 1973–74; F.R.S.C. 1985; Connaught Sr. Rsch. Fellow 1989–90; Killam Rsch. Fellow 1991–93; author: 'The Lucid Veil' 1987, 'Tennyson's Style' 1976, 'The Dialectical Temper' 1968 (MLA Book Club Selection), 'Victorians and Mystery: Crises in Representation' 1990 and more than 40 scholarly essays; Ed. Bd. Mem., 'Victorian Poetry' 1975– ; recreations: cycling, swimming, hiking; Home: 166 Grenadier Rd., Toronto, Ont. M6R 1R7; Office: Northrop Frye Hall 324, Victoria Coll., Univ. of Toronto, Toronto, Ont. M5S 1K7.

**SHAY, Ralph Howard,** B.Sc., LL.B., M.B.A.; lawyer; executive; b. Toronto, Ont. 3 Feb. 1951; s. the late Larry Samuel and Hilda (Hauer) S.; e. Univ. of Toronto, B.Sc. 1973; Osgoode Hall Law Sch. LL.B. 1977; York Univ., M.B.A. 1977; m. Heather Marie d. William and the late Dorothy McIntyre 31 May 1987; two d. Karen Dorothy, Julie Allison; EXEC. DIR. OF LISTINGS, TORONTO STOCK EXCHANGE 1985– , also Legal Counsel in litigation proceedings; joined T.S.E. 1979; read law with Fasken & Calvin, Toronto 1977–78; called to Bar of Ont. 1979; guest lectr. Univ. of Toronto, Univ. of W. Ont. and Queen's Univ. law schs.; speaker and panelist numerous seminars and confs. securities law; Exec. Bus. Law Sect. of Candn. Bar Assn. - Ont. 1981–84; mem., Law Soc. Upper Can.; Toronto Film Soc.; Bd. of Trade of Metro. Toronto; recreations: tennis, music, films; Home: 14 Sparwood Crt., Willowdale, Ont. M2M 4B8; Office: 2 First Canadian Place, Toronto, Ont. M5X 1J2.

**SHEA, Robert Edward,** B.Com.; executive; b. Boston, Mass. 8 June 1933; s. Joseph Clarence and Catherine Rossella (McKinnon) S.; e. St. Francis Xavier Univ. B.Com. 1956; Boston Coll. MBA 1960; m. Gertrude Marshall 27 Nov. 1965; children: Robert E. Jr. (deceased 15 June 1983), Kelly Ann, Joseph C. III; PROP. AND DIR., SHEA FINANCIAL GROUP INC., Deran Holding Company Inc., Balcam & Shea Insurance Agency, Inc., Consultant and Risk Managers, Inc.; Dir. Jack Mulqueen Ltd.; ACORN International Inc.; Longwood Professional Building Associates; Pizzeria Regina of America Inc.; National Sea Products Ltd.; Halifax-Dartmouth Industries Ltd.; MBB Helicopter Canada Ltd.; Southern Star Consolidated Corp.; Boston Restaurant Associates; JFRB Realty; Joslin Clinic; joined Connecticut General Life Insurance Co. 1958–60; Trustee, New England Baptist Hospital Corp.; St. Francis Xavier Univ.; Mem., Greater Boston Chamber of Commerce; New England-Canada Business Council; Clubs: Chief Executive Officer; Metropolitan; International Club of Washington; S.B.A.N.E.; Home: 1253 Commonwealth Ave., West Newton, Mass. 02165; Office: 205 Portland St., Boston, Mass. 02114.

**SHEA, Thomas Noble,** F.R.I., C.R.B.; trust and real estate executive; b. Toronto, Ont. 11 June 1932; s. Orville George and Ida Evelyn (Noble) S.; e. Ryerson Polytech. Inst. 1953; Fellow, Real Estate Inst. 1962; C.R.B.; M.T.C.I.; m. Catharine d. Lloyd and Marjorie Grant 17 July 1976; children: Courtney Jane, Cynthia Eliza, Hilary Dawn; PRES. & C.E.O., FAMILY TRUST CORP. (formerly Thos. N. Shea Limited) 1956– ; Past Pres., York Reg. Real Estate Bd.; Ont. Real Estate Assn.; Past Pres., Markham Kiwanis Club; Dir., Trust Cos. Assoc. of Can.; St. John's York Mills Anglican Ch.; mem., Cabbagetown Community Arts Centre Found.; recreations: tennis, skiing; Clubs: Queen's; Granite; Devil's Glenn Ski; Home: 82 Chestnut Park Rd., Toronto, Ont. M4W 1W9.

**SHEA, William René Joseph,** F.R.Sc., B.A., L.Ph., L.Th., Ph.D.; university professor; b. Gracefield, Que. 16 May 1937; s. Herbert Clement and Jeanne Thérèse (Lafrenière) S.; e. Univ. of Ottawa, B.A. 1959; Gregorian Univ., L.Ph. 1959, L.Th. 1963; Univ. of Cambridge, Ph.D. 1968; m. Evelyn d. Rudolf and Emma Fischer 1 May 1970; children: Herbert, Joan-Emma, Louisa, Cecilia, Michael; PROF., DEPT. OF PHILOSOPHY, MCGILL UNIV. 1974– and HYDRO-QUEBEC PROF. OF ENVIRONMENTAL ETHICS 1992– ; Lectr., Univ. of Ottawa 1963–65; Asst. Prof. 1968–72; Assoc. Prof. 1973; Fellow, Can. Counc. 1965–68; Harvard Univ. 1973–74; Assoc. Prof., present univ. 1974–82; Dir. d'études, Ecole des Hautes Etudes en Sci. Sociales, Paris 1982–83; Sec. Gen., Div., Internat. Union of Hist. & Philosophy of Sci. 1981–89 (Pres. 1990–93); Fellow, Inst. for Advanced Study Berlin 1988–89; Mem., Standing Cttee. for Hum., Eur. Sci. Found. 1989– ; Mem., Internat. Acad. of the Hist. of Sci. 1978; FRSC 1989; Knight of the Order of Malta 1993; Mem., Candn. Philos. Assn.; Candn. Soc. for the Hist. of Sci.; Hist. of Sci. Soc.; Philos. of Sci. Assn.; author: 'Galileo's Intellectual Revolution' 1972, 1977 (Ital., French & Span. transl.); 'Copernico, Cartesio, Galileo' 1989, 'The Magic of Numbers and Motion' 1991 (Ital., Span. & French transl.); co-author: 'Galileo's Florentine Residences' 1979; editor of 17 books incl. most recently 'Nature, Experiment, and the Sciences' 1990, 'Creativity in the Arts and Sciences' 1990, 'Persuading Science: The Art of Scientific Rhetoric' 1991; 'Interpreting the World, Science and Society' 1992; recreations: tennis, skiing; club: Faculty; Home: 217 Berkley, Saint Lambert, Que. J4P 3C9; Office: Dept. of Philosophy, McGill Univ., 855 Sherbrooke St. W., Montreal, Que. H3A 2T7.

**SHEAR, Neil Hartley,** B.A.Sc., M.D., FACP; university professor, physician, scientist; b. Toronto, Ont. 10 Dec. 1950; s. Meyer Abraham and Shirley S.; e. Univ. of Toronto B.A.Sc. (Hons.) 1973; McMaster Univ. M.D. 1976; Univ. of Toronto, Internal Medicine FRCP(C) & Am. Bds. 1980, Dermatology 1982; Hosp. for Sick Children, Clin. Pharm., MRC Fellow 1984; m. Suzann d. Edith and Alexander Kronovic; DIR., CLINICAL PHARMACOLOGY, UNIV. OF TORONTO, SUNNYBROOK HEALTH SCIENCE CENTRE AND DRUG SAFETY RSCH. GROUP; Founder & Dir., Adverse Drug Reaction Clinic, Sunnybrook & CosMedic Camouflage Clinic 1985; Dir., Univ. Clin. Pharm. Postgrad. program; Dep. Dir., Univ. Derm. program 1990– ; Dir., Candn. Derm. Assn. 1988–91; Mem./Cons., Drug Quality & Therapeutics Ctte., Ont. Min. of Health 1987– ; Derm. Adv. Bd., U.S. Pharmacopeial 1991– ; Barney Usher Award for Excellence in Derm. Rsch., Candn. Derm. Assn. 1986; Piafsky Young Investigator Award, Candn. Soc. for Clin. Pharm. 1989; Task Force, Sunsense Awareness, Candn. Cancer Soc. (Ont.) 1988–91; Nat. Adv. Ctte. on Risk/Benefit Mngt. of Drugs, Candn. Public Health Assn. 1990– ; Council Mem., Candn. Soc. for Clin. Investigation 1986–88; Sec.-Treas. 1998–91; Rsch. Ctte. Chair, Candn. Assn. of Profs. of Derm. 1988– ; author/co-author of 100 scientific pubs.; editor: 'Dermatologic Pharmacology,' 'Facts about Healthy Hair,' 'Cutaneous Adverse Drug Reactions' 1989; co-editor: 'Le guide-santé du cheveu, pour toutsavoir ...' 1989; Home: 11 Glencedar Rd., Toronto, Ont. M6C 3E9; Office: 2075 Bayview Ave., Toronto, Ont. M4N 3M5.

**SHEARD, Terence G.;** investment counsel; b. Toronto, Ont. 25 Feb. 1925; s. Terence Q.C., O.B.E. and Lorna Gordon (McLean) S.; e. Upper Canada College; Selwyn House School; Univ. of Toronto; m. Judith R. d. Lt. Col. E.A. Baker, M.C. 2 Sept. 1950; children: Gordon T., Robin J., Susan L.; PRESIDENT, SHEARD COULTER LIMITED 1986– ; joined Dominion Securities Ltd. Toronto 1947; London, England 1950–53; Montreal 1954–56; Research Dept. Toronto 1958–64; Partner 1960; elected Dir. 1962; Asst. Gen. Mgr., Investments, Eastern and Chartered Trust Toronto 1965–67; Partner, Martin, Lucas & Sheard 1968–79; Vice-Pres., McLean, Budden Ltd. Toronto 1980–86; Advisory Bd. and Past Pres., CJRT-FM Inc.; Trustee, Sir Ernest MacMillan Mem. Found.; Dir., Dr. R.L. Smith Memorial Fund; Anglican; clubs: Badminton and Racquet, Toronto, Toronto Golf, Craigleith Ski, Madawaska; Home: 6 Lawrence Cres., Toronto, Ont. M4N 1N1; Office: 372 Bay St., Suite 1906, Toronto, Ont. M5H 2W9.

**SHEARER, Robert,** B.Sc.; health agency executive; b. Peterborough, Ont. 15 April 1956; s. James Ronald and Jean Marion (Walker) S.; e. Trent University B.Sc. 1978; Extve. Dir., Candn. Hemophilia Society 1987; worked in non-profit voluntary health agencies in Canada for past 13 years; Home: 60 Riverbrook Rd., Nepean, Ont. K2H 7Z7.

**SHEARER, Ronald Alexander,** M.A., Ph.D.; educator; b. Trail, B.C. 15 June 1932; s. James Boyd Shearer; e. Rossland (B.C.) Primary and High Schs. 1950; Trail (B.C.) High Sch. 1951; Univ. of B.C., B.A. 1954; Ohio State Univ. M.A. 1955, Ph.D. 1959; m. Renate Elizabeth d. late Ernst Selig, Dayton, Ohio Dec. 1956 (divorced); two s. Carl Thomas, Bruce Stephen; PROF. OF ECON., UNIV. OF B.C. 1963– , Head of Econ. 1972–76, Asst. to Vice Pres. (Acad. Devel.) 1978–79; Asst. Prof. of Econ. Univ. of Mich. 1958–62; Research Econ. Royal Comn. Banking & Finance 1962–63; Assoc. Ed. Candn. Pub. Policy 1980–EM; 'Money and Banking' 1976; ed. 'Exploiting our Economic Potential: Public Policy and the British Columbia Economy' 1968; 'Trade Liberalization and a Regional Economy' 1971; co-author 'Economics of the Canadian Financial System' 1983; articles Candn. monetary hist. and Candn. monetary policy; mem. Candn. Econ. Assn.; Am. Econ. Assn.; Home: 3514 West 36th Ave., Vancouver, B.C. V6N 2S1; Office: 997, 1873 East Mall, Vancouver, B.C. V6T 1Y2.

**SHEBIB, Donald (Everett),** M.A.; film director; b. Toronto, Ont. 27 Jan. 1938; s. Moses and Mary Alice (Long) S.; e. De La Salle 'Oaklands' 1955; Univ. of Toronto, B.A. 1960; Univ. of Cal. (UCLA), M.A. 1965; PRESIDENT, EVDON FILMS LTD.; Director 'The Duel' (UCLA) 1962; 'Surfin' (CBC TV) 1963; 'Revival' (UCLA thesis) 1964; awarded 1st prize 'best short,' Montreal Film Festival and 3rd prize, Kenyon Film Festival, 1966; 'Plaza Gang' (CBC TV) and 'Satans Choice' (NFB) 1966; 'Basketball' (CBC TV), 'Search for Learning' (NFB) and 'This Land is People' (CTV) 1967; 'Haight Ashbury 1967' and 'Robert Stanfield' (CBC) 1968; Candn. Film Award for 'Good Times Bad Times' (CBC) 1969; 'Goin Down the Road' 1970; recreations: golf, surfing, music, football; Address: 312 Wright Ave., Toronto, Ont. M6R 1L9.

**SHEEHAN, John P.,** C.A., A.C.I.S., P. Admin.; executive; b. County Cork, Ireland 1 March 1931; s. John Maurice and Ellen (Russell) S.; e. Christian Brothers College and Univ. College, Cork, Ireland; ACIS (Chart. Secy.); C.A.; m. Bridget Mary, d. Timothy Harrington; children: Theresa Mary, Heather Elizabeth, Sonia Frances, Russell John; SENIOR VICE-PRES. AND CHIEF FINANCIAL OFFR., B.C. HYDRO AND POWER AUTHORITY 1992– ; Asst. Controller, George Weston Ltd. 1964–68; Extve. Vice-Pres. & Gen. Mgr., Chromium Mining and Smelting Ltd. 1968–72; Treasurer-Controller, Air Canada 1972–75; Vice-Pres., Petrosar Limited 1975–77; Asst. Gen. Mgr., Admin. & Finance, B.C. Hydro 1977–79, Vice-Pres., Finance & Administration 1979–88, Vice-Pres., Customer Service 1988–91; Vice-Pres., Environmental & Corporate Affairs 1991–92; Dir. & Past Chrmn., Holy Family Hospital; Dir., Energy Council of Can.; Past Chrmn., Candn. Electrical Assn.; mem.; Chart Inst. Secys. (Past Chrmn. Toronto Chapter); Ont. Inst. of Chartered Accountants; Inst. of Chartered Accountants of B.C.; Past Chrmn., Financial Executives Inst. of Can.; Club: Hollyburn Country; Office: 333 Dunsmuir St., Vancouver, B.C. V6B 5R3.

**SHEEHY, Hon. Gerald Earle,** M.L.A., D.V.Sc.; former politician; veterinarian; b. Noel, Hants Co., N.S. 24 June 1924; s. Basil Thomas and Iva (Miller) S.; e. elem. and jr. high schs. Upper Kennetcook, N.S.; Windsor (N.S.) Acad.; Ont. Veterinary Coll. Univ. of Toronto D.V.Sc.; m. Emma Grant d. George Davidson, Aberdeen, Scot. 20 Sept. 1945; children: Grant Earle, Patricia Kim, Theresa Georgene; veterinary med. practice Guelph, Ont. 1952–53, Erin, Ont. 1954–58, Middleton, N.S. 1958–78; former Town Councillor and Depy. Mayor, Middleton, N.S.; el. M.L.A. 1970, re-el. since; retired 1988; former Min. of Health, N.S. and Min. in Charge of Drug Dependency Act, Registrar Gen. 1978–86; Chrmn., N.S. Tidal Power Corp. 1986–89; former Gov., Dalhousie Univ.; Chrmn. Sch. Bd. Middleton; served with RCAF 1942–46, Navig.-Bomber Command, rank Flying Offr.; el. mem. Bd. of Govs., Candn. Corps of Commissionaires 1988; mem. Candn. Veterinary Med. Assn.; N.S. Veterinary Med. Assn.; P. Conservative; Anglican; recreations: golf, curling, cross-country skiing, swimming; Clubs: Rotary (Past Pres.); Middleton Curling (Past Pres.); Home: 181 Main St., Middleton, N.S. B0S 1P0.

**SHEETS-PYENSON, Susan,** Ph.D.; educator; b. Toledo, Ohio 9 Sept. 1949; d. Ted Charles and Martha Louise (Merrill) Sheets; e. Univ. of Mich. B.A. 1970; Univ. of Pa. Ph.D. 1976; m. Lewis s. Jacob and Regina Pyenson 18 Aug. 1973; children: Nicholas, Catharine, Benjamin; ASSOC. PROF. OF GEOG. CONCORDIA UNIV. 1990– , Dir. Sci. and Human Affairs Prog. 1984– ; joined present Univ. 1977; author 'Cathedrals of Science: The Development of Colonial Natural History Museums During The Late Nineteenth Century' 1988; 'Index to the Scientific Correspondence of John William Dawson' 1992; mem. Hist. Sci. Soc.; Brit. Soc. Hist. Sci.; Soc. Hist. Natural Hist.; Home: 8 Laberge, Senneville, Que. H9X 3P9; Office: 1455 de Maisonneuve Blvd. W., Montreal, Que. H3G 1M8.

**SHEFFER, Andra Lyn,** B.A.; arts administrator; b. Ottawa, Ont. 9 June 1951; d. Harry and Evelyn (Widman) S.; e. Nepean (Ont.) High Sch. 1969; Carleton Univ. B.A. (Hons.) 1973; m. Denis Hamel; one daughter: Kayla; EXTVE. DIR., MACLEAN HUNTER TELEVISION FUND 1991– ; Planning Offr. Strategic Planning Dept Sec. of State Ottawa 1973, Film Festivals Offr. 1974, Film Certification Offr. 1976–78; Mng. Dir. Toronto Festival of Festivals 1978–79; Extve. Dir., Acad. of Candn. Cinema & Television 1979–89; Freelance Arts Administrator and Consultant 1989–91; Address: 24 Hambly Ave., Toronto, Ont. M4E 2R6.

**SHEIN, Fraser,** M.Eng., P.Eng.; rehabiliation engineer; b. Hamilton, Ont. 13 Oct. 1956; s. Louis J. and Margaret E. (Pritchard) S.; e. Queen's Univ. M.Eng. 1978; McMaster Univ. P.Eng. 1981; REHABILITATION ENGINEER, HUGH MacMILLAN REHABILITATION CENTRE 1979– ; Rehab. Engr., Biofeedback Research Prog., The Hugh MacMillan Rehab. Ctr. 1979–82; Coordinator, Microcomputer Applications Prog. 1982–85, 1988– ; Principal Researcher, Ont. Consortium for Rehab. Research & Development 1992– ; PhD Fellow, National Health Research and Development Prog. 1985–88; designer / developer of innovative computer technology for people with physical disabilities; expertise lies in human factors & design; Mem., Assn. of Profl. Engrs., Prov. of Ont.; Rehab. Engr. Soc. of N. America; Ed. Bd., 'Augmentative and Alternative Communication,' 'Rehabilitation Technology'; Home: 56

Scarborough Rd., Toronto, Ont. M4E 3M5; Office: 350 Rumsey Rd., Toronto, Ont. M4G 1R8.

**SHEININ, Rose,** Ph.D., F.R.S.C., D.Hum. Lett., D.Sci.; university professor; b. Toronto, Ont. 18 May 1930; d. Harry and Anne (Szyber) Shuber; e. Univ. of Toronto, B.A. 1951, M.A. 1953, Ph.D. 1956; m. Joseph s. Bronia and Cecil S. July 1951; children: David M.K., Lisa B.J., Rachel S.R.; VICE-RECTEUR, ENSEIGNEMENT ET RECH., AND PROF., DEPT. OF BIOLOGY, CONCORDIA UNIV. 1989– ; Prof., Dept. of Microbiology, Univ. of Toronto 1982–90; Vice-Dean, Sch. of Graduate Studies, Univ. of Toronto 1984–89; Demonstrator, Dept. of Biochem., Univ. of Toronto 1951–53; Vis. Rsch. Assoc., Univ. of Cambridge 1956–57; Nat. Inst. for Med. Rsch. 1957–58; Rsch. Assoc. Fellow, Ont. Cancer Inst 1958–67; Asst. Prof., Dept. of Medical Biophysics, Univ. of Toronto 1967–72; Assoc Prof. 1972–78; Grad. Sec. 1973–75; Chrmn. & Prof., Dept. of Microbiol. & Parasit. 1975–82; Prof., Dept. of Med. Biophysics 1978–90; Cherch. Etr. d'INSERM, Dept. d'Enzym., IRSC/CNRS (France) 1982; Sr. Fellow, Massey Coll., Univ. of Toronto 1983–90, Continuing Fellow 1990– ; Cons., Z.L. Bochnek Labs. 1983–89; Canada Packers Ltd. 1985–87; Mem., Candn. Sci. deleg. to China 1973; mem. of numerous panels & cttes. incl. Cancer Grants, Med. Rsch. Counc. of Can.; Grants Panel A, Nat. Cancer Inst. of Can.; Prog. Ctte., XIth Internat. Cong. of Biochem. & NRC Adv. Ctte. on Biotech.; external review for several found., agy. (incl. Can. Counc. Killam Awards) & jours.; recipient of numerous burs., scholarships & fellowships; Vis. Prof., Univ. of Alta. 1971; Queen's Silver Jubilee Medal 1978; Fellow, Am. Acad. of Microbiol. 1978– ; Royal Soc. of Can. 1981– ; Josiah Macy Jr. Faculty Scholar 1981–82; Archibald Byron Macallum Mem. Lectr. 1981; NSERC delegate to Internat. Congress Biochem., Perth, Australia 1982; Vis. Lectr. several Candn. univs.; mem., Sci. Counc. of Can. 1984–87; Nat. Adv. Bd., 'Canadian Encyclopedia' 1985; featured in Flare Mag. 1984; Inaugural Award, Candn. Assn. for Women in Sci. & Candn. Biochem. Soc. 1985; Hon. Doctorate Human Letters, Mt. St. Vincent Univ. 1985; Hon. Doctorate Science, Acadia Univ. 1987; Univ. of Guelph 1991; Hon. Fellowship, Ryerson Polytechnical Institute 1993; Woman of Distinction Award, YWCA 1988; Mem., Sigma Xi, Am. Soc. for Virology; Candn. Assn. for Women in Sci.; Sci. for Peace; Internat. Assn. of Women Bioscientists; Candn. Soc. for Cell Biology (Past Pres.); Am. Soc. for Microbiol.; Am. Soc. for Virology; Candn Biochem. Soc. (Past Pres., Vice Pres., Ctte. Mem.); & past mem. of numerous other soc.; book reviewer; Assoc. Ed.: 'Intervirology' 1974–85; Past Assoc. Ed. of 2 jours.; Club: McGill, Mount Stephen Club; Office: 7141 Sherbrooke St. W., Montreal, Que. H4B 1R6.

**SHEKTER, Richard H.,** B.A., LL.B., LL.M.; lawyer; b. Hamilton, Ont. 24 March 1949; s. Benjamin Bernard and Dorothy (Taylor) S.; e. Hamilton C.I. 1967; Univ. of Toronto B.A. 1970; Osgoode Hall Law Sch., York Univ. LL.B. 1973 (Bronze Medalist); Univ. of California at Berkeley, Boalt Hall Law Sch., LL.M. (summa cum laude) 1975; one d.: Brooke Lesley; PARTNER, FOGLER RUBINOFF 1990– ; articled with Eddy Greenspan 1973–74; Law Clerk to Chief Justice of Ont. 1976–77; Assoc. & Partner, Blaney, Pasternak, Smela & Watson 1977–81; Founding Partner, Levitt, Shekter & Schnurr 1981–90; merged with Fogler, Rubinoff 1990; Head of Health Law Group & Criminal Law Group; Co-founded, Health Law Section, Candn. Bar Assn. 1985; Vice Chair, Civil Liberties Section CBAO 1981–83; Chair, Health Law Section CBAO 1987–89; Vice-Chair, CBAO Aids Ctte. Report 1986, 1991; Legal Columnist, 'Ontario Medicine' 1991– ; Legal Columnist, 'Dental Practice Management' 1993– ; num. legal lectures across N. Am.; frequent TV & radio appearances; has appeared before the courts at all levels; Candn. Bar Assn., Ont. Dedicated Service Award 1988; Canada Council & Laidlaw Foundation Scholarships; Mem., Advocate Soc.; Am. Trial Lawyers Assn.; Candn. Bar Assn.; Criminal Lawyers Assn.; Co. of York Law Assn.; Medical-Legal Soc.; author/contbr. of journal articles; co-author: 'Aids, the Disease & the Law' 1989; co-draftsman: CBAO Report on the Legal Implications of Aids 1986; recreations: musician, skiing, sailing, writing; Office: P.O. Box 95, Ste. 4400, Royal Trust Tower, T-D Ctr., Toronto, Ont. M5K 1G8.

**SHELEF, His Excellency Itzhak,** M.Law; diplomat; b. Jerusalem 28 Oct. 1936; s. Benjamin and Zahava Shliefer; Hebrew Univ. M.Law 1958; m. Malka Elkan April 1959; children: Michal, Nir, Alon, Yael; AMBASSADOR, EMBASSY OF ISRAEL, OTTAWA, CANADA 1991– ; Mem., Israel Bar Assn.; joined Min. of Foreign Affairs 1965; Asst., Internat. Coop. Div. 1965; First Sec., Addis Adaba, Ethiopia 1969; Counsellor, Tokyo, Japan 1973; Dep. Dir., Asian Div., Min. of Fgn. Affairs 1976; Sr. Asst. to Dep. Dir. Gen. in charge of N/A Affairs 1979; Min.-Couns., Embassy of Israel, Ottawa 1981; Dir., Internal Legal Div., Legal Bureau, Min. of Fgn. Affairs 1985; Dep. Dir.-Gen., Operations & Mngt. 1987; Office: 50 O'Connor St., Suite 1005, Ottawa, Ont. K1P 6L2.

**SHELL, Arnold Joseph,** FSA, FCIA, MA; insurance executive; b. Winnipeg, Man. 3 May 1949; e. Univ. of Manitoba B.A. 1971, M.A. 1972; Harvard Univ., Adv. Mngt. Prog. 1988; m. Barbara; children: Jonathan, Jeffrey, Sarah; SENIOR VICE-PRES., INSURANCE OPERATIONS, CROWN LIFE INSURANCE CO.; Scottish Widow's Fund & Life Assur. Soc. (Edinburgh, Scotland) 1972–73; various senior positions leading to current responsibilities since 1973; Office: 1901 Scarth St., P.O. Box 827, Regina, Sask. S4P 3B1.

**SHELL, Brian,** A.B., M.A., LL.B.; labour lawyer; b. Montreal, Que. 3 Nov. 1950; s. Hyman and Sophie (Cytrynbaum) S.; e. Brandeis Univ., A.B. 1972; Oxford Univ., B.A. 1974, M.A. 1976; Univ. of Toronto, LL.B. 1978; m. Barbara d. Bernie and Katie Ostroff 22 Dec. 1986; children: Laura Hava, Chaim Jeremiah, Adam Solomon; CANDN. COUNS., UNITED STEELWORKERS OF AM. 1980– ; resp. for legal affairs throughout Can.; call to Bar of Ont. 1980; appearances before Ont. Labour Relns. Bd. Supreme Ct. of Ont., Fed. Ct. of Appeal, Supreme Ct. of Can., var. admin. tribunals & arbitration panels; Rhodes Scholar (Que. & Balliol) 1972; Danforth Grad. Fellowship 1971; Phi Beta Kappa 1972; Dir., Toronto Econ. Devel. Corp.; Dir. & Sec., Steelworkers Humanity Fund Inc.; Mem., Candn. Bar Assoc.; Metro Toronto Assoc. for Community Living; Participating Families; Candn. Assoc. of Labour Lawyers; Georgian Bay Nonsuch Assoc.; recreations: sailing, skiing, swimming, cinema, theatre; Home: 615 Lonsdale Rd., Toronto, Ont. M5P 1R8; Office: 234 Eglinton Ave. E., Ste. 408, Toronto, Ont. M4P 1K7.

**SHELLEY, Gabriel Charles,** B.S.M.E., M.B.A., P. Eng., C.M.C; management consultant; b. Budapest, Hungary 11 Dec. 1950; s. Charles Ivan Shelley; e. Queen's Univ. B.S.M.E. 1972; York Univ. M.B.A. 1975; children: Paul Andrew; David James; MANAGING PARTNER, WESTERN REGION, PEAT MARWICK STEVENSON & KELLOGG MANAGEMENT CONSULTANTS since 1979; Process Engr. DuPont of Canada, Kingston 1972–74; Indust. Engr. Dominion Stores, Toronto 1974–75, Mgr. Indust. Engn. 1975–76; Associate Kearney: Management Consultants, Toronto 1976–77, Mgr. 1978–79; author various publs.; Mem. of Bd., Univ. of Alberta Hospitals; mem. Assn Prof. Engrs. Prov. Alta. and Ont.; Candn. Assn. Phys. Distribution Mang.; Nat. Council Phys. Distribution Mang.; mem. of Bd., SK/CF Inc.; past mem. of Bd. Nexus Theatre, Edmonton; recreations: photography, writing, tennis, squash; Home: 5603 Whitemud Rd., Edmonton, Alta. T6H 4Y3; Office: Suite 2610, Canada Trust Tower, Edmonton Centre, Edmonton, Alta. T5J 0H8.

**SHELTON, Ian Keith,** B.Sc., M.Sc.; astronomer; b. Winnipeg, Man. 30 March 1957; s. Peter James and Elizabeth (Malyska) S.; e. Univ. of Manitoba B.Sc. 1979; Univ. of Toronto M.Sc. 1990; ASTRONOMER, UNIVERSITY OF TORONTO 1990– ; Resident Astronomer, Univ. of Toronto Southern Observatory at Las Campanas, Chile 1981–83, 1985–87; Museum Technician, Manitoba Mus. of Man and Nature 1984; Mem., Candn. Astronomical Soc.; Mem., Order of the Buffalo Hunt (Prov. of Manitoba); Life Mem., Royal Astronomical Soc. of Canada; Hon. Life Mem., Science Teachers' Assn. of Manitoba; Royal Soc. of Canada; recreations: photography, hiking; Home: 43 Forest Park Dr., Winnipeg, Man. R2V 2R5; Office: Toronto, Ont. M5S 1A7.

**SHEMILT, Leslie W.,** O.C., M.Sc., Ph.D., D.Hon.C., D.Sc., F.R.S.C., F.C.A.E., H.F.C.I.C., F.A.I.Ch.E., F. E. I. C., P.Eng.; b. Souris, Man. 25 Dec. 1919; s. John Henry and Myrtle (Webster) S.; e. Univ. of Toronto, B.A.Sc. 1941, Ph.D. 1947; Univ. of Manitoba, M.Sc. 1946; Hon. D.H.C., St. Staszic Univ., Cracow, Poland 1992; Hon. D.Sc. McMaster Univ. 1994; m. Elizabeth MacKenzie, 25 May 1946; children: Roderick, Roslyn; PROFESSOR EMERITUS OF CHEM. ENGN., McMASTER UNIV. since 1987; Supervisor, Defence Industries Ltd., Winnipeg, 1941–44, Lectr., Univ. of Manitoba, 1944–45; Asst., Univ. of Toronto, 1945–46; Special Lecturer 1946–47; Asst. Prof., Univ. B.C. 1947–49, Assoc. Prof. 1949–57; Prof. 1957–60; Shell Visiting Prof., Univ. Coll. London, 1959–60; Prof. & Head, Dept. Chem. Engn., Univ. N.B. 1960–69; Dean of Engn., McMaster Univ. 1969–79; Prof. invité, Inst. génie chim., Ecole Polytech. Féd. de Lausanne 1975; Visiting Prof., Indian Inst. of Technol., Kanpur & Indian Inst. of Technol., Madras 1975; Univ. of Sydney, Australia 1981; Special Visiting Prof., Yokohama National Univ. 1987; Pres., Chem. Inst. of Can., 1970–71; Vice-Pres., Acad. of Sci., Royal Soc. of Can. 1990–91, Editor 1991– ; Dir., Can. Acad. of Engn. 1987–91, Treasurer 1991–92; Ed., 'Candn. Journ. of Chem. Engn.' 1967–85, Editor Emeritus 1987; Fellow, Roy. Soc. of Can.; Candn. Acad. of Engn.; Hon. Fellow, Chem. Inst. of Can.; Engn. Inst. of Can.; Am. Inst. Chem. Eng. mem., Am. Chem. Soc.; Am. Soc. for Engn. Educ.; Assn. of Prof. Eng. of Ont.; Sherlock Holmes Soc. of London; Can. Research Mgt. Assoc.; Fellow, Nat. Council on Relig. in Higher Educ.; mem., Nat. Research Council Can. 1966–69; Chrmn. N.B. Res. and Prod'y Council 1962–69; Tech. Adv. Comm. A.E.C.L. Waste Mgmt. Program 1979– ; recipient Canada Centennial Medal 1967; Queen's Jubilee Medal 1977; True Davidson Meml. Award 1978; T.P. Hoar Prize 1981; R.S. Jane Memorial Lecture Award 1985; McMaster Student Union Award for Teaching Excellence 1986; A.P.E.O. Engn. Medal 1986; Hamilton Engineer-of-the-Year 1989; Officer, Order of Canada 1991; 125th Anniversary of the Confederation of Canada Medal, 1992; Julian C. Smith Medal, Engineering Institute of Can. 1993; Engineering Alumni Hall of Distinction, Univ. of Toronto 1993; author of over 70 technol. papers and several reports & studies; editor of internat. volumes on chem. & food, fluidization, history of chem. engn.; N.D.P.; United Church; Home: 17 Hillcrest Court, Hamilton, Ont. L8P 2X7.

**SHENFIELD, Peter N.,** B.A.; executive search consultant; b. London, Eng. 25 Apl. 1946; s. Jack and Ethel (Brauerman) S.; e. Sir George Williams Univ. Montreal B.A. 1969; m. Eleanor d. Louis and Nina Cass 30 Aug. 1969; children: Eric Mitchell, Marion Debra; PARTNER, BAKER HARRIS & PARTNERS LIMITED (Executive Search Consultants) 1993– ; previously served Allstate Insurance; personnel consulting and exec. search practice Montreal 1969–77; sole practitioner Toronto 1977–80; Sr. Associate, E.L. Shore & Assocs. Corp. 1981–93; mem. Personnel Assn. Ont. (Pres. 1988–89, Dir. 1985– ); Personnel Assn. Toronto (previous Exec. and Bd. mem.); Sr. Vice Pres., Jewish Vocational Service of Metro. Toronto 1989– ; Home: 108 Hetherington Cres., Thornhill, Ont. L4J 2M2; Office: 130 Adelaide St. W., Suite 2710, Toronto, Ont. M5H 3P5.

**SHENNAN, Andrew T.,** M.B., MRCP(UK), FRCP(C); neonatologist; b. Aberdeen, Scotland 22 March 1943; s. Edward Theodore and Victoria (Trew) Shennan; e. Kings Sch. Worcester England; Aberdeen Univ. MB.Ch.B. 1967; m. Anne d. Harvey and Nancy Stewart 20 Jan. 1968; children: Michael, Catriona, Graeme; CHIEF, DEPT. OF NEWBORN & DEVELOPMENTAL PAEDIATRICS, WOMEN'S COLLEGE HOSPITAL 1991– ; General Paediatrics Training 1968–73; Neonatal Fellow, Hosp. for Sick Children 1974–75; Neonatal Dir., Perinatal Unit, Women's College Hosp. 1975– ; Assoc. Prof., Depts. of Paediatrics, Obstetrics & Gynaecology, Univ. of Toronto; Extve. Ctte., Commonwealth Assn. for Mental Handicap & Developmental Disabilities; Mem., Candn. Paediatric Soc.; Soc. of Obstetricians & Gynaecologists of Can., Ont. Medical Assn.; author/co-author of over 50 scientific papers dealing with treatment and outcome of premature babies; recreations: golf, travel; Home: 220 Windy Oaks Dr., Mississauga, Ont. L5G 1Z6; Office: Perinatal Unit, 76 Grenville St., Toronto, Ont. M5S 1B2.

**SHENNIB, Hani,** M.D., FRCS(C); surgeon, university professor; b. Tripoli, Libya 19 March 1953; s. Fouad and Ibtisam S.; e. Cairo Univ. 1975; London Univ. 1979; McGill Univ. 1983; Univ. of Toronto 1987; m. Awatef d. Ahmed Shihabeldeen 5 June 1976; children: Sarah, Faisal, Selma; DIRECTOR, MONTREAL LUNG TRANSPLANT PROGRAM & ASSOC. PROF., SURGERY, MCGILL UNIV. 1988– ; Cardiothoracic Surgeon, The Montreal General Hosp.; Fellow, Royal Coll.of Surgeons of Can.; Am. Coll. of Surgeons; Am. Coll. of Chest Physicians; author of over 60 publications; Office: 1650 Cedar Ave., Montreal, Que. H3G 1A4.

**SHENSTONE, Michael,** B.A., M.A.; diplomat; b. Toronto, Ont. 25 June 1928; s. late Prof. Allen Goodrich, O.B.E., M.C., F.R.S. and late Mildred Madeline (Chadwick) S.; e. Princeton New Jersey, 1933–41, Ashbury Coll., Ottawa 1941–45; Univ. of Toronto, Trinity Coll. B.A. 1949; Cambridge Univ., Trinity Coll., B.A., M.A. 1949–51; Univ. de Paris 1951–52; m. Susan Louise, d. late Archibald Leith Burgess, 8 Sept. 1951; children: Thomas Leith, Barbara Fairweather, Mary; FOREIGN AFFAIRS CONSULTANT (population, migration, Middle East, nuclear affairs etc.); joined Dept. of External Affairs 1952; Jan. 1954 Middle East Centre for Arab Studies, Shemlan, Lebanon; Third, then Second Secy. Candn. Legation, Beirut 1954; Middle East Div., Ottawa, 1957; Second, then First Secy., Candn. Embassy, Cairo, 1960; First Secy., Candn. Embassy, Washington, D.C. 1963, Counsellor 1964; Head, Peacekeeping and Mil. Assistance Div., NATO and North Amer. Defence Div., then Dir., Defence Relations Div. (all Ottawa) 1967; Royal Coll. Defence Studies, London, 1972; Principal Adv. to Candn. Ambassador, Helsinki, for Multilateral talks on Conf. on Security and Cooperation in Europe, 1972; Ambassador and Head of Candn. del. to C.S.C.E. 1973; Ambassador to Saudi Arabia 1974–76; Dir.-Gen., African and Middle Eastern Affairs (Ottawa) 1976–80; Assist. Under-Secy. of State for External Affairs, Africa and the Middle East, Oct. 1980–Aug. 1983; Asst. Depy. Min., Political & International Security Affairs, Dept. of External Affairs, 1983–85; Ambassador to Austria, Head of Delegation to Vienna talks on Mutual and Balanced Force Reductions in Europe, and Permanent Representative to the UN Office in Vienna, the Internat. Atomic Energy Agency, and the UN Industrial Develop. Organ. 1985–90; Special Advisor on Long Term Studies, Policy Planning Staff, Dept. of External Affairs and Internat. Trade 1990–92; Head, Candn. Del. to Prep. Cttee. for 1994 Internat. Conference on Population and Development 1993; Special Envoy of Canada for Middle East multilateral peace process 1993; Commandant, Confrérie des Chevaliers du Tastevin, Nuits-Saint-Georges, Côte d'Or, France; Ch. of Eng.; recreations: pottery-making, sailing, stamps, wine; Home: 10 Ellesmere Place, Ottawa, Ont. K1M 0N9.

**SHEPHARD, Roy Jesse,** M.D., Ph.D., D.P.E., F.A.C.S.M.; university professor; b. London, England 8 May 1929; s. Jesse and Esther Rose (Cummins) S.; e. Colwyn Bay Gr. Sch., Guy's Hosp. Med. Sch., Univ. of London, B.Sc. (Hons.) 1949, M.B.B.S. (Hons.) 1952, Ph.D. 1954 (Cardiac Rsch. Fellow & Univ. of London Post-Grad. Fellow 1952–54); M.D. 1959; D.P.E. (Hon. Causa) Univ. of Gent, 1989; Doct. (Hon. Causa) Univ. Montréal 1992; m. Muriel d. Fred and Dora Cullum 18 Aug. 1956; children: Sarah, Rachel; PROF. OF APPLIED PHYSIOLOGY, UNIV. OF TORONTO; Med. Offr./Flight Lt., RAF Inst. of Aviation Med. 1954–56; Fulbright Sch. & Asst. Prof., Univ. of Cincinnati 1956–58; Prin. Sci. Offr., UK Chem. Def. Exper. Establishment 1958–64; Prof. of Appl. Physiol. (sev. depts.) & Dir., Fitness Rsch. Unit, Univ. of Toronto 1964– ; Prof., Univ. de Qué. à Trois Rivières 1969–77; Dir., Ctr. des Sci. de la Santé, Trois Rivières 1973–74; Dir., Sch. of Physical & Health Edn., Univ. of Toronto 1979–91; Prof. Assoc., Univ. de Paris 1985–86; Cons., Toronto Rehab. Ctr.; Gage Rsch. Inst.; Def. & Civil Inst. of Environ. Med.; State Scholarship (UK) 1946; fellowships: Univ. of London post-grad. 1952, Beit Mem. 1954, Fulbright 1954, MRC travelling 1985; UNESCO Prize 1976, 1993; Prov. of Ont. Citation 1983; CASS Hon. Award 1985; Sir Adolphe Abrahams Medal 1988; Doctorates (honoris causa) Univ. of Gent, 1989; Univ. of Montreal 1992; Citation, Am. Coll. Sports Med. 1991; Former Pres., Am. Coll. of Sports Med.; Candn. Assn. of Sports Sci.; Former Vice-Pres., Internat. Cttee. for Physical Fitness Rsch.; Vice-Pres., Brit. Assn. for Sport & Med.; Un. Ch. of Can.; New Democrat; author: 'Economic Benefits of Endurance Exercise,' 'Fitness of a Nation,' 'Health and Fitness in Industry' 1986, 'Biochemistry of Physical Activity,' 'Carbon Monoxide – the Silent Killer' 1983, 'The Risks of Passive Smoking' 1982, 'Endurance Fitness' 1969, 1977 and many other books & articles; recreations: swimming, walking, stamp collecting, choral singing; Home: 29 Poplar Plains Rd., Toronto, Ont. M4V 2M7; Office: 320 Huron St., Toronto, Ont. M5S 1A1.

**SHEPHERD, Gordon Greeley,** M.Sc., Ph.D., F.R.S.C.; educator; b. Senate, Sask. 19 June 1931; s. George Frederick and Irene Eleanor (Thompson) S.; e. Luther Coll. Regina 1947; Univ. of Sask. B.Sc. 1952, M.Sc. 1953; Univ. of Toronto Ph.D. 1956; m. 1stly Marian Margaret d. Ida and Kasper Morgenroth 15 Aug. 1953; three s. Theodore Gordon, David Michael, Paul Ronald; 2ndly Marianna Genova d. Geno and Todorka Gerdjikova 19 Dec. 1987; PROF. OF EARTH AND ATMOSPHERIC SCIENCE and DIR., SOLAR TERRESTRIAL PHYSICS LABORATORY, INST. FOR SPACE AND TERRESTRIAL SCIENCES, YORK UNIV. 1969– ; Principal Investigator for WINDII instrument on the Upper Atmosphere Research Satellite; Asst. Prof. of Physics Univ. of Sask. 1957–64, Assoc. Prof. 1964–69; author over 100 publs. upper atmospheric physics, optical instruments, aurora and airglow; Fellow, Roy. Soc. of Can.; Candn. Aeronautics & Space Inst.; mem., Candn. Assn. Physicists; Am. Geophys. Union; Optical Soc. Am.; recreations: diving, swimming, boating; Home: 171 King High Dr., Thornhill, Ont. L4J 3N3; Office: 4700 Keele St., Toronto, Ont. M3J 1P3.

**SHEPHERD, Helen Parsons,** A.O.C.A., LL.D., R.C.A.; artist; b. St. John's, Nfld. 16 Jan. 1923; d. Richard Augustus and Bessie Parsons; e. Bishop Spencer Coll.; Mem. Univ. of Nfld.; Ont. Coll. of Art A.O.C.A. 1948; m. Reginald 9 Apr. 1948; s. Robert W. and Margaret Shepherd; one s. R. Scott; Co-Founder and Teacher Nfld. Acad. of Art 1949–61; painted in Europe 1957; solo exhn. Mem. Univ. of Nfld. 1975, exhn. toured Ont. and Atlantic regions 1975–76; solo exhn. at The Gallery (Mauskopf) 1982; Retrospective show, Memorial Univ. Art Gall. 1989; rep. in perm. colls. Beaverbrook Gallery, Mem. Univ. Nfld. and many private colls.; portraits incl. Gov.-Gen. & Mrs. Schreyer for Rideau Hall, Presidents of Mem. Univ. Nfld., Speakers of House of Assembly Nfld., Mayors City of St. John's, official portraits for Govt. House, St. John's; elected Hall of Honour, Arts Council, Govt. of Nfld. & Labrador 1990; mem. Arts Council Nfld. & Labrador; Anglican; recreations: swimming, sailing; Address: 26 Oxen Pond Rd., St. John's, Nfld. A1B 3J3.

**SHEPHERD, John Joseph,** M.A.; electronics executive; b. Lancashire, Eng. 20 Feb. 1929; s. William Albert and Angelina (Mulholland) S.; e. Univ. of London B.A. 1954; McMaster Univ. M.A. 1958; Ph.Eng. (h.c.) Carleton Univ.; Ph.D. Science (h.c.) RMC; m. Kathleen Joanna 19 May 1956; children: William Paul, Andrew Duncan, Adam John, Kristin Hamilton, Victoria Mary, Matthew Thomas; CHRMN., ERINTEC MANAGEMENT CORP. 1986– ; Former Chrmn., Leigh Instruments Ltd.; Science Council of Can. 1972–75; Trustee, Forum for Young Candns.; served U.K. and Candn. Civil Service 1947–55; Candn. electronics industry 1955–61; Founder, Pres. and Chrmn. of Bd. Leigh Instruments 1961–75; Dir. Candn. Patents & Development Ltd. 1970–75; Foreign mem. Royal Swedish Acad. Engn. Sciences; mem. Candn. Inst. Strategic Studies; Extve. Dir. and Vice Chrmn. Science Council of Can. 1972–79; Dir., Candn. Inst. for Econ. Policy 1979–81; Chrmn., Defence Science Advisory Bd. 1988–93; Fellow of Ryerson, 1982; R. Catholic; Home: 90 Kilbarry Rd., Toronto, Ont. M5P 1K7.

**SHEPHERD, Murray C.,** B.Ed., M.A.; university librarian; b. Saskatoon, Sask. 31 July 1938; Univ. of Sask. B.Ed. 1963; Univ. of Denver M.A. (Lib. Science) 1968; m. Ruth Maureen Bacon 3 March 1973; two s. Mark C., M. Craig; CHIEF LIBRARIAN, UNIV. OF WATERLOO 1973– ; Univ. of Waterloo Community Campaign Ctte. 1991– ; Univ. of Waterloo Staff Relations Ctte. 1991–93; Univ. of Waterloo Pascal Lectures Ctte. 1991–92; Council of Ont. Univs. Task Force on Educational and Rsch. Networking 1989–90; Teacher, Walter Murray Coll. Inst. Saskatoon 1963–64; Asst. Lib. Educ. Lib. Univ. of Sask. (Regina) 1964–67, Head Catalogue Dept. 1967–69; Head Tech. Services present Univ. 1969–71, Assoc. Lib. 1971–73; mem. Candn. Lib. Assn., 1963– ; Am. Lib. Assn. 1966– ; Assoc. Research Libs., 1985– ; Candn. Assn. Research Libs., 1973– ; OCUL, 1973– (Chrmn. 1975, 1976); CACUL; Sask. Assn. Sch. Libs. (Past Chrmn.); U.W. Faculty Club Exec. Comte. 1978–79; ACRL; Nat. Lib. Adv. Bd. Resource Network Comte., 1981–85; Trans Can. Telephone System, Computer Communication Group, iNet Gateway Trials, and Bibliographic Common Interest Group, 1981–84; Univ. of Waterloo Archives Bd. 1978– ; Councillor, COMLA 1981–89; Regional Vice-Pres., America's/Caribbean 1990–92; Adv. Ctte., Nat. Study on Photocopying in Candn. Libraries 1987–89; Home: 481 Branstone Dr., Waterloo, Ont. N2T 1P4; Office: Univ. of Waterloo, Dana Porter Library, Waterloo, Ont. N2L 3G1.

**SHEPHERD, Reginald,** A.O.C.A., LL.D., R.C.A., F.I.A.L.; artist and printmaker; b. Nfld. 28 March 1924; s. Robert Wilson and Margaret (Moore) S.; e. Ont. Coll. of Art A.O.C.A. 1949; studied in Europe on Candn. Govt. Fellowship awarded by Royal Soc. Can. 1956–57; m. Helen d. Richard A. and Bessie Parsons 9 Apr. 1948; one s. Reginald Scott; Dir., Nfld. Acad. of Art 1949–61; Visiting Lectr. in Art Mem. Univ. of Nfld. 1951–61; exhns. incl. 1st Biennial Nat. Gallery Can. 1955; Montreal Museum of Fine Arts 1964, 1968; London and Hamilton Galleries; N.B. Museum; St. Mary's Univ.; Zwickers Gallery; Trinity Coll. Univ. of Toronto 1969; Candn. Printmakers Showcase Carleton Univ. 1974; Gallery Graphics Ottawa; Burnaby Gallery; several exhns. Maritime Art Assn.; Mem. Univ. Nfld. 1972; Ont. Soc. Art Exhn. Toronto 1974; Travelling Print Show Univ. of Ore. 1976; Solo Exhn. London, Plymouth & Leeds, (Eng.) 1983, and Rome 1983–84; solo exhn. prints & watercolours shown at 8 galleries in Ireland 1984–85; Chrmn., Nfld. Arts & Letters Ctte. 1972–76; rep. in many pub. and private colls. Can., USA, Europe and Mexico; Prov. Vice Pres., R.C.A. 1978–83; Retrospective Show, Mem. Univ. Art Gall. 1989; elected, Hall of Honour, Arts Council, Govt. Nfld. & Labrador 1990; served with RCAF during World War II; Anglican; recreations: sailing, swimming, gardening; Address: 26 Oxen Pond Rd., St. John's, Nfld. A1B 3J3.

**SHEPPARD, Claude-Armand,** B.A., B.C.L.; b. Ghent, Belgium 26 May 1935; came to Can. 1950; e. McGill Univ. B.A. 1955, B.C.L. 1958; m. Claudine Proutat; children: Jean-Pierre, Michel, Marie-Claude, Stephane, Annabelle; PARTNER, ROBINSON SHEPPARD SHAPIRO; law lectr. at various acad. insts.; legal commentator for French and Eng. radio and TV networks of CBC; Past Pres., Candn. Civil Liberties Union; Counsel to Parlty. Comte. investigating Co. of Young Candns.; Prosecuting Atty. in Sir George Williams Univ. affair; Atty. for Eng.-speaking parents of St. Leonard since 1968; Dr. Henry Morgentaler's former defence counsel; Legal Supvr. and Counsel to Que. Royal Comn. of Inquiry on Situation of French Lang. and on Linguistic Rights in Que. (Gendron Comn.); Fellow on linguistic rights of the UN; called to Bar of Que. 1959; author of numerous legal studies in various legal and other learned journs.; other works incl. reports for various Royal Comns. (Bilingualism & Biculturalism Castonguay Comn.; Gendron Comn.); former mem., Federal Advisory Council on the Status of Women; mem., Bar of Que.; Candn. Bar Assn.; Am. Bar Assn.; Candn. Inst. for the Adm. of Justice; Fellow, The Foundation for Legal Rsch.; Soc. des amis de Jean Cocteau; Soc. des amis de Balzac; McGill Law Grad. Assn.; Soc. des amis de Montaigne; Soc. des amis de Marcel Proust; Soc. des Amis de Colette; Soc. des Amis de François Mauriac; Musée des Beaux-Arts de Montreal; Museum of Modern Art, N.Y.; N.Y. Metropolitan Museum of Art; Cinémathèque Québécoise; Memphremagog Conservation Inc.; Massachusetts Horticultural Soc.; Am. Horticultural Soc.; Dir., Les Ballets Jazz de Montréal; Pres., Internat. Inst. of Comparative Linguistic Law; Pres., Fondation André-Guérin; Vice-Pres., Fondation Montréal AN 2000; Office: #4700, 800 Place Victoria, Montréal, Qué. H4Z 1H6.

**SHEPPARD, John Douglas,** LL.B.; barrister and solicitor; b. Toronto, Ont. 6 Nov. 1938; s. John William and Nan (Matthews) S.; e. London Teacher's Coll. 1959; Univ. of West. Ont., LL.B. 1968; m. Diane Elizabeth Burnell 26 Aug. 1967; children: William Matthew Burnell, Elizabeth Leigh; PARTNER, SHEPPARD, MACINTOSH & LADOS 1970– ; Elem. Sch. Teacher (Etobicoke, Ont.) 1960–61; Teacher, Fed. Retraining Prog., Eng., Clark Rd. S.S., Ont. Vocational Ctr. (London, Ont.) 1963–67; Law, Farm Bus. Mngt. Prog., Fanshawe Coll. (Simcoe) 1972–87; called to Bar of Law Soc. of U.C. 1970; Past Pres., Rotary Club of Simcoe 1982–83; Past Dir., Children's Aid Soc. of Norfolk; Past Pres., Norfolk Law Assn.; Pres., Heart & Stroke Found. of Ont. 1988–90; recreations: sailing, curling; clubs: Long Point Bay Sailing, Simcoe Curling; Home: 7 Pinehurst Ave., Simcoe, Ont. N3Y 3T5; Office: 58 Peel St., Simcoe, Ont. N3Y 4T2.

**SHERBANIUK, Douglas John,** B.A., LL.M.; e. Univ. of Alta., B.A. (Hons. Modern Langs.) 1950, LL.B. 1953; Columbia Univ., LL.M. 1962; PROF. OF LAW, UNIV. OF TORONTO since 1965 and DIR., CANADIAN TAX FOUNDATION; called to Bar of Alta. 1954, Ont. 1971; mem. Research Staff (1963–64) and Sr. Staff (1965–67), Royal Comn. on Taxation; mem. Research Staff Ont. Select Comn. on Co. Law, 1967; mem., Fed. Govt. Task Force, Can. Corp. Act. 1967, and Legal Advisor to Fed. Govt. Task Force on Structure of Canadian Industry, 1967; Q.C. 1984; Law Society Medal 1990; mem., Canadian Bar Association; Candn. Assn. Univ. Teachers; Assn. Candn. Law Teachers; Office: Faculty of Law, Univ. of Toronto, 78 Queen's Park, Toronto, Ont. M5S 2C5.

**SHERBOURNE, Archibald Norbert,** M.S., M.A., Ph.D., D.Sc., F.R.S.A., P.Eng., C.Eng. (U.K.); educator; consultant; b. Bombay, India 8 July 1929; s. Maneckji Nowroji Bulsara and Sarah Agnes S.; e. Univ. of London, B.Sc. 1953, D.Sc. 1970; Lehigh Univ., B.S. 1955, M.S. 1957; Univ. of Cambridge, M.A. 1959, Ph.D. 1960; m. Jean Duncan, d. William Jeffrey Nicol, Comrie, Scot. 15 Aug. 1959; children: Mary Ann, Sarah Elizabeth, Jeffrey Andrew, Nicolas Duncan, Jonathan David, Simon Alexander; PROF. OF CIVIL ENGN., UNIV. OF WATERLOO since 1963; Dean of Engn. there 1966–74; Chrmn., Adv. Comtes. on Engineering Educ.; Dir., Sherbourne Consultants Ltd.; Engr., British Rlys., London, 1948–51; Engr. Local Govt., Greater London Council, UK, 1952–54; Instr., Lehigh Univ., 1954–57; Sr. Asst. in Research, Univ. of Cambridge, 1957–61; joined present Univ. as Assoc. Prof. 1961–63, Chrmn. Dept. of

Civil Engn., 1964–66, Dean of Engn. 1966–74; Visiting Sr. Lecturer, University Coll., University of London, 1963–64; Visiting OECD-DSIR Fellow, E.T.H. Zurich 1964; CIDA Visiting Professor, University of West Indies, Trinidad, 1969–70 and others; NRC Senior Research Fellow, LNEC Portugal, 1970; Visiting Prof., EPF Lausanne, 1975–77; DAAD Visiting Fellowship, West Germany, 1975; NATO Sr. Scientist Fellowship & Visiting Lectureship, 1975–76; Gledden Visiting Sr. Fellow, Univ. of Western Australia, 1978; Visiting Prof., Michigan Tech. Univ. 1980–83; Visiting Prof. of Ocean Engr., Florida Atlantic Univ., 1985; Visiting Prof., Architectural & Civil Engineering, North Carolina A & T State Univ. 1987; Visiting Prof., Civil Engr., Kuwait Univ. 1989; Visiting Prof., Aerospace Engr., I.I.Sc., Bangalore, India 1990; writings include over 250 papers, articles, reports in technical journals; awarded Engn. Medal, Assn. Prof. Engrs. Ont. 1975; Fellow, Institution Structural Engrs. London; mem., Internat. Assn. Bridge & Structural Engrs. Switzerland; Designated European Engr. (Eur.Ing.) 1990; R. Catholic; recreation: travel; Home: 131 Keats Way Pl., Waterloo, Ont. N2L 5H4; Office: Waterloo, Ont. N2L 3G1.

**SHERLOCK, Most Rev. John Michael,** D.D., J.C.L., LL.D.; bishop (Roman Catholic); b. Regina, Sask. 20 Jan. 1926; s. John Joseph and Catherine (O'Brien) S.; e. Brantford (Ont.) Coll. Inst.; St. Jerome's Coll. Kitchener; Univ. of Toronto B.A. 1946; St. Augustine's Semy. Toronto D.D. 1950; Cath. Univ. of Am. Washington, D.C. post grad. studies Canon Law 1950–52, J.C.L. 1952; Univ. of Windsor LL.D. (hon. causa) 1985; o. 1950; BISHOP OF LONDON 1978– ; Assoc. Pastor St. Eugene's Parish, St. Augustine's Parish (Dundas) and Cath. of Christ the King, Hamilton 1952–63; Pastor St. Charles Garnier Parish, Hamilton 1963–74; Auxiliary Bishop of London, Ont. 1974–78; Advocate Judge Regional Matrimonial Tribunal 1954–72; Chaplain McMaster Univ.'s Newman Club 1952–63, Nat. Chaplain 1963–66; Pres. Candn Conf. Cath. Bishops 1983–85, Liaison Bishop of Conf. with Cath. Health Assn. Can., Cath. Univ. Chaplains; Chrmn., St. Joseph's Hosp. Bd. Hamilton; Chrmn., Hamilton Wentworth R. Cath. Separate Sch. Bd. 1974, mem. 1966–74; Chrmn., Social Affairs Commission of the Ont. Conference of Catholic Bishops; CCCB Representative on Bd., Candn. Council of Churches 1989–91 (Vice-Pres. 1990–91); Mem. of Bd., Vision T.V. 1991; The World Community for Christian Meditation 1991; Office: 1070 Waterloo St., London, Ont. N6A 3Y2.

**SHERMAN, Geraldine Patricia,** B.A.; writer; former radio producer; b. Chatham, Ont. 17 June 1941; d. Philip Percy and Helen Katzman S.; e. Chatham C.I. 1958; McGill Univ., B.A. (Hons.) 1962; Grad. Sch. of Town Planning, Univ. of Toronto, Dip.TP 1963; m. Robert Fulford s. Albert and Frances F. 28 Nov. 1970; children: Rachel Sherman Fulford, Sarah Helen Fulford; radio producer 1966–88; Extve. Prod., CBC Radio, 'State of the Arts' & 'The Arts Report' 1985–88; Organising Prod., CBC Radio, 'Identities,' 'Rule & Revolution,' 'Soundings,' 'This is Robert Fulford,' 'The Arts This Week' 1966–74; Extve. Prof., 'Ideas' 1974–83; Co-Vice Chairperson, Ont. Govt. 'Spec. Ctte. on the Arts' 1983–84; Journalism Fellowship, Asia Pacific Found. 1987; Bd. mem. Ont. College of Art 1989–92; Energy Probe; Home: 19 Lynwood Ave., Toronto, Ont. M4V 1K3.

**SHERMAN, Jason Scott,** B.A.; writer, editor; b. Montreal, Que. 28 July 1962; s. Cyril Henry and Grace (Gangbar) S.; e. George S. Henry S.S. S.S.H.G.D.; York Univ. B.A. (Hons.) 1985; m. Melinda d. Merv and Florence Little 24 June 1989; one son: Noah Nathaniel; Fiction & Drama Editor, Coach House Press 1990– ; Playwright-in-Residence, Necessary Angel Theatre 1994 and Tarragon Theatre 1992– ; playwright: 'A Place Like Pamela,' 'To Cry Is Not So' 1990, 'The Serpent Woman' 1991, 'The League of Nathans' 1992, 'Three in the Back, Two in the Head' 1994; received Chalmers Candn. Play Award for 'The League of Nathans'; editor: 'What Magazine' 1985–90, 'Canadian Brash' 1990 (anthology, Coach House Press), 'Solo' 1993 (anthology, Coach House Press); Journalist/Broadcaster, various (Globe & Mail, Toronto Star, CBC, etc.); Office: c/o Tarragon Theatre, 30 Bridgman Ave., Toronto, Ont. M5R 1X3.

**SHERMAN, Kenneth,** M.A.; writer; educator; b. Toronto, Ont. 3 July 1950; s. Ted and Eve (Diamond) S.; e. York Univ. B.A. 1972; Univ. of Toronto M.A. 1973; author (poetry) 'Snake Music' 1978; 'The Cost of Living' 1981; 'Words for Elephant Man' 1983; 'Black Flamingo' 1985; 'The Book of Salt' 1987; 'Jackson's Point' 1989; 'Open to Currents' 1992; ed. 'Relations: Family Portraits' 1985; co-founded lit. jour. 'Waves' 1970; ed. Mosaic Press 1984–86; lectr. Min. of Culture Beijing, China 1986; Address: c/o Oberon Press, 400, 350 Sparks St., Ottawa, Ont. K1R 7S8.

**SHERMAN, Louis R. (Bud),** B.A.; communications executive; b. Québec City, Qué. 24 Dec. 1926; s. Louis Ralph and Carolyn Zerelda (Gillmor) S.; e. Kelvin H.S. 1944; Univ. of Man. B.A. 1949; m. Elizabeth Ann d. Grant and Ann Beaton 28 Dec. 1955; children: Cathy Diane, Christopher Grant, Todd Laurence; VICE CHRMN., TELECOMMUNICATIONS, CDN. RADIO-TV & TELECOMMUNICATIONS COMM. 1987– ; West. Can. Mgr., Un. Press Internat. 1950s; Dir., News & Public Affairs, CKY TV 1960–65; M.P. for Winnipeg S. 1965–68; M.L.A. for Ft. Garry 1969–84; Min. of Health, Prov. of Man. 1977–81; also Min. of Comm. Serv. & Corrections, Dep. Leader, P.C. Party of Man. 1982–84; Cons., Assoc. Health Planners 1985; Comnr., C.R.T.C. 1985; Acting Chrmn., Cdn. Radio-TV & Telecommunications Comm. (Mar.-Aug.) 1989; Candn. Centennial Medal 1967; Queen Elizabeth Jubilee Medal 1977; Mem., P.C. Party of Can.; Candn. Counc. of Christians & Jews; Anglican Ch. of Can.; Opera Lyra, Ottawa; author of several articles; recreations: music, reading, films, travel, profl. sports; Club: The Manitoba; Home: 204 – 60 McLeod St., Ottawa, Ont. K2P 2G1; Office: Ottawa, Ont. K1A 0N2.

**SHERMAN, Theodore I.,** C.A.; executive; b. Toronto, Ont. 22 Nov. 1926; s. Morris and Sara (Cohen) S.; e. Queen's Univ. C.A. 1952; m. Donna d. Lewis and Doris Fox 22 Sept. 1954; children: Leslie, Bradley, Mitchell; CHIEF EXEC. OFFR. & CHRMN. OF THE BD., REVENUE PROPERTIES CO. LTD. 1986– ; Dir. Slater Industries Inc.; St. Clair Paint and Wallpaper Corp.; Dominion Trust Co.; Pennington Stores Ltd.; acctg. practice forerunner firm of Laventhol & Horwath 1947–68; real estate devel. and financing of real estate 1968–85; Exec. Vice Pres. present Co. 1985; Dir. Mount Sinai Hosp.; mem. Adv. Ctte. Centre for Rsch. in Neurodegenerative Diseases Univ. of Toronto; me. Temple Sinai Synagogue; recreation: golf; clubs: Oakdale Golf & Country, Primrose, Oaks Golf & Country (Fla.); Home: 1103, 619 Avenue Rd., Toronto, Ont. M4V 2K6; Office: 300, 131 Bloor St. W., Toronto, Ont. M5S 1R1.

**SHERRINGTON, Amanda Lesley;** professional conference organizer; b. London, England 12 Feb. 1950; d. Sidney and Elaine (Surinamer) Finley; e. Streatham Hill Pub. Day Sch. (U.K.); m. John L. s. David and Isabella S. 11 March 1973; one s.: Alexander Jeremy; FOUNDER & PRES., CO-ORDINATION PLUS INC. 1976– ; Asst. to the Chrmn., SIS Serv. (U.K.) 1968–70; Administrator 1970–74; Personnel Cons., Peggy Dean & Assoc. 1974–76; Finalist, 1992 Candn. Woman Entrepreneur of the Year; Founding Mem., Meeting Planners Internat. Candn. Chapter; Mem., Metro. Toronto Convention & Visitors Assn. (Dir. 1982–87 and 1993–94; Chair, Convention Services Council); Bd. of Trade of Metro. Toronto (Founding Ctte. Mem.); 'Business Networking' and 'Tourism'; Chair, Community Issues; Vice-Chair, 'Business to Business Exposition'; Women Entrepreneurs of Canada; Appointments, Candn. National Exhibition Assn.; Ontario Tourism Strategy Task Force Regional Ctte.; Metro Toronto Convention Centre Site Selection Task Force; Metro Toronto Advisory Ctte. on Child Care; Ont. Chamber of Commerce Tourism Ctte.; Sunnybrook Foundation special events ctte.; Clubs: Bd. of Trade of Metro. Toronto, Toronto Cricket, Fitness Inst.; Office: Suite 3504, Aetna Tower, Toronto Dominion Centre, P.O. Box 68, Toronto, Ont. M5K 1E7.

**SHERRINGTON, John L.,** B.A., M.A., M.B.A.; investment banker; b. Southport, England 19 Feb. 1949; s. David and Isabella S.; e. Oxford Univ. B.A. 1970, M.A. 1975; City of London Business School (England) M.B.A. 1972; m. Amanda 11 March 1973; one s.: Alexander; SR. VICE-PRESIDENT & DIRECTOR, SCOTIAMcLEOD INC.; Hill Samuel, Merchant Bankers, London, Eng.; joined McLeod Young Weir 1976; Vice-Pres. 1979; Dir. 1982; Fellow, Candn. Securities Inst.; Sunnybrook Health Sci. Ctr.; club: Fitness Inst.; Home: 15 Cortleigh Blvd., Toronto, Ont. M4R 1K5; Office: P.O. Box 433, Toronto-Dominion Ctr., Toronto, Ont. M5K 1M2.

**SHEVEL, W. Lee,** B.Sc., M.Sc., Ph.D., F.I.E.E.E.; business executive; b. Monessen, Pa. 26 Oct. 1932; s. Wilbert Lee and Lillian Marie (Palomaki) S.; e. Carnegie Mellon Univ. B.Sc. 1954, M.Sc. 1955, Ph.D. 1960; m. Faye d. John and Ethel Johnston 20 Aug. 1954; children: Lynn Ann Mucci, Laurel Sue Heath, Kathleen Joy Shevel, Amy Beth Jaquess; VICE PRES., CORP. INFO SYSTEMS, UNISYS CORP. 1992– ; Research Scientist, IBM Corp. 1956–59; Mgr., Magnetics Device Rsch. 1959–61; Mgr., Memory Rsch. 1961–63; Mgr., Magnetics Memory & Materials Rsch. 1963–65; Mgr., Adv. Mem. Devel. 1965–69; Mgr., Component Systems & Technol. 1969–71; Dir., Strategy & Resource Planning 1971–73; Vice-Pres. & Asst. Gen. Mgr., Consumer Prod. Div., Motorola 1973–74; Vice-Pres. & Gen. Mgr., Home Electronics Div., Rockwell Internat. 1974–76; Pres., Omex 1976–80; Barrington Internat. 1980–82; Vice-Pres., Corp. Opns., Unisys Corp. 1982–84; System & Technol. 1984–88; Pres., Paramax Systems Canada, Unisys Corp. 1988–92; Dir., Air Indus. Assn. Can.; Outstanding Engr. of Nation 1961–64; F.I.E.E.E. 1969; Sigma Xi Sci. Rsch. Soc.; Adv. Bd., Sch. of Computer Science, Carnegie Mellon Univ.; Stratford Fest. Benefactor; recreations: golf, fishing; clubs: Renaissance, Bernardo Heights Country; Home: 1970A Villa Ridge Dr., Reston, VA 22091.

**SHIELDS, Carol;** writer; professor; b. Oak Park, Ill. 2 June 1935; d. Robert Elmer and Inez Adelle (Sellgren) Warner; e. Hanover Coll., B.A. 1957; Univ. of Ottawa, M.A. 1975; m. Donald Hugh s. Clarence and Agnes S. 20 July 1957; children: John, Anne, Catherine, Margaret, Sara; ASSOC. PROF., UNIV. OF MAN. 1980– ; Writer-in-Residence, Univ. of Winnipeg, 1988 Winter term; Writer-in-Residence, Univ. of Ottawa 1989; Edit. Asst., Candn. Slavonic Papers 1973–75; Lectr., Univ. of Ottawa 1976; Univ. of B.C. 1978–80; recipient, The Governor General's Award 1993; Booker Prize nomination 1993; Guardian Prize nomination 1992; The Marian Engel Award 1990; Governor General's Award nomination 1988; Arthur Ellis Award 1988; Canada Counc. A Grant 1986, 1991; Nat. Magazine Award 1984, 1985 (Gold); Man. Arts Counc. (Sr. Award) 1985, (Short-term award) 1984; CBC 2nd Prize for short fiction 1984; CBC Prize for Drama 1983; Candn. Authors Assn. Award 1977; CBC Young Poets Comp. 1965; Mem., Winnipeg Library Bd. 1984–85; New Democratic Party; Man. Writers' Guild; Writers Union of Canada; Man. Assn. of Playwrights; P.E.N.; author: 'Others' 1972; 'Intersect' 1974; 'Susanna Moodie: Voice and Vision' 1975; 'Small Ceremonies' 1976; 'The Box Garden' 1977; 'Happenstance' 1980; 'The View' 1982; 'A Fairly Conventional Woman' 1982; 'Women Waiting' 1983; 'Various Miracles' 1985; 'Not Another Anniversary' (with D. Williamson) 1986; 'Swann' 1987; 'Face Off' 1987; 'The Orange Fish' 1989; 'Departures and Arrivals' 1990; 'A Celibate Season' (with Blanche Howard) 1991; 'The Republic of Love' 1992; 'Coming to Canada' 1992; 'Thirteen Hounds' 1993; 'The Stone Diaries' 1993; recreations: France, reading, theatre; Home: 701 – 237 Wellington Cr., Winnipeg, Man. R3M 0A1; Office: Univ. of Man., Winnipeg, Man. R3T 2H2.

**SHIELDS, Donald Allen,** B.S.A., M.Ed.; b. Shelburne, Ont. 19 Jan. 1928; s. LLoyd Clifford and Leila Jane S.; e. Univ. of Toronto, B.S.A. 1950, M.Ed. 1972; m. Betty Julian d. Bessie and Burnett Butchart 2 Sept. 1950; children: Andrew, Marc, Julie; Retired 1992; Curriculum Consultant, Sabah Foundation, Kota Kinabalu, Borneo, Malaysia 1991–92; Dir., Dubai Women's College of Higher Technology, Dubai, United Arab Emirates 1989–91; Pres., Sheridan College 1981–88; Dist. Mgr., Massey-Ferguson 1950; Sales Rep., Ford of Can. 1953; Truck Sales Mgr. 1955; Sci. Teacher, North York Bd. of Edn. 1958; Head, Sci. Dept., Downsview C.I. 1962; Vice-Prin., Emery C.I. 1965; Dean, Sheridan Coll. 1967; Vice-Pres. 1972; Penlake Cottage Assn.; Nat. Sci. Found. Scholarship 1964; Shell Merit Fellowship 1962; recreations: tennis, skiing, travel; Home: 26 Government Rd., Toronto, Ont. M8X 1V9.

**SHIER, Harry;** retail executive; b. Toronto, Ont. 9 Nov. 1926; s. Joseph and Sadie S.; e. Central Tech.; married; PRESIDENT AND CHIEF EXECUTIVE OPERATING OFFICER, ONTARIO STORE FIXTURES INC.; Office: 5145 Steeles Ave. W., Weston, Ont. M9L 1R5.

**SHIER, Milton;** business executive; b. Toronto, Ont. 24 Nov. 1917; s. Joseph and Sadie (Shulman) S.; e. Bloor C.I.; m. Shoshana d. Peretz and Sadie Sherman 14 July 1946; children: Joy-Anne, Joseph, Judy; CHAIRMAN, OSF INC., ONTARIO STORE FIXTURES INC., BENWIND INDUSTRIES, OSF AMERICA 1943– ; joined Ontario Store Fixtures 1938; RCAF 1941–43; Dir., M. Shier & Assoc.; Adamhay Holdings Limited; Office: 5145 Steeles Ave. W., Weston, Ont. M9L 1R5.

**SHIER, Robert Michael,** B.Sc., M.D., FRCS(C); university professor; b. Toronto, Ont. 13 Dec. 1941; s. Crawford Beatty and Frances Claire (Page) Shier; e. Univ. of Toronto, B.Sc. 1964, M.D. 1968; F.R.C.S.(C) 1973; m. Sara d. Mildred and Ted Taman; children: Cortney, Jeremy, Adam, Ashleigh; CHIEF, DIVISION OF GYNAECOLOGY, THE WELLESLEY HOSP. 1986– ; Assoc. Prof., Fac. of Med., Univ. of Toronto 1987– ; Dir. of Undergrad. Edn. for Obstetrics & Gynaecology 1986– ; Secy. Treas., Soc. of Candn.

Colposcopists; Univ. of Toronto Aikins Award recipient for excellence in undergrad. teaching 1987 and 1992; AOA Hon. Med. Soc.; Mem., Soc. of Obstet. & Gyn. of Can.; Ont. & Candn. Med. Assns.; Soc. of Candn. Colposcopists; clubs: Craigleith Ski, Toronto Lawn Tennis; Office: Suite 441, Jones Bldg., 160 Wellesley St., Toronto, Ont. M4Y 1J3.

**SHIFF, Helaine G.;** volunteer; b. Toronto, Ont. 24 Oct. 1940; d. Murray and Rose (Warshawsky) Pulver; e. Huron St. Pub. Sch.; Downsview Coll. Inst.; m. Allan s. Morris and Rachael Shiff 18 June 1961; children: Lorne, Melissa; NAT. PRES. JUVENILE DIABETES FOUND. CAN. 1988–92; Acctg. Asst. 1958–62; co-devel. N. York Bd. Edn. Multi-Aged Grouping Unit 1970; orgn. Learning Disability Prog. City of Toronto Pub. Sch. System, John Ross Robertson Sch. 1973–75; devel. and adm. Local Initiatives Progs. Grant for parents & learning-disabled children; Dir. Havenbrook Realty; Founder, Toronto Chapter, Juvenile Diabetes Found. Can. 1974, Pres. 1981–83, Nat. Fundraiser and Dir. 1981; Dir., Juvenile Diabetes Foundation Internat. 1992–94; Dir., Sec.-Treas. Hadesh Found.; Dir. Secular Jewish Assn. 1975–79; Bd. Mem., Music Toronto 1991–94; Council Jewish Women Ctte. 'Council 17' 1981–90; recipient Candn. Volunteer Award 1987; Canada's Birthday Achievement Award Metrop. Toronto 1990; Juvenile Diabetes Foundation Internat. Volunteer of the Year Award 1992; Bd. Mem., The New Mount Sinai Hosp., Toronto 1993–94; Advisor, Candn. Found. for Infectious Diseases 1993–94; Chairperson, Conference in Ottawa for Juvenile Diabetes Found. Internat. 1994; Home: 86 Cortleigh Blvd., Toronto, Ont. M4R 1K6; Office: 108, 90 Sheppard Ave. E., North York, Ont. M2N 3A1.

**SHILLINGTON, Edward Blain,** B.A., LL.B.; politician; b. Moose Jaw, Sask. 28 Aug. 1944; s. Sterling Arthur and Dorathy Jessie (Henry) S.; e. Univ of Saskatchewan B.A. 1967, LL.B. 1967; m. Sonia Shirley d. John and Anna Koroscil 15 Aug. 1970; children: Ryan, Tara; MINISTER OF LABOUR, GOVERNMENT OF SASKATCHEWAN 1992– ; 1st elected to Sask. Legislature 1975; re-elected 1978, '82, '86, '91; served as Min. of Co-operatives, Edn. and Culture and Youth 1975–80; practiced law with Shillington-Dore Law Office 1980–92; is also currently Min. resp. for Sask. Computer Utility Corp.; recreations: reading, boating, fishing; Home: 2321 Argyle St., Regina, Sask. S4T 3T4; Office: Legislative Bldg., Room 307, Regina, Sask. S4S 0B3.

**SHILLINGTON, William M.;** employee benefits consultant; b. Chatham, Ont. 15 Jan. 1937; s. John Harold and Rowana Euphemia (McColl) S.; m. Margaret d. Bruce and Mary Krause 1 April 1961; children: Kristy, Jacki, Jane; PRINCIPAL, WILLIAM M. MERCER LIMITED 1963– ; Canadian Imperial Bank of Commerce 1957–61; Sun Life of Canada 1961–63; Mem., Human Resources Professionals of Ont.; London C. of C.; recreations: curling, golf, fishing; Home: R.R. 1, Morpeth, Ont. N0P 1X0; Office: 700 Richmond St., Suite 200, London, Ont. N6A 5C7.

**SHILTON, Elizabeth Jean,** B.A., M.A., LL.B., LL.M.; lawyer; b. Wolseley, Sask. 6 Nov. 1948; d. James Fraser and Jean Irving (Baynton) S.; e. Univ. of Toronto B.A. 1971, M.A. 1972; Dalhousie Univ. LL.B. 1977; Harvard Univ. LL.M. 1979; m. David Robert s. Robert and Sylvia Mackenzie 21 Sept. 1986; children: Graeme, Christina; FOUNDING PARTNER, CAVALLUZZO, HAYES & SHILTON (formerly Cavalluzzo, Hayes & Lennon) 1983– ; articled with Golden, Levinson 1977–78; Assoc. 1980–83; part-time fac., York Univ., Atkinson Coll. 1983; Osgoode Hall Law Sch. 1991; Univ. of Toronto 1980–82; Extve. Mem., Women's Legal Edn. & Action Fund (LEAF) 1987–88; Dir. 1987–90, 1992–93; Mem., LEAF Nat. Legal Ctte. 1987–93 (Chair 1987–90, 1992–93); Extve. Mem. & Founding Dir., LEAF Found. 1990–92; Mem., Law Soc. of U.C.; Candn. Bar Assn.; LEAF; N.D.P.; author of var. pub. articles on labour & employment law & women's equality issues; Office: 43 Madison Ave., Toronto, Ont. M5R 2S2.

**SHINER, Donald Victor,** C.D., B.Sc., M.B.A., Ph.D.; consultant; educator; b. Victoria, B.C. 12 Dec. 1948; s. John Edgar and Mardine (Ferrie) S.; e. Acadia Univ. B.Sc. 1969; Dalhousie Univ. M.B.A. 1980; Univ. of Bradford UK Ph.D. 1989; m. Nancy d. Thomas R. Power 17 July 1971; children: Christopher John Edgar, Jennifer Marie Francis; ASSOCIATE, PEAT MARWICK STEVENSON & KELLOGG 1989– ; Assoc. Prof. of Mktg. Mount Saint Vincent Univ. 1984– , served R.O.T.P.; Candn. Armed Forces 12 yrs. as Communications Electronics Systems Eng. (RC Signal Corps), UNEFME and C.D.; joined Bell Canada Internat. 1980; author 'Marketing Planning in High Technology Firms' 1989; various jour. articles; Board mem., Human Resources Devel. Assn.; mem. Am. Mktg. Assn.; recreation: restoring antique cars; Home: 19A Box 46, R.R.2 Armdale, N.S. B3L 4J2; Office: Office: 1507 Purdy's Wharf Tower One, 1959 Upper Water St., Halifax, N.S. B3J 3N2.

**SHIPLEY, Robert Jon Meyer,** B.A., M.A.; heritage planner; author; b. Toronto, Ont. 26 Feb. 1948; s. Capt. Vernon Meyer and Miriam Irene (Smith) S.; e. Westminster Secondary Sch. London, Ont.; Univ. of W. Ont., B.A. 1971, Hons. 1972; Univ. of Waterloo, M.A. 1992, Ph.D. in progress; m. Pamela Joan Fielding d. Dr. William and Doris Fielding 21 May 1983; one s. Ceilidh Jamieson Meyer; HERITAGE CONSULTANT 1990– ; Offr. Candn. Armed Forces 1972–76, serving Calgary, Chilliwack, Halifax, Atlantic, Caribbean, Eur., London, Ont.; freelance writer, edn. cons., playwright & journalist 1976–84; Exec. Adm. Welland Canals Preservation Assn. 1984–87; Sr. Develop. Consultant, Welland Canals Soc. 1987–90; Guest Lectr. Univ. of Waterloo, Mich. State Univ., Univ. of W. Ont., Brock Univ., Niagara Coll.; orgn. and Dir. Prov. Sch. Theatre Festival during Ont.'s Bicentennial 1984; author: 'Relationships' poetry, drawings 1984; 'St. Catharines – Garden on the Canal' illus. hist. 1987; 'To Mark Our Place – A History of Canadian War Memorials' 1987; author & illustrator: 'The Girl Who Got Stuck in the Mud' juvenile 1987; 'The Value of Heritage Properties' 1993; co-author: 'Schooners of the Great Lakes' 1990; 'Paddlewheelers of the Great Lakes' 1990; 'Wrecks & Disasters of the Great Lakes' 1992; 'Propellers of the Great Lakes' 1992; 'On Leaving Bai Di Cheng' 1993; numerous articles various newspapers & magazines; ed. 'History Through Drama' bibliog. Candn. Hist. Plays for Schs. 1984; Bd. Mem., Candn. Assoc. of Professional Heritage Consultants; provisional mem. Candn. Inst. of Planners; Editorial Bd. Mem., NC Press; mem. Ont. Hist. Soc.; Heritage Can. Found.; mem. and Founding Pres. Niagara Br., Candn. Author's Assn.; NDP, Riding Pres. 1979–85, Campaign Mgr. 1981–84; mem. Conestogo United Church; recreations: drawing, painting; Home: 89 King St., Conestogo, Ont. N0B 1N0; Office: School of Urban and Regional Planning, Univ. of Waterloo, Waterloo, Ont. N2L 3G1.

**SHIPOWICK, Taras,** B.F.A.; special event producer; b. Toronto, Ont. d. Michael and Irene (Kotelko) S.; e. York Univ., BFA; Julliard Sch. of Mus.; Royal Conserv. of Mus.; Banff Sch. of Fine Arts; PRES., SHOWMAKERS INC. 1984– ; Writer, Dir. & Creative Cons. for corp. & govt. special events; Dir., Queen Elizabeth II Jubilee perf.; Prod., Ont. Bicentennial Showcase Tour; Canada Day, Internat. Theatre Mosaic (UNESCO); Cons., Brooklyn Acad. of Mus.; NHL All Star; Sec. of State; Guest Teacher, York Univ., George Brown Coll.; Ryerson; Univ. of Man.; Banff Ctr. Scholarships; Mayors Award; Can. Counc. Arts Award; Special Event Magazine Award; Maxi Award; Office: P.O. Box 6288, Stn. A, Toronto, Ont. M5W 1P7.

**SHIPP, Harold G.;** community builder; b. Toronto, Ont. 21 Jan. 1926; s. late Gordon Stanley and Bessie Luella (Breeze) S.; e. Etobicoke (Ontario) Collegiate Inst.; m. June Catharine Ingram, 30 Sept. 1949; children: Victoria Haviland Shipp, Catharine Marjorie Wells, Gordon Harold; CHRMN. OF BD., CHIEF EXTVE. OFFR., SHIPP CORP. LTD.; Shipp Corp. Inc. (Fla.); Pres., Applewood Chevrolet Geo Oldsmobile Cadillac; Applewood BMW Inc.; joined father in home building business 1945; Chrmn., The Ont. Building Industry Strategy Bd. 1985–88; Dir. & former Vice-Chrmn., Bd. of Govs., Queensway Gen. Hosp.; Charter Dir. & Hon. Chrmn. of Bd., Mississauga Hosp. Foundation; Mem. Adv. Counc., Etobicoke Sch. of the Arts; Past Pres., Toronto Home Builders' Assn.; Candn. Home Builders' Assn.; Life Dir. & Liaison Director to National Assn. Home Builders U.S.; Trustee and Life Counc. Mem., Urban Land Inst. (U.S.); Dir., The Family Enterprise Found.; Dir., Candn. Assoc. of Family Enterprise (CAFE); Dir., Ont. Harness Horsemen's Assoc.; Trustee, Ont. Jockey Club; Pres., Kingsway Kiwanis Club, 1960 (Lt. Gov., Div. 4A, Eastern Canada and Caribbean Dist., 1964); helped to found Kiwanis Clubs in Caribbean; Gen. Campaign Chrmn., Un. Way Peel Region 1977; Pres., Mississauga City Bd. of Trade 1982; awarded, Silver Jubilee Medal; Commemorative Medal for 125th Anniversary of Candn. Confederation 1992; Paul Harris Award for community service, Rotary Club 1984; el. to Candn. Home Builders' 'Hall of Fame' 1986; Mississauga 'Citizen of the Year, 1988'; Knight of Grace, Sovereign Order of St. John of Jerusalem; awarded, Art Rooney Award, Harness Track of America 1992; City of Etobicoke Personal & Corporate Service Award 1992; Clubs: Mississauga Golf & Country; Granite; Port Credit Yacht; Tower (Fort Lauderdale); Home: 500 Comanche Rd., Mississauga, Ont. L5H 1W2; Office: Suite 1600, Mississauga Extve. Centre, 4 Robert Speck Pkwy., Mississauga, Ont. L4Z 1S1.

**SHIRLEY, Clifford J.,** B.A., M.B.A.; banker; e. Dalhousie Univ. B.A. 1962; Mass. Inst. Technol. M.B.A. 1966; EXEC. VICE PRES. CANADIAN IMPERIAL BANK OF COMMERCE 1982– ; joined present Bank St. John's, Nfld. 1951 serving in all 4 Atlantic provs. until 1962, Mgr. Main Br. Winnipeg 1966, Vice Pres.: Sask. 1967, Man. 1971, Internat. 1974, Ont. E. and N. 1976, B.C., Vancouver & Lower Mainland 1978, Sr. Vice Pres. B.C. and Y.T. 1981; Dir. Toronto Symphony; Assoc. Dir. Dalhousie Univ.; Clubs: Cambridge; Granite; Vancouver; Office: Commerce Court West, Toronto, Ont. M5L 1A2.

**SHIRLEY, Roger John,** B.A.; company executive; b. Bathurst, N.B. 7 Aug. 1921; s. Edgar Russell and Lydia (Le Marquand) S.; e. Pub. and High Schs., Bathurst, N.B.; Dalhousie Univ. 1939–41; Univ. of W. Ont., B.A. 1948; m. Janet Armour, d. Strachan Ince, Toronto, Ont. 14 Feb. 1953; children: Anne Lydia, David John, Peter Strachan; Depy. Chrmn., Bonar Inc.; joined J.D. Woods and Gordon, Ltd. as Consultant, 1948; apptd. Dir. 1957; opened Vancouver office 1957 and Calgary office 1960; Administrative Partner 1957–64; Partner, Woods, Gordon & Co., 1962; Administrative Partner, Montreal Office, 1964; Regional Partner, E. Can., 1969; Extve. Vice Pres. and Dir., Candn. Internat. Power Co. Ltd. and Chrmn. Investment Comte. 1970–73; Extve. Vice Pres. and Dir. C.I. Power Services Ltd. 1970–73; Pres., Bowater Canadian Ltd. 1974–79; served with R.C.N.V.R. 1941–45; rank Lt. Commdr.; Chairman, Red Feather Foundation 1974–79; Dir. and Treas., Centraide, Montreal 1970–79; Children's Aid Soc. Metrop. Toronto 1953–57; Un. Community Fund Vancouver 1957–64; Dir., Vancouver Internat. Festival 1963–64 (Vice Pres. 1964); Anglican; Clubs: Oakville Golf; Rideau (Ottawa); Address: 284 Gloucester Ave., Oakville, Ont. L6J 3W9.

**SHLESINGER, Joseph Charles,** B.A., M.B.A.; corporate strategy consultant; b. Toronto, Ont. 3 Oct. 1961; s. Harry and Hanna (Botnik) S.; e. Ryerson Polytechnical Inst. B.A. 1983; Univ. of Western Ont. M.B.A. 1986; single; MANAGING DIRECTOR, BAIN & COMPANY 1991– ; Casewriter, Univ. of Western Ont. 1985; joined Bain & Company London, U.K. 1986; transferred to Bain Boston U.S.A. 1987; returned to U.K. & promoted to Mgr. 1988; Co-founded Bain Canada 1989; specializes in consulting to service companies, to develop cost reduction & service enhancement strategies; Club: Ontario Club; recreations: golf, skiing, classic cars and car racing; Home: 11 Woodlawn Ave. W., Suite 2, Toronto, Ont. M4V 1G6; Office: 162 Cumberland St., Suite 300, Toronto, Ont. M5R 3N5.

**SHNIER, Allan;** manufacturing & distribution executive; b. Emerson, Man. 11 June 1928; s. Morris and Sarah (Bernstein) S.; e. Rhona d. Charles and Anne Ostrove; children: Clifford, Sarah, Jordy, Gary; Pres., Metropolitan Equities Limited; Metropolitan Equities U.S.A. Ltd.; United Fibre-Bond Inc.; United Wood Frame Inc.; Office: 1175 Sherwin Rd., Winnipeg, Man. R3H 0V1.

**SHNIER, Philip;** executive; b. Can. 12 May 1925; e. Queen's Univ.; Univ. of Okla. 1947; m. Shirley Abugov 16 Nov. 1952; children: Mark, Mitchell, Jeffrey, Karyn, Debbie; VICE-CHRMN., GESCO INDUSTRIES INC. 1983– ; Pres., Cardinal Leasing Ltd.; Vice Pres., Metropolitan Equities Ltd.; joined Canadian Resins and Chemicals, jt. venture Union Carbide and Shawinigan Water & Power, Shawinigan, Que. 6 yrs.; American Texolite Corp. Passaic, N.J. one yr.; Ind. Eng. special projects C.I.L. Inc. 10 yrs.; joined present Co. 1963; mem., Prof. Engs. Prov. Ont.; Bd. Trade Metrop. Toronto; recreations: golf, tennis, jogging; Home: 8 York Downs Dr., Downsview, Ont. M3H 1H8; Office: 1965 Lawrence Ave. W., Weston, Ont. M9N 1H5.

**SHOCTOR, Joseph H.,** O.C., Q.C., B.A., LL.B., LL.D.; b. Edmonton, Alta.; e. Pub. and High Schs. Edmonton; Univ. of Alta, B.A., LL.B.; COUNSEL, DUNCAN & CRAIG; Dir., Harvey Holdings Ltd.; and numerous Alta. Co.s in devel., construction and hospitality services; Assoc. Producer on Broadway 'Peter Pat' 1965, 'Henry Sweet Henry' 1967; Co-Producer Off-Broadway 'Hamp' 1966, on Broadway 'Billy' 1969, Nicol Williamson's 'Hamlet' 1969; Nat. Tour of 'Hamlet' 1969; Hon. Patron, National Screen Inst.; Dir., Edmonton Motion Picture & Television Bureau; Founder and Pres., Extve. Producer Citadel Theatre, Chrmn. Campaign and Bldg. New Citadel Theatre 1975–76; Life Gov., Nat. Theatre Sch. Can. 1993; Hon. Gov. Dom. Drama Festival; Panelist CFRN TV 'Wide Open' 2 seasons; Producer and Dir. Circle '8' Theatre; Red Cross Entertainment and Travelling N.W. Staging Route; regular Panelist CBC TV 'Sports Forum' 1972–74; impressario name bands, entertainers, concert artists Winnipeg to Vancouver early 1950's; originated first entertainment paper Edmonton 'Downtown Edmonton,' Original Founder/First Secy./Mgr. & Bd. mem. 13 yrs. Edmonton Eskimo Football Club; Vice Chrmn. Un. Community Fund 1969, Chrmn. Prof. Div. 1968, Legal Div. 1970, Gen. Campaign Chrmn. 1972; Chrmn., Mayor's Task Force on the Heart of the City of Edmonton, 1984; Chrmn., Edmonton Downtown Development Corp. 1986; Hon. mem. Edmonton Jewish Welfare Bd.; Hon. Dir., Edmonton Sports Foundation 1992; Past Pres. Edmonton Jewish Community Council; Past Nat. Secy. Fed. Zionist Organ. Can.; Past Nat. Vice Pres. Un. Jewish Appeal Inc.; Past Bd. mem. Candn. Council Jewish Welfare Funds; Hon. Life Mem., The Edmonton Klondike Days Assn. 1992; apptd. Queen's Counsel 1960; named CFRN TV 'Man of the Hour' 1966; B'Nai B'rith 'Citizen of the Year' 1966; Negev Dinner Honoree Edmonton 1967; City of Edmonton Performing Arts Award 1972; Prov. Alta. 'Achievement Award in recognition of Outstanding Service in Theatre Arts' 1975; Citadel Theatre names Main Auditorium 'The Shoctor Stage' 1976; Queen's Silver Jubilee Medal 1977; Mem., Order of Canada 1978; Prime Minister's Med. State of Israel 1978; City of Edmonton 75th Anniversary 'Builder of the Community' Award (16 only) 1979; Chosen by The Alberta Report (Alberta's Weekly Newsmagazine) one of 'The Twelve Top Albertans of the '70s'; Hon. LL.D. Univ. of Alta. 1981; Chrmn. Mayor's Task Force on the Heart of the City of Edmonton 1984; Silver Ribbon Award, City of Edmonton 1985; Officer, Order of Canada 1986; Hon. Dipl. in Theatre Admin., Grant MacEwan Community Coll. 1986; Builder, Edmonton Cultural Hall of Fame 1987; Performing Arts Publicists' Assoc. Award for Outstanding Contrib. to the Performing Arts 1989; The Alberta Order of Excellence 1990; Great Candn. Award 1992; Commemorative Medal for 125th Anniversary of Candn. Confederation 1992; Bd. of Dirs., The John G. Diefenbaker Memorial Found. Inc.; Gen. Chrmn./Chrmn. Legal Profession/Chrmn. Professional Div./Vice Chrmn., United Way 1968–72; Mem. Bd. of Advisors, Goodwill Rehabilitation Services of Alta. 1993; mem. Edmonton Bar Assn.; Law Soc. Alta.; Candn. Bar Assn.; Edmonton Chamber Comm.; Clubs: Edmonton; Centre Club; Home: 9022 Valleyview Dr., Edmonton, Alta. T5R 5T6; Office: 1501 Toronto-Dominion Tower, Edmonton, Alta. T5J 2Z1.

**SHOEMAKER, John Michael,** B.A., LL.B., Q.C.; civilian member, RCMP; lawyer; b. Toronto, Ont. 9 Oct. 1933; s. Wilfrid Henry and Helene Urania (Lanktree) S.; e. Trinity Coll., B.A. (Hons.) 1956; Univ. of Toronto, LL.B. 1959; m. Brenda d. Gilbert and Beatrice Nunns June 1967; children: Adam, Alexandra, John, David, Victoria; DEPUTY COMM., CORP. MNGT., ROYAL CANADIAN MOUNTED POLICE 1988– ; Fgn. Serv. Offr., Dept. of External Affairs, 1959–62; student at law, McDonald, Davies and Ward 1962–65; lawyer, Miller, Thomson, Hicks, Sedgwick, et. al 1965–67; Extve. Asst. to the Minister without Portfolio (Jean Chretien) 1967–68; various posts ending as Asst. Secy. to Cabinet, Privy Counc. of Can. 1968–74; Extve. Dir., CRTC 1974–79; Sr. Asst. Dep. Solicitor Gen., Dept. of Solicitor Gen. 1979–87; Extve. Dir., Appeals & Investigations, Public Serv. Comn. of Can. 1987–88; winner of several inter-scholarstic scholarships incl. World Univ. Serv. Summer Sch.; Univ. of Toronto 1956, War Mem. Sch.; Nesbitt Gold Medal 1952; Univ. of Toronto Schs.; Q.C. 1981; Mem., Law Soc. of U.C.; Candn. Inst. for the Admin. of Justice; RCMP Officers' Mess; Ctte. for Bravery Decorations, Govt. House 1973–74; recreations: squash, tennis; Home: 388 Mariposa Ave., Rockcliffe, Ont. K1M 0S9; Office: 1200 Vanier Parkway, Ottawa, Ont. K1A 0R2.

**SHON, Ronald C.,** B.A., M.B.A.; investor; real estate executive; b. Okinawa, Japan 2 Jan. 1953; s. Charles Chee and Gim Lan (Yip) S.; e. Choate Sch. Wallingford, Conn. 1971; Stanford Univ. B.A. 1975; Wharton Sch. of Finance Univ. of Pa. M.B.A. 1977; m. Sharon d. Theodore and Dorothy Chang 2 Aug. 1980; three s.: Jeffrey Charles, Christopher Theodore, Mathew Scott; PRES. AND CHIEF EXEC. OFFR. THE SHON GROUP OF COMPANIES 1977– ; Chrmn. Skyline Explorations Ltd.; Dir. Inel Resources Ltd.; Trustee, Dr. Sun Yat-Sen Garden Soc. (former Pres.); Vancouver Museum Found.; Dir., Candn. Cancer Soc. (B.C. & Yukon Div.); Vancouver Symphony Soc.; Pride Can.; Vancouver Bd. of Trade; mem. Young Pres.' Orgn. B.C. Chapter; recreations: golf, tennis, skiing, running; Clubs: Vancouver; Capilano Golf; Arbutus; Office: 2000 - 925 W. Georgia, Vancouver, B.C. V6C 3L2.

**SHOONER, Pierre;** B.A., M.Comm.; insurance executive; b. Pierreville, Aug. 1935; e. Univ. de Montréal B.A. 1958; École des hautes études commerciales, Univ. de Montréal M.Comm.(Econ.) 1961; Pres. & C.O.O., Cooperants Mutual Life Insurance Soc. 1983 and Cooperants Group; Chrmn. Exec. Ctte. and Dir., Guardian Trustco Inc.; Chrm. Extve. & Dir., Financière Entraide-Coopérants; Pres.: Les Cooperants, compagnie d'assurance général; Dir.: Epiciers-Unis; Metro-Richelieu Inc.; Guardian Financial Corp.; First Internat. Life Insurance Co.; IST (L'Industrielle Services Techniques Inc.); Gestion Sodiart Inc.; Gendron, Lefebvre Inc.; former Dir. Gen., Chambre de commerce de Montréal; Dir. and Ed.-in-Chief, Revue Commerce 1970–72; Asst. Dep. Min. of Ind. & Comm. Qué. 1975–79; first Dir. and Gen. Comnr. CIDEM (Comn. d'initiative et de développement économique de Montréal) 1979–83; Bd. Chrmn., I.D.U. Qué. (Inst. de développement urbain du Qué.); Vice Chrmn., Théâtre de la Marjolaine; Mem. Extve. Ctte., Chambre de commerce de la prov. du Québec; Dir.: Univ. of Montreal; Fondation CRUDEM Can.-Haïti Inc.; YMCA; Found. of Friends of the Catholic Inst. of Montreal; Clin. Rsch. Institute of Montreal; Montreal Internat. Music Competition; Montreal Sci., Tech. and Ind. Center; Life Mem., Chamb. de Comm. de Montréal; EPIC Health Centre; mem.: Cercle des officiers du régiment de Maisonneuve; Candn. Council of Internat. Chamb. of Comm.; Qué Ctte., C.D. Howe Inst.; Club: St-Denis; Address: 1540 Bernard, Apt. 28, Outremont, Que. H2V 1W8.

**SHORE, Jacques J.M.,** LL.L., LL.B.; lawyer; b. Montreal, Que. 13 Sept. 1956; s. Sigmond and Thérèse Lena (Herzig) S.; e. Univ. de Montréal LL.L. 1978; McGill Univ. LL.B. 1980; City of London (Eng.) Polytechnic Dip. Internat. Law summer 1977; m. Donna A. d William and Doris Cohen 19 March 1978; three d. Emily, Amanda, Victoria; PARTNER, SMITH LYONS TORRENCE STEVENSON AND MAYER 1991– ; called to Bar of Ont. 1982, Bar of Que. 1988; Criminal Justice Policy Analyst Solr. Gen. Can. 1981–83; Rsch. Prog. Adm. and Exec. Asst. to Dir. Legal/Constitutional Rsch. Royal Comn. Econ. Union & Devel. Prospects Can. (Macdonald Comn.) 1983–85; Dir. Rsch. Security Intelligence Review Ctte. 1985–87, Counsel; Associate, Heenan Blaikie 1987–90; General Counsel, Candn. Affairs, The Fairfax Group Ltd. (Falls Church, Virginia) 1990–91; Chief Negotiator Govt. of Canada, Golden Lake Algonquin Land Claim 1992– ; Mem. Medical Rsch. Ethics Ctte., Childrens' Hosp. of Eastern Ont. 1993; Mem. Extve., Canadian Club of Ottawa 1993; Chrmn. to the Superintendent's Adv. Bd. of the Ont. Insurance Commission 1991– ; Lectr. in Human Rights & Criminal Justice System Algonquin Coll. Ottawa 1983–84; Perm. mem., Legal Adv. to Med. Rsch. Ethics Ctte. Montreal Gen. Hosp. 1988–90; Former Chrmn. Community Relations Ctte. Candn. Jewish Cong. (Que. Region); Trustee Cong. Shaar Hashomayim 1988–90; Co-Founder and Dir. Que. Soc. Med. & Law; former mem. Bd. of Dirs., Lord Reading Law Soc.; Co-Founder and former extve. mem. Bar Admission Adv. Ctte. of the Law Soc. Upper Can. 1982–85; mem. Candn. Bar Assn.; Past Pres. New Edinburgh Community Assn.; author various publs. pub. policy, med. law, criminal justice issues; recreations: downhill skiing, squash, water skiing, painting; Home: 25 Cowichan Way, Ottawa, Ont. K2H 7E6; Office: 50 O'Connor St., Suite 1611, Ottawa, Ont. K1P 6L2.

**SHORT, Rt. Rev. Hedley Vicars Roycraft,** B.A., B.D., D.D. (Ang.); bishop; b. Toronto, Ont. 24 Jan. 1914; s. Hedley Vicars and Martha Hallam (Parke) S.; e. Private and Pub. Schs., Toronto; Univ. of Toronto, B.A. 1941; Trinity Coll., L.Th. 1943, B.D. 1945, D.D. 1964; D.D. (Hon. caus.) Univ. of Emmanuel Coll., Sask., 1983; m. Elizabeth Frances Louise, d. Russell Edward and Elsa Louise (Thorning) Shirley, Cochrane, Ont., 14 Apl. 1953; children: Martha Frances (Bowden), Elizabeth Helena (Rodgers), Janet Louise (De Giromlamo), Margaret Stephane (Zulkoskey), Desmond James Vicars; business career 1932–38; o. Deacon 1943; o. Priest 1944; Assistant Curate, St. Michael and All Angels, Toronto, 1943–46; Junior Chaplain, Coventry Cath., Eng., 1946–47; Lectr. and Sr. Tutor, Trinity Coll., Toronto, 1947–51; Dean of Residence 1949–51; Rector, Holy Trinity, Cochrane, Ont., 1951–56; during this period Examining Chaplain to Bishop of Moosonee (Extve. Comte. of Diocese; Prov. Synod; Gen. Synod; Rural Dean of Cochrane); Rector, St. Barnabas' Ch., St. Catharines, Ont., 1956–63; during this period Examining Chaplain to Bishop of Niagara (Extve. Comte. of Diocese; Prov. and Gen. Synods); Canon, Christ's Ch. Cath., Hamilton, Ont., 1962–63; Dean of Sask., Canon Residentiary of St. Alban's Cath., Prince Albert, 1963–70; Archdeacon of Prince Albert 1966–70; Bishop of Saskatchewan 1970–85; Chancellor, Univ. of Emmanuel Coll., 1974–79; Pres. of Council, Coll. of Emmanuel & St Chad, Saskatoon, 1973–80; Hon. Fellow, Univ. of Emmanuel Coll., Saskatoon, 1980; Past Chrmn., High Sch. Bd., Cochrane, Ont.; Past Chrmn., High Sch. Bd., Prince Albert; Past Chrmn. Bd. Govs., Prince Albert Regional Community Coll., Prince Albert; Chrmn., Doctrine and Worship Committee, Anglican Church of Can. 1973–83; Mem., Prov. Jubilee Ctte. Sask. 1979–80; Visiting Prof., Coll. of Emmanuel & St. Chad, 1982; mem., Northern Development Adv. Counc. (Govt. of Sakatchewan) 1985; recreations: music (violin), sketching, reading, travel; Address: 355 - 19th St. W., Prince Albert, Sask. S7V 4C8.

**SHORT, Martin,** B.S.W.; actor, comedian; b. 1951; s. Charles Patrick and Olive S.; e. McMaster Univ. B.S.W. 1972; m. Nancy Dolman; children: Katherine, Oliver, Henry; Actor: (feature films) 'Three Amigos' 1986, 'Innerspace' 1987, 'Cross My Heart' 1987; (TV series) 'The Associates' 1979, 'I'm a Big Girl Now' 1980–81, SCTV Network 1982–84, '90, 'Saturday Night Live' 1985–86; (TV movie) 'Martin Short's Consent for the North American' 1985, 'Really Weird Tales' 1987, 'Martin Short Goes to Hollywood' '987, 'Three Fugitives' 1989, 'The Big Picture' 1989; also numerous revues and cabaret appearances with Second City comedy troup 1977–78; Office: Rollins Joffe Mngt., 10201 W. Pico Blvd., No. 58, Los Angeles, Ca. 90064-2606.

**SHORT, Robert C.,** B.A.Sc., P.Eng.; executive; b. Toronto, Ont. 3 Dec. 1925; s. Charles Montague and Gertrude (Algie) S.; e. Pub. Schs., Toronto, Ont. 1937; Univ. of Toronto Schs. (Hons. Jr. and Sr. Matric.) 1943; awarded Nesbit Gold Medal and Bryce Engn. Scholar.; Univ. of Toronto, B.A.Sc. (Hons. Elect. Engn.) 1949; m. Ruth Virginia, d. late N.A. Myra, Sept. 1951; children: Douglas, Jane, David; R.C. SHORT & ASSOCIATES INC. 1990– ; served overseas with Royal Candn. Artillery 1943–45; with Ferranti Packard Ltd. as Sales Mgr., Que. and Ont. 1949; Pres., Edwards Co. 1960; Founding Pres., St. Lawrence Coll., Kingston, Ont. 1967; Pres., Candn. Cable TV Association 1971; Vice-Pres., Selkirk Communications Ltd. 1979; Pres., Candn. Satellite Communications Inc. 1981; Vice-Pres. Canada Wire and Cable Ltd. 1983; Depy. Chrmn., C.U.C. Ltd. 1987–89; Anglican; recreations: sailing, reading; Clubs: Royal Hamilton Yacht; Royal Canadian Military Inst.; Home: 1201 Northshore Blvd. E., Burlington, Ont. L7S 1Z5; Office: Burlington Office Centre, 2349 Fairview St., Burlington, Ont. L7R 2E3.

**SHORT, Roger John,** M.A., B.Sc., M.B.A.; business executive; b. England 17 Sept. 1939; e. Oxford Univ. B.A. 1961, M.A., B.Sc., 1963; Univ. of Toronto M.B.A. 1979; m. Susan; PRES. & CHIEF EXECUTIVE OFFICER, WAJAX LIMITED 1991– ; Vice-Pres., Planning, Canron Indus. Inc. 1981–85; Extve. Vice-Pres. 1985–87; Pres. 1987–89; Pres., Domtar Packaging, Domtar Chem. 1989–90; Pres. & Chief Op. Offr., Wajax Limited 1991; Mem., Business Council on National Issues; Bd. Mem., The Montreal Gen. Hosp.; clubs: Cambridge, The Mount Royal, Royal Montreal Golf, Vancouver; Home: 4700 St. Catherine St. W., Apt. 808, Westmount, Que. H3Z 1S6; Office: 770 Sherbrooke St. W., Ste. 1750, Montreal, Que. H3A 1G1.

**SHORTELL, Ann M.,** B.A.; author, feature writer; b. Kingston, Ont. 5 Sept. 1957; d. A. Vincent and Iris (Bartlett) S.; e. Regiopolis College, Lasalle S.S. 1975; Carleton Univ. B.A. 1979; m. Herbert H. Solway s. Alex and Fanny (Schwartz) Solway 28 Dec. 1991; CONTRIBUTING EDITOR, TORONTO LIFE MAGAZINE 1989– ; Staff Writer, The Financial Post 1979–84; Contbg. Ed., Maclean's 1986–88; Investment Editor, Columnist & Sr. Writer, The Financial Times of Canada 1988–89; Asia Pacific Foundation of Canada 'Japan Assignment' Award 1990; author: 'Money Has No Country' 1991; co-author: 'The Brass Ring' 1988, 'A Matter of Trust' 1985 (Inaugural Winner, Nat. Bus. Book Award 1985); clubs: McGill; Address: 24 Macpherson Ave., Toronto, Ont. M5R 1W8.

**SHORTER, Edward,** B.A., M.A., Ph.D.; university professor; b. Evanston, Illinois 31 Oct.1941; s. Lazar and Joan (Caperton) S.; e. Wabash College B.A. 1961; Harvard Univ. M.A. 1964, Ph.D. 1968; m. Dr. Anne Marie d. Anne and Patrick Sharkey 9 April 1983; HANNAH PROFESSOR IN THE HISTORY OF MEDICINE, FAC.OF MEDICINE, UNIV. OF TORONTO 1991– ; Asst. Prof., Dept. of History, Univ. of Toronto 1967–71; Assoc. Prof. 1971–77; Prof. 1977–91; cross appointed to depts. of History and Medicine 1991– ; Visiting Mem., Inst. for Advanced Study Princeton 1971–72; Prof. associé en visite, Univ. de Montréal 1974; Connaught Sr. Fellow, Univ. of Toronto 1981–82; Gastprof., Univ. Konstanz 1989; Edit. Bd. Mem., 'Hist. of Psychiatry'; Mem., Convening Ctte., Eur. Assn. for the Hist. of

Psych.; author: 'The Historian and the Computer' 1971, pbk. 1974, 'The Making of the Modern Family' 1975 (trans 7 languages), 'A History of Women's Bodies' 1982 (trans 6 languages), repub. as 'Women's Bodies' 1991, 'Bedside Manners' 1985 (trans Italian), repub. as 'Doctors and Their Patients' 1991, 'The Health Century' 1987, 'Das Arzt-Patient-Verhältnis in der Geschichte und Heute' 1991, 'From Paralysis to Fatigue' 1992 (2 trans forthcoming), 'From the Mind Into the Body' 1994 and num. articles; editor & contbr.: 'Work and Community in the West' 1973; co-author: 'Strikes in France, 1830–1968' 1974; Home: 6 Wychwood Park, Toronto, Ont. M6G 2V5; Office: 88 College St., Toronto, Ont. M5G 1L4.

**SHORTLIFFE, Glen Scott,** B.A.; federal civil servant; b. Edmonton, Alta. 12 Nov. 1937; s. J. Newton and Hazel Elizabeth (Higgins) S.; e. Univ. of Alta. B.A. 1960, postgrad. studies US Hist. 1962; Univ. of Ore. postgrad. studies US Hist. 1961; children: Newton, Scott; Clerk of the Privy Council & Secy. to the Cabinet, Privy Council Office 1992; Lectr. in Hist. Univ. of Ore. 1961, Univ. of Alta. 1962; various assignments Ottawa and abroad External Affairs 1962–71; Consul & Trade Comnr. San Juan, Puerto Rico 1971–73; Dep. Dir. then Dir. USA Div. External Affairs 1973–76; Special Asst. (Communications) to Secy. of State 1976; Dir. Security Services 1976–77; Ambassador to Indonesia 1977–79; Vice Pres. Policy, Cdn. Internat. Devel. Agency 1979–82; Asst. Dep. Min. Corporate Planning External Affairs 1982–83, Asst. Dep. Min. Policy Coordination 1983–86; Dep. Sec. to Cabinet (Ops) Privy Council Office 1986–88; Dep. Min. Transport Canada 1988–90; Assoc. Secy. to the Cabinet & Dep. Clerk of the Privy Council 1990–92.

**SHOYAMA, Thomas Kunito,** O.C., B.A., B. Com., LL.D.; Canadian public servant; b. Kamloops, B.C. 24 Sept. 1916; s. Kunitaro and Kimi (Wakabayashi) S.; e. Pub. and High schs. Kamloops; Univ. of B.C., B.A. 1938, B.Com. 1938; McGill Univ. Post-grad. reading 1948; m. Lorna A. d. Lorne Moore 18 Dec. 1950; one d. Kiyomi A. (dec'd); VISITING PROF., UNIV. OF VICTORIA; Dir., Hawker Siddeley Canada Inc.; Bank of Tokyo Canada; Greater Victoria Hosp. Soc.; B.C. Treasury Advisory Bd.; mem., Macdonald Royal Commission on Ec. Union & Development Prospects for Can.; Premiers Econ. Adv. Council of B.C.; Journalist and Publisher 1938–45; Candn. Army Intelligence Corps 1945–46; Research Econ. Govt. of Sask. 1946–48, Econ. Adviser 1950–64; Research Econ. Central Mortgage & Housing Corp. Ottawa 1949; Sr. Econ., Econ. Council of Can. 1964–67; Asst. Depy. Min. of Finance, Ottawa 1968–74, Depy. Min. 1975–79; Depy. Min. of Energy, Mines & Resources 1974–75; Chrmn. of the Bd., Atomic Energy of Canada Ltd., 1979; Constitutional Advisor, Privy Council Office, 1979; apptd. Officer, Order of Canada 1978; rec'd Outstanding Achievement Award Pub. Service Can. 1978; Vanier medal in public administration, 1982; LL.D. (h.c.) Univ. of B.C., Univ. of Windsor; mem. Candn. Tax Foundation; Inst. Pub. Adm. Can.; recreations: gardening, fishing, golf, curling; Home: 3030 Midland Rd., Victoria, B.C. V8R 6P1; Office: School of Public Administration, Univ. of Victoria, Box 1700, Victoria, B.C. V8W 2Y2.

**SHRIVE, Nigel Graham,** B.A., M.A., D.Phil.; university professor and administrator; b. 31 July 1949; e. Oxford Univ. B.A. 1971, D.Phil. 1974, M.A. 1976; m. Susan; children: Penelope, Fiona, Alex; PROFESSOR AND HEAD, DEPT. OF CIVIL ENGINEERING, UNIV. OF CALGARY 1989– ; Lecturer, Oxford Univ. 1973; Post-Doct. Fellow, Univ. of Calgary 1974–75; Asst. Prof. (part-time) 1975–76; full-time 1976–79; Asst. to Vice-Pres. (Services) 1977–80; Assoc. Prof. 1979–83; Assoc. Dean (Student Affairs) 1985–89; Prof., Civil Engr. 1983– ; Part-time Assoc. Prof., Surgery 1981– ; Dir., The Masonry Soc. 1986–92; Mem., Edit. Bd. The Masonry Soc. J.; Mem., Candn. Standards Assn. Ctte. S304; Chair, Candn. Standards Assn. Ctte. A179; APEGGA Vol. Serv. Award; Excellence in Rsch. Award, Am. Ortho. Rsch. Soc. for Sports Med.; Renee Redfern Hunt Mem. Prize, Inst. of Civil Engrs.; 'Superior Teacher' Engr.; Dir., W.G. (Bill) Howard Mem. Found. 1985–88; Mem., External Adv. Ctte., Calgary Sport Med. Ctr., Univ. of Calgary; co-author: 'Numerical Methods in Engineering and Applied Science (Numbers are Fun)' 1987, 'Finite Element Primer' 1983; Office: Calgary, Alta. T2N 1N4.

**SHUBER, Jack,** M.D., F.R.C.S.(C), F.A.C.O.G., F.S.O.G.C.; obstetrician and gynecologist; b. Toronto, Ont. 11 Mar. 1939; s. Harry Solomon and Anne (Szyber) S.; e. Harbord and Bathurst Hts. Coll. Inst. 1957; Univ. of Toronto M.D. 1963; m. Eleanor d. Jack and Sue Nelson 17 Dec. 1960; children: Carolyne, Jennifer, Matthew, Harry; DIRECTOR, REPRODUCTIVE BIOL. UNIT, MT. SINAI HOSPITAL 1971–88, mem. Active Staff 1969– ; Asst. Prof. Obstetrics & Gynecol. Univ. of Toronto 1977– , mem. In Vitro Fertilization Team 1982–87; mem. Courtesy Staff Toronto Gen. Hosp., Hillcrest Hosp. Toronto; Cons. Staff Central Hosp. Toronto; Internship Mt. Sinai Hosp., Toronto 1963–64, post grad. training Obstetrics & Gynecology, New York Hosp. – Cornell Medical Centre 1964–67; post grad. training Internal Med. Gen. Surg. Mt. Sinai Hospital 1967–68, Chief Resident Obstetrics & Gynecol. 1968–69; Trustee and Treas. The Genesis Rsch. Found.; former Pres. Parents Assn. and mem. Bd. Toronto French Sch.; author or co-author articles, book chapters and other med. publs.; mem. Soc. Obstetricians & Gynecols. Toronto; Candn. Fertility & Andrology Soc.; Am. Fertility Soc.; Am. Assn. Gynecol. Laparoscopists; Chrmn. Ont. Dist. Am. Coll. Obstetricians & Gynecols. 1982–85; mem. Holy Blossom Temple Toronto; recreations: athletics, ceramics, music, classical guitar, violin; Office: 457, 600 University Ave., Toronto, Ont. M5G 1X5.

**SHUEBROOK, Ronald Lee,** B.S., M.Ed., M.F.A.; artist; educator; b. Fort Monroe, Va. 29 July 1943; s. George Albert and Ruth Ellen (Nowling) S.; e. Kutztown Univ., Pa., B.S. (Art Edn.) 1965, M.Ed. 1969; Kent State Univ., M.F.A. 1972; m. Frances d. Francis and Margaret Gallagher 1968; children: Meghan, Paul; PROF. & COORD. OF MFA PROGRAM, UNIV. OF GUELPH 1992– ; Asst. to Dir., Provincetown Art Assn. 1969; Instr., Univ. of Sask. 1972–73; Asst. Prof., Art Dept., Acadia Univ. 1973–77; Assoc. Prof. & Prog. Coordinator of Art in Edn. and Visual Arts, York Univ. 1977–79; Assoc. Prof. of Studio, N.S. Coll. of Art and Design 1979–87, Chrmn. of Studio Div. 1980–83; Exec. Dir., Ottawa Sch. Of Art 1987–88; Chrmn., Dept. of Fine Art, present Univ. 1988–93; exhibiting prof. visual artist since 1965; solo and group exhns. in Can., U.S., and abroad; work in numerous pub. and priv. collections; represented by Olga Korper Art Gallery, Toronto and Galerie Maghi Bettini, Amsterdam; vis. artist at var. univ., schs., and galleries in N. Am. and Eng.; Participant, N.S. Coalition on Arts & Culture 1986–87; rcvd. Arts Grant A, Can. Counc. 1985–86; mem. Univ. Art Assn. of Can.; Candn. Assoc. of Univ. Teachers 1972–87; mem. of various Bds. incl. Bd. of Dirs., Visual Arts Nova Scotia 1975–77, 1986–87 (Chairperson); Bd. of Govd., N.S. College of Art and Design 1983–85; mem., Bd. of Dirs., Art Gallery of N.S. 1986–87; mem., Adv. Ctte. on the Arts, Ottawa Bd. of Education 1987–88; mem., Bd. of Dirs., Visual Arts Ont. 1988–92; served on numerous juries for Galleries and Cultural Agencies incl. The Canada Council; pub. numerous reviews, articles, and catalogue essays for var. Candn. publs. and galleries; Office: Dept. of Fine Art, Univ. of Guelph, Guelph, Ont. N1G 2W1.

**SHULMAN, Morton;** physician; b. Toronto, Ont. 2 Apr. 1925; s. David and Nettie (Wintrope) S.; e. Univ. Toronto, M.D. 1948; m. Gloria, d. Isadore and Lena Bossin, 30 May 1950; children: Dianne; Geoffrey; PRES., GUARDMAN MNGMT. SERVICES 1983– ; Coroner 1952; Chief Coroner 1961–67; M.P.P. Ont. 1967–75; Columnist, Toronto Sun 1975–85; Host, CITY-TV show 1975–84; Chief Writer, Hume Fund Mgmt. Inc. 1978–89; Board Chrmn., Deprenyl Rsch. Ltd. 1988–93; Pres. Guardian-Morton Shulman Precious Metals Inc.; author 'Anyone Can Make a Million' 1966; 'The Billion Dollar Windfall' 1968; 'The Coroner' 1971; 'Anyone Can Still Make a Million' 1972; 'Member of the Legislature' 1973; 'Anyone Can Make Big Money Buying Art' 1977; 'How to Invest and Profit from Inflation' 1979; recreations: bridge; travel; Office: 378 Roncesvalles Ave., Toronto, Ont. M6R 2M7.

**SHUMAK, Kenneth Howard,** B.Sc., M.D., M.Sc., FRCP(C); university professor, physician; b. Toronto, Ont. 1 June 1942; s. David John and Rose (Binstock) S.; e. Univ. of Toronto B.Sc. 1964, M.D. 1965, M.Sc. 1970; m. Rene d. Harry and Hilda Silverstein 1 Sept. 1963; children: Brian, Michael, Melanie; ASSOCIATE DEAN, UNDERGRADUATE MEDICAL EDUCATION, FAC. OF MED., UNIV. OF TORONTO & STAFF PHYSICIAN, TORONTO GENERAL DIV., THE TORONTO HOSP. 1990– ; Asst. Prof., Med., Univ. of Toronto 1972–78; Assoc. Prof. 1978–85; Prof. 1985 (cross-apptd. in Pathology & Immunology); Deputy Chair, Dept. of Med. 1986–88; Acting Chair, Dept. of Med. 1988–89; Mem., Inst. of Med. Sci., Sch. of Grad. Studies, Univ. of Toronto 1984– ; Staff Physician and Dir., Blood Transfusion Lab., Toronto Gen. Hosp. 1972–84; Dir., Apheresis Unit 1978–84; Physician-in-Chief, Women's Coll. Hosp. 1984–90; Centennial Fellow, Medical Rsch. Council of Canada 1970–72; FRCP(C); author/co-author of 59 pubns. in med. journals; recreation: golf; club: Emerald Hills Golf & Country; Home: 30 Gardiner Rd., Toronto, Ont. M5P 3B5; Office: Rm. 2115, Med. Sci. Bldg., Toronto, Ont. M5S 1A1.

**SHUMIATCHER, Morris Cyril,** O.C., Q.C., B.A., LL.M., S.J.D.; lawyer; b. Calgary, Alta. 20 Sept. 1917; s. A.I., Q.C. and Luba S.; e. Calgary Pub. and High Schs. (Gov. Gen.'s Medal), 1935; Mount Royal Coll., Calgary, 1936; Univ. of Alta., B.A. 1940, LL.B. 1941; Judge Green Medal 1940; Travelling Scholarship of the Foreign Office to Japan 1940; Univ. of Toronto, LL.M. 1942, S.J.D. 1945; Officer, Order of Canada, 1982; Order of the Sacred Treasure of Japan 1987; m. Jacqueline Clay 1955; called to the Bars of Alta. & B.C. (1942), Sask. (1945), Man. and N.W.T. (1956); K.C. 1948; Law Officer, Dept. of Atty.-Gen. (serving under Hon. J.W. Corman, Q.C.) Sask. 1945–49; various positions incl. Counsel to Cabinet of Sask., Personal Advisor and Asst. to Premier (Hon. T.C. Douglas); Counsel to Sask. Labour Relations Bd. and Econ. Adv. & Planning Bd.; Est. Sask. Air Ambulance Service; author: Sask. Bill of Rights, 1947 (abolishing discrimination on basis of race, religion, creed, colour or national or ethnic origin); Gen. practice of law in Sask., Alta., B.C. and Man.; sometime lectr., Regina College; Univ. of Sask.; Adult Educ., Univ. of West. Ont.; Dalhousie Univ. Law School; Univ. of Toronto Law Sch.; Univ. of B.C. Law Sch.; Law Sch., Univ. of Alta.; Univ. of Regina; Touring Guest Speaker & Lectr. to learned societies & service clubs in Canada and U.S.A., regular TV lecture series on internat. affairs, criminal law, adm. of justice and legislative policy; CBC lecture series on Indian Affairs, Civil Liberties, legal problems of farmers, University of the Air; daily radio program 'In Touch with Today'; served 1943–45 with RCAF (Air-Gunner) instr. in Military Law; lectr. in military law and education & vocational guidance; writings incl. 'Assault on Freedom' 1962; 'Welfare: Hidden Backlash' 1971; 'Man of Law: A Model' 1979; 'The Borowski Case and the Rights of the Unborn (1980-1987): I set before you Life and Death and wherever such a choice exists, I exhort you to choose not death but life'; Univ. of West. Ont. Law Review (1987) Vol. p. 24; author of numerous articles in leading professional journals and publications; mem., Law Societies of the Provinces of Alta., B.C., Sask., N.W.T., Man.; Candn. Bar Assn. (Nat. Chrmn. Gen. Practitioners Conf.; Nat. Chrmn. Civil Liberties Sec).; Internat. Assn. Jurists; Am. Trial Lawyers Assn.; Candn. Tax Found.; Inst. Internat. Affairs; Candn. Advocates for Human Rights (Chrmn. Province of Sask.), Duke of Edinburgh's Award, Candn. Challenge, Sask. President; Royal Commonwealth Soc., National Council; Candn. Council of Christians and Jews (Dir.); UN Assn. Can.; Sask. Centre of the Arts (Dir.); Regina Astron. Assn.; Plains Hist. Museum Soc.; Dom. Drama Festival; Sask. Drama Council; Norman McKenzie Art Gallery Assn. (Past Pres.); Regina Symphony Orch. (Past Pres.); John Howard Soc.; Sask. Wild Life Fed.; Sask. Music Festival Assn.; Eng.-Speaking Union Commonwealth in Can. (Hon. Pres. Regina); YMCA Polar Bear Club (founder); Dean Emeritus, Sask. Consular Corps 1992; Dean of the Corps 1977–91 (for 14 years Honorary Consul General for Japan in Saskatchewan); Chrmn., Schizophrenia Assn., Bd. of Dirs.; Candn. Civil Rights Assn.; Sask. Human Rights Assn.; Club: Assiniboia; United Services Institute, Regina; YMCA Health Club; Elks Club of Regina; endowed 'The Shumiatcher Annual Lecture Series' at College of Law, Univ. of Sask. on 'Law and Literature' (annual continuing presentation by leading Jurists, lawyers and members of the Academic Community; Dr. & Mrs. Shumiatcher donated 'The Shumiatcher Theatre' to the new MacKenzie Art Gallery; Home: 2520 College Ave., Regina, Sask. S4P 1C9; Office: 2100 Scarth St., Regina, Sask. S4P 2H6.

**SHUPE, The Hon. Terry William,** B.Comm., LL.B.; provincial court judge; b. Vancouver, B.C. 4 Mar. 1942; s. Roy William and Joan Emma (Ashton) S.; e. Univ. of B.C., B.Comm. 1966, LL.B. 1967; m. Yolanda d. Robert and Margaret McInnes 29 Sept. 1973; children, F. Philip, Eileen Joan, Shaun David; ASSOC. CHIEF JUDGE OF THE PROV. COURT OF B.C. 1989– ; DEPY. JUDGE, TERRITORIAL COURT OF YUKON 1989–94; called to bar 1968; Pres., Kamloops Bar Assn. 1973, 1974; Admin. Judge, Kamloops Reg. 1982–87; Edn. Ctte. Chrmn., Prov. Court of B.C. 1984–88; Founding Chrmn., Hon. Life Chrmn. (1980– ); & Mem., Bd. of Trustees, West. Can. Theatre Company; Adv. Trustee, Big Brothers, Kamloops; Mem., United Ch.; Scout Leader, 1st Cherry Creek Scout Troop 1987–91; Hon. Vice-Pres., Scouts Canada - BC and The Yukon 1991; recreations: fishing, flying, skiing, horseback riding, woodworking; Home: SS #2 Cherry Creek, Kamloops, B.C. V2C 6C3; Office: 455 Columbia St., Kamloops, B.C. V2C 6K4.

**SHURMAN, Peter Emil;** communications executive; broadcast acquisitions and management consultant; b. Montreal, Que. 18 Nov. 1947; s. Fred and Frances (Schneyer) S.; e. Montreal West H.S. 1964; Sir George Williams Univ.; m. Carole d. Norman and Libby Stoll 25 April 1971; children: Michael, Brian; VICE-PRES., SCOTPAGE CORP. LTD. (ONT.) 1988– and PRES., ULTRAMEDIA INC.; News Reporter, CJAD 1969–74; Acct. Extve. 1974–75; Stn. Mgr., CJFM 1975–76; Vice-Pres. 1976–81; Vice-Pres. & Gen. Mgr. CJAD Inc. 1981–83; Vice-Pres., Radio, Standard Broadcasting Corp. 1983–84; Pres., Radio, Standard Broadcasting Corp. Ltd. 1984–87; community work with Boy Scouts, Jewish Community Ctr.; Dir., Juvenile Diabetes Found.; Chrmn., Communications Comte., Temple Har Zion; Jewish; Mem., Opimian Soc.; recreations: ham radio, racquetball, swimming, running, skiing; Home: 104 Willowbrook Rd., Thornhill, Ont. L3T 5P5.

**SHUVE, Ainslie St.C.;** investment executive; b. Saint John, N.B. 18 Nov. 1922; s. John and Margaret (Moore) S.; e. N.B. Schs.; m. Anne Isobel, d. Arthur H. Washburn, 5 Oct. 1946; children: Dr. Sandra J. Messner, John A.; CHRMN. OF THE BOARD, THE DOMINION TRUST COMPANY 1993– ; began with Eastern Securities Company Limited, Saint John, M.B. 1947; Investment Mgr. Barclay's Trust Co. Montreal, Que. 1953; joined Crown Trust Co. as Invest. Offr., Montreal 1957, Asst. Treas. 1963, Mgr. Montreal 1965, Asst. Gen. Mgr. and Treas. Toronto 1966; Vice-Pres. Finance 1972; Extve. Vice Pres. 1973; Pres. and CEO 1978–80; Consultant, Jones Heward & Co. Ltd. 1980–84; Dir., The Dominion Trust Co. 1983–93; Anglican; recreation: golf; Clubs: National; Toronto Hunt; Granite; Address: 400 Walmer Rd., Suite 1409, Toronto, Ont. M5P 2X7 and Apt. 305, 3399 Gulfshore Blvd., North Naples, Fla 33940.

**SIBBALD, Cory V.,** B.A.Sc., M.B.A.; mining engineer; b. Fort Vermilion, Alta. 23 Jan. 1934; s. Walter Marshall and Rachel Estcourt (Harrison) S.; e. Univ. of B.C. B.A.Sc. 1960, M.B.A. 1970; m. Althea d. Norman and Irene Scott 10 Nov. 1956; children: Scott, Leanne, Regan; VICE-PRESIDENT, ENGINEERING, TECK CORPORATION 1970– ; Metallurgist then Mill Superintendent, Placer Development (Placer Dome) 1960–69 (Canex, Craigmont Mine, Endako Mine); CIM Fellow; Mem., AIME; B.C. Assn. of Profl. Engrs.; CIM (Chair, Vancouver Branch 1991); Home: 3883 W. 26 Ave., Vancouver, B.C. V6S 1P3; Office: 600-200 Burrard St., Vancouver, B.C. V6C 3L9.

**SIBBALD, R(onald) Gary,** B.Sc., M.D., F.R.C.P.(C); dermatologist; b. Toronto, Ont. 2 Nov. 1947; s. Ronald William and Marian Louise (Ginter) S.; e. Univ. of Toronto, B.Sc. 1969, M.D. 1974; m. Debra d. Gene and Dora Ricciatti Aug. 1978; children: Matthew, Timothy, Cathryn; ASSOC. PROF., MED. (DERMATOLOGY), UNIV. OF TORONTO; CONSULTANT, MEDICINE GROUP and ONTARIO COLLEGE OF PHARMACY; residency Med./Dermatol. 1975–79; Staff Phys. Toronto Gen., Women's Coll. and Mississauga Hosps.; McLaughlin Scholar St. Johns Hosp. for Diseases of the Skin, London, Eng. 1978–79; Cont. Med. Edn. Rep. Dermatol. Univ. of Toronto 1984–91; mem. Exec. Atlantic Dermatol. Conf. 1980–90; Samuel Straight Scholar Internal Med. 1974; Co-ordinator Adverse Dermatol. Reaction Prog. for Can. to Support Complete Labelling All Components; Acting Head Dermatology, Women's Coll. Hosp. 1990–92; Consultant, Health Protection Br., Ottawa 1990–92; Undergraduate Coordinator Dermatology, Univ. of Toronto 1992– ; mem. Adv. Council, Chiropody for Ont. 1990– ; mem. Workmen's Compensation Bd. Appeals Tribunal (Ont.); author various articles med. jours.; Contbg. Ed., Candn. Journal Dermatology and Contemporary Dermatology; mem. Toronto Dermatol. Soc. (Sec. 1980–85, Pres. 1985–89, Past Pres. 1990–92); Am. Acad. Dermatol. (Adv. Council 1985–88; 1st mem. for Can., Adv. Counc. Extve. 1989– ); Candn. Dermatol. Assn. (Dir. 1986–88); recreations: gardening, photography; Home: 2157 Autumn Breeze Dr., Mississauga, Ont. L5B 1R3; Office: 23–10, 1077 North Service Rd., Mississauga, Ont. L4Y 1A5.

**SIBBESTON, Hon. Nick G.,** B.A., LL.B.; former politician; b. Fort Simpson, N.W.T. 21 Nov. 1943; e. Fort Providence, Inuvik, Fort Smith and Yellowknife, N.W.T.; Univ. of Alta., B.A. 1970, LL.B. 1975; m. Karen Benoit 1968; children: Glen, Randy, Murray, Janice, Gerald, Laurie; private law practice Yellowknife 2 yrs.; Sec. Mgr. Fort Simpson 1970; el. M.L.A. for Nahendeh, N.W.T. 1970–74, 1979; first N.W.T. born lawyer; Min. of Culture & Local Govt. N.W.T. 1984–85, Aboriginal Rights and Constitutional Development 1984–87, Intergovernmental Affairs 1985–87, Culture & Communications 1986–87, Economic Development and Tourism 1987–88, N.W.T. Science Inst. 1987–88; Govt. Leader N.W.T. 1985–87; Min. of Govt. Services & N.W.T. Housing Corp. 1987–88; mem. Deh Cho Regional Council; N.W.T. Bar Assn.; R. Catholic; recreations: hockey, jogging; Office: Box 2488, Yellowknife, N.W.T. X1A 2P8.

**SIBLEY, John Thomas,** B.Math., M.D., F.R.C.P.C.; university professor, rheumatologist; b. Dundas, Ont. 4 May 1951; s. Norman Thomas William and Margaret Wilson (Allan) S.; e. Univ. of Waterloo B.Math 1973; Univ. of Western Ontario M.D. 1977; m. Betty d. Doris and Austin Schaefer 12 Aug. 1978; children: Kalle, David, Kevin, Brian; PROF. (MED.), UNIV. OF SASKATCHEWAN 1992– ; Intern, Ottawa Civic Hosp. 1977–78; Medical Resident, Univ. of Western Ont. 1978–82; F.R.C.P.C. (Internal Med.) 1982; Rheumatology Rsch. Fellow, Univ. of Sask. 1982–84; F.R.C.P.C. (Rheumatology) 1985; Asst. Prof., present univ. 1984–88; Assoc. prof. 1988–92; Consultant Rheumatologist; Med. Advr. to Lupus Erythematosus Soc. of Sask. & to Lupus Can.; Rsch. Grant Rev. Ctte., Arthritis Soc. & Sask. Health Rsch. Bd.; Reviewer, 'J. of Rheumatology'; Mem., Candn. Med. Assn.; Royal Coll. of Physicians & Surgeons of Can.; Candn. Arthritis & Rheumatism Soc.; Am. Coll. of Rheum.; author/co-author, rsch. pubns. involving rheumatic diseases; Office: University Hospital, Dept. of Med., Saskatoon, Sask. S7N 0X0.

**SIBLEY, William Maurice,** M.A., Ph.D., LL.D.; b. Saskatoon, Sask. 21 June 1919; s. John Cynddylan and Mary Stuart Isabella (Shaw) S.; e. Lord Byng High Sch. Vancouver 1935; Univ. of B.C. B.A. 1939 (Gov. Gen's Gold Medal), M.A. 1940; Brown Univ. Ph.D. 1943; Univ. of Man. LL.D. 1977; m. Margaret Jean d. William A. MacKenzie, Vancouver, B.C. 24 Apl. 1942; children: Robert William, John MacKenzie, Jean Elizabeth; SPECIAL ADVISER TO THE PRESIDENT, UNIVERSITY OF LETHBRIDGE 1988–93; Lectr. Queen's Univ. 1943–46; Asst. Prof. Univ. of Man. 1946, Assoc. Prof. 1947, Prof. and Head of Philos. 1948–69, Dean of Arts & Science 1961–69, Dir. of Planning 1969–70, Vice Pres. 1970–75; Chrmn. Adv. Bd. Educ. Man. 1962–65; Adv. Comte. on Univ. Planning, Assn. Univs. & Colls. Can. 1969–75; Vice Pres. Mount Allison Univ. 1975–78; Chrmn., Sask. Univs. Comn. 1978–83; Special Adv. to the Pres., Univ. of Saskatchewan, 1983–86; Dean Emeritus of Science Univ. Man. 1972 and of Arts 1975; Distinguished Visiting Lectr. Univ. Calgary 1978–79; Visiting Scholar, Univ. of California, Berkeley, spring semester 1987; Vice-Pres., Academic, University of Lethbridge 1987–88; rec'd Centennial Medal 1967; contributor 'Evaluating Institutions For Accountability' 1974; contrib. 'International Encyclopedia of Higher Education' 1977; various articles on aspects of univ. planning and adm., accountability and information systems; mem. Candn. Soc. Study Higher Educ. (Pres. 1977–78); Candn. Philos. Assn. (Founding mem.); Assn. Inst. Research; Phi Beta Kappa; Home: 71 Kings Crescent South, Lethbridge, Alta. T1K 5G6.

**SIBLIN, Herbert E.,** B.Comm., F.C.A.; chartered accountant; b. Montreal, Que. 25 April 1929; s. Morris S. and Lillian Helen (Kindestin) S.; e. McGill Univ. B.Comm. 1950; C.A. 1953; m. Jacqueline d. Lewis and Sylvia Rosenfeld 14 Aug. 1966; children: Judy, Eric, Steven, Jane; EXECUTIVE PARTNER, ERNST & YOUNG 1991– ; Formed Zittrer, Siblin with Jack Zittrer 1953; merged with Stein & Levine 1966; Mng. Partner, Zittrer Siblin Stein Levine until merger with Ernst & Young 1991; Fellow, Order of C.A.s of Que. 1984; Mem., Inst. of C.A.s of Ont.; has served on Council, Que. Order of C.A.s; Hon. Treas., Mem. of Extve. Ctte., Chairman of Audit & Finance Ctte. & Mem., Bd. of Gov., McGill Univ.; Dir. & Immediate Past Pres., Canadian Club of Montreal; Mem., Bd. of Dir. & Chair, Audit Ctte., Sir Mortimer B. Davis Jewish Gen. Hosp.; Mem. Bd. of Dirs., The Learning Centre of Quebec; clubs: Mount Royal, Montefiore, Elm Ridge Country; Home: 55 Aberdeen Ave., Westmount, Que. H3Y 3A6; Office: 3400 de Maisonneuve Blvd. W., Montreal, Que. H3Z 3E8.

**SICARD, Pierre P.,** C.A.; b. Montréal, Qué. 1 Apr. 1937; s. Roméo and Germaine (Valiquette) S.; e. McGill Univ. 1962; m. Solange d. Albert and Gisèle Therrien 1 July 1966; children: Hélène, Alain, Anne-Marie; CHRMN., BRONSON CONSULTING GROUP 1991– ; Special Advisor on Information Technology, Treasury Bd. of Canada 1987–91; Profl. Auditor McDonald, Currie & Co. 1954–63; Asst. to Treas. Candn. Internat. Paper Co. 1964; Treas. and Dir. Grissol Foods Ltd. 1965–68; Comptroller Montreal Constrn. Ind. Jt. Ctte. 1968–70; Dep. Gen. Mgr. Ivory Coast Ind. Devel. Bank 1970–72; Dir. and Vice-Pres. CIDA 1972–83; Dep. Min., Services, and Dep. Receiver Gen. 1983–84; Dep. Min. Veterans' Affairs Canada 1985–87; mem. Ordre des Comptables Agreés, Qué.; decorated Nat. Orders of Ivory Coast, Togo, Dahomey; Home: 430 Ave. Cannes, Gatineau, Qué. J8T 5M5; Office: Suite 610, 350 Sparks St., Ottawa, Ont. K1R 7S8.

**SIDDALL, D. Gene,** B.S.M.E., M.B.A.; b. Laurens, Iowa 5 May 1933; s. Lester Jessie and Hazel Jimmae (Trimble) S.; e. Iowa State Univ. B.S.M.E. 1954; Univ. of Iowa grad. studies Math. 1960–61; St. Louis Univ. M.B.A. 1963, grad. studies Servomechanisms 1963–67; m. Mary d. Michael and Bernice Grogan 11 Sept. 1954; children: Katherine R. Draper, Jane E. Lievense, Stephen G., Mary A. Parvaresh, William L., Mark D., John M.; Pres., Chief Exec. Offr. and Dir., McDonnell Douglas Canada Ltd. 1990–92 (Retired); Assoc. Eng. McDonnell Douglas St. Louis 1957–59, Sr. Eng. 1961, Chief Eng. Mich. 1967, Vice Pres. Gen. Mgr. Mich. 1981 and Tulsa 1988–90; Project Eng. Collins Radio Co. St. Louis 1960–61; served with U.S. Airforce 1954–57; comm. pilot; mem. of bd., Aerospace Industries Assn. of Can. 1990– ; mem. Candn. Manufacturer's Assn.; Candn. Aeronautics & Space Inst.; Aerospace Inds. Assn. Can.; Air Transport Assn. Can.; Candn. Export Assn.; Robotics Internat., Soc. Mfg. Engs. (Sr. mem.); Pres's. Assn.

**SIDDALL, Ernest,** B.Sc.(Eng.), D.Eng., P.Eng., FCAE; professional engineer; b. Halifax, England 10 Dec. 1919; s. Ernest and Charlotte Amelia (Jamieson) S.; e. Varndean Sch. 1937; Brighton Tech. Coll. B.Sc. (Eng.) (Hons. London Univ.) 1939; Banff Sch. of Adv. Mngt., dipl. 1967; Univ. of Waterloo, D.Eng. (h.c.) 1991; m. Irene d. Clement Owen and Violet Smith 17 Mar. 1945; children: Ann Judith, Jane Amelia, Robert Ernest; ADJUNCT PROF., DEPT. OF SYSTEMS DESIGN ENGINEERING, UNIV. OF WATERLOO 1989– ; PO Tel. system, Britain 1939–49; R. Corps of Signals, Brit. Army 1940–46, in 'secret radio war' to rank of major; High Explosive Rsch., Min. of Supply, Brit. 1949–51, devel. blast meas. instrumentation; Candn. Aviation Elect. Ltd. 1952–54, design, aircraft flight simulator; Atomic Energy of Can. 1954–58, rsch. & devel. of control & instrum. sys. for nuclear reactors; Founder-mem., Candu nuclear design team 1958–76; Canatom Inc. 1976–79, nuclear consultant; Inst. for Risk Rsch., Univ. of Waterloo 1985– ; Lectr., Univ. of Ottawa 1956–58; Mem., Ctte. on Safety of Nuclear Instal., OECD (Paris) 1982–84; internat. lectr., speaker & ctte. mem.; analyst, 'Ocean Ranger' loss & early remedial actions; W.B. Lewis medal 1982; Inaugural fellowship, Candn. Acad. of Engr. 1987; author of num. papers & articles; recreations: sailing (cruised 19,000 km in 14 months in 12 m. yacht with wife & family members as crew), music, reading, computers, making things; club: Port Credit Yacht; Home: 946 Porcupine Ave., Mississauga, Ont. L5H 3K5.

**SIDDON, Hon. Thomas Edward,** P.C., M.P., B.Sc., M.A.Sc., Ph.D., P.Eng.; politician; educator; b. Drumheller, Alta. 9 Nov. 1941; s. Ronald Victor and Gertrude Violet (Humfrey) S.; e. Univ. of Alta. B.Sc. (Mech. Eng.) 1963; Univ. of Toronto M.A.Sc. (Aerospace Eng.) 1965, Ph.D. (Aero Acoustics) 1968; m. Patricia Audrey d. Nick and Rose Yackimetz 1 Sept. 1962; children: Charles, David, Robert, Elizabeth, Katherine; Minister of Defence, Govt. of Canada 1993; Assoc. Prof. of Mech. Eng. Univ. of B.C. 1968–79; founded acoustical eng. firm and audiometric testing business; acoustical cons. Can. and U.S.A.; served as Ald. Richmond, B.C.; el. to H. of C. for Richmond-South Delta 1978; re-el. g.e. 1979, 1980, 1984, 1988; Parlty. Secy. to the Hon. James McGrath, Min. of Fisheries and Oceans, 1979; Caucus Spokesman on Pacific & Inland Fisheries, on Mines, on Econ. Devel. and Sci. & Technol.; Min. of State for Science & Technology 1984–85; Min. of Fisheries and Oceans 1985–90; Min. of Indian Affairs & Northern Devel. 1990–93; apptd. to Queen's Privy Council 1984; mem., Federal Cabinet Cttes.: Priorities and Planning; Environment; Human Resources; recipient Gov. Gen's. Bronze Medal 1955; Gold Medal in Mech. Eng. 1963; Assn. Prof. Engs. Award 1978; Professional Achievement Award, Fac. of Engr., Univ. of Alta. 1988; Fellow, Acoustical Soc. Am.; Anglican; Home: P.O. Box 118, Kaleden, B.C. V0H 1K0.

**SIDER, Robert Dick,** M.A., D.Phil.; educator; b. Cheapside, Ont. 10 Mar. 1932; s. Earl Morris and Elsie (Sheffer) S.; e. Univ. of Sask. B.A. 1955, M.A. 1956; Oxford Univ. (Rhodes Scholar) B.A. 1958, M.A. 1964, D.Phil. 1965; m. Lura Mae d. Harry and Edith Meeds 20 June 1959; children: Catherine Marie, Michael James, Robert Antony; CHARLES A DANA PROF. OF CLASSICAL LANGS, DICKINSON COLL. 1981– ; Assoc. Prof. of Biblical and Classical Lit. Messiah Coll. Grantham, Pa. 1962–68; Asst., Assoc. and Prof. of Classics present Coll. 1968–81; Visiting Prof. of Greek & Latin

The Catholic Univ. of Am. Washington, D.C. 1978–79; Univ. Coll. Univ. of Toronto 1982–83; author: 'Ancient Rhetoric and the Art of Tertullian' 1971; 'The Gospel and its Proclamation' 1983; co-author: 'A Decade of Patristic Studies 1970–1979' Vol. 1 1982, Vol. 2 1983; mem. Ed. Bd. 'Fathers of the Church' 1979– ; 'Studies in Christian Antiquity' 1981– ; 'Collected Works of Erasmus' 1981– ; 'Catalogus Translationum et Commentariorum' 1990 (Extve. Ctte. 1991– ); Mem. Advisory Bd., 'Journal of Early Christian Studies' 1993– ; Bd. of Dirs., Candn. Assn. of Rhodes Scholars 1987–91; Gen. Editor 'New Testament Scholarship' (CWE); ed. 'Paraphrases on Romans and Galatians' 1984; mem. Am. Philol. Assn.; N. Am. Patristic Soc. (Vice Pres. 1972–73, Pres. 1973–74); Toronto Renaissance & Reformation Colloquium; Erasmus of Rotterdam Soc.; Candn. Assn. Rhodes Scholars; Assn. Am. Rhodes Scholars; Fellow, Am. Counc. Learned Soc.'s 1974–75; Sr. Fellow Centre Reformation & Renaissance Studies Toronto 1982–83; Fellow-in-Residence, Netherlands Inst. for Advanced Study 1989–90; Anglican; recreations: cycling, gardening, music, theatre; Home: 902 Redwood Dr., Carlisle, Pa. 17013; Office: Dickinson Coll., Carlisle, Pa. 17013.

**SIDIMUS, Joysanne;** b. New York, N.Y.; d. Jerome Hillel and Bessie (Brodsky) S.; e. Adelphi Acad.; Barnard Coll.; separated; one d. Anya Janine; FOUNDER & EXTVE. DIR., DANCER TRANSITION CTR. 1985– ; Mem., N.Y. City Ballet; Soloist, London's Fest. Ballet; prin. dancer, Nat. Ballet of Can.; Pennsylvania Ballet; post-performing career incl. Ballet Mistress, Les Grand Ballets de Geneve, Ballet Repertory Co. (Now A.B.T.II); Teacher, A.B.T. Sch., Dance Theatre of Harlem, Briansky Saratoga Ballet Ctr., George Brown Coll., York Univ., Nat. Ballet Sch.; Fac. Mem., N. Carolina Sch. of Arts (7 yrs.); on-going relationship with Balanchine heritage incl. stagings of his work for Pennsylvania Ballet, Les Grands Ballets de Geneve, the N.C. Dance Theatre, National Ballet of Canada, National Ballet School; Mem., Bd. of Dirs., Performing Arts Lodges of Canada; Dance Ontario Award 1989; Vice-Pres., Internat. Organization for the Transition of Professional Dancers; Advisory Council, Dance Ontario; awarded Commemorative Medal for 125th Anniversary of Candn. Confederation (services to the arts community); author: 'Exchanges: Life After Dance' 1986; Office: 66 Charles St. E., Toronto, Ont. M4Y 2R3.

**SIDNELL, Michael;** university professor; b. London, England 29 Sept. 1935; s. Victor Thomas and Beatrice (Furness) S.; e. Pinner Gr. Sch.; King's Coll., Univ. of London; m. Felicity, divorced 1988; children: Michael Gustave, Anne Frances, Eleanor Jane, John Paul Sebastian; m. Natalie Rewa 1991; PROF., TRINITY COLL., UNIV. OF TORONTO 1969– ; Lt., Middlesex Regt. 1956–58; Asst. Prof., Mt. Allison Univ. 1958–64; Asst./Assoc. Prof., Trent Univ. 1964–60; Vis. Scholar, Corpus Christi Coll., Cambridge 1979–80; Dir., Grad. Ctr. for Drama, Univ. of Toronto 1976–81; Mem. (past & pres.), var. bd. of jours. incl. 'Canadian Forum,' 'Modern Drama,' 'Yeats Annual,' 'Themes in Drama'; Bd. of Gov., Trent Univ. 1967–71; Mem., Candn. Assn. for Irish Stud.; Internat. Fed. for Theatre Rsch.; Soc. for Theatre Rsch.; author: 'Dances of Death: the Group Theatre of London' 1984; editor: 'Sources of Dramatic Theory' 1991; co-editor: 'Druid Craft: Manuscripts of W.B. Yeats' 1978, 'The Secret Rose by W.B. Yeats' 1979; recreations: sailing, squash; Club: Collins Bay Yacht; Home: 100 Quebec Ave., Apt. 312, Toronto, Ont. M6P 4B8; Office: Trinity College, Toronto, Ont. M5S 1H8.

**SIEBEN, Don E.,** B.Comm., C.A.; financial executive; b. Edmonton, Alta. 29 June 1951; s. Mark John and Theresa (Riguedelle) S.; e. Univ. of Alta. B.Comm. 1976; C.A. 1981; m. Lorraine J. d. Stephen and Victoria Daciuk 3 Aug. 1974; children: Jeff, Melanie, Elisha; VICE-PRES., FINANCE & ADMIN., CHILDREN'S HEATLH CENTRE OF NORTHERN ALBERTA & CHIEF FINANCIAL OFFR., CHILDREN'S HEALTH FOUNDATION OF N. ALBERTA 1992– ; Assoc., Walter Zazula C.A. 1982–83; Sr. Partner, Sieben & Gauthier C.A.s 1983–87; Assoc., Peterson Walker C.A.s 1987–89; Extve. Dir., Children's Health Found. of N. Alta. 1989–91; Past Trustee, Winnifred Steward Sch.; Dir., Edmonton Assn. for the Mentally Handicapped 1980–87; Past Chair, Athabasca Reg. Econ. Devel. Council; Dir. & Vice-Chair, Alta. Hosp. Edmonton 1982–86; Dir. & Vice-Chair N. Alta. Children's Hosp. 1986–89; Mem., Bd. of Gov., Athabasca Univ.; Mem., Candn. Inst. of C.A.s; Alta. Inst. of C.A.s; Candn. College of Health Service Executives; Home: 4227 – 109A St., Edmonton, Alta. T6J 2R7; Office: Suite 1700, 8215 – 112 St., Edmonton, Alta. T6G 2C8.

**SIEBNER, Herbert Johannes Josef,** R.C.A.; artist; b. Stettin, Germany 16 Apr. 1925; s. Paul Hermann and Margarete Agnes (Resch) S.; e. elem. sch. Stettin 1931–1935; Dr. Schumacher's Private Gymnasium 35–1937; Schiller Real Gymnasium Stettin 37–1941; Atelier Max Richter Stettin 1941–43; Berlin Acad. 1946–49; m. Hannelore d. Willy Roehr 14 Oct. 1950; one d. Angela; came to Can. 1954; Teacher, Studio Group Victoria B.C. 1954–58; Art Gallery Victoria 1958–60; Univ. of B.C. Extension Travelling Lectr.; Visiting Prof. Univ. of Wash. 1963; Univ. of B.C. Summer Sch. Art 1964; Univ. of Alta. Painting Workshop 1966; Univ. of Victoria Graphics Lectr. 1967–68; over 100 solo exhns. Europe, Can. and USA; rep. Candn. Biennale 1959, 1962; Internat. Exhn. Graphics Lugano 1958; Yugoslavia 1959; Brussels World Fair 1957; Seattle World Fair 1962; Victoria Art Gallery Retrospective 1970, Univ. of Victoria 1979; Media Centre Vancouver 1980; 'Dualities' Victoria Art Gallery retrospective exhn., 30 years in Canada, 1984 (incl. special publication of artists work, illus.); retrospective exhn., The City of West Berlin 1986; 'Siebner Before Canada' Vancouver, Victoria 1989; H.S. Museum of Expressionism 1990–91; 4 Decades of Art, Calgary 1991; Trends of Expressionism, Weisenstein Gallery, Victoria 1992; Atelier Gallery & Winchester Gallery, Victoria 1993; 40 yrs in B.C. Victoria 1994; Representing Canada at the Graphic-Bienale in Lubljana 1989; recipient Design Award 1952, 1953 Berlin; Reid Award for Graphics Toronto 1956; Sculpture Award B.C. 1957; Seattle Art Museum 1957 Award; Painting Award Winnipeg 1959, Victoria 1960, 1961; Can. Council Sr. Grant 1962; Acad. in Berlin Guest of Honour 1963; Internat. Graphic Exhn. Medal 1969; named Hon. Citizen City of Victoria 1973; mural comns. incl. Crown House Victoria 1960; Univ. of Victoria 1964; Prov. Museum Victoria 1968; B.C. Govt. Centre Vancouver 1975 (Media); works in museum collections, Can. Europe, USA; served with German Army 1943–45, draughtsman, rank Cpl., Russian P.O.W. 1945; co-author 'Inscriptions' 1967; 'Color-Line & Form' 1970; 'Muse Book' 1972; biog. 'Herbert Siebner: 25 Years in B.C.' 1979 by R. Skelton; 'H. Siebner R.C.A. - A Celebration, Skelton, Bennett, Spreitz' 1993; Limners Soc.; Royal Canadian Academy; Home: 270 Meadow Brook Rd., Victoria, B.C. V8X 3X3.

**SIECIECHOWICZ, Krystyna Z.,** M.A., Ph.D.; university professor; b. London, U.K. 1 Dec. 1948; s. Wieslaw and Jadwiga A. (Pniewska) S.; e. Univ. of Toronto B.A. 1971, M.A. 1972, Ph.D. 1982; m. Jean-Louis s. Louis and Elizabeth de Lannoy 10 Dec. 1982; children: Maryna, Charles-François, Louise; CO-ORD., CANADIAN STUDIES PROGRAMME, UNIV. OF TORONTO 1990–93; Archaeologist-Researcher 1966– ; Asst. Prof., Anthropology, Univ. of Alta. 1979–80; Univ. of Toronto 1982–87; Assoc. Prof. 1987– ; Consultant, Anishnawbc-Aski, CKVR-TV Peterborough, CBC Newsworld, CBC Radio; Mem., Candn. Ethnol. Soc.; Assn. of Social Anthropologists; Candn. Assn. in Support of Native People; IWGIA; Royal Anthropological Inst. U.K.; participation in numerous confs. & lectures (by invitation); has served on several univ. cttes.; recipient of a number of grants, bursaries & fellowships; author: 'We Are All Related Here' forthcoming, 'The Kayahna Region Land Utilization and Occupancy Study'; several reviews, book chaps. & articles; Home: 7 Ranchdale Cres., Don Mills, Ont. M3A 2M1; Office: 15 King's College Circle, Toronto, Ont. M5S 1A1.

**SIEGEL, David T.,** B.Sc., M.A., Ph.D., C.G.A.; university professor; b. Louisville, Kentucky 18 Dec. 1947; s. Wesley C. and Catherine (Wilmot) S.; e. Univ. of Louisville, B.Sc. 1969; Carleton Univ., M.A. 1975; Univ. of Toronto, Ph.D. 1983; C.G.A. 1971; m. Nancy Jean d. William and Dora Kellaway 28 Aug. 1987; ASSOC. PROF., DEPT. OF POLITICS, BROCK UNIV. 1978– ; Chair, present dept. 1987–88, 1989–91; Pres., Candn. Assn. of Programmes in Public Admin. 1990–93; Dir. of Rsch., Niagara Reg. Review Comn. 1988–89; also worked for fed. govt. & City of Toronto; Nat. Extve., Inst. of Public Admin. of Can. 1985–88, 1989–93; Bd. of Dir., Ont. Municipal Mngt. Inst. 1983–93; co-author: 'Public Administration in Canada: A Text' 1987, revised 1991; author of scholarly articles & book chapters; recreations: nordic & alpine skiing; Home: 172 Highland Ave., St. Catharines, Ont. L2R 4J8; Office: St. Catharines, Ont. L2S 3A1.

**SIEGEL, William,** B.A., Ph.D.; business executive; b. Toronto, Ont. 24 Apr. 1943; s. Jack and Pearl S.; e. Univ. of Toronto, B.A. (Hons.) 1966; Univ. of Michigan, Ph.D. 1970; m. Jane Anna d. Myrle and Harold Alford 19 May 1978; children: Hallie Kirsten, Kathryn Rose; Pres., Longwoods International 1988; Asst. Prof., Univ. of West. Ont. 1970–76; Mgr., Mktg. Rsch., Bell Can. 1976–77; Dir. of Rsch., F.H. Hayhurst Co. Ltd. 1977–78; Pres., The Longwoods Rsch. Group Limited 1978– ; Distinguished Vis. Prof., Univ. of W. Australia; Adv. Bd. Mem., Ryerson Polytech. Inst.; Univ. of Waterloo; mem., Profl. Mktg. Rsch. Soc. of Can.; Travel & Tourism Rsch. Assn.; Candn. Inst. of Mktg.; recreations: antiques, boating, fishing; club: University; Home: 744 Duplex Ave., Toronto, Ont. M4R 1W3.

**SIFTON, Michael Clifford,** C.M., C.D.; publisher; b. Toronto, Ont. 21 Jan. 1931; s. Lieut.-Col. Clifford Sifton, D.S.O., and later Doris Margaret (Greene) S.; e. Public Schs., Toronto, Ont.; Trinity Coll. Sch., Port Hope, Ont.; Thornton Private Sch.; Univ. of Western Ont.; m. Heather Ann McLean, d. Hamilton A. McLean, 8 Sept. 1956; children: Clifford McLean, Michael Gregory, Derek Andrew; CHRMN., ARMADALE CO. LTD., since 1960; Chrmn., Armadale Publishers Ltd.; Saskatoon Star-Phoenix; Regina Leader-Post; Taber Times; Dauphin Herald; Yorkton This Week; Armadale Communications Ltd.; Toronto Airways Ltd.; Chrmn., Armadale Properties Ltd.; Highland Chev Olds Geo Cadillac Ltd.; while attending university worked with London Free Press Printing Co. Ltd., London, Ont.; employed with 'Peterborough Examiner' summer 1954, later that year joined Sifton family group of Co.'s as Extve. Asst.; elec. served as Offr. with Royal Canadian Armoured Corps. (Militia), Governor Gen. Horse Guards; Lieutenant 1954; Supplementary Reserve 1958; Former Hon. Colonel, 411 Air Reserve Sqdn. 1975; Mem.: Toronto Art Gallery; Candn. Daily Newspaper Publishers Assoc.; Candn. Assoc. of Airport Execs.; Am. Newspapers Publishers Assoc.; active Ctte. mem., Royal Winter Fair, Toronto 1950; responsible for revival of polo in Toronto after 2nd World War; Appt. Mem. of the Order of Canada 1988; Anglican; recreations: riding, skiing, water-sports; Clubs: Canadian; Empire; Toronto and N. York Hunt (Dir.); Toronto Polo (Chrmn.); Polo Canada (Founding Chrmn. & Pres.); Saskatoon (Sask.); Assiniboia (Regina); The Palm Beach Polo and Country; Home: Fox Den Farm, PO Box 610, Gormley, Ont. L0H 1G0; Office: 180 Renfrew Dr., Suite 100, Markham, Ont. L3R 9Z2.

**SIFTON, W. Mowbray;** real estate executive; b. London, Ont. 15 Oct. 1924; s. Harry L. and Tena M. (Mowbray) S.; e. Upper Canada College 1942; m. Doris d. Roy and Della Flanagan 3 Aug. 1946; children: Glen, Sherene, Carol, Paul, Richard; CHAIRMAN, SIFTON PROPERTIES LTD.; Chrmn. of Sifton Properties LTd. 1946–91; Named Laureate, London Business Hall of Fame 1992; recreations: golf; clubs: London Hunt & Country; Home: 1006 Hunt Club Mews, London, Ont. N6H 4R7; Office: Box 5099, Term. A, London, Ont. N6A 4M8.

**SIGAL, Israel Michael,** B.A., Ph.D., F.R.S.C.; university professor; b. Kiev, Ukraine 31 Aug. 1945; s. Moshe and Eva (Guz) S.; e. Gorky Univ. B.A. 1968; Tel Aviv Univ. Ph.D. 1976; m. Brenda d. Robert and Doris Tipper; children: Alexander, Daniel; PROFESSOR, DEPT. OF MATHEMATICS, UNIV. OF TORONTO 1985– ; Postdoctoral Fellow, ETH Zurich (Swiss Inst.of Technology), Inst. of Theoretical Physics 1976–78; Asst. Prof., Math., Princeton Univ. 1978–81; R.H. Revson Sr. Scientist, The Weizmann Inst.of Sciences, Math. 1981–85; Prof., Math., Univ. of Calif. 1984–90; Visiting Mem., Inst.for Advanced Study Princeton 1989, 1992–93; Mittaq-Leffler Inst. of Swedish Acad.of Sciences 1982, 1992–93; invited speaker at num. internat. profl. meetings, in particular Congresses of Math. Physics at Lausanne and Berlin, Addresses to AMS and CMS, Jeffrey Williams Address to CMS, Internat. Congress of Mathematicians in Kyoto, 50th Anniversary Conf., Candn. Math. Soc. (to be held); I.W. Killam Fellowship; John L. Synge Award, Royal Soc. of Canada; Fellow, Royal Soc. of Canada; Mem., Am. Math. Soc.; Candn. Math. Soc.; Internat. Assn. of Math. Physicists; editor: 'Duke Mathematical J.'; author: 'Mathematical Foundations of Scattering Theory' 1983; co-author: 'Spectral Theory of Schrödinger Operators,' 'Scattering Theory,' 'General Theory of Quantum Many-Particle' forthcoming; recreations: hiking, theatre, tennis, swimming, reading; Office: Toronto, Ont. M5S 1A1.

**SIGGINS, Maggie (Marjorie) May;** writer; b. Toronto, Ont. 28 May 1942; d. Elizabeth May; e. Ryerson Polytech. Inst. 1965; m. Gerald B. s. Sam and Lena Sperling 23 Aug. 1987; children: Shana, Adam, Carrie-May; Reporter, Toronto Telegram 1965–70; Political Reporter, City-TV 1971–73; TV interviewer-producer, CBC 1974–76; Prod., CITYPulsenews 1977–80; magazine writer 1969–89; TV documentarist 1972–93; Southam Fellowship for Journalists 1973–74; Max Bell Chair in Journalism 1983–84; Mem., Writers Union of Canda; ACTRA; Writers Guild of Sask.; Candn. Assn.

of Journalist; P.E.N.; author: 'A Guide to Skiing in Eastern North America' 1969, 'Bassett: His Forty Years in Politics, Publishing, Business and Sports' 1979, 'Brian and the Boys: A Study in Gang Rape' 1984, 'A Canadian Tragedy: JoAnn and Colin Thatcher: A Study of Love and Hate' 1985 (became CBC TV mini-series 1989; winner Crime Writers of Canada Award Arthur Ellis Award 1985)); 'Revenge of the Land: A Century of Greed: Tragedy and Murder on a Saskatchewan Farm' 1991 (1992 Gov. General's Lit. Award for Non-Fiction); 'Biography of Louis Riel' 1994; co-author: 'How to Catch a Man' 1970; Address: 2831 Retallack St., Regina, Sask. S4S 1S8.

**SIGLER, John H.;** university professor; b. Indianapolis, Ind. 22 Feb. 1932; s. Russell V. and Opal S. S.; e. Dartmouth Coll. B.A. 1953; Georgetown Univ. M.A. 1960; Univ. of S. Calif. Ph.D. 1968; m. Joan d. Alton and Alberta Myers 22 Aug. 1953; children: Jeffrey, David, Mary Anne; PROF., DEPT. OF POL. SCI., CARLETON UNIV. 1971– ; Strategic Analyst, US Air Force (Capt.) 1954–62; Rsch. Assoc., Univ. of S. Calif. 1962–67; Asst. Prof., Internat. Relns. 1967–68; Assoc. Prof., Pol. Sci., Macalester Coll. 1968–71; Dir., Norman Paterson Sch. of Internat. Affairs 1977–82; Dickey Fellow, Dartmouth Coll. 1988–89; Dir., Candn. Ctr. for Arms Control & Disarmament 1983–89; Candn. Inst. for Internat. Peace & Security 1984–88; Candn. Student Pugwash 1985–90; Vice-Pres., U.N. Assn. in Can. 1983–85; current events commentator, CTV & CBC; Adv. on Arms Control, Candn. del. to U.N. Gen. Assembly 1981; Ont. Fac. Excellence in Teaching Award 1973; Fulbright Scholar, Univ. of Grenoble 1953–54; Candn. citizen since 1977; Anglican; Mem., Group of 78 (Steering Ctte. 1986–88); co-author: 'Canadian-US Relations' 1979; co-editor: 'Canada and the United States' 1985, 'Conflicts Around the World' 1982–93; author of numerous scholarly articles; Club: Round Table; Home: 6 Rutherford Cres., Kanata, Ont. K2K 1M9; Office: Ottawa, Ont. K1S 5B6.

**SIGURDSON, Lorenz Willard,** B.A.Sc., M.S., Ph.D., P.Eng.; educator, scientist, engineer; b. Eriksdale, Man. 28 Jan. 1957; s. Johann Straumfjord and Gudrun Helga Julia (Holm) S.; e. Lundar Collegiate Inst.; St. John's Ravenscourt Sch. 1974 (Red River Scholarship); Univ. of Toronto B.A.Sc. 1978 (Varsity Nat. Scholarship); Cal. Inst. of Technol. M.S. 1980, Ph.D. 1986 (Special Scholarship); ASST. PROF. OF MECH. ENG. UNIV. OF ALTA. 1988– ; Rsch. Asst. Defence Rsch. Est. Atlantic 1978; Computer Applications Eng. Faculty of Med. Univ. of Man. 1978–79; Rsch. Asst. Caltech 1979–86; Rsch. Eng. Univ. of Cal. San Diego Inst. for Non-Linear Sci. 1986–88; guest lectr. Can., USA, India; author various papers structure & control turbulent fluids; syndicated photographs published in 'New Scientist,' 'Discover,' 'Outlook on Agriculture' and 'Current Science'; recipient Fac. of Engineering Teaching Award 1994; Bd. of Dir. Candn. Inst. Nordic Studies 1990–93; Hon. Chrmn., Engineering Students Soc. (ESS) 1991–92; Chrmn., APEGGA/Engineering Students Soc. Liaison Ctte., 1991–92; recipient APEGGA Appreciation Award 1992; mem. Sigma Xi, the Sci. Rsch. Soc.; Am. Phys. Soc.; Am. Inst. Aeronautics & Astronautics; Assn. of Professional Engrs., Geologists, and Geophysicists of Alta. (APEGGA); Office: Edmonton, Alta. T6G 2G8.

**SIGVALDASON, Oskar Thor,** B.Sc., D.I.C., Ph.D., P.Eng.; civil engineer; b. Arborg, Man. 8 Nov. 1937; s. Thorarinn Gudni and Adalbjorg (Simundson) S.; EXECUTIVE VICE-PRES. & CHIEF OPERATING OFFICER, DIR., ACRES INTERNATIONAL LTD.; Trustee, Brock Univ.; Vice-President, Consulting Engineers of Ontario; Home: 1238 Pelham Rd., R.R. 1, St. Catharines, Ont. L2R 6P7; Office: Box 1001, 5259 Dorchester Rd., Niagara Falls, Ont. L2E 6W1.

**SIKKUARK, Nick;** artist; b. Garry Lake, N.W.T. 21 May 1943; medium: sculpture, drawings, paintings; 19 group exbns. incl. most recent: Candn. Mus. of Civilization Hull, Que. 1992–92, Winnipeg Art Gall. 1992, The Isaacs/Innuit Gall. Toronto 1991, l'Iglou Art Esquimau, Douai (toured 5 cities) France 1990–91, Inuit Gall. of Vancouver 1990, 1991, York Quay Gall. & Leo Kamen Gall. (Earth Spirit Fest.) Toronto 1991, Art Space Gall. Philadelphia, Pa. 1991, Innuit Gall. of Eskimo Art Toronto 1990; solo exbns.: The Upstairs Gall. Winnipeg 1992, The Innuit Gall. of Eskimo Art 1988, Northern Images Cambridge Bay, N.W.T. 1981; collections: Sarick Coll., Art Gall. of Ont. Toronto, Winnipeg Art Gall.; award for craftsmanship 'Crafts from Arctic Canada' 1974; attended Cultural Olympics Montreal 1976; Delegate, 49th Annual Meeting, Can. Craft Council P.E.I. 1976; selected to carve ceremonial baton for opening of Commonwealth Games in Edmonton 1978; attended opening: solo exhbn. Northern Image, Whitehorse 1981; Instructor, carving workshop, Hall Beach 1989; attended Qatuujiqatgit Sanaguatit-Contemp. Carving/Sculpting Session, Ottawa Sch. of Art 1991, opening 'Indigena' Candn. Mus. of Civ. 1992; author of books, and subject of articles; Home: Pelly Bay, N.W.T.; Office: c/o Ingo Hessel, Indian and Northern Affairs Canada, Les Terrasses de la Chaudière, Ottawa, Ont. K1A 0H4.

**SILBER, Allan C.;** financial executive; b. Hamilton, Ont. 7 Dec. 1948; s. Godel and Cilka S.; e. Central H.S.; McMaster Univ.; Univ. of Toronto; m. Hinda d. Helen and Robert Rosen 24 May 1970; children: Joshua, Leah, Jay, David; CHRMN., PRES. & C.E.O., COUNSEL CORP. 1988– ; Chrmn., Counsel Financial Corp.; Diversicare Inc.; Dir., Mount Sinai Hosp.; Baycrest Hospital; recreations: tennis, skiing; Clubs: York Racquets; Primrose; Home: 106 Old Forest Hill Rd., Toronto, Ont. M5P 2R9; Office: 36 Toronto St., Suite 1200, Toronto, Ont. M5C 2C5.

**SILCOX, David Phillips,** M.A., F.R.S.A., LL.D.; art historian; arts administrator; b. Moose Jaw, Sask. 28 Jan. 1937; s. Albert Phillips Silcox; e. Univ. of Toronto B.A. 1959, M.A. 1966; Courtauld Inst. Univ. of London 1962–63; m. Linda Intaschi 1983; SR. RESIDENT FELLOW, MASSEY COLLEGE, UNIV. OF TORONTO 1991–94; Arts Consultant; Freelance writer and Broadcaster 1964–65; Visual Arts Offr. Can. Council 1965–66, Sr. Arts Offr. 1966–70; Asst. and subsequently Assoc. Dean of Fine Arts, York Univ. 1970–73, Assoc. Prof. 1970–77, Chrmn. of Music 1971–72, Chrmn. of Visual Arts 1972–73; Dir. of Cultural Affairs, Municipality of Metrop. Toronto 1974–83; Asst. Depy. Minister, Dept. of Communications, Ottawa, 1983–85; Depy. Min. of Culture and Communications, Ont. 1986–91; Asst. Dir. Candn. Conf. of Arts 1961, Bd. mem. 1976–81; Organizer, Toronto Outdoor Art Exhn. 1961 (first); Bd. mem. Candn. Film Devel. Corp. 1971–78; Vice Chrmn. 1975–78; Chrmn., 1981–83; Gov., Massey Hall 1972–83; Chrmn. Internat. Sculpture Conf. 1977–78; Bd. mem., Univ. of Toronto Sch. of Continuing Studies; Festival of Festivals; Founder, Toronto Theatre Festival 1981; past mem. various comtes. Art Gallery of Ont., Ont. Coll. of Arts, 1976–79; Can. Council, Vincent Massey Awards, Stratford Art Gallery; Bd. mem. Assn. Cultural Extves.; Koffler Arts Centre; Founding mem. Fed. Dept. Pub. Works Fine Arts Comte. 1968–70, Chrmn. 1978–79; Bd. mem., Stratford Festival 1981; Founder, Toronto Int'l Festival 1981–83; Trustee, Jack Bush Estate and Harold Town Estate; art consulting services incl.: Banff Sch. Fine Arts, Mem. Univ. Nfld., Metrop. Toronto, Govt. Alta., Toronto Transit Comn. (Spadina subway), Univ. of Toronto, Fed. Candn. Muns.; Special Advisor to Secy. of State on Fed. Cultural Policy 1978; special lectr. on Candn. art and Candn. Cultural Policy; rec'd Sir Frederick Banting Award 1962; Man of Yr. Globe & Mail 1962; Can. Council Arts Bursary 1962, Research Grant 1973, Research Fellowship 1974–75; Arts Award, 1979–80; McLean Foundation Research Grant 1970; York Univ. Research Grant 1972; co-author 'Tom Thomson: The Silence and the Storm' 1977; author 'Christopher Pratt' 1982; 'Jack Bush' 1984, contrib.; Guest Ed. 'Canadian Art' 1962; mem. Internat. Ed. Bd., 'Studio International' 1968–75; writer/producer/ed. various art catalogues; author various articles, essays and reports art mags. and newspapers; mem., American Friends of Canada 1990–94; mem., Praemium Imperiale Nominating Ctte. (Japan) 1992– ; Bd. Mem., Gardiner Museum 1992– ; Bd. Chair, Art Gallery of York Univ. 1992– ; recreations: canoeing, sailing, scuba diving; Home: Apt. 402, 70 Montclair Ave., Toronto, Ont. M5P 1P7.

**SILCOX, Peter,** B.A., M.A., Ph.D.; university professor; b. Dudley, U.K. 24 Aug. 1939; s. Arthur Matthew and Lilian Mary (Corneloues) S.; e. Bristol Univ. B.A. (Hons.) 1960; London Sch. of Economics Dipl. in Soc. Admin. 1961; Univ. of Toronto M.A. 1962, Ph.D. 1972; m. Antonia d. Hugh and Rose Stephens 27 Dec. 1966; children: Mark, Mary; PROFESSOR OF POLITICAL SCIENCE, ERINDALE COLLEGE, UNIV. OF TORONTO 1990– ; Lectr., Pol. Sci., Univ. of Toronto 1964–72; Asst. Prof. 1972–73; Assoc. Prof. 1972–90; ; Principal, Woodsworth College, Univ. of Toronto 1977–84; Assoc. Dean, Social Sciences & Vice-Principal, Student Services, Erindale College, Univ. of Toronto 1988–93; Visiting Prof., Dalhousie Univ. 1965; Univ. of West Indies 1966; Comnr., Essex Co. Local Government Restructuring Comn. 1974–76; Hon. Life Mem., Ont. Council for Univ. Continuing Education 1984; Mem., Gov. Council, Univ. of Toronto 1981–84; Chair, Presidents Ctte. on Edn. of Part-time & Mature Students, York Univ. 1985–87; Mem., Inst. of Public Admin. of Can. (Chair, Toronto Area Group 1976–77); Candn. Pol. Sci. Assn.; author: 'Report of the Essex County Restructuring Study' 1976; editor: 'Parties to Change' 1971; recreation: cricket; Home: 2535 Homelands Dr., Mississauga, Ont. L5K 1H5; Office: Mississauga, Ont. L5L 1C6.

**SILK, Frederick Charles Ziervogel,** B.Sc., C.A.(S.A.), F.C.A. (England & Wales); financial executive; b. Pretoria, S. Africa 29 July 1934; s. Frederick Charles and Edythe D'Olier (Ziervogel) S.; e. Rhodes Univ. B.Sc. 1954; Univ. of the Witwatersrand C.T.A. 1957; m. Margaret d. Earl and Phyllis Colbourne 12 May 1962; children: Michael, Alison, Jennifer; VICE-PRESIDENT & TREASURER, NABISCO BRANDS LTD. 1982– ; Auditing & Management Consulting, Deloitte Haskins & Sells (Johannesburg, London, San Francisco, N.Y.) 1954–64; Management Consultant, P.S. Ross & Partners 1964–68; Vice-Pres. Finance & Admin., J&P Coats (Canada) Ltd. 1968–74; Treas., Standard Brands Ltd. Montreal 1974–75; Asst. Treas., Standard Brands Inc. N.Y. 1975–78; Treas., Harlequin Enterprises Ltd. 1978–82; Vice-Pres. & Treas., RJR-Macdonald Inc. 1987– ; Mem., Financial Executives Inst.; Soc. of Internat. Treasurers; Office: Suite 1550, North Tower, P.O. Box 188, Royal Bank Plaza, Toronto, Ont. M5J 2J4.

**SILLCOX, Robert L.,** B.A.; investment executive; b. Toronto, Ont. 1931; e. Ridley Coll. St. Catharines, Ont. 1949; Williams Coll. Williamstown, Mass. B.A. 1953; m.; 3 children; Dir., Investment Div., OMERS (Ont. Municipal Employees Retirement System) 1988– ; Dir., Harris & Partners Ltd. 1956–70; Pres., McDunn, Sillcox & Co. Ltd. 1970–77 and founding Partner, Euro Brokers, Harlow & Co.; Sr. Vice Pres. Investments, Bank of Montreal 1977–79; Vice Pres., Metropolitan Life Insurance Co. 1979–88; Dir., Commercial Financial Corp. Ltd. 1986– ; Princeton Developments Ltd. 1989– ; Treas., Eye Research Inst. of Ont. 1984– ; Trustee, Lake Simcoe Conservation Authority Found.; Bd. Trade Metrop. Toronto; Financial Extves. Inst. Can.; recreations: horses, shooting, boating; Clubs: Toronto; University (N.Y.); Muskoka Lakes Golf & Country; Home: Grandview Farm, R.R. #3, King, Ont. L0G 1K0.

**SILLETT, Mary Jane,** B.S.W.; commissioner; b. Hopedale, Labrador, Nfld. 10 July 1953; d. Jerry and Esther (Tuttu) S.; e. Memorial Univ. of Nfld. B.S.W. 1976; divorced; children: Matthew and Martin Lougheed; COMMISSIONER, ROYAL COMMISSION ON ABORIGINAL PEOPLES 1991– ; Extve. Asst. to Pres., Labrador Inuit Assn. summer & full-time 1971–82; Nat. Co-ord., Inuit Ctte. on National Issues 1981–82; Sr. Policy Analyst, Native Citizens' Directorate, Sec. of State 1982–89; Pres., Pauktuutit (Inuit Women's Assn. of Can.) & Vice-Pres., Inuit Tapirisat of Can. 1989–91; extensive experience in aboriginal affairs, particularly on Inuit issues in both private & public sectors; Health & Welfare Canada Award for one of Canada's outstanding aboriginal women leaders 1992; Bd. Mem., Aborignal Women & Econ. Devel. 1991; Mem. & Vice Chair, Atii 1987–91; Mem., Joint Adv. Ctte. on Family Violence Initiatives Program 1981–91; Negotiator, Labrador Inuit Assn. Moravian Land Grants Negotiations 1983– ; Chair, First Northern Labrador Women's Conf. 1979; 'Annauqatigiit' 1977–79; Labrador Mem.s, Candn. Cons. Ctte. on Multiculturalism 1980– ; Bd. Mem., Native Women's Assn. of Canada 1979– ; Co-ord., Fishery Emergency Policy Ctte., Labrador 1979–80; Bd. Mem., Labrador Legal Services 1979– ; Home: 6745 Notre Dame St., Orleans, Ont. K1C 1H2; Office: 427 Laurier Ave. W., 5th fl., Box 1993, Stn. B, Ottawa, Ont. K1P 1B2.

**SILVA, Edward Timothy,** B.A., Ph.D.; university professor; b. New York, N.Y. 17 Nov. 1935; s. Obdulio and Anna (Pukanski) S.; e. Harpur Coll., State Univ. of N.Y., B.A. (cum laude) 1961; Univ. of Michigan, Ph.D. 1969; m. Susan E. d. Sylvia and Irving Warren 1961; divorced 1982; children: Nathaniel Warren, Adam Emmanuel Paul; PROF., DEPT. OF SOCIOLOGY, ERINDALE COLL., UNIV. OF TORONTO 1987– ; Asst. Prof., Sociology, Univ. of Wisconsin 1968–74; Assoc. Prof., Soc., Univ. of Toronto 1974–87; Rsch. Fellow, Inst. of Higher Edn. Law & Governance, Univ. of Houston 1984–85; Mem., Candn. Sociol. & Anthrop. Assn.; Candn. Assn. of Univ. Teachers; Counc., Univ. of Toronto Faculty Assn. 1984–86; co-author: 'Serving Power' 1984; co-editor: 'Social Movements / Social Change' 1988; 'Race, Class, Gender: Bonds and Barriers' 1989, 2nd Rev. ed. 1992; recreations: walking, swimming; club: Faculty Club, Univ. of Toronto; Home: 65 Henry Lane Terrace, Toronto, Ont. M5A 4B7; Office: Toronto, Ont. M5S 1A1.

**SILVER, Alfred Robert Leslie;** writer; b. Brandon, Man. 13 March 1951; s. Gerald John and Margarita Mary (Hoemsen) S.; e. Tech. Vocational High Sch. Winnipeg; m. Jane Buss d. John and May Holgate 24

Apl. 1989; first profl. prodn. as playwright Man. Theatre Workshop 1978 followed by 2 further plays; former Playwright-in-Residence Man. Theatre Centre, 3 plays produced; 8 radio scripts produced by CBC; author (novels) 'Good Time Charlie's Back in Town Again' 1978, French transl. 1979; 'A Savage Place' 1982; 'Red River Story' 1988; 'Lord of the Plains' 1990; 'Where the Ghost Horse Runs' 1991; (plays) 'Thimblerig' 1982; 'More of a Family 1984; 'Climate of the Times' 1987; recreation: hardscrabble gardening; Clubs: Louisville Sluggers; Belaying Pins; Address: RR 1, Ellershouse, N.S. B0N 1L0.

**SILVER, Malcolm D.,** M.B.B.S., M.Sc., M.D., Ph.D., FRCPC, FRCPA; pathologist; b. Adelaide, Aust. 29 April 1933; s. Eric Bertram and Stella Louise (Riley) S.; e. Univ. of Adelaide M.B.B.S. 1957; McGill Univ. M.Sc. 1961, Ph.D. 1963; Univ. of Adelaide M.D. 1972; m. Meredith d. Alan and Erica Galloway 19 Jan. 1957; children: Stuart Faulkner, Claire Eleanor, Caryl Louise; SENIOR STAFF PATHOLOGIST, THE TORONTO HOSPITAL 1992– and CHAIR IN PATHOLOGY, UNIV. OF TORONTO 1985– ; Resident Med. Offr., Royal Adelaide Hosp. 1957–58; Res. & Rsch. Training, Pathology, McGill Univ. 1958–63; Rsch. Fellow, Experimental Pathology, Australian Nat. Univ. 1963–65; Staff Pathologist, Toronto Gen. Hosp. & Mem., Dept. of Pathology, Univ. of Toronto 1965–79 (proceeding from Asst. to Full Prof. 1974); Chief of Pathology, Univ. Hosp. & Chair, Pathology, Univ. of W. Ont. 1979–85; Chief of Pathology, Toronto Gen. Div. (later The Toronto Hosp.) 1985–92; author of over 120 scientific articles; editor: 'Cardiovascular Pathoogy' 2 vols, 2nd ed. 1992; recreation: birdwatching; club: Franklin Fishing; Office: Room 110, 100 College St., Toronto, Ont. M5G 1L5.

**SILVERMAN, Hon. Judge Hugh W.,** B.A., M.A., LL.B., LL.M., Q.C.; judge; b. Oyen, Alta. 17 Dec. 1923; s. Dr. Abraham Hertz and Goldie (Fishman) S.; e. Univ. of Toronto B.A., M.A. 1947; Osgoode Hall Law Sch. Toronto LL.B. 1954; N.Y. Univ. Law Sch. LL.M. 1972; m. Anne M. d. Isaac and Lena Garlock 27 Aug. 1959; children: David, Judith, Nancy; ONTARIO COURT JUDGE, PROVINCIAL DIVISION 1982– ; called to Bar of Ont. 1954; Prof. of Law, Univ. of Windsor Law Sch. 1969–76; Rsch. Cons. Family Law, Law Reform Comn., Ottawa 1974–75; Ed. Chitty's Law Jour., Family Law Review, Legal Med. Quarterly; author numerous articles in law jours.; cr. Q.C. 1967; Home: 43 Blue Forest Dr., Downsview, Ont. M3H 4W4; Office: Old City Hall, 60 Queen St. W., Toronto, Ont. M5H 2M4.

**SILVERSTEIN, Alan Gary,** B.A., LL.B.; real estate lawyer, author, broadcaster; b. Toronto, Ont. 20 June 1951; s. Irving and Ethel (Rose) S.; e. York Univ. B.A. 1972; Osgoode Hall Law School LL.B. 1975; called to Bar of Ontario 1977; m. Hannah d. Aron and Frieda Rosenzweig 15 July 1973; children: Elliott, Darryl; practices law in Thornhill, Ont., specializing in the areas of real estate & mortgages; has written & lectured extensively on var. real estate & mortgage topics; participant in many public forums & seminars; num. radio & TV appearances across Canada; has taught mortgage financing & home-buying courses at Seneca, George Brown & Georgian colleges; Vice-Chair, Town of Vaughan Ctte. of Adjustment 1986–89; host of Canada's only real estate phone-in talk show 'The Real Estate Show' CFRB 1010 AM Radio; Mem., Candn. Bar Assn.; author: 'Hidden Profits in Your Mortgage' 1985, 'Home Buying Strategies for Resale Homes' 1986, 'Home Buying Strategies for Newly-Built Homes' 1987, 'The Perfect Mortgage' 1989; 'Save! - Guide to Mortgage Payment Tables' 1993; 'The Dotted Line' weekly column in Toronto Star; recreations: baseball, hockey; Office: 180 Steeles Ave. W., Unit 30, Thornhill, Ont. L4J 2L1.

**SILVERSTONE, Marc Jack;** lawyer & executive; b. Montreal, Que. 6 Feb. 1951; s. Ben and Esther Rachel (Abel) S.; e. McGill Univ., B.A. 1972, B.C.L. 1976, LL.B. 1978; Ecole de form. profl. du Barreau de Qué. 1976–77; m. Ann d. Max and Leah Muhlstock 23 June 1974; children: Gavriella, Simon, Lee; NAT. EXTVE. DIR. AND GEN. COUNSEL, CANDN. JEWISH CONGRESS 1985– ; Research Branch, Law & Govt. Div., Library of Parliament 1979–81; Spec. Asst., Senate Ctte. on Transp. & Communic. 1981–82; Vice Consul, Candn. Embassy, Mexico 1982–83; Legal Div., Dept. of External Affairs 1983; Vice Consul, Candn. Cons. Gen., Atlanta, Ga. 1983–85; Mem., Candn. Multicultural Advisory Ctte.; Mem., Law Soc. of Upper Can.; Candn. Society of Assn. Extves.; Candn. Bar Assoc.; Am. Soc. of International Law; Office: 1590 avenue Docteur Penfield, Montreal, Que. H3G 1C5.

**SILVERTHORNE, Leslie Nelles,** M.D.; paediatrician; b. Brantford, Ont. 24 Oct. 1901; e. Brantford C.I.; Univ. of Toronto Med. School 1926; CONSULTING PHYSICIAN, HOSP. FOR SICK CHILDREN; Hon. Consulting Physician, Wellesley Hosp.; Hon. Mem., Ecuadorian Pediatric Soc.; Candn. Pediatric Soc.; Am. Medical Assn.; Emeritus Fellow, Am. Acad. of Pediatrics; Mem., Am. Pediatric Soc.; Soc. for Pediatric Rsch.; Pediatric Travel Club; Christian Med. Soc.; Christian Business Men's Ctte. (Nat. & Internat.); Corp., Ont. Bible College; Faculty Club, Univ. of Toronto; Corp., Intervarsity Christian Fellowship; 50 Year Club, Air Travel Assn.; Bd. Chair, Scott Mission; several past executive positions; one of Canada's pioneers in preventive medicine; developed whooping cough vaccine, treatment for meningitis, anti-influenzal serum; first in Canada to treat a patient with penicillin 1942; has travelled worldwide to observe and discuss latest advances in treating infectious diseases; Address: 630 – 602 Melita Cres., Toronto, Ont. M6G 3Z5.

**SILVESTER, Peter P.,** B.S., M.A.Sc., Ph.D., Eng., F.I.E.E.E.; b. 25 Jan. 1935; e. Carnegie-Mellon Univ. B.S. 1956; Univ. of Toronto M.A.Sc. 1958; McGill Univ. Ph.D. 1964; m. Elizabeth V. Placek 1958; PROF. OF ELECT. ENG. McGILL UNIV. 1958– ; Dir. Infolytica Corp.; Sr. Rsch. Fellow General Electric 1978–79; Sr. Fellow SERC 1980–81; Visiting Fellow Commoner, Trinity Coll. Cambridge 1988–89; author: 'Modern Electromagnetic Fields' 1968; 'The Unix System Guidebook' 1988; 'Data Structures for Engineering Software' 1992; co-author: 'Finite Elements for Electrical Engineers' 1984; 'Computer-Aided Design in Magnetics' 1986; 'Computer Engineering' 1989; 'Finite Elements in Wave Electromagnetics' 1994; Fellow, IEEE (Inst. Electr. Electron. Eng.); mem. N.Y. Acad. Sci's; Assn. Computing Machinery; Candn. Soc. Hist. & Philos. Sci.; Royal Photographic Soc.; Sigma Xi; Office: 3480 University St., Montréal, Qué. H3A 2A7.

**SIM, L. Rodney,** B.Comm., M.B.A., C.F.A., F.C.S.I.; investment dealer; b. Ottawa, Ont. 30 Apr. 1950; s. Harry Yates and Phyllis Frances (Chu) S.; e. Xerox of Canada Scholarship 1971; Carleton Univ. B.Comm. 1972; Univ. of Toronto M.B.A. 1973; m. Yvonne d. Frank and Mia Verwimp 26 May 1984; children: Matthew Alexander; EXECUTIVE VICE-PRESIDENT & DIR., MIDLAND WALWYN CAPITAL INC. 1991– ; Investment Analyst A.E. Ames and Co. Ltd. 1973–76; Sales Exec. International Dominion Securities Corp., Harris & Partners Ltd. 1976; Investment Analyst A.E. Ames & Co. Ltd. 1977–78, Mgr. of Rsch. 1979, Vice-Pres. and Dir. Instl. Sales and Equity Rsch. 1980–81; Vice-Pres. and Dir. Equities Bell Gouinlock Ltd. 1981–84, Sr. Vice-Pres. and Dir. Equities 1984; Chrmn., Pres. & C.E.O., Capital Group Securities Ltd. 1984–91; Dir., W.I. Carr (U.K.) Limited 1988–91; author various investment rsch. reports; mem. Toronto Soc. of Fin. Analysts; mem. Assn. for Investment Management and Rsch.; Chartered Fin. Analyst (C.F.A.) 1979; Fellow, Candn. Securities Inst. (F.C.S.I.) 1978; recreation: golf, skiing; Clubs: Mississauga Golf & Country; Horseshoe Valley Golf; Heights of Horseshoe Ski; Fitness Institute; Office: BCE Place, Suite 500, 181 Bay St., Toronto, Ont. M5J 2V8.

**SIMAND-SEIDMAN, Carol,** B.A., M.S.W.; university administrator, educator; b. Montreal, Que. 22 March 1951; d. Mel J. and Leila E. Simand; e. Loyola Coll. B.A. (cum laude) 1972; State Univ. of New York M.S.W. 1974; Univ. of Toronto, Sr. Mngt. Program 1993; m. Peter s. Joe and Shirlee S. 4 June 1972; children: Joshua, Sarena; ASSISTANT DEAN, FAC. OF SOCIAL WORK, UNIV. OF TORONTO 1989– ; Teacher, Sch. of Cont. Studies, Univ. of Toronto 1982–90; Dir., Jewish Women's Fed. of Toronto & United Jewish Appeal Women's Div. 1986–89; Pres., Custom Seminars (consulting practice); Mem., Adv. Bd., Candn. Jewish News; Bd. Mem., Jewish Student's Union, Univ. of Toronto; Mem., Ont. Assn. of Profl. Social Workers; Ont. Coll. of Cert. Social Workers; Mem., Council for Advancement and Support of Edn.; Beth Avraham Yosef Cong.; Home: 485 Spring Gate Blvd., Thornhill, Ont. L4J 5B4; Office: 246 Bloor St. W., Toronto, Ont. M5S 1A1.

**SIMARD, André S.,** B.A., L.ès D.; diplomat; b. Montréal, Qué. 24 Aug. 1940; s. Barthélémy and Lucienne (Printemps) S.; e. Coll. Ste-Thérèse de Blainville B.A. 1963; Univ. de Montréal L.ès D. 1966; Acad. of Internat. Law The Hague Cert. in Internat. Law 1966; m. Sabine Théodas 1974; children: Marc-Antoine, Yusin; Ambassador to the Philippines 1989–93; lawyer 1967; Eur. Div. External Affairs 1967–68, Special Asst. Office of Under-Sec. 1968–69; Second Sec. Tokyo 1969–71; Cultural Affairs Div. Ottawa 1971; First Sec. Saigon 1972–73; Legal Adv. to ICSC Saigon 1973; Acting Commissioner to ICSC Laos 1973–74; Counsellor Tunis 1974–76; Head of Nuclear Sect. Transport, Communications & Energy Div. Ottawa 1976–77; Dept. Official Spokesman and Dir. Press Office Ottawa 1977–81; Counsellor and Consul Thailand 1981–84; Dir. Pacific Div. Ottawa 1984–86, Dir. Japan Div. 1986–87; Ambassador to Cameroun, Tchad & Central African repub. 1987–89; R.Catholic; recreations: tennis, golf, swimming; Clubs: Polo (Manila); Rotary (Manila); Office: Place Vanier, Tower A, 18th Floor, 333 River Rd., Ottawa, Ont. K1A 0G2.

**SIMARD, Claude A.,** A.O.C.A., R.C.A.; painter; university professor; b. Quebec City, Que. 9 July 1943; s. Alphonse and Noëlla (Rousseau) S.; e. Séminaire de Qué.; Académie de Qué.; Ont. Coll. of Art; m. Huguette d. Omer and Simone Moreau 24 June 1970; children: Rose-Mélanie, Roseline; PROF. WITH TENURE, VISUAL COMMUNICATIONS PROGRAM, LAVAL UNIV. 1975– ; Head of Communications & Design, Simons (Graphic Design) 1966–73; Head Designer, Communikart 1973–84; Sec., Fac. of Art, Laval Univ. 1985–89 and Vice-Dean, Fac. of Art, Laval Univ. 1988–89; 16 one-man shows, in galleries across Can. 1974–93; Show, Orangerie of Château Bagatelle, Paris, France 1991; mural works for Canada Parks, Esso; stamp designs for Canada Post, Christmas 1983 & 1987; Academician, Royal Candn. Acad. of Art 1983; elected mem., New York Soc. of Illustrators 1977; Founding Mem. Que. Graphic Designers Soc. 1974; Publication: 'Claude A. Simard' by André Juneau, 1991; recreations: skiing, walking, gardening; Home: 779 Bon Accueil, Ste-Foy, Que. G1V 2Z3; Office: Quebec City, Que. G1K 7P4.

**SIMARD, Jean-Claude,** B.A., M.S.; utilities executive; b. Delisle, Qué. 29 March 1945; s. Vincent Paul and Eglantine (Bergeron) S.; e. Univ. Laval B.A. 1966, C.E.S. 1969, Licence 1969; Univ. de Lyon M.S. 1970; Univ. St-Joseph of Beyrouth Ph.D. prog. Rural Econ. 1971; children: Geneviève, Pierre-Etienne; DIRECTOR OF DEVELOPMENT, HYDRO-QUÉBEC INTERNATIONAL 1987– ; Counsellor Middle E. and Asian Affairs Qué. Dept. Internat. Affairs 1972–74; Counsellor for Communications & Politics Qué. Del. Brussels 1974–77; Dir. Interdept. Bureau Qué. Nat. Assembly 1977–82; Rep. and Dir. Asia, Latin Am., Africa & Middle E. Qué. External Trade Dept. 1982–85, Dir. Ind. Goods & Internat. Projects 1986–87; First Counsellor and Chief Econ. Services Qué. Govt. Dels. Paris 1985–86; Sec. Jean-Charles Bonenfant Found. 1980–82; mem. Candn. Inst. Internat. Affairs; Home: 40 Querbes St., Outremont, Qué. H2V 3V6; Office: 800 De Maisonneuve E., Montréal, Qué. H2L 4L8.

**SIMARD, Jean-Jacques,** B.A., B.Sc., M.Sc., Ph.D.; university professor; b. Chicoutimi, Que. 15 Nov. 1945; s. Benoit and Marguerite (Mayrand) S.; e. Coll. de Jonquière, B.A.; Laval Univ., B.Sc., M.Sc., Ph.D.; m. Marie d. Maurice and Thérèse Mercier 10 June 1978; PROF. OF SOCIOL., LAVAL UNIV. 1987– ; field work amongst the Cree Indians, Wemindji, James Bay 1967–69; Prov. Civil Service, Dir. for Northern Que. 1969–71; Rsch. Assoc., present Univ. 1972–76, Asst. Prof., Dept. of Sociol. 1976, Assoc. Prof. 1981, Prof. 1987– ; cons. and lectr. on Que. society, contemporary social issues, northern and native affairs; rec'd Radio-Can. Prize for Young Writers 1962; R. Catholic; author: 'La Longue Marche des Technocrates' (essay) 1979; over 50 papers in scholarly and sci. jours.; ed. Recherches Sociographiques 1987–89; Dir., Groupe d'études inuit et circumpolaires 1988–91; recreation: outdoors; Home: 711 Clairmont, Ste-Foy, Que. G1V 3C5; Office: Dept. of Sociol., Laval Univ., Quebec City, Que. G1K 7P4.

**SIMARD, Léon;** industrialist; b. Sorel, Que. 21 Nov. 1920; s. Joseph Arthur, O.B.E., and Rose Blanche (Pontbriand) S.; e. Coll. Jean de Brébeuf, Mont Saint Louis, Que.; m. Jacqueline, d. Fernand Levasseur, Montreal, Que., 15 Nov. 1947; one d., Roseanne; PRESIDENT, SIMCOR INC.; Dir., Standard Paper Box Mfg.; La Cie de Charlevoix Ltée.; Dir., Marie-Enfant Hosp.; Greenshields Foundation; Quebec Labrador Foundation; Roman Catholic; recreations: golf, hunting, fishing, yachting; Clubs: Royal Montreal Golf; Mount Royal; Surf (Miami); Indian Creek Country (Miami); Home: 3110 Daulac Rd., Montreal, Que. H3Y 1Z9.

**SIMARD, Hon. (Rose Marie) Louise,** M.L.A., B.A., LL.B.; politician, lawyer; b. Val D'Or, Que. 17 April 1947; d. (Paul Eugene) Robert and (Mary Martha) Antoinette (Poitras) S.; e. Univ. of Sask. B.A. 1969, LL.B. 1970 (Award in Jurisprudence); children: Paul and Marin Simard-Smith; MINISTER OF SASKATCHEWAN HEALTH 1991– ; 1st elected to Sask. Leg. for Regina Lakeview g.e. 1986; re-elected 1991; articled with MacPherson, Leslie & Tyerman 1970–71; private &

public practice (incl. Legis. Counsel & Law Clerk 3 years; worked with num. community boards, agencies & comns.) 1971–86; Sessional Lectr., Univ. of Sask.; Vice-Chair, Human Rights Comn. 5 years; Lay Appt. to Council of the College of Physicans & Surgeons; Mem., Attorney General's Ctte. to Consolidate Queen's Bench & District Courts; Roman Catholic; N.D.P.; recreations: jogging, swimming, biking, skiing, skating, reading; Home: 2905 Hill Ave., Regina, Sask.; Office: Rm. 334, Legislative Bldgs., Regina, Sask. S4S 0B3.

**SIMARD, René**, M.D., F.R.C.S.(C); retired physician; university professor; b. Sillery, Que. March 1912; e. Que. Semy.; Laval Univ.; Univ. of Paris; m. Albina Petitclerc, Sorel, P.Q., 1937; children: Geneviève, Jacqueline; Past Prof. of Obstetrics, Head Dept. of OBS-GYN., 1957–71; Laval Univ.; Former Attending Gynecologist, Hôpital du St-Sacrament, mem., Soc. of Obstet. & Gynaecol. Can. Pres., 1955–56; Candn. Med. Assn.; recreations: reading, crosswords, scrabble; Home: 2590 Plaza, Apt. 411, Sillery, Que. G1T 1X2.

**SIMARD, René**, O.C., M.D., D.Sc., F.R.C.P., FRSC; university administrator; b. Montreal, Que. 4 Oct. 1935; s. Raoul and Alice (Lavoie) S.; e. Coll. de Saint-Laurent, B.A. 1956; Univ. de Montréal, M.D. 1962; Mount Sinai Med. Sch. (N.Y., U.S.A.), Residency (pathol.) 1965; Doctorat d'Etat, Univ. de Paris, D.Sc. 1968; m. Françoise d. Pierre and René Yven 9 Dec. 1967; children: Patrice, Sébastien, Caroline; RECTOR, UNIV. DE MONTRÉAL 1993– ; Pres., National Advisory Council on Pharmaceutical Rsch. 1990–93; Fellow, Med. Rsch. Counc. in Villejuif France 1965–68; MRC Scholar 1969–74; MRC Assoc. 1974–76; NCI Assoc. 1976–78; Dept. of Cell Biol. (Sherbrooke) 1968–75; Prof., present univ. 1975– , Vice-Rector, Acad. & Rsch. 1985–93; Dir., Montreal Cancer Inst. 1975–87; Pres., F.R.S.Q. 1975–78; Pres., Med. Rsch. Counc. of Can. 1978–81; Bd. of Dir., Nat. Cancer Inst. of Can. 1987–90; Sci. Adv. Counc., Alta. Heritage Found. for Med. Rsch. 1981–93; Gov. Counc., Internat. Agency for Rsch. on Cancer 1981–92; Sci. Adv. Bd., The Ciba Found. 1980– ; Extve. Ctte., Conference of Rectors & Principals of Quebec Universities 1993– ; mem., various grants cttes.; Prix Michel Sarrazin 1981; Queen Elizabeth II Silver Jub. Medal 1976; F.R.C.P. 1976; O.C. 1989; Fellow, Royal Soc. of Canada 1989; Docteur honoris causa, Université de Toulouse 1990; Scientific Advisory Council, Biotechnology Rsch. Institute, NRC 1989– ; Chrmn. of Bd., Institut de recherche en biologie végétale; Bd. mem., Research Institute on the History of Architecture; mem., Club des Ambassadeurs; Montreal Convention Ctr.; Bd. Mem., The Triumf Corp.; Revue Medecine-Sciences; author of over 250 sci. pubs.; Home: 53, ave. de Vimy, Outremont, Qué. H3S 2P9; Office: Univ. de Montréal, C.P. 6128, Succ. Centre-Ville, Montréal, Qué. H3C 3J7.

**SIMARD-LAFLAMME, Carole**, B.A., M.Museumology; artist; b. Baie St-Paul, Que. 16 March 1945; d. Lionel and Adrienne (Fortin) Simard; e. Univ. Laval B.A.(Arts) 1966, arch. studies 1966–68; Univ. of Montreal & McGill 1984–88; Univ. of Montreal & UQAM M.Musemology 1991; m. Denis K. s. Edouard Laflamme 9 Sept. 1967; children: Jo-Philippe, Alexis, Catherine; Candn. expositions & internat. contests incl.: Kyoto Japan 1989, Tournai Belgium 1990, London England 1983, Scandinavia & Spain 1983, Paris, Bordeaux, Lyon France 1981, Paris 1976, Grenoble, Strasbourg, Bruxelles, Luxembourg 1976, Vevey, Switzerland 1977; creation of more than 22 gigantic pieces of art integrated into Que. architecture 1972–83; 15 solo expositions in Que. & Ont. 1966–89; well rep. in collections in Canada & abroad; Stage in Africa & Prof., Nat. Inst. of Fine Arts (Bamako, Mali, Africa) 1968–70; Nat. Dir., Cons. can. de l'artisanat 1975–79; Mem., Bd. of Dir., Fond. du Musée Marsil 1980–86; Soc. québécoise de tapisserie contemporaine 1988–89; Galerie d'art Edouard-Montpetit 1987–90; the only Candn. artist selected to rep. Canada, 'Internat. Competition Textile '89' (Kyoto, Japan); 1st prize for sculpture, 'La force de l'énergie' orgn. by Gaz Metropolitan 1989; participant in many confs. & panels; selection ctte. extensive travel to Europe, the Middle-East & the Orient 1970–90; recreations: music, family; Home: 93 l'Espérance, St. Lambert, Que. J4P 1X4.

**SIMEON, Richard Edmund Barrington**, M.A., Ph.D.; educator; b. Bath, U.K. 2 March 1943; s. John Edmund Barrington and Anne Mary (Dean) S.; e. St George's Sch. Vancouver 1960; Univ. of B.C. B.A. 1964; Yale Univ. M.A. 1966, Ph.D. 1968; 1st m. A. Joan d. George and Marjorie Weld 6 Aug. 1966; divorced 1991; children: Stephen George Barrington, Rachel Elizabeth; 2nd m. Maryetta Cheney 17 April 1993; PROF., POLITICAL SCIENCE AND LAW, UNIV. OF TORONTO 1991– ; Asst. Prof. Queen's Univ. 1968, Assoc. Prof. 1972, Prof. of Political Studies 1977–91, Dir. Inst. Intergovt'al Relations 1976–83, Dir., Sch. of Public Administration 1986–91; Rsch. Coordinator (Insts.) Royal Comn. Econ. Union & Can.'s Devel. Prospects 1983–85; mem. Rsch. Council Candn. Inst. Advanced Rsch. 1982–86; Ont. Adv. Ctte. on Confed. 1977–81; Vice-Chair, Ont. Law Reform Commn., 1989– ; author 'Federal-Provincial Diplomacy: The Making of Recent Policy in Canada' 1972; 'A Citizen's Guide to the Constitutional Question' 1980; co-author 'Small Worlds: Regions and Parties in Canadian Political Life' 1980; 'Federalism & Economic Union in Canada' 1985; 'State, Society and the Development of Canadian Federalism' 1989; editor 'Must Canada Fail?' 1977; 'Confrontation or Collaboration' 1979; 'Division of Powers & Public Policy 1985; 'Intergovernmental Relations 1985; co-editor 'And Noone Cheered' 1983; 'Redesigning the State: The Comparative Politics of Constitutional Change' 1985; 'Tool Kits and Building Blocks: Constructing a New Canada' 1991; 'Canada and the United States: Changing Policy Agendas' 1991; mem. Candn. Pol. Sci. Assn.; Inst. Pub. Adm. Can.; Home: 20 Biggar Ave., Toronto, Ont. M6H 2N4; Office: 100 St. George St., Toronto, Ont. M5S 1A1

**SIMINOVITCH, David**, M.Sc., Ph.D., F.R.S.C.; research scientist (retired); b. Montreal, Que. 29 May 1916; s. Nathan and Goldie (Wachtman) S.; e. McGill Univ. B.Sc. 1936 (Maj. Hiram Mills Gold Medal in Biol. 1936), M.Sc. 1937 (Nat. Research Council Bursary & Studentship 1937, 1938), Ph.D. 1939; Univ. of Minn. Ph.D. 1946; m. Helen Elizabeth (dec.) d. late Fred and Gertrude Daubney 4 Sept. 1945; children: David Jonathan, Sara Jane, Michael Jeremy; Research Officer, Chem. & Biol. Research Inst., Agriculture Canada 1950–81; Rsch. Assoc., McGill 1939–40; Royal Soc. Can. Travelling Fellowship, Univ. of Minn. 1940–41, Herman Frasch Foundation Research Assoc. and Lectr. 1946–50; rec'd Candn. Soc. Plant Physiols. Gold Medal 1972; Mem., Royal Soc. of Can. 1973; Citation, Candn. Inventions Book (for development of a foam to insulate plants from frost) 1976; Ottawa Biological & Chem. Soc. Annual Award for Contribs. to Sci. 1984; Citation, Am. Cryobiology Soc. for pioneering work in freezing plants and plant cells; Governors' recognition of distinction, Soc. of Cryobiology 1988; author over 50 papers scient. journs. and symposia proceedings; mem. Candn. Soc. Plant Physiols.; Am. Soc. Plant Physiols. (past Ed. Bd.); Soc. Cryobiol. (past Ed. Bd., Gov.); Hebrew; recreations: gardening, swimming, reading, painting, natural history; Home: 202 - 2625 Regina St., Ottawa, Ont. K2B 5W8.

**SIMINOVITCH, Louis**, C.C., B.Sc., Ph.D., F.R.S.C. (1965), F.R.S. (1980); scientist and professor; b. Montreal, Que. 1 May 1920; s. Nathan and Goldie (Watchman) S.; e. McGill Univ., B.Sc. 1941, Ph.D. 1944; Memorial Univ., Nfld., D.Sc. 1978; McMaster Univ., Ont., D.Sc. 1978; obtained Arts & Science Scholar., 1939–40, Sir. Wm. McDonald Scholar. 1940–41, Anne Molson Prize in Chem. 1941, Nat. Research Council Studentship and Fellowship 1942–44, Nat. Cancer Inst. Can. Fellowships 1953–1955; m. Elinore, d. late Harry Faierman, 2 July 1944; children: Coco Jean, Katherine Ann, Margaret Ruth; PROF., DEPT. MEDICAL GENETICS, UNIV. OF TORONTO, since 1966; Prof., Dept. Med. Biophysics since 1960; Assoc. Prof., Dept. of Pediatrics, 1972–78; Geneticist-in-Chief, Hosp. for Sick Children 1970–85; University Professor, Univ. of Toronto 1976–85; University Professor, Emeritus 1985– ; Dir. of Research, Mount Sinai Hospital, Toronto 1983–89; Dir. of Rsch., Samuel Lunenfeld Rsch. Inst. of Mount Sinai Hosp. 1989– ; with N.R.C. at Ottawa and Chalk River, Ont., 1944–47; Roy. Soc. Fellow, Inst. Pasteur, Paris 1947–49; employed by Centre Nat. de la Recherche Scient., Inst. Pasteur, Paris, France, 1949–53; Connaught Med. Research Labs., Univ. of Toronto, 1953–56; Asst. Prof., Dept. of Medical Biophysics, U. of T. 1956–58; Head, Subdiv. of Microbiology, Div. of Biological Rsch., Ont. Cancer Inst. 1957–63; Assoc. Prof., Dept. of Medical Biophysics, Univ. of Toronto 1958–60; Prof. Dept. of Medical Biophysics, Univ. of Toronto 1960– ; Head, Div. Biol. Research, Ont. Cancer Inst. 1963–69; Chrmn., Dept. of Med. Cell Biol., Fac. of Medicine, Univ. of Toronto 1969–72; Dept. Med. Genetics 1972–79; contrib. over 190 scient. articles to learned journs.; former Ed., 'Virology'; 'Bacteriological Reviews'; founding mem. & former Pres., Ed. Bd. 'Science Forum'; former mem., Ed. Bd., 'Cell'; 'Somatic Cell Genetics'; 'Journ. Cytogenetics and Cell Genetics'; 'Mutation Research'; 'Annual Review of Genetics'; 'Cancer Genetics and Cytogenetics'; 'Genetics'; 'Journal Cell Science'; Adv. Bd., 'Molecular Biology and Medicine'; former mem., Cte. de Redaction, 'Journal de Microscopie et de Biologie Cellulaire'; 'Annales de Microbiologie'; former Ed. 'Journal of Molecular and Cellular Biology'; former mem., Ed. Bd., Journal Cancer Surveys (London); 'Somatic Cell and Molecular Genetics'; corresponding ed., Proc. of the Royal Soc. B 1989– ; mem., Health Research & Dev. Comte, Ont. Council of Health, 1966–82; (Chrmn. 1974); Convenor, Panel 5, Internat. Cell Research Orgn. (ICRO) 1970–85; served on Jury for the MOSST Award, Candn. Science Writers Assoc. 1972; mem., Bd. of Dir., Candn. Weizmann Inst. of Science 1972– ; mem., United Ch. of Can., General Counc. Comn. on Genetic Engineering 1974–78; Chrmn., Ad Hoc Ctte. on Guidelines for Handling Recombinant DNA Molecules and Certain Animal Viruses and Cells, Medical Research Counc. of Can. 1975–77; Bd. of Dir., Nat. Cancer Inst. of Can., 1975–85; Bd. of Dir., Mount Sinai Inst., Mount Sinai Hosp. (Toronto), 1975–82; mem., Working Group on Human Experimentation, Med. Research Council of Can., 1976–78, (mem. of Extve. 1977–83); mem. Adv. Comte. on Genetic Services, Prov. of Ont., 1976–82; Nat. Correspondent to the Internat. Counc. of Scientific Unions (ICSU) Ctte. on Genetic Experimentation 1977–85; mem., Ctte. on Science and the Legal Process: Science Counc. of Can. 1978–81; Adv. Comte., Nat. Cancer Inst., Nat. Inst. of Health (U.S.A.) 1978–83; mem. of Bd., Ont. Cancer Treatment & Research Foundation, 1979–93; mem. Scientific Adv. Comte. of the Connaught Research Inst., 1980–84; mem., The Rsch. Council, Candn. Inst. for Advanced Rsch, Toronto 1982–91; mem. Alfred P. Sloan, Jr., Selection Comte., General Motors Cancer Research Foundation, 1983–84; mem., Med. Adv. Bd., The Gairdner Found. 1983– ; Chrmn., Health Research and Development Counc. of Ont., Min. of Health 1983–86; mem., External Adv. Bd. Site Visit, Univ. of Southern California, Los Angeles, Cal. 1983– ; mem., Med. Planning Ctte., The Arthritis Soc. 1983–87; Chrmn., Scientific Adv. Ctte., Rotman Rsch. Inst. of Baycrest Centre 1990– ; mem., Scientific Adv. Bd. of the Huntington's Soc. of Can. 1984–89; Mem., Adv. Ctte., Coll. of Biol. Sciences, Guelph, Ont. 1986–90; Chrmn., Research Adv. Panel, Ont. Cancer Treatment and Rsch. Found. 1986– ; Chrmn., Adv. Ctte. on Evolutionary Biology, Candn. Inst. for Advanced Rsch., Toronto 1986– ; Mem., Bd. of Govs., Baycrest Centre for Geriatric Care, Toronto 1987– ; Chrmn., External Adv. Ctte., Loeb Inst. for Med. Rsch., Ottawa, Ont. 1987– ; Mem., Science-Technology-Services Sub-Ctte., Science Counc. of Can., Ottawa 1988–89; Hon. Pres., XVIth Internat. Congress of Genetics, Toronto 1988; Chrmn., Steering Ctte. for an Evaluation of the MRC Grants Program, Med. Rsch. Counc., Ottawa 1989–91; Mem., Adv. Ctte. on Evaluation of Rsch., Royal Soc. of Can. 1989– ; Mem., Candn. Institute of Academic Medicine 1992– ; Mem. Adv. Board, Montreal Neurological Institute Advisory Board, 1992– ; Mem., Genetics Soc. of Can.; Am. Assoc. for the Advancement of Sci.; Am. Assoc. for Cancer Research; Canadians for Health Rsch.; Genetics Soc. of America; Fellow, Roy. Soc. of Can. (F.R.S.C.) 1965; Centennial Medal, Canada 1967; Queen Elizabeth II Jubilee Silver Medal 1977; Flavelle Gold Medal, Roy. Soc. of Can. 1978; Univ. of Toronto Alumni Assoc. Award 1978; Fellow, Roy. Soc. (London) (F.R.S.) 1980; Officer of the Order of Canada 1980; Izaak Walton Killam Memorial Prize 1981; Gairdner Foundation Wightman Award 1981; Medal of Achievement Award, Inst. de Recherches Cliniques de Montreal 1985; Environmental Mutagen Soc. Award, Baltimore, Maryland 1986; R.P. Taylor Award of Candn. Cancer Soc., Nat. Cancer Inst. 1986; Companion of the Order of Canada 1989; Doctor, Honoris Causa, Univ. of Montreal 1990; McGill Univ. 1990; Univ. of Western Ont. 1990; Distinguished Service Award, The Candn. Soc. for Clinical Investigation 1990; Toronto Biotechnology Initiative Service Award 1991; awarded Commemorative Medal for 125th Anniversary of Candn. Confederation 1992; Hebrew; recreations: swimming, reading; Home: 106 Wembley Rd., Toronto, Ont. M6C 2G6.

**SIMMIE, Lois Ann**; writer; b. Edam, Sask. 11 June 1932; d. Edwin Maurice and Bessie Margaret (Thomson) Binns; e. Livelong H.S. 1950; Sask. Bus. Coll.; Univ. of Sask., mature student; divorced; children: Odell, Leona, Anne, Scott; Writer-in-Res., Saskatoon Pub. Lib. 1987–88; taught fiction at Sask. Summer Sch. of the Arts, Univ. of Sask. Extension Dept. & others; several prizes from Sask. Writers' Guild incl. major award for book-length story collection 1983; Sask. Arts Bd. Sr. Artist Grant 1983; Sask. Dept. Culture & Youth Award for story collection 1976; NDP; Mem., Sask. Writers' Guild; The Children's Book Ctr.; CANSCAIP; Writers Union of Canada; author: 'Ghost House' 1976 (short stories & poems); 'They Shouldn't Make You Promise That' 1981 (novel); 'Pictures' 1984 (short stories); 'Auntie's Knitting a Baby' 1984 (children's poems), 'An Armadillo Is Not a Pillow' 1986 (children's poems); 'What Holds Up The Moon?' 1987 (picture book; all Children's Book Ctr. Choices); 'Red Shoes' (a short story is an Atlantis Films Ltd. & NFB feature film which tied Art & Culture 2nd prize, Internat. Film Fest. 1987 and hon. mem., Internat. Children's Fest., Chicago (Live Action) 1987; 'Who Greased the Shoelaces?' (children's poems) 1989; 'Oliver's Chickens' (picture book) 1992; 'Betty Lee Bonner Lives There' (short stories) 1993; editor: 'Julie' 1985; 'The Doll' 1987; 'A Gift of Sky' 1988; works pub. in several anthologies & CBC broadcasts; recreations: walking, movies, beachcombing; Home: 1501 Carins Ave., Saskatoon, Sask. S7H 2H5.

**SIMMONDS, Monty M.,** Q.C., LL.B.; b. London, Eng. 8 June 1925; s. Harry and Esther (Pepper) S.; e. Hodgson Pub. Sch. and N. Toronto Coll. Inst.; Univ. of Toronto grad. 1946; Osgoode Hall Law Sch. grad. 1949; m. Judith Leah d. late Samuel B. Godfrey OBE, 23 Dec. 1951; children: Jillian Ruth (Cherniak), Catherine Lea (Perlmutter), Joy Elizabeth (MacAdam), Anne Harriet (Spence); PRESIDENT, GODFREY CORE INC.; Pres. York Mutual Investments Ltd.; Hon. Offr. and Life Dir., Mt. Sinai Hospital (Past Chrmn.); Life Dir., Jewish Home for the Aged; Past Pres. & Dir., Mt. Sinai Inst.; called to Bar of Ont. 1949; cr. Q.C. 1968; recreations: golf, sailing, skiing, tennis; Clubs: Devil's Glen Country (Past Pres.); Mad River Golf; Mulmur Hills Racquets (Past Pres.); Home: 149 Old Forest Hill Rd., Toronto, Ont. M5N 2N7; Office: Suite 1000, 2 St. Clair Ave. W., Toronto, Ont. M4V 1L5.

**SIMMONS, Alan B.,** M.A., Ph.D.; educator; b. Geraldton, Ont. 15 Oct. 1941; s. Harold B. and Tilhi A. (Paivio) S.; e. Nanaimo (B.C.) High Sch. 1959; Univ. of B.C., B.A. 1963, M.A. 1965; Cornell Univ. Ph.D. 1970; m. Jean d. Tony and Mary Turner 3 March 1961; children: Sean, Tica; ASSOC. PROF. OF SOCIOLOGY 1985– ; Asst. Prof. of Sociol. & Anthrop. York Univ 1970–75; Visiting Prof. UN Demographic Centre for Latin Am. Santiago, Chile 1972–73; Assoc. Dir. Health Sci's Div. Internat. Devel. Rsch. Centre Ottawa 1974–75, Assoc. Dir. Social Sci's Div. 1975–84; Visiting Investigator and Course Dir. Dept. Demography Univ. de Montréal 1980–81, Visiting Prof. 1981–82 and Course Dir. 1982–84 (part-time); Dir. Centre for Rsch. on Latin Am. & the Caribbean, York Univ. 1985–89; recipient rsch. grants The Population Council 1967–68, 1973; Can. Council 1971–72; Social Sciences and Humanities Council (SSHRC) 1988; Internat. Devel. Rsch. Centre 1972, 1985, 1989; Health & Welfare Can. 1975, 1987; cons. various orgns. incl. CIDA, Ford Found., Population Council, UN, U.S. Aid; co-author 'Family Planning in Colombia: Changes in Attitude and Acceptance' 1973; 'Social Change and Internal Migration' 1977; 'Destino La Metropoli' 1977; 'Cambio Social y Fecundidad en America Latina' 1982; author or co-author numerous articles, book chapters, conf. papers; mem. Candn Sociol. & Anthrop. Assn.; Internat. Sociol. Assn.; Internat. Union Sci. Study Population; Population Assn. Am.; Candn. Assn. Latin Am. & Caribbean Studies (Council 1990– ); Candn. Population Soc. (Exec. Council 1974–77; Vice Pres. 1984–86; Pres. 1986–88); Home: 45 Parkside Dr., Toronto, Ont. M6R 2Y7; Office: 142 Founders Coll., 4700 Keele St., North York, Ont. M3J 1P3.

**SIMMONS, Harvey G.,** B.A., M.A., Ph.D.; university professor; b. Boston, Mass. 21 Oct. 1935; s. Martin A. and Jean (Piken) S.; e. Brandeis Univ., B.A. 1956; Boston Univ., M.A. 1960; Cornell Univ., Ph.D. 1966; m. Eileen d. Benjamin and Jeanette Lavine 26 June 1960; children: Erica, Leah, Daniel; PROF., DEPT. OF POL. SCI., YORK UNIV. 1965– ; Hannah Medal for the Hist. of Med. awarded by Royal Soc. of Can. 1984; Mem., var. profl. assns.; author: 'French Socialists in Search of a Role: 1956–1966' 1970; 'From Asylum to Welfare' 1982; 'Unbalanced - Mental Health Policy in Ontario from 1930 to 1988' 1990; recreation: swimming; Home: 231 Glenview Ave., Toronto, Ont.; Office: 4700 Keele St., North York, Ont. M3J 1P3.

**SIMMONS, Phillip Jordan,** B.A.Sc., M.A.Sc., Ph.D.; chemical industry executive; b. Toronto, Ont. 30 June 1941; s. Clifford Frederick and Bernice Charlotte (Jordan) S.; e. Univ. of Toronto B.A.Sc. 1964, M.A.Sc. 1965, Ph.D. 1968; m. Louvain Piggott (Baldwin) d. John and Gwyneth Vickery 23 Aug. 1990; children: Craig Simmons, Kathleen Simmons, Christopher Piggott, Emma Piggott; PRES. & CHIEF EXTVE. OFFR., ECO-TEC LIMITED 1985– ; Rsch. & Devel. Mgr., WIX Inc. 1968–76; Vice-Pres. & Gen. Mgr., Eco-Tec Limited 1976–80; Pres. & Chief Extve. Offr., WIX and Eco-Tec Limited 1980–85; Dir., Eco-Tec Inc.; Eco-Tec Limited; Chrmn., Bd. of Dir., Eco-Tec (Eur.) Limited; Home: 8 Cree Ave., Scarborough, Ont. M1M 1Z2; Office: 925 Brock Rd. S., Pickering, Ont. L1W 2X9.

**SIMMONS, William Henry,** C.M.A., F.Inst.D.; company executive; b. Amsterdam, The Netherlands 27 Sept. 1942; s. Johan Andries and Johanna Wilhelmina (Sluyter) S.; e. St. Catharines Coll. Inst. & Vocational Sch. 1961; Candn. Securities Inst.; m. Jacoba Wilhelmina d. Engel and Johanna vanderGaauw 6 Oct. 1967; children: Joanne Jacqueline, Robert William, Monica Louise; CHRMN., PRES. AND CHIEF EXEC. OFFR., ATWICK FINANCIAL GROUP 1989– ; Dir., Crown-Capital International; Cromlix Holdings Inc.; joined Canadian Imperial Bank of Commerce 1961 becoming Corporate Banking Offr. Nat. Accts. 1967; Asst. Vice Pres. and Asst. Treas. Associates Capital Corp. 1972; Vice Pres. and Dir. Strathy & Simmons Ltd. 1979; Sr. Vice Pres. Corporate Finance, Sharwood and Co. Ltd. 1985; Pres. & C.E.O., The Regional Trust Co. 1987; Assoc., Inst. Candn. Bankers; Fellow, Inst. Corporate Dirs. Can.; Christian Reformed; recreation: golf; Clubs: Albany; Brampton Golf & Country.

**SIMMS, Glenda P.,** M.Ed., Ph.D.; association executive; b. Jamaica 25 Jan. 1939; d. Myrtle Francis Dennis; e. Univ. of Alta. B.Ed. 1974, M.Ed. 1976, Ph.D. 1985; children: Michelle Lois, Emil Alf, Shaun Alene; PRES. CANDN. ADV. COUNCIL ON STATUS OF WOMEN 1989– ; teacher Jamaica 1966; teacher Metis and Cree Aborigional Peoples 1966–74; taught Native Edn. Lethbridge 1977–80; Head of Native Edn. Dept. Sask. Indian Federated Coll. 1980–85; Supr. Intercultural Edn. Regina Pub. Sch. Bd. 1985–87; Assoc. Prof. of Edn. Nipissing Univ. Coll. 1987–89; recipient: 1988 Citizenship Citation for contrib. towards promotion cultural harmony; 1990 National Award, Canadian Council for Multiculture and Intercultural Education; inducted into the North Bay Human Rights Hall of Fame for her contribution to positive Race Relations in Canada 1991; recipient, 1992 Inter Amicus Human Rights Award for work in the area of aboriginal rights, women's rights and the rights of racial minorities; 1993 Ryerson Fellowship, Ryerson Univ., Toronto; Univ. of Alta., Distinguished Alumnus Award; Hon. Mem., Federation of Medical Women; Hon. Doctorate of Laws, Univ. of Man. 1994; Office: 110 O'Connor St., 9th Floor, P.O. Box 1541 Stn. B, Ottawa, Ont. K1P 5R5.

**SIMMS, Len,** M.H.A.; politician; b. Howley, Nfld. 23 Oct. 1943; s. Max and Emeline (Payne) S.; e. King's College School Windsor N.S.; Univ. of N.B.; Memorial Univ. of Nfld.; m. Sandra d. Thomas and Ruby O'Brien; children: Jacqueline, Douglas; ELECTED LEADER OF THE OPPOSITION and LEADER, NEWFOUNDLAND AND LABRADOR PROGRESSIVE CONSERVATIVE PARTY 1991– ; Extve. Assist., to Hon. John Lundrigan 1975–77, to Premier Frank Moores 1978–79, and Premier Brian Peckford 1979; el. M.H.A. for District of Grand Falls 1979, re-el. 1982, 1985 and 1989; el. Speaker of the House of Assem. 1979–82; Min. of Culture, Recreation, & Youth, Nfld. & Lab. 1982–84; Min. of Forest Resources and Lands, Nfld. & Lab. 1984–87; Min. Responsible for Status of Women, Newfoundland & Labrador, 1988; Min. of Development 1989; Pres. of Executive Council; Pres. of Treasury Bd.; Government House Leader 1989– ; Opposition House Leader 1989– ; Chrmn., Treasury Bd. Comte. of Cabinet; Mem. of Planning & Priorities Ctte. of Cabinet; Chrmn., Counc. of Ministers of Culture & Historic Resources for Canada 1983; Chrmn., Council of Ministers of Recreation for Canada 1984; Chrmn., Council of Forestry Ministers for Canada 1986–87; Apptd. Opposition House Leader 1989; mem., Kinsmen Club of Can.; Past District Gov., Kinsmen Clubs of the Atlantic Provinces; Past Natnl. Pres. Kinsmen Clubs of Canada 1979 (first Newfoundlander to hold position of Natnl. Pres. in first 60 yrs. (1920–1980); elected Life Mem., Assoc. of Kinsmen Clubs of Canada 1979; recreations: fishing, hunting; Home: 49 Sauve St., Mt. Pearl, Nfld. A1N 4K7; Office: Opposition Office, Fifth Flr., Confederation Bldg., House of Assembly, Nfld. & Labrador, St. John's, Nfld. A1B 4J6.

**SIMO, Zoltan Dominic,** B.Sc., M.B.A., P.Eng.; corporate director; b. Markinch, Sask. 3 May 1933; s. Dominic and Elizabeth (Huber) S.; e. Univ. of Sask. B.Sc. (Mech. Eng.) 1954; McMaster Univ. M.B.A. 1971; m.; five children; Past Chrmn. & Dir., Canadian Standards Assoc. (CSA); Sr. Extve. and Corporate Dir. and Grad., Young Presidents Organization; Dir., Bay Mills Ltd.; Shaw Industries Ltd.; Hammond Mfg.; Autrex Inc.; Past Dir., Electrohome Limited; Flakt Canada Ltd.; The Hugh MacMillan Med. Centre; Liv Canada; Bray Chromalox UK; Climatemaster Inc.; Candn. Corp. Mngmt. Co. Ltd.; EEMAC (Electrical & Electronic Manufac. Assn. of Can.); EEMAC rep., Ont. Exhibition Assn.; career: Canada Packers Ltd. Edmonton and Toronto 1954–67; Operations Mgr., Gen. Sales Mgr., Gen. Mgr. Ont. Sealtest Foods 1967–70; Pres., Chromalox Canada 1972–87; Senior Vice Pres., Sharwood and Co. 1989–92; Pres. & C.E.O., Electrohome Limited 1992–93; Group Vice Pres., Canadian Corporate Management Co. Ltd. and assoc. co's.; Bd. Chrmn. Hull-Thompson Ltd.; Delhi/Sheldons Inc.; Heron Cable Industries Ltd.; Easy Heat Inc. USA; Electrotherm Inc. USA 1978–87; Advisor to the Bd., Allan Smart Services Inc.; mem., World Business Council; XPO; PEO; Associate, Corporate Associates Inc. (C.A.I.); recreations: stock market, curling, water and snow skiing, sailing; Club: Boulevard; Mississaugua; Bd. of Trade; Home: 2280 Chancery Lane, Oakville, Ont. L6J 6A3.

**SIMON, Jerome B.,** M.D., F.R.C.P.C., F.A.C.G., F.A.C.P.; physician/teacher; b. Regina, Sask. 21 Aug. 1939; s. William and Aurora (Sussman) S.; e. Regina Central Coll. 1956; Queen's Univ., M.D. 1962; m. Cindy Boyer; children: David William, Nancy Lynne (previous marriage), Joel Stephen (previous marriage, dec'd.); PROF. OF MED., QUEEN'S UNIV. & FORMER HEAD, DIV. OF GASTROENTEROL., KINGSTON GEN. HOSP.; Internship & Residency in Internal Med., Montreal Gen. Hosp. 1962–65; Training Res. in Gastroenterol. 1965–66; post-doct. Fellow in Hepatol., Yale Univ. 1966–69; Consultant; Fellow, Royal Coll. of Physicians & Surgeons; Fellow, Am. Coll. of Gastroenterol.; Fellow, Am. Coll. of Physicians; several awards for rsch. & teaching; Bd. of Dirs., Ont. Medical Assn.; Mem., num. profl. soc. incl. Am. Assn. Study of Liver Diseases; Candn. Assn. of Gastroenterol.; Candn. Soc. for Clin. Invest. (Counc., Secy.-Treas.); Am. Gastroenterol. Assn.; Candn. Assn. Study of the Liver (Past-Pres.); author/co-author of over 80 sci. pubns.; recreations: photography (sev. awards); Home: 60 William St., Kingston, Ont. K7L 2C4; Office: Hotel Dieu Hospital, Kingston, Ont. K7L 5G2.

**SIMON, Norman Leon,** B.A.A.J.; energy executive; b. Toronto, Ont. 26 Jan. 1943; e. Ryerson Polytechnical B.A.A.J. 1964; m. Mary-Jane Holton; children: Rand, Alana; SENIOR VICE-PRES., CORP. & PUBLIC AFFAIRS, ONTARIO HYDRO 1993– ; Journalist, Toronto Telegram 1964–70; Dir. of Public Relns., Candn. Union of Public Employees 1967–79; Dir. of Info. & Communications Services, Toronto Govt. 1979–80; Chief of Staff to Federal NDP Leader 1980–82; Dir. of Communications, CBC 1982–88; Vice-Pres., Corp. Relns., Ont. Hydro 1988–91; Vice-Pres., Energy Mngt. & Corp. Relns. 1991–93; Mem., Bd. of Dir., TV Ontario; Adv. Bd., Ont. Investment Serv.; Joint Action Ctte. on Consultation,Public Policy Forum; Mem. & Extve., Friends of Candn. Broadcasting; Home: 509 Hillsdale Ave. E., Toronto, Ont. M4S 1V1; Office: 700 University Ave., 19th fl., Toronto, Ont. M5G 1X6.

**SIMON, Paul L.S.,** O.St.J., B.A., LL.B., C.H.R.M.; lawyer, business executive; b. Salgotarjan, Hungary 22 July 1946; s. Paul and Clara (Lengyel) S.; e. Lawrence Park C.I. 1965; York Univ., B.A. (Hons.) 1969; Osgoode Hall Law Sch., LL.B. 1972; children: Laura K., Paula S.; Pres., Edpro Education & Consulting Inc. 1987; practised litigation with Fitzpatrick & Poss 1974–77; Assoc. Couns., Candn. Gen. Electric 1977–81; Couns., Northern Telecom Can. Ltd. 1981–86; Dir., Health, Safety & Envir., Northern Tel 1986–87; sole practitioner specializing in employment law 1990– ; Mem., Public Edn. Ctte., Occupational Hygiene Assn. of Ont.; Cert. of Merit, Corpus Inform. Serv. for significant contrib. to occupational health & safety in Can. 1977; O.St.J. 1987; C.H.R.M. 1991; Pres., Preview Concerts for Young Candn. Artists; Extve., Pension & Benefits, Candn. Bar Assn. (Ont.) 1987–88; author: 'Hazardous Products' 1987, 'WHMIS Worker Handbook' 1988, 'Employment Law' 1988, 'Handbook of Occupational Health and Safety Law Reform in Ontario' 1990, ; co-author: 'Health and Safety in the Workplace' 1987; recreations: tennis, theatre, reading; club: St. Clair Club; Home: 1 Oriole Rd., #703, Toronto, Ont. M4V 2E6.

**SIMON, Peter C.,** B.M., M.M., D.M.A.; pianist; music administrator; b. Sajoszentpeter 8 June 1949; s. Paul and Clara (Lengyel) S.; e. Univ. of Toronto B.M. 1977; Univ. of Western Ont. M.M. 1981; Univ. of Michigan. D.M.A. 1983; m. Dianne d. Joseph Werner July 1980; children: Nicole, Justin; PRESIDENT, ROYAL CONSERVATORY OF MUSIC 1991; Pres., Manhattan School of Music, New York City 1989–91; Office: 273 Bloor St. W., Toronto, Ont. M5S 1W2.

**SIMONE, Walter;** insurance agent; b. Frosinone, Italy 3 Nov. 1949; s. Frank and Maria Teresa (Pecci) S.; e. Ryerson Polytech. Inst. Bus. Adm. 1971; Chart. Life Underwriter 1976; m. Cheryl Lynn d. Frederick and Alice Rausch 19 Aug. 1972; Registered Health Underwriter 1992– ; Chartered Financial Consultant 1989; Chartered Financial Services Broker 1993; Registered

Trust & Estate Practitioner 1993; Pres., Simone Internat. Insurance Services Inc.; Dir., The Oro Group Inc.; Willpine Developments Ltd.; Past Gov., Leonardo da Vinci Acad. Arts & Sci's; Past mem., Galleries Campaign Ctte. Royal Ont. Museum; St. Francis of Assissi Ch. Restoration Fund Ctte.; Multicultural Adv. Ctte. Toronto Hist. Bd.; Nat. Campaign Ctte. Palliative Care Found.; Maestro's Club Mem'ship Ctte. Toronto Symphony; Past mem., Fund Raising Ctte., The Desrosiers Dance Theatre; Treas. Nat. Cong. Italian Candn. Toronto Dist. Ctte. Monument to Multiculturalism; Founding mem. Candn. Italian Diabetic Assn.; Mem., Manresa Retreat House Fundraising Ctte.; Past Moderator Life Underwriters Assn. Can. Training Course; Founding Mem. and Past Pres., Nat. Fedn. Candn. Italian Bus. & Prof. Assns.; Past Pres. Candn. Italian Bus. & Prof. Assn. Toronto; mem. Life Underwriters Assn.; Independent Life Ins. Brokers of Can.; Million Dollar Round Table; Leading Producers Round Table; Candn. Assn. Financial Planners; Inst. Chart. Life Underwriters; Nat. Assoc. of Health Underwriters; Conference for Advanced Life Underwriting; Internat. Assn. for Financial Planning; Soc. of Trust and Estate Practitioners; recreations: skiing, tennis, sailing, golf, reading, fund raising; Clubs: Boulevard; Maestro; National Golf; Canadian; Empire; Etobicoke Yacht; Charlottetown Society; Società Gastronomica Italiana; Founders Club; Horseshoe Valley Golf & Skiing Country; Home: 3508 Ponytrail Dr., Mississauga, Ont. L4X 1W1; Office: 3100 Steeles Ave. E., Suite 601, Markham, Ont. L3R 8T3.

**SIMONEAU, Léopold,** O.C. (1971), B. ès. A., D.Mus.; singer; educator; b. Quebec, Que. 3 May 1918; s. Joseph and Olivine (Boucher) S.; e. Coll. de. Levis, B. ès L.; Laval Univ., B. ès. A.; Columbia Univ., Opera Sch. and Opera Work Shop; Univ. d'Ottawa, D.Mus. 1969; m. Pierrette, d. Sylva Alarie, 1 June 1946; two d., Isabell, Chantal; widely regarded as the most elegant Mozart tenor of his time; Teacher, San Francisco Conservatory of Music since 1972; leading singer of Metropolitan Opera; Paris Opera; Opera Comique; La Scala, Milan; Staatsoper, Vienna; Chicago Lyric Opera; guest artist with orchestras of world's capitals; sometime Artistic Dir., Que. Opera; recordings for Columbia, Victor, London, Angel, Deutsche Grammophon, Westminster; Officer of the Order of Canada, 1971; named Officer of the Ordre des arts et des lettres de France 1990; rec'd Centennial Medal; Dr. Mus., Laval 1973; Roman Catholic; recreation: golf.

**SIMONI, Arnold;** research consultant; b. Vienna, Austria 26 June 1911; s. Bernard and Theresa (Razdowitz) S.; e. Technol. Inst. Vienna; Univ. of Zurich; Univ. of Geneva; m. Cecile d. Jacob and Fanny Doliner 26 July 1939; children: Peter, Sylvia, Raymond; RESEARCH FELLOW, YORK UNIVERSITY, CENTRE FOR INTERNATIONAL AND STRATEGIC STUDIES (CISS) 1989– ; Dir. Devel. & Rsch. New Electronic Component Parts Vienna Tech. 1934–39; Dir. and Gen. Mgr. OHMAG Neuchatel, Switzerland 1940–49; Founder and Pres. Precision Electronic Components Ltd. Toronto 1950–76; Co-Founder Candn. Peace Rsch. Inst. 1964; holds 14 patents; tech. papers presented Eur., N. Am.; author 'Beyond Repair' 1972; 'Crisis and Opportunity' 1983; 6 booklets, 'Time of Transition' forthcoming; mem. Sci. for Peace (Superordinate Project); World Federalist (Past Pres.); Candn. Inst. Internat. Affairs; recreations: skiing, swimming, bicycling, hiking, music; Home: 89 Southill Dr., Don Mills, Ont. M3C 2H9; Office: York Univ., Centre for Internat. and Strategic Studies, 4700 Keele St., North York, Ont. M3J 1P3.

**SIMONS, John H.,** M.Eng., M.B.A.; electronics executive; b. Québec City, Qué 11 May 1939; s. Herbert A. and Catherine M. (Martin) S.; e. McGill Univ. B.Eng. 1961, M.Eng. 1963, Dip. in Mgmt. 1974, M.B.A. 1977; children: Christopher, Jonathan, Laura; PRES. & C.E.O., CANADIAN MARCONI CO. 1989– ; Design Eng. present co. 1963, Project Eng. 1966, Prog. Mgr. 1969, Group Mgr. 1974, Div. Mgr. Avionics Div. 1976, Vice Pres. Avionics Div. 1977, Group Vice Pres. Electronics 1982, Exec. Vice-Pres. 1982; mem. H.R.H. The Duke of Edinburgh's 5th Commonwealth Study Conf. Can. 1980; mem. Aerospace Inds. Assn. Can. (Chrmn. 1981–82, Dir. 1979– ); Order Engs. Qué.; recreations: squash, skiing; Clubs: Montreal Badminton & Squash; Home: 3514 ave. du Musee, Montréal, Qué. H3G 2C7; Office: 2442 Trenton Ave., Montréal, Qué. H3P 1Y9.

**SIMOURD, Micheal A.,** B.A.; insurance investment executive; b. Ottawa, Ont. 21 June 1951; s. Alexander J. and Eleanor S.; e. Ridgemount H.S. 1969; Carleton Univ. B.A. 1973; INVESTMENT VICE PRES. (MORTGAGES), THE MUTUAL LIFE ASSUR. CO. OF CANADA 1990– ; Asst. Treas. & Mortgage Mgr., Scotia Covenants 1973–77; Asst. Gen. Mgr., Wenagara Corp. 1977–81; Mgr., Real Estate & Mortgages, Northern Telecom Pension Fund 1981–83; Asst. Vice Pres., Mortgages & Real Estate, New York Life Insur. Co. 1983–88; Asst. Vice-Pres., Mortgages, present firm 1988–92; clubs: Toronto & Kitchener hockey clubs, Collingwood Lighthouse Point Yacht & Tennis; Home: 11 Maynard Ave., Kitchener, Ont.; Office: 227 King St. S., Waterloo, Ont. N2J 4C5.

**SIMPSON, Donald George,** B.A., M.A., Ph.D.; educator, entrepreneur, mgmnt. developer, hockey agent; b. Weston, Ont. 13 July 1934; s. George and Isobel (Sproule) S.; e. Univ. of Western Ont. B.A. 1957, M.A. 1964, Ph.D. 1971; m. Marion Virginia d. W. Cuyler and Eva Henderson 21 Dec. 1957; children: Janice, David, Christine, Craig; VICE-PRESIDENT & DIRECTOR, BANFF CENTRE FOR MANAGEMENT 1990– ; Secondary School Teacher 1957–65; Dir., West Africa Prog., Candn. Univ. Serv. Overseas 1967–68; established & directed Office of Internat. Programmes, Univ. of Western Ont. (UWO) 1969–72; Rsch. Dir. & Admin., Internat. Devel. Rsch. Centre 1972–76; Prof., Comp. Education, UWO (on loan to var. internat. orgns. & other UWO faculties much of the time) 1965–90; Dir., Centre for Internat. Business Studies, Sch. of Bus. Admin., UWO 1985–90; present mandate is to 'globalize' programming at Banff Centre for Mgmnt.; has lived and/or worked in close to 50 countries; Sr. Advr., Spec. Ctte. on Edn., Legis. Assembly, N.W.T. 1980–82; Chrmn., Salasan Assoc. Inc. 1982–87; Pres., Kanchar Internat. Inc. 1982–90; Professor Emeritus, UWO 1991; author & co-author of num. case studies, articles & reports in areas of internat. business, cross-cultural communication, edn. & training; co-author: 'Entrepreneurs in Education: Canada's Response to the International Human Resource Development Challenge' 1989; recreations: reading, hiking, watching hockey; Office: P.O. Box 1020, Banff, Alta. T0L 0C0.

**SIMPSON, Hamish Ian Fisher,** B.A.; educator; b. Victoria, B.C. 31 July 1936; s. James Ian and Florence Gerrard (Clark) S.; e. Glenlyon Sch.; Univ. Sch.; Victoria Coll.; Univ. of B.C. B.A. 1957; Oxford Univ. Dipl. in Educ. 1960; m. Patricia d. James and Lilian McNulty 25 July 1970; children: Andrew, Rachel, Sara; HEADMASTER, UPPER CANADA COLL. PREP SCHOOL Toronto, Ont. 1986– ; Teacher, Glenlyon Sch. Victoria, B.C. 1960–64, Headmaster 1964–82; Dir., Lester B. Pearson Coll. of the Pacific 1982–86; Past Pres. Independent Schs. Assn. B.C.; Pres. Univ. of Victoria Alumni Assn. 1966–67; Rotary of Oak Bay 1979–80; Presbyterian; recreations: tennis, golf, fishing; Club: Victoria Golf; Address: 220 Lonsdale Rd., Toronto, Ont. M4V 2X8.

**SIMPSON, Horace Birch;** executive; b. Kelowna, B.C. 17 March 1917; s. Stanley M. and Bertha E. (Birch) S.; e. Kelowna Pub. Schs.; City Park Coll. Inst. Saskatoon; m. Joan K. d. John M. Jennens 17 Nov. 1937; children: Sharron J., Alan G., G. Stanley; Dir., Okanagan Skeena Group Ltd.; Brenda Mines Ltd.; Central Okanagan Foundation (1967–75); Anglican; recreations: golf, fishing; Clubs: Gyro; Kelowna; Home: 4348 Hobson Rd., Kelowna, B.C. V1W 1Y3; Office: 102 – 565 Bernard Ave., Kelowna, B.C. V1Y 6N9.

**SIMPSON, Jeffrey Carl,** B.A., M.Sc.; journalist; b. New York City, N.Y. 17 Feb. 1949; s. Robert Lawrence and Eve Cloud (Matheson) S.; came to Can. 1959; e. Univ. of Toronto Schs. 1967; Queen's Univ. B.A. 1971; London Sch. of Econ. M.Sc. (Internat. Relations) 1972; m. Wendy Elizabeth d. William Everest Bryans, Dundas, Ont. 15 June 1974; children: Tait Bryans, Danielle Bryans, Brook Andrew Bryans; NATIONAL COLUMNIST, THE GLOBE AND MAIL 1984– ; National Newspaper Award, Column writing 1989; National Magazine Award for Political Writing; Parlty. Internship H. of C. Ottawa 1972–73; joined The Globe and Mail 1973; Ottawa Bureau Chief 1979–81; European Correspondent, The Globe and Mail 1981–83; author: 'Discipline of Power: The Conservative Interlude and the Liberal Restoration' 1981 (recipient Gov. Gen.'s Award Non-Fiction 1981); 'A Canadian's Guide to Britain' 1985; 'Spoils of Power: The Politics of Patronage' 1988; 'Faultlines: Struggling for a Canadian Vision' 1993; co-author: (with Ged Martin) 'Canada's Heritage in Scotland' 1989; contrib. 'Saturday Night'; Fellow at Univ. of B.C., Univ. of Alta. and Queen's Univ.; John S. Knight Fellow, Sanford Univ. 1993–94; Mem., Bd. of Trustees, Queen's Univ.; Anglican; recreations: skiing, tennis, music, reading; Office: 165 Sparks St., 3rd Flr., Ottawa, Ont. K1P 5B9.

**SIMPSON, John Joseph,** B.A.Sc., M.A., D.Phil., F.R.S.C.; educator; b. North Bay, Ont. 26 May 1939; s. John William and Teresa (Hagarty) S.; e. Scollard Hall North Bay 1957; Univ. of Toronto B.A.Sc. 1961, M.A. 1962; Oxford Univ. D.Phil. 1966; m. Marianne d. Cornelis and Maria Anna Van der Veen 5 July 1968; children: James R., Sarah J.; PROF. OF PHYSICS UNIV. OF GUELPH 1980– ; Rsch. Assoc. Oxford Univ. 1966, Weizmann Inst. 1966–68; Univ. of Toronto 1968–69; Asst. Prof. present Univ. 1969, Assoc. Prof. 1973, Gov. 1987–89; Visiting Rsch. Fellow Max Planck Inst. Heidelberg 1973, Niels Bohr Inst. Copenhagen 1975–76; Sci. Assoc. CERN 1982–83; Candn. Assn. Physicists Lectr. 1985; recipient Rutherford Meml. Medal for Phys. Royal Soc. Can. 1985; author various publs. nuclear and particle phys.; mem. Candn. Assn. Physicists; Am. Physical Soc.; recreations: cooking, skiing; Home: 36 Oxford St., Guelph, Ont. N1H 2M3; Office: Guelph, Ont. N1G 2W1.

**SIMPSON, Leo James Pascal;** writer; exemplary person; b. Limerick, Ireland 1934; s. Gerald Fitzgerald and Anne (Egan) S.; e. Clongowes Wood College (Winner of Titus Oates Memorial Scholarship), M.A. (Hons.) Poola McPhellimey Acad. 1954, two years post-grad. studies, Acme Correspondence (Ohio), completing epic thesis: 'Influences of the Heimskringla Saga of Snorri on the lyric poetry of Isabella Valancey Crawford,' described by thesis supvr. as 'exquisitely pointless'; m. Jacqueline Anne, d. of Jack Murphy, Belleville, 1964; children: one d. Julie Anne; played viola in Plovdiv Dazduv Quartetz, an emigré Bulgarian string ensemble based in Romke 1957–58; deported to London 1959 on suspicion of involvement in Hibbs-Düsskotop plot to 'fix' Papal elections of 1958; Foreign Correspondent and Fashion Ed., Putney T&B News, 1960; entered Canada 1961; Shepherd, Halton Hills 1961–62; Publicity Dir. and Ed., Macmillan of Canada 1962–66; Author: 'Mr. Tiddly and the Big Red Choo-Choo,' a dumb attempt to match the discipline of the Spenserian stanza (i.e. eight five-foot iambic lines followed by an iambic line of six feet, with a crazy rhyming scheme) to meet requirements of juvenile book market, ages 7–9; anthologies: 'New Canadian Stories' 1972–75; 'Best Canadian Stories' 1980; 'Small Wonders' CBC, 1982; 'The Norton Reader' 1983; novels: 'Arkwright' 1971; 'Peacock Papers' 1973; 'Kowalski's Last Chance' 1980; short stories: 'The Lady and the Travelling Salesman' 1976; Writer-in-Residence, Univ. of Ottawa 1973; Univ. of W. Ont. 1978; mem. The Wee Cooper o' Fife Club; Loons; Home: Moodie Cottage, 114 Bridge, St. W., Belleville, Ont. K8P 1J7.

**SIMPSON, Nancy E.,** B.P.H.E., M.A., Ph.D.; educator; human geneticist; b. Toronto, Ont. 29 Oct. 1924; d. William Norman and Jessie Isabelle (Knowles) S.; e. John Ross Pub. Sch., Lawrence Park Coll. Inst. Toronto; Univ. of Toronto, B.P.H.E. 1947, Ph.D. 1959; Colombia Univ., M.A. 1951; PROF. EMERITUS OF HUMAN GENETICS, DEPTS. OF PAEDIATRICS AND OF BIOLOGY, QUEEN'S UNIV. 1989– ; Dir. Biochem. Genetics Lab. Kingston Gen. Hosp. 1983–89; taught phys. edn. Dwight Sch. for Girls Englewood, N.J. 1947–50; joined phys. edn. staff Univ. of Toronto 1950–55; MRC Population Genetic Rsch. Unit Oxford, Eng. 1960–61 returning to Dept. of Pharmacol., Univ. of Toronto as Asst. Prof.; Asst. Prof. of Human Genetics present Univ. 1965, Assoc. Prof. 1967, Chrmn. Div. Med. Genetics 1975–80; Prof. of Human Genetics, Depts. of Paediatrics and of Biology, Queen's Univ. 1975–89; Research Prize, Queen's Univ.; Prof. Emeritus, Queen's Univ. 1989– ; Chrmn., Chromosome 10 Ctte., Human Gene Mapping 10.5–11 and CCM.92, 1990– ; named Queen Elizabeth II Sci. 1962–68; author or co-author articles, reviews and letters sci. jours.; mem. Genetics Soc. Can.; Am. Soc. Human Genetics; Candn. Coll. Med. Geneticists; Human Genome Organization (HUGO); recreations: sailing, skiing; Club: Kingston Yacht; Home: 32 Simcoe St., Kingston, Ont. K7L 2S6; Office: 20 Barrie St., Kingston, Ont. K7L 3N6.

**SIMPSON, Norman MacDougall,** Q.C., B.A., LL.B.; b. Vancouver, B.C. 25 July 1917; s. James Inglis and Jean Kinloch (MacDougall) S.; e. Roslyn Public and Westmount (Que.) High Sch.; Upper Can. Coll., Toronto, grad. 1936; Trinity Coll., Univ. of Toronto, B.A., 1940; Osgoode Hall Law Sch., Toronto 1947; m. Margaret B., d. R. B. Johnston, Q.C. of St. Catharines, Oct. 1948; children: Sandra Jean, James Norman, Elizabeth Margaret, Corey Isobel; PARTNER, BLAKE, CASSELS & GRAYDON; read law with present firm; called to Bar of Ont. 1947; cr. Q.C. 1966; with Imp. Chem. Industries, U.K., 1947–48; Candn. Industries Ltd., 1949–50; rejoined present firm 1951; served in R.C.N., 1941–45; C.O. Castle Class Corvette H.M.C.S. 'Petrolia'; now Lieut. Commdr. (Ret'd.); Councillor, Village of Forest Hill, 1961–64; Chrmn., Extve. Comte. Univ. of Trinity Coll., 1973–75; Chrmn., Care Canada 1985–88; Dir., Care Canada; The Rotary Foundation (Can.); Past Pres., Naval Offrs. Assn. of Can. (Silver

Medal 1970); Canada's Centennial Medal 1967; Queen's Jubilee Medal 1977; Pres., Fort York Br., Royal Candn. Legion 1986–87; Alpha Delta Phi; recreation: farming; Clubs: Badminton & Racquet; Golf Haven; Caledon Mountain Trout; National; Granite; Rotary (Pres. Toronto Club 1966–67, Foundation Pres. 1975–90, District Gov. 1982–83); Home: R.R.1, Alliston, Ont. L9R 1V1; Office: Suite 2500, Commerce Court W., Toronto, Ont. M5L 1A9.

**SIMS, Peter Harvey,** Q.C.; lawyer; b. Kitchener 20 Feb. 1933; s. James Kenneth, Q.C. and Mabel A. (Cameron) S.; e. Public Sch., Kitchener, Ont.; Ridley Coll., St. Catharines, Ont.; McGill Univ. 1955; Exchange Student, Univ. of British Columbia 1954; Osgoode Hall Law Sch., Toronto, Ont.; m. Elizabeth, d. Marshall Byers, 22 June 1957; children: Harvey James, Kenneth Marshall, Ellen, Margaret Roos, Alison Cameron; PARTNER, SIMS CLEMENT EASTMAN; Chrmn. and Dir., Chicopee Manufacturing Ltd.; Vice Pres. and Dir., Chicopee Securities Ltd.; Sims Investments Ltd.; Chairman and Dir., Economical Mutual Insurance Co.; The Missisquoi & Rouville Insurance Co.; Perth Insurance Co.; Waterloo Insurance Co.; called to the Bar of Ont., 1959; mem., Waterloo Bar Assn.; Candn. Bar Assn.; Presbyterian; Liberal; Home: 130 Aberdeen Road, Kitchener, Ont. N2M 2Y7; Office: 700 - 22 Frederick St., Kitchener, Ont. N2H 6M6.

**SINCLAIR, Alasdair Maclean,** B.A., B.Phil., Ph.D.; professor of economics; b. Valleyfield, P.E.I. 30 June 1935; s. Donald Maclean and Mary Baird (Jones) S.; e. Queen Elizabeth H.S.; Dalhousie Univ. B.A. 1956; Oxford Univ. B.A. 1958, B.Phil. 1959; Harvard Univ. Ph.D. 1966; m. Carol d. Audrie and Harold Vincent 19 Sept. 1959; children: Andrew, Peter, Douglas, Sarah; PROF., DEPT. OF ECONOMICS, DALHOUSIE UNIV. 1961– ; Vice-Pres., Academic & Research 1983–88; Consultant / Advisor on devel. projects in Tanzania, Ghana, Zimbabwe, O.E.C.S. countries, Nepal and Barbados; Home: 6422 Jubilee Rd., Halifax, N.S. B3H 2H1; Office: Halifax, N.S. B3H 3J5.

**SINCLAIR, Alastair James,** B.A.Sc., M.A.Sc., Ph.D., P.Eng., P.Geo.; university professor; b. Hamilton, Ont. 1 Aug. 1935; s. Burton Leslie and Grace (Isherwood) S.; e. Univ. of Toronto, B.A.Sc. 1957, M.A.Sc. 1958; Univ. of B.C., Ph.D. 1964; m. Elizabeth Mary Sylvia d. Grace and Frederick Hill 13 June 1964; children: Alison Trevena, Fiona Tamsin; PROF., DEPT. OF GEOL. SCIENCES, UNIV. OF B.C. 1974– ; Asst. Prof., Geology, Univ. of Washington 1962–64; Asst. Prof., present univ. 1964–68; Assoc. Prof. 1968–74; Head 1985–90; Dir., Geological Engineering 1992– ; Pres., Sinclair Consultants Ltd.; Dir., FSS Internat. Ltd.; Life Mem., C.I.M.M. 1987; Hon. Mem., Brazilian Geochem. Soc. 1987; Distinguished Service Award, Mineral Deposits Div., Geol. Assn. Canada 1990; Robert Elver Award (CIM) 1991; I.W. Killam Fellowship 1990–91; Profl. Engr. (B.C.); Treas., Mineral Deposits Div., Geol. Assn. Can. 1978–89; Mem., Assn. of Exploration Geochem. (Councillor 1992–94); Soc. of Econ. Geol.; Soc. of Geology Applied to Mineral Deposits; author: 'Applications of Probability Graphs in Mineral Exploration' 1976; authored over 150 scientific/tech. papers and over 170 consulting/professional reports; co-author: 'Exploration Geochemistry: Design and Interpretation of Soil Surveys' 1987; Home: 2972 W. 44th Ave., Vancouver, B.C. V6N 3K4; Office: Dept. of Geological Sciences, Univ. of B.C., Vancouver, B.C. V6T 1Z4.

**SINCLAIR, D'Alton Lally (Sandy),** B.A.Sc.; executive; b. Toronto, Ont. 27 Mar. 1925; s. Ian M.R. and Leah V. (McCarthy) S.; e. Upper Can. Coll. 1943; Univ. of Toronto B.A.Sc. 1949; Harvard Bus. Sch. A.M.P. 1972; m. Naomi d. the late Geoffrey and Miriam Carter 20 Nov. 1968; children: Katherine, Charles, Adam; PRES. & DIR., THE YORK INVESTMENT CORP.; Royal Candn. Artillery, N.W. Europe 1943–46; 27th Candn. Inf. Bde., Germany 1952–54; Canadian Gypsum Co. Ltd. 1949–52, 1954–56; Asst. to Pres. Charterhouse Canada Ltd. 1956–60, Pres. 1960–73; Sr. Assoc. Peat Marwick Mitchell & Co. 1974–82; Chrmn. Middlefield Ventures Ltd. 1984–87; Chrmn., Oasas Telecom Corp. 1987–88; Dir., Canadian Manoir Industries Ltd.; recreations: squash racquets, bridge; Club: Badminton & Racquet, Toronto; Home: 39 Roxborough St. W., Toronto, Ont. M5R 1T9.

**SINCLAIR, Duncan Gordon,** D.V.M., M.S.A., Ph.D.; university administrator; b. Rochester, N.Y. 2 Nov. 1933; s. Robert Gordon and Elizabeth Winter Marwick (Broadbridge) S.; e. Ont. Vet. Coll. Univ. of Toronto D.V.M. 1958; Ont. Agric. Coll. M.S.A. 1960; Queen's Univ. Ph.D. 1963; m. Leona Mae d. Edward Victor and Marjorie Payne 19 July 1958; one s. Robert Gordon; VICE-PRINCIPAL (HEALTH SCIENCES), AND DEAN, FACULTY OF MEDICINE, QUEEN'S UNIVERSITY 1988– ; U.S. Pub. Health Fellow Coll. of Phys. & Surgs. Columbia Univ. 1963; Meres Sr. Scholar in Med. Research St. John's Coll. and Dept. of Physiol. Cambridge Univ. 1964–66; Asst. Prof. of Physiol. Queen's Univ. 1966, Assoc. Prof. 1968, Prof. 1972, Dir. Acad. Planning Faculty of Med. 1971–74, Dean of Arts & Science 1974–83; Dir. Gen. Prog. Operations, Med. Rsch. Counc. of Can. 1983–84; Vice Princ. (Institutional Relations) Queen's Univ. 1984–86; Vice-Principal (Services) 1986–88; Markle Scholar in Acad. Med. 1966–71; Hon. Fellow, Royal College of Physicians & Surgeons of Canada 1989; Anglican (mem. Synod Ont. 1967–69); Home: 176 Churchill Cres., Kingston, Ont. K7L 4N2; Office: Botterell Hall, Queen's Univ., Kingston, Ont. K7L 3N6.

**SINCLAIR, Gordon M.,** B.Comm., C.A.; association executive; b. Ottawa, Ont. 29 July 1931; s. Milton Leslie and Annie Bernice (Condie) S.; e. Carleton Univ., B. Comm. 1952; Inst. of C.A.s 1955; m. Lorraine C. d. Martin and Gladys Black 14 Apr. 1956; children: Lesley, Barbara, Sandra, Nancy; PRES. & CHIEF EXTVE. OFFR., AIR TRANSP. ASSN. OF CAN. 1985– ; Auditor, Price Waterhouse & Co. 1952–58; Extve. Asst. to Vice Pres., Fin., Massey Fergsuon Ltd. 1958–61; Extve. Vice Pres., Candn. Pargas Ltd. 1961–63; Treas. & Contr., Pargas Inc. 1963–67; Dir., Fin. Mgmt., Dept of Fish., Govt. of Can. 1967–69; Asst. Dep. Postmaster Gen. 1969–76; Marine Admin., Dept. of Transp. 1976–82; Air Admin. 1982–85; recreations: fishing, curling; Club: Rideau; Office: #747, 99 Bank St., Ottawa, Ont. K1P 6B9.

**SINCLAIR, Gordon Maxwell,** B.S.A.; Chrmn. & Dir., The Co-operators Group Ltd.; Dir. Co-operative Energy Corp.; Federated Co-operatives Ltd.; Home: Box 215, Straphclair, Man. R0J 2C0.

**SINCLAIR, Helen K.,** M.A.; executive; b. Edmonton, Alta. 3 Apl. 1951; d. A. Richard and Sonja (Morawetz) S.; e. Coll. Marie de France and Havergal Coll. Toronto; York Univ. B.A. 1973; Univ. of Toronto M.A. 1974; Harvard Bus. Sch. Advanced Mgmt. Prog. 1989; m. James S. Coatsworth; children: Mark, Anna; PRES., THE CANADIAN BANKERS ASSOCIATION (CBA) 1989– ; she is the first woman and the youngest person to preside over the CBA; held various senior executive positions Bank of Nova Scotia, incl. Sr. Vice Pres. and Gen. Mgr. Planning & Legis. to 1980; Pub. Affairs Dir. CBA 1980–85; has been active in a number of public policy advisory boards, including the Financial Services Sectoral Advisory Group on Internat. Trade, Financial Services Institute; Policy Analysis Ctte., C.D. Howe Inst.; Chrmn. of the Bd. of Govs., YMCA of Greater Toronto 1992– ; Mem., Leadership Giving for the 1992 United Way Campaign for Greater Toronto (Chairperson 1991 Campaign); Dir. ABC Can. Found. for Literacy; Chair, Immigration Ctte. Can. Employment & Immigration Adv. Council 1986–89; mem. Pension Commn. Ont. 1984–86; Dir. and Vice Chrmn. Candn. Mothercraft Soc. 1980–85; mem. Internat. Labour Orgn. 1977, 1985; recreations: tennis, hiking, cross-country skiing; Clubs: Toronto Lawn & Tennis; York; Ticker; Rideau; Office: Suite 3000, 199 Bay St., P.O. Box 348, Commerce Court West, Toronto, Ont. M5L 1G2.

**SINCLAIR, Hon. Ian David,** O.C., Q.C., B.A., LL.B., LL.D.; former senator; b. Winnipeg, Man. 27 Dec. 1913; s. late John David and Lillian S.; e. Pub. Schs., Winnipeg, Man.; Wesley Coll. there; Univ. of Manitoba, B.A. (Econ.) 1937, Hon. LL.D. 1967; Manitoba Law Sch., LL.B. 1941; Laval Univ. Hon. D.B.A. 1981; Acadia Univ. Hon. D.C.L. 1982; m. Ruth Beatrice Drennan, 1942; two s. and two d.; Dir., Canadian Marconi Co.; Gov., Candn. Investment Protection Fund; read law with Guy Chappell & Co., Winnipeg, Man., 1937–41; called to Bar of Man., 1941; Lectr. in Torts, Univ. of Man., 1942–43; joined Canadian Pacific Ltd., Law Dept. as Asst. Solr., Winnipeg, Man. 1942, Solr. Montreal, Que. 1946, Asst. to Gen. Counsel 1951, Gen. Solr. 1953, Vice Pres. & Gen. Counsel Feb. 1960, Vice Pres. Law, July 1960, Vice Pres., Dir. and mem. Extve. Comte. 1961, Pres. 1966, Pres. & C.E.O. 1969, Chrmn. & C.E.O. 1972–81, Dir. 1961–84; Chrmn. & C.E.O. Canadian Pacific Enterprises Ltd. 1972–82, Chrmn. 1982–84, Dir. 1962–84; Chrmn. Canadian Pacific Airlines Ltd. 1969–82; Dir. and Vice Pres. The Royal Bank of Canada 1974–84; Dir., Sun Life Assurance Co. 1968–86; Canadian Investment Fund Ltd. 1972–89; mem. Extve. Comte., Internat. Air Transport Assn. 1975–81; Mem., Internat. Adv. Ctte., The Chase Manhattan Bank 1973–87; Public Dir., Investment Dealers Assn. of Can. 1984–88; summoned to The Senate of Canada, Dec. 1983; Mem., Candn. Business Hall of Fame; mem. Univ. of Man. Alumni Assn.; Fraser Inst., Vancouver (Lifetime Mem.); Engineering Inst. of Can. (Hon. Mem.); Clubs: Toronto Club; Office: 35 Cameo St., Oakville, Ont. L6J 5X9.

**SINCLAIR, John E. (Jack),** B.A.; b. Hamilton, Ont. 9 Dec. 1936; e. McMaster Univ. B.A. 1958; m. L. Patricia Miles; 4 children; Exec. Vice Pres. (Corporate Services), Bell Canada 1990–92 (Retired); joined Bell Canada 1958 serving various mgmt. positions Vice Pres. Systems 1977, Vice Pres. Regulatory Matters 1980, Exec. Vice Pres. (Corporate) 1983; Exec. Vice Pres. (Corporate), BCE 1985–88; Exec. Vice Pres. (Ont. Region) 1988–90; Past Chrmn., Candn. Chamber of Commerce; National Pres., Multiple Sclerosis Soc. of Can.; Chrmn. Territorial Advisory Bd. of the Salvation Army; International Commnr., Boy Scouts of Can.; Chrmn., The Concerned Kids (a substance abuse prevention program); Mem. Bd. of Dirs., Citizens Foundation for the Promotion of Police Community Relations in Metro Toronto (PROACTION); recipient, Hon. degree (LL.D.), McMaster Univ. 1991; Excellence in communications (EXCEL) Award, Internat. Assn. of Business Communicators 1992; recreations: cross-country skiing, hiking; Club: Ontario; Founders; Home: Toronto, Ont.

**SINCLAIR, John Gordon;** advertising executive; b. Toronto, Ont. 22 Dec. 1931; s. Daniel John and Mary Armorel (Silver) S.; e. Univ. of Toronto 1949–52; m. Jean Mary d. Charles and Jean Burgess 12 Sept. 1959; children: John, Anne Marie, Patricia, Michael, Peter, Rosemary; PRESIDENT, INSTITUTE OF CANADIAN ADVERTISING 1992– ; Account Extve., McKim Advtg. Group of Agencies 1958; Mngt. Supervisor 1965; Gen. Mgr., Case Assoc. (subs. of McKim) 1966; Pres. 1975; Extve. Vice-Pres., McKim holding co. 1988; over 32 years worked on advtg. assignments for General Foods, Warner Lambert, Ralston Purina, Govt. of Can., Suzuki, Spalding, Ont. Lottery & Avis Rent-a-car; Extve. Vice-Pres., Inst. of Candn. Advtg. 1990; Bd. of Dir., Candn. Advtg. Found.; Candn. Congress of Advtg. 1993; Molly Maid Internat.; Dir., North York Gen. Hosp. (Treas., Extve. Ctte.; Chair, Finance Ctte.); Muskoka Hist. & Steamship Soc.; YMCA of Metro Toronto; recreations: golf, skiing, swimming, travel; club: Rosedale Golf; Home: 171 Yonge Blvd., Toronto, Ont. M5M 3H3; Office: 30 Soudan Ave., Toronto, Ont. M4S 1V6.

**SINCLAIR, Lister,** O.C., B.A., M.A., LL.D., D.Litt., Litt.D.; actor, author, broadcaster; b. Bombay, India 9 Jan. 1921; s. W. Shedden (Chem. Engr.) and Lillie A. Sinclair; e. Colet Court and St. Paul's, London, Eng.; Univ. of British Columbia B.A. 1942, LL.D. 1972; Univ. of Toronto, M.A.; Mount Allison LL.D. 1970; Waterloo Lutheran D.Litt. 1970; Memorial Litt.D. 1971; York Univ. LL.D. 1992; Univ. of Victoria LL.D. 1992; Carleton Univ. LL.D.; m. Alice Mather, Vancouver, B.C., 24 Dec. 1942; one s.; 2ndly m. Margaret Watchman 2 June 1965; one s.; PRES., CANADIAN CONF. OF THE ARTS; Host, Festival of the Sound, Parry Sound 1983– ; Vice Pres. Program Policy & Development, C.B.C. 1975–80 (formerly Exec. Vice Pres. 1972); Host of C.B.C. 'Ideas'; widely known as author, actor (expert at languages and dialects), critic and mathematician; sometime Lect. in Maths., Univ. of Toronto for three yrs.; resigned to devote himself to freelance work, radio play writing and acting, stage play writing and editorial work; is one of the princ. contribs. to C.B.C. radio drama series and has produced a number of successful scripts for other programs, includ. shortwave broadcasts to Europe, institutional documentaries, also film scripts; taught radio writing at Acad. of Radio Arts, Toronto; engaged on Ways of Mankind for the Ford Foundation stage play 'Socrates,' produced Jupiter Theatre, Toronto, 1952; commissioned to write documentaries for Ford Foundation, 1953; apptd. to the teaching staff of the Royal Conservatory of Music of Toronto, 1952 and York Univ. Faculty of Fine Arts; played cricket and rugby in sch. days; hobby is collecting musical recordings of which he has more than 15,000 and birding; author of 'A Play on Words and Other Radio Plays' 1948; [Books] 'The Blood is Strong' 1950; 'Socrates' 1952; 'The Art of Norval Morrisseau' 1979; many radio and TV awards, including John Drainie Award for Contributions to Broadcasting; Sandford Fleming Medal, Royal Candn. Inst. 1984; Officer of the Order of Canada 1985; Office: CBC Ideas, Box 500, Terminal A, Toronto, Ont. M5W 1E6.

**SINCLAIR, Robert W.,** M.A., M.F.A., R.C.A., C.S.P.W.C.; artist; educator; b. Saltcoats, Sask. 9 Feb. 1939; s. Lorne Foster and Verita Florabelle (Kittle) S.; e. Univ. of Man. Sch. of Art B.F.A. 1962; State Univ. of Iowa M.A. 1965, M.F.A. 1967; m. Kathryn Anne d. Rev. Russell K. Vickers, Victoria, B.C. 28 Dec. 1961; m.

Katharine A. (Ord), Edmonton, Alta.; children: Shaun Kenyon, Andre Foster, Joel Bertrand; PROF. OF ART, UNIV. OF ALTA. 1965– ; Visiting Artist, Univ. of Iowa 1973, Banff Sch. of Fine Arts 1976; solo exhns.: Univ. of Iowa 1965; Univ. of Alta. 1966, 1969; Banff Sch. of Fine Arts 1966; W. Ill. Univ. 1967; Moorhead State Coll. Minn. 1968; maritimes travel exhn. 1968–69; Wynick/Tuck Gallery Toronto 1970–85; Edmonton Art Gallery 1972–73, 1982–83; Peter Whyte Art Gallery Banff 1973, 1991; The Gallery Stratford, Ont. 1976; Art Gallery of Ont. travel exhn. Ont. 1976–77; Chapman Gallery Red Deer 1977–78, 1980, 1982, 1991; Hett Gallery, Edmonton, 1982–84, 1992; Kathleen Laverty Gallery, Edmonton 1984–94; Thomas Gallery, Winnipeg 1988, 1990–91; Upstairs Gallery, Winnipeg 1992; Heffel Gallery, Vancouver 1986, Madison Gallery, Toronto 1987–88; Ingram Fine Art, Toronto 1990; Della Scala Gallery, Toronto 1992; rep. in over 60 group exhns. Can., USA, Europe and Japan since 1963; rep. in pub., corporate and private colls. incl. Can. Council Art Bank, Alta. Art Foundation, Prov. Alta. Museum; Royal Collection, Windsor Castle Royal Library, England; rep. various bibliogs.; mem., Royal Cdn. Acad.; Candn. Soc. Painters in Watercolour; Univs. Art Assn.; rec'd Elizabeth Greenshields Mem. Foundation Grant; Universalist; recreations: Tai Chi; Home: 10819 - 52 Ave., Edmonton, Alta. T6H 0P2; Office: Edmonton, Alta. T6G 2C9.

**SINCLAIR, Selby James,** D.F.C., C.A.; retired industrial executive; b. Toronto, Ont. 25 Sept. 1921; s. James Taylor and Elizabeth (Clelland) S.; e. C.A. 1948; m. Aileen Patricia Dogherty, 3 May 1953; children: Ann, Gail, Janet, Jane, Peter, John; served with RCAF Bomber Command during World War II; rank Flying Offr.; mem., Candn. Inst. C.A.'s; United Church; recreations: skiing, fishing; Clubs: Toronto Hunt; Devil's Glen Country; Key Largo Anglers; Home: 46A Chestnut Park Rd., Toronto, Ont. M4W 1W8.

**SINCLAIR PROWSE, Hon. Janet Ann,** B.A., LL.B.; supreme court judge; b. Toronto, Ont. 28 Feb. 1947; s. Alexander Boyd and Sheila Margaret (Grant) Sinclair; e. Univ. of Toronto, B.A. 1969; Dalhousie Univ., LL.B. 1972; m. D. Clifton s. D. Clifton and Edythe P. 1 Sept. 1972; children: Clifton Alexander, David Sinclair; JUSTICE OF SUPREME COURT OF BRITISH COLUMBIA 1990– ; worked with Crown Counsel at all court levels 1973–82; conducted the jointly funded Prov.-Fed. Pre-Trial Discovery Project 1978–79; private practice in crim. & civil law 1982–85; practised (mainly civil lit.) with Bourne Lyall (which became Lyall, McKercher) then Russell DuMeulin 1985–89; Judge of the County Court of Vancouver 1989–90; Dir., Lawyer's Inn; Extve. Mem., Vanc. Bar Assn.; Vice-Chrmn., Law Day Ctte.; author: 'Working Manual of Criminal Law' 1984 with yearly supplements; Office: Law Courts, 800 Smithe St., Vancouver, B.C. V6Z 2E1.

**SINGER, Irwin,** B.Com., LL.B.; corporation executive; b. Toronto, Ont. 8 Dec. 1935; s. Louis and Jennie (Sherman) S.; e. Univ. of Toronto B.Com. 1957, LL.B. 1960; m. Pamela d. James Norman Hird 22 Jan. 1964; children: Jason Ford, Galaen N.B.; CHRMN. & DIR., TM TECHNOLOGIES CORP.; Sec. and Dir., Arrowlink Corp.; Dir., Graph/Max Inc.; private law practice Toronto 1962–90; called to Bar of Ont. 1962; mem., Candn. Bar Assn.; Clubs: Lawyers'; Cambridge; Home: 1 Green Valley Rd., North York, Ont. M2P 1A4; Office: 906, 101 Richmond St. W., Toronto, Ont. M5H 1T1.

**SINGER, Ronald,** B.A., B.Ed.; educator; theatre, film, television producer; director; actor; b. Montréal, Qué. 11 June 1938; s. Morris and Yetta (Aidelbaum) S.; e. Sir George Williams Univ. B.A. 1960; Central Sch. of Speech & Drama London, Eng. 1960; McGill Univ. B.Ed. 1961; m. Yvonne d. Tibor and Agnes Vandor 18 Dec. 1966; children: Tamara, Sara, Hannah; PROF. OF THEATRE, YORK UNIV. 1973– , Assoc. Dean of Fine Arts, Dir. of Grad. Prog., Chrmn. of Theatre 1985–88; actor: Neighbourhood Playhouse New York 1962; Asst. to Producer Expo '67 Montréal 1967; Producer, Rediffusson TV London, Eng. 1968; Assoc. Producer Theatre Nat. Arts Centre Ottawa 1969, Dir. of Young Co's 1971; Dir. Actors' Workshops Stratford Festival 1970; Artistic Dir. Young People's Theatre Toronto 1972; Theatre Cons. Prov. Ont. 1973; Assoc. Dir., Toronto Arts Productions 1977; Entertainment Reporter CFRB Radio, Toronto 1980; Exec. Dir., Group W Television, Los Angeles 1981; Producer, City Pulse News, City TV Toronto 1982; Vice Pres., Entertainment, SAV Entertainment, Moscow 1988– ; Producer, Fundamentally Film Production Co. 1990–94; Extve. Producer, 'Jake & the Kid' (TV series, Global) 1994; mem. ACTRA; Equity; recreation: reading; Club: Mooredale; Home: 349 Wellesley St. E., Toronto, Ont. M4X 1H2; Office: 4700 Keele St., North York, Ont. M3J 1P3.

**SINGH, Arindra,** B.A., C.A.; financial executive; b. India 30 July 1947; e. St. Stephen's College India B.A. (Hons.) 1967; Fellow, Inst. of C.A.s in England and Wales 1981; SENIOR VICE-PRESIDENT, CHIEF FINANCIAL OFFICER & SECRETARY, INTER-CITY PRODUCTS CORP. 1990– ; Senior Manager, Coopers & Lybrand until 1985; Corp. Controller, Inter-City Products Corp. 1985; Vice-Pres., Chief Financial Officer & Sec. 1990; Dir., CHL Holdings Inc.; ICG Barriere Inc.; ICP Petroleum Inc.; ICP Property & Casualty Corp.; Inter-City Products Corp. (USA); Inter-City Products Corp. (Canada); Thompson Pipe & Steel Co.; Mem., Unicef Finance & Admin. Ctte.; Financial Executives Inst.; recreations: golf, tennis; clubs: St. George's Golf & Country, Fitness Inst.; Office: 20 Queen St. W., P.O. Box 32, Toronto, Ont. M5H 3R3.

**SINGH, Bhagirath,** M.Sc., Ph.D.; educator and researcher; b. Jaipur, Rajasthan, India 8 Feb. 1946; s. Shyam Lal and Laxmi Davi Yadav; e. Univ. of Rajasthan B.Sc. 1963, M.Sc. 1965 (Gold Medal 1965); Agra Univ. Central Drug Rsch. Inst. Ph.D. 1969; m. Rajkumari d. Raghubir and Margshri Yadav 6 May 1968; children: Gargi, Vivek, Somya; PROF. AND CHAIR, DEPT. OF MICROBIOLOGY AND IMMUNOLOGY, UNIV. OF WESTERN ONTARIO 1992– ; Co-Dir., Immunology Robarts Rsch. Institute 1992– ; Adjunct Prof. of Immunology, Univ. of Alta. 1993– ; Prof. of Immunology, Univ. of Alberta 1986–93, Acting Chrmn. of Immunol. 1988–90; Sci. Alta. Heritage Found. Med. Rsch. 1989–93; Jr. Rsch. Fellow 1966–69, Sr. Rsch. Fellow 1969–70 Div. Med. Chem. Central Drug Rsch. Inst. Lucknow, India; Postdoctoral Fellow Organic Chem. Univ. of Liverpool 1970–73; Rsch. Fellow Immunol. Univ. of Alta. 1974, Asst. Prof. 1977–81, Assoc. Prof. 1981–86; Prin. Investig. Med. Rsch. Council Can. Group on Immunoregulation 1982–87; Scholar of AHFMR 1985–89; Sci. Adv. Biomira Inc., Synthetic Peptide Inc. Edmonton; Exec. mem. Muttart Diabetes Rsch. & Training Centre Edmonton; ed. 'The Immunology of Diabetes Mellitus' 1986; Adv. Molec. Cell. Immunology 1993– ; mem. Candn. Soc. Immunol.; Candn. Fedn. Biol. Socs.; N.Y. Acad. Sci's; Fedn. Am. Socs. Exper. Biol.; Am. Assn. Immunols.; Am. Diabetes Assn.; Candn. Diabetes Assn.; recreations: camping, hiking, music; Home: 146 St. Bees Close, London, Ont. N6G 4B8; Office: 3014 Dental Sci. Bldg., Univ. of Western Ontario, London, Ont. N6A 5C1.

**SINGH, Gur Sharan,** M.B., B.S., FRSC(C), FACS, FICS; neurosurgeon, association executive; b. Jullundur, India 25 Sept. 1936; s. Partap and Gurdial S.; e. Punjab Univ. M.B., B.S.; Montreal Neurological Inst., McGill Univ. FRCS(C); m. Manju d. Harjit Grewal 4 Dec. 1966; children: Arjun, Sabina; DIRECTOR, NEUROLOGICAL INTENSIVE CARE UNIT, ROYAL INLAND HOSPITAL 1980– ; attending Neurosurgeon, Royal Inland Hosp. (Kamloops, B.C.) 1967– ; Chief of Surgery 1986–88; Mem., B.C. Medical Assn.; Bd. of Dir. 1979–86; Sec.-Treas. 1988–89; Chair, General Assembly 1989–90; President-Elect 1990–91; President 1991–92; Past Pres., Kamloops Med. Soc.; Section of Neurosurgery B.C.; Chair, Council of Health Policy and Economics, B.C. medical Assn.; Mem. Bd. of Dirs., Candn. Medical Assn.; Rotary Club; recreations: tennis, photography; clubs: Kamloops Tennis (Past Pres.); Office: #212 – 300 Columbia St., Kamloops, B.C. V2C 6L1; B.C. Medical Assn. Office: #115 – 1665 West Broadway, Vancouver, B.C. V6J 5A4.

**SINGH, Thimersingh Mohar,** B.A.; county court judge; b. Richmond, Natal, S. Africa 30 July 1933; s. Mohar Jugroop and Deoki Devi S.; e. Sastri Coll. (Natal) 1951; Springfield Traning Coll. (Natal), teacher's dipl. 1954; Univ. of S. Africa, B.A. 1960; Attorney's Adm. Dipl. (with distinction) 1963; m. Krishna Devi d. Balaram singh and Sukhdaye S. 7 Oct. 1956; children: Shaneela Devi, Umesh Thimer, Anilla Devi; JUDGE, COUNTY COURT OF WESTMINSTER, B.C. 1986– ; Primary teacher (Natal) 1955–56; Teacher, Windsor H.S. 1957–60; served articles with B.G. Choudree 1961–63; admitted Natal Law Soc. 1964; Partner (brother), M.M. Singh 1965–66; emigrated to Canada 1966; Teacher, Canwood H.S. 1966–67; served articles with Keith Taylor & Co. 1967–68; called to Man. Bar 1968; partner with P.D. Ferg, Q.C. 1968–73; called to B.C. Bar 1974; Partner, Williams, Davie, Singh & MacCarthy 1973–86; Mem., Child Welfare Soc. & Friends of the Sick Assn., Natal 1955–66; Kinsmen Club 1968–70; Candn. Bar Assn. 1984–86; Pres., Nanaimo Co. Bar Assn. 1978; B.C. Prov. Counc.; recreations: fishing, hunting, golf; Club: Cowichan Golf & Country; Home: Box 75, Duncan, B.C. V9L 3X1; Office: Court House, Begbie Sq., New Westminster, B.C. V3M 1C9.

**SINGLETON, Howard Barham,** B.Ed., M.A.; consultant; b. Edmonton, Alta. 7 Sept. 1928; s. Howard and Dorothy Violet (Barham) S.; e. Univ. of Alta. B.Ed. 1950, B.A. 1953; Oxford Univ. B.A. 1955, M.A. 1959; CONSULTANT 1990– ; joined Dept. of External Affairs 1956, Adv. Intnl. Control Comn. Hanoi, Vietnam 1957, Vientiane, Laos 1961–63, Second Sec. Helsinki 1958–60, Dept. External Affairs Far E., Press and Defence Liaison Divs. 1963–70, Dir. Rsch. & Planning Sec. of State's Dept. 1970–72, Counsellor Washington 1972–76, Chargé d'affaires Beirut 1976–78, Dir. E. Eur. Div. Ottawa 1978–79 and W. Eur. Div. 1979–80, Ambassador to Haiti 1980–83; Dir. Pacific Programs 1983–86; Adv. Personnel 1986–88; Depy. Chief of Protocol 1988–90; Anglican; recreations: tennis, skiing, sailing; Club: Britannia Yacht; Home: 502, 211 Wurtemburg St., Ottawa, Ont. K1N 8R4; Office: 502 – 211 Wurtemburg St., Ottawa, Ont. K1N 8R4.

**SINGLETON-WOOD, Allan James;** b. Newport, Monmouthshire, U.K. 13 Feb. 1933; s. Charles James and Violet Anne (Bond) S.; e. London Univ. 1949–51; m. Joan d. Henry and Florence Davies 23 June 1956; children: Ceri, Glendon; PRESIDENT, CANADIAN PRODUCTIVITY DIVISION, CB MEDIA LIMITED 1994– ; TV & Radio Mus. Dir. 1953–57; TV Prod. 1957–61; freelance Prod., BBC 1964–64; Indus. Advtg. Mgr., Western Mail (Wales) 1964; Advtg. Dir., Voice of Brit. Indus. Mags. (London) 1966; Mktg. Serv. Extve., The Sun and the People IPC Newspapers 1966–68; Mktg. Serv. Mgr., Financial Post (Toronto) 1969–71; Rsch. Dir. 1971–76; Nat. Sales Mgr. 1976–77; Pub., 'Financial Post' mag. 1978–79; Dir., Advtg. Sales, Financial Post Div. 1980–83; Pub., 'Small Business Magazine' 1983–87; Vice Pres., Publishing Bedford House Communications 1987; Publisher, 'Small Business' 1988–89; Vice Pres., C.B. Media Limited 1988–90; Corporate Publisher & Gen. Mgr., Sentry Communications 1990–91; Group Publisher, Business Publications Div., Maclean Hunter Ltd. 1991–93; lectr., var. univs.; pioneered 1st computer media evaluation prog. for Candn. advtg. indus. (now indus. standard); Anglican; Conservative; Dir., Candn. Club (Oakville) 1986–87; composer, contemp. music incl. title theme of 'Swing High' BBC Nat. Network series 1953–57; Home: 262 Vinova Court, Oakville, Ont. L6L 5X1; Office: Maclean Hunter Bldg., 777 Bay St., Toronto, Ont. M5W 1A7.

**SINHA, Ramesh Chandra,** Ph.D., D.Sc., F.R.S.C.; research scientist; b. Bareilly, India 10 Feb. 1934; s. Bhawani Prasada and Ram Pyari S.; e. Lucknow Univ., M.Sc. 1956; London Univ., Ph.D. 1960, D.Sc. 1974; m. Indu d. Chandradhari and Kamlavati Sinha 2 June 1957; children: Sanjeev, Sangita; PRINC. RSCH. SCI., AGRIC. CAN. 1965– ; Rsch. Scholar, Lucknow Univ. 1956–57; Ph.D. Student, Rothamsted Experim. Stn. 1958–60; Exper. Offr. 1959–60; Rsch. Assoc., Univ. of Ill. 1960–65; Adjunct. Prof., McGill Univ. 1979–83; F.R.S.C. 1985; Mem., Candn. Phytopathol. Soc.; Am. Phytopathol. Soc.; Indian Phytopathol. Soc.; Internat. Orgn. of Mycoplasmology; author of 87 sci. articles & 14 book chapters; Assoc. Ed.: 'Virology' 1971–73, 'Canadian Journal of Plant Pathology' 1981–85; recreations: badminton, golf; Home: 21 Barran St., Nepean, Ont. K2J 1G3; Office: Plant Rsch. Ctre., Agric. Can., Ottawa, Ont. K1A 0C6.

**SIREK, Anna,** M.D., M.A., Ph.D.; educator; b. Velke Senkvice, Czechoslovakia 12 Jan. 1921; d. Jan and Anna (Subik) Janek; e. Slovak Univ. of Bratislava M.D. 1946; Univ. of Toronto M. A. 1955, Ph.D. 1960; m. 27 July 1946; children: Ann, Jan, Peter, Terese; EMERITUS PROFESSOR since 1986; Intern, Detska klinika, Bratislava 1946–47; Research Fellow in Surg., Kronprinsessan Lovisas Barnsjukhus, Stockholm 1947–50 and Hosp. for Sick Children Toronto 1950–54; Research Assoc. Banting & Best Dept. Med. Research present Univ. 1954–60, Lectr. 1960–63, Asst. Prof. of Physiol. Univ. Toronto 1963–66, Assoc. Prof. 1966–72, Prof. of Physiol. 1972–86, Asst. Dir. Div. Teaching Labs. 1969–75, Dir. Div. Teaching Labs. 1975–86, rec'd Starr Medal Univ. of Toronto 1960; Centennial Medal 1966 Hoechst Co. Frankfurt/M, Germany; on the basis of expertise in expt. surg. has developed innovative procedures which have facilitated long term metabolic studies, resulting in solutions to numerous basic problems in the study of Diabetes in animals and humans; author over 100 articles published in scientific journals and as chapters in books; mem. Candn. Fed. Biol. Socs.; Am. Assn. Advanc. Science; Candn. Assn. Univ. Teachers; Fed. Med. Women Can; Internat. Diabetes Fed.; Toronto Diabetes Assn.; Candn. Soc. Endocrinol. & Metabolism; Candn. Diabetes Assn. Clinical & Scientific Section; Societa

Italiana Di Diabetologia; other biographical listings include: Am. Men and Women of Science; Internat. Scholars Directory; Dictionary of Internat. Biography; Who's of American Women; The World's Who's Who of Women; Who's Who in the East; Internat. Book of Honor; Who's Who in the Commonwealth; 5000 Personalities of the World; Women in Candn. Business and Finance; Internat. Directory of Distinguished Leadership; Directory of Distinguished Americans - Book of honor; Who's Who of Canadian Women; recreations: cooking, gardening, music, needlework; Home: 93 Farnham Ave., Toronto, Ont. M4V 1H6; Office: Medical Sciences Bldg., Toronto, Ont. M5S 1A8.

**SIREN, Paul,** C.M.; retired; b. Thunder Bay, Ont. 19 July 1917; s. Severi and Sofia Maria (Koistinen) S.; e. Ware Twp. Elementary Sch.; m. Natalie d. John and Helen Boychuk 31 Dec. 1936; children: Valerie, Kenneth, Gregory; Internat. Rep. United Automobile Workers Union 1942–60; freelance Cons. in Arbitration and Conciliation Services Labour matters 1960–64; Gen. Sec. Emeritus, Alliance of Candn. Cinema, Television and Radio Artists (ACTRA) 1965–86; Co-Chair, Task Force on the Status of the Artist, May-Aug. 1986; Pres., Candn. Conf. of the Arts 1988–90; Co-Chair, Candn. Adv. Ctte. on the Status of the Artist; 1987–91; served Candn. Armed Forces 1942–46; Member, Order of Canada 1987; Ace Award presented by Assn. of Cultural Extves. 1990; Diplomé d'Honneur 1992; Address: #1004, 820 Burnhamthorpe Rd., Etobicoke, Ont. M9C 4W2.

**SIRLUCK, Ernest,** M.B.E., M.A., Ph.D., LL.D., D. Litt., F.R.S.C.; educationist; b. Winkler, Man. 25 April 1918; s. Isaac and Rose (Nitikman) S.; e. Univ. of Man., B.A. 1940; Univ. of Toronto, M.A. 1941, Ph.D. 1948; m. Lesley Caroline, d. Wm. Carlton McNaught, Toronto, Ont., 10 Aug. 1942; children: Robert, Katherine; President, Univ. of Manitoba 1970–76; Lect., Univ. of Toronto 1946; Asst. Prof., Univ. of Chicago, 1947, Assoc. Prof., 1953, Prof. 1958; Professor English and Assoc. Dean, Sch. of Grad. Studies, Univ. of Toronto 1962, Dean 1964, Vice-Pres. & Grad. Dean 1968; Visiting Prof. of English (part-time) 1977–79; served overseas in U.K., France, Belgium, Holland, Germany with Candn. Army 1942–45; discharged with rank of Major; Guggenheim Fellow 1953–54; Fellow, Am. Council Learned Socs. 1958–59; Churchill Coll. Overseas Fellow (Cambridge Univ.) 1966; author of 'Complete Prose Works of John Milton' Vol. II 1959; 'Paradise Lost: A Deliberate Epic' 1967; Ed. (with others) 'Patterns of Literary Criticism' 1965–74; also articles in many prof. journs. in Can., U.S. and U.K. on Milton, Puritan Revolution, Spenser, Shakespeare, Jonson, and Univ. Policy and Admin.; Home: 153 Strathallan Blvd., Toronto, Ont. M5N 1S9.

**SIROIS, Hon. Allyre Louis,** M.B.E., B.A., LL.B.; judge; b. Vonda, Sask. 25 Aug. 1923; s. Paul Emile and Bertha (Pion) S.; e. Vonda, Sask., 1928–36, 1939; St. Anthony's Coll., Edmonton, 1937–1938; Radio Coll. of Can., Toronto, 1940–41; Univ. of Sask., B.A. 1948, LL.B. 1950; m. (late) Madeline Anne Marie Ehman, 14 Sept. 1948; children: Valerie, Richard, Guy, Marianne, Lisa, Norman; JUSTICE, COURT OF QUEEN'S BENCH, SASK., since 1964; apptd. to Court Martial Appeal Court, March 1985; apptd. to Pension Appeal Bd., May 1993; read law with Culliton & MacLean, Gravelbourg, Sask.; called to Bar of Sask. 1951; practised law Gravelbourg, Sask., 1951–64; served with Candn. Army 1941–45; on loan to War Office (M15) 1943–44; awarded Croix de Guerre avec Palme; Mem. of the Order of the Br. Empire (Mil.); served as Secy.-Treas. of Lib. organs. in local, prov. and fed. constits.; served on Gravelbourg Town Council, Sch. Bd. (Chrmn. for 10 yrs.), Bd. Trade and parish council; Prov. Pres., Assn. Culturelle Franco-Canadienne 1963–64; won scholarship to U.N. summer 1948; mem., Candn. Bar Assn.; K. of C. (Grand Kt.); Royal Candn. Legion; R. Catholic; recreations: reading, sports; Home: 1638 8th Ave. N., Saskatoon, Sask. SK7 2X9; Office: Court House, Saskatoon, Sask. S7K 3G7.

**SIROIS, Antoine,** B.A., L.èsl., B.Péd., D.d'U.; university professor; b. Sherbrooke, Qué. 28 Sept. 1925; s. Georges-Alfred and Marguerite (Campbell) S.; e. Sém. de Sherbrooke, B.A. 1945, Grand sém. de Sherbrooke, dipl. théo. 1949; Univ. de Sherbrooke, B.Péd. 1960; Univ. de Montréal, L.èsl. 1960; Univ. de Paris, D.d'U. 1967; PROF., FAC. DES LETTRES ET SCI. HUM., UNIV. DE SHERBROOKE 1967– ; Prof. & Prin., Ext. classique de Lac-Mégantic 1952–58; Sec. Gen., Univ. de Sherbrooke 1960–65; Head, French Dept. 1968–74; Vice-Dean (Rsch.) 1975–83; Extve. Mem., Candn. Fed. for the Hum. 1970–74, 1977–79 (Vice-Pres. 1973–74); Bd. Mem., Fonds pour la form. de cherch. et l'aide à la rech. 1975–81, 1984–87; Can. Counc. 1983–86; Pres., Killam Fellowship Jury 1984–87; Mus. of Fine Arts (Sherbrooke) 1985–87; mem., many lit. & art juries incl. those for the Gov. Gen. Award, Molson Prize, and Prix David; recipient, Prix Gabrielle-Roy 1986; Prix Juge-Lemay 1988; Certificat de mérite 1990 de l'ACS/AEC 1990; Prix d'excellence de la Ville de Sherbrooke 'carrière,' 1991; Priest, Roman Catholic Church; Mem., Royal Society of Canada 1993; Candn. Comp. Lit. Assn. (Pres. 1975–77); Candn. & Que. Lit. Assns.; Assn. for Candn. Studies; Internat. Comparative Lit. Assoc.; author: 'Montréal dans le roman canadien' 1968; co-author: 'Un homme et son péché' cr. edit. 1986; co-author & co-editor: 'A l'ombre de DesRochers' 1985, 'L'Essor culturel des Cantons de l'Est depuis 1950' 1985, 'Bibliography of Studies in Comparative Canadian Literature (1930–1987) 1989; 'Mythes et symboles dans le roman québécois' 1992; recreations: ski, golf; Home: 2497 Laurentie, Sherbrooke, Que. J1J 1L3; Office: Dépt. des lettres et communications, Fac. des lettres et sci. hum., Univ. de Sherbrooke, Sherbrooke, Qué. J1K 2R1.

**SIROIS, Gilles;** business executive; b. Fortierville, Que. 9 Feb. 1941; s. Arthur Leon and Antoinette (Laquerre) S.; e. Univ. of Moncton; VICE-PRES., SHERMAG INC. 1977– ; insurance broker 1970–77; Mem., Ch. Comm. of Que., Ch. Comm. de Sherbrooke; Membre du Conseil d'Administration et de l'executif de l'Association des fabricants de meubles du Quebec; recreations: fishing, hunting; Home: 2777 Cedar Bluff, Magog, Que. J1X 3W4; Office: 2171 King O., C.P. 2390, Sherbrooke, Que. J1J 2G1.

**SIROIS, Jean,** Q.C., LL.L.; lawyer; b. Québec, Qué. 14 Feb. 1938; s. Jean and France (Boutin) S.; e. Laval Univ. LL.L. 1961; children: Marie, Jean Jr.; SENIOR PARTNER, LEGRIS, LEFEBVRE 1991– ; called to Bar of Qué. 1962; Exec. Dir. Royal Comn. Adm. Criminal Justice Prov. Qué. 1967–69; Exec. Asst. to Prime Min. of Prov. Qué. 1969–70; Legal Adv. to Adv. Ctte. Bankruptcy & Insolvency Legis. Govt. Can. 1985–87; Vice Pres. and Dir. Nat. Film Bd. 1985–86; Pres. and Dir. Telefilm Canada 1986–88; Dir. Arbor Capital Inc.; Dir. Québec City Winter Carnival 1971–74; Québec City Summer Festival 1972–79; mem. Qué. Harbour Bd. 1979–80; Montréal C. of C.; Candn. Bar Assn. (Vice Pres. Young Candn. Lawyers Conf. 1969–70); recreation: golf; Clubs: Québec Garrison; Val Morin Golf; Home: 12L, 6100 Deacon, Montréal, Qué. H3S 2P3; Office: 1100 René-Lévesque Blvd. Ouest, Suite 2200, Montréal, Qué. H3B 4N4.

**SIROIS, Hon. Jean-Charles,** B.A., B.Ph.; judge; b. Ottawa, Ont. 5 Sept. 1930; S. Joseph A. and Marianne (Banville) S.; e. Univ. of Ottawa B.A., B.Ph. 1952; Osgoode Hall Law Sch. 1956; m. Françoise d. Hormidas Gariepy, Q.C. 1981; JUDGE, SUPREME COURT OF ONT. 1982– ; law practice Ottawa 1956–82; Q.C. 1974; Office: High Court of Justice, 161 Elgin St., Ottawa, Ont. K2P 1K2.

**SIROIS, Raymond,** C.M., M.Sc.Com.; telecommunications administrator; b. St. Epiphane, Que., 26 Jan. 1927; s. Georges-Emile and Bernadette (Levesque) S.; e. Que. Acad. 1945; Laval Univ. M.Sc.Com. 1948; m. Yolande, d. Télesphore Landry, 27 Nov. 1948; children: Michèle, Renée, Marie-Claude, Jean; DIRECTOR, QUEBEC TÉLÉPHONE 1969– ; Pres. and Chrmn., Bonaventure and Gaspe Telephone Co., Ltd. (subsidiary) 1974– ; Dir., General Trust of Canada; Ivanhoé Inc.; Industrial-Alliance Life Ins. Co.; Caisse de dépôt et placement du Québec; TM Multi-Regions Inc.; Laval Univ. Foundation; Gov., Que. Chamber of Comm.; Gov., Professional Corp. of Ch. Adminis. of Que.; Gov., Conseil du Patronat du Québec; Dir., Quebec Symphony Orchestra; Dir., Musée de la Civilisation; Dir., The Council for Candn. Unity; Hon. Col. Regiment 'Les Fusiliers du Saint-Laurent'; joined Québec-Téléphone in 1948 as Accountant; Dir. of Traffic 1965; Vice Pres. Operations 1967; Chrmn., Pres. & C.E.O. 1974–92; Chrmn. 1992–94; el. a Dir. 1969; Gov., Chart. Adms. of Que.; K. of C. Rimouski (4th Degree); Hermes trophy, Laval Univ. Administrative Science Faculty 1982; 'La Gloire de l'Escole' Laval Univ. 1989; Member of the Order of Canada 1991; Catholic; recreations: golf, fishing, hunting; Club: Bic Golf; Home: 241 Henri-Jacob St., Rimouski, Que. G5L 6V3; Office: 6 Jules-A.-Brillant St., Rimouski, Que. G5L 7E4.

**SIROIS, Venceslas,** B.A., B.Sc.; retired petroleum executive; b. St. Georges de Beauce, Que. 8 June 1920; s. Horace and Maria (Dionne) S.; e. Coll. Brébeuf, Montreal, 1937; Loyola Coll., B.A. 1939; Queen's Univ., B.Sc. (Chem. Engn.) 1943; m. Nancy, d. late C. H. Dickerson, 1943; one d., Anne Marie; Sr. Vice Pres. & Dir., Imperial Oil Ltd. (ret. Sept. 1980); joined Imperial Oil as Chem. Engr., Montreal E. Refinery, 1943; Process Supvr., Sarnia Refinery, 1952; Process Supt. Chems., Sarnia, 1956; Mang. Asst., Mfg. Dept., Toronto, 1959; Asst. Mgr., Refining Coordination, Toronto, 1961; Refining Advisor, Refining co-ordination, Standard Oil Co. (N.J.), N.Y., 1964; Mgr., Operations coordination, Mfg. Dept., Toronto, 1965; Asst. Gen. Mgr. Supply Logistics Dept., 1969; Vice Pres. and Gen. Mgr., Logistics Dept. 1971; mem. Assn. Prof. Engrs. Prov. Ont.; mem. Bd. of Adv., Concordia Univ., Sch. of Community & Public Affairs (Montreal); R. Catholic; recreations: golf, reading, Club: Donalda; Home: 3900 Yonge St., Ste. 803, Toronto, Ont. M4N 3N6.

**SIROISHKA, Victor M.,** B.S.P., M.B.A.; business executive; b. 1930; e. Univ. of Saskatchewan B.Sc.(Pharmacy) 1952; Univ. of Western Ontario M.B.A. 1958; m. Denyse; 3 children; TREASURER & VICE-PRESIDENT, FINANCE & ADMINISTRATION, SANDOZ CANADA INC. 1974– ; Reg. Mgr., Sandoz (Canada) Limited 1958–67; Corp. Planning Analyst , John Labatt Limited 1967–71; Treas., J.F. Hartz Ltd. 1971–74; Country Finance Coordinator, Sandoz Canadian Companies; Dir., Master Builders Technologies Ltd.; Mem., Candn. & prov. assns. of Pharmacy; Pharmaceutical Manufacturers' Assn. (former Chair, Fin. Section); Financial Executives' Inst.; Montreal Bd. of Trade; Candn. C. of C. (former Dir.); Swiss Candn. C. of C. (former Dir.); West Island C. of C.; recreations: curling, golf; clubs: Whitlock Golf & Country (Dir.); Office: 385 Bouchard Blvd., Dorval, Que. H9S 1A9.

**SIRRS, Robert Douglas,** B.A., B.J.; foreign service officer; b. Toronto, Ont. 18 May 1930; s. Robert Raymond and Consuelo (Spangler) S.; e. Am. High Sch., Buenos Aires, Argentina; Pickering Coll., Newmarket, Ont.; Carleton Univ., B.A., B.J.; m. Mary Margaret, d. Dr. A. B. Lucas, London, Ont., 29 Dec. 1956; children: Laurel Margaret, Reid Douglas, Owen Lucas; former Consul General of Canada in Atlanta, Ga. to S.E. USA, Puerto Rico and US Virgin Islands; Clk., Maclaren Advertising Co., Ottawa, 1950–53; Area Supvr. (Mexico, Colombia and Caribbean), Canadian Coleman Co., 1954–56; apptd. to Trade Commr. Service, Ottawa, 1956; Asst. Comm. Secy., Caracas, 1957–60; Consul and Trade Commr., New York, Defence Production Sharing Liaison Offr., 1960–64; Comm. Secy., Pakistan also accredited to Afghanistan, 1964–66; Chargé d'Affaires, Guatemala, & Commercial Counsellor to Central America & Panama, 1966–68; Consul and Sr. Trade Commr., Chicago, 1968–70; Acting Consul General and Trade Commr. 1970–71; Dir., Regional Marketing & Operations Trade Commissioner Service 1971–72; Counsellor, (Comm.), Candn. Embassy, Mexico, 1972–76; Dir. European Bureau, Dept. of Industry, Trade & Comm., 1976–79; Ambassador to Costa Rica, Panama, Nicaragua, Honduras and El Salvador, 1979–82; mem., Prof. Assn. Foreign Service Offrs.; recreations: sailing, tennis, skiing, camping; Clubs: University; Chicago Yacht.

**SISKIND, Barry,** B.A.; consultant/trainer; b. London, Ont. 3 Dec. 1946; s. Jack Allen and Esther Lorraine S.; e. McMaster Univ. B.A. 1972; m. Barbara 25 May 1980; children: Jillian, Geoffrey; N. Am.'s foremost sales trainer, speaker & best selling author specializing in helping companies that exhibit in trade/consumer shows; Mem., Candn. Assn. of Exposition Mgrs.; The Trade Show Bureau; author: 'The Successful Exhibitor' 1989; 'The Successful Exhibitors Handbook' 1990; 'The New Successful Exhibitor's Handbook' Revised ed. 1993; 'The Service Test' 1994; 'Making Contact: The Art of Networking' forthcoming 1995, and many bus. articles; Office: P.O. Box 38111, Castlewood Postal Outlet, 550 Eglinton Ave. W., Toronto, Ont. M5N 3A8.

**SISKIND, Robert Gary,** B.A., LL.B., Q.C., LL.D.; business executive/lawyer; b. London, Ont. 4 Aug. 1942; s. Abraham and Evelyn (Finkel) S.; e. Univ. of West. Ont. Law Sch., LL.B. 1965; Bar Adm. Course of Ont. 1967; m. Shelly d. Marie and Hyman Weisler 16 Aug. 1965; children: Catherine, Michael, Heather; FOUNDER & PRES., DECADE CORP. 1982– ; law practice, ending as Sr. Partner, Siskind, Cromarty 1967–82; part-time lectr., U.W.O. Law Sch.; Bar Adm. Course of Ont.; Pres., Quartel Mngt. Inc.; New England Hospitality Corp.; Q.C. 1980; var. constr. & restoration awards to Decade Corp.; Dir., London Community Foundation; Community Foundations of Canada; John Robarts Rsch. Inst.; Lonventure Capital Corp.; Bd. of Govs., U.W.O. 1978–86 (Chrmn. 1985–86); Former BD. Mem., Un. Way of Greater London; Chrmn., London Community Foundation; Explorations (Canada Counc.); Or Shalom Synagogue; Ont. Council of Regents; Pres. London Jewish Federation; John Robarts Rsch. Inst.; Steering Mem., Nat. Forum on Post-Sec. Edn.; Chrmn., Counc. of Chrmn., Ont. Univs. & Colls.; author of profl.

articles; recreations: golf, skiing, scuba, swimming; Clubs: University, London Hunt & Country; Wingate Lodge & Country; Home: 1498 Stoneybrook Cres., London, Ont. N5X 1C5; Office: 248 Pall Mall St., Ste. 400, London, Ont. N6A 5P6.

**SISLER, Rebecca Jean,** R.C.A.; sculptor; author; b. Mount Forest, Ont. 16 Oct. 1932; d. Byron Cooper and Mildred (Ramsden) Sisler; e. Anne St. Pub. Sch. and Belleville (Ont.) Coll. Inst. 1947; St. Thomas (Ont.) Coll. Inst. 1951; Ont. Coll. of Art 1951–52 (scholarship winner both yrs.); Royal Danish Acad. Fine Arts 1952–54; Curator, Erindale Campus Art Gallery, Univ. of Toronto 1986– ; Cultural Attaché to the Gov.-Gen. of Can. 1982–84; Extve. Dir., Royal Candn. Acad. of Arts 1978–82 (el. mem. 1973, mem. Nat. Counc. 1977–78); rec'd Can. Council Grant 1959 to visit Nubian treasures Upper Egypt; various visits Mayan and Incan sites; sculpture comns. incl. 'The Minstrels' Centennial Park St. Thomas, Ont. 1967; large walnut cross and candlesticks St. Paul's Ang. Cath. London, Ont. 1968; rep. in many private colls. across Can.; author 'The Girls: A Biography of Frances Loring and Florence Wyle' 1972; 'Passionate Spirits: A History of the Royal Canadian Academy of Arts 1880–1980'; 'Aquarelle! A History of the Canadian Society of Painters in Water Colour 1925–1985' 1986; various essays, articles; awarded 'Canadian Woman Artist of the Year' Medal, Ont. Soc. of Artists 1982; mem. Ont. Soc. Artists 1966; recreations: reading, walking, gardening, travel.

**SISSONS, Gordon H.,** B.Sc.; company chairman; b. Medicine Hat, Alberta 27 Jan. 1920; s. Herbert J. and Lissa R. Sissons; e. Public and High Schs., Medicine Hat, Alta.; Univ. of Alberta, B.Sc. (Mining Engn.) 1942; m. Isabelle D., d. Roy E. Newcombe, Medicine Hat, 28 June 1945; children: Wendy R., Clayton H.; CHAIRMAN, I-XL INDUSTRIES LTD. and associated Co's.; joined present interests in 1945; Past Pres., Medicine Hat Chamber Comm.; Freemason (Shrine); Presbyterian; recreations: hunting, golf, skiing; Home: 320 First St. S.E., Medicine Hat, Alta. T1A 0A6; Office: P.O. Box 70, Medicine Hat, Alta. T1A 7E7.

**SITAR, Daniel Samuel,** B.Sc.Pharm., M.Sc., Ph.D.; university professor; b. Fort William, Ont. 1 May 1944; s. Henry Andrew and Victoria (Jackimec) S.; e. Univ. of Manitoba B.Sc.Pharm. 1966, M.Sc. 1968, Ph.D. 1972; m. Maureen Elizabeth d. Andrew and Louise Crump 8 June 1968; children: Jamie Andrew, Scott Edward; PROFESSOR, CLINICAL PHARMACOLOGY SECTION, UNIV. OF MANITOBA 1987– ; Lic. Pharm., Prov. of Man. 1966– ; Asst. Prof., McGill Univ. 1973–78; Univ. of Man. 1978–80; Assoc. Prof. 1980–87; Rosenstadt Prof., Univ. of Toronto 1989–90; Edit. Bd., 'Clin. Pharm. & Therapeutics' 1986– ; Expert Adv. Ctte. on Drug Bioavailability, Health & Welfare Canada 1986– ; Dir., Program in Human Drug Studies, Internal Med., Univ. of Man. 1990– ; cons. to pharm. indus., govt. & legal profession with respect to drug related issues; Rh Inst. Award for outstanding contbns. to scholarship & rsch. in health sci. 1980; K.M. Piafsky Young Investigator Award in Clin. Pharm. 1981; Vice-Pres., Bd. of Dir., Preparatory Div. Assn., Sch. of Music, Univ. of Man.; Mem., Pharm. Soc. of Can. 1974– ; Soc. of Toxicology of Canada & Candn. Soc. for Clin. Invest. 1976– ; Am. Soc. for Pharm. & Exper. Therapeutics 1977– ; Candn. Soc. for Clin. Pharm. 1980– ; Am. Soc. for Clin. Pharm. & Therapeutics 1981– ; Gerontol. Soc. of Am. (Fellow) 1983– ; author/co-author of over 110 sci. manuscripts & more than 150 abstracts; recreations: tennis, golf; Home: 443 Bredin Dr., Winnipeg, Man. R2K 1N8; Office: Winnipeg, Man. R3E 0W3.

**SIVELL, John Norman,** B.A., M.Ed., Ph.D.; university professor; b. Toronto, Ont. 14 June 1946; s. Arthur Leslie and Josephine Ruth (Burgess) S.; e. Cedarbrae S.S. 1965 (Ont. Scholar); Trinity Coll., Univ. of Toronto B.A. 1969; King's Coll., Cambridge Univ., dipl. Engl. Studies 1970; Univ. of East Anglia Norwich Ph.D. 1974; Univ. of Wales M.Ed. 1983; m. Lucienne d. Georges and Albertine Issaly 1971; children: Vincent, Florent; PROF. OF APPLIED LANGUAGE STUDIES, BROCK UNIV. 1991– ; Asst. Prof., Jundi Shapur Univ. Iran 1974–78 (Dept. Chair 1975–77); Brit. Counc. English Lang. Teaching freelance cons. Iran 1977–78 & Morocco 1980–82; Asst. Prof. & Lang. Lab. Supvr., Univ. of Riyadh Saudi Arabia 1978–79; sabbatical year 1979–80; Maître de Conf., Rabat Fac. of Letters, Morocco 1980–82; freelance transl. & sess. lectr., Inst. for Am. Univs., Aix-en-Provence France 1982–83; Instr., present univ. 1983–84; Lectr., Asst. Prof., Assoc. Prof. 1984–91; Dir. of Non-Credit Programs 1986–88; Chair 1988–89, 1990–92; various scholarships incl. Can. Counc. doct. fellowship 1970–73; Bd. Dir., TESL Assn. of Ont. 1988–92; Ed. Bd., 'Language Teaching Strategies' 1991– ; Advisory Bd., Alpha Ontario 1992– ; Founding Organizer, Annual Colloquium on Lang. Teaching & Learning 1984; Symp. on Computer-Assisted Language Learning 1987; 1st N. Am. Conf. on Freinet Pedagogy 1990; Mem., TESL Can.; Internat. Assn. of Teachers of English as a Second Lang.; Internat. Reading Assn.; Candn. Assn. of Applied Linguistics; translator: Freinet: 'The Wisdom of Matthew' 1990; 'Education Through Work' 1993; co-trans. & co-ed.: 'Cooperative Learning and Social Change' 1990; author: 'From Near and Far' 1991 and num. articles, book chaps. & reviews; co-author: 'Jigsaw Reading and Writing Activities' 1993; recreations: gardening, fishing; Home: 95 Albert St., St. Catharines, Ont. L2R 2H4; Office: St. Catharines, Ont. L2S 3A1.

**SIVERTZ, Bent Gestur,** O.B.E., B.A.; b. Victoria, B.C. 11 Aug. 1905; s. Christian and Elinborg (Samuelson) S.; e. Public and High Schs., Victoria, B.C.; Univ. of British Columbia, B.A.; Victoria Normal Sch. (Teachers Cert.); m. Barbara Isabel, d. O. B. Prael, Portland, Oregon, 9 July 1948; Seaman and Ships Offr. in Merchant Marine, 1922–32; taught school in B.C. 1936–39; war time service, Royal Canadian Navy as Lieut. and Lt. Cdr. RCNR 1939–46; in charge, Navigation Sch. 1940–44; command, HMCS KINGS'S (Officer Training Establishment of the Candn. Navy, Halifax) 1944–45; awarded Offr. of the British Empire 1945; Foreign Service Offr., Dept. of External Affairs, 1946–50; joined Northern Affairs Dept. in 1950 as Staff Offr. in Depy. Minister's Office; apptd. Chief of Arctic Div., 1954; Dir. of N. Adm. Br., Dept. of N. Affairs, 1957–63; Commr. of N.W.T., 1963–67 (retired); Freemason; Protestant; recreations: travel, outdoors, reading, carpentry, stone work; Clubs: Union (Victoria); Thermopylae (Victoria); Home: 1159 Beach Dr., Apt. 302, Victoria, B.C. V8S 2N2.

**SJORGEN, Keith H.,** B.A., F.I.C.B.; bank executive; b. Birmingham, England 31 May 1945; e. Solihull School, England; Carleton Univ. B.A. 1971; F.I.C.B.; m. Dorothy; two children; SENIOR VICE-PRESIDENT, TRUST AND INTERNATIONAL PRIVATE BANKING, PERSONAL & COMMERCIAL BANK, CANADIAN IMPERIAL BANK OF COMMERCE; NM Rothschild & Sons 1964–67; joined Candn. Imperial Bank of Commerce 1967; Pres., Transatlantic Trust Corp.; Dir., CIBC Trust Co. (Bahamas) Limited; CIBC Bank & Trust Co. (Channel Islands) Limited; CIBC Bank & Trust Co. (Cayman) Limited; Candn. Opera Co.; recreations: squash, photography; clubs: Albany, Fitness Inst., Singapore Cricket; Office: Commerce Court West-4, Toronto, Ont. M5L 1A2.

**SKAGEN, Donald Glenn,** B.A.; resources executive; b. Glendive, Montana 1 Oct. 1925; s. Leonard Bernard and Mable Luna (Baillet) S.; e. Washington State Univ., B.A. (Bus. Admin.) 1948; m. Annika D. d. Howard and Maria Thoreson 13 Dec. 1951; children: Eric, Dane, Peter, Suzanne; CHRMN. OF THE BD., MOHAWK OIL CO. LTD.; Chrmn. Alta-Can Telecom Inc.; Dir. Telus Corp.; Ind. Rlns. Mgr. Husky Oil 1952–57; Exec. Asst. to Pres., Royalite Oil Co. Ltd. 1957–60; founding owner present firm 1960 (Pres. & C.E.O. 1977–85); Hon. Dir. Calgary Stampeder Football Club; Candn. citizen since 1965; recreation: golf; Clubs: Ranchmen's; Willow Park Golf & Country; Penticton Golf; Vancouver Golf & Country; The Springs Golf & Country, Radium Hot Springs, B.C.; Home: 1216 Killearn Ave. S.W., Calgary, Alta. T2V 2N4.

**SKAPINKER, Mark;** computer industry executive; b. Johannesburg, S.A. 24 Sept. 1954; s. Julius and Rachel (Sacks) S.; e. Univ. of Witwatersrand; m. Hazel d. Ralph and Freda Lanesman 15 Aug. 1980; children: Lisa, Rafael, Joshua; CO-FOUNDER & PRES., DELRINA CORPORATION; Dir. of Development & Marketing, 'Batteries Included'; Co-Founder & Pres., Schematix Computer Systems Inc.; Bd. of Dir., Bialik School; author of software products: 'Thunder' and 'Portfolio'; recreation: swimming: Home: 407 Glencairn Ave., Toronto, Ont. M5J 1V4.

**SKELDING, Neil D.,** M.B.A.; pharmaceutical executive; b. Etobicoke, Ont. 8 Sept. 1963; s. Shirley Rosemary Montgomery; e. McMaster Univ. M.B.A. 1988; m. Lisa d. Derek and Joan Kelly 18 July 1992; FOUNDER & PRESIDENT, PHARMEX CONTAINMENT SERVICES INC. 1992– ; Financial Analyst & Acct. Mgr., Xerox Canada Finance Inc. 1988–91; Pres., Skel Financial Inc. 1991–92; present company provides mail-order prescriptions to Candn. orgns.; Dir., Skel Financial Inc.; Pharmex Containment Services Inc.; Opera Hamilton (Chair, Finance Ctte.); Mem., Pharmaceutical Sub-Ctte., Oakville, Ont.; Project Business Consultant, Jr. Achievement; recreations: tennis, golf, alpine skiing; club: Cedar Springs Tennis and Athletic; Home: 227 Villagewood Rd., Oakville, Ont. L6L 5S6; Office: 353 Iroquois Shore Rd., Oakville, Ont. L6H 1M3.

**SKELTON, David,** M.B., B.S., D.M., M.R.C.P., M.R.C.S., M.R.C.G.P., F.A.C.P.; physician; university professor; b. Canterbury, Eng. 18 Nov. 1937; s. Robert Ernest and Florence Elizabeth May (Gilham) S.; e. King's coll., London Univ.; Westminster Hosp., London, Eng.; Westminster Hosp., London, Eng.; m. Mary Frances d. Edwin and Eileen Russell 12 Aug. 1961; children: Louisa Mary, Matthew David; PROF., DEPTS. OF MED. AND HEALTH SERVICES ADMIN. & COMMUNITY MED., UNIV. OF ALTA. 1980– ; House Surgeon, Westminster Children's Hosp. 1963– ; House Physician, Royal Victoria Hosp., Bournemouth 1964; Res. Pathologist, Westminster Hosp. 1965–66; Sr. Lectr., Univ. of Southampton 1968–73; Assoc. Prof. of Med., Univ. of Man. 1974–79; spl. cons. in geriatric med., Govt. of Alta.; Anglican; ordained priest, Anglican Church of Canada, 1978; author of numerous publs. in the field of geriatric med.; recreations: bird-watching, music, rugby football; Home: 9906 – 144 St., Edmonton, Alta. T5N 2T5; Office: 1160 – 10830 Jasper Ave., Edmonton, Alta. T5N 2T5.

**SKELTON, Robin,** M.A., F.R.S.L. (1966); university professor; poet; b. Easington, E. Yorks., Eng. 12 Oct. 1925; s. Cyril Frederick William and Eliza (Robins) S.; e. Pocklington Grammar Sch., Eng., 1936–43; Christ's Coll., Cambridge Univ. 1943–44; Leeds Univ., B.A. (1st Class Hons., Eng. Lang & Lit.) 1950, M.A. 1951; m. Sylvia Mary, d. P.W. Jarrett, Feb. 1957; children: Nicholas John, Alison Jane, Eleanor Brigid; Prof., Dept. Creative Writing, Univ. Victoria (Chrmn. 1973–76) Retired 1991; Prof. Dept. English 1966–73; Assistant Lecturer, University of Manchester, 1951–54; Lectr. 1954–63; joined present Univ. as Assoc. Prof. 1963; Dir., Creative Writing Programme, 1967; Visiting Centennial Lectr., Univ. of Mass., 1962–63; taught Summer Sch., Victoria Coll., B.C., 1962; Visiting Prof., Univ. of Mich., summer 1967; Examiner in Eng. Lit. for N. Univs. Matric. Bd., Eng., 1954–60 (Chrmn. of Examiners 1958–60); Dir., The Lotus Press 1950–51 and the Pharos Press since 1972; co-founder, Peterloo Group of Poets and Painters, 1957; founding mem. and 1st Hon. Secy., Manchester Inst. of Contemporary Arts, 1960 (Chrmn. Programme Comte. 1960–62); served with RAF in Eng., Pakistan, India and Ceylon, 1944–47; rank Sgt.; Poetry Critic 1956–57 and Theatre Critic 1958–60, 'Manchester Guardian'; has done many broadcasts for BBC, CBC and All India Radio; Art Columnist, 'Victoria Daily Times,' 1964–66; poetry readings given at various univs. in Eng., U.S., Ireland, Sweden and Can.; other activities incl. film making, collage (one-man show in Victoria 1966, 1968, 1980), libretti (composed words for 2 motets and 1 cantata), typography and book design, poetics; author poetry: 'Patmos and Other Poems' 1955; 'Third Day Lucky' 1958; 'Two Ballads of the Muse' 1960; 'The Dark Window' 1962; 'Valedictory Poem' 1963; 'An Irish Gathering' 1964; 'A Ballad of Billy Barker' 1965; 'Inscriptions' 1967; 'The Hold of Our Hands' 1968; 'Selected Poems 1947–67' 1968; 'Because of This' 1968; 'An Irish Album' 1969; 'The Selected Poems of Georges Zuk' 1969; 'The Hunting Dark' 1971; 'Private Speech' 1971; 'A Different Mountain' 1971; 'Remembering Synge' 1971; 'Timelight' 1974; Vol. 2 Georges Zuk 'The Underwear of the Unicorn' 1975; 'Callsigns' 1976; 'Because of Love' 1977; 'Landmarks' 1979; 'Collected Shorter Poems 1947–77' 1981; 'Limits' 1981; 'De Nihilo' 1982; 'Zuk' 1982; 'Wordsong' 1983; 'Distances' 1985; 'Collected Longer Poems 1947–1977' 1985; 'Openings' 1988; 'Words for Witches' 1990; 'Popping Fuchsias' 1992; 'Islands' 1993; 'A Formal Music' 1993; criticism: 'John Ruskin: The Final Years' 1955; 'The Poetic Pattern' 1956; 'Cavalier Poets' 1960; 'Poetry' 1963; 'The Practice of Poetry' 1971; 'The Writings of J.M. Synge' 1971; 'Poet's Calling' 1975; 'Poetic Truth' 1978; 'Herbert Siebner: A Monograph' 1979; 'Celtic Contraries' 1990; verse translation: 'Two Hundred Poems from the Greek Anthology' 1971; George Faludy 'Selected Poems 1933–1980' 1985; George Faludy 'Corpses, Brats and Cricket Music' 1987; 'F. Garcia Lorca: Songs and Ballads' 1992; ed., 'The Malahat Review' 1967–1983; 'J.M. Synge: Translations' 1961; 'J.M. Synge: Four Plays and The Aran Islands' 1962; 'J.M. Synge: Collected Works' Vol. 1 Poems 1962; 'David Gascoyne: Collected Poems' 1965; 'J.M. Synge: Riders to the Sea' 1969; 'David Gascoyne: Collected Verse Translations' (with Allan Clodd) 1971; 'Synge/Petrarch' 1971; 'The Collected Plays of Jack B. Yeats' 1971; 'The Selected Writings of Jack B. Yeats' 1991; anthols.: 'Leeds University Poetry 1949' 1950; 'Six Irish Poets' 1962; 'Five Poets of the Pacific Northwest' 1964; 'Poetry of the Thirties' 1964; 'Poetry of the Forties' 1968; 'Introductions from an Island' 1969, 1971, 1973, 1974, 1977,

1980; 'Six Poets of British Columbia' 1980; 'Earth, Air, Fire, Water' (with Margaret Blackwood) 1990; for schs.: 'Viewpoint: An Anthology of Poetry' 1962; 'Edward Thomas: Selected Poems' 1962; 'Selected Poems of Byron' 1964; occult: 'Spellcraft' 1978; 'Talismanic Magic' 1985; 'The Practice of Witchcraft Today' 1988; 'A Gathering of Ghosts (with Jean Kozokari 1989); 'The Magical Practice of Talismans' 1991; biography: 'J.M. Synge and His World' 1971; social history: 'They Call It The Cariboo' 1980; fiction: 'The Man Who Sang In His Sleep' 1984; 'The Parrot Who Could' 1987; Telling the Tale' 1987; The Fires of the Kindred' 1987; 'Hanky Panky' 1990; 'Aphorisms: A Devious Dictionary' 1991; 'Higgledy Piggledy' 1992; autobiography: 'Memoirs of a Literary Blockhead' 1988; 'Portrait of My Father' 1989; symposia: 'The World of W.B. Yeats' (with A. Saddlemyer); 'Irish Renaissance' (with D.R. Clark), 1965; 'Herbert Read: A Memorial Symposium' 1970; other writings incl. articles on 'Rhyme' and 'Poetry' in 'Encyclopedia Britannica'; also poetry, articles and reviews in various mags.; mem., Writer's Union Can. (Chrmn. 1982–83); The Limners; The Hawthorne Soc. of Arts & Letters; Home: 1255 Victoria Ave., Victoria, B.C. V8S 4P3.

**SKEOCH, Iris Marie,** B.A.; b. Regina, Sask. 5 June 1956; d. Llewellyn G. and Irene G. (Bucsis) S.; e. Nelson H.S.; Univ. of Guelph B.A. 1978 (Dean's Honour Roll); Univ. of Toronto 1979–87; m. G. Scott s. Holly and George Tupholme 7 Sept. 1985; children: Will Walker Tupholme, Sophie Rae Tupholme; CO-PUBLISHER AND EDITOR-IN-CHIEF, HARPERCOLLINS PUBLISHERS 1991– ; W.H. Smith Bookstores 1979–81; Production Editor/Project Editor, Prentice-Hall Can. 1981–85; Acquisitions Ed., Prentice-Hall Can. 1985–88; extve. Ed., Penguin Books Can. 1988–91; has worked with many wonderful writers incl. Timothy Findley, John Brady, Charles Foran, Thomas King, Stuart McLean, Ronald Wright; Mem., Book Publishers' Profl. Assn.; Office: 55 Avenue Rd., Toronto, Ont. M5R 3L2.

**SKIDMORE, Thomas Ernest;** business executive; b. Vancouver, B.C. 20 Oct. 1949; s. Arthur and Elsie (McLellan) S.; e. Trinity College 1968; m. Lorraine d. Harold and Thea Goodman 6 Feb. 1971; children: Cary, Lisa; VICE CHAIR, FINANCE & INVESTMENTS & C.E.O., COMMUNICATIONS GROUP, TCG INTERNATIONAL INC.; various positions, Trans Canada Glass Ltd. (now TCG Internat.) 1968– ; Vice Chair & C.E.O., Glentel Inc. (formerly Glenayre Electronics Ltd.) 1990–92; Pres. & C.E.O. 1992– ; Dir., TCG Internat.; Glentel Inc.; Franann holdings Ltd.; Autostock Inc.; Glenayre Technologies Inc.; Mem., Greater Vancouver Adv. Bd., Salvation Army; Adv. Council, Trinity Western Univ.; Variety Club; recreation: golf, fishing, skiing, music, clubs: Royal Vancouver Yacht, Hollyburn Country, Terminal City, Vancouver Golf; Address: 4710 Kingsway, 28th fl., Vancouver, B.C. V5H 4M2.

**SKILLING, H. Gordon,** A.T.C.M., M.A., Ph.D., F.R.S.C. (1970) LL.D.; university professor; b. Toronto, Ont. 28 Feb. 1912; s. William Watt and Alice (Stevenson) S.; e. Harbord Coll. Inst., Toronto, Ont.; Univ. Coll., Univ. of Toronto, B.A. (Pol. Science and Econ.) 1934; Rhodes Scholar for Ont. 1934; Christ Church, Oxford Univ., 1934–36, B.A., M.A. (Philos., Pol. and Econ.); Sch. of Slavonic and East European Studies, Univ. of London, Ph.D. (European Hist.) 1936–40; M.A. (Hon.) Dartmouth Coll., 1951; LL.D. (Hon.), Toronto, 1982; Dr. (h.c.) Prague 1990; m. Sara Conard (dec'd 1990) d. Horace Bright, 16 Oct. 1937; two s., David Bright, Peter Conard; PROF. EMERITUS UNIV. OF TORONTO 1981– ; Prof. of Pol. Science, Univ. of Toronto, 1959–81; Dir., Centre for Russian and E. European Studies there, 1963–75; with Czechoslovak Broadcasting Corp., 1938; B.B.C., 1939–40; Asst., United Coll., Winnipeg, Man., 1940–41; Asst. Prof. Pol. Science, Univ. of Wisconsin, 1941–47; Dept. of Govt., Dartmouth Coll., 1947–51 and Prof. there 1951–59; Sr. Fellow, Russian Inst., Columbia Univ. (on leave) 1949–51 and Visiting Prof. there 1952–53; Internat. Service, C.B.C., Supervisor of Central European Broadcasts, 1944–45 (on leave); U.N. Commentator, C.B.C., 1946 (on leave); Publications: 'Canadian Representation Abroad' 1945; 'Communism, National and International' 1964; 'The Governments of Communist East Europe' 1966; 'Czechoslovakia's Interrupted Revolution' 1976; 'Charter 77 and Human Rights in Czechoslovakia' 1981; editor: 'Czechoslovakia 1918–1988, Seventy Years From Independence' 1991; co-ed.: (with Peter Brock) 'The Czech Renascence of the Nineteenth Century: Essays in Honour of Otakar Odlozilik' 1970; (with Franklyn Griffiths) 'Interest Groups in Soviet Politics' 1971; (with Vilém Prečan) 'Parallel Politics: Essays from Czech and Slovak Samizdat' (special issue International Journ. of Politics, Spring 1981); 'Listy z Prahy, 1937–40' (samizdat in Czechoslovakia) 1985, Toronto 1989; 'Samizdat and an Independent Society in Central and Eastern Europe' 1989; (with Paul Wilson) 'Civic Freedom in Central Europe, Voices from Czechoslovakia' 1991; Hon. Life Mem. Candn. Assn. of Slavists; Amer. Assn. for Advancement of Slavic Studies; Candn. Inst. Internat. Affairs; Hon. Mem. Czechoslovak Soc. for Arts and Sciences, New York; mem. Ed. Bd.: Cross Currents; Killam Award, Canada Counc. 1971–72; Innis-Gérin Medal, Royal Soc. of Canada 1981; Susan Gross Solomon, ed. 'Pluralism in the Soviet Union: Essays in Honour of H. Gordon Skilling' 1983; Thomas G. Masaryk award, Czech. Assn. of Can. 1984; Award for distinguished contributions to Slavic Studies, Am. Assoc. for the Advancement of Slavic Studies 1988; recipient, Komenský Medal, Cominius Univ., Bratislava 1990; Order of White Lion, from President Havel, Czechoslovakia 1992; František Palacký Medal and Hlavka Medal, Czechoslovak Acad. of Sciences 1992; elected mem., Academic Assembly, Czech. Academy of Sciences 1994; Home: 40 Sylvan Valleyway, #630, Toronto, Ont. M5M 4M3.

**SKINNER, Cyril,** B.A.; publisher; b. Beverley, Yorks., Eng. 8 March 1920; s. Herbert and Violet (Davison) S.; e. Owen Sound (Ont.) Coll. Inst., 1939; Toronto Teachers' Coll., 1940; Univ. of Toronto, B.A. (Hons. Hist.) 1948; Ont. Coll. of Educ. 1948; m. Sydney Joyce (Woodhouse), 8 Oct. 1949; two s.: Brian and Colin; PRESIDENT, J.M. DENT & SONS (CANADA) LTD.; Dir. Malaby Holdings Ltd. London, Eng.; served with R.C.A.F., 400 Sqdn. 1940–45; with Book Society of Canada 1948–50; joined present Co. 1951; Anglican; recreations: golf, curling; Clubs: Bowmanville Golf & Country; York Downs Golf & Country; Home: R.R.#5, Bowmanville, Ont.; Office: 68 King Street East, Bowmanville, Ont.; Mailing Address: Box 374, Bowmanville, Ont. L1C 3L1.

**SKINNER, David Stewart,** B.Sc.; association executive; b. Ottawa, Ont. 19 May 1953; s. Stewart I. and Eleanor Ruth (Carmichael) S.; e. Carleton Univ. B.Sc. 1976; Tulane Univ.; m. Karen d. Dr. M. Patrick 21 Oct. 1984; PRES. NONPRESCRIPTION DRUG MFRS. ASSN. OF CAN. 1983– ; Rsch. Assoc. Candn. Internat. Devel. Agency 1976–77; Publs. Offr. Nat. Rsch. Council Can. 1977–79; Mgr. present Assn. 1979–83; Pres. Council on Family Health in Can.; Dir., World Fedn. Proprietary Med. Mfrs.; Council on Drug Abuse; mem. Candn. Pharm. Assn. (Ed. Bd.); Am. Med. Writers Assn.; Chem. Inst. Can., Pharm. Subgroup; Inst. Assn. Execs.; Profl. Speakers Assn.; co-author various articles sci. jours.; recreations: tennis, golf, oenology; Home: 4 Wellfleet Cres., Nepean, Ont.; Office: 830, 1600 Carling Ave., Ottawa, Ont. K1Z 8R7.

**SKINNER, Duncan S.,** C.A., B.Comm., B.A.; financial executive; b. Aberdeen, Scotland 3 March 1948; s. Duncan Stewart and Amelia Cobb (Ingram-Skinner) S.; e. York Univ. B.A. 1971; Univ. of Windsor B.Comm. 1973; C.A. 1975; m. Carole d. Rod and Muriel Nicoll 1 Oct. 1977; children: Fiona Lynne, Amanda Kirsteen; VICE PRESIDENT FINANCE, CANADIAN ULTRAMAR LIMITED, ULTRAMAR CANADA INC. 1991– ; Coopers & Lybrand C.A. 1975; various positions with Ultramar Canada 1979–84; General Manager, Group Acctg., Am. Ultramar Limited 1984–87; Dir., Financial Control, Candn. Ultramar Limited/Ultramar Canada Inc. 1987–88; Corp. Controller 1988–91; Dir., Gale's Gas Bars Ltd.; Geo. Williamson Fuels Ltd.; Oceanic Tankers Agency Ltd.; Ultramar Acceptance Inc.; Ultramar Credit Corp.; Universal Terminals Ltd.; Mem., C.I.C.A.; I.C.A.P.; St. Andrew's Soc. (Toronto); Royal Scottish Country Dance Soc. (Toronto & Montreal); recreations: golf, reading, Scottish Country dancing; clubs: Beaconsfield Golf; Office: 2200 McGill College, Montreal, Que. H3A 3L3.

**SKINNER, Thompson Elson,** B.Comm., C.A.; financial services executive; b. New York, N.Y. 16 Feb. 1949; s. Charles Elson and Marjorie (Waunderlich) S.; e. Loyola College B.Comm. (Hons.) 1973; McGill Univ., grad. dipl. in public acctg. 1975; C.A. 1977; m. Diane d. Dr. Rosario and Helene Rajotte 20 July 1968; children: Steven, Camille; VICE-PRES., FINANCE & ADMINISTRATION and CHIEF FINANCIAL OFFR., FEDERAL BUSINESS DEVELOPMENT BANK 1994– ; Shift Authorization Supvr., Chargex, Royal Bank of Canada 1970–73; Arthur Andersen & Co. 1973–80; Dir. of Auditing for Canada, Sun Life Asur. Co. of Canada 1980–83; Vice Pres., Finance & Admin. 1983–87; Vice Pres., Systems Strategy (Corp.) 1987–89; Vice-Pres., Finance for Great Britain & Ireland 1989–91; Vice-Pres., Financial Mgmnt. Information 1991–94; Mem., Candn. Inst. of C.A.s; Ont. Inst. of C.A.s; Order of C.A.s of Que.; Past Pres. & Chair, Bd. of Dir., Montreal Childrens Hosp. 1980–88; Dir., Montreal Childrens Hosp. Foundation 1980–88; recreations: golf, swimming; clubs: Dundas Valley Golf & Curling; Office: 777 Bay St., Toronto, Ont. M5G 2C8.

**SKOGGARD, Ross Mackay;** writer; publisher; b. Canton, China 4 Apl. 1949; s. Bengt Bruno and Mary Jean Mackay (Ross) S.; e. Bard Coll. Annandale-on-Hudson, N.Y.; Columbia Univ.; m. Esther d. Henry and Ruth Nordin 13 Nov. 1983 (sep.); one s. Nathaniel Henry Nordin; freelance writer maj. Candn. mags. and newspapers since 1975; staff writer 'Artforum' 1976–78; sr. ed. 'Print Collector's Newsletter' 1984–85; host, writer 'Art Buzz' cable TV series contemporary art, N.Y. 1983–85; ed.-in-chief 'Subway Link' Toronto 1986–87; antiques columnist 'Toronto Star' 1988– ; pub./ed. 'Sposa 2000' 1989– ; author: 'Collecting the Past: A Guide to Canadian Antiques' 1992; artist-in-residence New York Pub. Lib. 1983–84; recipient Author's Award arts & entertainment writing for 'Art of the State', 'Equinox' 1988; anthologized 'Looking Critically: 21 Years of Artforum Magazine' 1984; 'Greta Garbo' in 'Brushes with Greatness' 1989; Dir. Go Home Bay Assn. 1987–88; recreations: sailing, skiing; Address: 413, 77 Mowat Ave., Toronto, Ont. M6K 3E3.

**SKOREYKO, Alan M.H.,** B.Comm., M.B.A.; real estate executive; b. Edmonton, Alta. 16 July 1950; s. William Mike and Helen Marta (Dewald) S.; e. Univ. of Alberta B.Comm. 1974, M.B.A. 1975; m. Mary J. d. Francis Milne Cameron 4 Aug. 1984; children: Matthew, Joshua, Nicolas, Katherin, Sean; GENERAL MANAGER & CHIEF OPERATING OFFR., EDMONTON NORTHLANDS 1994– ; Extve. Asst. to Chief Deputy Min., Alberta Transportation 1975–79; Vice-Pres., N. Alta., Nu-West Devel. Corp. 1979–87; Partner, Devcon Group Limited 1987–89; General Manager, N. Alta., Intrawest Developments 1989–91; Pres., Crosspoint Developments Inc. 1991–93; General Mgr., Homes by Jayman, Edmonton 1993–94; Pres., Urban Development Inst. (Alberta) 1982, '87, '90 (Chair 1983, '88; Dir. 1988, '91); Dir., Nat. Assn. of Industrial and Office Parks 1982; Service Award, Alta. Summer Games 1989; Service & Achievement Award, Minor Hockey 1991; Dir., Edmonton Northlands 1990–94; Sr. Volunteer, Ducks Unlimited Canada; Dir., Elk Island P.C. Assn.; recreations: golf, skiing, fly-fishing; Home: 103 Manor Place, Sherwood Park, Alta. T8A 0S9; Office: Edmonton Northlands, Box 1480, Edmonton, Alta. T5J 2N5.

**SKOUTAJAN, Rev. Hanns Felix,** B.A., B.D., D.D.; retired minister; b. Czechoslovakia 13 March 1929; s. Felix and Gertrude (Mahner) S.; e. Queen's Unv., B.A. 1953; Queen's Theol. Coll., B.D. 1956; Post-grad. studies, Univ. of Muenster, West Germany & Ecumenical Inst., Switzerland; m. Marlene d. Fred and Helen Davison 6 Sept. 1958; children: Karla, Stephen; Minister, Knox United Church 1990–93 (Retired); Chaplain, Dalhousie Univ., 1957–60; Dir., World Refugee Comm., Un. Ch. 1960; Minister, Cooke's Un. Ch. 1960–64; Almonte Un. Ch. 1964–69, Wesley-Mimico Un. Ch. 1969–74; Minister, St. James-Bond United Church 1974–90; Comnr., Un. Ch. 1966, 1968, 1984, 1986, 1988, 1990, 1992; Initiator (1970) of relationship between United Church of Canada and Evangelical Church of the Union of Germany culminating in covenant partnership (1992); Chrmn., Ctte. on Ch. & Internat. Aff., Gen. Counc. 1979; Pres., Alumni Assn., Queen's Theol. Coll. 1982–84; Toronto Conf., Un. Ch. 1984–85; Ont. Coalition for Public Edn. 1985; Chrmn., Humber Area Residential Placement House 1972–74; B. Mem., Project Ploughshares; Mem, Bd. of Mgmt., Queen's Theol. Coll. 1983–92; Chairperson, Toronto South Presbytery, United Church of Can. 1986–87; mem. Adv. Ctte. to the Moderator, United Ch. of Can. 1986–88; Exec. Gen. Council, United Church of Canada 1990–94; Mem. Bd. of Dirs., Georgian Institute of Spirituality 1993– ; Mem., Christians Associated for Relationship with Eastern Europe 1993– ; Mem. Co-ordinating Ctte., Ont. Conferences (United Church) 1994– ; author & composer of numerous pub. hymns; broadcaster, 'Moments of Meditation,' CFRB 1983–85; recreations: camping; Address: 1940 - 8th Ave. E., Owen Sound, Ont. N4K 3C3.

**ŠKVORECKÝ, Josef Václav,** C.M., Ph.Dr., F.R.S.C.; writer; educator; b. Náchod, Bohemia 27 Sept. 1924; s. Josef Karel and Anna Marie (Kuráová) S.; e. Státní reálné gymnasium Náchod 1943; Charles Univ. Prague Ph.Dr. 1951; m. Salivarová d. Jaroslav Salivar Zdenka 31 March 1958; PROF. EMERITUS OF ENGLISH, UNIV. OF TORONTO 1990– ; Ed., Anglo-Am. Dept. Odeon Publishers, Prague 1953–56; Asst. Ed.-in-Chief, World Literature Magazine, Prague 1956–59; free-lance writer Prague 1963–68; Visiting Lectr. in Eng. Univ. of

Toronto 1968, Writer-in-Residence and Visiting Lectr. 1970, Assoc. Prof. of Eng. 1971–75, Assoc. Prof. Drama Centre 1972–75, Prof. 1975–90 (retired); Ed., Sixty-Eight Publishers Corp. Toronto 1972– ; Guggenheim Fellow 1980, recipient Neustadt Internat. Prize for Lit. 1980; Silver Award for Best Fiction Publ. in Candn. Mags. in 1980, 1981; Fellow, Roy. Soc. of Can. 1984; recipient of the 1985 City of Toronto Book Award; recipient, Governor General's Award 1985; D. Hum. Litt. (hon. causa), State Univ. of New York 1986; Ph.Dr., hon. causa, Masaryk Univ., Brno; Czechoslovak Order of the White Lion 1990; Echoing Green Foundation Literary Prize 1990; Dr. of Laws honoris causa, The Univ. of Calgary 1992; Dr. of Letters honoris causa, Univ. of Toronto 1992; Mem., Order of Canada 1992; author, novels (in Czech. and transl. into numerous langs.): 'The Cowards' 1958; 'The End of the Nylon Age' 1967; 'Miss Silver's Past' 1969; 'The Tank Corps' 1969; (English as 'The Republic of Whores' 1993); filmed 1991 Bonton, Prague 'The Miracle Game' 1972; 'The Swell Season' 1975; filmed 1993 Czech TV, Prague; 'The End of Lieutenant Borůvka' 1975; 'The Engineer of Human Souls' 1977; 'The Return of Lieutenant Borůvka' 1980; 'Dvorak in Love' 1986; 'The Bride from Texas' 1992; short story colls.: 'The Menorah' 1964; 'The Life of High Society' 1965; 'The Mournful Demeanor of Lieutenant Borůvka' 1966; 'A Babylonian Story' 1967; 'The Bitter World' 1969; 'Sins for Father Knox' 1973; filmed 1992 Czech TV, Prague; 'Oh, My Papa!' 1972; plays: 'The New Men and Women' CBC Radio 1977; 'God in Your House' 1980 (1st Prize Multicultural Theatre Festival Hamilton 1980); essays: 'Reading Detective Stories' 1965; 'They-Which Is We' 1968; 'All the Bright Young Men and Women' 1972; 'Working Overtime' 1979; 'Jiři Menzel and the History of the Closely Watched Trains' 1982; 'Talkin' Moscow Blues' 1988; travelogue: 'A Tall Tale About America' 1970; poetry: 'Do Not Despair' 1979; 'The Girl From Chicago' 1980; translator numerous publs. into Czech.; ed. various publs.; contrib. to many Czech. and Slovak lit., film, music and cultural mags.; honorary mem., Czechoslovak Soc. Arts & Sciences 1988; author various TV and feature film scripts; numerous articles, reviews, acad. addresses (Am. and Candn. univs.); over 190 lit. talks on Voice of Am. since 1973; mem. Candn. Writers' Union; Authors' League Am.; Crime Writers of Can.; Mystery Writers of Am.; The Internat. P.E.N. Club, Can. Branch; Czechoslovak Nat. Assn. Can. (mem. Presidium); Council Free Czechoslovakia (mem. Presidium); recreation: swing music.

**SLADE, Bernard;** playwright; b. St. Catharines, Ont. 2 May 1930; s. Frederick Newbound and Bessie Harriet (Walbourne) S.; e. John Ruskin Grammar Sch. Croydon, Eng.; Caernarvon (N. Wales) Grammar Sch.; m. Jill d. Harry and Amy Hancock 25 July 1953; children: Laurel, Christopher; began career as actor 1949 appearing theatres Toronto, Kingston, Vineland and CBC TV; began writing 1957 some 20 teleplays CBC TV and subsequently U.S. networks; spent 12 yrs. writing and creating various TV series Los Angeles incl.: 'Love on a Rooftop'; 'The Flying Nun'; 'Bridget Loves Bernie'; 'The Partridge Family'; author following plays: 'Simon Says Get Married' 1960 (produced Crest Theatre Toronto 1960); 'A Very Close Family' 1962 (produced Man. Theatre Centre Winnipeg 1962); 'Fling' 1970; 'Fatal Attraction' 1984 (World Premiere St. Lawrence Centre Toronto 1984, also presented at Theatre Royal Haymarket, West End of London); 'Return Engagements' (Westport Playhouse and Am. Tour) 1988; 'An Act of the Imagination' (Yvonne Arnaud Theatre, Guildford, and British tour 1987); 'Every Time I See You' (World premiere; Madach Theatre, Budapest, Hungary 1992); 'Same Time Next Year - The Musical' (World Premiere, Budapest); 'You Say Tomatoes'; 'Same Time, Another Year' (sequel to 'Same Time, Next Year'); Broadway plays incl.: 'Same Time, Next Year' 1975 (debut 1975; screenplay 1978; Tony Award Nomination Best Play 1975; Drama Desk Award 1975; Acad. Award Nomination Best Screenplay 1978); 'Tribute' 1978 (screenplay 1980); 'Romantic Comedy' 1979 (screenplay 1983); 'Special Occasions' 1982 (directorial debut W. End London 1983); screenplay 'Stand Up and Be Counted' 1971; starred with wife 'Same Time, Next Year' Citadel Theatre Edmonton 1977; anthologized various publs. incl. 'Best American Plays' 8th Series, 'The Most Popular Plays of the American Theatre' and 'Famous American Plays of the 1970s'; 'Same Time, Next Year,' 'Tribute,' 'Romantic Comedy,' Special Occasions,' 'Fatal Attraction,' 'Fling!,' 'An Act of the Imagination,' 'Return Engagements', all publ. by Samuel French; Broadway plays transl. most foreign langs. and presented world wide incl. London and Paris; mem. Dramatists Guild; Writers Guild Am.; Soc. Authors & Artists (France); Acad. of Motion Pictures Arts and Sciences; Office: 1262 Lago Vista Place, Beverly Hills, Calif. 90210.

**SLAIGHT, (John) Allan;** broadcaster; b. Galt, Ont. 19 July 1931; s. John Edgar and Florence Eileen (Wright) S.; e. Dickson Pub. Sch. and Galt (Ont.) Coll. Inst. 1946; Central High Sch. Moose Jaw, Sask. 1946; Univ. of Sask.; children: John Gary, Gregory Allan, Mrs. Jan Tasker; PRES., C.E.O. & DIR. STANDARD BROADCASTING CORPORATION LIMITED; PRES., C.E.O. & DIR. SLAIGHT COMMUNICATIONS INC. which includes URBAN OUTDOORS; news reporter/announcer CHAB Radio Moose Jaw, Sask. 1948; news reporter/ed. Radio CFRN Edmonton, Alta. 1950–52 and CJCA Radio 1952–54; News Dir. CHED Radio Edmonton 1954–56, Nat. Sales Mgr. 1956–58; Program Dir. CHUM AM Toronto 1958, Vice Pres. and Gen. Mgr. CHUM AM and FM 1965–66; Pres. and Gen. Mgr. Stephens & Towndrow Co. Ltd. 1967–69; estbd. Slaight Broadcasting Ltd. 1970, merged with IWC Communications Ltd. 1973; Pres. and CEO Global Communications Ltd. 1974–77; acquired Standard Broadcasting Corp. 1985; Mem., Toronto United Way (Campaign Chrmn. 1985); Chrmn., Shaw Festival 1985–86; Protestant; Clubs: Rideau; Home: 7 Sherwood Lane, Toronto, Ont. M4P 3B9; Office: 11th Flr., 2 St. Clair Ave. W., Toronto, Ont. M4V 1L6.

**SLAIGHT, (Carol) Annabel;** book and magazine publisher; film & television producer; b. Toronto, Ont. 11 Sept. 1940; d. John Stewart and Carol Elaine (Thompson) Gerald; e. Forest Hill Elem. Sch. and Deer Park Pub. Sch. Toronto 1950; Point Grey Jr. High Sch. Vancouver 1953; Crofton House Sch. Vancouver 1957; Univ. of B.C. 1957–60; m. Brian Wright Slaight 31 Aug. 1967; Founder, Greey de Pencier Books (Div. of Key Publishers Ltd.) 1974– , Co-Founder, 'Owl' mag. 1976– and 'Chickadee' mag. 1979– ; Exec. Prod. OWL Centre For Children's Film and Television; Dir., The Design Exchange; Dir., Key Publishers Ltd.; YTV; Children's Broadcast Inst.; Candn. Film and Television Producers Assn.; Pres., The Young Naturalist Foundation; Pres., Owl Centre for Children's Film and Television; taught elem. sch. Vancouver, B.C. and London, Eng. 1960–64; Mem., Order of Ontario; Winner, Environment Canada's Outstanding Communication Award; YWCA Woman of the Year Award 1990; mem. Assn. Candn. Publishers; Candn. Magazine Publishers Assn.; Acad. of Candn. Cinema and Television; Home: 120 Rosedale Valley Rd., Toronto, Ont. M4W 1P8; Office: 56 The Esplanade, Toronto, Ont. M5E 1A7.

**SLATER, C. Peter R.L.,** M.A., Ph.D.; theologian; b. Newcastle-upon-Tyne, UK 24 March 1934; s. Robert Henry Lawson and Alys Lennox Graham (Simpson) S.; e. St. Peter's Sch. Coll. Adelaide, Australia 1947; Trinity Coll. Sch. Port Hope, Ont. 1951; McGill Univ. B.A. 1954; Queens' Coll. Cambridge B.A. 1957, M.A. 1961; Harvard Univ. Ph.D. 1964; three d. Lynne Patricia, Ruth Anne, Claire Elizabeth; m. Joanne McWilliam 1987; PROF. OF SYSTEMATIC THEOLOGY 1985– ; Dean of Divinity, Trinity Coll. Univ. of Toronto 1985–90, Prof. Centre for Religious Studies 1983– , Prof. of Theol. Toronto Sch. of Theol. Grad. Faculty 1982– ; Hon. Asst. Parish of St. Clements, Eglinton 1983– ; o. Diocese of Montréal Ang. Ch. Can. 1958, Diocese of Toronto 1982; Chair, Inter-Faith Relations and Mem. Inter-Church and Inter-Faith Relations Ctte., Anglican Church of Canada; Asst. Prof. of Religion Haverford Coll. Pa. 1964–70; Assoc. Prof. of Religion Sir George Williams Univ. Montréal 1970–71; Assoc. and Full Prof. of Religion Carleton Univ. Ottawa 1971–82 (Chrmn. 1976–80); Prof. of Theol. Wycliffe Coll. 1982–85; recipient Gold Medal Philos. McGill 1954; Harvard Prize Fellow 1957; SSHRCC Sabbatical Fellowship 1980; Mather Meml. Lectr. Queen's Univ. 1983; Candn. Forces Chaplaincy Reserve; author 'The Dynamics of Religion' 1978; ed. 'Religion and Culture in Canada/Religion et Culture au Canada' 1977; co-ed. 'Traditions in Contact and Change' 1983; 'Toronto Journal of Theology' 1985– ; contbr. various prof. jours.; mem. Candn. Soc. Study Religion (Pres. 1978–80); Am. Acad. Religion (Regional Pres. 1975); Soc. Values Higher Edn.; Am. Theological Soc. (Program Chair 1991–93); Am. Soc. Study Religion; Candn. Theological Soc.; recreation: sailing, theatre; Office: Toronto, Ont. M5S 1H8.

**SLATER, David W.,** M.A., Ph.D.; retired public servant; b. Winnipeg, Man. 17 Oct. 1921; s. William and Jean Proudfoot (Halcrow) S.; e. Univ. of Man., B.Com. 1942; Queen's Univ., B.A. (Hons. Econ.) 1947; Univ. of Chicago, M.A. 1950, Ph.D. 1957; m. Lillian Margaret, d. George C. Bell, Sarnia, Ont., 3 May 1947; children: Barbara Jane, Gail Patricia, Carolyn Louise, Leslie Anne; Chrmn. (retired) Econ. Council of Can. 1980–85; Instr., in Econ., Queen's Univ., 1946–48; Stanford Univ., 1950–52; Asst. Prof., Queen's 1952–57; Assoc. Prof. 1957–61; Prof. 1961–70; Dean, Sch. of Grad. Studies 1968–70; Pres., York Univ. 1970–73; Dir. and Gen. Dir., Dept. of Finance, Can. 1973–78; Dir. and then Chrmn., Econ. Council of Can., 1978–85; Chrmn., Ont. Govt. Task Force on Insurance 1986; mem., Research Staff, Royal Commission on Canada's Econ. Prospects, 1955–56; Committee on University Affairs, Prov. of Ont.; served with Candn. Army in N.W. Europe, 1942–45; Mentioned in Despatches; author of 'International Trade and Economic Growth' 1968 and special studies for Royal Comn. on Can.'s Econ. Prospects, Candn. Trade Comte. and Econ. Council of Can.; some-time mem. of Extve., Candn. Assn. Univ. Teachers and Social Science Research Council of Can.; some-time mem. CANADA Council, Dir. of Bank of Can., Dir. of Ind. Dev. Bank; mem., Candn. Econ. Assn.; United Church; recreations: tennis, golf, skiing; Home: 199 Crocus Ave., Ottawa, Ont. K1H 6E7.

**SLATER, Gordon Frederick;** Dominion Carillonneur of Canada; b. Toronto, Ont. 22 Aug. 1950; s. James Boyd and Cecilia Florence (Mullins) S.; e. 3 yrs. study Univ. of Toronto Fac. of Music major in bassoon; 10 yrs piano study Royal Conservatory of Music of Toronto, Grade I highest mark in Can., Grade VIII 1st Class Hon.; Carillon study with his father James, and subsequently with Robert Donnell and Milford Myhre; m. Elsa Snelson d. James and Grace Kite 7 Apr. 1979; step-children: Julia, Caroline; DOMINION CARILLONNEUR, THE PEACE TOWER CARILLON, HOUSE OF COMMONS OF CANADA 1977– ; Organist and Choir Dir. Riverdale Presbyterian Ch. Toronto 1969–72; Carillonneur Soldiers' Tower Carillon Univ. of Toronto 1969–77; organ builder Legge Organ Co. Ltd. Islington, Ont. 1970–77; Carillonneur Rainbow Tower Carillon Niagara Falls, Ont. 1972–75; Carillonneur Carlsberg Carillon Candn. Nat. Exhbn. 1975–76; teacher of carillon; recordings: 'The Bells of Niagara' 1974; 'Bells and Brass/Carillon et cuivres' 1978; 'Peace Tower Christmas/Carillon Noël' 1979; 'Night Music' 1986; 'Soundtracks of the Imagination' 1989; Music Dir., Parkdale Orch. Ottawa 1982–86; Music Dir., Divertimento Orch. of Ottawa 1986– ; Carillonneur mem. Guild of Carillonneurs in N. Am. 1978– (co-ed. 'Bulletin' 1978–85); Bassoonist, Univ. of Ottawa Orchestra 1989– ; Bassoonist, Ottawa Symphony Orch. 1993– ; Office: House of Commons, Ottawa, Ont. K1A 0A6.

**SLATER, Robert Winston,** B.Sc., Ph.D.; civil servant; b. England 1 Jan. 1942; s. Edward John William and Madeleine S.; e. Royal Sch. of Mines B.Sc. 1963; Imperial Coll. Ph.D. 1967; m. Karen d. Ross and Mary Junke 20 May 1983; children: Vanessa, Mathew, Laura, Alexander; ASSISTANT DEPUTY MINISTER, ENVIRONMENTAL CONSERVATION SERVICE, ENVIRONMENT CANADA 1992–93; Senior ADM, DOE 1992; Teacher, W. Africa early sixties; Tech. Services Mgr., Aero Hydraulics Corp. 1966–9; Gen. Mgr., Pollutech Adv. Serv. 1969–71; Chief, Mining Div., Environ. Protection Serv. 1971–73; Regional Dir. 1973–78; Dir. Gen. Ont. Region 1978–81; Chief Negotiator, Canada-U.S. Great Lakes Water Quality Act 1978; Asst. Dep. Min., Environ. Protection Serv. 1982–85; Policy 1985–92; Chair, Air Pollution Control Assn. Ont. Section 1977; Internat. Joint Comn. Great Lakes Water Quality Bd. 6 years; Charleton Prize 1963; RTZ Scholarship 1964–67; Mem., Bd. of Dir., World Env. Ctr.; Home: 382 Chapel St., Ottawa, Ont.; Office: 351 St.-Joseph Blvd., Hull, Que. K1A 0H3.

**SLATOR, R.A. (Sandy),** C.A.; executive; b. Man. 10 July 1944; s. John and Diane S.; e. Univ. of Man., Inst. Chart Accts. Man. C.A. 1970; PRES., CHIEF EXEC. OFFR. AND DIR. VENCAP EQUITIES ALBERTA LTD. 1989– ; Sr. Acct. Clarkson Gordon & Co. Winnipeg 1970–71; Sr. Internal Auditor Candn. Nat. Rlys. Edmonton 1971–73; Controller, Byers Transport Ltd. Edmonton 1973–74, Gen. Mgr. 1975, Pres. and Chief Exec. Offr. 1975–82; Vice Pres. present Co. 1983, Exec. Vice Pres. and Chief Financial Offr. 1985–89; recipient Gary Winchell Prize and Runner-up to Outstanding Student Inst. C.A.'s Man. 1970; N. Alta. Transport. Man of Yr. 1981; Pres., Assn. of Candn. Venture Capital Companies; Dir., Hong Kong Canada Business Assn.; Mem., Univ. of Alberta Business Adv. Council; Mem., Univ. of Alberta Strategic Planning Task Force; recreations: handball, golf, jogging, reading; Clubs: Mayfair Golf & Country; Center; Office: 1980, 10180 – 101 St., Edmonton, Alta. T5J 3S4.

**SLAUNWHITE, Michael W.,** B.Comm.; business executive; b. Red Deer, Alta. 7 Nov. 1960; s. Ronald G. and Emily B. (Shippelt) S.; e. Carleton Univ. B.Comm. (Hons.); CHIEF FINANCIAL OFFICER, COREL CORP. 1988– ; Computer Cons., Ernst & Young 1984–87; independent consultant, Remped Corp. 1987–88; recreations: skiing, tennis, vollyball; Home: 21A Davidson Dr., Ottawa, Ont.; Office: 1600 Carling Ave., Ottawa, Ont. K1Z 8R9.

**SLAVUTYCH, Yar;** professor/poet/scholar; b. Blahodatne, Ukraine 11 Jan. 1918; s. Mykhailo and Tetiana (Bratunenko) Zhuchenko; e. Pedagogic Inst. of Zaporizhia, dipl. 1940; Univ. of Penn., M.A. 1954, Ph.D. 1955; m. Elwira d. Yakiv and Maria Cybar 10 Nov. 1948; children: Bohdan, Oksana; PROF. EMERITUS, UNIV. OF ALTA. 1983– ; Sr. Instr., U.S. Army Language Sch. 1955–60; Asst. Prof. then Prof., Univ. of Alta. 1960–83; Mgr., Slavuta Pubs. 1960– ; Ukrainian Poet Laureate Abroad; Shevchenko Gold Medal; Can. Counc. Resch. Award; Prize for text to music by S. Eremenko; Ukrainian Can. Centennial Medal; Franko 1st & 2nd prizes for poetry; Mem. & var. extve. posts incl. Pres., Candn. Soc. for the Study of Names; Ukrainian Shakespeare Soc.; West. Can. Br., Shevchenko Sci. Soc.; Ukrainian Lit. & Art Club (Edmonton); bibliographer: 'MLA Internat. Bibliography' 1968– ; author: 'Shabli topol' 1992; 'Zhyvi smoloskypy' 1983, 1992; 'Zibrani tvory' 1978 (poetry); 'U vyri bahatokul'turnosty' 1988; 'Mistsiamy zaporoz'kymy' 1985 (memoirs); 'Poemi scelti' 1994; 'Three Narratives and Six Poems' 1992; 'Oaza tęsknoty' 1989; 'Vybranae' 1989; 'Izbrannoe' 1986; 'Valogatott versek' 1983; 'L'Oiseau de feu' 1976; 'The Conquerors of the Prairies' 1974, 1984; 'Oasis: Selected Poems' 1959; 'The Muse in Prison' 1956 and two others (non-fiction); 'Rozstriliana muza' 1992; 'Ukraïns'ka literatura v Kanadi' 1992; 'Mech i pero' 1992; 'Ukraïns'ka poeziia v Kanadi' 1976; 'Moderna Ukraïns'ka poeziia' 1950 and two others (criticism); 'Standard Ukrainian Grammar' 1987, 2nd ed. 1990; 'Ukrainian for Beginners' 1962, 8th ed. 1993; 'Conversational Ukrainian' 1959, 5th ed. 1987 (textbooks); comp. & ed.: 'An Annotated Bibliography of Ukrainian Literature in Canada' 1984, 1986, 1987; 'Antolohiia ukraïns'koï poezii v Kanadi 1898–1973' 1975; 'Collected Papers on Ukrainian Settlers in Western Canada' 2 vols. 1973, 1975; almanac 'Pivnichne siaivo' 5 vols. 1964–71; 'Ukrainian Shakespeariana in the West' 2 vols. 1987, 1990; num. articles, etc.; symposium: Zyla: 'The Poetry of Yar Slavutych' 1978; Vira Slavutych: 'Bibliohrafiia pysan' pro Yara Slavutycha' 1986, 1987; Home: 72 Westbrook Dr., Edmonton, Alta. T6J 2E1.

**SLAYTON, Philip William,** B.C.L., M.A.; lawyer and educator; b. London, Eng. 19 July 1944; s. Harold Raymond and Valerie Adrienne (Stretton) S.; e. Kelvin High Sch. Winnipeg 1960; Univ. of Man. B.A. 1965; Oxford Univ. (Rhodes Scholar) B.A. 1968, B.C.L. 1969, M.A. 1972; one d. Gabrielle; PARTNER, BLAKE, CASSELS AND GRAYDON, TORONTO; Legal Secy. to Hon. Mr. Justice W. Judson Supreme Court of Can. 1969–70; Asst. Prof. of Law McGill Univ. 1970, Assoc. Prof. 1973; Assoc. Prof. of Law, Univ. W. Ont. 1977; Dean and Prof. of Law 1979–83; Chrmn., Ont. Law Deans 1982–83; part-time lecturer, York Univ., 1983; Univ. of Toronto, 1984–89; occasional consultant to various ministries Ont., Que. and Candn. Govts., Law Reform Comn. Can.; Tech. Adv. Comn. of Inquiry Relating to Dept. Manpower & Immigration Montreal 1973–75 (L'Heureux-Dubé Commission); Dir., Candn. Human Rights Foundation 1981–89; Candn. Rhodes Scholars Foundation 1981–88 (Pres., 1983–86); Mem. President's Council, Oxford Univ.; Co-Chrmn., Candn. Campaign for Oxford; recipient Woodrow Wilson Fellowship 1965; Can. Council Fellowship 1968; author 'The Anti-dumping Tribunal' 1980; co-author 'The Tariff Board' 1981; co-ed. 'The Professions and Public Policy' 1978; 'Non-Tariff Barriers After the Tokyo Round' 1982; 'Trade Law Topics' 1985–89; many articles in learned journals and other periodicals; recreations: reading, writing, music; Office: Box 25, Commerce Court W., Toronto, Ont. M5L 1A9.

**SLEEMAN, John Warren;** brewery executive; b. Toronto, Ont. 2 July 1953; s. George Warren and Jessie Marie (Henderson) S.; e. Julie d. Joan and Paul Edmiston 9 Nov. 1991; children: Jolae, Jemma, Cooper; PARTNER, PRESIDENT & CHIEF EXECUTIVE OFFICER, SLEEMAN BREWING & MALTING CO. LTD. 1985– ; Co-owner, builder of British Pub Oakville 1976–79; Partner, The Imported Beer Co. 1979–92; restarted original business with orig. patent, bottles, labels, recipes; also brewing Stroh's products in Can. & selling Sleeman Beer to U.S. (for distbn. by Stroh's); Mem., Young Pres. Assn.; Office: 551 Clair Rd. W., Guelph, Ont. N1H 6H9.

**SLEMON, Gordon R.,** M.A.Sc., D.I.C., Ph.D., D.Sc., F.C.A.E.; electrical engineer; professor emeritus; b. Bowmanville, Ont. 15 August 1924; s. Milton Everett and Selena Ethleen (Johns) S.; e. Univ. of Toronto, B.A.Sc. (Elect. Engn.) 1946, M.A.Sc. (Elect. Engn.) 1948; Univ. of London, D.I.C., Ph.D. 1952, D.Sc. 1967; m. Margaret Jean, d. late Rev. Dr. A. Dawson Matheson, 9 July 1949; children: Sally, Stephen, Mark, Jane; PROFESSOR EMERITUS, UNIV. OF TORONTO 1990– ; Dean, Fac. of Applied Sci. & Engrg. Univ. of Toronto 1979–86; Chrmn., Univ. of Toronto Innovations Foundation 1980–84, 1986–94; Chrmn., Univ. of Toronto Microelectronics Development Corp. 1983–87; Chrmn., Candn. Accreditation Bd. 1984–85; Pres., Elect. Engn. Consociates 1976–79; Head, Dept. of Elect. Engn., Univ. of Toronto 1966–76; Prof. 1964–90; Instr. (part-time), Univ. of Toronto, 1946–49; Assoc. Prof. 1955–63; Planning Engr. (part-time), Ont. Hydro, 1946–49; Lectr., Imperial Coll. of Science and Tech., London, Eng., 1949–53; Asst. Prof., N.S. Tech. Coll., Halifax, 1953–55; Tech. Advisor, Candn. Colombo Plan, Mangalore, India, to establish new engn. coll. 1963–64; Consultant to various U.S. and Candn. co's. on electric drives and energy conversion, since 1955; rec'd. Western Electric Award 1965; Centennial Medal 1967; Ross Medal 1978, 1983; I.E.E.E. Centennial Medal 1984; Engineering Alumni Medal 1986; George Sinclair Award, IEEE Nikola Tesla Award, Gold Medal of Yugoslav Union of Nikola Tesla Societies; Engineering Hall of Distinction 1992; Candn. Engineering Education Award 1992; co-author 'Scientific Basis of Electrical Engineering' 1961; 'Electric Machinery' 1979; 'Power Semiconductor Drives' 1984; author 'Magnetoelectric Devices' 1966; 'Electric Machines and Drives' 1992; over 140 tech. papers for various learned journs.; Fellow, Candn. Acad. of Engr.; Inst. Elect. Engrs. (U.K.); Inst. Elect. & Electronic Engrs.; Engn. Inst. of Can.; mem., Candn. Soc. for Elec. Engrs.; Am. Soc. for Engn. Educ.; Assn. Prof. Engrs. Ont.; United Church; Home: 40 Chatfield Dr., Don Mills, Ont. M3B 1K5.

**SLESSOR, Keith Norman,** B.Sc., Ph.D.; educator; b. Comox, B.C. 4 Nov. 1938; s. Norman and Margaret Dorothy (Brand) S.; e. Univ. of B.C., B.Sc. 1960, Ph.D. 1964; m. Marie d. William and Edna Goldack 20 Aug. 1960; children: Michael, Graham, Karen; PROF. OF CHEM. SIMON FRASER UNIV. 1981– ; Mgr. Trace Analysis Lab. Kennecott Copper Co. Ltd. N. Vancouver 1960–61; Overseas Postdoctoral Fellow Nat. Rsch. Council Can., Lister Inst./Royal Free Hosp. Med. Sch. London, Eng. 1964–65, Svenska Traforskningsinstitutet/Stockholm Univ. 1965–66; Asst. Prof. present Univ. 1966, Assoc. Prof. 1971, Dir. Workshops & Sci. Stores 1980–85, Prof. 1981, Excellence in Teaching Award 1985; Sr. Ind. Fellow Candn. Forest Service, Forest Mgmt. Inst. Natural Sci's & Eng. Rsch. Council Can. Sault Ste. Marie, Ont. 1978–79; Assoc. mem. Plant Biotechnol. Inst. Nat. Rsch. Council Saskatoon 1985– ; recipient, Simon Fraser Univ. Rsch. Professorship 1992; BC Science Council Gold Medal for Natural Sciences 1992; author or co-author over 80 publs. organic chem. and insect biochem. with special reference to insect semio-chems.; mem. Am. Chem. Soc.; Entomol. Soc. Am.; recreations: photography, choral singing, gardening; Club: Rhododendron Culture; Home: 10105 Rolley Cres., Whonnock, B.C. V2X 8X7; Office: Burnaby, B.C. V5A 1S6.

**SLETMO, Gunnar K.,** Ph.D.; Omer DeSerres Professor of Commerce; b. Sandefjord, Norway 3 Jan. 1937; s. Hans S. and Anna Andersen (Roed) S.; e. Univ. of Oslo, B.A. 1957; Norwegian Sch. of Econ. & Bus. Admin, Sivilokonom 1960; Columbia Univ., Ph.D. 1971; OMER DESERRES PROF. OF COMM., ECOLE DES HAUTES ETUDES COMMERCIALES 1989– ; Rsch. Fellow, Lectr., Norwegian Sch. of Econ. & Bus. Admin. 1960–67; Mem., Bus. Fac., Columbia Univ. 1969–77; Prof. of Bus. & Transp., Ecoles des Hautes Etudes Comm. 1977– ; Chrmn. of Federal Task Force on Deep Sea Shipping, Ottawa 1984–85; Dir., China-Management Program 1988–90; Coordinator, Poland Mngmt. Program 1990– ; has written extensively on internat. shipping & trade, and is author of numerous pubs. & books incl. 'Shipping Conferences in the Container Age: US Policy at Sea' (with E.W. Williams Jr.) 1981; 'Pacific Service Enterprises and Pacific Cooperation' (with Gavin Boyd) 1993; Office: 5255 ave. Decelles, Montreal, Que. H3T 1V6.

**SLIPPERJACK, Ruby;** see **FARRELL, Ruby Violet Marilyn.**

**SLOAN, David Edward,** B.Com.; corporate director; b. Winnipeg, Man. 29 March 1922; s. David and Annie Maud (Gorvin) S.; e. Univ. of Man. B.Com. 1942; m. Kathleen Lowry Craig d. John Hamilton and Jean 26 Dec. 1947; children: Pamela Jane, John David, Kathleen Anne; Pres. & Chief Exec. Offr. and Dir., Canadian Pacific Securities Ltd. 1985–88; Treas. Canadian Pacific Ltd. 1969–88; Dir., Chateau Insurance Co.; The Citadel General Assurance Co.; The Citadel Capital Corp.; General Insurance Corp. of New Brunswick; Kent General Insurance Corp.; Norma Products of Can. Ltd.; Winterthur Canada Financial Corp.; served with Royal Candn. Army Service Corps 1942–45, attached to Mil. Intelligence Pacific Command 1945, rank Lt.; joined Monarch Life Assurance Co. 1946–47; Canadian Pacific Ltd. 1947–88; Chrmn. 1974–76 and mem. 1967–76 Adv. Ctte. Can. Pension Plan, Candn. Govt.; mem. Financial Execs. Inst. (Pres. Montréal Chapter 1974–75); Soc. Internat. Treas.'s (Internat. Chrmn. 1985–86, mem. Adv. Ctte. 1977–87); Mem., Toronto Soc. of Financial Analysts; Nat. Assoc. of Business Economists; mem. Assn. for Investment Mngmt. and Rsch.; United Church; recreations: golf, gardening, theatre, music; Clubs: Royal Montreal Golf; Toronto Hunt; Home: 316 Rosemary Rd., Toronto, Ont. M5P 3E3.

**SLOAN, Douglas A.,** B.Sc., P.Eng., F.M.C., Ph.D.; management consultant; b. Toronto, Ont. 26 June 1920; s. Albert E. and Hazel A. (Townsend) S.; e. Carleton Univ. 1944–45; Queen's Univ., B.Sc. 1949; Urwick Mang. Centre (UK), 1956; Columbia Pac. Ph.D. 1985; m. E. Louise, d. late George B. Thomson, Sept. 1948; children: David A. G., Dianne J.; SR. PARTNER DOUGLAS A. SLOAN ASSOCIATES INC.; Professor, Univ. of Toronto; Pres., Probit Labs Inc.; Pinebrook Inc.; Dir., Dickenson Mines Ltd.; Goldcorp Inc.; Toronto East Gen. Hosp.; North York Symphony; Council, Queen's Univ.; Acct., Canadian Pacific Export Co., 1935–41; Engr., Buffalo Ankerite Mines Ltd., 1947; Metall. Concentrator, Noranda Mines, Ltd., 1948; Engr. Supvr., McIntyre Porcupine Mines Ltd., 1949–50; Supvr., Mang., Falconbridge (Hardy Mine, Falconbridge Mine, Boundary Mine) Mines Ltd., 1950–56; Urwick, Currie Ltd. (subsequently Coopers & Lybrand) 1956–85; served with Royal Candn. Corps of Signals (Reserve) 1935–39; Kent Regt. (Reserve) 1939; RCAF 1941–45 (Acct. AFHQ); Past Pres., Candn. Opera Co.; Fellow, Inst. Mang. Consultants (Pres. Ont 1969; Pres. Can. 1970); mem., Candn. Inst. Mining; author, 'Mine Management' textbook; CIM Award 1949; Queen's Jubilee Medal, 1977; Citizenship Award of Assoc. P. Eng. Ont., 1979; Dist. Lect. Award CIM 1986; recreations: skiing, equestrian, scuba, Taekwon Do; Clubs: Eglinton Hunt; Master of Fox Hounds; E. Galway Hunt (Ireland); Faculty; Mining (N.Y.); Chemists (N.Y.); Home: 25 Gormley Ave., Toronto, Ont. M4V 1Y9; Office: Suite 1002, 2200 Yonge St., Toronto, Ont. M4S 2C6.

**SLOAN, Hugh W., Jr.;** business executive; b. Princeton, N.J. 1 Nov. 1940; s. Hugh Walter and Elizabeth (Johnson) S.; e. Hotchkiss Sch., Lakeville, C.T. 1958; Aldenham Sch., England 1959; Princeton Univ., A.B.(Hons. History) 1963; m. Deborah Louise, d. William and Bette Jane Murray, 20 Feb. 1971; children: Melissa, Peter, Jennifer, William; PRESIDENT AUTOMOTIVE GROUP, WOODBRIDGE FOAM CORP. 1985– ; Dir. Cartex Corp.; Manufacturers Life Ins. Co.; Schneider Corp.; various mgmt. positions with Nat. Repub. Party 1965–68; White House Staff 1969–72; Treasr. Pres. Nixon's re-el. campaign 1971–72; purchasing, internat. and mktg. exec. positions with Budd Co., Troy, Michigan 1973–79; Pres. & Gen. Mgr. Budd Canada Inc. 1979–85; Dir., Junior Achievement of Can.; The Community House; Past Chrmn. & Dir., A.P.M.A.; World Presidents Organization; Soc. of Automotive Engs., Princeton Club, English Speaking Union; Anglican; recreations: golf, tennis, skiing; Club: Bloomfield Hills Country; Office: 2500 Meijer Dr., Troy, MI, U.S.A. 48084.

**SLOAN, James Joseph,** B.Sc. (Eng.), Ph.D.; professor of physics and chemistry; b. Lindsay, Ont. 5 Jan. 1943; s. James Victor and Olive May (Houghton) S.; e. Queen's Univ. B.Sc. 1965, Ph.D. 1969; PROF. OF PHYSICS & CHEM., UNIV. OF WATERLOO 1988– ; Rsch. Offr., Nat. Rsch. Counc. of Can. 1975–87; Adjunct Prof., Dept. of Chem., Carleton Univ. 1983–88; current rsch. in physical chem., reaction dynamics, atmospheric chem., chem. kinetics & transient spectroscopy; Mem., Guelph-Waterloo Ctr. for Grad. Work in Chem.; Guelph-Waterloo Prog. for Grad. Work in Physics; Mem., Chem. Inst. of Can.; Am. Chem. Soc.; Am. Physical Soc.; Am. Geophysical Union; author of more than 50 rsch. pubs. in phys. chem.; Home: 225 Benjamin Rd., #23, Waterloo, Ont. N2V 1Z3; Office: Dept. of Chemistry, Univ. of Waterloo, Waterloo, Ont. N2L 3G1.

**SLOANE, Richard Douglas,** B.Sc.; telecommunications executive; b. Stratford, Ont. 6 July 1930; e. Queen's University B.Sc. (Civil Engn.) 1953; Exec. Vice Pres., Bell Canada 1984–90; joined Bell Canada, Hamilton 1953 holding various line and staff mang. positions Chatham, Toronto, Kitchener and Montreal 1957–62;

Staff Engr., American Telephone and Telegraph Co., N.Y. 1963; Engr., Bell Laboratories, Holmdel, N.J. 1966; returned to Bell Canada as Constr. Program Engr., W. Area, Toronto 1966; Area Equipment Engr. 1967; Area Plant Extension & Transmission Engr. 1968; Chief Engr. Toronto 1969; Asst. Vice Pres. Engn. Ont. Region 1972; Vice Pres. North/East Area, Ottawa 1974; Vice Pres. (Operations Staff) Ont. Region, Toronto 1976; Vice-Pres. Bus. Devel. & Network Services 1977; Vice-Pres. (Saudi Arabia Project) 1978; Vice Pres. Marketing 1978; Vice-Pres. (Operations Performance) Hull, Que. 1980; Pres., Telecom Canada Ottawa 1982; Dir., Ont. Chamber of Comm.; Dir. Bell Northern Research Ltd.; Bell Canada Mgmt. Corp.; Maritime Tel. & Tel. Co. Ltd.; Jr. Achievement of Can.; Internat. Telecommunications Discovery Center; mem. Assn. Prof. Engrs. Prov. Ont.; Clubs: Ontario (Toronto); Mississauga Golf and Country; Rideau (Ottawa); Le Cercle Universitaire d'Ottawa; Home: 20 Taylorwood Dr., Etobicoke, Ont.

**SLONIM, Rabbi Reuben;** b. Winnipeg, Man. 27 Feb. 1914; s. Max and Gisela (Averbook) S.; e. Ill. Inst. of Tech., Chicago, B.S.A.S. 1933; ordained rabbi, teacher and preacher, Jewish Theol. Semy., N.Y. City, M.H.L. 1937; Albany Law Sch., N.Y. 1945–47; m. Rita, d. Jacob Short, Winnipeg Manitoba, 21 June 1936; one daughter, Rena; PRES., ASSOCIATION FOR THE LIVING JEWISH SPIRIT, (ALJS), TORONTO; Rabbi of Community Temple, Cleveland, Ohio, 1943–44; Temple Beth El, Troy, N.Y., 1944–47; McCaul St. Synagogue, Toronto, 1937–40 and 1947–54; Jewish Chaplain, N.Y. State Assembly, 1944–47; Rabbi, Beth Tzedec Cong., Toronto, 1954–55; Chairman, Synagogue Council, State of Israel Bonds, 1955–60; Rabbi, Cong. Habonim, Toronto, 1960–83; Extve. mem., Ont. Zionist Region (1947–60); Candn. Jewish Cong., Ont. Region (1947–60); Nat. Speakers' Bur., Zionist Organ. of Am.; Pres., Min. Assn. of Capitol Dist., N.Y. State, 1946; Pres., Toronto Zionist Council, 1947–51; Pres., Assembly of Jewish Organs., Toronto, 1947–52; Co-Chrmn., Interfaith Comte. of Metrop. Toronto Community Chest, 1953–55; mem. of World Soc. of Skippers of the Flying Dutchmen; Chaplain, Variety Club, Toronto, 1952–56; mem., Rabbinical Assembly of Am.; Assoc. Ed. 'The Telegram' Toronto 1955–71; author 'In The Steps of Pope Paul' 1965; 'Both Sides Now' 1972; 'Family Quarrel' 1977; 'Grand to be an Orphan' 1983; 'To Kill A Rabbi' 1987; Civilian Chaplain, RCAF 1940–43; Freemason; Home: 625 Roselawn Ave., Toronto, Ont. M5N 1K7.

**SLOOT, Rosemary,** M.V.A., B.A.; artist; b. Simcoe, Ont. 1952; e. Humber Coll. of Applied Arts, dipl. 1974; N.S. Coll. of Fine Art & Design B.A. 1976; Univ. of Alta. M.V.A. 1978; exhibitions: 'Priority of Truth' travelling solo exhibition – catalogue 1992–93: London Regional Art & Historical Museums; Rodman Hall Arts Centre, St. Catharines; Maclaren Arts Centre, Barrie; The Art Gallery of Algoma, Sault Ste. Marie; Definitely Superior, Thunder Bay; Kitchener-Waterloo Art Gallery; 39th, 40th, 42nd, 43rd, 44th Annual W. Ont. Exhib., London Reg. Art Gall. 1986, 87 (purchase award), 89, 90, 91; 'Beyond the Object' Brampton Pub. Lib. & Art Gall. 1990; Lynnwood Arts Ctr. Simcoe 1982 (purchase award), 86 87, 89, 90; Nancy Poole's Studio 1984, 86, 87, 88, 90, 91; McIntosh Gall. U.W.O. 1987, 88; Grimsby Public Art Gall. 1987; Premier's Office, Queen's Park Toronto 1986; 'Art Affairs North,' travelling exhib. (hon. mention) 1985–86; Lakehead Univ. 1982, 83, 84; juried exhib., Nat. Exhib. Ctr. Thunder Bay 1982, 83; St. Aloysius' Coll., Sydney, Australia 1981; collections: Victoria Hosp. London; The Best Corp.; Firestone Corp.; Smith, Lyons Corp.; Univ. of Alta., Lynnwood Arts Ctr.; Canada Council Art Bank; ViaRail Canada; awards: Ontario Arts Council grants 1982, 86, 88; Canada Council B Grant 1979– ; represented by Nancy Poole's Studio, 16 Hazelton Ave., Toronto, Ont.; Address: 47 Bruce St., London, Ont. N6C 1G5.

**SLUSARCHUK, William Alexander,** Ph.D., P.Eng.; civil engineer; b. Simcoe, Ont. 18 Apr. 1940; s. William and Ida (Kurchak) S.; e. Univ. of Toronto, B.Sc. 1963; Univ. of Guelph, M.Sc. 1967; Rutgers Univ., Ph.D. 1970; m. Mary d. Alan and Doris Glenny 21 Dec. 1963; one d. Cheryl; VICE-PRES., AGRA INDUSTRIES LTD. 1991– ; Pres. & C.E.O., AGRA Earth & Environmental Group 1991– ; Vice-Chrmn. of Bd. & C.E.O. HBT AGRA Ltd. 1985– ; Chrmn. of Bd. & C.E.O., RZA AGRA, Inc. 1990– ; Chrmn. of Bd. (1991– ) and C.O.O. (1992– ) SHB AGRA, Inc.; Shipboard Offr. & Base Devel. Offr., Royal Candn. Navy 1963–66; Grad. Student, Permafrost Engr. 1966–70; Rsch. Offr., Nat. Rsch. Counc. of Can. 1970–73; Sr. Geotech. Engr., Hardy Assoc. 1973–79; Geotech. Div. Mgr. 1979–81; Calgary Area Mgr. 1981–85; Gen. Mgr., Prairie Region 1985; has been involved in most oil & gas pipeline construction in Candn. North; served as expert witness in several north. pipeline hearings in Can. & U.S.; Dir., HBT AGRA Limited 1985– , RZA AGRA, Inc. 1990– , M&T AGRA, Inc. 1991– , SHB AGRA, Inc. 1991– ; Mem., Profl. Engrs. Assn. of Alta., Yukon & N.W.T.; Candn. Geotech. Soc.; Cons. Engrs. of Can. & Alta.; Calgary c of c.; author & co-author of many tech. papers; recreations: skiing, Pacific boating & fishing; Home: 3636 – 1A St. S.W., Calgary, Alta. T2S 1R5; Office: 221 – 18 St. S.E., Calgary, Alta. T2E 6J5.

**SLUTSKY, Samuel,** Q.C., LL.B.; tax lawyer, author, columnist; b. Winnipeg, Man. 10 Feb. 1956; s. Paul and Rose (Schwartz) S.; e. Univ. of Manitoba LL.B. 1979, 2 year arts program; m. Dr. Gloria Galant d. Nicholas and Anne G. 21 June 1980; PARTNER, CASSELS, BROCK & BLACKWELL 1989– ; In-house Counsel, Coopers & Lybrand (Calgary) 1980–81; Touche Ross & Co. 1981–84; specialty tax practice 1984–88; Partner, McMillan, Binch (Toronto) 1988–89; Columnist, 'Financial Post' 1982–90; Contbg. Ed. 1990– ; Mem., Candn. Bar Assn. Commodity Tax Ctte. 1987– (Vice-Chrmn. 1991– ); Revenue Canada's GST Adv. Ctte. 1990– ; Mem., Manitoba Bar 1980; Alta. Bar 1984; Ont. Bar 1988; Apptd. Q.C. by the federal government 1992; Univ. of Manitoba Alumni scholarship for high standing; Dean's honour list, Arts; Dir., Free Univ., Univ. of Manitoba 1973–74; Univ. Coll. Student Counc. Mem. 1972–74; author: 'Tax Aspects of Litigation' 1984, 'Tax Administration Reports' 1985, 'Tax Regulation Reports' 1986 (cont. tax reports, updated weekly), 'The Financial Post GST Handbook' 1990; 'Fraudulent Conveyances' in 'Canadian Encyclopedic Digest (West)' 1982; quoted nat. in Globe & Mail, Financial Post, The Financial Times of Canada, The Toronto Star, The Ottawa Gazette, Maclean's Magazine, The Canadian Lawyer Magazine; quoted internat. in Financial Times of London; TV commentator; frequent speaker for several orgns.; frequent contbr., 'Canadian Tax Journal'; recreations: travel, running; Home: 49 Lonsdale Road, Toronto, Ont. M4V 1W4; Office: 2100, 40 King St. W., Toronto, Ont. M5H 1B5.

**SLYKHUIS, John Timothy,** B.S.A., M.Sc., Ph.D., F.R.S.C.; plant pathologist; b. Carlyle, Sask. 7 May 1920; s. William and Emma (Hodgson) S.; e. Mountain Valley Pub. Sch. and Carlyle (Sask.) High Sch. 1938; Univ. of Sask. B.S.A. 1942, M.Sc. 1943; Univ. of Toronto Ph.D. 1947; m. 1stly (late) Ruth Enid d. late Russel Leisester Williams 6 July 1946; 2ndly Ellen Christine Light (nee Reinholdt) 26 Sept. 1983; children: Grace Emma, Margaret Janet, Dorothy Anne, Timothy Arthur, the late Alan Edward; Fruit Tree Virologist, Agriculture Can. 1976–85; ran a soil testing laboratory for apple replant disease at his home 1985–91; Research Plant Pathol. Agric. Can., Harrow, Ont. 1947–49, Lethbridge, Alta., 1952–57, Ottawa 1957–60 (Head, Plant Pathol. Unit 1957–60, Head, Plant Virology Sec. 1960–70), Cereal Virol. Ottawa Research Stn. 1970–76; Research Plant Pathol., S.D. State Coll. 1949–52; research discoveries incl.: 'spermatosphere' as a region surrounding seeds where soil fungi interact in specific ways 1947; identity of causes of sweet clover failure in Ont. 1947–49; wheat striate mosaic virus and its leafhopper vector 1949–52; mite vector of wheat streak mosaic virus 1952–55; wheat spot mosaic; European wheat striate mosaic virus, its insect vector and unique aspects of virus vector relations, ryegrass mosaic 1956–57; Hordeum mosaic virus and Poa semilatent virus in cereal crops, carrier of Agropyron mosaic virus, wheat spindle streak mosaic virus and its transmission by fungus in wheat soils 1957–76; Little cherry disease and apple replant disease 1976– ; author various articles scient. journs.; Fellow, Am. Phytopathol. Soc.; Royal Soc. of Canada, 1975; mem. Candn. Phytopathol. Soc. (Past Pres.); Agric. Inst. Can.; rec'd. Candn. Phytopathol. Soc. Award for Outstanding Research, 1983, Fellow, 1988; N.D.P.; Unitarian; recreations: gardening, hiking, curling, skiing, swimming, handicrafts, violin making, youth group activities; Home: R.R. 1, Site 2, Comp. 7, Summerland, B.C. V0H 1Z0.

**SMALE, Joanne R. Muroff,** B.A.; production, publicity and promotion executive; b. Brooklyn, N.Y. 20 June 1949; d. Walter and Renee (Rosenzweig-Rush) Muroff; e. Univ. of Miami B.A. (Psych., minor Anthrop. and Sociol.); PRESIDENT JOANNE SMALE PRODUCTIONS LTD. 1980– and VICE-PRES., DARK LIGHT MUSIC LTD.; Owner, Listening House Booking Agency 1974–80; has worked with a wide spectrum of people and projects from performers, cultural events, charities and benefits to industry conferences and awards; awarded 6 gold and 2 platinum albums for her work with Rough Trade, Murray McLauchlan and Bruce Cockburn; publicist, numerous theatre productions, nightclub openings, sports, cultural, and music industry events including: The Juno Awards, The CASBY Awards, WOMAD, The Moscow Circus (nat. tour), Caribana, Mariposa, The Toronto Jewish Film Festival, The Corel North Am. Indoor Tennis Championship and The Women's Snooker Assn. of Canada; charity & benefit events include: 'Rekindle The Light' Festival (held in conjunction with the Commonwealth Foreign Ministers Conference the aim was to heighten awareness of media censorship in S. Africa) 1988, 'Arts Against Apartheid' Toronto Arts Against Apartheid Foundation and acted as the Toronto base on behalf of the Nelson Mandela Reception Ctte. 1990, also worked with the United Way of Greater Toronto, Concert For Casey House, Squash Hunger, Council Fire Native Organization, Tears Are Not Enough, EcoFest and literacy related projects; media and industry organizations include: Toronto Star, NOW, CFNY, True North Records, Sam the Record Man, Molson Ontario Breweries Ltd. and Harbourfront Centre; formed an association with a U.S. based company, The Raleigh Group Ltd. and began Candn. representation for such events as: New Music Seminar (New York), The International Music and Media Conference (Montreux, Switzerland) and The American Video Conference and Awards (Los Angeles); Bd. mem., VideoFact; Candn. Independent Recording Producers Assn. (CIRPA); Internat. Federation of Festical Organizations (FIDOF); Extve. Bd., Candn. Women in Radio and Television (CWRT); recently: publicist, 'Road Movies' a CBC TV series and 'In The Key Of Oscar' a two-hour documentary, produced by CBC Television, the National Film Board and Elitha Peterson Productions Inc.; co-producer, 'Mondo Moscow' TV show and is in developmental stages with the National Film Bd. for a new documentary 'Un-Canadians'; Office: 51 Bulwer St., Main Level, Toronto, Ont. M5T 1A1.

**SMALL, William D.,** B.Com., C.A.; C.F.A.; banker; b. Cleveland, Ohio 28 May 1920; s. Roland B. and Mary W. (Pettet); e. Queen's Univ., B.Com. 1948; C.P.A. (Ont.) 1952; C.A. (Ont.) 1962; Chart. Financial Analyst (U.S.) 1965; m. Margaret C., d. J. Ernest Wright, Picton, Ont., 16 June 1945; children; Donald, Mary Ann, Nancy, Shelley; Vice Pres. Leg. & Govt., Bank of Montreal, 1973–78; joined Bank of Montreal, Picton, Ont., 1938; Kingston and Westport, Ont., 1947; Securities Dept., H.O., 1948–67; served as Research Analyst, Taxation Offr.; apptd. Asst. Mgr. 1954; Asst. Supt. 1957; Supt. 1959; Supt.-Adm., 1967–68; Vice Pres., Premises and Inspection, 1968–70; Vice Pres., Money Mang. 1970–71; Vice Pres., Investments 1971–73; served with RCAF 1942–45; Lectr. in Taxation (evenings), Sir George Williams Univ., 1951–54; Gov. 1971–73; mem. Adv. Bd. Concordia Univ. 1973–78; mem., Univ. Council, Queen's Univ. 1958–70, Adv. Council, Sch. of Business 1960–66, Invest. Comte. 1964–92, Pres., Montreal Alumni Assn. 1956–57; Trustee, Prince Edward County Meml. Hosp. 1981–91; Pres. Bd. of Gov. 1985–89; Gov., Kingston General Hosp. 1991– ; Mem., Hastings-Prince Edward District Health Council; Assoc., Candn. Bankers Assn., 1942; Pres., Montreal Soc. Financial Analysts, 1956–57; Vice Pres., Financial Analysts (U.S.) Fed., 1957–58; mem., Inst. Chart. Financial Analysts (U.S.); Inst. C.A.'s Ont.; Protestant; Home: P.O. Box 10, Picton, Ont. K0K 2T0.

**SMALLMAN, Beverley N.,** B.A., M.Sc., Ph.D., LL.D., F.R.S.C.; professor emeritus; b. Port Perry, Ont. 11 Dec. 1913; s. Benjamin and Ethel May (Doubt) S.; e. Port Perry elem. and sec. schs.; Queen's Univ. B.A. 1936; Univ. of W. Ont. M.Sc. 1938; Univ. of Edinburgh Ph.D. 1941; Trent Univ. LL.D. 1982; m. 1stly Hazel (dec. 1962) d. George and Alice Mayne 11 Dec. 1937; one d. Sylvia Gail; m. 2ndly Florence H. d. Thomas and Dorothy Cook 27 July 1965; PROF. EMERITUS OF BIOL., QUEEN'S UNIV. 1979– ; Prov. Apiary Insp. Ont. Co. Lennox & Addington 1981–92; Sci., Stored Grain Insect Investigations Bd. of Grain Comnrs., Winnipeg 1941–45; est. and Offr.-in-Charge Stored Products Lab. Agric. Can. Winnipeg 1945–50, Head Entomol. Sect. Sci. Service Lab. Agric. Can. London, Ont. 1950–57, Chief Entomol. Div. and subsequently Dir. of Entomol. & Plant Path., Rsch. Br. Agric. Can. Ottawa 1957–63; Prof. and Head of Biol. Queen's Univ. 1963–73, Prof. of Biol. 1973–78, mem. Senate 1968; Visiting Sci., Nat. Inst. Med. Rsch. London, Eng. 1954–56; CSIRO Labs. Brisbane, Australia 1970–71, 1976; Candn. del. Conf. Commonwealth Agric. Bureaus, Eng. 1960; Head Candn. del. FAO Conf. on Pesticides in Agric. Rome 1962; mem., Expert Ctte. Insect Resistance to Insecticides FAO Rome 1967–68; recipient Achievement Award & gold Medal Entomol. Soc. Can. 1967; elected F.R.S.C. 1968; author: 'Agricultural Science in Canada' 1970; 'Queen's Biology' 1992; co-author: 'Good-bye Bugs' 1983; author or co-author over 80 rsch. papers sci. jours.; Founding Pres., Entomol. Soc. Man. 1945; Pres., Entomol. Soc. Ont. 1953, Entomol. Soc. Can. 1964; Council, Zool. Sco. Can. 1963–65; recreations: mini-farming, beekeeping, writing popular sci. and reviews; Columnist, 'Harrowsmith' magazine; Address: R.R. 2, Yarker, Ont. K0K 3N0.

**SMART, Allan M.P. (Lord of Edingale),** B.A.; insurance executive; b. Hamilton, Ont. 22 Aug. 1933; s. Harry Allen and Jean Irene (Kohn) S.; e. McMaster Univ. B.A.; m. Ruth Mary d. Jacob Matthew and Augustine Elizabeth (Kelly) Seubert 24 Sept. 1960; two d. Kellie Ann, Kara Lee; CHAIRMAN AND DIR. ALLAN SMART SERVICES LTD. 1973– ; Chrmn. and Dir. Smart Insurance Services Ltd.; Smart Insurance Services Agency Inc. Lexington, Ky.; joined William M. Mercer Ltd. Toronto 1957, Asst. Mgr. Pension Consulting 1961, Mgr. Pension Consulting 1963, Asst. Vice Pres. 1965, Vice Pres. 1967; Pres. Alexander and Alexander Insurance Services 1970; el. Underwriting mem. Lloyd's of London 1976; recreations: walking, swimming, horse racing and breeding, travel; Clubs: Ascot (Eng.) Members Stand; Canadian (N.Y.); Los Flamingos Club (Puerto Vallarta, Mexico); Metropolitan (NY); Toronto Bd. of Trade; National; Royal Candn. Military Institute; New York Turf & Field; Turf, Ont. Jockey; Thoroughbred Club of Am. (Lexington, KY); Thoroughbred Owners and Breeders Assn.; Victoria Racing (Melbourne); Home: 67 Banbury Rd., Don Mills, Ont. M3B 2K9; Office: 730, 40 University Ave., Toronto, Ont. M5J 1T1.

**SMART, J. David,** B.A., M.B.A.; executive; b. Sarnia, Ont. 30 Jan. 1944; s. John Lennox and Margaret Lois (Patterson) S.; e. Univ. of W. Ont. B.A. 1966; York Univ. M.B.A. 1968; m. Joanne Sandra d. Jack and Ann Babb 7 Sept. 1968; two d. Christine Elizabeth, Caroline Shaleen; joined General Foods Ltd. 1969–73 serving as Financial Analyst, Financial Planning Mgr., Acctg. Services Mgr.; Slater Steel Industries Ltd. 1973–76, Financial Planning Mgr., Comptroller; joined Slacan Div. of Slater Industries 1976 serving as Mktg. Mgr., Field Sales Mgr., Gen. Sales Mgr., Vice Pres.-Gen. Mgr.; Vice-Pres., Sales & Mktg.; Home: 97 Salisbury Ave., Cambridge, Ont. N1S 1J6.

**SMART, Patricia (Purcell),** B.A., M.A., Ph.D.; university professor; b. Toronto, Ont. 3 Feb. 1940; d. Gillis Philip and Charlotte Frances (Fleming) Purcell; e. St. Anselm's Sch. 1952; Loretto Abbey 1957; St. Michael's Coll., Univ. of Toronto, B.A. 1961; Laval Univ., M.A. 1963; Queen's Univ., Ph.D. 1977; m. John s. Reginald and Madeline S. 22 June 1963; children: Mary Ann, Michael; PROF., FRENCH & CANDN. STUDIES, CARLETON UNIV. 1986– ; Winner, Marston Lafrance Leave Fellowship, Carleton Univ. 1986–87; joined Carleton Univ. 1971; Act. Dir., Inst. of Candn. Studies, Carleton Univ. 1987–88; Former Extve. Mem., Assn. for Candn. & Que. Lit.; Assn. for Candn. Studies; Ed. Bd., 'Voix et Images' 1986–89; Ed. Bd., 'The Canadian Forum'; Cons. Ed., 'Dalhousie French Studies,' 'Atlantis'; author: 'Hubert Aquin, Agent Double' 1973, 'Ecrire dans la maison du Père: l'émergence du féminin dans la tradition littéraire du Québec' 1988 (winner, Gov. General's Award, Fr. language non-fiction) and num. articles; 'Writing in the Father's House: the Emergence of the Feminine in the Quebec Literary Tradition' (trans. by author) 1991 (Gabrielle Roy Award); Ed. & Trans.: 'The Diary of André Laurendeau 1964–67' 1991 (finalist Gov. General's Award, Translation); elected, Royal Soc. of Canada 1991; Home: 11 Regent St., Ottawa, Ont. K1S 4R4; Office: Ottawa, Ont. K1S 5B6.

**SMEE, Kenneth A.,** B.Sc., M.Sc., M.B.A.; bank executive; e. Royal Military College of Canada B.Sc. 1962; McGill Univ. M.Sc. 1964; Queen's Univ. M.B.A. 1971; married; three children; EXECUTIVE VICE-PRES., SYSTEMS & TECHNOLOGY, ROYAL BANK OF CANADA 1992– ; Canadian Armed Forces (leaving as Captain) 1964–69; Supt. of Planning and Analysis, Alcan 1971–74; Mgr., Planning Coord., Control & Fin. Planning Dept., Royal Bank of Canada 1974; Finan. Analysis & Control 1975; Vice-Pres. & Compt. 1976; Vice-Pres., Retail Banking – Ont. 1982; Central Ont. 1984; Pres., Royal Bank de Puerto Rico, Royal Bank of Can. 1986; Sr. Vice-Pres., Retail Banking, Metropolitan Toronto 1987; Sr. Vice-Pres., Systems & Technol. 1991; Mem., Adv. Council, Queen's Univ. Sch. of Business; Chair, The Conservation Found. of Greater Toronto; Mem., Canadian Military Colleges Adv. Bd.; The Research Board (New York); Office: 8th floor, 315 Front St. W., Toronto, Ont. M5V 3A4.

**SMEENK, Brian Peter Leonard John,** LL.B., M.B.A., C.H.R.P.; labour and employment lawyer; b. London, Ont. 16 Dec. 1953; s. Theodore Joseph and Apolonia Cornelia (Bontje) S.; e. Catholic Central H.S. 1976; Univ. of Western Ont. 1974–76; Univ. of Ottawa LL.B. 1977; Univ. of Michigan, Indus. Relns. Prog. 1979, M.B.A. 1979; m. Margaret d. Anna and the late Levine Lansens 5 Aug. 1977; children: Christopher Theodore Lansens, Katharine Pauline Anna; COUNSEL, McCARTHY TÉTRAULT 1992– ; practice restricted to rep. of employers in labour & employment matters; Asst. Factfinder & Factfinder, Education Relations Comn. 1978–79; articled Student-at-Law, Cassels, Mitchell, Somers, Dutton & Winkler 1979–80; called to Bar of Ont. 1981; Assoc. Lawyer, Cassels, etc. 1981; Assoc. Lawyer, Winkler, Filion & Wakely 1982, Partner 1987–92; C.H.R.P. 1990; Full Mem., Human Resources Profl. Assn. of Ont. (Bd. of Dir. 1990–92, 1993– ; Vice-Pres. 1990–92; Sr. Vice-Pres. for Govt. Affairs 1992– ); Mem., Advocates' Soc.; Am. Soc. for Human Resource Mngt.; Inst. for Internat. Human Resources; Extve., Candn. Bar Assn., Edn. Law Section 1993– ; Mem., Candn. Bar Assn. (Labour, Admin., Edn. Law & Civil Lit. Sections); Co. of York Law Assn.; author/co-author of var. scholarly articles; recreations: tennis, cycling; clubs: Boulevard, Baby Point; Home: 44 Halford Ave., Toronto, Ont. M6S 4E9; Office: 4700, Toronto Dominion Bank Tower, Toronto, Ont. M5K 1E6.

**SMEENK, Theodore J. Sr.,** C.L.U.; retired; b. The Hague, Holland 22 March 1921; e. Municipal Business School (Holland); Extension Dept., Univ. of Toronto; C.L.U. (highest standing (Ont.), 2nd Canada-wide) 1962; Dunstall Mem. Medal for highest standing in ch. life underwriters exams (Ont.); m. Pauline 1946; 9 children; long-standing successful career with North American Life Assur. Co.; Former Dir., Moderator and later Educational Chair, Canadian Life Underwriters Assn. (London Chapter); taught quality, ethics and financial planning practices while consistently achieving Volume Leader & highest co. awards; proficient linguist handling Dutch, Flemish, German, French and English; extensive volunteer community involvement incl. Founding Sec. Treas., St. Willibrord Credit Union; Past Pres., Forest City Toastmasters; Saint Michael's and Catholic Central Parent-Teachers assns.; London's Oktoberfest Ctte.; Past Chair, London's Hist. Mus. Adv. Ctte.; Dormer Hist. Ctte.; Faithful Navigator, Dormer Gen. Assembly; Former Nat. Dir., Experiment in Internat. Living (student foreign exchange), Prov. of Ont.; 15 Year Government of Ontario Community Service Award 1990; declined candidacy for the Legislature; club: London; Address: 1 Scarlett Ave., London, Ont. N6G 1Z3.

**SMELLIE, Bruce Alan;** business executive; b. Toronto, Ont. 2 June 1933; s. Gordon and Mary Lillian (Topp) S.; e. Humberside Coll. Inst. 1950; m. M. Jane d. Eric and Margaret Bolton 20 May 1955; children: M. Catherine, J. Bruce, Christie Ann; PRES., LONGINES-WITTNAUER 1985– ; Salesman, D. Smellie & Sons Ltd.; 1950; Sales Mgr. & Partner 1962; Vice Pres. 1965; Pres. 1984; Chrmn., Candn. Jewellers Inst.; Pres., Candn. Jewellers Assn. 1980; Candn. Jewellery Travellers Assn. 1970; served 19 years on various indus. assn. bds. & cttes.; recreations: golf; Club: Weston Golf & Country; Home: 10 Kingsborough Cres., Weston, Ont. M9R 2T9; Office: 188 Wilkinson Rd., Unit 3, Brampton, Ont. L6T 4W9.

**SMELLIE, Robert Gordon,** Q.C.; b. Russell, Man. 23 Aug. 1923; s. Albert George and Jessie May (Cummings) S.; e. Public and High Schs., Russell, Man., 1942; Royal Mil. Coll., Aldershot, U.K., 1945; Brandon Coll., Univ. of Man., LL.B. 1950; m. Lois Evelyn, d. Robert Stuart Cochrane, 4 July 1946; children: Susan Lynn Kurushima, Carol Ann Gamby, Linda Darlene Gage; m. Jean Patricia (Stallwood) McIntyre, 23 Aug. 1980; PARTNER, AIKINS, MacAULAY & THORVALDSON; read law with Justice J.J. Kelly, K.C. and A. Lorne Campbell; called to Bar of Manitoba 1950; cr. Q.C. 1963; private practice of law, Russell, Manitoba, 1950–63; Smellie and Coppleman, 1963–66; joined present firm 1966; served with Royal Winnipeg Rifles in N.W. Europe during World War II; rank Lt.; def. cand. Man. g.e. 1958; el. Man. g.e. 1959; Min. of Mun. Affairs 1963–66; def. Man. g.e. 1966; Dir., Brandon Coll., 1959–61; Past Pres., Man. Heart Foundation; Dir. & Treasurer, Deer Lodge Centre Inc.; Chrmn. Local Govt. Boundaries Comn. 1966–70; mem., Man. Bar Assn.; Candn. Bar Assn.; Royal Candn. Legion (Past Dom. Pres.); Candn. Corps of Commissionaires, Past Man. Div., Chrmn. Nat., Vice Chrmn.; Hon. Lt. Col. Royal Winnipeg Rifles; P. Conservative; United Church; recreations: tennis, woodworking; Home: 100 Eastgate, Winnipeg, Man. R3C 2C3; Office: 360 Main St., Winnipeg, Man. R3C 4G1.

**SMELTZER, Walter William,** B.Sc., Ph.D., Dr.Hon.Causa (Dijon), F.R.S.C.; educator; b. Moose Jaw, Sask. 4 Dec. 1924; s. Harold Roland and Jean Marie (Haslam) S.; e. Queen's Univ. B.Sc. 1948; Univ. of Toronto Ph.D. 1953; Univ. of Dijon Dr. Hon.Causa 1981; PROF. EMERITUS OF METALL. AND MATERIALS SCI. McMASTER UNIV.; Rsch. Chem. Eng., Nat. Rsch. Council 1949–50, Aluminium Labs. 1953–55; Rsch. Metall. Eng. Carnegie Inst. of Technol. 1955–59; Visiting Sci., Max-Planck Inst. for Phys. Chem. 1965–66; Lawrence Berkeley Lab. 1972; Visiting Prof. Univ. of N.S.W. Australia 1968; France-Can. Exchange Prof. Univ. Limoges 1976; Brit. Council Sr. Rsch. Fellow Univ. Liverpool 1976; NATO Sr. Rsch. Fellow Univs. Dijon, Compiegne 1979; France-Can. Exchange Prof., Univ. Bourgogne 1986; Visiting Scientist, Cavendish Laboratory, Cambridge Univ. 1986–87; Chrmn., Gordon Conf. Advanc. Sci. Corrosion 1965; recipient Centennial Medal 1967; recipient Am. Soc. Metals Albert Sauveur Achievement Award 1986; 4th Candn. Metal Chemistry Award 1991, Candn. Materials Science Conference; ed. 'Zirconium and its Alloys' 1966; 'Metal-Slag-Gas Reactions and Processes' 1975; mem. various ed. bds.; Fellow, Am. Soc. Metals (Chrmn. Ont. Chapter 1966); mem., Electrochem. Soc.; Nat. Assn. Corrosion Engs.; Assn. Prof. Engs. Prov. Ont.; Home: 332 Newbold Court, Burlington, Ont. L7R 2Y6; Office: Hamilton, Ont. L8S 4M1.

**SMETHURST, Robert G.,** C.D., Q.C., LL.B.; b. Calgary, Alta. 28 May 1929; s. Herbert Guy Humphreys and Muriel Mary (Wilson) S.; e. Magee High Sch., Vancouver; Univ. of B.C.; Univ. of Man. Law Sch., LL.B. 1952; m. Carol Ann; children: Linda Anne, David Guy; EXTVE. DIR., B.C. BRANCH, CANADIAN BAR ASSOC.; former Partner D'Arcy & Deacon; read law with Albert H. Warner, Q.C.; called to Bar of Man. 1953; cr. Q.C. 1968; Partner, Warner, Billinkoff & Smethurst, Winnipeg, 1954–65; D'Arcy, Irving, Haig & Smethurst 1965–71; D'Arcy and Deacon 1971–87; Pres., Estate Planning Council of Winnipeg 1970–71; Commr. on Uniform Law Conference of Canada (Pres. 1978–79); drafted leg. for Condominium Act; served as an Offr. with Winnipeg Grenadiers (Militia) 1950–62 (second-in-command of regt. on retirement), Pres., V.O.N. for Man. Inc., 1966–70 and V.O.N. for Can., 1976–79; United Services Institute mem. (Pres. 1961–2), Man. Law Reform Comn.; mem., Man. Bar Assn. (Pres. 1969–70); Candn. Bar Assn. (Pres. of Man. Branch 1971–72); Pres., Candn. Bar Insurance Assoc. 1983–85; Law Soc. Man.; Phi Delta Theta; P. Conservative; Protestant; Home: 1597 Augusta Ave., Burnaby, B.C. V5A 4N9; Office: 10th Floor, 845 Cambie St., Vancouver, B.C. V6B 5T3.

**SMETHURST, Stanley Eric,** M.A.; university professor emeritus; b. Manchester, Eng., 19 Jan. 1915; s. Stanley and Anna (Linnert) S.; e. St. John's Coll., Cambridge, B.A. 1937, M.A. 1941; m. Viola Clara, d. Edward Butler, Cambridge, Eng., 22 Aug. 1938; children: Sandra, Anthony; came to Canada 1938; HEAD, DEPT. OF CLASSICS, QUEEN'S UNIV., 1961–1980; Prof. of Classics and Ancient Hist., Univ. of New Brunswick, 1938–47; apptd. Prof. of Classics, Queen's Univ., 1947; mem., Classical Assn.; Am. Philol. Assn.; Unitarian; recreations: writing, photography; Home: 305 – 1500 Merklin, Whiterock, B.C. V4B 4C5.

**SMILLIE, Robert Ian,** B.A.; writer; consultant; b. Toronto, Ont. 27 Dec. 1944; s. Robert and Ruth Aldyene (Watson) S.; e. Westmount (Qué.) High Sch.; McGill Univ. B.A. 1967; one s. Rowan Sean Wilson-Smillie; taught secondary sch. Sierra Leone 1967–68; Mgr. CUSO Tech. Assistance Prog. Nigeria 1968–71; Asst. Dir. Overseas Operations CUSO Ottawa 1971–72; Dir. CARE Housing Project Bangladesh 1972–74; Asst. Dir. Office Internat. Edn. Univ. of W. Ont. 1974–75; Founder and Dir. Inter Pares (internat. devel. agency) Ottawa 1975–79; Exec. Dir. CUSO 1979–83; writer and internat. devel. cons. since 1983; Bd. Mem., The Resource Foundation (N.Y.); Worldview Internat. Foundation (Colombo); recent or current cons. UNICEF, CIDA, EEC, NOVIB, CARE, OECD, Intermediate Technol. Devel. Group, Aga Khan Foundation; author: (non-fiction) 'Land of Lost Content' 1985; 'No Condition Permanent' 1986; 'Mastering the Machine' 1991; co-author: 'Sustainable Industrial Development' 1988; 'Stakeholders in Development' 1993; mem. Writers Union Can.; Brit. Soc. Authors; recreations: tennis, philately; Address: 618 Melbourne Ave., Ottawa, Ont. K2A 1X1.

**SMIT, Barry Edward,** Ph.D.; university professor/environmental consultant; b. Auckland, N.Z. 24 Sept. 1948; s. Albert Maurice and Shirley (Walters) S.; e. Univ. of Auckland, B.A. 1969, M.A. (Hons.) 1971; McMaster Univ. Ph.D. 1977; m. Ruthann d. Aubrey and

Bertha Buchner 11 Dec. 1975; children: Emily, Hannah; PROF. IN GEOGRAPHY, UNIV. OF GUELPH 1986– ; Jr. Lectr. in Geog., Univ. of Auckland 1972–73; Asst. Prof. in Geog., Univ. of Guelph 1976–80; Assoc. Prof. 1980–86; Mem., Candn. Climate Prog. Planning Bd.; Chrmn., Adv. Ctte. on Socio-Econ. Impacts of Climate Change; Adv./Cons., Energy, Mines & Resources, Can.; Environ., Can.; Agric. Can.; Food & Agric. Orgn., Rome; Environ. Min., Govt. of Norway; Internat. Inst. of Applied Sys. Analysis, Austria; Candn. Co-chair, FG3, IJC Ref. Study on Great Lakes' Water Levels; Mem., Candn. Assn. of Geog.; Assn. of Am. Geog.; Reg. Sci. Assn.; Candn. Agric. Econ. Soc.; Internat. Geog. Union; author of over 50 sci. articles & reports; co-editor: 'Demands on Rural Lands' 1987, 'Perspectives on Land Modelling' 1988; recreations: sports, photography, travel; Home: 19 Malvern Cres., Guelph, Ont. N1H 6H8; Office: Univ. of Guelph, Guelph, Ont. N1G 2W1.

**SMITH, Arthur J.R.,** B.A., M.A., Ph.D., D.U.C. LL.D.; economist; b. Simcoe, Ont. 7 Jan. 1926; s. Ralph Eugene and Mildred Helen (Johnson) S.; e. Pub. and High Sch. in India and in Simcoe, Ont.; McMaster Univ., B.A. (Math. & Pol. Econ.) 1947, LL.D. 1971; Harvard Univ., M.A. (Econ.) 1949, Ph.D. (Econ.) 1955; Hon. D.U.C., Univ. of Calgary; m. Ruth Frances Elizabeth, d. late H. Stanley Carey, 21 Aug. 1948; three d. Helen Alexandra, Deborah Ann, Barbara Jean; Visiting Prof., Brock Univ. since 1987; Dir., The Oshawa Group Ltd. since 1975; Teaching Fellow, Harvard University, 1949–50; Econ. successively in Monetary Research Div., Domestic Research Div. and Foreign Research Div., Fed. Reserve Bank of N.Y., 1950–54; Candn. Econ., Nat. Indust. Conf. Bd., Montreal, 1954–57; Lectr., Extension Dept., McGill Univ., 1955–56; Dir. of Research and Secy.-Treas., Private Planning Assn. of Can., Montreal, 1957–63; also Dir. of Research, Candn.-Am. Comte., 1957–63 and Secy., Candn. Trade Comte., 1962–63; Dir., Econ. Council of Can., 1963–67, Chrmn. 1967–71; Pres. Conference Brd. of Can. 1971–76; Vice Pres. Inco 1976–78; Asst. to Chrmn Inco 1978–79; Pres., Nat. Planning Assoc. 1979–81; Assoc., Woods Gordon 1981–83; Pres., Arthur J.R. Smith Assoc. Inc. 1983–84; C.E.O., Candn. Labour Mkt. and Productivity Centre, 1984–86; Visiting Prof., Brock Univ. 1986– ; mem., Cdn.-Am. Comm. 1971–81; Br.-N. Amer. Comm. 1979–81; Comm. on Changing Internat Realities 1979–81; United Church; Home: 4–375 Book Rd., Grimsby, Ont L3M 2M8; Office: Faculty of Business, Rm. TARO 336, Brock Univ., St. Catherines, Ont. L2S 3A1.

**SMITH, Arthur Ryan,** D.F.C., C.M.; executive; b. Calgary, Alta. 16 May 1919; s. Arthur LeRoy Smith; e. Shawinigan Lake Sch. B.C.; m. Betty Ann d. Bruce Walker 10 May 1964; three children; CHRMN., S.N.C. LAVALIN INC. (Chemical & Petroleum Div.); Dir., Asia Pacific Foundation; Calgary Airport Authority; Triton Energy Co. Ltd.; Calgary Cable TV Ltd.; Chief of Protocol, Calgary Olympic Winter Games 1988; Extve. Mem., Organizing Ctte., World Energy Congress, Montreal 1989; former Co-Chrmn., Calgary Economic Development Authority; Petrotech Lavalin Inc.; Ducks Unlimited Inc.; Invest. Counsellor, Tanner & Co. Ltd. 1945; Ed. 'Oil in Canada' and 'Petroleum Exploration Digest' 1952; Asst. to Pres. Anglo American Exploration Ltd. 1953, Pacific Petroleums Ltd. 1957; Pres. Ventures Management Ltd. 1965; Vice Pres. Foster Advertising Ltd. 1970; Pres. Arthur R. Smith & Associates Ltd., Can Trans Services (Malaysia) Ltd. 1973; Vice Pres., Allarco Developments Ltd. 1978; el. Ald. City of Calgary 1953, 1963; M.L.A. 1955; el. to H. of C. 1957, re-el. 1958, 1962; served as Chrmn. various parlty. comtes. 1957–63; Advisor, and Candn. Del. to UN 1957, 1959, 1961, 1963; mem. Royal Comn. on Fed. El. Expenses; served as RAF Pathfinder Pilot overseas 1939–44; Past Vice Pres. Alta. Chamber Comm.; Past Pres. Calgary Chamber Comm.; former Chrmn. Bd. Alta. Environmental Research Trust; Dir. Calgary Olympic Devel. Assn.; Pres. S. Alta. Recreation Devel. Assn.; mem. Chancellor's Club Univ. Calgary; former Dir. Calgary Philharmonic Soc., Calgary Exhn. & Stampede, Un. Services Inst., Stampeder Football Club, Gen. Hosp. Bd.; former Chrmn. Calgary Internat. Aviation Conf., Calgary Indust. Comn., Calgary Aviation Comn.; former Pres. Air Cadet League Can., Calgary Booster Club; rec'd Centennial Medal 1967; City of Calgary Award of Merit 1985; awarded Hon. LL.D., Univ. of Calgary 1988; Member, Order of Canada 1989; P. Conservative; Anglican; recreations: golf, tennis; Clubs: Calgary Golf & Country; Glencoe; Calgary Petroleum (Gov. and Pres.); Home: 1104 Beverley Blvd., Calgary S.W., Alta.; Office: 909–5 Ave. S.W., Calgary, Alta. T2P 3G5.

**SMITH, Hon. Brian Ray Douglas,** Q.C., M.A., LL.B.; lawyer; executive; b. Victoria, B.C. 7 July 1934; s. Douglas Edgar and E. Eleanor (Parfitt) S.; e. Victoria Coll., Univ. of British Columbia B.A., LL.B.; Queen's Univ. M.A.; m. Barbara; children; Claire E., Christopher C.; CHAIRMAN, CANADIAN NATIONAL RAILWAY COMPANY 1989– ; former provincial politician and formerly Associate Counsel, Pearlman & Lindholm (Victoria); el. M.L.A. for Oak Bay-Gordon Head prov. g.e. 1979, re-elected 1983, 1986; Min. of Education, B.C. 1979–82; Min. of Energy & Mines 1982–83; Attorney General 1983–88; Mayor of Oak Bay, B.C. 1974–79; Boards: Ballet B.C.; Tennis Canada; Vancouver Internat. Commercial Arbitration Centre; Clubs and Affiliations: Union Club; Oak Bay Tennis; Vancouver Lawn and Tennis; Vancouver Bd. of Trade; Extve. Office: Suite 1900, 1055 West Hastings St., Vancouver, B.C. V6E 2E9.

**SMITH, The Hon. Bruce Atherton,** CStJ; politician; b. Toronto, Ont. 3 May 1937; s. Hector MacDonald and Bertha Muriel (Dickie) S.; e. Peterborough C.V.S. 1956; Ryerson Polytech. Inst., Radio-TV arts 1959; children: Geoffrey, Stephen, Trevor; SOLICITOR GENERAL, PROV. OF N.B. 1991– ; var. posts from Prog. Dir. to Station Mgr., Carleton-Victoria Broadcasting (Woodstock, N.B.) 1959–87; elected MLA 1987; Min. of Supply & Services, Prov. of N.B. 1987–91; Past Dir., Atlantic Assn. of Broadcasters; Former Mem., Radio-TV News Dir. Assn.; Commander, Order of St. John; active work for St. John Ambulance; Mem., N.B. Liberal Assn.; recreations: golf, hockey; Clubs: Woodstock Golf & Curling, Woodstock Loafers Oldtimers Hockey; Home: Box 1768, Woodstock, N.B. E0J 2B0; Office: Box 6000, Fredericton, N.B. E3B 5H1.

**SMITH, C. Alan,** B.Comm., C.A.; executive; b. Olds, Alta. 19 July 1944; s. Thomas and Helen C. (Hartman) S.; e. Univ. of Alta. B.Com. 1967; C.A. 1971; m. Emily R. d. Van Buren Fleming 19 Aug. 1978; PRESIDENT, AEONIAN CAPITAL CORPORATION; Chrmn., Hillsborough Resources Ltd.; Plastifab Ltd.; Dir., Vector Industries Internat. Inc.; Dominion Explorers Inc.; joined Hudson's Bay Oil & Gas Ltd. 1965–67; articled with Peat, Marwick, Mitchell & Co. 1967–69; Bow Valley Industries Ltd. 1969–71; Vice Pres. & Dir., Paloma Petroleum Ltd. 1971–75; Pres., Conuco Ltd. 1976–79; Pres., Brinco Oil & Gas Ltd. 1979–81; Pres. & Chrmn., Consolidated Brinco Ltd. 1985–89; Chrmn. Bd. of Govs., Strathcona-Tweedsmuir School; Candn. Institute of Chartered Accountants; Former Dir., Independent Petrol. Assn. of Canada; mem. Candn. Assn. of Petroleum Landmen; recreation: outdoor sports; Clubs: Calgary Petroleum; Ranchmen's; Glencoe; Office: Suite 2150, 250 - 6 Avenue S.W., Calgary, Alta. T2P 3H7.

**SMITH, C. Linda,** B.A.; public relations executive; b. Montreal, Que. 18 Oct. 1957; d. Ian Donovan and Nancy St. Barbe (Kindersley) S.; e. Ryerson Polytech. Inst. B.A. (Journalism) 1981; GENERAL MANAGER & SR. VICE-PRES., FLEISHMAN-HILLARD 1993– ; Broadcast News Reporter-Editor 1981–82; joined Hill and Knowlton 1982; Vice-Pres. 1986; Sr. Vice-Pres. 1991; Sr. Vice-Pres. & Dir. of Candn. Health Care Practice 1992; expert in crisis health care, consumer prod. communications & issues mngt.; recreations: running, skiing, tennis, dog walking; Home: 165 Pape Ave., Toronto, Ont. M4M 2W1; Office: 360 Bay St., Toronto, Ont. M5H 2V6.

**SMITH, Cameron Mitchell,** B.A., LL.B.; writer; b. Kirkland Lake, Ont. 15 May 1935; s. George Edward and Margaret Cameron (Fitchett) S.; e. Sudbury H.S. 1954; Queen's Univ. B.A. 1957; Dalhousie Law Sch. LL.B. 1960; m. Muriel d. Wesley and Viola James 1962, div. 1981; two d. Vanessa Margaret, Alexandra Mitchell; law practice Blake, Cassels and Graydon, Toronto 1961–65; The Globe and Mail 1965–84 serving as reporter, ed. writer, asst. ed., exec. ed., mng. ed.; author 'Unfinished Journey: The Lewis Family' 1989; 'Love and Solidarity: A Pictorial History of the NDP' 1992; Assoc. mem. Internat. Club of Rome; Address: 147 Hamilton St., Toronto, Ont. M4M 2C9.

**SMITH, Carlton George,** M.D., M.Sc., Ph.D.; university professor; b. Ont. 8 Nov. 1905; s. Charles and Catherine (Wolfe) S.; e. Victoria Coll., Univ. of Toronto, B.A. 1928; Univ. of W. Ont., M.Sc. 1931; Ont. Coll. of Educ. (science specialist) 1932; Univ. of Toronto, M.D. 1935, Ph.D. 1936; m. Marquerite Harland, 1976; PROFESSOR EMERITUS OF ANATOMY, UNIVERSITY OF TORONTO 1979– ; Prof. Emeritus of Anatomy, Univ. of Toronto 1979; Visiting Prof. of Anatomy Uniformed Services Univ. of the Health Sciences 1979–81; served in World War 1939–45 as Surg. Lieut.-Commdr. with R.C.N.V.R.; awarded Reeve Prize for Med. Research; author: 'Basic Neuroanatomy' (textbook); 'Serial Dissections of the Human Brain' (atlas); 'The Eye in Childhood' (Chapter 1); 'Dissections of The Brain' (a series of videotapes in neuroanatomy); 'Sculptures of Brain Dissections as Teaching Aids'; mem., Am. Assn. of Anatomists; Candn. Physiol. Soc.; Acad. of Med., Toronto; Candn. Assn. Anats.; Candn. Neurol. Soc.; Alpha Kappa Kappa; United Church; Home: 10459 Resthaven Dr., Suite 313, Sidney, B.C. V8L 3H6.

**SMITH, Carlyle Taylor,** B.Sc., M.A., Ph.D.; educator; b. Brandon, Man. 20 Sept. 1941; s. William Walter and Annie Isobelle (Taylor) S.; e. Univ. of Man. B.Sc. 1964; Univ. of Waterloo M.A. 1969, Ph.D. 1971; reg'd Psychol. 1980; m. Mary Jane d. Ken and Dorothy Rutherford 11 Sept. 1971; two d. Danielle, Valerie; PROF. OF PSYCHOL. TRENT UNIV. 1986– ; Adjunct Prof. Carleton Univ. 1988– ; Postdoctoral Rsch. Fellow Sleep Lab. Univ. Claude Bernard Lyon, France 1971–72; Asst. Prof. of Psychol. present Univ. 1972, Assoc. Prof. 1977; Visiting Rsch. Prof.: Univ. de Nice, France 1979; Sleep Lab. Univ. of Ottawa 1980; Lab. de Psychophysiologie Univ. de Paris 1986; Lab. de Neurobiologie de l'Apprentissage et de la Memoire (CNRS) Université de Paris 1993; recipient Ont. Grad. Fellowships, Can. Council and Nat. Rsch. Council Travel Awards; rsch. supported by Natural Sci's & Eng. Rsch. Council; author or co-author over 50 acad. articles sleep and learning; mem. Candn. Sleep Soc. (Sec.-Treas. 1988–90); Assn. Profl. Sleep Soc's; Candn. Psychol. Assn.; recreations: fishing, curling; Home: R.R.11, Peterborough, Ont. K9J 6Y3; Office: Peterborough, Ont. K9J 7B8.

**SMITH, Carol Lynn,** Q.C., B.A., LL.B.; university administrator; b. Calgary, Alta.; d. Edward Charles and Edythe Alberta (Watters) S.; Central H.S. Calgary 1963; Univ. of Calgary B.A. (Hons.) 1967; Univ. of B.C. LL.B. 1973; m. Jon s. Norma and Harold Sigurdson 22 Dec. 1973; children: Elin Rebecca Smith Sigurdson, Krista Mary Smith Sigurdson; DEAN, FACULTY OF LAW, UNIV. OF B.C. 1991– ; Law Clerk to Chief Justice of B.C. 1973–74; called to Bar of B.C. 1974; practised general litigation at Shrum, Liddle & Hebenton (articled student, associate, then partner) 1974–81; Assoc. Prof., Univ. of B.C. 1981; Prof. 1990; Human Rights Bds. of Inquiry (B.C.); Continuing Legal Edn.; Continuing Judicial Edn.; YWCA Woman of Distinction Award 1990; Founding Dir., Women's Legal Edn. & Action Fund (Pres. 1989–91); Dir., Science World; Gov., Law Foundation of B.C.; Mem., Law Soc. of B.C. 1974– ; Candn. Bar Assn. 1974– ; Q.C. 1992; co-author: 'Civil Jury Instructions' 1990; Editor-in-Chief: 'Righting the Balance: Canada's New Equality Rights' 1986; Office: 1822 East Mall, Vancouver, B.C. V6T 1Z1.

**SMITH, Charles Haddon,** M.Sc., M.S., Ph.D., P. Eng., F.R.S.C., F.M.S.A.; geologist; b. Dartmouth, N.S. 3 Sept. 1926; s. Albion Benson and Dora Pauline (McGill) S.; e. Dalhousie Univ. B.Sc. and Dipl. in Engn. 1946, M.Sc. 1948; Yale Univ. M.S. 1951, Ph.D. 1952; m. Mary Gertrude d. late Dr. Jabez Ronald Saint 5 Sept. 1949; children: Dr. Charles Douglas, Richard David, Alan Michael, Timothy McGill; PRESIDENT, CHARLES H. SMITH CONSULTANTS 1982– ; Instr. in Engn. Dalhousie Univ. 1946–48; Geol. Cerro de Pasco Copper Corp. Morococha, Peru 1949; Geol. Survey of Can. Ottawa 1952–64, Chief Petrological Science Div. 1964–67, Chief Crustal Geol. 1967–68; Science Adviser, Science Council of Can. Ottawa 1968–70; Dir. of Planning, Dept. of Energy, Mines & Resources 1970–71, Asst. Depy. Min. (Science & Technol.) Dept. of Energy, Mines & Resources 1971–75; Sr. Asst. Depy. Min., Dept. of Energy, Mines & Resources 1975–80; Sr. Asst. Depy. Min. (Mines) Dept. of Energy, Mines & Resources 1980–82; Foreign Secy., Royal Soc. of Can. 1986–90; Science Adv., Candn. Commn. for UNESCO 1983–89; Gov., Candn. Institute for Radiation Safety 1983–86; Exec. Dir., Candn. Nat. Ctte., World Energy Conference 1984–90; Hon. Mem., Energy Council of Canada 1991– ; Coordinator, 150th Anniversary Geological Survey of Canada 1990–93; author over 60 publs. in earth sciences, energy and mineral fields; Fellow, Soc. Econ. Geols.; Past Vice Pres., Candn. Inst. Mining & Metall.; Past Pres., Candn. Geosci. Counc.; Mem., Geol. Assn. Can.; Prospectors and Developers Assn.; British Soc. for the History of Science; Prof. Eng. Prov. of Ont.; Dir., Rotary Club of Ottawa; United Church; recreations: cycling, swimming; Home: 2056 Thistle Cres., Ottawa, Ont. K1H 5P5.

**SMITH, Charles Murray,** D.V.M.; veterinarian, animal nutritionist; b. Blenheim, Ont. 19 July 1928; s. Percival Garnet and Loretta Mae (Riseborough) S.; e. Blenheim H.S. 1948; Univ. of Western Ont. 1950; Ontario Veterinary College D.V.M. 1956; m. Betty d. Ernest Campbell 1 Sept. 1948; children: Catherine, Douglas, David, Teresa, Michelle; PRESIDENT, HARVEST SPRING NUTRITIONAL SYSTEMS (CORP.) 1981 (manufacturs and sells complete environmental hydroponic growing chambers, to produce fresh cereal grass supplement daily for all livestock and poultry) 1989– ; veterinarian practice Charing Cross Animal Hospital 1956–63; imported Wessex Saddleback Swine from England & Scotland & devel. 3-way cross-breeding program; devel. Hydroponic Nutritional prog. for livestock & poultry; installed systems & set up nutritional programs for Fidel Castro in Cuba 1964; moved to U.S. late 1964 & devel. Hydroponic prog.; Pres., Autoponics Inc. (Dallas); patented complete auto. hydroponic system to produce fresh grass daily for livestock & poultry; Smith Animal Hosp. (London, Ont.) 1968–90; owner/operator, Fortune Farms (breeding & racing stable) 1975– ; Dir., Business Club of London; Candn. Trotting Assn.; Soc. of Ont. Vets.; Candn. Vet. Med. Assn.; Ont. Vet. Med. Assn.; Mem., Pres. Council, Univ. of Guelph; Mem., Kent Lodge 247 A.F.A.M. Blenheim, Ont.; Mocha Temple AAONMS London, Ont.; London Shrine Club; author of several feeding manuals incl.: 'Equine Nutrition' 1966, '90, 'Dairy & Beef Nutrition' 1966, 'Sheep & Swine Nutrition' 1966; recreations: hockey, breeding & racing standardbred horses; Home: Box 578, Lambeth, Ont. N0L 1S0; Office: Box 429, Lambeth, Ont. N0L 1S0.

**SMITH, (George Hayes) Clifford,** B.A.Sc., P.Eng.; b. Hamilton, Ont. 3 Apr. 1907; s. George M. and Russell Georgian (Hayes) S.; e. Delta Coll. Inst., Hamilton, Ont.; Univ. of Toronto, B.A.Sc. (Chem. Engn.) 1932; m. (Elizabeth) Wilma, d. W.B. Bate, Toronto, Ont. 15 June 1935; children: Stephen Clifford, Russell Bradnee, Fraser William; Dir., Bate Equities Ltd; PolyResins Inc.; Past Bd. Chrmn., Bate Chemical Co. Ltd.; Nuodex Products of Canada Ltd.; Hysol Canada Ltd.; mem., Assn. Prof. Engrs. Ont.; Past Dir., Chemical Producers Assn.; Lambda Chi Alpha; recreations: sailing, travel, music, colour-photography; Clubs: Granite; National; Rosedale Golf; Rotary; Caledon Mountain Trout; Home: 39 Strathgowan Crescent, Toronto, Ont. M4N 2Z8; Farm: R.R. #1, Terra Cotta, Ont. L0P 1N0.

**SMITH, Clive A.;** film producer; b. England 1944; e. sch. 1960; art school 1965; co-vivant: Melleny Melody; children: Zach Spider; emigrated to Can. 1967; CO-FOUNDER & VICE-PRES., NELVANA LTD.; PRES., CREATIVE DIR., BEARSPOTS INC.; Dir., numerous TV commercials, Animation and Live Combos.; Co-Extve. Prod.: 'Beetlejuice' (86 eps.) Animated TV Series 1989–92; 'Babar' (65 eps.) Animated TV Series 1990–92; 'Babar, The Movie' Animated Movie 1990; 'Tin Tin' (26 eps.) Animated TV Series 1991–92; 'Rupert' (26 eps.) Animated TV Series 1991–92; Director: 'Family Dog' (10 eps.) Animated TV Series 1992; Extve. Prod., 'The Edison Twins' (39 eps./Dir. 2 eps.) 1983–86; Co-Prod., 'T & T' (23 eps.) 1988, 'The Care Bears Family' (13 eps.) 1986, 'Ewoks' (13 eps.) 1985 (animated TV series); '20 Minute Workout' (120 eps., Co-Extve. Prod.) 1983 (TV series); 'The Care Bears Movie II' 1985–86, 'The Care Bears Movie' (Golden Reel Award 1986) 1985; Dir., 'Rock & Rule (Ring of Power)' 1983; Co-Prod.: 'The Care Bears Adventure in Wonderland' 1987 (animated movies), 'My Pet Monster' 1986, 'Mad Balls' 1986, 'The Great Heep' (& Dir.) 1985, 'The Ewok-Droids Adventure Hour' (& Dir.) 1985; Dir., 'Intergalactic Thanksgiving' 1979, 'The Star Wars Holiday Special' (Candn. inserts) 1978, 'Romie-0 & Julie-8' 1978, 'The Devil and Daniel Mouse' 1978, 'Cosmic Christmas' 1976–77 (animated TV movies/specials); num. awards incl. Mobius, Houston Int. Film Fest., Graphica, U.S. Indus. Film Fest., a Special Award from Candn. Film Awards 1978; Office: 32 Atlantic Ave., Toronto, Ont. M6X 1X8.

**SMITH, Cynthia McKay,** M.A., M.L.S.; rsch. director; b. Bracebridge, Ont. 3 Sept. 1942; d. Hon. Douglas Cameron and Margaret L. (McKay) Thomas; e. Univ. of Toronto B.A. 1964 (Trinity Coll.), M.A. 1966, B.L.S. 1968, M.L.S. 1979; m. 1st Richard Price Smith 18 June 1966 (div.); m. 2ndly Prof. J. T. McLeod 12 Apr. 1986; children: Andrew T. and Adrienne F. Price Smith; DIR., LEGIS. RSCH. SERVICE, ONT. LEGIS. LIBRARY 1984– ; Historian: Ont. Hist. Studies Series 1974–79, Ont. Min. of Culture & Recreation 1977–78; Chief Lib. Inco Ltd. Toronto 1979–82; Dir. of Placement Faculty of Lib. & Info. Sci. Univ. of Toronto 1982–84, Assoc. Instr. 1982–85; prin. ed. 'Sir John A.' anecdotal biog. 1989; assoc. ed. 'Oxford Book of Canadian Political Anecdotes' 1988; Univ. Affairs Bd., Governing Council, Univ. of Toronto 1991–92, 1993– ; Academic Bd., Governing Council, Univ. of Toronto 1992–93; Pres. Univ. Toronto Alumni Assn. 1990–91; Chair Univ. Toronto Coll. of Electors 1988–89; mem. Bd. Chamber Players Toronto 1978–89, Toronto Symphony 1974–75; Anglican; Home: 202 Inglewood Dr., Toronto, Ont. M4T 1H9; Office: 2520 Whitney Block, 99 Wellesley St. W., Toronto, Ont. M7A 1A2.

**SMITH, David C.,** C.M., M.A., Ph.D., LL.D., F.R.S.C.; educator; b. Ootacamund, India 12 Aug. 1931; s. Ralph Eugene and Mildred Helen (Johnson) S.; e. McMaster Univ. B.A. 1953; Oxford Univ. M.A. 1955; Harvard Univ. Ph.D. 1959; m. Mary Hilda d. late Kenneth W. Taylor 25 June 1955; children: Monica H., Geoffrey K.C.; PROF. OF ECON., PRINCIPAL AND VICE-CHANCELLOR, QUEEN'S UNIV. 1984– ; Dir. of Research (Economics) Royal Commission on the Economic Union and Development Prospects for Canada 1983–84; Chair of Council of Ontario Universities 1992– ; Honorary Doctorates: McMaster Univ. LL.D. 1991; Queen's Univ., Belfast LL.D. 1991; Mem., Order of Canada 1994; Home: 145 King St. W., Kingston, Ont. K7L 2W6; Office: Kingston, Ont. K7L 3N6.

**SMITH, David Edward,** M.A., Ph.D., F.R.S.C.; b. Springhill, N.S. 8 Aug. 1936; s. Sterling Truman and Doris (Haythorne) S.; e. Univ. of W. Ont. B.A. 1959; Duke Univ. M.A. 1962, Ph.D. 1964; m. Gene Anne d. Owen and Emma Gene (Allred) 10 May 1968; children: Joshua, Sarah; PROF. OF POL. SCI. UNIV. OF SASK. 1974– ; Asst. Prof. present Univ. 1966, Assoc. Prof. 1969, Asst. Dean of Grad. Studies 1975–78; Visiting Prof. of Candn. Studies in Japan 1981–82; Sask. mem. Historic Sites & Monuments Bd. Can. 1975–88; mem. Social Sci's & Humanities Acad. Adv. Panel 1982–84; Adv. Bd. Inst. Intergovt'al Relations Queen's Univ. 1978– ; Chrmn., Aid to Scholarly Publications Programme, Social Sciences Federation of Canada 1993– ; Pres.-elect, Candn. Political Science Assn. 1993–94; author: 'Prairie Liberalism: The Liberal Party in Saskatchewan, 1905–71' 1975; 'Regional Decline of a National Party: Liberals on the Prairies' 1981; co-author: 'James G. Gardiner: Relentless Liberal' 1990; 'Buildings Province: A History of Saskatchewan in Documents' 1992; Office: Saskatoon, Sask. S7N 0W0.

**SMITH, Hon. David Paul,** P.C., Q.C., B.A., LL.B.; lawyer; b. Toronto, Ont. 16 May 1941; s. Campbell Bannerman and Beulah (Argue) S.; e. Carleton Univ. B.A. 1964; Queen's Univ. LL.B. 1970; m. Madame Justice Heather Smith d. Rex and Norah Forster 30 May 1970; children: Alexander, Kathleen, Laura; PARTNER, FRASER & BEATTY; Tutor and Lectr. in Candn. Politics Queen's Univ. 1968–70; Asst. to Nat. Dir. Lib. Party of Can. 1964–65; Nat. Pres., Young Lib. Fed. Can. 1966; Exec. Asst. to Pres. of Privy Council and to Min. of Consumer & Corporate Affairs and Min. of Justice; called to Bar of Ont. 1972; Partner, Kaplan, Morris, Meagher & Smith; el. Ald. Toronto City Council 1972, re-el. Ald. and apptd. to Exec. Ctte. City of Toronto and Metro Toronto Council 1974, re-el. 1976 and apptd. Pres. Toronto City Council and Dep. Mayor of Toronto; Legal counsel Lyons, Arbus 1979; el. to H. of C. for Don Valley E. g.e. 1980; Chrmn. Special Ctte. Disabled and Handicapped 1980; Chrmn. Parlty. Ctte. Soviet Jewry; Parlty. Sec. to Pres. of Privy Council and Govt. House Leader 1981; Min. of State for Small Business and Tourism 1983–84; Bd. of Govs. Exhibition Place, Toronto; former Bd. mem. Toronto Gen. Hosp.; Mount Sinai Hosp.; George Brown Coll.; Retinitus Pigmentosa Foundation; Chrmn., Candn. Cancer Soc. Toronto Campaign 1980; Past Vice Chrmn., O'Keefe Centre for Performing Arts; St. George's College; Liberal; Baptist; Clubs: University; Empire; Churchill Soc.; National Liberal, London, Eng.; Home: 251 Russell Hill Rd., Toronto, Ont. M4V 2T3 and 93 Bagot St., Cobourg, Ont.; Office: 39th Floor, One First Canadian Place, Toronto, Ont. M5X 1B2.

**SMITH, David Todd,** B.B.A., M.B.A., C.G.A.; financial executive; b. Stamford, Conn. 19 Nov. 1953; s. Joseph m. and Ruth (Rolke) S.; e. Wilfrid Laurier Univ. B.B.A. 1976; McMaster Univ. M.B.A. 1978; C.G.A. Ont. 1980; m. Margaret d. George and Beryl Starke 30 Dec. 1978; children: Erik Joseph, Maximilian Peter; TREASURER, TORSTAR CORP. 1987– ; Financial Analyst, Economic Mutual Insur. Co. 1976–78; Portfolio Mgr., Merchant Trust Co. 1978–80; Treasury Offr., Harlequin Enterprises Ltd. 1980–82; Asst. Treas., Torstar Corp. 1982–87; Home: 141 Regent St., Richmond Hill, Ont. L4C 9P1; Office: 1 Yonge St., Toronto, Ont. M5E 1P9.

**SMITH, David Warner,** B.A., Ph.D.; educator; b. Loughborough, Eng. 14 Nov. 1932; s. John Sidney and Ellen (Wootton) S.; e. Univ. of Leeds B.A. 1953, Ph.D. 1961; m. Olaug Synnevåg 1963; two d. Ingrid Marie, Anne Catherine; PROF. OF FRENCH, VICTORIA UNIV. in the UNIV. OF TORONTO 1971– ; Asst. Prof. Meml. Univ. of Nfld. 1960–63; Asst. Prof. present Univ. 1963, Assoc. Prof. 1967, Chrmn. Combined Dept. French 1969–71, Chrmn. of French Victoria Coll. 1972–75, Chrmn. of French Univ. of Toronto 1975–80; Killam Rsch. Fellow 1980–81; Connaught Rsch. Fellow 1985–86; Guggenheim Rsch. Fellow 1986–87; author 'Helvétius: A Study in Persecution' 1965, reprinted 1982; 'Helvétius, Correspondance générale' Vol. I 1981, Vol. II 1984, Vol. III 1991; mem. Adv. Ctte. ed. Voltaire's Complete Works; mem. Editorial Bd. 'Studies on Voltaire'; Founder and 1st Pres., Candn. Soc. Eighteenth-Century Studies; Vice Pres., Internat. Soc. Eighteenth-Century Studies 1987–95; recreation: badminton; Home: 161 Colin Ave., Toronto, Ont. M5P 2C5; Office: Toronto, Ont. M5S 1K7.

**SMITH, Denis,** M.A., B.Litt., Litt.D.; professor; b. Edmonton, Alta. 3 Oct. 1932; s. Sidney Bruce and Doris Gertrude (Charlesworth) S.; e. McGill Univ., B.A. 1953; Oxford Univ., B.A. 1955, M.A. 1959, B.Litt. 1959; Trent Univ., Litt.D. 1989; m. Dawn Louise, d. Sir Donald Banks, K.C.B., D.S.O., M.C., Cadnam, Hampshire, 8 July 1961; children: Alastair, Stephen, Andrea; PROFESSOR OF POLITICAL SCIENCE, UNIV. OF WESTERN ONT. 1982– ; Instructor, Department of Pol. Econ., Univ. of Toronto, 1956–57; Lectr., 1957–58; Registrar and Lectr. in Pol. Science, York Univ., 1960–61; Asst. Prof., 1961–63; Assoc. Prof., 1964–68 Trent Univ.; Prof., 1968–82; Vice-Pres., Trent Univ., 1964–67, Chrmn. Dept., 1966–70; Ed. 'Journal of Canadian Studies' 1966–75; 'The Canadian Forum,' 1975–79; Master, Champlain Coll. 1969–71; Pres., Candn. Periodical Publishers' Ass'n., 1975–77; Dean, Social Science, Univ. of Western Ont. 1982–88; Chrmn., Lionel Gelber Prize Jury 1993; author: 'Bleeding Hearts, Bleeding Country' 1971; 'Gentle Patriot' (Univ. B.C. Medal for Popular Biog.) 1973; 'Diplomacy of Fear' (J.W. Dafoe Foundation Book Prize) 1988; Anglican; Home: 64 Augusta St., Port Hope, Ont. L1A 1G9.

**SMITH, Donald B.,** B.Sc., P.Eng.; manufacturing executive; B. Saskatoon, Sask. 14 May 1929; s. Frederic, W. and Adelaide C. (Jackson) S.; e. Eastwood High Sch. Edmonton; Univ. of Alta. B.Sc. (Civil Eng.) 1954; children: Christy Ann, Dean Marshall, Todd Fraser; VICE PRES. & GEN. MGR., ARMTEC INC. 1987– ; Dir. & Vice Pres. Court Galvanizing; Sales Eng. Armco Canada Ltd. 1954, Sales Mgr. 1959, Br. Mgr. 1960, Mgr. Alta. & Sask. 1965, Mgr. B.C. & Alta. 1970, Gen. Mgr. Constrn. Products 1977; Vice Pres. and Gen. Mgr. Constrn. Products, Armco Westeel Inc. 1983, Pres. & C.E.O. 1985–87; Past Chrmn. Edmonton Br. Egn. Inst. Can.; Past Pres. Corrugated Steel Pipe Inst.; Home: 362 Westwood Rd., Guelph, Ont. N1H 7P9; Office: P.O. Box 3000, Guelph, Ont. N1H 6P2.

**SMITH, Donald Cameron,** M.Sc., M.D., D.P.H., F.R.C.P. (C), F.A.P.H.A.; professor; b. Peterborough, Ont. 2 Feb. 1922; s. James Cameron and Clarice (Leighton) S.; e. Queen's Univ., M.D. 1945; Univ. of Toronto, M.Sc. (Med.) 1948 (Fellow in Physiol.), D.P.H. 1949; m. Ida Jean, d. late Earle Morningstar, 11 Sept. 1946; children: Douglas Frazer, Scott Earle, Donald Ian; Sr. Medical Advisor, Sisters of Mercy Health Corp., Farmington Hills, MI; Prof. of Psychiatry and Behavioural Sci., Northwestern Univ. Medical Sch.; Vice Pres. for Accreditation, Joint Comm. on Accreditation of Hosps. 1978–81; Internship, Victoria Hosp., London, Ont., 1945–46; Asst. Dir., E. York-Leaside (Ont.) Health Dept. 1949–50; Med. Dir., Kent Co. (Ont.) Health Dept., 1950–51; joined Univ. of Michigan as Commonwealth Fund Fellow in Pediatrics, 1952–55; Asst. Prof. of Maternal and Child Health, 1955–57; Assoc. Prof. 1957–61; Prof. at Maternal and Child Health, Sch. of Public Health, Prof. of Pediatrics, Med. Sch., Univ. of Michigan 1961–78; Med. Dir., Mich. Crippled Children Comn., 1962–64; overseas assignments incl. World Health Organ. Study of Child Health and Child Welfare Programs in Middle E., 1957; Review of New Devels. in W. Europe in Provision of Services for Handicapped Children and Youth, 1968; Integration of Maternal and Child Health & Family Planning Services, Repub. of S. Korea, 1969; Chrmn. Dept. Health Devel., Sch. Pub. Health Univ. Mich. 1964–72; Visiting Prof. Harvard Univ. 1969, 70, 71; Princ. Adv. Gov. Milliken (Mich.) Health & Med. Affairs 1972–78; Dir. Mich. Dept. Mental Health, 1974–78; Chrmn., Health Policy Bd., Mich. Dept. of Corrections 1976– ; Chrmn., Expert Ctte. on AIDS (Mich.) 1985–88; Public Health Adv. Council 1982– ; Medical Dir., Physicians Review Org. of Michigan 1992– ; Team Ldr., Cross-Nat. Study Health Care Services in Europe & Israel (Secy. H.E.W.) 1971; Pres., Mental Health Assn. in Michigan 1992; served with RCN 1946–47; rank Surg. Lt. on discharge; Chrmn., Med. Assistance Adv. Council, Secy. of Health, Educ. and Welfare; Examiner, Am. Bd. Preventive Med., Inc.; writings incl. numerous articles for prof. journs; Fellow, Am. Acad. Pediatrics; mem., Am. Med. Assn.; Mich. State Med. Soc.; Presbyterian; Home: 1000 Country Club Rd., Ann Arbor, MI 48105 USA.

**SMITH, Donald Maclean;** broadcast executive; b. Toronto, Ont. 25 June 1930; s. Donald Maclean and Annie Winnifred S.; m. Lorraine; children: Mary, Susan, Donald; PRES. & CHIEF EXTVE. OFFR., WESTCOM TV GROUP LTD. (1989– ) and WESTCOM ENTERTAINMENT GROUP LTD.; TV Time Salesman; Group Mgr.-Toronto Sales Mgr.-Vice Pres. Sales, All Canada Radio & TV Limited 1954–73; Vice-Pres., Sales/Extve. Vice-Pres., B.C. Television 1973–82; Pres. & Chief Extve. Offr., 1982–89; Dir., BBM Bureau of Measurement; Candn. Satellite Communications Inc. (Chrmn., Extve. Ctte.); Westcom Radio Group Ltd.; Westcom TV Group Ltd.; Westcom Entertainment Group Ltd.; Western Broadcast Sales Ltd.; WIC Western Internat. Communications Ltd.; Bd. Mem., Participaction; Assn. of Candn. Advertisers' Award 1977; clubs: Vancouver Bd. of Trade, Capilano Golf & Country, Hollyburn Country; Office: 1960 – 505 Burrard St., Vancouver, B.C. V7X 1M6.

**SMITH, Donald R.,** B.Sc., Ph.D., FCIC; scientist, administrator; b. Hamilton, Ont. 3 Sept. 1936; s. Milford Lorne and Gertrude Mae (Robertson) S.; e. McMaster Univ. B.Sc. (Hons.) 1958; Leeds Univ. Ph.D. 1961; m. Audrey d. Eva and Edward Gorst 2 April 1960; children: Mark, Sharon, Donald; DIRECTOR, STRATEGIC DEVELOPMENT, CANADIAN SPACE STATION PROGRAM, CANADIAN SPACE AGENCY 1991– Sept. 93; Consultant (Sept. 1993); Research Officer, Atomic Energy of Canada Ltd. 1961–82; Head, Physical Chem. Br. 1969–82; Dir., Nuclear Reactor, McMaster Univ. 1982–87; Prof. of Chem. (part-time) 1982–87; Pres., Nuclear Activation Services Ltd. 1984–87; Technology Devel. Mgr., Candn. Space Station Program, Nat. Rsch. Council 1988–90; Visiting Fellow, Emmanuel College, Cambridge Univ. 1975–76; elected Fellow, Chem. Inst. of Canada 1974; author of 44 scientific journal articles in radiation chem., electron spin resonance spectroscopy, far infrared laser magnetic resonance spectroscopy, laser photochem.; recreations: swimming, nordic skiing, music, reading, dogs; Office: 530 Leacock Dr., Barrie, Ont. L4N 7B3.

**SMITH, Donald W.,** B.A., M.A., Ph.D.; university professor; writer; editor; b. Toronto, Ont. 10 Aug. 1946; s. William Marshall and Evelyn Elizabeth (Coupland) S.; e. York Univ. (1 yr. Univ. Laval), Hons. B.A. (magna cum laude) 1968; La Sorbonne, France, m.ès arts 1969 (mention très bien, with high distinction); Univ. of Ottawa, Ph.D. 1979; m. Brigitte d. Marie-Françoise (Faure-Brac) and Francis Vincent 26 May 1984; PROF. OF QUE. & ACAD. LIT., DEPT. OF FRENCH, CARLETON UNIV.; instrumental in creation of B.A. in Candn. studies prog., Carleton Univ.; Chrmn., Dept. of French 1978–81; Suprvr., Grad. Studies 1984–85, 1987–88; active at all univ. levels; several scholarly achievement awards (Carleton Univ.); Ed. Bd. Mem., 'Lettres québécoises' 1976–86; Series editor, Editions Québec/Amérique: 'Littérature d'Amérique: traduction' (incl., in translation, works by authors such as Joan Barfoot, Robertson Davies, Jack Kerouac, Stephen Leacock, Lucy Maud Montgomery, Scott Symons, Guy Vanderhaeghe) 1985– ; Foreign Rights Editor, Editions Québec/Amérique 1986– ; Dir., Montreal Press (publ. house for Fr.-Candn. authors in translation); Cons., Que. lit. for sev. pubs.; author: 'L'Ecrivain devant son oeuvre' 1983 (interviews), 'Gilles Vigneault, poète et conteur' 1984 (biography, literary criticism); 'Voices of Deliverance' 1985 (rev. ed. of 'L'Ecrivain devant son oeuvre'), 'Gilbert La Rocque, l'écriture du rêve' (literary criticism) 1985, and num. articles on Qué. lit.; co-author: 'Pleure pas, Germaine' 1973 (textbook); 'Practical Handbook of Québec and Acadian French' 1984; 'Dictionary of Canadian French' 1990, 1992; copy editor: 'Harrap's Visual Dictionary' 1987; recreations: squash, golf, cycling; Home: 'La Grande Ourse,' 168 Chemin Pink, Cantley, Que. J8V 2Z5; Office: French Dept., Carleton Univ., Ottawa, Ont. K1S 5B6.

**SMITH, Douglas Burnet,** M.A., Ph.D.; educator; writer; b. Winnipeg, Man. 24 May 1949; s. Maurice Douglas and Annie (Nolan) S.; e. Univ. of Man. B.A. 1973, Ph.D. 1983; Carleton Univ. M.A. 1976; one s. Sean David; PROF. OF ENG. AND CREATIVE WRITING ST. FRANCIS XAVIER UNIV. 1984– ; Prof. of Eng. Univ. of Victoria 1981–82; Prof. of Eng. and Film Univ. of Man. 1982–84; Ed. Northern Light Mag. 1981–84; recipient Long Poem Prize The Malahat Review 1989; author (poetry) 'Thaw' 1977; 'Scarecrow' 1980; 'The Light of Our Bones' 1980; 'Living in the Cave of the Mouth' 1988; 'Ladder to the Moon' 1988; 'The Knife-Thrower's Partner' 1989; 'Voices From A Farther Room' 1992; Pres. League Candn. Poets 1988–90; nominated for Gov. General's Award for Poetry 1993; mem. Writers' Fedn. N.S.; Office: P.O. Box 162 St. Antigonish, N.S. B2G 1C0.

**SMITH, Hon. E.E.,** B.A., B.Ph.; judge; b. windsor, Ont. 19 Dec. 1928; s. Aldemard I. and Clarisse (Poisson) S.; e. Sudbury Coll., Laval Univ. Affiliate; Univ. of Ottawa B.A., B.Ph.; Osgoode Hall Law Sch. 1954; m. Jeannine A. Cote, B.A. 27 Oct. 1956; children: Patricia, Richard, Michelle, Marc; JUSTICE, ONT. COURT OF JUSTICE (GENERAL DIVISION); former Judge, Supreme Court of Ont. (Trial Div.) 1981; called to Bar of Ont. 1954; law practice Timmins, Ont. 15 yrs.; Dist. Court Bench, Cochrane-Timmins 1969; Ottawa-Carleton Co. Court 1973; Vice Chrmn., Pension Appeals Bd. 1973; Lectr. in Common Law and in Civil Law Univ. of Ottawa 1976–81; Office: 130 Queen St. W., Toronto, Ont. M5H 2N5.

**SMITH, Edward Herbert;** retired trust company executive; b. Saskatoon, Sask. 18 Jan. 1923; s. Herbert and Emily (Baxter) S.; e. City Park Coll. Inst., Saskatoon, Sr. Matric.; Univ. of W. Ont., Mang. Training Course 1972; m. Patricia Margaret, d. late James Powell, 31 Oct. 1944; two s., Richard Edward, Warren James; retired Sr. Vice Pres., Canada Permanent Trust Co.; served with RCNVR 1941–45; rank Lt.; named Serving Bro., Order of St. John; P. Conservative; Anglican; recreations: photography, music; Club: Donalda; Home: 52 Apollo Dr., Don Mills, Ont. M3B 2G8.

**SMITH, Elvie Lawrence,** C.M., M.S.; executive; born Eatonia, Sask. 8 Jan. 1926; s. Harry Burton and Laura Mae (Fullerton); e. Nutana Coll. Saskatoon 1943; Univ. of Sask. B.S. (Mech. Eng., Great Distinction) 1947; Purdue Univ., Indiana M.Sc. (Mech. Eng.) 1949; Hon. LL.D. Concordia Univ. 1983; Hon. Dr. Eng. Carleton Univ. 1984; Hon. Dr. Eng. Purdue Univ. 1987; CHAIRMAN, PRATT & WHITNEY CANADA 1985– ; Dir., DuPont of Can.; CAL Corporation; with National Research Council, Ottawa 1949–56: for five years of this period worked in the engine laboratory and was involved in projects on gas turbine anti-icing and thrust boosting, the remaining two years worked at the flight research section on flight testing of after-burning gas turbine engines; joined Pratt & Whitney Canada 1957; was part of the initial team assumbled to begin gas turbine design and development activity at Pratt & Whitney; Exec. V.P. Operations; Pres. & C.E.O. 1980; Chrmn. & C.E.O. 1984; el. Chrmn. 1985; el. Chrmn., Aerospace Ind. Assn. of Can. 1982–83; has written a number of papers on gas turbine development; Fellow, Candn. Aeronautics & Space Inst. from which he rec'd. McCurdy Award 1976 and C.D. Howe Award 1983 and was Rupert Turnbull Lecturer 1991; rec'd Thomas W. Eadie Medal, Royal Soc. of Can. 1985 and the Tom Sawyer Award, Am. Soc. of Mech. Engrs. 1986 for his work in the development of small aircraft gas turbines; Mem., Order of Canada 1992; inducted into Canada's Aviation Hall of Fame 1993; recreations: aircraft and glider flying, skiing; Home: St. Lambert, Que.; Office: 1000 Blvd. Marie-Victorin, Longueuil, Que. J4G 1A1.

**SMITH, Ernest Llewellyn Gibson;** executive; b. Goldaming, Eng. 21 June 1918; s. Brig. Armand Armstrong and Evelyn (Gibson) S.; e. Lake Lodge, Grimsby, Ont.; Trinity Coll. Sch., Port Hope, Ont.; Univ. of Bishop's Coll., Lennoxville, Que.; m. Elizabeth Ann, d. Col. Clifford Sifton, Toronto, Ont., 16 June 1945; children: Sharon Evelyn, Daphne June, Llewellyn Sifton; VICE-CHRMN., E.D. SMITH & SONS LTD. (estbd. 1882); served in 2nd World War with Royal Hamilton Light Inf. in Eng., France, Holland, Belgium and Germany as Co. Commdr.; Past Gov., Hillfield Strathallan Coll., Hamilton; Past Pres. Candn. Food Processors Assn.; Past Pres., Ont. Food Processors Assn.; Past Dir., Central Guaranty Trust Co. of Canada; Past Mem. Bus. Adv. Council, McMaster Univ.; Founding Mem., Conservation Found. Hamilton-Wentworth Region; Founding Dir., Candn. Assn. Family Enterprise; Mem., 'Knight of the Golden Pencil' Award; Patron, Parkinson Found. of Canada; Conservative; Protestant; recreations: golf, travelling; Clubs: Toronto; Hamilton Golf; The Toronto Hunt; Tamahaac-Hamilton (Past Pres.); Royal Cdn. Mil. Instit., Toronto; Home: 117 Glen Rd., Toronto, Ont. M4W 2W1; Office: Highway #8, Winona, Ont. L8E 5S3.

**SMITH, F. Margaret;** editor; b. Niagara Falls, N.Y. 30 May 1934; Canadian citizen 1972; d. Cecil M. and Lillian B. Hurd; e. Niagara Falls H.S. 1952; Algonquin Coll., journalism cert. 1969; m. Clarence G. Smith; children: Linda Clark, Cynthia Laprade, Melissa Lapensée, Alan Johnstone; EDITOR, CANADA YEAR BOOK (Statistics Canada) 1987– ; Public Relns. Offr., Algonquin Coll. 1969–71; Editor, Algonquin Coll. newspaper 1969–71; Editor: Canada: A Portrait (formerly Canada Handbook) which covers life in Canada in photos, text & tables 1972–92; Canada Year Book provides approx. 800 pages of text & tables covering a wide range of subjects related to Canada; latest publications: 'Canada: A Portrait' 1993, 'Canada Year Book 1992'; recreations: reading, writing, travel, needle crafts; Address: 1209 Firestone Cres., Ottawa, Ont. K2C 3E4.

**SMITH, Frank David,** P.Eng.; ocean research executive; b. England 18 Feb. 1936; s. Leonard Lewis and Jean (McGuffie) S.; e. Liverpool Tech., Dipl. Tech. Elect. 1957; m. Sheila d. Joseph and Elsie Formby 8 June 1969; children: Andrew, Leonard, Alexander, Krista, David; Pres. & C.E.O., Nordco Ltd. 1980; var. engr. positions, Candn. Marconi Co. 1959–70; Mgr. Telecontrol, Brinco Ltd. 1970–73; Mgr. Opn., Teleglobe 1973–75; Mgr. Telecontrol, Nfld. Hydro 1975–80; Chrmn. & Chief Extve. Offr., SeaForest Holdings Ltd.; Geonautics Ltd.; CAN AM Offshore Systems Ltd.; Chrmn. & C.E.O., ABB. NORDCO Inc.; CAN AM Simulation Ltd.; Chrmn., Fisheries Equip. & Technol. Ltd.; Hon. British Consul at St. John's; Dir. & Treas., Cerebal Palsy Assn. of Nfld.; Mem., Assn. of Profl. Engrs. of Nfld.; Ordre des Ingénrs. du Qué.; Sr. Mem., Inst. of Electrical & Electronic Engrs.; author of tech. papers; recreations; reading, walking, family; Club; Crows Nest; Home: 113 Topsail Rd., St. John's, Nfld. A1E 2A9.

**SMITH, Frank J.,** C.A.; real estate investment executive; b. 10 June 1938; s. John Donald and Edwinnia (Fry) S.; e. Univ. of Sask.; C.A. 1968; two s. Bradley Alexander, Neil Emmett William; DIR. & GEN. MGR. THE CANAPEN GROUP 1977– ; Pres. & Dir., Frank J. Smith & Associates Ltd. 1971– ; Dir., Canapen Investments Ltd.; Canapen (UCP) Ltd.; Can-Ray Holdings Ltd.; Gen. Mgr. Paragon Properties Ltd. 1968–71; Mem., Building Owners' & Managers' Assn.; Certified Environmental Inspector, Environmental Assessment Assn.; Alta. Arbitration & Mediation Soc.; Institute of Chartered Accountants of Alta.; Internat. Council of Shopping Centres; The Internat. Assn. of Corporate Real Estate Extves.; Alberta Real Estate Assn.; Club: Edmonton; Home: 304, 9737 – 112 St., Edmonton, Alta. T5K 1L3; Office: 300, 10020 – 101A Ave., Edmonton, Alta. T5J 3G2.

**SMITH, Garry John,** B.P.E., M.A., Ph.D.; university professor; b. Regina, Sask. 6 Feb. 1942; s. John Burr and Blanche Lillian (Peters) S.; e. Univ. of Alberta B.P.E. 1963; Univ. of W. Ont. M.A. 1968; Univ. of Alta. 1974; m. Dorothy d. Ken and Muriel McMillun 30 Aug. 1963; children: Darrell, Monica, Ryan; PROFESSOR, DEPT. OF SPORT STUDIES, UNIV. OF ALBERTA 1982– ; Teacher, Univ. of N.B. 1965–67; Faculty, Univ. of W. Ont. 1967–71; Univ. of Alta. 1972– ; coached univ. football & basketball 1965–79; Dir. of Athletics, Univ. of Alta. 1981–85; consultant for prov. govts.; provides professional counselling for compulsive gamblers; Mem., Univ. of Alta. 'Wall of Fame'; Coaching Staff, Men's Candn. Wheelchair Basketball Team (2 Olympics & num. internat. competitions); Bd. of Dir., Candn. Interuniv. Athletic Union 1983–86; Bd. Mem., Alta. Found. on Compulsive Gamblers; co-author: 'Sport in Canadian Society' 1991 and var. articles; recreations: running, golf, squash, reading; Home: 9111 – 142 St., Edmonton, Alta. T5R 0M8; Office: Edmonton, Alta. T6G 2H9.

**SMITH, Gary J.,** B.A.; diplomat; b. Toronto, Ont. 8 Aug. 1944; s. Herbert J. and Simone Stella (Desroches) S.; e. Riverdale C.I. 1964; Glendon College, York Univ. B.A. (Hons.) 1968; m. Laurielle d. Eric and Mabel Chabeaux 27 July 1968; children: Tatiana Alexandra, Eric Anthony; DIRECTOR GENERAL, ASIA PACIFIC BRANCH, EXTERNAL AFFAIRS CANADA 1993– ; Soviet Desk, Eur. Div., External Affairs Canada 1968; Arms Control & Disarmament Div. 1969; Candn. Forces Fgn. Language Sch. (Russian studies) 1970; Gen. Assembly of the U.N. N.Y. 1970–71; 1st Sec., Moscow, USSR 1971–74; Central Staff Ottawa 1974–75; Japan Desk, Pacific/N.E. Asian Div. 1975–77; Political Counsellor, Candn. Perm. Del. to NATO, Brussels 1977–81; Tel Aviv, Israel 1981–83; Prime Minister Trudeau's Task Force on Internat. Peace & Security Ottawa 1983–84; Dir., Arms Control & Disarmament Div. Ottawa 1984–86; Deputy High Commissioner, New Delhi, India 1986–89; Minister, Bonn, Germany 1989–93; Embassy Organizer & Liaison Offr. / Interpreter, 1st Canada-Soviet Profl. Hockey Series in Canada & USSR 1972; Mem., Wilton Park Assn.; contbg. author: 'Canada and the New Internationalism'; recreations: tennis, golf, skiing, riding; Office: 125 Sussex Dr. (A-5), Ottawa, Ont. K1A 0G2.

**SMITH, Geoffrey Macdonald,** LL.B.; building contractor; b. London, Ont. 26 Aug. 1955; s. Donald James and Joan Elizabeth (Macdonald) S.; e. Univ. of Toronto LL.B. 1979; m. Megan d. William and Evelyn Hagarty May 1986; children: Christopher, Rory, Adam; PRES. AND CHIEF OPERATING OFFR., ELLIS-DON INC.

1989– ; Field Eng. General Motors Distribution Centre Woodstock 1975; Project Eng. Univ. Hosp. Saskatoon 1976; Asst. Supt. Aquitaine Tower Calgary 1979–80; called to Bar of Ont. 1981; Corporate Lawyer Harrison, Elwood London, Ont. 1980–81; Dir. Corporate Affairs Ellis-Don Ltd. 1981–85; Vice Pres. W. Can. Ellis-Don Management Calgary 1985–89; mem. Univ. Hosp. Found. London; recreations: tennis, skiing; Clubs: London; London Hunt & Country; Home: 163 Wychwood Park, London, Ont. N6G 1S1; Office: 2045 Oxford St. E., London, Ont. N5V 2Z7.

**SMITH, Brig. Gerald Lucian Morgan,** C.B.E., C.D., M.A., M.D.; b. Toronto, Ont., 11 June 1909; s. late Dr. Lewis Gerald Smith and Laura Lavinia (Morgan) S.; e. Univ. of Toronto Schs., 1921–26; Trinity Coll., Univ. of Toronto, 1926–30; Med. Faculty, Univ. of Toronto, B.A., M.A., M.D.; m. Edith Emmeline West, 4 May 1936; children: Sarah, Gerald, Deborah; Anglican; Home: Goderich Place Manor, 30 Balvina Ave. E., Goderich, Ont. N7A 4L5.

**SMITH, Gordon A.,** LL.D.; artist; b. Hove, Eng. 18 June 1919; s. William George and Daisy (Appelbe) S.; came to Canada, 1933; e. Harrow County Sch., Eng.; Vancouver Sch. of Art (Grad.); California Sch. of Fine Arts; Harvard Univ.; LL.D. Simon Fraser 1973; m. Marion Katherine, d. Blair Fleming, White Rock, B.C., 15 Sept. 1941; PROFESSOR EMERITUS, FINE ARTS, UNIV. OF BRITISH COLUMBIA 1982– ; Council mem., R.C.A.; Past Pres., Canadian Group of Painters; rec'd. 1st Biennial Award, Nat. Gallery of Can.; Baxter Award, Ont. Soc. Artists; Centennial Medal, 1967; Queen's Medal, 1977; Allied Arts Medal, Roy. Arch. Inst. Can. 1978; executed murals, Vancouver Civic Theatre; Canadian Embassy, Washington, D.C.; paintings rep. in Nat. Gallery Can.; Toronto Art Gallery, London Art Museum, Queen's Univ., Hart House, Univ. of Toronto, Univ. of B.C., Vancouver and Victoria Art Galleries, etc.; rec'd. Arts Fellowship from Can. Council, 1960; paintings exhibited in Sao Paulo, Brazil 1961; Warsaw, Poland 1962; Candn. Biennial 1963; World's Fair, Seattle, 1963; (one man show), Agnes Lefort, Montreal, 1963; New Design Gallery, Vancouver, 1964; collab. with Arthur Erickson Osaka Worlds Fair 1970; solo exhns.: Toronto, Montreal, Vancouver 1974–75; Mira Godard Gallery, Toronto 1980, 1982, 1983, 1984, 1985; Bauxi Gallery, Vancouver 1981, 1983, 1984, 1986; Robertson Gallery, Ottawa 1986; Vancouver Art Gallery 1987, (46 new works) 1987–88; one man exhns. in Vancouver and Toronto 1990, 1991; group exhn.: The Vancouver Art Gallery 1983; designed Expo 86 poster, Vancouver; Expo 93, Seoul, Korea; completed 19' mural for new Canadian Chancery, Washington, D.C. 1988; new work purchased for Canadian collections, Vancouver Art Gallery, Art Gallery of Ontario; Art Advis. Comm., The Nat'l Capital Comm., Ottawa 1977–79; Chrmn., Jury for Sculpture Competition, R.C.A.F. Memorial 'Place of Tribute,' Ottawa 1983; rep. Can., Graphic Arts Portfolio, Prix Nobel, Sweden 1978; rep. Candn. Sec. Biennials in Yugoslavia, Germany, Spain, France, Norway; works acquired by Museum of Modern Art, N.Y.; Victoria & Albert Museum, London, Eng.; served Overseas with P.P.C.L.I., Intelligence Offr.; wounded Sicily, 1943; Bd. mem., Vancouver Art Gallery 1985; Counc. Ctte. on the Arts, Vancouver City Hall 1985–86; Anglican; Home: 5030 The ByWay, West Vancouver, B.C. V7W 1L7.

**SMITH, Gordon Scott,** Ph.D.; Canadian public servant; b. Montreal, Que. 19 July 1941; s. Gerald Meredith and the late Marjorie Helen (Scott) S.; e. Lower Can. Coll. Montreal; McGill Univ. B.A. 1962; Univ. of Chicago 1962–63; Mass. Inst. of Technol. Ph.D. 1966; m. Lise Grace Smith, d. Henri Lacroix; children: Derek Scott, Gavin Meredith, Sophie Ann and Henry Bennett; AMBASSADOR TO THE EUROPEAN UNION IN BRUSSELS, GOVT. OF CANADA 1991– ; joined the Defence Research Bd. 1966; transf. to External Affairs 1967; Defence Liaison Div. 1967–68; mem. Candn. Del. to NATO 1968–70; Special Adv. to the Min. of Nat. Defence 1970–72; joined the Privy Council Offc. 1972; Dir. of Planning Devel. 1972–73; Dir. of Gov't. Organization 1973–76; Sr. Assist. Secy. (Machinery of Gov't.) 1976–78; Dep. Secy. to the Cabinet (Plans) 1978–79; returned to External Affairs as Dep. Under-Secy. (Mgmt. & Planning) 1979; Assoc. Secy. to the Cabinet, Privy Council Office 1980–81; Secy., Min. of State for Social Development 1981–84; Assoc. Secy. to the Cabinet and Deputy Clerk of the Privy Council, Privy Council Office of Canada 1984; Depy. Min. for Political Affairs, Dept. of External Affairs 1985; Ambassador and Permanent Representative of Canada to NATO 1985–90; Secy. to the Cabinet for Fed.-Prov. Relations 1990–91; Bd. of Dirs., NATO Defence College, Rome; mem. Internat. Inst. Strategic Studies; Anglican; recreations: tennis, squash, sailing, skiing, antiques; Clubs: Five Lakes; several Classic Car Clubs, Jaguar; Rockcliffe Lawn Tennis; Home: 145 Ave des Dames Blanches, 1150 Brussels, Belgium; Office: Candn. Mission to the European Union, 2 Ave. de Tervuren, 1040 Brussels, Belgium.

**SMITH, Hugh Kelly,** B.Comm., LL.B.; business executive; b. Peterborough, Ont. 14 Nov. 1944; s. Mary Whipple K.; e. Queen Elizabeth H.S.; Dalhousie Univ. B.Comm. 1965, LL.B. 1968; m. Judith Ann d. William and Gloria Greenwood 18 Aug. 1967; children: Whipple, Amy, James, Victoria, Katie; PRES. & CHIEF EXTVE. OFFR., BUILDRITE CENTRES INC., HISTORIC PROPERTIES PHASE I LIMITED & FS INDUSTRIES LIMITED; admitted to Bar of N.S. 1969; joined Stewart, MacKeen & Covert (now Stewart, McKelvey, Stirling, Scales) 1969; Partner 1975–87; Counsel 1987; Q.C. 1984; entered partnership with John L. Bragg 1989; Dir., VIA Rail Canada Inc.; Clearwater Mngt. Serv. Ltd.; KB Electronics (1989) Ltd.; Green Waste Systems; Trustee, Royal Trust; Mem., Young Pres. Orgn.; Dir., Dalhousie Med. Rsch. Found.; Board Chrmn., Grace Maternity Hosp.; Mem., N.S. Counc. of the Duke of Edinburgh's Award; Reg. Adv. Bd., Natura Conservancy of Can.; Dir., Halifax Youth Found.; recreations: tennis, sailing, fishing; club: Waegwoltic; Home: 2201 Armcrescent East, Halifax, N.S. B3L 3C9; Office: 500 Windmill Rd., Box 816, Dartmouth, N.S. B2Y 3Z3.

**SMITH, Ian Cormack Palmer,** B.Sc., M.Sc., Ph.D., F.C.I.C., F.R.S.C.; biophysicist; b. Winnipeg, Man. 23 Sept. 1939; s. Cormack and Grace Mary (Palmer) S.; e. W. Kildonan Coll. Inst. Winnipeg 1956; United College, Winnipeg, 1958; Univ. of Man. B.Sc. 1961, M.Sc. 1962; Cambridge Univ. Ph.D. 1965; Stanford Univ. postdoctoral study 1966; m. Eva Gunilla d. late Sven and Siv Landvik 27 March 1965; children: Brittmarie Siv Grace, Sven Cormack, Duncan Fredrik, Roderick Bjoern; DIRECTOR GENERAL, INST. FOR BIODIAGNOSTICS, NAT. RESEARCH COUNCIL OF CAN. (WINNIPEG) 1992– ; Allied Scientist, Ottawa Civic Hosp. 1985– ; Ottawa Gen. Hosp. 1988– ; Ont. Cancer Foundation 1989– ; St. Boniface Hospital, Health Sci. Centre, Winnipeg; Adjunct Prof. of Chem. and Biochem. Carleton Univ., Univ. of Ottawa; Chemistry, Physics, Anatomy, Radiology, Univ. of Manitoba; Research Biophys. Bell Telephone Labs. Murray Hill, N.J. 1966–67; Asst. Research Offr. Nat. Research Council 1967, Assoc. Research Offr. 1970, Sr. Research Offr. 1974; Principal Research Offr. 1983; Trustee, Ottawa mem. Soc. 1969–70, 1980–82; Director General, Inst. for Biological Sciences, Nat. Research Council of Can. (Ottawa) 1987–92; rec'd Merck, Sharp and Dohme Award 1978; Ayerst Award 1978; Barringer Award 1979; Labatt Award, 1984; Herzberg Award 1986; Fil. Dr. (h.c.), Univ. of Stockholm, Sweden 1986; Organon Teknika Award, 1987; D.Sc. (h.c.) Univ. of Winnipeg 1990; author over 370 research papers biophys., med. and chem.; mem. Candn. Biochem. Soc.; Biophys. Soc. of Canada; Biophys. Soc.; Chem. Instit. Can.; Soc. for Magnetic Resonance in Medicine; Internat. Soc. for Magnetic Resonance; recreations: golf, tennis, curling; Home: 63 Shier Dr., Winnipeg, Man. R3R 2H2; Office: Winnipeg, Man. R3B 1Y6.

**SMITH, J. Herbert,** M.Sc., D.Sc.; professional engineer; b. Fredericton, N.B. 21 Nov. 1909; s. Charles Arthur and Amy (Marshall) S.; e. Pub. and High Schs., Fredericton, N.B.; Univ. of New Brunswick, B.Sc. (E.E.) 1932, M.Sc. (E.E.) 1942, D.Sc., 1958; Assumption Univ., D.Sc. 1961; m. Eldred Marian, d. F.J. Shaidle, Waterdown, Ont., 1937; Dir. Emeritus, Canadian Imperial Bank of Commerce and Sun Life Assurance Co.; Past Pres., Wellesley Hosp. Research Inst., Toronto; joined Canadian General Electric Co. Ltd. test course in 1932 and after experience in engn., hdqrs. and dist. sales work was apptd. Mgr. of Supply Sales for Ont. in 1945; Mgr. of Apparatus Sales for Ont. 1948; Gen. Mgr., Wholesale Divn., 1951, and Vice-Pres. and Gen. Mgr. 1953; Pres. and Chief Extve. Offr. 1957, Chrmn. of Bd. and Chief Extve. Offr. 1970–72; Chrmn. Bd., DeHavilland Aircraft of Can. Ltd. 1974–78; awarded Canada Centennial Medal 1967; awarded, Canada Volunteer Award Medal, 1989; awarded The Order of Ontario 1990; mem., Assn. of Prof. Engrs. of Ont. (Pres. 1953); Fellow, Am. Inst. of Elect. & Electronics Engrs.; mem., Engn. Inst. of Can.; Protestant; Clubs: National; Toronto; Address: Box 107, Commerce Court E., Toronto, Ont. M5L 1E2.

**SMITH, James Hamilton,** B.Com., F.C.A.; b. Montreal, Que. 14 July 1931; s. Alexander Laidlaw S.; e. Montreal W. High Sch. 1949; McGill Univ. B.Com. 1953; C.A. 1955; Fellow of the Ordre des comptables agréés du Qué. (F.C.A.) 1988; m. Lois Margaret d. late Fred Tanner 2 Oct. 1954; children: Sandra, Terri, Scott; President, C.E.O. & Dir. Domtar Inc. 1982–90 and Chrmn. of Bd. 1989–90; Dir., Mutual Life of Canada; joined Price Waterhouse & Co. Montreal 1953, Audit Supvr. 1960, Audit Mgr. 1963; managed the Domtar audit 1961–65; six months with Price Waterhouse, London, Eng. 1966; Asst. Controller Domtar Inc. Montreal 1966–68, Controller 1968–71, Vice Pres. Domtar Pulp & Paper Products 1971–74, Vice Pres. Finance Domtar Inc. 1974–78, Extve. Vice Pres. 1978, Pres. Domtar Packaging 1979, Pres. Domtar Inc. 1981; Bd. of Govs., Corporation des célébrations du 350e anniversaire de Montréal (1642–1992); Bd. of Govs., Concordia Univ.; Dir., The Montreal General Hosp. Rsch. Inst.; mem. Ordre des comptables agréés Qué.; Ont. Inst. C.A.'s; recreations: golf, skiing, baseball, swimming; Clubs: Royal Montreal Golf; The Forest and Stream.

**SMITH, Janet R.,** B.Comm., Ph.D.; public servant; b. Buckingham, Que. 3 Apr. 1940; e. Univ. of B.C., B.Comm. 1965; Univ. of Calif., Berkeley Ph.D. 1975; Nat. Defence Coll. 1978; DEPUTY MINISTER, WESTERN ECONOMIC DIVERSIFICATION 1993– ; Asst. Prof. Simon Fraser Univ. 1969–72; Liaison Offr. and Coordr. Office of Equal Opportunities for Women, Pub. Service Comn. 1972–74; Prog. Analyst Treas. Bd. Secretariat 1974–75; Dir. and Dir. Gen. Anti-Inflation Bd. 1977–79; Policy Adv. Treas. Bd. 1979–80; Dir. of Operations, Econ. and Regional Devel. Privy Counc. Office 1980–81; Asst. Sec. to the Cabinet, Econ. and Regional Devel., Privy Counc. Office 1981–84; Assoc. Depy. Min. Transport Canada 1985–86; Depy. Min., Privatization & Regulatory Affairs 1986–89; Extve. Dir., Royal Commission on National Passenger Transportation 1989–93; Deputy Min., Consumer & Corporate Affairs 1993; Office: Suite 1500, Canada Place, 9700 Jasper Ave., Edmonton, Alta. T5J 4H7.

**SMITH, Jean Edward,** A.B., Ph.D.; educator; b. Washington, D.C. 13 Oct. 1932; s. Jean McCollough and Mary Eddyth (Carter) S.; e. McKinley Tech. High Sch. Washington, D.C.; Princeton Univ., A.B. 1954; Columbia Univ., Ph.D. 1964; children: Sonja, Charles Christopher; PROF. OF POL. SCI., UNIV. OF TORONTO 1966– ; Capt., Field Artillery, U.S. Army 1954–61; Pres. Faculty Assn. Univ. of Toronto 1977–79; Visiting Prof., Princeton Univ. 1967–68, Univ. of Cal. 1978–82, Univ. of Va. 1987–88, Freie Universität Berlin 1989; Miss. State Univ. 1993–94; Pres. Roxborough Research Corp.; author 'The Defense of Berlin' 1964; 'Germany Beyond the Wall' 1969; 'Foreign Policy and the Constitution' 1987; 'General Lucius D. Clay: An American Life' 1989; 'George Bush's War' 1992; ed. 'The Papers of General Lucius D. Clay' 1974; 'Civil Liberties and Civil Rights' 1987; 'The Conduct of American Foreign Policy' 1989; Office: Toronto, Ont. M5S 1A1.

**SMITH, Jennifer Irene,** B.A., M.A., Ph.D.; university professor; b. Copper Cliff, Ont. 31 May 1950; d. John Henderson and Evelyn Mae (Dart) S.; e. McMaster Univ. B.A. (Hons.) 1972; Dalhousie Univ. M.A. 1975, Ph.D. 1981; m. Denis Winfield d. Gerald and Freda Stairs 17 July 1987; ASSOC. PROF., DEPT. OF POLITICAL SCIENCE, DALHOUSIE UNIV. 1980– ; Parliamentary Intern 1972–73; Lectr., Acadia Univ. 1978–80; SSHRCC Leave Fellowship 1986–87; Dep. Chair, The Electoral Boundaries Comn. for the Prov. of N.S. (Fed.) 1986–87; Dir., Candn. Pol. Sci. Assn. 1986–88; Presbyn.; author of scholarly articles; recreations: badminton, tennis, sailing, bridge; clubs: RNSYS; Home: 4 Rockwood, Halifax, N.S. B3N 1X5; Office: Halifax, N.S. B3H 4H6.

**SMITH, John Angus,** M.D., F.R.C.P.C.; physician, university professor; b. Scotland 6 Sept. 1936; s. John and Henrietta S.; e. Nicolson Inst. and Univ. of Aberdeen (both Scotland); m. Elizabeth d. George and Agnes Thomson 2 Oct. 1963; children: Fiona, Duncan; PHYSICIAN, VANCOUVER GEN. HOSP., PROF., UNIV. OF B.C. & DIR., PROV. LABORATORY, B.C.; trainee, Univ. of Aberdeen; Monash Univ., Australia; Univ. of Glasgow; formerly at Univ. of Toronto and Mt. Sinai Hosp.; Dir., ID Biomedical; Past Pres., St. Andrews & Caledonian Soc.; Un. Scottish Cultural Soc.; author of over 80 sci. pubns.; recreations: gardening; Home: 3540 Arthur Dr., Delta, B.C. V4K 3N2; Office: Vancouver Gen. Hosp., 855 W. 12th Ave., Vancouver, B.C. V5Z 1M9.

**SMITH, John Hillsdon,** B.Sc. (Hon.), M.B., Ch.B., F.R.C.P. (C); forensic pathologist; b. Leicester, Eng. 3 Mar. 1929; s. Alfred Herbert Morrison and Evelyn Vera (Hillsdon) S.; e. Univ. of Birminghan, Eng, B.Sc. (Hon.) 1949, M.B., Ch.B. 1952; m. Margaret d. Ernest and Ada King 18 Aug. 1951; children: Jeremy Peter, Mark Edward; Dir., Forensic Pathology Branch, Ministry of Solicitor General, Ont. 1973–94, retired; Major, R.A.M.C.

1954–58; Shepherd Res. Fell. in Experimental Immunopathology, Univ. of London 1959–60; Govt. Pathologist & Consultant Forensic Pathologist, Federation of Rhodesia & Nyasaland 1960–64; Senior Registrar, Pathology, Newcastle Upon Tyne, Eng. 1965–66; Lecturer, Forensic Med., Univ. of Edinburgh & Police Surgeon to S.E. of Scotland 1966–73; Prov. Forensic Pathologist, Ont. & Prof., Forensic Path., Univ. of Toronto 1973– ; Hon. Consultant, Forensic Path., Hosp. for Sick Children, Toronto; mem., Royal Soc. of Med.; British Assn. of Forensic Med.; Medicolegal Soc. of Toronto; Am. Acad. of Forensic Sc.; Internat. Acad. of Pathology; Queen's Jubilee Medal; recreations: photography, gundog breeding; Home: R.R. #1, Orton, Ont. L0N 1N0.

**SMITH, John Roxburgh;** b. London, Ont. 10 Nov. 1936; s. Hector Hugh Raleigh S.; e. Hillfield Coll. Hamilton 1957; Hamilton Teachers' Coll. 1958; McMaster Univ. B.A.; m. Judith d. George Pollard, Cambridge, Ont. 12 June 1976; children: Hayley Elizabeth, Drew Alexander, John Roxburgh; Ald. City of Hamilton 1963–67; MPP for Hamilton Mt. 1967–77, Min. of Correctional Services Ont. 1975–76, Min. of Govt. Service Ont. 1977; Alderman, City of Hamilton 1985–90; mem., Immigration and Refugee Bd.; rec'd Centennial Medal 1967; Bicentennial Medal 1984; Past Pres. Mountain Fund to Help the Boat People; Past Pres., Ont. Hortic. Assn.; Federal Citizenship Citation 1988; P. Conservative; Anglican; recreations: gardening, fishing, swimming, travel; Club: Albany; Home: 50 Sunninghill Ave., Hamilton, Ont. L8T 1B7.

**SMITH, John Webster Newton,** B.A.; film director; b. Montreal, Que. 31 July 1943; s. MacDonald Smith and Margot Marne (Fink) S.; e. West Hill H.S. 1960; McGill Univ., B.A. 1964, 1965–67; m. Cynthia d. Jack and Ena Scott 25 March 1974; children: Bruce, Morgan, Dylan; Film Dir., National Film Bd. of Canada 1973–93; Researcher & Prod., CBC TV Pub. Affairs, 'The Way It Is' 1967–68; Prod., CTV 'Face-to-Face' 1968; 'The Fabulous 60's' 1969–70; 'Here Come the Seventies' 1971; WNET (NY) 'The 51st State' 1972; Prod. & Dir., N.F.B. Films: 'The New Boys' 1973; 'Ready When You Are'; 'We Sing More Than We Cry' 1974; 'Bargain Basement' 1975; 'Happiness is Loving Your Teacher' 1976; 'No Day of Rest' 1977; 'First Winter,' 'Revolution's Orphans' 1978; 'For The Love of Dance,' 'River Journey' (IMAX), 'The Masculine Mystique' 1984; 'A Gift for Kate,' 'Gala,' 'First Stop, China' 1985; 'The Rebellion of Young David,' 'Sitting in Limbo' 1986; 'Train of Dreams' 1987; 'Welcome to Canada' 1989; 'The Boys of St. Vincent' 1992 (awards: Grand FIPA d'or Cannes 1993 for the Best Production; Golden Monitor for Best non-European mini-series and Award for Best Direction 1993; Grand Prize for Best Film, Television Festival, Banff 1993; Gold Medal for Best Drama, 36th Annual Internat. Television Programming & Promotion Award Ceremony, N.Y. 1994; Best Dramatic mini-series, Gemini Award 1994); 'Dieppe' 1993; awards: Nat. Film Fest.; Am. Film Fest.; Mannheim; Oscar nom.; Emmy; Spain; Italy; Toronto Film Fest.; France; Chicago; Cannes; Umbria; Columbus; Club: Dunany Golf; Home: 467 Grosvenor Ave., Westmount, Que. H3Y 2S5; Office: NFB, 3155 Cote de Liesse, Montreal, Que. H4N 2N4.

**SMITH, Joseph Percy,** Ph.D., D.Litt., LL.D.; b. Canora, Sask. 22 Mar. 1914; s. Rev. Percy and Alice (Hudson) S.; e. Univ. of Sask., B.A. 1940, M.A. 1945; Univ. of Cal., Berkeley, Ph.D. 1949; m. Morine Barbara, d. late Chris Baldwinson 30 June 1964; children (by previous marriage): Sylvia (Mrs. John Gill), Valerie (Mrs. L. Warke), Rhonda, Kevin; EMERITUS PROF. OF DRAMA, UNIV. OF GUELPH 1981– ; Vice Pres., Academic 1970–76; Prof. of Drama, Univ. of Guelph 1976–80; Bank of N.S. 1929–37; taught English, Univ. of Sask. 1945–64; Can. Council Sr. Research Fellowship, London, Eng., 1960–61; Extve. Secy., Candn. Assn. Univ. Teachers, 1964–69; Nuffield Travelling Fellowship in Humanities 1969; served with RCAF 1942–45; author 'The Unrepentant Pilgrim: A Study of the Development of Bernard Shaw' 1965; also essays and articles for various journs.; Gen. ed., 'Selected Correspondence of Bernard Shaw'; Hon. Life mem., Candn. Assn. Univ. Teachers (Milner Mem. Award 1973); D.Litt., Carleton Univ. 1970; LL.D. Univ. Windsor 1974; Hon. Fellow, Univ. of Guelph 1984; Ashley Visiting Fellow, Trent University 1986; By-Fellow, Robinson College, Cambridge Univ. 1992; Home: 15 Monticello Cres., Guelph, Ont. N1G 2M1.

**SMITH, Kenneth Carless,** Ph.D., F.I.E.E.E., P.Eng.; university professor; b. Toronto, Ont. 8 May 1932; s. Reginald Thomas and Viola Evelyn Clara (Carless) S.; e. University of Toronto, B.A.Sc. 1954, M.A.Sc. 1956, Ph.D. 1960; m. Laura Chizuko d. William and Dorothy Fujino 17 Sept. 1983; children: (Kenneth) David, Kevin Antony; PROF., ELECT. ENG., FACULTY OF ENGINEERING, UNIV. OF TORONTO 1970– ; Prof. Computer Sci. 1970– ; Prof., Lib. & Info. Sci. 1981– ; Prof., Mech. Eng. 1988– ; On leave: Dept. of Electrical and Electronic Engineering, Univ. of Science & Technology, Hong Kong 1993–94; Transmission Engr., Can. Nat. Telegraphs 1954–55; Rsch. Engr., Computation Ctr., present univ. 1956–58; Asst. Prof., Elect. Engr. 1960–61; Rsch. Asst. Prof., Elect. Eng., Univ. of Illinois 1961–64; Assoc. Prof., Elect. Eng., Comp. Sci. 1964–65; Chief Engr., Illiac II 1961–65, Illiac III 1962–65, Socrates Teaching Machine Project, Univ. of Ill. 1963–65; Assoc. Prof., Elect. Eng., Comp. Sci., present univ. 1965–70; Chrmn., Elect. Eng. 1976–81; Co-founding mem., Computer Systems Rsch. Group (and now Comp. Syst. Res. Inst.) 1968– ; Assoc. Mem., Inst. of Biomed. Eng. 1974– ; Advr. to Pres. & C.E.O., Semitech Microelectronics Inc. 1982– ; Co-chair, Adv. Ctte., Accelerated Processors (Calif.) 1985– ; cons. to several U.S. & Candn. cos.; Founding Dir., Electr. Eng. Consociates 1968–76, 1981–87 (Pres. 1974–76); F.I.E.E.E. 1978; Adv. Prof., Shanghai Inst. of Railway Tech. 1989– ; Dir., Candn. Soc. for Profl. Engrs. 1984– (Pres. 1988–90, Interim Pres. 1991); Mem., APEO, CSPE, CSEE, IEEE (encompassing CAS, CS, IMS, ES, RAS, ISSCC); several past & present extve. positions held in IEEE, CSPE, CSEE; Life Mem., ROM 1975– ; Mem., Pres. Ctte., present univ. 1987– ; author: 'Laboratory Explorations' 1991; 'Trial and Success' 1992; co-author: 'Microelectronic Circuits' 1982, 1st internat. ed. 1983, Spanish ed. 1985, 2nd ed. 1987, 2nd internat. ed. 1988, Hebrew ed. 1989, Korean ed. 1989, 3rd ed. 1991, 3rd internat. ed. 1991, Greek ed. 1994; author/co-author of 195 tech. pubs. & 14 book chapters; Anglican; recreations: power walking, bicycling, nordic skiing, skating, gardening, neighbourhood beautification (tree planting), tree farming; Home: 56 Torbrick Rd., Toronto, Ont. M4J 4Z5; Office: 10 King's College Rd., Toronto, Ont. M5S 1A4.

**SMITH, Kenneth Hugo,** C.A.; retired executive; b. Winnipeg, Man. 6 May 1917; s. William Alfred and Janie (Hugo) S.; e. Univ. Man.; C.A.; m. Annie Jean d. John and Louisa (Salmon) Arthur 1943; children: Barry, Roger, Craig, Lynda, Heather; Assessor, DNR Taxation, 1946–51; various positions to V.P., Treas., Contr. and Secy., Eddy Forest Products Ltd. (formerly the KVP Co. Ltd.) 1951–69; Secy. (V.P. 1977), Officer and Dir. of many subsidiaries, George Weston Ltd. 1969–79; Pres., Financial Extves. Inst. Can., 1979–83; R.C.A.F. 1942–45; mem. Candn., Ont., Man. Insts. of C.A.'s; Fin. Extves Inst.; Conservative; United Church; recreations: lawn bowling, reading, walking, singing; Home: 1762 Valentine Garden, Mississauga, Ont. L5J 1H5.

**SMITH, Lawrence Austin Hayne,** B.A., M.A., B.Litt.; diplomat; b. Vizagapatam, India 30 Oct. 1929; s. Rt. Rev. Ralph Eugene and Mildred Helen (Johnson) S.; e. McMaster Univ., B.A. 1951; Oxford Univ., M.A., B.Litt. 1955; Univ. of Toronto; m. Virginia d. Gen. Francis St.D.B. and Joyce M. Lejeune 2 June 1956; children: Adrian, Kelvin, Julian, Vanessa, Martin; Candn. High Commissioner to Kenya and Uganda 1990–93, Retired; Canadian Ambassador to Somalia and Comores 1990–93; Permanent Representative to the UN Environment Program (UNEP) 1990–93; Permanent Representative, UN Centre for Human Settlement (HABITAT) 1990–93; joined Dept of External Affairs 1957; Candn. High Comn., Pakistan 1958–61; on loan to External Aid Office Ottawa 1961–64; Candn. Perm. Mission to OECD Paris 1964–68; Dir., Aid & Devel. Div. & Dep. Dir. Gen., Bur. of Econ. Affairs 1968–73; Candn. High Comnr., Barbados & E. Caribbean Assoc. States 1973–77; Min. (Econ.), Candn. Embassy, Washington, D.C. 1977–78; Asst. Under-Sec., Ottawa 1978–81; Ambassador for N.-S. Relns. 1982–83; Candn. Ambassador to the Netherlands 1983–87; Candn. Ambassador to Thailand, Viet Nam and Laos 1987–90; author of jour. articles; co-author: 'Towards a New International Economic Order' 1976, 1977; recreations: reading, philately; Home: 383 Mariposa Ave., Rockcliffe Park, Ont. K1M 0S7.

**SMITH, Lawrence Berk,** B.Comm., A.M., Ph.D.; educator; b. Toronto, Ont. 10 Nov. 1939; s. Isadore Edward and Ruth (Berk) S.; e. Forest Hill Coll. Inst. 1958; Univ. of Toronto B.Comm. 1962 (Univ. Coll. Gov. Gen's. Medal 1962); Harvard Univ. A.M. 1964, Ph.D. 1966; children: Cynthia Joy, Ilyse Jan, Natalie Jill; PROF. OF ECON. UNIV. OF TORONTO 1972– ; Pres. High Value Consultants Ltd. 1968– ; Instr. in Econ. Harvard Univ. 1966; Asst. Prof. of Econ. present Univ. 1966, Assoc. Prof. 1969, Dir. of Econ. and Assoc. Chrmn. of Pol. Econ. 1975–79; Visiting Scholar Grad. Sch. Mgmt. UCLA 1973–74, Grad. Sch. Bus. Adm. Univ. Cal. Berkeley 1981–82; Cons.: Rsch. Dept. Bank of Canada 1967–68; Min. of Urban Affairs 1969–70; Canada Mortgage & Housing Corp. 1970–71, Dep. Chrmn. Task Force on CMHC 1979; Coopers and Lybrand 1975–81; Salomon Brothers Inc. 1986–88; Mem. Bd. of Dirs., Royal Trust Realty Inc. 1989– ; Woodrow Wilson Fellow 1962–63; Harvard Univ. Grad. Scholar 1963–64; Can. Council Fellow 1962–64; Ford Motor Co. Internat. Fellow 1964–65 and numerous other acad. awards and grants; mem. Policy, Planning & Govt. Relations Ctte. Un. Way Greater Toronto 1983– , Co-Chairperson 1989–91; mem., Bd. of Trustees 1989–92 and Mem. Exec. Ctte., United Way of Greater Toronto 1989–91; Mem. Bd. of Trustees, Community Information Centre 1993; author: 'Housing in Canada: Market Structure and Policy Performance' 1971; 'The Postwar Canadian Housing and Residential Mortgage Markets and the Role of Government' 1974; 'Anatomy of a Crisis: Canadian Housing Policy in the Seventies' 1977; co-author: 'Government in Canadian Capital Markets: Selected Cases' 1978; co-ed.: 'Canadian Economic Problems and Policies' 1970; 'Issues in Canadian Economics' 1974; author or co-author 3 other books and monographs, over 70 articles profl. jours. & anthols.; mem. ed. adv. bd. Fraser Inst. 1975– ; Editorial Review Bd., Am. Real Estate and Urban Economics Assn. Journal 1980– ; Editorial Bd., Journal of Real Estate Finance and Economics 1987– ; Editorial Bd., Journal of Housing Economics 1990– ; mem. Candn. Econ. Assn. (Exec. 1977–80); Am. Real Estate & Urban Econ. Assn. (Exec. 1980–83); Am. Econ. Assn.; Am. Finance Assn.; recreations: tennis, yoga, bridge, skiing, sailing; Home: 26 Eastbourne Ave., Toronto, Ont. M5P 2E9; Office: 150 St. George St., Toronto, Ont. M5S 1A1.

**SMITH, Lawrence Bernard,** B.A., M.B.A.; executive; b. Toronto, Ont. 17 Aug. 1946; s. William Bernard and Kathleen (Beacom) S.; e. Univ. of Toronto, B.A. (Hons.) 1969; York Univ., M.B.A. 1974; m. Arlene d. Arthur and Lillian Rayner 24 June 1967; children: Angela Louise, Tara Lynne, Darren Lawrence William; Pres. & C.E.O., Regional Cablesystems Inc. 1992; Xerox of Can. Inc. 1969–79; Gen. Mgr., Graham Cable 1979–82; Vice-Pres., Opns., Cablecasting Limited 1982–84; Vice-Pres. & Gen. Mgr., Cablenet Limited 1984–85; Pres., 1985–88; Sr. Vice-Pres., Corp. Devel., Cybermedix Inc. 1988–90; Pres., Kathbern Management Consultants Inc. 1990–92; Founding Pres., Cable Television Standards Found.; Past Pres., Ont. Cable Telecommunications Assn.; Home: 14 Tepee Court, Willowdale, Ont. M2J 3A9.

**SMITH, Lawrence Napier,** B.A.; journalist; b. Toronto, Ont. 17 Mar. 1919; s. the late Ruth (Langlois) and late Rev. George Napier S.; e. Lafayette High Sch., Buffalo, N.Y.; Ridley Coll., St. Catharines, Ont.; Univ. of Toronto, B.A. (Hon. Hist.) 1941, and John Moss Mem. Scholar. as Best All Round Student; m. Dorothy Joan (died 4 Dec. 1971), 2ndly Briar, d. late E. E. H. Wright, 19 May 1973; children: Sheila, Roger, Priscilla; RETIRED EDITOR-IN-CHIEF, 'ST. CATHARINES STANDARD' (Daily newspaper estbd. 1891); 1970–80 (Mang. Ed. 1955–70); Past Dir., The Canadian Press; Editor, 'The Varsity,' Univ. of Toronto 1940–41; Reporter for present Newspaper at various intervals, 1938–46 when he became Reporter and Columnist; in U.K., Europe as Winner of Kemsley Empire Journalist Scholarship, 1949–50; promoted to Asst. City Editor, 1950; City Editor, 1952; Mang. Ed. 1955–70; Ed.-in-Chief 1970–80; Winner, W. Ont. Newspaper Award for Spot News, 1957; Humorous Writing, 1980; Pres., Candn. Mang. Editors' Conf., 1959–60; mem. and Chrmn., St. Catharines Public Library Bd. 1952–64; C.O.T.C., Univ. of Toronto, 1940–41; 10th Field Batty. (R), St. Catharines, Ont., 1941–42; 23rd Field Regt. (SP), R.C.A. Overseas, rank of Capt., 1942–46; Pres., St. Catharines Rotary Club, 1977–78; Past Vice-Pres., St. Catharines Jr. Chamber Comm.; past mem., Bd. of Management, St. George's Ang. Ch., St. Catharines, Ont., Warden, 1962–64; Kappa Alpha (Pres. 1940–41); Anglican; Home: 27 Adelene Cres., St. Catharines, Ont. L2T 3C6.

**SMITH, Lois Irene;** O.C. ballerina; choreographer; b. Vancouver, B.C. 8 Oct. 1929; d. William and Doris (Newbery) Smith; e. Templeton Jr. High Sch. Vancouver; Rosemary Deveson Sch. and Mara McBirney Sch. ballet training, Vancouver; m. David Charles Adams 13 May 1950 (divorced); one d. Janine Dariel Adams; 1 grands. Mark; Freelance ballet teacher, choreographer, adjudicator and stained glass artist 1988–94; first prof. performance 1945; performed in light operas and musicals Can. and USA 1945–51; joined Nat. Ballet Co. 1951–69, performed as Ballerina 1951–55, became Can.'s First Prima Ballerina 1955–69; among her most acclaimed roles were those of the Swan Queen in Swan Lake and Caroline in Antony Tudor's Lilac Garden; performed various CBC TV Prod. 1954–69; estbd. Lois

Smith Sch. of Dance 1969; Chrmn. Sch. of Dance, George Brown Coll. of Applied Arts and Technol. 1975–88; Choreographer 3 TV Specials CBC; Choreographer, Candn. Opera Co. 'Aida and Eugene Onegin,' 1972, 'The Merry Widow,' 1973, 'Joan of Arc,' 1978, 'La Traviata,' 1982; ; Alberta Ballet Co. and Winnipeg Opera Co.; Florida Ballet Co. 1975; South West Ballet Co. 1977; Co-Dir. and Choreographer, Candn. Silent Players; Artistic Dir., Co-choreographer, 'The Dancing Circus' (with Earl Kraul), Dance Co. of Ont. 1979; many engagements as guest teacher in Can. and elsewhere; guest appearance Nat. Ballet of Can. as Black Queen in Swan Lake (Special Lois Smith Night) 1969; Guest Artist: as Carabose in Sleeping Beauty 1978; as Queen Mother in Sleeping Beauty Nov. 1979; as Giovanina in Napoli, Nat. Ballet of Can. 1981; in 'Quantum Leap' 1985; Toronto Dance Theatre Co. in Court of Miracles 1986, 1987; Guest Artist, Nat. Ballet Co. 1981 and 1982; rec'd Centennial Medal 1967; Internat. Women's Day Bronze Medal 1977; rec'd Dance Ontario Award for outstanding contribution to dance, 1983; received Order of Canada, Officer, 1980; awarded Service Medal City of Toronto 1985; mem. Dance in Can. Assn.; A.C.T.R.A.; Hon. mem., Cdn. Dance Masters of Amer.; rec'd., Life membership Actors Equity, 1983; Bd. Mem., Prologue to the Performing Arts 1986 and 1987; Encore Encore 1986; Gibsons Landing Theatre Project 1989; Hunter Gallery, Gibsons, B.C. 1991–94; Festival of the Written Arts, Sechelt, B.C. 1992; Trustee, Ballet British Columbia (Bd. Mem. 1991–94); Pres., Sunshine Coast Dance Society 1993– ; recreations: sewing, drawing; Home: s 15 c 12 RR #4, Gibsons, B.C. V0N 1V0.

**SMITH, Mallory,** A.B.; executive; b. Albany, N.Y. 10 Jan. 1931; s. Reveley Herbert Buller and Ruth Gaylord (Mallory) S.; e. Winchester (Mass.) High Sch.; Harvard Univ. A.B. 1952; m. Mary Ann d. William Filson 2 Oct. 1957; children: Baird, Katie, Janet, Dawn; Realtor, joined Metal Products Div. Koppers Co. Inc., Baltimore 1957, Sales Engr. New York 1958–61, Dist. Mgr. New York 1961–64, Vice Pres. and Gen. Mgr. Koppers Products Ltd. Toronto 1964–67; Nat. Field Sales Mgr. Baltimore 1967–69; Chrmn., Pres. and Chief Extve. Offr. Koppers International Canada Ltd. Vancouver 1969–82; Pres. & C.O.O. McGavin Foods Limited 1983–84; Pres. Methane Technologies 1985–86; Sr. Vice-Pres., C.E.O. & Dir., Continental Commercial Systems Corp. 1986–87; Realtor, Riddell Realty Ltd. 1988–90; Co-owner and Nominee, Bowen Island Realty Limited 1991– ; Dir., Bowen Island Realty Limited; Bowen Island Concrete Ltd.; Atlantic Industries Ltd.; served with U.S. Navy 1952–57, Carrier Command Pilot, rank Lt.; rec'd Queen's Silver Jubilee Medal; Past Pres. Bd. Govs. Jr. Achievement of B.C.; Chrmn. Salvation Army Red Shield Fund Drive 1984–85; Protestant; recreations: reading, boating; Club: Vancouver Lawn Tennis & Badminton; Home: 5, 4350 Valley Drive, Vancouver, B.C. V6L 3B5.

**SMITH, Mark L.S.,** B.Comm., C.A.; business executive; b. Toronto, Ont. 8 May 1960; s. John S. and Jane E. (Atkinson) S.; e. McGill Univ. B.Comm. 1982; SENIOR VICE-PRES., CLARIDGE INC. 1992– and CHIEF OPERATING OFFR., CLARIDGE ISRAEL INC. 1989– ; CEMP Investments (now Claridge) 1986– ; Vice-Pres., Claridge Inc. 1987–91; Touche Ross & Co. 1982–86; Dir., Medisys Inc.; Executive Health Group Inc.; Crowntek Business Centres Inc.; ECI Telecom Inc.; Osem Food Indus. Ltd.; Claridge Israel Inc.; Rhodes Scholar Finalist (Canada) 1982; recreations: tennis, skiing, golf, squash; clubs: Royal Montreal Golf, Mt. Royal Tennis, University; Home: 4006 Montrose, Westmount, Que. H3Y 2A4; Office: 1170 Peel St., Suite 800, Montreal, Que. H3B 4P2.

**SMITH, Melvin H.,** B.Comm., LL.B., Q.C.; public policy consultant; b. Winnipeg, Man. 8 Feb. 1934; e. Univ. of British Columbia B.Comm. 1956, LL.B. 1959; called to Bar of B.C. 1960; m. Beverley 1966; children: Darrell, Sandra; Departmental Solicitor, Dept. of Attorney Gen., Prov. of B.C. 1960–68; Dir., Constitutional and Administrative Law 1968–77; Depy. Min., Const. Affairs 1977–80; Depy. Min. of Intergovt. Relations 1980–87; Depy. Prov. Sec. & Depy. Min. of Govt. Serv. 1987; Sr. Constitutional Advr., Govt. of B.C. 1967–87 (longest serving govt. official in Can. on constitutional reform); Depy. Min. of Tourism & Dep. Prov. Secy., Prov. of B.C. 1988–89; Depy. Provincial Secretary 1989–90; Special Constitutional Advisor, B.C. Govt. 1990; left Govt. 1991; has also been involved in significant constitutional court cases & international issues; recognized authority on Senate reform; accomplished public speaker; Queen Elizabeth II 25th Anniv. Medal 1977; Q.C. 1983; Past Chrmn., Const. & Internat. Law Section, Candn. Bar Assn.; Dir., Can. West Foundation; Inst. of Intergovt. Relations, Queen's Univ.; Candn. Taxpayers' Federa-

tion; recreations: fishing, gardening, curling; Home: 4687 Amblewood Dr., Victoria, B.C. V8Y 1C4.

**SMITH, Michael,** B.Sc., Ph.D., F.R.S., F.R.S.C.; university professor; b. Blackpool, England 26 Apr. 1932; s. Rowland and Mary Agnes (Armstead) S.; e. Arnold Sch.; Univ. of Manchester, B.Sc. 1953, Ph.D. 1956; m. Helen Wood Christie d. Herbert Read Christie and Edith Germaine Wood 6 Aug. 1960; children: Tom, Ian, Wendy; PROF. OF BIOCHEMISTRY, UNIV. OF B.C. 1971– ; Dir., Biotechnology Laboratory, Univ. of B.C. 1987– ; post-doct. fellow, B.C. Rsch. 1956–60; Rsch. Assoc., Inst. for Enzyme Rsch., Univ. of Wisconsin 1960–61; Head, Vanc. Chem. Lab., Fisheries Rsch. Bd. of Can. 1961–66; Assoc. Prof., Dept. of Biochem., Univ. of B.C. 1966–71; Rsch. Assoc., then Career Investigator, Med. Rsch. Counc. of Can. 1966– ; Vis. Sci., Rockefeller Univ. 1971; M.R.C. Lab. of Molecular Biology (U.K.) 1975–76; Yale Univ. 1982; Found. Sci., ZymoGenetics Inc. (U.S.); Nobel Laureate in Chemistry 1993; Office: Biotechnology Lab., Univ. of British Columbia, Rm. 237, Wesbrook Bldg., 6174 University Boul., Vancouver, B.C. V6T 1W5.

**SMITH, Michael Dennis,** B.Sc.; business executive; b. Canada 22 March 1946; s. Leo and Jean S.; e. Forest Hill Coll. Inst. 1964; Univ. of Boston, B.Sc. in Business Admin. 1968; m. Lia d. Jack and Wilma Vander Klugt 1973; children: Morgan, Lindsay, Philip, Emily-Anne; PRES., NORTHERN FORTRESS LIMITED 1982– ; Dir., Northern Fortress Limited; Eaton's of Canada Limited; Tuckahoe Financial Corp.; Norwich Union Life Insurance Soc.; Lajambe Forest Products Limited; Champion Road Machinery; Trustee, Bishop Strachan Sch.; Bd. of Govs., Upper Canada Coll.; Clubs: Toronto; National; Office: 71 Steinway Blvd., Etobicoke, Ont. M9W 6H6.

**SMITH, Rev. Michael Joseph,** O.M.I., C.M.; Roman Catholic priest; b. Leduc, Alta. 1 Feb. 1911; s. Luke and Victoria (Halwa) S.; e. St. John's Coll. Edmonton 1925; St. Paul's Coll. Winnipeg 1927; Univ. of Alta. 1927–28; St. Charles Semy. North Battleford, Sask. 1933–36; Oblate Semy. Obra, Poland 1936–38; mem. Oblate Fathers of Assumption Prov.; Chrmn. Copernicus Lodge (sr. citizens complex); Dir. Candn. Polish Millenium Fund; Founder (1962–63) Queen of Apostles Renewal Centre; co-founder St. Stanislaus St. Casimir's Parish Credit Union 1946; Founder St. Casimir's Parish 1948; Founder of Copernicus Lodge, Sr. Citizens Apts.; K. of C.; R. Catholic; retired; Address: Queen of Apostles Renewal Centre, 1617 Blythe Rd. Mississauga, Ont. L5H 2C3.

**SMITH, Muriel Ann,** B.A., M.Ed.; educator; b. Britannia Beach, B.C. 9 May 1930; d. George Cherry and Mary (MacDonald) Lipsey; e. Univ. of Man. B.A. 1951, B.Ed., M.Ed. 1975; Oxford Univ. Dip. in Edn. 1953; m. Murray Rhodes s. C. Rhodes and Luella G. Smith 20 June 1952; children: Marta, Elaine, Carolyn, Cathryn; part-time instructor in social work, Winnipeg Edn. Centre 1988– ; Northern Access 1992; active mem. YWCA incl. Presidency, Winnipeg Assn. and mem. Nat. Bd. 1969–73; Chairperson Man. Action Ctte. Status of Women 1974–75; Comnr. Man. Human Rights Comn.; Lay Bencher Law Soc. Man., Gov. Univ. of Winnipeg 1974–78; Cand. for Man. NDP els. 1973, 1977, mem. Fed. Council 1977–82, 1984–89; mem. Winnipeg Teachers Assn. Exec. 1978–81; Counsellor Winnipeg High Schs. 1978–81; el. M.L.A. 1981, Dep. Premier of Man. 1981–88, Min. of Econ. Devel. & Tourism 1981–83, Min. of Community Services & Corrections 1983–87, Min. Responsible for Status of Women 1985–86, 1987–88, Min. of Housing, Labour 1987–88; Pres., Kinsmen Rehfit Centre Bd. (Vice-Pres. 1991–93) 1993– ; Candn. Inst. Internat. Affairs (Winnipeg Women's Br.); del. to Nairobi Conf. Status of Women; Pres., United Nations Assn. of Canada (Winnipeg Branch) 1990–93; Vice-Pres., UNA of Canada 1993– ; Secy., Women's World Finance - Manitoba; Secy., End of Decade Ctte. for Manitoba; Treasurer - LEAF Manitoba; mem. Steering Ctte., Coalition for Human Equality; mem. Soc. Planning Council Policy Ctte.; mem. of UNTAG election monitor team in Namibia 1989; delegate to UNCED/FORUM conferences in Rio de Janeiro 1992; to Vienna Conf. on Human Res. 1993; recreations: swimming, tennis, reading, writing; Address: 618 Oxford St., Winnipeg, Man. R3M 3K1.

**SMITH, Murray Rhodes,** B.A., B.A. Hon., M.A., M.Ed.; retired teacher; b. Winnipeg, Man. 12 June 1930; s. Charles Rhodes (also a Rhodes Scholar) and Luella Gertrude (Lick) S.; e. Daniel McIntyre H.S., Winnipeg 1944–46; Univ. of Manitoba B.A. 1950, B.Ed. 1956, M.Ed. 1978; Oxford Univ. B.A. Hon. 1952, Dip. in Edn. 1953; Univ. of London, Academic Dip in Edn. 1967; m. Muriel A. d. George and Mary Lipsey 20 June 1952;

children: Marta, Elaine, Carolyn, Cathryn; Pres. Manitoba Teachers' Soc. 1984–85; teacher, Winnipeg pub. schs.; Vice-Prin. and Acting Prin.; mem. Supt. Dept. and Asst. Supt. (8 yrs. total); Chairperson, Health Sciences Centre, Winnipeg 1975–78; Gov. Univ. of Man. 8 yrs.; mem. Man. Health Orgn.; Vice-Pres. Children's Aid Soc. of Winnipeg; NDP candidate, provincial election 1986; author numerous articles; awards: Rhodes Scholar for Man. 1950; 1st Class Hon. degree from Oxford; distinction in both Edn. Certificates 1953, 1967; recreations: cycling, swimming, running, music; Home: 618 Oxford St., Winnipeg, Man. R3M 3K1.

**SMITH, Nancy;** broadcast executive; b. Toronto, Ont. 22 Nov. 1949; d. Howard Vincent and Betty Lorraine (Sanderson) Baldasio; e. York Univ.; children: Jarett and Crystal Smith; PRESIDENT, SMITH MARSHALL MOTIVATIONS INC. 1993– and PRESIDENT, T'ELLE'VISION 1993– ; Teacher & Publications Marketing (8 years); built communications & marketing areas for innovative City TV, Much Music & Musique Plus; Vice-Pres. Communications, Global Television Network 1986–93; Chair, Broadcast Promotion & Marketing Executives (BPME) International (Los Angeles); Past Chair, Internat. Ctte., BPME; Co-Chair & Co-Founder, CWRT, Canadian Women in Radio & TV dedicated to advancing women in communications; YWCA Woman of Distinction; Broadcaster of the Year; Toronto Women in Film & TV Astral Award; Dir., Zoological Soc. of Metro. Toronto; recreations: skiing, travelling; clubs: McGill; Home/Office: 150 Balmoral Ave., Suite 605, Toronto, Ont. M4V 1J4; Alternative Office: 81 Barber Greene Rd., Don Mills, Ont. M3C 2A2.

**SMITH, Newman Donald,** C.A., C.M.A., P. Admin., F.C.I.S.; chartered accountant; b. Chesterville, Ont. 26 Dec. 1936; s. Clarke Harold and Ethelwyn Irene (Cross) S.; e. Chartered Accts. 1961; Certified Management Accountant 1966; Fellow Chartered Inst. of Secretaries 1967; m. Mary Elizabeth d. William and Mary Murdoch 27 June 1964; children: Clarke Murdoch, Brian Newman; Retired 1994, Sr. Extve. Vice-Pres., Sec. and Dir., Andres Wines Ltd.; Andres Wines (B.C.) Ltd.; Andres Wines (Alberta) Ltd.; Andres Wines (Manitoba) Ltd.; Les Vins Andres du Quebec Ltée; Andres Wines Atlantic Ltd.; Superior Wines Ltd.; Peller Wines of Calif.; Watleys Ltd.; Pelwin Agy. Ltd.; articled for Coopers & Lybrand 1956–63; Sec.-Treas. Deloro Smelting & Refining Co. Ltd. 1963–69; Sec.-Treas. M.J. O'Brien Ltd. 1965–69; mem. Fin. Execs. Inst.; Counc. on Road Trauma; Hamilton C. of C.; recreations: skiing, golf; Clubs: Hamilton Golf & Country; The Hamilton Club; Home: 463 Ontario St., Ancaster, Ont. L9G 3E1.

**SMITH, Peter C.,** B.Sc., M.Sc., Ph.D.; research scientist (physical oceanography); b. East Orange, N.J. 15 June 1944; s. Robert Irving and Shirley Colvin (Jones) S.; e. Brown Univ. B.Sc. 1966, M.Sc. 1967; MIT/Woods Hole Oceanographic Inst. Ph.D. 1973; m. Julia d. William and Jean Berry 17 June 1967; children: Benjamin Andrew, Jonathan Edward; RESEARCH SCIENTIST, BEDFORD INSTITUTE OF OCEANOGRAPHY 1975– ; NRC Postdoctoral Fellowship, Bedford Inst. 1973–75; Principal Investigator & Steering Ctte. Chair, DFO Fisheries Ecology Program 1983–85; Co-Chair, Sci. Steering Ctte., Candn. Atlantic Storms Program 1985–89; current primary activity is directing 2nd Candn. Atlantic Storms Program (Co-Chair, Organizing Ctte.); Oceanography Ed., 'Atmosphere-Ocean' 1992– ; Adjunct Prof., Oceanography, Dalhousie Univ. 1979– ; Hydrography Ctte., ICES 1977–87; Sci. Ctte., Candn. Meteorological & Oceanographic Soc. 1980–83; NATO Special Program Panel on Marine Sciences 1982–85; Adjunct Assoc. Prof. of Physics, Mem. Univ. of Nfld. 1983–86; DFO Merit Award 1989; Mem., Candn. Meteorological & Oceanographic Soc.; Am. Meteorological Soc.; Am. Geophysical Union; The Oceanographic Soc.; author of 10 sci. journal articles, 1 book chapter & 4 tech. reports; co-author: 24 sci. journal articles & 11 tech. reports; editor: 2 dedicated issues of sci. journals; recreations: swimming, cycling, tennis, jogging, sailing, ballroom dance; Home: 11 Hickory Lane, Dartmouth, N.S. B2V 2A2; Office: P.O. Box 1006, Dartmouth, N.S. B2Y 4A2.

**SMITH, Peter John,** M.A., Ph.D.; educator; b. Rakaia, N.Z. 18 Sept. 1931; s. late Sidney Charles and Ethel May (Pettit) S.; e. Ashburton High Sch. N.Z. 1948; Dunedin Teachers' Training Coll. N.Z. Cert. 1950; Univ. of Otago, N.Z. 1949–51; Canterbury Univ. Coll. N.Z. B.A. 1952, M.A. 1953; Univ. of Toronto Dipl. Town & Regional Planning 1959; Univ. of Edinburgh Ph.D. 1964; m. Sheana Mary d. late Alexander James Buchanan Lee, Bridge of Allan, Scot. 30 May 1959; children: Katrina Alison, Hugh Roger; PROF. OF GEOGRAPHY, UNIV. OF ALTA. 1969– ; various teaching positions N.Z. and Gt. Brit. 1952–55; Research Planner City of Calgary 1956–59; joined present Univ. 1959, Chrmn. of Geog. 1967–75; mem. Science Adv. Comte. Alta. Environment Conserv. Authority 1971–77; Vice Chrmn. and Chrmn. Grants Adv. Comte. Alta. Environment Research Trust, 1971–77; Chrmn. and mem. various awards comtes. Social Sciences & Humanities Research Council Can.; recipient Cert of Distinction Town Planning Inst. Can. 1959; Central Mortgage & Housing Corp., Can. Council and Social Sciences & Humanities Research Council Fellowships; Candn. Assn. of Geographers Award for Service to the Profession of Geography; author 'Population and Production' 1967; 'The Edmonton-Calgary Corridor' 1978; ed. 'The Prairie Provinces' 1972; 'Edmonton: The Emerging Metropolitan Pattern' 1978; 'Environment and Economy: Essays on the Human Geography of Alberta' 1984; 'A World of Real Places: Essays in Honour of William C. Wonders' 1990; over 60 essays, tech. reports urban planning, pollution, geog. Alta.; mem. Candn. Inst. Planners; Candn. Assn. Geogs. (Councillor 1966–70, Vice Pres., Pres., Past Pres. 1972–75, Ed. 'The Canadian Geographer' 1978–84); Soc. for the Protection of Architectural Resources in Edmonton (Treas. 1986– ); Internat. Planning History Soc. (Councillor 1993– ); Home: 64 Marlboro Rd., Edmonton, Alta. T6J 2C6; Office: Edmonton, Alta. T6G 2H4.

**SMITH, Philip Edward Lake,** A.M., Ph.D., D.Litt., F.R.S.C.; archaeologist; b. Fortune, Nfld. 12 Aug. 1927; s. late George Frederick and Alice M. (Lake) S.; e. Fortune U.C. High Sch., Acadia Univ. B.A. 1948; Harvard Univ. A.M. 1957, Ph.D. 1962; Thaw Fellow, Harvard, 1954, 56, 60; Univ. de Bordeaux Special Research 1958–59; Mem. Univ. of Nfld. D.Litt. (hon.) 1976; m. Dr. Fumiko d. late Rev. Dr. Jokei Ikawa, Osaka, Japan 1959; one s. Douglas Philip Edward; PROF. D'ANTHROPOLOGIE, UNIV. DE MONTREAL; served with 401 (Aux.) Fighter Squadron, R.C.A.F. 1949–51; Sun Life Assce. Co., Montreal 1948, 1953; Lecturer, Asst. and Assoc. Prof. Univ. of Toronto 1961–66; Assoc. Prof. and Prof., Univ. de Montréal since 1966; Dir., Can. Govt. Arch. Exped. to Egypt, 1962–3 in UNESCO NUBIAN SALVAGE Programme; Dir., 7 archaeol. expeditions (Egypt, Iran) since 1962; conducted archaeol. research in Mexico (1954), USA (1955–56), France (1957–59), Iraq (1957), W. Indies (1968, 1977); participant various local and internat. confs. prehistoric archaeol.; occasional consultant; Can. Council Graduate Fellowships 1958–60; rec'd N.R.C. 1967, Can. Council and S.S.H.R.C.C. Research Grants 1969, 1971, 1974, 1977, 1983, leave grant 1970–71, 1981–82; Rsch. visit to China under exchange prog. between Chinese Acad. of Soc. Sci. and Candn. Soc. Sci. Resch. Counc. 1984; Del. Perm. Council, Internat. Union Anthrop. & Ethnol. Sciences (Vice-Chrmn., Candn. Nat. Comte. 1981–84); Educational Foundation for Anthropology and the Public (Vice Pres. 1981–84); author 'Aboriginal Stone Constructions in the Southern Piedmont' 1962; 'Le Solutréen en France' 1966; 'Food Production and its Consequences' 1976; 'The Hilly Flanks and Beyond' (co-ed.) 1983; 'Origin of Agriculture and History of Mankind' (in Japanese) 1986; 'Palaeolithic Archaeology in Iran' 1986; contrib. Cambridge History of Africa, Vol. I, 1982; over 70 articles and reports prehistoric archaeol. research; mem. Internat. Union Prehistoric & Protohistoric Sciences (Candn. del. to Perm. Council 1978– ); Foreign Fellow, Am. Anthrop. Assn.; Current Anthrop. Assoc.; Soc. for Am. Archaeol.; mem., Comité de Lecture journal L'Anthropologie (Paris); mem. Comité Conseil international journal Anthropologie et Sociétés (Québec); Candn. Soc. Archaeol. Abroad (Vice-Pres., 1970–71; Pres., 1971–73); Nfld. Hist. Soc.; Royal Society of Canada (elec. 1978); East Coast Archaeological, Marching & Chowder Society; Comm., Candn. Inst. in Baghdad 1983– ; Soc. of Sigma Xi; recreations: walking, genealogy, reading and idleness; Home: 3955 Ramezay Ave., Montreal, Que. H3Y 3K3; Office: C.P. 6128, Succ. A, Montreal, Que. H3C 3J7.

**SMITH, Phyllis Anne Lowther,** Q.C., B.A., LL.B., LL.M.; lawyer; b. Ponoka, Alberta 27 April 1947; d. Frederick Arthur and Anne Margaret (Parkinson) Lowther; e. Univ. of Toronto, Trinity College B.A. 1968; Univ. of Alberta LL.B. 1974; Harvard Univ. LL.M. 1976; m. Patrick Frank s. Frank and Alice Smith 31 Aug. 1968; children: Morgan Elizabeth, Meredith Eden, Michael Patrick; PARTNER, EMERY JAMIESON 1982– ; admitted to Law Soc. of Alta. 10 July 1975; Solicitor, City of Edmonton Law Dept. 1976–80; Assoc., Emery Jamieson 1980–82; Sessional Instructor, Faculty of Law, Univ. of Alberta 1978–81, 1983–86; Q.C. 1985; Dir., Royal Alexandra Hospitals Found. 1985–87; Dir. (Vice-Chair), Alberta Cancer Board 1987–93; Dir., Legal Edn. Soc. of Alberta 1986; Oliver Daycare Soc. 1985– ; Mem., Law Soc. of Alberta (Bencher 1981–91; Pres. 1991); Dir., Fedn. of Law Soc. of Canada; Candn. Lawyers Insur. Assn.; Candn. Bar Assn. (Mem., Alta. Branch Council 1991); Home: 43 Patricia Cres., Edmonton, Alta. T5R 5N7; Office: 1700 Oxford Tower, Edmonton Centre, 10235 – 101 St., Edmonton, Alta. T5J 3G1.

**SMITH, R. Ross,** B.Eng., M.B.A., P.Eng.; executive; b. Three Rivers, Que. 28 July 1930; s. Frederick R. Mitchell and Elsie (Anderson) S.; e. Three Rivers (Que.) High Sch., 1947; McGill Univ., B.Eng. 1952; Stanford Univ., M.B.A. 1958; m. Dorothy Grace, d. Julius Milbrath, 18 Aug. 1956; SR. VICE PRES., JAMES RICHARDSON & SONS LIMITED; Dir., Pan Canadian Petroleum; Richardson Greenshields Limited; Wawanesa Mutual Insurance Co.; Engineer, Production Department, Shell Oil Co., Calgary, 1952–56; Mang. Assistant, Home Oil Co., Calgary 1958, Asst. to Pres. 1960–68; Vice Pres. and Gen. Mgr., Cygnus Corp., 1966–68; mem. Assn. Prof. Engrs. Man.; Christian; recreation: golf; Clubs: Manitoba; St. Charles Country; Home: Apt. C, 141 Wellington Cres., Winnipeg, Man. R3M 3X3; Office: One Lombard Pl., Winnipeg, Man. R3B 0Y1.

**SMITH, Ray,** M.A.; writer; teacher; b. Inverness, Cape Breton 12 Dec. 1941; s. Frederick Johnson and Jean (MacMillan) S.; e. Dalhousie Univ., B.A. 1963; Concordia Univ., M.A. 1985; m. Anja d. Adrie and Lois Mechielsen 12 June 1976; two s. Nicholas, Alexander; began teaching 1970, presently Teacher, Dawson Coll.; Writer-in-Residence, Univ. of Alta. 1986–87; Canada-Scotland Writer-in-Residence, Edinburgh 1987–88; recipient Can. Council and Ont. Arts Council grants; New Press Award Short Fiction 1985; author: 'Cape Breton is the Thought Control Centre of Canada' short stories 1968; 'Lord Nelson Tavern' novel 1974; 'Century' linked stories 1986; 'A Night At The Opera' novel (Winner of 1992 QSPELL Best Novel Award) 1992; Founding mem. Nat. Council, Writers Union of Can.; recreations: skiing, conversation; Address: Dawson College, 3040 Sherbrooke St. W., Montreal, Que. H3Z 1A4.

**SMITH, Ray Telford,** C.A.; financial executive; b. Toronto, Ont. 18 March 1942; s. Raymond Cameron and Ida Evelyn (Day) S.; e. C.A. Ont. 1969; m. E. Anne d. Arthur J. and Edith G. Cook 7 Sept. 1963; children: S. Craig, Katherine D.; VICE-PRESIDENT AND CONTROLLER, TRANSCANADA PIPELINES LIMITED 1983– ; Partner, Peat, Marwick, Mitchell & Co. 1975–83; Office: P.O. Box 1000, Stn. M., Calgary, Alta. T2P 4K5.

**SMITH, Raymond Victor;** forest products executive; b. Vancouver, B.C. 28 Apl. 1926; s. Stanley Victor and Kathryn Stewart (Hunter) S.; e. Magee High Sch.; Univ. of B.C. one yr.; Banff Sch. Advanced Mgmt. Prog.; m. Marilyn Joyce d. Alexander and Leah Meldrum 17 Oct. 1947; children: Vicki, Kathi, Stan; CHRMN. OF THE BD., MacMILLAN BLOEDEL LTD. 1990– ; Dir., KNP BT, Netherlands; CIBC; musician (trumpet) Dal Richards Band 1942; Candn. Army 1944; Partner, Warren McCuish (men's clothiers) 1947; Sales Rep., Vancouver Paper Box 1949; Home Oil Distributors 1954; Kraft Paper & Board Sales 1957, Asst. Mgr. 1961; Newsprint Rep. Powell River-Alberni Sales Corp. Pasadena 1965, Mgr. 1967; Mgr. Supply Control & Sales Adm. MacMillan Bloedel Ltd. 1968, Gen. Mgr. Mktg. Pulp & Paper 1970, Vice Pres. Mktg. Pulp & Paper 1971, Vice Pres. and Gen. Mgr. Newsprint 1973, Group Vice Pres. Pulp & Paper 1977, Sr. Vice Pres. Pulp & Paper 1979, Pres. & Chief Operating Offr. 1980; Pres. & C.E.O., 1983; Hon. Co-Chrmn., Western Wood Products Forum; Dir., Canadian Imperial Bank of Commerce; Adv. Bd. Salvation Army; recreations: music, golf; Club: Capilano Golf & Country; Home: 1488 Lawson Ave., W. Vancouver, B.C. V7T 2E8; Office: 925 W. Georgia St., Vancouver, B.C. V6C 3L2.

**SMITH, Robert Alexander,** Q.C., B.A., LL.B.; b. Montreal, Que. 10 June 1928; s. Alexander Guthrie and Agnes (Boyce) S.; e. Westmount (Que.) High Sch.; Dalhousie Univ. B.A., LL.B.; m. Joan Elizabeth d. James Myrden 10 May 1951; three s. Robert Bruce, James Stuart, David Alexander; PARTNER, SMITH, LYONS, TORRANCE, STEVENSON & MAYER; read law with Hon. Gordon S. Cowan; called to Bar of N.S. 1953, Ont. 1953; cr. Q.C. 1964; mem. Law Soc. Upper Can.; N.S. Barristers Soc.; Advocates Soc. Ont. (Dir. 1971–74); Candn. Bar Assn.; Fed. Ins. Counsel; Defense Research Inst.; Assoc. mem. Am. Bar Assn.; Fellow of Am. College of Trial Lawyers; Co. York Law Assn.; Lawyers Club Toronto; Phi Delta Theta (Pres. 1951); United Church; recreations: skiing, golf, tennis, sailing; Clubs: York Downs Golf & Country (Past Dir., Pres. 1968–69); Osler Bluffs Ski (Past Dir.); Willoughby Golf, Stuart Fla.; Home: 16 Blair Athol Cres., Islington, Ont. M9A 1X5; Office: Suite 6200, Scotia Plaza, 40 King St. W., Toronto, Ont. M5H 3Z7.

**SMITH, Very Rev. Robert Frederick,** B.A., B.D., Th.D., D.D.; clergyman; b. Montreal, Que. 25 May 1934; s. Reginald Douglas and Margaret Lorraine (Smyth) S.; e. Univ. of Alta. B.A. 1956, B.D. 1964; Boston Univ. Th.D. 1973; m. Margaret Ellen d. Dennis and Amy Maguire 2 Aug. 1958; children: Richard, Daniel, Margaret, Doris, Robert; MINISTER OF THE CONGREGATION, FIRST UNITED CHURCH; Moderator, United Church of Canada 1984–86; Minister: St. Luke's Fort St. John, B.C. 1958–61; Trinity Edmonton, Alta. 1961–65; Meml. Congregational Ch., N. Quincy, Mass. 1965–68; Richmond Hill United Ch. 1968–74; Eglinton United Ch., Toronto, Ont. 1974–82; Shaughnessy Heights United Church, Vancouver, BC 1982– ; Adjunct Prof. of Homilectics, Victoria Coll., Univ. of Toronto 1979–81; D.D. (h. causa) Victoria Univ. 1985; D.D. Stephen's Coll. 1990; Home: 3526 W. 2nd Ave., Vancouver, B.C. V6R 1J4; Office: 320 East Hastings, Vancouver, B.C. V6A 1P4.

**SMITH, Robert Henry Tufrey,** B.A., M.A., Ph.D.; educator; b. Walcha, N.S.W., Australia 22 May 1935; s. Robert Davidson and Gladys (Tufrey) S.; e. Farrer Meml. Agric. High Sch. N.S.W. 1952; Univ. of New Eng. N.S.W. B.A. 1957; Northwestern Univ., Ill. M.A. 1958; Australian Nat. Univ. Ph.D. 1962; m. Elisabeth d. Karl and Hannah Jones 8 Aug. 1959; children: Robert, Jennifer; EXTVE. DIR., AUSTRALIAN EDUCATION OFFICE, WASHINGTON, D.C. 1994– ; Lectr. Univ. of Melbourne 1961; Asst. Prof. of Geog. Univ. of Wis. 1962, Assoc. Prof. Geog. 1964, Prof. of Geog. 1967; Prof. and Head of Geog. Queen's Univ. Kingston 1970–72; Prof. of Geog. Monash Univ. Melbourne 1972, Chrmn. 1973–75, Assoc. Dean of Arts 1974–75; Prof. of Geog. 1975–85, Head of Geog. Univ. of B.C. 1975–80, Assoc. Vice Pres. Acad. 1979–83; Vice Pres., Acad. 1983–85; Pres. March-Nov. 1985; Vice-Chancellor, The Univ. of Western Australia Dec. 1985–Jan. 1989; Chrmn., National Bd. of Employment, Education and Training 1988–90; Vice-Chancellor, The Univ. of New England 1990–93; President, Australian Higher Education Industrial Assn. 1991–92; Vice Pres. & Bd. Mem., Australian Vice-Chancellors' Ctte. 1991–92; Pres., Australian Vice-Chancellor's Ctte. 1993– ; Fellow, Acad. Social Sci. Australia; Fellow, Australian Institute of Mgmnt.; Fellow, John Simon Guggenheim Meml. Found. 1964–65; author and ed. numerous books and articles internal trade and market-place systems Africa; Address: Australian Education Office, 1601 Massachusetts Ave. N.W., Washington, DC 20036.

**SMITH, Robert John,** B.Comm., M.B.A., FCCHSE; hospital executive; b. Vancouver, B.C. 23 Oct. 1944; s. Robert Sanford and Gladys (McHardy) S.; e. J. Lloyd Crowe H.S. 1962; Univ. of B.C. B.Comm. 1968, M.B.A. 1971; m. Patricia d. Patrick and Lillian Kelly 31 Dec. 1970; children: Andrea, Kelly, Jocelyn; PRES. & CHIEF EXTVE. OFFR., LIONS GATE HOSP. 1988– ; Extve. Dir., The Arthritis Soc. of B.C. 1977–80; Dep. Dir., Cancer Control Agency of B.C. 1980–88; Dir., Candn. Hosp. Assn. 1988– (Chrmn. 1993–94); Dir., B.C. Health Serv. Ltd. 1989– ; Dir., Western Interprovincial Network; Chrmn., B.C. Health Assn. 1985–86; Pres., U.B.C. Alumni Assn. 1980–81; Clinical Asst. Prof., Fac. of Med., Dept. of Health Care & Epid., Univ. of B.C.; Presidents Award, Health Admin. Assn. of B.C.; Life Mem., B.C. Health Assn.; Chrmn., Red Cross Bldg. Ctte. of B.C.; Fellow, Candn. Coll. of Health Serv. Extves.; recreations: skiing, ball, swim; Home: 3220 Del Rio Dr., North Vancovuer, B.C. V7N 4C2; Office: 231 East 15th Ave., North Vancouver, B.C. V7L 2L7.

**SMITH, Robert Thomas,** B.Sc., M.Sc., M.B.A., F.C.I.A., F.S.A., M.A.A.A.; insurance executive; b. Vancouver, B.C. 1 June 1943; s. Donald Arthur and Margaret Isabella (McFarlane) S.; e. Univ. of Victoria B.Sc. 1968; Univ. of Toronto M.Sc. 1969; Univ. of B.C. M.B.A. 1984; m. Kathleen d. Madelaine and Bernard Diemert 7 June 1979; children: Jason, Laura, Caitlin; PRESIDENT & CHIEF EXECUTIVE OFFICER, SEABOARD LIFE INSUR. CO. 1992– ; Group Actuary, The Mfr. Life Insur. Co. 1970–76; Vice-Pres., Storebrand Internat. Reinsur. 1976–79; Vice-Pres. & Actuary, Fidelity Life Assur. 1979–82; Partner, Paterson Cook Ltd. 1982–85; Sr. Vice-Pres., Seaboard Life Insur. Co. 1985–92; Mem., Extve. Council, Cdn. Inst. of Actuaries 1986–89; Vice-Pres., Extve. Council, Cdn. Inst. of Actuaries 1991– (Mem., Standards of Practice Ctte. 1987–91); Bd. Mem., Vancouver Community Coll. (Vice Chair) 1988–92; Bd. Mem., Physical Med. Rsch. Fdn. 1993– ; Mem., Financial Extves. Inst. of Cda. Vancouver Ch. 1985–91; Vancouver Actuaries' Club (Past Pres.) 1979– ; Bd. Mem., Seaboard Life Insur. Co. 1992– ; F.C.I.A. 1973; F.S.A. 1973; M.A.A.A. 1984; recreations: marine biology, scuba diving, underwater photography, travel, skiing; club: Arbutus; Home: 1125 W. 33rd Ave., Vancouver, B.C. V6M 1A3; Office: 2165 W. Broadway, P.O. Box 5900, Vancouver, B.C. V6B 5H6.

**SMITH, Robert W.,** B.Sc., P.Eng.; utilities executive; b. Boundary Creek, N.B. 8 Dec. 1912; s. Samuel Wallace and Ruth Celia (Mitton) S.; e. Moncton High Sch.; Univ. of N.B. B.Sc. 1934; m. Florence d. Murray and Annie Manuel 28 July 1940; children: Murray, Roberta, Sharon, Paul; Chrmn. of Bd., Maritime Electric Co. Ltd. 1984–93; served with R.C.E. 1943–45, rank Lt.; Asst. Prof. of Electrical Eng. Univ. of N.B. 1946–48; Sr. Design Eng. Montreal Engineering Co. Ltd. 1948–62; Gen. Mgr. Maritime Electric Co. Ltd. 1963, Dir. 1970– , Pres. 1978; Project Mgr. CIDA Nigeria 1971 (leave of absence); Dir. Queen Elizabeth Hosp. Found. 1985–90; Vice Chrmn. Rotary Club of Charlottetown Found. Ltd. 1987– , Dist. Gov. Rotary Internat. 1985–86; Campaign Chrmn. P.E.I. Un. Way 1969, Pres. 1973; Dir. Atlantic Provs. Econ. Council 1963–78, Vice Pres. 1966–68, 1972–74; Dir. Candn. C. of C. 1978–79, Chrmn. Atlantic Provs. C. of C. (P.E.I. Sec.) 1983–84; mem. Candn. Nat. Ctte. World Energy Conf. 1974–77; Dir. Industrial Enterprises Inc. 1977–79; Life Mem., Charlottetown Chamber of Commerce (Pres. 1978–79); Life mem. Inst. Elect. & Electronic Engs.; Hon. Life Mem., Assn. Profl. Engs. P.E.I.; Dir., Candn. Elect. Assn. 1978–79; Elder, Un. Ch. of Can. 1955–62, 1964–80, 1985– , Trustee 1983– ; recreations: reading, music, woodworking; Home: 135 Queen Elizabeth Dr., Charlottetown, P.E.I. C1A 3B2.

**SMITH, Roger S.,** B.A., M.A., Ph.D.; university professor and administrator; b. Oklahoma, U.S.A. 20 Oct. 1942; s. Theodore Harold and Elizabeth Stafford (McRoberts) S.; e. Oberlin College, Pomona College B.A. 1964; Harvard Univ.; Univ. of Calif. at Berkeley M.A. 1967, Ph.D. 1969; m. Elisabeth d. Joseph and Mary Sorkness 5 Aug. 1967; children: Christopher, Catherine, Theodore; PROFESSOR, UNIVERSITY OF ALBERTA; Economist, IMF 1972–74; Asst., Assoc. & Full Prof., Univ. of Alta. 1969– ; Dean, Fac. of Business 1976–88; Assoc. Vice-Pres. (Academic) 1992– ; Chair, Fed. of Business Deans 1986–88; Vice-Chair 1978–80, 1984–86; Chair, Banff Sch. of Advanced Mngt. 1993– ; Visiting Prof., Erasmus Univ. Rotterdam 1983–84; Visiting Scholar, Harvard Internat. Tax Prog. 1977–78, IMF 1988; Consultant to World Bank, Internat. Monetary Fund, Auditor Gen., USAID; Dir., Century Sales; Mem., Finan. Adv. Ctte., Alta. Securities Comn.; Distinguished Service Award, Alta. Inst. of C.A.s 1968; Woodrow Wilson Fellow 1964–65; Phi Beta Kappa; Dir. & Chair, Winspear Found.; Dir., Edmonton Concert Hall Found.; Dir. & Chair, Banff Sch. of Adv. Mngt.; Mem., Candn. Econ. Assn.; Candn. Tax Found.; Am. Econ. Assn.; Nat. Tax Assn.; author: 'Tax Expenditures' 1979, 'National Income Analysis and Forecasting' 1975, 'Personal Wealth Taxation' 1993, 'Local Income Taxes: Economic Effects and Equity' 1972; recreations: fishing, hiking, golf, jogging, reading; Home: 7811 – 119 St., Edmonton, Alta. T6G 1W5; Office: University Hall, Univ. of Alta., Edmonton, Alta. T6G 2J9.

**SMITH, Ronald E.,** B.B.A., C.A.; telecommunications executive; b. Shelburne, N.S. 26 May 1950; s. Edgar Earle and Ida Mae (Porter) S.; e. Acadia Univ. B.B.A. 1971; C.A. 1973; children: Sarah, Susan, Stephen; VICE PRES. FINANCE MARITIME TELEGRAPH AND TELEPHONE CO. LTD. 1987– ; Dir., The Island Telephone Co. Ltd.; Pres. and Dir. MT&T Leasing Inc.; Dir. MT&T Mobile Inc.; joined Clarkson Gordon Halifax and Toronto 1971–80; Woods Gordon 1980–87, Partner 1981; Nat. Past Pres., Candn. Assn. for Community Living; Vice Chrmn. of Bd. of Trustees, Grace Maternity Hosp.; Chrmn., Minister's Task Force on Physician Policy Development, N.S. Dept. of Health 1991–93; Chrmn., Atlantic Provs. Econ. Council; Mem., Acadia Univ. School of Business Advisory Ctte.; Mem., Dalhousie Univ. Investment Ctte.; mem. Council Financial Execs. Conf. Bd. Can.; Financial Execs. Inst.; mem. Inst. C.A.'s N.S. (Council member); Candn. Inst. C.A.'s; R.Catholic; Club: Ashburn Golf; Home: 57 Allison Dr., Dartmouth, N.S. B2V 1P8; Office: P.O. Box 880, Halifax, N.S. B3J 2W3.

**SMITH, Ronald Fenwick,** B.A., M.A.; publisher; writer; professor; b. Vancouver, B.C. 7 Aug. 1943; s. David Fenwick and Marguerite (Chester) S.; e. Univ. of B.C. B.A. 1969; Univ. of Leeds M.A. 1970; m. Patricia d. Tom and Lillian Murdoch 1 May 1969; children: Nicole, Owen; FOUNDER & PUBLISHER, OOLICHAN BOOKS 1975– ; Staff, Bookstore, Univ. of B.C. 1962–63; Instructor, U.B.C. 1970–71; Instr., English Dept., Malaspina College 1971– ; Fiction Ed., Douglas & McIntyre 1988–90; teacher in England 1977–78; has given readings & lectures at universities in U.S.A. and Britain; recipient of two Canada Council Arts Awards for writing; B.C. Cultural Arts Award for writing; Mem., Writers' Union of Can.; Assn. of Candn. Publishers; Literary Press Group; Assn. of Book Pubs. of B.C.; Internat. P.E.N.; Nanaimo District Youth Soccer Assn. (Registrar); author: 'The Silver Fox' 1981, 'Seasonal' 1984, 'A Buddha named Baudelaire' 1988; editor: 'Rainshadow: Stories from Vancouver Island' 1982, 'Collected Poems of Ralph Gustafson' 2 vols. 1987; recreations: golf, fishing, travel; club: Fairwinds Golf; Address: P.O. Box 10, Lantzville, B.C. V0R 2H0.

**SMITH, Ross;** motivational speaker, management seminar programmer and speech writer; b. St. Lambert, Que. 14 Aug. 1927; s. Henry Ernest and Dorothy Agnes (Ahern) S.; e. Hogg's Private Sch. for Boys; Montreal High Sch.; McGill Univ., Extension Courses; m. Pauline Marie, d. Anathine Jolicoeur, 5 March 1949; two d., Lynne, Roslyn; MOTIVATOR AT LARGE; Pres., Ross Smith Inc.; Past Pres., Grey Ronalds Smith Ltd.; joined Stevenson & Scott Ltd., Graphic Arts Dept., Montreal 1945; Radio-TV Dir. 1950; Asst. Mgr. Vancouver Office 1950, Creative Dir., Toronto 1953, Account Mgr., Montreal 1958–62, Vice Pres. 1963; merged with Crombie Advertising in 1964; Vice Pres. Creative 1965, Extve. Vice Pres. 1968, Pres., 1970; Formed Grey Ronalds Smith Ltd. 1983; former Sr. Vice Pres., Grey Advertising; daily nat. radio series 1965–69; Capitol Records comedy recording artist; Kiwanis International Ambass. of Goodwill 1967; professional speaker handled by Speakers' Bureau Int'l.; Grad. Dale Carnegie Institute, Dartnell Institute, NYC; served with Duke of Connaught Royal Candn. Hussars (R) 1945–49; rank Sgt.; rec'd Royal Humane Soc. Award for Bravery; received Outstanding Service Award from Assn. of Cdn. Advertisers, 1980; Past Dir., Inst. Can. Advertising; Past Dir., Quebec Soc. for Crippled Children; Past Pres., St. Bruno Riding Club; Past Pres. and Hon. Life Mem., Advertising & Sales Extves. Club Montreal; Advisor, Can. Exec. Serv. Org. (CESO); Past Dir., Chinguacousy Country; mem., Caledon Riding and Hunt Club; Regency Racquets Club; Presbyterian; recreations: riding, tennis; swimming; Home: Penthouse One, 53 Warrender Ave., Islington, Ont. M9B 5Z7.

**SMITH, Ross Siddall,** F.C.A.; chartered accountant; b. Winnipeg, Man. 22 Apr. 1939; s. Robert Guy and Greta Gordon (Scott) S.; e. Williams Lake Jr./Sr. H.S. Jr. Matriculation 1956; Institute of Chartered Accountants of British Columbia, C.A. 1962; Fellow 1990; m. Lillian Diane (nee Robinson) 24 Nov. 1962; children: Michelle Leanne, Kevin Ross; MANAGING PARTNER - BRITISH COLUMBIA, KPMG PEAT MARWICK THORNE (national firm of public accountants and auditors with predecessor firms going back over 100 years); Articled Student, Rickard Crawford & Co., Williams Lake 1956–59; Vancouver 1959–62; Staff Chartered Accountant 1962–63; joined Peat Marwick in Vancouver 1963; Partner 1973; Member of Executive Committee 1983–89; Managing Partner: Vancouver 1984–89; Vice-Chrmn. Vancouver and Lower Mainland Region, Member of Partnership Board and Management Committee of Peat Marwick Thorne 1989–93; Managing Partner - British Columbia and Member of Management Ctte. 1993– ; Member, Advisory Council to Faculty of Commerce and Business Admin., Univ. of B.C., President's Club of Simon Fraser Univ. and Vancouver Library Foundation; Dir. and Chrmn. of St. Christopher's School Foundation; Director of Endeavour Society; Campaign Chrmn., Chartered Accountants Education Foundation; Past Dir. & Treasurer of Vancouver Playhouse Theatre; Past Dir., Junior Achievement of British Columbia; recreations: skiing, golf, bridge; Clubs; Vancouver; Hollyburn Country; Homes: 5367 Esperanza Dr., North Vancouver, B.C. V7R 3W3 and 3325 Panorama Ridge, Whistler, B.C.; Office: P.O. Box 10426, Pacific Centre, 777 Dunsmuir St., Vancouver, B.C. V7Y 1K3.

**SMITH, Rowland James,** M.A., Ph.D.; educator; b. Johannesburg 19 Aug. 1938; s. John James and Gladys Spencer (Coldrey) S.; e. St. John's Coll. Johannesburg 1944–56; Univ. of Natal B.A. 1959, Ph.D. 1967; Oxford Univ. (Rhodes Scholar Transvaal 1960) M.A. 1967; m. Catherine Anne d. Richard and Hazel Lane 22 Sept. 1962; children: Russell Claude, Belinda Claire; McCULLOCH PROFESSOR IN ENGLISH, DALHOUSIE UNIVERSITY 1988– ; Lectr. English Dept. Univ. of the Witwatersrand, Johannesburg 1963–67; Asst. Prof. present Univ. 1967, Assoc. Prof. 1970, Prof. 1977, McCulloch Prof. 1988, Asst. Dean Fac. of Arts & Sci. 1972–74, Chrmn. Gen. Ctte. on Cultural Activities 1975–76, Dir. Centre for African Studies 1976–77, Chrmn. Dept. of Eng. 1977–83, 1985–86, Dean, Fac. of Arts and Social Sciences 1988–93, Provost, College of Arts and Sci. 1988–89, 1990–91, 1992–93; Visiting Fellow Dalhousie Univ. 1965–66; Visiting Mem. Sr. Common Rm., Lincoln Coll., Oxford 1974–75; Professeur, chercheur associé à l'Institut Plurisdisciplinaire d'Études Canadiennes, Université de Rouen 1994; mem. Aid to Scholarly Publications Ctte. Cdn. Fdn. for the Humanities 1979–85; Chair, N.S. Univ. Dept. of Educ. Liaison Ctte. 1990–93; Selection Ctte. for N.S., I.O.D.E. Meml. Scholarships 1969–71; Selection Ctte. for N.S. Rhodes Scholarships 1972–74; Gov. Halifax Grammar Sch. 1972–74; Gov., Neptune Theatre Found. 1977–78; mem. Education Ctte., Victoria Gen. Hospital 1986–90; Dir., Publicity and Promotion, Nova Scotia Rugby Football Union 1987–89; ACUTE (Sec.-Treas. 1968–70, Profl. Concerns Ctte. 1979–81); Modern Lang. Assn. of Am. (Chrmn. Div. 33, 1984); Cdn. Assn. of Chairmen of Eng. (Vice-Pres. 1981–82, Pres. 1982–83, Exec. Mem. 1985–86); CACLALS (Candn. Assoc. for Commonwealth Literature and Language Studies, Exec. Mem. 1989–92); Bd. of Dirs., Candn. Fdn. for the Humanities 1992– ; author: 'Lyric and Polemic' 1972; editor: 'Exile and Tradition' 1976; 'Critical Essays on Nadine Gordimer' 1990; Asst. Ed. 'English Studies in Africa' 1964–67; Editorial Advisory Bd., 'Ariel' 1991– ; recreations: squash, running, sleeping; Clubs: The Waegwoltic; Dalhousie Faculty; Home: 5683 Inglis St., Halifax, N.S. B3H 1K2; Office: English Dept., Dalhousie Univ., Halifax, N.S. B3H 3J5.

**SMITH, Selwyn M.,** M.B., B.S., M.D., F.R.C.P.(C), D.A.B.P.N.; D.P.M.; F.R.C.Psych. (U.K.), F.A.P.A.; psychiatrist; educator; b. Sydney, Aust. 12 Aug. 1942; s. Abraham and Lillian Gertrude (Greenwood) S.; e. Sydney Univ. Med. Sch., M.B., B.S. 1966; Univ. of Birmingham, M.D. (Hons.) 1974; London Univ., D.P.M. 1969; m. May D. Yiu-Kee and Fong-Yin Lau Tsang 5 Jan. 1968; children: Benjamin, Michelle; CONSULTANT IN PSYCHIATRY; Dir., Dept. of Forensic Psychiatry, Royal Ottawa Hosp. 1975–78; Psychiatrist-in-Chief, Royal Ottawa Hosp. & Prof. of Psychiatry, Univ. of Ottawa 1978–86; Consultant Psychiatrist, Brockville Psych. Hosp.; Consultant Psychiatrist, Community Care Systems Inc., Wellesley, Mass. U.S.A.; Courtesy Staff, Ottawa General Hosp.; Fellow, Royal Coll. of Psychiatrists, UK; Royal Coll. of Physicians and Surgeons of Can.; Royal Aust. & N.Z. Coll. of Psychiatrists 1983–92; Am. Psychiatric Assn.; Am. Coll. of Preventive Med. 1980–92; mem., Am. Coll. of Psychiatrists; Am. Acad. of Forensic Sci.; Diplomate, Am. Bd. of Forensic Psychiatry 1980–93; Certified Addiction Specialist 1991; Program Chrmn., Annual Meeting Am. Acad. of Psychiatry and the Law (San Diego and New York) 1981–82; Assoc. Ed., Bulletin of the Am. Acad. of Psychiatry and the Law; Pres., Am. Acad. of Psychiatry and the Law 1985–86; Advisor, various fed. & prov. funding agencies; mem., Bd. of Dirs., Internat. Acad. of Law and Mental Health 1984–87; Psychiatric Advisor, Med. and Health Care Adv. Ctte., Fed. Correctional Services of Can. 1984–87; Consultant Physician in Psychiatry, State of New South Wales, Australia; Bronze Medal, Royal Coll. of Psychiatrists 1974; author: 'The Battered Child Syndrome' 1975; editor: 'The Maltreatment of Children' 1978; co-author: 'Self-Assessment of Current Knowledge in Forensic & Organic Psychiatry' 1978; and numerous other articles on psychiatric topics; mem., Candn. Psychiatric Assns.; Am. Psychiatric Assn.; Internat. Adv. Bd., Am. Academy of Health Care Providers in the Addictive Disorders; mem., Am. Acad. of Psychiatry and the Law; mem. Rsch. Bd. of Adv., Am. Biographical Institute; recreations: tennis, skiing, running; Home: 39 Cedarhill Dr., Nepean, Ont. K2R 1C3; Office: Heritage Place, Suite 900, 155 Queen St., Ottawa, Ont. K1P 6L1.

**SMITH, Stephen Leonard J.,** M.A., Ph.D.; educator; b. Dayton, Ohio 20 Oct. 1946; s. Leonard Justinius and Edna Virginia (Jones) S.; e. Wright State Univ. B.A. 1968; Ohio State Univ. M.A. 1970; Texas A&M Univ. Ph.D. 1973; m. Carol d. Arthur and Dorothy Sidell 26 Aug. 1968; children: Kristin, Stephanie; PROF. OF RECREATION AND LEISURE STUDIES UNIV. OF WATERLOO 1976– ; Pres. Dauphin Associates; Asst. Prof. of Park & Recreation Resources Mich. State Univ. 1973–76; joined present Univ. 1976, Chrmn. of Dept. 1983–90, mem. Senate; Acad. Colleague Council Ont. Univs.; mem. Nat. Task. Force Tourism Data 1985–87; cons. prov. and fed. agencies tourism & recreation; Chrmn. Tourism Rsch. & Edn. Centre; Chrmn. of the Bd., Kitchener-Waterloo Area Visitor and Convention Bureau 1990–91; author 'Recreation Geography' 1983; 'Tourism Analysis' 1989; 'Dictionary of Concepts in Recreation and Leisure Studies' 1990; ed. Recreation Rsch. Review 1978–82; book review ed. Annals of Tourism Rsch. 1988– ; assoc. ed. Jour. Leisure Rsch. 1990–93; Leisure Sciences 1985–88; numerous scholarly articles and tech. reports; Fellow, Acad. Leisure Sci's; Internat. Study Tourism; mem. Travel & Tourism Rsch. Assn. (Dir. Can. Chapter); Candn. Assn. Geogs.; Council Hotel, Restaurant & Instnl. Edn.; R.Catholic; recreations: fishing, cooking, bicycling; Home: 31 – 375 Kingscourt Dr., Waterloo, Ont. N2K 3N7; Office: Waterloo, Ont. N2L 3G1.

**SMITH, Stuart H.B.,** B.A., C.A.; business executive; b. Montreal, Que. 29 Aug. 1945; s. the late Carl Henry and Gertrude Ann (Byers) S.; e. Royal York C.I.; Univ. of Western Ont., B.A. 1969; Univ. of Toronto, C.A. 1972; m. Wendy d. the late Stanley John and Lauleta Burk 27 June 1968; children: Kimberley, Stephanie, Stuart Jr.; EXEC. VICE-PRES. & DIR., THE OXFORD GROUP INC. 1989– ; Pres., Oxford Properties Inc. (U.S.) 1989– ; Touche Ross & Co. Toronto 1969–72; Pres., Shipp Corp. Ltd. Mississauga 1972–89; Dir., Appleby College; Past Chrmn., Mississauga Hosp.; Advr., Sheridan College Nursing; Mem., Candn. Inst. of C.A.'s; Acad. Acctg. Assn.; Am. Acctg. Assn.; Urban Land Inst. (U.S.); recreations: skiing, boating, golf; clubs: Mississaugua Golf & Country, Caledon Ski, Muskoka Golf & Country, The Candn.; Home: 2233 Shardawn Mews, Mississauga, Ont. L5C 1W6; Office: 1700, 120 Adelaide St. W., Toronto, Ont. M5H 1T1.

**SMITH, Stuart Lyon,** B.Sc., M.D., C.M., Dip.Psych., FRCP(C); psychiatrist, corporate executive; b. Montreal, Que. 7 May 1938; s. Moe Samuel and Nettie (Krainer) S.; e. McGill Univ. B.Sc. 1958, M.D., C.M. 1962, Dip.Psych. 1967; m. Patricia d. Arnold and Elsie Springate2 Jan. 1964; children: Tanya, Craig; PRESIDENT, ROCKCLIFFE RESEARCH & TECH. INC. 1987– ; Asst. then Assoc. Prof., McMaster Univ. Medical School 1967–75; Mem., Ont. Legislature 1975–82; Leader, Ont. Liberal Party 1976–82 & Leader of Opposition 1977–82; Chair, Science Council of Canada 1982–87; Chair, Peer Review & Implementation Cttes., Federal Networks of Centres of Excellence Competition 1989; Comn. of Inquiry on Candn. Univ. Edn. 1990–91; Bd. Chair, Ensyn Tech. Inc. 1990– ; Visiting Prof., Psychiatry, McMaster Univ. 1982–93; Adjunct Prof., Psychiatry, Univ. of Ottawa 1986– ; Decorated Knight, Nat. Order of Merit France 1988; McLaughlin Travelling Fellow 1964–65; Fellow, Royal College of Physicians & Surg. of Can.; Hon. LL.D. Mount Allison Univ. 1992; Hon. Fellow, Ryerson Polytech. Inst. 1987; Public Sector Award, Candn. Advanced Tech. Assn. 1987; Alpha Omega Alpha Hon. Med. Soc. 1961; Chair, Bd. of Trustees, Ottawa Gen. Hosp. 1991– ; Mem., Bd. of Gov., Univ. of Ottawa 1989– ; author: 'Technology and Work in Canada's Future' 1986; recreations: tennis; Home: 354 Cloverdale Road, RockCliffe Park, Ottawa, Ont. K1M 0X3; Office: 1000 – 280 Albert St., Ottawa, Ont. K1P 5G8.

**SMITH, Thomas Murray;** artist, lecturer; b. Vancouver, B.C. 25 May 1951; s. Robert Murray and Frances Verona (Pirzek) S.; e. Vancouver Sch. of Art 1971; m. Sonia d. Dillon and Tina Smith 27 Jan. 1990; one d.: Marissa Verona; solo exhibitions: Ferry Landing, West Vanc. 1991; Bau-Xi Gall. Vanc. & Toronto 1976, '78, '80, '82, '83, '89; group exhibitons: Bau-Xi Gall. Vanc. 1974, '75, '83, '84, '86, '87, '88; 'Graphite on Paper,' Art Gall. of Gr. Victoria 1977; '"50" Canadian Drawings,' Beaverbrook Art Gall. Fredericton; Olympic Exhib. Montreal 1976; Lectr., Gr. Vanc. Sch. Dist. 1982–88; Instr., Univ. of B.C. 1977; collections: B.C. Ferry Corp.; B.C. Prov. Collection; Saskatoon Gall. Corp.; Shell Oil Co. Collection; Gulf Oil Co. Collection; Art Gall. of Gr. Victoria; Imperial Oil Co. Collection; Air Canada; Home: 715 East 11th St., North Vancouver, B.C. V7L 2H9.

**SMITH, Victor Gordon,** M.Sc.F., Ph.D.; educator; b. Toronto, Ont. 24 May 1927; s. (late) Lewis Gordon and Florence Ione (Wilson) S.; e. John Ross Robertson Pub. Sch. and Lawrence Park Coll. Inst. Toronto 1945; Univ. of Toronto B.Sc.F. 1949, M.Sc.F. 1965; Iowa State Univ. Ph.D. 1972; m. Mary Taylor d. late Benjamin Franklin Avery 22 May 1954; children: Mary Anna, Elizabeth Ruth, Gordon Rymal, Susan Avery; EMERITUS PROF. OF FORESTRY, UNIV. OF TORONTO 1992– , Forest Engr. The KVP Co. Ltd. Espanola, Ont. 1949–63; Student Lectr. in Forestry present Univ. 1963–65, Assoc. Prof. 1970–76; Instr. Mich. Technol. Univ. 1965–66, Iowa State Univ. 1966–70; Visiting Fellow, Univ. of Canterbury, Christchurch, N.Z. 1977; Prof. of Forestry, present univ. 1976–92; mem. Acad. Bd. 1988–91; mem. Gov. Council 1978–84, Presidential Adv. Comtes. on Budget 1979–82 and Press 1979–84; Assoc. Dean, Fac. of Forestry 1984–86 and 1988–91; author or co-author numerous publs.; Tech. Comte. mem. Candn. Standards Assn.; mem. Ont. Prof. Foresters' Assn.; Candn. Inst. Forestry; Ont. Forestry Assn.; Soc. Am. Foresters; Sigma Xi; Gamma Sigma Delta; Xi Sigma Pi; United Church; recreations: curling, camping; Home: 13 Parkside Dr., Trenton, Ont. K8V 5L6; Office: 33 Willcocks St., Toronto, Ont. M5S 3B3.

**SMITH, Rev. Wilfred Cantwell,** M.A., Ph.D., D.D., LL.D., D.Litt., D.Lett., D.H.L., F.R.S.C. (1961); professor; b. Toronto, Ont. 21 July 1916; s. Victor Arnold and Sarah Cory (Cantwell) S.; e. Upper Canada Coll., Toronto, Ont. (Head Boy 1933); Univ. of Toronto, B.A. (with Hons. in Oriental Lang.) 1938; Westminster Coll., Cambridge (Theol.) 1938–40: St. John's Coll., Cambridge (Research Student) 1938–40; Princeton Univ., M.A. 1947 and Ph.D. (Oriental Lang. and Lit.) 1948; m. Muriel, d. Dr. and Mrs. R. Gordon Struthers, Toronto, Ont. 1939; children: Arnold, Julian, Heather, Brian, Rosemary; PROF. EMERITUS OF THE COMPARATIVE HISTORY OF RELIGION, HARVARD UNIV. 1984– ; Rsch. Assoc., Trinity Coll., Toronto 1986–91; Hon. Assoc., Centre for Religious Studies, Univ. of Toronto 1986–91; Sr. Killam Fellow, Univ. of Toronto 1985–86; Chrmn., The Study of Religion, and Prof., Comparative History of Religion, Harvard Univ. 1978–84; McCulloch Prof. of Religion, and Chrmn., Dept. of Religion, Dalhousie Univ. 1973–78; Prof. of World Religions and Dir., Center for Study of World Religions, Harvard Univ. 1964–73; W.M. Birks Prof. of Comparative Religion, McGill Univ., 1949–63; also Dir. of Islamic Inst. there, 1952–63; Lectr. in Islamic Hist., Forman Christian Coll., Lahore 1941–45; Instr. in Islamic Hist., Univ. of Punjab (Grad. Sch.), 1943–45; Advisory Ed., 'Muslim World' (Hartford, Conn.) 1956–84; 'Religious Studies' (Cambridge, Eng.) 1964–90; 'Studies in Religion' (Toronto) 1971–83; 'Dionysius' (Halifax) 1977–87; consulting ed., Encyclopaedia Britannica 1969–90; Visiting Prof.: Univ. of London 1960; Princeton Univ. 1966–67; Univ. of Toronto 1968, 1981; Chrmn., Islamics Sect., Int'l. Congress of Orientalists 1964; Pres., Am. Soc. for Study of Relig. 1966–69; Pres. Mid. East Studies Assn. of N. Amer. 1977–78; Pres., Cdn. Theological Soc. 1979–80; Pres. Am. Acad. of Religion 1982–83; Hon. Pres., Internat. Congress of Asian & N. African Studies 1990; author: 'Modern Islam in India: A Social Analysis' 1943 (rev. ed., 1947, 1964, 1972, 1979); 'Islam in Modern History' 1957, 1958, 1959, 1977; 'The Faith of Other Men' 1962, 1963, 1964, 1976; 'The Meaning and End of Religion' 1963, 1964, 1965, 1978, 1991; 'Questions of Religious Truth' 1967; 'Religious Diversity' 1976, 1982; 'Belief and History' 1977, 1985; 'Faith and Belief' 1979, 1987; 'Towards a World Theology' 1981, 1990; 'On Understanding Islam' 1981, 1984, 1986; 'What is Scripture?' 1993; articles chiefly on Islamic subjects, comparative religion, and theology to various journals; various of the books and articles have been published in translation in French, German, Swedish, Turkish, Arabic, Urdu, Indonesian, Chinese, Korean, and Japanese; F.R.S.C. (Pres. Humanities & Social Sciences 1972–73); Fellow, Am. Acad. Arts & Sciences; Chaveau Medal, Royal Soc. of Can., 1974; Home: 476 Brunswick Ave., Toronto, Ont. M5R 2Z5.

**SMITH, Wilfred Irvin,** O.C., C.D., M.A., Ph.D., D.C.L.; F.S.A.A.; archivist; b. Port La Tour, N.S. 20 May 1919; s. Albert Claude and Deborah S.; e. Nova Scotia Normal College, Superior 1st Class Teacher's Lic. 1937; Acadia University, B.A. (Honors), 1943, M.A., 1946, D.C.L., 1975; Univ. of Minnesota, Ph.D. 1968; m. Joan Eileen, d. Frank Capstick, Bebington, Cheshire, Eng., 27 Nov. 1946; children: Gordon Alan, Dorothy Heather, Helen Gail; Teacher, Schs. in N.S., 1938–40; Lectr., Hist., Univ. of Minnesota 1948; Instr., Hist., Univ. of Sask. 1948–50; joined Public Archives of Can. 1950; Head, various Secs. and Chief, Manuscript Div. 1963–64; Dir., Hist. Br. 1964–65; Asst. Dom. Archivist 1965–68, Acting Dom. Archivist 1968–70, Dominion Archivist 1970–84; served as Canloan Offr., R.C.I.C., with 4th Bn., Wiltshire Regt., 43 Div., in U.K. and N.W. Europe; Gov. Gen. Foot Guards, 1951–59; Maj. ret'd. list; published articles and book reviews in professional journals; chapters in internat. Festscrifts, military history 'Code Word Canloan'; Fellow, Soc. Am. Archivists (mem. Council 1968–71; Chrmn. Comte. on Internat. Archival Affairs 1969; Vice-Pres. 1971–72; Pres. 1972–73); mem. Candn. Hist. Assn. (Ed. Hist. Booklet Series 1964–67; Chrmn. Archives Sec. 1968–69; Hon. Life Mem. 1984); mem. Historic Sites and Monuments Bd. Can.; Candn. Perm. Comte. on Geog. Names 1968–84; Internat. Council on Archives (Extve. Comte. 1972–76; Depy. Secy. Gen. 1976–82; Sec. Gen. 1982–84; Hon. Life Mem. 1984); Assn. Candn. Archivists (Hon. Life Mem. 1984; Soc. of Archivists (U.K.); British Records Assn.; Canloan Assn.; mem. and Secy. International Comte. on Documentation, Libs. and Archives (UNESCO) 1972–76; mem. Nat. Lib. Adv. Bd. 1968–84; Am. Antiquarian Soc.; Friends of Canadian War Museum, Guards Assn.; Serving Brother O. St. J.; Hon. Pres., U.E.L. Assn. of Can.; Hon. Vice-Pres. Candn. Heraldry Soc.; apptd. Officer, Order of Canada; Public Service of Canada Outstanding Achievement Award; recipient Confed., Jubilee and Roy., Soc. of Can. Medals; recreations: curling, golf, historical research; Home: 201 – 71 Somerset W., Ottawa, Ont. K2P 2G2.

**SMITH, William John,** B.A.; investment counsellor; b. Chatham, Ont. 11 Dec. 1940; s. John Arthur and Lyla Mary (Dunlop) S.; e. Univ. of W. Ont. B.A. Econ. 1963; m. Margaret Ann d. R. Massey Williams 14 Feb. 1969; children: William Blair, Margaret Alison; PRESIDENT & C.E.O., SCOTIA INVESTMENT MANAGEMENT LTD. 1992– ; with Clarkson, Gordon & Co. 1963–67; Bank of Nova Scotia 1967–72; Vice-Pres., Toronto Investment Management 1972–76, Managing Partner 1976–91; mem. Toronto Soc. of Fin. Analysts; Chair, Bd. of Stewards, St. George's United Church; Protestant; recreations: golf, tennis, riding; Clubs: Rosedale Golf; Albany; Office: Scotia Plaza, Suite 602, 44 King St. W., Toronto, Ont. M5H 1H1.

**SMITH, William Y.,** M.A.; retired university professor; b. Saint John, N.B. 20 June 1920; s. Edward Hermiston and Mary Elizabeth (Young) S.; e. Saint John (N.B.) High Sch., 1937; Univ. of New Brunswick, B.A., 1946; Univ. Coll., Oxford, Eng. (Rhodes Scholar), B.A., 1948, M.A., 1953; m. Mary Joyce, d. late Maurice Edward Firmin, 20 Feb. 1949; children: Elizabeth Jean Young, William Young; formerly mem., Econ. Council of Can.; Defence Colls. Adv. Bd.; Consulting, Econ. Planning, Dept. of Finance and Econ., Govt. of Nova Scotia; Chrmn., Research Adv. Comte., Atlantic Provs. Econ. Council; Lectr. in Econ., St. Lawrence Univ., Canton, N.Y., 1948; Asst. Prof., Univ. of N.B., 1949; Head, Dept. of Econ. and Pol. Science, Univ. of New Brunswick, 1952–69; Econ. Advisor, Govt. of N.B., 1954–60; Chrmn., Royal Comn., N.B. Coal Mining Industry, 1960; Pres., Atlantic Provs. Econ. Council, 1961–62; named by Fed. Govt. 1st Chrmn. of the (new) Atlantic Devel. Council, 1969–73; served with Candn. Inf., 1940–1945; wounded in N. Africa while attached to Brit. 1st Army, 1943; Anglican; recreations: swimming, walking; Home: 3 Spruce Terrace, Fredericton, N.B. E3B 2S6.

**SMITH, Wycliffe Dalton;** graphic designer; b. Mandeville, Jamaica 30 Sept. 1947; s. Aubrey Malcolm and Edna Mae (Whyte) S.; e. Manchester High Sch.; Miami Dade Jr. Coll.; Ryerson Polytech. Inst. and George Brown Coll. Toronto; m. Yasmin d. Byron and Joyce Yapp 22 March 1975; children: Trisha, Amanda, Edward Jay; PRES. WYCLIFFE SMITH DESIGN OFFICE 1989– ; Design Dir. The Young Naturalist Found.; Art Dir. Owl Mag., Chickadee Mag., Grey De Pencier Books 1984–89; Dir. of Art & Design Holt, Rinehart and Winston of Canada Ltd., Assoc. Art Dir. Chatelaine Mag. 1981–84; Ed. Art Dir. Maclean Hunter Publications 1975–81; Art Dir. Spear Mag., Entertainment Mag. 1976–81; Graphic Designer The Rexall Drug Co. 1973–74; Cons. Designer to Harcourt Brace Jovanovich USA; McGraw Hill Ryerson; Scholastic Press; Kids Can Press; Marketing Mag.; recipient Silver Award Art Dirs. Club Toronto 1989, Merit Awards 1980–89; 2 Alcuin Citations Excellence in Book Design 1989; 6 Awards for Excellence in Design Ednl. Press Assn. Am. 1987–89; mem. Art Dirs. Club Toronto; Ednl. Press Assn. Am.; recreation: tennis; Club: Waterfront Tennis; Home: 15 McMaster Ave., Toronto, Ont. M4V 1A8; Office: 301, 56 The Esplanade, Toronto, Ont. M5E 1A7.

**SMITH, Y. Christine;** financial planner; b. Alton, England 17 Aug. 1939; d. Brian Desborough and Winifred Ida Elizabeth (Shrubsole) Ely; e. Convent of Our Lady of Providence; Cranescourt Sch. for Girls, Coll. of Preceptors Cert. 1955; m. Philip s. Robert and Myra Smith 10 June 1961; widowed 7 April 1983; children: Rachel Myra, Jason Philip, Aaron Daniel; OWNER, FINANCIAL DIRECTION INC. 1991– ; Extve. Sec. to Pres., Foister, Clay & Ward (U.K.) 1957–62; Extve. Sec. to Administrator, Dept. of Limnology, Univ. of Toronto 1962–64; full-time parent and volunteer 1964–84; Owner/Operator, Pembina Book Exchange (Winnipeg) 1982–87; Galleria Meeting & Convention Planning 1984–87; Financial Planner, Premier Cdn. Securities 1987–89; Summit Securities (purchased Premier) 1989–91; Creator & presentor of seminars: 'Women & Money'™ & 'RRSP Boot Camp'™ presented regularly; regularly referred by church ministers, family lawyers & accountants to counsel widowed & divorced women; Dir., St. John's College Council, Univ. of Manitoba (Finance & Fundraising cttes.); Winnipeg YW-YMCA; Manitoba Zoological Soc.; Fundraising Chair, Health Sciences Centre Winnipeg; Anglican; Mem., Greenpeace; Man. Humane Soc.; Candn. Assn. of Finan. Planners; World Vision (Emergency Child Relief); Prairie Public TV; recreations: nordic skiing, yoga, opera, theatre, symphony, crossword puzzles, reading; clubs: YW-YMCA Fitness Centre; Home: 934 Somerset Ave., Winnipeg, Man. R3T 1E7; Office: 320 – 35 King St., Winnipeg, Man. R3B 1H4.

**SMITH-WINDSOR, Arthur James;** insurance executive; b. Abernathy, Sask. 7 May 1939; s. Grenville and Lois Anne (Simpson) S. e. Kelvin H.S., Winnipeg, Man. 1957; m. Adrienne d. Frank and Ethel Hunt 7 Nov. 1959; children: Jennifer Anne, Brooke Arthur; SR. VICE-PRES., GEN. MGR. & DIR., LONDON AND MIDLAND GENERAL INSURANCE CO. and Sr. Vice-Pres. and Dir., Avco Financial Services Canada Ltd. 1984– ; Vice-Pres. and Dir., Provincial Trust Co.; Vice Pres. Info. Systems Div. 1981; Chief Agent, Balboa Life Insurance Co.; Chief Agent, Balboa Insurance Co.; Club: London Club; West Haven Golf & Country; Home: 549 Ridout St. N., PH1, London, Ont. N6A 5N5; Office: 201 Queens Ave., London, Ont. N6A 1J1.

**SMITS, Sonja;** actor; b. Sudbury, Ont. 13 April 1958; d. Joanus Albertus and Sophia Francesca (Hamelijnck) S.; e. Ryerson Acting Program Toronto; m. Seaton s. Lily and Alan McLean 10 Sept. 1989; one d.: Avalon Saskia McLean-Smits; Genie nominee for the films 'Videodrome' dir. by David Cronenberg and 'That's My Baby'; Gemini Award winner for TV series lead in 'Street Legal' CBC-TV (6 seasons); other roles: 'Morag' in 'The Diviners' based on Margaret Laurence's novel-film for CBC (Gemini nomination); 'War Brides' CBC-TV movie; American series work: 'Falconcrest', 'Fall Guy'; theatre roles: Helena in 'Midsummer Night's Dream' at M.T.C., 'Yelena' in 'Uncle Vanya' and 'Alma' in 'Summer & Smoke' by Tennessee Williams at Theatre Calgary; Founding Mem., ACTRA Women's Caucus; Office: c/o Great North Artists Management, 350 Dupont St., Toronto, Ont. M5R 1V9.

**SMYE, John Maurice,** B.Comm., C.A.; business executive; b. Hamilton, Ont. 13 Dec. 1942; s. Frederick Gervin and Dorothy Edna (Baseman) S.; e. Mcmaster Univ. B.Comm. 1966; m. Shirley Louise d. Stanley and Martina Meikle 5 June 1964; children: Carol-Suzanne, Michelle, Craig; PRESIDENT, MAYNE NICKLESS TRANSPORT INC. 1993– ; Pres., Am. Hosp. Supply Canada Inc. 1981–85; Dafoe & Dafoe Ltd. 1986–88; PCL Packaging Inc. 1989–91; Loomis Courier Service (Div. of Mayne Nickless Transport) 1991–93; Dir., Mayne Nickless Canada Inc.; recreations: golf, skiing; club: Hamilton Golf & Country; Home: 3107 Cedar Springs Rd., Burlington, Ont. L7R 3X4; Office: c/o Loomis Courier Service, 90 Matheson Blvd W., Mississauga, Ont. L5R 3R3.

**SMYTH, Delmar McCormack,** M.A., Phil.M., Ph.D.; educator; author; b. Toronto, Ont. 25 Jul. 1922; s. Charles Herman and Eva Etta (McCormack) S.; e. Univ. of Toronto Victoria Coll. B.A. 1944, Sch. of Grad. Studies M.A. 1959, Phil.M. 1970, Ph.D. 1972; m. Wanita d. Frank and Hazel Snelgrove 29 June 1946; SENIOR SCHOLAR, YORK UNIVERSITY 1993– ; Gen. Mgr. Elec. Heaters and Engn. Co. 1944–47; Pres. McCormack Smyth Ltd. 1947–51; Admin. Offr. Dept. of Trade and Commerce, Govt. of Can. 1951–56; Asst. Registrar Univ. of Toronto 1956–60, and Dir. of Admissions 1959–60; Fellow Commoner Churchill Coll., Univ. of Cambridge 1960–62; Asst. to Pres. and Lectr. in Pol. Sci. present Univ. 1962–63, Dean Atkinson Coll. 1963–69, Dir. Centre for Continuing Edn. York Univ. 1966–69; Comnr. on Govt., Ryerson Polytechnical Inst. 1969–70; Prof. of Admin., Atkinson College, York Univ. 1969–93; author: 'Government for Higher Learning' 1970; co-author: 'The House That Ryerson Built' 1984; 'Not for Gold Alone: Memoirs of a Prospector' 1989; 'Discovering and Developing Ontario's Mineral Wealth, 1791-1991' 1992; 'Pathfinders: Canadian Tributes' 1994; Founder and Chrmn. Churchill Soc. for the Advancement of Parlty. Democracy 1982–85; Vice-Chrmn. Ont. Counc. of Regents for Colleges of Applied Arts and Tech. 1966–73; mem. Ont. Ctte. on Student Awards 1966–70; Chrmn. Elliot Lake Centre for Continuing Edn. 1978–80; mem. Ed. Bd. Candn. Jour. of Higher Edn. 1973–76; mem. Internat. Bd. Yokefellow Movement, Richmond, Ind. 1971– ; Toronto Monthly Meeting Soc. of Friends (Quakers); mem. Kingsway Baptist Ch., Toronto; Chrmn. Social Concerns Ctte. Baptist Convention of Ont. 1975–78; mem. Counc., Bishop Strachan Sch. 1966–73; Ont. Region Ctte., Candn. Counc. of Christians and Jews 1965–70; Chrmn. Candn. Inst. for Radiation Safety 1980–85; Ford Found. Rsch. Scholar, Churchill Coll., Cambridge 1961–62; Life Fellow Atkinson Coll. York Univ. 1969; Staley Found. Lectr. 1976; Hon. Life Chrmn., Candn. Institute for Ra-

diation Safety (CAIRS) 1990; Hon. Gov., Eliot Lake Centre 1990; recreation: gardening; Clubs: Royal Commonwealth Soc.; Hawks,' Cambridge, England; Home: 51 Aberdeen Ave., Hamilton, Ont. L8P 2N7.

**SMYTH, Denis Paul,** B.A., Ph.D.; educator; b. Dublin, Ireland 29 Nov. 1948; s. James Paul and Patricia Marie-Elizabeth (Boland) S.; e. Blackrock Coll. Co. Dublin 1967; Univ. Coll. Dublin B.A. 1972; Cambridge Univ. Ph.D. 1978; m. Margaret d. Michael and Eileen (Byrne) Doody 9 Aug. 1974; PROF. OF HIST. UNIV. OF TORONTO 1990– ; Co-ordinator, Internat. Relations Programme, Trinity Coll., Univ. of Toronto 1989–92; Asst. Prof. 1985–87; Assoc. Prof. 1987–90; Tutor in Modern Hist. Univ. Coll. Dublin 1972–73; Supr. Contemporary Internat. Relations Bd. of Extra-Mural Studies Cambridge Univ. 1974–76; Lectr. in Modern Hist. Univ. Coll. Cork 1976–78, Coll. Lectr. 1978–85, Eur. Studies Co-ordinator 1981–85; recipient Univ. Coll. Dublin Hist. Scholarship 1972; Rsch. Studentship Peterhouse, Cambridge 1973–76; Rsch. Award Institut für Europäische Geschichte Mainz 1980 and Royal Inst. Internat. Affairs Chatham House London 1982–84; el. Fellow of Trinity College, Univ. of Toronto 1987; el. Fellow of the Royal Historical Soc., London 1989; author: 'Diplomacy and Strategy of Survival: British Policy and Franco's Spain 1940–41' 1986; co-author: 'Spain, the EEC and NATO' 1984; 'España ante la CEE y la OTAN' 1985; co-ed.: 'El Impacto de la Segunda Guerra Mundial en Europa y en España' 1986; numerous essays & articles internat. books and jours.; Reviewer: 'The Times Literary Supplement' London; mem. Candn. Inst. Internat. Affairs (Communications Ctte.); Am. Hist. Assn.; Candn. Assn. Security & Intelligence Studies; Eur. Community Studies Assn.; recreations: reading, classical music, sports; Home: 500 Sutherland Dr., Toronto, Ont. M4G 1K8; Office: Toronto, Ont. M5S 1H8.

**SMYTH, Harley Sandwith,** B.A., M.D., M.A., D.Phil., F.R.C.S.; b. Ottawa, Ont. 11 Sept. 1939; s. W.J. Earl and Isobel Maud (Sandwith) S.; e. Lisgar Coll. Inst. 1957; Queen's Univ. B.A. 1961, M.D. 1963; Oxford Univ. B.A. (Hons.I) 1964, M.A., D.Phil. 1967; Andrew Malcolm Scholarship 1957; Medical Rsch. Counc. Scholar 1960, 1961; Rhodes Scholar (Ont. and Balliol) 1963; Hon. Sch. of Animal Physiology, Oxford Univ. 1963–64; Rsch. Asst. to Reg. Prof. of Medicine 1964–67; Clinical Neurosurgical Training Univ. of Toronto 1967–72; m. Kathleen d. George and Elizabeth Koch 10 June 1967; children: Jeremy Harold, Benjamin Simeon Martyn, Anna Amy; NEUROLOGICAL SURGEON, WELLESLEY HOSPITAL 1973– ; Lectr. Surgery 1973–83; Asst. Prof. of Surgery, Univ. of Toronto 1983– ; Trustee, Wycliffe Coll.; Ctte. on Biomedical Ethics, R.C.P.S. 1980–84; Ont. Medical Assn.; Anglican Ch. (former mem. Exec., Diocese of Toronto); Cdn. Neurosurgical Soc.; Founding perm. Hon. Bd. mem., Toronto Central Christian School; Alpha Omega Alpha Honour Medical Soc. 1985; author: 'The Value of Human Life' 1979; recreations: sailing, music; Home: 408 Sumach St., Toronto, Ont. M4X 1V5; Office: Ste. 113, Elsie K. Jones Bldg., 160 Wellesley St. E., Toronto, Ont. M4Y 1J3.

**SMYTH, Norman Robert Anton,** O.M.M., C.D., M.Sc., P.Eng.; engineering executive; b. Tipperary, Ireland 3 July 1943; s. Walter M. and Lucy T. (Anton) S.; e. Kilkenny Coll. Ireland; Mountjoy Sch. Ireland; Univ. of Alta. B.Sc. 1963; U.S. Naval Postgrad. Sch. M.Sc. 1969; m. Joan d. Robert and Maxine Greenley 11 Sept. 1982; one s. Brendon; PRES. & DIR. THOMSON-CSF SYSTEMS CANADA INC. 1985– ; Dir. Thomson-CSF Canada Ltd.; Pres. & Dir. Candn. Defence Preparedness Assoc.; served with RCN 1960–83, retired with rank Capt. (N), Dir. of Eng. & Operations Candn. Patrol Frigate; Vice Pres. Eng. Norpak Corp. 1983–85; awarded O.M.M. 1976; mem. Assn. Prof. Engs. Prov. Ont.; recreations: sailing, skiing, squash; Clubs: HMCS Bytown Offrs. Mess; Rideau; Home: 69 Villa Cres., Ottawa, Ont. K2C 0H7; Office: 49 Auriga Dr., Nepean, Ont. K2E 8A1.

**SMYTH, Rev. Phyllis Norma,** B.A., B.D., Ph.D., D.D.; United Church Minister; b. Montreal, Que. 10 June 1938; d. John Norman and Norma Jeanette (Brown) S.; e. Elizabeth Ballantyne Sch., Montreal West; Montreal West H.S. 1955; McGill Univ. B.A. 1959, B.D. 1964; grad. studies in New Testament, St. Andrew's Univ., Scot. 1964–68, Ph.D. 1972; DIRECTOR OF PASTORAL SERVICES, ROYAL VICTORIA HOSPITAL, Montreal; Assoc. Prof. of Religion and Medicine, McGill Univ.; o. Minister, United Ch. of Can. 1964; served as Minister: combined Anglican/Un. churches Alma and Dolbeau, Lac St. Jean region 1968–70; Arvida First Un. Ch. 1970–72; St. Georges Un.

Church, Montreal 1972–74; Sr. Min., Dominion Douglas Ch. (Westmount, Que.) 1974–79; Asst. Prof. of New Testament, Univ. of Winnipeg 1979–80; Rsch. Asst. Fac. of Religious Studies present Univ. 1972–79; mem. Clincial Ethics Ctte., Royal Victoria Hosp. 1980– ; Cons. to Exec. Dir., Royal Victoria Hosp. in development of Pastoral Service 1984–85; author articles: 'Palliative Care: A Current Embodiment of New Testament Theology?'; 'La Pastorale aux Mourants'; numerous speaking engagements across Can. on palliative care 1980–85 and on pastoral care 1985– ; United Church: mem. Nat. Ctte. on Christian Faith 1972–76, Nat. Ctte. on Candidature for Min. 1976–78, Nat. Task Force on Theological Edn. 1978–80; mem. Nat. RC-UC Dialogue; mem. Cdn. Assn. for Pastoral Edn./C.A.P.E. (qualified Supr. as trained in Eng. and French-speaking hosp.); Vice-Pres. Que. Region 1984–85, Pres. Que. Region 1986–88); Co-Pres., Nat. Convention '95; mem. Exec. Carrefour des Chretiens du Que. pour la Santé (C.C.Q.S.) 1982– ; mem., Table de réflexion concernant la protection de la personne (org. par la curatrice publique); awarded D.D. (hon. causa) Victoria Coll. Univ. of Toronto 1984, Montreal Diocesan Theological College (Ang.) 1994; recreations: theatre, reading, travel, friends, summer sports; Home: 610, 201 ch. du Club Marin, Ile des Soeurs, Verdun, Que. H3E 1T4; Office: Pastoral Services, Royal Victoria Hospital, 687 Pine Ave. W., Montreal, Que. H3A 1A1.

**SMYTH, Ronald,** B.A., M.A., Ph.D.; geologist; b. Cahir, Ireland 27 Apr. 1946; s. Walter Michael and Lucy Theresa (Anton) S.; e. Trinity Coll., Dublin, B.A., M.A. 1968; Meml. Univ. of Nfld., Ph.D. 1973; m. Ruby d. Jim and Roxy Hudson 1974; children: Sheilagh, Jennifer; Chief Geologist, B.C. Min. of Energy, Mines and Petroleum Resources 1984; Proj. Geol., Nfld. Dept. of Mines & Energy 1973–75; Sr. Regional Geol. – Labrador 1975–78; Sr. Regional Geol. – Nfld. 1978–82; Sr. Geol. – Mineral Land Use, B.C. Min. of Energy & Mines 1982–84; Counc. mem., Geol. Assn. of Can. 1987– ; Pres., Pacific Sect. 1983–84; Pres., Nfld. Sect. 1980–81; author of var. articles in sci. jours.; recreations: cross-country skiing, swimming, sailing; Home: 1813 Lulie St., Victoria, B.C. V8R 5W9; Office: 106 – 553 Superior St., Victoria, B.C. V8V 1X4.

**SMYTH, Thomas Donald;** company executive; b. Trochu, Alta. 15 Aug. 1926; s. Thomas John and Margaret Ruth (Smith) S.; m. Maureen d. late J. M. Carphin and Sarah Greer (Harper) 15 Oct. 1955; children: Laurie, David; CHAIRMAN, H. J. HEINZ CO. OF CANADA LTD., since 1988; owns and operates purebred beef farm near Flesherton, Ont.; raises prominent blood line breeding stock of Charolais, Simmental; recipient, Ont. Dept. of Agriculture 'Outstanding Performance' Award 1990, 1991, 1992 for Simmenthal Breed in Ont.; joined present Co. as Office Asst., Calgary, 1946; apptd. Office Mgr., Edmonton, 1948 and Leamington (Ont.) 1951; Office Mgr., Toronto, 1953; Office Mgr., Vancouver, 1954; Staff Asst., Vice-Pres., Marketing, 1956; Sales Div., Assignment, Windsor, 1960; Mgr. Distribution, 1961; Gen. Mgr. Services, 1963; Vice Pres. Services & Dir., 1965; Vice Pres. Mfg. & Dir. 1968; Vice Pres., Marketing and Dir. 1969; Extve. Vice Pres. and C.O.O. 1976; Pres. & C.E.O. 1977–88; Chrmn. Membership Ctte. National Inst. of Nutrition; Past Chrmn. Grocery Product Mfrs. of Can.; Dir., Food Inst. of Canada; Dir., Versacold Canada Corp.; The Griffith Laboratories Ltd.; The Food Industry Assn. - Knight of the Golden Pencil; Dir., Fridays Child; Vice-Past Pres. and Dir., Leamington Dist. Chamber Comm.; mem. Ottawa Liaison Ctte., Candn. Chamber of Commerce; mem., Can.-U.S. Comte. Canadian Chamber of Commerce; mem. Agricultural Rsch. Institute of Ont. (Chair, Ontario Food Processing Rsch. Program); recipient, Governor General Commemorative Medal for 125th Anniversary of Candn. Confederation; Freemason; United Church; recreations: squash, golf; Clubs: Essex Golf and Country; Royal Canadian Yacht; Donalda Golf & Country; Home: 40 Restwell Cr., Willowdale, Ont. M2K 2A3; Office: 16th Flr., 5650 Yonge St., Toronto, Ont. M2M 4G3.

**SNAITH, Victor Percy,** M.A., M.Sc., Ph.D., Sc.D., F.R.S.C.; educator; b. Colchester, Eng. 15 March 1944; s. Harry Victor and Sylvia May (Botham) Yaraslaw-Paddon; e. Scunthorpe Grammar Sch.; Cambridge Univ. B.A. 1966, M.A. 1970, Sc.D. 1984; Warwick Univ. M.Sc. 1967, Ph.D. 1969; m. Carolyn d. Richard and Beryl Byers 25 July 1969; children: Anna, Nina, Daniel; BRITTON PROF. OF MATH. McMASTER UNIV. 1988– ; Coll. Lectr. Emmanuel Coll. Cambridge 1969–75; Visiting Prof. Purdue Univ. 1975–76; Assoc. Prof. Univ. of W. Ont. 1976–88; recipient Rayleigh Prize Cambridge 1968; Florence Bucke Prize for Rsch. Univ. W. Ont. 1987, Rsch. Professorship Faculty Sci. 1987–88;

author 'Topological Methods in Galois Representation Theory' 1989; 'The Yukiad' novel 1990; over 100 rsch. papers math.; ed. 3 conf. proceedings; ed. Candn. Jour. Math.; mem. Candn. Math. Soc. (Vice Pres.; Chrmn. Rsch. Ctte. 1980–82); Natural Sci. & Eng. Rsch. Council Granting Ctte. 1981–84; Rsch. Ctte. Fields Inst. Math. Rsch.; Office: Hamilton, Ont. L8S 4L8.

**SNART, Allen Edward,** B.Sc., M.Sc., CHRP, CMC; management consultant; b. Dauphin, Man. 8 July 1945; s. Bert and A. Doreen (Edward) S.; e. Univ. of Manitoba B.Sc. 1967; Brandon Univ. Cert.Ed. 1968; Univ. of Florida M.Sc. 1970; m. Myrna L. d. Mervin and Jean Graham 17 May 1969; children: Jason, Jennifer; DIRECTOR, WESTERN MANAGEMENT CONSULTANTS 1991– ; High school Biol. & Chem. Teacher (Man.) 1970–73; progressive human resource management and executive positions, in Canada and overseas, in natural resources, retail-wholesale and manufacturing 1973–82; concurrently Development Dir., N. Am. Wildlife Found. 1975–76; entered management cons. with Currie, Coopers & Lybrand 1982; Vice-Pres., Mktg., Edmonton Symphony Orch.; Mem., Candn. & U.S. comp. assns.; Human Resources Inst. of Alta.; Inst. of Cert. Mngt. Cons. of Alta.; recreations: golf, hockey, canoeing, running, symphony (pops); clubs: Edmonton Centre Club (Dir. Mktg. and Ctte. Chair), Glendale Golf & Country; 1500, 10250 – 101 St., Edmonton, Alta. T5J 3P4.

**SNEATH, George Edwin Ross,** B.B.A., I.A., LL.D., F.C.I.S., P. Admin.; financial executive; b. Regina, Sask. 19 March 1918; s. Isaac W. and Nellie C. (Ross) S.; e. Strathcona Pub. Sch. and Central Coll. Inst. Regina; Balfour Tech. Sch. Regina; Univ. of Minn. B.B.A. 1941; Harvard Grad. Sch. of Business Degree in Ind. Adm. 1942; Hon. LL.D. Univ. of Regina 1984; m. Marguerite T. d. William Thomas and Rachel Ellen Weir 7 May 1946; children: Shirley Mark, Heidi Martin, Susan Silvester, Isaac, Catherine, George (dec.); FOUNDING DIR., CANADIAN PIONEER MANAGEMENT LTD. (President and Chief Exec. Offr. 1969–84, former Chrmn. of the Bd.); Vice Pres., Western Surety Co. Regina; Mng. Dir., The Trianon Ltd. 1947–77; Mng. Dir., 2 Regina hotels 1947–55; Treas. and Dir., Canadian Devonian Petroleums 1951–61; exec. Glavebel Group of Co's 1960–68; served with Candn. Army 1942–45, rank Lt.; Partner, Regina Pats Hockey Club (1979–84); Consul of Belgium for Prov. Sask. 1964–86; Past Dir., Candn. Chamber of Commerce; Past pres., Chambers of Comm. Regina 1968; Sask. 1979; Dir., Fossil Resources Ltd. Calgary 1982–85; mem., Univ. of Regina Senate 1981–87; Bd. Regents and Senate, Athol Murray Coll. of Notre Dame Wilcox, Sask. 1983– ; Dir., Candn. Council Christians & Jews; named Sask. Salesman of Yr. by Sales & Mktg. Execs. Assn. 1972; Prof. Administrator Inst. Chart. Secs. & Administrators 1982; Life mem., Hotels Assn. Sask.; mem., Royal Un. Services Inst.; Regina Exec. Club; Royal Candn. Legion; Wa Wa Motor Patrol (Capt. 1964); Freemason; recreations: tennis, golf, swimming; Clubs: Assiniboia; Canadian; Home: P.O. Box 591, Fort Qu'Appelle, Sask. S0G 1S0.

**SNELL, Rt. Rev. George Boyd,** M.A., Ph.D., D.D. (Ang.); b. Toronto, Ont. 17 June 1907; s. John George and Minnie Alice Boyd (Finnie) S.; e. Trinity Coll., Univ. of Toronto, B.A. 1929, M.A. 1930, Ph.D. 1937; Oxford Univ., 1933–34; D.D. Trinity Coll. 1948, Wycliffe Coll. 1957, Huron Coll. 1968; m. Esther Mary, d. Robert Hartley, Toronto, Ont., 30 June 1934; o. Deacon 1931; Priest 1932; Asst. Curate, Ch. of St. Michael and All Angels, Toronto, Ont., 1931–39, and Rector there, 1940–48; Rector, St. Marks Port Hope, Ont. 1940; Rector, Cath. Ch. of the Redeemer, Calgary, Alta. and Dean of Calgary, 1948–51; Rector, St. Clements, Toronto, 1951–56; Archdeacon of Toronto, 1953–56; Suffragan Bishop of Toronto, 1956–59; Coadjutor Bishop 1959–66; Bishop 1966–72; Clubs: National; Albany; Home: 1210 Glen Rd., Mississauga, Ont. L5H 3K8.

**SNIDER, John Timothy;** retired executive; b. Lyon Co., Kansas 12 Jan. 1916; s. Carl George and Anna (Lyons) S.; e. Elem. Sch., Lyon Co., Kansas; High Sch., Greenwood Co., Kansas; Univ. of Houston; m. Julia Elizabeth, d. Harrold Chambers, March 1945; children: Linda, John Jr.; former Pres., Pinnacle Construction, Anchorage, Alaska; joined Constr. Dept. of Stearns Roger Corp. 1940; trans. to Can. 1956; left the Co. as Mgr., Constr. Dept. 1966; Co-founder, Delta Projects Ltd. 1966 (Co. acquired by Alaska Interstate Co. 1969); moved to Houston, Tex. 1974 to set up office for Pinnacle Construction; Roman Catholic; recreations: golf, fishing; Club: Ft. Bend Country; Home: 806 Foster Dr., Richmond, Tex. 77469.

**SNIDER, Robert F.,** B.Sc., Ph.D., F.R.S.C., F.C.I.C.; university professor; b. Calgary, Alta. 22 Nov. 1931; s. Edward C. and Agnes S. (Klaeson) S.; e. Univ. of Alta., B.Sc. 1953; Univ. of Wisconsin, Ph.D. 1958; children: Wendy A., Timothy J., Terry E., Geoffrey Y., Eric A.M. (Burrough); PROF. OF CHEM., UNIV. OF B.C. 1969– ; post-doct. fellow, Nat. Rsch. Counc. of Can. 1958; Instr., Univ. of B.C. 1958–60; Asst. Prof. 1960–65; Assoc. Prof. 1965–69; Vis. Rsch. Prof., Univ. of Leiden 1973–74; F.R.S.C. 1977; F.C.I.C. 1978; Mem., Am. Physical Soc.; Chem. Inst. of Can.; Candn. Assn. of Physicists; Royal Soc. of Can.; Home: 3952 West 29th, Vancouver, B.C. V6S 1T9; Office: Dept. of Chem., 2036 Main Mall, Vancouver, B.C. V6T 1Z1.

**SNIDER, Ronald Neil,** B.A., B.Ed., M.Ed., Ph.D.; university president; b. Westlock, Alta. 31 Aug. 1938; s. Charles Elmer and Anne (Rambold) S.; e. Briercrest Bible Inst. 1959; Univ. of Winnipeg B.A. 1962; Univ. of Manitoba B.Ed. 1969, M.Ed. 1970; Univ. of Oregon Ph.D. 1973; m. Marlie d. the late Leslie and Margaret Payne 3 Sept. 1960; children: Gloria Dawn, Dean Cameron, Dana Lynn; PRES., TRINITY WESTERN UNIV. 1974– ; High Sch. Instr., Winnipeg Sch. Div. 1963–64; Dir. of Music & Instructor, Winnipeg Bible Coll. 1964–71; Dean of Students 1968–71; Dean of Faculty 1973–74; Mem. of the Bd., Christian Children's Fund of Canada; Council of Reference for White Fields; Mem., Assn. of Univ. & Coll. of Canada; Counc. of Western Candn. Univ. Presidents; Evangelical Free Ch. of Can. (Leadership Devel. Council); Evangelical Free Ch. of Am. (Counc. of Administrators); ordained minister, Evangelical Free Ch.; Child Evangelism Fellowship; Contb. Ed., 'The Evangelical Beacon'; prolific speaker; recreations: tennis, racquetball; Home: 5993 – 243rd St., Langley, B.C. V3A 1B7; Office: Trinity Western Univ., 7600 Glover Rd., Langley, B.C. V3A 6H4.

**SNIDERMAN, Sam,** C.M.; entrepreneur; b. Toronto, Ont. 15 June 1920; s. Saul and Gertrude (Herman) S.; e. Harbord Coll. Inst.; two s. Jason, Robert; PRESIDENT, ROBLAN DISTRIBUTORS LTD.; Prop. Sam the Record Man; began selling records in brother's College St. radio store 1937, moving to Yonge St. location 1959; established franchise operation in 1969; began corporate growth 1980 Gov. Nat. Theatre Sch.; Former Dir. Animated Film Festival; former 2nd Vice Pres. and Dir., Candn. Academy of Recording Arts & Sciences; Dir. & Former Vice-Pres. & Gov., Candn. Nat. Exhn.; Dir. CHIN; 1985 Bach Piano Competitions; Toronto Sch. for Visually Impaired; estbd., The Sniderman Recordings Archive, Univ. of Toronto; mem. Federal Cultural Policy Review Comte.; Former Hon. Dir., CIRPA; Organizing Mem. Guitar Soc.; Member Mayor's Task Force on Drugs; Bd. Mem.: C.I.Q.M.; Glory of Mozart Festival, Music Building Restoration Ctte.; Can. Country Music Assoc.; Black Music Assoc. Can.; recipient, Order of Can. 1976; Ont. Bicentennial Medal 1984; Walt Grealis Award/CARAS 1989; Mem. Restoration Ctte. Music Bldg. Exhib. Place; Dir., Mozart Music Festival 1991; Ctte. Elgin Wintergarden Theatre; Mem., Variety Club of Canada; Mem., Advisory Bd. YMCA Substance Abuse Ctte.; 1992 Metro Citizen of the Year; Mem., Toronto 200 Advisory Ctte.; Mem. Mariposa Advisory Ctte.; Mem., United Way Advisory Ctte.; Mem., Metro Centre Opening Ctte.; recreation: tennis; Clubs: Variety; Empire; Home: 80 Front St. E., Toronto, Ont.; Office: 274 Church St., Toronto, Ont. M5B 1Z5.

**SNIEDZINS, Ernie,** B.A., Elec. Tech.; executive; b. Riga, Latvia 13 Feb. 1943; s. Karlis and Melita (Songailo) S.; e. Seneca Coll. Elec. Technologist 1971; York Univ. B.A. Econ. 1982; children: Sarah, Thomas, Scott; CENTRAL & WESTERN CANADA REGIONAL SERVICE MANAGER, QMS CANADA INC. and EXEC. CONSULTANT, CANADIAN RETT SYNDROME ASSN; Pres., Creative Concepts for Business; E.S. Publishing Enterprises Ltd.; E.S. Enterprises; Homegard Safety Products Ltd.; Customer Service Mgr. Xerox Canada Inc. 1980, National Product Mgr. 1983, Operational Support and Training Mgr. 1983–89; Founding Chrmn., Candn. Rett Syndrome Assn. (Pres. 1989–90); Founding author and publ.: 'Who's Who in Toronto: A Celebration of This City' 1984; mem. Adv. Bd., Seneca Coll.; Panelist Fed. Govt. Non-Traditional Occupations in Bus.; Chrmn. Community Homes for the Mentally Handicapped Assn.; mem. Inner City Angels (Chrmn. 1984); C.H.M.H.; M.T.A.M.R.; Creator and Climber, The 1991 Climb for Hope Mt. Everest Expedition and the National Everfitness Program to 18,000 Schools in Canada; winner Most Innovative Manager Award, Pres. & Master, Club Awards; Club: Toronto Japan Karate; Alpine Club of Canada; Home: 38 Helendale Ave., Toronto, Ont. M4R 1C4.

**SNOW, Hank** (Clarence Eugene); country music performer; b. Brooklyn, N.S. 9 May 1914; s. George Lewis and Marie Alice (Boutlier) S.; m. Minnie Blanche Aalders 2 Sept. 1935; one s. Jimmie Rodgers; star of 'Clarence Snow and His Guitar' radio stn. CHNS Halifax 1935; recording star RCA 1936–EM; performed as 'The Singing Ranger' U.S. and Can. 1946–50; mem. Grand Ole Opry, Nashville 1950–EM; owner Hank Snow Music Inc., Hank's Music Inc.; exclusive writer Hill & Range Songs Inc. New York 1948; Entertainer U.S. Armed Forces Korea 1953, Vietnam 1967; Founder, Hank Snow Internat. Foundation Prevention Child Abuse and Neglect of Children Inc. 1978; named Am.'s Favorite Folk Singer, Song Round-Up Mag. Billboard Mag. 1954; Top Country Singer Can. 1940; Songwriter's Hall of Fame 1978; Candn. Hall of Fame 1979; Country Music Hall of Fame 1979; Candn. Hall of Honor; presented with Millionaire Award for more than million airplays of song 'I'm Movin' On' which also holds all-time country music record 'Most Played Record by Disc Jockeys' 1985; recipient numerous citations, plaques, awards best-selling records; rec'd The Nat. Jewish Fund Tree of Life Award in recognition of his outstanding contributions to his community and the music industry and for his dedication to the cause of peace and the security of human life 1984; inducted into the Candn. Country Music Hall of Fame 1989; recorded numerous albums incl. 'My Early Country Favorites,' 'Hank Snow Souvenirs,' 'Hank Snow Sings Your Favorite Country Hits,' 'Heartbreak Trail,' 'Gospel Train,' 'My Nova Scotia Home,' 'This is My Story,' 'Cure for the Blues'; numerous singles; Home: 310 E. Marthonna Dr., Madison, Tenn. 37115; Office: (P.O. Box 1084) Nashville, Tenn. 37202.

**SNOW, Hon. James Wilfred;** contractor; industrialist; farmer; politician; b. Esquesing Twp. 12 July 1929; s. Wilfred Oliver and Margaret Florence (Devlin) S.; e. Milton, Ont. pub. and high schs.; m. Barbara Mae Joan, d. Alfred Hughes, 13 Sept. 1952; children: James Douglas, Julie Barbara, Jeffrey Owen, Jennifer Nancy; PRESIDENT, PINELAND FARM LTD. 1990– ; assumed mang. of family farm, Halton, upon leaving high sch.; estbd. Snow Construction Ltd. (gen. constr.), 1949; operated beef farm and feed lot, Hornby, Ont., 1959–75; el. M.P.P. for Halton E. in prov. g.e. 1967, 1971; elected M.P.P., Oakville, g.e. 1975, 1977, 1981; Dir., Ont. Housing Corp. and Ont. Student Housing Corp., 1970–72; Min. Without Portfolio 1971; Min. of Govt. Serv. 1972–75; Min. of Transport & Communications, Ont. 1975–85; Min. Without Portfolio Responsible for Urban Transportation, Feb. 1985–May 1985; Chrmn., Civil Aviation Tribunal 1985–90; rec'd Centennial Medal 1967; Past Pres., Halton Beef Improvement Assn.; Past Chrmn., Roads and Transportation Assoc. of Canada; Past Chrmn., Candn. Conference of Ministers responsible for Highway Safety; Past Dir., Ont. Beef Improvement Association; mem., Chamber Commerce; Candn. Owners & Pilots Assn. (elected Dir. & Treasurer 1992– ); elected Dir., Halton Region Conservation Foundation 1992– ; P. Conservative; United Church; recreations: hunting, fishing, computers, flying, woodworking; Clubs: Lions (Past Pres. Oakville; Past Dist. Gov. (A-11) Lions Internat.); Home: 8300 Trafalgar Rd., Hornby, Ont. L0P 1E0.

**SNOW, Jeffery Alexander,** B.Com., LL.B.; mining executive; b. Ireland 11 Nov. 1954; s. Walter W. and Elizabeth A. (Jeffery) S.; e. Queen's Univ. Kingston B.Com. 1976; Univ. of W. Ont. LL.B. 1979; m. Dr. Debbie G. d. William and Vina Ellis 25 Sept. 1982; VICE PRES. AND GEN. COUNSEL, NORANDA MINERALS INC. 1992– and PRES. & C.E.O., KERR ADDISON MINES LIMITED 1993– ; Labour Relations Supr. Central Can. Noranda Inc. 1981–84; Corporate Sec. Noranda Exploration Co. 1984–86; Legal Counsel, Kerr Addison Mines 1986, Gen. Counsel 1988, Vice Pres. & Gen. Counsel 1990–1992; mem. Law Soc. Upper Can.; Candn. Bar Assn.; Rocky Mountain Mineral Law Assn.; Candn. Inst. Mining & Metall.; Prospectors & Developers Assn.; recreations: golf, curling, tennis; Clubs: Engineers; Adelaide; Office: Suite 2700, 1 Adelaide St. E., Toronto, Ont. M5C 2Z6.

**SNOW, John Harold Thomas,** R.C.A.; artist; b. Vancouver, B.C. 12 Dec. 1911; s. Harold and Sophie (Thompson) S.; e. Gordon Sch.; Innisfail High Sch.; Life Drawing under Maxwell Bates 1947–49; Hon. LL.D. Univ. of Calgary 1984; Excellence Category, Alta. Achievement Award 1984; m. Kathleen Mary d. Thomas M. Allen 12 July 1963; one s. John Vance Forcade; Banker with Royal Bank of Canada 1928–71; solo exhns. incl. Gallery Pascal Toronto 1968, 1971, 1973, 1975, 1978; Dorothy Cameron Gallery Toronto 1963, 1964; Fleet Gallery Winnipeg 1965, 1972, 1977; Sarnia Pub. Lib. Gallery 1965; Medicine Hat Lib. Gallery 1965;

Calgary Allied Arts 1966; Univ. of Calgary 1966, 1967; Pandora's Box Gallery Victoria 1968; Travelling Exhn. Univs. of Maritime Provs. 1967–68; Man. Theatre Centre 1968; Opening Exhn. Gallery Trinity Coll. Sch. Port Hope 1968, 1970; Gallery 96 Ottawa 1970; Univ. of Toronto Erindale Coll. 1970; Godard Multiples Montreal 1971;. Calgary Galleries 1972–77; Studio Shop and Gallery Vancouver Opening Show 1973, 1975, 1980; Can. House Gallery London, Eng. 1973; Mendel Art Gallery Saskatoon 1974; Gallery 1640 Montreal 1975; Bau-Xi Gallery Victoria 1975; Attic Gallery Regina 1976; Lefebvre Gallery Edmonton 1976, 1977; Sundance Gallery Calgary 1978–80; Canadian Art Galleries, Calgary 1976, 1978; Candn. Art Galleries 1990, 1992; Kathleen Laverty Gall., Edmonton 1988, 1990; Atelier Gall., Vancouver 1993; rep. in various group exhns. Can., USA, Gt. Brit., Europe, Japan, S. Am., Australia incl. Première Expositions Bienale Internat. de Gravure à Tokio and Osaka 1957; Primera Bienal Interamerica de Pintura Y Grabada Mexico City 1958; 5th Internat. Biennial Colour Lithography Cincinnati 1958; Royal Soc. Brit. Artists London, Eng. 1960, 1962, 1967, 1968, 1969, 1972; Salon Des Beaux Arts Paris 1961, 1963, 1965, 1967, 1969, 1974, 1975; Candn. Print Exhn. Victoria and Albert Museum (travel) 1965; Annuale Italiani d'Arte Grafic Ancona, Italy 1968; Candn. Art in Britain, Canada House, London England 1982; rep. various pub., corporate and private colls. incl. Victoria and Albert Museum, Nat. Gallery Can., Art Gallery Ont., CHAR Internat. Puerto Rico, Royal Ont. Museum, Can. Council Art Bank, Can. House London; 'John Snow, Four Decades' retrospective Edmonton Art Gallery (catalogue) 1989; recipient Candn. Soc. Graphic Art Adrian Sequin Award 1957, 1969, C. W. Jeffreys Award 1961; Winnipeg Show Graphics Award 1961; Calgary Annual Graphics Exhn. Hon. Mention 1962, 1963; Montreal Museum Fine Arts Spring Show Jessie Dow Award 1962; Salon Des Beaux Arts Paris Hon. Mention 1965; Vancouver Print Internat. Purchase Award 1967; Medaglia e Diploma di Segnalzione Internat. Galleria D'Arte Moderna Ancona, Italy 1968; Can. Council comn. special lithograph 1966; cited various publs.; Film: 'The Sad Phoenician and Friends,' John Snow Sculptures, Robert Kroetsch reading from his works, Quenten Doolittle music, made by Ken Jones (a Clopton Film Production); served with RCAF and RAF as Navig. Gt. Brit., N. Africa, India World War II; Mentioned in Despatches; Fellow, Internat. Inst. Arts & Letters Switzerland; mem. Print & Drawing Council Can.; Address: 915 - 18th Ave. S.W., Calgary, Alta. T2T 0H2.

**SNOW, Michael James Aleck,** O.C.; artist; musician; photographer; film maker; b. Toronto, Ont. 10 Dec. 1929; s. Gerald Bradley and Marie Antoinette Carmen (Levesque) S.; e. Upper Can. Coll., Toronto 1948; Ont. Coll. Art (under John Martin) 1952; LL.D. (Hon.), Brock Univ. 1974; commissions: Mobile, Victoria Coll., Univ. of Toronto, Ont. 1954; Ont. Pavilion, Expo '67, Montreal, Que. 1967; Video-Photo Environ. Sculpture, Brock Univ. 1978; Gov. of Canada Bldg., North York 1978; 'Flightstop' Cadillac Fairview, Eaton's Centre, Toronto, Ont. 1979; Shaw Ind. Ltd., Toronto, Ont. 1981; 'The Spectral Image,' Expo '86, Vancouver, B.C. 1986; 'Audience,' SkyDome, Toronto, Ont. 1988–89; Via Rail, train installation 1989; Candn. Embassy, Washington, USA, proposed installation 1989; one-man exhns. incl.: Isaacs Gall. 1957, 58, 60, 62, 64, 66, 69, 74, 82, 84, 86, 87, 88; Poindexter Gall., N.Y.C. 1964, 65, 68; 'Michael Snow – A Survey,' Art Gall. Ont. 1970; XXV Biennale of Venice 1970; Bykert Gall., N.Y. 1970, 72; Centre for Inter-Am. Relations, N.Y. 1972; 'Projected Images,' Walker Art Center, Minneapolis 1974; Museum of Fine Art, N.Y. 1976; 'Sept Films et Plus Tard,' Centre Georges Pompidou, Paris (travelling) 1977–79; 'The Spectral Image' Expo '86, Vancouver, B.C. 1986; 'Visionary Apparatus' (with Juan Geuer), List Gall., MIT, Cambridge Mass. 1986; 'Ruine der Kunste Berlin, Germany 1988; Hara Museum of Contemporary Art, Tokyo, Japan 1988; 'The Michael Snow Project' a retrospective at Ont. Gallery of Art, The Power Plant and The Music Gallery 1994; one-man film showings: Edinburgh Film Festival 1969, 75; Jewis Museum, N.Y. 1970; Cinemateque Québecoise, Retrospective, Montreal 1975; Museum of Modern Art, N.Y. 1969, 70, 76; Anthology Film Archives, N.Y. 1975, 76; Film Retrospective Cinemateque Francaise, Paris, L'institut Lumiere, Lyon 1992; selected group exhns.: Biennial of Candn. Painting, Nat. Gall. Can. 1957, 1959, 1965; 'Canada 101,' Edinburgh Festival 1968; 'Art d'Aujourd-hui,' France, Italy, Holland 1968; 'Anti-Illusion: Procedures and Materials,' Whitney Museum, N.Y. 1969; 'Another Dimension,' Nat. Gall. Can. 1977; 'Photography and Art, 1984–86' Los Angeles County Museum of Art, CA 1987; 'Holography, Light in the Third Dimension' Ont. Sci. Centre, Toronto 1987; 'Toronto: Play of History' Power Plant, Toronto 1987; 'Images du Futur 88' Art et Nouvelles Tech., Montreal 1988; 'Festival des Arts Electroniques de Rennes' Rennes, France (travelling: Georges Pompidou Centre, France) 1988; 'Vanishing Presence,' Walker Art Center, Minn. (travelling: Detroit, Mich.; Winnipeg, Man.; Atlanta, GA; Ithaca, NY; Richmond, VA 1988–90; performances and group film showings: Cannes Film Festival 1969, 70; Montreux Film Fest., Switz. 1974; London Film Fest. 1973, 75; Edinburgh Film Fest. 1975, 76; 'Documenta,' Kassel, Germany 1977; CCMC Concert Tours, Europe 1978, 1979, 1980, 1981, 1983; Japan 1988; CCMC Biweekly and weekly performances. Music Gallery, Toronto 1976–93; Holland Festival 1985; New Music America, Montreal 1990; books: 'Michael Snow – A Survey' 1970; 'Cover to Cover' 1975; records: 'The Artists Jazz Band: Live at the Edge' 1977; 'Michael Snow: Music for Whistling, Piano, Microphone and Tape Recorder' 1975; CCMC, Vols. 1 to 5; 'The Last LP' 1988; Awards: Order of Canada 1982; Molson Prize 1981; Sr. Arts Grant, Can. Council 1966, 1973, 1979; Guggenheim Fellowship 1972; represented in many collections incl.: Museum of Mod. Art; Nat. Gall. Can.; Art Gall. Ont.; Montreal Museum of Fine Arts; Philadelphia Museum of Art; Art Galls. of Vancouver, Edmonton, Winnipeg; represented in many film archives incl.: Osterreichisches Film Museum, Vienna; Museum of Mod. Art; Nat Gall. Can.; Roy. Belgium Film Archive, Brussels; Rijkmuseum, Holland; Centre Pompidou, Musée des Beaux Arts, Paris; Carnegie Inst., Pittsburgh; Home: 176 Cottingham St., Toronto, Ont. M4V 1C5.

**SNOWDON, Kenneth G.,** B.A., M.P.A.; university administrator; b. Edmonton, Alta. 25 Jan. 1953; s. Emerson Laurie and Bernice Mary (Phinney) S.; e. Queen's Univ., B.A. 1975, M.P.A. 1976; m. Karen d. Howard and Phyllis Waldroff 5 May 1973; children: Jodi Lynne, Ryan Nelson; DIR., RESOURCES PLANNING, QUEEN'S UNIV. 1984– ; Finan. Analyst, Queen's Univ. 1976–80; Asst. Dir., Resources Planning 1980–84; Extve. Mem., Council on University Planning and Analysis; Home: R.R. 2, Gananoque, Ont. K7G 2V4; Office: Kingston, Ont. K7L 3N6.

**SNYDER, Beverly Wells,** B.Sc.; retired extve.; b. Toronto, Ont. 9 June 1908; s. Ross Wilbert and Mabel (Bowering) S.; e. Pub. and High Schs., Calgary, Alta.; Univ. of Alta., B.Sc.; m. 1stly Phyllis Jean (d. 1952), d. William E. Yeo, 15 June 1935; three children; m. 2ndly Jean Dutton d. Frederick D. Weir, Calgary, 21 Nov. 1953; three children; Jr. Engr., City of Calgary 1931; joined Candn. Western Natural Gas Co. Ltd. as Jr. Engr., 1933; Utility Engr. 1936; various engn. appts. with Candn. Western and Northwestern Utilities Ltd. 1945–56; Tech. Asst. to Pres. 1957; Dir. of Econ. and Rate Engineer 1961; Vice-Pres., Engineering & Rate Adm. 1968, Consultant 1973–76; Assoc. Consultant, Foster Research 1978–85; served with R.C.E. 1939–45 (Overseas 1940–45); Capt. 1942; Staff Offr., 1st Candn. Army HQ, 1942–45; Mentioned in Despatches; Order of Leopold II and Croix de Guerre (Belgium); Order of Orange Nassau (Netherlands); Life Mem., Engn. Inst. Can.; Assn. Prof. Engrs. Alta.; Pacific Coast Gas Assn.; Candn. Gas Assn. (Past Chrmn., Operating Div.); Candn. Standards Assn. (Past Chrmn., Sectional Comte.); Freemason (P.M.); P. Conservative; United Church; recreation: golf; Club: Earl Grey Golf; Home: 1743 Suffolk St. S.W., Calgary, Alta. T3C 2N4.

**SNYDER, Hugh R.,** B.Sc., P.M.D., P.Eng.; mining industry executive; b. South Africa 2 Jan. 1936; s. Erle Snider and Frances Dorothea (Enslin) S.; e. Univ. of Witwatersrand B.Sc. 1958;Harvard Univ., Bus: Sch. P.M.D. 1969; m. Jennifer d. Harold and Aileen Wells 17 Aug. 1962; children: Dalene, Jacqueline, Derek, Tom; CHRMN., GREENSTONE RESOURCES LTD. 1993– ; Chief Geol. & Agent for Johannesburg Consolidated Investments in Fed. of Rhodesia & Nyasaland 1962–64; Chrmn., Khan Mines (PUT), Namibia 1965–70; Pres., Western Mines Limited (Vancouver) 1974–78; Pres., Brinco Limited (Toronto) 1978–85; Pres., Southern Era Resources 1986–92; Pres., American Mineral Resources Inc. 1992–93; Dir., GBC North Am. Growth Fund; Dickenson Mines Ltd.; recreations: nordic skiing, classical music, Meso American Pre-History; club: Royal Candn. Yacth; Home: 4 Brule Cres., Toronto, Ont. M6S 4H9; Office: Suite 1000, 36 Toronto St., Toronto, Ont. M5L 2C5.

**SNYDER, Robert Bruce,** P.Eng.; petroleum executive; b. Edmonton, Alta. 16 Sept. 1936; s. Robert Selkirk and Lydia Jane (Bruce) S.; e. Univ. of Sask., B.Sc. (Mech. Eng.) 1958; m. Carol Ann Cooper 16 Sept. 1956; children: Susan, Tracy, Steven; DIV. SR. VICE PRES., ALBERTA GAS TRANSMISSION DIV., NOVA CORP. 1982– ; joined Northern & Central Gas Corp. 1958–76, Vice Pres. Operations, Eng., Constrn. 1972; joined NOVA group 1976, Vice Pres. Alberta Gas TrunkLine (Can.) Ltd. 1976–78, Div. Vice Pres. & Acting Gen. Mgr. A.P.D. 1978–80, Sr. Vice Pres. Foothills Pipe Lines (Yukon) Ltd. 1981–82; Mem., Candn. Gas Assn. (Dir.); Pacific Coast Gas Assn.; Assn. Profl. Engs. Prov. Ont.; Edmonton C. of C.; recreation: cross-country skiing; Club: Edmonton Petroleum; Home: 11108 – 64 St., Edmonton, Alta. T5W 4H1; Office: 9888 Jasper Ave., Edmonton, Alta. T5J 1P1.

**SOBERMAN, Daniel A.,** B.A., LL.M.; b. Toronto, Ont. 19 Oct. 1929; s. Joseph Allan and Rose (Offman) S.; e. Kirkland Lake (Ont.) C. & V. I., 1942; Harbord Coll. Inst., Toronto, 1943–45; Queen Elizabeth High Sch., Halifax, 1945–46; Dalhousie Univ., B.A. 1950, LL.B. 1952; Harvard Univ., LL.M. 1955; m. Patricia Margaret, d. Eric Charles Burrage, Morden, Surrey, Eng., 28 July 1958; children: David, Julia, Gail; UNIVERSITY PROFESSOR EMERITUS, QUEEN'S UNIV.; Dean of Law, Queen's Univ., 1968–77; Assoc. Dean there 1967–68; called to Bar of N.S. 1952, Ont. 1955; Instr., Dalhousie Univ., 1955–56; Asst. Prof. 1956–57; Asst. Prof., Queen's Univ., 1957–59; Assoc. Prof. 1959–65; former Dir., World Univ. Service of Can.; Pres., Social Science Research Council of Can. 1971–73; rec'd Sr. Postgrad. Research Fellowship, Univ. of Edinburgh, 1963–64; mem. of panel to hear human rights complaints, Ontario Human Rights Commission since 1978, Candn. Human Rights Commission since 1984; co-author of 'The Law and Business Administration in Canada,' 1964, 1968, 1976, 1983, 1987, 1991; mem., Law Soc. Upper Can.; Assn. Candn. Law Teachers (Pres. 1968–69); Candn. Bar Assn.; recreations: sailing, photography; Club: Kingston Yacht; Home: 143 Fairway Hill Cres., Kingston, Ont. K7M 2B5.

**SOBEY, David F.,** executive; b. Stellarton, N.S. 22 March 1931; s. Frank Hoyse and Irene (MacDonald) S.; m. Faye B. Naugle d. Mr. and Mrs. G.E. Harrison 2 June 1953; children: Paul David, Janis Irene Hames; CHRMN. AND DIR., SOBEYS INC. 1981– ; Deputy Chrmn. & Dir., Univa Inc. 1993– ; Dir., CHC Helicopter Corp.; Empire Co. Ltd.; Sobey Leased Properties Ltd.; Atlantic Shopping Centres Ltd.; Clover Group; Eastern Sign-Print Ltd.; Lumsden Brothers Ltd.; Dominion Textile Inc.; Evangeline Savings & Mortgage Co.; T.R.A. Foods Ltd.; Hannaford Bros. Co.; Versa Services Ltd.; joined present Co. 1949 holding various positions incl. Store Mgr., Dir. of Merchandising & Advertising, Vice Pres., Exec. Vice Pres. and Pres. and Deputy Chrmn. & C.E.O.; ; Dir. Jr. Achievement Can.; Retail Counc. of Can.; C.I.E.S. (Internat. Assn. of Chain Stores); Food Marketing Inst.; Tim Horton Children's Found.; The Atlantic Salmon Federation; mem., Bd. of Govs., St. Mary's Univ.; mem., Halifax Bd. Trade; Clubs: Royal N.S. Yacht Sqdn.; Halifax; City (New Glasgow); Abercrombie Golf & Country (New Glasgow); Home: 294 Linden Ave., New Glasgow, N.S. B2H 2A7; Office: 115 King St., Stellarton, N.S. B0K 1S0.

**SOBEY, Donald Rae,** B.Com., LL.D.; company chairman; b. Stellarton, N.S. 23 Oct. 1934; s. Frank H. and Irene (MacDonald) S.; e. Stellarton (N.S.) High Sch.; Queen's Univ., B.Com.; m. Elizabeth, d. George Purvis, Stellarton, N.S., 7 Sept. 1963; children: Robert George Creighton, Irene Elizabeth, Kent Richard; CHAIRMAN AND DIR., EMPIRE CO. LTD.; Dir., Atlantic Motors Ltd.; Atlantic Shopping Centres Ltd.; Crombie Insurance (U.K.) Ltd.; Foord Construction Ltd.; Jannock Ltd.; Lawtons Drug Stores Ltd.; Maritime Telegraph & Telephone Co. Ltd.; Merchant Private Ltd. (formerly Tuckahoe Financial Corp.); National Sea Products Ltd.; Paribas Participations Ltd., PPL; Sobey Leased Properties Ltd.; Sobey's Inc.; Tibbetts Paints Ltd.; Toronto-Dominion Bank; Univa Inc. (formerly Provigo Inc.); Wajax Ltd.; Underwriting mem., Lloyd's of London; Gov., Olympic Trust of Canada; mem., AIESEC; The Conference Bd. of Can.; Patron, 1986 World Congress on Education and Technology; Mem. Burns Commission, Privy Counsel; Bd. of Govs., Dalhousie Univ.; mem. Task Force on the Future of the Port of Halifax; Foundation Chrmn., Camp Hill Medical Centre; mem., Club de relations d'affaires Canada-France; recipient, LL.D. (honoris causa) Dalhousie Univ. 1989; recreations: skiing, squash, tennis, music, art, travel; Clubs: Toronto; Saraguay (Halifax); Halifax; Abercrombie Golf & Country (Trustee); Home: Birch Hill Dr., Stellarton, N.S. B0K 1S0; Office: King St., Stellarton, N.S. B0K 1S0.

**SOBEY, Frank C.;** real estate developer; b. Stellarton, N.S. 25 Jan. 1953; VICE-CHAIRMAN, ATLANTIC SHOPPING CENTRES LTD.; Dir., Empire Company Limited; Sobey Leased Properties Limited; Atlantic Shopping Centre Limited; Wajax Limited; Dir., Sobey Found.; YMCA (Pictou Co.); Dir., United Way of Pictou

County; Bd. of Govs., University College of Cape Breton; Office: 115 King St., Stellarton, N.S. B0K 1S0.

**SODEK, Jaroslav,** B.Sc., Ph.D.; university professor; b. Somerset England 4 Mar. 1943; s. Jaroslav and Phyllis (Willoughby) S.; e. King Edward VI Gram. Sch. 1961; Univ. of Sheffield, B.Sc. 1964; Univ. of Toronto, Ph.D. 1970; post-doct. work, Univ. of Alberta 1970–73; m. Joanne d. Joan and William Oliver 16 June 1969; children: Katharine Lise, Kevan Jaro Thomas; PROF. & DIR., MED. RSCH. COUNC. GROUP IN PERIODONTAL PHYSIOLOGY, FAC. OF DENTISTRY, UNIV. OF TORONTO 1983– ; joined MRC group as Asst. Prof., Univ. of Toronto 1973; Assoc. Prof. 1979; sabbatical, Nat. Institutes of Health, Bethesda, Maryland 1981–82; Internat. Assn. for Dental Rsch. Award for Basic Rsch. in Periodontal Disease 1989; mem. Univ. of Toronto Research Bd. 1989–92; Office: Toronto, Ont. M5S 1A8.

**SODEN, James Arthur,** Q.C.; financier; b. Montreal, Que. 20 Oct. 1922; s. late Robert and Violet (McNamara) S.; e. McGill Univ. (grad. with hons. in Law); m. Edna, d. late John McConkey, 30 June 1945; children: Ann, Robert, Margaret, Lesley; CHRMN. SONCO PROPERTY DEVELOPMENT AND SERVICES CORP.; The St. John's Development Corp. Ltd.; A.P. Property Management Co. Ltd.; 1718 Argyle Inc.; 167305 (Canada) Inc.; Franklin County Realty Corp.; Past Chrmn. & C.E.O., Trizec Corp.; Place Bonaventure Inc.; Trizec Equities Ltd.; Place Quebec Inc.; Tristar Western Ltd.; Mobile Home Communities, Inc.; Scarborough Shopping Centre Ltd.; Pres. and Dir., Tristar Developments Inc. (U.S.A.); Scotia Winnipeg Ltd.; Granite Holdings of Canada Ltd.; Dir., Covent Canada Corporation Limited; English Property Corporation Ltd.; Founding Chrmn. & Dir., Canadian Institute Public Real Estate Cos.; called to Bar of Que. 1950; cr. Q.C. 1968; upon grad. joined Montreal law firm of Wainwright, Elder, Laidley, Leslie, Chipman and Bourgeois; assoc. with firm of Phillips, Bloomfield, Vineberg & Goodman, 1957–76; former Lectr. in Law at McGill Univ. and Concordia Univ.; served with RCAF during World War II; discharged with rank Sqdn. Leader, 1945; twice Mentioned in Despatches; Dir., St. Mary's Hospital, Montreal; Honorary Life member York Finch General Hospital; member Quebec and National Councils, Boy Scouts Assn. of Can.; mem., Montreal and Candn. Bar Assns.; Clubs: Mount Royal; Royal Cdn. Military Inst.; Home: 80 Front St. E., #426, Toronto, Ont. M5E 1T4 and R.R. #1, Box 190, Montgomery Centre, Vermont 05471; Office: 1718 Argyle St., Halifax, N.S. B3J 3N6.

**SODERSTROM, Ingmar Gustav;** executive; b. Hofors, Sweden 2 Nov. 1920; e. Sweden – Engn. Degree; m. Margot; children: Lars, Monica; Retired Pres. & Chrmn. of Bd. SKF Canada Ltd.; Mem. of the Bd., SKF Steel Ltd.; former Consul General for Sweden in Toronto; recreations: fishing, skiing; Address: 35 Denver Cr., Willowdale, Ont. M2J 1G6.

**SOGANICH, John;** consultant; retired editor/journalist; b. Davidov, Slovakia, Aug. 3, 1928, came to Canada May, 1938. s. John and Susan (Nedzbala) S.; e. Elem. and High Schs. Sudbury, Ont., Ryerson Polytechnic Univ., Journalism (honours), Toronto 1952; editor and publisher, The Ryersonian, at Ryerson in 1952; Senior Editor, The Financial Post 1977–92; Assoc. Ed., Investor's Digest of Canada 1987–91; also former Candn. mining corr. The Financial Times, London, Eng. (1976–84); former contributor (investments) for Marketing and Style magazines; Ed. Asst. The Northern Miner 1952–60; Asst. Ed. The Financial Post 1960–77; mem., Canadian Club; Candn. Inst. Mining, Metall. & Petroleum; Candn. Slovak League; Slovak World Congress; Club: Ontario; Catholic; Home: 74 South Dr., Toronto, Ont. M4W 1R5.

**SOHM, Philip,** B.A., M.A., Ph.D.; university professor; b. Washington, D.C. 20 July 1951; s. Earl David and Myra (Lindsay) S.; e. Oberlin College B.A. 1973; Univ. of London M.A. 1974; Johns Hopkins Univ. Ph.D. 1978; m. Janet d. Gilbert and Harriet Stanton 21 Dec. 1974; one s.: Matthew; PROF., DEPT. OF FINE ART, UNIV. OF TORONTO 1990– ; Kress Fellow, Nat. Gallery of Art, Washington, D.C. 1976–78; Asst. Prof., Univ. of Toronto 1978–83; Assoc. Prof. 1983–90; Chair, Dept. of Fine Art 1989– ; Visiting Prof., Colorado Coll. (Getty Seminars) 1986; Bruce Sr. Fellow, Ctr. for Adv. Study in the Visual Arts, Nat. Gall. of Art (declined); Herodotus Fellow, Inst. for Adv. Study, Princeton 1992–93; Extve. Ctte., Candn. Soc. for Renaissance Studies 1981–82; Ed. Bd., RACAR 1990– ; Fellowships Ctte., SSHRCC 1986–88 (Chair 1987–88); Old Masters Collection Ctte., Art. Gall. of Ont. 1990– ; author: 'The Scuola Grande di San Marco: The Architecture of a Venetian Lay Confraternity' 1982, 'Pittoresco. Marco Boschini, His Critics and Their Critiques of Painterly Brushwork in 17th- and 18-Century Italy' 1991; editor: 'The Language of Gesture in the Renaissance' 1986; Home: 53 Hewitt Ave., Toronto, Ont. M6P 3A3; Office: Toronto, Ont. M5S 1A1.

**SOKOLOV, David Israel,** Q.C., B.A., LL.B.; b. Winnipeg, Man. 11 Dec. 1928; s. Hyman and Rebecca (Rusoff) S.; e. St. John's Tech. High Sch., Winnipeg, 1946 (Valedictorian); Univ. of Man., B.A. 1949; Man. Law Sch., LL.B. 1953; m. Rhoda Lorraine (economist), d. Oscar and Marion Aaron, Vancouver, B.C. 13 Feb. 1960; children: Stephen, Louis; PARTNER, FILLMORE & RILEY; Course Leader 'Solicitors Transactions' Faculty of Law, University of Manitoba 1979–83; Dir. Columbia Trust Co. (Vancouver) 1984–85; called to Bar of Man. 1953; cr. Q.C. 1966; Counsel for Man. Mun. Bd., 1961–65 and for Dept. of Mun. Affairs, 1961–69; Assoc. Ed. Fillmore & Riley Ctte. to prepare statement of Manitoba law for 'Insurance and Tort Desk Reference published by Am. Insurance Attorneys 1990– ; mem. Ramah Hebrew Sch. Bd., 1968–71 (Secy. 1970–71); Dir., Winnipeg Symphony, 1969–70; mem., P. Conserv. Assn., 1957–69 (Secy. S. Winnipeg Assn. 1960); mem. Law Reform Comte. 1962–65; mem. Comte. to Revise Man. Corp. Act 1977– ; Man. Bar Assn.; Dir., Firefighters Burn Fund Inc. 1979– (Chrmn. 1979–92); recreations: golf, chess; Club: Glendale Country (Dir. 1965–68; Secy. 1968): Office: 1700 – 360 Main St., Winnipeg, Man. R3C 3Z3.

**SOKOLSKY, Joel Jeffrey,** M.A., Ph.D.; educator; b. Toronto, Ont. 21 July 1953; s. Leonard and Rose Elizabeth (Pratz) S.; e. Univ. of Toronto, B.A. 1976; Johns Hopkins Sch. Advanced Internat. Studies, M.A. 1978; Harvard Univ., Ph.D. 1986; m. Denise d. Clyde and Mary Hudnall 21 June 1981; children: Jared, Mark, Rachel; PROF. OF POL. & ECON. SCI., ROYAL MIL. COLL. OF CAN. (Asst. Prof. 1986–88, Assoc. Prof. 1988); Sr. Fellow, Queen's Univ. Center for Internat. Affairs; Instr. in Candn. Studies Johns Hopkins Sch. of Advanced Internat. Studies 1980–84; Asst. Prof. (Rsch.) Centre for Foreign Policy Studies Dalhousie Univ. 1984–86; Cons. to H. of C. Standing Ctte. on External Affairs & Nat. Defence review Can.-U.S. N.Am. Aerospace Defence Agreement 1985–86; recipient Christian A. Herter Award Acad. Excellence Johns Hopkins 1977; NATO Rsch. Fellowship 1982–83; author, 'Defending Canada: U.S.-Canadian Defence Policies' 1989; co-author 'Canadian Defence: Decisions and Determinants' 1985; 'Canada and Collective Security: Odd Man Out' 1986; various articles Candn. defence policy & strategic studies; mem. Assn. Candn. Studies in U.S.; Jewish; recreation: cycling; Home: 229 Welborne Ave., Kingston, Ont. K7M 4G5; Office: Kingston, Ont. K7K 5L0.

**SOLDIN, Steven John,** M.Sc., Ph.D., F.A.C.B.; clinical biochemist; b. Johannesburg, S. Africa 20 Oct. 1940; s. Hans Leopold and Alexandra S.; e. Univ. of the Witwatersrand, Johannesburg M.Sc., Ph.D. 1968; Univ. of Toronto Dip. in Clinical Chem. 1976; Candn. Soc. of Clinical Chemists exams 1976; Am. Bd. of Clinical Chem. exams 1976; m. Offie Porat-Soldin; children: Beverley, Elana, Belinda, Danielle; DIR. OF CLINICAL CHEMISTRY, CHILDREN'S HOSP. NATL. MED. CTR., WASHINGTON, D.C.; Prof. Dept. of Child Health and Development, Pathology and Pharmacology, George Washington Univ.; author various book chapters and scientific papers; formerly Chrmn., Bd. of Dir. and Pres.: Nat. Acad. of Clinical Biochemistry U.S.A.; Pres., Am. Bd. of Clinical Chem.; recreation: music, chamber music (violinist); Home: 6335, 31st St. N.W., Washington, D.C. 20015; Office: 111 Michigan Ave., N.W., Washington, D.C. 20010.

**SOLE, Michael Joseph,** B.Sc., M.D., F.R.C.P.(C), F.A.C.C.; university professor/cardiologist; b. Timmins, Ont. 5 March 1940; s. Fred and Lillian (Sole) S.; e. Univ. of Toronto B.Sc. 1962, M.D. 1966; Fellow, Cardiovascular Rsch. Inst., S.F. 1969–71; P.B. Brigham Hosp., Harvard Univ. 1971–73; m. Susan K. d. Benjamin and Billie Samuels 26 May 1964; children: David, Leslie; DIR., DIV. OF CARDIOLOGY AND CARDIOVASCULAR PROGRAM, THE TORONTO HOSPITAL and THE CENTRE FOR CARDIOVASCULAR RSCH., UNIV. OF TORONTO 1989– ; Dir., Cardiology Rsch., Univ. of Toronto 1987–89; Rsch. Assoc., M.I.T. 1973–74; Instr. in Med., Harvard Med. Sch. 1973–74; Cardiologist, Toronto Gen. Hospital 1974– ; Asst. Prof., Univ. of Toronto 1974–78; Assoc. Prof. 1978–83; Prof. of Med. & Physiol. 1983– ; Dir., Cardiol. Rsch., Toronto Gen. Hosp. 1979–89; Staff, Inst. of Med. Sci., Univ. of Toronto 1979– ; Rsch. Assoc., Heart & Stroke Found. of Ont. 1979–89; Distinguished Rsch. Prof., Heart & Stroke Foundation of Ont., 1989– ; Extve. Comm., Internat. Soc. for Heart Rsch. 1979–88; Extve. Comm., Basic Sci. Counc., Am. Heart Assn. 1986–89; Fellow 1978– ; Chrmn., Rsch. Ctte. (Med.), Univ. of Toronto 1987–88; Dir., Heart & Stroke Found. of Ont. 1986– (Fin. Ctte. 1986– ); Review Panel, Gairdner Found. 1979– ; Rsch. Bd., Univ. of Toronto 1989– ; and several past extve. posts.; numerous acad. & med. awards incl. election to Am. Soc. for Clin. Invest. and Assoc. of Am. Profs.; Rsch. Achievement Award Canadian Cardiovascular Soc. 1989; Katz Mem. Lecturer, Univ. of Chicago 1989; over 20 vis. professorships & 30 invited lectureships; Mem., Metro Toronto Bd. of Trade; author/co-author of over 200 sci. pubs.; recreations: tennis, golf; Clubs: Mayfair Tennis, Bd. of Trade Country; Office: EN13 – 208, The Toronto Hospital, EN 13 - 208, 200 Elizabeth St., Toronto, Ont. M5G 2C4.

**SOLECKI, Sam Zdzislaw Zbigniew,** B.A., M.A., Ph.D; university professor; b. Doddington, England 21 Nov. 1946; s. Tadeusz Josef and Darinka Mijatovic S.; e. Niagara Falls C.I. 1965; Univ. of Toronto, B.A. 1969, M.A. 1970, Ph.D. 1974; m. Ursula Paula Bialas 14 June 1969; children: Vanessa Megan, Andre Zaria; PROF., DEPT. OF ENGLISH, ST. MICHAEL'S COLL., UNIV. OF TORONTO 1972– ; Host, 'Talking About Language' CJRT 1990; Editor: 'Canadian Forum' 1979–82 (Book Rev. Ed. 1977–84; Lit. Ed. 1980–84); Panelist, CBC radio 'Panning for Gold' 'In Other Words' 1980, 1981; Weekly book revr., CBC-FM 'Stereo Morning' 1979–84; author: 'Prague Blues: the Fiction of Josef Skvorecky' 1990; 'Volleys' 1990; editor: 'Spider Blues: Essays on Michael Ondaatje' 1986, 'Talkin' Moscow Blues: Josef Skvorecky's Essays and Interviews' 1988; 'The Achievement of Josef Skvorecky' 1994; recreations: basketball, chess, tennis, jazz; Home: 108 Manor Rd. E., Toronto, Ont. M4S 1P8; Office: 81 St. Mary St., Toronto, Ont. M5S 1J4.

**SOLER, Arthur R.;** confectionery industry executive; b. Malta 12 Feb. 1944; s. John and Helen (Parlato) S.; e. St. Albert's Coll., Malta (H.S. grad.) 1960; Ryerson Polytech. Inst., Hons. Bus. Admin. 1967; Univ. of Western Ont., Mktg. Mngt. course 1977; m. Elizabeth d. Helen and George Baker; children: Jonathon, Justine, Juliane; PRES., NEILSON CADBURY LTD. 1990– ; Clerk, Barclays Bank Internat. (Malta) 1960–64; Finan. Planning Sup. then Internal Audit Mgr., Procter & Gamble Canada 1965–70; Finan. Planning Mgr., Warner Lambert Canada 1970–72; Product Mgr. 1972–74; New Business Devel. (Europe) 1974–76; Dir. of Mktg., Health Care Div. (Can.) 1976–84; Vice-Pres., Mktg. Adams Brands, Warner Canada 1984–90; Vice-Chrmn., Confectionery Manufacturers Assn. of Can.; Marketing Man of Year Award runner-up 1989; recreations: chess, tennis, walking; club: Boulevard; Home: 162 Lake Driveway W., Ajax, Ont. L1S 4V7; Office: 277 Gladstone Ave., Toronto, Ont. M6J 3L9.

**SOLNTSEFF, Nicholas,** B.Sc., Ph.D., C.Eng., F.B.C.S.; university teacher; b. Shanghai, China 13 Dec. 1931; s. Nicholas and Anna (Rodionov) S.; e. Sydney Tech. H.S. 1948; Univ. of Sydney, B.Sc. 1952, Ph.D. 1957; m. June Hart 2 June 1967; one s.: Dominic; ASSOC. PROF., COMPUTER SCI., McMASTER UNIV. 1971– ; Teaching Fellow, Univ. of Sydney 1957–58; Reactor Physicist, Atomic Power Constr. Ltd. 1958–63; Lectr., Imperial Coll. 1963–67; Sr. Lectr., Univ. of N.S.W. 1967–70; Vis. Assoc. Prof., Univ. of Colorado 1970–71; Mem., IEEE, Assn. for Computing Machinery; author of rsch. papers in nuclear engr., extensible prog. languages & real-time expert systems; Home: 62 Sydenham St., Dundas, Ont. L9H 2T9; Office: Hamilton, Ont. L8S 4K1.

**SOLOMON, George Charles,** C.M., S.O.M., LL.D.; executive; b. Regina, Sask. 10 Apl. 1913; m. Doris Ilene Dean, 26 May 1932; three d. Mrs. Sharon D. Dyksman, Mrs. Vaughn C. Schofield, Mrs. Adrian I. Burns; PRESIDENT, WESTERN LTD.; Dir., YMCA; Salvation Army; rec'd Candn. Counc. of Christians and Jews Human Relations Award 1973; Jubilee Medal 1977; The Duke of Edinburgh's Award in Canada 1978; L.L.D., Univ. of Regina 1980; Saskatchewan Order of Merit 1985; Hon. Colonel, Royal Regina Rifles 1986; named Citizen of the Year, Regina B'Nai B'Rith 1986; Mem., Order of Canada 1994; United Church; Cert. of Life Mem., Salvation Army 1989; recreations: boating, swimming; Club: Assiniboia; Home: 5P, 1210 Blackfoot Dr., Regina, Sask. S4S 7G3; Office: Suite 200, 2184 - 12th Ave., Regina, Sask. S4P 0M5.

**SOLOMON, Lawrence;** writer, environmentalist; b. Bucharest, Romania 20 Feb. 1948; s. Isidor and Delicia (Mendel) S.; e. McGill Univ.; Officers, Partners & Directors Exam., Investment Funds Inst. of Can. 1987; m. Patricia d. Robert and Joan Adams 7 June 1985; CO-FOUNDER, AUTHOR & RESEARCH CO-ORDINA-

TOR, ENERGY PROBE RESEARCH FOUNDATION 1977– ; freelance writer 1968– ; Pres. & Founder, EIF Fund Management Ltd. 1987–93; Sr. Rsch. Assoc., Borealis Energy Rsch. Assn. 1991– ; Advisor, Pres. Task Force on Global Resources & Envir. (Global 2000 Report under Pres. Carter) 1979–80; Columnist, Globe & Mail 1981–82; syndicated columnist 1982–91; Advisor & Reviewer, Science Council of Canada; Donner Fellow 1991; Vice Chair, City of Toronto Planning Bd. 1979–81; author: 'Conserver Solution' 1978, 'Energy Shock' 1980, 'Breaking up Ontario Hydro's Monopoly' 1982, 'Power at What Cost' 1984; co-author: 'In the Name of Progress' 1985; editor: 'Odious Debts' 1991; contbr.: 'Economics' 6th ed. 1990, 'Microeconomics' 6th ed. 1990; Home: 193 Howland Ave., Toronto, Ont. M5R 3B7; Office: 225 Brunswick Ave., Toronto, Ont. M5S 2M6.

**SOLOMON, Maximilian,** B.A.; merchant banker; b. Cleveland, Ohio 19 Oct. 1946; s. Harry and Betty (Gerhardt) S.; e. Ohio State Univ. B.A. 1969; Stanford Univ. postgrad. 1979; m. Phyllis Gordon 18 Aug. 1974 (dec'd. 1979); m. Batya d. Isadore and Frieda Bastomski 18 Feb. 1990; PRES., CHIEF EXTVE. OFFR. & DIR., THE FIRST MERCANTILE CURRENCY FUND 1985– ; Dir., Inst. Adv. Serv., Friedberg Mercantile Group 1978– ; Mng. Dir., The First Toronto Mercantile Corp. 1979– ; The First Mercantile Corp., Toronto 1984– ; The First Mercantile Corp. of New York 1984–85; The First Mercantile Currency Corp., Toronto 1985– ; The First Mercantile (TFM) Global Corp. 1987– ; The First Mercantile Internat. Corp. (Toronto) 1992– ; Gen. Partner, TFM Partnership 1984– ; TFM Convertible Debenture Partnership 1986– ; TFM Global Partnership 1987– ; TFM Double Gold Plus Partnership I & II 1987–90; TFM Internat. Partnership 1988– ; TFM Am. Partnership 1988– ; TFM Currency Partnership 1990– ; TFM Global Currency Partnership 1990– ; The First Mercantile New Zealand Partnership 1992– ; The First Mercantile Global Capital Partnership 1993– ; Pres., Chrmn. of the Bd. of Govs., The Toronto Options and Futures Society 1984–85; Dir., The First Gulf Currency Corp., Toronto 1985–88; co-author of study on Argus Corp. for Royal Comn. on Corp. Concentration 1975–77; mem., The Toronto Society of Financial Analysts; Assn. for Investment Management and Rsch.; National Futures Assn.; Futures Industry Assn.; The Toronto Futures Exchange; Jewish; Home: 212 Strathallan Wood, North York, Ont. M5N 1T4; Office: The First Mercantile Currency Fund, 347 Bay St., Suite 404, Toronto, Ont. M5H 2R7.

**SOLOMON, Samuel,** M.Sc., Ph.D., F.C.I.C., F.R.S.C.; educator; research scientist; b. Brest, Poland 5 Dec. 1925; s. Nathan and Rachel (Greenberg) S.; e. McGill Univ. B.Sc. 1947, M.Sc. 1951, Ph.D. (Biochem.) 1953; m. Augusta Myers Vineberg 20 July 1974; three s. David, Peter, Jonathan; PROF. DEPTS. BIOCHEM., EXPER. MED. AND OBSTETRICS & GYNECOL., McGILL UNIV.; Dir., Endocrinology Lab., Royal Victoria Hosp. 1967– ; mem. Extve. Comte. Indust. Research McGill 1976–82, Bd. of Gov. 1974–77, McGill Planning Comn. 1971–75; Dir. of Rsch. Inst. Royal Victoria Hosp. 1982–84; Bd. Mem. Connaught Research Foundation 1980–82; Visiting Prof. Univ. of Vt.; mem. Research Comte. St. Mary's Hosp. 1980–82; Pres. Perinatal Research Soc. 1976–77; Chrmn. Endocrine Soc. Employment Service 1972–77, mem. Internat. Affairs Comte. 1972–77; Central Comte. Internat. Soc. Endocrinol. 1964–76; Program Comte. IV Internat. Cong. Endocrinology 1972; Prog. Chrmn. Soc. for Gynecologic Investigation 1980; Council, Soc. for Gynecological Invest. 1984–87; Chrmn. Steering Comte. Internat. Study Grp. for Steroid Hormones, Rome, Italy 1983–89; Co-Chrmn. 25th Anniversary Medical Research Council of Canada 1985; mem. Dubin Commn., Abuse of Drugs in Athletics 1988–89; Scientific Adv., Nat. Football League, U.S.A. 1990–91; Medical Rsch. Council of Canada Regional Dir., Que. 1993– ; co-ed. 'Chemical and Biological Aspects of Steroid Conjugation' 1970; over 200 articles endocrinology and metabolism, maj. journs.; Fellow, Roy. Soc. of Can. 1974; Schering Travelling Fellowship 1965; Hon. Fellow, Am. Gynecological and Obstetrical Soc. 1982; Joseph Price Oration, Am. Gynecological & Obstetrical Soc. 1982; MacLaughlan Gold Medal, Royal Soc. of Can. 1989; Hebrew; recreations: skiing, tennis; Club: M.A.A.A.; Ambassador's Club, Montreal Convention Center; Home: 239 Kensington Ave., Apt. 603, Montreal, Que. H3Z 2H1; Office: Endocrine Laboratory, Royal Victoria Hospital, 687 Pine Ave. W., Montreal, Que. H3A 1A1.

**SOLWAY, David,** B.A., Q.M.A., M.A.; professor; poet; b. Montreal, Que. 8 Dec. 1941; s. Samuel and Sylvia (Rabinovitch) S.; e. McGill Univ., B.A. 1962, Q.M.A. 1966; Concordia Univ., M.A. 1988; m. Karin d. Rudolf and Charlotte Semmler 23 Apr. 1980; one d.: Hannah; Prof., John Abbott Coll. 1971–90; President's Club, Univ. of Toronto; Sr. Can. Counc. grant; York Univ. Creative Writing Prize; QSPELL award for poetry 1988 and for non-fiction 1990; Bourse de Québec; mem., Internationl PEN; Union des écrivains québécois; Candn. Writers' Union; author: 'The Road to Arginos' 1976, 'Selected Poetry' 1982, 'The Mulberry Men' 1982, 'Modern Marriage' 1988, 'Bedrock' 1993 and others (poetry) as well as literary essays in 'Sewanee Review' 1987, 'Canadian Literature' (1988), etc.; author: 'Education Lost' 1989 (prose); 'The Anatomy of Arcadia' (prose) 1992; editor: '4 Montreal Poets' (poetry) 1972; Home: 4142 Beaconsfield Ave., Montreal, Que. H4A 2H3.

**SOLWAY, Lawrence Siegfried (Larry);** broadcaster; journalist; b. Toronto, Ont. 13 March 1928; s. Joseph Benjamin and Susan Gertrude (Gold) S.; e. Forest Hill Schs., Vaughan Rd. Coll. Inst.; Univ. of Toronto; m. Shirley d. Kalman and Mary Caplan 29 Nov. 1949; children: Joseph, Beth; broadcaster since 1947; joined CHUM Radio 1956–70, Vice Pres. and Dir. 1965–70, pioneered 'open line' radio 1960–70; TV Writer and Host various CBC documentaries incl. 'Railroads East Railroads West' 1975, 'Our Fellow Americans' 8 parts 1976; co-owner Marigold Playhouse, Whitby 1982–85; theatre producer, performer; appearances incl. Neptune Theatre, Halifax, Nat. Arts Centre Ottawa; newspaper columnist 'Sunday Star' 1977–84; Media Training Cons. to Govt. and Ind. Gabor Communications 1980– ; Teacher, Conestoga Coll. 1972–76; Talk Radio (CFRB Toronto) 1991–92; author (non fiction) 'The Day I Invented Sex' 1971; 'You Know Me I Never Interfere' 1988; recreations: sailing, skiing, music; Home: 217 Old Forest Hill Rd., Toronto, Ont.

**SOLY, Geneviève,** Doc.(Int.); musician; b. Montreal, Que. 14 Nov. 1957; d. Bernard and Mireille Bégin Lagacé; e. Conservatoire de Musique du Qué. à Montreal: 1st prize organ 1976, 2nd prize harpsichord 1977; Univ. de Montréal Doctorat, interpretation 1992; m. Jean Letarte 21 May 1988; children: Arnaud and Matthias Soly-Letarte; 200 solo recitals, organ and harpischord in Canada, France, Austria, Germany, Belgium, Switz.; in Canada: Place des Arts (Montreal), Roy Thompson Hall & O'Keefe Ctr. (Toronto), BCU and churches from east to west coast; over 200 CBC and Radio Canada performances; solo & continuo with MSO, McGill Chamber Orch., NBC, SMAM baroque groups & others; Harpsichordist with I Musici de Montréal 1982–89; Founder & Artistic Dir., 'Les Idées Heureuses' (successful Montreal concert series); 'Conférencière'; Dir., Early Music Week, CAMMAC Musical Camp (Que.) and Teacher for 15 years; Second Prize, 'Paul Hofhaimer' Internat. Comp. (Innsbruck) 1980; First Prize, 'John Robb' comp. (Montreal) 1976; Home: 1287 rue de la Visitation, Montreal, Que. H2L 3B6.

**SOMAIN, Jean-François;** see **SOMCYNSKY, Jean-François.**

**SOMCYNSKY, Jean-François,** M.A.; writer; diplomat; b. Paris, France 20 Apr. 1943; s. Paul and Marie Jenikova S.; e. Univ. of Ottawa, M.A. 1970; m. Micheline d. Ernest and Florine Beaudry 22 Aug. 1968; COUNSELLOR AND CONSUL, CANDN. EMBASSY, TOKYO, JAPAN 1992– ; Chief, Statistical Unit, Dept. of Finan. 1970–71; joined Dept. of External Affairs 1971; positions have included: Second Sec. & Vice-Consul, Buenos Aires 1973–75; First Sec. & Consul, Dakar, Senegal 1977–79; Dep. Dir., Francophone Africa 1980–84; Counsellor & Consul, Jakarta, Indonesia 1984–87; Dep. Dir., Programs in Europe 1987–92; Prix Solaris 1982; Prix Esso du Cercle du Livre de France 1983; Prix Louis Hémon de l'académie du Languedoc 1987; mem., Union des écrivains québécois; Centre québécois du P.E.N. Internat.; Profl. Assn. of Fgn. Serv. Offrs.; author (novels): 'Les rapides' 1966, 'Encore faim' 1970, 'Le diable du Mahani' 1978, 'Les incendiaires' 1980, 'La planète amoureuse' 1982, 'Vingt minutes d'amour' 1983, 'La frontière du milieu' 1983, 'Un tango fictif' 1986, 'Les visiteurs du pôle Nord' 1987, 'Sortir du piège' 1988, 'Dernier départ' 1989, 'Tu peux compter sur moi' 1990, 'La nuit du chien-loup' 1990; 'La vraie couleur du caméléon' 1991; 'Parlez-moi d'un chat' 1992; 'Le baiser des étoiles' 1992; 'Du jambon d'hippopotame' 1992; 'Le soleil de Gauguin' 1993; 'Le secret le mieux gardé' 1993; 'Moi, c'est Turquoise' 1994; (short stories): 'Les grimaces' 1975, 'Peut-être à Tokyo' 1981, 'J'ai entendu parler d'amour' 1984, 'Vivre en beauté' 1989; (poetry): 'Trois voyages' 1982; pen-name: Jean-François Somain; recreations: travel, painting, reading; Home: Canada Court #2401, 7-3-24 Akasaka, Minato-Ku, Tokyo 107, Japan; Office: Candn. Embassy, Tokyo, Japan.

**SOMERS, Emmanuel,** Ph.D., D.Sc., F.R.S.C.(UK); F.C.I.C.; public servant; b. Leeds, UK 3 July 1927; s. William and Sophia (Morris) S.; e. Roundhay Sch. Leeds; Leeds Univ. B.Sc. 1948, M.Sc. 1950, D.Sc. 1969; Bristol Univ. Ph.D. 1956; m. Rosemary d. Robert and Jane Norris 31 Aug. 1951; children: Sara Caroline, Andrew David Robert; SENIOR PROGRAMME OFFICER, INTERNAT. PROG. CHEM. SAFETY WORLD HEALTH ORGANIZATION, GENEVA 1994– ; Prin. Sci. Offr. Long Ashton Rsch. Station, Bristol Univ. 1951–67; Postdoctoral Fellow Pesticide Rsch. Inst. Agric. Can. 1957–58; Visiting Sci. Conn. Agric. Exper. Stn. New Haven 1963–64; joined Health and Welfare Canada 1967, Chief Food Div. Food & Drug Rsch. Labs. 1968–72, Dir. Food Rsch. Labs. 1972–74, Dir. Bureau Chem. Safety 1974, Dir. Gen. Environmental Health Directorate 1974–87; Dir. Gen. Drugs Directorate 1988–92; Expert Advisor, Life Sciences Institutes, National Rsch. Council 1993–94; initiated Internat. Prog. Chem. Safety World Health Orgn. 1980, mem. and Chrmn. Prog. Adv. Ctte., rep. Can. Governing Council Internat. Agency Rsch. Cancer 1983–92 serving as Vice Chrmn. and Chrmn.; consultant, UN Environment Prog. and Food and Agriculture Orgn.; consultant to World Health Orgn. on Environmental Health, Chemical Safety and Pharmaceuticals 1973– ; Chrmn., Sixth Internat. Conference of Drug Regulatory Authorities, Ottawa 1991; Dir. Toxicol. Forum USA 1988–92; Dir., Joseph Morgan Foundation 1993– ; Exec. mem. Sci. Group on Methodologies for Safety Evaluation of Chems. (WHO/UNEP/SCOPE) 1981–91; Nat. Conf. Chrmn. Candn. Inst. Food Sci. & Technol. 1976; Council mem.: Internat. Acad. Environmental Safety 1985–87; Internat. Soc. Ecotoxicol. & Environmental Safety 1979–83; author over 160 rsch., review papers, book chapters; co-ed. 'Short-Term Toxicity Tests for Non-Genotoxic Effects' 1990; recreations: reading, travel, walking, skiing; Office: IPCS, World Health Orgn., 1211 Geneva 27, Switzerland.

**SOMERS, Harry,** C.C. (1971), Hon. Doc. in Law (Univ. of Toronto), Hon. Doc. in Letters (York Univ.), Hon. Doc. of Music (Ottawa Univ.); composer; b. Toronto, Ont. 11 Sept. 1925; e. Royal Conserv. Music, Toronto; studied piano with Dorothy Hornfelt, Reginald Godden; theory and composition under John Weinzweig; piano study with Robert Schmitz 1948; composition under Darius Milhaud, Paris 1949; wrote his first String Quartet at age 17; other works incl., opera: 'Louis Riel' 1967; Chamber operas: 'The Fool' 1953; 'Enkidu' 1977; 3 ballet scores; 2 piano concertos; 3 string quartets; 5 piano sonatas and numerous other works for orchestras, chamber groups and soloists and music for T.V. and film; received numerous commissions and awards including Companion to the Order of Canada and Can. Council Sr. Arts Fellowship 1960; Assoc., Candn. Music Centre; Founding mem., Candn. League of Composers; Address: 158 Douglas Dr., Toronto, Ont. M4W 2B7.

**SOMERS, Stewart Douglas,** B.A., C.A.; financial executive; b. Hamilton, Ont. 3 March 1942; s. Harold and Tena (Weinstein) S.; e. Univ. of Toronto B.A. 1965; Coopers & Lybrand C.A. 1969; m. Margaret d. Fred and Isa Dalby 7 Sept. 1979; children: Johanna, Adam, Amanda, Lindsay; PRES., CAROUSEL CAPITAL CORPORATION 1993– ; CAROUSEL OPTICAL 1994– and CHIEF OPERATING OFFR., S.D. SOMERS & ASSOCIATES 1977– ; Pres., Concourse Building Ltd. 1990– ; Chief Operating Offr., Imperial Optical Co. Ltd. 1991–93; Extve. Vice-Pres. & Chief Financial Offr., Paja Group Inc. 1989–93; Pres., Claridge Apartments (1963) Limited and Clarendon Apartments (1963) Limited 1990–93; Extve. Vice-Pres., Tridont Health Care Inc. 1987–88; Vice-Pres., Finance, Algonquin Mercantile Group of Cos. 1970–76; has lectured extensively across Canada to var. bus. groups on pragmatic bus. subjects; Mem., Sigma Alpha Mu Frat.; Financial Extves. Inst.; Ont. Inst. of C.A.s; author of six CICA profl. devel. courses; recreations; golf, skiing; clubs: Donalda, The Meadows (Florida), Beaver Valley Ski; Home: 60 Brookshire Circle, Thornhill, Ont. L3T 7B3; Office: 1645 Bonhill Rd., Suite 3, Mississauga, Ont. L5T 1R3.

**SOMERVILLE, David Edward Triscott;** communications executive; b. Toronto, Ont. 2 Aug. 1950; s. William Lorne Northmore and Denise Madeleine (Church) S.; e. St. Andrew's Coll. 1968; Can. Jr. Coll., Switz. 1969; Univ. of Toronto 1983; m. Jennifer d. James and Ann O'Brian 23 June 1979; children: William, Madeleine, Elisabeth, Claire, Hilary, Margaret; PRES. & CHIEF EXTVE. OFFR., THE NATIONAL CITIZENS' COALITION 1987– ; Reporter/Columnist, The Toronto Sun 1974–77; Dir. of Rsch., Nat. Citizens' Coalition (NCC) 1978–79; Mgr., TCF/USCS Ltd. 1979–83; Vice-Pres., NCC 1983–86; Pres., NCC 1986– ; Co-founder, 'Peace with Freedom International' 1986–91; Co-founder, Ctte. for a Peaceful Transition to Democracy 1989; Dir., the Mackenzie Inst.; Trustee, The Philadelphia Soc.; author: 'Trudeau Revealed' 1978; recipient, Gold Cross of Merit (Poland); recreations: skiing, tennis, fishing, windsurfing; club: Osler Bluff Ski; Office: 100 Adelaide St. W., #907, Toronto, Ont. M5H 1S3.

**SOMERVILLE, Marc Jolliffe,** Q.C., B.A., LL.B.; lawyer; b. Toronto, Ont. 23 Apl. 1939; s. Jack B. and Sadie A. (Jolliffe) S.; e. Jarvis Coll. Inst.; Univ. of Toronto, Victoria Coll. B.A. 1962 (Honour Award 1962), LL.B. 1965 (Dean's Key 1965); Univ. of Toronto Law Sch.; m. Joan d. Leonard and Kay Graham 2 Feb. 1963; children: Jeffrey, Erinn, Graeme; PARTNER, GOWLING, STRATHY & HENDERSON 1986– ; Dir. The Equitable Life Insurance Co. of Canada; called to Bar of Ont. 1967; cr. Q.C. 1982; law practice Jolliffe, Lewis, Osler, Toronto 1967–69; Simmers, Edwards, Jenkins, Cambridge 1969–83; Simmers, Harper, Jenkins, Kitchener 1983–86; Dir. Kitchener-Waterloo Symphony Orch. 1984–88; Past Dir. Cambridge Un. Way; Ald. City of Galt 1970–72; City of Cambridge 1973; Regional Councillor Region of Waterloo 1973; Bencher, Law Soc. Upper Can. 1987, Chrmn. Profl. Conduct Ctte.; Hon. Trustee Waterloo Co. Law Assn.; mem. Prov. Council and Nat. Council Candn. Bar Assn. 1986–94; Pres. S.W. Ont. Br. Univ. of Toronto Law Alumni Assn.; Club: University (Toronto); Home: R.R.6, Shellard Rd., Cambridge, Ont. N1R 5S7; Office: 1100 Commerce House, 50 Queen St. N., Kitchener, Ont. N2H 6M2.

**SOMERVILLE, Margaret Anne Ganley,** A.M., F.R.S.C., A.u.A.(pharm.), LL.B.(hons.), D.C.L.; LL.D. Hon. causa (Windsor; Macquarie); university professor; b. Adelaide, S. Aust. 13 Apr. 1942; d. George Patrick and Gertrude Honora (Rowe) Ganley; e. Mercedes Coll.; Univ. of Adelaide, A.u.A.(pharm) 1963 (Pharm. Soc. of S. Aust. prize); Univ. of Sydney, LL.B. (Hons. I) 1973 (Univ. of Sydney Medal); McGill Univ., D.C.L. 1978; Honorary Doctor of Laws (LL.D.) Windsor Univ. 1992, Macquarie Univ. 1993; divorced; GALE PROF. OF LAW, MCGILL UNIV. 1989– ; PROF., FAC. OF LAW & FAC. OF MED., MCGILL UNIV. 1984– ; DIR., MCGILL CTR. FOR MEDICINE ETHICS & LAW 1986– ; Registered Pharmacist, S. Aust., Victoria, N.Z., N.S.W. 1963–69; Attorney, Mallesons (formerly Stephen, Jaques, and Stephen) Sydney, Aust. 1974–75; admitted to the Supreme Court of New South Wales as solicitor 1975; admitted to Que. Bar 1982; Consultant, Law Reform Commn. of Can. 1976–85; Asst. Prof., Fac. of Law, Inst. of Comparative Law, present univ. 1978, Assoc. Prof. 1979, Prof. 1984– ; Assoc. Prof., Fac. of Med., present univ. 1980, Prof. 1984–85; Chairperson, Graduate Studies Ctte. 1988–89; Clinical Ethics Ctte., Royal Victoria Hosp. 1980– ; Med. Scientist, Dept. of Med., & Mem. of Rsch. Inst., Royal Victoria Hosp., Montreal 1985– ; Prin. Investigator, Nat. Health Res. & Devel. Prog. grant to investigate var. aspects of AIDS in Can. 1986–89; Assoc. Mem., McGill AIDS Centre 1990– ; National Adv. Ctte. on AIDS (Min. of Health and Welfare, Canada) 1986–92; Chairperson, Research Ethics Ctte., National Research Council of Canada 1991– ; Reviewer, 'Journal of Clinical Epidemiology' 1988– ; 'Canadian Journal of Family Law' 1988– ; 'Journal of Pharmacy Practice' 1988– ; 'Community Health Studies' 1987– ; SSHRCC 1985– ; N.H.R.D.P. (National Health Rsch. Development Program of Health & Welfare Canada) 1989– ; 'Canadian Medical Association Journal' 1983– ; Internat. Adv., 'Medical Humanities Review' 1986– ; 'Bioethics Reporter' 1983– ; Ed. Bd., 'Bioethics' 1986– ; Adv. Ed., 'Social Science and Medicine' 1988– ; Editorial Bd., Kennedy Institute of Ethics Journal; Internat. Fellow, Hastings Ctr. 1986– ; Hon. Patron, Cult Project 1985– ; Assoc., Nat. Inst. on Mental Retardation 1985– ; Contbr. Ed., 'Health Law in Canada' 1979–87; Visiting Prof., Sydney Univ. 1984, 1986, 1990; Visiting Prof., Ctr. for Human Bioethics, Monash Univ. 1985–86; recipient of numerous acad. distinctions, scholarships, fellowships, prizes & rsch. grants incl. Univ. of Sydney Medal (for placing first over the four year course with sufficiently high merit) 1973; Australian Commonwealth Scholarship tenable in Canada, McGill Univ. 1975; Joseph Dainow Prize (for writing in the area of Civil Law) McGill Univ. 1976; Distinguished Service Award (for contributions to the enhancement of interdisciplinary medicolegal education through service on the Bd. of Dirs.) Am. Soc. of Law & Medicine 1985; 'Pax Orbis ex Jure,' Gold Medal (for support and dedication to the cause of world peace through law) Associates of the World Peace Through Law Center, Washington, D.C. 1985; Brockington Visitor 1988–89, Queen's Univ.; Gale Prof. of Law 1989; mem., Order of Australia 1990; Fellow, The Royal Society of Canada 1991; Cons. to num. orgns. including: Candn. Human Rights Found.; Dept. of Justice, Govt. of Can., Criminal Law Review; World Health Organization; United Way/Centraide Canada; Nat. Parole Bd., Govt. of Can.; Health & Welfare Can.; Candn. Council on Children & Youth; Dept. of Solicitor Gen. of Canada; Law Reform Commission of Ont.; UNESCO pres. & past ctte. mem., num. orgns.; Extve. Ctte., of Nat. Scientific & Planning Council, Candn. Mental Health Assn. 1984–90; Mem., Am. Soc. for Pharm. Law; Inst. of Soc., Ethics & Life Sci., Hastings Ctr.; Values Gr., McGill Univ.; Am. Soc. of Law & Med.; Assn. Henri Capitant; Assn. des Prof. de Droit du Qué.; Candn. Bar Assn.; Candn. Pharm. Assn.; World Assn. for Med. Law; Candn. Law Teachers Assn.; Soc. for Health & Human Values; Internat. Acad. of Comp. Law; Council Mem., World Jurists Assn.; McGill Study Gr. for Peace and Disarm.; Internat. Law Assn.; Nat. Adv. Ctte. on AIDS, Min. of Health, Can.; Bd. of Dirs., Am. Soc. of Law and Medicine 1989– ; Comité consultatif en génétique humaine au ministére de la Santé et des Services sociaux de Québec 1991– ; Bd. of Dirs., Candn. Centre for Drug-Free Sport 1992– ; Candn. National Legal Advisors Ctte., Choice in Dying 1992– ; author of num. articles, reviews, lectrs. & papers; Home: 2600 Pierre Dupuy, Habitat '67 Phase 3, Apt. 1025, Montreal, Que. H3C 3R6; Office: 3690 Peel St., Montreal, Que. H3A 1W9.

**SOMERVILLE, William Henry,** LL.D.; trust company executive; b. Blanshard Twp., Perth Co., Ont. 25 Apr. 1921; s. John and Mary (Taylor) S.; e. St. Marys (Ont.) Coll. Inst. 1939; Internat. Accts. Soc. 1953; m. Jean, d. Charles Fawcett 16 June 1945; children: John, Karen; CHRMN., ONTARIO PENSION BOARD and HONORARY CHAIRMAN, NATIONAL TRUST CO. 1989– ; National Trustco Ltd.; Dir.: Digital Equipment of Canada; Ellis-Don Inc.; E-L Financial Corp.; Dominion & Anglo Investments; Dominion of Can. Gen. Ins.; Empire Life Ins. Co.; Connecticut National Life Ins.; Newgrowth Corp.; St. Joseph's Health Centre; Prop., Drug Store, St. Marys, Ont. 1946–55; Executive, Drug Trading Co., London, Ont. 1956–62; Mgr., St. Marys Br., British Mortgage & Trust Co. 1962; Mgr., St. Marys Br. Victoria and Grey Trust Co. 1965, Mgr. Stratford Br. 1966, Asst. Gen. Mgr. 1968, Vice-Pres. 1973, Vice-Pres. Mortgages 1976, Extve. Vice-Pres. 1977; Pres. and CEO, Victoria and Grey Trustco, Victoria and Grey Trust 1978; Chrmn. & C.E.O., National Trust Company 1984; Chancellor Emeritus, Univ. of Windsor; Past Chrmn., Trust Co's Assn. of Can.; Past Pres. Stratford Shakespearean Festival; Perth Riding Liberal Assn.; Councillor, St. Marys 1962–64; Mayor, Town of St. Marys 1965–66; Lib. Cand. for Perth Riding Fed. g.e. 1968; Alderman, City of Stratford 1970–73; United Church; Clubs: Ontario; Toronto; Home: 30 Front St., Stratford, Ont. N5A 7S3; Office: 21 King St. E., Toronto, Ont. M5C 1B3.

**SOMERVILLE, William L.N.,** Q.C., B.A., LL.B.; b. Ottawa, Ont. 24 Aug. 1921; s. William Lorne and Olive Triscott (Northmore) S.; e. elem. and high schs., Collingwood, Ont.; Univ. of Toronto, Trinity Coll. B.A. 1943, LL.B. 1948; Osgoode Hall Law Sch. 1949; m. Mary Anne Burnett 18 Nov. 1988; children (by previous marriage): Fred, David, Sarah, William, Nancy; COUNSEL, CHRMN. AND PARTNER EMERITUS, BORDEN & ELLIOT; (Partner 1957–92; Chrmn. 1980–90); Chrmn. Candn. Bd., Norwich Union Life Insurance Soc. 1986–93; Dir., Eastern Utilities Ltd.; Hilti (Canada) Ltd.; read law with Fennell McLean & Davis; called to Bar of Ont. 1949, of Sask. 1971; cr. Q.C. 1960; served with RCA and Royal Candn. Intelligence Corps 1943–46; Can., USA and Japan; mem. Corp., Trinity Coll.; Churchwarden, St. James Cathedral 1977–80; Fellow, Am. Coll. of Trial Lawyers; Chrmn., Can.-U.S. Ctte. 1986–90; mem. first Canada/U.S. Legal Exchange; mem. Candn. Bar Assn. (Chrmn. Ont. Br. 1969–70, Nat. Pres. 1974–75); Governor, Candn. Inst. for Advanced Legal Studies; Advocates' Soc. (Past Dir.); Internat. Assn. Ins. Counsel; Zeta Psi (Pres.); Anglican; recreations: tennis, golf; Clubs: York; National; Osler Bluff Ski; Toronto Hunt; Cutten Club (Guelph); Home: 350 Lonsdale Rd., Apt. 109, Toronto, Ont. M5P 1R6; Office: Scotia Plaza, 40 King St. W., Toronto, Ont. M5H 3Y4.

**SONEA, Sorin,** M.D., F.R.S.C.; educator; b. Cluj, Romania 14 March 1920; s. Leonida Eusebiu and Cornelia (Chibulcuteanu) S.; e. Univ. of Bucharest M.D. 1944; Univ. of Paris Dip. in Hygiene 1949; m. Rodica d. Petre and Valeria Vlad 2 Feb. 1946; children: Ioana, Peter, Michael, Alex; EMERITUS PROF. OF MICROBIOLOGY, UNIV. DE MONTREAL 1993– ; Asst. Prof. Univ. de Montréal 1950, Assoc. Prof. 1955, Prof. 1960, Head of Microbiol. & Immunol. 1964–79; recipient Candn. Soc. Microbiols. Award for Outstanding Contributions 1978; D.U. (honoris causa) Univ. du Québec 1988; co-author: 'Introduction a la nouvelle bacteriologie' 1980; 'A New Bacteriology' 1983; author: 'Le Strutture Biologiche Batteri' 1993'; Home: 4282 Badgley St., Montréal, Qué. H4P 1N8; Office: (C.P. 6128 Succ. A) Montréal, Qué. H3C 3J7.

**SONGHURST, Ruth Ann,** B.A.; computer software sales and marketing executive; b. Ingersoll, Ont. 27 Jan. 1948; d. Leslie George and Kathleen Ruth (Tribe) S.; e. Ingersoll Dist. Collegiate; Wellington College, Univ. of Guelph B.A. (Hons.) 1970; children: Harold George and Nichole Aleena Songhurst Soulis; VICE-PRESIDENT OF SALES AND MARKETING, MORTICE KERN SYSTEMS (MKS) 1987– ; Researcher, NATO 1970; Librarian 1971–72; Social Worker, Brantford Children's Aid Soc. 1973–75; pursued travel, freelance writing and started her family; Public Interest Research Group, Univ. of Waterloo 1979–81; Co-ord., Inst. for Computer Rsch., Centre of Excellence, Univ. of Waterloo 1981–85; joined MKS 1985; Principal 1987– ; speaker on export marketing & entrepreneurialism for External Affairs, Univ. of Waterloo, Wilfrid Laurier Univ. & McMaster Univ.; Founder, Computer Technology Network of Waterloo, Kitchener, Guelph & Cambridge areas; recreations: travel, cottage, swimming, literature; Office: 35 King St. N., Waterloo, Ont. N2J 2W9.

**SONNENBERG, Hugo,** P.Eng., B.SC., D.B.A., M.B.A.; executive; b. 1938; s. Gustav and Susanne S.; e. Univ. of Alta. B.Sc. (Civil Engn.) 1963; Univ. of W. Ont. M.B.A. 1969, D.B.A. 1966; m. Christa d. Rev. W. Kowalski; two s. Jeffery, Christopher; Pres. & C.E.O., Foundation Company of Canada Ltd. 1990; Dir., Candn. Nuclear Assoc.; held various constr. engn. positions incl. Shawinigan Group of Companies, Techman Ltd. Calgary, Bechtel Corp. San Francisco, Northern Utilities Ltd. Edmonton; Pres., Lummus Canada Inc. 1982–90; mem. Engn. Inst. Can.; Candn. Inst. Mining & Metall.; Assn. Prof. Engrs. Prov. Ont.; Assn. Prof. Engrs., Geols. & Geophysicists Alta.; Order of Engrs. of Quebec; Assn. of Profl. Engrs of New Brunswick; Home: 1451 Warren Dr., Oakville, Ont. L6J 5T7.

**SONNENFELD, Frederick-Carl Peter,** Rer.Nat.Dr.; university professor; b. Berlin 20 Jan. 1922; s. Leon and Clara (Quast) S.; e. Comenius Univ., Bratislava, Absolutorium Rer.Nat. 1947; Charles Univ., Prague, Dr.Rer.Nat. 1949; m. Jean E. d. Alexander and Elizabeth Brown 10 Aug. 1959; children: Stephen Peter, Margaret Jean; PROF., UNIV. OF WINDSOR 1966–89; Prof. Emeritus 1989– ; Geologist, sundry oil & mining cos. 1949–53; Imperial Oil Ltd. 1953–57; Shell Can. Ltd. 1958–63; Asst. Prof., Texas A&I Univ. 1963–66; Life Mem., Assoc. of Prof. Engrs., Geologists & Geophys. of Alta.; Mem., Marine Geol. & Geophys. Ctte., Internat. Comn. for Sci. Explor. of the Mediterranean; author: 'Brines and Evaporites' 1984 ('Rassoli i Evapority,' Russian transl. 1988); co-author with J.P. Perthuisot 'Brines and Evaporites' Short Course Notes No. 3 of 28th Internat. Geological Congress 1989; editor: 'Tethys, The Ancestral Mediterranean' 1980; Home: 383 Rankin Blvd., Windsor, Ont. N9B 2R6; Office: 400 Sunset Ave., Windsor, Ont. N9B 3P4.

**SOPER, Warren Y.,** B.A.; corporate director; b. Montreal, Que. 24 Jan. 1919; s. Harold Warren and Alice (Ross) S.; e. Lower Canada Coll., Montreal, Que.; St. Andrews Coll., Aurora, Ont., McGill Univ., B.A. 1942; m. Lilianne Binard; children: Warren Y., Jr., Jane Isabel; Chrmn. Calmont Leasing Ltd.; Dir., Can. Reynolds Metals Ltd.; Saturn Solutions Inc.; with Defence Industries Ltd., 1943–46; Vice Pres. & Dir., Pitfield MacKay Ross Ltd. 1946–86; Sub-Lieut. R.C.N.V.R.; Protestant; recreations: fishing, golf; Clubs: Mount Bruno Country; Royal Montreal Golf; Gulfstream Golf (Delray Beach, Fla.); Gulfstream Bath & Tennis; Toronto Golf (Toronto); Home: 1174 Dunany Rd., R.R. 6, Lachute, Que. J8H 3W8

**SOPINKA, The Honourable Mr. Justice John,** B.A., LL.B.; supreme court justice; b. Broderick, Sask. 19 Mar. 1933; s. Metro and Anastasia (Kikcio) S.; e. elem. sch. Hamilton, Ont.; Saltfleet H.S.; grad. summa cum laude with scholarships to Queen's Univ. and Univ. of Toronto; Univ. of Toronto B.A. 1955, LL.B. 1958; m. Marie Ethel Wilson 22 Dec. 1956; children: Randall John, Melanie Anne; JUSTICE, SUPREME COURT OF CANADA 1988– ; practiced law in Toronto 1960–88; appointed Q.C., Prov. of Ont. 1974; formerly mem. of Bars of Ont. 1960, Nfld. 1973, N.B. 1975, Sask. 1984, Alta. 1987, Yukon 1987, N.W.T. 1987; Special Lectr. Civil Procedure, Osgoode Hall Law Sch. 1974–82 and Univ. of Toronto Law Sch. 1976–84; Chief Couns., Comn. of Inquiry on Aviation Safety 1979–81; Chrmn., Task Force on Equal Opportunity in Athletics (Ont.); Couns., Comn. of Inquiry on RCMP Relationship with DNR-Taxation; Commission Counsel to the Estey Bank

Inquiry; apptd. Judge, Supreme Court of Canada 1988; author: 'The Trial of an Action' 1981; co-author 'The Law of Evidence in Canada' 1992; 'The Conduct of An Appeal' 1993; Dir., Hockey Canada; Judicial Fellow, Am. Coll. of Trial Lawyers; Mem., Bd. of Foreign Advisors, Ukrainian Legal Found.; formerly: Bencher, Law Soc. of Upper Canada; Chrmn., Ctte. on Advertising and Certification Bd.; Chrmn., Metrop. Toronto Police Complaints Bd.; mem. Bd. of Edn., Town of Oakville 1967–69; Halfback Varsity Blues Intercoll. Champions 1954; Toronto Argonauts 1955–57; Montreal Allouettes 1957–58; recreations: squash, tennis, jogging; Clubs: University; Oakville; Boulevard; Home: 161 Carleton St., Rockliffe Park, Ottawa, Ont. K1M 0G6; Office: Supreme Court of Canada, Ottawa, Ont K1A 0J1.

**SOPKO, Michael D.,** B.Eng., M.Eng., Ph.D.; mining executive; b. Montreal, Que. 22 Jan. 1939; s. John and Mary S. (both dec.); e. McGill Univ. B.Eng. 1960, M.Eng. 1961, Ph.D. 1964; m. Mary Raatikainen 28 Dec. 1979; children: David, Stuart, Andrew; CHRMN. & C.E.O., INCO LIMITED 1992– ; Jr. Engineer/Mgr., Inco (Copper Cliff, Ont.) 1964–73; Operations Mgr., EXMIBAL (Guatemala) 1973–78; Mgr., Copper Refinery (Copper Cliff) 1978–79; Vice-Pres., Smelting & Refining 1980–84; Pres., Ont. Div. 1985–88; Vice-Pres., Human Resources (Toronto) 1989–91; Pres., Inco Limited 1991–92; Dir., Inco Limited 1991– ; Bd. of Dirs., Toronto-Dominion Bank 1992– ; Exploraciones Y Explotaciones Mineras Izabal, S.A. (EXMIBAL) 1991–92; First Vice Chrmn., The Mining Assn. of Can. 1992– ; Chrmn., Nicel Devel. Inst. 1992– ; Mem., Candn. Inst. of Mining & metallurgy; Am. Inst. of Mining & Metallurgical Engrs.; Assn. of Profl. Engrs. of Ont.; recreations: golf; club: Bd. of Trade, Woodbridge; Home: 2240 Chancery Lane, Oakville, Ont.; Office: P.O. Box 44, Royal Trust Tower, Toronto-Dominion Centre, Toronto, Ont. M5K 1N4.

**SORBARA, Gregory,** M.P.P., LL.B.; politician; b. Toronto, Ont. 4 Sept. 1946; s. Sam and Grace (Chirchiglia) S.; e. St. Michael's Coll. Sch.; Univ. of Toronto; York Univ., Glendon Coll., Osgoode Hall Law Sch. LL.B. 1981; m. Katharine d. Ted and Oda Barlow 1947; children: Lucas, Carla, Ginger, Noelle, Nicholas, Martina; re-el. M.P.P. for York C. prov. g.e. 1990 (Opposition Critic); Min. of Cons. & Comm. 1989–90; Min. of Colls. & Univs. and Min. of Skills Devel., Ont. 1985–87; Min. of Labour and Min. responsible for Women's Issues, Ont. 1987–89; el. M.P.P. for York N. prov. g.e. 1985; re-el. M.P.P. York Centre prov. g.e. 1987; prior to el. served as Solr. Law firms Stikeman, Elliott and Tanzola & Sorbara; leadership candidate, Ont. Lib. Party 1992; Home: 99 Highland Lane, Richmond Hill, Ont. L4C 3S1; Office: Legislative Bldg., Queen's Park, Toronto, Ont. M7A 1A4.

**SORBARA, Joseph Dominic,** B.A., M.A., LL.B., Q.C.; solicitor; real estate executive; b. Toronto, Ont. 4 Apr. 1942; s. Samuel and Grace (Chirchiglia) S.; e. St. Michael's Coll. Sch. 1959; Univ. of Toronto, B.A. 1963, M.A. 1965; Osgoode Hall Law Sch., LL.B. 1968; m. Antoinette d. Antonio and Domenica Memme 19 Dec. 1987; children: Paul, Julia, Thomas; PARTNER, TANZOLA, SORBARA, MCCLELLAN & HANDLER 1971– ; articled to Robertson, Lane, etc. 1968–69; called to Ont. Bar 1970; employed by Lorenzetti, Marianie & Wolfe 1970–71; taught real estate transactions course, Osgoode Hall, York Univ. in 1970s; Co-founder, Dir., Industrial Properties - Limited Partnership 1980; active interest & involvement in family real estate business; Dir. & Chrmn., Multilingual TV (Toronto) Ltd. to 1993; Dir., Dominion Trust Co. (Mem., Credit Approval Ctte.) to 1993; Pres. & Dir., Adriatic Insur. Brokers Ltd.; Vice-Pres. & Dir., N.H.D. Develop. Ltd.; Director & V.P., Sam Sorbara Real Estate Ltd.; Pres., Sam-sor Enterprises Inc.; Dir. & Hon. Chrmn., Security Trading Inc., & other personal & family corps.; Ont. Scholar 1959; Osgoode Hall Prize in Contract Law 1966; Ont. scholarship for grad. studies 1964; Vice-Chair and Gov., York Univ.; Dir., York Univ. Devel. Corp.; Dir., Toronto Symphony; Past Chrmn., Humber Coll. of Applied Arts & Technol.; Past Pres. (1974) Rotary Club of Toronto, Black Creek; recreations: boating, jogging, winemaking; clubs: Granite, Royal Candn. Yacht, Albany of Toronto; Island Yacht; Home: 19 Cedarwood Ave., Toronto, Ont. M2L 1L7; Office: 3700 Steeles Ave. W., Suite 800, Woodbridge, Ont. L4L 8M9.

**SORENSEN, Lynda;** executive asst.; consultant; nurse; b. Sask. 14 May 1947; d. Frederic Anthony and Christine Margaret (Ridd) Klotz; e. Battleford High Sch. 1965; Royal Alexandra Sch. of Nursing 1968; m. Arthur s. Isabel and Carl Sorensen 3 Feb. 1968; children: Ernestine, Jodi, Ridd; Exec. Asst. to Hon. S. Kakwi; Exec. Consultant Dene Nation 1985–87; el. M.L.A. for Yellowknife South NWT 1979–84; Dir. Canada Post Corp. 1981–84; Chrmn. Labour Standards Bd. NWT 1981–84; Standing Comte. on Finance & Pub. Accounts Chrmn. Leg. Assembly 1979–84; Mem. Bd. NWT Community Services Corp.; Chrmn. Sir John Franklin School Soc. 1985–87; Pres. and founding mem., Business and Professional Women's Assn. of Yellowknife; Former Pres. Nat. Women's Lib. Comm.; Pres. NWT Lib. Party 1981–83; Co-Chrmn. Nat. Lib. Policy Convention 1982; Pres. NWT Women's Liberal Comn.; Chrmn., Ethel Blondin MP Campaign 1988 and 1993; Co-Chrmn., NWT Turner Leadership Campaign 1984; Western Candidate Liberal Candidate 1984; prior to 1979 Dir. of Nursing, Stanton Yellowknife Hosp. and first Northern Consumer Advocate and Broadcaster; mem. Candn. Research Inst. Advanc. Women; Reg'd Nurses Assn. NWT; recreations: reading, cross-country skiing; Home: 9 Denison Court, Yellowknife, N.W.T. 3L3; Office: Box 1320, Yellowknife, N.W.T. X1A 2L9.

**SORENSEN, Stephen Harvey,** B.Comm.; mining executive; b. Toronto, Ont. 16 Nov. 1950; e. Queen's Univ., B.Comm. (Hons.) 1976; Chrmn., Pres. & C.E.O., Pioneer Metals Corp. 1989– ; Registered Rep., Pitfield McKay Ross Ltd. 1977–82; Nesbitt Thomson Bongard Ltd. (U.K.) 1982–86; Dir., Chief Finan. Offr. & Sr. Vice-Pres., Corp. Devel., present firm 1986–89; Pres. & Chief Extve. Offr., Big Bar Gold Corp. 1989– ; recreations: skiing, tennis, golf; club: Jericho Tennis Club (Vanc.); Home: 1160 Burrard St., Suite 804, Vancouver, B.C.; Office: 1770 – 401 W. Georgia St., Vancouver, B.C. V6B 5A1.

**SORESTAD, Glen Allan,** B.Ed., M.Ed.; writer; b. Vancouver, B.C. 21 May 1937; s. John and Myrtle Tillene (Dalshaug) S.; e. Teachers' Coll. 1956–57; Univ. of Sask., B.Ed. 1963, M.Ed. 1976 (Hons.); m. Sonia d. Stephen and Josie Talpash 17 Sept. 1960; Bank Clerk, CIBC 1954–55; Study Supr., Antelope Park Sch. 1955–56; Elem. Sch. Teacher, Yorkton 1957–60, 1963–67; Brooks, Alta. 1960–61; Saskatoon 1967–81; Co-founder & Pres., Thistledown Press 1975– ; Hilroy Fellowship for orgn. of Prairie Writers Workshop 1976; Founders Award from Sask. Writers Guild 1990; part-time creative writing teacher & semester lectr.; Writer-in-Res., Saskatoon Public Lib. 1988–89; Weyburn Public Library; Swift Current Sch. Dist.; public readings nationwide, California, Arizona, Minnesota, New Mexico, Nevada, Oklahoma, Texas, Wyoming, Washington State and in France; mem., Writers Union of Canada; Internat. P.E.N.; League of Candn. Poets (Extve. Mem. 6 yrs.); Sask. Writers Guild, Prairie Pubs. Group (Pres. 1984–86; Literary Press Group (Extve. Mem. 2 yrs.); Assn. of Candn. Pubs. (former Council Mem.); author: 'West Into Night' 1991; 'Air Canada Owls' 1990; 'Stalking Place: Poems Across Borders' (with Peter Christensen & Jim Harris) 1988; 'Hold the Rain in Your Hands' 1985, 'Jan Lake Poems' 1984, 'Ancestral Dances' 1979, 'Pear Seeds in my Mouth' 1977, 'Prairie Pub Poems' 1976, 'Wind Songs' 1975 (poetry); co-editor: 'Something to Declare' 1994; 'In Contexts: Anthology Three' 1990; 'More Strawberries' 1990; 'Contexts 3' 1984, 'Sunlight & Shadows' 1974, 'Tigers of the Snow,' 1973, 'Strawberries & Other Secrets' 1970 (anthol.); 'The Last Map is the Heart' (anthology of W. Candn. fiction) 1989; recreations: fishing, travelling; Home: 668 East Pl., Saskatoon, Sask. S7J 2Z5.

**SOROKA, Lewis Arthur,** M.A., Ph.D.; educator; b. Montreal, Que. 9 March 1943; s. Jack G. and Mildred (Solomon) S.; e. McGill Univ. B.A. 1964, M.A. 1967, Ph.D. (Econ.) 1970; m. Anne d. Ernest and Sara Bruker 17 Dec. 1967; two s. Stuart, Aaron; ASSOC. PROF. OF ECON., BROCK UNIV. 1974– ; Lectr. present Univ. 1967, Asst. Prof. 1969, Dean of Social Sciences 1981–91; Visiting Scholar Univ. of Kent, Canterbury 1974; consultant on prov. and mun. taxation; mem. Candn. Econ. Assn.; Candn. Tax Foundation; Candn. Regional Science Assn.; recreations: sailing, skiing; Club: Dalhousie Yacht; Home: 193 Woodside Dr., St. Catharines, Ont.; Office: St. Catharines, Ont. L2T 1X8.

**SOSKOLNE, Colin Lionel,** B.Sc., B.Sc.Hons., Ph.D., F.A.C.E.; epidemiologist; b. Johannesburg, S. Africa 17 Dec. 1946; s. Myer Lipe and Lily (Slabe) S.; e. Univ. of the Witwatersrand, Johannesburg B.Sc. 1970, B.Sc.Hons. 1971; Univ. of Pennsylvania, Pa. Ph.D. 1982; Fellow, Am. Coll. of Epidemiology 1988; DIR. EPIDEMIOLOGY PROGRAM, DEPT OF PUBLIC HEALTH SCIENCES, FACULTY OF MEDICINE, UNIV. OF ALBERTA 1985– and PROF. 1990– ; teaching, research, consulting, service; Assoc. Prof. Univ. of Toronto 1982–88; Assoc. Prof., Univ. of Alta. 1985–90; Statistician S. African Human Sci. Rsch. Counc. 1970–73; Biostatistician Univ. of the Witwatersrand Med. Sch. 1970–73; apptd. Head Dept. of Epidemiology and Biostatistics, S. African Med. Rsch. Counc. Nat. Rsch. Inst. for Occupational Diseases (where est. a computerized cardio-respiratory pathology info. system) 1973–77; Teaching Fellow, Univ. of Pennsylvania 1978–82; Dir. Epidemiology Research Unit, Ont. Cancer Treatment and Research Foundation, Univ. of Toronto 1982–85; public and professional education in AIDS 1982–87; studies of association between occupational exposure to sulfuric acid and the development of laryngeal cancer; author numerous publs. in profl. jours.; prime mover for establishing profl. ethics guidelines for epidemiologists since 1984; Dir. Metrop. Toronto Condominium Corp. No. 565 1983–85; Dir., Riverwind Strata Title Housing Co-operative Ltd., Edmonton 1989–91; awarded Annual Student Prize, Soc. for Epidemiologic Rsch. 1983; recreations: gym, philately, hiking; Home: 2107, 11135 - 83 Ave., Edmonton, Alta. T6G 2C6; Office: 13 – 103 Clinical Sciences Bldg., Univ. of Alberta, Edmonton, Alta. T6G 2G3.

**SOTEROFF, George B.,** B.A., B.J.; real estate executive; b. Toronto, Ont. 6 May 1943; s. John and Mary (Costas) S.; e. Lawrence Park Coll. Inst. 1962; Carleton Univ. B.A. 1966, B.J. 1967; Internat. Inst. Japan 1988; m. Susan d. Brig. Harold E. and Julia Brown 26 Aug. 1967; children: Tracey, Mark; SENIOR VICE PRESIDENT, COMMUNICATIONS AND CORPORATE AFFAIRS, Vice President, London Insurance Group; Asst. City Ed. The Toronto Telegram 1967–71; Chief of Info. Environment Can. 1971–72; Vice Pres. Pub. Relations Canadian Imperial Bank of Commerce 1972–84; Cons. Govt./Invest./Pub. Relations 1984–86; Vice Pres. Royal LePage Ltd. 1986–89; Pres. & Dir., Royal LePage Asia, 1989–91, Vice Pres. Asian Initiatives, London Life, Vice Pres. Shin Fu Life 1991–93; recreations: golf, tennis, sailing, oenology, literature; Clubs: Ontario; Home: 777 Wellington St., London, Ont. N6A 3S4.

**SOUBLIÈRE, Jean-Pierre,** B.Com., M.B.A.; executive; b. Ottawa, Ont. 10 Jan. 1947; s. Jean Horace and Cecile Marie (Blais) S.; e. Univ. of Ottawa, B.Com. 1967; Univ. of B.C., M.B.A. 1971; m. Cathie d. Andy and Marguerite Anderson 22 Nov. 1968; children: Daniel, Alexandre, Anna, Eric; CHAIRMAN, SHL SYSTEMHOUSE CANADA/ASIA, SHL SYSTEMHOUSE INC. 1988– ; Pres., SHL Systemhouse Canada 1988–93; Exec. Vice Pres., Candn. Operations 1986–88; Analyst/Programmer, Northern Telecom Ltd. 1967–69; Sr. Systems Analyst, Carleton Univ. 1969–70; Canada Post 1971–77, Acting Dir. Financial & Adm. Systems, Mgr. Environmental Forecasting, Mktg. Services; joined present Co. 1977 serving as Vice Pres. Human Resources, Gen. Mgr. Nat. Capital Region, Mng. Cons.; Lectr. MIS Univ. of Qué. 1977–78; Chrmn. High Technol. Div. Un. Way 1986–87; Campaign Chrmn., Un. Way 1989; Former Mem. of Bd. of Dirs., Ottawa Carleton Bd. of Trade; Former Mem., Ottawa Gen. Hosp. Found.; Pres., Harmony Foundation; Bd. of Govs., Montfort Hosp.; Mem. Bd. of Dirs., Information Tech. Assn. of Can. (ITAC); Ottawa-Carleton United Way; CENET (The Carlton Education Network Inc.); The World Trade Centre; OCEDCO; UniMédia; Presidential Advisory Council, Carleton Univ.; Club: Rideau; Home: 21 Condor Dr., Ottawa, Ont. K1V 9C1; Office: 50 O'Connor St., Ste. 501, Ottawa, Ont. K1P 6L2.

**SOUBRY, Paul Marie Alfons Joseph;** farm equipment executive; b. Bruges, Belgium 4 March 1930; s. Reginald and Jeanne (Persoons) S.; e. St. Hadelin Coll. Vise, Belgium; Univ. of Waterloo, McMaster Univ. Mgmt. & Mktg. Studies; The Warthon Sch.; Export Inst.; Univ. of Toronto; m. Louise Laurette d. Albert and Blanche (Sage) Fortier 21 Dec. 1957; children: Mark Reginald, Albert Gregory, Ann Marie, Paul Marie Jr., Marina Louise, Veronique Jeanne; DIR. & GEN. MGR., FORD NEW HOLLAND CANADA LTD. 1989– ; Export Trainee, Cockshutt Farm Equipment Ltd. 1951 becoming Br. Mgr. Montreal, Export Mgr., Mktg. Services Mgr. (Co. acquired by White Motor Corp. 1962, renamed White Farm Equipment Co. of Canada); apptd. Mktg. Devel. Mgr., Internat. Sales Mgr., Vice Pres. Mktg. Can., Pres. 1976; Pres. & C.E.O. Versatile Manufacturing Ltd. Winnipeg 1977; Vice Pres. Agric. Operations Versatile Corp. Vancouver 1978; Pres., Versatile Farm Equipment Co. 1978; Gen. Mgr., Versatile Farm Equipment Operations, Ford New Holland Canada Ltd. 1987; Past Chrmn. and Dir. Candn. Farm & Ind. Inst. 1990; Past Chrmn., Prairie Implement Manufacturers Assoc.; Bd. Trustee, Victoria Hospital; Centre for Internat. Bus. Studies for Univ. of Manitoba; mem. Winnipeg C. of C.; Mem., Industrial and Transportation Equipment SAGIT; Candn. Export Assn. (Chrmn. 1982–84, Dir.); Manitoba Economic Innovation and Technology Council, Winnipeg 1989; Dir., Fiatallis (Canada) Ltd.; recreations: golf, photography, gardening; Clubs: St. Charles Country; Manitoba; Home: 63

Ridgedale Cres., Winnipeg, Man. R3R 0B2; Office: 1260 Clarence Ave., Winnipeg, Man. R3T 1T3.

**SOUPCOFF, Murray,** B.A., M.A., Phil.M.; sociologist; writer; b. Toronto, Ont. 15 Feb. 1943; s. Louis Edward and Rose (Polien) S.; e. Univ. of Toronto, B.A. 1964, M.A. 1967, Phil.M. 1969; m. Bonnie d. Leon and Elsie Pape 29 Aug. 1966; one d.: Marni Joanne; PRESIDENT, M. SOUPCOFF & ASSOCIATES RESEARCH CONSULTANTS; Founding Mem. & Assoc. Cons., Ian Sone & Assoc. Ltd. 1969–81; Sr. Assoc., The Sutcliffe Group Inc. 1981–86; Creator, Head Writer & Prod., CBC Radio series, 'Inside from the Outside' 1969–76; Weekly CBC Radio, Panelist, 'Yes You're Wrong!' 1976–78; author: 'Canada 1984' 1979; co-author: 'Good Buy Canada' 1975; Commentator on such CBC Radio shows as 'Metro Morning,' 'Peter Gzowski Show,' 'Morningside,' 'Sunday Morning' and 'Commentary' 1974–80; associate ed.: 'Toronto Computes'; Innovations columnist: 'Globe & Mail'; Home: 79 Castle Knock Rd., Toronto, Ont. M5N 2J8.

**SOURKES, Theodore Lionel,** O.C., M.Sc., Ph.D., F.R.S.C.; educator; b. Montreal, Que. 21 Feb. 1919; s. Irving and Fanny (Golt) S.; e. McGill Univ. B.Sc. 1939, M.Sc. 1946; Queen's Univ. 1940–41; Cornell Univ. Ph.D. 1948; m. Shena d. Abraham Rosenblatt, Toronto, Ont. 17 Jan. 1943; children: Barbara May, Myra June; PROF. EMERITUS, McGILL UNIV. 1991– ; Dir. Lab. of Neurochem. Allan Mem. Inst. of Psychiatry; author 'Biochemistry of Mental Disease' 1962; 'Nobel Prize Winners in Medicine and Physiology' 1966; over 360 scient. articles biochem. of nervous system and mental disease; mem. many biochem., pharmacol. and neuroscience organs.; Recipient, 1st Heinz Lehmann Award, Can. College of Neuropsychopharmacology, 1982; awarded the Order of Andrés Bello, First Category, by the Govt. of Venezuela in recognition of his valuable contribution to the development of science, and particularly of neuroscience, in their country 1987; honoured by 'T.L. Sourkes (Internat.) Symposium' Montreal, 1988, and 'Internat. Symposium on 'Neurotransmitter Actions and Interactions' Albufeira, Portugal 1989; recip., 1990 Medal of the Can. Coll. of Neuropsychopharmacology; D.U. (honoris causa) Univ. of Ottawa 1990; Officer, Order of Canada 1993; awarded Commemorative Medal for 125th Anniversary of Candn. Confederation 1993; Office: 1033 Pine Ave W., Montreal, Que. H3A 1A1.

**SOUSTER, Raymond;** poet; b. Toronto, Ont. 1921; first works appeared in Montreal mag. 'First Statement' 1942 and later in 'Unit of Five' 1944; author of: 'When We Are Young' 1946; 'Go to Sleep, World' 1947; 'The Winter of Time' (novel pub. under psuedonym 'Raymond Holmes') 1949; 'City Hall Street' 1951; 'Shake Hands with the Hangman: Poems 1940–52' 1953; 'A Dream that is Dying' 1954; 'Walking Death' 1955; 'For What Time Slays' 1955; 'Selected Poems' (ed. by Louis Dudek) 1956; 'Crêpe-Hangers Carnival: Selected Poems 1955–58' 1958; 'A Local Pride' 1962; 'Place of Meeting: Poems 1958–60' 1962; 'The Colour of the Times' (Gov. Gen's Award for Poetry in English) 1964; 'Ten Elephants on Yonge Street' 1965; 'As Is' 1967; 'Lost and Found: Uncollected Poems' 1968; 'So Far So Good: Poems 1938–68' 1969; 'The Years' 1971; 'Selected Poems' 1972; 'On Target' (novel pub. under pseud. 'John Holmes') 1972; 'Change-up' 1974; 'Double-Header' 1975; 'Rain-Check' 1975; 'Extra Innings' 1977; 'Hanging In: New Poems' 1979; 'Collected Poems of Raymond Souster: Vol. One 1940–55' 1980, 'Vol. Two 1955–1962' 1981, 'Vol. Three 1962–1974' 1982, 'Vol. Four 1974–1979' 1983, 'Vol. Five 1977–82' 1984; 'Going the Distance: New Poems 1979–82' 1983; 'Queen City: Photographs by Bill Brooks and Poems by Raymond Souster' 1984; 'Jubilee of Death: The Raid on Dieppe, a poem for many voices' 1984; 'Flight of the Roller Coaster: Poems for Children' 1985; 'It Takes All Kinds: New Poems' 1986; 'The Eyes of Love' 1987; 'Asking for More' 1988; 'Collected Poems of Raymond Souster: Vol. Six 1982–86' 1989; 'Running Out the Clock' 1991; 'Collected Poems of Raymond Souster: Vol. Seven 1987–88' 1992; 'Riding the Long Black Horse' 1993; 'Old Bank Notes' 1993; co-author (with Douglas Alcorn) 'From Hell to Breakfast' 1980; Co-ed. mag. 'Direction' 1943–46; Ed. mags. 'Contact' 1952–54 and 'Combustion' 1957–60; Ed. 'Poets '56' 1956; 'New Wave Canada' anthology 1966; 'Windflower': Selected Poems of Bliss Carman, with introductions by Douglas Lochhead and Raymond Souster 1986; co-ed. (with Douglas Lochhead) 'Made in Canada' anthology 1970; '100 Poems of Nineteenth Century Canada' 1974; (with Richard Woollatt) 'Generation Now' (experimental high sch. poetry textbook) 1970; (with R. Woollatt) 'Sights & Sounds' (a jr. poetry text) 1972; 'These Loved These Hated Lands' 1975; 'Vapour and Blue' (poetry of W.W.

Campbell, selected and introd. by R. Souster) 1978; 'Comfort of the Fields' (poetry of A. Lampman, selected and introd. by R. Souster) 1979; (with R. Woollatt) 'Poems of A Snow-Eyed Country' (anthology) 1979; 'Powassan's Drum': Selected Poems of Duncan Campbell Scott, selected and introduced by Douglas Lochhead and Raymond Souster 1986; served in 2nd World War. R.C.A.F.; retired from Candn. Imperial Bank of Comm. after 45 yrs. service; apptd. Poet-in-Residence, University Coll., Univ. of Toronto 1984–85; former Chrmn. and a Co-Founder, League of Candn. Poets; Home: 39 Baby Point Rd., Toronto, Ont. M6S 2G2.

**SOUTHALL, Paul Albert,** B.A., C.A.; financial executive; b. Hamilton, Ont. 30 April 1934; s. Clarence G. and Rita M. (Brooke) S.; e. Royal Military College of Canada B.A. 1956; m. Barbara Jane d. Ralph and Phyllis Lumsden 19 Nov. 1960; children: Patricia, Peter, Andrew, Sarah; Managing Dir. and Chief Financial Offr., Commcorp Financial Services Inc. 1991; Clarkson Gordon & Co. 1956–67 (C.A. 1960); Vice-Pres. & Dir., The Hamilton Group Limited 1967–80; Vice-Pres. & Dir., Citibank Leasing Canada Limited 1980–87; Extve. Vice-Pres. & Dir., Norex Leasing Inc. 1987–91; Trustee, Chedoke McMaster Hospitals (Chair, Finance Ctte. & Hon. Treas.); Dir., Renascent Found.; Mem., Financial Extves. Inst. of Canada; Past Pres., Hamilton Chapter; recreations: sailing, travel; clubs: The Hamilton, Bronte Harbour Yacht; Home: 4476 Tremineer Ave., Burlington, Ont. L7L 1H7.

**SOUTHAM, (Mrs.) Audrey Goodwin,** B.A.; school principal (ret.); b. Montreal, Que. 12 Oct. 1919; d. William Carlyle and Ida Charlotte (Walker) Goodwin; e. Long Island, N.Y., 1925–37; McGill Univ., B.A. 1941; Ont. Coll. of Educ., Teaching Cert. 1965; m. 1stly, Surgeon Lieut. John E. Powell, R.C.N.V.R. (d. 1942); m. 2ndly, Basil G. Southam (div.); children: Sandra (Mrs. R.S. White), Linda (Mrs. D.W. Tait), Carlyle, Judith (Mrs. W.G. McMillan), Neal (Mrs. T.Y. O'Neill); Teacher of Eng. and Hist., Hillfield-Strathallan Colls., Hamilton, 1964–68; Headmistress 1968–72; Principal, Havergal Coll. 1972–75; served overseas with Candn. Red Cross Corps (V.A.D.) during World War II; loaned to Brit. Red Cross serving in Eng. hosp.; Address: 178 Blair Lane, Ancaster, Ont. L9G 1B7.

**SOUTHAM, Gordon Hamilton,** O.C. (1977), B.A.; retired public servant; b. Ottawa, Ont. 19 Dec. 1916; s. of Wilson Mills S.; e. Univ. of Toronto, B.A. 1939; Oxford, 1939 (Modern Hist.); LL.D., Trent 1977; Carleton 1978; D.C.L. King's Coll. 1981; D.U. Ottawa 1986; m. 1stly Jacqueline, d. Pierre Lambert-David, Paris, France, 15 April 1940 (divorced); children: Peter, Christopher, Jennifer, Michael; 2ndly Gro Mortensen, Oslo, Norway, 1968 (divorced); children: Henrietta, Gordon; 3rdly Marion Tantot, Paris, France, 1981; served in 2nd World War; Offr. Cadet, Royal Arty., 1939; Lieut., R.C.A., 1940; served in U.K., Italy, N.W. Europe; discharged, 1945 with rank of Capt.; Mentioned in Despatches; Reporter, 'The Times,' London, 1945–46; Edit. Writer, 'The Citizen,' Ottawa, 1946–47; joined Dept. of External Affairs 1948; Third Secy., Stockholm, Aug. 1949; Chargé d'Affaires a.i. Warsaw, March 1959, Ambassador to Poland, 1960–62; Head, Information Div., Dept. External Affairs, 1962; Coordinator, Candn. Centre for the Performing Arts (now National Arts Centre), Feb. 1964; Dir. Gen., Nat. Arts Centre 1967–77; Chrmn., Cdn. Mediterranean Inst. (Athens, Cairo and Rome) 1980–93, Hon. Fellow 1992, Hon. Chrmn. 1993; Chrmn. Official Residences Council 1985–93; Chancellor, Univ. of King's Coll. 1988; mem. ex officio of Canadiana Fund 1990–93; Co-Chrmn., Task Force on Military History Museums 1990; Hon. Chrmn., Rideau Canal Museum 1992; Dir., Canadian Battle of Normandy Foundation 1992; Club: Rideau; Anglican; Home: (Summer) 'All is Best' Portland, Ont. K0G 1V0 and (Winter) Le Mail, 26230 Grignan, France.

**SOUTHERN, Ronald D.,** B.Sc., industrial executive; b. Calgary, Alta. 25 July 1930; s. Samuel Donald and Alexandra Cuthill (MacDonald) S.; e. Stanley Jones Sch. (1936–44) and Crescent Heights High Sc. (1944–48), Calgary, Alta.; Univ. of Alta., B.Sc. 1953, LL.D. (Honoris Causa) 1991; LL.D. (Honoris Causa), Calgary Univ. 1976; m. Margaret Elizabeth, d. Charles Visser, Calgary, Alta., 30 July 1954; children: Nancy Christine, Linda Anne; CHAIRMAN AND CHIEF EXTVE. OFFR., ATCO LTD. (the parent of three companies active in the manufacture of transportable industrial shelters and related products, property management, electric utility operations, gas utility operations, oil and gas exploration and production, and gas marketing and processing); Chrmn. of the Bd. & Dir., Candn. Utilities Ltd.; Chrmn., Akita Drilling Ltd.; Dir., Candn. Pacific Ltd.; Lafarge Corp.; Royal Insurance Limited; Fletcher Chal-

lenge Canada Ltd.; Imasco Limited; PWA Corp.; Xerox of Canada Inc.; ATCO Ltd.; Fletcher Challenge Limited, New Zealand; Chrysler-Canada Ltd.; Hon. Assoc., Calgary Exhn. and Stampede Bd. in Can.; Mem. of Candn. Council Conference Bd. of Canada; Univ. of Calgary's Chancellor's Club; Assoc., Candn. German Chamber of Industry and Commerce Inc.; Hon. mem., Assn. of Prof. Engineers, Geologists & Geophysicists; Cdn. mem., Trilateral Commn.; rec'd The Candn. Tourism Medallion in recognition of significant contribution to Canada's tourism industry 1983; recipient Communications and Leadership Award (Toastmasters Internat.) 1988; Internat. Distinguished Entrepreneur Award 1990; Member of the Order of the British Empire; Member of the Order of Canada; Home: 67 Massey Pl. S.W., Calgary, Alta. T2V 2G7; Office: 1600 – 909 – 11th Ave. S.W., Calgary, Alta. T2R 1N6.

**SOUTHEY, Hon. James Bonham Strange,** B.A.; judge; b. Bowmanville, Ont. 26 Oct. 1926; s. Edmund Charles Clay and Mary Campbell (Strange) S.; e. Bowmanville (Ont.) High Sch.; Trinity Coll. Sch. Port Hope, Ont.; Queen's Univ. B.A. 1948; Osgoode Hall Law Sch. 1951 (Silver Medal); m. Winifred Mary Joyce d. Hugh M. Hughson, Ottawa, Ont., 27 June 1953; children: Sara Joyce, Robert George Hughson, Peter McBean, Edmund Campbell Armstrong, Michael Hugh Strange; ONTARIO COURT OF JUSTICE (GENERAL DIVISION); apptd. to High Court of Justice, Supreme Court of Ontario in 1975; Read law with the late C.F.H. Carson, Q.C.; called to Bar of Ont. 1951, Bar of Sask. 1964; cr. Q.C. 1966; practised law with Tilley, Carson & Findlay and predecessor firms Toronto 1951–75; served with Candn. Army 1945; Life Gov. Trinity Coll. Sch.; Past Pres., Candn. Judges Conf.; Past Pres. Lawyers Club Toronto; mem' Candn. Bar Assn.; Phi Delta Phi; Anglican; recreations: tennis, golf; Clubs: Toronto Golf; Badminton & Racquet; University; Home: 143 Rosedale Hts. Dr., Toronto, Ont. M4T 1C7; Office: Osgoode Hall, Toronto, Ont.

**SOWARD, Reginald Harvey,** Q.C.; b. Minden, Ont., 3 June 1907; s. Hubert Edward Thomas and Lue Alberta Victoria (Stinson) S.; e. Univ. of Toronto, B.A. (Mod. Hist.) 1928; Osgoode Hall, Toronto, 1931; m. Lillian Ruth, d. Prof. George A. Cornish, Toronto, 14 Oct. 1931; Counsel, McLaughlin, Markle, May, Phibbs (formerly McLaughlin, Soward, Morden, & Bales) 1984–91; Retired; Dir. and Vice-Pres. Victoria & Grey Trust Co. until 1982, Hon. Dir. 1983; mem. of Council, Wycliffe Coll., Toronto; Chancellor, Diocese of Toronto, 1949–75; Chancellor to the Primate 1977–86; mem., Gen. Synod of Ang. Ch., since 1943; Anglican Award of Merit 1986; read law with R.J. McLaughlin, K.C.; began practice with McLaughlin, Johnston, Moorhead & Macaulay 1931; mem. of firm 1939; mem., N. York Sch. Bd., 1937–40; Lawyers Club of Toronto (Pres. 1943–44); mem., Ruskin Lit. & Debating Soc. 1936– ; Assoc. Ed., 5th ed., Holmstead and Langton's 'Ontario Judicature Act' 1940; Ed., 5th ed., Bicknell & Seager's 'Division Court Manual' 1938; has contrib. articles to Canadian Encycl. Digest of Law (Ont.); I.O.F. (Past Chief Ranger); P. Conservative; Anglican; recreations: gardening, travelling, reading; Club: Albany; Home: 6 De Vere Gardens, Toronto, Ont. M5M 3E5.

**SOWERBY, Ronald E.,** B.Comm., C.A.; financial executive; b. New Westminster, B.C. 26 June 1943; s. Eric Grainger and Elsie Vera (Fulton) Sowerby; e. Lester Pearson H.S. 1961; Univ. of B.C. B.Comm. 1969; Inst. of C.A.s of B.C., C.A. 1969; m. Lynne d. Gustav and Tekla Bergman 26 Aug. 1967; children: Craig, Scott, Kevin; EXTVE. VICE-PRES., FINANC, CHIEF FINAN. OFFR. & SEC., TCG INTERNATIONAL INC. (formerly Trans Canada Glass Ltd.) 1970– ; articled with Chadwick Potts & Co., C.A. to 1969; Chief Finan. Offr., Sec.-Treas. & Dir., Glenayre Electronics Ltd.; Vice-Pres. & Dir., Autostock Inc.; Chrmn. Sapperton Baptist Ch.; Home: 2213 Sorrento Dr., Coquitlam, B.C. V3K 6H6; Office: 28th fl., 4710 Kingsway, Burnaby, B.C. V5H 4M2.

**SPAFFORD, Paul B.,** B.A.Sc., M.B.A.; investment banker; b. Toronto, Ont. 4 Apl. 1948; s. the late Harry D. and Doris I. (Watt) S.; e. Univ. of Waterloo, B.A.Sc. 1971; Univ. of W. Ont., M.B.A. 1976; VICE PRES. AND DIR. WOOD GUNDY INC. 1982– ; joined Corporate Finance Dept. present firm 1976, Dep. Mgr. 1982, Dir. (responsible for mergers and acquisitions) 1984; recreations: sailing, skiing; Clubs: Craigleith Ski; National Yacht; Fitness Inst.; Home: 52 Rochester Ave., Toronto, Ont. M4N 1N8; Office: BCE Place, Canada Trust Tower, P.O. Box 500, Toronto, Ont. M5J 2S8.

**SPALDING, J. Stuart,** C.A.; chartered accountant; b. Edinburgh, Scotland 23 Nov. 1934; came to Can. 1957;

e. C.A., Scotland, 1957; C.A., Montreal 1962; m. Louise Bourgeau 7 May 1960; children: Eric, Martin, Elizabeth, Valerie; Retired Exec. Vice Pres. Finance, BCE Inc. 1983–90; Vice Pres. and Treasurer, Bell Canada since 1979; Treasurer 1976; Gov., Candn. Investor Protection Fund; Past. Pres., Montreal Soc. of Financial Analysts; Past Chrmn., Financial Executive Institute, Canada; Clubs: Mt. Bruno Country; Montreal Indoor Tennis; Home: 54 Aberdeen Ave., Westmount, Que. H3Y 3A4.

**SPALDING, Jeffrey John,** B.A., M.A., M.F.A.; artist; b. Edinburgh, Scotland 5 Nov. 1951; s. John and Dolores Anderson Hunt (Laidlaw) S.; e. Univ. of Guelph, B.A. 1972; Ohio State Univ., M.A. 1975; Nova Scotia Coll. of Art & Design, M.F.A. 1976; m. Marianne d. Jack and Annette Gerlinger 13 June 1985; children: Lauren Adelle, Isa Renée, Margritte Raila, Yvonne Michele, Jennifer Lynn; DIR., ART GALLERY, UNIV. OF LETHBRIDGE 1981– ; exhibitor of paintings in solo & group exhibs. perennially since 1973; works incl. in key public collections: Nat. Gall. of Can., Art Gall. of Greater Vict., Vancouver Art Gall., Edmonton Art Gall., Art Gall. of Hamilton, Robert McLaughlin Art Gall., Mackenzie Art Gall., Glenbow Mus., Mendel Art Gall., Can. Counc. Art Bank, Banff Ctr., Alta. Art Found.; Canadn. Embassy Washington; Asst. Curator, Art Gallery of N.S. 1976; Dir., Anna Leonowens Art Gallery, N.S. Coll. of Art & Design 1977; Chief Curator of Art. Glenbow Mus. 1978–80; Art Teacher, Ohio State Univ. 1975; N.S. Coll. of Art 1976–77; Banff Ctr. 1983; York Univ. 1986; Univ. of Lethbridge 1981– ; Guest Curator/Adjudicator/Adv. for countless exhibs., comns., artist awards, art mags. & many nat. orgns. incl. 49th Parallel Ctr. for Contemporary Art (NY), Calgary 1988 Olympics, City of Lethbridge, City of Calgary Sculpture Comp.; author: 'Tim Zuck' 1976, 'Coasts, the Sea and Canadian Art' 1977, 'Max Ernst' 1979, 'Silversmithing in Canadian History' 1979, 'John Will' 1979, 'Aspects of Canadian Painting in the Seventies' 1980 (catalogues); Curator, Canada's Visual Arts Exhib. for EXPO 93, Korea: 'Reflecting Paradise'; Home: Oakshores, R.R. 3, Bobcaygeon, Ont. K0M 1A0; Office: 4401 University Dr., Lethbridge, Alta. T1K 3M4.

**SPANOS, Nicholas Peter,** Ph.D.; professor of psychology; b. Boston, Mass. 15 Jan. 1942; s. Peter Nicholas and Pauline (Demas) S.; e. Saugus H.S. 1960; Boston Univ. B.A. 1964; Northeastern Univ. M.A. 1968; Boston Univ. Ph.D. 1974; single; PROF., DEPT. OF PSYCHOL., CARLETON UNIV. 1981– ; Clin. Cons. & Psychother., Medfield State Hosp. 1967–75; Dir., Clin. Serv., Boston Psychol. Assoc. 1967–73; Rsch. Assoc., Medfield Found. 1967–73; Sr. Rsch. Scientist 1973–75; Lectr., Massasoit Community Coll. 1970–71; Dir., Lab. for Experimental Hypnosis, Carleton Univ. 1975– ; Asst. Prof. 1975–78; Assoc. Prof. 1978–81; Full Prof. 1981– ; Ed. Bd., 'Imagination, Cognition and Personality' 1980– ; Cons. Ed., 'Brit. J. of Exper. and Clin. Hypnosis' 1982– ; Carleton Univ. Scholarly Achievement Award 1977, 82, 83, 86, 87; rsch. grants from NSERC, SSHRCC, MRC & Ont. Min. of Health 1977– ; Mem., Am. Psychol. Assoc. (Co-Chrmn., Ethics & Conduct Ctte. 1986); Can. Psychol. Assn.; Soc. of Exper. Soc. Psych.; co-author: 'Hypnosis, Imagination and Human Potentialities' 1974; co-editor: 'Hypnosis' forthcoming; author of ca. 200 profl. articles/book chapters; recreations: reading, flying, horseback riding; Home: 311 Bell St., Ottawa, Ont.; Office: Room LA A307, 1125 Colonel By Dr., Ottawa, Ont. K1S 5B6.

**SPARKES, Carl Trevor,** B.Sc., M.B.A.; company president; b. Shearstown, Nfld. 11 June 1959; s. Garfield and Louise (Antle) S.; e. Memorial Univ. B.Sc. 1980; Saint Mary's Univ. M.B.A. 1987; DIRECTOR & PRESIDENT, EASTERN BAKERIES LTD. 1992– ; Dir., G.E. Barbour Co. Ltd.; Dir., Bakery Council of Canada; recreations: fishing, reading, travel; clubs: Union; Home: 11 Clark Rd., Fairvale, N.B. E2E 2H2; Office: P.O. Box 308, Saint John, N.B. E2L 3Z2.

**SPARLING, Maj.-Gen. H. Alan,** C.B.E., D.S.O., C.D., Officer, U.S. Legion of Merit; b. Toronto, Ont. 2 June 1907; s. Lt.-Col. Herbert Cosford, D.S.O., and Mabel Esther (Widner) S.; e. Elem. Schs., Saint John, N.B.; Roy. Mil. Coll., Kingston, Grad. 1929; Dalhousie Univ. 1932; Gunnery Staff Course, England 1933–34; m. Edith Blanche, d. James Archibald Hunter, Minneapolis, Minn. 30 Nov. 1935; one s.; Regimental Offr., Royal Canadian Horse Arty. 1929–33; Instr. in Gunnery, Kingston, Nov. 1934–Mar. 1935; Winnipeg 1935–37; 1938 with Nat. Defence Hdqrs., Ottawa, as G.S.O. III in Directorate of Mil. Operations; Jan.-Sept. 1939 attended Staff Coll., Camberley, Eng.; G.S.O. II 1939; Directorate of Mil. Training, N.D.H.Q. Oct. 1939–May 1940; apptd. Bgde. Maj., 2nd Candn. Div. Arty. and proceeded overseas 1940; Sr. Staff Offr., Directorate of Mil. Training in Can., with rank of Lt.-Col. 1941; Acting Dir. 1942; assumed commd. overseas of 13th Candn. Field Regt., R.C.A. 1942; specially employed in Sicily and later in Italy, 8th Army, and 13th (Br.) Corps 1943; promoted Brig. in command of Divn. Artillery of 3 Candn. Inf. Div. Oct.-Dec. 1943, then to 5 Candn. Armd. Divn., Italy Jan.-Dec. 1944; Corps Arty. Commdr., 1st Candn. Corps in Italy, Dec. 1944 and N.W. Europe to May 1945; returned to Can. to command Divn. Arty, of Candn. Army, Pacific Force 1945, on disbanding of which proceeded overseas as CRA, 3rd Candn. Inf. Divn., Candn. Army Occupation Force in Germany; on return to Can. June 1946 apptd. Dist. Offr. Commdg. Mil. Dist. No. 2, Toronto, then Brig. 1/c Admin. Central Command; Commdr., W. Ont. Area, London, Ont. 1947–49; Depy. Chief of Gen. Staff, Ottawa, Jun.-Dec. 1949; attended Imp. Defence Coll., London, England 1950; promoted Maj.-Gen. 1950; Vice-Chief of Gen. Staff, Candn. Army, NDHQ Nov. 1950–Dec. 1955; Chrmn., Candn. Joint Staff, Wash., D.C. 1956–58; G.O.C. Central Command 1958–62; retired Feb. 1963; Extve. Offr. Toronto Redevelopment Adv. Counc. 1963–1973; apptd. mem., of Ontario Police Comn. (part-time) 1962–78; retired; Col. Commandant, Roy. Regt. Candn. Arty. 1969–74; recipient, Queen Elizabeth II Coronation Medal 1953; Queen Elizabeth II Silver Jubilee Medal 1977; Hon. mem. Candn. Assn. of Chiefs of Police; Life Gov., Candn. Corps of Commissionaires (Toronto & Region); Life mem., Royal Candn. Artillery Assn.; Anglican; recreation: golf; Address: 1236 Cumnock Cres., Oakville, Ont. L6J 2N5.

**SPARLING, Sharon,** M.A.; writer; b. Montréal, Qué. 8 March 1951; d. Douglas Walter and Hazel Eileen (Clogg) Sparling; e. Miss Edgars and Miss Cramps Sch. 1969; McGill Univ., B.A. 1974; Concordia Univ., M.A. 1984; m. Robert René s. F.R. Graham 16 Aug. 1975; children: Morgannis Blithe, Max Huw, Hadley Margaret Renée; author 'The Glass Mountain' novel 1985; 'The Chinese Coat' short story 1983 (Author's Award for Mag. Fiction 1983); 'The Nest Egg' novel 1991; 'Homing Instinct' novel 1993; Home: 598 Victoria Ave., Westmount, Qué. H3Y 2R9.

**SPARROW, Hon. Herbert O.,** D.Sc.(Hon.); senator; businessman-farmer; m. Lois Irene, d. William J. Perkins, North Battleford, Sask. 31 Jan. 1951; children: Kenneth, Bryan, Robert, Ronald, Joanne, Lauren; Ald., City of North Battleford 1957–65; Founding Chrmn., Sch. for Retarded Children; Pres. & Founder of Soil Conservation Canada; Depy. Chrmn., Senate Finance Comte.; Chrmn. & Depy. Chrmn., Senate Agriculture, Fisheries and Forestry Comte.; mem., Senate Foreign Affairs Comte.; Senate Transportation and Communication Comte.; Special Comte. of Poverty; Special Comte. on Mass Media; Recipient, The Junior Chamb. of Comm. Outstanding Young Man of the Year Award; The Vanier Young Man of the Year Award; Soil Conservation Soc. of Am. Honor Award for Soil Conservation; UN Environmental Leadership Medal and Certificate of Distinction for Soil Conservation; Hon. Life Mem., Agricultural Inst. of Can.; Hon. Mem., Candn. Soc. of Soil Science; D.Sc. (hon. causa), McGill Univ.; Senate Comte. publications: Industry in Turmoil: Report on the Long Term Stabilization of the Beef Industry in Canada; Soil at Risk: Canada's Eroding Future; and, Herbicide Pricing; summoned to Senate of Can. 1968; Mem., Masons, Shriners and Kinsmen (Life mem.); Liberal; Home: 9113 Walker Dr., North Battleford, Sask. S9A 2Y2.

**SPARSHOTT, Francis Edward,** M.A., F.R.S.C.; educator; poet; b. Chatham, Eng. 19 May 1926; s. Frank Brownley and Gladwys Winifred (Head) S.; e. The King's Sch. Rochester, Eng. 1943; Corpus Christi Coll. Oxford Univ. B.A., M.A. 1950; m. Kathleen Elizabeth d. late W. Stewart Vaughan, Willowdale, Ont. 1953; one d. Pumpkin Margaret Elizabeth; Prof. of Philosophy, Victoria Coll. Univ. of Toronto 1964–91, retired; joined Univ. of Toronto 1950; appointed University Professor, University of Toronto, 1982; served with Brit. Army Intelligence Corps 1944–47; author 'An Enquiry into Goodness and Related Concepts' 1958; 'The Structure of Aesthetics' 1963; 'A Divided Voice' 1965; 'The Concept of Criticism' 1967; 'A Cardboard Garage' 1968; 'Looking for Philosophy' 1972; 'The Naming of the Beasts' 1979; 'The Rainy Hills' 1979; 'The Theory of the Arts' 1982; 'The Cave of Trophonius and Other Poems' 1983; 'The Hanging Gardens of Etobicoke' 1983; 'Storms and Screens' 1986; 'Off the Ground' 1988; 'Sculling to Byzantium' 1989; mem. Candn. Philos. Assn. (Vice Pres. 1974–75, Pres. 1975–76); Am. Soc. Aesthetics (Trustee 1973–75 and 1977–79, Vice Pres. 1979–80, Pres. 1981–82); League of Candn. Poets (Extve. Comte. 1970–76, Pres. 1977–79); Soc. of Dance Hist. Scholars (Bd. of Dirs., 1986–88); recreation: photography; Home: 50 Crescentwood Rd., Scarborough, Ont., M1N 1E4.

**SPEAK, Dorothy Eileen,** M.A.; writer; b. Seaforth, Ont. 22 Apl. 1950; d. Walter Phillip and Florence Elizabeth (Ryan) Speak; e. McMaster Univ. B.A. 1973; Carleton Univ. M.A. 1975; m. Paul C. s. Raymond C. and Margaret Wade LaBarge 1 Sept. 1973; two d. Monica Claire, Emily Margaret; Curator of Inuit Art, Indian & N. Affairs Ottawa 1978–80; Assoc. Curator of Inuit Art Glenbow Museum Calgary 1980–82; Instr. in Art Hist. Univ. of Calgary 1980–82; Instr. in Creative Writing Carleton Univ. 1983–87; recipient Can. Council Explorations Grant 1983–84; Can. Council Writer's Grant 1992; author: 'The Counsel of the Moon' short stories 1990; Contributing ed.: 'Inuit Art Quarterly' 1990–93; freelance articles art and lit. various mags. and newspapers; short stories Candn. and Am. lit. mags.; Club: Rideau Tennis; Address: 406 Wood Ave., Ottawa, Ont. K1M 1J9.

**SPEAKER, Hon. Raymond A.,** M.P., B.Ed.; politician; farmer; b. Enchant, Alta. 13 Dec. 1935; s. Mike and Olga S.; e. Enchant, Alta.; Univ. of Alta. B.Ed. 1962, grad. courses M.Ed. 1974; m. Ingrid Schwab 17 Dec. 1966; children: Kari, Mark; MEMBER OF PARLIAMENT (LETHBRIDGE) 1993– ; owner and operator irrigation and dry land farm Enchant, Alta.; Teacher, Taber Sch. Div. 1954–59, 1962–64; el. M.L.A. for Little Bow 1963, re-el. prov. g.e.'s 1967–89; served as cabinet min. 1968–71; Leader, Representative Party of Alta. 1984–89; apptd. Min. of Mun. Affairs 1989; Min. of Municipal Affairs, Govt. of Alta. 1989; 1st el. to House of Commons (for Lethbridge) g.e. 1993; Finance Critic for Reform Party of Canada 1993; Lutheran; recreations: golf, slowpitch, hockey; Home: P.O. Box 3032, Enchant, Alta. T0K 0V0; Office: Rm. 647-S, Centre Block, House of Commons, Ottawa, Ont. K1A 0A6.

**SPEAL, George N.,** B.Comm., Q.C.; lawyer; b. Kingston, Ont. 13 Feb. 1932; s. Nicholas and Anastasia (Geracimo) S.; e. Queen's Univ., B.Comm. 1954; Osgoode Hall 1958; m. Marina Stamos 30 June 1960; children: Edward, Stephanie, Allison; law practice, George N. Speal, Q.C., Kingston, Ont. 1959– ; Former Chrmn., St. Lawrence Parks Comn. 1986–92; Dir., Country Wide Kitchens & Floorings Inc.; Founding Chrmn., Healthcare Insurance Reciprocal of Canada; Chrmn., Reciprocal Insurance Management Ltd.; Chrmn., Crown Foundation, Queen's Univ. 1994– ; Life Mem., St. John Ambulance Assn.; Mayor of Kingston 1973, 74, 75, 76; Bd. of Gov., Kingston Gen. Hosp. (Chrmn. 1985–87); Bd. of Trustees, Queen's Univ. 1978–90 (Hon. Pres., Alma Mater Soc. 1975); Chrmn., Ont. Winter Games 1975; Pres., Frontenac Law Assn., 1978–79; Kiwanis Club of W. Kingston 1964; Dir., Candn. Club of Kingston 1985–87; Bd. of Dirs., K.G.H. Found.; recreations: golf, fishing; Clubs: Cataraqui Golf & Country; Fort Frontenac Officer's Mess; Queen's Univ. Fac.; Home: 237 Fairway Hill Cres., Kingston, Ont. K7M 2B5; Office: 74 Brock St., P.O. Box 81, Kingston, Ont. K7L 4V6.

**SPEARN, Gregory G.,** B.A.A.; real estate executive; b. Barrie, Ont. 15 Sept. 1952; s. Charles Franklin and Frances Eileen (Maxwell) S.; e. Univ. of Waterloo; Ryerson Polytech. Inst., B.A.A. 1975; SR. VICE-PRES., POLYGON GROUP LTD. 1993– and OWNER, SPEARN MANAGEMENT 1992– ; various positions, priv. corp. 1975–77; Gen. Mgr., S. Alta., Carma Developers 1977–85; Pres. York Univ. Devel. Corp. 1986–90; Sr. Vice Pres., Bramalea Ltd. 1990–92; Address: 4044 Lions Ave., North Vancouver, B.C. V7R 3S3.

**SPECHT, Wayne Gordon;** artistic director; b. Saskatoon, Sask. 8 Dec. 1946; s. Stephen Rudolph (dec'd) and Maria (Jaworski) S.; e. Prince Rupert Sr. Secondary Sch.; Nat. Theatre Sch. Can. Montréal; Ecole Jacques Lecoq Paris, France; children: August Anders, Tatiana Ellen; ARTISTIC DIR. AXIS MIME THEATRE 1975– ; Actor, Holiday Playhouse Tours 1968–70; 'Madelaine Is...' feature film 1970; Mime Artist, Dir. and Writer, Candn. Mime Theatre 1971–73; Mime Artist 'Salut' ednl. TV series 1978; Artistic Dir. Mime Fest '80; Chrmn. and Artistic Dir. Symposium Mime, Clown & Movement Theatre and Internat. Festival Beaux Gestes '86 and '88; Artists Rep. Bd. B.C. Touring Council 1987–88; Sessional Lectr. Theatre Dept., Univ. of B.C. 1987–89, 1991–92; co-author and performer: 'The Number 14' (multiple Jessie Award winning play) 1992–93; co-author: 'A Klondike Christmas' an animated TV christmas special; Bd. mem. and Sec. Firehall Arts Centre 1986–88; Theatre Adv. Bd Langara Coll. 1985– ; mem. Candn. Actors Equity Assn. (W. Coast Adv. Bd. 1984–85); Firehall Theatre Soc. (Founding Dir. 1983); Candn. Assn. Mime (Pres. 1979–80); recreations:

basketball & other sports; Office: 280 E. Cordova St., Vancouver, B.C. V6A 1L3.

**SPECK, Paul T.;** vintner, farmer; b. Toronto, Ont. 9 Dec. 1966; s. Paul S. and Bobbi S.; e. Annex Village Campus 1985; St. John's College Annapolis B.A. 1989; PRESIDENT, HENRY OF PELHAM FAMILY ESTATE WINERY; planted 65 acres of premium vineyards in 1984; production of first vintage wine 1988; Dir., Wine Council of Ont.; Vintners Quality Alliance; Mem., Grape Growers Marketing Bd.; Ont. Agric. Fed.; Office: 1469 Pelham Rd., St. Catharines, Ont. L2R 6O7.

**SPECTOR, Norman,** B.A., M.Phil., M.S., Ph.D.; public servant; b. Montréal, Qué. 6 Mar. 1949; s. Max and Gertrude (Schwartzbein) S.; e. McGill Univ., B.A. (Hons.) 1970; Columbia Univ., M.Phil. 1972, Ph.D. 1977; Syracuse Univ., M.S. 1974; AMBASSADOR TO ISRAËL and HIGH COMMISSIONER TO CYPRUS 1992– ; Prof., St. Paul's Coll., Univ. of Ottawa 1974–75; Successive positions in the Ont. Min. of Transp. and Communications as Manager, Director & Extve. Director 1975–80; Dir., Commun. Policy, 1977–78; Extve. Dir. 1979–80; Dep. Sec., Policy, B.C. Min. of Intergovt. Relns. 1980–81; Dep. Min., Office of the B.C. Premier 1982–86; Sec. to the Cabinet for Fed.-Prov. Relns, Govt. of Can. 1986–90; Chief of Staff, Office of the Prime Minister, Govt. of Can. 1990–1992; Woodrow Wilson Fellow; Can. Counc. Doct. Fellow; Newhouse Fellow; Office: P.O. Box 6410, Tel Aviv 61063, Israel.

**SPEED, Jeffrey Michael,** B.A.A.; photographer, photojournalist; b. London, Ont. 16 July 1959; s. Bernice Alberta (Polnik) S.; e. Westminster S.S. 1978; Ryerson Polytechnical Inst. B.A.A. 1986; regular contributions to: Equinox, Toronto Life, Maclean's, Ontario Living, Financial Times, World Magazine (London, England), London Magazine, Chatelaine, Financial Post, Canadian Business; clients: Ont. Ministry of Tourism, Promotion Dept., Canadian Imperial Bank of Commerce, Jim Ireland & Assoc., Kyocera Canada, Contax Cameras; Winner, Gold Magazine Award for Photojournalism 1990 for 'Day Break Diary' in Equinox Nov./Dec. 1990; Mem., Ont. News Photographers Assn.; recreations: hockey, wandering, working out; Mem., Canadian Frequent Flyer Club; Home: 650 Parliament St., Suite 317, Toronto, Ont. M4X 1R2.

**SPEERS, Douglas E.,** B.A.Sc., M.B.A.; building products executive; b. Barrie, Ont.; e. Univ. of Guelph, B.S.A. 1966; Univ. of Toronto B.A.Sc. 1967; Univ. of Western Ontario M.B.A. 1970; m. Kathy O'Rourke; children: Dana, Mandy; PRES., EMCO BUILDING PRODUCTS GROUP, BPCO INC. 1988– ; 17 years with Imperial Oil (Retail Div. Mgr.) incl. 2 yrs. with Exxon Internat., N.Y.C.; Profl. Engr. (Ont.); Office: Suite 110, 455 Boul. Fenelon, Dorval, Que. H9S 5T8.

**SPEERS, J. (John) Alvin,** A.C.E.; entrepreneur, accountant, financial consultant; b. Orangeville, Ont. 30 June 1930; s. Frank Alvin and Pauline (Albrecht) S.; e. Newspaper Inst. of Am., grad. 1966; Alexander Hamilton Inst., Modern Business Program, grad. 1967; registered Industrial Accountant, grad. 1972; m. Esther d. Samuel and Magdalena Roth 5 May 1962; children: Kelly Alvin, Craig John; ACCOUNTANT, CONSULTANT & CONTRACTOR, AARDVARK ENTERPRISES 1977– ; apprenticed Master Baker 1946–50; RCAF Intelligence Opns. Specialist 1951–56; Communications Installer 1956–59; small land developer 1959–60; Finance Branch Manager 1960–65; Credit Mgr. 1965–66; Acctg. Supvr. 1967–69; Insurance Mgr. & Agency Owner 1969–77; Editor & Publisher, 'Breakthrough! Magazine' 1986–92; Publisher, Catalogue of Books: Making Poetry Pay, Death of a Magazine, etc.; Mem., Alta. Writers Guild; Grass Roots Adv. Ctte. Mem., Accounting Soc. 1972–80; Pres., Home & School Assn. 1971–72; Hon. Degree, Nat. Retail Credit Inst. 1966; Church Treas. 1973–74; Cub Pack Leader 1972–74; author: 'Life of a Rolling Stone' 1991 (autobiography), 'First Collection of Short Stories 1991 (essays & cartoons), 'How to Operate Insurance Agency' 1978 (procedures manual), 19 poetry books – over 1200 poems 1984–94; short stories, articles & cartoons also widely published; editor: insurance newsletters 1969–73, 1977–78; mem., Canadian Poetry Assn.; recreations: square dancing, walking, reading; Address: 204 Millbank Dr. S.W., Calgary, Alta. T2Y 2H9.

**SPEIRS, Derek J.,** B.Com., C.A., M.B.A.; b. Montreal, Que. 21 Dec. 1933; e. McGill Univ. B.Com. 1954, M.B.A. 1959; C.A. 1956; Chart. Secy. 1956; children: Lara, Gregory, Scott; PRES., SPEIRS CONSULTANTS INC. 1992– ; Kruger Pulp 1960–65; Cynamid of Canada 1965–70; Domtar Ltd. 1970–72; Vice Pres. Finance & Secy., Dir., Consoltex 1972–76; Dir. Corporate Planning Domtar Inc. 1976–78; Sr. Vice Pres. Finance & Corporate Devel., Domtar Inc. 1978–91; recreations: travel, skiing; Home: 365 Stanstead, Ville Mont-Royal, Qué. H3R 1X5.

**SPEIRS, John Murray,** B.A., M.A., Ph.D.; teacher; b. Toronto, Ont. 7 April 1909; s. Robert Miller and Jennie (McClure) S.; e. Univ. of Toronto Schools 1926; Univ. of Toronto B.A. 1931, M.A. 1938; Univ. of Illinois Ph.D. 1946; m. Doris Louise d. Archibald Morrison and Florence Gooderham (Hamilton) Huestis 12 June 1939; Teacher, Danforth Tech. School Toronto 1932–33; Astronomy Demonstrator, Univ. of Toronto 1933; taught at var. high schools in Ont. 1935–38; Ecology Demonstrator, Univ. of Illinois 1939–41; Meteorologist, Royal Air Force (North Bay & briefly Camp Borden RCAF) 1943–45; worked on DDT rsch. at Eaglehead Lake, Ont. Dept. of Lands & Forests 1946; Staff, Library, Ont. Fisheries Rsch. Lab, Univ. of Toronto 1946; Sec., Great Lakes Fisheries Comn. (also worked on Lamprey Control Prog.) 1953–55; Sec., Candn. Ctte. on Freshwater Fisheries Rsch. 1950–58; Zoology & Ecology Teacher, Univ. of Toronto 1950s–74; ecology classes from Dept. of Zool. still come to study microclimates & succession at his home; Founding Mem., Fed. of Ont. Naturalists 1931; Toronto Ornithological Club 1930s (now Hon. Mem.); Toronto Field Naturalists; Founding Dir., Pickering Naturalists 1977 & several other small nat. hist. clubs; Mem., Am. Ornithologists' Union; Wilson Ornith. Soc.; Assn. of Field Ornith. Inc.; Cooper Ornith. Soc.; Brit. Ornith. Union; Soc. of Candn. Ornith.; author: 'Birds of Ontario County' 6 vols. 1973–79, 'Birds of Ontario' 2 vols. 1985; co-author: 'A Naturalists's Guide to Ontario' 1964 (several reprs); editor: 'The Bulletin' Fed. of Ont. Naturalists 9 yrs. (1950s); Life Science Consultant, 'The Illustrated Natural History of Canada' 12 vols. 1970; also author of over 100 articles in var. periodicals; recreations: playing bridge; Home: 1815 Altona Rd., Pickering, Ont. L1V 1M6.

**SPELLMAN, John Willard,** B.A., Ph.D.; educator; consultant; b. Mass., USA 27 July 1934; e. Northeastern Univ., Boston B.A. 1955; Univ. of London Sch. of Oriental & African Studies Ph.D. 1960; children: Suzanne Bharati, John Gilligan; HEAD, INST. OF ASIAN CULTURES, UNIV. OF WINDSOR 1975– , Prof. of Asian Studies 1967– ; Ford Found. Fellow 1958–61; Visiting Prof. Wesleyan Univ. 1962–63, Univ. of Kerala S. India 1963–64; Asst. Prof. Univ. of Wash. 1964–67; Head of Asian Studies present Univ. 1967–79; Asia Devel. Dir. CUSO 1981–82; Devel. Cons. Indian Cultural Devel. Centre Madras, India 1982– ; Cons. on Sikhism & Human Rights to Ont. Human Rights Comn. 1981, 1987, 1990; Alta. Human Rights Comn. 1986; Visiting Scholar, Human Rights, Harvard Law Sch. 1989–90; designed and co-directed prog. S. India internat. devel. funded by Govts. of W. Germany, Netherlands and Ford Found. 1982– ; author: 'Political Theory of Ancient India' 1964; ed. 'The Kamasutra of Vatsyayana' 1963; collector, ed. 'The Beautiful Blue Jay and Other Tales of India' 1967; Fellow, Royal Asiatic Soc. Gt. Brit. & Ireland; co-founder Candn. Soc. Asian Studies 1969; Dir. Shastri Indo-Candn. Inst. 1968–79; mem. Malden Hortic. Soc.; recreation: gardening; Office: Windsor, Ont. N9B 3P4.

**SPENCE, James M.,** Q.C., B.A., LL.B.; lawyer; b. Toronto, Ont. 7 Sept. 1940; s. George Hackland and Ruth Elizabeth (MacDonald) S.; e. Univ. of Toronto Schs. 1958; Univ. of Toronto B.A. 1962, LL.B. 1966; m. Katherine Elizabeth d. Rev. Prof. D.K. Andrews 15 June 1963; children: Sheila Elizabeth, Andrew George, Douglas Keith; PARTNER, TORY, TORY, DesLAURIERS & BINNINGTON 1979– ; Vice Pres. and Dir. Sechura Inc.; Sec. and Dir. Bose Ltd., Bose Investments Ltd.; Dir., Trygg-Hansa Reinsurance Co. of Canada; Tarkett Inc.; Hawley Group Canada Ltd.; Assoc. present firm 1968–74, Partner 1976–78; Chief, Legal Policy Foreign Investment Review Agency Ottawa 1974–75, Sr. Legal Adv. 1975–76; Gen. Counsel Torstar Corp. Toronto 1978–79; Dir. The Canadian Art Foundation; Syrinx Concerts Toronto; co-author 'A Guide to the Investment Canada Act' 1986; contbr. various profl. publs.; Treas., Law Soc. Upper Can.; Dir. Fedn. Law Socs. Can.; Chrmn. Candn. Bar Assn. Ctte. Trade & Invest.; recreations: swimming, painting; Clubs: Granite; Arts & Letters; Home: 115 St. Leonards Ave., Toronto, Ont. M4N 1K6; Office: P.O. Box 270 IBM Tower, Toronto-Dominion Centre, Toronto, Ont. M5K 1N2.

**SPENCER, Elizabeth,** M.A., DL, LL.D.; writer; educator; b. Carrollton, Miss.; d. James Luther and Mary James (McCain) S.; e. Belhaven Coll. Jackson, Miss. A.B. 1942; Vanderbilt Univ. Nashville, Tenn., M.A. 1943; Southwestern Univ. (now Rhodes) Memphis, Hon. LL.D. 1968; Concordia Univ, Montreal, Hon. DL 1988; Univ. of the South (Sewanee, Tenn.) Hon. LL.D. 1992; m. John Arthur s. Arthur and Frances Rusher 29 Sept. 1956; Prof. of Creative Writing, Concordia Univ. 1976–86; Teacher, Northwest Jr. Coll. Senatobia, Miss. 1943–44; Ward-Belmont Sch. Nashville 1944–45; Reporter 'The Nashville Tennessean' 1945–46; Instr. Univ. of Miss. 1948–51, 1952–53; Visiting Prof. of Creative Writing Univ. of N.C. 1986–92; recipient Recognition Award Am. Inst. Arts & Letters 1952; Guggenheim Fellowship 1953; Rosenthal Award Am. Acad. Arts & Letters 1957, Award of Merit Medal Short Story 1983; Kenyon Review Fiction Fellowship 1957; Lucy Donnelly Fellowship Bryn Mawr Coll. 1962; McGraw-Hill Fiction Award 1961; Bellaman Award 1968; National Endowment for the Arts Sr. Fellowship in Literature Grant 1988; Salem Award for Literature 1991; Dos Passos Award for Fiction 1992; 5 times selected for prize stories O. Henry Awards; 6 times selected Best Candn. Stories; author (novels) 'Fire in the Morning' 1948; 'This Crooked Way' 1952; 'The Voice at the Back Door' 1956; 'The Light in the Piazza' 1960; 'Knights and Dragons' 1965; 'No Place for an Angel' 1967; 'The Snare' 1972; 'The Salt Line' 1984; 'The Night Travellers' 1991; (short stories) 'Ship Island and other Stories' 1968; 'The Stories of Elizabeth Spencer' 1981; 'Marilee' 1981; 'Jack of Diamonds and Others Stories' 1988; 'On the Gulf' 1991; (interviews) 'Conservations With Elizabeth Spencer' 1991; (drama) 'For Lease or Sale' 1989 Playmakers Repertory Co.; el. mem. Am. Academy Dept. Lit. 1985; mem. P.E.N. Internat. Am. Center; Fellowship of Southern Writers 1987 (Vice-Chancellor 1993); Authors Guild; Anglican; recreations: yoga, swimming; Home: 402 Longleaf Dr., Chapel Hill, N.C. 27514, U.S.A.

**SPENCER, Elvins Yuill,** B.Sc., M.Sc., Ph.D., F.C.I.C.; research chemist; b. Edmonton, Alta. 28 Oct. 1914; s. Henry Elvins and Harriett Zella (Crowe) S.; e. Univ. of Alta. B.Sc. 1936, M.Sc. 1938; Univ. of Toronto Ph.D. 1941; m. Hanna, d. Adolf and Ella Fischl, 11 July 1942; children: Erica, Martin; Dir., Research Inst., Dept. of Agric., Univ. of W. Ont., 1960–78; (Principal Chemist, 1951–60); Hon. Prof. in Chem. 1951–79 and 1988–91, Hon. Lect. in Biochem., Univ. of W. Ont., 1951–79; Chief Chem., Fine Chemicals of Can., Toronto, 1941–42; Research Chem., Gelatin Products, Windsor, Ont. (later Detroit, Mich.) 1942–43; Consol. Mining & Smelting Co. Ltd., Trail, B.C. 1943–45; Prof. of Chem., Univ. of Sask., 1946–51; Co-ordinator of Research, Sask. Research Council, 1949–51; Visiting Prof., Cambridge Univ. 1956–57; Visiting Scholar, Rockefeller Conf. and Study Centre, Bellagio, Italy, spring 1976; Vice-Pres. and Dir. Jr. Un. Farmers of Alta., 1936–38; Consultant to Sask. Dept. of Natural Resources on potash problems, 1950; Ed., 'Pesticide Biochem. and Physiol.' 1978–90; Chrmn., Special Comte. on Dioxins, Ont. Min. of the Environment 1983–85; Science mem. Federal, Pest Management Adv. Bd. 1985–88; mem., Chem., Inst. Can.; Am. Chem. Soc.; Agric. Inst. Can.; Candn. Biochem. Soc.; Files in Univ. of Western Ont. archives library; Unitarian; recreations: photography, tennis, study of world affairs; Home: 7 Westview Dr., London, Ont. N6A 2Y2.

**SPENCER, Maj.-Gen. (ret.) George Hylton,** O.B.E., C.D., B.Sc., D.Eng., P. Eng.; b. Seaford, Sussex, Eng., 20 Nov. 1916; s. Angus Farquharson and Nora (Taylor) S.; e. Roy. Mil. Coll. Dipl. 1938; Queen's Univ., B.Sc. (civil eng.) 1939; Staff Coll., Camberley, 1943; Imp. Defence Coll., London, 1957; m. Jean Frances, d. M. D. Fitzgerald, Halifax, N.S., 5 Dec. 1939; children: Peter Fitzgerald, Kenneth George, Michael Hylton; Lieutenant serving at Kingston, Petawawa, Dundurn and Saint John, 1938–39; overseas in England, France, Burma, Belgium, Holland and Germany with R.C.E., 1940–45, in various regimental, command and staff capacities; Candn. Army Pac. Force, June to Sept. 1945; Asst. Dir. of Works and Constr., Army Hdqrs., Ottawa, 1945–46; mem. Dir. Staff, Candn. Army Staff Coll., 1946–49; Deputy Dir. Staff Duties, 1950–51; Dir. of Weapons & Devel., Army Hdqrs., Ottawa, 1951–54; Commdr., Candn. Base Units, Europe, 1954–56; Col. i/c of Adm., Hdqrs. Eastern Command, Halifax, N.S. 1958–61; Commandant, Royal Military Coll. of Can., Kingston, Ont. 1962–63; Commander and Chief Engr., Northwest Highway System, 1963–64; Dir. Gen. of Training and Recruiting, Candn. Forces Hdqrs., 1964–67; Asst. Chief of Staff for Plans and Policy, Supreme H.Q. Allied Powers Europe 1967–70; Depy. Comptroller Gen., Candn. Forces Hdqrs. 1970 till retired from Armed Forces 1971; Dir. Metric Conversion, Standards Council of Can. 1972–77; Management Consultant 1978–81; Col. Commandant, Candn. Military Engrs. 1978–82; hon. D.Eng. from Royal Military College of Can. 1982; mem., Engn. Inst. Can.; Candn. Soc. for Eng. Management; Assoc.

Prof. Eng. of N.S.; Military Eng. Assoc. of Can.; Roy. United Services Inst. of N.S. (Past Pres.); Extve. Ctte., RMC Club of Can. 1984–86; Hon. Pres., Atlantic Retired Sappers; Adv. Bd., Candn. Military Colleges 1983–88; N.S. Health Services and Insurance Comn. 1983–92; Dir., N.S. Assn. of Health Organizations 1983–87; Last Post Fund Maritime Br. 1985–90; The Army Museum, Halifax Citadel; National Vice-Chrmn. Fed. of Military and United Services Institutes of Can. 1983–88; Chrmn., Fishermen's Memorial Hosp., Lunenburg, N.S. 1984–87; Campaign Chrmn., South Shore Regional Hosp. Found. 1987–92; Chrmn., Health Services Assn. of the South Shore; awarded Commemorative Medal for 125th Anniversary of Candn. Confederation 1992; Anglican; recreation: golf; Home: Marriott's Cove, N.S. B0J 1K0.

**SPENCER, John Hedley,** B.Sc., Ph.D., F.R.S.C.; b. Stapleford, Eng. 10 Apl. 1933; s. Thomas and Eva (Johnson) S.; e. Univ. of St. Andrews, Scot., B.Sc. 1955, Hons. B.Sc. 1956; McGill Univ., Ph.D. 1960; m. Magdeliene Vera d. Joseph and Veronika Kulin 16 Sept. 1958; children: Robin Anne, David Thomas, Mark Stewart; PROF. OF BIOCHEM. QUEEN'S UNIV. 1978– ; Montreal Cancer Rsch. Soc. Studentship McGill-Montreal Gen. Hosp. Rsch. Inst., Dept. Biochem. McGill Univ. 1956–59; Damon Runyon Meml. Fund Postdoctoral Fellow Columbia Univ. 1959–61; Lectr. in Biochem. McGill Univ. 1961–63, Asst. Prof. 1963–66, Assoc. Prof. 1966–71, Prof. 1971–78; Prof. and Head, Dept. of Biochem, Queen's Univ. 1978–90; Visiting Scientist, Nat. Institute of Child Health and Human Diseases (NICHHD), Nat. Institutes of Health (N.I.H.) Bethesda, MD, U.S.A. 1987–88; Professeur invité, Département de biochimie, Faculté de médecine, Université de Montréal 1992–93; Cons. to Smith, Kline and French Labs. Montreal and Philadelphia 1967–76; to ENS Biols. 1978–82; mem. Sci. Adv. Bd. 1979–84 and to Q-Life Systems Inc. 1991– ; Dir., 1988–91; recipient Ayerst Award Candn. Biochem. Soc. 1972; el. Fellow, Royal Soc. of Can. 1985; author 'The Physics and Chemistry of DNA and RNA' 1972; mem. Biochem. Soc.; Am. Soc. Biochem. Mol. Biol.; Am. Assn. Advanc. Sci.; Candn. Biochem. Soc. (Treas. 1966–69, Pres. 1979–80); Candn. Fedn. Biol. Soc's (Pres. 1981–82); Royal Soc. of Can.; Sigma Xi, The Sci. Rsch. Soc.; Home: 21 Hillcroft Dr., Kingston, Ont. K7L 4E8; Office: Dept. of Biochemistry, Rm. 616, Botterell Hall, Kingston, Ont. K7L 3N6.

**SPENCER, Lyle Alexander,** B.Comm., C.A.; financial executive; b. Prince Albert, Sask. 4 Dec. 1946; e. Riverside C.I. 1964; Univ. of Saskatchewan B.Comm. (Hons.) 1968; Inst. of C.A.s of Sask. C.A. 1970; Univ. of Western Ont. Mngt. Training Course 1988; m. Beverley Garlick 13 July 1968; one s.: Christopher; CHIEF FINANCIAL OFFICER, SASKATCHEWAN WHEAT POOL 1990– ; Clarkson, Gordon & Co. 1968–71 (C.A. 1970); Budget Analyst, Sask. Wheat Pool 1971; Accountant, Thunder Bay opn. 1972; Terminal Elevator Div. Controller Winnipeg 1973; Mgr., Finance & Admin., Terminal Div. 1975; Controller, Country Elevator Div. Regina 1976; Corporate Controller 1981; Mem., Sask. Inst. of C.A.s; Candn. Inst. of C.A.s; Financial Extves. Inst. (Past President); has served on executives of various community and charitable orgns.; Treas., Hospitals of Regina Found. Inc.; Regina YMCA; Dir. Wasacana Country Club; (on behalf of Sask. Wheat Pool) AgPro Grain Inc.; CanAmera Foods; PrintWest Communications Ltd.; Prairie Malt Limited; Pool Insur. Co.; Pool Agencies Ltd.; Univ. of Sask. Entrance Scholarship; recreations: golf, aerobic fitness, reading, music, working with stained glass; Home: 3451 Olive Grove, Regina, Sask.; Office: 2625 Victoria Ave., Regina, Sask. S4T 7T9.

**SPENCER, Mary Eileen,** B.A., M.Sc., Ph.D., F.C.I.C.; F.R.S.C.; Univ. Professor; biochemist; educator; b. Regina, Sask. 4 Oct. 1923; d. John J., M.A., LL.B. and Etta Christina (Hamren) Stapleton; e. Regina Coll., Assoc. in Arts 1942; Univ. of Sask., B.A. with High Honours (Chem.) 1945; Bryn Mawr Coll., M.A. (Chem.) 1946; Univ. of Cal. (Berkeley), Ph.D. (Agric. Chem.) 1951; m. Henry Anderson Spencer, 3 July 1946; one d., Susan Mary; UNIV. PROFESSOR OF PLANT SCIENCE, UNIVERSITY OF ALBERTA 1984– ; Pres., Rootrainers Corp.; Chem., Ayerst, McKenna and Harrison Ltd., Montreal, summer 1945, full-time 1946–47; Nat. Canners Assn., San Francisco, 1948; Teaching Fellow, Univ. of Cal. (Berkeley) 1949, Instr. in Food Chem. 1951; joined present Univ. 1953; served as Instr., Asst. Prof., Assoc. Prof. and Acting Head, Biochem. Dept. 1960–61; Plant Science Dept. 1962; Prof. 1964–84; Univ. Prof. 1984– ; Mem. Nat. Research Council of Can. 1970, 1970–73; re-apptd. 1973–76; Mem. Task Force on Post-Secondary Educ., Alta. Govt. Comm. on Educ. Planning, 1970–72; Bd. of Govs., Univ. of Alta. 1976–79; Mem. Natural Sciences and Engineering Rsch. Council of Can. 1986–89; re-apptd. 1989–92; Mem., Minister's Adv. Ctte. on National Centres of Excellence 1988–92; Mem., Premier's Council on Sci. & Tech. 1990– ; author of book chapters and numerous scient. papers in field of plant biochem.; Chairman, National Advisory Comte. on Biol., Nat. Research Council 1973–76; Consultative Comte. on I.B.T. Pesticides, 1981; Mem. Candn. Soc. Plant Physiol. (Pres. 1971–72); Am. Soc. Plant Physiol.; Royal Soc. of Canada; Chemical Inst. of Can.; Candn. Assn. Univ. Teachers; Plant Growth Regulators Soc. of Am.; past Mem., Adv. Bd. NRC for Prairie Regional Laboratory; Adv. Bd. for NRC Atlantic Regional Laboratory; Chrmn. NRC ad hoc Visiting Comte. in Forestry Research 1975–76; recipient, Queen's Jubilee Medal; Commemorative Medal for 125th Anniversary of Candn. Confederation; Fellow, Chem. Inst. of Can. 1966; Fellow, Royal Soc. of Can. 1976; McCalla Rsch. Fellowship 1983; Gold Medal, Candn. Soc. of Plant Physiologists 1990; Home: 8005 – 137th St., Edmonton, Alta. T5R 0C1; Office: Dept. of Plant Science, Univ. of Alberta, Edmonton, Alta. T6G 2P5.

**SPENCER, Metta,** Ph.D.; university professor; b. Calera, Oklahoma 29 Aug. 1931; d. Howard Clayton and Gladys Occonna (Turner) Wells.; e. Univ. of Calif. at Berkeley, Ph.D. 1969; m. R.L. Spencer; divorced; 1 s. Jonathan Peter; SOCIOL. PROF., UNIV. OF TORONTO 1971– ; Rsch. Sociol., Center for Internat. Affairs, Harvard Univ. 1968–69; Survey Rsch. Center, Univ. of Calif. 1969–71; Founding Pres. & Dir., Candn. Disarmament Info. Service 1983– ; Ed., PEACE Magazine 1985– ; Dir., Hunger Proj. of Can. 1981–83; Science for Peace 1983– ; Consortium for Peace Rsch., Edn. & Devel. 1985– ; mem. Candn. Pugwash; The Group of 78; author 'Foundations of Modern Sociology' 1976, 1979, 1982, 1985; Candn. eds. 1981, 1985, 1990, 1992; co-author 'Adolescent Prejudice' 1975; Ed., 'Research in Social Movements, Conflict, and Change' vol. 13; Home: Apt. 201, 155 Marlee Ave., Toronto, Ont. M6B 4B5; Office: Erindale College, Mississauga, Ont. L5L 1C6.

**SPENCER, Robert Allan,** C.D., M.A., D.Phil.; educator; b. Montreal, Que. 9 Nov. 1920; e. High Sch. of Montreal 1937; McGill Univ. B.A. 1941; Univ. of Toronto M.A. (Hist.) 1947; St. John's Coll. Oxford D.Phil. (Hist.) 1950; m. Ruth Margaret Church 22 June 1948; children: Charles, Valerie Keyes, Katherine Ross; PROFESSOR EMERITUS 1987; Prof. of Hist., Univ. of Toronto 1964–87; Lectr. in Hist. present Univ. 1950, Asst. Prof. 1955, Assoc. Prof. 1961, Assoc. Chrmn. 1964–67; Assoc. Dean Sch. of Grad. Studies Div. I 1973–76; Dir., Centre for Internat. Studies, Univ. of Toronto 1976–86; mem. Adv. Comte. on Acad. Planning Ont. Council of Grad. Schs. 1968–72; served with Victoria Rifles of Can. 1942–43, 15th Candn. Field Regt. RCA 1943–45 Brit., N.W. Europe; Mentioned in Despatches 1945; Hist. Sec. Gen. Staff Br. Candn. Mil. HQ London 1945–46, rank Capt.; COTC Univ. of Toronto 1958–66, Lt. Col. and C.O. 1962–66; recipient Canada Decoration 1965; Queen's Silver Jubilee Medal 1978; Goethe Medal 1983; Commander's Cross of the Order of Merit (Fed. Republic of Germany) 1986; mem. Comte. on Atlantic Studies, Washington, D.C. 1966– , Chrmn. N.Am. Sec. 1970–72; Charter mem. Atlantic Council of Can., Secy.-Treas. and Secy. 1966–83, Vice Pres. 1983–90, Pres. 1990– ; Visiting Prof. Historische Kommission zu Berlin, Friedrich Meinecke Inst., Free Univ. of Berlin 1970; Visiting Prof. Univ. of Siena, May, June 1985; Sr. Assoc. mem., St. Antony's Coll., Oxford, Michaelmas Term 1986; Visiting Fellow, Dept. of Internat. Relations, Australian National Univ. Mar.-June 1987; rec'd Can. Council Research Grants 1959– , Sr. Research Fellowship 1960–61; Deutsche Akademischer Austauschdienst Research Grants 1966–67, summer 1970 (declined), 1978, 1983, 1986, 1992; co-author 'Canada and Western Security' 1982; ed. 'Iran, Iraq and the Gulf War' 1982; co-ed. 'International Journal' 1959–84; 'The International Joint Commission: Seventy Years On' 1982; 'The West and a Wider World' 1966; 'Modern German History' 4th ed. 1968; 'The Shaping of Postwar Germany' 1960; 'Canada in World Affairs: From UN to NATO 1946–1949' 1959; 'History of the Fifteenth Canadian Field Regiment, Royal Canadian Artillery 1941–45' 1945; contrib. to 'The European Community at the Crossroads: The First Twenty-five Years' (ed. N. Orvik and Charles Pentland) 1983; ed. & contrib. to 'Politics and Government in the Federal Republic of Germany: Basic Documents' 1983; 'Canada and the Conference on Security and Co-operation in Europe' 1984; 'Perceptions of the Federal Republic of Germany' (ed. & intro), 1987; contrib. to 'Bedrohung durch die Sowjetunion? Westliche Analysen der politischen Absichten Moskaus' (ed. Carl-Christoph Schweitzer) 1989; English translation 'The Changing Western Analysis of the Soviet Threat' 1990; contrib. to 'Auf der Suche nach der Gestalt Europas' (ed. Jochen Thies and Günther van Well) 1990; 'Kanada und die deutsche Einigung, 1989–90' in Josef Becker (ed), 'Wiedervereinigung in Mitteleuropa, Aussen- und Innenansichten zur staatlichen Einheit Deutschlands' München 1992; progress: 'Canada and the Federal Republic of Germany, 1948–1989'; mem. Ed. Comte. 'Canadian Historical Review' 1955–58; mem., Atlantik Brücke; mem. Sponsoring Comte., Candn. Council for European Studies; Candn. Hist. Assn.; Candn. Inst. Internat. Affairs; recreations: skiing, gardening, sailing; Club: Royal Candn. Mil. Inst.; Home: 52 Oriole Gardens, Toronto, Ont. M4V 1V7; Office: 208 Trinity Coll., Hoskin Ave., Toronto, Ont. M5S 1H8.

**SPENCER-DAVIS, Michael,** B.A., B.F.A.; actor; b. Regina, Sask. 23 May 1962; s. Royden Alfred Leonard and Angela Elizabeth (Pizzey) Davis; e. Kelvin H.S. 1980; Univ. of Winnipeg B.A. 1983; Univ. of Alberta B.F.A. 1986; m. Bonnie d. Earl and Jeanette Green 25 April 1991; working professional actor since 1986; selected resume: Theatre Network: 'The Third Ascent,' 'Gravel Run,' 'Adventures in Turning 40,' 'Skygeezers'; Worskhop West Theatre: 'The Ugly Man,' 'The Saints and Apostles,' 'Prairie Report,' 'The Rich Man'; Phoenix Theatre: 'Mad Forest'; The Citadel: 'St. Joan'; has worked with the following directors: Brad Fraser, Raymond Storey, Bernard Hopkins, Stephen Heatley, Jim Guedo, Robin Phillips; 1992 Sterling Award for Outstanding Performance of an Actor in a Lead Role (The Saints and Apostles); Mem., Candn. Actors' Equity Assn.; ACTRA; Past Instructor-Evaluator, Candn. Yachting Assn.; taught sailing for 10 summers in Manitoba; recreation: sailing; Address: 11404 - 71 Ave., Edmonton, Alta. T6G 0A7.

**SPENCLEY, Michael;** business executive; b. Sturgeon Falls, Ont.; e. Sheridan College of Aplied Arts & Technology, Bus.Admin. 1978; PRESIDENT & CHIEF EXECUTIVE OFFICER, HUDSON BAY TECHNOLOGY GROUP; Mgr., Oper./Corp. Mgr., Quality & Tech. Dev., S.K.D. Manufacturing; Dir., Quality Assurance, Tamco Ltd.; Gen. Mgr., Hudson Bay Diecasting Limited; Mem., N. Am. Diecasting Assn.; Am. Soc. for Quality Control; Soc. of Manufacturing Engineers; Automotive Parts Mfrs. Assn.; Devil's Pulpit Golf Assn.; author: 'Trout Secrets' 1980; recreations: books, art & wine collecting, golf, writing; Office: 230 Orenda Rd., Brampton, Ont. L6T 1E9.

**SPENSER, Ian Daniel,** Ph.D., D.Sc., F.R.S.C., F.C.I.C., C.Chem., F.R.S.C. (U.K.); university professor; chemist; b. Vienna, Austria 17 June 1924; e. schs. Vienna, Prague, Bournemouth, Hants. and Wem, Salop.; Univ. of Birmingham B.Sc. 1948; Univ. of London, King's Coll. Ph.D. 1952, D.Sc. 1969; m. Anita Fuchs 5 Sept. 1951; children: Helen Ruth, Paul Andrew; PROF. EMERITUS, McMASTER UNIV. 1989– ; Demonst. in Biochem. King's Coll. Univ. of London 1948–52; Asst. Lectr. in Biochem. Med. Coll. of St. Bartholomew's Hosp. Univ. of London 1952–54, Lectr. 1954–57; Post-doctoral Fellow Nat. Rsch. Council Can. Ottawa 1953–54; Asst. Prof. present Univ. 1957, Assoc. Prof. 1959, Prof. of Biochem. 1964–68; Prof. of Chemistry 1968–89; Akademischer Gast, Laboratorium für Organische Chemie, Eidgenössische Technische Hochschule, Zürich 1971, 1989; Visiting Prof. Inst. of Organic Chem. Tech. Univ. of Denmark 1977; Inst. für Organische Chemie Universität Karlsruhe, Fed. Repub. Germany 1981; Inst. für Pharmazeutische Biologie Universität Bonn, Fed. Repub. Germany 1989; recipient NATO Sr. Sci. Award 1980; Can. (NSERC)-Japan (JSPS) Exchange Award 1982–83; John Labatt Ltd. Award Chem. Inst. Can. 1982–83; Univ. Club of Hamilton Award 1990; author more than 100 rsch. publs. in bio-organic chem.; Fellow, Royal Soc. Chem.; mem., Biochem. Soc.; Am. Soc. Biochem. Mol. Biol.; Phytochem. Soc. N. Am.; Am. Soc. Pharmacognosy; recreations: squash, skiing, travel; Office: Hamilton, Ont. L8S 4M1.

**SPERRY, The Right Rev. John Reginald,** D.D.; bishop; b. Leicester, England 2 May 1924; s. William Reginald and Elsie Agnes (Priest) S.; e. Medway Jr.; Melbourne Secondary 1939; King's Coll., L.Th. 1950; Emmanuel – St. Chad, D.D. 1973; Wycliffe Coll., D.D. 1981; C.D. 1987; m. Elizabeth d. Andrew and Margaret Maclaren 24 Apr. 1952; children: Angela Elizabeth, John; Royal Navy 1943–46; Lt., Candn. Rangers 1952–69; Asst. Missionary, St. Andrew's Coppermine, NWT 1950–52; Missionary-in-Charge 1952–69; Canon, All Saints' Cathedral, Aklavik 1957–59; Archdeacon of Coppermine 1959–69; Missionary-in-Charge, St. John's, Fort Smith, Episcopal Dist. of Mackenzie 1969–74; Bishop of the Arctic, Anglican Ch. of Can. 1974–90;

Mem., Hist. Adv. Counc. of the N.W.T. 1968–72; Hon. Vice-Pres., Boy Scouts of Can. 1976–84; Candn. Bible Soc. 1986– (Pres. 1990– ); transl.; 'Anglican Prayer-book & Hymnary' 1962, 'Four Gospels and Acts' (Eskimo language copper dialect) 1972; recreations: gardening, sailing; Home: 1 Dakota Court, Yellowknife, N.W.T. X1A 2A4.

**SPICER, Erik John,** C.D., B.A., B.L.S., M.A.L.S.; retired librarian; b. Ottawa, Ont. 9 Apr. 1926; s. Clifford and Violet (Gundersen) S.; e. Model Sch., Lisgar Collegiate, Ottawa; Kenmore (N.Y.) Sr. H.S.; Victoria Univ., Univ. of Toronto, B.A. 1948; Univ. of Toronto Library Sch., B.L.S. 1949; Sch. of Grad. Studies, Univ. of Toronto, 1949–50; Univ. of Michigan, M.A.L.S. 1959; m. Mary Helen, d. late Dr. and late Mrs. W.G. Blair, 4 July 1953; children: Erika Anne, John Blair; Parliamentary Librarian Canada 1960–94, retired (longest continually serving official with the rank of Deputy Minister, serving under eight Prime Ministers and reporting to twelve Speakers of the Senate and ten Speakers of the House of Commons); Depy. Librarian, Ottawa Publ. Lib. 1954–60; Life Mem. Candn. Lib. Assn. (Pres. 1979–80); Life Mem. Ont. Lib. Assn. (Past Pres.); mem. Lib. Assn. of Ottawa (Past Pres.); Inst. of Profl. Librarians (Past Pres.); Candn. Assn. for Information Science; Candn. Political Sci. Assn.; Intl. Pol. Sci. Assn. (Paris); Hansard Soc.; Royal Candn. Air Force Assn.; Candn. Assn. of Journalists; Global Futures Network; Hon. Assoc. Mem., Candn. Br., Commonwealth Parl. Assn.; Life Mem. Ottawa Historical Soc.; Life Mem. Ont. Historical Soc.; Assn. of Parly. Librarians in Can. (Past Pres.); Candn. Correspondent, Intl. Centre for Parl. Documentation (Geneva); Candn. Correspondent, Parly. Libs. Sec., Intl. Fed. of Lib. Assns., The Hague; Dir. Special Libraries Sec. 1967–73; mem. Standing Adv. Comte. 1972–76; Pres. Parly. & Administrative Libraries Sec. 1972–76; Chrmn. Parly. Libraries Sec. 1976–80; mem. Comte. on Official Publications of the Standing Adv. Comte. 1972–78; del. to IFLA annual meetings 1966–92); del., European Conference on Intl. Exchange of Publications (Vienna, Apr. 1972); Intergovernmental Conf. on the Planning of National Documentation, Library & Archives Infrastructures, UNESCO (Paris, Sept. 1974); Rapporteur, Inter-Parliamentary Union, 3rd Intl. Symposium: 'The Member of Parliament: His Requirements for Information in the Modern World' (Geneva, Jan. 1973); Correspondent, European Centre for Parly. Research & Documentation Council of Europe (Strasbourg 1978; Luxembourg 1979; Bonn 1980; Rome 1981); Secy., Candn. Study of Parliament Group 1981–87; mem. Royal Candn. Mil. Inst., Toronto; Ex-officio Mem., Nat. Lib. Adv. Counc. 1960–69; Ex-officio Mem., Nat. Lib. Adv. Bd. 1969– ; Trustee, Ottawa Public Lib. 1970–73; has written for parly. and library periodicals; 2 papers publ. by C.L.A.; directed UNESCO workshop on Development of Parliamentary Libraries (Nigeria, 1982); invited part. & speaker at the Commonwealth Library Assn. Counc. Meeting and Seminar Nairobi, Kenya 1983; mem. R.C.A.F., R.C.I.C. 1944–45; Major (retired), Governor-General's Foot Guards; Library Service Fellowship, Univ. of Mich. 1953–54; Canada Council Fellowship 1959; mem. Club champêtre (Lucerne, Que.).

**SPICER, John H.,** B.Sc.; retired transportation executive; b. Moose Jaw, Sask. 12 Aug. 1924; s. Ralph Manley and Euphemia Alexander (Gow) S.; e. Greenway & Gen. Wolfe Sch., 1939 and Shellmouth & Daniel MacIntyre Sch., 1942, Winnipeg; Univ. of Man., B.Sc. (Civil Engn.) 1948; m. Irene, d. late Cuthbert Allison, Vancouver, 1 Sept. 1950; joined Canadian National Railways as instrumentman, Winnipeg, 1948; Office Engr., Vancouver, 1949; Asst. Engr., Winnipeg, 1950; Div. Engr., Prince Rupert, 1951; Dist. Engr., Edmonton, 1955 and Montreal, 1956; Asst. Gen. Supvr. of Budgets, Montreal, 1957, Chief Budget Offr. 1958, Chief of Engr. Econ. 1959, Coordinator of Analytical Services 1960; Area Mgr., Toronto, 1961; Asst. Vice Pres., Montreal, 1967; Vice-Pres., Mountain Region, April 1970; System Vice Pres., Planning & Admin. 1974; Corp. Vice Pres. 1976; Extve. Vice Pres. 1979–80; served with R.C.A.F. 1943–45; mem., Univ. of Man. Alumni Assn.; Order of St. John; Protestant; recreations: music, golf; Club: Kelowna Golf & Country; Canadian; Home: 13 Alameda Ct., Kelowna, B.C. V1V 1C6.

**SPICER, Keith,** O.C., Ph.D., LL.D.; journalist; broadcaster; professor; businessman; public official; b. Toronto, Ont. 6 March 1934; s. George James and Gertrude Grace (McMullen) S.; e. elem. and secondary schs. Toronto; Univ. of Paris Dipl. d'études de civilisation française, degré supérieur Sorbonne 1955, Dipl. de l'Institut d'Etudes Politiques (Internat. Relations) 1958; Univ. of Toronto B.A. 1956, Ph.D. 1962; LL.D. Laurentian Univ. 1973, York Univ. 1974, Univ. Ottawa 1977; children: Dag, Genevieve, Nicolas; CHRMN., CANADIAN RADIO-TELEVISION AND TELECOMMUNICATIONS COMMISSION 1989–90, 1991– ; Chrmn., Citizens' Forum on Canada's Future 1990–91; Pres., Spicer Communications Group Inc. 1983–88; Lectr. and Asst. Prof. of Pol. Science Univ. of Ottawa 1961–66; Assoc. Prof. of Pol. Science and Special Lectr. on French Can. Univ. of Toronto 1966–69; Visiting Assoc. Prof. of Pol. Science, Dartmouth Coll., U.S. 1967, Glendon Coll. York Univ. 1969–70; Visiting Prof. of Pol. Science Univ. of B.C. 1977–78; Adjunct Prof. of Candn. Studies, Simon Fraser Univ. 1983–84; Ed. Writer 'The Globe and Mail' Toronto 1966–69; Commentator on French TV and Radio networks CBC 1961–69, CBC Internat. Service in French 1968–69, 1977–84; Host and Interviewer CBOFT Ottawa 1965–66; Syndicated Columnist, 'The Vancouver Sun' 1977–84 (U.S. Syndication 1980–81); Editor, 'The Ottawa Citizen' 1985–89; Host TV Talk Show, 'Les invités de Keith Spicer' Radio-Québec 1978–80; Documentary Host, CBC-TV 1979; Documentary Host, TV Ontario 1984; Host of TV political show 'Sur la Colline,' TVA network, 1986–88; Staff Researcher on Armed Forces, Royal Comn. Bilingualism and Biculturalism 1964; Special Asst. to Min. of Justice and Pres. Privy Council 1964–65; Founder Candn. Overseas Volunteers (CUSO) 1960–61; Commr. of Official Langs. 1970–77; Dir. Katimavik; Canada World Youth; mem. Adv. Comte. Candn. Bilingual Dictionary Project; Comte. on Nuclear Issues in the Community (Royal Soc. of Canada and Science Council of Can. 1978–79); Officer, Ordre de la Pléiade 1980; author 'A Samaritan State? External Aid in Canada's Foreign Policy' 1966; 'Cher péquiste ... et néanmoins ami: propos pré-référendaires dans un esprit post-référendaire' 1980; 'The Winging It Logic System: How to Think and Make Sense' 1982; 'Think on Your Feet' 1985; various articles; Mem., Bd. of Govs., Univ. of Ottawa 1989–92; Office: CRTC, Ottawa, Ont. K1A 0N2.

**SPICER, Philip Michael;** investor; monetary analyst; consultant; b. Hamilton, Ont. 7 March 1937; s. Henry Siddall and Leanora May (Gunby) S.; e. Boston Univ. one yr. Business Adm.; m. Joanne d. Berend and Jantje Heuver 29 Oct. 1960; children: Michael, Michele, Stefan; FOUNDER AND PRESIDENT, CENTRAL FUND OF CANADA LTD. 1961– ; Founder, The Central Group 1961–92; Part Owner J.B. White & Co. Ltd.; mem., Toronto Stock Exchange 1966–70; Spicer Investment Counsel Ltd. 1971–76; Founder, Inst. for the Developent of Economic Advancement; Canadian Office: P.O. Box 7319, Ancaster, Ont. L9G 3N6.

**SPICKETT, R. Gyō-Zō;** painter, sculptor; b. Regina, Sask. 11 Apr. 1926; s. Hubert John and Catherine Georgina (Miller) S.; e. Calgary Prov. Inst. Tech. and Art; Ont. Coll. Art; Instituto Allende, Mexico; m. Anna Barbara Rose, d. late Michael Wingert, 29 June 1950; children: Ronald John, Richard James, Rae Janus; Sessional Instr., Univ. of Calgary, 1967–81; Display Artist. Simpson's, Toronto, 1949–51; Hudson's Bay Co., 1951–55; Instr., Alta. Coll. of Art, Calgary 1957–67; has exhibited in Ottawa, Mexico, Montreal, Toronto, Calgary, etc. in special shows; work rep. in coll. Edmonton, Toronto, London, Vancouver, Victoria Art Galleries, Sir Geo. Williams Univ., Rothman Coll., Albert Art Fdn., Can. Council Art Bank Coll., Nat. Gallery, Zack's Coll., C.I.L. Coll., Toronto-Dominion Bank Coll., Shell Oil, Firestone Coll., and others; work includes mural sculpture, free lance comn. work; won O'Keefe Award for Painting, 1951; Baxter Award, O.S.A., 1959; Canada Purchase Award Print, Vancouver, 1961; Can. Council grant for study in Japan, 1962; el. R.C.A. 1968; Arts Fellowship, Can. Council 1969; Sr. Arts Grant, Can. Council 1976; private publ.: 'Art as a Mirror of Tathagata Dhyana' 1974; 'Dokuritsu Zen: The Practice of Self Reliant Zen' 1986; 'Seeing Mind: One Hand' 1992; served overseas in 2nd World War with R.C.N.V.R. 1943–46; confirmed Zen Buddhist having received Zaike Tokudo (Soto Zen); Dharma Name: Gyō-Zō; Home: April Rain Zendo, 3427 Elbow Dr., Calgary, Alta. T2S 2J5.

**SPILSBURY, Ashton James (Jim);** writer; painter; b. Findern, Derbyshire, Eng. 8 Oct. 1905; s. Ashton Wilmot and Alice Maud (Blizard) S.; e. Savary Island, B.C. 1918; m. Winnifred Helen d. Edwin and Elizabeth Hope 24 Jan. 1970; children (by previous marriage) Ronald, David, Marie; radio service-repair and constrn. 1926–41; estbd. Spilsbury & Hepburn Ltd. 1941; Spilsbury & Tindall Ltd. 1943, later Spilsbury Communications Ltd., sold 1981; Queen Charlotte Airlines Ltd. 1944 (sold to Pacific Western Airlines 1955, now Canadian International Airlines); mem. Candn. Power Sqdns., instrn. 25 yrs.; Pres. B.C. Aviation Council 1953–56; Founder Western Can. Telecommunications Council, Jim Spilsbury Award estbd. by Council and Candn. Coast Guard Auxiliary 1982; recipient 75 Achievers Award W. Vancouver 1987; Inuksuk Award 'for outstanding application of information technology' Communications Can. 1988; B.C. Aviation Council Award 1988; B.C. Hist. Fedn. Cert. Merit 1988; B.C. Book Prizes, Bill Duthie Book Sellers Choice 1988; William H. Thompson Award Min. Regional Devel. & Electronics Mfrs. Assn. 1989; B.C. and Yukon Transportation Award of Achievement 1991; National Transportation Award of Achievement 1991; Order of British Columbia 1993; author (non-fiction) 'Spilsbury's Coast' 1987; 'Accidental Airline' 1988; 'Spilsbury's Album' 1990; mem. Fedn. Candn. Artists; recreations: boating, painting; Clubs: W. Vancouver Yacht; Point Grey Amateur Radio; Address: 6691 Madrona Cres., West Vancouver, B.C. V7W 2J9.

**SPINK, Marilyn (Lynn),** M.A.; union consultant; b. Batavia, N.Y. 2 Nov. 1938; d. E. Perry (dec.) and Arlene (Miller) S.; e. Queen's Univ. M.A. 1969; divorced; children: Sarah and Rachel Cox; co-author: (with Mary Cornish) 'Organizing Unions' 1994; Urban Project Coordinator, Pollution Probe (at Univ. of Toronto) 1971–74; Planner, City of Toronto Planning Bd. 1974–78; Extve. Asst. to Mayor John Sewell (Toronto) 1978–80; Consultant, Candn. Union of Public Employees (Toronto), Local 79 1981–90; Extve. Asst. to the Premier of Ontario 1990–92; Ed. Bd. Mem., 'This Magazine' 1986–90, 1993– ; Mem., Bloor Cinema; Home: 135 Albany Ave., Toronto, Ont. M5R 3C5.

**SPINKS, John William Tranter,** C.C. (1970), M.B.E., B.Sc., Ph.D., D.Sc., LL.D., D.M. Sc. F.R.S.C., F.C.I.C.; b. Norfolk, England, 1 January 1908; s. John William and Sarah Jane (Tranter) S.; e. King's College, London Univ., B.Sc.; Ph.D. 1930; Research in Spectroscopy, Darmstadt, Germany, 1933–34; came to Canada 1930; m. Mary Strelioff, 5 June 1939; President, University of Saskatchewan 1959–74 (formerly Dean of Grad. School and Head of Department of Chem. there); mem., Nat. Research Council Can.; Sask. Research Council mem., Sask. Oil & Gas Conservation Bd. since 1952; mem., Defence Research Bd.; The Canada Council; served in World War, 1939–45, as Operational Research Offr., R.C.A.F.; Candn. Atomic Energy Project, 1944–45; mem., Chem. Inst. Can. (Pres. 1953–54); Royal Inst. of Chem.; Faraday Soc.; Am. Chem. Soc.; Inst. of Internat. Affairs; transl. in co-operation with G. Herzberg, 'Atomic Spectra,' 1937, and 'Molecular Spectra,' 1939; co-author with R. J. Woods, 'Radiation Chemistry'; 'Two Blades of Grass,' 1980; Anglican; recreations: archaeology, reading; Home: 932 University Dr., Saskatoon, Sask. S7N 0K1.

**SPIRO, Peter Samuel,** B.A., M.A., A.M.; economist; b. Budapest, Hungary 25 Feb. 1952; s. Joseph and Susan (Fischer) S.; e. Univ. of Toronto B.A. 1975, M.A. 1976; Univ. of Chicago A.M. 1978; m. Frances d. Samuel and Helena Zimmerman 11 Dec. 1983; children: Jason, Deborah, Elias; SENIOR POLICY ADVISER, MACROECONOMIC POLICY, ONT. MIN. OF FINANCE 1991– ; Lecturer, Econ., Univ. of Toronto 1978–80; Economist, Wood Gundy Ltd. 1980–81; Project Leader, Financial Markets Analysis, Ont. Hydro 1981–83; Asst. Vice-Pres., Fixed Income Investments, Inco Limited 1984; Head, Econ. Forecasting, Ont. Hydro 1985–91 (described by Peter C. Newman as 'the best economic forecasting unit in Canada' during my tenure); Former Cons., Bank Credit Analyst Pubns.; Candn. Electrical Assn.; Polar Gas Project; Mem., Candn. Elect. Assn. Task Force on Elect. Trade 1989–91; Dir., Toronto Assn. of Bus. Econ.; Mem., Candn. Friends of Peace Now; Toronto Vegetarian Assn.; Nat. Assn. of Bus. Econ.; Am. Econ. Assn.; author: 'Real Interest Rates and Investment and Borrowing Strategy' 1989, 'Economic Analysis of Financial and Tax Policies in the Electricity Sector' 1988; author of num. journal articles & frequent book reviewer for 'Financial Analysts Journal'; recreations: bicycling, videography; Office: 95 Grosvenor St., 6th fl., Toronto, Ont. M7A 1Z1.

**SPITZER, Walter O.,** M.D., M.H.A., M.P.H., F.R.C.P.C., F.A.C.E.; university professor; b. Paraguay 19 Feb. 1937; s. Paul and Elsa (Wagner) S.; e. Univ. of Toronto M.D. 1962; Univ. of Michigan M.H.A. 1966; Yale Univ. M.P.H. 1969; m. Ursula Deckert; children: Paul, Pamela, Carl, Brenda, Marco; PROFESSOR, MCGILL UNIV.; estab. Health Serv. Rsch. Unit, McMaster Univ. 1971; Founder, Kellogg Centre for Studies in Primary Care, McGill Univ. 1976; Chair, Dept. of Epidemiology & Biostatistics 1973; created Epidemiology Rapid Response Unit; Past Chair, several govt. Task Forces; developed McGill Prog. in Pharmacoepidemiology 1987; seconded to Free Univ. of Berlin to create and direct a Eur. Inst. of Pharmacoepidemiology & Technology Assessment 1993–95; Adjunct Prof.

of Epidemiology, Free Univ. of Berlin & Karolinska Inst. Stockholm; Mem., Bd. of Dir., Phoenix Internat. Life Sicences Inc.; Founder, 'Clinical and Investigative Medicine' 1980; Editor, 'J. of Clin. Epidemiology' 1981–93; Anglican; Liberal; Mem., Am. Epidemiological Soc.; Soc. for Epid. Rsch.; Pres., Candn. Oncology Soc. 1987–89; author of 81 journal articles 1970–93; recreations: flying, music, tennis; Home: Ernst-Ring-Strasse 12, D-14129, Berlin, Germany; Office: Montreal, Que. H3A 1A2.

**SPIVAK, Sidney,** Q.C., b. Winnipeg, Man. 23 May 1928; s. late Malick David, Q.C. and Rose (Portigal) S.; e. Univ. of Man., LL.B. 1951; Harvard Law Sch., LL.M. 1952; m. Mira, d. Sam Steele, 29 May 1955; children: Lori, Harold, Diane; Min. of Industry & Comm., Man. 1966–69; Leader, Man. P. Conservative Party and Leader of Official Opposition, Man., Feb. 1971–5; Min. and Co-Chrmn. of Task Force on Gov's. Organization and Economy, Man., Oct. 1977–78; Min. Gov. Services, 1978–79; mem. Bd. of Govs., Miamedes Coll.; former Chrmn., Hillel Foundation Adv. Bd., Univ. of Man.; mem., Candn. Friends of Hebrew Univ.; Past Pres., Rainbow Stage; past Bd. mem., Man. Theatre Centre; Candn. Inst. Internat. Affairs; Man. Hist. Soc.; Harvard Club of Man.; Pres., Central Candn. Council, B'nai B'rith; Co-Chrmn., Mid-Western Adv. Bd., B'nai B'rith Foundation of U.S. and Can.; Chrmn., Winnipeg's Refugee Asst. Comm. Inc., 1979; Mem. Bd. of Governors, Univ. of Man.; Bd. of Dir., Citizenship Council of Man.; Hon. Counsellor Wpg. Chamber of Commerce; Mem. Bd. of Dir., Health Sciences Centre Research Foundation, Inc.; St. Boniface Gen. Hosp.; St. Boniface Rsch. Found.; Prairie Theatre Exchange; Man. Opera Foundation Conservative; Hebrew; recreation: tennis; Home: 703 Wellington Cres., Winnipeg, Man. R3M 0A7; Office: 527 - 1808 Wellington Ave., Winnipeg, Man. R3H 0Z4.

**SPLANE, Robert Arthur;** financial; b. Athabasca, Alta. 10 July 1935; e. Alta. pub. and secondary schs.; Seattle Pacific Coll. Sciences 1954; Carlton Univ. Sciences 1955–56; Univ. of Alta. Pub. Adm. 1967–70; Banff Sch. of Advanced Mang. 1970; Cert. Gen. Accts. Assn. 1970–74; m. Stella Grace Dafoe 1957; children: Coleen Mavis Taylor, Teresa Louise Lundell, Patricia Ann Imbeau, Robert Erwin; PRES. & MANAGING DIR., AGRICULTURAL FINANCIAL SERVICES CORPORATION 1988– ; Chrmn. & C.E.O., Northern Lite Canola Inc.; Owner, Bostel Salers Farms; Dir., Alberta Municipal Finance Corp.; Dir., Westcan Malting Ltd.; Gen. Mgr. Alberta Municipal Finance Corp. 1975–78; Asst. Depy. Prov. Treas. Prov. Alta. 1975–78; Vice Pres. Canadian Commercial Bank 1978–79, Extve. Vice Pres. and Chief Operating Offr. 1979–80, Vice-Chrmn. and Dir. 1980–83; Pres. & C.O.O., Bank of Alta. & Candn. Western Bank 1983–88; rec'd Queen's Silver Jubilee Medal 1977; Protestant; recreations: skiing, golf, farming; Home: 53577 Rg Rd. 223, Ardrossan, Alta. T0B 0E0; Office: 4910 - 52 St., Camrose, Alta. T4V 4E8.

**SPOONER, Malvin Charles,** B.A., M.A., M.B.A., C.F.A.; investment counsellor; b. Toronto, Ont. 28 Aug. 1955; s. George John and Barbara Anne (Morten) S.; e. Humberside Coll. 1974; Univ. of Toronto B.A. 1978; Univ. of West. Ont. M.A. 1979, M.B.A. 1981; m. Laila d. Ilga (Roze) and Arvids Marsons 23 Aug. 1980; children: Skaidrite, Erik, Sandra; PARTNER, MARQUEST INVESTMENT COUNSEL INC. 1992– ; Instr., Univ. of West. Ont. 1979; Cons., Econ. Counc. of Can. 1981; Analyst, Fgn. Equities, Candn. Pacific Ltd. 1981–82; Portfolio Mgr., Bolton Tremblay Inc. 1982–85; Vice-Pres., Elliott & Page 1985–89; Beutel, Goodman & Co. Ltd. 1989–92; CFA; Dir, Toronto Soc. of Financial Analysts; Mem., Candn. Pension Conf.; author: several published articles; one TV appearance; recreations: skiing, fishing, raquet sports; Club: Wellington; Home: 7 Birchcroft Rd., Islington, Ont. M9A 2L3; Office: 150 York St., Ste. 1816, Toronto, Ont. M5H 3S5.

**SPOONER, Michael Alan,** B.A., M.D., M.A.; physician; educator; b. Regina, Sask. 18 March 1937; s. Harold John and Inez L. (Rainer) S.; e. Univ. of Sask. B.A. 1958; Univ. of Toronto M.D. 1963; Mich. State Univ. M.A. 1972; m. Donna Marie Kernaghan d. Ernest A. Rice 17 May 1958; children: Peter Harold, Jane Elizabeth, Melinda Anne, Thomas Beattie; MEDICAL DIR., GERIATRIC SERVICE, PASQUA HOSPITAL 1988– ; Partner, Med. Arts Clinic, Regina 1964–71; Educ. Research Offr. Univ. of Sask. 1972–73, Head of Family Med. Plains Health Centre 1973–77; Prof. and Chrmn. of Family Med. 1977–88; service CFMS Militia, rank Capt.; mem. Sask. Med. Assn.; Candn. Med. Assn.; Coll. Family Phys. Can. (Past Pres.); Am. Educ. Research Assn.; Presbyterian; recreations: hunting, fishing, tennis; Office: 4101 Dewdney Ave., Regina, Sask. S4T 1A5.

**SPOONER, Steven E.,** B.Comm., C.A.; financial executive; b. Ottawa, Ont. 29 May 1958; s. Michael John and Madelyn Christine (Daye) S.; e. Carleton Univ. B.Comm. (Hons.) 1980; C.A. Ont. 1982; m. Donna d. Don and Lenora Piuni 3 Sept. 1977; children: Brendan, Stephanie, Emily; VICE PRESIDENT, CORPORATE CONTROLLER, SHL SYSTEMHOUSE INC.; Former Dir., Wang Canada; Mem., Financial Extves. Inst.; Home: 30 Stitt St., Stittsville, Ont.

**SPRACHMAN, Mandel Charles,** B.Arch., M.R.A.I.C., R.C.A.; architect; b. Toronto, Ont. 15 Jan. 1925; s. Abraham and Mina (Offenberger) S.; e. Univ. of Toronto B.Arch. 1951; m. Carol Nina d. Carl Frankel, Toronto, Ont. 28 Nov. 1953; children: Benjamin, Robert, Andrew, Barnett; PRINC., MANDEL SPRACHMAN, ARCHITECT; mem., Royal Candn. Academy of Arts, 1978; Home: 77 Highland Ave., Toronto, Ont. M4W 2A4; Office: 30 Roden Pl., Toronto, Ont. M5R 1P5.

**SPRAGGETT, Allen Frederick,** B.A., D.Min.; writer, broadcaster, psychical researcher and consultant; neo-astrologer; b. Toronto, 26 March 1932; s. Henry and Gertrude Lena (Brown) S.; e. Queen's Univ.; Queen's Theological College, Kingston, Ont., B.A. 1962; D.Min., International Coll. of Psychical & Spiritual Sciences, Montreal 1986; m. Marion, d. Joseph and Grace Martin, 26 June 1954; children: Stephen, Alanna, Sandra, Dennis, Kathryn; ordained to the ministry by the Open Door Evangelical Churches 1954; pastor in churches in Collingwood, Hamilton, Elk Lake and Frankville, Ont.; o. Spiritual Science minister 1986; with the 'Toronto Star': religion editor 1962–69, daily columnist 1969–71; wrote weekly syndicated column 'The Unexplained' 1972–77; presenter of several radio and tv. programs about the occult; made a Fellow of the College of Human Sciences 1976; founding pres., Toronto Soc. for Psychical Rsch. 1970–81; mem. of exec. counc., Spiritual Frontiers Fellowship, Chicago 1975–78; mem., internat. ctte., Centro Studi e Scambi Internazionali, Rome; author and co-author of several books, incl.: 'The Unexplained' 1967; 'Kathryn Kuhlman: The Woman Who Believes in Miracles' 1970; 'The Bishop Pike Story' 1970; 'Probing the Unexplained' 1971; 'Arthur Ford: The Man Who Talked With The Dead' 1972; 'The World of the Unexplained' 1973; 'New Worlds of the Unexplained' 1974; 'The Case for Immortality' 1974; 'The Psychic Mafia' 1976; many articles on religion, parapsychology and other exotica; contributer to the 'New York Times' & the 'Psychoanalytic Review'; recognized as 'expert witness' on voodoo by Ont. Supreme Court 1978; recreation: studying the social habits of the Mongolian gerbil; Home: 126 Thornridge Dr., Thornhill, Ont. L4J 1E3.

**SPRAGUE, John B.,** B.Sc., M.A., Ph.D.; biologist; b. Woodstock, Ont. 16 Feb. 1931; s. William John and Ada Mary S.; e. Univ. of West. Ont. B.Sc. 1953; Univ. of Toronto M.A. 1954, Ph.D. 1959; m. Lois d. Gordon and Ruby Stokes 22 June 1953; children: David John, Catherine Dee, Susan Mary, Christine Anne, Julia Kim; PRES., J.B. SPRAGUE ASSOC. LTD. 1975– ; Scientist-in-charge, Pollution Studies, Fisheries Rsch. Bd. of Can. (St. Andrews, N.B.) 1958–70; Assoc. Prof., Prof., Dept. of Zoology, Univ. of Guelph 1970–88; Adjunct Prof. 1988– ; co-editor: 'Cadmium in the Aquatic Environment' 1987; author/co-author 60 sci. articles or chapters in books and over 55 tech. reports/papers in conf. proceedings; Office: P.O. Box 20009, 20 Woodlawn Rd. E., Guelph, Ont. N1H 8H6.

**SPRAWSON, Barrie Gilbert;** management consultant; b. Sutton Coldfield, England 19 Nov. 1939; s. Gilbert Harry and Lily Anne (Archinstall) S.; e. King Edward VI Gr. Sch. 1957; Univ. of Toronto; Harvard Univ., Adv. Mngt. 1981; m. Gillian d. Baron and Joyce Spencer 25 Jan. 1958; children: Garry Clive, Jonathan David, Andrew Barrie, Julia Patricia, Tricia Laura Karen; MNG. PRIN., SIBSON & CO. 1984– ; Dir., Dellcrest Children's Centre 1992– ; Supvr., Group Records Dept., Nat. Life Assur. Co. 1959–61; Sr. Group Rep., Confederation Life Insur. Co. 1961–64; Vice-Pres., Johnson & Higgins Ltd. 1964–74; Vice-Pres. & Dir., Johnson & Higgins Equity Corp. 1971–74; Partner in Charge, Human Resource Practice, Peat Marwick & Partners 1974–84; Comnr., Pension Comn. of Ont. 1977–83; Chrmn., Toronto Jr. Bd. of Trade 1971–72; Survey Cttes., Bd. of Trade of Metro. Toronto 1973–93 (Counc. Mem. 1973–74 and 1989–93); Mun. of Metro Toronto, Compensation Ctte. for Elected Officials 1975–93; Mem., City of Toronto Comp. Ctte. for Elected Officials 1975– ; Fellow, Candn. Inst. of Employee Benefit Specialists (Pres. 1986–87); Queen's Scout 1955; Senator, Jr. Ch. Internat. 1974; Mem., St. Judes Anglican Ch.; Past Pres., Lakeside Res. Assn.; author or co-author of several reports and articles; Guest Lectr., Queen's Univ.; recreations: tennis, walking; Clubs: Albany; Oakville; Bd. of Trade of Metro. Toronto; Rotary Club, Toronto; Home: 1417 Lakeshore Rd. E., Oakville, Ont. L6J 1L9; Office: P.O. Box 110, Scotia Plaza, 40 King St. W., 15th Flr., Toronto, Ont. M5H 3Y2.

**SPRAY, Andrew Robert Lindsey,** B.Sc., D.Phil.; educator; b. Stamford, England 17 Aug. 1944; s. Robert Bernard and Beryl Joan (Fordham) S.; e. W. Vancouver H.S. 1961; Univ. of B.C., B.Sc. 1965; Oxford Univ. (Rhodes Scholar) D.Phil. 1968; m. Leslie Margaret d. John and Georgina Clark 20 Dec. 1969; children: Rebecca, Anna, Philippa, Jennifer; TEACHER, LESTER B. PEARSON COLLEGE OF THE PACIFIC 1975– ; Woodrow Wilson Fellow 1965; post-doctoral fellowship Simon Fraser Univ. 1969; Teacher, St. George's Sch. 1969–75, Head of Sci. Dept. 1971–75, Asst. Dir. of Studies 1974–75; Co-ordr. of Timetable and Search & Rescue Team, present Coll. 1975– ; Internat. Baccalaureate Mathematics Subject Ctte. 1986– ; Universities Advisor at L.B. Pearson College 1990– ; Anglican; Peoples' Warden, St. Mary's Church, Metchosin 1991–94; Life Mem., Vancouver Rugby Union (Vice-Pres. 1973–75); Pres. West Comm. Refugee Aid Soc. 1984; Mem., B.C. Search and Rescue Advisory Council 1990– ; recreation: hiking; Home: 3810 Duke Rd., R.R. #4, Victoria, B.C. V9B 5T8; Office: Lester B. Pearson Coll., R.R. #1, Victoria, B.C. V9B 5T7.

**SPROTT, David Arthur,** M.A., Ph.D., F.R.S.C.; educator; b. Toronto, Ont. 31 May 1930; s. Arthur Frederick and Dorothy (Barry) S.; e. Univ. of Toronto B.A. 1952, M.A. 1953, Ph.D. 1955; m. Muriel Doris Vogel 16 Dec. 1961; children: Anne Ellen, Jane Barry; PROF. OF STATISTICS, UNIV. OF WATERLOO; co-ed. 'Foundations of Statistical Inference' 1971; author numerous tech. papers; Fellow, Royal Photographic Soc.; Am. Stat. Assn.; Inst. Math. Stat.; mem. Internat. Stat. Inst.; Internat. Biometric Soc.; Royal Stat. Soc.; Statistical Soc. of Can.; recipient, Gold Medal for Rsch., Statistical Soc. of Can.; recreation: photography; Home: 295 Ferndale Pl., Waterloo, Ont. N2J 3X8; Office: Waterloo, Ont. N2L 3G1.

**SPROULE, Brian J.,** B.Sc., M.D., M.Sc., F.R.C.P.C., F.A.C.P. F.C.C.P.; physician; b. Calgary, Alta. 31 Oct. 1925; s. Robert Crawford and Dorothy Margaret (Jessup) S.; e. Univ. of Alberta B.Sc. 1949, M.D. 1951; m. Marion d. Tina and Jack MacKay 26 Feb. 1954; children: Timothy, John, Shannon, Erin; PROFESSOR, MEDICINE, UNIV. OF ALBERTA 1968– ; general practice 1953; Rsch. Fellowship, Cardiology 1954; Residency, Dalls Parkland Hops. 1954–58; Instr., Med. S.W. Med. Sch. 1959; Asst. Prof., Univ. of Alta. 1960–68; Acting Chair 1974–75; Dir., Resp. Div. 1960–88; Gov., Am. Coll. Physicians 1978–88; Am. Coll. Cert. Physicians 1973–78; Council, Royal College of Physicians & Surg. 1982–90; Vice-Pres. Royal Coll. 1988–90; Chair, Accred. Ctte. 1983–89; Council, Alta. Coll. Physicians 1989–92; Pres., Candn. Thoracic Soc. 1973–75; Pres. Garneau Lung Lab.; AOA Hon. Med. Soc.; RF Christie Lectr., Candn. Thoracic soc. 1989; Dinstinguished Friend of the Inst., NAIT 1992; Mem., Bd. of Dir., Univ. Hosp. 1992; Council, Candn. Council of Heatlh Facilities Assn. 1990– ; Clinical Dir., Alta. Asthma Centre 1993– ; author/co-author 6 books, 91 articles & 63 abstracts; recreations: golf, hiking, swimming, theater; Home: 12808 – 66 Ave., Edmonton, Alta. T6H 1Y7; Office: 2-E436 W.C. McKenzie Ctr., Edmonton, Alta. T6G 2E2.

**SPRUNG, Donald Whitfield Loyal,** B.A., Ph.D., D.Sc.; F.R.S.C.; physicist; university professor; b. Kitchener, Ont. 6 June 1934; s. the late Lyall MacAulay and Doreen Bishop (Price) S.; e. Kitchener Waterloo Coll. and Vocational Sch. 1949–53; Univ. of Toronto B.A. 1957; Univ. of Birmingham, Eng., Ph.D. 1961, D.Sc. 1977; m. Hannah Sueko Nagai 12 Dec. 1958; children: Anne Elizabeth, Carol Hanako; PROFESSOR OF PHYSICS, MCMASTER UNIV. 1971– ; Chair, Dept. of Physics & Astronomy 1991– ; (Dean, Fac. of Sci. there 1975–84 and 1989); Instr. Cornell Univ. 1961–62; Asst. Prof. McMaster Univ. 1962–66; Researcher Massachusetts Inst. of Tech. 1964–65; Assoc. Prof. McMaster Univ. 1966–71; Visiting Prof. Université de Paris-sud (Orsay) 1969–70; Gäst Prof. Univ. Tübingen, Germany, 1980–81; Univ. Mainz, 1990–91; Guest Scholar, Kyoto Univ. 1986; Visiting Rsch. Fellow, Univ. of Melbourne 1986; Visiting Prof., Univ. Barcelona (Spain) 1991–92; author of over 100 scientific papers in field of theoretical physics; mem. Inst. of Physics (London); Am. Physical Society; Candn. Assn. of Physicists; Fellow, Royal Soc. of Can; Lt.-Gov. Silver Medal, 1957; Rotary Foundation Fellow, 1957–58; C.D. Howe Memorial Fellow, 1969; Herzberg Medal of the Candn. Assn. of Physicists, 1972; recreations: cabinet making, bicycling, travel; Home: 15 Little John Rd., Dundas, Ont. L9H 4G5; Office: 1280 Main St. W., Hamilton, Ont. L8S 4M1.

**SPRUNG, Guy,** B.A.; theatre and television/film director; writer; b. Ottawa, Ont. 17 Apr. 1947; s. George Mervyn Carter and Ilse Erna (Grabenhorst) S.; e. Glebe Collegiate, Ottawa; McGill Univ. B.A. 1970; children: Kathleen, Trisanna, Northrop; Pres. McGill Players 1968–69; Asst. Dir. Schiller Theatre, West Berlin 1970; Founder and First Artistic Dir. Half Moon Theatre, London, Eng. 1971–75; freelance theatre dir. across Can. 1976–81; Artistic Dir., Toronto Free Theatre 1982–87; Assoc. Dir., Stratford Festival 1985–88; Artistic Dir., Vancouver Playhouse 1987–88; Co-Artistic Dir. and Co-Founder, Canadian Stage Co. 1988–90; brought to the stage 1st prodns. of: W.O. Mitchell's 'Back to Beulah' and 'Black Bonspiel of Wullie MacCrimmon'; David Fennario's 'Nothing to Lose' and 'Balconville'; 'Paper Wheat'; 'Les Canadiens'; Anne Chislett's 'Quiet in the Land'; Sharon Pollock's 'Doc'; Doug Rodger's 'Donut City' and 'How Could You Mrs. Dick'; Clinton Bomphray's 'Avro Arrow'; Marianne Ackerman's 'L'Affair Tartuffe'; directed: 'Damien'; 'Translations'; 'Death of a Salesman'; 'Fair Liberty's Call' (Stratford Festival); 'The Real Thing' and 'I'm Not Rappaport' (Manitoba Theatre Centre/The Royal Alex); has directed at Vancouver Playhouse, Manitoba Theatre Centre, Theatre Calgary, Centaur Theatre; CentreStage; Tivoli Theatre, Hamilton; establishing reputation in classical theatre for stagings of 'The Changeling,' 'Romeo and Juliet' and 'Hamlet'; founded TFT's Dream in High Park project bringing free Shakespeare to Toronto; Dir., 'A Midsummer Night's Dream' at Pushkin Theatre, Moscow; nominated for six Dora Mavor Moore Awards, winner of two Doras; Teacher, National Theatre School and Conservatoire de l'Art Dramatique; Co-author: (with Rita Much) 'Hot Ice'; Contributor to journals and newspapers on politics and the arts; Mem., Bd. of Dirs., Harbourfront; Vice-Pres., Barna/Alper productions; recreations: hockey, chess; Home/Office: 360 Sackville, Toronto, Ont. M4X 1S4.

**SPRY, Irene Mary,** O.C., M.A., LL.D., D.U., F.R.G.S.; professor emeritus; economic historian; b. Standerton, Transvaal, S. Africa 28 Aug. 1907; d. Evan E. and Amelia (Amie) Bagshaw (Johnstone) Biss; e. Bournemouth (Eng.) High Sch. for Girls; London Sch. of Econ. Intermediate Exm. 1925; Girton Coll. Cambridge B.A. 1928; Bryn Mawr Coll. Pa. M.A. 1929; Univ. of Toronto LL.D. (honoris causa) 1971; Univ. of Ottawa D.U. (honoris causa) 1985; m. Graham s. Maj.-Gen. Daniel William Bigelow and Ethalyn Alma (Rich) Spry 30 June 1938; children: Robert (Robin) Graham Michel, Richard Daniel Evan, Elizabeth (Lib) Ann de Gaspé; PROF. EMERITUS OF ECON. UNIV. OF OTTAWA 1974– ; Lectr. in Pol. Econ. and Asst. Prof. Univ. of Toronto 1929–38, Don Women's Residences Univ. Coll. 1929–35; Acting Dir. Studies in Econ. and Supr. students for Econ. Tripos, Girton and Newnham Colls. Cambridge 1938–39; Econ. Adv. to Nat. YWCA Can. 1940–41; Econ. Wartime Prices & Trade Bd. 1941–42, Commodity Prices Stabilization Corp. Ltd. 1942–45; Visiting Assoc. Prof. Univ. of Sask. 1967–68; Visiting Assoc Prof., Assoc. Prof. and Prof. Univ. of Ottawa 1968–73, part-time teaching 1973–79, mem. Senate 1970–71, Bd. Govs. 1973–76; Sr. Rsch. Assoc. Univs. Montréal and McGill GAMMA 1974–76; Rsch. Fellowship, Candn. Plains Rsch. Centre, Regina 1992–93; mem. Lord Tweedsmuir's Ctte. Inquiry Imperial Inst. 1950–52; mem. Bd. Govs., Exec. Ctte., Edn. Ctte. Commonwealth Inst. to 1967; Adv. Ctte. on Rsch. Dept. Transport Can. 1968–70; recipient Can. Council Award 1964; Silver Medal Royal Soc. Arts 1965; Officer, Order of Canada 1993; served with Assoc. Country Women of the World, Rep. Federated Women's Insts. Can. 1954–67, Chrmn. Exec. Ctte. & Gen. Purposes Ctte. 1959–65, Dep. World Pres. 1968–74, Co-opted mem. Council 1977–86, Member of Honour 1986; author 'The Palliser Expedition' 1964; co-author, 'The Records of the Department of the Interior' 1993; ed. 'The Papers of the Palliser Expedition 1857–1860' 1968; 'Buffalo Days and Nights' 1976; co-ed. 'Natural Resource Development in Canada' 1973; Assoc. Ed. 'The Musk-Ox' 1981–84; author various book chapters, papers; contbr. 'Dictionary of Canadian Biography' various yrs.; 'The Encyclopaedia of Canada 1935–37 and subsequent editions as the 'Encyclopaedia Canadiana'; "The Discoverers: An Encyclopedia of Explorers and Exploration' 1980; The Canadian Encyclopedia' 1985; festschrift 'Explorations in Canadian Economic History: Essays in Honour of Irene M. Spry' 1985; Hon. mem. Women's Corona Soc.; Alta. Historic Trails Soc.; Guest of Honour, Pol. Econ. Assn. 1984; Distinguished Canadian Award, Seniors' Univ. Group, Univ. of Regina 1987; mem. Royal Econ. Soc.; Candn. Econ. Assn.; Candn. Hist. Assn.; Candn. Pol. Sci. Assn.; recreations: gardening, ornithology, collecting western and arctic canadiana; Home: 446 Cloverdale Rd., Ottawa, Ont. K1M 0Y6; Office: 550 Cumberland, Ottawa, Ont. K1N 6N5.

**SQUARE, Paula Ann,** B.Sc., M.Sc., Ph.D.; university professor; b. Painesville, Ohio 20 Sept. 1948; d. Paul Joseph and Mary Elizabeth (Kulow) S.; e. Riverside H.S. 1966; Miami Univ. B.Sc. 1970; Kent State Univ. M.Sc. 1976; Mayo Clinic, Dept. of Neurology, Fellow 1978–80; Kent State Univ. Ph.D. 1981; ASSOC. PROF.& CHAIR, SPEECH PATHOLOGY, UNIV. OF TORONTO 1990– ; internationally recognized academician in area of acquired motor speech disorders due to brain damage in adults; Cons., Nat. Institutes of Health, Behavioural and Neuroscience; Honours, Candn. Assn. of Speech-Language Pathologists & Audiologists 1992; Bd. of Dir., Speech Found. of Ont.; Profl. Advisor, Aphasia Ctr.; Mem., AM. Speech-Language and Hearing Assn.; Ont. & Candn. Speech-Language Pathologists & Audiologists; Council of Grad. Programs in Communicative Disorders & Sciences (US); Chair, Cand. Council of Univ. Prog. in Communicaiton Sci. & Disorders; editor: 'Acquired Apraxia of Speech in Aphasic Afults: Theoretical and Clinical Issues'; recreations: gardening, riding; Home: 37 Rainsford Rd., Toronto, Ont. M4L 3N5; Office: Toronto, Ont. M5S 1A8.

**SQUIBB, Geoffrey Wayne,** B.A.; businessman; b. Saint John, N.B. 19 Jan. 1945; s. Reginald John and Mary Elizabeth (Leonard) S.; e. Fredericton H.S. 1964; Univ. of N.B. B.A. 1968; m. Maureen d. James and Joan Moffatt 15 Aug. 1988; children: Cristin, Jessica, Elizabeth, Geoffrey; CO-FOUNDER, PRESIDENT & CHIEF EXECUTIVE OFFICER, REALSTAR GROUP 1974– ; Trainee to Vice-President, Bank of Montreal 1968–78; several corporate and community organization directorships; Gov., Univ. of N.B.; Gov., Bishop Strachan School (Toronto); Mem., Little Trinity Anglican Church; Office: 2 St. Clair Ave. W., Suite 700, Toronto, Ont. M4V 1L5.

**SQUIRE, Anne Marguerite,** M.A., D.D.; retired church executive; b. Amherstburg, Ont. 17 Oct. 1920; d. Alexander Samuel and Coral Marguerite Park; e. Carleton Univ., B.A. 1972 (Senate Medal, B.A. Hons. 1974 (Judaic Studies Award), M.A. 1975, LL.D. 1988; Un. Theol. Coll. McGill Univ. D.D. 1980; Queen's Univ. D.D. 1985; m. William Robert children: Frances, Laura, Margaret; Teacher, Malden, Ont. 1939–40, Riverside, Ont. 1940–45; Curriculum Writer, Un. Ch. of Can. 1965–75; Adjunct Prof. Carleton Univ. 1975–82; Gen. Sec. Div. of Ministry Personnel & Edn. Un. Ch. Can. 1982–85; Moderator, United Church of Can. 1986–88; mem. Bd. Mgmt. Queen's Univ. Theol. Coll. 1980–85; Chairperson Ont. Conf. for Women 1979–80; author numerous publs.; Pres. Kappa Chapter, Delta Kappa Gamma Internat. 1977; Home: 731 Weston Dr., Ottawa, Ont.

**STABBACK, Jack Garry,** B.Sc., P.Eng., FCIM; b. Gleichen, Alta. 18 Aug. 1920; s. Robin Maxwell and Jessie Lavina (Eddie) S.; e. Pub. and High Schs., Calgary, Alta.; Univ. of Alta., B.Sc. (Chem. Engn.) 1949; m. Delphy, d. Martin Gronsdahl, deceased, 14 Nov. 1959; children: Lynne, Susan, Garry, Cheryl, Lynda, Kent; Energy Consultant 1985– ; Dir., Encor Energy Corp. Inc. 1982–88; Dir. United Canso Oil and Gas Ltd. 1986–88; joined Alta. Oil and Gas Conservation Board, 1949 and served as Field Engineer, Chief Gas Engineer and Adm. for Gas to 1964; on loan to Nat. Energy Board during 1960 as Acting Chief Engr.; carried out natural gas investigation for S. Australian Govt., 1964; joined Nat. Energy Board as Chief Engineer, 1964; appointed a member 1968; Assoc. Vice Chrmn. 1974; Vice Chrmn. of Bd. 1976; Chrmn. 1978–80; Sr. Vice Pres. Global Energy & Minerals Group, The Royal Bank Calgary, 1980–85; Chrmn., North Park Manor Soc. 1992– ; served with the Canadian Army and R.C.A.F. during World War II; mem., Canadian Institute Mining & Metall.; Assoc. of P. Eng. of Ont. and Alta.; Freemason; Shriner; Baptist; recreations: walking, swimming, travelling; Address: 406 – 1033 Belmont Ave., Victoria, B.C. V8S 3T4.

**STABLEFORTH, Nancy L.,** B.J., LL.B.; civil servant; b. Sault Ste Marie, Ont. 28 Nov. 1952; d. Arthur Edward and Eileen B. (McLarty) S.; e. Carleton Univ. B.J. 1975; Univ. of Windsor LL.B. 1978; m. Ronald B. s. Ronald R. and Mary C. Rose 24 Sept. 1983; EXECUTIVE VICE-CHAIRPERSON, NATIONAL PAROLE BOARD 1993– ; called to Bar, Prov. of Ont. 1980; Partner, Gaetz & Stableforth 1980–85; Extve. Asst. to Min. for Internat. Trade 1985–86; Extve. Asst. to Solicitor Gen. of Can. 1986–88; Mem., Appeal Div., Nat. Parole Bd. 1988–91; Vice-Chair 1991–93; Mem., Extve. Ctte. & Bd. of Dir., Council of Candn. Admin. Tribunals 1991– ; Sec., Algoma Dist. Law Assn. 1980–83; Librarian 1983–84; Dir. 1984–85; Pres. & Mem., Bd. of Dir., Gateway Children's Ctr. 1990– ; Mem., Bd. of Dir., Children's Mental Health Algoma 1981–83; John Howard Soc. 1981–82; editor 'The Oyez' 1976–77; recreations: sailing, skiing; club: Nepean Sailing; Home: 110 Falcon Brook Rd., Carp, Ont. K0A 1L0; Office: 340 Laurier Ave. W., Ottawa, Ont. K1A 0R1.

**STACEY, Anthony;** association executive; b. Southampton, England 3 Apr. 1920; s. Frederick Thomas and Rosina Maud (Leggett) S.; e. Pickering Cont. Sch.; m. Ada d. Joseph and Emma Galley 11 May 1979; children: Brian, Diane; served overseas with RCASC (mentioned in World War II despatches); operated refrig. serv. bus.; Life Mem., Highland Creek Br., Royal Candn. Legion (joined 1946; former br. pres. & zone & dist. comdr.); Dominion Vice-Pres. 1982–84; 1st Vice-Pres. 1984–86; Immed. Past Dominion Pres., 1986–88; Past Chrmn., Veterans Serv. Ctte. & Legion Sr. Prog.; Trustee, Sunnybrook Med. Ctr. 1975–81; Pres., RCL Care Cte. Inc.; Dir. 1971– ; Toronto Legion Homes Inc. 1967–84; Chrmn., Metro Legion Vill. 1971–83; Ont. Comd. Charitable Found. 1979–85; Candn. Centennial Medal; Jubilee Medal; Health & Welfare Can. Lifestyle Award; LMSM; Palm Leaf; recreations: curling, fishing, community service; Club: Royal Candn. Legion; Address: 4 Portia St., West Hill, Ont. M1E 1T5.

**STACKHOUSE, Reginald Francis,** M.A., L.Th., B.D., Ph.D., D.D.; b. Toronto, Ont. 30 Apl. 1925; s. Edward and Emmaline (McNeill) S.; e. Univ. of Toronto B.A. 1946, M.A. 1951; Wycliffe Coll. Toronto L.Th. 1950, B.D. 1954; Yale Univ. Ph.D. 1962; D.D. (hon.) Huron Coll., London, Ont. and Wycliffe Coll., Toronto; m. Margaret Eleanor d. Roland Allman, Toronto, Ont. 2 June 1951; children: Mary, Elizabeth, Ruth, John; PRES., STACKHOUSE CONSULTING INC.; Bd. of Dirs., Toronto Mutual Life Ins. Co. Ltd.; Professor, Toronto School of Theology 1969– and Principal, Wycliffe Coll. 1975–85; Principal Emeritus, Wycliffe Coll. 1991– ; Honorary Canon, St. James Cathedral, Toronto; Chaplain, Hospitaller Order of St. John of Jerusalem; Chrmn. Bd. of Govs. Centennial Coll. Scarborough 1966–69 (Hon. grad.); mem. Scarborough Pub. Lib. Bd. 1963–64; Scarborough Bd. Educ. 1965–72; M.P., Scarborough East, H. of C. 1972–74, Scarborough West 1984–88; Candn. Rep., UN Gen. Assembly 1986; Chrmn., H. of C. Standing Ctte. on Human Rights 1986–88; mem., Candn. Human Rights Commn. 1990–93; Ont. Council of Regents 1969–72; author 'Christianity and Politics' 1965; 'The God Nobody Knows' 1985; 'How Can I Believe When I Live In A World Like This?' 1990; 'You Don't Have to Be Neurotic to Feel Insecure' 1993; also various articles; P. Conservative; Anglican; Club: Empire (Pres. 1980–81); Albany; Home: R.R. 4, Bracebridge, Ont. P1L 1X2.

**STACKHOUSE, Richard G.,** B.Com., F.C.A.; chartered accountant; b. Ottawa, Ont. 26 Nov. 1929; s. A. Gilbert and Leone (Turner) S.; e. Queen's Univ. B.Com. 1953; C.A. 1956; F.C.A. 1976; m. Jean children: Brent R., Kerry J., Nancy E.; Retired Partner, Price Waterhouse; joined Price Waterhouse 1953, Partner 1967; Trustee, Queen's Univ. 1979– , Chrmn. of Bd. 1990– ; Chrmn. of Bd. Donwood Inst. 1982–86, Dir. 1978–86; Chrmn. of Bd. Ont. Safety League 1984–86, Dir. 1979–87; Dir. Candn. Nat. Exhn. 1985– , Vice Pres. 1987–90, Pres. 1990–92, Hon. Pres. 1992– ; Gov., Exhibition Place 1988– ; Gov., Shaw Festival 1991– ; Chrmn., Red Shield Appeal, Salvation Army 1992; Past Chrmn., Prof. Div., Un. Way; served with RCNVR 1949–53, rank Lt.; recreations: golf, antiques, philately, photography; Clubs: Mississaugua Golf & Country (Dir. 1976–78, 1980–84; Pres. 1982–84); National (Dir. 1981–88; Pres. 1986–87); Freemason (Treas. Harcourt Lodge 1983– ); Home: 1256 Woodland Ave., Mississauga, Ont. L5G 2X9; Office: P.O. Box 190, 1 First Canadian Place, Toronto, Ont. M5X 1H7.

**STADELMAN, William Ralph,** B.A.Sc., M.B.A.; b. St. Mary's, Ont. 18 July 1919; s. John Joseph and Lillian (Trachsell) S.; e. Univ. of Toronto, B.A.Sc. (Chem. Engn.) 1941; Univ. of Pennsylvania (Wharton Sch. of Finance & Econ.), M.B.A. 1949; m. Jean, d. late Walker MacLaren, Nov. 1951; one d. Laren; PRESIDENT, W.R.S. ASSOCIATES 1984– ; Dir., ICST, The Inst. of Chemical Sci. & Tech. 1985–89; with Defense Industries Ltd., Winnipeg, Man. 1941–43; apptd. Chief Devel. Engr. becoming Chief Process Engr., Candn. Synthetic Rubber Ltd., Sarnia, Ont. 1943–47; Lectr. in Marketing, Univ. of Pa. 1948–49; joined Pennsylvania Salt, Wyandotte, Mich. as Special Asst. to Mgr.; apptd. Secy.-Treas., Ont. Research Foundation 1950; Pres., Ont.

Research Foundation 1964–83; mem. Club of Rome; Fellow, World Academy of Art and Science; Assn. Prof. Engrs. Ont.; Toronto Bd. of Trade; Address: 31 Rykert Cr., Toronto, Ont. M4G 2T1.

**STAFFORD, David Alexander Tetlow,** B.A., M.A., Ph.D.; writer; professor; b. Newcastle upon Tyne, England 10 Mar. 1942; s. Norman and Edith Margaret (Cross) S.; e. Dame Allan's Sch.; Downing Coll., Cambridge, B.A. (Hons.) 1963, M.A. 1965; London Sch. of Econ. & Pol. Sci., Ph.D. 1968; SR. RSCH. FELLOW, CANDN. INSTITUTE OF INTERNAT. AFFAIRS 1992– ; Third Sec., Fgn. Off., London 1967; Second Sec. 1968; Rsch. Assoc., LSE, Ctr. for Internat. Stud. 1968–70; Asst. Prof., Univ. of Victoria, B.C. 1970–75; Assoc. Prof. 1976–83; Prof. 1984; Vis. Prof., Univ. of Toronto 1984–85; Adjunct Prof. 1986– ; Dir. of Stud., Candn. Inst. of Internat. Affairs 1985– ; Extve. Dir., 1986–92; Sr. Assoc. Mem., St. Antony's Coll., Oxford 1976; Vis. Assoc., Clare Hall, Cambridge 1982; Vis. Prof., York Univ., Glendon Coll. 1985–86; Cons., BBC-TV London, CBC-TV, Toronto; Chrmn., Candn. Assn. for Security & Intelligence Stud. 1987–91; author: 'From Anarchism to Reformism' 1970, 'Britain and European Resistance' 1980, 'Camp X' 1986, 'The Silent Game' 1988; co-author: 'Spy Wars' (with J.L. Granatstein) 1990; co-editor: (with S. Farson and W.K. Wark) 'Security and Intelligence Needs for the 1990s (1991); and num. articles & reviews in acad. jours., newspapers & mags.; Originator/Narrator, CBC radio series 'In From the Cold' 1981, 'History as Myth' 1985; 'The New Germany' 1990; Home: 267 Major St., Toronto, Ont. M5S 2L5; Office: 15 King's Coll. Circle, Toronto, Ont. M5S 2V9.

**STAFFORD, Gerard Simon;** insurance executive; b. Ottawa, Ont. 13 Dec. 1940; s. Alexandre and Pauline (Kingsbury) S.; CHAIRMAN, PRESIDENT AND CHIEF EXECUTIVE OFFICER, COMMERCIAL UNION ASSURANCE COMPANY OF CANADA; present firm since 1960; Chrmn. & C.E.O., Commercial Union Life Assurance Company of Canada; Director: Insurance Bureau of Can.; Underwriters Adjustment Bureau; Insurers' Adv. Organization; recreations: travel, painting; clubs: Toronto Club, National Club, World Trade Club, Adelaide Club; Home: 56 Brinloor Blvd., Scarborough, Ont. M1M 1L5; Office: P.O. Box 441, Toronto-Dominion Centre, Toronto, Ont. M5K 1L9.

**STAGER, David Arnold Albert,** B.Sc.A., M.A., Ph.D.; educator; b. Galt, Ont. 19 Sept. 1937; s. A. Oscar and Norma V. (McVittie) S.; e. Ont. Agric. Coll. Univ. of Toronto B.Sc.A. 1959; Johns Hopkins Univ. M.A. 1961; Oxford Univ. (Rhodes Scholar 1960) B.A. 1962, M.A. 1966; Princeton Univ. M.A. 1964, Ph.D. 1968; m. Beverly M. Hales 9 Oct. 1965; children: Andrea, Martha; PROF. OF ECON. UNIV. OF TORONTO 1988– ; Dean of Students New Coll. present Univ. 1964–69, Rsch. Assoc. Inst. Policy Analysis 1965–82, Asst. Prof. of Econ. 1965, Assoc. Prof. 1970, Assoc. Chrmn. of Econ. 1980–84; cons. several federal and provl. govt. depts., comns. policy devel. postsecondary edn., profl. labour mkts.; Comnr. and Chrmn. Parking Authority Toronto 1973–89; author 'Economic Analysis and Canadian Policy' 7th ed. 1992; 'Focus on Fees' 1989; 'Lawyers in Canada' 1990; numerous articles and reports econ. and financing higher edn.; mem. Candn. Assn. Rhodes Scholars (Treas.); Candn. Rhodes Scholars Found. (Dir.); Elder, Bloor St. Un. Ch.; Home: 84 Walmer Rd., Toronto, Ont. M5R 2X7; Office: 150 St. George St., Toronto, Ont. M5S 2E9.

**STAGG, Malcolm J.,** B.Sc.; business executive; b. 12 Aug.1947; e. Queen's Univ. B.Sc. 1972; two children; PRESIDENT & CHIEF EXECUTIVE OFFICER, PHILIPS CABLES LIMITED 1993– ; Marketing Engineer, Goodyear Canada 1972–74; Product Development Mgr., Fiberglas Canada 1974–80; Plant Mgr., Ottawa Fibre Indus. 1980–82; Manager Technical Services 1982–88; Pres., Vinyl Div., BPCO 1988–90; Pres., Utilities Div. & Vice-Pres. & Gen. Mgr., Phillips Cables Limited 1990–92; Dir., Phillips Cables Limited; Chrmn. of Board Phillips-Fitel Inc., BICC Cables Corp.; Mem., Bd.of Trade of Metro Toronto; Assn. of Profl. Engrs.; Bd.of Dir. & Chrmn. of Wire & Cable Section, Elect. & Electronic Mfrs. Assn. of Can.; Candn. Electrical Distributors Assn.; recreations: photography, golfing, curling; Office: 200, 100 Consilium Place, Scarborough, Ont. M1H 3G2.

**STAGG, Pamela Margaret Southwell,** B.A., A.O.C.A.; writer, botanical painter; b. Nottingham, England 22 April 1949; d. Prof. Geoffry Leonard and Amy Russell (Southwell) S.; e. St. Clement's School 1966; Ontario College of Art A.O.C.A. 1970; Univ. of Guelph B.A. 1974; PRES., PAMELA STAGG CREATIVE SERVICES 1984– ; Art Dir., Cockfield Brown & Co. 1975; Sr. Art Dir., Norman Craig & Kummel (Canada) 1980; Creative Dir., Product Initiatives 1981; solo shows of painting: Civic Garden Centre Toronto 1989, Royal Botanical Gardens Hamilton 1991; Park Walk Gall., London England 1993; Royal Horticultural Soc. Gold Medal for an exhibit of paintings of Candn. Garden Iris 1991; 7th Internat. Exhib., Botanical Painting & Illus. Pittsburgh April 1992; Royal Horticultural Soc. Grenfell Medal 1992; Special 70th Anniversary Exhib. of the British Iris Soc. 1991; Soc. of Botanical Artists Annual Exhibition, London 1992; rep. in private collections in Canada, U.S., Great Brit., France & Switz. incl. The Hunt Inst. for Botanical Documentation, Carnegie-Mellon Univ.; Mem., Royal Botanical Gardens; Candn. Iris Soc.; Brit. Iris Soc.; Soc. of Botanical Artists (London); Bd. of Dirs., Civic Garden Centre, Toronto; author: 'In the Spirit of Partnership' 1990; subject of several articles in 'The Times' (London), 'The Globe and Mail,' 'Applied Arts Quarterly,' 'Garden Design,' 'Pappus,' and 'Studio Magazine'; illustrations have appeared on covers of 'Pappus' & 'Harrowsmith'; illustrator: numerous articles for Canadian, American and British publications; taught Botanical Watercolour Workshop, Toronto 1992 & 1993, lectures on botanical illustration, London 1993; Home: 3 Bennington Heights Dr., Toronto, Ont. M4G 1A7.

**STAINER, Dennis William,** B.Sc., Ph.D.; consultant; b. Liverpool, U.K. 25 Aug. 1932; s. William Henry and Florence Jean (Davies) S.; e. Liverpool Univ. B.Sc. (Hons.) 1955, Ph.D. 1957; 1st. m. Anita (d. 1983) d. David and Clara Stewart 23 Nov. 1957; 2nd m. Inge Grethe d. Svend and Grethe Winslow 28 Sept. 1984; children: Mark Howard, Paul Jonathan, Jens Christian (stepson); PRESIDENT, STAINER ASSOCIATES 1992– ; Post-doctoral Fellow, National Research Council of Canada 1957–59; Dir., Bacterial Vaccines Div., Connaught Labs. 1960–87; Vice-Pres., Regulatory Affairs, Conpharma Vaccines 1987–92; Mem., Am. Soc. of Microbiology; Internat. Assn. of Biol. Standardization; Internat. Tetanus Soc.; author of 37 scientific papers and one chapter in 'Pathogenesis and Immunity in Pertussis' 1988; recreations: theatre, squash, music, opera; clubs: Richmond Hill Rotary (Past Pres.), Richmond Hill Racquet; Address: 109 Regent St., Richmond Hill, Ont. L4C 9P3.

**STAINES, David McKenzie,** A.M., Ph.D.; educator; b. Toronto, Ont. 8 Aug. 1946; s. Ralph McKenzie and Mary Rita (Hayes) S.; e. St. Michael's Coll. Sch. Toronto 1963; St. Michael's Coll. Univ. of Toronto B.A. 1967; Harvard Univ. A.M. 1968, Ph.D. 1973; PROFESSOR OF ENGLISH, UNIV. OF OTTAWA 1985– ; Teaching Fellow in Eng. Harvard Univ. 1968–73, Asst. Prof. of Eng. 1973–78, Visiting Assoc. Prof. summers 1980, 1982; Visiting Asst. Prof. of Eng. Univ. of P.E.I. summer 1975; Hon. Research Fellow, Univ. Coll. London 1977–78; Assoc. Prof. of English, Univ. of Ottawa 1978–85; recipient Can. Council Doctoral Fellowship 1968–72; Charles Dexter Travelling Scholarship 1971; Nat. Endowment for Humanities Fellowship Independent Study & Research 1977–78; Huntington Lib. Fellowship 1979; Newberry Lib. Fellowship 1980; Five College Prof. of Candn. Studies, Amherst, Mass. 1982–84; Ed. 'The Canadian Imagination: Dimensions of a Literary Culture' 1977; 'Responses and Evaluations: Essays on Canada by E.K. Brown' 1977; 'Reappraisals: The Callaghan Symposium' 1981; 'The 49th and Other Parallels: Contemporary Canadian Perspectives' 1986; 'Stephen Leacock: A Reappraisal' 1986; 'Stephen Leacock: My Financial Career and Other Follies' 1993; 'Journal of Canadian Poetry' 1985– ; Gen. Ed., New Canadian Library 1988– ; co-ed. (with A. Garrod) 'Illuminations: The Days of Our Youth' 1984; (with R. Scholes, C.H. Klaus, N.R. Comley) 'Elements of Literature' 1987; (with Neil Besner) 'The Short Story in English' 1991; author 'Tennyson's Camelot' 1982; trans. 'The Complete Romances of Chrétien de Troyes' 1990; various articles and reviews Arthurian lit., medieval drama & romance, Victorian poetry, Candn. lit.; mem. Medieval Acad. Am. (Chrmn. Comte. on Centers & Regional Assns. 1981–87); Internat. Arthurian Soc.; Modern Lang. Assn.; Assn. Candn. Univ. Teachers Eng.; Internat. Assn. Univ. Professors Eng.; R. Catholic; recreations: theatre, bridge; Home: 12 Galt St. Ottawa, Ont. K1S 4R4; Office: Ottawa, Ont. K1N 6N5.

**STAINES, Mavis Avril;** artistic director/ballet principal; b. Cownsville, Que. 9 Apr. 1954; d. David Russell and Betty (Knott) S.; e. The National Ballet Sch. 1968–73; Nat. Ballet Sch., Teachers Training Prog. 1981–83; m. Jyrki s. Unto and Miriam Virsunen 4 Feb. 1988; ARTISTIC DIRECTOR, THE NATIONAL BALLET SCHOOL 1989– ; Dancer, The National Ballet of Can. 1973–78; First Soloist 1975–78; Dancer, The Dutch National Ballet 1978–81; Artistic Staff, present institution 1982; Assoc. Artistic Dir. 1984; Office: 105 Maitland St., Toronto, Ont. M4Y 1E4.

**STAIRS, Denis Winfield,** M.A., Ph.D., F.R.S.C.; educator; b. Halifax, N.S. 6 Sept. 1939; s. Henry Gerald and Freda (Winfield) S.; e. Lachine High Sch. 1957; Dalhousie Univ. B.A. 1961; Oxford Univ. (Rhodes Scholar) B.A. 1964, M.A. 1968; Univ. of Toronto Ph.D. 1969; m. Jennifer Smith 18 July 1987; two s. (by previous marriage) Robert Woodliffe, Christopher Winfield; PROF. OF POL. SCIENCE, DALHOUSIE UNIV.; Asst. Prof. of Pol. Sci. 1966, Assoc. Prof. 1970, Prof. 1975– , Dir. Centre for Foreign Policy Studies 1971–75; Chair, Dept. of Pol. Science 1980–85; Vice-Pres. (Acad. & Rsch.) 1988–93; mem., Social Sci's. & Humanities Rsch. Council Can. 1981–87; Rsch. Co-ordinator for Royal Comn. on the Econ. Union and Development Prospects for Canada (Macdonald Comn.) 1983–85; Adv. Ctte. Acad. Relations Dept. External Affairs 1978– ; Dir., Atlantic Council Can. 1979– ; Rsch. Council, Candn. Inst. for Advanced Rsch. 1986– ; Can. Council Leave Fellow 1972–73; SSHRCC Leave Fellow 1979–80; mem., Bd. of Dirs., Institute for Rsch. on Public Policy 1989– ; author: 'The Diplomacy of Constraint: Canada, the Korean War and the United States' 1974; mem., Candn. Inst. Internat. Affairs; Internat. Studies Assn.; Candn. Pol. Sci. Assn. (Vice Pres. 1977–78, Pres. 1981–82); recreation: sailing; Clubs: Royal N.S. Yacht Sqdn.; Home: 4 Rockwood, Halifax, N.S. B3N 1X5; Office: Halifax, N.S. B3H 4H6.

**STAIT-GARDNER, Christopher E.,** B.A.Sc., P.Eng.; business executive; b. London, England 23 Dec. 1938; s. Eric Lucifer and May Marion S.; e. Univ. of Toronto, B.A.Sc. 1962; m. Myrna d. James and Lilly Saunders 5 Oct. 1963; children: Brent, Craig; CHRMN. OF THE BD, PRES. & C.E.O., SECURITY CARD SYSTEMS INC.; joined IBM Can. 1962 as Systems Engr.; left 1980 as Dir., Computing Serv.; Vice-Pres., Info. Systems, Hudsons Bay Co. 1980; Sr. Vice-Pres., Mktg. & Planning, The Bank of Montreal 1983; Pres., NBS Transaction Services 1987; formerly, Vice-Chrmn.: Interac Assn.; CIRRUS Systems; Mem., Can. Extve. Planning Ctte., Candn. Payments Assoc. & Interbank Opns. Ctte.; Pres., Mastercard Assn. of Can.; Dir., Security Card Systems Inc.; EFTA; York Technology Assn.; recreations: golf, curling; Club: Thornhill Country; Home: 220 Greenbrooke Dr., Woodbridge, Ont. L4L 1A6; Office: 399 Denison St., Markham, Ont. L3R 1B7.

**STAIT-GARDNER, Zane,** B.A.; insurance executive; b. Riga, Latvia 29 Sept. 1944; d. John and Zelma (Grinfelds) Brezinskis; e. Univ. of Toronto B.A. 1968; m. Keith s. Eric and May S. 15 May 1965; children: Christine, Lia; SENIOR VICE-PRES. & GEN. MGR., REINSURANCE OPERATIONS, MANULIFE FINANCIAL 1991– ; Dir., Manulife Internat. (P&C) Limited; Manulife (International) Reinsurance Limited; Manufacturers P&C Limited; Manulife Reinsurance Limited; Simcoe Erie Investors Limited; Dir., Clarke Institute of Psychiatry Foundation; Chrmn., Pacific Insurance Conference; Mem., Program Advisory Ctte., Internat. Insurance Soc. Inc.; joined Manulife Financial 1973; Systems Supervisor, Data Processing Div., 1975; Project Mgr. 1977; Mgr., Reinsurance Admin. 1978; Dir., Reinsurance 1980; Asst. Vice-Pres. 1982; Vice-Pres. 1984; Vice-Pres. & Gen. Mgr., Reinsurance Operations 1987; Office: 200 Bloor St. E., Toronto, Ont. M4W 1E5.

**STAMBROOK, Fred.,** B.A., B.Sc. (Econ.), Ph.D; educator; b. Vienna, Austria 16 Nov. 1929; s. Charles K. and Edith (Weiss) S.; e. Queen Elizabeth Grammar Sch. Alford, Eng.; Oxford Univ. B.A. 1950; Univ. of London B.Sc. (Econ.) 1951, Ph.D. 1960; children: Michael, David, Andrew; PROF. OF HISTORY, UNIV. OF MANITOBA 1968– ; Educ. Offr. RAF 1950–52; mem. German War Documents Project 1954–59; Lectr./Sr. Lectr. in Hist. Univ. of Sydney 1960–68; Assoc. Prof./Prof. present Univ. 1968– , Assoc. Dean of Arts 1975–77, Dean 1977–82, Vice Pres. (Acad.) 1982–91; Visiting Prof. Univ. of Ky. 1967; recipient Queen's Silver Jubilee Medal 1977; awarded Commemorative Medal for 125th Anniversary of Candn. Confederation 1992; author 'European Nationalism in the Nineteenth Century' 1969; various articles and reviews; co-ed. A Modern History Sourcebook 1966; Documents on German Foreign Policy 1918–1945, Series C and D (various vols.) 1956–66; Bd. of Dirs., Candn. Soccer Assn. 1975–79, 1982– (Pres. 1986–92, Vice Pres. 1984–86); Pres., Candn. Youth Soccer Assn. 1975–79; Pres., Man. Soccer Assn. 1980–86; Bd. of Dirs., Candn. Olympic Assn. 1986–92; Bd. of Dirs., Man. Multicultural Resources Centre 1992– , Vice-Chair 1993– ; Winnipeg Pan-Am Games Bid Ctte. 1990–91, 1993– ; FIFA Appeals Ctte.; recreations: swimming, walking; Home: 730 Waterloo

St., Winnipeg, Man. R3N 0T4; Office: University College, Univ. of Manitoba, Winnipeg, Man. R3T 2M8.

**STAMMATI, Gennaro,** LL.B.; banker; b. Naples, Italy 15 March 1945; e. State Univ. of Milan LL.B. 1975; m. Maria Antonietta 24 May 1975; children: Maria Chiara, Matilde, Margherita; PRESIDENT & CHIEF EXECUTIVE OFFICER, BANCA COMMERCIALE ITALIANA OF CANADA 1991– ; Human Resources, private industry Milan, Italy 1965; joined Banca Comm. Italiana Milan Main Br. 1969; Credit Officer N.Y. branch 1976; Asst. Treas. 1977; Manager, Off-Shore Lending Singapore Br. 1980; Sr. Vice-Pres., Banca Comm. Italiana of Canada 1984; Extve. Vice-Pres. 1987; Office: 1800, 130 Adelaide St. W., Toronto, Ont. M5H 3P5.

**STAMMLER, Herbert;** manufacturing executive; b. Yugoslavia 19 May 1944; s. William and Katherina S.; e. Univ. of Windsor; m. Crystal d. Fred and Dorothy Lake 17 Oct. 1969; children: Lori, Joseph, Katie; MFG. SUPT. GENERAL MOTORS OF CANADA LTD. 1980– ; Ind. Eng. H.J. Heinz Co. 1966; Ind. Eng. Supt. Chrysler Canada Ltd. 1968–80; Pres. Windsor Symphony Orch.; Past Pres. S. Windsor Girls Softball League; Cerebal Palsy Assn.; mem. C. of C.; Presbyterian; Liberal; Home: 2815 Skyline, Windsor, Ont. N9E 3A6; Office: 1550 Kildare Rd., Windsor, Ont. N8Y 4S1.

**STAMP, Robert Miles,** M.A., Ph.D.; writer; bookseller; b. Toronto, Ont. 11 Feb. 1937; s. Thomas Carson and Clarice Edith (Miles) S.; e. Port Colborne (Ont.) High Sch. 1955; Univ. of W. Ont. B.A. 1959, Ph.D. 1970; Univ. of Toronto M.A. 1962; m. Arlene Louise d. Gordon and Mary Smith 27 Aug. 1960; children: Shelley, David; FOUNDER, OWNER AND PRES. HERITAGE BOOKS 1983– ; Founder, Ed. and Author 'Canadian Obituary Record' 1988– ; Teacher London (Ont.) S. Secondary Sch. 1960–65; Asst. Prof. Univ. of W. Ont. 1965–69; Assoc. Prof. Univ. of Calgary 1969, Prof. 1973–83, Dir. Candn. Studies Prog. 1980–83; author 'School Days: A Century of Memories' 1975; 'The Schools of Ontario 1876–1976' 1982; 'The World of Tomorrow' 1985; 'QEW: Canada's First Superhighway' 1987; 'Kings, Queens and Canadians' 1987; 'Royal Rebels' 1988; 'Riding the Radials' 1989; 'Early Days in Richmond Hill' 1991; 'Bridging the Border' 1992; mem. Candn. Booksellers Assn.; Antiquarian Booksellers Assn. Can.; Address: 866 Palmerston Ave., Toronto, Ont. M6G 2S2.

**STANBRIDGE, Harry A.,** B.Ed., M.A.; artist, educator; b. Quesnel, B.C. 23 July 1943; s. Herbert Bruce and Dorothy Helen (Mannering) S.; e. Vancouver Sch. of Art, honors dipl. 1968; Univ. of B.C. B.Ed. 1974, M.A. 1982; m. Linda d. Alan and Hazel Morton 1 May 1971; children: Robin Morton, Jeremy Andrew; selected solo & curated shows: Art Gall. of Gr. Victoria 'Come Zion' 1987 (curator/author Nicholas Tuele); Art in Victoria 1986; Artists from the Island 1977; Victoria Kinesis 1975; Univ. of Victoria 'Passages' 1983; Surrey Art Gall. 1988; Bau-Xi Gall. Vanc. 1984, '85, '86, '88, '90, Toronto 1987, '89; North Park Gall. Victoria 1984, '85, '88; Burnaby Art Gall. 'Woman' 1972; C.C.A.C. Gall. Oakland CA 1970; San Diego Mus. of Art 1969; Open Space Victoria 1976, '77, '78; Simon Fraser Univ. 1968; Art Instr., Spectrum Community Sch. 1974– ; collections: Art Gall. of Victoria, Library Nat. Gall. of Can., Prov. of B.C., Mus. of Art Seattle Wash., Canada Council Art Bank, Civic Collection City of Vanc., Surrey Art Gall.; Purchase Prize, 40th Internat. Printmakers Exhib., Seattle Art Mus.; co-author: 'Mirrored Barriers' 1968 (limited ed. poetry & drawings); recreations: cycling; club: Victoria Wheelers Cycling; Home: 4256 Hughes Rd., R.R. #3, Victoria, B.C. V8X 3X1.

**STANBURY, Hon. Richard J.,** Q.C., LL.B.; senator; b. Exeter, Ont. 2 May 1923; s. Judge James George Stuart and Jane (Hardy) S.; e. Exeter (Ont.) Pub. Sch., 1935; St. Catharines (Ont.) Coll. Inst., 1940; Univ. of W. Ont., B.A. (Econ. & Pol. Science) 1944; Osgoode Hall Law Sch., LL.B. 1948 (granted 1991); m. Margaret F. M., d. T. F. Walker, Toronto, Ont., 14 Oct. 1944; two d.; Margaret Jane Baynham, Sally Barbara Day; PARTNER EMERITUS, CASSELS BROCK & BLACKWELL since 1988; Dir., Banco Central Hispanola of Canada; Beneficial Canada Inc.; Founder and Hon. Dir. Can-India Bus. Council, Can-Arab Bus. Co. and Can-Taiwan Bus. Co.; Canada-Poland Trade Council; mem. Internat. Com., Candn. Ch. of Commerce; read law with Aylesworth, Garden & Company; called to the Bar of Ont. 1948; cr. Q.C. 1961; Jr. Solr., Aylesworth & Co. 1948–52; Partner, 1952–54; Partner, Hollingworth and Stanbury 1955–73; Partner, Cassels Brock & Blackwell 1974–88; Lecturer Osgoode Hall Bar Admission Course, 1959–64; served with Candn. Inf. Corps, 1944–45; rank 2nd Lt.; summoned to Senate of Can., 1968; Pres., York Centre Liberal Assn., 1952–57; Toronto Dist. Lib. Assn., 1961–64; Lib. Fed. of Can., 1968–73; Chrmn., Nat. Policy Comte. Party, 1965–68; Chrmn., of Finance, Ont. Lib. Campaign, 1967; Chmrn., N. York Pub. Library Bd., 1958–63; Metro Special Lib. Comte., 1960–63; Secy., N. York Gen. Hosp. 1963–68; mem. Adm. Council, Presb. Ch. in Can. 1962–79 and 1984–92; Secy. Corp. of Synod of Toronto and Kingston 1959–71; Chrmn. Presb. Ch. Bldg. Corp.; Hon. Dir., Boy Scouts of Can.; mem., Candn. Bar Assn.; York Co. Law Assn.; Freemason; Liberal; Presbyterian; recreations: community work, swimming; Club: Ontario; Home: 268 Ridley Blvd., Apt. 515, Toronto, Ont. M5M 4N3.

**STANBURY, Hon. Robert Douglas George,** P.C. (Can.) 1969, Q.C. (Fed.), F. Inst. D., B.A., LL.B.; lawyer; b. Exeter, Ont. 26 Oct. 1929; s. James George Stuart and Elizabeth Jean (Hardy) S.; e. St. Catharines (Ontario) Collegiate Institute and Vocational School (1947); University of Western Ontario, B.A. (Journalism) 1950; Osgoode Hall Law Sch. 1955; York Univ. LL.B. 1991; m. Miriam, d. Oliver Voelker, Kitchener, Ont., 21 June 1952; children: Susan (Meloff), Carol (Vivian), Ian, Duncan; COUNSEL, INCH, EASTERBROOK & SHAKER, Barristers & Solicitors; Vice-Chrmn., Bd. of Dirs., Workers' Compensation Bd. (Ont.); Past Chrmn. & C.E.O., Firestone Canada Inc.; read law with Aylesworth & Co., Hollingworth & Stanbury; called to Bar of Ont. 1955; Account Extve., Public & Industrial Relations Ltd., Toronto, 1950–51; Partner, Hollingworth & Stanbury, Toronto, Ont., 1955–65; Pres., Candn. Univ. Lib. Fed., 1954; Trustee, 1961–64, (Vice-Chrmn. 1962, Chrmn. 1963–64) N. York Bd. of Educ.; mem. Metrop. Toronto Planning Bd., 1963; Metrop. Sch. Bd., Toronto, 1963–64; 1st el. to H. of C., 1965 (L. York-Scarborough), re-elected 1968, 1972, 1974; Chairman, House of Commons Standing Committee on Broadcasting, Films and Assistance to the Arts, 1966–68; Parlty. Secy. to Secy. of State 1968–69; Min. without Portfolio responsible for Citizenship Oct. 1969, additionally for Information Canada Feb. 1970; apptd. Min. Communications 1971; Min. Nat. Revenue 1972; Candn. Del. to U.N. Gen. Assembly 1974–76; Headed Canadian Delegations to U.N. Conf. on Prevention of Crime and Treatment of Offenders, Kyoto, Japan 1970; UNESCO 25th Anniversary Session, Paris 1971; Inter-Am. Devel. Bank annual meeting, Jamaica 1973; U.N. Conf. on Racism, Nigeria 1977; Chrmn., Candn. Group, Inter-Parlty Union 1974–77; Founding Chrmn. Candn. Parlty. Helsinki Group 1977; V.P. Gen. Counsel & Secy. 1977–83, Chrmn. & C.E.O. 1983–85, Firestone Canada Inc.; Dir., Inst. of Corporate Directors 1986–91 (Vice Pres. 1986–87, Pres. 1987–88, Vice Chrmn. 1988–91); Pres. & C.E.O., Candn. Counc. for Native Business 1988–91; Dir., Hamilton Foundation 1979–84 (Pres. 1983); Dir., Hamilton and Dist. Ch. of Comm. 1979–85 (Pres. 1983–84); National Finance Chrmn., U.N. Assn. in Can. 1983–85; mem. Bd. of Govs., Art Gallery of Hamilton (Dir. 1980–87, Vice Pres. 1984–85, Pres. 1985–86); mem., McMaster Univ. Bus. Advisory Council 1984–90 (ch. 1987–88); Dir., Chedoke-McMaster Hospitals 1984–92; Dir., Candn. Club of Hamilton 1986–90; mem., Bd. of Govs., Jr. Achievement of Hamilton 1988–91; Dir. and mem. Extve. Comte., Candn. Ch. of Comm. 1982–86; Ont. Bus. Adv. Council 1983–85; Fellow, Inst. of Dirs. (U.K.): mem., Intl. Comm. of Jurists; U.N. Assn. in.Can.; Law Soc. Upper Canada; Chrmn., Dir., Workers' Compensation Bd. (Ont.) 1985–88, 1991– ; mem., Candn. Broadcast Standards Council 1989– ; Kappa Alpha; Phi Delta Phi; Liberal; Presb.; Home: 607 Edgewater Cr., Burlington, Ont. L7T 3L8; Office: 1500, 1 King St. W., Hamilton, Ont. L8P 4X8.

**STANBURY, William Thomas,** B.Comm., M.A., Ph.D.; university professor; b. Winnipeg, Man. 14 Aug. 1943; s. William Alvin Cooper and Anne (Durward) S.; e. Univ. of B.C., B. Comm. 1966; Univ. of Calif. at Berkeley, M.A. 1968, Ph.D. 1972; UPS FOUND PROF. OF REGULATION & COMPETITION POLICY, UNIV. OF B.C. 1984– ; Asst. Prof., Fac. of Comm., Univ. of B.C. 1970–75; Assoc. Prof. 1975–81; Prof. 1981– ; Dir., Regulation Ref., Econ. Counc. of Can. 1978–80; Cons., Bur. of Comp. Policy; Dept. of Consumer & Corp. Affairs; Treasury Bd.; Law Reform Comn.; Macdonald Comn.; Ont. Comn. of Inquiry into Residential Tenancies; B.C. Min. of Forests; Dir., Regulation & Govt. Intervention Prog., Inst. for Rsch. on Public Policy 1977–81; Referee, various academic jours.; author: 'Money in Politics: Financing Federal Parties and Candidates in Canada' 1993; 'Business-Government Relations in Canada' 1986 and 1993, 'Reciprocal Buying Arrangements' 1978, 'Business Interests and the Reform of Canadian Competition Policy' 1977, 'Success and Failure: Indians in Urban Society' 1975, and over 200 articles in acad. journals and monographs; co-author: 'Rent Regulation: The Ontario Experience' 1990; 'Privatization and State-Owned Enterprise: Lessons from the United States, Great Britain and Canada' 1989 and several others; 'The Objectives of Canadian Competition Policy' 1984, 'Regulatory Reform in Canada' 1982; editor/co-editor: 'The Future of Telecommunications Policy in Canada' 1994; 'Global Perspective: Internationalizing Management Education' 1992; 'Canadian Competition Law and Policy at the Centenary' 1991; 'Mergers, Corporate Concentration and Power in Canada' 1988; 'Telecommunications Policy and Regulation' 1986; 'Papers on Privatization' 1985, 'Managing Public Enterprises' 1982, 'Government Regulation' 1980, 'Perspectives on the Royal Commission on Corporate Concentration' 1979 and 15 others; recreations: golf, reading; Office: Fac. of Comm. & Bus. Admin., Univ. of B.C., Vancouver, B.C. V6T 1Z2.

**STANFIELD, Right Hon. Robert L.,** P.C. (1967), Q.C., M.P., B.A., LL.D.; legislator; b. Truro, N.S., 11 April 1914; s. Frank and Sarah Emma (Thomas) S.; e. Colchester Acad. Truro, N.S.; Ashbury Coll., Ottawa, Ont.; Dalhousie Univ., B.A. (with high Hons. in Econ. and Pol. Science) 1936, winning Gov. General's Medal; Harvard Univ., LL.B. (with Hons.) 1939; Hon. LL.D.: Univ. of N.B. 1958, McGill 1967; St. Dunstan's Univ. 1967; St. Mary's Univ. 1968; Dalhousie Univ. 1981; McMaster Univ. 1985; Univ. de St. Anne 1987; Univ. of Acadia 1988; Univ. of Toronto 1988; Mt. Allison Univ. 1990; m. 1stly late Nora Joyce, d. late C. Weston Frazee, 5 June 1940; children: Sarah Jamesie, Robert Maxwell, Judith Joyce, Miriam Julia; 2ndly late Mary Margaret Hall 1957; 3rdly Anne Austin 10 Aug. 1978; called to the Bar of N.S. 1940; cr. K.C. Dec. 1950; 1st el. to N.S. Leg., g.e. 1949; Leader of the Opposition in Leg., 1949–56; Premier and various portfolios 1956–67; el. to Leader of P. Conservative Party of Can., 9 Sept. 1967; el. to H. of C. for Colchester-Hants. in by-el. 6 Nov. 1967; Leader of H.M. Opposition in H. of C. 15 Nov. 1967–22 Feb. 1976; M.P. for Halifax 1968–79; Special Rep. of Govt. of Can. to Middle East and North Africa July 1979–Feb. 1980; Chrmn., The Commonwealth Found. 1987–91; P. Conservative; Anglican; recreation: gardening; Clubs: Halifax; Saraquay; Albany (Toronto); Home: 136 Acacia Ave., Rockcliffe Park, Ont. K1M 0R1.

**STANFORD, James M.,** B.Sc.; petroleum executive; b. Montreal, Que. 2 Oct. 1937; s. Walter A. and Geraldine (O'Loghlin) S.; e. Loyola Coll. Montreal B.Sc. (Mining) 1958; Univ. of Alta. B.Sc. (Petrol. Eng.) 1960; children: Miriam, Kim, Jim; PRES. AND CHIEF EXECUTIVE OFFR. PETRO-CANADA 1993– ; Dir. & Offr., Petro-Canada; joined Mobil Oil Canada Ltd. 1960–78; Gen. Mgr. Conventional Prodn. Petro-Canada 1978, Vice Pres. and Sr. Vice Pres. Prodn. 1980, Pres. Petro-Canada Resources 1982–90; Pres. & Chief Operating Offr. 1990–93; Mem., Assn. of Profl. Engineers, Geologists & Geophysicists of Alta.; Candn. Inst. of Mining and Metallurgy; Dir., ICG Propane Inc. (Chair); Candn. Assn. of Petroleum Producers; Jr. Achievement of Canada and Alta. Theatre Projects; Past Chair, Calgary Philharmonic Soc.; Former Dir., Centre for Cold Ocean Rsch & Engr.; The Petroleum Recovery Inst.; Internat. Gas Union; Office: P.O. Box 2844, Calgary, Alta. T2P 3E3.

**STANFORD, Joseph Stephen,** Q.C., LL.B.; diplomat; b. Montreal, Que. 7 May 1934; s. Walter Albert and Geraldine (O'Loghlin) S.; e. St. Leo's Acad. Westmount, Que.; St. Mary's High Sch. Calgary, Alta.; Loyola Coll., Univ. of Montreal B.A. 1953; Univ. of Alta. LL.B. 1956; m. Agnes d. late Glen Walker 16 Nov. 1957; children: Kevin, Karen, Michael; SENIOR FELLOW (CONFLICT MANAGEMENT) CANADN. CENTRE FOR MANAGEMENT DEVELOPMENT 1993– ; called to Bar of Alta. 1957; private law practice Calgary 1957–60; joined diplomatic service 1960 serving in Paris 1961–64, Kingston, Jamaica 1964–66, Bonn 1970–73; Dir. Legal Adv. Div. Dept. External Affairs 1975–77, Dir. Gen. Bureau of Comm. and Commodity Relations 1977–79; Ambassador to Israel 1979–82; Asst. Depy. Min. (Africa and Middle East) 1983–85; Asst. Depy. Min. (Europe) 1985–87; Assoc. Under-Secy. of State for External Affairs, Dept. of External Affairs 1987–88; Deputy Solicitor General of Canada 1988–93; contrib. to learned journs. on treaty law, GATT, internat. nuclear relations, foreign invest. developing countries, application U.S. anti-trust law in Can.; mem. Candn. Council on Internat. Law; Phi Delta Theta; R. Catholic; recreations: tennis, canoeing; Home: 58 Amberwood Cres., Nepean, Ont.; Office: 373 Sussex Dr., Ottawa, Ont. K1N 8V4.

**STANGER, David E.;** advertising executive; b. Toronto, Ont. 26 June 1955; s. David Clifford and Olive Beatrice (Jones) S.; e. Leaside H.S. 1974; m. Mary d. Alonso and Ellen Bridgen 23 Sept. 1978; children: Kathryn-Leigh, Jennifer; NATIONAL MEDIA DIRECTOR, BAKER LOVICK, MCKIM BAKER

LOVICK/BBDO; J. Walter Thompson 1974–75, 1980; Media Buyer & Planner, Bristol Myers 1975–77; Assoc. Media Dir., Mgr. Broadcast Buying Unit, Ronald Reynolds 1977–79; Candn. Media Corp. 1980–82; joined present firm 1982; hired as Media Dir. and promoted from ranks to Vice-Pres., Sr. Vic-Pres. to pres. position; Dir., Candn. Outdoor Membership Bd.; Mem., BBM Radio Extve.; Lectr., York Univ. Extve. Series; co-author: 'Introduction to Media' 1985 (textbook); club: Marine Drive Golf & Country; Home: R.R. 1, 4417 No 1 Side Rd., Burlington, Ont.; Office: 2 Bloor St. W., Toronto, Ont. M4W 3R6.

**STANISZKIS, Joanna Katarzyna,** B.F.A., R.C.A.; tapestry artist; educator; b. Czestochowa, Poland 10 Apr. 1944; d. Stefan and Amelia (Krukowska) Kiljanski; e. elem. and high schs. Warsaw 1962; Acad. of Fine Arts Warsaw Interior Arch. 1962–64; Chicago Art Inst. (US Dept. State Scholarship) B.F.A. (Interior & Textile Design) 1967; Universidad Catholica Lima, Precolumbian Textiles 1965; m. Peter Hyndman 9 Dec. 1989; one s. Michael; ASSOC. PROF. OF DESIGN, SCH. OF HOME ECON., UNIV. OF B.C. 1973– ; Instr.-in-charge of Design Univ. B.C. 1969–73; Acting Head of Textiles Ont. Coll. of Art 1975–76; Founding Mem., Candn. Craft Museum (served on board 1980–91); selected solo exhibitions: Merton Gallery Toronto 1972, 1974, 1976; Mido Gallery Vancouver 1973; Equinox Gallery Vancouver 1978; Faculty Club, Univ. of B.C. Vancouver 1979; Cartwright Gallery, Vancouver 1988; UBC Museum of Anthropology, Vancouver 1989; Waikato Art Museum, Hamilton, New Zealand 1992; Ontario Craft Gallery 1992; group exhns. (partial list): 'Textiles into 3D,' organized and travelled by the Art Gallery of Ont. 1973–74; Internat. Tapestry Triennial, Lodz, Poland, Tapestry Exhib., Art Gallery of Windsor 1976; Internat. Tapestry Exhn., Vevey Switzerland 1976; Internat. Tapestry Triennial, Lodz, Poland 1978; Royal Candn. Acad. Centennial Exhn., Toronto 1980; Internat. Tapestry Triennial, Lodz, Poland 1981, 1983, 1985, 1992; Art Gallery of Windsor, 'Gregor, Rousseay-Vermette and Staniszkis 1981; Fashion Institute of Technology, New York 1986; Masters of Crafts, Candn. Museum of Civilization, Hull, Que. 1989; Kyoto Internat. Textile Competition 1992; over 40 large-scale architectural commissions in public buildings; Some of more recent projects include: Lloyd's Bank, Vancouver 1987; Commonwealth Tapestry, Vancouver Trade & Convention Centre 1987; Economic Summit, Toronto Convention Centre 1988; Citibank Tower, Phoenix, Arizona 1989; College of Dental Surgeons, Vancouver 1989; Owen Bird, Vancouver 1990; Providence Centre, Toronto 1990; Mississauga Hospital, Mississauga, Ont. 1992; Prize Competitions: Crown Life Vancouver; Daon Bldg. Vancouver; recipient, Saidye Bronfman Award for excellence in crafts, 1980; Liberal; R. Catholic; recreations: travel, skiing; Studio: 602 Stamps Landing, False Creek, Vancouver, B.C. V5Z 3Z1; Office: Family & Nutritional Science, 2205 East Mall, Vancouver, B.C. V6T 1Z4.

**STANLEY, Alan Douglas (Peter),** F.C.A.; consultant; b. Westmount, Que. 13 Aug. 1918; s. William Arthur and Alison (Greig) S.; e. The High Sch. of Montreal; m. Margaret Elizabeth Drysdale 16 Dec. 1940; children: Joanne Oake, Judith Gray, Pamela Harris; CONSULTANT, COOPERS & LYBRAND 1976– ; Dir., Northwest Freeholds Ltd.; Sans Changer Ltd.; Partner, Coopers & Lybrand Montreal 1949, Partner in Charge, W. Offices Vancouver, mem. Mgmt. and Exec. Cttes. 1961–76; Gov. Candn. Tax Foundation, Licensed Trustee in Bankruptcy 1957–82; Chrmn. B.C. Development Corp. 1973–76; served in R.C.N.V.R. 1939–45 (Lt. Cmdr.); Past Pres., BC-Yukon Candn. Red Cross; Un. Services Inst. Vancouver; Naval Offrs. Assn. B.C.; Pres., Inst. C.A.'s B.C. 1959–60; Hon. Life Mem., Vancouver Art Gall.; Can. Insolvency Assn.; United Church; former Gov., Vancouver Sch. of Theology; recreations: golf, billiards, chess; Clubs: Capilano Golf (Past Chrmn.); Vancouver (Past Pres.); Home: 2040 West 4th Ave., Vancouver, B.C. V6J 1M9; Office: 1111 West Hastings St., Vancouver, B.C. V6E 3R2.

**STANLEY, David Christopher Hall,** B.A., M. Comm.; b. Toronto, Ont. 12 July 1927; s. Oswald and Betty Blanche (Diamond) S.; e. Univ. of Toronto Schs., 1939–42; Upper Can. Coll., Toronto, 1942–45; Univ. of Toronto (B.A. 1949, M. Comm. 1954); m. Colleen Frances, d. Hugh C. Brown, Toronto, 17 Nov. 1950; children: Julia (Weaver), Christopher; Dir., The Thomson Corp.; joined Wood Gundy Ltd. 1949; el. Dir. 1966; Vice-Pres. 1969, mem., Exec. Comte., 1971; ret. 1979; former mem. Ont. Securities Comn. 1983–85; Past Pres. Toronto Soc. Financial Analysts; Bd. Mem., Toronto Mendelssohn Choir (Pres. 1986–88); Hon. Vice-Chrmn., Candn. Nat. Inst. for the Blind (Pres. 1976–79); Clubs: Toronto; National; Residence: 453 Russell Hill Rd., Toronto, Ont. M5P 2S6.

**STANLEY, Donald Russell,** S.D., P.Eng., D.Sc.(Hon.); engineering executive; b. Edmonton, Alta. 18 Oct. 1917; s. Russell and Frances Muriel (Sparling) S.; e. Univ. of Alta. B.Sc. 1940; Harvard Univ. S.M. 1948, S.D. 1952; D.Sc.(Hon.), Univ. of Alta. 1988; m. Joan d. Westgarth and Emily Bibby 23 Dec. 1960; children: Mary Louise, Russell Bruce, Donald Westgarth; HON. CHRMN., STANLEY TECHNOLOGY GROUP INC. 1993– ; Field Eng. Calgary Power Ltd. 1940–42; served with RCAF 1942–45; Dir. Sanitary Engineering Alta. Govt. 1946–50; Partner, Shareholder, Associated Engineering Services 1952–54; Chrmn., Stanley Technology Group Inc. 1954–93; Dir. Alta. Rsch. Council; mem. Constrn. Ind. Devel. Council, Edmonton Econ. Devel. Authority; Past mem. Expert Adv. Ctte. Environmental Health, World Health Orgn.; Past Dir. Candn. C. of C.; Past Pres. Edmonton C. of C.; Alta. C. of C.; Past Dir. Candn. German Chamber Ind. & Comm. (also Vice Pres.); Past Pres.: W. Can. Water & Sewage Conf.; Univ. of Alta. Alumni Assn., Past Gov. of Univ. of Alberta; recipient L.C. Charlesworth Award 1976 and Frank Spragins award 1982 Assn. Prof. Engs., Geols. & Geophys. Alta.; Carson F. Morrison Award 1984 Candn. Consulting Eng. Mag.; Julian C. Smith Medal 1986, Engn. Inst. of Can.; author or co-author numerous articles, papers; Fellow, Am. Soc. Civil Engs.; Life mem. Water Pollution Control Fedn.; Diplomate, Am. Acad. Environmental Engs.; mem. Assn. Prof. Engs. Alta. B.C. & Sask.; Am. Water Works Assn.; Am. Water Resources Assn.; Internat. Assn. Water Pollution Rsch.; Candn. Acad. of Engr.; recreations: golf, skiing, swimming; Club: Rotary; Home: 7127 Saskatchewan Dr., Edmonton, Alta. T6G 2A4; Office: 10160 – 112 St., Edmonton, Alta. T5K 2L6.

**STANLEY, The Honourable George Francis Gillman,** O.C. (1976), C.D., K.St.J., B.A., M.A., M.Litt., D.Phil., D.es.L., D.Litt., LL.D., D.C.L., D.U., F.R.S.C., F.R.Hist.S.; author, educator, soldier; b. Calgary, Alta. 6 July 1907; s. John Henry and Della Catherine (Lillywhite) S.; e. Univs. of Alta. and Oxford, B.A. 1931, M.Litt. 1933, M.A. 1936, D.Phil. 1936 (Rhodes Scholar 1929, Beit Sr. Research Scholar 1932; Royal Soc. Can. Scholar, 1934); Guggenheim Fellow, 1948; Canada Council Sr. Fellowship 1960; Hon. doctorates, Laval, 1965; Mount Allison, 1967; St. Dunstan's, 1969; Alberta, 1971; R.M.C., 1972; St. Francis Xavier, 1974; New Brunswick, 1975; Dalhousie, 1977; Calgary, 1980; Ottawa, 1983; Moncton, 1985; Saint Thomas, 1987; m. Ruth Lynette, B.A., B.C.L., LL.D., d. Alfred H. Hill, St. Lambert, Que., 24 Aug. 1946; children: Della Margaret Maude, M.A., Ph.D. (Mrs. Thomas Cromwell); Marietta Ruth Ellen, B.Sc., B.Ed., C.A.; Laurie Catherine Christina, M.A., Ph.D. (Mrs. John Blackwell); Lieutenant Governor, New Brunswick 1982–87; Emeritus Prof. R.M.C.; Emeritus Prof., Mount Allison Univ. (Dir. Canadian Studies there 1969–75; 1st such programme in any Canadian university); Professor of Hist., Mount Allison University 1936–46 (on military leave 1940–46); Professor of Cdn. Hist., University of B.C. 1947–49; Dean of Arts 1962–69, and Head of Hist. Dept., R.M.C., Kingston 1949–69; served in Candn. Militia (N.B. Rangers) 1938–40 as Lieut.; served in 2nd World War 1940–47; began as Capt. and retired as Lieut.-Col. and Deputy Dir., Hist. Sec. (Gen. Staff); Overseas 1942–45; Reserve of Offrs., 1947–67; Hon. Col., Royal N.B. Regiment 1982–92; War Service Medals 1934–45; awarded Tyrrell Medal by Royal Soc. Can. 1957; Centennial Medal 1967; Jubilee Medal 1977; Canada 125 Medal 1993; Médaille Commemorative de la Guerre 1939–45 de la République Française; apptd. Offr., Order of Canada 1976; Knight of Justice, Order of St. John 1982; Victoria Medal, St. John Ambulance 1984; Canadian Decoration 1991; author: 'The Birth of Western Canada' 1936 (repr. 1961); 'Canada's Soldiers' 1954 (rev. 1963, 1974); 'In Search of the Magnetic North' 1955, 'In the Face of Danger' 1960; 'For Want of a Horse' 1961; 'Louis Riel' 1963; 'The Story of Canada's Flag' 1965; 'New France: The Last Phase 1744–1760' 1968; 'A Short History of the Canadian Constitution' 1969; 'Mapping the Frontier' 1970; 'Canada Invaded 1775–1776' 1973; 'L'Invasion du Canada 1775–1776' 1975; 'The Military and Hospitaller Order of Saint Lazarus: A Short History of the Canadian Grand Priory' 1978; 'Nos Soldats, l'Histoire Militaire du Canada de 1604 à nos jours' 1980; 'The War of 1812: Land Operations' 1983, 'La guerre de 1812: operations terrestres' 1984; Gen. Ed., 'The Collected Writings of Louis Riel, Les écrits complets de Louis Riel' 1985; 'Toil and Trouble – Military Expeditions to Red River' 1989; 'Battle in the Dark – Stoney Creek, June 6, 1813' 1991; ed. 'Canadian Universities Today' 1963, and 'Pioneers of Canadian Science' 1966; articles in journals and reviews, also in 'Encyclopedia Americana' and 'Canadian Encyclopedia'; submitted basic design adopted as Canada's flag in Feb. 1965; Mil. and Hospitaller Order of St. Lazarus of Jerusalem (Kt. Grand Cross); Soberana Ordem dos Cavaleiros de Sao Paulo (Brazil) (Comendador); St. John Ambulance Assn. (Pres. N.B. Prov. Council 1979–82); 8th Candn. Hussars Regimental Assn. (Chrmn. Bursary Comte. 1975–81); N.B. Rangers Regimental Assn.; N.B. Army Cadet League (Vice-Pres. 1978–82); United Services Inst. (Moncton Br.) Vice-Pres. 1977–81; Maritime Automobile Assn. (Dir. 1979–82); Paul Harris Fellow, Rotary Internat., 1983; Fellow, Co. of Mil. Historians 1967 (Gov. 1968–74); Fellow, Candn. Heraldry Soc.; Hon. Mem., R.M.C. Club of Can. 1984; mem. Comn. de Planification Academique de l'Univ. de Moncton 1969–72; Candn. Hist. Assn. (Pres. 1955–56); Comte. on Hist. Sites & Monuments, Massey Comn. on the Arts, Letters & Sciences 1950–51; mem. Fed. Gov't. Adv. Bd. on Candn. Mil. Coll. 1973–79; Archaeol. and Hist. Sites Bd. of Ont. 1953–69; Kingston Historical Soc. (Pres. 1959–61); Atlantic Canada Inst. (founding mem. of the Bd. of Dirs.); Candn. Assn. of Rhodes Scholars (Dir. 1983–87); Mem. Adv. Bd. Candn. War Museum 1988–90; Fondation Laval; Inst. d'Histoire de l'Amérique Francaise; Anglican; Clubs: Garrison (Fredericton); Union (Saint John); Address: 18 Pond Shore Rd., P.O. Box 790, Sackville, N.B. E0A 3C0.

**STANLEY, James Paul;** printing company executive; b. Montreal, Que. 15 Aug. 1915; s. Paul Garton and Florence May (Tooke) S.; e. McGill Univ., B.Engr. 1938; m. Anne Seymour Raynsford, 28 May 1949; children: Marie, Susan, James, Sarah; Staff engr. Stevenson, Kellogg Ltd. 1938–41; plant mgr., Dow Brewery Ltd. 1947–53; Vice Pres., then Pres., Ronalds-Federated Ltd., Montreal 1954–77, Bd. Chrmn. & C.E.O. 1977–80; served with RCAF 1941–46; mem. Order Engrs. Que.; Fellow, Graphic Arts Tech. Found.; Clubs: St. James's; Home: 799 Wartman Ave., Kingston, Ont. K7M 4M3.

**STANLEY, Kathleen (Kay) Louise,** B.A.; civil servant; b. Ottawa, Ont. 24 Mar. 1942; d. Clarence Wellington Mulvagh and Florence Leanore (Barrett) M.; e. Ottawa Teachers' Coll., Ont. Teacher's cert. 1960; Carleton Univ., B.A. 1977; divorced; ASST. DEPUTY MINISTER, HEALTH PROGRAMS & SERVICES BRANCH 1993– ; Teacher, Eastview Pub. Sch. Bd. 1960–64; Teacher & Fed. Offr. (Pres.), Carleton Bd. of Edn. 1964–85; on loan to Min. of Nat. Defence, CFB Europe, Lahr W. Germany as teacher, DND Overseas Sch. 1971–74, 1978–80; Sr. Policy Advr., Min. Resp. for Status of Women 1985; Chief of Staff to Hon. W. McLean, Min. of State (Immigration) & Min. Resp. for the Status of Women 1985–86; Coordinator, Status of Women Can. 1986–93; Pres., Nepean Teachers' Fed. 1966–67; Teachers' Fed. of Carleton 1969–71; Overseas Teachers' Assn. 1972–74, 1979–80; Teachers' Fed. of Carleton 1982–85; Founding Pres., Fed. P.C. Women's Caucus of Ottawa 1981–82, re-elected 1982–83; Pres., Nat. P.C. Fed. 1983–86; Chairperson, Children's Aid Found. 1990– ; speaker, lectr., panelist on wide range of topics concerning women; mem., Inst. of Public Admin. of Canada; Assn. of Professional Execs. of the Public Service of Canada; The Elizabeth Fry Soc. of Ottawa; The Children's Aid Soc. of Ottawa-Carleton; recreations: travel, gardening, skiing; Clubs: Candn. Club of Ottawa; Univ. of Ottawa Phi Delta Kappa; Carleton Univ. Alumni; Home: 260 Russell Ave., Ottawa, Ont. K1N 7X5; Office: Rm. 540, Jean Manse Bldg., Tunney's Pasture, Ottawa, Ont. K1A 1B4.

**STANLEY-PAUL, Norman,** C.D., B.A.; retired company executive; b. Toronto, Ont. 14 Dec. 1926; s. Harold and Jean Conner (Cox) S-P.; e. Westhill High Sch. Montreal, Que.; N. Toronto Coll.; Univ. of Toronto, B.A.1948; m. Eleanore Vieve, d. Dr. Glenn T. Mitton, Markham, Ont., 5 May 1956; children: Harold Glenn, Maureen Anne; President & Dir., Mennen Canada Inc. 1977–90; retired; joined Lever Brothers Ltd. 1948–59 (Brand Mgr.); General Foods Ltd. 1959–67 (Product Group Mgr.); joined Canvin Products Ltd. as Vice-Pres. Marketing 1967; promoted to Extve. Vice Pres. and Dir., Pres. 1969–76; served with RCNR 1944–68; rank Lt. Comdr.; Past Chrmn., Stewards, Mem. Trustees, Humber Valley United Church; Past Pres., Mississauga Chapter; Regional Bd. Mem., Heart & Stroke Foundation; recreations: golf, carpentry; Clubs: Mississaugua Golf & Country; Home: 90 – 1725 The Chase, Mississauga, Ont. L5M 4N3.

**STANSBURY, Edward James,** M.A., Ph.D.; university professor; b. Oakville, Ont. 1 Aug. 1927; e. Univ. of Toronto, B.A. (Math. & Physics) 1949, M.A. (Physics) 1950, Ph.D. (Physics) 1952; m. Wilda Lee MacQuarrie; PROF. EMERITUS, METEOROLOGY, McGILL UNIV. 1986; joined present Univ. 1956, Prof. of Physics 1969;

Dean Faculty of Arts & Science 1969–71; Dean, Fac. of Science, 1971–76; Vice Princ., Planning 1976–86; Home: 11705 Lavigne St., Montreal, Que. H4J 1X4.

**STAPELLS, Richard Bredin,** Q.C., M.A., LL.B.; b. Toronto, Ont. 13 Aug. 1925; s. late Herbert Gordon, Q.C., and Edith (Bredin) S.; e. St. Andrew's Coll., Aurora, Ont.; Univ. of Toronto, B.A. 1946, M.A. 1949; London Sch. of Economics, 1947; Osgoode Hall, Toronto, Ont. (1950); Univ. of York LL.B. 1991; m. Beverley, d. late Erland S. Echlin, 25 May 1950; children: Victoria Louise, Alexandra Echlin, Elizabeth Bredin; COUNSEL, BLANEY, MCMURTRY, STAPELLS; Dir., The Counselling Foundation of Can.; read law with H.G. Stapells, Q.C.; called to the Bar of Ont., 1950; cr. Q.C. 1961; served in 2nd World War with R.C.A.F., 1944; Past Pres., Royal Life Saving Soc. Canada; Vice-Pres., Royal Life Saving Society (Commonwealth); Counsellor, Boy Scouts Greater Metro Toronto Region; Past Chrmn., Estate Planning Council of Toronto; Past Gov., Cdn. Tax Fdn.; Beta Theta Pi; Conservative-Independent; Anglican; recreation: gardening; Clubs: National; Albany; R.C.Y.C.; Coral Beach and Tennis (Bermuda); Caledon Ski (Past Bd. Chrmn.); Empire (Past Pres.); Royal Overseas League; Home: 107 High Street, Old Amersham, Buckinghamshire HP7 0DY, England.

**STAPLETON, Rev. John Francis,** B.A., B.L.S. (R.C.); teacher; librarian; pastor; b. Fitzroy Harbour, Ont. 24 Nov. 1921; s. Louis John and Mary Rita (McDermott) S.; e. St. Mary's Separate Sch., Collingwood, Ont. and Collingwood Coll. Inst. there; St. Michael's Coll., Univ. of Toronto B.A. 1944; St. Basil's Novitiate, Toronto 1940–41; St. Basil's Semy., Toronto 1941–43 and 1945–49; Library Sch., Univ. of Toronto, B.L.S. 1950; PASTOR, ST. PETER'S CHURCH, DURHAM, ONT. 1990– ; Asst. Dir. of Studies, Aquinas Inst., Rochester, N.Y., 1944–45; Asst. Librarian, Pontifical Inst. of Mediaeval Studies, 1946–49; Assoc. Lib., 1949–51, Lib. 1951–62; Librarian St. Basil's Seminary 1962–67 (Lectr. there 1959–72); Pastor St. Mary's Church, Owen Sound 1973–76; Pastor, St. Mary's Ch., Linwood, Ont. 1976–82; Pastor, Sacred Heart Church, Mildmay, Ont. 1982–90; Dean of Waterloo and Diocesan Consultor 1979–81; mem., Candn. Lib. Assn.; Ont. Lib. Assn.; Address: P.O. Box 14, Durham, Ont. N0G 1R0.

**STARK, Ethel,** C.M., LL.D., F.R.S.A.; conductor; concert violinist; educator; b. Montreal, Que. 25 Aug. 1916; d. Adolph and Laura (Haupt) Stark; e. McGill Conservatory Montreal, Violin studies 5 yrs. (MacDonald Scholarship); graduate Curtis Inst. Philadelphia (1st Candn. winner fellowship grant worldwide competition) studied with Fritz Reiner, Carl Flesch, Lea Luboshutz, Louis Bailly, Arthur Rodzinski; Concordia Univ. Montreal LL.D. 1980; Founder and Conductor, Montreal Women's Symphony Orchestra (1st Candn. orchestra invited Carnegie Hall, N.Y.), Montreal Women's Symphony Strings, Ethel Stark Symphonietta (men & women), N.Y. Women's Chamber Orchestra, Candn. Chorus (rep. Can. World Song Festival Israel); numerous appearances as guest conductor incl. Tokyo Asahi Philharmonic Orchestra, Nippon Hoso Kyokai Orchestra, Jerusalem Symphony Orchestra, Que. Symphony Orchestra, Toronto Symphony Orchestra, CBC Symphony Orchestra (Radio, TV), Miami Symphony Orchestra; numerous appearances as violin soloist incl. CBC Symphony Orchestra, Curtis Symphony Orchestra, Les Concerts Symphoniques, Les Petits Concerts, Montreal and Toronto Symphony Orchestras; host and soloist radio series on sonata N.Y. City; private recital Prokofieff 1st Violin Concerto Fritz Kreisler; Teacher of Music, Cath. Univ. Washington, D.C. (1st Candn. woman); Prof. of Violin Conservatoire Prov. de Musique, Montreal; mem. Music Faculty Sir George Williams Univ. Montreal; recipient Canada Counc. Rsch. Grant 1962; Concert Soc. Award 1976; Outstanding Citizenship Award, Montreal Citizenship Counc. 1977, appointed Member of the Order of Canada 1979; el. Fellow of the Royal Soc. of Arts, Eng. 1980; featured various articles maj. Candn. and Am. mags.; biographical film Nat. Film Bd. Can.; discography, interviews CBC Music Lib. Montreal; Nat. Archives Ottawa; Hon. mem. Musicians' Guild Montreal; Sigma Alpha Iota (Hon. Mem., Sigma Alpha Iota, USA).

**STARK, John Everett,** B.Com., M.B.A.; broadcasting executive; b. Vancouver, B.C. 21 May 1918; s. Everett Crawford and Caroline Myrtle (Cockreham) S.; e. Univ. of B.C. B.Com. 1940; Harvard Business Sch. M.B.A. 1942; m. Morva Jean d. William and Kitty Longfellow 25 July 1942; children: Carolyn Morva; Shirley Patricia Kathleen; John Everett Jr.; CHRMN. & PRESIDENT, CSVB RADIO STATION 1992– ; Pres. Memba Pectin Co. (Vancouver) 1932–50; V.P. and Mging. Dir. B.C.

Hardwood & Millwork Ltd. 1948–65; Dir. Hardwood Milling Co. Ltd. 1948–71; Pres. & Mging. Dir. Morrison Steel and Wire Co. Ltd. 1953–82; Pres., Q Broadcasting Ltd. 1973–90; mem. Vancouver Rotary Club; Vancouver Club; recreation: golf; Clubs: The Vancouver; Shaughnessy Golf & Country; Capilano Golf; Vancouver Lawn Tennis; Home: 1383 W. 32nd Ave., Vancouver, B.C. V6H 2J4; Office: 1134 Burrard St., Vancouver, B.C. V6Z 1Y8.

**STARK-ADAMEC, Cannie,** B.A., M.Sc.App., Ph.D.; university professor and administrator; b. Fredericton, N.B. 2 June 1945; s. Bazil Millan and Inez Muriel (Pearce) Stark; e. McGill Univ. B.A. (Hons.) 1966, M.Sc.Applied 1968, Ph.D. 1975; Regina Citizens' Police Acad., cert. 1990; American Critical Incident Stress Foundation, cert's. 1991; divorced; PROF. & DIR., ORGANIZATIONAL & SOCIAL PSYCHOLOGY RESEARCH UNIT, UNIV. OF REGINA 1992– ; Sr. Experimenter, Le Dain Comn. 1971; Asst. Prof., Dalhousie Univ. 1975–77; Sr. Investigator/Co-Dir., Scott Lab., Wellesley Hosp. 1977–84; Rsch. Assoc. 1983–84; Asst. Prof., Fac. of Med., Univ. of Toronto 1981–84; Assoc. Prof. & Head, Psychology, Univ. of Regina 1984–87, Prof. & Head, Dept. of Psychology 1987–92; Psych. Cons., Sask. Internat. Rescue Team & to individual police officers; Nat. Health Rsch. Scholar 1981–84; Candn. Psych. Assn. Applied Div. Award for Outstanding Contbns. to the Application of Psych. to Human Problems 1989; CPA Fellow 1983; Dir., Sask. Health Rsch. Bd. 1989–92; Mem., Candn. Psych. Assn. (Extve. 1977–79, 1981–86, 1990–93; Pres. 1991–92); Mem., Bd. of Dirs., Social Sci. Fedn. of Can. 1991–93 (Extve. 1993–95; Vice-Pres. 1993–95); Assoc. Mem., Candn. Police Canine Assn.; author/co-author of over 100 pubns. in areas of psych. of women, of work, of police, stress, etc.; contbg. editor: 'Resources for Feminist Research' 1979– ; editor/co-editor, 5 spec. issues 'Int. J. of Women's Studies' (also Science Editor 1980–86); editor: 'Sex Roles: Origins, Influences and Implications for Women' 1980; recreations: photography, walking, cats, reading, music (classical); Office: Organizational & Social Psychology Research Unit, CL340, Univ. of Regina, Regina, Sask. S4S 0A2.

**STARKEY, John,** B.Sc., Ph.D.; educator; b. Manchester, UK 11 Aug. 1936; s. John Henry and Alice (Davies) S.; e. All Saints Primary Sch. Manchester 1947; Manchester Central Grammar Sch. 1954; Liverpool Univ., B.Sc. 1957, Ph.D. 1960; m. Barbara Dawson 1958; children: Michael, Kathryn; PROF. OF GEOL., UNIV. OF W. ONT. 1979– ; Rsch. Fellow, Swiss Federal Inst. of Technol. Zurich 1960–62, Visiting Prof. 1979–80; Rsch. Assoc. Univ. of Cal. Berkeley 1962–65; Asst. Prof. present Univ. 1965, Assoc. Prof. 1969; Visiting Prof. Ruhr Univ. Bochum, Germany 1969, Imp. Coll. Sci. & Technol., London, UK 1971–72, Federal Univ. of Bahia, Salvador, Brazil 1975–77, Monash Univ. Melbourne, Australia 1979; recipient Manchester City Exhn. 1954–57; Leverhulme Eur. Scholarship 1960–61; NATO Rsch. Scholarship 1960–62; Miller Rsch. Fellowship 1963–65; Heinrich-Herz Fellowship 1969; Royal Soc. Bursary 1971–72; author or co-author over 70 sci. publs.; mem. Ont. Confedn. Univ. Faculty Assns. (Pres. 1986–89); Mineral Assn. Can.; Mineral Soc. Am.; Geological Assoc. of Canada; Geological Assn. of Canada, Tectonic Studies Div. (Vice Pres. 1988–92); Home: 32 Longbow Place, London, Ont. N6G 1Y3; Office: Geology Dept., Univ. of Western Ont., London, Ont. N6A 3B7.

**STARKMAN, Louise Evelyn;** community volunteer, conference travel planner, importer-sales; b. Toronto, Ont. 3 March 1941; d. Samuel and Gertrude (Yolleck) Rappaport; e. Oakwood C.I.; Toronto Teacher's College 1958; Seneca College 1984; m. Dr. Stanley E. s. Max and Bertha S. 3 Aug. 1961; children: Steven Michael, Robert Allan; active community volunteer; Teacher, Toronto Bd. of Edn. 1960–63; supply teacher for many years; Pres., The Roving Eye; Travel Planner & Leader; Founder of A.O.-Bahamas Dental Seminar 1990, '91, '92, '93; Pres., Flemingdon Dental Serv.; Former Mem., Bd. of Gov., Beth Tzedec Synagogue; Bd. of Dir., Bialik Sch.; United Jewish Appeal Women's Div.; currently on Bd. of Gov., Mount Sinai Hosp. 1985–93; Extve. & Bd. of Dir., Mount Sinai Auxiliary 1970–93; Mem., Hadassah; Alpha Omega Women; Baycrest Auxiliary; Brazilian Ball Committee; Hong Kong-Canada Business Assn.; Canadian Club; recreations: reading, travel, enjoying friends; Address: 9 Glencedar Rd., Toronto, Ont. M6C 3E9.

**STARKMAN, Stanley;** publishing executive; b. Toronto, Ont. 21 Oct. 1934; s. Morris and Hilda (Share) S.; e. Harbord Coll. Inst.; Univ. of Toronto, B.A. (Hons.) 1961; m. Ruth Marilyn d. Henry and Rose Weissburst 3 Nov. 1957; children: Shari Lynn (Stancer), Jodi Ellen

(Mendelsohn), Daryl Sue (Hersco), Melanie Joy (Rowe), Marshall Cory; PRES. AND OWNER, PIPPIN PUBLISHING LTD. (formerly Dominie Press) 1990– ; Mgr., Coll. Div., Holt, Rinehart & Winston of Can. Ltd. 1961–68; Found. Pres., D.C. Heath Can. Ltd. 1968–72; Chrmn. D.C. Heath Can. Ltd., & Vice Pres., Sales, D.C. Heath & Co. (U.S.A.) 1972–74; Vice Pres. & Mktg. Dir., Internat. Div., Addison-Wesley Pub. Co. (U.S.A.) 1974–75; Pres., Coronet Instructional Media Ltd. & Globe/Modern Curriculum Press 1975–90; Lectr., Centennial Coll. of Applied Arts & Tech. 1986–90; Pres., Candn. Book Pub. Counc. 1985–86; Pres., Thornhill Thunderbirds Minor Hockey Assn. 1982–88; led Trade Mission to Australia 1984 & China 1987; Keynote speaker, Printing & Publishing Opportunities, Singapore 1986; Lectr., Management in Book Publishing, Singapore Book Publishers Assoc. 1987; Dir., Assoc. for the Export of Candn. Books 1988–93; Chrmn., Candn. Book Publishers Council, Internat. Mktg. Ctte.; mem., Book Publishing Industry GST Sales Stabilization Ctte.; mem., Dept. of Communications Book Publishing Advisory Ctte.; (represented Candn. Publishing) 1988 & 1992 Beijing Internat. Book Fair; Member, Temple Har Zion; recreations: sports, Gilbert & Sullivan; Home: 185 Lyndhurst Dr., Thornhill, Ont. L3T 6T8; Office: 380 Esna Park Dr., Markham, Ont. L3R 1H5.

**STARNES, John Kennett,** B.A., D.C.L.; b. Montreal, P.Q. 5 Feb. 1918; s. Henry Kennett and Altha Ella (McCrea) S.; e. Selwyn House School, Montreal (1923–30); Trinity Coll. Sch., Port Hope, Ont. (1931–35); Instit. Sillig, Switzerland (1935–36); Univ. of Munich, 1936; Bishop's Univ., B.A. 1939, D.C.L. 1975; m. Helen Gordon, d. Guy de Lancey Robinson, 10 May 1941; two s., Colin John, Patrick Barclay; joined Department of External Affairs as 3rd Secretary; 1944; Canadian Legation Allied Governments, London, England, 1944–45; Ottawa, 1945–48; Adviser, Canadian Delegation to U.N., 1948–50; Ottawa, 1950–53; Counsellor, Canadian Embassy, Bonn, 1953–56; Deputy Extve. Secy., N. Atlantic Council, Paris, 1956–58; apptd. Acting Asst. Under Secy. of State for External Affairs, 1962; Ambassador to Fed. Republic of Germany and Head of Candn. Mil. Mission, Berlin, 1962–66; Ambassador to Un. Arab Republic and Sudan 1966–67; Asst. Undersecy. of State for External Affairs, Oct. 1967–70; Dir. Gen. RCMP Security Service 1970–73; mem. Council, Internat. Inst. for Strategic Studies, London, Eng. 1977–85; Dir., Themadel Foundation, N.B.; served in the 2nd World War, joined Black Watch of Can., 1939; discharged in 1944 with rank of Capt.; author of 'Deep Sleepers' (novel) and 'Scarab' (novel) 1982; 'Orion's Belt' (novel) 1983; 'The Cornish Hug' (novel) 1985; Anglican; Home: Apt. 9, 100 Rideau Terrace, Ottawa, Ont. K1M 0Z2.

**STAROWICZ, Mark M.,** B.A.; broadcasting executive; b. Worksop, UK 8 Sept. 1946; s. Stanley Marian and Barbara Jadwiga (Kielb) S.; e. Loyola Coll. High Sch. 1964; McGill Univ. B.A. 1968; m. Anne d. William and Sheila Wright 4 Dec. 1982; two d.: Caitlin-Elizabeth, Madeleine Anne; EXEC. PRODUCER TV DOCUMENTARIES CBC 1992– ; Reporter, Montreal Gazette 1964–68; Ed. McGill Daily 1968–69; Reporter, Toronto Star 1969–70; Co-founder, writer The Last Post mag. 1969–73; Producer 'Five Nights' series and 'Radio Free Friday' CBC Radio 1970–73; Documentary Producer 'The Battle of the Crossroads of the Sun' chronicle siege Phnom Penh 1973; Exec. Producer CBC Radio 'As It Happens' 1973–76; Creator and Exec. Producer 'Sunday Morning' 1976–80; Creator & Exec. Producer 'The Journal' CBC 1980–92; Producer-Dir. 'The Third Angel' 1991; 'Red Capitalism' 1993; Chrmn. Task Force to Reform CBC TV News & Current Affairs 1979; recipient Anik Award 1987; President's Award for contbr. to News Broadcasting, Radio Television News Directors' Assn. 1988; Golden Sheaf, Yorkton Film Festival, for Best Science Documentary 1992; Gemini Award (Best Information Series) 1987, 1989, 1990; recipient Cybil Award Candn. Broadcasting League 1973; Ohio State Documentary Award 1973; Pres.' Award CBC 1978; Atkinson Lectr. Ryerson Polytech. Inst. 1985; author numerous mag. articles, papers pol. and social issues; co-ed. 'Corporate Canada' 1973; mem. Assn. Toronto Producers & Dirs.; Candn. Broadcasting League; recreations: books, antiquarian newspapers; Home: R.R. 2, Cavan, Ont. L0A 1C0; Office: P.O. Box 500, Stn. A, Toronto, Ont. M5W 1E6.

**STARR, Colonel The Hon. Michael,** P.C. (Can.); b. Cooper Cliff, Ont. 14 Nov. 1910; s. Mathew and Mary (Matechuk) m. Anne, d. John Zaretsky, Toronto, Ont. 9 Sept. 1933; children: Robert, Joan; Alderman, City of Oshawa, 1944–49; Mayor of Oshawa, 1949–52; def. candidate for Ont. Legislature, g.e. 1951; el. to H. of C. for Ont., by-el. 26 May 1952; re-el. 1953, 57, 58, 62, 63,

65; Min. of Labour 1957–63; House Leader of P.C. Party 1965–68; Interim Leader, P.C. Party 1967–68; Chrmn. P.C. Caucus for 2 yrs; U.N. Observer to New York, 1955; Pres., Ont. Folk Arts Council, 1970–71; recipient Coronation Medal 1953; Centennial Medal 1967; Queen's Jubilee Medal 1977; Offr. Order of St. John Medal 1976; Commander Order of St. John 1978; def. g.e. June 1968 and 72; apptd. Citizenship Court Judge, Toronto, Ont. 1968–72; Chmrn., Bd. of Trustees, McLaughlin Art Gall. of Oshawa 1968–72; Chrmn. W.C.B. Ont. 1973–80; Gen. Chrmn., United Way for Oshawa-Whitby-Newcastle 1987; Mem., Refugee Status Adv. Ctte. 1987; Vice-Chrmn. & Dir., Liquor Licence Bd. of Ont.; Senator, Candn. Jr. Bd. of Trade; Hon. Mem., Rotary Club; Hon. Pres., Oshawa & District Boy Scouts' Assn.; Dominion Hon. Life Mem., Candn. Corps Assn.; Hon. Pres., Oshawa Folk Arts Council; P. Conservative; Home: 25 Olive Ave., Oshawa, Ont. L1H 2N7.

**STARR, Ronald E.,** B.Sc.Eng., P.Eng.; land development executive; b. Toronto, Ont. 1941; e. George Harvey Secondary Sch.; Mich. Tech. Univ. B.Sc.Eng. 1967; m. Elaine 1965; two d. Michele, Wendy; DIR. OF DEVEL. FIRST PROFESSIONAL MANAGEMENT INC. 1985– ; Pres. Deanlee Management Inc.; First Mississauga Property Corp.; Vice Chrmn. Mississauga Hydro Comn.; Pres. McAllister Charitable Found.; recipient Kentucky Col. Designation 1984; mem. Profl. Engs. Ont.; Theta Tau; recreation: outdoors; Club: Griffith Island; Home: 1665 Blythe Rd., Mississauga, Ont. L5H 2C3; Office: 300 - 1140 Burnhamthorpe Road West, Mississauga, Ont. L5C 4E9.

**STARRS, Roy Anthony,** B.A., M.A., Ph.D.; university professor; b. Birmingham England; 18 Nov. 1946; s. Edward Kenneth and Daisy May (Hay) S.; e. Earl Warren H.S. 1964; Univ. of B.C., B.A. 1971, M.A. 1980, Ph.D. 1986; Canadian citizen; m. Kazuko d. Tomekichi and Toshiko Yamaguchi 25 Aug. 1976; children: Sean Kenji, Serena Antonia; ASSOC. PROF. OF JAPANESE, AARHUS UNIV., DENMARK 1991– ; Teacher, Braidhurst H.S., Scotland 1969–70; Eng. Teacher, Japan 1972–74; Instr., Vanc. Comm. Coll. 1975–76; U.B.C. 1986–87; Postdoc. rsch. fellow, U.B.C. 1987–89; Asst. Prof. of Japanese, Union Coll., N.Y. 1989–91; fellowships: SSHRCC postdoct. 1987–89; SSHRCC doct. 1983–85; Japan Found. 1978–83; Nitobe-Ohira Grant 1981; student of Rinzai Zen Buddhist master, Joshu Sasaki Roshi 1970– ; NDP & Green (Rhinoceros in spirit); mem., Candn. Asian Studies Assn.; Am. Assn. of Asian Studies; European Assn. of Japan Studies; British Assn. of Japan Studies; Nordic Assn. of Japan Studies; asst. editor: 'Japan Studies in Canada: 1987' 1988; author: 'Deadly Dialectics: Sex, Violence and Nihilism in the World of Yukio Mishima' 1994, and of articles, book reviews & book chaps.; recreations: painting, hiking, tennis; Office: East Asian Institute, Aarhus Univ., DK-8000, Aarhus, Denmark.

**STARYK, Steven S.;** concert violinist; professor of violin; b. Toronto, Ont. 28 Apr. 1932; s. Peter and Maria S.; e. Harbord Coll.; Royal Conserv. of Music; priv. studies in New York; m. Ida d. Judith and Johannes Busch 17 May 1963; one d.: Natalie; Concert master, Royal Philharm. Orch. (U.K.) 1956–60; Concertgebouw Orch. Amsterdam, Amst. Chamber Orch. & Prof. of Violin, Amst. Conserv. 1960–63; Con. Master, Chicago Symph. Orch. 1963–67; Prof., Northwestern Univ. & Am. Conserv. in Chicago 1963–67; Prof., Oberlin Coll. Conserv. 1968–72; Head, String Dept., Vancouver Acad. of Music & Vis. Prof., Univ. of Victoria 1972–75; Prof., Royal Conserv. of Music & Univ. of Toronto Music Fac. 1975–87; Vis. Prof., Univ. of Ottawa 1975–77; Found. Mem., Quartet Can. 1976–81; Prof. & Quartet in Residence, Univ. of W. Ont. 1977–79; solo tours, N. Am., Europe & Far East; Concert Master, Toronto Symphony 1982–87; Prof. of Violin, Chair, String Div. Univ. of Washington, Seattle 1987– ; Jury mem., Internat. Music Comp. (1st Candn. invited as jury mem. to Tchaikovsky Internat. Comp., Moscow); Hon. Litt.D., York Univ.; Queen's Silver Jubilee Medal; Shevchenko Medal; Can. Counc. Arts awards, etc.; 180 compositions rec. on 20 labels; listed in numerous musical & biographical directories; Home: 5244 17th Ave. N.E., Seattle, Washington 98105; Office: The School of Music, Univ. of Washington, Mail Stop DN-10, Seattle, Washington 98195.

**STATHAM, Sidney James,** B.Sc., OLS, CLS; surveyor; hydrographer; b. Barrie, Ont. 21 Feb. 1943; s. Sidney John and Naomi Ann (McGibbon) S.; e. Nepean High Sch. Ottawa 1962; Erindale Coll. Univ. of Toronto Bachelor of Survey Sci. 1976; comnd. Ont. Land Surveyor 1979, Can. Lands Surveyor 1980; m. Annette d. Vincent and Jean Villenveuve 3 Sept. 1966; children: Michael, Kimberley; SENIOR VICE PRES. & DIR., MARSHALL MACKLIN MONAGHAN LTD.; Pres. & Dir., Marshall Macklin Monaghan Ontario Ltd.; Chrmn., Landata Internat. Services Inc.; with Candn. Hydrographic Service 1966–76; Marshall Macklin Monaghan 1976–83, Vice Pres. Surveying 1984; Gen. Mgr. Geodesy Div. Wild Leitz Canada Ltd. 1983; recipient Hans Klinkenberg Award Erindale Coll. 1976; mem. Adv. Bd. Survey Program Ryerson; invited speaker Internat. Fedn. Surveyors Cong. Sophia, Bulgaria 1983; author: 'Development of a Recreational Topographic/Bathymetric Map' 1982; mem. Candn. Inst. Surveying and Mapping; Candn. Hydrographers Assn.; Assn. Ont. Land Surveyors (Pres. 1992–93); Assn. Can. Land Surveyors; Home: 18 Copland Trail, Aurora, Ont.; Office: 80 Commerce Valley Dr. E., Thornhill, Ont. L3T 7N4.

**STÄUBLI, Jürg;** executif; né. Zurich, Suisse 13 nov. 1957; f. Ernst et Lydia (Blaser) S.; é. Diplôme sup. en écon. de Berne, diplôme en marketing (Zurich), diplôme cantonal en immobilier du canton de Berne, Suisse; trois enfants; ADMINISTRATEUR DELEGUE ET DIRECTEUR DE JS HOLDING SA; Prés. des conseils d'admin. suivants, J.S. Finance Canada Inc.; Les Indus. Fil Métallique Major Ltée.; Soc. d'Investissements de Genève Inc.; Le Centre Mondial du Comm. Qué.-Beauport Inc.; JS Genebeau Hockey Inc.; Propriétaire du Club de hockey sur glace 'Les Harfangs'; et en Europe, mem. des conseils d'admin. et prop. des soc. suivantes: JS Holding SA; JS Cons. SA, JS Finance SA; Peralco Constructions SA; Let Holding SA; Leysintours SA; Chatelan SA; WR Construction SA, Baluc SA, Surf SA, JS Luxembourg Holding SA, Fond. de Fribourg SA; Papival Holding SA; Papival Emballages SA; Valpaco SA; etc.; mem., Centre Européen de la Culture; Fond. suisse pour les dons d'organes; bur. des Gouv. de la Croix-Rouge, section Qué.; Gouv. de la C. du C. Qué.-Métro.; Fond. Harfang-Etudes; Fond. 'Les Muses'; bureau: C.P. 276, 9-11, rue Gautier, 1211 Genève 91, Suisse.

**STAVELEY, Michael,** M.A., Ph.D.; educator; university administrator; b. Swanland, Yorks., Eng. 21 July 1940; s. James Albert and Florence Mary (Carter) S.; e. Goole Grammar Sch. Yorks. 1959; Univ. of Reading B.A. 1962, M.A. 1965; Univ. of Alta. Ph.D. 1973; m. Anne Stewart d. Hugh and Anne Ford (McColl) Leslie 1 Aug. 1964; children: Victoria Anne, Alice Elizabeth, James Michael Hugh; PROF. OF GEOGRAPHY, MEML. UNIV. OF NFLD. 1983– , Head of Geog. 1979–83, Dean of Arts 1983–93; Visiting Fellow, Corpus Christi College, Cambridge 1993–94; Anglican; recreations: sailing, carpentry; Club: Royal Nfld. Yacht (Commodore 1983); Home: 59 Portugal Cove Rd., St. John's, Nfld. A1B 2M1; Office: St. John's, Nfld. A1C 5S7.

**STAVERT, The Right Reverend A. Bruce,** B.A., S.T.B., M.Th., D.D.; bishop; b. Montreal, Que. 1 April 1940; s. R. Ewart and Kathleen H. (Rosamond) S.; e. Lower Canada Coll. 1957; Bishop's Univ. B.A. 1961; Trinity Coll., Univ. of Toronto S.T.B. 1964, M.Th. 1976, Hon. D.D. 1986; m. Diana d. Donald and Elizabeth Greig 26 June 1982; children: Kathleen, Rosamond, Timothy; CONSECRATED BISHOP OF THE ANGLICAN DIOCESE OF QUEBEC 19 MARCH 1991; Incumbent, Mission of Schefferville, Que. 1964–69; Fellow & Tutor in Divinity, Trinity Coll., Univ. of Toronto 1969–70; Chaplain 1970–76; Incumbent, St. Clement's Mission E., St. Paul's River, Que. 1976–81; Chaplain, Bishop's Univ. & Champlain Reg. Coll. 1981–84; Dean & Rector, St. Alban's Cathedral, Prince Albert, Sask. 1984–91; recreations: swimming, skiing; club: Garrison Club of Que.; Home: 29 des Jardins, Quebec, Que. G1R 4L6; Office: 31 des Jardins, Quebec, Que. G1R 4L6.

**STAYSHYN, The Hon. Mr. Justice Walter Theodore,** B.A., LL.B.; superior court justice; b. Hamilton, Ont. 14 Nov. 1934; s. Theodore and Theresa (Chary) S.; e. McMaster Univ., B.A. 1958; Osgoode Hall Law Sch., LL.B. 1961; called to Ont. Bar 1963; m. Katherine d. Emile and Olive Dubois 17 June 1967; children: Katherine Theresa Olive, Walter Theodore Emile (Ted); SUPERIOR COURT JUSTICE, ONT. COURT OF JUSTICE (GENERAL DIV.) 1990– ; read law with John L. Agro, Q.C. 1961–62; Assoc., Agro, Cooper, Zaffiro, Parente & Orzel 1963–64; Founding Partner, Borkovich & Stayshyn 1964–75; Auditor, Hamilton Law Assn. 1970–74; District Court Judge, Ont. 1975–90; Chrmn., Legal Aid Area Ctte., Hamilton-Wentworth 1973; Dir., Legal Aid 1974; Pres., Hamilton Lawyers Club 1974; McMaster Univ. Letter, Football (1958), Basketball (1958); Vice-Chrmn., Bd. of Gov., Mt. Mary Acad. 1967–75; Ham./Went. Dist. Health Counc. & Extve. Ctte. 1986–92, Chrmn. 1989–90; Bd. of Trustees, St. Joseph's Villa Found. 1987– ; Chrmn. 1992– ; Chrmn. Hamilton Hospitals Joint Action Ctte. 1993– ; Chrmn., Ham./Went. AIDS Steering Ctte. 1987–90; Mem., Ont. Dist. Court Judges Assn. (Dir. 1987); Candn. Judges Conf.; Ontario Superior Court Judges Assn.; Internat. Commission of Jurists (Candn. Section); McMaster Alumni Assn.; McMaster Letterman's Assoc. (Hall of Fame Sel. Ctte. 1985– ); Past mem., several assns.; Roman Catholic; recreation: sports fan; Home: 114 Broadleaf Cres., Ancaster, Ont. L9G 3R8; Office: 50 Main St. E., Hamilton, Ont. L8N 1E9.

**STEACIE, J. Richard,** B.E.; electrical engineer; b. Montreal, Que. 22 Jan. 1927; s. Edgar William Richard and Dorothy Catalina (Day) S.; e. King's Sch. Montreal; Lisgar Coll. Inst. Ottawa; McGill Univ. B.E. 1951; m. Pamela Ann d. late Clarence Victor Putman 16 Sept. 1950; children: Pamela, Richard John, Adam Day; President, J.R.B. Steacie Investments Ltd.; Elect. Engr. Defence Research Bd. Ottawa 1951–56; Computing Devices of Canada 1956–62, Head Instrument Engn.; Co-Founder Leigh Instruments Ltd. 1961, Vice Pres. Engn., Pres. 1974, Chrmn., Pres. and Dir. 1975–79; served with RCNVR 1944–45; mem. Assn. Prof. Engrs. Prov. Ont.; recreations: sailing, golf; Club: Royal Ottawa Golf Club; Home: 600 Manor Ave., Ottawa, Ont. K1M 0K3.

**STEAD, Gordon Wilson,** D.S.C., B.Com., B.A., LL.D.; b. Vancouver, B.C. 4 Feb. 1913; s. late Frank and Ethel (Ritchie) S.; e. Univ. of B.C. B.Com. 1933, B.A. (Hons. in Econ.) 1934, LL.D. 1945; Univ. of California, Berkeley (Econ.) 1946–48; London Sch. of Econ., 1949–50; m. Lucy, d. late Harrison Rodgers Gore and Lucy (Sasscer) G, Upper Marlboro, Md., 24 June 1948; children: Frank Martin (Aller-Stead), Anne Harriet (Ms. Anne Lance); positions in accounting, market research, stock brokerage and geodetic surveying, 1933–36; managerial post with McKeen & Wilson Ltd., towboat operators, Vancouver, B.C., 1936–40; Lectr. in Econ., Univ. of B.C. 1946; Teaching Asst. in Accounting Univ. of Cal., 1946–47 and Lectr., 1947; Dept. of Finance, Ottawa, 1950–58, Asst. Secy. Treasury Bd. 1956–58; appointed to Dept. of Transport as Dir.-Gen., Marine Services 1958–60 and Asst. Depy. Min., Marine 1960–70 to do thorough reorganization resulting in creation of Canadian Coast Guard as a national professional Service, and establishment of Candn. Coast Guard College; Ldr. Candn. Del. to Intergovernmental Maritime Consultative Organ. 1965–69 and other international exchanges; mem. Candn. Ctte. on Oceanography 1959–69; Special Adv. (Transport.) Constitutional Review, Privy Council Office 1970–71; Prof. Sch. Community & Regional Planning, Univ. B.C. 1971–76; policy consult.; author various journal and newspaper articles, 'A Leaf upon the Sea' 1988 (Candn. Nautical Rsch. Soc. best book award); 2nd Lieutenant B.C. Regiment 1931–33; Lieutenant R.C.N.V.R. 1940; on loan to Royal Navy, 1940–43, serving mainly in the Mediterranean; Lt. Commdr. and Sr. Offr., 3rd Motor Launch Flotilla, 1943; served in H.M.C.S. 'Iroquois' in Bay of Biscay, W. Approaches and N. Europe, 1944–45; D.S.C. (Malta, 1942); and Bar (Salerno, 1943); Hon. Commodore, Candn. Coast Guard; Vice Pres. for Can., Inst. of Marine Engrs., 1968–71; Pres., Candn. Port and Harbour Assn., 1964–65; Pres., Le Cercle Universitaire d'Ottawa, 1970–71; recreations: sometime hiker, geography, history; Home: 117 - 2125 Eddington Dr., Vancouver, B.C. V6L 3A9.

**STEBBINS, Robert Alan,** M.A., Ph.D.; educator; b. Rhinelander, Wis. 22 June 1938; s. William Nelson and Dorothy May (Guy) S.; e. Macalester Coll. St. Paul, Minn. B.A. 1961; Univ. of Minn. M.A. 1962; Univ. of Minn. Ph.D. 1964; m. Karin Y. d. Oscar and Mary Olson 11 Jan. 1964; children: Paul, Lisa, Christi; PROF. OF SOCIOL. UNIV. OF CALGARY 1976– , Head of Sociol. 1976–82; Assoc. Prof. Presb. Coll. 1964–65; Asst. to full Prof. Meml. Univ. of Nfld. 1965–73, Head of Sociol. & Anthrop. 1968–71; Prof. Univ. of Texas Arlington 1973–76; Pres. Social Sci. Fedn. Can. 1991–92; Fellow, Calgary Inst. for Humanities 1987–88; Killam Resident Fellow 1990; Can. Council Sabbatical Leave Fellow 1971–72; author 'Commitment to Deviance: The Non-Professional Criminal in the Community' 1971; 'The Disorderly Classroom' 1974; 'Teachers and Meaning' 1975; 'Amateurs: On the Margin Between Work and Leisure' 1979; 'Fieldwork Experience' 1980; 'The Sociology of Deviance' 1982; 'The Magician' 1984; 'Canadian Football' 1987; 'Sociology: The Study of Society' 1987, 2nd ed. 1990; 'Deviance: Tolerable Differences' 1988; 'The Laugh-Makers: Stand-Up Comedy as Art, Business and Life-Style' 1990; 'Experiencing Fieldwork: An Inside View of Qualitative Research' 1991; 'Amateurs, Professionals and Serious Leisure' 1992; 'Predicaments: Moral Difficulty in Everyday Life' 1993; 'The Franco-Calgarians: French Language, Leisure, and Linguistic

Lifestyle in an Anglophone City' 1994; mem. Candn. Sociol. & Anthrop. Assn. (Pres. 1988–89); Candn. Assn. for Leisure Studies (Vice-Pres. 1993–94); Assn. Candn. Studies; Assn. canadienne des sociologues et anthropologues de langue française; Internat. Sociol. Assn.; Am. Sociol. Assn.; World Leisure and Recreation Assn.; Am. Fedn. Musicians (Can.); Assn. canadienne-française de l'Alberta; Club Inter; Calgary Civic Symphony; recreations: music, cross-country skiing; Home: 144 Edgemont Estates Dr. N.W., Calgary, Alta. T3A 2M3; Office: Dept. of Sociology, Univ. of Calgary, Calgary, Alta. T2N 1N4.

**STECK, Brian Jason,** B.Comm., M.B.A., C.F.A., F.C.S.I.; investment dealer; b. Montreal, Que. 26 Dec. 1946; e. Sir George Williams Univ. B.Comm. 1968; Wharton Grad. Sch. of Finance & Comm., Philadelphia PA, M.B.A. 1969; Univ. of Illinois Cert. Financial Analyst 1975; Fellow, Candn. Securities Inst. 1983; m. Ellen and has one child: Stephen; CHRMN. & C.E.O., NESBITT THOMSON CORPORATION LIMITED and subsidiaries; VICE-CHRMN., BANK OF MONTREAL; Mem., Bd. of Dirs., Nesbitt Thomson Corp. Ltd. and subsidiaries; BGR Precious Metals Inc.; Bankmont Financial Corp.; Bank of Montreal Investment Management Ltd.; Harris Nesbitt Thomson Securities Inc.; Bank of Montreal Investor Services; Bank of Montreal Investment Counsel Ltd.; Bank of Montreal Securities Canada Ltd.; The Trust Company of Bank of Montreal; Council for Candn. Unity and the Premier's Adv. Council of Ont.; began as Research Analyst, Nesbitt Thomson Inc., Montreal 1969; gained progressive experience and responsibility at Nesbitt Thomson Inc. and was apptd. President, 1977–87; Pres. & Chief Extve. Offr. 1987–90; Chrmn. & C.E.O. 1990– ; Vice-Chrmn., Bank of Montreal 1992– ; Past Chrmn.: Investment Dealers Assoc. of Canada; Canadian Securities Inst. and Security Industry Assn. of America, Canadian District; Past Gov., Toronto Stock Exchange; Mem., Bd. of Govs., North York Gen. Hosp., Concordia Univ. and Weizmann Institute of Science; Clubs: Oakdale Golf & Country; Beacon Hall; St. Andrews Golf, Boca Raton; Cambridge, Toronto and Founders; Office: Bank of Montreal, 68th Floor, First Canadian Place, 100 King St. W., Toronto, Ont. M5X 1A1.

**STECK, Warren Franklin,** A.R.C.T., B.Eng., Ph.D.; scientific researcher; b. Regina, Sask. 10 May 1939; s. Edgar and Dorothy (Start) S.; e. Univ. of Toronto A.R.C.T. 1956; McGill Univ. B.Eng. (Chem. Engr.) 1960; Univ. of Sask. Ph.D. (Org. Chem.) 1964; DIR. GEN., PLANT BIOTECHNOL. INST., NAT. RSCH. COUNC. OF CAN. 1990– ; Rsch. Offr., Prairie Regional Lab. 1965–77; Sr. Rsch. Offr. 1977–80; Assoc. Dir. 1981–82; Dir. 1983–89; Adv. Counc., Coll. of Agric., Univ. of Sask.; mem. Bd. of Mgmt., Nat. Centre for Protein Engr.; Candn. Agric. Servs. Coord. Comm.; Senate, Univ. of Sask.; Dir., Aspen Assoc.; mem., Phytochem. Soc. N. Amer.; Candn. Rsch. Mgmt. Assn.; author or co-author of more than 80 rsch. papers; holder of 6 patents; recreations: classical music performance; Home: 1326 Conn Ave., Saskatoon, Sask. S7H 3L1; Office: 110 Gymnasium Rd., Saskatoon, Sask. S7N 0W9.

**STEDMAN, Robert William,** M.C., B.A.Sc., M.E.I.C., P.Eng.; retired consulting engineer; b. Ottawa, Ont. 24 Sept. 1921; s. late Air Vice Marshal Ernest Walter, C.B., O.B.E. and late Ethel (Studd) S.; e. Ashbury Coll., Ottawa, 1939; Royal Mil. Coll., 1941; Univ. of Toronto, B.A.Sc. 1947; m. Elisabeth, d. late Rt. Hon. C. D. Howe, 8 June 1946; children: Robin Mary (Mrs. W. MacInnis), Charles E., William R., George F.; joined C. D. Howe Co. Ltd. 1947; President 1968–1982; Chairman, Howe International Ltd. 1978–1982; served with Brit. Army in N. Africa and Italy 1941–44; Reserve Army (Can.) 1947–60; rank Maj.; Anglican; recreation: boating (power and sail); Home: 130 Rideau Terrace, Ottawa, Ont. K1M 0Z2.

**STEDMOND, John Mitchell,** M.A., Ph.D., F.R.S.C. (1971); university professor; b. Leicester, England 14 May 1916; s. John Butler and Margaret Hunter (Mitchell) S.; came to Canada, 1924; e. Central Coll.; Moose Jaw, Sask.; Univ. of Sask., B.A. 1950, M.A. 1951; Univ. of Aberdeen, Ph.D. 1953; m. late Nona Fay, d. Ernest C. Horne, Moose Jaw, Sask., 14 Sept. 1940; EMERITUS JAMES CAPPON PROFESSOR OF ENGLISH, QUEEN'S UNIV. 1981– (Prof. there 1965–81 and Head of the Dept. 1968–77); Assoc. Dir., McGill-Queen's Univ. Pres. 1971–74; Editor, 'Queen's Quarterly' 1960–64; Asst. Lectr., Univ. of Aberdeen 1951–52; Instr. and Asst. Prof. of Eng., Univ. of Sask. 1953–58; served in 2nd World War with R.C.O.C., 1942–45, U.K. and N.W. Europe; author 'The Comic Art of Laurence Sterne' 1967, and numerous articles in scholarly journs.; Ed. 'The Winged Skull: Bicentenary Essays on Laurence Sterne' 1971; mem. Humanities Assn. Can. (Vice-Pres. 1958–60, Pres. 1972–73); Humanities Research Council Can. (Chrmn. 1972–74); Assn. Candn. Univ. Teachers of Eng.; Modern Lang. Assn.; Candn. Assn. Univ. Teachers; Home: 8 Barclay Road, Kingston, Ont. K7M 2S4.

**STEED, Graham (Percy),** B.Mus., F.R.C.O.; organist; b. Newcastle-on-Tyne, Eng. 1 March 1913; s. Percy Roland and Beatrice Evelyn (Hutchinson) S.; e. Royal Grammar Sch. Newcastle-on-Tyne 1930; Royal Coll. Organists (Fellow 1937); Univ. of Durham B.Mus. 1956; m. Rita G. d. R.G. and Olinda Ritchie 12 Nov. 1966; children (by previous marriage) Roger G., Christopher J., Brenda C. Laing; ORGANIST EMERITUS, ST. MARY'S CATH.-BASILICA, HALIFAX N.S. 1980–86; Organist and Dir. of Music Caths. and Chs. Saskatoon, Sask. 1949, Victoria B.C. 1949–58, Windsor Ont. 1959–65, New London, Conn. 1966–69, Hartford, Conn. 1969–73, Montreal 1974–75; Conductor Emeritus Victoria Choral Society, 1949–58; Founder & conductor Graham Steed Chorale, Windsor, 1959–65; Chrmn., Royal Candn. Coll. of Organists, Vancouver Island Chapt. 1987–89; adjudicator various festivals; numerous radio and TV appearances with Australian, Brit., Candn. and N.Z. Broadcasting Corps., also Austria, Belgium, France, Iceland, Switzerland; recording artist for R.C.A, Victrola and Red Seal, Vista and L'Oiseau Lyre Records, with over 600 recitals in 18 countries; author numerous articles various newspapers, journs.; recipient Critic's Choice Citation, Gramophone 1972, 1974, 1977; 3 record box organ works of César Franck named Best of Month, Stereo Review, N.Y. October 1981; Can. Counc. Grants 1977, 1983, 1986 for lectures in U.K. on Marcel Dupré; Golden Palms of Ste-Catherine of Alexandria 1983; served with RN 1941–46, rank Lt. Commdr. (S); recreations: travel, philately; Club: Rotary (Paul Harris Fellow 1989); Address: 9 - 4096 Torquay Dr., Victoria, B.C. V8N 3K7.

**STEED, Judy,** B.A.; writer; b. Wigan, Eng. 28 Aug. 1943; d. John Burke and Ethel Louisa (Mackenzie) Ewing; e. Univ. of Toronto Victoria Coll. B.A. 1965; m. Nicholas Steed 1965, div.; one d. Emily; film producer with Joyce Wieland 'The Far Shore' 1976 (winner 3 Candn. Film Awards); freelance mag. writer 1978–80; Feature Writer, Globe and Mail 1981–89, Toronto Star 1989– ; recipient Nat. Mag. Award 1980; Nat. Newspaper Award Citations 1981, 1987, 1989; Robertine Barry prize for best feminist article in popular print medium; author: 'Ed Broadbent: The Pursuit of Power' 1988; 'Our Little Secret: Confronting Child Sexual Abuse in Canada' 1994; Founding mem. The Ctte. for '94; recreations: sports, cross-country skiing, yoga; Office: Toronto Star, One Yonge St., Toronto, Ont. M5E 1E6

**STEEL, David A.B.,** B.A., M.A., B.C.L., M.B.A.; consultant; b. Cambridge, U.K. 15 June 1928; s. Anthony Bedford and Eileen Maud (Johnson) S.; e. Rugby Sch. 1946; Oxford Univ. B.A., M.A. 1952; McGill Univ. B.C.L. 1957; Univ. of Toronto M.B.A. 1965, M.A. 1972; m. Elisabeth Tesni d. Sir Wynne Cemlyn-Jones and Muriel Gwendolyn Cemlyn-Jones 27 July 1956, divorced 4 July 1990; m. Martica d. Arturo and Gloria Alberni 4 May 1991; children: Antony, Marion, Toby, Anita, Laura, Piers; Assoc. Counsel, Holden Day Wilson 1988–91; Borden & Elliot Toronto 1957–79; Vice-Pres. & Dir., McLeod Young Weir Toronto 1980–87; Pres., Platmast Charitable Found.; recreations: squash, rowing, tennis; clubs: R.C.Y.C.; Cambridge; Toronto Athletic; Office: 673 Euclid Avenue, Toronto, Ont. M6G 2T8.

**STEEL, Victor John,** B.A., F.C.I.M., F.R.S.A.; business executive; b. Keighley, England 19 Nov. 1938; s. John and May (Cope) S.; e. Holme Valley Grammar Sch. 1958; Liverpool Univ. 1958–61; m. Daphne d. John and May Russell 28 July 1962; children: John Russell, Richard Andrew, James Victor; CHAIRMAN, CONSUMERS DISTRIBUTING INC. & MGT. GROUP PARTNER, WESTBOURNE MNGT. GROUP 1991– ; Marketing Dir., J. Lyons & Co. (UK) 1964–71; SmithKline Beecham 1971–85 (Main Bd. Dir. 1983–85; Chair, Beecham Prod. Internat. Div.); Main Bd. Dir., Guinness PLC (UK) 1985–87; Chair, Woolworths PLC & Superdrug PLC, Kingfisher PLC (UK) 1987–91; Non-Extve. Dir., Mansfield Brewery Ltd. (UK) 1989– ; Trustee, British Dyslexia Edn. Trust 1987– ; recreations: tennis, swimming; Office: 6303 Airport Rd., Mississauga, Ont. L4V 1R8.

**STEELE, Clifford George;** executive; b. Vancouver, B.C. 30 March 1929; s. James Elder and Janet (Kinsman) S.; e. Lord Selkirk Sch., Vancouver, B.C.; Vancouver Tech Sch.; m. Margaret, d. Irvine H. Cook, 28 Nov. 1975; PRESIDENT, DIVERSIFIED ELECTRONICS OF CANADA LTD.; OWNER, WOODCHIPS CARVING SUPPLIES LTD., Vancouver; commenced as Business Servicer, radio and household appliances 1946; later Relieving Agent and Combination Operator, Dom. Govt. Telephone and Telegraphs; subsequently with Radio Station CKWX Vancouver, then Chief Engr. CKPG, Prince George, B.C.; prior to present position involved in supervisory capacity with tech. and engn. facilities of various sound and intercom equipment firms; developed specialty of buried metal location; equipment and water leak detection svces.; mem. Inst. Elect. and Electronic Engrs.; United Church; recreations: Amateur Radio (VE7LF); fishing, woodworking, woodcarving; Home: 8009 – 17th Ave., Burnaby, B.C. V3N 1M5; Office: 8521 East Lake Dr., Burnaby, B.C. V5A 4T5.

**STEELE, David Fraser,** MCIQS; construction executive; b. Montréal, Qué. 5 July 1936; s. David Broadfoot and Anne McPherson (Redfern) S.; e. Montréal West H.S. 1955; Full Mem., Candn. Inst. of Quantity Surveyors 1961; m. Carol d. George and Verna Haldimand 12 Sept. 1959; children: Linda Ann, Barbara Elizabeth; SR. VICE-PRES., EASTERN CONSTRUCTION CO. LTD. 1985– ; Asst. Chief Estimator, Richard & B.A. Ryan Ltd. 1955–68; Pres., Atlantic Masonry Ltd. 1968–71; Sr. Estimator & var. positions, then Sr. Vice-Pres. Eastern Construction 1972– ; Dir., Ont. Gen. Contractors Assn. (Pres. 1990–91); recreations: curling, golf; Clubs: Oakville Curling; Bd. of Trade Country; Home: 1530 Chasehurst Dr., Mississauga, Ont. L5J 3A8; Office: 4120 Yonge St., Suite 410, Toronto, Ont. M2P 2C8.

**STEELE, Hon. Donald Robert,** B.A.Sc.; judge; b. Toronto, Ont. 28 June 1925; s. late Harold Learoyd and late Gladys Ione (Bateman) S.; e. Upper Can. Coll. 1942; Univ. of Toronto B.A.Sc. 1946; Osgoode Hall Law Sch. 1949; m. Barbara L. d. late Carl A. Pollock 1 Oct. 1955; children: Victoria, Mark, Douglas; JUSTICE, SUPREME COURT OF ONT.; served with RCAF 1944; Lambda Alpha; Theta Delta Chi; Anglican; recreations: golf, skiing; Clubs: Toronto Golf; University; Osler Bluff; Muskoka Lakes Golf; Badminton & Racquet; Home: 14 May St., Toronto, Ont. M4W 2Y1; Office: Osgoode Hall, Toronto, Ont. M5H 2N5.

**STEELE, Granville George Ernest,** B.A., D.U.; b. Windsor, Ont. 11 Jan. 1920; s. Ernest and Ethel Isabel (Fordham) S.; e. High Schs., Montreal, Que. and Toronto, Ont.; Univ. of Toronto, B.A. (Hons. Pol. Science and Econ.) 1949; London Sch. of Econ., 1949–51; m. Edith Clare, d. late Frederick Hamilton Rutherford, Dec. 1948; children: Michael Ernest, Elizabeth Jean, John Peter, Graham Frederick; Pres., Candn. Assn. of Broadcasters 1978–85; former Pres., Grocery Products Mfrs. of Can., 1968; Life Trustee, Candn. Hunger Foundation; former Chrmn. Bd. Govs., Univ. of Ottawa; employed with Toronto Office of Simonds Canada Saw Co. Ltd. as Acct., 1937–41; joined Dept. of Finance, Ottawa, 1951; Asst. Depy. Min. and Secy. of Treasury Bd., 1960–64; Under-Secy. of State 1964 till resigned from public service, 1968; served in 2nd World War with R.C.A.F. 1941–45 (Overseas 1943–45); Pres., Candn. Assn. of Broadcasters; mem., Candn. Inst. Public Adm.; D.U. (h.c.) Univ. of Ottawa; Clubs: Canadian; Cercle Universitaire d'Ottawa; Home: Treasure Island, R.R. 1, Kingston, Ont. K7L 4V1.

**STEELE, Ian Kenneth,** B.A., Ph.D.; author, university professor; b. Edmonton, Alta. 10 Sept. 1937; s. Patrick and June S.; e. Univ. of Alberta B.A. 1961; Univ. of London Ph.D. 1964; m. Herta d. August and Ida Kleiner 8 July 1961; children: Kenneth, Colin; PROF. OF HIST. UNIV. OF WESTERN ONTARIO, 1975– ; lect. 1964; Asst. Prof. 1965–70; Assoc. Prof. 1970–75; Commonwealth Scholar 1961–64; Killam Fellow, 1980–81; SSHRC Fellow 1985–86; U.W.O. Research Professor 1988–89; author 'Politics of Colonial Policy' 1968; 'Guerillas and Grenadiers' 1969; 'The English Atlantic 1675–1740' (winner CSNR book award 1987); 'Betrayals: Fort William Henry and the Massacre' 1990 (winner SCWSNY book award 1992) rev. paperback 1993; ed. 'Atlantic Merchant Apothecary' 1977; recreation: gardening, woodworking, chess; Home: 433 Wortley Rd., London, Ont. N6C 3S7; Office: London, Ont. N6A 5C2.

**STEELE, John Wiseman,** B.Sc. (Pharm.), A.R.C.S.T., Ph.D. (Glas.); university professor; b. Motherwell, Scotland, 27 May 1934; s. James F.H. and Janet H.M. (Ogilvie) S.; e. Knowetop Public Sch.; Dalziel High Sch.; Univ. Glasgow, B.Sc. Hons. (Pharm.) 1955; Royal Coll. Sci. & Tech. (now Univ. Strathclyde), Glasgow, Assoc. 1958; Univ. Glasgow, Ph.D. 1959; Royal Inst. Chemistry, London, Assoc. 1966; m. Muriel, d. George and Ella Gribbon, 27 Dec. 1958; children: Colin; Alison; Graham; Alistair; PROF. OF PHARMACY, UNIV. OF MANI-

TOBA; Lectr. Sch. Pharm., Univ. Man. 1958; Asst. Prof. 1959; Acting Dir. 1963 (Jan.-Aug.); Prof. Faculty of Pharm. 1968– ; Acting Dean 1977; Dean 1981–92; author and co-author of 30 research publications related to pharmaceutical sciences; Visiting Fellow, Sch. Pharm., Chelsea Coll. Sci. & Tech., London, Eng. 1965–66; Visiting Prof., Medizinisch-chemisches Inst., Univ. Bern, Switzerland 1972–73 (funded through Visiting Scientist Award, Medical Research Counc.); Visiting Scientist, Nat. Inst. Environmental Health Sciences (Nat. Inst. Health, U.S.A.); Centennial Award, Manitoba Pharmaceutical Assn. 1979–80; Visiting Prof., Faculté de Pharmacie, Univ. de Montpellier, Montpellier, France 1986–87; Visitor to ADIS Internat. Ltd., Auckland, New Zealand 1992–93; mem. Candn. Pharmaceutical Assn.; Federation Internat. Pharmaceutique (F.I.P.); Assn. Faculties Pharm. Can. (Pres. 1975–76); Medical Research Counc. Can. 1970–72; Man. Pharmaceutical Assn. (mem. Counc. 1975–76, 1981–92); Man. Soc. of Pharmacists; club: Winnipeg Lawn Tennis; recreations: tennis, genealogy, philately, photography; Office: Faculty of Pharmacy, Univ. of Manitoba, Winnipeg, Man. R3T 2N2.

**STEELE, Richard Arthur;** newsprint marketing executive; b. Parry Sound, Ont. 2 Jan. 1947; s. John (stepfather) and Dorothy Eva (McG) Sinclair; e. Ryerson Polytechnical Inst. Dipl. of Bus. Admin. 1969; m. Mary d. Roy and Marion Waldeck 27 Dec. 1969; children: Zoe Katharine, Victoria Jane; VICE-PRESIDENT, REGIONAL SALES, QUNO CORPORATION 1985– ; Sales Rep., A.H. Robins 1971–76; Senior Sales Rep., IBM Canada 1976–79; Canadian Regional Mgr., Advanced Systems Inc. 1979–85; Home: 18 Barnsdale Lane, St. Catharines, Ont. L2N 7J5; Office: 80 King St., St. Catharines, Ont. L2R 7G2.

**STEELE, Robert,** M.D., D.P.H., F.F.C.M., F.R.C.P.(C); F.A.P.H.A.; F.R.C.P. (Ed.); b. Scotland, 16 Jan. 1929; s. John and Susan Halbert (Hunter) S.; e. Sch. of Med., Royal Colls., Edinburgh Univ., D.P.H. 1956; Univ. of Sask., M.D. 1960; m. Letitia Margaret, d. Robert A. Cuthbertson, Edinburgh, Scot., 30 July 1955; two s., Paul Robert, David Angus; PROF., DEPT. COMMUNITY HEALTH & EPID., QUEEN'S UNIV. 1968– and PROF., DEPT OF FAMILY MED. 1975– ; Consultant in Epidemiology, Kingston Gen. Hosp.; mem. Consulting Staff, Kingston Gen. and Hotel Dieu Hosps.; joined Dept. of Pub. Health and Social Med., Univ. of Edinburgh as Research Fellow in Epidemiology, 1956; apptd. Hon. Registrar to S.E. Scot. Regional Hosp. Bd., 1957; Asst. Prof., Dept. of Social and Preventive Med., Coll. of Med., Univ. of Sask. 1958; Med. Offr. Hosp. Div. of Scot. Home and Health Dept., Edinburgh, 1962–64; apptd. to present univ. as Assoc. Prof. of Preventive Med. and Dir. of Research, Child Health Programme, 1964; Prof. and Head, Dept. of Community Health & Epidemiol. 1968–87; served as Capt. with R.A.M.C. 1953–55; author of numerous articles in med. journs.; mem., Roy. Med. Soc.; Internat. Epidemiology Assn.; Candn. Assn. Teachers Social & Preventive Med.; Assn. Teachers Preventive Med.; recreations: golf, Indian cookery, opera; Address: 3rd Flr., Abramsky Hall, Queen's Univ., Kingston, Ont. K7L 3N6.

**STEELE, Thomas H.,** B.A.; utilities executive; b. Huntingdon, Que. 12 Aug. 1939; s. William Thomas and Margaret Helm (Irwin) S.; e. Sir George Williams Univ. B.A. 1972; m. Suzanne d. Joseph Absolom and Marie Adelina (Levert) Lanthier 11 June 1960; children: Kathleen, Patrick; VICE-PRES., CORP. OPERATIONS, BELL CANADA 1992– ; Asst. Vice-Pres., Customer Serv. Opns. Planning, Bell Canada 1981; Customer Serv. 1983; Gen. Mgr., Business Communications, Major Accts. 1983; Asst. Vice-Pres., Govt. & Nat. Systems 1984; Gen. Mgr., Saudi Telecom 1985; Asst. Vice-Pres., Corp. Performance 1988; Chair, Les Poteaux LPB Inc.; Dir., Canada-Ireland Chamber of Commerce; Mem., Telethon of Stars; Arthritis Soc.; clubs: St. James; Home: 346 Windermere, Beaconsfield, Que. H9W 1W5; Office: 1050 Beaver Hall Hill, Suite 1800, Montreal, Que. H2Z 1S4.

**STEEN, Peter,** P.Eng.; mining company executive; b. South Africa 8 Dec. 1930; e. Camborne School of Mines grad. 1956; m. Norma; children: Beverly, Gregory, Karen, Michael; Mine Superintendent, Anglo Am. Mining Co. Zambia 1956–68; Mine Supt., Anglo Rouyn Saskatchewan 1968–71; Gen. Mgr., Whitehorse Copper Mines 1971–73; Pres. & C.E.O., Cassiar Asbestos 1973; Pres. & Chief Extve. Offr. 1974–78; Inspiration Copper Arizona 1978–83; Consultant, Arizona 1983–85; President & C.E.O., International Corona Corp. 1985; Dir., Poco Petroleums; International Corona Corp.; Breakwater Resources; First Vice-Chrmn., Mining Assn. of Canada; clubs: Vancouver.

**STEER, Rt. Rev. Stanley Charles,** M.A., D.D. (Ang.); retired bishop; b. Aldershot, Hants, England; s. Stanley Edgar and Emma Grace (Comber) S.; e. Margate and Guildford Grammar Schs.; came to Canada 1922; Univ. of Sask., B.A. 1928; Oxford Univ., M.A. and General Synod, B.D. 1937; D.D. Wycliffe, 1946, Emmanuel Coll., Saskatoon, 1951, St. Chad's Coll., Regina, 1964; m. Marjorie Slater, 1936; Missy., Vanderhoof, B.C., 1929; Chaplain, St. Mark's Ch., Alexandria 1931; Chaplain, University Coll., Oxford, 1932–33; Tutor, St. John's Hall, Univ. of London, 1933; Vice-Principal there, 1936; Chaplain, The Mercers Company, City of London, 1937; Principal, Emmanuel Coll., Saskatoon, Sask., 1941; Hon. Canon of St. John's Cath., Saskatoon, Sask., 1943; Bishop of Saskatoon 1950–70; served in 1st World War with Imp. Army; 2nd World War, Chaplain, R.O.; Home: 2383 Lincoln Rd., Victoria, B.C. V8R 6A3.

**STEERS, Barry Connell,** B.A., LL.D.; diplomat; b. London, Ont. 15 Jan. 1927; s. late Connell Gerald and Kathleen Mary (Coles) S.; e. De La Salle Coll., London, Ont.; Univ. of W. Ont., B.A. 1951; m. Marta Molina-Vélez, d. late Arthur Molina, 16 Aug. 1952; children: Connell (Rio de Janeiro), Sara (London, Ont.), Gregory (Toronto, Ont.); Ambassador to Japan 1981–89; Nat. Research Council of Can., 1951–55; Partner in export/import business, Medellin, Colombia, 1955–57; joined Trade Commr. Service, Ottawa, 1957; Asst. Trade Commr. Singapore, 1958; Second Secy. (Comm.), Athens, 1960; First Secy. (Comm.), Tel Aviv, 1961; Consul and Trade Commr., New York City, 1966; Dir., Internat. Financing Br., Ottawa, 1968; also Alternate Dir., Export Devel. Corp., Ottawa; organ. Market Devel. Group, Ottawa and subsequently became Dir., 1970; Ambassador to Brazil 1971; apptd. Consul-Gen., New York, 1976 and concurrently Can.'s first Commr. to Bermuda, 1977; Asst. Deputy Min., Trade Commissioner Service and Int'l Marketing, Dept. Industry, Trade and Commerce, 1979–81; served with COTC, RCAC Militia; recipient Candn. Club of New York Gold Medal; Govt. of Canada Outstanding Achievement Award; Zeta Psi; R. Catholic; recreations: sports, history; Clubs: Chimo Group (Ottawa); Gatineau Fish and Game (Ottawa); Canadian (N.Y.); Canadian Soc. (N.Y.); Yacht (Rio de Janeiro); Tokyo Club, Japan; Home: 4 Sandfield Rd., North York, Ont. M3B 2B6.

**STEERS, Reginald F.,** C.A.; chartered accountant; b. Sudbury, Ont. 21 April 1938; s. Harold Thomas and Veronica (O'Connor) S.; m. Andrée d. Leontyne and Joseph Thériault 5 Sept. 1970; one d.: Isabelle; VICE-PRES., FINANCE, PRATT & WHITNEY CANADA INC. 1984– ; articled C.A. student, J.E. Beckett & Co. 1957–63; Accountant, Bell Canada 1964–66; various sr. level financial mngt. positions, Gillette Co. (Canada, U.S.A., France) 1966–78; Vice-Pres. Finance, Micom Co. 1978–81; Controller, Pratt & Whitney Canada Inc. 1981–84; recreations: golf, alpine skiing, tennis; club: Royal Montreal Golf; Home: 576 Chelsea Cr., Beaconsfield Que. H9W 4N5; Office: 1000 Marie-Victorin Blvd, Longueuil, Que. J4G 1A1.

**STEEVES, Keith E.,** F.C.A.; marketing executive; b. Saskatoon, Sask. 30 May 1932; s. Vaughn Orlo and Delilah Mae (Jolly) S.; e. primary and sec. schs. Saskatoon, Sask.; Alta. Inst. of Chartered Accts. C.A. 1963; B.C. Inst. of Chartered Accts. 1964; Banff Sch. of Advanced Mgmt. grad. 1967; m. Norma R. d. George and May Sparks 14 May 1955; one s., Terrence K.; VICE-PRES. MKTG., DIR. & MEM. EXEC. CTTE., TECK CORPORATION 1981– ; Chief Acct. Bethlehem Copper Corp. 1965, Sec.-Treas. 1966, Vice-Pres. Fin. and Treas. 1970, Sr. Vice-Pres. Fin. and Admin. 1976; mem., past Pres. and Dir. Fin. Execs. Inst. Vancouver Chapter; past Dir. Fin. Execs. Inst. of Can.; past mem. Counc., B.C. Inst. of Chartered Accts.; past Chrmn. Taxation Ctte., Mining Assn. of Can., Mining Assn. of B.C.; apptd. Fellow, B.C. Inst. of C.A.'s 1978; recreations: golf, fishing; Clubs: Point Grey Golf & Country; Semiahmoo Golf and Country (Blaine, Washington); Terminal City (Vancouver); Vancouver (Vancouver); Home: 1662 W. 52nd Ave., Vancouver, B.C. V6P 1J4; Office: Suite 600, 200 Burrard, Vancouver, B.C. V6C 3L9.

**STEEVES, Lea Chapman,** M.D., C.M., LL.D., D.Sc., F.R.C.P. (Can.), F.A.C.P.; b. New Westminster, B.C. 4 Nov. 1915; s. Harold Chapman, M.D. and Helen Anna (Lea) S.; e. Pub. and High Schs., New Westminster and Essondale, B.C., Moncton, N.B.; Mount Allison Univ., B.A. (MCL) 1936, LL.D. 1969; McGill Univ., M.D., C.M. 1940; m. Katharine Grace, d. Donald Fraser 19 Feb. 1942; children: Donald Chapman, M.D.; Alexander L., M.D.; Gordon F.; John M., M.D.; James I.; ASSOC. DEAN, FACULTY OF MEDICINE, DALHOUSIE UNIV. 1969–81 and Prof. of Med. there; Dir., Div. of Continuing Med. Educ., 1957–72; Hon. Med. consultant, Camp Hill Medical Centre, Halifax; served as Surg.-Lt. with RCNVR 1943–46; mem. Adv. Bd., Candn. Heart Foundation; Bd., N.S. Heart Foundation; Pres.; Med. Council Can. 1969–70; Candn. Assn. Continuing Med. Educ. 1968–69; Med. Soc. N.S. 1969–70; N.S. Div., Candn. Med. Assn.; Senior mem., N.S. Med. Soc. 1991– ; N.S. Soc. Internal Med.; Alpha Omega Alpha; Phi Rho Sigma; rec'd. D.Sc. Memorial Univ. 1974; LL.D. Dalhousie Univ. 1989; Emeritus Professor 1990; United Church; recreations: computing, photography, social dancing, travel, canoeing; Home: 51 Hazelholme Dr., Halifax, N.S. B3M 1N6.

**STEFFLER, John Earl,** B.A., M.A.; writer; university professor; b. Toronto, Ont. 13 Nov. 1947; s. Harold George and Dorothy Anne (Hoelscher) S.; e. Thornhill S.S. 1966; Univ. of Toronto, B.A. (Hons.) 1971; Univ. of Guelph, M.A. 1974; m. Shawn d. Nancy and Leslie O'Hagan 30 May 1970; children: Edith, Alban; PROF. OF ENGLISH, SIR WILFRED GRENFELL COLL., MEMORIAL UNIV. OF NFLD. 1975– ; W.H. Smith/'Books in Canada' First Novel Award, Thomas Raddal Atlantic Fiction Award, Joseph S. Stauffer Prize, Nfld. & Labrador Arts Council's Artist of the Year Award; Short-Listed for Gov. General's Award for Fiction, The Norma Epstein Award for Writing; Mem., Adv. Bd., MUN Art Gallery; mem., The League of Candn. Poets; PEN Internat.; The Writers' Alliance of Nfld. & Labrador; author: 'An Explanation of Yellow' 1981, 'The Grey Islands' 1985, 'The Wreckage of Play' 1988 (poetry); 'Flights of Magic' (illus. by Shawn Steffler) 1987 (children's fiction); 'The Afterlife of George Cartwright' 1992 (novel); began publishing poetry in literary periodicals in the late 1960s; work has appeared in many mags. & anthols. in Can. & abroad and has been broadcast on CBC & CJRT Radio; recreations: travel, films, music; Home: 5 Humber Park, Corner Brook, Nfld.; Office: University Dr., Corner Brook, Nfld. A2H 6P9.

**STEGER, Debra Pauline,** B.A., LL.B., LL.M.; lawyer; b. Oliver, B.C. 8 May 1952; d. Frank and Doreen (Cheveldave) S.; e. Univ. of B.C. B.A. 1975; Univ. of Victoria LL.B. 1979; Univ. of Michigan LL.M. 1983; m. Murray Smith s. Robert and Greta Smith 2 Sept. 1972; one s.: Nigel; one d.: Alexandra; GENERAL COUNSEL, CANDN. INTERNATIONAL TRADE TRIBUNAL 1991– ; Sec. to Cabinet Ctte., Govt. of B.C. 1979–80; Law Prof., Univ. of Victoria 1983; Cons., fed. govt. depts. & rsch. insts. 1983–85; on assignment to External Affairs and Internat. Trade Can. as Sr. Legal Counsel and Sr. Negotiator on Multilateral Trade Negotiations (Uruguay Round) 1989–94; Lawyer, McCarthy & McCarthy 1985–87; Lawyer, Fraser & Beatty 1987–91; part-time Law Prof., Univ. of Ottawa; Mem., Law Soc. of Upper Canada; Candn., Internat. & Am. Bar Assns; Am. Soc. of Internat. Law; author: 'A Concise Guide to the Canada-U.S. Free Trade Agreement' 1988 and several articles; editor: 'Canada-U.S. Trade Newsletter' 1988; 'Understanding the Canada-U.S. Free Trade Agreement' 1988; 'Living With Free Trade' 1990; 'In Whose Interest? Due Process and Transparency in International Trade' 1991; recreations: jogging, cycling, aerobics, swimming; Home: 66 Vaughan St., Ottawa, Ont. K1M 1X2; Office: 333 Laurier Ave. W., Ottawa, Ont. K1A 0G7.

**STEHR, Nico,** Diplom-Volkswirt, Ph.D., F.R.S.C.; university professor; b. Berlin 19 Mar. 1942; s. Dietrich and Mira (Lorent) S.; e. Univ. zu Köln, Diplom-Volkswirt 1967; Univ. of Oregon, Ph.D. 1970; m. Barbara Welge 1967; one s.: Sebastian; PROF. OF SOCIOL., UNIV. OF ALTA. 1979– ; Asst. Prof., Univ. of Alta. 1970–74; Assoc. Prof. 1974–79; Vis. Prof., Univ. of Zürich 1977, 1988; Univ. of Konstanz 1979–80; Eric-Voegelin Prof., Univ. of Munich 1984–85; Vis. Prof., Univ. of Augsburg 1990–91; F.R.C.S. 1985; author: 'Praktische Erkenntnis' 1991; 'Practical Knowledge' 1992; co-author: 'Karl Mannheim' 1984; 'Knowledge Society' 1986; 'Politisches Wissen' 1989; editor: 'Conservatism' 1986; 'Society and Knowledge' 1984; 'Modern German Sociology' 1987; 'Knowledge and Politics' 1988; 'The Power and Culture of Knowledge' 1992; 'Knowledge Societies' 1994; 'Arbeit, Eigentum und Wissen' 1994; 'Canadian Journal of Sociology'; Office: Dept. of Sociol., Univ. of Alta., Edmonton, Alta. T6G 2E5.

**STEIN, Harold A.,** M.D., M.Sc.Ophth., D.O.M.S., F.R.C.S.(C); ophthalmologist; b. Niagara Falls, Ont. 24 May 1929; s. Louis and Sadie (Levine) S.; e. Univ. of Toronto M.D. 1953; Univ. of Minnesota M.Sc.Ophth. 1957; Mayo Clinic 1953–57; Oxford, England 1958; m. Anne 17 Dec. 1952; children: Raymond, Gary, Laurie; PROF. OF OPHTHALMOLOGY, UNIV. OF TORONTO 1983– ; practicing ophthalmologist 1958– ; F.R.C.S. 1958; Chief of Ophthal., Scarborough

Gen. Hospital; Dir., Profl. Cont. Edn., Centennial Coll.; Staff, Scarborough Gen. & Mt. Sinai hosps.; Past Pres., Candn. Ophthal. Soc.; Joint Comn. on Allied Health (USA); Contact Lens Assn. of Ophth. (USA); Man of the Year Award, Bor. of Scarborough 1982; Javal Medal of Honour 1986; Am. Acad. of Ophth. Honour Award 1986; Man of the Year Award, JCHAPO 1991; co-author: 'The Ophthalmic Assistant' 5th ed. 1988, 'Ophthalmic Terminology' 3rd ed. 1994, 'Fitting Guide for Rigid & Soft Lenses' 3rd ed. 1990; 'Primer in Ophthalmology' 1994; recreations: tennis, boating; club: York Racquets; Home: 97 Douglas Dr., Toronto, Ont. M4W 2B2; Office: Bochner Eye Inst., 40 Prince Arthur Ave., Toronto, Ont. M5R 1A9

**STEIN, Joseph Charles,** Q.C., LL.D.; b. Rivière du Loup, Qué. 6 July 1912; s. Hon. Adolphe (former Justice, Superior Court of Qué.) and Alice (Hamel) S.; e. Petit Séminaire de Québec, B.A. 1931; Laval Univ., Ph.L. (summa cum laude) 1932 and LL.L. (summa cum laude) 1934 with Gov. Gen. Gold Medal and other prizes; m. Gabrielle, d. Eugène des Rivières, 15 Oct. 1938; children: Michel, Claire; former Counsel, Desjardins, Ducharme, Stein, Monast; read law with Antonio Langlais, K.C., Quebec; called to the Bar of Qué. 1934; c.r. (K.C.) 1947; practised his prof. at Québec City, 1934–38; Jr. Adv. Counsel, Dept. of Justice, Ottawa, 1938, and later Adv. Counsel and Sr. Adv. Counsel; Acting Asst. Depy. Min. of Justice, Sept. 1946; Asst. Depy. Min. of Justice, Feb. 1947 to Jan. 1949; Under Secy. of State & Deputy Registrar Gen. of Can., 1949–61; Roman Catholic; recreations; golf, tennis, jogging, reading; Clubs: Cap-Rouge Golf; Home: 4 Jardins de Merici (Apt. 302), Québec, Qué. G1S 4M4.

**STEINBERG, Blema S.,** B.A., M.A., Ph.D.; university professor, psychoanalyst; b. Montreal, Que. 4 Nov. 1934; d. Moe George and Dorita Bacal Salomon; e. McGill Univ. B.A. (1st class hons.) 1955; Cornell Univ. M.A. 1957; McGill Univ. Ph.D. 1961; m. H. Arnold s. Anne and Nathan S. 23 June 1957; children: Margot, Donna, Adam; ASSOC. PROF. WITH TENURE, MCGILL UNIV. 1972– ; Asst. Prof., McGill Univ. 1961–64; Assoc. Prof. 1964–67; Diploma in Psychoanalysis 1988; Mem., Candn. Psychoanalytic Soc.; author of numerous articles in various academic journals; co-editor: 'Superpower Involvement in the Middle East' 1985; Office: 855 Sherbrooke St. W., Montreal, Que. H3A 2T7.

**STEINBERG, David;** comedian, author, actor; b. Winnipeg, Man. 29 Aug. 1942; s. Jacob and Ruth S.; student Hebrew Theol. Coll.; Univ. Chicago; writer, actor 'Second City'; regular guest on Johnny Carson and David Letterman; directed 'Paternity' (starring Burt Reynolds) 1980; 'Going Berserk' (starring John Candy, with Joe Flaherty and Eugene Levy) 1982; currently director of episodes of 'Seinfeld,' 'Designing Women,' 'Evening Shade,' and 'It Had To Be You' (with Faye Dunnaway and Robert Urich); commercials incl.: Pizza Hut with Gary Shandling and Roseanne Barr for which he won a Clio Award; Jell-O Gelatin with Bill Cosby; NCR with Dom deLuise; Miller Lite with Rodney Dangerfield; IBM with 'M*A*S*H' Cast; Address: c/o William Morris Agy. Inc., 151 E. Camino, Beverly Hills, CA 90212.

**STEINBERG, H. Arnold,** C.M., B.Com., M.B.A.; retail merchant; b. Montreal, Que. 12 May 1933; s. Nathan Annie (Steinberg) S.; e. West Hill (Que.) High Sch.; McGill Univ. B.Com. 1954; Harvard Business Sch., M.B.A. 1957; m. Blema Solomon, 23 June 1957; children: Margot, Donna, Adam; PRINCIPAL, CLEMAN LUDMER STEINBERG INC.; Dir., Groupe Prenor Ltée; Teleglobe Canada Inc.; Teleglobe Inc.; Altamira Capital Corp.; joined Dominion Securities Corp. Ltd. 1957–58; joined Steinberg Inc. 1958–89 in various capacities including Dir., Extve. Ctte. and Chief Financial Officer; mem. Bd. of Mang., Montreal Children's Hosp.; Mem., Order of Canada 1994; Office: Suite 900, 2 Place Alexis Nihon, Montreal, Que. H3Z 3C1.

**STEINBRING, John H. (Jack),** B.A., M.A., Ph.D.; professor of anthropology; b. Oshkosh, Wisc. 1 July 1929; s. Arthur Edward and Lillian (Koller) S.; e. Wisc. State Univ., B.A. 1955; Univ. of Wisc., M.A. 1959; Univ. of Minn., Ph.D. 1975; m. Sandra d. Omar and Thelma Sund 14 June 1958; children: Lisa, Christian, Albert, Amelia, Frederick, Eric; Founder & Prof., Dept. of Anthropol., Univ. of Winnipeg 1967–90 (retired Jan. 1991); Senior Scholar 1991– ; archeol., mound site excavations, Wisc. 1956; ethnol. interest began 1958 with field work Red Cliff Chippews, n.w. Wisc.; 3 yrs., rural co. soc. worker & one yr. grad. study, Univ. of Minn.; Lectr., United Coll. 1963; Chrmn., Dept. of Anthropol., Univ. of Winnipeg 1967–74; active rsch. & pubn. in archaeol. & ethnol. field work 1963– ; specialty, prehist. rock art studies 1967– (rsch. all prov. w. of Qué. & 8 Am. states, Scotland, Yorkshire, Eng., Hawaii, Australia); Iden. & reported earliest evidence of metal working in Can. 1968; named and defined Reservoir Lakes Phase, Caribou Lake Complex, and Rush Bay Road Complex; Resp. for protection of Tie Creek petroform site 1978; arch. confirmed earliest Candn. rock art, Mud Portage Petroglyph site 1985; named & def. 'Lake-of-the-Woods' & 'Clearwater Bay' rock art styles 1980 and others; Co-ord., Native Alcohol Couns. Training Prog., Univ. of Winnipeg 1984–85; Rep. for the Americas, Steering Ctte., Internat. Congress on Rock Art, Co-Chrmn., Americas Session (Darwin, Australia) 1988; Keynote address, World Rock Art Congress, Cairns, Australia 1992 (Co-Chrmn., Symposium on Dating Rock Art); Chrmn., Symposium: Early Rock Art of the Americas, Internat. Rock Art Conference 1994; Nom. Ctte., Am. Rock Art Rsch. Assn. 1985–86; Pres., Rock Art Assoc. of Canada 1989–90; Pres., Rock Art Assoc. of Manitoba 1988, 1993– ; Vice Pres., Australian Rock Art Rsch. Assoc. 1988–92; num. past extve. appts. in var. assns.; Fgn. Fellow, Am. Anthropol. Assn. 1976; Who's Who in Rock Art 1986; author of over 150 papers, 9 book chapters & num. papers & addresses incl. Archaeol. Soc. of Man. (1985, 1987), of Wisc. (1984, 1988), of Ont. 1980; author: 'An Introduction to Archaeology on the Winnipeg River' 1980; 'A Review of TV Impact Research in the Canadian Sub-Arctic' 1984 (seconded by Candn. Comm. for UNESCO); co-author/co-editor: 'TV and the Canadian Indian,' 'Telecommunications in Transcultural Perspective,' 'Alcohol and the Native Peoples of the North' 1980, 'General Guidelines in the Development of Native TV Programming' 1981; 'Time and Space: Dating and Spatial Considerations in Rock Art Research' (edit.) 1993; 'The Rock Painting Sites of Manitoba' 1994; recreations: small-bore internat. rifle comp. & coach (Man. Prone MM Champ. 1979, 1980; Man. Precision Air Rifle Champ. Vet. 1986); Club: Assiniboia Sr. Rifle (Pres. 1979–90); Coach, Manitoba Prov. Rifle Team 1989–90; Home: 18 Browning Blvd., Winnipeg, Man. R3K 0L4; Office: 515 Portage Ave., Winnipeg, Man. R3B 2E9.

**STEINHOUSE, Herbert,** M.A.; author; retired broadcasting executive; journalist; public relations; broadcaster; b. Montreal, Que., 15 April 1922; s. Charles Mayer and Ray (Diamond) S.; e. McGill Univ., B.A. 1942; New Sch. for Social Research, New York City, M.A. (Internat. Affairs) 1948; m. Tobie Thelma Davis, artist; two s. Stephan Brock, Adam; served in 2nd World War with R.C.A.F.; three years overseas aircrew with R.A.F. Transport Command; France and Germany with UNRRA 1945–46; Reuters ed., London, and foreign correspondent, Western Europe 1948–49; CBC European Corr. and broadcaster from North Africa and Asia 1949–52; Information & Radio Consultant to WHO, Geneva 1950–54; broadcaster with special United Nations Info. mission to S.E. Asia 1951–52; Editor-Producer, UNESCO World Review (a weekly multiling. radio prog. broadcast in 125 countries) 1952–56; Sr. Producer, CBC Public Affairs, Montreal 1957–64; Dir. of Eng. Region, CBC Quebec 1964–66; Dir. Divisional Affairs, CBC French Networks 1966–73; Dir., Public Relations, CBC 1973–79 and Dir. Coverage Planning 1979–85; author of 'Ten Years After' (U.S. title: 'The Time of the Juggernaut') pol. novel on France and Algeria, 1958; formerly Secy., Fed. of Internat. Civil Servants' Assns., Geneva; Past mem., Nat. Union of Journs. (London); Foreign Correspondents Assn.; N.Y.; Amer. Acad. of Independent Scholars (Denver); Candn. Heritage Foundn.; Candn. Pub. Rel. Soc.; mem., Internat. P.E.N.; Canadian Club (Montreal); Candn. Inst. of Int'l Affairs; Trout Unlimited of Can.; Address: 208 Côte St. Antoine Rd., Montreal, Que. H3Y 2J3.

**STEINMAN, Mark C.,** B.Comm., M.B.A.; financial executive; b. Sherbrooke, Que. 11 Feb. 1948; e. McGill Univ. B.Comm. 1969; Univ. of Michigan M.B.A. 1971; m. Linda; children: Carly, Jon; CHIEF FINANCIAL OFFICER, ROGERS CABLESYSTEMS LTD. 1991– ; various financial positions, Xerox of Canada, Swift, IBM Canada Ltd. 1971–78; Vice-Pres. Finance, Gabriel of Canada Ltd. 1978–81; Cast North America Ltd. 1981–82; Regal Greetings & Gifts 1982–85; ROLM Canada Ltd. 1985–88; Chief Accountant, IBM Canada Ltd. 1988–90; Controller, Marketing & Service, IBM Canada Ltd. 1990–91; Mem., Financial Executives Inst.; recreations: golf, track, tennis; clubs: Fitness Inst.; Home: 29 Woodthrush Court, North York, Ont. M2K 2A9; Office: 1 Valleybrook Dr., Toronto, Ont. M3B 2S7.

**STEINMETZ, Peter E.,** Q.C., B.A., LL.B.; solicitor; b. Toronto, Ont. 2 Apr. 1941; s. Rev. Charles and Beatrice Margaret S.; e. Univ. of Western Ontario B.A. 1963; Univ. of Toronto LL.B. 1968; PARTNER, CASSELS BROCK & BLACKWELL 1974– ; Pres. (1983–92) and Dir. (1978–92) Candn. Acad. Recording Arts & Sci's; Pres. and Dir., Blackwell North America (Canada) Inc.; Vice-Chair, Ontario Film Development Corp.; called to Bar of Ont. 1970; cr. Q.C. 1983; joined Cassels Brock & Blackwell 1970, Partner 1974–83; Proprietor, Peter E. Steinmetz & Associates 1983–87; re-joined Cassels Brock & Blackwell, Partner 1987, Managing Partner 1990–91; Dir. Northern Lights for Africa; Exec. Producer, The Juno Awards 1984–92; lectr. entertainment law Candn. Bar Assn. 1977, 1978, 1981, 1985, 1989; York Univ. 1980; Ont. Festival of Festivals 1981; Insight Educational Services Ltd. 1980, 1987 and 1990; Law Soc. of Upper Can. 1989, 1991, 1993; Office: Suite 2100, Scotia Plaza, 40 King St. W., Toronto, Ont. M5H 3C2.

**STELCK, Charles Richard,** M.Sc., Ph.D.; educator; b. Edmonton, Alta. 20 May 1917; s. Robert Ferdinand and Florella Maud Mary (Stanbury) S.; e. Westmount Pub. and Victoria High Schs. Edmonton 1934; Univ. of Alta. B.Sc. 1937, M.Sc. 1941; Stanford Univ. Ph.D. 1951; m. Frances Gertrude d. late Rev. Francis McDowell 24 Apl. 1945; children: David, Brian, Leland, John; EMERITUS PROF. OF GEOL. UNIV. OF ALTA.; Geol. Exploration, Benedum & Trees 1939; Geol., Dept. Mines B.C. 1940–42; Canol Project U.S. Govt. 1942–43; Exploration, Imperial Oil 1943–49; Lectr. Univ. of Alta. 1946; author over 80 scient. articles cretaceous, devonian fossils, W. Can. biostratigraphy, ammonites, arenaceous foraminifera, pelecypods; Fellow Royal Soc. Can.; Assn. Prof. Engrs., Geologists and Geophysicists of Alta.; Candn. Soc. Petrol. Geols.; Geol. Assn. Can.; Geol. Soc. Am.; Paleontol. Soc.; Paleontol. Assn. (London); Cushman Foundation Foraminiferal Research; Sigma Xi; P. Conservative; Protestant; recreation: hunting; Home: 11739 – 91 Ave., Edmonton, Alta. T6G 1B1; Office: Edmonton, Alta. T6G 2E3.

**STELMASCHUK, Paul,** B.Sc., M.Ed., P.Ag.; university administrator; b. Spedden, Alta. 3 July 1923; s. Joseph and Sofia (Maciura) S.; e. Univ. of Alta. B.Sc. 1951; Univ. of N. Dakota M.Ed. 1964; post grad. work Univ. of Minnesota 1967; m. Anna C., d. Joseph and Eva Darahoj 29 June 1974; children: Anthony; Terry; Dean; Natalie; PROFESSOR AND DIR., SCH. OF AGRICULTURE, UNIV. OF MANITOBA 1972– ; farmer until 1947; Weed Inspector 1947–49; Weed Supervisor 1950; Vocational Agr. Instr. 1951–56; County Extension Agent & Assoc. Prof. 1956–64; Rural Develop. Specialist and Assoc. Prof., Univ. of Minnesota 1964–67; Rural Develop. Specialist, Prov. of Alta. 1967–72; author: 'Inventory of Community Resources in Alberta' 1972; 'Post Secondary, Non-Degree Agric. Education in Canada' 1979; as well as a number of pamphlets and articles in field; served on CIDA reconnaisance team, Indonesia 1973; delegate, conferences in Sao Paolo, Nairobi, and Bern; Dir., Senator and Chrmn. of the Bd., St. Andrew's Coll.; mem. Agricultural Inst. of Can.; Man. Inst. of Agrology (Councillor); Internat. Agric. Economists Assn.; Nat. Assn. of Colleges and Teachers of Agric. (Dir. 1976–79); Pres., Ukrainian Orthodox Church, Kelowna, B.C. (3 yrs.); Pres., Kelowna Branch of Ukrainian Candn. Congress (Vice-Pres. 4 yrs.); Conservative; recreations: golf; music; Club: Chamber of Commerce; Office: 306, Agriculture Bldg., Univ. of Manitoba, Winnipeg, Man. R3T 2N2.

**STEPHEN, Alison Mary,** B.Sc., Dip.Nut., Ph.D.; university professor; b. Vancouver, B.C. 12 Nov. 1951; d. David George Carnegie and Jessie Bernard (Williamson) Eggo; e. Morrison's Acad. for Girls (Scotland) 1962–70; Univ. of Edinburgh B.Sc. 1976; Univ. of Cambridge Dip.Nut. 1977, Ph.D. 1980; m. Bruce S. 17 Sept. 1977; divorced; one s.: James Duncan Stephen; ASSOC. PROF., DIV. OF NUTRITION & DIETETICS, COLL. OF PHARMACY, UNIV. OF SASKATCHEWAN 1990– ; currently on sabbatical in Australia; post-doctoral rsch., Gastroenterology Unit, Mayo Clinic (fellowship from Anna Fuller Found. for Cancer Rsch.); Rsch. Assoc., Dept. of Med., Case Western Reserve Univ. (fellowship from Mary B. Lee Fund for Diabetic Rsch.) 1982–83; Project Co-ord., Dept. of Environ. & Preventive Med., St. Bartholomew's Med. Coll. (U.K.) 1984–87; Asst. Prof., Univ. of Sask. 1987–90; Assoc. Prof. 1990– ; Head 1991–93; Cons., Pfizer (Groton, CT) & Sask. Pulse Crop Devel. Bd. (non-official basis); MRC Studentship (U.K.) 1976–80; Chair, Expert Ctte. on Human Nutrition, Agric. Canada; Sask. Heart Found. Edn. Bursary 1988–89, 1990–91; Mem., Nutrition Soc. (U.K.); Candn. Soc. for Nutritional Sciences; author of numerous books chapters & scientific articles; recreations: gardening, sewing, swimming, music; Offices: Univ. of Saskatchewan, Saskatoon, Sask. S7N 0W0 and Dept. of Surgery, Univ. of Adelaide, Queen Elizabeth Hospital, Woodville, South Australia 5011, Australia.

**STEPHEN, George,** F.T.C.I.; investment consultant; b. St. Cyrus, Scot., 4 March 1924; s. James Henderson and Katherine Henderson (Lindsay) S.; e. Montrose Acad., Scot., 1929–36; Aberdeen (Scot.) Grammar Sch., 1936–42; Aberdeen Univ., 1942–43; m. Dorothy Lorna, d. Rev. William A. Ross, Toronto, 22 July 1950; two s., Mark Lindsay, Ian Campbell; MANAGING PARTNER, BALANDRO CAPITAL CORP.; joined Montreal Trust Co. 1955, Vice Pres. 1969, Depy. Chrmn. & Mang. Dir., Trust Corp. of Bahamas 1970–73, Vice Pres. Montreal Trust 1973–80; Pres. Amedco Pacific 1980–82; served as Pilot-Air Br., R.N., 1943–50; United Church; recreations: golf, reading; Club: Lambton Golf & Country; Toronto; Address: 10 Thelma Ave., Toronto, Ont. M4V 1X9.

**STEPHEN, Hugh Roulston;** retired business executive; b. Guildford, Surrey, Eng. 25 Apl. 1913; s. Samuel and Margaret (Scott) S.; e. Bishop's Stortford Coll. Eng.; m. Barbara Leslie d. Richard Clwyd Williams, Victoria, B.C. 16 March 1942; children: Michael Clwyd, Susan Margaret, David Hugh; past Dir., British Columbia Telephone Co.; past Dir., Canada Trust; Mgr. and Owner New Method Laundries, Victoria 1946–63; Mayor of Victoria 1967–69; Pres. Victoria Chamber Comm. 1957–58; Past Pres. Victoria Art Gallery; Past Chrmn. Brentwood Coll. Bd. Govs.; Past Chrmn. Univ. of Victoria Bd. Govs.; Past Trustee, Fraser Inst. Vancouver; Past Dir. Victoria Foundation; Past Vice Chrmn. Victoria Adv. Planning Comn.; Chrmn. Capital Region Bd. 1969; Gov., Jaycees of Can.; Hon. mem. Community Planning Assn. Can.; Hon. Life mem. Victoria Conserv. of Music; served with 5th B.C. Coast Regt. R.C.A. 1939, subsequently trans. to Candn. Intelligence Corps and served with Psychol. Warfare Div. S.E. Asia Command on attachment to Brit. Forces; rec'd Candn. Centennial Medal 1967; LL.D. (Hon.), Univ. of Victoria 1986; recreations: golf, reading; Clubs: Union; Uplands Golf; Home: 208 - 1211 Beach Dr., Victoria, B.C. V8S 2N4.

**STEPHEN, Kenneth Alexander,** B.Com., C.A., F.C.I.S., F.R.I.; retired real estate executive; b. Toronto, Ont. 29 Aug. 1929; s. late Alexander and Mary J. (Simpson) S.; e. Vaughan Rd. Coll. Inst. 1947; Univ. of Toronto B.Com. 1951; C.A. 1954, A.C.I.S. 1960, F.C.I.S. 1964, F.R.I. 1966; m. Margaret d. late Angus MacTaggart, Toronto, Ont. 19 July 1952; children: Craig Alexander, Heather Margaret, Keith Fraser; DIR., CB COMMERCIAL REAL ESTATE GROUP CANADA INC. 1983– ; Dir. & Secy.-Treas., Candn. Automobile Sport Clubs 1987–89; Past Pres., Don Valley East P.C. Assoc. 1987; Past Pres., Don Valley North P.C. Assoc. 1988–89; Auditor, Clarkson Gordson & Co. 1951–54; Corporate Income Tax Assessor, Dept. of Nat. Revenue Taxation 1954–59; Comptroller A.E. LePage Ltd. 1959, Secy.-Treas. 1963, Dir. 1965, Secy. & Vice Pres., Finance, 1967; Sr. Vice Pres. Finance and Secy. 1971, Exec. Vice-Pres., Finance & Admin., 1975; Pres., A.E. LePage Asset Management Co. 1980–82; Financial and Real Estate Consultant (Retired) 1982–92; rec'd. MacDonald Cartier award from P.C.'s 1989; rec'd Nat. and Internat. prizes Chart. Inst. Secy. Course; Claude Leigh Mem. Scholarship, Candn. Inst. Realtors; Former Treas. and Hon. Life mem. Streetsville Community Centre; Fellow, Candn. Inst. of Realtors; Past Chrmn. Chart. Inst. Secys.; Past Finance Chrmn., Cdn. Real Estate Assoc.; Protestant; recreations: music, theatre, travel, vintage auto racing, golf; Club: Scarboro Golf; Bd. of Trade; Vintage Automobile Racing Assn. of Canada; Alfa Romeo Club of Can.; Home: 20 Guildwood Pkwy., Apt. 1414, Scarborough, Ont. M1E 5B6.

**STEPHEN, Michael A.,** B.A.; insurance executive; b. St. John, N.B. 17 Jan. 1929; e. Univ. of Montreal B.A.; High Sch. Teaching Licence, N.B.; Advanced Mgmt. Prog., Harvard; m. Beatrice Bourque; children: Christopher, Michael Jr., Joseph, Andrea; PRES., AETNA INTERNATIONAL INC. 1992– ; Dir., Aetna Internat. Inc.; Aetna Life Insurance Co. of Can.; Aetna Trust; Aetna Chile S.Pl.; Seguros Monterrey Aetna; Toronto Symphony; High Sch. Teacher, N.B. 1952–55; Agent London Life 1955–60, Br. Mgr. 1960–69; Dir. of Agys., Montreal and Dir. of Manpower Devel. Sun Life of Can. 1969–74; Vice-Pres. Life Div. Aetna Canada 1974–81, Exec. Vice-Pres. Ins. Operations 1981–83; Exec. Vice-Pres. & C.O.O. 1983–85; Pres. & C.O.O. 1985–87; Pres. and Chief Extve. Offr. 1987–92; mem. Toronto Bd. of Trade; mem. Toronto Harvard Alumni Assn.; recreations: jogging, swimming, gardening, politics; Clubs: Toronto; York; Home: 131 Blyth Cres., Oakville, Ont. L6J 5H5; Office: 151 Farmington Ave., Hartford, Conn. 06156.

**STEPHENS, Nigel,** B.A.; b. Ottawa, Ont. 10 Dec. 1925; s. Robert G. and Katie R. (Hinge) S.; e. Univ. of Toronto, B.A. 1948; children: Nigel D., Timothy M.; PAST PRES., NIGEL STEPHENS COUNSEL INC.; Past President & Founder, Stephens Management Inc.; Founding Dir. and former Vice Pres., Toronto Montessori Schs.; Past Pres., Investment Counsel Assn. of Can.; Past Pres., Candn. Figure Skating Assn.; former Candn. Singles Skating Champion; inducted into the Candn. Figure Skating Assn. Hall of Fame in the category of 'Official' 1994; Anglican; recreations: raising pure breed horses, skating, skiing; Clubs: Granite; Home: R.R. 1, Bowmanville, Ont. L1C 3K2.

**STEPHENS, Richard W.,** B.Comm., M.B.A.; business executive; b. Ottawa, Ont. 9 May 1956; s. Kenneth Arthur and Shirley May (Axford) S.; e. Univ. of Calgary B.Comm. 1978; Univ. of S. Calif., L.A., M.B.A. 1981; PRES., SPRING VALLEY WATER CO. 1988– ; Petroleum Marketer, Sundance Oil Co. (US) 1981–82; Vice-Pres., Stephens Energy Limited 1982–86; Founder & Pres., Spring Valley Water Corp. 1986–87; Pres. & C.E.O., Laurentian Spring Valley Inc. 1988– ; Laurentian Water Co. 1988– ; Spring Valley Water Co. 1988– ; Laurentian Water Co. (USA) 1990– ; Home: 76 Oriole Rd., Toronto, Ont. M4V 2G1; Office: 99 Rowntree Dairy Rd., Woodbridge, Ont. L4L 6C8.

**STEPHENSON, Bette M.,** O.C., M.D., F.C.F.P.(C); O.StJ.; (Mrs. G. Allan Pengelly) physician; b. Aurora, Ont., 31 July 1924; d. Carl Melvin and Clara Mildred (Draper) S.; e. Aurora (Ont.) Pub. Sch.; McKee Ave. Pub. Sch. and Earl Haig Coll. Inst., Willowdale, Ont.; Univ. of Toronto, M.D. 1946; m. Gordon Allan Pengelly, M.D., 1948; children: J. Stephen A., Elizabeth Anne A., C. Christopher A., J. Michael A., P. Timothy A., Mary Katharine A.; el. to Ont. Leg. for York Mills, Sept. 1975; re-el. June 1977, Mar. 1981 and May 1985; Min. of Labour 1975–78; Min. of Educ. & Min. of Colls. & Univs. 1978–85; Chrmn., Management Bd. of Cabinet and Min. of Economics, Treasurer and Dep. Premier, 1985; mem. Med. Staff, Womens Coll. Hosp., since 1950; Dir. of Outpatient Dept., 1952–56, Chief Dept. of Gen. Practice, 1956–64; mem. Med. Staff, N. York Gen. Hosp., 1967–76; Chrmn., Nat. Coordinating Comte. on Educ., Coll. of Family Physicians Canada, 1961–64 and Chrmn., Confs. on Educ. for Gen. Practice, 1961 and 1963; Dir., N. York Br. V.O.N. 1954–67; Fellow, Coll. Family Phys. Can.; Fellow, Acad. Med. Toronto; Ont. Med. Assn. (Bd. Dirs. 1964–72; Pres. 1970–71); Candn. Med. Assn. (Bd. Dirs. 1968–75; Pres. 1974–75); Pres., Gwillimbury Found.; Bd. of Dir., CIAR, Womens College Hosp.; mem. AGO, ROM, COC; Protestant; Address: 64 Forest Ridge Rd., Richmond Hill, Ont.

**STEPHENSON, Helga Mary Anna,** B.A.; film festival executive; b. Montreal, Que. 2 May 1947; d. Haraldur Jon and Mary Rita (Pickett) S.; e. McGill Univ., B.A. 1969; EXEC. DIR., FESTIVAL OF FESTIVALS and CINEMATHEQUE, ONTARIO 1986– ; Bd. of Dirs., John Labatt Ltd.; Public Relations Officer, Canada Council 1973–74; National Arts Centre 1971–73; Prof. of Eng., Univ. of Havana 1974–75; Vice Pres., Simcom Ltd. 1980–82; Dir. of Communications and Programmer, Festival of Festivals 1982–86; Bd. Mem., Candn. Film Centre; Nat. Film Bd. of Can.; Candn. Hearing Soc.; Metro Toronto Visitor and Convention Assn.; Expo '98; Bloor Yorkville Business Improvement Area; CulTech Collaborative Rsch. Center; Directors Guild of Can.; Candn. Foundation for the Americas (FOCAL); Home: 34 Farnham Ave., Toronto, Ont. M4V 1H4; Office: 70 Carlton St., Toronto, Ont. M5B 1L7.

**STEPHENSON, Olwen Diane,** B.A., M.D., F.R.C.P.; pathologist; b. Saskatoon, Sask. 31 Jan. 1943; d. James Norval and Olwen Eileen (Maule) S.; e. Univ. of Sask., B.A. 1965, M.D. 1969; CHIEF CORONER FOR SASK. 1987– ; Internship, Christchurch, N.Z. 1969–71; Path. Resident, Univ. Hosp., Saskatoon 1971–76; Path., Regina Gen. Hosp. 1976–87; Path., Pasqua Hosp. Regina 1987– ; Past Pres., Vice Pres. & Sec. Treas., Sask. Assn. of Paths.; mem. Candn. Assn. of Paths.; Internat. Assn. of Paths.; Am. Acad. of Forensic Scis.; Candn. Soc. of Forensic Sci.; Home: 2507 Philip Rd., Regina, Sask. S4V 1Z7; Office: 1874 Scarth St., Regina, Sask. S4P 3V7.

**STEPNEY, Philip Harold Robert,** B.Sc., M.Sc., Ph.D.; museum director; b. Alberta 19 Nov. 1947; s. Harold Albert and Elenor Blanche (Landals) S.; e. Univ. of Alberta B.Sc. (Hons.) 1969; Univ. of Toronto M.Sc. 1971, Ph.D. 1979; m. Donna Maureen d. James and Irene Kelly 4 Sept. 1967; children: Sean Philip Stuart, Erin Maureen, Lindsay Dawn; DIRECTOR, PROVINCIAL MUSEUM OF ALBERTA 1989– ; Wildlife Biologist, Renewable Resources Consulting Service Edmonton 1975; Project Mgr. 1976; Director, Business Devel. 1977; Curator of Ornithology, Prov. Museum of Alberta 1977–81; Asst. Dir., Natural History 1981–87; Asst. Dir., Curatorial 1987–89; Chrmn., Lakeland College Curriculum Adv. Ctte. 1984– ; Treas.-Membership Sec., Soc. of Candn. Ornithologists 1985– ; Edit. Bd., Alberta Studies Journal 1986–91; Co-Chair, Am. Ornithologists Union Collections Ctte. 1984–91; Elected Mem., Am. Ornithologists Union 1971– ; Mem., Cooper Ornithol. Soc. 1975– ; Wilson Ornithol. Soc. 1975– ; Soc. of Candn. Ornithol. 1985– ; Editor, 'The Scriver Blackfoot Collection' 1990 (exhib. catalogue); author of 20 published rsch. & tech. articles 1971– ; recreations: bonsai, hunting, fly fishing, taxidermy, landscape & nature photography and manufacturing & shooting blackpowder rifles; Home: 15 Lockhart Dr., St. Albert, Alta. T8N 2P9; Office: 12845 – 102 Ave., Edmonton, Alta. T5N 0M6.

**STERLING, Norman William,** Q.C., M.P.P., B.Eng., LL.B., P.Eng.; politician; b. Ottawa, Ont. 19 Feb. 1942; s. John Wesley and Marion Doris (Swerdfager) S.; e. Carleton Univ. B.Eng. 1964; Univ. of Ottawa LL.B. 1969; m. Janet d. Ian and Esther McArthur 22 June 1963; children: Ian Stuart, Sara Joanne; CHRMN., PROGRESSIVE CONSERVATIVE CAUCUS OF ONT. and PROGRESSIVE CONSERVATIVE CRITIC FOR INTERGOVERNMENTAL AFFAIRS; M.P.P., Carleton Grenville 1977–87; called to Bar of Ont. 1971; cr. Q.C. 1981; Eng., Dupont of Canada Ltd. 1964–66; Founder and Sr. Partner, Sterling, Clark & Young, Nepean, Ont. 1971–77; el. M.P.P. for Carleton Grenville Ont. g.e. 1977, re-el. 1981; Parlty. Asst. to Atty. Gen. 1978; Min. without Portfolio 1981; Prov. Sec. for Justice 1982; Min., Prov. Secretariat for Resources Development, Ont. 1983–85; re-el. 1985; re-el. M.P.P. for Carleton 1987, 1990; served Rideau Twp. Planning & Adv. Bd.; Past Pres., Manotick Home & Sch. Assn.; coached minor hockey and soccer; Club: Kiwanis; Home: 12 South Sunset Dr., Manotick, Ont. K0A 2N0; Offices: Legislative Office, Rm. 160, Legislative Bldg., Queen's Park, Toronto, Ont. M7A 1A8 and 1143A Mill St., P.O. Box 535, Manotick, Ont. K4M 1A5.

**STERLING, Theodore D.,** M.A., Ph.D.; educator; b. Vienna, Austria 3 July 1923; s. William and Sarah S.; e. Univ. of Chicago B.A. 1949, M.A. 1952; Tulane Univ. Ph.D. 1955; m. Nora Moskalik 1948; children: Elia, David; PROF. OF COMPUTER SCI. SIMON FRASER UNIV. 1972– ; Theodor D. Sterling Ltd.; Theodor D. Sterling and Associates; served as Prof. Univs. Ala., Mich. State, Wash. at St. Louis, Princeton, Cincinnati; cons. U.S. Govt., Vietnam, Kuwait agencies; Fellow, Am. Assn. Advanc. Sci.; Candn. Ctte. Sci's & Scholars; Fellow, AMSTAT; Am. Coll. Epidemiol.; author 8 books and over 300 sci. articles; Office; Burnaby, B.C. V5A 1S6.

**STERN, Michael I.,** B.A., M.A.Sc., C.M.C.; management consultant; b. Montreal, Que. 13 Feb. 1947; s. Samuel and Ethel (Freed) S.; McGill Univ. B.A. (Psych.) 1968; Univ. of Waterloo M.A.Sc., Psychol. & Human Relations 1972; PRESIDENT, MICHAEL STERN ASSOCIATES INC. 1982– ; Psychologist, Brantford Gen. Hosp. 1971; Program Consultant, Addiction Rsch. Found. 1972–77; Consultant, Andros Consultants Ltd. 1977; Cons. Price Waterhouse Associates 1978, Sr. Cons. 1980, Consulting Mgr. 1982; Partner, Urquhart, Preger & Stern 1982–85; author of monthly column on 'Managing' for the Globe & Mail's 'Report on Business'; author of a number of articles and pamphlets; Dir. Candn. Cancer Soc. (Ont. Div.) 1986–90; Affil.: Inst. of Certified Mgmt. Cons. of Ont. 1984– ; Mem., Bd. of Dirs. & Mem. Exec. Ctte., Internat. Assn. of Corporate & Professional Recruiters 1989– ; Special Cons. to the Ont. Legislature's Select Ctte. on Highway Safety 1977, Transport Canada 1975 and the Hamilton Automobile Club 1975–76; Advisor, R.I.D.E. Program 1975–77; Candn. Red Cross 1984–90; Mem., Canada-Japan Soc. of Toronto 1991– ; Personnel Assn. of Ont. 1977– ; recreations: skiing, jogging, tennis; Office: Ste. 370, 70 University Ave., Toronto, Ont. M5J 2M4.

**STEUART, David John,** B.Comm.; pulp and paper executive; b. Prince Albert, Sask. 6 July 1946; s. John Wallace and Betty (Hemmington) S.; e. Univ. of Sask., B.Comm. 1970; m. Catherine d. Leo and Patricia Haber 29 Feb. 1988; children: Sean, Liam, Dylan, Christian; PRES., PULP GROUP, AVENOR INC. 1993– ; Shipping Mgr. & Controller, St. Anne-Nackawic Pulp 1970–73; Sales Mgr., St. Anne Pulp Sales 1974–76; Vice-Pres. Sales 1976; Extve. Vice-Pres., St. Anne-Nackawic Pulp Co. 1985–86; Pres. 1986; Pres., St. Anne Pulp Sales Company Ltd. 1984–93; recreations: golf, tennis; clubs: The National Golf, Roseland, University, St. James (Montreal); Home: 120 Birett Dr., Burlington, Ont. L7L 2T1; Office: 5420 N. Service Rd., Burlington, Ont. L7L 6C7.

**STEVENS, Ernest Donald,** B.Sc., M.Sc., Ph.D.; university professor; b. Calgary, Alta. 5 July 1941; s. Douglas Ernest and Lorna (Stuart) S.; e. Univ. of Victoria B.Sc. 1963; Univ. of B.C. M.Sc. 1965, Ph.D. 1968; m. Elinor d. Walter and Mary Hagborg 21 Feb. 1964; children: Ken, Wendy; PROF., ZOOLOGY, UNIV. OF GUELPH 1986– ; Rsch. Assoc., Stanford Univ. 1968; Asst. Prof., Univ. of Hawaii 1968–72; Assoc. Prof. 1973–75; Univ. of Guelph 1975–86; Visiting Prof., St. Andrews 1972; Med. Coll. of Georgia 1982; Tohoku Univ. (Japan) 1983; Woods Hole Oceanographic Inst. 1989; Texas A & M Univ. 1990; Asst. Ed., 'Fish Physiology & Biochemistry'; author of approx. 80 sci. articles in var. sci. jours. (subject matter concerns comp. physiology, esp. of fish); Home: 17 Carnaby Cres., Guelph, Ont. N1G 2R6; Office: Guelph, Ont. N1G 2W1.

**STEVENS, (Thomas) Geoffrey (Stewart),** B.A.; journalist; b. London, Ont. 30 Jan. 1940; s. Stewart Nicol and Katherine Caroline (Guppy) S.; e. Ryerson Pub. Sch. London, Ont. 1953; Ridley Coll. St. Catharines, Ont. 1958; Univ. of W. Ont. B.A. 1962; children: Alexandra, Sean; PUBLISHER & EDITOR, SUN TIME OF CANADA; Reporter, The Globe and Mail, Toronto 1962–65, Ottawa Corr. 1965–68, Queen's Park Bureau Chief Toronto 1969–70, Ottawa Columnist 1973–81, Assoc. Ed. 1975, Nat. Ed. 1981–82, Sports Ed. 1982–83, Mng. Ed. 1983; Ottawa Corr., Time Magazine 1970–73; Political Columnist, Sunday Star 1989; ; author 'Stanfield' 1973; daily columnist 8 yrs.; Office: 515 West Bay St., Suite C, Tampa, Fl. 33606.

**STEVENS, George Richard,** A.B., M.A., Ph.D., F.G.S.A.; structural geologist; professor; b. Norfolk, Va. 28 May 1931; s. Glen F. and Maxine Elliott (Hancock) S.; e. Johns Hopkins Univ., A.B. 1951, M.A. 1955, Ph.D. 1960; m. Maeann, d. Oakland Ross Cameron, Findlay, Ohio, Feb. 1952; children: Eric Ross, Laurel Ann, Kirsten Allegra, Astrid Marie; Prof., Dept. of Geology, Acadia Univ., N.S. 1966 (retired); Head of Dept. 1966–82 and mem. of Univ. Senate; mem. Geol. Dept., Lafayette Coll., Pennsylvania, 1957–66; Visitor, Univ. Bergen, Norway 1973; Professional Assoc., Korea Inst. Energy and Resources 1982; served with U.S. Army Corps of Engrs. on Active Duty Korean War 1951–53 and Reserve to 1966; rank Capt.; author prof. papers and consultant reports; mem., Am. Assn. Advanc. Science; Fellow, Geol. Soc. America; Sigma Xi; Lutheran; recreations: golf, squash racquets, skiing, antiquarian books, maps; Home: 3 Victoria Ave., Wolfville, N.S. B0P 1X0.

**STEVENS, H.J.,** B.A., LL.B., M.P.A.; association executive; b. Manitoba May 1948; e. Defence Language Inst. (Monterey, Calif.) diploma (Hons.) 1969; Univ. of Winnipeg B.A. (Hons.) 1975; Osgoode Hall Law School LL.B. 1981; Univ. of Victoria M.P.A. 1983; m. Joan King 8 Sept. 1973; one d.: Katherine; PACIFIC REGIONAL DIR., INVESTMENT DEALERS ASSN. OF CANADA/THE CANDN. SECURITIES INST. 1984– ; U.S. Army Military Intelligence 1968–71; Candn. Naval Reserve, Lt.-Commander 1973–85; Policy Advisor, Govt. of B.C. 1978–81, 1982–84; articled with law firm of Pearlman & Lindholm Victoria 1981–82; called to B.C. Bar 1982; Dir., Career Education Soc. of B.C.; Candn. Club of Vancouver; Mem., Candn. Bar Assn.; Law Soc. of B.C.; B.C. C. of C.; Vancouver Chinatown Rotary Club; recreations: family outings, recreational sports, reading; Home: 1207 Plateau Dr., N. Vancouver, B.C. V7P 2J3; Office: P.O. Box 49151, Bentall Centre, Suite 944, 1055 Dunsmuir St., Vancouver, B.C. V7X 1J1.

**STEVENS, Lloyd Francis,** FCA; consultant; b. Toronto, Ont. 25 Apr. 1924; s. Frederic Roy and Anne (Sexton) S.; e. Riverdale C.I. 1942; C.A 1949; m. Margaret d. Hilliard and Ethel Flynn 7 Aug. 1948; children: Heather, Teresa, Sharon; CHRMN., STEBAR MACHINERY INC. 1982– ; joined Clarkson, Gordon & Co. 1942; Candn. army incl. overseas serv. 1943–46; rejoined Clarkson Gordon 1946; Partner 1954; pres., Allpak Limited 1962–78; Chrmn. & Chief Extve. Offr., Dale-Ross Holdings Ltd. 1978–82; Past Dir., Northern Life Insurance Co. of Canada, Dashwood Indus. Ltd., Livingston Indus. Ltd., Numac Oil & Gas Ltd. & several others; Dir., Prenor Group Ltd.; Avco Finan. Serv. of Canada Ltd.; Hon. Col. of 22 (London) Serv. Battalion 1987; Dir., Western Ont. Conservatory of Music; Dir., London Hosp. Linen Serv.; The Richard & Jean Ivey Fund; Former Chair., United Way of London; Family & Children's Serv. of London; Univ. Hosp. of London; Former V.P. & Dir., Westminster Coll., Mme. Vanier Children's Serv.; Parkwood Hosp. Found.; recreations: golf, tennis, fishing, trap-shooting; clubs: London Club Ltd., London Hunt & Country, Muskoka Lakes Golf & Country, Royal Candn. Military Inst.; Home/Office: 260 Baseline Rd. E., London, Ont. N6C 2P4.

**STEVENS, Peter Stanley,** M.A., Ph.D., university professor; poet; critic; b. Manchester, Eng., 17 Nov. 1927; s. Stanley Edgar and Elsie (Hill) S.; e. Burnage High Sch., Manchester, 1946; Univ. of Nottingham, B.A. (Eng.), Cert. in Educ., 1951; McMaster Univ., M.A. 1963; Univ. of Sask., Ph.D. 1968; m. June, d. late John Sidebotham, 13 Apl. 1957; children: Gillian, Kirsty, Martin Timothy; Assoc. Prof., Univ. of Windsor, 1969–76; Prof. since 1976; Co-founder and Co-dir., Sesame Press; Teacher, Eng. schs., 1951–57; Hillfield-Strathallan Coll., Hamilton, Ont., 1957–64 (Head of Eng. Dept. 1961–64); Part-time Lectr., McMaster Univ., 1961–64; Lectr. and Asst. Prof., Univ. of Sask., 1964–69; Poetry Ed., Canadian Forum, 1968–73; Ed., The McGill Movement 1969; Co-ed., Forum, 1972; Ed., 'The First Day of Spring by Raymond Knister'; author of 'Nothing But Spoons,' 1969; 'A Few Myths,' 1971; 'Breadcrusts and Glass,' 1972; 'Family Feelings And Other Poems' 1974; 'A Momentary Stay,' 1974; 'The Dying Sky Like Blood,' 1974; 'The Bogman Pavese Tactics,' 1977 (all poetry), 'Modern English-Canadian Poetry,' 1978; 'Coming Back,' 1981; 'Revenge of the Mistresses,' 1982; 'Out of the Willow Trees' 1986; 'Swimming in the Afternoon: New & Selected Poems' 1992; 'Dorothy Livesay: Patterns in a Poetic Life' 1992; other writings incl. book chapters, articles and reviews in various publs.; regular contributor to 'Jazz Radio Canada,' (CBC); Prairie Rep. 1968–69, Ont. Rep. 1969–74, League Candn. Poets; Finalist, Clifford E. Lee Playwriting Competition, 1979; recreations: jazz; canoeing; swimming; Home: 2055 Richmond St., Windsor, Ont. N8Y 1L3.

**STEVENS, Robert William;** barrister/solicitor; b. London, Ont. 30 Aug. 1926; s. John Harris and Alice Elizabeth (Martin) S.; e. Ridley Coll. 1937–44; Queen's Univ., B.A. 1949; Osgoode Hall Law Sch. 1953; m. E. Ann d. Harold and Madelaine Washington 23 Apr. 1955; children: John W., R. Michael H., Thomas A.C., Susann V.; PARTNER, BLAKE, CASSELS & GRAYDON 1959– ; called to Ont. Bar 1953; Jr. Solicitor, Blake Anglin, Osler & Cassels 1953; Dir. Can. Trust Co.; Can. Trustco Mortgage Co.; Emco Limited; Newmont Expl. of Can. Ltd.; Candn. Oxygen Ltd.; Revlon Can. Inc.; Bauer Indus. Ltd.; Wang Canada Ltd.; and 21 others; Dir. & Sec., Carlton Cards Ltd.; Dir. & Treas., Pumps & Softeners Ltd.; Dir. & Pres., Arva Investments Ltd.; Sec., Toronto Dist. Heating Corp.; Chrmn., Ludwig Inst. for Cancer Rsch., Toronto Br.; Ridley Coll.; Ridley Coll. Found.; Royal Ont. Mus.; Candn. Bar Assn.; Candn. Tax Found.; recreations: golf, tennis, skiing; Clubs: Toronto Golf; York; Toronto; Badminton & Racquet; Home: 208 Roxborough Dr., Toronto, Ont. M4W 1X8; Office: P.O. Box 25, Commerce Court W., Toronto, Ont. M5L 1A9.

**STEVENS, Hon. Sinclair McKnight,** P.C., Q.C., LL.B., B.A.; b. Esquesing Twp., Ont., 11 Feb. 1927; s. l. Robert Murray and l. Anna Bailey (McKnight) S.; e. Weston (Ont.) Coll. & Vocational Sch.; Oakwood Coll. Inst., Toronto; Univ. of W. Ont., B.A. 1951; Osgoode Hall Law Sch., 1955; m. Noreen Mary, d. Theophil A. Charlebois, 17 May 1958; SENIOR PARTNER, STEVENS & STEVENS (Newmarket, Ont.); former Min. of Regional and Industrial Expansion, Chrmn. of the Cabinet Cttee. on Economic And Regional Development, 1984–86; read law with Fraser & Beatty; called to Bar of Ont. 1955; cr. Q.C. 1971; el. to H. of C. for York-Simcoe in g.e. 1972, 1974; following redistribution elected in the riding of York Peel in 1979, 1980 and 1984; Apptd. Pres., Treasury Bd., 1979–80; Publisher, Canada's first environmental newspaper 'The Planet Today'; mem., Candn. Bar Assn.; Delta Sigma Phi; Phi Delta Phi; P. Conservative; Protestant; recreations: farming; Clubs: Albany; Toronto; Metropolitan; New York; Home: 4197 Niagara Parkway, R.R. 2, Stevensville, Ont. L0S 1S0.

**STEVENS, William H. Jr.;** film executive; musician; actor; b. Ottawa, Ont. 6 Oct. 1947; s. William Harris and Evelyn Mae (Whitney) S.; e. Ridgemont High Sch. Ottawa; m. Denise M. d. Maurice and Madeline Cloutier 10 Oct. 1970; children: William H. III, Caroline N.; ARTS & MEDIA CONSULTANT 1990– ; Pres. & C.E.O., Crawley Films Ltd. 1982– ; Partner, Stevens & Kennedy Inc. (10–piece band) 1979– ; Musician 1965– ; joined Crawley Films Ltd. 1967, edited sound effects, voice & music over 30 films 1968–74, wrote proposals and scripts 1969, film producer 1970, film dir. 1971; produced and/or dir. more than 23 films, videos and AV's; estbd. Atkinson Film-Arts Ltd. 1974; performs regularly in Montréal, Toronto and Ottawa as lead singer and percussionist with Stevens & Kennedy; performed for various heads of state and shared billing with many maj. artists; frequent guest speaker and panelist; mem., First Official Film Del. to China; Official Candn. Film Ind. Task Force; Chrmn. Local Bus. Div. Ottawa Un. Way 1986, 1987, Dep. Chrmn. Campaign 1987, Chrmn. Campaign 1988, Chrmn. Leaders Div. 1989; Founding Chrmn. Adv. Ctte. on Arts, Ottawa Bd. of Edn. 1987–90; award-winning producer films, TV Specials and Series incl. 'Tukiki and His Search for a Merry Christmas' 1981 Children's Broadcast Inst. Award; 'Heavy Metal: The Movie' Golden Reel Award 1980, Genie Awards 1982; 'Trolls and the Christmas Express,' 'The Care Bears in the Land Without Feelings' 1983, Internat. Film & TV Festival N.Y. Silver Medal, Platinum Cert. Home Video; 'The Care Bears Battle the Freeze Machine' ACTRA Award 1984 Best Children's Prog., Platinum Cert. Home Video; 'The Bestest Present' Gemini 1986 Best Animated Prog., ACTRA Award 1987 Prog. of Yr., Children's Broadcast Inst. Award Animation 1987, Am. Film & Video Festival Blue Ribbon Best Original Work Children 1987; 'The Velveteen Rabbit' Platinum Cert. Home Video; 'The Tin Soldier' Houston Internat. Film Festival Silver Cert. 1987, Internat. Film & TV Festival N.Y. Gold Medal 1987; 'Teddy Ruxpin' Best Children's Prog. U.S. Home Video Awards , Platinum Cert. Home Video 1987; 'Babar and Father Christmas' Internat. Film & TV Festival N.Y. Bronze Medal 1987, Gemini 1987 Best Animated Program; 'The Nightingale' First Official Canada/P.R. of China co-production, Internat. Film & TV Festival N.Y. Gold Medal 1988; sponsored and documentary award winning films incl. 'Child Behaviour Equals You' 1972 (ed.), 'Better Ways for Doing Work' 1973 (prod., dir., ed.), 'Make Fewer Motions' 1973, 'Roadways to Less Effort' 1973, 'Take Fewer Steps' 1973, 'Today's Firefighter' 1974 (prod., dir., ed.), 'Small Things' 1985 (actor); Dir., The Country Club 1981–83; Founding Pres. Ottawa Hull Film & TV Assn. 1984–85; Dir., Candn. Film Inst. 1986–87; Extve. Dir., Candn. Symphonic Pops of Gloucester 1989–90; Dir., Manotick Drama Fringe Festival 1990–91; Pres., Orchard Estates Community Assn. 1991– (Secy. 1990); Producer/Host United Way Community TV Talk Show 1992–94; mem., Candn. Acad. Recording Arts & Sci.; Candn. Acad. Film & TV; SOCAN; ACTRA; AFofM; Candn. Film & TV Assn.; recreations: reading, motorcycles, music, exercise; Clubs: Rideau; Canadian (N.Y.); Princeton (N.Y.); Address: P.O. Box 11069, Station H, Nepean, Ont. K2H 7T8.

**STEVENSON, Brian,** B.A., LL.B.; judge; b. Wakefield, Que. 12 Dec. 1939; e. Bishop's Univ. B.A. 1961; Queen's Univ. LL.B. 1965; m. Patricia; daughter, Melanie; JUDGE, PROV. CT. OF ALTA. 1974– ; practiced law with Fenerty & Co. 1966–67; Partner, Lutz, Westerberg, O'Leary & Stevenson 1967–74; Spl. Prosecutor Cdn. Dept. of Justice, Narcotic Control Act and Food & Drugs Act 1969–74; Pres., Alta. Provincial Judge's Assoc. 1978–79; mem. Calgary North East Eyeopener Lions Club 1966– ; has held most Club & District offices; Pres., Internat. Assn. of Lions Clubs 1987–88; Chrmn., Bd. of Trustees, Lions Clubs Internat. Found. 1988–89; Hon. Dir., Operation Eyesight Universal 1989– ; Dir., Soc. for Treatment of Autism 1984– ; Past Pres., Max Bell Soc.; Calgary Soc. Planning Counc.; Past Dir., Calgary United Way; Past Mem., City of Calgary Soc. Services Ctte.; Calgary Exhibition & Stampede Band Ctte.; Calgary Centennial Ctte.; United Church; Hon. Life Mem., Calgary Bar Assn.; Mem., Law Soc. of Alta.; Candn. Bar Assn.; Hon. Citizen numerous cities in North America; recreations: golf, literature, classical music; Club: Calgary Winter; Office: 323 – 6th Ave. S.E., Calgary, Alta. T2G 4V1.

**STEVENSON, Donald West,** B.A.; b. Stratford, Ont. 11 Feb. 1934; s. John Carter and Eva Kathleen (West) S.; e. Owen Sound pub. and high schs.; Univ. of Toronto, B.A. 1956; m. Ana d. Aleksa and Vasilija Tvrdišić 25 Aug. 1959; two d. Alida Nada, Yvonne Margot; ASSOC. TO THE PRINCIPAL, GLENDON COLL., YORK UNIV. 1989– and CONSULTANT, CANADIAN URBAN INSTITUTE (TORONTO) 1990– ; Foreign Service Offr. Dept. External Affairs 1956, Third Sec. and Vice Consul Belgrade 1957; Ont. Dept. Econ. 1959, Dir. Econ. Br. 1962, Dir. Econ. Planning & Federal Prov. Affairs 1965, Exec. Dir. Policy Planning Div. Treasury & Econ. 1968, Asst. Dep. Min. Treasury, Econ. & Intergovt'al Affairs 1972, Dep. Min. of Intergovt'al Affairs 1978, Dep. Prov. Sec. Resources Devel. 1983; Ont. Rep. to Que. and Federal Govts. 1985–89; Sec. Ont. Ctte. Portable Pensions 1960–63, Ont. Adv. Ctte. Confedn. 1965–71, 1977–79; Chrmn. Prov.-Mun. Grants Reform Ctte. 1976–77; Govt. Coordinator French Lang. Services 1977–83; Nat. Pres. Inst. Pub. Adm. Can. 1978–79; mem. Exec. Toronto Br. Candn. Inst. Internat. Affairs 1967; Adv. Council Queen's Univ. Inst. Intergovt'al Relations 1977– ; mem. Niagara Inst. Adv. Council 1980– ; mem., Chancellor's Council, Victoria Univ. 1986– ; mem. Advisory Council, Soc. for Educational Visits and Exchanges in Canada 1990– ; Adv. Bd. Inst.

Rsch. Pub. Policy 1978–79; mem. Ed. Bd. Candn. Pub. Policy 1975–81; Home: 99 MacPherson Ave., Toronto, Ont. M5R 1W7; Office: Glendon College, 2275 Bayview Ave., Toronto, Ont. M4N 3M6.

**STEVENSON, Garfield William;** farmer; executive; b. Whitewood, Sask. 15 May 1927; s. Norman Garfield and Winnifred Mary (Read) S.; e. high sch.; m. Christina d. Irvine and Christina McKay 20 Nov. 1950; children: Anne, Brian, Ronald, Allan; Pres., Sask. Wheat Pool 1987; Pres. CSP Foods Ltd.; Xcan Grain Ltd.; Vice Pres. Prairie Pools Inc.; Dir. Candn. Pool Agencies; Pool Insurance Co.; employed Dept. Natural Resources Sask. 1948; farmer since 1950; Pool Delegate 1959– , Dir. 1968– , Exec. mem. 1971, Vice Pres. 1981; mem. Sherwood & Whitewood Credit Union; former Dir. Western Co-operative Fertilizers Ltd.; former mem. Sask. Hog Mktg. Comn., Sask. Univ. Comn.; former Dir. Sask. Fedn. Agric., Candn. Fedn. Agric., Whitewood Rural Telephone Co., Whitewood Co-op Assn., Candn. Pork Council; Trustee, Evangelical Ch.; recreation: sports; Home: 2911 Truesdale Dr. E., Regina, Sask. S4V 0V2.

**STEVENSON, Henry F.,** B.Arch.; retired Canadian public servant; b. Winnipeg, Man. 5 Sept. 1911; s. Sydney S. Stevenson; e. Winnipeg schs.; Univ. of Man. B.Arch. 1932; m. Mary R. d. late Dr. Stanley T. Floyd 24 Sept. 1938; children: Cynthia Carsley, Alice Cooper, Douglas, Leigh Anne; joined Univ. of Toronto 1936–38; Imperial Oil 1938–57 serving as Gen. Operations Mgr.-Marketing and Asst. Gen. Mgr. Marketing; International Petroleum 1957–64, Dir. Marketing/Mfg. Petrochemicals 1957–62, Vice Pres. 1962–64; Standard Oil Co. (N.J.) 1964–71, Depy. Coordinator Europe 1964–65, Chief Extve. Offr. Greece 1965–68, Vice Pres. Esso Europe 1968–71, Pres. Esso Africa 1968–71; Anti-Inflation Bd. Can., Dir. Gen. Prices & Profits 1976–78, Commr. 1978–79; Chrmn., Energy Supplies Allocation Bd. Can. 1980–89; served with U.S. Army Air Force 1942–43, loaned from Imperial Oil; Trustee Emeritus, Sunnybrook Med. Centre Toronto; mem. Ont. Assn. Archs.; Anglican; recreations: golf, sailing, tennis; Clubs: Lambton Golf & Country; Beaumaris Yacht (Muskoka); Home: 18 Collegeview Ave., Toronto, Ont. M5P 1J3.

**STEVENSON, Ian,** B.Sc., M.D., C.M.; university professor; b. Montreal, Que. 31 Oct. 1918; s. John Alexander and Ruth Cecilia (Preston) S.; e. Lisgar Coll. Inst., Ottawa, Ont.; Bryanston Sch., Dorset, Eng.; Univ. of St. Andrews, Scotland; McGill Univ., B.Sc. 1941, M.D., C.M. 1943; m. 1) Octavia (dec.), d. late Gordon Reynolds 13 Sept. 1947; m. 2) Margaret Pertzoff 29 Nov. 1985; CARLSON PROF. OF PSYCHIATRY, UNIV. OF VIRGINIA, SCH. OF MED., since 1967; Interne, Royal Victoria Hosp., Montreal, Que., 1944–45; Interne and Resident, St. Joseph's Hosp., Phoenix, Ariz., 1945–46; Fellow in Internal Med., Ochsner Clinic, New Orleans, La., 1946–47; Commonwealth Fellow in Med., Cornell Univ. Med. Coll., 1947–49; Asst. Prof. of Med. and Psychiatry, Louisiana State Univ., 1949–52; Assoc. Prof. 1952–57; Prof. of Neurol. & Psychiatry, Univ. of Virginia and Chrmn. of Dept. 1957–67; Assoc. Mem., Darwin Coll., Cambridge, 1981– ; Life Fellow, Am. Psychiatric Assn.; Am. Soc. for Psychical Research; Am. Psychosomatic Soc.; author of 'The Diagnostic Interview' 1960 (2nd ed. rev. 1971); 'Twenty Cases Suggestive of Reincarnation' 1966, 2nd ed. rev. 1974; 'The Psychiatric Examination' 1969; 'Telepathic Impressions' 1970; 'Xenoglossy' 1974; 'Cases of the Reincarnation Type, Vol. 1 Ten Cases in India' 1975, 'Vol. 2 Ten Cases in Sri Lanka' 1977, Vol. 3 'Twelve Cases in Lebanon and Turkey' 1980, 'Vol. 4 Twelve Cases in Thailand and Burma' 1983; 'Unlearned Language' 1984; 'Children Who Remember Previous Lives' 1987; Home: Wintergreen Farm, Old Lynchburg Road, Route 1, Box 15, Charlottesville, Virginia, 22903.

**STEVENSON, Ian Garth,** B.A., M.A., Ph.D.; university professor; b. Montreal, Que. 7 Apr. 1943; s. Andrew Archibald and Ruth Scott (birthname) Swinton (adopted name) S.; e. Herbert Symonds Sch. & West Hill H.S. (Montreal); McGill Univ. B.A. 1963, M.A. 1965; Princeton Univ. Ph.D. 1971; 2nd m. Yvonne d. Albert and Jessie Brown; children: Colin, Fiona, Moira (1st m.), Jacqueline (2nd m.); PROF., BROCK UNIV. 1987– ; Asst. Prof., Carleton Univ. 1968–76; Assoc. Prof. 1976–78; Univ. of Alta. 1978–82; Prof. 1982–87; Adjunct Prof., York Univ. 1990– ; Visiting Fellow, Australian Nat. Univ. 1975–76, 1985; Visiting Prof., Duke Univ. 1992–93; Anglican; author: 'Mineral Resources and Australian Federalism' 1977, 'Rail Transport and Australian Federalism' 1987, 'The Politics of Canada's Airlines' 1987, 'Unfulfilled Union: Canadian Federalism and National Unity' 3rd ed. 1989; 'Ex Uno Plures: Federal-Provincial Relations in Canada 1867–1896' 1993; Home: 24 Marlatts Road, Thorold, Ont.; Office: Taro Building, Brock Univ., St. Catharines, Ont. L2S 3A1.

**STEVENSON, John Daniel,** Q.C.; b. Cobalt, Ont. 26 March 1929; s. late Carl Stanton and Norma (Cassidy) S.; e. Upper Canada Coll. and Toronto schs.; Trinity Coll. and Faculty of Law, Univ. of Toronto, B.A., LL.B., m. Joan Elaine d. late Rev. A.P. Gilles, 26 Sept. 1959; one s. John Gillies; two d. Norma Louise, Sarah Joan; read law with late K.B. Palmer, Q.C. 1953; called to Bar of Ont. 1955; cr. Q.C. 1969; PARTNER, SMITH, LYONS, TORRANCE, STEVENSON & MAYER since its inception 1962; Dir., CT Financial Services Inc.; Canada Trustco Mortgage Co.; Can. Trust Co.; Dana Corp.; Hayes-Dana Inc.; Holt, Renfrew & Co., Ltd.; George Weston Ltd.; Wittington Investments Ltd.; Chrmn. Bd. of Gov., Upper Can. Coll. 1982–87; Hon. Counsel, Candn. Educational Standards Inst.; mem., Internat. Bar Assn.; Candn. Bar Assn.; Candn. Tax Fdn.; recreations: golf, skiing; Clubs: Toronto; Toronto Golf; Osler Bluff Ski; Home: 166 Forest Hill Rd., Toronto, Ont. M5P 2M9; Office: Suite 6260, 40 King St. W., Toronto, Ont. M5H 3Z7.

**STEVENSON, Mary Margaret,** B.A., M.S., Ph.D.; research Ph.D.; b. Philadelphia, Penn. 10 Sept. 1951; d. George Andrew and Rita Rose (Badaracco) S.; e. Hood Coll. B.A. 1973; Catholic Univ. of Amer. M.S. 1977, Ph.D. 1979; m. Francis Rohland s. Betty Rohland Stark 4 Aug. 1990; ASSOC. PROF., MEDICINE, MCGILL UNIV. 1988– ; Asst. Prof. 1982–88; Expert Cons., U.S. Agency for Internat. Devel. Malaria Vaccine Devel. Program 1991– ; MRCC Scholarship 1982–87; Hood College Outstanding Young Alumnae Award 1985; Mem., Am. Soc. for Microbiol.; Am. Assn. of Immunol.; Candn. Soc. for Immunol.; Am. Soc. of Tropical Med. & Hygiene; editor/author of 1 book; recreations: alpine and nordic skiing, hiking, travel; Office: 1650 Cedar Ave., Montreal, Que. H3G 1A4.

**STEVENSON, Hon. Ronald Charles,** B.A., LL.B., D.Cn.L.; judge; b. Fredericton, N.B., 20 Dec. 1929; s. late Osley Vernon and Verna May (Burtt) S.; e. Univ. of N.B., B.A. 1951; Dalhousie Univ., LL.B. 1953; Univ. of King's Coll., D.Cn.L. (Hon.) 1987; m. Barbara Elizabeth, d. late Dr. J. A. M. Bell, Fredericton, N.B., 20 July 1957; three d., Barbara Christie, Nancy Verna (Craig), Sarah Elizabeth; JUDGE, COURT OF QUEEN'S BENCH OF N.B. since 1979; JUDGE, PROBATE COURT OF NEW BRUNSWICK since 1984; read law with F. D. Tweedie, Q.C.; called to Bar of N.B. 1953; cr. Q.C. 1972; Justice, Queen's Bench Div., Supreme Crt. of N.B., 1972–79; Home: 260 King's College Rd., Fredericton, N.B. E3B 2E8; Office: Supreme Court Chambers, Justice Bldg., P.O. Box 6000, Fredericton, N.B. E3B 5H1.

**STEWARD, David John,** M.B., B.S., F.R.C.P.(C); anaesthesiologist; educator b. Luton, Eng. 2 Feb. 1934; s. William John and Kathleen (Waterhouse) S.; e. Luton Grammar Sch. 1952; Univ. of London M.B., B.S. 1958; L.R.C.P., M.R.C.S. (Eng) 1958; D.A. (Lond) 1962; Univ. of Toronto 1964–68; F.R.C.P.(C) 1968; Dipl. Anaes. 1968; m. 2ndly Mary Louise d. Chester Roberts 18 March 1989; children (1st marriage): Jennifer Alexandra, Nigel Robert John; DIR. OF ANESTHESIOLOGY, CHILDRENS' HOSPITAL LOS ANGELES and PROF. OF ANESTHESIOLOGY, UNIV. OF SOUTHERN CALIFORNIA 1991– ; Consultant, Canada China Child Health Foundation 1992– ; Advisor in Anesthesiology, Guangzhou Children's Hosp., China 1992– ; joined Anaesthesia staff Toronto Sick Children's Hosp. 1968, Anaesthetist in Chief 1971–84; Prof. of Anaesthesia Univ. of Toronto 1975–84; Prof. of Anaesthesia Univ. of B.C. 1984–91; Anaesthetist in Chief, British Columbia Childrens' Hospital 1984–91; served with RCAF 1960–64 as Med. Offr., rank Flight Lt.; Joint Ed.: 'Anesthesia and Uncommon Pediatric Diseases' 1986, 2nd ed. 1993; 'Pediatrics For Anesthesiologists' 1993; author: 'Manual of Paediatric Anaesthesia' 1979, 4th ed. 1994; ed.: 'Some Aspects of Paediatric Anaesthesia' 1981; author several book chapters and over 80 articles gen. anaesthesia and paediatric anaesthesia; Comte. on Pediatric Anesthesia, World Fed. of Socs. of Anesthesiologists 1984–92; Comte. on Pediatric Anesthesia, Am. Soc. Anesthesiols 1993– ; mem., Candn. Med. Assn.; Ont. Med. Assn.; Candn. Anaesthetists Soc.; Am. Soc. Anaesthesiols.; Assn. of Paediatric Anaesthetists of Great Britain and Ireland; Assn. Candn. Univ. Depts. Anaesthesia; Methodist; recreations: photography, collecting antique cameras, sailing; Club: Arbutus; Royal Candn. Mil. Inst.; Office: 4650 Sunset Blvd., Los Angeles, CA 90027 U.S.A.

**STEWART, Alec Thompson,** B.Sc., M.Sc., Ph.D., LL.D., F.R.S.C., F.A.P.S.; scientist; educator; b. Windthorst, Sask. 18 June 1925; s. Arthur and Nelly Blye (Thompson) S.; e. Dalhousie Univ., B.Sc. 1946, M.Sc. 1949; Univ. of Cambridge, Ph.D. 1952; LL.D. 1986; m. Alta Ailene Kennedy, 4 Aug. 1960; children: A. James Kennedy, Hugh Donal, Duncan Roney; PROFESSOR OF PHYSICS, QUEEN'S UNIV. since 1968 (Head of Dept. 1968–74); joined Atomic Energy of Can. Ltd. 1952; Assoc. Prof. Dalhousie Univ., 1957; Assoc. Prof. and Prof., Univ. of N.C., Chapel Hill, 1960–68; Visiting Prof., Univs. in Canada, England, Germany, Switzerland and Japan; author, 'Perpetual Motion,' 1965; co-ed., 'Position Annihilation,' 1967; other writings incl. over 100 scient. articles in prof. journs.; mem., Candn. Assn. Physicists (Pres. 1972–73); recipient, Candn. Assn. Physicists Medal 1992; Canada 125 Medal 1992; Fellow, Am. Physical Society; Fellow, Royal Society of Canada, Pres., Academy of Science 1984–87; Japan S.P.S. Fellow 1990; Research in solid state physics, phonons, electrons, positrons and positronium in crystals and liquids; Public service: Royal Society cttes. on nuclear reactor safety, possible hazzards of power frequency electric and magnetic fields; recreation: racing and cruising yachting; Office: Queen's Univ., Kingston, Ont. K7L 3N6.

**STEWART, Anne Marie,** Q.C., B.Sc., LL.B.; lawyer; b. Nelson, B.C. 19 July 1951; d. Gordon Alexander and Agnes Nora Marie S.; e. Univ. of B.C. B.Sc. 1972, LL.B. 1975 (Gold Medal); Simon Fraser Univ. Cert. Health & Fitness; PARTNER, BLAKE CASSELS & GRAYDON 1989– ; Davis & Co. 1975–89; Dir. and Offc. numerous co's; lectr. many law related courses; Mem., Law Society Professional Standards Ctte. and Ad hoc Bencher; Extve. Comm., St. John Ambulance, B.C.; Past Dir.: Vancouver YWCA; Law Found. of B.C.; Office: 1700, 1030 West Georgia St., Vancouver, B.C. V6E 2Y3.

**STEWART, Barry Deane,** B.Sc., P.Eng.; petroleum executive; b. Winnipeg, Man. 5 May 1942; s. John Adam and Sybil May (Gilholme) S.; e. Queen's Univ., B.Sc. (Eng.Phys.) 1964; Univ. of W. Ont. Mgmt. Training Course 1977; m. Patricia Anne d. Carl and Margaret Hooge 20 Nov. 1992; children: Heather Joy, Larmer Deane, Deron John William; EXTVE. VICE PRES., RESOURCES GROUP, SUNCOR INC. 1991– ; joined Imperial Oil-Esso Resources 1964–83, Mgr. Eng. Esso Resources 1977–79, Mgr. W. Can. Operations 1979–81, Vice Pres. International Petroleum, Colombia, S. Am. 1981–83; joined Petro Canada 1983, Sr. Vice Pres. Prodn. Petro Canada Resources 1983–86; Sr. Vice Pres. W. Region, Petro Canada Products 1986–89; Pres., Petro Canada Products 1989–90; Past Dir., Syncrude Canada Ltd.; Panarctic Oil Ltd.; Alberta Products Pipeline Ltd.; ICG Propane Ltd.; mem. Assn. Prof. Engs., Geols. & Geophys. Alta.; Petrol. Soc. CIM (Dir. and Chrmn. Publs. Bd. 1978–81); Bd. of Govs., Candn. Petroleum Assn. 1991–92; Candn. Assn. of Petroleum Producers (CAPP) 1994– ; Chrmn., Majors Div., 1994 United Way Campaign, Calgary & Area; recreations: golf, skiing, reading, antique maps, photography; Clubs: Ranchmen's; Glencoe; Glencoe Golf & Country; Calgary Petroleum; Calgary Commerce; Home: 608 Crescent Rd. N.W., Calgary, Alta. T2M 4A6; Office: 112, Fourth Ave. SW, Calgary, Alta. T2P 2V5.

**STEWART, Cameron Leigh,** B.Sc., M.Sc., Ph.D., F.R.S.C.; university professor; b. Victoria, B.C. 29 Sept. 1950; s. Ross and Greta Marie (Morris) S.; e. Univ. of B.C. B.Sc. 1971; McGill Univ. M.Sc. 1972; Cambridge Univ. Ph.D. 1976; m. Ellen d. Eleftherios and Elisavet Papachristoforou 7 June 1980; children: Elisa Maria, Andrew Ross; PROF., DEPT. OF PURE MATHEMATICS, UNIV. OF WATERLOO 1986– ; Research Assoc., Mathematisch Centrum Amsterdam 1976–77; Inst. des Hautes Etudes Scientifiques, Bures-sur-Yvette, France 1977–78; Asst. Prof., Univ. of Waterloo 1978–82; Assoc. Prof. 1982–86; Visiting Prof., Univ. de Strasbourg; Univ. of Leiden; Univ. of Ulm; I.H.E.S.; Math. Inst. of the Hungarian Academy of Sciences; J.T. Knight Prize, Cambridge 1974; Fellow, Royal Society of Canada 1989; Killam Fellow 1990–92; author of many journal articles; recreations: golf, ice hockey; Home: 494 Heatherhill Place, Waterloo, Ont. N2T 1H7; Office: Waterloo, Ont. N2L 3G1.

**STEWART, Chester B.,** O.C. (1972), C.D., M.D., C.M., Dr. P.H., LL.D., D.Sc., F.R.C.P.(C), F.A.P.H.A.; b. Norboro, P.E.I. 17 Dec. 1910; s. Hugh Alexander and Lucy Ann (Bryant) S.; e. Pub. Sch., Norboro, P.E.I.; Prince of Wales Coll., Charlottetown, P.E.I.; Dalhousie Univ., B.Sc. 1936, M.D., C.M. 1938; Johns Hopkins Univ., M.P.H. 1946, Dr.P.H. 1953; Cert. in Pub. Health, R.C.P. & S. 1951; F.R.C.P.C. 1961; Hon. LL.D., Univ. P.E.I. 1973; Dalhousie Univ. 1979; Mount Allison Univ. 1983; Hon. D.Sc., St. Francis Xavier 1977; m. Kathleen, d. late William and Eva K. French, 20 Apl. 1942; two d.,

Joan Kathleen (Mrs. Lionel Teed), Moira Anne (Dr. Moira Stewart-Freeman); Assistant Secretary, Assoc. Committee on Medical Research, Nat. Research Council, 1938–40; Prof. of Epidemiology, Dalhousie Univ., 1946–76; Prof. Emeritus 1976– ; Dean of Med. 1954–71; Vice Pres. (Health Sciences) 1971–76; Dean Emeritus 1985– ; retired but active as consult. and in med. history; served with RCAF Med. Br., 1940–45; RCAF Reserve to 1962; rank Wing Commander; Bd. mem., Izaak Walton Killam Hosp. for Children, Halifax 1971–83; Pres., Dalhousie Alumni Assn., 1982–83; Mem. Bd. of Govs., Victoria Gen. Hosp. 1968–78; Univ. P.E.I. 1969–1972; Dalhousie Univ. 1981–85; Mt. St. Vincent Univ. 1981–82; author of numerous articles on aviation med., epidemiology, med. educ. and med. history; Pres., Assn. Candn. Med. Colls., 1962–64; mem. Council, Candn. Med. Assn. 1954–79, Sr. Mem. 1983; C.M.A. Medal of Service 1984; Candn. Pub. Health Assn. (President 1968, member emeritus 1976); Hon. Mem., Candn. Coll. of Family Physicians (1978); Queen Elizabeth II Coronation Medal 1952; Centennial Medal 1967; Queen Elizabeth Jubilee Medal 1977; awarded Commemorative Medal for 125th Anniversary of Candn. Confederation 1992; Presbyterian; recreations: med. history; gardening; Clubs: Rotary; Saraguay; Home: 6008 Oakland Road, Halifax, N.S. B3H 1N8.

**STEWART, Clair C.;** retired; b. Kenton, Man. 20 May 1910; s. Rev. Dr. Rupert and Lena (Johnson) S.; e. Pub. Sch., Man.; High Sch., Belleville, Ont.; Ont. Coll. of Art (Grad.): m. Amy, d. J. S. McLean, Toronto, Ont., 7 Sept. 1937; children: Michael, Timothy, John, James, Mary, Andrew; furthered art educ. in Europe, chiefly in Eng., 1932–36; returned to Toronto and engaged in graphic arts 1937–40; joined Rolph-Clark-Stone Ltd., Toronto, Ont. 1946; apptd. Creative Dir. 1948; el. a Dir., 1952; formed own firm of Stewart & Morrison Ltd., Industrial Designers, 1960, retired from co. 1982; currently Chrmn., Stewart Investments Inc.; served in 2nd World War with R.C.A.F.; mem., Roy. Cdn. Academy of Arts; Protestant; Clubs: Albany; York; Arts & Letters; Home: Highfields, RR #1, Caledon E., Ont. LON 1EO; Office: Stewart Investments Inc., Suite 202, 247 Davenport Rd., Toronto, Ont. M5R 1J9.

**STEWART, David James,** M.D., FRCPC; physician; university professor; b. Ottawa, Ont. 15 May 1950; s. Archibald McDiarmid and Iris Mary (Keenan) S.; e. Queen's University, M.D. 1974; m. Nancy d. John and Isabelle Hall 26 July 1975; children: Adam, Megan, Andrew; PROF. OF MED. & PHARMACOLOGY, UNIV. OF OTTAWA 1988– and HEAD, DIV. MED. ONCOLOGY, OTTAWA CIVIC HOSP. 1989– ; internship and residency, Internal Med., Royal Victoria Hosp. and McGill Univ. 1974–76; Fellowship in Med. Oncology, Univ. of Texas M.D. Anderson Hosp. & Tumor Inst. 1976–78; Fac. Assoc. & Instr. 1978–79; Asst. Internist & Asst. Prof. 1979–80; Clinical Asst. Prof. of Med., Univ. of Ottawa 1980–84; Assoc. Prof. of Med. 1984–87; Assoc. Prof. of Med. & Pharmocology 1987–88; med. oncologist, Ont. Cancer Treatment & Rsch. Fdn., Ottawa Regional Cancer Centre, Ottawa; FRCPC (Internal Med.) 1978; Diploma, Am. Bd. of Internal Med. (Med. Oncology) 1979; FRCPC (Med. Oncology) 1985; mem. Am. Soc. Clinical Oncology; Am. Assn. Cancer Rsch.; Candn. Oncology Soc.; Ont. Med. Assn.; Candn. Med. Assn.; author or co-author of more than 325 med. publs., abstracts, textbook chapters; recreations: skiing, fishing; Home: 207 Glebe Ave., Ottawa, Ont. K1S 2C8; Office: 190 Melrose Ave., Ottawa, Ont. K1Y 4K7.

**STEWART, Douglas B.;** business executive; b. Edinburgh, Scotland 13 Aug. 1940; e. The Royal H.S. of Edinburgh; Edinburgh Univ.; m. Catherine (Irene); children: Kate, Fiona, Douglas Jr.; PRESIDENT, SOBEYS INC. 1990– ; Dir., Empire Co. Ltd.; various executive positions with Steinberg Inc. 1970–84; Senior Vice-Pres. 1984–87; Mem., Bd. of Gov., Nat. Assn. of Wholesale Grocers of America; Mem., Extve. Ctte., Candn. Council of Grocery Distributors; Mem. of Extve. Ctte., Food Industry Assn. of Canada; recreations: sailing; clubs: Pictou Yacht, Oakville Yacht Squadron, Royal St. Lawrence Yacht; Home: P.O. Box 36, Pictou, N.S. B0K 1H0; Office: 115 King St., Stellarton, N.S. B0K 1H0.

**STEWART, Edward Emslie,** O.C., M.A., Ed.D., LL.D.; b. Montreal, Que. 11 Sept. 1930; s. Hector Emslie and Alice Mary (Matthew) S.; e. London (Ont.) Normal Sch.; Univ. of W. Ont., B.A. 1953; Univ. of Michigan, M.A. 1956; Univ. of Toronto, Ed.D. 1970; Univ. of Waterloo, LL.D. 1982; m. Victoria Elizabeth, d. Charles P. Lavis, Windsor, Ont. 24 Aug. 1956; Bd. of Dirs., Barclays Bank of Canada; Radio Station CJRT; taught in Pub. Schs., Windsor, Ont. 1949–56; on staff of Toronto and Lakeshore Teachers' Colleges 1956–60; Asst. Supt., Prof. Devel. Br., Ont. Dept. of Educ. 1960–62, Asst. Supt., Curriculum Br. 1963–64; Asst. Depy. Min., Dept. of Univ. Affairs 1964–67, Depy. Min. 1967–71; Depy. Min. Educ. 1971–73; Depy. Min. to the Premier, Ont. 1974–85; assumed additional duties as Secy. of Cabinet 1976–85 and Clerk of Extve. Council 1977–85; Exec. Vice Pres., Labatt Breweries of Canada, 1985–88; Vice Pres., Corporate Affairs, John Labatt Limited 1988–90; Bd. of Trustees, Royal Ontario Museum; Apptd., Officer of The Order of Canada 1991; Phi Delta Kappa; Club: Arts and Letters; Albany Club; Home: 8 Sunnylea Ave. W., Toronto, Ont. M8Y 2J7.

**STEWART, Hon. Fred A.,** B.Comm., C.L.U., LL.B.; politician; b. Maple Creek, Sask. July 1934; e. Univ. of Sask., B.Comm. 1955; C.L.U. 1962; Univ. of Toronto Law Sch., LL.B. 1965; m. Virginia; children: Doug, Gord; Minister, Technology, Rsch. & Telecommunications, Govt. of Alberta 1989; called to Alberta Bar 1966; established law practice in Calgary 1969 (has developed into a successful medium-sized firm); Q.C. 1980; el. M.L.A. for Calgary North Hill 1986; re-el. g.e. March 1989; has served on numerous legis. & caucus cttes.; Government House Leader; mem., various Cabinet cttes. incl. Priorities, Finan. & Coord., Econ. Planning & Energy; community service has incl. Vice-Chrmn., Bd. of Gov., Mount Royal Coll.; Pres., Alta. P.C. Assn.; Calgary Br., Candn. Cancer Soc.; Dir., Western Canada Summer Games; Calgary C. of C.; Home: 23 Coleridge Cres. N.W., Calgary, Alta. T2K 1X8.

**STEWART, George Calvert,** B.A. (Hon.); ret. investment dealer; b. Toronto, Ont. 27 Feb. 1915; s. late George Shipley and Anna Christena (Calvert) S.; e. Univ. of Toronto Schs.; Univ. of Toronto, B.A. (Hon.) Pol. Science and Econ., 1937; m. Shirley Pauline, d. Philip T. Lewis, Toronto, Ont., 19 June 1952; children: Susan Noreen, Jane Christena, George Lewis; joined Royal Securities Corp. Limited in 1937; apptd. Mgr. of Toronto Office, 1953, Vice-Pres. 1960, Extve. Vice-Pres. 1969; Pres., Merrill Lynch, Royal Securities Ltd. 1974; el. a mem., Toronto Stock Exchange, 1955; el. a Dir. of Royal Securities Corp. Ltd., Nov. 1955; Pres., Merrill Lynch, Royal Securities Ltd. 1973–1977, Vice-Chrmn., 1978; Sr. Adv., Merrill Lynch Canada Inc. 1985; Vice-Pres. and Dir., Aatco Travel Service (Richmond Street Ltd.) 1978–81; served in 2nd World War; Capt. with Toronto Scottish Regt. overseas (U.K., N.W. Europe) 1940–45; Group Chrmn., Candn. Comte. Investment Bankers Assn. 1969, 71; Gov., Investment Bankers Association 1972; Dir. and Chrmn., Investment Comte., Ont. Heart Found.; Trustee, M.D. Realty Fund; Dir., Ont. Golf Assoc. 1983– ; mem., Candn. Seniors' Golf Assoc.; Theta Delta Chi; Anglican; recreations: golf, sailing, fishing; Clubs: Lambton Golf; Boca Del Mar Golf; Boca Raton, Fla.; Address: 3 Woodmere Court, Islington, Ont. M9A 3J1.

**STEWART, Glendon Robert,** B.A.Sc., P.Eng.; marine executive; b. Victoria, B.C. 20 Sept. 1936; s. Robert John and Elsie Frances (Elkington) S.; e. Univ. of B.C. B.A.Sc. 1960; m. Joyce d. Norman and Lillian Coe 5 Sept. 1959; two d. Lori Ann, Andrea; PRES. AND CHIEF EXEC. OFFR. THE ST. LAWRENCE SEAWAY AUTHORITY 1990– ; Pres. The Jacques Cartier and Champlain Bridges Inc.; The Seaway International Bridge Corp. Ltd.; Dir. Thousand Islands Bridge Authority; mem. Lloyd's Register of Shipping Candn. Ctte.; Am. Bureau Shipping Candn. Ctte.; Eng. Marine Services Dept. Transport Victoria, B.C. 1960, Dist. Mgr. Prince Rupert, B.C. 1965; Exec. Asst. to Asst. Dep. Min./Comnr. Candn. Coast Guard Ottawa 1968–75, Chief Aids to Navig. Div. 1976, Regional Mgr. Aids & Waterways Maritime Region 1977, Regional Dir. Gen. Central Region 1980, Dep. Comnr. 1984, Regional Dir. Gen. W. Region 1987–89; mem. Assn. Profl. Engs. B.C.; Office: 1400, 360 Albert St., Ottawa, Ont. K1R 7X7.

**STEWART, Graham George,** B.Sc., Ph.D., D.Sc.; brewing executive; b. Cardiff, Wales 22 March 1942; s. Stanley Walter and Joan Hilder (Bennett) S.; e. Cathays High Sch. Cardiff 1959; Univ. of Wales, B.Sc. 1963; Bath Univ., Ph.D. 1967, D.Sc. 1983; m. Olga d. Samual and Dorothy Loveless 16 Sept. 1967; DIR. OF TECH. AFFAIRS, LABATT BREWERIES OF CANADA 1992– ; Lectr. in Biochem. Portsmouth Coll. of Technol. UK 1967–69; Rsch. Microbiol. John Labatt Ltd. 1969, Rsch. Mgr. 1974, Rsch. Dir. 1978, Dir. Rsch. & Quality Control 1982, Dir. of Tech. Affairs 1986, Dir. of Brewing Tech. Affairs 1989–92; Dir. Brewing & Malting Barley Rsch. Inst. Winnipeg; mem., Inter-Am. Ctte., Science and Technology of the Organization of American States (OAS), elected 1991; Adjunct Prof. Univs. of Guelph and Waterloo; Hon. Lectr., Univ. of W. Ont.; mem. Candn. Agric. Rsch. Council; recipient Hotpack Award Candn. Soc. Microbiols. 1980; Charles Thom Award Soc. Ind. Microbiol. 1987; Biotechnol. Div. Lectr. Am. Soc. Microbiol. 1983; co-author 'Current Developments in Yeast Research' 1981; 'Thermophilic Microorganisms for Ethanol Production' 1987; co-ed. 'Biological Research on Industrial Yeasts' 1987; 'Yeast Biotechnology' 1987; author over 150 papers, reviews, patents; Fellow, Inst. Brewing; Treas. Internat. Union Microbiol. Socs.; recreations: reading, jogging, music; Home: 32 Stuyvesant Pl., London, Ont. N6J 3S9; Office: 150 Simcoe St., London, Ont. N6A 4M3.

**STEWART, Greig,** B.A.; recreation consultant; writer; b. Glasgow, Scot. 25 July 1949; s. Robert McCullogh and Margaret Jeanie (McGregor) S.; e. Humber Coll. Toronto Dip. Journalism, Recreation Leadership 1971; York Univ. B.A. 1976( Hons. 1978), M.A. studies 1978; Pub. Relations Asst. Etobicoke Pub. Libs. 1972; Recreation Supr. City of N. York Parks & Recreation Dept. 1972–81; Recreation Cons. Min. of Culture & Recreation Ont. 1981–83, Min. of Tourism & Recreation Ont. 1983– ; recipient Nat. Bus. Book Award for Best Bus. Book in Can. 1989; author 'Shutting Down the National Dream: A.V. Roe and the Tragedy of the Avro Arrow' 1988; various articles; Founding mem. Simcoe Co. Recreationist Assn.; mem. Aerospace Heritage Found. of Canada; Writers Union Can.; Ontario Trails Council; Huronia Trails and Greenways; United Church; recreations: jogging, antique furniture, 50's music, golf; Home: P.O. Box 8, Crossland, Ont. L0L 1P0; Office: 302, 34 Simcoe St., Barrie, Ont. L4N 6T4.

**STEWART, Harold Brown,** M.D., Ph.D.; educator; b. Chatham, Ont. 9 March 1921; s. John Craig and Margaret Gertrude (Brown) S.; e. McKeough Pub. Sch. and Chatham (Ont.) Coll. Inst., 1938; Univ. of Toronto, M.D. 1944, Ph.D. 1950; Univ. of Cambridge, Ph.D. 1955; m. A. Pauline, d. Victor F. Blake, Toronto, Ont., 14 Oct. 1950; one d. Ann Margaret; EMERITUS PROFESSOR OF BIOCHEM., UNIV. OF WESTERN ONT.; Dean, Faculty of Grad. Studies there 1972–86; Intern, Toronto W. Hosp., 1944–45; Fellow in Biochem., Univ. of Toronto, 1946; NRC post-doctoral Med. Fellow 1947; Merck post-doctoral Fellow (NRC), Univ. of Cambridge, 1950; Elmore Fellow 1952–53; Med. Research Council Fellow (UK) 1953–55 and Visiting Scient. Dept. of Biochem. 1971–72; joined present univ. as Assoc. Prof. of Biochem. 1955–60; Prof. since 1960; Head of Dept. 1965–72; rec'd Starr Medal, Univ. of Toronto, 1950; served with RCAMC (Student) 1944–45; RCN Surg. Lt. 1945–46; rank Lt. Commdr.; author of numerous scient. papers; mem., Biochem. Soc.; Candn. Biochem. Soc.; Candn. Physiol. Soc.; Am. Soc. Biochem. Mol. Biol.; Alpha Omega Alpha; recreation: gardening; Home: 118 Baseline Rd. E., London, Ont. N6C 2N8.

**STEWART, Hilary M.;** writer; artist; b. St. Lucia, W.I. 3 Nov. 1924; d. Frank and Dorothy (Smith) S.; e. Meols Sch., Cheshire, Eng.; St. Martin's Sch. of Art, London, grad. 1951; worked as artist for interior designer 1951–56; costume designer, C.B.C.-TV 1956–60; Art Dir., BCTV Vancouver 1960–72; writer & illus. of bks. on Northwest Coast Indian cultures since 1972; publications: 'Artifacts of the Northwest Coast Indians' 1973; 'Indian Fishing' 1977; 'Looking at Indian Art' 1979; 'Robert Davidson: Haida Printmaker' 1979 (Pacific Northwest Booksellers Award 1980); 'Wild Teas, Coffees and Cordials' 1981; 'Cedar: Tree of Life to the Northwest Coast Indians' 1984 (B.C. Book Prizes Award 1985); 'The Adventures and Sufferings of John R. Jewitt' 1987 (B.C. Book Prizes Award 1988); 'Totem Poles' 1990; 'Looking at Totem Poles' 1993; curator several museum exhibits; has lectured extensively in N. Am. since 1973; mem. Archaeol. Soc. of B.C. 1966–90; Hon. Mem., Mus. of Anthrop., Univ. of B.C.; establised Hilary Stewart Foundation for First Nations Educational Programmes, Museum of Anthropology, Univ. of B.C.; mem. var. orgns. for preserv. of environmentally endangered areas of B.C.; recreations: crafts, paper making, nature printing, basketry, drumming, travel, photography, gardening; Address: P.O. Box 5, Quathiaski Cove, Quadra Island, B.C. V0P 1N0.

**STEWART, Ian G.;** business executive; b. Montreal, Que. 1 Oct. 1926; s. Henry J. and Irene Molson (Clerk) S.; e. Westmount (Que.) High Sch.; m. Carol d. Percy N. Soden 24 Sept. 1949; three d. Penelope, Wendy, Heather; Dir., Newell Industries Canada Inc.; Chrmn., Newell International; Pres. and Dir., Ian G. Stewart Holdings Ltd.; Stewart Holdings Ltd.; Dir. & Vice Pres., Brockridge Investments Ltd., Brockville, Ont.; Dir., The Fighting Stewarts Ltd.; Acrimo AB, Andersdorf, Sweden; Lionheart, plc, Knutsford, Cheshire, England; joined P.N. Soden & Co. Ltd. 1946–62, Pres. and Dir. 1953–62; Pres. and Dir.: Witco Chemical Co. Canada Ltd. 1959–64; Sonneborn Ltd. 1960–64; Delta Chemicals Ltd. 1962–64; Mng. Dir. Witco Chemical Co. Ltd. London, Eng. 1964–67; Vice Pres. and Gen. Mgr. Metal

Treating Chemicals Div. Witco Chemical Corp. New York 1967–71; Pres. and Dir.: Macco Products Corp. Chicago 1967–71; Aldridge Industrial Oils Inc. Cleveland 1968–71; WL. Spencer Mfg. Corp. Milwaukee 1970–71; H.S. Hunnisett Ltd. Toronto 1971–78; Chemspec Ltd. Toronto 1973–78; Candn. Comnr. The Stewart Soc. Edinburgh, Scot.; former Offr. Royal Candn. Armoured Corps; former mem., Young Presidents' Orgn.; mem. World Presidents' Organization; Chem. Inst. Can.; Candn. Assn. Corporate Growth; Royal Philatelic Soc. Can.; recreations: skiing, travel, philately, golf; Home: 60 Garfield Ave., Toronto, Ont. M4T 1E9.

**STEWART, Ian Hampton,** B.A., M.A., Ph.D.; university professor; b. Victoria, B.C. 2 July 1953; s. Ross and Greta Marie (Morris) S.; e. Prince of Wales H.S. 1970; Univ. of B.C. B.A. (Hons.) 1974; Queen's Univ. M.A. 1976, Ph.D. 1983; m. Audrey d. Doug and Elizabeth (Betty) Haig 10 June 1978; children: Duncan, Gavin, Robyn, Fraser; PROF., ACADIA UNIVERSITY 1993– ; Lecturer, Queen's Univ. 1977–78; Univ. of B.C. 1978–82 (summer school 1984, '87); Asst. Prof., Acadia Univ. 1982–87; Assoc. Prof. 1987–93; Head, Dept. of Political Science, 1991– ; Canada Council Doctoral Fellowships 1975–79; Univ. of Essex Summer Study Award from Candn. Pol. Sci. Assn. 1986; Commentator, CBC Halifax, NDP Leadership Convention 1989, N.S. P.C. Leadership Convention 1991; Chair, Senate, Acadia Univ. 1991– ; Dir., Johnson Water Co-op. 1988– ; Pres., Atlantic Prov. Pol. Studies Assn. 1985–86; Mem., APPSA; Candn. Pol. Sci. Assn. 1982– ; author of several journal articles and book chapters; recreations: curling, golf, horse racing; clubs: Wolfville Curling, Ken-wo Golf & Country; Home: R.R. #2, Wolfville, N.S. B0P 1X0; Office: Wolfville, N.S. B0P 1X0.

**STEWART, James F.C.,** B.Com., M.B.A.; merchant banking executive; b. Ottawa, Ont. 16 Feb. 1946; s. John Robert and Alice M. (Farrill) S.; e. Univ. of Ottawa B.Com. 1969; McMaster Univ. M.B.A. 1971; m. Kathleen d. Stuart and Eileen Murray 1967; children: Mark, James, Mike; PRES., C.E.O. & DIR., BAKOR INC. 1990– ; Pres., Chief Exec. Offr. and Dir., Canadian Venture Capital Corp. 1980– ; Chrmn., TMI Inc.; B.T.L. Industries Inc.; Div. Mgr., Simpson-Sears 1969–70; Invest Offr., RoyNat Ltd. 1971–72; Portfolio Mgr., TD Capital Group 1972–75; Vice Pres. Triarch Corp. Ltd. 1976, Sr. Vice Pres. 1978, Pres. & C.E.O. 1980–88; recreations: squash, tennis, skiing; Club: Cambridge; Mississauga Golf; Home: 929 Crozier Court, Mississauga, Ont. L5H 2T2; Office: 284 Watline Ave., Mississauga, Ont. L4Z 1P4.

**STEWART, John B.,** M.A., Ph.D.; senator; b. Antigonish, N.S. 19 Nov. 1924; s. George Harvie and Mary Elizabeth S.; e. Acadia Univ. B.A. (Hons.) 1945, M.A. 1946; Columbia Univ. Ph.D. 1953; unm.; Instr., Acadia Univ. 1945–47; Columbia Univ. 1950–53; Asst. Prof., Barnard College (Columbia Univ.) 1953–59; Consultant, The Rockefeller Foundation, 1953–55 and 1961; Assoc. Prof., Barnard Coll. 1959; Prof., St. Francis Xavier Univ., 1959–62 and 1969–85; Chrmn., Dept. of Govt., Barnard Coll. 1957–59; 1st el. to H. of C. for Antigonish-Guysborough in 1962; re-elect. 1963, 65; Parlty. Secy. to Secy. of State for External Affairs, to Min. of Pub. Works, and to Secy. of State; Leg. Adv. to Pres. of the Privy Council; mem. Adv. Comn. on Parlty. Accommodation; mem. Bd. Govs., Internat. Devel. Research Center; summoned to Senate of Can. 1984; Chrmn., Ctte. on Foreign Affairs 1988– ; author of 'Parliament and Executive in Wartime Canada,' 'The Moral and Political Thought of David Hume,' 'The Canadian House of Commons; Procedure and Reform' and 'Opinion and Reform in Hume's Political Philosophy'; Liberal; Baptist; Home: Bayfield, Antigonish Co., N.S. B0H 1R0.

**STEWART, John Douglas,** B.A., B.L.S., Ph.D.; art historian; b. Kingston, Ont. 28 Jan. 1934; s. Harold Huton and Frances Dunning (Crawford) S.; e. Kingston Coll. & Vocational Inst. 1951; Queen's Univ. B.A. 1955; McGill Univ. B.L.S. 1956; Courtauld Inst. Univ. of London Postgrad. Acad. Dipl. Hist. of Art 1961, Ph.D. 1968; m. Mary d. W. J. Cotterell, Kidderminster, Eng. 1 Sept. 1973; children: Georgiana 1976, Venetia 1978; PROF. OF ART HIST., QUEEN'S UNIV. 1980– ; Acting Head of Dept. of Art July-Dec. 1985; Librarian, Douglas Lib. Queen's Univ. 1956–58; Cadet Nat. Gallery Can. Museum Training Scheme 1958–59; Lectr. in Fine Art Univ. of Toronto 1964–65; Asst. Prof. of Art Hist. Queen's Univ. 1965, Assoc. Prof. 1970; served with Princess of Wales Own Regt. (Reserve) 1948–1951, Supplementary Reserve 1952, rank 2nd Lt.; rec'd Can. Council Grants 1958–60, 1968–69, 1973, 1977, Leave Fellowships 1974–75; 1981–2; co-author 'Heritage Kingston' 1973 (Best Local Hist. Award Candn. Hist. Assn. 1974); author 'Sir Godfrey Kneller and the English Baroque Portrait' 1983; 'Sir Godfrey Kneller' (catalogue) 1971; various articles Eng., Flemish and Dutch art, Candn. arch.; mem. Kingston Comte. Arch. Review 1972–73; Dir. Frontenac Foundation 1972–74; Dir., Cataracqui Archaeological Rsch. Found. 1983–88; mem. Kingston Hist. Soc.; Soc. Study Arch. Can.; P. Conservative; Anglican; Home: 11 Sydenham St., Kingston, Ont.; Office: Kingston, Ont. K7L 3N6.

**STEWART, John Leslie,** B.A.; banker; b. Toronto, Ont. 12 March 1947; s. John Leslie and Winifred Muriel (Gibson) S.; e. Univ. of Toronto Schools 1965 (Ontario Scholar); Yale Univ. B.A. 1969; m. Christine d. Wilf and Gladys Cutler 3 April 1974; children: Sarah Ashlyn Lisa, Christine Leslie; VICE-PRESIDENT & CORPORATE SECRETARY, DAI-ICHI KANGYO BANK (CANADA) 1986– ; Touche Ross & Co. 1981–86; recreations: tennis, golf; clubs: Badminton & Racquet; Office: Commerce Court W., Ste. 5025, Toronto, Ont. M5L 1H9.

**STEWART, Lester G.,** B.Sc.; petroleum industry executive; b. Reserve Mines, N.S. 30 April 1933; s. Lester Francis and Agnes Terisito (Hill) S.; e. New Glasgow N.S. H.S. 1950; St. Francis Xavier Univ. B.Sc. 1959; m. Yvonne d. Dr. Wilfred and Corinne Cormier 2 July 1960; children: Michelle, Lisa; VICE-PRESIDENT, ATLANTIC DIVISION, CANADIAN PETROLEUM PRODUCTS INST. 1990– ; Canadian National Railways 1950–59; Petro-Fina Canada Ltd. then Petro-Canada Ltd. 1959–89; has held var. middle management & extve. mngt. positions; Past Dir., Ont. Petroleum Assn.; Superlino Oil Ltd.; West Nova Fuels Ltd.; McGillvary Fuels Ltd.; recreations: golf, travel, swimming, gardening, curling; clubs: Oakfield Golf & Country; Home: 14 Chessvale Close, Halifax, N.S. B3M 4C7; Office: 45 Alderney Dr., Suite 703, Dartmouth, N.S.

**STEWART, Max Douglas,** B.A., B.Com., M.A., Ph.D.; educator; b. Edmonton, Alta. 6 June 1919; s. late Maurice Howard and late Mary Penn (Ritchie) S.; e. Glenora & Oliver Pub. Schs. 1934; Westmount High Sch. 1937, Edmonton; Univ. of Alta. B.A. 1941, B.Com. 1942; Univ. of Toronto M.A. 1946; Mich. State Univ. Ph.D. 1960; PROF. OF ECON., WILFRID LAURIER UNIV. 1974– ; served with RCA (Radar) and RCEME 1942–45; Travelling Secy. Delta Upsilon Fraternity, New York 1946–49; Invest. Analyst, Value Line 1949–50; N.Y. Stock Exchange Reg'd Rep., Shuman Agnew & Co. San Francisco 1950–51; Lectr. Royal Mil. Coll. Kingston 1953–56; Econ. Affairs Offr. UN, New York 1954; Asst. Prof. Waterloo (Ont.) Coll. 1956–59; Combines Investigation Offr. Dept. of Justice, Ottawa 1959–61; Prof. of Econ. Waterloo Lutheran Univ. 1961–65; Prof. of Econ. Univ. of Alta. 1965–74; Research Offr. Econ. Council Can. Ottawa 1967–68; Dean of Business & Econ. Present Univ. 1974–82; Academic Vice Pres. 1982–83; Internat. Liaison Officer 1985–92; Lectr., Banff Sch. Advanced Mang. 1966–82; Austrian Acad. of Advanced Mang. 1969; Visiting Prof. Michigan State Univ. 1985; Mem., Awards Comm., Delta Upsilon Educational Found. of Can. 1986– ; author 'Concentration in Canadian Manufacturing and Mining' 1970; various econ. articles; co-author 'UN Report on Restrictive Business Practices in International Trade' 1955; mem. Candn. Econ. Assn.; Am. Econ. Assn.; Royal Econ. Soc.; Commonwealth Trust; Financial Extves. Inst.; Internat. Cargo Handling Co-ordination Assn.; Delta Upsilon; Royal Military Coll. Club of Can. (Hon.); United Church; recreations: philately, photography, travel; Clubs: Kitchener-Waterloo Gyro; Royal Canadian Military Inst.; Address: Wilfrid Laurier Univ., Waterloo, Ont. N2L 3C5.

**STEWART, Nalini,** B.J.; freelance journalist; b. New Delhi, India 30 July 1944; d. Ranjit Singh and Dayavati Goel; e. Carleton Univ., B.J. 1964, grad. dipl., Publ Admin. 1965; m. Timothy s. Amy and Clair Stewart 28 June 1969; children: Tarun, Saira, Indira; var. positions with Govt. of Ont. & Ont. Hydro to 1973; volunteer, var. arts orgns. 1973– ; Dir., Writers Development Trust 1992; National Theatre School 1992; The Canadian Club 1992; Bd. of Govs., York Univ.; Former Chair, Ont. Arts Counc.; Founding Dir., Asia Pacific Foundation of Canada; Former Dir., Harbourfront Corp.; MTV; The Power Plant; Bd. Mem., Lester B. Pearson College of the Pacific; mem., Internat. Council of The Asia Society, New York; Hon. Dir., Toronto Film Fest.; recreations: reading, skiing, travelling; Club: Caledon Ski; Home: 2 Lamport Ave., Toronto, Ont. M4W 1S6.

**STEWART, Neil J.,** B.A., LL.B.; petroleum executive; b. Edmonton, Alta. 3 Oct. 1923; s. John N. and Catherine (MacLean) S.; e. Strathcona High Sch. Edmonton 1942; Univ. of Alta. B.A. 1948; Univ. of B.C. LL.B. 1951; Northwestern Univ. Business Adm. 1968; m. Sheila Moyra d. George Mackintosh, Edmonton, Alta., 17 May 1952; children: Ian M., Sandy B.; DIR., TRANSCANADA PIPELINES 1987– ; called to Bar of Alta. 1953; practiced law Edmonton 1952–53; joined Law Dept. of Amoco Canada 1953, Head Law Dept. 1956 and Adm. Dept. 1963, Vice Pres.-Finance and Adm. 1968; Assoc. Vice Chrmn. Nat. Energy Bd. 1971–74 Ottawa; Chrmn. Energy Supplies Allocation Bd., Ottawa 1974–76; Vice Pres., Finance & Admin. Amoco Canada, Calgary 1976–80, Dir. 1976–93; Vice Pres., Supply and Marketing and Dir. Amoco Can. 1980–86; Past Pres. Candn. Petroleum Tax Soc.; Past Chrmn. Tax Law Comte. Candn. Petroleum Assn.; Past Chrmn. Budget Allocation Comte. Calgary Un. Fund; Past Pres., Calgary Burns Club; Past Pres., Calgary Chapter Sir Winston Churchill Soc.; Past Chrmn., Calgary Military Museums Society 1988–92; served with Candn. Grenadier Guards as Tank Commdr. N.W. Europe during World War II; Hon. L. Col. King's Own Calgary Regiment 1990– ; author various articles on petroleum law and income tax law; P. Conservative; Presbyterian; recreations: fishing, swimming; Home: 2354 Windsor Rd., Victoria, B.C. V8S 3E5.

**STEWART, P.C.,** B.Sc., M.P.; politician, nurse; b. Hamilton, Ont. 3 Jan. 1941; d. Morris Alexander and Laura Anne (Doherty) Leishman; e. Univ. of Toronto B.Sc. 1963; m. David Ian s. Goldwin and Juliet S. 24 Aug. 1963; children: Douglas, John, Catherine; SECREATRY OF STATE (LATIN AMERICA & AFRICA), HOUSE OF COMMONS 1993– ; Public Health Nurse, Victorian Order of Nurses 1963–65; Nurse, Cobourg Dist. Gen. Hosp. 1965; mother at home 1966–71; volunteer doing charitable work in Honduras 1971–72; Founding Dir., Horizons of Friendship 1973–86; Extve. Dir., Horizons Devel. Agency 1986–88; 1st elected M.P. for Northumberland 1988; re-elected 1993; Opposition Critic for Candn. Internat. Development Agency 1988–93; Assoc. Critic for Human Rights, Vice-Chair Liberal Caucus Ctte. for External Affairs, Mem., House of Commons STanding Ctte. on External Affairs & Internat. Trade, Sub-Ctte. Devel. & Human Rights 1988–93; Paul Harris Fellow Award; Rotary Club; Hon. Bd. Mem., FEDECOH, Honduran Devel. Agency; Hon. Chair, Big Brothers & Big Sisters Assn., Trenton & Dist. Annual Fundraising Campaign 1989; Founding Dir. & Chair, Northumberland Co. Food Banks Program 1965–88; Trustee, Peterborough, Victoria, Northumberland & Newcastle R.C. Sep. Sch. Bd.; Bd. of Dir., Art Gall. of Northumberland; Roman Catholic; Mem., St. Michael's Parish Council; Mem., Liberal Party of Canada; Home: R.R. 2, Roseneath, Ont. K0K 2X0; Office: Rm. 484, Confederation Bldg., House of Commons, Ont. K1A 0A6.

**STEWART, Peter Beaufort,** B.Com., M.B.A.; b. Westmount, Que. 23 Aug. 1923; s. late Harold Beaufort and late Winnifred (Martin) S.; e. Selwyn House Sch., Montreal; McGill Univ., B.Com. 1942; Harvard Univ., M.B.A. 1947; m. Yolande Winifred, d. late William Bleecker Powell, 1955; two s. Thomas, Angus; Extve. Vice Pres., Corporate Services, The Molson Cos. Ltd. 1982, retired 1988; Dir., The Stewart Group Ltd.; with Building Products Ltd. 1947–62; joined Molson Breweries Ltd. as Dir. of Marketing, 1962; Vice-Pres., Marketing 1965; Pres., Molson's Western Breweries Ltd. 1966, Extve. Vice-Pres., Molson Breweries of Canada Ltd., and subsequently Pres. and Sr. Vice Pres., Brewing Group, Molson Industries Ltd. 1972–75; Extve. Vice Pres., The Molson Cos. Ltd. since 1975; retired 1988; served with Candn. Army 1942–45; rank Capt.; Anglican; Clubs: University (Toronto); Montreal Badminton & Squash; Home: 472 Russell Hill Rd., Toronto, Ont. M5P 2S7.

**STEWART, Peter Malcolm,** B.A.; b. Toronto, Ont. 10 Dec. 1931; s. Roy Alexander and Ruth Margaret (Kilbourn) S.; e. Upper Can. Coll., Toronto, 1939–48; Trinity Coll., Univ. of Toronto, B.A. 1952; m. Joan Temple, d. Wilfred Somers, 29 Jan. 1970; (by 1st m.) children: Elizabeth, Pamela, Richard; CONSULTANT, WICKETT & CRAIG OF AMERICA 1990– ; joined present Co. after grad.; apptd. Plant Mgr., 1957–60, Vice Pres., 1960–64, Pres. 1964–90; Dir., Tanners Assn. Can.; Alpha Delta Phi; Anglican; recreations: tennis, boating, skiing; Clubs: Queen's; Badminton & Racquet; Ojibway; Home: 19 Lower Village Gate, Apt. #702 B, Toronto, Ont. M5P 3L9.

**STEWART, Robert T.,** B.Comm.; business executive; b. Montreal, Que. 16 July 1932; s. James G. and Mary (Van Buren) S.; e. McGill Univ. B.Comm. 1955; m. Nancy Stewart 17 Oct. 1959; children: Robyn Norma, Susan Elizabeth, Carolyn Anne; CHAIRMAN, PRESI-

DENT AND CHIEF EXECUTIVE OFFICER, SCOTT PAPER LIMITED 1988– ; Sales Rep. and other positions, lastly Vice-Pres., Mktg., Scott Paper Limited 1957–68; Pres., Scott Paper Philippines 1975–79; Group Vice-Pres., Mktg. & Dir., Scott Paper Limited 1979; Extve. Vice-Pres. 1982; Pres. & C.E.O. 1987; Dir., Royal Bank of Canada; CBI Indus. Inc.; BC Gas Inc.; Conf. Bd. of Can.; Candn. Pulp & Paper Assn. (Mem., Extve. Bd.); Gov., Business Council of B.C.; Gov., Vancouver Bd. of Trade; Past Pres. & General Campaign Chairman, United Way of the Lower Mainland; Dir., Vancouver Found.; Trustee, B.C. Sports Hall of Fame & Museum; Council of Patrons, Outward Bound Can.; Mem., ADv. Ctte., Lions Gate Hosp. Found. Bd. of Dir.; Hon. ADv. Bd., W. Vanc. Memorial Library Found.; Univ. of B.C. Adv. Council, Fac. of Commerce; U.B.C. Fac. of Forest Adv. Ctte.; Simon Fraser Univ. Pres. Club; McGill Univ. Devel. Adv. Bd., Fac. of Engr.; Past Dir., Liquid Carbonic Ind. 1988–92; Candn. Club of Vanc. 1984–87; Seniors' Lottery Assn. of B.C. 1982–88; Candn. Inst. of Cultural Affairs 1985–89; Marketing Executiveof the Year, Sales & Mktg. Extves. of Vanc. 1987; Astra Award, Phoenix Food Group 1992; Canada 125 Medal 1993; Pres. Award of Distinction, United Way of the Lower Mainland 1993; recreations: golf, swimming, bridge, reading; clubs: Vancouver, Capilano Golf & Country; Home: 1395 Camridge Rd., West Vancouver, B.C. V7S 2M7; Office: P.O. Box 3600, Ste. 2300, 1066 W. Hasting St., Vancouver, B.C. V6B 3Y7.

**STEWART, Robert William,** O.C., Ph.D., D.Sc., LL.D., F.R.S., F.R.S.C.; administrator; b. Smokey Lake, Alta. 21 Aug. 1923; s. Robert Edward and Florence May S.; e. Queen's Univ. B.Sc. 1945, M.Sc. 1947; Cambridge Univ. Ph.D. 1952; McGill Univ. D.Sc. 1972; Dalhousie Univ. LL.D. 1974; m. Anne-Marie Robert 19 Apl. 1973; children: Anne, Brian, Philip, Colin; ADJUNCT PROF., UNIV. OF VICTORIA; Science Offr., Internat. Council of Scientific Unions (Paris); Rsch. Sci., Candn. Defence Rsch. Bd. Victoria, B.C. 1950–61; Prof. of Physics & Oceanography Univ. of B.C. 1960–71; Dir.-Gen., Inst. Ocean Sci's. Sidney, B.C., Dept. of Fisheries & Oceans, Can. 1970–79; Asst. Dep. Min. for Sci. & Technol. B.C. Ministry of Edn., Sci. & Technol. 1979; Dep. Min. B.C. Ministry of Univs., Sci. & Communications 1980–84; Pres. & C.E.O., Alberta Rsch. Counc. 1984–87; Dir., Centre for Earth & Ocean Rsch., Univ. of Victoria 1987–89; Pres., Intnl. Assn. Phys. Sci's. of Ocean 1975–79; mem. Jt. Organizing Ctte. Global Atmospheric Rsch. Prog. 1967–79, Vice Chrmn. 1967–71, Chrmn. 1971–75; mem., Ctte. Climatic Changes & the Ocean, World Climate Rsch. Prog. 1978–89, Chrmn. 1983–87; mem. Sci. Ctte., Int. Geosphere-Biosphere Prog. 1990– (Vice-Chrmn. 1990– ); recipient O.C. 1979; Sverdrup Gold medal Am. Meteorol. Soc. 1976; Patterson Medal Candn. Meteorol. Soc. 1973; Tully Medal, Candn. Meterol. & Oceanog. Soc. 1989; Visiting Prof. Dalhousie Univ. 1960–61, Harvard Univ. 1964, Pa. State Univ. 1964; Commonwealth Prof. Cambridge Univ. 1967–68; author numerous publs. turbulence, oceanog. and meteorol.; Fellow, Am. Meteorol. Soc.; Office: P.O. Box 3055, Victoria, B.C., V8W 3P6.

**STEWART, Ross,** M.A., Ph.D., F.R.S.C.; educator; b. Vancouver, B.C. 16 March 1924; s. Colin and Jessie (Grant) S.; e. Gen. Gordon Sch. and Kitsilano High Sch. Vancouver; Univ. Of B.C. B.A. 1946, M.A. 1948; Univ. of Wash. Ph.D. 1954; m. Greta Marie d. Pearce Morris, Vancouver, B.C. 7 Sept. 1946; children: Cameron Leigh, Ian Hampton; PROF. OF CHEM. UNIV. OF B.C. since 1962, Honorary Prof. of Chem. since 1989; mem. teaching staff Candn. Services Coll., Royal Roads 1949–55; joined Univ. of B.C. 1955; rec'd Lefevre Gold Medal 1946; el. to Royal Soc. of Can. 1971; author 'Oxidation Mechanisms' 1964; 'Investigation of Organic Reactions' 1966; 'Organic Chemistry, Methane to Macromolecules' 1971; 'The Proton: Applications to Organic Chemistry' 1985; over 100 scient. publs.; Pres. B.C. Thoroughbred Breeder's Soc. 1972–74; Vice Pres. Candn. Thoroughbred Horse Soc. 1975–76; Unitarian; recreations: golf, gardening, breeding thoroughbred horses; Club: Point Grey Golf; Home: 4855 Paton St., Vancouver, B.C. V6L 2H9; Office: University of B.C., Vancouver, B.C. V6T 1W5.

**STEWART, Thomas Henry MacKenzie,** M.B., Ch.B., F.R.C.P.(C); educator; b. Leavesden, Eng. 17 Aug. 1930; s. Roy MacKenzie and Agnes Maud S.; e. Univ. of Edinburgh M.B., Ch.B. 1955; m. Marie Paule Irene d. François Ouellet 20 Aug. 1960; children: Alexandre, James, Nicholas, Paul; DIR. NUCLEAR MED. UNIT. OTTAWA GEN. HOSP. 1964– , Geographic Full-Time Cons. 1964– ; Prof. of Medicine, Univ. of Ottawa 1977– ; Teaching Fellow, McGill Univ. 1960–61; Rsch. Fellow Univ. of Ottawa 1960–61; Asst. Coordinator Nuclear Med. Ann Arbor 1963–64; Chrmn., BR2 Protocol for Lung Cancer N.C.I. Can.; Co-Chrmn., NRC sponsored workshop prevention lung cancer Ottawa 1979; Invited Witness Select Ctte. on Aging U.S. House of Reps. 1979; Am. Cancer Soc. Sci. Writer's Seminar 1979; author or co-author various sci. publs.; mem., Candn. Med. Assn.; Candn. Soc. Immunol. (Founding mem.); Candn. Soc. Clin. Investig.; Soc. Nuclear Med.; recreations: skiing, sailing; Home: 1 Mount Pleasant Ave., Ottawa, Ont. K1S 0L6; Office: 501 Smyth Rd., Ottawa, Ont. K1H 8L6.

**STEWART, Walter Douglas;** author; journalist; b. Toronto, Ont. 19 April 1931; s. James Miller and Dorothy Margaret (McCall) S.; e. Univ. of Toronto; m. Joan d. Grace Finley 24 Sept. 1955; children: Craig, Sandra; Reporter, Picture Ed., Financial Feature Writer, Toronto Telegram 1953–62; Ottawa Corr., The Star Weekly 1964–68; Maclean's mag.: Ottawa Corr., Washington Corr., Managing Ed.; Nat. columnist, FP News Services 1981; Ed., Today Mag. 1981–82; Dir., Sch. of Journalism, King's College, Halifax 1984–86; Max Bell Prof., Univ. of Regina, Sch. of Journalism 1987–88; Editor, Policy Options Magazine 1988–93; author: 'Shrug: Trudeau in Power' 1971; 'Divide and Con' 1973; 'Hard to Swallow' 1974; 'But Not in Canada' 1976; 'As They See Us' 1976; 'Strike' 1977; 'Paper Juggernaut' 1979; 'Towers of Gold, Feet of Clay' 1983; 'True Blue' 1985; 'Uneasy Lies the Head' 1987; (with Prof. Eric Kierans) 'Wrong End of the Rainbow' 1988; 'Right Church, Wrong Pew' 1990; 'Hole in One' 1992; 'The Golden Fleece' 1992; 'Too Big to Fail' 1993; ed. and co-author: 'Canadian Newspapers: The Inside Story' 1981; recreations: reading, walking, arguing; Home: Sturgeon Point, Ont. K0M 1N0.

**STEWART, William Archibald,** O.B.E.; journalist; writer on Quebec affairs; b. Rivière-du-Loup, Que., 28 Feb. 1914; s. Charles Archibald and Anne Laura (Walsh) S.; e. Coll. St-Patrice, Rivière-du-Loup; Univ. of Ottawa; m. Katherine Elizabeth, d. Fred A. Young, Winnipeg, Man., 23 Apl. 1946; children: Dugald, Landon, Susan, John, Janet; GENERAL EXECUTIVE, THE CANADIAN PRESS (MONTREAL), 1975–79; joined C.P. 1934 and Corr. at Rivière-du-Loup, Sydney, N.S., P.E.I. and Quebec City, 1934–38; War Corr., London, Eng., 1941; reported campaigns in Sicily, July-Aug. 1943; Italy, Sept. 1943–Feb. 1944; Normandy invasion and W. European 1944; Southeast Asia 1945; Australian Corr. for CP 1946–47; Chief of Bureau, Quebec City, 1947–52; Chief of Bur. Montreal 1952–75; named to Candn. News Hall of Fame 1986; Roman Catholic; recreations: painting, cartooning; Home: 454 Oak Ave., Saint-Lambert, Que. J4P 2R1.

**STEWART, William R.,** B.Sc., C.A.; chartered accountant; b. Hartford, Conn. 5 June 1945; s. Peter R. and Elizabeth (Clement) S.; e. Upper Canada College 1963; Univ. of Toronto B.Sc. 1966; Inst. of C.A.s C.A. 1970; m. Sylvia d. Charles and Grace Davis 28 Dec. 1984; children: Geoffrey, Stephanie (1st m.); Kate, Sean (2nd m.); EXECUTIVE DIRECTOR, LONDON GOODWILL INDUSTRIES ASSN. 1993– ; joined Price Waterhouse 1966; C.A. 1970; Supervisor 1972; Manager 1975; Partner 1980–93; Head, Independent Business Service Dept. 1980– ; Campaign Chair, United Way, London 1991 (increase of 7% over 1990 campaign); Bd. Chair, United Way of London & Middlesex 1992–94; Dir., Salvation Army; Big Sisters of London; P.A.C.T.; Orchestra London; Heart-to-Heart; recreations: racquetball, hiking; clubs: YMCA; C. of C.; Home: 441 Victoria St., London, Ont. N5Y 4B1; Office: 554 First St., London, Ont. N5V 1Z3.

**STIEB, Ernst Walter,** M.Sc.Phm., Ph.D.; pharmacist; educator; historian; b. Windsor, Ont. 23 Aug. 1929; s. late Henry and late Elizabeth (Freund) S.; e. Univ. of Toronto, B.Sc.Phm. 1952, M.Sc.Phm. 1955; Univ. of Wis., Ph.D. 1959; m. Catherine, d. late Philip Spee, 22 May 1954; children: Susan Anne (Ashbourne), David Michael; ASSOC. DEAN, FAC. OF PHARMACY, UNIV. OF TORONTO since 1978; Curator, Niagara Apothecary Museum; Teaching Asst., Univ. of Toronto, 1953; Research Asst., Univ. of Wis., 1955, Instr. 1958, Asst. Prof. 1959, Assoc. Prof. 1964; Prof. of Hist. of Pharm., Univ. of Toronto since 1967 and Inst. for Hist. and Philos. of Sci. and Technol.; Asst. Dean, Fac. of Pharm. 1975–78; Acting Dean, 1978–79 and July to Dec. 1985 and 1993; rec'd Edward Kremers Award for 'distinguished historical writing,' Am. Inst. Hist. of Pharm., 1967; author 'Drug Adulteration: Detection and Control in Nineteenth Century Britain' 1966; 'The American College of Apothecaries: The First Quarter Century, 1940–67,' 1970; 'Pharmacy Museums and Historical Collections in Canada' 1988; other writings incl. book chapters and papers for various pharm. and historical journs.; Ed., 'One Hundred Years of Pharmacy in Canada' 1969; Ed., Faculty of Pharmacy 'Newsletter' 1977–87; Ed., 'Teaching the History and Sociology of Pharmacy [Newsletter]' 1983–88; mem., Candn. Acad. Hist. Pharm. (Extve. Dir. since 1968); Am. Inst. Hist. Pharm. (Pres. 1977–79, Sec. 1957–67); Assn. Faculties Pharm. Can. (Vice Chrmn. 1972–73, Chrmn. 1973–74); Brit. Soc. Hist. Pharm.; Candn. Pharm. Assn.; Internat. Acad. Hist. Pharm. (Hon.); Ont. Museum Assn.; Candn. Museums Assn.; Internat'l Soc. (German) of the Hist. of Pharmacy; Ont. Coll. of Pharmacists (Council, 1978–80, 1985, 1993–94); Cdn. Fdn. for Pharmacy (Bd. of Dir. 1978–87); Candn. Council on Continuing Educ. in Pharmacy (Council, since 1975); Rho Chi Hon. Soc.; United Church; recreations: music, pharmaco-medical philately, travel, photography; Home: 39 Kimbermount Dr., Agincourt, Ont. M1T 2Y1.

**STIKEMAN, Harry Heward,** O.C., Q.C., LL.D.; advocate; b. Montreal, Que. 8 July 1913; s. Harry Frederick Cawthorn and Dorothea (Horstmann) S.; e. Chestnut Hill Acad., Phila., Pa.; Selwyn House Sch., Montreal, Que.; Trinity Coll. Sch., Port Hope, Ont.; McGill Univ., B.A. 1935, B.C.L. 1938; LL.D. 1986; Univ. of Dijon, France, Diplome de Francais 1937; m. Virginia Eloise, d. Robert Dunbar Guy, Q.C., Winnipeg, Man., 16 Sept. 1939; children: Virginia Heward, Harry Robert Heward, Ann Heward, Elizabeth Heward; m. 2ndly, Mary Gertrude, d. Dr. M. R. Wilson, Perth, Ont., 14 Oct. 1967; one d. Roben Jane Heward; SR. PARTNER, STIKEMAN, ELLIOTT (Montreal, Que.; Toronto and Ottawa, Ont.; Vancouver, B.C.; Calgary, Alta.; London, England; Paris, France; Hong Kong; Taipei; New York; Prague, Budapest; Washington, DC); Dir., Federal Commerce & Navigation Ltd.; Rawson Trust, Nassau; Past Gov., Candn. Tax Foundation; Editor-in-Chief, Richard De Boo; collab. for Can., Internat. Bur. of Fiscal Documentation; read law with C. G. Heward, K.C.; called to the Bar of Que. 1938; entered Office of Income Tax Div., Dept. of Nat. Revenue, Ottawa, 1939, as Solr.; became Counsel and Extve. Asst. and finally Asst. Depy. Min. of Nat. Revenue, Legal; worked on all wartime budgets, and asst. in drafting most of the tax leg. during the war; left the Dept. 1946; apptd. Counsel to the Special Comte. of the Senate, investigating taxation; Author and Ed. in Chief, 'Canada Tax Cases, Annotated'; Tax Appeal Board Cases'; 'Canada Tax Service'; 'Canada Tax Manual'; 'Stikeman Canada Tax Acts Consolidated'; 'Doing Business in Canada'; has publ. lect. on taxation and articles in Candn. and foreign journs.; Officer of the Order of Canada 1991; Alpha Delta Phi; Conservative; Anglican; recreations: tennis, skiing, sailing, flying, painting; Clubs: Loxahatchee, Fla.; Lyford Cay (Nassau); Mount Royal; Rideau (Ottawa); The Toronto (Ont.); Confrerie des Chevaliers du Tastevin, France; Homes: 3940 Cote des Neiges, Montreal, Que. H3H 1W2, Shefford, Que. and Rideau Ferry, Ont.; Office: 1155 Réne Lévesque Blvd., Montreal, Que. H3B 3V2.

**STILES, Rev. Frank Bernard,** B.A., B.Ed., M.Div.; b. Truro, N.S. 28 Feb. 1935; e. Mount Allison Univ. 1957–62, B.A. (Arts and Theology), B.Ed.; Pine Hill Divinity Hall, B.Div. 1964, updated to M.Div. 1974; m. Louise Elsie Chappell, Amherst, N.S. 1 May 1961; three d.: Elizabeth, Patricia, Jane; Minister, St. Paul's United Church, Ottawa Presbytery 1970–87; Pres. & C.E.O., New Tech. Medical Internat.; o. Maritime Conf. Un. Ch. Can. 1964; active mem. of Presbytery and Church Outreach work; served as Chrmn. or mem. of Presbytery Pastoral Relations Cttes. 1967–87; Founder, Nat. Parent Youth Alert Corp. Can. 1969, Dir. Gen. Can. and Chrmn. Nat. Bd. Dirs. 1969–81; Founder and Dir. Companion Program for Alcoholics 1970–87; mem., former special affiliate mem., Candn. Psychology Assn.; former special affiliate mem., Candn. Psychiatric Assn.; Protestant Chaplain, Royal Candn. Legion, Huntley Sr. Citizens, Alcoholics Anonymous, 87; author 'Drugs, Trips and Tragedies' 1972; Reserve Army 1954–56; trained – licensed pilot; Inventions: Solid Rocket Fuel, functional 1945; Automobile Air Conditioner, 1958; Candn. Patent Office Caveat No. 27448; Automatic Paper-saver Dispenser, 1956; Emergency Helicopter Soft Landing System, 1954, Letters Patent, Canada No. 1246042; Self-lubricating concept for Hip-joint and other joints used in human implant, 1954; four-way Visual Speech Training Consol for deaf, siliscope and feed-back method, 1954; Ball-in-Basket Heart Valve, with surgical applicator 1958; Micro Quartz-Fibre Laser head for vaporizing plaque-cholesterol from blocked arteries, 1958; Medical Cardio-Vascular dilation instrument, used with or without guide wire 1959 (to include balloon-catheter for dilating arteries, heart valves); Medical Cardio-Vascular blood clot (and other) dissolving vacuuming system (U.S. Patent No. 4,692,139; Candn. Patent No. 1237482), Biological Duct Liner and Installation Catheter (Patent U.S. No. 5,089,006) (Patent pending Canada

No. 187P03CA) and family of varied specialized catheters 1958; Intraocular Micro Instrument for dissolving and removing cataracts, (and lens), ultrasonic-vacuum method; Automatic heart, lung, pulse computer (ausculation) analysis concept, 1961; Bionic Hearing Implant Device to include micro computation options, 1961; etc.; Address: P.O. Box 25, Northport, Cumberland Co., N.S. B0L 1E0.

**STILES, John A.,** B.Com.; diplomat (retired); b. Fredericton, N.B. 26 Jan. 1918; s. John Alexander and Margaret Campbell (MacVannel) S.; e. Glebe Coll. Inst., Ottawa, Ont.; Univ. of Toronto, B.Com. 1941; m. Margaret Celia, d. Douglas G. Buckley, Ottawa, 5 June 1948; two s. 1 d.; joined Trade Commissioner Service 1945; Assistant Trade Commissioner, New York, 1946; Caracas 1948; Asst. Dir., Trade Commissioner Service, Ottawa, 1954; Comm. Counsellor, Bonn, 1957, Sydney 1963; Min. (Comm.), Tokyo, 1967; High Commr. to Guyana 1970–73; Ambassador to Repub. of Korea 1974–77; Foreign Service Visitor 1977–81; Chief Inspector, Foreign Operations, Govt. of Canada 1981–83; served with the Canadian Army in England, France, Belgium, Holland Germany, 1941–45; rank Staff Capt. on discharge; United Church; author: 'Developing Canada's Relations Abroad' 1980; Mem., Canada-Korea Soc.; Retired Heads of Mission Assn.; recreations; golf, swimming, reading; Address: Apt. 91, 265 Botanica Lane, Ottawa, Ont. K1Y 4P9.

**STILLER, Calvin Ralph,** M.D., F.R.C.P.(C); physician; scientist; educator; business executive; b. Naicam, Sask. 12 Feb. 1941; s. Carl Hilmer and Mildred Ruth (Parsons) S.; e. Bedford Rd. Coll. Inst. Saskatoon 1958; Univ. of Sask. M.D. 1965; Univ. of W. Ont. postdoctoral studies 1965–71; Univ. of Alta. post doctoral studies 1971–72; m. Angelina children: Cynthia, Robert, Denise, Troy, Debra, Timothy; CHIEF, MULTIORGAN TRANSPLANT SERVICE UNIV. HOSP. 1984– ; Prof. of Med. Univ. of W. Ont. 1983; Asst./Assoc. Prof. of Med. above univ. and Chief of Nephrology & Transplantation above hosp. 1972–83, Dir. Transplant Lab. 1972– ; Chrmn. Centre for Transplant Studies 1981; mem. & Vice Chrmn., Bd. Dirs. Robarts Rsch. Inst., Dir. of Immunol. 1985– ; Chrmn. Min.'s Task Force Organ Donation 1984; Chrmn. Min.'s Adv. Ctte. Renal Disease 1984; Scientific Chrmn., Personnel Awards Com. M.O.H., Ont.; Mem. of Council, Extve. Ctte., Med. Rsch. Council of Canada (Queen's Appt.); Visiting Prof. over 60 locations including: Harvard Univ., UCLA. Univ. of Texas, Johns Hopkins Univ., Univs. Ottawa, Toronto, Sask., B.C., Oxford, London, Witwatersrand, Capetown, Durban, Munich, Warsaw; Chrmn. Bd. Chelsey Park Corp.; Past Chrmn., London Found., Kidney Found.; Dir., Transplant Internat. (Can.); Dir. & Co-Founder, Alan Thicke Centre for Juvenile Diabetes; cons. Ways & Means Ctte. U.S. Congress, Idea Corp. and other govt. and ind. orgns.; invited lectr. or Chrmn. numerous nat. and internat. confs.; recipient, rsch. awards Med. Rsch. Council Can., Kidney Found. and other orgns.; MEDIC Award of Canada 1992; Internat. Humanitarian Award Optimists Soc.; author or co-author over 200 sci. publs.; ed. or co-ed. several books; mem. ed. bd. various publs.; mem. Internat. Transplantation Soc. (past mem. Council, Dir.); Internat. Soc. Nephrol.; Candn. Soc. Nephrol. (Past Pres.); Internat. Soc. Immunol.; Candn. Med. Assn.; Internat. Heart Transplantation Soc.; Clubs: London; University; London Hunt & Country; Home: 6 Smallman Dr., London, Ont. N6G 4R3; Office: P.O. Box 5339, London, Ont. N6A 5A5.

**STINSON, Deane Brian,** F.C.A.; chartered accountant; b. Ottawa, Ont. 12 Nov. 1930; s. Earl Minto and Clara Edna (Acres) S.; e. Lisgar C.I.; Candn. Inst. of C.A.s, Queen's Univ. 5 year program 1954; F.C.A. 1985; m. Patricia Ann d. Richard John and Nan Paynter 25 Aug. 1956; children: Steven Wayne, Brian Richard, Andrew Alan; Clerk & Trouble Shooter, The Great A & P Tea Co. 1949; Student in Accounts, Arthur A. Crawley 1949–54; C.A., Peat Marwick Thorne 1954–58; Partner 1959–88; Managing Partner 1980–86; Sr. Extve. Partner 1986–88; Partner in Charge, Doane Raymond 1988–93; Ont. Mngt. Council, Peat Marwick Thorne 1979–85; Nat. Dir. of Credit Unions 1979–88; Dir. of Mktg. for Ont. 1984–88; Nat. Chair, Bus. Adv. Services, Mem., Partnership Bd. & Tax Standards Ctte., Doane Raymond 1989–93; Pres. & C.E.O., 985875 Ontario Inc.; Betwin Investments Inc.; Tolstar Management Inc.; Tille Investments Limited; Dir., Mark Four Resources Inc.; Mem., Candn. & Ont. Inst. of C.A.s 1954– ; Co-Founder & Pres., Sault Ste. Marie C.A. Assn. 1965; Mem., Rotary Club (Pres. 1978); Secy.-Treas., Sault Ste Marie Economic Development Corp.; Dir., Algoma Fall Festival Assn.; P.C. Assn. (Vice-Pres. 1982–87); author of several articles; recreations: philately, investment, golf; Home: 15 Atlas Ave., Sault Ste. Marie, Ont. P6A 4Z2; Office: 421 Bay St., Sault Ste. Marie, Ont. P6A 1X3.

**STINSON, Ford A.,** Ph.D; agriculturist; b. Norwood, Ont., 16 Sept. 1909; s. Richard John and Alice (Andrews) S.; e. Ont. Agric. Coll., B.S.A. 1934; Univ. of Toronto, M.S.A., 1938; North Carolina State Coll. of Agric., Ph.D. (Agron.-Soils) 1949; m. Margaret Dexter, d. late James Ross McLachlin, 24 Sept. 1938; children, Richard James, Martha Jane, Donald Andrew; Offr. i/c Dom. Exper. Stn., Delhi, Ont., 1935–49 (devel. of research on flue-cured tobacco); Prof. and Head, Dept. of Soils, Ont. Agric. Coll., 1949–51; (first) Dir., Tobacco Research Bd. of Rhodesia, 1951–56; Farmer, 1956–62; Gen. Mgr., Ont. Flue-cured Tobacco Growers' Mktg. Bd., 1957–58; Head, Field Crops Div., Kemptville Agric. Sch., 1962–66; mem., Ont. Agr. Research Inst., 1962–66; Chrmn., Ont. Flue-cured Tobacco Ind. Inquiry Comm., 1962–63; Princ., Kemptville Coll. of Agric. Tech. 1966–74; Prov. Leader, C.I.D.A. Tobacco Mktg. Study, Tanzania 1970; Consult., C.I.D.A. Study Team, Dry Land Agric., India and Sri Lanka 1975; Consult. C.I.D.A. Study Team, Natural Resources Coll., Malawi 1977; Sigma Xi, United Church; Address: Lanark, Ont. K0G 1K0.

**STINSON, Robert John Ross,** B.A., LL.B.; lawyer; b. Guelph, Ont. 7 Nov. 1953; s. Ivan Sparling and Margaret Catherine (Bolger) S.; e. Dalhousie Univ. LL.B. 1976; Univ. of Guelph B.A. 1979; m. Phyllis Lee d. Roderick and Hazel McLean 22 July 1978; children: Rebecca Bridgitte, Victoria Erin; PARTNER, FLINN MERRICK 1987– ; admitted to Bar of Ont. 1978; to Bar of N.S. 1980; Assoc., Payne, Smith, Campbell & Gazzola 1978–79; Assoc./Partner, Chandler Moore 1980–87; Pres., Howe Consulting Group; Chrmn., Candn. Exporters' Assn. N.S. Chapter 1988– ; New England Canada Bus. Council 1988– ; Chrmn., Britain Canada Trade Assn. (Atlantic Canada Chap.) 1989– ; N.S. New England Bus. Council 1990– ; Chrmn., Adv. Bd., Canada-Caribbean Bus. Coop. Office 1990– ; Internat. Trade Ctte., Halifax Bd. of Trade 1988–93; N.S. Export Achievement Award, Howe Cons. Group Limited 1990; Dir., Adv. Bd., Canada Pension Plan 1991–94; Dir., Nova Scotia Trade Council 1991– ; Dir., Atlantic Canada Plus Assn. 1992– ; Panel mem. U.S. Canada Bi-national Dispute Resolution Panel 1992– ; Dir., Council for Candn. Unity 1993– ; Comnr., Halifax Dist. Sch. Bd. 1985–91; Dir., Adv. Bd., Metro Volunteer Resource Ctr. (Halifax) 1990–92; Dir., Law Fdn. of N.S. 1984–89; Bd. of Dir., St. Paul's Ch. 1983–86; Mem., Osgoode Soc. 1984–90; Selden Soc. 1985–91; recreations: travel, sports; clubs: The Halifax; Home: 6327 Duncan St., Halifax, N.S. B3L 1K4; Office: P.O. Box 1054, Halifax, N.S. B3J 2X6.

**STINSON, Shirley M.,** R.N., B.Sc., M.N.A., Ed.D., LL.D., D.Sc.; b. Arelee, Sask. 10 Dec. 1929; d. James Edwin and Mary Luella (Ismond) S.; e. Univ. of Alta. B.Sc. Nursing 1953; Univ. of Minnesota M.N.A. 1958; Columbia Univ. Ed.D. 1969; PROFESSOR EMERITUS, FACULTY OF NURSING AND FACULTY OF MEDICINE, UNIV. OF ALTA.; Prof. Dept. of Health Services Admin. and Community Med., Univ. of Alta. 1969– , Prof., Fac. of Nursing & Fac. of Medicine 1969– ; Adjunct Prof. for Life, Univ. Calgary Fac. of Nursing 1991– ; Co-Chrmn., First Internat. Conference on Community Health Nursing Rsch. Planning Ctte. 1989–93; Consultant, World Health Organization 1991; Chrmn. Alta. Found. for Nursing Rsch. 1982–88; Dir., Winspear Found.; author over 70 articles on nursing rsch. and admin.; co-editor 'International Issues in Nursing Research' 1986; 'Graduate Education in Nursing' 1988; 'Policy Development for Consideration by National Nurses Associations' 1988; 'Education of Nurse Administrators in Canada' 1990; mem. Review and Adv. Cttes., Nat. Health Rsch. and Devel. Prog. 1978–87; manuscript reviewer for 'Nursing Research' 1979– ; Speaker, Rockefeller Invitational Health Management Conf., Italy 1988; Co-Dir. Internat. Nursing Rsch. Conf. 1986; Cons., Columbian Nurses Assn. 1984; Distinguished Visitor and Internat. Consultant, Health Sci. Center, Sch. of Nursing, Univ. of Oregon 1984–87; Visiting Prof., Sch. of Nursing, Univ. of Calif., San Francisco 1985; Nursing Rsch. Cons. Alta. Assn. of Reg'd Nurses 1976–84; Dir. Keyano Coll. Found. 1982–84; Pres. Candn. Nurses Assn. 1980–82; Candn. rep. Workgroup of European Nurse Researchers 1982, 1992; mem. Med. Rsch. Counc. Nursing Rsch. Ctte. 1982–84; first woman to receive Sr. Nat. Health Scientist Award 1972; Hon. LL.D. Univ. of Calgary 1982; Outstanding Achievement Award, Bd. of Regents, Univ. of Minnesota 1984; Edmonton YWCA Award 1982; Nursing Edn. Alumni Award, Columbia Univ. 1981; Candn. Nurses Assn. Jeanne Mance Award 1990; Candn. Nurses Found. Ross Award for Nursing Leadership 1990; Govt. of Alta. Sir Frederick Haultain Humanities Award 1990; Hon. Life Mem., Alta. Assn. Registered Nurses; Hon. Doctor of Science, Memorial Univ. 1991; 'The Dr. Shirley Stinson Ph.D. in Nursing Scholarship' estab. as a Tribute by the Univ. of Alta. Faculty of Nursing 1993; 'Stinson Rare Book Collection, Alberta Assn. of Registered Nurses Museum & Archives' estab. by Alta. Nurse Administrator Council 1993; recreations: gardening, music, golf; Home: 904, 11007 - 83 Ave., Edmonton, Alta. T6G 0T9; Office: 3rd Floor, Clinical Sciences Bldg., Univ. of Alta., Edmonton, Alta. T6G 2G3.

**STINSON, William W.,** B.A.; executive; b. Toronto, Ont. 29 Oct. 1933; e. Univ. of Toronto B.A. 1954; Univ. of W. Ont. Dipl. in Business Adm. 1955; CHRMN. & C.E.O., CANADIAN PACIFIC LTD. 1990– ; Dir., United Dominion Industries Ltd.; United Dominion Industries Inc.; Bank of Montreal; CP Ltd.; Canadian Pacific Enterprises Limited; Laidlaw Inc.; PanCanadian Petroleum Limited; PWA Corp.; Robco Inc.; Sun Life Assur. Co. of Canada; ADT Limited; Unitel Communications Inc.; joined Canadian Pacific Toronto 1950, held various positions 1950–66; Supt. Toronto Div. 1966, Asst. Gen. Mgr., Ops. and Maint., Pacific Region Vancouver 1969; Gen. Mgr., Oper. and Maintenance Pacific Region 1971 and Eastern Region 1972; Asst. Vice Pres. Operation and Maintenance Montreal 1974; Vice Pres., Oper. and Maint., Montreal, 1976; Exec. Vice-Pres., CP Rail 1979; Pres., Canadian Pacific Ltd. 1981, Pres. & C.E.O. 1985–89, Chrmn., Pres. & C.E.O. 1989–90, Chrmn. & C.E.O. 1990– ; Dir., The Van Horne Institute; mem., Business Council on National Issues; Clubs: Mount Royal; Mount Bruno Country Club; Office: P.O. Box 6042, Stn. A, Montreal, Que. H3C 3E4.

**STIRLING, Geoffrey William;** broadcasting and advertising executive; b. St. John's, Nfld. 22 March 1922; s. Edgar Weston and Mary Ethel (Uphill) S.; e. Grammar Sch., Ramsgate, Eng.; Bishop Feild Coll., St. John's, Nfld.; Univ. of Tampa; m. Joyce, d. James Cutler, 1957; children: Scott, Anne, Kim, Shawn, S. Greg; Newfoundland Television Network, CJON-TV (estbd. 1955) plus 30 other transmitters coast to coast; Newfoundland Broadcasting Co.; Chairman, Newfoundland Sunday Herald; Weston Enterprises; Newfoundland Enterprises; Newfoundland Television & Advertising Co.; Newfoundland Broadcasting Co. Ltd.; Pres., WWKC Holding Co.; Dir. and part owner, CTV Canadian National TV Network; Herald Publishing Corp.; Apache Film and Research Corp.; etc.; mem. of St. John's Beautification Board; Feildian Educ. Sports Comte.; Candn. Weekly Newspapers Assn.; Assn. of Radio & TV Broadcasters; Broadcast News; founded the Nfld. 'Sunday Herald' in 1946 and built it into the paper with the largest circulation in the Prov. within four yrs.; founded TV Stn. CJON and watched it triple its size within a two yr. period, now the NTV TV network of Nfld., the number one network in the prov. reaching 96% of the pop., Canada's first 24 hr. full TV network service; estab. OZ-FM Radio Network across Nfld. (the only Coast to Coast Commercial Network in Nfld.) 1977; worked as Freelance Journalist; author of several books incl.: 'In Search of the New Age'; 'The New Awareness'; 'The Lost Continent of Atlantis'; Film Maker & Dir. 28 TV Films incl.: 'India, Land of Yogi'; 'Waiting for Fidel'; 'Search for Enoch'; during 2nd World War worked with Lend-Lease Bd. in Wash., D.C.; Past Pres., St. John's Jr. Chamber of Comm.; Nfld. Press Club; Anglican; recreations: spear-fishing, speedboat racing, water-skiing; Clubs: Bd. of Trade; City (St. John's) Murray Pond Club; Royal Nfld. Yacht Club; N.Y. Authors Club; Arizona Riding; Address: P.O. Box 2020, St. John's, Nfld. A1C 5S2.

**STIRLING, Rear Admiral Michael Grote,** C.D. (retired); b. Kelowna, B.C. 29 June 1915; s. Grote and Mabel Katherine (Brigstocke) S.; e. Shawnigan Lake Sch., B.C.; Royal Naval Coll., Greenwich, Eng.; m. Sheelagh Kathleen, d. late Francis Xavier Russell, 3 Aug. 1942; children: Peter, Gillian, Andrew; joined R.C.N. 1933; specialized in communications in Eng., 1941; in command H.M.C.S. St. Laurent 1944–45 and HMCS Crusader 1945–46; HMCS Nootka 1947; Dir. of Naval Communications, 1949–51; attached to HQ of Supreme Allied Commdr., Atlantic, Norfolk, Va. and promoted to Capt., 1953; apptd. Naval mem. of Directing Staff, Nat. Defence Coll., Kingston, 1958; promoted to Commodore 1959; apptd. Sr. Candn. Offr. Afloat (Atlantic) in HMCS Bonaventure, 1961; promoted to Rear Admiral and Chief of Naval Personnel, 1962; Flag Offr. Pacific Coast and Sr. Off. in Chief Command and Maritime Commdr. Pacific, 1964–66; Dir., Univ. of Victoria Foundation 1967–68; Agent Gen. for B.C. in U.K. & Europe

1968–75; Address: 302 - 1280 Newport Ave., Victoria, B.C. V8S 5E7.

**STIRLING, Rev. R. Laird,** B.A., M.Div.; b. Noranda, Que. 22 Aug. 1938; e. McMaster Univ., Hamilton; Pine Hill Divinity Hall, Halifax; ordained, United Church of Canada 1963; m. Carolyn Wilson; two d. and one s.; Min. of Municipal Affairs 1987–88; Min. of Consumer Affairs and Min. Responsible for Residential Tenancies Act and Rent Review Act 1979–80 and 1981–87; Min. of Social Services, Min. responsible for co-ordinating native affairs 1979–81; Min. of Consumer Affairs, N.S. (Chrmn., Social Development Policy Bd. 1981–84) and Min. in charge of Human Rights Act 1981–87; Min. of the Environment 1987; the first clergyman el. to the N.S. Legislature; M.L.A. for Dartmouth North prov. g.e. 1978, re-el. 1981 and 1984; parish minister 1963–77; hosp. chaplain 1977–78; Interim Min., St. James United 1989 and Min., Stairs Mem. U.C. 1989– (Dartmouth Parishes); started publishing in 1993 (Piper Press); Past Pres. Ministerial Assn. Dartmouth and Yarmouth; Past Chrmn. Bd. Dirs. Dartmouth Boys & Girls Club; Past Pres. Rotary Dartmouth; recipient of Founders pin, Credit Union; orgn. Scout Assn. in N. Sask.; Past Pres., Metro Boys and Girls Club; Del. to World Council of Churches, Poverty Conf. 1968, World Lay Cong. Germany, C.P.A., London, Eng. 1979, World Welfare Conf. Hong Kong 1980, World Rehabilitation Conf. 1980; mem., Candn. Environmental Task Force 1987; P.C.; United Church; Address: 96 Chappell St., Dartmouth, N.S. B3A 3P8.

**STOBBE, Victor J.,** C.A.; oil & gas executive; b. Matsqui, B.C. 3 Sept. 1941; e. C.A. 1965; m. Margaret 27 Dec. 1971; children: David, Colleen; PRES. & CHIEF EXECUTIVE OFFICER, MANNVILLE OIL & GAS LTD. 1989– ; Public accounting 1965–78; Vice-Pres., Finance, Page Petroleums Ltd. 1978; Pres., Blue Anchor Resources Ltd. 1979–80; Vice-Pres. & Dir., Charlton Securities Ltd. 1980–82; Vice-Pres., Finance & Admin., Mannville Oil & Gas Ltd. 1982–89; Mem., Inst. of C.A.s of Alberta; Candn. Tax Foundation; Financial Executives Inst.; Office: 2400, 421 - 1 St. S.W., Calgary, Alta. T2P 3L8.

**STOCK, Brian Charles,** A.B., Ph.D.; university professor; b. U.S.A. 8 June 1939; s. Edward Sydney and Ada S.; e. Harvard Univ. A.B. 1962; Univ. of Cambridge Ph.D. 1967; separated; one d.: Maxime; PROF. OF HISTORY AND COMPARATIVE LITERATURE, UNIV. OF TORONTO; Distinguished Professor of Medieval Studies, Univ. of Calif. at Berkeley 1990; Distinguished Senior Fellow in the Humanities, Dartmouth College 1991; Senior Killam Fellow 1973–74; author: 'The Implications of Literacy' 1983 (major historical study); Home: 3 Laurier Ave., Toronto, Ont. M4X 1S2; Office: Toronto, Ont. M5S 1A1.

**STOCKFORD, Howard Roger,** B.Sc., P.Eng.; mining executive; b. Cuckfield, Sussex, Eng. 6 Apl. 1941; s. the late Frank Howard and Margery Ena (Fuller) S.; e. Rustington Primary Sch. Sussex 1952; Worthing High Sch. 1959; Royal Sch. of Mines Imp. Coll. Univ. of London B.Sc. 1962; m. Jean McCormack 20 Oct. 1962; children: Sally, Roger (dec. 1987); EXEC. VICE PRES. AND DIR. AUR RESOURCES INC. 1989– ; Vice Pres. and Dir. Thunderwood Resources Inc.; Vice Pres. Techdel International; Dir. Consolidated Abitibi Resources Ltd.; Jr. Mine Geol. Barnat Mines Ltd. Malartic, Que. 1962–63; Mine Geol. and Chief Geol. Coniagas Mine Desmaraisville, Que. 1963–65; Geol. Canadian Bechtel Ltd. Montreal 1965–67; Project Geol. Consolidated Morrison Explorations Ltd. Moosonee and Toronto 1967–70; Sr. Geol. Man. Falconbridge Nickel Mines Ltd. The Pas, Man. 1970–74, Exploration Mgr. Winnipeg 1974–81; Chief Geol. Can. Falconbridge Ltd. Winnipeg 1981–83; Vice Pres. present Co. 1983–89; co-recipient Prospector of Yr. Award 1989 Prospectors & Devels. Assn. Can.; Candn. citizen since 1968; author: 'The James Bay Pyrochore Deposit' 1972; 'Calculation of Geological Reserves Contained in the Louvicourt Copper-Zine-Gold Deposti' 1993; co-author: 'The Maskwa West Nickel Deposit' 1979; various profl. papers; mem. Assn. Profl. Engs. Prov. Ont.; Candn. Inst. Mining & Metall. (Chrmn. Winnipeg Br. 1979; Chrmn. Toronto Br. 1994); Geol. Assn. Can.; Prospectors & Developers Assn. Can.; Soc. Econ. Geols. U.S.; Instn. Mining & Metall. UK; Bd. Trade Metrop. Toronto; recreations: golf, painting; Club: Albany; Home: 160 Frederick St., PH4, Toronto, Ont. M5A 4H9; Office: 2501, 1 Adelaide St. E., Toronto, Ont. M5C 2V9.

**STOCKS, Robert J.,** B.A., B.C.L.; advocate / partner; b. Sweetsburg, Que. 15 Feb. 1934; s. John E. and Dorothy H. (Hall-Shepard) S. e. Bishop Univ. B.A. 1954; McGill Univ. B.C.L. 1959; m. Eleanor Ann d. George and Sheila Barker 9 Sept. 1960; children: Andrew D., Christopher G.; PARTNER, FASKEN MARTINEAU 1978– and MARTINEAU WALKER; practice in fields of commercial corp. & admin. law; Dep. Dir., Compliance Br., Fgn. Investment Rev. Agency 1978–79; Dir., AGFA Canada Inc.; J.J. Barker Co. Ltd.; J.J. Barker Holdings Ltd.; J.J. Barker Inc. (U.S.A.); Quebec Packers (1980) Inc.; Milded Holdings Inc.; Que. Explorers Ltd.; Legalett Canada Inc.; Hultdins Inc.; Scandia Steel Ltd.; Noss Canada Inc.; 131498 Can. Inc., Nat. Telephone Corp.; Goldstar Can. Ltd.; Yamato Transp. (Can.) Inc.; Sunkyong Can. Inc.; BC Bearing Engineers Ltd.; Gov., Montreal Gen. Hosp.; Mem., Bar of Montreal; Candn. Bar Assn.; Am. Bar Assn.; recreations: jogging, squash, biking; clubs: University, Montreal Badminton & Squash, Whiff of Grape; Home: 3 Commanche Dr., Nepean, Ont. K2E 6E8; Office: The Stock Exchange Tower, Suite 3400, P.O. Box 242, Place Victoria, Montreal, Que. H4Z 1E9.

**STOICHEFF, Boris Peter,** O.C., B.A.Sc., M.A., Ph.D., D.Sc., F.R.S.; F.R.S.C.; university professor emeritus; b. Bitol, Yugoslavia 1 June 1924; s. Peter and Vasilka (Tonna) S.; came to Canada 1931; e. Public and High Schs., Toronto, Ont.; Univ. of Toronto, B.A.Sc., 1947, M.A., 1948, Ph.D., 1950; m. Lillian Joan, d. William G. Ambridge, 15 May 1954; one s. Richard Peter; UNIV. PROF. EMERITUS, UNIV. OF TORONTO 1990– ; Prof. of Physics 1964–89; Univ. Prof. 1977– , Chrmn., Engn. Science 1972–77; Postdoctorate Fellow, Department of Physics, University of Toronto, 1950–51; Div. of Pure Physics, Nat. Research Council, Ottawa, 1951–53, and Research Offr. there 1953–64; Visiting Research Scientist, Dept. of Physics, Mass. Inst. of Tech., 1963–64; Visiting Scholar, Dept. of Physics, Stanford Univ., 1977; apptd. to Nat. Research Council of Can. 1977–83; author of over 170 publ. papers in prof. journs.; mem. Candn. Assn. of Physicists (Vice-Pres. 1982; President 1983); Fellow, Optical Soc. of Am. (Pres.-elect 1975; President 1976); Am. Phys. Soc.; Hon. Fellow, Indian Acad. Sciences; Macedonian Academy of Science and Arts; Hon. Foreign Fellow, Am. Acad. of Arts and Sciences 1989; Gold Medal, Canadian Assn. Physicists 1974; William F. Meggers Medal, 1981 and Frederic Ives Medal 1983 of Optical Soc. of Am.; Henry Marshall Tory Medal of the Royal Soc. of Canada 1989; awarded I. W. Killam Mem. Scholarship 1977–79; Sr. Fellow Massey Coll. 1979– ; Geoffrey Frew Fellow of the Australian Acad. of Sci., 1980; Honorary D.Sc. Univ. of Skopje 1981, York Univ. 1982, Univ. of Windsor 1989 and Univ. of Toronto 1994; H.L. Welsh Lecturer 1984; Elizabeth Laird Lectr., Univ. of Western Ont. 1985; Rsch. Fellow, Japan Soc. for the Promotion of Science 1986; UK-Canada Rutherford Lecturer (of the Royal Socs. of London and Canada) 1989; apptd. to Counc., Assn. Prof. Engrs. Ont. 1986–91; Extve. Dir., Ont. Laser & Lightwave Rsch. Ctr. 1988–91; Vice-Pres., Internat. Union of Pure and Applied Physics (IUPAP) 1993– ; discovered generation of sound by light; the inverse Raman effect; prof. interest, lasers, atomic and molecular spectroscopy and structure; Rayleigh, Brillouin and Raman light scattering; stimulated scattering processes, two photon absorption and nonlinear optics; Home: 66 Collier St., Apt. 6B, Toronto, Ont. M4W 1L9.

**STOIK, John L.,** B.E. (Chem); petroleum executive; b. North Battleford, Sask. 5 March 1920; s. late Mike and Barbara (Hoffmann) S.; e. Univ. of Sask. B.E. (Chem. Eng.) 1947; m. Margaret Mary d. late William B. Marshall, New Westminster, B.C., 23 Aug. 1943; two s. John H., Gary L.; joined Gulf Canada Ltd. (then B-A Oil) Moose Jaw (Sask.) refinery 1947, Asst. Refinery Mgr.-Moose Jaw 1957 and Clarkson (Ont.) 1961, Mgr. Moose Jaw refinery 1962, Mgr.-Planning and Services H.O. Toronto 1964, Gen. Mgr.-Mfg. H.O. 1965, Vice Pres.-Refining H.O. 1968; Extve. Vice Pres. and C.E.O. Korea Oil Corp. Seoul 1970; Sr. Vice Pres. Gulf Canada Ltd. 1974; Pres., C.O.O. and Dir. 1976–79; Pres. and C.E.O. 1979–85; served with RCAF 1942–45; mem. Engn. Inst. Can.; United Church; recreations: golf, curling; Home: 1100 – 5850 Balsam St., Vancouver, B.C. V6M 4B9.

**STOJKO, Elvis;** athlete; MEMBER, CANADIAN FIGURE SKATING ASSOCIATION; Silver Medal, Men's Figure Skating, 1994 Olympics, Lillehammer, Norway; Gold Medal, World Championship 1994; black belt in karate; Office: c/o Canadian Figure Skating Association, 1600 James Naismith Dr., Gloucester, Ont. K1B 5N4.

**STOJSIC, Dobri J.,** B.Comm.; university professor; b. Montreal, Que. 28 June 1947; e. McGill Univ. B.Comm.; Northeastern Univ., extve. devel. prog.; m. Nancy Gold 13 May 1971; children: Leslie, Carly; EXTVE.-IN-RESIDENCE, UNIV. OF TORONTO 1990– ; Sr. Vice-Pres., Corporate & Development, Aetna Canada; Bank of Montreal 1973–87 ending as Sr. Vice-Pres., Consumer Mktg.; Extve. Vice-Pres., Northeast Savings (Hartford, CT) 1987; Financial Practic Dir. (Consulting), Tandem Internat. 1988–90; Mktg. Prof., M.B.A. and E.M.B.A. Prog., Univ. of Toronto; Inst. of Mkt. Driven Quantity, U. of T.; Children's Aid Soc. Found. (Mktg. Ctte.); Children's Wish Found. (Former Nat. Bd. Mem.); recreations: squash, fishing, tennis; club: Fitness Inst.; Home: 26 Highview Cres., Richmond Hill, Ont.; Office: 145 King St. W., Toronto, Ont. M5H 3T7.

**STOLARIK, M. Mark,** B.A., M.A., Ph.D.; university professor; b. St. Martin, Slovakia 22 April 1943; s. Imrich and Margita (Vavro) S.; e. Univ. of Ottawa B.A. (Hons.) 1965, M.A. 1967; Univ. of Minnesota Ph.D. 1974; m. Anne d. John and Helen Ivanco 15 June 1968; children: Andrej, Matthew; PROF. & CHAIRHOLDER, CHAIR IN SLOVAK HISTORY & CULTURE, UNIV. OF OTTAWA 1992– ; Asst. Prof. of History, Cleveland State Univ. 1972–76; Head, Slavic & E. Eur. Prog., Nat. Mus. of Man Ottawa 1977–78; Pres. & Chief Extve. Offr., Balch Inst. for Ethnic Studies 1978–81; Pennsylvania Adv. Ctte. to U.S. Comn. on Civil Rights 1985–91; Mem., Penn. Hist. Records Adv. Bd. 1982–91; Extve. Bd. Mem., Slovak League of Am. 1990–93; Pres., Candn. Slovak League 1994–96; John Weldy Wasco Post-doctoral Fellowship, Lehigh Univ. 1976; Canada Council Fellowships 1967–72; Roman Catholic; Mem., Candn. Slovak League; Nat. Slovak Soc.; First Catholic Slovak Union; author: 'Immigration and Urbanization' 1989, 'Growing up on the South Side' 1985 (history), 'The Slovak Americans' 1988 (popular history); editor: 'Forgotten Doors' 1988 (history); co-editor: 'Making It In America' 1986 (history); recreations: swimming, skating; clubs: Faculty; Home: 22 Bren-maur Rd., Nepean, Ont. K2J 3Z7; Office: c/o Dept. of History, Univ. of Ottawa, Ottawa, Ont. K1N 6N5.

**STOLLERY, Arthur W.,** B.Sc.; retired; b. Toronto, Ont.; s. Frank and Annie Laurie (Watson) S.; e. Queen's Univ. B.Sc. 1939; m. Helen d. Wesley Ashton Gordon 1942; children: Arthur Gordon, Laurie Ann; VICE CHAIR & DIR., MORRISON PETROLEUMS LTD.; var. underground mining projects until 1942; RCAF & RAF Long-Range Transport Command flying out of UK to India 1942–55; various positions 1946–48; consultant, mineral & exploration 1948; staked claims which later became Denison Uranium Mine 1953; through Consolidated Morrison acquired potash interests in Sask. 1960, sold to Noranda Mines; connected with Morrison Limited (now Morrison Petroleums Ltd.) since 1956; Chair, Angus Glen Farm Limited; 50 Year Hon. Mem., Candn. Inst. of Mining & Metallurgy; clubs: Rosedale Golf, Beacon Hall Golf, York Downs Golf & Country, Lost Tree, Albany; Office: 4495 Major Mackenzie Dr. E., Markham, Ont. L6C 1K4.

**STOLLERY, Peter A.;** b. Toronto, Ont. 29 Nov. 1935; s. Alan Laurie and Jean Munro (Russel) S.; e. Toronto; Retail Merchant, on and off, for 24 years, Frank Stollery Ltd. (Toronto); travelled extensively Europe, Africa, Asia, Australasia, the Americas 1956–65; Teacher, Lycee Laperinne, Sidi-Bel-Abbes, Algeria 1958–59; Correspondent, Maclean's Magazine (Algeria) 1962; Founding mem., Toronto Municipal Liberal Assn.; elected House of Commons 1972, 1974, 1979, 1980; Organizational Chrmn., Toronto Waterfront Park 1973–74; Chrmn., Govt. Caucus 1976–78; Observer, U.N. Conference on Trade and Development IV (Nairobi) 1976; Can. Delegate to XXXIII U.N. Gen. Assembly 1978; Delegate to 21st Meeting Canada-U.S. Interparliamentary Group, (San Diego) 1980; Can. Delegate 2nd Session, MF (AM) Broadcasting Conference, Region 2 (Rio de Janeiro) 1981; Parliamentary Secy. to Secy. of State/Min. Communications 1980; Apptd. to Senate of Canada by Prime Minister Trudeau 1981; Founder and First Chrmn., Canada-Latin America Parliamentary Assn.; led delegation to Peru 1986; mem. National Democratic Institute for Internat. Affairs delegation to Nicaragua 1986; mem., Nauman Foundation delegation to El Salvador 1987; mem., delegation to the Conference on Security and Corporation in Europe (Spain) 1991; mem., National Democratic Institute for Internat. Affairs delegation to Senegal 1990; mem., Special Joint Cttee. on a Renewed Canada 1991–92; represented Pierre Trudeau on Carter Centre, Council of Freely Elected Heads of Government as Observer, 1992 Guyana elections; Fellow, Royal Geographical Soc.; mem., National Liberal Club, London, Eng.; languages spoken: English, French, Spanish; recreations: flyfishing; Arctic canoeing; long-distance cycling; Home: 148 Rusholme Rd., Toronto, Ont. M6H 2Y7; Office: The Senate of Canada, Ottawa, Ont. K1A 0A4.

**STOLLERY, Robert;** executive; b. Edmonton, Alta. 1 May 1924; s. William Charles and Kate Elizabeth

(Catlin) S.; e. Strathcona High Sch., Edmonton, 1941; Univ. of Alta., Bachelor of Civil Engn. 1949; m. Shirley Jean, d. late William Ernest Hopper, 11 June 1948; children: Carol Wendy, Janet Susan, Douglas Robert; DIRECTOR, PCL CONSTRUCTION GROUP INC. since 1979; Dir., Toronto-Dominion Bank; TransCanada PipeLines; Federal Industries Ltd.; Chrmn., Bus. Adv. Counc. and Dir., Bd. of Trustees, Univ. of Alta.; Sr. Mem., Conference Bd. of Can.; Chrmn., Edmonton Community Foundation; joined present Co. as Engr. 1949–53; Asst. Gen. Supt. 1953–57; Gen. Supt. 1957–60; Mgr., Edmonton, 1960–62; Vice-Pres. and Gen. Mgr. 1962–69; Pres. and C.E.O. 1969–1979; served with RCNVR 1942–45; rec'd hon. LL.D., Univ. of Alta 1985; Hon. LL.D., Concordia Univ., Montreal 1986; mem., Assn. Prof. Engrs. Alta.; Engn. Inst. Can.; United Church; recreations: golf, fishing, hunting; Home: 99 Westbrook Dr., Edmonton, Alta. T6J 2C8; Office: 5410–99 St., Edmonton, Alta. T6E 3P4.

**STONE, Hon. Mr. Justice Arthur J.,** B.A., LL.B., LL.M., Q.C.; judge; b. St. Peters, N.S. 1929; s. George and Charlotte Stone; e. St. Francis Xavier Univ., Antigonish, N.S. B.A. 1952; Dalhousie Law Sch. LL.B. 1955; Harvard Law Sch. LL.M. 1956; m. Anna M. 1956; JUSTICE OF APPEAL, FEDERAL COURT OF APPEAL 1983– ; read law with Stewart, Smith, McKeen, Halifax 1955 and 1956 and with Wright and McTaggart, Toronto 1957–58; called to Bar of N.S. 1956, Ont. 1958; Lawyer Wright and McTaggart and successor firms 1957–83; Lectr. Fac. of Law, Univ. of Toronto 1971–76; author several articles on Candn. jurisprudence; cr. Q.C. 1971; mem. N.S. Barristers' Soc.; Law Soc. of Upper Can.; N.B. Barristers' Soc. (occ. app.); Law Soc. of B.C. (occ. app.); Nat. Exec. Ctte., Candn. Bar Assn. 1971–73; Gov. Candn. Tax Found. 1977–79; Pres.: Toronto Marine Club 1977–78; Candn. Maritime Law Assn. 1978–81; Harvard Law Sch. Assn. of Ont.; Candn. Chrmn. Harvard Law Sch. Fund; Office: Supreme Court of Canada Bldg., Ottawa, Ont. K1A 0H9.

**STONE, J. Bruce,** B.S.A., M.S.A., Ph.D.; university professor; b. Forfar, Ont. 23 Sept. 1930; s. Talmage H. and Elva R. (De Wolfe) St.; e. Athens H.S. 1948; Ont. Agric. Coll., B.S.A. 1953, M.S.A. 1954; Cornell Univ., Ph.D. 1959; m. Nora d. Reginald and Constance Bowles 2 Oct. 1954; children: J. Douglas, Wendy A., Jeffrey M., J. Paul; ASSOC. DEAN, ONT. AGRIC. COLL., UNIV. OF GUELPH 1983– ; Asst. Prof., Ont. Agric. Coll. 1954–62; Asst. Prof., Cornell Univ. 1962–66; Assoc. Prof., Univ. of Guelph 1966; Prof. 1966– ; Mem., Bd. of Gov., Univ. of Guelph 1984–87; Cornell Univ. Counc. 1986–1990; Trustee, Harcourt Un. Ch.; Mem., Sigma Xi, Agric. Inst. of Can.; Ont. Inst. of Agro.; Am. Dairy Sci. Assn.; recreations: the visual arts; Home: 11 Mayfield Ave., Guelph, Ont. N1G 2L9; Office: University of Guelph, Guelph, Ont. N1G 2W1.

**STONE, Robert Ryrie,** B.Sc., C.A.; financial executive; b. Toronto, Ont. 25 March 1943; s. Frank Reid and Norah Isobel (Varey) S.; e. Univ. of Toronto B.Sc. 1964; m. Jacqueline d. Jerry and Genevieve Cogan 8 July 1966; children: Charles R., Tracy; VICE PRESIDENT FINANCE & CHIEF FINANCIAL OFFICER, COMINCO LTD. 1980– ; C.A., Clarkson Gordon & Co. 1967–69; Treas. & Dir. Finance, Great Northern Capital Corp. 1969–73; joined Cominco Ltd. 1973; Treas. 1978; Dir., Cominco Ltd.; Cominco Fertilizers Ltd.; Global Stone Corp.; Union Bank of Switzerland (Canada); Dir., Jr. Achievement of B.C. and Canada; Sunny Hill Hosp. for Children Found.; Mem., Financial Extves. Inst.; Inst. of C.A.s of B.C. & Ont.; recreations: tennis, skiing, golf, music; clubs: Vancouver Golf, Terminal City, Hollyburn Country; Home: 2319 Bellevue Ave., West Vancouver, B.C. V7V 1C9; Office: 200 Burrard St., Ste. 500, Vancouver, B.C. V6C 3L7.

**STONE, Ted,** B.Sc.; writer; b. Fawn River, Mich. 6 Aug. 1947; s. Edwin Tracy and Shirley Roberta (Blucker) S.; e. Central Michigan Univ., B.Sc. (cum laude) 1969; m. Patricia d. William and Hilda Pidlaski 3 Aug. 1981; children: Katherine Laura, Karen Suzanne, Heather Ann; author: 'Hailstorms and Hoop Snakes' 1984, 'It's Hardly Worth Talkin' If You're Goin' To Tell the Truth' 1986; '13 Canadian Ghost Stories' (editor) 1988; 'The Ghost of Peppermint Flats and Other Stories' 1989; 'The One That Got Away' 1990; 'Riding The Northern Range' (editor) 1993; stories & articles widely circulated in mags. & newspapers in Can. & U.S.; author of nationally syndicated newspaper column of humour & opinion: 'Ted Stone'; storyteller, performing for schools, libraries, festivals, var. community groups for children & adults, radio & TV progs. across country; occasional teacher, creative writing; Address: R.R. 1, C-50 Demetri Rd., Fulford Harbour, B.C. V0S 1C0.

**STONE-BLACKBURN, Susan Beth (Cole),** B.A., M.A., Ph.D.; Professor of English; b. U.S.A. 6 Oct. 1941; d. Lydon Briggs and Belva Alice (Stratton) Cole; e. Lawrence College (now Univ.) B.A. 1963; Univ. of Colorado M.A. 1967, Ph.D. 1970; 1st m. Michael G. Stone 1963; divorce 1976; 2nd m.: William G. Blackburn 1977; divorced 1983; children: Blake William Stone, Alan Paul and Lynn Elizabeth Blackburn; PROFESSOR OF ENGLISH, UNIV. OF CALGARY 1986– ; Asst. Prof., Univ. of Calgary 1973; Assoc. Prof. 1979; Assoc. Dean of Humanities 1985–89; Advisor to the President on Women's Issues 1989–91; Assoc. Dean of Graduate Studies 1993– ; Pres., Bd. of Dir., Maenad Theatre Productions 1991–93; Mem., Science Fiction Rsch. Assn.; Assn. for Canadian Theatre Research; Assn. of Candn. College & University Teachers of English; author: 'Robertson Davies, Playwright: A Search for the Self on the Canadian Stage' 1985; Home: 3323 Constable Pl. N.W., Calgary, Alta. T2L 0K9; Office: Calgary, Alta. T2N 1N4.

**STONECHILD, Alexander Blair,** B.A., M.A.; university professor and administrator; b. Fort Qu'Appelle, Sask. 9 Oct. 1950; s. Edward and Lucille (Poitras) S.; e. McGill Univ. B.A. 1974; Univ. of Regina M.A. 1988; m. Sylvia d. John and Betty Chaberek 23 June 1984; children: Michael, Rachel, Gabrielle; EXECUTIVE DIRECTOR OF PLANNING AND DEVELOPMENT, SASK. INDIAN FEDERATED COLLEGE, UNIV. OF REGINA 1993– ; Lectr. & Developer of Indian Studies, Sask. Indian Fed. College 1976–82; Head, Dept. of Indian Studies 1982–89; Dean of Academics 1989–93; Trustee, Candn. Museum of Civilization; Dir., Social Science Fed. of Canada; Past Pres., Candn. Indian/Native Studies Assn. 1982–87; Consultant to Indian orgns. on history, land claims & econ. devel.; Mem., Canadian Historical Assn.; Muscowpetung Band in southern Sask. (Cree); Contribution to Institutional Mission Award, Am. Indian Higher Edn. Consortium 1986; author: 'Saskatchewan Indians and the Resistance of 1885: Two Case Studies' 1986; Office: Regina, Sask. S4S 0A2.

**STONEMAN, John,** B.Sc., M.Sc., C.S.C.; film producer; cinematographer; b. Colchester, Eng. 12 Dec. 1939; s. John Brown and Rose (Hagar) S.; e. Frays Coll., Sebright Sch. Wolverhampton; South Western Univ. M.Sc. 1984; m. Sarah Libman 18 May 1974; children: Deborah Louise, Michael John; PRESIDENT AND EXEC. PRODUCER, MAKO FILMS LTD. 1972– ; Jr. Asst. Dir. Pinewood Studios Eng. 1957 becoming Producer, Dir., Writer, Cinematographer; specialist in underwater film particularly shark behaviour; producer over 180 films primarly for network and pub. TV, also Imax Film 'Nomads of the Deep' and 100 episodes of series 'The Last Frontier'; 'The Ocean World of John Stoneman' (TV series); Dir. Found. for Ocean Rsch. (John Stoneman Award estbd. 1974); recipient over 100 internat. film awards; numerous awards for conserv. marine environment; mem. Royal Candn. Inst.; Candn. Soc. Underwater Photogs.; Candn. Film & TV Assn.; Candn. Soc. Underwater Sci's; Candn. Soc. of Cinematog.; Candn. Racing Drivers Assn.; Home: 127 Confederation Way, Thornhill, Ont. L3T 5R8; Office: 70 East Beaver Creek Rd., Unit 19, Richmond Hill, Ont. L4B 3B2.

**STONER, (Oliver) Gerald,** B.A., LL.D.; public servant; b. London, Ont. 21 Aug. 1922; s. Oliver Christian and Ethel Stoner; e. Wortley Rd. Pub. Sch., London; London, (Ont.) S. Coll., 1933–38; Univ. of W. Ont., 1938–41; Queen's Univ., B.A. (Econ.) 1947; LL.D. (Hon), Univ. of W. Ont. 1980; m. Elizabeth Mary, d. W. G. Allen, Toronto, 1 Sept. 1951; one d.: Elizabeth Robyn; Chrmn., Restrictive Trade Practices Comn. 1979–91; former Deputy Min., Dept. Of Industry, Trade & Commerce 1975–77; joined Department of External Affairs 1947; 2nd Secretary, Paris, 1950–54; Dept. of External Affairs, 1954–56 (Responsible for Colombo plan and External Aid); Counsellor, Brussels, 1956 and Chargé d'Affaires, 1958–59; also 1st rep. of Can. to European Econ. Community; in charge of Econ. Affairs, External Affairs, Ottawa, 1959–64; Sr. Asst. Secy. of Cabinet and Asst. Clk. of Privy Council, 1964–67; Deputy Clerk of the P.C. and Deputy Secretary to the Cabinet, 1967–69; Acting Secretary to the Cabinet and Acting Clerk of the P.C. 1967–68; Depy. Minister of Transport 1969–75; Vice-Chrmn., Export Devel. Corp. 1975–77; Vice-Chrmn., Bd. of Dirs., DeHavilland Aircraft 1975–77; mem., Bd. of Dirs., Candn. Devel. Corp. 1975–77; Commissioner, Fed. Royal Comm. on Financial Management and Accountability (Lambert Comm.) 1977–79; served with the Canadian Armoured Corps, 1941–45; N.W. Europe, 1944–45; discharged with rank A/Maj.; Mentioned in Despatches; Protestant; recreations: tennis, reading, amateur hockey; Club: Rockliffe

Tennis; Home: 161 Maple Lane, Rockcliffe Pk., Ottawa, Ont. K1M 1G4.

**STOOKE, Philip John,** B.Sc., Ph.D.; university professor; b. Salisbury, U.K. 15 March 1952; s. Walter Kingsley and Hazel Mary (Shaw) S.; e. Bishop Wordsworth's Sch. 1970; Univ. of Victoria B.Sc. (Hons.) 1985, Ph.D. 1988; m. Rosamund d. Earl and Maude Ells 18 Aug. 1973; children: Anna Mai, Malcolm James; ASSOC. PROF., DEPT. OF GEOG., UNIV. OF WESTERN ONT. 1994– ; Asst. Prof. 1988–94; principle rsch.: cartography of irregularly-shaped worlds, history of lunar and planetary cartography, geology of planets and satellites; Gildea Scholarship Award, Nat. Counc. for Geog. Edn. 1983; Nat. Geog. Soc. Award in Cartography 1984; Mem., Royal Astron. Soc. of Can. (Vice-Pres., Victoria Section 1985–87); Candn. Cartographic Assn.; Planetary Soc.; Am. Geophysical Union; author: 'Landmarks and Legends of the North Island' 1978, 1979; numerous articles on planetary mapping and geology; inventor: morphographic map projections for non-spherical worlds; discoverer: neolithic lunar maps at Knowth, Ireland; recreations: hiking, map collecting; Home: 56 Forward Ave., London, Ont. N6H 1B7; Office: London, Ont. N6A 5C2.

**STOREY, Gary Garfield,** B.S.A., M.Sc., M.A., Ph.D., F.A.I.C.; university professor; b. Davidson, Sask. 9 March 1939; s. Robert Lincoln and Burna Rose (Townsend) S.; e. Univ. of Sask., B.S.A. 1963, M.Sc. 1966; Univ. of Wisconsin, M.A. 1968, Ph.D. 1970; m. Joelle d. John and Hilda Herbert 7 Aug. 1965; children: Kristin Jennifer, Lauren Caroline; ASST. DEAN OF AGRICULTURE 1992– and PROF., DEPT. OF AGRIC. ECON., UNIV. OF SASK. 1977– ; Rsch. Econ., Govt. of Sask. 1964–66; Asst. Prof., Univ. of Sask. 1970–72; operates 640–acre grain farm; Dir., IPSCO 1982–85; Dir, Agric. Credit Corp. of Sask. 1982–87; Bd. of Elders, Un. Ch.; Mem., Candn. Agric. Econ. & Farm Mngt. Soc. (Pres. 1977–78); Agric. Inst. of Can. (Nat. Counc. 1980–82); Assoc. of Faculties of Agric. in Canada (Pres. 1986–87); co-editor: 'International Agricultural Trade, Advanced Readings in Price Formation, Market Structure, and Price Instability' 1984; co-editor & author, 'The Political Economy of Agricultural Trade and Policy: Toward a New Order for Europe and North America' 1990; Fellow, Agricultural Institute of Canada 1991; recreations: canoeing, jogging, golf, skiing, music, painting; Home: 118 Mount Allison Cres., Saskatoon, Sask.; Office: Saskatoon, Sask. S7N 0W6.

**STOREY, Kenneth B.,** Ph.D., FRSC; university professor; b. Taber, Alta. 23 Oct. 1949; s. Arthur George and Madeline (Mawhinney) S.; e. Univ. of Calgary, B.Sc. (Hons.) 1971; Univ. of B.C. Ph.D. 1974; m. Janet d. Betty and Bill Collicutt 6 June 1975; children: Jennifer, Kathryn; PROF., DEPT. OF BIOL. AND CHEM., CARLETON UNIV. 1979; Asst. Prof., Duke Univ. 1975–79; Assoc. Prof., Carleton Univ. 1979–84; Fellow, Royal Soc. of Can.; Mem., Am. Soc. of Biol. Chem.; Soc. for CryoBiol.; Candn. Biochemical Soc.; Candn. Soc. of Zool.; The Explorers Club of N.Y.; Ed. Bd., 'Biochem. Cell. Biol.,' 'CryoLetters;' American J. Physiology; Environmental Reviews; E.W.R. Steacie Mem. Fellowship, NSERC; Ayerst Award, Can. Biochem. Soc.; Killam Senior Fellowship; author of over 300 jour. articles, review articles & book chaps. 1974– ; Home: 21 Seymour Ave., Nepean, Ont. K2E 6P4; Office: Ottawa, Ont. K1S 5B6.

**STORIE, Earl,** B.Comm., C.A.; investment manager; accountant; b. Vancouver, B.C. 21 March 1941; s. James Keith and Janet S.; m. Pamela d. John Hewsick 23 Sept. 1967; children: Bryce, Stephanie; MANAGING PARTNER, VENGROWTH CAPITAL FUNDS 1982– ; Dir. several venture-capital-backed cos. incl.: Aztec Resources Ltd.; Tri Link Resources Ltd.; Daltons Inc.; TD Capital Group 1973–79, Pres. 1979–82; Investment Mgr. RoyNat Ltd. 1969–73; C.A. Deloitte, Haskins & Sells 1966–69; mem. Candn. Inst. of Chartered Accts.; Assn. of Candn. Venture Capital Cos. (Pres. 1983–85); recreations: wood working, golf, reading, squash, tennis, skiing; Office: Suite 200, 145 Wellington St. W., Toronto, Ont. M5J 1H8.

**STORIE, The Hon. Jerry Thomas,** B.A., M.A.; sociologist; politician; b. Winnipeg, Man. 23 Mar. 1950; s. Clifford Earl and Iris Eliose (Young) S.; e. Brandon Univ., B.A. 1972; Univ. of Man., M.A. 1975, cert. of edn. 1975; m. Betty d. Murray and Irene Embury 12 Sept. 1970; children: Lindsay, Benjiman; M.L.A., FLIN FLON, PROV. OF MAN. 1988– ; Policy Analyst, Dept. of Edn. 1973–74; Teacher/Guid. Counc., Flin Flon Sch. Div. 1975–81; MLA, Flin Flon 1981– ; Min., Housing 1982–83; North. Affairs 1983–85; Bus. Devel. & Tourism 1985–86; Education 1986–87; Min. of Energy &

Mines 1987–88; Dep. Speaker 1982; past positions incl. Dep. Speaker 1982; Chrmn., Indus. Relns. Standing Ctte.; Treasury Bd. Mem.; Fellowship, Univ. of Man. 1973; Office: 123 Legis. Bldg., Winnipeg, Man. R3C 0V8.

**STORY, George Morley,** C.M., D.Phil., F.R.H.S., F.S.A., F.R.S.C.; educator; author; b. St. John's, Nfld. 13 Oct. 1927; s. George Errington and Dorothy Katharine (White) S.; e. Bishop Feild Coll. St. John's 1946; Mem. Univ. Coll. St. John's 1948; McGill Univ. B.A. 1950; Oriel Coll. Oxford Univ. (Rhodes Scholar) D.Phil. 1954; m. Laura Alice d. J. Ross Stevenson, Pickering, Ont. 16 May 1968; children: Katharine Alice, Lachlan Stevenson, Simon Jonathan; HENRIETTA HARVEY PROF. OF ENG., MEMORIAL UNIV. OF NFLD. 1979– ; Mem. Univ. Lectr. 1950–51, Asst. Prof. 1954, Assoc. Prof. 1959, Prof. 1962– , Secy. of Senate 1965–69, Chrmn. Ed. Adv. Bd. 1979–92, Public Orator 1960– ; Dir. and Chrmn. Bd., J.R. Smallwood Inst. of Nfld. Studies 1988– ; Chrmn. Ed. Adv. Bd. 'Encyclopedia of Nfld. and Labrador' 1989– ; Chrmn. Prov. Nfld. Task Force on Community Devel. 1972–74; Co-Chrmn. Comte. Fed. Regulations Relating to Seafisheries Nfld. 1973–74; Chrmn. Nfld. and Labrador Arts Council 1980–82; Ed. Bd., 'Collected Works of Erasmus' 1974– ; Chrmn., Ed. Bd., 'Nfld Studies' 1984–92; Adv. Bd. 'Acadiensis' 1984– ; Ed. Bd. 'New Oxford English Dictionary' 1984– ; Adv. Bd. 'Australian National Dictionary Centre' 1989– ; Bd. Dir. Candn. Inst. for Historical Microreproductions 1985–88; Adv. Bd. National Library of Can. 1986–90; Hist. Sites & Monuments Bd. of Can. 1993– ; Chrmn., Nfld. Heritage Found. 1993– ; mem. Counc. Academy II Royal Soc. Can. 1986–88; W.S. McNutt Lecturer, Univ. of New Brunswick 1985–86; rec'd Molson Prize (Can. Council) 1977; author 'Sonnets of William Alabaster' 1959 (with Helen Gardner); 'Study of English' 1960 (with E. R. Seary); 'Sermons of Lancelot Andrewes' 1967; 'Avalon Peninsula of Newfoundland' 1968 (with E. R. Seary, W. Kirwin); 'Christmas Mumming in Newfoundland' 1969, 3rd ed. revised 1990 (with H. Halpert); 'Dictionary of Newfoundland English' 1982, 2nd ed. with supplement 1990 (with W. Kirwin, J. D. A. Widdowson); 'Selected University Orations' 1984; editor 'Early European Settlement and Exploitation in Atlantic Canada: Selected Papers' 1982; co-editor 'A Festschrift for Edgar Ronald Seary' 1976; numerous papers and essays Tudor lit., Erasmus & Renaissance humanism, bibliog. & Textual criticism, Nfld. hist., lang. & lit.; mem. Bibliog. Soc. London; Champlain Soc.; Nfld. Hist. Trust (Pres. 1969–71); Nfld. Hist. Soc. (Pres. 1978–81); United Church; recreations: hunting, fishing, gardening, old books; Home: 335 Southside Rd., St. John's, Nfld. A1E 1A1; Office: St. John's, Nfld. A1C 5S7.

**STORY, Gertrude Elizabeth;** writer; b. Farm, E. of Saskatoon, Sask. 29 Sept. 1929; d. Rheinhold and Matilda (Jabusch) Wudrick; e. Sask. rural & town schs.; Univ. of Sask., B.A. 1981; m. Joseph LeRoy, s. Joseph and Gladys S. 3 July 1950; children: Ellen Louise, Joseph James; bank clerk, waitress, village sec.-treas., writer, protégé director, workshop conductor, storyteller, not a librarian (as she wanted to be), a shy & retiring person pretending to be an outgoing extrovert; 1st Resident Artist/Animateur, Prince Albert 1984–85; Mem., Bd. of Dir., Sask. Hist. & Folklore Soc.; Sask. Counc. of Cultural Orgns.; Sask. Sch. of Performing Arts; Pres. Medal & Arts Prize, Univ. of Sask. 1981; several Sask. Writer's Guild Literary Awards; CBC Nat. Radio Literary Award for Short Fiction 1980; Candn. Author & Bookman Okanagan Award 1981; etc.; author: 'The Book of Thirteen' 1981, 'The Way to Always Dance' 1983, 'It Never Pays to Laugh Too Much' 1984, The Need of Wanting Always' 1985, 'Black Swan' 1986; 'Rowena, Rowena, Rowena' 1986; anthologies: 'Saskatchewan Gold' 1983, 'More Saskatchewan Gold' 1984, 'Double Bond' 1984, '83: Best Canadian Stories' 1983, '100% Cracked Wheat' 1982; '86: Best Canadian Stories' 1986; author of many short stories pub. in periodicals; extensive radio broadcaster; recreations: meeting Canadians with bright, young, creative minds; cross country skiing; square dancing; walking; hiking; Clubs: not a joiner.

**STOTHERS, John Bailie,** M.Sc., Ph.D., F.C.I.C., F.R.S.C.; educator; b. London, Ont. 16 Apr. 1931; s. John Cannon and Florence Louise (Sleigh) S.; e. Univ. of W. Ont. B.Sc. 1953, M.Sc. 1954; McMaster Univ. Ph.D. 1957; m. Catherine d. Charles and Mabel Smith 6 June 1953; two d. Marta Louise, Margot Elizabeth; PROF. OF CHEM., UNIV. OF W. ONT. 1967– , Chrmn. of Chem. 1976–86; joined Imperial Oil Ltd. 1957–59; Lectr. present Univ. 1959, Asst. Prof. 1961, Assoc. Prof. 1964; recipient Merck, Sharpe & Dohme Lecture Award 1971; Fellow, Royal Society of Canada 1976; author over 200 rsch. papers; ed. 'Canadian Journal of Chemistry'; recreation: golf; Club: Sunningdale Country; Home: 45 Mayfair Dr., London, Ont. N6A 2M7; Office: London, Ont.

**STOTT, Michael Allan,** Ph.D., P.Eng.; aerospace executive; b. Southport, England 15 Feb. 1942; s. Frank Royden and Myra (Speight) S.; e. King George V Sch. 1960; Oxford Univ., B.A. 1963, M.A. 1966; Liverpool Univ., Ph.D. 1966; divorced; children: Claire, Alastair, Michael; CO-FOUNDER & SENIOR VICE PRES., CAL CORPORATION (formerly Candn. Astronautics Ltd.) 1974– ; Vice Pres., Electromagnetic Sciences Inc., Atlanta GA; Chrmn., CAL Systems Ltd. (UK); Trak-Sat Communications Ltd. (UK); CAL Systems Corp. (USA); Rsch. & Devel., Elect. Counc., U.K. 1966–69; Power Systems Engr., Candn. Dept. of Communications 1969–70; various mgr. pos., Telesat Canada 1970–73; Cons., Satellite Systems 1973–74; Co-Recipient, Ont. C. of C. Outstanding Bus. Achievement Award 1985; Mem., Assn. of Profl. Engr. of Ont.; Assn. of Old Crows (Extve. Dir., Col. By Chapter); co-author: 'Teach Yourself Acoustics' 1965; author and co-author of numerous sci. & tech. papers; holder of five patents; recreations: sailing, amateur radio, cross country skiing, music; Home: 15 Nesbitt St., Nepean, Ont. K2H 8C4; Office: 1050 Morrison Dr., Ottawa, Ont. K2H 8K7.

**STOUCK, David Hamilton,** B.A., M.A.; university professor; b. Beamsville, Ont. 28 Oct. 1940; s. John William Henry and Winnifred (Hamilton) S.; e. Beamsville Dist. S.S. 1959; McMaster Univ. B.A. 1963; Univ. of Toronto M.A. 1964; m. Mary-Ann d. George and Kathleen Quick 22 Aug. 1964; children: Jordan Wardell, John Hamilton; PROF., DEPT. OF ENGLISH, SIMON FRASER UNIV. 1983– ; Instr., Simon Fraser Univ. 1966–70; Asst. Prof. 1970–72; Assoc. Prof. 1972–83; Assoc. Chair, Dept. of English 1988–90; author: 'Willa Cather's Imagination' 1975, 'Major Canadian Authors' 1984, 1988, 'The Wardells and Vosburghs: Records of a Loyalist Family' 1986; editor: 'Ethel Wilson: Stories, Essays, and Letters' 1987; 'Sinclair Ross's "As For Me and My House": Five Decades of Criticism' 1991; Home: 354 Moyne Dr., W. Vancouver, B.C. V7S 1J5; Office: Burnaby, B.C. V5A 1S6.

**STOUGHTON, W. Vickery,** B.S., M.B.A.; hospital executive; b. Peoria, Ill. 1 March 1946; s. Warner Vickery and Mary Olive (McNamara) S.; e. St. Louis Univ. B.S. 1968; Univ. of Chicago M.B.A. 1973; m. Christine d. Benjamin and Rosemary Kreder 9 Aug. 1969; children: Zachary Benjamin, Samantha Elizabeth; PRES., SMITH KLINE BEECHAM CLINICAL LABS 1992– ; Dir., Sun Life of Canada 1988– ; Capt. U.S. Army Med. Service Corps 1970–72; Asst. Dir.: Boston Hosp. for Women 1974–76; Peter Bent Brigham Hosp. 1976–78, Dir. 1978–81; Asst. Prof., Univ. of Toronto 1981–91, Assoc. Prof. 1991– ; Chief Extve. Offr., Duke Univ. Hosp. and Vice Chancellor Health, Duke Univ. 1991–92; Pres., Toronto Gen. Hosp. 1981–86; Pres., Toronto Hosp. 1986–91; Lectr. Harvard Univ. 1978–81; mem. Bd. Toronto Symphony 1983–86; mem. Bd. Toronto United Way 1988–91; author or co-author various publs.; mem Ont. Hosp. Assn. (Bd. 1982–86); Am. Coll.; Soc. Health Service Execs.; recreations: tennis, music, reading; Clubs: Cosmos; York; Home: 7 Harford Ln., Radnor, PA 19087; Office: 620 Freedom Business Center, King of Prussia, PA.

**STOUT, Lawrence Thomas (Larry),** B.A.; journalist; b. Hamilton, Ont. 11 Sept. 1939; s. Thomas Michael and Reta (Gallagher) S.; e. Cath. High Sch. Hamilton; Assumption Univ. of Windsor B.A. 1960; m. Sheila d. John Allison and Evelyn Shotton 25 June 1987; three s. Michael, John, David; CTV NATIONAL NEWS SR. WRITER & ANCHOR; Newscaster: CKOC Radio Hamilton, Ont. 1960–61; CKEY Radio Toronto 1961–63; Reporter: Toronto Star 1963–64; CBC Nat. News, News Mag., News Specials 1964–87; Toronto Bureau Chief CTV News 1989; Partner, Fraser Kelly Corpworld; recreations: golf, reading; Clubs: Empire (Dir. 1987– ); Toronto Hunt; Toronto Press (Dir. 1986–90); Home: 159 Rosedale Hts. Dr., Toronto, Ont. M4T 1C7; Office: 42 Charles St. E., Toronto, Ont. M4Y 1T5.

**STOWE, David Howard Ross,** B.Comm.; marketing executive; b. Toronto, Ont. 16 Dec. 1932; e. Upper Can. Coll. 1953; Univ. of B.C., B.Comm. 1958; m. Mary-Anne d. William and Olive Johnstone 18 May 1957; children: Lesley Diane, Mary-Anne Emily, Craig Howard Ross; CORP. VICE-PRES., TRADE RELATIONS, SCOTT PAPER LTD. 1993– ; Sales Dept., Scott Paper Ltd. 1958; Dist. Mgr., East. Ont. 1960; Toronto Dist. Mgr., then Ont. Div. Mgr. and subsequently East. Can. Reg. Sales Mgr. 1966; Nat. Sales Mgr., then Vice-Pres., Consumer Sales 1972; Vice-Pres., Mktg. 1983; Corp. Vice-Pres., Mktg. 1986; Dir., Viceroy Resource Corp.; Channel Resources; PanAtlas Energy Inc.; great grandson of Dr. Emily Stowe, first woman to prac. med. in Can. (commemorative stamp); recreations: skiing, golf; Clubs: Vancouver Lawn Tennis; Shaughnessy Golf & Country; Home: 3607 Point Grey Rd., Vancouver, B.C. V6R 1B1; Office: P.O. Box 3600, Vancouver, B.C. V6B 3Y7.

**STRACHAN, Graham,** B.Sc.; pharmaceutical executive; b. Dundee, Scot. 12 Sept. 1938; s. Roualyn and Helen S.; e. Univ. of Glasgow B.Sc. 1961; PRES. AND CHIEF EXEC. OFFR. ALLELIX BIOPHARMACEUTICALS INC. 1988– ; Licencing Exec. Schering Eur. 1963–68; Vice Pres. Bus. Devel. John Labatt Ltd. 1968–82; Vice Pres. Comm. Devel. Allelix Inc. 1982–88; Fellow, Patent & Trademark Inst. Can.; Biotechnology Industry Organization, Washington, DC; Chrmn., Ind. Biotech. Assn. Can.; Chrmn., Nat. Biotechnol. Adv. Ctte.; Home: 118 West Deane Park Dr., Islington, Ont. M9B 2S3; Office: 6850 Goreway Dr., Mississauga, Ont. L4V 1V7.

**STRADWICK, John Conway,** B.A.; insurance executive; b. Hamilton, Ont. 20 May 1930; s. John Charles and Aileen (McIlwain) S.; e. Westdale Collegiate 1949; Cornell Univ. B.A. 1953; m. Janette; children: Pamela, John, Elizabeth, Cynthia, Katherine; CHRMN. & C.E.O., SIMCOE ERIE INVESTORS LTD. 1990– ; Pres., Simcoe & Erie General Insurance Co.; Gan Canada Insurance Co.; Chief Agent for Canada, New Rotterdam Insurance Co.; Dir., Stradwicks Ltd. 1954, Pres. 1960–65; Pres., Simcoe Erie Investors Ltd. 1971–90; Dir., Assoc. of Candn. Insurers; mem. Lloyds of London; Flying Offr., R.C.A.F.; mem. Phi Delta Theta; recreations: golf, skiing; Clubs: Hamilton Golf & Country; The Hamilton; The National; The Metropolitan; The Canadian; The Midocean; Home: 322 Lloyminn Ave., Ancaster, Ont. L9G 3X4; Office: 649 North Service Rd. W., Burlington, Ont. L7R 4L5.

**STRAIN, Edward Macdonald,** B.A.Sc.; electronics executive; b. Toronto, Ont. 18 Dec. 1935; s. David Edrich and Myrtle Winnifred (Hart) S.; e. Univ. of Toronto, B.Sc. (engr. physics) 1957; m. Janice Scott d. John Fraser and Isabel (Nimmo) McEwan 31 Aug. 1957; children: Robert David, Valerie Ellen, Thomas Edward, Marilyn Scott; PRES., VISION 2000 INC. 1991– ; Lt., Royal Candn. Corps. of Signals, Calgary Flight Training Rivers Man 1957–60; Design Engr. & Devel. Supvr., Ferranti Electronics Computer Div. 1960–65; Chief Engr., ESE Limited 1965–76; Pres., Motorola Information Systems (formerly ESE Limited) 1976–90; Chrmn., Motorola Canada Ltd. 1983–90; Mem., AFCEA Counc. of Advisers; Trio Bd. of Dir.; ITRC Bd. of Dirs.; recreations: sailing; Home: R.R. #1, Caledon East, Ont. L0N 1E0; Office: 294 Albert St., Ottawa, Ont. K1P 6E6.

**STRAITON, John S.,** B.A.; advertising consultant; b. Kapuskasing, Ontario; e. Queen's University, B.A. (Psychol.); m.; children: Kenneth, Susan; PARTNER, STRAITON/ENGE ADVERTISING since 1988; Chrmn., Ogilvy and Mather (Canada) Ltd. 1973; Dir. of Information, Federal Dept. Energy, Mines and Resources 1974; subsequently Pres., John Straiton & Partners from 1975; author, 'Of Women and Advertising'; recreations: swimming, painting, movie making; Home: 21 Allan St., Oakville, Ont. L6J 3M7.

**STRAKOWSKI, Patricia Elizabeth;** sculptor; b. Calgary, Alta. 19 May 1937; d. William and Kataryna (Krupa) Dmytrychyn; e. Central H.S. 1957; Alberta College of Art dipl. 1979; m. John s. Kasmir and Kathryn S. 17 Aug. 1957; children: Dorothy Jane, Linda Kathleen, Shirley Anne; visual art teacher, adult evening classes, grades 1 to 12, children's art classes at Muttart Gall. & Alta. Coll. of Art; organized art teacher workshops throughout Alta.; presently devoting total time to sculpting & prep. for further solo exhibs.; art works have appeared in group exhibs. since 1979 & solo exhibs. since 1986 locally, nationally & internationally; group exhibs. (selected) since 1979: 'Apocrypha - Mythic Images Outside of Orthodoxy' North Park Gall., Victoria, B.C.; 'Return to Exceptional Pass' Whyte Museum of the Candn. Rockies, Banff, Alta.; 'Alberta Vision' Alberta Soc. of Artists show travelling in Japan; 'Made in Canada' Virginia Christopher Gall., Calgary, Alta.; 'Beaten to a Pulp: Contemporary Paper Sculpture & Basketry' Internat. Gall., San Diega, CA; 'Visions of Alberta' Muttart Gall., Calgary, Alta.; 'Midnight Preview - Saturday Matinee' travelling show in Alta. & B.C.; 'Parallel & Affinities' Prairie Gall., Grand Prairie, Alta.; 'Western Canada Artists Showcase' Shayne Gall., Montreal, PQ; 'Reflections On Three Plains: Contemporary Crafts' Winnipeg Art Gall., Winnipeg, Man.; Candn. National Exhibition Show, Toronto, Ont.; collections: Alberta: Home Oil, Alberta Energy, Alberta

Art Found., Alberta Crafts Counc., Bass Ticket Serv. Ltd., Claridge Investments, Esso Canada Resources Ltd., Rice Brydone, Rockyview Hosp., MacKimmie Matthews, Norcen, Brit. Petrol. Can. Ltd., Kanesko Holdings Ltd., Edmonton Art Gall., Macleod Dixon; Montreal: Charles Bronfman Coll., Franklin Silverstone Fine Arts; Toronto: Marshall Cummings & Assoc., Imperial Oil Ltd.; Alex Chapman Design, British Petrol. Canada, Pan Continental, Peter Rice, Trizec Equities; plus numerous priv. collections; Home: 4908 – 21 Ave. N.W., Calgary, Alta. T3B 0X2.

**STRAND, Kenneth,** B.A., M.S., Ph.D.; consultant; b. Yakima, Washington 30 June 1931; s. Adolph D. Strand and Margaret Jean Morren Thomson; e. Wash. State Coll., B.A. (Econ.) 1953; Univ. of Wis., M.S. (Econ.) 1956, Ph.D. (Econ.) 1959; Simon Fraser Univ. LL.D. 1983; m. Elna Karen, d. John Tomaske, 22 Dec. 1960; PROFESSOR EMERITUS 1986; Prof. Econs., Simon Fraser Univ. 1966–86 (Pres. 1968–74); Instr. and Teaching Asst., Univ. of Wis.; 1956–58; Acting Assistant Professor, Washington State University, 1958–60; Oberlin College, Assistant Professor 1960–63; Economist, OECD 1964–66; Home: 3475 Main Ave., Belcarra, B.C. V3H 4R2.

**STRANGWAY, David W.,** M.A., Ph.D., F.R.A.S., F.R.S.C., P. Eng.; geophysicist; university administrator; Professional Engineer; b. Simcoe, Ont. 7 June 1934; s. Walter Earl and Alice Kathleen (Skinner) S.; e. Univ. of Toronto, B.A. 1956, M.A. 1958, Ph.D. 1960; Victoria Univ. (Univ. of Toronto) D.Litt.S. (h.c.) 1986; Memorial Univ. D.Sc. (h.c.) 1986; McGill Univ. D.Sc. (hon.) 1989; D.Sc. (hon.) Ritsumeikan Univ., Kyoto, Japan 1990; D.Ag.Sc. (hon.) Tokyo Univ. of Agriculture 1991; D.Sc. (hon.) Univ. of Toronto 1994; m. Alice Norine, d. Omer Gow, Fergus, Ont., 20 Sept. 1957; children: Richard Paul, Susan Kathleen, Patricia Ruth; PRES. UNIV. OF BRITISH COLUMBIA 1985– ; Dir.: MacMillan Bloedel Ltd.; Business Counc. of B.C.; BC Gas Ltd.; Internat. Inst. for Sustainable Development; Corporate-Higher Education Forum; Echo Bay Mines Inc.; Sr. Geophysicist, Dominion Gulf Co., May-Oct. 1956; Chief Geophysicist, Ventures Ltd., Toronto, 1956–57 and Consultant 1957–58, 1958–60; Research Geophysicist, Kennecott Copper Corp., Denver, 1960–61; Asst. Prof. of Geol., Univ. of Colo., 1961–64; Asst. Prof. of Geophysics, Mass. Inst. of Technol., 1965–68; Chief, Geophysics Br. NASA, Johnson Space Center, Houston, Texas 1970–72; Chief, Physics Br. 1972–73 and subsequently Acting Chief, Planetary and Earth Sci. Div. and Interim Dir., Lunar Sci. Inst., spring-summer 1973; Visiting Prof., Dept. of Geol., Univ. of Houston, 1971–73; former Chrmn., Dept. of Geology, Univ. of Toronto 1972; Assoc. Prof. of Physics 1968–71; Prof. of Physics since 1971; Vice Pres. and Provost 1980–83; Pres., Univ. of Toronto 1983–84; Prof. of Geology, Univ. of Toronto 1972–85; research as principal investigator or co-investigator: magnetic and elect. properties of lunar samples; surface elect. properties exper. (S-204) Apollo 17; magnetic and elect. properties of rocks and minerals; geophys. application of ELF and VLF signals; applications of radio frequency interferometry to glacier and permafrost sounding; lab. microwave radar and thermal emission studies of basalt soil in vacuum; continental crust and its min. deposits; audio magnetotelluric sounding; magnetism and stratigraphy in Blake River volcanics; awards: NASA Medal for Exceptional Scientific Achievement 1972; Virgil Kauffman Gold Medal, Soc. of Explor. Geophys. 1974; Fellow, Roy. Soc. Can. 1974; Pahlavi Lectr., Govt. Iran 1978; Hon. Mem., Candn. Soc. of Exploration Geophysicists 1979; Hon. Mem., Soc. of Exploration Geophysicists 1983; Logan Medal, Geological Assn. of Canada 1984; J. Tuzo Wilson Medal, Candn. Geophysical Union 1987; Hon. Prof., Changchun Coll. of Geology, Jilin Province, China 1985; Canada Council Senior Izaak Walton Killam Memorial Scholarship 1980; Fellow, Victoria College 1984–85; Hon. Prof., Guilin College of Geology, Guilin, China 1987; given the name Kil-Sly by the Haida Nation 1993; author, 'Electromagnetic Scale Modeling in Methods and Techniques in Geophysics' 1966; 'The History of the Earth's Magnetic Field' 1970; other writings (as author and co-author) incl. 1 book and 165 papers for various scient. journs., papers, book chapters; mem. Ed. Bd., 'Geoexploration' 1967–87; 'The Moon' 1972–81; Assoc. ed., 'Geophysical Research Letters' 1977–80; 'Canadian Journal of Earth Sciences' 1973–76; 'Geophysics' 1973–75; 'Proceedings of the 1st, 2nd, 3rd, 4th & 5th Lunar Science Conference; 'Physics & Chemistry of Minerals 1976–80; mem., Soc. Exploration Geophysicists; AGU; EAEG; Soc. of Geomag. and Geoelect.; Geol. Assn. Can.; Candn. Geophys. Union; Am. Assn. Advanc. Sci.; Candn. Explor. Geophys.; Scitec; Hon. mem., Cdn. Soc. of Exploration Geophysicists; mem., Canada-Japan Soc.; Chrmn., B.C. Task Force on Environment and Economy 1989; United Church; Home: 6565 N.W. Marine Dr., Vancouver, B.C. V6T 1Z2; Office: Univ. of British Columbia, 6328 Memorial Rd., Vancouver, B.C. V6T 1Z2.

**STRASBERG, Steven Martin,** M.D., F.R.C.S.(C), F.A.C.S.; university professor; b. Toronto, Ont. 10 Oct. 1939; s. Samuel and Freda S.; e. Univ. of Toronto M.D. 1963, F.R.C.S.(C) 1968; m. Yona d. Rose and Ben Ehrenworth 13 June 1963; children: Suzanne, Jennifer, Adam, Jessica; HEAD, DIVISION OF GENERAL SURGERY, MT. SINAI HOSP. 1984– ; Surgeon, Toronto Western Hospital 1971–83; Asst. Prof. of Surgery, Univ. of Toronto 1971–75; Assoc. Prof. 1975–81; Prof. 1981– ; Dir., Surgical Research, Univ. of Toronto 1982–86; Ed. Bd., 'Heapatology,' 'Gastroenterology,' 'Transplantation,' 'Journal of Clinical & Investigative Medicine'; Medallist, Royal College of Surgeons 1985; Peters Prize 1976; Lister Prize 1981; author of approx. 100 scientific articles; Home: 34 Forest Ridge Dr., Toronto, Ont. M6B 1H3; Office: 600 University Ave., Ste. 1225, Toronto, Ont. M5G 1X5.

**STRASSER, John Albert,** M.Sc., Ph.D., P.Eng.; corporate officer; b. Sydney, N.S. 28 Jan. 1945; s. Albert Gustav and Lillian (Tetanish) S.; e. St. Francis Xavier Univ. Eng. Dip. 1965; Tech. Univ. of N.S. Bach. Metall. Eng. 1967, Ph.D. 1972; Penn State M.Sc. 1968; Lasalle Assoc. Deg. Bus. Mgmt. 1977; m. Gayle d. Augustus Andrew Moore 15 Aug. 1970; two s. Andrew Albert, Kirby John; CHIEF, MATERIALS ENGINEERING, CANAC INC. 1993– ; Lectr., Dalhousie Univ. 1969–70; Rsch. Sci., EMR, Ottawa 1971–73; Pres., Sydney Steel 1988–91; mem. Atlantic Group for Rsch. in Ind. Materials; Am. Soc. of Metals; Candn. Institute of Mining and Metalluryg; mem. Ctte. Atlantic Coal Nat. Rsch. Council; recipient Bart Griffin Meml. Award 1965; author numerous publs. and presentations energy and metall.; mem., Prof. Engs. N.S.; recreations: golf, skiing, tennis; Club: Senneville Golf; Home: 17321 Brunswick Blvd., Kirkland, Que. H9J 1L2.

**STRATAS, Teresa (Anastasia Stratakis),** O.C., B. Mus.; singer; b. Toronto, Ont. 26 May 1938; d. Emmanuel and Argero Stratakis; e. studied Voice with Irene Jessner 1956–59; B. Mus; Univ. of Toronto 1959; LL.D. (h.c.) McMaster Univ. 1986; won Metropolitan Opera Auditions and joined Met. Opera 1959; has sung major roles with every major opera house in world; repetoire includes leading roles in operas 'La Boheme,' 'Eugene Onegin,' 'Marriage of Figaro,' 'Pagliacci,' 'Bartered Bride,' 'La Traviata,' 'Rusalka,' 'Mahogonny,' 'Lulu'; many recordings and films; Performer of Year Award, Can. Music Council 1979; 3 Grammy recording awards, 1 Emmy television citation (U.S.), 1 Tony Nomination, Drama Desk Award for Leading Actress in a Musical on Broadway 1986–87; Address: c/o Metropolitan Opera Co., Lincoln Centre Plaza, New York, N.Y. 10023.

**STRATE, Grant,** B.A., LL.B.; choreographer; b. Cardston, Alta. 7 Dec. 1927; s. Alfred R. and Mabel (Wilson) S.; e. High Sch., Cardston, Alta.; Univ. of Alta., B.A., LL.B.; Director, Centre for the Arts, Simon Fraser Univ. 1980–89; read law with Ford, Lindsay, Edmonton; called to Bar of Alta. 1951; choreographer, Nat. Ballet of Can. (20 ballets); Studio Ballet, Antwerp, Belgium; Julliard Sch. of Dance, N.Y.; Royal Swedish Ballet, Stockholm and several Candn. Dance Companies; Prof., Simon Fraser Univ.; rec'd Centennial Medal 1967; Queen's Jubilee Medal, 1978; Ontario Dance Award 1979; Dance in Canada Award 1984; Canada Dance Award 1988; Jean A. Chalmers Award for Creativity in Dance 1993; recreations: reading, film, music; Home: 128 West 13th Ave., Vancouver, B.C. V5Y 1V7; Office: Simon Fraser Univ., Burnaby, B.C. V5A 1S6.

**STRATFORD, Philip,** B.A., D. de l'U. (Paris); university professor; author; b. Chatham, Ont., 13 Oct. 1927; s. Dr. Reginald Killmaster and Phyllis (Coate) S.; e. Trinity Coll., Sch., Port Hope, Ont., 1945; Univ. of W. Ont., B.A. (Eng.) 1950 (Gold Medal in Eng.); Univ. de Paris, D. de l'U. 1954; m. Jacqueline, d. Vicomte de Puthod, Paris, 27 Sept. 1952; children: John, Catherine, Christopher, Peter, Anne, Marguerite; Prof. Titulaire, Univ. de Montreal 1967 and Dir., Dépt. d'Etudes anglaises, 1969–75; Lectr., Assumption Univ. of Windsor, 1954–56; Asst. Prof., Univ. of W. Ont., 1956–63; Assoc. Prof. 1963–64; joined present Univ. as Prof. Agrégé, 1964–67; Responsable, Programme de Littérature Comparée, 1967–69; Book Ed., 'Saturday Night,' 1964–65; monthly column on 'Quebec Books' for 'Globe Magazine,' Globe & Mail, Toronto; mem. Bd. Ed., 'English Studies in Canada'; received President's Medal, University of W. Ontario, for 'Best Scholarly Article in English,' 1964; author, 'Faith and Fiction: Creative Process in Greene and Mauriac,' 1964; 'Marie-Claire Elais,' 1971; trans. 'Convergence' by Jean Le Moyne, 1966; 'In an Iron Glove' by Claire Martin, 1968; 'The Madman, the Kite and the Island' by Félix Leclerc, 'Pélagie' by Antonine Maillet, 1976; Ed., 'The Viking Portable Graham Greene,' 1972; Ed. and transl. 'André Laurendeau: Witness for Quebec' 1973; Editor 'Stories from Quebec' 1974; Co-ed., 'Voices from Québec' 1977; Compiler, 'Bibliography of Canadian Books in Translation' 1977; other writings incl. articles for various journs.; mem., Assn. Candn. Univ. Teachers Eng.; Humanities Assn. Can.; Candn. Comparative Lit. Assn.; Founding mem., Lit. Translators' Assn.; Home: 31 Senneville Rd., Senneville, Que. H9X 1B7.

**STRATTON, Allan (John);** playwright; b. Stratford, Ont. 5 Mar. 1951; s. John Henry and Dorothy Annabelle (Avis) S.; e. Neuchatel Jr. Coll. (Switzerland) 1969; Univ. of Toronto, B.A. 1973, M.A. 1974; Actor, Stratford Fest., C.B.C & regl. theatres 1974–77; stage plays: '72 Under the O' 1977, 'Nurse Jane Goes to Hawaii' 1980 (over 200 prodns.), 'Rexy!' 1981 (Chalmers Award Best Play 1981, Dora Mavor Moore Award 1981; Candn. Authors' Assn. Award 1982), 'Joggers' 1982, 'Friends of a Feather' 1984 (1st Shaw prodn. televised by CBC, Award winner Columbus Internat. Film Fest.), 'Papers' 1985 (Chalmers Award Outstanding New Play 1985); 'The 101 Miracles of Hope Chance' (prem. Manitoba Theatre Centre) 1987; 'Bingo!' (prem. Gryhan Theatre) 1987; radio play: 'The Rusting Heart' 1968 (prod. C.B.C. 1974); teleplay: 'A Flush of Tories' 1983; publ. by Coach House Press, Playwrights Can., Samuel French Inc., Penguin Books, Bakers' Plays; Mem., Playwrights Union of Can. (Bd. Mem. 1982–83); Actors Studio; J.B. West Mem. Scholarship; Candn. Club Award 1981; recreations: squash, weights, reading, community service; Club: YMCA.

**STRATTON, Kerry,** B.Mus., M.Mus.; conductor, broadcaster; b. Belleville, Ont. 24 Oct. 1952; s. George Clayton and Lydia Jean (Stoliker) S.; e. McGill Univ., B.Mus. with distinction 1974; Univ. of Regina, M.Mus. 1976; Vienna Conserv. Conductors Mastercourse, dipl. 1981; divorced; one s.: Nicholas Francis Kyle; MUSIC DIR., NORTH YORK SYMPHONY ORCHESTRA 1988– ; after becoming conductor & music director of Canada's North York Symphony travelled to Europe to conduct the Hungarian State Symphony Orchestra in the world premier recording of Liszt's De Profundis (this program for piano & orchestra was released on compact disc in 1991 on the Hungaraton label); apptd. Music Dir., Huntsville Festival of the Arts (a summer festival in Ontario featuring internationally acclaimed artists) 1993; pupil of Sir Charles Mackerras, Michel Tabachnik and Franco Ferrara; long time devotee of Czech music, has managed to develop a considerable reputation in the field of classical music radio broadcasting; Am. Fed. of Musicians Scholarship, Univ. of Cincinnati 1970; Floyd Chalmers Award for Studies in Italy 1985; Mem., Conductors' Guild of Am. Symph. Orch. League; recreations: fly-fishing, military history; Home: P.O. Box 5002, Station A, Toronto, Ont. M5W 1N4; Office: 1210 Sheppard Ave. E., #109, North York, Ont. M2K 1E3.

**STRATTON, The Hon. Terrance Richard;** senator, consultant; b. Winnipeg, Man. 16 March 1938; s. George and Mary Ena (Sephton) S.; e. Univ. of Man. 2 years Arch.; m. Marie L. d. Louis and Ellen Wyatt 7 Oct. 1961; children: Mark Christopher, Shannon Laura, Geoffrey Sean; SENATOR, THE SENATE OF CANADA; Architect, Geo. A. Stewart 1961–69; Instructor, Red River Community College 1969–75; Managing Partner, The IKOY Partnership Architects 1975–93; Consultant, construction 1993– ; Partner, Airwest Charter Serv. 1991– ; Dir., Manitoba Hydro Electric Board 1991–93; Mem., Bd. of Regents, Univ. of Winnipeg 1981–86; Dir., United Way of Winnipeg 1991–93; Winnipeg Football Club 1988–90; Vice-Pres. Wester, P.C. Party of Canada 1991– ; Office: Room 902, Victoria Bldg., Ottawa, Ont. K1A 0A4.

**STRAUSS, Stephen,** B.A.; journalist; b. Pittsburgh, Penn. 31 Mar. 1943; s. Jack Ludwig and Natalie Kaye (Atkins) S.; e. Univ. of Colorado, B.A. history cum laude 1966; Phi Beta Kappa; m. Betty d. Yale and Sara White 25 June 1973; children: Simon, Anna; SCIENCE WRITER & COLUMNIST, THE GLOBE AND MAIL 1981– ; Social Worker, Can. & U.S. 1967–70; English Teacher, Rio de Janeiro 1971–72; Reporter, editor, translator, Montreal 1972–77; Editor, Montreal Star 1977–79; joined The Globe 1979 as feature writer; Hon. Fellow, York Univ., Norman Bethune Coll. 1989–91; Ford Found. Scholarship 1964–66; 1981 2nd prize, Candn. Petrol. Assn.; Candn. Sci. Writers' Assn. awards 1984, 1986, 1987, 1988, 1989; role model for Candn.

high sch. students in 'Understanding Chemistry' text 1988; contrib.: 'Encyclopedia of Scientific Biography' 1987; recreations: reading, bowling, golf; Home: 365 Sackville St., Toronto, Ont.; Office: 444 Front St. W., Toronto, Ont. M5V 2S9.

**STRAYER, Hon. Barry Lee,** B.A., LL.B., B.C.L., S.J.D., Q.C.; judge; b. Moose Jaw, Sask. 13 Aug. 1932; s. Carl John and Nina Naomi (Carr) S.; e. Luther Coll., Regina 1948–51; Univ. of Saskatchewan B.A. 1953, LL.B. 1955; Oxford Univ. B.C.L. 1957; Harvard Univ. S.J.D. 1966; m. Eleanor d. Wesley and Arlene Staton 2 July 1955; children: Alison Lee, Jonathan Mark, Colin James; JUDGE, FEDERAL COURT OF CANADA, TRIAL DIVISION 1983– ; Judicial Member, Competition Tribunal 1986–93; called to Bar of Sask. 1959; Crown Solicitor Dept. of Atty. Gen. of Sask. 1959–62; Prof. of Law Univ. of Sask. 1962–68; several positions in Govt. of Can., Ottawa; Dir. of Constitutional Review, Privy Counc. Office 1968–71; Dir. of Constitutional Law, Dept. of Justice 1971–74; Asst. Depy. Min. of Justice 1974–83; Lectr. Carleton Univ. 1973; Lectr. Univ. of Ottawa 1973–78; Cons. to Govts. of Sask. and Can. 1962–68; Constitutional Advr. to Republic of Seychelles 1979; cr. Q.C. 1974; Advr. to Government of Hong Kong on Bill of Rights 1989; author 'Judicial Review of Legislation in Canada' 1968, rev. and pub. as 'The Canadian Constitution and the Courts' 1983 (2nd ed.), 1988 (3rd ed.); 'The Patriation and Legitimacy of the Canadian Constitution' (Cronkite Lectures) 1982; numerous articles publ. in legal periodicals; mem. Law Soc. of Sask.; Internat. Comn. of Jurists; Internat. Law Assn.; recreations: golf, cross-country skiing, curling; Clubs: Rideau (Ottawa); Larrimac Golf (Chelsea, Que.); Home: 504 Queen Elizabeth Driveway, Ottawa, Ont. K1S 3N4; Office: Federal Court of Canada, Ottawa, Ont. K1A 0H9.

**STREATCH, Hon. Kenneth;** former politician; farmer; b. 27 Jan. 1942; e. N.S. Agric. Coll.; m. Barbara Blackburn; 5 children: Minister of Transportation and Communications, Govt. of N.S. 1991; Min. of Pub. Works 1978–79; Min. of Labour & Manpower 1978–81; Min. in Charge of Admininstration of Human Rights Act 1979; Min. of Fisheries 1981–83; Min. of Lands & Forests 1983–87; Min. of Mines & Energy 1987–89; Min. of Small Business Development 1989–91; Past Pres. Fed. Agric.; Co. Councillor 5 yrs.; el. M.L.A. for Bedford-Musquodoboit Valley prov. g.e. 1978, 1981, 1984, 1988; Mem., St. Andrews United Church Bd.; P. Conservative; Address: Elderbank, N.S. B0N 1K0.

**STREBEL, Max P.;** banker; b. Liverpool, UK 23 June 1950; e. Commercial Coll. Aarau, Switzerland 1967; m. Marianne Schaffer; children: Robert Charles, Fiona Caroline; PRES. AND CHIEF EXEC. OFFR. UNION BANK OF SWITZERLAND (CANADA) 1989– ; various executive positions with UBS in Zurich, London, Chicago, Paris, New York from 1967 to 1989; Mem. of the Bd., Swiss-Candn. Chamber of Commerce (Ont.) Inc.; Movel Restaurants Limited; Union Bank of Switzerland (Canada); UBS Securities (Canada) Ltd.; mem. Swiss-Canadian Cultural Assn.; Clubs: Granite, University; Board of Trade; Empire; Home: Toronto, Ont.; Office: 154 University Ave., Toronto, Ont. M5H 3Z4.

**STRECKER, James Albert,** M.A., B.A.; writer, college professor, consultant, publisher; b. St. Boniface, Man. 15 April 1943; s. William and Anna (Tantala) S.; e. Univ. of Toronto M.A. 1971; McMaster Univ. B.A. 1967; Dialogue House (N.Y.) advanced studies program cert. 1980; Internat. Graphoanalysis Soc. (Chicago) diploma 1983; m. Margaret d. Edgar and Anne Allison 23 June 1967; PROFESSOR OF ENGLISH & WRITING, SHERIDAN COLLEGE 1974– ; English Teacher, Hamilton Bd. of Edn. 1971–72; Co-ord. & Tutor for Min. of Edn., Cool School 1972–74; Intensive Journal Consultant, Dialogue House 1981– ; freelance writer & photographer for newspapers and magazines 1985– ; Co-publisher, Mini Mocho Press 1989– ; Columnist & Theatre Critic, 'Arts Beat' 1989– ; 'Arts & Entertainment Forum' 1985–86; Literary Consultant, St. Thomas Aquinas Sch. for the Arts 1988–89; Writing Program Coordinator, Sheridan College, summer School for the Arts 1992– ; Writer-in-Residence, Mohawk College 1986, '87; Definitely Superior 1988; Creative Arts 1986; extensive workshop presenter; Canada Council reading tours 1988, '89; over 100 poetry readings 1985– ; Poet-in-Residence, CBC radio; many radio & TV appearances; Hamilton Arts Award 1992 for contbn. to the arts; Mem., League of Candn. Poets 1984– ; Internat. Graphoanalysis Soc. of Chicago 1983– ; Focusing Inst. of Chicago 1991– ; author: 'Bones to Bury' 1984, 'Pas de Vingt' 1984, 'Corkscrew' 1986, 'Routes' 1986, 'Recipes for Flesh' 1989, 'Black' 1990, 'Echosystem' 1993 (poetry); co-author: 'Talks with Jackie Washington' 1987 (biography); editor: '17 Hamilton Poets' 1987, 'A Hamilton Anthology: Poetry' 1988, 'Image Fiction' 1988, 'Dead Time: Poems from Prison' 1989, 'Out of Incest: A Book of Hope' 1989, 'Shackles and Silence: Poems from Prison' 1992; 'The Golden Horshoe Anthology'; recreations: listening to music, travel, theatre, guitar, reading, concerts; Home: 48 Chedoke Ave., Hamilton, Ont. L8P 4N9; Office: 1430 Trafalgar Rd., Oakville, Ont.

**STREET, Brian Jeffrey;** writer; b. Hamilton, Ont. 8 May 1955; s. Bruce Morley and Barbara Jean (Slater) S.; e. Conestoga Coll.; McMaster Univ.; m. JoAnn d. Lorne and Dorothy Mallory; children: Taylor Alyssa, Colin Wright; documentary filmmaker since 1975; has written and directed films, videos for CBC-TV, Nat. Film Bd., govt. and private sector clients; freelance journalist 1973–87; writer/director and communications analyst/advisor, Royal Candn. Mounted Police 1991– ; author: 'The Parachute Ward: A Canadian Surgeon's Wartime Adventures in Yugoslavia' 1987; co-author: 'Champagne Navy: Canada's Small Boat Raiders of the Second World War' 1991; 'Invasions Without Tears: The Story of Canada's Top-Scoring Spitfire Wing in Europe During the Second World War' 1994; mem. Writers' Union of Can. 1987– ; ACTRA 1989– ; Address: c/o Sterling Lord Associates (Canada) Ltd., Suite 510, 10 St. Mary St., Toronto, Ont. M4Y 1P9.

**STREET, David John;** photographer; b. Shoreham-by-Sea, Sussex, Eng. 17 Apr. 1947; s. Albert Frederick and A. Mary Lorraine (Ramshay) S.; e. St. George's Sch. Royal Tunbridge Wells, Kent, Eng. 1964; Croydon Coll. of Art Dip. Photog. 1966; m. Margaret Leslie d. Reginald and Pearl Johnson 14 May 1977; two s. Tomas, Alexander; OWNER, DAVID STREET PHOTOGRAPHER; profl. photog. West Kent News Service 1964, freelancing London newspapers; ind. photog. 1965; emigrated to Can. 1966; Staff photog. Toronto Life 1967; freelancing as photo journalist 1967 various newspapers and mags. incl. The Globe and Mail Mag., Maclean's; portraiture, corporate and ind. journalism various comm. and artistic orgns. incl. Shell Canada, British Airways, Imperial Oil, Xerox, American Express, Nat. Ballet Can., Stratford Festival, Candn. Opera Co.; author: 'Karen Kain: Lady of Dance'; 'Horses: A Working Tradition'; 'Toller'; 'The Cabot Trail'; 'Craig Russell and His Ladies'; 'Peter Schaufuss: Dancer'; mem. Candn. Assn. Photog. & Illus. in Communications; recreations: gardening, renovation work; Home: 81 Percy Lane, Stouffville, Ont. L4A 7X9.

**STREET, His Hon. Thomas George,** b. Thorold, Ont. 4 Jan. 1916; s. James Cunard and Marjorie Marie (MacTavish) S.; e. Public and High Sch., Welland, Ont.; Osgoode Hall, Toronto, Ont.; m. Beverly Joan, d. John H. Rolph, Welland, Ont., 27 Dec. 1941; children: Douglas Alan, Linda Marjorie, Thomas George; JUDGE, COUNTY AND DIST. COURTS, ONT., since 1974; read law with John H. Flett; called to the Bar of Ont., Sept. 1939; cr. Q.C. 1960; joined the firm of Macoomb & Macoomb, later Macoomb, Macoomb & Street, Welland, Ont. till 1941, rejoining again after the war till 1948 when apptd. Magistrate for the City of Welland and area; apptd. Judge of Juvenile and Family Courts, April 1956; Chairman, Nat. Parole Bd. Can. 1959–74; former Chairman, Police Comn. for City of Welland, etc.; Pres., Jr. Chamber of Comm. and of Welland Badminton Club, 1941; mem. for 17 yrs. and Past Pres., Rotary Club of Welland; served in 2nd World War, 4 yrs. in Candn. Active Army, 3 yrs. Overseas; Saskatoon Light Inf., 1st Div., Sicily, Italy; Air Liaison Offr., Yugoslavia, Greece and Corsica; wounded in Sicily; 48th Highlanders, rank of Capt.; O.C. 170th Batty. of 57th Light anti-aircraft Regt., Welland, Ont., with rank of Major, 1947–52; awarded Centennial Medal, 1967; Hon. Life mem., Ont. Magistrates' Assn. (formerly mem. of Extve.); Pres., Assn. of Paroling Authorities; former Vice Pres., Am. Correctional Assn.; Fed. Lawyer's Club of Ottawa; Candn. Bar Assn.; Hon. mem., Candn. Assn. of Chiefs of Police; recreation: golf; Clubs: Royal Ottawa Golf; Whispering Oaks Golf, Fla.; Address: 621 Island Park Crescent, Ottawa, Ont. K1Y 3P4.

**STREIT, Mrs. J. Douglas.,** O.C. (1967), B.A., (Marlene Stewart); amateur golfer; b. Cereal, Alta. 9 Mar. 1934; d. Harold Stewart; e. High Sch.; Rollins, Coll., Winter Park, Fla., B.A. (Business Adm.) 1956; m. Douglas Streit, 5 April 1957; two d., Darlene Louise, Lynn Elizabeth; began golfing at Lookout Point Golf Club, Fonthill, Ont.; won Ont. Ladies' Championship, 1951, 56, 57, 58, 68, 69, 70, 72, 74, 76, 77; Ont. Jr., 1951; Candn. Ladies' Closed Championship, 1951–57 succesively and 1963; placed 1st in some 10 club tournaments, incl. invitation events in St. Catharines, Oshawa, Kingston, London, Brantford and Toronto, 1951; won Cdn. Ladies Amateur Championship 1951, 1954–56, 1958, 59, 63, 68, 69, 72, 73; semi-finalist, British Amateur 1954; Brit. Women's Amateur at Porthcowl, Wales, June 25th 1953; 42nd Candn. Ladies' Open Golf at Royal Colwood, Victoria, B.C., 1954; U.S. Women's Amateur at Meridian Hills Country Club, Indianapolis, 22 Sept. 1956 (first Candn.); U.S. Nat. Intercollegiate, 1956; North & South Amateur Golf Tournament 1956, 1974; Jasper Park, Alta. Totem Pole Tournament, also Medallist, 1956; U.S. Nat. Mixed Foursome with Hobart Manley 1953 and 1963, with Hillman Robbins 1958, Jack Penrose, 1959; Nat. Ladies' Two Ball, 1956 with Anne Casey Johnson; Candn. Commonwealth Team, 1953, 59, 63, 67, 79, 83; Helen Lee Doherty Championship 1959, 60, 61, 65; Mem. of Canada's World Golf Team 1966, 70, 72, 78, 80, 84; (CLGA) Candn. Ladies Golf Assn. Sr. Championship 1985–87, 1988–93; Ont. Ladies Sr. Championship 1985, 88, 90, 92; U.S.G.A. (U.S. Golf Assn.) Sr. Women's Championship (1st Candn.) 1985; runner-up U.S.G.A. Sr. Women's Championship 1986; runner-up U.S.G.A. Sr. Ladies' Championship 1988–90; mem. of N. American team (winners) Women's Senior Invitational Matches (N. Am. vs Europe) 1986–89, 1991, 1992; Winner, Sr. Div., Jones-Doherty Golf Championship 1988–90, 1993; Palm Beach Polo Four Ball (partner Gayle Borthwick) 1990; el. to Can.'s Sports Hall of Fame, 1962 (elected Gov. 1991); Cdn. Golf Hall of Fame 1974; voted Lou E. Marsh Trophy as Can.'s outstanding athlete, 1951 and 1956; Ont. Sportswriters and Sportscasters Assn., Ont. Outstanding Athlete of the Year, 1951, 1953, 1956; Candn. Woman Athlete of the Year, 1951, 53, 56, 60, 63; tied with Charlotte Whitton in Candn. Press Poll, Woman of the Year, 1953; named Outstanding Female Athlete of the Year in Nat. Poll of Sportswriters, 1951, 52, 53; Low Amateur U.S. Women's Open, 1961; won Australian Women's Amateur, 1963; Women's Amateur of Palm Beach, 1965; won (9th) Candn. Women's Amateur Golf title, 1969, (10th) 1972 Candn. Open (Duchess of Connaught Cup); 11th 1973; Playing Capt. of winning Candn. Team at Commonwealth Golf Tournament, Perth, Australia 1979; Non-playing Captain, 1992 Canadian World Amateur Team; Officer of The Order of Canada 1967; Kappa Alpha Theta Sorority; Dir., Ada Mackenzie Memorial Found.; Clubs: Granite; Craigleith Ski; Life mem. Lookout Point Golf; Scarborough Golf; Lambton Golf; Rosedale Golf; Toronto Ladies Golf; The Toronto Golf; St. George's Golf & Country; Summit Golf & Country; York Downs Golf and Country; Hon. Life Mem., Royal Porthcowl Golf Club, Wales; Home: R.R. 4, Stouffville, Ont. L4A 7X5.

**STREN, Richard Eli,** B.A., Ph.D.; university professor; b. Toronto, Ont. 16 Aug. 1939; s. John Jacob and Miriam Jaqueline (Garfunkel) S.; e. Univ. of Toronto Schools 1957; Univ. of Toronto B.A. 1961; Univ. of Calif., Berkeley Ph.D. 1971; m. Claude d. Abner and Esther Schetrit 9 Nov. 1970; children: Ariane, Olivia; DIR., CENTRE FOR URBAN & COMMUNITY STUDIES, UNIV. OF TORONTO 1989– ; Ford Found. Rsch. in Kenya 1966–68; Asst. Lectr., Univ. Coll. Tanzania 1969; Asst. Prof., Pol. Econ., Univ. of Toronto 1969– ; Chief Planning Offr., Min. of Lands, Housing & Urban Devel. Tanzania 1972–73; Rsch. Assoc., Univ. of Nairobi 1974; Prof., Pol. Sci., Univ. of Toronto 1986– ; Mem., Extve. Ctte., Candn. African Studies Assn.; Ed. Bd. 'Environment and Urbanization'; 'Cities'; Cons. for UNCHS (Habitat), World Bank, CIDA (Ottawa); USAID (in Côte d'Ivoire); fellowships & awards from Can. Counc., Ford Found., SSHRCC, IDRC; Rsch. Dir. of major projects during 1980s & 1990s: 'African Urban Mangement'; 'African Scholarly Publishing'; 'Urban Research in the 1990s'; author: 'Urban Inequality and Housing Policy in Tanzania' 1975; 'Housing the Urban Poor in Africa' 1978; 'Coping with Rapid Urban Growth in Africa' 1986; 'An Urban Problematique; 1992; co-editor: 'African Cities in Crisis' 1989; 'Sustainable Cities' 1992; recreations: golf, tennis, squash; clubs: Univ. of Toronto Faculty; Home: 185 Inglewood Dr., Toronto, Ont. M4T 1H8; Office: Toronto, Ont. M5S 2G8.

**STRINGER, Christopher John;** trust company executive; b. London, England 27 Oct. 1944; s. Reginald and Alice Margaret (Lailey) S.; e. St. Peter's Sch. Bournemouth England 1962; Univ. of West. Ont., MTC 1985; Associate, Chartered Inst. of Bankers (U.K.); m. Geraldine d. Ronald and Lynne Tyrrell 2 Dec. 1967; children: Justine, Jason; EXTVE. VICE-PRES., THE CANADA TRUST CO. 1986– ; Barclays Bank (U.K.) 1962–67; Royal Trust Toronto 1967–69; Trust Corp of Bahamas 1969–71; Chase Manhattan Trust Co. Bahamas 1971–72; Canada Permanent Trust Co. Toronto 1972–79, 1982–85; Halifax 1979–82; Dir., CT Mutual Fund Dealer Inc.; Trustee, CT Income Investment Trust; Past Pres., The Children's Aid Soc. of Metro. Toronto; recreations: running; club: The National; Home: 33

Corning Rd., Willowdale, Ont.; Office: 161 Bay St., Toronto, Ont. M5J 2T2.

**STRINGER, Marc T.,** M.A.; finance executive; b. Hemmingford, Que. 24 Feb. 1929; e. Univ. de Montréal B.A. 1950; Univ. Laval B.S.S. 1952, M.A. 1954; m. Micheline; children: Elaine, Claude, Michel; VICE CHRMN. & C.O.O., PARCAP MANAGEMENT INC.; Econ. Research Offr. Central Mortgage & Housing Corp. 1954–56; Market Analyst Squibb 1956–59; Adm. Asst. to Gen. Mgr. Pirelli 1959–63, Adm. Mgr. and Controller 1963–67, Dir. of Marketing 1967–69; Vice Pres. and Gen. Mgr. I.T.T. Wire & Cable 1969–73; Gen. Mgr. Outside Plant Div. Northern Electric 1973–76; Pres. and Gen. Mgr. Héroux Inc. 1976–82; Pres. & C.E.O., Clarke Transport Canada Inc. 1982–86; Dir. Northmonth Holdings and associated companies of Clarke; recreations: skiing, painting; Office: 1800 McGill Coll. Ave., Suite 2800, Montréal, Qué. H3A 3J6.

**STROINK, Gerhard,** M.Eng., Ph.D., P.Eng.; educator; b. de Bilt, The Netherlands 6 Oct. 1942; s. Gerhard and Lucienne (Douwes) S.; e. Tech. Univ. of Delft, M.Eng. 1967; McGill Univ., Ph.D. 1974; m. Maartje d. Frederick and Eline Schweigman 13 Sept. 1969; children: Joachim, Monica; PROF. OF PHYSICS, DALHOUSIE UNIV. 1988– , Adjunct Asst. Prof. of Physiol. & Biophysics 1985– ; Adjunct Assoc. Prof. of Eng. Phys. Tech. Univ. of N.S. 1984–89; Instr. in Phys. present Univ. 1973, Asst. Prof. 1979–83, Assoc. Prof. 1983–88; mem. Bd. Sci. for Peace; Halifax Children's Discovery Centre; co-author 'Biomagnetism: Applications and Theory' 1985; 'Advances in Biomagnetism' 1989; author or co-author various publs. material sci., biomagnetism and cardiology internat. sci. jours.; mem. Inst. of Electrical and Electronics Engineers (IEEE); Am. Assn. Phys. Teachers; Can. Assn. Phys.; Assn. Profl. Engs. N.S.; Home: 6246 Cedar St., Halifax, N.S. B3H 2K2; Office: Dalhousie Univ., Phys. Dept., Halifax, N.S. B3H 3J5.

**STROMBERG, E. Robert,** B.A., LL.B., Q.C.; lawyer; b. Montreal, Que. 25 Geb. 1942; e. Sir George Williams Univ. B.A. 1963; Univ. of Saskatchewan LL.B. 1968; m. Sandra d. Jack and Irene Scott 31 Dec. 1970; children: David, Jeffrey, Allison; COUNSEL, ROBERTSON STROMBERG; past involvements: Dir. & Pres., Persephone Theatre; Dir. & Trustee, Mendel Art Gall.; Dir., Pride Canada Inc.; School for Performing Arts; Mem. Soc. of Sask.; Saskatoon Visitor & Convention Bureau; Sec. to Bd., Cameco Corp.; Chair, Sask. Horse Racing Comn.; Hon. Chair, Candn. Mental Health Assn. 1991; present involvement: Mem., Sask. Place Bd. of Dir.; Bd. of Dir., Potash Corp. of Sask. Inc.; Mem., Bd. of Dir., Ctr. for Internat. Business Studies, Univ. of Sask.; Mem., Law Soc. of Sask.; Saskatoon Bar Assn.; Am. Bar Assn.; Candn. Bar Assn. (1st Vice Chair, Business Law Section); Home: 1710 – 14th St. E., Saskatoon, Sask. S7H 0B1; Office: 700, 122 – 1st Ave. S., Saskatoon, Sask. S7K 7E5.

**STRONACH, Frank;** automobile parts manufacturer; b. Austria; immigrated to Can. 1954; BD. CHRMN., MAGNA INTERNATIONAL INC. 1971– ; tool and machine engineer; formed Multimatic Investments, a tool and die co. 1957 (which subsequently prod. automative components, merged with Magna Electronics Corp. Ltd. 1969, was renamed Magna International Inc. 1973 ($12 million in sales 1971, $2.6 billion in sales 1993; mgmt. principle: employee equity participation and profit sharing); has served on numerous corp., govt. and univ. Bds. of Dirs.; Dir., Fishery Products International Ltd.; Mem.: GMI Engineering; Mgmt. Inst. Bd. of Trustees; Nat. Assoc. of Securities Dealers Inc., Corporate Adv. Bd., U.S.; Nat. Campaign Chrmn.: Big Brothers Orgn.; The York Finch Hosp.; The John Black Aird Corporate Ride; Office: 36 Apple Creek Blvd., Markham, Ont. L3R 4Y4.

**STRONG, David F.,** B.Sc., M.Sc., Ph.D., D.Sc., F.R.S.C.; university professor and administrator; b. Botwood, Nfld. 26 Feb. 1944; s. Chester George and Elva Frances (Granville) S.; e. Memorial Univ. of Nfld. B.Sc. 1965; Lehigh Univ. M.Sc. 1967; Univ. of Edinburgh Ph.D. 1970; m. Lynda Joan d. George and Joan Marshall; children: Eva Kimberley, Joanna Deryn; PRESIDENT & VICE-CHANCELLOR, UNIV. OF VICTORIA 1990– ; Asst. Prof., Geology, Memorial Univ. 1970–72; Assoc. Prof. 1972–74; Acting Head 1974–75; Prof., Earth Sciences 1974–90; Univ. Research Prof. 1985–90; Special Advisor to the Pres. 1986–87; Vice-Pres. (Academic) 1987–90; W.F. James Prof. of Pure & Applied Sciences, St. Francis Xavier Univ. 1981–82; Visiting Prof., Univ. de Montpellier 1976–77; Hon. D.Sc. Memorial Univ. of Nfld. 1990, St. Francis Xavier Univ. 1992; Univ. of Edinburgh Swiney Lecturer 1981; Geol. Assn. of Canada's Past President's Medal 1980; Candn. Inst. of Mining & Metal. Distinguished Service Award 1979; Barlow Medal 1987; Foreign Exchange Fellowships to Japan 1976, France 1976–77 (NRC); E.W. R. Steacie Fellowship 1975–77 (NRC); APICS Young Scientist Award (now Fraser Medal) 1973; Fellow, Royal Soc. of Canada; Geol. Assn. of Canada; Geol. Soc. of Am.; Soc. of Econ. Geologists; author of num. sci. papers & reports; Office: P.O. Box 1700, Victoria, B.C. V8W 2Y2.

**STRONG, Maurice F.,** O.C.; business, public servant; administrator; b. Oak Lake, Man. 29 Apr. 1929; s. Frederick Milton and Mary (Fyfe) S.; e. Oak Lake (Man.) High Sch.; Hon. degrees from 26 Universities in Can., U.S., & Europe; m. Pauline Olivette, d. Joseph Williams, Sidney, Man., 29 July 1950; div. 1980; m. Hanne Marstrand, 1981; children: Frederick Maurice, Maureen Louise, Mary Anne, Alice, Kenneth Martin; CHRMN., ONTARIO HYDRO 1992– ; Pres., The Baca Corp., Denver, Colorado; Vice-Chrmn. and Dir., Soc. Gén. pour l'Energie et les Ressources, Geneva; Chrmn., North-South Round Table; mem. World Commission on Environment and Development, Geneva, Switzerland; mem. Internat. Adv. Bd., Burroughs Corp. (U.S.); Chrmn., Adv. Comte., U.N. Nations Univ. (Tokyo, Japan) 1980–83; Under-Secy. General, United Nations 1985–87; Chrmn., Canada Development Investment Corp., Vancouver 1982–84; Chrmn., Internat. Energy Development Corp. 1980–83; Chrmn., AZL Resources Inc., Phoenix, Ariz.1978–83; Dir. and Vice-Chrmn., Canada Development Corp. 1981–84; Pres. Strovest Holdings Inc. (Vancouver); Chrmn., Petro Canada 1976–78; Chrmn. Bd. Dirs., Internat Devel. Research centre 1977–78; Pres., Canadian International Devel. Agency 1966–70; Trustee, Aspen Inst. for Humanistic Studies; Vice Pres., mem. Extve. Comte, World Wildlife Fund (Morges, Switzerland); Chrmn., Bureau of the Internat. Union for Conservation of Nature & Natural Resources (Geneva, Switz.); mem. Extve. Comte. & Founding Co. Chrmn., Internat. Foundation for Dev. Alternatives (Nyon, Switz.); mem. Adv. Bd., Inst. of Ecology, Padjadjaran. Univ. (Bandung, Indonesia); mem. Internat. Hon. Comte., Dag Hammarskold Foundation (Uppsala, Sweden); Trustee, Rockefeller Found. 1971–77; mem. Council, Rockefeller Univ. 1972–76; Accountant, Vincent Mining Corp., Toronto, 1945–47 (helped found New Horizons Explorations Ltd. of which was Dir. and Secy.-Treas); mem. of Secretariat of Un. Nations (N.Y.C.) 1947–48; Securities Analyst, James Richardson & Sons, Winnipeg and Calgary, 1948–51; Asst. to Pres., Dome Exploration (Western) Ltd., 1951–52; Vice-Pres. and Treas., Dome Petroleum Ltd. and assoc. cos., 1954–59; formed M. F. Strong Management Ltd., Calgary, and assumed mgmt. of Ajax Petroleums Ltd., reorganizing this co. to form Candn. Indust. Gas Ltd. (now Norcen); became Extve. Vice Pres., Power Corp. of Canada Ltd., Montreal, Que. 1961, and Pres. 1963; Pres. or Dir. of many corporations; Visiting Prof., York Univ., 1969; Montague Burton Prof. Internat. Relations, Univ. Edinburgh 1974; Extve. Dir., U.N. Environment Programme 1973; Tyler Ecology Award 1973; U.N. Environment Prize 1976; Nat. Audubon Soc. Award 1975; Mellon Award 1975; Freedom Festival Award 1975; Order of Can. 1976; Henri Pittier Order Venezuela; Order of the Golden Ark (Netherlands) 1979; 'Only One Earth' Award, N.Y 1980; Past Pres., Nat. Council of YMCAs of Can.; former mem. Extve. Comte. World Alliance of YMCAs; United Church; recreations: swimming, fishing, hiking; riding, photography; Clubs: Denver Petroleum; Yale (New York); Ranchmen's (Calgary); University (Vancouver); Mount Royal (Montreal); Rideau (Ottawa); Office: 700 University Ave., Suite H19 A27, Toronto, Ont. M5G 1X6.

**STRONG-BOAG, Veronica,** B.A., M.A., Ph.D.; university professor; b. Scotland 5 July 1947; d. John H. and Daphne M.L. (Bridges) S.; e. Univ. of Toronto B.A. 1970; Carleton Univ. M.A. 1971; Univ. of Toronto Ph.D. 1975; m. Douglas Ross; children: Christopher, Dominic, Gabriel; DIR., CENTRE FOR RESEARCH IN WOMEN'S STUDIES AND GENDER RELATIONS, UNIV. OF B.C. 1991– ; Historian / Women's Studies Scholar, Dept. of History, Trent University 1974–76; Concordia Univ. 1976–80; Dept. of History & Women's Studies Program, Simon Fraser Univ. 1980–91; Winner, John A. Macdonald Prize, Candn. Historical Assn. for best book in Canadian History 1988 ('The New Day Recalled'); author: 'The Parliament of Women' 1976, 'A Woman with a Purpose' 1980, 'The New Day Recalled: Lives of Girls and Women in English Canada, 1919–1939' 1988; co-editor: 'True Daughters of the North' 1980, 'Rethinking Canada' 1986, 1991; 'British Columbia Reconsidered' 1992; Pres., Candn. Historical Assoc. 1993–94; Office: Vancouver, B.C. V6T 1Z1.

**STRONGMAN, Wayne Cameron,** Mus.Bac., M.A.; conductor; organist; pianist; tenor; arranger; b. Hamilton, Ont. 9 Sept. 1948; s. William Cameron And Gladys Mary (Bonnallie) S.; e. Univ. of Toronto Mus.Bac. 1971, M.A. 1973; ARTISTIC DIR. THE TAPESTRY MUSIC THEATRE 1978– ; Artistic Dir., The Bach-Elgar Choral Soc. Hamilton 1984– ; Conductor/Lectr. McMaster Univ. 1977–88; Artistic Dir. Quinte Summer Music 1984–86; Chorus Master, Opera Hamilton 1984–85; guest contracts incl. Ontario Youth Choir 1990, Hamilton Orchestra, Symphony Nova Scotia, Orchestra London; Conductor World Premiere Harry Somers' Chura-Churum, New Music Concerts 1985; Faculty mem. Summer Inst. of Ch. Music 1983; Conductor Princess of the Stars, New Music Concerts 1982; mem. Ont. Choral Fedn.; Toronto Musicians' Assn.; Home: 255 Withrow Ave., Toronto, Ont. M4K 1E3; Office: 60 Atlantic Ave., Studio 112, Toronto, Ont. M6K 1X9.

**STROPLE, Stephen Berkley,** B.A., M.A.; university administrator; b. Halifax, N.S. 28 June 1948; s. Rev. Beverley Cecil and Ellen Madelaine (Van Buskirk) S.; e. Dartmouth H.S. 1965; Dalhousie Univ. B.A. (Hons.) 1970; York Univ. M.A. 1984; m. Margaret d. Ruth and Stuart McCallum 1 Dec. 1984; one d.: Emma Ruth; SECRETARY OF THE UNIVERSITY OF NEW BRUNSWICK 1992– ; Post-grad. study, Dalhousie 1970–72; Social Development Officer, City and County of Halifax & Dalhousie Legal Aid 1972–77; Private Woodlot Manager 1977–80; Member of team conducting evaluation of N.S. Legal Aid 1981; Post-grad. study, York Univ. 1981–85; Extve. Mem., Candn. Union of Educational Workers, York Univ. 1983–85; Academic Staff Relations Officer 1986–91; Academic Relations Officer, Univ. of N.B. 1991; Planning Coord. 1991–92; Sec. & Mem., Bd. of Gov., Maritime Forest Ranger School; Mem., Nat. Assn. of Univ. Bd. Chairs & Secretaries; Candn. Inst. Rsch. & Planning Assn.; North Colchester Forestry Co-op.; Editor, 'University of New Brunswick Undergraduate Calendar'; recreations: canoeing, hiking, fishing, music; Home: 117 Fleming Rd., Fredericton, N.B. E3B 5J8; Office: P.O. Box 4400, Fredericton, N.B. E3B 5A3.

**STROUD, Carsten Laurence;** writer; b. Hull, Qué. 10 July 1946; s. Casimir Laurence and Catherine Amanda (Potvin) S.; e. De La Salle 'Oaklands' Toronto; Univ. of Guelph; Univ. of Toronto (Art Hist.); m. Linda Patricia d. Robert and Audrey Mair 15 Apl. 1977; children: Danielle, Jay, Emily; career activities incl. military, creative dir. and mag. journalist; Partner, Mair, Stroud & Associates Inc. (communications); recipient various awards for mag. journalism incl. Nat. Mag. Awards, Author's Awards, Candn. Sci. Writers Award, Kans. Sch. of Journalism Award, New York City Mags. Award; author 'The Blue Wall: Street Cops in Canada' 1983; 'Close Pursuit: A Week in the Life of an NYPD Homicide Cop' 1987; 'A Sniper's Moon' (novel) 1989; 'Contempt of Court: the Betrayal of Justice in Canada' 1993; recreations: horses, sabre fencing; Home: 501, 2645 Bloor St. W., Toronto, Ont. M8X 1A3; Office: c/o Penguin Books Canada Ltd., Suite 300, 10 Alcorn Ave., Toronto, Ont. M4V 3B2.

**STRUK, Danylo Husar,** M.A., Ph.D.; educator; b. Lviv, Ukraine 5 Apl. 1940; s. Ostap and Daria (Bukachevska) S.; e. Rutgers Prep. Sch. New Brunswick, N.J. 1959; Harvard Univ. A.B. 1963; Univ. of Alta. M.A. 1964; Univ. of Toronto Ph.D. 1970; m. Oksana d. Danylo Pisetsky 11 Nov. 1978; children: from previous marriage, Boryslava, Ostap, Luka; step-children, Andriy, Youli, Tetiana Wynnyckyj; PROF. OF SLAVIC LANGS. AND LIT. UNIV. OF TORONTO 1982– ; Lectr. Univ. of Alta. 1964–65; Lectr. Univ. of Toronto 1967, Asst. Prof. 1970, Assoc. Prof. 1976; Woodrow Wilson Fellow 1963–64; elected Foreign Mem., Academy of Sciences of Ukraine 1992– ; awarded 'Higher Achievement in Ukrainian Studies' prize 1993; author 'Gamma Sigma' poetry 1963; 'A Study of Vasyl Stefanyk' 1972; 'Ukrainian for Undergraduates' 1978, 3rd ed. 1987; Book Ed. 'Canadian Slavonic Papers' 1980–82; Managing Ed. 'Encyclopedia of Ukraine' 1983–89; Editor-in-Chief, 'Encyclopedia of Ukraine' 1989– ; Dir. Encyclopedia of Ukraine Project Univ. Toronto 1982– ; Dir., Univ. of Toronto Publications Office for the Candn. Inst. of Ukrainian Studies 1990– ; Assoc. Dir., Candn. Institute of Ukrainian Studies 1990– ; Adv. Counc., Candn. Inst. Ukrainian Studies; Vice-Pres., Candn. Assn. Slavists 1989–90; Pres., Candn. Assn. Slavists 1991–92; Bd. of Dirs., Candn. Found. for Ukrainian Studies 1985– ; Assn. Teachers Slavic & E. European Langs.; Am. Assoc. for the Advancement of Slavic Studies (AAASS); recreation: squash; Home: 483 Runnymede Rd., Toronto, Ont. M6S 2Z4; Office: 21 Sussex Ave., Toronto, Ont. M5S 1A1.

**STRUTHERS, Betsy,** B.A.; poet; novelist; freelance editor; b. Toronto, Ont. 11 July 1951; d. Leslie Harrison and Susanne Evelyn (Day) Porter; e. Wilfrid Laurier Univ., B.A. 1972; m. James s. William and Irma S. 12 June 1971; one s.: Ned; an eclectic working career has incl. such jobs as secretary, bookseller, library clerk, advtg. mgr. for a dept. store, mng. ed. and extve. asst. to the editor of an academic journal; promotion manager for a publishing house; and currently freelance editor; has had poems published in literary journals and anthologies in Canada, the USA, and Australia; Can. Counc. Arts Grant B 1989; External Affairs Int'l Cultural Relations Grant 1992; Ont. Arts Counc. Writers Reserve Grants 1984, 1991, 1993; short-list, Arthur Ellis Best First Novel Award 1992; Milton Acorn People's Poet Runner-up 1994; mem. League of Candn. Poets; Candn. Centre Int'l. P.E.N.; Crime Writers of Canada; Sisters In Crime; author: 'Grave Deeds' 1994; 'Running Out Of Time' 1993; 'Found: A Body' 1992; 'Saying So Out Loud' 1988; 'Censored Letters' 1984; recreations: hiking, nordic skiing, travel; Home: 702 Ross St., Peterborough, Ont. K9H 2C9.

**STUART, Don R.,** B.A., LL.B., Dip.Crim., D.Phil.; law professor; b. S. Africa 2 Sept. 1943; s. Robert Maurice and Joy Muriel (Burchell) S.; e. Natal Univ. B.A. 1963, LL.B. 1965; Cambridge Univ., Dip. Crim. 1969; Oxford Univ. D.Phil. 1976; m. Pamela d. Meg and Dudley Bell 20 Sept. 1969; children: Lisa, Chloë, Joanne; PROF., FAC. OF LAW, QUEEN'S UNIV. 1978– ; Lectr., Univ. of Witwatersrand, S. Africa 1966–67; Teaching Fellow, Osgoode Hall, York Univ. 1970–72; Asst./Assoc. Prof., Univ. of Alta. 1971–75; Assoc. Prof., Queen's Univ. 1975–78; Part-time Cons., Law Reform Comn. of Can.; Rhodes Scholar for Natal 1967–70; Bd. of Dir., John Howard Soc. of Kingston 1975– ; author: 'Canadian Criminal Law' 2nd ed. 1987; 'Charter Justice in Canadian Criminal Law' 1992; co-author: 'Learning Canadian Criminal Law' 4th ed. 1993; 'Learning Canadian Criminal Procedure' 3rd ed. 1994; editor-in-chief: 'Criminal Reports' 1982– ; recreations: golf, canoeing; Home: 259 Willingdon Ave., Kingston, Ont. K7L 4J2; Office: Kingston, Ont. K7L 3N6.

**STUART, James G.,** B.A., B.Comm.; chartered accountant; b. Kenora, Ont. 24 Dec. 1954; s. James L. and Mary I. (Nickerson) S.; e. Univ. of West. Ont. B.A. 1976; Univ. of Windsor B.Comm. 1977; m. Carol d. Gerald and Rose Rushton 17 June 1978; children: Joanne, Richard, Michelle; PARTNER, ARTHUR ANDERSEN 1991– ; Employee, Manager, Clarkson Gordon 1977–87; Partner, Ernst & Young 1987–91; licenced trustee in bankruptcy; Office: 2300 - 1055 W. Hastings, Vancouver, B.C. V6E 2J2.

**STUART, Mary Alice,** C.M., O.Ont., B.A., LL.D.; company director; b. Toronto, Ont. 5 May 1928; d. Edgar Gordon and Clayton (Callaway) Burton; e. Branksome Hall Sch. Toronto 1945; Univ. of Toronto Univ. Coll. B.A. 1949 (Gold Medal Eng. Lang. & Lit.); m. Alexander Kyle s. Alexander Thomas and Isobel Elizabeth (Caldwell) Stuart 4 June 1949; children: Clayton Caldwell Scott, Alexander Edgar, James Merrill Kyle, Andrew Thomas Burton; CHRMN. & C.E.O., CJRT-FM INC. 1974– ; Dir., S.C. Johnson and Son, Limited, Brantford, Ont.; Dir., Bank of Montreal; The Electrolyser Corp. Ltd.; Dir.-at-Large, Junior Achievement of Canada; National Chairman, $100 million Breakthrough Campaign, Univ. of Toronto 1987–90; Mem., Bd. of Trustees, Candn. Museum of Civilization, Hull, Que. 1990– ; Hon. Mem., Canadiana Fund, National Capital Commission, Ottawa 1992– (Mem. 1990–92); Hon. Gov., Massey Hall & Roy Thomson Hall 1987– (Gov. 1975–87); National Co-Chrmn., Governor General's 1992 Celebrations; Mem. Adv. Ctte., Community Foundation for Greater Toronto 1991– (Trustee 1983–90, Vice-Chrmn. 1986–87); Pres., The Burton Charitable Foundation 1981– ; Dir., Bata Shoe Museum Foundation 1985– ; Mem. Bd. of Dirs., The Candn. Institute for Advanced Rsch.; Mem. Bd. of Govs., Candn. Scottish Heritage Found. 1985– ; Mem., Univ. Coll. Ctte. Univ. of Toronto 1982– ; mem. Adv. Ctte., The Nature Conservancy of Canada 1985– ; Mem. Patrons Council, Alzheimer Soc. for Metropolitan Toronto; Mem. Council of Ambassadors, The Museum for Textiles, Toronto; Founding Dir. 1979, Dir. 1979–83 and Hon. Dir. 1983– , Malignant Hyperthermia Assn.; Dir. 1979–86, Hon. Gov. 1986– , The Nat. Ballet of Can.; Assoc. mem. Bd. Trustees Art Gallery of Ont. 1967–84; Chrmn. 1971–73, Restoration The Grange (AGO); Chrmn. Grange Ctte. 1980–84; mem. Corp. Trinity Coll. 1970–84; Gov. Branksome Hall Sch. 1968–84; Chrmn. 1977–84, Hon. Chrmn. 1986– , Branksome Hall Foundation; Gov. Women's Coll. Hosp. 1975–83; Gov. Ryerson Polytech. Inst. 1978–84; Dir. and mem. Exec. Ctte. Toronto Internat. (Jubilee) Festival held in June 1984, 1981–84; Hon. Patron, mem. Campaign Ctte., Thérèse-F. Casgrain Foundation 1984–85; Vice Chrmn., 1985 Internat. Bach Piano Competition 1983–85; Vice-Chrmn., The 1989 Internat. Choral Festival 1987–89; Dir., Internat. Mozart Festival 1991; Chrmn., The 1993 Internat. Choral Festival; Pres., Candn. Club Toronto 1984–85; Fellow, The Ont. Inst. for Studies in Educ. 1986; Fellow, Ryerson Polytechnical Inst. 1989; Doctor of Laws (LL.D.), honoris causa, Univ. of Toronto 1990; Member of the Order of Canada 1991; Mem., Order of Ontario 1993; Clubs: Badminton & Racquet; Toronto Golf; Toronto Hunt; Home: 52 Binscarth Rd., Toronto, Ont. M4W 1Y4; Office: 150 Mutual St., Toronto, Ont. M5B 2M1.

**STUART, Peter A.,** B.Comm., C.F.A.; investment executive; b. Sydney, N.S. 26 Aug. 1943; s. Francis L. and Margaret H. (Kingstone) S.; e. Lower Can. Coll. 1960; Queen's Univ. B.Comm. 1965; Univ. of Virginia C.F.A. 1975; m. Barbara P. d. A.N. Francis 27 Feb. 1970; children: Christopher, Katherine; PRES., AETNA CAPITAL MNGT. 1988– ; Mgr., Money Market & Asst. Treas., Royal Trust 1978–80; Asst. Vice-Pres., Corp. Investments, Can. Permanent Trust 1980–84; Vice-Pres. & Treas., Yorkshire Trust 1984–88; Dir., Penreal Advisors; Aetna Capital Mngmt.; recreations: tennis, skiing; Clubs: Toronto Lawn Tennis; Home: 49 Duggan Ave., Toronto, Ont. M4V 1Y1; Office: 79 Wellington St. W., Toronto, Ont. M5K 1N9.

**STUART, Ronald Stiles,** M.A., Ph.D., D.Sc. (Hon.); university administrator; b. Tingley, N.B., 26 March 1919; s. Frederick Alvah and Flora Margaret (Tingley) S.; e. Univ. of N.B., B.A. 1940; Univ. of Toronto, M.A. 1941, Ph.D. (Organic Chem.) 1944 (Nat. Research Council Can. Scholar), D.Sc. (Hon.) Univ. of N.B. 1993; m. Mary Irene, d. Byron Samuel Vanstone, 21 Sept. 1946; four s., Brian, David, Robert, Craig; DIR. OF RESEARCH SERVICES AND DIR. OF THE CENTRE FOR RESEARCH IN ENGINEERING AND APPLIED SCIENCE, UNIVERSITY OF NEW BRUNSWICK, since 1982; Demonst. in Chem., Univ. of Toronto, 1940–42; Research Assoc., Nat. Research Council of Can., 1943–45; Asst. Dir. Research, Dom. Tar & Chem. Co., 1945–48; Mgr., Chem. & Biol. Control, Merck & Co., Ltd., 1948–53, Science Devel. 1953–60, Tech. and Prod. Operations, 1960–62, Dir. of Rsch. 1962–68; Dir. of Rsch., Charles E. Frosst 1965–68; Dir., and Extve. Dir. of Research, Merck Frosst Labs., 1968–81; Montreal Oral Sch. for the Deaf (Educ. Officer 1965–66; President 1967–71 and since Hon. mem. Board); Protestant; recreations: scouting, swimming; Club: Fredericton Golf & Curling; Home: Old Springhill Rd., R.R. #3, Fredericton, N.B. E3B 4X4; Office: Centre for Research in Engineering and Applied Science, P.O. Box 4400, University of New Brunswick, Fredericton, N.B. E3B 5A3.

**STUART-STUBBS, Basil Frederick,** B.A., B.L.S., F.R.S.C.; librarian; b. Moncton, N.B. 3 Feb. 1930; s. Thomas Edward and Amy (Jefferson) S.; e. Univ. of B.C. B.A. 1952; McGill Univ. B.L.S. 1954; F.R.S.C. 1984; PROF. EMERITUS, UNIV. OF BRITISH COLUMBIA 1992– ; Reference Librarian, McGill Univ. Lib. 1954–56; Catalogue Librarian, Univ. of B.C. Lib. 1956, Serials Librarian 1958, Head, Special Collections Div. 1960–62, Coordinator of Collections 1962–64; Univ. Librarian, Univ. of B.C. 1964–81; Dir., Sch. of Library, Archival and Information Studies, Univ. of British Columbia 1981–91; Bd., Council on Library Resources; co-author 'Interlibrary Loan in Canada' 1976; 'A Survey and Interpretation of the Literature of Interlibrary Loan' 1976; 'The Northpart of America' 1979; author: 'Library Resource Sharing in British Columbia' 1993; numerous articles, papers; mem. Candn. Lib. Assn.; B.C. Lib. Assn.; Home: 1847 Collingwood St., Vancouver, B.C V6R 3K4.

**STUBBS, John Owsley,** B.A., M.Sc., D.Phil.; university executive; educator; b. Sarnia, Ont. 1 May 1943; s. Frederick John and Caroline Eileen (Owsley) S.; e. Univ. of Toronto B.A. 1966; London Sch. of Econ. M.Sc. 1967; Oxford Univ. D.Phil. 1973; m. Mayling Pulsford d. William and Maria Weaver 19 Sept. 1970; one s. James Frederick; PRES. AND VICE CHANCELLOR, SIMON FRASER UNIV. 1993– , Prof. of Hist. 1993– ; Lectr. in Politics and Asst. to Master, Peter Robinson Coll. Trent Univ. 1967–69; Asst. and Assoc. Prof. of Hist. Univ. of Waterloo 1973–86, Dir. Applied Studies Faculty of Arts 1980–86, Assoc. Dean of Arts 1981–86; Visiting Lectr. St. Catherine's Coll. Oxford 1979–80, Visiting Fellow 1986–87; Pres. and Vice Chancellor, Trent Univ. 1987–93, Prof. of History 1987–93; Co-Dir. Waterloo Centre for New Oxford Eng. Dictionary 1984–86; mem. Exec. Ctte. Council Ont. Univs. 1990–93; Dir. Greater Peterborough Econ. Council 1987–93; Arbour Theatre Co. 1987–91; Gov. Sir Sandford Fleming Coll. 1987–90; Gov., Lakefield College School 1991–93; co-ed. 'MacKenzie King: Widening the Debate' 1978; author numerous articles, chapters and papers Brit. pol. hist. and hist. of journalism; recipient, 125th Anniversary of the Confederation of Canada Medal, 1992; Dir., The Laurier Institute; mem. Assn. Univs. & Colls. Can. (Dir. 1990–91); Business Council of British Columbia; The Candn. Club; Vancouver Board of Trade; Gov., The Olympic Trust of Can.; recreations: running, canoeing, skiing, reading; Office: Simon Fraser Univ., Burnaby, B.C. V5A 1S6.

**STUBBS, Thomas George;** real estate executive; b. Lichfield, Eng. 7 Nov. 1952; s. Denys Harvey and Margaret Jane (Cassidy) S.; e. King Edward VI Grammar Sch. Lichfield 1971; Univ. of Reading 1975; Pres., Knowlton Realty Ltd. 1985; Negotiator Calgary present co. 1975–78, Mgr. Denver & San Francisco offices 1979–81, Gen. Mgr. 1983–84; Pres. Jecco Development (USA) Inc. 1982–83; Assoc., Royal Inst. Chart. Surveyors.

**STUCKEY, Johanna Heather,** B.A., M.A., Ph.D.; university professor; b. Gananoque, Ont. 5 Sept. 1933; d. William Henry Stuckey and Mary M.F. Diplock (Smith) S.; e. Univ. of Toronto, B.A. 1956, M.A. 1960; Yale Univ., Ph.D. 1965; Co-ordinator, Women's Studies Prog., York Univ. 1986–89; Lectr., Eng., Univ. of Maryland (Overseas Div.) 1961–64; Asst. & Assoc. Prof., York Univ. 1964– ; Mem., Religious Stud. Prog. 1982– ; Women's Studies Prog. 1982– ; Acting Master, Founder College 1972–73; Chair, Div. of Hum. 1974–79; Adv. to Pres. on Status of Women 1981–85; Ed., 'Canadian Woman Studies Journal/Les cahiers de la femme' 1981–84; Vice-chair, York Univ. Fac. Assn. 1973–74; Chair, Senate Taskforce on Status of Women at York Univ. 1972–75; Teaching Excellence Award, Ont. Confed. of Univ. Faculty Associations 1984; Mem., Candn. Women's Studies Assn.; Soc. for Mesopotamian Studies; Soc. for Mediterranean Studies; Candn. Soc. for the Study of Religion; author of num. scholarly & popular articles; co-author: 'A Bibliography of Petronius' 1977; Gen. Ed., 'Senate Task Force Report on Status of Women' 1975, 'Equity for Women: the First Decade' 1985; recreations: stamp collecting, cooking, swimming; Club: The Goats Club, ISH, London, Eng.; Office: 314 Founders Coll., York Univ., 4700 Keele St., North York, Ont. M3J 1P3.

**STUEBING, Robert A.,** B.A., M.B.A., F.I.C.B.; trust company executive; b. Kitchener, Ont. 4 May 1946; s. Kenneth Allen and Marie Eleanor (Kudoba) S.; e. Univ. of Winnipeg B.A. 1968; Univ. of Western Ont. M.B.A. 1974; Inst. of Candn. Bankers, Fellow 1974; m. Eileen J. d. Clive and Lenore Roper 30 Jan. 1970; SENIOR VICE PRES., THE MUTUAL TRUST CO. (AND PRDEDECESSORS) 1980– ; Candn. Imperial Bank of Commerce 1968–74; Asst. Mgr. Toronto, Mercantile Bank of Canada 1974–76; Vice-Pres., Leaseguard Financial Services Limited 1976–78; Vice-Pres., The Merchant Trust Co. 1978–79; Pres. & Dir., Mutual Securities Inc.; recreations: Old Timer hockey, piano; Home: 22 Fairfield Rd., Toronto, Ont. M4P 1T1; Office: 400 – 70 University Ave., Toronto, Ont. M5J 2M4.

**STUEWE, Paul,** A.B., M.A.; writer; b. Rochester, N.Y. 5 Oct. 1943; s. Paul Burdette and Helen Joyce (Wood) S.; e. Columbia Univ., A.B. 1965; Univ. of Toronto M.A. 1993; m. Deanna d. Olive and Raymond Groetzinger 30 Aug. 1976; children: Matthew, Christina, Sarah; Social Worker 1966–71; Grad. Student in Sociol., York Univ. 1972–73; Secondhand & Antiquarian Bookseller 1974–86; writer of books & articles primarily in the area of Candn. lit. 1974– ; Ed., 'Books in Canada' 1990; Can. Counc. Explorations Grant 1979; Can. Counc. Arts Grant 1987; 'The Storms Below' shortlisted for City of Toronto Book Awards 1989; author: 'Clearing the Ground: English-Canadian Literature After Survival' 1984; 'Hugh Garner and His Works' 1985; 'The Storms Below: The Turbulent Life and Times of Hugh Garner' 1988; 'Don't Deal Five Deuces' (with Hugh Garner) 1992; mem., Candn. Soc. of Magazine Editors; Champlain Society; Crime Writers of Canada; recreations: collecting jazz records, computing; Home: 149 Essex St., Toronto, Ont. M6G 1T6.

**STUNDNER, Udo A.;** banker, investment advisor; b. Salzburg, Austria 9 Oct. 1942; s. Anton and Erda (Liebetegger) S.; e. Commercial School, Salzburg, Austria; m. Anne Françoise d. Guy and Rosette Bigaouette 4 July 1980; children: Antoine, Brigitte; MEMBER OF SENIOR MANAGEMENT, PRIVATE BANKING, CREDIT SUISSE (CANADA) 1993– ; bank training in private bank in Austria, universal banks in Berne and Neuchatel, Switz. 1960–67; Private Banking & Portfolio

Management, Swiss Corp. for Candn. Investments Ltd. 1968–73; Asst. Vice-Pres., New Bus. Devel. 1974; Vice-Pres. & Mgr. Toronto Br. 1975–77; Calgary Br. 1978–81; Montreal Br. 1982–87; Vice-Pres., Strategic Planning, Toronto Br. 1988–89; Dir. & Sec., SBC Portfolio Management (Canada) Inc. 1990–93; Sec. Chimo Region, Candn. Jaycees 1973–75; Dir., Swiss Candn. C. of C. Montreal; recreations: skiing, canoeing; clubs: St. James's; Rotary; Office: 1250 René Lévesque Blvd. West, Suite 3935, Montréal, Qué. H3B 4W8.

**STURGESS, Jennifer Mary,** B.Sc., Ph.D.; executive; professor; b. Hucknall, Nottinghamshire, Engl. 26 Sept. 1944; d. Daniel and Dorothy Joan (McKeand) Liptrot; e. Univ. of Bristol, Engl. B.Sc. (Hons.) Microbiology 1966; Univ. of London, Engl. Ph.D. Pathology 1970; m. Robert W.J. s. S. John and Barbara S. 2 Apr. 1966; children: Claire, Paul, Hugh; PRESIDENT, THE TORONTO HOSPITAL RESEARCH INSTITUTE 1993– and PROF., DEPT. OF PATHOLOGY, UNIV. OF TORONTO 1990– ; Assoc. Prof. Pathology, Univ. of Toronto 1973–90; mem., Medical Research Council 1990– ; mem., Science Counc. of Can. 1987–92; National Advisory Council on Pharmaceutical Rsch. 1990–91; Lectr. in Experimental Pathology, Univ. of London, Engl. 1966–70; Scientist, Hosp. for Sick Children Rsch. Inst., Toronto 1970–87; Dir., Warner Lambert/Parke-Davis Rsch. Inst. 1979–86; Vice Pres., Medical and Scientific Affairs, Warner Lambert (Canada) Inc. 1986–90; Assoc. Dean, Faculty of Medicine, Univ. of Toronto 1990–92; Bd. of Dirs. VS Services Ltd. 1982– ; Bd. of Dirs., Ont. Cancer Institute/Princess Margaret Hosp. 1992–93; Sr. Fellow, Massey College 1992– ; editor: 'Perspectives in Cystic Fibrosis' 1980; 'Electron Microscopy' 1978; Adv. Cons., World Health Organization; Ont. Ministry of Health; Health & Welfare Canada; Internat. Pediatric Assn.; National Inst. of Health, U.S.A.; Past Pres., Microscopical Soc. of Can.; Scholar, Medical Research Council 1974–79; Home: 68 King Georges Rd., Toronto, Ont. M8X 1L9.

**STURGESS, John Harry Douglas;** transportation executive; b. London, Eng. 18 Oct. 1936; s. Frederick John Howard and Dorothy Mount (Hughes) S.; e. Kingston Tech. Sch.; Kingston Tech. Coll.; Instn. of Civil Engs.; m. Mary d. Frank and Betty Lyons 13 May 1957; children: Jeremy, Teresa, Matthew, Daniel; SR. VICE PRES. & CHIEF OPER. OFFR., CANADIAN NATIONAL RAILWAYS 1987– ; joined Eng. Dept. CN Edmonton, Alta. 1958 holding various eng., rsch. & devel., gen. mgmt. and mktg. positions, Vice Pres. Mktg. 1980, Vice Pres. Great Lakes Region 1985; Commander, Order St. John; mem. Candn. Soc. Civil Eng.; Nat. Freight Transp. Assn.; Club: Beaconsfield Golf; Home: 223 Antoine Villeray, Beaconsfield, Qué. H9W 6E8; Office: 16th Floor, 935 de la Gauchetière St. W., Montréal, Qué. H3B 2M9.

**STURGESS, Robert William John,** B.Sc.; business executive; b. Morchard Bishop, Eng. 11 Nov. 1939; s. John and Barbara (Drew) S.; e. Queen Elizabeth Sch. 1958; London Sch. of Econ., B.Sc. 1961; m. Jennifer d. Daniel and Joan Liptrot 1966; children: Claire, Paul, Hugh; PRES., FITZPANE INVESTMENTS INC. 1988– ; Pres., Southport Foods; Grad. Trainee & Finan. Analyst, Ford Motor Co. 1961–63; Econ. Adv., S.W. Electricity Bd., Bristol, Eng. 1963–66; Corp. Planning Mgr., United Glass Limited 1966–69; Cons., Peat Marwick and Partners 1969–84; Partner 1974–84; Partner-in-charge Gen. Mgmt. Group 1976–84; Nat. Strategic Mgmt. Practice Dir. 1982–84; Vice Pres., Corp. Devel., Dominion Stores Limited 1984–85; Vice Pres., Retail Operations 1985–86; Vice-Pres. & Gen. Mgr., Permalite Automotive Group 1986–90; Pres., Rayonics Scientific Inc. 1990–92; recreations: tennis, skiing, squash, sailing; Clubs: Fitness Inst.; Caledon Ski; Royal Candn. Yacht Club; Longboat Beach and Tennis; Home: 68 King Georges Rd., Toronto, Ont.

**STURGESS, Maj. Gen. Roy,** C.M.M., C.D.; consultant; b. Toronto, Ont. 11 June 1929; s. William and Isobel (Alcock) S.; e. N. Toronto Coll. Inst.; RCAF Staff Coll. 1965; Nat. Defence Coll. 1976; U.S. Navy Postgrad. Sch. 1983; m. Dorothy d. William Dillon and Mary Kerr 16 Oct. 1976; children: Patricia Kim, William Scott, Ronald Alexander; Air Transp. and Training Operations RCAF and Sec. Air Council 1951–69; Base Commdr. Summerside, P.E.I. and Dir. Maritime Aviation 1969–75; Dir. Gen. Orgn. & Manpower, Commdr. Maritime Air Group and Chief of Operations Air Command 1976–80; Dep. Commdr. Air Command and Defence Attaché to U.S.A., Washington, D.C. 1980–84; Sr. Vice Pres. Operations CP Air, Dir. Eastern Provincial Airlines, and Dir. CP Consulting Services 1984–87; apptd. C.M.M. 1980; Assoc. Fellow, Candn. Aeronautics & Space Inst.; recreation: golf; Club: Shaughnessy Golf & Country; Arbutus Ridge Golf & Country; Address: 495 Marine View, Cobble Hill, B.C. V0R 1L1.

**STURSBERG, Peter;** writer and broadcaster; b. Chefoo, China 31 Aug. 1913; s. Walter Arthur and Mary Ellen (Shaw) S.; e. Canadian, British schools; McGill Univ.; m. Jessamy, d. J.H. Anderson Robertson, 5 Oct. 1946; children: Richard Barclay, Judith Mary (Mrs. J.R. Maus); began as Reporter with Victoria 'Daily Times,' 1934–38; Empire Press Union Exchange Reporter, 'Daily Herald,' London, Eng., 1938–39; Reporter, Vancouver 'Daily Province,' 1939–40; News Editor, Candn. Broadcasting Corp., Vancouver, B.C., 1941–43; War Corr., C.B.C., 1943–45, first to broadcast on Candns. in action (Sicilian invasion); Roving Foreign Corr., 'Daily Herald,' London, 1945–50 (travelled extensively in Europe, India, W. Indies, Africa); United Nations Corr., C.B.C., 1950–56; Ottawa Ed., Toronto Daily Star 1956–57; briefly, Research Offr. to Prime Min.; Secy., Candn. Trade Mission to U.K., 1957–58; Ottawa Newscaster, Commentator, CJOH, CTV 1960–73; corr., Maclean's, Saturday Night, Newsweek; Instructor, Cdn. Studies, Simon Fraser Univ., 1980–88; Adjunct Professor 1982–88; author: 'Journey Into Victory' 1944; 'Agreement in Principle' 1961; 'Those Were The Days' 1969; 'Mister Broadcasting' 1971; 'Diefenbaker Leadership Gained 1956–62' 1975; 'Diefenbaker Leadership Lost 1962–67' 1976; 'Lester Pearson and the Dream of Unity' 1978; 'Lester Pearson and the American Dilemma' 1980; 'EXTRA! When the Papers Had the Only News' 1982; 'Gordon Shrum' 1986; 'The Golden Hope' 1987; 'Roland Michener, The Last Viceroy' 1989; 'The Sound of War' 1993; received Candn. Radio Award 1950; mem. of Bd. of Govs., U.N. Internat. Sch., New York, 1952–55; Life mem., Press Gallery, National Press Club, Ottawa; Anglican; recreations: tennis, reading, stamps; Clubs: Hollyburn Country; Diamond Univ. (SFU); Home: 5132 Alderfeild Pl., W. Vancouver, B.C. V7W 2W7.

**STURSBERG, Richard Barclay,** B.A., M.A.; telecommunications executive; b. London, Eng. 27 July 1947; s. Peter and Jessamy (Robertson) S.; e. Carleton Univ. B.A. 1969; L'Université d'Aix-Marseilles 1970; Carleton Univ. M.A. 1974; Univ. of London 1979; m. Judi Tedlie 5 July 1979; children: James Alexander Peter, Jessamy Margaret; EXECUTIVE VICE-PRESIDENT, STRATEGIC PLANNING & EXTERNAL RELATIONS, UNITEL 1993– ; Ast. Dep. Min., Dept. of Communications, Govt. of Can.: Corp. Policy 1984–86, Telecommunications & Technology 1987–89, Broadcasting & Culture 1990; Sr. Vice-Pres., Unitel 1990–92; Dir., Vision 2000; Canarie; Agency for Instructional Technology; Mem., Sectoral Adv. Group on Internat. Trade; Dir., Friends of the Earth; Home: 128 Fentiman Ave., Ottawa, Ont. K1S 0T8; Office: 200 Wellington St. W., Toronto, Ont. M5V 3C7.

**STUSHNOFF, Cecil,** B.S.A., M.Sc., Ph.D.; university professor/administrator; b. Saskatoon, Sask. 12 Aug. 1940; s. Peter P. and Mary (Remizoff) S.; e. Vanscoy, XII 1959; Univ. of Sask., B.S.A. 1963, M.Sc. 1964; Rutgers Univ., Ph.D. 1967; m. Jeannette d. David and Mabel Baptist 20 July 1963; children: Shawna Marie, Stefan Bradley; PROF., DEPT. OF HORTICULTURE, COLORADO STATE UNIV., Ft. Collins, CO 1990– ; Asst. Prof., Univ. of Minn. 1967–70; Assoc. Prof. 1970–75; Prof. 1975–79, 1980; Vis. Sci., Tromso Univ. (Norway) 1976–77; Prof., Prin. Horticul., U.S.D.A., S.E.A., C.S.R.S., invited Admin. 1979–80; Prof. & Head, Dept. of Horticulture Sci., Univ. of Sask. 1981–89; Visiting Scientist, Dept. Biochemistry, Colorado State Univ., Ft. Collins 1987–88, Sr. Rsch. Scientist 1989–90; teaches horticul., plant breeding, plant stress physiology, plant sci., tech. writing, seminars; Dir., North Gro-Inc. 1970–79; Cons., Walter Butler Co. 1978–79; Partner/Mgr., White Rock Lake Farm 1970–80; NRC scholarship 1963–64; Phi Kappa Phi 1976–77; Shepard Award 1971, 1979; Gourley Best Paper Award 1973; Darrow Award 1980; Bishop Award 1989, 1992; Fellow, Am. Soc. Hort. Sci. 1993; Pres., Can. Soc. Hort. Sci. 1985–86; Vice-Pres. 1984–85; U.S. Nat. Acad. of Science Working Ctte. to review Nat. Seed Storage Lab. 1987–88; Chrmn., Fin. Ctte., Am. Soc. Horticul. Sci. 1983; Prairie Potato Counc., Rsch. Ctte. 1984–87; Expert, Ctte. Plant Gene Resources 1985–87; Expert Ctte. Hort. 1985–87; Apptd. as member of the Editorial Bd., 'Plant Stress' 1993; USDA/CSRS Affiliate Faculty Administrator 1992, 93, 94; Chair, CSU Plant Biotechnology Task Group Strategic Planning 1993; author: 'Potential Use of in vitro Storage for Temperate Fruit Crops'; 'Prairie Garden Notebook' 1988; and num. sci. & rsch. papers, book chaps., pubs. & reports; editor: 'Hort-Hints' 1985; Assoc. Ed., 'Canadian Journal of Plant Science' 1983–87; recreations: curling, downhill and cross-country skiing; Home: 1217 Springfield Dr., Ft. Collins, CO 80521; Office: Dept. of Horticulture, Colorado State Univ., Fort Collins, CO 80523.

**STUSS, Donald T.,** Ph.D., C.Psych, ABPP, ABCN; university professor / administrator; b. Sudbury, Ont. 26 Sept. 1941; s. Nicholas and Anne (Maga) S.; e. Univ. of Ottawa, B.A. 1967; St. Paul's Univ., B.Ph. 1967; Univ. of Ottawa, Ph.D. 1976; Post-doct. training, Boston Univ., Sch. of Med.; m. Kaaren d. Helena and Oliver Kummer 23 Aug. 1969; children: David Paul, Leanne Elizabeth; VICE-PRES. OF RESEARCH, BAYCREST CENTRE FOR GERIATRIC CARE 1991– ; DIR. OF RSCH. ROTMAN RSCH. INST. & PROF., UNIV. OF TORONTO, DEPTS. OF PSYCHOL. AND MED. (NEUROLOGY) 1989– ; Asst. Prof., Univ. of Ottawa 1978–83; Assoc. Prof. 1983–88; Prof., Schools of Med. & Psych., Univ. of Ottawa, 1988–89; Co-ord., Neuropsychol. Serv., Ottawa Gen. Hosp.; Dir. of Psych. 1988; Fellow, Am. Psych. Assn., Div. 40 1984, Div. 6 1990; Fellow, Am. Psychological Soc. 1990; Fellow, Stroke Council of the Am. Heart Assn. 1990; Fellow, Candn. Psych. Assn. 1992; Internat. Neuropsych. Soc.; Candn. Neurol. Soc.; Acad. of Aphasia; Candn. Rsch. Management Assn.; Memory Disorders Rsch. Soc.; Soc. for Neuroscience; Pres., Internat. Neuropsychological Soc. 1994; author of 56 sci. articles & 20 book chapters; co-author: 'The Frontal Lobes' 1986; Office: Rotman Rsch. Inst. of Baycrest Ctr., 3560 Bathurst St., North York, Ont. M6A 2E1.

**STYLES, Richard Geoffrey Pentland,** B.Comm.; banker; b. Regina, Sask. 3 Dec. 1930; s. Alfred G. and C. Ila (Pentland) S.; e. Univ. of Saskatchewan B.Comm. 1951; Prog. for Mgmt. Devel. Harvard Univ. 1964; m. Jacqueline Joyce Frith 31 Oct. 1959; children: Leslie Diane, David Patrick; former Vice-Chrmn., The Royal Bank of Canada, retired 1987; joined Royal Bank Victoria B.C. 1951; Asst. Rep. Chicago 1957; Credit Offr. Dist. HQ Toronto 1959; Asst. Mgr. Main Br. London Ont. 1960; Asst. Mgr. Toronto Main Br. 1961; Asst. Supr. Internat. Div. Montreal 1964, Supr. Internat. Div. 1966, Asst. Gen. Mgr. Internat. Div. 1968; Sr. Rep. and Dir. Orion, Orion Royal Banking Group, London, Eng. 1970; Dep. Gen. Mgr. Internat. Div. Montreal 1973; Gen. Mgr. Metrop. Toronto District 1974; Chrmn. Bd. of Supr. Dirs. RBC Holdings B.V. and RBC Houdstermaatschappij B.V., holding cos. for 22 internat. subsidiaries 1979; Exec. Vice-Pres. World Trade & Merchant Banking Div. Toronto 1980; Sr. Exec. Vice Pres., Internat. & Corporate Banking 1983; Vice-Chrmn. 1986; Chrmn. & Dir.: Grosvenor International Holdings Ltd.; Drivers Jonas (Canada) Ltd.; Dir.: Echo Bay Mines Ltd.; Onex Corp.; Fortis Inc.; Fairwater Capital Corp.; ProSource Distribution Services; The Royal Trust Co.; Scott's Hospitality Inc.; Working Ventures Candn. Fund Inc.; Gov., Mount Sinai Hosp.; Chrmn., Toronto Symphony Foundation; Dir., Niagara Inst.; The Inst. of Corp. Dirs. in Can.; recreations: golf, photography; Clubs: Rosedale Golf; Toronto Club; Office: Suite 3115, Royal Bank Plaza, Toronto, Ont. M5J 2J5.

**SUBRAMANIAM, Venkateswarier,** B.Sc., M.A., Ph.D.; educator; b. Tuticorin, India; s. Mahedeva and Gomathy (Ananthakrishna) s.; e. Saraswathy Anglo-Vernacular High Sch. Tuticorin 1936; Madras Univ., B.Sc. 1941, M.A. 1954; Australian Nat. Univ., Ph.D. 1959; m. Jaya Subramaniam 26 Feb. 1956; one s. Gautam; DISTINGUISHED RESEARCH PROF. OF POL. SCI., CARLETON UNIV. 1993– ; lectr. in chem. 1941–54; journalist and ed. 1954–55; Lectr. in Pol. Sci. Univ. of Queensland 1959; Simon Sr. Fellow Manchester Univ. 1960; Sr. Lectr. Univ. of W. Australia 1961–65, on loan as Prof. of Pol. Sci. Nat. Acad. Adm. India 1964–65; Sr. Fellow, Australian Nat. Univ. 1966; Prof. Indian Inst. Pub. Adm. New Delhi 1967; Found. Prof. of Pub. Adm. Univ. of Zambia 1968–74; Prof. of Pol. Sci., Carleton Univ. 1974–92; Consultant, Candn. Internat. Devel. Agency; Shastri Indo-Candn. Inst.; regular lectr. Madras Classical Music Festival; awarded First Prize Haldane Essay Royal Inst. Pub. Adm. 1956; Simon Sr. Fellow 1960; Visiting Prof. Heidelberg Univ. 1977; Australian Grad. Sch. Mgmt. 1981; Leningrad Univ. 1983; author (dance dramas in Sanskrit) 'Pancha Kanya Tarangini' 1975; 'Veera Kanya Vahini' 1980; 'Kinkini Mala' 1983; 'Dima Panchakam' 1985; 'Arya Satyam' 1993; (social sci's) 'Social Background of India's Administrators' 1971; 'The Managerial Class of India' 1971; 'Indian Administration' 1972; 'Transplanted Indo-British Administration' 1977; 'Cultural Integration in India: A Socio-Historical Analysis' 1978; ed. 'The Sacred and the Secular in India's Performing Arts' 1980; 'Problem Recognition in Public Policy and Business Management' 1986; 'Hindu Syncretism: Cause & Context'; 'Mother Goddesses & Other Goddesses'; 'Socio-historical Context of Asian Political Theorizing'; 'Public Administration in the Third World' all in 1990; 'Buddhist-Hindu

Interactions: Sakyamuni to Sankaracarya' 1993; 'Classes and Elites in Afro-Asia: The Colonial Legacy' 1993; 'Dominant Historical Influences on Indian Society and Polity' 1993; mem. Internat. Sociol. Assn.; Candn. Assn. Sanskrit & Related Studies; S. India Cultural Assn. (Founder Pres. Ottawa 1976–79); Internat. Pol. Sci. Assn.; Life mem., Indian Inst. of Public Admin.; recreations: yoga, classical music, sculpting; Home: 2044 Chalmers Rd., Ottawa, Ont. K1H 6K5; Office: Ottawa, Ont. K1S 5B6.

**SUDDICK, Patrick J.,** B.A.Sc., P.Eng.; retired company executive; b. London, Ont. 27 Sept. 1923; s. late Percy Edward and late Mrs. Eva (Jones) S.; e. Univ. of Toronto, B.A.Sc. (Engn. & Business) 1949; m. Mary, d. late Joseph Walsh and late Mrs. Agnes (Lang), 7 July 1951; children: Paul, Peter, Michael, Jane, Mark; Past Dir., Gandalf Technologies Inc., Ottawa (retired); Engn. Sales for 2½ yrs., B.F. Goodrich Rubber Co.; joined Honeywell 1953; Sales Rep., Indust. Div., Toronto, 1953; estbd. and headed up Candn. Transport Div., Montreal, 1954; Candn. Rep., Boston Div. (formerly Doelcam), 1955; Head, Candn. Ordinance & Marine Divs., 1956; Asst. Mgr., Service Engn. Dept. Candn. Aeronautical Div., 1957; Comm. Div., Sales, 1958; Gen. Mgr., EDP Div., 1965; Vice Pres., EDP Div., 1968; Vice Pres. & Gen. Mgr., Information Systems 1970; retired 1984 as Vice Pres., Defence Systems Organization and Dir. of Honeywell Ltd., Dir. Honeywell Holdings Ltd.; Past Chrmn., Candn. NIAG, Delegation to NATO; served with RCA in Can., Eng., Holland and Germany during World War II; Past Chrmn., Bd. Govs., Seneca Coll.; Past Chrmn., Candn. Nat. Business Show, Data Processing Conf.; mem., Assn. Prof. Engrs. Ont.; Past Pres. Candn. Business Equipment Mfrs. Assn.; Bd. Trade Metrop. Toronto; R. Catholic; recreations: golf, gardening, bridge, squash; Summer Address (May-Oct.): 25 Austin Dr., Ste. 419, Unionville, Ont. L3R 8H4; Winter Address: 5548 Chanteclaire, Sarasota, Fla. 34235.

**SUEDFELD, Peter,** B.A., M.A., Ph.D., F.R.S.C.; university professor; b. Budapest, Hungary 30 Aug. 1935; came to Can. 1972; s. Leslie John Field and Jolan (Eichenbaum) S.; e. Univ. of the Philippines, 1956–57; Queen's Coll., City Univ. of N.Y., B.A. 1960; Princeton Univ. M.A. 1962, Ph.D. 1963; m. Gabrielle Debra Guterman 11 June 1961; div. 1980; children: Michael Thomas, Joanne Ruth, David Lee; m. Phyllis Jean Johnson 19 Oct. 1991; PROF., UNIVERSITY OF B.C. 1972– ; Head, Dept. of Psychology 1972–84; Dean, Faculty of Graduate Studies 1984–90; Research Assoc., Princeton Univ. 1963–64; Visiting Asst. Prof., Univ. of Illinois, 1964–65; Asst. to Prof. and Chrmn., Dept. of Psych., Univ. Coll., Rutgers Univ., 1965–72; served with U.S. Army, 1955–58; U.S. Air Force Reserve, 1958–72, discharged 1st Lieut.; Invited Lectr. in inst. and meetings North, Central and South America, Europe, Australia, N.Z., Japan; author of 'Social Processes' 1966; 'Personality Theory and Information Processing' 1971; 'The Behavioral Basis of Design' 1976–77; 'Attitude Change: The Competing Views' 1971; 'Restricted Environmental Stimulation' 1980; 'Psychology and Torture' 1990; 'Psychology and Social Policy' 1991; Ed., 'Journal of Applied Social Psychology' 1976–82; other writings incl. over 150 scientific articles and book chapters in anthologies on intellectual functioning, decision making, the effects of environmental factors on human behaviour, health maintenance and enhancement, international and political problem solving; mem. of various ed. bds., assn. cmtes.; Representative to Scientific Ctte. on Antarctic Rsch.; Chrmn., Candn. Antarctic Rsch. Program; grant reviewer and consultant for US and Candn. govt. agencies; manuscript reviewer for professional jnls. and book publs.; Fellow, Royal Soc. of Canada; Fellow, Am. Psychol. Soc.; Fellow, Candn. and Am. Psychol. Assns.; Fellow, Acad. of Behavioral Medicine Research; Fellow, N.Y. Acad. of Sciences; Fellow, Soc. of Behavioural Med.; mem. Soc. for Explt. Social Psychol.; Interamerican Soc. of Psychol.; Amer. Assn. for the Advancement of Science; Psychonomic Soc.; recreations: skiing, scuba diving, target shooting, fishing; Home: 201 – 1311 Beach Ave., Vancouver, B.C. V6E 1V6; Office: Vancouver, B.C. V6T 1Z4.

**SUGDEN, Roy,** F.C.A.; retired executive; b. England 12 Feb. 1935; s. Herbert and Lilly (Mills) S.; e. Chartered Acct., F.C.A. (England and Wales) Leeds 1958; Advanced Mgmt. Program, Harvard Bus. Sch.; m. Mona d. Hilda and Charles Edward Clegg 21 Dec. 1957; children: Carol, Michael, Jill; Pres., Nestle Canada Inc. 1989–90, Retired; Dir. Rowntree plc York, Engl.; Chrmn., Rowntree Ltd.; Dir., Mmmuffins Ltd. 1993– ; Salesman IBM 1960–62; joined Rowntree Mackintosh plc, York Engl. 1962 as successively Data Processing Mgr., Finance Dir. UK Confectionery Div., Finance Dir. Transport and Distribution Div., Finance Dir. Overseas Div., Depy. Chrmn. Overseas Div.; Pres. of Rowntree Mackintosh Canada Ltd. Toronto 1974; Pres. Rowntree Mackintosh Inc. 1979; Chrmn. & C.E.O., Rowntree North America 1985–89; actively involved in the acquisitions of The Original Cookie Company, Inc. (Cleveland, OH); Sunmark Companies (St. Louis, MO); Tom's Foods Inc. (Columbus, GA); Laura Secord Ltd. (Toronto, Ont.); Rowntree DeMet's Inc. (Chicago, IL); Hot Sam Co.; Garant Candies; Pres. Confectionery Mfrs. Assn. of Can. 1977–78; Dir., Midland Bank of Canada 1985–88; Dir. Grocery Products Mfrs. of Can. 1975–79 (mem. Exec. Ctte. 1976–79, Treasurer 1977–79); recreation: golf; Club: Credit Valley Golf & Country; Home: 2334 Bennington Gate, Oakville, Ont. L6J 5N6.

**SULATYCKY, Hon. Allen,** B.A., LL.B.; judge; b. Hafford, Saskatchewan, 13 June 1938; s. Dmytro and Polly (Bodnarchuk) S.; e. Univ. of Saskatchewan, B.A., LL.B. 1962; m. Marylin Joyce, d. Irvin and Evelyn Perkins, Calgary, Alta, 17 Feb. 1962; children: Warren, Robert, Annemarie, Donald; JUSTICE, COURT OF QUEEN'S BENCH OF ALBERTA 1982– ; called to Bar of Alta 1963; formerly practised law with firm of Parlee, Irving, Henning, Mustard & Rodney at Edmonton and Calgary; candn. in fed. by-el. for Jasper-Edson 1967; el. to H. of C. for Rocky Mountain, g.e. 1968; apptd. Parlty. Secy. to Min. of Energy, Mines & Resources, 1971; Parlty. Secy. to Min. of Indian Affairs and Northern Devel., 1972; def. g.e. 1972; Greek Orthodox; Office: Court House, 611 – 4th Street S.W., Calgary, Alta. T2P 1T5.

**SULIMMA, Hans-Guenter,** Dr.; diplomat; b. Hirschwalde, Germany 22 Oct. 1933; s. Ewald and Erna S.; e. Freiburg Univ. studies of Law & Econ. 1953–57; 1956 1st Law State Exam.; Harvard Law School studies of Law 1958–59; Master of Laws 1959; Asst. to a Prof. of Law, Techn. Univers. Darmstadt 1960–62; Dr. of Laws 1961; 2nd Law State Exam. 1962; Training at Diplomatic School Bonn 1962–64; m. Helge Müller Aug. 1962; children: Maryse, Wulf; AMBASSADOR OF THE FEDERAL REPUBLIC OF GERMANY TO CANADA 1993– ; Foreign Office Bonn 1964–65; Dep. Head of Mission, Embassy of Conakry 1965–67; Foreign Office Bonn 1967–71; Embassy Paris 1971–73; since 1973 Foreign Office Bonn; Head of Div., Dept. of Econ., Min. of Fgn. Affairs 1975–81; Head of Delegation for North-South Negotiations; Ambassador-at-large 1981–83; Commissioner for North South Negotiations and Dir.-Gen. 1983–84; Dir.-Gen. for African Affairs 1984–93; Home: 290 Coltrin Rd., Rockcliffe Park, Ont. K1M 0A6; Office: 275 Slater St., 14th floor, Ottawa, Ont. K1P 5H9.

**SULLIVAN, Alan William,** B.Sc., LL.B.; diplomat; b. Winnipeg, Man. 27 March 1938; s. Dr. William C. and Marjorie (Smith) S.; e. Inst. des Etudes politiques Paris 1959; Georgetown Univ. B.Sc. 1961; Queen's Univ. LL.B. 1964; CANADIAN CONSUL GENERAL, NEW YORK & COMMISSIONER TO BERMUDA 1991– ; has served in Saigon, Port of Spain, Geneva, Beirut & London; Ambassador to Ireland 1981–82; to Austria & Perm. Rep. & Ambassador to the Internat. Orgns. in Vienna & Gov., Internat. Atomic Energy Agency 1983–85; var. positions in Ottawa incl. Asst. Sec. to Cabinet (Fgn. & Defence Policy) & Sr. Dept. Asst. to Sec. of State for External Affairs; Asst. Dep. Min., Pol. & Internat. Security Affairs 1985–87; Asst. Dep. Min., Personnel 1987–88; Ambassador to Italy with concurrent accreditation as Ambassador to Libya & High Comnr. to Malta 1988; Spec. Rep., Sec. of State for External Affairs, Cambodian peace process 1989; recreations: skiing, music; clubs: Economic / Metropolitan / Canadian (New York); Stephen's Green (Dublin), Five Lakes (Ottawa); Office: 1251 Ave. of the Americas, New York, N.Y. 10020.

**SULLIVAN, Daniel F.,** B.A., M.B.A., M.A.; investment banking executive; b. Minneapolis, Minn. 13 Sept. 1942; s. Frank and Margaret S.; e. Columbia Univ. B.A. 1966, M.B.A. 1967; Univ. of Toronto M.A. 1968; m. Sandra 1971; children: John Douglas, Jennifer; DEPY. CHRMN., SCOTIA McLEOD INC. 1990– ; Dir. & Extve. Vice Pres., Scotia McLeod Inc. 1968–90; Schneider Corp.; William R. Barnes; Family Trust; Trustee and Vice-Chrmn., St. Michael's Hosp.; Gov., Branksome Hall; Dir., Conf. of Independent Schools; Past Chrmn., Investment Dealers Assoc.; author numerous papers corporate finance and real estate financing; Clubs: Muskoka Lakes Golf & Country (Past Pres.); Toronto Golf; Tamahaac; Toronto Club; York Club; Toronto Golf; Badminton & Racquet, Toronto; Office: P.O. Box 433, Toronto-Dominion Centre, Toronto, Ont. M5K 1M2.

**SULLIVAN, Kevin Roderick,** B.Sc.; film producer; director; writer; b. Toronto, Ont. 28 May 1955; s. Glen Alexander Q.C. and Helen Ann (O'Grady) S.; e. Univ. of Toronto, B.Sc. (Hon.) 1978; m. Trudy C. d. Mary Gertrude and John Morgan Grant 4 July 1981; PRES., SULLIVAN ENTERTAINMENT INC.; Guest Lectr. univs. & colls.; award winning films & series incl.: 'Krieghoff' 1981 (Chris Award, Columbus Festival); 'Megan Carey' 1982 (Canadian Showcase Award); 'The Fir Tree'; 'Sight Unseen'; 'Katya's Gift'; 'The Wild Pony' (1983 Candn. Film Television Assoc. Best Feature Film Award); 'Anne of Green Gables' 1986 (numerous awards incl: (1986) Emmy Award - Outstanding Children's Program; Peabody Award for Outstanding Contribution to Broadcasting in U.S., 1st Candn. drama to receive such an award; 9 Gemini Awards; TV Guide Award - Most Popular Program; Emily Award - Highest Honour of Festival, Am. Film & Video Festival; Grand Award of Festival, Internat. Film & TV Film Festival NY; Chris Award, Columbus Internat. Film Festival; Silver Hugo Award, Chicago Internat. Film Festival; (1987) CFTA Award, Outstanding Personal Achievement in TV; The Ruby Slipper, Best TV Special; Parents Choice Award for TV Programming; Golden Apple Award, Best of the Nat. Educational Film & Video Festival; (1988) Prix Jeunesse - Best Drama, West Germany); 'Anne of Green Gables – The Sequel' (numerous awards incl.: (1987) Best New TV Production Award, CFTA; 2 ACE Awards; (1988) 6 Gemini Awards; Best Children's Production, TV Movie Awards, NJ; TV Guide, Best Family Series); 'Looking for Miracles' (numerous awards incl.: (1989) Ollie Award for Best Outstanding Family Programming, Am. Children's TV Festival; Silver Medal Teen Special Category, NY Film Festival; 3 ACE Award Nominations; (1990) Emmy Award; Gemini Award; Internat. Monitor Award N.Y., Best Director; (1991) Best Children's Film, Candn. Film Celebration; European Jury Prize, Umbriafiction TV Festival, Italy - Best Screenplay); 'Lantern Hill' 1988 (awards incl.: ACE Award 1990; 2 Gemini Awards 1991; Crystal Heart Award, Heartland Film Festival 1992); 'Road to Avonlea' Extve. Producer (13 part television series) 1994, into sixth season (numerous awards incl.: (1990) 4 Gemini Awards; John Labatt Classic Award, Most Popular Program in Canada; 3 ACE Award nominations; Emmy nomination; (1991) ACE Award, Best Dramatic Series; 2 Gemini Awards; (1992) Emmy Award; Golden Monitor Award, Umbriafiction TV Festival - Best Series; 3 Gemini Awards; (1993) Emmy Award, Best Children's Programme; Ace Award, Best Dramatic Series; Golden Gate Award, Best of Category - Television Drama); 'By Way of the Stars' 1993 (Bronze Plaque Award, 41st Columbus Internat. Film Festival; 2 Gemini nominations); Bd. Mem., Candn. Film Inst.; Adv. Bd., Trade Forum; Roman Catholic; Mem., ACTRA; Dir. Guild of Can.; recreations: all sports, painting; Club: Royal Candn. Yacht; Office: 110 Davenport Rd., Toronto, Ont. M5R 3R3.

**SULLIVAN, Robert E.;** politician, labourer; b. Penetanguishene, Ont. 8 Aug. 1946; s. Alan Anthony and Leona (Dubeau) S.; e. Forest Hill Coll.; St. Michael's Coll.; Trent Univ.; m. Elinor d. John and Doreen Scott 9 July 1976; children: Ian Alan; Elizabeth Elinor; COUNCILLOR, TOWN OF PENETANGUISHENE 1988– ; Mayor 1988–91; varied career, currently working as labourer, Canada Post Corp.; mem., Loyal Order of Raccoons; Candn. Union of Postal Workers; recreations: flying, sailing, tennis; club: Penetanguishene Tennis; Home: 8 Water St., Box 1081, Penetanguishene, Ont. L0K 1P0; Office: 10 Robert St. W., Penetanguishene, Ont. L0K 1P0.

**SULLIVAN, Rosemary,** M.A., Ph.D.; university professor/writer; b. Montreal, Que. 29 Aug. 1947; d. Michael Patrick and Leanore Marjorie (Guthrie) S.; e. McGill Univ., B.A. 1968; Univ. of Conn., M.A. 1969; Univ. of Sussex, Ph.D. 1972; PROF. OF ENGLISH, UNIV. OF TORONTO 1977– ; Maitre Asst.-Assoc., Univ. de Dijon 1972–73; Univ. de Bordeaux 1973–74; Univ. of Victoria 1974–77; Asst. Prof., Univ. of Toronto 1977; Assoc. Prof. 1980; Full Prof. 1991; founding mem., Toronto Arts Group for Human Rights; Co-ord., Internat. Congress 'The Writer and Human Rights' in aid of Amnesty Internat. 1981; Vis. Lectr., Shastri Inst. 1982; Ed. Bd. Mem., 'Descant' 1982–84; 'This Magazine' 1982–88; Gerald Lampert Award for Poetry 1986; Brascan Silver Medal for Culture, Nat. Mag. Awards 1986; Guggenheim Fellow 1992; author: 'The Garden Master: The Poetry of Theodore Roethke' 1975, 'The Space a Name Makes' 1986; 'By Heart: Elizabeth Smart/A Life' (biography) 1991 nominated for Gov. General's Award for non-fiction; 'Blue Panic' (poetry) 1991; editor: 'The Pool in the Desert' 1983, 'Stories by Canadian Women' 1985, 1987; 'Poetry by Canadian Women' 1989; co-editor: 'Elements of Fiction' (Canadian ed.) 1982; 'The Writer and Human Rights' 1982; 'Poetry in English: An Anthology' 1987; other writings incl. poems & num. acad. articles on Candn. & Am. lit. in var. mags. & jours.; Office: Erindale Coll., Univ. of Toronto, Mississauga, Ont. L5L 1C6.

**SULLIVAN, Timothy,** B.Mus., M.Mus.; composer; teacher; administrator; b. Ottawa, Ont. 16 Dec. 1954; s. Charles Anthony Lawrence and Prudence Eva (White) S.; e. Univ. of Toronto B.Mus., M.Mus. 1980; Royal Conservatory of Music, comp. with Dr. S. Dolin 1974–78; Dept. of Music, Nazareth College, Rochester, N.Y.; Head, Composition Div., Royal Conservatory of Music 1986; formerly with Dept. of Music, Univ. of Victoria, Victoria, B.C.; selected premieres: 'Pro Tempore' Lontano Ensemble, France 1980, New Music Concerts (CBC broadcast) 1981; 'Music from Nowhere' Arraymusic (CBC) 1984; 'Tomorrow and Tomorrow' Ctr. for Contemp. Opera, N.Y. 1987 (1st Candn. opera to prem. in N.Y.), produced by CBC for television (broadcast Feb. 19th 1989); 'Dream Play' Candn. Opera Co. 1988 (1 of first 'composers-in-res.' at C.O.C.); Comissioned by Three Centuries Festival to compose an opera for 1990 season; profiled: 'Music' magazine, autumn 1988; 'Music Scene' Jan. 1988; 'Maclean's' Apr. 1987; see also 'Opera Monthly' (N.Y.) August 1988 for lengthy article on composer-in-residence programme, criticism of compositions; Teacher, Royal Cons. 1979; Mem., Candn. League of Composers (past bd. mem.); Assoc. Comp., Candn. Music Ctr.; Mem., P.R.O. Can.; Past Extve., Fac. Assn., Royal Cons.; Bd. of Dir., Church Isabella Housing Co-op. 1982–85, 1987.

**SULTAN, Ralph George Martin,** B.A.Sc., M.B.A., M.A., Ph.D.; executive; b. Vancouver, B.C. 6 June 1933; s. John Edward Sultan; e. Univ. of B.C. B.A.Sc. 1956; Harvard Business Sch. M.B.A. 1960; Harvard Univ. M.A. 1964, Ph.D. (Econ.) 1965; m. Shirley Anne Steele 1956; children: Nels, Kirsten, Christina, Karla; PRES., NORTHERN INVESTORS INC. and CHRMN., CARIBOO FIBREBOARD LTD.; Teaching Fellow in Econ. Harvard Univ. 1962–63, Assoc. Prof. Harvard Grad. Sch. Business Adm. 1964–73; Chief Economist, Sr. Vice-Pres. Global Energy & Minerals Group, Royal Bank of Canada 1973–80; Extve. Vice-Pres., Hudson Bay Mining & Smelting 1981; Vice Pres., Starlaw Holdings Ltd. 1982; Extve. Vice Pres., Curragh Resources 1986; Baker Scholar, Harvard Univ. 1960; Ford Foundation Fellow in Econ. 1962–64; Dir., Discovery Enterprises Inc.; author 'Pricing in the Electrical Oligopoly' (Vol. I: 'Competition or Collusion' 1974; Vol. II 'Business Strategy' 1975); 'Problems in Marketing' 1969; mem. Assn. Prof. Engrs. Ont.; Beta Theta Pi; Lutheran; recreations: skiing; Homes: 7165 Rockland Wynd, West Vancouver, B.C. V7W 2L2 and 199 Lang Farm Rd., Stowe, Vermont 05672.

**SUMARAH, John Charles,** B.A., M.Ed., Ed.D.; university professor; b. Newcastle, N.B. 24 April 1948; s. George William and Amanda Helen (Asoyuf) S.; e. St. Francis Xavier Univ. B.A. (1st class hons.) 1969; Univ. of Toronto (OISE) M.Ed. 1981, Ed.D. 1984; m. Colleen d. John and Laura Walsh 26 June 1976; one d.: Sheena; PROFESSOR, FACULTY OF MANAGEMENT AND EDUCATION, ACADIA UNIV. 1982– ; L'Arche Internat. France, India 1971–76; Psychology Consultant, Atlantic Behavioural Science Applications Inc.; Dir., Robert Pope Found.; author: 'On Becoming a Community' 1989; editor: 'A Network of Friends' 1992; co-editor: 'Images of Love, Words of Hope' 1991; Home: P.O. Box 1224, Wolfville, N.S. B0P 1X0; Office: Wolfville, N.S. B0P 1X0.

**SUMMERS, Joe;** music executive; b. Detroit, Mich. 4 May 1940; s. Joseph M. and Margaret (Wilson) S.; e. York Univ.; Queen's Univ.; m. Gloria d. David and Edna Laface 2 May 1959; children: Michelle, Lori, Veronica, Joseph, Christine, Jeremy; PRESIDENT, A&M/ISLAND/MOTOWN RECORDS 1972– ; Capitol Records 1957–59; Decca Records 1960–68; Motown Records 1968–72; Chair, Canadian Assn. Recording Ind.; Dir., Canadian Assn. Recording Arts & Sci.; Black Music Assn. Canada; recreations: sports, music; Home: 1498 Concession Rd. #4, R.R. 1, Box 1498, Hamton, Ont. L0B 1J0; Office: 1345 Denison St., Markham, Ont. L3R 5V2.

**SUMMERS, Rear-Admiral Kenneth James,** B.A., OMM, MSC, CD2; naval officer; b. St. Thomas, Ont. 20 July 1944; s. Kenneth and Margaret (Parker) S.; e. Nepean H.S. 1963; Royal Military College B.A. 1967; m. Joanne d. Ross and Beatrice Thompson 16 Dec. 1967; children: Edward (Ted) James, Kimberley (Kim) Leigh, Kenneth 'David' Andrew; COMMANDER, CANADIAN DEFENCE LIAISON STAFF (WASHINGTON) 1992– ; Junior Officer training, West Coast 1971; completed Operations Officer Course 1971; Operations Offr., HMCS Iroquois 1972–75; Extve. Offr., HMCS Athabaskan & Commanding Offr., HMCS Algonquin; served as Staff Offr., Nat. Defence H.Q. 3 times between 1975–88; returned to sea as Commander, Second Candn. Destroyer Squadron 1988; Commodore 1989; Commander, Candn. Fleet & Chief of Staff Opns., Maritime Command H.Q. Halifax 1989; Commander, Candn. Naval Task Group ordered to Arabian Gulf Aug. 1990; Commander, Candn. Forces Middle East based in Bahrain Oct. 1990; Chief of Staff, Maritime Forces Pacific 1991–92; Order of Military Merit (Cda) 1988; Order of Bahrain Medal (1st class) 1991; Bronze Star (U.S. govt.) 1991; King Abdul Aziz Medal (3rd class), Saudi Arabia Govt. 1991; Meritorious Service Cross (Cda) 1991; Key to City of Ottawa 1991; recreations: sailing, jogging, golf; Home: 3539 Williamsburg Lane N.W., Washington, D.C. 20008; Office: Canadian Embassy, 501 Pennsylvania Ave. N.W., Washington, D.C. 20001.

**SUMMERS, Merna;** writer; b. Mannville, Alta.; d. Lewis Edward and Anna (Modin) S.; author: (short stories) 'The Skating Party' 1974; 'Calling Home' 1982; 'North of the Battle' 1988; faculty mem., writing program, Banff Sch. of Fine Arts 1989, 1990; writer-in-residence, St. Albert Public Lib. 1989; Winnipeg Library 1990–91; Univ. of Alta. 1991–92; recipient Ohio State Award Ednl. Broadcasting 1968; Katherine Anne Porter Fiction Prize 1979; Writers Guild Alta. Award for Excellence 1982, 1988; Marian Engel Award 1989; mem. PEN Internat.; Writers' Union Can.; Writers' Guild Alta.; Enoch Emery Soc.; Address: No. 201, 11455 – 41 Ave., Edmonton, Alta. T6J 0T9.

**SUMSION (GILL), Thelma H.,** B.Sc., M.Ed.; association executive; occupational therapist; b. Woodstock, Ont. 28 Aug. 1947; d. Frank William Charles and the late Helen May (Corman) S. (dec.); e. Univ. of Toronto Dip. Physical & Occupational Therapy 1969, B.Sc. (O.T.) 1979; Univ. of W. Ont. M.Ed. 1982; PAST PRES. CANDN. ASSN. OF OCCUPATIONAL THERAPISTS 1990–91; presently Faculty mem. Prog. in Occupational Therapy Univ. of W. Ont. and OT Co-ordinator for Northern Outreach Program; Dir. Occupational Therapy London Psychiatric Hosp. 1976–78; Dir. of Occupational Therapy Clarke Inst. of Psychiatry 1984–89; apptd. Asst. Prof. to Dept. of Psychiatry Univ. of Toronto 1988, Asst. Prof. (status only) Div. Occupational Therapy 1985; lectr. many facilities, univs., nat. & internat. confs.; held various positions provl. and nat. profl. assns. incl. Chrmn. Membership Credentialling Ctte. and Conf. Adv. present Assn. and Vice Pres. Ont. Soc. Occupational Therapists; Muriel Driver Lectureship present Assn. 1985; Candn. Delegate to World Federation of Occupational Therapists 1991– ; author numerous articles and book reviews various jours.; Home: 366 Victoria St., London, Ont. N6A 2C9; Office: Northern Outreach Program, Univ. of Western Ont., London, Ont. N6A 5C1.

**SUN, Anthony Mien-Fang,** M.Sc., Ph.D.; research scientist; educator; b. Nanking, China 10 Apr. 1935; s. Pei Chien Sun and Tung Hsin Wang-Sun; e. Nat. Taiwan Univ. B.Sc. 1958; Univ. of Toronto M.Sc. 1965, Ph.D. 1972; m. Irene Lin-Lin d. Kung-Lian 20 June 1964; children: Alexander, Elizabeth; ASSOC. PROF. OF PHYSIOLOGY, UNIV. OF TORONTO 1978– , Lectr., Asst. Prof. 1965–68; Rsch. Sci./Cons. Toronto Hosp. for Sick Children 1972–78; Sr. Rsch. Scientist, Connaught Rsch. Inst., Connaught Labs. Ltd. and Head of Islet & Hormone Rsch. 1974; Hon. Prof. Shanghai Med. Univ. 1985– ; Assoc. Ed. CRC CRitical Reviews in Therapeutic Drug Carrier Systems; author or coauthor numerous articles; Section Ed., Biomaterial, Artificial Cells and Artificial Organs 1986– ; mem. Internat. Soc. Artificial Organs; Candn. Diabetes Assn.; Candn. Physiol. Soc.; Toronto Diabetes Assn.; Internat. Controlled Release Soc.; Banting & Best Diabetic Centre; Am. Diabetes Assn.; Am. Soc. Artificial Internal Organs; recreations: tennis, art; Home: 1001 Bay St., Apt. 1703, Toronto, Ont. M5S 3A6; Office: Dept. of Physiology, Med. Sciences Bldg., Univ. of Toronto, Toronto, Ont. M5S 1A8.

**SUNDARESAN, Mosur Kalyanaraman,** M.Sc., Ph.D.; university professor; b. Madras, India 2 Sept. 1929; s. Mosur Ramanathan and Mosur (Kanakavalli) Kalyanaraman; e. Delhi Univ., B.Sc. (Hons.) 1947, M.Sc. 1949; Cornell Univ., Ph.D. 1955; m. C.S. Bharathy d. of C.S. Rao 7 June 1957; children: Sudhir, Sujata; PROF., DEPT. OF PHYSICS, CARLETON UNIV. 1961– ; Rsch. Offr., Atomic Energy Establishment (India) 1955–57; post-doct. fellow, N.R.C. 1957–59; Reader in Physics, Panjab Univ. (India) 1959–61; Mem., Candn. Assn. of Physicists; Am. Physical Soc.; Am. Assn. of Physics Teachers; Inst. of Particle Physics of Can.; recreations: classical music; Home: 11 Brockington Cres., Nepean, Ont. K2G 4K7; Office: Colonel By Dr., Ottawa, Ont. K1S 5B6.

**SUNTER, Robert Henry Anthony;** broadcasting executive; b. Liverpool, Eng. 20 Nov. 1931; s. Thomas and Elizabeth (Gee) S.; e. St. Francis Xavier's Coll. Liverpool; Simon Fraser Univ. Burnaby, B.C.; m. Cynthia Fung Feb. 27th 1993; DIR. OF RADIO FOR BRITISH COLUMBIA REGION 1987– ; Reporter, 'Lakeshore Advertiser' Toronto 1954, Mng. Ed. 1956–59; Ed. 'Weston Times and Guide' 1955–56; Asst. Ed. 'Peterborough Examiner' 1959–64; News Ed. and Ed. 'Vancouver Times' 1964–65; Music Critic 'Vancouver Sun' 1965–68; Head of Music, Ont. Arts Council 1968–76; Head of Radio Music CBC 1976–81; Assoc. Head, TV Arts, Music & Science, CBC 1984–87; co-author and ed. 'English Radio Development Project Report' 1983; Founding Bd. mem. Assn. Candn. Orchs. 1971– ; Founding mem. Ont. Choral Fedn. 1971–76; recreations: tennis, cooking; Clubs: West Vancouver Tennis; Vancouver Bd. of Trade; Home: 2195 Lawson Ave., West Vancouver, B.C. V7V 2E1; Office: Box 4600, Vancouver, B.C. V6B 4A2.

**SUOPANKI, Kari Johannes;** forest industry executive; b. Helsinki, Finland 19 Sept. 1940; s. Eero Johannes and Mary Regina (Henriksson) S.; e. HSYK H.S. (Finland) 1958; Forest Industry School Sweden diploma 1959; Military Serv., Officer School Finland, 2nd Lieutenant 1960; SLK Finnish Businessman's College Finland diploma 1962; children: Robin Johannes, Thomas Bryden; President, Enso Forest Products Ltd. 1990–93; Salesman, Soc. Copap France 1963–65; Marketing Mgr., Eurocan Pulp & Paper Co., B.C. 1966–69; Dir., Rauma-Repola (U.K.) Ltd. 1969–74; Managing Dir., Enso (U.K.) Ltd. 1974–82; Pres., Enso Internat. Inc. New York 1982–83; Pres. & Chief Extve. Offr., Eurocan Pulp & Paper Co. B.C. 1983–88; Pres. 1991–93; Managing Dir., Soc. Copap France 1988–90; Chair, Papeteries R. Soustre & Fils France 1990–92; Bd. Mem., Council of Forest Industries of B.C.; Pulp & Paper Indus. Relns. Bureau; B.C. Forest Alliance; recreations: golf, skiing; clubs: Vancouver Club, SF Club (U.K.); Home: 402 – 1012 Beach Ave., Vancouver, B.C. V6E 1T7.

**SUPER, Donald E.,** M.A., D.Sc., Ph.D.; psychologist; b. Honolulu, Hawaii 10 July 1910; s. Paul and Margaret Louise (Stump) S.; e. La Chataigneraie, Geneva, Switz.; Oxford Univ. B.A. (Hons.) 1932, M.A. 1936, D.Sc. 1985; Columbia Univ. Ph.D. 1940; Hon. Doct. Univ. of Lisbon 1983; Univ. de Sherbrooke 1989; m. Anne-Margaret d. Marion Russell and Althea Baker 12 Sept. 1936; children: Robert Marion, Charles McAfee; PROF. EMERITUS, COLUMBIA UNIV. 1975– ; Instr., Fenn Coll. & Asst. Sec., YMCA Cleveland 1932–36; Asst. & Assoc. Prof., Edn. Psych., Clark Univ. 1938–42; Aviation Psychol., US Air Force 1942–45, 1951; Assoc. Prof., Columbia Univ. 1942–49; Prof. 1949–75; Dir., Div. Psych. & Edn. 1965–75; Chrmn., Dept. of Psych. 1971–75; Visiting Prof., Univ. of Paris 1958–59, 1976–78; Fellow, Wolfson Coll. & Nat. Inst. for Careers Edn. & Counselling (Cambridge) 1975–79; Cons. or Vis. Prof., Univ. of Georgia, Univ. of N.C., Armstrong State Coll.; Former Cons., Canada Employment & Immigration Occupational Analysis Br. 1978–80, Canada Council and other orgns.; Distinguished Sci. Cont. Award 1983; Outstanding Rsch. Award 1961; Career Devel. Profl. Award 1989 and others; several past extve. positions with assns. (played a part in bringing Candn. anglo- & francophone guidance & psych. assns. together, and is still active); author/co-author, editor of monographs and articles as well as prefaces for francophone books; an American who values his Canadian connections; recreations: reading, travel, gardening; clubs: United Oxford & Cambridge, Princeton; Home: 23 Mulberry Bluff, Savannah, GA 31406.

**SUPERINA, Riccardo Antonio,** B.Sc., M.D., C.M., F.R.S.C.(C); university assoc. prof.; attending surgeon; b. Trieste, Italy 30 July 1950; s. Giuliano Alessandro and Maria (Ivis) S.; e. St. Pius Tenth H.S. 1967; McGill Univ., B.Sc. (Hon.) 1971, M.D., C.M. 1975; University Scholar 1973; m. Lori d. Phil and Veronica Acal 1 May 1993; children: Nicholas, Gabriella, Stefan, Simone; CONS. SURGEON, HOSP. FOR SICK CHILDREN 1985– ; Staff, Toronto Gen. Hosp.; Chief Res., Hosp. for Sick Children 1982–83; R. Samuel MacLaughlan Surg. Fellow 1983–85; Asst. Prof., University of Toronto; Rsch. Fellow, Univ. of Oxford 1983–85; Medical Dir., Transplantation Services; Dir., Liver Transplant Serv., Hosp. for Sick Children; Mem., Royal Coll. of Phys. & Surg. of Can.; Candn. Assn. for Pediat. Surgs.; Transplantation Soc.; Am. Soc. of Transplant Surgeons; Candn. Transplant Soc.; Am. Pediatric Surgical Assn.; Candn. Assn. for Trauma; Royal Soc. of Med. (U.K.); Candn. Med. Assn.; Fellow, Am. Coll. of Surgs.; recreations: opera, tennis; Home: R.R. 1, King City, Ont. L0G 1K0; Office: 555 University Ave., Toronto, Ont. M5G 1X8.

**SUREAU, Real,** F.C.A.; financial executive; b. Val d'Or, Que. 18 Nov. 1940; s. Bruno and Alice (Ouellet) S.; e. Coll. St-Joseph Sr. H.S. 1957; McGill Univ., summer sch. in accountancy 1961, 1963; m. Huguette d. Roland and Rita Naud 27 July 1963; children: Nathalie, Christine, Sophie; President, Sureau Management Limited since 1976; ADVISOR, CAISSE CENTRALE DESJARDINS 1993– ; Partner & Mng. Dir., Belanger, L'Houmeau, Sureau & Assoc. 1963–73; Sec. Treas. & Vice-Pres. Finan., Forex Inc. 1973–82; Vice Pres., Canam Manac Group Inc. 1982–91; Advisor 1992– ; C.A. 1963; F.C.A. 1986; Dir., Ordre des C.A. du Québec 1993–95; Dir., Inst. de Readaptation de Montréal 1990; Home: 90 Berlioz, Suite 1701, Ile des Soeurs, Que. H3E 1N1.

**SURRIDGE, Marie Elizabeth,** M.A., D.Phil.; educator; b. London, Eng. 13 March 1931; d. Edward Kenneth and Olwen Watkins (Roberts) Thomas; e. Brondesbury and Kilburn High Sch. London 1950; Oxford Univ. (State Scholar, Exhibitioner Somerville Coll.) B.A. 1953, Dip. in Comparative Philol. 1955, M.A. 1957, D.Phil 1962; m. David Henry Crossley s. Rex and Roy Surridge 23 July 1955; daughters: Michela, Lisa, Siân; PROF. OF FRENCH STUDIES, QUEEN'S UNIV. 1987– , Head of French Studies 1983–93, mem. Senate 1979–83, 1990–91; part-time teaching St. John's and other Oxford Colleges 1955–67; Asst. Prof. present Univ. 1970, Assoc. Prof. 1977; author various linguistics articles; Pres. Candn. Linguistic Assn. 1988–90; recreations: family activities, walking, sailing; Home: 831 Wartman Ave., Kingston, Ont. K7M 4M3; Office: Kingston, Ont. K7L 3N6.

**SUSSMAN, Henry B.,** B.Sc.; real estate syndication; b. Toronto, Ont. 21 Jan. 1922; s. David and Rachel (Cohen) S.; e. Pub. and High Schs., Toronto, Ont.; St. John's Mil. Acad., Delafield Wis., Grad. 1941; Coll. of Business Adm., Syracuse Univ., Grad. 1945 B.Sc.; PRES., DELAFIELD INVESTMENTS LTD.; PRES., HENRY SUSSMAN REAL ESTATE LTD.; entered family business 1946; joined real estate firm of L.G. Candler Associates Ltd. 1954; Partner 1956; resigned 1958; formed own firm, H.B. Sussman Associates Ltd. and assumed Presidency 1958; Pres. and Dir., The Sussman Realty Corp. Ltd. 1962–73; served with U.S. Army; Dir., Mt. Sinai Hosp.; Zeta Beta Tau; recreations: golf, tennis, reading; Clubs: Oakdale Golf & Country; Primrose; York Raquets; Office: Suite 607, 2 St Clair Ave. W., Toronto, Ont. M4V 1L5.

**SUTCLIFFE, Simon Bruce,** B.Sc., MBBS, M.D., FRCP, FRCP(C); physician, clinical oncologist; b. Hitchin Herts., U.K. 12 May 1946; s. Jack and Hannah Catherine S.; e. St. Bartholomew's Hosp., Univ. of London B.Sc. (Hons.) 1966, LRCP MRCS 1970, MBBS (Hons.) 1970; MRCP (U.K.) 1973; Univ. of London, M.D. 1979; FRCP(C) 1981; FRCP(U.K.) 1985; m. Margaret Ann d. Bernard and Florence Armitage 17 Feb. 1973; children: Siobhan, Sian, Catherine; PRES. & CHIEF EXTVE. OFFR., PRINCESS MARGARET HOSP. 1994– ; internship St. Bartholomew's, Hammersmith, Churchill hospitals, Albert Einstein Coll. of Med. 1971–78; Vis. Asst. Prof., Tulane Univ. 1979; Resident, Radiation Oncol., present hosp. (P.M.H.) 1979–81; Staff radiation oncol. P.M.H., Sr. Sci. Staff Mem., O.C.I., Prof., Radiol., Univ. of Toronto 1989– ; Vice-Pres., Oncology Prog., Princess Margaret Hosp. 1989–94; Mem., Sci. Adv. Bd., Imreg Inc. (U.S.); Mem., Sci. Adv. Bd., Cangene; Cons., Wellesley & Toronto Gen. hosps.; Assoc. Prof., Dept. of Hematol./Oncol., Hosp. for Sick Children; Mem., Candn. Assn. of Radiation Oncol.; Am. Fed. of Clin. Rsch.; N.Y. Acad. of Sci.; author: 'Immunology of the Lymphomas' 1985; recreations: music; Home: 67 Metcalfe St., Toronto, Ont. M4X 1S1; Office: Rm. 187, 500 Sherbourne St., Toronto, Ont. M4X 1K9.

**SUTHERLAND, Daniel Rae,** B.Sc., P.Eng., C.L.S., A.L.S., S.L.S.; consulting engineer; executive; b. Edmonton, Alta. 4 March 1926; s. Daniel Robert and Stella Mary (Boyle) S.; e. Pub. and High schs.; Univ. of Alberta, B.Sc. (Civil Engn) 1948; m. Lorna Phylis Pearce 1 Sept. 1951; children: Terry Ingrid, Kim Joanne, Barbara Gail; PRESIDENT, SPATIAL INFORMATION SERVICES LTD.; Pres., C.E.S. Surveys Ltd.; Candn. Engineering Services Ltd.; Canadian Databank; Sutherland Airship Corp.; Mercantile Ventures Holding Ltd.; Codavision Dev. Ltd.; Former Chairman, Pay Television Corp.; Mystery Lake Broadcasting Ltd.; CESM-TV Ltd.; Western Coded Television Ltd.; Smart Management Systems Ltd.; Former Chrmn. and Dir. Western Industrial Research Training Centre; Canadian Rural Television Network CRTN Ltd.; Former Dir., Unity Bank of Canada; Chrmn., Kiwanis Children's Home; Pres., Windsor Pk. Home & School; mem. Alta. Prof. Engrs. & Geol. Assn.; Canadian Inst. of Surveying; Dom., Alta. & Sask. Land Surveyors; Phi Kappa Pi; Presbyterian, recreations: skiing, golf, swimming, climbing, hiking; Clubs: Kiwanis; Edmonton; Mayfair; Petroleum; Derrick; Home: 220 Brookside Terrace, Edmonton, Alta. T6H 4J6.

**SUTHERLAND, Donald,** O.C.; actor; b. Saint John, N.B. 17 July 1935; e. Univ. Toronto; m. Shirley Douglas (div.); Theatre appearances incl.: 'The Male Animal'; 'The Tempest'; 'August for People' (London debut); 'On a Clear Day You Can See to Canterbury'; 'The Shewing Up of Blanco Posnet'; 'The Spoon River Anthology'; films incl.: 'The Castle of the Living Dead'; 'Dr. Terror's House of Horrors'; 'The Dirty Dozen'; 'Oedipus the King'; 'Interlude'; 'Joanna'; 'The Split'; 'Start the Revolution Without Me'; 'The Act of the Heart'; 'MASH'; 'Kelly's Heroes'; 'Little Murders'; 'Alex in Wonderland'; 'Klute'; 'Steelyard Blues'; 'Alien Thunder'; 'The Master'; 'Don't Look Now'; 'Lady Ice'; 'SPYS'; 'The Day of the Locust'; 'Casanova'; 'The Eagle Has Landed'; 'The Great Train Robbery'; 'Murder by Decree'; 'Invasion of the Body Snatchers'; 'Animal House'; 'A Man, A Woman and A Bank'; 'Ordinary People' (winner Best Picture Oscar 1981); TV appearances: 'Marching to Sea'; 'The Death of Bessie Smith'; 'Hamlet at Elsinore'; 'The Saint'; 'The Avengers'; Gideon's Way'; 'The Champions'; formerly with London Acad. Music and Dramatic Art, Perth Repertory Theatre, Scotland; also repertory at Nottingham, Chesterfield, Branley, Sheffield.

**SUTHERLAND, Fraser,** B.J.; writer; b. Pictou, N.S. 5 Dec. 1946; s. Russell and Mary S.; e. Univ. of King's Coll.; Carleton Univ., B.J. (Hons.) 1969; m. Alison d. Dr. W.E. and Althea Armour 20 Oct. 1978; one s.; Malcolm Patrick; Reporter/Staff Writer, Wall Street Journal, The Globe & Mail, Toronto Star, etc. 1965–70; Founding Ed., 'Northern Journey' 1971–76; Columnist, 'Quill & Quire' 1974–75; Mng. Ed., 'Books in Canada' 1984–86; regular reviewer, The Globe & Mail 1984– ; Lit. Ed., 'The Idler' 1986; Ed. Funk & Wagnalls 'Canadian College Dictionary' 1992– ; lectr., speaker, panelist/participant, num. seminars/workshops on pub., edit. & writing 1971– ; Orgnr., Scottish-Candn. Lit. Celeb. 1979; Teacher, D. Thompson Univ. Ctr. 1982–83; Contbr., num. anthol. & jours. (worldwide); several writing grants, Can. Counc., Nova Scotia Department of Tourism and Culture & Ont. Arts Counc. 1973– ; Writer-in-Res., Univ. of Edinburgh 1981–82; Presbyn.; Mem., League of Candn. Poets 1974–87 (Extve. Mem. 1979–80); Writers' Fed. of N.S. 1977– (Extve. Mem. 1978–80, 1987–90, 1991–92); Writers' Union of Canada 1988– (Extve. mem. 1990–91); Internat. P.E.N.; Chrmn., N.S. Writers Counc. 1979–80, 1991–92; Freelance Editors' Assn. of Canada 1991– ; author: 'The Monthly Epic: A History of Canadian Magazines' 1989; 'In the Village of Alias' 1986, 'Whitefaces' 1986, 'John Glassco' 1984, 'Madwomen' 1978, 'The Style of Innocence' 1972; Home: 39 Helena Ave., Toronto, Ont. M6G 2H3.

**SUTHERLAND, Harry,** Q.C., LL.B.; lawyer; b. Toronto, Ont. 26 Apl. 1930; s. Harry and Anne Collingwood (Johnston) S.; e. Upper Can. Coll.; Univ. of Toronto (Trinity Coll.) 1947–48, LL.B. 1952; Osgoode Hall Law Sch.; PARTNER, FRASER & BEATTY 1962– ; Dir. Blue Streak-Hygrade Motor Products Ltd.; Capitol-EMI Industries Inc.; Dunn & Bradstreet Canada Holding Ltd.; Finlayson Enterprises Ltd.; Fisons Corporation Ltd.; Great Lakes Biochemical (Canada) Ltd.; Grote Manufacturing Ltd.; ITC Television Cinema Distribution Inc.; MEPC Canadian Properties Ltd.; Nabco Technologies Ltd.; Nor-Am Agricultural Products Ltd.; Coats Canada Inc.; Reed Exhibition Companies Inc.; Rouse Service Canada; Tenneco Heavy Duty Brake Ltd.; Woodchem Inc.; TEMI Canada Inc.; articled with Fraser & Beatty 1952–54; called to Bar of Ont. 1954; cr. Q.C. 1972; recipient Centennial Medal Can.; Queen's Silver Jubilee Medal; mem. Vincent Graves Greene Philatelic Rsch. Found.; Philaprint Inc.; co-author 5th, 6th and 7th eds. Fraser's Handbook on Company Law; 6th ed. Fraser and Stewart Company Law of Canada; co-ed. 2nd ed. Candn. Abridgement on Corporations; mem. Royal Philatelic Soc. Can.; Toronto Assn. Philatelic Exhns. Inc.; Presbyterian; recreations: philately, reading, backgammon, bridge; Clubs: Toronto; York; National; Rosedale Golf; East India (London, Eng.); Home: 155 Forest Hill Rd., Toronto, Ont. M5P 2N2; Office: P.O. Box 100, 1 First Canadian Place, Toronto, Ont. M5X 1B2.

**SUTHERLAND, Ian,** B.Comm., C.A., C.F.A.; b. Ottawa, Ont. 29 Jan. 1945; s. Hugh W. and Jocelyn M. (Campbell) S.; e. Univ. of Man., B.Comm. 1966; C.A. 1968; C.F.A. 1976; m. Judy d. Miller and Marjorie Stewart 16 June 1967; three s. Ian W., Derek, James; PRESIDENT & CHIEF EXECUTIVE OFFR., THE NORTH WEST COMPANY 1993– ; Dir., The North West Company; MFP Technology Services Inc.; MTC Mortgage Investment Corp.; MTC Leasing Inc.; Acct. Price Waterhouse 1966–69; Treas. Commercial Trust 1969–75; Vice Pres. Mercantile Bank 1975–78; Pres., Merchant Trust 1978–81; Extve. Vice Pres., The Mutual Trust Co. 1981–93; Office: 77 Main St., Winnipeg, Man. R3C 2R1.

**SUTHERLAND, R.J. (Bob);** banker; b. Ottawa; EXECUTIVE VICE-PRESIDENT, HUMAN RESOURCES 1992– ; joined Royal Bank Ottawa 1958; various posts in Ottawa, Montreal, Toronto and Vancouver 1958–82; Vice-Pres., Planning & Devel. Nat. Accounts 1982; Nat. Accounts - Ont. 1983; Commercial Banking & Nat. Accounts for B.C. District 1985; Sr. Vice-Pres., Corp. & Govt. Banking 1986; Sr. Vice-Pres. & Gen. Mgr., Atlantic provinces 1988; Office: Box 6001, 1 Place Ville Marie, Montreal, Que. H3C 3A9.

**SUTHERLAND, Ronald,** B.A., M.A., Ph.D.; writer, university professor, journalist; b. Montreal, Que. 10 Nov. 1933; s. (by adoption) Alexander John and Janet Hunter (Goudie) S.; e. Montreal H.S. 1950; McGill Univ., B.A. 1954, M.A. 1955; Univ. of Glasgow; Wayne State Univ., Ph.D. 1960; m. Velma-Jean d. Lillian and Luther Carter 7 June 1958; children: Janet, Katherine, Velma, Winona, Colin; PROF. TITULAIRE, UNIV. DE SHERBROOKE 1973– ; Lectr., Wayne State Univ. 1957–59; Prof., present univ. 1959– ; dir., études anglaises 1963–69, 1970–73; Guest Prof., Stirling Univ. 1969; Leeds Univ. 1970; Calgary Univ. 1979; Colorado Coll. 1979, '80, '83, '89; Univ. Augsburg 1984; Univ. canadienne en France 1988; Award of Merit, Assn. of Candn. Studies 1984; Pres., N. Hatley Sch. Comn. 1966–68; Mem., P.E.N.; author: 'Frederick Philip Grove' 1969, 'Second Image' 1971, 'The New Hero' 1977 (monographs); 'Lark des Neiges' 1971, 'Where Do the MacDonalds Bury Their Dead' 1977 (novels); co-author: 'L'Esprit de la langue anglaise' 1965; editor: 'The Romaunt of the Rose and le Roman de la Rose' 1967; Contbr. 'The Encyclopedia of World Literature' 1973, 'Understanding Canada' 1982, 'La Storia della civiltà letteraria inglese' 1990; recreations: bag-piping, pool; Home: C.P. 223, North Hatley, Que. J0B 2C0; Office: Sherbrooke, Que. J1K 2R1.

**SUTHERLAND, Sandra D.,** Q.C., B.Com., LL.B.; lawyer; b. Vancouver, B.C. 12 June 1944; d. C.R. and Lucille S.; e. Kitsilano High Sch. 1959–61; Univ. of B.C., B.Com. 1968, LL.B. 1969; called to Bar of B.C. and admitted as solicitor 1970; apptd. Q.C. 1984; Partner, Freeman & Company 1979; preferred field of practice, CORPORATE AND COMMERCIAL LAW; Dir.: The Imperial Life Assurance Company of Canada 1984– ; Vancouver Opera Assn. (Dir. 1984– ); Vancouver Opera Found. (Trustee 1987– ; Chrmn. 1988– ); Power Smart Inc. 1990–92; Chrmn., Personal Property Security Act Consultative Ctte. 1992– ; Chrmn., Solicitors' Legal Opinions Ctte. 1988– ; mem., Personal Property Security Ctte., a Sub-ctte. of the Bus. Law Sect., Candn. Bar Assoc. (B.C.) 1976– ; Assoc., Campney & Murphy 1970–73, Partner 1973–79; Dir., Vancouver City Savings Credit Union 1974–85 (Vice-Chrmn. 1977–81, Chrmn. 1981–83); B.C. Central Credit Union 1976–81 (First Vice-Chrmn. 1980–81); Insur. Corp. of British Columbia 1977–81; Yorkshire Trust Co. 1985–87; Eaton Trust Co. 1986–88; British Columbia Hydro & Power Authority 1981–92; Tutor, Company Law Course, Bar Admission 1975–80 (Head Company Law Course 1979–80); Continuing Legal Education Panels: Debentures, Family Relations Act 1979–80, Solicitors Opinions 1985 and 1990; Personal Property Security Act 1989; Personal Property Security Act 1990–91; Public Gov.: Vancouver Stock Exchange 1977–80; former mem. Adv. Bd., M.B.A. Programme, Simon Fraser Univ. 1978–82; former mem. Adv. Bd., Fac. of Business Admin., Simon Fraser Univ. 1982–85; mem.: Law Soc. of B.C.; Candn. Bar Assn.; SPCA; Candn. Wildlife Fedn.; Credit Union Found. of B.C.; Clubs: University Women's; The Canadian (Vancouver); Arbutus; America Contract Bridge League; Address: 3937 W. 12th Ave., Vancouver, B.C. V5Z 4G3.

**SUTHREN, Victor James Henry,** B.A., M.A., F.R.S.A.; museum director; writer; b. Montréal, Qué. 2 Mar. 1942; s. Joseph William and Emily Anne (Roberts) S.; e. Bishop's Univ., B.A. 1965; McGill Univ. 1966; Concordia Univ., M.A. 1970; m. Lindsay d. Haldane and Jean Scott 12 July 1969; children: Scott, Caedi, Amy; DIR. CANADN. WAR MUSEUM 1986– ; Navy Res. Offr. 1964–71; Curator, 'La Maison Del Vecchio' Mus.,

Old Montreal 1967–68; Staff Hist., Fortress of Louisbourg, N.S. 1971–73; Rsch. Hist., Parks Can. 1973–75; Curator of Art, War Mus. 1975–76; Curator, Exhibit Planning & Design 1976–81; Dep. Chief Curator 1981–86; Bd. of Adv., Am. Clipper Trust; Adv. Bd., Maritime Mus. of B.C.; Bd. B.C. Vintage Vessel Registry; Fellow, Co. of Military Hist. 1978; Royal Soc. of Arts (U.K.) 1980; Mem., N. Am. Soc. for Oceanic Hist.; Internat. Hist. Watercraft Soc.; Candn. Mus. Assn.; Secy., Candn. Sail Training Assn.; Naval Offrs. Assn. Can.; Candn. Nautical Rsch. Soc.; author: 'In Perilous Seas' 1983, 1984, 'A King's Ransom' 1980, 1982, 'The Black Cockade' 1977, 1978, 1981; 'Royal Yankee' 1988; 'The Golden Galleon' 1989; 'Admiral of Fear' 1990; 'Captain Monsoon' 1992 (novels); 'The Oxford Book of Canadian Military Anecdotes' 1989; 'Canadian Stories Of The Sea' 1993; currently writing hist. novels based on career of Capt. James Cook, R.N., and Venetian Republic of 1494 (agent: Lucinda Vardey); recreations: sailing, light opera, ski touring, writing; Home: 36 Bellwood Ave., Ottawa, Ont. K1S 1S7; Office: 330 Sussex Dr., Ottawa, Ont. K1A 0M8.

**SUTTER, Morley Carman,** M.D., B.Sc.(Med.), Ph.D.; educator; pharmacologist; b. Redvers, Sask. 18 May 1933; s. Christian Benjamin and Amelia (Duke) S.; e. Redvers (Sask.) High Sch. 1950 (Gov. Gen.'s Medal); Univ. of Man. M.D., B.Sc.(Med.) 1957 (Isbister Scholarship 1952), Ph.D. 1963; m. Virginia F. M. d. Robert Laidlaw, Winnipeg, Man. 29 June 1957; children: Gregory Robert, F. Michelle, Brent Morley; PROF. OF PHARMACOL. & THERAPEUTICS, UNIV. OF B.C. since 1971 (Head of Dept. 1971–87); gen. med. practice Souris, Man. 1957–58; Med. Resident Winnipeg Gen. Hosp. 1958–59; Med. Research Council Fellow Univ. of Man. 1959–63; Imperial Chemical Industries Fellow, Cambridge Univ. 1963–65; Asst. Prof. of Pharmacol. Univ. of Toronto 1965–66; Med. Research Scholar Dept. Pharmacol. present univ. 1966–71, Asst. Prof. 1966, Assoc. Prof. 1968; Wellcome Foundation Travel Fellow 1963; mem., Comte. on Ethics of Exper. on Human Subjects Univ. of B.C.; author various articles scient. journs.; Sec., Pharmacol. Soc. of Can. 1986–89; mem., Br. Pharmacol. Soc.; Amer. Soc. Pharmac. and Exp. Therapy; Candn. Soc. Clin. Investigation; AAAS; New York Acad. of Sciences; recreations: reading, fishing, music, gardening, baseball, tennis; Office: Univ. of B.C., Vancouver, B.C. V6T 1Z3.

**SUTTON, Gerald Dudley;** economist; b. Uckfield, Sussex, Eng., 23 July 1925; s. John Reginald and Mildred Anne (Lockyer) s.; m. Margaret Lilian, d. James Scally, Kingston, Ont., 15 May 1948; children: Brian Dudley, Malcolm Robert, Christine Mary, Deborah Anne; Chrmn., Serenpet Inc.; Dir., Cassidy's Ltd.; Continental Manufacturers Canada Ltd.; Unican Security Systems Inc.; with Bank of Montreal 1943–58; apptd. Asst. Econ. Adviser, 1955; joined Nesbitt, Thomson and Co., Ltd. as Dir. of Research, 1958–64; became Gen. Mgr. of Canadian Enterprise Development Corp. Ltd. 1964; Vice Pres. and Gen. Mgr. 1966; Pres. to 1986; served with RCAF 1943–45 as Pilot Offr. (Pilot); past Pres., Child Care & Child Guidance Centres Inc.; Montreal Econs. Assn.; Montreal Jr. Bd. Trade; Que. Assn. for Mentally Retarded Children; Anglican; Clubs: National (Toronto); Home: 230 Morrison Rd., Oakville, Ont. L6J 4J4.

**SUTTON, Most Rev. Peter Alfred,** OMI; b. Chandler, Gaspé 18 Oct. 1934; s. Cornelius and Mabel (Greene) S.; e. St. Patrick's Coll, Ottawa; Loyola Univ., Chicago, M.Ed.; ARCHBISHOP OF KEEWATIN-LE PAS 1986; entered Cong. Missionary Oblates Mary Immaculate 1953; final profession as Oblate 1957; ordained 1960; Teacher, St. Patrick's Coll. High Sch. (Ottawa) 1961; Catholic Central High Sch. (London, Ont.) 1963; R.C. Bishop, Labrador-Schefferville 1974–86; Accompanying Bishop of Communities of L'Arche International of Jean Vanier since 1983; Archbishop of Keewatin-Le Pas 1986; Address: P.O. Box 270, The Pas, Man. R9A 1K4.

**SUTTON, Robert John,** B.Gen.Studies, M.B.A.; consultant; b. Edmonton, Alta. 4 April 1959; s. Percival and Dorothy Bertha (Wright) S.; e. Univ. of Michigan B.Gen.Studies 1981; Univ. of W. Ont. M.B.A. 1985; PARTNER, THE CALDWELL PARTNERS AMROP INTERNATIONAL (EXECUTIVE SEARCH) 1988– ; Vice-Pres., Regional Drilling 1981–82 (self-employed); Sales Rep., Procter & Gamble 1982–83; Product Mgr., then Vice-Pres., Sales & Marketing, Madison Chem. Indus. Ltd. 1985–88; Assoc., The Caldwell Partners Amrop Internat. 1988–89; Consultant 1989–90; Home: 3202 Vercheres St. S.W., Calgary, Alta.; Office: 3450, 400 Third Avenue S.W., Calgary, Alta. T2P 4H2.

**SUVIN, Darko R.,** Ph.D., F.R.S.C.; educator; writer; b. Zagreb, Yugoslavia 19 July 1932; s. Miroslav and Gertrude (Weiser) S.; e. Univ. of Zagreb. B.A. 1954, M.Sc. (equiv.) 1956, Ph.D. 1970; Bristol Univ.; The Sorbonne; Yale Univ.; PROF. OF ENGLISH, McGILL UNIV. 1976– ; Lectr. in Theatre Arts, Zagreb Univ. 1959–67; Visiting Lectr. Univ. of Mass. Amherst 1967–68; Asst. Prof. present Univ. 1968, Assoc. Prof. 1970; Prof. of English and Comparative Lit. 1976–92; Visiting Prof. Comparative Lit. Indiana Univ. 1968; Univ. of Rome Eng. and French Insts 1982; Afd. Literaturwetenschap Kath. Univ. Leuven 1986; Institut für Theaterwiss. Ruhr-Univ. Bochum 1989; Dept. of Comparative Lit., Univ. of Alta. 1992; Killam Fellowship of the Canada Council 1992–94; mem. various profl. execs. and bds., chair sessions or confs. incl. Internat. Cong. Sci. Fiction Criticism 1978; Vice Pres. Union Internat. des Théâtres Universitaires 1962–65; mem., MLA, Sci. Fiction Rsch. Assn. (Vice-Pres. 1977–78); Internat. Brecht Soc. (Vice-Pres. 1984–88); Can. Comparative Lit. Assn.; Can. Soc. of Semiotics; Can. Centre ITI; Haiku Soc. of America; Hon. Fellow Clare Hall Coll. Cambridge 1973–74, Univ. Coll. London 1980–81; Visiting Rsch. Fellow, Tokyo Univ. 1990–91; recipient Pilgrim Award Sci. Fiction Rsch. Assn. 1979; author 'Dva vida dramaturgije' 1964; 'Od Lukijana do Lunjika' 1965; 'Uvod u Brechta ' 1970; 'Russian Science Fiction 1956–1974' 1976; 'Dramatika Iva Vojnovića' 1977; 'Metamorphoses of Science Fiction' 1979 (chosen one of Outstanding Acad. Books 1979 by Choice mag. 1980); 'Victorian Science Fiction in the United Kingdom' 1983; 'To Brecht and Beyond' 1984; 'The Long March' (poems) 1987; 'Positions and Presuppositions in Science Fiction' 1988; 'Armirana Arkadija' (poems) 1990; over 400 critiques, essays and studies lit., theatre and culture various books and periodicals; ed. 'Literary Research/Recherche littéraire'; over 15 books or special issues; contbg. ed. 'Science Fiction Studies' (co-ed. 1973–81, publisher 1978–81); Office: Dept. of English, Montréal, Que. H3A 2T6.

**SUZUKI, David T.,** O.C. (1977), Ph.D., F.R.S.C.; scientist; educator; b. Vancouver, B.C. 24 March 1936; s. Kaoru Carr and Setsu Sue (Nakamura) S.; e. Amherst Coll. (Scholarship 1954–58) B.A. 1958; Univ. of Chicago (John M. Prather Fellowship 1960–61) Ph.D. 1961; Hon. degrees: Univ. of P.E.I. 1974, Acadia Univ. 1979, Univ. of Windsor 1979, Trent Univ. 1981, Lakehead Univ. 1986, Univ. of Calgary 1986, Governors State Univ. (U.S.) 1986, Queen's Univ. 1987, McMaster Univ. 1987, Carleton Univ. 1987, Amherst Coll. (U.S.) 1989; m. Joane Sunahara, London 1958; div. 1965; children: Tamiko Lynda, Troy Takashi, Laura Miye; m. 2ndly Tara Elizabeth Cullis, Vancouver, B.C. 1972; children: Severn Setsu Elizabeth, Sarika Freda; PROF. OF ZOOLOGY, UNIV. OF BRITISH COLUMBIA, since 1969; Teaching Asst. Biol. Amherst Coll. 1957; Research Asst. Univ. of Chicago 1958; Teaching Asst. Zool. 1959; Research Assoc. Biol. Div. Oak Ridge (Tenn.) Nat. Lab. 1961; Asst. Prof. Genetics Univ. of Alta. 1962; joined present Univ. as Asst. Prof. Zool. 1963; Assoc. Prof. 1965; Visiting Assoc. Prof. Zool. Univ. of Cal. Los Angeles 1966; Visiting Prof. Univ. of Cal. Berkeley 1969, 1976, 1977; Hon. Prof. Biol. Univ. of Utah 1971–72; Visiting Prof. Biol. Univ. of Puerto Rico 1972; Visiting Prof. Zool., Univ. of Toronto 1978; has rec'd grants Nat. Research Council Can., U.S. Atomic Energy Comn, Nat. Cancer Inst. Can.; Nat. Inst. of Health, U.S.; Supply & Services Can.; Candn. Del. Internat. Congress Genetics The Hague 1963, Chrmn. Tokyo 1968 and Berkeley 1973; NRC Exchange Scientist France 1969; U.S.S.R. 1973; NATO Research Fellow W. Germany 1974; Univ. Ccl. of B.C. Exch. Prog., People's Rep. of China 1982; internat. speaker and lectr. various univs. scient. confs. meetings; has served as Host and Moderator on various TV programs and films incl. PEMC 'Interface – Science and Society' 1974–75 CBC 'Suzuki on Science' 1971–72, 'Science Magazine' 1974–79; 'Quirks and Quarks' (radio) 1974–79; 'Nature of things' since 1979; 'Futurescan' 1984–85; 'A Planet for the Taking' 1985; 'It's A Matter of Survival' (Radio) 1989; E.W.R. Steacie Memorial Fellowship (Outstanding Research Scientist in Can.) 1969–72; mem. Grant Comte. Nat. Research Council Can. 1969–72; named 'Outstanding Japanese Canadian of the Year' 1972; Candn. Human Rights Foundation Award 1975; Royal Bank Award 1986; Bell-Northern Award for radio 1976, 1978, 1979 and for TV 1983; ACTRA Award for TV 1985; GEMINI Award for TV 1986, 1992; Cybil Award, Candn. Broadcasters League 1977; Royal Candn. Inst. Sanford Fleming Medal 1982; Candn. Medical Assn. Medal of Honour 1984; Quill Award (Press) 1985; UN Envir. Prog. Medal 1985; Gov. Gen. Award for Conservation 1985; UNESCO Kalinga Prize 1986; UN Envir. Prog. Global 500 1989; Biol. Soc. of Can. Gold Medal Award 1986; Assoc. Ed. 'Genetics' 1976–78; Pres. Candn. Soc. Cell Biol. 1969–70; mem., Sci. Council of Can. 1978–84; Secty., Genetics Soc. of Amer. 1980–82; Dir., Candn. Civil Liberties Assn. 1982–87; Hon. Life mem. Univ. of B.C. Alumni Assn; Fellow, Amer. Assoc. for Advancement of Sci. (AAAS) 1980; Royal Society of Canada 1978; Officer, Order of Canada 1977; recreations: scuba diving, skiing, fishing, camping; Home: 2477 Point Grey Rd., Vancouver, B.C. V6K 1A1; Office: 219 - 2211 West 4th Ave., Vancouver, B.C. V6K 4S2.

**SVENDSEN, Melvin Henry;** executive; b. Radway, Alta. 17 Feb. 1949; s. Ola and Eliese Johanna (Friebe) S.; e. Newbrook (Alta.) High Sch.; S. Alta. Inst. of Technol. Dip. in Technol. 1968; m. Marlene Dianne d. Sigurd and Margaret Foster Lorence 24 March 1972; children: Cathy Anne, Dianne, Brenda, Jennifer, Christopher, Erin; VICE PRES., GEN. MGR., CHIEF OPERATING OFFR. AND DIR. STANDEN'S LTD. 1990– ; Joint founder, Vice Pres. & Dir., Smartmaint Software Inc. 1991– ; Dir. Standen's Management Inc.; joined present Co. 1968, Supr. of Mfg. 1971, Plant Supt. 1974, Gen. Mgr. 1985; jt. founder Standen's Management Inc. 1990; devel. moisture saving tillage tine; Dir. Spring Rsch. Inst. 1985–90, Chrmn. 1987–89; Dir., Canadian Labour and Productivity Centre 1991– ; mem. Candn. Mfrs. Assn. (Dir. 1986–90); Candn. Leaf Spring Mfg. Assn. (Pres. & Dir. 1986–88); Soc. Automotive Engs.; Calgary Family Leisure Center; recreations: golf, racquetball, skiing; Club: Cottonwood Golf & Country; Home: 528 Willacy Dr. S.E., Calgary, Alta. T2J 2C4; Office: P.O. Box 67, Stn. T, Calgary, Alta. T2H 2G7.

**SVOBODA, Josef,** B.Sc., Ph.D.; professor of botany; b. Praha, Czechoslovakia 16 July 1929; s. Josef and Alžbeta (Kaderabkova) S.; e. Masaryk Univ. (Brno, Czech.) & Univ. of Western Ont. B.Sc. 1970; Univ. of Alta. Ph.D. 1974; m. Miu-Yin Lewina d. Ming Chun and Shuen-Yung (Leung) 27 March 1976; children: Michael Yan, Andrew Yin; PROF., DEPT. OF BOTANY, UNIV. OF TORONTO, ERINDALE COLLEGE 1985– ; Political Prisoner, Communistic Czech. 1949–58 (significantly delayed academic, scientific & profl. career; most profl. achievements were accomplished after age 45); Animal Caretaker, Brno Zoo 1958–61; Technician, Hydrological Survey, Brno 1961–64; Rsch Asst., Botanical Inst., Czech. Acad. of Sciences 1964–68; Special Student, Univ. of Western Ont. 1969–70; Grad. Student & Teaching Asst., Botany, Univ. of Alta. 1970–73; Visiting Asst. Prof., present univ. 1973–74; Asst. Prof. & apptd. to Grad. Sch. 1973–74; Assoc. Prof. (tenure) 1978–85; Assoc. Chrmn. 1990–92; Chrmn., Biol. Extve. Ctte., Erindale Coll. 1991–92; Arctic Working Group, Univ. of Toronto; Mem. of Council & U. of T. rep., Assn. for Candn. Univs. for Northern Studies; supervised 18 grad. students in Arctic Ecology incl. 3 Ph.D.s; organized 20 rsch. expeditions to Candn. High Arctic; orgn. Symposium on Arctic Ecophysiology 1989; Symposium on Devel. of Arctic & Alpine Ecosystems, INTECOL Congress (Japan) 1990; Candn. Representative and National Coordinator of ITEX (International Tundra Experiment) for monitoring global change in the Circumpolar regions 1990– ; Member of Long-term Ecosystem Rsch. and Monitoring Panel Candn. Global Change Program 1992– ; estab. & dir., world's most northern Agric. Rsch. Stn., Ellesmere Island 79$N 1981–85; elected Fellow, Arctic Institute of North America 1993; subject of 19-page article 'Canadians Who Made a Difference' in vol. 98, 'Queen's Quarterly' 1991; personal profile in 'Your Body Works' (textbook) 1990; listed in Who is Who in Education, Who is Who in Frontiers of Science & Technology, Who is Who in Toronto, American Men and Women of Science (15th ed.); NATO Senior Fellowship 1979; Mem., Arctic Inst. of N. Am. 1972– ; Ecol. Soc. of Am. 1974– ; Inst. of Arctic & Alpine Research 1973– (Assoc. Journal Ed. 1985– ); The Arctic Soc. 1985– ; Assn. of Candn. Univ. for Northern Studies 1977– (Council Mem. 1988–91); Candn. Botanical Assn. 1974– ; Soc. for the Study of Human Ideas on Ultimate Reality & Meaning 1985– ; co-author: 'Climatic Change and Ecosystem Response: The Role of Ecophysiology' 1992 and 'Ecology of Polar Oasis, Alexandra Fiord, Ellesmere Island, NWT, Canada' 1994 and scholarly articles; recreations: naturelore, hiking; clubs: Boy Scouts of Canada; Home: 943 Phyllis St., Burlington, Ont. L7R 3W1; Office: 3359 Mississauga Rd., Mississauga, Ont. L5L 1C6.

**SWAIN, Harry S.,** B.A., M.A., Ph.D.; public servant; b. Prince Rupert, B.C. 26 July 1942; s. Lyle A. and Wilma E. (Huddleson) S.; e. Univ. of B.C. B.A. (Hons.) 1964; Univ. of Minnesota M.A. 1967, Ph.D. 1970; m. Julie B. d. Albert and Dorothea Dettman 17 July 1965; DEPUTY MINISTER, INDUSTRY CANADA 1992– ; various positions in the university and public sector 1968–80; Dir. & Dep. Sec. (Ops.), Min. of State for Econ. Devel. & for Econ. & Reg. Devel. 1981–84; Asst. Dep. Min., Plans, Dept. of Reg. Ind. Expansion 1984–85; Asst. Sec.

to Cabinet, Econ. & Reg. Dev. Policy, Privy Council Office 1985–87; Dep. Min., Indian Affairs & Northern Devel. 1987–92; Bd. of Dir., Federal Bus. Devel. Bank; Bd. Mem. & Exec. Ctte., Public Policy Forum; Mem., Can. Assn. of Geographers; Am. Asn. for the Advancement of Sci.; co-author: 'St. Croix Border Country' 1968, 'Issues in the Management of Urban Systems' 1975, 'Canada North' 1992; recreations: sailing, hiking; club: Britannia Yacht; Home: 175 Waverley St., Ottawa, Ont. K2P 0V5; Office: C.D. Howe Bldg., 235 Queen St., Ottawa, Ont. K1A 0H5.

**SWAIN, Robert Francis;** art museum director; b. Halifax, N.S. 25 Oct. 1942; s. Robert Francis and Mary Elizabeth (Joyce) S.; e. Carleton Univ., B.A. 1966; m. Wendy, d. T.A. Kines, 2 Nov. 1968; children: Deirdre Siobhan, Moira Elizabeth; MUSEUM CONSULTANT; Nat. Mus. of Science and Technology, Ottawa: rsch. officer 1967–68, registrar 1968–73; Dir., Gallery/Stratford 1973–78; Dir., Agnes Etherington Art Centre 1978–90; Dir., Art Gallery of Hamilton 1990–92; Councillor, Candn. Museums Assn. 1990–94; past Pres., Can. Art Museum Directors' Organization; past pres., Ontario Assn. of Art Galleries; author of portions of Gallery Development Handbook, and numerous exhibition catalogue essays; contributor to ArtsCanada, Queen's Quarterly; Home: 43 Jorene Dr., Kingston, Ont. K7L 3X5.

**SWAMY, Srikanta M.N.,** M.Sc., Ph.D., Ing., F.E.I.C., F.I.E.E.E., F.I.E.E.; educator; b. Bangalore, India 7 Apl. 1935; s. Nanjundiah M.K. and Mahalakshamma (Kashipathiah) Mayasandra; e. Mysore Univ. B.Sc.(Hons.) 1954; Indian Inst. of Science D.I.I.Sc. 1957; Univ. of Sask. M.Sc. 1960, Ph.D. (Elect. Engn.) 1963; m. Leela d. K. P. and Lalithamma Sitaramiah 5 June 1964; children: Saritha, Nikhilesh, Jagadish; PROF. OF ELECTRICAL ENGINEERING, CONCORDIA UNIV. 1968– ; Adjunct Prof. of Elect. Engn. Penn State Univ. 1982–84; Adjunct Prof. of Electrical Engn., City Coll., City Univ. of N.Y. 1990– ; Sr. Research Asst. Indian Inst. of Science 1957–59; Part-time Lectr. in Math. Univ. of Sask. 1961–63, Asst. Prof. of Math. 1964–65; Govt. of India Scient. Indian Inst. of Technol. Madras 1963–64; Asst. Prof., Assoc. Prof. and Prof. of Elect. Engn. N.S. Tech. Coll. 1965–68; Prof, of Elect. Engn. Univ. of Calgary 1969–70; Chrmn. of Elect. Engn. present Univ. 1970–77; Dean of Engineering and Computer Sci. 1977–93; co-author 'Graphs, Networks and Algorithms' 1981; 'Graphs: Theory and Algorithms' 1992; author or co-author over 200 research articles in scient. journs. on circuits, systems and signal processing; Assoc. Ed. 'Journal on Circuits, Systems and Signal Processing' 1982– ; 'Fibonacci Quarterly' 1967– ; 'IEEE Transaction on Circuits and Systems' 1985–87; Fellow, Inst. Elect. & Electronic Engrs. (Vice Pres. Circuits and Systems Soc. 1976); Inst. Engrs. (India); Inst. Electronics & Telecommunications Engrs. (India); Engrg. Inst. of Canada; Inst. of Elect. Engrs. (U.K.); Depy. Gov., Am. Biog. Inst.; Intl. Biographical Assn.; mem. Candn. Soc. Elect. Engn.; Am. Soc. Engn. Educ.; Eta Kappa Nu; recreations: duplicate bridge, classical music; Home: 275 des Landes, St. Lambert, Que. J4S 1V9; Office: 1455 Maisonneuve Blvd. W., Montreal, Que. H3G 1M8.

**SWAN, Conrad Marshall John Fisher,** C.V.O. (1986), L.V.O. (1978), M.A., Ph.D., F.S.A. (1971); b. Duncan, Vancouver Island, B.C. 13 May 1924; s. Henry Peter, M.D., C.M. and Edna Hanson Magdalen (Green) S. Cross of Honour, 'Pro Ecclesia et Pontifice,' 1979; e. Queen Margaret's Sch., Duncan, V.I., B.C.; St. George's Coll., Weybridge, Surrey, Eng.; Univ. of London; Univ. of Western Ont., B.A. 1949, M.A. 1951; Univ. of Cambridge (Peterhouse), Ph.D. 1955; m. The Lady Hilda Susan Mary Northcote, Dame of Honour and Devotion of Sovereign and Mil. Order of Malta, Dame of Justice of Sacred and Mil. Order of Constantine St. George, younger d. Earl of Iddesleigh and cousin of H.R.H. the Princess of Wales and Field Marshal the Viscount Montgomery of Alamein, K.G., 28 Dec. 1957; children: Andrew Conrad Henry Joseph, Mary Elizabeth Magdalen Herring, Hilda Juliana Mary Galvin, Catherine Sylveria Mary Walters, Anastasia Cecilia Mary Hatvany; GARTER PRINCIPAL KING OF ARMS since 1992; York Herald of Arms 1968–92; Registrar and Senior Herald-in-Waiting, College of Arms 1982–92; Genealogist: Order of the Bath, 1972– ; of Grand Priory, Most Ven. Order of St. John, 1976– ; 1st Hon. Genealogist, Order of St. Michael & St. George 1989– ; Inspector of Regimental Colours 1993– ; joined Assumption Univ., Windsor, Ont. as Lectr. in Hist., 1955; Lectr. in Pol. Science, 1955–57; Asst. Prof. of Hist., 1957–61; Univ. Beadle, 1957–61; Guest Lecturer at universities etc. in U.K., Europe, Canada, U.S., Australia, South Am., Iceland, Thailand, Japan, Poland; Woodward Lectr., Yale 1964; Confed. Centennial Lectr., Univ. of Sask. 1967; Inaugural Sir Wm. Scott Mem. Lect. (Ulster-Scot Hist. Foundation) 1968; George M. Beley Mem. Lectr. (Heraldry Soc. of Can.) 1983; 60th Anniversary Lectr., St. Joseph's Coll., Univ. of Alta. 1987; Constance Egan Lectr., Heraldry Society 1991; Rouge Dragon Pursuivant of Arms, 1962–68 (Offr. of Arms-in-Ordinary to H.M. the Queen, and as such a mem. of the Royal Household – first Candn. to be so apptd.); on Earl Marshal's Staff for State Funeral of Sir Winston Spencer-Churchill, K.G., 1965; Investiture of Prince of Wales 1969; attended upon H.R.H. the Prince of Wales, at his Installation as Great Master of the Order of the Bath, 1975; and upon H.M. The Queen at Silver Jubilee Service, St. Paul's Cathedral, 1977; First Herald of Crown to execute duties in Tabard on W. side of Atlantic (Bermuda 1969), in Southern Hemisphere (Australia Silver Jubilee tour 1977); to complete round world tour 1970, to visit New Zealand 1976, and to be Herald-in-Waiting upon the Sovereign in Canada (Commonwealth Heads of Government Conf., Vancouver) 1987; Gentleman Usher-in-Waiting to H.H. Pope John-Paul II, Papal Visit to the United Kingdom, 1982; invited by Secy. of State of Can. to participate in the nat. forum on heraldry in Canada 'Heraldry – a Nation and its Symbols' Ottawa 1987; Co-founder (with Lady Hilda Swan) Heraldic Garden, Boxford, Suffolk 1983; served in 2nd World War in Europe and the Far East in the Indian Army (Madras Regt.) rank of Capt.; author, 'Heraldry: Ulster and North American Connections' 1972; 'Canada: Symbols of Sovereignty' 1977; 'The Chapel of the Order of Bath, Westminster Abbey' 1978; and a number of monographs and articles (armorial, historical, sigillographic) in various journs.; co-author: 'Blood of the Martyrs' (with Peter Drummond-Murray of Mastrick, Slains Pursuivant of Arms) 1993; Kt. of Honour and Devotion of Sovereign and Mil. Order of Malta (Geneal., Brit. Assn. and has Cross of Commander-of-Merit, both of that order); Kt. of Justice of Sacred and Mil. Order of Constantine St. George; Hon. Citizen of Texas; Freeman of Shreveport, La.; Birmingham, Ala.; Loudoun Co., Virginia; St. George, Bermuda, City of London; mem. of the Court, Freeman and Liveryman, Master 1993–94 of Gunmakers Company of City of London; Vice-Pres. and Founder mem. of Heraldry Soc. of Can.; Hon. Vice-Pres., U.E.L. Assn. of Can.; K. St. J. (1976); Fellow, Zoological Soc. of London 1986; Roman Catholic; recreations: riding, rearing ornamental pheasants & waterfowl, beagling; Home: Boxford House, Suffolk, C010 5JT England.

**SWAN, John,** LL.B., B.C.L.; b. Belfast, N. Ireland 10 Oct. 1938; s. Thomas McDermott and Lydia Mary (White) S.; e. Univ. of B.C., LL.B. 1963; Oxford Univ., B.C.L. 1965; m. 1stly Jane Westcott; 2ndly Margaret Angevine; children: William John, Philippa Jane, Ellen Victoria, Jacqueline Amanda; DIR. OF LEGAL RSCH. & PROFL. EDN., AIRD & BERLIS 1987– ; joined Univ. of Toronto 1965; Commonwealth Scholar 1963–65; Prof. of Law, Univ. of Toronto 1973–88; co-author (with B.J. Reiter) 'Studies in Contract Law' 1980; 'Contracts: Cases, Notes and Materials' 1991; Office: Aird & Berlis, 181 Bay St., Toronto, Ont. M5J 2T9.

**SWAN, Rev. Peter Julian Michael,** M.A., Ph.D. (R.C.); priest, professor; b. Folkestone, Kent, Eng., 21 May 1919; s. Henry Peter (Major RCAMC and RAMC) and Edna Hanson (Green) S.; e. Queen Margaret's Sch., Duncan, B.C.; Duncan (B.C.) Grammar and High Schs.; St. Michaels Coll., Univ. of Toronto, B.A. 1938; Sch. of Grad. Studies, Univ. of Toronto, M.A. 1942, Ph.D. 1946; St. Basil's Semy., Toronto. 1940–44; Dean, St. Joseph's Coll., Univ. of Alta. 1985–91; retired; o. Priest 1943; Assoc. Prof. of Philos., Assumption Univ. of Windsor, 1946–61, Registrar 1949–61, Acad. Vice Pres. 1958–61 and Secy. and mem. of Bd. of Govs. there 1953–61; Princ. and Prof. of Philos., St. Thomas More Coll., Univ. of Sask., 1961–77; Superior, Basilian Fathers of St. Thomas More Coll., 1961–67; Gen. Councillor, Basilian Fathers, 1970–73; Vice Pres. 1977–78, Pres. & Vice Chancellor 1978–84, Univ. of St. Michael's Coll.; Councillor, Internat. Federation of Catholic Universities 1980–88 and Pres., Can. Assoc. of IFCU 1983–87; mem. Heraldry Soc. Can.; Chaplain Kts. of Malta 1968; recreation: reading; Club: Faculty; Address: St. Michael's Coll., 81 St. Mary St., Toronto, Ont. M5S 1J4.

**SWAN, Susan Jane,** B.A.; writer; b. Midland, Ont. 9 June 1945; d. Dalton Churchill and Jane Pardee (Cowan) S.; e. McGill Univ. B.A. 1967; m. Barry s. Muriel and Kenneth Haywood 1969; divorced; 1 d.: Samantha; Prof. of Creative Writing, York Univ. 1985– ; Writer-in-Res., Haliburton 1987; Playwright-in-Res., 'Necessary Angel' 1985–86; author: 'Queen of the Silver Blades' (play) 1975; 'Unfit for Paradise' (short stories) 1982; 'The Biggest Modern Woman of the World' (novel) 1983 Canada, 1986 U.S., 1988 UK; 'The Last of the Golden Girls' (novel) 1989 (U.S. ed. 1991); 'Frictions Anthology' (short story) 1989; co-author: 'Tesseracts' (science fiction anthology) 1985, Mondadori, Italy 1990; Ed., 'Language in Her Eye' (anthology of essays by women writers) 1990; co-editor: 'Mothers Talk Back' (non-fiction) 1991; 'Slow Hand' (Women Writing Erotica) 1992; 'The Wives of Bath' 1993 (published in Canada, USA & Granta, UK); articles, poems, and short stories have appeared in numerous Candn. publs. and is a contributor to TVO's Book Show, Imprint; recreations: tennis, yoga; Club: Toronto YMCA; Address: 151 Robert St., Apt. 2, Toronto, Ont. M5S 2K6.

**SWANICK, Brent W.,** B.Comm., LL.B., LL.M.; lawyer; b. Toronto, Ont. 2 Nov. 1950; s. Robert Wilmot and Mary (Klapchuk) S.; e. Univ. of Toronto B.Comm. 1972, LL.B. 1975; York Univ., Osgoode Hall LL.M. 1986; m. Gail Oikawa 17 July 1976; children: Kalen, Mariko; OWNER/MANAGER, SWANICK SHNIER D'OLIVEIRA (tax practice); called to Bar 1977; has run approx. 25 marathons, all but one in less than 3 hrs.; personal best is 2:26:14; Past Pres., Parkinson Found. of Canada; Office: 101 – 225 Duncan Mill Road, Don Mills, Ont. M3B 3K9.

**SWANN, Peter Charles;** Retired; b. London, Eng., 20 Dec. 1921; e. Tottenham Grammar Sch., London, 1939; Oxford Univ., read Chinese (1st Class Hons., Scarborough Scholarship); London Univ., 1942; Leyden Univ., 1947–48; Hon. Doctorate Brock Univ., Queen's Univ., Wilfrid Laurier Univ., Univ. of Waterloo; m. Elizabeth Hayden, 9 Aug. 1952 (now divorced); m. 2ndly Susan McPhee, 3 Nov. 1980; children: Sebastian Paul, Toby Nicholas, Geron Matthew, Francesca, Claire; Alexander McPhee Mayer Swann; DIRECTOR EMERITUS, EAST ASIAN STUDIES, RENISON COLL., UNIV. OF WATERLOO 1992– , Dir. 1989–92 (retired); Dir., J.E. Seagram and Sons Ltd.; first Dir., Seagram Museum; founder and Honourary Pres., Assoc. of Cultural Executives; studied in Japan 1950–51; apptd. to Ashmolean Museum 1952; in charge of Dept. 1956; planned new dept. and made Keeper 1961; former Dir., Royal Ont. Museum 1966–June 1972; Mem. Fed. Task Force on Role of National Museums 1986; served with R.N. 1942–46, destroyer service, Japanese Intelligence, Combined Chiefs of Staff, Washington; author of 'Introduction to Japanese Art'; 'Hokusai'; 'Chinese Painting'; 'The Monumental Art of China'; 'Japanese Art'; '2,000 Years of Japanese Art' (with Y. Yashiro); 'The Arts of China, Korea and Japan'; 'A Concise History of Japanese Art'; Ed., 'Oriental Art' 1955–68, Vice Pres. 1968–92; transl. 'Yün-Kang' (15 vols.); mem., Worshipful Co. of Turners; Exec. Dir. (First) Samuel and Saidye Bronfman Family Foundation; rec'd Candn. Museums Assn. Award of Merit 1985; Address: 133 Claremont Ave., Kitchener, Ont. N2M 2P9.

**SWANSON, A.L.,** B.A., M.H.A., M.D., C.M., F.A.C.H.E.; retired; b. Red Deer, Alta., 29 Sept. 1918; s. William Frederick and Clara Isabella (Pierce) S.; e. Univ. of British Columbia, B.A., 1940; McGill Univ., M.D., C.M. 1943; Northwestern Univ., Master of Hosp. Adm., 1949; m. Joan Maurine, d. Leslie Stuart Hawkins, Vancouver, B. C., 9 April 1942; children: Stuart, Karen, Wendy, David, Eric, Patricia; Past President, Saskatchewan Hosp. Assn.; mem. of Med. Staff, Prov. Mental Health Services, B.C., 1946–49; Deputy Med. Supt. 1949–52; Hosp. Accreditation Surveyor 1949–87; Extve. Dir., Candn. Hosp Assn., also Editor of 'Canadian Hospital,' also Asst. Prof., Dept. of Hosp. Adm., Sch. of Hygiene, Univ. of Toronto, 1952–54; Extve. Dir., Univ. Hosp., Saskatoon, and Asst. Prof., Univ. of Sask., 1954–65; Extve. Dir. Victoria Hosp., London, Ont. 1965–70; Adm., Queen St. Mental Health Centre and Asst. Prof. Psychiatry, Univ. of Toronto 1970–75; Exec. Dir., Canadian Council on Hospital Accreditation 1975–82; consultant, UBC Health Sciences Centre Hosp. 1982–84; Capt., Royal Candn. Army Med. Corps. 1944–46; retired mem. Candn. Med. Assn.; Coll. of Phys. and Surg. of B.C. and Ontario; Retired Mem. B.C. Med. Assn.; Fellow,, Am. Coll. of Healthcare Execs. (mem. Bd. of Govs. 1964–68, Past Chrmn. 1970); Life mem., Sask. Hosp. Assn., 1966; Founding mem. Candn. Coll. of Health Service Execs., 1974; Pres. McGill Undergrad. Soc. 1943; Alpha Kappa Kappa (Pres. 1943); mem. Rotary Club since 1955; Anglican; recreations: swimming, walking, bridge; Address: 16 – 185 Woodridge Dr. SW, Calgary, Alta. T2W 3X7.

**SWARD, James F.;** communications executive; b. Toronto, Ont. 17 Apr. 1945; s. James and Betty (Dancy) S.; m. Gail d. Russell and Elaine Bloomfield 17 June 1967; children: Paul James, Sarah Gail; PRESIDENT & CHIEF EXTVE. OFFR., GLOBAL TELEVISION NETWORK 1993– ; Dir.: Canwest Global Communications Corp.; Rogers Broadcasting Ltd.; Candn. Assn. of

Broadcasters; Vice-Pres. and Gen. Mgr., Maisonneuve Broadcasting 1970–77; Pres. & C.E.O., Rogers Broadcasting Ltd. 1977–89, Pres. & C.E.O. Rogers Cantel Communications Inc. 1989–93; recreations: sailing, skiing, fishing; Home: 15 Nanton Ave., Toronto, Ont.; Office: 81 Barber Greene Rd., Don Mills, Ont. M3C 2A2.

**SWARNEY, Paul Richard,** M.A., Ph.D.; educator; b. Fairfield, Conn. 10 Jan. 1937; s. Paul and Anna (Marak) S.; e. Fairfield Coll. Prep. Sch.; Coll. of Holy Cross B.A. 1959; Yale Univ. M.A. 1960, Ph.D. 1965; m. Jane d. John and Alice Hyland 3 Sept. 1964; children: Ann, Matthew, Katharine; DIR. OF CLASSICAL STUDIES, YORK UNIV. 1979– , Assoc. Prof. 1970– ; Lectr. Yale Univ. 1961–64; Lectr., Asst. Prof. Dartmouth Coll. 1964–67; Asst. Prof. York Univ. 1967; Fellow, Univ. Coll. London 1973–74; Researcher, Instituto Papirologico 'G. Vitelli' Firenze 1980–81; recipient SSHRC Leave Fellowship 1973–74; author 'The Ptolemaic and Roman Idios Logos' 1972; Pres. Rathnally Area Residents' Assn. 1972–73; Home: 3 McMaster Ave., Toronto, Ont. M4V 1A8; Office: Vanier Coll., 4700 Keele St., Downsview, Ont. M3J 1P3.

**SWARTOUT, Douglas Reyburn,** C.I.B.; insurance executive; b. Prince Albert, Sask. 10 Oct. 1948; s. Douglas Benjamin and Helen Campion (Klasen) S.; e. Calgary petroleum engineering technology 1969; Chartered Insur. Broker Alberta 1979; York Univ. Extve. Mngt. Program 1988; m. L. Jo-Anne d. John and Lois Devine 19 July 1969; children: Stephanie, Nicole; EXECUTIVE VICE-PRES., REED STENHOUSE LIMITED 1992– ; Vice-Pres. & Partner, J.T. O'Bryan & Co. 1971–75; Vice-Pres. & Asst. Mgr., Tomonson Saunders Whitehead 1975–80; Vice Pres. & Asst. Mgr., Reed Stenhouse Edmonton 1980–82; Sr. Vice Pres. & Asst. Mgr. 1982–87; Sr. Vice-Pres. & Manager Northern Region 1987–91; Managing Dir., Central Region 1991–92; Mem., Inst. of Corp. Dirs. 1991– ; recreations golf, hunting, curling; clubs: Windermere Golf & Country (Past Pres.), Lambton Golf & Country, Griffith Island Hunting Club; Home: 1290 Lindburgh Court, Mississauga, Ont. L5H 4J2; Office: 24th floor, 20 Bay St., Toronto, Ont. M5J 2N9.

**SWARTZMAN, Stanley Brian;** executive; b. Johannesburg, S. Africa 13 Oct. 1939; s. David Henry and Hetty (Loon) S.; e. Parktown Boys High 1957; Univ. of the Witwatersrand; m. Ruth d. Isadore and Gertrude Altbeker 16 Dec. 1963; children: Gavin, Elana, Lisa; PRESIDENT, IPCF PROPERTIES, INC. 1983– ; E.A. Gaisford, Chartered Inst. of Quantity Surveyors 1958; Bldg. and Equipment Buyer, O.K. Bazaar (1929) Ltd. 1960; self-employed (manufacturing, supplying and servicing capital items to supermarket industry in S. Africa) 1970; Vice-Pres., Loblaws Supermarkets Ltd. (Canada) 1977; Vice-Pres. National Grocers Inc. 1985; Home: 24 Swansdown Dr., Willowdale, Ont. M2L 2N1; Office: 22 St. Clair Ave. E., Toronto, Ont. M4T 2S5.

**SWEATMAN, Alan,** Q.C., B.A., LL.B.; b. Winnipeg, Man. 9 Dec. 1920; s. Travers and Constance Winnifred (Newton) S.; e. Pub. and High Schs., Winnipeg, Man.; Univ. of Manitoba, B.A. 1942, LL.B. 1948; m. Lorraine Mary, d. late David Cluness MacDonald, 26 June 1943; children: Alan Travers, Wynn David, Paul, Margaret Lisa, Elizabeth, Scott; PARTNER, THOMPSON, DORFMAN, SWEATMAN; Dir., Hudson Bay Mining & Smelting Co. Ltd.; Greyhound Lines of Can. Ltd.; read law with Isaac Pitbaldo, Q.C.; called to Bar of Man. 1948; cr. Q.C. 1962; served in 2nd World War with RCNVR, 1942–45; discharged with rank of Lieut.; recreations: golf, sailing, skiing; Club: St. Charles Country; Home: 266 Kingsway Ave., Winnipeg, Man. R3M 0H3; Office: 2200 - 201 Portage Ave., Winnipeg, Man. R3B 3L3.

**SWEATMAN, Margaret Lisa,** M.A.; writer; b. Winnipeg, Man. 13 May 1953; d. Alan and Lorraine Mary Alice (MacDonald) S.; e. Loyola, Concordia Univ., postgrad. dipl. Communications Arts 1976; Simon Fraser Univ. M.A. 1985; children: Bailey, Hillery; author: 'Fox' 1991 (novel), 'Private Property' 1988 (chap book); also short stories and poetry in Prairie Fire, Border Crossings, NeWest Review, Dandelion, Prose-Jazz dramas for CBC-Radio; currently; 'Kore in Hell' (a jazz text, full-length drama); teaches creative writing workshops for young people; Extve. Mem., Manitoba Writers' Guild; Office: c/o Turnstone Press, Suite 607, 100 Arthur St., Winnipeg, Man. R3B 1H3.

**SWEDE, George,** B.A., M.A.; writer; educator; b. Riga, Latvia 20 Nov. 1940; s. Valdis and Virginia Irmgard (Seeberg) Purins; Valdis Purins killed in war; mother remarried in 1944 to Arnold Swede who became adoptive father, name change from Juris Purins to George Swede; e. Univ. of B.C., B.A. 1964; Dalhousie Univ., M.A. 1965; m. 1stly, Bonnie d. Robert and Evelyn Lewis June 20 1964; divorced June 1969; m. 2ndly, Anita d. Ida and Gothards Krumins 23 July 1974; children: Juris, Andris; PROF. OF PSYCHOL., RYERSON POLYTECH. UNIV. 1973– ; Instr., Vancouver City Coll. 1966–67; Sch. Psychol., Scarborough Bd. of Ed. 1967–68; Instr., Ryerson 1968–73; Dept. Chrmn. 1974–75; Co-Dir., Radiostudy, CJRT 1969–70; Dir., Devel. Psych., Open Coll. 1973–75; Poetry and things 1969–71; Mem., Candn. Authors Assn.; P.E.N.; Candn. Soc. for Children's Authors, Illus. & Performers (Extve. Mem. 1981–84); Haiku Canada (co-founder, 1977); League of Candn. Poets; Writers' Union of Can.; author: 'Leaving My Loneliness' 1992; 'I Want To Lasso Time' 1991; 'Holes in My Cage' 1989; 'I Throw Stones At The Mountain' 1988; 'Leaping Lizard' 1988; 'I Eat A Rose Petal' 1987; 'Writing Children's Poetry' 1986 (audio tape); 'High Wire Spider' 1986, 'Time Is Flies' 1984, 'Night Tides' 1984, 'Bifids' 1984, 'Frozen Breaths' 1983, 'Tick Bird' 1983, 'Flaking Paint' 1983, 'A Snowman, Headless' 1979, 'Tell-Tale Feathers' 1978, 'Unwinding' 1974 and others (poetry); 'Dudley and the Christmas Thief' 1986, 'Dudley and the Birdman' 1985, 'Undertow' 1982, 'Downhill Theft' 1982, 'Seaside Burglaries' 1981 and others (children's fiction); 'Creativity: A New Psychology' 1993; 'The Modern English Haiku' 1981 (non-fiction); co-author: 'Where Even The Factories Have Lawns' 1988; 'The Space Between' 1986; 'Quillby' 1979; ed.: 'There Will Always Be A Sky' 1993; 'The Universe Is One Poem' 1990; 'Brussels Sprout' 1988; 'Cicada Voices' 1983, 'Candn. Haiku Anthol.' 1979; Poetry Ed.: 'Poetry Toronto' 1980–81; co-editor: 'Writer's Magazine' 1982–90; Judge: Japan Air Lines Haiku Contest 1990, 1987; Haiku Soc. of Am. Henderson Award 1990; Mirrors Internat. Tanka Award 1991; recipient: 3rd Place, Poetry Soc. of Japan's Internat. Tanka Contest 1990; Wind Chimes Press Minibook competition runner-up 1988; The Canadian Children's Book Centre 'Our Choice' Award 1984, 1985, 1987, 1991, 1992; Museum of Haiku Literature Award, 1983, 1985, 1993; High/Coo Press Chapbook Competition Winner 1982; Haiku Soc. of Am., Book Award 1980; recreations: tennis; Club: The Waterfront Tennis & Squash; Home: 70 London St., Toronto, Ont. M6G 1N3; Office: 350 Victoria St., Toronto, Ont. M5B 2K3.

**SWEENEY, John,** B.A., M.Ed.; former politician; b. Saint John, N.B. 20 June 1931; s. Frank and Winnifred (Crowley) S.; e. Univ. of Toronto B.A. 1960, M.Ed. 1964; m. Kay Doran 27 Dec. 1952; ten children; served as teacher and prin. Toronto 1952–62; Prov. Inspr. of Schs. Kitchener 1962; Dir. of Edn. Waterloo Co. Separate Sch. Bd. 1968; el. M.P.P. for Kitchener-Wilmot 1975, re-elect. since; Min. of Community & Social Services, Ont. 1985–89; Min. of Housing & Min. of Municipal Affairs 1989–90; served as Critic for Mins. of Edn., Ind. & Trade and Health; Home: 36 Shadywood Cres., Kitchener, Ont. N2M 4J2.

**SWEETING, Dennis,** D.S.O., B.A., M.C.; broadcaster, director, actor; b. Calgary, Alta. 23 Nov. 1915; s. John Findlay and Jessie Craven (Dickens) S.; e. St. Johns Coll. Sch., Winnipeg, Man., 1922–29; Univ. of Manitoba (Arts) 1931–33; B.A., Trent Univ. 1978; m. Margaret Elaine Palmer, 21 July 1962; children: (by previous m.) Derek, Pamela, Barbara, (adopted s.) Christopher; PRES., SWEETING MANAGEMENT SERVICES (independent theatrical producers and consultants); with Hudson's Bay Co., Merchandising and Stat. Depts., Winnipeg, 1933–39 (also free lance actor, dir., radio and theatre); after was Announcer, CJAT, Trail, B.C.; with CBC Vancouver, and other posts before appt. as Extve. Secy., Assn. Candn. Radio and Television Artists and Actors Equity Assn., Toronto, Ont., 1954; Gen. Mgr., Candn. Players Ltd., 1958–60; Producer, Kawartha Festival Foundation 1970–90; Founding Artistic Dir., Kawartha Festival Foundation; Deputy Reeve, Town of Lindsay 1979–82 and 1986–88; Reeve, Town of Lindsay 1989–91; Warden of Victoria County 1989; withdrew from Municipal politics 1991 election; served in 2nd World War with Queen's Own Cameron Highlanders, Winnipeg, 1939; staff appts. with Air Staff, Candn. Army, returning to unit to conclude war with rank of Major; awarded D.S.O., Czechoslovakian M.C.; Publications: T.V. and radio plays, articles, scripts for CBC radio; first Secy., Candn. Theatre Centre, which devel. the Nat. Theatre Sch. of Can.; Hon. Fellow in Applied Education, Sir Sandford Fleming Coll. 1986; Hon. LL.D., Trent Univ., Peterborough 1990; Anglican; recreation: boating; Office: Box 184, R.R. 3, Sunderland, Ont. L0C 1H0.

**SWENSON, Robert Charles,** B.A.; executive; b. Winnipeg, Man. 11 Feb. 1928; s. Carl Elmer and Hazel Margaret (O'Neill) S.; e. Kelvin High Sch.; Lawrence Park Coll. Inst. Toronto; Univ. of W. Ont., B.A. 1950; CHRMN. AND CHIEF EXEC. OFFR. SWENSON CANADA INC. 1950– ; Pres. and Dir. Avenheath Apartments Ltd.; Vice Pres. and Dir. Wahl Clipper Corp. of Canada; Dir. Mill Bros. Distributors Ltd.; C.C.I.C.; Dir., Treas. and Pres. Allied Beauty Assn. (over 25 yr. span); former Pres. Keystone Acceptance Corp.; mem. Muskoka Lakes Assn.; Bd. Trade Metrop. Toronto; Hon. Life Mem., C.T.A.; Anglican; P. Conservative; recreations: swimming, boating, golf; Clubs: Granite; Empire; Sea (Hillsboro Beach, Fla.); Home: 1102–3, 581 Avenue Rd., Toronto, Ont. M4V 2K4; Office: 80 Orfus Rd., Toronto, Ont. M6A 1M1.

**SWIDLER, John J.,** B.Comm., B.C.L., F.C.A.; legal executive; b. Montreal, Que. 8 Feb. 1993; s. Samuel and Gertrude (Segal) S.; e. McGill Univ. B.Comm. 1965, B.C.L. 1969; m. Vickied d. Irving Engleman 7 Aug. 1966; children: Gary, Darren, Todd; CHAIRMAN OF EXECUTIVE CTTE., RICHTER, USHER & VINEBERG 1990– ; Lawyer, Phillips & Vineberg 1970–72; Chartered Accountant, Richter, Usher & Vineberg 1972– ; Partner 1974– ; Lecturer, McGill Univ. 1968–72; Fellow, Inst. of C.A.s of Que. 1992; Pres., Candn. Insolvency Assn. 1984; Founder Dir., Insolvency Inst. of Can. 1989; author of Articles of the Practise of Insolvency Seminar; recreation: golf; club: Elmridge Country; Home: 3 Fallbrook Rd., Hampstead, Que. H3X 3W1; Office: 2 Pl. Alexis Nihon, Montreal, Que. H3Z 3C2.

**SWIFT, Catherine Susan,** B.A., M.A.; economist; b. Toronto, Ont. 21 Oct. 1952; d. Harold Edgar and Susan (McPherson) S.; e. Univ. of Toronto (undergrad.); Carleton Univ. B.A. (Hons.) 1977; Carleton Univ. M.A. 1980; divorced; children: Alexander, Nicolas; SENIOR VICE-PRES., CANADIAN FED. OF INDEPENDENT BUSINESS 1987– ; Economist, Consumer & Corp. Affairs Can. & Dept. of Communications 1976–83; Sr. Econ., Toronto-Dominion Bank 1983–87; Dir., Le Cercle Canadien; Office: Suite 401, 4141 Yonge St., Willowdale, Ont. M2P 2A6.

**SWIFT, Michael David,** M.A.; archivist; b. Minto, N.B. 23 May 1936; s. Victor Michael and Madeline Agatha (Cullen) S.; e. Minto Meml. High Sch. 1954; St. Dunstan's Coll. Charlottetown B.A. 1958; Univ. of N.B. M.A. 1964; m. Ann d. Henry and Mary McGreevy 18 Aug. 1962; three s. Peter, David, Andrew; ASSISTANT NATIONAL ARCHIVIST, NATIONAL ARCHIVES OF CANADA 1986– ; served family retail business 1959–60; high sch. teacher Minto and CFB Gagetown, N.B. 1961–64; Staff Archivist, Pub. Archives of Can. 1964–71; Prov. Archivist of N.B. 1972–78; Director General, Archives Branch, Public Archives of Can. 1978–86; mem. Assn. Canadn. Archivists; Soc. Am. Archivists; Candn. Hist. Assn.; recreation: curling; Home: 90 Craig Henry Dr., Nepean, Ont.; Office: 395 Wellington St., Ottawa, Ont. K1A 0N3.

**SWIGGUM, Susan Mary Margaret,** B.Sc., M.D., F.R.C.P.(C.); physician, university professor, association executive; b. Halifax, N.S. 16 June 1951; d. Harry Louis and Barbara (Chipman) S.; e. Univ of Ottawa B.Sc. (summa cum laude) 1969, M.D. (magna cum laude) 1976; m. Jack s. Helen and Albert Adam 16 Dec. 1988; children: David Geoffrey, Alison Margaret; PRES., FEDERATION OF MEDICAL WOMEN OF CANADA; residency in med. & dermatology; Fellowship in Derm. 1987; Staff, Ottawa Civic Hosp.; Asst. Prof., Med., Univ. of Ottawa; Nat. Spokesperson, Candn. Derm. Assn.; Jean Jacque Lussier Gold Medal; Univ. of Ottawa Silver Medal; Mosby Awards for Excellence; Chair, Maude Abbott Found.; Margaret Owen Waite Memorial Found.; Mem., Alpha Omega Alpha Hon. Med. Soc.; Sunday School Teacher, St. James Anglican Ch.; MiLady Doctor, 78th Fraser Highlanders; recreations: golf, traveling; club: Rideau View Country; Home: 1095 Brevar Dr., Manotick, Ont. K4M 1G2; Office: No. 106, 1815 Alta Vista Dr., Ottawa, Ont. K1G 3Y6.

**SWIM, Peter Evan Thomas,** B.Sc., B.Eng.; seafood industry executive; b. Shelburne, N.S. 23 March 1957; s. Cyril Bruce and Josephone Joan (Nickerson) S.; e. Acadia Univ. B.Sc. 1978; N.S. Technical Univ. B.Eng. 1980; Maritime Fisheries Centre, Class III Fishing Masters Licence 1982; m. Barbara d. Richard and Mildred Crowell 4 Sept. 1983; one s.: Evan; MANAGER, ISLAND MARINE 1981– ; devel. market & supply of bluetin tuna industry in S.W. N.S.; devel. individual lobster facility for long-term high-quality supply of live lobster; Mem., Internat. Conservation Comn. for Atlantic Tuna 1991–92; Atlantic Bluefin Tuna Advisory Ctte. of S.W. N.S. 1990–92; Home: P.O. Box 40, Clark's Harbour, N.S. B0W 1P0.

**SWIMMER, Eugene Roy,** B.A., M.A., Ph.D.; university professor; b. New York, N.Y. 8 Sept. 1946; s. Andrew and Ann (Karp) S.; e. Bronx H.S. of Sci. 1963; City Coll. of N.Y., B.A. 1967; Univ. of Chicago, M.A. 1968; Cornell Univ., Ph.D. 1972; one s.: Adam; PROF., CARLETON UNIV. 1985– ; Asst. Prof., Univ. of Alta. 1971–74; Assoc. Prof., present univ. 1975–84; Dir., Sch. of Public Administration 1985–92; Chair, Ontario Emergency Medical Services Review 1991–92; Adjudicator, Office of Social Contract Adjudication 1993– ; Fact Finder & Mediator, Ont. Edn. Relns. Comn. & College Relations Comn.; Guest lectr. on Police Labour Relns., Candn. Police Coll.; on Public Sector Collective Bargaining, Indus. Relns. Inst.; mem., Inst. of Public Admin. in Canada; Candn. Indus. Relns. Assn.; Candn. Econ. Assn.; co-author: 'Wage Controls in Canada' 1980; co-editor: 'Conflict or Compromise: The Future of Public Sector Industrial Relations' 1984; Home: 155 Belmont Ave., Ottawa, Ont. K1S 0V4; Office: Colonel By Dr., Ottawa, Ont. K1S 5B6.

**SWINTON, George,** C.M., B.A., LL.D.; artist, author; b. Vienna, Austria 17 April 1917; s. Alfred and Elisabeth Victoria (Helsinger) Schwitzer; e. Hochschule für Welthandel Vienna 1936–38; McGill Univ. B.A. 1946; Montreal School of Art & Design 1946–47; Art Students' League 1949–50; children: Moira, Nelda; PROFESSOR EMERITUS OF ART HISTORY, CARLETON UNIV. 1986– ; Curator, Saskatoon Art Ctr. 1947–49; Instructor, Smith College 1950–53; Artist-in-residence, Queen's Univ. 1953–54; Asst. Chief of Industrial Design 1954; Prof. of Art, Univ. of Man. 1954–74; Adjunct Prof. of Anthropology 1970–74; Prof. of Art Hist., Carleton Univ. 1973–81; Adjunct Prof., Dept. of Art Hist., Carleton Univ. 1981–85; Capt., Candn. Intelligence Corps., Candn. Army 1941–46; Visiting Prof., Simon Fraser Univ. 1972; Univ. of Wisconsin 1974; Univ. of Leningrad 1981; 31 one-man shows in Canada & US; 4 retrospective exbns.; many other group exbns. & prizes; rep. in Confed. Art Ctr., Beaverbrook Art Gall., Nat. Gall., Hamilton Art Gall., Winnipeg Art Gall., Mendel Art Gall. Saskatoon, Glenbow Found., Vancouver Art Gall. & many other private & institutional collections; Consultant on Inuit Traditions, Inuit Cultural Inst., Arviat 1974–78; Nat. Capital Comn., Adv. Ctte. on the Visual Arts; Bd. of Gov., Winnipeg Art Gall. 1972–73; Candn. Eskimo Arts Council 1967–73; Western Rep., Candn. Soc. for Graphic Arts 1960–63; Dir., Exbns., Univ. of Man. 1965–71; Visual Arts Rep., Candn. Univs., Centennial Comn. 1966–67; Bd. of Dir., Ottawa Sch. of Art 1981–83; recipient: Centennial Medal 1967; Mem. of the Order of Canada 1979; The 125th Anniversary Medal 1992; recipient of several arts grants; author: 'Eskimo/Sculpture/Esquimaude' 1965, 'Sculpture of the Eskimo' 1972, 2nd ed. 1975, 3rd ed. 1982, (French ed.) 'Sculpture Esquimaude' 1976; 'Sculpture of the Inuit' 1992; co-author: 'What is Good Design?' 1954; illus./des.: 'Red River of the North' 1969; recreations: music, art collecting and books; Home: 647 Strathcona St., Winnipeg, Man. R3G 3E9;

**SWINTON, Katherine Edna,** B.A., LL.B., LL.M.; university professor; b. East York, Ont. 14 Aug. 1950; d. Robert James and Laura Edna (Anderson) S.; e. Univ. of Alberta B.A. (Hons.) 1971; Osgoode Hall Law School, York Univ. LL.B. 1975; Yale Univ. LL.M. 1977; Mem., Ont. Bar 1979– ; m. Kenneth s. Harry and Violet Swan 23 Aug. 1983; children: Michael Daniel Swinton Swan, Laura Katherine Swinton Swan; PROFESSOR, FACULTY OF LAW, UNIV. OF TORONTO 1988– ; Parliamentary Intern, House of Commons 1971–72; Law Clerk to the Rt. Hon. R.G.B. Dickson, Supreme Court of Canada 1975–76; Asst. Prof., Osgoode Hall Law Sch. 1977–79; Asst. Prof., Univ. of Toronto 1979–82; Assoc. Prof. 1982–87; Consultant in constitutional law; Chair, Education Relations Comn. of Ont. 1987–91; Labour Arbitrator; Bd. Mem. and Vice-Pres., Candn. Civil Liberties Assn. 1986– ; author: 'The Supreme Court and Canadian Federalism: The Laskin-Dickson Years' 1990; co-editor: 'Competing Visions of Constitutionalism: The Meech Lake Accord' 1988, 'Studies in Labour Law' 1983; Home: 345 Glengrove Ave. W., Toronto, Ont. M5N 1W4; Office: 78 Queen's Park Cres., Toronto, Ont. M5S 2C5.

**SWINTON, Robert Timothy,** B.A., M.B.A.; oil industry executive; b. Orillia, Ont. 13 Nov. 1946; s. Robert J. and Laura E. S.; married Mary Anne 1974; children: Robin Michael, Lindsay Anne; PRES., C.E.O. & DIR., ENSERV CORP.; Mem., Calgary Petroleum Club; Calgary Winter Club; Young Presidents' Organization; Office: 1505, 505 - 3 St. S.W., Calgary, Alta. T2P 3E6.

**SWINTON, William Elgin,** Ph.D., D.Sc., LL.D., F.R.S.E., F.R.S.C., F.R.G.S., F.R.A.I., F.L.S., F.Z.S., F.S.A. (Scot.); univ. professor; b. Kirkcaldy, Fifeshire, Scotland, 30 Sept. 1900; s. William Wilson and Rachel Hunter (Cargill) S.; e. Whitehill Sch., Glasgow, Scot.; Trinity; Coll., Glenalmond, Scot.; Univ. of Glasgow, B.Sc. 1922 (Strang-Steel Prize), Ph.D. 1931; D.Sc. 1971; Hon. LL.D., Toronto 1975; Hon. D.Litt., Western 1977; Hon. D.Sc., Queens Univ., 1982; unm.; Demonst., Univ. of Glasgow, 1922–24; mem. Scottish Spitsbergen Expedition, 1920 mem. Scient. Staff, Brit. Museum (Nat. Hist.), London, 1924–61; Hon. Assoc., Royal Museum of Central Africa (Belgium), since 1950; Dir., Life Sciences, Royal Ont. Museum, 1961–63; Dir., Royal Ont. Museum, 1963–66; Prof. of Zool., Univ. of Toronto 1962–66, now Prof. Emeritus; Centennial Prof. (History of Sci.) 1966; Visiting Prof., Prince of Wales Coll., P.E.I. 1967; Visiting Prof., Waterloo Univ. 1974; Visiting Prof., Queen's Univ., Anatomy and Biol. 1977 and 1978; Fellow, Massey Coll., since 1966; Life Mem., Trinity Coll. Common Rooms 1982; served in 2nd World War, 1939–45, with Naval Intelligence, Lieut. Commdr., R.N.V.R.; Publications: 'The Dinosaurs,' 1934; 'Corridor of Life,' 1946; 'Geology & the Museum,' 1941; 'Wonderful World of Prehistoric Animals,' 1961; 'Animals before Adam,' 1961; 'Fossils,' 1961; 'Digging for Dinosaurs,' 1962; 'Giants,' 1966; 'The Dinosaurs,' 1970; and many Brit. Museum Handbooks; has edited prof. journs. and written articles for 'Illustrated London News,' 'Nature,' 'New Scientist,' 'Canadian Medical Association Journal,' etc.; many broadcasts and TV programmes for BBC (mem., Schools Broadcasting Council 1956–61); has broadcast on CBC, CFRB, TV Ont. and CTV; mem., Metropolitan Educational TV Assn. 1964–66; mem. Adv. Comte., Science & Medicine, Expo 67; Dir., Candn. Audubon Soc. 1967–69; Trustee, Ont. Science Centre 1965–85; Hon. Trustee, Royal Ont. Museum; Hon. Fellow, Hon. Curator, Acad. Museum; Hon. Chrmn., Sect. of Med. Anthropology and Archaeology, Acad. of Med., Toronto; Pres., Brighton Natural Hist. Soc. 1957–58; Pres., Museums Assn. (UK), 1958–60 (Hon. fellow 1981); Hon. Gen. Secy., Brit. Assn. for Advanc. of Science, 1959–61 (Pres. Section X 1953); rec'd. Darwin Medal (upon giving address on centenary of 'Origin of Species') Acad. of Sciences, Moscow 1959; mem., N.Y. Acad. of Sciences; Am. Inst. of Biol. Sciences; Soc. of Authors, London, Eng.; Corresp. mem. Geol. Soc. of Belgium; Hon. mem. Royal Antwerp Zool. Soc.; Case Mem. Lecturer, Univ. of Michigan, 1966; Sr. Fellow, Hannah Inst. for Hist. of Medicine, 1977–79; hon. mem., Royal Candn. Inst.; Admiral of Nebraska 1957; hon. Fellow, Museum of Arts and Sci., Rochester, N.Y.; Hon. Fellow, Roy. Coll. Phys. & Surg. Can. 1978; Hon. Mem., Ont. Medical Assn., 1982; Hon. Officer, 78th (Fraser) Highlanders; Silver Jubilee Medal; Clubs: Athenaeum (London, Eng.); Arts & Letters (ex-Pres.); R.C.Y.C.; Royal Canadian Military Institute (Life mem.); Home: 276 St. George St. (Apts. 604–605), Toronto, Ont. M5R 2P6; Office: Massey College, Toronto, Ont. M5S 2E1.

**SWIRSKY, Benjamin,** B.Comm., LL.B., F.C.A.; executive; b. Corner Brook, Nfld. 9 Oct. 1941; e. Dalhousie Univ. B.Comm. 1963; Queen's Univ. LL.B. 1968; PRES. & C.E.O., SLATER INDUSTRIES INC. 1993– ; Chrmn., Trilea Centres Inc.; Dir., Four Seasons Hotels Limited; The Horsham Corp.; Slater Ind. Inc.; Consolidated Talcorp Ltd.; former Sr. Tax Partner with Peat, Marwick, Mitchell & Co.; joined Bramalea Ltd. as Exec. Vice Pres. 1979, Pres. & C.E.O. 1988–90; Vice-Chrmn. & C.E.O. 1990; former Gov. Candn. Tax Found.; Vice-Chrmn. and mem. Exec. Ctte., Baycrest Hosp. Foundation; author numerous articles and books on financial and tax matters; mem., Candn. Inst. C.A.'s; recreations: tennis, jogging, skiing; Clubs: Donalda; Maple Downs Golf & Country; Office: 4100 Yonge St., Suite 410, Toronto, Ont. M2P 2B5.

**SWITZER, Clayton Macfie,** M.S.A., Ph.D.; educator; b. Melbourne, Ont. 17 July 1929; s. Wilford H. and Marion V. (Macfie) S.; e. Ont. Agric. Coll., B.S.A. 1951; Univ. of Toronto, M.S.A. 1953; Iowa State Coll., Ph.D. 1955; Dalhousie Univ., LL.D. 1987; m. Dorothy Jean, d. late Roger Allan, Windsor, Ont., 28 July 1951; children: John, Karen, Robert; PRES., CLAY SWITZER CONSULTANTS LTD. 1989– ; joined Ont. Agricultural Coll., Univ. of Guelph as Lectr. 1955–56; Asst. Prof. 1956–60, Assoc. Prof. 1960–62, Prof. 1963–67, Prof. and Chrmn., Dept. of Bot., 1967–70, Assoc. Dean of Coll. 1971–72, Dean 1972–83; Depy. Min., Ont. Min. of Agriculture & Food 1984–89; Extve. Dir., Confederation of Candn. Faculties of Agriculture and Veterinary Med. 1993– ; Chrmn., Ont. Pesticides Advisory Comm. 1993– ; Visiting Prof., Univ. Nat. del Sur, Argentina, 1968; visiting Prof., Hawkesbury Agr. Coll. Australia 1975, 1978; Lincoln Coll., New Zealand 1978; author of over 150 scient. papers, reports and articles; Fellow, Weed Science Soc. Am.; Fellow, Agric. Inst. of Can.; Mem., Candn. Soc. Plant Physiol.; Can. Pest Mgmt. Soc.; Am. Assn. Advance. Science; Weed Science Soc. Am.; Past Pres., Internat. Turfgrass Soc.; Agric. Inst. Can.; Ont. Inst. Agrols.; former mem., Science Council Can. (1977–82); Candn. Agric. Research Council; Ont. Econ. Council; Dir. and former Exec. mem., Royal Agric. Fair; former Dir., Foundation for Rural Living; Hon. mem.: Ont. Golf Superintendents Assn.; Candn. Golf Superintendents Assn.; Ont. Assoc. of Landscape Architects; Candn. Seed Growers Assoc.; Alumnus of Honour, Univ. of Guelph 1985; United Church; recreations: golf, curling; Clubs: Guelph Country; Guelph Curling; Home: 16 Tamarack Pl., Guelph, Ont. N1E 3Y6.

**SWITZER, John Harcourt,** B.A., LL.B.; Q.C.; lawyer, land developer, builder; b. Toronto, Ont. 31 Jan. 1931; s. Norman Grafton and Maud Hannah (McBride) S.; e. Humberside Collegiate; McMaster Univ. B.A. (Hons) 1955; Univ. of Toronto Law Sch. LL.B. 1958; Q.C. 1973; m. Lynne Jeffe d. Marjorie and Lawrence Stoll 20 July 1983; children: John Harcourt Jr., David Grafton, Jeffery Maxwell; CHRMN. & CHIEF EXTVE. OFFR., J.H. SWITZER CORP.; Pres., The Urban Devel. Inst. of Ont. 1987–89; Dir., Law Alumni, Univ. of Toronto 1989–92; Mem., Governing Council, Univ. of Toronto 1988–91 (Dep. Chrmn., Bus. Bd.); Trustee Art Gallery of Ont. & Co-Chrmn., Curator's Circle 1990–93; Dir., The National Ballet of Can. 1990–93; Dir., Canadian Opera Co. 1990–93; Dir., Canadian Stage Company; Arbor Award for outstanding voluntary serv. to Univ. of Toronto 1990; Cross of Malta 1991; Master Mason, Zeta Lodge (Toronto); clubs: Mississauga Golf & Country, Ontario Jockey, Albany, Breakers (Palm Beach); Home: 1527 Mississauga Rd., Mississauga, Ont. L5H 2J7; Office: 2902 South Sheridan Way, Oakville, Ont. L6J 7L6.

**SWITZER, Maurice H.;** publisher; b. Toronto, Ont. 28 March 1945; s. Harold and Ruby (Marsden) S.; e. Trent Univ. 1964–65; m. Mary Helen Pavlik; children: Andrea, Adin, Lisa; PUBLISHER, WINNIPEG FREE PRESS 1992– ; Journalist, Belleville Intelligencer 1965–67; Sports Editor 1967–72; Managing Editor 1972–79; Oshawa Times 1979–81; Publisher, Timmins Daily Press 1981–86; Sudbury Star 1986–92; Bd. of Dir., Canadian Press; Bd. Mem., Man. Art Gall. 1992–93; Man. Opera 1992– ; Health Science Centre Foundation 1992– ; author: 'Bruno Cavallo A Conversation' 1991; clubs: Manitoba, St. Charles Country, Carleton; Home: 7A – 221 Wellington Cres., Winnipeg, Man. R3M 0A1; Office: 1355 Mountain Ave., Winnipeg, Man. R2X 3B6.

**SWITZER, Ronald H.;** insurance executive; b. Montreal, Que. 11 March 1938; e. Carleton Univ.; Univ. of Syracuse; Univ. of New Hampshire; m. Barbara A. (nee Ball); children: Mark, David; SENIOR VICE-PRES. & MANAGER FOR CANADA, LIBERTY MUTUAL INSURANCE GROUP 1990– ; Underwriter, Employers' Liability Insur. Co. 2 years; Broker, Richards, Melling Insur. Brokers 2.5 years; Sales Rep., Liberty Mutual Insur. Co. Montreal 1962–70; various sales mngt. positions Don Mills 1970–87; Vice-Pres. & Mgr. for Canada 1987–90; Dir., Underwriters' Labs. of Canada; Facility Assn.; Mem., Ont. Adv. Comm.; Assoc., Insur. Inst. of Canada; recreations: golf, skiing, cabinetmaking; clubs: The Granite; Horseshoe Valley Golf & Country; Home: 17 Highland Dr., R.R. 1, Shanty Bay, Ont. L0L 2L0; Office: 675 Cochrane Dr., Unionville, Ont. L3R 0S7.

**SWITZER, William John,** B.A., M.B.A., F.C.A.; management consultant; b. Ottawa, Ont. 18 June 1946; e. Univ. of Toronto B.A. 1970; York Univ. M.B.A. 1974; C.A. Ontario 1974; F.C.A. 1991; PRINCIPAL, ERNST & YOUNG 1994– ; Deloitte, Haskins and Sells, Toronto 1970–74; York Univ., Fac. of Admin. Studies 1974–79; Deputy Comptroller, The Bank of N.S. 1976–85; Senior Vice-Pres., National Trust Co., Toronto 1985–92; Independent Consultant 1992–93; Chair, The Christopher Robin Home Foundation; Chair, Dept. of Treas., United Church of Canada; Dir., Ecos Environmental Health Found.; recreations: competitive running; clubs: Fitness Inst.; Office: P.O. Box 251, Toronto-Dominion Centre, Toronto, Ont. M5K 1J7.

**SWORD, John Howe,** M.A., LL.D.; educator (retired); b. Saskatoon, Sask. 22 Jan. 1915; s. Martha (Morrison) and William Brown S.; e. Pub. and High Schs., Winnipeg, Man.; Univ. of Manitoba, B.A., 1935; Univ. of Toronto, M.A. 1950; LL.D. (Hon.), Univ. of Manitoba 1970; LL.D. (hon. causa), Univ. of Toronto 1988; m. Constance A., d. late Thomas W. Offen, Rivers, Man.; children: Stephen John, Linda May; began career in educ. as teacher, jr. high and high schs., Man., 1936–42; Secy., Man. Royal Comn. on Adult Educ., 1945–46; Asst. Secy., Sch. of Grad. Studies, Univ. of Toronto, 1947–48, Secy., 1948–60; Extve. Asst. to the Pres., Univ. of Toronto, 1960–65; Vice-Provost, 1965–67; Acting Pres., 1967–68; Extve. Vice Pres. (Academic) and Provost 1968–71, Acting Pres. 1971–72, Vice Pres., Inst. Relations & Planning 1972–74; Special Asst. to Pres. 1974–80; Chrmn. of the Press Bd. (U. of T. Press) 1977–80; Retired 1980; Acting Dir., School of Continuing Studies, 1980–81 and 1983–84; Mgmt. Bd., Geneva Park 1972–85; Trustee, Toronto Sch. of Theology 1978–83; Mem., Bd. of Stewards, Hart House, Univ. of Toronto 1988– (Chrmn. Art Comte. 1980–83; Chrmn., Finance Comte. 1983–88); Royal Candn. Inst. 1981–93; Dir., Univ. of Toronto Oral History Project 1981–90; mem., Prov. of Ont. Addiction Research Fdn. 1981–87; mem., Toronto District Heating Corp. 1982–87; Vice-Pres. and Dir., Associated Medical Services 1983–92; Chrmn. Certificate Review Advisory Cttee., Ministry of Ed. 1984– ; Jr. Trustee, Wychwood Park Heritage Conservation District 1986–90; Co-ordinator, Toronto Round Table 1991–93; served as Aircrew Instr. R.C.A.F., 1942–45; recipient, Queen's Silver Jubilee Medal 1977; United Church; Clubs; Arts and Letters; Faculty, Queens; Home: 8 Wychwood Park, Toronto, Ont. M6G 2V5.

**SWYER, Paul Robert,** M.A., M.D.(Cantab), F.R.C.P.(C), F.R.C.P.(L), D.C.H.; neonatologist; b. London, Eng. 21 May 1921; s. Robert and Kathleen (Rodwell) S.; e. Bedford Sch. UK 1938; Christ's Coll. Cambridge M.B. 1943; Univ. of Lausanne M.D. (Hon.) 1984; m. Fernande Hélène Rumbaut 7 June 1947; children: Sandra, Michèle; Prof. of Paediatrics, Univ. of Toronto 1975–86; Prof. Emeritus, Univ. of Toronto; Hon. Consultant Physician, The Hosp. for Sick Children, Toronto; former Chief, Div. of Neonatal Med., Consultant Physician, The Hosp. for Sick Children, Toronto 1965–86; Chrmn. Perinatal Complex Ctte. Univ. of Toronto and affiliated hosps. (Mount Sinai, Toronto Gen., Women's Coll. Hosp. and Hosp. for Sick Children) 1984–86; internship Middlesex Hosp. (Univ. of London), Brompton Hosp. for Diseases of the Chest, Hosp. for Sick Children Great Ormond St. and in Birmingham region of Eng.; Oxford & Cambridge Univ. Scholar, Middlesex Hosp. Med. Sch. 1940; Brit. Council Fellow in Cardiol. The Hosp. for Sick Children Toronto 1953, later served as part-time Rsch. Assoc. Rsch. Inst. in Neonatology becoming full-time 1961; organized Intensive Care Unit The Hosp. for Sick Children 1961; various rsch. sabbaticals Univs. Oxford, Stockholm, Cambridge, Lausanne; recipient World Health Orgn. Fellowship 1985; author 'The Intensive Care of the Newly Born: Physiological Principles and Practice' 1974; author or co-author 102 original articles, 113 abstracts, 9 books and 34 book chapters; served with RAMC N.W. Eur. World War II; Scientific Ctte., Hospital for Sick Children Foundation; Mem., Maternal-Newborn-Child Steering Ctte. and Chair, Hospital Integration Sub-Ctte. of the Metro Toronto District Health Council; mem. Candn. Paediatric Soc.; Candn. Med. Assn.; Ont Med. Assn.; Fellow, Am. Acad. Pediatrics; Am. Pediatric Soc.; Founding Mem., Soc. Critical Care Med.; Soc. Pediatric Rsch.; Scientific Ctte., Candn. Found. Study Sudden Infant Death Syndrome; Past Chrmn. and mem., Ont. Prov. Adv. Ctte. Reproductive Med. Care; recreations: tennis, fencing (Ont. Jr. Gold Medal, sabre; Silver Medal, foil 1961), skiing, music, photography, computer technology; Office: The Hospital for Sick Children, 555 University Ave., Toronto, Ont. M5G 1X8.

**SYKES, Brian D.,** B.Sc., Ph.D., F.R.S.(C); university professor; b. Montreal, Que. 30 Aug. 1943; s. Douglas Lehman and Mary (Anber) S.; e. Univ. of Alta., B.Sc. (Hons.) 1965; Stanford Univ., Ph.D. 1969; m. Nancy d. Clarence and Elsie Sengelaub 25 May 1968; children: David, Michael; PROF. OF BIOCHEMISTRY, UNIV. OF ALBERTA 1980– ; Asst. Prof. of Chem., Harvard Univ. 1969–74; Assoc. Prof. 1974–75; Univ. of Alta. 1975–80; Ayerst Award, Candn. Biochem. Soc. 1982; Steacie Prize 1982; Fellow, Royal Soc. of Can. 1986; J. Gordin Kaplan Award for Excellence in Rsch. 1992; Pres., Candn. Biochem. Soc. 1989–90; Mem., Counc. Biophysical Soc. 1989–92; author of over 200 sci. papers; recreations: hockey; clubs: South Side Athletic, SouthWest United Sports; Home: 11312 – 37 Ave., Edmonton, Alta. T6J 0H5; Office: Dept. of Biochem., Univ. of Alta., Edmonton, Alta. T6G 2H7.

**SYKES, Ralph Leonard,** B.A., M.B.A., F.C.A.; chartered accountant; b. Calgary, Alta. 7 May 1939; s. Leonard and Dorothy Mary S.; e. Royal Military Coll. B.A. 1961; Inst. of C.A.s C.A. 1968; York Univ. M.B.A. 1987; m. The Rev'd Barbara A. d. Stuart and Edna Robb 11 Nov. 1961; children: Robb, Cynthia; EXECUTIVE PARTNER & CHIEF EXECUTIVE OFFICER, DOANE RAYMOND 1987– ; C.A. Student, Doane Raymond Fredericton N.B. 1965–68; Resident Manager Bathurst N.B. 1968–70; Consulting Partner Halifax N.S. 1970–72; Resident Partner Moncton N.B. 1972–75; Office Mng. Partner Dartmouth N.S. 1975–77; Profl. Standards Partner Halifax 1977–79; Admin. Partner 1979–82; Office Mng. Partner Toronto 1982–87; Dir., Grant Thornton Internat.; Fellow, Inst. of C.A.s of Ont. 1985; Trustee, Wycliffe College, Univ. of Toronto; recreations: golf, skiing, travel; clubs: National Golf, Albany, Royal Military College (life mem.); Home: 12 Whitman St., Willowdale, Ont. M2M 3H8; Office: Ste. 1100, North Tower, Royal Bank Plaza, 200 Bay St., Toronto, Ont. M5J 2P9.

**SYLVAIN, John,** B.Comm., F.I.I.C.; Senator, Senate of Canada; insurance executive; b. London, Eng., 7 June 1924; s. John Albert and Alice (Carriere) S.; e. Univ. Ottawa, B.Com. 1950; m. Yolande, d. Ernest Maranger, 22 Dec. 1947; five d., one s.; CONSULTANT, DALE-PARIZEAU INC; Dir., Corp. of the Children's Hospital of Montreal; with The Travelers Insurance Co., Hartford, Conn. 1950, Montreal, Que. 1951, Br. Mgr. Ottawa 1952, Br. Mgr., E. Can., Montreal 1964; Vice-Pres., Marsh & McLennan, Montreal 1968; Pres., Robert Hampson and Son Ltd. 1970; Vice Pres., Maryland Casualty Co., Baltimore, Md. 1970; Pres., Gen. Mgr. and Dir., United Provices Ins. Co., Montreal 1975–82; served in 2nd World War, R.C.A.F. in Europe, Africa and Asia; Fellow, Insurance Inst. of Canada; formerly: Chrmn. Cartier Fisheries Inc.; Dir., Insur. Bureau of Canada; Canada Development Investment Corp.; Groupement des Assureurs Automobile du Quebec; Insurers' Advisory Organization; recreations: golf, gardening; Clubs: Beaconsfield Golf; M.A.A.A.; St. James; Home: 335 Berwick Drive, Beaconsfield, Que. H9W 1B8.

**SYLVAIN, Noel;** administrator; né Thetford-Mines, Qué. 13 juin 1928; f. Pierre et Blanche (Boulet) S.; é. Ecole secondaire St.-Frédéric de Drummondville 1946; Univ. d'Ottawa cours sur 'La Mutualité' 1950; ép. Lucille Chainey 15 juillet 1950; enfants: Odette, Guy, Yves, Marielle; ADMINISTRATOR, L'UNION VIE; entrait au service de L'Union-St-Joseph de Drummondville (fondée en 1889, maintenant sous le nom de L'Union-Vie) 1946, promoteur des ventes 1957, surintendant des agences 1959, directeur général-adjoint, administrateur de la compagnie 1972; président du conseil d'administration de L'Union-Vie depuis août 1985; président de la Corporation du Centre Culturel; membre Chambre de Comm. Drummond; récreations: fermier, acériculteur (produits d'érable); Adresse: 70 Des Châtaigniers, Drummondville, Qué. J2C 3J4; Bureau: 142 rue Hériot, Drummondville, Qué. J2C 1J8.

**SYLVESTRE, Claude;** commissioner; b. Montreal, Que. 18 Feb. 1927; COMMISSIONER, CANADIAN RADIO-TELEVISION AND TELECOMMUNICATIONS COMMISSION 1992– ; Former TV Prod., Radio-Canada 20 years; Former Dir., Radio Network Prog., Radio Canada & Co-ord., News Broadcasts (Paris); Former Vice-Pres., Prog., Radio-Québec; Former Pres., Prod. Dix-huit Ltée. produced projects by Gilles Carle, Jean-Pierre Lefebvre, Michel Moreau and a feature film on La Bolduc; Co-founder, Cinéma 16; Home: 37 av. Lorne, Ottawa, Ont. K1R 7G6; Office: Ottawa, Ont. K1A 0N2.

**SYLVESTRE, Jean-Guy,** O.C., L.Ph., M.A., D.Bibl., D.Litt., LL.D., F.R.S.C.; librarian, writer; b. Sorel, P.Q., 17 May 1918; s. Maxime Arthur and Yvonne (Lapierre) S.; e. Coll. Ste-Marie, Montreal, P.Q.; Univ. of Ottawa, B.A. 1939, L.Ph. 1940, M.A. 1941; D.L.S. (Hons.) Ottawa; D. Litt. (Hons) Mount Allison; LL.D. (Hons) Toronto; LL.D. (Hons.) Prince Edward Island; LL.D. (Hons.) Memorial; LL.D. (Hons.) Concordia; m. Françoise, d. Eugene Poitevin, Ottawa, Ont., 27 Feb. 1943; one d. Marie, two s. Jean, Paul; Ed., Wartime Information Bd. 1944–45; Private Secy. to Rt. Hon. Louis S. St. Laurent, 1945–50; Book Reviewer, Le Droit, Ottawa, Ont., 1939–48; Assoc. Parlty. Librarian, Lib. of Parliament, 1956–68; National Librarian of Canada 1968–83; Pres., Candn. Inst. for Historical Microreproductions 1983–86; Chrmn., Ottawa Valley book Festival 1988–92; Past Chrmn. of Comte. for Gov.-Gen. Lit. Awards; Past Chrmn., Candn. Writers Foundation; past Pres., Royal Society of Canada; mem. Académie Canadienne-française; Pres. World Poetry Conf., 1967; Officer, Order of Canada; Commdr., Ordre internat du Bien public; Ordre du mérite de Pologne; IFLA Medal; Candn. Rep., Intergovernmental Council for General Info. Prog., Unesco 1979–83; Candn. Del. to UNESCO Conferences 1949, 70, 72, 74; Chrmn., Conference of Dirs. of Nat. Libraries, 1974–77; Chrmn. Nat. Libraries Section, IFLA., 1977–81; Outstanding Public Service Award 1983; author of 'Louis Francoeur, journaliste' 1941; 'Situation de la poésie canadienne' 1942; 'Anthologie de la poésie canadienne d'expression française' 1943; 'Poètes catholiques de la France contemporaine' 1944; 'Jules Laforgue' 1945; 'Sondages' 1945; 'Impressions de théâtre' 1950; 'Panorama des lettres canadiennes françaises' 1964; 'Canadian Writers/Ecrivains canadiens' 1964; 'Un siècle de littérature canadienne' 1967; 'Guidelines for national libraries' 1987; Life mem., Candn. Library Assn. (CLA); Assn. des Sci. et Tech. de la Documentation; Hon. Life mem. Ont. Library Assn. (OLA); mem. & First Pres., Candn. Assn. for Information Sci.; Roman Catholic; recreation: Clubs: Seigniory (Montebello); Home: 2286 Bowman Rd., Ottawa, Ont. K1H 6V6.

**SYLVIA, Mark A.,** F.I.I.C., F.L.M.I.; insurance executive; b. Montreal, Que. 13 Jan. 1956; s. Gordon Edward and Leila Angela (Pollard); e. F.I.I.C. 1978; F.L.M.I. 1993; Duke Univ., Exec. Educ. Dipl. 1993; Fairfield Univ., adv. mngt. dipl. 1984; Univ. of Toronto; m. Bonnie Heather d. Gordon and Florence Robertson March 1977; children: Robyn, Ellyn, Graeme; PRES. & CHIEF EXTVE. OFFR., ABBEY LIFE INSUR. CO. OF CANADA 1988– ; Dir., Compcorp 1993– ; var. underwriting & mktg. positions, Commercial Union Assur. Co. of Canada 1973–82; Market Devel. Offr., Aetna Canada 1982–85; Vice-Pres., Mktg., Laurier Life Insur. Co. 1985–87; Extve. Vice-Pres., Royal Agencies Limited (Royal Trustco Ltd. subs.) 1987–88; Instr., Insur., Algonquin College Ottawa 1977–80; Home: R.R. 4, Tottenham, Ont. L0G 1W0; Office: 3027 Harvester Rd., Burlington, Ont. L7N 3G9.

**SYMES, Lawrence Richard,** B.A., M.S., Ph.D.; university professor; b. Ottawa, Ont. 3 Aug. 1942; s. Oliver Lawrence and Maybell Melita Blanche (Gilliard) S.; e. City Park Collegiate (Saskatoon) 1960; Univ. Sask., Honours Cert. Math. 1964; Purdue Univ., M.S. 1966; Ph.D. 1969; m. Evelyn, d. Fredrick and Jean Hewett, 2 May 1964; children: Calvin Richard; Michelle Louise; Erin Kathleen; PROF., FACULTY OF SCIENCE, UNIV. REGINA 1974– ; Asst. Prof. Computer Sci. Purdue Univ. 1969–70; Assoc. Prof. Univ. Regina 1970–74, Dir. Computer Centre 1970–75, Head Computer Sci. Dept. 1972–81, Dir. Academic Computing 1980–81; Dean, Faculty of Science 1982–92; Invited Lectr., Xian Jiaotong Univ., Xian, China 1983; Invited Lectr., Shandong Acad. of Sciences, Jinan, Shandong China 1987; author and co-author 27 technical papers, primarily on programming languages and computer system performance; mem. Bd. Dirs., Hosp. Systems Study Group (Chrmn. 1980–83); mem. Mgmt. Bd., Data Processing Centre Sask. Sch. Trustees' Assn.; Tech. Consultant, Prov. Computer Rationalization Mgmt. Comte. 1972–73; mem. Assn. for Computing Machinery (Self-Mgmt. Comte. 1974–79); Adv. Ctte. to Data Processing Prog. Sask. Tech. Inst. (Moose Jaw) 1971–91; mem. Candn. Information Processing Soc. (Nat. Pres. 1979–80, Accreditation Ctte. 1988– ); Adv. Council, Mngmt. Ctte., Canada-Sask. Advanced Tech. Agreement 1985–87; mem. Sask. Agriculture Rsch. Fund Bd. 1987–88; The Steering Ctte. IBM/Sask. Agreement 1990– ; mem., Bd. Sask. Ada Assn. 1991– ; recreations: hockey; water skiing; wind surfing; Home: 4 Arlington St., Regina, Sask. S4S 3H6; Office: Faculty of Science, Univ. of Regina, Regina, Sask. S4S 0A2.

**SYMINGTON, John Marston,** B.D.S., M.Sc., Ph.D., F.D.S., R.C.S., F.I.C.D.; university professor; b. Blackhill, Durham, Eng. 22 Nov. 1933; s. Marston Granville and Gladys Mary (Milne) S.; e. Consett Grammar Sch.; Merchant Taylors Sch.; Crosby Liverpool Univ. of Durham B.D.S.; Univ. of Manchester M.Sc. 1973, Ph.D. 1977; m. Hildegarde d. William and Laura Marshall 13 Sept. 1958; children: Owen, Alison, Amanda, Joanna; PROF. & HEAD, DEPT. OF ORAL & MAXILLOFACIAL SURG., UNIV. OF TORONTO 1978– ; entered hosp. serv. in U.K. culminating in appt. as Cons. Dental Surg., Sheffield Reg. Hosp. Bd. 1966; Sr. Lectr., Univ. of Manchester 1968; author/co-author numerous sci. papers; internat. lectr.; Pres., Bone Anchorage Systems; Mem., Candn. & Ont. Dental Assns.; Candn. & Ont. Socs. of Oral and Maxillofacial Surg.; recreations: 3D photography, canoeing; Home: 17 Norbert Cres., Etobicoke, Ont. M9C 3J8; Office: 124 Edward St., Toronto, Ont. M5S 1A1.

**SYMONS, Al P.,** Hon. B.A.; insurance executive; b. Sudbury, Ont. 8 May 1936; s. Peter and Agnes (Duhaime) S.; e. Univ. of West. Ont. B.A. (Hons.) 1958; m. Rosemary d. Peter and Francis Casey 1 Aug. 1959; children: Monique, Marc, Sean, Kearan; EXTVE. VICE-PRES. & DIR., CANDN. DIV., CANADA LIFE ASSURANCE CO. 1991– ; various sales positions, present firm 1969–72; Dir. of Group Sales, Canada 1972; Vice-Pres., Group Pension 1976; Group Div. 1982; Vice-Pres. & Dir., Group Div. (U.S. & Canada) 1985; Chair & C.E.O., Canada Life Casualty Co. 1985; Dir., Canada Life Investment Management Limited; club: Toronto

Cricket, Meadowbrook Golf & Country; Home: 58 Heatherwood Cres., Unionville, Ont.; Office: 330 University Ave., Toronto, Ont. M5G 1R8.

**SYMONS, Gerald Gordon;** executive; b. Quebec; s. Wilfred Gerald and Nellie Shaw (Howarth) S.; e. Lachine High Sch.; Sir George Williams Univ.; Chairman & Chief Extve. Offr.: Goran Capital Inc. (Canada); Granite Reinsurance Co. (Barbados); Symons Internatonal Group Ltd., Canada; Pafco General Insurance Co., U.S.A.; Symons International Group Inc., U.S.A.; Granite Insurance Company, Canada; IGF Insurance Company, U.S.A.; Served with RCAF 1941–45; pilot overseas, attached R.A.F. Squadron 143, Anti-Shipping Coastal Command; joined Lloyd's broker, Stewart Smith Canada Ltd. 1947, Ont. Mgr. 1951; joined Morgan Insurance Services Ltd. 1953, Dir. 1956, Vice-Pres. 1958; formed G. Gordon Symons Co. Ltd. (predecessor of present firm) 1964; mem. Candn. Schizophrenic Found., Lakeshore Gen. Hosp.; Life Gov. Montreal Gen. Hosp.; Hon. Life Mem. Soc. for Emotional Development in Children; recreations: golf, writing, painting; Clubs: Mid Ocean (Bermuda); Kanawaki Golf; Lambton Golf & Country; John's Island Club (Fla.), Bent Pine Golf & Country (Fla.); Residence: Bermuda.

**SYMONS, Thomas H.B.,** O.C., B.A., M.A., LL.D., D.U., D. Litt., F.R.S.C., F.R.G.S.; educator; b. Toronto, Ont. 30 May 1929; s. Harry Lutz and Dorothy Sarah (Bull) S.; e. Upper Can. Coll.; Univ. of Toronto Schs.; Univ. of Toronto, B.A. 1951; Oxford Univ. B.A. 1953, M.A. 1957; independent studies at Paris, Leyden, Rome 1953; Rockefeller Grant, Harvard Univ. 1956; LL.D., Wilfrid Laurier 1971, N.B. 1972, York 1973, Trent 1975, Laurentian 1977, Mount Allison 1979, Concordia 1981, P.E.I. 1983, Dalhousie 1983, Manitoba 1989; D.U. (Ottawa) 1974; D. Litt. (Colombo) 1985; Distinguished Service to Education Award, Council for the Advancement and Support of Education, Washington, D.C., 1982; Hon. Fellow, Oriel College, Oxford 1988; m. Christine, d. late Harvey Ryerson, 17 August 1963; children: Mary, Ryerson, Jeffrey; Cumming Fellowship and Asst. Dean of Men, Trinity Coll. and Instr., Dept. of Hist., Univ. of Toronto 1953–55; Dean, Devonshire House, Univ. of Toronto 1955–63; founding Pres. and Vice-Chancellor Trent Univ. 1961–72; Chrmn., Comm. on Cdn. Studies 1972–84; Chrmn., Historic Sites and Monuments Bd. of Can. 1986– ; Visiting Fellow, Calgary Instit. for the Humanities 1977; Vanier Prof., Trent Univ., 1979– ; Assoc. of Australian Studies Centre, Univ. of Queensland, Australia, 1980; Candn. Co-Chrmn., Australia-Canada Colloquium, Canberra, 1981; Visiting Fellow, Clare Hall, Cambridge 1984; Visiting Scholar, Scott Polar Rsch. Institute, Cambridge 1984, 1992–93; Visiting Fellow, Centre for Internat. Studies, Cambridge 1992–93; Bye Fellow, Robinson College, Cambridge 1992–93; Dir., Celanese Canada Inc.; Dir., Gilbey Canada Inc.; Founding mem., Council of Ont. Univ. 1961–72; mem. Council, Assn. Commonwealth Univs. 1970–88 (Chrmn. 1971–72; Hon. Treas. 1973–88); Chrmn., Candn. Commonwealth Scholarship and Fellowship Ctte. 1983–87; mem., Commonwealth Standing Ctte. on Student Mobility 1982–88; Chrmn., Internat'l Bd. of United World Colleges 1980–86; mem. Bd., Pearson Coll.; Mem. Adv. Comte. Academic Relations, Dept. of External Affairs, 1978– ; Chrmn., Candn. Polar Rsch. Commission Study 1988; Trustee, Oriel Coll., Oxford Univ.; Chrmn., Ont. Human Rights Comn. 1975–78; Chrmn., Min. Comn. on Fr. Lang. Educ. in Ont. 1971–72; mem., Adv. Comte. on Confed. to Prime Min. of Ont. 1965–72; Pres., Candn. Assn. in Support of Native Peoples 1972–73; mem., Adv. Comte. on Land Claims of Native Council of Can. 1972–73; Co-Chrmn., Candn. Conf. on Multiculturalism 1973; mem., Ont. Arts Council 1974–76; mem., Can. Council 1976–78; mem., Nat'l Library Bd. 1978–90 (Chrmn. 1987–90); Vice Pres., Soc. Sci. and Humanities Research Council 1978–84; Special Adv. on higher educ. to Secy. of State 1976–84; mem., Federal Cultural Policy Review Comte. 1979–82; Co-Chrmn., Colloquium on the State of the Official Languages 1982; Chrmn., National Statistics Counc. 1986– ; Chrmn. Adv. Comte on the Nat. Atlas of Canada 1983– ; mem. National Capital Planning Comte. 1987– ; mem. Confederation Birthplace Commission P.E.I. 1990–91; Chrmn. Candn. Educational Standards Inst. 1987–91; Adv. Bd., Lakefield Coll. Sch.; Gov., Upper Can. Coll. 1969–82; chart. mem. Bd. Govs., Sir Sandford Fleming Coll. 1964–69; Loyalist Coll. 1964–67; Chart. mem., World Univ. Service of Can.; Chart. mem., Candn. Bureau for Internat. Education; founding mem. Ed. Bd., Journ. of Candn. Studies; Founding mem., Candn. Soc. for Study of Higher Educ.; Founding mem., Candn. Civil Liberties Assn.; Chrmn., Policy Adv. Committee to Hon. R. L. Stanfield 1968–75; rec'd. Candn. Centennial Medal 1967; Civic Award of Merit, Peterborough 1969; Queen's Jubilee Medal 1977; O.C. 1977; awarded Commemorative Medal for 125th Anniversary of Candn. Confederation 1992; Award of Merit, Candn. Bureau for Internat. Education 1993; Hon. Dipl. from Sir Sandford Fleming Coll. 1970; Diplôme d'Etudes Collégiales, Dawson Coll., 1981; author 'Report of the Ministerial Comn. on Fr. Lang. Educ. in Ont.' 1972; 'To Know Ourselves: the Report of the Comn. on Candn. Studies' 1976; 'Report of the Canadian Polar Research Commission Study' 1988; 'Canada - Italy Relations' 1989; co-author 'Some Questions of Balance: Human Resources, Higher Education, and Canadian Studies' 1984; 'Report of the Federal Cultural Policy Review' 1982; 'Life Together: a Report on Human Rights in Ontario' 1977; contrib. chapters to: 'Demographic Currents' 1991; 'The Contribution of Universities to National Development' 1989; 'Political Education in Canada' 1988; 'Postsecondary Education in Canada' 1986; 'Human Rights and Peace' 1985; 'Ontario Universities: Access, Operations, and Funding' 1985; 'Technological Innovation: University Roles' 1984; 'Archives, Libraries, and the Canadian Heritage' 1983; 'Public Policy in Two Federal Countries; Canada and Australia' 1982; 'A Century of Canada's Arctic Islands, 1880–1980' 1981; 'Britain and Canada' 1980; 'Issues in Higher Education' 1979; 'Canadian Confederation Forum' 1978; 'Cartographica' 1979; 'A History of Peel County' 1967; 'Peterborough' 1967; 'The Confederation Challenge' Vol. I 1967, Vol. II 1970; 'Fighting Men' 1967; 'One Country or Two' 1971; 'The Dictionary of Canadian Biography' Vol. X 1972; 'Native Rights in Canada' 1970, rev. ed. 1972; articles and reviews; Nat. Adv. to the Canadian Encyclopedia 1980–85; Clubs: University (Toronto); Rideau (Ottawa); Athenaeum (London); Home: 361 Park St. N., Peterborough, Ont. K9H 4P7.

**SYNAN, Rev. Edward A.,** M.A., Ph.D. (R.C.); educator; b. Fall River, Mass. 13 Apr. 1918; s. late Edward A. and late Mary Frances (McDermott) S.; e. Seton Hall Coll. South Orange, N.J. B.A. 1938; Coll. Américain Univ. de Louvain 1938–40; Cath. Univ. Washington, D.C. STL 1942; Pontifical Inst. Mediaeval Studies Toronto MSL 1951; Univ. of Toronto M.A., Ph.D. 1952; PROF., INST. OF MEDIAEVAL STUDIES AND SCH. OF GRAD STUDIES, UNIV. OF TORONTO 1959– ; Pres. of Inst. 1973–79, Acting Pres. 1989–90; Parish Priest Montclair, N.J. 1942–44; Chrmn. Dept. of Philos. Seton Hall Univ. 1952–59; served as Chaplain USAAF 1944–48 Zone of Interior and Overseas; rec'd Can. Council Research Grant 1965; author 'The Popes and the Jews in the Middle Ages' 1965; 'The Works of Richard of Campsall' Vol. 1 1968, Vol. 2 1982; 'The Fountain of Philosophy' 1972; also various articles and reviews in learned journs.; Hon. Prelate, 1979; Fellow Royal Soc. of Can., 1980; mem. Mediaeval Acad. Am.; Am. Cath. Phil. Assn. (recipient, Aquinas Medal for 1990); Candn. Philos. Assn.; recreations: art, films; Address: 59 Queen's Park Cres. E., Toronto, Ont. M5S 2C4.

**SYRON, Martin Bernard;** executive; b. Sask. 27 Sept. 1936; CHRMN. AND CHIEF EXECUTIVE OFFR., CARA OPERATIONS LTD. 1990– ; Office: 230 Bloor St. W., Toronto, Ont. M5S 1T8.

**SZABO, Denis,** O.C., Ph.D., FRSC; criminologist; educator; b. Budapest, Hungary 4 June 1929; s. Jenö and Catherine (Zsiga) S.; came to Can. 1958; e. Univ. of Budapest; Univ. of Louvain, Ph.D. 1956; La Sorbonne, France, Dipl. in Criminology 1958; Univ. of Siena (Italy) Doctor (honoris causa) 1983; Univ. of Budapest (Hungary) Doctor (honoris causa) 1985; Doctor (honoris causa) Univ. d'Aix-Marseille (France) 1992; m. Sylvie, d. Gustave Grotard, Brussels, Belgium 25 July 1956; children: Catherine; Marianne; PROFESSOR, SCH. OF CRIMINOLOGY, UNIV. DE MONTREAL 1966– ; DIR., INTERNAT. CENTRE FOR COMPARATIVE CRIMINOLOGY 1969–83; Chrmn., Bd. of Dir. ICCC 1984– ; Asst. in Sociology, Univ. of Louvain 1951; Lectr. in Sociology, Catholic Univs. of Paris and Lyon 1956; Asst. Prof. Sociology, Univ. of Montreal 1958; Founder and Dir., Dept. of Criminology there 1960–70; author 'Crimes et villes ...' 1960; 'Délinquance juvénile ... ' 1963; 'Criminologie' 1965; 'Criminologie et politique criminelle' 1978; 'Science et Crimes' 1986; co-author (with J.L. Baudouin and J. Fortin) 'Terrorisme et justice' 1971; (with D. Gagne and A. Parizeau) 'Face à face: l'adolescent et la société' 1972; (with A. Parizeau) 'Le traitement de la criminalité au Canada' 1976; (with Marc Leblanc) 'Traité de criminologie empirique' 1993; 'De l'anthropologie à la criminologie companée' Paris 1993; 'La criminologie empirique au Québec' 1985; author of numerous articles in field; Commander, Nat. Order of Ivory Coast; awarded Beccaria Gold Medal, German Soc. of Criminology; Sutherland Award, Amer. Soc. of Criminol.; recipient of scientific distinctions from several learned societies; Hon. Pres., Internat. Soc. of Criminol.; Pres., Assoc. Internat. des Criminologues de Langue Française, Geneve 1989– ; mem. Bd. of Dir., Internat. Soc. of Social Defence; Internat. Assn. of Penal Law; Founder & mem., Ed. Bd., Revue Criminologie; Sci. Dir., Revue internationale de criminologie et de police technique; Fellow, Royal Society of Canada 1974; Officer of the Order of Canada (1985); La Médaille de la Ville de Paris (Echelon vermeil) 1986; mem. Ed. Bd., Annales internationales de criminologie; R. Catholic; recreations: swimming, gardening, traveling; Home: Georgeville, Qué. J0B 1T0; Office: I.C.C.C., Univ. de Montréal, C.P. 6128, Succ. 'A,' Montreal, Que. H3C 3J7.

**SZAMOSI, Geza,** Ph.D., D.Sc.; educator; physicist; b. Budapest, Hungary 23 March 1922; s. Ludwig and Rosalia (Hartmann) S.; e. Berzsenyi High Sch. Budapest; Pazmany Univ. of Budapest, Ph.D. 1947; Hungarian Acad. of Sciences, D.Sc. 1956; m. Asnat d. Jonathan and Margaret Sternberg 21 July 1944; children: Michael, Anne; VISITING SCHOLAR AND PRINCIPAL OF SCIENCE COLL., CONCORDIA UNIV., Montreal, Que. 1987– ; Prof. of Physics Emeritus, Univ. of Windsor 1989– ; Assoc. Prof. Eotvos Univ. Budapest 1948–55, Prof. 1955–56; Prof. Israel Inst. of Technol. Haifa 1957–61, A. Alberman Visiting Prof. 1970–71; Rsch. Assoc. Nat. Labs. of Italy, Frascati 1961–64, Visiting Sci. 1979; Prof. of Physics, Univ. of Windsor 1964–88; Nuffield Fellow 1970; Visiting Sci.: Inst. Henri Poincare, Paris 1974, 1980–81; Inst. for Theoretical Physics, Nagoya, Japan 1981; recipient Schmidt Prize Hungarian Phys. Soc. 1955; author 'The Twin Dimensions: Inventing Time and Space' 1986; over 60 publs. theoretical physics; mem. Candn. Assn. Phys.; Am. Phys. Soc.; recreation: music; Home: 6307 Westbury, Montreal, Que. H3W 2X4; Office: 1455 De Maisonneuve West, Montreal, Que. H3G 1M8.

**SZATHMÁRY, Emőke Jolàn Erzsébet,** B.A., Ph.D.; university professor; b. Ungvár, Hungary 25 Jan. 1944; d. Károly Béla and Lenke Etelka (Legány) Szathmáry; e. Univ. of Toronto, B.A. 1968, Ph.D. 1974; m. George Alexander s. Arthur and Violet Reilly 14 Feb. 1974; children: Colleen Tünde Frances, Géza Arthur George; PROVOST AND VICE-PRESIDENT (ACADEMIC), MCMASTER UNIV. 1994– ; PROF. DEPT. OF ANTHROPOLOGY 1994– and PROF. DEPT. OF BIOLOGY 1994– ; Asst. Prof., Trent Univ. 1974–75; joined McMaster Univ. 1975; Prof. of Anthrop. 1983–88; Assoc. Mem., Dept. of Biol. 1985–88; Chrmn., Dept. of Anthrop., McMaster Univ. 1985–88; Chrmn., Pres.'s Ctte. on the Ethics of Rsch. on Human Subjects 1987–88; Chrmn., Arts Rsch. Bd., McMaster Univ. 1984–86; mem. Univ. Bd. of Govs. 1986; Senate 1977–78; mem. Adv. Counc. to Bd. of Trustees, Wenner-Gren Found. for Anthrop. Rsch. 1986–89; Dean, Faculty of Social Science, Univ. of Western Ont. 1989–94; Prof., Dept. of Anthropology 1989–94; Hon. Prof., Dept. of Zoology 1989–94; ed. Yearbook of Phys. Anthrop. 1987–91; Past Pres., Candn. Assn. for Phys. Anthrop.; mem. Exec. Ctte., Am. Assn. of Phys. Anthrops. 1987–91; Secy.-Treas., Biological Anthrop. Section, Am. Anthrop. Assoc. 1987–89; Exec. Ctte., Human Biol. Counc. 1985–89; Pres.-Elect 1989–90; Pres. 1990–92; Permanent Counc., Internat. Assn. for the Study of Human Paleont.; Am. Soc. of Human Genetics; Genetics Soc. of Can.; Can. Soc. for Circumpolar Health; R. Catholic; co-ed. 'Diseases of Complex Etiology in Small Populations' 1985; 'Out of Asia' 1985; author and co-author of numerous articles in sci. jours.; recreations: swimming, knitting, embroidery; Office: Hamilton, Ont. L8S 4L8.

**SZENDROVITS, Andrew Zoltan,** M.A., M.Pharm.Sc., Ph.D.; educator; b. Budapest, Hungary 18 March 1919; s. William and Olga (Klem) S.; e. Univ. of Kolozsvar Ph.D (Dr.oec.pub.) and M.A. 1945; Univ. of Budapest M.Pharm.Sc. 1946; m. Margaret d. George and Iren Luntzer 3 Apl. 1945; one s. William Zoltan; PROF. EMERITUS, MCMASTER UNIV. 1985; HONORARY PROF., TECHNICAL UNIV. OF BUDAPEST 1992; Dir., Effort Trust Co. Hamilton; Adjunct Prof. Tech. (Eng.) Univ. of Budapest 1953–56; Supr. Candn. SKF Co. Ltd. Toronto 1957–61; Prof. of Prodn. & Mgmt. Sci., McMaster Univ. 1962–85, Chrmn. 1971–77; Dean of Business, 1979–84; author of numerous scientific papers and books: 'Models and Solutions in Connection with Organization and Planning in the Machine Industry' 1955; 'Introduction to Production Management-Technical Notes' 5th ed. 1981; 'Business Simulation Participants' Manual' 6th ed. 1988; co-author 'Organization and Management of Industrial Enterprises' 1958; mem., Inst. Mgmt. Sci.; recreations: swimming, tennis, photography; Home: 1966 Main St. W., Hamilton, Ont. L8S 1J6; Office: Hamilton, Ont. L8S 4M4.

**SZLAZAK, Anita Christina,** B.A.; Canadian public servant; b. Fulmer, Bucks., Eng. 1 Jan. 1943; d. Jan P. and Christina W. (Matecz) S.; e. Univ. of Toronto B.A. 1963; Coll. of Europe, Bruges Cert. Advanced European Studies (Econ.) 1964; Harvard Grad. Sch. of Business Admin., Boston Advanced Management Program, 1981; DIRECTOR GENERAL, SPECIAL PROJECTS, ATMOSPHERIC ENVIRONMENT SERVICE, ENVIRONMENT CANADA 1992– ; Research Econ. Devel. Centre, Organ. Econ. Coop. and Devel. Paris 1964–67; Foreign Service Offr. Dept. of External Affairs Ottawa 1967–72; Depy. Dir. Gen. Internat. Telecommunications, Dept. Communications Ottawa 1972–73, Dir. Gen. 1973–76; Commr., Public Service Comn. of Can., 1976–82; Extve. Dir. Govt. of Canada Office for the 1988 Olympic Winter Games 1982–84; Spec. Advr., Dept. of External Affairs 1984–86; Sr. Policy Advr., Treas. Bd. of Can. 1986–88; Spec. Advr., Internat. Relns., Can. Mortgage & Housing Corp. 1988–90; Director General, Program Management, Canadian Parks Service, Environment Canada 1990–92; mem. Inst. Pub. Admin. Can. (Extve. Comte. 1976–80); Internat. Inst. of Admin. Sciences, Brussels (Extve. Comte 1983–86, Vice Pres. for North Am. 1986–89); Nat. Capital Harvard Bus. Sch. Alumni Club (Vice-Pres. 1990–92); R. Catholic; Clubs: Rockcliffe Lawn Tennis; Home: 60 Belvedere Cres., Ottawa, Ont. K1M 2G4; Office: 11th Floor, 45 O'Connor St., Ottawa, Ont. K1P 1A4.

**SZONYI, Andrew John,** Ph.D., P.Eng., M.B.A.; university professor (retired); administrator and management consultant; b. Budapest, Hungary 30 May 1934; s. Andor and Marta (Hajdu) S.; e. Polytech. Univ. of Budapest, Dip.Eng. 1956; Univ. of Toronto, M.A.Sc. 1958, Ph.D. 1962, M.B.A. 1971; children: Michael Andor, Janos Eric; Prof. of Mngt. & Engr. 1981–90; Sr. Cons., Ont. Devel. Corp. 1971–81; Program Dir., Mngt. Edn. Program, Huazhong Univ. of Sci. & Technol., People's Rep. of China 1983–86; extensive consulting practice in fin. & bus. mngt., etc.; extensive lectr.; Dir., Engr. & Mngt. Ctr., Univ. of Toronto 1983–86; Zenon Environmental Inc.; Devjo Industries Inc.; RockCliffe Research and Technology Inc.; Biologistics, Inc.; Altai Resources Inc.; Candn. Resource Mngt. Ltd.; Tackla Canada Inc.; The MacLachlan Sch. Educational Found.; Hungarian Candn. Chamber of Commerce; Cons. Prof., Huazhong Univ. of Sci. & Technol., People's Rep. of China; Vis. Prof., Univ. Linz, Austria; External Exam./Assessor, Univ. of the West Indies; fellowships: Ont. Rsch. Found. 1958–61, Ford Found. Sr. 1963–64; Mem., Sci. Counc. of Can. (mem. Extve. Ctte. 1985–92); Assn. of Profl. Engrs. of Ont.; Candn. Soc. of Chem. Engr.; Am. Assn. of Cost Engrs.; Chem. Inst. of Can.; Ed. Bd., 'Journal of Small Business and Entrepreneurship'; Mem., Assn. of Candn. Venture Capital Cos. (Profl. Devel. Program Dir. 1984–88); author: 'Small Business Management Fundamentals,' 4th ed. 1991; 'State of Small Business 1988' 1989; senior author: 'Principles of Engineering Economic Analysis' 1982, 2nd ed. 1989; contbr.: 'The Technical Entrepreneur' 1980; recreations: rowing, sailing, skiing, reading, badminton, music; Clubs: Royal Candn. Yacht (former Vice-Commodore); Home: 746 Avenue Rd., Toronto, Ont. M5P 2K2.

**SZPL, Thaddeus;** see **THADDEUS.**

**SZUMIGALSKI, Anne (Howard Davis);** writer; b. London, Eng. 3 Jan. 1922; d. Herbert Edward and Mary Winder (Allen) Davis; e. privately; m. Jan Wacław (dec. 1985) s. Józef and Katarzyna Szumigalski 31 Mar. 1946; children: Katharine, Elizabeth, Anthony, Mark; Writer-in-Residence, Saskatoon Public Library 1980–81; Winnipeg Centennial Library 1987–88; author: 'BOooOM' 1969; 'Woman Reading in Bath' 1974; 'A Game of Angels' 1980; 'Risks' 1983; 'Doctrine of Signatures' 1983; 'Instar' 1985; 'Dogstones' 1986; 'The Word, The Voice, The Text' 1990; 'Rapture of the Deep' 1991; works performed 'Eyes of the Fishes' 1972; 'Wild Man's Butte' 1975; 'The Exile's Catalogue' 1980 (all radio); 'Litany of the Bagladies' 1983 (dance); 'Z' (stage) 1994; co-author: (with Terrence Heath) 'Wild Man's Butte' 1979; (with Terrence Heath) 'Journey/Journée' 1988; ed. 5 anthols., 15 books, Grain mag., N.W.R.; Founding mem. AKA (artist-run centre); Saskatoon Moving Collective (dance); Sask. Writers Guild; Sask. Writers & Artists Colonies; recipient: SAB Lifetime Excellence in the Arts Award 1990; YWCA W.O.Y. Award 1989; Saskatchewan Order of Merit 1989; short listed Gov. Gen's Award 1983, 1985; Writers Choice 1986, 1987; Silver Mag. Award 1986, 1991; SWG Founders Award 1984; Okanagan Short Story Award 1979; Lifetime Mem., LCP 1990; Lifetime Mem., ACTRA 1991; mem. Writers Union of Canada; League Candn. Poets; P.E.N. Internat.; M.W.G.; Address: 9 Connaught Place,. Saskatoon, Sask. S7L 1C7.

**SZWEC, Terry W.;** business executive; b. Canada 15 March 1951; s. James Eugene and Stephanie Anne (Naumowich) S.; e. York Univ. 1982; m. Louise d. Leo and Zita Clare 13 Oct. 1981; children: Julia Clare, Jonathan James; EXTVE. VICE-PRESIDENT, RIGHT ASSOCIATES 1985–92; Sales Rep., Bristol Myers Canada Ltd. 1981–83; Manager, Human Resources, De Havilland Aircraft 1980–83; Dir., Human Resources, Control Data Corp. 1973–83; Consultant 1983–85; Bd. of Dir., Right Human Resources Inc.; York Condominium Bd.; Dir., HRPAO, Employment Services Group; E.E.O. Award Winner 1982; Mem., Our Lady of Sorrows Parish; author of articles; frequently quoted in Globe & Mail and Financial Post; recreations: tennis, equestrian sports; clubs: Bd. of Trade Toronto and Mississauga, The Boulevard Club; Office: 1033 Bay St., Toronto, Ont. M5S 3A5.

# T

**TABARROK, Behrouz,** B.Sc., D.Phil., P.Eng., F.EIC, F.CSME; university professor; b. Tehran, Iran 16 June 1938; s. Mohammad Taghi T.; e. Wolverhampton Polytechnic (U.K.) B.Sc. 1962; Oxford Univ. D.Phil. 1965; m. Carolyn d. H. and P. Croft 20 April 1963; children: Alexander, Nicholas, Jeremy; FOUNDING CHAIR & PROF., DEPT. OF MECHANICAL ENGINEERING, UNIV. OF VICTORIA 1987– ; Ford Foundation Fellow, Univ. of Toronto 1965–66; Asst. Prof., Dept. of Mech. Engr. 1966; Assoc. Prof. 1970; Prof. 1976; Alexander Von Humboldt Fellow, Univ. of Hannover 1970; Senior Rsch. Fellow, Univ. of Bristol 1974; Consultant, Atomic Energy of Canada Ltd. 1980–88; Fellow, Engineering Institute of Canada; Fellow, Candn. Soc. for Mechanical Engineering; Pres., Candn. Society for Mech. Engineering 1993–94; author of over 100 scientific papers; recreations: gardening; Home: 3005 Beach Dr., Victoria, B.C. V8R 6L3; Office: Victoria, B.C. V8W 3P6.

**TADDEO, Donat J.,** Ph.D.; educator; university administrator; b. Montreal, P.Q. 30 May 1946; s. Donat and Loretta (Di Giovanni) T.; e. Loyola Coll. B.A. 1967; Stanford Univ. (Calif.) Ph.D. 1972; Annenberg Sch. of Communications, Comm. Mgmt., Univ. of South. Calif. M.A. 1986; m. Brigitte Marie Cécile St-Laurent 9 Feb. 1985; two d. (twin): Francesca Maria, Julia Monica; ASSOC. PROF., DEPT. OF COMMUNICATION STUDIES, CONCORDIA UNIV. 1985– ; Dean of Div. I, Fac. of Arts & Sci. 1980–85; Dean, Faculty of Engineering & Computer Sci. 1993–95; apptd. Délégué du Québec en Italie (Rome) 1988–92; el. Commr., Montreal Cath. Sch. Comm. 1973; re-el. 1977; l. Delegate of MCSC to Sch. Counc. for Island of Montreal 1976; re-el. 1977; el. Mem. Extve., Sch. Counc. for Island of Montreal 1976; re-el. 1977; el. Delegate of MCSC to Fed. of Que. Cath. Sch. Commns.; Admin. Asst. to Dean of Arts and Sci., Loyola Coll. 1975–77 (Trustee, Dept. of Economics, July 1975); Admin. Asst. to Vice-Rector, Academic, Arts and Sci., Concordia Univ. 1977–79; Acting Dean, Div. I, Fac. of Arts and Sci. Aug.-Dec. 1979; former mem. Comité Conjoint; Que./Calif. Universities Exchange Prog.; co-Pres., Comité du Non, St. Henri 1980; mem. Comm. des Groupes Ethniques, Parti Liberal du Qué. (Sec. 1980–81; Pres. 1981–85); founding mem. Consiglio Educativo Italo-Canadese 1974–77; Positive Action Comte. 1977–79; English-Speaking Catholic Counc. 1980–82; named as Ethnic Rep. for Gov. of Que. to Appeals comte. for Application of Bill 22 1975–76; el. as 'Hospitals' rep., Ville Marie Social Services Bd. of Dirs.; el. Vice-Pres. of Bd., Chrmn. of Programmes and Services Comte. 1981–83; Pres., Nat. Congress of Italian-Canadians, Que. Region (Dir. & Vice-Pres. 1982–84) 1984–85; mem. Candn. Communications Assn. (CCA); Internat. Communications Assn. (ICA); Speech Communication Assn. (SCA); Candn. Italian Profl. and Businessmen's Org.; awarded Cavaliere al Merito della Republica Italiana, Rep. of Italy 1992; co-author (with Raymond Taras) 'Le débat linguistique au Québec: La communauté italienne et la langue d'enseignement' 1987; Home: 4394 de Maisonneuve O., Westmount, Que. H3Z 1L5; Address: Concordia Univ., 7141 Sherbrooke St. W., Montreal, Que. H4B 1R6.

**TADROS, Constance Dilley,** B.A., M.A.; social worker/magazine editor/journalist; b. Cleveland, Ohio 16 Jan. 1941; d. Charles Albert and Gretchen Wilma (Widmann) Dilley; e. Cleveland Heights H.S. 1958; Mount Holyoke Coll. B.A. 1962; Case West. Res. Univ. M.A. 1965; m. Jean-Pierre s. Aubrey and Yolande T. 30 Dec. 1965; children: Patricia, Catherine; Editor, Cinema Canada 1975; Prof. of Phys. Edn., Le Coll. Cévènol (France) 1962–63; English teacher, U.S. Serv., Beirut, Lebanon 1965–66; Med. Caseworker, Royal Victoria Hosp., Montreal 1966–67; Family Caseworker, Soc. de serv. social aux familles 1967–71; Group Worker, Univ. Settlement & Supvr., McGill Univ. Sch. of Soc. Work 1971; Community Worker, Comn. des écoles cath. de Montréal 1971–72; Prof., Dawson Coll. 1974–75; Extve. Sec., Assn. des prod. de films du Qué. 1973–75; Ed., CineMag 1978–80; Cons., Fed. Dept. of Communications; broadcaster, commentator, reviewer, Candn. Broadcasting Corp. 1975– ; freelancer for film/TV fests.; Jury duty: Candn. Student Film Fest. 1978; ACTRA Awards 1980–86; Atlantic Film Fest. 1978; Alta. Motion Picture Indus. Awards 1981; Can. Counc. 1988; Jr. Arts Grant, Can. Counc. 1981.

**TAFLER, David;** communications executive; b. Montreal, Que. 6 Apr. 1943; s. Abraham and Sarah (Shetzer) T.; e. Adath Israel, Montreal; McGill Univ.; m. Susan d. Nathan Shtull 30 June 1966; children: Jonathan, Jason; PRES., TAFLER COMMUNICATIONS (product development and consulting in media and communications); Reporter, McGill Daily, Montreal 1961–62; Journalist, Montreal Star 1963; Reporter and Columnist, Montreal Gazette 1963–69, Asst. City Ed. 1969–70, Financial Ed. 1972–75; Ed., Financial Times of Canada 1975–79, Asst. Publisher 1980–82, Publisher, 1982–88; C.E.O., Infomart 1987–89; Pres., Financial Times Group, Southam Inc. 1988–89; author 'Trapped' (with Dr. Morton Korenberg); commentator in print and broadcast, on business and financial affairs; recreations: golf, tennis; Clubs: Donalda Golf & Country; The Boulevard; Office: One Yonge St., Ste. 1801, Toronto, Ont. M5E 1W7.

**TAGGART, Hon. John David,** LL.B.; judge; b. Regina, Sask. 20 Sept. 1921; s. James Gordon and Mary (Birkett) T.; e. Univ. of Sask., 1939–41; Univ. of B.C., LL.B. 1949; m. late Marian Joyce, d. late Capt. Walter Wingate, 5 Jan. 1946; children: James Lawton, Anne Elizabeth, John David, Ian Gordon; m., Her Honour Judge Valerie Jean, d. late V. Manning, 18 June, 1981; JUDGE, COURT OF APPEAL, B.C., since 1968; read law with Senator J. W. de B. Farris, Q.C.; called to Bar of B.C. 1949; cr. Q.C. 1964; practiced with Farris & Company, 1949–68 (Partner from 1958); served with Royal Candn. Engrs. in Can. 1941–42 and with 5 Candn. Armoured Div. in U.K., Italy, N.W. Europe, 1943–45; Mentioned in Despatches; Pres., Vancouver Bar Assn., 1967; mem. B.C. Council, Candn. Bar Assn.; Protestant; recreations: golf, sailing; Club: Royal Vancouver Yacht; Home: 6021 Collingwood Place, Vancouver, B.C. V6N 1V2; Office: Law Courts, 800 Smithe St., Vancouver, B.C. V6Z 2E1.

**TAGGART, Hon. Valerie Jean,** LL.B.; judge; b. Cranbrook, B.C. 9 Aug. 1926; d. Viril Zenis Manning; e. Univ. of B.C. LL.B. 1949; m. 1stly 9 July 1949; m. 2ndly Hon. Mr. Justice J.D. Taggart 18 June 1981; children: Deborah Jean Meredith, Guy Manning Meredith, Daphne Louise Meredith; PROVINCIAL COURT JUDGE, B.C.; called to Bar of B.C. 1949; Acting Dir. Continuing Legal Educ.; Research Dir. Law Foundation of B.C.; served with W.R.C.N.S. 1945; Past Pres. Vancouver Jr. League; Gamma Phi Beta; recreations: golf, skiing; Club: Shaughnessy Golf; Home: 6021 Collingwood Place, Vancouver, B.C. V6N 1V2.

**TAGUCHI, Yosh,** B.Sc., M.D.C.M., Ph.D., F.R.C.S.(C); urologist/university professor/author; b. Japan 25 Sept. 1933; s. Zenichi and Fumiko (Kawasaki) T.; e. McGill Univ. B.Sc. 1955, M.D.C.M. 1959, Ph.D. 1970; m. Joan d. Elsie and Aiden Hogan Oct. 1963; children: Kathleen, Edwin, Jocelyn, Carolin; UROLOGIST, ROYAL VICTORIA HOSP. 1966– ; Assoc. Prof. of Surgery (Urology) and Programme Dir. (Urology) McGill Univ.; author: 'Private Parts: An Owner's Guide,' McClelland and Stewart 1988, Les parties intimes de l'homme traduit de l'anglais par Pierre-Louis Gelinas Vlb éditeur; Privato-Partsu, Japanese edition, Konansha, ed: Osamu Yoshida, MD; Partes Privadas, traduccion: Elsa Mateo, Ediciones, Spain, 1991; Columnist, Globe 'Dr. Josh' Family Health 1980– ; Office: S686, 687 Pine Ave. W., Montreal, Que. H3A 1A1.

**TAHEDL, Ernestine,** R.C.A.; artist; b. Austria 12 Oct. 1940; d. Heinrich and Elisabeth (Leutgeb) Tahedl; e. Acad. for Applied Art Vienna, Masters Degree in Graphic Art 1961; m. Richard Ian Ogilvie 9 Oct. 1965; children: Degen Elisabeth, Lars Ian; Asst. to Prof. of Graphic Arts Acad. for Applied Arts Vienna 1961–63; Teacher, Edmonton Art Gallery 1963–64; Univ. of Alta. Art Extension Courses 1964–65; Stewart Hall Cultural Center Pointe Claire, Qué. 1968; solo exhns. (paintings) Edmonton 1963, 1965, 1973, 1977–78, 1980, 1982–83, 1986, 1990; Calgary 1965, 1989, 1990, 1993; Montreal 1967–68, 1970, 1972–73, 1976–78, 1980, 1983, 1987; Toronto 1976, 1978, 1982, 1984, 1986–88, 1990, 1992,

1993; Ottawa 1972, 1974, 1977; Vienna Wiener Secession 1971; Ecole des Beaux-Arts Montpellier, France 1975; Cultural Center Lower Austria 1975; group exhns. (internat.): Rockford Internat. Biennial 1983; 15th Internt. Biennial of Graphic Art, Ljubljana Yugoslavia 1983; Internat. Biennial Print Exhibit, Taipei Taiwan 1985, 1987; Hanga Annual Print Exhibit, Metropolitan Museum of Fine Art, Tokyo Japan 1985, 1987; maj. works in stained glass incl. Sisters of Holy Cross Edmonton 1964; St. Timotheys Ang. Ch., McKernan Bapt. Ch. Edmonton 1965; The Sanctuary, Candn. Pavilion Expo '67; Carefree Lodge Toronto 1969, 1971; Fed. Revenue Bldg. Qué. 1971; Centre d'Accueil St. Bruno 1982; Bibliotheque de Varennes 1982; Municipal Library Greenfield Park Que. 1982; Annunciation of the Lord Church, Ottawa, Ont. 1987; 7th Street School, Etobicoke, Ont. 1989; restoration, Christkoenigs Church, Klagenfurt, Austria 1989; St. Peters Estonian Lutheran Church, Toronto 1990; arch. murals incl. Fed. P.O. Terminal Edmonton 1964–66; W.W. Cross Cancer Clinic Hosp. Edmonton 1969; rep. in pub. galleries Vienna, Montpellier, Hamilton, London (Ont.), Musée du Qué.; cited various bibliogs.; limited edition portfolio of etchings 'Circle of Energy' published 1981, Artworld International; recipient Austrian Govt. Grad. Prize 1961; Vienna Internat. Exhn. Painting Bronze Medal 1963; Royal Arch. Inst. Can. Allied Arts Medal 1966; Concours Artistique du Qué. Purchase Award 1966; Can. Council Arts Award 1967; awarded Commemorative Medal for 125th Anniversary of Candn. Confederation 1993; mem. Royal Candn. Acad. of Arts 1977; mem. Council RCA 1980–82; First Vice-Pres. 1988–90; mem. Ont. Soc. of Artists 1984 (mem. Counc. 1986–88, Vice-Pres. 1988–89); Bd. of Dirs., Arts Foundation of Greater Toronto 1992–94; Address: 79 Collard Dr., King City, Ont. L7B 1E4.

**TAISIA;** artist; b. Russia 6 May 1925; d. Paul and Klaudia (Losewa) Silin; m. Jan s. Joseph and Stefany Paczkowski 10 Nov. 1946; children: Nicholas, Peter, John; self taught water-colour artist known for her wildflower paintings; presently exhibiting in galleries Gallery on the Lake Buckhorn, Ont.; Koyman Gallery, Ottawa: Trojanowska Gallery San Francisco, Ca.; featured on cover and in article 'Art Treasurers of the Woods' by Jan Anderson of Reader's Digest May 1979; Home: 34 Dove Lane, Thornhill, Ont. L3T 1V9.

**TAIT, George Edward,** B.A., B.Paed., Ed.D.; retired professor; author; b. Sarnia, Ont. 19 July 1910; s. James Edward and Maude Eliza (Harrower) T.; e. Watford (Ont.) High Sch.; London Normal Sch. (Grad. 1931); Univ. of W. Ont. B.A. 1939; Univ. of Toronto, B.Paed., 1945, Ed.D., 1957; m. Reginae Mae, d. Maj. R.H. Stapleford, Watford, Ont. 31 Aug. 1938; one s. Gary Edward Stapleford M.A., B.Ed.; PROF. EMERITUS, FACULTY OF EDUCATION, UNIV. OF TORONTO 1973– ; Teacher in London, Ont., Pub. Schs., 1931–41; Dir. of Anglo-Am. Sch., Bogotá, S.A. 1941–44; Inspector of Pub. Schs, Huntsville, Ont. 1944–47; Welland, Ont. 1947–50; mem. of Pub. Library Bd., Welland, Ont. 1947–50; Prof. Educ., Univ. of Toronto 1950–73; mem. Senate there 1964–72; accompanied Comnr. N.W.T. on tour of Eskimo Settlements; mem. Franklin Probe II 1974; wrote two reports for Government of the Northwest Territories re observations in the high Arctic, 1974; Publications: 'The Saddle of Carlos Perez' 1949; 'The Silent Gulls' 1950; 'Ideas for Junior Grade Teachers' 1951; 'Wake of the West Wind' 1952 (dramatized by C.B.C. in 13 progs. 1954); 'Famous Canadian Stories' 1953 (used as a special prizebook by the I.O.D.E.); 'Breastplate and Buckskin' 1953; 'The World Was Wide' 1954; 'The Upward Trail' 1956; co-author of '100 Types of Primary Seatwork' 1948; 'Peach Tree Farm' 1950; 'What To Do, Reading Workbook' 1949; 'Proud Ages' 1958; 'Fair Domain' 1960; 'One Dominion' rev. ed. 1973; co-ed., 'Aldine World Atlas' 1961; 'Mathematics Enrichment' 1966; 'Young Teacher's Handbook' 1967; 'The Eagle and the Snake' 1968; 'The Unknown People: Indians of North America' 1974; 'Here & There in Teacher Education' (co-author) 1974; awarded the McGraw-Hill Ryerson Special Book Award, to mark the outstanding contribution that his books have made to Canadian education, 1978; miscellaneous articles in educ. mags.; presented to Her Majesty Queen Elizabeth I, Buckingham Palace, 1971; mem., Candn. Educ. Assn.; Candn. Authors' Assn. (Pres., Toronto Br., 1954–55; mem., Nat. Extve.); Candn. Assn. Profs. of Educ.; Mem. of Bd., John Graves Simcoe Mem. Foundation, 1975– ; Un. Church; recreation: landscape painting; Home: 105 Golfdale Rd., Toronto, Ont. M4N 2B8.

**TAIT, John C.,** Q.C., B.A., B.C.L.; lawyer; public servant; b. Montreal, Que. 4 Dec. 1945; s. John Watterson and Eleanor (Raymond) T.; e. Lower Can. Coll., Sr. Matric. 1963; Princeton Univ. B.A. 1967; New Coll., Oxford Univ. B.A. 1969; McGill Univ. B.C.L. 1972; m. Sonia d. Maurice and Colombe Plourde 30 June 1978; DEPUTY MINISTER OF JUSTICE AND DEPUTY ATTORNEY GENERAL OF CANADA 1988– ; Officer and Asst. Sec. to the Cabinet with Legis., Privy Counc. Offr. 1974–80; Asst. Depy. Min. Dept. of Indian Affairs and Northern Devel. 1980–83; Asst. Depy. Min. Public Law, Dept. of Justice, Govt. of Canada 1983–86; Depy. Solicitor General of Can. 1986–88; mem. Bar of Que.; cr. Q.C. 1984; Rhodes Scholar 1967; recreations: tennis, windsurfing, sports; Clubs: Royal Montreal Golf; Home: 901, 333 Chapel St., Ottawa, Ont. K1N 8Y8; Office: Rm. 350, 239 Wellington St., Ottawa, Ont. K1A 0H8.

**TAIT, Reginae M.;** teacher; b. Watford, Ont. 9 July 1910; d. Richard Homer and Lily Mae (Williamson) Stapleford; e. London Normal School 1930–31; ART SPECIALIST DEPT. EDUC., undergraduate courses at Univ. of Western Ont.; m. George Edward Tait s. Edward and Maude T. 31 Aug. 1938; child: Gary Edward Stapleford; Teacher and art supervisor, Gordon McGregor Sch., Windsor 1931–38; Pres., Jr. Mary Grant Soc., Windsor 1934–36; Pres., Women Teachers Federation, Windsor 1935–36; Art Instr. for summer and evening courses for teachers; Asst. Dir., Anglo-American School, Bogota, Colombia 1941–44; Pres., Bedford Park Home and School Assn. 1956–57; Program Chrmn., Toronto Home and School Assn. 1957–59; Natl. Pres., I.O.D.E. 1970–72 (Hon. National Vice Pres. 1973– ); Gov. and first woman Extve. Mem., Frontier Coll. 1969–79; Pres., Health League of Can. 1979–82; Candn. Natnl. Exhibition Assn., mem., 1969–80, Dir., 1980–87; Hon. Dir., 1987– ; Vice-Pres. for Can., The Commonwealth Countries League, London Eng. 1970–94; Extve. Mem., Natl. Action Comte., Status of Women 1965–79; Bd. mem. and Dir., Council for Candn. Unity 1974–81; Dir., Sir William Campbell House Found. 1978–80; Lay Bencher, The Law Soc. of Upper Can. (one of two women first acting as Benchers in Ont. since founding of society in 1797) 1974–87; responsible, as Chrmn. of a ctte., for project involving ten large stained windows illustrating the Hist. of Law in Can.; establishment of an archives and a Museum of Law for The Law Soc. of Upper Can.; Bd. & Extve. Mem., John Graves Simcoe Found.; Queen's Jubilee Medal 1977; Fell. of Frontier Coll. 1980; has written various articles for educational journals; mem., The Osgoode Soc.; United Church; recreations: travel, art, crafts; Home: 105 Golfdale Rd., Toronto, Ont. M4N 2B8.

**TAKANO, Azuhiko,** B.A.; business executive; b. Tokyo, Japan 3 Apr. 1939; s. Tomijiroh and Eiko T.; e. Tokyo Metrop. Univ. B.A. (Bus. Adm.) 1962; m. Takako 1965; children: Atsushi, Hiroshi, Satoshi; Chrmn. & C.E.O., Oe Inc. and Vice Chrmn., Canon Canada Inc. 1988; Acctg. Clk. Canon, Tokyo 1962, Asst. Mgr. 1970, Mgr. Acctg. 1974, Exec. Vice Pres. present Co. 1980; Dir. Japanese Bus. Assn. Toronto; recreation: golf; Home: 73 Prince George Dr., Etobicoke, Ont. M9A 1V5.

**TAKEFMAN, Earl,** B.Sc.Architecture, M.B.A.; consumer products executive; b. Montréal, Qué. 8 March 1950; s. Joseph and Annette (Tower) T.; e. West Hill H.S. 1967; McGill Univ., B.Sc.Architecture 1971, M.B.A. 1973; m. Mona-Lee d. Judith Friend 28 Aug. 1971; children: Jay, Robert, Keri; CO-C.E.O. SLM INTERNATIONAL, INC. (US public company), C.E.O., SLM Inc. (US subsidiary of SLM Internat.) and C.E.O., SLM CANADA (Candn. subsidiary of SLM Internat.); Pres. & Dir., Charan Indus. Inc. 1984–89; McGill Grad. Fellowship for Acad. excellence 1972; Mem., Toy Mfrs. Assn.; recreations: golf, skiing; Club: Hillsdale Golf & Country; Home: 68 Belvedere Rd., Westmount, Qué.

**TAKLA, Michael George,** B.Comm., B.A.; management consultant; b. Montreal, Que. 1 April 1949; s. George and Yvette (Azem) T. (stepfather: Raymond Salim); e. St. Patrick's H.S. 1963–67; Loyola Coll., Univ. of Montreal B.Comm. 1971, B.A. 1977; m. Johanne d. Sylvio and Rita St. Jean 31 Dec. 1983; one d.: Lyia; PRINCIPAL & NAT. PRACTICE LEADER, HUMAN RESOURCES MGMT. & EFFECTIVENESS CONS. SERV. IN CANADA, TOWERS PERRIN 1983– ; Asst. to Mgr., Prudential Assur. Co. Ltd. 1971–74; Employee Relns. Advr., Esso Canada 1974–77; Eastern Region Coord., Human Resources Planning & Devel., Gulf Canada Ltd. 1977–81; Corp. Dir., Human Resources Planning & Devel., Federal Business Devel. Bank 1981–83; Bd. Mem., Secy. and Pres., Human Resource Planning Soc. 1989–95; Mem., Adv. Bd., Candn. Human Resource Planners (Chrmn. 1981–85); Montreal C. of C.; Pres., Human Resource Planning Soc. (HRPS); OD Canada; Bd. of Trade; co-author of articles on mgmt. succession & devel., human resource issues in Canada, 'Focus' 1989–90; 'Canadian Survey of Workforce 2000 Issues and Programs'; recreations: skiing, hockey, baseball; Home: 111 Cragmore Rd., Pointe Claire, Que. H9R 3K7; Office: 1800 McGill College Ave., Montreal, Que. H3A 3J6.

**TALBOT, David A.,** FCMC, B.A.Sc., P.Eng.; certified management consultant; b. Guelph, Ont. 28 Oct. 1940; s. Barney and Ruth (Brown) T.; e. Univ. of Toronto, B.A.Sc. 1965; Cert. Mgmt. Consultant; m. Mary-Anne d. Sam and Ruth Silverstein 23 May 1963; children: Kevin Lowell, Susan Meryl; PRESIDENT & C.E.O, TALBOT & COMPANY 1992– ; Systems Eng. and Mktg. Rep. International Business Machines Co. Ltd. 1965–68; Systems Cons. AGT Data Systems Ltd. 1968–70; Mgr. Financial Adm. Info. Systems, York Univ. 1970–72; Vice Pres. Corporate Services, Gozlan Bros. Ltd. 1973–76; Mgmt. Cons. David A. Talbot & Associates 1976–81; Dir., Special Projects Group, Laventhol & Horwath 1981–89; Assoc. Consultant, Western Management Consultants 1989–92; Asst. Prof. of Strategic Planning Candn. Sch. Mgmt.; Fellow, Inst. Cert. Mgmt. Cons. Ont.; Past mem. Pres.'s Adv. Ctte. Continuing Edn., Computer Studies & Info. Systems, Centennial Coll.; Bd. Mem., Candn. Industrial Innovation Ctr. Waterloo; Past Pres., Inst. Cert. Mgmt. Cons. Ont., Honour Roll 1983; Past Dir., Inst. Cert. Mgmt. Cons. Can.; Past Trustee, Internat. Counc. of Mgmt. Consulting Inst.; author various articles; mem. Assn. Profl. Engs. Prov. Ont.; Candn. Export Assn. (Devel. Aid Ctte.); Human Factors Assn. Can.; Inst. Elect. & Electronics Engs.; Home: 21 Belcourt Rd., Toronto, Ont. M4S 2T8; Office: 49 Wellington St. E., Suite 400, Toronto, Ont. M5E 1C9.

**TALBOT, David Brian,** C.M.A.; manufacturing executive; b. Hamilton, Ont. 16 July 1948; s. Everett Gordon and Winnifred (Vickers) T.; e. McMaster Certified Management Accountant 1976; Yale School of Orgn. & Management 1987; m. Donna E. d. Wesley and Marion Malstrom 21 March 1970; children: Jeremie, Justin; Pres. & General Mgr., Stanley Tools, Div. of Stanley Canada Inc. 1982; joined Stanley Works Ltd. 1969; Controller Stanley Taymouth 1975; Plant Manager 1975; Asst. Controller Stanley Tools U.S.A. 1976; Controller, Stanley Works Ltd. 1978; Vice-Pres. Sales & Mktg., Stanley Tools, Div. of Stanley Canada Inc. 1980; Dir., Stanley Canada Inc.; Ont. C. of C.; Business Edn. Adv. Group, Halton Indus. Edn. Council; Past Dir., Iatco Indus. Inc.; Mem., Burlington Cultural Ctr.; Ont. C. of C.; Candn. Mfrs. Assn.; The Soc. of Mngt. Accountants of Ont.; Automotive Assn. of Canada; Candn. Hardware & Housewares Mfrs. Assn.; Am. Supply & Machinery Mfrs. Assn.; Assoc. Mem., Candn. Retail Hardward Assoc.; Young Pres. Orgn.; recreations: golf, fishing; clubs: Glendale Golf & Country (Past Dir.), Heritage Golf (Bd. of Gov.); Home: 1000 Old Mohawk Rd., Ancaster, Ont. L9G 3K9.

**TALLIS, Hon. Calvin F.,** B.A., LL.B.; judge; b. Borden, Sask. 5 March 1930; s. Ernest Forrester and Beryl Irene T.; e. Borden (Sask.) High tch. 1946; Saskatoon Normal Sch. 1949; Univ. of Sask. B.A. 1952, LL.B. 1954; m. Dorothy Irene d. L. Poppl, Humboldt, Sask., 24 Dec. 1955; JUSTICE, COURT OF APPEAL FOR SASKATCHEWAN 1981– ; Depy. Supreme Crt. Judge of N.W.T. 1981– (Justice, Supreme Crt. of N.W.T. 1976–81); Depy. Judge of the Supreme Court of the Yukon Territory; Justice of Appeal, Court of Appeal, N.W.T.; former Justice of Appeal, Y.T.; Lectr. in Civil Procedure Univ. of Sask.; read law with J.M. Goldenberg, Q.C.; called to Bar of Sask. 1955; cr. Q.C. 1968; former partner, Goldenberg, Taylor & Tallis, Saskatoon; former Vice Chrmn., Sask. Prov. Police Comn.; mem. Med. Complaints Comte. Coll & Phys. & Surgs. (Sask.); Bencher Law Soc. Sask.; mem. Law Soc. B.C.; mem. Candn. Bar Assn.; Protestant; Home: Regina, Sask.; Office: Court House, 2425 Victoria Ave., Regina, Sask. S4P 3E4.

**TALLMAN, Fredrick Wallace,** B.Comm (Hons.), F.C.I.A., A.S.A., F.L.M.I.; executive; b. Winnipeg, Man. 16 Feb. 1922; s. James Wallace and Emma Jane (Hipple) T.; e. Gladstone Sch., Earl Grey Sch. and Kelvin Tech. High Sch., all Winnipeg 1930–38; Univ. of Man., Winnipeg 1938–43; Alice Selina, d. Rupert E. Noakes, 26 Aug. 1944; children: S. Jane Lockley, Fred R. J., Bruce W., Ross F.; PRES., TALLMAN ENTERPRISES, actuarial, investment and management consultants; Past Dir. and Past Chrmn. of the Investment Ctte., The Citadel Life Assurance Co.; The Citadel General Assurance Co.; Fire Insurance Co. of Canada; Kent General Insurance

Co.; General Insurance Corp. of New Brunswick; Winterthur Canada Financial Corp.; Financial Analyst, Lightcap Securities, Winnipeg 1943–44; Lectr. Maths., Univ. Man. 1944–45; Supv., Monarch Life Assurance Co. 1945–57; Asst. Actuary, The Citadel Life Co. 1957–63, Assoc. Actuary 1963–67, Actuary 1967–70, Vice Pres. and Actuary 1970–74, Sr. Vice Pres. and Actuary 1974–75, Pres. 1975–84; mem. (1982–93) Adv. Ctte. on Rehabilitation Courses, York Univ./Seneca College; Chrmn. (1975) Winnipeg Econ. Devel. Bd.; Premier (1940) Older Boys Parliament Winnipeg; Pres. (1942–43) Univ. of Manitoba Student Union; Treas. (1945) Univ. of Man. Alumni Assn.; Treas. (1952) Soc. for Crippled Children Winnipeg; Pres. (1951–52) Jr. Chamber of Comm. Winnipeg; mem. Extve. Winnipeg Chamber Comm. 1978; Treas. (1972) Candn. Inst. Actuaries; Life Office Management Assoc. (Chrmn. Examination Cttee. 1981–84); mem. Candn. Inst. Actuaries; Soc. Actuaries; United Ch.; recreations: fishing, stamp collecting; Clubs: Manitoba; Rotary; St. Charles Country; Rosedale Golf; Address: 27 Tanbark Cres., Don Mills, Ont. M3B 1N7 and Baysport, Big Whiteshell Lake, Manitoba.

**TALMAN, James Davis,** B.A., M.Sc., Ph.D.; b. Toronto, Ont. 24 July 1931; s. James John and Ruth Helen (Davis) T.; e. London Central C.I. 1949; Univ. of West. Ont. B.A. 1953, M.Sc. 1954; Princeton Univ. Ph.D. 1959; m. Ragnhild Bruun d. Andreas and Liv Nilssen 2 Feb. 1957; children: Liv E., Stephen J., Marianne R., Eric A.; PROF., DEPT. OF APPLIED MATH., UNIV. OF WEST. ONT. 1967– ; Instr., Princeton Univ. 1957–59; Asst. Prof., Am. Univ. of Beirut 1959–60; Dept. of Math., Univ. of West. Ont. 1960–62; Assoc. Prof. 1962–65; Prof. 1965–67; Rsch. Assoc., Physics Dept., Univ. of Calif., Davis 1963–64; Vis. Prof., Phys. Dept., Univ. of Florida 1978–79; Phys. Dept., Univ. of Oslo 1986–87; Dir., Ctr. for Chem. Physics, Univ. of West. Ont. 1983–85; Chrmn., Dept. of Applied Math. 1987–92; Mem., Candn. Assn. of Physicists; Candn. Applied Math. Soc.; Am. Physical Soc.; Soc. for Indus. & Applied Math.; Am. Assn. for the Advancement of Sci.; author: 'Special Functions: A Group Theoretic Approach' 1968; Clubs: London Squash Racquets; Home: 29 Lonsdale Dr., London, Ont. N6G 1T4; Office: London, Ont. N6A 5B7.

**TALON, Jean-Denis;** insurance executive; b. Sherbrooke, Que. 6 April 1941; s. Gaston and Simone (Lapointe) T.; e. Sherbrooke Univ.; PRESIDENT & CHIEF EXECUTIVE OFFICER, AXA ASSURANCES INC.; Vice-Pres., Mktg. & Claims, IARD 1979; Vice-Pres., Mktg. & C.E.O. 1982; Pres. & C.E.O. 1982; Pres. & Dir., Axa Caanda Inc.; Chair, C.E.O. & Dir., Axa Home Insur. Co.; Pres., Chair & Dir., Les Services Financiers Provinces-Unies Inc.; Dir., Anglo Canada Gen. Insur. Co.; Provinces Unies Com. d'assur.; Pres., Comité BAC/Que.; Dir., GAA; recreations: golf, tennis, alpine skiing, jogging; clubs: Saint-Denis, de golf LongChamp; Home: 60 William Paul, No. 408, Ile des Soeurs, Que. H3E 1N5; Office: 2020 University St., Ste. 600, Montreal, Que. H3A 2A5.

**TAN, Y.H.,** B.Sc., Ph.D.; university professor; b. Singapore 2 Sept. 1941; s. Thian Sek and Seet Kwan (Tay) T.; e. Raffles Inst.; Univ. of Singapore, B.Sc. (Hons.) 1965; Univ. of Man., Ph.D. 1969; m. Catherine Pallen; children: Lin Tan, Sien Mackie-Tan, Jonathan Robert Shen Li Tan; FIRST DIR., INST. OF MOLECULAR & CELL BIOL., NAT. UNIV. OF SINGAPORE 1987– ; Founder, West East Center for Microbial Diversity, Univ. of B.C., Vancouver 1993; First Chrmn., Nat. Biotechnology Ctte., Singapore 1988– ; Dir., Singapore Bio-Innovations Pte. Ltd. 1990– ; Dir., Singapore Bio-Innovations America 1991– ; Dir., Centre for Natural Product Rsch., IMCB; Bd. of Dirs., Technology Parks Pte. Ltd. 1990– ; Obr., Amylin Pharmaceuticals Inc., San Diego, Ca. 1991– ; Mem., National Science & Technology Board 1991– ; Gen. Adv., Glaxo EDB Rsch. Fund 1989– ; Asst. Prof., Johns Hopkins Univ. Sch. of Med. 1974–75; Assoc. Prof., Fac. of Med., Univ. of Calgary 1975–83; Prof. 1983–87; Sci. Adv. Bd. Mem., Candn. Broadcasting Corp.; Singapore Sci. Counc.; Inst. Molecular & Cell Biology; Cetus Corp.; Editorial Bd. Mem., J.IFN Res. and Biotech & Applied Biochemistry; Rep., Internat. Soc. for Interferon Rsch. for Can.; MRC Fellow, Univ. of Pittsburgh 1969–71; NIH Fellow, Yale Univ. 1972–73; NIH Vis. Scholar, U.S.A. 1974–75; NCI Scholar Award 1976; Alta. Cancer Bd. Sci. Award 1980; Hon. Prof., Chin. Acad. Med. Sci., Beijing 1982; National Sci. & Tech. Medal for Distinguished Contbr. in Biotechnology, Singapore 1993; Inaugural Firkin Orator, Australian Soc. Med. Rsch., Adelaide 1993; Inventor of procedure for human Beta interferon prodn. (U.S. patent 1973); reported the genetics of IFN's, its isolation & signalling, as well as IL-1, TNF and growth factor signal transduction, initiated IFN beta clinical trials; author of numerous sci. pubns. in jrnls. incl., J. Exp. Med., Science, Nature, TIBS, La Recherche, Virology, Proc. Natl. Acad. Sci. U.S.A., Current Opinion Cell Biology and J. Biol. Chem.; current research interest includes transgenic amylin rat as a model for Human Type II Diabetes conducting clinical trial of genetically engineered tumor cell vaccines with the British Columbia Cancer Agency, setting up high through-put screens for bioactive compounds and the discovery of TNF & IL-1 mimics; recreation: cross-country skiing, jogging, reading; Home: 67 Gables Ct., Beaconsfield, Que. H9W 5H3; Office: I.M.C.B., National Univ. Singapore, Kent Ridge Cres., Singapore 0511.

**TAN-WILLMAN, Conchita,** B.Ed., M.A., M.A., Ph.D.; university professor; b. Rizal, Philippines; d. Francisco Cruz and Elena (Abella) Tan; e. Philippine Normal College B.Ed. (magna cum laude & Salutatorian, elem. teacher's cert.) 1960; Philippine Women's Univ. M.A. 1962; Univ. of Minnesota M.A. 1964, Ph.D. 1967; m. Andrew s. Jerzy and Halina Willman 28 June 1968; PROF., FACULTY OF EDN., UNIV. OF TORONTO 1983– ; part-time Instr., Phil. Normal College 1960–61; Phil. Women's Univ. 1960–62; Psychometrician, Phil. Women's Univ. 1960–61; Dir., Rsch. Dept., Phil. Psych. Corp. 1960–62; Rsch. Asst., Univ. of Minnesota 1962–64; Instr., Rhode Is. Coll. 1964–65; Lectr., Queen's Coll., City Univ. of N.Y. 1967–68; Asst. Prof., McArthur Coll. of Edn., Queen's Univ. 1968–69; Asst. Prof. Fac. of Edn., Univ. of Toronto 1969–76; Assoc. Prof. 1976–82; Pres. & Founder, PRIME Mentors of Canada; Pres., Finan. Public Relations; Co-Founder, Chopin Soc. of Canada; Co-Founder & Chair, Filipino-Candn. Youth Participation Prog.; Dir., Astone Incorp.; recipient of num. scholarships & fellowships, rsch. grants & leadership awards; mem. of var. profl. organs.; included in num. internat. Who's Who publications; presenter & speaker at many national and internat. conferences; author: 'Mentor: Guidebook'; 'Canadian Achievers & Their Mentors'; and over 40 monographs & articles; co-author: 'Useful Citizens in Action' (3 levels) 1969, 'General Clerical Civil Service Exam' 1964; recreations: travel, music, cooking; Home: 400 Walmer Rd., Penthouse 22, Toronto, Ont. M5P 2X7; Office: 371 Bloor St. W., Toronto, Ont. M5S 2R7.

**TANABE, Takao;** artist; b. Prince Rupert, B.C. 16 Sept. 1926; s. Naojiro and Tomie T.; e. Winnipeg Sch. of Art 1946–49; Brooklyn Museum Art Sch. N.Y.C., Hans Hofmann, N.Y.C. 1951–52; Central Sch. of Arts & Crafts London, UK 1954; Isao Hirayama, Tokyo Univ. of Fine Arts 1959; Emily Carr Coll. of Art & Design Hon. Dip. in Fine Arts 1990, Emily Carr Found. Scholarship 1953; m. Patricia Anne d. Hugh and Zilla White 1956, div. 1983; m. Anona Thorne 1992; solo exhns. incl. Coste House Calgary 1953; Gallery of Contemporary Art Toronto 1957–58; Vancouver Art Gallery 1957; New Design Gallery Vancouver 1959, 1961, 1964, 1966; Nihonbashi Gallery Tokyo 1960; Winnipeg Art Gallery 1962; Agnes Lefort Gallery Montreal 1962, 1966, 1968; Mira Godard Gallery Toronto 1971–93; Equinox Gallery Vancouver 1974–92; Marlborough Roma Gallery Italy 1975; Norman Mackenzie Art Gallery Regina 1975; Glenbow Museum Calgary 1979; Art Gallery of Hamilton 1980; Windsor Art Gallery 1980; Bernice Steinbaum Gallery N.Y.C. 1985; Paul Kuhn Fine Arts Calgary 1985–92; Can. House UK 1987; Dominion Gallery Montreal 1989, 1990; group exhns. incl. maj. Candn. galleries since 1951, Sao Paolo Bienal 1953, 1957, Caracas Exhn. 1953, Guggenheim Internat. Paris and N.Y.C. 1956, Smithsonian Inst. 1956, Milan Triennale 1957, Brussels World Fair 1958, 1st Inter-Am. Biennial Arts & Crafts Mexico 1958, Brooklyn Museum 1959, Seattle World's Fair 1962 and Art Museum 1964–65, Philadelphia Art Museum 1971, Albright-Knox Gallery Buffalo 1974, Galerie d'arte Pescara Italy 1976, Hokkaido Museum of Modern Art Japan 1990; rep. colls. maj. Candn. art galleries; estbd. Periwinkle Press 1963; comns. incl. Sir John Carling Bldg. Ottawa mural, Winnipeg Concert Hall 6 silk hangings, nylon banners Univ. of Alta., Univ. of Regina, Candn. Chancery Mexico; teacher Vancouver Sch. of Art 1962–67; Banff Centre Sch. of Fine Arts, Head of Art Dept. and Artist-in-Residence 1973–80; mem. Fine Art & Design Cttes. Nat. Capital Comn. Ottawa 1979–84, 1982–84 respectively; R.C.A. 1967–79, resigned; recipient Queen's Silver Jubilee Medal 1977; Can. Council Bursary 1959, Sr. Scholarship 1969; Order of British Columbia 1993; Home: 1926 Swayne Rd., Errington, B.C.; Office: P.O. Box 969, Parksville, B.C. V9P 2H1.

**TANENBAUM, Joseph Manuel,** B.A.Sc.; P.Eng.; executive; b. Toronto, Ont. 1932; s. the late Max Tanenbaum and Anne (Wolff) T; e. Runnymede Pub. Sch., Humberside Coll. Inst. and Forest Hill High Sch. Toronto; Univ. of Toronto B.A.Sc.; m. Toby Hochman 1955; children: Michael, Alan, Martin, Susan, Robert; CHRMN. & C.E.O., JAY-M ENTERPRISES LTD.; Hydro-Pontiac Inc.; Jay-M Holdings Ltd.; LOC-Pipe; Pres., Pembroke Electric Light Co.; Dir., The Ballet-Opera House; First Calgary Petroleum Ltd.; Sunnybrook Medical Centre Inst.; Candn. Psychiatric Research Found.; Candn. Opera Company; joined Runnymede Iron & Steel, Toronto as Labourer 1943; York Steel 1951, Asst. Supt. 1955, Production Mgr. 1957, Vice Pres. & Production Mgr. 1965; Pres. & Chief Extve. Offr. Bridge & Tank, Hamilton 1975; York Steel Construction Ltd. 1978; Past Chrmn., Old Masters Comte. and mem., Bd. of Trustees, Art Gallery of Ont.; Hon. Trustee, Ont. Coll. of Art Foundation; Mem., Bd. of Trustees, Royal Ontario Museum; Sunnybrook Health Sciences Centre; Past Chrmn. Comte. of Friends Israel Museum; Hon. Dir., National Ballet School; rec'd Roy A. Phinnemore for Accident Prevention Award; Lescarbot Award 1993; Ont. Assn. of Art Galleries 1993 Partners/Individual Award; mem. Assn. Prof. Engrs. Prov. Ont.; B'nai B'rith Forest Hill; mem. Adv. Bd., Banting and Best Inst., Univ. of Toronto; and Fac. of Engr., Univ. of Toronto; mem., Menachem Begin Heritage Foundation; Candn. Ctte. for the Fiftieth Anniversary of the United Nations; recreation: collecting 19th century French Art; Clubs: Beth Tzedec Men's; B'nai B'rith Forest Hill Empire Lodge; The Toronto; Home: 2 Lynwood Ave., Toronto, Ont. M4V 1K2; Office: 2 St. Clair Ave. E., Suite 700, Toronto, Ont. M4T 2T5.

**TANENBAUM, Lawrence Murray,** B.Sc.; construction executive; b. Toronto, Ont. 8 July 1945; e. Cornell Univ. B.Sc. 1968; PRES., KILMER VAN NOSTRAND CO. LIMITED; Chrmn. The Warren Paving and Materials Group Ltd.; Dir. CUC Group (Scarborough & Trillium Cable); Vice-Chrmn. Mount Sinai Hospital Board; Treas., Mount Sinai Hosp. Foundation; Mem. Bd. of Govs., Baycrest Centre; Mem., National Bd., The Candn. Soc. for the Weizmann Institute of Science; Mem. Adv. Bd., York-Wharton-Recanati; Office: 50 Ashwarren Rd., Downsview, Ont. M3J 1Z5.

**TANG, Alex Oi Shung,** B.A., B.Tech.; seafood industry executive; b. China 13 Aug. 1957; s. Shui Tim and Shui Kwan (Choy) T.; e. St. Andrew's Coll. 1976; Univ. of Toronto, B.A. 1980; Ryerson Polytech. Inst., B.Tech. 1984; m. Melinda Wai Sau Lee; PRES., MANHATTAN KING SEAFOOD INC. 1988– ; Extve. Dir., Midland Seafoods Inc. 1983–88 & Extve. Dir., Midland Superior Seafoods Inc. (N.Y. City) 1987–88; Instructor-Trainer, C.P.R., Candn. Heart Found. 1983–85; Toronto Internat. Salon of Photography, gold medal 1976; exhibitor in var. internat. salons of photography; Mem., Instr. & Examiner, St. John Ambulance 1976–84; Life Mem., Photographic Soc. of Am.; Mem., Aircraft Owners & Pilots Assn.; recreations: flying, reading, photography; Office: 22 Clinton Ave., Brooklyn, N.Y. 11205.

**TANNENBAUM, Hon. Louis S.,** B.A., B.C.L.; judge; b. Montréal, Qué. 8 July 1932; s. Hyman and Ida (Avrich) T.; e. Edward VII Sch. 1945; Baron Byng High Sch. 1949; McGill Univ. B.A. 1953, B.C.L. 1956; m. Diane d. Frank and Sarah Gersovitz 28 June 1959; children: Carolyn Gail, Joani Ellen, Robert Peter; JUDGE, SUPERIOR COURT OF QUE. 1982– ; called to Bar of Que. 1957; cr. Q.C. 1976; Candn. Intercollegiate Welterweight Boxing Champion 1950; awarded Paris Medal by Batonnier of Paris Bar (1st in Civil Law Que. Bar Exam) 1957; Office: 1est, Notre Dame, Montréal, Qué. H2Y 1B6.

**TANNER, Jack William,** M.S.A., Ph.D.; educator; b. Eden, Ont. 25 Aug. 1932; s. John William and Elsie Edyth T.; e. Eden Pub. Sch., Tillsonburg High Sch.; Ont. Agric. Coll. B.S.A. 1957, M.S.A. 1959; Iowa State Univ. Ph.D. 1962; m. Melba d. Cyril and Grace Baker 1 Aug. 1982; children: Robert, Richard, Rebecca; step-children Carol, Sharon; PROF. OF CROP SCI., UNIV. OF GUELPH 1959– , Chrmn., Dept. of Crop Science 1976–1987, former mem. Bd. Govs.; Prof. and Head of Crop Sci. Univ. of Ghana 1970–72, Leader Univ. Guelph Prog. there 1970–72; Visiting Prof. Univ. of Reading, UK 1982; Iowa State Univ. 1968; Internat. Agric. Cons.; mem. Candn. Agric. Hall of Fame; Dir. Royal Agric. Winter Fair 1987– ; Bd. of Trustees, Centro Internat. de Agricultura Tropical 1988–94; Chrmn. Can. Ctte. Crop Prodn. Services; mem. Agric. Council Ont. 1984–88; Chrmn. Ont. Task Force Longterm Future Ont. Wine & Grape Ind. 1984–86; recipient Ont. Agric. Coll. Alumni Assn. Distinguished Teaching Award 1974; Fellow, Am. Soc. Agronomy; Crop Sci. Soc. Am.; Hon. Life Mem., Candn. Seed Growers' Assn. 1992; mem. Agric. Inst. Can.; Ont. Inst. Agrols.; Phi Kappa Phi; Sigma Xi; Gamma Sigma Delta; author or co-author 5 book chapters, over 60 sci. papers and reports; recreation: writing poetry; Home: 165 College Ave. W., Guelph, Ont. N1G 1S5; Office: Guelph, Ont. N1G 2W1.

**TANNIS, Ralph G.;** business executive; b. Ottawa, Ont. 17 Sept. 1944; s. George Tannis and Patricia Marie (Zarbatany) Nesrallah; e. Lisgar Coll. Inst. Ottawa 1963; CHRMN., FAT ALBERT'S & RALPH'S INC. 1990– ; Co-Founder, Snow Suit Fund and Chrmn. 1982–93; Asst. Acct. Royal Bank of Canada 1964–66; Sales Rep. Investors Overseas Services 1966–67; Programmer, Teacher IBM Canada Ltd. Ottawa 1967–71; Pres. and Founder Fat Albert's/Ralph's/Randa Food System Co. Ltd. Ottawa 1968–90; Dir. CHEZ-FM Ottawa 1977–86; Dir. Children's Hosp. of E. Ont. 1985–88; Un. Way Ottawa-Carleton 1986–88; Central Can. Exhn. 1987– ; Better Bus. Bureau 1978–80; Comnr. Nat. Capital Comn. 1989– ; mem. Ottawa Rough Rider Adv. Bd. 1983–88; P. Conservative; recreations: racquet ball, cycling, softball; Residence: 80 Presland Rd. W., Ottawa, Ont. K1K 2C3.

**TANSER, Paul Harry,** M.D., F.R.C.P.(C), F.A.C.P.; cardiologist; educator; b. Chatham. Ont. 7 Dec. 1938; s. Harry Ambrose and Isabelle Grace (Saporito) T.; e. Chatham Coll. Inst. 1956; Univ. of Ottawa M.D. 1962; m. Catherine d. Jacob and Phyllis Weaver 1 Sept. 1962; two s. Christopher, Carl; CHIEF OF MEDICINE, ST. JOSEPH'S HOSP. and Prof. of Med. McMaster Univ. 1981– ; internship Internal Med., Cardiol., Cardiac Research and Cardiac Pathol. Royal Victoria Hosp. and McGill Univ. 1962–69; mem. McGill Med. Sch. faculty, staff Royal Victoria Hosp. and Queen Elizabeth Hosp. 1969–75; Chief of Medicine, St. Joseph's Hosp. Hamilton and Prof. of Med. McMaster Univ. 1975–81; mem. Prof. Ed. Comm. & Mem. Bd. of Dirs., Heart & Stroke Found., Ont.; Affiliate Staff Phys. Hamilton Civic Hosps. and McMaster Med. Centre; mem. Cardiovascular Faculty M.S.D. Can.; Major, Cdn. Armed Forces (Reserve), District Surgeon, Hamilton Militia Dist., M.O., Royal Hamilton Light Infantry, D.C.O. 23 Med. Coy.; violinist, Oakville Symphony Orchestra, Dundas Valley Orchestra, Dundas Valley Quartet; author over 55 scient. papers; ed. bd. 'The Merck Manual'; F.A.C.C.; F.I.C.A.; C.S.P.Q.; recreations: tennis, sailing; Club: Cammac; Home: 488 #8 Hwy., Dundas, Ont.; Office: 50 Charlton Ave. E., Hamilton, Ont. L8N 4A6.

**TAPPER, Max;** arts administrator; b. Winnipeg, Man. 4 Nov. 1944; s. Sam and Sylvia (Karpel) T.; e. Univ. of Man.; children: Evan, Jason, Simon, Jonathon; MANAGING DIR., TORONTO SYMPHONY ORCH. 1992– ; Asst. Gen. Mgr., Man. Theatre Ctr. 1971–79; Devel. Dir., Royal winnipeg Ballet 1979–83; Devel./Mktg. Cons. to Can. Counc., Royal Winnipeg Ballet, Roy Thomson Hall 1983–85; Extve. Dir., Winnipeg Symphony Orch. 1985–92; Lectr., Banff Ctr. 1980– ; Mem., Fed. Cultural Policy Review Ctte. 1981–83; Cons., Theatre Calgary & Edmonton Symphony Orch. 1985– ; Bd. Mem., Winnipeg Folk Fest.; Mem., Candn. Actors' Equity; Assn. of Candn. Radio & TV Artists; Assn. Cultural Extves.; Nat. Soc. of Fund Raising Extves.; recreations: reading, travel; Office: 60 Simcoe St., Suite C116, Toronto, Ont. M5J 2H5.

**TAPSCOTT, H. Donald,** B.A., B.Sc., M.Ed.; business executive; b. Toronto, Ont. 1 June 1947; s. Donald Frederick and Mary Catherine (Borisuk) T.; e. Trent Univ. B.A. 1969, B.Sc. 1970; McGill Univ.; Univ. of Alta. M.Ed. 1978; m. Ana P. d. Antonio and Gertrude Lopes 2 April 1983; children: S. Nicole, Alexander D.; PRESIDENT, NEW PARADIGM LEARNING CORPORATION 1993– and VICE-PRES., DMR GROUP 1986– ; Independent Information Technology Cons. 1973–78; Dir., Office Information Communication Systems, Bell Northern Rsch. 1978–81; Vice-Pres., Trigon Systems Group Inc. 1981–86; Pres., Emerald City Research Inc. 1984–86; internationally sought author, consultant, speaker & writer on information technology; Chair, Adv. Ctte. on a Telecommunications Strategy for Ont.; Vice-Chair, Council for an Ontario Information Infrastructure; keynote speaker at over 200 conferences; Mem., Candn. Mental Health Assn.; Antique and Classic Boat Soc.; author: 'Office Automation: A User-driven Method' 1981 and over 50 articles, reports, etc.; co-author: 'Paradigm Shift: The New Promise of Information Technology' 1992; 'Planning for Integrated Office Systems: A Strategic Approach' 1985; Home: 11 Connaught Circle, Toronto, Ont.; Office: 252 Adelaide St. E., Toronto, Ont. M5A 1N1.

**TARAS, David,** Ph.D.; university professor; b. Montreal, Que. 7 June 1950; s. Irwin and Sheila T.; e. Sir George Williams Univ., B.A. 1972; Univ. of Toronto, M.A. 1974, Ph.D. 1983; m. Daphne d. David and Betty Gottlieb 23 May 1983; children: Matthew Ari, Joel Asher; PROF. & ASSOC. DEAN (GRADUATE PROGRAMS & RESEARCH), FACULTY OF GENERAL STUDIES, UNIV. OF CALGARY 1994– ; Ont. Legislative Intern 1976–77; Asst. Prof. of Pol. Sci., Univ. of Toronto 1982–83; Asst. Rsch. Dir., Candn. Inst. of Internat. Affairs 1982–84; Assoc. Prof. & Dir., Candn. Studies Prog., Univ. of Calgary 1984–93; Prof. & Asst. Dean (Research), Faculty of General Studies 1993–94; Commentator, CBC TV on 1989 and 1993 Alberta elections on 1991 federal consitutional package and during the 1993 federal election; author: 'The Newsmakers: The Media's Influence on Canadian Politics' 1990; editor: 'Parliament and Canadian Foreign Policy' 1985; co-editor: 'Passion for Identity' 1987, 1992; 'Prime Ministers and Premiers' 1988; 'The Domestic Battleground' 1989; 'Seeing Ourselves: Media Power and Policy in Canada' 1992; Home: 2016 Bayshore Rd. S.W., Calgary, Alta. T2V 3M1; Office: 2500 University Dr., N.W., Calgary, Alta. T2N 1N4.

**TARDIF, Monique Bernatchez,** B.A.; former politician; b. Québec City, Qué. 8 Jan. 1936; d. Henri and Aline (Larue) Bernatchez; e. Coll. des Ursulines Québec City B.A.; Univ. Laval Law Studies; m. Louis (dec.) s. Ulric Tardif 31 May 1956; children: François, Michel, Dominique; Parlty. Secy. to Solicitor General of Canada 1991–93, retired; el. to H. of C. for Charlesbourg g.e. 1984, re-el. 1988; Parlty. Secy. to Min. of Regional Industrial Expansion 1984–86; Parlty. Secy. to Min. of National Health and Welfare 1986–88; Parlty. Secy. to Min. of Supply and Services 1989–91; Counsellor, Service de la protection du consommateur automobiliste, Club automobile du Qué. 1973, Dir. 1976–80; mem. Bd. Govs. Office de la protection du consommateur 1980–81, Vice Pres. 1981–84; Gen. Sec. Interministerial Council on Road Security 1980–81; mem. Bd. Govs. Régie de l'assurance automobile du Qué. 1978–81; mem. Bd. Govs. Les Grands Ballets Canadiens, Montréal, Pres. Qué. Sect. 1969–70; Home: P.O. Box 97, Cap Rouge, Que. G1Y 3C6.

**TARDIF, Paul,** LL.L., M.B.A.; banking executive; b. Quebec 1 Oct. 1949; s. Jean-Paul and Madeleine (Latraverse) T.; e. Laval Univ. LL.L. 1970; Univ. of Western Ont. M.B.A. 1974; m. Carol Turgeon; children: Catherine, Pierre Olivier, Philippe; CHAIRMAN OF THE BOARD, PRES. & CHIEF EXECUTIVE OFFICER, TRUST PRÊT ET REVENUE 1987– ; Sec. & Dir., Legal Dept., Trust Prêt et Revenue 1974–78; Extve. Vice-Pres. & Gen. Mgr. 1978–85; Pres. 1985–87; Dir., J.S. Finance Canada Inc.; Aeterna-Vie Compagnie d'Assurance; Pres., Fund Raising Campaign; Pres., Hôpital St-Sacrement Foundation; recreations: tennis, skiing; clubs: Cercle de la Garnison de Québec; Home: 313 Chemin du Tour du Lac, Lac Beauport, Que. G0A 2C0; Office: 850, place d'Youville, Quebec, Que. G1R 3P6.

**TARDIF, Paulin,** B.A., B.Sc.Com., M.B.A.; né Courcelles, Qué. 13 juillet 1943; f. Jean-Marie et Marie-Paule (Fortin) T.; é. Pétit Séminaire de Québec B.A. 1963; Univ. Laval B.Sc.Com. 1966; Univ. Sherbrooke M.B.A. 1968; ép. Gaby f. Georges et Thérèse Quirion 24 juin 1966; enfants: Michèle, Simon. Martin; PRÉS. DU CONSEIL, PRÉS. ET CHEF DE LA DIRECTION, BESTAR INC. 1986– ; Contrôleur Bestar Inc. 1969, Dir. général 1972, Prés., dir. général 1980–85; mem. Assn. des fabriquants de meubles du Qué. (Administrateur); L'A.M.A.Q.; N.A.D.A.U.S.; Adresse: 172 Val Chenaie, Rosmère, Qué. J7A 4B6; Bureau: 3171 Louis Amos, Lachine, Qué. H8T 1C4.

**TARR, Hugh Lewis,** M.S.A., Ph.D., F.R.S.C.; scientist; b. Clevedon, Eng. 17 Nov. 1905; s. Gilbert Cecil and Florence Isabel (Coates) T.; e. North Vancouver schs.; Royal Naval Coll.; Univ. of B.C. B.S.A. 1926, M.S.A. 1928; McGill Univ. Ph.D. 1931; Emmanuel Coll. Cambridge Ph.D. 1934 (1851 Overseas Scholarship and External Rsch. Studentship); m. Patricia d. Arthur Garry 1 Feb. 1955; children: Robin, Michael, Garry; Hon. Investigator, West Vancouver Laboratory, Dept. of Fisheries & Oceans 1970–1991, retired; Hon. Lectr. in Zool. and Agric. Univ. of B.C.; Bacteriol. Rothamsted Exper. Stn. Harpenden, Herts. 1934–38; Fisheries Rsch. Bd. Can. Asst. to Prin. Microbiol. Prince Rupert, B.C. 1938–42, Vancouver Lab. 1942–70, Stn. Dir. 1955–70; recipient Prof. Inst. Gold Medal in Sci. 1957 and Deputy Minister's Commendation 1991; author or co-author over 250 sci. and tech. papers and reviews various jours. and texts; Fellow, Inst. of Food Technols. (recipient, 50 yr. Silver Medal); el. into Federated Soc's (Biochem.) U.S.A. 1953; recreations: sailing, swimming, hiking; Home: 5696 Eagle Harbour Rd., West Vancouver, B.C. V7W 1P5.

**TARR, Robert Haggart,** B.A., LL.B.; executive (retired) ; b. Winnipeg, Man. 19 July 1909; s. Edgar Jordan and Kathleen Anderson (Burke) T.; e. Univ. of Man., B.A. 1930, LL.B. 1934; m. Barbara, d. Brig.-Gen. R. W. Paterson, 1 Aug. 1936; children: Beverley, David, Valerie; former Vice-Pres., Canadian National Railways; read law with Messrs. Craig, Tarr, Hughes & Macleod, Winnipeg; called to Bar of Man. 1934; practised law with firm of Craig, Tarr, Hughes & Macleod, Winnipeg, 1934–39; joined Bank of Canada 1939 and loaned to Foreign Exchange Control Bd. on its estab., 1939; Asst. Secy., 1939–41; Secy., 1941–52; joined C.N.R. as Asst. Secy., 1952; Secy., 1954; Vice-Pres., 1958; Zeta Psi; Home: 3449 Capilano Rd., North Vancouver, B.C. V7R 4H9.

**TARTE, Yvon C.,** B.A., LL.B.; lawyer, civil servant; b. Ottawa, Ont. 6 Sept. 1947; s. Louis Olivier and Simonne (Bastien) T.; e. Univ. of Ottawa B.A. 1968, LL.B. 1971; m. Roberta d. Lois and Robert Gonyer 14 Feb. 1987; children: Marc-André, Kris (step-son); DEPUTY CHAIRMAN, PUBLIC SERVICE STAFF RELATIONS BOARD 1992– ; Asst. City Solicitor, City of Ottawa 1973–76; Counsel, Public Serv. Alliance of Can. 1976–78; McDonald Royal Comn. (RCMP) 1978–81; Candn. Human Rights Comn. 1981–83; Counsel & Extve Dir., Elections Can. 1983–92; Mem., Council on Govt. Ethics Law 1983–92; Ordre du mérite coop. de l'Ont.; Mem., Candn. Observer Team, Namibia 1989; leader, Candn. Teams, Bénin & Burkina Faso 1990; Speaker on Electoral Reform, Sophia, Bulgaria 1990; several former directorships; recreations: tennis, ski; Home: R.R. 2, P.O. Box 521, Masham, Que. J0X 2W0; Office: Box 1525, Stn. B, Ottawa, Ont. K1P 5V2.

**TASCHEREAU, Maurice E.,** B.Eng.; industrialist; b. Noranda, Que. 5 Jan. 1930; s. Rogers H. and Louise (Rolland) T.; e. McGill Univ. B.Eng. 1953; m. Louise Y. d. Frederic Hébert, Montreal, Que. 5 Sept. 1953; children: Denise, Claire, Madeleine, Lucille; former PRES. & C.E.O., ASBESTOS CORP. LTD.; served Noranda Group 25 yrs. various positions incl. Pres. Gaspé Copper Mines Ltd.; Vice Pres. Brunswick Mining and Smelting Ltd.; mem. Candn. Inst. Mining & Metall.; Am. Inst. Mining & Metall.; Corp. Prof. Engrs. Que.; recreations: golf, swimming, skiing, gardening; Home: 5 Davidson Dr., Ottawa, Ont. K1J 6L7.

**TASCHEREAU, Pierre,** Q.C.; b. Quebec City, Que. 13 Jan. 1920; s. late Edouard, Q.C. and Juliette (Carroll) T.; e. Garnier Coll., B.A. 1938; Laval Univ., LL.L. 1941; Univ. of W. Ont., Mang. Training Course, 1952; m. Yseult, d. Laurent Beaudry, LL.D., Montreal, Que., 13 Aug. 1945; children: Paule, Laurent, Francois; read law with late Hon. A. Fournier, Hull, Que.; called to Bar of Que. 1941; cr. Q.C. 1955; Secretary, Adv. Comtes., Department of Justice, Ottawa, 1941–42; Asst. Solr., Solr. & Asst. Gen. Solr., Law Dept., C.N.R., 1946–63; Sr. mem., Geoffrion & Prud'homme, Montreal, 1963–67; Vice Pres., Candn. Transport Comn. 1967–71; joined Candn. National as Vice-Pres. and Gen. Counsel 1971, Extve. Vice Pres.-Corp. Affairs 1972–74; Chrmn., 1974–77; Chrmn. of Bd., Air Canada, 1975–81; served in Canada 1942–46, Inf. and permanent Prosecutor; retired with rank of Capt.; Gov., Hôpital Marie Enfant, Montreal and Montreal Gen. Hosp. Foundation; Life Gov., Douglas Hosp. Corp.; Hon. Dir., UQAM Foundation; Home: 4350 Sherbrooke St. W., Westmount, Que. H3Z 1E3.

**TASCONA, Antonio (Tony),** R.C.A.; artist; b. St. Boniface, Man. 16 March 1926; s. Sebastiano and Nunziata (Sanfillipo) T.; e. Winnipeg Sch. of Art 1947–50; Univ. of Man. Sch. of Fine Arts 1948–52; m. May Gilchrist 1 June 1951; children: Lorenzo, Martin, Christopher, Catherine; joined Canadian Aerospace Industries 1953–56; Trans Canada Airlines metal-plating technician 1956–70; solo exhns.: Univ. of Man. 1958; Winnipeg Art Gallery 1960, 1962, 1967, 1974; Allied Arts Centre Brandon 1962; La Gallerie Soixante Montreal 1964; Calgary Allied Arts Centre 1962; Confed. Art Centre Charlottetown 1965; Mem. Art Centre St. John's, Nfld. 1965; Blue Barn Gallery 1966; Carmen Lamanna Gallery Toronto 1968; Griffith Gallery Vancouver 1969; Grant Gallery 1961 and Yellow Door Gallery Winnipeg 1965; Atlantic Art Circuit, Maritimes 1972–73; Art Gallery of Brant, Brantford 1973–74; La Gallerie Internationale 1976 Ribe, Denmark; Rodman Hall Art Gallery St. Catharines 1976; Art Gallery of Windsor 1976; Kesik Gallery Regina 1979; rep. in numerous group exhns. Can., USA and Europe incl. Nat. Gallery Biennial 1965 and 7th Biennial Exhn. 1968; Candn. Artists Exhn. Habitat Expo '67; Survey 68 Montreal Museum of Fine Arts; Montreal Olympics 1976; Cardiff Commonwealth Arts Festival Wales 1965; Nat. Gallery Exhn. Australia 1967; Travel Exhn. Paris, France 1976–77; Royal Candn. Acad. Centennial Exhn., Winnipeg Art Gallery, 1980; rep. in pub., corporate and private colls. incl. Nat. Gallery Can.; Can. Council Art

Bank; Univ. of Man. Tony Tascona Perm. Exhn. cert. by Cultural Property Review Bd. 1978 and 17 works 1949–77; comns. incl. murals Man. Centennial Art Centre 1967, YWCA Bldg. Univ. Man. 1969, and Fletcher Argue Bldg. 1970–71, Windsor, Ont. 1973; Hanging Mobile Freshwater Inst. Univ. Man. 1971–72; 2 murals Centennial Concert Hall Winnipeg 1967; Winnipeg Centennial Lib. sculpture 1977; rec'd Can. Council Grant (Materials) 1967–79, Sr. Arts Award 1972–73; Bethzedec Competition Toronto 1969; Royal Arch. Inst. Arts Medal 1970; Man. Arts Council Sr. Arts Award 1976–77; Queen's Silver Jubilee Medal 1977; Academia Italia Del Arti e Del Lavoro Gold Medal 1980; Gov., Winnipeg Art Gallery; mem. Art Adv. Bd. Man. Dept. Pub. Works Mural Competitions 1975–78; Dir. Univ. Man. Faculty Arch. Endowment Fund 1980; mem. Candn. Artists' Representation; Candn. Conf. of Arts; served with Candn. Army 1944–46; R. Catholic; recreation: walking.

**TASKER, Ronald Reginald,** M.D., M.A., F.R.C.S.(C); neurosurgeon; educator; b. Toronto, Ont. 18 Dec. 1927; s. Reginald and Lillian Gilberston (Tarberton) T.; e. Model Sch. Toronto 1939; E. York Coll. Inst.; Univ. of Toronto, Victoria Coll. B.A. 1948, M.D. 1952, M.A. 1954, postgrad. course in neurosurg. 1953–59; m. Mary Morris d. James Henry and Grace Morris Craig 1 Oct. 1955; children: Moira, James, Ronald, Alison; former Head, Neurosurgical Div. Toronto Gen. Hosp.; Prof. of Surg. Univ. of Toronto 1978– ; jr. rotating interne Toronto Gen. Hosp. 1952–53, Neurosurg. 1961– ; McLaughlin Travelling Fellow, 1959–61; Markle Scholar 1961–66; Rsch. Asst. Banting & Best Dept. Med. Rsch. Univ. of Toronto 1950–52, Clin. Teacher 1961–63, Assoc. 1963–66; Asst. Prof. 1966–73; Assoc. Prof. 1973–78 Dept. Surgery, mem. Grad. Faculty Inst. Med. Sci. 1974– ; Neurosurg. Cons. Workers Compensation Bd. Ont. 1978–90; co-author 'The Human Somesthetic Thalamus with Maps for Physiological Target Localization During Stereotactic Surgery' 1975; 'The Thalamus and Midbrain of Man' 1982; editor: 'Stereotactic Surgery' State of the Art Reviews in Neurosurgery, vol. 2, no. 1, May 1975; Vice Pres. Am. Soc. Stereotactic & Functional Neurosurg. 1976–77, Pres. 1980–81; Pres. World Soc. Stereotactic & Functional Neurosurg. 1985–89; Chrmn.: IX Meeting World Soc. Stereotactic & Functional Neurosurgery, Toronto 1985; mem. Council Internat. Assn. Study of Pain 1984–90; Ed. Bd., Applied Neurophysiology; Chrmn. Med. Adv. Bd. Parkinson Found. Can. 1962–70, 1978–84; mem., Sci. Adv. Ctte., Candn. Pain Found. 1987– ; Pres. Candn. Pain Society (Vice-Pres. 1989–91) 1991– ; awarded Spiegel and Wycis Medal of the World Soc. Stereotactic & Functional Neurosurgery 1993; mem. Exec. Fedn. Ont. Naturalists 1982–84; mem. Bd., Long Point Bird Observatory 1975–80, 1982–90, 1991– , Chrmn. 1978–80, 1983–87, 1988–90; mem. Bd., Nature Conservancy of Can. 1987– ; recreations: natural history, environmental preservation; Home: 12 Cluny Dr., Toronto, Ont. M4W 2P7; Office: 399 Bathurst St. - 2 McL – 431, Toronto, Ont. M5T 2S8.

**TASSÉ, Jean-Louis;** business executive; b. Bellevue, Qué. 14 July 1932; s. Louis and Georgette (Plamondon) T.; e. Loyola Coll., Montreal, Qué.; m. Hélène, d. Joseph Cuierrier, 26 May 1956; three s. Louis-Joseph, Jean-Baptiste, Thomas Emmanuel; three d. Héloise, Sophie, Catherine; PRES. & C.E.O., TASSÉ & ASSOCIATES, LIMITED, Stockbrokers and Investment Dealers; mem. Montreal (Gov. 1972, 1978, 1979) Toronto and Vancouver Stock Exchanges and Investment Dealers' Assn. Can. (Vice-Pres. 1976, 1977); Chrmn., Challenge Securities Inc.; mem. NYSE, AMEX & NASD; Pres., Autobus Terremont Ltée.; joined Royal Securities Corp. 1951, later with W. C. Pitfield & Co. Ltd. and other nat. and Montreal dealers until 1967 when founded present Co.; Pres. (1972 and 1977) Montreal Bond Traders' Assn.; Past Vice-Pres., Montreal Jr. Chamber Comm.; mem. Chamber Comm. Que.; Catholic; recreations: travel, swimming; Clubs: M.A.A.A.; St. James's (Montreal); Home: 600 Rabastalière E., St. Bruno, Qué. J3V 1Z9; Office: 630 René-Lévesque Blvd. West, Suite 1200, Montreal, Qué. H3B 1S6.

**TASSÉ, Roger,** O.C., Q.C.; counsel; b. Montreal, Que. 5 June 1931; e. Coll. Ste-Marie B.A. 1952; Univ. de Montréal LL.L. 1955; Univ. d'Ottawa, Dipl. Grad. Studies in Law 1957; m. Renée Marcil; 4 children; COUNSEL, FRASER & BEATTY (Ottawa); called to the Bars: Québec 1956; Yukon 1977; Ont. 1986; cr. Q.C. 1971; Univ. de Montréal, Fac. of Law, Dipl. of Merit 1978; Officer of the Order of Canada 1981; Career: Combines Offr., Restricitive Trade Practices; Civil Law Sect., Dept. of Justice; Supt. of Bankruptcy, Asst. Depy. Min., Dept. Consumer and Corporate Affairs; Depy. Solr. Gen. of Can., Dept. of the Solicitor Gen. 1972–77; Depy. Min. of Justice and Depy. Attorney Gen. of Can. 1977–85; Partner: Lang Michener Lash Johnston, Ottawa, Ont.; Noël, Décary, Aubry et Associés, Hull, Québec; Extve. Vice-Pres. (Legal & Environmental Affairs) Bell Canada 1988–91; Chrmn. Study Comte. on Bankruptcy and Insolvency Legis.; report made public June 1970; Chrmn. Comte. 'Young Persons in Conflict with the Law'; report July 1975; former lectr. part-time, Law Faculty and the Public Administrative Law Inst., Univ. of Ottawa; Affil: Candn. Bar Assoc.; Trustee, La Commission Scolaire Outaouais-Hull 1972–74; Vice-prés., Collège d'Enseignement Général et Professionnel (CEGEP) de l'Outaouais 1974; Chrmn., Fed.-Prov. Continuing Ctte. of Depy. Ministers and Depy. Attorneys Gen. 1977–85; mem., Citizens' Forum on Canada's Future (1991); Principal Internat. Advisor, Special Joint Ctte. on a Renewed Canada (1992); Home: 25 Chemin de la Mine, Chelsea, Que. J0X 1N0; Offices: 180 Elgin St., Ste. 1200, Ottawa, Ont. K2P 2K7.

**TASSEOR TUTSWEETOK, Lucy;** sculptor; b. Nunalla, Manitoba 1934; 60 group exbns. incl. most recent: Candn. Mus. of Civilization Hull, Que. 1992–93, Marion Scott Gall. Vancouver 1992, Galerie Saint Merri France 1992, Arctic Artistry Hastings-on-Hudson, N.Y. 1992, Nat. Gallery of Canada 1992, l'Iglou Art Esquimau, Douai (toured 19 cities) France & Belgium 1987–92, Vancouver Inuit Art Soc. 1991, York Quay & Leo Kamen galls. (Earth Spirit Fest.) Toronto 1991, Maison Hamel-Bruneau Ste-Foy, Que. 1990–91; works in collections incl. art galleries of Ontario (Klamer Family & Sarick colls.) and Winnipeg (Millard, Swinton & Twomey colls.), Candn. Mus. of Civilization, Inuit Cultural Inst. Rankin Inlet, N.W.T., Nat. Gallery of Can., Prince of Wales Northern Heritage Ctr. Yellowknife, N.W.T.; attended openings: 'Sculpture/Inuit: Masterworks of the Canadian Arctic' Philadelphia, Pa. 1973, Nat. Gallery of Can. (gala) 1988, 'Indigena' Candn. Mus. of Civ. 1992; comnd. by Earth Spirit Festival to carve a piece for Visions of Power exhbn. Toronto 1991; subject of several articles and catalogues; Home: Arviat, N.W.T.; Office: c/o Ingo Hessel, Indian and Northern Affairs Canada, Les Terrasses de la Chaudière, Ottawa, Ont. K1A 0H4.

**TATA, Sam Bejan,** R.C.A.; photographer; b. Shanghai, China 30 Sept. 1911; s. Bejan Dadabhoy and Naja Tata; e. Shanghai Pub. Sch.; Univ. of Hong Kong 2 yrs.; came to Can. 1956; formerly m. to Marketa Langer; one d. Antonia; as photojournalist has contributed to maj. Candn. mags. since 1956 incl. Time Can.; exhn., National Gallery, 'Shanghai 1949,' 1981; rep. in exhns. Shanghai, Bombay, Phoenix, George Eastman House Rochester, Boston, Paris, Toronto, Ottawa and Montreal; recipient various Can. Council grants incl. 3 Sr. Arts Grants; Queen's Silver Jubilee Medal 1977; Hon. LL.D., Concordia Univ. 1982; Lifetime Achievement Award, Candn. Assn. of Photogs. & Illus. in Commun. (CAPIC) 1990; Award of Excellence, Fraternity Ahuramazdyan Ont. 1990; co-author 'Montreal' (photographs) with late Frank Lowe 1963; Canadian Fiction Magazine 50 portraits Candn. writers 1958–78, 1979; 'A Certain Identity' 50 portraits 1983; Canadian Fiction Magazine 33 portraits 'Sam Tata's Colleagues' (internat. as well as Candn. photographers) 1985; Descant 58 'Land of My Fathers: India' 32 photographs, text by Mulk Raj Anand, Fall 1987; 'The Tata Era -- L'Époque Tata' a retrospective exhbn., Candn. Museum of Contemporary Photography 1988; co-author: 'Shanghai 1949 The End of an Era' 63 photos. with Ian McLachlan 1989; 'Portraits of Canadian Writers' 50 portraits 1991; mem. Royal Photographic Soc. (Eng.); Liberal; Zoroastrian; recreations: classical music, reading; Address: 4361 Beaconsfield Ave., Montreal, Que. H4A 2H5.

**TATE, Donald McLean,** M.A., Ph.D., F.R.G.S.; federal civil servant; b. Portage la Prairie, Man. 3 Sept. 1943; s. Cecil Marcus and Winnifred Grace (Wilson) T.; e. York Univ. B.A. 1965; Univ. of W. Ont. M.A. 1968; Univ. of Ottawa Ph.D. 1984; m. Sharron Margaret d. Newton and Lauretta Edey 27 June 1970; children: Christopher Donald Newton, Jonathan Cecil Douglas; HEAD, ENVIRONMENTAL ECONOMICS, ENVIRONMENT CANADA 1992– ; Am. Water Works Assn. Water Conservation Ctte.; Dir. Ottawa Foyers Partage 1986– ; Mississippi River Conserv. Authority 1986–93; Field Geol., Geol. Survey of Can. 1968; Water Resource Planner, Environment Can. 1969, Water Use Specialist 1976–81; Sr. Economist 1981–91; Sr. Econ. Environment Canada 1981–91; Head, Water Resource Economics 1991–92; Sessional Lectr. in Geog. Univ. of Ottawa 1982, 1983, 1988, 1989, 1991; Adjunct Prof. of Geog., Univ. of Ottawa; author or co-author over 90 sci. papers and monographs water resources mgmt. Can.; Assoc. Ed. Water Internat. 1984–89, Candn. Water Resources Jour. 1988– ; Fellow, Royal Geographic Society; recreations: model railroads, jazz music; Home: 74 Penfield Dr., Kanata, Ont. K2K 1M1; Office: Candn. Wildlife Service, Ottawa, Ont. K1A 0H3.

**TATILON, Claude D.,** Ph.D.; university professor; b. Marseille, France 3 Jan. 1938; s. Paul and Mireille (Gerbi) T.; e. Lycée Thiers; Univ. de Provence, licence, maîtrise, D.en Linguistique 1973; PROF. OF LINGUISTICS, YORK UNIV. 1972– ; Asst. Prof. of French, Eastern Wash. State Coll. 1966–68; Asst. Prof. of French, Univ. of W. Ont. 1968–72; Vis. Prof., Univ. d'Ottawa 1976–77; Founding Dir., Sch. of Transl., York Univ. 1979–83; Dir., MA Programme in Translation; Pres., Union des Français de l'Etranger, section de l'Ont. 1984–86; author: 'Sonorités & texte poétique' 1976; 'Traduire: pour une pédagogie de la traduction' 1986; 'Helena' 1991; co-author: 'Interprétations orales' 1984; Home: 55 Kappele Ave., Toronto, Ont. M4N 2Z4; Office: 2275 Bayview Ave., Toronto, Ont. M4N 3M6.

**TATOSSIAN, Armand,** R.C.A.; artist; b. Alexandria, Egypt 26 Sept. 1948; e. Cath. Coll. of St. Marc, Alexandria; Montreal High Sch. 1967; McGill Univ. Art Hist. 1967–69; drawing and sculpture under J. Majzner; pupil of A. S. Scott, R.C.A. 1966–69; Cararra Acad. Bergamo, Italy mural painting 1970; Paris, France 1971; m.; children: Anais, Charles; assisted in restoration of murals Bank of Montreal St. James St. Br. Montreal; Prof. of Art Educ. Concordia Univ. 1971–74; solo exhns. incl. Double Take Art Gallery New York 1968; Galerie Gauvreau Montreal 1968, 1970, 1971; Molesworth Gallery New York 1969; Mount Stephen Club Montreal 1972; Studio des Artistes Canadiens Inc. Quebec City 1973; Galerie Bernard Desroches Montreal 1973, 1975, 1980, 1983, 1985; Galerie Peintre Québécois Baie St-Paul 1974; Galerie St. Laurent Ottawa 1976; Nat. Gallery of Armenia, Yerevan, U.S.S.R. 1976; A.G.B.U. Gallery New York 1977; Dominion Corinth Ottawa 1978; Kaspar Gallery Toronto 1978, 1979; Menasen Gallery Sherbrooke 1978; Pub. Archives Can. Ottawa 1980; Lindchrist Gallery Windsor, Ont. 1980; rep. various group exhns.; rep. numerous perm. colls. incl. Museum of Fine Arts of Soviet Armenia, Musée de Québec, Nat. Gallery Can.; work cited various publs.; mem. Conseil de la peinture du Québec; recreations: music, travel, reading; Clubs: Montreal Art; Arts & Letters Toronto; Address: 2121 Tupper St., Apt. 416, Montreal, Que. H3H 1P1.

**TATRALLYAY, Geza P.Z.,** B.A., M.A., M.Sc.; banker; b. Budapest, Hungary 11 Feb. 1949; s. Peter A. and Livia (Baitz) T.; e. Univ. of Toronto Schools 1967; Harvard Univ., B.A. 1972; Oxford Univ., M.A. 1974; London Sch. of Econ. & Pol., M.Sc. 1975; m. Marcia d. Arne and Mary Ethel Nousanen 18 Oct. 1980; children: Alexandra, Nicholas; VICE PRES., GERMANY & CENTRAL/EASTERN EUROPE, ROYAL BANK OF CANADA 1991– ; Tech. Asst. to Extve. Dir. for Can., Inter-American Devel. Bank 1977–80; Asst. Mgr., Project Finance, Royal Bank of Can.; Extve. Dir., Orion Royal Bank Limited 1983–86; Mgr., Corp. Planning 1986–87; Vice-Pres. 1987–89; Vice Pres., Business Serv. & Mktg., U.S.A. 1989–91; Rhodes Scholar; Office: Lyoner Strasse 15, 60528 Frankfurt, Germany.

**TATTERSALL, Robert,** M.A., M.B.A., C.F.A.; investment counsellor; b. Clitheroe, England 8 Nov. 1947; e. St. John's Coll., Cambridge, M.A. 1969; Ohio State Univ., M.B.A. 1971; CO-OWNER & DIR., HOWSON TATTERSALL INVESTMENT COUNSEL LTD. 1985– ; Vice Pres., Pension Fund Investments, Confederation Life Insur. Co. 1977; Sr. V.P. & Dir., Bolton Tremblay Inc. 1981; Lecturer, Humber Coll.; Office: Suite 1904, Cadillac Fairview Tower, 20 Queen St. W., Toronto, Ont. M5H 3R3.

**TATTRIE, Gordon Lewis;** banker; b. Westville, N.S. 15 Feb. 1936; s. Lewis Layton and Marion Olive (Bezanson) T.; e. Stellarton (N.S.) High Sch. 1953; m. Shirley d. Walter Snyder 11 May 1957; two d. Tracey, Janice; Sr. Vice Pres. E. Can. Candn. Comm. Credit, The Bank of Nova Scotia 1987; joined The Bank of Nova Scotia, Stellarton, N.S. 1953, various assignments Can., trans. to Jamaica as Mgr. Main Br. 1974, Asst. Gen. Mgr. Credit Caribbean Regional Office 1976, Gen. Mgr. Loan Audit/Loan Adm. 1979, Sr. Vice Pres. and Gen. Mgr. Caribbean Region 1983; recreation: golf; Clubs: Cedarbrae Golf & Country; Ontario; Home: 37 Dunsdale Square, Agincourt, Ont. M1S 2L7.

**TAYLOR, Alastair MacDonald,** B.A., M.A., D.Phil.; professor emeritus; writer; b. Vancouver, B.C. 12 March 1915; s. James and Bertha Elizabeth (Redman) T.; e. Univ. of S. Cal. B.A. (summa cum laude) 1937, M.A. 1939; Columbia Univ. 1941–42; Oxford Univ. D.Phil. 1955; m. Mary E. d. Charles and Elizabeth Clements 17

July 1944; three s. Angus, Graeme, Duncan; Teaching Asst. and Lectr. Univ. of S. Cal. 1937–41; Nat. Film Bd. Can. 1942–44; UN Relief & Rehab. Adm. Secretariat 1944–46, UN Secretariat 1946–52, sr. ed. Dept. Pub. Info. and Official Spokesman Security Council UN Comn. Indonesia 1949–50; Visiting Prof. of Geog. Edinburgh Univ. 1959–60; Assoc. Prof. Depts. Pol. Studies & Geog. Queen's Univ. Kingston 1960, Prof. 1965, Prof. Emeritus 1980– ; UNITAR Prof. Inst. Internat. Relations Univ. of W. Indies 1967; Visiting Prof. Bermuda Coll. 1980; Adjunct Prof. Antioch-Seattle Univ. 1983– ; Visiting Prof. Univ. of Guelph 1987; author 'Indonesian Independence and the United Nations' 1960; 'For Canada: Both Swords and Ploughshares' 1963; 'Evolution-Revolution: Patterns of Development in Nature, Society, Man' 1971; co-author 'Civilization, Past and Present' 1942 (single vol. format in 7th edn., 2 vol. format 8 edns.); 'The Development of Civilization' 2 vols. 1962; 'Promise and Perils' 1965; 'Peacekeeping: International Challenge and Canadian Response' 1968; 'Integrative Principles of Modern Thought' 1972; 'Evolution and Consciousness: Human Systems in Transition' 1976; 'Goals for Mankind: A Report to the Club of Rome' 1977; 'Unity in Diversity' 1977; 'From Rhodesia to Zimbabwe: The Politics of Transition' 1981; 'Peacekeeping: Appraisals and Proposals' 1982; 'World Religions and the Environment' 1989; 'Poles Apart: Winners and Losers in the History of Human Development' 1992; 'Science and Causality: An Historical Perspective' 1992; Pres.: Candn. Assn. Am. Studies 1966; Candn. Centre Integrative Edn. Kingston; mem. Centre Integrative Edn. N.Y.; UN Assn. Can.; Candn. Institute of Internat. Affairs; Affiliation: Club of Rome 1977; Internat. Devel. Rsch. Centre Ottawa 1989–91; Inst. Noetic Sci's Sausalito 1990– ; Phi Beta Kappa; Phi Kappa Phi; recreations: golf, tennis, walking, reading, writing poetry; Address: 2855 Lansdowne Rd., Victoria, B.C. V8R 3P8.

**TAYLOR, Albert William,** B.A., H.B.A., M.Sc., Ph.D., D.Sc., D.P.E.; educator; b. Brantford, Ont. 18 Sept. 1939; s. Raymond William and Gertrude Helen (Lamb) T.; e. Univ. of W. Ont. B.A. 1962, H.B.A. 1963; Univ. of B.C. M.Sc. 1964; Wash. State Univ. Ph.D. 1967; London Inst. of Technol. D.Sc. 1972; m. Carole June d. Edward and Joan Turner; children: Mary-Jill, Andrew Scott Ryan, Taryn-Lise, Edward Todd; DEAN, FACULTY OF KINESIOLOGY, UNIV. OF W. ONT. and Prof. of Med. 1982– ; joined Dept. Nat. Health & Welfare Fitness Research Unit Univ. of Alta. 1967–70, Assoc. Prof. of Phys. Educ. and Research Assoc. Surgical-Medical Research Inst. of Univ. 1970–73; Visiting Prof. of Clin. Physiol. Karolinska Hosp. Stockholm 1973–74; Assoc. Prof. and Prof. Educ. Physique Univ. de Montréal and Hon. Prof. of Occupational & Phys. Therapy McGill Univ. 1974–81; Reader, Dept. Human Movement Studies and Assoc., Dept. Anat. Univ. of Queensland 1981–82; consultant numerous firms, corps. and sport governing bodies; recipient numerous acad. and sport honours; ed. or author over 30 books and manuals sports med., Olympic wrestling, sport science; over 250 scient. papers various journs.; past ed.-in-chief several journs.; Fellow, Am. Coll. Sports Med.; Fellow or Mem., 32 profl. assns., Dir. and mem. Extve. of 6; Pres., Sports Medicine Council of Canada; D.P.E. (Hon.) Université de Sherbrooke 1993; recreation: swimming, racquetball, Olympic wrestling, bridge; Home: 1686 Louise Blvd., London, Ont. N6G 2R3; Office: 118 Thames Hall, London, Ont. N6A 3K7.

**TAYLOR, Allan Richard;** banking executive; b. Prince Albert, Sask. 14 Sept. 1932; s. Norman and Anna Lydia (Norbeck) T.; m. Shirley d. late Ellis K. Ruston 5 Oct. 1957; children: Rodney Allan, Leslie Ann; CHRMN. & C.E.O., ROYAL BANK OF CAN. 1986– ; Dir., Royal Bank of Canada; TransCanada Pipelines Ltd.; Canadian Pacific Ltd.; General Motors of Canada Ltd., Oshawa, Ont.; Founding Dir., Corporate Higher Education Forum; Past Pres., Internat. Monetary Conference; Vice Chrmn. Business Council on National Issues (BCNI) and serves on the Extve. and Policy Cttes.; mem., Advisory Council, Candn. Extve. Service Overseas; Trustee, Queen's Univ., Kingston, Ont.; mem. adv. ctte., Sch. of Bus. Admin., Univ. of Western Ont.; mem. Adv. Bd., Assoc. Internationale des Étudiants en Sciences Économiques et Commerciales (AIESEC) Canada; joined Royal Bank in Prince Albert 1949; served at various posts in Saskatchewan, Ontario, New York and Montreal; apptd. Extve. Offr. 1970; Mgr., Toronto Main Branch 1971; Deputy Gen. Mgr., Intl. Div., Head Office, Montreal 1974; Sr. Vice Pres., Intl. Div. 1977; Extve. Vice Pres. Intl. Div. 1978; Pres. & C.O.O. 1983; Hon. LL.D., Univ. of Regina 1987; Hon. LL.D., Concordia Univ. 1988; Hon. LL.D., Queen's Univ. 1991; Hon. Doctorate of Business Admin., Laval Univ. 1990; Hon. Doctorate of the University, Univ. of Ottawa 1992; Chrmn., Junior Achievement of Canada; Gov., Olympic Trust of Canada; Mem., National Adv. Council of IMAGINE (former Chrmn. Corporate Program); mem. Council of Patrons, Candn. Outward Bound Wilderness Sch.; mem. Advisory Bd., Candn. Foundation for AIDS Rsch. (CANFAR); Clubs: Granite; National; Toronto; York; Rosedale Golf; Forest and Stream; Saint James's; Mount Royal; Royal Montreal Golf (Montreal); recreations: golf, tennis; Office: Royal Bank Plaza, Toronto, Ont. M5J 2J5.

**TAYLOR, Andrew Russell,** B.Sc., M.Sc., Ph.D.; university professor of astrophysics; b. London, England 2 April 1953; s. Alice and Joseph Russell T.; e. Osgood H.S. 1971; Univ. of W. Ont. B.Sc. (Hons.) 1976; Univ. of B.C. M.Sc. 1978, Ph.D. 1982; m. Janis d. Gloria and William Milligan 13 Oct. 1984; children: Jessica and Morgan Milligan-Taylor; ASSOC. PROF., PHYSICS & ASTRONOMY, UNIV. OF CALGARY 1987– ; NSERC Postgrad. Scholar, U.B.C. 1976–82; NSERC Postdoct. fellowship, Univ. of Toronto 1982–84; Rsch. Sci., Rijksuniversiteit Groningen 1984–86; Univ. of Manchester Radio Astronomy Lab. (U.K.) 1987; NSERC Univ. Rsch. Fellow, Univ. of Calgary 1987– ; Dir., Candn. Astronomical Soc. 1990–93; Chair, Subctte. for Radioastronomy 1992–94; Adv. Bd., NRC, Herzberg Inst. of Astrophysics 1992–95; User's Ctte., U.S. Nat. Radio Astronomy Observatory 1991–94; Internat. Science Steering Ctte., Japanese VSOP Space Mission; Core Sci. Team for Russian-led Radioastron Space Mission to be launched 1996; Maud Holt Kingston Medal for Excellence (U.W.O.); discoverer: radio jets from the Star CH CYGNI 1985; many new supernova remnants in our galaxy, Westerbork Galactic Plane Radio Survey 1991; Mem., Candn. & Am. Astron. societies; Nederlandse Astronomenclub; author/co-author of over 50 pubns. in profl. jours.; recreations: camping, outdoors, guitar, music; Home: 344 Ranchridge Ct. N.W., Calgary, Alta. T3G 1W6; Office: 2500 University Dr. N.W., Calgary, Alta. T2N 1N4.

**TAYLOR, Arthur Leonard;** travel executive; b. Vancouver, B.C. 5 May 1929; s. Henry James and Marie Jean Jeanette (Biggs) T.; e. Magee H.S. (scholarship); Univ. of B.C., 3 yrs.; Price Waterhouse, C.A.; m. Marie d. Dan and Agnes Holland 21 Dec. 1978; children: Michael, Karyn, Christina, Sean, David, Melissa; Comptroller, Scott Paper Limited 1955–65; Sr. Finan. Analyst, McMillan Bloedel 1965–68; Vice-Pres., McCan Franchises (McDonald's Can.) 1968–71; Extve. Vice-Pres., Burkes World Wide Travel 1971–79; Vice Pres., Global Travel Computers Ltd. 1979–83; Pres., Hallmark Resources & Ramm Venture Corp. 1983–84; Vice-Pres., Marlin Travel 1984–91; Pres., Alliance of Candn. Travel Assns. 1989–91; N. Am. Dir., Universal Federation of Travel Agents' Assn. (UFTAA) 1991– (elected First Vice-Pres. 1992); recreations: fishing, scuba diving, photography; club: The Vancouver; Home: #4 – 2206 Folkestone Way, West Vancouver, B.C. V7S 2X7; Office: #100 – 10711 Cambie Rd., Richmond, B.C. V6X 3G5.

**TAYLOR, Bruce,** B.A., M.A., Ph.D.; poet; b. Vancouver, B.C. 1 March 1960; s. David Earl and Janet Belle (Ferrier) T.; e. McGill Univ. B.A. 1981, M.A. 1986; Univ. of Toronto Ph.D.; m. Maggie d. Scott and Dorothy Odell 5 Dec. 1985; one s.: Elias David; author: 'Getting on with the Era' 1987, 'Cold Rubber Feet' 1989 (poetry), 'Marionette Magic' 1989 (non-fiction); QSPELL award for Poetry 1989 (shared with Erin Mouré); Norma Epstein Award 1988; E.J. Pratt Medal and Prize 1988; Shapiro Award 1981; Office: 4646 Hutchinson, Montreal, Que. H2V 3Z9.

**TAYLOR, Charles,** B.A., D.Phil.; educator; b. Montreal, Que. 5 Nov. 1931; s. Walter Margrave and Simone (Beaubien) T.; e. Selwyn House Sch. 1946; Trinity Coll. Sch. Port Hope, Ont. 1949; McGill Univ. B.A. 1952; Oxford Univ. B.A. 1955, D.Phil. 1961 (Fellow All Souls' Coll. 1956–61); m. Alba d. Tadeusz Romer, 2 Apl. 1956; children: Karen, Miriam, Wanda, Gabrielle, Gretta; PROF. OF POL. SCIENCE and PROF. OF PHILOSOPHY, McGILL UNIV. 1973; joined McGill Univ. as Asst. Prof. 1961; Prof. of Philos. Univ. de Montréal 1962–71; Visiting Prof. Princeton Univ. 1965, Univ. of Cal. Berkeley 1974; mem., Inst. for Advanced Study, Princeton, 1981–82; el. Chichele Prof. of Pol. and Social Theory, Univ. of Oxford 1976–81; Fellow, All Souls Coll. 1976–81; mem., Inst. for Advanced Study, Princeton, 1981–82; former Vice Pres., fed. NDP, Pres. Que. NDP; author 'Explanation of Behaviour' 1964; 'Pattern of Politics' 1970; 'Hegel' 1975; 'Hegel and Modern Society' 1979; 'Philosophical Papers' v. 1 and 2, 1985; 'Sources of the Self' 1989; 'The Malaise of Modernity' 1991; articles fields of philos. and pol. theory in various learned journs. mags.; mem. Candn. Pol. Science Assn.; Candn. Philos. Assn.; Royal Soc. Can.; British Academy; NDP; R. Catholic; recreations: swimming, skiing, hiking; Home: 344 Metcalfe Ave., Montreal, Que. H3Z 2J3; Office: Dept. of Philosophy, Stephen Leacock Bldg., Rm. 908, 855 Sherbrooke St. W., Montreal, Que. H3A 2T7.

**TAYLOR, Charles Patrick Stirling,** M.A, Ph.D.; educator; b. Toronto, Ont. 11 May 1930; s. Thomas Mayne Cuninghame and Barbara Davidson (Howell) T.; e. Univ. of Toronto Schs.; Univ. Hill, Vancouver; Univ. of B.C., B.A. 1952; Oxford Univ. (Rhodes Scholar) B.A. 1954, M.A. 1957; Univ. of Pa. Ph.D. 1960; m. Elizabeth d. J. Frank S. and Muriel Sowerby 20 Aug. 1955; children: John, Ann, Christopher, Ruth; PROFESSOR OF MEDICAL BIOPHYSICS, UNIV. OF W. ONT. 1974– ; Fellow, Jane Coffin Childs Meml. Fund Med. Rsch. Dept. Theoretical Chem. Cambridge Univ. 1960–61; Asst. Prof. of Physics Univ. of B.C. 1961–67; Assoc. Prof. of Biophysics present Univ. 1968; Corp. mem. Inter-Varsity Christian Fellowship Can., sometime Faculty Adv. to Univ. of Western Ont. Chapt. and to Univ. of B.C. Chapter; teacher great highland bagpipe; speaker on sci. and Christian faith, biblical creation; author various tech. articles; Anglican; recreations: piping, English country dancing; Home: 61 Lloyd Manor Cres., London, Ont. N6H 3Z4; Office: London, Ont. N6A 5C1.

**TAYLOR, Charles Plunket Bourchier,** B.A.; writer; horse breeder; b. Toronto, Ont. 13 Feb. 1935; s. Edward Plunket and Winifred Thornton (Duguid) T.; e. Upper Can. Coll.; Trinity Coll. Sch. 1951; Queen's Univ., B.A. 1955; PRES., WINDFIELDS FARM LIMITED 1983– ; Reporter, Toronto Telegram 1952–53; Sub-Ed., Reuter's News Agency 1955–56; Pub. Relns. Offr., Stratford Shakespearian Fest. 1956–57; Freelance journalist (U.K.) 1957–62; Fgn. Corr., The Globe and Mail 1962–69; Vice-Pres., Windfields Farm Limited 1969–82; Dir., New Providence Devel. Corp.; Lyford Cay Co.; Trustee, Ont. Jockey Club; Chief Steward, Jockey Club of Can.; Mem., The Jockey Club (N.Y.); Dir., The Breeders' Cup Ltd.; Keeneland Assoc.; Chrmn., Writers' Union of Can. 1977–78; author: 'Radical Tories' 1982, 'Six Journeys' 1977, 'Snow Job' 1974, 'Reporter in Red China' 1965; editor: 'China Hands' 1984; Office: P.O. Box 67, Oshawa, Ont. L1H 7K8.

**TAYLOR, Claude I.,** O.C.; transportation executive; b. Salisbury, N.B. 20 May 1925; s. Martin Luther and Essie (Troope) T.; e. Salisbury (N.B.) High Sch., 1941; Robinson Business Coll., N.B., 1942; McGill Univ. Extension, R.I.A. 1950–53; Hon. D.C.L. Univ. of N.B. 1980; Hon. LL.D. McMaster Univ. 1983; m. Frances Bernice, d. late Robert Watters, 4 Nov. 1947; children: Peter, Karen; CHRMN. EMERITUS, AIR CANADA 1993– ; has served Air Canada as Vice Pres. Strategic Devel., Vice Pres., Govt. & Industry Affairs, Vice Pres. Pub. Affairs; Pres. and C.E.O. 1976–84; Bd. Chrmn. 1984–92; Chrmn., Pres. & C.E.O. 1990–92; Past Pres., Internat. Air Transport Assn. 1979–80; Past Mem. of Exec., Ctte. of I.A.T.A. 1977–88, 1990; Past Pres., Travel Industry Assn. of Can. 1972–73; Past Chrmn., Air Transport Assn. Can. 1975–76; Bd. Chrmn., Internat. Aviation Mgmt. Training Inst.; Internat. Business Counc. of Can.; Sr. Mem., The Conf. Bd.; Life Gov., Douglas Hosp. Found.; Gov., Montreal Gen. Hosp.; mem. Bd. of Govs., Concordia Univ.; Commander of the Order of St. John; Hon. Pres., Boy Scouts of Canada; mem. Adv. Bd., Salvation Army; rec'd. Gordon R. McGregor Trophy, Royal Candn. Airforce Assn., 1980; Excellence in Communications Leadership Award, Internat. Assn. of Business Communicators 1982; B'Nai Brith Canada Award of Merit 1984; McGill Management Achievement Award 1985; Human Relations Award, Candn. Counc. of Christians and Jews; Gold Medal Award, Administrative Mgmt. Soc.; National Transportation Person 1987; Tony Jannus Award 1988; C.D. Howe Award 1989; Officer of the Order of Canada; Fellow, Soc. of Mgmt. Accts. of Can. 1985; Fellow, Chartered Inst. of Transport 1985; inducted into Canada's Aviation Hall of Fame 1986; Baptist; Clubs: Mount Stephen; Mount Royal; Forest and Stream (Mtl.); Office: Air Canada Centre, Montreal, Que. H4Y 1H4.

**TAYLOR, Colin,** C.A.; chartered accountant; b. Glasgow, Scotland 17 March 1946; s. William Bilsland and Catharine (Montgomery) T.; e. Inst. of C.A.'s (Scotland) and Ontario 1969; Harvard A.M.P. 1987; m. Anthea d. John and Violet Mill 2 Dec. 1972; children: Kevin, Mark; DEPUTY MANAGING PARTNER, DELOITTE & TOUCHE; Supervisor, Ernst & Whinney UK 1971–72; joined Touche Ross (now Deloitte & Touche) 1972; Partner 1977; Toronto 1978; Partner-in-Charge 1987; Group Managing Partner, Metro Toronto Offices 1990; Mem., Mngt. Ctte.; Adv. Council to Dean of Business Sch., Queen's Univ.; Mem., Brit.-Cdn. Trade Assn.;

Toronto Scottish C.A.s Soc.; Bd. of Dir. & Extve. Ctte., Multiple Sclerosis Soc. of Can., Ont. Div. (Past Chair, Finance & Executive cttes.); recreations: golf, tennis, soccer; clubs: St. George's Golf & Country, York, Ontario, Boulevard; Home: 14 Ridgevalley Cres., Islington, Ont. M9A 3J6; Office: 181 Bay St., Ste. 1400, BCE Pl., Toronto, Ont. M5J 2V1.

**TAYLOR, Cora Lorraine,** B.A.; author; b. Fort Qu'Appelle, Sask. 14 Jan. 1936; d. Harvey Traub and Edith Mary (Kalbfleisch) T.; e. Univ. of Alta., B.A. 1973, teaching cert. 1973; m. Russell s. Harry and Evelyn T.; children: Durward Granger and Gwendolyn Marie Thomas, Clancy Grant and Randall Sean Livingston; step-children: Kenneth Allan, Mary Evelyn (Sullivan), James Robert; Terrance Russell Taylor; City of Edmonton Arts Award 1987; Anglican (Vestry, St. Faith's 1981–87); Mem., Candn. Authors Assn. (Alta. V.P. 1980); CANSCAIP; author: 'Julie' (Candn. Lib. Assn. Book of the Year for Children award 1985; Can. Counc. Award for Children's Literature 1986) 1985 (novel); 'The Doll' 1987 (Ruth Schwartz Award 1988); 'Julie's Secret' 1991 (Internat. Youth Library White Raven Book); 'Ghost Voyages' 1992; several short stories, musical plays & articles; editor: 'Poetry Yearbook' 1980–85; recreation: reading; Club: Seven Arts; Home: P.O. Box 3196, Spruce Grove, Alta. T7X 3A5.

**TAYLOR, David A.,** B.Comm., C.A.; financial executive; b. Penticton, B.C. 28 Nov. 1950; e. Univ. of B.C. B.Comm., C.A. 1975; m. Dana; children: Jeffrey, Christopher; GROUP EXTVE. VICE-PRES. & CHIEF FINANC. OFFR., GROSVENOR INTERNAT. HOLDINGS LIMITED; Office: 2100 – 1040 West Georgia St., Vancouver, B.C. V6E 4H1.

**TAYLOR, Douglas Graham,** B.Ed.; former politician; b. Wolseley, Sask. 4 July 1936; s. Robert Douglas and Isabella Roy (Graham) T.; e. Candiac Elem.; Wolseley High Sch.; Univ. of Regina B.Ed. 1966, Dip. in Ednl. Adm. 1972; m. Katherine Isabel d. John Robson Garden 3 Oct. 1959; children: Robert Douglas, Katherine Isabel Marie, Susan Joan, Peter Samuel; former Min. of Public Participation also responsible for Sask. Govt. Insurance, the Liquor Bd., and Sask. Property Mgmt. Corp.; Teacher Kipling (Sask.) High Sch. 1962–64; Prin. Wolseley (Sask.) High Sch. 1967–79; el. M.L.A. for Indian Head-Wolseley prov. g.e. 1978, re-el. 1982, 1986; Cand. Leadership P. Conservative Party Sask. 1979, Opposition House Leader Sask. 1979, Opposition Critic for Edn. and Continuing Edn.; Min. of Health, Sask. also responsible for the Sask. Medical Care Insur. Comm., Sask. Cancer Found., and Sask. Alcohol and Drug Abuse Comm. 1982–86; Min. of Tourism, Small Business and Co-operatives, also responsible for SEDCO, Sask. Property Mgmt. Corp. and Sask. Liquor Bd. 1986–88; Dir. and Founder, Qu'Appelle Valley Sci. Fair; Past Pres., Indian Head Superintendency Teachers' Assn.; mem., Qu'Appelle Valley Prins. Assn.; United Church; recreations: horses, golf; Club: Wolseley Lions; Home: P.O. Box 159, Wolseley, Sask. S0G 5H0.

**TAYLOR, Eric John;** business executive; b. Bracebridge, Ont. 19 Dec. 1952; m. Debra; CHAIRMAN OF THE BOARD, CANADA MOTOROLA CANADA LTD.; Home: R.R. 22, Golden Lane, Cambridge, Ont. N3C 2V4; Office: 4000 Victoria Park Ave., North York, Ont. M2H 3P4.

**TAYLOR, Gladys Maime;** publisher; writer; b. Swan River, Man. 25 June 1917; d. Alfred Earnest and Maime (Jordan) Tall; e. Bowsman High Sch.; Swan River High Sch.; Winnipeg Normal Sch.; m. Lorne E. s. Leslie and Dorothy 27 Aug. 1940; divorced 1968; children: Barry (dec.), Dennis, Lorne, Susan; OWNER & PUBLISHER, ROCKY VIEW FIVE VILLAGE WEEKLY, CARSTAIRS COURIER, WHEEL & DEAL 1975– ; taught school 1936–40; Candn. Women's Army Corp. 1943–45; freelance writer 1950– ; Ed., Book Page, Sherbrooke Daily Record 1955–65; TV show host, CHLT, Sherbrooke 1958; Ed., Eng. sect., Thetford Mines Le Canadian 1958–62; Ed., Canadian Author & Bookman 1963–67; Columnist, Toronto Telegram 1963–67; Past Columnist, United Church Observer; Nat. Sec., Candn. Authors Assn. 1958–62; mem., Ed. Adv. Bd., Quill & Quire 1965–66; Bd. Mem., Journalism Bd., Southern Alta. Inst. of Technol. 1973–76; Ryerson All-Canada Fiction Award 1955, 1958; Calgary Businesswoman of the Yr. 1983; United Church; Dir., Bow River Prog. Cons. Assn. 1983–84; speaker to many groups on writing, newspaper pub., etc.; author: 'Pine Roots' (novel) 1955; 'The King Tree' (novel) 1958; 'Alone in the Australian Outback' 1984; 'Alone in the Boardroom' 1987; first and only woman to run in Canada's first Senate Election (Alta. 1989) - ran as an Independent; recipient, Candn. Community Newspapers Assn.'s Gold Quill Award, for service to the publishing industry 1992; recreation: travelling; Address: Box 40, Irricana, Alta. T0M 1B0.

**TAYLOR, Gordon E.,** F.R.S.A.; politician; b. Calgary, Alta. 20 July 1910; s. John Thomas and Hannah (Gillis) T.; e. sr. matric.; univ. (sch. teacher); bus. coll.; Sr. Whip, House of Commons and mem. Transport and Veterans' Cttes. 1985–87, retired 1988; el. M.L.A. Alta. g.e. 1940, re-el. to 1979; el. as an Independent 1975; Min of Railways & Telephones 1950, Acting Min. of Pub. Works; Min. of Highways & Transport 1951–71; retained Telephones portfolio until 1959 and served as Min. of Youth 1970; el. to H. of C. for Bow river g.e. 1979, re-el. 1980, 1984; served as sch. teacher 13 yrs.; estbd. bus. Drumheller area 1946; served with RCAF World War II, rank Flying Offr. on discharge 1945; Co-founder Candn. Highway Safety Council; Founder and Pres. Camp Gordon Soc. (for underprivileged boys) 1932–86; Fellow, Rosebud Sch. of the Arts (hon. degree in recognition of 48 yrs. of devoted public service to the citizens of Alberta) 1989; mem. Boy Scouts Prov. Council, former cub and scout master, dist. comnr. and rover mate; recreations: hockey, baseball, hunting; Home: 13412 Buena Vista Rd., Edmonton, Alta. T5R 5R2.

**TAYLOR, Harry William,** B.Sc., M.Sc., Ph.D.; university professor; b. Sturgeon Valley, Sask. 28 Sept. 1925; s. Wm. and Gladys Muriel (Evans) T.; e. Univ. of Manitoba B.Sc. 1951, M.Sc. 1952, Ph.D. 1954; m. Wanda Jason 18 June 1949; children: Allison Leslie, Karen Elizabeth; PROF. OF PHYSICS, UNIV. OF TORONTO, 1969– ; Lectr. Univ. of Manitoba, 1952–53; Post-doctoral Fellow NRC, Ottawa, 1954–55; Lectr., Asst. Prof. Queen's Univ., 1955–61; Assoc. Prof. Univ. of Alta., 1961–65; Assoc. Prof. of Physics, Univ. of Toronto; served with RCNVR, active service, 1944–45; awarded Candn. Volunteer Service Medal, War Medal 1939–45; has written scientific papers with special reference to nuclear spectroscopy, environmental radioactivity; Fellow, Am. Physical Society; Fellow, Inst. of Physics; Fellow, Inst. of Nuclear Engn.; Fellow, Am. Assoc. for Advancement of Science; mem., Candn. Assn. of Univ. Teachers; recreations: military history, tennis; Home: 3525 Grand Forks Road, Mississauga, Ont. L4Y 3N2; Office: Toronto, Ont. M5S 1A7.

**TAYLOR, Hugh;** retired insurance executive; b. Edinburgh, Scotland 23 Jan. 1925; e. Glasgow Univ. m. Mary-Lee (Hubbs) T.; children: Ian, Graham, Trudy, Joseph, Kelly-Ann; Dir. Canadian-Scottish Philharmonic Foundation; joined Norwich Union Life, Scot. 1941, held various appts. after World War II service UK, Mgr. E. Africa 1956, Asst. Gen. Mgr. Can. 1961, Gen. Mgr. Can. 1977–81; Pres. 1981–86; recreations: automobile racing, sports, music.

**TAYLOR, Hugh Alexander,** O.C., M.A.; consulting archivist; b. Chelmsford, England 22 January 1920; s. Hugh Lamport and Enid Essex (Horrocks) T.; e. St. Christopher's School Bath 1930–33; Tynemouth Sch. 1933–36; Keble Coll., Oxford Univ. B.A. 1949, M.A. 1953; Liverpool Univ., dipl. in archive admin. 1951; m. Daphne d. Dr. William and Margery Johnson 3 Jan. 1959; children: Madeline Hildreth, Mary Margery, Ruth Enid; Royal Air Force 1939–46, Flight Lt. 1945; Archivist, Leeds Public Libraries 1951–54; Liverpool Public Libraries 1954–58; County Archivist of Northumberland (U.K.) 1958–65; Prov. Archivist of Alta. 1965–67; of N.B. 1967–71; Dir., Archives Branch, Public Archives of Canada 1971–77; Prov. Archivist of N.S. 1978–82; Adjunct Prof., School of Library, Archival & Information Studies, Univ. of B.C. 1982–86; Officer of the Order of Canada 1990; Hon. Life Mem., Assn. of Candn. Archivists 1983; Pres., Soc. of Am. Archivists 1978–79; Mem., Candn. Council of Archives 1985–88; Bd. of Dir., Candn. Inst. for Historical Microreproductions 1980–86; Co-Founder, Veterans against Nuclear Arms 1982; Editor, 'The Canadian Archivist' 1968–70; author of several articles on the nature & future of archives in 'Archivaria,' 'The American Archivist,' etc. 1970– ; recreations: walking, cycling, gardening; Home: #19 - 3987 Gordon Head Rd., Victoria, B.C. V8N 3X5.

**TAYLOR, J. Allyn,** O.C., LL.D.; retired trust and loan company executive; b. Winnipeg, Man. 10 Apr. 1907; s. John and Florence Elizabeth (Poyntz) T.; e. Pub. Schs. and Model Sch., Winnipeg, Man.; St. Michael's Sch., Victoria, B.C., Kelvin High Sch., Winnipeg, Man.; Univ. of Manitoba, B.A. 1928; m. Elizabeth C., d. Hon. Senator John T. Haig, Winnipeg, Man., 15 Oct. 1938; children: Ann, Lynn, John; retired Chairman, The Canada Trust Co. & Canada Trustco Mortgage Co. since 1978; Dir., Canada Trust 1957; Pres. & Gen. Mgr. 1958; Chrmn. & Pres. 1968; Chrmn. 1973; Chrmn. Interim Steering Ctte., The Candn. Medical Hall of Fame; Retired Chrmn. Ont. Press Council; Retired Chrmn. John P. Robarts Medical Research Inst.; Past Pres., Trust Co's. Assn. of Can.; Past Pres. (1969–70) Candn. Chamber of Comm.; Past Chrmn., McMichael Candn. Collection; former Chancellor, Univ. of Western Ont.; Past Pres., London Health Association (Univ. Hospital); Hon. Chrmn., London Foundation; Anglican; recreations: golf, bridge, billiards; Clubs: The London; London Hunt; Home: 1117 The Parkway, London, Ont. N6A 2X2; Office: 275 Dundas St., London, Ont. N6B 3L1.

**TAYLOR, James A.F.,** B.A., D.D.; writer; editor; b. Indore, India 1 Sept. 1936; s. William Stephens and Mary Oberlin (Frackleton) T.; e. Univ. Hill High Sch. 1954; Univ. of B.C. B.A. 1958; United Coll., Montreal D.D. (honoris causa) 1990; m. Joan K. d. Canute and Florence Anderson 2 July 1960; children: Stephen (dec.), Sharon; CO-FOUNDER, OWNER, ED. AND CREATIVE DIR. WOOD LAKE BOOKS INC. 1981– ; writer, producer CJOR Radio Stn. Vancouver 1958–61; sales rep. CBU Radio and TV CBC Vancouver 1961–64; prog. prodn. and supervision CFPR Radio CBC Prince Rupert 1964–68; Mng. Ed. The United Church Observer Toronto 1968–81; mem. Faculty McLuhan & Davies Communications Toronto 1984– ; Chair, Book & Periodical Devel. Council 1989–90, Vice Chair 1988–89, Past Chair 1990–91; Fellow, Candn. Inst. Speech; author (non-fiction) 'An Everyday God' 1981; 'Lifelong Living' 1983; 'Canadian Religious Travelguide' 1983; 'Two Worlds in One' 1985; 'Last Chance' 1989; 'Surviving Death' 1993; several hundred mag. articles; editor 'PMC: Practice of Ministry in Canada' (journal) 1983– ; Sec. Freelance Eds. Assn. Can. 1981–83, Treas. 1983–86; Dir. Faith at Work Can. 1985– , King-Bay Chaplaincy (ecumenical) 1983–92; United Church (various nat. bds. & cttes.); Home: Box 10, 1300 6th St., Okanagan Centre, B.C. V0H 1P0; Office: P.O. Box 700, 10162 Newene Rd., Winfield, B.C. V0H 2C0.

**TAYLOR, James B.,** B.Sc., M.Sc.; geologist; b. Harrisburg, Pa. 12 April 1938; s. Dr. James B. Taylor Sr.; e. Univ. of Redlands, Calif. B.Sc. 1960; U.C.L.A., Calif. M.Sc. 1963; m. Sarah Williams; children: Dale, Karen; EXTVE. VICE-PRES. & CHIEF OPERATING OFFICER, CANADIAN OCCIDENTAL PETROLEUM LTD. 1990– ; worked in Alaska, Calif. & South America for Texaco 1963–68; var. positions for Occidental International Exploration and Production Co. incl. Vice-Pres. of Colombian Opns., Vice-Pres. of Latin American Opns. & most recently, Vice-Pres., Eastern Hemisphere Opns. 1968–90; recreations: karate, hunting; clubs: Calgary Petroleum, Pinebrook Golf & Country; Office: 1500, 635 – 8th Ave. S.W., Calgary, Alta. T2P 3Z1.

**TAYLOR, James Dudley,** B.E., M.Sc.; executive; b. Winnipeg, Man. 23 Feb. 1944; s. Dudley Robert and Viola May (Thomson) T.; e. McGill Univ. B.E. (Elect. Engn.) 1966; Stanford Univ. M.Sc. (Aeronautics & Astronautics) 1969; m. Mary B. (Hughes); children: Allan James, Katherine Anne; Chrmn. of Bd. and C.E.O., Cal Corporation 1974; Flight recorders and controls research Air Canada 1963–65; Flight Controls Engr. SST and 737 Projects The Boeing Co. 1966–67; Systems Engr. Missile Projects Lockheed Missiles and Space Co. 1967–68; Systems Engr. responsible for launch vehicles, mission analysis and spacecraft control systems, Launch Operations Mgr. Anik Al and Anik A2, Telesat Canada 1969–74; Dir. Aerospace Industries Assn. Can. 1980–83; Fellow, Candn. Aeronautics & Space Inst.; mem., Am. Inst. Aeronautics & Astronautics; recreations: hockey, skiing; Home: 22 Kingsford Cr., Kanata, Ont. K2K 1T4.

**TAYLOR, James Edgar;** writer/broadcaster; b. Nipawin, Sask. 16 Mar. 1937; s. James Edgar and Ethel Florence (Quinton) T.; e. Victoria H.S. 1955; m. Deborah d. Carman and Lilian Easton 29 Oct. 1960; children: Teresa, Christopher; SPORTS COLUMNIST, 'VANCOUVER PROVINCE' 1978– ; Sports Writer, 'The Daily Colonist' 1955–63, 1965; 'Vancouver Times' 1964; 'Vancouver Sun' 1966–70; Sports Columnist 1979–78; Sports Editorialist, CBC TV 1978–81; CKWX Radio 1975– ; co-author: 'Dirty 30' 1974, 'Inside the Dynasty' 1983; 'Gretzky, from the Backyard Rink to the Stanley Cup' 1984, 'Rick Hansen, Man in Motion' 1987; recreations: music, books; Home: 1277 W. 39 Ave., Vancouver, B.C. V6M 1S9; Office: 2250 Granville St., Vancouver, B.C. V6H 3G2.

**TAYLOR, James Hutchings,** M.A., LL.D.; retired diplomat; b. Hamilton, Ont. 25 Mar. 1930; s. John Douglas and Mabel (Pugh) T.; e. pub. and high schs. Hamilton, Ont.; McMaster Univ. B.A. 1951; Oxford Univ. (Rhodes Scholar) B.A. 1953, M.A. 1983; McMaster Univ. LL.D. 1989; m. Mary d. Bruce and Jean Cosh 18 Oct. 1957; children: Andrew, Sarah, Katherine, Pegatha, James; CHANCELLOR, MCMASTER UNIV. 1993– ; joined Dept. of External Affairs 1953 serving in Vietnam, India, France, U.S.S.R., Belgium (Ambassador to NATO 1983–85) and Japan (Ambassador 1989–93); served in Ottawa as Dir. Gen. Eur. Affairs, Asst. Under-Sec., Depy. Under-Sec., Under-Secy. of State for External Affairs 1985–89; Prime Minister's Personal Representative for the 1989 Economic Summit 1989; Baptist; recreations: reading, sailing, skiing, fishing; Clubs: Five Lakes; Rideau; Home: 541 Manor Ave., Ottawa, Ont. K1M 0J1.

**TAYLOR, James Renwick,** B.A., M.A., Ph.D.; university professor; b. Little Shemogue, N.B. 13 Dec. 1928; s. Hugh Stephen and Bertie (Morton) T.; e. Mount Allison Univ., B.A. (cum laude) 1949, M.A. 1950; Univ. of London (Eng.), Lord Beaverbrook Overseas Scholar 1950–51; Univ. of Pennsylvania, Ph.D. 1978; m. Elizabeth d. Alan and Janet Van Every 4 July 1966; children: Matthew Stephen, Gavin James; DEPARTMENTAL CHRMN. 1991– and PROF. OF COMMUNICATION, UNIV. DE MONTRÉAL 1971– ; Radio/TV Prof., CBC 1956–65; Supr. Prod., CBC Pub. Affairs TV Ottawa 1959–63; Reg. Supr. 1963–65; seconded to Royal comn. on Bilingualism & Biculturalism 1965–66; Lectr. & Dir., TV Lab., Univ. of Penn. 1966–71; Founder & First Chrmn., Dept. of Commun. Sci., Univ. de Montréal 1971–75; Spec. Advr., Planning, Fed. Depy. Min. of commun. 1982–84; Sci. Advr., Candn. Workplace Automation Rsch. Ctr. 1984–86; Cons., Dept. of Commun. 1986–87; Scholar in residence, The Inst. for Rsch. on Public Policy, Jan.-June 1988; Mem., Sci. Counc. of Can. Task Force on Computerization of Commun. 1980–82; Commun. Rsch. Advr. Bd. 1981–83; SSHRC Task Force on Technol. & Commun. of Rsch. 1984–86; Central Mort. & Hous. scholarship 1966–70; Pres., Visual Arts Ctr. of Montréal 1975–77; Pres., Candn. Communication Assn. 1992–93; Mem., Sub-Commission on Communication, Information and Informatics; Participant and mem. of Secretariat Roundtable on Governing in an Information Soc.; Mem., Internat. Commun. Assn.; Assn. de la rech. en commun. du Qué.; Internat. Assn. of Mass Commun. Rsch.; Assn. of Computing Machinery; Office Systems Rsch. Assn.; Standing Ctte., Organizational Symbolism; Am. Soc. for Cybernetics; Speech Communication Assn.; Acad. of Mgmt., Social Science Fedn. of Canada; Association canadienne française pour l'avancement des sciences; author: 'L'organisation n'est qu'un tissu de communications' 1988; 'Rethinking the Theory of Organizational Communication' 1993; co-author: 'The Dynamics of Adaptation' 1971; 'The Vulnerable Fortress' 1993 and num. book chapters & articles; Ed. Bd. Mem., 'Communication Theory' and 'Canadian Journal of Communication'; recreations: tennis, gardening, guitar; Clubs: Mount Royal Tennis; Home: 3051 Cedar Ave., Montréal, Qué. H3Y 1Y8; Office: C.P. 6128, Succ. 'A,' Montréal, Qué. H3C 3J7.

**TAYLOR, John Nicholas;** lumber executive; b. Melton Mowbray, England 7 June 1951; s. John Leslie and Cynthia Maureen (Ledwidge) T.; e. Hull Coll. of Comm. (UK) 1970; m. Joan d. Rene and Olive Cusack 27 July 1974; children: Kate, Vivienne, Caroline; EXTVE. VICE-PRES., GREEN FOREST LUMBER CORP. 1975– ; David Samuel Trust Ltd. (UK) 1970–74; Bank of N.S. 1974–75; Dir., JBO Distrib. Ctr., Inc.; recreations: squash, tennis, sailing; Home: 85 Airdrie Rd., Toronto, Ont. M4G 1M4; Office: 194 Merton St., Toronto, Ont. M4S 3B5.

**TAYLOR, John Roderick Stanley,** B.A., M.A.; utility executive; b. Niagara Falls, Ont. 14 Oct. 1953; s. William Stanley and Bettie (Giddens) T.; e. Univ. of Toronto B.A. (Hons.) 1975, M.A. 1977; m. Laurie d. Robert and the late Marilyn Brown; children: Hadley, Will; DIRECTOR OF CORPORATE STRATEGIC PLANNING, ONTARIO HYDRO 1993– ; Public Hearings Officer, Ont. Hydro 1986–87; Acting Mgr. of Communication Services 1987–88; Mgr. of Corp. Relns. Strategic Planning 1988–89; Dir. of Extve. Office 1989–93; Ont. Hydro Staff Rep. to E7 Group 1991– ; recreations: travel, music; Home: Toronto, Ont.; Office: 700 University Ave., H19-G1, Toronto, Ont. M5G 1X6.

**TAYLOR, Kenneth Douglas,** O.C., M.B.A., LL.D.; diplomat; b. Calgary, Alta. 5 Oct. 1934; s. Richard Taylor; e. Univ. of Toronto B.A. 1957; Univ. of Cal. Berkeley M.B.A. 1959; Laurentian Univ. LL.D.; m. P. E. Lee 1 Oct. 1960; one s. Douglas; joined Candn. Foreign Service 1959; Guatemala 1960, Detroit 1963, Karachi 1966, Counsellor London, Eng. 1967, Ottawa 1971 (various assignments incl. Asst. Secy. Interdepartmental Comte. on External Relations, Dir. Finance and Personnel Trade Commr. Service 1972, Dir. Gen. Foreign Trade Service 1973); Candn. Ambassador to Iran 1977; When U.S. Embassy was taken by Iranians in 1979 and its occupants captured, six escaped and were successfully hidden by the Canadian Embassy staff, directed by Mr. Taylor, and later escaped from Iran posing as Canadians; Candn. Consul Gen., New York, and Candn. Comr. to Bermuda 1981–84; Sr. Vice Pres. Gov't Affairs, Nabisco Brands Inc. 1984–89; Sr. Vice Pres., RJR Nabisco Inc. 1987–89; recipient U.S. Congressional Gold Medal; Officer, Order of Canada; Haas Internat. Award Univ. of Cal. Berkeley; Detroit-Windsor Internat. Freedom Festival Award; Candn. Club N.Y. Gold Medal Award; Am. Acad. Achievement Gold Plate Award; N.Y. Police Dept., St. George's Assn. Golden Rule Award; State of Cal. Medal of Merit; Ave. of Americas Assn. N.Y. Gold Key Award; Key to City of N.Y.; Am. Friendship Medal, Freedoms Foundation Valley Forge, Pa.; Harry S. Truman Good Neighbor Award; Sigma Chi; recreations: tennis, squash, golf; Club: Canadian (N.Y.); Home: 146 West 57 St., N.Y. 10019.

**TAYLOR, Kent Dallas,** B.A.; real estate executive; b. Winnipeg, Man. 17 Apr. 1936; s. Cecil Harry and Thelma M. (Dallas) T.; e. Concordia Coll., B.A.; m. Diane M. d. Clarence H. Smith 23 Sept. 1962; children: Robert David, Susan Daphne; Pres., The Edgecombe Group 1977; several years in real estate & investment indus. before joining Edgecombe Group as Vice-Pres., Eastern Opns. 1970; Extve. Vice-Pres. & Dir. 1975; Dir., Edgecombe Investment Serv. Limited; Edgecombe Properties Limited; Edgecombe Realty Limited; Princeton Devel. Ltd.; Mem., Internat. Counc. of Shopping Ctrs.; Ont. Mortgage Brokers Assn.; recreations: sailing, skiing, reading, music; Clubs: Boulevard; Caledon Ski; Mimico Cruising.

**TAYLOR, Larry Douglas,** C.M.A., C.M.C.; business executive; b. Cambridge, Ont. 1 April 1957; s. Douglas George and Marion May (Brethauer) T.; e. Fanshawe Coll. 1976; Certified Management Accountant 1984; Certified Management Consultant 1988; m. Patricia d. Bryant and Gail Langmuir 19 June 1992; DIRECTING PARTNER, ERNST & YOUNG FOOD INDUSTRY PRACTICE 1992– ; 6 years of food industry experience for large Candn. food co.; Partner, Ernst & Young (at age 32) 1990; Partner, Ernst & Young Performance Improvement Consulting Practice 1992; Mem., Soc. of Mng. Accountants of Ont.; Bd. of Trade of Metro Toronto; author of numerous articles; recreations: tennis, cycling; clubs: Fitness Inst., Royal Canadian Yacht; Office: P.O. Box 251, Ernst & Young Tower, Toronto, Ont. M5K 1J7.

**TAYLOR, Malcolm Gordon,** M.A., Ph.D., LL.D.; b. Alberta 31 Aug. 1915; s. Charles G. and Ora E. T.; e. Calgary (Alta.) Normal Sch., 1933–34; Univ. of Calif., B.A., M.A., Ph.D. (1949); LL.D. Alberta 1965; LL.D. York 1987; m. Helen Doris Taylor 1983; children: Deanne Elizabeth, Burke Gordon; PROF. EMERITUS OF PUBLIC POLICY, YORK UNIV.; with Indust. Relations Dept., Henry Kaiser Corp., Calif., 1941–43; subsequently Assoc. Prof. of Pol. Econ., Univ. of Toronto; Principal, Univ. of Alberta (Calgary), 1960–64; Research Consultant, Royal Comm. on Health Services 1961–64; Pres., Univ. of Victoria (B.C.), 1964–68; Pres., Candn. Soc. for Higher Educ. 1974–75; Chrmn., Nat. Manpower Council for Mental Retardation 1972–76; Research Consultant (Hall) Health Services Review, 1978–80; Publications: 'Administration of Health Insurance in Canada,' 1956; 'Financial Aspects of Health Insurance,' 1958; 'Health Insurance and Canadian Public Policy' 1978 (2nd ed. 1988); 'Insuring National Health Care: The Canadian Experience' 1990; and articles in prof. and learned journs.; Ed., 'Canadian Journal of Public Administration,' 1958–60; mem., Inst. Public Adm. Can. (Pres., 1959–60); Awarded Roy. Soc. of Canada J.A. Hannah Book Medal, 1980; Hannah Lecturer, 1980–81; Nat. Health Scientist Award 1981; Candn. Pol. Science Assn.; Phi Beta Kappa; Pi Sigma Alpha; Address: Royal Quays, 308 – 11 Cooperage Pl., Victoria, B.C. V9A 7J9.

**TAYLOR, Mark Rushbrooke Forbes,** B.A., M.A.; certified health executive (Canada); public sector manager; b. Bristol, U.K. 6 Dec. 1943; s. Frank Robert Forbes and Caroline Dora (Rushbrooke) T.; e. Oriel College, Oxford Univ. B.A. 1965, M.A. 1970; 1st m. Judith Hamilton Sandison; 2nd m. Anna d. Margaret and Edward Spicer 28 Jan. 1989; daughter (from prev. m.): Caroline; PRESIDENT, ADDICTION RESEARCH FOUND. 1989– ; Nat. Admin. Trainee, Nat. Health Serv. U.K. 1965–67; Lectr./Tutor, Univ. of Aston in Birmingham U.K. 1968–70; Admin., Aga Khan Hosp. Kenya 1970–74; Manager, Peat Marwick & Partners Canada 1974–79; Extve. Sec., Aga Khan Found. East Africa 1979–81; Principal, Woods Gordon (Ernst & Young) Canada 1981–84; Sr. Vice-Pres. then Pres., Toronto Western Hosp. 1985–86; Chief Extve. Offr., Cromwwell Hosp. U.K. 1987–89; Preceptor, Univ. of Toronto 1982– and Kellog School of Management (Canada & U.K.) 1985–89; Dir., Independent Hospitals Assn. U.K. 1987–89; Chair, Toronto Academic Health Sci. Council 1991– ; Dir., Crossmatch Health Corp. U.K. 1987; Mem., Internat. Hosp. Fed.; Hon. Vice-Pres., Internat. Council on Alcohol & Addictions; author of articles in profl. journals; recreations: sailing, travel; clubs: Leander, R.A.F. Yacht (both U.K.); Home: 107 Mineola Rd. E., Mississauga, Ont. L5G 2E6; Office; 33 Russell St., Toronto, Ont. M5S 2S1.

**TAYLOR, Hon. Martin Rapson,** LL.B.; judge; b. Harrow, Eng. 18 May 1931; s. Henry Archibald, C.B.E. and Muriel Kathleen (Little) T.; e. Univ. of B.C. LL.B. 1962; m. Carolyn Frances d. Frank W. Harvie, Vancouver, B.C. 1960; children: Michael, Alexandra, Susan; JUDGE, COURT OF APPEAL OF B.C. 1989– ; read law with C. W. Brazier, Q.C.; called to Bar of B.C. 1963; law practice Davis & Co. Vancouver and at Prince George 1963–78; Counsel for Atty. Gen. B.C. 1965–75; Advisor to Govt. of B.C. on estab. of B.C. Energy Comn. and on other pub. utility and energy matters 1973–77; Counsel for B.C. Energy Comn. on Inquiry into B.C. Natural Gas Industry 1973; mem. B.C. Del. to First Mins. Conf. on Energy 1974; Dir. B.C. Petroleum Corp. 1973–74, Secy. 1973–77; Chrmn. B.C. Motor Carrier Comn. 1973–74; Counsel to Royal Comn. on B.C. Rly. 1977–78; Chrmn. Univ. of Calgary Faculty Remuneration Arbitration Bd. 1978; Judge, Supreme Court of B.C. 1978–89; mem. Extve. Vancouver Bar Assn. 1976–78; Dir. The Lawyers' Inn 1972–74; mem. Ed. Bd. 'The Advocate' 1971–78; Home: 941 Belvedere Dr., North Vancouver, B.C. V7R 2C2; Office: The Court House, Vancouver, B.C. V6Z 2E1.

**TAYLOR, Neville G.,** B.Sc., M.B.A.; banker; b. London, England 23 Aug. 1953; s. Alan Frederick Bragg and Doris Evelyn Beatrice (Byles) T.; e. Upper Can. Coll., SSHGD 1972; Univ. of Guelph, B.Sc. 1976; York Univ., M.B.A. 1981; m. Kathryn d. Gordon and Jeannette Plamondon 13 June 1981; children: Carolyn, Bryan, John; SENIOR VICE PRES., BARCLAYS CANADA OF CANADA 1991– ; Indus. Comm. Leasing, IAC Limited 1976–80; Corp. Comm. Acct. Mngt., Barclays Bank 1980–86; Vice-Pres., Credit 1986–88; Pres., Barclays Canada Leasing Corp. 1989–91; Finan. Advr. to United Way Allocation Ctte.; club: Royal Candn. Yacht; Home: 86 Melrose Ave., Toronto, Ont. M5M 1Y7; Office: 304 Bay St., Toronto, Ont. M5H 2P2.

**TAYLOR, Nicholas William,** M.L.A., B.Sc.; politician; geologist; b. Bow Island, Alta. 17 Nov. 1927; s. Frederick David and Marie Louise (Ancion) T.; e. Bow Island High Sch.; St. Theresa's Coll., Medicine Hat 1944; Univ. of Alta. B.Sc. (Geol. & Engr.) 1949; m. Margaret d. Lemuel and Gladys Davies 1 Oct. 1949; children: Patrice, Jennifer, Terrance, Cayt, Ian, Sheila, Alison, Susan, Sarah; LEADER ALTA. LIBERAL PARTY 1974–88; M.L.A. for Westlock-Sturgeon, Alberta 1986–93; for Redwater, Alberta 1993– ; Pres., Cariad Exploration Ltd.; Northwest Sulphur Ltd.; Chief Geologist, Canada-Cities Service 1949–55; Chief Geologist, Honolulu Oil Corp. 1955–60; Pres., Taylor Mgmt. 1960–68; Pres., N.W. Taylor Exploration Ltd., Citizens Pipeline Ltd. 1961, Lochiel Exploration Ltd. 1971–86; served RCNVR 1944–45; Vice Chrmn., Separate Sch. Bd., Calgary 1959–63; former Pres.: North Calgary Rotary Club; Calgary Social Planning Counc.; former Co-Chrmn., Western Counc. of Christians and Jews; awarded Medal of Merit, Profl. Engrs., Geophysicists & Geologists of Alta. 1984; mem. Alta. Profl. Engrs.; recreations: sailing, reading, skiing; Home: Box 779, Bon Accord, Alta. T0A 0K0.

**TAYLOR, Patrick J.,** M.D., F.R.C.S.(C), F.R.C.O.G.; physician; educator; rsch. worker; b. Blackpool, Lancs., Eng. 23 Aug. 1941; s. James and Winnifred May (Malcolm) T.; e. Campbell Coll. Belfast 1958; Queen's Univ. Belfast M.B.,B.Ch. 1964, M.D. 1985; m. Kathleen d. Jack and Norah Withers 1 Apl. 1967; children: Sarah, David; PROF. OF OBSTETRICS AND GYNECOL. UNIV. OF B.C. 1991– and CHRMN. DEPT. OF OBSTETRICS AND GYNECOL. ST. PAUL'S HOSP., VANCOUVER 1991– ; Univ. of Calgary Asst. Prof. of Obstetrics & Gynecol. 1971, Assoc. Prof. 1976, Prof. 1981–87, Dir. Reproductive Endocrinol. 1975–87; Bourn Hall Clinic (Cambs.) Dep. Med. Dir. 1987, Dir. 1988; Prof. of Obstetrics & Gynecol. Univ. of Man. 1989–1991; Chief Section of Reproductive Endocrinol. 1989–91; co-author 'Laparoscopy and Hysteroscopy in Gynecologic Practice' 1986; 'Unexplained Infertility' 1992; 'Practical Hysteroscopy' 1993; 'Practical Laparoscopy' 1993; transl. 'Hysteroscopy Atlas and Text' by J. Hamou 1990; over 170 articles sci. jours.; editor-in-chief, Journal Soc. 1990– ; mem. various ed. bds.; F.S.O.G.C. (Vice Pres. 1985–87); F.A.C.O.G.; Soc. Reproductive Surgs. (Charter mem.); Candn. Fertility Soc.

(Pres. 1980–81); Candn. Fertility & Androl. Soc. (Pres. 1981–82); Am. Fertility Soc.; Brit. Fertility Soc.; recreation: sailing, fly-fishing; Office: St. Paul's Hosp., 1081 Burrard St., Vancouver, B.C. V6Z 1Y6.

**TAYLOR, Paul Albert,** B.A., M.B.A.; banker; b. Saint John, N.B. 17 June 1943; s. Albert and Mary Kathleen (McCullough) T.; e. Univ. of W. Ont. B.A. 1966; Univ. of Windsor M.B.A. 1971; div.; children: Beth Ellen, Brian Paul, Stephen Charles; EXEC. VICE PRES. TREASURY AND INVESTMENT BANKING, ROYAL BANK OF CANADA 1990– ; Dir., Royal Bank Investment Management Inc.; RBC Dominion Securities Limited; joined present Bank 1966; various br. positions Toronto 1966–69; Asst. Mgr. Toronto Main Br. 1971–74; Area Exec. Orion Royal Bank Ltd. London, Eng. 1974–77 and Exec. Dir. 1977; Sr. Mgr. Global Finance RBC H.O. Montreal 1978–80 and Asst. Gen. Mgr. 1980; Asst. Gen. Mgr. Nat. Accts. 1980–82 becoming Sr. Vice Pres. 1982; Sr. Vice Pres. World Corporate Banking 1983–86; Sr. Vice Pres. Invest. Banking Internat. London, Eng., also Dep. Chrmn. Orion Royal Bank Ltd. 1986–88; Exec. Vice Pres. Invest. Banking H.O. Toronto 1988–90; Co-Chrmn., Financial Sector, Canada-Japan Business Ctte.; Chrmn., Candn. National Institute for the Blind Nationwide Campaign Cabinet; mem., The Founders Club; Zeta Psi Fraternity; Home: 30 Wellington St. E., Suite 1702, Toronto, Ont. M5E 1S3; Office: Royal Bank Plaza, 200 Bay St., Toronto, Ont. M5J 2J5.

**TAYLOR, Richard,** B.A.; writer; b. Winnipeg, Man. 25 Feb. 1953; s. Thomas Robert and Eleanor Ruth T.; e. Handsworth Sr. Secondary 1971; Simon Fraser Univ. 1972; Carleton Univ., B.A. 1976; m. Dale d. Patricia and Ernest Gosselin 9 Aug. 1975; children: Sky, Quinn; author: 'Blue Mornings' forthcoming, 'Cartoon Woods' 1988 (novels); 'Tender Only to One' 1984 (short stories); 'Last Resort' 1981 (prose poems); combines writing career with that of being a full-time househusband; travelled with wife around the world 15 months 1978–79; travelled with wife & daughter around the world 1 year 1987–88; lived one year in Hong Kong 1992–93; recreations: wood sculptor; club: Masters Swim; Home: 61 Rueter St., Nepean, Ont. K2J 3Z9.

**TAYLOR, Richard E.,** B.Sc., M.Sc., Ph.D.; physicist; b. Medicine Hat, Alta. 2 Nov. 1929; s. Clarence Richard and Delia Alena (Brunsdale) T.; e. Univ. of Alta., B.Sc. 1950, M.Sc. 1952; Stanford Univ., Ph.D. 1962; m. Rita Jean Bonneau 25 Aug. 1951; one s.: Norman Edward; PROFESSOR, STANFORD LINEAR ACCELERATOR CTR. 1968– ; Boursier, Lab. de l'Accelerateur Lineaire (France) 1958–61; Phys., Lawrence Berkeley Lab. 1961–62; Staff Mem., Stanford Linear Accelerator Ctr., Stanford Univ. 1962–68; Prof., 1968– , Assoc. Dir., 1982–86; J.S. Guggenheim Fellowship, Geneva, Switzerland 1971–72; Docteur (Honoris Causa), Univ. of Paris 1980; D.Sc. Univ of Alta. 1991; LL.D. (hon.) Univ. of Calgary 1993; D.Sc. Univ. of Lethbridge 1993; Sr. Sci. Award, DESY Hamburg, W. Germany, von Humboldt Found. 1982; D.Sc. Univ. of Alta. 1991; Mem., Candn. Assn. of Physicists; Foreign Assoc., U.S. National Acad. of Sciences; Fellow, Am. Assn. for the Advancement of Sci.; Fellow, Am. Physical Soc. (Counc., Div. Particles & Fields, 1983–84); F.R.S.C. 1985; Fellow, Am. Acad. of Arts & Science; Awards: W.K.H. Panofsky Prize (with H.W. Kendall & J.I. Friedman), Am. Physical Soc. (Div. Particles & Fields) 1989; Nobel Prize in Physics (with J.I. Friedman and H.W. Kendall) 1990; Home: 757 Mayfield Ave., Stanford, CA 94305; Office: P.O. Box 4349, Mail Stop 96, Stanford, CA 94309 U.S.A.

**TAYLOR, Robert Berkeley,** B.A., LL.D., F.C.A.; b. St. Thomas, Ont. 22 Sept. 1914; s. late Charles Berkeley and late Christine Elliot Bowes (Coyne) T.; e. St. Thomas (Ont.) Coll. Inst. (Sr. Matric. 1933); Univ. of Western Ont., B.A. 1941; McMaster Univ. LL.D. 1976; Univ. of Western Ont. LL.D. 1981; m. Marian Elizabeth, d. late Judge A. A. Ingram, St. Thomas, Ont., 13 Feb. 1943; children: Patricia, Margaret, Paul; began as Clerk, Dominion Bank, 1934–37; Faculty, Dept. of Business Adm., Univ. of W. Ont., 1941–42, 1945–49 (rank on leaving Assoc. Prof.); joined The Steel Co. of Canada 1949, Vice-Pres. and Treas. 1959–74; joined Ont. Hydro as Vice-Chrmn. 1974, Chrm. 1975–79; served in 2nd World War with Royal Candn. Navy (Lieut.) 1942–45; Dir., Engineering Interface Ltd.; past mem., Ont. Council on University Affairs; past mem. Ont. Econ. Council; Past mem. and Chrmn Bd. Govs. McMaster Univ.; Delta Upsilon; recreations: tennis, golf, skiing, fishing; Clubs: Toronto; Toronto Cricket; Home: 121 Beechwood Ave., Willowdale, Ont. M2L 1J8.

**TAYLOR, Ronald Wesley,** B.A.Sc., P.Eng., M.D.; medical doctor; b. Toronto, Ont. 13 Dec. 1937; s. Wesley Walter and Maude Elizabeth (Evans) T.; e. North Toronto C.I. 1956; Univ. of Toronto, B.A.Sc. (Hons.) 1961, M.D. 1977; m. Rona d. Roland and Shirley Douglas 26 Sept. 1981; children: Drew Wesley, Matthew Roland; FOUNDER & DIR., S.C. COOPER SPORTS MED. CLINIC, MT. SINAI HOSP. 1981– ; played major league baseball & pitched 500 major league games incl. World Series 1962–72 (world champ. St. Louis Cardinals 1964, New York Mets 1969); Team Physician, Toronto Blue Jays Baseball Club; Family practice, Toronto; Staff Physician, Mt. Sinai Hosp.; Lectr., Univ. of Toronto Med. Sch.; Mem., Candn. Baseball Hall of Fame 1985; Canada's Sports Hall of Fame 1993; Mem., Ont. Med. Assn.; Coll. of Family Physicians of Can. & of Ont.; Acad. of Med.; Assn. of Profl. Engrs. of Ont.; Assn. of Profl. Baseball Players of Am.; Assn. of Major League Baseball Team Physicians; recreations: skating, swimming, sailing, baseball; Clubs: Granite; Caduceus; Home: 3 Red Oaks Cres., Toronto, Ont. M4G 1A4; Office: 19 Alvin Ave., Toronto, Ont. M4T 2A7.

**TAYLOR, Stephen Ainsley,** B.A., F.S.A., F.C.I.A.; insurance executive; b. Belleville, Ont. 21 March 1945; s. Clarence Milton and Thelma 'Vivian' Muriel (Maracle) T.; e. Queen's Univ. B.A. 1967; m. Margaret d. Kenneth and Rose Dudley 3 Sept. 1966; children: Kevin, Lysa, Wendy; PRESIDENT & CHIEF EXTVE. OFFR., LUTHERAN LIFE INSURANCE SOC. OF CANADA 1990– ; Empire Life Insur. Co. 1967–74; Mgr. of Actuarial Services, Lutheran Life Insur. Soc. of Canada 1974–76; Asst. Actuary 1976–77; Vice-Pres. & Actuary 1977–88; Sr. Vice-Pres. & Actuary 1988–90; Sr. Vice-Pres. 1990; Bd. of Dir., Wilfrid Laurier Univ.; Mem., Rsch. Council, Life Office Mngt. Assn.; Mem., Bd. of Dir., Candn. Gospel Music Assn.; Mem., Bd. of Deacons of a 600-member church; Bd. of Gov., Lutherwood; F.S.A.; F.C.I.A.; recreations: music, sports, canoeing, camping; Home: 179 Golf Course Road, Conestoga, Ont. N0B 1N0; Office: 470 Weber St. N., Waterloo, Ont. N2J 4G4.

**TAYLOR, Stephen Joseph,** B.A.; business executive; b. Hamilton, Ont. 11 Apr. 1948; s. John Joseph and Mary Patricia (Brady) T.; e. Sir George Williams Univ., B.A. 1972; m. Bonnie Lee Williams 5 Sept. 1981; one s.: Stephen Joseph Linton; one d.: Cathrine Meredith Patricia; Pres. & Founder, Atien Enterprises Inc.; Mngt. Trainee, T. Eaton Co. 1972; Buyer, Men's Clothing (Mtl.) 1973; Merch. Mgr., All Men's Wear 1975; Vice-Pres., Merch., Crossley Karastan Carpets 1977; Atien produces men's skin care products & is largest and 1st. co. of its kind in Can.; Roman Catholic; recreations: tennis, Squash, skiing; Clubs: Toronto Lawn & Tennis; Montreal Badminton & Squash.

**TAYLOR, William E.;** investment counsellor; b. Toronto, Ont. 20 Nov. 1915; s. William and Lilliane (Ashton) T.; e. Duke of Connaught; Riverdale Collegiate 1927–32; m. Audrey d. Sara and Charles Emerson 7 June 1941; children: Wm. Robert, Joan Elizabeth; Pres. & Gen. Mgr., Wm. E. Taylor Canada Ltd.; Vice-Pres. & Sales Mgr., Marshalls Co. Ltd. 1933–53; Pres., WETCO Leasing 1976–83; WETCO Sanitation 1979–83; Past Chairman of the Board, Toronto East General Hospital (TEGH); Dir., TEGH Foundation; Vice-Chrmn., Hospital Council of Metro. Council; Past Dir., St. Lawrence Foods 1986–89; Black Diamond Cheese 1953–70; Brooke Bond 1971–74; Nat. Food Brokers of Am. 1981; Past Pres., Candn. Food Product Assn. 1972; Ont. Food Product Assn. 1968; Food Products Assn. 1965; Am. Food Product Assn. 1981; Past Grand Offr., Masonic AF&AM 1965; Past Warden, St. Aidans Anglican Ch.; St. Johns Norway Anglican Ch.; Trustee, St. Johns Norway Endowment Fund; Dir., St. Johns Norway Cemetery; recreations: golfing, boating; clubs: Toronto Bd. of Trade, Granite, Scarboro Golf & Country, Hunt, R.C.Y.C., JDM Country (Florida); Home: 10 Guildwood Parkway, PH23, Scarborough, Ont. M1E 5B5.

**TAYLOR, William E., Jr.,** A.M., Ph.D., F.R.A.I., F.R.G.S., F.S.A.S. (hons.), F.R.S.C., LL.D., D.Litt.; archaeologist; b. Toronto, Ont. 21 Nov. 1927; s. William E. and Margaret (Patrick) T.; e. Univ. of Toronto, B.A. 1951; Univ. of Ill., A.M. 1952; Univ. of Mich. Ph.D. 1965; LL.D. Univ. Calgary; D.Litt. Meml. Univ.; m. Joan Doris, d. John Elliott, Scarborough, Ont., 12 Sept. 1952; children: Alison, Beth, William E.; DIRECTOR EMERITUS, CANADIAN MUSEUM OF CIVILIZATION, Ottawa 1991– ; Pres., Social Sciences and Humanities Rsch. Counc. of Can. 1982–88; Dir., National Museum of Man. 1967–83; Dir., Candn. Centre for Anthrop. Research; Past Chrmn., Bd. Govs., Candn. War Museum; made several discoveries in Eskimo archaeol. between 1950 and 1966; author of 'The Arnapik and Tyara Sites' 1968; other writings incl. over 100 prof. papers in archaeol. mostly of Arctic Am.; Bd. mem. Museum of Archeology, U. of Western Ont.; Advisory Panel Comm. of Canadian Studies; Mem., Visiting Comm., The Glenbow Museum, Calgary; Research Comm., German Inst. of Archaeology, Bonn; Assoc. Mem., Medical Research Council of Can.; Mem., National Adv. Council on Sci. and Tech., Ottawa; Candn. Eskimo Arts Counc.; Ed. Bd. 'Journal of Canadian Studies' Trent Univ.; Res. Scholar, School of American Research, Sante Fe, New Mexico, 1977–78; Jury member, Guild of Northwest Coast Artists; Perm. Council mem., Internat. Union Anthrop. and Ethnol. Sciences and Internat. Union Prehist. & Protohist. Sciences; Fellow, Am. Assn. Advanc. Science; Ashley Fellow, Trent Univ. 1989; Fellow, Am. Anthrop. Assn.; Arctic Inst. N. Am.; Hon. Fellow Society of Antiquaries of Scotland; Hon. Fellow, Champlain College; Sigma XI; Unitarian; recreations: skiing, bicycling, reading; Home: 509 Piccadilly, Ottawa, Ont. K1Y 0H7; Office: Ottawa, Ont. K1A 0M8.

**TCHORZEWSKI, Hon. Edwin Laurence,** B.A., M.L.A.; politician; b. Alvena, Sask. 22 April 1943; s. Ezydor and Francis (Deptuch) T.; e. Hudson Bay Comp. H.S. 1962; Univ. of Sask. B.A. 1968; m. Shirley Ann d. Steve and Olga Stasiuk 6 Aug. 1966; children: Dion, Raquel, Sharla, Shaunda; DEPUTY PREMIER AND PROVINCIAL SECRETARY and MINISTER RESPONSIBLE FOR SASK TEL, GOVT. OF SASKATCHEWAN 1993– ; Teacher, Humboldt Roman Catholic Separate School Division 1965–67, 1968–71; 1st elected M.L.A. Humboldt constituency g.e. 1971; re-elected g.e. 1975, '78; defeated g.e. 1982; re-elected in by-election 1985, for Regina North East constituency g.e. 1986, '91; Minister of Culture & Youth 1971–77; Min. of Consumer Affairs & Prov. Secy. 1971–75; Min. of Edn. 1975–77; Min. of Continuing Edn. 1975–76; Min. of Health 1977–79; Min. of Finance 1979–82; Deputy Premier and Min. of Finance 1991–93; Roman Catholic, 4th Degree Knights of Columbus; NDP (Deputy Leader since 1989); recreations: curling, baseball, basketball, badminton, golf; Home: 3110 Parkland Dr. E., Regina, Sask. S4V 1E6; Office: Room 361, Legislative Bldg., Regina, Sask. S4S 0B3.

**TEAL, Joel Douglas,** B.Comm., M.B.; real estate executive; b. Saskatoon, Sask. 2 Apr. 1947; s. Harold Vernon and Claribel Laidley (Hicks) T.; e. Univ. of Saskatchewan B.Comm. 1969; m. Twila d. Bruce and Vivian Murray; one s.: Mark Douglas; PRES. & CHIEF EXTVE. OFFR., PRESTON DEVELOPMENTS INC. 1990– ; Dir., Saskatoon Economic Development Authority; Mem., Advisory Bd., Dynatek Automation Systems Inc.; various mngt. positions, Canada Mortgage & Housing Corp. 1969–75; Gen. Mgr., Cairns Devel. Inc. 1976–88; Extve. Vice-Pres., Boychuk Devel. Inc. 1989–90; recipient, Canadian Medal of Bravery; Homebuilder Member of the Year C.H.B.A. 1983; Mem., Candn. Home Builders Assn.; recreations: golf, curling, hunting, piano; clubs: Riverside Country (Dir.), Nutana Curling, Saskatoon; Home: 339 Whitewood Rd., Saskatoon, Sask. S7J 4K8; Office: 300, 2100 8th St. E., Saskatoon, Sask. S7H 0V1.

**TEATERO, Leo Vincent;** social activist; s. Leo James (dec.) and Francis Rose (Brown) T.; e. Carleton Univ.; TREASURER, BRUCE M. HICKS EDUCATION FOUNDATION 1993– ; Pres., Leo Teatero Holdings 1988–92; Admin. Asst., 'The Financial Post' Info. Serv. 1988–89; Co-Founder, Sec. & Membership Chair, Shefford Heritage Housing Co-op. 1989–92; Participation Chair 1992– ; Asst. Ed., 'The Financial Post' Dir. of Govt. 1989–90; Assoc. Ed. 1990–91; Tender Contract Clerk, Defence Construction Canada 1990; Co-ord. (Computers), Campaign to Elect Richard Cannings, 1991 Municipal Election; Admin. Asst., House of Commons 1991–93; Special Asst. 1993– ; Co-ord. (Computers), Liberals for Sidney Hicks 1992; Co-Founder, V.P. & Acct. Extve. (Municipalities), Candn. Parly. Serv. 1992–93; Fundraising Chair, ALGO 1992–93; Co-ord., Nat. Liberal Adv. Team 1993 Gen. Election; Treas., Gidney News & Pub. Limited 1993– ; Liberal; Home: 300 Cooper St., Ottawa, Ont. K2P 0G7; Foundation Office: P.O. Box 1450, Station B, Montreal, Que. H3B 2L2; House of Commons Office: 561, Confederation Bldg., Ottawa, Ont. K1A 0A6.

**TEDLIE, Maj.-Gen. Alfred James,** D.S.O., K. St. J., C.D., B.A., M.A. (hist.); b. Montreal, Que., March 1916; e. Sir George Williams Univ.; Candn. Army Staff Coll., Kingston, Nat. Defence Coll., Kingston; Univ. of Victoria; m. Margaret Mary Brown, Feb. 1940; children: Jane, Judith and Jennifer; enlisted 17th Duke of York's Candn. Hussars, 1939; Royal Montreal Regt. (Machine Gun), 1940; served in Brit. with 32 Reconnaissance Regt., Royal Candn. Armoured Corps 1941–44; later served in N.W. Europe with 28 Cdn. Armd. Regt.

(B.C.R.) and commanded 3rd Btn., Cameron Highlanders of Ottawa during occupation of Germany; following war served as Staff Offr., Army H.Q.; Commandant, Fort Churchill, Man., 1948–50; apptd. G.S.O. and Depy. Dir. of Mil. Training Army H.Q. 1950–54; Mil. Adviser, Mil. Component Candn. Del., Indochina, 1954–55; Chief of Staff, Prairie Command, Winnipeg 1956; Commandant, Royal Candn. Armoured Corps Sch., Camp Borden, 1958; Dir. of Armour, Army HQ, 1960; Dir. of Combat Devel., 1961; Commdr., 2nd Candn. Inf. Bgde. Group, Camp Petawawa, 1963; Commdr., Nicosia zone, U.N. Forces in Cyprus, 1964 and 4th Candn. Inf. Bgde. Group, Germany, Dec. 1964; Chief of Staff (Training) and Depy. Commdr., Training Command, 1966–68; Depy. Chief of Defence Staff for Force Devel. 1968–70, for Intelligence & Security for the Armed Forces 1970–Oct. 1971 when retired; B.C. Prov. Commr., St. John Ambulance Bgde. 1973–76, Depy. Chief Commr. for Can. 1976–81; recreations: golf; swimming; Clubs: R.U.S.I. of V.I.; Address: 2289 Adela Place, Sidney, B.C. V8L 1R1.

**TEED, Eric Lawrence,** O.C., C.D., Q.C., Kt.o.D.,B.Sc., B.C.L., B.A.; lawyer; b. Saint John, N.B. 19 May 1926; s. John Francis Hanington and Muriel Vivian (Wetmore) T.; e. Saint John High Sch. 1943; Univ. of N.B. B.Sc. 1947, B.C.L. 1949, B.A. 1972; m. Lois A. d. Ebenezer and Wilda Smith Aug. 1949; children: Robert C.G., Peter E.L., J.P. Christopher, Terrence L.S., David D.G.; SR. PARTNER, TEED, TEED & BROWN; called to Bar of N.B. 1949; cr. Master of Supreme Court 1958; cr. Q.C. 1966; commenced law practice family firm (estbd. 1884) in 1949; lectr. environmental law, municipal law, labour law, civil liberties law Univ. N.B. Saint John Campus; Mayor, City of Saint John 1960–62, 1962–64; served as M.L.A. of N.B. 1970–74; Comnr. of Inquiry into Municipal Labour Relations in N.B. 1986; Hon. Consul of Denmark; awarded Kt. Order of Dannebrog; awarded Candn. Forces Decoration; recipient Queen's Silver Jubilee Medal 1977; Officer, Order of Canada 1987; Commemorative Medal for 125th Anniversary of Candn. Confederation; Nat. Scout Medal of Merit for services to Scout movement, 35 yrs. Scout service Medal, Hon. Counsel for Prov.; Citizenship Merit Award Candn. Citizenship Fed. (Past Nat. Pres.); mem. Nat. Extve. Ctte.; served with Candn. Militia, rank Capt. Royal N.B. Regt.; author 'Canada's First City' 1963; 'Handbook for Commissioner of Oaths' 1964; numerous legal and non-legal articles and book reviews; ed. N.B. Hist. Soc. Colls.; Founding Ed. Univ. of N.B. Law Journal; past Prov. Ed. Candn. Bar Review; past Gov. Univ. of N.B.; Past Pres., N.B. Hist. Soc.; Founding mem. and Past Pres. Saint John Br. John Howard Soc.; founding mem., Elizabeth Fry Soc.; Dir., Candn. Criminal Justice Assn. (Past Pres., N.B. Chapt.); Past Pres. Saint John Br. Candn. Cancer Soc.; Past Pres. Animal Rescue League; Historian and Past Pres., St. George's Soc. Saint John; past mem. Council Saint John Bd. Trade; Hon. mem. Bricklayers, Masons & Plasterers Internat. Union; Del., Commonwealth Law Conf. Delhi 1971, Edinburgh 1976, Hong Kong 1983; Past Chrmn., Internat. Assn. Penal Law; 1st Nat. Chrmn. jt. Legal-Med. Comte. Candn. Bar and Candn. Med. Assn.; Chrmn. Special Candn. Bar Comte. on Parole; mem. Saint John Law Soc. (former Council Mem.); Law Soc. of N.B.; Candn. Bar Assn. (Council); past Nat. Chrmn.: Young Lawyers Conf.; Criminal Law Sec.; Labour Law Sec.; Civil Liberties Sect., National Secy. Wills & Trusts Section; Mem. & Past Chrmn. National Legal Aid Liaison Comte.; Past Chrmn., Employment Law Ctte.; Candn. Bar Assn.; Section Co-ordinator, N.B. Branch Candn. Bar Assn.; past mem. Provincial Legal Aid Adv. Ctte.; past mem., Legal Aid Ctte., N.B. Law Soc.; past mem. Uniform Law Commissioners of Can.; Past Chrmn., Citizens Advisory Ctte., Correctional Services of Canada; Nat. Dir. Candn. Civil Liberties Assn.; Past Pres. Saint John Charter Rights Civil Liberties Assn.; Sec., N.B. Human Rights Assn., Past Pres., Multicultural Assn. of Saint John; Vice Pres., N.B. Multicultural Council; Vice-Pres., Atlantic Multicultural Council; past Dir., Candn. Rights and Liberties Fedn.; Atlantic Vice Pres., Arbiters Inst. Can.; Pres. N.B. Branch and Vice-Pres. Atlantic Region, United Nations Assn. of Can.; Chrmn., Saint John Canada Day Ctte.; Chrmn., N.B. World Food Day Ctte.; Chrmn., Loyalist City Festival; Dir. Anderson-McTague & Associates; past Mem. of Senate, Univ. of N.B.; past mem., Saint John Senate, Univ. of N.B.; Dir., Saint John College Development Inc.; Past Pres., Univ. of N.B. Alumni (Saint John Chapt.); Vice Pres., Saint John Horticultural Assn.; mem., Rockwood Park Advisory Board; Freemason (P.M.); Anglican (past mem. Diocesan Synod); recreations: hiking, camping, canoeing, fishing; Clubs: Union; Chisholm Lake Fishing; Home: 1019 Seawood Lane, Saint John, N.B. E2M 3G8; Office: 127 Prince William St., PO Box 6639, Stn. A, Saint John, N.B. E2L 4S1.

**TEES, Miriam Hadley,** M.L.S.; librarian; educator; b. Montreal, Que. 24 Feb. 1923; d. Frederick James and Beatrice Mary (Armstrong) T.; e. McGill Univ. B.A. 1944, B.L.S. 1951, M.L.S. 1975; Assoc. Prof., Grad. Sch. of and Information Studies, McGill Univ. 1979–88; now retired; Lib., McGill Univ. Med. Lib. 1951; Internat. Civil Aviation Organ. 1951–53; Chief Lib. The Royal Bank of Canada 1953–79; mem. Comn. des bibliothèques publiques de la Prov. de Qué. 1974–78; Nat. Comte. on Liturgy Un. Ch. Can. 1980–86; author various articles librarianship; Fellow, Special Libs. Assn. (N.Y., Pres. 1975–76); Corp. des Bibliothécaires professionnels du Qué. (Pres. 1971–72); Internat. Fed. Lib. Assns. (Chair, Lib. Schs. Sec. and Div. Education & Research; Mem., Prof. Bd. 1987–89); Am. Library Assn, Comte. on Accreditation 1982–84; United Church; recreations: early music, choir, gardening; Home: 24 Holton Ave., Westmount, Que. H3Y 2E8.

**TEES, Richard Chisholm,** B.A., Ph.D.; university professor and administrator; b. Montréal, Qué. 31 Oct. 1940; s. Ralph C. and Winnifred H. (Chisholm) T.; e. McGill Univ., B.A. 1961; Univ. of B.C., Ph.D. 1965; m. Kathleen d. Edmund and Dorothy Coleman 1 Sept. 1962; children: Susan, Carolyn; PROF. & HEAD, DEPT. OF PSYCHOL., UNIV. OF B.C. 1984– ; Asst. Prof., Univ. of B.C. 1965–69; Assoc. Prof. 1969–74; Prof. 1975– ; Vis. Rsch. Prof., Univ. of Sussex 1972–73, 1977–78; Mem., Candn. Psychol. Assn.; Inter. Soc. Develop. Psychobiol.; Am. Psychol. Assn.; Psychonomic Soc.; Soc. Neuroscience; Sigma Xi; Exper. Psychol. Soc. (Hon. Fgn. Mem.); fellowships: Can. Counc. 1972–73, Killam Sr. Rsch. 1971–73, 1978–79; Rsch. Prof., Univ. of Sussex 1978–79; Fellow, Candn. Psychol. Assn. 1980; Fellow, Am. Psychol. Assn.; Fellow, Am. Psychol. Soc.; Mem., Grants Panel, NSERC, MRC, B.C. Health Found.; U.B.C. Senate; author: 'Cerebral Cortex of Rat' and approx. 60 scholarly articles & invited chapters; recreations: skiing, sailing; Clubs: UBC Faculty; Jericho; Sailing; Home: 1856 Acadia Rd., Vancouver, B.C. V6T 1R3; Office: Dept. of Psychol., Univ. of B.C., Vancouver, B.C. V6T 1Z4.

**TEFS, Wayne A.,** B.A., M.A., Ph.D.; writer, teacher; b. St. Boniface, Man. 17 Nov. 1947; s. Armin Alexander and Stella (Spelchak) T.; e. Univ. of Manitoba B.A. (Hons.) 1970; Univ. of Toronto M.A. 1971, Ph.D. 1978; one s.: Andrew Armin; WRITER; Lectr., Univ. of Regina 1971–74; St. John's College 1975–78; Teacher, St. John's-Ravenscourt School 1978–92; freelance writer 1975– ; Fiction Columnist, 'Border Crossings' 1988– ; reviews in mags., articles in newspapers & mags. on divers subjects; short stories in mags.; freelance editor for lit. publishers; Contbr. Ed., 'Broder Crossings' 1985– ; Founding Editor, 'The Sphinx' 1974; Turnstone Press 1975; Pachyderm Press 1991; jury member for prairie arts bodies; author: 'Figures on a Wharf' (Books in Canada First Novel Prize nom.) 1983, 'The Cartier Street Contract' 1985, 'The Canasta Players' (McNally Robinson Manitoba Book Prize nom.) 1990, 'Dickie' 1993 (novels); editor: 'Made in Manitoba' 1990; 'Hearts Wild' 1993; Western Magazine Fiction Prize for short story 'Red Rock and After' 1989; recreations: hockey, tennis; Home and Office: 191 Wildwood Park, Winnipeg, Man. R3T 0E2.

**TEICHROB, Hon. Carol;** business person; b. Saskatchewan 27 Aug. 1939; d. J. Delbert and Elizabeth (Spenst) Sproxton; e. Notre Dame Convent H.S.; Univ. of Sask. Profl. Court Reporter; m. Donald P. s. John and Aganetha T. 1 March 1958; children: Lori, Sharon, James; Education Minister, Govt. of Saskatchewan 1992; Dir., V.I.D.O. 1980–86; Sask. Rsch. Council 1983–91 Farm Credit Corp. 1980–83; Candn. Egg Marketing Agency 1986–91; Extve. Mem., Can. & Sask. Federations of Agriculture 1976–81; Chair, Candn. Turkey Mktg. Agency 1980–81; Plains Poultry Ltd. 1981–88; Reeve, R.M. of Corman Park, Sask. 1981–91; Senate, Univ. of Sask. 1981–86; Mem., Saskatoon C. of C. 1980– ; Founding Partner, Primrose Books Inc. 1988– ; Partner, Amberlea Farm Ltd. & Moonvale Farms; YWCA Saskatoon Woman of the Year Award (Business) 1981; Saskatoon Rotary Club, Golden Wheel Award for Excellence in Business & Industry 1990; Address: 10B, 234 Primrose Dr., Saskatoon, Sask. S7K 6Y6.

**TEITEL, Jerome,** M.D., F.R.C.P.(C); physician; educator; b. Toronto, Ont. 15 June 1949; s. Irvin and Rose (Hauer) T.; e. Univ. of Toronto, M.D. 1973; m. Patricia L. d. Kenneth and Virginia Leary 4 Apr. 1981; one d. Amy Shira; PHYSICIAN, DIV. OF HEMATOL. DEPT. OF MED. ST. MICHAEL'S HOSP. 1981– ; Asst. Prof. of Med. Univ. of Toronto 1983– , Lectr. 1981–83; Assoc. Dir. Toronto & Central Ont. Regional Comprehensive Hemophilia Prog. 1983– ; Rsch. Assoc. Sidney Farber Cancer Inst. Harvard Univ. 1978–81; Med. Rsch. Council Can., Heart & Stroke Found. Ont. Rsch. Fellowships & Grants 1979– ; prin. or co-author over 29 sci. publs.; mem. Candn. Hemophilia Soc. (Med. & Sci. Adv. Ctte. Ont. Chapter 1983– , Med. Dir. Ont. Chapter 1986– , Chrmn. MSAC Info. Subctte. 1987– ); mem. Beach Hebrew Inst. Toronto; Office: 30 Bond St., Toronto, Ont. M5B 1W8.

**TELEGDI, Andrew Peter,** B.A., M.P.; politician; b. Budapest 28 May 1946; s. Alexander Sandor and Elenora Maria (Friedrich) T.; e. Royal York Collegiate 1966; Univ. of Waterloo B.A. 1980; m. Nancy Curtin-Telegdi d. James and Madeline Curtin 28 Dec. 1985; one child: Erin; MEMBER OF PARLIAMENT FOR WATERLOO 1993– ; Extve. Dir, Youth in Conflict with the Law 1976–93; Co-ord., Justice Week, Waterloo Region 1979– ; Pres., Fed. of Students, Univ. of Waterloo 1973–75; City of Waterloo Councillor 1985–93; Regional Mun. of Waterloo Councillor 1988–93; Vice-chair & Regional Licencing Ctte.; Regional Finance & Admin. Ctte.; Regional Health & Social Serv. Ctte.; Chair, Reg. Water Sub-ctte.; Mem., Reg. Engr. Ctte.; Initiator & Mem., Mayor's Race Relations Ctte.; Waterloo Reg. Crime Prevention & Community Safety Ctte.; Mem., Waterloo Reg. Social Resources Council; Senate & Senate Extve. Mem., Univ. of Waterloo 1973–75; Mem., Bd. of Gov., Wilfrid Laurier Univ. 1990–93; Bd. Mem., The Working Centre & St. John's Soup Kitchen 1986– ; Kitchener House 1979– ; Pres., K.W. Multicultural Centre 1987–89; Chair, Conestoga College Basic Job Readiness Training Advisory Group 1980–84; Mem., Clin. Adv. Ctte. for Catholic Family Counselling Centre 1986–87; Chair, People Working and Learning Inc. 1984–86; Home: 275 Lincoln Rd., Waterloo, Ont. N2J 2P6; Office: 22 King St. S., Waterloo, Ont. N2J 1N9.

**TELFER, Ian William,** B.A., M.B.A., C.A.; business executive; b. Oxford, Eng. 19 March 1946; s. John Deans and Isobel (Livingston) T.; e. Univ. of Toronto, B.A. 1968; Univ. of Ottawa, M.B.A. 1976; C.A. 1978; m. Nancy Anne d. Joseph and Joanne Burke 23 Oct. 1976; two s. John Burke, Bradley James; PRES. & DIR., VENEZUELA GOLDFIELDS LTD. 1993– ; Exec. Vice-Pres. & Dir., TVX Gold Inc. 1983–93; recreations: tennis, skiing, golf; Clubs: Granite Club; Beacon Hall Golf; Home: 5524 Parthenon Place, West Vancouver, B.C. V7W 2V7.

**TELFER, Nancy Ellen,** B.A., B.Mus.; composer; b. Brampton, Ont. 8 May 1950; d. James N. and Margaret Jean (Duff) Lindsey; e. Univ. of Western Ont. B.A. 1971, B.Mus. 1979; London Teachers' College 1972; m. Stuart Beaudoin 20 March 1981; children: David, Michael; Teacher 1972–76; Composer of Classical Music 1979– ; Assistant Prof., Univ. of Western Ont. 1991; Guest Lectr., Summer Kodaly Course, UWO 1990–92; frequently invited as a clinician or guest conductor thorughout N. America; music is performed & broadcast in many parts of the world; author: 'Contemporary Warmups' 1985, 'Successful Sightsinging' Book 1 1992 and Book 2 1993 (textbooks); over 100 individual octavos & short books of music published in Canada & U.S. 1980– ; Home: 629 Queen St., Newmarket, Ont. L3Y 2J1.

**TELLIER, Bernard Robert;** financial executive; b. Joliette, Que. 20 Aug. 1928; s. Maurice and Marie-Eva (Bouvier) T.; m. Colette Lamothe; SR. VICE-PRES. and DIR., RICHARDSON GREENSHIELDS OF CANADA LIMITED; chief extve. offr. & controlling shareholder of an engineering & mining equipment co. 1952–63; owner, real estate redevel. firm 1963–69; joined Corp. Finan. Dept. of present firm 1969; Mem., Extve. Ctte.; Dir., Sico Inc.; Former Gov., Montreal Stock Exchange; Gov., Candn. Securities Inc.; Office: 4 Place Ville Marie, Montreal, Que. H3B 2E8.

**TELLIER, Lt.-Gen. Henri,** D.S.O., C.M., C.D.; retired; b. Montreal, Que. 1 Sept. 1918; s. Henry Joseph and Jeanne(St. Cyr) T.; e. St. Leo's Academy, Westmount, Que.; University of Montreal 1935–40; Univ. of Ottawa 1946–47; Candn. Army Staff Coll. 1942–43; Imp. Defence Coll., London, Eng. 1966; Dept. of Defence Computor Inst., Washington, D.C. (Sr. Business Mang. Course), 1968; m. Virginia Ann Wright, 23 July 1945; children: Pierre, Michele, Suzanne, John, Nicole; commnd. in C.O.T.C. Univ. of Montreal 1940; served with Le Regt. de Joliette, Le Regt. de la Chaudiere, Le Royal 22e Regt., in Can., U.K., Mediterranean Theatre and N.W. Europe as both Commdr. of troops and staff offr.; awarded D.S.O., C.M., C.D., Queen's Medal (Netherlands); Commander, Order of Merit, Italy; Mentioned in Despatches; Officer, Order of the Red Cross; Asst. Mil. Secy. to Min. of Nat. Defence 1945–

48; C.O. Royal 22e Regt. 1948–51; Instr., Candn. Army Staff Coll. 1951–54; Army mem., Jt. Intelligence Staff, 1954–57; Mil. Adviser, Viet Nam 1957–58; Chief of Staff, Quebec Mil. Dist. 1958–60; Mil. Attaché, Rome, Italy 1960–63; Dir. Mil. Operations and Plans, Army 1963–64; Dir. Internat. Plans 1964–65; Commdr. Candn. Contingent, Cyprus 1965–66; Dir. Gen. Plans, 1966–69; Vice Chief Plans 1969–71; Candn. Mil. Rep. to NATO Brussels, 1971–73; retired Nov. 1973; Assoc. Nat. Comnr., Candn. Red Cross Soc. 1973, 1975, Nat. Comnr. Jan. 1975, 1982; Secretary General 1982–83, Private mem., Refugee Status Adv. Comte 1984–88; Hon. Vice Pres. Candn. Red Cross Soc.; member Mil. Co-op Comte.-Can.-U.S. (Chrmn. Candn. Sec.); Commr., Comn. for Strategic and Internat. Studies; mem. Perm. Jt. Bd. on Defence-Can.-U.S.; mem. Candn. Inst. Internat. Affairs; Assn. Roy. 22e Regt.; mem. U.N. Assn. in Can.; mem. Adv. Counc., Candn. Exec. Service Organization (C.E.S.O.); mem. Candn. Soc. of Assn. Execs.; mem. Empire Club of Can.; R. Catholic; recreations: aquatic sports, cycling; Address: 19 Bay Hill Ridge, Stittsville, Ont. K2S 1B9.

**TELLIER, Paul M.,** P.C., C.C., Q.C., LL.L., B.Litt.; executive; b. Joliette, Que. 8 May 1939; s. late Maurice and late Eva (Bouvier) T.; e. Univ. of Ottawa B.A. 1959, LL.L. 1962; Oxford Univ. B.Litt. 1966; m. Andree d. Jean-Paul Poirier 6 June 1959; children: Claude, Marc; PRES. & C.E.O., CANDN. NATIONAL RAILWAYS 1992– ; Apptd. Secy. to Cabinet for Federal Prov. Relations 1991–92; Chrmn., Governing Bd., International Energy Agency 1985; Dir. Petro Canada 5 yrs.; Atomic Energy of Canada Ltd. 3 yrs.; called to Bar of Que. 1963; Asst. Prof. of Law, Univ. of Montreal 1966–67; Extve. Asst. to Min. of Energy, Mines & Resources Ottawa 1967–68; Privy Council Office. Constitutional Review, Ottawa 1968, Asst. Secy. to Cabinet 1968–70; Depy. Clerk to Cabinet, Extve. Council, Govt. of Que. 1970–72; Dir. Gen. Urban Policy Br. Ministry of State for Urban Affairs, Ottawa 1972–73; Extve. Dir., Pub. Service Comn. Ottawa 1974–75; Sr. Asst. Depy. Min. of Fisheries and the Environment 1976; Depy. Secy. to Cabinet (coordination) Fed.-Prov. Relations Office 1977–79; Depy. Min. of Indian and Northern Devel., 1979–82; Depy. Min. of Energy, Mines and Resources 1982–85; Clerk of the Privy Council and Secretary to the Cabinet, 1985–92; apptd. Q.C. 1981; apptd., Queen's Privy Council 1992; elected Companion of the Order of Canada 1993; author various articles on pub. adm.; mem. Inst. Pub. Adm.; R. Catholic; recreations: squash, skiing, tennis; Home: 458 Wood Ave., Westmount, Que. H3Y 3J2; Office: Lagauchetière St., Box 8100, Montreal, Que. H3C 3N4.

**TELMER, Frederick H.,** B.A., M.A.; steel executive; b. Edmonton, Alta. 28 Dec. 1937; s. Ingar and Gertrude (Floen) T.; e. Univ. of Alta., B.A. 1961, M.A. 1964; m. Margaret d. Frank and Margaret Hutchings 30 Oct. 1959; children: Christopher, Kevin, Colin; CHRMN. AND C.E.O., STELCO INC. 1991– ; joined Stelco Inc. 1963; trans. from Ind. Relations Dept. to Mktg. Div., where held var. mgmt. positions prior to becoming Gen. Mgr., Field Sales 1982; Gen. Mgr., Corp. Affairs & Strategic Planning 1984; Vice Pres., Corp. Affairs & Strategic Planning 1985; Pres., Stelco Steel 1988–90; Bd. of Dirs., Stelco Inc. 1989– ; Dir., INCO Ltd.; CT Financial Services Inc.; Am. Iron and Steel Inst.; Internat. Iron and Steel Institute; Founding Dir., The Japan Society; mem., Bd. of Govs., McMaster Univ., Hamilton; recreations: tennis, golf, skiing, cycling, piano, woodworking; Clubs: Hamilton; Toronto; Hamilton Golf & Country; Burlington Golf & Country; Home: 4451 Lakeshore Rd., Burlington, Ont. L7L 1B3; Office: P.O. Box 2030, Hamilton, Ont. L8N 3T1.

**TEMPLE, Chris,** A.O.C.A.; artist; b. Ajax, Ont. 18 June 1957; s. Alan George and Jean Emily (Brothwell) T.; e. St. Michael's Coll. Sch. 1976; Ontartio College of Art A.O.C.A. 1981; m. Nadia d. Dr. Sol and Hajira Boorany 28 June 1980; one s.: Mackenzie; professional painter since 1982; solo exhibitions: Gallery 76 Toronto 1981; Bau Xi Gallery Toronto 1982, '83, '85, '86, '88; Waddington and Shiell Toronto 1989; Mira Godard Gallery Toronto 1991; collection highlights (public): Corp. of the City of Toronto; Canada Council Art Bank; Carleton Univ.; Univ. of Toronto; Peel Bd. of Edn.; (corporate): Imperial Oil, Maclean Hunter Publishing, Toronton Sun Publishing, Xerox Canada; Bell Canada; Sun Life; Crown Life; First City Financial Corp.; Home: 6 Neepawa Ave., Toronto, Ont. M6R 1V2.

**TEMPLE, David J.,** B.Sc.; business executive; b. Oshawa, Ont. 23 May 1945; s. Herbert W. and Jessie W. (Cunliffe) T.; e. Leaside H.S. 1964; Univ. of Guelph, B.Sc. 1968; m. Lynne M. d. William A. and Bernice Taylor 29 Nov. 1969; PRES. & CHIEF EXTVE. OFFR., CANPLAS INDUS. LTD. 1984– ; Gen. Mgr., Gen. Steel Wares, Bldg. Prod. Div. 1972–78; Canplas Indus. Ltd. 1978–80; Vice-Pres. 1980–84; Dir., Forsco Ind.; Barrie Dist. C. of C.; Dir., Barrie Royal Victoria Hosp.; recreations: golf, sports, hunting; Club: Nat. Golf Club, Woodbridge; Home: 16 Royal Oak Dr., Barrie, Ont. L4M 4S6; Office: 31 Patterson Rd., Barrie, Ont. L4N 3V9.

**TEMPLE, Walley John,** M.D., FRCS(C), FACS; university professor; b. Ann Arbor, Mich. 8 May 1946; s. Victor Clarence and Marna (Walley) T.; e. Queen's Univ., M.D. 1970; m. Doreen Helen d. Willet Jay and Kathleen Farley Sept. 1966; children: Larissa, Claire, Philip, Martha; DIR. OF SURGERY, TOM BAKER CANCER CTR. 1983– & PROF., DEPT. OF SURGERY, UNIV. OF CALGARY 1988– ; Royal Coll. Fellowship in Gen. Surgery 1976; Surgical Oncology Fellowship 1978–80; Fellowship, Am. Coll. of Surgeons 1979 and 1989; Asst./Assoc. Prof., Dept. of Surgery, Univ. of Miami 1980–83; Chief, Div. of Surg. Oncol., Univ. of Calgary 1983– ; of General Surgery 1986–92; Dir., Gen. Surg. Residency Training Prog., present univ. 1986–91; Mem., Am. Radium Soc. Extve. Counc. 1988–90; NCIC Extve. Ctte. for Clinical Trials 1986–89; Chrmn., Local Rsch. Assessment Ctte. Funding, Alta. Cancer Bd. 1988–90; James IV Surgical Traveller for 1987; Vice Pres., World Federation of Surgical Oncology Societies; Mem., Soc. of Surg. Oncol.; Soc. of Head & Neck Surgeons; of Pelvic Surgeons; Candn. Oncol. Soc.; Candn. Assn. of Clin. Surgeons; of Gen. Surgeons; Pres., Candn. Soc. of Surgical Oncology 1991–93; Examiner for Royal College of Physicians and Surgeons of Canada for General Surgery; author/co-author of 68 med. articles & 4 book chapters; recreations: equestrian sports, canoeing, sailing; Home: Box 19, RR 12, Site 22, Calgary, Alta. T3E 6W3; Office: 1331 – 29 St. N.W., Calgary, Alta. T2N 4N2.

**TEMPLETON, Carson Howard,** O.C., B.Sc., L.L.D., D.E.S.; professional engineer; b. Wainwright, Alta. 9 Sept. 1917; s. Ellen Florence (Porteous) and late Samuel Howard T.; e. Central Coll. Inst., Calgary, Alta. (Sr. Matric.); Univ. of Alberta, B.Sc. (Applied Science) 1943; Alberta Inst. of Technol. (Dipl.); hon. L.L.D., Univ. of Man. 1982; hon. D.E.S., Univ. of Waterloo 1983; m. Laurie Jean, d. late Rory MacLachlan, 29 April 1948; children: Colleen, Neil; PRES., C.H. TEMPLETON & ASSOC., (consulting Engrs.); Pres., Northern Environment Foundation; Chrmn., Alaska Hwy. Pipeline Panel 1975–81; Dir., Winnipeg Children's Hosp. 1958–81; Dir., Canada-West Foundation; Chrmn. of Environmental Impact Review Bd. for Western Arctic 1986–89 (set up by the Invialuit Land Claims Settlement); Vice Chrmn., Bd. of Govs., Univ. of Man. 1968–71; Pres. (1968–69) Assn. of Consulting Engrs. of Canada; began engn. experience in the field in Yukon and N.W.T.; subsequently Asst. Chief Engr. of Fraser Valley Dyking Bd., Chief Engr. of Winnipeg Dyking Bd., Dir. (1956) of Greater Winnipeg Flood Protection Comte., Found. of Templeton Eng. Co. and Teshmont Consult. Inc.; mem., Assns. of Prof. Engrs. of B.C., Manitoba, Alta.; Fellow, Engn. Inst. Can.; recipient, Gold Medal, Candn. Council of Professional Engineers 1989; Protestant; Home: 4969 Georgia Park Terrace, Victoria, B.C. V8Y 2B8.

**TEMPLETON, Charles B.,** D.D.; broadcaster, author; b. Toronto, Ont. 7 Oct. 1915; s. William Loftus T.; e. Parkdale Coll. Inst., Toronto, Ont., 1927–31; Princeton Theol. Semy., 1948–51; Lafayette Coll., D.D. 1953; m. Madeleine, d. late Leroy DesBrisay Stevens, 21 Dec. 1980; children: Deborah A., Michael D., Bradley S., Tyrone M.; Sports Cartoonist, Toronto 'Globe & Mail' 1932–36; o. Ch. of the Nazarene 1938; Minister, Avenue Rd. Ch., Toronto, Ont. 1941–48; Secy. of Evangelism, Nat. Council of the Churches of Christ, U.S.A. 1952–54; Host: 'Look Up and Live,' CBS television network 1952–55; Dir. of Evangelism, Presbyterian Ch. USA 1955–57; moderator, performer many CBC, CTV-TV programs 1957–72; Exec. Managing Ed. 'Toronto Star' 1959–64; resigned to contest Liberal Party Leadership in Ont. (def.); Vice-Pres., Liberal Party of Ont. 1964–65; Pres., Technamation Canada Ltd. 1966; Dir., News and Public Affairs CTV Television Network 1967–69; 'Dialogue' (with Pierre Berton) CFRB 1964–66, CKEY 1966–83; B'nai B'rith Award 1967; ACTRA award 'Integrity and Outspokeness in Broadcasting' 1972; ACTRA Award, 'Best Public Affairs Broadcaster: Radio' 1978; Editor, Maclean's Mag. 1969; has had numerous plays performed on CBC, BBC and Aust. Broadcasting Corp.; author: 'Life Looks Up' 1953; 'Evangelism for Tomorrow' 1954; 'Jesus-His Life' 1973; 'The Kidnapping of the President' (novel) 1975; 'Act of God' (novel) 1977; 'The Third Temptation' (novel) 1980; 'An Anecdotal Memoir' 1983; 'The Queen's Secret' (novel) 1986; 'World of One' (novel) 1988; 'Succeeding' 1989; 'Succeeding - What it Takes' (Audio book) 1990; 'End Back Attacks' 1991; Inventor: two Candn., one US patent; recipient, 125th Anniversary of the Confederation of Canada Medal, 1992; recreations: reading, sculpting, drawing, conversation; Address: 701 Don Mills Rd., Apt. 2600, Toronto, Ont. M3C 1R9.

**TEMPLETON, Ian Malcolm,** M.A., D.Phil., F.R.S.C., F.Inst.P.; research physicist; b. Rugby, Eng. 31 July 1929; s. late William and late Eleanor Clayton (Butcher) T.; e. Rugby (Eng.) Sch.; Univ. Coll. Oxford Univ. M.A. 1950, D.Phil. 1953; m. Elsa d. late John Victor Wood, Sedbergh, Eng. 11 Aug. 1956; children: Nicola Jean, Jennifer Jane; PRINC. RESEARCH OFFR., NAT. RESEARCH COUNCIL OF CAN. since 1971, Head Electronic Structure & Calorimetry Group 1976–87; Postdoctoral Fellow, Physics Div. Nat. Research Council of Can. 1953–54, Asst. Research Offr. 1957–60, Assoc. Research Offr. 1960–64, Sr. Research Offr. 1964–71, Jt. Head Metal Physics Group 1969–76; Staff mem. Research Lab. Associated Electrical Industries, Rugby, Eng. 1955–57; author over 90 scient. papers low temperature metal physics, focussed ion beam processing; mem. Candn. Assn. Physicists; Home: 17 Dunvegan Rd., Ottawa, Ont. K1K 3E8; Office: Ottawa, Ont. K1A 0R6.

**TEMPLETON, Robert Bruce,** C.L.U., C.H.F.C.; insurance executive; b. Toronto, Ont. 4 Aug. 1937; s. Robert and Olive Marjorie (Harrison) T.; e. Weston Coll. Inst. 1956; Ryerson Inst. of Technol. 1959 (Gold Medal Mdse. Adm.); C.L.U. 1966; C.H.F.C. 1989; children: Patricia, Susan, Kelly, Robin, Jonathan; BR. MGR. PRUDENTIAL ASSURANCE 1970– ; joined present Co. as Agt. 1961, Asst. Mgr. 1965; Dir. Life Underwriters Assn. Toronto 1970–78, Pres. 1977; Chrmn. Ont. Sales Cong. 1978; Dir. Life Underwriters Assn. Can. 1977– , Vice Chrmn. 1984–85, Chrmn. & Chief Exec. Offr. 1986–87, Past Chrmn. 1988–89; Pres. Toronto Unit Candn. Cancer Soc. 1977–78; recreations: farming, fishing; Home: 11 Glamis Pl., Thornhill, Ont. L3T 3G7; Office: Suite 800, 251 Consumers Rd., Willowdale, Ont. M2J 4R3.

**TENACE, Louis M.,** B.A.; public servant; e. Univ. of Ottawa B.A. 1960; Queen's Univ. Ont. Teaching Cert. 1961; m. Michèle Gaudreau; children: Lisa Ann, Michael Anthony; VICE CHAIRMAN, PUBLIC SERVICE STAFF RELATIONS BOARD 1990– ; School Teacher 1961–70; joined federal public service 1970; held a variety of progressively senior positions in personnel & labour relations with depts. of Industry, Trade and Commerce, Nat. Defence, Transport & the Treasury Bd. Secretariat 1970–78; Supt. of Personnel, Ottawa Bd. of Edn. 1978–84; Dir. of Collective Bargaining, Staff Relations Br., Treasury Bd. 1984–85; Dep. Sec. 1985–90; Office: Box 1525, Stn. B., Ottawa, Ont. K1P 5V2.

**TEN CATE, Arnold Richard,** B.Sc., Ph.D., B.D.S., D.Sc.(Hon) McGill, D.Sc.(Hon) UWO; educator; b. Accrington, Lancs., Eng. 21 Oct. 1933; s. Gijs Johan Ten Cate; e. London Hosp. Med. Coll. Univ. of London B.Sc. 1955; Ph.D. (Anat.) 1957, B.D.S. 1960; m. Alice Annie d. Charles Mitchell, Markham, Ont. 7 Apl. 1956; children: Pauline Ann, Jill Elaine, Ian Richard; PROFESSOR OF DENTISTRY, UNIV. OF TORONTO 1994– ; Chair, About Face; Leverhulme Fellow, Royal Coll. of Surgs. London 1961–63; Sr. Lectr. (Anat.) Guy's Hosp. Univ. of London 1963–68; Prof. Univ. of Toronto 1968, Prof. and Chrmn. Biol. Sciences (Dent.) 1971–77; Dean, Faculty of Dentistry, Univ. of Toronto 1977–89; Vice-Provost, Health Sciences, Univ. of Toronto 1989–94; rec'd Colyer Prize Royal Soc. med. 1962; Milo Hellman Award Am. Assn. Orthodontists 1975; Isaac Schour Mem. Award Internat. Assn. Dental Research 1978; author 'Oral Histology: Development, Structure & Function' 1994 (4th ed.); co-author 'Techniques in Photomicroscopy' 1963; 'Advances in Dental Histology' 4th ed. 1983; over 70 scient. papers, articles and chapters; Pres. Internat. Assn. Dental Research 1984; P. Conservative; recreation: cottaging; Home: 50 Squire Bakers Lane, Markham, Ont. L3P 3G9; Office: Rm. 222 Simcoe Hall, 27 King's College Circle, Toronto, Ont. M5S 1A1.

**TENISON, Robert Blake;** executive; b. Houston, Texas, 26 Jan. 1924; s. Jack R. and Auban (Blake) T.; e. Univ. of Texas, 1942–46; m. Willie Mae; children: Robert B. Jr., William B., John Thomas, Susan; PRES. & C.E.O., TENISON OIL CO. 1989– ; Chrmn., Triton Canada Resources Ltd. 1967–89; Pres., Triton Oil & Gas Corp. 1986–89; Dir. and Extve. Vice Pres., Triton Energy Corp. 1986–89; Operations Mgr. for Independent Oil Operator Texas and Okla., 1947–51; Independent Oil Operator and Drilling Contractor, Texas, Colo., Mont., Wyo. and N. Dak., 1951–59; Vice Pres., Consolidated Oil & Gas, Inc., Denver, 1959–67; joined Worldwide Energy Corp. Co. (then Cold Lake Pipe Line Co. Ltd.), 1965; Pres. & C.E.O., Worldwide Energy Corp. 1976–86; served with USN 1943–46; rank Lt.-jg; Anglican; recreations: hunting, fishing, golf, tennis; Clubs: Bent Tree Country, Dallas; The Energy Club, Dallas; Dallas Petroleum Club; Garden of the Gods, Colorado Springs; Home: 12516 Matisse Lane, Dallas, TX 75230; Office: 8140 Walnut Hill Lane, Suite 601, Dallas, TX 75231.

**TENNANT, Howard Edward,** B.B.A., M.B.A., Ph.D.; university professor & administrator; b. Lethbridge, Alta. 13 May 1941; s. Rex J. and Jean S. T.; e. Gonzaga Univ., B.B.A. 1963; Univ. of Oregon, M.B.A. 1964, Ph.D. 1970; m. Sharon "Buckley" d. John and Marie Buckley 7 Sept. 1963; children: Carmen, Patricia, Daniel; PROF. OF MANAGEMENT, PRES. & VICE-CHANCELLOR, UNIV. OF LETHBRIDGE 1987– ; Asst. Prof. of Mngt., Univ. of Sask. 1966–70; Assoc. Prof. 1970–74; Prof. 1974–87; Assoc. Dean of Grad. Studies & Rsch. 1977–83; Assoc. Vice-Pres. (Rsch.) & Dean of Grad. Studies & Rsch. 1983–87; Dir.: CATV Advisory Bd.; Royal Trust Advisory Bd.; Alberta Rsch. Council; Assn. of Univ. & Coll. of Can.; Univ. of Lethbridge Bd. of Gov.; Univ. of Lethbridge Foundation; Tennant Devel. Ltd.; Beta Gamma Sigma 1964; adopted 'Kainai Chief' with given name of Young Eagle (Blood Indian Band) 1987; mem. 'Univ.' Co-ord. Counc.', Prov. of Alta.; Candn. Plains Rsch. Ctr.; Mem., Am. Mktg. Assn.; C. of C.; Admin. Sci. Assn. of Can.; author: 'Readings in Consumer Behavior' 1970, 'Consumers Preferences for Non-structural Wood Products in New Home Construction' 1970, 'A Glossary of Behavioral Science Terminology for Marketing Decision Makers' 1975; recreations: fishing, camping; club: Rotary; Home: 61 Ridgewood Cres. W., Lethbridge, Alta. T1K 6C3; Office: A760 University Hall, Lethbridge, Alta. T1K 3M4.

**TENNANT, John Martin,** B.A., LL.B.; barrister and solicitor; b. Vancouver, B.C. 29 Jan. 1928; s. James Leonard and Emily Rosalie (Paquette) T.; e. Kitsilano High Sch. 1945; Univ. of B.C., B.A. 1949, LL.B. 1953; m. Joan d. Frederick and Violet Billington 10 Sept. 1954; children: Craig Martin, Susan Joan Climie; PARTNER, LAWSON LUNDELL LAWSON & MCINTOSH, BARRISTERS AND SOLICITORS; Pres. and Dir. Realwest Energy Corp.; Dir. Munich Reinsurance Co. of Can.; The Great Lakes Reinsurance Co.; Nike Canada Ltd.; Evans Forest Products Ltd.; called to Bar of B.C. 1954; Hon. Lectr., Fac. of Law, Univ. of B.C. 1975–81; Past Chrmn. B.C. Sports Hall of Fame and Museum; Patron, Rick Hansen Man in Motion World Tour; mem. Cdn. Bar Assn.; Law Soc. of B.C.; Psi Upsilon Frat.; Sigma Tau Chi Hon. Frat.; recreations: shooting, fishing, tennis; Clubs: Vancouver; Shaughnessy Golf & Country; Vancouver Lawn Tennis and Badminton; Evergreen Rugby; Mens Canadian; U.B.C. Big Block; Homes: #11 – 4350 Valley Dr., Vancouver, B.C. V6L 3B5 and Woods Rd., Bowen Island, B.C. V0N 1G0; Office: 1600 Cathedral Place, 925 W. Georgia St., Vancouver, B.C. V6C 3L2.

**TENNANT, Paul Richard,** B.A., M.A., Ph.D.; university professor; b. Indian Head, Sask. 6 Sept. 1938; s. James Walton and Gertrude Elizabeth (Gray) T.; e. Kamloops H.S. 1956; Univ. of B.C. B.A. 1961; Univ. of Chicago M.A. 1962, Ph.D. 1970; m. Susan d. Ralph and Mary Carey 1961; divorced 1989; children: Christopher, Douglas, Matthew, Jonathan; PROF., DEPT. OF POLITICAL SCIENCE, UNIV. OF B.C. 1966– ; Woodrow Wilson Fellow 1961; 1st Candn. to hold U.S. Congressional Fellowship 1964; Asst. to E.D. Fulton, M.P. 1965; specializes in local govt., B.C. & Yukon politics & politics of tribal peoples; Colombo Plan Adviser, Malaysia 1971–73; Adviser, Council for Yukon Indians 1980–91; Consultant to Yukon & Candn. govts. on native claims; Dir., B.C. Legislative Internship Prog.; UBC Master Teacher Award 1990; B.C. Lt. Governor's Medal for Historical Writing 1991; Co-Founder, Vanc. Civic Party the Electors' Action Movement (TEAM) 1967; Pres. 1975; author: 'Aboriginal Peoples and Politics: The Indian Land Question in British Columbia' 1990; Office: Univ. of B.C., Vancouver, B.C. V6T 1Z1.

**TENNANT, Veronica,** O.C. (1975), LL.D. (1985), D.Litt. (1987); ballerina; b. London, England 15 Jan. 1947; d. Harry and Doris (Bassous) T.; e. Bishop Strachan School, Toronto; National Ballet School, Toronto, graduated 1964; m. Dr. John Robert Wright, 11 June 1969; one d. Jessica Robin Wright; joined National Ballet Company as principal dancer 1965; danced 'Juliet' in CBC TV production 'Romeo and Juliet' 1965 (production rec'd René Bartlélémy Prix de Monte Carlo); danced 'Cinderella' in Emmy winning CBC TV production 1967; created leading role in 'Kraanerg' by Ronald Petit at opening of Nat. Arts Centre, Ottawa 1969; danced 'Juliet' in Osaka at Expo 70; guest artist, Jacob's Pillow Internat. Dance Festival, USA, 1971; danced opposite Rudolf Nureyev in world premiere of his 'Sleeping Beauty,' Ottawa 1972 (TV production of ballet rec'd Emmy Award 1973); danced premiere performance of 'La Sylphide' for Princess Anne in London, Eng. (first European engagement for Nat. Ballet Co.); danced opposite Rudolf Nureyev in premiere performance at Metrop. Opera House, N.Y. 1973 (Co.'s N.Y. debut) and throughout N. Am. tour; performed at Newport Music Festival, R.I., summer 1973; 1974 roles incl. 'Aurora' in 'The Sleeping Beauty' opposite Rudolf Nureyev and leading roles in 'Giselle,' 'Le Loup' and Erik Bruhn's productions of 'Les Sylphides,' 'La Sylphide,' 'Swan Lake'; 'The Dream'; 'La Fille Mal Gardée' and 'Etudes' and John Neumeier's 'Don Juan'; featured on CBC's 'Telescope' (1970), 'Impressions' (1973), and 'Arts Magazine' (1974); also various TV talk programmes; has lectured on dance, Waterloo and York Univs.; C.B.C./TV production 'La Sylphide' July 1974 with Mikhail Baryshnikov (first Western ballerina to dance with him after his defection from Soviet Union); live performance with Baryshnikov at Ontario Place Aug. 1974; cr. role 'Swanhilda' in world premier Erik Bruhn's 'Coppelia,' O'Keefe Centre, Toronto Feb. 1975; several guest appearances U.S. 1975–76; other lead roles in Balanchine's 'Serenade'; 'Kettentanz,' 'Dark Elegies,' and Brian MacDonald's 'Newcomers'; danced Role of 'Teresina' to Peter Schaufuss' 'Gennaro' in production of August Bournoville's Ballet 'Napoli,' in the National Ballet of Canada's 30th Anniversary Performance, O'Keefe Centre, Toronto 1981; Officer of the Order of Canada 1975; danced at Birthday Gala Stratford Shakespearean Festival 1978; created role of 'Catherine Sloper' in world premiere of 'Washington Square,' by James Kudelka, Toronto 1978; stage acting debut at the Young Peoples Theatre, Toronto, in 'Hans Christian Andersen' 1978; starred in the film 'Mad Shadows' 1979; starred in 'La Sylphide' with Fernando Bujones as guest of American Ballet Theatre. Lincolm Centre, N.Y. 1979; danced in world premieres of Kudelka's 'All Night Wonder' and Vicente Nebrada's 'Portrait of Love and Death' in, respectively, the National Ballet's 1981 and 1982 Galas; during the 1981–82 season, danced 'La Sylphide' in Puerto Rico; accompanied resident choreographer Constantin Patsalas to L'Aquila, Italy where she danced world première of his 'Liebestod'; debuted as 'Kitri' in National Ballet's newly acquired production of 'Don Quixote' and danced with Anthony Dowell in 'The Dream' Nov. 1982; debut as 'Tatiana' in 'Onegin' by John Cranko 1984; toured Italy's dance festivals with choreographer David Allan to great acclaim summer 1985; danced at Shaw Festival's 25th Anniversary 1986; added 'Hanna' in Ronald Hynd's 'The Merry Widow' to repertoire and danced lead role in David Allan's 'Masada' 1987; performed 'Botticelli Pictures' with Rex Harrington at Opening of the Tampa Bay Arts Centre in Florida 1987; danced 'Tchaikowsky Pas de Deux' and 'Four Last Songs' with Henny Jurriens on tour with Royal Winnipeg Ballet in U.S. and Canada 1987; added lead role in Jiri Kylian's 'Forgotten Land' to repertoire, danced role of 'Tatiana' in 'Onegin' with National Ballet at Metropolitan Opera House in New York, and danced world premiere of David Allan's 'Rendezvous des Coeurs' at Floyd Chalmers 90th birthday Gala 1988; subject of CBC documentary 'Veronica Tennant: A Dancer of Distinction' Feb. 1983; CBC-TV documentary 'Veronica: Completing the Circle' on Adrienne Clarkson's Summer Festival 1989; hosted live Gala for Queen Elizabeth II, Roy Thomson Hall, Toronto (broadcast on CBC-TV) Oct. 1984; hosted 'Tribute to Norman McLaren' for CBC and NFB 1985; hosted 'The Dance-Makers' series for CBC and TVOntario 1988; retired from National Ballet in Farewell Performance of Romeo and Juliet, O'Keefe Centre, Feb. 1989; Veronica Tennant 25th Anniv. Gala Tribute performance, O'Keefe Centre Nov. 1989; Host Writer and Creative Consultant for 'Sunday Arts Entertainment' for CBC-TV 1989–90; rec'd Award of Merit, City of Toronto 1989; author 'On Stage Please' 1977; 'The Nutcracker' 1985; recorded 'The Nutcracker' on cassette with Toronto Symphony 1987; recorded 'On Stage Please' on cassette 1989; LL.D. (h.c.) Brock Univ. 1985; D.Litt. (h.c.) York Univ. 1987; Toronto Arts Award in the Performing Arts category 1987; Dancers' Rep. Bd. Dirs. Nat. Ballet Co. 1970–73, and 1984–85; served on Ont. Arts Counc. 1975–78; Bd., Toronto Arts Awards 1989; Bd., Glenn Gould Foundation 1989; Hon. Chairperson, Ont. March of Dimes 1989–90; Adjunct Prof., Faculty of Fine Arts, York Univ. 1989; recreations: writing, theatre, textile design; Studio: 157 King St. E., Toronto, Ont. M5C 1G9.

**TENNYSON, Roderick C.,** M.A.Sc., Ph.D., P.Eng.; educator; b. Toronto, Ont. 7 June 1937; s. Clarence A. and Rosalie (Calderone) T.; e. Univ. of Toronto, B.A.Sc. (Eng. Phys.) 1960, M.A.Sc. 1961, Ph.D. 1965; m. Judith Grace d. Edwin and Margaret Williams 17 June 1961; children: Shân, Marc, Kristin; DIR., INST. FOR AEROSPACE STUDIES, UNIV. OF TORONTO 1985– , Prof. 1974– , Chrmn., Eng. Sci. 1982–85; selected as Candn. Experimenter on Space Shuttle Flights; cons. to ind. and govt. depts. aerospace technol.; Dir. Candn. Airworthiness Adv. Bd.; Past Dir. Ont. Centre Advanced Mfg.; Dir. Centre of Excellence for Inst. Space & Terrestrial Sci.; Chrmn., Candn. Found. for Internat. Space Univ.; author or co-author over 150 jour. articles, tech. reports, 7 book chapters; Fellow, Candn. Aeronautics & Space Inst.; recreations: sailing, writing; Home: 104 McClure Dr., King City, Ont. L0G 1K0; Office: 4925 Dufferin St., Downsview, Ont. M3H 5T6.

**TEOLI, Ida,** B.A., M.B.A.; executive; b. Italy 27 Sept. 1955; d. Antonio and Carmela (Delli Colli) T.; e. McGill Univ. B.A. 1977, M.B.A. 1980; m. Doug P. Bertoia s. Douglas and Gabrielle Bertoia 5 May 1984; children: Edward Douglas, Bianca Chloé; ASST. VICE PRES., CORPORATE COMMUNICATIONS, BCE INC. 1993– ; Nordair Inc. 1980–84; joined Montreal Trust 1984; Vice Pres. Communications, Montreal Trust 1990–93; Dir. Muscular Dystrophy Assn. Can.; Dir., YWCA Montreal; Dir., St. Mary's Hospital Center, Montreal; Home: 8 Burgundy, Baie D'Urfé, Que. H9X 3E8; Office: 1000, rue de la Gauchetière Ouest, Bureau 3700, Montreal, Que. H3B 4Y7.

**TEPPERMAN, Lorne Jay,** Ph.D.; educator; b. Toronto, Ont. 21 July 1943; s. Isadore James and Molly (Rosenberg) T.; e. Royal Conserv. of Toronto A.R.C.T. 1961; Univ. of Toronto B.A. 1965; Harvard Univ. Ph.D. 1970; Princeton Univ. Cert. in Demography 1973; m. Sandra d. William and Marjorie Wain 5 Aug. 1977; three s. Andrew, Charles, Alexander; PROF. OF SOCIOL., UNIV. OF TORONTO 1978– ; joined present Univ. 1970; Visiting Researcher, Princeton Univ. 1972–73; Harvard Univ. summer 1973; Yale Univ. 1983; Sorokin Lectr. Univ. of Sask. 1980; recipient grants and fellowships Harvard Univ. 1965–67, Can. Council 1967–69, Russell Sage Found. 1969, Population Council 1972–73, Social Sci's & Humanities Rsch. Council Can. 1972–73, 1976–77, 1982–87; Health and Welfare Canada 1987–88, 1989–90; McGillicuddy Gold Medal in Sociol., Univ. of Toronto 1965; mem. Adv. Ctte. on Social Sci's, Candn. Comn. for UNESCO 1983–90, Chrmn. 1988–90; Cons. to National Defence (Can.) 1989–90; Health and Welfare (Can.) 1987–90; I.B.M. 1986; Hosp. for Sick Children 1984–85; Ont. Ministry Community & Social Services 1982, 1984, 1986; Candn. Encyclopedia 1981–82; City of St. Albert, Alta. 1980; Ont. Assn. Family Service Agencies 1981; Solr. Gen. Can. 1976 and others; author 'Social Mobility in Canada' 1975; 'Crime Control: The Urge to Authority' 1977; 'Choices and Chances' 1989, rev. ed. 1994 (U.S. edition, 1990, rev. ed. 1996); co-author 'The Roots of Disunity' 1979; 'Making Sense in Social Science' 1986; 'False Alarm: The Computerization of Eight Social Welfare Organizations' 1990; 'Macro/Micro: An Introduction to Sociology' 1991, rev. ed. 1995; 'Lives of Their Own' 1990; co-ed. 'The Social World: An Introduction to Sociology' 1986 (2nd ed. 1991, 3rd ed. 1995); 'An Introduction to the Social World' 1987; 'Understanding Canadian Society' 1988; 'Readings in Sociology' 1988; 'Images of Canada' 1990; 'Everyday Life' 1992; 'Next of Kin' 1993; 'Small World' 1994; 'Haves and Have-nots' 1994; ed. McGraw-Hill Ryerson Series in Candn. Sociol. 1972–88; assoc. ed. Candn. Jour. Sociol. 1974–88; Social Indicators Research 1988– ; Canadian Studies in Population 1985– ; Candn. Review of Sociology and Anthropology 1992– ; mem. Candn. Sociol. & Anthrop. Assn.; Candn. Population Soc.; Internat. Sociological Assoc.; World Futures Studies Federation; Pop. Assoc. of Am.; recreations: music, reading; Home: 22 Cardinal Place, Toronto, Ont. M4N 2S1; Office: New College, Toronto, Ont. M5S 1A1.

**TERASMAE, Jaan,** Ph. D.; educator; b. Estonia 28 May 1926; s. Enn and Virge (Lepik) T.; e. elem. and secondary educ. Estonia and Sweden; Univ. of Uppsala Bachelor's degree 1951; McMaster Univ. Ph.D. 1955; m. Vaike d. Mihkel Jurima, Estonia 31 July 1954; PROF. EMERITUS OF GEOL. SCIENCES, BROCK UNIV. 1991– ; Head of Pleistocene Palynology Lab., Mines & Tech. Surveys, Geol. Survey of Can. 1955–67, Head of Paleoecology and Geochronology Sec., Energy, Mines & Resources 1968; Prof. of Geol. Sciences, Brock Univ. 1968–91, Chrmn. of Geol. Sciences 1969–73, 1975–76; author or co-author book chapters and over 100 papers and reports quaternary geol., palynology and paleoecology; Ed. 'Quaternary Research in Canada' 8 yrs.; Pres. Candn. Assoc. of Palynologists 1985; served many nat. and internat. scient. comtes. incl. Nat. Research Council; Candn. del. several internat. confs. and congs.; mem. Am. Assn. Advanc. Science; Am. Assn. Stratigraphic

Palynols.; Am. Quaternary Assn.; Arctic Inst. N. Am.; Candn. Assn. Palynols.; Candn. Quaternary Assn.; Geol. Assn. Can.; Geol. Soc. Am.; Internat. Assn. Gt. Lakes Research; Internat. Glaciol. Soc.; Internat. Peat Soc.; Royal Candn. Geog. Soc.; Royal Soc. Can.; Tree-Ring Soc.; Lutheran; recreation: photography; Home: 196 Woodside Dr., St. Catharines, Ont. L2T 1X6.

**TERON, William;** O.C., F.R.A.I.C. (Hon.); executive; b. Gardenton, Man. 15 Nov. 1932; s. George and Sadie (Sandul) T.; e. St. John's High Sch. Winnipeg; m. Jean Miriam d. Rev. H.K. Woodwark 5 Sept. 1955; children: Christopher Noel, Kim Allison, William George, Bruce Charles; CHIEF EXTVE OFFICER, URBANETICS INC. and TERON INC.; Chrmn. & Pres., Central Mortgage & Housing Corp. 1973–76; Chrmn. of C.M.H.C. and Secy., Ministry of State for Urban Affairs 1976–79; Chief Extve. Offr., Teron International, Teron Construction Co. Ltd., Carleton Towers Hotels Ltd., Marina City (Kingston) Ltd., Golden Ridge Developments Ltd. (Kanata), 1955–73; Chrmn. of Bd. Commerce Capital Corp. 1970–73; former Trustee, Nat. Arts Centre; Past Gov. Carleton Univ.; Past Gov. Lester B. Pearson Coll. of the Pacific; Ashbury Coll.; Past Dir. Candn. Council on Urban & Regional Research, Candn. Housing Design Council; Past Chrmn. African Students Foundation, Nat. Capital Arts Alliance; Officer, Order of Can. 1982; Hon. Fellow, Royal Arch. Inst. Canada 1978; rec'd 2 Nat. Awards, 4 Regional Awards and Nat. Award for Community Design (Kanata), Candn. Housing Design Council; Home: Suite 505, 111 Echo Dr., Ottawa, Ont. K1S 5K8.

**TERREAULT, Charles R.,** B.A., B.A.Sc., P.Eng., D.H.C.; university professor; b. Montréal, Qué. 21 Mar. 1935; s. Charles and Antonia (Clark) T.; e. Coll. Stanislas Montréal B.A. 1954; Ecole Polytechnique Montréal B.A.Sc. 1959; Bell Labs OETP Holmdel, N.J. 1967; Univ. du Qué. D.H.C. 1986; m. Marie d. René and Marie-Jeanne Rolland 10 Sept. 1960; children: Geneviève, François, Patrick, Hugues; JVR CYR PROFESSOR OF MANAGEMENT OF TECHNOLOGY, ECOLE POLYTECHNIQUE DE MONTRÉAL 1991– ; joined Bell Canada 1959 holding various eng. and mktg. positions with Bell, Northern Telecom, Telebec and Bell Northern Research (BNR); Vice Pres. Systems Div. BNR 1973; founded BNR Nun's Island lab. 1974, Bell's quality lab. Longueuil 1986 and outside plant rsch. facility Varennes 1987; Asst. Vice Pres., Network Tech. Rsch. 1988–91; retired from Bell Canada Aug. 1991; estbd. INRS-Telecom, Univ. du Qué. 1974; mem. Conseil de la Science et de la Technologie du Qué. 2 terms; Gen. Chrmn. Internat. Switching Symposium 1981; recipient Prix des Télécommunications du Gouvernement du Qué. 1983; Armstrong Medal Inst. Elect. & Electronic Engs. 1985; ADRIQ Industry Award 1992; author or co-author tech. papers telecommunications; mem. Assn. Canadienne Française pour l'Avancement des Sciences (Pres. 1987–88); Ordre des Ingénieurs du Qué.; Qué. Assn. Ind. Rsch. (ADRIQ); Fellow, Inst. Elect. & Electronics Engs.; mem. Natural Sciences and Engineering Rsch. Council (NSERC) (Exec. Ctte. Mem.); Chrmn., Targeted Rsch. Ctte.; recreations: music, reading, skiing, cycling; Home: 1665 Victoria Ave., Apt. 804, St-Lambert, Qué. J4R 2T6; Office: Dept. de génie industriel, CP 6079, Succ. A, Montréal, Qué. H3C 3A7.

**TERRIS, Andrew David,** B.A.; artist, arts administrator, cultural policy consultant; b. Albany, N.Y. 28 March 1943; s. Milton and Rema (Lapouse) T.; e. Antioch Coll. B.A. 1967; Univ. of Edinburgh; McGill Univ.; m. Rejene Allyn d. Reginald and Elrene Stowe 2 March 1970; EXECUTIVE DIRECTOR, VISUAL ARTS NOVA SCOTIA; Internat. Touring Shows: 'Atlantic Visions' 1982–86, 'Old Paths, New Ways' 1985–87; Nat. Shows: 'Can. Glass Invitational' Toronto 1986, 'Restless Legacies' Calgary 1988; Halifax Shows: Fire Works Gall., Art Gallery of N.S., Mt. St. Vincent U. Art Gall., Anna Leonowens Gall., Eye Level Gall., Centre for Art Tapes, Mary Black Gall. 1980–91; Major Commissions: Dalhousie Law Sch. 1983, Halifax Sheraton Hotel 1985, Mt. St. Vincent Univ. 1992, Purdy's Wharf Tower 2 1994; Dir., N.S. Designer Craftsmen 1979–82; N.S. Coalition on Arts & Culture 1985–94; Arts and the Cities 1990; NovaKnowledge 1993; President, Cultural Feds. of N.S. 1994; Cons., Atlantic Prov. Art Gall. Assn. 1987–88; N.S. Coalition on Arts & Culture 1988–89; Arts Nova 1989–91; National Film Board 1992; Canada Council grants 1984, '85, '86, '87; Juror, Can. Council Explorations Prog. 1987–89; Art Allocation Ctte., City of Halifax 1987–90; N.S. Arts Adv. Ctte. 1991–92; Arctic Awareness Prog., Otto Fjord 1990; Mngt. Ctte., Assessment of the Cultural Feds. of N.S. 1992–93; Mem., Candn. Conf. of the Arts 1988–94; NovaCulture 1993; Chair, CULTURE WORKS! Campaign 1993; editor: 'Does Nova Scotia Need a Provincial Arts Council?' 1988, 'Public Art Competitions' 1989; author: 'Artnews' 1988, 'Public Policy and Cultural Development in Nova Scotia' 1991, 'Beyond Excellence' 1991; computer animation: 'Deus Ex Machina' 1990; recreations: film, theatre, music; Home: 2182 Gottingen St., Halifax, N.S. B3K 3B4; Office: 1809 Barrington St., Ste. 901, Halifax, N.S. B3J 3K8.

**TERRY, John Bruce,** B.A., M.B.A.; food industry executive; b. Toronto, Ont. 24 April 1954; s. John Wilfred and Anne Margaret (Campbell) T.; e. York Univ. B.A. (hons.) 1978; Univ. of B.C. M.B.A. 1980; m. Anna d. Zenon and Gabriela Gasowska 2 July 1977; children: Fiona, Julie, Vanessa; VICE-PRES. & CHIEF FINANCIAL OFFICER, McCAIN FOODS LIMITED 1990– ; Analyst, Corp. Finance, Imperial Oil Limited 1980–82; Cash Planning Mgr., Canada Development Corp. 1982–84; Manager, Bank of America 1984–85; Div. Mgr., Corp. Finance, Gulf Canada Corp. 1985–88; Vice-Pres., Finance & Planning, Tricaster Mngt. Inc. 1988–90; recreations: golf, skiing, family recreation; Home: Riverview Dr., Florenceville, N.B. E0J 1K0; Office; Main St., Florencville, N.B. E0J 1K0.

**TERRY, John Everard,** B.E., B.Ed., P.Eng.; mining executive; b. Calcutta, India 23 Jan. 1925; s. John Eustace and Maisie Amelia (Martinelli) T.; e. St. Edmund's Coll. 1943; Univ. of Calcutta B.E. (Mech.) 1948; St. Francis Xavier Univ. B.Ed. 1971; m. Janet d. Russell and Pat Kallak 5 Aug. 1961; children: John, Brian, Yvonne, Jennifer; CHRMN. & C.E.O., SYDNEY TARPON CLEAN-UP INC.; Dir. N.S. Rsch. Found. Corp.; N.S. Small Bus. Devel. Corp.; joined Dominion Coal Co. (now present Co.) 1950, Design Eng., Special Projects Eng.; Founding Prin. N.S. Eastern Inst. of Technol. Sydney 1967; Sr. Vice Pres. Univ. Coll. of Cape Breton 1974, Vice Pres. 1984; Pres. 1990; Chrmn. Maritime Provs. Higher Edn. Comn. Fredericton 1982; Chrmn. Bd. of Dirs., Cape Breton Development Corp. 1989; Commdr. (Col.) Cape Breton Militia Dist. 1970–73; Hon. Col. 45 Field Eng. Sqdn. 1981– ; Gov. N.S. Div. Candn. Corps Commissionaires; Trustee Alexander Graham Bell Inst.; Dir. Un. Way Cape Breton; mem. Min.'s Nat. Adv. Ctte. to CANMET 1987– ; Nat. Rsch. Council IRAP Ctte. 1988– ; Northern Telecom Nat. Edn. Prog. Steering Ctte. 1986– ; Min.'s Adv. Bd. Candn. Mil. Colls. 1982–86; Chrmn. Sydney Ctte. Fed. Ind. & Labour Adjustment Prog. 1981–82; Adv. Bd. Tech. Univ. of N.S. 1981–85; mem. 3 N.S. Missions to UK and Norway offshore oil/gas operations 1980–81; Chrmn. Mining Sector N.S. Voluntary Planning Bd. 1977–78; Maritime Mun. Training & Devel. Bd. 1974–79; Maritime Provs. Higher Edn. Comn. 1974–84; Chrmn. Red Cross Financial Campaign Cape Breton 1985; Past Chrmn. St. John Ambulance Cape Breton; author various papers profl. jours., confs.; mem. Assn. Profl. Engs. N.S. (Pres. 1978–79); Mining Soc. N.S. (Pres. 1971–72); Eng. Inst. Can. (Chrmn. Cape Breton Br. 1967); Assn. Candn. Community Coll. Adms. (Pres. 1979); Candn. Vocational Assn. (Vice Pres. 1977–78); Mil. Engs. Assn. Can.; Royal Un. Services Inst.; N.S. Council Applied Sci. & Technol.; recreations: golf, fishing, hiking; Club: Rotary; Home: 129 Howe St., Sydney, N.S. B1P 4V3; Office: 500 George Place, Suite 250, Box 12, Sydney, N.S. B7P 1K6.

**TERRY, Mark,** B.A.; producer; theatre general manager; b. Toronto, Ont. 16 Sept. 1958; s. Herbert J. and Catherine (Enright) T.; e. De La Salle Coll.; York Univ. Glendon Coll. B.A. 1980; children: Herbie Guy Mark, Mary Anne Catherine T.; freelance film critic 1972–80; Asst. to Copy Ed. Toronto Sun 1979; Reporter Toronto Star 1980; Ont. News Ed./Youth Ed. The Canadian Register 1980–83; actor 1973– ; stage crew Young People's Theatre 1980; Founder, Publisher and Editor, Hollywood Canada Magazine 1986–91; Producer, Writer, Dir. 'A Lesson for the Bogeyman' Glendon Theatre Toronto 1980; Producer, Dir. (TV) 'Come and Go' 1980; General Manager, The Bayview Playhouse Toronto 1989–94; Pres., Hollywood Canada Productions, Inc. 1989– ; Co-Founder, Producers Network Associates (C.E.O. 1991–94); Producer (Theatre): 'The Servant' 1990; 'Reflections' 1990; 'The Best of Times, The Worst of Times' 1990; 'Sinners' 1991; 'Pinocchio' 1991; 'Alice in Wonderland' 1991; 'Mump & Smoot in CAGED ... with Wog' (off Broadway) 1991; 'Mump & Smoot in FERNO' (Canadian tour) 1992; Producer (Film), 'Replikator'; 'Strange Horizons'; 'Clive Barker: The Art of Horror'; Television: 'Timestorm Theatre'; 'Lives Lived'; Audio: 'The Best of Charles Dickens'; Judge, Juno Awards 1986– ; Genie Awards 1992– .

**TESCHKE, William R.,** C.D., B.Com., M.B.A.; consultant; corporate director; b. Winnipeg, Man. 3 Sept. 1929; s. John Jacob and Margaret Frederica T.; e. Univ. of Toronto B.Com. 1951; Mich. State Univ. M.B.A. 1963; m. Katherine d. Harper and Dorothy Kress 4 Aug. 1951; children: Katherine, Jill, Eric, Ann; Dir. Varity Corp.; Canada Development Investment Corp.; Westinghouse Canada; Pratt & Whitney Canada; Theratronics International Ltd.; Gore Mutual Insurance Co.; served with Candn. Armed Forces 1951–65, rank Wing Commdr.; Chief Acct. Pub. Works Can. Ottawa 1966–69; Dir. Gen. Finance Ind. Trade & Comm. 1969–72, Assoc. Dep. Min. 1978–82; Dep. Sec. to Cabinet Privy Council Office 1972–78; Sec. Econ. Devel. 1981–83; Dep. Min. Regional Ind. Expansion 1983–85; Adv. to Bank of Nova Scotia 1986–92; recreation: golf; Home: 1103, 1967 Barclay St., Vancouver, B.C. V6G 1L1.

**TESKEY, Gordon;** judge; b. Toronto, Ont. 18 May 1932; s. Luke and Evelyn (Lilly) T.; e. Oakwood C.I. 1951; Victoria Coll. 1954; Osgoode Hall 1958; m. Pat d. Gage and Isabelle Campbell 27 June 1957; children: Campbell, Nancy, Elizabeth; JUDGE, TAX COURT OF CANADA 1988– ; Boys Seagram & Rowe 1958–62; F.W. Woolworth Co. Ltd. 1963–64; Sr. Partner, Teskey Heacock Ferguson & Main 1965–88; former Dir., Bruin Engineered Parts Inc.; St. Andrew's Gen. Hosp.; former mem., Bd. of Gov., Georgian Coll.; former trustee, St. Paul's Un. Ch.; former mem., Barrie Public Sch. Bd.; mem., Ramesis Shrine Club; club: Craigleith Ski; Home: Apt. 1603, 1510 Riverside Dr., Ottawa, Ont. K1G 4X5; Office: 200 Kent St., Ottawa, Ont. K1A 0M1.

**TESKEY, John David,** B.A., M.L.S.; librarian; b. Regina, Sask. 14 July 1949; s. Floyd William and Ester (Beaton) T.; e. Univ. of Guelph B.A. 1971; Univ. of W. Ont. M.L.S. 1973; m. Theresa d. Peter and Stella Bertin 17 April 1971; children; David, Genea, Taisha; DIRECTOR OF LIBRARIES, UNIV. OF N.B. 1991– ; Asst. to the Univ. Librarian, Univ. of Sask. 1974–80; Library Personnel Officer, Univ. of Alta. 1980–85; Head, Admin. Services 1986–88; Acting Chief Librarian 1989–90; Area Coordinator Admin. Services 1990–91; Sessional Lectr., Fac. of Library & Info. Studies, Univ. of Alta. 1989–90; Mem., Candn. Lib. Assn.; Am. Lib. Assn.; Candn. Assn. of Rsch. Libs.; Atlantic Provinces Lib. Assn.; Home: 205 Coburn Court, Fredericton, N.B. E3B 7A6; Office: P.O. Box 7500, Fredericton, N.B. E3B 5H5.

**TESKEY, Robert Hugh,** Q.C.; lawyer; b. Red Deer, Alta. 25 June 1946; s. Willis Thomas and Ruth Eleanor (Richardson) T.; e. Rocky Mountain House Alta. 1964; Univ. of Alta. B.A. 1969, LL.B. 1970; Queen's Counsel 1990; m. Hazel d. Joe and Helene Kuehn 28 Dec. 1976; children: Kent James, Karen Michelle; PARTNER, FIELD & FIELD PERRATON (previously Field Hyndman) 1973– ; Managing Partner, Field & Field 1989– ; articled Field Hyndman 1970–71, Assoc. 1971–73; Dir., Oxford Development Group Inc. 1981– ; DFG Limited Partnership 1980– ; Dir., Candn. Diabetes Assn. 1974–82; Trustee and Legal Counsel, Diabetes Can. 1982–91; mem., Conduct Ctte., The Law Soc. of Alberta 1991– ; ed. Alberta Law Review 1969–70; Home: 14019 – 91A Ave., Edmonton, Alta. T5R 5A8; Office: 2000 Oxford Tower, 10235 – 101 Ave., Edmonton, Alta. T5J 3G1.

**TESLYK, Donald S.,** B.A.; banker; b. Edmonton, Alta. 1 Jan. 1941; e. N.A.I.T. B.A. 1967; m. Darlene Lee children: Kevin John, Jo-Lynn Marie; SENIOR VICE-PRESIDENT, CANADIAN COMMERCIAL CREDIT, THE BANK OF NOVA SCOTIA 1992– ; various senior positions in credit admin. extve. offices, Bank of N.S. 1978–86; Reg. Sr. Vice-Pres. & Gen. Mgr. Saskatchewan 1986–87; Vice-Pres., Credit, Prairie Reg. Office 1987–92; Office: 11th fl., 44 King St. W., Toronto, Ont. M5H 1H1.

**TESSIER, Jean Michel,** B.A., M.Comm.; transportation executive; b. 6 Apr. 1941; e. Laval Univ., B.A., M.Comm. 1964; Univ. of B.C. post-graduate studies in transportation (M.B.A. level) 1965; Sherbrooke Univ. post-graduate studies in marketing (M.A. level) 1973; Laval Univ. Ph.D. student Operations Management 1975; m. Michelle d. Louis Philippe Goulet 20 June 1964; children: Jean-François, Marie-Hélène, Jean-Bernard; PRESIDENT & CHIEF EXTVE. OFFR., CANADA PORTS CORPORATION (PORTS CANADA) 1987– ; Dir., Ridley Terminals Inc. 1987– ; with CP Rail as Asst. Supvr. of Labour Relations, a Marketing and Planning Analyst and District Manager, Sherbrooke and Quebec City 1967–77; Dir., Planning & Devel., National Harbours Bd., Quebec City 1977–81; Asst. Vice-Pres., Mktg., National Harbours Bd. 1981–83; Dir., Corporate Policies, Ports Canada 1983–85; Dir., Planning & Devel. 1985; Gen. Mgr. & C.E.O., Port of Quebec Corp. 1985–87; Chrmn., Candn. Council of the Chartered Institute of Transport 1992; Pres., National Transportation Week 1993–95; Dir., Am. Assn. of Port Authorities 1988– ; Internat. Assn. of Ports and Harbours 1991– ; Mem., Transport Canada Management Ctte. 1987– ; Profl.

Corp. of Chartered Administrators of Que.; Distinguished Alumnus, Transportation Div., Univ. of B.C. 1992; Lectr. on marketing, transportation and admin. rsch. at McGill, Sherbrooke and Laval universities; Home: Gatineau, Que.; Office: 99 Metcalfe St., Ottawa, Ont. K1A 0N6.

**TESSIER, Pierre,** B.A., LL.L., D.E.S.; judge; b. Montreal, Que. 11 Nov. 1939; s. Paul and Lucile (Deslauriers) T.; e. Univ. of Montreal, B.A. 1961, LL.L. 1964, D.E.S. 1966; m. Claude d. J.-Rene and Doris Girard 4 Sept. 1967; children: Paul, Julie; JUDGE, SUPERIOR COURT OF QUE. 1988– ; Mem., Bar of Que. 1966–88 (Gen. Counc. 1972–73); Bar of Montreal (Treas. 1972–73); Chrmn., Ctte. on the Admin. of Civil Justice, Bar of Montreal 1986–88; , Trial attorney in civil & admin. law; Prof., Evidence & Trial Techniques, Bar Admission Course 1975–86; Lectr., Edn. Prog. of the Bar of Que. 1983– ; Guest Speaker on civil evidence & procedure, trial proceedings, charter of rights, family law, tech. issues, admin. law, professional law, bioethics and labor law at legal seminars 1984–94; Dir., Y.M.C.A. 1970–77; mem., Candn. Bar Assn. (Mem., Nat. Extve. 1983–85; Pres., Que. Br. 1985–86); Candn. Inst. for the Admin. of Justice; Candn. Conf. of Judges; author: 'La preuve devant la cour civile' 1978 with annual updates (law book) and several articles; recreations: skiing, tennis, golf; Home: 262 Morrison Ave., Town of Mount-Royal, Que. H3R 1K6; Office: 1 Notre-Dame St. E., Montreal, Que. H2Y 1B6.

**TESSIER, Robert,** B.A., B.Sc.; business executive; b. Montréal, Qué. 5 March 1945; s. Fernand and Lucie (Normandeau) T.; e. Univ. de Montréal B.A. 1965, B.Sc. 1967, M.A. courses completed 1968; m. Denyse d. R. Ouimet 11 Oct. 1969; children: Geneviève, Godefroy; Dir., Domtar Inc.; Sintra Ltd.; Sec. Gen. Univ. du Qué. 1969–74, Vice Pres. Adm. Affairs (interim) 1973–74, Vice Pres. 1974–76; Asst. Sec. Adm. Policy Treasury Bd. Qué. 1976–79, Assoc. Sec. Adm. Policy 1979–80, Sec. 1980–84; Dep. Min. Energy & Resources Qué. 1984–87; Exec. Vice Pres. Le Groupe SGF 1987; Pres., C.E.O. & Dir., The Mil Group 1988; Mem. Bd., Chambre de commerce du Montréal métropolitain 1989– ; mem. Candn. Maritime Industries Assoc.; Candn. Chamber of Commerce; R. Catholic; recreations: swimming, skiing; Club: Mount-Royal; Home: 174 Edison Ave., St-Lambert, Qué. J4R 2P5; Office: 4984 place de la Savane, Montreal, Qué. H4P 2M9.

**TESSIER-LAVIGNE, (Trevor) Marc,** B.Sc., B.A., Ph.D.; neurobiologist; b. Trenton, Ont. 18 Dec. 1959; s. Yves Jacques and Sheila Christine (Midgley) T.-L.; e. Lycée Français de Belgique, Brussels 1977; McGill Univ. B.Sc. 1980; Oxford Univ. (Rhodes Scholar) B.A. 1982; Univ. Coll. London Ph.D. 1986; m. Mary Alanna Hynes 4 Feb. 1989; two sons: Christian, Kyle; ASST. PROF., PROGRAMS IN DEVELOPMENTAL BIOLOGY AND NEUROSCIENCE, DEPT. OF ANATOMY, UNIV. OF CALIFORNIA AT SAN FRANCISCO 1991– ; Postdoctoral Fellow, Medical Rsch. Counc. (MRC) Developmental Neurobiology Programme, Univ. Coll. London 1986–87; Rsch. Assoc., Howard Hughes Med. Inst. and Center for Neurobiology and Behavior, Columbia Univ., New York 1987–91; Founding mem. Candn. Student Pugwash 1980, Nat. Coordinator (Exec. Dir.) 1982–83; recipient Gold Medal in Physics McGill 1980; Commonwealth Scholar 1983; Shafer Prize for distinction in research in Physiology, Univ. Coll. London 1986; Lucille P. Markey Scholar in Biomedical Sci. 1989; Searle Scholar 1991; McKnight Scholar 1991; Klingenstein Fellow 1992; author various sci. papers biophysics & neurobiol., articles sci. and social issues; recreations: cinema, history; Address: 1000 Chenery St., San Francisco, CA 94131 USA; Office: Dept. of Anatomy, Univ. of California, San Francisco, CA 94143-0452 USA.

**TESTER, Frank James,** B.Sc., M.E.Des, M.S.W., D.Phil.; university professor; b. Dundas, Ont. 26 Oct. 1949; s. Frank and Jeanne (Issac) T.; e. Univ. of Western Ont. B.Sc. (Hons.) 1971; Univ. of Calgary M.E.Des 1975, M.S.W. 1976; Waikato Univ. (Hamilton, N.Z.) D.Phil. 1987; PROFESSOR, SCHOOL OF SOCIAL WORK, UNIV. OF B.C. 1989– ; social worker / mental health worker, Hamilton Psych. Hosp., Hamilton-Wentworth Health Unit, Chedoke Hosp., A.Y. Canada (Hamilton) 1968–72; researcher & community development worker, Resolute Bay & Arctic Bay, N.W.T. 1973–74; Research Assoc., Kananaskis Centre for Environ. Research & Sch. of Social Work, Univ. of Calgary 1976; Co-ord. of Social, Econ., Eviron. Impact Assessment, proposed Polar Gas Pipeline, Keewatin Dist., N.W.T. 1977–79; Research Assoc., Arctic Inst. of N. Am. 1984; Prof., Fac. of Environ. Studies, York Univ. 1984–89; Mem., Regional Bd., CUSO B.C.; Steering Ctte., Tin Wis Coalition B.C.; Edit. Collective, 'New Directions' mag.; Columnist: 'Canadian Dimension Magazine'; Mem., Social Planning & Rsch. Council of B.C.; editor: 'Social Impact Assessment, Theory, Method and Practice' 1981, 'Socio-Economic and Environmental Impacts, Polar Gas Pipeline, District of Keewatin, N.W.T.' 1979; co-author: (with P. Kulehyski) 'Tammarniit (Mistakes): Inuit Relocation in the Eastern Arctic 1939–63' 1994; recreations: sailing, nordic skiing, climbing, hiking, canoeing; Home: #308, 2410 Cornwall St., Vancouver, B.C. V6K 1B8; Office: 2080 West Mall, U.B.C., Vancouver, B.C. V6T 1Z2.

**TETLEY, Glen,** B.Sc.; choreographer; b. Cleveland, Oh. 3 Feb. 1926; s. Glenford and Eleanor (Byrne) T.; e. Franklin & Marshall Coll. 1946; New York Univ., B.Sc. 1948; cont. dance stud., Hanya Holm, Martha Graham 1946; class. ballet stud., Margaret Craske, Antony Tudor, Met. Opera Ballet Sch. 1949; Artistic Assoc., Nat. Ballet of Can. 1987–89; Guest Instr., Yale Dramatic Workshop 1947–48; Colorado Coll. 1946–49; Hanya Holm Sch. Cont. Dance 1946–52; Ballet Rambert 1966–68; Netherlands Dance Theatre 1962–65 (art. dir. 1969); B. De Rothschild Found., Israel 1965–67; Featured dancer, 'Kiss Me Kate' 1949, 'Out of This World' 1950, 'Juno' 1958; premiered in Menotti's 'Amahl' & 'The Night Visitors,' NBC Opera 1951; soloist, NYC Opera 1951–54; John Butler's Am. Dance Th. 1951–55; Robert Joffrey Ballet 1955–56; Martha Graham Dance Co. 1957–59; Am. Ballet Th. 1959–61; Jerome Robbins' Ballets: USA 1961–62; Netherlands Dance Th. 1962–65; own co. 1962–69; govt.-sponsored tour of Eur. 1969, appearing at Spoleto Fest, all maj. Am. dance fests.; guest choreographer, Netherlands Dance Th. (former art dir.); Am. Ballet Theatre; Ballet Rambert; Batsheva Co.; Robert Joffrey Ballet; Alvin Ailey Co.; Univ. Utah Rep. Dance Th.; Vanc. Fest.; Royal Danish Ballet; Royal Ballet Covent Garden; Royal Swedish Ballet; Pacific Northwest Ballet; San Francisco Ballet; Dance Theatre of Harlem; Norwegian National Ballet; Hamburg Ballet; Stuttgart Ballet (former art. dir.); produced: 'The Rite of Spring,' National Ballet of Canada 1992; ballets incl.: 'Dialogues' 1991; 'Tagore' 1989; 'La Ronde' 1987, 'Orpheus' 1987, 'Alice' 1986, 'Dream Walk of the Shaman' 1985 and num. others; Patron, Benesh Inst. of Choreol.; served with USNR 1944–46; German Critics award for Die Feder; Queen Elizabeth II Coronation Award, Royal Acad. Dancing 1981; Prix Italia Rai Prize 1982; Tennant Caledonia Award, Edinburgh Fest. 1983; Ohioana Career Medal 1986; Achievement Award, Alumni Assoc., Washington Square Coll. 1988; Home: 15 W. 9th St., New York, NY 10011.

**TETLEY, William,** Q.C., LL.L., B.A.; b. 10 Feb. 1927; e. Pub. Sch., Montreal; Royal Candn. Naval Coll., 1st Class Cert. and Sword; served with R.C.N.V.R.; rank of Lieutenant; McGill Univ., B.A. (Econ. & Pol. Science); Laval Univ., LL.L.; m. Rosslyn Marjory; children: Pauline, Jane, Priscilla, William; PROF. OF LAW, McGILL UNIV. since 1976; called to the Bar of Quebec 1952; Q.C. 1968; practised law 18 yrs. with Martineau, Walker, Allison, Beaulieu, Tetley & Phelan, becoming Senior Partner; Municipal Councillor, Town of Mount Royal, 1965–68; el. M.N.A. for Notre-Dame-de-Grâce in by-el. 1968, re-el. 1970, 73; apptd. Min. of Revenue, May 1970; Min. of Consumer Affairs Cooperatives & Financial Insts. 5 yrs.; Min. of Pub. Works & Supply 1 yr.; resigned 1976 to become Prof. of Law, McGill Univ.; Distinguished Visiting Prof. of Maritime and Commercial Law, Tulane Univ., New Orleans; one of three Hon. Members, Maritime Law Assoc., U.S.A.; has taken active interest in Boy Scouts Can., his church Sunday Sch. and the YMCA; awarded Boy Scout Medal of Hon. 1968; rep. Can. at internat. law conventions; lit. critic, 'Montreal Gazette' 1952–65; is editor, and has publ. in internat. law journs. in Italy, Belgium, Spain; U.K., France and U.S.; Speaker at internat. law conf. in Athens, London, New York, Capetown, Hong Kong, Buenos Aires, Rome, Cartagena, Vancouver and Halifax; author 'Marine Cargo Claims' 1966, 2nd ed. 1978, publ. in English, Russian and Japanese; 'Maritime Liens and Claims,' 1985; 'Marine Cargo Claims' 3rd E. 1988 to be publ. as well in Chinese; Judge of the Candn. Human Rights Tribunal; Pres., International Maritime Arbitration Organization (Paris); Past Pres., Candn. Maritime Law Assn.; Past Chrmn., Bd. of Gov., Frontier College; Pres., The Assn. of Maritime Arbitrators of Canada; Vice-Pres., Comité Maritime Internat., Brussels; Pres., La Société Pro Musica, Montréal; Internat. Pres., Collectors Anonymous; Clubs: Athenaeum, London; Vive La Nouvelle-Orléans Libre, New Orleans; University, Montreal; Anglican; recreations: swimming, collecting souvenir china, antique furniture, books and other Canadiana; Home: 112 Cornwall Ave., Montreal, Que. H3P 1M8; Office: 3644 Peel St., Montreal, Que. H3A 1W9.

**TETREAULT, Robert,** B.A., M.Com., C.A.; b. Granby, Que. 1925; s. Leon and Marie-Emma (Valcourt) T.; e. St.-Hyacinthe Semy. B.A. 1947, M.Com. 1955; C.A. 1956; m. Madeleine d. A. Domingue 23 June 1956; Children: Gilles, Julie, Louise; Sr. Consultant, Zins Beauchesne & Associates, Marketing Rsch. Firm, Secor Group, Retired 1992; former Sr. Consultant, Cogem Inc.; Marketing Research Firm; joined Marchands En Quincaillerie 1958; Comptroller Metro Food Stores Ltd. 1966, Gen. Mgr. 1970; former Extve. Vice-Pres., Metro-Richelieu Inc.; R. Catholic; Recreations: golf, swimming, sailing, skiing, cycling; Home: 154 Greenwood, Dollard-Des-Ormeaux, Que. H9A 1E8.

**TEVLIN, John D.,** B.Comm., M.B.A.; business executive; b. Toronto, Ont. 3 Jan. 1957; s. Thomas Anthony and Jesse Carol (Wood) T.; e. Queen's Univ. B.Comm. 1978; York Univ. M.B.A. 1980; m. Kathleen d. Rodney and Louise Lammers 14 March 1987; children: Thomas William, James Rodney; PRESIDENT, CN TOWER LTD. 1992– ; Asst. to Dir. of Creative Services, Foster Advtg. Ltd. 1978; Product Supvr., Warner-Lambert Canada Ltd. 1980; Product Mgr., Pepsi-Cola Canada Ltd. 1981–83; Category Mgr. then Dir. of Grocery Merchandising, Loblaws Supermarkets Ltd. 1983–86; Mktg. Mgr. Can., then Dir. of Mktg. Middle East and lastly Dir. of Operations Africa, Pepsi-Cola Internat. Ltd. 1986–92; Bd. Mem., Metro Toronto Convention & Visitors Assn. (Chair, Revenue Devel.; Ambassadors Ctte.); Bd. Mem., Ryerson School of Hospitality & Tourism Advisory Bd.; Mem., World Fed. of Great Towers (Steering Ctte.); recreations: golf, bridge, reading; Home: 102 DeVere Gardens, Toronto, Ont. M5M 3G2; Office: 301 Front St. W., Toronto, Ont. M5V 2T6.

**THACKER, Blaine Allen,** B.Sc., LL.B., M.P.; barrister & solicitor/member of parliament; b. Taber, Alta. 11 Jan. 1941; s. Herbert Frederick and Madeline Ferna (Weatherhead) T.; e. Olds, Alta., Hon. Dipl.Ag. 1960; Univ. of Edmonton B.Sc.Agriculture 1964, LL.B. 1968; m. Suzanne Evans; children: David, Michelle, Todd, Tynan; lawyer 1968–79; M.P. 1979; re-elected 1980, 1984, 1988; Chrmn., Standing Ctte., for Justice & Solicitor Gen. 1984–87; Parlty Sec., to Min. of Transport 1987–88; Parliamentary Sec. to Min. of Consumer and Corporate Affairs 1989–91; Chrmn., Special Ctte., Review of the Access to Information and Privacy Ad. 1984– ; Chrmn., Special Ctte., Review of the CSIS and Security Offences Act 1989– ; Mem., Law Soc. of Alta.; recreations: golf, fishing, skiing; Club: Lethbridge Country; Home: 200, 220 - 4th St. South, Lethbridge, Alta. T1J 4S7.

**THACKRAY, The Hon. Mr. Justice Allan Douglas,** B.Comm., LL.B., Q.C.; supreme court judge; b. Moose Jaw, Sask. 19 Oct. 1932; s. Allan Douglas and Alexina (Miller) T.; e. Univ. of B.C. B.Comm. 1957, LL.B. 1958; m. Maureen d. William and Bessie Bromley 19 Sept. 1957; children: Michael Allan, Victoria Anne; JUDGE, SUPREME COURT OF BRITISH COLUMBIA 1990– ; Dept. of External Affairs 1959–61; Medical Litigation Specialist, Harper, Grey & Easton 1961–90; Q.C.; recreations: golf; club: Shaughnessy Golf & Country; Home: 4246 Staulo Cres., 1367 Dogwood Ave., Vancouver, B.C.; Office: 800 Smithe St., Vancouver, B.C. V6Z 2E1.

**THACKRAY, James Carden,** B.Sc.; telecommunications company executive; b. Granby, Que. 25 Feb. 1924; s. Carden Cousens and Maud Stewart (Macpherson) T.; e. Westmount (Que.) High Sch., 1939; McGill Univ., B.Sc. 1946; m. Marie Therese, d. Dr. David Stephenson, Scarborough, Yorks., Eng., 6 March 1948; children: David, Anne, Elizabeth, James; DIR., BELL CANADA; Bank of Montreal; Canadian Reinsurance Co.; Canadian Reassurance Co.; Served with R.C.N.V.R. N. Atlantic, Mediterranean and Far E., 1942–46; rank Lt.; Gov. Montreal Gen. Hosp. Foundation; Past Pres. Can. Safety Council, 1970–72; Past campaign Chrmn., Metro Toronto United Way; Anglican; recreations: skiing, golf; Clubs: Toronto; York; Mount-Royal; Lambton Golf & Country; Home: 503–63 St Clair Ave. W., Toronto, Ont. M4V 2Y9; Office: Bell Trinity Sq., F10S, Toronto, Ont. M5G 2E1.

**THADDAEUS;** sculptor; b. Toronto, Ont. 15 Jan. 1955; s. the late George Nickolas and Mary Barbara (Luczynski) Szepielewicz; e. Univ. of Waterloo, 1st yr. architecture 1973; self-taught sculptor; m. Susan d. Evelyn and Carl Strahlendorf 5 June 1976; divorced 1982; one d.: Kirsten April; selected commissions: Bell Canada, Bell Trinity Square 1983; Belmont Construction 1982; I.D.J. Devel. Group 1981; Market Sq. Condominiums 1985; Horizon on Bay Condominiums; Ronto Devel. 1984; Telegenic Prog. Ltd. 1979, 1987; Tridel Devel. Corp. 1978, '81, '83; Trizec Equities Ltd. 1980; Yorkdale

Mall 1979; Yonge Walker Place 1981; 2000 & 2010 Islington Ave. Condos. 1978, '82; 1331 Bay St. Condos. 1986, 130 Carlton Ave. Condos. 1984; 25 The Esplanade Condos. 1990 (all Toronto); Buwalda Construction (London, Ont.) 1983; McDonalds Restaurants (Toronto/Montreal) 1979; Royal Bank of Can. (Stratford) 1979; Westin Hotel (Ottawa) 1981; selected collections: Ont. Govt. Art Collection; Right Hon. William Davis; Andreas Papandreaus (Pres. of Greece); Mr. Martens (Premier of Belgium); Robert Noakes; Jack Winston; Albert Latner; Jeffrey J. Smyth; Thomas Galt; Godfrey Jacobs; Max Sherman; Bill Ridpath; Henry Gotfryd; David Margulis; David Ruben Piquton; Leo Delzotto; Don Watt & numerous others; museums: Art Gall. of Ont.; Hakone Open Air Museum; exhbns. incl.: Ont. Potters Assn. 1972–80; La Chasse Gall. 1980; Beaux Arts Gall. 1989, '90; Evelyn Amis Fine Art Gall. 1982–86; Festival of Festivals, The Fourm 1987; River St. Studio 1980– ; Humewood II Gall. 1987; Chess Set Unveiling Game with Walter Moos, Gall. Moos 1990 (all Toronto); Poland Travelling Exhib. 1983, '89; Ottawa Convention Ctr. 1987; Altamira Gall. (Ottawa) 1989; Galleria Renata (Chicago) 1988; The Shanyne Gall. (Montreal) 1988; Apple Gall. (Boardman, Ohio) 1989; Ontario Arts Council grant 1980; Aviva Art Award 1984; 7th Henry Moore Grand Prize, The Utsukushi-ga-hara Open-Air Museum, Japan (where his sculpture sits with and overlooks all the masters); created first sterling silver lapel pin 1986 & continued to make different pins 1987, '88, '90; subject of articles: 'Canadian Datasystems' April 1991, 'The Globe and Mail' summer 1989, 'Sculpture' Oct. 1988, 'Canadian Art' Fall 1988, 'T.O.' July/Aug. 1988; 'The Current' Summer 1988; Studio: 17 River St., Toronto, Ont.; Address: P.O. Box 115, Adelaide St. P.O., Toronto, Ont. M5C 2H8.

**THAIN, Donald Hammond,** M.B.A., D.B.A.; university professor; b. Toronto, Ont. 6 May 1928; s. William Edwards and Lucy May (Marsden) T.; e. Univ. of Toronto Schs.; Univ. of Toronto; Harvard Univ., M.B.A. 1953, D.B.A. 1955; m. Helen Margaret, d. Kenneth Steeves, 28 Aug. 1952; children: Peter Marsden, Carol Ann, John Fraser; PROF. OF BUSINESS ADM., UNIV. OF WESTERN ONT.; apptd. to Magna Internat. Chair in Business Admin., present Univ. 1987; former Dir. of many companies; Account Extve., Spitzer, Mills & Bates Ltd., Toronto, 1948–51; Research Asst., Instr. Harvard Business Sch., 1953–56; joined present Univ. as Asst. Prof. 1956; Assoc. Prof. 1959–64; Prof. of Gen. Mang., IMEDE (l'Institut pour l'Etude des Methodes de Direction de l'Enterprise), 1965–66; Instr. in Marketing Mang. course for extves.,and in Mang. Training for sr. mang.; has planned and taught mang. training programs for many co.'s and assns.; consultant on problems of strategic management, corporate governance, government relations, marketing and mang. devel. with numerous internat. co.'s; mem., Fed. Task Force on Agric. 1968–70; Project Dir. on study of Candn. Aero-Space Indust. for Dept. of Indust., Trade & Comm., 1968–69; mem. Fed. Computer-Communications Industry Task Force 1971–72; Petrochem. Sector Task Force Dept. Indust. Trade & Comm. 1978; author 'Corporate Long Range Planning in Canada' 1963; co-author 'Marketing in Canada' 1959; 'How Industry Buys' 1960 (Media-Scope Award); 'Business Administration in Canada' 1961; 'Canadian Cases in Business-Government Relations' 1985; 'Business Policy: A Canadian Casebook' 1988; contrib. author 'Internationalizing the Traditional Business Curriculum' 1968; recipient: P.S. Ross Award for best article 'Business Quarterly' 1970, 1977, 1990 and 1992; Protestant; recreations: golf, hockey; Home: 31 - 1200 Riverside Dr., London, Ont. N6H 5C6.

**THALL, Burnett M.,** B.A.Sc., M.A.Sc., Ph.D., P.Eng.; b. Toronto, Ont. 27 Sept. 1922; s. Henry Rosenthal and Selina (Harris) T.; e. Harbord Coll. Inst., Toronto, Ont.; Univ. of Toronto, B.A.Sc. 1945, M.A.Sc. 1947, Ph.D. 1950 m. Eleanor, d. M. Langbord, Toronto, Ont., 23 Sept. 1945; two s., Nelson Spencer, Martin Evan; SR. VICE PRES., TORSTAR CORP.; Dir. Toronto Star Newspapers Ltd.; Ont. Cancer Inst.; Gov. Council, Univ. of Toronto; Ont. Cancer Treatment & Research Foundation; Trustee, Atkinson Charitable Foundation; Princess Margaret Hosp. Found.; Hon. Treas., Women's Coll. Hosp., Toronto; named to Hall of Distinction Engineering Alumni, Univ. of Toronto 1990; recipient, Medal for Citizenship, Assn. of Professional Engineers of Ont. 1991; Urgent Care Centre named in his honour Women's Coll. Hosp. 1989; Assoc. with Nat. Research Council in Montreal at Univ. of Montreal in 1945 where initial engn. work and research for Can. first atomic reactor was conducted; Research Physicist at Deep River, Ont., engaged in fundamental research at Chalk River Atomic Energy Plant; apptd. Lectr. in Dept. of Applied Science & Engn., Univ. of Toronto, 1947 and Special Lectr.; joined present interest in 1947 as Consulting Engr. dealing specifically with production problems; el. a Dir., Dec. 1956; mem., Assn. of Prof. Engrs. Ont.; Home: 15 Rosemary Lane, Toronto, Ont. M5P 3E7; Office: One Yonge St., Toronto, Ont. M5E 1E6.

**THEAKSTON, Franklyn H.,** B.Sc., B.E., M.E.; civil engineer/consultant; b. Halifax, N.S. 1 Sept. 1919; s. Arthur Cook and Mabel (Lawson) T.; e. Acadia Univ., B.Sc. 1941; N.S. Tech. Coll., B.E. 1948; N.S. Tech. Coll. & Dalhousie Univ., M.E. 1950; m. Ethel d. James and Nettie Cameron 21 June 1946; children: Patricia, Janet, Kathryn, Elizabeth; Pres., F.H. Theakston & Assoc. 1987; Pres., Guelph Manufacturing Group 1987– ; Lt., Royal Candn. Engrs. Eur. Theatre 1942–46; Asst. Prof., Univ. of Guelph 1950–53; Assoc. Prof. 1953–56; Prof. 1956–81; Vice-Pres., Morrison, Herschfield, Theakston & Rowan Ltd. 1972–81; Pres., Guelph Mfg. Group 1982–87; Pres., Frank H. Theakston & Assoc. Inc. 1982– ; Fellow & Past Chrmn., Engr. Inst. of Can.; Am Soc. of Agric. Engrs.; Can. Soc. of Agric. Engrs.; Chrmn., Bd. of Trustees, Dublin St. Un. Ch.; Chrmn., Can. Farm Bldg. Plan Serv.; Bd. of Dir., J. Steckle Heritage Homestead; Mem. Bd. of Dirs., Winter Cities Assn. 1990– ; Dir., Candn. Snow and Wind Institute 1991– ; Mem., Candn. Extve. Serv. Overseas (serv. in Inner Mongolia); Acadia Univ. Athletic Hall of Fame; Home: 32 University Ave. W., Guelph, Ont. N1G 1N4.

**THEALL, Donald F.,** M.A., Ph.D.; educator; b. Mount Vernon, N.Y. 13 Oct. 1928; s. Harold A. and Helen A. (Donaldson) T.; e. A.B. Davis High Sch., Mount Vernon, N.Y. 1946; Yale Univ., B.A. 1950; Univ. of Toronto, M.A. 1951, Ph.D. 1954; m. Joan Ada, d. Frederick Benedict, Staten Island, N.Y., 14 June 1950; children: Thomas, Margaret, John, Harold, Lawrence, Michael; PROF. OF ENGLISH AND CULTURAL STUDIES, TRENT UNIV. 1980– ; Adjunct Prof. of Graduate Communications, McGill Univ. 1988–91; Adjunct Graduate Prof. of English, Queens Univ. 1981–87; Lectr. to Prof., Univ. of Toronto, 1953–65; Chrmn., Jt. Depts. of Eng., 1964–65; Molson Prof. of English, McGill Univ. 1972–80 (Chrmn. of Dept. 1966–74, Dir. Grad. Program in Communications 1975–80); Pres., Trent Univ. 1980–87; Secy. and mem. Culture & Communications Seminar 1953–54; mem. comte. exam. second lang. teaching 1956–59; Eng. Sub-comte., Toronto Bd. Educ. Curriculum Study, 1960–61; Prof. and Chrmn., Dept. of Eng. (Atkinson) and Dir. of Communications, York Univ., 1965–66; Dir., special 16 week seminar 'Human Communications: The Structure of Interaction,' 1965–66; Dir., project on audio-visual and multi media exhibits, Expo '67, 1967–69; mem. co-op. Educ. TV Bd. of Can. and U.S.; Candn. UNESCO rep., Conf. on Student Participation in Univ. Govt., Dubrovnik, 1970; First Cultural Exchange Professor, People's Republic of China 1974–75; consultant in fields of education, communication; author (with Robinson and Wevers) of 'Let's Speak English,' 4 volumes (translated into 21 languages), 1962; Educational T.V. Hon. Mention, Ohio State Univ., for 'Let's Speak English' series, C.B.C., 1962; Report on the Creation of a Visual Arts Info. Service for Canada, 1968; Report on Cultural Effects of Advertising to Que. Ministry of Communications, 1978; 'The Medium is the Rear View Mirror' 1971; Co-ed. (with G.J. Robinson) 'Studies in Canadian Communications' 1975; Chrmn., Ed. Comte., 'Arts Canada,' 1966–68; Past Vice Pres., Soc. Arts Publs.; Past Dir., Ont. Council Teachers Eng.; Assn. Teachers Eng., Quebec; Founding Chrmn., Candn. Assn. of Chairmen of Eng. 1971–74; mem., Candn. Assn. for Irish Studies; Internat. James Joyce Foundation; Cinémathèque Canadienne; Modern Lang. Assn.; Philol. Soc. Gt. Brit.; Internat. Inst. of Communications; Internat. Communications Assn. (Dir. 1978–81); Ed. Bd. of Science Fiction Studies 1976– ; 'Canadian Journal of Communication' 1979– (Treas. 1986–91); 'Culture and Content' 1979– ; 'Journal of Canadian Studies' 1980–87; mem. Adv. Bd., 'Semiotic Inquiry' 1982– ; Chrmn. Comte. to Form Candn. Communication Assn. 1978, elected Founding Pres., Candn. Communication Assn. 1979–80; Corr. Fellow, Acad. Medicine Toronto; mem. Greater Peterborough Economic Council 1982–87; mem. Bd. of Dir., Candn. Fed. for the Humanities, 1984–87; mem. Fed. Employment Adv. Counc. (for Peterborough Area) 1985–87; mem., Massey College, U. of T. 1991– ; recreations: swimming, films, theatre; Clubs: Elizabethan (Yale); University C. of Toronto; McGill Faculty; Yale (Toronto); Home: 1604 Champlain Drive, Peterborough, Ont. K9L 1N6.

**THEBERGE, John Bedford,** B.Sc.A., M.Sc., Ph.D.; university professor; b. Hamilton, Ont. 11 Oct. 1940; s. Clifford Bingham and Elaine (Bedford) T.; e. Oshawa C.V.I. 1959; Univ. of Guelph, B.Sc.A. 1964; Univ. of Toronto, M.Sc. 1966; Univ. of B.C., Ph.D. 1971; m. Mary d. Josie and Edward Kotynski 1 July 1963; children: Jeannette Christine, Michelle Marie; PROF. OF WILDLIFE ECOL. & RESOURCE MNGT., UNIV. OF WATERLOO 1970– ; pure rsch. spec., predator; applied rsch. spec., wildlands planning & mngt. esp. nat. parks; Former Vice-Pres., Nat. & Prov. Parks Assn. of Can.; Former Extve. & Bd. Mem., Fed. of Ont. Naturalists (Hon. Life Mem.); Chrmn., Task Force for Fed. Min. of Environ. on New Park Establishment 1986; Fellow, Arctic Inst. of N. Am.; author: 'Wolves and Wilderness' 1975; num. sci. papers on large mammals & predator ecol. following rsch. in Ont., Yukon, Labrador; also many pop. mag. articles on resource mngt. issues and children's nature articles illus. by Mary Theberge; editor: 'Kluane: Pinnacle of the Yukon' 1980; 'Legacy: The Natural History of Ontario' 1989; Home: R.R. #2, New Hamburg, Ont. N0B 2G0; Office: Fac. of Environ. Studies, Univ. of Waterloo, Waterloo, Ont. N2L 3G1.

**THÉRIAULT, The Hon. Camille Henri,** M.L.A.; politician; b. Baie-Ste-Anne, N.B. 25 Feb. 1955; s. Norbert L. and Joséphine (Martin) T.; e. Baie-Ste-Anne; m. Gisèle; children: Sophie, Sébastien; MINISTER OF FISHERIES & AQUACULTURE, GOVT. OF N.B. 1991– ; 1st elected to Legislative Assembly of N.B. as M.L.A. for Kent South 13 Oct. 1987; served as Chairman, Public Accts. Ctte. & Mem., Standing Ctte. on Estimates; re-elected 23 Sept. 1991; Mem., Bd. of Management; Regional Dir., Liberal Party, Kent Region; Home: P.O. Box 38, Bouctouche, N.B. E0A 1G0; Office: P.O. Box 6000, Fredericton, N.B. E3B 5H1.

**THERIAULT, Hon. L. Norbert;** senator; b. Baie Ste-Anne, N.B. 16 Feb. 1921; s. Edmour and Céline (Turbide) T.; e. St. Thomas Univ.; St. Xavier Univ.; m. Joséphine d. Raphael and Charlotte Martin 26 Aug. 1941; children: Raoul, Ginette, Monette, Aurel, Berthe, Jean-Marie, Gilles, Camille, Nicole, Mario; el. to Mun. Council Northumberland Co. 1955, re-el. 1957, 1959; Chief Warden 1957; el. M.L.A. g.e. N.B. 1960, re-el. 1963, 1967, 1970, 1974, 1978; Min. of Mun. Affairs 1965; Min. of Health & Welfare 1967–70; summoned to Senate of Can. 1979; Home: P.O. Box 7, Baie Ste-Anne, N.B.; Office: Rm 274, East Block, The Senate of Canada, Ottawa, Ont. K1A 0A4.

**THÉRIAULT, Michel,** B.Phil., M.L.S., J.C.D.; university professor; b. Toronto, Ont. 2 Dec. 1942; s. Yves and Germaine Michelle (Blanchet) T.; e. Univ. de Montréal B.Phil. 1962; McGill Univ. M.L.S. 1976; Pontifical Univ. of Saint Thomas Rome Italy J.C.D. 1971; ASSOCIATE PROFESSOR, FACULTY OF CANON LAW, SAINT PAUL UNIVERSITY 1992– ; Head, Acquisitions Dept., Univ. de Montréal Libraries 1969–75; Chief, Retrospective Nat. Bibliography Div., Nat. Library of Canada 1975–85; Asst. Prof., Faculty of Canon Law, Saint Paul Univ. 1985–92; Secretary 1987– ; Judge, Canadian Appeal Tribunal, Roman Catholic Church; Mem., Candn. Canon Law Soc. (Sec.-Treas. 1988–90); Soc. for the Law of the Eastern Churches (Del. for Canada 1987– ); Corp. of Profl. Librarians of Quebec (Pres. 1972–73); Bibliographical Soc. of Canada (Assoc. Sec. 1981–86); author: 'Le livre religieux au Québec depuis les débuts de l'imprimerie jusqu'à la Confédération 1764–1867' 1977, 'The Institutes of Consecrated Life in Canada from the Beginning of New France up to the Present' 1980, 'Néo-vagin et impuissance' 1971; editor: 'Choix et acquisition des documents au Québec' vol. 1 1977; co-editor: 'Proceedings of the 5th Internat. Congress of Canon Law' 1986, 'Code de droit canonique' (éd. bilingue et annotée) 1990, 'Canonical Studies Presented to Germain Lesage' 1991, 'Studia Canonica, Index 1-25 1967–1991' 1992, 'Code of Canon Law Annotated' 1993; Home: 2069 – 56 Jasmine Cr., Ottawa, Ont. K1J 7W2; Office: 223 Main St., Ottawa, Ont. K1S 1C4.

**THERIEN, Emile-J.,** M.A.; association executive; b. Aylmer, Qué. 6 Oct. 1942; s. Rene Jos and Ruth T.; e. St. Lawrence Univ. Canton, N.Y. B.A. 1966; Univ. of N.B. pre-M.A. 1967; Carleton Univ. M.P.A. 1969; m. Beth d. Jack and Lillian Bowie 30 July 1966; children: Sarah Beth, Christopher Bowie; PRES. CAN. SAFETY COUNCIL 1988– ; Mgmt. Trainee Met Life 1969–71; Dir. Govt. Relations Automotive Industries Assn. Can. 1971–73; Exec. Vice Pres. Candn. Home Mfrs. Assn. 1973–75; Exec. Dir. Candn. Assn. Fire Chiefs 1975–88; Office: 2750 Stevenage Dr., Unit 6, Ottawa, Ont. K1G 3N2.

**THÉRIO, Adrien,** M.A., Ph.D.; éducateur; auteur; né St-Modeste, Qué. 15 août 1925; f. Charles-Eugène et Eva (Bouchard) T.; é. Univ. d'Ottawa B.A. 1950; Univ. Lavl M.A. 1951, Ph.D. 1952; Harvard Univ. Rockefeller Foundation Fellowship Studies in Am. Lit. 1953–54; Notre Dame Univ. M.A. 1959; Univ. of Toronto Studies in Pol. Science 1959–60; PROFESSEUR DE LETTRES

FRANCAISES, UNIV. D'OTTAWA; Fondateur et dir. de 'Lettres Québécoises' 1976–90; Fondateur et dir. de 'Livres et auteurs québécois' 1961–72; Head of French, Royal Mil. Coll. Kingston 1962–69; auteur: 'Les brèves années' (roman) 1953; 'La soif et le Mirage' (roman) 1958; 'Mes Beaux Meurtres' (nouvelles) 1961; 'Le Printemps qui pleure' (roman) 1962; 'Ceux du Chemin-Taché' (contes) 1962; 'Le Mors aux flancs' (récit humoristique) 1965; 'Soliloque en hommage à une femme' (roman) 1968; 'Un païen chez les pingouins' (récit) 1970; Les Fous d'amour' (roman) 1973; 'La Colère du père' (récit) 1974; 'La Tête en fête' (histoires) 1975; 'C'est ici que le monde a commencé' (récit-reportage) 1978; 'Marie-Ève! Marie-Ève! (roman) 1983; pour adolescents: 'Contes des belles saisons' 1958; 'Flamberge au vent' (roman) 1958; études: 'Jules Fournier, journaliste de combat' 1955; 'Mon encrier de Jules Fournier' 1965; 'Conteurs canadiens-français' (anthologie) 1968; 'L'Humour au Canada français' (anthologie) 1968; 'Conteurs québécois 1900–1940' (anthologie) 1988; théâtre: 'Les Renégats' (pièce en trois actes) 1964; 'Le Roi d'Aragon' (pièce en 2 actes) 1979; traduction: 'Un Yankee au Canada de Henry David Thoreau' 1962; mem. Union des écrivains québécois; Soc. Royale du Can.; Bureaux: 165, La Gauchetière ouest, #504, Montréal, Qué. H2Z 1X6.

**THIBAUDEAU, Colleen,** B.A., M.A.; writer; b. Toronto, Ont. 29 Dec. 1925; d. John Stewart and Alice (Pryce) T.; e. St. Thomas Coll. Inst. 1944; Univ. of Toronto, Univ. Coll. B.A. 1948, M.A. 1949; L'Univ. Cathol. de l'ouest Angers, dipl. 1951; m. James C. s. James N. and Elizabeth (Crerar) Reaney 29 Dec. 1951; children; James Stewart, John Andrew (dec.), Susan Elizabeth (Reaney); joined Mktg. Dept., McClelland & Stewart 1949–50; Assistante, Lycée Joachim Du Bellay, Angers, France 1950–51; author: Poetry collections in 'Ten Letters' 1975 etc., 'My Granddaughters Are Combing Out Their Long Hair' poetry 1977; 'The Martha Landscapes' poetry 1984 and stories & poetry in many anthologies & on radio, etc.; 'The Artemesia Book: Poems Selected and Now' 1991; Lit. Cons.; several Candn. & U.S. tours & readings; Eva McCulley Mem. Award (Wellington P.S.) 1939; shared scholarship in Eng. & Hist., Univ. Coll. 1944; shared prize 1st yr. English Lang. & Lit. 1945; Mem., League of Candn. Poets 1969– ; Mem., United Church; NDP; Address: c/o Brick Books, P.O. Box 38, Postal Station B, London, Ont. N6A 4V3.

**THIBAULT, J. Laurent,** B.A., M.A.; b. Sturgeon Falls, Ont. 31 Dec. 1944; s. J. Rene and Leone T.; e. Laurentian Univ. B.A. Econ. 1966; Univ. of Toronto M.A. Econ. 1968; m. Paulette d. Jean Paul Lalonde 4 June 1966; children: Alain, André; CO-CHAIR, CAN. LABOUR FORCE DEVELOPMENT BOARD 1991– ; Consultant Kates, Peat, Marwick Toronto 1968–72; Mgr. Econ. Dept. The Candn. Manufacturers' Assn. 1972–76, Dir. Econ. and Communications 1976–81, Exec. Vice-Pres. 1981–84, Sr. Exec. Vice-Pres. 1984, Pres. and Exec. Dir. 1985–91; mem. Candn. Assn. for Bus. Econ.; Candn. Found. for Econ. Edn.; Mem. of the Bd., Skills Canada; Mem. Bd. of Govs., McMaster Univ.; recreations: hiking, canoeing, hockey, scuba diving; Home: 24 Cindebarke Terrace, Georgetown, Ont. L7G 4S5.

**THIBERT, Patrick A.,** B.F.A., M.F.A.; college professor; b. Windsor, Ont. 25 Feb. 1943; s. Ernest Ferdnand and Anna Exilda (Robinet) T.; e. Western. Ont. Inst. of Technol., Chem. Technol. 1965; Univ. of Windsor B.F.A. 1972; Florida State Univ. M.F.A. 1974; m. Muriel (Billie) d. Muriel and Joseph O'Rourke 27 July 1968; children: Victoria (Tori), Muriel (Molly), Katie; PROFESSOR, FANSHAWE COLL. OF APPLIED ARTS & TECHNOL. 1975– ; selected one-man shows: Olga Korper Gallery Toronto 1983, '87, '90, '92; touring to Art Gall. of Hamilton, Kitchener-Waterloo Art Gall. 1986 & Gall. 'O' Toronto 1977, '79, '81; London Regional Art and Historical Museum 1992; selected group shows: Columbia Plaza Sculpture Show Washington, D.C. 1980; Outdoor Sculpture Show, Aquarium of Niagara Falls, N.Y. 1981 (1 year); Contemporary Outdoor Sculpture, Guildwood Hall Toronto 1982; Toronto Sculpture Garden: 'Down the Garden Path' 1982 'Visual Rhythms' 1984; Sculpture Tour 1983–84, '84–85, '87–88 Univ. of Tennessee; Artscape Burlington Cultural Ctr. 1987; two-man show: N.A.M.E. Gall. Chicago 1979; A.C.T. Harbourfront Art Gall. Toronto 1976; Grad. Teaching Position, Florida State Univ. 1973, 1973–74; Sessional position, St. Clair Coll. of Applied Arts & Technol. 1974–75; Guest Lectr., Laurentian Univ. Mus. & Art Ctr. 1984; Brock Univ. 1984; Univ. of Windsor 1985; Art Gall. of Hamilton 1986; Univ. of Calgary 1989; Emily Carr Sch. of Art & Design 1989; Kitchener-Waterloo Art Gall. 1986, '90; Ontario Arts Council Material Grant 1975–85, 1992; Mem., Forest City Gallery; Home: R.R. 1, Mt. Brydges, Ont. N0L 1W0; Office: 1460 Oxford St. E., London, Ont. N5W 5H1.

**THIBERT, Roger Joseph,** B.A., M.S., Ph.D., F.C.I.C.; university professor; b. Tecumseh, Ont. 29 Aug. 1929; s. Charles and Violet (Hebert) T.; e. Assumption High Sch., Windsor, Ont. 1948; Univ. of Western Ont. Assumption Coll., B.A. 1951; Univ. of Detroit, M.S. 1954; Research Fellow. Mich. Heart Assn. (1956–57); Wayne State Univ. Ph.D. 1958 (excellence Prize in Phys. Sc.); m. Audrey M. (R.T., B.A.) d. Robert Orville Wissler, Windsor, Ont. 10 July 1954; children: Mark, M.D.; Robert, M.D.; DIR. OF CLIN. CHEM., UNIV. OF WINDSOR since 1973; Prof. Pathol., Wayne State Univ. Sch. Med., since 1972; Assoc. Div. Head, Clin. Chem., Detroit Receiving Hosp.-University Health Centre since 1972; began career as Quality Control Asst., Green Giant Co. of Can., Tecumseh, Ont., summers 1948–53; Clin. Chem., Grace Hosp., Windsor, Ont., summer 1954; Detroit Mem. Hosp. summer 1955; Lectr. in Chem., Assumption Univ. of Windsor, 1953–57; Asst. Prof. 1957–61, Univ. of Windsor, Assoc. Prof. 1961–67, Prof. since 1967; Assoc. Dean Faculty of Arts and Science 1964–70; Instr. Nursing Chem., Grace Hospital School of Nursing 1954–73; Research Associate, Dept. of Pathology, Wayne State Univ. Sch. of Med. 1971–72; rec'd: Union Carbide Award of the Chemical Inst. of Canada for Chem. Educ. 1978; Smith Kline Clinical Laboratories Award, Am. Assn. for Clinical Chem., for Outstanding Efforts for Educ. & Training, 1980; Univ. of Windsor Alumni Award for Distinguished Contributions to University Teaching 1988; The Ames Award, Candn. Soc. of Clinical Chemists for Outstanding Achievement in the Field of Clinical Chem. 1988; Ont. Confederation of Univ. Faculty Assoc. (OCUFA) Teaching Award 1990; Beckman Education Excellence Award, Candn. Soc. of Clinical Chemists 1992; Publications: various articles in chem. and learned journs.; Fellow, Am. Assn. Advanc. Science; Nat. Acad. Clin. Biochem.; Candn. Acad. of Clin. Biochem.; Chem. Inst. of Can.; mem., Am. Chem Soc.; Am. Soc. for Biochem. and Molecular Biol.; Am. Assn. Clin. Chem.; Candn. Soc. Clin. Chems.; Candn Soc. for Chem.; Candn. Assn. Univ. Teachers; Candn. Biochem. Soc.; Sigma Xi; Roman Catholic; recreation: music (guitar); Home: 445 Randolph Ave., Windsor, Ont. N9B 2T5.

**THIBODEAU-DeGUIRE, Michèle,** ing.; business executive; b. Montreal, Que. 6 Sept. 1941; d. Jean J. (architect) and Patricia (Savard) T.; e. Sacred Heart School 1957; Ecole Polytechnique, civil engineer 1963; m. Pierre-André (C.A.) s. Lucie and J. Armand D. 21 Dec. 1963; children: Caroline, Bernard; PRES. & EXTVE. DIR., CENTRAIDE OF GREATER MONTREAL 1991– ; Structural Engr., Groupe LGL 1963–75; Cons. Engr., F. Boulva & Assoc. 1975–82; General Delegate to New England, Que. Govt. 1982–84; Dir. of Public Relations, Ecole Polytechnique 1985–91; Doctorat Honoris Causa (Human Sciences) Rivier College, New Hampshire; Prix Mérite, Assn. des diplômés de Polytechnique 1994; Fellow, Candn. Acad. of Engineering; Mem., Natural Sciences and Engineering Rsch. Council of Can.; Mem., Candn. Centre for Philanthropy; Gov., Assn. des diplômés de Polytechnique (Pres. 1977); Home: 1450 Cap-Eternité, Duvernay, Laval, Que. H7E 3K2; Office: 493 Sherbrooke St. W., Montreal, Que. H3A 1B6.

**THIESSEN, Abram J.;** transportation executive; b. Rosenfeld, Man. 12 Dec. 1910; s. Abram and Susanna (Braun) T.; e. elem. sch. Rosenfeld and high sch. Steinbach, Man.; m. Lenora, d. Bernhard Friesen, 28 July 1935; children: Ronald, Bernard, William, Irvine, Carolyn; Secy., Grey Goose Bus Lines Ltd.; with Rosenfeld Trucking 1931–45; Partner, G. H. Fast Automobile & Farm Machinery dealership, Rosenfeld and Altona 1936–59; began bus transport, business 1946; estbd. and became first Pres. and Gen. Mgr., Radio Stn. CFAM, Altona 1957; rec'd Coronation Medal 1953, Centennial Medal 1967; P. Cons. cand. g.e. 1953 and 1962; Past Pres., Man. Assn. Sch. Trustees; Candn. Sch. Trustee Assn.; Rosenfeld Chamber Comm.; mem., Man. Mennonite Hist. Soc.; past Chrmn., Mennonite Coll. Inst., Gretna, Man.; P. Conservative; Mennonite; recreations: curling, golf, fishing, reading; Club: St. Charles Country; Home: 1201 – 200 Tuxedo Blvd., Winnipeg, Man. R3P 0R3; Office: 301 Burnell St., Winnipeg, Man. R3G 2A6.

**THIESSEN, George J.,** M.Sc., Ph.D., F.R.S.C.; retired research physicist; b. Russia 7 May 1913; s. Rev. Jacob G. and Sara (Goetz) T.; came to Canada, 1923; e. Saskatoon Normal Sch., Sask.; Univ. of Sask., B.Sc. 1935, M.Sc. 1937; Columbia Univ., Ph.D. 1941; m. Isabel, d. Arthur Clendenan, 12 Aug. 1946; children: Edwin George, Carol Isabel, Randolph Richard; author of more than 50 scient. papers; Fellow, Acoustical Soc. Am., Fellow. Royal. Soc. of Can.; Home: 242 Roger Road, Ottawa, Ont. K1H 5C6.

**THIESSEN, Gordon G.,** M.A., Ph.D.; economist; b. South Porcupine, Ont. 14 Aug. 1938; s. David Jacob and Ella Susie (Shultz) T.; e. Moosomin (Sask.) High Sch. 1955; Univ. of Sask. B.A. 1960, M.A. 1961; London Sch. of Econ. Ph.D. 1972; m. Annette Hillyar 3 Oct. 1964; two children; GOVERNOR, BANK OF CANADA 1994– and Chrmn. of the Bd. of Dirs.; joined Royal Bank of Canada, Wapella and Eyebrow, Sask. 1955–56; Lectr. in Econ. Univ. of Sask. Saskatoon 1961–62; Econ. in Rsch., Monetary and Financial Analysis Depts. Bank of Canada Ottawa 1963–73, Chief Dept. Monetary & Financial Analysis 1975–79, Adviser to Gov. 1979–84; Deputy Gov. 1984–87; Sr. Deputy Governor, Mem. of the Bd. of Dirs. and Mem. of the Extve. Ctte. of the Bd., Bank of Canada 1987–94; Visiting Econ. Reserve Bank of Australia, Sydney 1973–75; recreations: sailing, swimming, skiing, skating; Office: 234 Wellington St., Ottawa, Ont. K1A 0G9.

**THIRSK, Robert Brent,** B.Sc., S.M., M.D.C.M.; P.Eng.; astronaut; b. New Westminster, B.C. 17 Aug. 1953; s. Lester Wayne and Christina Eva (Jansson) T.; e. Univ. of Calgary B.Sc. 1976 (Mech. Engn.); Mass. Inst. of Technol. S.M. (Mech. Engn.) 1978; McGill Univ. M.D.C.M. 1982; m. Brenda d. Attilio and Lina Biasutti 7 Jan. 1984; children: Lisane, Elliot; ASTRONAUT, CANADIAN SPACE AGENCY 1983– ; began rsch. in biomedical engn. while at M.I.T. and McGill Univ.; one of six astronauts Dec. 1983; served as back-up crew mem. for 5 Oct. 1984 mission of Space Shuttle Challenger; recipient Gold Medal, Assn. of Profl. Engrs., Geols. & Geophysicists of Alta. 1976; Distinguished Alumni Award, Univ. of Calgary 1985; co-recipient, F.W. (Casey) Baldwin Award, Candn. Aeronautics & Space Inst. 1985; mem. Candn. Aeronautics & Space Inst.; Aerospace Med. Assn.; Assn. of Profl. Engrs. of Ont.; Candn. Coll. of Family Physicians; recreations: flying, scuba diving, piano, spending time with family; Home: Ottawa, Ont.; Office: Canadian Space Agency, 6767, Route de l'aéroport, Saint-Hubert, Que. J3Y 8Y9.

**THODE, Henry George,** C.C. (1967), M.B.E. (1946), M.Sc., D.Sc., Ph.D., LL.D., F.R.S. (1954), F.R.S.C. (1943), F.C.I.C. (1948); b. Dundurn, Sask. 10 Sept. 1910; s. Charles Herman and Zelma Ann (Jacoby) T.; e. Univ. Sask., B.Sc. 1930, M.Sc. 1932; Univ. Chicago, Ph.D. 1934; Columbia Univ. (Research) 1936–39; LL.D. Univ. of Sask. 1958; Univ. of Regina 1983; D.Sc., Univ. of Toronto 1955, Brit. Columbia 1960, Acadia 1960, Laval 1963, Royal Mil. Coll. 1964, McGill 1966, Queen's 1967, York 1972, McMaster 1973; m. Sadie Alicia, d. John A. M. Patrick, 1 February 1935; children: John Charles, Henry Patrick, Richard Lee; mem. of Defence Research Board, 1955–61; National Research Council of Canada, 1955–61; Research Consultant, Atomic Energy of Canada 1952–65; Asst. Professor of Chemistry, McMaster Univ., 1939–42, Assoc. Prof. 1942–44, Prof. 1944–79; Dir., of Research, 1947–61; Head of Dept., 1948–52, Vice Pres. of the Univ. 1957–61, (Principal of Hamilton Coll. there 1949–63), Pres. and Vice Chancellor July 1961–30 June 1972, cont. as Prof. Emeritus of Chem.; on leave of absence for War Research with Nat. Research Council of Can. 1943–45; Pres., sec., 111, Roy. Soc. of Can., 1950–51 and Pres. of Soc. 1960; mem. Comn. on Atomic Weights, Inorganic Chem. Div. 1963–79 & mem. Canadian National Committee 1975–79, International Union Pure and Applied Chem.; Dir., Western New York Nuclear Research Centre 1965–73; Atomic Energy of Canada, Ltd. 1966–81; Stelco Inc. 1969–85; Gov., Ontario Research Foundation 1955–82; Royal Bot. Gardens 1961–73; mem., Chem. Inst. of Can. (Pres. 1951–52, Medal 1957); Am. Chem. Soc.; mem., Ed. Adv. Bd. 'Journal of Inorganic & Nuclear Chemistry'; has written articles relating to separation of isotopes, mass spectrometry, & isotope abundances in terrestrial, meteoritic and lunar materials, etc.; awarded H.M. Tory Medal by Royal Soc. Canada 1959; Nat. Science Foundation Sr. Foreign Scientist Fellowship 1970; Hon. Shell Fellow 1974; Sherman Fairchild Distinguished Scholar, Caltech 1977; awarded Arthur L. Day Medal by Geolog. Soc. of Am., 1980; Centenary Medal, Royal Soc. of Can. 1982; The Sir William Dawson Medal, Royal Soc. of Can. 1989; Order of Ontario 1989; Montreal Medal, Chemical Institute of Can. 1993; Sigma Xi; Gamma Alpha; United Church; recreations: swimming, farming; Club: Rotary; Address: McMaster University, Nuclear Research Bldg., 1280 Main St. W., Hamilton, Ont. L8S 4K1.

**THOM, Bing Wing,** B.Arch, M.Arch, FRAIC; architect; b. Hong Kong 8 Dec. 1940; s. Wesley C. and Millicent (Chan) T.; e. Univ. of B.C. B.Arch. 1966; Univ. of Calif. at Berkeley M.Arch. 1970; m. Bonnie d. Jim and Teanna Koo 21 May 1966; SOLE PRINCIPAL, BING THOM ARCHITECTS INC. 1980– ; Fumihiko Maki Arch. 1971; Personnel & Project Dir., Arthur Erickson Architects 1972–80; Past Chair, Planning & Building Ctte., Vancouver Public Library; Past Chair, Planning & Building Ctte., Bd. of Gov., Univ. of B.C.; Mem., Asian Pacific Initiative Advisory Ctte.; Founding Mem., Chinese Cultural Ctr.; Sessional Lectr., Univ. of B.C., Univ. of Singapore, Univ. of Calif. at Berkeley; Guest Lectr., McGill Univ., Tech. Univ. of N.S., Univ. of Calif. at L.A., Ching Hua Univ., Chongqing Arch. & Engr. Inst., Tong Ji Univ. and at Louvain La Neuve Univ.; Co-founder, Asian Am. Studies Program, Third World Studies Dept., Univ. of Calif. at Berk.; CMHC Fellowship for Grad. Studies 1968–70; CMHC Travelling Scholarship 1965; Arch. Inst. of B.C. Design Prize, 1966; firm has received Gov. Gen. Medal, Gov. Gen. Award, Lt. Gov. of B.C. Medal, Cdn. Wood Council Award, Am. Hotel/Motel & Restaurant Gold Key Award, Excellence on the Waterfront Award; Cdn. Architect Design Awards (2); Interior Designers' Institute of B.C. Award; Cdn. Travel & Tourism Award; Commissions: Canada Pavilion, Expo '92; Chan Centre for the Performing Arts, UBC; Office: 1430 Burrard St., Vancouver, B.C. V6Z 2A3.

**THOM, Donald Cullen,** B.A.Sc.; government relations consultant; b. Vernon, B.C. 6 May 1934; s. William Archibald and Lillian Eileen (Hembling) Thom; e. Univ. of B.C., B.S.Sc. 1959; m. Linda d. Neill and Cara Malcolm 26 Sept. 1972; children: Samantha, Murray; PRES., THOM, MALCOLM & ASSOC. INC. 1984– ; Dept. of Def. Prodn., Govt. of Can. 1959–63; Extve. Asst. to Dep. Min. & Div. Chief, Mech. Transp. Div., Dept. of Indus. 1963–68; Dir., Econ. Devel., Dept. of Fin. 1968–72; Dep. Perm. Candn. Rep, Orgn. for Econ. Co-op. & Devel. 1972–75; Gen. Dir., Min. of State for Sci. & Tech. 1975–77; Asst. Sec. (Indus.), 1978–84; Home: 19 - 551 Riverdale Ave., Ottawa, Ont. K1S 1S3.

**THOM, James Lewis;** transportation executive; b. Paterson, N.J. 23 Oct. 1921; s. James Balfour and Florence Roberts T.; came to Canada 1921; e. West Hill H.S., Sir George Williams Coll. (Montreal); American Univ. Washington (Transp. Extension Course); m. Martine Merlevede; children from previous marriage: James Colin, Eugene Graeme; retired Pres. & Dir., Montreal Shipping Inc. 1990; Pres. & Dir. Montship Lines, Ltd; Vice-Pres. and Dir., Allied Steamship Lines Ltd.; served as Dir., Candn. Comte., Pacific Basin Economic Council; Canada-India Business Council; Mem., Inst. of Chart. Shipbrokers (London); Canada-China Trade Council; Montreal Port Authority 1971–83; Dir., Canada Ports Corp., Ottawa 1983–87; Mem. Extve. Counc., Shipping Fed. of Can. 1965–75 (Chrmn. 1970); Dir., Candn. Export Assoc. 1964–68; Dir., Westmount Municipal Assn. (Pres. 1970–71); Alderman, City of Westmount 1972–75; Dir., Montreal Sailors' Inst. 1966–68; Pres., Mariners House 1968; Protestant; Clubs: Shaughnessy Golf & Country (Vancouver); The Vancouver; Homes: 1101 – 2075 Comox St., Vancouver, B.C. V6G 1S2; Poipu Crater 22, 2330 Hóohu Rd., Koloa, Kauai, HI 96756.

**THOM, Linda M.,** CM, B.J.; athlete; real estate sales rep.; b. Hamilton, Ont. 30 Dec.; d. John Neill and Carissima (Lundin-Stanhope) Malcolm; e. Carleton Univ. B.J. 1967; Le Cordon Bleu (France), Dep. d'Enseignement Culinaire Superieur 1975; La Rép. Française, cert. d'Aptitude Profl. en Cuisine 1975; m. Donald s. Archibald and Lillian T. 26 Sept. 1972; children: Samantha, Murray; SALES REPRESENTATIVE, ROYAL LEPAGE 1989– ; Vice-Chairperson, Candn. Advisory Council on Firearms 1990– ; Mem., Candn. Shooting Team, participant in numerous internat. comps. 1970–75 and 1982–87 and winner of 6 gold, 4 silver, 3 bronze medals; Cooking teacher, caterer, writer about food & restaurants 1975–83; Founder, Soc. for Am. Wines 1980–81; 1984 Olympic Gold Medalist, Los Angeles, Sport Pistol; former Chrmn., Ont. Sport Med. & Safety Adv. Bd.; Mem., Order of Canada; Velma Springstead Trophy 1984 (Candn. Woman Athlete of the Year); Key to the City of Ottawa; Mem., Candn. Amateur Sports Hall of Fame; Mem., Canada's Sports Hall of Fame 1992; Hon. Mem., numerous gun clubs; Candn. Fed. of Chefs de Cuisine; Life Mem., Shooting Fed. of Can.; Ont. Handgun Assn.; author of numerous articles & reviews; Club: Civil Serv. Recn. Assn.; Home: 19 – 551 Riverdale Ave., Ottawa, Ont. K1S 1S3.

**THOM, Stuart Douglas,** Q.C., B.A., LL.B., LL.D.; b. Regina, Sask. 7 Sept. 1906; s. Douglas John and Mabel (Chown) T.; e. Victoria Coll., Univ. of Toronto B.A. 1927; Univ. of Sask. LL.B. 1929; m. Lian, d. Harold Douglas Stephen 8 Nov. 1935; one s. Stephen; PARTNER, OSLER HOSKIN & HARCOURT 1956– ; called to the Bar of Sask. 1930, Ont. 1947; c. Q.C. 1957; Legal Extve. Asst., Dept. of Nat. Revenue, Taxation 1945–47; joined firm Smith, Rae & Greer, Toronto 1947; present firm 1954; a Gov. (1953–55) Candn. Tax Foundation (Chrmn. 1959–60); el. a Bencher, Law Soc. Upper Can. 1966, 71 (Chrmn. Admissions Comte. 1968–70, Discipline 1971–74, Treas. 1974–76); served R.C.N.V.R. 1940–45, convoy duty in N. Atlantic, rank Lt. Commdr.; mem. Candn. Bar Assn.; Liberal; recreations: reading, walking; Clubs: National; Lawyers; Home: 27 Ridgevalley Cres., Islington, Ont.; Office: First Canadian Place, King St. W., Toronto, Ont. M5X 1B8.

**THOMAS, Arthur Roy Hugh,** B.A., B.Ed., M.A.; educator; writer; b. St. Catharines, Ont. 30 Apl. 1922; s. Charles Edgar and Charlotte Norah (Moon) T.; e. Ridley Coll. St. Catharines, Ont. 1941; Royal Naval Coll. Greenwich 1942; McGill Univ. B.A. 1951; Univ. of Toronto B.Ed. 1956; Waseda Univ. Tokyo 1966; Univ. of Ottawa M.A. 1973; served with RNVR 1941–45, Mediterranean and Atlantic, rank Lt.; High Sch. Teacher Ottawa 1955–80, Head of Hist. 1960, sabbatical to S.E.Asia, China and Japan 1965–66; compiled Can.'s first high sch. course on E. Asian Hist., approved for use Ont. 1968; rsch. leave 1969–70; frequent guest speaker; scripted and narrated TV progs. 'Living in Japan and China: The Cultural Revolution' CJOH Ottawa; radio interviews CBC Ottawa 1978; field and ednl. tours China and Japan 1977, 1979, 1982, 1985; author (text) 'Japan: The Rise of an Industrial Power' 1971; 'China: The Awakening Giant' 1971, rev. 1981; 'Japan, The Blighted Blossom' (non-fiction) 1989, transl. into Japanese Tokyo 1990, Korean Ed. Seoul 1992; other writings incl. articles in various journs.; Researcher, Diet Lib. Tokyo 1974, 1979; mem. The Royal Over-Seas League (London); The Foreign Corr's Club Japan; Ont. Coll. Teachers; Candn. Asian Studies Assn.; Club: Jericho Tennis (Vancouver); recreations: tennis, skiing, swimming; Address: 1205, 1348 Barclay St., Vancouver, B.C. V6E 1H7.

**THOMAS, Audrey Grace,** B.A., M.A.; writer; b. Binghamton, N.Y. 17 Nov. 1935; d. Donald Earle and Frances Waldron (Corbett) Callahan; e. Smith Coll. B.A. 1957; Univ. of B.C., M.A. 1963; m. Ian Thomas 1958 (now div.); children: Sarah, Victoria, Claire; author: 'Ten Green Bottles' (stories) 1967; 'Munchmeyer' and 'Prospero on the Island' (2 short novels) 1972; 'Mrs. Blood' (novel) 1970; 'Songs My Mother Taught Me' (novel) 1973; 'Blown Figures' (novel) 1975; 'Ladies and Escorts' (stories) 1977; 'Two in the Bush and Other Stories' (a selection) 1980; 'Latakia' (novel) 1979; 'Real Mothers' (stories) 1981; 'Intertidal Life' (novel, nominated for Gov. Gen's. Award in Fiction) 1984; 'Goodbye Harold, Good Luck' (stories) 1986; 'The Wild Blue Yonder' (stories) 1990; 'Graven Images' (novel) 1993; also many radio dramas for CBC; recipient: Ethel Wilson Prize (best fiction, B.C. Book Prize for 'The Wild Blue Yonder' and 'Intertidal Life'); The Marian Engel Award; Canada-Australia Literary Prize 1990; Visiting Prof., Concordia Univ. 1989–90; Visiting Prof. in Creative Writing, Dartmouth College, Hanover, N.H. (winter term) 1994; Visiting Lectr. in Creative Writing: Univ. of B.C., Univ. of Victoria, Concordia Univ.; Writer-in-Residence: Simon Fraser Univ., David Thompson University Centre; Canada-Scotland Literary Fellow 1985–86; Writer-in-Residence, Univ. of Ottawa; mem. Writers Union of Can.; P.E.N.; Amnesty Internat.; ACTRA; Address: R.R. 2, Galiano, B.C. V0N 1P0.

**THOMAS, Mrs. Clara McCandless,** M.A., Ph.D., F.R.S.C., D.Litt., LL.D.; b. Strathroy, Ont. 22 May 1919; d. Basil and Mabel Elizabeth (Sullivan) McCandless; e. Univ. Western Ont., B.A. 1941, M.A. 1944; Univ. of Toronto, Ph.D. 1962; York Univ., D.Litt. (Hon) 1986; Trent Univ. D.Litt. (Hon.) 1991; Brock Univ. LL.D. (Hon.) 1992; m. Morley Keith, s. Morley Thomas, 23 May 1942; two s. Stephen Morley, John David; PROFESSOR EMERITUS OF ENGLISH, YORK UNIVERSITY 1984– (Lecturer there 1961; Prof. 1969); Candn. Research Fellow, York University Libaries 1984– ; Pres., A.C.U.T.E. 1971–72; Killam Awards Bd. 1978–81; Aid to Pub. Bd. of Judges, C.F.H. 1979–82; Acad. Adv. Panel, SSHRCC, 1981–84; Univ. of Man., Dist. Prof. Selection Bd. 1982–85; Ed. Bd., 'Literary History of Canada' (2nd rev.); 'Journal of Canadian Studies'; 'Journal of Canadian Fiction'; 'Short Stories Series' Univ. of Ottawa; Recipient, Northern Telecom Internat. Candn. Studies Prize 1989; author 'Canadian Novelists 1920–45'; 'Love and Work Enough: The Life of Anna Jameson'; 'Margaret Laurence'; 'Ryerson of Upper Canada'; 'Our Nature: Our Voices'; 'The Manawaka World of Margaret Laurence'; 'William Arthur Deacon: A Canadian Literary Life' (with John Lennox); articles in 'Canadian Literature,' 'Journal of Canadian Studies,' 'Journal of Canadian Fiction' and numerous other journals and collections; Charter Secy., Drama Guild of Can.; Protestant; Home: 15 Lewes Cres., Toronto, Ont. M4N 3J1.

**THOMAS, Gordon;** author; journalist, screenwriter, film director, producer; b. U.K. 21 Feb. 1933; s. Gwynfor Rees and Helena Alice (Griffith) T.; e. Cairo H.S. for Boys; Bedford School (U.K.); m. Edith (Kraner); children: Catherine, Alexander, Lucy, Nicholas, Natasha; Fgn. Corresp. for the London Daily Express and Sunday Express in Middle East, Algeria, Cyprus, Kenya, and Uganda 1955–60; Writer, Dir. & Prod., BBC in London, Germany, S. & N. Africa, U.S.A., Canada 1961–69; News Features Correspondent, The Press Assoc., London 1984– ; contbr. corres. to: Sunday Star, Toronto Star 1984– ; Toronto Globe and Mail 1982–84; author: 'Descent into Danger' 1954; 'Physician Extraordinary' 1955; 'Bed of Nails' 1956; 'Heroes of the Royal Air Force' 1956; 'Miracle of Surgery' 1957; 'The National Health Service and You' 1958; 'The Parents Home Doctor' 1959, (4th ed. 1971); 'The Day the World Ended' 1965; 'Earthquake' 1966; 'Shipwreck' 'The Strange Fate of the Morro Castle' 1968; 'Voyage of the Damned' 1970; 'Guernica: The Crucible of World War Two' 1973; 'Issels: The Biography of a Doctor' 1975; 'Ruin From the Air' 1977; 'Enola Gay' 1977; 'The Day the Bubble Burst' 1979; 'Trauma' 1981; 'The Year of Armageddon' 1984; 'The Operation' 1985; 'Desire and Denial' 1986; 'The Trial' 1987; 'Journey into Madness' 1988; 'Enslaved' 1989; 'Chaos Under Heaven' 1991; 'Deadly Perfume' 1991; 'Godless Icon' 1992; Films: 'Voyage of the Damned' 1974; 'Time Ran Out' 1976; 'A Bit of an Experience' 1978; 'The Heart Man' 1979; 'Go Climb a Mountain' 1980; 'The Day the Bubble Burst' 1980; 'Chaos Under Heaven' 1991; Awards: The Jury's Prize, Monte Carlo Film Festival 1979; The Critics Prize, Monte Carlo Film Festival 1979; The Mark Twain Soc. Award for Historical Reportage 1980, 1983, 1985; Mem., Inst. of Journalists, London; Offices: Scott Meredith Literary Agency, 845 Third Ave., New York, NY 10022, USA and Contemporary Artists Ltd., Contemporary Artists Bldg., 132 Lasky Dr., Beverly Hills, CA 90212, USA.

**THOMAS, Gordon W.,** O.C. (1970), M.D., C.M., D.C.L., F.R.C.S.(C), F.A.C.S.; surgeon; b. Ottawa, Ont. 28 Dec. 1919; s. Russell Henry and Florence Mabel (Waddell) T.; e. Lachine (Que.) High Sch., 1936; McGill Univ., B.A. 1940, M.D., C.M. 1943; Acadia Univ., D.C.L., 1969; Mem. Univ. Nfld., D.Sc. (Hon.) 1979; Dalhousie Univ., LL.D. (Hon.) 1979; Officer of the Order of Canada 1970; Officer of the Order of St. John; m. Thora Patricia, d. late Lawrence E. Lister, 27 May 1944; children: (Mrs.) Patricia Ruth Simpson, Leonard Lister, Mrs. Pamela Jane Colbourne; Country Practitioner, Mabou, N.S.; on staff as Surgeon, Inverness County Mem. Hosp.; Surgeon-in-Chief and Extve. Dir., Internat. Grenfell Assn., 1959–78; Clin. Prof. of Surg., Memorial Univ. of Nfld.; Lectr., Dalhousie Sch. Outpost Nurses; Surg., Grenfell Hosp. St. Anthony, 1946–57; Acting Supt. and Surg.-in-Chief, 1957–59; Teaching Fellow Surg. Pathol., McGill Univ., 1953–54; Fellow, Thoracic Clinic Karolinska Inst., Stockholm, 1957–58; Teaching Fellow and Clin. Asst. Cardiovascular Surg., Univ. of Toronto, 1961–62; Clin. Asst. Surg. and Paediatric Surg., Dalhousie Univ., 1965–66; served with RCAMC 1942–46; rank Capt.; rec'd Centennial Medal 1967; Queen's Jubilee Medal 1976; Royal Bank Award for work in Nfld. and Labrador, 1977; Starr Award Can. Med. Assoc. 1985; awarded Commemorative Medal for 125th Anniversary of Candn. Confederation 1993; Hon. Chrmn., Bd. Internat. Grenfell Assoc.; Part-time mem. Candn. Radio & TV Comn. 1967–76; J.P., Nfld.; Past Chrmn., Grenfell Sch. Bd.; author 'From Sled to Satellite' 1987; author of various med. papers and articles; Fellow Victoria Inst.; former Gov-at-large, Am. Coll. Surgs.; former mem. Council, Royal Coll. of Physicians (Can.) & Surgs. (Canada); mem., Prov. Med. Bd., N.S.; Exec. Ctte. N.S. Med. Soc.; Can. Cancer Inst.; American Assn. of Thoracic Surg.; Thoracic Soc.; Candn. Thoracic Soc.; Protestant; recreations: riding, fishing, flying; Address: P.O. Box 99, Mabou, N.S. B0E 1X0.

**THOMAS, Ian Frederick,** B.A., A.A.S.A., A.C.I.S., A.F.A.I.M.; management consultant; b. Sydney, Australia 23 Oct. 1945; s. Dr. James Frederick Noel and Angela (Gordon) T.; e. Newington Coll.; York Univ., B.A. 1975; Assoc. Australian Soc. Accts. 1970; Chart. Inst. Secs. & Adms. 1970; m. Felicity Ashton 22 Oct. 1977; children: Trevor Martin Ashton, Rosalyn Ruthann; PRES. THOMAS CONSULTANTS INC. 1979– (offices in Vancouver, Toronto, Singapore, Sydney & Gold Coast,

Australia); Chrmn. Thomas Consultants Pty. Ltd.; Audit Clk. A. Jelfs & Co. C.A.'s 1964–68; Sec. Treas. Watts Griffis & McOuat Ltd. 1969–71 Australia, trans. Toronto 1971–74; Sr. Cons. Geoffrey Still Assoc. Toronto 1975–77, Mgr. Vancouver Office 1977–79; Partner, Retail Management Consultants Inc. 1986– ; frequent speaker profl. seminars, radio, TV; Dir., Downtown Parking Corporation; Future Shop; Internat. Council of Shopping Centers (N.Y.) Education Foundation; Vancouver Opera; Vancouver Opera Foundation; Downtown Vancouver Assn. (Past Dir.); Urban Devel. Inst. (Past Dir.); Urban Land Inst.; Australian Inst. Mgmt.; mem. St. David's Un. Ch.; recreations: skiing, golf, tennis, swimming, opera, reading; Clubs: Hollyburn Country; Vancouver; Palm Beach; Home: 2319 Westhill Dr., West Vancouver, B.C. V7S 2Z2; Office: 910, 700 West Pender, Vancouver, B.C. V6C 1G8.

**THOMAS, Jacob Ezra;** educator; b. Grand River Country 6 Jan. 1922; s. late David and late Elizabeth (Sky) T.; e. S.S. No. 6 Sch., Pub. Sch. gr. 5; m. 1stly Doris d. John and Annie Keye 1943; children: Jake, John, Dave, Clarence, Janice, Karen, Dorothy, Donna, Darvis, Gene, Milton, Garfield; m. 2ndly Yvonne Frances Hill; stepchildren: Phyllis Hill, Wayne Hill; Associate Professor of Native Studies, Trent University 1976; Chrmn., Council of Elders 1987– ; Bd. of Dir., Iroquoian Inst. 1987– ; Consultant in Residence, Iroquoian Inst. 1987– ; Special Instr. on Mohawk Lang. and Iroquois culture and traditions, Native Studies Dept., Trent Universy 1975; Cultural Coordinator, North Am. Indian Travelling College 1974–75; original Museum Curator Woodland Indian Cultural Ednl. Centre 1972–74; assoc. with Am. Indian Centre, Niagara Falls, N.Y.; Consultant to Museum of Man, Ottawa on Great Law and Treaties of the Six Nations Iroquois Confederacy; Faithkeeper in the Longhouse; Confederacy Lord, condoled 1973; transcribes Indian manuscripts; documenting the Great Law with Dept. of Ethnoloy, Museum of Man, Ottawa; involved in making six audio-visual works, many incl. in collections of Woodland Indian Cultural & Ednl. Centre; musical work incl. Iroquois Social Dance records (Nos. 1, 2, and 3); films: 'My Hands are the Tools of My Soul'; 'Ganonsio nni'; 'False Face Masks'; videotape: Jake Thomas reciting Condolence Rituals 1989; several exhbns. incl. The McMichael Candn. Collection, Kleinberg; Minneapolis Inst. of Arts; Royal Ontario Museum; Gall. of Am. Indian Community House; carvings incl. in numerous permanent colls. (museums, private colls.); Address: R.R. #1, Wilsonville, Ont. N0E 1Z0.

**THOMAS, John A.,** B.Comm., M.Sc.; financial executive; b. Vancouver, B.C. 11 Dec. 1945; e. Univ. of B.C. B.Comm. 1969; Massachusetts Inst. of Technology M.Sc. 1971; CHIEF FINANCIAL OFFICER, LIGNUM LTD. 1989– ; Royal Bank of Canada 1971–77; Bank of Montreal 1977–80; Bank of B.C. 1980–86; Kaiser Resources Ltd. 1986–89; Office: 1200, 1090 West Georgia St., Vancouver, B.C. V6E 3V7.

**THOMAS, John Edward;** university professor; b. Wales (Merthyr Tydfil) 9 April 1926; s. David Llewellyn and Ann (Olwen) T.; e. McMaster Univ., B.A. 1951, B.D. 1954; Duke Univ., M.A. 1958, Ph.D. 1964; m. Moreen Duff du Jean and William Muir 1 Sept. 1947; children: David William, Ian Campbell; WRITER & LECTURER, EMERITUS PROFESSOR, PHILOSOPHY, MCMASTER UNIV. 1991– ; Minister, Renforth Baptist Ch. 1952–56; Lectr. in Philosophy, McMaster Univ. 1959–61, Asst. Prof. 1961–66, Assoc. Prof. 1966–73, Prof. 1973–91; Chrmn., Dept. of Philos., McMaster Univ. 1966–72; Chrmn. & Pres., Ctte. on Ethics of Rsch. Rel. to Human Subjects; Chrmn. & Pres., Ctte. on Social Responsibility; Mem., Clinical Ethics Ctte., McMaster Med. Ctr. & Hamilton Civic Hosps.; Adjuct Prof. of Med., Fac. of Health Sci., McMaster Univ. 1985–91; Resident Ethicist, Fac. of Health Sciences 1991–93; Columnist 'The Canadian Doctor' 1986–88; Columnist 'Canadian Family Physician' 1991– ; a pioneer of medical ethics in Can.; worldwide lectr.; McMaster Univ.: McCrimmon Scholarship 1951, Hoyes LLoyd Memorial Prize 1952, John MacNeill Scholarship 1953; John Roberts Scholarship 1954, S.S. Bates Scholarship 1954, Ker Scholarship for Post-Graduate Study 1956–58; Duke Univ.: Graduate Scholarship 1956–59; Religious Council Scholarship 1957–59; Canada Council Predoctoral Scholarship 1962, 1963; Commonwealth Fellow, Inst. of Classical Stud. 1973; Social Sci. & Human. Rsch. Award 1982; Charles Johnson Found. Rsch. Award 1986–89; Distinguished Alumni Award for Creative Contribution to Arts and Sciences, McMaster Univ. 1988; Mem., Bd. of Dirs., The Hamilton Found. 1988–90; Mem. Bd. of Dirs., Found. for Health in the Arts 1990– ; Mem., Candn. Philos. Assn.; Am. Catholic Philos. Assn.; Soc. of Promotion of Hellenic Studies; Soc. for Bioethics Consultation; author: 'Matters of Life and Death' 1978, 'Musings on the "Meno"' 1980, 'Medical Ethics and Human Life' 1983; co-author: 'Well and Good' 1987, Rev. ed. 1990; co-editor: 'Russell in Review' 1976; recreations: miniature model making; Home: 9 Edenbridge Court, Dundas, Ont. L9H 3Y2; Office: Philos. Dep., McMaster Univ., Hamilton, Ont. L8S 4K1.

**THOMAS, Kenneth Carl,** B.Sc.; professional argologist; venture capitalist; b. Leoville, Sask. 19 Sept. 1954; s. Leo and Miriam Elizabeth T.; e. Univ. of Sask., B.Sc. 1976; m. Dorothy d. Lawrence Myo 29 June 1974; PRES., SASK. INDIAN LOAN CO. 1985– ; Prog. Mgr., Sask. Indian Argricul. Prog. 1977; Chrmn., Candn. Aboriginal Economic Develop. Program 1985– ; Outstanding Agrol., Univ. of Sask. 1986; Dir., Mem., Duke of Edinburgh Study Conf. 1980; Home: 314 Braeburn Cres., Saskatoon, Sask. S7V 1A5.

**THOMAS, Lewis Gwynne,** B.A., M.A., Ph.D., F.R.S.C.; university professor emeritus; b. Okotoks, Alta. 12 Mar. 1914; s. Edward Harold and Edith Agnes Louise (Lewis) T.; e. Mount Royal Coll.; Univ. of Alta., B.A. (Hons.) 1934, M.A. 1935; Harvard Univ., Ph.D. 1954; m. Muriel E. d. George F. and Anna B. Massie 22 Oct. 1943; children: Dennis Roland Gwynne, Gregory Edward Gwynne; PROF. EMERITUS, UNIV. OF ALTA. 1975– ; Teaching Fellow, Univ. of Alta. 1938–39; Instr. 1939–42; Lectr., Asst. Prof., Assoc. Prof., Prof. 1945–75; R.C.N.V.R. 1942–45; Vis. Prof., Univ. of Mass.; Trent Univ.; Univ. of Guelph; Pres., Candn. Hist. Assn. 1972–73; F.R.S.C.; Keeper, Rutherford House; Anglican; author: 'The University of Alberta in the War of 1939–45' 1948, 'The Liberal Party in Alberta, 1905–1921' 1959; 'Our Foothills' 1975 (also editor); editor: A.S. Morton 'History of the Canadian West to 1870–71' 1973; 'Ranchers' Legacy,' ed. P.A. Dunae, Univ. of Alta. Press 1986; recreation: gardening; Club: Univ. of Alta. Fac.; Address: 210, 10148 - 118 St. N.W., Edmonton, Alta. T5K 1Y4.

**THOMAS, Lionel Arthur John,** R.C.A.; artist; b. Toronto, Ont. 3 Apr. 1915; s. Arthur Edward and Ida Mae (Mooney) T.; e. John Russel Sch. Fine Arts Toronto 1933–35; Ont. Coll. Art 1936–37; Karl Godwin Sch. Illustration Toronto 1937; Candn. Coll. Music Dipl. 1930; Hans Hofman Sch. Fine Arts Provincetown, Mass. grad. 1947; Calif. Sch. Fine Arts San Francisco grad. 1949; m. Patricia Simmons 10 Sept 1940; children: Aurora Elyse Stewart, Michael Tristan John, Anthony Brian; former Instr. Vancouver Sch. Art; Instr. Sch. of Arch. Univ. of B.C. 1950–59, Asst. Prof. of Arch. 1959–64, Assoc. Prof. of Fine Arts 1964–80; guest speaker/lectr. 1950–79; Chrmn. Comte on Applied Design B.C. Archives & Centennial Museum Project Victoria 1965–67; maj. exhns. incl. Vancouver Art Gallery 1942, 1948; Univ. of B.C. 1947, 1948, 1951; 200 drawings & paintings Zan Art Gallery Victoria 1973; 136 enamels Spatial Concepts & Origin of Constellations Univ. Calgary 1973; U-Frame-It Gallery Toronto, Exposition Gallery Vancouver and Ward Plaza Gallery Honolulu (88 intaglio etchings) 1976; Students Union Bldg. Univ. B.C. 1977; Northland Plaza Gallery and Southland Gallery Edmonton 1977; Vancouver Planetarium & Museum (226 framed works) 1977; Harrison Galleries Vancouver 1978; Omniplex Museum Oklahoma City 1978; Strasenburgh Planetarium Rochester 1978; Fleischmann Atmospherium Planetarium Univ. Nevada 1978, 1979; Hansen Planetarium Gallery Salt Lake City 1978; Russell C. Davis Planetarium & Science Centre Jackson, Miss. 1978–79; Reading Museum & Art Gallery, Pa. 1979; William Penn State Mem. Museum & Archives Bldg. 1979; 282 framed works, The Pacific Science Centre Foundation, Seattle, Wash., April 4 – May 25, 1980; rep. in numerous group exhns. and travelling exhns. Can., USA, Europe and S. Am.; rep. in various pub. and private colls. incl. Nat. Gallery Can., Art Gallery Ont., Vancouver Arts Gallery, Univ. Victoria, Fla. S. Coll.; comns. incl. bronze fountain Edmonton City Hall; copper and bronze doors St. Thomas More Coll. Univ. Sask.; diarama carved wood 'Nootka Whaling Scene' and door panels B.C. Prov. Museum Victoria; numerous bas relief, murals, sculptures; 'The Pacific Rim' mural Student Union Bldg. Univ. B.C.; co-author (illustrations) forthcoming book 'Firmaments: The Story of the Constellations'; recipient John Russel Sch. Fine Arts Scholarship 1935; Emily Carr Trust Fund Scholarship 1949–50; Fla. Internat. Art Exhn. Award; Royal Arch. Inst. Can. Allied Arts Medal 1956; Pacific Northwest Artists Exhn. Award 1952; served with Seaforth Highlanders Regt. 1941–44; mem. B.C. Soc. Artists; Candn. Group Painters; Pacific Artists Assn.; Northwest Inst. Sculptors; Royal Astron. Soc.; Soc. Am. Archaeols.; Am. Craftsmen Council; cited numerous bibliogs.; recreations: swimming, walking.

**THOMAS, (John Warren) Nevil,** B.Com., M.A., M.B.A., C.F.A.; executive; financial analyst; b. Toronto, Ont. 7 Feb. 1938; s. late Charles Cleeve Nevil and Margaret Lillian (Jones) T.; e. pub. and private schs. Ont.; Trinity Coll. Univ. of Toronto B.Com.; Queen's Univ. M.A. (Econ.); York Univ. M.B.A.; Univ. of Va. Chart. Financial Analyst (C.F.A.); m. Susanne Elizabeth d. late F. Claude Passy, Ottawa, Ont. 12 Sept. 1964; children: Rebecca Susanne, Jeremy Christopher Nevill, Julian David Nevill, Ryan John Nevill; CHRMN. AND DIR., BEDFORD CAPITAL CORP.; Chrmn. & Dir., Pet Valu Inc.; French Fragrances Inc.; Pres. and Dir., Nevcord Inc.; Dir., Bedford Capital Financial Corp.; Simcoe Erie Investors Ltd.; Reliable Life Insurance Co. (Old Republic Group U.S.); Chatham Intl. Ltd. (Jacquin Distilleries); Ennisteel Corp.; Micrographic Tech. Inc.; joined Dominion Securities Ltd. Toronto and London, Eng. 1963–65; Pitfield Mackay 1965–67; Midland Doherty 1967–79; mem. Inst. Chart. Financial Analysts; Anglican; recreations: sailing, travel; Clubs: Toronto Club; Metropolitan (N.Y.); R.C.Y.C.; Lyford Cay (Bahamas); Home: 110 Sandringham Dr., Downsview, Ont. M3H 1C9; Office: Scotia Plaza, Suite 4712, 40 King St. W., Toronto, Ont. M5H 3Y2.

**THOMAS, Paul Griffith,** M.A., Ph.D.; educator; b. Winnipeg, Man. 24 Dec. 1943; s. Clifford Robert and Bernice Duret (Bateman) T.; e. Univ. of Man. B.A. 1966, M.A. 1968; Univ. of Toronto, Ph.D. 1976; m. Roberta d. William and Marion Johnson 13 Aug. 1966; three s. Hugh, Neal, Bryan; PROF. OF POL. STUDIES, UNIV. OF MAN. 1986– ; Chrmn., Bd. of Commissioners, Man. Telephone System 1987–89; Rsch. Offr. Finance Dept. Govt. Man. 1966–68; Parlty. Intern H. of C. Ottawa 1971–72; Asst. Prof. present Univ. 1969, Assoc. Prof. and Head of Pol. Studies 1973–78; Cons. to Royal Comn. Financial Mgmt. & Accountability 1979, to Royal Comn. Econ. Union & Devel. Prospects for Can. 1984 and Royal Comn. on Electoral Reform and Party Financing 1990–91; mem. Fed. Boundaries Comn. for Man. 1982; City of Winnipeg Act Review Ctte. 1984–85; Chrmn. Rsch. Ctte. Inst. Pub. Adm. Can. 1983–85; Chrmn. Exec. Bd. Inst. for Social & Econ. Rsch. 1981–84; Chrmn. Jt. Masters in Pub. Affairs 1984–87; Acad. Dir. Man. Legis. Internship 1985–87; Mem., Fed. Boundaries Comm. for Man. 1993–94; recipient Social Sci's & Humanities Fellowship 1979–80; Univ. Man. Excellence in Grad. Teaching Award 1983; co-author 'Canadian Public Administration: Some Problematic Perspectives' 1982, 2nd ed. 1987; Editor: 'Canadian Public Administration' 1993–96; Assoc. ed., 'Canadian Public Administration'; numerous articles; mem. Inst. Pub. Adms. Can.; Candn. Pol. Sci. Assn.; Man. Assn. Rights & Liberties; recreations: fishing, golf, cross-country skiing; Home: 817 Ash St., Winnipeg, Man. R3N 0R7; Office: Winnipeg, Man. R3T 2N2.

**THOMAS, Raye Edward,** B.Sc., Ph.D., D.I.C., P.Eng.; electronics executive; b. Greenhill, N.B. 5 June 1938; s. Stanley Edward and Hazel Augusta (Sellick) T.; e. Univ. of N.B., B.Sc.E.E. 1961; London Univ., Ph.D. 1966; Imperial Coll., D.I.C. 1966; married; children: Linda Christine, Kevin William; PRES. & CHIEF EXTVE. OFFR., MEGASOL CORP. 1993– and PRES., DARENTEK CORP. 1988– ; Mem., Sci. Staff, Northern Electric R&D Labs 1966–69; Mgr., Phys. of Devices, 1969; Asst. Prof., Electronics, Carleton Univ. 1969–71; Assoc. Prof. 1971–77; Prof. 1977–84; Acting Chrmn. 1979–80; Vis. Prof., Katholieke Univ. of Leuven, Belgium 1976–77; Adjunct Prof., Carleton Univ. 1984– ; Cons., Bell North. Rsch. 1973–76, 1978–81; Mitel Corp. 1979–81; Energy, Mines & Resources Canada 1985–92; CIDA 1991, 1992; Pres., TPK Internat. Inc. 1979–88; Pres., Astropower Canada Ltd. 1988–90; Mem., Candn. Sub-Ctte. of IEC TC82 (photovolatic standards), Chrmn. 1984–86; CSA Ctte. for Photovolatic Standards 1980– ; Sr. Mem., Inst. of Electrical & Electronics Engs. Inc. (Chrmn., Ottawa Sect. 1978–79; Pres. Conf. Inc. 1979–80; Gen. Chrmn., Internat. Electron Devices Meeting, Washington, D.C. 1978; Tech. Prog. Chrmn., 1st Candn. Semicond. Technol. Conf. 1982); Assn. of Profl. Engs. of Ont.; Vice-Pres., Solar Energy Soc. of Can. 1988–89, Pres., 1989–90, Past Pres. 1990–91; Vice Pres., Can. Photovoltaics Industry Assoc. 1987–91; Dir., Candn. Solar Industries Assn. 1992– (Vice-Pres. 1993– ); Chrmn., Renewable Energy Sub-Ctte., ISTC Alt. Energy Sector Campaign 1991–92; author of over 60 tech. papers; co-author: 'Solar Energy Conversion' 1979; Home: 5 Frederick Place, Ottawa, Ont. K1S 3G1.

**THOMAS, Richard James,** B.A., M.P.A., P.Adm.; financial services executive; b. Bristol, Eng. 10 March 1951; s. Clifford Thomas and Margaret Grace (Thomas) R.; e. Univ. of Victoria B.A. 1972, M.P.A. 1976; m. Christine; one s.: Neil; VICE-PRESIDENT, GOVERNMENT RELATIONS, B.C. CENTRAL CREDIT UNION

1990– ; Branch Accountant, Bank of N.S. 1972–74; Rsch. Officer, Saskatchewan Govt. 1976–77; B.C. Govt. 1978–80; Dir. of Govt. Affairs, B.C. Central Credit Union 1980–85; Corp. Sec. 1985– ; Pres. & Gen. Mgr., Cupp Services Ltd.; Sec. & Dir., Central Financial Serv. Ltd.; Dir., B.C. Lottery Corp.; Pres., Grad. Students' Soc., Univ. of Victoria 1975–76; Office: 1441 Creekside Dr., Vancouver, B.C. V6J 4S7.

**THOMAS, Robert**, B.A., M.B.A., C.G.A., F.I.C.B.; financial executive; b. Sheffield, England 4 March 1944; s. George William Curtis and Edith (Francis) T.; e. Concordia Univ. B.A. 1982, M.B.A. 1987; F.I.C.B. 1969; C.G.A. 1977; m. Suzanne d. John and Susan Hoare 4 June 1966; children: Jason, Claire; VICE-PRESIDENT, ACCOUNTING & FINANCIAL INFORMATION DEVELOPMENT, ROYAL BANK OF CANADA 1988– ; Manager, Float Management & Control, Royal Bank of Canada 1981–83; Deputy Chief Accountant 1983–88; Mem., Nat. Assn. for Bank Cost & Management Accounting; Certified General Accountants Assn. (Quebec & Ontario); has written and presented papers on a variety of topics incl. Off-Balance-Sheet Disclosure, International Payment Systems, Funds Evaluation & Management Acctg.; Club: Whitlock Golf & Country; recreations: skiing, scuba diving, golf; Office: Box 6001, Stn. A, Montreal, Que. H3C 3A9.

**THOMASON, Tommy H.**; aviation executive; b. Chattanooga, Tenn. 8 Aug. 1944; s. Tommy and Jean (Wilson) T.; e. R.P.I., Harvard, USC; m. Marylee 11 Sept. 1971; children: Fletcher, Gregory, Michael; PRES., BELL HELICOPTER TEXTRON CAN. 1992– ; Mem., Am. Helicopter Soc.; AIAC; recreations: golf, fitness; Office: 12,800 rue de l'Avenir, Mirabel, Que. J7J 1R4.

**THOMLISON, Ray J.**, B.Sc., B.S.W., M.S.W., Ph.D.; educator; b. Edmonton, Alta. 22 Jan. 1943; s. Herbert MacLeod and Margaret Patricia (Hagen) T.; e. Univ. of Alta. B.Sc. 1963; Univ. of B.C., B.S.W. 1964, M.S.W. 1965; Univ. of Toronto, Ph.D. 1972; m. Barbara d. Howard and Jean Buckler 22 Aug. 1964; two d. Lynn, Breanne; DEAN AND PROF. OF SOCIAL WORK, UNIV. OF CALGARY 1983– ; joined Dept. of Pub. Welfare (Child Welfare) Edmonton 1964, (Social Allowance) 1965; Psychiatric Social Worker Mental Health Centre Burnaby, B.C. 1965–67; Cons. in Mental Health Lower Mainland and N. Brit. Columbia 1967–68; Assoc. Prof. of Social Work, Wilfrid Laurier Univ. 1971–73, Sessional Faculty 1974–83; Prof. of Social Work, Univ. of Toronto 1973–83; mem. Sessional Faculty Lakehead Univ. Cont. Edn. Series Family Life Edn. 1979–82, Atkinson Coll. York Univ. Dept. Social Work 1978–83; Visiting Prof., Univ. of Regina 1977, Univ. of B.C. 1980–81; Dir. Metrop. Toronto Children's Aid Soc. 1979–83; Employee Assistance Prog. Adv. Bd. Family Service Assn. Metrop. Toronto 1977–83; recipient Univ. of Toronto Faculty Teaching Fellowship 1974; Health League of Can. First Annual Jackman Lectr. 1985; editor: 'Perspectives on Industrial Social Work Practice' 1983; co-editor: 'Perspectives on Social Services and Social Issues' 1987; 'Child Sexual Abuse: Critical Perspectives on Prevention, Intervention and Treatment' 1991; 'Action-Oriented Evaluation in Organizations: Canadian Practices' 1992; author or co-author various book chapters, articles, reports and papers; mem. Alta. Assn. of Social Workers; Assn. of Social Workers of Russia; Council Social Work Edn.; Assn. Advanc. Behavior Therapy; Assn. for Behavioural Social Work; Rsch. Inst. on Social Work, The People's Republic of China; Home: 1139 Varsity Estates Dr. N.W., Calgary, Alta. T3B 3B5; Office: 2500 University Dr. N.W., Calgary, Alta. T2N 1N4.

**THOMPSON, Alan G.**; investment dealer; b. Winnipeg, Man. 23 Nov. 1927; s. Henry H. and Gladys R. (Holland) T.; e. Woodsworth Elementary School; Brooklands Collegiate; Cecil Rhodes High School, Winnipeg, Man.; m. Doreen E. d. W.B. Gibson, Winnipeg, 3 June 1950; children: Randall J., Derek W.; Chrmn. and Dir., B.Y.G. Natural Resources Inc.; Chrmn. & Dir., Liberian Iron Ore Ltd.; Dir.: Crestbrook Forest Industries Ltd.; Granges, Inc.; Past Pres. and Chrmn., Investment Dealers' Assn. Can. 1971–72; past Chrmn. (1966) Vancouver Stock Exchange; Conservative; Protestant; recreations: sailing, golf; Clubs: Terminal City (Vancouver); The Vancouver (B.C.); Royal Vancouver Yacht; Home: 1124 Eyremount Dr., West Vancouver, B.C. V7S 2C2; Office: 801 - 602 W. Hastings St., Vancouver, B.C. V6B 1P2.

**THOMPSON, Hon. Andrew E.**, M.S.W., B.A.; senator; b. Ireland 14 Dec. 1924; s. Joseph Stanley and Edith (Magill) T.; e. Monkton Combe Sch., Eng.; Oakwood Collegiate, Toronto Ont., 1940–42; Univ. of Toronto, 1942–43; Queen's Univ., B.A. 1947; Univ. of B.C., M.S.W. 1949; m. Amy, d. Edward Riisna, Toronto, Ont.; one d. Katherine Anne (Anya); Dir. CHIN Radio (Toronto); Past Chrmn., Transair; Canadian Foods Ltd.; Past Dir., Tridel; CanDutch Fund.; with Dept. Atty. Gen., B.C. 1949; Candn. Citizenship and Immigration 1951–57; Special Asst. to Hon. L. B. Pearson 1958; Lectr. Univ. Man. 1953; Nat. Program Organizer CBC 1957; el. M.P.P. Dovercourt (Toronto, Ont.) 1959; former editorial consultant Toronto Star; el. Leader, Liberal Party in Ont., 1965; summoned to Senate of Canada April 1967; enlisted in RCNVR, 1943; discharged with rank of Lieut., 1946; mem., Candn. Commonwealth Parlty. Assn.; NATO Parlty. Assn.; World Fed. Parlty. Union; Hon. mem., Ethnic Press Assn. Ont.; Baltic Fed. Can.; Homes 12 Ava Cres., Toronto, Ont. M5P 3B1 and Kendal, Ont. L0A 1E0.

**THOMPSON, Colin Keith**, B.A.; employment & labour relations consultant; b. Hopetown, Que. 20 Jan. 1933; s. James W. and Jessie Mae (McRae) T.; e. McMaster Univ. B.A. 1963; m. Joan d. George H.P. Woodall 12 April 1958; children: Colin Bradley, Paul Cameron, Jeffrey Ross; CONSULTANT/OWNER, THOMPSON RESOURCES 1990– ; Mgr., Credit Bureau of Niagara Falls 1953–60; Teacher, Stamford Collegiate 1963–65; Dir. of Personnel, Fleet Mfg. 1965–69; Vice-Pres., Human Resources, Harding Carpets 1970–90; Address: Box 778, 323 Mississauga St., Niagara-on-the-Lake, Ont. L0S 1J0.

**THOMPSON, David A.**, B.Sc., (Econ.); mining executive; b. London, England 6 May 1939; e. London Sch. of Econ., B.Sc.; Harvard Business Sch., AMP; m. Gail Marie Harper; children: Julia Elizabeth, Adrian David; SR. VICE-PRES. & CHIEF FIN. OFFR., TECK CORP.; C.E.O., QUINTETTE COAL LIMITED; C.E.O, ELKVIEW COAL LIMITED; Chrmn., Golden Knight Resources Inc.; Dir., Teck Corp.; Cominco Ltd.; Dresdner Bank Can.; Quintette Coal Limited; Trilogy Resource Corp.; St. Paul's Hospital Foundation; Mem., Vancouver Bd. of Trade; Terminal City Club; Home: 420 Keith Rd., West Vancouver, B.C. V7T 1L7; Office: Suite 600, 200 Burrard St., Vancouver, B.C. V6C 3L9.

**THOMPSON, David Allan**, B.Sc., Ph.D., C.Eng.; educator; b. Oxford, UK 28 Apr. 1942; s. Allan Charles and Elizabeth Anne (Orchard) T.; e. Reading Univ. B.Sc. 1963, Ph.D. 1967; m. Elizabeth d. Thomas and Dorothy Hart 25 July 1964; children: Michael, Jennifer, Susan; PROF. OF ENG. PHYSICS, McMASTER UNIV. 1981– ; and Chrmn. of Dept. 1981–87; Dir., Centre for Electrophotonic Materials and Devices 1987– ; Rsch. Engineer 1967–70 and Mgr. Process R & D Solid State Devices 1970–73 Westinghouse Canada Ltd.; Asst. Prof. (part-time) Eng. Phys. present univ. 1970–72, Asst. Prof. 1972–75, Asoc. Prof. 1975–81; Visiting Assoc. Cal. Tech. 1980; Rsch. Fellow Reading Univ. 1973; author over 130 sci. publs.; mem. Böhmische Physical Soc.; Materials Rsch. Soc.; Inst. Physics; Candn. Assn. Physicists; Home: 5 Birch Cres., Greensville, Ont. L9H 6A6; Office: Hamilton, Ont. L8S 4L7.

**THOMPSON, Donald N.**, B.A., B.Com., M.B.A., Ph.D., LL.M.; university professor; management consultant; b. Winnipeg, Man. 1939; s. Laurence Ernest and Margaret (Neill) T.; e. Univ. of Man. B.A. 1959, B.Com. (Hon.) 1960; Univ. of Cal. M.B.A. 1962, Ph.D. 1968, LL.M. 1988; children: Neil, Michael, Sarah, Elizabeth; PRES., DONALD N. THOMPSON & ASSOCIATES; Dir. Research, and Chief Economist, Royal Comn. Corporate Concentration; served Procter and Gamble Ltd., Coca Cola Ltd.; Lectr. Harvard Univ., London Sch. of Economics and York Univ.; consultant to various business organs. Can. and US and to govts. of Can., US, Israel, Thailand, Laos, the United Nations and Internat. Monetary Fund; rec'd Research Grants from Can. Council, Nat. Science Foundation; author 'Franchise Operations and Antitrust' 1971; 'Contractual Marketing Systems' 1971; 'The Economics of Environmental Protection' 1973; 'Canadian Marketing Problems and Prospects' 1973; 'Problems In Canadian Marketing' 1977; 'Conglomerate Mergers' 1978; 'Macromarketing: A Canadian Perspective' 1979; other writings incl. articles in various prof. journs. newspapers and mags.; mem. Am. Econ. Assn.; Am. Marketing Assn.; Address: Faculty of Admin. Studies, York Univ., 4700 Keele St., North York, Ont. M3J 1P3.

**THOMPSON, Douglas Terrence (Terry)**, B.A., M.S.W., M.S.O.D.; social worker; b. Vantage, Sask. 22 Oct. 1938; s. Douglas and Patricia Faith (Cowan) T.; e. Univ. of Sask., B.A. 1961; Univ. of B.C., M.S.W. 1965; Pepperdine Univ., M.S.O.D. 1981; m. Agatha d. Michael and Mary Trohak 29 Oct. 1960; children: Tanya, Chad; ASST. DEP. MIN., SASK. DEPT. OF JUSTICE 1987– ; various social work & sup. positions with Sask. Social Serv. in Moose Jaw, Weyburn, Prince Albert & Melfort, Sask. 1961–71; Dir. of Community-Training Prog., Sask. Social Serv. 1968–71; Extve. Dir. of Corrections, Sask. Justice 1971–87; awarded Lieut.-Gov's. Medal of the Inst. of Public Admin. of Canada (Public Servant of the Year Award) 1990; Past Mem., Bd. of Dir., Candn. Assn. of Social Workers; recreations: cross country skiing, curling, golfing, camping; Home: 4 Hudson Dr., Regina, Sask. S4S 2W2; Office: 1874 Scarth St., Regina, Sask. S4P 3V7.

**THOMPSON, Edward Gerald**, B.A., M.A., Ph.D.; educator; b. Toronto, Ont. 1 Aug. 1945; s. John Roland and Hilda Frances (Dyson) T.; e. Univ. of Toronto B.A. 1967, M.A. 1973, Ph.D. 1979; spouse: Mary Helen Barron d. Gordon and Jean Tracy; COORDINATOR, CONTINUING STUDIES, SCHOOL OF PHYSICAL & HEALTH EDUCATION, UNIV. OF TORONTO 1982– ; Dir., Research Projects, Ont. Inst. for Studies in Edn. & Div. of Community Health, Fac. of Med., Univ. of Toronto 1977–83; Asst. Dir., Dept. of Alumni Affairs 1984–89; Lecturer in Sociology, Univ. of Toronto, York Univ, Ryerson Polytech. Univ. & Sheridan Coll. 1982– ; Teacher of Seniors, Toronto Bd. of Edn. 1992– ; Inst. Council, OISE 1991– ; Community Outreach & Education Ctte., Nat. Ballet of Canada 1991–93; Advisory Bd., St. Lawrence Centre Forum 1993; Pres., Ont. Folk Dance Assn. 1983–85 (Extve. 1982–87; Mem., several folk dance performing groups incl. La Troupe Folklorique de la Chasse Gal. and Settlement/Folkfest Dancers 1976–88; author of research articles; editor: 'The New Senior Network News' Adult Edn. Cons. to teachers of seniors; recreations: folk and baroque dance, reading, running, travel; Home: 312 Berkeley St., Toronto, Ont. M5A 2X5; Office: 320 Huron St., Toronto, Ont. M5S 1A1.

**THOMPSON, Eugene Mayne**, B.A., M.Div., D.Min.; minister; b. Oxford, N.S. 5 Jan. 1931; s. Curry Allison and Hortense Elsie (Mayne) T.; e. Acadia Univ., B.A. 1954; Acadia Div. Coll., M.Div. 1976; Southern Baptist Theol. Sem., D.Min. 1979; m. Rhoda d. Howard Mitchell 21 May 1955; children: Adrian Calvin, Nancy Lynn, Howard Allison; EXTVE. MIN., UN. BAPTIST CONVENTION OF THE ATLANTIC PROVS. 1984– ; Pastor, S. End Bapt. Ch. 1954–58; Assoc. Sec. of Christian Edn., Un. Bapt. Conv., Atl. Provs. 1958–61; Pastor, Immanuel Bapt. Ch. 1961–65; Hillcrest Bapt. Ch. 1965–68; Area Min. for Man., Bapt. Union of W. Can. 1968–74; Area Min. for West Nova Scotia, Un. Bapt. Conv., Atl. Provs. 1974–84; Counc. & Extve., Candn. Bapt. Fed.; Bd. of Dir., Atl. Bapt. Sr. Citizens Homes Inc.; Atl. Bapt. Found.; Bd. of Gov., Atl. Bapt. Coll.; Bd. of Trustees, Acadia Div. Coll.; Mem., Candn. Bapt. Internat. Ministries Bd.; author: 'Baptist Youth Fellowship Handbook' 1958; 'New Design for a Dynamic Church' 1973; recreations: music, gardening, cross country skiing; Home: Box 37, Site 10, Chalmers Dr., Saint John, N.B. E2L 3W7; Office: 1655 Manawagonish Rd., Saint John, N.B. E2M 3Y2.

**THOMPSON, Garry D.**; plumbing executive; e. North Vancouver S.S.; Univ. of B.C.; Univ. of Toronto, mngt. course; married; 4 children; SR. VICE-PRES., NORTH AMERICA - PLUMBING, WESTBURNE INC. 1989– ; Sales, Vanc., American Standard Canada 1957; Sask. Sales Rep. 1961; Ont. Architect & Eng. Rep. 1963; Branch Mgr., Man. & Sask. 1965; Branch Mgr., B.C. 1967; Nat. Mgr., Specialized Products & Sales 1968; Gen. Mgr., Cronkhite Companies 1969–73; Mktg Mgr., Mfg. Div., Emco Limited 1973–76; Vice-Pres. & Gen. Mgr., Delta Faucet of Can. Ltd. (a div. of Emco), 1976–88; mem., Candn. Ski Instructors' Alliance; Chrmn. of the Bd., Candn. Inst. of Plumbing & Heating (Former Nat. Chrmn., Peronal Devel. Counc.; Former Pres., Ont. Reg.; Nat. Bd. Dir.); Candn. Environ. Exposition (Chrmn. 1986); clubs: Thornhill Golf, Devil's Glen Country, Glencoe; Home: 571 Village Pkwy., Unionville, Ont. L3R 6C1; Office: 1001 Corporate Dr., P.O. Box 5034, Burlington, Ont. L7R 3Y8.

**THOMPSON, Glenn R.**, B.A., M.S.W., C.S.W.; association executive; EXECUTIVE DIRECTOR, CANADIAN MENTAL HEALTH ASSOCIATION 1991– ; Social Worker, John Howard Soc. of Metro. Toronto; Social Work & Admin., Ont. Ministyr of Correctional Services 20 years; Deputy Ministry, Govt. of Ontario, ministries of Correctional Services, Energy, Government Services, Municipal Affairs, Labour & Housing; Centennial Medal 1967; Office: 56 Wellesley St. W., Suite 410, Toronto, Ont. M5S 2S3.

**THOMPSON, Gordon Edward**, B.A., LL.B.; lawyer; b. Montreal, Que. 27 Oct. 1943; s. George Carson and Aileen Mary (Dawson) T.; e. elem. and high schs. Montreal; Univ. of Bishop's Coll. B.A. 1964; Queen's

Univ. LL.B. 1967; m. Margaret Ann d. Douglas Charles Melville, Toronto, Ont. 30 May 1970; Children: Sara Kerr, Timothy Gordon, Patrick Douglas Carson; PARTNER, BORDEN & ELLIOT; Dir., Zurich Life Ins. Co. of Can. and other Zurich Ins. companies; Rhône-Poulenc Rorer Consumer Inc.; Freudenberg-NOK, Inc.; Translogic Ltd.; Visionwall Tech. Inc.; Gates Canada Inc.; Alco Capital Resource Canada Ltd.; J.D. Carrier Sr. Charitable Found.; North Toronto Hockey Assn.; called to Bar of Ont. 1969; publs. incl. 'Manual on Legal Citation' 1967; mem. and Hon. Dir. Candn. Inst. for Adm. Justice; Law Soc. Upper Can.; Candn. Bar Assn.; Co. York Law Assn.; Fellow, Amer. Coll. of Investment Counsel; Liberal; Anglican; recreations: swimming, tennis, skiing; Home: 112 Cortleigh Blvd., Toronto, Ont. M4R 1K6; Office: Suite 4200, Scotia Plaza, 40 King St. W., Toronto, Ont. M5H 3Y4.

**THOMPSON, Harold**, B.Com., F.S.A., F.C.I.A.; retired insurance executive; b. Winnipeg, Man. 18 Aug. 1922; s. Harry and Hrodny (Finson) T.; e. Univ. of Man., B. Com.; m. Beatrice May, d. Henry J. Shipman, Victoria, B.C., 21 Sept. 1946; children: Patricia Lynn, Gordon Douglas; Chrmn., Newflyer Industries Ltd.; served with RCAF, Fleet Air Arm-RN, during World War II; Chrmn., Winnipeg Rh Institute Inc.; Past Pres., Winnipeg Lions Club; Past Pres., Candn. Cancer Soc. (Man. Div.); Past Chairman of Board Univ. of Winnipeg; Protestant; Clubs: Manitoba; St. Charles Country; Home: 1402, 160 Tuxedo Blvd., Winnipeg, Man. R3P 1B2.

**THOMPSON, John**, B.A.Sc., P.Eng., M.B.A.; merchant banker; b. Liverpool, England 12 Feb. 1942; s. John and Dorothy Winnifred (Duffy) T.; e. Univ. of Ottawa B.A.Sc. Chem. Engn. 1964; Univ. of W. Ont. M.B.A. 1966; m. Mary Patricia d. Mary and Pierce O'Gorman 3 July 1965; children: Robert, Darren, Erinn; PRINCIPAL, GORNITZKI, THOMPSON & LITTLE 1987– ; Consultant Touche Ross & Partners 1966–68; Vice-Pres. Greyhound Leasing 1968–72; Vice-Pres. Merban Capital 1972–74; Pres. R.C. Baxter Ltd. 1974–83; Pres. Baxter Technologies Corp. 1976–85; Pres. The Jaunty Corp. 1985–86; Clubs: Albany; Weston Golf & Country; Home: 29 Lynngrove Ave., Toronto, Ont. M8X 1M5; Office: Suite 2004, 200 King St. W., Toronto, Ont. M5H 3T4.

**THOMPSON, John D.**, B.Eng., M.B.A.; financier; b. Montreal 28 Sept. 1934; s. William Douglas and Anne F. (Whebby) T.; e. McGill Univ., B.Eng. (Mining Engn.) 1957; Univ. of W. Ont., M.B.A. 1960; m. Jocelyne Vanasse; children: Jacqueline, Catherine, Peter, Anne-Marie, François; PRES. & C.E.O., MONTREAL TRUST and CHRMN., ROYNAT INC.; Chrmn.: Montrusco and Associates Inc.; Dir.: AXA Assurances; BCE Mobile; Domtar Inc.; J.S. Redpath Holdings Inc.; Société générale de financement du Québec; Macdonald Stewart Found.; Atwater Fund; Mem. of the Dean's Advisory Council, Univ. of B.C.; Mem. Audit Ctte., McGill Univ.; Chrmn., Salvation Army Montreal Adv. Bd.; Gov., St. Mary's Hosp. Center (Past-Pres.); Past Pres., St. Mary's Hosp. Found.; Past-Chrmn., The Trust Companies Assn. of Can.; mem., Assn. Prof. Engrs. Ont. and Que.; recreations: skiing, golf; Clubs: Mount Royal; Royal Montreal Golf; Montreal Amateur Athletic Assn.; Office: Place Montreal Trust, 1800 McGill College Ave., Montreal, Que. H3A 3K9.

**THOMPSON, John Herd**, M.A., Ph.D.; educator; b. Winnipeg, Man. 18 Sept. 1946; s. Joseph Whyte and Gladys Kate (Campain) T.; e. pub. and high schs. St. James, Man.; Univ. of Winnipeg, B.A. 1968; Univ. of Man. M.A. 1969; Queen's Univ. Ph.D. 1975; m. Katrin d. Ants and Hilda Partelpoeg 15 Jan. 1977; children: Anne Marie, Mark Thomas; PROF. OF HISTORY, DUKE UNIV. 1990– ; Prof. of History, McGill Univ. 1971–90; Exchange Prof. Simon Fraser Univ. 1982–83; Exchange Prof. Duke Univ. 1987–88; recipient Margaret McWilliams Medal, Man. Hist. Soc. 1968; W.L. Morton Gold Medal Univ. Man. 1969; Candn. Hist. Assn. Regional Hist. Prize 1981; author: 'Ethnic Minorities During Two World Wars' 1991; 'The Harvests of War: the Prairie West 1914–1918' 1978; sr. author: 'Canada 1922–39: Decades of Discord' 1985; 'Canada and the United States: Ambivalent Allies' 1994; co-ed. 'Loyalties in Conflict: Ukrainians in Canada During the Great War' 1983; mem. Candn. Hist. Assn.; Soc. Am. Baseball Rsch.; United Church; NDP; recreation: baseball; Home: 39 York Ave., Westmount, Qué. H3Z 1M7.

**THOMPSON, Judith Clare Francesca**, B.A.; playwright; screenwriter; b. Montréal, Qué. 20 Sept. 1954; d. William Robert and Mary Therese (Forde) T.; e. Queen's Univ., B.A. (Drama & English) 1976; Nat. Theatre Sch., Montréal grad. 1979; m. Gregor Duncan s. John and Edith Campbell 28 Oct. 1983; children: Ariane Francesca Forde, Elias, Grace; toured with TAP 1979; mainstage MTC 1980; Instr. Playwriting, Univ. of Toronto 1983–84; workshops & seminars in various Universities & Secondary Schs. 1980–90; Playwright's Unit, Tarragon Theatre 1984–86; Fifty Hour Seminars, 'KINGFEST,' Kingston, Ont. 1985, 1987; Resident Instr. & Dir., Univ. of New Brunswick 1989–90, directed full production of Miller's 'The Crucible'; Writer (TV & Airwaves (series) 'Turkey'; 'Turning to Stone' CBC (2hr. TV); 'Life With Billy' (2hr. TV movie); 'Taking Care of Angela (2hr. TV); 'Life of Elizabeth Smart,' dir. Patricia Rozema (in progress); Writer (Stage): 'Lion in the Streets' (Chalmers Award) (French Transl.) (Dir., Tarragon Theatre, Toronto; duMaurier Festival, Toronto); 'I Am Yours' (also French and Swedish translation); 'White Biting Dog' (Governor General's Literary Award 1984); 'The Crackwalker' (Dir., Touchstone Theatre, Vancouver; Hudson's Guild Theatre N.Y.); Director: 'Hedda Gabler' Shaw Festival 1991 (and adaptor); Radio: 'Quickening & A Kissing Way'; 'Sugarcane' (1 hr. drama); 'Yellow Canaries' (1/2-hr. for children); recipient Nellie Award for Best Radio Drama for 1 hr. play 'Tornado') (CBC 1988) 1988; Toronto Arts Award (Writing & Editing) 1988; Governor General's Literary Award for 'The Other Side of the Dark' 1990; B'nai Brith Award for 'White Sand'; Assoc. Prof., Drama, Guelph Univ.; Office: Great North Artists Mngmt. Inc., 350 Dupont St., Toronto, Ont. M5R 1V9.

**THOMPSON, Kent Elgin**, M.A., Ph.D.; educator; writer; b. Waukegan, Ill. 3 Feb. 1936; s. Maurice Madison and Clarice Laverne (Graves) T.; e. Salem, Ind. High Sch. 1953; Hanover Coll. Ind., B.A. 1957; Univ. of Exeter, Eng. 1954–55; State Univ. of Iowa, M.A. 1962; Univ. of Wales, UK, Ph.D. 1965; m. Michaele d. Charles and Hildred Fowler 1 Aug. 1960; children: Kevin, David; PROF. OF ENG. UNIV. OF N.B. 1974– , Asst. Prof. 1966, Assoc. Prof. 1968; Teacher, Ripon Coll. Wis. and Colo. Woman's Coll. Denver; came to Can. 1966, Candn. citizen 1971; joined present Univ. 1966; Fiction Ed. 'The Fiddlehead' 1982– , Ed. 1967–70; freelance radio broadcaster since 1970, radio plays broadcast by CBC; Candn. Writer-in-Residence in Scot. 1982–83; recipient Woodrow Wilson Fellowship 1957–58; Fullbright Jr. Fellowship 1963–65; Can. Council Arts Bursary 1972–73, Sr. Arts Grant 1976–77; author 'Shotgun and Other Stories' 1979; 'A Local Hanging and Other Stories' 1984; 'Leaping Up Sliding Away' 1986; 'The Tenants Were Corrie and Tennie' novel 1973; 'Across From the Floral Park' novel 1974; 'Shacking Up' novel 1980; 'Married Love' 1988; ed. 'Stories from Atlantic Canada' 1973; 'Open Windows' 1988; 'Engaged Elsewhere' 1989; 'Playing in the Dark' novel 1990; Office: (P.O. Box 4400) Fredericton, N.B. E3B 5A3.

**THOMPSON, Lilian Umale**, B.Sc., M.Sc., Ph.D.; university professor; b. Cavinti, Laguna, Philippines 20 Aug. 1940; d. Francisco Umale and Crescencia Lavador; e. Mapua Inst. of Technology B.Sc. 1960; Univ. of the Philippines M.Sc. 1964; Univ. of Wisconsin Ph.D. 1969; m. Walter Garvin s. Walter and Amy Thompson 28 Dec. 1968; children: Sylvan Xerxes, Ryhna Sheryne; PROF., DEPT. OF NUTRITIONAL SCIENCES, UNIV. OF TORONTO 1988– ; Chemist, Inhelder Laboratories 1961; Research Instructor, Univ. of the Philippines 1964–65; Research Asst., Univ. of Wisconsin 1965–69; Asst. then Assoc. Prof., Univ. of Toronto 1969–88; Most Outstanding Univ. of the Philippines Alumnus (in Canada) 1991; Fulbright Fellowship 1965–69; Nat. Science Devel. Bd. Fellowship 1961–64; College Scholarship 1955–60; High School Valedictorian 1956; Mem., Strategic Grant Ctte., NSERC 1990–92; Operating Grants Ctte. for Plant Biol., NSERC 1986–90; Expert Ctte. on Plant Products, Agric. Canada 1981–84; Chair, Academic Panel, Ont. Grad. Scholarship, Ont. Min. of Colleges & Univs. 1986–87; Edit. Bd. Mem., 'J. of Food Sci.' 1985–88, 'Meat Probe' 1986–90; Chair, Nutrition Interest Group, Candn. Inst. of Food Sci. & Tech. 1985–86; Mem., Candn. Soc. for Nutritional Sci.; Am. Inst. of Nutrition; Am. Oil Chem. Soc.; Am. Chem. Soc.; Am. Assn. of Cereal Chems.; Inst. of Food Technologists; author of over 100 scientific papers; recreations: travel, reading, playing piano; Home: 83 Caines Ave., North York, Ont. M2R 2L2; Office: 150 College St., Toronto, Ont. M5S 1A8.

**THOMPSON, Margaret Anne Wilson**, C.M., B.A., Ph.D.; geneticist; b. Northwich, Cheshire, Eng. 7 Jan. 1920; d. late David Heywood and Essie Margaret (Moore) Wilson; e. Univ. of Sask., B.A. 1943; Univ. of Toronto, Ph.D. 1948; m. (late) Dr. James Scott Thompson, 19 Aug. 1944; two s., Gordon Moore, David Bruce; PROF. EMERITUS, UNIV. OF TORONTO and Consultant in Genetics, Hosp. for Sick Children, Toronto; Faculty mem. Univ. of Toronto 1944–48, Univ. of W. Ont. 1948–50, Univ. of Alta. 1955–62; Univ. of Toronto 1963– , and Geneticist, Hosp. for Sick Children 1963–88; Visiting Investigator, Jackson Lab. Bar Harbor, Me., 1962–63; Hon. Research Associate, Univ. Coll., London, Eng. 1977–78; Saul Lehmann Visiting Prof., SUNY Downstate, Brooklyn, 1981; Fellow, Canadian College of Medical Geneticists (Pres. 1983–85); Dir., Muscular Dystrophy Assn. Can. 1963–80; Trustee, Queen Elizabeth II Fund for Research on Diseases of Children 1971– ; Gov. Counc. Univ. of Toronto 1974–77; Eugenics Bd. of Alta. 1959–62; rec'd Ramsay Wright Fellowship in Zoology 1943–44; Muscular Dystrophy Assn. Can. Post-doctoral Fellowship 1962–63; apptd. Member, Order of Canada 1988; awarded Commemorative Medal for 125th Anniversary of Candn. Confederation 1992; co-author, 'Genetics in Medicine,' 1966, 2nd ed. 1973, 3rd ed. 1980, 4th ed. 1986, 5th ed. 1991; other writings incl. scient. publs. in human and med. genetics; mem., Genetics Soc. Can. (Pres. 1972–73); Am. Soc. Human Genetics; Royal Candn. Inst. (Pres. 1986–87); Home: 7 Danville Dr., Willowdale, Ont. M2P 1H7; Office: 555 University Ave., Toronto, Ont. M5G 1X8.

**THOMPSON, Margaret Joan**, B.A.; arts executive; b. Toronto, Ont. 6 May 1925; d. Francis Gordon and Zaidee Emily (Watt) Venables; e. St. Clement's Sch. 1943; Univ. of Toronto, B.A. 1949; m. the late Austin Seton s. Stanley Seton and Anna Kathleen Thompson 12 May 1951; children: Austin Evan Seton, James Austin Seton; DEP. CHRMN. ROYAL ONT. MUSEUM 1985–89; W.R.C.N.S. 1943–45; var. extve. positions, The Junior League of Toronto 1946–60; extensive sr. level ctee. work, Members' Volunteer Ctte., Royal Ont. Mus. 1959– ; ROM Renovation & Expansion Campaign 1978–82; Mem., Bd. of Trustees ROM 1983–89 (Communications Ctte. 1974–77, 1980–83); Mem., Mus. Ctte., Toronto Hist. Bd. 1979– ; Bd. of Dir., CARE Can. 1986–88; Bd. of Trustees, G.R. Gardiner Mus. of Ceramic Art 1988– ; Bd. of Gov., Hillcrest Hosp.; Club: Badminton & Racquet; Home: 171 Cortleigh Blvd., Toronto, Ont. M5N 1P6; Office: 100 Queen's Park, Toronto, Ont. M5S 2C6.

**THOMPSON, Michael**, B.Sc., Ph.D., D.Sc., F.R.S.C.(UK), F.R.I.C.; educator; b. Rotherham, U.K. 8 July 1942; s. Maurice and Nancy Freda (Green) T.; e. Univ. of Wales, Swansea B.Sc. Hon. Chem. 1966; McMaster Univ. Ph.D. Analytical Chem. 1970; m. Avril d. Donald and Phyllis Coffey 8 Aug. 1966; children: Samantha Elizabeth, Allister Neal; PROFESSOR OF ANALYTICAL CHEMISTRY, UNIVERSITY OF TORONTO 1982– ; Staff Rsch. Scientist, Toronto Gen. Hosp. 1989– ; post-Doctoral Fellow Univ. Coll. of Swansea, U.K. 1970–71; Lectr. in Instrumental Analysis, Loughborough Univ., U.K. 1971–76; Asst. Prof. present Univ. 1976, Assoc. Prof. 1978; Visiting Prof., Univ. of Utah, Salt Lake City 1983–84; Visiting Prof. Universität der Bundeswehr, München 1987; co-author 'Auger Electron Spectroscopy' 1985; Assoc., IGEN Corp., U.S.; Cons.: Squibb Corp., U.S.A.; Paradigm Biotechnology, Ont. (joint-founder); mem. Ed. Bds.: Analytical Chem., Biosensors and Bioelectronics; Talanta, The Analyst, Analytica Chimica Acta; Chemical Sensor Technology; Fellow: Royal Soc. of Chem., U.K.; Chem. Inst. of Can.; D.Sc. Univ. of Wales; recipient Teaching Award, Ont. Confdn. of Faculty Assns. 1982; Fisher Scientific Lecture Award 1989, Candn. Soc. for Chem.; recreations: cooking, jogging, philosophy; Office: University of Toronto, Toronto, Ont. M5S 1A1.

**THOMPSON, Michael**, B.F.A.; artist; b. Montreal, Que. 23 Mar. 1954; s. Arthur S. and Cecile (Paquette) T.; e. Concordia Univ., B.F.A. 1976; m. Carol DeGrandis 21 July 1979; one-man exhibitions: Sir George Williams Gall. 1978; The Art Gall. of N.S. 1979; Saidye Bronfman Ctr. 1979; The Mena'Sen Gall. 1979; Univ. of N.B. 1979; Gallery Moos 1981, 82, 84, 86, 88; Art Gall. of Hamilton 1983; Drabinsky Gallery 1990; Kitchener-Waterloo Art Gallery 1994; public collections: London Regional Art Gallery; Kitchener-Waterloo Art Gallery; Beaverbrook Art Gallery; Sun Life Insurance Co.; Memorial Univ. Art Gallery; Art Gallery of Ont.; Cineplex Odeon Corp.; Musée d'Art Contemporain; N.B. Mus.; Sarnia Art Gall.; Newcourt Credit Group; Greenshields Found.; Guaranty Trust Co.; Banque Nat.; Concordia Univ.; Univ. of Sherbrooke; City of North Bay; Gluskin, Sheff and Assoc.; Art Gallery of Algoma; Counsel Trust Co.; The Vivian and David M. Campbell Collection; numerous priv. collections in Eur. & N. Am.; awards: Chancellor's Associates Society Memorial Univ., Nfld.; Greenshields Found. 1977, 1978; Can. Counc. 1982; Ont. Arts Counc. 1984, 86; Ont. Art Council Grant 1994; selected publications: 'Dictionary of International Biography' Cambridge, England; Burnett, David (catalogue essay) 'Michael Thompson: A Ten Year Survey' Drabinsky Gallery 1990; Moos, David (catalogue essay) 'Crisis and Triumph of the Real: The Paintings of Michael Thompson' 1988; Duval, Paul (catalogue essay), 'Michael Thompson – Recent Works' 1984, Burnett David, and Marilyn Schiff, 'Contemporary Canadian Art' 1983 (170–1), Rondos, Spyros, 'The Work of Michael Thompson' (Discussion, spring 1985 12–13); Home: 213 Reynolds St., Oakville, Ont. L6J 3L2.

**THOMPSON, Patricia Anne;** editor; publisher; writer; b. Portsmouth, England 28 June 1927; d. William Albert and Florence Lucy (Brazier) T.; e. gen. edn. & 2–yr. bus. course; EDITOR/PUB., FILM CANADA YEARBOOK 1986– ; Dir., Toronto Film Soc. 1958–66; Sec. 1962–66; Mem., Founding Ctte. & Co-ord., Nat. Film Theatre 1966–69; Film & Info. Offr., Candn. Fed. of Film Soc. 1968–70; Co-founder & Co-ord., Ont. Film Inst. & Theatre, Ont. Sci. Ctr. 1969–72; Co-ord., Stratford Internat. Film fest. 1971–74; Pub. Dir., Women & Film Fest. in Can. 1973; Rsch., 'Index of Feature Films Available in Canada' 1973–81; Extve. Dir., Candn. Film Awards (now Genie Awards) 1977–78; Short Film Prog., Cineplex Cinemas 1978–81; Ed., Canadian Film Digest Yearbook 1977–85; Bd. Mem., Candn. Filmmakers Distr. Ctr. 1982–84; Columnist/writer, 'Cinema Canada' 1983–89; Candn. Ed. 'International Motion Picture Almanac' and 'International Television & Video Almanac' 1989– ; Writer, 'Take One' (magazine) 1992– ; Queen's Silver Jubilee Medal 1977; Mem., Toronto Film Soc.; Candn. Picture Pioneers; recreations: movies, theatre, travel; Home: 57 Mallory Crescent, #4, Toronto, Ont. M4G 3L6; Office: Box 152, Stn. R, Toronto, Ont. M4G 3Z3.

**THOMPSON, Robert Norman,** O.C., B.Sc., M.A., D.C., Ph.D., LL.D., F.R.G.S., F.C.G.A., G.C.L.J.; b. Duluth, Minn. 17 May 1914; s. Theodore Olaf and Hanna Josephine (Olufson) T.; e. Calgary Normal Sch. Univ. of Alta. Life Cert. Teacher 1934; Palmer College D.C. 1939; Bob Jones Univ. B.Sc. 1953; Univ. of B.C. grad. studies in edn. 1953; Wheaton Coll. LL.D. 1972; Biola Univ. LL.D. 1987; Northgate Grad. Sch. M.A. 1987, Ph.D. 1989; m. the late Hazel Maxine d. George and Cora Kurth Monroe 4 May 1939; 8 children; m. Evelyn May Brant Jan. 1993; teacher 1934–47; served Commonwealth Air Training Scheme 1940–43, rank Flt. Lt.; Lt. Col. 78th Fraser Highlanders 1968–79; Imp. Ethiopian Air Force Commdr. 1944–45, rank Col.; Headmaster Haile Selassie Secondary Sch. 1945–46; Supt. of Edn. Kaffa Prov. Ethiopian Govt. 1946–47; Assoc. Dep. Min. of Edn. Ethiopia 1947–51; SIM Internat. Chrmn. of Edn. Comn. for E. Africa and Dir. Sheshemane Leprosarium Ethiopia 1952–59; freelance univ. lectr. African affairs 1959–60; Pres. Social Credit Party Can. 1960–61, Nat. Leader 1961–67; el. to H. of C. for Red Deer 1962–72; Visiting Prof., Wilfrid Laurier Univ. 1968–72; Prof. of Pol. Sci. Trinity Western Univ. Langley, B.C. 1973–84; Chief of Del. Ont. Fedn. Agric. to China 1973; mem. Parole Bd. Can. and B.C. 1984–88; mem. Bd. Roman Corp. Toronto 1972–90; Headmaster, Fraser Academy (Langley, B.C.) 1979–1982; Chief Exec. Offr. Mardel Internat. Trading Corp. 1988–90; Pres. Freedom Council Can. 1967–92; Officer, Order of Canada 1990; recipient Star of Ethiopia, Grand Offr. 1967; G.C.L.J.; C.M.L.J.; The Military and Hospitaller, Order of St. Lazarus of Jerusalem; Knight of Honour, The Sovereign Order of St. John; author 'Canadians - Face Facts' 1962; 'Commonsense for Canadians' 1965; 'From the Market Place' 1978; 'A Model Constitution' 1982; 'Liberation, The First To Be Freed' 1988 (memoirs E.African Campaign WW2); 'A House of Minorities' 1990 (pol. memoirs 1957–72); 'Letters From Life's Way' 1992; exec. various professional orgns.; Life mem. Surrey C. of C., former exec. mem. C. of C. Can.; Fellow, Candn. Guild Authors; Life mem. Candn. Bible Soc.; mem. Gideon Internat. Can.; Evangelical Free Ch. Can.; Rotary Internat.; The Legacy Foundation of Fort Langley; recreations: reading, internat. consulting, hiking; Address: P.O. Box 430, Fort Langley, B.C. V0X 1J0.

**THOMPSON, Robert Shirley,** B.Sc.; executive consultant; b. Ottawa, Ont. 26 Oct. 1925; s. Victor Wentworth and Katharine Shirley T.; e. Lakefield (Ont.) Coll. Sch.; Ryerson Inst. of Tech. B.Sc. 1948; m. Ruth d. Lyda and Oulton Hammond 14 May 1949; children: Catherine, Robin, Geoffrey; President, Candn. Sugar Institute 1982; Mgr. Marketing, Canadian General Electric 1962, Vice Pres. and Gen. Mgr. 1970; Pres. General Tire Canada 1978–80; Depy. Min. of Econ. Devel. and Tourism, Man. 1980–82; Chrmn. Manitoba Trading Corp. 1981–82; Dir. Man. Design Inst.; served with RCN(R) 1950–60, rank Lt.; Dir. Un. Appeal Barrie 1978–80; Dir. and Treas. Rubber Mfg. Assn. 1978–80; Chrmn. Portable Appliance Mfrs. Assn. 1972–74; Dir. Food Mfg. Assn. Extves.; Bd. Trade Metrop.; recreations: tennis, skiing; Home: 331 Codrington St., Barrie, Ont. L4M 1S9.

**THOMPSON, Ronald Paul,** B.A., M.A., Ph.D.; university professor; b. Toronto, Ont. 14 Dec. 1947; s. Lewis and Gladys Olive (Greenaway); e. Univ. of Toronto, B.A. 1970, M.A. 1972, Ph.D. 1979; m. Jennifer d. David and Regina McShane 23 Dec. 1971; children: Jonathan Michael, Erinn Rebecca, Kerry Morgan; PRINCIPAL AND DEAN, SCARBOROUGH CAMPUS, UNIV. OF TORONTO 1989– ; Asst. Prof., Dept. of Phil., Univ. of Toronto 1977–83; Assoc. Prof., 1983–88; Prof. 1988– ; Chrmn., Div. of Hum., Scarborough Campus 1987–89; Visiting Assoc. Prof., Univ. of Calif., Davis, 1983; Univ. of Guelph 1985; Prin. Cons., TV Ontario series 'The Moral Question'; Dir. & Extve. Mem., Ont. Confed. of Univ. Fac. Assns. 1986–87; SSHRCC post-doct. fellow 1981–82; Mem., Philos. of Sci. Assn.; Candn. Soc. for Hist. & Phil. of Sci.; Candn. Phil. Assn.; author: 'The Moral Question' 1983, 'The Structure of Biological Theories' 1989, and numerous scholarly articles; Ed. Bd. Mem., 'Biology and Philosophy'; recreations: canoeing, sailing, winemaking; Home: R.R. 1, Uxbridge, Ont. L9P 1R1; Office: Scarborough Campus, Univ. of Toronto, Toronto, Ont. M5S 1A1.

**THOMPSON, Wayne H.,** B.Comm., C.A.; chartered accountant; b. Kenaston, Sask. 31 Mar. 1942; s. Dave and Florence (Butler) T.; e. Univ. of Sask. B.Comm. 1963; Chartered Acct. 1966; Banff Sch. of Advanced Mgmt.; m. Eleanor d. Joe and Anne Lasco 18 July 1964; children: Joanne, Kevin, Kelly; CHIEF EXEC. OFFR., FEDERATED CO-OPERATIVES LTD. 1984– ; Dir., Cooperative Energy Corp.; Supr. Touche Ross & Co. 1966; Controller Smith Roles Ltd. 1968; joined present firm as Internal Auditor 1970, Controller 1972, Distrbn. Div. Mgr. 1975, Treas. 1977; recreations: curling, fastball; Club: Masonic Lodge; Home: 23 Riel Cres., Saskatoon, Sask. S7J 2W7; Office: 401 - 22nd St. E., Box 1050, Saskatoon, Sask. S7K 3M7.

**THOMPSON, Wesley Duncan,** B.A.; grain merchant; b. Blenheim, Ont. 18 Oct. 1926; s. Wesley Gairdner and Anna Corneil (McCallum) T.; e. Univ. of W. Ont. B.A. 1950; m. Patricia d. Frank and Bernice Coatsworth 6 July 1957; children: Wesley, Jennifer, Frank; PRESIDENT AND CHIEF EXEC. OFFR., W.G. THOMPSON & SONS LTD. 1951– ; joined present Co. 1950; Vice Pres., Hyland Farms Ltd.; Office: 122 George St., Blenheim, Ont. N0P 1A0.

**THOMPSON, William David,** B.Sc., M.B.A.; business executive; b. Brantford, Ont. 5 Dec. 1952; s. William Charles and Eileen (Fulmines) T.; E. Univ. of Toronto B.Sc. 1975, M.B.A. 1979; m. Sandra Hawkins May 1982; children: David, Stefanie, Jeffrey; MANAGER, HRIM, TPF&C CANADA & MANAGER, RETIREMENT ADMIN., TPF&C U.S. 1991– ; joined T.A. Associates 1975; Vice-Pres. 1981; joined Towers Perrin (TPF&C) 1983; Principal 1986; Vice-Pres. 1990; Office: 1100, 250 Bloor St. E., Toronto, Ont. M4W 3N3.

**THOMPSON, William Grant,** F.C.A., C.M.C., C.M.A., F.C.I.S., P.Adm.; business executive; b. Westville, N.S. 27 June 1925; s. Harvey Alden and Jessie (MacGregor) T.; e. Maritime Business College 1944; Inst. of C.A.s of N.S.; C.A. 1950; Soc. of Mngt. Accountants C.M.A. 1951; Inst. of Mngt. Consultants Atlantic Canada C.M.C. 1983; Inst. of Chartered Secretaries & Administrators F.C.I.S., P.Adm. 1963; m. Margaret d. Herbert and Anne Mackenzie 24 Sept. 1952; children: Heather, Anne, Carole, Andrew; PRESIDENT & DIRECTOR, REVENUE MANAGEMENT LTD. 1987– ; Treasurer, Maritime Steel & Foundries Ltd. 1951–58; Financial Dir. to Vice-Pres. & Gen. Mgr., EMI Electronics Canada Ltd. 1958–69; Partner, Price Waterhouse & Price Waterhouse Assoc. 1970–87; Vice-Pres. & Dir., Price Waterhouse Ltd. 1977–87; Pres. & Dir., MacCulloch & Co. Ltd. & Oakwood Investments Ltd. 1983–87; Gold Medal, Maritime Business College; Fellow, Inst. of CA's of N.S.; Dir., Treas. & Chair Investment Ctte., Financial Services, United Ch. of Canada; Chair, Bd. of Gov., Pine Hill Divinity Hall 1974–79; Atlantic Sch. of Theology 1982–85; Maritime Bd. of Trusts, United Ch. of Canada 1982–88; Finance Ctte. & Dir., Waterfront Development Corp. 1977–81; Comnr., Food Prices Review Board Ottawa 1974–77; Chair, Bd. of Dir., Windsor Elms Seniors' Home 1983–87; club: Sauguay; Office: 2184 Connaught Ave., Halifax, N.S. B3L 2Z3.

**THOMSON, Alexander John,** Ph.D.; banking executive; b. Glasgow, Scotland 21 Dec. 1943; s. Alex and Jeanie (Wright) T.; e. Univ. of Toronto B.A. (Econ./Pol. Sci.) 1967; Cornell Univ. Ph.D. (Econ. theory) 1973; m. Ursula d. Eleanora and George Lummis 17 Aug. 1968; children: Julia Eleanora, Andrew Alexander, Michael Edward; VICE PRES. ECONOMICS, ROYAL BANK OF CANADA 1987– ; Asst. Chief, Monetary & Fin. Analysis, Bank of Can. 1973–80; Sr. Econ., Econ. Dept., Royal Bank of Can. 1980–85; Deputy Chief Econ., 1985–87; Club: Summerlea Golf & Country; Home: 430 Concord Dr., Beaconsfield, Que. H9W 5S9; Office: P.O. Box 6001, Montreal, Que. H3C 3A9.

**THOMSON, Alistair S.,** M.A.; investment consultant; b. Stirling, Scotland 18 Dec. 1939; s. William Alexander and Janet McLaren (Young) T.; e. Stirling H.S. (Scotland) 1956; Univ. of St. Andrews, Scotland M.A. (Hons.) 1963; m. Janet Tevere 12 May 1979; PRESIDENT, TOUCHE THOMSON & YEOMAN INVESTMENT CONSULTANTS LTD. 1973– ; Former Pres., Economic Society of Alberta; Calgary Soc. of Investment Analysts; Mem., Vancouver Soc. of Financial Analysts; recreations: tennis, hiking, travel; club: Vancouver Lawn Tennis; Home: 1961 Tolmie St., Vancouver, B.C. V6R 4C1; Office: 4000 – 350 7th Ave. S.W., Calgary, Alta. T2P 3W5.

**THOMSON, Brent Robert,** B.Comm., C.A.; executive; b. Calgary, Alta. 13 Nov. 1951; s. Alan Robert and Vivian Ruth (Goss) T.; e. McMaster Univ. B.Comm. 1974; m. Diane d. Desmond and Sarah Thompson 13 Dec. 1980; children: Christine, Sean, Kevin; VICE-PRES. CENTRAL REGION & CHIEF FINANCIAL OFFR., WESTROC INDUSTRIES LIMITED 1993– ; Peat Marwick Mitchell 1974–77; various finan. positions, present firm 1977–84, Vice Pres. Finance & Treas. 1984–93; Dir. 1985– ; Dir., Lochinvar Finance Inc.; Western Gypsum (1980) Ltd.; Mem., Inst. of C.A.s of Ont.; Finan. Extves. Inst. of Can. (Hamilton Chap.); recreations: golf; clubs: Hamilton Golf & Country; Home: 2029 Barlow Cres., Burlington, Ont. L7P 4N8; Office: 2424 Lakeshore Rd. W., Mississauga, Ont. L5J 1K4.

**THOMSON, Dale Cairns,** D.F.C., B.A., D.ès L.; educator; b. Westlock, Alta. 17 June 1923; s. Walter James Cairns and Margaret Charlotte (Falkson) T.; e. Fort Assiniboine (Alta.) Pub. Sch. 1928–38; Barrhead (Alta.) High Sch. 1938–41; Univ. of Alta. B.A. 1948; Univ. de Paris, Dipl., Inst. d'Etudes Pol. 1950, D.ès L. 1951; PROF. OF POL. SCIENCE, McGILL UNIV. 1974– ; Prof. of Pol. Sci., Univ. de Montréal 1960–69, Chrmn. Dept. of Pol. Sci. 1963–67; Prof. Internat. Rlns. & Dir. Center Candn. Studies, Sch. of Advanced Internat. Studies, Johns Hopkins Univ., Washington, D.C. 1969–73; Vice Princ. (Planning) McGill Univ. 1973–76; served with R.C.A.F. 1941–45 as Pilot, rank Flt. Lt.; participated in D-Day and liberation of W. Europe, awarded DFC; Secy. to Prime Min. St. Laurent, 1953–58; def. cand. for Jasper-Edson in g.e. 1958; author: 'Alexander Mackenzie: Clear Grit' 1960; 'Louis St. Laurent: Canadian' 1967 (French ed. 1968); 'Jean Lesage and the Quiet Revolution' 1984 (Fr. & Eng. eds.); 'Vive le Québec libre' 1988 (Fr. ed. 1990); numerous articles; co-author (with Roger F. Swanson) 'Canadian Foreign Policy: Options and Perspectives' 1971; ed. 'Quebec Society & Politics: Views from the Inside' 1973; mem. Candn. Pol. Sci. Assn.; Am. Pol. Sci. Assn.; Internat. Soc. for Political Psychology; Mem., Bd. of Dirs., Internat. Centre for Ethnic Studies, Colombo, Sri Lanka; founding Pres., Assn. for Candn. Studies in the U.S. 1971–73; mem. Gov. Counc., Montreal Mus. of Fine Arts 1974–82, mem. Exec. Ctte. 1974–77; Liberal; United Church; recreations: skiing, sailing, swimming, scuba diving, squash; Home: 458 Elm Ave., Westmount, Que. H3Y 3J1; Office: 855 Sherbrooke St. W., Montreal, Que. H3A 2T7.

**THOMSON, Donald Walter,** LL.B., LL.D.; author; b. Edmonton, Alta. 18 Jan. 1906; s. George and Anna (McRae) T.; e. King Edward P.S. 1919; Strathcona H.S. 1923; Univ. of Alta. LL.B. 1926, LL.D. (Hon.) 1970; m. Theresa (dec. 1975) d. Horace and Emily Meeres 5 Sept. 1936; m. Wanda d. Frank and Marie Boleyn 2 Oct. 1976; admitted to Alta. Bar 1927; Staff, Law Branch, Can. House of Commons 1928–31; served as Private Sec. to Hon. James Gardiner (Agric. Min.) 1936–39; Hon. James MacKinnon (Trade & Comm. Min.) 1939–48; Hon. George Prudham (Mines. & Tech. Surveys Mins.) 1950–57; freelance writer, Candn. periodicals 1927– ; Life Fellow, Royal Geographical Soc. (U.K.); Hon. Life Mem., Candn. Inst. of Surveying & Mapping; Winner, Alan Sangster Award, Candn. Author's Assn. 1970; Dr. Don W. Thomson Award 1986; Nat. Pres., Candn. Authors Assn. 1960–62; Hon. Life Mem. 1980– ; Hon. Pres. 1989– ; Dir., Candn. Writers Found., Inc. 1963– ; Pres. 1970–73; Hon. Pres. 1989– ; continues as active Dir.; Nat. Treas., Candn. Youth Hostels Assn. 1958–60; Ordained Lifetime Elder, Un. Ch. of Can. 1943; Mem., Sr. Citizen's Activity Ctr. Ottawa 1988– ; author: 'Men and Meridians' (3 vols. Eng. &

Fr. versions) 1961–67, 'Skyview Canada Q.P.' 1975 (story of aerial surveys of Canada); co-author: 'Silver Light' 1955, 'River and Realm' 1959, 'Myth and Monument' 1957, 'Starway and High Orbit' 1974 (poetry); editor: 'Totem Poles' by Marius Barbeau 1950; recreations: travel, reading, writing correspondence; Home: 2055 Carling Ave., Apt. 1016A, Ottawa, Ont. K2A 1G6.

**THOMSON, Douglas Ferguson Scott,** M.A.; professor (emeritus); b. Renfrewshire, Scot., 13 Oct. 1919; s. James Scott and Louise Ferguson (Pearson) T.; e. Glasgow (Scot.) Acad., 1928–38; Merton Coll., Oxford Univ., B.A., M.A., 1946; m. Eleanor Mary, d. late A. E. Hodgkins, M.C., Tunbridge Wells, Eng., 27 June 1953; children: James Fetherston Scott, Sarah Mary Scott, Jessica Jane Scott; PROFESSOR EMERITUS, UNIV. OF TORONTO; Resident Tutor, Univ. Coll. Men's Residence, 1950–53; Lect. Univ. Coll. 1948–56, Asst. Prof. 1956–62, Assoc. Prof. 1962–69; Nuffield (Travelling) Fellow, London and Oxford, 1959–60; Visiting Prof., Univ. of N.C., 1967–68; Prof. of Classics, Univ. Coll., Univ. of Toronto, 1969–85; served with RA (Field and Mtn. Batteries), Europe, Middle East, Burma, 1939–45; rank Capt.; COTC, Univ. of Toronto, 1954–60; rank Maj.; Chrmn., Inter-Univs. Council on Grade 13 Latin (Ont.) 1963–64; author/editor, 'Catullus; a critical edition' 1978; co-author, (with H.C. Porter) 'Erasmus and Cambridge' 1963; (with E. Limbrick) 'That Nothing is Known (*Quod Nihil Scitur*)' (works of F. Sanches) 1988; other writings incl. articles and book chapters; translator 'Collected Works of Erasmus'; Past mem. Ed. Comte. 'Phoenix' 1958–71; mem., Am. Philol. Assn.; Soc. Promotion Roman Studies; Classical Assn. Can. (mem. of Counc. 1985–87); Ont. Classical Assn. (Past Vice Pres.); recreations: reading, music; Home: 116 Manor Rd. E., Toronto, Ont. M4S 1P8.

**THOMSON, The Honourable Mr. Justice Gordon Ian,** B.A., LL.B., Q.C.; judge; b. Windsor, Ont. 5 Oct. 1939; s. Walter Gordon and Lillian Margaret (Macarthur) T.; e. Univ. of Windsor B.A. 1964; Univ. of Ottawa LL.B. 1967; m. Carol d. June and Ernest Little 19 Aug. 1978; children: Trisha Dawne, Deni Hall, Victoria Anne; JUDGE, ONTARIO COURT OF JUSTICE, GENERAL DIV. 1992– ; Asst. Crown Attorney Ont. 1969–70; private practice 1970–73, 1976–83; Law Partner with Michael J. Neville 1973–76; Crown Counsel (Standing AGent), Attorney Gen. of Can. 1979–82; apptd. to Ont. Municipal Bd. 1983; Dir., Ont. Heritage Found.; Friendship Concept (half-way house); Ottawa Rideau Kinsmen Club; Robin Sea House; Guest Lectr., Criminal Trial Tactics, Univ. of Windsor and Ottawa; Q.C. 1981; Mem., Law Soc. of U.C.; Candn. Judicial Inst.; Ont. Superior Court Judges Assn.; recreations: skiing, building, reading; Home: 443 Norfolk St. S., Simcoe, Ont. N3Y 2W8; Office: 530 Queensway W., Simcoe, Ont. M3Y 4N4.

**THOMSON, John,** C.A.; chartered accountant; b. Stonehouse, Scotland 18 June 1937; e. Larkhall Academy (Scotland) 1955; Inst. of Scotland 1960; Inst. of C.A.s of Scotland (Member); VICE-PRESIDENT & COMPTROLLER, CANADIAN PACIFIC LIMITED 1988– ; joined Canadian Pacific 1969; Asst. Dir. of Taxation 1974; Mgr., Taxation 1975; Dir. of Taxation 1977; Asst. Comptroller 1981; Comptroller 1983; Office: P.O. Box 6042, Stn. A., Montreal, Que. H3C 3E4.

**THOMSON, Kenneth R., The Rt. Hon. Lord,** of Fleet of Northbridge in the City of Edinburgh; newspaper proprietor; b. Toronto, Ont. 1 Sept. 1923; s. late Rt. Hon. Lord Thomson of Fleet; (Founder of the Thomson Newspapers); e. Upper Can. Coll. Toronto; Univ. of Cambridge B.A., M.A. 1947; m. Nora Marilyn d. A. V. Lavis June 1956; children: David Kenneth Roy, Peter John, Lesley Lynne; CHRMN. OF THE BD. AND DIR., THE THOMSON CORP.; The Thomson Corp. plc.; The Woodbridge Co. Ltd.; Thomson U.S. Inc.; Pres. & Dir., Thomson Works of Art Ltd.; Dir., Hudson's Bay Co.; Markborough Properties Inc.; Began in editorial dept. of Timmins Daily Press, 1947; Advertising Dept. Cambridge (Galt) Reporter, 1948–50; Gen. Mgr., 1950–53; Returned to Toronto Head Office to take over direction of Company's Canadian & Am. operations; Served in 2nd World War with R.C.A.F.; Baptist; Clubs: York Downs; National; Toronto; York; Granite; Toronto Hunt; Recreations: Collecting paintings and works of art, walking; Residences: 8 Castle Frank Rd., Toronto, Ont. M4W 2Z4; and 8 Kensington Palace Gardens, London W8, England; Offices: 65 Queen St. W., Toronto, Ont. M5H 2M8; and The Quadrangle, P.O. Box 4YG, 180 Wardour St., London, W1A 4YG, England.

**THOMSON, Murray McCheyne,** M.A.; foundation executive; b. Honan, China 19 Dec. 1922; s. Andrew and Margaret Smith (Mackay) T.; e. Univ. of Toronto B.A. 1947; Univ. of Mich. M.A. 1953; m. Suteera d. Sukonta and Niphon Vichitranond 6 June 1964; one d. Sheila; CO-FOUNDER AND EXEC. SEC. PEACEFUND CANADA 1986– ; served 6 yrs. with UNESCO Thailand, and as Assoc. Dir. Confs. for Diplomats & Internat. Seminars Am. Friends Service Ctte. S. Asia; served 7 yrs. CUSO as Field Staff Offr. Thailand becoming Asian Regional Dir. and subsequently Exec. Dir. Ottawa; Co-Founder Project Ploughshares, The Group of 78, Candn. Srs. for Social Responsibility and Peace Brigades Internat.; Pres. Candn. Council for Internat. Co-op. 1976–79; mem. UN Group Experts producing report est. World Disarmament Campaign, adopted by UN Gen. Assembly 1982; received Pearson Peace Medal Award 1990; author 'Militarism 1969: Global Trends' 1970; 'A Daring Confidence: the Life and Times of Andrew Thomson in China' 1992; co-author 'A Time to Disarm' 1978; mem. Religious Soc. Friends (Quakers); NDP; recreations: tennis, music, hiking; Home: 554 Orkney, Ottawa, Ont. K2C 3M7; Office: 206, 145 Spruce St., Ottawa, Ont. K1R 6P1.

**THOMSON, Nancy Gordon,** B.A.; educator; investment executive; d. Ewart Kenneth and Marjorie (Forbes) Fockler; e. Blythwood Pub. Sch. and Lawrence Park Coll. Inst. Toronto 1951; Univ. of Toronto Victoria Coll. B.A. 1954; Ont. Coll. of Educ. 1955; Candn. Securities Course Toronto; m. Ralph M. Barford 18 Dec. 1993; children: Lynn, Laurie, Greg; HONORARY CHRMN., NANCY THOMSON, INVESTING FOR WOMEN 1979– ; Dir. The National Trust Co.; MacLean Hunter Ltd.; GSW Inc.; Adv. Ctte., Sch. of Bus. Admin., Univ. of Western Ont.; author: 'Basic Course – Investing For Women'; co-author 'Course II – Investing For Women'; United Church.

**THOMSON, Pamela A.;** judge; b. Timmins, Ont. 27 Aug. 1942; d. James Withell and Ruth Bernice (Ashkanase) Thomson; e. Queen's Univ., B.A. 1964; Univ. of Toronto, LL.B. 1966; m. judge, E. Gordon Hachborn; children: Eric, Gregory; PROVINCIAL JUDGE 1981– ; co-ordinator, Case Flow Mngmt. Program, Ont. Court of Justice (Gen. Div.) Small Claims Court Branch 1990– ; law practice 1968–71, 1975–81; Co-Dir., Ctr. for Public Interest Law 1971–75; called to Qué. Bar 1972; Mem., Candn. Assn. of Prov. Court Judges (Extve. Dir., Secy./Treas., Chrmn., Civil Courts Ctte., Assoc. Dir., Judges' Edn. Conf.); Pres., Ont. Prov. Court (Civil Div.) Judges Assn. 1993– and formerly Chrmn., Police Complaints Bd. 1982–86; author; 'Consumer Access to Justice' 1976; Clubs: University Alumnae Dramatic Club; Office: 400 University Ave., Toronto, Ont. M5S 1S8.

**THOMSON, Peter,** B.J.; transportation executive; b. Miami, Man. 13 Apr. 1930; s. John Ray and Annie Kennedy (Stirling) T.; e. Carleton Univ. B.J. 1953; m. Patricia Marie d. Huntley and Marie Reid 27 Dec. 1963; children: Peter Reid, Robert Huntley; ADM. GRAIN TRANSPORTATION AGENCY 1988– ; reporter daily newspaper 1953–58; pub. relations exec. 1958–64; financial reporter, columnist, Ottawa Bureau Chief daily newspapers 1964–77; Exec. Asst. Min. of Ind., Trade & Comm. Ottawa 1977–79; Sr. Policy Adv. Min. of Transport, Min. Responsible for Candn. Wheat Bd. 1979–80; Exec. Asst. Candn. Wheat Bd. 1981–85; Dep. Adm. present Agency 1985–88; recreations: golf, gardening, hunting; Clubs: Manitoba; Mousetrap (Winnipeg); Niakwa Country (Winnipeg); Winnipeg Press Club; Office: 3rd Flr., 200 Graham Ave., Winnipeg, Man. R3C 4L5.

**THOMSON, Reginald George,** D.V.M., M.V.Sc., Ph.D., Dip.A.V.C.P.; b. Woodstock, Ont. 7 Apr. 1934; s. George Douglas and Kathleen (Smith) T.; e. Ont. Vet. Coll., Univ. of Toronto, D.V.M. 1959, M.V.Sc. 1963; Cornell Univ., Ph.D. 1965; Diplomate, Am. Coll. of Vet. Path. 1965; m. Helen d. Wilfred and Corinne Ure 25 May 1957; children: Joanne, Carol, Kathy; Retired 1990; Dean, Faculty of Veterinary Med., Univ. of P.E.I. 1983; Gen. Vet. Prac., Fisherville, Ont. 1959–61; Assoc. Prof., Univ. of Guelph 1965–67; Prof. 1967–79; Chrmn., Path. Dept. 1969–79; Planning Coordinator, proposed Atlantic Vet. Coll., Univ. of P.E.I. 1979–81; Prof., Dept. of Vet. Path., Western Coll. of Vet. Med., Univ. of Sask. 1982–83; Vis. Prof., Univ. Nairobi 1975; Univ. of Ibadan; External Exam. 1972, 1981–82; Exam. Ctte., Am. Coll. of Vet. Path. 1978–83; Chrmn., Vet. Path. section 1978–83; AVMA Womes Aux. award for outstanding achievements 1959; Borden Co. Scholarship 1962; Norden Distinguished Teacher Award 1971; Award for Teaching Excellence 1972; Alumnus of the Year Award, Univ. of Guelph 1986; awarded C.L. Davis Foundation Award for sustained excellence in teaching Veterinary Pathology 1992; rec'd. Hon. Doctor of Laws, Univ. of P.E.I. 1993; rec'd. Hon. Doctor of Science, Univ. of Guelph 1994; Sunday Sch. Supt. 1972–75; Chrmn., Harcourt Un. Ch.1977; Supr., Youth Group, Spring Park Un. Ch. 1979–80; Supr., Ctte. Mem. & Supervisor for numerous graduate students; 70 presentations given, 66 refereed and 4 non-refereed; author: 'General Veterinary Pathology' 1st ed. 1976, 2nd ed. 1984; Ed.: 'Canadian Journal of Comparative Medicine' 1970–82 (Asst. Ed. 1983–85); 'Special Veterinary Pathology' 1988; recreations: camping, boating; Club: Charlottetown Rotary; Home: 1215 Sprucedale Rd., Woodstock, Ont. N4T 1N1.

**THOMSON, Richard Murray,** B.A.Sc., M.B.A.; banker; b. Winnipeg, Man. 14 Aug. 1933; s. late Harold W. and Mary (Lees) T.; e. Univ. of Toronto B.A.Sc.(Eng.) 1955; Harvard Business Sch. M.B.A. 1957; Queen's Univ. F.I.C.B. 1958; CHRMN., C.E.O. & DIR., THE TORONTO DOMINION BANK 1978– ; Dir., Cadillac Fairview Corp. Ltd.; CGC Inc.; S.C. Johnson & Son, Inc.; Inco. Ltd.; The Thomson Corp.; Prudential Ins. Co. of America; Hosp. for Sick Children; joined T-D Bank in 1957 and served in several Brs. in various positions in Toronto and Montreal; Asst. to Pres., H.O. 1963; Chief Gen. Mgr. 1968; Vice Pres., Chief Gen. Mgr. & Dir. 1971; Pres. 1972; Pres. & C.E.O. 1977; Chrmn. & C.E.O. 1978; Office: P.O. Box 1, Toronto-Dominion Centre, Toronto, Ont. M5K 1A2.

**THOMSON, Robert,** E.D., F.C.I.S., P.Adm.; executive; b. Aberdeen, Scotland 16 May 1904; s. Robert and Mary (Brodie) T.; came to Canada, 1914; e. William Dawson and Comm. High Sch., Montreal Que.; m. Annabel Scott, d. Robert Doig, Lachute, Que., 30 June 1934; one s. Robert Graham; VICE-PRES. AND DIR., YALE PROPERTIES LTD. since 1969; Treas. & Dir. Nationwide Capital; joined Standard Life Assurance Co. as a Jr. Clerk, 1919; apptd. Secy. for Canada, 1937, Asst. Mgr. 1956, Depy. General Manager 1957 Extve. Dir. 1966; served in 2nd World War, 1940–45 Overseas with 17th Duke of York's Royal Candn. Hussars, Candn. Mil. Hdqrs., Eng.; discharged with rank of Major; Freemason; Conservative; Protestant: recreations: golf, gardening, reading; Clubs: Mount Royal; Kanawaki Golf; Home: 4555 Montclair Ave., Montreal, Que. H4B 2J8; Office: 2015 Peel St., Montreal, Que. H3A 1T8.

**THOMSON, Robert Holmes (R.H.),** B.Sc.; actor; b. Toronto, Ont. 24 Sept. 1947; s. Woodburn Stratford and Cicely Evelyn (Holmes) T.; e. Richmond Hill H.S. 1965; Univ. of Toronto, B.Sc. 1969; Nat. Theatre Sch. of Can.; London Acad. of Music & Dramatic Art; m. Laurie d. Donald and Betty Matheson 28 Nov. 1983; children: MacIntosh Wildy, Andrew Matheson; extensive work in stage, film and television; Gemini Award; Dora Mavor Moore Award; Genie Award; Home: 201 Albany Ave., Toronto, Ont. M5R 3C7.

**THOMSON, Shirley Lavinia,** O.C., Ph.D.; art gallery director; b. Walkerville, Ont. 19 Feb. 1930; d. Walter Cull; e. Univ. of West. Ont., B.A. (Hons.) 1952; Univ. of Maryland, M.A. 1974; McGill Univ., Ph.D. 1981; DIR., NATIONAL GALLERY OF CANADA 1987– ; Editor, NATO, Paris 1956–60; Asst. Sec.-Gen., World Univ. Serv. WUSC 1960–63; Assoc. Sec.-Gen., Candn. Comn. for UNESCO 1964–67; Rsch. Coord. & Writer for memoirs of Sen. Thérèse Casgrain 1968–70; Dir. & Dep. Comnr., UNESCO Pavilion, Man & His World, Montreal 1978–80; Special Coord., Largillierre Exhib., Montreal Mus. of Fine Arts 1981; Dir., McCord Mus. 1982–85; Sec.-Gen., Candn. Commn. for UNESCO 1985–87; Doctorat Honoris Causa, Univ. of Ottawa 1988; Doctorat Honoris Causa, McGill Univ. 1989; Doctorat Honoris Causa, Mount Allison Univ. 1990; Doctorat Honoris Causa, Univ. of W. Ont. 1990; Chevalier des Arts et des lettres, Govt. of France 1990; Officer, Order of Canada 1994; Office: 380 Sussex Dr., Ottawa, Ont. K1N 9N4.

**THOMSON, William Edward,** B.Com., C.A.; consultant; b. Halifax, N.S. 19 June 1941; s. Ronald Douglas and Barbara Cora (Zinck) T.; e. Dalhousie Univ. B.Com. 1961; Inst. C.A.'s N.S. 1963; m. C. Janice Cameron 6 Oct. 1962; children: Ronald William, Tracey Elizabeth; PRES. WILLIAM E. THOMSON ASSOCIATES INC. 1978– ; Chrmn., Accommodex Franchise Mgmnt. Inc.; Votek Systems Ltd.; Pres., Epton Industries Ltd.; Dir., Electrical Contacts Ltd.; Elegant Communications Ltd.; Med-Emerg Ltd.; BMDX Medical Waste Systems; Tucker Plastics Ltd.; Evaz Investments Ltd.; David Wood Food Shop Ltd.; Mgr. Peat Marwick Mitchell & Co. 1961–66; Asst. Sec.-Treas. Industrial Estates Ltd. 1966–68; Sec.-Treas: Clairtone Sound Corp. Ltd. 1968–70; Gage Educational Publishing Ltd. 1971–73; Vice Pres. Upper Lakes Shipping Ltd./Leitch Transport Ltd. 1973–81; Pres. I P Sharp Associates Inc. 1985–87; Anglican; recreations: riding, reading; Clubs:

Toronto & North York Hunt; Granite; Address: 33 Daffodil Ave., Thornhill, Ont. L3T 1N3.

**THORBURN, Hugh Garnet,** A.M., Ph.D.; university professor b. Toronto, Ont. 8 Feb. 1924; s. Hugh and Delia Amanda (Jacobs) T.; e. Univ. of Toronto, B.A. (Pol. Science & Econ.) 1949; Columbia Univ., A.M. 1950, Cert. of European Inst., 1951, Ph.D. 1958; m. Gwendolyn Alice Montgomery, 8 July 1950; children: Janet, Julie, Hugh A.R. (Sandy), John, Maria, Malcolm; PROF. DEPT. OF POL. STUDIES, QUEEN'S UNIV. (Head of Dept. 1968–71); Lectr. in Pol. Science and Econ., Mount Alison University 1952–53; Assistant Professor 1953; apptd. Asst. Prof. University of Sask. (granted 1 yr. leave of absence from Mount Allison), 1954–55; returned Mount Allison 1955–56; joined present Univ. 1956; served with Candn. Army 1943–46; enlisted as Pte. in Inf.; commnd. 2nd Lt. 1944; trans. to Candn. Intelligence Corps attached to Candn. Mil. HQ. London; served as Intelligence Offr. to HQ 1st Candn. Army, HQ 2nd Candn. Corps, HQ 30 Brit. Corps; served as Field Security Offr., Holland and Germany; discharged 1946 with rank Capt.; author: 'Politics in New Brunswick' 1961; 'Party Politics in Canada' 1963 (6th rev. ed. 1991); co-author: 'Canadian Anti-Combines Administration 1952–60' 1963; 'Planning and the Economy' 1984; 'Interest Groups in the Canadian Federal System' (a monograph for Roy. Comn. on the Economic Union and Develop. Prospects for Can. 1985); has written numerous articles for various learned journs. and has completed 2 studies for Royal Comn. on Bilingualism and Biculturalism; prepared 'Political Science in Canada; Graduate Studies & Research' for Comn. on Grad. Studies in Humanities & Social Sciences 1975; awarded grants for research from Canadian Social Science Research Council, Can. Council, Soc. Sci. & Humanities Research Counc. of Can., Queen's Univ. and French Govt. (Bourse d'Etude 1961); awarded Centennial Medal 1968; Queen's Jubilee Medal 1978; Vice-Chrmn. Research Ctte. on Socio-Political Pluralism of the Internat. Pol. Sci. Assn. 1976–85 (Chrmn. 1985–91); Mem. Bd. of Dir., Social Science Federation of Canada, 1979–80; Pres., Candn. Pol. Science Assn., 1977–78 (mem. Extve. Comte. 1965–67, Vice Pres. 1968–69); Pres., Social Science Research Council Can., 1967–69 (Chrmn., Publs. Comte., 1965–67); Chrmn., Kingston Br., Candn. Inst. Internat. Affairs, 1965–67; Delta Chi; Home: 194 Johnson St., Kingston, Ont. K7L 1Y1.

**THORFINNSON, Arthur Rodney,** B.A., D.H.A., FACHE; health care administrator; b. Kandahar, SK 30 Nov. 1934; s. Arthur Sigurjon and Wilhelmine Bernice (Krause) T.; e. Univ. of Sask., B.A. 1958; Univ. of Toronto, D.H.A. 1960; m. Kathleen d. Harold and Sadie Fennell 10 Sept. 1957; children: LeAnne Elizabeth, Rodney Michael, John Douglas; PRES. & CHIEF EXTVE. OFFR., HEALTH SCI. CTR. 1985– ; various admin. positions in hospitals & assns. 1961–70; Extve. Dir., Victoria Hosp. 1970–77; Pres. & Chief Extve. Offr., Victoria Hosp. Corp. 1977–85; Past Bd. Mem., Man. Health Orgn.; Past Bd. Mem., Candn. Hosp. Assn.; Past Chrmn., Assn. of Candn. Teaching Hosps.; Ont. Counc. of Admin. of Teaching Hosps.; Past Bd. Mem., Ont. Hosp. Assn.; Past Regent, Am. Coll. of Healthcare Extves.; Past Chrmn., The M.I.S. Group; Past Chrmn., Candn. Assn. of Pediatric Hospitals; Assoc. Prof., Univ. of Man. & Univ. of Toronto; recreations: trap shooting, flying, boating; clubs: Manitoba, Winnipeg Flying; Home: 95 Shier Dr., Winnipeg, Man. R3R 2H2; Office: 820 Sherbrook St., Winnipeg, Man. R3A 1R9.

**THORLAKSON, James Allan,** B.A.Sc., P.Eng.; lumber industry executive; b. Edmonton, Alta. 27 Jan. 1940; e. Univ. of B.C. B.A.Sc. 1964, P.Eng. 1967; m. Marlene; children: Brad, Shane, Dean; PRES. & CHIEF EXTVE. OFFR., TOLKO INDUSTRIES LTD. 1971– ; Engr., Weldwood of Canada 1964–67; Plant Mgr., Lavington Planer Mill 1967–71; Interim Pres., Westar Timber Ltd. 1990; Dir., Gilbert Smith Forest Prod.; Home: R.R. #1, Site 3, Comp. 35, Vernon, B.C. V1T 6L4; Office: Box 39, Vernon, B.C. V1T 6M1.

**THORN, Rev. Jean,** B.A., S.T.L., LL.L., J.C.D.; university administrator; b. Montreal, Que. 4 April 1927; s. William and Jeanne (Lauzon) T.; e. Univ. of Montreal B.A. 1948, S.T.L. 1952, LL.L. 1964; St. Thomas Aquin Univ. (Rome) J.C.D. 1955; DEAN, FACULTY OF CANON LAW, SAINT PAUL UNIVERSITY 1984– ; Notary, Ecclesiastical Tribunal of Montreal 1955–60; Judicial Vicar (Pres.) 1964–85; Chancery Office (Diocese of Montreal) 1983–84; Consultor, Pontifical Council for the Interpretation of Legislative Texts 1986– ; Episcopal Comn. Canon Law/Inter-Rite 1973– ; Role of Law Award, Canon Law Soc. 1990; Hon. Mem., Candn. Canon Law Soc.; Mem., Canon Law Soc. of Great Britain & Ireland; Canon Law Soc. of Australia & N.Z.; Canon Law Soc. of Am.; Assoc. Ed., 'Studia canonica' 1984– ; editor: 'The New Code of Canon Law' (proceedings) 1986, 'Code de droit canonique' 1990, 'Code of Canon Law Annotated' 1993, 'Unico Ecclesiæ servitio' 1991, 'Studia canonica' (index of vols. 1–25); recreations: skiing, golf, travel, reading; Home: 912 – 1551 Riverside Dr., Ottawa, Ont. K1G 4B5; Office: 223 Main St., Ottawa, Ont. K1S 1C4.

**THORNE, Douglas;** food manufacturing executive; b. Moncton, N.B. 26 Aug. 1951; s. Wendel Douglas and Beulah Berdina (MacLeod) T.; e. Riverview H.S. 1968; m. Jane d. Tom and Kaye MacNeil 18 Oct. 1974; children: Douglas, Christopher; VICE-PRESIDENT & GENERAL MANAGER, COBI FOODS INC. 1991– ; various sales positions, Cobi Foods Inc. 1969–86; Eastern Canada Sales Mgr. 1986–89; Private Label Sales Mgr. 1989–90; Vice-Pres., Sales & Mktg. 1990–91; Home: 15 Dalhousie Ave., Kentville, N.S. B4N 5E5; Office: Box 10900, Port William, N.S. B0P 1T0.

**THORNHILL, Roland John;** former politician; b. Grand Bank, Nfld. 3 Sept. 1935; s. Archibald and Ruth (Williams) T.; e. Memorial and Dalhousie Univs.; m. Mary MacLeod; two s. Christopher, Jeffrey; el. to Dartmouth City Council 1961; Mayor 1967–73; el. to N.S. House of Assembly for Dartmouth S. 1974, re-el. 1978, 1981, 1984 & 1988; apptd. Sr. Cabinet Min. 1978; Minister of Tourism & Culture 1989–91; formerly Min. of Development and Min., N.S. Research Foundation Corp.; Depy. Premier, N.S. and Min. of Industry, Trade and Technology, Min. of Environment and is presently Min. of Community Services, Chair of the Senior Citizens Secretariat, Min. Responsible for Reporting on Disabled Persons and the Disabled Persons Commission, Min. Responsible for the Administration of the Advisory Council on the Status of Women Act; rec'd Vanier Award 1974; Past Pres. and Senator, Dartmouth Chamber of Comm.; Chrmn., Flowers of Hope Campaign, Candn. Assoc. for Community Living; Mem., Salvation Army Adv. Bd. for Can. and N.S.; Mem., Masonic Order; P. Conservative; United Church; recreations: curling and reading history and biography; Clubs: Kiwanis; Brightwood Golf; Dartmouth Curling; Office: P.O. Box 696, Halifax, N.S. B3J 2T7.

**THORNLEY, Ronald F.;** security systems executive; b. 13 Aug. 1938; married; children: two; PRES., ADT CANADA INC. & SR. VICE-PRES., ADT SECURITY SYSTEMS INC. 1979– ; Salesman, ADT 1964; Sales Mgr., 1969; Gen. Sales Mgr. 1972; Gen. Mgr., Candn. Cos. 1974; Pres. & Gen. Mgr., Dominion Electric Protection Co. & subs. 1978– ; Clubs: Summit Golf & Country; Office: 5734 Yonge St., Willowdale, Ont. M2M 4E7.

**THORNLEY, Shirley Blumberg,** B.Arch., O.A.A., M.R.A.I.C.; architect; b. Cape Town, South Africa 4 Feb. 1952; d. Alec and Anne (Minkowitz) Katz; e. Ellerslie Girls H.S.; Univ. of Cape Town; Univ. of Toronto B.Arch. (Hons.) 1976; m. Scott s. Charles and Margaret (Gleadon) Thornley; one s.: Charles R.; ARCHITECT, KUWABARA PAYNE MCKENNA BLUMBERG ARCHITECTS; Assoc., Barton Myers Assoc. 1977–87, selected projects: Hazelton Townhouses Toronto 1983; Unionville Library Markham 1984; Hasbro Corp. H.Q. Phase One R.I. 1986; selected projects, present firm: Hasbro Corp. H.Q. Phase Two, R.I. 1994; King James Place Toronto 1991; The Design Exchange Toronto 1994; Stauffer Library Interiors, Queen's Univ. 1994; Min. of Culture, Tourism & Recreation Niagara Falls 1995; Mem., Ont. Assn. of Architects; Royal Arch. Inst. of Can.; Adjunct Asst. Prof., Univ. of Toronto 1987, '90; Guest Critic, Carleton Univ., Univ. of Ottawa & Univ. of Waterloo; Toronto Arts Award for Arch. & Design 1993; Gov. Gen. Award of Merit, King James Place 1992; Bd. Mem., Royal Arch. Inst. of Can. 1990–93; Bd. of Trustees, Ont. Sci. Centre 1988–91; Home: 6 Braemore Gardens, Toronto, Ont. M6G 2C8; Office: 322 King St. W., Toronto, Ont. M5V 1J2.

**THORNTON, Archibald Paton,** M.A., D.Phil., F.R.Hist.S., F.R.S.C.; university professor; b. Glasgow, Scotland 21 Oct. 1921; s. John Joseph and Margaret (Paton) T.; e. Kelvinside Acad., Glasgow, 1929–39; Univ. of Glasgow 1939–41, 1945–47 (M.A. 1947); Univ. of Oxford, Trinity Coll., 1947–50 (D.Phil. 1952); two s.: Roderick Charles Stuart and Andrew Rohan George; PROF. OF HISTORY, UNIV. OF TORONTO since 1960 and Chrmn. of Dept. 1967–72; Capt., E. Riding Yorks. Imp. Yeomanry, 1942–45 (D-Day Landing 6 June 1944); Lect. in Modern Hist., Trinity Coll., Oxford 1948–50; Lect. in Imp. Hist., Univ. of Aberdeen 1950–57; Prof. and Chrmn. of Hist. and Dean of Arts, Univ. Coll. of W. Indies 1957–60; mem., H.M. Colonial Service Appts. Bd. 1952–57; Commonwealth Fellow of St. John's Coll., Cambridge 1966; Visiting Smuts Fellow in Commonwealth Studies, Univ. of Cambridge 1965–66; Visiting Fellow, Sackler Inst., Tel Aviv Univ., Israel 1986; Fellow, Roy. Soc. of Can.; author 'West-India Policy under the Restoration' 1956; 'The Imperial Idea and its Enemies' 1959 (repr. 1966, 2nd ed. 1985); 'Doctrines of Imperialism' 1965; 'The Habit of Authority' 1966; 'For the File on Empire' 1968; 'Imperialism in the 20th Century' 1978; ed. G. Martel 'Studies in Imperial History in honour of A.P. Thornton' 1986; over 70 articles, reviews in learned journs.; mem. Am. Hist. Assn.; Candn. Hist. Assn.; Hakluyt Soc.; Reform Club (London); Presbyterian; recreations: chess, G.A. Henty, theatre; Office: University College, Toronto, Ont. M5S 1A1.

**THORPE, Trevor Alleyne,** B.Sc., M.S, Ph.D.; educator; b. Barbados, W. Indies 18 Oct. 1936; s. Mitchell Livingstone and Violet Eudora (Alleyne) T.; e. Harrison Coll. Barbados 1956; Allahabad Agric. Inst. India B.Sc. 1961; Univ. of Cal. Riverside M.S. 1964, Ph.D. 1968; m. Rosita Yvonne d. Calvert and Violet Cumberbatch 10 Aug. 1963; children: Anthony Ricardo, Jennifer Michelle; PROF. OF BOTANY, UNIV. OF CALGARY 1978– ; joined Min. of Agric. Lands & Fisheries Barbados 1961–63; Rsch. Asst. Dept. Hortic. Sci. 1964–67, Vegetable Crops 1967–68 Univ. of Cal. Riverside; Rsch. Plant Physiol. Agric. Rsch. Service US Dept. Agric., Fruit & Vegetable Chem. Lab. Pasadena, Cal. 1968–69; Asst. Prof. of Botany present Univ. 1969, Assoc. Prof. 1973, Asst. Dean of Arts & Sci. and of Sci. 1974–76, Head, Dept. Biological Sciences 1988, Assoc. Dean (Rsch.), Faculty of Science 1989–92; Adjunct Prof. of Forest Sci. Univ. of Alta. 1986; Affiliated Sci. Nat. Rsch. Council Can. Plant Biotech. Inst. Saskatoon 1987–92; mem., Sci. Adv. Bd. DNA Plant Tech. Corp. N.J. 1981–86; Cons., Internat. Devel. Rsch. Centre Ottawa 1983– ; Internat. Atomic Energy Agency 1987; Pres. 4th Internat. Cong. Plant Tissue & Cell Culture, Univ. Calgary 1978, ed. Proceedings: 'Frontiers of Plant Tissue Culture'; Govt. of India Cultural Scholar 1957–61; Fulbright Scholar 1963–64; Frank and Ivy Meyers Scholar 1967–68; Nat. Rsch. Council USA Postdoctoral Rsch. Associateship 1968–69; NATO Sr. Fellow France & Belgium 1977; Killam Resident Fellow Univ. Calgary 1978; Japan Soc. Promotion Sci. Rsch. Fellow 1982; ed. 'Plant Tissue Culture – Methods and Applications in Agriculture' 1981; co-author 'Peroxidases: A Survey of Their Biochemical and Physiological Roles in Higher Plants' 1982; author or co-author over 200 articles profl. jours.; mem. various ed. bds.; Chrmn. Internat. Assn. Plant Tissue Culture 1974–78; Covenor, Panel Plant Cell Biol. & Technol. Internat. Cell Rsch. Orgn. UNESCO 1979–85; Exec. Ctte. W. Dir., Candn. Soc. Plant Physiols. 1986–88 (Vice-Pres. 1991–93); Sigma Xi (Past Pres.); recreations: baseball, cricket, hockey; Home: 5843 Dalford Hill N.W., Calgary, Alta. T3A 1L5; Office: 2500 University Dr. N.W., Calgary, Alta. T2N 4N4.

**THORSELL, James Westvick,** Ph.D.; conservation executive; b. Wetaskiwin, Alta. 5 Dec. 1940; s. Arnold and Irene (Westvick) T.; e. Univ. of Alta., B.Sc. 1962; Univ. of W. Ont., M.A. 1967; Univ. of B.C., Ph.D. 1971; SR. ADVISOR, INTERNAT. UNION FOR CONSERVATION OF NATURE & NATURAL RESOURCES, WORLD CONSERVATION UNION 1984– ; Planner, Parks Can. 1966–68; priv. environ. cons. 1971–76; Asst. Prof., Univ. of Alta. 1977–79; Planner, Kenya Wildlife Dept. 1979–81; Sr. Lectr., Coll. of Afr. Wildlife Mgmt. Tanzania 1982–83; numerous cons. projects for U.N. and other aid agencies; Vice Pres., Storm Mt. Lodge Ltd. 1975–79; Rsch. Assc., Island Resources Found.; Instr., Banff Centre 1971–75 (seasonal); author/editor of 75 publ reports & books incl. (au.) 'Managing Protected Areas in Eastern Africa' 1984, (ed.) 'Conserving Asia's Natural Heritage' 1985, (co-au.) 'Protected Areas in the Tropics' 1987; recreations: skiing, hunting, horses, photography; Home: Box 1374, Banff, Alta.; Office: Rue Mauverney 28, 1196 Gland, Switzerland.

**THORSON, Kim,** B.S.A., B.A., LL.B., Q.C.; lawyer; b. Macoun, Sask. 2 March 1932; s. Miles and Ethel (Sinclair) T.; e. Univ. of Sask. B.S.A. 1954, B.A., LL.B. 1963; m. Myrtle d. George and Catherine Lipsett 12 Oct. 1957; children: Eric, Janet, Vanessa; LAWYER, HARDY & THORSON 1990– ; Research Economist, Govt. of Sask. 1955; Member of the Legislative Assembly, Sask. 1956–60; articling law student, Saskatoon 1963–64; practice of law Estevan, Sask. 1964–71; Mem. of the Legislative Assembly & Extve. Council, Sask. 1972–75; practice of law Regina 1975–90; Dir. & Chair, Estevan Co-op. Assn. Ltd. 1968–71; Dir., IPSCO Inc. 1980– ; Cameco Corp. 1992– ; Weyburn Security Co. Ltd. 1990– ; Weyburn Co-op. Assn. Ltd. 1993– ; World Univ. Serv. Study Tour Scholarship to Eur. & W. Africa 1954; Trustee & Chair, Estevan Comprehensive Sch. Bd.

1970–71; Dir. & Chair, Sask. Centre of the Arts Regina 1978–83; Mem., Bd. of Regents, Luther College Regina 1986– (Chair 1989– ); author of one article in 'Sask. LR'; Mem., Weyburn Rotary Club 1991– ; Dir., Weyburn Humane Soc. Inc. 1992– ; Dir., Weyburn C. of C. 1994– ; Home: 1621 Warren Ave., Weyburn, Sask. S4H 0M5; Office: 102 Coteau Ave., Weyburn, Sask. S4H 2Z5.

**THORSSEN, Robert William;** business owner; b. Edmonton, Alta. 13 April 1948; s. Dr. Leroy A. and Gwendolyn B. (Weir) T.; e. Henry Wise Wood H.S.; Mount Royal College; Univ. of Calgary; m. May C. Chavez 12 Sept. 1993; MANAGING DIRECTOR, CITYSPCE ASIA LTD. 1993– ; Dir., Roylyn Investments Ltd. 1970– ; Pres. & Dir., Northrim trading INc. 1978–93; Dir., Hong Kong Canada Business Assn. 1988– ; Pres. & C.E.O., Jungle Interiors Canada Ltd. 1981–88; Dir. & Pres., Orient Express Enterprises Canada 1987–93; Extve. Consultant, Hutchison Bldg. Materials Hong Kong 1989–90; Canadian Entrepreneur of the Year, Hong Kong C. of C. 1993; Businessman of the Year, Calgary C. of C. 1987; Award of Excellence, Marketing, Candn. Govt. 1981; Dir., IFMA Hong Kong; IDA Hong Kong; recreations: sailing, racing; clubs: Royal Hong Kong Yacht, Rotary Club of Wanchai Hong Kong; Home: Box 12, Aberdeen Marina Club, Hong Kong; Office: 12th Floor, 24-34 Hennessey Rd., Hong Kong.

**THORSTAD, Linda E.,** M.Sc., P.Geo.; geologist; business executive; b. Vancouver, B.C. 21 Apr. 1954; e. Univ. of B.C., B.Sc. 1977, M.Sc. 1983; CONSULTANT 1991– ; Geol., Geol. Survey Can. 1975–79; Ventures West Minerals Ltd. 1979–82; Thorstad Consulting 1982–83; Pres. Questore Consultants Ltd. 1983–86; Pres., Interaction Resources Ltd. 1986–91; Business & Communications Consultant 1991–92; Assoc., B.C. Commission on Resources and Environment 1992– ; Fraser Basin Management Program 1993– ; author or co-author numerous publs.; Assn. of Professional Engineers and Geoscientists; recreations: skiing, cycling, tennis; Office: 5340 Marine Dr., W. Vancouver, B.C. V7W 2P8.

**THORSTEINSON, Arni Clayton,** B.Comm., C.F.A.; real estate executive; b. Rosetown, Sask. 14 Oct. 1948; s. Johann and Mayme June (Griffiths) T.; e. Univ. of Man. B.Comm.(Hons.) 1969; Chartered Fin. Analyst 1974; m. Susan Jane d. Helen and Floyd Robert Glass Jr. 28 Oct. 1984; PRESIDENT SHELTER CANADIAN PROPERTIES LTD. 1979– ; Dir. Bird Construction Company Limited, Toronto; CanWest Broadcasting Ltd. (CKND-TV) Winnipeg; CanWest Communications Corp. Winnipeg; Centra Gas Manitoba Inc.; Manitoba Hydro Electric Bd., Winnipeg; Onex Corp. Toronto; Petro-Canada Limited, Ottawa; Vision Capital, Winnipeg; Montreal Federal Industries Ltd., Winnipeg; Sr. Rsch. Analyst and Securities Underwriter Richardson Securities of Canada, Toronto and Winnipeg 1969–76; Exec. Vice-Pres. Shelter Corp. of Canada Ltd. 1976–79; past Chrmn. Associates of Fac. of Management, Univ. of Man. 1984–87; past Pres. Winnipeg Soc. of Fin. Analysts 1972; former Trustee Inst. of Chartered Fin. Analysts 1975–77; Chrmn. P.C. Manitoba Fund; Vice-Pres., Candn. Area, Young Presidents' Orgn.; Protestant; Progressive Conservative; recreations: golf, boating, reading; Clubs: Manitoba; St. Charles Country; Royal Lake of the Woods Yacht; Home: 12D-221 Wellington Cres., Winnipeg, Man. R3M 0A1; Office: 2600 Seven Evergreen Place, Winnipeg, Man. R3L 2T3.

**THORSTEINSSON, Raymond,** O.C., B.A., M.A., F.R.S.C.; research scientist; b. Wynyard, Sask. 21 Jan. 1921; e. Univ. of Sask. B.A. 1944; Univ. of Toronto M.A. 1950; Univ. of Kans. Ph.D. 1955; m. Jean Kristjansson 23 Dec. 1944; children: Eirikur, Anna Ingrid; EMERITUS RESEARCH SCIENTIST, INST. OF SEDIMENTARY & PETROLEUM GEOL., GEOL. SURVEY OF CAN. 1992; served entire prof. career with Geol. Survey of Can. Contbr. memoirs, bulletins, papers, geological maps; geology and paleontology, Western and Arctic Canada; recipient, Founder's Medal Royal Geog. Soc. (London) 1968; Willet G. Miller Medal Royal Soc. Can. 1973; Logan Medal Geol. Assn. Can. 1979; Massey Medal Royal Candn. Geog. Soc. 1981; R.J.W. Douglas Medal Candn. Assn. Petrol. Geols. 1982; C.M. 1983; Gold Medal Scie. Profl. Inst. Pub. Svc. Can. 1987; O.C. 1989; Commemorative Medal for 125th Anniversary of Candn. Confederation 1992; mem. Geol. Assn. Can.; Arctic Inst. N. Am., Vertebrate Paleontol.; Home: 10 Varsville Pl. N.W., Calgary, Alta. T3A 0A8; Office: 3303 – 33rd St. N.W., Calgary, Alta. T2L 2A7.

**THRANE, Poul Ovesen;** artist; b. Denmark 14 June 1925; s. Hartwig and Karen (Ovesen) T.; e. evening classes under John Alfsen and Geo. Pepper, Ont. College of Art; m. Audrey d. Cyril and Elizabeth Archer 5 Feb. 1949; children: Linda, Ann, Teresa; self taught oil & watercolour painter; style: traditional to impressionistic; left Denmark 1946 to serve in British army; emigrated to Canada 1951; opened Poul Thrane Art Studio near Tweed, Ont. 1973 and has painted full time since; Past Membership Chair, East Central Ontario Arts Assn.; Teacher, Loyalist College Extension Staff; Buckhorn School of Fine Art; has taught at several worskhops; 1st Prize East Central Arts Assn. juried show 1993; num. prizes & hon. mentions in many shows; Address: R.R. 3, Tweed, Ont. K0K 3J0.

**THRASHER, Richard Devere,** Q.C., B.A.; Retired 1992; b. Amherstburg, Ont. 5 Mar. 1922; s. Charles Devere and Irene Agnes (Richard) T.; e. Assumption Coll., B.A. 1948; Osgoode Hall, Toronto, Ont.; m. Norma Jeanne, d. Francis Edwin Whittal, Amherstburg, Ont., 23 Nov. 1940; children: Linda, Heather, Richard, Jr., Bradley, Daniel; read law with McKenzie, Wood & Goodchild, Toronto, Ont.; called to the Bar of Ont., 1951; cr. Q.C., 1962; served in 2nd World War with R.C.A.F. 1942–45, rank Flying Offr.; Past Secy., S. Essex P. Cons. Assn.; el. to H. of C. for Essex S. in g.e. 1957 and re-el. 1958; apptd. Parlty. Secy. to Minister of Labour, Nov. 1959; def. in g.e. June 1962; Special Asst. to Prime Min. of Can. 1962; named Chief Adm. Offr., P. Cons. Party Nat. Hdqrs. and Nat. Dir. of Party, June 1963; def. cand. (Essex S.) to H. of C. in g.e. Nov. 1965; a Magistrate for Windsor, Ont. area 1966–67; mem., Royal Candn. Legion; K. of C.; P. Conservative; Roman Catholic; Home: 41 Woodbridge Drive, Amherstburg, Ont. N9V 1T9.

**THRESHER, John,** F.C.A.; real estate executive; b. Merton, Surrey, England 16 Dec. 1939; s. Ernest Edwin and Mabel Thresher (Bagshaw) T.; e. Raynes Park Co. Grammar Sch. 1956; Assoc., Inst. of C.A.s in England and Wales 1963; Fellow 1973; m. Mavis d. Wallace and Eileen Fraser 13 June 1970; children: Hannah, Neil, Ian; SENIOR VICE-PRES., CAPITAL MARKETS, EDGECOMBE GROUP INC. 1991– ; articled with Nevill, Hovey Gardner & Co. C.A.s (U.K.) 1958–63; Chief Accountant, Ronald Lyon Group 1964–71; Capital & Counties Property Group 1972–73; Finance Dir., Property Group, Bovis Corp. 1973–75; Sec. Treas., McCallum Hill Group Canada 1975–78; Vice-Pres., Finance, Imperial Group 1979–82; Vice-Pres., Equion Group 1982–91; Pres. & Founder, Assn. of Candn. Real Estate Syndicators 1984–90; Dir. of Fair Rental Policy Orgn. of Ont. 1988–90; Mem., Ont. Securities Comn. Private Sector Ctte. on Securities Reform; English Track International 1963–69; Olympic Games Qualifying Standard (5000 metres) 1968; Mem., British Olympic Research Squad 1967 Font Romeu, France; ranked Canadian Master 1980–83; recreations: running, cycling, nordic skiing; clubs: Belgrave Harriers, Adelaide; Home: 51 Macdonell Ave., Toronto, Ont. M6R 2A3; Office: 655 Bay St., Suite 1200, Toronto, Ont. M5G 2K4.

**THRIFT, Eric W.,** M.Arch., F.R.A.I.C. (1961), F.C.I.P., A.I.C.P.; educator; b. Winnipeg, Man. 23 Aug. 1912; s. William David and Amy Eveline (Daw) T.; e. St. James (Man.) Pub. and Coll. Inst.; Univ. of Manitoba, B.Arch. 1935 (Gold Medal); Mass Inst. of Technol., M.Arch. 1938; m. Melba Maude (dec. Jan. 1987), d. Tilley W. Belyea, 22 Aug. 1941; children: Kristin Elizabeth, Murray Eric, William David, Dennis Gordon; m. 2ndly Monnie Lucile Raven; d. the late L. McK. Robinson 24 Sept. 1988; currently PROFESSOR EMERITUS, QUEEN'S UNIV. (1981– ) and Private Planning Consultant; Travelling Fellow, Engineering & Architecture, Univ. of Manitoba 1936; with Hudson's Bay Co. Buildings Office, 1938–42; Lectr. in Arch. & Planning, 1942–50, Univ. of Manitoba; Tech. Adviser on Planning to Postwar Reconstr. Comte., Prov. of Man., 1943–44; Planning Consultant, advising and assisting on the estab. of urban and regional planning programs and staff in city of Calgary, Alta., Calgary Region, Yorkton, Sask., Brandon, Man., Sudbury, Ont. and district, and city of Kingston, Ont. 1948–60; Dir., Metrop. Planning Comn. of Greater Winnipeg 1945–60; Gen. Mgr., Nat. Capital Comn. 1960–70; Dir., Prov. of Man. Planning Service, 1957–60; private Indust. Design Consultant & Arch.; Chrmn., Gter. Winnipeg Transportation Study 1955–56; Vice-Chrmn., Winnipeg Renewal Bd. 1958–60; Extve. Ctte., Commercial and Industrial Development Corp., Ottawa 1965–71; Chrmn., Local Adv. Ctte. on Architectural Conservation, City of Kingston 1979–80; mem. Man. Assn. of Archs. (Pres. 1949); Roy. Arch. Inst. Can.; Am. Inst. Planners; Urban Land Inst.; Roads & Transport. Assn. Can. 1961–71; Urban & Regional Information Systems Assn., 1970–75; Town Planning Inst. Can., (Pres. 1953–54, 1961–62); Am. Soc. of Planning Officials (Pres. 1964–65); mem. Ottawa Planning Area Bd. 1960–71; Candn. Council on Urban and Regional Research, 1963–66; Pres., Univ. of Man. Alumni Assn. 1950; Pres., Nat. Gallery Assn. 1968–71; Pres., Seasoned Spirits of Kingston 1985–87; Bd. Mem., Independent Living Centre of Kingston; Chrmn., Property, Cooke's-Portsmouth United Church, Kingston 1976–87; rec'd First Medal, R.A.I.C. 1935; Hon. Citizen, City of Winnipeg 1960; Mem., Order of the Buffalo Hunt, Manitoba 1960; Centennial Medal of Can. 1967; Queen's Jubilee Medal 1977; Fellow, Royal Arch. Inst. of Canada 1961; Fellow, Canadian Inst. of Planners 1978; Hon. Life Mem., Am. Planning Assn. 1978; Charter Mem., Amer. Inst. of Certified Planners 1978; publications: 'Town and Community Post-War Planning' 1944; series of reports on comprehensive plans for Greater Winnipeg 1946–50; numerous articles on arch. and planning contrib. to mags; mem. Kiwanis Club, Winnipeg 1952–60, Ottawa 1961–68; United Church; recreations: music, art, books; Home: 165 Ontario St., #808, Kingston, Ont. K7L 2Y6.

**THROOP, Gerald Charles,** B.Math., C.A., M.B.A.; financial executive; b. Ottawa, Ont. 23 Jan. 1958; s. Elmer Gerald and Muriel Lorraine (Tompkins) T.; e. Univ. of Waterloo B.Math. 1981; C.A. 1982; Harvard Univ. M.B.A. 1988; m. Diane d. Helen and Vincent Zdrilich 22 Dec. 1984; children: Brandon James, Alanah Diane; VICE PRES. & CHIEF FINANCIAL OFFICER, CALL-NET ENTERPRISES INC. 1991– ; Co-op Student, Thorne Riddell C.A.s 1976; Audit Manager 1982; Vice Pres., Finance, TIE/Telecommunications Canada Limited 1984; Consultant, Monitor Co. Boston 1987; Senior Consultant & Treas., Monitor Co. Canada Limited 1988; Dir., TIE/Telecommunications Canada Limited; Mem., Candn. & Ont. Insts. of C.A.s; Harvard Business School Club of Toronto; recreations: squash, golf; clubs: Granite; Home: 48 Wanless Cres., Toronto, Ont. M4N 3B9; Office: 105 Gordon Baker Rd., Willowdale, Ont. M2H 3S1.

**THROOP, Jean Louise;** association executive; b. St. John, N.B. 29 Oct. 1929; d. Harry and Ruth Crawford; e. Hampton, N.B., Niagara Falls, Ont. and Etobicoke, Ont.; m. Thomas Dwight T. 19 Dec. 1953; children: Harry Bruce, David Thomas; Pres., Nat. Chapter of Can. IODE 1990–92; Home: 6 Spencely Ct., Etobicoke, Ont. M9P 1N5.

**THURSTON, Frank Russel,** O.C.(1982), B.Sc., F.C.A.S.I.; b. Chicago, Ill. 5 Dec. 1914; s. Charles William and Emma Louise (Connor) T.; e. Univ. of London, B.Sc. (Physics) 1940; m. Olive, d. Alfred Cullingworth, 23 Nov. 1940; one s., Peter Russel; joined Nat. Phys. Lab., Teddington, Eng. 1937–47; joined National Rsch. Council of Canada, Div. of Mech. Engn. 1947; former Dir., Nat. Aeronautical Estab., N.R.C. 1959–79; joined Candn. Aviation Safety Bd. 1984; Dir. of many nat. and internat. comtes. and organs. in field of science and engn.; author of numerous publs. on theory of structures, fatigue of materials and structures, materials research and aerodynamics; mem., Inst. Physics; Candn. Aeronautics & Space Inst.; former Chrmn., Adv. Group for Aerospace Research & Devel. (N.A.T.O.); Commonwealth Adv. Aeronautical Research Council; recipient, McCurdy Award; Von Karman Medal; Officer, Order of Canada 1982; N.A.S.A. Public Service Medal; Home: 793 Hemlock Rd., Ottawa, Ont. K1K 0K6.

**THURSTON, Harry Kenneth,** B.Sc.; writer; b. Yarmouth, N.S. 3 March 1950; s. Kenneth Alvin and Elizabeth Madeline (Gillis) T.; e. Acadia Univ. B.Sc. 1971; m. Catherine d. Vernon and Ruth Rideout 1 July 1972; one d.: Meaghan Ruth; Editor/Pub., 'Germination' a hotbed of verse culture 1977–83; Field Correspondent & Contbg. Ed. 'Equinox,' 1982–94; Instructor, Writing Poetry & Writer-in-Residence, St. Mary's Univ. 1988; Visiting Writer, Mt. Allison Univ. 1993–94; Contract Ed., Nat. State of Envir. Report, Environment Canada 1990–91; freelance writer, editor, poet, playwright 1977–92; Instructor, Science & Environmental Reporting, Univ. of King's College, School of Journalism 1994; Dir., Evelyn Richardson Mem. Literary Soc. 1978–80; Founding Chair, The Ship's Co. Theatre 1984; Chair, Writers' Council, Writers' Fed. of N.S. 1980; Publications Bd., Atlantic Salmon Journal 1993–94; Evelyn Richardson Mem. Lit. Award 1991; City of Dartmouth Book Award 1991; Atlantic Bookseller's Choice Award 1991; num. mag. awards incl. Author's Award 1982, '87, Nat. Mag. Award 1983, Science Journalism Awards 1986, '87; author: 'Against Darkness and Storm, Lighthouses of the Northeast' 1993, 'Tidal Life, A Natural History of the Bay of Fundy' 1990, 'Atlantic Outposts' 1990, 'Clouds Flying Before the Eye' (poetry) 1985, 'Barefaced Stone' (poetry) 1980; co-author: 'Black River Miracle' (two-act play) 1992; feature articles have appeared in major magazines; poetry has appeared in Candn. & Am. lit. magazines & anthologies; recreations: bird watching, fly-fishing; Home: R.R. 2, Amherst, N.S. B4H 3X9.

**TIBERIUS, Richard Gordon,** B.Sc., M.A., Ph.D.; educator; b. New York, N.Y. 3 May 1941; s. Dennis Edward and Anna Elizabeth (Mayer) T.; e. Brown Univ. Providence, R.I. 1959–61; Univ. of Toronto B.Sc. 1964, M.A. 1966, Ph.D. 1975; m. Joyce Marie Slingerland d. Frank and Doreen Slingerland 7 Aug. 1983; three d. Valerie, Paula, Corinne; ASSOC. PROF., DEPT. OF PSYCHIATRY, FACULTY OF MED., UNIV. OF TORONTO 1991– ; Lectr. Grad. Sch. of Edn. Univ. of Pa. 1969–70; teacher Audubon Jr. High Sch. Los Angeles 1971; Asst. Prof. Div. Studies in Med. Edn. present Univ. 1973, Ednl. Devel. cons., Office of Ed. Develop., U. of T. 1976–79, Asst. Prof. of Family & Community Med. 1977, Centre for Studies in Medical Education 1986–91; former Dep. Dir. Centre Studies Med. Edn.; author 'Small Group Teaching: A Trouble Shooting Guide' 1990; co-ed. 'To Improve the Academy: Resources for Student, Faculty and Institutional Development' 1988; various articles, tech. reports profl. jours.; presentations Candn., U.S. and Eur. univs.; mem. Am. Ednl. Rsch. Assn.; Am. Assn. Higher Edn.; Assn. Study Higher Edn.; Assn. Study Med. Edn.; Candn. Assn. Med. Edn.; Generalists in Med. Edn.; Profl. & Orgn. Devel. Network Higher Edn.; Alliance for Teaching in Med.; recreations: landscape oil painting, backpacking, sailboarding; Home: 131 Winchester St., Toronto, Ont. M4X 1B3; Office: The Toronto Hosp., Western Division, 399 Bathurst St., ECW-3D-032, Toronto, Ont. M5T 2S8.

**TIBO, Gilles;** illustrator; author b. Nicolet, Qué. 18 July 1951; s. Bernard and Henriette (Vandemeulebrooke) Thibault; children: Simon, Marlène; author and/or illus. 'Annabell Lee' 1987; 'Maria Chapdelaine' 1987; 'Simon and the Snow Flakes' 1988; 'Simon and the Wind' 1989; 'Giant' 1989; 'Simon et la ville de carton' winner Gov. Gen.'s Award 1992 for illustration (French category); books published Can., USA, Eur., Japan; cartoonist numerous Que. newspapers since 1970; illus. over 40 books nat. and internat. presses; recipient numerous awards incl. 1st Prize Illus. Tokyo 1989; nominated Gov. Gen.'s Award 1989; recreations: tennis, bicycling; Home: 4303 de Lanaudière, Montréal, Qué. H2J 3N8.

**TICOLL, David,** B.A.; management consultant; b. Montreal, Que. 3 July 1947; s. Louis and Elsie (Yancovich) T.; e. McGill Univ. B.A. 1968; Simon Fraser Univ. Computer Sci. Prog.; Univ. of Toronto Mktg. Rsch.; m. Tracey Ann Macey d. Hope M. Rust 19 Aug. 1976; one d. Amy Louise; EXTVE. DIR., ALLIANCE FOR CONVERGING TECHNOLOGIES CORPORATION 1994– ; Pub. Affairs Broadcaster CBC and Radio-Can. Vancouver 1972–76; mktg. exec. positions Philips Information Systems 1977–83; Dir., Dmr. Group Inc. 1988; Co-Founder The Transition Group Inc. initiating Candn. prog. Gartner Group Inc.; recipient Oustanding Achievement Award DMR 1989; ed. and co-author 'Strategies for Open Systems' 4 vols. 1990; various reports, articles; mem. YMCA Toronto; Home: 11 Annesley Ave., Toronto, Ont. M4G 2T5.

**TIESSEN, Paul Gerard,** M.A., Ph.D.; educator; b. Kitchener, Ont. 28 Jan. 1944; s. Henry Bernard and Helen (Reimer) T.; e. Waterloo Lutheran Univ. B.A. 1966; Univ. of Alta. M.A. 1968, Ph.D. 1973; m. Hildegard d. Abe and Mary Froese 15 Aug. 1969; children: Matthew, Christopher; PROF. OF ENG. WILFRID LAURIER UNIV. 1987– , Chrmn. of Eng. 1988– ; Dir. Sand Hills Books Inc. (publishers) St. Jacobs, Ont.; Asst. Prof. of Eng. Univ. of Man. 1973–74; Asst. Prof. of Eng. present Univ. 1974, Assoc. Prof. 1980; recipient various Can. Council and Social Sci's & Humanities Rsch. Council grants; guest lectr. various univs. N. Am. and Eur.; editor: 'The Malcolm Lowry Review' est. 1977; editor or co-editor twenty books, incl.: 'The 1940 Under the Volcano by Malcolm Lowry' 1994; 'A Sunday Afternoon: Paintings by Henry Pauls' 1991; 'The Cinema of Malcolm Lowry' 1990; 'Apparently Incongruous Parts: The Worlds of Malcolm Lowry' 1990; 'The Road to Victory: Radio Plays of Gerald Noxon' 1989; 'The Letters of Malcolm Lowry and Gerald Noxon' 1988; 'A Public and Private Voice: Essays on the Life and Work of Dorothy Livesay' 1988 (1986); mem. various profl. assns.; Home: 85 Rusholme Rd., Kitchener, Ont. N2M 2T5; Office: Waterloo, Ont. N2L 3C5.

**TIFFIN, Robert Joseph,** B.A., M.A.; university administrator; b. Wingham, Ont. 31 Oct. 1950; s. William Joseph and Pearl Olive (Mathers) T.; e. Univ. of W. Ont. B.A. 1973, M.A. 1975; m. Suzanne d. Harry and Ruth Lucan 25 June 1988; children: Tamara, Robert, Andrew, Matthew; REGISTRAR, UNIV. OF WESTERN ONT. 1986– ; Teacher, Spanish 1973–75; Secondary School Liaison Officer, Univ. of W. Ont. 1975; Dep. Registrar 1980; Dir., Western 1/Bell Canada Partnership; Official Observer, Univ. Senate; Ctte. on Academic Programs & Policy; on Univ. Admissions, Univ. Enrolment Policy & Planning; Chair, Planning Ctte. on Admin. Systems 1993; Senate Review Bd. Acad.; Acad. Counselling Adv. Ctte.; Instruction for First Year Experience & Orientation Course 1988–93; Bd. of Gov.; Governing Council, King's College; Chair, Council on Univ. Admission 1994–96; Ont. Rep., Assn. of Registrars of Univs. & Colls. of Can. 1988–90; Pres., Ont. Univ. Registrars' Assn. 1986–88; Mem., Am. Assn. of Registrars & Admission Offrs.; London C. of C.; author of 1 article; recreations: golf; clubs: Amici dell'enotria; Home: 28 Southgate St., London, Ont. N6K 4H1; Office: 165 Stevenson-Lawson Bldg., London, Ont. N6A 5B8.

**TIFFOU, Etienne D.;** professeur titulaire; né. Oran 15 septembre 1935; f. Augustin E. et Marcelle A. (Barcelo) T.; é. Agrégation de grammaire 1961; Sorbonne Doctorat d'Etat 1971; ép. Maylis f. Jean et Madeleine Noyer 26 décembre 1960; enfants: Benoît, Marie, Denis, Augustin; PROFESSEUR, DÉP. DE LINGUISTIQUE ET DE TRADUCTION, UNIV. DE MONTRÉAL 1977– ; Professeur agrégé 1969; auteur: 'Essai sur la pensée Morale de Salluste à la lumière de ses prologues' 1974; co-auteur: 'Contes du Yasin' 1989, 'Dictionnaire complémentaire du bourouchaski du Yasin' 1989, 'Hunza Proverbs' 1993; loisirs: tennis, bridge; domicile: 3140 Kent, Montréal, Qué. H3S 1N1; bureau: C.P. 6128, Succ. A., Montréal, Qué. H3C 3J7.

**TIGER, Lionel,** M.A., Ph.D., F.R.A.I.; social scientist; b. Montreal, Que. 5 Feb. 1937; s. Martin and Lillian (Schneider) T.; e. McGill Univ., B.A. 1957 (with Distinction), M.A. (Sociol.) 1959; London Sch. of Econ. Ph.D. (Pol. Sociol.) 1963; m. Virginia Marie, d. Gordon Conner, Toronto, Ont., 19 Aug. 1964; one s., Sebastian Benjamin; PROF. OF ANTHROPOLOGY, RUTGERS UNIVERSITY 1972– ; Charles Darwin Professor of Anthropology 1990– ; Research Director, H. F. Guggenheim Foundation 1972–84; Lectr. on Bureaucracy and Adm., Inst. of Pub. Adm., Ghana and Visiting Lectr., Univ. of Ghana, 1961; Asst. Prof. of Sociol., Univ. of B.C., 1963–68; mem. Dean's Comte. study B.A. Degree 1963–64; gave lecture series in Nursing Educ., Vancouver Gen. Hosp., 1964–65; Rep., McGill Univ. Student Soc., World Univ. Senate Study Seminar, W. Africa, 1957; rec'd. Nat. Council of Jewish Women Bursary, 1956; Chester McNaughton Prize for Creative Writing, 1956; McGill Univ. Fellowship 1957; Can. Council Fellowships 1958 and 1960, Grant 1965, Special Award 1966–67 and Killam Bequest Inaugural Award 1968, renewed 1969; I.O.D.E. First World War Mem. Overseas Post-grad. Fellowship for Que., 1959; Comte. on Comparative Bureaucracy of S.S.R.C. Grant-in-aid, 1960; Ford Foundation Foreign Area Training Fellowship 1962; Univ. of B.C. Pres.'s Research Fund Grant 1965; Nat. Research Council of Can. Grant-in-aid 1966–67; John Simon Guggenheim Mem. Foundation Fellowship 1968; Rockefeller Fellowship, The Aspen Inst. for Humanistic Studies 1979; H.F. Guggenheim Research Fellowship 1972–84; Warren Sussman Award for excellence in teaching, Rutgers Univ. 1985; H.F. Guggenheim Research Fellowship 1987–90; author 'Men in Groups' 1969, 2nd ed. 1987, French transl. 1970; 'The Imperial Animal' (with Robin Fox) 1971, 2nd ed. 1989; 'Der Mannergruppe' 1972; 'Women in the Kibbutz' (with J. Shepher) 1975; 'Optimism: The Biology of Hope' 1979; 'China's Food' with R. Wolf; 'The Manufacture of Evil: Ethics, Evolution and the Industrial System' 1987; Ed. 'Female Hierarchies' 1978; co-ed., 'Man and Beast Revisited' 1991; 'The Pursuit of Pleasure' 1992; other writings incl. numerous articles in Candn. and foreign journs.; mem. Ed. Bd., 'Journal of African Studies in Canada' 1966–68; 'Social Science Information'; 'Ethology & Sociobiology'; Fellow, Soc. for Study of Evolution; Assn. for Study of Animal Behaviour; Am. Assn. Advanc. Science; Am. Anthrop. Assn.; P.E.N., U.S.A., Secy. Extve. Bd. 1981–83, mem. Extve. Bd. 1983–85, Treasurer 1988–91; Vice Pres. 1991– ; Mem. Bd. of Dirs., David R. Graham Foundation, Toronto 1993– ; The Century Assoc.; Address: Douglass Coll., Rutgers Univ., New Brunswick, N.J. 08903-0270.

**TIGERT, Douglas John,** B.Com., M.B.A., Ph.D.; educator; b. St. Catharines, Ont. 22 Apl. 1938; s. Arthur James and Marion Jean (Barnard) T.; e. Queen's Univ. B.Com. 1960; Northwestern Univ. M.B.A. 1961; Purdue Univ. Ph.D. 1966; m. Mary Jane d. Sam and Louise Quattrocchi 31 Aug. 1963; two d. Sandra Jeanne, Susan Jill; CHARLES CLARKE REYNOLDS PROFESSOR OF RETAIL MARKETING, BABSON COLLEGE, Wellesley, Mass. U.S.A. 1986– ; Asst. Prof. Univ. of Chicago 1967–70; Assoc. Prof. Univ. of Toronto 1970, Prof. 1974–80, Dean of Mgmt. Studies 1980–85; mem. Bd. of Dirs., Smith's Food & Drug Centers, Inc., Salt Lake City, Utah; Bd. of Dirs., Hudson's Bay Company, Toronto; Mem. Bd. of Advisors, Country Road (USA); mem. Am. Marketing Assn.; Assn. Consumer Rsch.; recreations: tennis, skiing, photography; Home: H.C. 60, Box 63, Waldoboro, ME 04572; Office: Babson College, Babson Park, Mass. 02157

**TIGHE, Jim C.;** newspaper executive; b. Edmonton, Alta.; s. James Donald T.; m. Barbara; children Teresa, Jason; VICE PRES. AND PUBLISHER, TORONTO SUN PUBLISHING CORP. 1988– ; Circulation Supr. Edmonton Journal 1967–73; Circulation Mgr. Nanaimo Free Press 1973–75; W. Can. Circulation Supr. Thomson Newspapers Calgary 1975–78; Circulation Dir. Edmonton Sun 1978–81, Gen. Mgr. 1981–82; Gen. Mgr. United Press Can. 1982–84; Publisher Calgary Sun 1984–88; Dir., Newspaper Mktg. Bureau Can.; Candn. Advertising Foundation; mem. Newspaper Assn. of America; recreations: sports, golf; Club: Wyldewood Golf; Home: 1282 Hollyfield Cres., Oakville, Ont. L6H 2T6; Office: 333 King St. E., Toronto, Ont. M5A 3X5.

**TILBY, Wendy Joy;** D.F.A.; filmmaker; b. Edmonton, Alta. 28 March 1960; d. Sidney Edward and Joy Doreen (Evers) T; e. Univ. of Victoria; Emily Carr Coll. of Art D.F.A. 1986; DIRECTOR, NATIONAL FILM BOARD OF CANADA 1991– ; Dir., 'Tables of Content' (animated film) 1986; animation segment for 'Sesame Street' CBC Van. 1986; 'Strings' (animated film) NFB Montreal 1987–91; Prof. of Film Animation, Concordia Univ. 1991– ; Jury Mem., Edinburgh Internat. Film Fest. 1992; Internat. Fest. of Animation Film Stuttgart 1992; Yorkton Short Film & Video Fest. 1988; Candn. Student Film Fest. 1986; Festivals at which 'Tables of Content' has been awarded incl. Montreal World Film, Annecy Internat. Animation, Shanghai Animation, Espinho Internat., Ottawa Internat. Anim., Yorkton Short Film & Video, Canadian Academy of Cinema and Television (Genie Award nom.); Festivals at which 'Strings' has been awarded incl. Annecy Internat., Hiroshima Internat. Anim., Espinho Internat. Anim. Film, Ottawa Internat. Anim., Am. Film & Video, Atlantic Film, N.Y. Expo of Short Film & Video, Internat. Film Fest. of Columbus Ohio, 64th Annual Acad. Awards (Oscar nom.), Canadian Academy of Cinema & Television (Genie award); Home: 5163 Clark, Montreal, Que. H2T 2V1; Office: Box 6100, Stn. A, Montreal, Que. H3C 3H5.

**TILEY, Jim (James Henry);** artist; educator; b. London, Eng. 22 Sept. 1933; s. Herbert Henry and Maud Alice Kate (Morrison) T.; e. Harrow Sch. of Art; Royal Coll. of Art London, Eng. A.R.C.A. 1958; m. Sarah R. d Harry A.M. and Rosa K. Downes 28 Aug. 1961; children: Kate, Mark, Alison; solo exhns. incl. Hart House Univ. of Toronto 1964, Scarborough Coll. 1967, Sch. of Arch. 1970; Merton Gallery Toronto 1973, 1975; Meml. Univ. Nfld. touring Atlantic Provs. 1973–74; A.C.T. Gallery Toronto 1978, 1980; Rosenberg Galleries Toronto 1984; Klonaridis Inc. Gallery, Toronto 1986, 1988; rep. numerous group exhns. since 1956; Art Master Belmont Sch. 1958–60; Holloway Sch. London, Eng. 1960; joined Young & Rubicam London 1960–61; teacher Ont. Coll. of Art 1961, mem. Gov. Council 1970–71, 1985–88, Chrmn. Exper. Arts 1985–88 and presently Instr. there; teacher Hart House Univ. of Toronto 1967–74; Founding mem. and Dir. 'Workscene' Co-op Studio 1969–76; Chrmn. Dundas Valley Sch. of Art Curriculum Ctte. 1975; rep. Ont. Univs. on Min. of Edn.'s SERP/ROSE Ctte. 1984; rep. liaison ctte. Ont. Confedn. Ont. Univs. 1984–86; mem. 4 person ctte. planning visual arts courses Scarborough Bd. Edn., new O.A.C. courses; author various articles art jours.; Bd. mem. and Ed. 'Artists' Review' mag. 1980–81; presented with A.J. Casson Award for distinguished service, O.C.A. Alumni Assn. 1991; recreations: tennis, sailing; Clubs: Downtown Tennis; Kew Gardens Tennis; Home: 26 Waverley Rd., Toronto, Ont. M4L 3T1; Office: 100 McCaul St., Toronto, Ont. M5T 1W1.

**TILL, James Edgar,** O.C., M.A., Ph.D., F.R.S.C.; scientist; b. Lloydminster, Sask. 25 Aug. 1931; s. late William and Gertrude Ruth (Isaac) T.; e. Univ. of Sask. B.A. 1952, M.A. 1954; Yale Univ. Ph.D. 1957; m. Marion Joyce d. late Alfred Victor Sinclair 6 June 1959; children: David William, Karen Sinclair, Susan Elizabeth; MEM., SEN. SCIENTIFIC STAFF, ONT. CANCER INST. since 1957; Head of Biol. Research 1969–82; University Professor, Univ. of Toronto 1984– (Prof. there 1965– ); Postdoctoral Fellow, Connaught Med. Research Labs. Toronto 1956–57; Asst. Prof. Univ. of Toronto 1958, Assoc. Prof. 1962; Assoc. Dean, Life Sciences, School of Grad. Studies, 1981–84; co-recipient Gairdner Foundation Internat. Award 1969; Officer, The Order of Canada 1994; author or co-author over 200 scient. publs. various aspects of cancer research; Candn. Bioethics Soc.; Royal Soc. of Canada; Office: 500 Sherbourne St., Toronto, Ont. M4X 1K9.

**TILLARD, Rev. Jean-Marie Roger,** D.Ph., D.Th.; educator; priest (Dominican); b. Saint-Pierre-et-Miquelon, France 2 Sept. 1927; s. Ferdinand and Madeleine (Ferron) T.; e. Angelicum, Rome D.Ph.; Le Saulchoir Paris D.Th.; Magisterium in Sacra Theologia Rome; Trinity Coll. and St. Michael's Coll. Univ. of Toronto D.Th.; PROF. OF THEOL. DOMINICAN COLL. OF PHILOSOPHY AND THEOLOGY 1959– , Maitre des Etudes; Vice Chrmn. Faith & Order World Council Chs. Geneva; mem. Ang.-R.C. Internat. Comn.; Orthodox-R.C. Internat. Comn., R.C.-Disciples of Christ; Consultor of Vatican for Ecumenical Affairs; mem. Internat. Comn. of Theologians (counselling the Vatican); mem. Bd. Tantur (Jerusalem); invited lectr. Laval Univ., St. Stephen's Oxford Univ., Univ. of Nottingham, Univ. of Genève; visiting prof. Louvain, Brussels; Fribourg 1982; author 'L'Eucharistie Pâque de l'Eglise' 1964; 'Adaption et Renovation de la Vie Religieuse' 1967; Devant Dieu et Pour le Monde' 1974; 'L'evêque de Rome' 1982; 'Eglises d'Eglises' 1987; 'Chair de l'Eglise' 1992; various articles; mem. N. Am. Ecumenists; Alcuin Club; Soc. Promotion Religious Studies; R. Catholic; Address: 96 Empress Ave., Ottawa, Ont. K1R 7G2.

**TILLEY, Alexander Joseph,** B.A.; b. Newmarket, Ont. 8 Jan. 1938; s. Joseph Allen and Audrey Margaret (Smith) T.; e. Univ. of B.C., B.A. 1962; m. Susan Corrigan; children: Karen, Alison; PRES. AND FOUNDER, TILLEY ENDURABLES INC. 1984– ; Office: 900 Don Mills Rd., Don Mills, Ont. M3C 1V8.

**TILLEY, Donald Egerton,** B.Sc., Ph.D., D.Sc.; retired educator; physicist; b. Flushing, N.Y. 6 July 1925; s. Arthur and Florence Mary (Fortier) T.; came to Can. 1938; e. Mahwah (N.J.) Grammar Sch. 1938; Lakefield Coll. Sch. 1942; McGill Univ., B.Sc. (Hons. Math & Physics) 1948, Ph.D. (Physics) 1951; Royal Military Coll. of Can., D.Sc. (hon. causa) 1988; m. Margaret Elizabeth d. late James Ferrier Torrance, 5 June 1948; children: James Arthur, Margaret Anne, Peter Donald; Research Assoc., McGill Univ. 1951; joined Coll. militaire royal as Asst. Prof. 1952, Assoc. Prof. 1953–57, Prof. of Physics 1957–78, Head Dept. of Physics 1961–71, Dean Science and Engn. 1969–78; Principal, Royal Military Coll. of Canada 1979–84; retired Feb. 1984; Professor Emeritus 1984– ; served in 2nd World War Flying Offr., R.C.A.F. 1942–45; mem. Candn. Assn. Physcists; Am. Phys. Soc.; Am. Assn. Physics Teachers; mem. St. Johns Prot. Sch. Bd. 1964–72; Gov. Lakefield Coll. Sch. 1983– ; recipient Centennial Medal 1967; has researched in fields of nuclear physics and physics of dielectrics; co-author 'Physics: A Modern Approach' 1970; 'College Physics: A Text with Applications to the Life Sciences' 1971; 'Physics in Medicine' 1972; 'Physics for College Students' 1974; author 'University Physics for Science & Engineering' 1976; 'Contemporary College Physics' 1979; United Church; recreation: golf; Clubs: RMC Club of Canada, Club des Anciens du CMR; Address: 44 Faircrest Blvd., RR #1, Kingston, Ont. K7L 4V1.

**TIMBRELL, Hon. Dennis Roy;** b. Kingston, Ont. 13 Nov. 1946; s. Walter William Sydney and Beryl (Clark) T.; e. Elem. and High Schs., Kingston and Scarborough, Ont.; Toronto Teacher's Coll.; Atkinson Coll., York Univ.; m. Janet Mary Lees, 1 Feb. 1980; 6 children; PRES., ONTARIO HOSPITAL ASSN.; taught Don Mills (Ont.) Jr. High Sch. 1967–70; Ald., City of N. York, 1969–72; el. M.P.P. prov. g.e. 1971, 1975, 1977, 1981 and 1985; Parlty, Asst. to Min. of Colls. and Univs. 1973–74; Min.-without-Portfolio, Ont., responsible for Youth Secretariat, 1974, becoming the youngest Minister in the history of Ont.; apptd. Min. of Energy Jan. 1975; Min. of Health, 1977–82; Min. of Agriculture and Food 1982–85; Min. of Municipal Affairs and Housing, and Min. Responsible for Women's Issues, 1985; Dir., Ontario Blue Cross; Confederation Trust; CCG Equipment Ltd.; Progressive Conservative; Protestant; recreations: squash, tennis; Clubs: Albany; Home: 23 Anewen Dr., Toronto, Ont. M4A 1R9; Office: 150 Ferrand Dr., Don Mills, Ont. M3C 1H6.

**TIMMS, Arthur Murray,** B.Sc., Ph.D., CAE; association executive; b. Hespeler, Ont. 28 May 1944; s. Arthur Frederick Murray and Nellie Anna (Jones) T.; e. McMaster Univ., B.Sc. (Hons.) 1967, Texas A & M Univ., Ph.D. 1972; Candn. Soc. of Assn. Extves., C.A.E. 1985; EXTVE. DIR., ONT. ASSN. OF LANDSCAPE ARCHITECTS 1989– ; Teaching Fellow, Univ. of W. Ont. 1973–74; Extve. Dir., Conservation Counc. of Ont. 1974–83; Extve. Dir., Candn. Cerebral Palsy Assn. 1984–89; Dir., Rene Marcil Found.; Former Mem. Nat. Bd., Candn. Soc. of Assn. Extves. (Past Pres., Toronto Chapt.); former Fellow, Am. Acad. for Cerebral Palsy & Devel. Med.; former Dir., Great Lakes Tomorrow, Inc.; Three Trilliums Community Place Inc.; Sierra Club of Ont.; Chair, Advisory Ctte., Kempenfelt Centre, Georgian College 1990– ; Home: 49 Wendover Rd., Etobicoke, Ont. M8X 2L2; Office: 75 The Donway West, Suite 302, Don Mills, Ont. M3C 2E9.

**TIMS, Michael J.,** B.Comm., M.B.A.; investment banker; b. Calgary, Alta. 3 July 1954; s. Joseph Henry and Marion Eileen T.; e. Univ. of Calgary B.Comm. (with distinction) 1976; Harvard Univ. M.B.A. 1978; m. Renae N. d. Leslie and Irene Weir 25 Feb. 1984; 2 children; PRES. & CHIEF OPERATING OFFICER, PETERS & CO. LIMITED 1990– ; Corp. Finan. Dept., Wood Gundy Limited 1978–80; Head, Corp. Finan., Peters & Co. Limited 1980–83; Pres. & Mng. Dir., Tims & Co. Capital Inc. 1984–85; various offices, present firm 1986–90; Dir., Candn. Mountain Holidays Inc.; Investment Dealers Assn. of Canada; Former Lecturer, Univ. of Calgary; Finan. Extves. Inst. Gold Medal 1976 (Univ. of Calgary); Uhlmann Rsch. Prize 1978 (Harvard Univ.); Senate Mem., Univ. of Calgary 1982–88; Mem., Chancellor's Club, Univ. of Calgary; Institutional Adv. Ctte., S. Alta. Inst. of Technology; mem., Leadership Giving Team, United Way; recreations: tennis, martial arts, reading; clubs: Ranchmen's; Glencoe; Office: 2500, 350 Seventh Ave. S.W., Calgary, Alta. T2P 4N1.

**TINDALE, John T.;** retired business executive; b. Toronto, Ont. 13 May 1930; s. Charles and Muriel (Royle) T.; e. var. profl. courses incl. Sch. of Bus. Admin., Univ. of West. Ont. M.T.C. prog.; m. Joyce Lillian d. James Goldie 21 Apr. 1951; children: Mark, Deborah, Dianna; Retired from all positions 1990; Chrmn., Pres. & C.E.O., Candn. Oxygen Ltd.; Pipeline Welder 1948–55; Trade Instr., Govt. of Ont. 1955–60; Tech. Serv. Rep., Candn. Oxygen Limited 1960; then Salesman, Prod. Supvr., Reg. Mgr., Gen. Mgr., Vice-Pres. Opns., Chrmn. Pres. & C.E.O.; Pres. & Dir., Candn., Helium Ltd.; Past Dir., Candn. Oxygen Ltd.; Compressed Gas Assn.; Protestant; recreations: golf, skiing; Clubs: Credit Valley Golf & Country; Univ. of West. Ont. Bus. Sch. Club of Toronto; Home: 1485 Tecumseh Park Dr., Mississauga, Ont. L5H 2W7.

**TINGLEY, The Hon. Daniel Harper,** B.S.L., B.A., Q.C.; judge; b. Winnipeg, Man. 25 Nov. 1937; s. Hall William Frederick and Grace Elizabeth (Quigley) T.; e. McGill Univ. B.S.L. 1963, B.A. 1963 (Fac. of Law Prize, Best Public Law Essay; Scarlet Key Hon. Soc., Zeta Psi Frat. (Pres. 1959–60); inter-collegiate football & rugby); m. Sara d. Harold and Chella Thornton 8 June 1963; children: Hall Nicholas, Chella Elizabeth, Charles Eric; JUDGE OF THE SUPERIOR COURT OF THE PROVINCE OF QUEBEC 1992– ; labourer in sawmills, fish canneries & railway construction, tugboat deck-hand, brokerage researcher, naval officer traiining 1953–63; articled with Lafleur & Brown 1963–64; Assoc. Lawyer 1965–73; Partner, Lafleur, Brown, de Grandpré, Kronstrom 1973–92; Lecturer, McGill Univ. 1978–81; Concordia Univ. 1983–85; Sr. Rulings Officer, Extve. Interchange Can. attached to Corp. Rulings Directorate, Revenue Canada 1982; Mem., Candn. Human Rights Comn. Panel 1986–92; Q.C. 1987; Councillor (elect), City of Westmount 1987–92; Mem., Barreau du Qué.; Barreau de Montréal (Council Mem. 1984–86); Candn. Bar Assn. (Council Mem., Que. Div. 1979–82); Candn. Tax Found.; Internat. Fiscal Assn.; Dir., Westmount Municipal Assn. 1972–77 (Pres. 1976–77); Candn. Club of Montreal 1974–80 (Pres. 1979–80); Legal Ctte., Positive Action 1978–82; Metis Beach Community Assn. 1979–91 (Pres. 1986–91); Westmount Housing Bureau 1985–88; Queen Elizabeth Hosp. 1992; Grad. Gov., McGill Univ. 1992–97; Chair, Reunion-Class Ctte., Mcgill Alma Mater Fund 1989–90; Dir. & Hon. Sec., McGill Grad. Soc. 1989–91; Dir. & Chair, Appeals Ctte. & Mem., Extve. Ctte., Montreal Assn. for the Blind 1985–92; Toujours Ensemble Inc. 1980–89; fundraiser: Salvation Army, Quebec Student Debating Assn., Centraide, McGill Univ. and others; author: 'The Declaratory Power of the British North America Act' 1962, 'Casebook for Intermediate Business Law' 1978–82, 'Tax Aspects of Aircraft Financing Techniques' 1989; 'Notes and Case Study on Tax Issues in Planning for Continuity of a Family Business' 1990; co-author: 'The Disregard of a Legal Entity for Tax Purposes' 1989; clubs: Montreal Indoor Tennis (Pres. & Dir. 1989–91), Mount-Bruno Country (Pres. 1993–94; Dir. 1989–94), Cascade Golf & Country, Univ. Club of Montreal (Finance Ctee. Mem. 1990–91), Whiff of Grape, Orleans Fish & Game (Dir. 1979); Home: 16 Thornhill Ave., Westmount, Que. H3Y 2E2; Office: Court House, 1 Notre-Dame St. E., Room 6.43, Montreal, Que. H2Y 1B6.

**TINGLEY, S. Phillip,** B.Com.; investment dealer; b. Vancouver, B.C. 2 May 1937; s. Stephen A. and Joy M. (Major) T.; e. Univ. of B.C., B.Com. 1961; m. Maureen L. d. J. Norman and Gretchen Hyland 17 Aug. 1963; children: S.J. Patrick, Fiona S.; SENIOR VICE PRES. AND DIR. SCOTIA McLEOD INC. 1961– ; joined present firm after grad.; Clubs: Union (Victoria, B.C.); Tamahaac (Ancaster, Ont.); Home: 53 Binscarth Rd., Toronto, Ont. M4W 1Y3; Office: Box 433, Toronto-Dominion Centre, Toronto, Ont. M5K 1M2.

**TINKER, David Owen,** B.Sc., Ph.D.; university professor; b. Toronto, Ont. 25 Jan. 1940; s. Stanley Francis and Patricia Ann (Jerred) T.; e. Richmond Hill H.S.; Univ. of Toronto B.Sc. 1961; Univ. of Washington Ph.D. 1965; m. Sheila d. Richard and Alice Wilcox 16 May 1962; children: Nicholas, Timothy, Michael, Katherine; PROF., DEPT. OF BIOCHEMISTRY, UNIV. OF TORONTO 1982– ; Rsch. Fellow, Univ. of London (U.K.) 1965–66; Asst. Prof., Dept. of Biochem., Univ. of Toronto 1966–71; Assoc. Prof. 1971–82; Fellow, Trinity Coll. 1986– ; Assoc. Ed., 'Canadian Journal of Biochemistry' 1974–82; Mem., Candn. Biochem. Soc.; The Biophysical Soc.; Soc. of Sigma Xi; The N.Y. Acad. of Sci.; IEEE Computer Soc.; Gabriel's Anglican Ch., Richmond Hill; Woodrow Wilson Fellow 1961–62; author of approx. 40 rsch. articles; recreations: sailing; Home: 16 Victoria St., Markham, Ont. L6C 1A7; Office: Toronto, Ont. M5S 1A8.

**TINKER, Edward Brian,** B.E., M.Sc., Ph.D., F.C.I.C., P.Eng.; retired university administrator; b. Yorkton, Sask. 22 Jan. 1932; s. Percy and Lily (Woodhead) T.; e. Yorkton C.I. 1949; Univ. of Sask., B.E. (Chem. Eng.) 1953, M.Sc. 1954, Ph.D. 1962; m. Elizabeth Yvonne d. James and Viva Fraser 11 Dec. 1954; children: Wayne Michael, Susan Patricia; Prod. Engr., Shell Oil Co. 1954–57; Asst. Prof., Univ. of Sask. 1957–62; Assoc. Prof. 1962–68; Regina Campus 1968–69; Prof. 1968–74; Vice Principal 1972–74; Vice-Pres. & Prof., Univ. of Regina 1974–81; Vice-Pres. (Admin.), Univ. of Sask. 1981–85; Vice-Pres. (Finan. & Services), The Univ. of Calgary 1985–91; Hon. Mem., Candn. Assn. of Univ. Business Offrs. (Past Dir.); Queen Elizabeth II Silver Anniversary Medal 1977; Fellow, Chem. Inst. of Can. (Past Dir.); Candn. Soc. for Chem. Engr. (Pres. 1975–76); recreations: hiking, skiing, sailing; Home/Office: 18 – 1255 Wain Rd., Sidney, B.C. V8L 4R4.

**TINNING, George Campbell,** R.C.A.; artist; b. Saskatoon, Sask. 25 Feb. 1910; s. George Richard and Caroline Georgina (Campbell) T.; e. St. Johns and Earl Grey Schs. Winnipeg; Regina Coll. Inst.; attended the Eliot O'Hara N.A. water-colour classes in Maine and the Art Student's League in New York City; came to Montreal 1939; enlisted 1942 in the Candn. Army; apptd. an Official War Artist, Candn. Army, Historical Sect. (General Staff), rank Lt. 1943; painted in the Maritimes, Eng. Italy and Holland, rank Capt. 1944; has painted in every province of Can.; paintings in perm. colls. Nat. Gallery, Ottawa; Nat. War Museum, Ottawa; Charlottetown Art Gallery, Charlottetown, P.E.I.; Robert McLaughlin Gallery, Oshawa, Ont.; The Candn. Club, New York; McGill Univ., Montreal; Univ. of Manitoba; Bank of Montreal; Royal Bank of Can., Montreal and other pub., corporate and private colls.; National Archives of Canada recently acquired most of the memorabilia of this artist done on his postings in Canada, England, Italy and Holland, including paintings, sketchbooks, drawings, photographs, scrapbooks and his War Diary 1943–46; el. Royal Canadian Academy of Arts, 1954; retrospective exhbn. at The Dominion Gallery (Montreal) June 1994; recreation: genealogy, reading; Address: The Linton, Apt. 52, 1509 Sherbrooke St. W., Montreal, Que. H3G 1M1.

**TINTNER, Georg Bernhard;** music director; conductor; b. Vienna, Austria 22 May 1917; s. Alfons and Marie Elizabeth (Horowitz) T.; e. Vienna State Acad. of Music Dips. in Composition and Conducting 1936, 1937; Dalhousie Univ., LL.D. (honoris causa) 1989; m. (1) Rosa Muriel Norman; children: Demas Franz, Boris Norman, Tulin Paul, Ariadne Georgina; m. (2) Cecilia Gretel Lawrence; children: Chrysothemis Magdalena, Esmeralda Irit Miriam, Hephzibah Wanda; m. (3) Tanya Ruth d. Hans and Pamela Buchdahl 27 May 1978; MUSIC DIR. AND RESIDENT CONDUCTOR, SYMPHONY NOVA SCOTIA 1987– , Music Dir. and Prin. Conductor Nova Scotia Youth Orch. 1988–89; Asst. Conductor Vienna Volksoper 1938; Resident Conductor & Musical Dir.: Auckland String Players 1947–54,

Auckland Choral Soc. 1946–54, Nat. Opera of Australia 1954–55, Elizabethan Opera 1956–63, 1965–67, N.Z. Opera 1964, Cape Town Mun. Orch. 1967–68, Sadlers Wells Opera 1968–70, W. Australian Opera Co. 1971–73, Australian Opera 1973–76, Queensland Theatre Orch. 1977–87; Guest Musical Dir.: Nat. Youth Orch. Can. 1971, 1973, 1974, 1977, 1979, 1982, 1986, 1989; Hong Kong Youth Orch. 1982, 1984, all Australian and New Zealand orchestras, Australian Youth Orch. and N.Z. Youth Orch. several appearances; appearances: London Symphony, London Mozart Players, Bournemouth Symphony, Singapore Symphony, Hong Kong Philharmonic, Hong Kong Sinfonietta, Candn. Chamber Orch., Vancouver Symphony, Toronto Symphony, Montreal Symphony, CBC Vancouver Orchestra, Kitchener-Waterloo Symphony, Candn. Opera Co. Ensemble, Winnipeg Symphony, Calgary Philharmonic, Candn. Brass with principal brass New York Philharmonic and Boston Symphony, Orchestre des jeunes du Quebec, National Arts Centre Orchestra, Chamber Players of Toronto, Orchestra London, Michigan Opera Theatre, Edmonton Symphony, Saskatoon Symphony, several Czech & Slovak orchestras; conducting master classes Czech Republic 1991, 1993; regular appearances all Australian and N.Z. orchs. and opera companies; soundtracks ten operas Australian Broadcasting Corp. TV and Broadcasting Corp. N.Z. TV; broadcast talks Australia; recordings Philips; ABC and Festival (Australia), Jubal (Can.); CBC SM5000 series; lecture series composers CBC 1977; mem. Vegan Soc.; Amnesty Internat.; recipient, Grosses Ehrenzeichen (Officer's Cross) for services to the Austrian Republic 1992; awarded Commemorative Medal for 125th Anniversary of Candn. Confederation 1993; recreation: bicycling; Office: 1646 Barrington St., #401, Halifax, N.S. B3J 2A3.

**TIPPETT, Maria Wendy,** B.A., Ph.D.; historian; b. Victoria, B.C. 9 Dec. 1944; d. George Deeble and Violet Ellen (Wheeler) T.; e. Victoria H.S. 1962; Vancouver City Coll., Simon Fraser Univ. (Hons.) B.A. 1972; Univ. of London Ph.D. 1982; m. Dr. Douglas Cole 1971, dissolved 1984; m. Prof. Peter Clarke July 1991; work and travel in Europe and Mid. East 1964–66, 1969; writer and curator 1972– ; Guest Curator, Simon Fraser Univ. Art Gall. 1974, 1978 (two exhibits), 1983; Guest Curator, Clare Hall Art Gall. (5 exhibits) 1992 and 1993; Consultant, C.B.C.-TV 1975, TV Ont. 1980, Cygnus Comm. 1980; Sess. Lectr. Simon Fraser Univ. 1976–82, Univ. of B.C. 1983–84; Sess. Lectr., Univ. of B.C., Simon Fraser Univ. 1984–85; Robarts Professor of Canadian Studies, York Univ. 1986–87; recipient Eaton's B.C. Book Award 1978; Gov.-Gen.'s Award (non-fiction) 1979; Sir John A. Macdonald Prize for Canadian History 1979; Canadian Studies Writing Award 1982; Hon. Mention, Francois-Xavier Garneau Medal 1985; B.C. Book Prize, finalist 1993; awarded Commemorative Medal for 125th Anniversary of Candn. Confederation; Bd. Chrmn. 1986–87, mem. Adv. Bd. Canadian Historical Review; mem. of Non-Fiction Jury for the Governor General's Literary Awards 1987–89; Pres. of all Juries 1988–89; mem. Candn. Historical Assn.; Mem., Royal Over-Seas League; Candn. Writers' Union; author: 'Emily Carr' 1979; 'Art at the Service of War' 1984; 'The Making of English-Canadian Culture 1900–1939: The External Influences' 1988; 'Breaking the Cycle and other stories from a Gulf Island' 1989; 'Making Culture, English-Canadian Institutions and the Arts before the Massey Commission' 1990; 'By A Lady: Celebrating Three Centuries of Art by Canadian Women' 1992; co-author: 'From Desolation to Splendour' 1977; 'Phillips in Print' 1982; exhib. catalogue and guest curator 'Lest We Forget' London Regional Art Gallery, London, Ont. 1989; Visiting Fellow, Clare Hall, Cambridge Univ., England 1991; elected to the Faculty of History, Cambridge Univ. 1992; Life Mem., Clare Hall, Cambridge Univ. 1992; Rsch. Associate, Scott Polar Rsch. Institute, Univ. of Cambridge 1993– ; elected, Royal Society of Canada 1992; recreations: swimming, music, hiking; Home: 'Foxbarn,' Windjammer Rd., Bowen Island, B.C. V0N 1G0 and 71 Wimpole Rd., Barton, Cambridge CB3 7AB England.

**TISDALL, John Charles Woodland;** retired public relations consultant; b. Toronto, Ont. 8 May 1919; s. Frederick FitzGerald Tisdall and Betty Alberta (Woodland) Tisdall Burton; e. St. Andrew's Coll., Aurora, Ont.; m. Diana Gage, d. William Martin Griffith, 29 Sept. 1951; twin d., Martha Gage Smith, Marilee Carmen MacFarlane; Ed-Announcer, Radio Stn. CHML, Hamilton, Ont., 1938–39; Dept. of Pub. Information, Ottawa, in charge of Consumer Information Service, 1940; later with Wartime Information Bd. becoming Assoc. Dir. of Indust. Information; scenario writer and Film Dir., J. Arthur Rank Organization, 1947; Dir. of Pub. Relations, Tandy Advertising Agency, Toronto, 1949; with partner formed Tisdall, Clark and Co. 1952; el. Chairman of Board 1967; merged with Continental Public Relations 1985; Vice Chrmn. and Sr. Counsel, Continental Public Relations Ltd. 1985; rec'd Centennial Medal 1967; mem., Candn. Pub. Relations Soc. (Toronto) Inc. Pres. 1956–57; Candn. Pub. Relations Soc. (Accredited Mem., Nat. Pres. 1963–64 and Chrmn., Nat. Accreditation Bd., 1968–71); Pub. Relations Soc. Am. (Accredited mem.); Foundation for Pub. Relations Research and Educ., N.Y. (Trustee 1965–68); Trustee, International Public Relations Found., London, Eng.; named one of world's 40 outstanding p.r. extves. by internat. publication 'P.R. News' 1984; elected mem. College of Fellows PRSA (1990); Anglican; recreations: music, reading, art; Home: 64 South Dr., Toronto, Ont. M4W 1R5.

**TITLEY, Edward Brian,** M.Ed., Ph.D.; university professor; b. Cork, Ireland 8 Jan. 1945; s. Edward and Nora (Hanlon) T.; e. Nat. Univ. of Ireland, B.A. 1966; Univ. of Man., B.Ed., 1970, M.Ed. 1975; Univ. of Alta., Ph.D. 1980; m. Jane d. John and Mary O'Dea 26 Dec. 1972; children: Marcia, Deirdre; PROF., FACULTY OF EDUCATION, UNIV. OF LETHBRIDGE 1993– ; H.S. teacher, Man. 1967–70; Elem. Sch. Prin., Dept. of Indian Affairs 1971–74; Lectr., Univ. of Alta. 1980–86; Asst. Prof., 1986–89; Assoc. Prof. 1989–90; Assoc. Prof., Univ. of Lethbridge 1991–93; Mem., Candn. Hist.Assn.; Candn. History of Education Assn. (Pres. 1990–92); Candn. Soc. for the Study of Education; Writers' Guild of Alta.; author: 'Church, State and the Control of Schooling in Ireland, 1900–1944' 1983, 'A Narrow Vision: Duncan Campbell Scott and the Administration of Indian Affairs in Canada' 1986; co-editor: 'Education in Canada: An Interpretation' 1982; editor: 'Canadian Education: Historical Themes and Contemporary Issues' 1990; Review Ed., 'Historical Studies in Education/Revue d'Histoire de l'Education'; recreations: swimming, chess, gardening; Home: 2312 – 19 Ave. South, Lethbridge, Alta. T1K 1E6; Office: Lethbridge, Alta. T1K 3M4.

**TITTLER, Robert,** B.A., M.A., Ph.D., F.R.H.S.; university professor; b. New York, NY 7 Dec. 1942 (Naturalized Canadian Citizen 1992); s. Irving Albert and Sylvia (Isseks) T.; e. Oberlin Coll., B.A. 1964; New York Univ., M.A. 1965, Ph.D. (highest distinction) 1971; m. Anne d. D.W. and Pearl H. Kelso 2 Apr. 1966; children: Andrew, Rebecca; PROF. OF HIST., CONCORDIA UNIV. 1981– ; Vis. Asst. Prof., Bloomsburg State Coll., summer 1968; Haskell Fellow & Penfield Fellow, England 1968–69; Asst. Prof., Hist. Loyola Coll. 1969–74; Assoc. Prof. 1974–75; Can. Counc. Leave fellowship 1975–76; Assoc. Prof. of Hist., Concordia Univ. 1975–81; Chrmn., Hist., Loyola Campus 1976–77; Co-Chrmn., united Dept. 1977–78; SSHRC Rsch. grant, sabb. (UK) 1982–83; 1987–89; 1991–94; (US) NEH Fellowship 1991; Dir., Concordia Hist. Grad. Prog. 1986–89; sometime reader, Folger Shakespeare Lib.; Ctr. for Ren. & Ref. Stud.; Inst. of Hist. Rsch.; Andrew H. Mellon Lectr., Princeton 1987; Conf. Brit. Stud. (Nat. Nom. Ctte. 1987–89); Pre-Mod. Towns Group; Econ. Hist. Soc.; Toronto Ren. & Ref. Colloq.; Soc. 16th C. Stud.; Friends Oberlin Coll. Lib.; Records of Early English Drama (Ed. Adv. Bd.); Ed. Adv. Bd., Cent. Renais./Ref'n. Stud.; Past & Pres. Soc.; Econ. Hist. Soc.; Dir., London Goodenough Assn. of Canada 1991– ; Acad. Ed.-in-Chief: 'History of Urban Society in Europe' (4 vol. series) forthcoming; author: 'Nicholas Bacon, The Making of a Tudor Statesman' 1976, 'The Reign of Mary I' 1983 (2nd ed. 1991); editor: 'Accounts of the Roberts Family of Ticehurst, Sussex' 1979; co-ed.: 'The Mid-Tudor Polity, c. 1540–1560' 1980; author: 'Architecture and Power, the Town Hall and the English Urban Community, 1500–1640' 1991; recreations: newspapers, canoeing, ornithology, gardening; Club: London House; Home: 4078 Hampton Ave., Montreal, Que. H4A 2K9; Office: 7141 Sherbrooke St. W., Montreal, Que. H4B 1R6.

**TITUS, Richard Ford,** B.Sc., B.E.; construction executive; b. Moncton, N.B. 22 Mar. 1921; s. late Harrison Burrill and Annie Belle (Ford) T.; e. Moncton (N.B.) High Sch. (Grad. 1939); Mount Allison Univ., 1939–40 (course interrupted by war), B.Sc. 1948; N.S. Tech. Coll., 1948–50, B.E. 1950; m. Annabel (Nancy), d. late Alexander S. Donald, 11 July 1942; children: Barbara Catherine, Richard Hugh; former Vice-Pres., Standard Industries Ltd. (retired); Pres., Hillsvale Farms Ltd.; joined Standard Paving Maritime Ltd., Halifax N.S., as Constr. Engr., 1950; apptd. Asst. Mgr., 1955; Mgr., Standard Paving Ltd., Toronto, Ont., 1956; Vice-Pres.-Constr., Standard Paving Maritime Ltd., 1959–65; Pres., 1965–86; Lieut, R.C.N.V.R., 1940–45; Lieut., R.C.N.(R), 1949–52; Past Pres, N.S. Road Builders Assn.; Halifax Metro Centre Ltd.; Past Chrmn. Halifax Metro Centre Comn.; Bd. of Govs., Technical Univ. of N.S. 1986; Bd. Chrmn., Halifax Citadels Hockey Club (Am. Hockey League); Past Pres., Nova Scotia Oilers (Am. Hockey League); mem., Assn. Prof. Engrs. Ont. and N.S.; Freemason; United Church; recreations: swimming, yachting, farming; Club: Saraguay; Home: 1752 Dunvegan Dr., Halifax, N.S. B3H 4G1.

**TIVY, Robert C.,** E.M., C.D., B.Sc., P.Eng.; executive; b. Fenelon Falls, Ont. 16 Oct. 1923; s. Clifford and Meta M. (Moffat) T.; e. Central Pub. and Peterborough (Ont.) Coll. Inst.; Queen's Univ., B.Sc. (Hons., Elec. Engn.) 1951; Am. Mngmt. Inst., New York Diploma in Business Admin. Mngmt.; m. Ethel V., d. Thomas Wilson, Brockville, Ont. 2 June 1945; children: Jane W. (Johnston), Mary E.; Business Consultant; Adjunct Prof., Univ. of South Florida 1983–85; Pres. and Founder, Quail Creek Cable TV Inc.; holds directorships in Candn. and Amer. companies; with Automatic Electric (GTE) 1951–70; joined Black & Decker Canada Inc. 1970, Vice Pres. and Gen. Mgr. 1972; Pres., Gen. Mgr. and Dir. 1974, Chrmn., Dir. and Vice-Pres. (Candn.-Pacific Operations) 1979–83; Dir. Black & Decker Canada, Japan, Australia, New Zealand, McCulloch Australia 1979–83; served with Prince of Wales Rangers (Militia) 1939–41; Royal Candn. Inf. Active Service 1942–46; rank Lt; Brockville Rifles; retired rank Lt. Col., C.O.; mem. Brockville Dist. High Sch. Bd. 1960–64; Business Council on Nat. Issues; Anglican; Clubs: Bel Air Country Club, Los Angeles, California; Royal Candn. Mil. Inst.; Brockville Country (Past Pres.); Quail Creek (Naples, Fla.); Sapphire Lakes CC, Sapphire North Carolina; Address: 10330 Quail Crown Dr., Naples, Florida 33999.

**TJADEN, Arthur Kenneth;** farmer, marketing board executive; b. Carman, Man. 27 March 1943; s. John Jacob and Anna Jean (McConnell) T.; e. Sperling H.S. 1965; Univ. of Man., Dipl.Agric. 1965; m. Marlene d. Louie and Winnie Duvenaud 23 Oct. 1965; children: Lynda, Tracy, Brenda; CHAIRMAN, BD. OF DIR., CANADIAN EGG MARKETING AGENCY 1990– ; Asst. Grain Buyer, Manitoba Pool Elevators 1962–63; Feed Salesman, Feed Rite Mills 1965–68; Full-time farming, grain & egg prodn. operation, Sperling, Man. 1968–90; Dir., Manitoba Egg Producers Mktg. Bd. 1984–89; Univ. of Man. Cert. of Merit 1991; Chair, Agric. Ctte., Manitoba C. of C. 1989–91; School Trustee, Midland Sch. Div. 1972–81; recreations: golf, curling; clubs: Carman Golf & Curling; Home: Box 333, Carman, Man. R0G 2M0; Office: 1900 – 320 Queen St., Ottawa, Ont. K1R 5A3.

**TOBE, Stephen S.,** Ph.D., F.R.S.C.; university professor; b. Niagara-on-the-Lake, Ont. 11 Oct. 1944; s. John Harold and Rose (Bolter) T.; e. Queen's Univ., B.Sc. 1967; York Univ., M.Sc. 1969; McGill Univ., Ph.D. 1972; m. Martha d. Moritz and Celia Reller 1969; PROF., UNIV. OF TORONTO, DEPT. OF ZOOL. 1982– ; Rsch. Fellow, Univ. of Sussex 1972–74; Asst. Prof., present univ. 1974–78; Assoc. Prof. 1978–82; Assoc. Chair 1986–87; Assoc. Dean, Sci., Fac. of Arts & Sci., present univ. 1988–93; Vis. Prof., U. of Calif. 1981; Nat. Univ. of Singapore 1987, 1993–94; Univ. of Hawaii 1988; E.W.R. Steacie Fellow, NSERC 1982–84; Mem., Animal Biol. Grant Selection Ctte., NSERC 1986–89 (Chair 1988–89); Ed. Bd., 'J. of Insect Physiol.,' 'Physiol. Entomol.,' 'Life Science Advances'; Sec.-Treas., Internat. Fed. of Comp. Endocrin. Soc. 1989–93; consultant in hydroponics; C. Gordon Hewitt Award, Entomol. Soc. of Can. 1982; FRSC 1987; Opening Lectr., Internat. Cong. of Entomol. 1988; Gold Medal, Entomol. Soc. of Canada 1990; Pickford Medal 1993; Mem., Am. Assn. for the Advancement of Sci.; Am. Soc. of Zool.; Entomol. Soc. of Can.; Royal Entomol. Soc., London (Fellow); Soc. for Exper. Biol.; for Neurosci.; for Sigma Xi; author/co-author of 150 refereed sci. pubs. & 17 refereed book chaps.; editor: 'Insect Biochemistry' 1987 (conf. proceedings); Home: 467 Soudan Ave., Toronto, Ont. M4S 1X1; Office: 25 Harbord St., Toronto, Ont. M5S 1A1.

**TOBIAS, Kal,** B.A.; business executive; b. New York, N.Y. 1 Feb. 1946; e. City Univ. of N.Y., B.A. 1967; m. Karen Liberty 11 Mar. 1967; children: Kristopher, Kirk; PRES. & CHIEF EXTVE. OFFR., DHL INTERNAT. EXPRESS LTD. (world-wide air courier co.) 1983– ; var. mngt. positions, Volkswagen Can. 1969–74; Mngt. Cons. 1974–80; Vice-Pres., Burmah Oil Co. 1980–83; Pres., C.E.O. & Dir., Candn. Courier Assn.; Office: 6205 Airport Rd., Bldg. B., Ste. 400, Mississauga, Ont. L4V 1E1.

**TOBIN, Hon. Brian Vincent,** M.P.; politician; b. Stephenville, Nfld. 21 Oct. 1954; s. Patrick Vincent and Florence Mary (Frye) T.; e. Memorial Univ.; m. Jodean d. Joseph and Edith Smith 27 Aug. 1977; children:

Heather, Adam, Jack; MINISTER OF FISHERIES AND OCEANS CANADA 1993– ; 1st elected to House of Commons as M.P. Humber-St. Barbe-Baie Verte, Nfld. 1980; re-elected 1984, '88, '93; parly. sec. to Min. of Fisheries & Oceans 1981; Official Opposition Forestry Critic & Assoc. Critic for Transport 1984; Critic for Regional Indus. Expansion & Privatization 1987; Party Critic for Transp. & Chair, Nat. Liberal Caucus 1989; Party Critic for Employment 1990; Chair, Caucus Ctte. on Communications, Mem. of Nat. Campaign Ctte. & Nat. Platform Ctte. 1992; served on several govt. cttes.; recreations: reading, music, sports; Office: Room 807, Confederation Bldg., Ottawa, Ont. K1A 0A6.

**TOD, Joanne;** artist; b. Montréal, Qué. 12 Feb. 1953; d. Andrew Clark and Georgina Bernadette (Srogen) T.; e. Ont. Coll. of Art A.O.C.A. 1974; regular exhns. Carmen Lamanna Gallery since 1982; numerous exhns. galleries and maj. instns. Can. and USA; rep. colls. various galleries incl. Nat. Gallery Ottawa, Art Gallery Ont., numerous private colls.; frequent lectr. Candn. univs. and instns.; mem. Adv. Ctte. Gallery 76, Ont. Coll. of Art; Bd. mem. YYZ Artists' Outlet Toronto 1982–89; Visual Arts Ont. Toronto 1985–89; mem. 'Flaming Dono' W. African Music & Dance 1980– ; recreation: N. Indian music (Tabla); Address: 20 Brockton Ave. Unit 1, Toronto, Ont. M6K 1S5.

**TODD, Rosalie Daly,** A.B., M.S., LL.B.; lawyer; b. Wisconsin, 11 Aug. 1947; d. Charles Martin and Mary Jane (Monroe) Daly; e. Marquette Univ. A.B. 1969; American Univ. M.S. 1978; McGill Univ. LL.B. 1982; m. David e. s. Ernie and Doris T. 28 Oct. 1978; one stepson: Thomas; EXECUTIVE DIRECTOR & LEGAL COUNSEL, CONSUMERS' ASSN. OF CANADA 1990– ; Management Intern, U.S. Govt. 1969–72; Editor, Amtrak 1972–75; Dep. Dir., Maryland Dept. of Transportation 1975–78; Editor, Royal Bank of Canada 1978–79; Assoc., FitzPatrick, Bennett, Trombley, Owens & Lahtinen 1982–86; Inst. for Rsch. on Public Policy 1986–87; Legal Dept., City of Ottawa 1987–90; Mem., N.Y. State Bar (Mem., Ctte. on Internat. Law & Trade); Law Soc. of U.C.; Publications Awards from I.A.B.C. and Candn. Public Relns. Soc.; recreation: portrait artist; Home: 6431 Clingin Lane, Manotick, Ont. K4M 1B3; Office: 307 Gilmour St., Ottawa, Ont. K2P 0P7.

**TODD, William L.,** B.Eng.; b. Huntingdon, Que. 3 May 1916; s. late Elizabeth Arnton (McEwen) and late William Stewart Todd; e. Elem. and High Schs., Huntingdon, Que.; McGill Univ., B.Eng. (Mech. Engn.) 1941; m. Ruth Katherine Winnifred Loken, 10 July 1948; children: Marilyn Heather Todd; Bruce, B.Sc., M.D.C.M. (Meridy Black, B.N.); Bryan, B.Comm., C.G.A.; Kevan, B.Eng. (Lyne Jussaume, B.Ed.); retired Vice President, Stadler Hurter, Ltd. (Consulting Engineers); prior to joining Stadler Hurter, served in various capacities with Canadian Hoosier Engineering Company, Quebec Roads Dept., Malinckrodt Chemical Works, Defence Industries Ltd., St. Lawrence Corp., R. A. Rankin & Co.; served with RCN for 4 yrs. as Engr. offr. during WWII; discharged with rank of Lt. Commdr. (E) RCNVR; mem., Assn. Consulting Engrs. Can. Inc.; Candn. Pulp & Paper Assn.; Engn. Inst. Can.; Order of Engrs. Que.; Assn. Prof. Engrs. Ont.; Protestant: Home and Office: 377 Church St., Beaconsfield, Que. H9W 3R3.

**TOLLEFSON, Edwin Archer,** Q.C., D.Phil.; consultant; b. Moose Jaw, Sask. 30 July 1933; s. Lars and Lily (Archer) T.; e. Univ. of Sask. B.A. 1954; LL.B. 1956; Oxford Univ. B.C.L. 1958; D.Phil. 1976; children: Christopher; Mark; Claire; Sr. General Counsel, Federal Dept. of Justice, retired 1993; mem. Faculty of Law, Univ. of Saskatchewan 1958–71; joined Federal Dept. of Justice, Research & Planning Sect. 1971; Dir. Programmes and Law Information Develop. Sect. 1974–80; Chrmn. Federal/Provincial Task Force on Uniform Rules of Evidence 1979–81; Co-ordinator, Criminal Law Review, Dept. of Justice Canada 1981–90; Senior General Counsel 1986– ; Sessional Lectr., Univ. of Ottawa Fac. of Law (Common Law Sect.) 1974–77; mem. Social Sciences and Humanities Research Counc. Consultative Grp. on Legal Research and Educ. 1980–82; Chargé de cours, Faculté de droit-Maîtrise, Univ de Montréal, hiver 1986; mem. Sask. Bar 1961– ; Federal Queen's Counsel 1980; author 'Bitter Medicine: The Saskatchewan Medicare Feud' 1964; 'Cases and Comments on the Law of Evidence' 1966, 1972; co-author: (with Bernard Starkman) 'Mental Disorder in Criminal Proceedings' 1993; United Church; recreations: music, bricolage; Home: #1, 15 Olympia Ave., Victoria, B.C. V8V 2N3.

**TOLLEFSON, Eric Lars,** B.A., M.A., Ph.D., FCIC, P.Eng.; university professor, professional engineer; b. Moose Jaw, Sask. 15 Oct. 1921; s. Lars and Lavinia (Lily) (Archer) T.; e. Univ. of Sask. B.A. 1943, M.A. 1945; Univ. of Toronto Ph.D. 1948; m. Jean d. John and Etta Andrews 14 June 1947; children: Beverley Jean, Janet Elizabeth, Susan Grace; PROF., DEPT. OF CHEMICAL & PETROLEUM ENGINEERING, UNIV. OF CALGARY 1967– ; Rsch. Asst., NRC 1948–51; Chemist & Sr. Chemist, Stanolind Oil & Gas 1951–56; Head, Physical Chem. Section, Chemcel Ltd. 1956–64; Chem. Development Dept. 1964–65; Technical Mgr. 1965–67; joined Staff, Dept. of Chem. Engr., Univ. of Calgary 1967; Head, Dept. of Chem. & Petrol. Engr. 1971–81; Alta. Oil Sands Technol. & Rsch. Authority Professor 1982–87; Pres., Tollefson Engr. Enterprises Ltd.; Consultant, Alta. Energy Conservation Bd. 1974–84; Aqua Tech. Ltd. 1971–74; Councillor & Dir., Chem. Inst. of Can. 1971–74; Grant Selection Ctte., NSERC 1970–73, 1985–88; Winner, Chem. Inst. of Canada Award in Industrial Practice sponsored by Esso Petroleum Canada 1987; Extve. Mem., Canadian Pugwash Group 1987– ; Mem., Un. Ch. of Canada; Canadian Pugwash Group; Group of 78; author of num. scientific papers & tech. reports; has shared in writing 16 patents as an inventor; recreations: skiing, hiking, tennis; clubs: University of Calgary Faculty; Home: 3219 24 Ave. N.W., Calgary, Alta. T2N 1N5; Office: Dept. of Chem. and Petrol. Engr., Univ. of Calgary, Calgary, Alta. T2N 1N4.

**TOLMIE, J. Ross,** Q.C., M.A., B.C.L.; b. Hartney, Man., 24 Aug. 1908; s. Dr. J.A. and Maude Emma (Ross) T.; e. Univ. of Brit. Columbia, B.A. 1929; Oxford Univ., B.A. (Juris.) M.A. and B.C.L. 1932; m. Hélène Louise, d. Leon J. Ladner, Q.C., Vancouver, B.C. 6 July 1936; two d. and four s.; former Counsel, Osler, Hoskin & Harcourt, retired; called to the Bar of British Columbia 1932, and of Ontario, 1945; cr. Q.C. 1955; Solr. and Counsel to Income Tax Divn., Ottawa, 1935–41; Solr., Dept. of Finance, Ottawa, 1941–46; mem., Law Soc. of B.C.; Law Soc. of Upper Can.; Candn. Bar Assn.; Can.-U.S. Comte. of the Chamber of Comm.; author of 'Canadian Tax Service,' 1938; Liberal; Presbyterian; recreations: skiing, fishing, hunting; Clubs: Rideau; Home: Apt. 101, 5750 Larch St., Vancouver, B.C. V6M 4E2.

**TOLMIE, Kenneth Donald;** B.F.A. Hons.; artist; b. Halifax, N.S. 18 Sept. 1941; s. Archibald and Mary Evelyn (Murray) T.; e. Mt. Allison Univ. Sch. Fine Arts. B.F.A. Hons. 1962; m. Ruth, d. George and Heloise MacKenzie, 8 Aug. 1962; children: Sarah Katherine; Jane Marianna; painted extensively in Europe and across Can.; many one-man shows, incl. nat. travelling exhn. 'Ken Tolmie: The Bridgetown Series' 1982–84; works held by Nat. Gall. Can.; Art Gall. N.S.; N.S. Art Bank; Bronfman Coll., Montreal Mus. F.A.; Confed. Centre for the Arts Mus.; Owens Gall., Mt. Allison Univ.; Univ. Western Ont.; DOFASCO; Husky Oil; Procter and Gamble; subj. of 3 CBC-TV films, incl. 'Profile of Ken Tolmie' for series 'Seeing It Our Way'; subj. TV-Ont. documentary for series 'Visions'; author 'Tale of an Egg' 1974 (children's book; chosen by Nat. Library Can. one of ten best children's books 1975); and art book 'A Rural Life: An Artist's Portrait' 1986; mem., Writers' Union of Canada; 1st Hon. Life Mem., Bridgetown Historical Soc.; mem. Bridgetown Hist. Soc. (Dir. 1979–81); Art Gall. N.S. (Mem. Bd. 1979–81); Chrmn., Visual Arts Ottawa, 1975–76; Visual Arts Ontario; Visual Arts Nova Scotia; Writers Federation of Nova Scotia; represented by: Beckett Gallery, Hamilton, Ont.; Kaspar Gallery, Toronto; Prog. Conservative Party; recreations: tennis; reading; Home: 6229 Regina Terrace, Halifax, N.S. B3H 1N4.

**TOLSTOY, Paul,** Ph.D.; educator; anthropologist; b. Versailles, France 20 Sept. 1929; s. André and Mary (Shuvalov) T.; e. Columbia Coll. B.A. 1951; Columbia Univ. Ph.D. 1959; Univ. Paris I Doctorat d'Etat 1984; PROF. OF ANTHROPOLOGY, UNIV. DE MONTRÉAL 1977– ; Asst. Prof. present Univ. 1961–64, Assoc. Prof. 1964–66, Dir. of Anthrop. Dept. 1977–81; Assoc. Prof. Queens Coll. City Univ. of N.Y. 1966–73, Prof. and Dir. Archaeol. Lab. 1973–77; recipient Can. Council, Nat. Science Foundation (U.S.A.) and Research Foundation City Univ. of N.Y. grants field research Mexico 1963–77, SSHRCC Ecuador 1984–87; author or co-author numerous publs.; mem. Soc. Am. Archaeol.; Am. Anthrop. Assn.; Am. Assn. Advanc. Science; Sigma Xi; Office: (C.P. 6128 Succ. A) Montréal, Qué. H3C 3J7.

**TOLTON, John Bertrum,** B.Com.; executive; b. Toronto, Ont. 7 May 1933; s. Bertrum Edward and Helen Mary (Nelson) T.; e. Humberside Coll. Inst. Toronto; Univ. of Toronto, B.Com. 1955; m. Margaret d. Percival and Catherine Kirby 6 July 1957; children: Susan, John, Paul; Vice-Pres., Merrill Lynch Canada Inc. 1975–89 (retired); self-employed mfr./distributor 1955–58; writer/researcher Candn. Bus. Service 1958–60; Secondary Sch. Teacher 1960; joined Merrill Lynch Canada Inc. 1960; Trustee, City of Etobicoke Bd. of Edn. 1970–88, Chrmn. 1975–76; Trustee, Metrop. Toronto Sch. Bd. 1975–88, Chrmn. 1981–86; mem. Intercollegiate Hockey Champions (U of T Blues) 1955–56, Bronze T Holder; Coach, Humber Valley Hockey (MTHL) 1975–85; Theta Delta Chi (Treas. Grand Lodge 1966, mem. Adv. Ctte. 1967); Founder, Dody's Tennis, Fishing & Sailing Club 1976; United Church; recreations: tennis, fishing, reading; Club: Lambton Golf & Country; Home: R.R. 1, Port Elgin, Ont. N0H 2C5.

**TOMAN, Adolf Jan,** M.A.; artistic director; producer; b. Pardubice, Czechoslovakia 19 Feb. 1942; s. Adolf, M.D. and Vera (Frickova) T.; e. Acad. of Fine Arts Prague M.A. 1967; Owner and Artistic Dir., Limelight Dinner Theatre 1978; came to Can. 1968; Artistic Dir. 'New Theatre' Colonnade Theatre Toronto 1971–72, 'Classical Stage Prodns.' Toronto 1972–74; Owner and Artistic Dir. Aladdin Theatre Toronto 1975; Dir. and Producer 1st Candn. prodns. Broadway musical hits 'Annie,' 'Best Little Whorehouse in Texas,' 'Evita' (nat. tour), 'Chorus Line' (nat. tour), 'Sophisticated Ladies,' '42nd Street,' 'Singing in the Rain,' 'Me and My Girl'; Guest Dir. McMaster Univ., Dalhousie Univ.; Artistic Dir. Czech New Theatre past 20 yrs.; recipient 3 awards Best Dir. Ont. Theatre Festival, New Candn. Play 'After Baba's Funeral' (Candn. rep. World Theatre Festival Monte Carlo); Dir. over 150 shows across Can.; contbg. ed. 'How To Become An Actor And Survive'; recreation: horseback riding; Address: Miczpiewiczova 6, Prague 6, Czechoslovakia.

**TOMARIN, Harry Paul;** executive; b. Russia 17 Jan. 1916; s. Samuel Paul and Millie (Rudolph) T.; came to Can. 1926; e. St. Catharines, Ont. pub. and high schs.; m. late Adelle Eudice d. Maurice Slepkov 22 Nov. 1939; children: Seymour, Larry; remarried 1984; Hon. Chrmn., TecSyn International Inc.; Subsidiaries: TecSyn Canada Limited (divisions: Poli-Twine, Polytech Netting Industries, Omnisport International, Kenarin Agencies), Polyloom Corp. of America; Lecofilms, Ozite Canada (1981) Inc.; Tuftbond Carpet Mills, Instant Tuft Industries Inc.; Playfield Inc.; All Pro Athletic Surfaces Inc.; joined Revzen & Tomarin, St. Catharines, Ont. 1937, estbd. Steel Warehouse br. 1946 and Steel Fabricating Plant 1948; formed Niagara Structural Steel Co. 1949 (inc. 1952; Preference shares listed on TSE, 1962; name changed to TecSyn Int'l. Inc. Dec. 1983; Non-voting shares listed on TSe Jan. 1986); Pres. until becoming Chrmn. 1977; gentleman farmer (Tomarin Acres); served 4 yrs. Lincoln and Welland Regt. (Militia), rank Sgt.; Dir. Brock University; Lifetime Hon. Mem., Shaw Theatre; mem. Candn. Chamber Comm.; Candn. Inst. Steel Constr. (Dir.); Affil.: B'nai B'rith, Lord Melchett Lodge; P. Conservative; recreations: golf, tennis, fishing; Clubs: Lookout Point Golf (Fonthill, Ont.); Primrose (Toronto); Canadian (Toronto); St. Catharines; St. Catharines Golf and Country; Home: R.R. 1, St. Catharines, Ont. L2R 6P7.

**TOMBALAKIAN, Artin S.,** B.A., M.A.Sc., Ph.D., F.C.I.C., P.Eng.; educator; b. Jerusalem, Palestine 4 Nov. 1929; s. Sarkis and Mary T.; e. Am. Univ. of Beirut, B.A. 1952; Univ. of Toronto, M.A.Sc. 1954, Ph.D. (Chem. Engn.) 1958; m. Mary, d. Krikor Pandjardjian, 23 Aug. 1959; three d. Lisa Mary, Nora Jane, Celia Margaret; PROF. AND DIR., SCH. OF ENGN., LAURENTIAN UNIV. OF SUDBURY 1968–79, and Prof. of Chem. there; Head, Dept. of Chem., Univ. of Sudbury, 1958–60 and of Laurentian Univ. of Sudbury, 1960–70; mem. Bd. of Govs., Cambrian Coll. of Applied Arts & Technol. 1971–78; research activities incl. diffusion and mass transfer across ion-exchange membranes, treatment of indust. waste waters, sorption of crude oil derivatives on Arctic terrain, processing of copper & nickel sulphide ores; Fellow, Chemical Inst. of Can. 1966; designated Specialist in Chem. Processes 1973; author of various articles in prof. journrs.; mem. Assn. Prof. Engrs. Ont.; Chem. Inst. Can.; Armenian Apostolic Church; recreations: music, swimming, table tennis, bridge, fishing, hunting; Home: 172 Walford Rd., Sudbury, Ont. P3E 2G9.

**TOMBLIN, Stephen G.,** M.A., Ph.D.; educator; b. Calgary, Alta. 5 Jan. 1955; s. William Alfred and June Francis (MacDonald) T.; e. Univ. of Calgary B.A. 1977; Dalhousie Univ. M.A. 1979; Univ. of B.C. Ph.D. 1985; Essex Univ. Colchester, Eng. Quantitative Analysis Course 1981 (Candn. Pol Sci. Assn. Scholarship); m. Lesley L. d. Kenneth and Barbara Burluck Tomblin 21 Dec. 1974; one d. Leah Renee; ASSOC. PROF. OF POL. SCI. MEML. UNIV. OF NFLD.; Asst. Prof. 1985; regular contbr. radio and TV; recipient various rsch. grants and scholarships incl. Inst. Social & Econ. Rsch. 1987, 1990; author various articles profl. jours.; mem. Candn. Political Science Assn.; IPAC; APPSA; YM/YWCA; recreations: running, aerobics, scuba diving, hiking, weight lifting; Home: 11 Whiteford Pl., St. John's, Nfld. A1B 2A3; Office: Dept. of Political Science, Memorial Univ. of Nfld., St. John's, Nfld. A1B 3X9.

**TOMKINSON, Constance (Lady Weeks);** author; b. Canso, N.S. 22 June 1915; d. Rev. Harold Tomkinson, a minister of the Un. Ch. who held leading charges in E. Can., and Grace (Avard) Tomkinson, D.Litt; e. Public Schs. in McAdam and Moncton, N.B., and Yarmouth, N.S.; Yarmouth High Sch., Grad. 1935; attended the Neighborhood Playhouse, N.Y. as a Scholarship Pupil in 1933 and grad. in 1935; m. Sir Hugh Weeks, Kt., C.M.G. 19 Nov. 1949; one d. Jane Avard Weeks; appeared as an actress on Broadway in the play 'Libel' in 1935, and in repertory companies in Maryland and N.Y. state; appeared as a dancer in various shows in Eng., Sweden, France, Germany, Italy and Holland; during the war yrs. was a temporary Civil Servant in charge of the Dir. General's Office of the Brit. Min. of Supply in N.Y.; in 1945 engaged with the S. Command Entertainments Br. entertaining the troops in Eng.; in 1946 became Secy. of the Sadlers Wells Ballet at the Royal Opera House till 1948; in 1949 joined the staff of the Old Vic Theatre, London, and worked with them till 1952; since then has engaged in writing; author of: 'Les Girls' (autobiography) 1956, Italian and Spanish eds. 1957; 'African Follies' 1959; 'What a Performance!' 1962; 'Dancing Attendance' 1965; Protestant; recreation: travel; Address: 14 St John's St., Chichester, West Sussex, England.

**TOMLIN, Brian William,** B.A., M.A., Ph.D.; university professor; b. London, Ont. 24 Sept. 1944; s. Alfred William and Hazel Muriel (Ross) T.; e. McMaster Univ. B.A. 1966; York Univ. M.A. 1969, Ph.D. 1972; m. Georgia d. Alfred and Phyllis Farwell 24 May 1969; children: Paula Anne, Amanda Kate, Benjamin Alfred Ross; PROFESSOR OF INTERNATIONAL AFFAIRS, CARLETON UNIV.; Dir., The Norman Paterson Sch. of Internat. Affairs, Carleton Univ. 1982–88; Centre for Negotiation & Dispute Resolution, Carleton Univ. 1986– ; Pres., Cambria Assoc. Limited; Sr. Acad. Advr., Candn. Foreign Service Institute, Dept. of Foreign Affairs & International Trade; Honorary Fellow, Candn. Inst. for Conflict Resolution; co-author: 'Faith and Fear: The Free Trade Story' 1991 (winner, National Business Book Award; short-listed for the Lionel Gelber Prize for best English-language book on internat. relns.); 'Canada as an International Actor' 1979, 'Canadian-U.S. Relations: Policy Environments, Issues and Prospects' 1979, 'Canadian Politics: An Introduction to Systematic Analysis' 1977; editor: 'Canada's Foreign Policy: Analysis and Trends' 1978; co-editor: 'Canada Among Nations' 1985, '86, '87, '88, '89, 'The Integration Question: Political Economy and Public Policy in Canada and North America' 1984; Home: 11 Monkland Ave., Ottawa, Ont. K1S 1Y7; Office: Ottawa, Ont. K1S 5B6.

**TOMLINSON, George Herbert,** Ph.D., F.R.S.C.; b. Fullerton, La. 2 May 1912 (came to Canada 1914); s. late George Herbert and Irene Loretta (Nourse) T.; e. Cornwall (Ont.) Coll. & Vocational Sch., 1928; Bishop's Univ., B.A. 1931 (Gov. Gen.'s and Lt. Gov.'s Medals 1931); McGill Univ., Ph.D. 1935; D.C.L. (Hon.) Bishop's 1986; m. Frances Louise, d. late Samuel S. Fowler, Riondel, B.C., 17 July 1937; children: Peter, David, Susan; AUTHOR AND CONSULTANT 1990– ; Research Assoc., Dept. of Indust. & Cellulose Chem., McGill Univ., 1935–36; Chief Chem., Howard Smith Chemicals, 1937–40; Dir. of Research, Howard Smith Paper Mills, 1940–61; joined Domtar Ltd. as Dir. of Research 1961–70, Vice Pres. Research & Environmental Technol. 1970–77; Sr. Scientific Advisor, Domtar Inc. 1977–90; inventor of no. of processes in pulp and paper indust.; awarded Weldon Medal 1947; Tappi Medal 1969; John S. Bates Gold Medal 1991; Hon. Life Mem., Tech. Assn. Pulp & Paper Indust.; Fellow, Candn. Inst. Chem.; Royal Soc. Can.; Hon Life Mem., Candn. Pulp & Paper Assn. (Tech. Sec.); Am. Chem. Soc.; Internat. Academy of Wood Science; Fellow, Am. Assn. Advanc. Science; mem., New York Academy of Sciences; named Laureate of 'Global 500' of UN Environment Program (UNEP) 1987; Delta Sigma Phi; Anglican; recreations: skiing, swimming, canoeing; Home: 920 Perrot Blvd. N., Ile Perrot, Que. J7V 3K1; Office: Domtar Rsch. Centre, Senneville, Que. H9X 3L7.

**TOMPA, Frank William,** Ph.D.; university professor; b. New York, N.Y. 5 Nov. 1948; s. Peter Michael and Elizabeth (Feiks) T.; e. Brown Univ., Sc.B. 1970, Sc.M. 1970; Univ. of Toronto, Ph.D. 1974; m. Helen d. Phyllis and Harold Lomas 1 July 1972; children: David, Karen, Andrea; PROF., DEPT. OF COMPUTER SCIENCE, UNIV. OF WATERLOO 1974– ; Dept. Chair 1992– ; Lectr., Univ. of Toronto 1974; Mem., Technical Staff, Bellcore, Morristown, N.J. 1987–88; Dir., Waterloo Ctr. for the New OED and Text Rsch., Univ. of Waterloo 1984– ; Mem., Bd. of Dir., Open Text Corp. 1989– ; Mem., Bd. of Dir., Info. Tech. Rsch. Cntr. 1992– ; Mem., Assn. for Computing Machinery; author/co-author of many papers in area of data structuring & databases, esp. as related to text databases, hypertext, videotex systems & relational databases; Home: 481 Claywood Ct., Waterloo, Ont. N2T 2C6; Office: Waterloo, Ont. N2L 3G1.

**TOMPKINS, Patricia Anne,** B.A., B.Mus.; music administrator; b. Denver, Colo. 26 Nov. 1922; d. Orville Cyrus and Hazel Maud (Hopkins) Spore; e. Ponca City, Okla. High Sch.; Nat. Music Camp Interlochen, Mich.; Coll. of Emporia, Kans.; Univ. of Mich., B.A., B.Mus. 1944; m. James Burnet s. Leslie Jay and Jean Burnet Tompkins 27 Oct. 1946 (dec.); children: Leslie Jay, James Burnet (dec.), Teresa Spore; Pres. Candn. Music Council 1984–87, Dir. 1981–87; Mgr. Toronto Mendelssohn Choir 1967–89; music specialist and teacher Dearborn, Mich. 1945–46; music therapist with Dr. Gordon Bell, Toronto 1946–47; chamber music rsch. Candn. Music Centre 1963–64; Dir. Victoria Day Nursery 1957–61; Travellers' Aid Soc. 1962–64; mem. Jr. League Toronto 1950– ; mem. Assn. Cultural Execs.; Internat. Soc. Contemporary Music 1984–85; Internat. Yr. Candn. Music 1985–86; Gamma Phi Beta; Mu Phi Epsilon; Anglican; Club: Arts & Letters; Home: 20 Glen Cedar Rd., Toronto, Ont. M6C 3G1.

**TONDINO, Gentile,** R.C.A.; artist; educator; b. Montreal, Que. 3 Sept. 1923; s. Antonio and Lucia (Liberatore) T.; e. full-time apprenticeship with A. S. Scott 1942–47; Montreal Sch. of Art 1947–48; Montreal Museum of Fine Arts Sch. of Art & Design (under Dr. Arthur Lismer) Dipl. 1950, Art Centre Child and Adult Art Teaching 1952–53; m. Livia Helen d. Mario Martucci 14 Nov. 1945; children: Guido, Tristan, Lisa; ASSOC. PROF. OF DRAWING & PAINTING, FACULTY OF EDUC., McGILL UNIV. 1977– , Sch. of Arch. 1959– and Part-time Instr. in Sketching Summer Sch. 1966– ; Asst. in Adult Teaching Montreal Museum of Fine Arts 1952–53, Instr. in Basic and Advanced Drawing & Painting 1953–67; Instr. in Drawing & Painting McGill Univ. Dept. Fine Arts 1964–69; recipient Montreal Museum of Fine Arts Scholarship 1951; rep. in numerous exhns. since 1940's incl. Art Gallery of Ont., Brussels World Fair, Vancouver 1940's incl. Art Gallery of Ont., Brussels World Fair, Vancouver Art Gallery, Spring Exhns. Montreal Museum of Fine Arts, Candn. Group of Painters, R.C.A., Candn. Biennial Exhns.; mem. Candn. Group of Painters; Home: 4594 Earnscliffe, Montreal, Que. H3X 2P2; Office: 817 Sherbrooke St. W., Montreal, Que. H3A 2K6.

**TONKS, Alan,** M.A., M.Ed., B.A.; politician; b. Toronto, Ont. 2 Apr. 1943; s. Christopher Alexander and Anna (Young) T.; e. Upper Canada Coll. and York Memorial Collegiate 1958–62; Lakeshore Teachers Coll. 1963; Waterloo Lutheran Univ., B.A. 1969; York Univ., B.A. Hons.; M.A. 1975; Univ. Toronto, M.Ed. 1978; m. Cecile, d. James and Florence Kong; children: Christopher James; Matthew Alan, Alison Jean; METRO CHRMN., METROPOLITAN TORONTO 1988– ; Dir., Federation of Candn. Municipalities 1989– and Chrmn., International Program Ctte. 1991– ; Pres., North Am. Section, Internat. Union of Local Authorities 1993; Vice Pres., Internat. Union of Local Authorities World Extve. 1993; Mayor, City of York 1982; Metro Councillor, Metro Ward York-Humber; Commnr., Toronto Transit Commn.; Commnr., Bd. of Commnrs. of the Metro. Toronto Police Force; Mem., Toronto Area Transit Operating Authority; Volunteer Teacher, Candn. Univ. Services Overseas (CUSO) Jamaica, 1965; Teacher, Scarborough (Ont.) Bd. Ed. 1967–76; Bd. Mem., Metro Toronto Children's Aid Soc. 1976–78; elected Controller, Borough York (Ont.) 1976; Mem. Metro (Toronto) Counc., Metro Transportation Comte., Metro Toronto & Region Conservation Authority, 1976–80; Chrmn., Metro Toronto Special Comte. on Human Relations (Pitman Report) 1976–78; Chrmn., Finance & Budget Comte. Ont. Pub. Sch. Men Teachers Assn. 1981; Budget Chief, Borough York 1978–79; Deputy Mayor, York 1979–80; Mem. Metro Toronto T.T.C. Joint Comte. on Transportation 1979–80; Teacher, Chrmn. of Curriculum, Gooderham Public Sch. 1981; Mem. Jt. Bd. Affiliate (Scarborough) Comte. on Education Policy and Curriculum Development 1981– ; Gov. Humber Coll. 1982; Dir., Weston Lions Club 1971–81; York Community Services 1971–81; York-Weston Meals on Wheels 1974–81; West Park Hosp. for Chronic Care 1976–80; St. Hilda's Towers for Sr. Citizens 1979–81; Dir., Assoc. of Municipalities of Ont. 1984–86; mem. Assn. of Municipalities of Ont. Fiscal Policy Ctte. 1985–86; Hon. Mem. of Counc., Boy Scouts of Can. 1984–86; Hon. Chrmn. St. Joseph's Health Centre Fund 1984; Master Mind, Masters Games 1984; Chrmn. Metro Toronto Task Force on Functional Relationships of the Council, Committees, Boards & Commissions 1984–86; Dir., Catholic Children's Aid Soc. 1986; Mem., Bd. of Govs. Exhibition Place; Dir., Candn. National Exhib. Assn.; Dir., Bd. of Dirs., Sick Children's Hosp.; Home: 50 Greenbrook Dr. Toronto, Ont. M6M 2J9; Office: Station 1070, 7th Floor, Metro Hall, 55 John St., Toronto, Ont. M5V 3C6.

**TONKS, Robert Stanley,** B.Pharm., Ph.D., F.P.S.; F.I.Biol.; educator; pharmacologist; b. Aberystwyth, Wales; s. (late) Robert Patrick Dennis and Prudence Violet (Williams) T.; e. Univ. Coll. Cardiff; Welsh Coll. of Pharm. and Welsh Coll. of Med.; Univ. of Wales B.Pharm.; Welsh Coll. of Med. Ph.D. (Pharmacol.); m. Diana M. Cownie; children: Pamela Mary, Julia Rosalind, Robert Michael, Sara Katharine; PROF., DIV. OF GERIATRIC MEDICINE, DALHOUSIE UNIV. 1988– ; Dean of Health Professions, 1977–88, Dir. Coll. of Pharm. 1973–77, Prof. of Pharm. 1973–88; formerly: Organon Post Doctoral Fellow, Med. Sch. Cardiff; Nat. Health Service Post Doctoral Fellow, Med. Sch. Cardiff, Nevill Hall Hosp. Abergavenny; Univ. Lectr. in Pharmacol. Univ. of Wales; Visiting Research Fellow Faculté de Médecine, Paris, Sr. Lectr. in Materia Medica, Pharmacol. and Therapeutics, Med. Sch. contrib. to various prof. journs.; recipient Cert. of Merit N.S. Pharm. Soc. 1977; Hon. Life mem. Pharm. Assoc. N.S. 1985; Fellow, Inst. of Biol. (London); Fellow, Royal Pharm. Soc. (London); Hon. mem., Candn. Soc. Hosp. Pharm.; N.B. Pharm. Soc.; Co-Chrmn. N.E. Candn./Am. Health Council; mem. Candn. Soc. Clin. Investig.; Internat. Soc. Thrombosis & Haemostasis; Brit. Pharmacol. Soc.; Clin. Pharmacology Soc. (London); Soc. Pharmaceutical Med. (London); Candn. Assn. Gerontol.; Gerontol. Soc. Am.; Am. Soc. Clin. Pharmacol. Therap.; Med. Soc., Prov. Govt. Working Group on Pharmacare Issues; Nat. Adv. Panel on Risk/Benefit Management of Drugs; Joint MRC-NHRDP Ctte. on Rsch. in Nursing; Career Awards Ctte., NHRDP; Adviser to US Public Health Service on estab. joint projects and information sharing on health care in Western US and Canada; Co-ord. drugs/medical supplies for Ethiopia Airlift 1984–85; Cons., Pew Charitable Trusts, Philadelphia; Anglican; recreations: skiing, hiking, horseback riding, music; Home: 62 Kingsway Dr., Haliburton Hills, Halifax County, N.S. B0J 3J0; Office: Div. of Geriatric Med., Fac. of Med., 8th Flr., Abbie Lane Bldg., Halifax, N.S. B3H 3G2.

**TOOKOOME, Simon;** artist; b. Chantrey Inlet 9 Dec. 1934; medium: prints, printmaking, sculpture; 96 group exbns. incl. most recent: National Gall. of Canada Ottawa 1991, 1992, l'Iglou Art Esquimau, Douai (toured 9 cities) France 1989–92, Albers Gallery San Francisco, Calif. 1991, Bunkamura Art Gall. Tokyo, Japan 1992, Snow Goos Assoc. Seattle, Wa. 1991, Maison Hamel-Bruneau, Ste-Foy, Que. 1990–91; solo exbns.: Inuit Galerie Mannheim, Germany 1992, McMichael Candn. Coll. Kleinburg, Ont. 1983, Inuit Gall. of Vancouver 1980, Theo Waddington New York, N.Y. 1980; works in 19 collections incl. art galleries of Greater Victoria, Nova Scotia, Ontario (Klamer Family Coll.), Winnipeg Art Gallery (Swinton Coll.), Amon Carter Mus. of Western Art Fort Worth, Texas, Canada Council Art Bank Ottawa, Candn. Mus. of Civilization Hull, Que., Inuit Cultural Inst. Rankin Inlet, N.W.T., Nat. Gall. of Can.; attended openings: 'Baker Lake Print Coll.' Winnipeg 1975, 'The People Within' Art Gall. of Ont. 1976, 'Imprint 76' Montreal (also invitee to Eskimo Games, Cultural Olympics) 1976, Minneapolis, Minn. 1979, 'Masters of the Arctic' N.Y. 1989; 'The World of Man and the World of Animals Come Together in the Shaman' reproduced on Candn. stamp 1980; visual arts grant, Canada Council 1985; 1st prize poster contest 1988 Winter Olympics Calgary 1988; subject of several articles and catalogues; Home: Baker Lake, N.W.T.; Office: c/o Ingo Hessel, Indian and Northern Affairs Canada, Les Terrasses de la Chaudière, Ottawa, Ont. K1A 0H4.

**TOOLE, David George,** B.Sc.M.E., M.Sc.Bus.Admin.; financial executive; b. Winnipeg, Man. 22 April 1942; s. George Edwin and Kathleen Mary (Wood) T.; e. Univ. of Manitoba B.Sc. Mech. Engr. 1964; The City Univ., London, England M.Sc.Bus.Admin. 1968; m. Bette d. James and Dorothy Smith 28 Aug. 1965; children: Jennifer Kathleen, Simon David; SENIOR VICE-PRES. AND CHIEF FINANCIAL OFFR., CANADIAN PACIFIC FOREST PRODUCTS; formerly Gen. Mgr., Canadian Pacific (Bermuda); Vice-Pres., Canadian Pacific

Limited; Athlone Fellow; Dir., Alpine Club of Can.; Home: 497 Mountain Ave., Westmount, Que. H3Y 3G3; Office: 1250 René-Lévesque Blvd. W., Montréal, Que. H3B 4Y3.

**TOOLE, John L.,** B.A., C.A.; transportation executive (retired); b. London, Ont. 16 Feb. 1913; s. late Mabel (Leary) and Wade T.; e. Public and High Schs., Guelph, Ont.; Univ. of Toronto, B.A. (Comm. & Finance); C.A., Ont.; m. late Elaine Patricia, d. late C.A. Callen, 9 Sept. 1943; Retired (1977) Dir., The Mortgage Insurance Company of Canada; MICC Investments Ltd.; Morguard Mortgage Investment Co. of Canada; Toronto College Street Centre Limited; Seachel Accommodations Ltd.; Markborough Properties Ltd.; Auditor with Sholto Scott, C.A., 1938–40; Asst. to Group Acct., Canadian Industries Ltd. 1940–42; Asst. Controller, and later Control Mgr., Dominion Rubber Co. Ltd., 1942–49; Asst. Controller, Ford Motor Co. of Canada Ltd., 1949–54; Asst. Comptroller, Canadian Nat. Rlys., 1954–57, and Comptroller, 1957–59; Vice Pres., Acct. & Finance, 1959–68; Vice Pres. & Chrmn. CN Invest. Div. Candn. Nat. Rlys. 1968–77; Past mem. of Assn. of Am. Railroads; Inst. Chart. Accts. of Ont. and Que.; Sigma Chi; United Church; recreations: golf; Home: 1000 Vicar's Landing Way, Apt. A310, Ponte Vedra Beach, Florida 32082.

**TOPPING, Frederick Victor,** B.A.Sc.; company president; b. Toronto, Ont. 13 Apr. 1924; s. Victor, B.A.Sc., M.A., M.Sc. and Agnes (White) Topping, M.B., B.S.; e. Pub. Schs., Toronto; Trinity Coll. Sch., Port Hope, Ont.; Univ. of Toronto (1947–51), B.A.Sc., 1951; m. Doris (dec'd.) d. Fred E. Pearson, Aug. 1947; three s. Christopher, Edward, Douglas; one d. Marilyn; m. 2ndly Georgina d. Emmanuel Quinn; PRESIDENT AND DIR., TOPPING TECHNICAL AND MARINE LTD. 1989– ; Pres. Spectrac Ltd. Holding Co.; Research Enterprises, Toronto, as Radar Inspr. 1940–42; Engineer, Canadian Radio Mfg., Toronto, 1951–54; Project Engr., Radio Condenser Ltd., Toronto, 1954–56; Pres. & Dir., Topping Electronics Ltd. 1956–89; served with R.C.A., Staff Sgt., Radar Instr.; discharged 1945 (C.V.S.M.); mem., Fed. Govt. Electronic Trade Mission to S.E. Asia (1966); mem., Assn. Prof. Engrs. of Ont.; Candn. Mfrs. Assn.; contrib. of articles to mags. and journs. in field of electronics; articles on guns to 'American Rifleman'; holder of patents re electronics; Anglican; recreations: boating, target shooting; Home: 3 Kirkton Rd., North York, Ont. M3E 1K6.

**TORCHINSKY, Benjamin Bernard,** B.Sc., M.Sc., P.Eng.; business executive; b. Calgary, Alta. 24 Sept. 1926; s. Max and Rosa (Frandt) T.; e. Univ. of Alta., B.Sc. 1947, M.Sc. (Civ. Engr.) 1949; m. Sarah R. d. Abraham Pearlman 17 Aug. 1947; children: Alan, Raymon; CHRMN., AGRA IND. LTD. 1994– ; Instr., Univ. of Alta. 1947–49; Asst. Prof. of Civ. Engr., Univ. of Sask. 1949–53; Assoc. Prof. 1953–56; founded B.B. Torchinsky & Assoc. 1953; this was inc. into Agra Vegetable Oil Products Ltd. 1959 whose name was changed to AGRA Industries Ltd. 1970 (a public co.); Chrmn., Pres. & C.E.O., AGRA Ind. Ltd. 1959–89; Chrmn. & C.E.O. 1989–93; mem. Am. Soc. of Civ. Engrs.; Home: 1201 Old Mill Towers, 39 Old Mill Rd., Toronto, Ont. M8X 1G6; Office: 400 – 2233 Argentia Rd., Mississauga, Ont. L5H 2K6.

**TORNO, Noah,** M.B.E.; executive; b. Toronto, Ont. 27 Nov. 1910; m. Rose Rein (Laine), 10 April 1950; one stepson, Michael Laine; Dir., 1001 Trust, World Wildlife Fund; Mount Sinai Hosp.; former Dir., Distillers Corp. Seagrams Ltd.; Canada Trust; Consumers Gas; Carling O'Keefe Breweries; Hiram Walker Resources; O'Keefe Centre for the Performing Arts; Hon. Trustee Canada Trust Co.; Treas., Mount Sinai Inst.; Past Chrmn., Royal Ont. Museum; served in 2nd World War with RCN, 1942–45 with rank of Lieut.; Life mem., Art Gallery Ont.; Royal Candn. Inst.; Haida, Inc.; Candn. Guild Crafts; Arch. Conserv. Ont.; Naval Offrs. Assn. Can.; Home: 155 Cumberland St., Toronto, Ont. M5R 1A2; Office: 122 Scollard St., Toronto, Ont. M5R 1G2.

**TORODE, John Arthur;** real estate executive; b. Big Spring, Tex. 22 July 1949; s. Arthur Reginald and Betty Walker (Roberts) T.; e. Royal Roads Military Coll.; Royal Military Coll.; children: Reece, Cole; FOUNDER & PRES., TORODE REALTY LTD. 1973– ; Dir., Circa Communications; Top 50 Fastest Growing Companies 1989; Former Dir., Theatre Calgary; Calgary Centre for Performing Arts; recreations: squash, golf, car racing; clubs: Glencoe; Bow Valley; Home: 2211 – 7th St. SW, Calgary, Alta. T2T 2X3; Office: 2400, 421 - 7 Ave. SW, Calgary, Alta. T2P 4K9.

**Toronto Blue Jays;** see **Blue Jays Baseball Club.**

**TORRANCE, James Grayson,** Q.C., LL.B.; solicitor; b. Toronto, Ont. 9 Sept. 1928; s. Melvin James and Ellen Louisa Jean (Grayson) T.; e. Univ. of Toronto LL.B. 1952; Osgoode Hall Law Sch. 1954; m. Beverley Elaine d. Clarence C. and Florence I. Downey 12 Sept. 1953; children: Nancy Rebecca, Robert James, Patricia Jean; PARTNER EMERITUS, SMITH LYONS TORRANCE STEVENSON & MAYER 1962– ; Dir., D'Arcy, Masius, Benton & Bowles Canada Inc.; Blackwood Hodge (Canada) Ltd.; Dynacare Inc.; H & S Reliance Limited; Mitsui & Co. (Canada) Ltd.; Potash Company of Canada Ltd.; Sakura Bank (Canada); Toyota Canada Inc.; Wintershall Canada Ltd.; called to Bar of Ont.; recreation: golf; Clubs: Albany; Lambton Golf & Country; Boca del Mar Country; Mono Hills Country; Home: 100 North Dr., Etobicoke, Ont. M9A 4R2; Office: Suite 6200, Scotia Plaza, 40 King St. W., Toronto, Ont. M5H 3Z7.

**TORREY, David L.,** B.A.; investment dealer; b. Ottawa, Ont. 6 Oct. 1931; s. Arthur Starratt and Josephine E. (Leonard) T.; e. Vermont Acad.; St. Lawrence Univ., B.A. (Econ.) 1953; Univ. of W. Ont., Grad. Sch. of Business Adm. Dipl. 1954; m. 17 Sept. 1955 (divorced); three s., two d.; Chrmn., Phillips Cables Ltd.; Dir., ICI Canada Inc.; Canadian Stebbins Engineering & Manufacturing Co. Ltd.; Total Petroleum (N.Am.) Ltd.; Wajax Ltd.; Vice-Chrmn., RBC Dominion Securities Inc. 1984–93; Chrmn., Bd. of Mgmt., Montreal (Downtown) YMCA 1972; mem. Council, Montreal Bd. Trade, 1968–70; Trustee, Vermont Acad. 1976–79; Chrmn., Bd. of Govs., Montreal Stock Exchange 1972; Gov., Securities Indust. Assn. (N.Y.) 1971; Trustee, St. Lawrence Univ.; Dir., Montreal General Hosp. Found.; Past Pres., Multiple Sclerosis Soc. of Can.; Beta Theta Pi; United Church; recreations: sailing, golf; Clubs: Royal Montreal Golf; Mount Royal; Toronto Club; Home: 389 Carlyle Ave., Montreal, Que. H3R 1T3; Office: 2000 McGill College Ave., Suite 300, Montreal, Que. H3A 3H5.

**TORRIE, Ralph Douglas,** B.Sc.; consultant; environmentalist; b. Toronto, Ont. 24 Aug. 1952; s. Keith MacGregor and Edna Letitia (Wansborough) T.; e. Univ. of Waterloo B.Sc. 1979; m. Judy d. Frank and Pauline Smith, Sault Ste. Marie, Ont. 30 June 1979; children: Alison, James; PARTNER, TORRIE SMITH ASSOCIATES 1979– ; mem. Adv. Panel Candn. Sustainable Soc. Project; Asst. Co-ord. Energy Rsch. Group Internat. Devel. Rsch. Centre and UN Univ. 1984–86; Tech. Adv. Panel Ont. Nuclear Safety Review 1987–88; Rep. Candn. Peace, Environ. & Devel. Orgns. before Candn. Hearings World Comn. on Environ. & Devel. 1986; Founding mem. Friends of the Earth 1978; Nat. Adv. Bd. Cedar Investments Inc. 1986– ; Co-Founder Candn. Council Internat. Co-op. Task Force Environ. & Devel. 1986; Pres. Alternet Communications Assn. 1988–89; author numerous articles energy, environ., sustainable devel.; mem. ed. adv. bd. 'Energy Studies Review'; Home: 1697 Des Perdrix, Orleans, Ont. K1C 5E2; Office: 255 Centrum Blvd., Suite 302, Orleans, Ont. K1E 3V8.

**TORSNEY, Michael J.,** F.R.A.I.C., O.A.A., MRIAI; architect, athlete; b. Dublin, Ireland 23 April 1930; s. Michael and Jane (Roche) T.; e. Blackrock College & Dublin Inst. of Tech. 1955; m. Marie T. d. Malachi and Ann O'Gorman 14 Nov. 1955; children: Brian, Michelle, Patricia (Paddy) (M.P. Burlington), Sean; emigrated to Canada 1957; ARCHITECT, TORSNEY GRAFF ARCHITECTS INC. 1962– ; notable buildings: St. Joseph's Villa Dundas, Ont., East End Police Station and Unified Family Court Hamilton, Ont.; Past Dir., Federal Bus. Devel. Bank (Ont.); Past Pres., Rotary Club of Hamilton; Fellowship, Royal Arch. Inst. of Can.; World Class Masters Swimmer; World Championships: 2 gold, 1 silver, 2 bronze (relay); U.S. Championships: 1 gold, 2 silver, 3 bronze; Canadian Championships: 5 times-5 gold medals winner; Mem., St. Joseph's Hosp. Bd.; Past Dir., Social Planning & Rsch. Council of Hamilton-Wentworth; Past Chair, Hamilton Auto Assn.; Mohawk College Adv. Bd.; Pres., Burlington South Liberal Assn. 1975; Vice-Pres., Candn. Water Polo Assn.; club: Hamilton; Home: 866 Danforth Pl., Burlington, Ont. L7T 1S2; Office: 144 James St. S., Hamilton, Ont. L8P 2A3.

**TORY, John A.,** Q.C., LL.B.; DEPY. CHRMN. & DIR. THE THOMSON CORPORATION; Pres. & Dir., The Thomson Co. Inc.; Thomson Equitable Company Inc.; The Woodbridge Co. Ltd.; Vice-Chrmn. and Dir., Thomson U.S. Inc.; Depy. Chrmn., & Dir., Markborough Properties Inc.; Dir., Royal Bank of Canada; Sun Life Assurance Co. of Canada; The Thomson Corporation PLC (U.K); Abitibi-Price Inc.; Hudson's Bay Co.; Rogers Communications Inc.; Hon. Solr., Candn. Mental Health Assn.; Office: 65 Queen St. W., Toronto, Ont. M5H 2M8.

**TORY, John Howard,** Q.C., B.A., LL.B.; b. Toronto, Ont. 28 May 1954; s. John Arnold and Elizabeth Emma (Bacon) T.; e. Univ. of Toronto Schs. 1972; Univ. of Toronto Trinity Coll. B.A. 1975; Osgoode Hall Law Sch. LL.B. 1978; m. Barbara d. Donald and Yvonne Hackett 27 May 1978; children: John Alexander Donald, Christopher Hackett, Susan Kathleen, George Marshall; PARTNER, TORY TORY DesLAURIERS & BINNINGTON 1986– ; Mem. Exec. Ctte. 1989– ; Dir., CamVec Corp.; John Labatt Limited; Multilingual Television (Toronto) Ltd.; Rogers Broadcasting Ltd.; Chrmn., Bd. of Govs., Candn. Football League; called to Bar of Ont. 1980; joined Tory, Tory 1980; Prin. Sec. to Premier of Ont. and Assoc. Sec. Ont. Cabinet 1982–85; P. Cons. Campaign Mgr. 1976, 1977, 1979, 1980, 1981; Ont. Campaign Chrmn. 1987; Dir. of Tour and Sr. Policy Adv. to Prime Min. 1988 Fed. el.; Dir. Salvation Army Metro Toronto; St. Michael's Hosp. Found.; Outdoor Canada (Sportsmen's Shows); United Church; recreations: golf, skiing, tennis, politics; Home: 37 Stratheden Rd., Toronto, Ont.; Office: P.O. Box 270, Suite 3000, Aetna Tower, T-D Centre, Toronto, Ont. M5K 1N2.

**TORY, Martha Jane,** B.Comm., C.A., CMC; chartered accountant; b. Toronto, Ont. 25 Sept. 1954; d. James Marshal and Marilyn Alice (Yorath) T.; e. St. Clement's Sch. 1972; Univ. of Toronto, Trinity Coll., B.Comm. 1976; C.A. 1978; CMC 1984; m. William s. William and Edith Orr 8 Sept. 1979; PARTNER, ERNST & YOUNG 1985– ; joined Ernst & Young 1976; Past Pres., Family Serv. Assn. of Metro. Toronto; Past Chrmn., Extve. Ctte. of Corp., Trinity Coll.; Mem., Extve. Ctte. of Pres. Ctte., Univ. of Toronto; Chair, St. Clement's Sch. Found.; Bd. Mem., Orthopaedic and Arthritic Hosp.; Audit Ctte., Baycrest Centre for Geriatric Care; Bd. of Dirs., Conference of Independent Schools; Home: 63 Teddington Park Ave., Toronto, Ont. M4N 2C5; Office: P.O. Box 251, Ernst & Young Tower, Toronto-Dominion Centre, Toronto, Ont. M5K 1J7.

**TOSSELL, William Elwood,** M.S.A., Ph.D.; educator; agronomist; b. Binbrook, Ont. 3 Jan. 1926; s. Franklin Edward and Elizabeth (Shannon) T.; e. Ont. Agric. Coll. (Univ. of Toronto), B.S.A. 1947, M.S.A. 1948; Univ. of Wis., Ph.D. 1953; m. Jean Anne, d. Wilfrid Laurier Callander, 27 Dec. 1947; children: Karen Jean (Mrs. J. Vandergrift), David William, John Franklin; PROF. EMERITUS, UNIV. OF GUELPH 1991– ; joined the Univ. (then Ont. Agric. Coll.) as Lectr. 1948, Asst. Prof. 1950–52, Prof. 1952–91, Chrmn., Crop Science Dept., 1961–66, Assoc. Dean of Coll. 1966–70; Dean of Research for Univ. 1970–85; Dir., Centre for Food Security for Univ. 1987–89; Professor Emeritus 1991– ; Visiting Prof. (Nuffield Fellow), Cambridge Univ., 1973–74; author of over 50 scient. and tech. papers; Internat. Recognition Award, Agricultural Institute of Canada; Hon. Life Mem., Candn. Seed Growers Assn.; mem., Candn. Soc. Agron. (Past Pres.); Candn. Assn. Univ. Research Adms. (Past Pres.); Internat. Center for Tropical Agriculture in Columbia (Past Chrmn. of Bd.); Internat. Plant Genetic Resources Institute in Rome (Chrmn. of Bd.); Ctte. of Bd. Chairs, Consultative Group on Internat. Agric. Rsch. (Past Chrmn.); Dir., Candn. Industrial Innovation Centre, Waterloo; mem., Agric. Inst. Can.; Sigma Xi (Past Pres., Guelph); Baptist; recreations: cottaging, woodwork, antiques; Home: 22 Karen Ave., Guelph, Ont. N1G 2N9.

**TOTEN, John Ernest,** B.A.; economist; banker; b. London, Ont. 4 May 1918; s. late Mabel Winifred (Bugler) and Alfred George T.; e. Univ. of W. Ont. B.A. (Pol. and Econ. Science) 1948; m. Mary R., d. late Andrew Sweeton, Perth County, Ont. 19 Sept. 1942; children: Kenneth, Janet; Retired, Bank of Montreal; joined Bank of Montreal at London, Ont. 1935 (returned after army service and univ.); apptd. Secy. Asst. to the Pres. 1951; a Br. Mgr. in Montreal 1953; in 1955 engaged with Royal Comn. on Canada's Econ. Prospects (compiling survey of Candn. Service Industries); Asst. Mgr., Hamilton, Ont. Br. 1956; Asst. Supt. of W. Credit Dept., at H.O., Montreal 1958; Associate Econ. Advr. 1959, Econ. Advr. 1961, Vice Pres. Planning and Econ. 1965–75, Chief Economist 1975–78, Ret. Vice-Pres. Legisl. & Gov. 1982; served in 2nd World War; enlisted in Royal Candn. Engrs. Sept. 1939; discharged 1945 with rank of Q.M.Sgt.; Vice-Chrmn., Business and Ind. Adv. Comte. to OECD, Paris, France 1982–86; Anglican; Home: 2241 All Saints Cres., Oakville, Ont. L6J 5N1.

**TOTH, Hon. Thomas;** judge; b. Budapest, Hungary 27 June 1925; s. Nicolas and Claire (Czájlik) T.; e. Pères

Piaristes Coll., Budapest, Baccalauréat classique 1943; Univ. of Budapest (Law and Pol. Science) 1943; Univ. of Fribourg (Post-Grad. studies in Law), Dr. Utriusque Iuris 1949; came to Can. 1950; m. Thérèse, d. Arsène Fournier, Granby, Qué., 3 Aug. 1954; children: Marie-José, François; JUSTICE, SUPERIOR COURT QUE. 1971; Pres. (1967–71) Bd. Examiners, Bar of Que.; Pres. (1969–70) Assn. des Avocats du Province de Que.; called to Bar of Que. June 1956; R. Catholic; Office: Court House, 77 Main St., Granby, Que. J2G 9B3.

**TOUPIN, Fernand,** R.C.A.; artiste; né Montréal, Qué. 12 nov. 1930; f. Anatole et Albertine (Lapointe) T.; é. Mont-Saint-Louis Montréal; Ecole des Beaux-Arts de Montréal 1949; étudie la peinture avec Jean-Paul Jérôme 1949–53; ép. Yolande Labelle 28 août 1950; enfants: Pierre (d.), Ginette Toupin-Benoit; expositions personnelles: à Montréal: Galerie Denyse Delrue 1959; Galerie Agnès Lefort 1962; Galerie Camille Hébert 1965; Musée d'art contemporain 1967 (Quinze ans de peinture de Fernand Toupin), 1974; Galerie Gilles Corbeil 1970, 1980; Galerie Bernard Desroches 1974, 1976, 1988, 1990; Place des Arts 1977; Les jeunesses musicales du Can. Mont-Orford, Qué. 1977; Claude Gadoury Art Moderne 1979; Galerie Arnaud Paris 1970, 1972 and 1976; Centre Culturel canadien Paris (Rétrospective) 1972; Galerie Frédéric Palardy, St-Lambert 1979; Galerie Lacerte Guimont, Sillery, 1982; Galerie Frédéric Palardy, St-Lambert 1983, 1986; Musée d'Art de Joliette (Retrospective) 1986; expositions de groupe comprenant Musée des Beaux-Arts de Montréal 1958 (Lauréat du ler prix de cette exposition); Pavillon du Qué. Exposition Universelle d'Osaka 1970; IVe Festival Internat. de Peinture Cagnes-sur-Mer, France 1972 (Lauréat du prix national pour le Can.); Candn. Canvas exposition itinérante de tableaux grands formats dans neuf musées canadiens 1975; Musée d'art contemporain Montréal Jauran et les premiers plasticiens 1977; Internat. Art Exhn. N.Y. 1980; 10 ans de propositions géométriques Musée d'art contemporain 1980; Ouverture du nouveau Musée d'art contemporain de Montréal 1992; Winnipeg Art Gallery 1992; Musée National du Canada, Ottawa 1992; Musée de Québec 1992; collections publiques comprenant Musée du Qué., Galerie nationale du Can., Musée d'art contemporain, Statische Kuntsgalerie Bochum, Allemagne, Centre national d'art contemporain Paris; création de tapisseries, ateliers Pierre Daquin Paris 1970–72; création d'un décor aux Grands Ballets Canadiens 1974, 1977; sérigraphies: 'Errances' album de sept sérigraphies sur des poèmes de Fernand Quellette 1975; 'Prochain Episode' livre d'art comprenant quatorze sérigraphies et une gravure sur le roman d'Hubert Aquin 1978; mem. fondateur du groupe Les Plasticiens et co-signataire du manifeste des Plasticienss1955; Dir. des Expositions au Conseil Exécutif de l'Assn. des artistes non-figuratifs de Montréal 1957–58; mem. Assn. des Artistes Professionnels du Qué.; Opimian Soc.; Addresse: 4175 Deauville St., Terrebonne, Qué. J6X 3E6.

**TOURIGNY, L'Honorable Christine,** B.A., LL.L.; lawyer; b. Quebec City 18 June 1943; d. Emile and Yvette (LeBel) T.; e. Coll. Jesus-Marie de Sillery B.A.; Univ. Laval Fac. de Droit LL.L. 1966; APPT'D TO THE QUEBEC COURT OF APPEAL 1987; APPT'D TO THE SUPERIOR COURT OF QUEBEC 1985; Atty.-at-law with Bard, L'Heureux, Philippon & Tourigny; Philippon, Garneau, Tourigny & Associes; Garneau, Tourigny, Doyon & Guimont 1969–79; Assoc. Sec. Gen. of Exec. Counc. (Status of Women), Govt. of Que. 1979–82; Assoc. Depy. Min. of Justice (Litigation), Govt. of Que., 1982–85; Lectr. Univ. Laval Fac. de Droit (Family Law) 1976, 1978–79; mem. Consultative Ctte. Trust Général du Can. 1979; Dir.: Ecole Nationale d'Admin. Publique 1980–84; Régie du Grand Théatre de Que. 1979–82; CEGEP Francois-Xavier Garneau 1969–72; Centre de Loisirs St. Sacrement 1973–75; Centre Jeunesse de Till 1973–74; mem. Bar of Que. 1967– (and mem. Gen. Counc. 1974); Sec. Que. Bar. Assn. 1974–75; recreations: tennis, golf; Clubs: de Tennis Montcalm; de Golf de Cap Rouge; Home: 910, Gérard-Morisset #506, Quebec, Que. G1S 4V7; Office: 300, boul. Jean-Lesage (R. 457), Quebec, Que. G1K 8K6.

**TOUSIGNANT, Claude,** O.C.; artist; b. Montréal, Qué. 23 Dec. 1932; s. Alberic and Gilberte (Hardy-Lacasse) T.; e. The Montreal Museum of Fine Arts Sch. of Art & Design 1948–51; m. Judith d. Neville and Trudy Terry, Wantage, Berks., Eng.; 2 children: Isa and Zoë; rec'd Candn. Inst. Rome Prize 1973–74; Prix Borduas 1989; Home: 4678 St. André, Montréal, Qué. H2J 3A1; Studio: 181 Bourget St., Montréal, Qué. H4C 2M1.

**TOVELL, Vincent Massey,** M.A., R.C.A.; writer; television producer; b. Toronto, Ont. 29 July 1922; s. Harold Murchison and Ruth Lillian (Massey) T.; e. Crescent Sch. Toronto; Washington Hall Brussels; Upper Can. Coll. Toronto 1940; Univ. of Toronto Schs. 1941; Univ. Coll. Univ. of Toronto B.A. 1945, M.A. 1946; Columbia Univ. 1948–50; Extve. Producer, TV Arts, Music & Science, CBC until 1987; Lectr. in Eng. Univ. Coll. Univ. of Toronto 1946–48; Actor/Dir., New Play Soc. Toronto 1946–48; Dir., Hart House Theatre 1946–48; CBC Radio 1942–48; Radio Producer, Writer, U.N., New York 1950–53 and CBC Radio/TV Producer, Writer U.N., New York 1953–57; TV Producer, Writer and Performer CBC/TV since 1957; lectr. on TV York Univ., Ont. Inst. for Studies in Educ.; various lectures and panel seminars incl. Couchiching Conf.; Chrmn. 25th Anniversary Internat. Seminar Nat. Ballet Co. of Can. 1976, 20th Anniversary Internat. Seminar Nat. Ballet Sch. 1978; Trustee, Art Gallery of Ont. 1961–82; Nat. Ballet Sch. of Can. 1970–80; mem. Nat. Theatre Sch. Montreal; Bd. mem., Glenn Gould Found.; Couchiching Inst. on Public Affairs; Chrmn. Adv. Arts Panel Can. Council 1966–70; Vice Pres. Royal Candn. Acad. Arts 1980–82; co-author 'Success of a Mission: Lord Durham in Canada' (3 TV scripts) 1960; author various theatre reviews, scripts for radio and TV and documentaries; T.V. Producer/Director created 'Images of Canada' CBC TV 1970–76; 'The Masseys' 1978; 'The Owl and the Dynamo: The Vision of George Grant' 1980; 'Fire & Sand: The Mysteries of Glass' 1981; 'Hand and Eye: Seven Hours on Seven Arts' 1982–84; 'Glenn Gould: A Portrait' 1984–85; 'Glenn Gould Plays...' 1986–87; 'Thirty Years of the Nature of Things' 1990; rec'd Centennial Medal 1967; Queen's Silver Jubilee Medal 1978; Gemini Award 1986; mem. Candn. Conf. of Arts (Past Vice Pres.); Candn. Museums Assoc.; Senior Fellow, Massey College, Univ. of Toronto 1985– ; Past Pres. Candn. Soc. of the Decorative Arts; Founding Bd. Mem., The Design Exchange, Toronto; Home: Apt. 701, 190 St. George St., Toronto, Ont. M5R 2N4.

**TOWE, Peter Milburn,** M.A.; executive; b. London, Ont. 1 Nov. 1922; s. Allen Milburn and Clare (Durdle) T.; e. Univ. of W. Ont., B.A. (Econ.); Queen's Univ. M.A. (Econ.); Hon. LL.D. Univ. of W. Ont. 1981; m. Carol, d. Walter Krumm, Sioux City, Iowa, 2 Aug. 1953; children: Christopher, Fredericka, Jennifer; Sr. Adviser, International Affairs, Petro-Canada 1991; served with Dept. of External Affairs, 1947–81 in Washington, Bonn, Beirut, Paris (OECD); Depy. Dir. Gen., External Aid Office (now Candn. Internat. Devel. Agency) 1962–67; Min., Candn. Embassy, Washington, D.C. 1967–72; Ambassador and Perm. Rep. to OECD, Paris 1972–75; Asst. Under-Secy. of State for External Affairs 1975–77; Ambassador to U.S.A. 1977–81; Chrmn., Petro-Canada International Assistance Corp. 1981–91; served overseas as an Offr. with R.C.A.F. Bomber Command, 1942–45; recreations: golf, fishing; Clubs: Royal Ottawa Golf; Five Lakes; Home: 32 Charles St., Ottawa, Ont. K1M 1R2.

**TOWERS, George Hugh Neil,** M.Sc., Ph.D., F.L.S., F.R.S.C.; educator; b. Bombay, India 28 Sept. 1923; s. George William and Kathleen (Thompson) T.; e. McGill Univ. M.Sc. 1951; Cornell Univ. Ph.D. (Bot.) 1954; m. 1stly Lorna Lynn 8 Dec. 1944; m. 2ndly Elizabeth Gonzales d. Guadalupe and Marie Gonzales 28 Dec. 1982; children: Christopher, Cedric, Charles, Kathleen, Jane, Neil, Thomas, Lily Elena; PROF. OF BOTANY, UNIV. OF B.C. 1964– ; Assoc. Prof. of Bot. McGill Univ. 1953–62; Rsch. Assoc. Nat. Rsch. Council Can. Ottawa 1954, Saskatoon 1958, Sr. Rsch. Offr. 1962–64; Head of Bot. present Univ. 1964–70; Visiting Prof., Hungarian Acad. of Sciences 1970; Commonwealth Visiting Prof. Univ. of East Anglia 1970–71; Killam Fellow 1970–71; Visiting Scientist, Indian Inst. of Sci., Bangalore 1975; Special Killam Sr. Rsch. Scholarship 1975–76; mem., a-Helix Expedition to the Amazon 1976; Visiting Lectr. and Cons., Univ. of Khartoum and Univ. of Juba, Sudan 1981; Distinguished Prof., Instituo Technologico y Estudios Superiores de Monterrey, Mexico 1983; Visiting Scientist, Univ. of Tripoli, Libya 1984; Visiting Erskine Fellow, Univ. of Canterbury, Christchurch, N.Z. 1988; recipient Candn. Soc. Plant Physiols. Gold Medal 1973; Flavelle Medal, Royal Soc. of Canada 1986; Special Killam Sr. Rsch. Scholarship 1975–76, 1987–88; invited lectr. N. and S. Am., Europe, Australia, China, India, Japan, Africa, W. Indies phytochem. topics; author or co-author over 330 rsch. publs.; Assoc. Ed. 'Phytochemistry'; mem. various ed. bds.; Life Mem., Phytochem. Soc. N.Am. (Pres. 1974, 1986–87); Pres., Candn. Soc. Plant Physiols. 1965–66; mem., Am. Soc. of Photobiology; Am. Soc. Pharmacognosy; Phytochem. Soc. Europe; recreations: classical guitar, tennis, raquetball, gardening, travel; Home: 3874 W. 13th Ave., Vancouver, B.C. V6R 2S8; Office: Dept. of Botany, Univ. of B.C., 6270 University Blvd., Vancouver, B.C. V6T 1Z4.

**TOWERS, The Hon. Gordon,** LL.D., K.St.J.; lieutenant governor of Alberta; b. Red Deer, Alta. 5 July 1919; s. Thomas Henry and Janet (Morrison) T.; e. at Willowdale; Univ. of Alberta LL.D. 1992; m. Doris Roberta d. R.J. Nicholson 27 Dec. 1940; children: Thomas Robert, Gary Lee, Lynda Marie, Ross Gordon, Leona; SWORN IN AS LIEUTENANT GOVERNOR OF ALBERTA 11 MARCH 1991; Cand. to the H. of C. g.e. 1963 and 1965 (defeated); 1st elected to the H. of C. ge. 1972; re-elected g.e. 1974, 1979, 1980, 1984; apptd. Deputy Critic Veterans Affairs 1984; Parl. Sec. to Solicitor Gen. & to Min. of State for Science & Technol.; Deleg. to U.N. Gen. Assembly 1978; Deleg., Candn. Br., Commonwealth Parl. Assn., 29th Parl., Westminster 1980; a farmer involved in the Red Deer farming community throughout his career; patron of num. assns.; Past Pres., Red Deer Exhbn. Assn.; Prairie Fairs Assn.; Red Deer 4-H Council; River Glen Home & School Assn.; Deputy Grand Master & Grand Master, Red Deer Dist. Ancient Order of Free & Accepted Masons 1963–64, 1967–68; Chancellor of the Alberta Order of Excellence; K.St.J.; Paul Harris Fellow, Rotary Internat. 1989; Citizen of the Year, Red Deer C. of C. 1990; Presbyn.; Home: 58 St. Georges Cres., Edmonton, Alta.; Office: 3rd Floor, Legislative Bldg., Edmonton, Alta. T5K 2B6.

**TOWLE, Roderick M.L.,** B.A., C.A., M.B.A.; accountant; b. Montreal, Que. 2 Oct. 1941; s. Roderick Duerst and Frances Mary (Lamb) T.; e. Univ. of N.B. B.A. 1965; Inst. of C.A.s of Quebec (McGill Univ.) C.A. 1968; Univ. of Western Ont. M.B.A. 1970; m. Maryl d. Richard and Gladys Reeves 28 June 1975; PRESIDENT, JAYTOWL INC. 1980– ; Budget and Forecast Administrator, Nordair Ltd. 1970; Manager, Aircraft Services 1972; Asst. Treas. 1974; Vice Pres., Finance 1974; Vice Pres., Finance & Secretary 1978; Mem., Order of C.A.s of Que.; Financial Extves. Inst. of Canada; clubs: Montreal Amateur Athletic Assn., Royal Montreal Golf Club; Home: 1017 Habitat '67, Montreal, Que. H3C 3R6; Office: 2060 Drummond St., Ste. 300, Montreal, Que. H3G 1W9.

**TOWNSEND, G. Leigh,** B.Com., M.B.A., C.A.; consultant; b. Charlottetown, P.E.I. 2 Sept. 1932; s. late William Arthur and Edna Jane (Cloutier) T.; e. Sir George Williams Univ., B.Com. 1961, Business Adm. 1962; C.A. 1964; m. Phyllis Earla, d. late Alfred Newbatt, 22 Dec. 1956; children: Bruce, Brian, Cynthia, Barry; PRES., CONCEPT AUTO G.L.T. INC. 1992– ; Concept Auto P.E.T. Inc. 1992– ; Concept Cellulaire Plus G.L.T. Inc. 1992– ; Leigh Townsend Consultants Inc. 1990– ; Pres., Leigh Townsend Business Expertise Inc. 1990– ; Supvr., Dupont of Canada 1954–63; Mgr., McDonald, Currie & Co. 1964, Extve. Vice Pres., Credico 1966; Pres., Vilas Industries Ltd. 1968–78; Pres. Consolidex Inc., 1978–80; Gen. Mgr., South Shore Ind. Ltd. 1980–89; mem. Order C.A.'s Que.; Que. Furniture Mfg. Assn. (Pres.); Conseil du Patronat du Que. (Dir.); recreations: flying, boating, skiing; Home: 743 Le Payeur, Ste-Foy, Que. G1X 3K2.

**TOYE, William Eldred,** C.M.; editor; b. Toronto, Ont. 19 June 1926; s. Eldred Dalston and Clarenda (Steenson) T.; e. North Toronto Collegiate; Victoria Coll, Univ. Toronto, B.A.; Editorial Dir., Oxford Univ. Press Can. 1969–91; retired; joined Oxford Univ. Press Can. 1948, became Trade Ed. 1963; author: 'The St. Lawrence,' 1959; 'Cartier Discovers the St. Lawrence,' 1970; 'How Summer Came to Canada,' 1969; 'The Mountain Goats of Temlaham,' 1969; 'The Loon's Necklace,' 1977; 'The Fire Stealer,' 1979; editor: 'A Book of Canada,' 1962; 'Supplement to the Oxford Companion to Canadian History and Literature,' 1973; 'The Oxford Companion to Canadian Literature,' 1983; founding ed. The Tamarack Review (1956–82); co-ed. (with Robert Weaver) 'The Oxford Anthology of Canadian Literature,' 1973 (2nd ed. 1982); co-ed. (with Matie Molinaro & Corinne McLuhan) 'Letters of Marshall McLuhan' 1987; winner, 2 Book-of-the-Year medals from Candn. Assn. Children's Librarians: for 'The St. Lawrence,' 1959; 'Cartier Discovers the St. Lawrence,' 1970; Vicky Metcalf Award (Candn. Author's Assn.) 1972; I.O.D.E. Book Award 1978; Eve Orpen Award for Publishing Excellence 1981; Mem., Order of Canada 1994; Pres., Soc. Typographic Designers Can. (now Graphic Designers Can.) 1961–63; mem., PEN Internat., Candn. Centre; Club: Royal Candn. Yacht; Home: 139 Collier St., Toronto, Ont. M4W 1M2.

**TOZER, Edward Timothy,** C.M., M.A., Ph.D., F.G.S., F.G.S.A., F.G.A.C., F.R.S.C.; geologist; b. England 13 Jan. 1928; s. Alfred and Olive Vera (Bicknell) T.; e. Cambridge Univ., B.A. 1948, M.A. 1952; Univ. of Toronto, Ph.D. 1952; m. Ruth Jane d. Keith A.B. Wilson, Sussex, Eng., 7 Oct. 1958; children: Paul Alfred,

Sally Jane; SENIOR RESEARCH SCIENTIST, GEOLOGICAL SURVEY OF CANADA, NATURAL RESOURCES CANADA; Lectr. in Geol., Univ. of W. Ont. 1948–52; with Geol. Surv. of Canada since 1952; Author of about 30 reports published by the Geol. Surv. of Canada and about 30 articles in scientific journals on geology of Canadian Arctic Islands, Triassic Ammonoidea and biochronology; awarded Founders Medal, Royal Geographical Soc., 1969; Willet G. Miller Medal, Royal Soc. of Canada, 1979; Billings Medal, Geological Assn. of Canada, 1989; Mem., Order of Canada 1994; recreations: sailing, skiing; Home: 4476 West First Ave., Vancouver, B.C. V6R 4J4.

**TRABANDT, Joachim,** LL.D., B.Sc. (Econ.); executive; b. Ruegenwalde, Germany 14 Dec. 1935; s. Paul and Charlotte (Ziebell) T.; e. Katharineum zu Luebeck (Coll.) 1956; Univ. of Hamburg Law Degree 1962; Faculté Internationale de Droit Comparé, Strasbourg, France, Diplôme de Droit Comparé 1963 and Diplôme de Droit Européen; University of Hamburg Doctorate in Law 1971; Univ. of London B.Sc. (Econ.) 1972; m. Hanna M. Wulf 6 June 1961; two s. Jorg Joachim, Jan Uwe; PRESIDENT AND DIR., TRAFOR CORPORATION and QUADRA INTERNATIONAL S.A.; Commissioner for Oaths and Affidavits; Apprentice, Feder & Berg Export House, Hamburg 1956; Deutsche Bundesbank, 1963; Asst. to the Bd. Gerling-Konzern Globale, Cologne 1966; Asst. Mgr. Gerling Global Reinsurance Co. Ltd. London, Eng. 1967; Mgr. Gerling Insurance Service Co. Ltd. London 1969; Direktor, Concordia Lebensvers. A. G., Cologne 1970; Gen. Mgr. and Chief Agt. for Can. Concordia Life Insurance Co. Toronto 1971; Pres., Colonia Life Ins. Co. and Colonia Life Holdings Ltd., 1977; Past Dir., Candn.-German Chamber Indust. & Comm.; German-Candn. Business & Prof. Assn.; mem., Mensa; Schlaraffia; recreations: sports, boating, reading; Office: 225 Davisville, Toronto, Ont. M4S 1G9.

**TRAHAN, Anne-Marie,** B.A., LL.L., Q.C.; lawyer; b. Montréal, Qué. 27 July 1946; d. Marcel and Émélie (Bourbonnière) T.; c. Coll. Marie-de-France, B.A. 1964; Univ. of Montréal, LL.L. 1967; admitted to Qué. Bar 1968; ASSOC. DEPY. MIN. CIVIL LAW AND LEGISLATIVE SERVICES OF JUSTICE, GOVT. OF CAN. 1986– ; law practice, Lavery, De Billy 1968–79; Legal Offr., Un. Nations, Vienna 1979–81; Comnr., Candn. Transp. Comn. 1981–86 (Chrmn., Water Transp. Ctte. 1984–86; Joint Govt. & Indus. Task Force to study bias Candn. airlines Computer Reserv. Systems 1984–85); Lectr., Univ. of Montréal, McGill Univ., Qué. Real Estate Assn.; Profl. Sch., Qué. Bar; Qué. Bar Prize for Comml. Law 1967; Great Montrealer of the future in the field of Law 1983; Q.C. 1983; certificat de l'Association des diplômés de l'V. de M. le 30.10.92; recipient, 125th Anniversary of the Confederation of Canada Medal, 1992; Mem., Bar of Montréal and of Hull; Qué. Bar; Candn. Bar; Internat. Assn. of Young Lawyers (Pres. 1977–78; Hon. Pres. 1979– ); Internat. Bar Assn.; mem. Sect. Counc., Sect. on Gen. Practice 1988–92); Internat. Union of Lawyers; mem., Comité consultatif relatif aux contrats de vente et d'échange du projet de recherche sur les contrats internationaux & le droit civil du Québec; mem. of Bd. of Govs., UNIDROIT 1988–93; Vice-Pres., Uniform Law Conference of Can.; mem. Comité de patronage of the Centre Internat. de Common Law en français, Moncton; nominated by Canada on the list of persons who can be apptd. under the CSCE Procedure for Peaceful Settlement of Disputes; Ctte. Dir., Centre de recherche en droit public of the Univ. of Montréal; Mem. Bd. of Dirs., Candn. Inst. for Advanced Legal Studies; Hon. Vice-Pres., Assn. Canada-France, of Ottawa; Candn. Fed. of Univ. Women; has held num. past extve. positions in above assns.; Roman Catholic; recreations: reading, opera, hiking; Home: 110, chemin du Château – #2309, Hull, Qué. J9A 1T4; Office: 239 Wellington St., #250, Ottawa, Ont. K1A 0H8.

**TRAINOR, Lynn E.H.,** M.A., Ph.D.; educator; b. Chamberlain, Sask. 4 Dec. 1921; s. Anthony Reginald and Aline Marguerite (Souply) T.; e. Univ. of Sask. B.A. 1946, M.A. 1947; Univ. of Minn. Ph.D. 1951; m. Anne d. Frank and Marguerite Fidler 7 July 1984; children (from previous marriage to Helen Dixon Trainor): Patricia, Laurel, Charles; PROF. OF PHYSICS, UNIV. OF TORONTO 1963– ; Teacher, Valor, Sask. 1940–42; Nat. Rsch. Council Postdoctoral Fellow 1952–53; Asst. Prof. Queen's Univ. 1952–55; Assoc. Prof. Univ. of Alta. 1956, Prof. 1963; Visiting Prof. Univ. of B.C. 1955–56, Univ. of Sussex 1977, Oxford Univ. 1984, 1987, 1992; Lady Davis Fellow Technion, Israel 1976; Trustee, N. York Bd. Edn. 1969–76, Chrmn. 1970–72, 1973–74; Trustee, Metro Toronto Bd. Edn. 1970–74, 1975–76; Hon. mem. Theoretical Physics Inst. Univ. of Alta.; mem. Bd. Toronto Montessori Schs.; Co-Chrmn. Hiroshima-Nagasaki Relived; Dir., Allergy and Environmental Health Assoc. of Ont.; co-author 'From Physical Concept to Mathematical Structure: An Introduction to Theoretical Physics' 1979; mem., Candn. Assn. Physicists (Nat. Sec. 1967–71); Am. Physical Soc.; Science for Peace; Pugwash Canada; recreations: music, art, drama, farming; Home: 281 Briar Hill Ave., Toronto, Ont. M4R 1J3; Office: 60 St George St., Toronto, Ont. M5S 1A7.

**TRAINOR, Hon. Richard Gerald,** Q.C.; judge; b. Star City, Sask. 8 July 1930; s. Martin Gerald and Bertha May (McKenna) T.; e. St. Thomas Sch. and Sudbury (Ont.) High Sch. 1950; Univ. of Toronto 1953; Osgoode Hall Law Sch. Toronto 1958; m. Jacqueline St. Denis 24 Sept. 1955; children: Patricia, Therese, Martin, Jackie May, Susan, Jennifer; Apptd. REGIONAL SENIOR JUSTICE OF THE ONTARIO COURT OF JUSTICE (GENERAL DIVISION), METROPOLITAN TORONTO REGION Sept. 1st 1990– ; called to Bar of Ont. 1958; cr. Q.C. 1974; Judge, Supreme Court of Ontario 1979–90; R. Catholic; Home: 2170 Marine Dr., #1407, Oakville, Ont.; Office: Osgoode Hall, 130 Queen St. W., Toronto, Ont. M5H 2N5.

**TRAINOR, Hon. William Joseph,** B.Sc., LL.B.; judge; b. Peace River, Alta. 11 Jan. 1923; e. Peace River Pub. and High Schs. 1939; Vermilion (Alta.) Sch. of Agric. 1939–40; Univ. of Alta. B.Sc. 1943; Univ. of B.C. LL.B. 1950; m. Gwendolyn Elizabeth Williams, Halifax, N.S. 1945; children: Michael, Brian, Monica, Niall, Christine; JUDGE, SUPREME COURT OF B.C. 1977; called to Bar of B.C. 1951, NWT 1971; cr. Q.C. 1972; Devel. Engr., Canadian Marconi Co., Montreal 1943–47; law practice Vancouver 1951–63; Police Magistrate and Judge of Juvenile Court – Y.T., Dist. Magistrate of Prov. Court B.C. 1963–68; Sr. Adv. Counsel, Dept. of Justice Ottawa 1968–73; Judge, Co. Court of Vancouver 1973, Sr. Judge 1975; Judge, Court Martial Appeal Court 1979; Lib. Cand. Burnaby-Richmond Riding Fed. g.e. 1962, 1963; R. Catholic; Home: 3416 Cedar Cres., Vancouver, B.C. V6J 2R3; Office: Law Courts, 800 Smithe St., Vancouver, B.C. V6Z 2E1.

**TRÄSS, Olev,** B.S.E., Sc.D., F.C.I.C., P.Eng.; educator; b. Estonia 9 Oct. 1931; s. Aleksander and Adele (Poksi) T.; e. Kungsholmens h.a.l. Stockholm Studentexamen 1951; Princeton Univ. B.S.E. 1955; Mass. Inst. of Technol. Sc.D. 1958; Doctor Honoris Causa, Univ. Rerum Technicarum Tallinensis 1993; m. Elvi d. Leon and Edna Jürisson 14 Jan. 1961; children: Ulle-Merike, Toivo; PROF. OF CHEM. ENG. AND APPLIED CHEM., UNIV. OF TORONTO 1968– ; Asst. Prof. present Univ. 1958, Assoc. Prof. 1962, Assoc. Chrmn. Div. Eng. Sci. 1974–77, Speaker Faculty Council 1978–82; Dir. and Cons. Chemical Engineering Research Consultants Ltd. 1963– ; Dir. and Vice Pres. General Comminution Inc. 1975–86, Dir. and Chrmn. 1986– ; Dir., FRC Composites Ltd. and Tapecrete Ltd. 1975– ; former Dir. Esto Mutual Fund Ltd. and Esto Management Co. Ltd. 1969–87; Grimms Foods Ltd. 1982–89; Visiting Prof. Eidgenossische Technische Hochschule Zurich 1968–69; Ecole National Superieur des Industries Chimiques 1978; Dir. Tartu Inst. 1969–83, Dir. & Pres. 1983– ; Dir. Tartu Coll. 1979–87 (alternate yrs.), Dir. & Vice Pres., 1987– ; Pres., Free Estonian Publishers Ltd. 1983–93; Dir. & Treas., Univ. of Tartu Fund 1988– ; Dir. Chair Estonian Studies Found. 1983– ; Founder & Chrmn. Estonian Forest Univ. Muskoka 1967–72, 1985– ; mem., Estonian Central Council in Canada 1960–70 (Vice-Chrmn. 1966–68); author or co-author over 110 publs. transp. phenomena, coal technol., comminution; Patents: (assigned to Univ. of Toronto) 'Method of Separating Solids by Simultaneous Comminution and Agglomeration' USA Patent No. 4,730,783 (1988), Candn. Patent No. 1,249,986 (1989), Australia (1989), Belgium, France, Germany, India, Italy, Netherlands, Sweden and U.K. (1990), pending in Japan; (assigned to General Comminution Inc.) 'Multiple Stage Comminution Device' Can. Patent No. 1,134,336 (1982), Belgium, Finland, France, Italy, Netherlands, S. Africa, Sweden, Germany, U.K. (1981–86) and Japan (1989); Fellow, Chem. Inst. Can.; mem. Candn. Soc. Chem. Eng.; Am. Inst. Chem. Engs.; Am. Chem. Soc.; Fine Particle Soc.; Assn. Profl. Engs. Prov. Ont.; Assn. Advanc. Baltic Studies (Chrmn. Candn. Ctte. 1972–83); Estonian Soc. Toronto (Pres. 1960–64); Chrmn., League of Estonian Fraternities in Canada 1961–62, 1969–70; Alumnus mem., Fraternitas Liviensis (Chrmn. Candn. Section 1961– ; Mem., Phi Beta Kappa (academic); Sigma Xi (scientific); Phi Lambda Upsilon (chemistry); recreations: swimming, skiing, reading; Home: 4 Conrad Ave., Toronto, Ont. M6G 3G5; Office: Toronto, Ont. M5S 1A4.

**TRAVERS, Brian Claude,** B.Comm., C.A., C.M.C.; chartered accountant; b. Montreal, Que. 4 Sept. 1944; s. Claude Douglas Roy and Margaret Shaw (Gittus) T.; e. Lachine H.S. 1961; Carleton Univ. B.Comm. 1965; m. E. Diane d. Hazel and Gordon Gibson 27 July 1968; children: Andrew David Douglas, Heather Leanne; PARTNER, ERNST & YOUNG, EDMONTON 1990– ; Student, McDonald Currie & Co. 1965–69; Controller, Lab Volt Limited 1969–70; C.A., Coopers & Lybrand 1970–74; Partner in Charge of the Ottawa Office, Laventhol & Howarth 1974–76; Partner, Ernst & Ernst Ottawa 1976; Edmonton 1979; Partner in Charge, Corp. Adv. Services, Thorne Ernst & Whinney 1986–90; Mem., Office of the Auditor Gen. of Canada on Executive Interchange (participant, Financial Management Control Study 1974, '75 and Principal 1978, '79); Communications Ctte., Inst. of C.A.s of Alta. 1987–89; Bd. of Gov., Centre Club; Dir. & Treas., Edmonton Opera; Mem., Presidents Adv. Ctte., Carleton Univ.; Inst. of C.A.s of Alta.; Inst. of Mngt. Consultants of Alta.; Treas., Manotick United Ch. 1973–78; Mem., St. Pauls Un. Ch. Finance Ctte. 1980, '81; Dir., Manotick Kiwanis Club 1978–79; recreations: golf skiing; clubs: Centre, Derrick Golf & Winter; Home: 2823, 118th St., Edmonton, Alta. T6J 3R1; Office: 1800 Esso Tower, Scotia Place, 10060 Jasper Ave., Edmonton, Alta. T5J 3R8.

**TRAVES, Thomas Donald,** B.A., M.A., Ph.D.; university professor; administrator; b. Winnipeg, Man. 5 June 1948; s. Samuel and Marjorie (Kay) T.; e. Univ. of Man, B.A. 1970; York Univ., M.A. 1971, Ph.D. 1976; m. Karen d. Ben and Leah Posner 1970; children: William, Julie; VICE PRES. (ACADEMIC) and PROF. DEPT. OF HISTORY, UNIV. OF NEW BRUNSWICK 1991– ; Lectr., York Univ. 1974; Asst. Prof. 1976; Assoc. Prof. 1976–91; Chrmn., Div. of Soc. Sci. 1981–83; Dean, Faculty of Arts 1983–91; Mem., Ont. Crown Empl. Grievance Settlement Bd. 1982–91; Chrmn., Ont. Counc. of Deans of Arts & Sci. 1985–87; Mem., N.B. Minister's Council on Education; author: 'The State and Enterprise' 1979, 'Essays in Canadian Business History' 1984; Home: 89 Kingswood Dr., Fredericton, N.B. E3B 6Z8; Office: P.O. Box 4400, Fredericton, N.B. E3B 5A3.

**TRAVIS, Vance Kenneth;** executive; b. Coriander, Sask. 30 Jan. 1926; s. Roy Hazen and Etta Orilla (Anderson) T.; e. Westglen High Sch. Edmonton; Business Coll. Edmonton; m. Mildred Elaine d. Stanley and Florence Webber 29 June 1979; children: Stuart, Gordon, Donald, Shirley, Marian; stepchildren: Susan, Nancy, Gordon, Sandra, Karen; Pres., Beaver Geophysical Services Ltd. 1954–71; Drilling Fluid Services Ltd. 1956–68; Oilex Industries Ltd. 1973–76; Chrmn., Turbo Resources Ltd. 1970–83; Challenger International Services Ltd. 1977–83; Bankeno Mines Ltd. 1977–83; Queenston Gold Mines Ltd. 1977–83; Triad International Inc. 1985– ; Dir., Health Risk Management, Inc. 1984– (Chrmn. 1984–86); recipient Petroleum Fastball League Best Pitcher Award; Jr. Achievement S. Alta. Presidential Pin; Past Chapter Chrmn. Young Pres. Organ.; mem., World Presidents Organization; Un. Appeal; cubs and scouts; recreations: music, sports, hiking, travel; Clubs: Calgary Petroleum; Ranchmen's; Home: #2310 – 720 – 13th Ave. S.W., Calgary, Alta. T2R 1M5; Office: #200 4600 – 5th St. N.E., Calgary, Alta. T2E 7C3.

**TREDGETT, Roy Gordon,** B.A.Sc., P.Eng.; executive; b. Toronto, Ont. 20 July 1925; s. Frank and Lucy (Cruikshank) T.; e. Public and High Schs. Toronto; Univ. of Toronto, B.A.Sc. 1947, Advanced Structural Hons. 1947; m. April, d. George Wilen 12 Oct. 1962; children: David, Judith, Martha, Mark, Jonathan; CONSULTING ENGINEER; joined Proctor & Redfern Inc., 1947, retired as Dir., Pres. & Gen. Mgr. 1980; Am. Water Works Assn.; Candn. Inst. Pollution Control; Assn. Prof. Engrs. Ont.; Cons. Engr. designate, Consulting Engrs. Ont.; recreation: golf; Club: Thornhill Golf & Country; Home: 82 Highland Cres., Willowdale, Ont. M2L 1G9.

**TRELEAVEN, Richard Lloyd,** Q.C., B.A., LL.B.; barrister and solicitor; former member of provincial parliament; b. Goderich, Ont. 11 July 1934; s. Richard Lane and Ena Rachel Arabella (Switzer) T.; e. Univ. of West. Ont., B.A. 1956; Osgoode Hall Law Sch., Barrister-at-Law 1960; m. Donna d. Roy and Kathleen Bean 11 Aug. 1957; children: Christine Gail, Richard Lane, Patricia Marena, Janine Elizabeth, Angus Roy; Depy. Speaker & Chrmn. of the Committees of the Whole House of Ont. Legislature 1985–87; Partner, Treleaven, Graham, White, Coad & Patience 1960–80; elected Prog., Cons. M.P.P. 1981; re-elected 1985; defeated 1987; Chrmn., Standing Ctte. on Justice 1981–83; on Procedural Affairs 1983–85; Trustee, Oxford County Bd. of Education; Pres., Vice-Pres., Dir. & Mem. of many

Woodstock & Oxford Co. serv. clubs & charitable & athletic orgns.; Mem., Un. Ch. of Can.; Clubs: Woodstock Curling, Wellington-Waterloo Hunt, Standardbred Breeder & Farmer; Home: R.R. 4, Woodstock, Ont. N4S 7V8.

**TRELEAVEN, Wesley Allan,** B.Comm., C.A.; business executive; b. Toronto, Ont. 29 Sept. 1949; s. Allan Wesley and Beatrice Maud (Clark) T.; e. Queen's Univ., B.Comm. 1972; C.A. (Ont.) 1974; m. Lorraine d. Don and Isabel Clemes 30 Sept. 1972; children: David, Ryan; PARTNER, DELOITTE & TOUCHE AND SENIOR VICE-PRES. OF DELOITTE & TOUCHE INC. 1990– ; joined Clarkson Gordon 1972; C.A. 1974; trans. to Clarkson Gordon Inc. 1975; apptd. Mgr. 1976; Trustee's Licence (for bankruptcy practice) 1980; Partner, Clarkson Gordon, and Vice-Pres., Clarkson Gordon Inc. 1981; Exec. Vice-Pres., Caravan Trailer Rental Co. Ltd. & Trailerent Mfg. Ltd. 1987–90; Pres., Caravan Fin. Corp. 1987–90; Past Lectr., York Univ.; Past Dir. and Treas., Children's Aid Soc. of Metrop. Toronto; Past Pres., C.M. Hincks Treatment Centre; mem. Toronto Bd. of Trade; recreations: golf, sailing; Clubs: Cedar Brae Golf & Country; Toronto Cricket; Office: 390 Bay St., Suite 2400, Toronto, Ont. M5H 2Y2.

**TREMAINE, Scott Duncan,** B.Sc., M.A., Ph.D.; professor; b. Toronto, Ont. 25 May 1950; s. Vincent Joseph and Beatrice Delphine (Sharp) T.; e. McMaster Univ., B.Sc. 1971; Princeton Univ., M.A. 1973, Ph.D. 1975; DIR., CANDN. INST. FOR THEORETICAL ASTROPHYSICS, UNIV. OF TORONTO 1985– ; Rsch. Fellow, Cal. Tech. 1975–77; Rsch. Assoc., Cambridge Inst. of Astron. 1977–78; Long-Term Mem., Princeton Inst. for Adv. Study 1978–81; Assoc. Prof., Physics, M.I.T. 1981–85; Prof., Univ. of Toronto 1985– ; Albert Einstein Prof., Inst. for Adv. Study 1983; Morris Loeb Lectureship, Harvard Univ. 1988; Alfred P. Sloan Fellow; Helen B. Warner prize of Am. Astron. Soc. 1983; E.W.R. Steacie Fellowship 1988; Steacie Prize 1989; Carlyle S. Beals Award of Candn. Astronomical Soc. 1990; Rutherford Medal in Physics 1990; Foreign Hon. Mem., Am. Acad. of Arts and Sciences 1992; Office: C.I.T.A., McLennan Labs., Univ. of Toronto, Toronto, Ont. M5S 1A7.

**TREMBLAY, A. Rodrigue,** B.Sc.A.; land surveyor; b. St-Paul du Nord, Qué. 28 Apr. 1939; s. Emile Charles and Calixte (Emond) T.; e. Univ. Laval B.Sc.A. 1965; m. Yvette d. Robert Emond 13 July 1968; children: Hugues, Pierre-Yves, Mélanie; R. TREMBLAY & ASSOCIÉS 1972– ; Pres. Service Multidisciplinaires Sodex Ltée; joined Aero-Photo, Qué. 1965; Candn. Tech. Asst. Lagos, Nigeria 1966; Samson, Tremblay & Associates, Qué. 1967–68, 1970–71; Service Photogrammétrie, cartographie Gouvernement du Qué. 1969; Trustee, Nat. Museums Can. 1984–90; Vice-Chrmn., Candn. Museum of Nature; Corp. de L'Hopital de Sept-Iles; mem. Ordre des Arpenteurs-géomètres du Qué.; Canada Land Surveyor Assn.; Assn. Canadienne des sciences Géodésiques; Assn. Québécoise d'Urbanisme; Société Historique Côte-Nord; Institut Canadien Affaires Internationales; Clubs: Ski Gallix; Richelieu; Home: 614, Franquelin, Sept-Iles, Qué G4R 2M3; Office: 522, avenue Brochu, Sept-Iles, Qué. G4R 2X3.

**TREMBLAY, André-Marie,** Ph.D.; university professor; b. Montréal, Qué. 2 Jan. 1953; d. Emile and Marie-Anna (Lépine) T.; e. Univ. de Montréal, B.Sc. 1974; Mass. Inst. of Technol., Ph.D. 1978; m. Guylaine s. Guy and Jane Séguin 26 Dec. 1975; children: Noémie and Rachel Séguin-Tremblay; PROF., UNIV. DE SHERBROOKE 1988– ; summer stud., Atomic Energy of Canada 1973, 74; Hydro Qué. 1975; Teaching Asst., MIT 1975; post-doct. fellow, Cornell Univ. 1978–80; Asst. Prof. (NSERC), Univ. de Sherbrooke 1980–84, Assoc. Prof. 1984–88; Full Prof. 1988– ; Assoc. Prof., Univ. de Provence (France) Jan. 1982, May-June 1983; Invited Sci., Brookhaven Nat. Lab (NY) Aug. 1984; Vis. Sci., C.R.T.B.T. Grenoble June 1985; Cornell Univ., Sept. 1986–Aug. 1987; I.T.P. Santa Barbara 1989; recipient, Herzberg Medal 1986; E.W.R. Steacie Fellowship 1987–88; Assoc., Candn. Institute of Advanced Research 1988– ; Killam Fellowship 1992–94; Dir., Centre de recherche en physique du solide 1991– ; Mem., Candn. Assn. of Physicists; Am. Physical Soc.; Union of Concerned Sci.; Amnesty Internat.; author/co-author of about 80 sci. pubs.; recreations: swimming, piano; Home: 1179 Portland, Sherbrooke, Qué. J1H 1J1; Office: Dépt. de physique, Univ. de Sherbrooke, Qué. J1K 2R1.

**TREMBLAY, Hon. Arthur,** O.C., O.Q., M.A., M.Ed.; senator; b. St. Bruno, Qué. 18 June 1917; s. Édouard and Flore (Girard) T.; e. Laval Univ., B.A. 1937, M.A. 1942; Harvard Univ., M.Ed. 1945; Univ. of Paris 1949–51; m. Pauline d. Vincent Dubuc 27 May 1944; children: Suzanne, Simon-Pierre; Co-Founder, Laval Inst. Vocational Guidance 1941, Asst. Dir., Laval Univ. Teacher's Sch. 1945, Prof. 1949; Special Adv. Min. of Youth Qué. 1960–64; Dep. Min. of Edn. 1964–69; Pres. and Dir. Gen., Qué. Planning & Devel. Bureau 1969–72; Dep. Min. Intergovt'al Affairs 1971–77; Lectr. Ecole nationale d'adm. publique Univ. of Qué. 1977–79; summoned to Senate of Can. 1979; Special Adv. to Prime Min. Constitutional Affairs & Fed.-Prov. Relations 1984; mem. Special Jt. Ctte. Senate & H. of C. Constitution of Can. 1980–81; Special Senate Ctte. Senate Reform 1983–85; Pres. Senate Ctte. Social Affairs, Sci. & Tech. 1984–88; Co-Chrmn. Special Jt. Ctte. Senate & H. of C. 1987 Constitutional Accord; Retired from Senate June 1992; Apptd. to Privy Council July 1992; Founding mem. and Vice Pres. Qué. Edn. Assn. 1957–60; Assoc. mem. Royal Comn. Edn. 1961–64; mem. Royal Soc. Can.; author several books and numerous articles; P. Conservative; R. Catholic; Hon. Doctorate, Univ. of Sherbrooke 1976; Hon. Doctorate, Univ. of Qué. 1977; Hon. Doctorate, York Univ. 1978; Hon. Doctorate, Univ. of Waterloo 1983; Hon. Doctorate, Laval Univ. 1989; Hon. Doctorate, Montreal Univ. 1990; Officer of the Order of Canada 1976; Recipient of the Édouard Montpetit Medal 1988; Officer of the Ordre national du Québec 1991; Home: 115 Laurier Ave., Québec, Qué. G1R 2K8.

**TREMBLAY, Edmond-Louis;** industrial executive; b. Metabetchouan, Que. 4 March 1935; s. Louis and Albertine (Simard) T.; c. Coll. Candn. des Travailleurs; Univ. de Montréal 1966; m. Madeleine d. Osias and Bernadette Lalancette 22 June 1957; children: Mario, Jocelyn, Serge, Stephane, Nathalie; PRES., LAR MACHINERIE (1983) INC. 1983– ; Prés., Gestion Immobiliere Mbel Inc. 1987– ; Lar Machinerie Matagami 1988– ; Les Construction Lar Machinerie 1988; Les Entreprises LarMachinerie Matagami inc. 1990; Pres., PDG Equipements Indus. Edmond-Louis Tremblay 1971–87; Les Immeubles Metabetchouan 1975–81; Leo Laprise Inc. 1976–79; Instr. Minier 1963–66; Vice-Pres., Syndicat des Metallos U.S. (Local Patino Mining, Chibougamau) 1964–67; Pres., Cercle des Affaires 1983–86; Home: 179, rue St-Andre, Metabetchouan, Qué. G0W 2A0; Office: 63, Rang Caron, Metabetchouan, Qué. G0W 2A0.

**TREMBLAY, Hon. Francois;** juge; né. Québec, Qué. 28 janv. 1938; f. Juge Thomas et Anne-Marie (Dupuis) T.; é. Université de Moncton; Université de Sherbrooke; Université Laval, admission au Barreau 1966; JUGE, COUR SUPERIEURE DU QUEBEC 1988– ; Substitut du Procureur général 1967–75; Sous-ministre associé 1975–80; Juge en chef associé de la Cour des Sessions de la Paix 1980–88; Office: Palais de Justice, R-331, 300, boul. Jean Lesage, Québec, Qué. G1K 8K6.

**TREMBLAY, Gérald,** M.A., F.C.A.; business executive; b. Kenogami, Que. 25 May 1941; s. Rosaire and Gertrude (Harvey) T.; e. Univ. Laval M.A. 1966; m. Margot Ménard; children: Steve, Lucie, Jean-Philippe, Sabrina; EXECUTIVE VICE-PRESIDENT, WHOLESALE, METRO-RICHELIEU INC. 1993– ; Managing Partner Montreal Office, Arthur Andersen & Co. 1966–89; Pres. & Gen. Mgr., Héroux Inc., Longueuil Div. 1989–92; Mem., Quebec C.A.s Inst.; Ont. C.A.s Inst.; Dir., Jr. Achievement of Quebec; Fellow, Quebec C.A. Inst.; co-author: 'Direction's report in the Annual Report to the Shareholders'; recreations: golf, snowmobiling, fishing, hunting; club: Islesmere Golf; Home: 3844, Draper, Montreal, Que. H4A 2P1; Office: 11011 boul. Maurice Duplessis, Montreal, Que. H1C 1V6.

**TREMBLAY, Louise,** B.Sc., C.A.; senior executive; b. Laval, Que. 21 Nov. 1954; d. Germain and Thérèse (Bourelle) T.; e. Ecole des Hautes Etudes Commerciales B.Sc. 1978; C.A. 1980; CHIEF OPERATING OFFR., CANADIAN SATELLITE COMMUNICATIONS INC. 1994– ; Accountant in construction industry 1973–79; articled with Clarkson Gordon 1979–80; Controller, Telemedia Communications Inc. 1980; Dir. of Finance & Admin., Canadian Satellite Communications Inc. 1984; Vice Pres. Finance & Admin. 1987; Vice-Pres., Finance & Admin. & C.F.O. 1990; Sr. Vice-Pres. & C.F.O. 1993; past teacher of financial case studies, Univ. of Quebec; Coach for Certified Gen. Accountant students for final finance exam; actively involved in a number of proceedings before C.R.T.C.; expert witness at several public hearings; recreations: country home; Office: 50 Burnhamthorpe Rd. W., Missisauga, Ont. L5B 3C2.

**TREMBLAY, Marc-Adélard,** O.C., B.A., L.S.A., M.Soc., Ph.D.; anthropologue; né Les Eboulements, Comté de Charlevoix, Qué. 24 avril 1922; f. Willie et Laurette T.; é. Univ. de Montréal B.A. 1944, L.S.A. 1948; Univ. Laval M.Soc. 1950; Cornell Univ. Ph.D. 1954; Doctorats honorifiques, Ottawa 1982; Guelph 1984; Prix Molson 1987 du Conseil des Arts du Canada; Prix Marcel Vincent (ACFAS) 1988; International Order of Merit 1990; Prix Esdras Minville 1991; ép. Jacqueline f. Georges Cyr 27 décembre 1949; enfants: Geneviève, Lorraine, Marc, Colette, Dominique, Suzanne; Dean, Grad. School, Laval Univ. 1971–79, et Prof. d'Anthropologie; Conseiller en recherche, Comn. d'enquête sur la santé et le bien-être Qué. 1967–69; Dir. des études sur l'enthnographie de la Côte Nord du Saint-Laurent 1965–71, co-dir. 1971–76; Prés., Soc. Royale du Canada 1981–84; Prés., Assn. universitaire canadienne d'études nordiques 1985–89; Prés., Conseil Québécois de la recherche sociale 1987–1991; auteur 'Initiation à la recherche dans les sciences humaines' 1968; 'L'Identité québécoise en péril' 1983; 'L'anthropologie à l'université Laval: Fondements historiques, pratiques académiques, dynamismes d'évolution' 1989; 1Les fondements historiques et théoriques de la pratique professionnelle en authropologie' 1990; co-auteur 'People of Cove and Woodlot: Communities from the Viewpoint of Social Psychiatry' vol. 11 1960; 'Etude des conditions de vie, des besoins et des aspirations des familles salariées canadiennes-françaises' 1962; 'Les comportements économiques de la famille salariée du Québec' 1964; 'Les fondements sociaux de la maturation chez l'enfant' 1965; 'Rural Canada in Transition' 1966; 'Etude sur les Indiens contemporains du Canada' 1969; 'Les changements socio-culturels à Saint-Augustin' 1969; 'Famille et parenté en Acadie' 1971; 'Changements dans l'organisation économique et sociale à Tête-à-la-Baleine' 1971; 'Le jeu des cartes d'identité' (Télé-université) 1976; éd. 'The Individual, language and Society in Canada/L'individu, la langue et la Société au Canada' 1977; en collaboration 'Une décennie de recherches au Centre d'études nordiques 1961–1970' 1971; éd. 'Communities and Culture in French Canada' 1973; 'Les Facettes de l'identité amérindienne' 1976; 'Conscience et Enquête: l'ethnologie des réalités canadiennes' 1983; rédacteur, 'Nouvelles Technologies et Société' 1985; rapports, articles, chapîtres de livres; mem. Assn. Internat. des Sociologues de langue française; Soc. Applied Anthrop.; Soc. Med. Anthrop.; Assn. Can. de Sociologie et d'anthropologie (Pres. fondateur); Soc. canadienne d'anthropologie (ancien prés.); Assn. des Sociologues et anthropologues de langue française; mem., Académie des Lettres et des Sciences Humaines de la Soc. Royale du Canada (ancien prés.); Sec., Acad. des Sciences Morales et Politiques (Montréal); catholique; Adresse: 835 Nouvelle Orléans, Sainte Foy, Qué. G1X 3J4; Bureau: Sainte Foy, Qué.

**TREMBLAY, Michel;** writer; b. Montréal, Qué. 25 June 1942; s. Armand and Rhéauna (Rathier) T.; e. Graphic Arts Inst. Québec; linotypist 1963–66; author 20 plays, 3 musical comedies, 9 novels, one coll. tales, 7 film scripts, song lyrics, opera libretto; plays incl. 'Le train' 1959 (CBC 1st Prize for young writers 1964); 'Les Belles Soeurs' 1965 premiered Montreal 1968, Paris prodn. 1973 declared 'best foreign production of the year', Chicago 1982; 'Bonjour là, bonjour' New York 1980, Tokyo 1981; films incl.' Françoise Durocher, waitress' (awarded 3 Genie Prizes 1972); 'Il était une fois dans l'Est' 1972 (rep. Can. Cannes and Chicago Film Festivals 1974); novels incl. 'Chroniques du Plateau Mont-Royal' 5 books 1978, 1980, 1982, 1984, 1989; opera libretto 'Nelligan' 1989, prodn. Opéra de Montréal 1990; transl. and adapted plays by various authors incl. Tennessee Williams, Tchekhov, Gogol; recipient 6 grants Can. Arts Council; named 'Chevalier de l'Ordre des Arts et des Lettres de France' French Govt. 1984, promoted to Officier in 1991; cited numerous nat. and internat. newspapers, mag. and books incl. 'Michel Tremblay' by Renata Usmiani; recipient various awards incl. Trophee Meritas 1970, 1972; Etrog 1971 (2); Chalmers Award 1972, 1973, 1974, 1975, 1978, 1986, 1989; Prix Victor Morin 1974; Lt. Gov. Ont. Prize 1976 (2); Prix France Qué. 1981; Selections des lectrices de la revue elle France 1983; 1ère selection Prix Medicis 1983; Prix Qué.-Paris 1985; Athanase-David 1988; Prix Anik CBC 1988; Prix Gemeau 1988 and 1992; Meilleur long metrage 1989; Chevalier de l'Ordre du Québec 1990; Doctorat Honoris Causa, Concordia Univ. and McGill Univ. 1991; Stirling Univ. (Scotland) 1992; Windsor Univ. 1993; Address: c/o Agence Goodwin, 839 est, Sherbrooke, no. 2, Montréal, Qué. H2L 1K6.

**TREMBLAY, Paul-Gaston,** O.C., B.A., M.C.S., C.A., Ph.D.; chartered accountant; b. Chicoutimi, Que. 8 Aug. 1928; s. Edouard and Flore (Girard) T.; e. Laval Univ. B.A. 1949, M.C.S. 1953; Univ. of Quebec Ph.D. (honoris causa) 1980; m. Fernande d. Alfred and Germaine Morisset 2 July 1955; children: Michel, Mireille, Chantal; PRES., PRIMO-GESTION INC. 1983– ; Auditor, Samson & Bélair (now merged with Touche & Ross)

1952–57; Sr. Partner, Laroche & Tremblay (merged to become Gagnon, Bergeron, Laroche & Tremblay) 1957–80; Gauthier, Tremblay et al. 1980–83; Vice-Rector (Admin.), Univ. du Qué. à Chicoutimi 1969–72; Income Tax & Mngt. Teacher, Ecole de comm. et de génie (affil. Laval Univ.) 1957–69; Dir., National Bank of Canada 1978– ; Price Brothers Co. 1979–84; Abitibi Price Inc. 1981–93; Bell Canada 1984– ; UniMédia Inc. 1987– ; Union canadienne 1985–90; Mem., Order of Canada 1982; Pres., Fond. de l'Univ. du Qué. à Chicoutimi 1972– ; Fond. Sagamie 1979– ; Inst. sci. du Saguenay-Lac St-Jean 1983– ; Pres., C. de C. de Chicoutimi 1964–65; Ecole de comm. de Chicoutimi 1965–67; Ecole de Génie-Comm. 1967–69; C. de C. de la Prov. de Qué. 1975–76; Home: 1048 D'Avaugour, Chicoutimi, Qué. G7H 2T1; Office: C.P. 574, Chicoutimi, Qué. G7H 5C8.

**TREMBLAY, Rodrigue,** B.Sc., M.A., Ph.D.; economist; b. Matane, Qué. 13 Oct. 1939; s. George and Germaine (St.-Louis) T.; e. Laval Univ., B.A. 1961; Univ. de Montréal, B.Sc. 1963, Stanford Univ., M.A. 1965, Ph.D. 1968; m. Carole d. Ernest and Clarion Howard 5 Sept. 1964; children: Jean-Paul, Alain, Joanne; PROF. OF ECON., UNIV. DE MONTREAL 1967– ; Min. of Indus., Trade & Commerce, Govt. of Qué. 1976–79; Pres., N.A. Econ. & Fin. Assn. 1987; Canada-U.S. Free Trade Dispute Settlement Panels 1989; Bd. of Dirs., Assumption Mutual Life Co. 1990–93; Woodrow Wilson Fellow 1964–65; author: 'Economie et Finances Publiques' 1982, 'Le Québec en Crise' 1981; 'L'Economique' 1969, 1971, 1975; ed. 'Issues in North American Economics and Finance' 1987; 'Macroéconomique Moderne' 1992; Home: 68 ch. les Chenaux, Vaudreuil, Qué. J7V 1G3; Office: Univ. de Montréal, Montréal, Qué. H3C 3J7.

**TRENT, John Elliot,** M.A.; educator; b. Toronto, Ont. 12 May 1936; s. Gordon Chapman and Dorothy Agnes (Bell) T.; e. St. Andrew's Coll. Aurora 1953; Harvard University A.B. 1958; Sorbonne and Inst. d'Etudes Politiques 1963–64; Univ. de Montréal M.A. 1968; Queen's Univ. doctoral studies, 1969; m. Colette d. Antonio Alepins, Montréal, Qué. 26 June 1965; children: Deborah Marie, Andrew Powell, Patrick Leduc; ASSOC. PROF. OF POL. SCIENCE, UNIV. OF OTTAWA 1971– ; Extve. Dir., Social Science Federation of Canada 1979–82; Visiting Scholar, Science Council of Can. 1982–83; Bank of Toronto and Burns, Bros. & Denton, Toronto 1953–55; Pub. Relations Counsellor, Public and Industrial Relations Ltd. Toronto 1958–62; Lectr. in Pol. & Econ. Science Royal Mil. Coll. Kingston 1969–71; Press, Radio and TV Commentator, consultant, guest lectr.; most recent publication: 'Social Science in Canada: A National Resource' for Dept. of Secretary of State; Secy.-Gen. Internat. Political Science Association 1976–88; mem. International Social Science Council 1978–90; Secy.-Treasr., Canadian Political Science Assn. 1969–76; Dir., Toronto Jr. Bd. Trade 1960–62; mem. Constitutional Comn. and Policy Comn. Que. Lib. Party 1978–79 and 1984–85; Dir. Alliance Quebec 1983–85; Pres. Outaouais Alliance 1982–85; Prés., Conseil de développement touristique Hull Chelsea-La Pêche; Chrpn., Council of Canadians 1987; Dir., Centraide de l'Ouest québécois 1986–89; Founding Co-Chair, Action Canada Network 1987; Founding Pres., Dialogue Canada; Home: (C.P. 165) R.R. 1, Chelsea, Qué. J0X 1N0; Office: Dept. of Political Science, University of Ottawa, Ottawa, Ont. K1N 6N5.

**TRENTMAN, John Allen,** B.A., M.A., Ph.D.; university professor; b. Willmar, Minn. 17 Feb. 1935; came to Can. 1963; Canadian citizen; s. John Libory and Johannah Marie Violet (Johnson) T.; e. Univ. of Minn. B.A. 1956, M.A. 1958, Ph.D. 1964; Lunds Universitet, Lund, Sweden, 1958–59; Yale Univ. 1960–61; m. Florine Opal d. Oliver B. Tweeten 16 July 1955; children: Anne Elisabeth, Karna Marie, John Stefan Per, Denise Erika; PROFESSOR, HURON COLLEGE, UNIV. OF WESTERN ONT.; Gov. Mtl. Diocesan Theol. Coll. 1978–84; Instr. Univ. of Minn., 1961–63; at Huron Coll., Univ. W. Ont., Lectr. 1963–64, Asst. Prof., 1964–67, Acting Head, Dept. of Phil., 1965–67; came to McGill Univ. as Assoc. Prof., 1967–70, Chrmn. Dept. of Phil. 1967–72; Vice Dean, Humanities, Faculty of Arts and Science, 1968–71, Prof. of Philosophy 1971–84; Principal, Huron College, Univ. of Western Ont. 1984–85; Visiting Prof. and Lectr. at Univ. of Minn., 1966; O.I.S.E., Univ. of Toronto, 1972; Institut for Graesk og Latinsk Middelalder-filologi, Koebenhavns Universitet 1974; Harvard Univ. 1977; Dir. McGill-Queen's Univ. Press 1976–77; author of 'Vincent Ferrer: Tractatus De Suppositionibus' 1977; 'Scholasticism in the Seventeenth Century' Cambridge Hist. of Later Medieval Phil.; 'Ferrer, Vincenz,' Theologische Realenzyklopädie; other writings incl. contributions to books and professional jnls. on late medieval logic, metaphysics, ethics, natural law theory in the late middle ages and renaissance, and critical editions of medieval latin texts; rec'd. undergrad. athletic and academic scholarships; sometime Fellow, American-Scandinavian Foundation; Kent Fellow; Can. Council Leave Fellowship (1974–75); SSHRCC Leave Fellowship (1981–82); Corresponding Mem. HRCC; mem. Société Internationale pour l'Etude de la Phil. Médiévale; Soc. for Medieval and Renaissance Phil.; Soc. of Christian Phil.; Cambridge Bibliographical Soc.; Am. Catholic Phil. Assn.; Candn. Phil. Assn. (Co-Chrmn., Programme Cmte. 1978) Vice Pres. 1986–87, Pres. 1987–88; Assn. for the Advancmt. of Scandinavian Studies in Can.; Phi Beta Kappa; Anglican; Club: McGill Univ. Faculty (Pres. 1971); recreations: running, music, mediocre golf; Home: 1 Foxchapel Rd., London, Ont. N6G 1Z1; Office: Huron Coll., London, Ont. N6G 1H3.

**TRÉPANIER, Hon. Violette;** politicienne; née Montréal, Qué. 14 mars 1945; f. Georges et Lucienne (Dionne) Briand; é. Univ. de Montréal Baccalauréat en pédagogie 1966; ép. André f. Guy Trépanier 15 juillet 1967; enfants: Guy, Jean-François; MINISTRE DE LA SÉCURITÉ DU REVENU 1994– ; MINISTRE DÉLÉGUÉE à LA CONDITION FÉMININE et MINISTRE RESPONSABLE DE LA FAMILLE 1989– ; Professeure de français, de littérature et d'histoire Coll. Ville Marie et Commission scolaire Lignery 1966–76; Attachée politique pour un député de l'Assemblée nationale du Qué. 1981–82; Vice-présidente du Parti libéral du Qué. 1982–85; Députée de la circonscription électorale de Dorion depuis 1985; Adjointe parlementaire au ministre des Affaires municipales responsable de l'Habitation 1985–89; Membre de la Commission de l'aménagement et des équipements 1985–89; Présidente du caucus des députés de l'Est de Montréal 1988–89; Ministre déléguée aux Communautés culturelles, 1989; Bureau: 425, Saint-Amable, 4e étage, Québec, Qué. G1R 4Z1.

**TREVITHICK, John Richard,** B.Sc., Ph.D.; university professor; b. St. Thomas, Ont. 30 Nov. 1938; s. Garnet Walker and Jean Yvonne (Salmoni) T.; e. Queen's Univ. B.Sc. (Hons.) 1961; Univ. of Wisconsin Ph.D. 1965; m. Katharine A. (dec'd.) d. Headrick and Arnetta Allan 8 Aug. 1962; m. Donna N. d. Lawrence and Blanche Copeland 27 Dec. 1967; children: Caroline, Scott, Colleen; PROF., DEPT. OF BIOCHEMISTRY, FAC. OF MEDICINE, UNIV. OF WESTERN ONT. 1979– ; postdoctoral study with Dr. G.H. Dixon, Univ. of B.C. 1965–67; MRC Scholar & Asst. Prof., Univ. of Western Ont. 1967; Sabbatical, Berne, Switz. with Dr. R. Braun 1972–73; Assoc. Prof. 1972; studies on 'Neurospora crassa' enzyme invertase, nuclear proteins in differentiation, lens differentiation & cataract prevention by antioxidants, sunburn treatment using topical vitamin E acetate; France-Canada Exchange Scholarship with Dr. Y. Courtois 1984; Mem., Un. Ch. of Canada; Candn. Biochem. Soc.; Editor, CFBS News 1973–76; Chrmn., U.W.O. Faculty Assn. 1978; Treas. 1988–92; Mem., Internat. Soc. of Eye Rsch.; Internat. Soc. Ocular Toxicol.; ARVO; author of 60 sci. papers & 5 book chapters; Home: 557 Leyton Cres., London, Ont. N6G 1S9; Office: Biochemical Dept., Medical Sciences Bldg., Room M316, London, Ont. N6A 5C1.

**TREVORS, Jack T.,** B.Sc., M.Sc., Ph.D.; university professor of microbiology; b. Berwick, N.S. 24 Feb. 1953; s. Ronald J. and Ethel M. (Corbett) T.; e. Acadia Univ. B.Sc. 1978, M.Sc. 1979; Univ. of Waterloo Ph.D. 1982; m. Karen E. d. Doug and Pauline Saunders 1 Sept. 1979; one child: A.K.; PROFESSOR, ENVIRONMENTAL BIOLOGY, UNIV. OF GUELPH 1982– ; Adjunct Prof., Biology Dept., Univ. of WAterloo; Researcher, Candn. Network of Toxicology Centres; Mem., Global Rsch. Network on Sustainable Devel.; conducted collaborative research in Scotland, The Netherlands and U.S.A.; Microbial Ecology Section Ed., 'Can. J. of Microbiol.' 1990–93; Edit. 'Microbial Releases,' 'Molecular Ecol.,' 'Envir. Toxicity and Water Quality,' 'Biometals'; Principal, J.T. Trevors, Consulting Serv.; Imperial Oil Canada Rsch. Excellence Award 1990; Am. Men & Women of Science 1988; NSERC Scholar 1981; Ont. Grad. Scholar 1980; Univ. of Waterloo Grad. Scholarship 1979; Acadia Univ. Gra. Sch. 1978; Mem., Candn. Soc. Microbiol. (Past Chair, Envir. Microbiol. Div.); co-editor: 'Nucleic Acids in the Environment' 1994, 'Modern Soil Microbiology' 1994; author of 7 textbook chapters, 35 review papers and over 100 sci. rsch. papers; recreations: gardening, cycling, reading, computing; Home: 48 Freshmeadow Way, Guelph, Ont. N1K 1S1; Office: Guelph, Ont. N1G 2W1.

**TREVORS, John D.,** B.B.A., LL.B.; barrister & solicitor; b. Chatham, N.B. 14 Feb. 1945; s. Carmen Lloyd and Helen (Brown) T.; e. Univ. of N.B. B.B.A. 1967, LL.B. 1973; Officer, Royal Canadian Navy 1963–70; private law practice 1973–87; Mem., Nat. Parole Board 1987– ; major shareholder, Miramichi Agricultural Exbn. Assn. Limited; Mem., P.C. Party; Home: 80 Henderson St., Chatham, N.B. E1N 2R7; Office: 1045 Main St., 1st Floor, Moncton, N.B. E1C 1H1.

**TRIANO, (Howard) Jay,** B.A., PDP; university head basketball coach; assistant coach Canadian National Team; b. Tillsonburg, Ont. 21 Sept. 1958; s. Howard A. and Muriel L. (Peoples) T.; e. A.N. Myer S.S.; Simon Fraser Univ. B.A. 1982; m. Beth d. Bob and Isobel Dovey 18 June 1988; children: Courtney, Jessica; HEAD BASKETBALL COACH, SIMON FRASER UNIV.; A.N. Myer S.S. Basketball Player 1974–77 (one of top players in Canada); Simon Fraser Univ. Basketball Player 1977–82; set 15 school records (all time leading scores); NAIA All Am. School Number '12' retired only athlete; Mem., Canada's National Team 1978–89; Assistant Coach, Canadian National Team 1992–93; three Olympic teams (two as Captain); all time leading scorer for Canada; played in Mexico and Istanbul; drafted by Los Angeles Lakers and Calgary Stampeders; inducted Canada's Basketball Hall of Fame 1993; Home: 10233 - 172nd St., Surrey, B.C. V4N 3L4; Office: Burnaby, B.C. V5S 1S6.

**TRIANTIS, Stephen George,** B.A., M.A., LL.B., Ph.D.; educator, author; b. Patras, Greece; s. George N. and Stefanie (Stefanou) T.; e. Gymnasium, Patras; Univ. of Athens B.A. (Pol. Science & Econ.), LL.B.; Univ. of Toronto M.A. (Econ.), Ph.D.; m. Danae d. Andrew D. Nicoletopoulos 16 Sept. 1959; two s. George Gregory, Alexander John; PROF. OF ECON., UNIV. OF TORONTO 1964– ; Barrister and Solicitor 1939–44; Secy., Supreme Economic Counc. of Greece 1944–45; joined Univ. of Toronto 1947; Dir., Diploma Course in Econ. Development 1965–67; Mem. Governing Council 1978–84; Adviser, Dept. Econ. & Devel. Govt. Ont. 1962; Pearson Comn. on Internat. Develop. 1968–69; Candn. Internat. Devel. Agency, Government of Canada 1969; Select Comte. Ont. Leg. on Econ. & Cultural Nationalism 1972; Visiting Prof. Univ. of Calif. 1963; Consultant, Smith Comte. on Taxation in Ont. 1964; Unemployment Insurance Comn., Govt. of Can. 1969; World Bank 1977; Econ. Adviser to Govt. of Greece 1965, 1983–88; Bank of Greece 1984–88; National Bank of Greece (Can.) 1984–90; Pres. Univ. of Patras 1965; Dir. Harvard Univ. Devel. Adv. Service 1966–67; Dir. January Sch. Toronto 1969–70; Dir. Mosslaw Growth Fund 1972–77; Mem., Ont. Commercial Registration Appeal Tribunal 1986–92; served with Greek Navy 1939–41, Brit. Army 1944–45; rec'd Athens Acad. Arts & Letters Prize 1944; awarded Fellowships, King's College, Cambridge Univ., 1945–47, Rockefeller Foundation Grant 1954, Can. Council Grants 1959, 1960, 1962, 1965; Mem. Ed. Adv. Bd. 'International Encyclopedia of the Social Sciences' 1965–67; Ed. Bd., 'Commentator' 1961–64; author 'Common Market and Economic Development' 1965; 'Cyclical Changes in Trade Balances of Countries Exporting Primary Products 1927–1933: A Comparative Study of Forty-Nine Countries' 1967; numerous contribs. to books and scholarly journs.; press, radio and TV commentator, guest lecturer in Canada and abroad; Mem. Candn. Econ. Assn.; Candn. Inst. Internat. Affairs; Inter-Am. Stat Inst. (Constituent Mem. 1965–76); Extve. Comte., Candn. Chapter of Society for International Development 1965; Candn. Operational Research Soc. 1959–63; Am. Econ. Assn.; Royal Econ. Soc.; Mem., Bd. for Metropolitan Toronto, Candn. National Inst. for the Blind 1990– ; Internat. Programmes and Development Education Ctte., Toronto Branch, Candn. Red Cross Soc. 1990–93; Chrmn. Task Force on Child Sponsorship 1982–83, Mem. Bd. of Dir., 1983–89, Chrmn. Program Comte. 1983–85, and Vice Pres., Chrmn., Extve. Comte. 1985–87, Save the Children - Canada; Chrmn., Consultation Advisory Group on Long Term Care in Ont., Govt. of Ont. 1991–92; Mem. Bd. of Dirs., Candn. Pensioners Concerned (Ont. Div.) 1989–93; Mem., Steering Comte., Ont. Coalition of Senior Citizens Organizations 1989–92; Toronto Mayor's Subcommittee on Seniors and the Law 1991–93; Hellenic-Candn. Federation of Ont. (Hon. Chrmn. 1983–85); Hellenic-Candn. Cultural Soc. (Vice Pres. 1960–63); Chrmn., Adv. Bd., Hellenic Home for the Aged 1983–84; Dir., Oriole Park Assn. 1981–83, 1988–89; recreations: reading, music, philately; Home: 32 Elmsthorpe Ave., Toronto, Ont. M5P 2L6; Office: 150 St. George St., Toronto, Ont. M5S 1A1.

**TRIGG, Eric Austin,** B.Com., M.B.A.; industrialist; b. Verdun, Que. 5 Dec. 1923; s. Walter A. L. and Winifred (Tupling) T.; e. McGill Univ., B.Com. 1944; Harvard Business Sch., M.B.A. 1947; m. Marjorie Evelyn, d. John Berry, Dorval, Que., 20 Aug. 1949; children: Linda Joyce, Heather Ann, Eric Bruce, David Michael; former Sr. Vice Pres., Dir., Alcan Aluminium Ltd.; Dir., Hunter Douglas N.V.; Dai-Ichi Kangyo Bank (Canada); served as Pilot Officer, R.C.A.F. during the 2nd World War; Patron, Lester B. Pearson College of the Pacific; Protestant; recreations: golf, hiking, reading; Clubs: Wentworth (Virginia Water, Eng.); University (Montreal and N.Y.); Mt. Royal; Mt. Bruno, Montreal; Home: 57 de Lavigne Rd., Westmount, Que. H3Y 2C3.

**TRIGGER, Bruce Graham,** B.A., Ph.D., D.Sc., D.Litt., F.R.S.C., F.S.A.S. (Hon.); anthropologist & archaeologist; educator; b. Cambridge (Preston), Ont. 18 June 1937; s. late John Wesley Dodd and Gertrude Elizabeth (Graham) T.; e. Preston (Ont.) and St. Marys (Ont.) Pub. Schs. 1950; St. Marys Coll. Inst. 1951; Stratford (Ont.) Coll. Inst. 1955; Univ. of Toronto B.A. 1959; Yale Univ. Ph.D. 1964; m. Barbara Marian d. Edgar S. Welch, Marlow, Eng. 7 Dec. 1968; children: Isabel Marian, Rosalyn Theodora; PROF. OF ANTHROP. McGILL UNIV. since 1969; Asst. Prof. Northwestern Univ. 1963–64; Asst. Prof. McGill Univ. 1964, Assoc. Prof. 1967, Chrmn. of Anthrop. 1970–75; Chief Archaeol. Pa.-Yale Expdn. to Egypt 1962; Staff Archaeol. Oriental Inst. Sudan Expdn. 1963–64; rec'd Queen's Silver Jubilee Medal; Cornplanter Medal for Iroquois Research, 1979; Innis-Gérin Medal, Royal Soc. of Can. 1985; D.Sc. (hon. causa), Univ. of New Brunswick 1987; D.Litt. (hon. causa) Univ. of Waterloo 1990; Prix Victor-Barbeau 1991; Prix Léon-Gérin (Prix du Qué.) 1991; J.R. Wiseman Book Award, Archaeological Institute of Am. 1991; Fourth Gordon Childe Mem. Lecture, Univ. of London 1982; Seagram Lectures, Univ. of Toronto 1986; Lansdowne Visitor, Univ. of Victoria 1987; Harry Hawthorn Distinguished Lecture 1988; Distinguished Lecture in Archeology, Am. Anthropological Assn. 1990; adopted mem., Huron Great Turtle clan with name Nyemea 1990; Distinguished Visiting Prof., Am. Univ. in Cairo 1992; Woodrow Wilson Fellowships 1959, 1963; Killam Rsch. Fellowships 1971, 1990, 1991; Can. Council Leave Fellowships 1968, 1977; Soc. Sci. and Humanities Research Counc. of Can. Leave Fellowship 1983; Adv. Bd., 'World Archaeology' since 1968; 'Ontario History' 1980– ; 'History of Anthropology' 1982– ; 'Journal of Field Archaeology' 1986– ; 'Journal of Archaeological Research' 1991– ; mem. Bd. of Govs., McGill-Queen's Univ. Press 1988– ; ed. 'Native and Northern Series' McGill-Queen's Univ. Press 1988– ; author 'History and Settlement in Lower Nubia' 1965; 'The Late Nubian Settlement at Arminna West' 1967; 'Beyond History: The Methods of Prehistory' 1968; 'The Huron: Farmers of the North' 1969 (2nd ed. 1990); 'The Meroitic Funerary Inscriptions from Arminna West' 1970; 'Cartier's Hochelaga and the Dawson Site' 1972 (co-author); 'The Children of Aataentsic: A History of the Huron People to 1660' 2 vols. 1976; 'Nubia Under the Pharaohs' 1976; 'Time and Traditions: Essays in Archaeological Interpretation' 1978; 'Gordon Childe: Revolutions in Archaeology' 1980; 'Natives and Newcomers: Canada's "Heroic Age" Reconsidered' 1985; 'History of Archaeological Thought' 1989; 'Early Civilizations: Ancient Egypt in Context' 1993; vol. ed., 'Handbook of North American Indians' (Vol. 15: Northeast) 1978; numerous articles ethnohist., African archaeol., Meroitic lang., theory & hist. of archaeol.; Fellow, Sigma Xi; Foreign Fellow, Am. Anthrop. Assn.; Hon. Mem., Prehistoric Soc. (UK) 1991; Hon. Fellow, Soc. of Antiquarians of Scotland 1993; recreations: sandcastles, goldfish; Home: Apt. 603, 3495 Mountain St., Montreal, Que. H3G 2A5; Office: 855 Sherbrooke St. W., Montreal, Que. H3A 2T7.

**TRIGGLE, Christopher Robert,** B.Sc., Ph.D.; university professor; administrator; b. London, England 27 Feb. 1946; s. William John and Maud Florence (Henderson) T.; e. Leyton Co. H.S. 1964; Univ. of East Anglia B.Sc. (Hons.) 1967; Univ. of Alta. Ph.D. 1972; m. Cecile d. Eugene and Margaret Rocque 16 Aug. 1969; children: Gillian Nicole, Meghan Christina, Marc Christian; RSCH. PROF., MEMORIAL UNIV. OF NFLD. 1989–94; Prof. of Pharmacology and Head of Department of Pharmacology and Therapeutics, Univ. of Calgary and the Chair of Cardiovascular Rsch. of the Alberta Heart Foundation 1990– ; Dir. of Rsch., CIBA Geigy Canada Ltd.; H.S. teacher (U.K.) 1967–68; post-doct. fellow, Dept. of Biochem. Pharmacol., Buffalo, N.Y. 1972–73; Asst. Prof. of Pharmacol., Mem. Univ. of Nfld. 1973–78; Assoc. Prof. 1978–83; Prof. of Pharmacol. & Assoc. Dean of Basic Med. Sci. 1983–90; Mem., Pharmacol. Soc. of Can. (Vice Pres. 1987–89, Pres. 1989–91); Candn. Physiol. Soc.; Hypertension Soc. of Can.; Candn. Soc. for Clin. Investig.; Am. Soc. of Pharmacol. & Experimental Therapeutics; Internat. Soc. of Hypertension; co-author: 'Pharmacology of the Peripheral Nervous System' 1976; recreations: running, hiking, skiing; Home: 7007 Silverview Rd. N.W., Calgary, Alta.; Office: H1627 Fac. of Med., Univ. of Calgary, 3330 Hospital Dr. N.W., Calgary, Alta. T2N 4N1.

**TRILLWOOD, Leslie Denys;** business executive; b. London, England 4 Nov. 1935; e. Aston Univ., Birmingham, England; m. Betsy Sullivan; EXTVE. VICE-PRES., POWER SYSTEMS GROUP, INTERNATIONAL SALES AND MARKETING, ALCATEL CANADA WIRE INC. 1987– ; var. positions in Sales, Mktg. & Gen. Management, Canada Wire 1969–87; Dir., Canada Wire & Cable (Internat.) Ltd.; Office: 250 Ferrand Dr., North York, Ont. M3C 3J4.

**TROLLOPE, Robert Woodland;** association executive; b. Toronto, Ont. 11 June 1914; s. Robert Hambly and Charlotte Louise (Woodland) T.; m. Eileen Lillian d. Albert H. and Louise Graham; children: Robert Graham, Anthony Woodland, Thomas Heath, Rowlin Kent, Charlotte Deborah Adderley, Elizabeth Jill; CHRMN., WESTMINSTER FINANCIAL SERVICES LTD.; Chrmn., Dominion Automobile Assn.; North Am. Automobile Assn. Ltd.; L'Assn. de l'Automobile Que.; Clubs: Brooks's (UK), Granite, London, London Hunt & Country, Royal Candn. Yacht, Royal Thames Yacht (UK), Toronto, Wellington-Waterloo & Trollope Hunt, M.F.H.; Home: Darwood, Hyde Park, Ont. N0M 1Z0; Office: 201 King St., London, Ont. N6A 4T3.

**TROTT, Ralph Edward;** retail executive; b. Campbellford, Ont. 14 Dec. 1950; s. Albert Charles and Rita Alice (Baker) T.; m. Deborah d. James and Theresa Nicholls 26 July 1975; children: Jeff, David; PRESIDENT & CHIEF EXECUTIVE OFFICER, BEAVER LUMBER COMPANY LIMITED 1993– ; Dir., The North West Company 1993– ; Managing Director, Automotive, Canadian Tire Corp. 1985–89; Pres. & C.E.O. The North West Co. 1989–93; Mem., Young Presidents' Orgn.; recreations: auto racing; clubs: Manitoba, Winnipeg Winter; Office: 7303 Warden Ave., Markham, Ont. L3R 5Y6.

**TROTTER, Bernard,** M.A.; university officer (retired); b. Palo Alto, Cal. 24 March 1924; s. Reginald George and Prudence Hale (Fisher) T.; e. McMaster Univ. B.A. 1945; Acad. of Radio Arts Toronto 1946–47; Queen's Univ. M.A. 1948; Nat. Defence Coll. Can. Course V 1951–52; m. Jean Cairns, d. James Findlay, Eng. 16 Sept. 1948; children: Reginald James, Victoria Jane; various posts Queen's Univ. 1963–88; Dir. Canadian Broadcasting Corp. 1975–80; joined CBC as Asst. Talks Producer Winnipeg 1948, rep. at UN 1950–51, Head Eng. Lang. Sec. Internat. Service 1952, European Rep. London 1954, Supervising Producer TV Pub. Affairs Toronto 1957, Gen. Supvr. Pub. Affairs 1960–63; Extve. Asst. to Princ., Queen's Univ. 1963–68, Head of Academic Planning, 1968–81, Special Asst. to the Principal 1981–88; mem. sub-comte. Comte. of Pres's Ont. Univs. to develop funding system for Ont. univs. 1967; Chrmn. Assn. Univs. and Colls. Can. Adv. Comte. on Univ. Planning 1972–73; Co-Chrmn. Council Ont. Univs. Comte. on Instructional Devel. 1972–75; Past Pres., Kingston Symphony Assoc.; author 'Television and Technology in University Teaching' 1970; co-author 'Towards 2000: the Future of Post-Secondary Education in Ontario' 1971; 'Planning for Planning: Relationships Between Universities and Governments in Canada: Guidelines to Process' 1974; numerous other writings and broadcasts; mem. Candn. Soc. Study Higher Educ.; Internat. Inst. Communication; Club: Arts & Letters (Toronto); Home: 320 King St. W., Kingston, Ont. K7L 2X1.

**TROTTER, James,** Ph.D., D.Sc., F.R.S.C., F.R.S.Chem., F.C.I.C.; educator; b. Dumfries, Scot. 15 July 1933; s. James and Annie (Burns) T.; e. St. Modan's High Sch. Stirling; Univ. of Glasgow B.Sc. 1954, Ph.D. 1957, D.Sc. 1963; m. Ann d. James and Isabella Ramsay 14 Sept. 1957; two s. Martin, David; PROF. OF CHEM., UNIV. OF B.C. 1960– ; Postdoctoral Fellow Nat. Rsch. Council Ottawa 1957–59; Visiting Prof. Oxford Univ., Cambridge Univ., E.T.H. Zurich, Univ. of Christchurch (N.Z.); Meldola Medallist Royal Inst. Chem.; Alfred P. Sloan Fellow; Killam Sr. Fellow; Fellow of Clare Hall Cambridge; ed. 'Structure Reports' 1972–81; Home: 4225 Doncaster Way, Vancouver, B.C. V6S 1W1; Office: Vancouver, B.C. V6T 1Y6.

**TROTTER, Kate,** B.A. (Hons.); actress; b. Toronto, Ont. 5 Feb. 1953; d. Johnston Mervin and Audrie Jean (Dempsey) T. e. Brock Univ. B.A. (Hons.) 1975; Nat. Theatre Sch. Montréal 1975–78; one d. Kathleen; guest appearances numerous TV progs. incl.: 'Beyond Reality,' 'E.N.G.,' 'Dracula: the Series,' 'First Season,' 'Night Heat,' 'Philip Marlow Private Eye,' 'Diamonds,' 'Street Legal,' 'The Campbells,' 'Friday's Curse,' 'Alfred Hitchcock Presents,' 'Kung Fu - The Legend Continues,' 'Material World'; starred: 'Glory Enough For All' Thames TV, CBC TV; various CBC progs. incl. lead: 'Kate Morris V.P.,' 2 episodes 'The Judge' and 'For the Record,' mystery drama 'Suicide Murders'; played lead 'Connection' Atlantis Films, also appeared in 'The Playground'; leading roles feature films incl. 'First Season,' 'Entry in a Diary,' 'Joshua Then and Now,' Martha, Ruth and Edie,' 'Les Plouffes'; Am. TV appearances incl. 'Clarence' (Family Channel), 'Murder in Space,' 'Conspiracy of Love'; stage credits incl.: 'Dancing at Lughnasa,' 'The Stillborn Lover,' 'The Affections of May,' 'The Silver Dagger,' 'Summer and Smoke,' 'Hamlet,' 'The Marriage of Figaro,' 'Andromache,' 'The Cocktail Hour,' 'The Father,' 'Man and Superman and Don Juan in Hell,' 'Sullivan and Gilbert,' 'The Grace of Mary Traverse,' 'Top Girls,' 'Holiday,' 'Translations,' 'The Real Thing,' 'Playboy of the Western World,' 'Doc,' 'Quiet in the Land,' 'Romeo and Juliet,' 'The Tempest,' 'Mrs. Warren's Profession,' 'Twelfth Night,' 'Yesteryear,' 'Of Mice and Men,' various Candn. theatres incl. Shaw and Stratford Festivals, National Arts Centre (Ottawa), The Grand Theatre (London), The Kennedy Centre (Washington), Tarragon Theatre, Royal Alex, CentreStage, Toronto Free Theatre, Opera Atelier (Toronto), Aldeburgh Connection (Toronto), Bastion Theatre (Victoria), Theatre New Brunswick; radio dramas incl. narrations and pub. readings; directed short film 'David' Nat. Film Bd.; recipient Guthrie Scholarship 1975; Dora Award 1983 'Translations,' nominated 1984 for 'Top Girls'; nominated 1989 'The Father'; nominated 1992 'Summer and Smoke'; nominated Am. ACE Award, 1988 for 'Alfred Hitchcock Presents: Hunted'; recreations: photography, reading, sewing, gardening, people, films, theatre; Office: Oscars and Abrams Associates, 59 Berkeley St., Toronto, Ont. M5A 2W5.

**TROTTIER, Armand;** retired; b. Québec, Qué. 7 Oct. 1923; s. Philippe and Alice (Hamel) T.; e. Coll. St-François d'Assise, Qué.; Séminaire St-Alphonse, Ste-Anne de Beaupré, Que.; Ecole Technique Qué.; m. Janine, d. Edmond Bolduc, 26 June 1946; children: Louise, Claude, Jean-Marc, Hélène, François, Stéphane; Past Pres., Philippe Trottier Inc. (indust. constr.); Past Pres., Candn. Construction Assn. Past Pres. Quebec Urban Community; Commr., Mun. Comn. Que.; R. Catholic; recreations: theatre; swimming; Address: 175 Blvd. Benoit XV, Quebec, Que. G1L 2Y8.

**TROTTIER, James P.,** B.A., M.D., F.R.C.P.(C); radiologist; b. Val d'Or, Qué. 12 Dec. 1945; s. Clément and Etiennette (Tanguay) T.; e. Univ. of Ottawa B.A. 1966, M.D. 1970; children: Eric, Joel, Julie; CHIEF RADIOL. OUTAOUAIS REGIONAL HOSP. 1987– ; Radiol. C.H.R.N. 1975–81; Prés. C.M.D. Hôpital Rouyn Noranda 1980; Radiol. present hosp. 1981; devised first system X Ray transmission with M Mode for partial digital integration of all imaging modalities in one imaging room; recreation: squash; Office: 116 Lionel Emond St., Hull, Qué. J8Y 1W7.

**TROUBETZKOY, Alexis Serge,** B.A.; educator; b. Paris, France 6 Mar. 1934; s. Prince Serge Gregory and Princess Luba Alexeyvna (Obolensky) T.; e. Sir George William Univ., B.A. 1959; Bishop's Univ., Grad. Faculty of Ed., 1960; m. Helene, d. Wladimir and Maria de Klebnikoff, 8 July 1967; children: Anne; Andrew; Housemaster, Bishop's College Sch., P.Q., 1960; Asst. to H.M., St. Stephen's Sch., Rome, Italy 1966; Asst. to H.M., Appleby Coll. 1968; Headmaster, Selwyn House Sch., Montreal 1971–81; Headmaster, Appleby College, Oakville 1981–87; Headmaster, Toronto French School 1987–92; Extve. Dir., The Tolstoy Foundation 1992– ; mem. Candn. Headmaster's Assn. (Pres. 1973–74); Candn. Assn. of Independent Schools (Extve. 1979–85; Pres. 1982); Que. Assn. of Independent Schs. (Pres. 1979–81); Conference of Independent Schs. (Chrmn. 1983); Headmaster's Conference, U.K. (since 1978); Orthodox Church of Amer.; Amities Internationales Napoleoniennes (Honour Comte.); Bd. of Overseers, CARE; Cathedral Bd. of Regents, St. John the Divine, NYC; Soc. of Russian Scholars in America; author of extracts from 'The Esquimalt Naval Establishment Record' 1958; 'The Road to Balaklava' 1986; served with Royal Candn. Navy (Reserve) 1954–65; commissioned Lieut. 1956; recreation: history; Address: 50 Rosehill Ave., Apt. 1611, Toronto, Ont. M4T 1G6 and 7 East 75th St., New York, NY 10021.

**TROWER, Peter (Gerard);** writer; b. St. Leonards, Eng. 25 Aug. 1930; s. Stephen Gerard Herbert and Gertrude Eleanor Mary (Gilman) T.; e. high sch.; Vancouver Sch. of Art 2 yrs.; author (poetry) 'Moving Through the Mystery' 1969; 'The Sky and The Splinters' 1974; 'The Alders and Others' 1976; 'Ragged Horizons' 1978; 'Bush Poems' 1978; 'Goosequill Snags' 1982; 'The Slidingback Hills' 1986; 'Unmarked Doorways' 1989; 'Grogan's Cafe' (novel) 1993; 'Rough and Ready Times' (history) 1993; 'Where Roads Lead' (poems) 1994; forthcoming books: 'Chainsaws in the Cathedral' (logging poems); 'Upwind From Yesterday' (poems); 'Holy Herb - The Safecracker King (biog.); 'Odysseys' (travel stories incorp. some poetry); 'Way Stations' (selected short prose); 'Dead Man's Ticket' (novel); prose and poetry contbr. numerous mags.; rep. various anthols.; singer and songwriter 2 musical groups; weekly columnist and book reviewer'Sunshine Coast News' 1977– ; assoc. ed. 'Raincoast Chronicles' 1972– ; recipient 8 Can. Council Grants since 1974; Eatons Book Award 1978; MacMillan and Bloedel Award newspaper column 1977; mem. Fedn. B.C. Writers; recreations: collecting jazz, blues & swing records; studying film; Home: R.R. 1 S-6 C-6, Gibsons, B.C. V0N 1V0; Office: 407, 205 W. First Ave., North Vancouver, B.C. V0N 1V0.

**TRUDEAU, Clarence E.;** b. Springfield, Mass. 8 June 1912; s. Ernest E. and Delia (Gemme) T.; e. Chicopee (Mass.) High Sch. (Grad. 1930); Bay Path. Inst., Springfield, Mass. (Grad. 1932); m. Rosina (d. 1976), d. late Michael Kamrad, 21 Sept. 1937; two d. Mary Rosina Bratty, Jo Anne Cloudsdale; m. Margaret d. late James McDevitt 19 Feb. 1977; Auditor, Taylor Bunker & Co., C.P.A.'s Springfield, Mass., 1932–33; R. G. Rankin & Co., C.P.A.'s, New York City, 1933–34; Office Mgr., The Goodyear Tire & Rubber Co., Akron, Ohio, 1934–36; Sales Supv. 1936–39; Sales and Sales Supervision Work, CIT Corp., N.Y.C. 1939–43, Sales Supervisor, 1946–47, Assistant Vice-President, 1947–55; apptd. Vice-President, Canadian Acceptance Corp. Ltd., 1955, President and Director 1961, Chrmn. and Chief Extve. Offr. 1975–77; served in the 2nd World War with U.S. Army, 1943–46; European Theatre of Operations, August, 1944–March 1946; with 29th Inf. Div. as Staff Sgt.; mem., K. of C.; Roman Catholic; recreations: curling, golf; Clubs: Donalda; American; Home: 10 Kenneth Ave., Apt. PH 6, North York, Ont. M2N 6K6.

**TRUDEAU, Rt. Hon. Pierre Elliott,** P.C., C.C., C.H., Q.C., M.A., LL.L., LL.D., M.R.S.C.; b. Montreal, Que. 18 Oct. 1919; s. Charles-Emile and Grace (Elliott) T.; e. Querbes Primary Sch., Montreal; Jean de Brébeuf Coll., Montreal, B.A. (Hons.) 1940; Univ. of Montreal, law degree with Hons. 1943; Harvard Univ., M.A. (Pol. Econ.) 1946; Ecole des sciences politiques, Paris and London Sch. of Econ., post-grad. studies in law, econ. and pol. science; Hon. LL.D. Univ. of Alta. 1968; Queen's Univ. 1968; Duke Univ. 1974; Univ. of Ottawa 1974; Keio Univ., Japan 1976; St. Francis Xavier Univ. 1982; Notre Dame Univ. 1982; Dalhousie Univ. 1983; McGill Univ. 1985; Univ. of B.C. 1986; Univ. de Montréal 1987; Univ. of East Asia 1987; Mount Allison Univ., New Brunswick 1989; Univ. of Toronto 1991; Hon. Litt.D., Univ. of Moncton 1969; m. Margaret, d. late Hon. James Sinclair, P.C., W. Vancouver, B.C. 4 Mar. 1971 (div. 1984); three sons: Justin Pierre James, Alexandre Emmanuel (Sacha), Michel Charles-Emile; called to Bar of Que. 1944; Q.C. 1969; joined P. Council Office, Ottawa as Econ. and Policy Advisor 1949; began practice of law specializing in labour law and civil liberties cases in Que. 1952; apptd. Assoc. Prof. of Law, Univ. de Montréal and mem. staff, Institut de Recherches en Droit Pub. 1961; el. to H. of C. for Mount Royal in g.e. 1965; re-el. g.e. 1968, 1972, 1974, 1979, 1980; served on Justice and Legal Affairs, External Affairs, Broadcasting and Assistance to Arts, and Divorce Comtes.; apptd. Parlty. Secy. to Prime Min. 1966, 1967; Min. of Justice and Atty. Gen. of Can. 1967; Leader of Lib. Party of Can. 1968–1984; Prime Minister of Can. 1968–79, 1980–84; del. to France-Can. Interparlty. Assn., Paris 1966; rep. Can. at 21st Session of U.N. Gen. Assembly 1966; toured French-speaking African states in 1967 on behalf of Prime Min. and Secy. of State for External Affairs; travelled extensively in Europe, Middle East and Asia 1948–49; attended Internat. Econ. Conf., Moscow 1952; co-founded, co-directed and major contrib. to 'Cité Libre' (monthly review); author of 'Federalism and the French Canadians' 1968; 'Réponses' 1967; co-author 'Deux Innocents en Chine' 1961; contrib. to 'Canadian Dualism/La Dualité Canadienne' 1960; 'The Future of Canadian Federalism' 1965; 'Politics: Canada' 1966; co-editor (with Thomas Axworthy) 'Toward a Just Society: The Trudeau Years'; has written numerous articles and papers in socio-econ. and pol. fields for many publs.; Hon. Fellowship, London Sch. of Economics 1968; Order of Merit, Univ. of Montreal 1975; Freeman of City of London 1975; Hon. Dean, Fac. of Law, Univ. of Poitiers 1975; Berkeley Citation, Univ. of Calif. 1977; Family of Man Award, N.Y. City Council of Churches 1981; Albert Einstein Internat. Peace Prize 1984; Companion of Honour 1984; Companion of the Order of Canada 1985; J.H. Ralston Prize, Faculty of Law, Stanford Univ. 1990; Founding mem., Montreal Civil Liberties Union; mem., InterAction Counc. 1985; recreations: skiing, scuba-diving, canoeing; Address: c/o Heenan Blaikie, 1250 René-Lévesque Blvd. W., Suite 2500, Montréal, Qué. H3B 4Y1.

**TRUDEL, L'honorable Clément,** B.A., LL.L.; juge à la cour supérieure du Québec; né à L'Assomption, Qué. le 7 juillet 1943; f. Joachim Trudel et Elianne Malo; é. Séminaire de Joliette, B.A. 1964; Faculté de Droit de l'Université d'Ottawa, section droit civil, LL.L. 1967; ép. Lise f. Albert Perreault et Gilberte Neveu 24 juin 1967; enfants: Benoit, Jean-François; JUGE À LA COUR SUPÉRIEURE DU QUÉBEC; admis au Barreau du Qué. en 1968; pratique du droit à Joliette 1968–87; nommé Conseiller de la Reine (C.R.) en 1985; Bâtonnier du Barreau des Laurentides en 1979, Vice-président du Barreau du Québec 1984 et Bâtonnier du Québec, en 1985; Chargé de cours à l'Ecole du Barreau 1974–81, Président de l'Ecole du Barreau 1981–83; Représentant du Barreau du Québec à la Fédération des professions juridiques du Canada 1984 et 1985; membre du comité permanent Ministère de la Justice – Barreau du Québec 1984–87; membre du comité tripartite (Magistrature – Ministère de la Justice – Barreau) 1984–87; Membre du conseil d'administration de la Société québécoise d'information juridique (SOQUIJ) 1986 et 1987; Membre de l'Association du Barreau canadien depuis 1975; Membre de l'American Bar Association depuis 1983; récréations: lecture, chasse, pêche, golf; Adresse: 822, rue Bordeleau, Joliette, Qué. J6E 2J5; Bureau: 1 rue Notre-Dame est, Montréal, Qué. H2Y 1B6.

**TRUDEL, Marcel,** O.C. (1971), Docteur ès lettres (1945); né St-Narcisse-de-Champlain, Qué. 29 mai 1917; é. Univ. Laval, B.A., 1938; L.ès lettres, 1941; d.ès lettres summa cum laude, 1945; Univ. Harvard, recherches, 1945–47; ép. Anne Chrétien, 11 Juil. 1942; enfants: Jeanne, Madeleine, Marc.; ép. Micheline d'Allaire, 27 août 1970; DIR. DEPART. D'HISTOIRE, UNIV. D'OTTAWA de 1966 à 1968; prof. Coll. Bourget, Rigaud, 1941–45; prof. d'hist. du Can., Univ. Laval 1947–65; Univ. Carleton 1965–66; sec., Inst. d'Hist. et Géog., Laval 1948–54; dir. 1954–55; dir., Inst. d'Hist., Laval 1955–64; sec., Fac. des lettres, Laval 1952–58; dir., Inst. of Candn. Studies, Carleton Univ. 1965–66; conférencier; Inst. Scient.fr.-can. 1957; a la Sorbonne et l'Inst. cath. de Paris, a l'Univ. de Poitiers, France; Gray Lectures, Univ. de Toronto 1966; prés., Candn. Hist. Assn. 1963–64; dir. gén. adj. de vol I 'Dict. biogr. du Can.'; dir., 'Revue canad. d'hist. soc.'; dir. de collection, 'Hist. de la Nlle-Fr.'; dir. adj., 'Centre de recherche en hist. relig. du Can.'; co-dir. de collect., 'Fleur de Lys'; prés., Conseil des Arts de Qué.; membre: Acad. can-fr.; Acad. berrichonne; bur. comm. des Monuments et lieux hist. du Can.; jury, Aff. univ. dans Conseil des Arts du Can.; prix David 1945 et 1951; prix Casgrain 1961; prix Concours Litt. du Qué. 1963 et 1966; prix Duvernay 1966; prix Gouv. Gén. 1967; prix Molson 1980; prix Macdonald 1984; doct. hon. causa de l'Univ. du Qué.; Univ. Laval; Chevalier de L'Ordre National du Québec; Médailles: Léo-Pariseau 1960; Tyrrell 1964; ouvrages: 'L'influence de Voltaire au Canada' 1945; 'Vézine' 1946; 'Louis XVI, le Congrès américain et le Canada' 1949; 'Carte seign. de la Nouvelle-France' 1950; 'Histoire du Canada par les textes' 1952; 'La régime milit. dans le Gouvernement des Trois-Rivières' 1952; 'L'affaire Jumonville' 1953; 'Chiniquy, Les Trois-Rivières' 1955; 'Le régime seigneurial' 1956; 'Champlain' 1956; 'L'Eglise canadienne sous le régime milit.' (2 vol) 1956, 1957; 'L'esclavage au Can.fr.' 1960; 'Atlas hist. du Can.fr.' 1961; 'Hist. de la Nlle-Fr.' vol I 1963, vol. II 1966; 'Canada: Unity and Diversity' 1967; 'Initiation à la Nlle-Fr.' 1968; 'Jacques Cartier' 1968; 'Le Terrier du Saint-Laurent en 1663' 1972; 'La Population du Canada en 1663' 1973; 'The Beginning of New France' 1972; 'Les débuts du régime seigneurial au Canada' 1974; 'La formation d'une Société: Montréal 1642–1663' 1976; 'La révolution américaine' 1976; La seigneurie des cent-associés' (tome 1: 'Les événements' 1979; tome 2: 'La Société' 1983); 'Catalogue des immigrants: 1632–1662' 1983; 'Mémoires d'un autre siècle' 1987; 'Au Canada français Dictionnaire des esclaves et de leurs propriétaires; 1990; 'Histoire du Montréal de Dollier de Casson' 1992; résidence: 560, Saint-Laurent ouest, app. 632, Longueuil, Qué. J4H 3X3.

**TRUDEL, Rémy,** M.Ed., Ph.D.; éducateur; né St-Thècle, Qué. 20 avril 1948; f. Martin et Béatrice (Veillette) T.; e. Univ. du Québec Trois Rivières B.S.Ed. 1973, M.Ed. 1975; Univ. d'Ottawa Ph.D. 1979; ép. Nicole f. Philippe Dubé 28 Janvier 1969; enfants: Myriam, Maud, Jacinthe; DEPUTÉ EN ROUYN-NORANDA; Recteur, Université du Québec en d'Abitibi-Temiscaminque 1981; Directeur général Univ. du Québec Rouyn 1980; Directeur de la vie étudiante Nicolet, Qué. 1971–74; Directeur du Module des sciences de l'éducation Univ. du Québec Rouyn 1974–75, Directeur du Département des sciences de l'éducation 1975–76, Directeur de l'enseignement et de la recherche 1979–80; Consultant, Institut des Banquiers Canadiens 1976; membre Comm. de l'enseignement et de la recherche et Comm. administrative du réseau Univ. du Qué. 1981; Prés. du Conseil régional de développement de l'Abitibi-Témiscamingue 1981–82; auteur 'Théories de la personnalité: fondements, postulats de base et implications pour la pratique' 1979; membre Conseil d'adm. de l'Assn. canadienne des éducateurs de langue française 1969–70; membre Assn. canadienne des chercheurs en éducation; Assn. canadienne des fondements de l'éducation; Résidence: 380, Rang 5 Ouest, Granada, Qué. J9X 2C0; Bureau: 74 Taschereau E., Rouyn-Noranda, Qué. J9X 3E4.

**TRUEMAN, Stuart Douglas,** LL.D., D.Lit.; writer; b. Saint John, N.B. 6 Nov. 1911; s. John Macmillan and Annie May (Roden) T.; e. Saint John High Sch. 1928; St. Thomas Univ. LL.D. 1970; Univ. of N.B. D.Lit. 1975; m. Mildred d. Riley and Kate Stiles 2 Dec. 1937; two s. Dr. Douglas Hugh M., Stuart Macmillan; early career comm. artist, newspaper cartoonist and reporter; Ed.-in-Chief New Brunswick Telegraph-Journal and Evening Times-Globe, Saint John 20 yrs.; only Maritime Provinces humorist in Stoddart Publishing Co.'s 'That Reminds Me ... Canada's Authors Relive Their Most Embarrassing Moments' (tribute to the late Marta Kurc); co-discoverer Magnetic Hill, Moncton 1933; Hon. Life mem. Saint John Regional Lib.; N.B. Museum; Saint John Press, Radio and TV Club; Candn. Alternate mem. Roosevelt Campobello Internat. Park Comn. 27 yrs.; former mem. Lord Beaverbrook Overseas Scholarship Ctte. and Beaverbrook Playhouse Ctte. Fredericton; recipient Stephen Leacock Award 1969; author (humour) 'Cousin Elva' 1955; 'You're Only as Old as You Act' 1969; 'My Life as a Rose-Breasted Grosbeak' 1972; 'Don't Let Them Smell the Lobsters Cooking' 1982; 'Add Ten Years to Your Life' 1989; (history) 'The Ordeal of John Gyles' 1966; 'An Intimate History of New Brunswick' 1970; 'Tall Tales and True Tales from Down East' 1979; (travelogue) 'The Fascinating World of New Brunswick' 1973; (coll. legends) 'Ghosts, Pirates and Treasure Trove' 1975; (animal & bird stories) 'The Wild Life I've Led' 1976; 'Life's Odd Moments' 1984; (art photos, bilingual text) 'The Colour of New Brunswick' 1981; co-author 'Favorite Recipes from Old New Brunswick Kitchens' 1983; 'Mildred Trueman's New Brunswick Heritage Cookbook' 1986; over 300 articles Candn. and US mags.; guest speaker; Addresses: (Summer) R.R.2, 71 Kennebecasis River Rd., Hampton, N.B. E0G 1Z0 and (Winter) 9016 Mission Oaks Blvd., Seminole, FL 34646.

**TRUEMAN, William Peter Main;** freelance journalist; broadcaster; b. Sackville, N.B. 25 Dec. 1934; s. Albert William and Jean Alberta (Miller) T.; e. Univ. of N.B.; Carleton Univ.; m. Eleanor d. Anne and Norman Wark 22 Dec. 1956; children: Anne, Mark, Victoria; COLUMNIST, STARWEEK MAGAZINE 1988– and THE KINGSTON WHIG-STANDARD 1990– ; Contbr. editor, 'This Country, Canada' and 'Pathways' magazines 1993– ; Copy boy, Ottawa Journal 1953, Jr. Reporter 1953–56; PR, CNR 1956–57; N.Y. Corr., Montreal Star 1957–62, Washington Corr. 1962–64; Ottawa Corr., Toronto Star 1964–65; National Dir., United Nations Assn. of Can. 1966–67; Writer, CBC National News 1968–69, Exec. Producer 1969–70; Head News & Information Programming CBC Network 1970–72; Reporter, CBC Weekday 1972–73; Anchorman, Global Television News 1973–88; Host, 'North South' Vision TV 1988–90; columnist, 'The Catholic Register' 1988–93; recipient Bowater Award for Journalism 1963; Sam Ross Award, RTNDA 1983; author: 'Smoke and Mirrors'; recreations: landscape painting, photography, bicycling, cross-country skiing; Address: R.R. 1, Stella, Ont. K0H 2S0.

**TRUSS, Jan;** writer; b. Stoke-on-Trent, England 3 May 1925; d. William Edwin Degg and Catherine (Spragg) D.; e. Longton H.S. & Thistley Hough; Goldsmiths' Coll., Univ. of London; Univ. of Alta.; Univ. of Calgary; m. Donald; s. Harry and Edith T. 6 July 1946; children: Martin Jon, Sally Virginia; School teacher, England 1945–57; School & univ. teacher, Alta. 1957–72; Winner, First Alta. Search for a New Novelist 1974; Ruth Schwartz Award for Children's Literature 1983; Winner, First prize, short poem, Alberta Poetry Yearbook 1984; Mem., Writers' Union of Can.; Playwrights Union of Can.; CANSCAP; ACTRA; author: 'Bird at the Window' 1973 (novel); 'A Very Small Rebellion' 1977, 'Jasmin' 1982, 'Summer Goes Riding' 1987, 'Peter's Mocassins' 1987 (children's novels); 'Red' (Y.A. novel) 1988; 'Rocky Mountain Symphony' 1983 (non-fiction); 'The Judgement of Clifford Sifton' 1979 (play); 'A Very Small Rebellion & Oomerahgi Oh!' 1977 (plays for young audiences); recreations: theatre goer, wilderness walker; Address: c/o General Publishing Co. Ltd., 30 Lesmill Rd., Don Mills, Ont. M3B 2T6.

**TRYGGVASON, Bjarni V.,** B.A.Sc.; astronaut; b. Reykjavik, Iceland 21 Sept. 1945; e. elem. and high schs. N.S. and B.C.; Univ. of B.C., B.A.Sc. 1972; Univ. of W. Ont. postgrad. work applied math. & fluid dynamics; m. Lily-Anna Zmijak 1984; children: Michael Kristjan, Lauren Stephanie; PAYLOAD SPECIALIST, CANDN. ASTRONAUT PROG. 1983– ; Meteorol. Cloud Physics Group, Atmospheric Environment Service, Toronto 1972–73; Rsch. Assoc. Boundary Layer Wind Tunnel Lab. Univ. of W. Ont. 1974–78 (projects included C.N. Tower in Toronto, the Sears building in Chicago and the Haj Terminal in Saudi Arabia), Lectr. in Applied Math. 1979–82; Guest Rsch. Assoc. Kyoto Univ. Japan and James Cook Univ. of N. Queensland Australia 1978; Assoc. Rsch. Offr. Low Speed Aerodynamics Lab. nat. Rsch. Council Can. 1982 becoming mem. special team assembled to study sinking of Ocean Ranger oil rig; Lectr. in dynamic analysis, stats. & spectral analysis random vibrations Univ. of Ottawa 1982– ; Lectr., Carleton Univ. 1988– ; part-time flying instr. basic, instrument & multi-engine ratings since 1979; holds airline transport license; recipient B.C. Govt. Scholarships 1969–72; Icelandic Candn. Club B.C. Undergrad. Scholarship 1970; Assn. Prof. Engs. B.C. Graduating Book Prize 1972; Ont. Grad. Scholarship 1979; Mem., Assn. of Professional Engineers of Ont.; Engineering Institute of Can.; Candn. Aeronautics and Space Inst.; Candn. Owners and Pilots Assn.; Co-Founder and former Pres., Tuniit Flying Club; Mem., Aerobatics Canada Chapter 5, Ottawa 1986– ; mem. Assn. Prof. Engs. Prov. Ont.; Eng. Inst. Can.; Candn. Aeronautics & Space Inst.; Candn. Owners & Pilots Assn.; recreations: flying (including aerobatic flight jogging), skiing, scuba diving, sky diving; Office: Candn. Space Agency, 6767 Route de l'aéroport, Saint Hubert, Que. J3Y 8Y9.

**TRYNCHY, Hon. Peter, Jr.,** M.L.A.; businessman, farmer; b. Rochfort Bridge, Alta. 22 Aug. 1931; s. Peter and Anna (Roszko) T.; e. Rochfort Bridge (Alta.) Schs.; m. Lorraine Mary d. Frank Wilkinson Sr., Mayerthorpe, Alta. 29 Oct. 1952; children: Darlene Annette, Marlin Peter; MINISTER OF TRANSPORTATION AND UTILITIES, responsible for ALBERTA PUBLIC SAFETY SERVICES 1992– ; owner Mayerthorpe Mar. and various farms; served Mayerthorpe Town Council 6 yrs.; first el. M.L.A. Alta. g.e. 1971, re-el. g.e. 1975, 1979, 1982, 1986, 1989; Min. of Recreation & Parks, Alta. 1979–89; Min. Resp. for Occupational Health & Safety, Min. Resp. for Alta. Public Safety Services and The Workers' Compensation Bd. 1989–92; Past Chrmn., Alta. Hail and Crop Insurance Bd.; Past Pres. Mayerthorpe Chamber Comm.; mem. Royal Cndn. Legion; Freemason (P.M.); Kinsman; P. Conservative; United Church; recreations: baseball, curling, golf; Club: Mayerthorpe Curling (Dir.); Home: (P.O. Box 449) Mayerthorpe, Alta. T0E 1N0; Office: 420 Legislature Bldg., Edmonton, Alta. T5K 2B6.

**TRYON, Valerie Ann,** A.R.C.M., L.R.A.M., F.R.A.M.; pianist; university professor; b. Portsmouth, England 5 Sept. 1934; d. Kenneth Montague and Iris Winifred (Lunan) T.; e. Royal Academy of Music 1949–54; studied with Jacques Fevrier 1954–55; ASSOC. PROF. OF MUSIC, McMASTER UNIV. 1986– ; first BBC solo piano broadcast 1946; Cheltenham Festival recital 1959; Promenade concerts, concertos at the Royal Halls, London, and the other major British concert halls 1959–71; moved to Canada 1971; Artist in Residence, McMaster Univ. 1978– ; adjudicated and performed at numerous music festivals and competitions in N. America and Europe; has broadcast frequently for BBC and N. American stations; recorded for Virtuoso Series of Pye and (solo) for BBC Enterprises, Omnibus, Pye, Argo, Lyrita, Educo, Dorian and the CBC; Assoc. Bd. Scholarship to Royal Academy of Music 1949; Dove Prize (R.A.M.) 1954; Boise Scholarship for Study Abroad 1954; Harriet Cohen Award for Service to Music 1967; F.R.A.M. 1984; Ferencz Liszt Medal of Honour 1986; mem. Hamilton Musicians Guild Local, A.F.M.; Club: R.A.M. (London); Home: 609 Tuscarora Dr., Ancaster, Ont. L9G 3N9; Office: Music Dept., McMaster Univ., Hamilton, Ont. L8S 4L8.

**TRYON, Victor Weld, Jr.,** B.A.; company executive; b. Manhattan, Montana 2 Feb. 1914; s. Victor W. and Grace (Brown) T.; e. (came to Canada, 1918) Winnipeg (Man.) Pub. and High Schs.; Univ. of Manitoba, B.A. 1933; m. Constance Janet, d. late Travers Sweatman, K.C., 13 Nov. 1943; children: Alix Tremaine, Victor W. 3rd; Vice President, Pratt & Whitney Aircraft of Canada Ltd., 1976–79; after grad. employed by International Petroleum Co. Ltd. and posted to Colombia, S.A.; left in 1946 to join present Co. as Gen. Acct.; promoted to Treas., 1947; el. a Dir., 1960; mem., Montreal Chapter, Financial Extves. Inst. (Past Pres.); Delta Kappa Epsilon; recreation: golf; Clubs: Royal Montreal Golf; Hamilton Golf and Country; Home: 148 Colonial Court, Burlington, Ont. L7L 5K8.

**TSUBOUCHI, Daniel T.;** financial executive; b. Toronto, Ont. 16 July 1955; SENIOR VICE PRESIDENT, CORPORATE AFFAIRS AND FINANCE, MARK RESOURCES INC.; Office: 1300, 800 – 5th Ave. S.W., Calgary, Alta. T2P 4A4.

**TSUCHIYA, Takehiko,** B.A.; business executive; b. 5 Feb. 1930; e. Tokyo Shooka Univ. B.A.; PRESIDENT & CHIEF EXECUTIVE OFFICER, NISSHO IWAI CANADA LTD.; Executive Vice-Pres., Nissho Iwai Corp. Japan; Office: 1506, 150 King St. W., Box 106, Toronto, Ont. M5H 1J9.

**TSUI, Lap-Chee,** O.C., B.Sc., M.Phil., Ph.D., DCL, D.Sc., F.R.S.C.; geneticist; b. Shanghai, China 21 Dec. 1950; s. Jing-Lue and Hui-Ching (Wang) Hsue; e. New Asia Coll. The Chinese Univ. of Hong Kong B.Sc. 1972, M.Phil. 1974 (Yale-in-China Scholarship 1968–69); Univ. of Pittsburgh Ph.D. 1979; DCL (hon.) 1991; D.Sc. (hon.) 1991, 1992; m. Lan Fong Ng d. Wing Wah and Sui Sum 11 Feb. 1977; two s. Eugene, Felix; SR. SCIENTIST, RSCH. INST. HOSP. FOR SICK CHILDREN 1988– (Scientist 1983–88); Medical Rsch. Council Scientist 1989– ; Prof. of Med. Genetics, Univ. of Toronto 1990– (Asst. Prof. 1983–88, Assoc. Prof. 1988–90); Post-doctoral Investigator Biol. Div. Oak Ridge Nat. Lab. Tennessee 1979–80; Postdoctoral Fellow in Genetics Hosp. for Sick Children 1981–83; recipient Candn. Cystic Fibrosis Found. Fellowship 1982–83 and Scholarship 1984–89; discoverer of the gene responsible for Cystic Fibrosis 1989; Sellers Chair, Cystic Fibrosis Rsch. 1990– ; author or co-author numerous sci. papers, abstracts; Editorial Boards: Internat. Journal of Genome Rsch. 1990– ; PCR Methods and Application 1991– ; Clinical Genetics (Assoc. Editor) 1991– ; Human Mutation (Communicating Editor) 1991– ; Human Molecular Genetics 1991– ; European Journal of Human Genetics (Advisor) 1992– ; Assoc. Fellow, Massey Coll., Univ. of Toronto; Fellow, The Royal Society of London; Royal Society of Canada; recipient of numerous awards including: Award of Merit, Educ. Found., Federation of Chinese Candn. Professionals (Ont.) 1985; Chinese Candn. Achievement Award, Chinese Community Centre of Ont. 1986; The Paul di Sant'Agnese Distinguished Scientific Achievement Award, Cystic Fibrosis Found. (USA) 1989; Royal Soc. of Canada Centennial Award 1989; Toronto City Award of Merit 1990; Metro Toronto Gardiner Award 1990; Doris Tulcin Cystic Fibrosis Rsch. Achievement Award, Cystic Fibrosis Found. (USA) 1991; Etobicoke City Hall of Fame 1991; Officer of the Order of Canada 1991; The Cresson Medal, Franklin Institute 1992; The Mead Johnson Award 1992; Distinguished Scientist Award, Candn. Soc. of Clinical Investigators 1992; Commemorative Medal for 125th Anniversary of Candn. Confederation 1992; Sarstedt Rsch. Prize 1993; XXII Sanremo Internat. Award for Genetic Rsch. 1993; Mem., Am. Soc. Human Genetics (Bd. Mem.); Assn. of Chinese Geneticists in Am. (Past-Pres.); Chinese Candn. Assn. of Biomedical Professionals (Past-Pres.); The Federation of Chinese Candn. Professionals (Ont.); The Human Genome Organisation; Academia Sinica; Trustee of the FCCP Education Foundation; Office: 555 University Ave., Toronto, Ont. M5G 1X8.

**TSUJITA, Masaru James,** Ph.D., P.Ag.; university professor; b. Whonnock, B.C. 26 Feb. 1935; s. Takeni and Hide (Goryo) T.; e. Olds Coll., dipl.Ag. 1956; Utah State Univ., B.Sc. 1962; Univ. of Alta., M.Sc. 1964; Ohio State Univ., Ph.D. 1974; m. Miyuki Lilly d. Yoshio and Sueno Ikeda 27 June 1964; children: Cameron, Kimberly; PROF., DEPT. OF HORTICULTURAL SCI., UNIV. OF GUELPH 1985– ; Farming, Alta. 1953–58; Instr. in Plant Sci., Olds Coll. 1964–66; Sr. Instr. 1966–74; Co-ord., Crop & Soils Technol. 1968–70; Asst. Prof., Univ. of Guelph 1974–79; Assoc. Prof. 1979–84; Prof. 1985– ; Mem., Univ. of Guelph Senate 1985–87; Cons.: hort. rsch., edn., indoor illumination; Assoc. Ed., 'Canadian Journal of Plant Science'; Flowers Can. Person of the Year Award for Excellence in Rsch. 1985; Henry E. Heiner Award for Excellence in Teaching & Rsch. 1985; Pres., Candn. Ornamental Plant Found. 1987–88; Candn. Soc. for Hort. Sci. 1986–87; Candn. Rep., Internat. Comn. for Illumination 1985–87; Mem., Am. Soc. for Hort. Sci.; Agric. Inst. of Can.; Ont. Inst. of Agrol.; Flowers Can.; Candn. Orn. Plant Found.; Cec. Delworth Found.; Roses Inc.; Prof. Plant Growers Assn.; Candn. Soc. Hort. Sci; Internat. Soc. for Hort.; author: chapters in 'Rose Manual,' 'Potted Chrysanthemum'; recreations: golf, skiing, fishing, hiking; Clubs: Masonic Lodge; Sigma Xi; Phi Kappa Phi; Home: 75 Durham St., Guelph, Ont. N1H 2Y4; Office: Guelph, Ont. N1G 2W1.

**TUCK, John A.,** Q.C., B.A., LL.B.; executive; b. Niagara Falls, Ont. 12 Feb. 1913; s. Dr. John R. and Elizabeth (Cleghorn) T.; e. Univ. of Alberta, B.A. 1932, LL.B. 1935; m. Dorothy, d. William Reed, Toronto, Ont., 10 Aug. 1938; children: John, David, Margaret, Barbara; Past. Pres., Toronto Rehab. Centre; Past Chairman, Ins. Law Sec., Candn. Bar Assn.; read law with Woods, Field, Craig & Hyndman, Edmonton, Alta.; called to Bar of Alta., 1936, and to Bar of Ont., 1947; cr. Q.C. 1955; practised law with Woods, Field, Craig & Hyndman, Edmonton, Alta., 1936–37; joined staff of Candn. Life Ins. Assn. as Legal Asst., Dec. 1937; apptd. Asst. Gen. Counsel 1948, Gen. Counsel 1955, Mang. Dir. & Gen. Counsel 1961, Mang. Dir. 1966; Extve. Dir. 1972–78; Dir., Arbitrators' Inst. of Canada 1978–80, Secy. 1980–88; Hon. Dir., Equitable Life Ins. Co. of Can.; Toronto Rehabilitation Centre; Delta Upsilon; Un. Church; recreations: golf, curling; Clubs: Rosedale Golf; Toronto Cricket, Skating & Curling; Home: 177 Alexandra Blvd., Toronto, Ont. M4R 1M3.

**TUCKER, Brian,** Ph.D., M.B.A., B.Eng.; university professor; stress researcher; management consultant; b. Liverpool, Eng. 25 July 1941; s. Richard Owen and Evelyn (Pickering) T.; e. Liverpool Coll. Sch.; Univ. of Liverpool, B.Eng. 1963; Univ. of Alta., M.B.A. 1974; Cornell Univ., Ph.D. 1986; children: Christie Marie, Dana Wendy Cherie, Janet Leona; ADJUNCT PROF. OF ORGN. BEHAVIOUR, SIMON FRASER UNIV./CARIBOO COLL. 1989– ; Training Offr., Assoc. Electr. Indus. 1965–66; Tech. Training Offr., Rank Xerox Limited 1966–67; Engr., B.C. Tel. Co. 1967–70; Staff Devel. Offr., Govt. of Alta. 1970–75; Orgn. Effectiveness Coord., Esso Petrol. Can. 1976–81; Rsch. Fellow, Tavistock Inst. for Human Relns. 1983–84; Vis. Asst. Prof., Bucknell Univ. 1985–86; Assoc. Prof., Univ. of Sask. 1986–89; Pres., Western O.D. Cons. Limited 1975– ; introduced multi-dimensional model of the stress experience; scholarships: Civil Serv. Assn. of Alta. Grad. 1973; Izaac Walton Killam Grad. Mem. 1974; Wilfrid R. May Career Devel., Alta. Heritage Trust Fund 1982, 1983; SSHRCC doct. 1984, 1985; Cornell Univ. Rsch., Tuition & Fees 1982–85; Mem., Acad. of Mngt.; Am. Psychological Assoc.; Candn. Psychol. Assoc.; Soc. for Industrial and Organizational Psychology; United Church; author: 'Components of Stress' 1986 and var. articles; recreations: golf, skiing, climbing, photography.

**TUDOR, Dean Frederick,** B.A., M.L.S.; educator; author; b. Toronto, Ont. 26 May 1943; s. Frederick and Jean (Pasquantonio) T.; e. Univ. of Toronto Schs. 1962; Univ. of Toronto (York Coll.) B.A. 1965; McGill Univ. M.L.S. 1967 (G.R. Lomer Scholar 1965); George Brown C.A.A.T. Dip. Haute Cuisine 1974; m. Ann d. Myron and Eileen Johnson 17 June 1978; stepchildren: Coleman, Mary and Ross Harwell; PROF. OF JOURNALISM, RYERSON POLYTECH. UNIV. 1984– and FACILITIES CO-ORDINATOR, ROGERS COMMUNICATION CENTRE'S RESOURCES CENTRE 1992– ; Princ. Gothic Epicures; Bus. Mgr. Honest Threads; Reference Lib. York Univ. Libs. Toronto 1967–68; Dir. Lib. Br. Ont. Dept. of Revenue 1968–72; Rsch. Lib. Ont. Min. of Treasury, Econ. & Intergovt'al Affairs 1972–73; Chrmn. Lib. Arts Dept. present Inst. 1974–80, Prof. of Lib. Arts 1980–83; recipient H.W. Wilson Award for Special Libs. 1972; author: 'Wines, Beers and Spirits' 1975, 2nd. ed. 1985; 'Cooking for Entertaining' 1976 (Am. Lib. Assn. Notable Reference Book Award 1976); 'Black Music' 1979; 'Contemporary Popular Music' 1979; 'Jazz' 1979; 'Grass Roots Music' 1979; 'Popular Music' 1983 (Lib. Jour. Reference Book Award 1984); 'Finding Answers' 1993; ed. Candn. Book Review Annual 1975– ; Annual Index to Popular Music Record Reviews 1972–79; (Am. Lib. Assn. 'Choice' Award 1974); Popular Music Periodicals Index 1973–79; Informatics consultant, 'Sources' 1993– ; Internat. Wine & Food Soc. 'Grapevine' newsletter; wine columnist, 'Viewpoint 50'; mem. Am. Lib. Assn.; Indexing & Abstracting Soc. Can.; Nat. Book Critics Circle; Candn. Assn. of Journalists; Investigative Reporters and Editors (IRE); Soc. Wine Educators; Wine Writers' Circle, Toronto; Winetasters of Toronto; Toronto Vintners; recreations: food & wine, music, writing; Home: 51 Gothic Ave., Toronto, Ont. M6P 2V8; Office: 350 Victoria St., Toronto, Ont. M5B 2K3.

**TUDOR, Sir James Cameron,** B.A., M.A.; diplomat; b. Clapham, St. Michael, Barbados 18 Oct. 1918; e. Harrison Coll.; Keble Coll., Univ. of Oxford B.A. 1943, M.A. 1948; single; HIGH COMNR. FOR BARBADOS, GOV. OF BARBADOS 1990– ; Founder/Mem., Democratic Labour Party (1st Gen. Sec.); 1st Black to become Pres. of Oxford Union 1942; Sr. History Master, Queen's Coll. Guyana 1949–52; Mem. of Parl. 1954–71; of Senate 1971–72, 1986– ; Rep. for St. Lucy 1954–71; Min. of Edn. 1961–67; Dep. Premier 1965–67; Dep. P.M. 1966–71; Leader of the Senate 1971–72, 1986–89; High Comnr. to Britain 1972; Ambassador to France, Cyprus, W. Germany, Holland, Belgium & Israel 1972–75; Perm. Rep. to U.N. 1976; Min., Fgn. Affairs 1986–89; Silver Cross, Order of Christopher Columbus (Govt. of Dominican Rep.) 1969; Companion of the Most Distinguished Order of Saint Michael & Saint George (Queen Elizabeth II) 1970; Knight Commander 1987; Order of the Liberator (Govt. of Venezuela) 1987; recreations: Masonry, Forestry, reading, cooking, music; Home: 368 Lisgar Rd., Rockcliffe Park, Ont. K1M 0E9.

**TUER, Robert Burton,** LL.B., Q.C.; lawyer; b. Toronto, Ont. 14 June 1934; s. Clarence Frederick and Helen Isabel (Ross) T.; e. Osgoode Hall 1958; m. Lynne d. Geoffrey and Hester Beament 25 June 1960; children: James, Carolyn, John; MANAGING PARTNER, FASKEN CAMPBELL GODFREY 1991–94 and PARTNER & DIR., FASKEN MARTINEAU 1986– ; articled to W.R. Ramsay, Q.C. 1952–54; Fasken Robertson Aitchison Pickup & Calvin 1956–58; called to Bar of Ont. 1958; Assoc., present firm 1958; Partner 1964; Q.C. 1971; occasional guest lectr. & panelist, Law Soc. of U.C. and Candn. Bar Assn.; Dir., St. Lawrence Cement Inc.; Seaboard Surety Co. of Can.; Mem., Candn. Bar Assn.; Advocates' Soc. (Past Dir.); Co. of York Law Assn.; recreations: golf, skiing, reading; clubs: Ontario, Huntsville Downs Golf & Country; Home: 80 Highbourne Rd., Toronto, Ont. M5P 2J4; Office: Box 20, T-D Ctr., Toronto, Ont. M5K 1N6.

**TUGMAN, Laurie Alan,** B.A., C.A.; financial executive; b. Kingston, Ont. 31 March 1954; s. W. Lindsay and Mildred Irene (Caldwell) T.; e. Univ. of Western Ont. B.A. 1975; C.A. 1977; m. Teresa Fitzmaurice 6 Aug. 1977; children: James, Jeffrey, Jonathan; VICE PRESIDENT FINANCE & CHIEF FINANCIAL OFFICER, DYNATEC INTERNATIONAL LTD. 1990– ; articled Thorne, Riddell & Co. 1975; C.A. 1977; Manager, Corp. Acctg., Famous Players Ltd. 1978; Corp. Accountant, Suncor (Toronto) 1979; Manager, Financial Accounting (Fort McMurray, Alta.) 1981; Manager, Performance Analysis 1982; Corp. Controller, Tricil (Mississauga) 1985; Regional Manager (Hamilton) 1988; Mem., Candn. Inst. of C.A.s; Inst. of C.A.s of Ont.; Financial Extves. Inst.; Christ Church United Ch. (Treasurer & Bd. Mem. 1986–88); club: Richmond Hill Country; Home: 1410 Marshwood Place, Mississauga, Ont. L5J 4J5; Office: 2 East Beaver Creek Rd., Building No. 2, Richmond Hill, Ont. L4B 2N3.

**TUGWELL, Maurice Arthur John,** C.B.E., Ph.D.; writer; institute president; b. Totland, Isle of Wight, U.K. 24 June 1925; s. William Basil Pope and Marion Bryce (Cousens) T.; e. Bedford Sch. 1943; King's Coll., Univ. of London, Ph.D. 1979; m. C. Claire d. Norman and Peggy Johnstone 11 Jan. 1975; children: Andrew Hamilton, Julia Alexandra; PRES., THE MACKENZIE INST. FOR THE STUDY OF TERRORISM, REVOLUTION AND PROPAGANDA 1986– ; enlisted, British Army 1943 (age 17); commissioned, Parachute Regt. 1944; served N.W. Eur. (Rhine crossing) 1945, India 1945, Palestine 1945–48, Malaya 1950–52, Cyprus 1957–59, 1963–64, Bahrain & Aden 1965, N. Ireland 1971–73, Iran 1973–75; Brigadier, retired 1978; Founding Dir., Ctr. for Conflict Studies, Univ. of N.B. 1980–86; speaker, broadcaster & writer; C.B.E. 1973 (for serv. in N. Ireland); Mem., Royal Un. Serv. Inst. for Defence Studies; Ed. Adv. Bd., 'Conflict Quarterly'; author: 'Airborne to Battle' 1971, 'Arnhem, A Case Study' 1975, 'Skiing for Beginners' 1977, 'Peace with Freedom' 1988; editor/contbr.: 'The Unquiet Peace' 1957, 'Armies in Low-Intensity Conflict' 1989, 'Deception Operations: Studies in the East-West Context' 1990; recreations: reading, walking, photography; clubs: Royal Candn. Military Inst.; Home: 3546 Redwood Ave., Victoria, B.C. V8P 4Z7; Office: P.O. Box 338, Adelaide Postal Stn., Toronto, Ont. M5C 2J4.

**TULANDI, Togas,** M.D., F.R.C.S(C); obstetrician/gynecologist; b. Indonesia; e. Univ. of Indonesia M.D. 1971; McGill Univ.; DIR. DIVISION OF REPRODUCTIVE ENDOCRINOLOGY/INFERTILITY, MCGILL UNIV. 1988– , Prof. of Obstetrics & Gynecol. 1991– ; Attending Staff, Jewish Gen. Hosp. and Royal Victoria Hosp.; Charter mem. Soc. Reproductive Surgs. 1984; Pres.-Elect, Candn. Fertility & Andrology Soc. 1994– (Secy.-Treas. 1990–93); Office: 687 ave. des Pins ouest, Montreal, Que. H3A lAl.

**TULIP, John,** B.Sc., Ph.D.; university professor; b. Durham, England 2 Sept. 1943; s. John and Lillian T.; e. Sheffield, B.Sc. 1965; University Coll., London 1969; m. Jennifer Shaw-Pethers; children: Karen, Andrea; HON. PROF., MED. FAC., UNIV. OF ALTA. 1982– ; Prof., Elect. Engr. 1974; cons., Govts. of Can. & U.S. and others; Tech. Dir., Aurora Laser Inc.; leading specialist in med. laser tech.; Founding Dir., Alta. Laser Inst.; author of 70 sci. pubs.; Home: 11625 Edinboro Rd., Edmonton, Alta.; Office: Edmonton, Alta. T6G 2E5.

**TULLY, James Hamilton,** B.A., Ph.D.; university professor; b. Nanaimo, B.C. 17 April 1946; s. John Patrick and Ethel Lorraine (Hamilton) T.; e. Univ. of B.C. B.A. 1974; Univ. of Cambridge Ph.D. 1977; m. Debra d. Harold and Catherine Higgins 1990; children: Cynthia, Erin; PROFESSOR OF PHILOSOPHY, MCGILL UNIV. 1992– ; Professor of Political Sci. & Philosophy, McGill Univ. 1977–92; taught and lectured at several U.S., Candn. & U.K. univs.; Advisor, Royal Comn. on Aboriginal Peoples 1992–94; Sir John Seeley Distinguished Lecturer, Univ. of Cambridge 1993–94; author: 'A Discourse on Property' 1980, 'An Approach to Political Philosophy' 1993; editor: 'John Locke' 1983, 'Meaning and Context' 1988, 'Puferndorf' 1991, 'Philosophy in an Age of Pluralism' 1994; Home: 167 Beacon Hill Rd., Beaconsfield, Que. H9W 1T5; Office: 855 Sherbrooke O., Montreal, Que. H3A 2T7.

**TULLY, R. Brent,** Ph.D.; astronomer; b. Toronto, Ont. 9 March 1943; s. William Munro and Margaret Jean (Eaton) T.; e. Univ. of B.C. B.Sc. 1964; Univ. of Md. Ph.D. 1972; ASTRONOMER, INST. FOR ASTRONOMY UNIV. OF HAWAII 1975– ; Discoverer 'Tully-Fisher' relation (method for measuring scale and age of universe); author 'Nearby Galaxies Atlas' 1987; 'Nearby Galaxies Catalog' 1988; Office: Honolulu, Hawaii.

**TULVING, Endel,** M.A., Ph.D., D.Litt., F.R.S.C., F.R.S.; cognitive psychologist; educator; b. Estonia 26 May 1927; s. Juhan and Linda T.; e. Univ. of Toronto B.A. 1953, M.A. 1954; Harvard Univ. Ph.D. 1957; Yale Univ. M.A. (h.c.) 1969; Univ. of Umea, Sweden Ph.D. (h.c.) 1982; D.Litt., Univ. of Waterloo 1987; D.Litt., Laurentian Univ. 1988; Doctor of Psychology (h.c.) Tartu Univ., Estonia 1989; m. Ruth d. Eduard and Hilda Mikkelsaar 24 June 1950; two d. Elo Ann Tulving-Blais, Linda; ANNE AND MAX TANENBAUM CHAIR IN COGNITIVE NEUROSCIENCE, ROTMAN RSCH. INSTITUTE OF BAYCREST CENTRE 1992– ; UNIV. PROFESSOR EMERITUS IN PSYCHOLOGY, UNIV. OF TORONTO 1992– ; Lectr. to Prof. of Psychol., Univ. of Toronto 1956–70, 1972–92, Univ. Prof. 1985–92, Chrmn. 1974–80; Prof. of Psychol. Yale Univ. 1970–75; Fellow, Center for Advanced Study in Behavioural Sciences Stanford, Cal. 1972–73; Sr. Rsch. Fellowship, Nat. Rsch. Council 1964–65; Visiting Scholar Univ. of Cal. Berkeley 1964–65; Commonwealth Visiting Prof., Oxford Univ. 1977–78; recipient Izaak Walton Killam Meml. Scholarship Can. Council 1976; Howard Crosby Warren Medal Soc. Exper. Psychols. 1982; Distinguished Sci. Achievement Award Am. Psychol. Assn. 1983, Candn. Psychol. Assn. 1983; Foreign Hon. Mem., Am. Acad. of Arts and Sciences 1986; Guggenheim Fellowship 1987; Foreign Assoc., U.S. Nat. Acad. of Sciences 1988; Foreign mem., Royal Swedish Acad. of Sciences 1989; Fellow, Royal Soc. of London 1992; Izaak Walton Killam Memorial Prize, Canada Council 1994; Gold Medal Award for Life Achievement in Psychological Science, Am. Psych. Foundation 1994; author 'Elements of Episodic Memory' 1983; ed. 'Organization of Memory' 1972; 'Journal of Verbal Learning and Verbal Behaviour' 1969–72; Mem., Ed. Bd., Oxford Psychology Series 1979– ; numerous articles sci. jours.; William James Fellow, Am. Psychol. Soc.; Fellow, Am. Psychol. Assn.; Candn. Psychol. Assn.; Am. Assn. Advanc. Sci.; Soc. of Experimental Psychologists; mem., Psychonomic Soc. (Gov. Bd. 1975–80); Internat. Neuropsychol. Soc.; Soc. for Neuroscience; Home: 45 Baby Point Cres., Toronto, Ont. M6S 2B7; Office: Rotman Rsch. Institute of Baycrest Centre, 3560 Bathurst St., North York, Ont. M6A 2E1.

**TULVING, Ruth,** R.C.A.; artist painter/printmaker; b. Estonia; e. Ont. College of Art grad. 1962; L'Academie de la Grande Chaumiere, Paris; California College of Art (printmaking) 1963–44; Taught painting and printmaking, Ontario College of Art 1965–73; Pres. of Ont. Soc. of Artists 1983–84; Solo exhibs. in Canada, U.S.A., France, England, Sweden, Estonia and China; recipient Lieutenant Governor's Medal 1962; National Academy of Design (U.S.A.) Award 1966; many other awards and prizes; elected mem., Royal Candn. Academy of Arts 1977; Address: 45 Baby Point Cres., Toronto, Ont. M6S 2B7.

**TUMASONIS, Elizabeth,** B.A., M.A., Ph.D.; university professor and administrator; b. Charleston, W. Va. 1 Sept. 1941; d. Thomas Kesley and Christyne (Bowman) Barnes; e. Coll. of William and Mary B.A. 1963; New York Univ. M.A. 1967; Univ. of Calif. at Berkeley Ph.D. 1979; m. Rimas P. s. Dr. Venceslaus P. and Vida T. 26 dec. 1978; CHAIR, DEPT. OF HISTORY IN ART, UNIV. OF VICTORIA 1991– ; Instr., Univ. of Missouri 1966–7; DePauw Univ. 1967–69; Indiana Univ. 1967–69; Univ. of S. Calif. 1973–75; in Europe on dissertation rsch. 1975–76; Visiting Asst. Prof., Univ. of New Mexico 1977–78; Asst. Prof. (part time), Calif. State Univ. 1978–81; joined Dept. of History in Art, Univ. of Victoria 1981; tenure 1986; Assoc. Prof. 1991; 3M Teaching Fellowship 1992; Univ. of Victoria Alumni Award for Excellence in Teaching 1989 (1st recipient); Samuel H. Kress Found. Grant 1975–76; Mem., Universities art Assn. of Can.; Coll. Art Assn.; German Studies Assn.; author of several journal articles; recreations: gardening, bird-watching, dog-walking; clubs: Victoria Horticultural Soc.; Home: 367 Irving Rd., Victoria, B.C. V8S 4A3; Office: P.O. Box 1700, Victoria, B.C. V8W 2Y2.

**TUMMON, Ian S.,** M.D., F.R.C.S.(C); university professor, physician; e. Univ. of Toronto M.D. 1971–75; Resident, Toronto Western Hosp. 1975–77; Univ. of Ottawa 1977–81; Rush-Presbyn.-St. Lukes Medical Ctr., Fellow, Section of Reproductive Endocrin. & Infertility 1985–87; Univ. of Illinois at Chicago, postgrad. studies 1986; ASST. PROF., DEPT. OF OBSTETRICS & GYNAECOLOGY, UNIV. OF WESTERN ONT. & STAFF, DEPT. OF GYNAECOLOGY & REPRODUCTIVE MED., UNIVERSITY HOSP. 1988– ; Chrmn., Continuing Medical Education Ctte., Dept. OB/GYN, Univ. of W. Ont. 1993– ; Active Staff, Grace Gen. Hosp.; Courtesy Staff, Ottawa Gen. Hosp.; Clin. Assoc. Staff, Ottawa Civic Hosp. 1981–85; Instr., Rush Medical Coll.; Adjunct Attending Staff, Rush-Presbyn.-St. Lukes Med. Ctr. 1985–87; Asst. Prof., Rush Medical Coll.; Asst. Attending Staff, Rush-Presbyn.-St. Lukes Med. Ctr.; Assoc. Attending Staff / Chief, Section of Repro. Endocrin. / Dir. of Edn., Obs./Gyn., St. Francis Hospital 1987–88; FRCS(C) 1981; Am. Bd. Osb./Gyn. Inc., dipl. 1985; Cert. of Special Qualification in Repro. Endocrin. 1990; recipient of several researh awards and grants; Mem., Soc. of Obs. & Gyn. of Can.; Bioscreen Inc.; Am. Soc. of Androl.; Candn. Fertility & Androl. Soc.; Am. Fert. Soc.; Am. Coll. Obs. & Gyn.; Ont. Med. Assn.; member of 4 ad hoc review committees; has made several presentations at hospitals, seminars, TV & radio; author/co-author of num. medical articles, abstracts & newsletters; Office: 339 Windermere Rd., London, Ont. N6A 5A5.

**TUNNICLIFFE, Verena Julia,** B.Sc., M.Phil., Ph.D.; university professor; b. Deep River, Ont. 6 June 1953; d. Philip Robert and Patricia Maria (Brown) T.; e. McMaster Univ. B.Sc. 1975; Yale Univ. M.Phil. 1978, Ph.D. 1980; m. John F. s. John and Louise Garrett 8 May 1987; one d.: Arielle K.; ASSOC. PROF., DEPT. OF BIOLOGY & SCHOOL OF EARTH & OCEAN SCIENCES, UNIV. OF VICTORIA; on faculty at Univ. of Victoria since 1982; major field of research: evoluton & ecology of marine communities; has worked in coral reef, fiord & deep-sea habitats; major achievement: discovery & documentation of animals that live at hydrothermal vents (hot water springs) on the ocean floor off B.C.; major research tool: deep-diving submersibles; author of many scientific articles; Office: Victoria, B.C. V8W 2Y2.

**TUNNILLIE, Ovilu;** artist; b. Cape Dorset, N.W.T.; d. Toonoo and Sheojuke T.; medium: sculpture, jewellery; 20 group exbns. incl. most recent: Marion Scott Gallery Vancouver 1992, Surrey Art Gallery Surrey, B.C. 1992, The Isaacs/Innuit Gallery Toronto 1991, l'Iglou Art Esquimau, Douai (toured 3 cities) France 1991, Inuit Gallery of Vancouver 1991, Feheley Fine Arts Toronto 1990; solo exbns.: Canadian Guild of Crafts Quebec Montreal 1981; works in 8 collections incl. art galleries of McMaster Univ. and Winnipeg, Canada Council Art Bank Ottawa, Candn. Guild of Crafts Quebec, Candn. Mus. of Civilization Hull, Que., GE Canada, Hermitage Mus. Leningrad, Soviet Union, Nat. Gallery of Canada Ottawa; art collector Sam Sarick donated carving of an eagle by Ovilu to Hermitage Mus. in Leningrad which was displayed at 'Hermitage-89: New Exhibits'; attended opening: 'Women in the North' exbn. Marion Scott Gall. 1992; subject of articles and catalogues; Home: Cape Dorset, N.W.T.; Office: c/o Ingo Hessel, Indian and Northern Affairs Canada, Les Terrasses de la Chaudière, Ottawa, Ont. K1A 0H4.

**TUNNILLIE, Qavaroak;** artist; b. 15 June 1928 children: Peter, Letia; medium: sculpture, printmaking; 60

group exbns. incl. most recent: l'Iglou Art Esquimau, Douai (toured 14 cities) France 1987–92, Inuit Gall. of Vancouver 1991, Feheley Fine Arts Toronto 1991, Candn. Mus. of Civilization Hull, Que. 1990, 'Masters of the Arctic' UN Gen. Assembly N.Y. 1989; solo exbns.: Inuit Gall. of Vancouver Ltd. 1992, Feheley Fine Arts Toronto 1990, Inuit Galerie Mannheim, Germany 1981, Waddington Galleries Toronto 1980, Theo Waddington Montreal 1973, 1979; collections: McMaster Univ. Art Gall. Hamilton, Canada Council Art Bank, Candn. Mus. of Civilization, Dennos Mus. Ctr., N.W. Michigan Coll. Traverse City, Mich., GE Canada Mississauga, Musée des beaux-arts de Montréal, Sunnybrook Medical Ctr. Toronto, Toronto-Dominion Bank Coll.; sculpture 'Mother & Child' appeared on cover of 'Canadian Labour' Dec. 1968; subject of articles and catalogues; Home: Cape Dorset, N.W.T.; Office: c/o Dorset Fine Arts, 33 Belmont St., Toronto, Ont. M5R 1P9.

**TUOHY, Carolyn J.,** B.A., M.A., Ph.D.; university professor and administrator; b. Toronto, Ont. 29 Oct. 1945; d. Carman Russell and Marjorie May (Valliant) Hughes; e. Univ. of Toronto B.A. 1966; Yale Univ. M.A. 1968, Ph.D. 1974; m. Walter s. Walter and Mary T. 5 May 1973; children: Laura, Kevin; VICE-PROVOST, UNIV. OF TORONTO 1992– ; Asst. Prof., Univ. of Toronto 1970–76; Assoc. Prof. 1976–88; Prof. 1988– ; Vice-Chair, Adv. Council on Occupational Health & Occupational Safety, Govt. of Ont. 1982–91; Mem., Academic Adv. Ctte., Ont. Council on Univ. Affairs 1991– ; Mem., Bd. of Dir., Candn. Pol. Sci. Assn. 1986–88; Sr. Fellow, Massey College; author: 'Policy and Politics in Canada: Institutionalized Ambivalence' 1992; co-author: 'Opting out of Medicare: Private Medical Markets in Ontario' 1980; Office: 27 King's College Circle, Toronto, Ont. M5S 1A1.

**TUPPER, Allan James Arthur,** B.A., M.A., Ph.D.; university professor; political scientist; b. Ottawa, Ont. 19 Dec. 1950; s. Thurman Arthur and Kathleen Agnes (Rodgers) T.; e. Carleton Univ., B.A. 1970, Pub.Admin.dipl. 1971, M.A. 1972; Queen's Univ., Ph.D. 1977; m. Peggy d. George and Janey Shelfoon 1 July 1972; children: Joshua, Adam; ASSOC. DEAN OF ARTS, UNIV. OF ALTA. 1993– ; Admin. Offr., Telesat Can. 1972–73; Asst. Prof., Dept. of Pol. Sci., Univ. of Alta. 1976–81; Assoc. Prof. 1981–86; Prof. 1986– ; Assoc. Chrmn. 1983–85; Chrmn. 1985–92; Sr. Cons., 'The Canadian Encyclopedia'; frequent pol. commentator, local & nat. media; Mngt. Bd., Ctr. for Constitutional Studies, Univ. of Alta.; Anglican; Mem., Candn. Pol. Sci. Assn. (Bd. of Dir. 1985–87; Ed. 'Bulletin' 1982–86); Inst. of Pub. Admin. of Can.; author: 'Public Money in the Private Sector' 1982 & num. scholarly articles; coeditor: 'Public Corporations and Public Policy in Canada' 1981; 'Privatization, Public Corporations and Public Policy' 1989; 'Government and Politics in Alberta' 1992; 'Corruption, Character and Conduct' 1993; recreation: baseball; Home: 672 Romaniuk Rd., Edmonton, Alta. T6R 1A6; Office: Edmonton, Alta. T6G 2E8.

**TURBIDE, Diane Mary,** B.A.; editor, writer; b. Montreal, Que. 10 Feb. 1954; d. Charles Joseph and Mary Eileen (Deegan) T.; e. McGill Univ. B.A. 1981; Banff School of Fine Arts Fall 1981; m. Hugh s. Michael and Pauline Ashton 1 May 1987; one s.: Leo; ASSOCIATE EDITOR, ENTERTAINMENT, MACLEAN'S MAGAZINE 1988– ; various freelance work with CBC Radio, CBC-TV, Radio Guide, Cottage Life; Senior Editor / Book Review Editor, Quill & Quire 1981–88; Bd. of Dir., Stanley Knowles Housing Coop. 1989–91; Mem., Southern Ont. Newspaper Guild (CLF & AFL-CIO) Local 87; Home: 38 Orchard View Blvd., #1207, Toronto, Ont. M4R 2G3; Office: 777 Bay St., Toronto, Ont. M5W 1A7.

**TURCOT, Lt.-Gen. G.A.,** C.M.M., C.D., B.A.; b. Québec, Que. 9 Dec. 1917; s. René and Yvonne (Légaré) T.; e. Laval Univ., B.A.; m. Helen, d. William P. Mitchell; two d.; with N.P.A.M., Les Voltigeurs de Québec, 1935–39 (2nd Lieut., Lieut.); Active Army, Royal 22e Regt., 1939; served in U.K. (1939), Sicily (1943), Italy (1943–44), France, Netherlands, Germany (1945); apptd. C.O., R22eR., 1945; awarded Croix de Guerre; attended Candn. Staff Coll., 1946, Gen. Staff Appt., Army Hdqrs., Ottawa, 1947; re-apptd. C.O., R22eR, 1948–49; Candn. Joint Staff, London, Eng., 1950–52; attended Jt. Services Staff Coll., Eng., 1952; Dir. of Mil. Operations, AHQ Ottawa, 1952–56; attended Nat. Def. Coll., Canada, 1956; Mil. Adviser, Internat. Supervisory Comn., Indo China, 1957–58; Offr. in charge of Adm., Hdqrs. Quebec Command, Montreal, Que., 1958–59; Commdr., 1st Canadian Inf. Brigade Group, Calgary, Alta., 1959–62; Dir.-Gen. of Mil. Training, AHQ Ottawa, 1962–64, G.O.C., E. Command, Halifax 1964–66; Commdr. of Allied Command Europe Mobile Force, 1966–69; Commdr., Mobile Command 1969 till retired 9 Dec. 1972; Capt. 1940, Major 1941, Lieut.-Col. 1943, Col. 1952, Brig. 1959, Maj.-Gen. 1964, Lt.-Gen. 1969; Col. of the Regiment, Royal 22e Regiment 1974–1978; Dir.-Gen. Services, Organising Comte. of Olympic Games Montréal 1976; Past Pres. The Last Post Fund Que. Br. 1978; Past National Pres., Cdn. Corps of Commissionaires; Gov., Montreal Div., Can. Corps of Commissionaires; National Past Pres., The Last Post Fund; Roman Catholic; Clubs: United Services (Hon. Vice Pres.); Montreal; The Hermitage, Magog; Address: 'La Redoute,' 96 Laurendeau Rd., R.R. 3, Magog, Que. J1X 3W4.

**TURCOTTE, Guy Joseph,** B.Sc., M.B.A., P.Eng.; financial executive; b. Wainwright, Alta. 14 Feb. 1952; s. Lionel Alfred and Louise Malvina T.; e. N. Alta. Inst. of Technol. (Hons.) 1972; Univ. of Tulsa B.Sc. (Hons.) 1975; Univ. of Alta., M.B.A. 1976; CHRMN., CHIEF EXECUTIVE OFFR. & DIR., CHAUVCO RESOURCES LTD. 1981– ; Dir., Gendis Inc.; Project Offr., Fed. Bus. Devel. Bank 1976–78; Pres. & Gen. Mgr., Kassel-Steiner Indus. Ltd. 1978–80; Sr. Investment Offr., Cavendish Investing Ltd. 1980–81; Mem., Assn. of Profl. Engineers, Geologists, & Geophyysicists; recreations: skiing, golf, hockey; clubs: Calgary Petroleum, Silver Springs Golf & Country; Home: 1103 Varsity Estates Dr. N.W., Calgary, Alta. T3B 3B1; Office: 2900, 255 – 5th Ave. S.W., Calgary, Alta. T2P 3G6.

**TURCOTTE, J. Marc,** L.Sc.Comm., C.A.; exécutif; né Sherbrooke, Qué. 12 août 1933; f. Alphonse et Alfrédine (Gosselin) T.; é. Ecole des Hautes Etudes Commerciales L.Sc.Comm. 1954; ép. Raymonde f. Adrien Simard septembre 1959; enfants: Martine, Robert; PRES. ET CHEF DE LA DIRECTION, TIOXIDE CANADA INC. 1965– ; Price Waterhouse 1954–57; Ludger Gravel & Fils Ltée 1958–64; Prés. du conseil de l'hôpital Hôtel-Dieu de Sorel 1975–80, Prés. de la Fondation 1985–88; Prés. fondateur de l'Assn. des grandes industries de la région de l'acier 1986–87; Prés. div. du Qué. de l'Assn. des manufacturiers canadiens 1980–81, mem. de l'exécutif et du conseil national 1981–85; mem. Ordre des comptables agréés; Soc. Chem. Ind.; récreations: ski alpin, golf; Clubs: Saint-James's; Saint-Denis; Adresse: 366 ave. Ellerton, Ville Mont-Royal, Qué. H3P 1E2; Bureau: 9999 boul. Cavendish, Bureau 100, Montréal, Qué. H4M 2X5.

**TURCOTTE, John Gerald,** B.Eng.; research executive; b. Ottawa, Ont. 8 July 1939; s. John Orville and Constance (Belaire) T.; e. Royal Military Coll., Dip. Engr. 1961; McGill Univ., B.Eng. 1962; m. Ernestine d. Ernest and Madeleine Lambert 3 June 1961; children: Raymond, Andrew, Gordon, John, George; PRES., OTTAWA CARLETON RSCH. INST. 1984– ; Dir., OCRInet Inc.; OPCOM; Naval Offr. 1961–65; Engr. Mgmt., Computing Devices of Can. 1965–74; Chrmn., Electronics/Computing Sci. Tech., Algonquin Coll. 1974–84; Mem., APEO; IEEE; Dir., various ch. orgns.; Roman Catholic; recreations: scuba diving, white water canoeing; Home: 1640 Bear Hill Rd., Carp, Ont. K0A 1L0; Office: 340 March Rd., Suite 400, Kanata, Ont. K2K 2E4.

**TURGEON, Robert Louis,** B.Comm., LL.B.; lawyer; corporate executive; b. Montréal, Qué. 16 Jan. 1943; s. Roger and Marthe (Lamarre) T.; e. Sir George Williams Univ., B.Comm. 1967; Univ. de Montréal, LL.B. 1970; called to Qué. Bar 1972; one d. Michèle; PRES., DIR. & MEM., EXTVE. CTTE., TRANS QUÉBEC & MARITIMES PIPELINE INC. 1985– ; Lechter & Segal 1971; Legal Couns., Zellers Inc. 1972; Partnership, Beaudry, Turgeon & Rancourt 1974; Legal Couns., SNC Group 1977; Sr. Couns., Trans Québec & Maritimes 1981; Assoc. Gen. Couns., then Asst. Sec.; Vice-Pres., Admin. & Sec. 1983; Pres. 1985; Mem., Candn. Bar Assn.; Qué. Bar Assn.; c. of c. of Montréal; c. of c. of the Prov. of Qué.; Vice-Chrmn., Bd. of Dirs., Le Musée d'art contemporain de Montréal; Mem. Bd. of Dirs., l'Orchestre Symphonique de Trois-Rivières; L'Opéra de Montréal; Mem., Admin. Managing Ctte., Candn. Gas Assn.; recreations: golf, skiing; Club: Country Club of Montréal; Home: 10 Bayard St., Candiac, Qué. J5R 2C4; Office: 1 Place Ville Marie, Suite 2220, Montréal, Qué. H3B 3M4.

**TURL, Stephen Edward;** M.C.I.Q.S.; professional quantity surveyor; construction executive; b. England 12 Jan. 1934; s. Frank Edward and Julia Pantalei (Cardaleva) T.; e. Maidstone Grammar Sch. for Boys, Eng.; London Univ. Matric. Cert. 1950; m. Patricia d. Richard and Doris Luckhurst 24 Apr. 1954; two s. Nigel, Graeme; one d. Kim; PRES. AND DIR., CASEY-HEWSON CONSTRUCTION LIMITED 1987– ; Quantity Surveyor Kent Co. Council, Eng. 1950; emigrated to Can. 1967; joined present Co. 1980, Vice Pres. and Dir. 1981; mem. Toronto Bd. of Trade; Markham Bd. of Trade; Toronto Constrn. Assn. (Edn. Ctte.); Candn. Inst. Quantity Surveyors; Am. Assn. Cost Engs.; Am. Soc. Profl. Estimators; recreation: amateur theatre; Clubs: Kiwanis (Past Pres. Markham); Markham Little Theatre (Past Pres.); Home: 28 Sir Lancelot Dr., Markham, Ont. L3P 2H8.

**TURMEL, Hon. Gerard,** B.A., LL.L.; judge; b. Beauce Co., Que. 26 June 1926; s. Leon and Marie-Ange T.; e. La Verendrye Sch. and Lebrun Sch. Montreal; Ste-Therese Coll.; Ste-Croix Coll. B.A.; Univ. of Montreal LL.L. 1954; m. Suzanne d. late Hon. L. A. Giroux 18 Aug. 1956; children: Helene, Benoit, Lucie, François, Antoine; JUDGE, SUPERIOR COURT OF QUE.; called to Bar of Que. 1954; cr. Q.C. 1969; R. Catholic; Club: Cowansville Country; Home: 116 Pine, Cowansville, Que. J2K 2G6.

**TURMEL, Jean B.,** B.Comm., M.B.A.; b. Ste-Justine, Que. 17 Dec. 1944; s. Joseph N. and Rose (Chabot) T.; e. Laval Univ. B.Comm. 1966, M.B.A. 1967; m. Lorraine d André and Bernadette (Bisson) Langevin 4 June 1966; children: Andrée, Elaine, Johanne; SENIOR EXTVE. VICE-PRES., TREASURY, BROKERAGE & TRUST SERVICES, NATIONAL BANK OF CANADA 1989– ; Marketing, MacMillan Bloedel 1967–68; Vice-Pres., Money Market, Dominion Securities 1968–78; Merrill Lynch Royal Securities 1978–81; Vice-Pres., Treas. & Fgn. Exchange, Nat. Bank of Can. 1981–82; Sr. Vice-Pres. 1982–86; Etve. Vice-Pres., Treas. 1986–89; Chair, Nat. Bank Securities; Natcan Investment Mngt. Inc.; Dir., Levesque Beaubien Geoffrion Inc. (Mem., Extve. Ctte.); Outside Adv. Investment Ctte., Assn. de bienfaisance et de retraite de la comm. urbaine de Montréal; Fonds de pension de Hydro-Qué.; Chairman of the Board, Sherbrooke Trust, General Trust; recreations: squash, fishing, music, reading; clubs: Nautilus, St-James and St-Denis; Home: 1067 boul. Mont-Royal, Outremont, Que. H2V 2H5; Office: 600 de la Gauchetière St. W., Montreal, Que. H3B 4L2.

**TURNBULL, A.M. Gordon,** M.A., LL.B., C.A.; financial executive; b. Dumfries, Scot. 29 Dec. 1935; s. late Catherine R. and late Rev. R. W. Turnbull, B.D.; e. Univ. of Edinburgh M.A. 1956, LL.B. 1958; Inst. of C. A.'s Scot., C.A. 1960; m. Karen M. d. Fred B. Walker, York, Eng. 1965; children: Candida, Andrew; SENIOR VICE PRES., FINANCE & CHIEF FINANCIAL OFFICER, HAWKER SIDDELEY CANADA INC. 1994– ; joined Price Waterhouse & Co. Paris 1960–62; U.S. Time Corp. (Timex) Besancon, France 1962–63 and Waterbury, Conn. 1963–64; Group Financial Controller, Formica International Ltd., London, Eng. 1965–70; Finance Dir. Donald Macpherson Group Ltd., London 1970–77; Controller & Asst. Treas., Indal Ltd., 1978–81; Vice-Pres. & Treas., Indal Ltd. 1981–90; Vice-Pres., Finance & Chief Financial Offr., Hawker Siddeley Canada Inc. 1990–94; Home: 2610 Hammond Rd., Mississauga, Ont. L5K 2M3; Office: 3 Robert Speck Parkway, Mississauga, Ont. L4Z 2G5.

**TURNBULL, John W.,** B.A., LL.B.; judge; b. Montréal, Qué. 8 Jan. 1936; s. Hugh H. and Jessie L. (Gladwin) T.; e. Bishop's Coll. Sch. Lennoxville, Qué.; Univ. of N.B., B.A. 1957, LL.B. 1960; m. Kathryn d. Eugene and Vera Mutch 14 July 1956; children: Vera, Caroline, Hugh; JUDGE, COURT OF QUEEN'S BENCH, N.B. TRIAL DIV. 1985– ; Dir. G.E. Barbour Co. Ltd.; former Partner, Palmer, O'Connell, Leger, Turnbull & Turnbull; apptd. to Court of Queen's Bench Family Div. 1983; e. M.L.A. for City of Saint John 1973–74, Saint John Harbour 1974–78; Dir. Candn. Council Christian & Jews; mem. Candn. Bar Assn. (Council); N.B. Barristers' Soc. (Council); recreation: salmon fishing; Home: Reynar Dr., Quispamsis, N.B.; Mailing Address: 22 Reynar Dr., Quispamsis, N.B. E2G 1J8; Office: 110 Charlotte St., Saint John, N.B. E2L 2J4.

**TURNBULL, Robert S.,** C.M.A.; business executive; b. North Dumfries, Ont. 19 Dec. 1929; s. Leslie William and Marjorie Clara (Scott) T.; e. Galt (Ont.) Coll. Inst. 1950; R.I.A. 1959; m. Dawna Sinclair 17 Feb. 1956; PRESIDENT & DIR., CANADIAN GENERAL-TOWER LTD. 1980– ; joined present Co. 1950, Comptroller 1964, Dir. of Mktg. 1969, Vice Pres. and Gen. Mgr. 1977; Dir., Chem. Fabrics & Films Assn.; Dir., Society of Plastics Industry; Home: 26 Lansdowne Rd. S., Cambridge, Ont. N1S 2T3; Office: 52 Middleton St., Cambridge, Ont. N1R 5T6.

**TURNER, David Howe,** B.A., Ph.D.; university professor; b. England 18 July 1941; s. Norman and Maud (Bullock) T.; e. Carleton Univ., B.A. 1965; Univ. of W.

Australia, Ph.D. 1971; 1st m. Ruth d. Walter and Mary Charles 1966–88; children: Graeme, Bryan (dec.), Michelle, Iain (dec.); PROF. OF ANTHROP., UNIV. OF TORONTO 1982– ; Post-Doctoral Rsch. Fellow, Australian Inst. of Aboriginal Studies 1971–72; Lectr., Australian Nat. Univ. 1972–74; Asst. Prof., Univ. of Man. 1974–75; joined Univ. of Toronto as Assoc. Prof. 1975; consultant, Min. of Community Devel., N. Territory Govt. of Australia 1986; Med. Rsch. Team, Univ. of New South Wales 1987; Fellow, Netherlands Inst. for Advanced Studies; Australian Inst. of Aboriginal Studies; author: 'Tradition and Transformation: A Study of Aborigines in the Groote Eylandt Area of Northern Australia' 1974; 'Life Before Genesis: A Conclusion' 1985, 1987; 'Return to Eden: a journey through the Promised Landscape of Amagalyuagba' 1989; recreations: hockey, soft-ball, music; Address: Trinity Coll., Toronto, Ont. M5S 1A1.

**TURNER, David Samuel,** B.A., M.A.; management consultant; b. Saskatoon, Sask. 18 March 1961; s. Ronald Jamieson and Evelyn Marie (Parker) T.; e. Univ. of Victoria B.A. 1985; Univ. of B.C. M.A. 1991; m. Madeleine d. Dr. Harry and Dorothy Sullivan 10 June 1991; SENIOR RETAIL DEVELOPMENT CONSULTANT, THOMAS CONSULTANTS INC. 1988–91, 1993–present; Partner, 'The Franchise Store' 1992; Mem., Real Estate Inst. of B.C.; Internat. Council of Shopping Centres; Urban Land Inst.; Downtown Vancouver Assn.; frequently interviewed & quoted in the popular press (newspapers, radio, TV); Editorial Bd. Mem., 'Journal of Retailing and Consumber Services'; co-author: 'Vancouver Metropolitan Area' 1990 Urban Land Institute; author of 2 articles in Monday Report on Retailers; recreations: squash, hiking, skiing; Home: 2215 Vine St., Vancouver, B.C. V6K 4K5; Office: 910 – 700 West Pender St., Vancouver, B.C. V6C 1G8.

**TURNER, Edward Giles (Ted);** business executive; b Toronto, Ont. 12 May 1932; s. the late Edward Giles and Violet Evelyn (Post) T.; m. Patricia d. the late Allan Joseph and Maude Elizabeth Sutherland 20 June 1980; children: Loren, Leslie, Amy, Joseph; PRESIDENT & C.E.O., HUNT PERSONNEL and TEMPORARILY YOURS, operated by Business Aid Inc. 1973– ; Pres., SKILLSET Training Systems Inc. 1993– ; Partner, ADR Practice 1994– ; Premier Ind. Corp. 1961–73; Mem., Fed. of Temporary Help Services 1977– (Pres. 1985–89); Bd. Mem., ABC Canada 1990– ; Bd. Mem., Canadian Stage Company 1990– ; Corporate Sponsor, Public Policy Forum; Operation Lifeline 1978–80; Radio Broadcaster 1984– ; author of articles on various subjects; Founder & Pres., Toronto Vintners Club 1975– ; recreations: food, wine, tennis, reading, writing, photography; Clubs: Royal Candn. Yacht; Internat. Wine and Food Soc.; Baron de Forrester Society; Home: 655 Broadview Ave., PH1, Toronto, Ont. M4K 2P3; Office: 365 Bloor St. E., Suite 1902, Toronto, Ont. M4W 3L4.

**TURNER, Edward Kerr,** C.M., LL.D.; agricultural executive; b. Maymont, Sask. 6 Apr. 1927; e. Sch. of Agric., Univ. of Sask. 1948; Banff Sch. of Advanced Mgmt. 1968; m. Patricia Melville Bright 5 July 1950; three d.: Janice, Joy, Jill; CHANCELLOR, UNIV. OF SASK. 1989– ; Chrmn., Bioriginal Food & Science Corp., Saskatoon; Bd. of Govs., Univ. of Sask.; Senate, Univ. of Sask.; Consultant, Agriculture Plus; Former Dir., Philom Bios Inc.; Former Chrmn., Chamber of Maritime Commerce; Former Dir., Conference Bd. of Can.; Former mem., Internat. Trade Adv. Ctte.; Pres., Sask. Wheat Pool 1969–87; Extve. Dir., Prairie Pools Inc. 1987–89; Bd. of Govs., Plant Biotechnology Inst.; toured India as mem. agric. group to observe agric. production and marketing and Candn. aid programs 1966; mem. Duke of Edinburgh's Third Commonwealth Conf., Australia 1968; Hon. Vice-Chrmn., Sask. Campaign for establishment of Rt. Hon. John G. Diefenbaker Centre, Saskatoon; Trustee, Sports Fund for the Physically Disabled; Un. Ch.; recreation: sports; Home: 2638 Ehman Bay, Regina, Sask. S4V 0L6.

**TURNER, Francis Joseph,** D.S.W.; educator and social worker; b. Windsor, Ont. 3 Jan. 1929; s. Frank Michael and Mary Germaine (Gendron) T.; e. Assumption High Sch. Windsor; Univ. of W. Ont. B.A. 1949; Univ. of Ottawa B.S.W. 1953, M.S.W. 1955; Columbia Univ. D.S.W. 1963; m. Joanne d. John and Madeline Housley 26 July 1958; children: Francis John, Sarah Elizabeth, Anne Marie; DEAN, FACULTY OF SOCIAL WORK, WILFRID LAURIER UNIV. 1993– ; Social Worker, Cath. Children's Aid, Windsor, Ont. 1952–53, Toronto 1956–57; Asst. Dir. Cath. Social Service Bureau Peterborough 1957–59; Chief Social Worker Ont. Hosp. New Toronto 1960–63; Asst. Prof. Sch. Social Welfare Univ. of Ottawa 1963–66; Assoc. Prof. of Social Work Waterloo Lutheran Univ. 1966–68; Prof. and Head of Social Work Mem. Univ. of Nfld. 1968–69; Dean of Social Work Wilfrid Laurier Univ. 1969–73, 1974–79; Visiting Prof. Dept. Social & Adm. Studies Oxford Univ. 1973; Vice Pres. (Acad.) and Prof. of Social Work, Laurentian Univ. of Sudbury 1979–83; Prof. of Social Work, Laurentian Univ. of Sudbury 1979–85 (and Extve. Vice Pres. of Univ. 1983–84); Prof. and Chair, Sch. of Social Work, York Univ. 1985–92; Distinguished Moses Visiting Internat. Prof., Hunter Coll., City Univ. of N.Y. 1984–85; Chrmn., Sch. of Social Work, York Univ. 1985–88; Bd. mem. Ottawa Welfare Council 1964–66; Pres. Kitchener-Waterloo Social Planning Council 1976–79; Pres. Un. Way of Sudbury 1981–84; mem. Nat. Academies of Practice 1985; mem. Prov. Adv. Bd. Addictions Research Foundation 1977–80; mem. Ed. Bd., 'Canada's Mental Health' 1983; author 'Psychosocial Therapy' 1978; 'Adult Psychopathology' 1983; 'Child Psychopathology' 1989; 'Mental Health and the Elderly' 1992; co-author 'Catholic Social Work' 1965; ed. 'Differential Diagnosis and Treatment in Social Work' 1969, 2nd ed. 1976, 3rd ed. 1983; 'Social Work Treatment' 1974, 3rd ed. 1986; 'Social Worker' 1966–68; Ed. 'International Social Work' 1987– ; co-ed. 'Canadian Social Welfare' 1981, 2nd ed. 1986; Nat. Pres. Candn. Assn. Social Workers 1973–75; Chrmn. Bd. Accreditation Candn. Assn. Schs. of Social Work 1970–73; Bd. mem., Family Service Canada 1986– ; External Examiner, Univ. of Hong King 1987–90; Visiting Researcher, Mandel Sch. of Applied Social Studies, Case-Western Reserve Univ. 1988–89; recreations: sailing, flying, tennis; Clubs: Gyro; Northfield Tennis; Home: 186 Claremont Ave., Kitchener, Ont. N2M 2P8; Office: Wilfred Laurier Univ., 75 Univ. Ave. W., Waterloo, Ont. N2L 3C5.

**TURNER, Gary Edmund,** F.I.C.B.; bank executive; b. Minnedosa, Man. 20 Oct. 1938; s. James Edmund and Charlotte Catherine (McAree) T.; e. Univ. of Manitoba, F.I.C.B. (Fellow, Inst. of Candn. Bankers); m. Pamel d. Melville and Eileen Hughes 28 June 1980; children: Sheri, Richard, Russell, Allison; VICE-PRESIDENT, EXTERNAL RELATIONS (ONTARIO), ROYAL BANK OF CANADA 1991– ; numerous positions in retail & corp. banking as well as district & head office positions, Royal Bank 1956–80; General Manager, Tokyo Japan Br. 1980–86; Leader 'Team Japan' Corp. Banking in Toronto 1986–91; Dir., Ontario C. of C.; Dir., Children's Oncology Care of Ontario; Past Pres. & Dir., Canada-Japan Soc. of Toronto; Dir., Marshall McLuhan Centre on Global Communications; clubs: Canadian; Empire; Toronto Bd. of Trade; Toronto Triumph; Ontario Club; Office: 11th floor, 20 King St. W., Toronto, Ont. M5H 1C4.

**TURNER, Harold Melvin, Jr.,** B.A.; b. Toronto, Ont. 20 Jan. 1927; s. Harold Melvin and Esther (Joel) T.; e. Public and High Schs., Toronto, Ont.; Tufts Univ. B.A. 1950; m. Gloria, d. Arthur Coops 30 Sept. 1950; children: Judith, Jeffrey; PRES., HMT INVESTMENTS LTD.; Pres., J & J Turner Associates; with General Electric, N.Y., Corp. Advertising & Public Relations 1950; joined McLaren Advertising as Media Space Buyer 1952, Radio and TV Dept. 1953, Acct. Extve. 1954, Acct. Mgr. Corp. Develop., Vice Pres. 1962, Pres., C.E.O. & Chrmn. 1974; Hon. Trustee, Royal Ont. Museum; Museum Trustees Assoc.; Delta Tau Delta; recreations: tennis; sailing; Clubs: Toronto; RCYC; Tuft's (Boston); Hyannis Yacht (Hyannis, MA); Beach (Centerville, MA); Address: Suite 3406, 99 Harbour Sq., Toronto, Ont. M5J 2H2.

**TURNER, Rt. Hon. John N.,** P.C., Q.C., M.A., B.C.L.; b. Richmond, England 7 June 1929; s. Leonard and Phyllis (Gregory) T.; came to Canada 1932; e. Normal Model Pub. Sch., Ottawa, Ont. 1934–39; Ashbury Coll., 1939–42; St. Patrick's Coll., 1942–45; Univ. of B.C., B.A. (Pol. Science, Hons.) 1949; Rhodes Scholar, Oxford Univ., B.A. (Juris) 1951, B.C.L. 1952, M.A. 1957; Univ. of Paris 1952–53; m. Geills McCrae Kilgour, 11 May, 1963; one d. Elizabeth; three s. Michael, David, Andrew; PARTNER, MILLER THOMSON (Toronto law firm); Bd. of Dirs.: Beatrice Foods Inc.; Curragh Resources Inc.; The Dominion of Canada Gen. Insur. Co.; The Empire Life Insur. Co.; Noranda Forest Inc.; E-L. Financial Corp.; Harvard Capital Corp.; The Loewen Group Inc.; Purolator Courier Ltd.; Mount Sinai Hospital; The Canadian Club of Toronto; Leader of Her Majesty's Loyal Opposition 1984–90 (until resigned); read law with Stikeman & Elliott, Montreal, Que., and practised with them after being called to English Bar 1953; Bar of Quebec 1954, of Ont. 1968, of B.C. 1969, of Yukon and N.W.T. 1969; cr. Q.C. 1968; el. to H. of C. 1962; resigned 1976; Partner, McMillan, Binch (Toronto law firm) 1976–84; el. Leader of Lib. Party of Can. 16 June 1984; resigned 1990; Prime Minister of Can. 30 June-17 Sept. 1984; during early parliamentary career held post of Parliamentary Secretary to Min. of Northern Affairs and Nat. Resources; Min. without Portfolio; Registrar General; Min. of Consumer and Corp. Affairs; Sol. Gen; Min. of Justice and Attorney Gen.; Min. of Finance; el. M.P. for Vancouver Quadra 1984; re-elected M.P. for Vancouver Quadra 1988; mem. Eng. Bar, Grey's Inn, London; and Bars of Ont., Que., B.C., Barbados, Trinidad; Chrmn., Metro. Toronto Community Foundation; Liberal; R. Catholic; recreations: tennis, canoeing, skiing; Clubs: Mt. Royal; Montreal Racquet; Cercle Universitaire d'Ottawa; Country Club, Aylmer, Que; Queen's; Badminton & Racquet; York (Toronto); The Vancouver; Home: 27 Dunloe Rd., Toronto, Ont. M4V 2W4; Office: 20 Queen St. W., Box 27, Suite 2700, Toronto, Ont.
M5H 3S1.

**TURNER, Larry Philip,** B.A., M.A.; historian; writer; b. Toronto, Ont. 2 Feb. 1952; s. Philip Sydney and Frances (Dickinson) T.; e. Trent Univ. B.A. 1976; Queen's Univ. M.A. 1984; PRINCIPAL HISTORIAN, COMMONWEALTH HISTORIC RESOURCE MGMT. LTD. 1987– ; Rsch. Asst., Trent Univ. 1977–78; Tutorial Asst., Queen's Univ. 1979–80; Asst. Dir., Wanapitei Co-ed Camps 1981–83; contract writer & historian, Parks Can., Ont. Reg. 1983–87; Assoc., Cardinal Rsch. & Design 1985–87; Anglican; mem. Candn. Hist. Assn.; Ont. Hist. Soc.; Ont. Genealog. Soc.; Douglas-Coldwell Found.; Fedn. of Ont. Naturalists; Long Point Bird Observatory; Friends of the National Gallery of Canada; Manotick Classic Boat Club; American Canal Soc.; author: 'Ernestown: Rural Spaces, Urban Places' 1993; 'Perth: Tradition and Style in Eastern Ontario' 1992; Voyage of a Different Kind: The Associated Loyalists of Kingston and Adolphustown' 1984; co-author: 'Historic Mills of Ontario' 1987; co-editor: 'On a Sunday Afternoon... Classic Boats on the Rideau Canal' 1989; author of var. articles, biographies for the Dictionary of Candn. Biog., Parks Canada Microfiche Reports; Bd. of Dirs., Wanapitei Co-Ed Camps Ltd.; Big Rideau Lake Assn.; Chrmn., Rideau Waterway Co-ordinating Assoc. (Friends of the Rideau); recreations: Camp Wanapitei; canoeing, travel, local history, book collecting, Pethern Point Cottage; Home: 504 – 60 MacLaren St., Ottawa, Ont. K2P 0K7; Office: 53 Herriott St., Perth, Ont. K7H 1T5.

**TURNER, Peter Merrick,** B.A.Sc., M.B.A.; executive; b. Toronto, Ont. 4 July 1931; s. William Ian MacKenzie and Marjorie Hilda (Merrick) T.; e. Univ. of Toronto, B.A.Sc. 1954; Harvard Univ., M.B.A. 1956; m. Beverley (dec'd) d. late Harold Miller Brophey, 13 Sept. 1958; m. Alix Houston d. late Norman A. Robertson 17 Aug. 1991; children: Peter Merrick Jr., Christopher Harold, David MacKenzie; VICE-PRES. CORPORATE PLANNING & DEVELOPMENT, SPX CORP. 1992– ; Dir., Grand Trunk Corp.; Grand Trunk Western Railroad Co.; Domestic Four Leasing Corp.; joined Bridgeport Brass Co., Bridgeport, Conn., 1956; Secy.-Treas., Perkins Paper Products Ltd., Montreal, 1957; Asst. to Mang., Texaco Canada Ltd., 1958, Adm., Marketing Research, 1959, Adm., Planning, 1962, Asst. Treas. 1964, Treas. 1966 also Treas., Montreal Pipeline Co. Ltd. and Treas. and Dir., Public Fuel Transmission Systems Ltd., Ottawa; joined Molson Breweries Ltd. as Budgeting and Planning Dir., Corporate Devel., 1968; Vice Pres., Planning Molson Breweries of Canada Ltd., 1968; Vice-Pres. Corporate Devel., Molson Industries Ltd. 1970; Extve. Vice Pres., Bennett Pump Co. 1972; Pres. 1973–78; Vice-Pres., Corp. Planning & Develop., Sealed Power Corp. 1978; Group Vice Pres., International 1981; Group Vice Pres., General Products 1984; Vice Pres., Business Development 1989; Vice-Pres. Operations 1991; Chrmn., Salvation Army Campaign for Montreal, 1969–70; Lectr. in Extension Dept., McGill Univ., 1960–67; Chairman, McGill Assn. 1969–70; Chrmn., Muskegon Area Chamber of Comm. Long Range Planning Comte.; Muskegon Community College Long Range Planning Comte.; Lectr. in Extension Dept., Grand Valley State College; Dir., Hackley Hosp.; West Shore Symphony Orchestra; Hackley Public Library; mem., Assn. Prof. Engrs. Ont.; Zeta Psi; Anglican; recreations: reading, hiking; Clubs: Mount Royal; Granite; Lake O'Hara Trails; Muskegon Country; Home: 524 Lake Drive, North Muskegon, Mich. 49445; Office: 700 Terrace Point Drive, Muskegon, Mich. 49443.

**TURNER, R(obert) Edward,** M.D., F.R.C.P.(C); psychiatrist; educator; b. Hamilton, Ont. 8 June 1926; s. late Robert William and Alice May (Johnson) T.; e. McMaster Univ. B.A. 1948; Univ. of Toronto M.D. 1952, Dipl. in Psychiatry 1957; Univ. of Bristol postgrad. studies Psychiatry 1953–55; m. Gene Anne d. late Robert Boys Stewart 27 Sept. 1952; children: Margaret Anne, John William, Robert Paul, Richard James; PROF. EMERITUS, UNIV. OF TORONTO 1991– and HON. MEM.,

MEDICAL STAFF, CLARKE INSTITUTE; Dir. and Psychiatrist-in-Charge, Metro. Toronto Forensic Service (METFORS) 1977–87; Pres., Kenneth G. Gray Foundation 1971– ; Interneship Hamilton Gen. Hosp. 1952–53; Asst. Prof. of Psychiatry, Univ. of Toronto 1964, Assoc. Prof. 1968, Prof. 1973–77, Prof. of Forensic Psychiatry 1977–91; mem. Bd. of Dirs.: Clin. Inst. Addiction Resch. Foundation Ont. 1973–84 (Chrmn. 1985–86); Addiction Research Foundation 1983–86; Chrmn. Ethics Comte. Research Adv. Comte. Clarke Inst. Psychiatry 1976–83; Lt.-Gov.'s Bd. of Review Ont. 1976–88, 1988–90, 1990–93, 1994–96; Legal Task Force Comte. Mental Health Services Ont., Ont. Council Health 1978–79; Adv. Council Candn. Inst. Law & Med.; Consultant in Psychiatry Law Reform Comn. Can. 1972–84; co-author 'Pedophilia and Exhibitionism' 1964; numerous book chapters, articles Forensic Psychiatry; mem. Council, Medico-Legal Soc. Toronto 1980–82; Pres. Ont. Psychiatric Assn. 1975–76, Council 1972–74; Dir. Candn. Psychiatric Assn. 1974–77; Life Fellow, Am. Psychiatric Assn.; Royal Coll. Psychiatrists (UK); Life mem., Ont. Psychiatric Assn. 1991; Life Mem., Candn. Psychiatric Assn. 1991; Anglican; recreations: photography, history, art, music, theatre, travel; Home: 18 Rolph Rd., Toronto, Ont. M4G 3M6; Office: Clarke Inst. of Psychiatry, 250 College St., Toronto, Ont. M5T 1R8.

**TURNER, Ross J.;** company executive; b. Winnipeg, Man. 1 May 1930; s. James Valentine and Gretta H. (Ross) T.; e. Univ. of Man. Extension, C.M.A. 1951; Banff Sch. of Advanced Mang. 1956; children: Ralph, Rick, Tracy; CHRMN., GENSTAR INVESTMENT CORP. 1987– ; Chrmn./Pres., C.E.O. and Dir. Genstar Corp. 1976–86; Sr. Operating and Management Positions, Genstar Corp. 1961–76; Dir., Rio Algom Ltd.; Western Corporate Enterprises, Inc.; The Great West Life Assurance Co.; Guy F. Atkinson Co. of Calif.; Blue Shield of California; Fellow, Soc. Mgmt. Accts. Can.; Protestant; recreation: sports; Clubs: Toronto Club (Toronto); Pacific Union Club (San Francisco); Peninsula Golf and Country Club (San .Francisco); Rancho Santa Fe Golf Club (Rancho Santa Fe); Office: Metro Tower, Suite 1170, 950 Tower Lane, Foster City, CA 94404-2121.

**TURNER, Wesley Barry,** B.A., M.A., Ph.D.; university professor; b. Toronto, Ont. 17 May 1933; s. Henry Frederick and Margaret (Elliot) T.; e. Weston Collegiate 1952; Univ. of Toronto B.A. 1956; Ont. College of Edn. 1957; Univ. of Toronto M.A. 1962; Duke Univ. Ph.D. 1971; m. Diane d. Clifford and Beryl Parsons 22 July 1961; children: Douglas, Gordon, Jennifer; ASSOCIATE PROF., HISTORY DEPT., BROCK UNIV. 1977– ; Teacher, Toronto area high schools 1957–59, 1960–65 (one year as head, history dept.); Lecturer, Brock Univ. 1967–69; Asst. Prof. 1969–77; Chair, History Dept. 1985–88; Mem., University Senate 1985–87; Founder & Owner, Goturn Enterprises; Mem., Ont. Historical Soc. (Extve. Mem. 1979–85; Pres. 1983–84); St. Catharines Historical Mus. (Mem., Bd. of Trustees 1984–85; Chair 1985); Candn. Historical Assn.; Champlain Soc.; Candn. Canal Soc.; Friends of Fort George; Candn. Military History Group; author: 'Life in Upper Canada' 1980, 'Album of Upper Canada' 1987, 'The War of 1812: the War for Canada' 1982, 'The War of 1812: The War that Both Sides Won' 1990 and 7 biographies in 'Dictionary of Canadian Biography'; editor: 'The Military in the Niagara Peninsula' 1990; assistant editor: 'The Defended Border: Upper Canada and the War of 1812' 1964; recreations: Scottish country dancing, golfing; Home: 248 Riverview Blvd., St. Catharines, Ont. L2T 3M8; Office: St. Catharines, Ont. L2S 3A1.

**TURNER, William Ian MacKenzie, Jr.,** C.M., B.A.Sc., M.B.A., P.Eng.; b. Sharon, Pa. (Canadian citizen) 17 Jan. 1929; s. William I.M. T. Sr.; e. University of Toronto, B.A.Sc. (Hons. Mech. Engn.) 1951; Harvard Business School, M.B.A. (with Distinction) 1953; Mount Allison Univ., LL.D. (hon.) 1984; Bishop's Univ. D.C.L. (hon.) 1987; m. Nancy Herman: two s. William, James; two d. Julia, Carol; CHRMN. & C.E.O., EXSULTATE INC. 1990– ; Chrmn., Canadian Marconi Company; SNC Lavalin Inc.; Axel Johnson Canada; Dir., A. Johnson & Co., Inc.; Baca Resources; Bombardier Inc.; Celanese Canada Inc. (Chrmn, Exec. Ctte.); Newmont Mining; Power Corp. of Canada Ltd.; Provigo Inc.; Remington Energy Ltd.; Repap Enterprises; Schroders p.l.c.; Internat. Adv. Council, Wells Fargo Bank; Advisory Council, Alexander Proudfoot; Ingersoll-Rand Canada; Chancellor, Bishop's Univ.; Asst. to Pres., Willys-Overland Export Corp., Toledo, Ohio 1953; Controller, Canadian Ingersoll-Rand Co. 1954; Vice-Pres., Power Corp. of Canada Ltd. 1963, Extve. Vice-Pres. 1964, Pres. 1966; Pres., Consolidated-Bathurst Inc. 1970, Pres. & C.E.O. 1971–82, Chrmn. & C.E.O. 1982–89; Chrmn. & C.E.O., PCC Industrial Corp. 1989–90; Senator, Stratford Shakespearean Festival Fdn.; Member of the Order of Canada; Trustee, Carnegie Institution of Washington; World Economic Forum; Trilateral Commission; recreations: racquets, squash, reading; Clubs: Brook; Knickerbocker (both New York); National; York (both Toronto); Toronto; Mount Royal; St. James's; M.A.A.A.; Montreal Racket; Hillside Tennis (Montreal); Home: 4294 Montrose Ave., Westmount, Que. H3Y 2A5; Office: 1981 McGill College Ave., Suite 575, Montreal, Que. H3A 2X1.

**TURPEL, Mary Ellen;** university professor, barrister & solicitor; b. Niagara Falls, Ont. 15 Feb. 1963; d. William Loosely and Shirley Mae (Logan) T.; e. Carleton Univ.; Univ. of Strasbourg; Osgoode Hall Law School 1985; Cambridge Univ. 1987; Harvard Univ. 1988; ASSOC. PROFESSOR OF LAW, DALHOUSIE UNIV. 1989– ; Lawyer, Indian Law Resource Ctr. (U.S.) 1985; Legal Counsel, Native Women's Assn. of Can. 1986–87; Assoc., Buchan, Derrick and Ring 1991–93; Sr. Rsch. Assoc., Royal Comn. on Aboriginal Peoples 1993–94; Mem., N.S. Barrister's Soc.; Indigenous Bar Assn.; Visiting Prof., Univ. of Notre Dame Law Sch.; Legal Counsel, Assembly of First Nations; Medalist, Osgoode Hall Law Sch.; Laidlaw Scholar; Harvard Law Sch. Fellowship/ Pegasus Scholar of Inner Temple; Thérèse F-Casgrain Fellowship; Mem., Bd. of Editors, 'Can. J. of Fgn. Affairs,' 'Nat. J. of Constitutional Law,' 'Can. J. of Women and the Law' 1989–91; Mem., Internat. Comn. on Folk Law & Legal Pluralism; Lawyers for Social Responsibility; co-author: 'In the Rapids' 1993; author of several articles and book chapters; recreations: birding, sea kayaking, pow-wows; Home: Box 71, Prospect, N.S. B0J 2V0; Office: Halifax, N.S. B3H 3J5.

**TURRITTIN, Anton H.,** Ph.D.; association executive; university professor; b. El Paso, Texas 27 Feb. 1938; s. Hugh Lonsdale and Adele (Fritz) T.; e. Univ. of Minnesota, B.A. 1959, M.A. 1960, Ph.D. 1969; m. Linna Jane d. Burton Russell and Marjorie Craig Sawyer 1963; children: Stacey Lynn, Thomas Hugh; ASSOC. PROF., DEPT. OF SOCIOLOGY, FACULTY OF ARTS, YORK UNIV. 1981– ; Lectr., St. Paul's College, Univ. of Man. 1964–66; York Univ. 1966–69; Asst. Prof. 1969–81; Vice-Pres. for Sociol., Candn. Soc. & Anthropol. Assn. 1977–79; Mng. Ed., 'Canadian Review of Sociology and Anthropology' 1979–82; Chairperson, Dept. of Sociology 1983–86; Pres., Transport 2000 Ont. 1984–87; Nat. Sec., Transport 2000 Canada 1984–87, Pres., 1987–89; Pres., Better Transportation Coalition 1993– ; author/co-author of 3 jour. articles and 6 book chapters; author 'Report of the Sheppard Subway Citizens Task-force' 1990; co-author: 'Is the Die Cast? Educational Achievements and Work Destinations of Ontario Youth' 1980; Home: 100 Albertus Ave., Toronto, Ont. M4R 1J7; Office: Dept. of Sociology, Vari Hall, York Univ., North York, Ont. M3J 1P3.

**TUSHINGHAM, A. Douglas,** B.A., B.D., Ph.D., LL.D., F.S.A., F.R.S.C.; b. Toronto, Ont. 19 Jan. 1914; s. Arthur Douglas and Lottie Elizabeth (Betts) T.; e. Univ. of Toronto, B.A. 1936; Univ. of Chicago, B.D. 1941, Ph.D. 1948; m. Margaret McAndrew, d. Henry Thomson, Toronto, Ont., 9 April 1948; children: Margaret Elizabeth, Ian Douglas David (dec.); HEAD, JERUSALEM PROJECT OFFICE AND HONORARY TRUSTEE, ROYAL ONTARIO MUSEUM; Lectr., Pine Hill Divinity Hall, Halifax, N.S. 1941–42 and 1946; Lectr., University of Chicago 1948–51; Annual Prof., American Sch. of Oriental Research, Jerusalem, Jordan 1951–52, and Dir. 1952–53; Assoc. Prof., Queen's Theol. Coll., Kingston, Ont. 1953–55; Head, Art and Archaeology Div., Royal Ont. Museum 1955–64; Chief Archaeologist, R.O.M. 1964–79; Mem. Bd. of Trustees 1984–90; Prof. Dept. of Near Eastern Studies, Univ. of Toronto 1955–79; was Asst. Dir. of Excavation of Jericho in 1952, 1953, and 1956; participated in and directed excavations at Dhiban, Jordan in 1951–53; Assoc. Dir., excavations in Jerusalem, Jordan 1962–67; Hon. Curator, Marine Museum; former Chrmn., Toronto Hist. Bd.; Bd. mem., Palestine Archeol. Museum, Jerusalem, Jordan 1951–53; served in 2nd World War with Royal Candn. Navy 1942–45; Lieut., R.C.N.V.R.; 1st Lieut. of Frigate; Publications: 'Masks: the Many Faces of Man' 1959; 'The Beardmore Relics: Hoax or History?' 1966; (with V.B. Meen) 'The Crown Jewels of Iran' 1968; (with A. Denis Baly) 'Atlas of the Biblical World' 1971; 'The Excavations at Dibon (Dhibân) in Moab' 1972; 'Gold for the Gods' 1976; 'Studies in Ancient Peruvian Metalworking' 1979; 'Excavations in Jerusalem 1961–1967' vol. 1 1985; has contrib. many archaeol. and Old Testament studies to 'Nat. Geog. Mag'; 'Bull.' of Am. Schs. of Oriental Research; 'Journ. of Near Eastern Studies'; 'Biblical Archaeology'; 'Zeitschrift des Deutschen Palästinavereins'; etc.; Fellow, Canadian Museum Assn. (Pres. 1964–65); Victoria College (1975–81); Royal Soc. of Canada; Soci. of Antiquaries of London; Silver Service Medal of the City of Toronto; Gold Award of Merit of the City of Toronto; Gold Medal presented by Govt. of Iran; Silver Jubilee Medal; mem., American Schools of Oriental Research; Archaeol. Inst. of Am. United Church; Home: 20 Baif Blvd. #501, Richmond Hill, Ont. L4C 8T1.

**TUTTE, William Thomas,** B.A., M.Sc., Ph.D., F.R.S.C., F.R.S.; educator; b. Newmarket, Eng. 14 May 1917; s. William John Tutte; e. Cambridge and Co. High Sch. Eng. 1935; Trinity Coll. Cambridge Univ. B.A. 1938, M.Sc. 1941, Ph.D. 1948; m. Dorothea Geraldine Mitchell 8 Oct. 1949; EMERITUS PROFESSOR; Prof. of Math. Univ. of Waterloo 1962–85 (retired); Dept. of Math. Univ. of Toronto 1948–62; author 'Connectivity in Graphs' 1966; 'Introduction to the Theory of Matroids' 1971; 'Graph Theory' 1984; rec'd Tory Medal, Royal Soc. Can. 1975; rec'd Izaak Walton Killam Memorial Prize 1982; Fellow, Royal Soc. of London 1987; mem. London Math. Soc.; Cambridge Philosophical Soc.; Am. Math. Soc.; Candn. Math. Soc.; Home 16 Bridge St., W. Montrose, Ont. N0B 2V0; Office: Waterloo, Ont. N2L 3GL.

**TUTTON, James Wilfred Frank,** B.Com.; real estate executive; b. Iroquois Falls, Ont. 5 March 1939; s. Wilfred Reid and Doris May (Russell) T.; e. Univ. of B.C. B.Com. 1965; div.; children: Sarah Lea, Christopher James, Kathleen Mary; Pres., Webb & Knapp (Canada) Ltd. 1981– ; Dir. Wolstencroft Insurance Agencies Ltd.; Butec International Chemical Corp.; Golden Dragon Resources Ltd.; served Knowlton Realty Ltd. as Real Estate Negotiator, Br. Mgr. Edmonton, Asst. to Pres. Calgary; purchased Wolstencroft Agencies Ltd. 1968; Vice Chrmn., Fraser Burrard Hosp. Soc.; Regimental Council Royal Westminster Regt.; Fellow, Real Estate Inst. Can.; mem. Real Inst. B.C.; Fraser Valley Real Estate Bd.; Urban Devel. Inst.; Urban Land Inst.; Nat. Assn. Ind. & Office parks; recreations: skiing, backpacking, boating.

**TUZ, Paul John,** C.M., C.D., S.B.St.J., M.B.A., D.B.A., P.Eng.; association executive; b. Vienna, Austria 20 Oct. 1929; came to Can. 1943; e. Univ. of Detroit M.B.A. 1971; Ind. Univ. D.B.A. 1973; PRES. AND DIR., BETTER BUSINESS BUREAU OF METROP. TORONTO INC. 1977– and PUBLISHER, CANADIAN BUSINESS LIFE; Hon. Consul General and Head of Post, Republic of Mali, 1989; Hon. Consul and Head of Post, Republic of Togo 1990; Interim Pres., Candn. Counc. of Better Business Bureaus 1985–87; Sec., Consular Corps Assoc. of Toronto 1989–91; held various engn. positions Can. and abroad 1954–58; Controller, Emergency Measures for Muns. of N. York, Leaside and Weston 1958–62; Dir. of Educ., Constr. Safety Assn. Ont. 1962–64; Dir. of Safety & Workmen's Compensation, Chrysler Corp.'s Candn. operations 1964–74; Extve. Vice Pres. and Chief Operating Offr. present Bureau 1975; mem. Bd. on Curriculum Planning in Business Adm. Univ. of Detroit 1972–77, mem. Alumni Council; Columnist 'The Toronto Sun' 1975–77; present Columnist 'The Oshawa Times'; host MTV 'moneywise' 1981; served with militia Candn. Intelligence Corps, Royal Candn. Army Service Corps, Royal Candn. Corps of Signals, commanded Essex & Kent Scottish, rank Lt. Col.; invested as mem. of Order of Canada, 1979; former Trustee N. York Lib. Bd.; Past Vice Chrmn. N. York Safety Council; N. York Community Council; Riverview Hosp. Bd.; Past Chrmn. Court of Revision City of Windsor; Essex Co. Div. and Metal Trades Div. Indust. Accident Prevention Assn. Ont.; mem. of Extve., St. John Ambulance, Metropolitan Toronto; Safety Dirs.' Comte. Motor Vehicle Mfrs.' Assn.; Gov., Army Cadet League Can.; Former Gov., The Doctors Hospital; Dir. Credit Counselling Services of Metropolitan Toronto; Goodwill Industries Ltd.; Past Gov. Tau Kappa Epsilon; recreations: photography, chess, shooting; Home: 519 Spadina Rd., Toronto, Ont. M5P 2W6; Office: 1 St. Johns Road, Toronto, Ont. M6P 4C7.

**TWA, Craighton Oliver,** B.Sc., P.Eng.; power company executive; b. Drumheller, Alta. 15 Oct. 1937; s. Joe Philander and Freda Alice (Fowler) T.; e. Univ. of Alberta B.Sc. 1959; m. (Eva) Irene d. James and Grace Adam 7 May 1960; children: Tracy, Robert, Carey; PRESIDENT, CU POWER, DIVISION OF CANADIAN UTILITIES LIMITED 1988– ; joined Alberta Power Limited (subs. of Canadian Utilities Limited) 1959; Vice-Pres., Customer Services 1980; Senior Vice-Pres. & General Manager 1985; Pres. 1986– ; Dir., Alberta Power Limited; Northland Utilities Enterprises Limited; The Yukon Electrical Co. Limited; Frontec Logistics Corp.; CU Power Internat. Limited; Mem., Assn. of Profl. Engr., Geologists & Geophysicists of Alta.; Past Pres., N.W. Electric Light & Power Assn. 1988–89; recreations: golf; clubs: Mayfair Golf & Country, Edmonton; Home: 4107 Ramsay Cres., Edmonton, Alta. T6H 5M9; Office: 10035 – 105 St., Edmonton, Alta. T5J 2V6.

**TWA, Ritchie E.;** businessman, entrepreneur; b. Calgary, Alta. 12 March 1942; s. Hugh F. and Verna A. (Preston) T.; e. Grande Prairie H.S.; m. Elizabeth A. d. Allen and Dorothy Currier 17 April 1992; children (from prev. marriage): Christopher, Patrick, Jamie; Pres., Nahanni Land Co. Ltd. 1975– ; Denwood Enterprises Ltd. 1977– ; 270021 Alberta Ltd. 1984– ; Dir., Frenger Canada Inc.; Canada Mortgage & Housing Corp.; Wainwright & District Devel. Corp.; Partner & Sec.-Treas., Denwood Motors (1972) Ltd. 1972–85; Pres., Denwood Motors (1985) Ltd. 1985–89; frequent public speaker / Master of Ceremonies; Chair, Alta. Recreation Parks & Wildlife Found.; Trustee, Rotary Fair Play Award; Supporter, Rotary; Canadian Volleyball Assn.; Big Brothers & Sisters; Friends of NAIT; Ducks Unlimited; Chamber of Commerce; Frontier & Agric. Soc.; recreations: golf, walking, coaching, hunting, fish & game; clubs: Wainwright Golf & Country; Address: Box 2361, Wainwright, Alta. T0B 4P0.

**TWADDLE, The Hon. Mr. Justice Archibald Kerr;** judge of appeal; b. Glasgow, Scotland 7 Nov. 1932; s. Archibald Ferguson and Mary Kerr (Harris) T.; e. Hillhead H.S., Glasgow 1937–50; Inns of Court School of Law, London, England 1950–54; m. Susan d. Kenneth and Mary Bowden 17 Aug. 1957; children: Katherine, Iain; JUDGE OF APPEAL, MANITOBA COURT OF APPEAL 1985– ; called to English Bar 1954; to Manitoba Bar 1961; Q.C. 1966; Founding Pres., Man. Opera Assn.; Home: 224 Rouge Rd., Winnipeg, Man. R3K 1K1; Office: Court of Appeal, Winnipeg, Man. R3C 0V8.

**TWEEDY, Robert J.,** B.A., M.B.A.; executive; b. Toronto, Ont. 29 June 1942; s. James Donald and Barbara Margaret (Ault) T.; e. Univ. of Toronto Schs. 1960; Univ. of Toronto Trinity Coll. Hon. B.A. 1964 Stanford Univ. M.B.A. 1966; m. Diana Maria d. Humphrey B. Style 27 Aug. 1965; two d. Laura Anne Lisa Diana; CHRMN. & C.E.O., SKLAR-PEPPLER FURNITURE CORP.; SKLAR-PEPPLER OF AM. and CHRMN. & C.E.O., STEPHENSON'S RENT-ALL INC.; Chrmn., Multivans Inc.; Emerson Summers Co. Ltd.; Infocon Technologies Inc.; Dir., Arrow Electronics, Ltd.; Nutech Precision Metals Ltd.; The Toronto Hospital Found.; The Environmental Inst.; joined McKinsey and Co. Inc. (mgmt. consultants) Cleveland, Toronto and Paris 1966–72; Extve. Holderbank Financiere, Glaris, Switzerland 1972–73; Pres. DCP Group, Toronto 1973–77; Pres. Bata Shoe Co. Inc. (U.S.A.) and Regional Co-ordinator, Bata Caribbean, 1977–80; Pres. & C.E.O., PCL Industries Ltd. 1980–90; mem. Ont. Govt. Adv. Comte. for CAD/CAM and Robotics Technical Centre 1982; Chrmn. Prov. Task Force on Reorgan. Ont. Ministry of Indust. and Tourism 1976; mem. Chief Extves. Organization Inc.; World Presidents' Organization Inc.; Am. Marketing Assn.; Delta Kappa Epsilon: Anglican; recreations: tennis, golf, squash, fishing, reading; Clubs: Toronto Club; Rosedale Golf Club; Badminton & Racquet Club of Toronto; Big Bay Point Golf & Country; Mississaugua Golf & Country; Ocean Reef Club (Key Largo, Fla.); Home: 155 Rosedale Hts. Dr., Toronto, Ont. M4T 1C7.

**TWIGG, Alan Robert;** writer, editor, publisher, and film producer; b. West Vancouver, B.C. 11 Feb. 1952; s. Arthur and Olive (Thomson) T.; m. Tara d. Fred and Phae Farnsworth 2 Sept. 1973; children: Jeremy, Martin; EDITOR & PUBLISHER, B.C. BOOKWORLD 1987– ; Extve. Dir., West Coast Book Prize Soc. 1993– ; Contbg. Ed., Quill & Quire 1979–88; Books Columnist, The Province 1979–88; and Vancouver Mag. 1988–89; Theatre Critic, CBC Radio 1983–86 and Georgia Straight 1980–85; Publisher, Prairie Bookworld 1990–91; freelance contbr. to var. Candn. publs.; author: 'For Openers: Conversations with 24 Canadian Writers' 1981; 'Hubert Evans: The First Ninety-Three Years' 1985; 'Vancouver & Its Writers' 1986; 'Vander Zalm: From Immigrant to Premier' 1986; 'Strong Voices: Conversations with 50 Canadian Writers' 1988; 'Twigg's Directory of 1,001 B.C. Writers' 1992; film producer: 'Spilsbury's Coast' (nationally screened on CBC) 1992; 'And The Winners Are...' (documentary on the B.C. book industry) 1994; Home: 3516 W. 13th Ave., Vancouver, B.C. V6R 2S3.

**TWINN, Hon. Walter Patrick,** LL.D.; Cree chief, senator, businessman; b. Slave Lake, Alta. 29 March 1934; s. Paul and Irene (Cunningham) T. (both Cree); e. Athabasca Univ. Hon. LL.D.; m. Catherine May Cameron 23 Nov. 1984; children: Irene, Roland, Arlene, Ardell, Paul, Cameron, Patrick, Samuel, Issac; SUMMONED TO SENATE BY RIGHT HON. B. MULRONEY 27 SEPT. 1990; Chief, Sawridge Band 23 June 1966– ; Pres., Sawridge Holdings Ltd.; Sawridge Developments Co. (1977) Ltd.; Sawridge Enterprises Ltd.; TAI Resources Ltd.; Sawridge Energy Ltd.; Sawridge Enterprises Inc.; Sawridge Glacier Investments Ltd.; Glacier Bay Exploration Ltd.; 352736 Alberta Ltd.; Sawridge Manor Ltd.; Sawridge Administration Ltd.; Sawridge Hotels Inc.; Sawridge Plaza Corp.; Optima Engineers and Constructors Inc.; TAI Energy Resources Ltd.; Plaza Food Fare Inc.; Sawridge-Shuswap Resort Corp.; Past Dir., PetroCanada; Indian Equity Found.; Native Venture Capital; Founding Dir., Peace Hills Trust Co.; Dir., Indian Assn. of Alta.; Founding Pres., Lesser Slave Lake Indian Regional Council; Past Dir., Native Econ. Devel. Program; Slave Lake Developments Ltd.; Lifetime Mem., Native Friendship Centre; P.C.; Roman Catholic; clubs: Edmonton, Edmonton Petroleum, Centre; Office: 162N Centre Block, The Senate, Ottawa, Ont. K1A 0A4.

**TYERMAN, David McIntyre,** Q.C., LL.B.; b. Prince Albert, Sask. 14 Nov. 1906; s. Peter David and Jessie (Thompson) T.; e. Pub. and High Schs., Prince Albert, Sask.; Univ. of Sask., LL.B. 1928; m. Emilia Hedwick, 7 July 1945; children: Jane, Peter, Nancy; retired MacPHERSON, LESLIE & TYERMAN (estbd. 1921); read law with M. A. MacPherson, Q.C. and E.C. Leslie, Q.C.; called to the Bar of Saskatchewan 1930; cr. Q.C. 1956; served with RCN 1939–45; rank Commdr. (S); former Trustee, Found. for Legal Rsch.; former Gov., Candn. Tax Foundation; Candn. Petroleum Assn.; mem., Candn. Bar Assn.; Sask. Law Soc.; Regina Bar Assn.; Freemason (P.M.); Liberal; United Church; recreations: golf, curling, fishing; Clubs: Assiniboia; Wascana Country; Canadian; Homes: 2254 Wascana Greens, Regina, Sask. S4V 2M3 and 122 Caryl Way, Oldsmar, Florida 34677; Office: 1500 - 1874 Scarth St., Regina, Sask., S4P 4E9.

**TYLER, Douglas Owen;** politician; b. Chipman, N.B. 19 Aug. 1954; s. Charles and Joan (Lloyd) T.; e. Chipman H.S.; Saint John Comm. Coll.; m. Sandra Egers; three children; MINISTER OF STATE FOR MINES AND ENERGY, GOVT. OF N.B.; employed in auto sales industry for several years; 1st elected to Legislative Assembly of N.B. (Queens North) 1987; served on standing and special committees 1987–91; re-elected 1991; Mem., Extve. Council 1991; Mem., Liberal Party (Past Pres., Queens North Liberal Assn.); Royal Candn. Legion Branch 74; Former Extve. Mem., local rec. council and Kinsmen Club; Past Mem., Chipman Curling Club; Grand Lake Region Crime Stoppers; Elder, Chipman United Ch.; recreations: minor hockey; Home: Chipman, N.B. E0E 1C0; Office: Legislative Bldg., Fredericton, N.B. E3B 5H1.

**TYLER, Jonathan Mahon,** Ph.D.; university professor; b. Raleigh, N.C. 1 Feb. 1954; s. Lloyd Parry and Phyllis Aileen (Mahon) T.; e. Swarthmore Coll., B.A. 1976; Harvard Univ., Ph.D. 1980; m. Wilhelmina d. George and Wilhelmina Kearns 26 May 1976; children: Justine, Hannah, Rebecca; DIR., BIOMEDICAL DESIGN CENTRE, FAC. OF MED., UNIV. OF ALBERTA 1986– ; Jane Coffin Childs Med. Rsch. Scholar 1980–81; Alta. Heritage Med. Rsch. Scholar 1981–86; Asst. Prof. of Genetics, present univ. 1981–86; Assoc. Prof. of Med. 1986– ; Pres. & C.E.O., Tyler Rsch. Instruments Corp. 1981– ; Dir. & Sci. Adv. Bd., Tyler Rsch. Corp.; Phi Beta Kappa; Soc. of Sigma Xi; postdoctoral awards: Nat. Sci. Found. (U.S.), N. Atlantic Treaty Orgn., Killam Found., Helen Hay Whitney Found., Jane Coffin Childs; Bd. Mem. & Dir., Edmonton Counc. for Advanced Technol.; club: The Little Club of Edmonton; Home: 11704 – 91 Ave., Edmonton, Alta. T6G 1A9; Office: 750 Heritage Clin. Rsch. Bldg., Edmonton, Alta. T6G 2S2.

**TYMCHAK, Michael John,** B.A., Ph.D.; university professor and administrator b. Edam, Sask. 28 Fe. 1943 s. Dr. Zane Alexander and Johanna (Vreke) T.; e. Aden Bowman Collegiate 1960; Univ. of Sask. B.A. (Hons.) 1964; Univ. of Manchester Ph.D. 1974; m. Beryl d. Edward and Nora Wear 19 Aug. 1967; children: Rachel Ellen, Mark Edward; DEAN OF EDUCATION, UNIV. OF REGINA 1992– ; Asst. Lecturer, Philosophy, Univ. of Manchester 1967–68; Lay Minister, United Ch. of Canada 1968–69; Instructor, Philos., Univ. of Regina 1969–71; Ethnohistorian, SASKED 1974–75; Asst. Prof., Philos., Regent Coll. (U.B.C. affiliate) 1976; Assoc. Prof. (Phil. & Gen. Studies), Candn. Bible Coll. 1985–88; Extve. Dir., Northern Education Program & Prof., Univ. of Regina 1977–85, 1988–92; Bd. of Dir., Gabriel Dumont Inst.; Mem., Indian and Metis Edn. Adv. Ctte.; Commonwealth Scholar 1964–67; Canada 125 Medal 1992; Adjunct Prof., Coll. of Grad. Studies, Univ. of Sask.; Mem., Christian and Missionary Alliance; Candn. Soc. for Studies in Education; author: 'Our Heritage' 1975, 'Saskatchewan Internship and Field Experiences Review' 1988; recreations: music, camping, canoeing, skiing; Home: 39 Dunning Cres., Regina, Sask. S4S 3V9; Office: Regina, Sask. S4S 0A2.

**TYNAN, Kathleen,** B.A.; writer; b. London, Eng. 25 Jan. 1939; d. Matthew Henry and Jean Joslin (Campbell) Halton; e. Queen's Hall Vancouver 1943–45; Queen's Coll. Harley St. London 1952–55; Sorbonne Paris 1955; Oxford Univ. 1956–59; London Univ. B.A. 1959; m. Kenneth s. Sir Peter Peacock and Rose Tynan 30 June 1967; children: Roxana Nell, Matthew Blake; Researcher 'Newsweek' mag. N.Y. 1960; Features Writer and Reporter Arts Column. 'London Observer' 1962–64; Features Writer 'London Sunday Times' 1964–67; freelance jour. and TV interviewer since 1967; author 'The Summer Aeroplane' novel 1975; 'Agatha' novel 1979, screenplay 1978; 'The Life of Kenneth Tynan' biog. 1987, paperback 1988; 'Editor Profiles by Kenneth Tynan' 1989; Runner-up NCR Lit. Award Non-fiction; recreations: reading, travel.

**TYNKALUK, William G.,** B.A., C.F.A.; executive; b. Sault Ste Marie, Ont. 7 Dec. 1929; e. Univ. of Toronto B.A. 1953; m. Marguerite Brown; children: Gregory W., Gail M.; PRESIDENT, LEON FRAZER & ASSOCIATES LTD.; Vice Pres. & Dir., Associate Investors Ltd.; Dir. Goldfund Ltd.; mem. Bd. Trade Metrop. Toronto; Clubs: Gyro; Empire; Albany; Home: 46 Palomino Cres., Willowdale, Ont. M2K 1W3; Office: 8 King St. E., Suite 2001, Toronto, Ont. M5C 1B5.

**TYRIE, Anne,** B.Sc., M.Sc., Ph.D.; university professor and administrator; b. Edinburgh, Scotland 10 Oct. 1954; d. Thomas Palmer and Isabella Wilkie (Smilie) T.; e. Manchester Univ. B.Sc. (Hons.) 1977, M.Sc. 1979, Ph.D. 1981; Centre for Research in Applied Creativity, Creative Problem Solver Level III 1992; m. Michael W. s. William and Winifred Horsfall (c.l.) 1 Sept. 1985; children: Ross and Blair Tyrie-Horsfall; DIRECTOR, INDUSTRY SUPPORT, INFORMATION TECHNOLOGY RESEARCH CENTRE 1993– ; Trainee C.A., Arthur Andersen & Co. (U.K.) 1977; Geologist, Geophysicist, Scientific Editor, Ministry of Northern Devel. & Mines 1980–83; Prof., Surveying Science, Univ. of Toronto 1983–90; Vice-Pres., R&D, Real/Data Ontario Inc. 1988–90; Pres., Anne Tyrie & Assoc. 1986– ; Dir., Real/Data Ontario Inc. 1987–93; consultant, Carleton Profl. Devel. Centre 1991–92; Philip A. Lapp Ltd. 1987–90; Mem., Internat. Soc. for Photogrammetry & Remote Sensing; Am. Soc. of Photogrammetry; Nat. Adv. Council on Surveys & Mapping 1990–92; Candn. Aeronautics & Space Inst.; Pres., Ont. Assn. of Remote Sensing 1986–88; Dir., Women in Sci. & Engr. 1984–86; Financial Mgr., Candn. Hydrographic Journal 1985–87; co-editor: '2nd Internat. Proc.' 1987 J. of Geodynamics; author of 24 journal papers, technical reports, etc.; Home: 2236 Grenville Dr., Oakville, Ont. L6H 4W7; Office: Suite 286, D.L. Pratt Bldg., 6 King's College Rd., Toronto, Ont. M5S 1A1.

**TYRRELL, Frances Claire;** illustrator; b. Kirkland Lake, Ont. 1 July 1959; d. Donald Henry and Avril Joyce (Tyler) T.; m. Colin J. s. Joan and Alex Philip 2 June 1990; Illustrations for 'The Huron Carol' 1990 (Finalist, Governor General's Award for book illustration); 'The Worker in Sandalwood' 1991; 'Kates Castle' 1992; 'Joy to the World' 1992; 'The Christmas Clown' 1993; 'The Dragon's Egg' 1994; Home: 448 Caesar Ave., Oakville, Ont. L6J 4E5.

**TYRRELL, Robert John Charles;** publisher; b. Dawson Creek, B.C. 8 June 1948; s. Gordon Patrick and Jean McBeth (Rae) T.; e. Univ. of Victoria 1970; Simon Fraser Univ. 1976; m. Avril I.M. Malone 18 Dec. 1987; one d.: Alexandra Jean; FOUNDER & PUBLISHER, ORCA BOOK PUBLISHERS LTD. 1984– ; High School Teacher, Kelowna, Nanaimo & Victoria 1976–85; Orca publishes 15-20 titles per year; an Orca book, 'Waiting for the Whales' won Governor General's Literary Award 1992; Publisher of the Year, Candn. Booksellers Assn. 1992; Pres., Assn. of Book Publishers of B.C.; co-author: 'Rumrunner: The Life & Times of Johnny Schnarr' 1988, 'Island Pubbing' 1984; recreations: squash, flyfishing; Home: 1702 San Juan Ave., Victoria, B.C. V8N 5E4; Office: P.O. Box 5626, Stn. B, Victoria, B.C. V8R 6S4.

**TYRWHITT-DRAKE, The Hon. Montague Lawrence,** LL.B.; judge; b. Victoria, B.C. 14 Oct. 1922; s. Brian Halsey and Constance Laetitia (Lawrence) T-D.; e. Victoria Coll., Victoria, B.C., 1939–40; McGill Univ., 1940–43; Univ. of B.C., LL.B., 1949; m. Nancy Elizabeth, d. Daniel Webster Lang, K.C., 7 June 1946; children: Elizabeth Laetitia (Holovsky), Montague Daniel,

Guy Lawrence; JUDGE, SUPREME COURT OF BRITISH COLUMBIA; served in 2nd World War, Black Watch of Canada and in CANLOAN Scheme, 1942–46; discharged with rank of Capt.; Kappa Alpha; recreation: fishing; Clubs: Union of B.C.; Victoria Golf; Home: 404 Lands End Rd., R.R. 4, Sidney, B.C. V8L 5L9; Office: Law Courts, 850 Burdett Ave., Victoria, B.C. V8W 1B4.

**TYSALL, John Robert,** B.A., M.B.A., M. Sc.; financial executive; b. London, Eng. 9 Feb. 1938; s. Frank John and Lillian Doris (Hornby) T.; e. York Univ. B.A. 1969; London Sch. of Econ. M.Sc. 1971; Univ. of Chicago M.B.A. 1974; three s. Innis, David, Steven; m. Wendy Doris Cottrell d. Cyril and Vera Cottrell, December 30, 1984; VICE PRES. AND TREASURER, CANADA TRUST 1993– ; Sr. Econ. Ministry of Treasury, Ont. 1976; Vice Pres. Underwriting McLeod, Young, Weir Ltd. Toronto 1976–79; Dir. of Treasury, Gulf Canada 1979–82; Vice Pres. and Treas., Gulf Canada Resources Ltd., GW Utilities Ltd. 1987–93; mem. Financial Extves. Inst.; recreations: skiing, collecting antique cars; Home: 18 Owen Blvd., North York, Ont. M2P 1E9.

**TYSOE, The Hon. Mr. Justice David F.,** LL.B.; judge; b. Victoria, B.C. 19 June 1951; s. John Franklin and Joan May (Welchman) T.; e. Univ. of Victoria; Univ. of B.C. LL.B. 1975; m. Louise d. Galt and Joyce Smith Feb. 1980; children: Avril, Claire, Brent; JUDGE, SUPREME COURT OF B.C. 1992– ; articling student, Farris, Vaughan, Wills & Murphy 1975; Associate 1976; Partner 1981; Office: Law Courts, 800 Smithe St. Vancouver, B.C. V6Z 2E1.

**TYSON, Ian D.;** song writer, entertainer, rancher, cowboy historian; b. Victoria, B.C. 25 Sept. 1933; s. George Dawson and Margaret Gertrude (Campbell) T.; e. Vancouver School of Art 1958; 1st. m. Sylvia Fricker 1961; one s. Clay Dawson Tyson; 2nd m. Twylla d. Fred and Lydia Biblow 26 Sept. 1986; one d.: Adelita Rose Tyson; OWNER, FOUR STRONG WINDS LTD.; Ian Tyson is one of a kind ... authentic and durable; his brilliant career has spanned decades, from internat. fame in the 1960s folk boom to the forefront of the current revival of tradition in country music; along the way, he has perfected skills as a cowboy on his ranch in the foothills of the Rocky Mountains (fulfilling his boyhood dream); Graphic Artist Toronto while playing folk club circuit with performers such as Gordon Lightfoot and Joni Mitchell; former partnership with Sylvia Fricker began 1961; cut over a dozen albums becoming pioneers of country rock with their band Great Speckled Bird; Co-hosts, 'Nashville North' (later host, 'The Ian Tyson Show') 1970s; classic songs incl. 'Four Strong Winds,' 'Someday Soon,' 'Summer Wages,' 'The Gift,' 'Fifty Years Ago,' 'Navajo Rug,' 'Springtime in Alberta,' 'Black Nights'; most recent albums: 'And Stood There Amazed,' 'I Outgrew the Wagon,' 'Cowboyography'; currently developing pops orchestra format in western Canada; extensive tours 1989– ; opened Calgary Olympics with Gordon Lightfoot; inducted Canadian Country Music Hall of Honour, Candn. Country Music Assn. (CCMA) 1989; CCMA Awards: Male Vocalist of the Year, 1987, '88, '92; Single of the Year (Navajo Rug) 1987; Album of the Year (Cowboyography) 1987; Video of the Year (Springtime in Alberta) 1991; 1st Male Country Vocalist to Achieve 2 Gold Albums in Canada 1992; Juno Awards: Induction, Juno Hall of Fame 1992; Male Vocalist of the Year 1987; numerous awards from Big Country (RPM Mag.), Alta. Recording Industry Assn., Country Music Assn. of Calgary; Office: P.O. Box 5607, High River, Alta. T1V 1M7.

**TYSON, John Edward Alfred,** M.D., F.R.C.S.(C), F.A.C.O.G., F.A.C.S., F.S.O.G.C.; physician; university professor; corporation president; b. Hamilton, Ont. 27 May 1935; s. Alfred Bousefield and Grace (Hughes) T.; e. Univ. of W. Ont., M.D. 1960; Fellow, Ob./Gyn., Univ. of W. Ont. 1961–65; Johns Hopkins Univ., Post-Doct. Fellow 1966–68; m. Patricia E. d. Henry and Marjorie Capes 15 Dec. 1962; children: Alicia G., Suzanne D., John A.W.; PROF., OB./GYN., UNIV. OF TORONTO 1985– ; Active Staff, The Toronto Hospital – Toronto General Division; Toronto Western Division 1986– ; mem., Obstetrics & Gynecology Task Force on Reproductive Health Care, The College of Physicians and Surgeons 1990– ; Med. Dir., C.A.R.E. Health Resources; Intern, Hamilton Gen. Hosps. 1960–61; Residency, Westminster Vet. Hosp. & Hamilton Civic Hosps. 1962–66; Cons. & Acting Chief of Obstet. & Gynec., Norfolk Gen. Hosp. 1966; Fellow, Johns Hopkins Univ. Sch. of Med. 1966–68; Instr. 1968–69; Asst. Prof. 1969–71; Assoc. Prof. 1971–78; Prof. and Chrmn. 1978–84; Obstet./Gynec. in Chief, Women's Hospital, Winnipeg 1978–84; Prof. and Chrmn., Univ. of Man. 1978–84; Adjunct. Prof., Univ. of N. Dakota 1979–84; Pres., Direction South Media 1984; Vice Pres., Direction South Mgmt. 1984; Cons., CTV Television Ltd. 1984–88; Candn. Broadcasting Corp. 1984–86; Pres., The Life Channel Inc. 1984–86; and prev. others; Mem., Am. Fed. for Clin. Rsch.; Soc. of Obstet. & Gynec. of Can.; Soc. for Gynec. Investig. (Prog. & Local Arrangements Chrmn., 1986/93 mtg.) and Chrmn. Finance & Development Ctte.; Endocrine Soc.; Ont. Med. Assoc.; Assn. of Profs. of Gynec. & Obstet. (both U.S. & Candn.); Dipl., Am. Bd. of Obstet. & Gynec.; Bd. Mem., Candn. Fertility & Andrology Soc.; Amer. Fert. Soc.; past mem., several assns.; extensive instl. & community ctte. work; recipient of numerous awards & rsch. grants; sci. reviewer several med. jours.; Guest Ed.: 'Seminars in Perinatology,' 'MEDICINE North America'; produced & directed over 600 audio visual pieces; author of numerous abstracts, jour. articles & book chapters; recreations: skiing, farming; Home: 1532 Point-O-Woods Rd., Mississauga, Ont. L5G 2X7.

**TYTANECK, Robert W.,** B.A., M.A.; transportation executive; b. St. Catharines, Ont. 18 Dec. 1949; s. William Nicholas T. and Theodosia (Zelinsky) T.; e. Sir Winston Churchill S.S. 1967; Univ. of Waterloo, B.A., M.A. 1974; m. Margaret d. Douglas and Ruth Morton 6 Oct. 1972; children: Janice Ruth, William Morton; VICE-PRES., OPERATING DIVISION, CANADA PORTS CORPORATION 1993– ; Econ., St. Lawrence Seaway Auth. 1974–80; Dir., Info. Serv., Canada Ports Corp. 1980–86; Gen. Mgr. & C.E.O., Prince Rupert Port Corp. 1986–90; Vice-Pres., Finance and Admin., Canada Ports Corp. 1990–93; Mem., Chartered Inst. of Transp.; recreations: fishing, curling, woodworking, automotive enthusiast; Home: 1686 Teslin Court, Ottawa, Ont. K1C 4W9; Office: 99 Metcalfe St., Ottawa, Ont. K1A 0N6.

# U

**UBALE, Bhausaheb,** M.A., Ph.D.; consultant; b. Bawchi, India 28 Feb. 1936; s. Maruti Krishna and Ganga U.; e. St. Andrews Univ. Scot. post grad. Dip. in Econ. Devl. 1970; Univ. of Leeds M.A. 1971; Univ. of Bradford Ph.D. 1975; m. Pramila d. D.N. Khedekar 24 Nov. 1963; children: Priti, Amol; Comnr., Ont. Human Rights Comn. 1978–85; Comnr., Candn. Human Rights Comn. 1986–89; former Dir. Indian Inst. of Pol. Studies, Bombay, India; Sec. Indo-Plast Ltd. Bombay; Mgr. Zenith Publishing Co. London, Eng.; Cons. Seneca Coll. Toronto; Race Relations Comnr. Prov. Ont.; Dir. Internat. Assn. Official Human Rights Agencies; Trustee, Un. Way Metro Toronto; Hon. Fellow, Biographical Acad. Commonwealth; author 'Equal Opportunity and Public Policy' 1978; 'Politics of Exclusion: Multiculturalism or Ghettoism' 1992; Home: 83 Kingslake Rd., Willowdale, Ont. M2J 3E6.

**UCHIDA, Irene Ayako,** O.C., Ph.D.; educator; b. Vancouver, B.C. 8 Apr. 1917; d. Sentaro Uchida; e. Univ. of Toronto Ph.D. 1951; PROF. EMERITUS, DEPTS. OF PEDIATRICS AND PATHOLOGY, MCMASTER UNIV.; DIR. OF CYTOGENETICS, OSHAWA GENERAL HOSPITAL 1991– ; Research Assoc. Hosp. for Sick Children Toronto 1951–59; Rockefeller Fellow, Univ. of Wisc. 1959; Dir. Med. Genetics Children's Hosp. of Winnipeg; 1960–69, Asst. Prof. Pediatrics 1962, Assoc. Prof. 1967–69 Univ. of Man.; Dir. Regional Cytogenetics Lab., McMaster Univ. 1969–91; mem. Organizing Comte. on Standardization of Human Cytogenetics (Internat.) 1966; Visiting Prof. Univ. of Alabama Medical Sch. 1968; Med. Research Council Visiting Scient. Univ. of London and Harwell 1969; mem. Science Council of Can. 1970–73; MRC Genetics Grants Comte. 1970–73; MRC Visiting Prof. Univ. of W. Ont. 1973; Consultant to Internat. Program in Radiation Genetics, NEA of OECD, Paris 1973; Organizing Comte. Candn. Coll. Med. Genetics 1976; Task Force on Cytogenetics for Adv. Comte. on Genetic Services 1977; mem. Adv. Comte. on Genetic Services for Ontario, 1979; Am. Bd. of Medical Genetics (Consultant) 1980; Mental Retardation Research Comte, Nat. Inst. of Child Health & Human Dev., Nat. Inst. of Health, H.E.W., U.S.A. 1980–84; Ont. Med. Assn. Lab. Proficiency Testing Programme, Genetic Cell Culture Comm. Chrmn. 1981; Ont. Med. Assn. Lab. Proficiency Testing Programme Steering Comte. 1981; Sci. Advy. Comte., N.Y. State Inst. for Basic Rsch. 1984; author various reports on genetics and cytogenetics in scient. and med. journs. and monographs; Ramsay Wright Scholar, Univ. of Toronto 1947; Woman of the Year, Winnipeg, Manitoba 1963; Woman of the Century 1867–1967, Manitoba 1967; Achievement Award, Winnipeg, Man. 1969; Queen Elizabeth II Speaker, Winnipeg, Man. 1971; 25 Outstanding Women, Internat. Women's Year, Gov't of Ont. 1975; 1000 Canadian Women of Note, 1867–1967, 1983; Emeritus Fellow, Candn. Coll. Med. Geneticists (Chrmn., Quality Control of Cytogenetics Laboratories 1979; Bd. mem. 1980–84); Emeritus Fellow, Am. Coll. of Medical Genetics 1993; Officer, Order of Canada 1993; mem. Am. Soc. Human Genetics (Pres. 1968); Assn. Genetic Counsellors Ont.; Genetics Soc. Can.; Home: 20 North Shore Blvd. W., #1210, Burlington, Ont. L7T 1A1; Office: 1200 Main St. W., Hamilton, Ont. L8N 3Z5.

**UFFEN, Robert James,** O.C.(1983), B.A.Sc., M.A., Ph.D., D.Sc., F.R.S.C., F.G.S.A., P.Eng., F.A.A.A.S., F.C.A.E.; b. Toronto, Ont. 21 Sept. 1923; s. James Frederick and Elsie May (Harris) U.; e. Univ. of Toronto, B.A.Sc. (Engn. Physics) 1949, M.A. (Geo. physics) 1950; Univ. of Western Ont., Ph.D. (Physics) 1952; D.Sc. Queen's 1967, W. Ont. 1970; R.M.C. 1978; McMaster 1983; m. Mary Ruth, d. John Ross Paterson, Toronto, Ont., 3 May 1949; children: Joanne Grace, Robert Ross; PROF. EMERITUS, QUEEN'S UNIV. 1989– ; Prof. of Geophysics, Queen's Univ. 1971–89; Dean, Faculty of Applied Science, 1971–80; Co-ordinator, Summer Program for Science Teachers 1986–89; Chrmn. Candn. Engn. Manpower Council 1972–74; mem. Fisheries Research Bd. Can. 1975–79; mem. Bd. of Dir., Ont. Hydro 1973–79 (Vice Chrmn. 1975–79); Commissioner Ont. Royal Commission on Asbestos, 1980–84; Commissioner, Ont. Comm. on Truck Safety, 1981–83; Chrmn., Exploration Technology Devel. Fund, Ont., 1981–83; Cons. to E.E.C. on energy rsch. 1987–88; Waddell Lectr., R.M.C., 1982; joined Univ. of W. Ont. 1953; Princ. Univ. Coll. of Arts & Science U.W.O., 1961–65; Dean, Coll. of Science, 1965–66; mem. Nat. Research Council Can. 1963–66; mem., Defence Research Bd., Can. 1964–69 (Chrmn. 1967–69); mem., Science Council Can. 1967–71; Chief Science Adviser to the Cabinet, Privy Council Office, Ottawa, 1969–71; mem. Council of Regents, Colls. Applied Arts & Technol. Ont. 1966–69, 72–75; Visiting Fellow, Sci. Policy Research Unit, Univ. of Sussex 1976–77 and 1983–84; Bd. of Dir., Centre for Resource Studies, 1973–77, 1980; mem., Comm. of Ont. Deans of Eng. 1971–80 (Chrmn, 1977–78); N.R.C. Assoc. Comm. on Environment 1979–82; mem., Comm. on Nuclear Waste Management, A.E.C.L. 1988–91; Bd. of Dirs., Harbour Place, Kingston, Ont. 1989–91; Fellow, Royal Soc. of Can. 1964; mem., Candn. Assn. Physicists; Assn. Prof. Engrs. Ont. (Council mem. 1975–79); Am. Geophys. Union; Geol. Soc. Am. (Fellow 1967); Candn. Inst. Mining & Metall.; Club of Rome (1969–84); Fellow, Am. Assoc. for the Advancement of Science 1986; Fellow, Candn. Acad. of Engr. 1988; co-discoverer of Allard Lake titanium deposits, Que.; served in 2nd World War with R.C.A. as Pte., 1942, Lieut. 1943; C.I.C. Lieut., 1944–45; has written numerous articles on geophysics, evolution, science policy, nuclear waste and occupational safety; awarded Centennial Medal, Canada 1967; Officer, Order of Canada 1983; Public Service Medal, Assn. of Prof. Engr. of Ont. 1985; Distinguished Service Award, Queen's Univ. 1990; Engineering Hall of Distinction, Univ. of Toronto 1990; 125th Anniversary of the Confederation of Canada Medal, 1992; John Orr Award, Queen's Univ. 1993; Sigma Chi; recreation: painting; Home: 185 Ontario St., #1504, Kingston, Ont. K7L 2Y7.

**ULLMAN, Gary Wesley,** B.B.A.; business executive; b. Toronto, Ont. 29 Aug. 1941; s. Wesley Art and Marion Lois (Lawson) U.; e. Weston/Riverdale Collegiate; York Univ. B.B.A. 1962; m. Cindy d. Edna and Harry Saville 20 July 1985; children: Kenneth, Kim, Kristopher, Danielle, Brett; CHIEF EXECUTIVE OFFICER, CCL CUSTOM MANUFACTURING 1993– and EXTVE. VICE-PRES., CCL INDUSTRIES INC. 1991– ; Salesman, Charles Albert Smith (Toronto) 1961–62; General Mgr., Rexall Drug, Carnegie Labs. 1962–64; Vice-Pres., Gen. Mgr. & Pres., CCL Chempac Div. 1966–81; Pres., Kleen-Stik Fasson Limited & Extve. Vice-Pres. & Chief Operating Offr., CCL Custom Mfg. Div. 1981–83; Pres., Custom Mfg. & Product Identification Divisions 1983–90; Pres. & C.O.O., CCL Consumer Products Group 1990–93; Chrmn., CCL Industries Ltd.; CCL Indus. (UK) Ltd.; Advanced Monobloc Inc.; CCL Label Inc.; Haventrail Ltd.; Osmond Ltd.; Pres. & Dir., CCL Management Inc.; Chempac Inc.; EnviroSpray Canada Inc.; Interneecom Mfg. Ltd.; Vice-Pres. & Dir., CCL Internat. Ltd.; Dir., CCL Indus. Inc.; Kolmar Internat. Ltd.; Kolmar de Mexico S.A.; Mem., Sales & Marketing Extve., North Am., The Soap and Detergent Assn. of Canada; C.M.C.S. Assn.; recreations: jogging, tennis, cycling; clubs: Boulevard; Home: 420 Woodland Acres Cres., Maple, Ont. L6A 1G2; Office: 6133 N. River Rd., Suite 800, Rosemont, IL 60018 U.S.A.

**ULLULAQ, Judas;** sculptor; b. Thom Bay, north-east of Spence Bay, N.W.T. 1 July 1937; 37 group exbns. incl. most recent: Galerie Saint Merri Paris, France 1991, 1992, Inuit Gall. of Vancouver 1990, 1991, l'Iglou Art Esquimau, Douai (toured 3 cities) France 1991, Albers Gall. San Francisco, Ca. 1991, Vancouver Inuit Art Soc. 1991, Orca Aart, Chicago, Ill. 1991; solo exbns.: The Upstairs Gall. Winnipeg, Man. 1987, Northern Images Edmonton, Alta. 1985, Alaska Shop, Gall. of Eskimo Art New York, N.Y. 1983, The Innuit Gall. of Eskimo Art Toronto 1983; works in 8 collections incl. art galleries of Ontario (Klamer Family Coll.), Winnipeg, Inuit Cultural Inst., Rankin Inlet, N.W.T., Musée des beaux-arts de Montréal, Nat. Gall. of Canada; attended openings: 'Contemporary Indian and Inuit Art of Canada' and Alaska Shop opening, N.Y. 1985, 'Mother & Child' Marion Scott Gall. Vancouver 1988, 'In the Shadow of the Sun' Dortmund, Germany 1988, 'Masters of the Arctic' N.Y. 1989; carving 'Legendary Woman' appeared on front cover 'Up Here' Oct./Nov. 1991; subject of articles and catalogues; Home: Gjoa Haven, N.W.T.; Office: c/o Ingo Hessel, Indian and Northern Affairs Canada, Les Terrasses de la Chaudière, Ottawa, Ont. K1A 0H4.

**ULMER, Ralph C.;** business executive; PRESIDENT, CO-OPERATORS DATA SERVICES LIMITED; Office: CDSL Tower, 1900 Albert St., Regina, Sask. S4P 4K8.

**UMBRICO, Judy Loman;** harpist; b. Goshen, Ind. 3 Nov. 1936; d. Herschel Gilmour and Sabra Pauline (Waltz) Leatherman; came to Can. 1957; e. Carlos Salzedo, Camden,. Ma. and Curtis Inst. of Music Diploma 1949–56; m. Joseph U. 25 June 1956; children:. Pennie, Linda, Julie, Joey; HARPIST, TORONTO SYMPHONY ORCHESTRA; Adjunct Prof., Univ. of Toronto; Asst. Prof. Harp, McGill Univ.; Instr., Royal Conservatory of Music; Instr., Fenelon Falls Harp Sch.; harp soloist; has recorded for RCA, CBC, Aquitane, CBS and EMI; soloist in Eur., U.S.A., Can. with Tor. Symphony, Shaw Festival, Stratford Festival, CBC Radio and TV; Juno 1979; Grand Prix du Disque 1980; commissioned new works for harp; Home: 38 Burnside Dr., Toronto, Ont. M6G 2M8.

**UMEZAWA, Hiroomi,** B.E., D.Sc., F.R.S.C.; university professor; b. Saitama-ken, Japan 20 Sept. 1924; s. Junichi and Takako (Sato) U.; e. Univ. of Nagoya, Japan, B.E. 1947, D.Sc. 1952; m. Tamae d. Akio and Tatsue Yamagami 30 July 1958; children: Rui, Ado; KILLAM PROF. EMERITUS, DEPT. OF PHYSICS, UNIV. OF ALTA. 1992– ; Killam Memorial Prof. of Science, Prof. of Physics, Univ. of Alta. (Retired) 1975–92; Rsch. Assoc., Univ. of Nagoya 1947–53; Assoc. Prof. 1953–55; Univ. of Tokyo 1955–60; Prof. 1960–64; Univ. of Napoli 1964–66; Dir., Inst. of Theoretical Physics, Finland 1965; Leader, Group on Structure of Matter, Ctr. of Nat. Rsch., Naples Div. 1964–66; Prof., Univ. of Wisconsin 1966–67; Disting. Prof. 1967–75; Vis. Prof., Max Planck Inst. 1980; Univ. of Wisconsin 1976–78 (March yearly); Tohoku Univ. 1977; Univ. of Salerno 1967–76 (May yearly); Univ. of Marseille 1959; of Iowa 1957; of Maryland 1957; of Washington 1956; Lady Davis Sr. Scholar, Israel 1989; F.R.S.C. 1989; Fellow, N.Y. Acad. of Sci. 1976; Fellow, Am. Physical Soc. 1968 (Life Mem. 1987); ICI Fellow, Univ. of Manchester 1953–55; Life Mem., Japan Physical Soc. 1990; author/co-author of 7 books most recent incl. 'Quantum Mechanics' 1985, 'Thermo Field Dynamics and Condensed States' 1985 (Russian translation 1985), and 302 refereed scientific pubs.; Home: 14116 52 Ave., Edmonton, Alta. T6H 0P8; Office: Edmonton, Alta. T6G 2J1.

**UMHOLTZ, David,** B.F.A.; artist; b. Harrisburg, Penn. 4 Nov. 1943; s. Charles David and Viola (Hughes) Um; e. Kutztown State Coll.; Penn. Acad. of Fine Art; Univ. of Penn. B.F.A. 1970; children: Ewan B., Damon J., Noah D., Zoë M.; Founder / Dir., Moosehead Press 1977– ; Advisor, Holman Eskimo Co-op. 1985– ; Former Asst. Head, Art Studio, Banff Centre; solo exhibitions incl. Ottawa Sch. of Art, Univ. de Moncton, Virginia Christopher Gall. Calgary, Beaverbrook Fredericton 1988; Norman Mackenzie Art Gall. Regina 1987; Gallery Connection Fredericton, W.A.G. Winnipeg 1986; North of Sixty St. Andrews 1985; Granville Island Graphis Vanc., Virginia Christopher Gall. 1984; Gallery Don Stewart Montreal, Anna Leonowens Gall. Halifax 1982; Brian Melnychenko Gall. Winnipeg 1981, '83, '84, '85, '86 and 11 others prior to 1980; collections incl.: Winnipeg Art Gall., James Richardson & Sons Ltd., Pioneer Grain, Metropolitan Properties (Winnipeg); Mendal Art Gall., Univ. of Sask. (Saskatoon); Nickel Art Gall. (Sackville); Nova Corp., Husky Oil, Petro-Can., Sceptre Resources (Calgary); Steinberg Collection, Alcan Aluminum (Montreal); Portland Mus. of Art; Beaverbrook Art Gall. (Fredericton); Toronto-Dominion Bank; N.B. Govt. Art Bank; Univ. of N.B.; Canada Council Art Bank; Shell Oil Collection (Toronto & Calgary); participant in over 50 group exhibitions incl.: 'Boston Printmakers,' Boston, Mass. 1983–85, '91; 'Printshops in Canada,' MacDonald Stewart Centre, Guelph 1987, '88, '89; 'Within Range,' Moscow, Idaho 1990; 'British International Print Biennale,' Bradford, London 1990, Glasgow 1991; recipient of several arts grants; silk screen & etching printer, photographer, journalist, lecturer, lithographer, teacher, technical consultant; participant in over 20 workshops; rep. by Brian Melnychenko Winnipeg; Virginia Christopher Gall. Calgary; Concept Art Gall. Pittsburgh; Open Studio Toronto; North of Sixty St. Andrews, N.B.; Lumley Cazalet London, England; Home: Fairhaven, Deer Island, N.B.

**UNDERHILL, Anne Barbara,** M.A., Ph.D., D.Sc., F.R.S.C; honorary professor; b. Vancouver, B.C. 12 June 1920; d. Frederic Clare and Irene Anna (Creery) U.; e. Univ. of B.C. B.A. 1942, M.A. 1944, D.Sc. 1992; Univ. of Chicago Ph.D. 1948; York Univ. D.Sc. 1969; HON. PROF. UNIV. OF B.C. 1985– ; Rsch. Sci. Dom. Astrophys. Obs. Victoria 1949–62; Prof. of Astrophys. Univ. of Utrecht 1962–70; Chief, Lab. for Optical Astron. NASA Goddard Space Flight Center Greenbelt, Md. 1970–77, Sr. Sci. 1978–85; author 'The Early-Type Stars' 1966; co-author 'B Stars With and Without Emission Lines' 1982; 'O Stars and Wolf-Rayet Stars' 1988; over 200 rsch. papers; co-ed. several conf. proceedings; mem. Internat. Astron. Union; Am. Astron. Soc.; Candn. Astron. Soc.; Royal Astron. Soc.; Royal Astron. Soc. Can.; Astron. Soc. Pacific; Anglican; recreation: church choir singing; Office: Dept. Geophysics and Astronomy, Univ. of B.C., Vancouver, B.C. V6T 1Z4.

**UNDERHILL, Herbert Stuart;** journalist; b. Vancouver, B.C. 20 May 1914; s. Harold John and Helena (Ross) U.; e. elem. and high schs. B.C.; m. Emma Gwendolyn d. late J. T. MacGregor 23 July 1937; childen: Carol, James Stuart; President, Victoria Press 1978–79; Publisher, Victoria Times and Vice Pres. Victoria Press (Div. of F. P. Publications (Western) Ltd.) 1971–78; Corr. and Ed. The Canadian Press, Vancouver, Toronto, New York and London 1937–50; N. Am. Ed. Reuters (London, Eng.) 1950, Asst. Gen. Mgr. 1958, Mang. Ed. 1965–68, Depy. Gen. Mgr. (N. and S. Am., Caribbean) 1963–70; Asst. Publisher Financial Times of Canada 1970; winner Candn. Newspaper Award for Corr. 1950; Dir. The Candn. Press 1972–78; Candn. Newspaper Publishers Assn. 1972–76; Anglican; Home: 308 Beach Dr., Victoria, B.C. V8S 2M2.

**UNGER, Frank Michael,** Ph.D.; pharmaceutical executive; b. Vienna, Austria 1 July 1940; s. Guenther Karl and Maria Anna (Walcher) U.; e. Akademisches Gymnasium Vienna 1958; Univ. of Vienna 1964; Georgetown Univ. Washington, D.C. Ph.D. 1968; m. Judit Maria d. Imre and Gizella Brand 2 June 1971; children: Judith Christine, Annemarie Sophie, Peter Imre; ALBERTA RESEARCH COUNCIL; Pres. & C.E.O., Chembiomed Ltd. 1990; mem. Inst. Exper. Cancer Rsch. Univ. of Vienna 1968, Universitaetsdozent 1982; Inst. Organic Chem. Univ. of Basel 1968–69; Sandoz Rsch. Inst. Vienna 1970–87, Sr. Sci. 1979; Vice Pres. Rsch. and Devel. present Co. 1987, Sr. Vice-Pres. Rsch. & Devel. 1988–90; holds 6 patents; invited speaker Gordon Conf. on Carbohydrates 1985; author or co-author numerous publs. Carbohydrate Rsch., Biochem. & Biophys. Rsch. Communications; mem. Eur. Carbohydrate Orgn. (Pres. 1981–83); Am. Chem. Soc.; Rotary Club of Edmonton; Assn. Biotechnol. Co's; Advisory Bd. of the Institute of Biological Sciences, National Research Council Canada; R. Catholic; recreations: woodcarving, music, swimming; Home: 11602 – 77 Ave., Edmonton, Alta. T6G 0M3.

**UNGER, Israel,** B.Sc., M.Sc., Ph.D.; university professor and adminsitrator; b. Tarnow, Poland 30 March 1938; s. David and Hinda (Fisch) U.; e. Sir George Williams Univ. B.Sc. 1958; Univ. of N.B. M.Sc. 1960, Ph.D. 1963; m. Marlene Parker 6 July 1964; chjildren: Sharen, Sheila; PROFESSOR, UNIV. OF NEW BRUNSWICK 1974– ; CIL Fellow, Univ. of N.B. 1962–63 Welsh Post, Doctoral, Univ. of Texas 1963–65; Asst. Prof., Univ. of N.B. 1965–69; Assoc. prof. 1969; Dean of Science, 1986–91, 1991– ; Pres., Candn. Assn. of Univ. Teachers 1980–81; Mem., Council of Trustees, Inst. for Rsch. on Public Policy 1981–86; Judge, Telesat Getaway Special Contest, Space Shuttle Atlantis 1984; Chair, Adv. Bd. on Sci. & Tech. Information on NRC 1991; Mem., Prime Minister's Ctte. for Awards in Excellence in Edn. 1993; Merit Award, Univ. of N.B. 1984; Pres., B'nai Brith, Fredericton Chapter 1981–83; Mem., Nat. Bd. of Dir. of Science for Peace 1982–85; Chair, Dr. Everett Chalmers Hosp., UNB Liaison Ctte. 1988– ; co-author: 'Singlet and Triplet States: Benzene and Simple Aromatic Compounds' 1966; Home: 66 Cameron Court, Fredericton, N.B. E3B 2R9; Office: P.O. Box 4400, Fredericton, N.B. E3B 5A3.

**UNGER, Richard W.,** Ph.D.; university professor; b. Huntington, W. Virginia 23 Dec. 1942; s. Abraham I. and Marion Patterson (Simons) U.; e. Haverford Coll., B.A. 1963; Univ. of Chicago, A.M. 1965; Yale Univ., M.A. 1967, M.Phil. 1969, Ph.D. 1971; m. Katharine d. Charles H. III & Sallie Lawrence 4 June 1966; one d.: Emily Patterson; PROF., DEPT. OF HISTORY, UNIV. OF B.C. 1980– ; Asst. Prof., present univ. 1969–76; Assoc. Prof. 1976–80; Dept. Head 1985–91; author: 'Dutch Shipbuilding before 1800' 1978, 'The Ship in the Medieval Economy, 600–1600' 1980; 'The Art of Medieval Technology: Images of Noah the Shipbuilder' 1991; co-editor: 'Nautical Archaeology, Progress and Public Responsibility' 1982; Office: 1297 – 1873 East Mall, Vancouver, B.C. V6T 1Z1.

**UNRAU, John,** M.A., D.Phil.; university teacher and writer; b. Saskatoon, Sask. 13 May 1941; s. John and Mary (Klassen) U.; e. McKernan Jr. High Sch. Edmonton; Soham Grammar Sch. Eng. 1957–58; Rosthern (Sask.) Jr. Coll. 1959; Univ. of Alta. B.A. 1962; Oxford Univ. (Rhodes Scholar) B.A. 1965, M.A., D.Phil. 1969; m. Olive d. Maurice and Susan Foley 14 Aug. 1965; children: Cathleen, John Ivan; PROF. OF ENGLISH, ATKINSON COLL. YORK UNIV. 1985– , mem. Faculty Grad. Studies 1971– , Asst. Prof. 1969–73; Assoc. Prof. 1973–85; Robert Browning Student in 19th Century Eng. Lit. Pembroke Coll. Oxford 1967–69; author 'Looking at Architecture with Ruskin' 1978; 'Ruskin and St. Mark's' 1984; 'The Balancings of the Clouds: Paintings of Mary Klassen' 1991; recreations: hockey, tennis, fishing, photography; Home: 136 Clifton Rd., Toronto, Ont. M4T 2G6; Office: 4700 Keele St., Downsview, Ont. M3J 2R7.

**UNRUH, William George,** B.Sc., M.A., Ph.D., F.R.S.C.; university professor; b. Winnipeg, Man. 28 Aug. 1945; s. Benjamin and Anna (Janzen) U.; e. Univ. of Man., B.Sc. (Hon.) 1967; Princeton Univ., M.A. 1969, Ph.D. 1971; Rutherford Mem. Fellow 1971; NRC PDF (Birbeck Coll., U.K.) 1971–72; m. Patricia d. Ralph and Brina Truman 19 Apr. 1974; one s.: Daniel; PROF., UNIV. OF BRITISH COLUMBIA 1982– ; Miller Rsch. Fellow, Univ. of Calif. 1973–74; Asst. Prof., McMaster Univ. 1974–76; Assoc. Prof., Univ. of B.C. 1976–82; Dir., Cosmology, Candn. Inst. for Adv. Rsch. 1986– ; var. worldwide univ. appointments & lectrs. since 1972; main rsch. achievements: understanding gravity & black holes, early cosmology, quantum phenomenon, devel. of low noise gravity wave detectors; Alfred P. Sloan Rsch. Fellowship 1978–80; Rutherford Medal, Royal Soc. of Can. 1982; Hertzberg Medal, Candn. Assn. of Physics 1983; Steacie Prize 1984; Steacie Fellowship, NSERC 1984–86; F.R.S.C. 1984; Rutherford Lectr., R.S.C. 1985; Fellow, C.I.A.R. 1986– ; Japan Soc. for Promotion of Science Fellow 1986; B.C. Science Council Gold Medal 1990; author of num. scholarly articles & book chapters; recreations: fishing, boating; Office: 6224 Agriculture Rd., Vancouver, B.C. V6T 2A6.

**URIE, Hon. John J.,** B.Com; judge; b. Guelph, Ont. 2 Jan. 1920; s. late Dr. George Norman and Jane A. (Ballantyne) U.; e. Lisgar and Glebe Coll. Insts., Ottawa; Queen's Univ., B.Com. 1941; Osgoode Hall Law Sch. LL.B. 1948; m. Dorothy Elizabeth, d. late Dr. Ivan W. James, 2 Sept. 1946; children: John David, Janet Elizabeth, Alison Jill; COUNSEL, SCOTT AND AYLEN (OTTAWA) 1991– ; read law with McIlraith & McIlraith, Ottawa; called to Bar of Ont. 1948; cr. Q.C. 1961; assoc. with McIlraith & McIlraith, Ottawa, 1948–50; Ewart, Scott, Kelley & Burke-Robertson, 1950–54; Partner, Burke-Robertson, Urie, Butler & Chadwick, 1954–73; Justice, Appeal Div., Federal Court of Canada 1973–90; Counsel, Scott & Aylen (Ottawa) 1991– ; served with Cameron Highlanders of Ottawa, Overseas, 1942–45; mem. Candn. Bar Assn.; Royal Candn. Mil. Inst. (Toronto); Phi Delta Phi; Protestant; recreations: golf, curling, skiing and other sports; Clubs: Rideau; Ottawa Hunt & Golf; Home: 1291 Parkhill Circle Ottawa, Ont. K1H 6K2; Office: 60 Queen St., Ottawa, Ont. K1P 5Y7.

**URQUHART, Anthony (Tony) Morse,** B.F.A.; artist; educator; b. Niagara Falls, Ont. 9 Apr. 1934; s. Henry Archer Marsh and Maryon Louise (Morse) U.; e. Barker St. Pub. Sch. and Stamford Coll. & Vocational Inst., Niagara Falls, Ont. 1953; Yale Univ. Summer Sch. 1955; Albright Art Sch. Dip. 1956; Univ. of Buffalo B.F.A. 1958; m. Mary Jane Keele d. W.A. and Marian Carter May 1976; one d. Emily Jane; children by previous marriage: Mary Allyson, Robin Anne, Joseph Marsh, Anthony Aidan; PROFESSOR OF FINE ART, UNIV. OF WATERLOO 1972– , Chrmn. of Dept. 1977–79, 1982–85, 1994–96; Artist-in-Residence Univ. of W. Ont. 1960–63, 1964–65; Asst. Prof. 1967–70, Assoc. Prof. 1970–72; Lectr. McMaster Univ. 1966–67; paintings, drawings, sculpture rep. various nat. and internat. galleries incl.: Nat. Gallery Can.; Art Gallery Ont.; Montreal Museum Fine Art; Museum Modern Art N.Y.; Victoria & Albert Museum, London, England; Walker Art Center, Minneapolis, Minn.; Vancouver Art Gallery; Bibliotec National, Paris, France; recipient Can. Counc. Jr. Fellowship 1963, Sr. Fellowship 1979, travel grants 1969, 70, 74, 75, 76, 88, 91 and project cost grants 1981, 82; recipient Baxter Award Ont. Soc. Artists 1961; Winner, Outdoor Sculpture Contest, McDonald Stewart Art Center, Guelph, Ont. (45′ x 25′ sculpture 'Magic Wood') 1987; Editions I Award Arts Counc. Ont. 1974; author: 'The Urquhart Sketch Book' 1960; illustrator: 'The Broken Ark: A Book of Beasts' (editor: Michael Ondaatje) 1962; 'False Shuffles' (poems by Jane Urquhart) 1982; 'I Am Walking in the Garden of His Imaginary Palace' (poems by Jane Urquhart) 1982; 'In Search of Leonardo' (with Mat Cohen) 1986; 'Cells of Ourselves' (with Gary Michael Dault) 1989; 'Memories of a Governor General's Daughter' (with Joan Michener-Rohr & Terry Heath) 1991; Chrmn. Jack Chambers Meml. Found. 1978–85; Sec. and Founding mem. Candn. Artists Representation 1968–71; mem. CAR-FAC; recreations: golf, music; Home: 24 Water St., Wellesley, Ont. N0B 2T0; Office: Waterloo, Ont. N2L 3G1.

**URQUHART, Jane,** B.A.; writer; b. Geraldton, Ont. 21 June 1949; d. Walter Andrew and Marian (Quinn) Carter; e. Havergal Coll., Toronto 1967; Univ. of Guelph, B.A. (English) 1971, (Art History) 1976; m. Tony s. Archer and Maryon U. 5 May 1976; one d. Emily Jane; WRITER-IN-RESIDENCE, MEMORIAL UNIV., NFLD. 1992– and UNIV. OF OTTAWA 1990– ; recipient, Can. Counc. & Ont. Arts Counc. grants; began writing full time 1978; author: 'False Shuffles' 1981, 'I am Waking in the Garden of His Imaginary Palace' (Tony Urquhart, illus.) 1981, 'The Little Flowers of Mme de Montespan' 1984 (poetry); 'The Whirlpool' 1986 (novel, awarded: France's 'Prix de Meilleur Livre Etranger' 1992); 'Storm Glass' (short fiction) 1987; 'Changing Heaven' (novel) 1990; 'Away' (novel) 1993; books published in Canada, Britain, France, U.S.A., Germany, Italy and Norway; mem., Writer's Union of Canada; P.E.N. Internat.; League of Candn. Poets; recreation: tap dancing; Home: P.O. Box 208, Wellesley, Ont. N0B 2T0.

**URQUHART, John Cameron,** B.A.; writer, editor; b. Ottawa, Ont. 25 June 1956; s. John Gordon and Phyllis Cameron (Convery) U.; e. Lorne Park S.S. 1975; Carleton Univ. B.A. 1980; m. Patricia d. Bower and Barbara Hutton 8 Aug. 1987; one s.: Michael Vieira; MANAGING EDITOR, THE CANADIAN FORUM 1989– ; freelance writer and editor 1982– ; Information Officer, Inuit Tapirisat of Canada 1985–87; recreations: book collecting, loafing; Home: 650 Tweedsmuir Ave., Ottawa, Ont. K1Z 5P6; Office: 804 – 251 Laurier Ave. W., Ottawa, Ont. K1P 5J6.

**URQUHART, Malcolm Charles,** B.A., D.C.L., LL.D., F.R.S.C.; educator; b. Islay, Alta. 12 Dec. 1913; s. William Gordon and Mary Louise (Marlow) U.; e. elem. sch. Islay, Alta.; Strathcona High Sch. Edmonton, Alta.; Edmonton Normal Sch. Teacher's Cert. 1932; Univ. of Alta. B.A. 1940; Univ. of Chicago 1940–42, 1948–49 (Invited Fellow); London Sch. of Econ. and Cambridge Univ. 1962–63; Univ. of Cal. (Berkeley) 1969–70; m. Mary Elizabeth d. Howard Paige Rowell 8 June 1969; step-children: Elizabeth Anne Arrowsmith, John David Arrowsmith; Sir John A. Macdonald Prof. of Econ., Queen's Univ. (retired); Instr. Mass. Inst. of Technol. 1942–43; Asst. to Dir. Gen. Econ. Research, Dept. of Finance, Dept. of Reconstruction & Supply 1943–45; Asst. Prof. Queen's Univ. 1945 becoming Assoc. Prof. and Prof. of Econ., Dir. Inst. for Econ. Research 1960–66, Head of Econ. 1964–68, Acting Head of Econ. 1970–71; Adv. on Forecasting Models, Econ. Research Br. Ottawa 1945–47; Adv. to Govt. of Pakistan on 1st Econ. Devel. Program 1954–55; mem. Comte. on Healing Arts Ont. 1966–70; mem. Extve. Comte. Conf. on Research in Income and Wealth, Nat. Bureau of Econ. Research 1967–70; co-founder Conf. on Quantitative Econ. Hist. in Can. 1964; mem. Subcomte. on Research Grants, Comte. on Health Research, Ont. Council of Health 1968–72; Visiting Prof., Centre of Candn. Studies, Univ. of Edinburgh, 1979–80; co-author 'Public Investment and Capital Formation: A Study of Public and Private Investment Outlay, Canada, 1926–41' 1945; 'Economics' 1959; Mgr. and Contrib. Ed. 'Historical Statistics of Canada' 1959–65; author, with associates, 'Gross National Product, Canada, 1870–1926: The Derivation of the Estimates' 1993; author or co-author book chapters, reports, articles, papers; rec'd Gov. Gen.'s Gold Medal Alta. 1940; Innis-Gerin Medal, Royal Soc. of Can. 1983; D.C.L., Bishop's Univ. 1985; Hon. LL.D., Queen's Univ. 1991; Pres., Candn. Econ. Assn. 1968–69; Acad. Humanities & Social Sciences, Royal Soc. Can. 1975–76, mem. Gen. Council 1974–77; mem. Art Collection Soc. Kingston (Secy., Pres.); Community Chest Kingston (Chrmn. Budget Comte.); Anglican; recreation: curling; Club: Cataraqui Golf & Country; Home: 94 Beverley St., Kingston, Ont. K7L 3Y6; Office: Queen's University, Kingston, Ont. K7L 3N6.

**URSELL, Geoffrey Barry,** B.A., M.A., Ph.D.; writer; composer; editor; b. Moose Jaw, Sask. 14 Mar. 1943; s. Barry Alexander and Irene Phyllis (Motta) U.; e. Nutana C.I. 1961; Univ. of Man., B.A. (Hons.) 1965, M.A. 1966; Univ. of London, Ph.D. 1973; m. Barbara d. Bill and Rose Davies 8 July 1967; Teacher, Univ. of Man. 1971–73; Univ. of Regina 1975–83; Co-founder & Dir., Thunder Creek Publishing Co.; Writer-in-Res., Saskatoon Public Library 1984–85; Assoc. Artistic Dir., 25th Street Theatre 1989– (Playwright-in-Residence, 1987–88, 1988–89); Writer-in-Res., Winnipeg Public Library 1989–90; Nat. Playwriting Award, Clifford E. Lee 1977; Persephone Theatre 1981; First Novel Award, 'Books in Canada' (Perdue) 1984; Sr. Artists Award, Sask. Arts Bd.; Can. Counc. grants; Mem., A.F. of M.; ACTRA (Vice-Pres. Sask. 1979–83, 1984–85); SOCAN; P.E.N.; Playwrights Union of Canada; Sask. Playwrights Ctr. (Pres. 1984–85); Sask. Writers Guild (Pres. 1975–77); Writers Union of Can.; author: 'Saskatoon Pie!' 1993 (play); 'Way Out West!' 1989 (fiction); 'The Look-Out Tower' 1989 (poetry); 'Perdue, or How the West Was Lost' 1984 (fiction); 'Trap Lines' 1982 (poetry); 'The Running of the Deer' (play) 1981; co-author: 'Black Powder,' 'Superwheel' 1979 (plays); editor: 'Saskatchewan Gold' 1982, 'More Saskatchewan Gold' 1984, 'Sky High' 1988 (anthols.); co-editor: '200% Cracked Wheat' 1992 (humour anthol.); 'Jumbo Gumbo' 1989; 'Prairie Jungle' 1985 (children's anthols.); 'Grain' (magazine) 1990– ; recreations: reading, music, badminton; Address: c/o Coteau Books, 401 - 2206 Dewdrey Ave., Regina, Sask. S4R 1H3.

**USHER, Dan,** B.A., Ph.D.; university professor; b. Montréal, Qué. 15 May 1934; s. Abraham and Rose (Leventhal) U.; e. Westmount H.S. 1950; McGill Univ., B.A. 1955; Univ. of Chicago, Ph.D. 1960; m. Samphan d. Phong (Han Tong Phong) and Sudchit Chayaraks 27 July 1962; children: Ann, David; PROF., QUEEN'S UNIV. 1967– ; Jr. Bureaucrat, U.N. (Bangkok) 1960–61; Rsch. Fellow, Univ. of Manchester & Nuffield Coll. 1961–66; Asst. Prof., Columbia Univ. 1966–67; Cons., Candn. Internat. Devel. Agency 1969; Stats. Can. 1970; Econ. Planning Unit (Malaysia) & Min. of Fin. (Indonesia) under auspices of Harvard Inst. of Internat. Devel.; Killam Fellow 1971–72; Nat. Fellow Hoover Inst. on War, Revolution & Peace 1978–79; Mem., Candn. Econ. Assn.; Am. Econ. Assn.; Royal Soc. of Can.; Jewish; author: 'The Price Mechanism and Meaning of National Income Statistics' 1969, 'The Measurement of Economic Growth' 1980, 'The Economic Prerequisite to Democracy' 1981, 'The Measurement of Capital' 1980, 'The Welfare Economics of Markets, Voting and Predation' 1993; 'The Collected Papers of Dan Usher; Volume 1: National Accounting and Economic Theory; Volume 2: Welfare Economics and Public Finance' 1994, and scholarly articles; Home: 168 Churchill Cres., Kingston, Ont. K7L 4N2; Office: Dept. of Econ., Queen's Univ., Kington, Ont. K7L 3N6.

**USHER, F. Barrie,** B.Com.; insurance executive; b. North Shields, Eng. 16 March 1942; s. Fred. Spires and Mary (Turnbull) U.; e. McGill Univ. B.Com. 1974; m. Nancy d. Grant and Muriel Bradley; children: Laura, Mark, Amy; PRES. NEW YORK LIFE INSURANCE CO. OF CAN. 1989– ; joined Royal Bank of Canada 1960–78; The Mercantile Bank of Canada 1978–85, Sr. Vice Pres.; National Bank of Canada 1985–88, Sr. Vice Pres.; mem. Bd. Trade Metrop. Toronto; recreations: golf, skiing; Clubs: Weston Golf & Country; National; Cambridge; Home: 261 Inglewood Dr., Toronto, Ont. M4T 1J2; Office: 1600, 121 Bloor St. E., Toronto, Ont. M4W 3N2.

**USHER-JONES, Brian,** B.Comm., C.A.; financial executive; b. Montreal, Que. 6 Jan. 1946; PRESIDENT, THOMSON KERNAGHAN & CO. LTD. 1993– ; Manager, Coopers & Lybrand 1966–77; various functions, Nesbitt Thomson Inc. 1977–92; Chief Financial Offr., Telular Canada Inc. 1992–93, Dir. 1992– ; recreations: squash, tennis, skiing; clubs: Adelaide, Cricket, Georgian Peaks Ski; Home: 81 Glengowan Rd., Toronto, Ont. M4N 1G5; Office: 2nd Floor, 365 Bay St., Toronto, Ont. M5H 2V2.

**USSELMAN, Anton M.;** executive; b. Sask. 9 March 1922; s. Fred and Caroline (Fetch) U.; e. Univ. of Man., Agric.; various business and pub. speaking courses; German and Spanish studies; m. Olive Doreen Donaldson 24 March 1950; one s. Paul; Pres., Anton Developments Ltd.; owns commercial real estate for lease or development, also owns & manages extve. office bus.; Past Chrmn. Carma Developers Ltd.; Appraiser, Prudential of America, Winnipeg 1950–53; Past Builder, Lumberman, Rooftrussman; Past Chrmn. Alta. Housing Council; Past Pres. Calgary Hudac; served 3 yrs. RCAF; recreations: travel, bridge, chess, golf, music; Club: Rotary (Past Pres. & Charter mem.); Home: 2560 Toronto Cres., Calgary, Alta.; Office: 1700 Varsity Estates Dr. N.W., Calgary, Alta. T3B 2W9.

**UYEDE, Joseph John,** B.Sc., C.A.; production company executive; b. St. Boniface, Man. 29 Apr. 1946; s. Samuel and Hideko (Nakata) U.; e. Univ. of Toronto B.Sc. 1968; C.A. 1971; m. Joanne d. Albert and Augusta Kress 26 June 1970; children: Michael, Jessica, Lisa; CO-OWNER, EXEC. VICE PRES. AND DIR. RAWI SHERMAN FILMS INC. 1988– ; Dir. Rawifilm Inc.; Triumph Entertainment Corp.; joined Thorne Gunn Helliwell & Christenson 1968–72; Mgr. Resnick, Wintraub & Co. 1972, Partner 1975–85; Partner, Touche Ross & Co. 1985–88; Past Dir. & Treas. Pauline McGibbon Cultural Centre; former Leader, Boy Scouts Can.; Chrmn., C.A. Sect. Un. Way 1982–83; Coach, N. Toronto Hockey Assn. 1980–89, Dir. 1983–88, Pres. 1986–87; Dir. N. Toronto Meml. Arena 1987–92; Anglican; recreations: skiing, hockey, squash, golf; Clubs: Granite; Weston Golf & Country; Home: 14 Cortleigh Blvd., Toronto, Ont. M4R 1K6.

# V

**VACCARINO, Franco Joseph,** B.Sc., M.Sc., Ph.D.; university professor; b. Italy 29 Nov. 1955; s. Leonardo and Alfonsina (Vella) V.; e. Univ. of Toronto B.Sc. 1978; McGill Univ. M.Sc. 1981; Ph.D. 1983; m. Cosmina d. Constantin and Cristina Ionescu 11 Sept. 1982; children: Oriana, Elysia; ASSOC. PROF., PSYCHOLOGY & PSYCHIATRY 1990– ; undergrad. training in Psychobiology 1977–79; grad. training in psychopharm. 1979–83; postdoctoral training, Selk Inst. for Biol. Sci. & Scripps Clinic (Calif.); Asst. Prof., Psychol. & Psychiatry, Univ. of Toronto 1984–90; Psychopharm. & Research Consultant; Dir., Grad. Studies, Psychol., Univ. of Toronto 1990– ; Young Investigator Award, Candn. Coll. of Neuropsychopharm. 1989; Office: Toronto, Ont. M5S 1A1.

**VACHON, André,** B.A., B.Ph., L. ès L., M.A., Docteur en histoire, F.R.S.C.; historian, writer; b. Quebec City, 2 Dec. 1933; s. René and Germaine (Boutin) V.; e. Séminaire de Québec, B.A. 1954; Univ. Laval, B.Ph. 1954, L. ès L. 1956, M.A. 1962; m. Rita, d. Alphonse and Alphonsine Huot, 8 July 1957; children: Francois, Normand; archivist, Quebec Prov. Archives 1956–61; Sec. Gen. and Assoc. Ed. D.B.C./D.C.B. 1961–71; Dir. des Editions 1962–64, Dir. adjoint 1964–66, Dir. gén. 1966–71 des Presses de l'Univ. Laval; Dir. of Quebec Nat. Archives 1971–76; freelance hist., ed. and writer 1976–82, 1985– ; Titulaire, Chaire d'Etudes Acadiennes, Univ. de Moncton 1982–85; Doctorat en histoire (hon. causa) Univ. d'Ottawa; mem. La Soc. des Dix; author: 'Histoire du Notariat canadien, 1621–1960' 1962; 'Eloquence indienne' 1968; 'Francois de Laval' 1980; 'Rêves d'empire, Le Canada avant 1700' (transl. in English) 1982; 'L'enracinement, Le Canada de 1700 à 1760' (transl. in English) 1985; Address: 866 Boul. Pie XII, Sainte-Foy, Que. G1X 3T8.

**VACHON, François,** B.A., B.Sc., F.S.A., F.I.C.A.; actuaire; né Montréal, Qué. 8 juillet 1935; f. Irénée et Aimée (Masson) V.; é. Coll. de Saint Laurent B.A. 1953; Univ. de Montréal B.Sc. (Math) 1956; ép Marie Andrée f. Rodrique Lefebvre 9 nov. 1968; enfants: André, Bernard, Pierre; ACTUAIRE CONSEIL, ECKLER ASSOCIÉS LTÉE depuis 1990; au service de Produits Forestiers Canadien Pacifique Limitée de 1979 à 1990; de Sun Life du Canada de 1956 à 1979; Chargé de cours, Faculté des Sciences, Univ. de Montréal 1956–59; Trésorier, Confédération des Sports du Qué 1973–75; mem. du Conseil, Inst. Canadien des Actuaires 1973–75; Prés. Club des Actuaires de Montréal 1975–76; Résidence: 323 ave. Stuart, Outremont, Qué. H2V 3G9.

**VACHON, Cardinal Louis-Albert,** C.C. (1969), D.Th., D.Ph., LL.D., F.R.S.C.; b. St. Frederic (Beauce), Que., 4 Feb. 1912; s. Napoleon and Alexandrine (Gilbert) V.; e. Que. Semy., B.A. 1934; Laval Univ., D.Ph. 1947; Angelicum, Rome, D.Th. 1949; Hon. degrees from Montreal, McGill, Victoria 1964, Guelph 1966, Moncton 1967, Bishop's, Queen's, Strasbourg 1968, Notre Dame 1971, Carleton 1972, Laval 1982; ARCHEVÊCHE ÉMÉRITE 1990– ; Prof. of Philos. Laval Univ., 1941–47; Prof. of Theol. 1949–55; Superior of Grand Seminary of Quebec, 1955–59; Vice Rector of Laval Univ. 1959–60, Rector 1960–72; Supt. gén. séminaire de Québec 1960–77; Auxiliary Bishop of the Diocese of Quebec 1977–81; Archbishop of Quebec and Primate of Canada 1981–90; apptd. Cardinal with the title of St. Paul of the Cross 1985; Offr. de l'Ordre de la Fidélité française (1963); author of: 'Espérance et présomption' 1958; 'Verité et Liberté' 1962; 'Unité de l'Université' 1962; 'Apostolat de l'universitaire catholique' 1963; 'Mémorial' 1963; 'Communauté universitaire' 1963; 'Progrés de l'université et consentement populaire' 1964; 'Responsabilité collective des universitaires' 1964; 'Les humanités, aujourd'hui' 1966; 'Excellence et loyauté des universitaires' 1969; Several pastoral letters, 1981– ; President of 'L'Entraide universitaire mondiale du Canada'; 'Conf. (1965–68) des recteurs et des Principaux des Universités du Québec'; mem. Assn. des Univ. et Coll. de Can. (Pres. 1965–66); Conseil d'administration de la Fédération Internationale des universités catholiques' (FIUC); Conseil d'adm. de l'Assn. des universités partiellement ou entièrement de langue française (AUPELF); Candn. Educ. Assn.; 'Société Canadienne de l'histoire de l'Eglise catholique'; Catholic Theol. Soc. Am.; Société Canadienne pour l'histoire et la philosophie des sciences; Union mondiale des enseignants catholiques; Pres. de l'Association canadienne des éducateurs de langue française (ACELF); Assn. Commonwealth Univs.; Société des écrivains canadiens; mem. L'Ordre des francophones d'Amérique; del. by C.C.C.B. to 'Synod of Bishops on Reconciliation and Penance in the Mission of the Church' (Rome, October 1983); Prés. de l'Assemblée des évêques du Qué. 1981–85; mem., Adm. Bd. of CCCB 1981– ; Gov., Candn. Bible Soc. 1985; Mem. of Sacred Congregation for Clergy, Vatican 1985– ; mem., Adm Bd., l'Ordre national du Québec 1985– ; Hon. Pres., Laval Univ. Fund Drive 1986; Hon. Fellow, Royal Coll. Phys. & Surgs. (Canada) 1972; mem. de la Soc. royale du Canada; Centennial Medal of Confederation 1967; Companion of Order of Canada 1969; Prix '3 juillet 1608' du Conseil de la langue française 1983; Kt. 'Great Cross,' Ordre équestre du Saint-Sépulchre de Jérusalem 1985; Officier, Ordre national du Québec 1985; Bailli Great Cross and Devotion, Knights of Malta (Can.) 1987; Officier de la Legion d'honneur, France 1988; Address: Séminaire de Québec, 1 Rue des Remparts, Québec, Qué. G1R 5L7.

**VADAS, Peter,** M.D., B.Sc., Ph.D., FRCP(C), FACP; clinical immunologist and allergist; b. Budapest 5 Aug. 1953; s. Steven and Veronica (Radnoti) V.; e. Univ. of Toronto B.Sc. 1976, Ph.D. 1980, M.D. 1983; FRCP(C) 1990, FACP 1992; m. Louise; ACTIVE STAFF, DEPT. OF MEDICINE, WELLESLEY HOSPITAL; Asst. Prof., Div. of Immunology, Dept. of Med., Univ. of Toronto: Asst. Prof., Dept. of Immunology, Fac. of Med., Univ. of Toronto; Mem., Inst. of Med. Sci., Univ. of Toronto; School of Grad. Studies; Deputy Director, Inflammation Research Group; Mem., Steering Ctte., Internat. Assn. of Inflammation Societies; N.Y. Academy of Sciences; Fellow, Candn. Soc. of Allergy & Clin. Immunology; Mem., Sci. Adv. Bd., Salix Pharmaceuticals; author of 75 scientific pubns. & 6 book chapters; Office: 160 Wellesley St. E., Toronto, Ont. M4Y 1J3.

**VAILLANCOURT, François,** B.Sc., Ph.D.; educator; b. Montréal, Qué. 9 Nov. 1950; s. Roland and Fleurette (Belair) V.; e. Univ. de Montréal B.Sc. 1972; Queen's Univ. Ph.D. 1978; m. Louise d. Gilford and Elise 29 Dec. 1979; children: Luc, Alain; PROF. OF ECON. UNIV. DE MONTREAL 1989– ; Lectr. present Univ. 1976, Asst. Prof. 1978, Assoc. Prof. 1983; Rsch. Coordinator MacDonald Comn. 1983–85; Prof., Policy Modelling, Inst. for Policy Analysis, Univ. of Toronto and Visiting Fellow, Federalism Rsch. Centre, Australian National Univ. 1991; Visiting Lectureship, Candn. Studies (Economics), Shastri Institute, India 1993; cons. various govt. and other orgns. incl. Law Reform Comn., Stats. Can., Econ. Council Can., Dept. of Finance, Candn. Tax Found., Office et Conseil de la Lanque Française, World Bank; author or co-author of 16 monographs, 35 book chapters, 53 articles; mem. Candn. Econ. Assn.; Office: P.O. Box 6128, Montréal, Qué. H3C 3J7.

**VAILLANCOURT, Louise Brais;** b. Montreal, Que. 12 Aug. 1926; d. Hon. F. Philippe Brais, C.C., C.B.E., Q.C., LL.D., and Louisette (Doré) OBE, Brais; e. The Mother House Business Coll. 1946; Couvent du Sacré-Coeur, Sault au Récollets, Montréal 1944; m. Paul Vaillancourt jr. (dec'd) 14 June 1947; children: Michèle (wife of Jean René de Cotret), Louise (wife of Pierre-Yves Châtillon), Marie, Paul III (m. Birgit Fliege); Dir., Air Canada; Atomic Energy of Canada Ltd.; B.C.E. Inc.; Banque Nationale du Canada; Université de Montréal; AXA Assurances Inc.; Institut de Recherches Cliniques de Montréal; Past Pres., Fondation Armand-Frappier; Past Pres., Vanier Inst. of the Family; Gov., Hôpital Marie-Enfant; Douglas Hosp.; Mem. Adv. Bd., Royal Soc. of Canada; recipient: Cross of Merit; Order of Malta; Member, Order of Canada; Doctorat Honoris Causa (U.Q.); Commemorative Medal for 125th Anniversary of Candn. Confederation; Medal for exceptional merit, Clinical Rsch. Institute of Montreal; R. Catholic; Liberal; recreations: skiing, reading; Home: #702, 115 Côte Ste Catherine Rd., Outremont, Que. H2V 4R3.

**VALASKAKIS, Gail,** B.Sc., M.A., Ph.D.; educator; b. Ashland, Wis. 9 May 1939; d. Benedict Matthew and Miriam Adele (Van Buskirk) Guthrie; e. Univ. of Wis., B.Sc. 1961 (Outstanding Sr. Women Award 1961); Cornell Univ., M.A. 1964; McGill Univ., Ph.D. 1979; children: Ion, Paris; DEAN, FACULTY OF ARTS & SCI. (1992– ) and PROF. OF COMMUNICATION STUDIES, CONCORDIA UNIV. (1989– ); Lectr. in Communication Arts Loyola Coll. 1969–71, Co-ordinator Prog. Candn. Studies Loyola Campus 1978–79; Assoc. Prof. of Communication Studies, Concordia Univ. 1979–89; Fellow, Sch. of Community & Pub. Affairs 1979–83; Trustee, Simone de Beauvoir Inst. (Women's Studies) 1985; Asst. Prof. of Communication Studies present Univ. 1971, Chair 1983–85, Dir. MA Prog. Media Studies 1982–84, Vice Dean of Acad. Planning, Faculty of Arts & Sci., 1985–90; recipient various grants & fellowships; Kappa Kappa Gamma Internat. Alumnae Award Ednl. Innovation 1972; mem. Advisory Bd., New Initiatives in Film for Women of Colour and Women of the First Nations, National Film Bd. of Canada; Adv. Council Asia-Pacific Project Broadcasting in Devel. CIDA, Ryerson Internat. Devel. Centre 1986–90; Adv. Bd. Centre Rsch. Action Race Relations 1984–87, Dir. 1987– ; Dir. Candn. Council Christians & Jews Qué. Region 1981–83; Founding mem. Montreal Native Friendship Centre (Dir. 1974–82, Sec. 1976–79, Pres. 1979–80); Native N. Am. Studies Inst. Montréal and Manitou Community Coll. (Dir. 1970–75); author various articles; mem. Candn. Communication Assn. (Vice Pres. 1984–85, Pres. 1985–86); Canadian Journal of Communication (Dir. 1986–89); Internat. Soc. Intercultural Edn., Training & Rsch. (Gov. Council 1979–82; Annual Conf. Prof. Ctte. 1981); Candn. Assn. Support Native Peoples (Dir., Second Vice Pres. 1978–79); Office: 7141 Sherbrooke St. W., Montréal, Qué. H4B 1R6.

**VALASKAKIS, Kimon,** Ph.D.; educator; b. Egypt 29 Sept. 1941; s. Platon and Marie-Claire (Zalzal) V.; e. Cornell Univ. Ph.D.; Univ. de Lyons French Law Degree; m. Iris d. John Fitzpatrick 25 May 1981; children: Ian, Paris, Andrew; PROF. OF ECON. UNIV. DE MONTREAL 1966– ; Founding Pres. Gamma Inst. 1975– ; Chrmn. ISO Group 1989– ; cons. maj. corps. and govts.; Asst. Dir. Centre de Recherches et Développement Economique 1970–71; mem. Bd. Nat. Bank of Greece (Can.); Max Bell Found. Prize winner 1987; Auguste Frigon Lectr. Ecole Polytechnique 1985; author 'The Conserver Society' 1980; 'Le Québec et son Pestin International' 1981; 'Canada in the Nineties: Meltdown or Renaissance?' 1990; mem. World Future Studies Fedn.; Am. Econ. Assn.; recreations: squash, judo, tennis, theatre acting; Home: 4555 Bibaud, Montreal, Que. H3W 2E1; Office: 1514 Penfield, Montreal, Que. H3G 1X5.

**VALBERG, Leslie S.,** M.D., F.R.C.P.(C); physician/university adminstrator; b. Churchbridge, Sask. 3 June 1930; s. John Stephen and Rose (Vigfusson) V.; e. Queen's Univ., M.D. 1954, M.Sc. 1958; m. Barbara d. Harry and Linda Torhurst 1954; children: John, Stephanie, Bill; PHYSICIAN, UNIV. HOSPITAL 1992– ; Fac. Mem. & Career Sci., Queen's Univ. 1960–75; Chrmn., Dept. of Med., Univ. of West. Ont. & Chief of Med., Univ. Hosp. 1975–85; Dean, Faculty of Medicine, Univ. of West. Ont. 1985–92; author of over 100 med. articles & papers; Home: 1496 Stoneybrook Cres., London, Ont. N5X 1C5; Office: Univ. Hospital, London, Ont. N6A 5A5.

**VALCOUR, Pierre;** film executive; b. Montreal, Que. 8 July 1931; e. Univ. of Montreal, 1952; m. Jose Leduc 16 Sept. 1954; children: Bertrand, François, Genevieve, Antoine, Nicolas, Dominique, Kateri, Gregoire; producer of over 125 feature films and TV programs; PRES., CINE MUNDO since 1972; Dir., Comundo Inc.; P.V. Assoc.; Auvidec Inc.; Valemo Inc.; Hon. Gen. Consul of Rwanda since 1965; Comdr., Ordre de St. Hubert (Quebec); Offr., Ordre de la Paix (Rwanda); mem. several assocs.; recreations: tennis, golf; Office: 1600 De Lorimier Ave., Montreal, Que. H2K 3W5.

**VALCOURT, Hon. Bernard,** P.C., B.A., LL.B.; b. St-Quentin de Restigouche, N.B. 18 Feb. 1952; s. Bertin Valcourt and Géraldine Allain; e. Académie St-Joseph, St-Quentin, N.B.; Coll. St-Louis-Maillet, Edmundston, N.B.; Univ. of N.B.; two children: Annie, Edith; Min. of Employment and Immigration 1991–93 & Min.-Designate of Human Resources and Labour 1993; el. to H. of C. g.e. (Madawska-Victoria) 1984; re-el. 1988; apptd. Parlty. Secy. to Min. of State for Science and Technology; apptd. Parlty Secy. to the Min. of Revenue 1985; Min. of State (Small Businesses and Tourism) and sworn to the Privy Council 1986; Min. of State (Indian Affairs and Northern Development) 1987; Min. of Consumer and Corp. Affairs 1989; Min. of Fisheries and Oceans 1990; mem., Candn. Bar Assoc.; N.B. Lawyers Assoc.; P.C.; Catholic; Address: 90 - 48th Ave., Edmundston, N.B. E3V 3C9.

**VALDES, Mario James,** B.A., M.A., Ph.D., F.R.S.C.; university professor; b. Chicago, Ill. 28 Jan. 1934; s. Mario Luis and Juanita (San Martin) V.; e. Univ. of Ill., B.A. 1956, M.A. 1959, Ph.D. 1962; m. Maria Elena d. Consuelo and Miguel Diaz-Barriga 13 Aug. 1955; children: Mario Teótimo, Michael Jordi; PROF., UNIV. OF TORONTO 1971– ; Instr., Univ. of Michigan 1962–63; Asst. Prof., Univ. of Toronto 1963–66; Assoc. Prof. 1966–71; Fellow, Univ. College 1985– ; Head, Spanish Dept., Univ. of Illinois 1976–78; Dir., Ctr. for Comp. Lit., Univ. of Toronto 1978–83; Chrmn., Appraisals Ctte., Ont. Counc. of Grad. Studies 1978–83; Ph.D. Selection Ctte. SSHRCC 1982–83; Pres., Candn. Assn. of Comp. Lit. 1981–83; F.R.S.C. 1983– ; Vice-Pres., Modern Lang. Assn. 1989–90; Pres., Modern Lang. Assn. 1991; Bd. of Dir., Am. Council of Learned Soc. 1989–97; Mem., Nat. Acad. of the Lang., Mexico 1986– ; Mem., Academy of Literary Studies (USA); Modern Lang. Assn.; Internat. Comp. Lit. Assn. (Pres., Publications); Internat. Assn. of Hispanists; author: 'Worldmaking: A Study of the Truth-Claim in Literature' 1992; 'Phenomenological Hermeneutics and the Study of Literature' 1987, 'Shadows in the Cave' 1982, 'Death in the Literature of Unamuno' 1964, also several critical eds. of novels pub. in Spain and num. scholarly articles & lectures; co-author: 'An Unamuno Source Book' 1973; editor: 'Comparative Literary History as Discourse' 1992; 'Reflection and Imagination: A Ricoeur Reader on Literary Theory and Criticism' 1991; 'Toward a Theory of Comparative Literature' 1990; 'Approaches to Teaching Garciá Márquez's "One Hundred Years of Solitude"' 1990; 'Interamerican Literary Relations' 1985, 'Identity of the Literary Text' 1985, 'Interpretation of Narrative' 1978; Ed.: 'Canadian Review of Hispanic Studies' 1976–92; Home: 80 Dale Ave., Toronto, Ont. M4W 1K9; Office: 14045 Robarts Library, Univ. of Toronto, Toronto, Ont. M5S 1A1.

**VALE, Don M.J.;** business executive; b. London, England 25 Apr. 1941; s. Ernest James and Violet Dorothy (Mills) V.; e. Downhills Sch. 1957; City of London Coll. 1965; Univ. of Toronto; Western Business School, Univ. of Western Ont. M.B.A.; m. Beverley d. Elsie and Campbell Hood 16 June 1967; children: Jill, Trevor; SENIOR VICE-PRES., SHARP CORPORATION 1993– ; Asst., Chief Gen. Mgr.'s Office, NatWest (U.K.) 1962; joined Shell Canada 1965; moved to N.V. Philips (Holland) 1968–81; Pres., C.O.O. & Dir., Heritage Silversmiths Inc. 1981–82; Dir., Internat. Marketing Rush Hampton Industries (U.S.A.) 1982–83; Gen. Mgr., Matsushita Electric (Canada) 1983–88; Extve. Vice-Pres. & C.O.O., National Business Systems Ins. 1988–89; Vice-Pres. & Gen. Mgr., Sharp Corporation (Tokyo, Japan) 1990–93; progressively sr. mktg. & gen. mngt. positions in three of the world's largest corporations; Home: 68 Carondale Cres., Agincourt, Ont. M1W 2B1; Office: 335 Britannia Rd. E., Mississauga, Ont. L4Z 1W9.

**VALENTA, Zdenek,** M.Sc., Ph.D., F.R.S.C.; university professor; b. Havlickuv Brod, Czechoslovakia 14 June 1927; s. Karel and Jindra (Komers) V.; e. E.T.H., Zurich, Switz., Dipl. Ind. Chem. 1950; Univ. of N.B., M.Sc. 1952, Ph.D. 1953; m. Noreen Elizabeth d. Elizabeth and Frank Donahoe 29 July 1957; children: Katherine Elizabeth, Richard Karel, Michael Francis; RSCH. PROF., CHEM. DEPT., UNIV. OF N.B. 1990– ; Spec. Lectr., Chem. Dept., Univ. of N.B. 1953–54, Lectr. 1954–56; Asst. Prof. 1957–58; Assoc. Prof. 1958–63; Prof. 1963–90; Dept. Head 1963–72; Cons., Delmar Chem. 1970– ; Ayerst Rsch. Labs. 1980–85; Torcan Chem. 1980– ; U.N.B. Excellence in Teaching Award

1974; Fellow, Chem. Inst. of Can. (Merck Sharp & Dohme Award 1967); APICS/Northern Telecom Science Teaching Award for 1987; Union Carbide Award for Chem. Educ. 1989; author of num. sci. articles; recreations: gardening, sports, mushroom collecting; Home: 872 Windsor St., Fredericton, N.B. E3B 4G5; Office: Bag Serc. #45222, Fredericton, N.B. E3B 6E2.

**VALENTE, Francesca,** Dott. Lingue e Letterature Straniere, M.A.; b. Vicenza, Italy 24 Oct. 1943; d. Francesco and Cristina V.; e. Univ. of Ca' Foscari, Venice, Dott. Lingue e Letterature Straniere 1968; Univ. of Toronto, M.A. 1977; m. Branko s. Francesco and Sonia Gorjup 5 Dec. 1979; one s.: Francesco; Dir., Istituto Italiano di Cultura, Toronto 1985–91; Asst. Dir. present Inst. 1977–79; Acting Dir. Italian Cultural Inst. (San Francisco) 1980–81, Vice Dir. San Francisco 1982, Dir. San Francisco 1983–85; Fellow, Massey Coll.; recipient Italian Min. of Foreign Affairs & Can. Council Fellowship, Univ. of Toronto 1976–77; Brit. Council Fellowship in Applied Linguistics, Essex Univ. 1974; Scholarship Yeats Internat. Sch. Ireland 1970; Proclamation Mayor of San Francisco 1985; Gold Medal recipient for the promotion of Italian culture abroad, Chamber of Commerce, Vicenza 1990; Proclamation Mayor of Toronto 1992; author various publs. incl. articles and translator into Italian of noted Candn. writers works: Margaret Atwood 'The Edible Woman'; Leonard Cohen 'The Favorite Game'; Northrop Frye 'The Fearful Symmetry, Mito, Metafora, Simbolo' (selected essays), 'The Double Vision'; Irving Layton 'The Tamed Puma' (selected poems) and 'The Baffled Hunter' (fifty poems); Marshall McLuhan 'The Mechanical Bride, From Cliche to Archetype, Through the Vanishing Point, Letters of Marshall McLuhan (selected with Matie Molinaro and Corinne McLuhan), The Global Village, The Man and His Message; 'For the Cause of Architecture' (selection of essays) by Frank Lloyd Wright (with intro. by Paolo Portoghesi); an anthology of English Candn. short stories and a short anthology of English-Canadian poetry; transl. into English 'Rolls Royce and Other Poems' by Giorgio Bassani (in collaboration with Greg Gatenby and Irving Layton, with introduction by Northrop Frye); 'Roman Poems' by Pier Paolo Pasolini (in collaboration with Lawrence Ferlinghetti, with introduction by Alberto Moravia) and 'Words of Enzo Cucchi'; and orgn. reading tours in Italy for Irving Layton 1975, Leonard Cohen 1976, Northrop Frye 1979 (also Cal. 1984); Project Dir., 'Italy on Stage,' 1987, and 'Italy in Canada' 1990–91, two multi-media festivals of Italian culture for Ontario and Manitoba; Dir., The Candn. Club of Toronto 1989–91; Mem., Exhibition Ctte., Design Exchange, Toronto 1989–91; Mem. Adv. Bd., Northrop Frye Centre, Toronto; Initiator of the 'Fountain of Italy' project by Enzo/Cucchi, York Univ. Toronto; Address: 496 Huron St., Toronto, Ont. M5R 2R3.

**VALENTINE, George Douglas,** B.A.; diplomat; b. Calgary, Alta. 5 Feb. 1932; s. John C. and Evelyn Mary (Lamarche) V.; e. Univ. of B.C. B.A. 1952; m. Beverly d. Carlton and Phyllis Alexander 26 July 1963; children: Deborah, Christopher, Mark; CONSUL GENERAL FOR CANADA IN CHICAGO 1989– ; Sales Mgr. Halford and Valentine Ltd. 1952–63; Vice Consul Duesseldorf, W. Germany 1963–67, Counsellor Bogota, Colombia 1967–69, Rio de Janeiro 1969–73, Dir. Foreign Invest. Review Agency Ottawa 1973–75, Counsellor Tehran 1975–78, Consul Dallas 1978–80; Ambassador to Colombia 1980–83; Dir. Gen. Latin America, Dept. External Affairs, Ottawa 1983–85; Ambassador to Saudi Arabia 1985–89; recreation: golf; Office: Consulate General, 180 N. Stetson Ave., Chicago, Ill. 60601 U.S.A.

**VALGARDSON, William D.,** B.A., B.Ed., M.F.A.; writer; university professor; b. Winnipeg, Man. 7 May 1939; s. Alfred Herbert and Raechel Iris (Smith) V.; e. Univ. of Man., B.A. 1961, B.Ed. 1966; Univ. of Iowa, M.F.A. 1969; divorced; children: Nancy Rae, Val Dempsey; Chrmn., Dept. of Creative Writing, Univ. of Victoria 1982–87; High school teacher, Man. 1961–67; Assoc. Prof., Cottey Coll. 1970–74; Prof., Univ. of Victoria 1974–92; CBC first prize for fiction; 'Books In Canada' best novel award; CAA $5000 prize, drama; first prize, CBC annual literary prize, drama 1987; mem., AWP; TWUC; PWAC, CACLALS, CAA (Pres. 1985–86); author: 'The Girl With The Botticelli Face' 1992; 'What Can't Be Changed Shouldn't Be Mourned' 1990; 'The Carpenter of Dreams' 1986, 'Gentle Sinners' 1980, 'Red Dust' 1978, 'In the Gutting Shed' 1976, 'God is Not A Fish Inspector' 1975, 'Bloodflowers' 1973, (books); 'The Cave,' 'An Unacceptable Standard of Cockpit Practice,' 'Bloodflowers,' 'Granite Point,' 'The Burning' (radio plays); recreations: rock climbing, folk dancing, hiking; Home: 1908 Waterloo Rd., Victoria, B.C. V8P 1J3; Office: Box 1700. Dept. of Creative Writing, Univ. of Victoria, Victoria, B.C. V8W 2Y2.

**VALIANT, Jonathan J.,** B.A., F.R.I., M.B.A.; real estate executive; b. Sturgeon Falls, Ont. 1948; e. Carleton Univ. B.A. (Hons.) 1972; Univ. of Toronto M.B.A. 1989; EXECUTIVE VICE-PRESIDENT, CAMDEV PROPERTIES INC. 1992– ; Senior Vice-Pres., The Cadillac Fairview Corp. Limited 1983–92; Mem., The Real Estate Inst. (Fellow); licensed Real Estate Broker, Ont.; United Way Cabinet, Ottawa 1993; Presidents Adv. Council, Carleton Univ.; Office: Suite 1500, 112 Kent St., Ottawa, Ont. K1P 5P2.

**VALKO, Andrew;** artist; b. Prague, Czechoslovakia 1957; e. Forum Art Inst. 1971–77; Red River Comm. Coll. dipl. course 1975–78; Woodblock Printing Studies (Toshi Yoshida, Japan) 1983, 1985; Candn. citizen since 1968; solo exhibitions incl.: Nancy Poole's Studio Toronto 1990, 1991, 1993; Gal. Franklin Silverstone Montreal 1989, Thomas Gall. Winnipeg 1984, Assiniboia Gall. Regina 1980, '82, Cardigan Milne Gall. Winnipeg 1979, '81; group shows incl.: 'Oh Canada,' R.S.V. Gallery, South Hampton, Long Island, NY 1992; 8th Internat. Print Exhib. Frechen, West Germany; 4th Internat. Biennial Print Exhib. Taiwan, Republic of China 1989, Boston Printmakers 41st N. Am. Print Exhib. 1988, '89 (Andrew Nelson Whitehead Award); N.Y. City Internat. Art Comp. #6 1989, 'Contemporary Block Prints' Memorial Univ., St. John's, Nfld.; Nancy Poole's Studio 1989, 1990, 1991, 1992, 'Contemporary Western Woodblock Prints' Muttart Public Art Gall. Calgary 1989, Yoshida Annual Print Exhib. Kabatoja Gall. Japan 1988, '89 and others; has exhibited extensively in both private & public galls. in Manitoba, as well as nationally & internationally; collections incl.: Via Rail Canada Inc. (Montreal, Que.), Esso Petroleum Alberta, The Canada Council Art Bank, Memorial Univ., Manitoba Govt., Alliance Française Winnipeg Claridge Collection Montreal, Great West Life & priv. collections in N. Am. & Europe & Hong Kong; Office: c/o Nancy Poole's Studio, 16 Hazelton Ave., Toronto, Ont. M5R 2E2.

**VALLANCE, James G.,** B.A., M.B.A., C.A.; chartered accountant; b. Hamilton, Ont. 20 Aug. 1948; e. McMaster Univ. B.A. 1974, M.B.A. 1976; Candn. Inst. of C.A.s C.A. 1976; CONTROLLER, IVAX INDUSTRIES CANADA, INC. 1993– ; Clarkson Gordon 1975–77; Controller & Treas. then Sec.-Treas., Bd. of Dir., M & T Chemicals Limited 1977–90; Controller & Treas., Elf Atochem Canada Inc. 1991–93; Office: 666 Appleby Line, Suite C-106, Burlington, Ont. L7L 5Y3.

**VALLANCE, Ret. Col. Mary Graham,** O.M.M., C.D., A-de-C.; b. Atwood, Ont. 6 Feb. 1924; d. Lloyd Duncan and Anne Campbell (Lochead) V.; e. Sr. Matric. Listowel, Ont. 1942; Westervelt Sch. (Extve. Secretarial Course) London, Ont. 1944; 1st yr. Univ. of Western Ont. (Soc. Sciences); Dir., Women Personnel, Dept. of Nat. Defence 1971–76.; Secy. McCormick's Ltd. London, Ont. 1944; Teacher, Westervelt Sch., London 1949–53; enlisted RCAF 1954 rank Flight Cadet; attended Offrs.' Sch., London, Ont. later becoming Adj. there 1955–57; Adj. Radar & Communications Sch. Clinton, Ont. 1954–55; Recruiting Offr. Regina, Sask. 1957; Personnel Adm. Offr., 3 (F) Wing, Zweibrucken, Germany 1958; served in Personnel Adm. and Training, Parent, Que., St. Jean, Que., Camp Borden, Ont. and Winnipeg, Man. 1961–67; Personnel Adm. Offr., 4 (F) Wing, Baden Soellingen, Germany 1967; Base Personnel Adm. Offr., CFB Rockcliffe, Ont. 1968 and CFB Toronto-Downsview 1969–71; promoted Col. 1974; Mem., Bd. of Govs., Candn. Corps of Commissionaires (London); Elder, Presbyterian Church; recreations: cycling, reading, spectator sports; Clubs: RCAF Assn.; Atwood Lioness Club; Home: 211 King St., Atwood, Ont. N0G 1B0.

**VALLANCE-JONES, Alister,** B.Sc., M.Sc., Ph.D., F.R.S.C.; physicist; b. Christchurch, N.Z. 4 Feb. 1924; s. Frederick Edmund and Nellie Marion (Vallance) J.; e. St. Andrews Coll. Christchurch 1941; Canterbury Coll. Univ. of N.Z. B.Sc. 1945, M.Sc. 1946; Univ. of Cambridge Ph.D. 1950; m. Catherine d. James Fergusson, Farr, Scot. 1 Dec. 1951; children: Elizabeth Marie Jones-Villeneuve, Catriona Anne Gallant, Alasdair Frederick Vallance-Jones; PHYSICIST, NAT. RESEARCH COUNCIL OF CAN.; Post-Doctoral Fellow, Physics Div. Nat. Research Council 1949–51; Prof. of Physics Univ. of Sask. 1952–68; author 'Aurora' 1974; over 96 publs. on research spectroscopy, aurora and airglow; Assoc. Ed. Aeronomy and Space Physics, Candn. Journal of Physics 1981– ; Chrmn., Div. II, Internat. Assoc. of Geomagnetism and Aeronomy 1987–91; Ed. 'Physics in Canada' 1963–66; Protestant; recreations: sailing, skiing; Club: Britannia Yacht; Home: 2145 Fillmore Cres., Ottawa, Ont. K1J 6A1; Office: Herzberg Inst. of Astrophysics, Ottawa, Ont. K1A 0R6.

**VALLEE, Francis Gerald,** Ph.D., F.R.S.C.; anthropologist; educator; b. Montreal, Que. 27 July 1918; s. Richard Boulanger and Clara (Dempsey) V.; e. D'Arcy McGee High Sch. Montreal; McGill Univ. B.A. 1950; Univ. of London Ph.D. 1955; m. Anna Mathilde d. Hette Kerst Hylkema, Bilthoven, Holland 2 Aug. 1947; children: Richard Kerst, Frances Margaret, Martine Claire, Paul Nicholas; PROF. EMERITUS; PROF. OF ANTHROP. CARLETON UNIV.; Lectr. Univ. of Edinburgh 1953–55; Chief, Research Div. Dept. Citizenship & Immigration Ottawa 1955–57; Asst. to Assoc. Prof. McMaster Univ. 1957–64; Assoc. to Full Prof. Carleton Univ. since 1964; Visiting Prof. Univ. of Hawaii 1970–71, Australian Nat. Univ. 1978; mem. N.W.T. Leg. Council 1964–67; rec'd Candn. Centennial Medal 1967; served with RCA 1940–45, 14th Field Regt.; author 'Kabloona and Eskimo' 1967; 'Survey of the Contemporary Indians of Canada' Vol. II 1967; 'Eskimo of the Canadian Arctic' 1968; 'Language Use In Canada,' 1980; various articles ethnic relations, lang. and soc.; mem. Candn. Ethnol. Soc. (Pres.); Candn. Sociol. & Anthrop. Assn.; Candn. Ethnic Studies Assn.; Am. Anthrop. Assn.; NDP; recreations: music, sports, reading; Home: 2022 Rideau River Dr., Ottawa, Ont. K1S 1V2; Office: Colonel By Dr., Ottawa, Ont. K1S 5B6.

**VALLÉE, Pierre Michel,** FCMC; management consultant; b. Montréal, Qué. 20 June 1941; s. Joseph Archie and Kathleen Elizabeth (Tellier) V.; m. Louise d. Pierre and Jeanne Gendron 22 Feb. 1964; children: Peter, Lisa; PRES. & C.E.O., NYNEX DPI COMPANY 1994– ; Mngt. Cons., Stevenson & Kellogg 1965–71; Vice-Pres., Human Resources, The Price Co. 1971–79; Partner, Stevenson Kellogg Ernst & Whinney 1979–85, Pres. 1985–89; Extve.-in-Residence, School of Business, Dalhousie Univ. 1989–91, Dir. of Co-op Education 1991–92; Pres. & C.E.O., Atkinson Tremblay & Assoc. Inc. 1992–93; Pres. & C.E.O., AGS Information Services, Inc. 1993–94; Mem., Extve. Mgmnt. Ctte., AGS/NYNEX; Mem., Federal Minister's Advisory Ctte. on The Goods & Services Tax; recreations: trap shooting, photography; Clubs: Royal Nova Scotia Yacht Squadron; Home: 569 Colonial Ave., Westfield, NJ 07090; Office: 1139 Spruce Dr., Mountainside, NJ 07092 USA.

**VALLE-GARAY, Pastor,** A.A., B.A.; educator; b. Managua, Nicaragua 12 Jan. 1936; s. late Pastor and Rosa (Garay de) Valle-Quintero; e. Christian Brothers De La Salle Primary & Secondary Schs. Managua 1953; San Jose (Cal.) State Coll. Univ.; City Coll. San Francisco Assoc. of Arts degree, San Francisco State Coll. Univ.; Univ. of Toronto B.A. 1968; Ont. Coll. Edn. Dip. Secondary Edn. 1969; m. Angela Bocchicchio; children: Jacqueline, Michelle, Nicole, Alejandro, Claudio; PROF. OF LANGUAGES, LINGUISTICS & LITERATURES, YORK UNIV. 1968– , Fellow of Bethune Coll. 1976– ; taught Eng. as second lang. Adult Edn. Centre Employment & Immigration Can. and George Brown Coll. Applied Arts 1967–69; joined present Univ. 1968 lectr. in Spanish Lang. & Culture and Latin Am. & Caribbean Studies Prog., Spanish Course Dir. and Spanish Course Coordinator; Prof., Advanced Business Spanish, International MBA Graduate Programme, Faculty of Administrative Studies 1990– ; Prof. and Course Dir., Advanced Business Spanish, Internat. MBA; Instructor and Consultant, Spanish Programme, Continuing Education, Humber College of Applied Arts and Technology; mem. Univ.'s Speakers' Bureau, Centre Rsch. Latin Am. & Caribbean; mem. 'Nuestra Gente' Spanish TV Prog., Dir. 1970–75; Cons. Multi-Lingual TV Progs., Candn. Internat. Devel. Agency, Can. Save the Children, OXFAM Can.; Chargé d'Affaires for Govt. Nicaragua to Ottawa 1979; Consul Gen. of Nicaragua in Toronto 1982–90; Cons. to Deltonic Trading Corp.; mem. Hispanic Cong.; frequent guest lectr. various orgns. & Candn. univs.; TV and radio interviews CBC and CTV progs.; author (poetry): 'Doce poemas y una esperanza' 1978; current rsch. for publication: short stories 'This Damn Revolution Had Better Be Funny,' on the light side of the Nicaraguan revolution; publications: Foreword, 'Nicaraguan Portfolio' by Doug Wicken 1990; numerous articles nat. and internat. newspapers and mags since 1954; mem. Consular Corps. Assn. Toronto; Sandinista National Liberation Front, Nicaragua; York Univ. Faculty Assoc.; Hon. mem., World Trade Club; recreations: travel, collection of jazz and Latin Am. music; Home: 54 Van Horne Ave., North York, Ont. M2J 2S9; Office: S-570 Ross Building, 4700 Keele St., North York, Ont. M3J 1P3.

**VALLELY-FISCHER, Lois M.,** M.A., Ph.D.; educator; b. Capreol, Ont. 8 May 1931; d. John Michael and Theresa Ann (Ready) Vallely; e. St. Joseph's Coll. Sch. Toronto; Univ. of Toronto B.A. 1953; McGill Univ. M.A. 1962, Ph.D. 1965; m. Gabriel s. Joseph Fischer 1 Aug. 1974; children: Lia, Joseph; DEAN OF ARTS, ACADIA UNIV. 1982, Assoc. Prof. of Hist. 1973; Lectr. Sir George Williams Univ. 1961–62; Asst. Prof. Marianopolis Coll. Montreal 1964–68; Asst. Prof. present Univ. 1968–73; Home: 26 Chestnut, Wolfville, N.S.; Office: Wolfville, N.S. B0P 1X0.

**VALLENTYNE, John Reuben Way (a.k.a. 'Johnny Biosphere');** ecologist; b. Toronto, Ont. 31 July 1926; s. Harold James and Alice (Laurie) V.; e. Queen's Univ. 1945–49; Yale Univ. 1949–52; Nat. Defence Coll. Can. 1974–75; m. Ann V., d. Herman Lloyd Tracy, 30 Aug. 1947; children: Peter L.; Stephen W.; Jane L.; Anne Marie; Geoffrey G.; SCIENTIST EMERITUS, DEPT. FISHERIES & OCEANS, CAN. CENTRE FOR INLAND WATERS since 1992; Lectr., Queen's Univ. 1952; Asst. Prof. 1955; Fellow, Carnegie Inst. Washington 1956; Assoc. Prof. Cornell Univ. 1958; Prof. 1964; Scientific Leader, Eutrophication Sect., Fisheries Research Bd. Can., Freshwater Inst. 1966–72; Adjunct Prof., Univ. Man. 1968–72; Sr. Scientist, Freshwater Inst. 1972–74; Sr. Scientific Advisor, Ocean & Aquatic Sciences and Sci. Adv. Fisheries Research Bd. Can. 1975–77; Sr. Scientist, Dept. Fisheries & Oceans (Govt. Can.), Can. Centre for Inland Waters 1977–92; Candn. Co-Chrmn., IJC Great Lakes Science Adv. Bd. 1986–91; host, joint NHK (Japan) – TVO (Ont.) eight episode series 'The Miracle Planet'; author 'The Algal Bowl,' 1974; rec'd. various fellowships, incl. Sheffield (Yale) 1950–51; Visiting, Carnegie Inst. Washington 1956–57; Guggenheim for Study in Italy 1964–65; Journal Fund Award 1955–59; Hamilton and Dist. Environmentalist of the Year Award 1989; Merit Award, Dept. of Fisheries & Oceans 1992; Rachel Carson Award, Soc. of Environmental Toxicology and Chemistry 1992; served as L CPL., Candn. Army 1943–45; Fellow, Am. Assn. for the Advancement of Sci.; Fellow, Indian Soc. of Naturalists; mem., Am. Soc. Limnology & Oceanography (Member-at-large 1956–57; Vice-Pres. 1964–65; Ed. Bd. 1966–69); Internat. Assn. Limnology (Pres. 1974–80); Ecological Soc. Am.; Geochemical Soc. (Secy. Organic Group 1962–64; Chrmn. 1967–68); Internat. Assn. for Great Lakes Research; Internat. Assn. for Ecology; Internat. Union Biological Sciences (Rep. Environmental Biology 1979–82); N. Am. Assoc. for Environmental Educ.; Rawson Acad. for Aquatic Sciences (Chrmn. 1980–82); recreations: tennis; skiing; Home: 36 Longwood Rd., N., Hamilton, Ont. L8S 3V4; Office: 867 Lakeshore Rd., P.O. Box 5050, Burlington, Ont. L7R 4A6.

**VALLERAND, The Hon. André,** B.A., M.A.; economist; b. Québec, Qué. 9 June 1940; s. Louis-Olivier and Marguerite (Bélanger) V.; e. Concordia Univ., B.A. 1967, M.A. 1970; m. Denyse d. Yvon and Pauline (Boyer) Tassé 7 Sept. 1963; one d.: Natalie-Andrée; MINISTER OF REVENUE, PROVINCE OF QUEBEC 1994– ; Gen. Mgr., Edutec Form. Internat. 1977–79; Extve. Vice-Pres. & Gen. Mgr., C. of C. of Montréal & Pres., World Trade Ctr. Montreal 1979–85; el. MNA 1985, 1989; Min. Resp. for Small & Medium-Sized Businesses, Govt. of Qué. 1985; Min. responsible for International Affairs 1987; Min. of Supply and Services 1988; Min. of Tourism 1989–94; served as mem. Treas. Bd., Cabinet Standing Ctte. on Purchasing, Standing Ctte. on Econ. develop.; taught econ. at a number of univs. & insts. in Montréal 1970–81; Mem., Qué. Liberal Party; Qué. Econ. Assn.; Candn. Econ. Assn.; author: 'L'inflation et la technique d'indexation' 1975, 'La sociale démocratie' 1974, 'Pour une politique commerciale continentale' 1982; recreations: jogging, tennis, racketball; Office: 800 Sq. Victoria, Ste. 316, Montréal, Qué. H4Z 1B7.

**VALLERAND, Hon. Claude,** B.A., LL.L.; judge; b. Montreal, Que. 1 Sept. 1932; s. René and Claudine (Simard) V.; e. Coll. Stanislas, Montreal, B.A. 1949; Univ. de Montréal, LL.L. 1954; m. Lucie, d. Rolland Rinfret, Montreal, Que., 10 Sept. 1955; children: René, François, Josée; JUSTICE, QUÉ. COURT OF APPEAL (apptd. March 1983); Depy. Judge of the Supreme Court of the Yukon Territory 1983– ; read law with Blain, Piché, Godbout, Emery, Blain & Vallerand; called to Bar of Que. 1955; service with RCAF (Reserve); rank Flying Offr.; appt'd. to Superior Court of Que. Dec. 1971; R. Catholic; recreations: skiing, music, theatre; Home: 6100 Deacon Rd., App. 06K, Montreal, Que. H3S 2V6; Office: Court House, Montreal, Que. H2Y 1A2.

**VALPY, Michael Granville;** journalist; b. Toronto, Ont. 13 Aug. 1942; s. Charles Dupré and Vivian Grenfell (Walkem) V.; e. Vancouver pub. schs.; Univ. of B.C.; two children: Leslie Amanda, Francis Edward Walkem; COLUMNIST & DEPUTY MANAGING EDITOR, THE GLOBE AND MAIL 1987– ; Associate Editor, Vancouver Sun 1975–78, Nat. Pol. Columnist 1978–81; mem. Ed. Bd., present newspaper 1970–75, Nat. Pol. Columnist 1981–84; Africa Correspondent 1984–87; Winner 1985 and 1986 National Newspaper Awards for foreign reporting; co-author 'The National Deal – The Fight for a Canadian Constitution' 1982; Anglican; Office: 444 Front St. W., Toronto, Ont. M5V 2S9.

**VAN AERDE, Michel,** M.A.Sc., Ph.D.; educator; b. Tillsonburg, Ont. 7 May 1960; s. Omer Joseph and Germaine (Verstraeten) V.; e. Univ. of Waterloo B.A.Sc. 1983, M.A.Sc. 1984, Ph.D. 1985; m. Maureen d. William and Lois Cooke 28 May 1988; PROF. OF CIVIL ENG. QUEEN'S UNIV. 1986– ; Rsch. Project Mgr. Inst. Risk Rsch. Univ. of Waterloo 1985; Assoc. Prof. present Univ. 1986, devel. Q-Route (traffic responsive in-vehicle route guidance system); created INTEGRATION, the first computer simulation model for estimating potential benefits of various types of route guidance systems; evaluator of the Trav Tek and Pathfinder route guidance systems in Orlando and Los Angeles, respectively; evaluator of V.S. IVHS architecture study; cons. Rsch. & Devel. Br. Min. of Transp. Ont.; GM Research Labs; Federal Highway Admin.; mem. Candn. Soc. Civil Eng.; Inst. Transp. Engs.; Assn. Profl. Engs. Prov. Ont.; Home: 86 Point St. Mark, Kingston, Ont. K7K 6X8; Office: Kingston, Ont. K7L 3N6.

**VAN ALSTYNE, Thelma Selina,** R.C.A.; artist; b. Victoria, B.C. 26 Jan. 1913; d. Alpha Thomas and Rosetta Schoch (Cooper) Scribbans; e. Miss Seymours Sch. for Girls Vancouver; Duffus Sch. of Business 1929; Vancouver Sch. of Art 1944–46; Doone Sch. of Art, studied with Jock MacDonald; m. late E. Lloyd Van Alstyne 12 June 1953; one step-d.; solo exhns. incl. Pollock Gallery 1960–80; Le Fevre Gallery Edmonton 1981; Quan Gallery Toronto 1982, 1983, 1984, 1987; Masters Gallery Calgary 1993; rep. in numerous group exhns. incl. Candn. Group of Painters Montreal Museum of Fine Arts 1961; Colour and Form Soc. Toronto 1968–70; Bryan Robertson White Gallery London, Eng. (Centennial Purchase) 1967; Art Gallery of Ont. 1968, 1971; Birmingham, Ala. Can. Council Group 1979; rep. in pub., corporate and private colls. incl. Can. Council Art Bank, OISE Coll.; recipient Hadassah Auction Prizes 1972–80; Can. Council Grant 1972; profiled in 'World Who's Who for Women' 1984; Buddhist; recreations: gardening, travel, religions; Address: 81 Bramley St. S., Port Hope, Ont. L1A 3K6.

**VAN ANDEL, Hendrikus Willem Helenius,** B.Sc., M.Sc., Ph.D.; college executive; b. Soest, The Netherlands 2 July 1940; s. Hendrikus and Wilhelmina A.M. (Fernhout) Van A.; e. Univ. of B.C. B.Sc. 1962, M.Sc. 1963, Ph.D. 1966; m. Hendrika d. Derk Jan and Gerda Heinen 24 Aug. 1963; children: Kenneth, Eric, Harmen, David, Julie; PRES. THE KING'S COLL., EDMONTON 1985– , Prof. of Physics 1985– , Dir. Coll. Found.; post-doctoral fellowship The Netherlands 1966–68; Rsch. Offr. FOM Inst. Plasma Physics Nieuwegein, Holland 1968–69, Visiting Sci. 1976–77; Rsch. Assoc. Univ. of Sask. 1969–70; Prof. of Physics Univ. de Montréal 1970–84; Visiting Sci. Inst. fur Plasma Physik KFA Julich, W. Germany 1984; Mem., Candn. Assn. of Physicists, Plasma Div. 1970–85 (Extve. 1972–75, 1979–81; Chrmn. 1980); Lectr., Candn. Assn. of Physicists 1981; Trustee, Inst. for Christian Studies 1977–83; Gov., Redeemer Coll. (Ancaster) 1978–84; author numerous articles sci. jours.; Chair Plasma Physics Div. Candn. Assn. Physicists 1980; Home: 13607 – 109 Ave., Edmonton, Alta. T5M 2G8; Office: 9125 – 50 St., Edmonton, Alta. T6B 2H3.

**VAN BAREN, Catherine,** B.A.; editor; b. Brantford, Ont. 9 Feb. 1951; d. Cornelis and Metje Cornelia (deKoning) V.; e. York Univ. B.A. (Hons.) 1974; SENIOR EDITOR, EXHIBITION & DESIGN DEPT., ART GALLERY OF ONTARIO 1982– ; Editorial Asst., Trade Dept., Macmillan of Canada 1978; Managing Editor, Personal Library Publishers 1979–82; editor: 'Art Gallery of Ontario: Selected Works' 1991; Office: 317 Dundas St. W., Toronto, Ont. M5T 1G4.

**VAN BEEK, Keith C.;** executive; b. Amsterdam, Netherlands 20 April 1946; s. Kees and May (Borgman) Van B.; m. Beverly d. David Pinnock 2 Oct. 1971; children: Ries, Nick, Dan; Pres., C.E.O. & Dir., MacLeod-Stedman Inc. 1987; Pres., Gambles Canada Acceptance Ltd.; Homeguard Insurance Agency Inc.; Davis Automotive Centre (1982) Ltd., Davis Div.; Crestliner Transport; Stedmans 1985–87; Dir., Stanley Mutual Insur. Co.; joined Zellers in 1967 as Mgmt. Trainee; Store Mgr. 1972; Dist. Mgr. 1976; Merchandise Mgr. 1980; Dir., Sales & Mktg. 1981; Pres., 738558 Ont. Ltd.; Dir. 689377 Ont. Ltd.; Dir., Amyotrophic Lateral Sclerosis Soc. of Can. 1989; Past Dir., Nat. Retail Merchandising Inst.; recreation: squash.

**van BRIDGE, Tony;** actor; director; writer; b. London, Eng., 28 May 1917; s. Arthur Stanley and Edith Christina (Drane) Bridge; e. Elmhurst Coll., Kingston-on-Thames, Eng.; Royal Acad. of Dramatic Art; m. Elizabeth Adamson Tully (deceased, 11 July 1979); children: Peter, David, Shona Elizabeth; m. Stacey Stewart Curtis 30 Aug. 1987; acting career incls. 15 yrs. with Stratford (Ont.) Festival (notably as Falstaff in all 3 plays in which that character appears); Old Vic Co.; 10 yrs. with Shaw Festival, of which he is an associate director, Niagara on the Lake, notably for Capt. Shotover in 'Heartbreak House,' 1968, and as director of 'Man and Superman,' 1977; Lincoln Center, N.Y.; Stratford, Conn.; Houston, Texas; TV work in Hollywood; wrote original play 'The Old Ones' which appeared on CBC TV and did adaption of 'Diary of a Scoundrel'; appears frequently in his one-man show 'GKC,' based on G.K. Chesterton; appeared for 3 seasons as 'Judge' on CBC-TV, for which he received an Actra Award; served with Brit. Army 1940–46; rank Capt. on discharge; Queen Elizabeth Silver Jubilee Medal; Clubs: Arts & Letters, recreations: golf, astronomy; Address: 450 Merton St., Toronto, Ont. M4S 1B3.

**VAN CAMP, Hon. Mabel Margaret;** judge; b. Blackstock, Ont. 11 May 1920; d. William John Weir and Mary Jane (Smith) Van Camp; e. Blackstock Pub. and High Schs.; Univ. of Toronto, Victoria Coll. B.A. 1941; Osgoode Hall Law Sch. 1947; JUDGE, ONT. COURT OF JUSTICE (GENERAL DIVISION); read law with Macdonald & Macintosh; called to Bar of Ont. 1947; cr. Q.C. 1965; joined Gerard Beaudoin law practice 1947 becoming Partner, Beaudoin, Pepper & Van Camp; Pres. YWCA Metrop. Toronto 1965–68; del. to World Conf. Australia 1967; former mem. Goal Setting Comte. & Allocations Comte. Un. Community Fund; Past Regent, Fudger House Chapter IODE; Past Pres. Women's Law Assn. Ont.; former Council mem. Candn. Bar Assn.; former Chancellor and Dean, Alpha Mu Chapter of Kappa Beta Pi; Anglican; Clubs: Royal Candn. Mil. Inst.; Women's University; Home: 7 Jackes Ave., 1608, Toronto, Ont. M4T 1E3 and 1 Church St., Blackstock, Ont. L0B 1B0; Office: Osgoode Hall, 130 Queen St. W., Toronto, Ont. M5H 2N5.

**VANCISE, The Hon. Mr. Justice William John,** B.A., LL.B.; b. Regina, Sask. 10 Jan. 1938; s. Albert John and Jean Finlayson (Sclater) V.; e. Luther Co., 1956; Univ. of Sask., B.A. 1958, LL.B. 1960; m. Joy Yvonne, d. William Watson, 26 Aug. 1961 (div. 1990); children: Robert William, John Allen, Nancy Jean; m. Sybile Tremblay 30 Mar. 1990; JUDGE OF COURT OF QUEEN'S BENCH 1982; JUDGE OF COURT OF APPEAL 1983; Former Partner, Balfour, Milliken, Moss, Laschuk, Kyle, & Vancise; Dir., CN Railways 1972–82; Paragon Business Forms (Western) Ltd. 1975–82; The H.A. Roberts Group Ltd. 1975–82; Bird Machine Canada Ltd.; read law with R.M. Balfour, Q.C.; called to Bar of Sask. 1961; assoc. with Balfour & Balfour 1961–62, Balfour MacLeod, MacDonald, Laschuk & Kyle, 1962–63; named Partner of Balfour, MacLeod in 1963; appptd. Q.C. 1979; Dir., YMCA Regina; mem., Regina Bar Assn.; Sask. Law Soc.; Candn. Bar Assn. (Sec. Chrmn.); Luther Coll. Alumni Assn. (Past Pres.); Freemason; Protestant; recreation: skiing, tennis; Club: Rotary (Pres. Eastview 1973–74); Home: 98 Lockwood Rd., Regina, Sask. S4S 3G2.

**VAN DAMME, Paul Joseph,** C.A., B.Comm., M.B.A.; financial executive; b. Toronto, Ont. 6 Jan. 1950; s. George Raymond and Lorraine Loretta V.; e. Univ. of Toronto B.Comm. 1972, M.B.A. 1988; m. Deborah d. Gordon and Betty LeBarre 24 May 1991; children: Angela, Susannah, Christopher; SENIOR VICE-PRESIDENT & CHIEF FINANCIAL OFFICER, TELEZONE CORPORATION 1994– ; Corporate Controller, Canada Systems Group Limited 1983–85; Treasurer 1985–87; Divisional Vice-Pres. 1987–88; Vice-Pres., Finance 1988; Vice-Pres. & Chief Financial Officer, STM Systems Corp. 1988–91; Vice-Pres., Controller, Laidlaw Inc. 1991–94; Mem., Financial Executives Inst. 1987– ; American Management Assn. 1986– ; Inst. of C.A.s of Ont. 1974– ; recreation: sailing, tennis, golf; clubs: Mississaugua Golf & Country, Fitness Inst.; Home: 76 Aldershot Cres., Willowdale, Ont. M2P 1M1; Office: 181 University Ave., Suite 1210, Toronto, Ont. M5H 3M7.

**van den BERGH, Sidney,** A.B., M.Sc., Dr.rer.nat.; astronomer; b. Wassenaar, Holland 20 May 1929; s. Sidney J. and S.M. (van den Berg) van den B.; e. Leiden Univ. 1947–48; Princeton Univ. A.B. 1950; Ohio State

Univ. M.Sc. 1952; Univ. Göttingen Dr.rer.nat. 1956; children: Peter, Mieke, Sabine; Adjunct Prof. Univ. Victoria 1978– ; Principal Research Officer 1977– and Dir., Dominion Astrophysical Observatory 1977–86; Asst. Prof. Ohio State Univ. 1956–58; Prof. Univ. of Toronto 1958–77; mem. Internat. Astron. Union (Vice-Pres. 1976–82); Am. Astron. Soc.; Fellow, Royal Soc. London; Royal Soc. Can.; Associate, Royal Astron. Soc.; Pres., Candn. Astron. Soc. 1990–92 (Sr. VP 1988–90); Killam Laureate 1990; recreations: photography, archaeology; Home: 418 Lands End Rd., Sidney, B.C. V8L 5L9; Office: 5071 W. Saanich Rd., Victoria, B.C. V8X 4M6.

**VANDEN BORN, William H.,** M.Sc., Ph.D.; educator; b. Rhenen, Netherlands 17 Nov. 1932; came to Canada 1949; e. Univ. of Alta., B.Sc. (Agric.) 1956, M.Sc. 1958; Univ. of Toronto, Ph.D. (Bot.) 1961; m. Edigna Wierenga, 6 June 1958; 5 children; DEPT. OF PLANT SCIENCE, UNIV. OF ALBERTA; joined present Univ. as Asst. Prof. 1961, Assoc. Prof. 1966, Prof., 1972; Chrmn., Dept. of Plant Science, 1970–75, 1982–87; author of numerous articles in various scient. journs.; Home: 14011 – 89A Ave., Edmonton, Alta. T5R 4S4; Office: Rm 4-16 C, Agriculture Forestry Bldg., Edmonton, Alta. T6G 2E1.

**VANDEN BRINK, Antonie (Tony);** industrial executive; born Enschede, Holland, 10 Oct. 1928; e. Enschede, Holland; m. Kathleen Rose Archibald, 18 July 1953; children: Paul B., Stephen R., Sandra J.; PRESIDENT, TOKAY RESOURCES LTD.; Dir., Trimac Limited 1976– ; Mark Resources Inc.; Transwest Energy Inc.; Chauvco Resources Ltd.; Intera Information Technologies Corp.; Wascana Energy Inc.; Dir., Calgary Advisory Bd. of Salvation Army; came to Can. 1950 serving in drilling industry; Field Supt. Peter Bawden Drilling Ltd. 1958; Operations Mgr. Jennings Drilling 1960; co-founder Petrolia Drilling Co. 1963; merged with Kenting Group 1967; became Vice Pres. Kenting Drilling & Dir. Kenting Limited; Pres. Kenting Ltd. 1973–88 (Kenting acquired by Trimac 1977); Pres. & Chief Operating Offr., Trimac 1980–88; Mem., Calgary Petroleum Club; Calgary Golf & Country; Ranchmen's; Home: Calgary, Alta.; Office: Bow Valley Postal Outlet, P.O. Box 20007, Calgary, Alta. T2P 4H3.

**VANDERBURGH, Rosamond Moate,** B.A., M.A., Ph.D.; university professor (anthropology); b. Arlington, Mass. 2 Oct. 1926; d. Herbert Arthur and Katharine (Eberhardt) Moate; e. Forest Hill Collegiate 1944; Radcliffe Coll. B.A. 1948; Northwestern Univ. M.A. 1951; Univ. of Pennsylvania Ph.D. 1989; m. Albert s. Albert and Kathryn V. 11 Sept. 1954; children: Matthew, Katharine; PROF. EMERITUS, ERINDALE COLLEGE, UNIV. OF TORONTO IN MISSISSAUGA 1992– ; Curatorial Asst., Ethnology, Royal Ont. Mus. 1954–56; Spec. Lecturer, Anthrop., Erindale Coll., Univ. of Toronto 1967–71; Asst. Prof. 1971–77; Tenured Assoc. Prof. 1977–90; Prof. of Anthropology 1990–92; Founding Dir., Mississauga Heritage Found. 1960–87; Mem., Candn. Ethnol. Soc.; Native Art Studies Assn. of Can.; author: 'I am Nokomis, too: the biography of Verna Patronella Johnston' 1977; co-author: 'Shaman's Daughter' 1980, 1981 (novel), 'A Paint-brush in My Hand: Daphne Odjig' 1992; recreations: gardening; Home: 21 Regency Court, Oakville, Ont. L6H 2P6; Office: Mississauga, Ont. L5L 1C6.

**VANDERBURGH, William G.,** B.A., LL.B., A.R.C.T.; lawyer; b. Ottawa, Ont. 8 March 1947; s. William Crichton (dec.) and Jeanne Marietta (Glover) V.; e. Univ. of Toronto B.A. 1969, LL.B. 1972, Royal Conservatory of Music A.R.C.T.; m. Dr. Sarah R. d. W. Edward and Joyce Jones 17 June 1988; children: Ian & David VanderBurgh, Simon & Jane Isbister; PARTNER, AIRD & BERLIS 1977– ; Assoc., present firm 1974–77; Mem., Law Soc. of U.C.; Candn. Bar Assn.; Internat. Bar Assn.; Dir. & Sec., Candn. Worcester Controls Limited; Fasco Motors Limited; Geonor Investments Limited; Mt. Hope Machinery Co. Limited; Scharr Indus. Can. (1991) Inc.; Teltone Limited; Twentieth Century Fox Canada Limited; Weavexx Corporation; 164113 Canada Inc.; 164226 Canada Inc.; Dir. & Asst. Sec., Kee Indus. Products Ltd.; Stewart Warner Corp. of Can., Limited; Dir., ACF Canada Limited; Beaufort Air-Sea Equipment Inc.; Brook Hansen (Canada) Inc.; Daily Racing Form of Canada Ltd.; Dunlop Aviation Can. Inc.; Dunlop-Beaufort Can. Ltd.; EPS Entertainment Prog. Serv. Ltd.; FoxVideo Can. Limited; Hamilton Kent of Can. Limited; Hansen Commun. Ltd.; Hoffman Indus. of Can. Limited; McDonnell Douglas Information Systems Can., Inc.; Schlegel Can. Inc.; Stryker Can. Inc.; Church of St. Clement, Eglinton; recreations: hockey, swimming, piano, children's sports; club: The Royal Candn. Yacht; Home: 5 Bryce Ave., Toronto, Ont. M4V 2B3; Office: BCE Place, Suite 1800, Box 754, 181 Bay St., Toronto, Ont. M5J 2T9.

**VANDERHAEGHE, Guy Clarence,** B.A., M.A., B.Ed.; writer; b. Esterhazy, Sask. 5 Apr. 1951; s. Clarence Earl and Alma Beth (Allen) V.; e. Esterhazy High Sch. 1968; Univ. of Sask. B.A. 1971; Univ. of Sask. M.A. 1975; Univ. of Regina B.Ed. 1978; m. Margaret d. Gottlieb and Emma Nagel 2 Sept. 1972; Visiting Prof. of Creative Writing, Univ. of Ottawa 1985–86; archivist, rscher. and high sch. teacher 1975–79; Writer-in-Residence Saskatoon Public Library 1983–84; Writer-in-Residence, Univ. of Ottawa 1985–86; author 'Man Descending' (short stories; won Gov.-Gen.'s Award for Fiction 1982; Geoffrey Faber Memorial Prize, Gt. Britain 1987) 1982; 'The Trouble with Heroes' (short stories) 1983; 'My Present Age' (novel) 1984; 'Homesick' (novel) 1989; mem. Sask. Arts Bd. 1984; recreations: basketball, hockey, tennis, golf.

**VANDERKAMP, Joan Rosemary Ruth,** M.A., Dip.Lib.; editor; b. St. Andrews, Scotland 15 April 1931; d. George Herbert and Elizabeth (Bladen) Bushnell; e. St. Leonards School; Univ. of St. Andrews M.A. (Hons.) 1953; Univ. of London, postgrad. dipl. in librarianship 1985; m. John (dec.) s. Henk and Gertruida Vanderkamp 4 Aug. 1960; children: Nicholas Henry, Fiona Yvonne, Christa Joan; BUSINESS EDITOR, CANADIAN PUBLIC POLICY/ANALYSE DE POLITIQUES 1974– ; Librarian, County Library, Warwickshire 1953–54; Bonar-Law Bennett Library Fredericton, N.B. 1955–56; Research Asst. to Lord Beaverbrook 1956–58; Librarian & Rsch. Asst., Assn. of Univs. & Colleges of Canada 1958–62; Production Mgr., 'Can. Rev. of Sociology & Anthropology' 1985– ; Managing Editor, 'Can. J. on Aging' 1990– ; Business Ed., 'J. of Agric. & Envir. Ethics' 1990– ; Bd. Mem., Candn. Periodical Publishers Assn.; Treas., College Women's Club, Univ. of Guelph; Corresponding Sec., Univ. Women's Club of Guelph 1984–86; author: 'Provincial Programs of Aid to University Students 1957–58 to 1960–61,' 'University Study in Canada' 1961, 'Study Research and Travel Grants for University Professors' 1961; co-author (with John Vanderkamp): 'The Impact of Computer Technology on the Production of Scholarly Journals and Books' 1988; recreations: tennis; clubs: Cutten; Home: 27 Lynwood Place, Guelph, Ont. N1G 2V9; Office: Room 039, MacKinnon Bldg., Univ. of Guelph, Guelph, Ont. N1G 2W1.

**VANDERKUUR, George,** B.Sc.; headmaster; b. Harlingen, Holland 2 Sept. 1942; s. Jan and Maria Christina (Schumacher) V.; e. Royal Mil. Coll.; Carleton Univ. B.Sc. 1967; m. Mary d. Osborne and Helen Orr 31 July 1964; children: Mark, Jeffrey, Jennifer; HEADMASTER, HOLY TRINITY SCH. 1990– ; Physics Teacher Courtice Secondary Sch. 1965–71; Sci. Museum Educator Ont. Sci. Centre 1971, Chief Sci. 1983, Assoc. Dir. Gen. 1987, Mgr. of Sci. and Design 1988–89; Adm. of Evaluation Premier's Council 1989–90; co-author 'Science Ways' 7 1978 and 8 1979; Life mem. Am. Assn. Physic Teachers; recreation: cycling; Home: 812 Fairview Ave., Pickering, Ont. L1W 1M8.

**VAN DER LEE, Charles Wesley,** B.Comm.; retail executive; b. Edmonton, Alta. 18 July 1953; s. Earl Wesley and Dorothy Elizabeth Lorraine (McCullough) V.; e. Bonnie Doon H.S. 1971 (R.V. Clark Citizenship Award); Univ. of Alberta B.Comm. 1975; m. Debra d. Basil and Elsie Davies 11 June 1983; children: Erin Christine, Matthew Wesley; PRESIDENT & CHIEF OPERATING OFFICER, ROGERS VIDEO 1992– ; Dist. Mgr., Texaco Canada Inc. 1975–84; Real Estate Mgr., Silcorp. 1984; Director Real Estate 1984–85; Dir. Opns. 1986–88; Vice-Pres. Opns. 1988–90; Vice-Pres. Sales & Opns., Rogers Video 1990–92; Dir., Candn. Bd. of Gov., Video Software Dealers Assn.; Business Candn. Video Retailer of the Year 1993; recreations: squash, skiing; club: California; Home: 13894 – 18A Avenue, White Rock, B.C. V4A 9E9; Office: 10100 Shellbridge Way, Unit 100, Richmond, B.C. V6X 2W7.

**van der MEULEN, Emiel Georg,** B.Sc., M.L.A., R.C.A.; landscape architect; b. Rheden, The Netherlands 6 Oct. 1928; s. Daniel and A.C.E. (Kelling) van der M.; e. High Sch. Zutphen, Netherlands 1947; Mich. State Univ. B.Sc. (Landscape Arch.) 1959, postgrad. Fellowship 1960; Harvard Univ. Master Landscape Arch. 1961; children: Coral Ann Amanda, Emil George; m. Catherine van Steen; child: Daniel; CHIEF LANDSCAPE ARCHITECT, DAR AL RIYADH, RIYADH, K.S.A.; Consultant, Arriyadh Development Authority, Riyadh, S.A. 1987–88; Royal Gardens Jeddah, Riyadh, Urban Design Projects Jubail, Yanbu, Riyadh, S.A.; Assoc. Prof. in Landscape Arch. Univ. of Toronto 1968–70; Dir. Landscape Arch. Dept. Ryerson Polytech. Inst. Toronto 1972–74; Prof. of Environmental Design King Abdul Aziz Univ. Jeddah, Saudi Arabia 1979–80; Associate, Talal Kurdi Consultants, Jeddah, S.A. 1981–87; Princ., van der Meulen Associates Ltd. Toronto 1969–76; Princ., EVM Ltd. Landscape Architects 1976–83; maj. projects 1970–80 incl. Trent Univ.; Queen's Univ.; Shaw Festival Theatre; Courtyard York Univ.; First Canadian Place Toronto; Royal Bank Plaza H.O. Toronto; New Massey Hall Toronto; Downtown West, Toronto; Harbourfront, 74, Toronto; Royal Ont. Museum Courtyard; Bank of Canada, Ottawa; mem. Art Adv. Comte. City Hall Toronto 10 yrs.; Design Comte. Nat. Capital Comn. Ottawa, Chrmn. Fine Arts Comte.; Past Councillor Stratford Seminar Civic Design; mem. Royal Ont. Museum; served with Royal Netherlands Marines 1947–49; rec'd Civic Award City of Toronto 1979; Design Awards, Landscape Ont.; author various articles Landscape arch.; Fellow, Candn. Soc. Landscape Archs.; Past Pres., Ont. Assn. Landscape Archs.; Am. Soc. Landscape Archs.; Beta Alpha Sigma (Past Pres.); Academician, Royal Candn. Acad. of Arts; recreations: scuba diving, sculpting, archeology; Home: 38 Scarborough Cres., Scarborough, Ont. M1M 2J4; Office: P.O. Box 5364, Riyadh, 11422 Saudia Arabia.

**Van der ZALM, Hon. William Nick;** b. Noordwykerhout, Holland 29 May 1934; s. Wilhelmus Nicholaas and Agatha C. (Warmerdam) Van der Z.; e. St. Josephs Noordwykerhout, Holland; Bradner and Mt. Lehman, B.C.; Phillip Sheffield, Abbotsford, B.C.; m. Lillian B. 27 June 1956; children: Jeffrey, Juanita, Wim, Lucia; Premier, Province of British Columbia 1986–91 (Retired); Ald. Surrey, B.C. 4 yrs., Mayor 6 yrs.; Min. of Human Resources, B.C. 1975–78; Min. of Municipal Affairs 1978–81; Min. of Education 1981–83; Pres., B.C. Chamber Comm. 1986; mem. K. of C.; Social Credit; R. Catholic; recreations: gardening, fishing, soccer; Home: 3553 Arthur Dr., Delta, B.C. V4K 3N2.

**van de WATER, Frank,** B.Com., C.A.; executive; b. Amsterdam, The Netherlands 7 June 1941; s. late J.H.A. van de Water; came to Can. 1947; e. West Hill High Sch. Montreal 1957; Sir George Williams Univ. B.Com. 1961; C.A. 1963; m. Jean Dulcie d. late Fraser McIntosh, N.Z. 27 Sept. 1975; children: Melanie, Christopher; CHIEF EXTVE. OFFR. & DIR., EXPERTEXT SYSTEMS LTD. 1991– ; joined Coopers & Lybrand, Montreal and London, Eng. 1957–66; Controller, Patino, N.V., Toronto and London, Eng. 1966–73; Vice Pres. and Group Controller, Hambro Canada Ltd., Toronto 1973–75; Pres., Peel-Elder Developments Ltd. 1974–75; Vice Pres. Finance and Treas. Y & R Properties Ltd. 1976–79; Vice Pres., Finance and Secy., CAE Industries Ltd. 1979–87; Vice Pres. and Controller, Polysar Energy & Chemical Corp. 1987–88; Vice Pres. & C.F.O., Pamour Inc. 1989–90; Vice Pres. & Chief Finan. Offr., Giant Yellowknife Mines Ltd. 1989–90; ERG Resources Inc. 1989–90; Pamorex Minerals Inc. 1989–90; mem. C.A.'s Inst. Que. and Ont.; Protestant; recreations: squash, skiing; Clubs: Granite; Ontario; Cambridge; Georgian Peaks; Home: 99 Otter Cres., Toronto, Ont. M5N 2W9.

**VAN DUSEN, Tom F.J.;** communications consultant; b. 13 Feb.1948; s. Thomas Walter and Shirley (Hogan) V.; e. Univ. of Ottawa H.S.; Univ. of Ottawa; m. Carol Ann Stockley; children: Allison, Victoria, Oliver; PRESIDENT, VAN DUSEN MEDIA MANAGEMENT 1994– ; Reporter, 'Ottawa Citizen' 1972–82; Copy Editor 1982–83; Reporter, CTV 1983; Press Sec., Min. of Transport 1984–87; Press Sec., Leader of the Govt. in the House of Commons & Pres. of the Privy Council 1986–88; Press Sec., Pres. of the Treas. Bd. 1987–88; Owner, Castor Country Gallery & Bed & Breakfast 1989–93; Dir. of Communications, Min. of Agric. 1989–91; Dir. of Communications, Min. of Finance 1991–93; Press Sec. & Dir. of Communications, Pres. of the Treas. Bd. 1993; Dep. Press Sec., Prime Minister of Canada 1993; Columnist, 'The Villager'; Vice-Pres., Bruce M. Hicks Edn. Foundation; Chairman, Boyd Community Museum; Founding Mem., Russell Heritage & Core Devel. Ctte.; Community Artist Co-op.; Russell Twp. Hist. Soc.; club: National Press, Russell Writer's; Office: 98 Mill St., Box 322, Russell, Ont. K4R 1E2; Office: 112 Mill St., Box 716, Russell, Ont. K4R 1E2.

**van DUYVENDYK, Nicolaas,** M.Ed., C.A., C.M.A., C.I.A.; federal public servant, retired; b. Holland 4 Sept. 1923; Royal Dutch Shell Indonesia 1947–53; oil ind. Can. 1954–68; Fed. Govt. 1968–91 serving Supply & Services, Consumer & Corporate Affairs, Veterans Affairs, Transport Can.; Dir., Marine Atlantic; Dir., C.N.I.B. Ontario; Dir., Redeemer College; Dir., Calvin College; Home: 467 Richardson Ave., Ottawa, Ont. K2B 5G9.

**VANEK, David,** B.A., LL.B.; retired provincial court judge; b. Pine Orchard, Ont. 17 Feb. 1915; s. Jacob and Jessie (Oster) V.; e. Richmond Hill H.S., Harbord C.I. 1932; Univ. of Toronto, B.A. (Hon.) 1936, LL.B. 1949; Osgoode Hall Law Sch. 1939; admitted to Ont. Bar 1939; m. Joyce d. Samuel and Leah (Lily) Lester 28 Nov. 1942; children: Peter, Nancy, Howard; Judge of the Prov. Court of Ont. (Crim. Div.) 1969–90; retired; priv. practice (Toronto) 1939–42; military serv., Candn. Intelligence Corps. 1942–46; Lectr., Univ. of Toronto 1946–50; Gen. Couns., Principal Investments Limited 1950–57; priv. practice (Toronto) 1958–68; apptd. Queen's Counsel 1958; apptd. Magistrate, Prov. of Ont. 1968; reported judgements incl. 'Regina v. Squires' 1986, 'v. Susan Nelles' 1982, 'v. Weightman and Cunningham' 1978, 'v. Lawson and Slavnick' 1975; Candidate, Ont. Legisl. 1963; Hon. Life Dir., The Credit Couns. Serv. of Metro. Toronto (Orgnr. & Past Pres.); Assoc. of Provincial Criminal Court Judges of Ont. (Past Pres.); Chrmn., The Provincial Criminal Court Judges Special Ctte. to Report on Criminal Justice in Ont. 1986–87; The Internat. Acad. of Trial Judges; Temple Sinai Cong. of Toronto (Past Pres.); Ed. Staff, 'Canadian Law Abridgement 1936–38'; contbr.: 'Univ. of Toronto Law Journal,' 'The Criminal Law Quarterly'; recreations: golf, tennis, raquetball, music; Club: Markham Golf & Country; Home: North York, Ont.

**VAN EVRA, Judith Page,** B.A., M.A., Ph.D.; university professor; b. Neenah, Wisc. 20 Sept. 1939; d. William Gerhardt and Bernice Martha (Wolf) Page; e. Valparaiso Univ. B.A. 1960; Bowling Green State Univ. M.A. 1961; Michigan State Univ. Ph.D. 1966; m. James W. s. Robert and Esther V. 2 Sept. 1961; children: Stephanie, Susan, Jennifer; PROF., PSYCHOLOGY, UNIV. OF ST. JEROME'S COLLEGE 1992– ; joined St. Jerome's College 1975; Chair, Dept. of Psych. 1981–87; Assoc. Dir., Inst. for Studies in Learning Disbilities 1981– ; has served on several cttes. & Bd. of Gov.; Sexual Harassment Advisor; lecturer on and off campus; media inverviews; reg. Ont. Bd. of Examiners in Psych. 1970– ; private clin. work; Cons., Waterloo Regional Sep. Sch. Bd. 1985–90; Part-time teacher, Univ. of Waterloo 1980–83; several past executive academic, association & community positions; Invited Guest, Educational Testing Serv., 20th Anniversary 'Sesame Street' 1989; Symposium Participant, 'Children and War Coverage' 1991; Mem., Can., Ont. & Am. Psychological Assns.; Learning Disabilities Assn.; Am. Orthospych. Assn.; author: 'Television and Child Development' 1990 (extensive media coverage); 'Psychological Disorders of Children and Adolescent' 1983 and articles, book reviews and 1 book chapter; recreations: travel, sailing, cooking; club: YMCA Health; Home: 97 Claremont Ave., Kitchener, Ont. N2M 2P7; Office: St. Jerome's College, Waterloo, Ont. N2L 3G1.

**van GINKEL, Blanche Lemco,** B.Arch., M.C.P., F.R.A.I.C., M.C.I.P., R.C.A.; architect; educator; b. London, Eng. 14 Dec. 1923; d. Myer and Claire Lemco; e. McGill Univ. B.Arch. 1945; Harvard Univ. M.C.P. 1950; m. 1956; children: Brenda Renée, Marc Ian; PARTNER, van GINKEL ASSOCIATES 1957– ; Prof. of Architecture, Univ. of Toronto 1977– (Dir., Sch. of Arch. there 1977–80, Dean of Arch. & Landscape Arch 1980–82); Pres. ACSA 1986–87; Mgr. City Planning Office Regina, Sask. 1946; Arch. Atelier Le Corbusier, Paris 1948; Asst. Prof. Univ. of Pa. 1951–57; Visiting Prof. Harvard 1958, Univ. de Montréal 1961–63 and 1969, McGill 1973–77; mem. Nat. Capital Planning Comte.; Planning Commission, Province of Québec; Adv. Council Sch. of Arch. Princeton Univ., G.S.D. Harvard, Univ. of Miami; recipient Lt. Gov.'s Medal 1945; Grand Prix for Film, Internat. Fed. of Housing & Planning 1956; Massey Medal for Arch. 1962; Candn. Arch. Award for Excellence 1972; Queen's Silver Jubilee Medal 1977; ACSA Distinguished Professor 1989; Citizenship Citation 1991; author various articles; Past Offr. Royal Architectural Inst. of Can.; Prov. Que. Assn. Archs.; Town Planning Inst. Can.; Corp. Urbanists Que.; Candn. Housing Design Council; Bd. Internat. Film Festivals Montreal; Pres., Assn. of Collegiate Schs. of Arch.; Office: 79 Woodlawn Ave. E., Toronto, Ont. M4T 1B9.

**van HERK, Aritha,** M.A.; writer; educator; b. Wetaskiwin, Alta. 26 May 1954; d. Willem and Maretje (van Dam) van H.; e. Univ. of Alta., B.A. 1976, M.A. 1978; m. Robert Sharp 14 Sept. 1974; PROF., DEPT. OF ENGLISH, UNIV. OF CALGARY 1991– , Asst. Prof. 1983–85, Assoc. Prof. 1985–91; author (novels): 'Judith' 1978; 'The Tent Peg' 1981; 'No Fixed Address' 1986; 'Places Far From Ellesmere' 1990; (criticism): 'In Visible Ink' 1991; 'A Frozen Tongue' 1992; editor: 'Alberta Rebound' 1990; 'Boundless Alberta' 1993; co-editor: 'West of Fiction' 1983; 'More Stories from Western Canada' 1980; Office: Calgary, Alta. T2N 1N4.

**VAN HOUTEN, Ronald,** M.A., Ph.D.; educator; b. Brooklyn, N.Y. 3 Aug. 1944; e. State Univ. of N.Y. Stony Brook B.A. 1968, Dalhousie Univ. M.A. 1969, Ph.D. 1972; m. Joy 21 Sep. 1986; children: Lisa, Jason, Courtney, Jonathan, Ashleigh, Andrew; PROF. OF PSYCHOL., MOUNT SAINT VINCENT UNIV. 1971– , Chrmn. of Psychol. 1979–82; Dir., Behavior Analysis Family Centre; Chrmn., Right to Effective Treatment Task Force, Assn. for Behavior Analysis; Pres., Internat. Assn. for the Right to Effective Treatment 1991– ; mem. N.S. Min.'s Ctte. Highway Safety 1981–82; Dir., N.S. Safety Council 1982–85; mem., Prov. Med. Adv. Ctte. Driver Licensing 1982– ; Premier's Task Force Against Drunk Driving 1984–87; Dir. Soc. for the Experimental Analysis of Behavior 1984–92; mem. Organizing Ctte., Prog. Subctte., and Chrmn. Papers Ctte. First Candn. Multidisciplinary Highway Safety Conf. 1982; mem., Sch. Psychol. Adv. Bd. 1981– ; mem., Univ. Subctte. Nat. Rsch. Council 1973–79; Consultative Assembly Social Sci. Rsch. Council Can. 1973–78; Social Sci. Fed. Can. 1977–78; author 'Learning Through Feedback' 1980; 'How to Motivate Others Through Feedback' 1980; 'How to Use Reprimands' 1980; 'The Correct Use of Sensory Irritant Aerosol Weapons' 1982; co-author 'Managing Behavior: Measuring Behavior' 1983; 'Training Guide for the Correct Use of Sensory Irritant Aerosol Weapons' 1982; 'Auto Control Plus' 1992; co-editor 'Behavior Analysis and Treatment' 1993; author or co-author numerous articles, book chapters, papers prof. jours.; Assoc. Ed., 'Journ. of Applied Behavior Analysis'; mem., various ed. bds.; recipient Nat. Rsch. Council Grant 1973–75; Can. Council Grant 1975–77, 1977–78, 1978–79, 1979–82; Social Sciences and Humanities Resch. Counc. Grant 1982–85, 1985–87, 1988–90, 1990–92; Prov. Govt. Safety Belt Study Grant 1979–80; Imperial Oil Grant 1981–82, 1982–84; Insurance Institute for Highway Safety Grant 1994; Alcoholic Beverage Medical Rsch. Found. Grant 1994–95; Pres. Law Enforcement Consultants 1980–87; Vice-Pres., Centre for Education and Rsch. in Safety; RCMP, Dept. Transport Contract 1981–82, 1982–83, 1985–86; Solicitor Gen.'s Crime Prevention Award 1984; Co-Chrmn. Psychol. Sect. Atlantic Provs. Ctte. on Sci's. 1978–82; mem., Assn. Behavior Analysis; Candn. Psychological Assn.; Home: 17 John Brenton Dr., Dartmouth, N.S. B2X 2V5; Office: Halifax, N.S. B3M 2J6.

**VAN HOUTEN, Stephen Harris,** B.A., LL.B., LL.M.; business executive; b. Toronto, Ont. 2 March 1951; s. William Henry and Doris Theresa (Webster) Van Houten; e. Univ. of W. Ont., B.A. 1974; Univ. of Ottawa, LL.B. 1977; Osgoode Hall Law Sch., LL.M. 1984; m. Mary E. d. Francis and Bette Brennan 22 Aug. 1975; children: Sarah, Graham, Owen; PRES., CANADIAN MANUFACTURERS' ASSOCIATION 1991– ; called to Ont. Bar 1979; solicitor, Ricketts, Jewell, Angus & Michael 1979–80; joined legal staff of General Motors of Canada 1980; Mgr., Bus. Planning 1984–87; Dir., Govt. Relations and Trade Policy 1987–88; Dir., Public Relations 1988; Pres., Automotive Parts Manufacturers' Assn. 1989–91; Dir., Traffic Injury Rsch. Found.; Manufacturing Rsch. Corp. of Ont.; Candn. Mfg. Tech. Source; Candn. Industry Program for Energy Conservation; Candn. Labour Market & Productivity Centre; Candn. Environmental Council; mem. Law Soc. of Upper Can.; Candn. Bar Assn.; Am. Bar Assn.; Osgoode Soc.; Internat. Trade Advisory Ctte.; Internat. Steering Ctte. on Intelligent Mfg. Systems; author 'Letters of Credit and Fraud,' Candn. Bar Rev. 1984; contbr. 'Current Issues in Canadian Business Law' 1986; recreations: fly-fishing, cross country skiing, golf, history, reading; Club: Lambton Golf & Country; Office: 75 International Blvd., 4th Floor, Toronto, Ont. M9W 6L9.

**VANÍČEK, Petr,** Ph.D., Dr.Sc.; educator; b. Sušice, Czechoslovakia 18 July 1935; s. Ivan and Irena (Blahovcová) V.; came to Can. Oct. 1969; e. Czech Technical Univ., Degree Geodetic Engr. 1959; Czechoslovak Acad. of Sciences, Ph.D. (Mathematical Physics) 1968; Dr.Sc. (Mathematical and Physical Sciences) 1993; children: Filip; Štěpán; Naninka; PROFESSOR, DEPT. OF GEODESY & GEOMATICS, UNIV. OF NEW BRUNSWICK 1976– ; Adjunct Prof., Univ. of Toronto (Survey Science, Physics, Civil Engrg.) 1983–89; Consultant and Instr., Dept. of Computer Science, Czech. Tech. Univ. 1963–67; Sr. Research Fellow & Sr. Scientific Offr., Tidal Inst., Liverpool, England 1967–69; Post-doctoral Fellow, Nat. Res. Counc. of Can. 1969–71; Assoc. Prof., Univ. of N.B. 1971–76; Prof., Univ. of Toronto 1981–83; Visiting Prof., Univ. of Paraná, Brazil Summers 1975, 1976, 1979, 1984, 1987; Sr. Visiting Scientist, U.S. National Acad. of Sciences, Nat. Geodetic Survey 1978; Visiting Prof., Univ. of Saõ Paolo, Brazil Summer 1981, 88; Visiting Prof., Univ. of Stuttgart, Germany Summers 1981, 82; Visiting Scientist, Royal Inst. of Technology, Stockholm, summer 1986; CSIR Rsch. Fellow, South Africa, summer 1986; co-author: 'Basic Programming for Ural 1' 1964; 'Programming for Ural 2' 1965; 'Geodesy: The Concepts' 1982, 2nd ed. 1986; 'Guide to GPS Positioning' 1986; editor: 'Proceedings of International Symposium on Problems Related to the Redefinition of North American Geodetic Networks' 1974, 'Proceedings of 1975 CGU Symposium of Satellite Geodesy and Geodynamics'; 'Geoid and Its Geophysical Interpretations' 1993; co-editor: 'Slow Deformation and Transmission of Stress in the Earth' 1989; author over 270 articles, conference papers, reviews, etc.; recipient Humboldt Foundation Distinguished Senior Scientist Award (Germany) 1990; Fellow, Geological Assn. of Can.; Amer. Geophysical Union; mem., Candn. Inst. of Surveying; Candn. Geophysical Union (Past Pres.); Prof. Engrs. of N.B.; Editor-in-Chief, 'Manuscripta Geodaetica'; Vice-Pres., IUGG Commn. on Recent Crustal Movements; mem. of Extve., Geoid Comn. of IAG; Czech. Soc. for Arts & Sciences; Sigma Xi; Conservative; recreations: sports, bridge, travel, classical music, photography, carpentry; Club: Explorers (Fellow); Home: 667 Golf Club Rd., Fredericton, N.B. E3B 4X4; Offices: Dept. of Geodesy & Geomatics Engineering, Univ. of N.B., Fredericton, N.B. E3B 5A3.

**VANIER, Jacques,** M.Sc., Ph.D., F.A.P.S., F.I.E.E.E., F.R.S.C.; scientist; b. Dorion, Qué. 4 Jan. 1934; s. Henri and Emma (Boileau) V.; e. Coll. Bourget Rigaud, Qué. B.A. 1955; Univ. de Montréal B.Sc. 1958; McGill Univ. M.Sc. 1960, Ph.D. 1963; m. Lucie d. Médéric and Blanche Beaudet 8 July 1961; children: Lyne, Pierre; Lectr. McGill Univ. 1961–63, Univ. de Montréal 1962–63; Eng. Varian Associates Beverly, Mass. 1963–67, Hewlett-Packard 1967; Prof. of Elect. Eng. Univ. Laval 1967–83; Prin. Rsch. Offr. Nat. Rsch. Council 1983–85, Head Elect. & Time Standards 1985–87, Dir. lab. for Basic Standards 1986–90; Dir., Gen. Inst. for Nat. Meas. Standards, Nat. Rsch. Council Can. 1990–93; Cons. Communication Comp. Corp. Costa Mesa, Ca. 1974–76, EG & G Salem, Mass. 1979–82; Chrmn. CNO Study Group 7 Comité consultatif internat. radio communications 1985–90; Chrmn. Comn. A Union radio scientifique internat. 1990–93; Visiting Sci. Univ. de Paris, Nat. Bureau of Standards USA 1974–75, 1981–82; Instituto Electrotecnico Nationale Torino, Italy 1974–75; mem. Comn. de la Recherche Qué. 1982–85; various grant cttes.; Initiator and Co-founder series internat. confs. 'Symposium on Frequency Standards and Metrology'; Mem. Admin. Ctte., Inst. of Electrical & Electronics Engineers (IEEE) and Instrumentation & Measurement Soc. 1986–93; Chrmn. 1990 Conf. Precision Electromagnetic Measurements Ottawa; Chrmn. Extve. Ctte. Precision Electromagnetic Measurements 1990– ; mem., Comité Internat. des Poids et Mesures 1992– ; author: 'Basic Theory of Lasers and Masers' 1971; co-author 'The Quantum Physics of Atomic Frequency Standards' 1989; over 90 sci. articles; Fellow, Royal Society of Canada 1989; Inst. Elect. & Electronic Engs. Fellow 1983, Centennial Medal 1984; Mem., Candn. Assn. Physicists 1970; Fellow, Am. Phys. Soc. 1989; recreations: skiing, boating, painting, reading, music; Club: Candn. Power & Sails Squadrons; Home and Office: 6149 Rivermill Cres., Orléans, Ont. K1C 5N3.

**VAN IERSSEL, Harry,** B.A. (Econ.), C.A.; administrator; b. Breda, The Netherlands 25 July 1936; s. Harry Cornelis and Josephina Constanza Van I.; e. Holy Heart Pub. Sch., Breda, Holland, 1948; Gymnasium B, Canisius Coll., Nymegen, Holland, 1954; Sch. of Econ., Tilburg, Holland, B.A. (Econ.) 1958; C.A. (Ont.) 1963; children: Marcus, Jacqueline; m. Linda Speth; Vice President, Finance & Secretary-Treasurer, Univ. of Toronto Press Incorporated 1992–93; Financial Adm. 1967–79; Asst. Director Finance and Gen. Mgr., Downsview Div. 1979–89; Interim Dir., 1989–90; Asst. Director Finance 1990–92; joined Deloitte Haskins & Sells as student-in-accts. Toronto, 1958, trans. to Montreal office 1963 and apptd. Supvr.; Asst. Comptroller, Associated Textiles Ltd., Montreal 1965; joined Clairtone Sound Ltd. to set up accounting system, Stellarton, N.S., 1966, trans. Toronto as Asst. to Vice Pres. Finance and apptd. to Group Comptroller of various Clairtone Co.'s 1967; Treas. (1975–76) Am. Univ. Press Services Inc. and Assn. of Am. Univ. Presses; Treasurer, Assn. of Candn. Publishers, 1978–82; co-author, 'Publishing: The Creative Business' 1974; Chrmn., Stat. Comte., Assn. Am. Univ. Presses 1971–73 (mem. Stats. Comte. 1974–80); mem. Journals Comm. 1979–81; Treas., Candn. Book and Periodical Counc. 1985–93; Treas., Candn. Telebook Agency 1986–88; Chrmn., Business Reports Comte., Assn. Am. Univ. Presses 1986–93; Treas., Assoc. for Export of Candn. Books 1990–93;

Treas., Assn. of Candn. Univ. Presses 1992– ; Home: 14 Tranby Ave., Toronto, Ont. M5R 1N5.

**VANKOUGHNETT, Allan LeRoy (Roy),** B.E.Sc., M.A.Sc., Ph.D.; b. London, Ont. 7 Nov. 1941; s. Roy Bertram and Vera Loreen (Abbott) V.; e. Univ. of West. Ont. B.E.Sc. 1963; Univ. of Toronto M.A.Sc. 1964, Ph.D. 1967; m. Carol Anne; d. Carl and Mary Little 18 July 1964; children: Carl Andrew, Kimberly Ann; DIR. GENERAL, INSTITUTE FOR NATIONAL MEASUREMENT STANDARDS, NATIONAL RESEARCH COUNCIL CANADA 1993– ; Rsch. Offr., NRC Div. of Electrical Engr. 1968–73; Mgr., Microelect. Lab., Communications Technol. Satellite Project; Commun. Rsch. Ctr., Dept. of Commun. 1973–77; Mgr., Surveillance Satellite project, Can. Ctr. for Remote Sensing 1977–80; Assoc. Dir., NRC Can. Ctr. for Space Sci. 1980–86; Dir., Space Rsch. Opns., NRC Space Div. 1986–90; NRC Science Affairs Off. 1990–91; NRC Inst. for Microstructural Sciences 1991–92; Assn. of Profl. Engrs. of Ont. Gold Medal Award 1963; recreations: men's hockey; Home: 58 Centrepark Dr., Gloucester, Ont. K1B 3C1; Office: Ottawa, Ont. K1A 0R6.

**VAN LAARE, Fred Kenneth,** B.Comm.; retail executive; b. Vancouver, B.C. 14 Feb. 1941; s. John and Nellie Tena (Kool) V.; e. Univ. of B.C., B.Comm. 1965; m. Evelyn d. Charles and Sadie Timestra 22 Aug. 1964; children: Bradley John, Brent Kenneth, Darrell Lee; SR. EXTVE. VICE-PRES., OPNS. (TORONTO), SHOPPERS DRUG MART 1987– ; Sears 1965–67; Personnel Co-ord., Cunninghams Drug Stores 1967; Dir. of Opns. (Vancouver), Shoppers Drug Mart 1971; (Prairies) 1976; Vice-Pres., Opns. (Prairies) 1978; Extve. Vice-Pres. (Florida) 1982; Extve. Vice-Pres., Oper. Serv. (Toronto) 1985; Trustee, Bethesda Hosp. (Colorado); Dir., Holland Christian Homes; recreations: boating, travel, reading; Home: 87 Torran Rd., Woodbridge, Ont.; Office: 225 Yorkland Blvd., Willowdale, Ont. M2J 2Y7.

**VAN NEST, Norman Gary,** B.Comm.; b. Windsor, Ont. 22 July 1936; s. William Norman and Elmira Van N.; e. Patterson Coll., Windsor, Ont.; Univ. of Windsor, B.Comm.; PRESIDENT, CHIEF EXTVE. OFFR. & DIRECTOR, LANDMARK CORPORATION; Offr. & Dir., Aquarius Coatings Inc.; Conserve Energy Corporation; LMK Energy Inc.; Parvus Mines Ltd.; Southwestern Water Exploration Co.; Dir., D.A.C. Davis Investment Counsel Inc.; Hospice Calgary Soc.; Noble China Inc.; Salesman, Royal Securities, Montreal 1957–67; Dir., Widener and Partners, Toronto 1967–72; Pres. & Dir. 1972–74; Chrmn. 1974; Consultant 1975; Pres. & Chief Extve. Offr., Triarchy Corporation Ltd., Toronto 1975–80; Pres. & Dir., Heritage Securities Corp., Toronto 1980–83; Chrmn. & Pres., Pathfinder Financial Corporation, Toronto 1983–86; Pres. & Dir., Bridgebank Capital Corporation (now Aquarius Coatings Inc.) 1986–90; Chrmn. & Dir. 1990–92; recreations: golf, squash, tennis, skiing; Clubs: Bow Valley Club, Calgary; Calgary Petroleum; Cambridge, Toronto; Earl Grey, Calgary; Glenmore, Calgary; Lambton Golf & Country, Toronto; National, Toronto; St. Jame's, Montreal; Home: 2918 Champlain St. S.W., Calgary, Alta. T2T 3J6.

**VAN OYEN, Gerry,** B.Sc., M.B.A.; retired chemical industry executive; b. Amsterdam, Holland 2 Nov. 1932; s. Gerrit and Lysbeth (Van de Klundert) V.; e. Sir George Williams (Concordia) Univ. B.Sc. 1958; Univ. of Toronto M.B.A. 1978; m. Mariene A. d. Henk and Marie Elzinga 15 Oct. 1955; children: Audrey Rowena, Karen Astrid, Bryan Fitzgerald; Chief Chemist, Technical Director, Shareholder & President, Halltech Inc. 1969–93, Retired; Production Manager, Nacan 1956–60; Polymer R&D Chemist & Manager, Technical Serv. Dept., Polyresins (Div. of Bate Chemical) 1960–69; Chair & Dir., Polycol Ltée.; Dir., Halltech Inc.; Consultant in Canada and Switzerland 1970s; Mem., A.P.E.O.; Royal Ont. Museum; recreations: cottage, travel, gardening; Home: 10 Longhope Place, Willowdale, Ont. M2J 1Y2.

**VAN PARYS, Frederick Charles;** business executive; b. Simcoe, Ont. 1941; s. Herman and Jean Van P.; e. Ryerson Poly. Univ. (Bus. Admin.) 1962; m. Constance Jane 1962; children: Frederick Drew, Garner Todd; Pres. & C.E.O., Saskatchewan Telecommunications Ltd. (Sasktel) 1993–94; formerly Pres. & C.E.O., Granada Canada Ltd. 1989–91, Laura Secord Inc. 1983–89, U.C.S. Group 1976–82; Dir., ISM Canada, Stentor Canada, SRCI Canada, Alouette Communications, Telesat Canada, Human Resources Professionals of Ont., Candn. Council for Aboriginal Business; Clubs: Boulevard (Toronto); Bayview C.C. (Toronto); Wascana C.C. (Regina); Assiniboia Club (Regina); Home: 5144 Wascana Vista, Regina, Sask. S4V 2S3.

**VAN RJNDT, Philippe,** B.A., M.A.; novelist; b. Montreal, Que. 12 July 1950; e. McGill Univ. B.A. 1971, M.A. 1973; author 'The Tetramachus Collection' 1976; 'Blueprint' 1977; 'The Trial of Adolf Hitler' 1978; 'Samaritan' 1983; 'Last Message to Berlin' 1984; 'Eclipse' 1986; recreation: scuba diving.

**VANSANT, Richard Douglas,** B.A., M.A.; retail executive; b. Ogdensburg, N.Y. 18 June 1949; s. Merton Lee and Ava Natalie (Burt) V.; e. Gov. H.S. (Regents Hon. dipl.; Nat. Merit Scholar); Colgate Univ., B.A. (Hons.) 1971; St. Lawrence Univ., M.A. 1975; m. Joan d. Douglas and Janet (Moore) Kallmeyer 24 Nov. 1984; one s.: Adam Zachary; PRES. & FOUNDER, MONEYSWORTH & BEST QUALITY SHOE REPAIR 1984– ; Dir., Edn. Comm., St. Law Co. Bd. of Edn. 1971–74; Nabisco Brands 1974–77; Vice-Pres., G.M. Dovers Ltd. 1977–79; Foodex Inc. 1979–81; Pres., Opportunities Can. 1981–84; Co-founder, Firehall Restaurant 1978; Scives Inc. 1972; Mem., Young Presidents Organization 1993– ; Planning Ctte., Retail Counc. of Can. 1987–88; Candn. Franchise Assn., Bd. of Dir. 1989–92; Chrmn., Program Ctte. 1989–90; Extve. Ctte. 1990–92; Treas. 1990–92; Republican Abroad (Chrmn. 1982 campaign); Un. Ch. of Can.; Un. Fund of St. Law Co. (Publicity Chrmn.); recreations: skiing, tennis, sailing; Club: Royal Candn. Yacht Club; Office: 10 – 80 Galaxy Blvd., Rexdale, Ont. M9W 4Y8.

**Van SCHAIK, Gerard,** M.Sc., M.A., P.Eng.; executive; b. Eindhoven, Holland 17 Nov. 1930; s. John A. and (Sophia Kraan) Van S.; e. Carnegie Inst. of Technol., B.Sc. (Mech. Engn.) 1957; Ecole Polytechnique, M.Sc. 1959; McGill Univ., Dipl. in Mang. 1964; Univ. of Sherbrooke, M.A. (Econ.) 1967; m. Henriette C.H. d. the late Gerard Veldhuis, Groningen, Holland 4 Apl. 1959; children: André Louis, Clare Frances; PRESIDENT & CHIEF EXTVE. OFFR., TIDECO INDUSTRIES (Langley, B.C.) since 1986; Past President, Beloit Canada Ltee/Ltd. 1974–78; Asst. Gen. Mgr., Velan Engineering, Montreal 1960; Vice Pres. of Mfg., B. K. Johl 1963; Production Mgr., Canadian Ingersoll-Rand 1965; Plant Mgr., Canadian Allis Chalmers 1966–69; self employed mang. consultant, Vancouver 1970–74; mem. Assn. of Prof. Engrs. of Ont. & B.C.; Am. Soc. Mech. Engrs.; R. Catholic; recreations: reading, photography; jogging; Home: 676 Linton St., Coquitlam, B.C. V3J 6K3; Office: 20151 Logan Ave., Langley, B.C. V3A 4L5.

**VAN SETERS, Arthur,** B.A., B.D., Th.M., Th.D.; principal; professor; b. Bronte, Ont. 26 March 1934; s. Hugo and Anna (Hubert) V.; e. Univ. of Toronto B.A. 1958; Westminster Theol. Sem. B.D. 1961; Union Theol. Sem. Th.M. 1962, Th.D. 1965; m. Rowena d. Winnifred and Arthur Elliott; PRINCIPAL & PROF. OF BIBLICAL INTERPRETATION AND PREACHING, KNOX COLLEGE, TORONTO 1993– ; Asst. Min., Knox Presbyn. Ch. 1961–62; Min. of the pastoral charge of Port Elgin, Sackville & Dorchester, N.B. 1965–68; Min., St. Andrew's Presbyn. Ch. (St. Lambert, Que.) 1968–74; Instr., Old Testament, Fac. of Rel. Studies, McGill Univ. 1976–83; Principal & Prof. of Biblical Interpretation and Preaching, Vancouver School of Theology 1983–93; Extve. Dir., The Montreal Inst. for Ministry 1974–83; Teacher of Preaching 1973–83; Bd. Mem., Ecumenical Ctr. for Stewardship Studies 1979–83 (Chair, Prog. Ctte.); Mem., Soc. for the Advancement of Cont. Edn. (3 yrs.); Acad. of Homiletics 1978– ; Comn. on Accrediting the Assn. of Theol. Schs. 1984–90; Cons., Internat. Globalization of Theological Education Project 1988–94; author of numerous journal articles; ed. & contbr.: 'Preaching as a Social Act' Feb. 1988; recreations: wood and stone carving, reading, gardening; Home: c/o Knox College, 59 St. George St., Toronto, Ont. M5S 2E6.

**VANSTONE, Scott Alexander,** B.M., M.M., Ph.D.; university professor; b. Chatham, Ont. 14 Sept. 1947; s. Gordon Lyle and Margaret Lillian (Alliston) V.; e. Univ. of Waterloo, B.M. 1970, M.M. 1971, Ph.D. 1974; m. Linda d. Thomas and Bernice Gall 16 May 1970; one d.: Andrea Lynn; PROF. OF MATHEMATICS, ST. JEROMES COLL., UNIV. OF WATERLOO 1985– ; Asst. Prof. of Math., St. Jerome's Coll., Univ. of Waterloo 1974; Assoc. Prof. 1981; Prof. 1985; Dir., Cryptech Systems Inc.; Editor in Chief: 'Ars Combinatoria' 1976– ; Home: 333 Auburn Dr., Waterloo, Ont.; Office: Math and Computer Bldg., Rm. 6056, 200 Univ. Ave. W., Waterloo, Ont. N2L 3G1.

**VANT, The Hon. T. Neil,** M.L.A., B.A., M.Div.; politician; b. Nelson, B.C. 11 July 1944; s. Thomas Edgerton and Helen Isabel (Simpson) V.; e. Quesnel H.S. 1962; B.C. Vocational Sch. 1964; Univ. of B.C., B.A. 1972; Vanc. Sch. of Theol., M.Div. 1975; m. Jeanie d. Ralph and Jean Panrucker 25 July 1970; children: Pamela, Timothy; Min. of Transportation & Highways, Prov. of B.C. 1988–89; elected M.L.A. for Cariboo 1986–91; Canon, Ang. Cath. & Diocese of Cariboo 1982– ; Last Resident Anglican Vicar of Barkerville 1974; Vicar, St. Timothy's Ang. Mission 100 Mile House, B.C. 1975–84; Extve. Sec., Diocese of Cariboo 1976–86; Rector, St. Peter's Ang. Ch., Williams Lake, B.C. 1984–86; prospecting & mineral explor. 1966– ; constr. of new pulp mills & oil refineries throughout B.C. 1965–74; Noranda Mines, Boss Mountain Molydenum Mine start-up 1964–65; Pres., Vant Explor. 1966– ; Dir. & Corp. Sec., Triple Creek Resources Ltd. 1983–88; 60th Anniv. Royal Candn. Legion Medal; B.C. Comnr. of Human Rights 1978–81; Chrmn., 100 Mile Dist. Gen. Hosp. Bd. 1980–84; Chrmn., Western Transportation Adv. Council (WESTAC) 1989; Wor. Master, Mt. Begbie Lodge No. 183 A.F. & A.M. of B.C. 1985–86; Grand Chaplain 1979, 1983; Mem., Rocky Mountain Rangers, R.C.A.C. 1958–61, 1975–83 (Chaplain); Captain 31st B.C.H. (Cariboo Regt.) 1985– ; recreations: square dancing, hunting, canoeing; Clubs: Williams Lake C. of C.; Home: P.O. Box 561, 150 Mile House, B.C. V0K 2G0; Office: P.O. Box 8, Barkerville, B.C. V0K 1B0.

**VAN TIGHEM, Clarence Joseph,** B.Com.; retired diplomat; b. Strathmore, Alta. 12 March 1921; s. Joseph L. and Jane (Kelly) Van T.; e. Queen's Univ.; Univ. of Manitoba, B.Com. 1942; m. Noëlle Mary, d. late George Frederick Waters, 23 April 1949; children: Paul Gregory, Mark David, John Michael; joined Fed. Dept. Trade and Comm. 1945; Comm. Secy., Candn. Embassy, Lima, Peru 1945; Consul and Trade Commr., Sao Paulo, Brazil 1949; Comm. Secy., Rio de Janeiro, Brazil 1954; Comm. Counsellor, Mexico City, Mexico 1956; Dir., Trade Publicity Br., Dept. Trade and Comm., Ottawa 1959; Comm. Counsellor, Vienna, Austria 1962; Depy. Consul. Gen. (Comm.) New York 1964; Min. Comm., Candn. High Comn., London, Eng. 1969; Ambassador to Venezuela and concurrently to Dominican Republic 1972; Consul General, Milan, Italy, 1975; Chief of Protocol, Department of Industry, Trade and Commerce, 1981; Special Adviser for Trade Promotion Activities, Public Affairs Branch, Dept. of External Affairs, 1982; Depy. Coordinator, Davos Task Force, Dept. of External Affairs, 1983; served in R.C.N.V.R., Lt. 1942–45; recipient Coronation Medal 1953; Centennial Medal 1967; R. Catholic; recreation: golf; Home: 172 Rodney Cres., Ottawa, Ont. K1H 5J9.

**VAN VLIET, Maurice Lewis,** O.C., M.S., Ed.D., LL.D.; educator; b. Bellingham, Wash., 3 Aug. 1913; s. Frank Davis and Nellie (Booker) V.; e. Univ. of Ore., B.S. 1936, M.S. 1939; Univ. of Cal., Los Angeles, Ed.D. 1950; Univ. of W. Ont., LL.D. 1973; Univ. of Windsor, LL.D. 1978; Univ. of Alta., LL.D. 1979; Dalhousie Univ., LL.D. 1979; Queen's Univ., LL.D. 1980; Univ. of Victoria, Ed.D. 1982; m. Virginia, d. Capt. William Peace Gaddis, Cal., 9 Sept. 1936; children: Maury, Victoria, Pieter, Katharine; HONORARY PROFESSOR, UNIV. OF VICTORIA 1986; Dir. of Phys. Educ., Univ. of B.C. 1936–45 and Univ. of Alta. 1945–62; Dean, Fac. of Physical Educ., Univ. of Alberta 1962–78; served with Candn. Reserve Forces; rank Maj. on retirement; rec'd Centennial Award 1967; Premier's award for Excellence 1978; Edmonton's 75th Anniversary Award; Cert. of Meritorious Service, City of Edmonton; Candn. Parks & Recreation Assn. Honor Award; Fed. Scholarship for Advanced Study; Nat. Fitness & Amateur Sport Travel Fellowship; Alumnus of the Yr. (1967), Citrus Coll., Cal.; mem. Edmonton Sportsmen Hall of Fame; mem. Univ. of Alberta 'Wall of Fame,' Univ. of Alberta Alumni Golden Jubilee Award 1985; Univ. of B.C. Sports Hall of Fame; 125th Anniversary of the Confederation of Canada Medal, 1992; author 'Physical Education for Junior and High Schools' 1956; co-author 'Physical Education and Recreation in Europe' 1963; 'Physical Education Activities for Secondary Schools' 1967; ed. 'Physical Education in Canada' 1965; Pres., XI Commonwealth Games; Bd. mem., Digital Equipment of Canada; Past Chrmn., Alta. Prov. Recreation Bd.; Fellow, Am. Coll. Sports Med.; Past Pres., B.C. Phys. Educ. Assn.; Alta. Assn. Health, Phys. Educ. & Recreation; W. Candn. Intercoll. Athletic Assn.; Alta. Paraplegic Assn.; Candn. Intercoll. Athletic Union; Candn. Assn. Health, Phys. Educ. & Recreation (Honor Award, Hon. Pres.); Alta. Recreation Assn.; Chrmn., Candn. Wheelchair Sports Assn.; mem., Candn. Assn. Sports Sciences; Am. Assn. Health, Phys. Educ. & Recreation; Nat. Coll. Phys. Assn. Men.; Pres. (1974–75), Candn. Council Univ. Phys. Educ. Adms.; B.C. Sports Hall of Fame, 1981; Kappa Sigma; Protestant; recreations: golf, swimming, tennis; Club: Edmonton Centre (Founding Chrmn.); Rotary; Round Table Club of Victoria; Home: 1035 Belmont Ave., Apt. 701, Victoria, B.C. V8S 3T5.

**VARDEY, Lucinda Mary;** literary agent/writer/reviewer; b. London, England 1 April 1949; d. Lewis George and Edwina Mary (Hollingshead) V.; e. Merrow Grange Grammar Sch.; Guildford Tech. Coll.; Trinity Coll. of Mus.; PRES., LUCINDA VARDEY AGENCY LTD. 1977– ; Partner, Vardey & Brunton Assoc. (U.K.) 1985– ; Partner, Hickson Vardey & Brunton (Australia) 1990– ; Ed. Asst., Secker & Warburg Pub. 1967–68; Music Pub. Asst., Oxford Univ. Press 1968–69; Extve. Asst., Pallas Gall. of Fine Prints 1969–70; Promotion Mgr., Collins Pubs. 1970–77; Office: 297 Seaton St., Toronto, Ont. M5A 2T6.

**VARI, George W.,** P.C., O.C., C.L.H., Ph.D., Eng., LL.D. (Hon.); b. Hungary 14 Aug. 1923; s. Steven and Ida (Grang) V.; e. Lausanne 1940; Univ. of Szeged 1945; Univ. of Joseph Nador Budapest 1948; m. Helen de Fabinyi 1967; left Hungary as refugee and immigrated to Canada 1957; estab. Vari Construction 1959; participated in Expo '67, Metropolitan Blvd., Urban Devel. Project in Montreal; built Montparnasse Tower in Paris; developed internat. activities in real estate on 4 continents (Moscow, Paris, Africa, South America, Asia, etc.); Member of Her Majesty's, Elizabeth II, Privy Council for Canada; Order of Canada; recipient, Commemorative Medal for 125th Anniversary of Candn. Confederation; Knight of Legion of Honour of France; Doctor of Law Honoris Causa, York Univ.; Co-Chair, George and Helen Vari Foundation, and various other humanitarian organizations, associations and international companies; recreations: collector of arts, sports, walking, swimming; clubs: York; National; Cercle de l'Union des Interallies in France; Home: Toronto and Cobourg, Ont.; Office: 55 St. Clair Ave. W., Suite 100, Toronto, Ont. M4V 2Y7.

**VARLEY, Christopher John,** B.A.; art historian; curator; private art dealer; b. Vancouver, B.C. 19 Sept. 1950; s. Peter and Sarah Jane (Watt) V.; e. Simon Fraser Univ. B.A. 1972; m. Sandra d. David and Shirley Shaul 18 Apl. 1986; children: Emma, Robin (by previous marriage); Asst. Curator Vancouver Art Gallery 1974–77; Head Curator The Edmonton Art Gallery 1979–83; private art dealer specializing in hist. Candn. art and freelance curator since 1983; recipient Can. Council Travel Grant 1982; W. Can. Art Assn. Publs. Award 1984; mem. Rsch. & Ed. Ctte. Candn. Museums Assn. 1982–83; Hist. Resource Sub-ctte. Alta. Assn. Archs. 1982–83; Private Art Dealers Assn., New York 1992– ; author 'The Contemporary Arts Society: Montreal 1939–1948' 1980; 'F.H. Varley: A Centennial Exhibition' 1981; 'Winnipeg West: Painting and Sculpture in Western Canada 1945–1970' 1983; 'William Nicoll Cresswell' 1986; 'Aba Bayefsky Revisited' 1989; Mem., Curator's Circle (Art Gallery of Ont.); recreations: hiking, golf, art collecting; Address: 6 Kendal Ave., Toronto, Ont. M5R 1L6.

**VARNAI, George;** public servant; b. Budapest, Hungary 3 Sept. 1942; s. Andor and Helena (Kepes) V.; e. Baron Byng H.S.; Sir George Williams Univ.; m. Shelley d. Jack and Pearl Pascal 18 Dec. 1980; children: Sarah, Yiska, Avraham, Perl Leah, Miriam, Rochel, Levi, Rivka, Chaya; REGIONAL MANAGER, CITIZENSHIP & SETTLEMENT OPERATIONS B.C., CANADA EMPLOYMENT & IMMIGRATION 1976– ; joined Dept. 1968; Observant Jew (Chabad/Lubavitch); Dir., The Candn. Immigration Historical Soc.; mem., var. rel. & soc. orgns.; Home: 6411 Cambie St., Vancouver, B.C. V5Z 3B2; Office: P.O. Box 11145, 1055 W. Georgia St., Vancouver, B.C. V6E 2P8.

**VARSHNI, Yatendra Pal,** M.Sc., Ph.D., F.A.P.S., F.Inst.P., F.R.A.S.; educator; b. Allahabad, India 21 May 1932; s. Harpal; e. Univ. of Allahabad B.Sc. 1948, M.Sc. 1952, Ph.D. 1956; PROF. OF PHYSICS, UNIV. OF OTTAWA 1969– ; Asst. Prof. of Physics Univ. Allahabad 1955–60; Postdoctorate Fellow, Nat. Research Council, Ottawa 1960–62; Asst. Prof. present Univ. 1962, Assoc. Prof. 1965; recipient Ward-Vidyant Gold Medal 1952; Univ. Jubilee Silver Medal 1952; Candn. Assn. of Physicists Lectr. 1984–85; author numerous research publs. astrophysics, nuclear structure, molecular structure, solid-state physics; Fellow, Indian Physical Soc.; mem. Candn. Assn. Physicists; Candn. Astron. Soc.; Royal Astron. Soc. Can.; Am. Astron. Soc.; Astron. Soc. Pacific; Am. Assn. Physics Teachers; Am. Assn. Advanc. Science; European Physical Soc.; Assoc. Mem., Roy. Soc. of Chemistry (U.K.); Hindu; recreations: reading history of science, biographies; Home: Apt. 702, 333 Chapel St., Ottawa, Ont. K1N 8Y8; Office: 150 Louis Pasteur, Ottawa, Ont. K1N 6N5.

**VARTANIAN, Sona;** prima ballerina, choreographer, master teacher; b. Alexandria, Egypt 16 Jan. 1947; d. Bedros and Vartanouch (Shamlian) V.; e. State Ballet Academy of Erevan; m. Samuel Abramian 25 Nov. 1989; fondatrice et directrice de L'Academie de Ballet Vartanian 1982; fondatrice et directrice et 1ère danseuse de Ballet Classique de Montréal de Sona Vartanian 1987, Principal Dancer, State Opera House of Erevan (Armenian) 1964–73 (reportoire: Swan Lake, Odette Odile, Gisele, Romeo & Juliette, Don Quichotte, Nut Cracker); Les Grands Ballets Canadien (repertoire: all the classic and Balanchine Four Temperments Serenade, Alegro Brillante, Concerto Barocco, A. Dolin – Pas de quatre, MacDonald – Tam Di Delam, jeux de Cartes, Diabelli Variations); Cleveland Ballet; current repertoire of her company: L'autre Tango, Barcelona, Adieu, Symphonie, Dying Swan, Rossiniana, Priere, invitation to the Danse, avec Gagnon, etc.); Guest artist & teacher, Nat. Ballet of Portugal teacher, Tokyo Ballet, Tokyo City Ballet, Shishouaka Ballet, Cleveland Sch. of Ballet and others 1990; Dir. & Master Teacher, Acad. of Nevada Danse Theatre 1991; awards for ballet competitions for Soviet artists in the Soviet Union; Artistic Dir., Tekeyan Armenian Danse Group; future projects: Video for daily ballet classes for students and teachers and a book of ballet courses for ballet teachers; recreations: reading, opera, theatre; Home: 2196 René Lévesque Ouest, Montreal, Que.; Office: 486 St. Catherine St. W., Montreal, Que. H3B 1A6.

**VARUGHESE, Sugith,** B.A., M.F.A.; film writer, director, actor; b. Cochin, India 25 Apl. 1957; s. George and Susan (Zachariah) V.; e. Evan Hardy Coll. Inst. Saskatoon 1974; Univ. of Minn. B.A. 1978; York Univ. M.F.A. 1981; TV screenwriter since 1979; progs. incl. 'The Phoenix Team', 'Fraggle Rock', 'Mount Royal', 'Best of Both Worlds'; film writer/dir. since 1981; films incl. 'The Crush', 'Kumar and Mr. Jones'; 'Mela's Lunch'; 'Salutin'; film, TV and radio actor since 1982 incl. 'Blindside', 'Inside Stories', 'Night Heat'; recipient Gov. Gen.'s Medal 1974; York Trillium Award Most Promising Writer TV 1989; ACTRA Award nominations Best Writer (Fraggle Rock), Best Writer, Actor, Prog. (Best of Both Worlds); Dir., Candn. Film Centre 1990–91; mem. Writers' Guild of Canada; mem. ACTRA Performers Guild; mem. Acad. Candn. Cinema & TV; mem. Metro Central YMCA; recreations: golf, squash, karate; Home: 806, 123 Scadding Ave., Toronto, Ont. M5A 4J3.

**VAS, Stephen I.,** M.D., Ph.D.; physician; university professor; b. Budapest, Hungary 4 June 1926; came to Can. 1957; s. Gyula and Ilona (Rosenberg) V.; e. Univ. of Budapest M.D. 1950, Ph.D. 1956; m. Magdalene d. Stephen Raditz 25 April 1953; PHYSICIAN, TORONTO WESTERN HOSP.; PROF., UNIV. OF TORONTO; author of over 60 scientific articles; Home: 46 King Georges Rd., Etobicoke, ON M8X 1L5; Office: 399 Bathurst St., Toronto, ON M5T 2S8.

**VASSANJI, Moyez G.,** B.S., Ph.D.; writer; b. Nairobi, Kenya 30 May 1950; s. Gulamhussein Vassanji and Daulatkhanu Mitha (Manji) Nanji; e. H.H. The Aga Khan Boys' Sch. Dar es Salaam, Tanzania 1969; Mass. Inst. Technol. B.S. 1974; Univ. of Pa. Ph.D. 1978; m. Nurjehan d. Abualy and Taj-Bibi Aziz 14 July 1979; children: Anil, Kabir; Rsch. Fellow Chalk River Nuclear Lab. 1979–80; Rsch. Assoc. and Lectr. Univ. of Toronto 1980–89; ed. Tsar Publications (part-time) 1981– ; full-time writer 1989– ; Internat. Visiting Writer Univ. of Iowa 1989; recipient Commonwealth First Novel Award Africa Region 1990; author (fiction) 'The Gunny Sack' 1989; 'No New Land' 1991; 'Uhuru Street' 1991 (UK) 1992 (Canada); 'The Book of Secrets' 1994 (Canada); Sigma Xi; Home: 39 Woburn Ave., Toronto, Ont. M5M 1K5; Office: P.O. Box 6996 Stn. A, Toronto, Ont. M5W 1X7.

**VAUGHAN, J. Bryan,** C.M.; communications counsel; b. Toronto, Ont. 19 June 1914; s. Joseph McCarthy and Margaret (Stewart) V.; m. Dorothy (dec.) d. Harold and Evelyn Truax 20 Nov. 1937; children: Michael B., Seanna Ross, J. Joseph, Alan T., Steven M. (dec.), Julie Sharpe, Timmi; CHRMN., J. BRYAN VAUGHAN ASSOC. INC.; Chrmn. Vaughan Ventures; served 'Toronto Star' Copy Boy to City Ed.; Depy. Dir., Information Wartime Prices & Trade Bd.; Dir., Rsch. and Promotion Merchandising Publs. Maclean-Hunter; Cofounder to Chrmn. emeritus, Public & Industrial Relations Ltd.; Mng. Dir. to Chrmn. Emeritus Vickers & Benson Ltd.; Trustee Emeritus, Sunnybrook Med. Centre; Hon. Trustee, Princess Margaret Hosp. Ont. Cancer Inst.; Hon. Ch., Candn. Geriatrics Rsch. Soc.; Nat. Advertising Benevolent Soc.; Awards: mem., Order of Can.; Gold Medal, Assn. Candn. Advertisers; Lamp of Service, Candn. Pub. Relations Soc.; Good Servant, Candn. Council Christians & Jews; United Church; Liberal; recreations: family, canoeing, writing; Clubs: Primrose; Ontario; Arts & Letters; Muskoka Lakes Golf & Country; Address: 71 Clarendon Ave., Toronto, Ont. M4V 1J2.

**VAUX, Robert G.,** B.Comm., C.A.; financial executive; b. Montreal 14 Oct. 1948; m. Diana; VICE-PRESIDENT, DOMTAR INC.; Mgr., Contract Div., Amseco 5 yrs.; Corp. Controller, Ivaco Inc. 5 yrs.; Treas. & Controller, John Labatt Limited 2 yrs.; Vice-Pres., Finance, Labatt Brewing Co. 3 yrs.; Extve. Vice-Pres., Ault Foods 1 yr.; Vice-Pres., Finance, John Labatt Limited 3 years; Dir., Allelix Crop Technologies; Canada Malting Co. Limited; Mico Investments; Home: 105 Charleswood, Hudson Heights, Que. J0P 1J0; Office: 395 de Maisonneuve Blvd. W., Montreal, Que. H3A 1L6.

**VAYDA, Eugene,** B.S., M.D., F.R.C.P.(C), F.A.C.P., F.A.C.P.M., F.A.P.H.A.; educator; b. Cleveland, Ohio 1 Aug. 1925; s. Sol Aren and Sophie (Berman) V.; e. Case Western Reserve Univ. B.S. 1948, M.D. 1951; m. Elaine Ruth d. Philip E. Jacobs, Cleveland, Ohio 18 June 1949; children: Joseph Marc, Paul Andrew; DIRECTOR OF EVALUATION, ONTARIO BREAST SCREENING PROGRAM, ONTARIO CANCER TREATMENT AND RESEARCH FOUNDATION; EMERITUS PROF. OF HEALTH ADMIN. AND MED., UNIV. OF TORONTO since 1991 (and Assoc. Dean, Community Health 1981–88); Intern, Resident and Teaching Fellow Dept. Med. Univ. Hosps. Cleveland 1951–55; Boston Veteran's Hosp. 1953–54; private practice Internal Med. Cleveland 1955–64; Med. Dir. Community Health Foundation Cleveland 1964–69, concurrently Asst. Prof. Depts. Internal Med. and Preventive Med. Case Western Reserve Univ.; Visiting Fellow, Epidemiol. and Pub. Health Yale Univ. 1969–70; Assoc. Prof. and Prof. Depts. Clin. Epidemiol. and Biostats. & Med. McMaster Univ. 1970–76; Prof. and Chrmn. Dept. of Health Admin. Univ. of Toronto 1976–81; rec'd Faculty Fellowship Award Milbank Mem. Fund 1966–73; served with US Army 1944–46; Home: 407 Walmer Rd., Apt. 502, Toronto Ont. M5R 3N2; Office: University of Toronto, McMurrich Bldg., Toronto, Ont. M5S 1A8.

**VEILLEUX, Gérard,** B.Comm., M.Pub.Admin., D.U.; broadcasting executive; b. East Broughton, Que. 8 May 1942; e. Laval Univ., B.Comm. 1963; Carleton Univ., M.Pub.Admin. 1968; m. Céline Bisson; one d. Elaine; SENIOR VISITING FELLOW, HARVARD BUSINESS SCHOOL 1994– ; Bd. of Dirs., Industrial-Alliance Insurance Co.; Manitoba Dept. of Finan. 1963–65; Fed. Dept. of Finan. 1966–70; Dir. Gen., Fed.-Prov. Relns., Que. Dept. of Intergovt. Affairs 1970–71; Asst. Sec. (Cabinet Cttes.), Treasury Bd. Sec. (fed. govt.) 1971–72; Dept. of Finan. 1973–76; Asst. Depy. Min., Dept. of Nat. Health & Welfare 1976–77; Dir. Gen., Tax Policy & Fed.-Prov. Relns. Br., Dept. of Finan. 1977–79; Asst. Depy. Min., Fed.-Prov. Relns. & Social Policy 1979–80; seconded to Privy Council 1980–82; Assoc. Depy. Min., Min. of State for Econ. Devel. 1982; Sec. to the Cabinet, Fed.-Prov. Relns. & Depy. Clerk, Privy Counc. 1982–86; Sec., Treasury Bd. 1986–89; active in a number of govt., profl. & cultural orgns; Bd. of Dir., Can. Mortgage & Housing Corp. 1980–85; Bd., Fed. Bus. Devel. Bank 1983–86; Inst. for Rsch. on Public Policy 1987–89; Pres. & C.E.O., Candn. Broadcasting Corp. 1989–93; Sr. Visiting Fellow, Candn. Centre for Management Development (CCMD) Nov. 1993–Mar. 1994; scholarships: Candn. John's Manville 1960; Royal Trust 1961; Mem., Banff Sch. of Mngt.; Roman Catholic; author: 'Les relations intergouvernementales au Canada, 1867–1967' 1971; rec'd., honorary doctorate degree (Administration), Univ. of Ottawa 1990, D.U., honoris causa 1990; awarded Outstanding Achievement Award, the highest award in the Public Service of Canada; awarded Prix Hermès, Faculty of Admin., Laval Univ. 1991; Address: 1321 Sherbrooke St. Ouest, #F-101, Montréal, Qué. H3G 1J4.

**VEITCH, Edward,** M.A., LL.B.; educator; b. Markinch, Scot. 26 Oct. 1941; s. Edward and Jean (Fairfield) V.; e. Bell-Baxter High Sch.; Edinburgh Univ. M.A. 1963, LL.B. 1966; m. Dorothy d. Edward and Dorothy Frazier 14 Dec. 1968; children: Nicholas, Fraser, Laura; COUNSEL, GILBERT, MCGLOAN GILLIS and EDITOR, CANADIAN BAR REVIEW 1994– ; Dean of Law, Univ. of N.B. 1979–84; called to Bar of N.B. 1980; Gilbert, McGloan, Gillis, Fredericton, N.B.; joined Ahmadu Bellow Univ. 1966–69; Makerere Univ. 1969–71; Queen's Univ. 1971–73; Univ. of Ill. 1973–74; Univ. of Windsor 1974–79; Univ. of N.C. 1976; mem. Acad. Panel SSHRC 1983–93; author various articles nat. and intnl. prof. jours.; Home: R.R. 6, Kelly Creek, N.B. E3B 4X7; Office: P.O. Box 4400, Fredericton, N.B. E3B 5A3.

**VEIZER, Ján,** Ph.D., F.R.S.C.; educator; b. Pobedim, Slovakia 22 June 1941; s. Victor and Brigita (Brandstetter) V.; e. Tech. Coll. for Geol. & Mining Spisska Nova

Ves 1955–59; Comenius Univ. Bratislava P.G. (Promovany geol.) degree (M.Sc.) 1964, Dr.rer.nat. degree (Ph.D.) 1968; Slovak Acad. of Sci's Bratislava Cand. Geol. Sci. (Ph.D.) 1968; Australian Nat. Univ. Canberra Ph.D. 1971; m. Elena d. Mikulas and Jolana Ondrus 30 July 1966; two s. Robert, Andrew; PROF. OF GEOL. UNIV. OF OTTAWA 1979– ; Prof. and Chair Ruhr Univ. Bochum, Germany 1988– ; Lectr. Comenius Univ. 1964–66; Rsch. Sci. Slovak Acad. Sci. Bratislava 1966–71; Visiting Asst. Prof. Univ. of Cal. Los Angeles 1972; Visiting Sci. Göttingen Univ. 1972–73; Rsch. Sci. Tübingen Univ. 1973; Asst. Prof. present Univ. 1973, Assoc. Prof. 1975; Founder and Head Derry Lab. Sedimentary Geochem. & Mineral Deposits Ottawa-Carleton Geosci. Centre 1983–86; Visiting Prof. or Fellow Australian Nat. Univ. 1979; Univ. of Adelaide 1979; Univ. of Strasbourg 1980; Hebrew Univ. 1981; Northwestern Univ. Evanston, Ill. 1983; mem. Grant Review Panel & Steering Ctte. NASA's Early Crustal Genesis Project; SCOPE/UNEP Internat. Sulfur Unit; Internat. Lithosphere Prog.; recipient Killam Award 1986; Past Pres. Medal Geol. Assn. Can. 1987; named Prof. of Yr. Univ. of Ottawa 1987; W.G. Miller Medal, Royal Society of Canada 1991; G.W. Leibniz Prize, German Research Foundation (Deutsche Forschungsgemeinschaft) 1992; invited lectr. numerous sci. meetings, rsch. projects; author over 90 articles various profl. jours., book chapters, reviews, reports; Fellow, Geol. Soc. Am.; Geol. Assn. Can.; mem. Geochem. Soc. Am.; recreation: skiing; Home: 29 Burrows Rd., Ottawa, ON K1J 6E5; Office: Ottawa, ON K1N 6N5.

**VELAN, A. Karel,** M.E.; industrial executive; b. Ostrava, Czechoslovakia 8 Feb. 1918; e. M.E.; m. Olga; children: Ivan, Peter, Tom; PRESIDENT & FOUNDER, VELAN INC.; Canada Export Award 1991; author: 'The Multi-Universe Cosmos' 1992; recreations: tennis, skiing; clubs: Rotary Club of Montreal; Home: 49 Aberdeen, Westmount, Que. H3Y 3A5; Office: 2125 Ward Ave., Montreal, Que. H4M 1T6.

**VELK, Thomas James,** B.Sc., M.Sc., Ph.D.; university professor and journalist; b. Milwaukee, Wisconsin 25 June 1938; s. Harry Florian and Sally Ann (Rozga) V.; e. Univ. of Wisconsin B.Sc. 1960, M.Sc., Ph.D. 1967; m. Dr. Linda Jane d. Kenneth and Lily Fraser 17 July 1975; FACULTY MEMBER, MCGILL UNIV. 1966– ; Faculty Mem., Dartmouth College 1964–66; Visiting Prof. & Consultant; Bd. of Governors; Federal Reserve System (Washington D.C.); Consultant, Joint Econ. Ctte., Congress of the U.S.; Economics Ed., CFCF TV Montreal; Contbr., Toronto Globe and Mail, Montreal Gazette, Financial Post, Wall Street Journal, Canadian Forum Magazine; Chairman & Co-Dir., McGill Univ. program in N. Am. Studies; Undergrad. Honors in Am. Literature and Econ.; Grad. Honours in Contract Law; co-author: 'Canadian-American Free Trade: Historical, Political and Economic Dimensions' 1987, 'Canadian American Free Trade: The Sequel' 1988, 'Federalism in Peril: The Fraser Institute' 1992; author of 500–600 TV scripts (news, editorial opinion & economic advice) along with many newspaper & mag. stories dealing with econ. & public policy; Home: 1321 Sherbrooke St. W., Apt. D111, Montreal, Que. H3G 1J4; Office: Montreal, Que. H3A 2T5.

**VENETSANOPOULOS, Anastasios,** M.S., M.Ph., Ph.D., F.E.I.C., F.I.E.E., P.Eng.; b. Athens, Greece 19 June 1941; s. Nicolaos A. and Elli Ch. (Papacondylis) V.; e. Athens Coll. 1960; Nat. Tech. Univ. of Athens Dip. in Mech. & Elect. Eng. 1965; Yale Univ. M.S. 1966, M.Ph. 1968, Ph.D. 1969; PROF. OF ELECT. ENG., UNIV. OF TORONTO 1981– ; Adjunct Prof. of Elect. Eng. Concordia Univ. 1981–84; Asst. in Instruction Yale Univ. 1966–68, Asst. in Rsch. 1968–69; Lectr. in Elect. Eng. present Univ. 1968, Asst. Prof. 1970, Assoc. Prof. 1973, Chrmn. Communications Group 1974–78, 1981–86, Assoc. Chrmn. of Elect. Eng. 1978–79; rsch. leave Imp. Coll. of Sci. & Technol. Univ. of London 1979–80; Nat. Tech. Univ. of Athens 1979–80; Swiss Federal Inst. of Technology 1986–87; Univ. of Florence 1986–87; invited lectr. George Washington Univ. 1980– ; invited lectr., Univ. of Calif. (UCLA) 1989; nat. and internat. guest lectr.; Cons., Electrical Engineering Consociates Ltd. 1970– ; cons. various ind. and govt. depts.; recipient numerous grants and awards incl. Province of Ont. Center of Excellence on Information Technology (ITRC), Candn. Institute for Telecommunications Research Network (CITR), Nat. Sci's & Eng. Rsch. Council Can., Defence Rsch. Bd. Can., Nat. Sci. Found. (U.S.), J.P. Bickell Found.; NATO; AGARD; Fulbrigh Scholar 1965; Arthur F. Schmitt Scholar 1978; John Vakis Award for Greatest Progress in Sci. 1969; author over 460 papers tech. jours. and conf. proceedings, 43 tech. reports, 236 scholarly addresses, contrib. to 20 books; ed. Candn. Elect. Eng. Jour. 1981–83, Asst. Ed. 1979–81; Assoc. Ed., IEEE Transactions on Circuits and Systems 1985–87, Guest Editor, special issue, IEEE Transactions on Circuits and Systems in Image Processing 1987; Fellow, Inst. Elect & Electronics Engs. for contributions to digital signal and image processing (Chrmn. Toronto Sect. 1977–79; Chrmn. Central Can. Council 1980–82); Fellow, Eng. Inst. Can. (Vice Pres. 1983–86); mem., N.Y. Acad. Sci's; Candn. Soc. Elect. Eng. (Chrmn. Toronto Sect. 1975–77; mem., Nat. Bd. Dirs. 1976– , Pres. 1982–86); Tech. Chamber of Greece; Am. Assn. Advanc. Sci.; Sigma Xi; recreations: travel, photography; Home: 60 Heathdale Rd., Toronto, Ont. M6C 1M8; Office: 10 King's College Rd., Toronto, Ont. M5S 1A4.

**VENIOT, Harvey A.,** Q.C., M.H.A., B.A., LL.B.; judge; b. Pictou, N.S. 18 Nov. 1915; s. Alexander R. and Gladys (Maclean) V.; e. Pictou (N.S.) Acad., 1934; St. Francis Xavier Univ., B.A. 1936; Dalhousie Law Sch.; Univ. of Sask., LL.B. 1939; m. Rhoda Marion, d. Jack and Nettie MacLeod, Montague, P.E.I., 10 Feb. 1942; children: James Stewart, Susan Rhoda; JUDGE OF PROVINCIAL COURT OF NOVA SCOTIA 1979– ; read law with J. Welsford MacDonald, Q.C.; called to Bar of N.S. 1940; cr. Q.C. 1960; def. in Prov. g.e. 1953; 1st el. 1956; re-el. since; apptd. Speaker of N.S. Assembly 1961; Min. of Agric. 1968; Min. of Municipal Affairs, 1969; defeated in prov. el. 1974, returned to law practice; appt'd judge Jan 1979; former Solr., Town of Pictou; mem., N.S. Bar Assn.; P. Conservative; mem. Knights Columbus; recreations: swimming, golf; Clubs: Pictou Lions (Past Pres.); Pictou; Home: 56 Faulkland St., Pictou, N.S. B0K 1H0.

**VENN, Richard Ernest,** B.AppSc., M.B.A.; financial executive; b. Manchester, England 3 Apr. 1951; s. Mervyn Ernest and Brigitte Melanie (Pollak) V.; e. Univ. of Toronto, B.App.Sc. 1973; Harvard Business Sch., M.B.A. 1975 (scholarship); m. Carol Robin Mitchell d. Marvin and June Mitchell; children: Madeleine Venn-Mitchell; CHRMN. & C.E.O., WOOD GUNDY INC.; EXTVE. VICE-PRES., INVESTMENT AND CORPORATE BANK, CANDN. IMPERIAL BANK OF COMMERCE; summer assoc. prog., Wood Gundy 1974; permanent post in Corp. Fin. 1975; Asst. Vice-Pres. 1978; Vice-Pres. 1980; Dir. 1981; Mgr. of Corp. Finan. Dept., Toronto 1981–84; Head of Capital Markets Worldwide 1988; Vice Chrmn. (Wood Gundy Inc.) 1989, President 1990; Mem., Mngt. Ctte., Investment and Corporate Bank, CIBC; recreations: camping skiing, tennis; Home: 377 Glencairn Ave., Toronto, Ont. M5N 1V2.

**VENNAT, Michel,** Q.C., LL.L., M.A. (Oxon.); business executive; b. Montreal, Que. 17 Sept. 1941; s. André and Annette (Brisebois) V.; e. Coll. Jean-de-Brébeuf B.A. 1960; Univ. of Montreal LL.L. 1963; Merton Coll. Oxford (Rhodes Scholar) M.A. (Oxon.) 1965; m. Marie-Anne d. Edouard and Lydia Tawil 19 June 1987; children: Catherine, Charles-Alexandre, Frédéric, Michèle; CHRMN. AND C.E.O., UNITED WESTBURNE INC. 1993– ; Dir. Dumez North America Inc.; Meloche Monnex Inc.; Sidbec-Dosco Inc.; National Bank of Greece (Can.); Bastos du Canada Ltée; Foreign Affairs Offr. External Affairs Ottawa 1965; Special Asst. to Min. of Finance 1966–68; Special Asst. to Prime Min. 1968–70, Special Counsel to Prime Minister, Energy & Constitutional questions 1977; mem. Bd. and Chrmn. Canadian Film Development Corp. Montreal 1976–81; Sr. Partner law firm Stikeman, Elliott, Montreal 1970–90; cr. Q.C. 1983; Vice Chrmn. & C.E.O., Westburne Inc.; 1991–93; mem. Barreau du Québec; Cdn. Bar Assn.; The Candn. Chamber of Commerce; Chambre de comm. française au Canada; recreations: squash, golf, tennis, skiing; Clubs: Mount-Royal; Hermitage; Mount-Bruno Country; Hillside Tennis; Montreal Badminton & Squash; Home: 22 Claude Champagne Ave., Outremont, Que. H2V 2X1; Office: 400, 6333 Decarie Blvd., Montreal, Que. H3W 3E1.

**VENNE, Lionel,** B.A.; artist; b. Verner, Ont. 2 July 1936; s. Orien Edward and Maria Lise (Gauthier) V.; e. New Liskeard (Ont.) High Sch.; Sacred Heart Coll. Sudbury B.A. 1957; Self-taught: works in watercolour, mixed-media collage, and tapestry in an impressionistic style; works included in private and corporate collections in Canada, the United States, England, Scotland, Germany, Belgium, Norway, France, Italy and Australia; solo exhns. incl.: La Galeruche Galerie d'Art Timmins 1979, 1991–94; The Temiskaming Art Gallery Haileybury 1980–83, 1986–93; Timmins Museum & Nat. Exhn. Centre 1982, 1988, 1991, 1992; McGugan Gallery, Hess Village, Hamilton 1982; Angel Gallery Toronto 1983–85; Algonquin Art Gallery Bancroft 1984; Queen Charlotte Museum & Art Gallery Queen Charlotte Islands 1986; Meta Gallery, Sault-Ste-Marie 1990; Emma Ciotti Gallery, Iroquois Falls 1991; Bancroft Art Gallery 1991; Centre des Arts, Rouyn-Noranda, Que. 1992; Salle Augustin-Chénier, Ville-Marie, Que. 1993; Englehart Museum Gallery 1993; White-Water Gallery, North Bay 1993; two-person shows: Cobble Stone & Red Brick Galleries, Niagara-on-the-Lake 1983; La Galerie du Nouvel-Ontario, Sudbury 1984; La Galeruche, Timmins 1984; White Water Gallery, North Bay 1993; group and juried exhibs. incl: Toronto Dominion Centre, Toronto 1977, 1979–80; City Hall, North Bay 1978–79, 1983; 'Ontario North Now,' Ontario Place, Toronto 1980, 1986–90; The Temiskaming Art Gallery, Haileybury 1981–94; 'Image North' Mid-Canada Television 1982; 'NorArt,' Laurentian Univ. Museum and Arts Centre, Sudbury 1982–87; White Water Gallery, North Bay 1985–86, 1988, 1990–91; Science North, Sudbury 1986; 4th Internat. Exhib. of Miniature Art (1989) and F.E.D. North (1991) Metro Toronto Convention Centre; 8ième Biennale: Rouge 90, Rouyn, Que. 1990; Premier Exhibition: Society of Night Artists, Among Friends' Gallery, Queen Charlotte Is. 1992; Look '93, Lambton Gallery, Sarnia; Northern Telephone Exhib. 1993; Northern Impressions Exhib. 1989–94; Sodarco Internat. Fall Exhib. (1st award, Mixed Media) Montréal, Qué.; The American Artist 10th Annual Internat. Juried Exhib. (Finalist) Cincinnati, Ohio; collections: Agnico-Eagle Mines Ltd., Cobalt (Ont.); Assn. of Optometrists of Ont.; Bancroft Art Gallery Permanent Collection; Christopher Walken Collection, Hollywood, CA; City of Timmins (Ont.); Continental Bank, NY; Englehart and Dist. Hospital; Fiset and Sons, Elk Lake (Ont.); Four Seasons/Sheraton Hotel, Toronto; Grant Forest Products, Englehart (Ont.); Internat. Platinum Corp., Toronto; Little Gallery, Haileybury (Ont.); Michael Benson Assoc., Windsor; N.O.R.P. Art Acquisitions, Min. of Northern Development and Mines; N.O.R.P., Provincial Govt. Bldgs. North Bay & Sudbury; Northern Telephone Ltd.; Ontario Northland Transportation Commn.; Ont. Provincial Govt. Collection, North Bay & Sudbury; Ottawa Roman Catholic Separate School Bd.; Queen Charlotte Museum (B.C.); Roger Lemire Assoc., Montreal; The Temiskaming Art Gallery Permanent Collection, Haileybury; Timiskaming Roman Catholic Separate Sch. Bd.; Wypich, Illsley & Assocs., Toronto; commissioned tapestries: Ont. Assn. of Optometrists 1984; Internat. Platinum Corp. 1985, 1986; Agnico Mines Ltd. 1986; Ont. Northland Transp. Commn. 1991; Govt. of Ont. 1992; Ascension Parish, Matachewan 1992; recipient various awards: Ont. Craft Council 1974 (Excellence), 1975 (Merit); NorArt Award Laurentian Univ. Museum and Arts Centre 1981; N.O.A.A. Graphics l5, Denison Mines Award 1982; Ont. Arts Council Grant 1983–91; Invitation, Hinterland Award (best in mixed media), David B. Milne Award 1984 (best in show), Special Hon. Mention 1985, Algonquin Art Gallery; Timmins Museum 1986 Exhn. Award, Hon. Mention 1987, 'Northern Impressions du Nord' First Prize 1990, 1991; Northern Telephone du Nord, Hon. Mention 1987; N.O.A.A. Annual Juried Exhib., Timmins, Kidd Creek Award 1990, INCO Award 1991; Winner, Northern Telephone Cover 1993; grants: Ont. Arts Council (Material Assistance Grants): 1981–82, 1982–83, 1984–85, 1986–92, 1993–94; Canada Arts Council (Exploration Grant) 1984, (Visiting Artist Grants) 1986, 1988; Individual Artist Grant, O.A.C. 1993; Jury: Impressions 93, Timmins Museum 1993; Festival of the Arts, Sault Ste. Marie 1987; Invitational '86 Exhib., Bancroft, Ont.; Tem. Art Gallery 1986; N.O.A.A. Pres. 1986–89, Dir. 1984–86, 1989–94; Address: Box 283, Elk Lake, Ont. P0J 1G0.

**VENNEMA, Alje,** O.C. (1967), M.D., C.M., M.P.H.-T.M.; b. Leeuwarden, The Netherlands 11 Aug. 1932; s. Sytze and Tryntje (Hiemstra) V.; came to Can. 1951; e. Western Reserve Univ., B.A. 1958; McGill Univ., M.D.C.M. 1962; Tulane Univ., M.P.H.-T.M. 1969; Hammersmith Post-grad. Med. Sch., London, Eng., Internal Med. 1969; Welsh Nat. Sch. of Med., Dipl. in Tuberculosis and Chest Diseases (D.T.C.D.) 1970; CLINICAL DIR., B.C. DIV. OF TUBERCULOSIS CONTROL, MIN. OF HEALTH, Vancouver, B.C. 1988– ; Med. Offr., Cottage Hosp., Govt. of Nfld., 1963–64; Team Capt., Volunteer Med. Team CARE-MEDICO, Prov. Hosp., Quang-Ngai, S. Vietnam, 1964–65; Tech. Adviser to Govt. of S. Vietnam under Candn. Colombo Plan, assigned to Prov. Hosp., 1965–66; Dir. of Candn. Med. Assistance to S. Vietnam, 1966–68; mem. Faculty of Med., Univ. of Dar es Salaam, Tanzania 1970–72; Univ. London, Sch. Tropical Med. & Hygiene and Sch. Econs., research in demography 1972–74; 1982 Diplomate, Am. Bd. of Pediatrics; Fellow, Am. Academy of Pediatrics 1992; Dept. Pediatrics, Tulane Univ., New Orleans; Assoc. Prof. Pediatrics, New York Univ. Sch. Med.; Dir., Pediatric Education, N.Y. Infirmary; Director, Bureau of Tuberculosis, N.Y. City Dept. of Health;

Medical Dir. (USA), Tom Dooley Heritage Inc. rec'd Order of Merit, Govt. of S. Vietnam, 1965; Distinguished Grad. Award, McGill Univ., 1966; Order of Distinguished Service to Vietnamese People, Govt. of S. Vietnam, 1968; co-author 'Harvest of Death' 1972; author 'The Viet Cong Massacre at Hue' 1975; author of various articles for prof. journs.; Order of Canada 1967; mem., Candn. Med. Assn.; Ont. Med. Assn.; mem. American Thoracic Soc. Home: 630 E. Carisbrooke Rd., N. Vancouver, B.C. V7N 1N9.

**VENTER, Ronald Daniel,** B.Sc., M.Eng., Ph.D., P.Eng.; mechanical engineering professor; b. East London, South Africa 3 Jan. 1944; s. the late Daniel Frans and Myrtle (Quirk) V.; e. Univ. of Witwatersrand, B.Sc. 1966; McMaster Univ., M.Eng. 1969, Ph.D. 1971; m. Beryl d. June and the late William Kent 17 July 1975; VICE DEAN, FACULTY OF APPLIED SCIENCE AND ENGINEERING, UNIVERSITY OF TORONTO and WALLACE G. CHALMERS PROFESSOR OF ENGINEERING DESIGN 1993– ; Head, Mech. Div., deBeers Indus. Diamond Div. 1971–72; Head, High Pressure Systems for Diamond Synthesis 1972–74; Asst. Prof., Dept. of Mech. Engr., Univ. of Toronto 1975–78; Assoc. Prof. & Assoc. Chrmn. 1978–81, Chrmn. 1981–91; Prof., Dept. of Mech. Engr. 1981– ; Mem., Bd. of Dirs.: Ont. Ctr. for Automotive Parts Technol. 1983–89; Ind. Res. & Dev. Inst. 1990– ; Ont. Centre for Materials Rsch. 1993– ; engaged in numerous cons. & contract rsch. activities for indus. & fed. Dept. of Justice; Chamber of Mines Gold Medal Award for Outstanding Engr. Grad. in S. Afr. 1966; Mem., Robotics Internat.; Soc. of Mgr. Engrs.; Am. Soc. of Mech. Engrs.; Assn. of Profl. Engrs of Ont.; author of numerous tech. pubns. in internat. jours.; co-author: 'Plane Strain Slip Line Fields' 1982; Home: 55 Thorncrest Rd., Islington, ON M9A 1S8; Office: 5 King's College Rd., Toronto, ON M5S 1A4.

**VERDUN, John Robert (Bob);** editor; b. St. Thomas, Ont. 21 Dec. 1948; s. Jan and Gladys (Agar) V.; e. Univ. of Waterloo (engineering) 1966–68; FOUNDER AND EDITOR, ELMIRA INDEPENDENT (weekly newspaper) 1974– ; Founder and Editor, The Farm Gate (monthly agric. jour.) 1977– ; The National Independent (monthly) 1986– ; Elora Sentinel 1990– and Fergus Thistle 1992– (combined weeklies); Co-founder, the Amani Working Group (non-profit organization providing paper and other support for education in African refugee camps); Co-founder, Theatre on the Grand (professional summer theatre in Fergus, Ont.); tour leader to unusual Third World locations; occasional media commentator and university lecturer, principally on news media, environment, municipal politics, and community development; shareholder activist; campaigner against junkmail; recipient, Merit Award Ont. Fedn. Agric 1987; twice named to the 'Golden Dozen' ed. writiers of Internat. Soc. of Weekly Newspapers Editors; Elmira Independent received the Michener Award for meritorious public service in journalism, Canada's highest honour for news organizations 1990; numerous awards in provincial and national community-newspaper competitions; recreation: Stratford Festival, Kitchener-Waterloo Symphony, African safari photography, ice dancing; Office: 15 King St., Elmira, Ont. N3B 2R1.

**VERDUYN, Christl,** M.A., Ph.D.; educator; b. Amsterdam, Netherlands 2 Apr. 1953; d. Frans and Stintje (Wagenmakker) V.; e. Trent Univ. B.A. 1975; Univ. of Ottawa M.A. 1976, Ph.D. 1979; m. Robert Malcolm s. Dougald and Claire Campbell 10 Oct. 1981; children: Malcolm, Lachlan, Colin, Frances; CHAIR, CANADIAN STUDIES PROGRAM, TRENT UNIV. 1993– ; Asst. Prof. of French, Queen's Univ. 1979–80; Founding Chair, Women's Studies Prog., Trent Univ. 1987–90, Assoc. Prof., French and Women's Studies 1986– , Asst. Prof. of French 1980–86; Resident-Dir., Trent-Univ. of Waterloo Year Abroad Program, Univ. de Nantes, France 1990–91; ed. 'Margaret Laurence: An Appreciation' 1988; mem. ed. bd. Jour. Candn. Studies 1983–93; RFR/DRF 1986–88; Home: 749 Bethune St., Peterborough, Ont. K9H 4A5; Office: Trent Univ., Peterborough, Ont. K9J 7B8.

**VERGE, Pierre,** B.A., M.A., LL.L., LL.M., LL.D.; professeur titulaire; né. Québec, Qué. 9 janv. 1936; f. Francis et Régina (Roy) Verge; é. Coll. des Jésuites, B.A. 1956; Univ. Laval, LL.L. 1959, LL.D. 1970; Univ. of Toronto, LL.M. 1968; McGill Univ., M.A. 1962; Univ. of Cambridge, M.A. 1977; ép. Colette d. Maurice Habel 29 juin 1963; enfants: Marc, Caroline, Louis; PROFESSEUR, FACULTE DE DROIT, UNIV. LAVAL 1967– ; Bar. du Qué. 1961– ; Q.C. 1977– ; Doyen, Fac. de droit, Laval 1973–77; Prés., Candn. Assn. of Law Teachers 1972–73; Commonwealth Fellowship, St. John's Coll., Cambridge Univ. 1977; Mem., Royal Soc. of Can. 1986– ; co-auteur: 'Droit du travail' 1987, 2nd ed. 1991; auteur: 'Le droit de grève, fondements et limites' 1985; 'Le droit et les syndicats' 1991; résidence: 2547, de la Falaise, Sillery, P.Q. G1T 1W3; bureau: Fac. de droit, Univ. Laval, Québec, P.Q. G1K 7P4.

**VERJEE, Shaffique,** M.A.; banker; b. Kampala, Uganda 31 May 1954; s. Jimmy and Roshan (Devji) V.; e. Haileybury Coll. (Hertford, Eng.) 1967–71; Cambridge Univ., B.A. 1975, M.A. 1978; m. Nilusha d. Maleksultan Harjee 25 Aug. 1979; children: Jehad, Mishal; CHIEF EXTVE. OFFR., PETRUS FINANCIAL CORP. 1992– ; Mng. Dir., Internat. Advisory Serv. (Kenya) 1976–82; Pres., Shadow Point Investments Ltd. 1982–85; Pres. & C.E.O., Seel Mortgage Investment Corp. 1985–92; Vice-Pres. & C.E.O., The Equitable Trust Co. 1983–90; Dir., Pacific Nat. Finan. Corp.; Ismaili Muslim; mem., The Inst. of Corp. Dir. in Canada; recreations: bridge; clubs: Donalda; Cambridge; Mad River Golf; Home: 7 Alderbrook Dr., Don Mills, Ont. M3B 1E3; Office: 150 York St., Ste. 1100, Toronto, Ont. M5H 3S5.

**VERNEY, Douglas V.,** M.A., Ph.D.; university professor; b. Liverpool, England 21 Jan. 1924; s. John Henry and Olive Shirley (Barritt) V.; e. Oriel Coll., Oxford, B.A. 1947, M.A. 1948; Liverpool Univ., Ph.D. 1954; m. Diana Mary Read, d. William Robinson, Cheshire, Eng., 24 June 1950 (deceased 1974); two s.; Andrew John Edmund, Jonathan Edward; m. Prof. Francine Ruth Frankel, 28 Nov. 1975; PROF. OF POL. SCIENCE, YORK UNIV. (Retired 1992); Chrmn. of the Dept., 1962–67; Lektor, Svenska Handelhogskolan, Helsinki, 1948–49; Asst. Lectr. and Lectr. in Pol. Science, Univ. of Liverpool, 1949–61; Commonwealth Fund Fellow, Columbia Univ., 1953, and Univ. of Cal. (Berkeley), 1954; Visiting Assoc. Prof., Univ. of Florida, 1958–59; Assoc. Prof. of Pol. Science, York Univ., 1961–62; Visiting Grad. Prof., Columbia Univ. 1967; Can. Council Sr. Fellow 1967–68, 1974–75; served as Capt., W. Somerset Yeomanry (R.A.); Publications: 'Parliamentary Reform in Sweden 1866–1921' 1957; 'Public Enterprise in Sweden' 1959; 'The Analysis of Political Systems' 1959; 'Political Patterns in Today's World' (with Prof. Sir Denis Brogan) 1963, 1968; 'British Government and Politics' 1966, 1971, 1976; 'Three Civilizations, Two Cultures, One State: Canada's Political Traditions' 1986; and various articles to journs.; Ed. 'Canadian Public Administration' 1970–74; Dir., Soc. Sci Research Council of Can. 1972–74; mem., Inst. for Advanced Study, Princeton, N.J. 1977–78; Shastri Indo-Canadian Inst. Senior Long-Term Fellowship 1983–84; SSHRCC Fellowship 1984–85; Jules and Gabrielle Leger Fellowship 1984–85; Adjunct Prof., South Asia Regional Studies, Univ. of Pennsylvania 1991– ; Visiting Prof. of Public and Internat. Affairs, Princeton Univ. 1993; mem., Pol. Studies Assn. of U.K.; Am. Pol. Science Assn.; Candn. Pol. Science Assn. (Pres. 1969–70); Internat. Pol. Science Assn.; Anglican; Club: University; Home: 104 Pine St., Philadelphia, PA 19106-4312; Office: York Univ., North York, Ont. M3J 1P3.

**VÉRONNEAU, Guy;** business executive; b. Montreal, Que. 8 June 1937; s. Robert and Marie (Blondin) V.; e. Ecole Sacré Coeur de Sorel 1956; Sir George Williams Univ. 1962; Inst. for Cert. of Computer Profls. 1963; Ecole des hautes études commerciales 1968; Am. Mngt. Assn. 1971; m. Huguette d. Léo and Germaine Léonard 17 June 1961; children: Marie, Louis; PRES., MIL GROUP INC. 1991– ; Mgr., Data Processing, Labatt Brewery Ltd. 1959–64; Dir., D.P., La Presse Ltée 1965–69; Dir., D.P., Soc. Générale de Finan. 1970–72; Vice-Pres., Shipbuilding, Marine Indus. Ltée 1973–87; Vice-Pres., Mktg. & Sales, Bombardier Inc. 1987–89; Vice-Pres., Opns., MIL Group 1989; Pres. & C.E.O., MIL Davie Inc. 1989–91; Chrmn., Candn. Maritime Industries Assn.; Pres., Candn. Institute of Marine Engineers; mem., Candn. Ctte., Lloyd's Register of Shipping; Home: 11, rue Fraser, Lévis, Qué. G6V 3R4; Office: P.O. Box 130, Lévis, Qué. G6V 6N7.

**VERREAULT, Denise,** B.Ed.; executif; née Matane, Qué. 18 oct. 1958; f. Borromée et Anita (Dumaresq) V.; é. Cegep de Matane, D.E.C. en Sciences admin. 1975–77; Univ. de Sherbrooke, Etudes en admin. 1977–78; Univ. du Qué. à Rimouski, B.Ed. 1981, etudes en Gestion des Ressources Humaines 1981; PRESIDENT, GROUPE MARITIME VERREAULT INC. 1989– ; emplois d'été chez Verreault Navigation Inc. étés 1976–81; Vice-prés., construction et réparation de navires 1982–89; Dir., Compagnie de Gestion de Matane 1990– ; Assurance-Vie Desjardins 1992– ; Société Québécoise de Développement de la Main-d'Oeuvre 1992– ; Chambre de Commerce du Qué. 1994– ; a reçu Prix de la Femme de l'Année (catégorie Affaires), Salon de la Femme de Montréal 1991; loisirs: ski alpin, ski de randonnée, marche, lecture, voyages; bureau: 264 rue Principale, Les Méchins, Matane, Qué. G0J 1T0.

**VERRIER, William Lawrence,** B.A., M.A.; transportation executive; b. Montréal, Qué. 30 May 1930; s. Edward John and Helen (Houston) V.; e. Concordia Univ., B.A. 1962; McGill Univ., M.A. 1965; Royal Naval Coll. 1955; m. Honor d. William and Norah Constable 21 June 1982; children: Hugh, Wendy, Linda, Richard; CHRMN., SKIPBURN LTD. 1993– ; CHRMN. & PRES., SCOTCAN INTERNAT. LTD. 1990– ; Dir., Stagecoach Internat. Services Ltd., Scotland; Extve. Offr., Royal Candn. Navy 1951–60; Nat. Training Co-ordr., BP Can. 1965–68; Corp. Mgr., Personnel, Can. Steamship Lines 1968–72; Dir., Admin. & Personnel, Gen. Mgr., Atlantic Reg., Gen. Mgr., UK & Ire., Air Can. 1972–80; Extve. Vice-Pres. & Chief Op. Offr., Eastern Prov. Airways 1980–83; Pres., C.E.O., & Dir., Gray Coach Lines 1985–90; C.E.O. & Dir., Trentway-Wagar Properties 1987–90; Chrmn., Internat. Travel Group 1988–89; Vice Chrmn., Gray Coach Lines Inc. 1990–92; Chrmn., Inst. of Corporate Directors in Can.; Clubs: Royal N.S. Yacht Squadron; Ontario Club; Home: 123 King St., Niagara-on-the-Lake, Ont. L0S 1J0; Office: 77 Gerrard St. W., Ste. 1004, Toronto, Ont. M5G 2A1.

**VERSTEEG, Hajo Nicolaas,** B.A., LL.B., M.Jur.; lawyer; b. netherlands 7 Feb. 1951; s. Karel Laurens and Elmyre Marie (Gans) V.; e. St. Michael's Coll. Toronto 1968; Candn. Jr. Coll. Switzerland Sr. Matric. 1969; Univ. of W. Ont., B.A. 1973; Univ. of W. Ont., LL.B. 1976; Univ. of Auckland, N.Z., M.Jur. 1978; m. Jean d. Mark and Elsie Myszakowski 10 May 1975; one s. Menno André; ENVIRONMENTAL LAW AND POLICY ANALYST 1991– ; Asst. Prof. of Law Univ. of N.B. 1980, Assoc. Prof. 1985; Chrmn., Federal Pest Mgmt. Adv. Bd. 1985–89; Dir. of Secretariat, Candn. Pesticides Registration Review 1989–91; mem. N.B. Task Force Cancer & the Environment 1982–84; Pres. and Dir. Conserv. Council of N.B. 1980–85; Regional Ed. Candn. Environmental Law Reports 1980–85; mem. Adv. Bd. Atlantic Inst. of Criminol. Dalhousie Univ. 1982–85; author: 'Handbook of Environmental Law for New Brunswick' 1983; 'The Spruce Budworm Spray Programme and the Perception of Risk in New Brunswick' 1984; 'Public Consultation: A Comprehensive Practice Manual' 1992; 'Final Report Recommending Ways to Improve Pesticide Policy in the Philippines' 1992; 'Examining the Potential of the Canadian Environmental Protection Act to Incorporate Pollution Prevention Principles' 1993; author or co-author various articles, papers, reports; mem. Barristers' Soc. N.B.; Candn. Bar Assn.; Mem., Permanent Advisory Group on Environmental Law to the Law Reform Comn. of Can. 1989–92; recreations: skin-diving, hiking, photography; Home & Office: 5365 Hilltop Dr., Manotick, Ont. K4M 1G4.

**VERSTRAETE, Ursula Mary,** R.N., B.A.S., M.Ed., C.H.E.; health administration executive, nurse; b. Derby England 25 Aug. 1943; d. John Bernard and Catherine (Whelan) Woodward; e. The Pines Ursuline College (Hons.) 1962; Hôtel-Dieu Hosp. Sch. of Nursing R.N. 1965; York Univ. B.A.S. 1984; Candn. Coll. of Healthcare Executives C.H.E. 1986; Brock Univ. M.Ed. 1993; m. William s. George and Irene V. 11 Sept. 1965; children: Sarah Irene Elodie, Jared William Joseph; DIRECTOR OF NURSING PRACTICE, SCARBOROUGH GENERAL HOSPITAL 1989– ; various staff positions in hospitals in Ont. 1965–76; Admin. Supervisor, Nursing Div., York County Hosp. 1976–80; Dir. of Nursing, Shouldice Hosp. 1980–89; Mem., Medical Research Council of Canada 1990– ; Educational Consultant, Nursing Management Prog., Candn. Nurses' Assn. Ottawa 1986–92; Mem., Candn. College of Health Care Extves.; Registered Nurses' Assn. of Ont.; College of Nurses of Ont.; recreations: travel, bridge, reading; clubs: Candn. Fed. of University Women North Toronto Club (Vice-Pres. 1993–94; Pres. 1994–95); Home: 9 Dutch Myrtle Way, Toronto, Ont. M3B 3K7; Office: 3050 Lawrence Ave. E., Scarborough, Ont. M1P 2V5.

**VEZINA, Christopher Lyall Jon,** B.A., A.O.C.A.; painter, sculptor, designer (of furniture, marble products); b. North Bay, Ont. 1955; s. Lyall Joseph and Ellen Jean (Cousineau) Vezina; e. Wilfrid Laurier Univ. B.A. 1973; Nipissing Univ. 1973–74; Ont. Coll. of Art A.O.C.A. 1976–80; numerous trips & extensive study and work in Pietrasanta, Italy in marble, terra cotta and granite 1979–90; exhibits in private collections in Canada, London, England, Italy, France, and Bermuda; private exhibit Widdifield S.S. North Bay Ont. 1970; Ont. Coll. of Art Student Exhibit 1981; Artisan's Alley London Ont. (1st pub. exbn) 1981; Libbey's of Toronto 1982; Outdoor Toronto, Ont. Art Exbn 1982–92; Columbus Centre Comn. of Christopher Columbus 1986; Toronto Comp. Winner Statue in Bronze marking Italian World Cup Soccer Win 1982; private collection, Lord Thomson of Fleet (var. works & furniture in marble & stone) 1982–92; Campbell House Gall. Georgetown Ont. 1989; subject of several newspaper articles; Address: 282 Labreche Dr., North Bay, Ont. P1A 4J5.

**VÉZINA, L'Hon. Monique,** P.C., M.P.; politician; b. Rimouski, Que. 13 July; e. Comml. dipl. 1950; Min. of External Relations and Internat. Development 1993; Min. of State for Seniors 1988–93 and Min. responsible for La Francophonie 1993; elected Rimouski-Témiscouata riding 4 Sept. 1984; Min. of External Relations 1984–86 (and min. resp. for orgn. of 1st Francophone summit and CIDA); Min. of Supply & Services, Receiver Gen. for Canada & Min. Resp. for Statistics Can. 1986–87; Min. of Transport 1987; Min. of State for Employment and Immigration 1988–93; Chrmn., Lower St. Lawrence Sch. Bd. parents ctte. 1964–77; Nat. Pres., Dames Hélène de Champlain 1976–79; Dir. & Pres., OFAQ 1974–81; Mem., Cons. sup. de l'édn. du Qué. & Chrmn., Comn. de l'enseignement secondaire 1978–82; Pres., Conf. des Caisses pop. et d'écon. Desjardins (CCPED) du Bas St-Laurent 1976–84; Dir., CCPED du Qué. 1977–84; Chrmn., Inst. coop. Desjardins & Pres., Fond. Girardin-Vaillancourt 1981–84; Vice-Chrmn., Régie de l'assur. auto. du Qué. 1978–81; Mem., Qué. Real Estate Bd. 1978–81; Address: C.P. 788, Rimouski, Que. G5L 8G1.

**VICCARI, Benedetto George Silvestro,** APR; editor; journalist; b. London, England 2 July 1918; s. Cavaliere Benedetto and Florence Honor (Bartholomew) V.; e. St. Francis Xavier Coll. (U.K.); APR 1970; 1st m. Margaret Brookes July 1949; 2nd m. Anne Welch Oct. 1967; children: Beverleigh, Brenda, Cheryl, Paul; MANAGING EDITOR, 'CANADIAN SCENE' 1989– ; served with Royal Artillery, France, U.K., Italy 1939–44; military mission to Italian Army (Allied Control Comn., Italy) 1944–46; Story Analyst, Paramount Pictures & J. Arthur Rank Orgn. 1946–47; emigrated to Can. 1947; Pub. Relns. Mgr., Turnbull Elevator Ltd. 1947–56; General Foods Ltd. 1956–60; Pres., Mentor Public Relations 1960–61; Viccari Public Relations Ltd. 1961–80; Publisher, 'Oggi Canada' 1980–81; Cons. 1981– ; Editor, 'Canadian Scene' 1986–89; Past Lectr., Harvard Sch. of Bus., Univ. of Toronto, Wilfred Laurier Univ., Ryerson Polytech. Inst., Humber Coll., etc.; Pres., Candn. Pub. Relns. Soc. (Toronto) Inc. 1960–61 (Award of Attainment 1971); Toronto Press Club 1982–83; rec'd.: Award of Distinction, SOFADECA (Soc. for Assistance and Defence of New Canadians and Ethnic Groups in Canada) 1987; Candn. Ethnic Journalists' and Writers' Club Annual Award 1989; author of var. articles; recreation: reading; Clubs: Toronto Press; Candn. Ethnic Journalists & Writers (1st Vice Pres.); Home: 22 Walmer Rd., Toronto, Ont. M5R 2W5; Office: 73 Simcoe St., Toronto, Ont. M5J 1W9.

**VICKERS, Jon,** C.C. (1968), D. Mus., D.C.L., LL.D.; opera singer; b. Prince Albert, Sask. 1926; e. Royal Conservatory Music Toronto (with George Lambert); LL.D. Sask.; D.C.L. Bishop's; D. Mus. Univ of Western Ont.; Brandon Univ.; Laval Univ.; Univ. of Illinois; McMaster Univ.; Univ. of Guelph Ont; mem. Royal Acad of Music; m. Hetti Outerbridge 1953; five children; operatic debut with Toronto Opera Festival 1952; a winner of Singing Stars of Tomorrow and 1st Prize 'Nos Futures Etoiles,' Montreal; internat career began 1956; appearances at Festivals of Stratford (Ont.), Bayreuth, Orange, Vancouver, Salzburg, Tanglewood, Israel and Guelph (Ont.); appeared at Opera Companies of Toronto, Covent Garden, Vienna State, Dallas Civic, Rio de Janeiro, Berlin, Paris, Munich, Metropolitan (N.Y.C.), Philadelphia, Florence, Houston, Miami, Venice, San Francisco, La Scala (Milan), Chicago Lyric, Montreal Expo, Quebec City, Colon Beunos Aires; roles include: Trojans, Samson et Delilah, Tristan and Isolde, Bartered Bride, Fidelio, Aida, Masked Ball, Jenufa, Andre Chenier, Parsifal, Don Carlos, Pagliacci, Norma, La Forza del Destino, Handel's Samson, Benvenuto Cellini, Coranazione de Poppea, Trovatore, Rigoletto, La Traviata, Carmen, die Walkure, Otello, Peter Grimes; films include: Carmen, Fidelio, Tristan and Isolde, Norma, Pagliacci, Otello; numerous recordings, oratorio, concert, symphony and CBC appearances.

**VIEHBACHER, Christopher A.,** B.Comm., C.A.; pharmaceutical executive; b. Kitchener, Ont.; e. Queen's Univ. B.Comm. 1983, C.A. 1985; m. Alison Glossop; two children; PRESIDENT, BURROUGHS WELLCOME INC. 1993– ; Price Waterhouse Toronto 1983–86; Price Waterhouse GmbH Hamburg Germany 1986–88; Wellcome GmbH Finance Dir. 1988–90; Finance Director Central Europe 1990–93; Mem., Inst. of C.A.s of Ont.; recreations: golf, skiing; club: Forest & Stream; Office: 16751 TransCanada Rd., Kirkland, Que. H9H 4J4.

**VIEN, Paul G.,** B.Sc.Comm.; financial executive; b. Montréal, Qué. 18 Nov. 1934; s. Thomas and Anna (Dionne) V.; e. Univ. of Montréal, B.Sc.Comm. 1959; m. Françoise B. d. Philippe de Gaspé and Lucille Beaubien 25 June 1960; children: Thomas Jr., Nicole, Patrick; PRESIDENT, ST. JAMES FINANCIAL CORP. INC. 1990– ; var. positions 1959–65; joined Nesbitt, Thomson Inc. 1965; Sr. Assoc., Vice-Pres., Sr. Vice-Pres. & Chrmn., Nesbitt Thomson Securities Ltd.; purchased Television TéléMédia assets 1979 to start Pathonic Commun. Inc. & Tele-Capital Inc. (merged 1986 to form Pathonic Network) sold to Télé-Métropole 1990; Pres. & Dir., Pathonic Inc., Pathonic U.S.A., Inc., Pathonic Real Estate Inc.; Dir. & member of the Extve. Ctte. and of Compensation Ctte., Auberges des Gouverneurs Inc.; Dir. & Member of Audit Ctte. and of Compensation Ctte., Commercial Union Holdings Ltd.; Dir.: Commercial Union Assurance Company of Canada; Commercial Union Life Assurance Company of Canada; Groupe Univers Info; Mitel Corp.; Somiper Inc.; Telecite Inc.; Founder, Fondation Pathonic; Gov., Ctr. Hosp., Univ. de Sherbrooke; Assoc. Gov., Univ. of Montreal; recreations: golf, skiing, yachting; Clubs: Mount Royal; Beaconsfield Golf; Sailfish Point Golf; Home: 166 Chartwell Cr., Beaconsfield, Qué. H9W 1C3; Office: 910 Sherbrooke St. W., #300, Montréal, Qué. H3A 1G3.

**VIGER, André,** O.C.; marathonien en fauteuil roulant; conférencier-motivateur; né Windsor, Ont. 27 septembre 1952; f. Lucien et Madeleine (Goulet) V.; ép. Louise f. Leo et Cecile Scalabrini 20 septembre 1975; DIR. MAISON ANDRÉ VIGER (ORTHOPÉDIE); Dir. Bijouterie André Viger; Vainqueur de marathons celebres: Boston, Paris, Montréal, Oïta (Japan); record internat. au 1500 métres; Chevalier de l'ordre du Québec; Officier de l'ordre du Canada 1990; outstanding young people Jaycees Internat.; Dir. fondation André Viger; Président d'honneur féte du Can. 1989; Adresse: 6700 St. Denis, Montreal, Que. H2S 2S2.

**VIGOD, Toby Elaine,** B.A., LL.B.; lawyer; b. Toronto, Ont. 19 Nov. 1951; d. Norman and Florence (Nesbitt) V.; e. Univ. of Toronto B.A. 1973; Queen's Univ. LL.B. 1977; m. Joseph F. s. Alberto and Mary Castrilli 10 May 1986; COMMISSIONER, COMN. ON PLANNING & DEVELOPMENT REFORM IN ONTARIO 1991– ; Counsel, Candn. Environmental Law Assn. 1980–86; Extve. Dir. 1986– ; casework emphasis on wide var. of environ. matters; appearances before admin. tribunals & courts; num. speaking engagements; Spec. Lectr., Queen's Univ., Faculty of Law 1986– ; Instr. School of Public Administration 1990– ; Spec. Lectr., Univ. of Toronto, Faculty of Law 1991; Mem., Ont. Roundtable on Environment & Economy; author of 1 journal article & 1 book chapter as well as num. briefs & submissions on environ. law matters; co-author: 'Pesticides in Canada: An Examination of Federal Law and Policy' 1987; Home: 98 Borden St., Toronto, Ont. M5S 2N1.

**VIGRASS, Laurence William,** B.E., M.Sc., Ph.D., P.Eng.; geologist; educator; b. Melfort, Sask. 9 May 1929; s. Victor Laurence and Anna Wilhelmina V.; e. Univ. of Sask. B.E. 1951, M.Sc. 1952; Stanford Univ. Ph.D. 1961; m. Glenna d. Ben and Elsie Graham 11 Sept. 1954; children: Richard, Lauren, Mark; PROFESSOR EMERITUS, DEPT. OF GEOLOGY, UNIV. OF REGINA 1991– ; Geol. Chevron Standard (Canada) 1952–55; Geol. Humble Oil & Refining Co., Ore. 1956–57; Rsch. and Staff Geol. Imperial Oil Ltd. Calgary 1958–65; Consulting Geol. 1965–68; Assoc. Prof. Univ. of Regina 1968–73, and Prof. Dept. of Geology 1973–91, Dir. of Energy Research Unit 1976–87; Chrmn., Saskatchewan Oil & Gas Conservation Board 1991– ; mem., Sask. Natural Gas Conserv. Bd. 1977–80; Cons. Offshore Geol. Govt. Nfld. 1974–75; Chrmn. Bd. Dirs. and Special Tech. Cons., Sask. Oil & Gas Corp. 1973–74, Cons. 1985; recipient Candn. Soc. Petrol. Geols. Medal of Merit 1979, Link Award 1965; Shell, Chevron and NRC grad. fellowships; co-author 'Fifty Years of Canadian Petroleum Geology 1928–78' 1978; author or co-author numerous tech. reports, papers; mem., Am. Assn. Petrol. Geols.; Assn. Prof. Engs. Sask.; Candn. Inst. Mining & Metall.; Candn. Soc. Petrol. Geols.; Sask. Geol. Soc.; recreations: canoeing, camping, carpentry; Home: 9 Bryant St., Regina, Sask. S4S 4S5; Office: Regina, Sask. S4S 0A2.

**VIJH, Ashok K.,** O.C., C.Q., K.C.St.J., M.Sc., Ph.D., LL.D. (h.c.), F.C.I.C., F.R.S.Chem., FInstP, Fellow APS, Fellow IEEE, Assoc. Fellow TWAS, F.R.S.C.; scientist; university professor; b. Multan, India 15 Mar. 1938; s. Bishamber Nath and Prem Lata (Bahl) V.; e. Panjab Univ., B.Sc. (Hons.) 1960, M.Sc. (Hons.) 1961; Univ. of Ottawa, Ph.D. 1966; LL.D. (hon. causa) Concordia Univ. 1988; D.Sc. (hon. causa) Waterloo Univ. 1993; divorced; one s.: Aldous Ian; MAîTRE-DE-RSCH., HYDRO-QUÉBEC RSCH. INST. 1973– ; Sr. Chem., Sprague Electric Co. 1966–69; Group leader, Hydro-Qué. Inst. of Rsch. 1969–73; Group Leader & Maître-de-Rsch. 1973–74; Prog. Leader & Maître-de-Rsch. 1974–81; Vis. Prof. & Thesis Dir., INRS-Ener., Univ. of Qué. 1970–78, 1981– ; Lash Miller Award, F.C.I.C., F.R.S.Chem., Fellow, IREQ 1973; Noranda Lecture Award 1979; Fellow IEEE 1982; Prix Urgel – Archambault of ACFAS, FInstP 1984; F.R.S.C. 1985; Fellow APS 1986; Order of Quebec 1987; Izaak Walton Killam Memorial Prize 1987; Assoc. Fellow, Third World Academy of Sciences 1987; Fellow, The National Acad. of Sciences (India) 1987; Thomas W. Eadie Medal, Royal Soc. of Can. 1989; The Chemical Inst. of Canada Palladium Medal 1990; Officer of the Order of Canada 1990; elected Dir., Applied Sciences and Engr. Div., Academy of Science of the Royal Soc. of Canada 1990; Xerox Lecture Award, Univ. de Montréal 1991; elected Academician, European Academy of Arts, Sciences and Humanities 1991; elected Hon. Mem., Materials Rsch. Society of India 1991; Founding Fellow, Académie Francophone d'Ingenieurs (Paris) 1993; honoured with a Biography in 'In Celebration of Canadian Scientists: A Decade of Killam Laureates' 1991; Distinguished Guest Speaker at first 'Science and Technology Workshop' of CEMAID (Centres of Excellence in Molecular and Interfacial Dynamics), Toronto 1991; Knight Commander of Merit, Sovereign Military Order of Saint John of Jerusalem (Knights of Malta) 1992; Founding Fellow, Acad. Francophone d'Ingenieurs (Paris) 1993; Foreign Fellow, India National Science Acad. 1994; author: 'Electrochemistry of Metals and Semiconductors' 1973; editor & co-editor: 'Oxides and Oxide Films,' vol. 3–6 1976–81; Ed. Bd. Mem., 'Materials Chemistry and Physics,' 'International Journal of Hydrogen Energy,' 'Bulletin of Electrochemistry' and 9 others; Office: C.P. 1000, Varennes, P.Q. J0L 2P0.

**VIKIS-FREIBERGS, Vaira,** B.A., M.A., Ph.D., LL.D.; educator; b. Riga, Latvia 1 Dec. 1937; d. Karlis and Annemarie (Rankis) Vikis; e. Coll. Mers-Sultan, Casablanca, Morocco; Univ. of Toronto Victoria Coll. B.A. 1958, M.A. 1960; McGill Univ. Ph.D. 1965; m. Imants F. s. Augusts and Marta (Gravelis) Freibergs 16 July 1960; children: Karlis Roberts, Indra Karoline; PROFESSOR OF PSYCHOLOGY, UNIV. DE MONTREAL 1977– ; Vice Chrmn. Sci Council Can. 1984–89; Clin. Psychol. Toronto Psychiatric Hosp. 1960–61; Sessional Lectr. McGill Univ. and Sir George Williams Univ. 1964–65; Asst. Prof. of Psychol. Univ. de Montréal 1965, Assoc. Prof. 1972; Candn. mem. Special Prog. Panel Human Factors, NATO Sci. Ctte. 1979–82, Chair 1980–81; recipient Prof. Anna Abele Meml. Prize distinguished work Latvian philol. 1979; Distinguished Contribution Prize of the World Assoc. of Free Latvians (U.S.) 1989; Hon. LL.D., Queen's Univ. 1991; Marcel-Vincent prize and medal for disting. contrbn. in the social sciences, ACFAS (Assn. canadienne-française pour l'avancement des sciences) 1992; Recipient, Killam Rsch. Fellowship, Canada Council 1993–95; Trustee, Latvian Heritage Cultural Seminars Divreizdivi (Chair 1979); Fellow, Royal Soc. of Canada 1990; Foreign Mem., Academy of Science of Latvia 1990; author 'Fréquence lexicale des mots au Québec' 1974; 'Dzintara kalna (On the Amber Mountain)' 1989; 'Pret Straumi' (Against the Current) 1993; co-author 'Latvian Sun Songs' 1988; Boston/Montreal data base of 72,000 Latvian folk song texts 1982; of the Montreal data base of Latvian Sun songs 1976–86; Editor 'Linguistics and poetics of Latvian folk songs' 1989; author or co-author over 100 articles, book chapters, tech. reports; Pres.: Candn. Psychol. Assn. 1980–81; Social Sci. Fedn. Can. 1980–81; Assn. Advanc. Baltic Studies (U.S.) 1984–86; mem. Bd. and Exec. Ctte. Candn. Humanities Fedn. 1980–82; recreations: travel, gardening; Home: 444 Grenfell Ave., Montréal, Qué. H3R 1G5; Office: C.P. 6128, Succ. A., Montréal, Qué. H3C 3J7.

**VILLA, Brian Loring,** A.B., Ph.D.; university professor; b. Bogota, Colombia 8 Nov. 1940; s. Jorge and Marie Vivian (de Villa) Villa S.; e. Harvard Univ. B.A. 1962, Ph.D. 1969; single; PROF., UNIV. OF OTTAWA 1970; educated in Europe & South America; graduated from Harvard magna cum laude, Phi Beta Kappa 1962; Fulbright Scholar, Univ. of Rome, Ph.D. Harvard 1969; Asst. Prof., West Point 1967–70; awarded five prizes for scholarship incl. 1989 Dafoe Prize, Soc. of Historians of American Foreign Relations; Consultant & Historical Advisor to several CBC programs; author: 'Unauthorized Action, Mountbatten and the Dieppe Raid' 1989, '90; Home: 474 Wilbrod St., Ottawa, Ont. K1N 6M2;

Office: Rm. 305, 155 Séraphin Marion, Ottawa, Ont. K1N 6N5.

**VINAY, Jean-Paul,** C.M. (1987), M.A., Agr. Univ., D.Lett., D. Laws, F.R.S.C.; b; Paris, France, 18 July 1910; s. Maurice and Blanche (Leconte) V.; e. University of Paris, Licence 1930; University of London, M.A. (Linguistics and Phonetics) 1937; Agrégé, Univ. of France, 1941, Titular Sch. of Higher Studies, 1945; Officier d'Acad. 1952; D. Lett. Univ. of Ottawa 1975; D. Laws (Hon. Causa) Concordia; Candn. Confederation Medal 1967; Alexander Gode Medal, A.T.A. 1973; Queen's Jubilee Medal 1977; Chevalier Légion d'Honneur 1978; Member, Order of Canada 1987; 125th Anniversary of the Confederation of Canada Medal, 1992; m. Marie-Paule, d. Pierre Amidieu du Clos, Marquis de Fontaine, 13 Nov. 1940; children: Marie-Elisabeth, Patrick, François, Marie-Emmanuelle; EMERITUS PROF. OF LINGUISTICS, UNIV. OF VICTORIA 1976– ; began teaching career, Swansea Grammar School for Boys 1932; Assoc. Lectr., Dept. of Phonetics, University Coll., London 1937–39; Prof., Chartres High Sch. 1941–42; Inspector-Gen. Modern Lang., City of Paris 1942–46; joined staff of Univ. of Montreal in 1946; Head, Dept. of Linguistics and Dean, Fac. of Arts & Sci., Univ. of Victoria 1968–69, 1972–75; Consultant, I.C.A.O., Montreal, on Internat. Spelling Alphabets, 1948–51; Consultant with I.A.L.A., New York, 1946–48; Publications: 'A Basis and Essentials French Reader' 1946; 'A Basis and Essentials Welsh Grammar' 1947; 'Fluent English' Vol. 1 and 2, 'Stylistique comp. français & anglais' 1958; 'The Canadian Dictionary' (Editor in Chief) 1962; further research in biling. lexicogr. with support from Donner Foundation, 1971 and Canada Council, 1975–76; co-author 'Le Français international' 1966–71; mem., Internat. Phonetic Assn. (Mem. Council); Internat. Council French Language (Paris); Inst. of Translation, Montreal (Vice-Pres.); Soc. of Translators & Interpreters of Can. (Past Pres.); Past Editor, Translators' Journal & Candn. Journ. of Linguistics; Hon. mem., Linguistic Soc. of Am.; Emer. Mem. Int. Soc. of Phonetic Sciences; Visiting Prof., Univ. of Strasbourg, 1964–65; Conservative; Roman Catholic; Home: 2620 Margate Ave., Victoria, B.C. V8S 3A5.

**VINCELLI, Stanley John Frank,** B.Sc., P.Eng.; professional engineer; business executive; b. Ottawa, Ont. 25 Jan. 1947; s. Frank and Sophie (Briganti) V.; e. Loyola H.S. 1963; Lower Can. Coll. 1965; Queen's Univ., B.Sc. (Hons.) 1972; m. Lyne Millette; children: Marc Alexandre, Nicholas, Jonathan; CHRMN. & C.E.O., MADISON AVENUE RETAIL BRANDS INC. 1990– ; Order desk clerk, warehouseman, inventory clerk, Norton Steel Co. Ltd. 1965–72; Vice-Pres. 1972–78; Pres. & C.E.O. 1978–90; Vice-Pres., Qué. Heart Found. 1989–91; Dir., Lower Canada College; Candn. Counc. of Christians & Jews (Qué. reg.) 1984– ; Cedars Cancer Found. R.V.H.; Chrmn. Am. Soc. for Metals (Qué. reg.) 1979–80; Chrmn., Candn. Steel Serv. Ctr. Inst. 1988–90; recreations: golf, fishing; Clubs: Royal Montréal Golf; Montréal Amature Athletic Assn.; Univ.; Young Presidents' Organization; Home: 300 Pine Tree Cres., Beaconsfield, Qué. H9W 5E1; Office: 1320 Graham Blvd., Suite 120, Montréal, Qué. H3P 3C8.

**VINCENT, Anthony Gustave,** B.A.; diplomat; b. Beaconsfield, Eng. 9 Nov. 1939; s. George Gaston and Lady Noel Stratheden (Viner) V.; e. Shawnigan Lake Sch., B.C.; Univ. of Minn. B.A. 1967; m. Lucie d. Maurice and Yvette Houle 9 Aug. 1985; one d. Alexandra Genevieve; AMBASSADOR TO PERU AND BOLIVIA 1994– ; joined Dept. of External Affairs Ottawa 1969, Third/Second Sec. The Hague 1971, First Sec./Counsellor New Delhi 1976, Dep. Dir. S. and S.E. Asia Relations Div. 1980, Dir. of Div. 1983; former High Comnr. for Can. to Bangladesh and Ambassador to Burma 1985–88; Department of External Affairs, Ottawa 1988–93; Anglican; recreations: tennis, gardening, golf, skiing; Home: 10 Kilbarry Cres., Ottawa, Ont. K1K 0G7; Office: c/o Dept. of External Affairs, Lester B. Pearson Bldg., 125 Sussex Dr., Ottawa, Ont. K1A 0G2.

**VINCENT, Jean Denis;** corporate director; b. Kapuskasing, Ont. 15 Apr. 1930; s. late Gaston and Robertine (Gauthier) V.; e. Univ. of Ottawa B.A., B.Ph. 1951; m. Denyse d. late Alphonse Ouimet, Pointe Claire, Que. 13 Aug. 1960; children: Denis, Josée; Dir., Ault Foods Ltd.; Liquid Carbonic Inc.; John Labatt Ltd.; Amoco Can. Petroleum Company Ltd.; Québec-Téléphone; Canada World Youth; The Arthritis Soc.; Trustee, Le Devoir; joined Quebec Trust Co. (Fiducie du Québec), Montreal 1964–67, Depy. Gen. Mgr. and Mgr. Le Fonds Desjardins; Saving and Investment Ltd. Quebec 1967–69, Vice Pres. and Dir.; Philips Electronics Ltd. 1969–81, Vice Pres.; Alliance Mutual Life Insurance Co. 1981–86, Pres. & C.E.O. & Dir.; Vice-Chrmn., Pres. & C.E.O., Industrial-Alliance Financial Inc. 1987–91; Vice-Chrmn., Pres. & C.E.O., General Trustco of Canada 1991–93; service with RCN rank Lt.; Past Chrmn., Consulting Ctte., Court of Quebec 1988; Past Pres. and Dir. United Way Canada, Ottawa; conferred Hon. Doctorate, Univ. of Ottawa 1991; R. Catholic; Clubs: Mount-Royal; St-James; Saint-Denis; Address: 3450 Redpath Rue, #003, Montreal, PQ H3G 2G3.

**VINCENT, Marc-Aurèle,** M.A., M.Th., D.Sc.; educator; b. Hull, Que. 6 Apl. 1934; s. Aurèle and Germaine (Lacourcière) V.; e. Univ. of Ottawa B.A., B.Ph. 1956, B.A., L.Ph. 1957, B.Sc. 1961, B.Th. 1963, M.A. 1965, M.Th., L.Th. 1965, M.Sc. 1966; Univ. de Paris D.Sc. 1971; m. Françoise d. Wilfrid and Valeda Desjardins 20 March 1976; children: Jean-Luc, Brigitte, Benoît; OFFICE OF THE VICE-RECTOR ACADEMIC, UNIV. DU QUE. à HULL 1987– ; Research Fellow Centre d'études nucléaires de Saclay, France 1966–71; Post-doctoral Fellow, Lectr. in Math and Head Supvr. Labs. Dept. Physics Univ. of Ottawa 1971–72; Asst. Dir. Centre de recherches en sciences appliquées à l'alimentation 1972–76, mem. Bd. Dirs. 1973–82; Exec. Secy. 2nd Internat. Symposium on Ozone Technol. Montréal 1975; Dean of Studies and Research Dir. present Univ. 1977–80, Internat. Coop. Agt. 1978–86; Dean of Graduate Studies and Research, present univ. 1980–86; mem. Bd. Dirs., present univ. 1981–86; mem., Groupe de travail des études avancées et de la recherche and Comn. des programmes d'études avancées gérées conjointement (Chrmn., 1984–86), Univ. du Qué. 1977–86; Secy. Public Image Ctte., present univ. 1987–88; mem., Comité de concertation sur les impacts et la maîtrise sociale des transformations technologiques, Univ. du Qué. 1987–92; Dir., Module Arts et lettres, present univ. 1988– ; mem., Assn. des Cadres, present univ. 1988– (Chrmn. 1991– ); Vice Chrmn. Assn. des propriétaires de Perkins-sur-le-lac 1982–85; mem. Bd. Dirs. Fondation des aînés de l'Outaouais 1985–86; mem. Bd. Dirs., Vanier Pub. Lib. 1983–88 (Vice Chrmn. 1984–86); mem. Bd. Dirs. Académie de gérontologie de l'Outaouais 1983–84; mem. Bd. Dirs., Notre-Dame du Saint-Esprit parish 1989– (Chrmn. 1991–93); mem., World Assn. for Cooperative Education 1989– ; Chrmn., Div. de la Formation of Centraide Outaouais 1990– ; Vice-Chrmn., Multiressources 1990– ; mem., Bureau canadien de la main d'oeuvre en génie 1991– ; recipient numerous awards and grants 1963–79; author or co-author various publs.; mem. Internat. Ozone Assn. (Dir. 1975–86, Vice Chrmn. N.Am. Exec. Ctte. 1975–76 and Chrmn. 1976–79); Soc. France-Can.; Soc. Française de Physique; Soc. Européenne de Physique; Assn. Canadienne-Française pour l'Avancement des sciences; Soc. d'Astronomie du Qué. Inc.; Studio d'Arts des Jeunes de Vanier; Confrérie des Amis de St-Vincent France; Club Internat. 'Blanc de Mer' France; Soc. canadienne pour l'étude de l'enseignement supérieur; R. Catholic; recreations: sports, music, chess; Home: 226 Ave. Greensway, Vanier, Ont.; Office: P.O. Box 1250, Stn. B, Hull, Qué. J8X 3X7.

**VINCENT, Roger,** B.A., LL.B., C.R., j.c.s.p.; judge; b. Ville-Marie, Qué. 31 Oct. 1927; s. Joseph Adélard and Thelma (McGuire) V.; e. Bourget Coll., B.A.; Univ. of Montréal, LL.B.; m. Clairette d. Armand Lafrenière 4 July 1959; children: Michel, Pierre-Jean; JUDGE, COURT OF THE PROVINCIAL COURT, CRIMINAL DIV., MONTREAL 1976– ; admitted to Qué. Bar Assn. 1954; gen. practice 1955–68; Crown Prosecutor, Ville-Marie & Val d'Or 1966–76; Office: 1 est, Notre Dame, Montréal, Qué. H2Y 1B6.

**VINCENT, Thomas Brewer,** B.A., M.A., Ph.D.; university professor; b. Fredericton, N.B. 27 Jan. 1943; s. Carl Eugene and Clara Elizabeth (Brewer) V.; e. Kings College School; Kings College B.A. 1965; Queen's Univ. M.A. 1968, Ph.D. 1972; m. Nora d. Bishop George and Mary Arnold 20 Aug. 1966; children: Charles Thomas, Douglas George; PROF., DEPT. OF ENGLISH AND PHILOSOPHY, ROYAL MILITARY COLLEGE 1984– ; joined Dept. of English & Phil., Royal Military Coll. 1969; Assoc. Prof. 1979; Head of Dept. 1993; extensive rsch. activity & pubs. in early Candn. lit. culture & computerized bibliograhy & indexing; Dir., Early Candn. Cultural Journals Project, RMC 1982–92; Mem., Anglican Ch. of Canada; vice-Pres., Bibliographical Soc. of Canada; Assoc., John Carter Brown Lib.; author: 'Narrative Verse Satire in Maritime Canada, 1779–1814' 1978, 'Eighteenth-Century Canadian Poetry' 1981, 'Index to Pre-1900 English Language Canadian Cultural and Literary Magazines' 1993; recreations: canoeing, hiking; clubs: Kingston Field Naturalist, Randolph Mountain; Home: 304 Olympus Ave., Kingston, Ont. K7M 4T9; Office: Kingston, Ont. K7K 5L0.

**VINCENT, Maj.-Gen. William Horace,** CMM, CD(2); air force officer; b. Winnipeg, Man. 31 Jan. 1922; s. Horace Gordon and Alice Mina (Leeder) V.; e. Lord Byng H.S. Vancouver B.C.; m. Margaret d. Elsie and Charles Lancaster Harrison 18 Nov. 1943; children: Ann, Peter, John; Pilot, wartime RCAF 1941–45 (WW II Eur. Theatre of Opns., Night Fighter Pilot) served two tours; transferred to peacetime RCAF 1946; var. training assignments Can. & U.S. 1946–56; Commanding Offr., CF 100 Weapons Practice Unit, RCAF Station, Cold Lake, Alta. 1956; Sr. Dir., Seattle Air Def. Control Ctr., NORAD 1960; Chief Controller, North Bay Underground NORAD Control Ctr. 1963; Com. Offr., 409 All Weather Squadron, RCAF Station Comox 1965; Base Comdr., Cold Lake, Alta. 1967; Candn. Air Attache, London, England 1971; Chief of Staff, Air Def. Command H.Q. 1972; Comdr., Air Def. Command & 22 NORAD Region then Comdr., Air Def. Group 1975; promoted to Group Captain 1967, Brig. Gen. 1972, Major Gen. 1975; has served all facets of Air Def. specialty in air & ground positions of operational command & control; Comdr., Order of Military Merit 1974; Cert. of Achievement, NORAD 1964; U.S. Airforce Air Def. Achievement cert. 1961; Dir. & Chrmn., St. Joseph's Hosp. Bd. 1982–92; Dir. & Pres., Comox Valley Assn. for Mentally Handicapped 1977– ; Alderman, Town of Comox 1977– ; Dir., Comox-Strathcona Dist. 1982–85, 1987–92; Chrmn., Comox Valley Sanitary Sewer Comn. 1977–85, 1987– ; recreations: outdoor leisure, golf, fishing; Clubs: RCAF Assn.; Royal Candn. Legion; Comox Masonic Lodge 188 of B.C.; Address: 167 Carthew St., Comox, B.C. V9N 5C9.

**VINER, Anthony Peers,** B.A.; broadcast executive; b. Colombia, S. America 24 Feb. 1947; s. Douglas Samuel and Ruth Marjorie (Peers) V.; e. Univ. of W. Ont., B.A. 1968; m. Catherine d. John and Catherine Madden, 4 June 1976; children: Gregory, Michael, Elizabeth; PRES., ROGERS BROADCASTING 1989– ; Marketing, Sun Oil Co. Ltd. 1969–73; Broadcast Sales, Paul Mlvihill Ltd. 1973–77; Pres., Radio., Slaight Broadcasting 1977–81; Extve. Vice Pres., Rogers Broadcasting 1981–89; Past Chrmn., Radio Bureau of Canada; Chrmn. Radio Extve. Ctte., and Chrmn. Bd. of Dirs., Bureau of Broadcast Measurement; Chrmn., Special Events, United Way of Greater Toronto 1988; Candn. Assoc. of Broadcasters; Club: Thornhill Country; Office: 25 Adelaide St. E., Toronto, Ont. M5W 1A8.

**VINER, Peter Douglas,** C.A.A.P.; communications executive; b. Bogata Columbia, S.A. 23 Aug. 1945; s. Douglas Samuel and Ruth Majorie (Peers) V.; e. Gordon Graydon H.S. 1965; C.A.A.P. 1970; Harvard PMD 39 1980; divorced; one d.: Christine Lynn; PRES. & C.E.O., CANWEST BROADCASTING LTD. 1990– ; Extve. Vice-Pres., English Pub. & Broadcasting, Telemedia Inc. 1988–90; Sales Extve., Maclean Hunter 1968; Radio TV Reps. 1969–73; Vice-Pres., Mktg., Global Commun. 1974–80; Pres. & C.E.O., Western Approaches Ltd., CKVU Vancouver 1980–84; Extve. Vice-Pres., Engl. Broadcasting, TCOI 1984; Pres., Engl. Broadcasting, Telemedia Commun. Ont. Inc. 1986; Dir., TV Bur. of Can. 1979; Radio Bur. of Can. 1989–90; Radio Extve. Mem., Bur. of Broadcast Measurement 1987– ; Marketing Man of the Year, Am. Mktg. Assn. 1979; recreations: golf, tennis, bridge; clubs: Toronto Cricket, Skating & Curling, Emerald Hills Golf & Country; Home: 456 Moberly Rd., #914, Vancouver, B.C. V2S 4L7; Office: 180 West 2nd Ave., Vancouver, B.C. V5Y 3T9.

**VINETTE, Paulette G.;** association executive; b. Montréal, Qué. 9 Oct. 1953; d. Laurier Joseph and Yvonne Elizabeth (Leblanc) V.; e. Concordia Univ.; Fellow, Am. Soc. Assn. Exec.; Cert. Assn. Exec.; PRES. CANDN. SOFT DRINK ASSN. 1986– ; Exec. Dir. Candn. Frozen Food Assn. 1979–81; Pres. Inst. Assn. Execs. 1983–86; Office: 55 York St., Suite 330, Toronto, Ont. M5J 1R7.

**VINH, Sinh,** B.A., M.A., Ph.D.; professor of Japanese history; b. Hue, Vietnam 4 July 1944; s. Tuyen Buu and Nhan Phan; e. Tokyo Internat. Christian Univ. B.A. 1970; Univ. of Toronto M.A. 1974, Ph.D. (Japanese History) 1979; m. Kyoko d. Hung-sang and Ki-dal Cho 3 May 1970; one child: Bao Tan; PROF. OF JAPANESE HISTORY, UNIV. OF ALBERTA 1986– ; Asst. Prof., Dept. of East Asian Studies, Univ. of Toronto 1979–82; Japan Found. Fellow, Inst. of Social Science, Univ. of Tokyo 186; Visiting Prof., Meiji Univ. (Tokyo) 1991; Adv. Bd., 'Can. J. of History'; Ed. Bd., Lac-Viet Monograph Series, Yale Internat. & Area Studies; Chrmn., East Asian Studies Ctte., Univ. of Alta. 1990– ; recipient, Canada Council Canada-Japan Book Award 1990; Tokutomi Soho Soc. (Tokyo) Award 1990; Mem., Japanese Studies Assn. of Can.; Am. Assn. of Asian Studies; Tokutomi Soho Soc. (Japan); Fukuzawa Yukichi Soc. (Japan); author: 'Tokutomi Soho: The Later Career' 1986, 'The Rise of Modern Japan' 1991, 'Japan and Vietnam in the Context of East Asia' 1993; editor & contbr.: 'Phan Boi Chau and the Dong Du Movement' 1989; transl. & co-editor: 'The Future Japan' 1990; recreations: tennis; Home: 5212 – 111A St., Edmonton, Alta. T6H 3G9; Office: Edmonton, Alta. T6G 2H4.

**VINING, Leo Charles,** Ph.D., F.C.I.C., F.C.S., F.R.S.C.; microbiologist; educator; b. Whangarei, N.Z. 28 March 1925; s. Charles Hildrup and Ruby Robina (Withers) V.; e. Whangarei (N.Z.) High Sch. 1941; Auckland Univ. B.Sc. 1948, M.Sc. 1949; Cambridge Univ. Ph.D. 1951; Kiel Univ. Germany 1951–52; Rutgers Univ. 1953–54; children: Robert Charles, Michael Taylor, Deborah Lee, Russell James; Prof. of Biology, Dalhousie Univ. 1990–92; Instr. Rutgers Univ. 1954–55; Research Offr. Prairie Regional Lab. Nat. Research Council Can. 1956–62, Sec. Head Atlantic Regional Lab. Nat. Research Council Can. 1963–71; Prof. of Biol. Dalhousie Univ. 1971–86; Killam Prof., 1986–90; Visiting scientist, Massachusetts Inst. of Technology 1977–78; Univ. of Alberta 1984–85; Merck Sharp and Dohme Lectr. Chem. Inst. Can. 1965; rec'd Harrison Prize in Microbiol. Royal Soc. Can. 1972; CSM Award, Candn. Soc. Microbiol. 1976; John Labatt Ltd. Award, Chem. Ins. of Can. 1985; Charles Thom Award, Soc. Industrial Microbiol. 1985; served with Royal N.Z. Navy (Fleet Air Arm) 1943–45; Emeritus Ed., Journal of Antibiotics; Section Ed., Candn. Journal of Microbiology; Mem. of Ed. Bd., Journal of General Microbiol.; Assoc. Ed., Applied Microbiol. & Biotechnol.; author various articles and over 200 research papers chem., biochem. and microbiol. of natural products especially antibiotics produced by fungi and actinomycetes; Trustee, Internat. Fdn. for Sci. 1981–87; Dir. Chem. Inst. Can. 1972–77; mem. Am. Chem. Soc.; Candn. Soc. Microbiols. (Extve. 1972–76, 1990–93, Pres. 1992–93); Am. Soc. Microbiol.; N.S. Inst. Science (Pres. 1980–81); Soc. for General Microbiol.; Home: 6121 Regina., Halifax, N.S. B3H 1N4; Office: Halifax, N.S. B3H 4J1.

**VIRTUE, The Hon. Mr. Justice C.G.,** Q.C., B.A, LL.B.; b. Lethbridge, Alta. 30 May 1926; s. Abner Gladstone and Marian (Ells) V.; e. McMaster Univ., B.A. 1947; Univ. of Alta., LL.B. 1950; m. Mary Irene, d. Charles Greenwood, 21 June 1952; children: Marni, George, Carol, Jephson, Judson, Marian Jane; JUSTICE OF THE COURT OF QUEEN'S BENCH OF ALBERTA and DEPUTY JUSTICE, COURT OF NORTH WEST TERRITORIES 1985; Former Partner, Virtue & Co.; read law with A. Gladstone Virtue; called to Bar of Alta. 1951; Past Pres., Lethbridge YMCA; Past Distr. Gov. of Y Men's Club (1960–62); cr. Q.C. 1968; Past Pres., Lethbridge Bar Assn.; Past Chrmn. (1968–69) Lethbridge Mun. Hosp.; Past Pres., Alta. Hosp. Assn. (1970); mem., Alberta Hosp. Services Comm., (1970–78); Pres., 1975 Canada Winter Games; Past Chrmn. Alta. Law Found. (1980–84); Past Pres., Law Soc. of Alta. 1984–85; Zeta Psi; Baptist; recreations: sailing, skiing, golfing; Office: Court of Queen's Bench, 611 - 4th St. S.W., Calgary, Alta. T2P 1T5.

**VISANO, Livy Anthony,** M.A., Ph.D.; educator; b. Naples, Italy 27 July 1949; s. Gino and Mary (Bosna) V.; e. Univ. of Toronto B.A. 1973, M.A. 1974, Ph.D. 1986; m. Robynne d. M. Portnoy & Henry Neugebauer 1992; one s. Anthony; ASSOC. PROF. OF SOCIOL. YORK UNIV. 1984– ; Lectr. Ryerson Polytech. Inst. 1974–78, Univ. of Toronto 1984–85, 1990–93; Cons. Min. of Community & Social Services, York Reg. Police, Metrop. Toronto Police, Sec. of State; Candn. Rep. N.E. Criminal Justice Assn.; Vice Pres. Social Planning Council Metrop. Toronto 1985–86, mem. Bd. 1985– ; Adv. Bd., Centre for Justice Studies; Chair, Security Advisory Ctte. 1992; Citizens Adv. Ctte. Corrections Can. 1987–90, Charter of Rights Action Group 1989; Cofounder, Race Relations Certif. Prog.; Resource, Mayor's Ctte. Community & Race Relations 1982– ; Patron, J. of Human Justice; mem. Bd. Urban Alliance Race Relations 1989; Chair, Task Force on Race Relations, S.P.C. 1989– ; mem. Consortium on Youth Empowerment; mem. Bd. Vita Nova Found.; mem. Extve. YUFA; mem. Adv. Group Italian Candn. Benevolent Corp.; Extve. Editor, J. of Int. Sociol.; Editor, J. of Developing Societies; J. of Race and Ethnic Studies; J. of Asian and African Studies; mem. Access Action Council; Awards Ctte. Am. Acad. Criminal Justice Sci.'s; recipient Solr. Gen. Can. Fellowship Grants 1977–81; Univ. of Toronto Open Scholarship 1982; Puntzen Internat. Acad. Arts, Sci. & Lit. Publ. Award 1988; Dean's Award Outstanding Contributions in Teaching York Univ. 1987–88; O.C.U.F.A. Award for Outstanding Teaching 1990; author 'This Idle Trade' 1987; co-author 'Deviant Designation' 1983; 'A Time for Action; Access to Health and Social Services' 3 vols. 1987; 'Canadian Penology'; 'Understanding Policing' 1992; 'Beyond The Text' 1994; numerous book chapters, jour. articles, nat. & internat. presentations tech. reports; Assoc. Ed., Int. J. of comp. soci.; mem. various ed. bds., reviewer; mem. Am. Criminol. Assn.; Candn. Critical Criminol.; Acad. Criminal Justice Sci.'s; Ethics Ctte., C.S.A.A.; Criminal Justice Assn. (Can.); recreations: chess, photography, swimming; Office: Room 2150, Vari Hall, York Univ., 4700 Keele St., North York, Ont. M3J 1P3.

**VISSER, Harry J.,** B.A., M.B.A.; information technology executive; b. The Netherlands 11 March 1945; s. Hilbrand J. and Neltje W. (Stork) V.; e. Univ. of Toronto B.A. 1983; York Univ. M.B.A. 1988; m. Hendrika M. d. Karel Waversveld 22 April 1967; children: Matthew, Mark; SENIOR VICE-PRESIDENT, EDS CANADA 1989– ; Application Software Devel. 1969–73; Systems Software Devel. 1974–75; Computer Opns. Mngt. 1975–77; Financial Mngt. 1978–84; Comptroller, EDS Canada 1985–86; Vice-Pres. & Chief Financial Offr. 1986–88; Dir., EDS Canada; Capsco Software Canada Ltd.; Pres., EDS Canada Leasing, Ltd.; Vice-Chrmn., Consortium Members, Real Data Ontario Inc.; recreations: golf, reading; clubs: Toronto Bd. of Trade; Office: 300 Consilium Place, Suite 800, Scarborough, Ont. M1H 3G2.

**VISSER, Margaret Agar Barclay,** B.A., M.A., Ph.D.; writer, broadcaster, university lecturer; b. S. Africa 11 May 1940; d. John Holland Barclay and Ruby Margaret Agar (O'Connell) Lloyd; e. Univ. of Toronto, B.A. (Hons.) 1970, M.A. 1973, Ph.D. 1980; m. Colin Wills s. Johannes and Anna Mazzena V. 8 June 1962; children: Emily, Alexander; Course Dir., York Univ. 1976–79, 1982–88 and Canada Research Fellow, Dept. of Classics 1988–93; broadcaster, CBC 'Morningside' 1982–91; CBC 'The Arts Tonight' 1991– ; many other TV & Radio progs. in Can., U.S., Australia & U.K.; Contrib. Ed. & Columnist, Saturday Night Magazine: 'The Way We Are' 1988–94; public lectr., Canada, Britain, Australia & USA; series, CFTO TV 'Lifetime' 1986–89; subject of CBC TV's 'Monitor' 1987 and of TVO's 'A comme Artiste' 1992; Gold Medal for Classics, Univ. of Toronto 1970; Roman Cath.; author: 'Much Depends on Dinner' 1986 (French trans. 1988, Italian trans. 1989; pub. U.S. & Britain 1989, Glenfiddich Award, Food Book of the Year, Britain 1989); 'The Rituals of Dinner' 1991 (Pub. U.S. 1991, Britain 1992; recipient, Internat. Assn. of Culinary Professionals' Literary Food Writing Award 1992, Jane Grigson Award for Scholarly Distinction 1992); 'The Way We Are' 1994; recreations: music, theatre, film, novels, poetry, painting, architecture; Address: Wylie, Aitken & Stone, 250 West 57th St., Suite 2114, New York, NY 10107.

**VIVASH, John Alfred;** banker; b. Toronto, Ont. 22 June 1931; s. Alfred Thomas and Rubina Crichton (Tait) V.; m. Barbara d. Edward and Dorothy Williams 8 Feb. 1958; children: Mary Elizabeth, Catherine Anne, John Michael; PRES. & CHIEF EXECUTIVE OFFICER, CIBC SECURITIES INC. 1990– ; Vice-Pres. & Dir., Midland Doherty Limited 1975–87; Pres. & C.E.O., Fidelity Investments Canada Limited 1987–90; Pres. & Sr. Cons., Vivash Consulting Inc.; Guest Lectr., Univ. of Toronto, Univ. of Alta., Univ. of W. Ont. Sch. of Business; Advisory Bd. Mem., The Am. Assn. of Individual Investors 1978–89; The Candn. Shareowners Assn. 1987–89; Home: 184 Castlewood Rd., Toronto, Ont. M5N 2L7; Office: Commerce Court, Toronto, Ont. M5L 1A2.

**VIZINCZEY, Stephen;** writer; b. Káloz, Hungary 12 May 1933; s. István and Erzsébet (Mohos) V.; e. Benedictine Gymnasium Esztergom; Gymnasium Univ. of Budapest; Univ. of Budapest 1949–50; Acad. of Theatre Arts Hons. Grad. 1956; m. Gloria d. Murray and Martha Fisher 27 Sept. 1963; three d.: Martha Harron, Mary Harron, Marianne Vizinczey; fought in Hungarian Revolution 1956; came to Can. 1957, Candn. citizen; learned Eng. writing Nat. Film Bd. scripts Montréal; ed. 'Exchange' mag. 1961–62; radio writer/producer CBC Toronto 1962–65; moved to England, wrote extensively for 'The Times,' 'Sunday Telegraph,' and 'Observer'; author: 'In Praise of Older Women' (novel) 1965; 'The Rules of Chaos' (essays) 1969; 'An Innocent Millionaire' (novel) 1983; 'Truth and Lies in Literature' (reviews & essays) 1986; recreations: classical music, walking; Home: 70 Coleherne Court, Old Brompton Rd., London SW5 OEF, England.

**VLASIC, Ivan A.,** B.C.L., LL.M., J.S.D.; university professor; b. Gorizia, Italy 29 July 1926; e. Univ. of Zagreb, B.C.L. 1949; McGill Univ., LL.M. 1955; Yale Univ., LL.M. 1958, J.S.D. 1961; m. Katherine C.; d. Vernon and Claire Parker 1956; children: Edward, John; PROF., MCGILL UNIV. 1969– ; Sr. Fellow, Yale Law Sch. 1959–62; Asst. Prof., Univ. of Florida 1958–59; Univ. of Ottawa 1962–63; Assoc. Prof., McGill Univ., 1963–69; Dir., Inst. of Air & Space Law, McGill Univ. 1971–75; Mem., Candn. Counc. on Internat. Law; Am. Soc. of Internat. Law; Internat. Law Assn.; co-author: 'Law and Public Order in Space' 1963; editor: 'Explorations in Aerospace Law' 1968; Home: 669 Warwick, Baie d'Urfé, Qué. H9X 2P4; Office: 3644 Peel St., Montréal, Qué. H3A 1W9.

**VOGEL, Barbara,** M.Arch.; architect; b. Slupsk, Poland 24 Dec. 1945; d. Antoni and Ludwika (Böhm) Mielnik; e. Dept. of Arch., Univ. of Technol., Cracow, Poland M.Arch. 1969; m. Jacek s. Marian Vogel 27 June 1970; one d.: Kaija Vogel; PRINCIPAL, VOGEL ASSOCIATES, DESIGN AND PLANNING CONSULTANTS 1988– ; Asst. Prof., Dept. of Arch., Univ. of Technol., Cracow 1969–72; Arkkitehtitoimisto Prof. E. Krakstrom, Helsinki Finland, Arch.-Designer 1972–76; Principal, Vogel & Vogel Designers 1978–84; Design Dir., Arthur Erickson Architects 1980–88 (Candn. Chancery, Washington, D.C.; Provincial Govt. Bldg. Thunder Bay; King Ranch Health Spa, Ont.); Tutor in Sch. of Arch., Univ. of Toronto; profile in num. mags. in Europe & Can.; winner of arch. awards & competitions in Poland and Finland; Roman Catholic; Mem., Polish Assn. of Arch., SARP; Finnish Assn. of Arch., SAFA; Nordic Register of Arch.; Address: 33 Bernard Ave., Toronto, Ont. M5R 1R3.

**VOGEL-SPROTT, Muriel Doris,** M.A., Ph.D.; university professor; b. Waterloo, Ont. 20 Aug. 1934; d. Henry and Anne Ellen (Stroh) Vogel; e. McMaster Univ. B.A. 1955; Univ. of Toronto M.A. 1957, Ph.D. 1960; m. David Arthur Sprott, 16 Dec. 1961; two d. Anne Ellen, Jane Barry; PROF. OF PSYCHOL. UNIV. OF WATERLOO since 1969, mem. of Senate and Bd. of Govs. (Extve.) 1976–78; Acting Dean of Graduate Studies, 1978; Research Assoc. Addiction Research Foundation Toronto 1959–61; Asst. Prof. present Univ. 1961, Assoc. Prof. 1965, Assoc. Dean of Grad. Affairs Arts Faculty 1971–78; Visiting Scholar Pharmacol. Dept. Univ. Coll. and Psychol. Dept. Bedford Coll. London, Eng. 1969–70; mem. Science Council Can. 1973–79; author numerous research papers in prof. journs., book and book chapters on topics of human learning, alcoholism and alcohol effects on behaviour; Fellow, Am. Psychol. Assn.; Fellow, Candn. Psychol. Assn.; Registered Psychol. Ont.; Home: 295 Ferndale Pl., Waterloo, Ont. N2J 3X8.

**VOGLER, Kersten H.O.;** business executive; b. Muenster, W. Germany 20 Sept. 1934; s. Helmuth O. and Hildegard (Althoff) V.; e. elem. and high schs. Germany; McGill Univ.; Concordia Univ.; Northwestern Univ.; m. Eva S. d. Sandor and Berta Szenassy; one s. Ralph; CORPORATE VICE PRES. HOECHST CANADA INC.; joined Internat. Trade present Co. 1960, Product Mgt. – Sales Coordination 1960, Gen. Mgt. Sales Dept. 1967, Gen. Mgt. Sales Div. 1973– ; mem. Candn. Chem. Producers Assn.; Soc. Chem. Ind.; Candn. Agric. Chems. Assn. (Past Dir.); Bd. Trade Toronto; recreations: sports, sailing, practical hobbies; Home: R.R. 2, Kettleby, Ont. L0G 1J0; Office: 100 Tempo Ave., Willowdale, Ont. M2H 2N8.

**VOGT, Erich Wolfgang,** O.C.; Ph.D., F.R.S.C.; physicist; b. Steinbach, Man., 12 Nov. 1929; s. Peter Andrew and Susan (Reimer) V.; e. Steinbach (Man.) Pub. and High Schs.; Univ. of Man., B.Sc. 1951 (Gold Medal in Hon. Science), M.Sc. 1952, D.Sc. 1982; Princeton Univ., Ph.D. 1955; Queen's Univ., D.Sc. 1984; Univ. of Regina, LL.D. 1986; Carleton Univ., D.Sc. 1988; m. Barbara Mary, d. Edward Herbert and Edith Mary (McCann) Greenfield, Vancouver, B.C., 27 Aug. 1952; children: Edith Susan, Elizabeth Mary, David Eric, Jonathan Michael, Robert Jeremy; Physicist, Univ. Of Brit. Columbia; Vice Pres. (Faculty & Student Affairs) there 1975–81; First Chrmn., Sci. Council of B.C. 1978–80; Chrmn., Bd of Management, TRIUMF Project 1974–80; Dir. since 1981; recipient Centennial Medal 1967; Fellow, Royal Society of Canada 1970; Officer, Order of Canada 1976; Queen Elizabeth Jubilee Medal 1977; CAP Medal for Achievement in Physics, Candn. Assn. of Physicists 1988; co-editor 'Advances in Nuclear Physics' (Vols. 1–19, 1969– ); other writings incl. over 70 scient. papers; Mem., Candn. Assn. Physicists (Pres. 1970–71); Liberal; recreations: hiking, tennis; Club: Canadian; Home: 1816 Wesbrook Cr., Vancouver, B.C. V6T 1W2.

**VOLGYESI, Elizabeth;** business executive; b. Hungary; d. Joseph and Elizabeth (Bodak) Nemes; e. Hungary m. Andrew Stephen s. Dr. Francis Andrew Volgyesi 3 Sept. 1963; children: Christina, Lara; Founder (1977) and Pres., Treats Inc. 1986–90, franchized 1979; guest speaker Univ. of Toronto and various entrepreneurial orgns.

**VOLKOFF, George Michael,** M.B.E. (1946), M.A., Ph.D., D.Sc., F.R.S.C. (1948); retired university professor; b. Moscow, Russia, 23 Feb. 1914; s. Michael and Elizabeth (Titoff) V.; came to Can. 1924; e. Univ. of Brit. Columbia, B.A. 1934, M.A. 1936; D.Sc. (honoris causa) 1945; Univ. of Cal., Ph.D. 1940; Princeton Univ., 1940; m. Olga, d. Joseph Okulitch, Vancouver, 22 June 1940; children: Elizabeth, Alexandra, Olga; PROFESSOR EMERITUS AND DEAN EMERITUS, UNIV. OF B.C. since 1979; mem. Bd. of Trustees (and Chrmn. 1984–85), Vancouver Gen. Hosp. 1979–86; mem. Tech. Adv. Comte. to AECL on Nuclear Fuel Waste Management Program 1979–89; mem., Nat. Research Council Can. 1969–75; Research Physicist i/c of Theoretical Physics Br., Atomic Energy Divn., Nat. Research Council, Chalk River, Ont., 1945–46; Asst. Prof. of Physics, Univ. of B.C., 1940–43; Assoc. Research Physicist, Montreal Lab., Nat. Research Council, 1943–45; Prof. of Physics, Univ. of B.C., 1946 and Head of the Dept. 1961–71; Dean, Fac. of Sci. 1972–79; Editor, 'Canadian Journal of Physics' 1950–56; 'Soviet Physics-Uspekhi' 1979–93; Fellow, Am. Phys. Soc.; Am. Assn. Advanc. Science; mem., Am. Assn. of Phys. Teachers; Candn. Assn. of Phys.; Phi Beta Kappa; Sigma Xi; Gamma Alpha; Greek Orthodox; Home: 1776 Western Parkway, Vancouver, B.C. V6T 1V3.

**VOLPÉ, Peter G.,** C.F.P., R.F.P.; financial advisor; b. Toronto, Ont. 3 April 1958; s. Dr. Robert and Ruth (Pullan) V.; e. McMaster Univ. 1981; Canadian Securities Inst. (CIF) 1987; Chartered Financial Planner 1983; Registered Financial Planner 1987; VICE-PRES., INTEGRA CAPITAL MANAGEMENT CORPORATION 1994– ; Advisory Bd., Acuman Financial Inc. (Cambridge, MA); Women and Money, Inc.; Lectr., York Univ. 'Personal Finance' Atkinson College; Financial Planner, Financial Concept Group 1982–84; Manager, Finan. Planning Serv., Royal Trust Corp. 1984–88; Nat. Dir., Finan. Planning & Adv. Serv., Central Guaranty Trust 1988–90; Mem., Task Force on Finan. Regulation, Trust Cos. Assn. 1989–90; Edn. Ctte., Trust Cos. Inst. 1989–90; Vice-Pres., Kerr Financial Corporation 1991–93; Guest Lectr. at several colleges & univs.; popular speaker at trade shows & conventions across Canada; Co-host & Speaker at 1st IAFP/CAFP Conference on Finan. Planning in Canada, Toronto 1991; Candn. Rep., Assoc. Naz. Agenti Servizi Financiale conf. Italy 1990; involved with Terry Fox Run 1985–88; Extve. Campaigner, United Way 1986–87; Nat. Pres., Candn. Assn. of Financial Planners (C.A.F.P.) 1989–91; Ont. Pres. 1987–89; Nat. Chrmn. 1991–93; Mem., Assn. of Fellows, Candn. Securities Inst.; contbr. to financial press, TV & radio as host and technical consultant; author of several articles published worldwide; contbr., 'The Only Retirement Guide You'll Ever Need' 1993; co-author, 'How to Retire Young & Wealthy' 1994; Contbg. Ed., Hume Pub. 1985–87; recreations: skiing, tennis, canoeing, photography; club: Alpine Ski; Home: 42 Elm Rd., Toronto, Ont. M5M 3T3; Office: 55 University Ave., Suite 1100, Toronto, Ont. M5J 2H7.

**VOLPÉ, Robert,** M.D., F.R.C.P.(C.), F.R.C.P.(Edin.); F.A.C.P.; physician; educator; b. Toronto, Ont. 6 Mar. 1926; s. Dr. Aaron G. and Esther (Shulman) V.; e. Univ. of Toronto M.D. 1950; postgrad. studies Univ. of Toronto 1950–57; m. Ruth Vera Pullan 5 Sept. 1949; children: Catherine Lillian; Elizabeth Anne; Peter George; Edward James; Rose Ellen; PROF. EMERITUS, UNIVERSITY OF TORONTO 1991– ; Dir., Endocrinology Research Lab., Wellesley Hosp. 1965– ; mem. Ed. Bd., 'Annals of Internal Medicine' 1976–80; 'Clinical Endocrinology' 1976–83; 'Clinical Medicine' 1981–86; 'Journal of Clinical Endocrinology and Metabolism' 1982–87; 'Endocrine Pathology' 1989–94; Sr. Research Fellow, Univ. of Toronto 1957–62; Asst. Prof. 1962–68; Assoc. Prof. 1968–72; Prof. of Medicine 1972–91; Active Staff, St. Joseph's Hosp. 1957–65; Wellesley Hosp. 1965– , Physician-in-Chief 1974–87; Dir., Div. of Endocrinology, Univ. of Toronto 1987–92; Chrmn., Undergrad. Educ. Comte. (Period II) 1967–70; Postgrad. Comte. 1973–75; Centennial Comte. 1987–88; State of Art Lectr., Endocrine Soc. 1975; Goldie Medal for Medical Research, Univ. of Toronto 1972; Jamieson Medal, Candn. Nuclear Medicine Soc. 1980; State of Art Lectr., Dept. of Med., Univ. of Toronto 1981; Baxter Prize, Toronto Soc. Clin. Research, 1984; Sandoz Prize, Can. Soc. Endocr. & Metab., 1985; Gold Medal, Japan Endocrine Soc. 1986; Squires Club Award, Wellesley Hosp. 1987; Distinguished Service Award, Can. Soc. Endocr. Metab. 1990; Novo-Nordisk Prize, Irish Endocrine Society 1990; Medicine North American Lectureship, Can. Soc. Int. Med. 1990; Parke-Davis Distinguished Lectureship, American Thyroid Assoc. 1991; Symposium on thyroid autoimmunity honoree, McGill Univ., Montreal 1991; Hashimoto Memorial Lecturer, Kyushu Univ., Fukuoka, Japan 1992; Wightman Visiting Prof., Royal College of Physicians (Canada) 1994; many visiting professorships in universities in this country and abroad; author 'Systematic Endocrinology' 1973 (2nd ed. 1979); 'Thyrotoxicosis' 1978; 'Autoimmunity in the Endocrine System' 1981; 'Autoimmunity in Endocrine Diseases' 1985; 'Thyroid Function and Disease' 1989; 'Autoimmunity and Endocrine Diseases' 1990; over 280 articles in scientific journals, mostly on autoimmunity in the endocrine system (esp. thyroid); R.C.N.V.R. 1943–45; mem. Candn. Soc. Endocrinology & Metabolism (first Pres.); Amer. Thyroid Assn. (past Pres.); Toronto Soc. Clinical Research (past Pres.); Endocrine Soc.; Assoc. Americ. Physicians; Amer. Fed. Clin. Res.; Candn. Soc. Clinical Investigation; Royal Coll. of Physicians and Surgeons, Canada (Counc. 1988– ); Amer. Coll. of Physicians (Gov. for Ont. 1979–83); Fellow, Royal Coll. Phys. Edinburgh 1992; Can. Inst. Acad. Med.; Royal Soc. of Med.; A.A.A.S.; European Thyroid Assn.; Latin Amer. Thyroid Assn.; (hon.) Chilean Endocrine Soc.; Japan Endocrine Soc. (Hon.); Endocrine Comte., Med. Research Counc. of Can. 1976–80; U.S. Nat. Inst. of Health Task Force on the funding of endocrine research 1979–80; Nat. Inst. of Health Endocrine Study Section 1993; Chrmn., Ann. Mtg. Comte., RCPS(C) 1988– ; Rsch. Comte. RCPS(C) 1990– ; has served on many other profl. comtes., particularly in R.C.P. and A.C.P.; mem. Bd. of Dirs., Wellesley Hosp. 1979–85 (and Chrmn., Med. Advy. Comte. 1981–85); Alpha Omega Alpha; recreations: skiing, tennis, sailing; Clubs: Alpine Ski (mem., Bd. Dirs. 1987–89); Donalda; Faculty; Home: 3 Daleberry Pl., Don Mills, Ont. M3B 2A5; Office: Dept. of Med., Wellesley Hospital, 160 Wellesley St. E., Toronto, Ont. M4Y 1J3.

**von BAEYER, Edwinna Louise,** B.A., M.A.; writer; b. Detroit, Michigan 22 Aug. 1946; d. James Edwin and Vera G. (Gorrell) Clappe; e. Univ. of Michigan B.A. 1968; Univ. of Pennsylvania M.A. 1970; m. Cornelius s. Hans Jakob and Renata v. 11 Oct. 1970; children: Eliza Corinna, Jakob Edwin; freelance writer, researcher and editor since 1978 specializing in Candn. landscape history; compiled first bibliography of Candn. garden history sources 1981; Canada Council Explorations Grant 1981; SSHRCC grant 1983; Bd. of Dir., Ottawa Independent Writers Assn. 1989– ; author: 'Rhetoric and Roses: A History of Canadian Gardening, 1900–1930' 1984, 'Garden of Dreams: Kingsmere and Mackenzie King' 1990; co-author: 'The Reluctant Gardener' 1992; 'The No-Garden Gardener' 1993; writes articles on Candn. landscape history, heritage, the environment and forestry, and edited Canada's first newsletter on garden history; recreations: reading, gardening, skating; Address: 131 Sunnyside Ave., Ottawa, Ont. K1S 0R2.

**von BOSE, Baron Botho;** stockbroker; b. Berlin, Germany 23 July 1941; s. Hasso Carl Georg Thilo and Juliane Henriette Lotte (von Boettinger); e. Kreuzgasse, Cologne 1961; Banking exam, Chamber of Commerce, Hamburg 1963; m. Susan d. Lord and Lady Cecil Douglas (Lord Cecil was the younger son of the 10th Marquis of Queensberry) 23 June 1965; VICE-PRESIDENT & DIRECTOR, LOEWEN, ONDAATJE, McCUTCHEON LIMITED; entered banking with Donner Bank Hamburg 1961; Trainee, William Brandt's & Co. London 1964; Banque Worms & Cie, Paris 1964–65; Banque de Paris & des Pays-Bas London 1965–68; Inst. Rep., Jones Heward & Co. Ltd. 1969–71; Dir., Mgr. of Institutional Sales 1972; joined Loewen, Ondaatje, McCutcheon 1973; transferred to European Head Office, Geneva 1975; Pres. 1977; returned to Canada 1983; Knight of Justice, Johanniterorden, Bailiwick of Brandenburg, Knightly Order of the Hosp. of St. John of Jerusalem; Lutheran; Vice-Pres. & Dir., Johanniter Aid Assn.; recreations: high speed driving and instructing, antiques; clubs: White's – London (England), University Club of Montreal; Home: 1166 Bay St., Apt. 1203, Toronto, Ont. M5S 2X8; Office: 55 Avenue Rd., Suite 2250, Toronto, Ont. M5R 3L2.

**von KARSTEDT, Joachim Albrecht (Jock);** automotive executive; b. Wismar, Germany, 10 July 1930; s. Baron Wilhelm A. and Countess Maximiliana (Mycielska) von K.; e. High Sch., Arts & Science, West Berlin, Sr. Matric. 1948; Tech. Univ., Indust. Mang. 1948–51, W. Berlin; various special courses in business mang., marketing, langs.; m. Mary Kathryn Jean, d. William Basil George and Mary Kelly; children: Heidi Ann vK.-Curl, Angela vK.-Jones, Mary Kelly vK. dec. 1986; four grandchildren: Alexandra, Jamie vK.-Curl, Meghan, Brendan vK.-Jones; SR. CONS., MANAGEMENT CONSULTING GROUP, HATCH ASSOC. 1990– ; Authorized dealer, Pan-Abode Internat. 1990– ; Pres., Inter-Lock Cedar Homes Inc.; joined White Motor Co. of Can. 1951; Industrial Acceptance Corp. Ltd. 1953; Volkswagen Canada Ltd., Toronto 1956–71, Gen. Mgr. Operations, 1970; Volkswagen of America, Inc. Englewood Cliffs, N.J. 1971–72; Gen. Sales and Marketing Mgr., Volkswagen Do Brasil S.A. 1972–76; Marketing Coordinator for Can.; Mgr., Business Development, Volkswagen Can. Ltd. 1976–79; Sr. Internat. Investment Counselor, Ministry of Industry & Trade, Ont. Gov't. since 1981; Pres., IntervestCan Ltd.; Vice-Pres., Gen. Mgr. Edscha of Can. 1987–89; Sr. Cons., present company 1989–90; Dir., Niagara Development Corp.; Mem., Candn. Adv. Bd. to Auto Parts Industry of Can.; Gen. Mgr., The Candn. Council For The Americas; R. Catholic; recreations: photography, tennis, tree farming, sailing; Clubs: Granite (Toronto); Royal St. Lawrence Yacht (Montreal); Homes: 81 Balliol St., Toronto, ON M4S 1C2 and (Country) Island View Dr., Golden Lake, ON K0J 1X0; Office: 2800 Speakman Dr., Mississauga, ON L5K 2R7.

**VON LOESECKE, David S.,** B.A., M.B.A., M.E.; business executive; b. 7 March 1952; e. Dartmouth College B.A., M.B.A., M.E.; PRESIDENT AND GENERAL MANAGER, FOXBORO CANADA INC.; Home: 291 Pinetree Cres., Beaconsfield, Que. H9W 5E2; Office: 4 Lake Rd., Dollard-des-Ormeaux, Que. H9B 3H9.

**VON PALLESKE, Heidi;** actor; b. Toronto, Ont. 9 Nov. 1960; d. Wolfgang Arnold Kurt Friedrich and Doreen Elaine (Strachan) V.; e. Ajax H.S. 1977; George Brown Coll., honours grad. 1979; CO-OWNER AND PRODUCER, PIG DOG PRODUCTIONS INC. 1990– ; dialogue coach for feature films 1984–87; acted in films: 'Wetworks' 1987, 'Dead Ringers,' 'Blind Fear,' 'Blue Moon,' and 'Renegades' 1988; 'Ramona' 1989; 'White Light' 1990; 'A Fist, A Nail, Two Windows' 1990; 'Shadows of the Past' 1990; 'Deceived' 1991; 'Hidden Room' 1991; Presenter, Genie Awards 1989, 1990; Aerobics Instructor of the Year (Toronto) 1986, 1987; mem., The Core Group Talent Agency; ACTRA; co-author: 'Sweatship' a situation comedy (pilot script); wrote first draft 'Love and Suicide' 1992; Home: Toronto, Ont.

**von SASS, Peter E.,** B.Com., M.B.A.; business executive; b. Riga, Latvia 11 Sept. 1930; s. Baron Werner A. and Baroness Vera L. (von Gizycki) von Sass; e. Univ. of Alta. B.Com. 1960; Sir George Williams Univ. B.Com/M.B.A. 1970; m. Ilona M. d. Count Alexander von Koskull 30 Mar. 1963; children: Benita, Carola, Peter Jr., Katrina; CHRMN., C.E.O. & DIR., SASKO GROUP OF COMPANIES 1981– ; Asst. Acct. Grocery Wholesale Edmonton 1955–57; Chief Acct. and Office Mgr. H.J. Kaiser Co. (Canada) Ltd. Montréal and Edmonton 1957–63; Controller and Chief Acct. Farr Co. Ltd. Montréal 1963–66; Corporate Controller RCA Ltd. Montréal 1966–71, also served as Asst. Treas., Mgr. Internat. Finance and Chief Financial Negotiator during this period; Vice Pres. Finance & Internat. Operations, Dir. (parent Co. and subsidiaries) VS Services Ltd. Toronto 1971–73; Pres. and Chief Exec. Offr., Dir. Allont Ltd. Toronto 1973–76, also served as Vice Pres. Finance & Adm., Chief Operating Offr.; mem. Exec. Ctte. Elco Mining Ltd. Calgary 1976–82; Partner, The Merbanco Group Calgary 1980–83; Pres., Chief Exec. Offr. and Dir. General Minerals Corp. Calgary 1983–86; Pres., C.E.O. & Dir., Nortek Capital Corp. (formerly Nortek Energy Corp.) 1986–89; Comnr. for Oaths Prov. Alta.; Lectr. in Internat. Bus. McGill Univ. and in Internat. Finance & Franchizing Princeton Rsch. Inst.; author 'Financing, Credit and Insurance in Canada's International Trade' 1977; 'Protective Measures for Corporations in a Floating Exchange Environment' 1978; 'Handbook of Economics and Taxation' 1979; 'Restructuring the Corporation' 1985; 'Financial Business Expansion' 1993; 'The Virtual Corporation' 1993; various other publs. econ., philos., metaphysics; Past Chrmn. Econ. & Taxation Ctte. Coal Assn. Can.; Internat. Finance Ctte. FEI; Finance & Taxation Ctte. CRA; mem. Financial Execs. Inst.; Candn. Inst. Mining & Metall.; Dir., Found. for Higher Learning Calgary; Home: 1525 – 32nd Ave. S.W., Calgary, Alta. T2T 1V7; Office: c/o River Lodge, R.R. 5, Stony Plain, Alta. T0E 2G0.

**von SCHILLING, Kurt K.,** B.Sc., F.S.A., F.C.I.A.; insurance executive; b. Latvia 30 June 1939; s. Bodo Peter and Ingeborg Adelhai S.; e. Univ. of Toronto B.Sc. 1963; m. Stephanie Ann d. Douglas and Evelyn Brace 3 July 1965; children: Peter, Michelle, Erik, Alexander; VICE-PRESIDENT & CHIEF ACTUARY, MUTUAL LIFE ASSURANCE CO. 1989– ; attained F.S.A. and F.C.I.A. 1970; joined Mutual Life Assurance 1963; President-Elect, Candn. Inst. of Actuaries 1993–94; Home: 283 Glenridge Pl., Waterloo, Ont. N2T 3Y1; Office: 227 King St. S., Waterloo, Ont. N2J 4C5.

**VOSE, John Randal,** B.Sc., Ph.D.; research executive; b. Manchester England 21 June 1941; s. Henry F. and Doris (Lucas) V.; e. Univ. of Wales, B.Sc. 1964; Univ. of Alta., Ph.D. 1968; m. Nancy L. d. Edward and Mildred Nelson 13 May 1967; children: Robin, Susanna, John

Gwyn; DIRECTOR, REGULATORY & GOVT. AFFAIRS - EUROPE, PASTEUR-MERIEUX MSD (Lyon, France); post-doct. fellow, Biochem. Dept., Univ. of Liverpool & Botany Dept., U.B.C. 1968–70; Mgr., Reckitt & Colman Ltd. (Montreal) and R.T. French Co. (Rochester, N.Y.) 1970–75; Sr. Rsch. Offr., then Gen. Mgr. (IRAP), Nat. Rsch. Counc. of Can. 1975–87; Asst. Vice-Pres., Regulatory & Tech. Affairs, Connaught Labs. Ltd. 1987–91; Vice-Pres. 1992–94; recreations: mountaineering, photography; Office: Allee du Mas, Charbonnieres, Lyon 69620 France.

**VOSS, Walter Arthur Geoffrey,** B.Sc., Ph.D., P.Eng., C.Eng. (U.K.); engineer; educator; b. Westcliff-on-Sea, England 4 June 1935; s. Walter Arthur Staehling and Winfred Joyce (Burgess) V.; came to Canada 1959; e. Brentwood Sch., Eng. 1954; B.B.C. Scholar., Univ. of London, Queen Mary Coll., B.Sc. (Hons. Engn.) 1959, Ph.D. 1961; Univ. of Brit. Columbia (NATO Exchange Scholar) 1960–61; m. Carole Jane, d. Victor Dougherty, 13 April 1963; children: Jeremy David, Graham Miles, Shauna Elizabeth; Prof. of Elect. Engn., Univ. of Alta. 1969; Prof. (formerly Dir.) of Biomedical Engr., Fac. of Medicine; Princ., Voss Assoc. Engineering Ltd. (Victoria, B.C.); joined University of British Columbia as Assistant Prof., Dept. Elect. Engn. 1961; Assoc. Prof., Univ. of Alta. 1964; Private Consultant in practice of Voss Tinga Associates, Vancouver, B.C. 1966; Past Chrmn. and Past mem. Bd. Govs., Internat. Microwave Power Inst.; past Ed., 'Journal of Microwave Power'; mem. Inst. Elect Engrs. (U.K.); Assn. Prof. Engrs. B.C. and Alta.; Mem., Soc. for Cryobiology (US); staff instructor, Alta. Soccer Assn; co-author of 'Microwave Power Engineering' 1968; contrib. to 'Handbuch der Elektrowärme' 1973' and other books; published research papers in biology, physics, and engineering; Anglican; recreations: walking, swimming, squash, soccer; Home: 2601 Dufferin Ave., Victoria B.C. V8R 3L5.

**VOYER, Roger D.,** B.Sc., M.Sc., D.Ing.; consultant; b. Cornwall, Ont. 24 May 1938; s. John Albert and Alma Marie (Lebrun) V.; e. Queen's Univ., B.Sc. 1961, M.Sc. 1962; Univ. de Grenoble France, D.Ing.; FOUNDING PARTNER, NORDICITY GROUP LTD. 1979– ; Rsch. Engr., Candn. Liquid Air Ltd. 1965–68; Sci. Advr., Sci. Counc. of Can. 1968–69, 1973–75; Sci. Attache, Candn. Permanent Delegation to the OECD 1969–72; Dir. of Rsch., Sci. Council of Can. 1975–79; Extve. Dir., Candn. Inst. for Econ. Policy 1979–84; Candn. del. to OECD Ctte. on Sci. & Tech. Policy; Dir., Candn. Ocean Indus. Assn.; del. to TV Ont. Long Range Planning Ctte.; Mem. Rsch. Mgmnt. Bd., Ottawa-Carleton Rsch. Institute; Lectr., Univ. of Montreal and Carleton Univ.; Mem., Candn. Advanced Technol. Assn.; author: 'Offshore Oil' 1983; co-author: 'Global 2000' 1984, 'A Technology Assessment System' 1974; contrib.: 'The Canadian Encyclopedia' (indus. section) 1985, 1988; Home: 601 Dovercourt Ave., Ottawa, Ont. K2A 0V5.

**VRANIC, Mladen,** M.D., D.Sc., F.R.C.P.(C.); professor; b. Zagreb, Croatia 3 April 1930; s. Vladimir and Anna (Berger) V.; e. Univ. of Zagreb M.D. 1955, D.Sc. 1962; m. Linda M. d. John and Margaret Swallow 11 Aug. 1983; children: Iva, Claire, Anne; PROF., PHYSIOLOGY, UNIV. OF TORONTO 1972– ; Chair, Physiology 1991– ; Prof., Med. 1978– ; Mem., Inst. Med. Sci., U. of T. 1973– ; Staff, Div. of Endo. Metab., Toronto Gen. Hosp. 1977– ; Chair, Comm. on National and Internat. Relations, Banting & Best Diabetes Centre, U. of T. 1981–93; Cair, Grants Ctte., C.D.A. 1985–88; Dir., C.H. Best Found.; Extve. Mem., Banting Best Diabetes Centre; extensive ctte. work; organizing chair/co-chair of num. nat. & internat. symposia incl. joint U. of T. / Karolinska / Joslin Center-Harvard Symp. on Persp. in Diab. Res. comm. 75th Ann. of Discovery of Insulin 1996; Sat. Symp. of 15th IDF Cong., Nara, Japan; 2nd Toronto / Stockholm Symposium on Perspectives in Diabetes Rsch. 1992; Sat. Symp. of 14th IDF Cong. 1991; Assoc. Edit.: 'Am. J. Physiol.' 1982–88, 'Cdn. J. Physiol. Pharm.' 1976–82, 'Metabolism' 1976–82; Edit. Brd. A.J.P. 1976–82; Foreign Adjunct Prof., Karolinska Inst. Stockholm 1992–98; Mizuno Inaugural Lect. & Award Osaka, Japan 1992; Hon. D.M. Karolinska Inst. 1992; Am. Diabetes Assn. Banting Medal & Lect. for Dist. Sci. Achievement, 14th IDF Cong. Washington 1991; Canada Council Killam Scholar 1988, '89; F.R.C.P.(C) 1986; MRC Visiting Sci. Award 1986; Visiting Rsch. Fellow, Merton Coll., Univ. of Oxford 1986; Inaugural Banting and Best Mem. Lect. & Cdn. Diab. Assn. Award, 12th IDF Cong. Madrid 1985; Pfizer Lect. Clin. Rsch. Inst., Univ. of Montreal 1985; Upjohn Lect., Univ. of Ottawa 1980; Vuk Vrhovac Mem. Lect. Univ. of Zagreb Croatia 1977; Fac. Scholar of Josiah Macy Found. and Visiting Prof., Univ. of Geneva 1976; Am. Chairmen of Physiology; Internat. Diabetes Fed.; Am. Diabetes Assn.; Am. Physiol. Soc.; Endocrine Soc. (USA); N.Y. Acad. of Sci.; European Assn. for Study of Diabetes; Cdn. Physiol. Soc.; Cdn. Soc. for Clin. Rsch.; Candn. Soc. of Endocrinology; Cdn. Diabetes Assn.; Toronto Diab. Assn. (Pres. 1978–79); Toronto Clin. Rsch. Soc. (1975–76); author of 144 sci. papers, 58 book chapters, 187 abstracts; editor/co-editor of 9 conf. proceedings or books; recreations: hiking, skiing, tennis; Office: Room 3358, Med. Sci. Bldg., Toronto, Ont. M5S 1A8.

**VROOMAN, Wallace Muir,** B.Sc., P.Eng.; forest industry executive; b. Niagara Falls, Ont. 17 March 1939; s. Harry Connell and Jessie Gladys (Muir) V.; e. Niagara Dist. H.S. 1958; Queen's Univ. B.Sc. 1962; m. Nancy d. Edward and Vera Cope 29 June 1963; children: Stephen, Leslie, Kelly; VICE-PRES., ENVIRONMENT, AVENOR INC. 1990– ; Engr., Quality Control Supvr., Continental Can Co. 1962–69; various positions ending as Regional Director, N.W. Region, Ministry of the Environment, Govt. of Ontario 1969–88; Mgr., Environmental Affairs, Great Lakes Paper 1988–90; Mem., Candn. Pulp & Paper Assn.; Conf. Bd. of Canada; Ont. Forest Industries Assn.; Council of Great Lakes Indus.; Assn. of Profl. Engrs. of Ont.; recreations: skiing, golf, fishing, tennis; Home: 234 Hinton Ave., Thunder Bay, Ont. P7A 7E1; Office: 2001 Neebing Ave., Thunder Bay, Ont. P7C 4W3.

# W

**WACHOWICH, Hon. Mr. Justice Allan H.,** B.A., B.L.; judge; b. Edmonton, Alta. 8 March 1935; s. Phillip Wachowich; e. Opal, Alta.; St. John's, Grandin and St. Josephs High Schs., Edmonton, Alta.; Univ. of Alta. B.A. 1957, B.L. 1958; m. Elizabeth Louise d. Dr. John Byers, Ponoka, Alta. 8 Aug. 1959; children: David, Patrick, Jane, Nancy; ASSOC. CHIEF JUSTICE, COURT OF QUEEN'S BENCH ALTA. 1993– ; Deputy Judge, Supreme Court of Y.T. 1979– ; Judge, Supreme Court of the Northwest Territories 1992– ; Chrmn., Education Comte., Court of Queen's Bench of Alta.; called to Bar of Alta. 1959; Bar of Northwest Territories 1963; Bar of Yukon 1964; Partner, Kosowan, Wachowich 1959–74; Apptd. to Dist. Court of Alta. 1974; Apptd. to Court of Queen's Bench of Alta. 1979; Past Pres. in Can. and Chrmn. Bd. Govs. Candn. Cath. Organ. Devel. & Peace; Past Pres. Cath. Charities and Alta. Cath. Welfare Assn.; Past Mem. Bd. of Dirs., United Way of Edmonton 1968–71; Past Dir. Nat. Cath. Council Social Services; Past Pres. Edmonton E., Fed. Lib. Assn.; mem. Adv. Bd. XI Commonwealth Games Foundation; Past Pres. St. Thomas Moore Lawyers Guild; Pres. of Friars 1974–75; Past Chrmn., of the Bd. Edmonton Gen. Hosp. (Bd. Mem. 13 yrs.); Chrmn. Education Cttee. Ct. of Queen's Bench, Alberta 1985–90; Past Pres. Bd. Govs., Alta. (Edmonton) Coll.; Past Pres. Edmonton Medico-Legal Soc.; Chair, Alta. Automobile Insurance Bd. 1978–93; Bd. of Govs., International Insurance Soc. Inc.; Arbitrator, Players Salaries Canadian Football League; Chrmn. of Henry Singer Memorial Hockey Scholarship Fund; Judicial Advisor, St. Thomas Moore Lawyers Guild; Mem. Adv. Bd., Redemptorist Fathers; Dir., Henri M. Toupin Medical Found.; Judicial Supr., Judicial District of St. Paul, Alta.; Lectr., Bar Admission Course, Alta.; Mem., Court of Queen's Bench List Mgmnt. Ctte.; Court of Queen's Bench Annual Meeting Ctte.; Mem. of Judiciary seized with all applications relating to the liquidation of the Candn. Commercial Bank; Bankruptzy Judge, Court of Queen's Bench of Alta.; Mem. Bd. of Dirs. and Curriculum Ctte., Cambridge Conference, Candn. Institute for Advanced Legal Studies; Ctte. mem., 1991 World Junior Basketball Championships Inc.; Hon. Dir., Citadel Theatre; Dir. YMCA; mem. Hon. Order Blue Goose Internat.; Mem. Candn. Bar Assn.; Ducks Unlimited; Knights of Columbus; Candn. Judges Conference; Candn. Inst. for the Admin. of Justice; Skilex Internat.; Zeta Psi (Past Pres.); R. Catholic; recreations: golf, hockey, baseball; Clubs: Highlands Golf; Centre (Edmonton); Home: 12043 - 91 Ave., Edmonton, Alta. T6E 2T9; Office: The Law Courts, Edmonton, Alta. T5J 0R2.

**WACHTEL, Eleanor;** writer; broadcaster; b. Montreal, Que. 18 Nov. 1947; d. Meyer Samuel and Celia (Gottlieb) Zornberg; e. McGill Univ., B.A. 1969; Syracuse Univ., grad. work at Newhouse Sch. of Communication; HOST, 'WRITERS AND COMPANY,' CBC RADIO 1990– ; Freelance Journalist 1976– ; contbr. of articles to numerous Candn. publs.; regular contbr. to network and local CBC radio; mem., ed. collective, Room of One's Own 1976–89; Adjunct Prof. of Women's Studies, Simon Fraser Univ. 1982–87; Host, 'Monitor,' CBC-B.C. 1985; Literary Commentator, 'State of the Arts,' CBC Radio 1987–88; Writer, Broadcaster 'The Arts Tonight,' CBC Radio 1988–92; mem. Adv. Ctte., Graphic Communications Prog., Selkirk Coll.; West Coast Magazine Award 1985; Journalists Panel, Nat. Leaders Debate on Women's Issues 1984; mem. Nat. Counc., Human Rights Found.; Vice-Pres., Candn. Periodical Pubs. Assn. 1979–81; Founding Bd. Mem., West Coast LEAF 1985–86; Bd., Mem., National Magazine Awards Found. 1989–91; author of study of feminist periodicals in Can. 1982 and 1985; co-author: 'A Feminist Guide to the Canadian Constitution' 1992; 'Writers & Company: Conversations with Eleanor Wachtel' 1993; co-ed. 'The Expo Story' 1986; 'Language in Her Eye' 1990; Office: Writers & Company, CBC Radio, Box 500, Stn. A, Toronto, Ont. M5W 1E6.

**WADDAMS, Stephen Michael,** M.A., LL.M., S.J.D., F.R.S.C.; professor of law; b. U.K. 30 Sept. 1942; s. Herbert Montague and Margaret Mary (Burgess) W.; e. Trinity Coll., Toronto, B.A. 1963; King's Coll., Cambridge, M.A. 1969; Univ. of Toronto, LL.B. 1967; Univ. of Michigan, LL.M. 1968, S.J.D. 1972; m. Suzanne d. Phyllis and Keith Ball 4 Aug. 1967; children: Alison, Michael; PROF. OF LAW, UNIV. OF TORONTO 1976– ; Asst. Prof., Univ. of Toronto 1968; Assoc. Prof. 1971; Vis. Fellow, Jesus Coll., Oxford 1981–82, All Souls Coll. 1988; Vis. Sr. Lectr., Univ. of Otago 1985; Fellow, Trinity Coll., Assoc. Fellow, Massey Coll.; Hurst Prize in Law 1965; Angus MacMurchy Gold Medal 1967; mem., Law Soc. of Upper Can.; Candn. Bar Assn.; Candn. Assn. of Law Teachers; Walter Owen Book Prize (shared) 1987; Fellow, Royal Soc. of Can. 1988; Candn. Assoc. of Law Teachers - Law Reform Commission of Canada Award 1989; Student Teaching Award 1990; author: 'Products Liability' 1974, 1980, 1993; 'The Law of Contracts' 1977, 1984, 1993; 'Introduction to the Study of Law' 1979, 1983, 1987, 1992; 'The Law of Damages' 1983, 1991; 'Law Politics and the Church of England: the Career of Stephen Lushington 1782–1873' 1992; and essays & articles on legal subjects; editor: 'Milner's Cases and Materials on Contracts' 1969, 4th ed. 1985; Home: 58 Russell Hill Rd., Toronto, Ont. M4V 2T2; Office: 78 Queen's Park, Toronto, Ont. M5S 2C5.

**WADDELL, David Edward,** C.I.M., F.C.S.I.; stockbroker; b. England 12 Jan. 1940; s. Herbert John and Eileen Ella (Leak) W.; e. Oldershaw Grammar Sch.; Birkenhead Tech. Coll.; York Univ.; m. Susan d. Richard and Alma Shaw 6 June 1967; children: Nicholas David, Amanda Jane; VICE-PRES., WOOD GUNDY INC. 1985– ; investment dealer for past 21 years; Past Pres., Toronto Soc. Investment Dealers Assn.; Past Alternate Gov., Candn. Securities Inst.; original publisher & editor: 'Mersey Beat' magazine ca. 1959 (Liverpool, U.K.); mem., Candn. Masters Internat. Track Team; recreations: sprinter, long/triple jumper; Office: 2005 Sheppard Ave. E., Suite 718, Willowdale, Ont. M2J 5B4.

**WADDELL, Ian Gardiner;** former politician; b. Glasgow, Scot. 21 Nov. 1942; s. John and Isabel (Dickie) W.; came to Can. 1947; e. Alderwood Coll. Inst. Toronto 1960; Univ. of Toronto B.A. 1963, LL.B. 1967; Ont. Coll. of Educ. 1964; London Sch. of Econ. LL.M. 1968; called to Bar of B.C. 1969, N.W.T. 1975; Asst. City Prosecutor Vancouver 1969–71; Dir. Storefront Lawyers Vancouver 1971–73; Special Counsel Berger Inquiry Mackenzie Valley Pipeline 1974–77; Partner, De Cario & Waddell 1977–80; el. to H. of C. for Vancouver Kingsway 1979; re-el. 1980, 1984, 1988 (for Port Moody - Coquitlam); Justice Critic; recreations: skiing, yoga, theatre.

**WADDELL, James Patterson,** M.D., F.R.C.S.(C); orthopaedic surgeon; b. Edmonton, Alta. 9 June 1943; s. James Munroe and Evelyn Margaret (Gault) W.; e. CCI 1961; Univ. of Alta., M.D. 1967; Univ. of Toronto, F.R.C.S.(C) 1972; m. Barbara d. Elizabeth and Thomas Currie 27 Sept. 1969; children: Jennifer, Andrea; MEDICAL DIRECTOR, TRAUMA PROGRAM, ST. MICHAEL'S HOSP. 1993– ; Attending Staff, St. Michael's & St. Joseph's Hosps. 1973; Asst. Prof., Dept. of Surg., Univ. of Toronto 1977; Assoc. Prof. 1982; Prof. 1988– ; Assoc. Chrmn., Dept. of Surg. 1989–92; Chief, Div. of Orthopaedic Surg., St. Michael's Hosp. 1980; Surgeon-in-Chief 1983–93; Prog. Dir., Div. of Orthopaedic Surg., Univ. of Toronto 1984–89, 1991– ; North Am. Travelling Fellow 1972; ABC Travelling Fellow 1983; Dir., St. Michael's Hosp. 1986–89; Mem., Candn. & Am. Ortho. Assns.; Am. Acad. of Ortho. Surgs.; Trauma Assn. of Can.; Am. Assn. for the Surgery of Trauma; S.I.C.O.T.; recreations: photography, gardening; club: Duck (Pres., Ont. Chap.); Home: 38 Kingsway Cres., Toronto, Ont. M8X 2R4; Office: 55 Queen St. E., Ste. 800, Toronto, Ont. M5C 1R6.

**WADDINGTON, John G.,** B.Sc., P.Eng.; atomic energy executive; b. Ruislip, Middlesex, England 13 Aug. 1941; s. Gilbert Fettes and Eileen Effie (Warren) W.; e. Univ. of Bristol B.Sc. 1963; m. Pamela d. Derek and Joyce Hornby 24 Sept. 1966; children: Geoffrey Mark, Louise Helen, Tom Andrew, Michael David; DIRECTOR GENERAL, DIRECTORATE OF ANALYSIS AND ASSESSMENT, ATOMIC ENERGY CONTROL BOARD 1990– ; Teacher, Dar-es-Salaam, Tanzania 1963–65; Rolls-Royce & Assoc., England 1965–75; Sci. Advisor, Atomic Energy Control Bd. 1975–77; Mgr., Safety Analysis Div. 1977–85; Admin. Div. 1986–88; Operator Cert. & Research Facility Div. 1988–90; recreations: active with Ottawa Scouts Assn.; Office: P.O. Box 1046, Ottawa, Ont. K1P 5S9.

**WADDINGTON, Miriam,** M.A., M.S.W., D.Litt.; teacher, poet; b. Winnipeg, Man. 23 Dec. 1917; d. Isidore and Mussia (Dobrusin) Dworkin; e. Machray (Winnipeg) Sch. and Jr. High Sch.; Lisgar (Ottawa) Coll. Inst., Univ. of Toronto, B.A., 1939, Sch. of Soc. Work Dipl., 1942, M.A. 1968; Univ. of Pennsylvania, M.S.W., 1945; D.Litt. Lakehead 1975; D. Litt. York Univ. 1985; m. Patrick Donald s. John Frushard W., London, Eng., 1939 (divorced, 1965); children: Marcus, Jonathan; began career in social work as Caseworker, Jewish Family Service, Toronto, 1942–44; Student and Caseworker, Philadelphia Child Guidance Clinic, 1944–45; Asst. Dir., Jewish Child Service, Montreal, 1945–46; Lectr. and Supervisor, Fieldwork, McGill Sch. of Soc. Work, Montreal 1946–49; Caseworker, Speech Clinic, Montreal Children's Hosp. 1950–52; John Howard Soc. 1955–57; Jewish Family Service 1957–60; Supv., N. York Family Service, Toronto, 1960–62; Sr. Fellowship in Writing, Canada Council, 1962–63, 1971–72 and 1979–80; Can. Council Academic Leave Fellowship 1968–69; Lectr., Dept. of English, York Univ. 1964, Prof. 1973; Prof. Emeritus 1983; Senior Scholar; Writer-in-Residence, Univ. Ottawa 1974; Borestone Mountain Prize for Best Poem 1974; Canada Council Wales Exchange Poet 1980; Writer-in-residence, Metro Toronto Reference Library 1986; Advisory Ed., Journal of the Otto Rank Assoc. 1973–83; Publications: 'Green World' 1945; 'The Second Silence' 1955; 'The Season's Lovers' 1958; 'The Glass Trumpet' 1966; 'Call Them Canadians' 1968; 'Say Yes' 1969; 'A.M. Klein' 1970; (ed.) 'John Sutherland: essays, controversies, poems' 1972; 'Driving Home: Poems, New & Selected' 1972 (won J.I. Segal Award, 1973); 'The Dream Telescope' 1973; 'The Price of Gold' 1976; (ed.) 'The Collected Poems of A.M. Klein' 1974; 'Mister Never' 1978; 'The Visitants' 1981; 'Summer at Lonely Beach and Other Stories' 1982; 'Collected Poems' 1986 (won the J.I. Segal award 1987); 'Apartment Seven: Selected Essays' 1989 (rec'd Rachel Bessin Hochman prize for scholarship in non-fiction 1991); 'The Last Landscape' poems 1992; Ed., 'Canadian Jewish Stories' (anthology) 1990; poems and articles in various anthols., and journs.; has transl. and published poems and stories from Yiddish, and some of own work has been transl. into Spanish, Romanian, Hebrew, Italian, Bulgarian, Hungarian, French and Chinese; has lectured on Candn. lit. in Germany and England, and read her poetry at internat. festivals in Yugoslavia and France; manuscripts have been acquired by Public Archives in Ottawa; mem., Candn. Assn. of Candn. Studies; National Yiddish Book Centre, Amherst; Amer. Assn. of Professors of Yiddish; Canadian Centre, Internat. PEN; League of Canadian Poets; Writers Union of Canada; ACUTE; Address: 625 West 27th Ave., Vancouver, B.C. V5Z 4H7.

**WADDS, Jean (Mrs. A.C. Casselman),** B.A., O.C.; b. Newton Robinson, Ont. 16 Sept. 1920; d. Hon. William Earl and Treva (Lennox) Rowe; e. Newton Robinson Public and Cookstown Cont. Schs.; Barrie (Ont.) High Sch.; Univ. Coll., Univ. of Toronto B.A. 1940; Weller Business Coll.; m. late Arza Clair Casselman, 24 May 1946; children: Nancy, Clair; Dir. Bell Canada; Former Dir., Canadian Pacific; Celanese Canada Inc.; Royal Trustco Lt.; Air Canada; Royal Winnipeg Ballet; M.P. for Grenville-Dundas 1958–68; Del. to United Nations 1961; Parlty. Secy. to Min. of Nat. Health & Welfare 1962–63; Nat. Secy., Prog. Cons. Party 1971–75; mem., Ont. Municipal Bd. 1975–79; Candn. High Commissioner to Gt. Britain 1979–83; rec'd Freedom of the City of London 1981; Hon. D.C.L., Acadia Univ., N.S. 1981; Hon. Patron and mem. Bd. of Advisors, Grenville Christian Coll., Brockville, Ont. 1981; Hon. Fellowship Award, Breton Hall Coll., Yorkshire, Eng. 1982; apptd. Officer, Order of Canada 1982; Hon. LL.D., St. Thomas Univ., Fredericton, N.B. 1983; Commander, Military and Hospitaller Order of St. Lazarus of Jerusalem 1983; Hon. LL.D. Univ. of Toronto 1985; Hon. LL.D. Dalhousie Univ. 1985; Kappa Kappa Gamma; P. Conservative; United Church; Clubs: Albany (Toronto); Rideau (Ottawa); Address: P.O. Box 579, Prescott Ont. K0E 1T0.

**WADE, Adrian Paul,** B.Sc., Ph.D.; educator; b. Amersham, Bucks., UK 7 Apl. 1960; s. Malcolm Edward and Jean Margaret (Payne) W.; e. Ashlyns Sch. UK 1978; Southampton Univ. B.Sc. 1981; Univ. of Wales Ph.D. 1985; m. Susan d. Alan and Sheila Nash 22 May 1982; children: Toby James William, Andrew David Edward, Samuel Benjamin Peter; ASST. PROF. OF CHEM. UNIV. OF B.C. 1987– ; Faculty Associate, Pulp & Paper Rsrch. Inst. of Canada; Extra-mural rsch. assoc. Univ. Coll. Swansea on secondment to BP Rsch. Centre 1984–85; Rsch. Chem./Computer Sci. BP Rsch. Centre Sunbury-on-Thames, UK 1985–87; Visiting Rsch. Assoc. Mich. State Univ. 1985–87; founded Lab. for Automated Chem. Analysis present Univ.; Dir. Pyrapalm Ltd. 1979–82; recipient BP Rsch. Studentship 1981–84; Harry Hallam Meml. Prize Distinguished Work Physical/Inorganic Chem. 1985; author or co-author 60 sci. publs.; presenter/co-author 150 lectures confs., ind. labs. and univs.; contbg. ed. 'Trends in Analytical Chemistry'; corresponding ed. 'J. Automatic Chem.'; mem. various ed. bds.; mem. Candn. National Network of Centres of Excellence for High Quality Wood Pulps; mem. Royal Soc. Chem. and Chart. Chem.; Can. Soc. Chem.; Chem. Inst. Can.; Fellow, Instn. Analysts & Programmers; Anachems; Technical Sect., Can. Pulp & Paper Assn.; recreations: angling, scrabble, darts; Home: 30, 11551 Kingfisher Dr., Richmond, B.C. V7E 3N5; Office: 2036 Main Mall, Vancouver, B.C. V6T 1Z1.

**WADSWORTH, His Excellency Michael Andrew,** Q.C., B.A., LL.B.; diplomat; b. Ottawa, Ont. 4 June 1943; s. John Bernard and Catherine Teresa (Kehoe) W.; e. Univ. of Notre Dame B.A. 1966; Osgoode Hall Law Sch. LL.B. 1969; Harvard Grad. Sch. of Bus. AMP 1985; m. Bernadette d. William and Bernadette Apted 19 June 1965; three d. Carolan, Mary, Jane; AMBASSADOR OF CANADA TO THE REPUBLIC OF IRELAND 1989– ; Sr. Vice Pres. U.S. Operations Crown Life Insurance Co. 1987–89; Exec. Vice Pres. and Corp. Secretary, Crownx Inc. 1984–87; Vice Pres. Adm. Tyco Laboratories Inc. 1981–83; law practice with late Arthur E. Maloney, Q.C. 1971–81; cr. Q.C. 1982; Player, Toronto Argonaut Football Club 1966–70; Football Commentator and Columnist 1971–81; Lectr. in Criminal Procedure Bar Admission Course 1973–80; Chrmn. Provl. Judges Benefit Bd. Ont. 1985–89; Dir. Ireland Fund Can.; R.Catholic; P. Conservative; recreations: reading, walking, golf, tennis, swimming; Clubs: Granite; Beacon Hall Golf; Portmarnock Golf & Country (Ireland); Harvard; Notre Dame Monogram; Stephen's Green (Ireland); Home: Strathmore Hill, Killiney, Co. Dublin, Ireland; Office: 65 St. Stephen's Green, Dublin 4, Ireland.

**WAELTI-WALTERS, Jennifer Rose,** B.A., L.èsL., Ph.D.; university professor; b. Wolverhampton, U.K. 13 March 1942; s. Thomas Gilbert and Joan Ellen (Mills) Walters; e. Dudley Girls' H.S. 1960; Univ. College, Univ. of London B.A. (Hons.) 1964; Univ. de Lille L.èsL. 1965; Univ. of London Ph.D. 1968; DIRECTOR OF WOMEN'S STUDIES AND PROFESSOR OF FRENCH, UNIV. OF VICTORIA; author: 'Alchimie et litterature' 1975, 'JMG Le Ciezio' 1977, 'Michel Butor' 1977, 'Icare ou l'evasion impossible' 1981, 'Fairytales and the Female Imagination' 1982, 'Feminist Novelists of the Belle Epoque' 1990; co-author: 'Jeanne Hyvrard' 1989; co-editor: 'Feminisms of the Belle Epoque' 1994 (anthology); recreations: photography, singing; Home: 1934 Crescent Rd., Victoria, B.C.; Office: Victoria, B.C. V8W 2Y2.

**WAGAMESE, Richard;** newspaper columnist; b. Minaki, Ont. 14 Oct. 1955; s. Stanley and Marjorie Alice (Wagamese) Raven; e. grade 9; studied with traditional elders in 1980s who told him his role was to be a storyteller; began to write despite lack of education focussing on traditional native teachings; Native Issues Columnist, Calgary Herald 1989; odd jobs throughout Canada 1970s; freelance work, CBC-Radio and independent stations in mid-1980s; wrote cultural column for 'Windspeaker' (native newspaper out of Edmonton) 1987–91; First Aboriginal Canadian to win Nat. Newspaper Award for Column Writing 1990; nominated 1989; Mem., Adv. Ctte., Native Communications Program, Grant McEwen College; Journalism Arts, S. Alta. Inst. of Technol.; Bd. of Gov., Old Sun Community College, Siksika Indian Reserve, Gleichen, Alta.; Native Am. Press Assn. Award for Column Writing 1988; Nat. Aboriginal Communications soc. Award for Column Writing 1988–89; mem., native militant orgns. 1970s; participant in ceremony, ritual; recreations: sports, collecting music, reading.

**WAGNER, Norman Ernest,** O.C., Ph.D., LL.D.; energy company executive; educator; b. Edenwold, Sask. 29 March 1935; s. Robert Eric and Gertrude Margaret (Brandt) W.; e. Luther Coll. Regina 1952–53; Univ. of Sask. 1953–58; Univ. of Toronto 1958–63, M.A. 1960, Ph.D. 1965 (Near Eastern Studies); Hon. LL.D., Wilfrid Laurier Univ. 1984; Officer of the Order of Canada 1989; President Emeritus, Univ. of Calgary 1990; m. Catherine Caroline d. Jacob E. Hack, Grenfell, Sask. 16 May 1957; children: Marjorie Dianne, Richard Roger, Janet Marie; CHRMN., ALBERTA NATURAL GAS CO. LTD; former Pres., Univ. of Calgary; author 'Canadian Biblical Studies' 1967; co-author 'The Moyer Site: A Prehistoric Village in Waterloo County' 1974; Chrmn. of Canadian Museum of Nature; serves on bd., Alta. Natural Gas; CFCN Communications Ltd.; formerly, Adv. Council on Adjustment; Nat. Adv. Bd. on Science and Technol.; Selection Ctte., Centre of Excellence, CIDA; Dir., OCO '88 (organizing ctte.); Chrmn., Alberta Univs. Coordinating Council; Council of Western Candn. Univ. Presidents; Founding Trustee, Alberta Heritage Foundation for Medical Rsch. Candn. Centre for Learning Systems; a founder, Calgary Rsch. & Development Authority; Lutheran; recreations: music and sports; Home: Box 5, Site 33, R.R. 12, Calgary, Alta. T3E 6W3; Office: 2900, 240 Fourth Ave. S.W., Calgary, Alta. T2P 4L7.

**WAGNER, Sydney,** Ph.D.; physicist; retired Canadian public servant; b. Montreal, Que. 1 Nov. 1919; s. late Carl and late Jennie (Herscovitch) W.; e. McGill Univ., Ph.D. (Physics) 1951; m. Marie Flore Madeleine, d. late Charles Edouard Vaillancourt, 11 Nov. 1961; one d., Janet; Dir. Gen., Research Planning, Dept. of Communications, 1980–84; Counselor (Scientific) Canadian Embassy, Paris France; past Gen. Dir., Office of Science and Technol., Dept. of Industry, Trade and Comm.; Prof. of Physics, McGill Univ., 1948–55; Assoc. Dir. Research, RCA Victor Co. Ltd., 1955–62; Pres., Simtec Ltd., 1962–68; served with RCN 1941–46; Sr. mem., Inst. Elect. & Electronic Engrs.; mem., Electrochem. Soc.; Candn. Assn. Physicists; Sigma Xi; Jewish; Home: 4476 Ste. Catherine West, Apt. 103, Westmount, Que. H3Z 1R7.

**WAGNER-BARTAK, Claus G.J.,** M.Sc., Ph.D.; consultant; polymath; b. Munich, Germany 9 Sept. 1937; s. Friedrich and Johanna A. W-B. (v. Bartach); e. Ludwig-Maximilian Univ. Munich B.Sc. 1962, M.Sc. (Dipl.Phys.) 1966, Ph.D. (Dr. rer.nat.) 1969; Tech. Univ. Munich Business Adm.; m. Maria Helene d. Karl and Elisabeth Reich, Arlington, Va. 23 Aug. 1969; children: Natalie, Nicolaus, Nadine; PRES. & C.E.O., STRUCTURED BIOLOGICALS INC., TORONTO 1988– ; Pres., Spanex Capital Inc. 1990– ; Pres., Energy Dynamics Inc. 1983– ; Rsch. Asst. Electronics, Siemens AG, Germany 1962; Rsch. Scient. Atomic and Molecular Physics Univ. Munich 1966–69; Project Scient., Project Mgr., Consultant on Advanced Technology Projects, Messerschmitt-Boelkow-Blohm GmbH, Munich 1969–74; Program Mgr., Engn. Mgr., Space Shuttle Remote Manipulator System ('Canadarm'), Spar Aerospace Ltd., Toronto 1974–80, Vice Pres. and Gen. Mgr. RMS Div. 1980–82, Corp. Vice Pres. 1982–83; Consultant to govt. and business in frontier technologies 1983– ; recipient Engn. Medal Assn. Prof. Engrs. Prov. Ont. 1982; Pub. Service Medal NASA 1982; NASA Astronauts Award, 1983; Group Achievement Award NASA-KSC 1982; Group Achievement Award NASA-JSC 1982; Joseph F. Engelberger Award 1986; mem. Assn. Prof. Engrs. Prov. Ont.; Bd. Trade Metrop. Toronto; Home: 32 Woodgreen Dr., Woodbridge, Ont. L4L 3B3.

**WAHL, Barbara,** B.A., R.N.; nurse; b. Schwerin, Germany 12 June 1949; d. Josef and Annelise Wahl; e. Nightingale School of Nursing R.N. 1970; Univ. of Waterloo B.A. 1990; children: Amy, David; HOME CARE CASE MANAGER, MINISTRY OF HEALTH 1986– ; Nurse, Kitchener-Waterloo Hospital 1970–71; Victorian Order of Nurses 1971–86; Bd. of Dir., Ont. Nurses' Assn.; Wilfrid Laurier Univ.; District Health Council Waterloo Region; Nursing Adv. Ctte., Min. of Health; recreations: watercolourist; clubs: Central Ont. Watercolour Soc.; Home: 220 Corrie Cres., Waterloo, Ont. N2L 5W4; Office: 175 Columbia St. W., Waterloo, Ont.

**WAHL, Ivan Stanley,** M.B.A.; trust company executive; b. Saskatoon, Sask. 19 May 1946; s. Cornelius Peter and Mary (Enns); e. York Univ., M.B.A. 1976; m. Sharon Craig 27 Sept. 1980; children: Richard, Kimberley, Sean; CHRMN., FIRSTLINE TRUST CO. 1987– ; Mgr., Group Claim Dept., Aetna Life & Casualty 1965–68; Mktg. Rep. 1968–71; Pres., Y & B Ins. Agen. Ltd. 1971–77; Mortgage Ctr., Metmar Finan. Corp. 1977–80; Extve. Vice-Pres., Fidelity Trust Co. 1980–83; Pres., GMC Investors Corp. 1983–87; Dir., FirstLine Finan.

Corp.; Home: 3 Sussex Dr., Etobicoke, Ont.; Office: 600, 20 Toronto St., Toronto, Ont. M5C 2B8.

**WAHL, John E.;** insurance executive; b. Kitchener, Ont. 27 Oct. 1934; s. Edgar Albert and Mary Winfred (Vogel) W.; e. St. Jerome's College; Wells Business Academy; m. Doreen d. Duncan and Mary Crawford 13 Feb. 1971; children: Scott Alexander, Andrew John; Agency Manager, Great-West Life Assurance 1985; Banking Industry 1952–67; Fellow, Candn. Banker's Assn. 1967; Securities Rep./Mgr. 1967–74; Fellow, Canadian Securities Assn. 1971; Insurance Indus. 1974– ; Chartered Life Underwrite 1980; Chartered Financial Consultant 1989; Chrmn. & Chief Extve. Offr., Life Underwriters Assn. of Canada; Past Chrmn., Inst. of Chartered Finan. Cons. & Chartered Life Underwriters; lectr., many insur. schools & seminars; Life Mem., Million Dollar Round Table; author of insurance pubn. articles; Past Chrmn., Sarnia & Dist. United Way; Sarnia & Dist. Lung Assn.; Sarnia Seaway Kiwanis Club; recreations: photography, travel, physical fitness; Home: 66 Penrose Ave., Kitchener, Ont. N7A 1G2.

**WAHLE, Elliott,** B.S.; retail executive; b. New York, NY 27 July 1951; s. Harold Lawrence and Renee (Altfest) W.; e. Rider Coll., B.S. 1973; m. Helene d. Elinor and Edwin Fishman 9 June 1973; children: Melissa Beth, Elyse Michelle; PRES., TOYS 'R' US (CAN.) LTD. 1983– ; Internal Auditor, Warner Commun. 1973–74; Asst. Dir., Minor League Opns., New York Yankees Baseball Club 1974–76; Dir., Player Personnel, Toronto Blue Jays Baseball Club 1976–83; Bd. of Dir., Assoc. Hebrew Day Schs.; Bd. of Gov., Baycrest Hosp. for Geriatric Care; Toy Indus. Group Chrmn., Hosp. for Sick Children Capital Campaign; Mem., Toronto Freedom Lodge, B'nai Brith Can.; Candn. Div., Internat. Council of Shopping Centres; Home: 2621 Bayview Ave., Willowdale, Ont. M2L 1B6; Office: 2777 Langstaff Rd., Concord, Ont. L4K 4M5.

**WAHN, Ian Grant,** Q.C., LL.B., M.A.; b. Herbert, Sask. 18 Apr. 1916; s. Edgar Valentine and Florence Margaret (Reid) W.; e. Swift Current (Sask.) Pub. Sch. 1922–28; Swift Current Coll. Inst. 1928–32; Univ. of Sask, 1932–37; Queen's Coll., Oxford Univ. 1937–39; Osgoode Hall Law Sch. 1939–42; m. Pearl (dec.), d. George Lychak, Aberdeen, Sask., 15 Dec. 1942; children: Ian G. V., Gordon D. A.; Dir., Candn. Badger Co. Ltd.; read law with Fraser & Beatty; called to Bar of Ont. 1942; practised law with Borden & Elliot 1942–61; with Smith, Lyons, Torrance, Stevenson & Mayer 1962–80; served in 2nd World War with Queen's Own Rifles in Holland and Germany; mem., H. of Commons for Toronto-St. Paul's 1962–1972; mem., Law Soc. of Upper Can.; Club: National; Home: Suite 201, 61 St. Clair Ave. W., Toronto, Ont. M4V 2Y8.

**WAINWRIGHT, John Andrew,** B.A., M.A., Ph.D.; university professor/writer; b. Toronto, Ont. 12 May 1946; e. Univ. of Toronto B.A. (Hons.) 1969; Dalhousie Univ. M.A. 1973, Ph.D. (cum laude) 1978; m. Marjorie Stone; children: Michael, Eric, Christopher; PROF., DEPT. OF ENGLISH, DALHOUSIE UNIV. 1979– ; Mem., Writers' Fed. of N.S.; Assoc. of Candn. Universities Teachers of English; editor: 'Notes for a Native Land' 1969 (anthology); author: 'Moving Outward' 1970 (poetry), 'The Requiem Journals' 1976 (poetry); 'After the War' 1981 (poems & short stories); 'Flight of the Falcon: Scott's Journey to the South Pole 1910–12' 1987 (long poem); 'World Enough and Time: Charles Bruce, A Literary Biography' 1988; 'Landscape and Desire: Poems Selected and New' 1992; Home: 6176 Pepperell St., Halifax, N.S.; Office: Dept. of English, Dalhousie Univ., Halifax, N.S. B3H 3J5.

**WAINWRIGHT, Robert Barry,** R.C.A.; artist; educator; b. Chilliwack, B.C. 29 June 1935; s. Ralph and Ethel Irene (Kipp) W.; e. Vancouver Sch. of Art 1962; Atelier 17 (with S.W. Hayter) Paris 1962–64; assn. with Atelier Libre des Recherches Graphiques Montréal 1965–67; m. Frances Elizabeth d. Hans and Elsbeth Heinsheimer, New York, N.Y. 7 Oct. 1967; children: Carla Elise, Julian Abram; ASSOC. PROF. OF FINE ARTS, & CHAIR, DEPT. OF PRINTMAKING, CONCORDIA UNIV.; solo exhns. incl. Concordia Univ. 1969, 1976, 1980; Galerie Martal Montreal 1972; Mazelow Gallery Toronto 1977; Galerie Elca London, Montreal 1984; rep. in numerous nat. and internat. group exhns. incl. Vancouver Print Internat. 1967; Internat. Biennale of Graphic Art Cracow 1968, 1970; Brit. Print Internat., Bradford, Eng. 1970; Premio Internazionale Biella per l'Incisione Italy 1971, 1973, 1976; Creation Que. au Salon Internat. Art 3/72, Basel, Switzerland 1972; III Biennale de Gravure de Paris 1972; Spectrum Can. R.C.A. Tour Exhn. 1976; Estampe Québécoises Actuelles 1979; 'Celebrating Spring' Invitational Exhn. Continental Gallery, Montreal 1986; Karnak Temple/Shriners Art Auction, Montreal 1990; rep. in pub., corporate and private colls. incl. Nat. Gallery Can., Art Gallery Ont., Musée d'Art Contemporain Montreal; Musée du Québec; Can. Council Art Bank; Montreal Museum of Fine Arts; recipient Emily Carr Travel Study Scholarship 1962; Leon & Thea Koerner Foundation Grant 1963; Can. Council Grant 1963, 1967; Internat. Exhn. Graphics Montreal Prize 1971; Concours Artistique du Que. 1971; Hadassah Nov. Art Auction Prize 1981; Hadassah Nov. Art Auction Hon. Mention 1982; Home: 4248 Hampton Ave., Montreal, Que. H4A 2K9; Office: Dept. of Printmaking, Concordia Univ., 1455 de Maisonneuve Blvd. W., Montreal, Que. H3G 1M8.

**WAISBERG, Lorie,** Q.C., M.A., LL.M.; lawyer; b. Sudbury, Ont. 2 May 1941; s. Harry and Madelin (Tarshis) W.; e. Univ. of Toronto B.A. (Hons.) 1963, M.A. 1964, LL.B. 1967; Harvard Univ. LL.M. 1969; m. Marie d. John and Anna Plishka 17 June 1969; children: Noah, Hannah; LAWYER, GOODMAN & GOODMAN 1970– ; Q.C. 1983; Former Instr. & Lectr., Bar Admission Course; Mem., Candn. Bar Assn., Ont. (Former Chrmn., Bus. Law Section); Dir., Autrex Inc.; Bay Mills Ltd.; Harris Steel Group Inc.; Home: 33 Welland Ave., Toronto, Ont. M4T 2H8; Office: Suite 2400, P.O. Box 24, 250 Yonge St., Toronto, Ont. M5B 2M6.

**WAISGLASS, Harry J.,** B.Com., M.A.; economist, professor, mediator, arbitrator, industrial relations consultant; b. Toronto, Ont. 19 May 1921; s. Nathan and Tammy (Henechovitch) W.; e. Univ. of Toronto, B.Com. 1944, M.A. 1948, Ph.D. studies 1947–50; m. Mari Joseph, 13 June 1943; children: Elaine, Barry, Karen, David; Prof. of Industrial Relations, Fac. of Business, McMaster Univ., 1976–79, and Founder and Dir., Labour Studies Prog. there 1976–81; Vice Chrmn., Grievance Settlement Bd., Ont. Public Service 1980– ; former Candn. Vice Pres., Soc. of Prof. in Dispute Resolution; arbitrator and mediator in various labour disputes; mem. Candn. Human Rights Tribunal; previously served as Rsch. Consultant to Special Planning Secretariat, Privy Council Office, Ottawa; Rsch. Dir. (Can.) for United Steelworkers of Amer.; Educ. and Resch. Dir. (Can.) for Amalgamated Clothing Workers of Am.; Lectr. in Indust. Relations and Research Fellow in former Indust. Relations Inst., Univ. of Toronto; Researcher, Dept. of Labour and Indust. Production Co-op. Bd., 1944–47; Internat. Labour Office Consultant, Singapore Govt. and trade unions, 1963–64; served on Voluntary Planning Bd. for N.S., 1964–67; Financial Adv. Comte. of Ont. Govt's Devel. Agency, 1963; apptd. Dir. Gen. Research & Devel., Dept. of Labour Can. 1968–74; Visiting Prof., Indus. Relations, McMaster Univ. 1974–76; Dir., Cdn. Foundation for Econ. Educ.; numerous bds. of conciliation and arbitration in labour disputes; author 'Towards Equitable Income Distribution: Some Social and Economic Considerations for Union Wage Policies' 1966; contrib. articles to various journals.; Office: 67 Caroline St. S., Ste. 6D, Hamilton, Ont. L8P 3K6.

**WAISMAN, Allan Harvie,** B.Arch., F.R.A.I.C. (1968), A.R.I.B.A., A.I.C.P., P.I.B.C., M.A.I.B.C.; architect (registered in the state of California, Washington and Texas); b. Winnipeg, Man. 24 Jan. 1928; s. Rubin and Bessie W.; e. Mulvey and Gordon Bell Schs., Winnipeg, Man.; Univ. of Man., B.Arch. 1950; m. Faigie; children: Sheera, Yail, Tully, Dean; PARTNER, WAISMAN, DEWAR, GROUT, CARTER INC., Archs. & Planners, since 1971; Chrmn. Intercon. Group Ltd.; Dir. several Cdn. cos. including Internat. Care Corp. (a London Life Co.); formed Partnership of Waisman, Ross & Assoc. 1953; Waisman Ross Blankstein Coop Gillmor Hanna 1964; mem. B.C., Ont., Calif., Texas and Washington Arch. Assns.; Dir., Royal Winnipeg Ballet; Past Dir., Winnipeg Art Gallery; former Chrmn., Vancouver Playhouse Theatre; Industrial Devel. Bd.; Dir., Urban Development Inst.; Dir. Education UDI Pacific; Regional Chrmn., RAIC College of Fellows; Awards incl. Internat. Stainless Steel Design Award; several Massey Medals for Arch.; Royal Arch. Inst. award for Anchor Point high density housing and for Hudson's Bay Dept. Store, Coquitlam Shopping Centre, IKEA Warehouse, Pacific Marine Training Inst., Vancouver Hosp. Parking and Park Facility; planning award for Whistler Town Centre; City of Seattle award for Seattle Trade Centre; Design Competition Winner for the Province of British Columbia Host Pavilion at Expo '86; Project Award, and Awards of Excellence by the Urban Develop. Inst. for Windsor Square Shopping Centre; Award of Excellence in Interior Design and Award of Excellence by the Urban Development Inst. for Parkwood Manor Seniors Residence; CMHC Award for the Victoria Congregate Hotel; Office: 1505 W 2nd Ave., Vancouver, B.C. V6H 3Y4.

**WAIT, Mrs. Arthur H.,** B.A.; b. Vancouver, B.C. 1 Aug. 1913; d. late Chief Justice Malcolm Archibald and Ida Lena (Baird) Macdonald; g.d. of the late Senator Geo. T. Baird of Andover, N.B.; niece of the late Senator J. H. King, P.C., former Min. of Public Works, Leader of the Senate, Speaker of the Senate, etc. and Mrs. King; e. Royal Victoria Coll. 1930–32; Univ. of British Columbia, B.A. 1934; m. late R. Reginald Arkell, former Vice-Pres. and Gen. Mgr., Kelly, Douglas & Co. Ltd. Vancouver, B.C., 16 Sept. 1939; one d., Elena Angela; 2ndly the late Arthur H. Wait, Toronto, Ont.; founding mem. of Can. Council (apptd. 1957); former Dir., Vancouver Festival Soc.; Vancouver Centennial Comte.; Past Pres., Jr. League of Vancouver; Past Pres., Community Arts Council of Vancouver; Past Dir., Vancouver Symphony Soc.; Nat. Ballet Guild of Can.; Community Chest & Council; Volunteer Bureau of Greater Vancouver; Women's Auxiliary of Vancouver Art Gallery; Red Cross Lodge; Friends of Chamber Music; Vice-President, Bureau of Municipal Research (Toronto); Delta Gamma; Liberal; Anglican; recreation: gardening; Home: 7 Cluny Drive, Toronto, Ont. M4W 2P8.

**WAITE, Larry Michael,** B.A., C.M.A., C.F.E.; public servant; b. Toronto, Ont. 20 April 1946; e. York Univ. B.A. 1973; The Soc. of Mngt. Accts. of Ont. C.M.A. 1976; Ryerson Polytechnical Inst., Business Admin. 1970; Certified Fraud Examiner 1992; m. Diane; children: Michael, Lindsay; DIRECTOR, ENFORCEMENT BRANCH, ONTARIO SECURITIES COMN. 1990– ; Audit Supervisor, Office of the Provincial Auditor 1970–78; Staff Forensic Accountant, Enforcement Br., Ont. Securities Comn. 1979–86; Chief Forensic Accountant 1986–90; Chair, Enforcement Ctte., Candn. Securities Administrators 1990– ; Mem., Internat. Enforcement Ctte., N. Am. Securities Admin. Assn. Inc. 1991– ; Enforcement Ctte., Internat. Orgn. of Securities Comns. 1990– ; Candn. & Ont. assns. of Chiefs of Police 1990– ; Chair, Supervisory Ctte., Queen's Park Credit Untion 1978–84; Dir. 1985–86; recreations: photography, travel; Office: 20 Queen St. W., Suite 1800, Box 55, Toronto, Ont. M5H 3S8.

**WAITE, Peter B.,** O.C., Ph.D., D.Litt., LL.D., F.R.S.C.; b. Toronto, Ont. 12 July 1922; s. Cyril and Mary (Craig) W.; e. Saint John (N.B.) High Sch., 1937; Univ. of B.C., B.A. 1948, M.A. 1950; Univ. of Toronto, Ph.D. 1954; Univ. N.B., Memorial Univ. of Nfld. and Carleton Univ. D. Litt.; Dalhousie Univ. LL.D.; m. Masha, d. Dr. Ante Gropuzzo, Rijeka, Yugoslavia, 22 Aug. 1958; children: Alice Nina, Anya Mary; PROF. OF HIST., DALHOUSIE UNIV., since 1961 and Head of Dept. there 1960–68; appt'd Thomas McCulloch Professor, 1985; Professor Emeritus 1988– ; with Dom. Bank 1937–41; served with R.C.N. 1941–45, rank Lt.; apptd. Lectr. in Hist. at present Univ., 1951, Asst. Prof. 1955, Assoc. Prof. 1960; visiting Prof., Univ. W. Ont. 1963–64, J.B. Smallman Prof. 1988–89; Dartmouth Coll., Hanover, U.S. 1967; author of 'The Life and Times of Confederation, 1864–1867' 1962 (50th Anniv. Certificate of Merit, Social Sci. Federation of Canada 1990); 'The Confederation Debates in the Province of Canada, 1865' 1963; 'Pre-Confederation' (Vol. II Candn. Hist. Documents) 1965; 'Canada 1874–1896: Arduous Destiny' vol. 13 Candn. Centenary Series 1971; 'Confederation, 1854–1867' 1972; 'Macdonald: His Life and World' 1975; 'Years of Struggle, 1867–1896' vol. 1, Century of Canada Series, 1985; 'The Man from Halifax: Sir John Thompson, Prime Minister' 1985; 'Lord of Point Grey: Larry MacKenzie of U.B.C.' 1987; 'The Loner: Three Sketches of the Personal Life and Ideas of R.B. Bennett, 1870–1947' 1992; 'The Lives of Dalhousie University, 1818–1980: Vol. I, 1818–1925' 1994; Ed., 'Candn. Parlty. Debates, 1867–1870'; Great-West Life Lecture, Centre for Cdn. Studies, Univ. of Edinburgh, May, 1980; Winthrop Bell Lecture, Mt. Allison Univ., 1981; Visiting Candn. Fellow, Macquarie Univ., Sydney, Australia, 1983; British Columbia Historical Federation Medal 1989; W. Stewart MacNutt Memorial Lectures, Univ. of N.B. 1990; 1991 Goodman Lectures, Univ. of W. Ont.; Chrmn., Macdonald Prize Comte., Candn. Hist. Assn. 1976–80; mem. Canadian Historical Assn. (President 1968–69); Humanities Research Council (Chrmn. 1968–70); mem. Hist. Sites & Monuments Bd. Can. (1968–77); Nat. Archives Appraisal Bd. 1979–89; Chrmn., Aid to Scholarly Publications Programme, Soc. Sci. Fed. of Can. 1987–89; Officer, Order of Canada 1993; Home: 960 Ritchie Dr., Halifax, N.S. B3H 3P5.

**WAITE, William Barrie;** electrical engineering executive; b. Brantford, Ont. 12 Dec. 1937; s. Dr. Wilford I. and Florence (Gowman) W.; e. Electrical Engineering in Toronto with postgrad. studies in Elect. Eng. and Physics in Germany; m. Ursula von Horn 1967; children; Steffen, Russell; PRESIDENT & CHIEF EXECUTIVE OFFICER, SIEMENS ELECTRIC LIMITED 1981– ;

National Research Council Ottawa 1959; joined Siemens Canada 1963; spent 6 years working in Germany and 3 years in Edmonton before assuming current position; Dir. of various Siemens cos. in N. Am.; Dresdner Bank Canada; Gerling Global Life Insur. Co.; Alberta Microelectronic Centre; Dir., Candn. German Chamber of Industry and Commerce, Inc.; Dir., Electrical and Electronic Manufacturers Assn. of Can.; Mem., Premier's Council on Economic Renewal; Business Council on National Issues; Bd. of Govs., Ryerson Polytechnical Institute; Faculty of Music Adv. Bd., McGill Univ.; Mem. Adv. Bd., Centre for Internat. Studies of Univ. of Toronto; Mem. Adv. Bd., Internat. MBA Program; clubs: Toronto, Forest and Stream; Home: Toronto, Ont.; Office: Montreal and 1180 Courtney Park Dr. E., Mississauga, Ont. L5T 1P2.

**WAITZER, Edward James,** LL.B., LL.M.; lawyer; b. Norfolk, Virgina 24 Jan. 1954; s. Paul Lawrence and Valorie Pera (Levine) W.; e. Univ. of Toronto, LL.B. 1976, LL.M. 1981; called to Ont. Bar 1978; N.Y. Bar 1986; m. Smadar Peretz children: Jonathan, David; CHAIRMAN, ONTARIO SECURITIES COMMISSION 1993– ; Prof. (part-time), Osgoode Hall Law School 1990– ; Policy Consultant 1970–77; Vice-Pres., Toronto Stock Exchange 1977–81; Partner, Stikeman, Elliott 1981–93; Mem., Candn. & Am. Bar Assns.; author of numerous articles on legal & pub. policy issues; Home: 50 Forest Hill Rd., Toronto, Ont. M4V 2L3; Office: Suite 800, Box 55, 20 Queen St. W., Toronto, Ont. M5H 3S8.

**WAITZER, Paul L.;** investment executive; b. New York, N.Y. 2 April 1927; came to Can. 1956, citizen 1967; e. Schs., Norfolk, Va.; William & Mary Univ.; m. Valorie Levine 15 March 1953; two s., Edward, Michael; one d., Sloane; Pres. Pebble Enterprises Inc.; Yorkvest Ltd.; Bd. of Govs., Baycrest Centre for Geriatric Care; founded and assumed Pres. Chempac Ltd. 1959 until sale in 1967; Vice-Pres. and Dir., E. H. Pooler & Co. (former name of Yorkton Securities Ltd.) 1969; Pres., Yorkton Securities Ltd. 1970; Chrmn. and CEO 1972–79; Bd. of Govs., Mount Sinai Hosp.; served in 2nd World War as Hosp. Corpsman, U.S.N.; hon. discharge 1945; Jewish (Past Pres. Temple Sinai Cong.); recreations: sailing, tennis, swimming, bridge, walking; Clubs: Ontario; Island Yacht; Home: 40 Rosehill Ave., Toronto, Ont. M4T 1G5; Office: Suite 607, One St. Clair Ave. East, Toronto, Ont. M4T 2V7.

**WAKEFIELD, Donald Ernest,** C.D., B.A., LL.B.; lawyer; b. Toronto, Ont. 23 Oct. 1936; s. Ernest Arthur and Ruth Jeanette W.; e. E. York Coll. Inst. 1955; Univ. of Toronto B.A. 1959 (Victoria Coll.), LL.B. 1962; m. Elizabeth d. William and Elizabeth Thompson 3 Sept. 1960; two s. David Thompson, Mark Ernest; PARTNER, OSLER, HOSKIN & HARCOURT 1973– ; Dir. Amax Gold (B.C.) Ltd.; The Aristocrat Manufacturing Co. Ltd.; Besser Canada Ltd.; Santa Fe Pacific and Cyprus Minerals Candn. subsidiaries; GenCorp Canada Inc.; Lincoln Electric Co. of Canada Ltd.; Universal Forest Products of Canada Inc.; Consolidated Hydro Ltd.; Intalco Aluminum Co.; H & J Properties Ltd.; Candn. Institute of Resources Law; called to Bar of Ont. 1964; active RCNR until retirement 1969, rank Lt. Commdr.; Mem., Candn. Bar Assn.; Am. Bar Assn.; Internat. Bar Assn.; recipient Nat. Defence Telescope 1958; Trustee-at-Large Rocky Mountain Mineral Law Found. 1980–90 and 1993; mem. Naval Offrs. Assn. Can.; UNTD Assn. Upper Can.; United Church (Trustee Trinity St. Paul's Un. Ch.); recreations: scuba diving, golf; Mem., Ontario Club; Home: 19 Kingsmill Rd., Toronto, Ont. M8X 2N7; Office: 1 First Canadian Place, P.O. Box 50, Toronto, Ont. M5X 1B8.

**WAKEFIELD, Wesley Halpenny;** evangelist; b. Vancouver, B.C. 22 Aug. 1929; s. late Pastor William James Elijah and Jane Mitchell (Halpenny) W.; m. Mildred June Shouldice; Calgary, Alta., 24 Oct. 1959; el. Internat. Leader (a bishop-general), Bible Holiness Movement since inception 1949; author 'Bible Doctrine'; 'Bible Basis of Christian Security' 1957; 'Jesus is Lord' 1977; 'Foundation of Freedom' 1979; 'Fire from Heaven' 1987; 'Bringing back the Ark' 1987; 'John Wesley – The Burning Heart' 1988; 'Like Lightning' 1990; 'Antinomianism, the Curse of the Ages' 1990; Ed., 'Wesleyan Annotated Edition Bible' 1980– ; 'Hallelujah' (hymnal) 1981–83; 'Truth on Fire' ( now 'Hallelujah' magazine) since 1949; 'Christian Social Vanguard' 1960–61; 'Canadian Church and State' 1977–90; 'Miniature Railways' quarterly 1988– ; Dir., 'Bible Broadcast' 1952–56; researcher on effects of marijuana and youth 1969; labour leg. conscience clauses 1973, also religious liberty leg.; Vice Pres., Candns. United for Separation of Church and State 1977–90; Chrmn., Concerned Christians for Racial Equality; Religious Freedom Conf. 1978–79; Bd. mem., Candn. Council of Japan Evangelistic Band; Nat. Comte mem., Christian Holiness Assn.; West Can. rep., Canadians for the Protection of Religious Liberty; Chrmn., Religious Information Centre; Pres. & Founder, Double Dial Lock Co.; Manual Offset Printing Press Co.; Pres., Imperial Security Guard Service Ltd.; Bd. mem., Agarwal Resources Ltd.; Pres., Cumo Resources Ltd.; Secy., NP Energy Corp.; Mrg., Liberty Press; Evangelistic BookServ.; Aldersgate Advertising Agency; honoured twice for activity in religious liberty (Religious Freedom Crusade); honoured twice with Internat. Community Service Award (Gt. Britain); mem. Anti-Slavery Soc.; Candn. Bible Soc.; Creation Science Assn.; Evangelicals for Social Action; Salvation Army Historical Soc.; Nat. Assn. Advanc. Coloured People; Internat. Platform Assn.; Bible Advisory Ctte., Wesley Bible 1988–90; recreation: model railways; Address: P.O. Box 223, Postal Stn. A., Vancouver, B.C. V6C 2M3.

**WAKELING, Thomas C.,** Q.C., LL.B.; judge; b. Saskatoon, Sask. 19 May 1924; s. Bertram M. and Keith (Pennington) W.; e. Nutana Collegiate, Saskatoon grade XII 1942; Univ. of Sask. LL.B. 1948; m. Margaret L. d. William and Levina Munro 31 Aug. 1946; children; Thomas W., Robbie M., Margaret E.K.; JUDGE, SASKATCHEWAN COURT OF APPEAL 1984– ; Flying Instr. RCAF F/O 1943–45; called to Bar of Sask. 1950; practiced law in Lloydminster 1950–57, Regina 1957–84; cr. Q.C. 1971; Pres. (Sask.) Candn. Bar Assn. 1970–72; Bencher Law Soc. of Sask. 1973–79, Pres. 1978–79; Chrmn. Sask. Police Comn. 1975–84; past Pres.: YMCA; Sask. Div. Candn. Red Cros; Regina Kiwanis Club; recreation: golf; Club: Wascana Country; Home: 865 McNiven Ave., Regina, Sask. S4S 5X9; Office: 2425 Victoria Ave., Regina, Sask. S4P 3V7.

**WAKIM, Arthur Samuel,** B.Sc., BCL, Q.C.; lawyer; b. Saint John, N.B. 13 Feb. 1937; s. Arthur Samuel and Emma Maryanne (Emin) W.; e. St. Malachy's Mem. H.S. 1955; St. Francis Xavier Univ. B.Sc. 1959; Univ. of N.B. Law Sch. BCL 1962; m. Mary Martin d. Ted and Mona Robertson 2 Sept. 1963; children: Saleem, Mary Martin, Charles, Emma, Mona, Ted; ASSOCIATE, WEIR & FOULDS 1980– ; Priv. Sec., Min. of N. Affairs & Nat. Resources 1962–63; called to Ont. Bar 1965; Asst. Crown Attorney, Co. of York; SNR Investigation Couns., Ont. Securities Comn. 1967–73; private practice of law; M.P. (House of Commons) 1979–80; Dir., PWA Limited; FT Capital; Q.C. 1977; Bd. of Dir., Candn. Opera Co.; Roman Catholic; recreations: skiing; clubs: Albany, National, Rideau; Home: 43 Denver Cres., Willowdale, Ont. M2J 1G6; Office: Suite 1600, Exchange Tower, 2 First Canadian Place, P.O. Box 480, Toronto, Ont. M5X 1J5.

**WALCOT, Donald Thomas,** B.A., M.B.A.; investment executive; b. Montréal, Qué. 5 Dec. 1942; s. Thomas Callam and Eveline Mai (Jousse) W.; e. McGill Univ. B.A. 1963; Univ. of W. Ont. M.B.A. 1968; Chart. Financial Analyst 1975; CHIEF INVESTMENT OFFICER, BIMCOR 1992– ; Personal Trust Offr. Royal Trust 1963–66; Asst. Treas. Pension Fund Invests., Ontario Hydro 1968–87; Pres., Sunimco 1987–92; recreations: cycling, skiing, wine-tasting, music; Home: 2162 Sherbrooke St. W., #19, Montreal, Que. H3H 1G7.

**WALDEN, Charles Edward,** B.A., LL.B.; lawyer; b. Ontario 22 June 1933; s. Carroll Edison and Kathleen Maude (MacGrotty) W.; e. Univ. of West. Ont., B.A. (Hons.) 1956; Univ. of Vienna, dipl. 1956; Osgoode Hall Law Sch., LL.B. 1962; m. Maxine d. Willis and Beatrice Thompson 27 Dec. 1957; children: Jennifer Carol, Francis Scott, Donna Beth, Megan Ann; PARTNER, McCARTHY TÉTRAULT, BARRISTERS & SOLICITORS 1989– ; Partner, Thomas and Walden 1963–70; Counsel, Smith, Lyons, Torrance, Stevenson & Mayer 1970–88; Speaker or Chairperson for Candn. Bar Assn., Internat. Counc. of Shopping Centres, Univ. of B.C., Real Estate Inst. of Can., Insight Edn. Serv., Urban Devel. Inst., Real Estate Counc. of B.C., Candn. Bar Assn., Law Soc. of U.C.; Beta Theta PI; author of section in 'Shopping Centre Leases' 1982 & 4 chaps. in a U.B.C. text 'Principles of Cdn. Real Estate' and 'Appraisers and the Law' 1984; recreations: mountain hiking, canoeing, jogging, piano, music history; Home: 137 First Ave., Toronto, Ont. M4M 1W9; Office: Suite 4700, Toronto Dominion Bank Tower, Toronto-Dominion Centre, Toronto, Ont. M5K 1E6.

**WALDERMAN, David Bruce,** B.A., M.B.A.; business executive; b. Toronto, Ont. 13 July 1954; s. Murray and Elaine Doris W.; e. Univ. of Toronto B.A. 1977; York Univ. M.B.A. 1979; m. Linda d. Leslie and Minda Feldman 19 June 1980; children: Daniel, Paul, Rachel; PRESIDENT & CHIEF EXECUTIVE OFFICER, BELMONT MEAT PRODUCTS LTD. 1988– ; consultant, Arthur Anderson & Co. 1979–80; Asst. Vice-Pres. Finance, Vickers & Benson Advtg. 1980–81; joined Belmont Meat Products Ltd. 1981; Pres. & C.E.O., 230 Signet Drive Ltd.; Park Avenue Meat Sales; Walderman Holdings Ltd.; Walderman Brothers Holding; recreations: golf, tennis, swimming; club: Maple Downs Golf & Country; Home: 37 Gordon Rd., Willowdale, Ont. M2P 1E2; Office: 230 Signet Dr., Weston, Ont. M9L 1V2.

**WALDMAN, Lorne,** LL.B.; barrister & solicitor; b. Toronto, Ont. 28 Sept. 1952; s. Harvey and Toby (Goldwasser) W.; e. York Univ., Osgoode Hall Law Sch. LL.B. 1977; m. Maria Susana d. Alberto and Beatriz Munarriz 14 Oct. 1981; children: Clarisa Denise, Martin Rolando; BARRISTER & SOLICITOR, LORNE WALDMAN 1979– ; specializes in immigration and refugee cases; more than 1000 refugee claimants from over 20 countries represented; lobbyist for ethnic legal & religious groups & in opposition to govt. refugee policy; spokesperson, Nat. Coalition for A Just Refugee & Immigration Policy; frequent public speaker; Dir., Candn. Jesuit Refugee Prog. 1986–89; Observer, U.N. Human Rights Comn. 1980; regular contb. to newspaper on immigration, racism and human rights issues; Mem. of Extve., Candn. Bar Assn. (Ont. Immigration Section) 1989– ; recipient, Law Found. grant to write book on Immigration & Refugee Law; recreations: jogging, swimming; Home: 286 Bessborough Dr., Toronto, Ont. M4G 3K8; Office: 281 Eglinton Ave. E., Toronto, Ont. M4P 1L3.

**WALDO-BALTZER, Carolyn;** synchronized swimmer; b. Montreal, Que. 11 Dec. 1964; d. Stuart and Sally W.; e. Univ. of Calgary; m. Tom Baltzer 15 Mar. 1989; daughter: Brittany Baltzer; SPORTS REPORTER AND ANCHOR, CJOH TV; Double Olympic Gold Medalist 1988; Olympic Silver Medalist 1984; World Cup Champion 1985, 1987; World Solo, Duet, Team Champion 1986; Candn. Female Athlete of the Year 1985, 1986, 1987, 1988; fitness consultant; television appearances; Clothing Collection at Sears 1988, 1989, 1990, 1991; Spokesperson for Lupus 1989, 1990; Chrmn. Candn. Lung Assn. 1985–86; participant, anti-drug awareness prog. 1987–90; rec'd. Officer of the Order of Canada 1989; Honorary Depy., United Way 1990; Address: c/o CJOH TV, 15 Merivale Rd., Ottawa, Ont. K2C 3G6.

**WALDOCK, Peter John,** B.A.; book publisher; b. Lincoln, Eng. 26 Feb. 1945; came to Can. 1967; s. Norman Bruce and Norah (Dransfield) W.; e. Glyn Grammar Sch., W. Ewell, Eng., 1956–63; Keele Univ., Staffordshire, Eng., BA 1967; m. Diane Lynn; children: Christopher James, Sarah Elizabeth; entered publishing with Longman Canada Ltd.; PRES., NORTH 49 BOOKS 1992– ; Pres., Penguin Books Can. Ltd. 1974–83; Pres., Candn. Telebook Agency 1981–84; Exec. Vice Pres., McClelland & Stewart 1985–87; Chief Executive Offr., Cannon Book Distribution 1987–92; Protestant; recreations: tennis, golf, basketball; Home: 10 Divadale Dr., Toronto, Ont. M4G 2N9.

**WALDON, David George;** retired executive; b. Toronto, Ont. 24 Aug. 1916; e. North Toronto Coll. 1935; Shaw Business Sch. 1935–37; m. Mary Eileen Moore, Toronto, 21 Oct. 1944; one s., Robert David; Dir., Canuck Well Servicing Ltd.; Zeta Oilfield Rentals Ltd., (Edmonton); Jr. Clerk, Andian National Corp. Ltd. 1935; trans. to operating H.Q., Cartagena, Colombia, S.A., 1936, Asst. Chief Acct., 1941, Asst. to Mgr., 1947; joined Interprovincial Pipe Line Ltd. as Office Auditor, Edmonton, Alta. 1950, Asst. Treasr. 1953; trans. to Toronto, apptd. Treasr. 1954; trans. to Edmonton as Asst. Gen. Mgr. 1959, Gen. Mgr. 1964; returned to Toronto as Vice-Pres., el. a Dir. 1966; Pres. 1967; Chrmn and Dir. 1977–78 (when ret.); Hon. Life Mem., Candn. Petroleum Assn.; Clubs: National; York Downs Golf; Home: 469 Oriole Pky., Toronto, Ont. M5P 2H9.

**WALE, Norman Edward,** B.Sc., M.A.; diversified company executive; b. Montreal, Que. 14 Dec. 1947; s. Edward George and Anita Louise (Laniel) W.; e. Univ. de Montréal B.Sc. 1968, M.A. 1970; m. Marta d. Kenneth and Juanita Atkinson 8 Oct. 1982; children: Julie, Andrea, Olivier, Rémi, Zoë; VICE PRES. PLANNING AND ANALYSIS, CANADIAN PACIFIC LTD. 1991– ; Staff Econ. Royal Bank of Canada 1970; Dir. Performance Group Econ. Council of Can. 1971; Dir. Gen. Min. of State for Sci. & Technol. Ottawa 1975; Dir. Econ. & Bus. Analysis present Co. 1976, Asst. to Comptroller 1982–83, Asst. Comptroller 1983–87 Finance & Acctg., Gen. Mgr. Planning 1987–88, Vice Pres. Investor and Industry Relations 1988–91; Lectr. Ecole des Hautes Etudes Commerciales Univ. de Montréal 1978–80; Mem., Economic Council of Canada 1987–90; recipient Hon. E.L. Patenaude Award and

Montreal Econ. Assn. Prizes Outstanding Acad. Achievement 1968–70; author various publs.; Dir., Culinar Inc.; Candn. Chamber of Commerce; Centre de recherche et développement en économique (CRDE); Univ. de Montréal; Home: 41 Northridge, Ile Bizard, Que. H9E 1A9; Office: 800, Place du Canada, P.O. Box 6042 Stn. A, Montreal, Que. H3C 3E4.

**WALKER, Alan,** D.Mus., F.R.S.C.; university professor; writer; b. Scunthorpe, Lincolnshire 6 Apr. 1930; s. Henry James and Dorothy Elizabeth (Whitby) W.; e. Gainsboro' Gr. Sch. 1945–48; Guildhall Sch. of Music, L.G.S.M. 1948; Univ. of Durham, B.Mus. 1956, D.Mus. 1965; PROF. OF MUSIC, MCMASTER UNIV. 1971– ; Lectr., Guildhall Sch. of Music 1959–61; London Univ. 1954–70; Prod., Brit. Broadcasting Corp. 1961–71; Chrmn., McMaster Univ., Music Dept. 1971–80; Distinguished Vis. Prof., City Univ., London 1984–87; Hungarian Liszt Soc. Medal 1980; Am. Liszt Soc. Medal 1984; F.R.S.C. 1984; Contbr., BBC & CBC Radio progs.; author: 'Franz Liszt: Volume One' (James Tait Black Award 1983; Yorkshire Post Music Book of the Year Award 1984) 1983, 'Franz Liszt Volume Two' 1989 (Volume 3 forthcoming), 'Robert Schumann' 1976, 'Franz Liszt' 1971, 'An Anatomy of Musical Criticism' 1968, 'A Study in Musical Analysis' 1962; co-author: (with Gabriele Erasmi) 'Liszt, Carolyne, and the Vatican: the Story of a Thwarted Marriage' 1991; editor: 'Symposium on Liszt' 1970, 'Symposium on Schumann' 1972, 'Symposium on Chopin' 1967; over 100 articles for learned journals; recreation: watching old movies; Home: 151 McNiven Rd., Ancaster, Ont.; Office: Arts II, No. 429, McMaster Univ., Hamilton, Ont. L8S 4M2.

**WALKER, Arthur William,** FCA; executive; b. Brantford, Ont. 12 Feb. 1930; s. William and Emily Doris (Turner) W.; e. Brantford Coll. Inst. 1948; C.A. 1953; m. Doris Ann d. Frank and Edythe Howell 5 Apl. 1952; children: Paul Howell, Christopher Arthur, Pamela Ann, Susan Lee, Carol Elizabeth; CHRMN., C.E.O. & DIR., CAMVEC CORPORATION 1992– and MID-NORTHERN APPLIANCE INDUSTRIES CORP. 1991– ; Dir., Lange Transportation & Storage Ltd.; National Enterprises Inc. (Texas); Rand Malartic Mines Ltd.; NSR Resources Inc.; Chartered Accountant 1953; Glendinning, Campbell, Jarrett & Dever (subsequently Price Waterhouse) Brantford & Toronto, Ont. 1953–62; Vice Pres. Finance, Hardee Farms Internat. Ltd. Toronto 1962–69, Exec. Vice Pres. 1970–72, Pres. & Dir. 1973–86; Pres. & Dir., Algonquin Mercantile Corp. 1973–90; Chrmn., C.E.O. & Dir., Austin Health Care Corp. 1986–90; Chrmn., C.E.O. and Dir., Dominion Citrus & Drugs Inc. 1986–90; Chrmn., C.E.O. & Dir., Vector Inc. 1991–92; Chrmn., Consultative Task Force on Processed Fruit & Vegetable Industry Ont. 1980; Gov., North York Gen. Hosp. 1973– (Chrmn. 1982–88); Chrmn., North York General Hosp. Found. 1991– (Gov. 1982– ); Fellow, Inst. of Chartered Accountants of Ontario (1985); recipient, (for community service) 125th Anniversary of the Confederation of Canada Medal, 1992; Clubs: National; Aurora Highlands Golf & Country; Bd. Trade Metrop. Toronto; Baptist; recreations: golf, cottaging, waterfowl carving, history; Home: 25 Cranberry Lane, Aurora, Ont. L4G 5Y2; Office: 1190 Meyerside Dr., Mississauga, Ont. L5T 1R7.

**WALKER, Charles A.,** B.A., M.B.A.; business executive; b. Montreal, Que. 29 April 1944; s. Arthur and Laurette (Gauthier) W.; e. Univ. of Montreal B.A. 1966, M.B.A. 1969; m. Louise d. Martial Lemieux Oct. 1969; children: Eric, Caroline; VICE-PRES. FINANCE & ADMIN., REYNOLDS ALUMINUM CO. OF CANADA 1984– ; Bank of Montreal 1969–80; Vice-Pres. Finance, Delisle Foods Ltd. 1980–83; Dir. of Foundation, Ste. Marie Hospital; Dir., Ste. Marie Hospital; Mem., Financial Executives Inst.; Home: 4885 Des Chenaux Blvd., Trois Rivières, Que. G8Y 1A9; Office: 290 Blvd. St-Laurent, Cap-De-La-Madeleine, Que. G8T 7W9.

**WALKER, David Charles,** B.A., M.A., Ph.D.; University professor; b. Sudbury, Ont. 1 Aug. 1947; s. William Brown and Dorothy May (Nesbitt) W.; e. Carleton Univ., B.A. 1970; Queen's Univ., M.A. 1974; McMaster Univ., Ph.D. 1976; m. Debra Shaen; children: Jeffrey, Andrew; PARLIAMENTARY SECRETARY TO FINANCE 1994– ; el. Mem. of Parliament (Winnipeg-North Centre) 1988, re-el. 1993; Critic for Social Policy; Chair, Northern and Western Caucus; Chair, Caucus Committee on Health and Social Development; Prof. of Pol. Sci., Univ. of Winnipeg 1981–88; Spl. Asst., Min. of Justice 1969–70; joined Univ. of Winnipeg 1974; Spl. Asst., Off. of Vice Pres. (Academic) 1980–87; Adv., Off. of Min. of Employment & Immigration 1980–83; Chrmn., Task Force on Native Employment in Man. 1981; Adv., Off. of Min. of Transp. 1983–84; Chrmn., Via Rail Task Force, Transp. Can. 1983–84; Rsch. Dir., Angus Reid Assoc. 1985–86; Pres., West-Can Cons. Ltd.; Adjunct Prof., Univ. of Man.; Dir., C. Rhode Smith Found.; Bd. Mem., Soc. Sci. & Humanities Rsch. Counc. of Can. 1978–83; prov. candidate, Lib. party 1977; mem. Nat. Policy Ctte. 1978–80; mem. Carleton Univ. Nat. Fundraising Ctte.; author 'Great Winnipeg Dream' 1979; regular contbr. to CBC Radio and Winnipeg Free Press; Offices: 892 Sargent Ave., Winnipeg, Man. R3E 0C7 and Rm. 433-C, Centre Block, House of Commons, Ottawa, Ont. K1A 0A6.

**WALKER, Hon. David James,** P.C. (Can.), Q.C., LL.D.; b. Toronto, Ont. 10 May 1905; s. David James and Margaret (Robertson) W.; e. Winchester Pub. Sch., Toronto Model Sch.; and Jarvis Coll. Inst., Toronto, Ont.; Univ. of Toronto, B.A. 1928; Osgoode Hall, Toronto, 1928–31; m. Elizabeth Joyce, d. Irving W. Smith, Toronto; Ont., 2 Sept. 1933; children: David James, Margaret Joyce (Mrs. W.D. McKeough), Diane Elizabeth (Mrs. R.B. Walters); former Bencher, Law Soc. of Upper Can.; read law with Tilley, Johnston, Thomson & Parmenter; called to Bar of Ont. 1931; cr. K.C. 1944; Special Crown Prosecutor for Dom. Govt., 1931–35; Secy. of Royal Comn. Investigating H.E.P.C. of Ont., 1932; Past Pres. of following: Macdonald-Cartier Club of Univ. of Toronto; Osgoode Hall Cons. Club; Toronto P. Cons. Business Men's Club; nominated John Diefenbaker for leadership of National P.C. Party 1942; Diefenbaker Campaign Mgr. at Leadership Convention 1948, and his official agent in 1956 when he was elected Leader, and 1957 when he became Prime Minister's agent responsible for initial drafting of Bill of Rights; def. cand. for Rosedale to H. of C., g.e. 1953; el. to H. of C. g.e. 1957 and re-el. 1958; Parlty. Asst. to Min. of Justice, 1957–58; apptd. Min. of Public Works, 20 Aug. 1959, also Min. of Housing and Nat. Capital Comm.; def. g.e. June 1962; summoned to Senate of Can., Feb. 1963; P. Conservative; Anglican; recreations: riding, skiing; Clubs: Albany (Pres. 1949–52); Rideau Club (Ottawa); Toronto Lawyers (Pres. 1951–52); Toronto Hunt; Badminton & Racquet; Advocates Society; Home: 65 Glen Edyth Dr., Toronto, Ont. M4V 2V8.

**WALKER, David Moffatt,** B.A., M.S.; teacher and consultant; b. Ottawa, Ont. 18 Dec. 1927; s. Harry James and Olive Kennedy (Moffatt) W.; e. Queen's Univ., Hon. B.A. 1950; Inst. World Affairs, Conn., 1951; Columbia Univ., M.S. 1951; m. Moyra Margaret, d. late John Wilson, Cal., 13 Nov. 1954; children: Stephen, Hilary, Nicholas; Communications Consultant; Adjunct Prof., Social Science, York Univ.; Extve. Director, Ontario Educational Communications Authority 1975–85; Editor, Yale Reports, Yale Univ., 1966–71; Producer, Radio & TV, C.B.C., 1951–56; Producer, WGBH-TV, Boston for Ford Foundation and Harvard Univ., 1956; Program Organ., C.B.C. Toronto, 1957–61; Supv., Information and Adult Educ., CBC, 1962–66; Dir., Corp. Affairs, O.E.C.A 1971; Poynter Fellow, Yale, 1978, Lustman Fellowship, Yale, 1981; Candn. Comn. for UNESCO; mem. Cdn. Assoc. for Adult Educ.; recreation: gardening; Home: 2 Rose Park Dr., Toronto, Ont. M4T 1R1.

**WALKER, Donald J.,** B.A.Sc., P.Eng.; business executive; b. London, Ont. 29 Aug. 1956; s. Cyril Reginald and Margaret Marilyn (Wallace) W.; e. Univ. of Waterloo B.A.Sc. 1980; m. Belinda d. Frank and Elfriede Stronach 18 Aug. 1990; PRESIDENT & CHIEF OPERATING OFFICER, MAGNA INTERNATIONAL INC. 1992– ; Sr. Engineer & Supt. of an assembly plant, General Motors 8 years; Asst. to Chair, Magna Internat. 1987; Dir. of Corp. Mktg. & Strategic Planning 1988; Vice-Pres. of Product Development 1989; Extve. Vice-Pres. & C.O.O. 1990; Mem., Automotive Parts Manufacturers Assn. (Bd. of Dir. 1993–96); Dir., Humber College Found.; Mem., Assn. of Profl. Engrs. of Ont.; Office: 36 Apple Creek Blvd., Markham, Ont. L3R 4Y4.

**WALKER, Doreen Elizabeth,** B.A., M.A.; art historian; b. Vancouver, B.C. 4 Sept. 1920; d. Edward John Wilson (D.S.O.) and Lila May (Wood) Ryan; e. Univ. of B.C. B.A. 1942, M.A. 1969; m. the late Colin B. s. Edwin and Fanny W. 21 Dec. 1944; children: Coleen, Nancy, Michael; SENIOR INSTRUCTOR EMERITA, CANADIAN ART HISTORY, UNIVERSITY OF B.C. 1986– ; Instr., Art History, Univ. of B.C. 1969–86; Trustee, Vancouver Art Gallery 1985–91; editor: '"Dear Nan": Letters of Emily Carr, Nan Cheney and Humphrey Toms' 1990; clubs: Vancouver Lawn Tennis & Badminton, Shaughnessy Golf & Country; Home: 4490 Pine Crescent, Vancouver, B.C. V6J 4L1.

**WALKER, Edward Arthur,** B.Sc., M.B.A.; financial consultant; b. Digby, N.S. 9 Jan. 1923; s. Charles Ernest and Muriel Violet (Swabey) W.; e. Queen's Univ. B.Sc. 1946; Harvard Business Sch. M.B.A. 1950; Univ. of Va. Chartered Financial Analyst 1970; m. Shirley d. Harry Hambleton 26 Dec. 1959; children: Susan Meris, Charles Henry; Structural Eng. Canadian Industries Ltd. 1946–53; Financial Asst. Technical Mine Consultants 1953–55; Mgr. of Rsch., Gairdner & Co. Ltd. 1957–68; Pres. and Portfolio Mgr. Canadian Gas & Energy Fund, Canadian Security Growth Fund and AGF Japan Fund 1968–78; Sr. Vice Pres. Finance National Trust Co. 1978–84; Pres. and Dir. Sentinel Investment Management Ltd.; MOF Mgmt. Ltd.; All Canadian Mgmt. Ltd.; Natural Resources Growth Fund; G.T. Management (Canada) Ltd. 1984–88; formed Edward Walker Financial Placements 1989–90; Sr. Advisor (Investment) Candn. High Commn., London, England 1990–92; author various articles; mem. Eng. Inst. Can.; Inst. of Chartered Financial Analysts; recreations: sailing, golf; Clubs: RCYC; The Toronto Hunt; Home: 330 Russell Hill Rd., Toronto, Ont. M4V 2T8.

**WALKER, G. Andrew,** B.A., LL.B.; lawyer; b. Summerside, P.E.I. 5 Jan. 1954; s. Kenneth Alexander and Florence Willene (McLean) W.; e. Dartmouth Coll. B.A. 1976; Cornell Law Sch.; Dalhousie Law Sch. LL.B. 1980; m. Carol d. George and Mabel MacLanders 1 Sept. 1979; children: Luke Andrew, Rebecca Anne, Victoria Katherine, Hannah Alexandra; SR. PARTNER WALKER & AYLWARD 1988– ; Partner and Associate, Campbell, McEwen 1980–88; el. M.L.A. for 5th Prince P.E.I. 1987–89; Pres. P. Cons. Assn. P.E.I. 1985–87; Dir., Candn. Scholarship Found. of Phillips Exeter Academy; Mem., Law Found. P.E.I.; recreations: running, golf; Home: 141 Victoria Rd., Summerside, P.E.I. C1N 2G6; Office: 82 Summer St., Summerside, P.E.I. C1N 3H9.

**WALKER, George F.;** playwright; b. Toronto, Ont. 23 Aug. 1947; s. Malcolm and Florence (Braybrook) W.; m. Susan d. Walter and Courtenay Purdy 23 Aug. 1980; two d., Renata, Courtney; RESIDENT PLAYWRIGHT, NEW YORK SHAKESPEARE FESTIVAL 1981– ; Pres. Playwright Factory Theatre, Toronto 1972–75; author of 15 plays incl.: 'Zastrozzi'; 'Beyond Mozambique'; 'Ramona and the White Slaves'; 'Gossip'; 'Filthy Rich'; 'The Art of War'; 'Rumours of Our Death'; 'Criminals in Love'; plays have been produced in Can., U.S.A., Australia, New Zealand and Gt. Brit.; publ. by Coach House Press, Playwrights Press, Penguin Books, Talon Books; mem. Playwrights Union of Can.; recipient three Chalmers Awards for Outstanding Playwrighting; Dora Mavor Moore Award for Directing; Sr. Arts Award Can. Counc.

**WALKER, George Rutherford,** M.D., M.S., F.R.C.S.(C), F.A.C.S.; surgeon; b. Bolton, Ont. 16 Oct. 1915; s. Robertson Roy and Mary Rebecca (Rutherford) W.; e. Deer Park P.S.; Oakwood Coll.; Victoria Coll. 1933–34; Univ. of Toronto, M.D. 1941; post-grad. surg. training 1945–49 (incl. Gallie Course 1945–48); Dip. American Bd. of Surgery 1960; m. Mary Eastwood d. Wilfred J. and Hilda Ripley 16 Dec. 1944; children: Mary Louise, George Alexander, Robertson Roy, Alan Ripley, Jamieson Scott; Intern, Toronto Gen. Hosp. 1941; Am. Hosp. in Brit. 1942; Royal Candn. Navy 1942–45 (on loan to Royal Navy 1942–44); Acting P.M.O., HMCS York 1944; retired as Ltd. Col., Candn. Forces 1970; priv. practice, Surgery, Sudbury 1950– ; Surg. Staff, Hosp. for Sick children & Univ. of Toronto 1957–58; Chief of Staff, Sudbury Meml. Hosp. 1982–87; Past Dir., Sudbury C. of C. (Past pres.); Emergency Orgns., City of Sudbury; Sudbury Red Cross; Coroner, Prov. of Ont. 1970–86; F.R.C.S.(C), F.A.C.S.; Mem., Soc. for Thoracic Surgs.; Am. Assn. for Thor. Surg.; author: 'Penicillin in Suppurative Tenosynovitis, Essays in Surgery' 1950, and several med. articles; Paul Harris Fellow, Rotary 1990; Order of Ontario 1991; recreations: sailing, travel, flying; Clubs: Rotary; Gallie; Home: 306 Stewart Dr., Sudbury, Ont. P3E 2R8; Office: Ste. 407, 65 Larch St., Sudbury, Ont. P3E 1B8.

**WALKER, Gordon Arthur Hunter,** Ph.D.; educator; b. Kinghorn, Scot. 30 Jan. 1936; s. Frederic Thomas and Mary (Hunter) W.; e. The Edinburgh Acad. 1954; Edinburgh Univ. B.Sc. 1958; Cambridge Univ. Ph.D. 1962; m. Sigrid Helene Fischer 21 Apl. 1962; two s. Nicholas Ian, Eric Gordon Thomas; PROF. OF ASTRONOMY, UNIV. OF B.C. 1972–EM; NRC Postdoctoral Fellow, Dom. Astrophysical Observatory, Victoria 1962–64, Research Scient. II 1962–69; Assoc. Prof. present Univ. 1969–72; author over 80 scient. papers astron. prof. journs.; mem. Candn. Astron. Soc. (Pres. 1980–82); Am. Astron. Soc.; Astron. Soc. Pacific; Royal Soc. Can.; recreations: skiing, hiking, tennis; Home: 2499 West 35th Ave., Vancouver, B.C. V6M 1J7; Office: Vancouver, B.C. V6T 1W5.

**WALKER, Gordon Wayne,** Q.C., B.A., LL.B.; lawyer; b. St. Thomas, Ont. 10 Sept. 1941; s. Albert Cornwall and Ruby Pearl (Stansell) W.; e. elem. and secondary schs. St. Thomas, Ont. 1961; Univ. of W. Ont. B.A. 1964, LL.B. 1967; m. Harriet Emmeline d. Harold Whitfield Hedley and Emmeline Amelia, Woodstock, Ont. 21 Dec. 1968; two d. Wynsome Harriet, Melanie Jennifer; COUNSEL, HOLDEN, DAY, WILSON, Toronto; Commissioner, Internat. Joint Commission (Canada-U.S.A. Boundary Waters); Dir., First Candn. Properties Ltd.; In-Flight Phone Canada Inc.; called to Bar of Ont. 1969; cr. Q.C. 1979; Partner, Walker & Wood, London, Ont.; former Min. of Correctional Services 1978–81 and 1985; Prov. Secy. for Justice, Ont. 1979–82; Min. of Consumer & Commercial Relations, 1981–82; Min. of Industry & Trade 1982–83; Ont. Provincial Secretary for Justice 1983–85; Ald. City of London 1967–71; el. M.P.P. for London North 1971, def. 1975, re-el. for London South 1977, 1981, def. 1985; past director of several private and crown corporations; awards: rec'd Centennial Medal 1967; Queen's Silver Jubilee Medal 1977; awarded Commemorative Medal for 125th Anniversary of Candn. Confederation 1993; author: 'A Conservative Canada' 1983; mem. Law Soc. Upper Can.; senior corporate fundraiser; Progressive Conservative; United Church; mem., Albany Club of Toronto; Home: 47 Elm Ave., Toronto, Ont. M4W 1N6.

**WALKER, Graham H.;** investment dealer; b. Sask. 24 Aug. 1931; s. George Keys and Anne Viola (Sled) W.; e. High Sch.; children: Michael, Alison, Sandra, Erin; DIR., RBC DOMINION SECURITIES LTD.; Dir., Saskoil; Co-Enerco; Newgrade Energy Inc.; Atlantic Council of Can.; CKCK Children's Fund; YMCA; Protestant; Clubs: Optimist; Assiniboia; Wascana; Chamber Comm.; Home: 2007E Cunning Cres., Regina, Sask. S4V 0M7; Office: 600, 2103 – 11th Ave., Regina, Sask. S4P 3Z8.

**WALKER, Ian Lawrence,** B.Sc., P.Eng.; b. Plymouth, Eng. 25 May 1937; s. Clifford Lawrence and Lillian (Marwood) W.; came to Canada 1968; e. Clifton Coll., Bristol, Eng. 1955; Woolwich Polytech., London, Eng. B.Sc. (Hons.) (Mech. Engn.) 1955–59; Brit. Inst. Mang., Dipl. Mang. Studies 1965; m. Marianela Carolina Rojas-Valenzuela; children: Kevin, Jeremy, Eve; Pres., Cami Management Inc.; has held various directorships inc.: Shawinigan Integ; Integ; Vancouver Board of Trade; Balfour Beatty Canada; CH2M-Integ Canada; Westwood Polygas Ltd.; Aquatech Inc.; Lakewood Forest Products Lts.; Wild Horse Industries Inc.; with General Electric Co. Ltd., U.K. as Operational Service Engr. 1959, Project Mgr. 1960, Test Engr. 1962, Contract Mgr. 1964; Sr. Mech. Engr., Balfour, Beatty & Co. Ltd. 1966; Mgr. Balfour Beatty Power Consultants Canada Ltd., Vancouver, B.C. 1968; Pres. INTEG (Intercontinental Engineering Ltd.) 1971; Pres. Shawinigan Integ 1985; Chrmn. & C.E.O., Shawinigan Integ Inc. (Lavalin) 1988; mem. Assns. Prof. Engrs. B.C., Alta. and Sask.; Chart. Engrs. Gt. Brit.; Inst. Mech. Engrs. (U.K.); Assoc. mem. Brit. Inst. Mang.; recreations: sculpture, sailing, scuba diving, travel; Home: 2245 Chairlift Rd., West Vancouver B.C. V7S 2T4.

**WALKER, Irwin R.,** M.B., B.S., F.R.C.P.(C); physician; educator; b. Melbourne, Australia 11 Dec. 1941; s. Charles Z. and Gertrude (Teichert) W.; e. Scotch Coll. Melbourne 1959; Univ. of Melbourne M.B., B.S. 1965; m. Susan d. Gordon and Margaret Patrick 1 Sept. 1974; two s. Matthew, Timothy; PROF. OF MED. McMASTER UNIV. 1973– ; Clin. Hematol. Chedoke-McMaster Hosp. Hamilton 1973– ; Dir. Hamilton-Niagara Regional Hemophilia Clinic 1978– ; Head, Internal Medicine Sect., Chedoke-McMaster Hosps., Hamilton; Fellow, Royal Australasian Coll. of Phys.; Chrmn., Candn. Hemophilia Clinic Dirs. Group; Past Pres., Ancaster Alligators Swim Club; recreations: tennis, soccer (coach); Clubs: Mohawk College Tennis; Ancaster Youth Soccer; Home: 39 Park Lane, Ancaster, Ont. L9G 1K9; Office: Chedoke-McMaster Hospitals, P.O. Box 2000, Stn. A, Hamilton, Ont. L8N 3Z5.

**WALKER, Kenneth Francis,** B.A., M.D., F.R.C.S.(C); surgeon; syndicated medical columnist; b. Croydon, Eng. 28 Feb. 1924; s. Walter Francis and Annie Mabel (Harrison) W.; e. Univ. of Toronto B.A. 1946; Harvard Med. Sch. M.D. 1950; post-grad. training: Strong Meml. Hosp., Univ. of Rochester; Montreal Gen. Hosp., McGill Univ.; Harvard's Hosp. for Women; Banting Inst., Univ. of Toronto; m. Susan d. Harold and Esther Turner 8 Feb. 1956; children: Robert, John, Brett, Diana; SURGEON, TORONTO WESTERN HOSPITAL; TORONTO GENERAL HOSPITAL; Pres., W. Gifford-Jones Ltd.; Giff Holdings Ltd.; author weekly column 'The Doctor Game' (under pseudonyn W. Gifford-Jones; syndicated to 90 Candn. newspapers, 324 in U.S., transl. into French by Montreal's La Presse; transl. into German by Die Deutsche, Toronto and into Chinese by Sing Tao newspaper, Toronto and Hong Kong, readership 18,000,000); books: 'Hysterectomy: A Book for the Patient' 1961; 'On Being a Woman' 1969; 'The Doctor Game' 1975; 'What Every Woman Should Know About Hysterectomy' 1977; 'Medical Survival' 1985; Pres. W. Gifford-Jones Foundation; Dir. and mem. Exec. Ctte., Founding Mem. Lincoln Trust Co.; mem., Toronto Adv. Bd., National Trust V & G; mem.: Gynecological Soc. of Toronto; Med. Legal Soc. of Toronto; recreation: tennis; Club: The University (Toronto); Toronto Press; Downtown Tennis; Homes: 65 Harbour Sq., Ste. 1110, Toronto, Ont. M5J 2L4; Bristol Harbour Village, 135 Cliffside Dr., Canandaigua, N.Y., U.S.A. 14424; Office: Commerce Ct. Med. Centre, PO Box 37, Commerce Ct. E., Toronto, Ont. M5L 1A1.

**WALKER, Michael A.,** M.A., Ph.D.; economist; b. Corner Brook, Nfld. 11 Sept. 1945; s. Augustus Francis and Pauline Frances (Sullivan) W.; e. St. Francis Xavier Univ. B.A. 1966; Univ. of W. Ont. M.A. 1967, Ph.D. 1969; m. Janet d. Ralph and Rosella Busche 19 Aug. 1967; children: Margot, Joel; DIR. THE FRASER INST. 1974– ; joined Univ. of W. Ont. 1969; Bank of Canada, Ottawa 1969–73; Carleton Univ. 1971; Dept. of Finance, Ottawa 1973–74; Guest Host CBC 'As It Happens,' 'Easy Money' 1976; Columnist: Financial Post 1981–89, Toronto Sun 1983, Vancouver Province 1983–84; Ottawa Citizen 1986–89; syndicated daily radio show B.C. and Alta. 'Perspective' 1982–91; frequent speaker various worldwide orgns.; Cons. on Future Studies, Stanford Rsch. Inst. 1978–79; Participant KNOW Network Econ. TV series 1978–79; mem. City of Vancouver Econ. Adv. Ctte. 1980–81; Dir., Collingwood Sch. 1986–89; Bd. mem., Candn. Club; mem. Bd. of Dirs., Canada-Ukraine Chamber of Commerce; Founder & Dir., Buthelezi Educational Foundation for Black Africa; Bd. of Dirs., Mackenzie Fiemann; mem. Rsch. Adv. Group Econ. & Social Issues & Ideas, Royal Comn. on Econ. Union & Devel. Prospects Can.; Mem. Internat. Trade Adv. Ctte.; Acad. Adv. Bd. The Atlas Found.; recipient Woodrow Wilson, Can. Council and Ont. Grad. Fellowships; Winner, Colin M. Brown Freedom Medal and Award 1992; author/ed. numerous publs.; mem. Candn. Econ. Assn.; Candn. Assn. for Business Economics; Am. Econ. Assn.; Internat Assn. Energy Econs.; Société Canadienne de Sciences économique; Escuela Superior de Economia y Adm. de Empresas Buenos Aires (Assoc. Council); Center for the New West Health Care Council, Denver, CO; Mem. Bd. of Dirs., Mount Pelerin Society; recreations: squash; Club: Hollyburn Country (Dir. 1990– ); Office: F2, 626 Bute St. Vancouver, B.C. V6E 3M1.

**WALKER, Michael Barry,** B.Eng., D.Phil.; educator; b. Regina, Sask.; e. McGill Univ., B.Eng.; Oxford Univ., D.Phil.; m. Elizabeth Peterson 1967; children: David, Mark; PROFESSOR, DEPT. OF PHYSICS, UNIVERSITY OF TORONTO; Chair of Department 1987–92; Office: Toronto, Ont. M5S 1A7.

**WALKER, Michael C.,** S.C.A., O.S.A.; artist; b. Kingston, Ont. 28 May 1957; s. Peter Michael and Greta Yvonne (Byers) W.; e. St. Lawrence Coll. 1979; Art Students' League 1981; Queen's Univ. 1991; m. Debbie Louise d. Lino and Gloria Cavasin 19 June 1993; Teacher, Loyalist C.V.I. Kingston 1984–85; Tennessee Fine Arts Centre 1985–86; St. Lawrence Coll. 1988; Diversional Art Therapist, Inst. of Psychotherapy, 1991– ; 10 solo exbns 1982–93; group exbns 1981–92 incl. Drabinsky Gallery, Toronto 1992; Prince Galleries, Chicago 1992; National Arts Club, New York 1989, '92; Salmagundi Club, New York 1988, '89, '90, '91; Agnes Etherington Art Centre, Queen's Univ., Kingston 1981, '86; winner of several awards in Canada and U.S.A.; awarded several Ontario Arts Council grants; member Ont. Soc. Artists; Soc. Candn. Artists; recreation: travel; Address: Golf Course Rd., Amherstview, Ont. K7N 1W6.

**WALKER, Michael Gordon;** media executive; b. San Francisco, Calif. 28 Jan. 1933; s. Harold Frederic and Bessie Jean (Risk) W.; e. Woodstock C.I. 1953; Univ. of West. Ont.; Univ. of Michigan; m. Judith Anne d. Ronald and Norah Murray 1 June 1957; children: Christopher, Catherine, Rebecca; CORPORATE SECRETARY AND GROUP VICE PRESIDENT, HUMAN RESOURCES, THE BLACKBURN GROUP INC. 1982– ; various positions, present firm 1953–92 (incl. writer, columnist and later admin. positions); Mem., Bd. of Newspaper Personnel Relns. Assn. (U.S.); Vice-Pres., Orchestra London; Pres., Pioneer Park Assn.; Candn. Daily Newspaper Pub. Assn. (Employee Relns. Ctte.); Trustee, First St. Andrews Un. Ch.; Past Dir., Family Serv. Bureau; Past Pres. & Dir., Children's Aid Soc.; Past Chrmn., C. of C. Prov. & Nat. Affairs Ctte. & Civic Affairs Ctte.; Past Pres., Wm. Proudfoot House; recreations: music; clubs: Baconinan, London; Home: 950 Colborne St., London, Ont. N6A 4A6; Office: 369 York St., P.O. Box 2280, London, Ont. N6A 4G1.

**WALKER, Philip H.,** B.Sc., P.Eng.; engineer; consultant; b. High Prairie, Alta. 4 Feb. 1931; s. late Harry George and late Mary W.; e. Univ. of Alta. B.Sc. Civil Engn. 1956; Am. Mgmt. Assn. Exec. Course 1970; Queen's Univ. Inst. of Municipal Govt. 1971; Sloan Sch. of Mgmt., M.I.T. 1975; Aspen Inst. for the Humanities 1982; m. Eileen d. late Robson and Madeleine Press 4 Aug. 1956; children: Gregory, Kevin, Michael, Monica, Theresa, Derek; MEMBER, WORKMAN'S COMPENSATION APPEALS COMMISSION; Member, Alta. Water Resources Comn. 1986– ; Chrmn., Construction Industry Advisory Council of Alberta 1984; various positions with City of Edmonton in engn., admin. of water and sewer, land devel. co-ordination branch 1957–76; Comnr. City of Edmonton Utilities, Engn. and Protective Services 1976–84; Dir. St. Joseph's Hosp. (Chrmn. 1981–82); mem. Rotary Internat. (Chrmn. Youth Ctte.); past Dir. Edmonton Family Service Assn.; mem.: Area 14 Recreational Counc.; Edmonton Community Concerts; Assn. Profl. Engrs., Geologists & Geophysicists Alta.; R. Catholic (Chrmn. Parish Counc.; mem. Diocesan Ministries Ctte.); recreations: bridge, dancing, opera, theatre; Clubs: Rotary; Knights of Columbus; Home: 9236 - 58 St., Edmonton, Alta. T6B 1L6.

**WALKER, Richard D.,** B.A.Sc., P.Eng.; pipeline utility executive; b. Sault Ste Marie, Ont. 21 Feb. 1932; e. Univ. of Toronto, B.A.Sc. 1954; Harvard Bus. Sch., AMP 1979; children: Dr. D.A., M.J., A.E., Dr. R.P., G.M.; CHRMN. & PRES., CENTRAL GAS ONTARIO INC.; Vice-Pres., Univ. of Toronto Engineering Alumni Council; Sr. Vice-Pres., TransCanada Pipelines 1983–90; joined TransCanada PipeLines 1956; Gen. Mgr., Nat. Gas PipeLines Authy. of S. Australia 1967–70; Vice-Pres. 1972; Sr. Vice-Pres. 1980; Sr. Vice-Pres. & Chief Operating Officer 1983; Chief Executive Officer of IPEL Kopp Companies and International PipeLine Engineering Ltd., Toronto (TCPL Subsidiaries) 1987; Dir., Internat. PipeLine Engr. Ltd.; Past Chrmn., Candn. Gas Assn.; Mem., Univ. of Toronto Engr. Alumni Counc.; Assn. of Profl. Engrs. of Ont.; Inst. of Engrs. Aust.; Fellow, Inst. of Gas Engrs. (U.K.); Clubs: Ontario; Donalda; Home: 47 Burbank Dr., Willowdale, Ont. M2K 1N1; Office: 200 Yorkland Blvd., North York, Ont. M2J 5C6.

**WALKER, Roger G.,** B.A., D.Phil., F.R.S.C.; educator; b. London, Eng. 26 March 1939; s. Reginald N. and Edith A. (Wells) W.; e. Oxford Univ. B.A. 1961, D.Phil. 1964; Johns Hopkins Univ. NATO Postdoctoral Fellow 1964–66; m. Gay d. John and Isabella Parsons 18 Sept. 1965; children: David John, Susan Elizabeth; PROF. OF GEOL. McMASTER UNIV. 1973– ; Asst. Prof. present Univ. 1966, Assoc. Prof. 1969; Visiting Sci., Denver Rsch. Center, Marathon Oil Co. 1973–74; Amoco Canada Petroleum Co. Calgary 1982; Visiting Prof. Australian Nat. Univ. 1981; cons. and lectr. various petroleum co's and profl. orgns.; mem., Earth Scis. Grant Selection Ctte. Natural Scis. & Eng. Rsch. Council Can. 1981–84; recipient Past Pres.' Medal Geol. Assn. Can. 1975; Soc. Scholars Johns Hopkins Univ. 1975; R.J.W. Douglas Memorial Medal, Candn. Soc. Petroleum Geologists 1990; Hon. mem., Soc. Econ. Paleont. & Mineral. 1991 (Councillor for Mineral.), Pres. Eastern Section; Am. Assn. Petrol. Geols. (Distinguished Lectr. 1979–80); Candn. Soc. Petrol. Geols. (winner Link Award 1983; National Lectr. 1984); Internat. Assn. Sedimentols.; Geol. Assn. Can. (ed. 'Facies Models' 1979, 2nd ed. 1984, 3rd ed. 1992); Assoc. ed., Journal of Sedimentary Petrology; Canadian Journal of Earth Sciences; author over 130 tech. papers various sci. jours.; recreations: skiing, classical music, model railroading, photography; Office: 1280 Main St. W., Hamilton, Ont. L8S 4M1.

**WALKER, Ross Allan;** transportation executive; b. Lindsay, Ont. 8 Aug. 1929; s. Charles William and Emily Christine (Kerr) W.; e. Lindsay Coll. Inst. 1947; m. Sylvia d. Mendal and Emily Smith 29 Apr. 1950; children: Jon, Lynne, Craig; SR. VICE PRES., WEST CAN., CN 1984– ; Telegrapher, agent & train dispatcher, CN 1947–56; Trainmaster, Asst. Supt.-Opns. Mgr. & Area Mgr. 1956–70; Dir., Accident Prevention & Safety 1970; Chief of Transp. 1971–79; Vice Pres., Mountain Region 1979–84; Dir., West. Transp. Adv. Counc.; CN Explorations; Mem. Bd. of Govs., Junior Achievement of Northern Alta.; Offr., Order of St. John; recreations: golf, ranching, reading; Clubs: Edmonton Petroleum, Mayfair Golf & Country; Home: 24 Wellington Cres., Edmonton, Alta. T5N 3V2; Office: 10004 – 104 Ave., Edmonton, Alta. T5J 0K2.

**WALKER, Stanley,** M.A., D.Phil., D.Sc., F.R.S.C.(UK); professor emeritus; b. Padiham, Lancs. UK 21 May 1923; s. David and Ellen (Shaw) W.; e. London Univ. B.Sc. 1944 (King's Coll.) D.Sc. 1964; Exeter Coll. Oxford B.A. 1950, M.A. 1952, D.Phil. 1952; m. Kathleen d. William and Hannah Preston 30 July 1951; children: Heather, Michael Stanley; PROF. EMERITUS OF CHEM. LAKEHEAD UNIV. 1988– ; Rsch., Materials Sci. Div. Royal Aircraft Est. Farnborough, UK 1944–46 and Dept. Applied Chem. Imp. Coll. London Univ. 1946–47; Lectr. Woolwich Polytechnic, UK 1952–56; Sr. Lectr. Phys. Chem. Leicester Polytech. UK 1956–62; Reader in Chem. Univ. of Aston, Birmingham, UK 1962–67; Prof. and Chrmn. of Chem. Lakehead Univ. 1967–75, Dean of Grad. Studies 1975–86; Adjunct Prof. Univ. of Man. 1969–76; mem. Ont. Council Grad. Studies 1969–86; co-author 2 books 'Spectroscopy' 1964; jt. ed. and author 'Spectroscopy' 3 vols. 1974; over 140 sci. papers; mem. Royal Inst. Chem. (UK); Dielectrics Soc. (UK); recreations: walking, travel; Club: Overseas League (UK); Home: 2893 Haughton Ave., Ottawa, Ont. K2B 6Z4.

**WALKER, Susan,** B.A., M.A.; editor; publisher; b. Victoria, B.C. 11 June 1948; d. William Frederick and Catherine Dunbar (King) W.; e. Oak Bay H.S. 1966; Univ. of Victoria, B.A. (Hon.) 1970; Univ. of Sussex, M.A. 1971; common law husband: Colin Vaughan; children: Thomas, Samuel, and Jenny Vaughan; Book Review Editor, The Toronto Star 1988–91; joined Quill & Quire 1972, Ed. 1978–83, Publisher 1983–88; Editor, 'Canadian Art' 1984–88; Commonwealth scholar 1970–71; Home: 70 Coolmine Rd., Toronto, Ont. M6J 3E9.

**WALKER, Tennyson Arnold;** accountant; b. Moncton, N.B. 22 July 1927; s. Trueman Harry and Viola Myrtle (Graves) W.; e. Moncton H.S.; Success Business Coll., Moncton; m. Hilda H. d. Naomi and Roy Thorne 9 Oct. 1948; one s., William Tennyson; President, Lounsbury Co. Ltd. 1979–94; Dir. APM Ltd.; with Lounsbury Co. Ltd. since 1945, Dir. and Sec. Treas. 1969, Vice-Pres. Finance 1976; Dir. Baptist Found.; mem. Highfield Baptist Church; Gideon's Internat. in Can.; Home: 36 Bedford Ave., Moncton, N.B. E1E 4C5; Office: 1655 Mountain Rd., P.O. Box 2129, Stn. A., Moncton, N.B. E1C 8H7.

**WALKER, Victor H.J.,** B.A.Sc.; retired consultant; b. Stratford, Ont. 24 Jan. 1926; s. George Edward and Eva Victoria (Saunders) W.; e. Univ. of Toronto, B.A.Sc. (Ceramic Engn.) 1950; m. Kathleen Sheila Patricia, d. David Keogh, 8 May 1948; children: Gina, Bruce, Lloyd; engng. and supervisory positions with General Steel Wares (London, Ont.) 1950–54; Prod. Mgr., 1954; Plant Acct. and Office Mgr., 1960; Chief Inspr., 1961; Dir. Mfg. & Engn., Brantford Washing Machines Co. Ltd. (Toronto) 1962; Mgr. of Mfg., Hupp Canada Ltd. (L'Assumption, Que.) 1965; Mfg. Mgr., John Inglis Co. Ltd. (Toronto) 1969; Vice-Pres. Mfg. and C.E.O., Brunswick of Canada Ltd. (Mississauga) 1970; Vice-Pres. and Dir. Mfg., Sunbeam Corp. (Can.) Ltd. (Toronto) 1973; Dir., Doon and Cambridge Campuses, Conestoga College (Kitchener) 1979; Pres., Mobile Consulting Services 1981–84; mem. Assn. Prof. Engrs. of Ont.; former Nat. Gov. and Candn. Regional Vice-Pres., Soc. for Advancement of Mang.; recreations: music, travel, photography; Address: 805 Valetta St., London, Ont. N6H 2Z2.

**WALKER, Wayne Stanley,** C.A., M.B.A., C.F.P.; financial executive; b. Brandon, Man. 17 Nov. 1941; s. Frank Irvin and Margaret Evelyn (Burton) W.; e. Cdn. Inst. of C.A.s C.A. 1963; Univ. of Manitoba M.B.A. 1976; Cdn. Inst. of Finan. Planning C.F.P. 1982; m. Astrid d. Enoch and Erma Overgaard 30 Dec. 1989; children: David, Leslie; EXECUTIVE VICE-PRESIDENT, SALES & MARKETING, INVESTORS GROUP INC. 1993– ; Tax Specialist, Deloitte Haskins & Sells (Winnipeg) 1963–67; Mgr., Tax Services, Investors Syndicate Limited 1967–72; Gen. Mgr., Marketing Services 1972–75; Vice-Pres., Mortgage Operations 1975–79; Vice-Pres., Executive & Corp. Sales 1979–86; Sr. Vice-Pres., Marketing, Investors Group Inc. 1986–93; Lectr., Certified Gen. Accountants 7 years; Dir., Winnipeg C. of C.; Silver Medallist & Honour Roll C.A. 1963; recreations: curling, golf; Clubs: Wildewood; Manitoba Club; Home: 336 Lindenwood Dr. E., Winnipeg, Man.; Office: 447 Portage Ave., Winnipeg, Man. R3C 3B6.

**WALKER, William Ross,** B.Comm., FCA; chartered accountant; b. Winnipeg, Man. 15 Apr. 1934; s. Edwin and Mary Margaret (MacCharles) W.; e. Univ. of Alta. B.Comm. 1956; C.A. Alta. 1959; m. Audrey d. Albert Erickson 20 Nov. 1959; children: Jayne, Karen, Graham, Douglas; CHRMN. & CHIEF EXTVE., KPMG PEAT MARWICK THORNE 1989– ; joined present firm 1956, Partner 1964, Mng. Partner Ottawa 1972–77, Mng. Partner Toronto 1977–84, mem. Exec. Ctte. 1975– , Sr. Partner & Chief Extve. 1984–89; mem.: KPMG International Extve. Comm. and Counc.; Panel of Sr. Advrs. to Auditor Gen. of Can.; Chrmn., Univ. of Waterloo Accounting Adv. Council; past Chrmn. Ind. Adv. Ctte. Auditor Gen. of Can.; Vice-Chrmn. & Bd., Candn. Comprehensive Auditing Found.; past Chrmn., Clarke Inst. of Psychiatry; past Chrmn. Ottawa Gen. Hosp.; Past Pres., Inst. of Chartered Accts. of Ont.; Past Mem. Extve. Ctte. & Bd. of Govs., Candn. Inst. of Chartered Accountants; awarded Fellow, Inst. of Chartered Accts. of Ont. 1973; Life Mem., ICAO 1990; Queen's Jubilee Medal 1977; recreations: skiing, travel; Clubs: Toronto; National; York; Rosedale Golf; Home: 34 Wilket Rd., Willowdale, Ont. M2L 1N8; Office: P.O. Box 122, Scotia Plaza, Toronto, Ont. M5H 3Z2.

**WALKOM, Thomas Lawrence,** B.A., M.A., Ph.D.; journalist; b. Kirkland Lake, Ont. 17 Aug. 1950; s. Lawrence Kew and Phyllis Elizabeth (Rogers) W.; e. Dome Pub. Sch. 1963; Ridley Coll. 1968; Univ. of Toronto B.A. 1973, M.A. 1974, Ph.D. 1983; m. Charlotte Anne Montgomery d. Robert and Mary M. 31 Aug. 1986; QUEEN'S PARK COLUMNIST, TORONTO STAR 1989– ; Co-Editor, Univ. of Toronto 'Varsity' 1971–72; Lectr. in Econ. Univ. of Guelph 1978–80; Econ. Reporter Ottawa Bur., Globe & Mail 1981–85; Tokyo Bureau Chief, Globe & Mail 1985–88; Provincial Affairs Columnist, Globe & Mail 1988–89; Office: One Yonge St., Toronto, Ont.

**WALL, Glenn G.,** B.A., B.P.E., M.Ed.; public servant; b. Ottawa, Ont. 25 July 1936; s. Roland and Anne (Gordon) W.; e. Carleton Univ., B.A. 1962; McMaster Univ., B.P.E. 1963; Univ. of Ottawa, M.Ed. 1969; m. Gillian 27 June 1963; children: Christopher, Andrea, Susan; DIR. OF EDUCATION PROGRAMMES, ASIA PACIFIC FOUNDATION OF CANADA 1993– ; Secondary Sch. Teacher & Vice-Principal, Ottawa Bd. of Edn. 1963–69; Asst. Supt. of Schools, Greater Victoria Sch. Dist. 1970–80; Asst. Deputy Minister of Education, Prov. of B.C. 1980–93; Trustee, Lester B. Pearson Coll. of the Pacific; Bd. of Dirs., Internat. Baccalaureate North America; Past Pres., Oak Bay Rotary Club; Past Gov., Brentwood Coll. Sch.; Sessional Lectr., Univ. of Victoria; Office: 1175 Douglas St., Suite 200, Victoria, B.C. V8W 2C9.

**WALLACE, Christopher John,** B.Comm. (Arts); entrepreneur; b. Toronto, Ont. 14 Aug. 1951; s. William and Phyllis Adele (Cork) W.; e. Mount Royal Catholic H.S. (Hons.) 1968; Concordia Univ. B.Comm. Arts (cum laude) 1977; m. Pauline d. Paul and June Thompson 17 Sept. 1993; one s. Adam Paul William; PRESIDENT & FOUNDER, TOPIX COMPUTER GRAPHICS AND ANIMATION INC. 1987– ; Assistant to the Director, Quest Film Productions 1977–79; Assoc. Prod., CBC Radio 1979–82; Director of Programming, Nabu Network Corp. 1982–84; Pres., MediaWare Marketing Inc. 1984–87; Vice-Pres. of Marketing, First Course Software Inc. 1985–87; ImageWare R+D Inc. 1987– ; Home: 846 Carlaw Ave., Toronto, Ont. M4K 3L2; Office: 567 Queen St. W., 3rd fl., Toronto, Ont. M5V 2B6.

**WALLACE, Ian,** A.O.C.A.; author/illustrator; b. Niagara Falls, Ont. 31 Mar. 1950; s. Robert Amiens and Kathleen Elizabeth (Watts) W.; m. Debra Wiedman; e. Ont. Coll. of Art 1973; Assoc. of Ont. Coll. of Art/Grad. Stud. OCA 1973–74; Teaching Asst. 1973–74; author/illus.: 'Julie News' 1974; 'The Sandwich' (with A. Wood) (City of Toronto Book Award runner-up 1976) 1975; 'The Christmas Tree House' 1976; 'Chin Chiang and the Dragon's Dance' (I.O.D.E. Book Award 1984, A.F. Howard Gibbons Award 1984, IBBY Hon. List 1986) 1984, 'The Sparrow's Song' 1986, 'Morgan the Magnificent' 1987; 'Mr. Kneebone's New Digs' 1991; illus.: 'Very Last First Time' (J. Andrews) (ALA Notable Book list 1987, White Raven Book – Bologna 1987) 1985; 'The Architect of the Moon' (T. Wynne-Jones) 1988; 'The Name of the Tree' (C. Lottridge) 1989; recipient Mr. Christie Book Award (illus.) 1990; Elizabeth Cleaver Award (illus.) 1990; Runner-up, Amelia Francis Howard Gibbon Award 1990; 'The Year of Fire' (Teddy Jam) 1992; 'The Mummer's Song' (Bud Davidge) 1993; 'Hansel & Gretel' (The Brothers Grimm) 1994; Hans Christian Anderson Medalist nominee (illustration) 1994; toured extensively reading to over 200,000 kids & adults across Canada, the U.S. and Australia; keynote/conf./seminar/workshop speaker, guest univ. lectr., storyteller; Ont. Arts Counc. grants 1985, 1986, 1989, 1992; Can. Counc. grants 1980, 1981, 1983, 1986, 1987; Mem., Writers' Union of Can.; Candn. Children's Book Ctr.; Home: 184 Major St., Toronto, Ont. M5S 2L3.

**WALLACE, Jack Leslie,** C.D.; retired insurance executive; b. Regina, Sask. 18 Sept. 1913; s. William Leslie and Mildred (Ross) W. (both dec.); e. Central C.I. Regina 1931; m. Joyce d. L.A. and Agnes Thornton 2 June 1945; children: George Thornton, Brian Ross; HON. CHAIR, MORRIS & MACKENZIE INC. 1990– ; joined Northern Assurance Co. Ltd. Winnipeg 1931; Asst. Br. Mgr., Union Insur. Soc. of Canton Ltd. 1933–40; Partner, Wallace & Milne Regina 1947; joined Morris & Mackenzie Inc. 1948; Vice-Pres. 1956; Pres. 1964; Chair & Chief Extve. Offr. 1972; served overseas Second World War 1940–45; 17 Field Reg't RCA 1940–43; 5 Cdn. Armoured Div. 1944; Staff, Candn. Army Overseas 1945; Militia: 2nd Field Reg't, RCA Montreal 1945–53; Retired Lieut-Colonel; joined Montreal Children's Hosp. Board 1957; Chairman of Bd. 1970; Founding Pres., Montreal Children's Found. 1973; Mem., First St. Andrew's Un. Ch. of Canada; Freemason, St. Paul's Lodge; Mem., Kiwanis Club of Middlesex; Pres. Insurance Inst. of the Prov. of Que. 1963; Council Mem., Montreal Bd. of Trade 1971–73; recreations: golf; clubs: Sunningdale Golf; Home: 10 – 65 Fiddlers Green Rd., London, Ont. N6H 4V5.

**WALLACE, John H.,** B.A., LL.B.; legal executive; b. Toronto, Ont. 22 June 1950; s. William and Kathleen A. (Hall) W.; e. Univ. of Toronto B.A. 1972; York Univ. LL.B. 1975; SENIOR VICE-PRES., LEGAL & CORP. SEC., OXFORD DEVELOPMENT GROUP INC. 1987– ; various positions incl. Vice-Pres., Legal, Oxford Development Group Companies since 1980; also Senior Vice-Pres., Legal & Corp. Sec., Oxford Properties Canada Limited 1987– ; Mem., Candn. Bar Assn.; Candn. Corp. Counsel Assn.; Am. Corp. Counsel Assn.; Office: Suite 1700, 120 Adelaide St. W., Toronto, Ont. M5H 1T1.

**WALLACE, Kenneth William;** artist; instructor; b. Penticton, B.C. 7 July 1945; s. Samuel Hugh and Alfreda Clara (Beakes) W.; e. Alta. Coll. Art Calgary Dip. 1970; Vancouver Sch. of Art Dip. in Fine Arts Film & Painting 1973; children: Julia, Montane Procter; Instr. Emily Carr Coll. of Art & Design 1980– ; solo exhns. incl. Vancouver Art Gallery 1974, Bau-Xi Gallery 1975–78, 1980–81, 1986–87, 1990–1992, Vancouver and Toronto, Lefebvre Gallery Edmonton 1981; rep. numerous group exhns. USA and Can. since 1973; rep. various nat. and internat. film exhns.; recipient Internat. Critics Prize Annecy Film Festival, FIRRESCI Prize, N.Y. Film Festival 1975; Can. Council Grants & Travel Grants 1975–76, Film Awards 1977, 1983; Home: 2603 Dundas St., Vancouver, B.C. V5K 1R1; Office: 1399 Johnston St., Granville Island, Vancouver, B.C. V6H 3R9.

**WALLACE, Lawrence James,** O.C.(1972), C.V.O.(1983), LL.D. B.A., M.Ed., C.St.J.; B.C. civil servant; b. Victoria, B.C. 24 Apr. 1913; s. John and Mary E. B. (Parker) W.; e. Victoria (B.C.) Public and High Schs.; Univ. of Brit. Columbia, B.A. 1938; Univ. of Washington, M.Ed. 1945; m. Lois d. Arthur Leeming, Duncan, B.C., 24 April 1942; children: Marilyn, Gillian, Wendy; Deputy Minister to the Premier of British Columbia 1980–81; Agent General in U.K. and Europe 1977–80; joined B.C. Govt. Service 1953 as Dir., Community Programmes Br. and Adult Educ.; Dept. of Educ.; joined R.C.N.V.R. 1941; trained in Extve. Br., Royal Roads; Lt.-Commdr. 1945; Depy. Prov. Secy., B.C. 1959–77 and Depy. to premier, 1969–72; Gen. Chrmn. four centennial celebrations, marking founding of Crown Colony of B. C. in 1858, union of Crown Colonies of Van. Is. and B.C., 1866, Cdn. Confedn. 1867 and joining into confedn by B.C. in 1871; Past Chrmn., Inter-Provincial Lottery Corp., Queen Elizabeth II Schol. Comte. and Nancy Greene Schol. Comte.; Hon. Trustee, B.C. Sports Hall of Fame; Pres., Duke of Edinburgh Awards in B.C. & Yukon; BC Forest Museum; Adv. Bd. Salvation Army; Cdn. Council of Christians and Jews; Chrmn. Cedar Lodge Soc.; Chrmn., Official Bd., First Un. Church, Victoria; Chrmn. McPherson Foundation, Victoria; Depy. Chrmn. Provl. Capital Comn.; Depy. Chrmn. B.C. Press Council; Dir. Goodwill Enterprises for Handicapped; Dir. Craigdarrock Castle Soc.; Dir. Horticultural Centre of the Pacific; Hon. Co-Chrmn., Operation Eyesight Universal, B.C.; named B.C. Man of the Year 1958; Greater Vancouver Man of the Year 1967; Cdn. Centennial Medal 1967; Comdr. Brother, OStJ 1969; City of Victoria Citizenship Award 1971; Officer, Order of Canada 1971; Queen's Jubilee Medal 1977; Freeman of the City of London 1978; Hon. LL.D., Univ. of B.C. 1978; Good Servant Award, Cdn. Council of Christians & Jews 1980; Comdr., Victorian Order 1983; Hon. Life Mem. B.C. Legislative Press Gallery 1984; Hon. Mem., BC High Sch. Basketball Assn.; BC Recreation Assn.; Hon. Chief, Alberni, Gilford and Southern Vancouver Is. Indian Bands; recreations: gardening, community activities; Address: 1345 Fairfield Rd., Victoria, B.C. V8S 1E4.

**WALLACE, Mary Elisabeth,** B.A., Ph.D., F.R.S.C.; professor emeritus; b. Oak Park, Ill. 27 July 1910; d. Malcolm William and Lillie May (Pitkin) W.; e. Univ. of Toronto B.A. 1931, Dip. in Social Sci. 1935; Oxford Univ. B.A. 1934; Columbia Univ. Ph.D. 1949; held various social work positions 1935–45; Staff mem. Sch. of Social Work 1945–46, Lectr. to Prof. of Pol. Sci. Univ. of Toronto 1946–76, Prof. Emeritus of Pol. Sci. 1976– ; mem., Art Gallery of Ont.; Shaw Festival; Stratford Festival; Candn. Nature Fed.; Candn. Assn. Internat. Affairs; Candn. Wildlife Fed.; ed. 'Readings in British Government' 1948; author 'Goldwin Smith: Victorian Liberal' 1957; 'The British Caribbean: From the Decline of Colonialism to the End of Federation' 1977; various articles learned jours.; United Church; recreations: ornithology, music; Address: 421 Heath St. E., Toronto, Ont. M4G 1B4.

**WALLACE, Peter L.,** B.A., M.B.A.; investment executive; b. Montreal, Que. 8 April 1953; s. Robert and Phyllis (Lloyd) W.; e. McGill Univ. B.A. 1976; Univ. of Western Ont. M.B.A. 1978; m. Kimberlee Nolan; children: Nolan, Kristin, Emma; PRESIDENT, MIDLAND WALWYN CAPITAL INC. 1991– ; Corp. Finance Wood Gundy Vancouver / Syndication, Retail Sales Toronto 1979; Chief Operating Officer, Walwyn Stodgell Cochran Murray 1987; Executive Vice-Pres. & Dir., Midland Walwyn; Dir., Midland Walwyn Inc.; Bd. of Govs., Toronto Stock Exchange; Office: 40 King St. W., Suite 3300, Toronto, Ont. M5H 4A1.

**WALLACE, Philip Russell,** M.A., Ph.D., F.R.S.C.; professor; b. Toronto, Ont. 19 Apr. 1915; s. George Russell and Mildred (Stillwaugh) W.; e. Univ. of Toronto, B.A. 1937, M.A. 1938, Ph.D. 1940; m. Jean Elizabeth, d. late Albert Young, 15 Aug. 1940; children: Michael David, Kathryn Joan, Robert Philip; PROFESSOR EMERITUS IN PHYSICS, MCGILL UNIVERSITY 1982– ; Principal, Science Coll., Concordia Univ. 1984–87; Fellow in Applied Math., Univ. of Toronto, 1937–40; Instr. in Math., Univ. of Cincinnati, 1940–42; Mass. Inst. Tech., 1942; Assoc. Research Physicist, Nat. Research Council Can. (Div. of Atomic Energy), 1943–46; Assoc. Prof. Applied Math., McGill Univ. 1946–49; Prof. of Applied Math. 1950–61; Professor of Physics 1962–82; Dir., Inst. of Theoretical Physics 1966–1970; Visiting Prof., Laboratoire de physique des solides, Université Paul Sabatier, Toulouse 1972–73; Prof., Laboratoire de Physique des Solides, Univ. Paul Sabatier, Toulouse 1981–82; MacDonald Prof. of Physics, McGill Univ. 1973–82; author of 90 scientific papers on relativity, nuclear and solid state physics; author 'Mathematical Analysis of Physical Problems' 1972 (repr. 1984); 'Physics: Imagination and Reality' 1991; ed. 'Superconductivity (2 vols) 1969; co-ed. 'New Developments in Semiconductors' 1973; Founder and first Chrmn., Theoretical Physics Div., Candn. Assn. of Physicists; mem., Intl. Adv. Comm., Intl. Conference on Narrow Gap Semiconductors, Warsaw 1977; Intl. Adv. Comm., 14th Intl. Conference on Semiconductors, Edinburgh 1978; 15th Intl. Conference on Semiconductors, Kyoto 1980; 16th Intl. Conference on Semiconductors, Montpellier, 1982; Ed., Candn. Journ. Physics 1972–80; mem., Ed. Adv. Bd., McGill-Queen's Press 1975–78; mem., Commission de l'enseignement supérieur, Conseil de l'éducation du Québec 1970–72; mem., Univ. Grants Comm. for Physics, Nat. Research Coun. of Canada 1972–76; mem., 1967 Centennial Scholarships Comte, NSERC, 1980–83 (Chrmn., 1982–83); Candn. Assn. Physicists; Am. Physical Soc., Candn. Assn. Univ. Teachers; Am. Assn. Physics Teachers; New York Acad. of Sciences; Honorary F.N.A.S. (India); Sigma Xi; Home: 104 – 1039 Linden Avenue, Victoria, B.C. V8V 4H3.

**WALLACE, Robert A.,** B.Comm.; food industry executive; b. Toronto, Ont. 31 Jan. 1953; s. John C. and Ruth G. (Cope) W.; e. John Rennie H.S. 1970; Capilano College 1973; Univ. of B.C. B.Comm. 1977; m. Nancy d. Peter and Rosemary Marson 17 May 1975; children: Michelle, Patrick, Daniel; PRES., INDUSTRIAL FOODS, ROBIN HOOD MULTIFOODS INC. 1991– ; joined Robin Hood Multifoods Inc. 1977; Product Mgr. 1979–81; Group Product Mgr., Robin Hood Flour Consumer 1982–84; Mktg. Mgr., Indus. Bakery Ingredients 1984–85; Gen. Mgr. 1986–88; Senior Vice-Pres., Indus. Foods 1989–90; Chrmn., Candn. Nat. Millers Assn. 1991–92; Chairman., Sharelife, St. Xavier Parish 1988–89; Mem., Mayor's Task Force, Markham 1991; recreation: golf, skiing; clubs: Yorkdown Golf & Country, Markham Suites Fitness; Home: 73 Eastwood Cres., Markham, Ont. L3P 6A1; Office: 60 Columbia Way, Markham, Ont. L3R 0C9.

**WALLACE, Robert S.,** B.A., M.A.; university professor; writer; editor; b. Montreal, Que. 21 Aug. 1943; s. John George and Vera May (Sunderland) W.; e. Delbrook Sr. High 1961; Univ. of B.C. B.A. 1966, M.A. 1970; PROF., DEPT. OF ENGLISH, GLENDON COLLEGE, YORK UNIV.; worked for CBC 1966–68; hired as Dramatic Arts Teacher, Glendon Coll. 1970; simultaneously began career as writer / broadcaster writing stage plays, radio & TV scripts and later theatre criticism; as critic & editor worked for var. nat. institutions such as the CBC; Assoc. Artist, Theatre Direct 1990– ; Drama Editor, Coach House Press 1982– ; Theatre Critic, CBC Radio 1986– ; Editor, 'Canadian Theatre Review' 1982–88 (edited over 60 plays for pub. incl. numerous volumes of plays for CHP, many of which were awarded Gov.-Gen.'s Awards for Drama pub. in English); Rédacteur invité, 'Cahiers de théâtre Jeu' 1987–89; Maclean-Hunter Fellowship in Arts Journalism 1989; Canada Council 'B' grant Arts Award 1987; author: 'Producing Marginality: Theatre and Criticism in Canada' 1990; co-author: 'The Work: Conversations with English-Canadian Playwrights' 1982; editor: 'Quebec Voices' 1986; 'Making, Out: Plays by Gay Men' 1992; Home: 127 Albany Ave., Toronto, Ont. M5R 3C5; Office: 2275 Bayview Ave., Toronto, Ont. M4N 3M6.

**WALLACE, William Laurie,** B.A.Sc., P.Eng.; industrial executive; b. Toronto, Ont. 24 June 1934; s. late William James and Jean (Wilson) W.; e. Normal Model Sch.; Rosedale Publ Sch.; Jarvis Coll. Inst.; Univ. of Toronto B.A.Sc. 1956; m. Joyce M. d. late Harold K. Hillier 1 March 1957; children: Laurie Gordon, Beth, Grant, Scott, Bruce; CHAIRMAN, LIQUID CARBONIC INC. 1993– ; Dir. Liquid Carbonic Inc.; The B.F. Goodrich Company, U.S.A.; Woodbridge Foam Corp.; Gov. Stratford Festival Found.; YMCA; joined Dofasco Inc. as Metall. 1956, Staff Asst. to Works Mgr. 1962, Asst. Works Mgr. 1964, Works Mgr. 1970, Vice Pres. and Works Mgr. 1979, Vice Pres. Operations 1981; Extve. Vice Pres. 1983; Extve. Vice Pres. & C.O.O. 1987–90, Pres. & C.O.O. 1990–91; Chairman, Pres. & C.E.O. 1992; retired 1992; joined Liquid Carbonic Inc. as Chairman – designate Dec. 1992; mem. Candn. C. of C.; Ont. C. of C. (Pres. 1985, Chrmn. 1986); Hamilton & Dist. C. of C.; Past Dir. Am. Iron & Steel Institute; Internat. Iron & Steel Inst.; Mem. Ont. Business Advisory Council; Assn. Prof. Engs. Prov. Ont.; Assn. Iron & Steel Engs. (Dir.); Candn. Inst. Metall.; United Church; recreations: skiing, photography, water sports; Clubs: Hamilton, Toronto, Hamilton Golf & Country, Hidden Valley Highlands Ski; Home: 159 Nicholson Court, Burlington, Ont. L7N 3N5; Office: 255 Brimley Road, Scarborough, Ont. M1M 3J2.

**WALLER, Dalton McFarlane;** management consultant; b. Toronto, Ont.; s. Stanley McFarlane and Mary Elizabeth (McCutcheon) W.; e. Lawrence Park Coll., Toronto; Queen's Univ.; m. Margaret Patricia, d. Charles Grover Cleveland; three s., Grant McFarlane, Garfield Dalton, Andrew Jay; Pres. and Dir. Dalmar Foods Ltd. 1963–84, Chrmn. 1984–90; served in 2nd World War with R.C.N.; Past Pres., Metrop. Toronto Convention & Visitors Assoc.; Past Pres., Candn. Restaurant Assn.; Tourism Industry Assn. Can.; mem. Bd. Trade Metrop. Toronto; Anglican; recreations: golf, tennis, squash; Club: Badminton & Racquet; Home: 61 St. Clair Ave. W., Toronto, Ont. M4V 2Y8.

**WALLER, Harold Myron,** S.B., M.S., Ph.D.; university professor; b. Detroit, Mich. 12 Oct. 1940; s. Allan L. and Lillian R. (LeVine) W.; e. M.I.T. S.B. 1962; Northwestern Univ. M.S. 1966; Georgetown Univ Ph.D. 1968; m. Diane d. Eugene and Pearl Goodman 28 June 1966; children: Sharon, Dahvi, Jeffrey; PROFESSOR, POLITICAL SCIENCE, MCGILL UNIV. 1993– ; Asst. Prof., Pol. Sci., McGill Univ. 1967–71; Assoc. Prof. 1971–93; Chair 1969–74, 1980–81, 1986–87, 1989–90; Assoc. Dean (Academic), Faculty of Arts 1991– ; National Jewish Book Award (US) 1991; Fellow, Jerusalem Center for Public Affairs; Dir., Candn. Centre for Jewish Community Studies; Chair, Edit. Bd., 'Viewpoints'; Jewish; Mem., Candn. Pol. Sci. Assn.; Am. Pol. Sci. Assn.; Chair, Nat. Extve., Candn. Professors for Peace in the Middle East 1975–85; co-author: 'Maintaining Consensus: The Canadian Jewish Polity in the Post-War World' 1990; co-editor: 'Canadian Federalism: From Crisis to Constitution' 1987; recreations: travel, sports; club: Faculty; Home: 6885 Emerson Rd., Montreal, Que. H4W 1G6; Office: 855 Sherbrooke St. W., Montreal, Que. H3A 2T7.

**WALLER, Irvin,** M.A., Dip.Crim., Ph.D.; university professor; b. Hovingham, England 24 July 1944; s. George Stanley and Elisabeth Margery (Hacking) W.; e. Cambridge, Univ. B.A. 1965, Dip.Crim. 1966, Ph.D. 1973; 1st m. Myriam d. Elizabeth and Pierre de Bie 1966; divorced 1981; 2nd m. Susan Gwen d. Doris and Chester Tanner 1983; children: Ann Virginie, Marie Katherine (Waller); James Byron, Mark Patrick (Tanner Waller); PROF., DEPT. OF CRIMINOLOGY, UNIV. OF OTTAWA 1980– ; rsch. & teaching posts incl. Assoc. Prof., Ctr. of Crim., Univ. of Toronto 1966–74; Dir., then Dir. Gen., policy relevant rsch. & stats., Min. of Solicitor Gen. of Can. 1974–80; Assoc. Prof., Univ. of Ottawa 1980–82; frequent public appearances & cons. worldwide 1980– ; pioneered Declaration on Justice for Victims of Crime and Abuse of Power adopted by UN Gen. Assembly 1985; Advisor to Montreal Urban Community on Internat. Centre for Prevention of Crime, Montréal 1992– ; planned European and North Am. Conference on Urban Safety and Crime Prevention 1989, that developed the 'Agenda for Safer Cities'; Internat. Advisor, Eur. Forum for Urban Security 1987– ; Vice-Pres., World Society of Victimology 1988– ; elected member, executive board, Internat. Scientific and Professional Advisory Council of the United Nations Crime Prevention and Criminal Justice Programme 1992– ; several past extve. posts; Pres., Irvin Waller Cons. Inc. 1983– ; Donald Santarelli Award 1987; Marlene Young Award 1987; Anglican; Mem., Ctte. on Justice & Corrections 1985–88; author: 'Men Released from Prison' 1974; co-author: 'Burglary, the Victim and the Public' 1978; recreations: personal fitness; Home: 136 Brighton Ave., Ottawa, Ont. K1S 0T4; Office: Ottawa, Ont. K1N 6N5.

**WALLER, T. Gary,** Ph.D.; educator; b. 26 Dec. 1939; s. William T. and Ruth G. W.; e. Vanderbilt Univ. Ph.D. 1967; m. Jacquelyn d. Lester and Wanda Scott 31 March 1962; children: James S., Amy E.; PROF. OF PSYCHOL. UNIV. OF WATERLOO 1968– ; Rsch. Assoc. Human Resources Rsch. Orgn. 1961–64; Teaching and Rsch. Asst. Vanderbilt Univ. 1964–67, Asst. Prof. 1967–68; private cons.; author, co-author, co-ed. 8 books, 25 jour. articles; Office: 200 University Ave. W., Waterloo, Ont. N2L 3G1.

**WALLING, David Robertson;** electronics executive; b. Lindsay, Ont. 5 Nov. 1930; s. Oscar Henry and Daisy Jane (Robertson) W.; e. Tri-State Univ.; m. Jane d. George and Doris Wells 29 Oct. 1960; children: Gregory, Peter, Amy, Mary; CHRMN. & PRES., D.R. WALLING CO. LTD. 1960– ; secondary edn. to Royal Candn. Navy 1948–53; Tri-State Univ. to Sales Mgr., Lindsay Specialty Products Ltd. 1953–60; Pres., Rosedale Furniture Co. Ltd. 1971–80; Grey Electronics Ltd. 1973; Canam Internat. Ltd.; Chrmn. & C.E.O., Walling Corp.; U.N. Medal; Korean Medal; Paul Harris Fellow; Trustee, Cambridge St. Un. Ch.; Gov., Sir Sandford Fleming Coll.; Past Pres., Rotary Club of Lindsay; Mem., The Pres. Assn.; Nat. Elect. Dist. Assn.; Past Dir. & Chrmn., Small Business Ctte. of Candn. C. of C.; Past Vice-Chair, Eastern Ont. Development Corp.; Royal Candn. Legion; Founding Mem., Friends of H.M.C.S. Haida; author: 'Federalism or Provincialism for Canada' (monograph) 1982; recreations: golf, curling, skiing, sailing, reading; clubs: Rotary Club of Lindsay, Toronto Bd. of Trade, Ontario Club; Home: 54 Bond St., Lindsay, Ont. K9V 3R2; Office: 205 St. David St., Lindsay, Ont. K9V 4S5.

**WALLIS, Diana Lynn;** b. Windsor, England 11 Dec. 1946; d. Dennis Blackwell and Joan Williamson (Gatcombe) W.; e. Tonbridge (Eng.) Grammar Sch. for Girls; ARTISTIC DIR., ROYAL ACADEMY OF DANCING 1994– ; Royal Ballet Sch. 1962–65; Royal Ballet Touring Co. 1965–68; Artistic Coordinator, Nat. Ballet of Can. 1984–86; Assoc. Artistic Dir. 1986–87; Co-Artistic Dir., The Nat. Ballet of Can. 1987–89; Deputy Artistic Dir., English National Ballet 1990–94; Fellow, Imp. Soc. Teachers Dancing (Cecchetti Soc. Br.); Residence: 41 Musard Rd., London W6 8NR England.

**WALLOT, Jean-Pierre,** O.C., L.ès L., M.A., Ph.D., F.R.S., ALQ; educator; archivist; b. Valleyfield, Qué. 22 May 1935; s. Albert and Adrienne (Thibodeau) W.; e. Univ. de Montréal B.A. 1954, L.ès L. 1957, M.A. 1957, Ph.D. 1965; m. Denyse d. Benoît Caron 7th Sept. 1990; children (previous marriage): Normand, Robert, Sylvie; NATIONAL ARCHIVIST 1985– ; Chrmn. d'histoire, Univ. de Montréal 1973–75; Vice Dean, Studies, Fac. of Arts and Sciences 1975–78; Vice Dean, Research, Fac. of Arts and Sci. 1979–1982; Vice-President (Academic), U. of Mtl. 1982–85; el. mem., Univ. Council 1981–82; mem. Faculty of Arts & Science Council, Univ. of Toronto 1970–71; mem. Can. Council Acad. Panel 1973–76; Soc. Sci. and Humanities Rsch. Counc. Acad. Panel 1983–84; Negotiated Grants Comte. 1975–1980 (Chrmn. 1978); Dir. de recherche associé Ecole des Hautes Etudes en Sciences Sociales, Paris 1975, 1979, 1981, 1983, 1984, 1985, 1987, 1989, 1994; Guest Lectr. Univ.

of Sherbrooke 1967, 1968; UQUAM 1972; Univ. of B.C. 1972; Laval Univ. 1973, 1977; Univ. of Ottawa 1986–94; Assoc. Prof., Univ. of Toronto 1969–1971, Prof. Concordia U. 1971–73; rec'd yearly research grants Can. Council and Qué. Govt. 1961–88; Shawinigan Prize best feature (reportage) Candn. Weeklies Assn. Newspapers 1957–58, 1958–59; Marie Tremaine Medal, Soc. canadienne de bibliog. 1973; author 'Intrigues françaises et américaines au Canada (1800–1802)' 1965; 'Un Québec qui bougeait' 1973; co-author 'Les Imprimes dans le Bas-Canada 1801–1810' 1967; 'Patronage et pouvoir dans le Bas-Canada 1794–1812' 1973; Ed. 'Mémoires d'un Bourgeois de Montréal' 1980; ed. 'France de l'Ouest et Québec' 1982; ed. 'Evolution et éclatement du monde rural' 1986; mem. various ed. comtes.; author over 100 articles econ. and social hist. Qué.; Ed. 'Le Progrès de Valleyfield'; mem., sec., Academy I, Royal Soc. Can. (Pres. 1985–87); Candn. Hist. Assn. (Dir. 1970–73, Vice-Pres. 1981–1982; Pres. 1982–1983); Inst. d'histoire de l'amérique française (Dir. 1970–83, Vice Pres. 1971–73, Pres. 1973–77); Pres. Assn. canadienne-française pour l'avancement des sciences (1982–1983); Pres., Bd. of Dir., forming C.L.S.C., Côte-des-Neiges, Montreal 1984–85; Chevaliers de colomb; Mem., Can. Cultural Property Comm. (1981–1984); Tyrrell Medal of Royal Society (1982); el. mem. Acad. des lettres du Québec (1983); Doctorate (honoris causa) and University Medal, Univ. of Rennes (France) 1987; Officier, Ordre des Arts et Lettres de la République française 1987; el. mem., Amer. Antiquarian Soc. 1987; Fellow, Royal Society; Officer, Order of Canada 1991; Mem. Bd. of Govs., Univ. of Ottawa 1988–90; Vice Pres., Internat. Counc. of Archives 1988–92, Pres. 1992–96; mem. ex-officio: Historic Sites & Monuments Bd. of Canada; Nat. Library Adv. Bd.; Catholic; recreation: music (drums); Home: 32 St-Cyr, Hull, Que. J9A 1G8; Office: 395 Wellington St., Ottawa, Ont. K1A 0N3.

**WALMAN, Bernard S.,** S.M.F.C., M.T.C.I.; trust officer; b. Toronto, Ont. 21 Sept. 1928; m. Anita; children: Nadine, Terry, Glenn; CHRMN., INCOME FINANCIAL CO.; former Pres. & Chrmn., Income Trustco & Income Trust Co.; Mortgage and Trust Office for 35 years; Home: 101 Bertram Dr., Dundas, Ont.; Office: 231 Main St., W., Box 999 Hamilton, Ont. L8P 3N9.

**WALMSLEY, Norma E.,** O.C., B.Comm., M.A., LL.D.; professor (retired); social activist; b. Winnipeg, Man. 12 Apr. 1920; d. Henry John and Bertha Mary (Franzmann) W.; e. McGill Univ., B.Comm. 1950, M.A. 1954; Carleton Univ. LL.D. 1983; Brandon Univ. LL.D. 1988; MEM. BD. OF DIRS. & EXEC. COMM., INTERNAT. CENTRE FOR HUMAN RIGHTS AND DEMOCRATIC DEVELOPMENT, Montreal 1990– ; Mem. Exec. Group, Can. Ctte. for the Fiftieth Anniv. of the United Nations 1993– ; Hon. Vice-Pres. Can. Ctte. for UNIFEM 1993– ; served with RCAF (W.D.) 1941–45, Sr. Offr. in Charge Women's Div. Supplies Can. & Overseas; Prof. of Pol. Sci. Brandon Coll. Man. 1955–67, Registrar 1962–64; Social Sci. Rep. Candn. Govt. Del. to 11th and 12th Gen. Conf. UNESCO Paris 1960, 1962; Rsch. Prof. Royal Comn. Bilingualism & Biculturalism Ottawa 1965–66; Dir. Univ. Resources Study Assn. Univs. & Colls. Can. Ottawa 1967–70; Founding Pres. and Life Mem. Bd. of Dirs. MATCH Internat. Centre; mem. Candn. Govt. Del. to World Conf. UN Decade for Women Copenhagen 1980; Soc. Internat. Devel. (Internat. Governing Council 1975–82, Exec. Ctte. 1977–82, North South Round Table 1978– ); mem.-at-large Candn. Comm. for UNESCO 1980– , Chair Sub-Comn. Status Women 1982–84; mem. Group of 78, Adv. Council Can.-S. Africa Cooperation; has promoted and served as voluntary mem. various bds. & cttes. incl. UN Assn. Can., World Univ. Service Can., CUSO, Candn. Bureau Internat. Edn., Candn. Council Internat. Co-op., World Food Day Assn. Can., Can. World Youth, mem. Adv. Ctte. North-South Inst. Study Women in Devel.; recipient Queen's Silver Jubilee Medal 1977; The Governor General's Awards in Commemoration of the Persons Case 1987; Lewis Perinbam Award Internat. Devel. 1988; Officer, Order of Canada 1994; mem. Royal Candn. Legion; author: 'Some Aspects of Canada's Immigration Policies' 1966; 'Canadian Universities and International Development' 1970; Anglican; recreations: golf, photography, travel, skiing; Club: Larrimac Golf & Tennis; Address: P.O. Box 68, Wakefield, Qué. J0X 3G0.

**WALPOLE, Noel Gavin;** insurance executive; b. Burton-on-Trent, Staffordshire, England 30 Dec. 1944; s. Hugh and Joan Grace (Gill) W.; e. Aylesbury Gr. Sch.; m. Susan d. Kenneth and Margaret Grant 1 Nov. 1967; children: Jeffrey, Michael; PRES. & CHIEF EXTVE. OFFR., ANGLO CANADA GENERAL INSUR. CO. 1986– ; Pres. & C.E.O., AXA Insurance 1991– ; var. pos. incl. Mktg. Mgr. for Can., Underwriting Mgr., & Claims Mgr., SAFECO Insur. Co. 1969–83; Resident Vice-Pres., Fireman's Fund Insur. Co. 1983–85; Extve. Vice-Pres., Halton-Caird Insur. Brokers Limited 1985–86; Fellow & Mem., Soc. of Fellows, Insur. Inst. of Can.; recreations: running, sailing, golf, tennis; Clubs: The London Club; Sunningdale Country; Home: 27 Debbie Lane, London, Ont. N5X 3H1; Office: 217 York St., London, Ont. N6A 5P9.

**WALSH, Hon. Allison Arthur Mariotti,** B.A., B.C.L.; retired judge; b. Montreal, Que. 30 June 1911; s. James Francis and Isabel (Mariotti) W.; e. High Sch. of Montreal 1929; McGill Univ., B.A.1933 (Oliver Gold Medal in Econ. & Pol. Science), B.C.L. 1936; Univ. De Grenoble, Cert. d'Etudes Francaises 1936; m. Carol, d. Albert Edward Stevens, 27 Dec. 1939; two d. Julia Kelly, Diana Allison Lockwood; Puisne Judge, Federal Court of Can. 1964–86; Judge, Court Martial Appeal Court 1968–86; read law with late Aubrey H. Elder, Q.C.; called to Bar of Que. 1936; cr. Q.C. 1960; practised law in Montreal with Creelman, Edmison & Beullac, later known as Creelman and Walsh 1939–54 and with Campbell, Weldon, McFadden & Walsh which became Laidley, Campbell, Walsh & Kisilenko until 1964; has served as Commr. of Senate in connection with Resolutions for Dissolution of Marriage and as Umpire under Unemployment Ins. Act.; Past Pres., Hampstead Mun. Assn.; Hampstead Home & Sch. Assn.; Iverley Community Centre, Montreal; McGill Alumni Inter-Fraternity Council; rec'd Centennial Medal 1967; Queen's Jubilee Medal 1976; Hon. mem. Phi Delta Phi Legal Fraternity; Sigma Chi; Protestant; recreations: golf, billiards, travel; Clubs: Rideau; Royal Ottawa Golf; Kiwanis (Past Dir.); University (Montreal); Montreal Badminton & Squash; M.A.A.A. (Life mem.); Home: Apt. 1411, 10 The Driveway, Ottawa, Ont. K2P 1C7.

**WALSH, David Allan,** B.A.; opera stage director; b. Toronto, Ont. 12 Sept. 1947; s. Francis Lorimer and Margaret Allan (Brown) W.; e. Patterson C.I.; Univ. of Windsor, B.A. 1969; Theatre Tech. Course, Univ. of Toronto, grad. 1972; common law wife: Kim d. Joseph and Beatrice Tymkow; two d.: Vanessa Andrea, Siobhan Marie; Head of Prod., Scottish Opera 1988–91; Stage Dir., Vancouver Opera 1984–87; Stage Mgr., Candn. Opera; Stratford Fest.; Guelph Spring Fest.; Scottish Opera; Asst. Dir., English Music Theatre; English Nat. Opera; Covent Garden; Frankfurt Opera; Freelance Dir., Germany, England, France, Canada and U.S.; Dir., Opera Studio, Victoria Conservatory of Music; recreations: tennis, hiking; Home: 1251 Victoria Ave., Victoria, B.C. V8S 4P3.

**WALSH, F. Michael,** B.A., M.A., M.B.A., Ph.D.; b. Maryfield, Sask. 7 Feb. 1947; s. Frederick Michael and Alice Marguerite (McDonald) W.; e. Univ. of Guelph B.A. 1969, M.A. 1970, Ph.D. 1992; York Univ. M.B.A. 1975; m. Virginia d. William B.S. Trimble 1 May 1971; children: Thomas Philip, Alan Michael; VICE PRESIDENT & DIR., FIRST MARATHON SECURITIES LTD. 1993– ; Investment Analyst, Merrill Lynch Royal Securities Ltd. 1977–78; Mgr., Rsch. 1978; Senior Underwriting Rep. 1978–81; Senior Underwriter, Burns Fry Limited 1981–82; Vice-Pres., Merrill Lynch Canada Inc. 1982–84; Vice-Pres. & Dir., First Marathon Securities Ltd. 1984–89, 1993– ; 1992 Sr. Policy Consultant, Ont. Securities Commission; Chrmn. of Trustees, Samuel Rogers Memorial Trust; Steering Ctte., Friends of the Thomas Fisher Rare Book Library, Univ. of Toronto; Mem., Religious Soc. of Friends (Quakers); Life. Mem., Am. Philos. Assn.; recreations: book collecting; clubs: University Club of Toronto; Home: 117 St. Leonard's Ave., Toronto, Ont. M4N 1K6.

**WALSH, Lieut.-Gen. Geoffrey,** C.B.E., D.S.O., C.D., B.Eng., D.M.Sc.; b. Brantford, Ont. 19 Aug. 1909; s. late Harris Leamon and late Bertha Ione (Benson) W.; e. St. Catharines (Ont.) Coll. Inst.; Royal Mil. Coll. (Dipl.) 1926–30; Nova Scotia Tech Coll. 1930–31; McGill Univ., B.Eng. (Elect.) 1932, D.M.Sc. 1971; Nat. Defence Coll. 1948; m. Gwynn Abigail, d. late Robert S. Currie 14 Sept. 1935; one s., Robert Geoffrey; Lieut., R.C.E. 1930; served in 2nd World War, proceeding Overseas in May 1940 and returning in Aug. 1945; served in Spitzbergen, Sicily, Italy, N.W. Europe; Commanded a Field Co.; C.R.E., 1 & 4 Divs.; Chief Engr., 2 Corps; Chief Engr., Candn. Army; awarded C.B.E., D.S.O.; Mentioned in Despatches (twice); Commdr., Order of Orange Nassau (Netherlands); Legion of Merit (U.S.); organ. N.W. Highway System to take over Alaska Rd. from U.S. Army and operated it two yrs.; O.C., Eastern Ont. Area at Kingston, Ont., for three yrs.; Commanded 27th Bgde. on.its formation and trained and Commanded it in Germany for one yr.; Dir.-Gen. of Mil. Training 1953–55; Quartermaster General 1955–59; G.O.C. Western Command. 1959–61; Chief of the Gen. Staff, Oct. 1961–Aug. 1964 when apptd. Vice Chief Candn. Defence Staff on integration of 3 services; Col. Commandant, R.C.A. Cadets 1970–74 and as such, organized Army Cadet League of Can.; Anglican; recreations: fishing, golf; Address: 201 Northcote Place, Ottawa, Ont. K1M 0Y7.

**WALSH, Harry,** Q.C., B.A., LL.B.; b. Old Kildonan, Man. 14 Aug. 1913; s. Philip and Fanny (Mastensky) W.; e. King Edward Sch., Isaac Newton Sch. and St. John's Tech. Sch., Winnipeg; Univ. of Man., B.A. 1932, LL.B. 1937; m. Irene d. Vasily Oleinikov of Belgrade, Yugoslavia 14 Aug. 1964; children: Paul Victor Q.C., Arlyne; FOUNDING PARTNER, WALSH, MICAY AND CO. (estbd. 1937); read law with The Hon. Edward James McMurray, P.C., Q.C.; called to Bars of Man. 1937, Ont. 1949, Sask. 1955, B.C. 1963, Alta. 1970, N.W.T. 1972; cr. Q.C. 1953; served with RCA as Lance Bombardier during World War II; Life Bencher, and of Standards Comte. Law Soc. of Man. (Vice-Chrmn., Legal Aid Comte.); Nat. Chrmn., Wills and Bequests, United Israel Appeal of Can. Inc.; Chrmn., Jud. Comm. of Benchers, Law Soc. of Man.; Gov., Ben-Gurion Univ., Negev, Israel; Bd. mem., and Senior Vice-Pres., Candn. Assocs., Ben-Gurion Univ.; Harry Walsh Q.C. Chair on Law and Morality, est. Ben-Gurion Univ. of the Negev; Past Pres., Winnipeg N. Lib. Assn.; Hon. Pres., YMHA Community Centre, Winnipeg; Head of Bar Admission Course in Criminal Law, Law Soc. of Man. and Lectr. in Continuing Legal Educ.; Dir., Legal Aid Services Soc. Man.; recipient of 1985 award of Canadian Bar Assoc. (Manitoba Branch) in recognition of 47 years of Distinguished Service to the Legal Profession and the Internat. Community; former Nat. Chrmn., Criminal Justice Sec., Candn. Bar Assn.; Nat. Chrmn. of Comte. on Evidence and Nat. Chrmn. of Legal Aid Liaison Comte., Candn. Bar Assn.; el. Hon. Life Mem., Candn. Bar Assn. 1987; Liberal; Hebrew; recreations: reading, cycling, golf; Club: Hon. Life Mem. & Legal Counsel of Glendale Golf & Country; Home: 425 Scotia St., Winnipeg, Man. R2V 1W3; Office: 10th Flr., Richardson Building, Portage and Main, One Lombard Place, Winnipeg, Man. R3B 3H1.

**WALSH, Henry Michael,** C.D.; association executive; b. Quebec City, Que. 13 May 1920; s. the late Edward Patrick and the late Clara (Bussieres) W.; e. St. Patrick's High Sch., Que. City; Laval Univ.; RCAF Staff Coll. Inst. 1953–56; NATO Defence Coll. 1961; m. Anne. d. Yves and Monique Suberbielle 8 Mar. 1975; children: (1st m., wife dec.) Nicholas, Teresa Brescacin, Kathleen; (2nd m.) Aurelie, Stephanie, Melanie; Pres. and C.E.O., Candn. Shipbuilding and Ship Repairing Assn. 1976–87; RCAF Navigator 1940–45, promoted to Squadron Leader 1944; served in U.K., Middle East and Far East; obtained regular RCAF comn. 1946; served Air Transport Command 1946; Directorate of Air Training 1947; promoted to Wing Cmdr. 1951; Chief Admin. Offr. Gros Tenquin, France 1952–53; Planning Staff RCAF HQ 1956–61; promoted to Group Capt. 1961; C.O. RCAF Station Bagotville, Que. 1961–65; NORAD HQ. Tacoma and San Francisco 1965–6; Dir. Continental Plans NDHQ 1967–69; transf. to Dept. of Transport as Special Asst. to Depy. Min.; Dir. Bur. of Internat. and Environmental Affairs, Dept. of Transport 1971–74; Dir. Gen. Marine Policy and Plans 1974–75; R. Catholic; mentioned in Dispatches 1943; recreations: skiing, skating; Home: 2051 Thistle Cr., Ottawa, Ont. K1H 5P4.

**WALSH, John B.,** B.S., M.A., Ph.D., F.R.S.C.; mathematician; b. Rochester, N.Y. 12 Sept. 1938; s. John Joseph and Elizabeth Ann (Bradstreet) W.; e. S. Ariz. High Sch. 1956; Cal Tech B.S. 1960; Univ. of Ill. M.A. 1962, Ph.D. 1966; m. Johanna d. Jochem and Pauline Albrecht 1961; children: Owen, Kevin; PROF. OF MATH., UNIV. OF B.C. 1975– ; Instr. Stanford Univ. 1966–68, Asst. Prof. 1968–69; Visiting Prof., Univ. de Strasbourg 1969–71; Ecole Polytechnique Federale de Lausanne 1971–72; Assoc. Prof. present Univ. 1972; Visiting Prof. Univ. of Paris 1976–77; author numerous articles math.; Assoc. Ed. 'Annals of Probability' 1972–80; mem. ed. bd. Candn. Math. Soc. publs.; recreations: sports, music, reading; Office: Vancouver, B.C. V6T 1W5.

**WALSH, John Stanley;** artist; b. Brighton, England 16 Aug. 1907; s. John and Ethel Edith (Pickwell) W.; e. Brighton Grammar Sch.; Brighton Tech. Coll.; Univ. of London; art schs. Eng., Can., Mexico; m. Marion Louise Cowie d. James Laurence and Mary Cowie 16 July 1942; one d. Patricia Marion; during World War II served in Brit. Admiralty as eng. offr. guns & ammunition production Eng. & Can.; has held 27 solo exhns. Can. and USA; rep. perm. colls. Montreal Museum of Fine Arts, Art Gallery of Ont., Winnipeg Art Museum and McGill Univ.; specializes city scenes and eng. subjects; comns.

Can., Eur., India and Panama; painting of Idikki Dam, India presented to Mrs. Ghandi 1974; water colour chosen for the Queen's Diamond Jubilee Coll. Windsor Castle, England 1986; water colour chosen for internat. collection of water colours assembled from three countries (Canada, U.S.A. & Gt. Britain) for a travelling exhibition in Canada, U.S.A. & Gt. Britain 1991; author numerous articles painting and travel Candn. and USA publs.; recreations: fishing, swimming; Club: Montreal Amateur Athletic; Home: 142 – 52nd Ave., Lachine, Qué. H8T 2W9.

**WALSH, Patrick G.,** B.A., M.Sc., M.B.A., Ph.D.; investment dealer; b. Toronto, Ont. 14 Apr. 1949; s. Gerald Francis and Catherine Agnes (Shea) W.; e. Univ. of Toronto, B.A. 1972 (Bruels Gold Medal in Econ.); London Sch. of Econ. M.Sc. 1973; Univ. of Pa. Wharton Sch. of Finance, M.B.A. 1976, Ph.D. 1978; m. Sharon H. Sallows d. Cefni and Darlene Sallows 3 July 1976; two d. Caitlin Meghan, Meghan Taylor; PRES., RESEARCH CAPITAL CORP. 1986– ; Corporate Finance Associate, Dominion Securities Ltd. 1977–78; Salesman, Partner, Dir. and Pres. Canavest House Ltd. 1978–85; Pres. Andras Canavest Hetherington Ltd. 1985–86; Dir. Financial Rsch. Found. Can. 1984–86; recreations: yachting, hockey; Home: 40 Edgar Ave., Toronto, Ont. M4W 2A9; Office: P.O. Box 265, Ernst & Young Tower, Suite 1500, 222 Bay St., Toronto, Ont. M5K 1J5.

**WALTER, Donald Paul,** B.Com.; fabricating distributor company executive; b. Montréal, Qué. 17 Sept. 1929; s. Arthur William and Anna (Boronow) W.; e. Westmount (Qué.) High Sch. 1947; McGill Univ. B.Com. 1951; Univ. of W. Ont. Mgmt. Training Course 1968; m. Margaret d. Howard and Dorothy Boulden 1 June 1957; children: Heather, Kathryn, Timothy; PRES. E.F. WALTER LTD. 1986– ; joined present co. 1951 holding various positions incl. Corporate Sec., Exec. Vice Pres.; Treas. & Dir., Candn. Mfrs. Assn.; mem. Metro Toronto Econ. Devl. Corp. Adv. Council; Metrop. Toronto Bd. Trade; Past Pres. Stony Lake Cottagers Assn.; Past Warden, St. Peters' on the Rock Ch., Stony Lake, Ont.; Dir., St. Hilda's Towers; recreations: skiing, squash, sailing, swimming, tennis, music, reading, theatre; Clubs: Badminton & Racquet; Montreal Badminton & Squash; Stony Lake Yacht; Home: 126 Alexandra Blvd., Toronto, Ont. M4R 1M2; Office: 51 Wingold Ave., Toronto, Ont. M6B 1P8.

**WALTER, John A.,** B.Comm., C.A., M.B.A.; project finance executive; b. Montreal, Que. 17 Apr. 1956; s. Arthur Richard and Diane Adele (Robertson) W.; e. Concordia Univ., B.Comm. (magna cum laude) 1979 (awarded Finance Medal); Univ. of Toronto, M.B.A. 1984; m. M. Leith Maclaren d. Fred and Nancy Maclaren 21 June 1986; two s. Christopher Maclaren, S. Jeffrey Maclaren; VICE PRESIDENT, BECHTEL FINANCING SERVICES INC. 1990– ; Vice-Pres., Middlefield Ventures Ltd. 1986–89; Mgr., Project Fin., Bank of Montreal 1983–86; Audit & insolvency practice, Ernst & Young (formerly Clarkson Gordon) 1979–83; recreations: sailing, gardening; Club: Royal Canadian Yacht; Office: P.O. Box 193965, 50 Beale St., San Francisco CA 94119-3965 USA.

**WALTERS, Jack Henry,** M.D., F.R.C.S.(C), F.A.C.O.G., D.A.B.O.G., F.R.C.O.G.; obstetrician-gynaecologist; educator; b. Toronto, Ont. 2 Apl. 1925; s. Henry Melville and JosephineIsabella (O'Donnell) W.; e. St. George's Pub. Sch. and London (Ont.) Central Coll. Inst. 1943; Univ. of W. Ont. B.A. 1946, M.D. 1951 (Teaching Fellow in Physiol. 1946–47, Nat. Research Council Fellow 1952–53), Post-grad. Program Obstetrics-Gynaecol. 1951–58; m. Mary Joan (dec'd) d. late Dr. Frank Robert Clegg, London, Ont. 7 Sept. 1949; children: Joan Anne, John Frank, Janet Patricia; remarried: Carol Louise Moyer; PROF. & CHRMN., DEPT. OF OBSTETRICS/GYNAECOL., KING FAHAD HOSP., RIYADH, SAUDI ARABIA 1990– ; (Prof. and Chrmn. 1978–82); Chief of Obstetrics/Gynaecol. Ottawa Gen. Hosp. 1978–82; Prof. of Obstetrics & Gynaecol. Univ. of W. Ont. 1960–73, mem. Senate 1967–68; Prof. and Chrmn. of Obstetrics & Gynaecol. Med. Coll. of Ohio 1973–78; Prof. of Obstetrics/Gynaecol., Univ. of Ottawa 1978–90; Chief of Obstetrics & Gynaecol. St. Joseph's Hosp. 1960–73, Dir. of Cytol. 1958–73; John S. McEachern Mem. Traveling Fellow 1956–58 (Stockholm, Amsterdam, Austria, Eng., Buffalo); mem. Bd. Dirs. London Symphony Orchestra 1970–73; London Art Gallery 1970–73; Film Task Force Ont. Dept. Indust. & Tourism 1972; Chrmn. Ont. Film Festival Comte. 1972; London Music Scholarship Foundation 1971–72; Perinatal Consultant Ohio Dept. Health 1974–78; Consultant Perinatal Units Alta. Hosp. Comn. 1973; Chrmn., Fed. Task Force, High Risk Pregnancies 1980–90; served with RCAF (Reserve), rank Sqdn. Leader; Co-Chrmn., Comm. on Reproductive Care, Ont. Min. of Health 1979–80; author 'Perinatal Problems' 1971; various publs. and papers; Fellow, Am. Coll. Obstetricians & Gynaecols.; diplomate Am. Bd. Obstetricians & Gynaecols.; Central Assn. Obstetricians & Gynaecols.; N. Am. Gynaecol. Soc. (past Pres.); Ont. Med. Assn. (Pres. 1970); Candn. Med. Assn. (Extve. Comte. 1967–70); Chrmn., Task Force on Imaging 1980; Specialized Services, High Technology Comte. 1981; Chrmn. Advy. Comte. Reproductive Physiology, Federal Health Protection, National Health Welfare 1983–90; Chrmn., Publications Ctte., Candn. Med. Assn. 1983–90; Ont. Council Health; Candn. Cancer Soc. (Dir. Ont. Div. 1970–73); Soc. Obstetricians Gynaecols. of Can.; Am. Cancer Soc. (Ohio Div. Bd. 1976–78); Laser Soc., and other med. assns.; Alpha Omega Alpha (Pres. Toledo Chapter 1977); Alpha Kappa Kappa; Bayfield Internat. Croquet Assn.; P. Conservative; Anglican; recreations: music, fishing, croquet; Club: London Hunt & Country; Address: c/o 61 Chartwell Rd., Oakville, Ont. L6J 3Z3.

**WALTERS, Paul Scott,** B.Comm.; marketing executive; b. Edmonton, Alta. 30 Mar. 1954; s. Kenneth Ernest and Elizabeth June (McWhinnie) W.; e. Univ. of B.C., B.Comm. 1978; m. Darla d. Lloyd and Olive Abotsway 19 June 1976; children: Sarah Lynn, Christopher Scott; PRES., ZELLERS INC. 1989– ; Vice-Pres., Human Resources, Hudson's Bay Co. 1986; Extve. Vice-Pres., The Bay 1987; Pres., Simpsons' Ltd. 1988–89; Home: 443 Lakeshore Rd., Beaconsfield, Que.; Office: 5100 De Maisonneuve W., Montreal, Que. H4A 1Y6.

**WALTON, John Sheppard,** B.E.; business executive; b. Toronto, Ont. 7 Dec. 1930; s. John Ruskin and Doris Armstrong (Sheppard) W.; e. Ridley Coll. St. Catharines, Ont. 1949; McGill Univ. B.E. (Civil) 1953; m. Joan d. Bob and Dorothy Watson; two s. Ross, Stuart; CHRMN., ENDEAVOUR FINANCIAL CORP., VANCOUVER 1989– ; Dir. Candn. Imperial Bank of Commerce, Toronto; MacMillan Bloedel Ltd., Vancouver; Chrmn., Vengold Inc., Vancouver; Victoria Commonwealh Games (1994) Soc., Victoria; Gov. Ridley College; joined Robertson-Irwin Ltd. Montreal 1955–63; Gen. Mgr. Atlas Titanium Ltd. Welland 1963–65; Mgr. Mktg. and mem. Mgmt. Ctte. Atlas Steels Co. Ltd. Welland 1965–70; Exec. Vice Pres., Chief Operating Offr., Dir. and mem. Exec. Ctte. Canadian Liquid Air Ltd. Montreal 1970–76; Chief Exec. Offr., Dir. and mem. Exec. Ctte. Amalgamated Metal Corp. London, Eng. 1977–79; Pres., Chief Exec. Offr. and Dir. Cia. Estanifera do Brasil, Rio de Janeiro 1979–82; Exec. Vice Pres., Dir. and Mem. Exec. Ctte. Westmin Resources Ltd. 1982–85; Pres., C.E.O., Dir. & Mem. Exec. Ctte., Placer Development Ltd., Vancouver 1985–87; Pres., C.E.O., Dir., & Mem. Exec. Ctte., Placer Dome Inc., Vancouver 1987–88; recreations: golf, fishing, travel; Clubs: Royal Collwood; Toronto; York; Victoria Golf; Shaughnessy Golf; Union; Vancouver; Office: Ste. 404, 1111 West Georgia St., Vancouver, B.C. V6E 4M3.

**WANG, Hon. Kechin,** M.A., B.C.L., Ph.D., Q.C.; family division judge; b. Peking, China 16 Aug. 1919; s. Chin-Chun and Wen-Jung (Meng) W.; e. Oxford Univ., M.A., B.C.L.; London Univ., Ph.D.; Barrister-at-Law, Middle Temple, London Eng.; called to Ont. Bar 1958; m. Loretta Lai d. Ah-Heng Yuen 5 May 1956; children: Sandra, Steffanie, Sheila, Lani, Timothy, Winson; JUDGE, FAMILY DIV., PROV. COURT OF ONT. 1955– ; First Sec. & Chargé d'Affaires, Chinese Embassy, Ottawa to 1955; Occasional Lectr., law schs. & facs., Univ. of Toronto, Univ. of W. Ont., Univ. of Windsor, Univ. of Hong Kong, Chinese Cultural Univ. (Taipei, Rep. of China), Tunghai Univ., Law School, Taichung, Taiwan; Dir., First Bd. of Dirs., Mon Sheong Found.; Former Trustee, Bd. of Edn., North York; Former Local Pres., Civitan Club; Past Pres., Internat. Law Assn.; Mem., Bd. of Dir., Chinese Interpreter & Info. Serv.; former member, Ch. Bd., Victoria Village Un. Ch.; Bd. of Management, St. Andrews Presbyterian Church, Aurora; Bd. of Dirs., Central Hospital; Masonic Lodge; Shrine; Clubs: Granite; Bayview Country; 23 Boulding Dr., Aurora, Ont. L4G 2V9.

**WANSBROUGH, John Christopher Counsel,** B.A., C.F.A., C.T.C.I.; b. Montreal, Que. 30 Apr. 1932; s. late Victor Counsel and the late Ruth (Barrett) W.; e. St. Andrew's Coll., Aurora, Ont.; Univ. of Toronto B.A. 1955; m. Jean Elizabeth, d. late Harold R. Lawrence, Brampton, Ont. 14 Sept. 1957; three d., Susan, Jane, Ruth; CHRMN., OMERS REALTY CORP. 1989– ; Chrmn. Munich Reinsurance Co. of Can.; Munich Holdings Ltd.; Munich-Life Mgmt. Corp. Ltd.; The Great Lakes Reins Co.; National Trustco Ltd.; United Corporations Ltd.; Dir., Rogers Communications Inc.; St. Mary's Cement Ltd.; Rogers Broadcasting Ltd.; Wellesley Hospital; Trustee, R.S. McLaughlin Foundation; Invest. Underwriting, Wood Gundy, Toronto 1956–63; joined National Trust Co. Ltd. as Invest. Offr. 1963, Mgr.-Vancouver 1966, Asst. Vice Pres.-Finance Toronto 1970, Vice Pres.-Finance 1972; Extve. Vice-Pres. 1974; Pres. 1977; Pres. & CEO 1984; Vice Chrmn. & Dir. 1986–89; mem., Inst. of Chartered Financial Analysts; recreations: tennis, golf; Clubs: Toronto; Toronto Golf; Badminton & Racquet; Home: 132 Warren Rd., Toronto, Ont. M4V 2S1; Office: 161 Bay St., Ste. 2220, P.O. Box 508, Toronto, Ont. M5J 2S1.

**WANSBROUGH, Michael Barrett,** B.A., M.Ed.; headmaster; b. Montréal, Qué. 10 Aug. 1935; s. Victor Counsel and Ruth Fleming (Barrett) W.; e. St. Andrew's Coll. Aurora, Ont. 1954; Bishop's Univ. B.A. 1961; Univ. of W. Ont. M.Ed. 1978; children: Michael, Connie, Gwyn; m. Michaele Robertson 1986; HEADMASTER, HILLFIELD-STRATHALLAN COLL. 1969– ; Teacher: Ashbury Coll. Ottawa 1961–63; Upper Can. Coll. Toronto 1963–69, Sr. Housemaster; recipient Queen's Silver Jubilee Medal 1977; Conf. Dir. CAIS 1983; Chrmn. Conf. Independent Schs. 1985–86; Pres., CAIS 1990–91; mem. Clin. Ethics Ctte. Chedoke – McMaster Univ. 1981–86; Business Adv. Counc., McMaster Univ.; co-author 'Great Canadian Lives: Profiles In Heroism to 1867' 1985; mem. Candn. Assn. Independent Schs.; Headmasters' Conf., U.K.; recreations: tennis, arts, travel, reading; Clubs: Rotary; Hamilton; Badminton & Racquet (Toronto); Home: 313 Queen St. S., Hamilton, Ont. L8P 3T6; Office: 299 Fennell Ave. W., Hamilton, Ont. L9C 1G3.

**WAPPEL, Thomas (Tom) William,** B.A., LL.B.; politician; b. Toronto, Ont. 9 Feb. 1950; s. Leslie and Margaret W.; e. North Toronto C.I.; Univ. of Toronto, B.A. 1971; Queen's Univ., LL.B. 1974; m. Glenda Joyce 26 May 1973; children: Monica, Christopher, Veronica, Victoria, Vanessa; Official Opposition Critic for Solicitor General 1992–93; Official Opposition Critic for Immigration 1991; Official Opposition Critic for Revenue 1990; Past Co-Chrmn., Joint House of Commons and Senate Standing Ctte. on the Scrutiny of Regulations; Past Vice Chrmn., Standing Ctte. on Labour, Employment and Immigration; lawyer; el. to H. of C. for Scarborough West g.e. 1988; Candidate for Leader of the Liberal Party of Canada 1990; Advocate & Mem., K. of C., Knight of Grace, Knights of Malta; Mem. and Past Pres., Ruskin Literary & Debating Soc.; Liberal; Roman Catholic; Home: Scarborough, Ont.; Office: Room 115, East Block, House of Commons, Ottawa, Ont. K1A 0A6.

**WARD, Hon. Brad,** M.P.P.; politician; b. Brantford, Ont. 23 Nov. 1956; s. Edward Arthur and Elsie Marie (Hienni) W.; e. Sir Sanford Fleming Coll. 1978; Labour Coll. of Canada 1982; m. Cindy d. Harry and Patricia Bullock 30 Sept. 1989; one d.: Amber; MINISTER WITHOUT PORTFOLIO FINANCE, GOVT. OF ONT. 1993– ; elected City Councillor 1985; re-elected 1988; 1st elected M.P.P. for Brantford, Govt. of Ont. 6 Sept. 1990; Parly. Asst., Skills Devel. 1990; Industry Trade & Technology 1991; Labour Citizen of the Year 1989; Chair, United Way 1989; Riverfest 1988; Mem., Gov. General's Study Conf. 1988; committees served: Ont. Legis. Finance Ctte., City Council Grants, Restructuring, Parks, Rec. & Lakefront Cttes.; Mohawk Lake Clean-up Ctte. 1990–93; Mem., Candn. Centre for Policy Alternatives; Extve. Mem., Local 45 Communications Energy & Paperworkers Union 1978–90; Brantford & Dist. Labour Council 1979–90; Brantford Help Ctr. 1986–88; Bd. of Gov., Brantford Gen. Hosp. 1988; Children's Aid Soc. 1986; recreations: all sports, reading, music, politics; club: Dunsdon Legion; Home: 6 Elmwood Ave., Brantford, Ont. N3R 2J8; Office: 7 Queen's Park Cres., 7th fl.; Toronto, Ont. M7A 1Y7.

**WARD, David,** B.Sc., Ph.D., F.R.S.C.; physicist; b. Wakefield, U.K. 5 Aug. 1940; s. Kenneth and May (Horrobin) W.; e. Univ. of Birmingham B.Sc. 1961; Univ. of Manchester Ph.D. 1965; children: Hazel, Jonathon; SCIENTIST, ATOMIC ENERGY OF CANADA LTD., CHALK RIVER LABS. 1968– ; postdoctoral fellow, Univ. of Manchester 1965–66; Univ. of Calif. at Berkeley 1966–68; Visiting Fellow, Univ. of Calif. at Berkeley 1974–75; Australian Nat. Univ. 1982–83; Consultant, Univ. of Chicago; Fellow, Am. Physical Soc. 1988; Fellow, Royal Soc. of Canada 1991; author/co-author of over 140 pubns. in nuclear and atomic physics; recreation: chamber music; club: American Contract Bridge League; Office: Chalk River Labs, Chalk River, Ont. K0J 1J0.

**WARD, David Anthony,** Q.C., B.Comm., LL.B.; b. Calgary, Alta. 24 March 1931; e. Queen's Univ. B.Com.; Osgoode Hall Law Sch. LL.B.; m. Nancy Ruth 12 July 1958; two d. Martha Jane, Mary Ruth; PARTNER,

DAVIES, WARD & BECK; called to Bar of Ont. 1958; gen. ed. 'Ward's Tax Law and Planning' 1983; author 'Taxation of Income of Foreign Affiliates' 1983; 'Current Tax Planning' 1971; 'Current Estate Planning' 1971; mem. Extve. Ctte. Internat. Fiscal Assn. 1987–92; Past Pres., Candn. Br., Internat. Fiscal Assn. 1983–85; mem. Candn. Bar Assn.; Candn. Tax Found.; Internat. Bar Assn.; Delta Chi; Anglican; recreations: skiing, sailing; Clubs: Ontario; Granite; R.C.Y.C.; Georgian Peaks Ski; Home: 28 Daleberry Place, Don Mills, Ont. M3B 2A7; Office: 44th Flr., 1 First Canadian Place, Toronto, Ont. M5X 1B1.

**WARD, David G.,** B.Bus.Admin, C.A., F.C.A.; investment banker; b. Montreal, Que. 11 May 1938; s. Dr. R.V. Ward; e. Univ. of N.B. B.Bus.Admin. 1962; C.A. 1965; F.C.A. 1982; m. Anne Paterson 6 Sept. 1968; children: Robin, Colin; VICE CHRMN. & MANAGING DIR., MERGERS & ACQUISITIONS, BURNS FRY LIMITED 1984– and Mem. of Extve. Ctte.; Partner, Coopers & Lybrand 1962–81; C.F.O. Barrick Resources 1981–82; Vice Chrmn. & Dir., Hongkong Bank of Canada 1982–85; Dir., Armbro Holdings (Brampton) Ltd. 1982–90; Candn. Inst. of C.A.s (Acctg. Rsch. Ctte. 1976–81; Chrmn. 1980–81; Dir., The Queen Elizabeth Hosp. Found. 1990; Fund Raising Adv. Ctt., The Easter Seal Soc.; Gov., Stratford Shakespearean Fest. Found. of Can. 1986–88; Extve. Ctte. & Dir., Candn. UNICEF Ctte. 1983–87; Dir., The Young Naturalist Found. 1981–85; Vice-Commodore, Finan., The Royal Candn. Yacht Club 1981–83; Home: 'Stonelea', 7328 30th Side Rd., R.R. 3, Caledon East, Ont. L0N 1E0; Office: P.O. Box 150, Ste. 5000, 1 First Canadian Place, Toronto, Ont. M5X 1H3.

**WARD, G. Kingsley,** B.A., B.Comm., C.A.; businessman; b. Bathurst, N.B. 29 Aug. 1932; s. George Raymond and Elsie Elizabeth (Smith) W.; e. Queen's Univ., B.A., B.Comm. 1955; Price Waterhouse, C.A. 1958; m. Adele Eleanor d. John and Eleanor Hartman 18 July 1959; children: Julie, Kingsley Jr.; CHRMN., THE VIMY RIDGE GROUP 1961– ; Adrem Ltd.; Nucro-Technics; SMS Marine; Pilgrim Creek Ltd.; Canhart Industries; Past Pres., Candn. Found. of Pharm. 1988; Chrmn., Proprietary Assn. of Can. 1974–75, 1977; Candn. Cosmetic, Toiletries & Fragrances Assn. 1984; Gov., St. Andrew's Coll.; St. Michaels Hosp. Cardiac Found.; Vice Chrmn., St. Michaels Hosp. Found.; mem. Bd. of Regents, Mount Allison Univ.; author: 'Letters of a Businessman to his Son' 1985; 'Letters of a Businessman to his Daughter' 1988; 'Courage Remembered' 1988; recreation: bush pilot; Clubs: Granite; Royal Candn. Military Inst.; Home: 650 Stouffville Rd., Richmond Hill, Ont. L4E 3P5; Office: 140 Renfrew Dr., Suite 205, Markham, Ont. L3R 6B3.

**WARD, Jeffrey Kenyon;** executive; b. Manchester, Eng. 26 July 1943; s. John Bradley and Marjorie (Crabtree) W.; e. Burnage Grammar Sch. Manchester 1959; Manchester Coll. of Comm. 1962; m. Brenda d. Harold and Nancy Horne 9 Aug. 1965; children: Samantha Jane, Louise Kate; PRESIDENT/MANAGING PARTNER, ACADEMY BRANDS INTERNATIONAL INC. 1993– ; Sales Exec. Courtenay Wines London, Eng. 1969–73; Ont. Sales Mgr. Barnes Wines Ltd. 1974, Sales Dir. 1976, Dir. 1979, Vice Pres. 1978, Pres. 1980–88; Vice-Pres., Ridout Wines Ltd. (subsidiary of John Labatt) 1988–89; Extve. Vice-Pres., Labatt International Brands (subsidiary of Labatt Brewing Co.) 1989–93; Chrmn., Wine Council Can. 1982–84; recipient Wine & Spirit Edn. Trust (U.K.) Dip. 1964; recreation: tennis; Club: Cedar Springs; Home: Sandy Lane, Oakville, Ont.; Office: 700 Dorval Dr., Suite 300, Oakville, Ont. L6K 3V3.

**WARDLAW, Janet Melville,** B.A., M.S., Ph.D.; educator; b. Toronto, Ont. 20 June 1924; d. James Macallum and Mary Stark (Law) W.; e. Etobicoke (Ont.) High Sch. 1942; Univ. of Toronto B.A. 1946; Univ. of Tenn. M.S. 1950; Pa. State Univ. Ph.D. 1963; DEPT. OF FAMILY STUDIES, UNIV. OF GUELPH 1987– ; Dietetic Internship Royal Victoria Hosp. Montréal 1946–47; Dietitian, Sch. Meal Study, Candn. Red Cross Soc. 1947–49; Nutritionist Mich. Dept. of Pub. Health, Lansing 1950–53, Dept. of Pub. Health City of Toronto 1953–56; Asst./Assoc. Prof. of Food Sci. Univ. of Toronto 1956–66; Prof. Macdonald Inst. Univ. of Guelph 1966–67, Dean Designate of Inst. 1968, Dean, Coll. of Family & Consumer Studies 1969–83, Assoc. Vice Pres. Acad. 1984–87; Chrmn. Bd. Govs. Internat. Devel. Rsch. Centre 1985–92; recipient Stuart Achievement Award Candn. Dietetic Assn. 1972; Alumni Recognition Award Coll. of Human Devel. Pa. State Univ. 1985; Alumni Fellow, Pennsylvania State Univ. 1988; Fellow, Univ. of Guelph 1989; Distinguished Alumnus Award, Pennsylvania State Univ. 1990; mem. Candn. Soc. Nutritional Sci's; Candn. Dietetic Assn.; Home: 20 Suffolk St. W., Guelph, Ont. N1H 2H8; Office: Dean's Office, FACS, Univ. of Guelph, Guelph, Ont. N1G 2W1.

**WARDLE, Frederick David;** book publisher; b. Belleville, Ont. 18 March 1939; s. Reginald Albert and Catherine (McCallum) W.; e. Cornwall (Ont.) Coll. & Vocational Sch. 1958; Sir George Williams Univ. 1962; m. Maxine (div.); 2ndly Susan Traer, 30 Dec. 1981; children: Jennifer Lesley, Jonathan Frederick, Emma Charlotte; PUBLISHER & C.E.O., CANADIAN ALMANAC & DIRECTORY 1989– ; Dir. Carswell Co. Ltd. 1972–88; Assn. for the Export of Candn. Books 1979–87; joined McGraw-Hill Co. of Canada 1962–66, McGraw-Hill Book Co. (UK) 1966–67; joined Methuen Publications 1967, Pres. 1971–89; Pres., Methuen Inc. (USA) 1978–80; Pres., Canadian Book Publishers Council 1978 (Chrpn. Internat. Marketing Comte. 1984–85, Exec. Ctte. 1974–78); Home: 382 Balliol Street, Toronto, Ont. Office: 55 St. Clair Ave. W., Suite 225, Toronto, Ont. M5W 2J8.

**WARE, Tracy,** B.A., M.A., Ph.D.; university professor; b. Victoria, B.C. 17 June 1956; s. Eric Tracy and Gladys (Riches) W.; e. Univ. of Victoria, B.A. (Hons.) 1978; Univ. of West. Ont., M.A. 1980, Ph.D. 1984; m. Brenda d. David and Anne Reed 22 Aug. 1985; ASSOC. PROF., DEPT. OF ENGLISH, BISHOP'S UNIV. 1987– ; Asst. Prof., English, Univ. of W. Ont. 1984–85, 1986–87; Killam Postdoct. Fellow, English, Dalhousie 1985–86; SSHRCC postdoct. fellow 1987; Sch. of Criticism & Theory, Dartmouth Coll. 1989; Editorial Adv. Bd. 'Canadian Poetry'; referee & organizer, Assn. of Canadian Univ. Teachers of English, the 'Dalhousie Review,' 'Canadian Poetry' & the N.E. Modern Languages Assn.; SSHRCC doct. fellowship 1981–84; Mem., Assn. of Candn. & Que. Lits.; Keats-Shelley Assn. of Am.; Modern Lang. Assn. of Am.; Poe Studies Assn.; author of several articles; recreations: golf, travel; Home: 105 Oxford Cres., Lennoxville, Que. J1M 2G3; Office: Lennoxville, Que. J1M 1Z7.

**WARING, George Ernest,** B.Sc.; company president; b. Saint John, N.B. 29 Apl. 1927; s. George Ramus and Sarah (Martin) W.; e. Univ. of N.B., B.Sc.; children: Patricia, Peter, Michael; CHRMN., WARNAN CONSULTANTS INC. 1983– ; Pres., Ocean Maid Foods until retirement in June 1983; Pres., Star-Kist Canada Inc.; Past Commr., Internat. Comn. for Conserv. of Atlantic Tunas and Inter-Am. Tropical Tuna Comn.; mem., Am. Chem. Soc.; Chem. Inst. Can.; Sugar Indust. Technols.; Freemason; Anglo-Catholic; recreations: sailing, reading; Home: 187 Splinter Court, Kingston, Ont. K7M 7Z3.

**WARK, Wesley K.,** B.A., M.A., Ph.D.; university professor; b. Edmonton, Alta. 31 Dec. 1952; s. Kenneth A. and Noreen (Wellman) W.; e. Carleton Univ. B.A. 1975; Cambridge Univ. M.A. 1977; London Sch. of Econ. Ph.D. 1984; m. Dr. Christine d. Capt. Ian Bold; ASSOC. PROF., UNIV. OF TORONTO 1988– ; Alta. Heritage Scholar 1979–83; Vis. Prof., McGill Univ. 1983–84; Assoc. Prof., Univ. of Calgary 1984–88; Founding Mem., Candn. Assn. for Security & Intelligence Studies; Mem., Brit. Study Group on Intelligence; author: 'The Ultimate Enemy' 1985; 'Spy Fiction, Spy Films and Real Intelligence' 1991; 'Espionage: Past, Present, Future?' 1993; editor: 'Intelligence and National Security Journal' since 1986; recreations: reading spy fiction, Inuit art; Home: 37 Shadybrook Cresc., Guelph, Ont. N1G 3G8; Office: Trinity Coll., Toronto, Ont. M5S 1A1.

**WARKENTIN, Germaine Therese,** M.A., Ph.D.; educator; b. Toronto, Ont. 20 Oct. 1933; d. Gerard Patrick and Therese Mary (Reilly) Clinton; e. Oakwood Coll. Inst. 1951; Univ. of Toronto B.A. 1955 (Univ. Coll.), Ph.D. 1972; Univ. of Man. M.A. 1965; m. John Henry s. Isaac and Mary Warkentin 26 Dec. 1956; one d. Juliet Mary; PROF. OF ENG. VICTORIA COLL. UNIV. OF TORONTO 1990– ; freelance film critic 1953–62; ed. Candn. Newsreel: Bulletin of Candn. Fedn. Film Soc's 1954–57; Advt. Sec. Univ. of Toronto Press 1956–57; Instr. in Eng. Un. Coll. Winnipeg 1958–59; Chrmn. Candn. Fedn. Film Soc's 1964–65; Lectr. in Eng. present Coll. 1970, Asst. Prof. 1972, Assoc. Prof. 1976, Dir. Centre for Reformation & Renaissance Studies 1985–90; editor: 'Poems' by J. Reaney 1972; 'Canadian Exploration Literature' in English 1993; Dir. and Ed., Penshurst Lib. Ed. Project (in progress); numerous scholarly articles Renaissance Eng. Lit. and Candn. Lit.; mem. Assn. Candn. Univ. Teachers Eng.; Modern Lang. Assn.; Candn. Soc. Renaissance Studies; Renaissance Soc. Am.; Medieval Acad. Am.; Bibliog. Soc.; Assn. Candn. & Que. Lit.; Candn. Soc. Hist. Rhetoric; Bibliog. Soc. Can.; Internat. Assn. Neo-Latin Studies; Renaissance Eng. Text Soc. (Internat. Adv. Bd.); NDP; recreations: ballet, cooking, travel; Home: 71 Poplar Plains Cres., Toronto, Ont. M4V 1G1; Office: Victoria College, Univ. of Toronto, Toronto, Ont. M5S 1K7.

**WARKENTIN, John Henry,** B.Sc., M.A., Ph.D., LL.D., F.R.S.C.; professor of geography; b. Lowe Farm, Man. 3 Mar. 1928; s. Isaac and Mary (Warkentin) W.; e. Univ. of Man., B.Sc. 1948; Univ. of Toronto, M.A. 1954, Ph.D. 1961; m. Germaine d. Gerard and Therese Clinton 26 Dec. 1956; one d.: Juliet; PROF., YORK UNIVERSITY 1963– ; Instr., Univ. of Maryland 1956–57; Asst. Prof., Winnipeg United Coll. 1957–59; Asst./Assoc. Prof., Univ. of Man. 1959–63; Guggenheim Fellow 1970; Award for Scholarly Distinction, Candn. Assn. of Geographers 1975; F.R.S.C. 1982; LL.D., Univ. of Brandon 1987; Massey Medal, Royal Candn. Geographical Soc. 1988; Pres., Champlain Soc. 1974–79; author: 'The Western Interior of Canada' 1964; co-author: 'Canada Before Confederation' 1974, 'Manitoba Historical Atlas' 1970; editor: 'Geological Lectures by Dr. John Richardson' 1979, 'Canada: A Geographical Interpretation' 1968; Home: 71 Poplar Plains Cres., Toronto, Ont. M4V 1G1; Office: Dept. of Geog., York Univ., Ross Bldg., Rm. North 424A, North York, Ont. M3J 1P3.

**WARNER, The Hon. David,** B.A., M.P.P.; politician; b. Toronto, Ont. 18 Nov. 1941; s. William John and Margaret Eleanor (Brown) W.; e. York Univ. B.A. 1972; m. Patricia d. Gordon and Hatti Draper 26 June 1965; children: Sherri-Anne Beverly, Barbara Elizabeth; SPEAKER OF THE LEGISLATIVE ASSEMBLY OF ONTARIO 1990– ; Teacher, Scarborough Bd. of Edn. 1964– (excluding terms of political office); 1st elected to Ont. Leg. g.e. 1975 for the riding of Scarborough-Ellesmere); re-elected 1977, 1985, 1990; as M.P.P. travelled to Nicaragua on a fact-finding mission 1987; went to India as Mem., Candn. team, Project Overseas 1990; Critic for Ministries of Coll. & Univ., Attorney General, Skills Devel. & Metro. Toronto Affairs; Pres., Ont. Br., Commonwealth Parl. Assn.; Co-Pres., Ont.-Que. Parl. Assn.; Chair, Bd. of Dir., Agincourt Community Serv. 1973–75; Scarborough Community Legal Serv. 1980–85, 1987–90; Bd. of Dir., Youth Assisting Youth 1974–77, 1981–85; recreations: beermaking, bridge, sports, music, theatre, reading; Home: 833 Huntingwood Dr., Scarborough, Ont. M1T 2L8; Office: Room 180, Legislative Bldg., Queen's Park, Toronto, Ont. M7A 1A2.

**WARNER, Harold Albert;** businessman; b. Wawota, Sask. 8 Nov. 1951; s. James Arthur and Aline Emily (Rey) W.; e. St. Francis H.S. (Calgary) 1968; Grande Prairie Reg. Coll. 1970; m. Vicki d. Rodney and Vera Worrall 5 Dec. 1981; children: Tera, Graham, Stephen, Jenna; OWNER, AERO DYNAMICS, AEROSTATS & PROMOTION INC. 1981– ; Sales 1970–81; Candn. Hot Air Balloon Champion 1980, 1982; World Record distance Hot Air Balloons 1985; Paul J. Tissandier Diplome; recreations: ballooning, trail riding; Home: Box 4, Site 23, R.R. 8, Calgary, Alta. T2J 2T9; Office: 3413 – 8 St. S.E., Calgary, Alta. T2G 3A4.

**WARNHOFF, Edgar W.,** Ph.D.; university professor; b. Knoxville, Tenn. 5 May 1929; s. Edgar William and Mabel Catherine (Huth) W.; e. Washington Univ., A.B. 1949; Univ. of Wisc., Ph.D. 1953; m. Patricia Catherine, d. late Samuel Reynolds 1956; three s. Mark, Andrew, Rolf; PROF. OF CHEM., UNIV. OF WESTERN ONT. since 1966; Postdoctoral Fellow, Birkbeck Coll., London 1953–54; Asst. Scientist, U.S. Pub. Health Service 1954–56; Post-doctoral Fellow Faculté de Pharmacie, Paris 1957–58; Research Assoc., Mass. Inst. of Technol. 1958–59; Asst. Prof., Univ. S. Cal. 1959–62; joined present Univ. as Asst. Prof. 1962; Assoc. Prof. 1963; rec'd Merck Sharp and Dohme Lecture Award of Chem Inst. Can. 1969: co-author 'Molecular Rearrangements' 1964; co-author 'Rearrangements in Ground and Excited States' vol. 1 1980; other writings incl. over 80 papers in chem. journs.; ed. the Canadian Journal of Chemistry 1982–88; mem., Chem. Inst. Can.; Chem. Soc. London; Am. Chem. Soc.; Address: London, Ont. N6A 5B7.

**WARRACK, Dr. Allan Alexander,** B.Sc., M.S., Ph.D.; professor; b. Calgary, Alta. 24 May 1937; s. Alexander Low and Alice Katherine (Christensen) W.; e. Strathmore High Sch. 1955; Olds Sch. of Agric. 1956; Univ. of Alta. B.Sc. (Agric.) 1961; Iowa State Univ. M.S. (Agric. Econ.) 1963, Ph.D. (Econ.) 1967; m. Linda Jean d. Gordon Herbert Rennie, Edmonton, Alta. 18 Aug. 1962; children: Lauren Jean, James Allan, Daniel Gordon Alexander; PROF. OF BUSINESS, UNIV. OF ALTA. 1992– ; operates A & A Farms, Langdon, Alta.; Sales Rep. Upjohn Co. Madison, Wis. 1963–64; Asst. Prof. Univ. Alta. 1967, Assoc. Prof. 1969–71; el. M.L.A. for Three Hills 1971, re-el. 1975, declined re-el. 1979;

Min. of Lands and Forests 1971–75; Min. of Utilities and Telephones 1975–79; Prof. of Rural Econ., Univ. of Alta. 1979–81; Assoc. Dean & Dir. MPM Program, Fac. of Bus. 1981–85; Vice Pres. (Administration), University Hall, Univ. of Alta. 1986–91; rec'd Queen's Silver Jubilee Medal 1977; author numerous agric. econ. and public mgmt. articles in various tech. and other publs.; Bd. Mem., Edmonton Telephones Corp.; Canada West Foundation; mem. Inst. of Public Admin. of Canada; Alta. Inst. Agrology; Candn. Agric. Econ. Soc.; Am. Agric. Econ. Assn.; Internat. Assn. Agric. Econ.; Agric. Inst. Can.; W. Agric. Econ. Assn.; Am. Econ. Assn.; Phi Kappa Phi; Delta Upsilon (Pres., Field Secy.); Gamma Sigma Delta; P. Conservative; United Church; recreations: squash, racquetball, golf, tennis, skiing; Clubs: Gyro; Derrick Golf & Winter; Home: 91 Fairway Dr., Edmonton, Alta. T6J 2C2; Office: Faculty of Business, Univ. of Alta., Edmonton, Alta. T6G 2R6.

**WARREN, Bernie,** B.A.(Hons.), Ph.D., F.R.S.A.; university professor; b. London, U.K. 27 Dec. 1953; s. David Jack and Freda Ruth (Shulman) W.; e. Manchester Metro. Univ. B.A. (Hons.) 1980; Columbia Pacific Univ. Ph.D. 1985; m. Julie d. Orest and Alice Ortynsky 27 July 1990; PROFESSOR, SCHOOL OF DRAMATIC ART, UNIV. OF WINDSOR 1992– ; Dept. Dir., Ludus Special Schools Project (U.K.) 1980–82; Instr., Drama, Univ. of Calgary 1982–84, 1986–87; Asst. Prof., Theatre, Concordia Univ. 1988–90; Assoc. Prof. 1990–92; Visiting Instr., Gaza City summer 1985; Visiting Prof., Antioch Univ. winter 1986; Artistic Dir., Prospero's Fools (Barrier) Free Theatre Co. 1992– ; Co-artistic Dir., 50-50 Theatre Co. 1988–92; Adjunst Prof., Edn. Psych., McGill Univ. 1992– ; Univ. of Calgary 1986–88; Acad. Cons., Inst. of Dramatherapy, Stratford-Upon-Avon 1990–91; Fellow, Royal Society of Arts; Registered Dramatherapist U.K. 1980– , U.S. 1986– ; Mem., British Actors Equity Assn. 1981– ; Brit. Assn. for Dramatherapists 1979– ; editor/contbr.: 'Using the Creative Arts in Therapy' 1993, 'A Theatre in Your Classroom' 1991; co-author: 'Drama Games' 1989, 'Social Drama' 1986; author: 'Disability and Social Performance' 1989, 'Drama Games for Mentally Handicapped People' 1981; author/co-author (plays): 'Not Just Another Blind Date' 1993, 'The Demon of Experiment' 1992, 'Cross Border' '1992, 'Paradiso Stultorum' 1991, 'The Last Forest' 1990 and four others; recreations: cricket; martial arts; clubs: St. John's Zingari Cricket, Rose City Cricket; Home: 2202 Victoria Ave., Windsor, Ont. N8X 1R1; Office: Windsor, Ont. N9B 3P4.

**WARREN, David Holmes;** journalist; b. Toronto, Ont. 29 Apr. 1953; s. James Frederick and Florrie Alice W.; e. Georgetown Dist. H.S., grade 10; m. Lynne d. George and Barbara Rigley 29 Oct. 1983; children: Jonathan, Matthew; FOUNDER AND EDITOR, THE IDLER 1985– ; Women's & Social Ed., The Bangkok World (daily) 1970–71; various other posts on English-language papers in various countries; Anglican (St. Mary Magdalene's Ch., Toronto); Tory; Home: 104 Montreal St., Kingston, Ont. K7K 3E8; Office: 255 Davenport Rd., Toronto, Ont. M5R 1J9.

**WARREN, Frederic Michael Patrick,** B.A., LL.B., Q.C.; lawyer; e. Univ. of B.C., B.A. 1957, LL.B. 1960; Chrmn., International Murex Technologies Corporation; Chrmn. and Chief Extve. Offr., Murex Diagnostics Limited, London, England; Chrmn., Murex Corporation, Atlanta, Georgia; Dir., Medi-Physics Inc., an Amersham company, Chicago, Illinois; Dir., Glyko BioMedical Ltd., Toronto, Ont.; Chrmn. Biotechna Environmental Ltd., Toronto, Ont.; of Counsel, Owen, Bird, Barristers and Solicitors, Vancouver, B.C. 1991– .

**WARREN, Harry Verney,** O.C. (1971), O.B.C. (1991), D.Sc., D.Phil., F.R.S.C., F.G.S.A., F.R.C.G.P.(U.K.); retired professor; former consulting geological engineer; b. Anacortes, Wash. 27 Aug. 1904; s. Victor Mackenzie and Rosamond Ellice Burrell (Campion) W.; e. Univ. of Brit. Columbia, B.A. 1926 (Rhodes Schol. for B.C. 1926–29), B.A.Sc. 1927; Oxford Univ., M.Sc. 1928, D.Phil. 1929; Commonwealth Fund Fellow at Cal. Inst. of Tech. 1929–32; D.Sc. Univ. Waterloo 1975 and Univ. of B.C. 1978; m. Margaret Bessie, d. Charles Edward and Edith Bessie Tisdall (White) 14 July 1934; children: Charlotte Louisa Verney, Victor Henry Verney; Pres. B.C. & Yukon Chamber of Mines 1952–54; mem. Senate, Univ. B.C. 1939–60, 1963–72; Tech. Adviser, Vancouver Stock Exchange 1938–40; Lectr., Dept. of Geol. & Geog., Univ. of B.C. 1932–35; Asst. Prof. 1935–39; Assoc. Prof. 1939–45, Prof. 1945–73; Hon. Prof. 1973–93; Consultant 1942–76; Pres., Third Resources Conf. (B.C.) 1949–50; Pres., Un. Nations Assn. of Can. (Vancouver Br.) 1955, 1956, 1957; Fellow, Geol. Soc. of Am.; Geol. Soc. of Finland; Fellow Inst. of Mining & Metall. (Gt. Britain); Am. Inst. Mining & Metall. Engrs.; Soc. of Econ. Geols.; Mineral. Soc. (Gt. Brit.); Walker Mineralogical Soc.; Life Mem., Assn. of Prof. Engrs.; Assn. of Prof. Engrs. B.C.; Hon. Fellow, Royal Coll. Gen. Practice (Gt. Brit.) 1973; Founding mem., Assn. Exploration Geochems.; Soc. Environmental Geochem. & Health; has written 198 articles contrib. to scient. journs.; mem. Council, Vancouver Bd. Trade variously 1939–81; B.C. & Yukon Ch. of Mines Extve. 1939– (Pres. 1952–54); Co-founder, 'Save Our Parklands' 1954; B.C. Rep., Alaska Chamber of Mines 1959; Founding Pres., Candn. Field Hockey Assn. 1961–64; Order of Canada 1971; H.H. 'Spud' Huestis Award for excellence in prospecting & mineral exploration 1986; Distinguished Pioneer Award, City of Vancouver 1986; Distinguished Service Award, Prospector & Developer's Assn. of Canada 1990; inducted B.C. Sports Hall of Fame 1990; Order of British Columbia 1991; awarded Commemorative Medal for 125th Anniversary of Candn. Confederation 1992; inducted U.B.C. Sports Hall of Fame 1993; Sigma Xi; Anglican; recreations: cricket, field hockey, rugby; Club: Faculty; Brock House; Home: 1816 Western Parkway, Vancouver, B.C. V6T 1V4; Office: Univ. of B.C., 6339 Stores Rd., Vancouver, B.C. V6T 2B4.

**WARREN, Jack H.,** O.C.; trade policy advisor; b. Howard Township, Ont. 10 Apr. 1921; e. Queen's Univ. BA 1941, LL.D. (Hon.) 1974; m. Hilary J. Titterington, 7 May 1953; children: Hilary Nicolson, Martin, Jennifer Part, Ian; ADVISOR, Government of Que. 1986– ; served with Royal Canadian Navy 1941–45; public service with Departments of External Affairs, Finance, Trade & Comm., Industry Trade & Comm.; diplomatic postings Ottawa, London, Washington, Paris, Geneva; Asst. Depy. Min. Dept. of Trade & Comm. 1958; Chrmn. Council of Reps. Gen. Agreement on Tariffs & Trade 1960; Chrmn. Contracting Parties GATT 1962–1964; Depy. Min. Dept. of Trade & Commerce 1964; Depy. Min. Dept. of Industry Trade & Comm. 1969; Candn. High Commr. to U.K. 1971–74; Canadian Ambassador to U.S.A. 1975–77; Ambassador & Co-ordinator for the Multilateral Trade Negotiations 1977–79; Vice-Chrmn. and Dir., Bank of Montreal 1979–86; Principal trade policy advisor, Govt. of Que. 1986– ; Depy. North Am. Chrmn., Trilateral Comn. 1986–90; rec'd. Outstanding Achievement Award Pub. Service Can. 1975; Officer of the Order of Canada 1982; Home: P.O. Box 282, R.R. 1, Chelsea, Que. J0X 1N0.

**WARREN, James Douglas,** B.A., M.A.; teacher, winemaker; b. Hamilton, Ont. 6 Aug. 1942; s. James Alfred and Mary Christine (Pease) W.; e. McMaster Univ. B.A. 1964, M.A. 1965; m. Charlotte d. John and Susan Toffin 10 Aug. 1962; one s.: Marshall; CO-OWNER & PRESIDENT, STONEY RIDGE CELLARS 1985– ; Head of Language Dept., Glendale Sec. School until 1990; Gallery Mem., McMaster Univ.; OGGMB Award of Merit 1982; recreations: travel; Home: 9 Crozier Court, Hamilton; Office: 1468 Highway 8, Winona, Ont. L8E 5K9.

**WARREN, Myles,** B.F.A.; arts manager, theatre designer; b. Saskatoon, Sask. 7 Jan. 1954; s. Thomas Edward and Elizabeth Helen (Scott) W.; e. Univ. of Alberta B.F.A. (Hons.); m. Judith Debra d. Nathan Rudakoff 29 Dec. 1978; ARTS MANAGER & THEATRE DESIGNER, DANCE UMBRELLA OF ONT. 1992– ; Producer, Muskoka Festival 1984–86; Assoc. Artistic Dir. 1987–89; General Manager, Desrosiers Dance Theatre 1989–92; theatre designs incl. Robert Desrosiers' 'Incognito' 1990, 'Full Moon' 1991, 'Arc en Ciel' 1989 as well as productions with Crow's Theatre, Tarragon, Muskoka Festival, Nat. Arts Centre, Theatre Passe Muraille and others; Extve. Dir., Dance Umbrella of Ont.; Chair, Coalition of the Ont. Dance Service Orgns.; Adv. Mem., Harbourfront Centre's Dance Prog.; Fringe Festival of Independent Dance Artists; Cultural Advisor, Can.-Cuba Sport and Cultural festivals; Office: 490 Adelaide St. W., Ste. 201, Toronto, Ont. M5V 1T2.

**WARREN, Robert Michael,** B.Com.; investment and consulting company executive; b. Montreal, Que. 10 Apr. 1937; s. late John Edward Leslie and Isabelle Sophie Janie (Dodwell) W.; e. Lower Can. Coll., Selwyn House and Montreal W. High Sch.; Sir George Williams Univ. B.Com. 1956; children: Stephen Gregory, Scott Edward Kenneth, Sarah Ashley Claire; CHRMN., C.E.O., & DIR., THE WARREN GROUP INC. 1987– ; Dir., MDS Health Group Ltd.; Canadian Direct Marketing Assoc.; Ontario Internat. Corp.; Royal LePage Advisory Council; Former Pres., C.E.O. & Dir., Canadian Investors Corp. Debentures Ltd.; Sales Engr. Lincoln Electric, Toronto 1958–60; Sales Mgr. S. Coorsh & Sons, Toronto 1960–62; Indust. Devel. Offr. Trade & Devel. Govt. Ont., Extve. Asst. to Min. of Labour Ont., Extve. Dir. Manpower Services Ont., Depy. Prov. Secy. and Depy. Min. of Citizenship Ont., Depy. Solr. Gen. Ont., Depy. Min. of Housing Ont. 1962–75; Pres., R. Michael Warren & Associates Ltd., Consultants 1975; Chief Gen. Mgr. Toronto Transit Comm., Dir. Gray Coach Lines 1975–81; Pres. Candn. Urban Transit Assn. 1980–81; Pres., C.E.O. & Dir., Canada Post Corp., Ottawa 1981–85; recipient Candn. Centennial Medal 1967; Dir., Toronto Arts Awards Found.; mem., Elgin & Winter Garden Council; Dir., YMCA, Metro. Toronto; recreations: farming, skiing, squash; Office: One First Canadian Place, Suite 5900, P.O. Box 24, Toronto, Ont. M5X 1K2.

**WARREN, Trumbull,** O.B.E.; manufacturer; b. Montreal, Que. 1 Aug. 1915; s. Trumbull W. and Marjorie Laura (Braithwaite) Snively; e. Crescent Sch., Toronto, Ont. (1922–24) Upper Canada Coll., Toronto, Ont. (1924–27); Lakefield Coll. (1927–30); Ridley Coll., St. Catharines, Ont. (1930–34); m. Mary, d. Gerald W. Wigle, Hamilton, Ont., 9 Sept. 1939; children: Mary Trumbull (Mrs. G. Rapley Bunting), Margaret Ann (Mrs. John Lang), Joan Trumbull (Mrs. Grant Fisher); PAST CHRMN. & DIR., RHEEM CANADA INC. (Mfrs. of Steel Shipping Containers, Domestic, and Commercial Water Heaters, Estbd. 1946); joined 48th Highlanders of Can., N.P.A.M., 1934 served in 2nd World War with rank of Lieut.-Col. in Eng., W. Desert, Sicily, Italy, France, Belgium, Holland and Germany; O.B.E.; Mentioned in Despatches; American Bronze Star; Hon. Col. 1973–76; Conservative; Anglican; recreation: skeet-shooting; Clubs: Tamahaac; University (Toronto); Home: Corwhin Acres, R.R. 1, Puslinch, Ont. N0B 2J0.

**WARRILLOW, James Keith;** communications executive; Pres., Candn. Publishing, Maclean Hunter Ltd. 1988; Pres. & C.E.O., CB Media Ltd. 1990– ; Chrmn., Industrial Trade & Consumer Shows; Dir., The Financial Post Company; Toronto Life Publising Company; Canadian Magazine Publishers' Assn.; Today's Parent Group; ABC Canada; Member: Bd. of Trustees, The Clark Institute of Psychiatry; Advisory Bd., Queen's Univ., Business School; Past Pres., Candn. Club of Toronto; Office: Maclean Hunter Bldg., 777 Bay Street, Toronto, Ont. M5W 1A7.

**WARRILOW, Clive B.;** automotive executive; b. London, England 8 Oct. 1938; e. Grey High Sch., Port Elizabeth, South Africa; Graduate Sch. of Business, Univ. of Cape Town; m. Barbara children: Kirsty, Brigid, William, David; PRES., VOLKSWAGEN CANADA INC. 1989– and PRES., VOLKSWAGEN OF AMERICA, INC. 1994– ; Accountant, South Africa 1956–63; joined Volkswagen South Africa, Uitenhage, Accounting 1963–69, Parts and Accessories 1969–77, General Sales Manager 1977–79, Marketing Dir. 1979–89; Home: Beacon Hall Dr., Aurora, Ont.; Office: 1940 Eglinton Ave. E., Scarborough, Ont. M1L 2M2.

**WARWICK, Earl Joseph,** B.A.; public relations executive; b. Petrolia, Ont. 2 Sept. 1945; s. Ross Thompson and Helen Marie W.; e. Woodstock C.I. (Hons.) 1966; Univ. of West. Ont., B.A. 1970, dip.Jour. 1972; m. Janice d. Cardiff and Mabel Cline 14 Aug. 1970; children: Sara Lynn, Jennifer; CHRMN., WARWICK & ASSOCIATES PUBLIC RELNS.; Pub. Affairs Dir., Pollution Probe 1972–73; Dir. of Mktg. & Pub. Relns., Can-Sports Inc. 1974–76; Vice-Pres., Prom. Serv., Vickers & Benson Advtg. Ltd. 1976–80; Pres., Warwick & Assoc. Pub. Relns. 1980–86; Warwick & Associates, Pub. Relns.; recreations: thoroughbred racing, fishing, cross-country skiing; Club: OJC Turf; Home: 29 Playter Blvd., Toronto, Ont. M4K 2W1; Office: 1133 Yonge, St., Toronto, Ont. M4T 2Z3.

**WASHBURN, Jon Spencer,** B.S.(Music Ed.); conductor, composer, arranger, musician, editor, lecturer; b. Rochelle, Illinois 4 July 1942; s. Richard Millard and JoAnne Hubert (Broens) W.; e. Illinois State Univ. 1960–63; Univ. of Illinois B.Sc. 1965; Northwestern Univ. 1966–67; Univ. of B.C. 1967–70; m. Linda Lee d. Winnifred and Fielding Thomas; children: Susan Gail Terry, Michael Sebastian Washburn; FOUNDER, CONDUCTOR, ARTISTIC & EXTVE. DIRECTOR, VANCOUVER CHAMBER CHOIR 1971– ; Conductor, Artistic Dir., Phoenix Bach Choir, Phoenix, Arizona 1992– ; Unitarian Ch. of Vancouver 1967–71; Jon Washburn Singers 1969–71; Vancouver Bach Choir 1969–77; Hortulani Musicae 1969–79; Amity Singers (Victoria) 1975–80; CBC 1977–80; Univ. of B.C. 1982; Vancouver Community College 1974–87; Co-Artistic Dir., Masterpiece Chamber Music 1987–92; Conductor, Vancouver Chorale 1977– ; Mem., Chorus America; Internat. Music Festivals; Assn. of Candn. Choral Conductors; B.C. Choral Fed.; Candn. Music Ctr.; ACTRA; Am. Choral Dir. Assn.; Am. Fed. of Musicians; Candn.

Conf. of the Arts; Soc. of Composers, Authors & Music Publishers of Canada; Canadian Silver Jubilee Medal 1977; Vancouver Awards 1988; Willan Award (BCCF) 1982; Fellowship, Univ. of B.C. 1968–69; Bronze Tablet, Univ. of Illinois 1964; Internat. Choral Prizes: Holland, Poland, England 1971–77; composer, arranger, editor of num. choral compositions; Choral Music Editor, Jaymar Music Ltd.; 16 recordings conducting the Vancouver Chamber Choir plus other misc. recordings as conductor, composer, & instrumentalist; editor, 'Canadian Choral Records List' 1979; Home: 186 West 18th Ave., Vancouver, B.C. V5Y 2A5; Office: 1254 West 7th Ave., Vancouver, B.C. V6H 1B6.

**WASON, John Stuart Munro,** F.F.A.; F.C.I.A.; A.S.A.; actuary and consultant; b. St. Helen's, Eng. 30 Aug. 1922; s. Thomas Stewart and Mary Ross (Munro) W.; came to Canada 1950; e. The Leys Sch., Cambridge, Eng.; m. Winifred Marjorie, d. Frank Horsfall, Pudsey, Yorks., Eng., 5 June 1948; one s. Stuart; FORMER DIR. AND GEN. MGR. SHIELD LIFE INSUR. CO.; FORMER DIR., SHIELD INSUR. CO., DUBLIN; previously President, the Empire Life Insurance Company; joined Standard Life Assurance Co., Edinburgh, Scot. as Actuarial Student 1946; Actuarial Asst., later Secy. and Actuary, Maritime Life Assurance Co., Halifax, N.S. 1950–60; joined Dom. of Can. Gen. Ins. Co. as Actuary, Toronto, Ont. 1961; Assistant General Manager and Actuary 1967, General Manager, Life Insurance and Actuary 1969; served in 2nd World War; enlisted as Gunner and later commissioned in R.H.A. 1941; served Overseas with Surrey & Sussex Yeomanry, N. Africa, Italy and N.W. Europe 1943–45; Staff Offr., Rhine Army 1945–46; retired with rank of Captain; member International Actuarial Association; mem. Candn. Planning Comte., Life Office Mang. Assn. 1964–70; P. Conservative; United Church; recreations: golf, bowling, travel; Clubs: Granite; National (Toronto); Cataraqui Golf & Country (Kingston); Home: #1404, 1000 King St. W., Kingston, Ont. K7M 8H3.

**WASSER, Larry,** B.A. (Hons.); business executive; b. Toronto, Ont. 2 Dec. 1955; s. Leonard and Mary (Cohen) W.; e. Univ. of Toronto B.A. (Hons.) 1978; m. Marla d. Albert and Anita Kerzner June 1986; children: Justin Samuel, Derek Spence; PRES. & C.E.O., BEAMSCOPE CANADA INC. 1982– ; employed at Sam the Record Man for two years; Incorporated Beamscope Canada Inc. 1982; completed initial public offering Nov. 5, 1993; subject of numerous newspaper & magazine articles, most recent: 'Financial Times' Jan. 1994, 'Financial Post' Oct. 1993 and Dec. 1992, 'Computing Canada' Feb. 1992, 'Canadian Computer Reseller' Dec. 1991, 'Marketnews' June 1991, Oct. 1993, 'Computing Canada' June 1991, 'Computing Now' Dec. 1991 and Sept. 1989, 'Computer Dealer News,' 'Playback Strategy,' 'Business Computer Reseller News,' 'The Computer Paper' May 1991, 'Video Industry Monthly' Feb./Apr. 1991; Sponsor, Home Office Show Mar. 23/24 1994; National Ballet Sch. 1993 & 1994; 'March Building Break' Art Gallery of Ont. (A.G.O.) 1991–94; Guido Molinari show, A.G.O. June-Sept. 1990; recreations: antique automobiles, contemporary art, sports; clubs: Oakdale Golf; Home: 249 Warren Rd., Toronto, Ont. M4V 2S7; Office: 35 Ironside Cres., Scarborough, Ont. M1X 1G5.

**WASSERMUHL, Sol,** B.Arch., MRAIC, OAA; architect; b. Poland 26 March 1946; s. Benjamin and Mathilda W.; e. McGill Univ. B.Arch. 1969; m. Goldie d. Leon and Eva Greenbaum Sept. 1969; children: Kevin, Beth; ARCHITECT & SR. PARTNER, PAGE+STEELE ARCHITECTS PLANNERS 1926 with offices in Toronto, Ottawa & Hong Kong; received number of awards for design, heritage awards & competitions in Canada & overseas for a var. of commerical, instit. & residential projects; local projects incl.: Commercial: Madison Centre, 30 St. Clair, New York Life, 70 York Hongkong Bank, 525 University Credit Suisse, One Queen Street East & 1 Richmond St. W. (all Toronto); Residential: The Ports on Yonge St., The Dunhill Club at 95 Prince Arthur, The Renaissance at Bloor & Avenue Rd. and the award winning Marina Del Rey in Etobicoke; other: award winning Markham Suites Hotel, new Library Resource Ctr. & Technol. Bldg. at Humber College, and restoration / reconstruction of Sandford Fleming Bldg., Univ. of Toronto; current projects incl. major mixed use waterfront developments for San Diego Calif., a Marina & Resort project for Shanghai, Davisville Centre, The York City Centre, an office hotel complex for Dalian China, & a 50-acre residential-office-retail-industrial village in North York; Mem., Royal Architectural Inst. of Can.; Ont. Assn. of Architects; Toronto Soc. of Architecture; Visiting Arch. Lectr. & Guest Critic, Universities of Toronto & Waterloo; Past Mem., Ont. Building Code Task Force; Office: 110 Eglinton Ave. E., Suite 600, Toronto, Ont. M4P 2Y9.

**WASYLYCIA-LEIS, Klazina Judith,** B.A., M.A.; former politician; b. Kitchener, Ont. 10 Aug. 1951; d. Harry and Klazina (Nielsen) Wasylycia; e. Univ. of Waterloo, B.A. (Hons.) 1974; Carleton Univ., M.A. 1976; m. Ronald s. Harold and Ruth Leis 26 Aug. 1972; two s.: Nicholas and Joseph; re-el. MLA for St. John's, Sept. 1990; re-el. M.L.A. for St. Johns, Apr. 1988; Parl. Intern 1976–77; Women's Co-ord., Fed. NDP 1977–80; Extve. Asst. to Ed Broadbent, Fed. NDP Leader 1980–82; Co-ord., Premier's Secretariat, Prem. of Man. 1982–84; Policy Co-ord. Group, Govt. of Man. 1984–85; Extve. Dir., Women's Directorate 1985–86; Min. resp. for Status of Women 1986–87; Min. Resp. for Culture, Heritage & Recreation; Lotteries Found., Govt. of Man. 1986–88; NDP candidate, Ont. prov. constituency of Carlton 1977, 1980, 1981; Assoc. Pres., Federal NDP 1983; Mem., NDP; Un. Ch.; Home: 59 Bannerman Ave., Winnipeg, Man. R2W 0T1.

**WATANABE, Mamoru,** B.Sc., M.D., C.M., Ph.D., F.R.C.P.(C); physician; educator; b. Vancouver, B.C. 15 March 1933; s. Takazo and Nao (Suginobu) W.; e. McGill Univ. B.Sc. 1955, M.D.,C.M. 1957, Ph.D. 1963; m. Marie d. Oliver and Katie Bryndzak 1 June 1974; one s. David; Dean of Medicine, Univ. of Calgary 1982–92; internship and residency Royal Victoria Hosp. Montreal 1957–63; Research Assoc. Dept. Molecular Biol. Albert Einstein Coll. of Med. Yeshiva Univ. New York 1963, Assoc. 1965, Asst, Prof, 1966–67; Assoc. Prof. of Med. and Biochem. Univ. of Alta. 1967, Head Div. of Endocrinol. & Metabolism 1968–74, Prof. of Med. 1970–74; Research Assoc. Med. Research Council Can. 1969–74; Prof. and Head of Internal Med. present Univ. and Dir. of Med. Foothills Hosp. 1974–76, Assoc. Dean (Educ.) of Med. 1976, Assoc. Dean (Research) of Med. 1980, Acting Dean of Med. 1981–82, Dean of Med. 1982–92; recipient Research Fellowship Med. Research Council Can. 1959–62, Research Assoc. 1969–74; Ayerst Fellowship Endocrine Soc. 1963–64; Research Fellowship Am. Coll. Physicians 1964–67; author or co-author numerous med. publs.; mem. Candn. Med. Assn.; Candn. Biochem. Soc.; Candn. Soc. Clin. Investig.; Candn. Soc. Endocrinol. & Metabolism (Council mem. 1972–77, Pres. 1976); Candn. Hypertension Soc. (mem. Bd. 1982); Office: 3330 Hospital Dr. N.W., Calgary, Alta. T2N 1N4.

**WATCHORN, C.L.F. (Lee),** B.Sc.; F.S.A.; insurance executive; b. Montreal, Que. 13 Jan. 1945; e. McGill Univ. B.Sc. (Hons.); Fellow, Soc. of Actuaries; m. Nancy Prichard 12 Feb. 1971; children: Christopher, Katherine; SENIOR VICE-PRES. & GENERAL MANAGER FOR CANADA, SUN LIFE ASSURANCE CO. OF CANADA 1991– ; Sun Life 1965; Asst. Actuary 1970; Supt. Policy Admin. 1973; Sr. Underwriting Offr. for Can. 1978; Vice-Pres., Admin. for Can. 1980; Vice-Pres., Group Insur. for Can. 1982; Vice-Pres. & Asst. Gen. Mgr. 1987; Vice-Pres. & Assoc. Gen. Mgr. 1990; Chair, Chief Extve. Offr. & Trustee, Spectrum Bullock Financial Services Inc.; Chair, C.E.O. & Dir., Sun Life of Canada Benefit Mngt. Ltd.; Spectrum Bullock Finds Inc.; Chair & C.E.O., Sun Life Investment Mngt. Ltd.; Dir., Calvin Bullock Ltd.; Glengarry and Stormont Railway Co.; Bd. Mem., Internat. Mathetmatical Olympiad; Sr. Vice-Pres., St. John Ambulance Ont.; Adv. Bd. Mem., Chair in Insur. & Risk Management, Univ. of Calgary; Audit & Finance Ctte., Bd. of Gov., McGill Univ. and Mem. McGill Fund Council; Office: 225 King St. W., Toronto, Ont. M5V 3C5.

**WATCHORN, William Ernest,** C.A.; financial executive; b. Toronto, Ont. 8 Aug. 1943; s. Roy Elgin and Josephine (Swyrida) W.; e. William Lyon MacKenzie Coll. Inst. North York 1962; C.A. Ont. 1967; m. Maureen d. Muriel and Dudley Emmett 28 Dec. 1967; one d. Meghan; PRES., CHIEF EXECUTIVE OFFR. & DIR., ENSIS CORPORATION INC. 1991– ; Dir., Carte Internat. Inc.; Delhi Industries Inc.; Heron Cable Industries Ltd.; Milltronics Ltd.; Neo Europe S.A.; Neo Industries Ltd.; Mgr. Financial Planning & Analysis, Foundation Group of Companies 1968–72; Controller, Selkirk Holdings Ltd. 1972–75; Corporate Controller, Torstar Corp. 1975–78; Vice Pres. Finance, Canwest Capital Corp. 1978–82; Exec. Vice Pres. Kaiser Resources Inc. 1982; Sr. Vice Pres., Chief Financial Offr., Federal Industries Ltd. 1982–88; Pres. & C.E.O., Federal Industries Industrial Group 1988–91; Vision Capital Fund Adv. Bd.; Past Chrmn., Bd. of Govs., Balmoral Hall Sch.; Dir., C.D. Howe Inst.; Mem. Extve. Ctte., Winnipeg 2000 Leaders Comm.; Dir., ARCOR; Dir., Canadian Standards Assn.; recreations: squash, tennis, reading, travel; Clubs: Carleton; Winnipeg Winter; Home: 6453 Southboine Dr., Winnipeg, Man. R3R 0B7; Office: 1120, 200 Graham Ave., Winnipeg, Man. R3C 4L5.

**WATERHOUSE, Alan,** B.A., M.Sc., Dr.Ing.; educator; planning consultant; b. Sheffield, Eng., 13 Apr. 1936; s. Herbert and Jessie (Whelpton) W.; e. Univ. of Manchester, B.A. (Arch.) 1959; Univ. of Toronto, M.Sc. (Urban & Regional Planning); Univ. of Berlin, Dr. Ing. (City Planning) 1968; m. Karin-Maria, d. Friedrich Seidel, Univ. of Cologne, 3 Jan. 1960; PROF. AND CHRMN., DEPT. URBAN & REGIONAL PLANNING, UNIV. OF TORONTO since 1972; Tech. Consultant, U.N., since 1969; Asst. Arch., London (Eng.) Co. Council, 1959; Arch./Planner, Central Mortgage & Housing Corp., 1961–63; Dir., Planning Dept., Canadian Michell Assoc., 1964–66; joined present Univ. as Lectr. 1965–66, Asst. Prof. and Assoc. Prof. 1969–72; Housing Consultant, Govt. ofEthiopia, 1966–67; Dozent, Technische Universitat Berlin, 1966–67; author, 'Terms of Reference for a Proposed Low Income Housing Study' 1967; 'Urban Development in Medieval Europe,' 1971; 'Visual Change in Cities' (Die Reaktion der Bewohner auf die aussere Veranderung der Stadte), 1972; co-author, 'A National Housing Program for the Empire of Ethiopia,' 1966; other writings incl. papers in prof. journs.; tech. and research reports; several planning reports for communities and agencies in Can., U.S.A., Bahamas, Germany and Africa; Office: 230 College St., Toronto, Ont. M5T 1R2.

**WATERMAN, Anthony Michael Charles,** M.A., L.Th., Ph.D.; university professor; b. Southampton, England 4 June 1931; s. Bernard Charles and Doris Maude (Longland) W.; e. King Edward VI Sch. 1949; Selwyn Coll., Cambridge Univ. B.A. 1954, M.A. 1958; St. John's College Winnipeg L.Th. 1962; Australian Nat. Univ. Ph.D. 1968; m. Margaret d. Laughlin and Margaret Sinclair 3 Sept. 1955; children: Andrew, Michael, Caroline, Alice; DIRECTOR, UNIV. OF MANITOBA, INST. FOR HUMANITIES 1992– ; 2nd Lt., Royal Artillery 1950–51; Lt., Queen's Own Dorset Yeomanry 1951–54; Auditor, Fred Page Higgins & Co. 1954–56; Economic Analyst, C-I-L 1956–59; Fellow, St. John's College Winnipeg 1959– ; ordained (Diocese of Rupert's Land) Deacon 1962; Priest 1963; resigned orders 1982; Rsch. Scholar, Australian Nat. Univ. 1964–67; Prof. of Econ., Univ. of Man. 1972– ; Head 1972–76; Maurice Reckitt Fellow, Univ. of Sussex 1979–80; Bye Fellow, Robinson College, Cambridge Univ. 1986–87; Consultant, Candn. Prices & Incomes Comn. 1969–70; Chair, Gen. Synod Nat. Task Force on the Econ. 1973–76; Edit. Bd. Mem., 'Can. J. of Econ.' 1973–75, 1979–82, 'Can. Pub. Policy' 1974–76; Forkosch Prize for Intellectual History 1992; St. John's College Councill 962–64, 1967–69, 1991– ; Pres., Winnipeg Bach Fest. 1983–86; Vice-Pres. 'GroundSwell' 1991– ; Mem., Joint External Affairs, AUCC Candn. Commonwealth Scholarships & Fellowship Ctte. 1983–86; Mem., Anglican Ch. of Can. (del. to Gen. Synod 1973–74; Nat. Extve. Council 1974); Candn. Econ. Assn.; Assn. for Social Econ.; Assn. of Christian Economists; Hist. of Econ. Thought Soc.; author: 'Economic Fluctuations in Australia, 1945–1964' 1972, 'The Measurement of Economic Fluctuations in Canada' 1973, 'Revolution, Economics and Religion' 1991; co-author: 'Poverty in Canada' 1978; co-editor: 'Collected Economic Papers of C.L. Barber' 1982, 'Economics and Religion' forthcoming; recreations: music, walking, bridge, golf; Home: 171 Brock St., Winnipeg, Man. R3N 0Y7; Office; Winnipeg, Man. R3T 2N2.

**WATERS, Donovan William Mockford,** Q.C., M.A., Ph.D., D.C.L., F.R.S.C.; educator; lawyer; b. Brighton, Eng. 23 Apl. 1928; s. James William and Marjorie M. (Mockford) W.; e. Xaverian Coll. Brighton, Eng.; Varndean Sch. Brighton; Wadham Coll. Oxford B.A. 1952, B.C.L. 1953; Univ. Coll. London Ph.D. 1963; Oxford, D.C.L. 1990; m. Maria (Maryla) d. Bronislaw and Barbara Zakrzewski 18 March 1961; children: Catherine Alexandra, Anne-Marie, Alastair Donovan; SCHOLARS PROFESSOR OF LAW, UNIV. OF VICTORIA 1993– ; Assoc. Couns., Douglas Symes & Brissenden, Barristers and Solicitors, Vancouver, B.C. 1989– ; called to English Bar, Lincoln's Inn, Eng. 1958, Bar of B.C. 1980; Lectr. New Coll. Oxford 1954–56; Visiting Prof. Univ. of Chicago 1956; Lectr. Univ. of London, Univ. Coll. 1956–64, Reader in Eng. Law 1964–67; Visiting Prof. Univ. of Sask. 1965–66; Prof. of Law, McGill Univ. 1967–74, Gale Prof. of Law 1974–77; Candn. citizen 1977; Prof. of Law, Univ. of Victoria 1977–93; Queen's Counsel 1989; author 'The Constructive Trust' 1964; 'Law of Trusts in Canada,' 2nd ed. 1984; Pres., Internat. Acad. Estate & Trust Law; Mem., Royal Soc. of Can.; Am. Coll. of Trust and Estate Counsel; Candn. Assn. Law Teachers; recreations: walking, reading; Club: Union; Home: 1031 Falkland Rd., Victoria, B.C. V8S 4M3; Office: (P.O. Box 2400) Victoria, B.C. V8W 3H7.

**WATERS, Peter David;** banker; b. England 11 Aug. 1935; e. England; m. Charlotte 16 May 1959; children: Caroline, Trevor, Gerry and Beverley; HEAD OF REAL ESTATE LENDING and SR. VICE PRES., CORPORATE & INSTITUTIONAL FINANCIAL SERVICES, BANK OF MONTREAL; Home: 1400 Goldthorpe Rd., Mississauga, Ont. L5G 3R3; Office: 1 First Canadian Place, Toronto, Ont. M5X 1A1.

**WATERS, Robert Galbraith,** B.A., LL.B.; lawyer, board member; b. London, Ont. 29 July 1947; s. Donald Galbraith and Clover Marguerite (McLachlan) W.; e. Univ. of West. Ont. B.A. 1969, LL.B. 1972; m. Jayne Elizabeth d. Allan and Joan Kenny 30 Oct. 1970; children: Donald M., Andrew A., Mark C.K., Jennifer E.; CHAIR, FARM PRACTICES PROTECTION BOARD 1990– ; called to Ont. Bar 1974; sole practitioner 1974–75; Partner, Waters & Sinker 1976–90; Lawyer, Robert G. Waters 1990– ; frequent speaker/lectr. on agricultural law; Chair, Study Team, Recreation Master Plan, Town of Strathroy 1984–86; Chair/Pres., Strathroy-Middlesex Multi-Service Centre 1980, '81; Chief Financial Offr., Middlesex Lib. Assn. 1975–78; C.F.O. Donald Nisbet 1977, Maurice Platts 1975 campaigns; recreation: skiing; club: Strathroy Aquatic; Home: 7 Kittridge Ave. E., Strathroy, Ont. N7G 2A9; Office: 72 Frank St., P.O. Box 58, Strathroy, Ont. N7G 3J1.

**WATERSTON, Elizabeth Hillman,** B.A., M.A., Ph.D.; university professor; b. Montreal, Que. 18 April 1922; d. Lt-Col. Daniel and Bertha Jean (Smith) Hillman; e. Univ. of Toronto B.A. 1944; Bryn Mawr Coll. M.A. 1945; Univ. of Toronto Ph.D. 1950; m. Douglas s. Edward and Dorothy W. 17 Nov. 1949; children: Daniel, Jane, Christina, Charlotte, Rosemary; PROFESSOR EMERITUS, UNIVERSITY OF GUELPH 1989– ; Asst. Prof., Sir George Williams College 1945–47; Assoc. Prof. 1950–58; Chair, English Dept. 1956–58; Assoc. Prof., English Dept., Univ. of W. Ont. 1958–67; Assoc. Prof., Univ. of Guelph 1967–71; Prof. 1971–87; Chair, English Dept. 1974–77; Founding Mem., Assn. of Candn. Univ. Teachers of English; Assn. of Candn. & Que. Literatures; Founding & Life Mem., Assn. of Candn. Studies; Edit. Bd. Mem., 'Scottish Tradition,' 'English Studies in Canada'; Founder & Editor: 'Canadian Children's Literature'; Canada Council & SSHRC grants 1962–88; assessor, consultant & external examiner for Candn. publishers & univs.; Anglican; N.D.P.; Nat. Pres., Humanities Assn. of Canada 1977–79; author: 'Children's Literature in Canada' 1992, 'Canada to 1900' 1989, 'Gilbert Parker' 1989, 'Brush up Your Basics' 1981, 'Survey' 1973, 'Composition for Canadian Universities' 1964; co-author: 'Silenced Sextet' 1993, 'John Galt' 1985; editor: 'Some Scots' 1982, 'Bogle Corbet' 1976, 'Seats of the Mighty' 1968; co-editor: 'Selected Journals of L.M. Montgomery' vol 1 1985, vol 2 1987, vol 3 1992; recreations: music, gardening; Addresses: (Summer) 535 Colborne St., London, Ont. N1B 3E8 and (Winter) 9436 Trinity Circle, Bradenton, Florida 94210.

**WATKINS, Charles Gaylord;** lawyer; b. Calgary, Alta. 25 Mar. 1941; s. Albert Drummond and Gertrude Evelyn (Roebuck) W.; e. McGill Univ. B.Sc. 1962; Osgoode Hall LL.B. 1967; Yale LL.M. 1971; Strasbourg Dip. en Droit Compare 1966; m. Pamela May d. Leslie Bond and the late Jean (Try-Ferguson) Bond 26 Aug. 1967; two d. Adrianna Gay, Amelia Gabrielle; PARTNER, HADIPUTRANTO, HADINOTO & PARTNERS, CORRESPONDENT OFFICE OF BAKER & McKENZIE, ATTORNEYS-AT-LAW, JAKARTA, INDONESIA; Cons., Task Forces on Canadian Ownership & Labour Relations 1967–68; Lectr. Law, Univ. of Singapore 1967–69; Fellow, Yale Univ. Law 1969–70; Counsel, ILO/BIT Geneva 1970–72; Cons., Admin. Law, Law Reform Comn. 1972–76; Lectr. Law, Univ. of Ottawa 1974–78; Lectr. Pub. Adm. Carleton Univ. 1973–76; Counsel, Hewitt Nesbitt Reid, Ottawa 1977–79; Counsel, Royal Comn. N. Environment (Ont.) 1977–79, 1981–83; Partner, Parlee, Calgary 1980–86; Adj. Prof. Law Univ. of Calgary 1982–87; Public Interest Advocacy Centre, Director 1976–92, Chair of Bd. 1990–92; Member Nat. Council, Chair, Nat. Section Communications Law, Cdn. Bar Assn. 1984–88; Dir., Calgary Opera 1984–87; Dir., Alberta Law Reform Inst. 1986–92; Trustee & Counsel, Candn. Mediterranean Inst. 1980–92; Dir., Cdn. Business Assn. of Jakarta 1992– ; Clubs: Yale (N.Y.); Tanglin (Singapore); Lake Louise Ski; Mercantile (Jakarta); Hilton Executive; Office: The Landmark Centre, Tower A, 24th Floor, Jl. Jend. Sudirman No. 1, Jakarta 12910, Indonesia.

**WATKINS, Melville Henry,** B.Com.; educator; b. McKellar, Ont. 15 May 1932; s. Wilmot Henry and Sadie Evelyn (Kirkham) W.; e. Univ. of Toronto B.Com. 1952; Mass. Inst. of Technol. grad. studies in Econ.; m. Kelly d. Harold and Pat Crichton 28 May 1971; children: Kenneth, Matthew, Emily; PROF. OF ECON. & POL. SCI. UNIV. OF TORONTO 1970– , mem. Faculty since 1958; Head, Fed. Govt. Task Force Structure Candn. Ind. 1967–68, chief author report 'Foreign Ownership and the Structure of Canadian Industry' (Watkins Report); Econ. Cons. to Indian Brotherhood of NWT, Yellowknife 1974–76; Cons. on free trade to Candn. Labour Cong. Ottawa 1987–88; Pres. Harold Innis Found. 1969–70; author numerous acad. articles and essays Candn. econ. hist. and policy; guest speaker Candn. policy issues; commentator, radio and TV; author: 'Madness and Ruin: Politics and the Economy in the Neoconservative Age' 1992; editor: 'Dene Nation – The Colony Within' 1977; 'Canada: Handbooks to the Modern World' 1993; co-ed. 'Economics Canada' 1963; 'Approaches to Canadian Economic History' 1967; 'Gordon to Watkins to You' 1970; 'Canadian Economic History' 1993; 'Canada Under Free Trade' 1993; co-ed. and columnist 'This Magazine' 1978– ; Co-Founder Waffle Movement NDP 1969, Vice Pres. Fed. NDP 1969–71; Home: 103 Browning Ave., Toronto, Ont. M4K 1W2; Office: Toronto, Ont. M5S 1A1.

**WATMOUGH, David Arthur;** writer; b. London, U.K. 17 Aug. 1926; s. Gerald Arthur and Ethel Florence (Bassett) W.; e. Coopers Co. Sch.; King's Coll., Univ. of London 1945–49; Prod., BBC Third Prog. 1955–56; Feature Writer, San Francisco 'Examiner' 1957–60, Visual Arts & Drama Critic, 'Vancouver Sun' 1965–67; freelance writer, England, France, U.S., Can.; Mem., Vancouver Art Gallery; Fed. of B.C. Writers (Founding Pres.); TWUC; author: 'The Unlikely Pioneer' 1986 (opera); 'A Church Renascent' 1951 (non-fiction); 'The Time of the Kingfishers' 1994; 'Thy Mother's Glass' 1992; 'The Year of Fears' 1987; 'Vibrations in Time' 1986, 'Fury' 1984, 'The Connecticut Countess' 1984, 'No More Into the Garden' 1978, 'From a Cornish Landscape' 1975, 'Love & the Waiting Game' 1975, 'Ashes for Easter' 1972 (fiction); 'Names for the Numbered Years' 1967 (plays); Ed.: 'Vancouver Fiction' 1985 (anthology); recipient, two Can. Counc. Sr. Arts Grants (Creative Writing); recreations: opera, symphonic and chamber music, theology, murder trials, dog & cat obedience training; Home: 3358 West First Ave., Vancouver, B.C. V6R 1G4.

**WATSON, A. John,** M.A., Ph.D.; executive; b. Ottawa, Ont. 28 July 1948; s. Alexander and Helenora (Slater) W.; e. Univ. of Toronto, B.A. 1969, M.A. 1973, Ph.D. 1981; m. Roshanara d. Omar and Famida Majeed 28 Nov. 1986; two s. Max, Slater; EXEC. DIR. CARE CANADA 1987– ; Assoc. Dir. World Univ. Service Can. 1975–78, Field Dir. Candn. Tech. Assistance & Training Prog. Zimbabwe 1981, Dir. Prog. Devel. 1983, Dep. Exec. Dir. 1985–87; 1st Pres. Standing Conf. Candn. Orgns. Refugees 1977; Can. Council Fellow 1973–75; Soc. Sci's & Humanities Rsch. Council Fellow 1978–81, Postdoctoral Fellow 1981; author various publs.; recreations: squash, skiing, photography; Home: 111 Banner Rd., Nepean, Ont. K2H 9L1; Office: P.O. Box 9000, Station T, Ottawa, Ont. K1G 4X6.

**WATSON, Alexander Gardner,** C.M., M.D., F.R.C.S.(C), F.A.C.S.; ophthalmologist; educator; b. Scot. 28 March 1918; s. Capt. John Salter and Lilias (Gardner) W.; m. Patricia Jane Brown d. late Senator Prentiss Brown, St. Ignace, Mich. 30 May 1953; children: Dr. John Brown, Alexander Gardner; PROF. EMERITUS OF OPHTHALMOL., UNIV. OF OTTAWA; Cons., Ophthalmol. Ottawa Gen. Hosp.; Extve. Dir. Sally Letson Foundation for Eye Research; Consultant to Candn. Forces Medical Council; retired from Council, Rockcliffe Park Village, 1985; served with RCAF Med. Services, rank Wing Commdr.; Mgr. Candn. Olympic Hockey Team 1948; el. to Candn. Armed Services Sports Hall of Fame; Member, Order of Canada 1988; mem. Candn. Olympic Assn.; author or co-author numerous publs.; mem. Candn. Ophthal. Soc.; Ottawa Acad. Med.; Internat. Soc. Eye Surgs. (Founding mem.); Ont. Med. Assn.; Candn. Med. Assn.; Royal Coll. Phys. & Surgs. and mem. various Ophthalmol. comtes.; Alpha Omega Alpha; Presbyterian; recreations: golf, hockey; Office: 267 O'Connor St., Ottawa, Ont. K2P 1V3.

**WATSON, Colin D.,** B.A.Sc., M.B.A.; broadcasting executive; b. Kettering, Eng. 5 July 1941; s. Harry John W.; e. Public Sch. Kettering, Eng.; High Sch. N. Vancouver, B.C.; Univ. of B.C., B.A.Sc. 1963; Univ. of W. Ont. M.B.A. 1970; m. Barbara d. Russel J. Preeter; children: Christopher, Kevin, Matthew; PRES., C.E.O., AND DIR., ROGERS CABLESYSTEMS LIMITED 1979– ; Dir., Rogers Communications; Candn. Satellite Communications Inc. (Cancom); Canadian Cable Television Assn. (CCTA); Conwest Exploration Co. Ltd.; Calmeadow Charitable Found.; Devel. Engr., Polymer Corp., Sarnia, Ont. 1963; Product Mgr. Trane Co. of Canada Ltd. 1964–68; Asst. to Vice-Pres. Industrial Devel., Brascan Ltd. 1970–72; Vice-Pres. Triarch Corp., Treas. Jonlab Investments Ltd. and Pres. Canadian Venture Capital Corp. 1972–74; Pres. and Dir., Metro Cable TV Ltd., 1974–76; Sr. Vice Pres., Operations, Candn. Cablesystems Ltd. 1976–78; mem. Assn. Prof. Engrs. Ont.; Anglican; recreations: tennis, cycling, skiing; Clubs: York; Toronto Lawn Tennis; Home: 72 Chestnut Park Rd., Toronto, Ont. M4W 1W8; Office: 1 Valleybrook Dr., 5th Flr., Toronto, Ont. M3B 2S7.

**WATSON, David Barr,** M.B.E., E.M., C.D., B.Com; management consultant; b. Swansea, U.K., 5 Sept. 1920; s. Thomas and Winnifred (Davies) W.; e. Haileybury Coll., Eng. (Sr. Matric.) 1938; Univ. of London, B.Com. 1941; London Polytech. (Sales) Dipl. 1946; Univ. of W. Ontario (Mang. Training Course) Dipl. 1953; m. Nancy Roberta, d. R. P. Cretney, Toronto, 3 Nov. 1973; children: Nigel, Ian; ret. PARTNER, WOODS, GORDON & CO. (Management Consultants, estbd. 1932), since 1954; Asst. Export Sales Mgr., Philips Radio, England, 1946–47; with Remington-Rand Ltd., Toronto, Ont., 1947–49; joined present Co. 1949, apptd. Supervisor, 1951, Secy., 1953, Partner, 1954, ret. 1980; served with Hon. Arty. Co. (U.K.) 1938–40; served in 2nd World War; Major, Royal Corps of Signals (Airborne), 1940–46; M.B.E., M.I.D.; Lieut.-Col., Royal Candn. Signals (Militia), Toronto, Ont., 1947–62; ret. Hon. Col., 709 Communications Regt.; mem., Inst. Mang. Consultants Ont.; Anglican; Address: 292 Morrison Rd., Oakville, Ont. L6J 4J4.

**WATSON, Don Allan,** B.A.Sc.; power company executive; b. Lethbridge, Alta. 15 May 1935; s. Allan Kerr and Pearl Almira (Moir) W.; e. Univ. of B.C. B.A.Sc. 1959; m. Vera Mary d. Steven and Tillie Malahoff 6 Sept. 1958; children: Mark, Scott, Kim, Kristi; PRESIDENT & CHIEF EXECUTIVE OFFICER, GREAT LAKES POWER 1990– ; progressed from Junior Engineer to Manager, Health Physics & Manager, Safety Services, Ontario Hydro 1959–85; Dir., Eastern Region, Ontario Hydro 1985–90; Chrmn., Pres. & Dir., 956868 Ontario Limited; Lake Superior Power Inc.; Vice-Pres. Utilities, Great Lakes Power Inc.; Dir., Great Lakes Power Ltd.; Great Lakes Power Inc.; Dir., United Way Sault Ste. Marie; Mem., Assn. of Profl. Engrs. (Ont.); Past Pres., Power Reactor Health Physicists; Candn. Radiation Protection Assn.; recreations: canoeing, biking; Home: 33 Nokomis Beach Rd., Sault Ste. Marie, Ont. P6A 5K6; Office: 122 East St., Sault Ste. Marie, Ont. P6A 5L4.

**WATSON, Donald,** M.A.; b. Bristol, Eng., 19 May 1919; s. Herbert Ernest and Violet Gertrude May (Forse) W.; e. Oxford Univ., B.A. (Physics) 1940; m. Mary, d. late J. P. Plenderleith, Belfast, N.I., Dec. 1945; children: Peter, Shirley; with Telecommunications Research Establishment, Eng., 1940–45 and trans. to India, 1945; joined Chalk River Project, Atomic Energy of Can. Ltd., Canada, 1946; Asst. to Vice-Pres., Research & Devel., 1948–55; Secy., 1956–63; Vice Pres. Adm. 1963–74; Anglican; Home: 2342 Rembrandt Rd., Ottawa, Ont. K2B 7P5.

**WATSON, Garry Richard,** B.Sc., Ph.D.; cultural executive; b. Toronto, Ont. 27 Sept. 1944; s. Walter Stewart and Marian (Blake) W.; e. Humberside C.I. 1963; Univ. of Toronto B.Sc. (Hon.) 1967, Ph.D. 1975; m. Sharon Lynne d. Albert and Marjorie Hargreaves 11 Oct. 1969; children: Lindsay Meredith, Blake Alexander; DIRECTOR, ROYAL BOTANICAL GARDENS; Sr. Career Counsellor, Univ. of Toronto 1972–75; Registrar, Div. of Sciences, Erindale College, Univ. of Toronto 1975–79; Registrar, George Brown College of Applied Arts & Technol. 1979–92; Dir. of Student Services 1988–91; Acting Dir. of Computer Services 1990; National Research Council Scholarships 1968–71; Recognition Award by Ctte. of Registrars, Admissions & Liaison Officers of Ont.; Mem., Un. Church; Beta Theta Pi Frat.; recreations: cottage, gardening, crafts; Home: 2495 Glamworth Cres., Mississauga, Ont. L5K 1G4; Office: Box 399, Hamilton, Ont. L8N 3H8.

**WATSON, George Nelson,** B.A., F.S.A. (1945), F.C.I.A., M.A.A.A.; actuary; b. Toronto, Ont. 21 Oct. 1914; s. Harold and Alice Florence (Elliott) W.; e. Malvern Coll., Inst., Toronto, Ont.; Victoria Coll., Univ. of Toronto, B.A. 1936 (Hon. Math. and Physics); 1stly m. the late Hylda d. Samuel Hayhurst, 4 Dec. 1937; one s., Cameron Nelson; 2ndly m. Clare McClafferty d. John

McClafferty 11 June 1993; PRES., G.N. WATSON LTD.; Vice Pres. & Actuary, Creative Personnel Systems Inc.; Fellow, Candn. Inst. of Actuaries; The Society of Actuaries; Mem., Am. Acad. of Actuaries; Past Pres., Candn. Assn. Accident and Sickness Insurers (1965–66); Candn. Pension Conf. (1971–73); Conservative; Protestant; recreation: golf; Clubs: The Ontario Club; The Metro Toronto Bd. of Trade; Home: RR #1, Palgrave, Ont. L0N 1P0; Office: 629 The Queensway, Toronto, Ont. M8Y 1K4.

**WATSON, George W.,** B.Sc.Eng., M.B.A., A.M.P.; petroleum executive; b. Leamington, Ont. 31 May 1947; s. Grant Murray and Janke Klaus (deJong) W.; e. Queen's Univ., B.S.Eng. 1970, M.B.A. 1972; Harvard Univ., A.M.P. 1988; m. Sheila Smith 29 Apr. 1972; children: Eric, Tara, Scott; PRESIDENT, TRANSCANADA PIPELINES 1993– ; various positions in Toronto, Ottawa & Calgary ending as Asst. Gen. Mgr., Oil & Gas Div., Cdn. Imperial Bank of Commerce 1972–81; Dir. then Vice-Pres., Finance, Dome Petroleum Ltd. 1981–88; Pres. & C.E.O., Intensity Resources Ltd. 1988–90; Chief Financial Offr., TransCanada PipeLines 1990–94; Pres. 1993– ; recreations: sports; clubs: Bow Valley, Calgary Winter; Office: 2900, 111 - 5th Ave. SW, Calgary, Alta. T2P 3Y6.

**WATSON, Ian,** B.A., B.C.L.; consultant, govt. & parliamentary affairs; b. Howick, Que. 10 April 1934; s. Wilfred, D.V.M. and late Jean (Whillans) W.; e. Howick (Que.) High Sch.; Bishop's Univ., B.A.; McGill Univ., B.C.L.; m. Monique d. late Leopold Carle, M.D., 20 Nov. 1965; children: Mark, Chantal, Yannie, Anik; Extve. Dir., Nat. Counc. on Canada-Arab Relations; Rapporteur, Scient. and Tech. Comtes., North Atlantic Parl. Assembly, 1978–81; Co-Chrmn., Canada U.S. Interparliamentary Group, 1980–82; Vice-Chrmn., Canada-Arab World Parliamentary Group 1983–84; called to Bar of Que. 1959; 1st el. to H. of C. for Chateauguay-Huntingdon-Laprairie 1963, re-el. 1965; re-el. for Constit. of Laprairie 1968, 1972 and 1974; re-elect. Const. of Chateauguay, 1979 & 1980; Vice-Chrmn., H. of C. Comte. on Mines, Forest & Waters 1963–64; Parlty. Observer, Candn. Del. to U.N., New York 1965 and 1966; Chrmn., H. of C. Comte. on Citizenship, Immigration, Indian Affairs & Human Rights 1965; Jt. Chrmn., H. of C. and Senate Comte. on Penitentiaries 1966–67; Chrmn. H. of C. Standing Comte. on Indian Affairs and N. Devel. 1968–72, 1976–79; Parlty. Secy. to Min. of Nat. Revenue 1972; Parlty. Secy. to Min. State for Urban Affairs 1973–74; Chrmn., H. of C. Comte. Nat. Resources & Public Works 1980–84; Liberal; Presbyterian; Address: 425 Sussex Dr., Ottawa, Ont. K1N 9M6.

**WATSON, Ian Stuart;** business executive; b. Wellingborough, U.K. 20 Jan. 1955; s. Ronald and Joan Elizabeth (Fosket) W.; e. Grammar Sch. U.K.; 1 yr. community college, Sudbury; m. Marie d. Lloyd and Eleanor Cunningham 27 Aug. 1977; children: Stephanie, Joshua; PRESIDENT, ELASTO VALVE RUBBER PRODUCTS (subsidiary of Devjo Industries Inc.); emigrated to Canada in 1971 with parents; Draftsman / Plant Manager, Elliott Rubber & Plastic 1975–81; Partner, Abraflex Ltd. 1981–84; joined Elasto Valve as Manager, Manufacturing 1984; Home: 2064 Southlane Rd., Sudbury, Ont.; Office: 1691 Pioneer Rd., Sudbury, Ont. P3G 1B2.

**WATSON, John Hamilton,** B.Com., M.B.A.; insurance executive; b. Toronto, Ont. 15 Nov. 1943; s. Gordon McKay and Kathleen (Hamilton) W.; e. Vaughan Rd. Coll. Inst. Toronto 1962; Univ. of Toronto B.Com. 1966, M.B.A. 1967; m. Denise Florence d. Thomas A. Humphrey, Thornhill, Ont. 21 Sept. 1968; one s. Andrew Gordon; Dir. Fairbank Lumber Co. Ltd.; PRESIDENT, SPRUCEGROVE INVESTMENT MANAGEMENT LIMITED 1993– ; joined Confederation Life Insur. Co. as Invest. Analyst Trainee Bond Dept. 1967, Invest. Analyst Bond Dept. 1969 and Stock Dept. 1970, Invest. Mgr. US Common Stocks 1971, Asst. Vice-Pres. Invest. Research 1973; Vice-Pres., Investments 1977; Sr. Vice-Pres., Investments 1983–90; Pres., Confed Investment Counselling Ltd. 1990–93; Fellow Life Mang. Inst.; C.F.A. 1973; mem. Toronto Soc. Financial Analysts; Freemason; United Church; recreations: hockey, golf, table tennis; Club: Thornhill Country; Home: 22 Nevada Ave., Toronto, Ont. M2M 3N8; Office: 350 Bloor St. E., Toronto, Ont. M4W 1H4.

**WATSON, Patrick,** O.C., M.A., D.Litt., LL.D.; television journalist; filmmaker; writer; b. Toronto, Ont. 23 Dec. 1929; s. Stanley Alvin and Lucy Lovell (Bate) W.; e. Univ. of Toronto B.A. 1951, M.A. 1953; Univ. of Mich. doctoral studies 1954–55; m. Beverly Holmes, Toronto, Ont. 11 June 1951 (div. 1983); children: Christopher, Gregory, Andrea; m. Caroline Bamford 30 Nov. 1985; CHRMN., CANADIAN BROADCASTING CORPORATION 1991– ; Ed., W.J. Gage & Co. Toronto 1953–56; TV Producer CBC Toronto and Ottawa 1956–66 (program series incl. 'Close-Up,' 'Inquiry,' 'This Hour Has Seven Days'); Adjunct Prof. of Pol. Science Univ. of Waterloo 1966–67; Ed. and Anchorman 'The Fifty-First State' N.Y. Pub. TV 1972–73; documentary films incl. 'The Seven Hundred Million,' 'Search in the Deep' (with Jacques Cousteau), 'The Struggle for Democracy'; Pres., Patrick Watson Enterprises Ltd., since 1968; Rideau Broadcasting Ltd., 1979–84; Vice. Pres. Programming, Bushnell Communications Ltd. 1969–70; Vice Pres. Immedia Inc. 1975–77; Dir., Candn. Centre for Arms Control & Disarmament 1983–89; Trustee, National Film Bd. of Can. 1984–87; Pres., Democracy Films Ltd. 1984–89; Host, 'Witness to Yesterday' 1973–75; 'Some Honourable Members' 1973–75; 'The Watson Report' 1975–81; 'Titans' 1981; The CBS Cable Network (all programming) 1981–82; 'Live from Lincoln Centre' (PBS) 1982– ; Venture (CBC) 1985–86; author 'Alter Ego' 1978; 'Zero to Airtime' 1974; 'Fasanella's City' 1973; 'Conspirators in Silence' 1969; co-author 'Alexander Dolgun's Story' 1975; 'The Struggle for Democracy' 1988; numerous articles on science, religion, broadcasting, educ.; numerous film and TV scripts; Chrmn., The Abilities Found.; mem., Assn. Candn. Radio & TV Artists; Officer of Order of Canada, 1981; Address: 1500 Bronson Ave., P.O. Box 8478, Ottawa, Ont. K1G 3J5.

**WATSON, Peter D.,** B.A., M.Sc.; insurance executive; b. Winnipeg, Man. 6 June 1942; s. W. Roy and Mary Elizabeth (Ostrander) W.; e. Royal Mil. Coll. Can. B.A. (Comm.) 1963; London Sch. of Econ. M.Sc. (Econ.) 1968; Harvard Grad. Sch. of Bus. Mktg. Mgmt. 1973; m. Elaine Frances d. Douglas and Marjorie Wilson 19 Sept. 1964; two s. Craig Duncan, Colin Michael; PRES., WILLIS CORROON MELLING LTD. 1992– ; served 3 yrs. RCAF assigned to UN Middle E., Asia and NATO Eur.; served Air Canada as Financial Analyst becoming Dir. Corporate Planning and mem. Ctte. Mgmt.; joined Roy Henry Insurance Ltd. Edmonton 1976, purchased majority control 1980; Merged with Richards Melling 1988; and Willis Corroon 1991; Past Chrmn. Misericordia Hosp. Edmonton; Chrmn. Edmonton Regional Airports Authority; Past Chrmn. Western Ind. Rsch. & Training Centre Edmonton; recreations: skiing, sailing; Clubs: Edmonton; Centre; Home: 81 St. George's Cres., Edmonton, Alta. T5N 3M7; Office: 1200 Scotia Place, 10060 Jasper Ave., Edmonton, Alta. T5J 3R8.

**WATSON, Peter James Scott,** B.Sc., Ph.D.; university professor; b. Basingstoke, Eng. 26 Aug. 1947; s. William Robert and Marian Ruby (Bliss) W.; e. Sedbergh Sch. 1960; Edinburgh Univ., B.Sc. (Hons.) 1964; Durham Univ. Ph.D. 1967; m. Margaret d. Jack and Margaret Mason 1 Sept. 1967; children: Genefer, Marcus; CHRMN., PHYSICS DEPT., CARLETON UNIV. 1990– ; Rsch. Asst. in Theor. Physics, Oxford Univ. 1968–70; post-doct. fellow, Univ. of Guelph 1970–71; Asst. then Assoc. Prof., Carleton Univ. 1971–84, Prof. 1984– ; Vis. Prof., Ahmadu Bellow Univ., Nigeria 1977–78; Schweizerische Inst. f. Nuclearfurschung, (sabbatical) 1983–84; University of Edinburgh 1989; CERN 1990; Cons., legal prof.; Dir., Ottawa-Carleton Inst. for Physics; Mem., Candn. Assn. of Physicists; Am. Physics Soc.; Inst. of Particle Physics Counc. 1983–86; author of 40 articles; TV series 'The Nature of Matter' shown on Univ. of the Air; recreations: skiing, windsurfing; Home: Box 254, Wakefield, Que. J0X 3G0; Office: 1125 Colonel By Drive, Ottawa, Ont. K1S 5B6.

**WATSON, Robert George,** M.Sc., P.Eng.; company president; b. Creemore, Ont. 17 Sept. 1917; s. Norman and Ella Jane (Blackburn) W.; e. Queen's Univ.; M.Sc., Harvard Univ.; m. Florence Irene Pearce, 4 Sept. 1948; children: Linda, William, Calvin, Shirley, Nancy; PRES. & DIR., R.G. WATSON CO. LTD. since 1956; practised civil engn. in Can. 1947–51; organized own engn. firm, 1951; inc. as R. G. Watson Co. Ltd. 1956; mem., Assn. Prof. Engrs. of Ont.; life mem., Amer. Soc. Civil Engrs.; recreations: golf, hunting; Clubs: Rosedale Golf; Granite; Muskoka Lakes Golf & Country; Goodwood; Homes: #1, Scotch Elmway, Toronto, Ont. M4N 3N4.

**WATSON, Robert William,** B.A.Sc., P.Eng.; utilities executive; b. Vancouver, B.C. 25 March 1947; s. William John and Beverly Mildred (Curry) W.; e. Univ. of B.C. B.Sc. 1970; m. Julie d. Andrew and Ruth Remple 3 Sept. 1982; one s.: Kris Ryan; PRESIDENT & CHIEF OPERATING OFFICER, CANADIAN NIAGARA POWER CO. LTD. 1992– ; Electrical Project Engineer, M.A. Thomas & Assoc. 1970–74; Asst. Electrical Supt., City of Penticton B.C. 1974–77; Manager, Transmission & Distribution, West Kootenay Power 1977–90; Extve. Vice-Pres., Candn. Niagara Power 1990–92; Mem., Profl. Engineers of B.C.; Profl. Engineers of Ont.; Niagara Falls Economic Development Agency; Niagara Peninsula Development Steering Ctte.; recreations: golf, skiing, sailing; clubs: Bridgewater Country; Home: 7107 Mt. Forest Lane, Niagara Falls, Ont. L2J 3Z3; Office: P.O. Box 1218, Fort Erie, Ont. L2A 5Y2.

**WATSON, (Donald) Scott,** B.A., M.A.; curator, writer, critic; b. Vancouver, B.C. 22 May 1950; s. Ross Ward and Helen Ardis (Ross) W.; e. Univ. of B.C. B.A. 1975, M.A. 1978; DIRECTOR, FINE ARTS, GALLERY, UNIV. OF B.C. 1987– ; Registrar, Vancouver Art Gallery 1978–80; Curator, Surrey Art Gallery 1980; Vancouver Art Gallery 1980–87; became active as an art critic in 1979 with pub. of 1st work in 'Vanguard' magazine; has since pub. over 50 articles on contemporary art in Canada & abroad; author: 'Stories' 1974, 'Platonic Love' 1980 (short stories), 'Jack Shadbolt' 1990 (non-fiction); B.C. Book Award for Non-Fiction for 'Jack Shadbolt' 1990; recreations: weight-lifting; Home: 1836 Venables, Vancouver, B.C. V5L 2H7; Office: 1956 Main Mall, Vancouver, B.C. V6T 1Z1.

**WATSON, Wilfred,** Ph.D.; writer; b. Rochester, England 1 May 1911; s. Frederick Walter and Louisa (Claydon) W.; e. Univ. of B.C. B.A. 1943; Univ. of Toronto M.A. 1946, Ph.D. 1951; m. Sheila d. C.E. Doherty 1941; PROF. EMERITUS, UNIV. OF ALTA. 1976– ; author 'Friday's Child' (verse) Faber & Faber 1955; 'Cockcrow and the Gulls' (verse play) directed Gordon Peacock, performed Studio Theatre Univ. of Alta. 1962; 'The Trial of Corporal Adam' directed Michael Tait, performed Coach House Theatre Toronto 1964; 'O holy ghost DIP your finger in the blood of Canada and write, I LOVE YOU' directed Thomas Peacocke, Studio Theatre 1967; 'Lets murder Clytemnestra according to the principles of Marshall McLuhan' directed Bernard Engel, Studio Theatre 1969; 'The Sorrowful Canadians' (verse) 1972; 'I Begin with Counting' (number-grid verse) 1978; 'Mass on Cowback' (number-grid verse) 1982; 'Gramsci x 3' (play) published Longspoon Press 1983 performed, Thomas Peacocke director, Studio Theatre 1986; 'Poems collected unpublished, new' introduction Thomas Peacocke, Longspoon/NeWest 1986; 'Plays at the Iron Bridge: The Autobiography of Tom Horror' ed. Shirley Neuman, introduction Gordon Peacocke, Longspoon/NeWest 1989; co-author 'From Cliché to Archetype' (with Marshall McLuhan) Viking 1970; 'The woman taken in adultery' one of a number of short plays, published and unpublished in 'Prairie Performance: An Anthology of Short Plays' ed. Diane Bessai NeWest 1980; Collection of short stories, ed. Shirley Neuman NeWest forthcoming; recipient Gov. Gen.'s Medal for Poetry 1955; Candn. Govt. Grant for theatre study in Paris 1956; Assoc. Marshall McLuhan Centre for Culture & Technol. Univ. of Toronto 1968–69; invented number-grid verse form 1976; mem. Studio Theatre Players; Home: 3612 Place Rd., Nanaimo, B.C. V9T 1M8.

**WATSON HENDERSON, Ruth,** ARCT, LRCT; composer; b. Toronto, Ont. 23 Nov. 1932; d. Frederick W. and Margaret T. (Hehn) W.; e. Royal Conservatory of Music ARCT 1950, LRCT 1952; Mannes College of Music 1952–54; formerly married to Donald S. s. Stuart and Orba Henderson 23 June 1956; children: Karen, Deborah, Anne-Marie, David; studied at Royal Conservatory with Viggo Kihl and Alberto Guerrero until 1952; concert pianist with many solo appearances on the CBC; Accompanist, Festival Singers of Canada under Elmer Iseler 1968–78; Toronto Children's Chorus 1978– ; Ont. Youth Choir 1980s; as well as choral compositions has written for piano, organ, string orch., winds, brass, & percussion; compositions are pub. in Canada and U.S. & performed internationally; Organist, Eglinton Un. Ch.; has written commissioned works for Guelph Spring Festival, the Oriana Singers, the Ont. Youth Choir, the Toronto Children's Chorus, the Elora Festival; Prize Winner, Internat. Comp. for Women Composers, Mannheim, Germany 1989; recipient, Assn. of Canadian Choral Conductors National Choral Award for 'Voices of Earth' as the outstanding choral composition for 1990–92; Mem., Candn. Music Centre; Candn. League of Composers; Assn. of Candn. Women Composers; Royal Candn. College of Organists; SOCAN; selected compositions: 'Missa Brevis' 1974; 'Musical Animal Tales' 1979; 'Through the Eyes of Children' 1981; 'Songs of the Nativity' 1984; 'Creation's Praise,' 'Crazy Times' 1986; 'The Last Straw' 1990; 'Five Ontario Folk Songs,' 'Voices of Earth' 1991; 'The Travelling Musicians' 1994; Home: 23 Birchview Blvd., Toronto, Ont. M8X 1H4.

**WATT, Donald Richard;** stockbroker; b. Raymore, Sask. 5 Feb. 1912; s. Richard Paul and Minnie Agnes

Burns (Lee) W.; e. High Sch., Raymore, Sask. (Grad. 1930); Reliance Sch. of Comm. Regina, Sask.; m. Edna Mae, d. James Tate, 23 May 1935; HON. DIR., WATT CARMICHAEL INC.; Hon. Dir., Consolidated Morrison Explorations Ltd.; Salesman, Beatty Washing Machines, Toronto, 1931–32; Manager, Dominion Stores Ltd., Toronto, 1932–34; Manager and Comptroller, Williams, McLean & Bell, Stockbrokers, Toronto, 1934–37; Asst. Comptroller and Manager, H. R. Bain & Co., Stockbrokers, Toronto, 1937–40; Gen. Mgr., Yolles Furniture Co. Ltd., Toronto, 1940–49; Sales Mgr., Wallace Silversmiths, Wallingford, Conn., 1949–53; Special Rep., Newling & Co., Stockbrokers, Toronto, July 1953–Mar. 1954; Pres., G. W. Nicholson & Co. Ltd. 1954–69; Salesman, Grant Johnston Ltd. 1969–71; Chrmn. of Bd., Watt Carmichael Securities 1971–81; Protestant; recreations: golf; Clubs: Portmarnoch Golf (Ireland); Rosedale Golf; Pine Tree Golf (Fla.); Home: One Benvenuto Place, Apt. 605, Toronto, Ont. M4V 2L2.

**WATT, Douglas G.D.,** B.Sc., M.Sc., M.D., Ph.D.; research scientist; b. Montreal, Que. 30 Sept. 1944; s. Bruce L. and Doris E. (Dodds) W.; e. McGill Univ. B.Sc. 1965, M.Sc. 1969, M.D. 1969, Ph.D. 1974; m. Suzanne d. Louis and Anna Gauthier 31 May 1969; children: Katherine, Heather, Kirsty, Richard; DIRECTOR, AEROSPACE MEDICAL RESEARCH UNIT, MCGILL UNIV. 1988– ; Intern, Royal Victoria Hosp. 1969–70; Medical Research Council Fellow, McGill Univ. 1970–74; M.R.C. Postdoctoral Fellow, Univ. of Arizona 1974–75; NASA, Ames Rsch. Ctr. 1975–76; M.R.C. Scholar, McGill Univ. 1976–81; Assoc. Prof. 1981–87; Prof. 1987– ; Mem., Soc. for Neuroscience; Candn. Physiological Soc.; Candn. Soc. of Aerospace Med.; Aerospace Med. Assn.; Profl. Corp. of Physicians (Que.); recreations: sailing, skiing; clubs: Beaconsfield Yacht; Home: 137 Chartwell Cres., Beaconsfield, Que. H9W 1C2; Office: 3655 Drummond St., Montreal, Que. H3G 1Y6.

**WATT, Duncan Ray,** B.Eng., M.B.A., P.Eng.; university administrator; b. Saskatchewan; e. Royal Military College of Can. B.Eng. (First Class Hons.) 1974; Univ. of Ottawa M.B.A. 1982; married with two children; ASSOCIATE VICE-PRESIDENT (FACILITIES), UNIV. OF REGINA 1985– ; Consulting Engineer, Candn. Forces Winnipeg 1974–76; Project Engr., Eagle River Bridge, Yukon 1976–77; Unit Commander, Chilliwack, B.C. 1977–79; Staff Officer, Nat. Defence H.Q. 1979–80; Facility Engineer, Dept. of Nat. Defence, Candn. Forces Base, Calgary, Alta. 1982–83; Facility Planner, Sask. Advanced Edn. & Manpower 1984–85; Mem., Sask. Assn. of Profl. Engineers; Assn. of Physical Plant Administrators; Council of Educational Facility Planners; Office: Regina, Sask. S4S 0A2.

**WATT, Fergus William,** B.Sc.; association executive; b. Lachine, Que. 24 May 1957; s. William George and Shiela Mary (Barron) W.; e. Ohio Univ. B.Sc. (Hons.) 1980; EXECUTIVE DIRECTOR, WORLD FEDERALISTS OF CANADA 1985– ; freelance writing, travel 1980–83; Rsch. Assoc., Optima Consultants in Applied Soc. Rsch. 1983–85; Mem. of Council, World Federalist Movement (main governing body of 22 World Federalist orgns.; Dir., World Federalist Found.; editor: 'Canadian World Federalist' (quarterly jour.); recreations: soccer; clubs: Lusitania Soccer Club of Ottawa (player & coach), Algonquin College Women's Soccer Team (coach); Home: Box A4, Ch. des Sables, RR 1, Wilson's Corners, Que. J0X 3J0; Office: Suite 207, 145 Spruce St., Ottawa, Ont. K1R 6P1.

**WATT, Frank William,** B.Litt., M.A., Ph.D.; educator; writer; b. Humboldt, Sask. 1 Sept. 1927; s. Cecil Dennis and Esther Kathleen (Balsam) W.; e. Kitsilano High Sch. Vancouver 1946; Univ. of B.C., B.A. 1950; Oxford Univ. (Rhodes Scholar) B.A. 1952, B.Litt. 1954, M.A. 1956; Univ. of Toronto, Ph.D. 1957; m. June d. Peter and Dushi Reilly 19 June 1954; children: Tessa, Nicholas; PROF. EMERITUS OF ENGLISH, UNIV. COLL., UNIV. OF TORONTO; Lectr. Univ. of Toronto 1956; Visiting Commonwealth Prof. Leeds Univ. 1960–61; Prof. of English, Univ. Coll., Univ. of Toronto 1964; author: 'Steinbeck' 1962; 'It's Over It's Beginning' poetry 1986; ed. 'Matthew Arnold, Poetry' 1964; co-ed. 'Essays in English Literature From the Renaissance to the Victorian Age' 1965; assoc. ed. Univ. of Toronto Quarterly 1960–65; ed. 'Letters in Canada' Univ. of Toronto Quarterly 1959–66; various articles, reviews Candn. lit., Candn. labour hist., poems and short stories numerous mags.; mem. League Candn. Poets; Candn. Equestrian Fedn.; Ont. Tennis Assn.; recreations: riding (show-jumping), tennis, squash; Club: Aurora Highlands; Home: R.R. 1, Schomberg, Ont. L0G 1T0; Office: University College, Univ. of Toronto, 15 Kings College Circle, Rm. H012, Toronto, Ont. M5S 1A1.

**WATT, Gordon E.,** CLU; retired insurance executive; b. Toronto, Ont. 10 Oct. 1930; s. Robert and Marion Anne Viola (Durnford) W.; e. York Mem. C.I. 1949; m. Vera d. Walter and Violet Pitts 25 Aug. 1951; children: Cheryl, Kenneth, Deborah, Stephen; Extve. Vice-Pres. & C.O.O., Life Underwriters Assn. of Can. 1987–90; Bookkeeper, Life Underwriters Assn. of Can. 1949–52; Office Mgr. 1952–56; Extve. Sec. 1956–63; Dir. of Admin. 1964; Dir., Field Serv. 1965–72; Asst. Gen. Mgr. 1972–80; Vice-Pres. & Gen. Mgr. 1980–84; Sr. Vice-Pres. & Gen. Mgr. 1984–86; Grad., Chartered Life Underwriter 1973; Chrmn., Adv. Bd., Christ Church (Anglican) Stouffville 1985–86; recreations: boating, snowmobiling; Clubs: Toronto Bd. of Trade; Inst. of Assn. Extves.; Home: R.R. 2, Stouffville, Ont. L4A 7X3.

**WATT, Graham McTavish;** advertising writer; b. Montréal, Qué. 6 Feb. 1934; s. James Stewart and Marjorie Helen (Annett) W.; e. West Hill and Westmount High Sch. Montréal Sir George Williams Univ.; m. Wendy d. James and Dorothy Maclaren 17 Sept. 1966; children: Kate Maclaren, Alexander McTavish, Thomas Mackenzie, Emily Graham; PRES. WATT BURT ADVERTISING INC. 1981– ; Montréal Sr. Writer McKim Advertising 1960–63; Grey Advertising Montréal and New York 1963–70, Vice Pres. and Assoc. Creative Dir. 1968; Vice Pres. Creative Services McKim Advertising, Montreal 1970, Vice Pres. & Creative Dir. 1977; Candn. Juror, Cannes World Advertising Film Festival 1978; co-recipient; Candn. TV Festival Silver Bessie for The Long Distance Feeling 1977; Internat. Gold Clio Best Copywriting 1977; World Advertising Film Festival Cannes Bronze Lion for Thank You Very Much Milk 1980; Advertising Club of New York ANDY for Milk 1980; Mktg. Awards Gold for Best Campaign Milk 1980; Bessie, Gold for Best Comm. Irreplaceable Milk 1983; Toronto Art Dirs. Club Gold Medal, Milk 1983; Mktg. Awards, Gold for Milk 1984; Judges Choice Award milk animation 1984; Internat. Film & TV Festival New York Gold Medal for Irreplaceable Milk; Bronze Bessie Irreplaceable Milk 1985; Toronto Art Directors Club Gold Medal for Television 1985; conceived, wrote and directed 5-part TV series on Cross-Country Skiing, PBS Network U.S.A., winner Silver Medal Internat. Film & TV Festival New York 1982; Co-winner 1991 Bronze Bessie for Lambada Bread Dance; Co-winner 1991 Fritz Speiss Award for lifetime contribution to television advertising; Dir., ECS School; recreations: cross-country skiing, sailing, sea kayaking; Home: 1545 Docteur Penfield, Apt. 602, Montréal, Qué. H3G 1C7; Office: 1110, 1350 Sherbrooke St. W., Montréal, Qué. H3G 1J1.

**WATT, Keith Gary,** B.A.; writer, broadcaster; b. Winnipeg, Man. 8 June 1951; s. Gordon Lloyd and Jean Eva W.; e. Trent Univ. B.A. 1976; m. Melanie d. Robert and Mary (Twigg) White 28 Dec. 1977; children: Morgan Boyle, Ursula Watt, Aureol Watt; independent broadcaster, journalist & film-maker for CBC, Globe & Mail & other nat. pubns. 1987– ; 1980–87: Producer, CBC Radio (Prince Rupert & Edmonton), Broadcast & Journalism Instr., CBC Radio, Bd. of Dir., Western Canada Magazine Awards Found., Pres., 123 Swim Productions Ltd.; Candn. Assn. of Journalists Award 1991; Jack Webster Award as B.C.'s top journlaist 1990; B'nai Brith Media Human Rights Award 1989; author: '123 Breathe! The Way to Teach Freestyle' 1990; co-author & editor of book on new approach to swim instructon; recreations: swimming, running; Home: 4345 Jericho Circle, Vancouver, B.C. V6R 1G1; Office: 305 – 1110 Hamilton St., Vancouver, B.C. V6B 2S2.

**WATT, Lynn Alexander Keeling,** M.S., Ph.D., D.Eng.; educator; b. Winnipeg, Man. 25 Oct. 1924; s. Alexander Robb and Mary Isabelle (Keeling) W.; e. Elem. and High Schs. Winnipeg, Man.; Univ. of Man. B.Sc. 1947; Univ. of Chicago M.S. 1951 (Univ. Fellowship 1947); Univ. of Minn. Ph.D. 1959; Carleton Univ. D.Eng. (honoris causa) 1989; m. Pauline Marion d. late Christian Oliver Einarson 18 Aug. 1948; children: Martha Bjorg Isabel (Mrs. J. Jurkovic), Laura Geraldine (Mrs. K. Nyback), Paula Lynn, Graham Alexander Kristinn; Pres., Waterloo County Unitarian Fellowship 1993– ; Extve. Vice Chrmn., Ont. Council on Grad. Studies 1983–86; Dean of Grad. Studies, Univ. of Waterloo 1972–83, Acting Dean of Rsch. 1988–89 and Prof. of Elect. Engn. 1966–90, Adjunct Prof. (retired) 1990– ; Lectr. Dept. Physics Univ. of Man. 1948–49, 1951–52; Asst. Research Offr. Atomic Energy of Canada Ltd. Chalk River Nuclear Labs. 1952–55; Research Fellow Dept. Elect. Engn. Univ. of Minn. 1955–59; Asst. Prof. of Elect. Engn. Univ. of Wash. 1959, Assoc. Prof. 1962, Prof. 1966; Chrmn. Ont. Council on Grad. Studies 1976–78; Co-ordinator, Ont. Centres of Excellence 1987– ; author various research papers on magnetics and semiconductor materials and devices; Pres. Candn. Assn. Grad. Schs. 1977–78 (Vice Pres. 1976–77); mem. Inst. Elect. & Electronics Engrs.; Am. Phys. Soc.; Candn. Assn. Physicists; Candn. Soc. Higher Educ.; Sigma Xi; Unitarian; recreations: tennis, cross-country skiing, gardening, reading; Home: 193 Mohawk Ave., Waterloo, Ont. N2L 2T4.

**WATT, Roland Browning,** Q.C., B.A., LL.B.; barrister and solicitor; b. Toronto, Ont. 27 Sept. 1944; s. Matthew Raymond and the late Juanita Beatrice (Browning) W.; e. Upper Can. Coll. 1962; Univ. of West. Ont., B.A. 1965; Univ. of Toronto Law Sch., LL.B. 1968; called to Bar of Ont. 1970; cr. Q.C. 1982; Counsel, Raymond & Honsberger 1990–92 (Partner 1970–90); read law with Blake, Cassels & Graydon 1968–69; former Chrmn., Ont. Licence Suspension Appeal Bd.; Dir. & Past Pres., Don Mills Found. for Sr. Citizens, Inc.; Mem., Professional Advisory Council, North York General Hospital Foundation; Mem., United Ch. of Can.; Law Soc. of Upper Can.; Candn. Bar Assn.; Co. of York Law Assn.; Council of Candn. Administrative Tribunals; recreations: art, music; Club: Granite; Home: 78 DeVere Gardens, Toronto, Ont. M5M 3E9.

**WATTS, Reginald Michael,** B.A.Sc., P.Eng.; business executive, managment consultant; b. Ottawa, Ont. 28 Aug. 1937; s. Captain Reginald Wallace and Eugenia Rose (Chudyk) W.; e. St. Patrick's Coll. H.S. 1956; Royal Roads, Candn. Services Coll. 1958; Royal Military Coll., dipl. in engr. 1960; Univ. of Toronto B.A.Sc. 1961; children: Bryan Michael, Suzanne Patricia, Stephen William; PRESIDENT, THE STRATQUEST GROUP LTD. 1987– ; Navigator / Flight Lt., 405 Squadron R.C.A.F. 1961–64; engineering & marketing positions, Litton Systems & Barringer Rsch. 1964–71; Vice-Pres., Huntec '70 Ltd. 1971–76; Div. Dir., Trench Electric & Vice-Pres. & Gen. Mgr., Highway Trailers Ltd. 1976–81; Vice-Pres., VMR Corporate Planning Group 1981–87; Dir., Tesla 10 Holdings Ltd.; APEO Council Commendation Cert. 1968; John Griner Award, Candn. Soc. of Assn. Extves. for Outstanding Service 1991; Chrmn. of the Bd., The Amyotrophic Lateral Sclerosis (Lou Gehrig's Disease) Soc. of Canada; Mem., Assn. of Profl. Engrs. of Ont. 1966–80 (York Chapter Extve.); Candn. Soc. of Assn. Extves. 1986– (var. nat. cttes.); Planning Forum; frequent author of articles & monographs such as 'The Role of Volunteers in Non-Profit Organizations' 1990; recreations: sailing, scuba diving; clubs: Royal Military Coll. Club of Canada (Toronto Branch); Home: 1039 Fair Birch Dr., Mississauga, Ont. L5H 1M4; Office: Suite 130, 5925 Airport Rd., Mississauga, Ont. L4V 1W1.

**WATTS, Ronald Lampman,** O.C., M.A., D.Phil., LL.D.; educator; b. Japan 10 March 1929; s. Candn. missy. parents; e. Univ. of Toronto, B.A. 1952; Oxford Univ., Oriel Coll. (Rhodes Scholar), B.A. 1954, M.A. 1959, D.Phil. 1963 (Can. Council Fellowships 1959–61); LL.D. Trent Univ., Queen's Univ. 1984, Royal Military Coll. of Can. 1986, Univ. of Western Ont. 1987; m. Donna Catherine Paisley 1954; PROF. OF POLITCAL STUDIES, QUEEN'S UNIV. 1965– ; joined Queen's University as Lecturer in Pol. Philosophy 1955, Warden, Men's Residences 1956–59, Asst. Prof. of Pol. Studies 1961, Assoc. Prof. 1963; Asst. Dean, Fac. of Arts and Sci. 1964–66, Assoc. Dean 1966–69, Dean 1969–74; Principal and Vice Chancellor 1974–84; Dir., Institute of Intergovernmental Relations 1988–93; Nuffield College, Oxford University (on leave from Queen's) 1959–61, 1985; Candn.-Commonwealth Exchange Scholar to Australia 1968; Visiting Fellow, Australian Nat. Univ., Canberra 1968; Ford Foundation Visiting Prof., Inst. of Adm., Univ. of Ife, Ibadan, Nigeria 1969; Consultant, Uganda Govt. re E. African Fed. 1963; consultant, Dept. of Secy. of State, Canada, re citizenship in fed. systems 1970–74; consultant, Constit. Planning Comte., Govt. of Papua New Guinea 1974–75; mem., Task Force on Cdn. Unity 1978–79; consultant, Fed-Prov. Rel. Office, Gov't. of Can., re constitutional conferences, 1980; Asst. Secretary to the Cabinet (Constitutional Affairs) Federal-Provincial Relations Office, Government of Canada 1991–92; Visiting Lectr., Britain, USA, Australia, N.Z., Belgium, Germany, Switzerland, Nigeria, India, Malaysia, South Africa, Asia and Canada; has been active in univ. affairs at prov. and nat. level incl. Chrmn. Council Deans Arts & Science Ont. 1971–73; Chrmn., Council of Ont. Univ. 1979–81; Exec. Assn. of Univ. and Coll. of Can., 1975–77, 1979–81, 1982–84; mem., Council Assn. of Commonwealth Universities, 1978, 1982–84; mem., Secondary Education Review Comte. (Ont.) 1980; Comte. on Future Role of the Universities (Ont.) 1980–81; Commission on Future Devel. of Univs. of Ont. 1984; mem. Commonwealth Adv. Group on Distance Ed. 1986–87; Chrmn., New Zealand Univs. Review Ctte. 1987; Pres., Council for Canadian Unity 1983–84, Vice-Chrmn. 1990–91; Chrmn. Adv. Bd. of Encounters with

Canada 1982–91; Gov. Donner Canadian Foundation 1979–88; Pres., Can. Assn. of Rhodes Scholars 1991–93; mem., Ed. Adv. Bd., 'Publius: the Journal of Federalism' 1988– ; Pres., Internat. Assn. of Centres for the Study of Federalism 1991– ; Bd. Mem. and Chrmn. Rsch. Ctte., Institute for Research on Public Policy (Canada) 1989–91, 1992– ; Officer, Order of Canada 1980; author: 'New Federations: Experiments in the Commonwealth' 1966, rev. ed. 1968; 'Multicultural Societies and Federalism' 1970; 'Administration in Federal Systems' 1970; co-author: 'Intrastate Federalism in Canada' 1985; co-ed.: 'Canada: The State of the Federation' 1988, 1989, 1990, 1993; 'Options for a New Canada' 1991; also book chapters, comnd. reports and articles in various learned and prof. journs.; recreation: sailing (Past Vice-Commodore, Kingston Yacht Club 1966; Chief Class Offr., Sailing, Olympics 1976), aviation history and modelling (Secy., Kingston R.C. Modellers 1988–89); Home: Apt. 105, 185 Ontario St., Kingston, Ont. K7L 2Y7; Office: Inst. of Intergovernmental Relations, Queen's University, Kingston, Ont. K7L 3N6.

**WAUGH, Douglas Oliver William,** M.Sc., Ph.D., M.D.C.M., F.R.C.P.(C), LL.D.; educator; essayist and writer; b. Hove, Sussex, Eng. 21 Mar. 1918; s. Oliver S., M.D. and Helen A. (Champion) W.; e. Pub. and High Schs., Winnipeg, Man.; Univ. of Man., 1935–38; McGill Univ., M.D.C.M. 1942, M.Sc. (Path.) 1948, Ph.D. (Path.) 1950; Dalhousie Univ., LL.D. (honoris causa) 1992; m. Sheila Louise, d. late Dr. G. Lyman Duff, 16 Jan. 1971; ESSAYIST AND WRITER 1983– ; Extve. Dir., Assn. Candn. Med. Colls. 1975–83; Demonst. Path., Asst. in Surg. Path., Path. Inst., McGill Univ. 1946–47; Grad. Med., Research Fellow, N.R.C. of Can., Dept. of Path., Path. Inst., McGill Univ. 1947–50; Assoc. Prof. of Path., Univ. of Alta. 1950–51; McGill Univ., 1951–58; Assoc. Prof. of Pathol., Queen's Univ. 1958–61, Prof. 1961–64, and Pathol., Hotel Dieu Hosp., Kingston 1958–64; Prof. and Head, Dept. of Pathol., Dalhousie Univ. and of V.G. Hosp. N.S., Pathol. Inst. 1964–70; Dean, Faculty of Med., Queen's Univ. 1970–75 Vice Princ., Health Sciences there 1971; served in 2nd World War, 1942–46 with R.C.A.M.C.; service in Can. and N.W. Europe; Dir., Nat. Cancer Inst. (Pres. 1974–76); Candn. Cancer Soc.; Medical Adviser, N.S. Div., Candn. Heart Foundation; Chrmn. (1964–65) Candn. Cytology Council; Chrmn., Medical Research Council Assessment Group for Pathology, 1967–68; mem., Nat. Comte. on Physician Manpower 1974–83; Council Roy. Coll. of Physicians and Surgeons of Can. 1969–70; mem., Behav. & Soc. Adv. Council, Alcoholic Beverages Medical Res. Found. 1982–86; Nat. Vice Pres., Can. Authors Assn. 1991– ; author: 'Maudie of McGill: Dr. Maude Abbott and the Foundations of Heart Surgery'; co-author: (with Robert B. Kerr) 'Duncan Graham: Medical Reformer and Educator'; recipient, Queen's Jubilee Medal; 'Professor of the Year' Dalhousie Medical Faculty 1967; Mem. Bd. of Accreditation, Candn. Assoc. University Schs. of Nursing; Candn. Assn. of Pathol.; Am. Assn. of Path. & Bacter.; Internat. Acad. Path.; Am. Soc. for Exper. Path.; Alpha Omega Alpha; Home: 183 Marlborough Ave., Ottawa, Ont. K1N 8G3.

**WAUGH, Richard E.,** B.Comm. (Hons.), M.B.A., F.I.C.B.; banker; b. Winnipeg, Man. 23 Dec. 1947; s. Earl F. and Francis M. (Richardson) W.; e. Univ. of Man. B.Comm. (Hons.) 1970; York Univ. M.B.A. 1974; m. Lynne d. Victor and Winifred Zenone April 1974; children: David, Stephen, Christopher; SENIOR EXTVE. VICE PRES. CORPORATE BANKING, BANK OF NOVA SCOTIA 1992– ; Dir., ScotiaMcLeod Inc. 1993– ; Sr. Vice Pres., Corporate Banking, Bank of Nova Scotia 1983–91, Extve. Vice Pres. 1991–92; ; Pres. and Dir. Bank of Nova Scotia Trust Co. 1985–92; Clubs: National; Granite; Metropolitan; Office: Scotia Plaza, 44 King St. W., Toronto, Ont. M5H 1H1.

**WAVERMAN, Leonard,** B.Com., M.A., Ph.D.; university professor; b. Toronto, Ont. 18 Oct. 1941; s. Solomon and Edith (Cargotch) W.; e. Univ. of Toronto, B.Com. 1964, M.A. 1965, M.I.T., Ph.D. 1969; m. Hélène d. Marie-Jeanette Paré and André Boiziau 2 Feb. 1984; PROF. OF ECON., UNIV. OF TORONTO 1977– ; Dir., Centre for Internat. Studies 1989– ; Rsch. Assoc., Inst. for Policy Analysis, Univ. of Toronto 1968– ; Asst. Prof. of Econ. 1968–72; Assoc. Prof. 1973–77; Extve. Counc., Internat. Assn. of Energy Econ. 1979–82; Bd. Mem., Ont. Energy Bd. (Part-time); Bd. Mem., Ont. Telephone Service Commn. 1989– ; Mem., Nat. Assn. of Regulatory Utility Commns. 1978–80, 1989– ; Mem., Candn. Cooperation Law and Policy Ctte., Candn. Council for Internat. Business 1992– ; Dir., PROFMEX, The Consortium for Rsch. on Mexico 1992– ; Visiting Scholar, Sloan Sch., M.I.T. 1976; Dept. of Econ., Stanford Univ. 1976; Visiting Prof., INSEAD Jan-June 1991, ESSEC April-June 1993; Mem., Am. Econ. Assn.; Candn. Econ. Assn.; Ed. Bd., 'Energy Economics' 1979– ; Assoc. Ed., 'Canadian Journal of Economics' 1976–80; Editor, 'The Energy Journal' 1990– ; co-author: 'The Energy Question' 2 vols. 1974; 'Petro-Canada, An Analysis of Control, Accountability and Financial Viability' 1988; 'Costs and Productivity in the Automobile Industry' 1992; Home: 52 Poplar Plains Rd., Toronto, Ont. M4V 2M8; Office: 170 Bloor St. W., 5th Floor, Toronto, Ont. M5S 1T9.

**WAXMAN, Albert Samuel,** B.A.; actor; director; producer; b. Toronto, Ont. 2 March 1935; s. Aaron and Tobie (Glass) W.; e. Univ. of W. Ont. B.A. 1957; Univ. of Toronto Law Sch.; Neighbourhood Playhouse Sch. of the Theatre, New York; London (Eng.) Sch. of Film Technique; m. Sara d. Manuel Shapiro, Winnipeg, Man. 24 Oct. 1968; children: Tobaron, Adam Collier; PRES., ADAMCORP. LIMITED and TOBARON PRODUCTIONS LTD.; actor/dir. or writer on over 500 TV episodes and films, commercials, documentaries and industrials London, New York, Hollywood, Montreal, Toronto, theatre in London and New York; repertory theatre Eng. and summer stock New Eng. and Can.; TV series incl. 'King of Kensington' C.B.C. 1975–80; 'Circus International with Al Waxman' C.B.C. 1979, 1980; 'Moments In Time with Al Waxman' P.B.S. 1983–84; 'Cagney & Lacey' (1981–88) 1988; 'Missing Treasures: The Search For Our Lost Children with Al Waxman' Global TV Network 1991–92 and 1992–93; recipient Actra awards Best Performance in a Continuing Role 1976, Best Acting Performance in TV (Earle Grey Award) for 'The Winnings of Frankie Walls' 1981; Metro Toronto Community Involvement Award 1980; Queen's Silver Jubilee Award 1977; recipient Luminous Award, Am. Women in Film 1986; Nancy Susan Reynolds Award, Ctr. for Population Options 1988; Scott Newman Award for Directing 'Maggie's Secret', CBS TV 1990; Nat. Campaign Chrmn. Candn. Cancer Soc. 1979–81; Big Brothers: Variety Club; Official Spokesman for the Heart & Stroke Found. of Ont. 1987–88; Chrmn., Acad. of Candn. Cinema & Television 1988–92; Medical Centre for Maternal and Fetal Medicine in Jersusalem's Shaare Zedek Hospital named for Albert Waxman and his wife Sara; recipient, B'nai Brith Canada Humanitarian Award 1989; Audio-Visual Library estab. in Al and Sara Waxman's names at B'nai Brith Canada's Nat. Human Rights Bldg. in Toronto 1989; Mem. Bd. of Dirs., Stratford Festival; Mem., Founders' Council of the Candn. Film Centre; Mem. Dirs. Guild Can.; Acad. Candn. Cinema; Assoc. of Candn. T.V. & Radio Artists; Screen Actors Guild, Directors Guild of America; recreations: tennis, travel; Address: 138 Rosedale Valley Rd., Toronto, Ont. M4W 1P7.

**WAYE, John Stewart,** Ph.D.; scientist; molecular geneticist; b. Hamilton, Ont. 14 May 1958; s. the late John Walter and Vivian I. (Stewart) W.; e. Univ. of Guelph, B.Sc. 1981; McMaster Univ., M.Sc. 1984; Univ. of Toronto, Ph.D. 1986; m. Jane d. Bud and Irene Richardson 15 Oct. 1983; children: Andrew Walter, Stacey Marie; CIVILIAN MEM., ROYAL CANADIAN MOUNTED POLICE, MOLECULAR GENETICS SECTION 1988–90; responsible for devel. & implementation of DNA analysis; expert witness in 1st Candn. court case in which DNA evidence was introduced April 1989; Adjunct Prof., Univ. of Ottawa; Assoc. Mem., Rsch. Inst., Children's Hosp. of E. Ont. 1990– ; Asst. Prof., Dept. of Pathology, McMaster Univ.; Co-Director, Provincial Hemoglobinopathy DNA Diagnostic Laboratory; author/co-author over 50 rsch. articles; recreations: ice hockey, fishing: Home: 164 Quaker Cres., Hamilton, Ont.; Office: 1200 Main St. W., Hamilton, Ont. L8N 3Z5.

**WAYGOOD, Ernest Roy,** M.S.A., Ph.D., F.C.I.C., F.R.S.C.; educator; b. Bramhall, Cheshire, Eng. 26 Oct. 1918; s. Edward Samuel and Alice (Harrison) W.; e. Macclesfield, Cheshire Mill Hill Elem. Sch. and Cheadle Hulme Secondary Sch. 1935; Reaseheath Agric. Coll. 1936; Ont. Agric. Coll. B.S.A. 1941 (Cheshire Co. Univ. Scholarship in Agric. 1937–41, Whitehead Scout Scholarship 1937–39); Univ. of Toronto M.S.A. 1947, Ph.D. 1949; m. Adorée Magdalyn Woolf-LeBrooy 30 Dec. 1950; one d. Pamela Mimi; PROF. EMERITUS, UNIV. OF MAN. since 1979; Assoc. Dir. Biomass Energy Inst. Winnipeg; Asst. Prof. of Bot. McGill Univ. 1949–52, Assoc. Prof. 1952–54; Research Assoc. Nat. Research Council 1950; Prof. and Head of Bot. Univ. Man. 1954–74; Prof. 1974–79 (ret. Emeritus); Visiting Prof. of Agron. Univ. of Ill. 1958; Dir. Algal Project (Nat. Research Council Devel. Grant) 1974–77; Lalor Foundation Research Award 1956; served with RCAF 1941–45, Pilot RAF Transport Command 24 Sqdn., 512 Sqdn. Mediterranean & W. Africa Theatres, Ferry Command Dorval, Que.; Assoc. Ed. 'The Plant Biochemical Journal' (India) 1974; 'Canadian Journal Botany' 1971; over 85 scient. publs.; mem. Candn. Soc. Plant Physiols. (Pres. 1960); Anglican; recreations: swimming; Home: #802 - 1245 Quayside Dr., New Westminster, B.C. V3M 6J6.

**WAYMAN, Morris,** Ph.D., F.R.S.C., F.C.I.C., F.A.A.A.S., P.Eng.; educator; consultant; b. Toronto, Ont. 19 March 1915; s. Harry and Martha (Alt) W.; e. Univ. of Toronto B.A. 1936, M.A. 1937, Ph.D. 1941; m. Sara d. Joseph and Margaret Zadkin 9 Jan. 1937; two s. Michael Lash, Thomas Ethan; ADJUNCT PROF. OF CHEM. ENG., UNIV. OF ALBERTA 1993– ; Pres. and Prin. Morris Wayman Ltd. 1966– ; consulting assignments Can., U.S.A., Brazil, Sweden, UN; mem., Pioneering Rsch. Canadian International Paper Co. 1941–52; Tech. Dir., Columbia Cellulose Co. Ltd. 1952–58; Rsch. Dir., Sandwell International, Consultants 1958–63; Prof. of Chem. Eng. & Applied Chem. and Prof. of Forestry, Univ. of Toronto 1963–93; Hon. Fellow, Innis Coll. Univ. Toronto; Chrmn., Candn. Wood Chem. Symposium 1982; author & prin. ed. 'Guide for Planning Pulp and Paper Enterprises' 1973; author 'Wealth and Welfare' 1978; 'Biotechnology of Biomass Conversion: fuels and chemicals from renewable resources' 1990; over 160 sci. papers; holds 16 patents; Office: Suite 206, 11650 79th Ave., Edmonton, Alta. T6G 0P7.

**WAYNE, Hon. Elsie Eleanore,** LL.D., D.P.A.; politician; b. Shediac, N.B. 20 April 1932; d. Paxton Lee and Ada Catherine (Cook) Fairweather; e. Saint John H.S. grad.; Saint John Vocational Business College; St. Thomas Univ. Hon. LL.D.; m. Richard s. Harry and Betty W. 4 July 1956; children: Stephen Paxton, Daniel Alan; MEMBER OF PARLIAMENT (Saint John) 1993– ; 1st elected to Saint John Common Council 1977; served three, three-year terms; 1st elected as Mayor, City of Saint John 1983; re-elected 1986, 1989, 1992; first woman Mayor in Canada's first incorporated city; 1st elected to H. of C. (Saint John) 1993; operates family business with husband; life-long community activist incl. charitable and church work & establishment of a workshop for the physically handicapped; Maclean's Magazine list of top 10 upcoming politicians in Canada 1987; only civic leader invited to make submission to 'If I Were Prime Minister'; recipient of several awards incl. Red Triangle Award, YM-YWCA (for outstanding service to the community) 1992; Comnr., Citizen's Forum on Canada's Future; Mem., Bd. of Gov., Univ. of N.B.; Econ. Devel. Adv. Bd., City of Saint John; Salvation Army Adv. Bd.; Fed. of Candn. Municipalities (2 cttes.) Saint John Boys' & Girls' Club Endowment Fund; 2nd Battalion Delancey's Brigade; Extve. Mem., Cities of N.B.; Dir., Market Sq. Corp.; Saint John Found.; Saint John Harbour Devel. Comn.; United Way of Greater Saint John; Saint John Non-Profit Housing; Hon. Pres., Chair & Mem. of num orgns.; P.C.; Home: 25 Holland St., Saint John, N.B.; Office: House of Commons, Ottawa, Ont. K1A 0A6.

**WAYNE, Jack,** B.A., M.A., Ph.D.; university professor, publisher; b. Windsor, Ont. 25 April 1939; s. Irving and Eva (Slopen) W.; e. Univ. of Toronto B.A. 1961; Univ. of Michigan M.A. 1963; Univ. of Toronto Ph.D. 1971; m. Susan d. Irving and Silvia Warren 1982; children: Andrew, Timothy, Ian, Nathaniel Silva, Adam Silva, Sarah; DIRECTOR, TRANSITIONAL YEAR PROGRAMME, UNIV. OF TORONTO 1986– ; Prof., Dept. of Sociology 1968– ; taught at Univ. of Dar es Salaam 1969–71; Visiting Fellow, Cambridge Univ. 1977–78; Founder & Publisher, Canadian Scholars Press Inc. 1986– ; Bd. of Dir., Woodgreen Community Centre 1966–68; Vice-Pres., Univ. of Toronto Fac. Assn. 1984–85; Home: 211 Grenadier Rd., Toronto, Ont. M6R 1R9; Office: 49 St. George St., 2nd Floor, Toronto, Ont. M5S 1A1.

**WEARING, Joseph,** D.Phil.; university professor; b. London, Ont. 15 Sept. 1936; s. Joseph and Marjorie Eleanor (Thompson) W.; e. London Central C.I.; Univ. of West. Ont., B.A., Mus.G.Paed 1958; Univ. of Toronto, M.A. 1959; Oxford Univ., B.A. 1961, D.Phil. 1965; m. Susan d. Harold and Dorothy Soanes 1964; divorced; children: Peter Thompson, Alison Jane, Timothy Soanes; PROF., POL. STUDIES DEPT., TRENT UNIV. 1967– ; Asst. Prof., Pol. Sci., Bishop's Univ. 1963–67; Dept. Chair 1990–93; Special Advisor on Policy, Sec. of State 1973; S.F. Glass Gold Medal, Econ. 1958; IODE War Mem. scholarship 1959–61; dinner guest of Govt. of Can. in Honour of Canadians who have achieved excellence in the Arts & Sciences (H.M. The Queen & H.R.H. The Duke of Edinburgh were present) 1977; Bd. of Dir., Peterborough Symph. Orch. 1976–81; Conductor, Coventry Singers 1967–75;

Toronto Gay Men's Chorus 1989–92; Anglican; mem., Candn. Pol. Sci. Assn.; author: 'The L-Shaped Party: The Liberal Party of Canada' 1981, 'Strained Relations: Canadian Parties and Voters' 1988; 'The Ballot and its Message: Voting in Canada' 1991; recreations: music, cooking, swimming, cycling; clubs: Downtown Swim Club; Mayfly; Home: 38 Walmsley Blvd., Toronto, Ont. M4V 1X6; Office: Peterborough, Ont. K9J 7B8.

**WEATHERILL, John Frederick William,** B.A., LL.B., LL.M.; labour relations executive; b. Oakville, Ont. 3 Aug. 1932; s. John Frances and Elda Evelyn (Stinson) W.; e. Univ. of Toronto, B.A. 1954, LL.B. 1957; Harvard Univ., LL.M. 1958; called to Bar of Ont. 1960; m. Stephanie d. Douglas and Elaine Goodman 1957; divorced 1985; children: Timothy, Andrew, Katherine; CHRMN., CANADA LABOUR RELATIONS BOARD 1989– ; Asst. Prof., Osgoode Hall Law Sch. 1960–63; Univ. of West. Ont., Law 1963–64; part-time Prof., Univ. of Ottawa, Law 1975–78; Vice-Chrmn., Ont. Labour Relations Bd. 1964–67; full-time practice as labour-mngt. arbitrator 1968–89; Chrmn., Crown Employees Grievance Settlement Bd. (Ont. 1980–84); Arbitrator, Candn. Railway Off. of Arbitration and Grievance Comnr., Inco Metals Limited & United Steelworkers of Am. 1968–83; Bd. Mem. & Adjudicator, PSSRB 1970–86; Bd. of Gov., Nat. Acad. of Arbitrators 1974–77 (Vice-Pres. 1971–76; Chrmn. (Can.) 1971–76; Co-Chrmn. 1986–89; Dir., Rsch. & Edn. Found. 1985–89); Fellow, Chartered Inst. of Arbitrators (U.K.); Anglican; Past Pres., Ont. Labour Mngt. Arbitrators Assn.; Internat. & Candn. Bar assns.; author: 'A Practical Guide to Labour Arbitration Procedure' 1987 and num. periodical articles; recreations: reading, music, tennis; clubs: Cercle univ. d'Ottawa; Home: 24 Belvedere Cres., Ottawa, Ont.; Office: C.D. Howe Bldg., 4th Floor W., Ottawa, Ont. K1A 0X8.

**WEATHERILL, Timothy Douglas Stinson,** A.O.C.A.; artist, writer, composer; b. Toronto, Ont. 8 Mar. 1960; s. John Frederick William and Stephanie Ann (Goodman) W.; e. Lakefield Coll. Sch. 1979; The Exeter Coll. of Art & Design; Ontario College of Art A.O.C.A. 1990; single; showing sculpture and painting since 1984 in Canada and England; collections in Canada, England, France and the United States; compositions used in educational-commercial videos; major sculpture comn. for private firm 1989; work in collection of the Art Bank of Canada, Ottawa; George A. Reid Scholarship, Ont. Coll. of Art; Office: c/o Bau-Xi Gallery Ltd., 3045 Granville St., Vancouver, B.C. V6H 3J9.

**WEAVER, Donald Fredric,** M.D., Ph.D., FRCP(C); university professor; b. North Bay, Ont. 12 July 1957; s. Douglas Andrew and Betty May (Hartrick) W.; e. Queen's Univ. M.D. 1981, Ph.D. 1986; Dalhousie Univ. FRCP(C) 1989; m. Cheryl Anne d. Donald and Claudine Beaton 22 Aug. 1981; children: Colin Alexander, Ian Nicholas; ASSOC. PROF., NEUROLOGY & CHEM., QUEEN'S UNIV. 1992– ; Asst. Prof., Med. & Chem., Queen's Univ. 1989–92; Founder & Dir., Queen's Univ. Epilepsy Clinic 1989– ; Dir., Queen's/IBM Quantum Pharm. Lab. 1992– ; Ont. Min. of Health Career Scientist 1989– ; Vice-Pres., Epilepsy Kingston; Med. Dir., Epilepsy Kingston and Epilepsy Ont.; Dir., Neuroconvulsive Clinic, Rideau Rg. Ctr. for the Developmentally Delayed; S. Weir Mitchell Award, Am. Acad. of Neurology; IBM Supercomputing Award in Health Sci. Rsch. 1991; A. Barbeau Award, Candn. Neurol. Soc. 1991; European Gowers Award, Internat. League Against Epilepsy 1992; Mem., Candn. & Ont. Med. Assns.; Candn. Neurol. Soc.; Am. Acad. of Neurol.; Candn. League Against Epilepsy; Am. Epilepsy Soc.; Candn. Soc. for Chem., Am. Chem. Soc.; Epilepsy Ont.; Edit. Bd. Mem., 'Seizure'; author of journal articles; Home: 27 Collegeview Cres., Kingston, Ont.; Office: Queen's Univ., Kingston, Ont. K7L 3N6.

**WEAVER, John Trevor,** B.Sc., M.Sc., Ph.D.; university professor and administrator; b. Birmingham, England 5 Nov. 1932; s. Hubert Edward and Muriel (Smith) W.; e. Solihull School 1950; Univ. of Bristol B.Sc. (Hons.) 1953; Univ. of Sask. M.Sc. 1955; Univ. of Göttingen Geophysics 1955–56; Univ. of Sask. Ph.D. 1959; m. Ludmilla d. Alexander and Antonina Krawchenko 8 May 1960; children: Andrew, Anthony, Alexandra; PROFESSOR OF PHYSICS, VICTORIA UNIV. 1972– ; Asst. Prof. of Math, Univ. of Sask. 1959–61; Scientific Officer, Defence Rsch. Establishment Pacific Victoria B.C. 1961–66; Asst. Prof., Univ. of Victoria 1966; Assoc. Prof. 1967; Acting Chair, Dept. of Physics & Astronomy 1978–79; Chair 1980–88; Acting Dean of Science 1988–89; Prof., School of Earth & Ocean Sciences 1991– ; Dean of Science 1993– ; Visiting scholar, Cambridge Univ. 1972–73; Univ. of Edinburgh 1979–80, '89 Collaborateur Scientifique, Observatoire Cantonal, Neuchâtel, Switz. 1984, '90; Coronation Medal 1953; German Acad. Exchange Scholarship 1955–56; Royal Soc. & Nuffield Found. Commonwealth Bursary 1979; NSERC/Royal Soc. Bilateral Exchange Grant 1989; NSERC/Swiss Nat. Sci. Found. Bilateral Exchange grant 1990; B.C. Asia Pacific Univ. Scholars Award 1991; NSERC operating grants annually 1966– ; Fellow, Royal Astronomical Soc.; Mem., Am. Geophysical Union; Candn. Geophysical Union; Eur. Geophysical Soc.; Candn. Assn. of Physicists; author: 'Mathematical Methods for Geo-Electromagnetic Induction' 1994; guest editor: 'Geophysical Surveys' vol. 6, nos. 1/2 1983; author/co-author of num. sci. papers in geophysical & physical journals; Home: 1651 St. Francis Wood, Victoria, B.C. V8S 1X5; Office: Div. of Science, Fac. of Arts & Sci., Univ. of Victoria, Victoria, B.C. V8W 3P4.

**WEBB, Anthony Allan,** B.A., B.I.M.; banker; b. Lincoln, Nebraska 24 May 1943; s. Robert McGraw and Ruth Irene (Good) W.; e. Univ. of Colorado, B.A. 1965; Thunderbird Grad. Sch. of Internat. Mngt., B.I.M. 1970; m. Micheline d. Marcel and Yvette Touchette 10 July 1971; children: Annie, Christian; PRESIDENT AND C.E.O., ROYAL TRUST CORPORATION OF CANADA 1993– ; Lt., U.S. Navy 1965–69; joined Royal Bank, held var. positons in Montreal, London, England & Toronto 1970–80; Vice-Pres., Merchant Banking 1980; Sr. Vice-Pres. 1982; Dir. Gen., Royal Bank of Can. (Suisse) 1984; Sr. Vice-Pres., Corp. Banking (Europe) 1988; Chrmn., Royal Bank of Canada (Suisse); (Channel Islands); Sr. Vice-Pres., Personal Financial Services 1992; clubs: Baur au Lac (Zurich), Overseas Bankers Club (London, Eng.); Home: 48 Suncrest Dr., Don Mills, Ont. M3C 2L3; Office: Royal Trust Tower, 3rd Floor, P.O. Box 7500, Station A, Toronto, Ont. M5W 1P9.

**WEBB, Clifford Wellington,** M.A., Ph.D.; educator; b. Prescott, Ont. 21 May 1925; s. Walter George and Ruby Marguerite (Lake) W.; e. Prescott High Sch. 1943; Univ. of W. Ont. B.A. 1951, M.A. 1952; Univ. of Toronto Ph.D. 1956; children: Marianne Elizabeth, Jane Penelope, Thomas Neil Walter; RETIRED PROF. OF PHILOS., UNIV. OF TORONTO; served with RCAF 1943–46; Prof. of Philos., Univ. of Waterloo summer 1966; Adm. Offr. Govt. Can. 1952–53; cons. various rsch. foundations; journalist, ednl. subjects 'The Globe and Mail,' 'Maclean's' and other publs.; frequent contbr. 'Journal of Philosophy' and 'Idealistic Studies'; recipient Sir Joseph Flavelle Fellowship; Univ. of Toronto Open Fellowship; Royal Soc. Fellowship; mem., Candn. Philos. Assn.; affiliation Un. Empire Loyalist Soc.; Anglican; Liberal; recreations: piano, hiking, chess, mathematics; Home: 66 Oakmount Rd., Apt. 1102, Toronto, Ont. M6P 2M8.

**WEBB, Donald Irving,** B.A., B.Com., F.C.A.; financial consultant; b. Saskatoon, Sask. 1 Feb. 1920; s. Lewis Charles and Alice (Hyslop) W.; e. Kennedy Coll. Inst., Windsor, Ont.; Queen's Univ., B.A. (Hons. Math. and Econ.) 1943, B.Com., 1946; C.A. (Ont.) 1949; m. Dorothy Isobel, d. Andrew Nesbitt, Kingston, Ont.; 22 May 1943; children: Ian Donald Andrew, Barbara Allison; with Clarkson, Gordon, Chart. Accts., Toronto, Ont., 1946–55 latterly as a Partner; Partner, J.H. Crang & Co., Stock Brokers, Toronto, Ont., 1955–59; Pres. Merrill Lynch, Pierce, Fenner & Smith of Canada Ltd. 1969 and subsequently Chrmn., Merrill Lynch Royal Securities Ltd. till 1972 since when a Financial Consultant; served in 2nd World War; R.C.N.V.R., 1942–45 (N. Atlantic); mem., Inst. Chart. Accts. Ont.; recreation: golf, tennis; Clubs: National; Granite; Rosedale Golf; Lost Tree (Fla.); Address: 23 Country Lane, Willowdale, Ont. M2L 1E1.

**WEBB, Phyllis,** O.C., B.A.; poet; b. Victoria, B.C. 8 Apr. 1927; d. Alfred Wilkes and Mary (Patton) W.; e. St. Margaret's Sch.; Univ. of B.C., B.A. 1949; McGill Univ.; Officer of The Order of Canada 1992; CCF candidate 1949 (youngest nominated at that time); Adjunct Prof., Creative Writing Dept., Univ. of Victoria 1989–92; sec., freelance broadcaster 1954–74; Teacher, Univ. of B.C. 1960; Pub. Affairs Dept., CBC 1964; Co-Creator & Extve. Prod. 'Ideas' (radio prog.) 1967; Teacher, Creative Writing, Univ. of B.C.; Univ. of Victoria; The Banff Ctr.; Upper Can. Writers Workshop; Writer-in-Res., Univ. of Alta. 1980–81; Gov.-Gen's Award for poetry 1982 ('The Vision Tree: Selected Poems'); Can. Counc. Sr. Arts Award 1987, 1981, 1969; Greatest contrib. to poetry in B.C., B.C. Library Assn. 1972; Can. Counc. Bursary 1963; Candn. Government Overseas Award 1957; Mem., Amnesty Internat. (Candn. Eng. – speaking); The League of Candn. Poets; author: 'Water and Light' 1984, 'The Vision Tree' 1982, 'Sunday Water' 1982, 'Wilson's Bowl' 1980, 'Selected Poems 1954–65' 1971, 'Naked Poems' 1965, 'The Sea Is Also A Garden' 1962, 'Even Your Right Eye' 1956, 'Trio' 1954 (poetry); 'Talking' 1982 (essays); 'Hanging Fire' 1990 (poetry); Home: 128 Menhinick Dr., Salt Spring Island, B.C. V8K 1W7.

**WEBBER, Patrick Neil,** B.Sc., B.Ed., M.A., Ph.D.; business executive; b. Hanna, Alta. 17 Apr. 1936; s. late Charles and Katherine (McAuliffe) W.; e. Univ. of Alta. B.Sc. 1957, B.Ed. 1962, Ph.D. 1973; Univ. of Toronto Meteorol. Office 1962; Univ. of Mont. M.A. 1963; m. Dorothy d. late John and Anna Platzer 3 Aug. 1957; children: Barbara, Carol, Len, Lorne, Dianne; CHRMN., TELUS CORP.; Chrmn., AGT Ltd.; Bd. of Dirs., SNC-Lavalin Group Inc.; Calgary Rsch. and Development Authority; estab. Neil Webber Consulting Ltd. 1989– ; formerly: Min. of Energy, Alta.; Min. of Education, Alta.; Min. of Soc. Serv. & Community Health, Alta.; Assoc. Min. of Telephones for Prov. of Alta.; Chrmn. Alta. Govt. Telephones Comn.; el. M.L.A. Alta. 1975, re-el. 1979, 1982, 1986; Past mem. Mount Royal Coll. Bd. Govs.; Candn. Math. Cong.; Assn. Inst. Research; P. Conservative; R. Catholic; recreation: golf; Home: 210 Edgeview Dr. N.W., Calgary, Alta. T3A 4X5; Office: Floor 26, 411–1 Street S.E., Calgary, Alta. T2G 4Y5.

**WEBBER, William Alexander,** M.D., F.R.C.P.; educator; b. Nfld. 8 Apr. 1934; s. William Grant and Hester Mary (Constable) W.; e. Univ. of B.C. M.D. 1958; m. Marilyn Joan d. late William M. Robson 17 May 1958; children: Susan Joyce, Eric Michael, George David; ASSOC. VICE PRES. ACADEMIC, UNIV. OF B.C. 1990– ; Intern, Vancouver Gen. Hosp. 1958–59; Fellow, Cornell Med. Coll. 1959–61; Asst. Prof. of Anat. present Univ. 1961, Assoc. Prof. 1966, Prof. 1969– , Dean of Medicine 1977–90; author various publs. on structure and function of kidney; mem. Candn. Assn. Anatomists; B.C. Med. Assn.; Candn. Nephrol. Soc.; Am. Assn. Anatomists; recreation: soccer; Office: Vancouver, B.C. V6T 1Z2.

**WEBER, George Brian,** B.Ed., M.A., C.A.E.; association executive; b. Montreal, Que. 18 Apr. 1946; s. Harry and Johanna (Alexopoulos) W.; e. McGill Univ. B.Ed. 1970, M.A. 1974; Advanced Mgmt. Prog., Harvard Univ. 1989; m. Mary d. Frank and Frances Morris 8 May 1976; SECRETARY GENERAL OF THE INTERNAT. FEDERATION OF RED CROSS AND RED CRESCENT SOCIETIES, GENEVA 1993– ; part-time Teacher Protestant Sch. Bd. Greater Montreal 1967–73; contract diver and instr. Dominion Diving Co., Que. 1967–73; voluntary instr./examiner, etc. Candn. Red Cross 1963–73; internat. assignments with Red Cross incl.: team mem. in Vietnam; field delegate in Vietnam with Indochina Operational Group, Internat. Red Cross 1973–74; Disaster Relief Offr. and Chief Del. of League of Red Cross Societies, Geneva 1974–76; Nat. Dir., Internat. Affairs, Candn. Red Cross 1976–81, Nat. Dir. of Programmes 1981–83; Secretary General & C.E.O., Canadian Red Cross 1983–93; Hon. Vice Pres., Candn. Red Cross 1993– ; mem.: Candn. Inst. of Internat. Affairs; Amnesty Internat.; Am. College of Sports Medicine; Candn. Soc. Assn. Execs.; Candn. Comprehensive Auditing Found.; Bd. of Dirs., Nat. Capital Harvard Business Sch. Alumni Club; author various articles on disaster relief, physiol. and phys. edn.; recipient Vanier Award 1984; Communication and Leadership Award, Toastmasters Internat. 1985; recreations: diving, tennis, squash, skiing; Clubs: Rideau, Harvard, Five Lakes; Home: 29 avenue Budé, 2e étage, 1202 Petit-Saconnex, Switzerland; Office: P.O. Box 372, 1211 Geneva 19, Switzerland.

**WEBER, Irvin E.;** business executive; b. Waterloo, Ont. 28 Oct. 1923; s. Irvin K. and Irene E. (Bingeman) W.; e. Ont. Agric. Coll. 1942–43; m. Dorothea d. R.V. Alles 1947; children: Donald, Brent, Cheryl; VICE-CHRMN., KAUFMAN FOOTWEAR; Bombadier, RCAF 1943–45; United Ch. of Can.; recreations: racquet sports, fishing, motor cycling; Clubs: Westmount Golf & Country; YMCA; Home: 59 Duchess Ave., Kitchener, Ont. N2M 2K2; Office: 410 King St. W., Kitchener, Ont. N2G 4J8.

**WEBER, Stanley G.,** B.Comm., C.A.; financial executive; b. Wilkie, Sask. 18 March 1945; s. Anton and Matilda (Wirachowsky) W.; e. St. George H.S. Wilkie 1963; Univ. of Sask. B.Comm. with distinction 1967; Inst. of C.A.s of Alta. C.A. 1970; m. Sally d. Norman and Mickey Jones 22 July 1972; children: Travis, Bryce, Lydia, Krista, Blain; VICE-PRESIDENT, FINANCE, CHIEF FINANCIAL OFFICER & CORPORATE SECRETARY, SCEPTRE RESOURCES LIMITED 1980– ; Manager of Auditing, Riddell Stead & Co. 1967–73; Asst. Treasurer, Trimac Limited 1973–76; Manager of Auditing, Peat Marwick Thorne 1976–80; recreations: running, tennis, golf; clubs: Calgary Petroleum, Calgary

Winter; Home: R.R. 1, Airdrie, Alta. T4B 2A3; Office: 2000, 400 – 3rd Ave. S.W., Calgary, Alta. T2P 4H2.

**WEBSTER, Alexander Robertson (Sandy),** B.A.; actor; b. Fort William, Ont. 30 Jan. 1923; s. William and Sarah Jane (Stewart) W.; e. Sr. Matric. Fort William Coll. Inst.; Queen's Univ. B.A. (Hons. Hist., Pol., Eng.) 1949; Grad. Lorne Greene Acad. Radio Arts, Toronto, 1950; m. Ruth Marie, d. Harry S. Fennell, Brantford, Ont. 16 Oct. 1959; children: Bruce, Gail, Craig; served with R.C.A.F. 1942–45; comnd. Air Bombardier, discharged with rank of Flying Offr.; an actor in Candn. radio, television, film and theatre since 1950; leading roles in CBC 'Stage Series'; Thomas Craig, Head of Farm Family in CBC Ont. Farm Broadcast; frequent appearances in Toronto and Candn. regional theatres; mem. both Shaw and Stratford Festival Cos.; Pres., Candn. Actors Equity Assn. 1982–85; mem., Bd. of Dirs., Equity Showcase Theatre, Toronto; mem. of the Corp., Candn. Theatre Sch., Montreal; Pres., Actors' Fund of Canada; recipient, 'The Silver Ticket Award,' Toronto Theatre Alliance for distinguished contrib. to the theatre 1991; Talent Group, 387 Bloor St. E., Agent; United Church; recreations: swimming, golf; Home: 178 Bingham Ave., Toronto, Ont. M4E 3R3.

**WEBSTER, Hon. Arthur V.,** B.Sc., M.Sc.; cabinet minister; b. Toronto, Ont. 31 Dec. 1946; s. Arthur V. and Mary J. (Holowaty) W.; e. Runnymede Collegiate Institute; Univ. of Waterloo, Ont.; Dalhousie Univ., N.S.; m. 30 May 1981, separated 1989; children: Matthew, Arbor; Min. of Tourism & Min. of Renewable Resources 1989; Administrator; Extve. Dir., Yukon Sports Federation 1976–79; Councillor, Dawson City Council 1984–85; First elected to Yukon Legis. Assembly for Klondike Riding g.e. 13 May 1985; re-el. g.e. 1989; Deputy Speaker & Ch. Comm. of the Whole 1985–89; N.D.P. House Leader 1991– ; Party Pol.: N.D.P.; Religion: United.

**WEBSTER, Donald Dickson;** financial executive; b. Winnipeg, Man. 12 June 1933; s. William John and Margret Cathlene (Dickson) W.; e. articled with Miller, MacDonald & Co., predecessor firm to Deloite, Plender Haskins and Sells, CA 1956; m. Islay Marion d. Louis W. and Florence Irene Roppel 26 Sept. 1959; children: Craig Donald, Dean Alan, Blair Edward, Noreen Ellen; PRES., WEBSTER MANAGEMENT INC. 1990– ; Deloitte, Haskins & Sells 1950–58; Chevron Standard Limited 1958–72; Dir. of Fin. & City Treas., City of Calgary 1972–74; Vice-Pres., Fin. & Treas., Westmin Resources Limited 1974–85, Extve. Vice-Pres., Fin. & Admin. 1985–90; Dir., Trilogy Resource Corp. 1992– ; Dir., Co-Enerco Resources Ltd. 1993– ; Past Dir., Westmin Resources Limited; F.C.A. (Alta.); Past Chrmn., Fin. Extve. Inst. of Can.; Past Dir., Arthritis Soc. of Alta.; recreations: golf, curling, gardening; Clubs: Ranchmen's; Calgary Petroleum; Calgary Winter; Silver Springs Golf; Home: 140 Varsity Cres., N.W. Calgary, Alta. T3B 2Z4.

**WEBSTER, Gordon Bruce,** F.C.A.; chartered accountant; b. Kilmarnock, Scot. 23 Sept. 1938; s. Gordon and Margaret Gracie W.; e. Churchill High Sch. Man. 1957; Univ. of Man. C.A. 1963; F.C.A. Ontario 1985; m. Maris d. Lillian and Henry Keil 28 Jan. 1961; children: Bruce, Blair, Heather; PARTNER, PRICE WATERHOUSE 1974– ; joined present firm Winnipeg 1958, Supr. 1965, Mgr. 1967, trans. Toronto 1972, Partner 1974, Mng. Partner Mississauga 1977–86, Mng. Partner Winnipeg 1991– ; Vice Pres. Finance and Adm. Lease Corp. Ltd. 1986–88; recipient Community Service Award City of Winnipeg 1972; Chrmn. Credit Valley Hosp. 1986–90, Vice Chrmn. 1979–86; Gov. Metro Toronto YMCA 1987–90; Campaign Chrmn. Un. Way Peel 1986; Pres. Mississauga Bd. Trade 1981; Chrmn. Bus. Devel. Adv. Bd. City of Mississauga 1982; mem. Pan Am. Games Ctte. Winnipeg 1967; mem. Inst. C.A.'s Ont. (Chrmn. Practical Experience Requirements 1984–86); Candn. Inst. C.A.'s; Inst. C.A.'s Man.; Campaign Comm. United Way, Winnipeg 1992 and 1993; Inst. C.A.'s Man. Council 1992– ; Bd. of Dirs., Winnipeg Health Sciences Centre 1992– ; Bd. of Dirs., Royal Winnipeg Ballet 1992– ; Bd. of Management, Manitoba Club 1993– ; Premier's Internat. Business Advisory Council 1993– ; recreations: golf, curling; clubs: Credit Valley Golf & Country; Mississaugua Golf & Country; St. Charles Country Club; Manitoba Club; Office: 2200 One Lombard Place, Winnipeg, Man. R3B 0X7.

**WEBSTER, Jill R.,** B.A., M.A., Ph.D., F.R.S.C.; university professor; b. London, U.K. 29 Sept. 1931; d. Harold James and Dora Elena (Andreini) W.; e. St. Mary's Hall and Brighton & Hove H.S.; Univ. of Liverpool B.A. 1962; Univ. of London B.A. 1978; Univ. of Nottingham M.A. 1964; Univ. of Toronto Ph.D. 1969; PROF., UNIV. OF TORONTO 1968– ; St. Michael's College 1979– ; Assoc. Dean, Fac. of Arts & Science, Univ. of Toronto 1978–81; Dir., Centre for Medieval Studies 1989–94; Chair, Grad. Dept. of Spanish & Portuguese 1993–94; Fellow, Royal Soc. of Canada 1991; Pres., Am. Acad. of Research Historians of Medieval Spain 1990– ; author of publications on Francesc Eiximenis, Mendicant Orders in Spain esp. 'Els Menorets: The Franciscans in the Realms of Aragon from St. Francis to the Black Death (1348)' 1993; Home: Apt. 403, 158 Crescent Rd., Toronto, Ont. M4W 1V2; Office: 81 St. Mary St., Toronto, Ont. M5S 1J4.

**WEBSTER, John Bruce,** B.A., B.F.A.; artist; b. Ottawa, Ont. 9 June 1947; s. Gilbert Sutton and Margaret Alena (Bruce) W.; e. Nepean H.S. Ottawa; Carleton Univ. B.A. 1968; Mount Allison Univ. B.F.A. 1972; m. Valerie d. Thomas and Mary Roos 21 Nov. 1987; step-d. Laura Hull; solo exhns. incl. Robertson Galleries Ottawa 1974–77 inclusive, 1979, 1981 1983, 1986, 1989, 1991, 1993; Shaw-Rimmington Gallery Toronto 1976; Welch Gallery McLaren's Landing, Ont. 1982, 1984; Andrew Dickson's Gallery Pakenham, Ont. 1987, 1988, 1990, 1991; Galerie Franklin Silverstone Montreal 1989; Kaspar Gallery Toronto 1990; rep. various pub., corporate and private colls. incl. Agnes Etherington Gallery Kingston, Can. Council Art Bank, City of Ottawa Coll., Rideau Club; recreations: reading, gardening; Address: General Delivery, Burnstown, Ont. K0J 1G0.

**WEBSTER, John Malcolm,** B.Sc., Ph.D., D.Sc., D.I.C., F.L.S.; educator; b. Wakefield, Eng. 5 May 1936; s. Colin Ernest and Marion (Waterhouse) W.; e. Imp. Coll. Univ. London B.Sc. 1958, Ph.D. 1962, D.Sc. 1988, A.R.C.S., D.I.C.; m. Carolyn Ann d. Hon. George Argo McGillivray, Toronto, Ont. 15 May 1970; children: Gordon John, Sandra Jane; PROF., SIMON FRASER UNIV.; Mem. Science Council of Can. 1982–89; Premier's Advisory Council on Science & Technology 1991– ; Agric. Research Council Scholar, Imp. Coll. Univ. London 1958–61; Research Scient. Rothamsted Exper. Stn. Eng. 1961–66; Canada Dept. of Agric., Belleville, 1966–67; Assoc. Prof. of Biol. Sciences present univ. 1967, Prof. 1971–, Chrmn. 1974–76, Dean of Science 1976–80; Assoc. Vice Pres., Academic, and Dean of Grad. Studies 1980–85; Ed. 'Economic Nematology' 1972; Co-editor: 'Plant Parasitic Nemotodes in Temperate Agriculture' 1993; author over 200 publs. in parasitology and nematology; mem., TRIUMF project 1976–85 (Chrmn. Bd. Mgmt. 1982–84); Pres., West. Cdn. Univ. Marine Biol. Station Soc. 1979–83; Past Pres., Soc. of Nematologists; mem. Candn. Soc. Zool.; Candn. Phytopathol. Soc.; European Soc. Nematology; and other nat. and foreign socs.; Fellow of the Soc. of Nematologists; Fellow of the Inst. Biol.; Fellow of the Linnean Soc. of London; Dir., Arts, Sciences and Technology Centre, Vancouver (Pres. 1981–82); Tynehead Zoological Soc., Vancouver; Mem. Bd. of Govs., Vancouver Public Aquarium (Pres. & Chrmn. 1990–92); Home: 5551 Molina Rd., North Vancouver, B.C. V7R 4P3; Office: Burnaby, B.C. V5A 1S6.

**WEBSTER, Lorne C.,** B.E., LL.D.; company officer; b. Montreal, Que. 19 Sept. 1928; s. Colin Wesley and Jean (Frosst) W.; e. St. Georges Sch., Westmount, Que.; Lower Canada Coll., Montreal, Que.; McGill Univ., B.E. (Mech.); Concordia Univ. LL.D. (honoris causa); m. Beverley Meredith Evans 17 Oct. 1969; children: Adam Wesley, Lorne Howard, Beverley Meredith, Tegan Ruth; by former marriage Feb. 1954, children: Linda Ann, Brenda Alice, Lorne Campbell; CHRMN. AND CHIEF EXEC. OFFR. PRENOR GROUP LTD.; Chrmn., Bolton Tremblay Funds Inc.; Canaprev Inc.; RHW Foundation; Pres., Bolton Tremblay Planned Resources Fund; Bolton Tremblay Taurus Fund; Canabam Ltd.; Cartier Tower Ltd.; Imperial Windsor Group Inc.; Montreal Securities Corp.; Dir., Bank of Montreal; Bankmont Financial Corp. (Chicago, Ill.); Consumers Packaging Ltd.; Murphy Oil Co. Ltd.; Calgary, DSMA-TATA Inc. (Bombay, India); Dale Parizeau Inc.; H.B. Fuller Co. Ltd. (St. Paul, Minn.); Helix Investments Ltd.; Kativo Chemical Industries Ltd. (Costa Rica); Murphy Oil Corp. (El Dorado, Arkansas); National Reinsurance Co. of Canada; Schaenen Wood & Assoc. Inc. (New York); Vulcan Assets (Dominion) Ltd.; Wyant & Co. Ltd.; Chrmn., Lower Canada College Foundation; Pres., Julius Richardson Convalescent Hospital; Old Brewery Mission; Gov., Olympic Trust of Canada; Trustee, Stanstead College; Advisory Bd., McGill Faculty of Medicine; Montreal Neurological Inst.; TVX Gold Inc.; Univ. of Vermont, School of Business Adm.; INCAE (Instituto Centroamericano de Administracion de Empresas-Managua, Nicaragua; mem., United Church; recreations: skiing, tennis, golf, racquets, squash; Clubs: Montreal Badminton & Squash; Montreal Racket; Mount Royal; Royal Montreal Golf; University Club of Montreal; Boston Tennis & Racquet (Mass.); The Brook Club (N.Y.); Cambridge Club (Toronto); Cercle de l'union Interalliée (Paris); Hillside Tennis; Jesters; Société Sportive du Jeu de Paume et de Racquets (Paris); York Club (Toronto); Home: 56 Belvedere Circle, Westmount, Que. H3Y 1G8; Office: 1100 University St., Suite 1200, Montreal, Que. H3B 3A4.

**WEBSTER, Norman Eric,** M.A.; journalist; b. Summerside, P.E.I. 4 June 1941; s. Eric and Elizabeth (Paterson) W.; e. Bishop's Coll. Sch. Lennoxville; Bishop's Univ. B.A. 1962; St. John's Coll. Oxford (Rhodes Scholar) M.A.; m. Pat Roop 1966; children: David, Andrew, Derek, Gillian, Hilary; PRES., R. HOWARD WEBSTER FOUNDATION; Corr. Que. Legis. Assembly for The Globe and Mail newspaper 1965, Ottawa bureau 1966, Ed. The Globe Magazine 1967–68, Peking Corr. 1969–71, Queen's Park bureau chief Toronto 1972–78, Eur. Corr. London 1978–81, Asst. Ed. 1981–83; Ed.-in-Chief, 1983–89; Ed-in-Chief, The Montreal Gazette 1989–93; recipient Nat. Newspaper Award 1971, 1988; author 'Discovering Today's China' 1972; 'The Pope in Poland' 1979; recreations: hockey, triathlon; Office: Suite 2912, 1155 René Lévesque Blvd. W., Montréal, Que. H3B 2L5.

**WEBSTER, William Graham,** B.Sc., M.A., Ph.D.; educator; b. Ottawa, Ont. 6 Jan. 1944; s. Edward Clark and Inez Graham (Patton) W.; e. McGill Univ. B.Sc. 1965; Cornell Univ. M.A. 1966; Pa. State Univ. Ph.D. 1970; m. Anne L. Godden-Webster; children: Audrey Reiko, Christine Yumi, Heather Joyce Godden; DEAN, FACULTY OF SOCIAL SCIENCES and PROF. OF PSYCHOL. BROCK UNIV. 1991– ; Cons. in Psychol. Ottawa Rehab. Centre 1984–91; Sci. Cons. Inst. for Stuttering Treatment & Rsch. Univ. of Alta. 1986– ; Asst. Prof. Carleton Univ. 1969, Assoc. Prof. 1974, Prof. 1982–91, Chrmn. of Psychol. 1979–86; Woodrow Wilson Fellow 1965–66; mem. Bd. of Dirs., Niagara Rehabilitation Centre 1992– ; mem. and Chair, Mental Health Bd. Ottawa-Carleton Regional Dist. Health Council 1988–91; author: 'Principles of Research Methodology in Physiological Psychology' 1975; co-author: 'Facilitating Fluency: Transfer Strategies for Adult Stuttering Treatment Programs' 1989; over 30 sci. articles profl. jours., book chapters; Fellow, Candn. Psychol. Assn.; mem. Am. Psychol. Assn.; recreations: bicycling, swimming; Home: 34 Millbridge Cres., Fonthill, Ont. L0S 1E1; Office: St. Catharines, Ont. L2S 3A1.

**WEDEPOHL, Leonhard Martin,** B.Sc., Ph.D., F.I.E.E., P.Eng.; electrical engineer; educator; b. Pretoria, S. Africa 26 Jan. 1933; m. Sylvia Andréa Lise (St. Jean); s. Martin Willie and Liselotte (Franz) W.; e. Grey Coll. Bloemfontein 1949; Univ. of Witwatersrand B.Sc. 1953; Univ. of Manchester Ph.D. 1957; two s. Martin, Graham; PROF. OF ELECTRICAL ENGINEERING, UNIV. OF B.C. 1985– ; Vice Pres., Quantic Labs., Winnipeg 1985–86; mem. Science Council, B.C. 1975–79; Gov. B.C. Hydro 1981–84; Gov., B.C. Arts, Sci. and Technology Soc. 1981–84; Dean, Fac. of Engineering, Univ. of Man. 1974–1979; Vice-Chrmn. Manitoba Hydro Electric Bd., Dec. 1978–Aug 1979; Dean, Faculty of Appl. Sci., Univ. of B.C. 1979–85; Chrmn., Implementation Team, Candn. Inst. for Indust. Tech., Winnipeg, July-Dec. 1985; Telecommunications Planning Engr. S. African Electricity Supply Comn. 1954–61; Mgr. L.M. Ericsson, Pretoria 1961–62; Sec. Leader Protection Relay A. Reyrolle & Co., Eng. 1962–64; Lectr. Fac. of Technology, Univ. of Manchester 1964–66, Prof. of Power Systems Engrg. 1967–70, Chrmn. of Dept. 1970–74, Bd. of Govs. 1968–71; mem. N.W. Council for Higher Educ. 1968–72; Gov. Bolton Coll. 1972–74; holds 4 patents on electronic relays for protecting high voltage transmission lines; developed first transistorised protection relay system which went into field service on high voltage transmission line 1958; author numerous papers; Fellow, Inst. of Electrical Engineers, London; Lutheran; recreations: skiing, camping, music; Club: University, Vancouver; Address: Dept. of Elect. Engr., Univ. of B.C., Vancouver, B.C. V6T 1W5.

**WEEDON, Michael G.,** B.A., M.B.A.; executive; b. Toronto, Ont. 7 May 1953; s. Garth Francis Charles and Joan Marie (Ingram) W.; e. Univ. of Toronto B.A. 1974; Univ. of W. Ont. M.B.A. 1976; m. Nora d. Bill and Peggy Dale 24 Aug. 1974; children: Chris, Ryan, John, Robert; PRES., C.E.O., DIR., EPTON INDUSTRIES INC. 1983– ; Vice-Pres. Fin. and Treas. B.F. Goodrich Canada Inc. 1976–83; mem. Bd. of Advrs. Waterloo Wellington Western Bus. Sch. Club; Dean's Hon. List Univ. of W. Ont. Sch. of Bus. 1975, 1976; recreations: squash, tennis, cycling; Club: Waterloo Wellington Western Bus. Sch.; Home: 296 Castlefield Ave., Waterloo, Ont. N2K 2N1; Office: 521 King St. W., Kitchener, Ont. N2G 1C5.

**WEEDON, R. Peter,** B.Sc., M.B.A., FCMC; management consultant; b. Toronto, Ont. 27 Jan. 1949; s. Garth F.C. and Joan M. (Ingram) W.; e. Univ. of Toronto Schools 1967; Univ. of Toronto B.Sc. 1970; York Univ. M.B.A. 1972; m. Diana L. d. Emerson and Muriel Wallace 16 May 1970; children: Amy Jane, Amanda Emily, Alexandra Kate; OFFICE MANAGING PARTNER FOR ATLANTIC REGION, DOANE RAYMOND MANAGEMENT CONSULTANTS 1991– ; Management Trainee, Oshawa Group 1972; entered management consulting profession with H.R. Doane & Co. (predecessor of present firm) 1975; Partner 1980; Dir., Victoria General Hosp. Centre for Clinical Research Limited; Fellow, Certified Mngt. Consultant 1989; Chair, Victoria General Hospital 1992; Pres. Inst. of Cert. Mngt. Cons. of Atlantic Canada 1982; Pres., Inst. of Cert. Mngt. Cons. of Canada 1993–94; Vice-Pres., Jr. Achievement of Mainland N.S. 1988; recreations: masters swimming, golf, genealogy; club: Ashburn Golf; Home: 6 Reed Court, Halifax, N.S. B3M 3L2; Office: P.O. Box 426, Halifax, N.S. B3J 2P8.

**WEERASINGHE, Asoka,** B.Sc., M.Sc., FGAC; poet, communications executive; b. Colombo, Sri Lanka 13 Feb. 1936; s. Arnolis and Janet Matilda W.; e. Univ. of Wales B.Sc. 1967; Memorial Univ. of Nfld. M.Sc. 1970; World Univ. Arizona Hon. Ph.D 1992; m. Jean Y. d. Albert and Florence Guy 21 March 1980; children: Kokila Nelun, Anikka Maya; DIR. OF COMMUNICATIONS AND CULTURAL AFFAIRS, SRI LANKA HIGH COMMISSION; Head, Thematic Research, Nat. Museums of Canada; Head, Exhibits, Nat. Museum of Natural Sciences Canada; Exhibits Mgr., Dept. of Fisheries & Oceans Canada; Major County Award, Greater London Council (U.K.) 1964–67; Dept. Fellowship, Memorial Univ. of Nfld. 1968–70; Brit.-Nfld. Co. Scholarship for Geology 1970; Manifold Poetry Award (U.K.) 1962, '67, '68; Welsh Univ. Eisteddfod Poetry Award 1966; Taras Shevchenko Poetry Award (U.K.) 1967; Govt. of Nfld. & Lab., Arts & Letters, Gold Medal for Poetry 1969; John Lewis Paton Hon. Soc. for Poetry 1968–69, 1969–70; Ont. Arts Council grants 1976, '78, '79, '80, '83, '85, '86; Past Chair, Project Peace for a United Sri Lanka; Pres., Ottawa Buddhist Assn. (1980–81, 1992–93); author: 'Lotus & Other Poems,' 'Another Goodbye for Alfie,' 'Spring Quartet,' 'Poems for Jeannie,' 'Poems in November,' 'Exile 1956–78,' 'Hot Tea and Cinnamon Buns,' 'Home Again Lanka,' 'Selected Poems 1958–1983,' 'Kitsilano Beach Songs' (all poetry); Asst. Editor, 'Vesta's Who's Who of North American Poets'; Home: 2066 Kings Grove Cres., Gloucester, Ont. K1J 6G1; Office: 85 Range Rd., Suite 102–104, Ottawa, Ont. K1N 8J6.

**WEESE, Robert Donald,** B.A., M.Sc.Econ.; corporate executive; b. Chatham, Ont. 4 Feb. 1945; s. Donald James and Alma Irene (Smale) W.; e. Lambton-Kent Dist. H.S.; Univ. of W. Ont. B.A. (Hons.) 1967; Univ. of Wales M.Sc.Econ. 1970; Univ. of London; m. G. Menna d. Wynford and Margaret Jones 15 Aug. 1969; children: Dylan, Bryn; VICE-PRESIDENT, GOVERNMENT AND EXTERNAL RELATIONS, GE CANADA 1991– ; Parliamentary Intern Ottawa 1972–73; Research Asst., House of Commons, NDP Caucus 1973–75; Extve. Dir., Fed.-Prov. & Constitutional Affairs, Govt. of Sask. 1976–82; Asst. Dep. Min., Govt. of Can. Supply & Services 1982–89; Business/Govt. Extve. Exchange 1989–91; Bd. of Dir., Electrical & Electronic Mfrs. Assn. of Can; Chair, Govt. Affairs Ctte.; Commonwealth Scholarship; Canada Council Doctoral Award; U.S. State Dept. Foreign Visitor; Dir., Eye Research Inst. of Can.; Mem., Runnymede United Ch.; Humber Valley Minor Hockey Assn.; United Way of Peel Region; recreations: golf, cottage; Home: 290 Runnymede Rd., Toronto, Ont. M6S 2Y6; Office: 2300 Meadowvale Blvd., Mississauga, Ont. L5N 5P9.

**WEETMAN, Gordon Frederick,** B.Sc.F., M.F., Ph.D.; university professor; b. York, U.K. 24 Apr. 1933; s. Reginald George and Marie (Lawson) W.; e. Univ. of Toronto, B.Sc.F. 1955; Yale Univ., M.F. 1958, Ph.D. 1962; m. Anna Buyko May 1967; children: Joanne, Roger, George; PROFESSOR, FACULTY OF FORESTRY, UNIV. OF B.C. 1978; Rsch. Forester, Pulp & Paper Rsch. Inst. of Can. 1955–71; Prof., Fac. of Forestry, Univ. of N.B. 1971–78; Mem., Assn. of B.C. Profl. Foresters; Assn. des Ing. forestiers du Qué.; Past Pres., Candn. Inst. of Forestry; author of 80 tech. publications; Home: 3567 West 50th Ave., Vancouver, B.C. V6N 3Y3; Office: Vancouver, B.C. V6T 1W5.

**WEGENER, John Frensel,** B.Comm.; financial executive; b. Montreal, Que. 21 Dec. 1939; s. John F. and Molly Jean (Smith) W.; e. Sir George Williams Univ. B.Comm.; m. Jean d. James and Maureen Macklin 1957; children: Deborah, John, Robert, Nancy, Christopher; Extve. Vice-Pres., CIBC Toronto 1990; Canadian Pratt & Whitney Aircraft 1955–71; Nordsen Corp, Amherst, Ohio 1971–74; RJR Macdonald Tobacco 1974–83; Wood Gundy Inc. 1983–90; recreations: golf; clubs: Lambton Country Club; Royal Montreal Country Club; Home: 4 Hartfield Court, Etobicoke, Ont. L9A 3E3.

**WEHRLE, Ernest,** B.Eng., LL.B.; lawyer; b. Winnipeg, Man. 1 Jan. 1940; s. Max A. and Rosa M. (Kirner) W.; e. Royal Military College B.Eng. (Civil) 1962; Univ. of Manitoba LL.B. 1969; m. Erika d. Heinrich and Johanna Holtmann 30 July 1964; children: Deborah, Deanna, Heather, John; PARTNER, D'ARCY AND DEACON; RCAF Navigator 1962–66; stationed in Greenwood N.S. 1963–65; Air Navigation Instructor Winnipeg 1965–66; called to Bar of Man. 1970; Lawyer, Walsh Micay 1970–72; Founding Partner, McJannet Rich 1972; Dir., Inventronics Ltd. 1971–93 (Sec.-Treas. 1971–89); Lecturer, Man. Corp. & Comm. Law/Bar Adm. Course 1976–82 (Course Dir. 1979–82); Lecturer, Winnipeg Real Estate Bd. 1978–86; Mem., Candn. & Man. Bar assns. 1970– ; Dir., Age & Opportunity Centre Inc. 1973–81 (Pres. 1979–81); Catholic Health Assn. of Canada 1984–86; Mem., 5 Govt. Trade & Investment Delegations to W. Germany (2), U.S. (2), China (1); Bd. Chair, Catholic Health Assn. of Man. 1990–92; Chief Candn. Legal Counsel to Mother Teresa 1983– ; recreations: skiing, fishing, sailing, travel; clubs: German Canadian Club of Winnipeg; Office: 1200 - 330 St. Mary Ave., Winnipeg, Man. R3C 4E1.

**WEICHEL, William Lewis,** B.A., B.P.E.; journalist, educator, politician; b. Elmira, Ont. 23 May 1931; s. Hilbert Lewis and Gertrude Elizabeth (Schedewitz) W.; e. Elmira H.S. 1949; Waterloo College 1951; Valparaiso Univ. 1952; Univ. of W. Ont. B.A. 1953; Univ. of Waterloo B.P.E. 1966; Ont. College of Edn. Phys.Ed. (Spec. A) 1954; m. Muriel d. Albert and Vera Hilliard 28 July 1956; children: Blain L., Laurie C., Craig W.; COUNCILLOR, WILMOT TWP. & REGIONAL COUNCILLOR, WATERLOO REGION 1988–94; Journalist, United Press 1952–54 (Montreal, Halifax, Toronto); Teacher, Dept. Head, South Grenville Dist. H.S. 1954–56; Waterloo-Oxford Dist. H.S. 1956–89 (English, History, Geography, Phys. & Health Ed.); Vice-Chair, Region of Waterloo (R.O.W.), Planning & Culture and Water Liaison cttes.; Chair, Envir. Adv. Ctte., R.O.W.; Public Works, Finance, Fire & Emergency, Planning, Parks & Rec. cttes., Twp. of Wilmot; Ecol. & Envir. Adv. Ctte and Tree By-Law cttes., R.O.W.; Board, Laurel Creek Watershed Study; Ont. Traffic Conf.; Bd. of Dir., Grand River Cons. Authority; Bd. of Gov., Wilfrid Laurier Univ. 1988–94; Bd., Festival Country; Steering Bd., K-W Visitors' Convention Bureau; Assn. of Mun. of Ont.; Adv. Bd., Min. of Envir. & Energy; Charter Bd. Mem., Central W. Ont. S.S. Athletic Assn. 1958; Royal Candn. Legion (New Hamburg Br.); recreations: tennis, golf, alpine & nordic skiing; Home: R.R. 2, Petersburg, Ont. N0B 2H0; Office: 150 Frederick St., Kitchener, Ont.

**WEIL, Francis,** M.Sc., Ph.D.; educator; b. Sélestat, France 5 Nov. 1938; s. Gilbert and Claire Simone (Dreyfuss) W.; e. E.N.S. Télécommunications Paris D. Ing. 1961; Dalhousie Univ. M.Sc. 1962, Ph.D. 1968; m. Shiella d. Samuel and Reva Lipton 24 May 1964, divorced; children: Olivier, Sarah-Nadine; PROF OF PHYSICS, UNIV. OF MONCTON 1979– ; joined present Univ. 1968, Chrmn. of Physics 1973–79, Dean of Sciences and Engineering 1980–90, Judge 'Génies en Herbe' Radio Can.; Pres., Conseil francophone pour l'éducation Interculturelle au N.B.; Vice Pres. and Dir. Cadmi Inc.; mem., Tiferes Israel Synagogue; author various publs. math. edn., discrete equations, energy conservation, elem. particles physics; mem., Candn. Assn. Physicists (Counsellor); groupe Dév. Energ. Envir. et Econ., Instut de l'Energie des Pays Francophones (IEPF); APICS (Treas.); Counsellor, ACFAS (Assn. canadienne française pour l'avancement des Sciences) Home: 221 Ave. McBeath, Moncton, N.B. E1C 7A2; Office: Université de Moncton, N.B. E1A 3E9.

**WEILBRENNER, Bernard,** M.A.; archiviste; né à Verdun, Qué. 3 nov. 1929; f. Wilfrid et Alma (Morency) W.; é. Collège de St. Laurent, B.A. 1949; Univ. de Montréal, M.A. (Histoire) 1951; Comm. de la Fonction Publique, Ottawa, Cert., cours en adm. 1958; American Univ., Washington, D.C., cert. en archivistique 1958; ép. Renée Beaulne 4 août 1956; ARCHIVISTE CONSULTANT 1988; Archiviste, Archives Publiques du Canada 1952–63; Dir., Archives Nat. du Qué. 1963–67; Dir., Direction des Archives Historiques, 1967–71; Archiviste fédéral adjoint 1971–86; Conseiller Spécial de l'Archiviste National 1986–88; Prof. d'Archivistique, Univ. Laval 1965–67 et Ecole des bibliothécaires, Univ. d'Ottawa 1970–71; Editeur, 'Rapport des Archives du Québec' 1964–66; 'Etat général des archives publiques et privées,' Archives du Québec 1968; biographies dans 'Dictionnaire biographique du Canada,' tomes I et II; mem., Soc. hist. du Canada (Conseil 1961–62, secrétaire de langue française 1962–69, vice-prés. sec. des archives 1969–70, prés. 1970–71); mem., Conseil Internat. des Archives depuis 1959, corr. pour le Canada 1970–86, membre, comité pour le développement 1976–88; mem., Soc. of Archivists (U.K.) depuis 1960; Soc. hist. de Québec (vice-prés. 1966–67), Féd. des Soc. hist. du Québec (vice-prés. 1967); Assn. des Archivistes du Qué. (prés. 1981); Assn. of Candn. Archivists; Soc. of Amer. Archivists; prés. comité des Archives de l'Inst. pan-am. de géog. et d'hist. 1973–90; Prix de l'Association des Archivistes du Qué. 1983, membre émérite 1987; Médaille de la reine Elisabeth 1977; catholique; residence: 272 avenue Crocus, Ottawa, Ont. K1H 6E9.

**WEILER, Hon. Karen Merle Magnuson,** B.A., LL.B., LL.M., LL.D. (Hon.); judge; b. Regina, Sask. 13 June 1945; d. Edgar Theodore and Rose Emma (Beliveau) Magnuson; e. Spiritwood, Sask.; Nutana Coll. Saskatoon, Sask. (rec'd Assn. Franco-Canadien Prov. Prize in French Lit. 1960; Sask. Govt. Scholarship 1962); Univ. of Sask. B.A., Law Sch 1964–65; Osgoode Hall Law Sch. Toronto LL.B. 1967, LL.M. 1974; m. Robert David Weiler 29 July 1967; two d. Nancy Elizabeth, Catherine Victoria; JUSTICE, ONTARIO COURT OF APPEAL 1992– ; read law with Blake, Cassels & Graydon; called to Bar of Ont. 1969; law practice Weiler, Weiler & Maloney 1969–72; Lectr. in Business Law Lakehead Univ. Sch. of Business evening 1970–72; Instr. in Family Law Bar Admission Course 1975–79; Solr. Ministry of Community & Social Services Legal Services Br. 1973–74; Counsel, Policy Devel. Div. Ministry of Atty. Gen. 1974 becoming Sr. Counsel to 1980; District Court Judge, 1980–89; Justice, Supreme Court of Ontario (Trial Div.) 1989–90; Justice (General Div.) 1990–92; former mem. Ont. Status Women Council; Ont. Comte. Candn. Council on Children & Youth; Ont. Comnr. Uniform Law Conf.; co-author 'Law and Practice Under the Family Law Reform Act (Ontario) to 1988'; author or co-author various articles book chapters; Hon. mem. Phi Delta Phi; participant First Candn. Am. Legal Exchange 1987; Speaker, Nat. Conf. Women's Bar Assoc., Am. Bar Assoc. Annual meeting 1988 and at Am. Judges Assoc. Annual meeting 1988, 'Women in the Judiciary,' 'Comparative Constitutional Rights under the American Constitution and the Canadian Charter of Rights and Freedoms'; mem. The Lawyers Club; Candn. Bar Assn. (mem. Counc. Ont. Br. 1985–86, 1987–88); Candn. Judges Conf.; Candn. Inst. Adm. Justice; Women's Law Assn.; l'Association des juristes d'expression française; R. Catholic; recreations: reading, swimming, golf, tennis, skiing; Home: 11 Anderson Ave., Toronto, Ont. M5P 1H2.

**WEILER, Paul C.,** M.A., LL.M.; b. Port Arthur, Ont. 28 Jan. 1939; s. Gerard Bernard and Mary Marcella (Cronin) W.; e. St. Patrick's High Sch., Fort William, Ont., 1956; Univ. of Toronto, B.A. 1960, M.A. 1961; Osgoode Hall Law Sch., LL.B. 1964; Harvard Law Sch., LL.M. 1965; Univ. of Victoria, hon. LL.D.; m. Florrie Darwin; children: Virginia, John, Kathryn, Charles; HENRY J. FRIENDLY PROFESSOR OF LAW, HARVARD LAW SCHOOL; apptd. Prof. of Law, Osgoode Hall Law Sch., York Univ. 1972; called to Bar of Ont. 1967; joined Faculty Osgoode Hall Law Sch. 1965; Labour Arbitrator 1965–73; Chrmn., Labour Relations Bd. of B.C. 1973–78; Research Consultant, McRuer Royal Comn. on Civil Rights, 1966–67, Woods Task Force on Labour Relations, 1968–69, LeDain Comn. on Drugs, 1971–72, Chief Reporter, Am. Law Institute's Reform of Personal Injury Liability Law 1986–92; Mem., Public Rev. Bd. of the United Auto Workers 1980– ; Impartial Umpire, AFL-CIO 1986– ; Mem., Softwood Lumber Panel - Free Trade Agreement 1992–93; Chief Counsel, President's Commission on the Future of Worker Management Relations 1993– ; author, 'Labour Arbitration and Industrial Change' 1970; 'In the Last Resort: A Critical Study of the Supreme Court of Canada' 1974; 'Reconcilable Differences: New Directions in Canadian Labour Law' 1980; 'Reshaping Workers' Compensation in Ontario' 1980; 'Protecting the Worker from Disability: Challenges for the Eighties' 1983; 'Governing the Workplace: The Future of Labor and Employment Law' 1990; 'Medical Malpractice on Trial' 1991; 'A Measure of Malpractice' 1992; also numerous articles in law journs.; Co-ed., 'Labour Relations Law,' 2nd ed. 1974; 'Cases, Materials and Problems on the Law and Sports' 1993; co-author 'Studies in Sentencing' 1974; 'Enterprise Responsibility for Personal Injury' 1991; mem.

Candn. Bar Association; Candn. Law Teachers; Candn. Assn. Univ. Teachers; Nat. Acad. Arbitrators; Royal Soc. of Canada; National Academy of Sciences, Institute of Medicine; R. Catholic; recreations: golf, skiing, squash, tennis; Home: 7 Follen St., Cambridge, Mass. 02138; Office: Harvard Law School, Cambridge, Mass. 02138.

**WEINER, Hon. Gerry,** P.C., B.A., B.Sc., Ph.M.; former politician; b. Montréal, Qué. 26 June 1933; e. McGill Univ., B.A.; Univ. of Montréal, B.Sc., Ph.M.; St. Thomas Univ., N.B. Honorary LL.D.; m. Judith Rosen 1959; children: Roberta, Mark; Pharm., Norgate Pharmacy 1950–60; Ayerst Labs. 1960–62; Former Sr. Partner, Apothapharm Pharms. 1963–84; City Counc. & Planning Ctte. Mem. Dollard-des-Ormeaux 1978–82; Mem., Rég. intermun. des bibliothèques Pierrefonds 1978–84; Mayor 1982–84; elected M.P. Dollard 1984; Parl. Sec., External Affairs 1984; Employment & Immigration 1985; Min. of State (Immigration), Govt. of Can. 1986–88; Min. of State (Multiculturalism) 1988; Min. of State (Multiculturalism and Citizenship) 1988–89; Secy. of State and Min. of State (Multiculturalism & Citizenship) 1989–91; Min. of Multiculturalism and Citizenship 1991–93 (Min.-Designate of Citizenship 1993); Sworn to the Privy Council 1986; Dir., West Island Bus. Devel. Counc. 1982–84; Co-Chrmn., Emergency Med. Serv. Counc., Dollard-des-Ormeaux 1978–82; Former West Island Co-ord., Urgence Pharmacien; Initiator, 1st Neighbourhood Watch Program, Isl. of Montréal 1978; past extve. mem. of 4 other orgns.; Mem., Cong. Beth Tikvah; Cong. Rodeph Shalom (Founding Pres.); recreation: tennis; Home: 40 Fredmir St., Dollard-des-Ormeaux, Qué. H9A 2R3.

**WEINER, Harvey,** B.A.; association executive; b. Montreal, Que. 20 Feb. 1943; s. Levy and Fanny (Sapolsky) W.; e. Macdonald Coll. Ste-Anne de Bellevue Teaching Dip. 1966; Sir George Williams Univ. B.A. 1969; m. Margaret Rose d. William Edward and Rose Laycock 30 June 1973; one d. Kimberley; DEP. SEC. GEN. CANDN. TEACHERS FEDN. 1988– ; Teacher Prot. Sch. Bd. Greater Montreal 1966–71; Exec. Asst. Montreal Teachers' Assn. 1971, Pres. 1976–80; Pres. Prov. Assn. Prot. Teachers Que. 1980–88; Exec. mem. CEQ-PAPT-PACT Negotiations Comn. 1980–88; Pub. Sector Negotiating Ctte. regarding changes to Que. Legis. on Negotiations 1985; mem. Steering Ctte. Que. Estates Gen. on Quality of Edn. 1985–86; CTF Rep.: UN Assn. in Can. Adv. Ctte. Internat. Literacy Yr. 1988–89, Action Can. Network 1988– ; National Education Organizations Ctte. 1991– ; Mem. Steering Ctte., Candn. Forum on Learning 1993; Steering Ctte. Readers Digest Leadership in Edn. Awards 1989–91; Dir. Alliance Que. 1983–88, mem. Adv. Council 1990; Home: 14 Beaumont, Kirkland, Que. H9J 2R4; Office: 110 Argyle Ave., Ottawa, Ont. K2P 1B4.

**WEINER, Mervyn L.,** B.Com., M.Phil.; consultant; retired development banker; b. Montreal, Que. 30 Oct. 1922; s. Louis and Beatrice W.; e. Strathcona Acad. 1939; McGill Univ. B.Com. gold medallist, 1943; Royal Canadian Artillery 1943–46; Balliol Coll., Oxford Univ. (Rhodes Scholar) M.Phil. 1948; Univ. of Pennsylvania (instructor) 1948–49; Johns Hopkins Univ., Johnson Scholar 1949–51; m. Shirley R. d. Freda and Isadore Hurwitz 26 Aug. 1951; children: Risa Ellen, Lewis Richard; joined World Bank 1951; Gen. and Country Econ. Studies 1951–62; Loan Officer, Operations Div. Chief 1962–65; Econ. Advr., Chief Economist W. Hemisphere 1965–69; Dir. Public Utilities Projects Dept. 1969–72; Dir. Asia Region Projects Dept. 1972–74; Regional Vice-Pres. South Asia 1974–75; Dir.-Gen. Operations Evaluation 1975–84; retired from World Bank 1984; International Consultant 1984– ; Home: 3206 Cummings Lane, Chevy Chase, Maryland 20815.

**WEINFELD, Morton Irwin,** B.A., Ed.M., Ph.D.; university professor; b. Montreal, Que. 20 Sept. 1949; s. Arnold and Irene (Alstock) W.; e. McGill Univ., B.A. 1970; Harvard Univ., Ed.M. 1973, Ph.D. 1977; m. Phyllis d. Sigmund and Nina Zelkowitz 15 June 1975; children: Rebecca, David, Joanna; PROF., SOCIOLOGY DEPT., McGILL UNIV. 1992– ; Assoc. Prof. 1982–92; researcher & cons., govt. & priv. agencies on ethnic relns. & pub. policy; Jewish; Mem., Am. Soc. Assn.; Candn. Assn. of Anthropol. & Sociol.; Candn. Ethnic Studies Assn.; apptd. Mem., Candn. Multiculturalism Adv. Ctte. 1990; author of num. acad. & popular articles on ethnicity, immigration & other topics; co-author (with Harold Troper): 'Old Wounds': Jews, Ukrainians, and the Hunt for Nazi War Criminals in Canada' 1988; (with John J. Sigal) 'Trauma and Rebirth: Intergenerational Affects of the Holocaust' 1989; editor: 'The Jews in Canada' 1993; 'Canada's Jews' 1993; co-editor: 'The Canadian Jewish Mosaic' 1981, 'An Introduction to Sociology' 2nd ed. 1987; Home: 31 Banstead Rd., Montreal W., Que. H4X 1P1; Office: 855 Sherbrooke St. W., Montreal, Que. H3A 2T7.

**WEININGER, Otto,** B.A., M.A., Ph.D.; clinical child psychologist; b. Montreal, Que.; s. Ben and G. (Brazier) W.; e. McGill Univ. B.A. 1950; Univ. of Toronto M.A. 1952, Ph.D. 1954; m. Sylvia d. Morris and Bertha Singer 22 June 1952; children: Lisa Nan, Erica; PROFESSOR OF CHILD-CLINICAL PSYCHOLOGY, ONT. INSTITUTE FOR STUDIES IN EDUCATION, UNIV. OF TORONTO 1970– ; Lectr., Dept. of Psychol., Univ. of W Ont. 1954–56; Clin. Psychol., Mental Health Clinic, St. Thomas, Ont. 1955–66; Lectr. and Rsch. Assoc., Dept. of Psychol., Univ. of Toronto 1956–60; private practice 1956–68; Dir. St. Joseph Treatment Ctr. for Boys 1959–61; Asst. Prof. Inst. of Child Study, Univ. of Toronto 1969–70; developed and directed Madison Ave. Sch. and Clinic 1971–79; Clinical Cons., W. End Creche and Family Serv. 1980–85; developed and cons. to Peel Family Court Clinic 1972–85; Gold Medal Educator of 1980s, Project Innovation, Chula Vista, Calif.; Teaching Award, Ont. Confed. of Univs. (OCUFA) 1986; Ont. Psychological Assn., Div. of Psychoanalysis, 1989 Award for contribution to Psychoanalysis; Stein Award, Ontario Psychological Assoc.; mem. various bds., govt. cttes.; Chrmn. Early Childhood Prog. O.I.S.E. 1981; Sch. and Comm. Psychol. Prog., Dept. of Applied Psychol 1971–74, 1981–82; Hon. Advr. for Rsch., Orgn. Mondiale pour l'Educ. Prescholaire; The Inst. for the Prevention of Child Abuse; ed. 'J. Melanie Klein and Object Relations'; 'International Journal of Early Childhood'; author: 'Play and Education' 1979; 'Out of the Minds of Babes' 1982; 'The Clinical Psychology of Melanie Klein' 1984; 'The Differential Diagnostic Technique: A Visual Motor Projective Test: Research and Clinical Use' 1986; 'Children's Phantasies: The Shaping of Relationships' 1989; 'Third-R Structures: The Math Research Program in Primary Grades' 1991; 'Melanie Klein: From Theory to Reality' 1992; co-author: (with S. Daniel) 'Playing To Learn: The Young Child, the teacher and the classroom' 1992; 'View From the Cradle: Children's Emotions in Everyday Life' 1993; recreations: the arts, antiques of the Art Nouveau and Art Deco periods; Office: 252 Bloor St. W., Toronto, Ont. M5S 1V6.

**WEINMAN, Richard F.,** B.Sc., LL.B., M.B.A.; barrister & solicitor, business executive; b. Heidelberg 6 July 1936; s. J. John and Christine (Schoger) W.; e. Univ. of B.C. B.Sc. 1961, LL.B. 1964; City Univ. Seattle, WA M.B.A. 1990; m. Kay P. d. Miles and H. McCorley 28 Aug. 1965; children: Janine, Michelle, Jason, Michael; VICE-PRES. & SEC., CANFOR CORP. 1969– ; Barrister & Solicitor, Andrews & Co. 1965–69; Dir., B.C. Lung Found. 1985– (Pres. 1989–90); B.C. Lung Assn. (Pres. 1989–90); recreations: golf, squash, skiing; clubs: Vancouver, Mt. Seymour Golf & Country; Home: 1190 Russell Ave., North Vancouver, B.C. V7G 2C3; Office: 3000 – 1055 Dunsmuir St., P.O. Box 49420, Bentall P.S., Vancouver, B.C. V7X 1B5.

**WEINRICH, Peter Henry Moore,** F.R.S.A.; association executive; b. Kelvedon, Eng. 20 May 1932; s. Henry Albert and Kathleen (Moore) W.; e. Earls Colne Grammar Sch.; Leeds Univ.; Brit. Inst. Mgmt. Dip.; m. Sybil Grace d. William and Grace Strachan 6 June 1959 (divorced 1988); children: Heather M., John G., David S.; EXEC. DIR. CANDN. CRAFTS COUNCIL 1974– ; Ex-Dir. M. Joan Chalmers Cultural Centre Foundation Canada Ltd.; Trustee Artisan Business Trust; craftsman, crafts adv. and cons. 1957–74 incl. adv. to govts. & non-govt. agencies Africa, Asia & Caribbean; Internat. Trade Centre/UNCTAD/GATT 1971–73; Govt. of Tanzania 1971–72; Haiti 1975; World Univ. Service Can. 1958–61; Christian Aid (UK) 1963–65; Nat. Service RAF 1950–52; Antiquarian Bookseller 1968–76; mem. Bd. Visitors Boston Univ. 1975–80; recipient Queen's Silver Jubilee Medal 1977; Commemorative Medal for 125th Anniversary of Candn. Confederation 1992; author: 'Social Protest in Canada 1870–1970' bibliog. 1984; 'Bibliographic Guide to Books on Ceramics' 1976; numerous reports, briefs, studies; mem. Assn. Cultural Execs.; former mem. & Sec. Antiquarian Booksellers Assn. Can.; recreations: book-collecting, music, watercolours; Home: 4 Harvard Ave., Ottawa, Ont. K1S 4Z1; Office: 189 Laurier East, Ottawa, Ont. K1N 6P1.

**WEINSTEIN, Deborah,** B.A.; public relations executive; b. Prince Albert, Sask. 26 Oct. 1949; d. Saul Arnold and Florence (Cosman) W.; e. Ecole Vincent D'Indy, Sr. Dip. Music 1966; McGill Univ., B.A. 1970; daughter: Sadie Mae; PRES. & PARTNER, STRATEGIC OBJECTIVES INC. 1983– ; Freelance prod., CBC Radio Network 1971–74; Prod., 'N. Am. Transmission,' Radio Can. Internat. 1974–76; Prod., 'Nightcap,' CBC Radio Network 1976–79 (ACTRA Award, Best Radio Prog. 1977); Feature Reporter, 'The City at Six,' CBC TV News 1979–80; Critic/Entertain. Rep., 'Newshour' 1980–81; Location prod., 'Thrill of a Lifetime,' CTV TV Network 1981–83; Ohio State Award for 'Stroke – A Family Portrait' 1975; Strategic Objectives awards: Assn. for Multi-Image of Can., Gold, Script 1984; Best of Show, Gold and Silver, Script 1983; IABC Award of Merit, Speech Writing 1986; Assn. for Multi-Image of Can., Gold, Video Transfer 1986; IABC Gold Quill Award of Excellence, Media Relations 1987; Retail Counc. of Can., Mktg. Communications Award 1987; IABC Silver Leaf Award, Promotions/Marketing Campaign 1989; IPRA Awards: IPRA Golden World Trophy, Total Communications Program 1990, IPRA Golden World Trophy, Marketing New Product 1992; IPRA Certificates of Excellence: Total Communications Program 1990, Marketing Communications 1990, Public Service 1992, Marketing New Product 1992, Marketing Established Product 1992, Marketing New Service 1992; Extve., Fashion Group Internat., Toronto; mem., ACTRA; IABC; IPRA; Retail Council of Canada 1994 Convention Committee; Office: 184 Front St. E., Suite 701, Toronto, Ont. M5A 4N3.

**WEINSTEIN, Harvey Marvin,** B.Sc., M.D.,C.M.; psychiatrist; b. Montreal, Que. 15 Feb. 1942; s. Louis W. and Bertha (Gertsman) W.; e. McGill Univ. B.Sc. 1963, M.D.,C.M. 1967; Yale Univ. Postdoctoral Fellow in Psychiatry 1968–71; m. Rhona d. Alex and Lotte Strasberg 17 Dec. 1967; DIR. COWELL STUDENT HEALTH CENTER STANFORD UNIV. 1989– ; PRIVATE PRACTICE OF PSYCHIATRY 1993– ; Asst. Prof. of Psychiatry Univ. of Conn. 1971–72; Dir. of Training and of Evaluation & Brief Treatment Dept. of Psychiatry Pacific Med. Center San Francisco 1972–76; Asst. Prof. in Residence, Asst. Chief Psychiatry Service San Francisco VA Hosp., Dept. of Psychiatry Univ. of Cal. San Francisco 1976–77; Clin. Assoc. Prof. of Psychiatry & Behavioral Sci's present Univ., Sr. Staff Psychiatrist present Centre 1977–87, Dir. Counselling & Psychol. Services 1987–89; mem. Rsch. Bd. Spring Found. 1987–89; author 'A Father, A Son, and the CIA' 1988; over 20 publs. med., psychiatry; Fellow, Am. Psychiatric Assn.; mem. Assn. Acad. Psychiatry; Am. Med. Assn.; N. Cal. Psychiatric Soc.; Am. Coll. Health Assn.; Home: 855 Chimalus Dr., Palo Alto, Ca. 94306; Office: Stanford, Ca. 94305.

**WEINSTEIN, William,** B.Sc., P.Eng.; executive; b. Brooklyn, NY 19 Sept. 1925; s. Harry Louis and Bess Helen (Brodach) W.; e. Univ. of Mo., Sch. of Mines, B.Sc. (Civil Engn.); m. Marilyn, d. Louis Hillman, Brooklyn, N.Y., 22 June 1952; children: Lawrence Mark, Judi Lynne, Andrea Jo; EXEC. DIR., CONSULTING ENGINEERS OF ONTARIO 1984– ; Dir., Better Roads Coalition; Community Building Coalition; Past Dir., Toronto Transit Consultants Ltd.; President, SNC/GECO Can. Inc. 1978; Past Chrmn. & Dir. Sandford Fleming Found. (Life Mem. Award); Past Chrmn. Extve. Ctte. & Treas., Found. for Internat. Training; joined U.S. Dept. of Interior, Alaska, as Engr. (Jr.) 1950; Engr. (Field), F. R. Harris, Inc., N.J., 1951, Engr. (Design), N.Y., 1952; Project Engr., Fenco-Harris, Toronto, 1955; Div. Engr. Transport. of FENCO 1959, Vice Pres. Foreign Operations 1965, Sr. Vice Pres. 1968; Pres. and Dir., Fdn. of Can. Engn. Corp. Ltd. (FENCO), 1974; served with U.S. Army during World War II; rank Staff Sgt.; mem. Assn. Prof. Engrs. Mo.; Assn. Prof. Engrs. Ont. (Past Chrmn. Communications Advy. Comte.; Past Chrmn. Consulting Engrs. Div.), Engineering Award for Citizenship; Ed. Bd., Elec. Systems Engineering Publication; recipient Sons of Martha Medal, Officer; Assn. of Consulting Engrs. Ont. (Past Dir.); Roads and Transport Assn. Canada (Past Chrmn. Design Comte., Geom. Design Comte., Tech. Council); Assn. of Consulting Engrs. of Can. (Past Dir.); Ont. Engrg. Heritage Records Found.; Bd. Trade Metrop. Toronto; Tau Kappa Epsilon; Theta Tau, Blue Key; recreations: golf, theatre, music; Clubs: Ontario; Home: 30 Whittaker Cres., Willowdale, Ont. M2K 1K8.

**WEINTHAL, Arthur,** B.A.; broadcast executive; b. Montreal, Que. 12 Jan. 1932; e. McGill Univ., B.A. 1953; VICE-PRES. & DIR., ENTERTAINMENT PROG., CTV TELEVISION NETWORK LTD. 1973– ; News Ed., CFCF Radio 1953–54; Prod. & Prom. Mgr. 1954–55; Radio-TV Prod., Harold F. Stanfield 1955–57; Mgr., Radio-TV Dept., Ronalds Advtg. 1957–59; Dir. 1959–60; Ronalds-Reynolds Advtg. 1960–62; Extve. Prod., CTV TV Network Ltd. 1962–66; Nat. Prog. Dir. 1966–73; program Chrmn., Judging Ctte., CANPRO 1976, 77; Dir. & Vice-Pres., Broadcast Extves. Soc. 1973–76; Dir. & Chrmn., Planning & Policy Ctte., Children's Broadcast Inst.; Mem., Adv. Bd., Telefilm Can. for Candn. Assn. of Broadcasters; Extve. Ctte. Dir.,

Banff TV Found.; Mem., Internat. Council, NATAS; Mem., CTV Mgmt. Ctte.; Office: 42 Charles St. E., Toronto, Ont. M4Y 1T5.

**WEINTRAUB, Stephen Allen,** B.Comm., C.A., LL.B.; business executive; b. Buffalo, N.Y. 29 Sept. 1947; s. Aaron and Bessie (Miller) W.; e. Univ. of Toronto B.Comm. 1969; C.A., Clarkson, Gordon 1972; Osgoode Hall Law Sch., York Univ. LL.B. 1975; m. Teresa d. Ben and Adele Albaum 20 Dec. 1970; children: Aaron, Debra, Robyn; SR. VICE-PRESIDENT & SECRETARY, COUNSEL CORPORATION 1989– ; Treas. & Chief Financial Offr., Unicorp Financial Corp. (now Unicorp Canada Corp.) 1975–80; Sec.-Treas., Pinetree Devel. Co. Limited 1980–83; Vice Pres., Finance & Chief Finan. Offr., Counsel Corp. 1983–89; recreations: golf, tennis, skiing; Home: 36 Mossgrove Trail, Willowdale, Ont. M2L 2W3; Office: Exchange Tower, Suite 1300, P.O. Box 435, 2 First Canadian Place, Toronto, Ont. M5X 1E3.

**WEINTRAUB, William,** B.A.; film producer; script writer; novelist; b. Montreal, Que. 19 Feb. 1926; s. Louis and Mina (Blumer) W.; e. McGill Univ. B.A. 1947; m. Magda d. Henryk and Lila Landau 26 Nov. 1967; Reporter and Copy Ed. 'The Gazette,' Montreal 1948–50; Freelance Journalist & Broadcaster 1950–52; Staff Writer & Chief Copy Ed., 'Weekend Magazine,' Montreal 1952–55; Freelance Writer, Magazine Articles & Film Scripts 1955–65; Producer, National Film Board 1965–86; Dir., N.F.B. studio Nairobi, Kenya, set up to assist African film-makers 1975–76; Dir., English Programming, N.F.B. 1976–78; has written and/or produced more than 100 documentary films, incl. 'Commonwealth of Nations' series 1957; 'Between Two Wars' series 1960; 'Nahanni' (winner of 7 awards, incl Silver Bear at Berlin Film Fest.) 1962; 'Turn of the Century' 1964; 'Struggle for a Border' series 1969; 'A Matter of Fat' (first prize 'Etrog' in Candn. Film Awards) 1970; 'Challenge for the Church' 1972; 'The Aviators of Hudson Strait' 1973; 'Margaret Laurence: First Lady of Manawaka' 1978; 'Arthritis: A Dialogue with Pain' 1980; 'The Rise and Fall of English Montreal' 1993; wrote and produced feature film 'Why Rock the Boat?' (winner of first prize 'Etrog' for screenplay in Candn. Film Awards) 1974; has lectured or conducted seminars on screenwriting at Memorial Univ., Nfld.; Stanford Univ., Calif.; St. Cloud State Univ., Minn.; Ryerson Inst.; McGill Univ.; Concordia Univ.; Candn. del. to U.N.E.S.C.O. Conf. on Films & Television, Morocco 1955; Can. Council Sen. Arts Fellowship 1962; Mem., Intl. Jury, Cracow Film Fest., Poland 1973; mem., Candn. delegation visiting film industry in China 1977; mem., Bd. of Dir., Conseil québécois pour la diffusion du cinéma 1971; author' 'Why Rock the Boat?' (winner of Prov. of Quebec Literary Award) 1961; 'The Underdogs' 1979; Jewish; Home: 433 Wood Ave., Westmount, Que. H3Y 3J4.

**WEINZWEIG, Daniel Gilbert;** motion picture distributor/producer; b. Toronto, Ont. 23 July 1947; s. John Jacob and Helen (Tenenbaum) W.; e. North Toronto C.I.; children: Noah, Joshua; PRES., SELLULOID SCREEN SERVICES INC.; Film and T.V. Producer; Mem., Bd. of Dirs., Windsor Court Holdings Inc.; Head Booker, Internat. Film Dist. 1964–67; Sales Mgr., Astral Films Limited 1968–69; Pres., Danton Films Limited 1969–80; Chief Buyer & Booker, Cineplex Corp. 1980–83; Sr. Vice-Pres. 1983; Pres., Norstar Releasing Inc. 1984–86; Pres., Selluloid Screen Serv. Inc. & Independent Prod. 1986–88; Producer Adviser, Candn. Ctr. for Advanced Film Study 1989–90; Chrmn., Cinephile Limited 1989–93; apptd. to Industry Task Force, Fed. Min. of Communication 1986; Co-chairperson, Trade Forum, Fest. of Fests. 1987; Co-Chrmn., Nat. Assn. of Candn. Distbrs. 1986–91; elected Bd. of Dir., Candn. Film Inst. 1982; Mem., Candn. Assn. of Motion Picture Prod. 1979–81; Founding Mem. & Sec., Motion Picture Inst. of Can.; Founding Mem. & Pres., Assn. of Independent & Candn. Owned Motion Picture Distbrs.; author of chapter in 'Making It – The Business of Film and Television in Canada'; recreations: running, swimming, tennis, movies; Club: YMCA; Address: 10 Olive Ave., Toronto, Ont. M6G 1T8.

**WEINZWEIG, John,** O.C. (1974), D.Mus.; composer; b. Toronto, Ont. 11 Mar. 1913; s. Joseph and Rose (Burshtyn) W.; e. University of Toronto, Mus.B. 1937; Eastman School of Music, University of Rochester, Mus.M. 1938; D.Mus., Ottawa 1969; Hon. LL.D., Univ. of Toronto, 1982; m. Helen Tenenbaum, 19 July 1940; children: Paul, Daniel; began as Teacher Composition and Orchestration, Royal Conservatory of Music of Toronto 1939; Professor of Composition, University of Toronto, 1952; Prof. Emeritus 1978; has trained many of the new generation of Canadian composers; Pres., Dir. and Founder (1951), Canadian League of Composers; Pres. Emeritus, Candn. League of Composers, 1981; Founder and Conductor of the University of Toronto Symphony Orchestra, 1934–37; has conducted his own compositions with Toronto Philharmonic, Vancouver Symphony, etc., his compositions broadcast and performed in many countries; comn. by Nat. Film Bd. to write musical scores for 4 films; has written over 100 scores for C.B.C. radio plays; compositions incl. music for Ballet 'Red Ear of Corn,' sonatas for piano, cello, violin, etc.; won highest award (silver medal) for Chamber Music in Arts Div. of London Olympiad for his 'Divertimento' for flute and string orchestra, 1948; Violin Concerto completed 1954 and received first performance 30 May 1955, C.B.C. broadcast; Commissions include: 'Wine of Peace' for soprano and orchestra (CBC) and dedicated to the United Nations, premiered by CBC Symphony 1958; 'Symphonic Ode' (Saskatoon Symphony); 'Divertimento No. 3' (Saskatoon Festival); 'Divertimento No. 5' (American Wind Symphony of Pittsburgh); 'Piano Concerto' (CBC) 1966; 'Harp Concerto' (Candn. Centennial Commission) 1967; 'Pieces of Five' Brass Quintet (comn. by Canadian Brass for the cultural celebrations of the 1976 Montreal Olympics) 1976; 'Dummiyah' (CBC) 1969; 'Divertimento No. 6' (Intl. Saxophone Cong.) 1972; 'Riffs' (New Music Concerts Toronto) 1974; 'Contrasts for solo guitar' (Guitar Soc. of Toronto) 1976; 'Anthology' recorded works issued by Radio Canada International 1978; 'Divertimento No. 7' (Ont. Arts Council) 1979; 'Divertimento No. 8, Tuba & Orch.' (for 21st anniv. of Canadian Music Centre) 1980; 'Divertimento No. 9 for Orchestra' (commd. by Toronto Symphony for inaugural season in Roy Thomson Hall) 1982; '15 Pieces for Harp' 1983; 'Conversations for Three Guitars' (comm. by Amsterdam Guitar Trio) 1984; 'Hockey Night in Canada' (mixed chorus) 1985; 'Prisoner of Conscience' (dedicated to 25th Anniversary of Amnesty Internat.) 1985; 'Tango for Two' piano solo, comm. by Music Gallery of Toronto for Tango Marathon, Nov. 1986; Resident composer for Toronto Internatonal Guitar Festival and awarded certificate for dedication on behalf of Canadian music 1987; Adjudicator, Internat. Accordion Celebration, Toronto 1993; 'Tremologue for viola solo' comm. by Rivka Golani 1987; 'Divertimento No. 10 for Piano and Strings' comm. by Jon Kimura Parker 1988; 'Divertimento No. 11 for Eng. Horn and Strings' comm. by Hamilton Philharmonic 1989; Duologue 'for Piano Duo' comm. by Petowska-Sokol Piano Duo 1990; 'Sounds and Reflections' (a collection of essays and lectures) pub. by Pool Hall Press 1990; 70th birthday was celebrated with a concert of his music in Roy Thomson Hall 6 Mar. 1983; 75th birthday was celebrated with a concert of his music at the Jane Mallet Theatre and the launching of a documentary film on his life and music by Rhombus Media 19 March 1988; World Premiere 'The Radical Romantic' (the Rhombus Media documentary film), St. Lawrence Centre, Toronto Nov. 1989; 'Prime Time' (music theatre) premiere by Sunday Stage, Toronto April 26, 1992; 80th birthday concert was celebrated with a concert of his music in Walter Hall, Univ. of Toronto March 11, 1993; Gemini Award for Best Arts Program 1990; week-long Retrospective of his music on radio CJRT-FM (Toronto) Nov. 1989; rec'd. Can. Council Sr. Arts Award 1968, 1975; Order of Canada 1974; Order of Ontario 1988; Victor M. Lynch-Staunton Award 1975; Medal, Cdn. Music Council 1978; Molson Prize from Canada Council 1981 ($20,000 for exceptional achievement in music); Roy Thomson Hall Award 1991; 125th Anniversary of the Confederation of Canada Medal, 1992; Hon. Mem. Amer. Harp Soc. (Toronto Br.) 1984; Chrmn., Intl. Jury, Intl. Soc. for Contemporary Music, 1984 Canada World Music Days; Dir., Canadian Music Centre (Ont. region); Composers Authors Assn. Can. (Pres. 1973–75); served in 2nd World War in R.C.A.F. 1943–45; Hebrew; Home: 107 Manor Rd. E., Toronto, Ont. M4S 1R3; Office: Edward Johnson Bldg., Univ. of Toronto, Toronto, Ont. M5S 1A1.

**WEIR, John Angus,** B.Com., M.B.A., Ph.D.; President Emeritus; b. Charlottetown, P.E.I. 29 Oct. 1930; s. John Angus and Mary Isabel (Kilfoy) W.; e. St. Dunstan's (P.E.I.), B.Com., 1953; Univ. Western Ont., M.B.A. 1955; Notre Dame Univ., Ph.D. 1964; m. Ann, d. David and Constance Dooley, 29 Aug. 1959; children: John; David; Michael; Gregory; Pres., Wilfrid Laurier Univ. 1982–92; Teacher, St. Paul's Coll. Univ. Man., 1961; joined present univ. as Assist. Prof. Economics 1965; Chrmn., Dept. Econ. 1968; Vice-Pres. Academic 1978; Kitchener-Waterloo Symphony Orchestra; mem. Kitchener Rotary Club; Roman Catholic; recreation: sailing; Clubs: Westmount Golf & Country; Conestoga Sailing; University; Home: 315 Batavia Pl., Waterloo, Ont. N2L 3W1; Office: 75 University Ave. W., Waterloo, Ont. N2L 3C5.

**WEIR, John P.,** B.Comm., LL.B., LL.M.; lawyer; educator; public servant; b. 22 Nov. 1947; e. McMaster Univ., B.Comm. (Hons.) 1976, Queen's Univ., LL.B. 1979; called to Ont. Bar 1981; York Univ., LL.M. 1983; ASSOC. DEAN 1993– & PROF. 1983– , FACULTY OF LAW, UNIV. OF WINDSOR (on leave 1986–88); Hearing Officer (Income Tax Act), Min. of National Revenue (Can.) 1988–92; Corp. Legal Couns., Can. Life Assur. Co. 1981–83; Supt. of Insur. 1986–88, & Asst. Depy. Min. 1987–88, Min. of Fin. Insts., Govt. of Ont. 1986–88; Adv. Ctte., Mr. Justice Coulter Osborne, Royal Comn., 'Inquiry Into Motor Vehicle Accident Compensation in Ontario' 1987–88; Adv. Ctte., Ont. Law Reform Comn., 'Compensation for Personal Injuries & Death' 1986–87; Senator, Univ. of Windsor 1985–92; Trustee, Candn. Assn. of Univ. Teachers, 1984–86; Mem. of Bd., Windsor-Essex Dist. Health Council 1993– ; Capitol Theatre & Arts Centre 1993– ; Mem., Candn. Counc. of Superintendents of Insur.; Nat. Assoc. of Insur. Comnrs. (U.S.A.); Law Soc. of Upper Can.; Candn. Bar Assn.; Candn. Tax Found.; Essex Law Assn.; York Law Assn.; Hamilton Law Assn.; Internat. Bar Assn.; Am. Bar Assn.; Assn. of Trial Lawyers of Am.; Candn. Assn. of Law Teachers; Candn. Assn. of Univ. Teachers; Ins. Inst. of Can.; author: 'The Annotated Insurance Act of Ontario', 'Structured Settlements', 'Norwood on Life Insurance Law In Canada' (2nd ed.); various journal articles; Club: University Club of Toronto; R.C.M.I.; Office: Faculty of Law, Univ. of Windsor, Windsor, Ont. N9B 3P4.

**WEIR, Robert Harold,** B.A., LL.B., M.B.A.; lawyer; b. Calgary, Alta. 10 June 1931; s. Robert Henry and Stella Blanche (McLean) W.; e. Univ. of B.C. B.A. 1953; Univ. of W. Ont. M.B.A. 1955, LL.B. 1962; m. Georgette d. Paul and Sylvia Parr 1 June 1964; VICE PRES., GEN. COUNSEL AND SEC. JANNOCK LTD. 1973– ; Dir. 153810 Canada Inc.; 359856 Alberta Ltd.; 554836 Ontario Ltd.; 745674 Ontario Ltd.; 873805 Ontario Inc.; Acadia-Atlantic Sugar Co. Ltd.; Alamo Clay Products Co., Inc.; Allanson Manufacturing Industries Ltd.; Armtec Inc.; Boren Clay Products Co.; Brazos Brick Co. Inc.; Canada Brick Industries Ltd.; Cemfort Inc.; Dumbarton Construction Ltd.; Enameltec Porcelain Industries (1989) Ltd.; Holly Springs Brick & Tile Co., Inc.; Jannock Imaging Companies, Inc.; Jannock Inc.; Real Brick Products, Inc.; Richtex Corp.; Sipple Brick, Inc.; Sonco Steel Tube, Inc.; St. Lawrence Brick Industries Ltd.; Tiffany Brick, Inc.; U.S. Brick, Inc.; U.S. Westeel, Inc.; Westeel-Rosco Industries Ltd.; Trust Offr. Crown Trust Co. 1955–59; Sec.-Treas. North-West Line Elevators Assn. Winnipeg 1963–69; Sec. Atlantic Sugar Refineries Co. Ltd. Montreal 1969–73; recreation: golf; Clubs: St. George's; Mid-Ocean (Bermuda); Home: 1603, 39 Old Mill Rd., Toronto, Ont. M8X 1G6; Office: Suite 5205, Scotia Plaza, P.O. Box 1012, 40 King St. W., Toronto, Ont. M5H 3Y2.

**WEIR, Ron Douglas,** C.D., B.Sc., D.I.C., Ph.D., P.Eng.; educator; b. Saint John, N.B. 10 Jan. 1941; s. Ronald Albert Stanley and Hazel Eleanor (Burger) W.; e. Univ. of N.B. B.Sc. 1963 (Lt. Gov.'s Medal); Imp. Coll. of Sci. & Technol. D.I.C. 1966; Univ. of London Ph.D. 1966 (Athlone Fellow 1963–65, NATO Fellow 1965–66, Lessing Medal 1966); Nat. Rsch. Council Can. postdoctoral rsch. 1966–68; Oxford Univ. rsch. visitor 1978–79; m. Barbara A. d. Kenneth and Lois Kierstead 10 May 1963; two d. Michele M., M. Lynn; PROF. OF CHEM. AND CHEM. ENG. ROYAL MIL. COLL. OF CAN. 1981– ; Adjunct Prof. of Chem. Queen's Univ. 1986– ; served with Candn. Forces Royal Candn. Engs. 1958–75, rank Maj.; Asst. Prof. present Coll. 1968, Assoc. Prof. 1975, Head of Chem. and Chem. Eng. 1990– ; Visiting Prof. of Chem. Univ. of Mich. 1985– ; Visiting Sci. Nat. Bureau of Standards Boulder, Colo. 1987 (recipient, Award for Teaching Excellence 1993); mem. St. Lawrence Islands Nat. Park Adv. Ctte. Govt. Can. 1976–78, 1982–86; author 'Birds of Prince Edward County, Ontario' 1984; 'Birds of the Kingston Region' 1989; Ont. ed. 'American Birds' 1982–92; ed. 'Orientational Disorder in Solids' 1983–90; over 100 papers sci. jours.; Fellow, Royal Soc. Chem. (UK); Fellow, Chem. Inst. Can.; mem., Am. Soc. Eng. Edn.; Assn. Profl. Engs. Prov. Ont.; Calorimetry Conf. 1968– (Chrmn. 1990–91); Chart. Chem. (UK); Thermodyn. Comn. Internat. Union Pure & Applied Chem. 1989–93; Titular Mem. & Comn. Secretary 1994–98; Editorial Adv. Bd., J. Chem. Thermodynamics 1988–93, Editor 1993– ; recreations: bird watching, ballet, opera, philatelist, pianist; Home: 294 Elmwood St., Kingston, Ont. K7M 2Y8; Office: Kingston, Ont. K7K 5L0.

**WEIR, Stephen James,** C.A., M.B.A.; executive; b. Calgary, Alta. 22 March 1940; s. Jack W. and Elizabeth T. (Speirs) W.; e. Univ. of Manitoba C.A. 1962; Univ. of W.Ont. M.B.A. 1967; m. Janet R. d. late James H. Suggitt 8 July 1961; children: James S., Jennifer J.; EXTVE. VICE PRES. and C.F.O., TELEMEDIA INC. 1988– ; C.A., Robison, Green & Co., Winnipeg 1957–63; Mgr. Credit and Data Process Control, 3M Co., London 1963–65; joined Bank of Mtl., Special Projects, Head Off. 1967–69; Planning and Analysis 1969–70; Asst. Credit Mgr. (Mtl. Main Branch) 1970–71; Asst. Cr. Mgr. (Corp. Cr.) 1971–72; joined Dominion Textile Inc. as Asst. Treasr. 1972–73; Treasr. 1973–77; Corp. Comptroller 1977–81; Vice Pres., Asst. Gen. Mgr., Intl. Div. 1981–83; Vice-Pres., Consumer Products Div. 1983–84; Vice Pres. Operation Services 1984–85; Vice Pres., Finance and Operation Services, Apparel/Industrial Fabrics Div. 1985–87; Vice Pres., Finance, Candn. Operations 1987–88; mem., Financial Extve. Inst.; Inst. of C.A.; Club: Mtl. Amateur Athletic Assn.; recreations: squash, hockey, golf, skiing, tennis; Office: 1411 Peel St., Suite 500, Montreal, Que. H3A 1S5.

**WEIS, Lyle,** M.A., Ph.D.; association executive; b. Beardmore, Ont. 8 Nov. 1947; s. Glen and Sylvia (Radomske) W.; e. Simon Fraser Univ. B.A. 1970; Univ. of B.C. M.A. 1977; Univ. of Alta. Ph.D. 1983; m. Donna d. Larry and Julia Dietrich 1969; children: Jared, Erica; Extve. Dir., Writers Guild of Alta. 1987; sch. teacher Richmond, B.C. 1969–71; high sch. teacher Vernon, B.C. 1974–76; Teaching Asst. Univ. of Alta. 1976, Killam Scholar 1980–83, Sessional Instr. 1983–87; author novels, short stories, poetry and articles; Home: 11607 – 49 Ave., Edmonton, Alta. T6H 0G9.

**WEISBART, Melvin,** B.Sc., M.A., Ph.D., F.A.A.A.S.; educator; b. Toronto, Ont. 28 Dec. 1938; s. Albert and Clara (Satok) W.; e. Forest Hill Coll. Inst. 1957; Univ. of Toronto B.Sc. 1961, M.A. 1963; Univ. of B.C. Ph.D. 1967; m. Marilyn d. Harry and Fay Greenwood 30 June 1963; children: Cindy Elizabeth, Michael James, Caren Jennifer; PROF. OF BIOL. UNIV. OF REGINA 1989– ; Postdoctoral Fellow Fisheries Rsch. Lab. Halifax 1967–69; Asst. Prof. Wayne State Univ. Detroit 1969–76; Rsch. Assoc. Univ. of Wash. Seattle 1976–78; Asst. Prof. St. Francis Xavier Univ. 1976, Assoc. Prof. 1977, Prof. 1986–89, Chrmn. of Biol. 1983–89; Head of Biology, Univ. of Regina 1989–92; Visiting Rsch. Sci. Marine Sci's Rsch. Lab. Meml. Univ. of Nfld. 1982; recipient Nat. Rsch. Council Can. Postdoctorate Fellowship 1968–69; Faculty Rsch. Award Wayne State Univ. 1970–71; author or co-author over 30 publs.; Chrmn. Zool. Edn. Trust 1988–89; mem. Candn. Soc. Zools. (Pres. 1988–89); Am. Soc. Zools.; Am. Physiol. Soc.; Soc. Promotion Old Fishes; B'nai Brith Regina (Vice Pres. 1990–92; Pres. 1993– ); Bd. of Dirs., Regina Symphony Orchestra 1992– ; Chrmn. Ritual Ctte., Beth Jacob Synagogue 1992– ; Home: 2074 Wascana Greens, Regina, Sask. S4V 2L7; Office: Regina, Sask. S4S 0A2.

**WEISDORF, John,** Q.C., B.A., LL.B., LL.M.; b. Toronto, Ont. 23 Dec. 1929; s. Louis and Bella W.; e. Univ. of Toronto B.A. 1952; Osgoode Hall LL.B. 1956; New York Univ. LL.M. 1970; m. Stella d. Rudolph von Vittorach 1971; children: Christopher, Ashley; MEMBER, IMMIGRATION AND REFUGEE APPEAL BOARD 1984– ; private law practice 1956–60; Dir. of Legal Aid 1960–66; Immigration Attache, The Hague 1967–69; New York Univ. 1969–70; Crown Atty. Toronto 1970–76; Sr. Duty Couns. Legal Aid 1976–80; private practice 1980–84; United Nations Human Rights Fellowship to study Admin. of Justice in Scandinavia, France 1964; Ford Found. Grant to study at N.Y. Univ. Criminal Law Edn. & Rsch. Centre 1969; Home: 165 Chaplin Cres., Toronto, Ont. M5P 1B1; Office: 1 Front St., Toronto, Ont. M5J 1A5.

**WEISDORF, Mark A.,** B.Comm., C.A., C.F.A., C.B.V.; investment executive; b. Swidnica, Poland 31 Aug. 1957; s. Jack and Helen Julia (Adamczyk) W.; e. Univ. of Toronto B.Comm. 1979; C.A. 1981; m. Lorraine D. d. Harry and Hilda Bell 12 Oct. 1981; children: Lisa, Kayla; VICE-PRES. & DIR., WOOD GUNDY INC. INVESTMENT BANKING 1986– ; Audit Supervisor, Touche Ross & Co. 1979–83; Ont. Securities Comn. (seconded from Touche Ross) 1981–82; Vice-Pres., Corp. Finance, Walwyn Stodgell Cochran Murray Limited 1983–86; Trustee, Health Care & Biotechnology Venture Fund; Lectr., Univ. of Toronto 1981–82; Pres., Univ. of Toronto Alumni Assn.; Dir., Kid's Help Found.; Mem., Candn. Inst. of C.A.s; Inst. for C.A.s of Ont.; Assn. for Investment Mngt. & Rsch.; Toronto Soc. of Finan. Analysts; Candn. Inst. of Chartered Business Valuators; author of 1 book chapter; recreations: skiing, fitness; club: Fitness Institute; Home: 74 Glengowan Rd., Toronto, Ont. M4N 1G4; Office: 161 Bay St., 6th fl., BCE Pl., Toronto, Ont. M5J 2S8.

**WEISGERBER, The Hon. John Sylvester (Jack);** politician; b. Barrhead, Alta. 12 June 1940; s. Sylvester and Eva Harrison (Kilshaw) W.; e. Northern Alta. Inst. of Technol., Bus. Adm. 1962; m. Judith Muriel d. Alfred and Muriel Janke 30 June 1961; children: Joanne Melissa, Pamela Jane; MEMBER B.C. LEGISLATURE (PEACE RIVER SOUTH) 1986– ; Auditor, Imperial Oil Ltd. 1962–64; Claims Adjuster, Motors Ins. Corp. 1964–69; Reg. Sales Mgr. 1969–74; Pres. & Gen. Mgr. Dawson Carlantl Ltd. 1975–82; Reg. Econ. Devel. Comm., Peace River Reg. 1982–84; Gen. Sales Mgr., Timberline Pontiac Buick Ltd. 1984–86; past Dir., B.C. Rail; B.C. Rail Ltd.; B.C. Rail Properties Ltd.; B.C. Hydro; Pres., Dawson Creek & Dist. Fall Fair 1980–86; Chair, B.C. Petroleum Corp. 1991; 1st el. to B.C. Leg. (Peace River South) g.e. 1986, re-el. 1991; Minister of State for Nechako and Northeast, Responsible for Native Affairs, Govt. of B.C. 1988–89; Minister of Native Affairs, Govt. of B.C. 1989–91; Minister of Energy, Mines and Petroleum Resources 1991; Interim Leader, Social Credit Opposition 1992–93; recreations: hunting, fishing, curling, downhill skiing; clubs: Rotary (Pres. 1979–80); Home: #305, 10709 - 13st., Dawson Creek, B.C. V1G 3W7; Parliament Bldgs., Victoria, B.C. V8V 1X4.

**WEISMAN, Ronald Gary,** Ph.D.; university professor; b. Detroit, Mich. 14 Sept. 1937; s. Samuel Howard and Martha Selma (Rostein) W.; e. Michigan State Univ., B.A. 1960, M.A. 1961, Ph.D. 1964; m. Colleen Cairns 27 June 1987; children: Mitchell A., Bess K., Dwight W.; PROF., DEPT. OF PSYCHOLOGY, QUEEN'S UNIV. 1976– ; Assoc. Prof., present univ. 1968–76; Asst. Prof. 1964–68; Vis. Prof., Fellow or Scientist: Univ. of Calif. at Santa Barbara; at San Diego; Sussex Univ.; Cambridge Univ.; author/co-author of over 90 sci. articles; research: the evolution of auditory pattern recognition & decision making; recreations: sailing; Home: 58 William St., Kingston, Ont. K7L 2C4; Office: Humphrey Hall, Kingston, Ont. K7L 3N6.

**WEISS, Norman Allen;** b. Edmonton, Alta. 23 Dec. 1935; s. Alfred and Matilda W.; e. Edmonton P.Schs.; Victoria Comp. H.S.; m. Carol Dittberner; one d.: Jill; Minister of Career Development & Employment 1989–93, retired as member of the legislature; bus. experience incl. zone mgr. for farm equipment mfr.; mkt. devel., oil & gas indus.; co-owner, restaurant, real estate co., car wash/serv. stn. & sporting goods retail store; elected Alta. Legisl. for Lac La Biche/McMurray 1979; re-elected 1982, 1986, 1989 (Ft. McMurray); Minister for Alta. Recreation & Parks 1986–89; Assoc. Minister of Family & Social Services 1989; Dir., Alta. Oil Sands Technol. Research Authority; Oil Barons Hockey Club; Candn. Chinese Cult. Assn.; Alberta '85 Summer Games; Keyano Coll. Found.; Ft. McMurray Interpretive Ctr.; North. Alta. Devel. Counc.; Past Vice-Pres., Jr. & Sr. C. of C., Ft. McMurray; Past Pres., Lac La Biche/McMurray P.C. Assn.; recreations: all spectator sports; Clubs: Kinsmen; Rotary.

**WEISS, (Ephrum) Philip;** retired Canadian public servant; designer; b. Montreal, Que. 19 Apr. 1924; s. Hyman and Gertrude (Vogel) W.; e. Central Tech. Sch., Toronto, grad. Comm. Art 1941; Ont. Coll. of Art, Toronto, grad. Fine Art 1947; m. Nancy Johanna, d. late Klaas Raven, 28 Dec. 1945; children: Paul Raymond, Stephen Roy, Karl Raven, Benjamin Ronald; Secy. Gen., Nat. Design Council, 1970–76 Sr. Designer, Candn. Govt. Exhn. Comn., 1947–61; Asst. Dir.; Nat. Design Br., Depts. Trade & Comm. and Indust., Can., 1961–65; Gen. Dir., Office of Design, Depts. of Indust. and Indust. Trade & Comm. 1965–70; Dir., Nat. Design Council, 1961–70; Cdn. Exec. Serv. Overseas volunteer for advancement of ind. design in developing countries; served with Candn. Army (Overseas) in Can. and Europe 1943–46; designer of 10 Candn. postal stamps; contrib. to estab. of Standards Council of Can.; mem. Fed. Govt. Adv. Comtes. for improvement of design and standards in govt. accommodation and constr., procurement and graphics; taught art and design in extension courses, Ottawa Tech. High Sch., Univ. of Toronto, Carleton Coll.; speaker and contrib. to Candn. publs. on subject of design; Hon. mem., Assn. Candn. Indust. Designers; recreations: art, sculpture; Home: 1000 King St. W., Suite 1503, Kingston, Ont. K7M 8H3.

**WEISS, Vladimir Stanley,** P.Eng.; engineering executive; b. Yugoslavia 23 Aug. 1931; s. Bogdan Michael and Gjurgjica Duda (Von Layer) W.; B.Sc. 1954; M.Sc. 1956; M.Sc. 1957; m. Branka-Marie, d. Peter and Slavica Papa 26 Jan. 1957; children: Theodore Daniel; Tamara Duda; PRES. & C.E.O., WEISS GROUP OF ENGINEERING COMPANIES (Weiss & Assoc. 1965– ; Weiss Engineering Corp. 1985– ; Weiss Systems Inc. 1987– ); mem. Amer. Assn. of Engrng. Socs.; Amer. Inst. of Chem. Engrs.; Assn. of Profl. Engrs., Geophysicists and Geologists of Alberta; Assn. of Profl. Engrs. of Ont.; Candn. Pulp & Paper Assn.; Candn. Soc. for Profl. Engrs.; Instrument Soc. of Amer.; Massachusetts Soc. of Profl. Engrs.; Natl. Soc. of Profl. Engrs.; New York State Soc. of Profl. Engrs.; Order of Engrs. of Que.; received Distinguished Society Service Award, Instrument Soc. of Amer. 1973, and Distinguished Service to the Community Award of its Montreal Sect. 1976 and 1983; el. Pres., Instrument Soc. of America (1st Candn. in 42 yr. history of Instr. Soc. to be so honoured) 1986–87; Mem., Am. Soc. for Quality Control; Home: 120 Blackfoot Trail, Mississauga, Ont. L5R 2G7; Office: 505 Queensway E., Mississauga, Ont. L5A 4B4.

**WEISZ, Thomas James,** B.A., LL.B., LL.M.; trust company executive; b. Moson Hungary 12 June 1946; s. Arthur and Margaret W.; e. McMaster Univ. B.A. (Dean's Hon. List) 1967; Osgoode Hall Law School LL.B. 1970 (Silver Medal for standing first in final year; Prize in Insurance and Prize in Estate Planning); Harvard Univ. LL.M. 1971; m. Sasha d. Rose Swaye 5 Aug.; children: Eric O. and Danna E.; PRESIDENT, THE EFFORT TRUST COMPANY; McCarthy Tetrault Toronto to 1979; Sr. Partner, Weisz, Rocchi & Scholes Hamilton; Instr. in Income Tax & Estate Planning Sections, Bar Admission Course; in Income Tax Prog., Law Soc. of U.C.; author of various articles in periodicals & journals; Bd. of Dir., St. Joseph's Hosp.; Philharmonic Orch.; Temple Anshe Sholom; Nat. Bd. of Dir., State of Israel Bonds; Weitzman Inst. of Science; Jewish Nat. Fund of Canada; clubs: President's (McMaster Univ.), Beverly Golf & Country, The Hamilton Club, Harvard Club of Toronto; Office: 242 Main St. E., Hamilton, Ont. L8N 1H5.

**WEITZ, Jeffrey I.,** M.D., F.R.C.P.(C), F.A.C.P.; physician; scientist; educator; b. Ottawa, Ont. 14 Oct. 1952; s. Harry and Clare (Shankman) W.; e. Univ. of Ottawa M.D. 1976; Univ. of Toronto, post-grad.; Columbia Univ., Rsch Scholar; m. Julia d. Harold and Ursula Masterson 10 Aug. 1979; children: Daniel, Caileen; PROF. OF MED., MCMASTER UNIV. 1992– ; Intern/Res., Internal Med., Toronto Gen. Hosp. 1976–78; Res., Hematol./Oncol. 1978–80; Rsch. Fellow, Hematol., Columbia Univ. 1980–82; Instr. in Med. 1983; Asst. Prof. of Med. 1983–86; Asst. Prof. of Med., McMaster Univ. 1986–88; Assoc. Prof. of Med., 1988–92; Cons., Genentech Can.; Biogen Inc.; CIBA-Geigy; Rsch. Fellowship, N.Y. Heart Assn.; Career Investigator, Heart & Stroke Found. of Ont.; Mem., Candn. & Am. Soc. for Clin. Investig.; Ont. Med. Assn.; Candn. & Am. Colls. of Phys.; Am. Soc. for the Adv. of Sci.; Am. Soc. of Hematol.; Am. Soc. of Clin. Oncol.; Am. Fed. for Clin. Rsch.; Am. Heart Assn.; Internat. Soc. on Thrombosis & Hemostasis; N.Y. Acad. of Sci.; recipient, Medal in Medicine, Candn. Coll. of Phys. 1991; author/co-author of num. rsch. papers, book chapters & review articles; Home: 54 Carluke Rd. E., Ancaster, Ont. L9G 3L1; Office: Henderson Gen. Hosp., 711 Concession St., Hamilton, Ont. L8V 1C3.

**WEIZEL, Harold Aaron Eliot,** M.D., F.R.C.S.(C), F.A.C.S.; surgeon; b. Toronto, Ont. 2 Sept. 1925; s. Paul and Sarah W.; e. Harbord Coll. Inst.; Univ. of Toronto M.D. 1947; Harvard Med. Sch. post-grad. surgery; m. Eleanor d. A. Bogen 22 Jan. 1950; children: Jonathan, Laurence, Pamela; DIR. BREAST CLINIC, TORONTO WESTERN HOSP. 1987– ; Surgeon 1977– ; Assoc. Prof. of Surgery Univ. of Toronto 1987– ; Assoc. Surg.-in-Chief Doctors Hosp. Toronto 1957–69, Surg.-in-Chief 1969–76; Lectr. Univ. Toronto 1977, Asst. Prof. of Surg. 1982; Cons. Hillcrest Hosp. Toronto; Workmen's Compensation Appeal Bd. Ont.; Pres. Acad. of Med. Toronto 1980–82, Chrmn. Bd. Trustees; Home: 51 Hawarden Cres., Toronto, Ont. M5P 1M8; Office: 200 Elizabeth St., M.L.W. 2-014, Toronto, Ont. M5G 2C4.

**WEKERLE, Gerda R.,** M.A., Ph.D.; educator; b. Heidelberg, Germany 1947; d. Adam Jakob and Eva (Kramer) W.; e. York Univ. B.A. 1968; Northwestern Univ. M.A. 1969, Ph.D. 1974; m. Slade s. William Hall and Margaret Slade Lander 1972; one child: Bryn; PROF. OF ENVIRONMENTAL STUDIES YORK UNIV. 1990– ; Lectr. present Univ. 1972, Asst. Prof. 1974, Assoc. Prof. 1978, Exec. Ctte. Faculty Grad. Studies 1990–93 and Faculty Assn. 1977–78, 1986–87, Co-Chair Senate Tenure and Promotions Ctte. 1992–93; Visiting Scholar, Massey College; cons. City of Toronto Planning & Devel. Dept. & Mgmt. Services Dept.; Canada Mortgage and Housing Corp.; recipient Ont. Scholarship, Gov. Gen.'s Medal and York Univ. Gov.'s Scholarship 1965; Woodrow Wilson Hon. Mention 1968; Can. Council Grad. Fellowship 1969–71; Laidlaw Found. Advanced Studies Fellowship 1970–71; CMHC External Rsch. Grant 1984, 1988; Social Sci's & Humanities Rsch. Council Rsch. Grants 1984–89, 1993–96 inclusive; Dir. Social Planning Council Metrop. Toronto 1980–82; mem. Exec. Nat. Action Ctte. Status of Women 1980–81; Chair Interdisciplinary Adjudication Ctte. SSHRC 1990–91; Mem., Safe City Ctte. City of Toronto 1991–93; Co-founder, Pub. and Ed. 'Women and Environments' 1976–84; author: 'Women in the Urban Environment' 1980; 'Responses to Austerity: the Miniaturization of the Urban Neighbourhood' 1987; 'Canadian Women's Housing Cooperatives' 1988; 'The Mobility of Capital and the Immobility of Female Labour: Responses to Economic Restructuring' 1989; 'Developing Two Women's Housing Cooperatives' 1989; co-author: 'Gender and Housing in Toronto' 1991; 'A Working Guide for Planning and Designing Safer Urban Environments' 1992; 'Gender Politics in Local Politics' 1993; co-ed. 'New Space for Women' 1980; Co-author: 'Safe Cities' 1994; numerous articles and book chapters various scholarly jours. and publications; mem. Am. Sociol. Assn. (mem. Robert Parks Book Award 1986); Am. Planning Assn.; Candn. Women's Studies; recreations: gardening, bicycling, canoeing, cross-country skiing, reading; Home: 144A Lawton Blvd., Toronto, Ont. M4V 2A5; Office: 350 Lumbers Building, North York, Ont. M3J 1P3.

**WELBOURN, Pamela Mary,** B.Sc., Ph.D.; university professor; b. Hertford, U.K. 24 June 1935; d. George Walter and Daisy (Stokes) Hepden; e. Ware Grammar Sch. for Girls 1946–53; Bristol Univ., B.Sc. 1953–56, Ph.D. 1956–59; m. O. Rex s. William and Gertrude Welbourn 8 Dec. 1989; children: Michael Wilfrid Joy, David Andrew Joy; MCLEAN VISITING PROF. IN ENVIRONMENTAL STUDIES 1991–92 and CONJUNCT PROF., TRENT UNIV. 1989– ; Teacher, Sir John Cass Coll., Univ. of London 1960–63; Asst. Prof. of Botany, Univ. of Toronto 1970–73; Assoc. Prof. 1973–81; Prof. 1981–90; Conjunct Prof., Envir. Studies, Trent Univ. 1989– ; Dir., Program in Toxicology, Univ. of Toronto 1989–90; Dir., Envir. Studies Inst., Univ. of Toronto 1984–89; Board, Candn. Inst. in Atmospheric Chem. 1988–89; OCUFA teaching award 1976; U. of T. Alumni Fac. award 1989; Chrmn., Ont. Pesticides Adv. Ctte., Ont. Min. of Envir. 1989–90; Mem., Ontario Round Table on Envir. & Econ. 1989–90; Office: Peterborough, Ont. K9J 7B8.

**WELCH, Herbert John Richardson,** B.A.; financial executive; b. Rochester, Minn. 27 March 1956; s. Herbert Clark and Geraldine Joan (Richardson) W.; e. Univ. of B.C. B.A. 1978; Fac. des lettres et sci. humaine, Besançon, France 1979; m. Wendy d. John and Doris Baxter 9 Aug. 1986; children: Baxter Clark, Sam Richardson; PORTFOLIO MANAGER & VICE-PRESIDENT, DUNCAN ROSS ASSOC. 1988– ; Wood Gundy Inc. 1981–88; recreations: skiing, boating, fishing; clubs: Vancouver; Home: 3365 W. 27th Ave., Vancouver, B.C. V6S 1R5; Office: 301 – 325 Howe St., Vancouver, B.C. V6C 1Z7.

**WELCH, Robert S.,** Q.C., LL.D.; b. St. Catharines, Ont. 13 July 1928; s. John Robert Charles and Edna Rebecca (Groombridge) Kemp-Welch; e. St. Catharines (Ont.) Pub. and High Schs.; McMaster Univ., B.A. 1949, LL.D. 1984; Osgoode Hall Law Sch., grad. 1953; Brock Univ., LL.D. 1971; m. Margaret Emily (Rita) d. William James Boston and Margaret Jane Low, Montreal, Que., 18 July 1953; children: Robert William Peter, Christine Elizabeth Anne, Willa Mary-Jayne; called to Bar of Ont. 1953; cr. Q.C. 1966; Counsel, Lancaster Mix & Welch, St. Catharines, Ont.; first el. M.P.P. for Lincoln in Prov. g.e. 1963; represented Lincoln Riding from 1963 to 1975; represented Brock Riding (after redistribution) 1975 to May 1985 on which date retired from Legis.; present; Pres., Lincoln Co. P. Cons. Assn. 1957–63; served on Select Comte. on Youth 1964–65 and Select Comte. on Co. Law 1965–66; Prov. Secy., Min. of Citizenship and Registrar Gen., 1966–71; mem. Treasury Bd. 1968–71; Govt. House Leader 1969–71; Min. responsible for Civil Service Comn. and Dept. of Civil Service 1969–71; cand. for Leadership of Ont. P. Cons. Party Feb. 1971; Min. of Educ. 1971–72; Prov. Secy. for Social Devel. 1972–74; Min. Housing 1973–74; Prov. Secy. for Justice and Atty. Gen. 1974–75; Govt. House Leader 1975–79; Min. Culture and Recreation 1975–78; Depy. Premier 1977–85 (position assigned Cabinet rank 1983); Prov. Secy. for Justice 1978–79; Minister of Energy 1979–83; Min. Responsible for Women's Issues 1983–85; Attorney Gen., 1985; mem., St. Catharines Recreation Comn. 1953–54; St. Catharines Bd. of Educ.1955–63 (Chrmn. 1958, 1961 and 1962); Campaign Chrmn., Un. Appeal, 1960; Chancellor Emeritus, Anglican Diocese of Niagara; Chancellor, Brock Univ. 1985; Chrmn. of the Bd., Consumers' Gas; mem., Lincoln Co. Law Assn.; Ex-officio Bencher, Law Soc. of Upper Canada; Club: The St. Catharines; Home: 72 Johnson St., Niagara-on-the-Lake, Ont. L0S 1J0; Office: 55 King St., St. Catharines, Ont. L2R 6Z1.

**WELDON, David Black,** B.A., LL.D.; b. London, Ont. 27 June 1925; investment dealer; s. Douglas Black and Margaret (Black) W.; e. Pub. Sch., London, Ont.; Ridley Coll.; Univ. of W. Ontario, B.A. (Hons.), Business Adm.; m. Ina G., d. late Fred Perry, 7 July 1951; two s., three d.; Vice-Pres. and Dir., Goderich Elevators Limited; Dir., Grafton Group Limited; Silcorp Ltd.; Dover Industries Ltd; Emco Limited; Chancellor, Univ. of W. Ont. 1984–88; Trustee, Ont. Jockey Club; Pres. Past Royal Agricultural Winter Fair; started as Clerk with Dominion Securities Corp. Ltd., Montreal, Que., 1947–49; Stat. Clk., Bank of Montreal, Montreal, Que., 1949–50; Securities Trader, Midland Securities Corp. Ltd., Toronto, Ont., 1950–51, Securities Salesman, London, Ont., 1951, Dir. and Treas., 1955, Vice-Pres. and Treas., 1959; Extve. Vice-Pres., Midland-Osler Securities Ltd. (merger), 1963, Pres. and Dir. 1966; Pres. & Chrmn., Midland Doherty (merged cos.) 1974–89; served with Canadian Infantry, 1944–45; Pres., P. Cons. Assn., London, Ont., 1963–65; mem., Invest. Dealers Assn. Can.; Conservative; Anglican; recreations: fishing, golf, horses, hunting; Clubs: The London; London Hunt & Country; The Toronto; Toronto Golf; York; Caledon Mountain Trout; Griffith Island: Ristigouche Salmon; Homes: Prospect Farms, Arva, Ont. N0M 1C0 and Apt. 408, Hazelton Lanes, 18A Hazelton Ave., Toronto, Ont. M5R 2E2; Office: c/o Denison Mines Ltd., National Bank Building, 150 York St., Suite 1508, Toronto, Ont. M5H 3S5.

**WELDON, William J.;** accounting executive; b. Jamestown, N.Y.; s. Robert and Marie W.; e. Mich. State Univ.; m. Arlene Levesque 21 June 1961; three d. Karen, Cynthia, Kathleen; MNG. PARTNER, ARTHUR ANDERSEN CANADA 1987– ; joined Audit Div. Arthur Andersen N.Y. 1959, apptd. Mgr. London, Eng. Office, Partner 1969; Partner (Audit) Hartford, Conn. 1972; Mng. Partner Toronto Office 1983; Trustee Un. Way Greater Toronto; mem. Bus. Bd. and Chair of Audit Ctte. Governing Council, Univ. of Toronto; Bd. Dirs. Nat. Ballet of Can.; Patrons Council, Toronto Symphony Orch.; recreations: tennis, golf, squash; Clubs: Toronto; Avon Golf & Country; The Queen's; Adelaide; Lambton Golf & Country; Home: 33 Crescent Rd., Toronto, Ont. M4W 1T4; Office: 19F, 79 Wellington St. W., Toronto, Ont. M5K 1B9.

**WELIN, Dennis Alfred;** b. Timmins, Ont. 27 Mar. 1947; s. Eric G. and Janice (Lundquist) W.; e. Univ. of Toronto Teacher's Coll.; m. Diana d. Tiami and Urho Kivioja 26 June 1969; children: Larry, Allan; Mayor, Corp. of the City of Timmins 1989–91; operated own mechanical business for 12 yrs.; served as alderman for 8 yrs; school board, 4 yrs (2 yrs as Chrmn.); Bd. of Dir., St-Mary's Hosp.; Timmins Dist. Hosp.; Timmins Econ. Devel. Corp.; Chrmn. for Seniors non-profit Housing; Mem., Timmins Kinsmen; Porcupine Dante Club; Timmins Moose; recreations: fishing, hunting, hockey; Home: R.R. 2, 21 Wallingford Rd., Timmins, Ont. P4N 7C3.

**WELLER, Geoffrey R.,** B.Sc., M.A.; university professor and administrator; b. Tonbridge, Kent, U.K. 25 Jan. 1942; s. Raymond Henry and Edith Letitia W.; e. Univ. of Hull (U.K.) B.Sc. (Econ.) (Hons.) 1964; McMaster Univ. M.A. 1967; m. Jean B. d. Evelyn and William Carley 14 Sept. 1963; children: Duncan, Eric, Alexander; PRES., UNIVERSITY OF NORTHERN BRITISH COLUMBIA 1991– ; Asst. Prof., Bishop's Univ. 1965–71; Asst. Prof., Assoc. Prof., Prof., Lakehead Univ. 1971–90, Dean of Arts 1983–85, Vice-Pres. (Academic) 1985–90; Vis. Prof., Univ. of Ottawa 1977–78; Past Chrmn., Thunder Bay Dist. Health Counc.; Chrmn., Candn. Assoc. for Security and Intelligence Studies 1991–93 (Secy./Treas. 1989–91); mem. Social Sciences and Humanities Rsch. Council of Canada (SSHRC); author of many articles in academic journals and book chapters; recreation: hiking; Home: 2482 Panorama Cres., Prince George, B.C. V2K 4B9; Office: Bag 1950, Station A, Prince George, B.C. V2L 5P2.

**WELLINGTON, William George,** M.A., Ph.D., F.R.S.C.; educator; b. Vancouver, B.C. 16 Aug. 1920; s. George and Lilly (Rae) W.; e. Univ. of B.C., B.A. 1941; Univ. of Toronto M.A. 1945, Ph.D. 1947; m. Margret d. Samuel and Rose Reiss 1959; children: Katherine Jean, Stephen Ross; HON. PROF. PLANT SCIENCE AND PROF. EMERITUS OF PLANT SCIENCE AND RESOURCE ECOLOGY, FAC. AGRIC. SCIENCES, UNIV. OF B.C. 1986; Meteorol. Offr. Candn. Meteorol. Service 1942–45; Rsch. Entomol. Agric. Can. Sault Ste. Marie, Ont. 1946–51; Head, Bioclimatol. Sect. Dept. Forestry Can. Sault Ste Marie, Victoria, B.C. 1951–67, Princ. Sci. Victoria 1964–68; Prof. of Ecology Univ. of Toronto 1968–70; Prof. of Plant Science & Resource Ecology, Inst. of Animal Resource Ecology, Univ. of B.C. 1970–86; Dir. Inst. Animal Resource Ecology present Univ. 1973–79, Killam Sr. Rsch. Fellow 1980–81, Chrmn. Resource Ecology & Planning Council 1976–78; mem. various grant selection comtes. NSERC 1975–86; Biometeorol. Cons. Jt. Can./U.S. Spruce Budworms Program, W. 1981–82; External Reviewer Grad. Programs Appraisals Comte. Ont. Council Grad. Studies 1982; Visiting Prof. N.C. State Univ. 1972, 1975, 1981; San Diego State Univ. 1975; Laval Univ. 1981; Univ. of Calgary 1983; Simon Fraser Univ. 1987; 1st C.E. Atwood Memorial Lectr., Dept. of Zool., Univ. of Toronto, March, 1993; author over 110 rsch. papers refereed sci. jours., various book chapters; Assoc. Ed. 'Canadian Journal of Zoology' 1983–86; Fellow, Royal Soc. Can.; Entomol. Soc. Can. (Gold Medal 1968; Pres. 1976–78); Explorers Club; mem. Am. Entomol. Soc. (C.J. Woodworth Award 1979); Am. Meteorol. Soc. (Award Outstanding Achievement Biometeorol. 1969); Candn. Soc. Zools.; Entomol. Soc. of Can.; Japanese Soc. Population Ecology; Biol. Council Can. (Exec. Council 1977–79); Am. Philatelic Soc.; recreations: nature photography, mountain natural history; Home: 2350 – 130A St. Surrey, B.C. V4A 8Y5.

**WELLMAN, Barry,** B.A., M.A., Ph.D.; university professor; b. New York City, N.Y. 30 Sept. 1942; s. Philip and Rosalind (Levine) W.; e. Bronx H.S. of Science 1959; Lafayette College B.A. 1963; Harvard Univ. M.A. 1965, Ph.D. 1969; m. Beverly d. Irving and Sadie Meyrowitz 6 July 1965; RSCH. ASSOCIATE, CENTRE FOR URBAN & COMMUNITY STUDIES, UNIV. OF TORONTO 1970– ; Asst. Prof. of Sociology, Univ. of Toronto 1967; Assoc. Prof. 1973; Prof. 1979; Visiting Prof., Surrey Univ. 1974–75; Fellow, Netherlands Inst. of Adv. Studies 1978–79; Visiting Prof., Univ. of Calif. at Berkeley 1984; Rsch. Assoc., Clarke Inst. of Psych. 1967–69; Partner, Back Seat; Wellman Assoc.; The Palmerston Group; Distinguished Keynote Speaker, Internat. Sunbelt Social Network Conference 1994; Edit. Bd. Mem., 'Cultural Analysis Methods,' 'Connections,' 'Am. J. of Soc.,' 'Soc. Networks,' 'J. of Soc. and Personal Relationships'; Ed., 'Connections' 1976–88; 'SAS Success Story' 1990; 2nd Prize, Theory, Am. Soc. Assn. 1984; num. research grants; Bd. Mem., Univ. of Toronto, Ctr. for Urban & Comm. Studies, Telepresence Project; Founding Coord., Internat. Network for Social Network Analysis 1976–88; Internat. Coord. 1988–94; Comm. Rsch. Council, Internat. Soc. Assn. 1984–88; author: 'The Community Question' 1979, 'Men in Networks' 1992; co-author: 'The Network City' 1973, 'Different Strokes from Different Folks' 1990, 'Domestic Affairs and Network Relations; co-editor: 'Social Structures: A Network Approach' 1988; recreations: computers, cars, books; Clubs: BMW CCC, BMW CCA; Home: 818 Palmerston Ave., Toronto, Ont. M6G 2R9; Office: 455 Spadina Ave., Toronto, Ont. M5S 1A1.

**WELLS, Honourable Clyde Kirby,** Q.C., B.A., LL.B., M.H.A.; b. Buchans Junction, Nfld. 9 Nov. 1937; s. Ralph Pennell and Maude (Kirby) W.; e. All Saints Sch. Stephenville Crossing, Nfld. 1953; Memorial Univ. of Nfld. B.A. 1959; Dalhousie Univ. Law Sch. LL.B. 1962; m. Eleanor d. Arthur and Daisy Bishop, Stephenville Crossing, Nfld. 20 Aug. 1962; three children: Mark, Heidi, David; two grandchildren; PREMIER OF NEWFOUNDLAND & LABRADOR 1989– ; acclaimed as M.H.A. for Bay of Islands 1989, re-el. 1993; Leader of the Liberal Party of Nfld. and Lab. June 1987– ; former Sr. Partner, Wells and Company; former Dir. & Bd. Chrmn., Newfoundland Light & Power Co. Ltd.; former Dir., Humber Valley Broadcasting Co. Ltd.; private law practice since 1964; el. M.H.A. 1966, Min. of Labour 1966, resigned from Cabinet 1968 and from House of Assembly 1971; called to Bar of N.S. 1963, Bar of Nfld. 1964; Q.C. 1977; mem. Candn. Bar Assn.; served with Candn. Army, Judge Advocate Gen.'s Office 1962–64, rank Capt.; recreations: golf, skiing, sailing; Home: 3 Glenridge Cres., St. John's, Nfld.; Office: 8th Flr., Confederation Bldg., St. John's, Nfld. A1B 4J6.

**WELLS, Colin Michael,** M.A., D.Phil., F.S.A.; educator; b. West Bridgford, England 15 Nov. 1933; s. Alfred Henry and Ada (Nicholls) W.; e. Nottingham High Sch. 1952; Oriel Coll. Oxford, B.A. 1958, M.A. 1959, D.Phil. 1965; m. Catherine d. Richard and Frances Hughes 23 July 1960; two s. Christopher William Llewellyn, Dominic Richard Alexander; T. FRANK MURCHISON DISTINGUISHED PROFESSOR OF CLASSICAL STUDIES, TRINITY UNIV., San Antonio, Texas 1987– ; Classical VIth Form Master, Beaumont Coll., Old Windsor, Eng. 1958–59; joined Univ. of Ottawa 1960, Asst. Prof. 1964, Assoc. Prof. 1966, Chrmn. of Classical Studies 1967–72, Prof. of Classical Studies

1971–88, Vice Dean of Arts 1974–77; Visiting Fellow, Brasenose Coll. Oxford 1973–74; Visiting Prof. Univ. of Cal. Berkeley 1978; Adjunct Professor, Carleton Univ. 1985–88; professeur invité, Institut d'Histoire Romaine, Strasbourg 1990; Dir. Candn. Excavations Carthage (2nd Candn. Team) since 1976; Pres. Ottawa Montessori Schs. 1966–72; Del. Fédération internationale des études classiques 1970–75; author: 'The German Policy of Augustus: An Examination of the Archaeological Evidence' 1972; 'The Roman Empire' 1984, transl. German, Italian, Spanish; ed. 'L'Afrique Romaine/Roman Africa' 1982; 'Echos du Monde Classique' 1965–81; mem. Classical Assn. Can. (Council); Archaeol. Inst. Am. (Pres. Ottawa-Hull Soc. 1976–78, Southwest Texas Soc. 1988– ); recreations: cricket, squash, books, music, friends; Home: 129 E. Summit Ave., San Antonio, Texas 78212; Office: San Antonio, Texas 78212.

**WELLS, Donald Otis,** B.S., M.S., Ph.D.; university president and professor of physics; b. McKeesport, Pa. 3 Apr. 1933; s. Otis Henry and Ottilie Hilda (Bostak) W.; e. Stanford Univ., B.S. 1955, M.S. 1956, Ph.D. 1963; m. Deborah Ann Dewar; children: Eric Donald, Valana Lorraine, Vanessa Ottilie, Vanita Diana, Barrett Otis, Barton Stanislaus; PRES., UNIV. OF REGINA 1990– ; Rsch. Sci., Lockhead Missile & Space Div. 1956–57; Rsch. Asst., Stanford Univ. 1957–61; Asst. Physics Prof., Univ. of Oregon 1961–67; Assoc. Physics Prof., Univ. of Man. 1967–86; Physical Edn. Prof. 1982–86; Asst. Vice-Pres. 1971–74; Vice-Pres. 1975–86; Physics Prof., Mount Allison Univ. 1986–90; Pres. 1986–90; Cons., Lockheed Missile & Space Div.; Univ. of Sask.; Univ. of Lethbridge; Univ. Grants Comn. (Man.); Carleton Univ.; Saint Boniface Gen. Hosp.; Dir., High Voltage Direct Current Rsch. Ctr. 1981–86; Univ. of Manitoba Research, Inc. 1984–86; Dir., Regina Economic Development Authority 1990– ; Chair, Ctte. on Education for Sustainable Development 1991–92; Westinghouse War Meml. Scholar 1951–55; Alfred P. Sloan Found. Fellow 1957–58; Mem., Candn. Soc. for Studies in Higher Edn.; Candn. Assn. of Univ. Bus. Offrs. (Pres.); Am. Phys. Soc.; Candn. Assoc. of Phys.; Assoc. of Atlantic Univs. (Extve. Ctte.); Sigma Xi; Candn. Amateur Swimming Assn. (Vice-Pres. Man.); Candn. Swim Coaches Assn.; Am. Assn. of Phys. Teachers; Mgr., Candn. Swimming Championships & Olympic Trials 1968, 69, 70, 71, 72; Chrmn., United Way Subcampaign 1984; author or co-author of 45 papers; recreations: running, skiing, golf, tennis, music; Office: Office of the Pres., Univ. of Regina, Regina, Sask. S4S 0A2.

**WELLS, Donald Smith,** B.A., M.B.A., C.A.; banker; b. Montreal, Que. 28 Oct. 1935; s. John M. and Stella M. (Smith) W.; e. Bishop's Univ. B.A. 1955; Univ. of Western Ont. M.B.A. 1957; Inst. of C.A.s C.A. 1960; m. Mary E. d. Wayne Hall 6 July 1963; children: Michael, Nancy, Susan; SENIOR VICE-PRES., CORPORATE PLANNING & ORGANIZATION, ROYAL BANK OF CANADA 1990– ; C.A., Touche Ross & Co. 1957–72 (Partner 1966–72); Corp. Comptroller & Chief Acct., Royal Bank of Canada 1972–77; Asst. Gen. Mgr., & Mgr., Montreal Main Br. 1977–78; Vice-Pres., Commercial Lending 1981–83; Pres. & Chief Extve. Offr., Industrial Credit Insur. Co. 1983–84; Vice-Pres., Strategic Investments, Royal Bank of Canada 1984–86; Vice-Pres. & Comptroller, Banking Network 1986–87; Sr. Vice Pres., Business Planning 1987–90; Dir., Royal Bank Mortgage Corp.; The Montreal Gen. Hosp. Found.; Piggery Theatre; Dir. & Past Chair, McGill Assoc.; former Pres., Corp. of Bishop's Univ. 1988–91; Montreal Gen. Hosp. Ctr. 1984–86; recreations: golf, tennis; clubs: University Club of Montreal, Beaconsfield Golf, Montreal Indoor Tennis; Home: 145 Stonehenge Dr., Beaconsfield, Que. H9W 3X6; Office: 1 Place Ville Marie, Montreal, Que. H3B 4R7.

**WELLS, Lyle E.,** B.Sc., P.Eng.; insurance executive; b. Aultsville, Ont. 23 March 1936; s. Sandford G. and Lois M. (Van Allen) W.; e. Queen's Univ. B.Sc. 1959; m. Marilyn d. Charles and Hilda Daly 10 Oct. 1959; children: Kent, Karen, Kevin; EXTVE. VICE-PRESIDENT, FRANK COWAN COMPANY 1973– ; Asst. County Engineer, S, D & G Counties 1959–60; County Engineer, Lanark County 1960–72; Office: Princeton, Ont. N0J 1V0.

**WELLS, Robert;** provincial supreme court justice; b. Badgers Quay, Nfld. 28 Aug. 1933; s. Warwick and Dorcas May (Parsons) W.; e. Prince of Wales Sch. 1949; Memorial Univ. of Nfld., B.A. 1953; Oxford Univ., B.A. (Hons.) 1956, M.A. (Oxon) 1961; called to Bar of England & Wales 1958; Bar of Nfld. 1959; Rhodes Scholar (Nfld. & Keble) 1953; m. Lucy d. Chesley and Annie Pilgrim 1 March 1985; children: Sally (Dicarlo), Louise, Robert H.W., David, Nancy (Desaulniers); JUSTICE, SUPREME COURT, NEWFOUNDLAND, Trial Div.; Staff Mem., Dept. of Justice, Govt. of Nfld. 1959–63; Queen's Counsel 1972; Treas. (Pres.), Nfld. Law Soc. 1977–81; Bencher 1974– ; Pres., Candn. Bar Assn. 1985–86; Mem., House of Assembly, Nfld. 1972–79; Min. of Health 1976; Govt. House Leader 1976–77; Chrmn., Janeway Child Health Ctr. 1977–87; Chancellor, Diocise Eastern Nfld. & Labrador 1976–84; Past Pres., Candn. Institute for the Administration of Justice; Pres., Internat. Commission of Jurists (Candn. Section) 1993–94; recreation: sailing; Club; Terra Nova Sailing; Office: Box 937, St. John's, Nfld. A1C 5M3.

**WELLS, Hon. Thomas Leonard,** Litt. D.; diplomat; b. Toronto, Ont. 2 May 1930; s. Leonard and Lillian May (Butler) W.; e. Malvern Coll. Inst., Toronto, Sr. Matric., 1948; Univ. of Toronto, 1949–51; m. Audrey Alice, d. Arthur C. Richardson, 24 April 1954; children: Andrew Thomas, Brenda Elizabeth, Beverley Gail; CONSULTANT, TLW CONSULTING 1992– ; Trustee, Scarborough, (Ont.) Bd. of Educ., 7 yrs., (Chrmn. 1961, 1962); Scarborough Rep., Metro. Sch. Bd., 1962, 1963; (Chrmn. Finance Comte., 1963); el. to Ont. Leg. for Scarborough N. in g.e. in 1963; re-el. in g.e. in 1967, 1971, 1975, 1977 and 1981; Minister without Portfolio, 1966–69, Minister of Health, 1969–71, of Social & Family Services, 1971–72; Min. of Education 1972–78; Min. of Intergovernmental Affairs, 1978–85; Min. of Municipal Affairs 1978–80; Gov't House Leader 1979–85; Agent General for Ontario in the United Kingdom 1985–91; Commissioner, EXPO-98 Canada Bid Corp. 1991–92; Hon. mem., Bd. of Govs., Scarborough Gen. Hosp.; mem., Albany Club of Toronto; mem., Empire Club & Royal Commonwealth Society; Royal Over-Seas League; Guild of Freemen of the City of London; Company of Freeman of the City of London of North America; Hon. Fellow, Ont. Teachers Fedn. 1976; Litt. D. (h.c.) Univ. of Windsor 1985; Freeman of the City of London 1985; P. Conservative; United Church; recreations: walking, photography, movies; Office: 808 – 65 Spring Garden Ave., North York, Ont. M2N 6H9.

**WELSH, Sydney Wallis;** executive; b. Vancouver, B.C. 24 Nov. 1913; s. Frederick Wallis and Alice Maude (Robinson) W.; e. Vancouver Tech. Sch.; m. Jeannette Millicent d. late Bert M. Cope, Vancouver, B.C. 2 March 1937; children: Frederick Wallis, Wendy Jeannette Marshall, Barbara Lyne Anderson; PRES., WELSH CABLE VISION LTD.; Chrmn. of Bd., Fred Welsh Ltd.; Chrmn. of Bd., Central Heat Distribution Ltd.; Dir., North West Sports Ltd.; Western International Communications Ltd.; PeBen Oil Field Services Ltd.; former mem. Bd., Vandusen Botanical Guardens; former Ald., Dist. of W. Vancouver; Past Chrmn., Town Planning Adv. Comn. W. Vancouver; former Dir. Lions Gate Hosp. N. Vancouver and Grace Hosp. Vancouver; Commr., Royal Comn. on B.C. Rly. 1977–78; Past Pres. World Council Young Men's Service Clubs 1952–54; Past Pres. and Life mem. Vancouver Bd. Trade; Amalgamated Constr. Assn. B.C.; Past Nat. Pres. and Life mem. Candn. Plumbing & Mech. Contractors Assn.; Past Vice Pres. for B.C., Candn. Constr. Assn.; Freemason; Kinsmen (Past Nat. Pres. 1951–52); Anglican; recreations: fishing, horticulture; Clubs: Vancouver; Pennask Lake Fish & Game; Rotary; Vancouver Club; Home: 9811 Kearns Rd., Whonnock, B.C. V0M 1S0; Office: 3755 Wayburne Dr., Burnaby, B.C. V5G 3L4.

**WELSH-OVCHAROV, Bogomila,** B.A., M.Phil., Ph.D.; university professor, art historian; b. Sofia, Bulgaria; d. Konstantin and Slavka (Natcheva) O.; e. Univ. of Toronto B.A. 1964, M.Phil. 1971; Univ. of Utrecht Ph.D. (cum laude) 1976; m. Robert Paul s. Edward and Victoria Welsh 1 Oct. 1966; one s.: Christopher Edward Konstantin; PROF., DEPT. OF FINE ART, UNIV. OF TORONTO 1989– ; studied Art History, Sorbonne 1964–65; joined Dept. of Fine Art, Erindale College, Univ. of Toronto 1975; organized exbn. 'Vincent Van Gogh & the Birth of Cloisonisim,' Art Gall. of Ont. and Rijksmuseum Vincent Van Gogh Amsterdam 1981; 1st non-French guest curator, the Louvre 1987; Canada Council grants; SSHRCC awards; Canada Council & Dept. of External Affairs Grant for Exchange of Rsch. Scholars with France & Soc. Sciences; author: 'The Early Work of Charles Angrand and his Contact with Van Gogh' 1971, 'Van Gogh in Perspective' 1973, 'Van Gogh: His Paris Period: 1886–88' 1976, 'Vincent Van Gogh & the Birth of Cloisonism' 1981, 'Emile Bernard: Bordellos and Prostitutes in Turn-of-the-Century French Art' 1988, 'Van Gogh à Paris' 1988, 'Charles Pachter' 1992; Home: 84 Chestnut Park Rd., Toronto, Ont. M4W 1W9; Offices: 100 St. George St., Toronto, Ont. M5S 1A1 and Erindale College, 3359 Mississauga Rd. N., Mississauga, Ont. L5L 1C6.

**WELWOOD, Ronald Joseph Adrian,** B.A., B.L.S.; library director; b. Penticton, B.C. 14 Feb. 1940; s. Joseph Roy and Alice Marie (Bonthoux) W.; e. Univ. of B.C., B.A. 1966, B.L.S. 1967; m. Frances Josephine, d. late Albert Edward Clay, 8 Oct. 1966; children: Gregory Joseph, Michael Edward; ASST. LIBRARIAN – PUBLIC SERVICES, SELKIRK COLLEGE 1984– ; Chrmn., Nelson Heritage Advisory Comte., 1981– ; ed. Union List of Candn. newspapers held by Candn. libs. 1968–69; Nat. Lib. of Can. (acting head, newspaper section 1968–69) 1967–69; ed. 'Centennial Issues of Candn. Newspapers' and 'Kootenainana' 1976; author 'Flexible working hours' (Candn. Lib. Journal, Aug. 1976); 'Book budget allocations' (Candn. Lib. Journal, June 1977); 'Management indicators for B.C. learning resource centres' (Candn. Lib. Journal, June 1982); text for 'Architectural Heritage Walking Tour, Nelson, B.C.' 1984, rev. ed. 1993; 'Architectural Heritage Motoring Tour: Historic Nelson, B.C.' 1986; 'Heritage Cemetery Tour: Historic Nelson, B.C.' 1991; 'Wilby in the Kootenays' (B.C. Historical News, Fall 1987); 'The University Club of Nelson and the Provincial University Question, 1903–1910 (B.C. Historical News, Spring 1989); 'The Wilby Hoax' (B.C. Historical News, Winter 1990); 'The All Red Route Through the Kootenays' (Canadian West, Spring 1991); 'Selkirk College Comprehensive Planning Report' 1992; 'Gone But Not Forgotten: The Nelson Club, 1896–1925' (B.C. Historical News, Winter 1992–93); mem., B.C. Lib. Assn.; Candn. Lib. Assn.; Roman Catholic; recreations: hiking, photography, skiing, golf; Home: R.R. 1, S22 C1, Nelson, B.C. V1L 5P4.

**WENDEBORN, Richard Donald;** retired; b. Winnipeg, Man. 16 Sept. 1929; s. Curtis Ernest and Rose Elizabeth (Lysecki) W.; e. Elma (Man.) elem. and high schs.; Univ. of Man. 2 yrs.; Colo. Sch. of Mines, Engr. of Mines 1952, Distinguished Achievement Award 1973; Advanced Mgmt. Prog., Harvard Univ. 1974; m. Dorothy Ann d. late R.S. Errol Munn 24 Aug. 1957; children: Margaret Gayle, Beverley Jane, Stephen Richard, Peter Donald, Ann Elizabeth; joined Ingersoll-Rand Canada Inc. as Sales Engr., Sydney, N.S. and St. John's, Nfld. 1952–56, Mgr. Carset Bit Div. Montreal H.O. 1956, Mgr. Rock Drill Div. H.O. 1957, Mgr. Moncton Br. 1959, Mgr. Mining Constr. & Indust. Sales 1961, Mgr. Montreal Br. 1963, Gen. Mgr. Sales H.O. 1965, Vice Pres. and Gen. Mgr. 1968, Pres., C.E.O. and Dir. 1969; Chrmn. 1975–89; Extve. Vice Pres., Ingersoll-Rand Co., Woodcliff Lake, NJ 1976–89; mem. Machinery & Equipment Mfrs. Assn. Can.; US-USSR Trade & Econ. Council; Colo. Sch. Mines Alumni Assn.; Dir., Town & River Civic Assn.; Tau Beta Pi; U.S. citizen 1988; recreation: golf, boating; Clubs: Royal Palm Yacht, Ft. Myers, FL (Fleet Captain and Dir.); Useppa Island Club; Home: 9990 Cypress Lake Dr., Fort Myers, FL 33919.

**WENMAN, Wanda Mary,** M.D., F.R.C.P.(C); physician/university professor; b. Flin Flon, Man. 1 Aug. 1950; d. Frederick Arthur and Mathilda Margaret (Reid) W.; e. Univ. of Calgary M.D. 1974; PROF., DEPT. OF PEDIATRICS & DEPT. MED. MICRO & INFECT. DIS., UNIV. OF ALTA. 1988– ; postgrad. training in pediatrics, Univ. of Ottawa 1974–76; Infect. Dis., Univ. of Glasgow 1976–77; Univ. of Man. 1977–80; Molecular Biol., UCLA 1980–81; Assoc. Prof., Dept. of Pediatrics, Univ. of Alta. 1981–88; Dir., Div. Infect. Dis. 1984– ; Division Head, Provincial Laboratory of Public Health, Edmonton, Alta.; Adjunct Prof., Dept. Microbiol. 1983– ; Assoc. Prof., Dept. Med. Micro. & Infect. Dis. 1987–88; Ped. Infect. Dis. Cons., Univ. of Alta. Hosp. 1983– ; Royal Alexandra Hosp. 1987– ; Fellowship, Med. Rsch. Counc. of Can. 1979–81; Scholarship, Alta. Heritage Found. Med. Rsch. 1981– ; Exch. Sci., Alta.-Hokkaido Exchange Agreement 1985; Fellow, RCPSC; Fellow, Infectious Diseases Soc. of Am.; Fellow, Pediatric Infectious Diseases Soc.; Mem., Candn. Infectious Diseases Soc.; Am. Soc. for Microbiol.; Candn. Soc. for Clinical Investigation; Soc. for Pediatric Rsch.; author of jour. articles & holder of internat. patents related to vaccine devel.; recreations: racquet sports, cycling, music; Home: 1811 – 91st Ave., Edmonton, Alta.; Office: 2C3.77 Walter Mackenzie Ctr., Edmonton, Alta. T6G 2R7.

**WENTE, Margaret,** M.A.; editor; b. Evanston, Ill. 15 Feb. 1950; d. William Z. and Barbara M. (McNeill) W.; e. Univ. of Mich. B.A. 1971; Univ. of Toronto M.A. 1972; ED., REPORT ON BUSINESS, THE GLOBE AND MAIL 1991– ; Ed. Canadian Business mag. 1980–84; Sr. Ed. Venture CBC TV 1984–86; Ed., Report on Business Magazine, The Globe and Mail 1986–91; Dir., Scarborough Grace Hosp.; recipient Nat. Mag. Award Bus. Writing 1980; Home: 10 Balsam Ave., Toronto, Ont. M4E 3B4; Office: 444 Front St. W., Toronto, Ont. M5V 2S9.

**WENZEL, Werner,** J.M.; executive; b. Guatemala, C.A. 16 Feb. 1934; s. Walter F. and Maria E. (Heil) W.; e. Univ. of Frankfurt, Engn. Physics; m. Johanna K. d. Wilhelm and Emma Sulzmann 8 Dec. 1955; children: Rolf, Alexander, Derek; PRES., C.E.O. AND DIR., WEGA-D GEOPHYSICAL LTD. 1984– ; Pres., C.E.O. & Dir. Intcan Economic Development and Finance Associates Ltd. 1975– ; Dir., Industrial Research & Management Ltd.; 244687 Alberta Ltd.; Hurricane Hydrocarbons; Eming Inc., Canadian-Russian J.V.; Pres., Turan Petroleum, Canadian-Kazakh J.E.; joined Imperial Oil 1955–65, Geophys. Engn. Research; Mang. Dir. Brimstone Export Ltd. 1965–69; Vice Pres. Finance and Corporate Development, Vennard & Ellithorpe Ltd. 1969–72; Asst. Depty. Min. of Industry & Comm., Alta. 1972–75; Pres. & C.E.O. Chancellor Energy Resources Ltd. 1981–83; Past Pres. Calgary Safety Council; Candn. Automobile Sport Club Prairie Region; Past Chrmn., Alta. Roadbuilders & Heavy Construction Assn.; author various papers and articles sulphur research, markets, handling, forming and transport.; mem. Candn. German Chamber Comm.; CANADA-U.S.S.R. Business Council; Internat. Soc. for Strategic Management and Planning; recreations: hiking, swimming, hunting, fishing, photography; Clubs: Ranchmen's; Calgary Petroleum; Office: 100, 1301 – 8th St. S.W., Calgary, Alta. T2R 1B7.

**WERMELINGR, Heinz B.;** publishing executive; b. Lucerne, Switz. 24 June 1946; s. Josef and Alice Hermine (Kuhn) W.; e. Zurich Commercial; m. Beatrice d. Rudolf and Hanna Merian 25 Sept. 1982; children: Frank, Remo; EXTVE. VICE-PRES., OVERSEAS, HARLEQUIN ENTERPRISES LIMITED 1987– ; Product Mgr., Juvena S.A. Cosmetics 1962–72; Mktg. Mgr., Wella Internat. 1972–75; Mktg. Dir., Reader's Digest 1975–86; recreations: tennis, skiing, soccer, wine; Home: 70 Erskine Ave., Apt. 103, Toronto, Ont. M4P 1Y2; Office: Baar, Switz.

**WERNHAM, Richard Stephen,** B.A., LL.B.; investment manager; b. Toronto, Ont. 25 Sept. 1953; s. Prof. James C.S. and Rosemary M. (Soutter) W.; e. Carleton Univ. B.A. 1973; Univ. of Toronto LL.B. 1976; m. Julia E.A. West d. Bernard and Margaret West Aug. 1976; children: Nicholas James Richard, Emma Margaret Julia, Simon Thomas West; PRES., FOUNDER AND DIR. GLOBAL STRATEGY FINANCIAL INC. 1983– ; called to Bar of Ont. 1978; Corporate Lawyer, Tory, Tory, DesLauriers & Binnington 1978–83; Policy Counsel, Toronto Stock Exchange 1979–80; Special Lectr. in Law Trinity Coll. Univ. of Toronto 1977– ; Gov. Invest. Funds Inst. Can.; Assoc., Massey Coll. 1988– ; recreations: golf, music; Office: 1600 – 33 Bloor St. E., Toronto, Ont. M4W 3T8.

**WESENBERG, Ray;** business executive; b. Edmonton, Alta. 10 Jan. 1939; s. William Henry and Martha (Martin) W.; e. Similkameen Jr. & Sr. High; Univ. of B.C.; m. Ruth d. Richard and Alicia O'Neill 25 Nov. 1967; children: Sean, Erin; CHAIRMAN, WESTERN INVENTORY SERVICE LTD. 1967– ; purchased Small Inventory Co. Dec. 1967 with offices in Wpg. & Vanc.; Western Inventory is the largest & only nat. Candn. co. of its kind with 52 offices & 1800 employees; Past Mem., Y.P.O.; Mem., MENSA; W.P.O.; recreations: golf, walking, swimming; clubs: Capilano Golf & Country, Hollyburn Country; Home: 1319 Chartwell Dr., W. Vancouver, B.C.; Office: 510 – 1380 Burrard St., Vancouver, B.C. V6Z 2H3.

**WESSON, Paul S.,** B.Sc., M.Sc., Ph.D.; university professor; b. Nottingham, England 11 Sept. 1949; s. Stephen and Betty Irene W.; e. Univ. of London B.Sc. 1971; Univ. of Cambridge M.Sc. 1972, Ph.D. 1979; m. Ellen d. Havard and Erna Stauborg 12 Sept. 1980; children: Amanda, Emily, Jasper; PROF., UNIV. OF WATERLOO 1988– ; Asst. Prof., Univ. of Alta. 1980–84; Assoc. Prof., Univ. of Waterloo 1984–88; Visiting Prof., Univ. California at Berkeley 1990–91; Visiting Prof., Stanford Univ. 1991–94; Mem., Cambridge Astron. Soc.; Royal Astron. Soc. of London; Internat. Astron. Union; author: 'Cosmology and Geophysics' 1978, 'Gravity, Particles and Astrophysics' 1980; co-author: 'Gravitation, A Banff Summer Institute' 1991; author/co-author of approx. 140 rsch. papers in journals; recreations: ice hockey, boating; Office: Dept. of Physics, Univ. of Waterloo, Waterloo, Ont. N2L 3G1.

**WEST, Allen Sherman, Jr.,** B.Sc., Ph.D.; university professor; b. Worcester, Mass. 13 Aug. 1909; s. Allen Sherman and Grace May (Booth) W.; e. Mass. State Coll., B.Sc. 1931; Yale Univ., Ph.D. 1935; m. Mary Lucille, d. Dr. Harry Quinn, 30 Nov. 1946; Mgr. Environmental Policy, Nfld. and Labrador Hydro, 1975–78; Emeritus Prof. of Biology, Queen's Univ., 1974; Prof. of Biology, Queen's Univ., 1949–74; Forest Entomol. with U.S. Dept. Agric., engaged in research and control work in Ariz. and Cal. 1935–39; Prof. of Forest Entomol., Univ. of New Brunswick, 1939–43 (1st chair of forest entomol. in Can.); Assoc. Prof. of Biol., Queen's Univ., 1946–49; served in World War, 1943–46, with Candn. Army in Chem. Warfare Service with rank of Capt.; mem. Entomol. Soc. of Ont.; Entomol. Soc. of Can.; Am. Mosquito Control Assn.; Entomol. Soc. of Am.; United Church; Home: 208 Albert St., Kingston, Ont. K7L 3V3.

**WEST, William A.,** B.A.Sc., M.B.A.; consultant; b. Toronto, Ont. 19 Oct. 1934; s. Arthur Currie and Ruth Wilhelmina (Frankish) W.; e. Univ. of Toronto, B.A.Sc. 1956; Univ. of West. Ont., M.B.A. 1958; m. Geraldine Barran d. Arthur Vickers 7 Mar. 1987; children: Jennifer, James, Sharon, Andrew; Div. Mgr., Exxon Internat. Inc. 1969–71; Asst. Gen. Mgr., Imperial Oil, Logistics 1971–73; Vice-Pres. & Gen. Mgr., Mktg. 1974–76; Extve. Asst. to Chrmn., Exxon Corp. 1976–77; Sr. Vice Pres., Exxon Internat. Inc. 1977–78; Vice-Pres. & Gen. Mgr., Logistics, Imperial Oil Limited 1978–81; Pres., Esso Petrol. Can. 1981–82; Pres., Petro-Can. Prod. 1982–85; Consultant 1986–89; Pres. & Chief Extve. Offr., Junior Achievement of Canada 1989–93; St. George's Golf & Country Club; recreations: golf; Home: 17 Thornbury Cres., Islington, Ont. M9A 2M1.

**WESTBURY, Richard (George) S(elby),** C.D., B.Sc., F.R.G.S., F.G.S., C.Geol., P.Geol.; business executive/professional geologist; b. Windsor, Berkshire, England 17 June 1926; s. Major Bertram Selby and Beatrice Elizabeth (Pope) W.; e. Imperial Serv. Coll., Windsor, Eng.; Queen Mary Coll., Univ. of London, B.Sc. (Spec. Hons.) 1952; m. Nancy d. Jean and Keith McAllister J.P. 18 Dec. 1954; children: John, Elizabeth, Eleanor, Fiona; DIR., PRES. & FOUNDER, ALBURY RESOURCES LTD. 1980– ; Royal Navy 1944–47; Home & Brit. Pacific fleets, Hon. Artillery Co. Inf. Bn. 1948–52; Candn. Militia, Staff Offr. 1974–82 (Major); Geologist, Phillips Petroleum & Texaco Can. 1952–60; Petroleos Brasileiro S.A. 1960–63; Cons. & management of independent companies 1964–80; Dir. & Pres., Madison Oils Ltd. 1973–83; P. Geol., Assn. of Engr., Geol. & Geophysicists 1965; Candn. Forces Decoration 1980; Silver Jubilee Medal 1977; admitted to Order of St. John 1979; promoted to Commander 1986; Dir., Royal Alta. United Serv. Inst. 1983–89 and 1990–94; Gov., Alta. Army Cadet League 1980– ; Mem., Geol. Assn. 1949– ; Fellow, Geol. Soc. of London (F.G.S. C.Geol.) 1951– ; Royal Geog. Soc. 1969; Mem., Royal Candn. Legion 1953; associated with work of Order of St. John for many years: Chrmn., Calgary Br. 1978–81, Prov. Commnr. St. John Ambulance Brigade 1986–88; recreations: reading, work; Clubs: Royal Commonwealth Soc. (fellow) 1944, Royal Alta. Un. Serv. Inst.; Home: 111 Wimbledon Cres. S.W., Calgary, Alta. T3C 3J2; Office: 508, 630 – 8th Ave. S.W., Calgary, Alta. T2P 1G6.

**WESTCOTT, James William,** B.A., M.A., M.B.A.; management consultant; b. Saskatoon, Sask. 16 June 1928; s. Herbert and Grace (Chamberlain) W.; e. Univ. of Saskatchewan B.A. 1949; McGill Univ. M.A. 1950; Univ. of Pennsylvania M.B.A. 1954; m. Nancy d. Thomas and Anne Curran 10 July 1954; children: Mark Curran, Grace Ann, Donna Mary; PRES., ANGLO FIDELITY FUNDING INC. 1989– ; CHRMN. EMERITUS, WESTCOTT, THOMAS & ASSOC. LTD. 1986– ; Clinical Psychol. Montreal Gen. Hosp. 1950–51; Personnel Asst. Imperial Tobacco, Montreal 1954–55; Supr. Methods and Time Study, Noranda Copper and Brass, Montreal 1955–58; Dir. Western Div., P.S. Ross & Partners, Mgmt. Cons. 1959–63; Gen. Mgr. Lamond, Dewhurst, Westcott & Fraser Ltd., Ind. Psychologists 1963–69; Pres., James W. Westcott & Assoc. Ltd. 1969–86; Chrmn. Emeritus, Westcott, Thomas & Associates Ltd. 1986– ; mem. Adv. Counc., Toronto Symphony; Dir., Northwestern Health Campus Corp.; Vice Chrmn., Northwestern Health Centre Found.; Past Pres., Candn. Counc. of Christians and Jews; Dir., Turning Point Youth Services; Clifton Youth Services; Strings Across the Sky; mem. Associates, Consulting and Audit Canada; past Pres. Univ. of Pennsylvania Canadian Alumni Fund; past Vice-Pres., Metro Toronto Big Brothers Assn.; recreations: reading, collecting art, cottage, family history, music; Club: Granite; Home: 84 Weybourne Cres., Toronto, Ont. M4N 2R7.

**WESTCOTT, Joan Marlene,** B.A., M.Ed., F.O.T.F.; educator; b. London, Ont. 1 Apr. 1945; d. Roylance Arthur (dec.) and Elsie Margaret (Robins) W.; e. South Huron Dist. High Sch., Exeter, Ont.; London (Ont.) Teachers' Coll. 1964; Univ. of W. Ont. B.A. 1970; Univ. of Toronto (OISE) M.Ed. 1991; Exec. Dir., Federation of Women Teachers' Assns. of Ont.; elem. sch. teacher 1964–85; Vice-Princ. 1975–78; Princ. Kindergarten-gr. 5 1979–84; Pres. Waterloo County Women Teachers' Assn. 1973–74, mem. Exec. 1970–84; Dir. Fedn. of Women Teachers' Assns. of Ont. 1974– , mem. Exec. 1976– , Pres. 1978–79; Gov. Ontario Teachers' Fedn. 1976– ; Pres. 1984–85; Exec. Mem. 1981– ; Gov. Ontario Institute for Studies in Education 1990– ; Dir. Alliance for Children, Ont. 1983–88; adult leader Children's Internat. Summer Villages 1970–74; Office: 1260 Bay St., Toronto, Ont. M5R 2B8.

**WESTDAL, Christopher William,** B.A., M.B.A.; diplomat; b. Winnipeg, Man. 13 Sept. 1947; s. Swain Neilson and Margaret Mary (Badger) W.; e. St. John's College, Winnipeg B.A. 1968; Univ. of Manitoba M.B.A. 1970; m. Sheila d. Paul and Nuala Hayes 22 Feb. 1992; children: John, Ruth; Economic Advisor (Univ. of Toronto team), Tanzania 1970–73; CIDA Ottawa-Asia Br. 1973–75; Privy Council Office Ottawa 1975–77; E. Africa Reg. Dir., CIDA 1978–82; High Comnr. to Bangladesh & Ambassador to Burma 1982–85; Asst. Sec. to Cabinet Ctte. on Defence & Fgn. Policy, Privy Council Office 1985–87; Dir. Gen., Internat. Orgns., Dept. of External Affairs 1987–91; Canadian Ambassador to South Africa 1991–93; Diplomat-in-Residence, Royal Roads Military College 1993–94; Office: Royal Roads Military College, FMO Victoria, B.C. V0S 1B0.

**WESTELL, Anthony;** journalist; b. Exeter, Devon, Eng., 27 Jan. 1926; s. John Wescombe and Blanche (Smedley) W.; e. Mount Radford Sch., Exeter, Eng.; m. Jeanne Margaret Collings, 10 Jan. 1950; children: Dan, Tracy; began career as Apprentice Reporter, 'Express and Echo,' Exeter, Eng., 1942–43, 1946–48; joined 'Evening World,' Bristol, Eng., 1948–49; Northcliffe Newspaper Group, London, Eng., 1949–55; apptd. Pol. Corr. for Group 1950–55 and occasional Columnist and Ed. Writer, 'Sunday Express,' London; became Dipl. Corr., 'Evening Standard,' London, 1955–56; joined 'Globe & Mail,' Toronto, as Reporter, 1956–59; mem. Ed. Bd., Chief Ed. Writer, Asst. to Ed. 1959–64; Chief, Ottawa Bureau 1964–69; Ottawa Ed., 'Toronto Star' 1969–71, 73–74; Ottawa columnist, Ed. Page 1974–86; Prof. of Journalism, Carleton Univ., 1972–73, 1975–92; Supervisor of Grad. Stud., Sch. of Journal., Carleton Univ., 1981–82, Acting Dir. 1983–84, Dir. 1988–91; Assoc. Dean of Arts, 1985–86; Retired 1992; Inducted into 'Canadian News Hall of Fame' 1992; Assoc. Ed. (N. Amer.), World Paper, Boston since 1978; Visiting Fellow, Inst. Candn. Studies, Carleton Univ., 1974–75; Senior Associate, Carnegie Endowment for Internat. Peace, N.Y. 1980; Visiting Assoc., Center for Inter-Amer. Rel., N.Y. 1983; author, 'Paradox – Trudeau as Prime Minister' 1972; 'The New Society,' 1977; (with A. Frizell) 'The Canadian General Election of 1984–Politicians, Parties, Press and Polls' 1985; 'The Canadian General Election of 1988' (with A. Frizzell & J. Pammett) 1989; served in 2nd World War with Royal Navy, 1943–46; recreations: reading, sailing; Home: 44 Charles St. W., Apt. 4402, Toronto, Ont. M4Y 1R8.

**WESTON, Hilary M.;** fashion industry executive; b. Dublin, Rep. of Ireland; m. W. Galen 1966; two children; DEPUTY CHAIRMAN, HOLT RENFREW & CO. LIMITED; Dir., Brown Thomas & Co. Limited (Ireland); The Windsor Club (US); Co-Founder & Chair, Candn. Environ. Edn. Found.; Co-Chair, Winter Garden Show, The Royal Agricultural Winter Fair; Founding Chair, The Ireland Fund of Canada; The Mabin School; Past Co-Chair, The Elgin & Winter Garden Theatre Found.; Adv. Bd. Mem., Sothebys of Canada; co-author: 'In a Canadian Garden' 1989; Office: 22 St. Clair Ave. E., Ste. 2001, Toronto, Ont. M4T 2S3.

**WESTON, W. Galen,** O.C.; diversified holdings executive; b. England 29 Oct. 1940; s. W. Garfield Weston & Reta L. Howard; m. Hilary Frayne 1966; 2 children; B.A. & LL.D. (hon. causa) Univ. of Western Ont.; CHRMN. & PRES., GEORGE WESTON LTD., and Wittington Investments, Limited, (holding co. of Weston companies); Chrmn.: Holt Renfrew & Co. Ltd.; Lester B. Pearson Coll. of the Pacific & United Colleges Inc.; Loblaw Companies Limited; Weston Foods Limited; Weston Resources Limited; Vice-Chrmn.: Fortnum & Mason plc (U.K.); Pres.: The W. Garfield Weston Found.; Dir.: Assoc. British Foods plc (U.K.); Brown Thomas Group Ltd.; Candn. Imperial Bank of Commerce; George Weston Holdings Limited (U.K.); United World Colleges (U.K.); Life Mem.: Art Gallery of Ont.; Royal Ont. Museum; Officer of the Order of Canada; recreations: polo, tennis; Clubs: Badminton & Raquet (Toronto); Guards Polo (U.K.); Lyford Cay (Bahamas); Toronto; York (Toronto); Windsor Club (Florida); Address: Ste. 2001, 22 St. Clair Ave. E., Toronto, Ont. M4T 2S3.

**WESTWATER, George Traill,** M.A., F.F.A., F.C.I.A., A.S.A.; actuary; b. Hawick, Roxburghshire, Scot., 26 June 1911; s. Alexander and Christina (Henderson) W.; e. Edinburgh Inst.; Edinburgh Univ., M.A. (1st Class Hons.) 1933; m. Phoebe Mary (dec.), d. George E. Moss, St. Helena, 12 Jan. 1944; one d. Judith Margaret; with present Standard Life Assnce. Co., Edinburgh, Scot., 1933–39; Montreal Que., 1946; Gen. Mgr., 1957; apptd. Extve. Dir., 1 Sept. 1966; retired 1976; served in World War, 1939–45, with R.N.V.R., Naval Meteorol. Service; Fellow, Candn. Inst. Actuaries; past Vice Pres., Faculty of Actuaries (Scotland); Anglican; recreation: golf; Clubs: Mt. Royal; Royal Montreal Golf; Home: 14 Willow Ave., Westmount, Que. H3Y 1Y2.

**WESTWOOD, Bruce Malcolm;** business executive; venture capitalist; b. Montréal, Qué. 25 Apr. 1940; s. George Smythe and Pearl Grace (Nicholls) W.; e. Montréal West H.S.; Sir George William Coll.; Univ. of Toronto; m. Lyn d. Geraldine and Clifford Sifton 3 Sept. 1966; children: Ashton Clifford, Whitney Martha; PRESIDENT & CHIEF EXTVE. OFFR., STERLING LORD ASSOCIATES LTD. 1993– ; Chrmn.: Westwood Lord Inc. 1993– ; Lucinda Vardey Agency 1994– ; McLuhan Program in Cultural & Technology, Univ. of Toronto; Shawinigan Chem. 1956–58, 1961–65; Imasco 1958–60; Planned Investments Ltd. 1966–68; Founder & Extve. Vice-Pres., Venturetek Internat. 1969–72 (Chrmn., Unidata (London, England)); Chief Extve. Offr., Pop Shoppes Internat. 1973–78; Founder, Chrmn. & Chief Extve. Offr., Meridian Technol. Inc. 1978–85 (Dir., Jutras Die Casting Ltd.; Microdesign Ltd.; CEMCORP; CompAS & Solartech Limited); Pres. & C.E.O., Royal Gold Enterprises Inc. 1985–90; former Chrmn., Roscomag Industries Ltd. 1987–89; Bittner Packers Limited 1987–90; CNC Machine Inc. 1987–91; Myod Industries Ltd. 1988–89; former Dir., ESP Edn. Software Products Inc. 1985–88; David Wood Food Shop 1985–88; Guest Speaker, Univ. of West. Ont.; York Univ.; Chrmn., Harbourfront Lit. Bd.; Past Chrmn., Toronto French Sch. (Chrmn., Curriculum, Extve. & Nom. Cttes.); Past Chrmn., Candn. Solar Indus. Assn.; co-author: 'Toronto French School' brochure (NCA Typographic Excellence Award 1986; Toronto Art Dir. Club); Vice-Chrmn., The Candn. Centre for Global Security; recreations: tennis, skiing, gardening, squash, reading; Clubs: Royal Candn. Yacht; The Queen's Club; Home: 67 Sussex Ave., Toronto, Ont. M5S 1J8.

**WETMORE, The Hon. Douglas Tupper,** LL.B.; supreme court judge; b. Trail, B.C. 23 June 1927; s. Douglas Stevenson and Alice Tupper (Ellis) W.; e. Univ. of B.C. LL.B. 1950; m. Catherine d. Henry and Catherine Giegerich 5 May 1952; children: Mara Elizabeth, Catherine Alison, Douglas Henry; JUDGE, SUPREME COURT OF BRITISH COLUMBIA 1990– ; practice, Trail, B.C. 1950–75; Bencher of Law Society 1973–75; Judge, County Court of Vancouver 1975–90; author of seminar papers & leader of national conf. of County & District Court Judges, 'Papers on Criminal Law' for 9 years; recreations: golf; clubs: Pt. Grey Golf; Home: 3996 West 38th Ave., Vancouver, B.C.; Office: 800 Smithe St., Vancouver, B.C. V6Z 2E1.

**WETMORE, Rt. Rev. James Stuart,** B.S.Litt., D.D.; retired bishop (P. Epis.); b. Hampton, N.B. 22 Oct. 1915; s. Charles Talbot and Alberta Mae (McCordic) W.; e. Hampton (N.B.) Consol. Sch.; Sussex (N.B.) High Sch. (Matric.); Univ. of King's Coll., B.A. 1938, L.Th. 1939, B.S.Litt. 1949, D.D.1960; Yale Divinity Sch. 1947; m. Frances Howard, d. E. Wallace Robinson, Annapolis Royal and Bear River, N.S., 4 July 1940; children: Nancy Faulds, Charles Edward, Stuart Andrew, Mrs. J. Bohun, Mrs. David Gulotta; SUFFRAGAN BISHOP, DIOCESE OF NEW YORK, 1960–87; retired; made Deacon, All Saints Cath., Halifax, 1938; Curate, St. Anne's Parish Ch., Fredericton, N.B., 1939–41; o. Priest, Christ Ch. Cath., Fredericton, 1939; Rector, Westfield, N.B., 1941–43; St. James Ch., Saint John, N.B., 1943–47; Eastern Field Secy., Gen. Bd. of Religious Educ., Ch. of Eng. in Can., 1947–51, and Asst. to the Gen. Secy., 1951–53; Dir., Christian Educ., Epis. Diocese of New York, 1953–60; Canon (Hon.), Cath. of Saint John the Divine, N.Y.C.; el. Suffragan Bishop, Diocese of N.Y., 1959, consecrated, 1960; served in Princess Louise (N.B.) Hussars, 1929–32; King's O.T.C., Co. Commdr. and Adjt., 1933–39; Chaplain, No. 7 Dist. Depot, Fredericton, N.B., 1939–41, Reserve Chaplain, No. 7 Mil. Dist., 1943–47; Pres., Soldier Comfort Assn., Fredericton, 1939–40; mem., Bd. of Trustees, Windham House, N.Y.C., 1955–58; Vice-Pres., Metrop. Chapter, Relig. Educ. Assn., 1958–60; Vice-Pres., Prot. Epis. City Missions Soc., N.Y. 1960–86; Pres., Richmond Fellowship of America, 1973–78; Convenor, Metrop. Mission Task Force, N.Y. Met. Area; mem., Presiding Bishop's Comte. on Evangelism; the Pilgrims of U.S.; Dept. Christian Educ. of Nat. Council, Prot. Epis. Ch. (1960–65); Secy., House of Bishops of Second Prov. 1960–1966; Chrmn. Extve. Comm., Internat. Council of Religions; mem., Bd. of Dir., N.Y. State Council of Churches; Prot. Council of N.Y.; mem. Dept. of Ch. Renewal, Nat. Council of Chs.; Secy.-Treas. Assn. for Christian Mission in City of N.Y.; Vice Pres., Ch. Plan Comn. for N.Y. Metrop. Area; Pres. (1958) Friends of Kings Coll., Halifax Inc.; Pres., Episcopal Housing Corp.; Good Shepherd-on-the-Island Corp.; St. Peter's School, Peekskill, N.Y.; Anglican Soc.; Second Province of Episcopal Ch.; Chrmn., House of Bishops Comte. on Educ.; Sub-Prelate, Order St. John Jerusalem (Am. Chapter); Secy., Council of Diocese of N.Y.; Affiliate, Soc. of the Atonement; Home: 10 Meadowview, Millbrook, N.Y. 12545.

**WETMORE, John D.,** B.Math.; financial executive; b. 30 Oct. 1949; e. Univ. of Waterloo B.Math 1973; m. Karen Gibson; children: Gregory, Cameron, Sean; VICE-PRES., FINANCE & PLANNING, IBM CANADA LTD. 1993– ; joined IBM as Sales Trainee 1973; progressed through various mktg. & branch mgmt. positions; assignment in N.Y., in Latin America HQ, and as Administrative Assistant to A/FE Corp. Chairman; 1986 Vice-Pres. of Mktg. for Western Canada; 1990 Assignment to N.Y. as WW Mktg Dir for A1X & RS/6000; Financial executive position in N.Y. in Credit Corp., Corp. Controller's Office and Corp. Bus. Development; Bd. of Dirs., ISM Information Systems Mgmt.; Office: 3600 Steeles Ave. E., Dept. 938, Stn. C4, Markham, Ont. L3R 9Z7.

**WETSTON, Howard I.,** Q.C., B.Sc., LL.B.; judge; b. Ulm, Germany 3 June 1947; s. Abe and Freda W.; e. Mt. Allison Univ., B.Sc. 1969, Dalhousie Univ. LL.B. 1974; JUDGE, FEDERAL COURT OF CANADA, TRIAL DIVISION 1993– ; articled with Stewart, McKeen, Covert 1974–75; Crown Couns., Attorney-General's Office (N.S.) 1975–76; Dept. of Justice Ottawa 1976–80; Legal Counsel, National Energy Bd. 1980–81; Gen. Couns., Consumers' Assn. of Can. 1981–82; Asst. Gen. Couns., Nat. Energy Bd. 1982–83; Gen. Couns., Candn. Transport Comn. 1983–85; Lawyer, Burnet, Duckworth & Palmer - Phillips & Vineberg 1985–86; Sr. Depy. Dir. of Inv. & Rsch., Consumer & Corp. Affairs Can. 1986–89; Part-time Prof. of Law, Univ. of Ottawa 1981–89; Dir. of Investigation & Rsch., Competition Policy, Consumer & Corp. Affairs Can. 1989–93; Mem., The Law Soc. of Alta. 1986; The Law Soc. of U.C. (Ont.) 1978; N.S. Barristers Soc. 1975; Candn. Bar Assn.; author of 3 jour. articles & 5 book chaps.; recreations: tennis, music; Home: Ottawa, Ont.; Office: Supreme Court Bldg., Wellington St., Ottawa, Ont. K1A 0H9.

**WEVERS, John William,** Th.D., D.D., D.H.C., F.R.S.C.; educator; b. Baldwin, Wis. 4 June 1919; s. Ben and Wilemina (Te Grootenhuis) W.; e. Calvin Coll. B.A. 1940; Calvin Semy. Th.B. 1943; Princeton Theol. Semy. Th.D. 1945 and Princeton Univ. post-doctoral work Arabic, Islamic Hist., Indo-European Philol., Sanskrit 1945–47; Dropsie Coll. work in Akkadian, Aramaic Dialects, Ugaritic 1947–48; Knox Coll. D.D. 1973; Univ. of Leiden D.H.C. 1985; m. Grace Della d. late Rev. Samuel G. Brondsema 22 May 1942; children: Robert Dick, John William Jr., Harold George, James Merrit; PROFESSOR EMERITUS OF NEAR EASTERN STUDIES, UNIV. OF TORONTO 1984– ; Teaching Fellow, Dept. Biblical Langs. Princeton Theol. Semy. 1944–46, Lectr. in Old Testament and Semitic Langs. 1946–48, Asst. Prof. 1948–51; Asst. Prof. of Oriental Langs. Univ. Coll. Univ. of Toronto 1951 becoming Assoc. Prof. and Prof. of Near E. Studies 1963; Chrmn. Grad. Dept. Near E. Studies 1972–75; Chrmn. Dept. Near E. Studies 1975–80; Fellow Rockefeller Foundation studying Modern Arabic Dialects and Modern Islamic Movements in Near East 1954; CBC Teacher series 'Let's Speak English' 1961–62; Site Supvr. Archaeol. Excavations of Jerusalem summers 1962, 1963; Lectr. Theol. Faculty Univ. of Leiden 1954, Lund 1954, Göttingen 1971, Uppsala 1971, Groningen 1972, Madrid 1972, Helsinki 1983, Stellenbosch 1990; Gov. Central Hosp. Toronto since 1963 (Chrmn. 1967–80); Pres., Central Hosp. Foundation, since 1980; Vice Chrmn. Hosp. Council Metrop. Toronto 1973–74 (Chrmn. 1974–75); Gov., Ont. Hosp. Assn. (Pres. 1978–79); el. Corr. mem. Akademie der Wissenschaften in Göttingen, Philologisch-historische Klasse 1972; el. Fellow, Royal Soc. of Canada 1976; el. member Accademia Mediterranea della Scienza, artistic-lit.-philos. class 1982; Ed.-in-Chief 'Canadian Journal of Linguistics' 1960–67; author 'The Way of the Righteous' 1961; 'A Commentary on the Book of Ezekiel' 1969; 'Genesis, Septuaginta' 1973; 'Text History of the Greek Genesis' 1974; 'Deuteronomium, Septuaginta' 1977; 'Text History of the Greek Deuteronomy' 1978; 'Numeri, Septuaginta' 1982; 'Text History of the Greek Numbers' 1982; 'Leviticus, Septuaginta' 1986; 'Text History of the Greek Leviticus' 1986; 'Notes on the Greek Text of Exodus' 1990; 'Exodus, Septuaginta' 1991; 'Text History of the Greek Exodus' 1992; 'Notes on the Greek Text of Genesis' 1993; co-author: 'Let's Speak English' 4 vols. 1960; reviews and articles on linguistics, Hebrew studies, Semitic Grammar, Septuagint in various internat. journs.; mem. Oriental Club Toronto; Internat. Organ. Septuagint & Cognate Studies (Pres. 1972–80, Honorary Pres. 1985– ); Presbyterian; recreation: Scottish country dancing; Club: Arts & Letters; Home: 116 Briar Hill Ave., Toronto, Ont. M4R 1H9; Office: Dept. of N.E.S., 4 Bancroft Ave., Toronto, Ont. M5S 1A1.

**WEXLER, Muriel Ines Korngold,** B.A., LL.L.; labour lawyer, arbitrator, public service executive; b. Lyon, Rhône, France 18 April 1948; d. Joseph and Berthe (Weill) Korngold; e. Pontifica Universidad de Lima Peru B.A. (equivalent) 1968; Univ. of Ottawa LL.L. 1971; m. Michael S. s. Irving and Diane Wexler 6 Nov. 1971; children: Audrey Françoise, Shawn Andrew; DEPUTY CHAIRPERSON, PUBLIC SERVICE STAFF RELATIONS BOARD 1988– ; Lawyer, Cutler, Castiglio and Langlois 1971–72; Legal Counsel, Immigration Appeal Board 1973–74; Senior Legal Counsel, Professional Inst. of the Public Service of Canada 1974–83; Bd. Mem., Public Service Staff Relations Board 1983–88; Mem., Quebec Bar; Candn. Bar Assn.; Past President, Beth Shalom Sisterhood (President 1987–88; Bd. of Dir. 1987–88); Office: 240 Sparks St., West Tower, Ottawa, Ont. K1P 5V2.

**WEYANT, Robert George,** M.A., Ph.D.; educator; b. Jersey City, N.J. 27 July 1933; s. late Edgar Merrill and late Emma Henrietta (Haberdenk) W.; e. Lafayette Coll., B.A. 1955; Kent State Univ., M.A. 1957; Univ. of Iowa, Ph.D. 1960; m. Doris Joan, d. late John J. Barry, Aug. 1955; two s., Stephen Barry, David Thomas; Prof. of Psychol., Univ. of Calgary since 1970 and mem. Bd. of Govs.; Asst. Prof., St. Lawrence Univ., 1960, Assoc. Prof. 1964–65; Assoc. Prof. present Univ. 1965–70, Asst. Dean present faculty 1967–68, Vice Dean 1968–69, Dean 1972–75; mem. Council, Banff Sch. of Fine Arts; Bd. Dirs., Archives Hist. of Psychol., Univ. of Akron; rec'd Prov. of Alta. Achievement Award in Psychol.; Nat. Science Foundation, Nat. Research Council and Can. Council Grants; Ed. Bd., 'The Journal of the History of Behavioral Sciences'; 'An Essay on the Origin of Human Knowledge' (by Etienne Bonnot), 1971; author of numerous papers; Fellow, Am. Psychol. Assn.; Candn. Assn. Deans Arts & Science (Chrmn. 1973–74); Am. Assn. Advanc. Science; Hist. of Sci. Soc.; Internat. Soc. Hist. Behavioral & Social Sciences; Psi Chi; Sigma Xi; Bd. of Dirs., Candn Club, Calgary; Home: 2015 7th St. S.W., Calgary, Alta. T2T 2X1.

**WEYMAN, C. David,** M.A., F.C.A.; chartered accountant; b. London, Eng. 16 June 1936; s. J. Stanley and Rose (Hellinger) W.; e. City of London Sch.; Trinity Coll. Cambridge, B.A. 1959, M.A. 1962; children: Karen, Jacqueline, Michael, Debra; C.A. London, Eng. 1962, B.C. 1964, Ont. 1974; F.C.A. B.C. 1974; joined Peat Marwick Mitchell & Co. (now Peat Marwick Thorne), Vancouver, B.C. 1967, Toronto Office 1974, Partner 1971–93, Sr. Tax Partner and mem. Exec. Ctte. 1980–84 and 1986–89; Asst. Dep. Min. Tax Policy and Legislation Branch, Dept. of Finance 1984–86; Adviser on tax reform to the Standing Ctte. on Finance and Economic Affairs, H. of C. 1986–89; Vice-Pres., Treas. & Dir., Cabbagetown Community Arts Centre; Chrmn.-Finance Ctte., Friday's Child; Treas. & Dir., Classical Cabaret; recreations: hiking, sailing, cross-country skiing, photography; Clubs: Granite; Ontario; Home: 361 Wellesley St. E., Toronto, Ont. M4X 1H2; Office: Suite 1200, One Toronto Street, Toronto, Ont. M5C 2V5.

**WEYNEROWSKI, Witold Maciej,** M.A.; foreign service officer; b. Bydgoscsz, Poland 20 Nov. 1937; s. Witold Klemens and Julia Hermane (Kessler) W.; e. Ridley Coll. St. Catharines, Ont. 1955; Univ. of Toronto Trinity Coll. B.A. 1959; Univ. Laval B.S.S. 1960; Oxford Univ. B.A., M.A. 1962; Univ. of Geneva Institut des Hautes Etudes Internationales 1965–66; m. 1stly Mary Gael McCarthy 11 July 1959 (div. 1980); m. Evelyn d. Diosdado and Delfina Serrano 29 Aug. 1981; children: Timothy, Juliana, Genevieve, Alexandra, Carolyn; DIR., FRANCOPHONE AFRICA AND MAGHREB, DEPT. OF EXTERNAL AFFAIRS 1989– ; joined Internat. Affairs Div. Dept. Finance Ottawa 1963–64; Research Asst. Candn. Assn. Univ. Teachers 1964–65; Foreign Service Offr.Hist., Legal and Fed.-Prov. Relations Divs. 1966–68; First Secy. NATO Brussels 1968–71; First Secy. and Consul Tunis 1971–74; Comm. Policy Div. Dept. External Affairs Ottawa 1974–75, Depy. Dir. Middle E. Div. 1977–78; secondment to Internat. Programs Div. Dept. Finance Ottawa 1978–80; Candn. Ambassador to Iraq 1980–83; Canadian Ambassador to Tunisia and Libya 1983–86; Dir., Anglophone Africa, Dept. of External Affairs 1986–89; mem. Candn. Del. to UNCTAD V 1979; UN Common Fund Negotiations 1979–80; author various articles working conditions Candn. univ. teachers 1964–65; Hon. Patron of Soc. for Mesopotamian Studies 1980–83; Pres. Conserv. Gatineau 1978–79; mem. Oxford & Cambridge Golfing Soc.; Anglican; recreations: gardening, poetry, golf, squash; Club: Cascades Squash (Wakefield, Que.); Address: R.R. 3, Wakefield, Qué. J0X 3G0.

**WHALEN, John Hubert (Hugh),** B.Sc., M.Sc.; pulp and paper industry executive; b. Trois-Rivières, Qué. 14 July 1930; s. Thomas Fitzgerald and Loretta Alma (Le Boutillier) W.; e. Three-Rivers H.S. 1947; Univ. of N.B., B.Sc. 1952; Mass. Inst. of Technol., M.Sc. 1954; m. Mary d. Antonio and Helen Leblanc 12 Oct. 1957; children: Michael, Nancy, Maryanne; joined Candn. Internat. Paper Co. (now Canadian Pacific Forest Products Limited) 1955; Overseas Newsprint Div. 1960; Vice-Pres., Mktg., Internat. Paper Sales 1969; Pres. 1972; Vice-Pres. & Gen. Mgr., CIP Newsprint & Pulp Businesses 1981; Exec. Vice-Pres., Mktg. CIP Inc. 1986; Extve. Vice-Pres. Mktg., Canadian Pacific Forest Products Ltd. 1988; Chrmn., Canadian Pacific Forest Products (Europe) Ltd.; Canadian Pacific Forest Services Ltd.; Canadian Pacific Forest Products (Asia) Ltd.; Dir., NBIP Ltd.; Chrmn., Candn. Export Assn. 1982–85; Mem., Candn. Pulp & Paper Assn. (Chrmn., Newsprint Section 1987–88); Dir., St. Mary's Hosp. Ctr.; St. Patrick's Orphanage; recreations: skiing, golf, tennis; Clubs: Forest & Stream; Mount Royal; Royal Montreal Golf; Home: 54 White Pine Dr., Beaconsfield, Qué. H9W 5E3.

**WHALEN, Twila M.,** B.A., LL.B.; lawyer; b. Dalhousie, N.B. 29 Aug. 1944; d. Reginald E. and Clarissa G. (Perrott) W.; e. Eel River Crossing Sch.; Dalhousie H.S. 1961; Hotel Dieu Hosp. Sch. of Nursing 1964; St. Michael's Hosp. 1966; Univ. of N.B. B.A. (Hons.) 1977, LL.B. 1980; CHAIRMAN, VETERANS APPEAL BOARD CANADA 1991– ; Clinical Instructor, Hotel Dieu Hosp., Campbellton, N.B. 1966–68; various positions in Nursing in Canada 1968–78; called to Bar of N.B. 1981; private law practice 1981–85; Deputy Clerk & Admin., Court of Queen's Bench 1982–85; Member, Pension Review Bd. 1985–87; Veterans Appeal Bd. 1987–90; Deputy Chrmn. 1990–91; Chrmn., East Restigouche Community Health Care Centre 1984–85; Mem., Restigouche Barristers' Soc. 1981–85 (Sec. 1982–84); Law Soc. of N.B.; Candn. Bar Assn. 1981; Roman Catholic; recreations: nordic skiing, walking, reading; Home: P.O. Box 141, Charlottetown, P.E.I. C1A 7K2; Office: P.O. Box 7700, Charlottetown, P.E.I. C1A 8M9.

**WHALEY, John A.,** Q.C., B.A., LL.B.; financial executive; b. Woodstock, Ont. 23 Mar. 1940; s. Albert C. and Helen I. (Gardner) W.; e. Univ. of Western Ont. B.A. 1961; LL.B. 1966; children: Heather, Dianne, Janice; VICE-PRES., GENERAL COUNSEL & SECY., CT FINANCIAL SERVICES INC. 1981– ; Officer, Personnel & Planning, London (Ont.) Life 1961–63; private practice London 1968–81; Mem., Am. & Candn. Bar assns.; Law Soc. of Upper Canada; Conference Bd. of Canada; Council of Senior Legal Extves.; recreation: fitness; clubs: London; Fitness Inst. (Toronto); Office: 161 Bay St., 35th Fl., Toronto, Ont. M5J 2T2.

**WHALLEY, Edward,** Ph.D., D.I.C., D.Sc., F.C.I.C., F.R.S.C.; chemist; b. Darwen, U.K. 20 June 1925; s. Edward and Doris (Riding) W.; e. St. Mary's Coll. Blackburn 1936–41; Blackburn Tech. Coll. 1941–43; Imp. Coll. London B.Sc., A.R.C.S. 1945, Ph.D., D.I.C. 1949, D.Sc. 1963; m. Isabel Elizabeth d. late James Gillespie 25 Aug. 1956; children: Brian, Monica Mary, Kevin; Lectr. Royal Tech. Coll. Salford, U.K. 1948–50; Post-doctoral Fellow, Nat. Research Council Can. Ottawa 1950–52, Asst. Research Offr. 1952, Assoc. Research Offr. 1955, Sr. Research Offr. 1959, Principal Rsch. Offr. 1961; Sessional Lectr. Univ. of Ottawa Dept. Chem. Engn. 1954, Dept. Chem. 1967, 1969; Head of High Pressure Rsch., Div. of Chem., Nat. Rsch. Council Can. 1961–90; Guest worker, Nat. Rsch. Council, Ottawa 1990– ; Visiting Prof. Univ. of W. Ont. 1969; Univ. of Kyoto 1974–75; co-editor: 'Physics and Chemistry of Ice' 1973; 'High Pressure in Science and Technology' 1984; author or co-author of more than 335 research papers on phys. chem. high pressures and related topics; Candn. Ed. 'Accidents in North American Mountaineering' 1976–80; Alpine Club of Canada (A.C.C.): Mem. 1950– , Chrmn. Ottawa Sec. 1970–74, Chrmn. Safety Comte. 1975–80, Eastern Vice Pres. 1978–80, Silver Rope 1979, Pres. 1980–84, Immed. Past Pres. 1984–88; A.C.C. Repr. to the U.I.A.A. (Union Internat. des Association d'Alpinisur) General Assembly 1976–80; General Camps 1951, '52, '60, '70; Family Camp 1972; Ski Camps 1955, '74; Leader A.C.C. Alpine Climbing Camp, Baffin Island 1979; A.C.C. Representing the Advisory Ctte. on Glaciological and Alpine Nomenclature, became Pres. 1983; climbed extensively in the U.K., Europe, Africa, New Zealand and Japan; Fellow, Royal Soc. Can. (Life Mem. 1951– , Assoc. Hon. Treas. 1969–71, Assoc. Hon. Secy. and Chrmn. Awards Comte. 1971–74, Hon. Sec. 1974–77, Ed. Acad. III 1972–74, Chrmn. Devel. Comte. 1981–82, Centennial Medal 1983); Fellow, Chem. Inst. Can. 1968 (Chrmn. Phys. Chem. Div. 1971–72); Internat. Glaciol. Soc.; Am. Phys. Soc.; Internat. Assn. Advanc. High-Pressure Science & Technol. (Hon. Treas. 1977–85); Internat. Assn. Properties Steam; Candn. Nat. Comte. Properties Steam (Founding mem. and Chrmn. 1973–83, Secy. 1983–90, Member 1990–92); recipient, Queen's Silver Jubilee Medal 1977; Mem., Alpine Club (London), and reporter for the Alpine Journal (U.K.) for climbing in the Candn. Arctic and Alaska; Mem. Arctic Circle, Ottawa 1970– , mem. Exec. Ctte. 1990– ; Fellow, Explorer's Club, New York 1987; R. Catholic; recreations: mountain climbing, skiing; Home: 175 Blenheim Dr., Ottawa, Ont. K1L 5B8; Office: Ottawa, Ont. K1A 0R6.

**WHEALE, Ivan Trevor,** LL.D.; artist; b. Sunderland, Eng. 8 Nov. 1934; s. Arthur Christie and Doris (Parker) W.; e. Barnes Sch. (UK); m. Jean d. Thomas and Winifred Livingstone 3 Nov. 1956; children: Geoffrey, Michael, Kathleen, June; 70 solo exhibitions 1960–91; touring exhib. to 7 pub. art galls. 1987–88; 48 group exhibs. 1966–91; 38 corp. collections inc. Govt. House, Prov. Parl. Bldgs., Nfld.; Parl. Bldgs., Ottawa; Can. Counc. Art Bank; The Royal Collection & The Dean Collection, Windsor Castle, England; 3 touring exhibs.; Book Reviewer, Manitoulin Expositor; Bd. mem., Little Current-Howland Lib.; Adv. Bd. Mem., Laurentian Univ. Mus. & Arts Centre; Judge, Temiskaming Art Gall., Dir. Cover Art Comp. 1987; Panel Mem., Visual Arts Ont., 'Art Means Business'; Jury Mem., O.A.C. awards 1979; Judge, N.O.A.A. Graphics Exhib. 1978; MCTV, 'Almost Noon' 1991; CBC Radio 1990–91; MCTV, 'Image North' 1990; MCTV, 'Don Marks Show' 1989–90; CKSO TV, Image North 'Ivan Wheale' 1989; MCTV, The Today Show 'Ivan Wheale' 1989; MCTV, 'Image North' 1984; CBC Radio, 'Ivan Wheale' 1983; CBC TV, Conlons Ontario 'Ivan Wheale' 1979; Sudbury Cable TV, The Spirit of Art 'Ivan Wheale' 1978; CKSO TV, 'Inco Presents Ivan Wheale Artist' 1975; True North – 'Profile of Ivan Wheale' 1973; Listed in 1991–94 International Who's Who; 1990–94 American Who's Who; Laurentian Univ., LL.D. 1982; awards: Can. Counc. 1979; Ont. Arts Counc. 1976, 78; Creative Artists in Schools 1977, 78; Best of Show, 5th Toronto Outdoor Toronto City Hall 1965, Best of Show, Toronto Fest. of Art 1965; N.O.A.A. 1963; served 3 yrs. in R.A.F. 1952–55; Judge, Onaping Cavalcade of Colour 1993; Elliot Lake Deer Trail Printing Comp.; Trustee, Little Current Public Library; Bd. Mem., Laurentian Cancer Care Hospital (Sudbury); Bd. Mem., Northern Cancer Rsch. Foundation; Hon. Patron., N. Ont. Cancer Care Treatment Centre; Past Mem., Candn. Soc. of Painters in Watercolour; Past Mem., Soc. of Candn. Artists; recipient, Rotary Internat. Paul Harris Award 1993; recreations: sailing, skiing; Home: Box 40, Little Current, Manitoulin Island, Ont. P0P 1K0.

**WHEALY, Hon. Mr. Justice Arthur Carrick,** LL.B.; judge; b. Toronto, Ont. 30 July 1929; s. Arthur Treloar, D.S.C. and bar, D.F.C. and Margaret Agnes (Carrick) W.; e. Upper Can. Coll. Toronto 1948; Royal Mil. Coll.; Univ. of Toronto; Dalhousie Law Sch. LL.B. 1958; m. Elizabeth Helen Richardson 1954; m. Anna Bokor 1979 (dec. 1987); two d. Elisabeth Honore 1959, Victoria Anne Marie 1963; ONTARIO COURT OF JUSTICE 1990– ; called to Bar of N.S. 1958, Ont. 1961; cr. Q.C. 1975; Sr. Adv. Counsel, Dept. of Justice (Can.) 1958–67; private law practice Toronto 1967–78; Judge, District Court of Ont. 1978–90; Lieut. with Q.O.R. Reserve 1949–51, Active Service 1951–54; Major (ret.); Lectr. Bar Admission Course Osgoode Hall 1970–78; Founding Dir. and Past Pres. Criminal Lawyers Assn.; mem. Advocates Soc. (Dir. 1970–71); mem. Royal Candn. Military Inst.; Home: 1803 – 33 Harbour Sq. Toronto, Ont. M5J 2G2; Office: Osgoode Hall, 130 Queen St. W., Toronto, Ont. M5H 2N5.

**WHEATON, Donald Harold;** automobile dealer; b. Saskatoon, Sask. 7 Oct. 1923; s. Albert Joseph and Electa Jane (Rutledge) W.; e. Univ. of Sask.; m. Marion d. Dr. William Sparling 7 July 1948; children: Jane, Ann, Donald, William, David, Ruth, Ross, Herbert; PROP., DON WHEATON LTD. 1961– ; Dir., First Canadian Insurance Corp.; Morningstar Air Express; North West Trust; Edmonton Telephones; Triathlon Leasing Toronto; G.M. dealership in Victoria, B.C.; General Motors Dealer with controlling interests in dealerships Regina, Saskatoon, Calgary, Edmonton, Red Deer, Camrose, New Westminster, Prince George, Vancouver, Victoria and Nanaimo; Dir. & Campaign Chrmn., Un. Way Edmonton; Dir., Alta. Heritage Resource Found.; Past Pres. Edmonton Motor Dealers; Alberta Motor Dealers; Lions Club Edmonton; former Bd. mem. Family Services and St. Joseph's Hosp. (Past Chrmn. Lay Bd.); Dir. Alta. Motor Assn.; United Church; club: Edmonton Flying (sustaining mem., Past Dir.); Home: 15F, 11826 – 100 Ave., Edmonton, Alta. T5K 0K3; Office: 10727 – 82 Ave., Edmonton, Alta. T6E 2B1.

**WHEATON, Mark G.,** B.A., M.B.A.; financial executive; b. Sarnia, Ont. 18 May 1942; s. Hugh Philip and Dorothy B. (Hackney) W.; e. Univ. of Manitoba B.A. 1962; Univ. of West. Ont. M.B.A. 1969; m. Marilyn d. Albert and Winnifred Byrne 20 Jan. 1979; PRESIDENT, LANCASTER FINANCIAL CORP. 1991– ; Banker, Royal Bank (Montreal, Winnipeg, Toronto) 1962–75; Associate, Burns Fry 1975–80; Dir. 1980–86; Lancaster Financial Inc. 1986–91; recreations: aerobics, running, tennis; Home: 94 South Dr., Toronto, Ont. M4W 1R6; Office: 1 First Cdn. Pl., Ste. 5700, Toronto, Ont. M5X 1A9.

**WHEELER, Anne;** film director; producer; writer; b. Edmonton, Alta. 23 Sept. 1946; d. Benjamin Morrill and Nell Rose (Pawsey) W.; DIR. WHEELER-HENDREN ENTERPRISES LTD. 1983– ; Co-owner, Filmwest Associates Ltd. 1971–76; freelance filmmaker, broadcaster, media instr., writer and performer 1976–78; Producer, Dir., Writer N.W. Studio Nat. Film Bd. Can. 1978–83; guest lectr. various acad. instns.; film prodns. incl. 'Other Women's Children' Dir. 1992/93; 'The Diviners' Dir. 1991/92; 'Mom P.I.' Dir. (two episodes 'Through the Door Quickly' and 'A Fist of Fate') 1991/92; 'The Martian' Dir. (Bradbury Theatre) 1991/92; 'Angel Square' Writer, Dir., Prod. 1990; 'Bye Bye Blues' Writer, Dir., Prod., Ed. 1989; 'Cowboys Don't Cry' Writer, Dir., Co-Prod. 1987 (Best Film of Festival, Best Drama Over 30 Minutes, Best Dramatic Direction, Best Dramatic Script, Alta. Motion Picture Industry Awards (A.M.P.I.A.) 1988); 'Loyalties' Dir. & Co-producer 1985 (Critics Choice, Quebec City Film Festival 1986; Best Film of Festival, Best Performance, Best Direction, N. Am. Indian Festival, San Francisco; Best Film, Best Dir., Best Performance, Best Script, Alta. Motion Picture Industry Awards (A.M.P.I.A.) 1987); 'To Set Our House in Order,' Dir. & Writer 1984 (Best Dramatic Script, Best Direction and Best Dramatic Film Under 30 Minutes, A.M.P.D.C. 1986); 'One's A Heifer' Dir. & Co-writer 1984; 'A Change of Heart' Dir. 1983 (Alta. Motion Picture Ind. Awards-AMPIA Best Script, Best Dir., Best Film TV, Best Film of Festival 1985; Blue Ribbon Award Am. Film Festival 1986); 'A War Story' Producer, Dir., Writer 1981 (Best Hist. Documentary Man's Humanity 10th Annual Film Festival Flander-Ghent 1983; Blue Ribbon Award Am. Film Festival 1983; Best Dir., Best Musical Score, Best Feature Length Film & Best Film of Festival AMPIA 1983); 'Teach Me To Dance' Dir. 1978 (Best Performance AMPIA 1979, Dip. of Honour Milano, Italy 1979); 'Welfare Mothers' Cinematog. 1978; 'Krajina and His Forests' co-ed. 1977; 'The Red Dress' ed. 1977; 'Augusta' Dir., Ed., Writer 1976 (Special Recognition Award San Francisco Film Festival 1978; Best Dir. AMPIA 1978); 'Happily Unmarried' Producer, Dir., Ed., Cinematog. 1976; 'Great Grand Mother' Dir., Researcher, Cinematog., Writer 1975 (Blue Ribbon Award Am. Film Festival 1977; Best Dir., Best Ed., Best Cinematog., Best Documentary, Best Film of Festival AMPIA 1976); 'Marie Campbell' and 'Little Startlers' Cinematog. 1975; 'A Grain of Truth' Cinematog., Ed., Instr. 1975 (Best Script Award AMPIA 1975); 'Three Minutes to Live' ed 1974 (Blue Ribbon Am. Film Festival 1975; Best Film of Festival AMPIA 1975); 'Bruce Cockburn' ed. 1974; 'Every Saturday Night' Asst. Dir. 1974; producer: 'Children of Alcohol' 1983; 'It's Just A Test' 1983; 'From Bears to Bartok' 1982 (Best Documentary AMPIA 1983); 'Aux (Twin Boys)' 1980; 'Byron Harmon' 1980; 'Never A Dull Moment' 1979; 'Triangle Island' 1978; 'Priory The Only Home I've Got' 1977 (Best Short Documentary Genie Awards 1979; Red Ribbon Award Am. Film Festival 1979); awards: YMCA 'A Tribute to Women' Edmonton 1988; Alta. Achievement Award in Filmmaking 1988; Achievement Award, Candn. Film and Television Assn. 1989; Lifetime Achievement Award, Festival of Candn. Films, Calgary; 'Woman of the Year,' Edmonton Business & Prof. Womens Club 1989; Honorary Roll, Macleans Magazine 1989; Cultural Hall of Fame, City of Edmonton, Dramatics 1993; Honorary degrees: Univ. of Alta. Litt.D. 1990; Doctor of Univ., Athabasca Univ.

1990; Univ. of Calgary LL.D. 1991; Univ. of Lethbridge LL.D. 1993; Univ. of Brock LL.D. 1993; Office: R.R. 1, 212 Sunset Dr., Ganges, B.C. V0S 1E0.

**WHEELER, John Oliver,** B.A.Sc., Ph.D., F.G.S.A., F.R.S.C.; geologist, b. Mussoorie, India 19 Dec. 1924; s. Edward Oliver and Dorothea (Danielsen) W.; e. Shawnigan Lake Sch. Vancouver Island, B.C. 1942; Univ. of B.C. B.A.Sc. (Geol. Engn.) 1947; Columbia Univ. Ph.D. (Geol.) 1956; m. Nora Jean d. late James H.C. Hughes 17 May 1952; two d. Kathleen Anna (Mrs. T.R. Hunter), Jennifer Margaret (Mrs. R.D. Crompton); EMERITUS RESEARCH SCIENTIST, CORD. DIV. GEOL. SURVEY OF CANADA 1990– ; Geol., Geol. Survey of Can. Ottawa, 1951–61, Vancouver 1961–65, Research Scient. Vancouver 1965–70, head of Cordilleran & Pacific Margin Sec. 1967–70, Research Mgr. Ottawa 1970–79, Chief of Regional & Econ. Geol. Div. 1970–73; Depy. Dir. Gen. 1973–79; Rsch. Scientist, Vancouver 1979–90; Visiting Prof. Univ. of Toronto 1972; Instr. Mountain Warfare Sch., Pacific Command 1944; rec'd Queen's Silver Jubilee Medal 1977; author various scient. papers, monographs and geol. maps on geol. of Central and S. Yukon, S.E. B.C., glacial geol. S. Yukon, tectonics and structure S. part W.Candn. Cordillera, recent glacial fluctuations in Selkirk Mts.; Fellow, Geol. Assn. Can. (Pres. 1970–71; Logan Medal 1983); Dir. Can. Geol. Foundation (Pres. 1975–79); Candn. Geoscience Council (Pres. 1981); mem. Candn. Inst. Mining & Metall.; Alpine Club Can.; Am. Alpine Club; Anglican; recreations: mountaineering, skiing, hiking; Home: 3333 Mathers Ave., W. Vancouver, B.C. V7V 2K6; Office: 100 West Pender St., Vancouver, B.C. V6B 1R8.

**WHEELER, John St. Clair,** executive; b. Brackley, Eng.; s. John and Clara Elizabeth W.; e. Univ. of Mich.; Univ. of Toronto post-grad. studies, Ch. Eng.; Pacific Western Univ. Ph.D.; m. Mary Katherine Bothwell; children: Peter Alexander, Paul Frederick, Wendy Elizabeth, James Stuart Bothwell; PRESIDENT, SAXONY COURT ESTATES INC.; Standards Development Consultants on G.A.T.T.; Military Service RCASC; Founding Chrmn. and mem. Adv. Bd., St. Georges Coll., Toronto; Past Pres., Am. Soc. for Testing & Materials; mem., Candn. Standards Assn.; former Pres. & Owner, Ont. Bldg. Materials Grp. of Cos.; author numerous papers in U.S. and Can. on brick mfg., calcium silicate units, acrylic coatings and electrical properties of surfaces; Inventor, holding numerous patents on calcium silicate products, and on composit fibre structures; Fellow, A.S.T.M.; mem., Royal Candn. Legion, Post 60; Anglican; recreation: flying, choral musician, guncollector; Clubs: Boulevard; Toronto Lions (Past Pres. Runnymede); Bd. of Trade, Metro Tor.; Gulf Harbours Yacht, New Port Richey, Fl; Power Boat Squadron; Address: 3 Greenfield Dr., Ancaster, Ont. L9G 1M2; Winter residence: 3923 Marine Pkwy., Gulf Harbours Woodlands, New Port Richey, FL 34652.

**WHEELER, Lucile,** O.C.; skier; b. 1935; m. June 1960; one d., one s.; finished third in Womens Downhill at Cortina d'Ampezzo, Italy 1956, winning Canada's first Olympic Medal for skiing; won Women's Downhill, Hohnekamm Tournament, Kitzbühel, Austria 1957, also combined Title there; World Championship Downhill Title, and Giant Slalom Title, Bad Gastein, Austria, 1958; served on Nat. Fitness Council for 2 years; named Canadian Athlete of the Year, 1958; 1st Canadian to receive Perry Medal awarded by Ski Club of Gt. Britain; 1st skier to win Lou Marsh Trophy (1958); mem., Candn. Athletic Hall of Fame; U.S.A. Ski Hall of Fame; Candn. Honour Roll of Skiing; Laurentian Hall of Fame; Quebec Hall of Fame; Mem. of The Order of Canada; Address: Knowlton, Que. J0E 1V0.

**WHELAN, Hon. Eugene Francis,** P.C. (1972); former politician; farmer; b. Amherstberg, Ont. 11 July 1924; s. Charles B. and Francis L. (Kelly) W.; e. Separate Schs., Anderdon Twp., Ont.; Gen. Amherst High Sch., Windsor, Ont.; Walkerville (Ont.) Vocational & Tech. Sch.; m. Elizabeth, d. Frank Pollinger, Kingsville , Ont., 30 Apl. 1960; children: Theresa Ann, Susan Elizabeth, Catherine Frances; el. Pres., U.N. World Food Counc. 1983–85; returned as Min. of Agriculture, Can. Feb. 18, 1980–84; Candidate for Leadership of Liberal Party of Canada 1984; def. Lib. Cand. for Essex S., Prov. g.e. 1959; el. to H. of C., g.e. 1962 and re-el. until 1984 when he did not run; Parlty. Secy. to Min. of Forestry and to Min. of Fisheries 1968–70; Min. of Agric. Fed. Gov. 1972–79; Pres. & C.E.O., Agricultural Internat. Associates of Canada, Inc. 1985– ; Hon. Col., 21st (Windsor) Service Battalion 1976; Hon. LL.D., Univ. of Windsor 1983; Hon. Life Mem., Ont. Inst. of Agrologists (P.Ag.) 1986; apptd. Officer of the Order of Canada 1987; author: 'Whelan – The Man in the Green Stetson' (memoirs) 1986; Former Reeve; Twp. of Anderdon; Warden, Essex Co., Ont. 1962; Past mem. Bd. Govs., Ont. Fed. of Agric.; Past Pres., Essex Co. Fed. of Agric.; Past Dir., Un. Co-ops. of Ont.; Harrow Farmers Co-op; Ont. Winter Wheat Producers Marketing Bd.; Past mem. Local Sch. Bd.; Kt. of Columbus; Liberal; R. Catholic; Club: Lions; Home: 727 Front Rd. N., Amherstberg, Ont. N9V 2V6.

**WHELAN, John Paul Joseph,** B.Sc., M.D., F.R.C.S.(C); physician; b. Barrie, Ont. 1 Dec. 1956; s. Joseph Bernard and Margaret Mary (Brennan) W.; e. McMaster Univ. B.Sc. 1978, M.D. 1981; Univ. of Western Ont. F.R.C.S.(C); Univ. of Florida F.R.C.S.(C); m. Angela d. Evan and Florence Mazza 5 June 1982; children: Lauren Alexandra, Jordan Joseph, Kaitlyn Florence; clinical practice in Urology since 1987 with specific interest in treatment of kidney stone disease; Chief of Urology, St. Joseph's Hosp., Hamilton, Ont.; Co-Founder, Hamilton Stone Treatment Clinic 1989; has been involved in devel. of Extracorporeal Shock Wave Lithotripsy facilities throughout the world; Clinic Dir., Hamilton Stone Treatment Clinic; Med. Dir., TransAmerica Lithotripsy Centres Inc.; Dir., American Internat. Medical Services; TLC de Mexico Inc.; Asst. Clin. Prof., Dept. of Surgery, McMaster Univ.; Coll. of Physicians & Surgeons of Ont.; Dir. of Rsch., Division of Urology, Dept. of Surgery, McMaster Univ.; Inventor, Whelan Steri-Shield – Cook (Canada) Inc.; Whelan ESWL Retrograde Lavage Catheter – Cook (Canada) Inc.; Roman Catholic; Mem., Ont. Med. Assn.; Candn. Urologic Assn.; Am. Lithotripsy Soc.; Am. Urologic Assn.; Hamilton Academy of Medicine; author of num. pubns. in peer-reviewed journals of urologic surgery 1986– ; recreations: golf, tennis; club: Hamilton Golf & Country; Office: 662 Concession St., Hamilton, Ont. L8V 1B8.

**WHELAN, William John,** C.A.; financial executive; b. Perth, Ont. 4 June 1928; s. Reginald Vincent and Francis Margaret W.; e. Univ. of Toronto 1947–48; Queen's Univ. extension, C.A. 1953; m. Margaret Elizabeth Harris; children: Jerrold Douglas, Blair William, Thomas Richard, Elizabeth Ann; PRES. & DIR., SYLVA RESOURCES LTD. 1985– ; Controller & Extve. Vice-Pres., Warren Bitulithic, 1954–70; Vice-Pres. then Exec. Pres., Ashland Oil Can. Limited 1970–78; Pres., Kaiser Petroleum Ltd. 1979–80; Pres. & Chief Extve. Offr., Carlyle Energy Ltd. 1980–86; Sr. Vice-Pres. & Chief Finan. Offr., Encor Energy Corp. Inc. 1986–88; Retired Sr. Oil and Gas Advisor, Price Waterhouse 1988–91; Dir., Rayrock Yellowknife Resources Ltd.; Morrison Middlefield Petroleum Ltd.; Zargon Oil & Gas Ltd.; Mem., C.I.C.A.; recreations: golf, bridge, reading; Clubs: Calgary Petroleum; Canyon Meadows Golf & Country; Wigwam Golf & Country (Phoenix); Home: 6 Willow Park Green S.E., Calgary, Alta. T2J 3L1.

**WHILLANS, Morley Gray,** M.D.; b. Manitoba 22 Aug. 1911; s. Rev. James William and Olive (Dryden) W.; e. Univ. of Liverpool and Univ. of Toronto, M.D. 1935; m. Olive ('Obi'), d. John Noble, Toronto, Ont. 1 July 1939; children: Ian M., Penelope J., Timothy P.; Interne, Hamilton Gen. Hosp., 1935–37; Fellowships, Banting Inst., Univ. of Toronto, Pathology, 1937–38; Neuropathology, 1938–39; Harvard Univ. Neurology, 1939–40; Consultant Neurology, Ont. Dept. of Health, 1940–41; Head, Dept. of Pharmacol., Dalhousie Univ., 1945–48; Dir., Biol. Research, Defence Research Bd., 1948–50; Supt., Defence Research Med. Labs., 1950–55; Prof. Banting & Best Dept. of Med. Research, Univ. of Toronto, 1954–55; National Defence College 1955; Asst. Chief Scientist and Dir. of Biosciences Research, Defence Research Bd., 1955–63; Vice Chrmn., Aerospace Med. Panel AGARD (NATO), 1952–55; Chief, Canadian Defence Research Staff, London (Eng.), 1963–68, Adv. Career Devel., DRB, 1968–72, when retired; served in 2nd World War with R.C.A.F., 1941–45, engaged in aviation med. research; has publ. papers on pathology, aviation med., pharmacology, physiol., survival techniques, colour vision and safety; Hon. mem., Phi Rho Sigma; Founder and Exec. Secy., Colour Blind Ctte.; recreations: photography, sketching; Home: 401 – 2800 Blanshard St., Victoria, B.C. V8T 5B5.

**WHITAKER, Ian (Rice),** B.A., M.A., Dr.Phil.; university professor, anthropologist; b. Lenton, U.K. 4 July 1928; s. Thomas Rice and Gertrude (33rd Baroness de la Ville de Beaugé) W.; e. Univ. of St. Andrews; Cambridge Univ. B.A., M.A.; Univ. of Oslo Dr.Phil.; m. Margaret d. William and Agnes Easson 17 Dec. 1955; children: Kythe Siobhan, Ronan Easson Jeffreys; SENIOR RESEARCH ASSOCIATE, SCOTT POLAR RESEARCH INSTITUTE, UNIV. OF CAMBRIDGE (U.K.) 1993– and PROFESSOR EMERITUS OF ANTHROPOLOGY, SIMON FRASER UNIV. 1993– , Professor 1972–93; Research Fellow, Sch. of Scottish Studies, Univ. of Edinburgh 1952–59; Assoc. Prof. of Soc. & Anthrop., Memorial Univ. of Nfld. 1959–62; Prof. 1962–64 Co-founder & Dir., Inst. of Social & Econ. Rsch. 1961–64; Prof. of Soc., Univ. College, Cardiff 1964–65; Reader in Soc., Univ. of York 1964–73; Visiting Scholar, Scott Polar Rsch. Inst., Univ. of Cambridge 1976–93; anthrop. fieldwork among Sami (Lapps), Scottish & Icelandic fishers, Albanophones, Inuit, Chinese Evenki & Tajiks; worked as reindeer herder for 2 years; Candn. Army (Militia) Capt. (now Supplementary Reserve); Consultant, Mackenzie Valley Pipeline Inquiry 1974–77; Visiting Prof., univs. of Durham, N.B., Carleton; elected Royal Gustav Adolf Academy (Sweden) 1981; Tennant Studentship (Cambridge) 1951–52; Wallenberg Prizeman (Cambridge) 1952; Wygard Award 1962; Anglican; Social Democrat; Mem., Edit. Bd. 'Studies in Polar Research,' 'Polar Record'; author: 'Social Relations in a Nomadic Lappish Community' 1956; editor: 'Small-Scale Agriculture in Selected Newfoundland Communities' 1964; 70 academic papers; recreations: travel, skiing; Home: 3571 Marine Dr., W. Vancouver, B.C. V7V 1N3; Office: Scott Polar Rsch. Institute, Lensfield Rd., Cambridge, England CB2 1ER.

**WHITAKER, William Denis,** D.S.O., C.M., E.D., C.D.; company president; b. Calgary, Alta. 27 Feb. 1915; s. Guy S. and Bertha (Moore) W.; e. Univ. of Toronto Schs., grad. 1933; Roy. Mil. Coll. of Can., grad. 1937; comnd. as Lieut., Royal Hamilton Light Inf. (WR); m. Shelagh Dunwoody; children: Gail, Clarke, Michael; PRES., W. DENIS WHITAKER & ASSOCIATES LTD.; Consultant, Burns Fry Ltd.; Dir., Scintrex Ltd.; Asst. to Supt., Stanley Works of Can., Hamilton, Ont., 1937–39; Extve. Dir., Hamilton Centennial Celebration, 1946; Comm. Mgr., Radio Stn. CHML, 1946–61; Vice-Pres., O'Keefe Brewing Co. Ltd., Toronto, Apl. 1962, Pres., 1962–65; Pres., Radio Sales Bureau, 1965–67; served in 2nd World War, 1939–46; discharged with rank of Brigadier; C.O. Third Infantry Brigade till retired, 1951; Hon. Colonel, Royal Hamilton Light Infantry since 1973; Mem., Canada's Sports Hall of Fame; Dir., Candn. Olympic Trust; co-author 'Tug of War,' winner 1984 John W. Dafoe Award for best book on internat. and Can. affairs; co-author: 'Rhineland: The Battle to End the War' 1989; 'Dieppe: Tragedy to Triumph' 1992; Anglican; recreations: hunting, squash, water skiing; Clubs: Hamilton Club; Royal Hamilton Military Inst.; Hamilton Hunt (Ex-Master); Badminton and Racquet (Toronto); Home: 2094 Lakeshore Rd. E., Oakville, Ont. L6J 1M3; Office: Burns Fry Ltd., Suite 5000, First Canadian Place, P.O. Box 150, Toronto, Ont. M5X 1H3.

**WHITE, Adrian M.S.,** F.C.A.; financial executive; b. Kent, Eng., 15 Aug. 1940; Canadian citizen; e. C.A. 1964, F.C.A. 1982; m. Elaine Margaret 10 Sept. 1966; children: Malcolm, Catherine; CHRMN., WHITEMAVEN CORPORATION and MANAGING PARTNER, SCALLYWAGS GROUP; articled with Coopers & Lybrand 1962–64; Acting Treas. Rothesay Paper Corp. 1965; Asst. Treas. Genstar Ltd. 1967–71; Treas. Brinco Ltd. and Churchill Falls (Labrador) Corp. 1971–75; Treas. Algoma Steel Corp. Ltd. 1975–80; Vice Pres. Finance Little Long Lac Gold Mines, Toronto 1980; Vice Pres., Capital Markets Group, Bank of Montreal 1981–88; Extve. Vice-Pres., Finance and Chief Financial Officer & Mem. Bd. of Dirs., Curragh Inc.; mem. Bd. of Govs., C.I.C.A. 1983–86; Ont. Inst. C.A.'s (Council 1977–82, Extve. 1979–82, Planning Comte., 1982–87); Que. Inst. C.A.'s; Financial Extves. Inst. Can. (Pres. Toronto Chapter 1984–85); Chrmn. Task Force on Capital Adequacy and Liquidity, Canadian Bankers' Assn. 1984–87; Chrmn. & Bd. mem., Doctors Hosp. Found., Toronto; Bd. Mem., Doctors Hosp.; Club: Cambridge, Boulevard; United Church; Home: 72 Sir Williams Lane, Islington, Ont. M9A 1V3.

**WHITE, Calvin John,** B.Comm.; zoological executive; b. Twillingate, Nfld. 28 Feb. 1948; s. Harold and Meta Blanche (Abbott) W.; e. Victoria Coll., Univ. of Toronto, B.Comm. 1971; m. Lorna d. Isabel and John Maclachlan 21 Nov. 1987; GENERAL MANAGER, METROPOLITAN TORONTO ZOO 1986– ; Finan. Analyst, Candn. Gen. Electric Co. Ltd. 1971–72; Ford Motor Co. of Can. Ltd. 1972–74; Sr. Finan. Analyst, Municipality of Metro. Toronto 1974–77; Asst. Dir., Budget & Opns. Analysis 1977–81; Dir., Budget Analysis & Internal Control 1981–86; Dir., Metro. Toronto Convention & Visitors Assn.; Reptile Breeding Found.; Inst. of Public Admin. of Can.; Mem., MENSA; Toronto Sportsmen's Assn.; Candn. & Am. Assns. of Zool. Parks & Aquariums; Am. Assn. of Zoo Keepers; The Inst. of Public Admin. of Can.; Office: P.O. Box 280, West Hill, Ont. M1E 4R5.

**WHITE, Donald Allen;** retired manufacturer; b. Toronto, Ont., 7 June 1913; s. late Frederick Charles and late Mabel Claire (Griswold) W.; e. Stratford (Ont.) Coll. Inst.; Shaw Business Schs.; m. late Zeita Alberta, d. the late James D. Mason, 6 Aug. 1938; children: Donald Richard, Dennis James Frederick; m. 2ndly Myrtle Anne Bond, d. the late William Waterland, 22 May 1985; PAST PRESIDENT, HUNTINGTON LABORATORIES LTD.; Past Pres., Donald A. White Manufacturing Co. Ltd.; former Chrmn., Bd. Govs., Humber Coll. of Applied Arts & Technol.; with C.N. Rlys., 1929–31; engaged in sales work, 1932–34; Clerk and later Dept. Mgr., Standard Tube Co. Ltd., Woodstock, Ont., 1934–39; Gen. Mgr., Metal Fabricators Ltd., Woodstock and Tillsonburg, 1939–49; served in Reserve Army as Capt.; Past Pres., Candn. Sanitation Standards Assoc.; Past Pres., Kiwanis Music Festival Assoc. of Greater Toronto; Past Pres., Bd. of Rexdale Community Information Directory & Legal Services; Pres., Rexdale Community Legal Clinic 1993/94; Conservative; United Church; recreations: philately, sailing; Clubs: Kiwanis, Kingsway (Past Pres.); Home: 58 Riverwood Parkway, Etobicoke, Ont. M8Y 4E5.

**WHITE, Douglas Perry,** B.A., M.A., Ph.D.; university professor; b. Kingston, Ont. 24 March 1947; s. Dr. Edwin Perry and Marjorie Wilson (McBride) White; e. Queen's Univ. B.A. (Hons.) 1969, M.A. 1971, Ph.D. 1979; m. Mary Elizabeth d. Evelyn and Louis Ahern 28 June 1975; children: Christopher Perry, Elizabeth Justina; PROFESSOR, DEPT. OF BUSINESS AND TECHNICAL COMMUNICATION, RYERSON POLYTECHNIC UNIV. 1985– ; Instructor, Dept. of English, Ryerson 1979–84; Chair, Dept. of Business and Tech. Communication 1991– ; various service activities for faculty associations and/or univ. cttes.; currently Vice-Chair, Academic Standards Ctte. of Academic Council; Mem., Assn. for Business Communication; Candn. Assn. of Teachers of Technical Writing; recreations: reading, piano, cottaging; Home: 61 Westholme Ave., Toronto, Ont. M6P 3B9; Office: 350 Victoria St., Toronto, Ont. M5B 2K3.

**WHITE, Edward B.,** B.A., F.C.S.I., OLJ; investment executive; b. Toronto, Ont. 29 March 1944; s. Henry Francis Q.C. and Helen Elizabeth (Baker); e. Upper Canada College; Victoria College, Univ. of Toronto B.A. 1966; m. Francoise d. Georges and Simone Delabre 2 Sept. 1972; one d.: Delphine; OTTAWA BRANCH MANAGER, WOOD GUNDY INC. 1990– ; Royal Securities Corp. 1967–68; Branch Mgr., Merrill Lynch Canada London, England 1968–78; Toronto 1978–80; Ottawa 1981; Fellow, Candn. Securities Institute; Officer, Order of St. Lazarus of Jerusalem; Dir., Ottawa Ballet; Chair, Canada Dance Festival; Co-chair, Ottawa Citizens Task Force on Culture 1991–92; Anglican; recreations: skiing, swimming, theatre, dance; clubs; Rideau; Home: 14 Birch Ave., Rockcliffe Park, Ont. K1K 3G6; Office: Metropolitan Life Bldg., 99 Bank St., Suite 200, Ottawa, Ont. K1P 6B9.

**WHITE, Evan William;** real estate executive; b. Verdun, Que. 3 Sept. 1934; s. Charles Herbert and Gladys Victoria (Lewis) W.; e. Westmount (Que.) High Sch.; m. Maureen Ann Rowell 16 Aug. 1958; children: Jennifer, Joanne, Evan, Jeffrey, David; CHRMN. & PRES., CB COMMERCIAL REAL ESTATE GROUP CANADA INC. since incorporation in 1983; Dir. CB Commercial Real Estate Group Canada Inc.; Upper Canada Airways; mem. Candn. Inst. Realtors; Protestant; recreations: horseback riding, polo, golf, skiing, tennis; Clubs: National; Beacon Hall Golf; Toronto & North York Hunt; Palm Beach Polo & Country; Home: Tannery Hill, Concession 8, R.R. 2, King, Ont. L0G 1K0; Office: 145 King St. W., Ste. 600, Toronto, Ont. M5H 1J8.

**WHITE, Franklin Marshall Matthews,** M.D., C.M., M.Sc., F.R.C.P.C.; educator; b. Perth, Australia 7 June 1946; s. Frank Thomas Matthews and T. Marian (Nunn) W.; e. Ch. of Eng. Grammar Sch. Brisbane; Univ. of Queensland; McGill Univ. M.D., C.M. 1969; Univ. of London M.Sc. 1973; m. Sharon d. William and Winifred Carlyle 21 Nov. 1970; children: Genevieve, Bernard, Alexander; DIR., CARIBBEAN EPIDEMIOLOGY CENTRE, (PAHO/WHO) 1989– ; Clinical Prof., Health Care and Epidemiology, Univ. of B.C. 1990– ; Prof. of Community Health & Epidemiology, Dalhousie Univ. 1982– ; Chief Examiner (Community Medicine) Royal Coll. of Phys. and Surg. of Can. 1986–88; Asst. Dir. Boundary Health Unit B.C. 1970–71; Lectr., Asst. Prof. McGill Univ. 1972–74; Physician Community Clinic Royal Victoria Hosp. Montréal 1974; Chief, Communicable Disease Div. Bureau of Epidemiol. Nat. Health & Welfare Ottawa 1974–77; Hon. Sr. Lectr. Univ. of Ottawa 1974–77; Dir. Communicable Disease Control & Epidemiol. Alta. Social Services & Community Health 1977–80; Hon. Assoc. Clin. Prof. Univ. of Alta. 1977–80; Hon. Assoc. Prof. Univ. of Calgary 1979–80; Dir. Div. Epidemiol. B.C. Min. of Health 1980–82; Hon. Clin. Assoc. Prof. Univ. of B.C. 1981–82; Dir. Halifax Sr. Citizens Housing Corp. 1983–84; recipient Commonwealth (Australia) Scholarship 1965; McGill Bursary 1965–69; Breakthrough Award for Creativity, U.S. Acad. for Educational Development 1989; author or co-author approx. 200 publs. and reports; ed. and mem. ed. bd. various prof. jours.; mem. Candn. Soc. Internat. Health (Dir. 1992– ); Candn. Pub. Health Assn. (Past Pres. 1988–90, Pres. 1986–88, 1st Vice Pres. 1984–86, Dir. 1982– ); Family Planning Assn. B.C. (Dir. 1970–71); recreations: sailing, track and field, music; Club: Trinidad & Tobago Yachting Assn.; Address: Box 164, Port of Spain, Trinidad, West Indies.

**WHITE, Howard;** author and publisher; b. Abbotsford, B.C. 18 April 1945; s. Franklin and Kathleen W.; e. Pender Harbour H.S.; m. Mary d. Jim and Pat Lee; children: Silas, Patrick; FOUNDER, PRES. & PUBLISHER, HARBOUR PUBLISHING 1974– ; Founder, Editor & Publisher 'The Peninsula Voice' 1969–74; 'Raincoast Chronicles' 1972– ; Pres., Assn. of Book Publishers of B.C. 1988–90; Dir., Indian Isle Construction (1981) Ltd. 1981– ; has given many readings of his poetry and prose works in all parts of Canada; has conducted seminars & workshops on writing & publishing incl. Dawson College, Univ. of Sask., Simon Fraser Univ., etc.; Best Magazine Feature, Candn. Media Club Awards 1975, '77; Eaton's BC Book Award 1976; Bill Duthie Prize, BC Book Awards (shortlist) 1987; BC Hist. Fed. Cert. of Merit for Hist. Writing 1987; Candn. Hist. Assn. Career Award for Regional History 1989; Stephen Leacock Medal for Humour 1990; J.P. Wiser Cash Award 1990; author: 'The Men There Were Then' 1983, 'Writing in the Rain' 1990 (BC Bestseller List 13 weeks), 'Patrick and the Backhoe' 1991; 'Ghost In The Gears' 1993; co-author: 'A Hard Man to Beat' 1983, 'Spilsbury's Coast' 1987 (BC Bestseller List 31 weeks), 'The Accidental Airline' 1988 (BC Bestseller List 26 weeks); editor/contbr.: 'Raincoast Chronicles First Five' 1975, 'Raincoast Chronicles Six-Ten' 1983; anthologies: 'Raincoast Chronicles First Five' 1975, 'A Government Job at Last' 1975, 'Raincoast Chronicles Six-Ten' 1983, 'Going for Coffee' 1983, 'The New Canadian Poets' 1985, 'Paper Work' 1991; also published in Macleans, Readers Digest, B.C. Outdoors, Event, Poetry Canada Review, etc.; Office: Box 219, Madeira, Park, B.C. V0N 2H0.

**WHITE, His Hon. J.A.;** retired judge; b. St. John's, Nfld. 22 Dec. 1921; s. Stanley and Charlotte (Knight) W.; e. Prince of Wales Coll.; Boston Univ., trustee scholar, journalism; traffic law, Univ. of Nevada & Tulane Univ.; m. Joan d. James and May Shears 5 June 1950; children: Jennifer Elizabeth May, Edwina Alexandra, Bliss, Heather Ruth; volunteered 1941 for De-Gaulle's Free French Navy; first Newfoundlander to be fgn. news corr./reporter with 'Daily News' then CJON Radio & CJON TV; appt. Magistrate 1957 then Prov. Court Judge of Specialized Traffic Court; Queen's Silver Jubilee Medal; extensive traveller; Church of England; Asst. Chrmn., The Nfld. Monarchist League; Onetime Chief Protocol Offr. for Nfld. Govt. at Gander Internat. Airport; Press Offr., H.M. the Queen's visit to Nfld. West Coast; arranged details for various Lieutenant-Governor's tours of Nfld.; Editor books/column 'The Streets of St. John's' (historic stories of each street in the oldest white-settled city in the western hemisphere); Past Chrmn., num. sch. bds., farm fairs, etc.; recreations: cricket, war games, reading, English soccer fan; Home: 98 Campbell Ave., St. John's, Nfld. A1E 2Z6.

**WHITE, Jerry S.,** B.A., Dip.B.A., M.A., M.B.A., D.Litt.; professor; writer; broadcaster; consultant; b. Toronto, Ont. 25 Aug. 1946; s. Louis and Lillian (Potash) W.; e. Univ. of Toronto, B.A., Dip.B.A. 1969, M.B.A. 1970; City Coll. (U.K.), M.A. 1982; IMCB (U.K.), D.Litt. 1983; m. Lilli d. Abraham and Sarah Kurtz 23 June 1968; children: Ian, Cayle, Hartley, Mariam, Jonathan; PROF. OF MANAGEMENT, COLLEGE FOR HUMAN SERVICES, NEW YORK 1992– ; Chrmn., J. White & Associates Inc.; Mktg. Mgr., Toronto Dominion Bank 1968; Econ., Candn. Bankers Assn. 1969; Dir., Cont. Bus. Edn., Univ. of Toronto 1970–74; Sr. Teaching Master, George Brown Coll. 1974–76; Vice-Pres. & Dir., MacMillan of Can., Finan. Post Books 1976–78; Nat. Dir., Thorne Riddell 1979–82; Dir., Strategic Serv., Laventhol & Horwath 1983–86; Pres., Mothers Restaurants 1986–88; Prof. of Entrepreneurial Studies, Univ. of Toronto 1988–92; Chrmn., J. White & Assoc. Inc. Investment Bankers 1988– ; F.B.I.M., F.Inst. Dir., F.C.A.M., F.R.S.A.; Nat. Journalism Award, F. Hostelry Inst. 1984; Chrmn., New College Alumni Fund; Dir., Ont. Hostelry Inst.; Special Olympics; author of over 26 books incl. 'The Canadian Accountant' & 'Management Consultsnts Practice Guide'; 'The Art and Science of Small Business Management'; 'Managing in the Fourth Dimension'; 'Strategic Personal Investing' 1992; 'Ultimate Money Guide for Canadians' 1994; National Business Columnist, Thomson Newspapers (for 160 U.S. & Candn. daily newspapers); recipient, Gold Medal, New York Festival of Radio 1991, 1992; recreations: golf, antiques, food; club: Bd. of Trade; Office: 233 E. 62nd St., New York, NY 10021.

**WHITE, John,** M.A., D.Litt.; financial executive; b. Chicago, Ill. 16 Aug. 1925; s. Howard Rivers and Margaret Lyell (Johnston) W.; e. Univ. of W. Ont. B.A. 1946, Dipl. Business Adm. 1949, M.A. (Econ.) 1966; D. Litt. (hon. causa) Carleton Univ.; m. Beatrice Elizabeth d. Charles Ivey, Port Dover, Ont., 15 June 1957; two d. Martha Nancy, Emily Barbara; PRESIDENT, CANADIAN DEVELOPMENT CO. LTD.; Chrmn. & C.E.O., First Canadian Money Market Fund; First Canadian Fixed Income Fund; First Canadian Equity Index Fund; First Canadian Balanced Fund; First Candn. Internat. Growth Fund; Chrmn., First Candn. Mortage Fund (Bank of Montréal); el. to Ont. Leg. 1959, re-el. 1963, 1967, 1971; Min. of Revenue 1968–71; Min. of Colls. and Univs. 1971–72; Min. of Industry & Tourism 1972–73; Treas. Min. of Econ. & Intergovernmental Affairs 1973–75; former Chrmn. and C.E.O., Candev Financial Services Ltd.; served with RCNVR 1943–45, rank Sub-Lt.; Hon. Chrmn., Inst. for Pol. Involvement; Chrmn., Springdale Found.; Delta Upsilon (Past Pres.); P. Conservative; Anglican; recreations: travel, reading, gardening; Clubs: London; Home: 119 Base Line E., London, Ont. N6C 2N6; Office: 357 Dufferin Ave., London, Ont. N6B 1Z5.

**WHITE, John Cecil,** B.Sc.; mining executive; b. Margate, Kent, Eng. 10 March 1933; s. Cecil and Lillian (Bushell) W.; e. Royal Sch. of Mines, Imp. Coll. Univ. of London B.Sc. 1954; m. Margaret d. Joseph and Edith Barrow, Retford, Eng. 21 May 1956; children: Andrew, Michael, Philip, Timothy; EXTVE. VICE PRES., MINE DEVELOPMENT AND ENGINEERING, NORANDA MINERALS INC. and MANAGING DIRECTOR, FALCONBRIDGE CHILE 1993– ; Chrmn. & Dir., Brunswick Mining and Smelting Corp. Ltd. 1990– ; Pres. & Dir., Novicourt Inc., Mattabi Mines Ltd.; Chrmn., Mine Environment Neutral Drainage (MEND); joined Madsen Red Lake Gold Mines 1954–59; Gaspe Copper Mines 1959–70, Asst. Mgr. 1969–70; Mattabi Mines Ltd. 1970–76, Mgr.; Mines Gaspe 1976–78, Mgr.; Gen. Mgr.-Mines present Co. 1978–80; Vice-Pres., Mines. 1980–82; Group Vice Pres. 1982–86; Vice Pres., Noranda Minerals Inc. and Pres., Noranda Zinc 1986–89; Sr. Vice-Pres., Noranda Minerals Inc. and Pres., Eastern Mining Group 1989–90; Pres., Chrmn. & Dir., Brunswick Mining and Smelting Corp. Ltd.; Pres., Candn. Electrolytic Zinc Ltd.; Heath Steele Mines Ltd. 1986–89; rec'd Leonard Medal, Engn. Inst. Can. 1968; mem. Assn. Prof. Engrs. Prov. Ont.; Soc. Mining Engrs. A.I.M.E.; Candn. Inst. Mining & Metall.; United Church; recreations: pottery, gardening, golf; Club: Ontario; Home: 323 Warminster Dr., Oakville, Ont. L6L 4N1; Office: 1 Adelaide St. E., Suite 2700, Toronto, Ont. M5C 2Z6.

**WHITE, Hon. John Gerald Michael,** B.A.; judge; b. Hamilton, Ont. 3 June 1921; s. John Michael and Lena (Thompson) W.; e. Holy Family and St. Augustine's Separate Schs.; Cathedral High Sch.; McMaster Univ. B.A. 1944; Osgoode Hall Law Sch. 1947; m. Mary Elizabeth d. Wilfred and Florence Valencourt; children: John Michael, Thomas Gerrard, Stephen Joseph; SUPERNUMERARY MEMBER, ONTARIO COURT OF JUSTICE (GENERAL DIVISION) 1992– ; called to Bar of Ont. 1947; cr. Q.C. 1961; law practice W. Schreiber, Q.C. and Wm. Momotiuk, Q.C., Hamilton 1947; White & Paikin and successor firms 1948–81; Judge, High Court of Justice, Supreme Court of Ont. 1981–90; Sr. Regional Justice for the Central South Region of the Ontario Court of Justice (General Div.) 1990–92; recipient Bronze Medal and Mathew Wilson Meml. Scholarship 1947; Past Pres. Lawyers' Club; Past Pres. Hamilton Med. Legal Soc.; Past Trustee Hamilton Law Assn.; Judicial Fellow Internat. Soc. Barristers; mem. Advocates Soc.; Bencher, Law Soc. Upper Can. 1971–81; mem. St. Thomas More Lawyers Guild; K. of C.; R. Catholic; Club: Hamilton; Home: 111 Judith Cres., Ancaster, Ont. L9G 1L3; Office: Osgoode Hall, Toronto, Ont. M5H 2H5.

**WHITE, John Kennedy,** M.A.; retired textile executive; b. Tasmania 10 Aug. 1928; s. James Bishop and Joan Meiklem (Thomson) W.; e. Edinburgh Acad. Scot.; Cambridge Univ. M.A.; m. Jane d. Selwyn and Barbara

Pumphrey 18 Aug. 1962; three s. Andrew, Nigel, Roger; PAST CHRMN., PATONS & BALDWINS CANADA INC.; joined Patons & Baldwins, Scot. 1951, mgmt. appts. Eng., S. Africa and Belgium, Chrmn., Patons & Baldwins Canada Inc. 1988–90; Past Chrmn. Candn. Textiles Inst.; Club: Toronto Cricket Skating & Curling; Home: 12 Brooke Ave., Toronto, Ont. M5M 2J6.

**WHITE, Kerr Lachlan,** M.D., F.A.C.P.; educator; physician; b. Winnipeg, Man. 23 Jan. 1917; s. John Alexander Stevenson and Ruth Cecelia (Preston) W.; e. McGill Univ., B.A. (Econ.) 1940, M.D., C.M. 1949; Yale Univ. Grad. Sch., Cert. in Econ. 1941; Univ. of London and London Sch. of Hygiene & Tropical Med., 1959–60; hon. Dr. Med., Univ. of Leuven 1978; Hon. Doctor of Sciences, McMaster Univ., 1983; m. Isabel Anne, d. Clarence Pennefather, 26 Nov. 1943; two d., Susan Isabel, Margot Edith; Deputy Director for Health Sciences, Rockefeller Foundation, retired 1984; Interne, Mary Hitchcock Mem. Hosp., Hanover, N.H., 1949–50; Resident in Med., Dartmouth Med. Sch., Mary Hitchcock Mem. Hosp. 1950–52; Hosmer Research Fellow, McGill Univ., Royal Victoria Hosp.; Asst. Prof. of Med. and Preventive Med., Univ. of N.C., 1953–57; Assoc. Prof. 1957–59 and 1960–62; Chrmn. and Prof., Dept. of Epidemiol. and Community Med., Univ. of Vermont 1962–65; Prof., Dept. of Health Care Organization, John Hopkins Univ. Sch. of Hygiene and PublicHealth 1965–77 (Chrmn. 1965–72); served with Candn. Army Overseas 1942–44; Consultant: Nat. Center for Health Stat.; World Health Organ.; Dir., Foundation for Child Devel.; mem., Health Adv. Comm., off. of Technology Assessment, U.S. Congress; mem., Visiting Committee, Sch. Public Health, Harvard University; mem. various councils, U.S. Department of Health Education and Welfare; Expert Panel of Organization of Medical Care, World Health Organization; received Oliver Gold Medal, McGill Univ.; author numerous books and scient. papers for various prof. journs.; Fellow, Am. Coll. of Physicians; Am. Assn. Advanc. Science; Am. Heart Assn.; Am. Pub. Health Assn. (Gov. Council 1964–68 and 1971); mem., Am. Med. Assn.; Am. Hosp. Assn.; Am. Fed. Clin. Research; Am. Sociol. Assn.; Assn. Am. Med. Colls.; Group Health Assn. Am. Inc.; Internat Hosp. Fed.; N.Y. Acad. Sciences; N.Y. Acad. of Med.; Soc. Epidemiol. Research; Internat. Epidemiol. Assn.(mem. Council; Treas. 1964–71, Pres. 1974–77, Hon. Mem. 1984); Inst. Med., National Acad. Sciences (mem. Council 1973–76); Hon. mem., Nat. Acad. of Med. of Argentina, 1980; Curtis Hames Award for Primary Care Research 1986; Distinguished Career Award, Assoc. for Health Services Rsch. 1987; Robert J. Glaser Award, Soc. for General Internal Medicine 1990; Hon. Fellow, The Royal Soc. of Medicine, London 1990; Hon. Dir., Royal Soc. of Medicine Foundation 1993; Sigma Xi; Alpha Omega Alpha; recreations: gardening, travel, reading; Clubs: Century Assn. (N.Y. City); Cosmos (Washington D.C.); Home: 2401 Old Ivy Rd., #1410, Charlottesville, Virginia 22903-4858.

**WHITE, Mary Anne,** B.Sc., Ph.D.; educator; b. London, Ont. 28 Dec. 1953; d. Myron Russell and Mary Patricia (Donnelly) Millar; e. Univ. of W. Ont., B.Sc. 1975 (Alumni Gold Medal); McMaster Univ., Ph.D. 1980; m. Robert Lester s. Harry James and Phyllis Evangeline White 27 Aug. 1977; children: David Ian, Alice Patricia; PROF. IN CHEM. AND PHYS. DALHOUSIE UNIV. 1992– ; Postdoctoral Fellow in Inorganic & Phys. Chem. Labs. Oxford Univ. and concurrently Jr. Rsch. Fellow St. Hilda's Coll. Oxford 1979–81; Rsch. Asst. Prof. in Chem. Univ. of Waterloo 1981–83; Asst. Prof. in Chem. Dalhousie Univ. 1983–87; Assoc. Prof. in Chem. and Phys., Dalhousie Univ. 1987–92; NSERC Rsch. Fellow 1981–91; Dir. Calorimetry Conf. 1984–86; Dir, Discovery Centre 1987–93; Dir., Canadian Soc. for Chemistry 1992–95; mem. NSERC Ctte. Grants & Scholarships and Rsch. Manpower Task Force and Women's Faculty Award Ctte.; recipient NSERC 1967 Centennial Sci. Scholarship, Postdoctoral Fellowship and rsch. grants since 1981; rsch. grants and contracts Candn. Ind. Innovation Center, S.C. Johnson and Son, Dept. Supply & Services, NSERC, NATO; CNC-IUPAC Award 1989; Dalhousie Univ. Alumni Award for Excellence in Teaching 1993; Dalhousie Univ. Faculty of Science Award for Excellence in Teaching 1993; author over 60 sci. papers refereed jours.; mem. Chem. Inst. Can.; Candn. Assn. Phys.; Am. Phys. Soc.; Home: 6670 First St., Halifax, N.S. B3L 1E4; Office: Chemistry Dept., Dalhousie Univ., Halifax, N.S. B3H 4J3.

**WHITE, Patrick,** B.A.; poet; b. Campbell River, B.C. 15 Sept. 1948; s. William and Nina (Kostin) W.; e. Univ. of Victoria, B.A. 1973; m. Joanne Kearney 1970 (div.); children: Jody Shannon, Aaron Jesse Garcia; poet since 1966; gallery-quality landscape painter since 1978; Ed., Anthos; apptd. Poet Laureate of Ottawa 1987–90; literary radio host; Pub., Anthos Books 1981; worked as social worker for approx. 6 yrs.; author of poetry collections: 'Poems' 1974; 'The God in the Rafters' 1978; 'Stations' 1978; 'Seventeen Odes' 1981; 'Homage to Victor Jara' 1985; 'Orpheus on High Beam' 1987; 'Poems New and Selected' 1988; 'Gardens and Underground Rivers' 1988; 'Habitable Planets' 1988; 'Stars Smile Back' 1992; 'The Benjamin Chee Chee Elegies' 1992; poems pub. in over 150 N. Am. lit. periodicals; recipient: Benny Nicholas Award for Creative Writing 1973; Candn. Literature Award 1978; Silver Medal, Milton Acorn People's Poet Award 1983; Archibald Lampman Poetry Award 1989; founder of Transformalism, Candn. lit. movement; recreations: tennis, gardening, weights, astronomy; Address: c/o General Store Publishing House, 1 Main St., Burnstown, Ont. K0J 1G0.

**WHITE, Paul Cameron,** B.Sc., M.B.A., P.Eng., F.M.C.; consultant; b. Winnipeg, Man. 18 Aug. 1934; s. Richard Whitney and Lenore Cameron (Thompson); e. Univ. of Man. B.Sc.; Univ. of W. Ont. M.B.A. 1960; m. Marilyn d. W.D. Hurst 15 Sept. 1956; children: Cynthia, Leslie, Valerie; VICE PRESIDENT, MANAGEMENT CONSULTING, HATCH ASSOCIATES 1990– ; Coll. Apprentice Metrop. Vickers Electric Co. Ltd., Trafford Park, Manchester 1956–58; Mgmt. Cons. Peat, Marwick, Mitchell & Co., Toronto 1960–63; Mgmt. Service Rep. IBM 1963–64; Project Mgr. Massey Ferguson Ltd. 1964–66; Partner and Dir., Currie, Coopers & Lybrand Mgmt. Cons. 1966–81; PRES., Arthur D. Little of Canada Ltd. 1981–89; Pres. Inst. of Mgmt. Cons. of Can. 1978–79; Fellow Inst. of Mgmt. Cons. of Ont. (Pres. 1976–77); mem. Counc., Assn. of Profl. Engrs. 1979–81; Dir. The Canadian Stage Co.; Pres., Lake Rosseau North Assn. 1992/93; past Dir.: Winnipeg Symphony; Candn. Opera Co.; Children's Home of Greater Winnipeg; recreations: squash, tennis, music; Clubs: Granite; Ontario; Home: 3 Stratheden Rd., Toronto, Ont. M4N 1E2; Office: 2800 Speakman Dr., Mississauga, Ont. L5K 2R7.

**WHITE, Peter G.,** B.A., M.B.A.; b. London, Eng., 1 Aug. 1939; s. Cyril Grove Costley and Elizabeth Katherine Mary (Delmore) W.; e. Eton Coll. 1957; Univ. of W. Ont. B.A. 1966, M.B.A. 1970; m. Faye A. Marks 16 Apr. 1988; children: Richard, Sarah, Annabelle, Brooke, Devon; Dir., Canada Trust 1984–91; Goodhead Canada Ltd. 1988–91; formerly Aluminum Co. of Canada Ltd. 1961–63, 1966–68; joined The London Free Press as Marketing Services Mgr. 1970, Planning and Devel. Mgr. 1972, Asst. to Pres. and Publisher 1975, Pres. 1976–84; Pres., C.E.O. & Dir., The Blackburn Group Inc. 1984–86; Chrmn. & Dir., Ontario Development Corp. 1987–89; served with 1st Greenjackets UK 1958–60; recreation: winter and summer sports; Club: London, Ojibway.

**WHITE, Richard Leonard,** B.Sc., M.Sc.; director; artist; curator; b. Hamilton, Ont. 6 Mar. 1954; s. Leonard Roscoe and Marie W.; e. McMaster Univ., B.Sc. (Hons.) 1976; Univ. of Man., M.Sc. 1977; McMaster Univ., Ph.D. studies 1977–79; m. Brenda d. Russell and Elyse Kisyk 12 July 1980; DIR./CURATOR, MUTTART ART GALLERY 1984– ; Profl. artist, over 39 critically acclaimed exhbns. 1979– (most recent 'Echoes in the Gap,' Medicine Hat Art Gallery); Compiler 'Street Art For Gleichen' Project; exhibs.: 'GAP II' Gulf Gallery, Calgary, Alta. 1989; Recent Works, U. of C. Fine Arts Gallery, Calgary, Alta. 1989; Co-ordinator, Univ. Prog., Univ. of Calgary at Old Sun Community Coll., Blackfoot Indian Reserve; Curator, Calgary Allied Art Foundation 1988– ; Pres., Western Canada Art Assn. 1988– ; numerous community & fund-raising positions incl. Mem., Gleichen Town Counc., Parks & Recn. Bd., Lib. Bd. 1983; Bd. of Dir., Prairie Gallery, Valleyview Cultural Soc. 1981; Alta. Parks & Recn. Major Cultural & Recn. Grant 1984; Alta. Culture Project Grant 1984; Nat. Rsch. Counc. Scholarship 1978; Sigma-Xi Grant in Aid of Rsch. 1977; Spec. Achievment in Sci. 1976; Mem., Alta. Art Gallery Assn.; West. Assn. of Art Galleries; Candn. Mus. Assn.; Alta. Mus. Assn.; co-author of several scholarly articles; newsletter contrib.; recreations: squash, reading; Home: 304, 1305 Glenmore Trail S.W., Calgary, Alta. T2V 4Y8; Office: 1221 2nd St. S.W., Calgary, Alta. T2R 0W5.

**WHITE, Richard Paul,** O.B.E., C.M., V.R.D.; retired; b. Ottawa, Ont. 29 May 1915; s. Louis Talbot and Dorothy Gordon (Brown) W.; e. Normal-Model Sch. (1928) and Lisgar Coll. Inst. (1933), Ottawa, Ont.; Univ. of W. Ont. (Management Training) 1952; m. June Ruth, d. F.W. White, Ottawa, Ont. 6 Apr. 1940; children: Martha Jocelyn, Gordon Paul, Phyllis Jane; Pres., Harry P. Ward Found.; joined Naval Reserve, 1934; served in 2nd World War on active service, 1939–46; at Sea in N. Atlantic, Mediterranean and Pacific, and Ashore in Can. and U.K.; awarded O.B.E. 1945; Order of Canada 1976; Hon. Gov. Candn. Corps of Commissionnaires; Hon. Dir., The Perley Hosp; Dir. Royal Candn. Naval Benevolent Fund; Capt., R.C.N.(R.) (retired); Anglican; recreations: skiing, fishing, golf; Clubs: Rideau; Royal Ottawa Golf; Maganasippi Fish and Game; Home: #10, 251 Bruyère St., Ottawa, Ont. K1N 5E5.

**WHITE, Robert (Bob),** O.C.; labour leader; PRESIDENT, CANADIAN LABOUR CONGRESS 1992– ; began career in the union movement & organizing with United Auto Workers; Pres., UAW Local 636 1959; Internat. Rep. assigned to organizing duties in Canada 1960; Admin. Asst. to UAW Dir. for Canada 1972; First Pres., Canadian Auto Workers Union 1985; Co-Chair, Canadian Labour Market & Productivity Centre 1992–93; Hon. doctorates: York Univ.; Univ. of Windsor; St. Francis Xavier; recipient, City of Toronto Award of Merit; Officer, Order of Canada 1990; Office: 2841 Riverside Dr., Ottawa, Ont. K1V 8X7.

**WHITE, Robert Carley,** B.A., C.A.; chartered accountant; b. Trail, B.C. 26 March 1934; s. Henry Carley and Amelia Jessie (Wallbaum) W.; e. Univ. of B.C. B.A. 1956; Inst. of C.A.'s of B.C. C.A. 1960; single; PARTNER, OLIPHANT + WHITE 1980– ; Winspear, Hamilton, Anderson & Co. (now Deloitte & Touche) 1956–60; Communications Dir., Candn. Inst. of C.A.s 1961–74; Nat. Practice Devel. Mgr., Thorne Riddell (now Peat Marwick Thorne) 1974–79; works primarily with individuals in arts & non-profit orgns in arts, soc. serv. & advocacy; Canada 125 Medal; Bd. Mem., The Wellesley Hosp. 1992– (var. cttes.); Former Bd. Mem., Community Information Centre of Metro Toronto; Mid-Toronto Community Serv.; Second Mile Club; Assn. for Native Devel. in the Performing & Visual Arts; Oxfam Canada; Past Chair & Bd. Mem., Cabbagetown Community Arts Ctr.; Toronto Sch. of Art; Oxfam Trading Ltd.; Co-ord., Cabbagetown Cultural Fest. 1987–91; Past Pres. & Bd. Mem., Open Studio; Organizing Ctte., Candn. Artists Rep., Copyright Collective; author: 'The Newspaper as a Business' 1981; recreations: cycling; Address: 37 Amelia St., Toronto, Ont. M4X 1E3.

**WHITE, Robert George,** C.M.A.; university executive; b. Niagara Falls, Ont. 5 Sept. 1937; s. Philip Jackson and Goldie May (Lorenz) W.; e. Stamford Collegiate 1955; Certified Management Accountant C.M.A. 1966; Univ. of Western Ont., Sr. Univ. Administrators Program 1976; m. Jacqueline d. John and Mona McGeachie 21 Sept. 1957; children: Mark Robert, Sharon Ann, Brian Douglas; ASSISTANT VICE-PRES., FINANCE & CHIEF FINANCIAL OFFICER, UNIV. OF TORONTO 1982– ; Controller, Anthes Equipment Ltd. (Div. of Molson Indus.) 1964–69; Extve. Asst. to Chief Accountant, Univ. of Toronto 1969–71; Asst. Comptroller 1971–73 Budget Manager 1973–75; Comptroller 1975–82; Mem., Candn. Assn. of Univ. Business Officers (active in ctte. work); Council of Finance Officers, Univs. of Ont. (Chair 1989–90); Dir., Toronto District Heating Corp.; Univ. of Toronto Press Inc.; Midland Golf and Country Club Limited; Mem., St. Hilary's Anglican Ch.; Candn. Club of Toronto; Empire Club of Toronto; recreations: golf, nordic skiing, photography, theatre, ornithology; clubs: Midland Golf & Country; Office: Room 216, Simcoe Hall, 27 King's College Circle, Toronto, Ont. M5S 1A1.

**WHITE, Roger William Buchanan,** B.A., B.C.L.; lawyer; b. Montreal, Que. 18 Sept. 1939; s. Arthur Ogilvy and Audrey I.P. (Buchanan) W.; e. Lower Can. Coll. 1946–58; McGill Univ. B.A. 1961, B.C.L. 1964; m. Marlyn Frances d. Burton and Geraldine Matchett 3 May 1971; children: Jennifer Lynne Matchett, Geoffrey Arthur Buchanan; SR. VICE PRES. CORPORATE AFFAIRS AND SECRETARY, NATIONAL BANK OF GREECE (CANADA) 1973– ; joined Foster, Watt, Leggatt & Colby 1964–67; Crown Trust Co. 1968–72; Offr. The Black Watch (RHR) of Can. 1961–67; mem. Barreau du Que.; Candn. Bar Assn.; Presbyterian; recreations: golf, squash, cross-country skiing; Clubs: St. James; Seigniory; Home: Apt. D-41, The Gleneagles, 3940 Cote des Neiges Rd., Montreal, Que. H3H 1W2; Country Residence: 'Whitehall', Montebello, Que. J0V 1L0; Office: 1170 Place du Frère André, Montreal, Que. H3B 3C6.

**WHITE, Ronald Lorne,** B.A., B.Ed., M.Phys.Ed., M.Sch.Admin., D.D.h/c; retired teacher, administrator, actor; b. Halifax, N.S. 16 Dec. 1928; s. William Andrew and Izie Dora W.; e. Queen E. H.S. 1947; Acadia Univ. B.A. 1951, B.Ed. 1952; Dalhousie Univ. M.Phys.Ed. 1955; M.Sch.Admin. 1975; Hon. D.D. Acadia

Univ.1993; m. Ann Mary d. Wilfred and Dina Hennigar 19 Nov. 1955; children: Holly Michele, Shelly Ann, Rosalie Joan; taught physical education, health & math. 1952–73; Vice-Principal, Elementary/Jr. H.S. (Bloomfield), Halifax 1973–86; N.S. Appeals Bd., Dept. of Social Serv.; Mem., Bd. of Dir., Canada World Youth; Shelburne Youth Centre; N.S. Home for Coloured Children; Student Adv. Council of N.S.; N.S. Talent Trust; N.S. Sports Heritage Centre; Acadia Univ. Senate; Acadia Univ.; Acadia Univ. Alumni; Halifax Memorial Bells Ctte.; Cox Cup & Medal for most outstanding record in intercollegiate athletics and other awards & scholarship; Canadian Centennial Medal, Queen Elizabeth II's Silver Jubilee Medal; Canada 125 Medal; principal performer on several CBC shows, movies and various roles on stage; ensemble mem., Olympic Arts Festival production of 'Porgy & Bess' 1988; Mem., Candn. Bap. Fed. Council 1988–94; several past volunteer church positions including soloist, N.S. Prayer Breakfast & Baptist World Alliance; participant in many religious Crusades & Festivals in Bermuda & the Atlantic provinces; recreations: music, golf, tennis, badminton; club: Chester Golf; Home: 18 Winona Cres., Halifax, N.S. B3M 1Z1.

**WHITE, Terrence Harold,** B.S., M.A., Ph.D.; educator; b. Ottawa, Ont. 31 March 1943; s. William Harold and Shirley Margaret (Ballantine) W.; e. Univ. of Toronto Ph.D. 1972; m. Susan Elizabeth Hornaday; children: Christine Susan, Julie Pamela; PRESIDENT, BROCK UNIV. 1988– ; Head of Sociol. and Anthrop Univ. of Windsor 1973–75; Chrmn. of Sociol. Univ. of Alta. 1975–80, Dean of Arts and Prof. of Sociol. there 1980–88; Pres. T.H. White Organization Research Services Ltd.; Dir. Labatt's Alberta Brewery; Tri Bach Festival Foundation; Alberta Ballet Company; Edmonton Symphony Orchestra Soc.; Alta. Assn. of Registered Nurses Counc.; Edmonton Convention and Tourism Authority; Vice Pres., Edmonton Symphony Orch. Soc.; Niagara Symphony; YMCA (St. Catharines); United Way (St. Catharines); Fox Foundation; Canada-United States Business Assn. (Niagara/Buffalo); Bd. of Govs., Univ. of Alta., Ridley College; Chrmn. Arch Enterprises Ltd.; Chair, St. Catharines United Way Campaign 1992; author 'Power or Pawns: Boards of Directors in Canadian Corporations' 1978; 'Innovative Work-Sites in Alberta' 1978; 'Organization Size as a Factor Influencing Labour Relations' 1977; 'Quality of Working Life: Contemporary Case Descriptions' 1983; awarded Commemorative Medal for 125th Anniversary of Candn. Confederation 1992; Delta Tau Kappa; Alpha Kappa Delta; Presbyterian; Clubs: St. Catharines; Rotary (Pres. S. Edmonton); Home: 15 Deer Park Cres., Fonthill, Ont. L0S 1E0; Office: P.O. Box 1445, 32 Church St., St. Catharines, Ont. L2R 7J8.

**WHITE, William Eugene,** B.E., M.Sc., Ph.D., CET., P.Eng.; b. Toronto, Ont. 25 July 1939; s. Eugene and Reta (Seaton) W.; e. Fenelon Falls (Ont.) High Sch. 1957; Ryerson Polytech. Inst. Dip. Metall. Eng. 1966; Univ. of Sask. B.E. 1971, M.Sc. 1973, Ph.D. 1977; m. Denna d. Stan and Annie Marles 9 July 1960; children: Kim Michelle, Andrea Lynne; DEAN, FACULTY OF ENGINEERING AND APPLIED SCIENCE, RYERSON POLYTECH. UNIV. 1987– ; Lab. Tech. Canadian General Electric Peterborough 1957–60; Radiographer, Canadian Curtiss-Wright 1960; Foreman, Canadian Vac-Hyd Processing 1960–62, Dep. Chief Inspr. 1962–66; Dept. Mech. Eng. Univ. of Sask. 1966–77; Asst. Prof. Univ. of Calgary 1977, Assoc. Prof. 1980, Adjunct Assoc. Prof. 1982–87; Sr. Rsch. Specialist, Petro Canada Exploration 1982–86; Supvr. and Sr. Rsch. Specialist, Petro Canada Resources 1983–87, Sr. Eng. Specialist and Group Leader 1986–87; cons. to bus. and ind. materials behaviour, selection, environmental and corrosion phenomena; recipient Carveth Prize 1966; Internat. Metallographic Soc. Best Rsch. Paper Award 1980; Nat. Assn. Corrosion Engs. Candn. Region Distinguished Service Award 1987; Internat. Metallographic Soc. Presidents Award 1990; author or co-author numerous sci. publs.; Mngmt. Ctte. Chrmn., University Space Network (USN); mem. Assn. Profl. Engs. Provs. Ont., Alta., Sask.; Internat. Metallographic Soc. (Past Pres.); CFISU (Dir.); ASM; IMS; MCSME and other profl. assns.; Home: 15 Darbyshire Court, Ajax, Ont. L1T 1W9; Office: 350 Victoria St., Toronto, Ont. M5B 2K3.

**WHITE, William F.,** B.A.Sc., M.B.A.; investment dealer; b. London, Ont. 24 April 1944; e. Univ. of B.C., B.A.Sc. 1967; Univ. of W. Ont. M.B.A. 1969; m. Gale Rosanne Wilcock, 27 May 1967; children: Vivien, Michael, Kristopher; PRESIDENT, IBK CAPITAL CORP.; Dir., Burns Fry Ltd. 1969–82; Founder and Dir. Vanguard Trust of Canada Ltd. 1974–88; Dir. Energy & Precious Metals Inc. 1979–85; Dir. and Senior Vice-Pres., Corporate & Government Finance, Merrill Lynch Canada Inc. 1983–88; Dir. Colortech Corp. 1988– ; Vice Chrmn. Market Functions Comte., Toronto Stock Exchange 1976–77, mem. Market Access Comte. 1980–82, mem. Listing Comte. 1987–90; Gov., Montcrest Sch. 1979–87; Elder of The People's Ch.; Vice Chrmn., Greater Europe Mission; Gov., The Sunnybrook Foundation; recreations: tennis, golf, junior hockey, oriental art; Home: 108 Forest Hill Rd., Toronto, Ont. M4V 2L7.

**WHITE, William R.,** Ph.D.; economist; b. Kenora, Ont. 17 May 1943; s. Fredrick T. and Helen E. (McCann) W.; e. Kenora-Keewatin Dist. High Sch. 1961; Univ. of Windsor B.A. 1965; Univ. of Manchester Ph.D. 1969 (Commonwealth Scholar); m. Margaret d. James and Doris Philson 2 Jan. 1971; children: Matthew James, Katherine Louise; DEP. GOV. BANK OF CANADA 1988– ; Econ. Bank of England 1970–72; joined present Bank 1972, Chief Rsch. Dept. 1979, Adv. to Gov. 1984; special adv. on macro econ. policy Dept. of Finance 1985–86; author numerous acad. articles and reviews; recreation: fitness; Home: 39 Putman Ave., #7, Ottawa, Ont. K1M 1Z1; Office: 234 Wellington St., Ottawa, Ont. K1A 0G9.

**WHITEFORD, Gary Thomas,** B.A., M.A., Ph.D.; university professor; b. Toronto, Ont. 17 July 1941; s. William Barbour and Elsie (Lister) W.; e. Lawrence Park Inst. 1961; York Univ., B.A. 1964; University of Toronto 1964–65; Clark Univ., M.A. 1968; Univ. of Oklahoma, Ph.D. 1972; m. Carole Ann d. Elmer and Ruby McIntyre 7 Aug. 1967; children: Jennifer Ann, Thomas William; PROF., FAC. OF EDUCATION – GEOGRAPHY, UNIV. OF N.B. 1974– ; Teacher, Burford Dist. H.S. 1967–68; Rsch. Asst., NOAA summer 1969; Prof., West Texas State Univ. 1970–72; Instr., Champlain Reg. Coll. (Lennoxville, Que.) 1972–74; Prof., Concordia Univ. summer 1973; St. Mary's Univ. intersession 1974; Rsch. Asst., NASA Ames Rsch. Ctr. (Calif.) 1980–81; Guest Prof., Tezukayama Gakuin Univ., Osaka, Japan 1991–92; mem., Candn. Assn. of Geographers; Nat. Counc. for Geographic Edn.; co-author: 'Kings Landing. A Geography Guide' 1980; co-editor: 'Gage Atlas of the World' 1985; author of numerous profl. articles; Home: 434 Dufferin St., Fredericton, N.B. E3B 3A7; Office: Fredericton, N.B. E3B 6E3.

**WHITEHALL, Ivan George,** Q.C., B.A., LL.B., P.Grad.Dipl.; lawyer; b. Hungary 21 March 1942; s. Alexander S. Weiss; e. Univ. of B.C., B.A. 1964, LL.B. 1967; Univ. of Alta. Post Grad. Dipl. 1981; m. Georga d. J.E. Henderson 10 Nov. 1966; children: Stephanie-Ann, Andrea, Geoffrey; CHIEF GEN. COUNSEL, DEPT. OF JUSTICE CAN. 1988– (Sr. Gen. Counsel 1981–88); called to Bar of B.C. 1968; Bar of Alta. 1976; Bar of Ont. 1985; joined Dept. of Justice 1971; recreations: sailing, tennis; Club: OAC; Home: 2210 Bowman Rd., Ottawa, Ont. K1H 6V5; Office: Ottawa, Ont. K1A 0H8.

**WHITEHEAD, Francis Edward Paxton;** actor; director; b. Kent, Eng., 17 Oct. 1937; s. Charles Parkin and Louise (Hunt) W.; e. Rugby Sch., Eng.; Webber-Douglas Sch. of Singing and Dramatic Art, 1957; m. Patricia d. Heather Gage; came to Canada 1965; Artistic Dir., Playhouse Theatre, Vancouver, 1971–72; Shaw Festival, 1967–77; theatre work incls. Shaw Festival, Candn. Players, Manitoba Theatre Centre, Citadel and U.S. Regional Theatres, and tours, 'You Never Can Tell,' 'Major Barbara,' 'Charleys Aunt,' 'Devils Disciple,' 'The Bed before Yesterday,' 'Thark'; and Broadway ('Beyond the Fringe,' 'The Affair,' 'Candida'; 'Habeas Corpus' and Sherlock Holmes in 'Crucifer of Blood'; U.K., USSR with Royal Shakespeare Theatre, Stratford-on-Avon; CBC and BBC TV; co-author 'The Chemmy Circle' (play; world premiere 1968); 'There's One in Every Marriage' (play; world premiere 1970); Council mem., Candn. Actors Equity Assn.; Hon. LL.D., Trent Univ. 1978; Anglican; recreations: tennis, skiing; Club: Players (N.Y.); Address: Box 1234, Niagara on the Lake, Ont. L0S 1J0.

**WHITEHEAD, James Rennie,** B.Sc., Ph.D., F.R.S.C.; consultant; b. Barrow (near Clitheroe), Lancashire, England, 4 Aug. 1917; s. William and Beatrice Cora (Fenning) W.; e. Barrow Elem. Sch., Eng.; Clitheroe Royal Grammar Sch., Lancs., Eng.; Univ. of Manchester, B.Sc. (Hons. Physics), 1939; Camb. Univ. (Gonville and Caius), Ph.D. (Physics), 1949; m. Nesta Doone, d. Robert Roberts James, Malvern, Eng., 1 Nov. 1944; children: Valerie Lesley (dec.), Michael James Rennie; CONSULTANT ON SCIENCE POLICY AND RESEARCH; Scientific Officer, Telecommunications Establishment (TRE), Dundee, Swanage and Malvern, England, 1939–44 (designed airborne radar identification transponder fitted to all allied ships and aircraft); on loan to Brit. Air Comn., Wash., D.C. on Scient. Liaison, 1944–45; Headed Research Div. at TRE Malvern on millimeter waves and pulsed-light radar, 1945–46; on loan to Physics and Chem. of Surfaces Research Group, Univ. of Cambridge as Consultant on Electronics 1946–49; Head Physical Electronics Div., TRE Malvern, 1949–51; came to Canada, 1951; joined Physics Staff, McGill Univ. (Headed experimental work incl. trials, on Mid-Canada Line (McGill Fence) from Jan. 1952 to the start of its implementation in 1955); Dir. of Research RCA Victor Co. Ltd., 1955–65 ; Princ. Science Adviser, Science Secretariat, Privy Council Office 1965–71; Asst. Secy. Min. of State for Science and Tech. 1971–73; Special Advisor 1973–75; Sr. Vice-Pres., Philip A. Lapp Ltd., 1976–82; Dir., Lapp-Hancock Associates Ltd. 1983–89; Cdn. mem. of Science Policy Committees of NATO, OECD, ECE, and Commonwealth during period 1965–75; Life mem., Institute of Electrical and Electronic Engrs.; Fellow, Royal Soc. of Canada; Inst. Elect. Engrs.; Inst. of Physics; Canadian Aero. and Space Inst.; mem., Candn. Assn. Physicists; Candn. Research Mgmt. Assn.; Prof. Engrs. Ont.; Club of Rome; Anglican; recreations: automobiles, hi-fi, carpentry, philately, stage management; Clubs: Royal Auto. of Can.; Home: 1368 Chattaway Ave., Ottawa, Ont K1H 7S3.

**WHITEHEAD, Michael Anthony,** Ph.D., F.R.S.C. (U.K.), F.C.I.C., F.R.S.A.; educator; b. London, Eng. 30 June 1935; s. Francis Henry and Edith Downes (Rotherham) W.; e. Kilburn Grammar Sch. London, Eng. 1953; Queen Mary Coll. Univ. of London, 1st Class Hons. Degree in Special Chem. 1956, Ph.D. (Chem.) 1960, D.Sc. 1974; Univ. of Cincinnati Postdoctoral studies 1960–61; one s. Christopher Mark; PROF. OF THEORETICAL CHEM., McGILL UNIV. 1974– ; Asst. Lectr. Queen Mary Coll. Univ. of London 1958–60; Asst. Prof. of Chem. Univ. of Cincinnati 1961–62; Asst. Prof. of Chem. present Univ. 1962, Assoc. Prof. 1966, Assoc. Prof. with tenure 1971; Visiting Prof. of Theoretical Chem. Cambridge Univ. 1971–72, Oxford Univ. 1972–74; Visiting Prof. Fellow in Chem. Univ. Coll. of Wales 1980; Prof. Invité Chimie-Physique, Univ. de Genève, C.H. 1983–84; Life Guest Prof., National Univ. of Defence, Technology Changsha, Hunan, PRC 1988; Visiting Prof., Dept. of Theoretical Chemistry, Oxford Univ., England 1990–91; Co-Chrmn., 7th Intl. Symposium on Nuclear Quadruple Resonance Spectroscopy, Kingston, Ont. 1983; author over 200 research papers quantum chem. and nuclear quadrupole resonance spectroscopy; mem. Am. Physical Soc.; Am. Chem. Soc.; Fellow, Roy. Soc. of Chem.; Fellow, Candn. Inst. of Chem.; Fellow, Royal Society of Arts; mem., Intl. Comte. on Nuclear Quadruple Resonance Spectroscopy, 1974–77, 1980–85; Sigma Xi (Pres. 1970–71, 1981–82, Programme Vice-Pres. 1992–93, Pres. 1993–94); Eng. Speaking Union (Vice Pres. Montreal Br. 1970–72); Pres., James McGill Soc. 1993–95; Anglican; recreation: music, models, cross country skiing, hill walking; Office: 801 Sherbrooke St. W., Montreal, Que. H3A 2K6.

**WHITEHEAD, Robert;** theatre producer; b. Montreal, Que.; 3 March 1916; s. William Thomas and Lena Mary (Labatt) W.; e. Lower Can. Coll., Montreal, Que.; Trinity Coll. Sch., Port Hope, Ont. (1927–34); m. late Virginia, d. late Ross Bolen, Colorado, 16 April 1948; 2ndly, Zoe Caldwell; former Producing Dir., Lincoln Centre Repertory Theatre, till resigned, Dec. 1964; Past Pres. and Gov., League of New York Theatres; Dir., Neighborhood Playhouse, N.Y.; Trustee, Shakespeare Festival, Stratford, Conn.; Dir., Shakespeare in Park, N.Y.C.; V.P., Am. National Theatre & Acad.; produced on Broadway; 'Medea' (w. Judith Anderson) 1947; 'Crime & Punishment' (w. John Gielgud) 1947; 'Member of the Wedding' (prize-winning play by Carson McCullers) 1949; 'Golden Boy' (by Clifford Odetts) 1951; 'Desire Under the Elms' (O'Neill) 1951; 'Mrs. McThing' (w. Helen Hayes) 1951; 'Time of the Cuckoo' (w. Shirley Booth) 1952; 'Bus Stop' (by Wm. Inge) 1954; 'The Remarkable Mr. Pennypacker' 1955; 'Separate Tables' (by T. Rattigan) 1956; 'Waltz of the Toreadors' (by Jean Anouilh) 1957; 'Orpheus Descending' (by Tennessee Williams) 1957; 'A Hole in the Head' 1957; 'The Visit' (w. Alfred Lunt, Lynn Fontaine) 1958; 'A Touch of the Poet' (by E. O'Neill) 1959; 'The Cold Wind and the Warm' (by S.N. Behrman) 1959; 'Much Ado About Nothing' (w. Sir John Gielgud); 'A Man for All Seasons' (by Robert Bolt, w. Paul Scofield; won 5 Tony Awards, Drama Critics Award) 1961; 'The Price' (by Arthur Miller) 1968; 'The Prime of Miss Jean Brodie' (by Jay Allen) 1968; 'Sheep on the Runway' (by Art Buchwald) 1970; served in 2nd World War with Am. Field Service attached to Brit. 8th Army in Africa and Italy, 1942–45, and Brit. 14th Army, Burma, 1945; mem., Am. Arbitration Soc.; Anglican; recreation: fishing; Clubs: Players; Century.

**WHITEHEAD, William Frederick,** M.A.; retired; writer; b. Hamilton, Ont. 16 Aug. 1931; s. Berkeley Kyle and Marjorie Jacqueline (Robinson) W.; e. Central Coll. Inst. Regina 1949; Univ. of Sask. B.A. 1953, M.A. 1955; actor/producer 1957–62, Stratford 1958, Candn. Players 1958–59, Red Barn Theatre Jackson's Point 1959, 1960, 1962; film and documentary writer CBC, TVO, NFB since 1963 incl. over 100 episodes 'The Nature of Things' series, 3 episodes 'Planet for the Taking', 3 'Images of Canada'; 'Dieppe 1942'; 'Dimensions in Science'; co-writer with Timothy Findley 'The National Dream'; recipient ACTRA Award best documentary (with Timothy Findley) 1975; Prince Rainier Prize Monaco Film Festival 1975; Wilderness Award (now Anik Award) 1973, 1979; Bell Northern Prize for Sci. Journalism 1974, 1975, 1976; Ohio Award 1965 (Radio), 1976, 1979; recreations: cooking, volunteer work; Address: P.O. Box 419, Cannington, Ont. L0E 1E0.

**WHITELAW, Donald Mackay,** B.A., M.D., C.M.; physician; educator; b. Vancouver, B.C. 20 Oct. 1913; s. William Albert and Ann Elizabeth (Mackay) W.; e. Univ. of B.C., B.A. 1934; McGill Univ., M.D./C.M. 1939; m. Jean Agnes, d. Wm. A. Berger, Franklin, N.J., 21 Sept. 1940; children: William Albert, John Peter, Bruce Andrew; EMERITUS PROF. OF MED., UNIV. OF BRIT. COLUMBIA, since 1978; Hon. physician, Shaughnessy Hosp. and Cancer Control Agency of B.C.; Physician, B.C. Cancer Inst.; private practice of Med., 1948; Assoc. Prof. of Med., Univ. of British Columbia, 1953, and Prof. 1960–61; subsequently Assoc. Prof. of Med., Univ. of Toronto; Prof. of Med., U.B.C., 1964–77; mem. of Senate, Univ. of B.C., 1959–61; served in 2nd World War with R.C.N.V.R. 1941–46, Surgeon Lieut.-Commander; Fellow, Royal Coll. Phys. of Canada; Zeta Psi; recreation: bird-photography; Home: 6848 Hudson St., Vancouver, B.C. V6P 4K5.

**WHITELAW, John Coghlan,** C.M., Q.C., B.A., LL.B.; retired executive; b. Montreal, Que. 16 June 1907; s. John and Norah (Coghlan) W.; e. Loyola Coll., Montreal, B.A.; Univ. of Montreal (law); m. Yolande, d. late C. N. Moisan, Montreal, Que. 1 June 1940; called to the Bar of Que. 1932; cr. K.C. 1946; practised his prof. in Montreal, Que., before becoming Mgr. of CMA's Que. Div. which position he held for 13 yrs. before his appt. as Extve Vice Pres. and Gen. Mgr. in 1953–74 and life member, 1976; retired mem., Candn. Bar Assn.; Order of Canada 1973; Roman Catholic; Clubs: Mississauga Golf & Country; Imperial Golf and Country (Naples).

**WHITELY, Jack B.,** B.A.; executive; b. Toronto, Ont. 13 Apr. 1930; e. Victoria Coll., Univ. of Toronto, B.A., Pol. Sci. & Econ. 1953; m. Eleanor Mae Trimming 1954; three children; CHRMN., BEACON CAPITAL CORP.; Dir., Evcon Holdings, Inc.; Rapid-Aid Ltd.; Research Officer, Research Dept., Bank of Canada, Ottawa 1954–57; Account Exec., R.D. Steers & Co. Ltd., Investment Dealers, Ottawa 1957–58; Investment Asst. to the Treasurer, Canada Council, Ottawa 1958–59; Vice-Pres. and Dir., Annett & Co. Ltd., Investment Dealers, 1959–68; Vice-Pres., Finance, Canadian Interurban Properties Ltd. 1968–69; Pres. & C.E.O., Commerce Capital Corp. Ltd. 1970–79; Pres. & C.E.O., Crown Trust Co. 1980–81; Chrmn. & C.E.O., Argyll Energy Corp. 1981–86; Home: 3087 Balmoral Ave., Burlington, Ont. L7N 1E5.

**WHITEMAN, (David) Bruce,** M.A., M.L.S.; librarian; writer; b. Brampton, Ont. 18 June 1952; s. Ralph David and Marguerite June (Kibbey) W.; e. Trent Univ. B.A. 1975; Univ. of Toronto M.A. 1977, M.L.S. 1979; m. Deborah d. John and Myrtle Scharbach 31 Aug. 1973; children: Thera Emily, Jesse David; HEAD, RARE BOOKS AND SPECIAL COLLS. McLENNAN LIB. McGILL UNIV. 1988– ; author '12 Poems 12 Drawings' 1978; 'The Sun At Your Thighs, The Moon At Your Lips' 1978; 'Inventions' 1979; 'Ten Lessons in Autobiography' 1981; 'Recesses in the Heart: The Thera Poems' 1984; 'The Invisible World is in Decline' Book 1 1984, Books 2–4 (poetry) 1989; 'Raymond Souster and His Works' 1984; 'Raymond Souster: A Descriptive Bibliography' 1985; ed. 'A Literary Friendship: The Correspondence of Ralph Gustafson and W.W.E. Ross' 1984; 'The Collected Letters of John Sutherland' 1992; Poetry editor, ECW Press; mem. Bibliog. Soc. Can.; Bibliog. Soc. Am.; Bibliog. Soc. UK; Am. Lib. Assn.; League Candn. Poets; Home: 4834 Westmore Ave., Montreal, Que. H4V 1Z3; Office: 3459 McTavish St., Montreal, Que. H3A 1Y1.

**WHITEN, Grover Timothy,** B.S., M.F.A., F.R.C., F.A.H.S.; university professor, artist; b. U.S. 13 Aug. 1941; s. Tom and Mary E. (Glaze) W.; e. Central Michigan Univ. B.S. 1964; Univ. of Oregon M.F.A. 1966; m. Colleen d. James T. and Viola Bush Sept. 1968; PROF., FINE ART & GRADUATE STUDIES, DEPT. OF VISUAL ARTS, YORK UNIV.; Graduate Teaching Fellowship, Univ. of Oregon & Teacher, Maude I. Kerns School of Art 1965–66; served U.S. military 1966–68; began teaching at York Univ. 1968; served as Dir. of Co-Curricular Art, Chrmn., Dept. of Visual Arts & Dir., M.F.A. Program; selected exhibitions incl.: solo: Jerrold Morris Gallery 1972–74, The Bau-XI Gallery 1976–79, '81, '83, '85, Olga Korper Gallery 1987–90 (all Toronto); group: 5th Annual Dalhousie Drawing Exhbn., Dalhousie Univ. 1980, 'Post Modernist Metaphors,' The Alternative Mus., N.Y. 1981, 'Sculptural Density,' Mus. of Visual Arts, N.Y. 1981, 'Down Under,' Harbourfront Gall. Toronto 1981, 'Art Across the Park, Central Park 1982, 'Remains to be Seen,' John M. Kohler Arts Ctr., Wisconsin 1983, 'International Arts Fair,' Chicago 1987; Internat. Art Fair, Cologne, Germany 1988, 'Site Memory,' Contemp. Art from Canada, Clevelend Ctr. for Contemp. Art Guelph 1991 & several others prior to 1980; Distinguished Leadership Award for Extraorindary Service to the Arts & Edn., Am. Biographical Inst. 1989; listed in 5,000 personalities of the world; Who's Who in American Art; 'Who's Who in the East; subject of articles incl. 'Overlay' by Lucy Lippard 1983, 'Art Across the Park: Tim Whiten' by Gilbert Coker 1982, '20th Century Canadian Drawing' by Jerrold Morris 1981, 'Site Memory' by Ingird Jenkner 1991; Office: York Univ., CFA II, Room 246, 4700 Keele St., North York, Ont. M3J 1P3.

**WHITESIDE, Kenneth George,** F.C.A.; financial executive; b. London, Ont. 6 Aug. 1944; s. Harold Seymour and Gladys (Goodwin) W.; e. C.A.; Harvard Business School, Adv. Mngt. Program; m. Carolyn d. Murray and Margaret Christie 16 Aug. 1969; children: David, Catherine; MANAGING DIR., OSLER, HOSKIN & HARCOURT 1990– ; Peat, Marwick, Mitchell & Co. 1962–67; Internat. Utilities Corp. 1967–72; Chief Admin. Offr. or Financial Extve., TransCanada Pipelines 1972–90; Dir., Women's College Hosp. Foundation; Mem., Financial Executives Inst.; clubs: National, Granite, Bd. of Trade of Metro. Toronto; Home: 35 Hilldowntree Rd., Islington, Ont. M9A 2Z7; Office: P.O. Box 50, 1 First Canadian Place, Toronto, Ont. M5X 1B8.

**WHITHAM, Kenneth,** M.A., Ph.D., F.R.S.C.; consultant; b. Chesterfield, Eng. 6 Nov. 1927; s. Joseph and Evelyn (Murphy) W.; e. Cambridge Univ. B.A. 1948, M.A. 1952; Univ. of Toronto M.A. 1949, Ph.D. 1951; m. Joan Dorothy d. Arthur and Dorothy Glasspool 21 Nov. 1953; three d. Melanie Judith, Katherine Hilary, Stephanie Frances; Geophys. Dominion Observatory Ottawa 1951–59, 1960–64; UN Tech. Asst. Expert, Brit. E. Africa 1959–60; Dir. Div. of Seismology & Geothermal Studies, Earth Physics Br. 1964, Dir. Gen. Earth Physics Br. 1973, Asst. Depy. Min. Conserv. & Non-Petroleum Energy 1980; Asst. Depy. Min. Research & Technol. 1981–87, Chief Scientific Adv., Energy, Mines and Resources, Can. 1987; recipient Merit Award Pub. Service of Can. 1971; author over 50 tech. articles, book chapters; Anglican; recreations: reading, philately; Office: 1367 Morley Blvd., Ottawa, Ont. K2C 1R4.

**WHITING, Allan Leslie,** B.Comm., D.H.A., F.A.C.H.E., C.H.E.; health executive; b. Ottawa, Ont. 22 Sept. 1943; s. Leslie Edward and Evelyn Mary (Ferguson) Whiting; e. Univ. of Ottawa B.Comm 1966; Univ. of Toronto D.H.A. 1969; m. Jane d. Dr. Thomas and Bonnie McCarthy 8 June 1968; children: Elizabeth, Joseph, Kathryn, Matthew; PRESIDENT & CHIEF EXECUTIVE OFFICER, CENTENARY HEALTH CENTER 1980– ; Admin. Resident-Asst., Kingston General Hosp. 1969–70; Asst. Admin., Support Profl. Services, Oakville Trafalgar Memorial Hosp. 1970–73; Assoc. Admin., Profl. Services, The Mississauga Hosp. 1973–76; Extve. Vice-Pres. 1976–80; Asst. Prof., Dept. of Health Admin., Fac. of Med., Univ. of Toronto; Fellowship, Am. Coll. Health Care Extves; Cert. Candn. Coll. Health Care Extves.; Surveyor, Candn. Council on Health Facilities Accreditation; Dir., Hospital Council of the Greater Toronto ARea; Home: 730 Meadow Wood Rd., Mississauga, Ont. L5J 2S6; Office: 2867 Ellesmere Rd., Scarborough, Ont. M1E 4B9.

**WHITMAN, Linley (Lin) Vail,** B.Com.; retired insurance executive; b. Emerson, Man. 27 March 1929; s. Charles Alfred and Alic May (Dowswell) W.; e. Univ. of Man. B.Com. 1950; m. Catherine d. Donald Sinclair 15 Aug. 1953; children: Catherine Alice, John David, Karen Louise; Dir. of Insurance, Law Society of Upper Canada and Pres., Lawyers' Professional Indemnity Co., Toronto 1990–93, Retired; Bank Credit Clk. Bank of Commerce Winnipeg 1950; Liability Underwriter The Canadian Indemnity Co. Winnipeg 1955, Br. Casualty Mgr. Toronto 1958, Br. Mgr. Toronto 1973, Regional Vice Pres. Ont. 1978, Vice Pres. Underwriting 1982, Exec. Vice Pres. 1983; Pres. & Dir., 1983–85; Art Gallery Owner and Operator 1986–90; Mem: Bd. Trade Metrop. Toronto; recreations: music, sculpting; Home: 89 Botany Hill Rd., Scarborough, Ont. M1G 3K6.

**WHITMORE, Gordon Francis,** M.A., Ph.D.; scientist; educator; b. Saskatoon, Sask. 29 June 1931; s. Ernest Francis and Mary Anne (MacLean) W.; e. Univ. of Sask. B.A. 1953, M.A. 1954; Yale Univ. Ph.D. 1956; m. Margaret Dawn d. William D. Stuart, Victoria, B.C. 1 Sept. 1954; children: Christine, Elinor, Meredith; PHYSICIST, PHYSICS DIV. ONT. CANCER INST. since 1956; Prof. and Head of Med. Biophys. Univ. of Toronto since 1971; Asst. Prof. of Med. Biophys. Univ. of Toronto 1958, Assoc. Prof. 1962, Prof. 1965, Assoc. Dean Basic Sciences & Research Faculty of Med. 1974–77; rec'd David-Anderson-Berry Gold Medal Royal Soc. Edinburgh 1966; Failla Award 1978; co-author 'Radiobiology of Cultured Mammalian Cells' 1967; numerous works in areas radiation phys., radiation biol., somatic cell genetics, action of chemotherapeutic agts.; mem. Candn. Assn. Phys.; Candn. Assn. Cell Biols.; Biophys. Soc.; Radiation Research Soc.; Am. Assn. Advanc. Science; Protestant; recreations: swimming, skiing, travel; Home: 78 Roxborough St. W., Toronto, Ont. M5R 1T8; Office: 500 Sherbourne St., Suite 732-A, Toronto, Ont. M4X 1K9.

**WHITTAKER, Herbert William,** D.Litt, O.C.; designer, columnist, drama critic, author; b. Montreal, Que. 20 Sept. 1910; s. George Herbert and Eleanor (Trappitt) W.; e. Strathcona Acad., Outremont, Que.; Ecole des Beaux Arts, Montreal, Que.; D.Litt., York 1971; D.Litt. McGill 1991; as Critic; 'Globe & Mail,' Drama Critic there 1949–75; formerly 'The Gazette,' Montreal, radio, film and stage critic; has also written criticism for 'New York Times,' 'New York Herald-Tribune,' 'Christian Science Monitor,' etc.; as Director; Little Theatre of 'The Y.', Montreal Repertory Theatre, Brae Manor Playhouse, Knowlton, Que., Trinity Coll., Victoria Coll., Univ. of Toronto, Hart House, Univ. Alumnae Dramatic Club, Jupiter Theatre, The Crest Theatre, Drama Centre, Univ. of Toronto; as Designer: Everyman Players (Montreal), Shakespeare Soc. of Montreal, Univ. Alumnae Dramatic Club, Canadian Players, Montreal Festivals; as Adjudicator: Dom. Drama Festivals and regional festivals in B.C., Alta., W. Ont., etc.; twice winner of Louis Jouvet Trophy for direction; Martha Allan Award for Design; Bessborough and Sir Barry Jackson Awards, D.D.F.; also Candn. Drama Award; Drama Bench (Toronto) Award 1975; Silver Ticket, Toronto Theatre Alliance 1981; Ontario Dance Award 1985; Publications: 'The Stratford Festival 1953–58,' 'Canada's National Ballet' 1967; 'Whittaker's Theatre 1944–1975' ed. by Ronald Bryden 1985; Preface, Modern Canadian Drama (Penguin) 1984; co-author 'Winston's: The First Fifty Years' 1988; 'Whittaker's Theatricals' 1993; special articles for 'Encyclopaedia Brittanica,' 'Encyclopaedia Americana,' The Culture of Canada, 'The Saturday Review,' 'Theatre Arts,' 'The Stage' (London), 'Hemisphere,' Canberra, Contemporary Canadian Theatre: New World Visions (CTCA), L'Ecole/The School, Nat. Theatre Sch.; Robertson Davies, Can. Studies, Trent Univ.; Film: 'Canada at 8.30' 1971; Bd. of Trustees, Nat. Arts Centre Corp. 1976–82; mem. First Canada Counc. Conf., Kingston 1957; mem. Extve. Comte., Dom. Drama Festival 1957–68, and Gov. 1949–69; Candn. Play Contest, organized for Stratford Festival and Globe and Mail 1958; mem., Expl. Comte., Nat. Theatre Sch, w. Michel Saint-Denis 1958; First Chairman, Drama Bench (Toronto) 1972–75; First Chrmn., Nat. Bd., Cdn. Theatre Critics Assn., 1980; final judge, Theatre Ont. Playwrights Showcase Competition, 1980; judge ACTRA Awards (various); mem., Am. Newspaper Guild; First Life mem., Candn. Actors' Equity Assn. 1976; Expl. Comte., Nat. Play Award 1983; Expl. Comte., Candn. Theatre Museums; First Hon. mem., Associated Designers of Can. 1982; Hon. mem., Assn. Candn. Theatre History 1982; Founder Chrmn., Candn. Theatre Critics Assn., Montreal 1985; Chrmn., Ethics Comte., Candn. Theatre Critics Assn., Ottawa 1986; part-time faculty mem., Bishop's Univ., Oct.-Nov. 1986; Nat. Chrmn., Friends of Candn. Theatre Museums (mem., feasibility study group 1986), a project of Assn. Candn. Theatre History 1987; Fellow, Ryerson Polytechnical Inst. 1988; mem., Archives Comte., Candn. Opera Co.; major contributor, Oxford Companion to Canadian Drama and Theatre 1986; Adv. Bds.: Amer. Shaw Festival, George Brown Theatre Dept., Danny Grossman Dance Co.; 1992 DuMaurier Ltd. World Theatre Fest; Int'l. Theatre Inst., Canada (English Division); Foreign Affairs Special Overseas Media Visitor (SOVF) Australia, 1982; Initiating Comte. Jane Mallett Theatre, St. Lawrence Centre, 1985; Prayer for All Artists comm. St. Martin's In-the-Fields, London memorial service 1987; First Vice

Chrmn., Theatre Museum Inc. 1990; Heritage citation, Royal Alexandra 1989; Publisher's Award and Citation, Globe and Mail 1990; Birthday Celebration, Drama Bench C.T.C.A. at Hart House 1990; Instig. Morley Callaghan Bridge; Tribute Gratien Gelinas, Arts and Letters Club 1991; recreation: theatre; Club: Arts & Letters (Toronto); Home: 10 Lamport Ave., Apt. 301, Toronto, Ont. M4W 1S6.

**WHITTAKER, Sheelagh Dillon,** B.Sc., B.A., M.B.A.; communications executive; b. Ottawa, Ont. 9 Apl. 1947; d. Dean and Tessie (Sadlier-Brown) W.; e. Univ. of Alta. B.Sc. 1967; Univ. of Toronto B.A. 1970; York Univ. M.B.A. 1975; m. William John Morgan s. William and Josephine (Ryan) M.; children: Meghan, Matthew and Daniel Whittaker-Van Dusen, Nicholas Whittaker-Morgan and Abigail and Emily Morgan; PRESIDENT, EDS CANADA 1993– ; Hon. Fellow, Ryerson Polytech. 1992; CWRT Woman of the Year 1992; Dir. General Trust Corp.; Dir., Royal Bank of Canada; Trustee, Internat. Inst. of Communications 1990– ; Asst. to Provost Univ. of Guelph 1971; Comm. Offr. Consumer & Corporate Affairs Can. 1975; Cons. The Canada Consulting Group 1979, Cons. and Dir. 1983; Vice Pres. Planning & Corporate Affairs CBC 1986; Sr. Vice Pres., Candn. Satellite Communications Inc. 1988, Exec. Vice Pres. 1989, Pres. & C.E.O. 1989–93; Office: 300 Consilium Place, Suite 800, Scarborough, Ont. M1H 3G2.

**WHITTALL, Hubert Richard,** D.F.C.; b. Vancouver, B.C. 3 April 1923; s. Norman Reginald and Glen Margaret (McLennan) W.; e. Brentwood Coll., V.I., B.C. (Grad. 1940); m. Jocelyn Hamilton, d. Mr. Justice C. Gerald O'Connor, 29 Oct. 1949; children: Gerald Bruce, Richard O'Connor, Pamela Glen, Virginia Ann; Dir., Placer Dome Inc.; Lafarge Corp.; Trans Mountain Pipe Line Co. Ltd.; Noranda Inc.; B.C. Sugar Refinery Ltd.; Weldwood of Canada Ltd.; Grosvenor International Holdings Ltd.; BC Gas Inc.; Alberta Energy Co. Ltd.; served in 2nd World War with R.C.A.F., 1941–45; awarded D.F.C. and Bar; Anglican; recreations: tennis, fishing; Clubs: The Vancouver; Shaughnessy Golf; Home: 3410 Marpole Ave., Vancouver, B.C. V6J 2S1; Office: Suite 1100, 885 West Georgia St., Vancouver, B.C. V6C 3E8.

**WHITTEN, John A.,** B.A.Sc., P.Eng.; business consultant; b. Toronto, Ont. 23 Aug. 1922; s. Alfred R. and Gladys Aileen (Weese) W.; e. Humberside Coll. Inst., Toronto, Ont.; Univ. of Toronto, B.A.Sc. 1947; m. Margaret Jean, d. W.E. Webster, Niagara-on-the-Lake, Ont. 16 June 1951; children: Robin Jill, Janet Ann; CHRMN., FREDERICK HARRIS MUSIC CO.; joined Christie Brown and Co. Ltd. 1948 as Plant Engr.; Chief Engr. 1953; Dir. of Production and Engn. 1955; Vice-Pres., Production and Dir. 1958; Vice Pres. and Gen. Mgr., Nabisco Foods Div. 1971–79; Sr. Vice-Pres., Christie, Brown 1979–82; served overseas in 2nd World War with Royal Candn. Arty. 1943–45; Past Councillor, World Packaging Organ.; Past Pres., N. Am. Packaging Fed.; Packaging Assn. Can.; Past Chrmn., Univ. of Toronto Governing Council; Conservative; Anglican; recreations: sailing, golf; Clubs: R.C.Y.C.; Toronto Golf; Home: 1122 Balmoral Place, Oakville, Ont. L6J 2C9.

**WHITTINGTON, Stuart Gordon,** M.A., Ph.D.; educator; b. Chesterfield, Eng. 16 Apl. 1942; s. Frank and Eva May (Gretton) W.; e. Chesterfield Sch.; Queens' Coll. Cambridge, B.A. 1963, M.A. 1966, Ph.D. 1972; m. Ann d. Ronald and Phyllis Fretwell 3 Aug. 1964; children: Graeme, Megan; PROF. OF CHEM. UNIV. OF TORONTO 1980– , Chrmn. of Chem. 1985–88; Rsch. Sci. Unilever Rsch. Eng. 1968–70; Asst. Prof. present Univ. 1970, Assoc. Prof. 1975; Visiting Prof. Univ. of Newcastle, Australia 1977; Sci. Rsch. Council Sr. Rsch. Fellow Univ. of Bristol 1977–78; Visiting Fellow Trinity Coll. Oxford 1983–84; Visiting Rsch. Fellow, Univ. of Melbourne, Australia 1990; author or co-author numerous sci. papers; recreation: natural history, music; Home: 173 Airdrie Rd., Toronto, Ont. M4G 1M7; Office: Toronto, Ont. M5S 1A1.

**WHYARD, Florence Esther,** C.M., B.A., LL.D.; journalist; b. London, Ont. 13 Jan. 1917; d. William and Henrietta Elliott; e. Univ. of W. Ont. B.A. 1938; LL.D. (Hon.) 1979; named Mem., Order of Canada 1983; m. James Herbert Whyard 22 July 1944; children: Mary Ellen (dec'd), Judith, William Elliott; apptd. ADMINISTRATOR OF YUKON, Dec. 23, 1988; former Assoc. Ed. 'Fort Erie Times-Review'; freelanced for CBC-IS and Cndn. programs, Yellowknife; 'News of the North' N.W.T.; became Ed. 'Whitehorse Star' 7 yrs., Candn. Ed. Alaska Northwest Publishing Co. 4 yrs.; resigned when el. M.L.A. for Whitehorse West, Yukon Leg. Assembly 1974; mem. Extve. Comte. Y.T. Govt. 1975–78, Mem. responsible for Health, Welfare & Rehabilitation; Mayor, Whitehorse (Y.T.) 1981–83; served with WRCNS Naval Information Br. Ottawa during World War II, rank Lt.; Chrmn. Yukon Found.; Past Pres., Yukon Transp. Museum Soc.; Mem., RCN Benevolent Fund; Hon. Life mem. W.A. Ang. Ch.; Hon. Life mem. Golden Age Soc. Yukon; Hon. Life mem., Whse. Ch. of Commerce; publs. incl.: 'My Ninety Years' 1976; 'Canadian Bush Pilot: Ernie Boffa' 1984; 'Martha Black' 1986; 'Ninety Years North' (history of Yukon Electrical Co.) 1991; ed., pamphlets: 'Five Pioneer Women in Yukon' 1964; 'Kiwi in the Klondike' 1972; 'Hilda Hellaby's Story' 1983; 'Welcome to Beringia!' (Yukon Historical and Museums Assoc.) 1986; Publisher Beringian Books 1986; Yukon Colouring Books; Kappa Alpha Theta (Gamma Epsilon Chapter); P. Conservative; Anglican; recreations: research/writing, northern history, reading, travel; Address: 89 Sunset Dr. N., Whitehorse, Yukon Y1A 3G5.

**WHYTE, Anne Veronica Tennant,** M.A., Ph.D., F.R.S.C.; social scientist; research director; b. Thorne, Eng. 14 Apl. 1942; d. Philip and Grace Grant Mathieson (Tennant) W.; e. The Dame Alice Harpur Sch. Bedford, Eng.; Cambridge Univ. B.A. 1963, M.A. 1967 (Open Exhn. & State Scholar Girton Coll. 1961–63); Johns Hopkins Univ. Ph.D. 1971 (Fulbright Scholar 1963–65); children: David, Clare, Joanna; DIR. GEN. ENVIRONMENT AND NATURAL RESOURCES DIV. INTERNAT. DEVEL. RSCH. CENTRE 1986– ; Geographer, Smithsonian Instn. 1965–67; Rsch. Fellow Cambridge 1967–68; Rsch. Assoc. Univ. of Bristol 1968–74; Lectr. in Geog. Univ. Coll. Univ. of London 1974–75; Assoc. Prof. of Geog. Univ. of Toronto 1976–86 and Dir. Environmental Studies Prog. Innis Coll. 1978–86, Assoc. Inst. Environmental Studies; Prog. Specialist Sci. Sector UNESCO Paris 1984–86; Chair, Candn. Nat. Ctte. for Man & the Biosphere Prog., African Econ. Rsch. Consortium 1987–92; Chair, Candn. Global Change Prog. 1989–93; Vice-Pres., Candn. Assn. of Geographers; mem. Internat. Adv. Ctte. for Environment, Internat. Council of Scientific Unions (ICSU); mem. Ont. Roundtable on Environment and Economy; mem. Working Group on Science, Technology and Training of China Council; mem. Internat. Steering Ctte., Environmental Leadership Program; Dir., LEAD Inc.; mem. Exec. Bd. Candn. Comn. for UNESCO; mem. Hammarskjöld Internat. Comn. for UNESCO; Candn. Del. to UNESCO Gen. Conf. 1979, 1989; author 'The Use of Land and Water Resources in the Past and Present Valley of Oaxaca, Mexico' 1973; 'Guidelines for Field Studies in Environmental Perception' 1977; 'Guidelines for Planning Community Participation' 1986; co-author 'Environmental Risk Assessment' 1980; 'The Mississauga Evacuation' 1981; over 50 articles, book chapters; Fellow, World Acad. Art & Sci.; mem. Candn. Assn. Geogs.; Am. Assn. Geogs.; Inst. Brit. Geogs.; Soc. Human Ecol.; Sigma Xi; recreations: farming, mountain walking, ferns; Clubs: Cambridge (UK); McGill (Toronto); Home: White House Farm, R.R. 2, Russell, Ont. K4R 1E5; Office: P.O. Box 8500, 250 Albert St., Ottawa, Ont. K1G 3H9.

**WHYTE, Francis Rae,** B.A., M.A., Ph.D.; university administrator; b. Felstead, Essex, Eng. 17 Aug. 1943; s. Albert and Barbara Birkbeck (Wood) W.; e. Northcote Coll., Auckland, N.Z. Univ. Entrance 1960; Univ. of Auckland B.A. 1964, M.A. 1966; Laval Univ. Ph.D. 1969; m. Margaret d. William Arthur and Mary Jocelyn Brown 18 Dec. 1967; children: Rohan Christopher, Anik Christiane; DIRECTOR-GENERAL, COUNC. OF MINISTERS OF EDUCATION, CANADA 1988– ; Lectr. in French Univ. of Waikato, N.Z. 1969–71; Comml. Transl. Bombardier Ltée, Valcourt, Que. 1971–72; Prof. of Transl. Univ. du Que. à Trois-Rivières 1972–76; Dean, Graduate Studies & Rsch., Univ. du Qué. à Trois-Rivières 1978–79; Assoc. Vice-Rector for Fac. and Student Affairs, Laval Univ. 1979–85; Vice-Rector (Academic), Concordia Univ. 1985–88; Vice-Pres. Laval Univ. Pension Fund.; Dir. St. François d'Assise Hosp., Que.; co-transl. 'Promotion: communication en marketing' 1975; recreations: sailing, aviation, reading; Home: 430 Donnybrook Rd., Oakville, Ont. L6J 4Y3; Office: 252 Bloor St. W., Ste. 5–200, Toronto, Ont. M5S 1V5.

**WHYTE, John Donaldson,** B.A., LL.B., LL.M.; educator; b. Owen Sound, Ont. 26 June 1940; s. W. Donaldson and Elisabeth Eileen Priscilla (Talbot-Crosbie) W.; e. Univ. of Toronto Trinity Coll. B.A. 1962; Queen's Univ. LL.B. 1968; Harvard Univ. LL.M. 1969; m. Tessa d. Michael and K.S. Davies 12 Dec. 1964; three d. Naomi Rebecca, Vanessa Catriona, Laura Nathalie; PROF. OF LAW QUEEN'S UNIV. 1977– ; Exec. Offr. Pub. Trustee Office London 1963–65; Asst. Prof. of Law present Univ. 1969–73, Assoc. Prof. 1973–77, Prof. 1977–79, 1982– ; Visiting Scholar Yale Univ. 1975–76; Constitutional Adv. Govt. of Sask. 1979–80; Dir. Constitutional Law Br. Dept. of Atty. Gen. Sask. 1980–82; Visiting Prof. Osgoode Hall Law Sch. York Univ. 1987; Dean of Law, Queen's Univ. 1987–92; Constitutional Advisor, Govt. of the Yukon 1992; Visiting Prof., Univ. of Melbourne 1993; author 'The Constitution and Natural Resource Revenues' 1982; co-author 'Canada ... Notwithstanding' 1984; co-ed. 'Canadian Constitutional Law' 1977; United Church; Home: 418 Earl St., Kingston, Ont. K7L 2J8; Office: Kingston, Ont. K7L 3N6.

**WHYTE, Shannon Ralph;** insurance executive; b. Dunedin, New Zealand 4 Feb. 1937; s. Stanley Ralph and Honor Margaret W.; e. King's H.S. Dunedin, New Zealand; University Entrance 1953; m. Madeleine d. Réne and Marta Geneux 3 July 1965; children: Jason Bruce, Nikki Danielle; SR. VICE PRES. & DIR., WILLIS CORROON AEROSPACE OF CANADA LTD. 1991– ; various training positions, Royal Insurance Co. (N.Z.) 1954–60; Inland Marine Underwriter, Co. Fieldman, Hartford Insur. Group Vanc. 1960–63; Aviation Insur. Broker, Back & Bevingtons Ltd. 1964–72; Br. Mgr., Johnson & Higgins Willis Faber Ltd. 1988–91; recreations: tennis, skiing, collecting art; Home: 182 Panorama Pl., P.O. Box 27, Lions Bay, B.C. V0N 2E0; Office: 1100 – 555 W. Hastings St., Vancouver, B.C. V6B 4N6.

**WICIJOWSKI, J. Gordon,** B.Comm., F.C.A.; chartered accountant; e. Univ. of Sask. B.Comm. 1955; articled with present firm C.A. 1958, F.C.A. 1973; m. Ardella; 3 children; SENIOR PARTNER, ERNST & YOUNG; Trustee, Clarkson Gordon Found.; Gov., Law Found. of Sask.; Mem., Inst. of C.A.s of Sask. (Pres. 1971–72), CICA (Gov. 1971–72); Regina C.A. Assn. (Pres. 1963–64); Past Mem., Mgmnt. Ctte., Ernst & Young; Dir. & Chrmn., Audit Ctte., Sask. Roughrider Football Club (mem., Plaza of Honor Selection Ctte.); Treas., Inst. for Sask. Enterprise; Mem. of the Extve. Ctte. and Founding Mem., Business Advisory Council, College of Commerce, Univ. of Saskatchewan; Past. Chrmn., Bd. of Gov., Univ. of Regina; Past Vice-Chrmn., Norman MacKenzie Art Gallery; Past Pres., Rotary Club; Office: 2103 – 11th Ave., Suite 900, Regina, Sask. S4P 3Z8.

**WICK, Donald,** M.A., F.L.A.; librarian; b. Enfield, Eng. 15 Feb. 1928; s. Ernest Charles and Marjorie Joyce (Ridler) W.; e. Enfield (Eng.) Grammar Sch.; Cambridge Univ., B.A. 1952, M.A. 1956; Loughborough Coll., Sch. of Librarianship; children: Adrian, Jonathan, Patricia; LIBRARIAN EMERITUS, UNIV. OF LETHBRIDGE; Br. Librarian, Worthing Pub. Libs., 1954; Interne Librarian, Toronto Pub. Libs., 1955; Bookmobile Librarian, Etobicoke (Ont.) Pub. Libs., 1956, Head of Reference Dept. 1959; Coll. Librarian, Selkirk Coll., Castlegar, B.C., 1965–67; Chief Librarian, Univ. of Lethbridge, 1967–74, 1979–81, Univ. Archivist 1968–83; Collection Development Librarian, Univ. of Lethbridge 1981–85; served with Royal Elect. and Mech. Engrs. 1948–49; Chrmn., Comte. for Survey of Ont. Reference Services, Ont. Lib. Assn. Workshop, 1964–65; Vice Chrmn., Council of Prairie Univ. Libs., 1972–73; author bibliogs., research papers, articles; mem., Bibliog. Soc. Can.; Home: 1117 – 18th St. S., Lethbridge, Alta. T1K 2A4.

**WICKENS, George Michael,** M.A., F.R.S.C.; educator; b. London, Eng. 7 Aug. 1918; s. George William and Annie (White) W.; e. Holloway Sch. London, Eng. 1929–36; Trinity Coll. Cambridge B.A. 1939, M.A. 1946 (Maj., Sr. & Research Scholar); m. the late Ruth Joyce d. the late William Thomas Lindop 9 Nov. 1940; children: Maxim, Anna, Simon, Clare, Andrew, Giles, Stephen, Paul; UNIVERSITY PROFESSOR EMERITUS OF MIDDLE E. & ISLAMIC STUDIES, UNIV. OF TORONTO 1984– ; Lectr. Univ. of London 1946–49; Lectr. in Oriental Studies, Cambridge Univ. 1949–57; Assoc. Prof., Univ. of Toronto 1957–60, Prof. 1960, Chrmn. of Middle E. & Islamic Studies 1961–68; appt. Univ Prof. 1980; served with RAPC 1939–41, Intelligence Corps 1941–46 Middle E., rank Capt., Mentioned in Despatches; author 'Avicenna: Scientist and Philosopher' 1952; 'Booklist on Asia For Canadians' 1961; 'The Nasirean Ethics' 1964; 'Morals Pointed and Tales Adorned' 1974; 'Introduction to Islamic Civilisation' 1976; 'Háji Ághá' 1979; 'Arabic Grammar' 1980; numerous articles and reviews in learned journs. on Middle E. lit., thought and hist.; Founding Fellow, Middle E. Studies Assn. Am.; mem. Am. Oriental Soc.; Home: 50 Prince Arthur Ave., Apt. 506, Toronto, Ont. M5R 1B5; Office: Toronto, Ont. M5S 1A1.

**WICKHAM, Robert B.,** B.Comm., C.M.A., C.A.; financial executive; b. Hamilton, Ont. 20 Jan. 1957; s. Edward Murray Baye and Marlene Joyce (Howie) W.; e. McMaster Univ. B.Comm. 1979; Certified Management

Accountant 1981; Chartered Accountant 1982; m. Donna Fukumoto 19 June 1982; children: Cameron, Midori; VICE PRESIDENT, FINANCE & CHIEF FINANCIAL OFFR., AMERICAN BARRICK RESOURCES CORP. 1983– ; Ernst & Young (formerly Clarkson Gordon) 1979–83; Home: 1253 Springwood Cres., Oakville, Ont.; Office: Royal Bank Plaza, South Tower, Suite 2700, 200 Bay St., P.O. Box 119, Toronto, Ont. M5J 2J3.

**WICKS, Ben;** C.M.; cartoonist, writer; b. London, Eng. 1 Oct. 1926; s. Alfred and Nell (Davies) W.; left sch. aged 14; m. Doreen, d. Jack Curtis 31 Mar. 1957; children: Vincent, Susan, Kim; fruit seller, clog maker, wallet maker, army, shipping clerk, musician; emigrated to Canada 1957; weekly newspaper subscription seller, commercial artist, janitor, window cleaner, milkman, army musician; in 1962 began drawing for Saturday Evening Post, then Toronto Star Syndicate, Los Angeles Times Syndicate, King Features N.Y.; television progs.: World of Wicks, Dear Mum, Wicks; author of 'Ben Wicks Canada' 1976; 'Ben Wicks Women' 1977; 'Book of Losers' 1978; 'Wicks' 1979; 'Ben Wicks Book of Etiquette' 1980; 'More Losers' 1982; 'Ben Wicks Book of Dogs' 1983; 'So You Want to be Prime Minister' 1984; 'Wicksys' 1984; 'No Time to Wave Goodbye' 1988; 'The Day They Took The Children' 1989; 'Nell's War' 1990; 'The Boys Came Marching Home' 1991; 'Promise You'll Take Care of My Daughter' 1992; 'Stop Smoking with Ben Wicks' 1992; 'My Kid on Drugs? Never!' 1993; illustrator for 'Katie and Orbie Save the Planet' (childrens books) 1991; 'Wicks' line of greeting cards; Labatt's 'Know Where To Draw the Line' Anti-Drinking and Driving TV Campaign 1990–91; articles for sev. magazines; Member, Order of Canada; Home: 77 Harbour Sq., Suite 3201, Toronto, Ont.; Office: 449–A Jarvis St., Toronto, Ont. M4Y 2H2.

**WICKWIRE, Wendy Cochrane,** B.Mus., M.A., Ph.D.; anthropologist; writer; b. Liverpool, N.S. 17 Dec. 1949; d. James Alexander and Grace King (Cochrane) W.; e. Univ. of W. Ont., B.Mus. (Hons.) 1972; York Univ., M.A. 1978; Wesleyan Univ., Ph.D. 1983; m. R. Michael s. Arthur and Margaret M'Gonigle 26 Mar. 1982; children: Leithen King, Patrick Finian; freelance writer: anthropology, folklore, music; I.W. Killiam post-doct. fellow, Dept. of Anthropol. 1982–84; Sessional Lectr., Native Indian Teacher Edn. Prog., Univ. of B.C. 1986–88; B.C. Book of the Year Award 1989; recipient, Canada Research Fellowship, Social Sciences & Humanities Research, Council of Canada & Dept. of Social & Educational Studies, UBC, Vancouver 1990–93; co-author: 'Nature Power: In the Spirit of An Okanagan Storyteller' 1992 (winner, Roderick Haig-Brown BC Book Award 1993); 'Write It On Your Heart: The Epic World of An Okanagan Storyteller' 1989; 'Stein, The Way of the River' 1988; recreations: hiking, swimming; Home: 3555 W. 2nd Ave., Vancouver, B.C. V6R 1J5.

**WIDDRINGTON, Peter Nigel Tinling,** M.B.A.; executive; b. Toronto, Ont. 2 June 1930; s. Gerard Nigel Tinling and Margery (MacDonald) W.; e. Pickering Coll. Newmarket, Ont. 1949; Queen's Univ. B.A. (Econ.) 1953; Harvard Business Sch. M.B.A. 1955; m. Betty Ann Lawrence 12 Oct. 1956; two d. Lucinda Ann, Andrea Stacy; CHRMN., TORONTO BLUE JAYS BASEBALL CLUB and CHRMN., LAIDLAW INC.; Dir., Talisman Energy Inc.; Brascan Ltd.; Ellis-Don Inc.; Hayes-Dana Inc.; Laidlaw Inc.; ADT Ltd.; Toronto Blue Jays; Canadian Imperial Bank of Commerce; The SNC-Lavalin Group Inc.; Hon. Dir., John Labatt Ltd.; Salesman, Labatt's 1955; Asst. Regional Mgr. S. Ont. Region, Labatt's Ontario Breweries Ltd. 1957, Regional Mgr. 1958; Gen. Mgr. Kiewel and Pelissiers, Winnipeg 1961, Labatt's Manitoba Breweries Ltd. 1962, Labatt's B.C. Breweries Ltd. 1965; Pres. Lucky Breweries Inc. San Francisco 1968; Vice Pres. Corporate Devel. John Labatt Ltd. 1971, Sr. Vice Pres. 1973, Pres. & C.E.O. 1973–89; Chrmn. 1987–91; recreations: tennis, hockey, golf, swimming; Clubs: London; London Hunt & Country; Granite (Toronto); Shaughnessey Golf & Country (Vancouver); Olympic (San Francisco); York (Toronto); London; Home: 1 Doncaster Ave., London, Ont. N6G 2A1; Office: Suite 400, 248 Pall Mall St., London, Ont. N6A 5P6.

**WIEBE, Donald,** B.Th., B.A., M.A., Ph.D.; professor of the philosophy of religion; b. Niagara Falls, Ont. 29 Apr. 1943; s. David K. and Helen (Braun) W.; e. Mennonite Brethren Coll. of Arts, B.Th. 1967; Wilfred Laurier Univ., B.A. 1967; Univ. of Guelph, M.A. 1970; Univ. of Lancaster, Ph.D. 1974; m. Gloria d. Clarence and Hilda Willems 28 Dec. 1965; one s.; Geoffrey Donald K.; PROF., TRINITY COLL., UNIV. OF TORONTO 1987– ; Asst. Prof., Candn. Nazarene Coll. 1965–67, 1975–77; Winkler Bible Inst. 1967–69; Sessional Lectr., Univ. of Guelph 1969–70; Univs. of Winnipeg & Man. 1977–80; Tutorial Fellow, Univ. of Lancaster 1974; Asst. Prof., Trinity Coll. 1980–82, Assoc. Prof. 1982–87, Prof. 1987– ; Assoc. Dir., Centre for Religious Studies, Univ. of Toronto 1990–92; Mem., Internat. Assn. for the Hist. of Religions (Extve. Bd. Mem. 1985– ; Extve. Dir., XIVth Quinquennial Cong. 1980); Candn. Soc. for the Study of Religion (Extve. Bd. 1980–83); Am. Acad. of Religion; N.A. Assn. for the Study of Religion (Pres. 1986–87, 1991–92; Extve. Bd. 1987– ); Soc. for the Scientific Study of Religion; Can. Counc. Fellow 1970–74; SSHRCC Leave Fellowship 1986–87; Sr. Rsch. Scholar, Corpus Christi Coll., Cambridge 1986–87; Ed. Adv. Bd., Peter Lang Press 1987– ; Ed. Bd. Mem.: 'Religion,' 'Method and Theory in the Study of Religion,' 'Numen'; author: 'Religion and Truth' 1981; 'The Irony of Theology and the Nature of Religious Thought' 1991 and over 60 articles; editor: 'Concept and Empathy' 1986; 'Toronto Studies in Religion' (series); co-editor: 'Traditions in Contact and Change' 1983; Home: 9 Douglas Ave., Toronto, Ont. M5M 1G4; Office: 6 Hoskin Ave., Toronto, Ont. M5S 1H8.

**WIEBE, John P.,** B.Sc., Ph.D.; educator; endocrinologist; e. Univ. of B.C., B.Sc. 1963, Ph.D. 1967; PDF, Leeds, U.K.; PROF. OF ZOOLOGY, UNIV. OF W. ONT. 1972– , Hon lectr. in Physiol.; Offr.-in-Charge I.G.Y. Meteorol. Rsch. Stn. Banks Is., Can. Arctic Div. 1958–59; Biol. Arctic Biol. Survey 1962; Nat. Rsch. Council Fellow UK 1968–69; Asst. Prof. Inst. of Life Sci. Texas A&M Univ. 1970–72; Visiting Prof., Dept. of Biomed., Turku Univ., Finland 1986; James Chair Prof. of Pure and Applied Science 1988; recipient Nat. Rsch. Council Scholarships and Postdoctorate Fellowship; McLean Fraser Scholarship N.S.E.R.C. New Rsch. Ideas Award; Kroc Found. Award Advances Med. Sci.; numerous research grants from NSERC, Health & Welfare Can., Med. Rsch. Counc., Bickell Found. for Med. Rsch., U.S. Agency for Internat. Develop., NATO & NSERC Grants for Collaborative Rsch. (Internat.); author or co-author over 100 papers reproductive endocrinol. and other related subjects; holds patent on male contraceptive; mem. Am. Soc. Androl.; Soc. Advanc. Contraception; N.Y. Acad. Sci's.; Soc. Study Reproduction; Candn. Soc. Cell Biols. Candn. Biochem. Sco.; Sigma Xi; recreations: tennis, photography, skiing; Office: London, Ont. N6A 5B7.

**WIEBE, Rudy Henry,** B.A., Th.B., M.A., D.Litt.; educator; author; b. near Fairholme, Sask. 4 Oct. 1934; s. Abram Jacob and Katerina (Knelsen) W.; e. Alta. Mennonite High Sch. 1953; Univ. of Alta. B.A. 1956, M.A. 1960; Univ. of Tuebingen (W. Germany) 1958; Mennonite Brethren Bible Coll. Th.B. 1961; Univ. of Man. 1961; Univ. of Iowa 1964; m. Tena F. d. Jacob and Sara Isaak 4 March 1958; children: Adrienne, Michael, Christopher; PROFESSOR EMERITUS OF ENGLISH AND CREATIVE WRITING, UNIV. OF ALTA. 1992– ; Rsch. Offr. Glenbow Foundation Calgary 1956; Grad. Teaching Asst. 1958–60; Foreign Service Offr. Govt. of Can. 1960; High Sch. Teacher Selkirk, Man. 1961; Ed. 'Mennonite Brethren Herald' Winnipeg 1962–63; Asst. and Assoc. Prof. of English Goshen (Ind.) Coll. 1963–67; Asst. Prof. Univ. of Alta. 1967, Assoc. Prof. 1971, Prof. 1977; lectr. Sask. Sch. for Arts; Univ. of B.C.; Concordia Univ. Montreal; Banff Sch. Fine Arts; Univ. of Calgary; Univ. of Augsburg and Univ. of Kiel, W. Germany; Univ. of Copenhagen, Denmark; recipient Gov. Gen.'s Award for Fiction 1973; Prov. Alta. and City of Edmonton Arts Achievement Award 1974, 1975; D. Litt., Univ. of Winnipeg 1986; Lorne Pierce Medal, Royal Soc. of Can. 1987; D.Litt., Wilfred Laurier Univ. 1991; LL.D. Brock Univ. 1991; various individual awards for novels, stories; author, novels: 'Peace Shall Destroy Many' 1962; 'First and Vital Candle' 1966; 'The Blue Mountains of China' 1970; 'The Temptations of Big Bear' 1973; 'The Scorched-Wood People' 1977; 'The Mad Trapper' 1980; 'My Lovely Enemy' 1983; 'Chinook Christmas' 1992; 'A Discovery of Strangers' 1994; story collections: 'Where is the Voice Coming From?' 1974; 'Alberta/A Celebration' 1979; 'The Angel of the Tar Sands' 1982; drama: 'Far as the Eye Can See' 1977; essays: 'A Voice in the Land' 1981; 'Playing Dead: A Contemplation Concerning the Arctic' 1989; ed. 'The Story-Makers' (short stories) 1970, rev. ed. 1987; 'Stories from Western Canada' 1971; 'Getting Here' 1977; 'Double Vision' 1976; co-ed. 'Stories from Pacific and Arctic Canada' 1974; 'More Stories from Western Canada' 1980; 'West of Fiction' 1983; "War in the West,' Voices of the 1885 Rebellion' 1985; mem. Writers Adv. Comte. to Min. of Culture Alta. 1980–82; mem. Arts Panel Can. Council 1974–77; Fed. Cultural Policy Review Comte. 1981–84; Alta. Found. for the Literary Arts 1984–87; Founding Pres. Writers Guild Alta. 1980; Founding Vice Chair Writers Union Can. 1973 (Chair 1986–87); President, NeWest Press 1989; Mennonite Brethren Ch.; recreations: reading, travel; Address: 105, 10610 - 83 Ave., Edmonton, Alta. T6E 2E2.

**WIELAND, Joyce,** O.C.; artist/filmmaker; b. Toronto, Ont. 30 June 1931; e. Central Tech. Sch.; animator, Graphic Films 1957–59; exhibits: Film retro., Georges Pompidou Ctr. (France) 1989; Nat. Film Theatre 1988; AGO Candn. Nat. touring retrospective of art & film 1987; 'Toronto Painting '84' AGO 1984; '20th Century Candn. Painting' Nat. Mus. of Modern Art, Japan 1981; 'True Patriot Love' NGC 1971; 'Eight Artists from Canada' Tel-Aviv Mus., Israel 1970; 'Five Films by Joyce Wieland' Mus. of Modern Art, N.Y. 1968; 'Canada Art d'Aujourd hui' Mus. Nat. d'Art Moderne, Paris (travelled through Eur.) 1968 and many more exhibs.; film festivals: Edinburgh Internat. 1988; Ann Arbor (2nd prize) 1986; Oberhausen 1986; London 1985; Berlin 1985; Candn. Film, Hong Kong Arts Ctr.; Cannes 1976; Sonsbeek 1972; Philadelphie Internat. Fest. of Short films (award for exceptional merit) 1971; films: 'Far Shore' (2 Candn. film awards 1977; German TV Fest. of Fest. 1986); 'O Kanada' 1983; multiple comns., world wide exhibs., extensive biblio. of books, mags., newspapers & rsch. papers incl. 'Artist on Fire' by Kay Armitage 1987; Artist-in-Res., Univ. of Toronto, Architecture 1988–89; Instr., N.S. Coll. of Art & Design 1971; San Francisco Art. Inst. 1985–86; Can. Counc. grant 1966, 68, 72, 84, 86; Offr., Order of Can. 1983; Toronto Arts Award 1987; YWCA Woman of Distinction Award 1987; Mem., Royal Acad. of Arts 1973; Can. Counc. Victor M. Staunton Award 1972; Office: 497 Queen St. E., Toronto, Ont. M5A 1V1.

**WIELER, Diana Jean;** writer; b. Winnipeg, Man. 14 Oct. 1961; d. Heinz Egon and Jean Florence (Zebrasky) Petrich; e. Lord Beaverbrook Senior High 1979; m. Larry John s. John and Edith W. 2 May 1981; one s.: Benjamin; author: 'Last Chance Summer' 1986, 'To the Mountains by Morning' 1987, 'Bad Boy' 1989; editor: 'A Question of Courage' 1988, 'Dog Runner,' 'The Freedom Run' 1990; Major Award, Sask. Writers' Guild Lit. Awards 1985; 1st Place, CBC Literary Comp., children's lit. 1984; Vicky Metcalf Award, best short story for children 1986; Max and Greta Ebel Memorial Award ('Last Chance Summer') 1986; Gov.-Gen.'s Lit. Award for Children's Lit. ('Bad Boy') 1989; Internat. Bd. on Books for Young People, Internat. Hon. List; Ruth Schwartz Award for Excellence 1990; Candn. Booksellers Assn., Young Adult Book of the Year ('Bad Boy') 1990; Office: c/o Douglas & McIntyre, 1615 Venables St., Vancouver, B.C. V5L 2H1.

**WIENS, The Honourable Bernhard Henry,** B.S.A., M.Sc., M.L.A.; farmer, politician; b. 2 Sept. 1945; e. Rosthern Jr. College; Univ. of Saskatchewan B.S.A. 1967, M.Sc. 1972; m. Cheralyn d. Irwin and Muriel Krug 1968; children: Devin, Nicole, Lauren, Stacey, Teresa; MINISTER OF ENVIRONMENT AND RESOURCE MANAGEMENT, GOVT. OF SASKATCHEWAN 1992– ; mixed farming operation 1969–; 1st elected to Sask. Legis. g.e. 1991; Mem., Sask. Ctte. on Rural Area Devel. 1989–90; Agriculture in the Classroom Reference Ctte. 1989–91; Minister of Agriculture & Food and Minister of Highways & Transportation, Govt. of Saskatchewan 1991–92; Soc. for Educational Visits & Exchanges in Canada 1990; Canada Farm Labour Pool Adv. Bd. 6 years; Chair, Sask. Wheat Pool Ctte.; Rosetown Co-op Implements Bd.; Nat. Farmers' Union; Rosetown School Div. Bd. (Chair 1984–87) 1975–91; Herschel Local School Board 1991– ; Sask. Sch. Trustees Assn. (Br. Rep. 1982–84; Vice Pres. 1984–87; Pres. 1987–89; Life Mem.); Candn. School Bd. Assn. (Bd. of Dir. 1987–89; Vice Pres. 1989–90; Pres. 1990–91; Past Pres. 1991–92, Life Mem.); Social Studies Task Force 1981; mem., Honorary Bd., Candn. Council for Multicultural and Intercultural Education 1991– ; Core Curriculum Adv. Ctte. 1985; Wheatlands Project, Coord. Serv. for Handicapped 1982–84; Chair, Govt. Trustee Bargaining Ctte., Prov. Teachers Negotiations 1989–90; Mem., Herschel Mennonite Ch.; recreations: church choir, male choir, mechanics; Home: Box 70, Herschel, Sask. S0L 1L0; Office: Room 348, Legis. Bldg., Regina, Sask. S4S 0B3.

**WIERSMA, John,** B.E., P.Eng.; utilities executive; b. Diever, The Netherlands 2 Nov. 1944; s. Paul and Grace (Mulder) W.; e. Hill Park Secondary Sch. Hamilton 1964; McMaster Univ. B.E. 1968; m. Louise d. Gerrit and Joanne Muys 1967; children: Bradley Paul, Amanda Joyce, Edward John, Robert Peter; GEN. MGR. PICKERING HYDRO-ELECTRIC COMN. 1979– ; Distribution Eng. Hamilton Hydro System 1968–72; Mgr. Streetsville Pub. Utilities Comn. 1972–76; Gen. Mgr. Wasaga Beach Hydro-Electric Comn. 1976–79; Pres. Mun. Electric Assn. 1990–91; Past Pres., Mun. Electric Assn. 1991–92; mem. Bd. Govs. Redeemer Coll. Hamilton 1987–91; mem. Assn. Profl. Engs. Prov. Ont.; Assoc. Gospel Churches; recreations: cross-country skiing, golf, outdoors; Home: 1014 Mountcastle Cr., Pickering, Ont. L1V 5J2; Office: 1920 Bayly St., Pickering, Ont. L1W 3R7.

**WIESEL, Robert C.,** B.Sc.E., M.Sc.E.; engineering and construction industry executive; b. Springfield, Mass. 23 Aug. 1950 e. Univ. of Massachusetts B.Sc.E. 1972; Northeastern Univ. M.Sc.E. 1978; m. Lynne Lippmann 13 Sept. 1975; children: Jared, Lindsey; STONE & WEBSTER ENGINEERING CORP. (Boston, Mass.); Structural Engineer, Stone & Webster Engr. Corp. Boston 1978; Sr. Structural Engr. 1982; Supvr. of Projects 1984; Asst. Chief Engr., Structural 1986; Chief Engineer, Civil-Structural 1988; Vice Pres., Stone & Webster Canada Limited 1990; Extve. Vice-Pres. 1991; Pres. & C.E.O. 1991– ; Mem., Am. Soc. of Civil Engrs.; Boston Soc. of Civil Engrs.; Structural Stability Research Council; Office: 245 Summer St., Boston, Mass. 02210.

**WIESENTHAL, David Lawrence,** Ph.D.; university professor; b. New York, NY 28 Oct. 1945; s. Charles I. and Debora (Goldman) W.; e. CCNY, B.A. 1966; State Univ. of NY, Ph.D. 1971; m. Sandra d. James and Betty Young 2 July 1972; children: Naomi, Joshua; ASSOC. PROF. OF PSYCHOLOGY, YORK UNIV. 1977– ; post-doct. fellow, York Univ. 1970; Asst. Prof. 1971; Coordinator, Social/Personality Graduate Programme 1987–89; Fellow, La Marsh Programme on Violence and Conflict Resolution 1988–89, Extve. Ctte. Mem. 1990; Can. Counc. Leave Fellow 1977; Vis. Prof., Hebrew Univ. of Jerusalem; SSHRCC leave fellow 1984; Scandinavian Leave Fellow 1991; Rsch. citation, N. York Chap., Candn. Red Cross Soc. 1981; N.Y. State Regents Scholarship 1962–66; Mem., Candn. Assn. of Univ. Teachers; York Univ. Fac. Assn.; author: 'Studies in Residential Vandalism' 1987 & num. scholarly articles & papers; participant in several workshops; Cons., Candn. Red Cross Soc. Blood Donor Prog.; Can. Mortgage & Housing Corp.; Eye Bank of Can.; Ont. Min. of Transp.; Office: 4700 Keele St., North York, Ont. M3J 1P3.

**WIGDOR, Blossom T(emkin),** C.M., B.A., M.A., Ph.D.; psychologist & gerontologist; b. Montreal, Que. 13 June 1924; d. Solomon and Olga (Gilels) Temkin; e. McGill Univ. B.A. 1945, Ph.D. 1952; Univ. of Toronto M.A. 1946; m. Leon Wigdor 31 May 1945 (dec'd. 1991); one child Mitchell; PROFESSOR EMERITUS OF PSYCHOL. & BEHAVIOURAL SCIENCE, UNIV. OF TORONTO 1991– ; Dir., Prog. in Gerontology 1979–89; Dir., Centre for Studies of Aging 1989–90 and current member; Mem., Nat. Adv. Counc. on Aging 1988–93 (Chair Person 1990–93); Trustee, Inst. for Research on Public Policy 1983–89 and of the Ont. Psychological Found. 1987–90; joined Dept. of Veterans Affairs 1946, Psychol. Christie St. Hosp. and Sunnybrook Hosp. 1946–47, Ste. Anne de Bellevue and Queen Mary Veterans Hosps. 1947–78; Consultant in Psychol., Maimonides Hosp. and Home for Aged Montreal 1954–68; participated in organ. of Multi disciplinary Geriatric Clinic, Jewish Gen. Hosp. Montreal 1955–56; Sr. Consultant in Psychol. Queen Elizabeth Hosp. Montreal 1963–74; Dir. of Psychol. Services Centre Hospitalier Cote des Neiges (formerly Queen Mary Veteran Hosp.) 1961–79, Dir. Psychiatric-Psychol. Research Unit 1965–78, M.B.O. Advisor (Mang. & Organ. Devel.) 1971–78; Consultant in Psychol. to Asst. Depy. Min. D.V.A. Ottawa 1965–78; Assoc. Prof. of Psychol. McGill Univ. 1972–79; Prof. of Psychol. & Behavioural Science, Univ. of Toronto 1979–91; Chrmn. Grad. Faculty Comte. on Aging; mem. Science Council Can., 1973–79; Bd. of Dir., Candn. Geriatics Rsch. Soc. 1980–86; External Consultant, Soc. Sci. and Humanities Research Council of Can. and Health & Welfare Can.; conducted many seminars for med. and grad. students in psychol., nurses and others on topics in clin. psychol. and aging; named Woman of Achievement YWCA Montreal 1975; apptd. Member of the Order of Canada 1989; Candn. Assn. of Gerontol. Award for outstanding contrib. to gerontol. 1989; Hon. D.Sc., Univ. of Victoria 1990; awarded Commemorative Medal for 125th Anniversary of Candn. Confederation 1993; Ed. 'Canadian Gerontological Collection I' 1977; 'Planning Your Retirement' 1985, 2nd ed. 1988; Vice-Chrmn. & Dir., Gerontological Research Council of Ont. 1980–90; Gov., Baycrest Centre for Geriatric Care; Gov., Mount Sinai Hosp.; Bd. of Dirs., Candn. Stage Company 1992– ; Candn. Memorial Services 1993– ; Editor-in-Chief, Candn. Journal on Aging 1981–85; mem. Ed. Bd. 'Psychiatric Journal of the Univ. Ottawa'; author or co-author various articles, papers, reports and of the recent book 'The Over Forty Society'; Fellow, Candn. Psychol. Assn.; Gerontol. Soc. of America; Fellow, American Psychological Assn.; mem. Candn. Assn. Gerontol. (2nd Vice Pres., 1977–81; E. Psychol. Assn.; Sigma Xi (Toronto Chap.); recreations: theatre, reading; Home: Apt. 708, 21 Dale Ave., Toronto, Ont. M4W 1K3.

**WIGGINS, Chris;** actor; writer; b. Lancs., Eng., 13 Jan. 1931; s. Walter and May (Ellor) W.; m. Erica Margaret, d. Max Montesole; stage career incls. Stratford (Ont.) Festival, Alley Theatre (Houston), Crest and Museum Theatres (Toronto), Globe Theatre; over 1450 TV roles for CBC, CTV and Nat. Film Bd. in Can.; various networks in U.S.; over 120 film roles incl. Spearfield in 'Spearfield's Daughter'; Yardley in 'Two Solitudes'; Lyle Bishop in 'Why Shoot the Teacher'; John Sheardown in 'Escape from Iran'; over 1000 radio roles and over 200 roles in educ. TV; rec'd Telegram Theatre Award for Best Candn. Actor 1964; 'Etrog' Candn. Film Award for Best Actor 1969; Ohio State Competition Award for Host-Narrator; Jessie De Rivers Award for Dramatic Writing, Candn. Authors' Assn. 1973; Andrew Allan Award for Best Radio Drama Performance, ACTRA 1976; author 'Sinbad and the Mermaid' and 'Sleeping Beauty' (children's plays) 1965; other writings incl. plays for TV, radio and film incl. 'The Ballad Master,' 'Spaniard's Rock'; 'Five Unpleasant Canadian Stories' (radio); 'The Subject is the Dog,' Radio Internat.; title role 'Paul Bernard, Psychiatrist' and Father Robinson, 'Swiss Family Robinson' (TV series); also educ. series for film, TV and radio; named Hon. Chief of Stoney Indian Tribe of Alta. under title 'Swift-Running Bear Cub'.

**WIGGINS, John R.;** brewery executive; b. Vancouver, B.C. 19 Oct. 1931; s. Reginald Heber and Mary-Jane (Hendry) W.; e. Lisgar Collegiate; Ottawa Technical Special Art Course; Northern Vocational, special art course; m. Sylvia J. d. Elgin and Lydia vanSteenburgh 28 Aug. 1954; children: Christopher, Sheralie, Lisa; PRESIDENT, CREEMORE SPRINGS BREWERY 1987– ; Art Dir. & Mgr. for several design studios 1950–58; Creative Dir. & Art Dir. for several advtg. agencies 1958–66; Pres., Embryon Limited 1966–78; Corp. Communications Consultant to Bell Canada, Polysar Ltd., Allied Chem., Bahamas Tourism Min., Lake Ont. Cement, Toronto Stock Exchange, Chemical Bank 1979–85; Chair, Ont. Small Brewers Assn. 1989–92; Lecturer, Ont. College of Art 1985–91; recreations: skiing, golf, painting: clubs: Devil's Glen, Mad River; Home: The Mill Privilege, Box 338, Creemore, Ont. L0M 1G0; Office: 139 Mill St., Box 369, Creemore, Ont. L0M 1G0.

**WIGHTMAN, David P.,** C.M.M., B.Eng.; public servant; b. Toronto, Ont. 20 Dec. 1931; s. Lyall M. and Dorothy A. (Hurcomb) W.; e. Royal Roads; Royal Military Coll.; McGill Univ., B.Eng. 1955; m. Tannis d. Gustav and Margaret Carlson 5 June 1954; children: Carol, David, Janet, Judith, John; ASST. DEPY. MIN., AVIATION, DEPT. OF TRANSPORT 1989– ; 36 years in Royal Candn. Air Force; retired as Commander, Candn. Forces Europe in rank of Major General; Sr. Vice-Pres., Eur. Helicopter Indus. (Can.); Past Chrmn., Air Force Offrs. Adv. Group; Mem., Candn. Aeronautics & Space Inst.; recreations: skiing, music; club: RCAF Ottawa Officers Mess; Home: 3426 Greenbank Rd., Nepean, Ont. K2J 4H7; Office: Place de Ville, Ottawa, Ont. K1A 0N8.

**WIGHTMAN, Joseph A.O.,** B.Comm., C.A.; financial executive; b. Napanee, Ont. 10 Aug. 1950; s. Henry Duncan and Ruth Naomi (Singleton) W.; e. Queen's Univ. B.Comm. (Hons.) 1972; C.A. (Ont.) 1974; m. Christine d. Wallace and Elaine Finley 24 June 1972; children: Andrew, Elizabeth, Peter; VICE-PRESIDENT, FINANCE, DAVIS + HENDERSON LTD. 1983– ; Chartered Accountant, Thorne, Riddell 1972–83; recreations: skiing, sailing; clubs: Skyloft Ski; Home: 47 Addington Sq., Unionville, Ont. L3R 7N4; Office: 2 Lansing Sq., Suite 701, North York, Ont. M2J 4P8.

**WIGLE, Donald Theodore,** M.D., Ph.D., M.P.H.; physician; b. Canada 15 Dec. 1942; s. John Theodore Nelson and Jean McBeth (Rae) W.; e. South Collegiate, London 1960; Univ. of West. Ont., M.D. 1966; Rotating Internship, Victoria Hosp., London 1966–67, Univ. of B.C., Ph.D. 1970; Univ. of Calif. at Berkeley, M.P.H. 1974; m. Elizabeth M.J. d. William H. and Alice P. McLean 28 Aug. 1965; children: Jacqueline Patricia, Jeffrey Theodore Nelson, Jason McLean; DIRECTOR, BUREAU OF CHRONIC DISEASE EPIDEMIOLOGY, HEALTH & WELFARE CAN. 1990– ; MRC Fellow 1967–70; postdoct. fellow, Inst. for Molecular Biol., Aarhus, Denmark 1970–72; Med. Offr., Health & Welfare Can. 1972–74; Chief, Cancer Section 1974–81; Chief, Chronic Disease Div. 1981–86; Chief, Surveillance and Risk Assessment Div. 1986–90; Adjunct Prof., Epidem. & Biostat., McGill Univ.; Epidem. & Community Health, and Kinanthropology, Univ. of Ottawa; Epidem. & Community Health, Queen's Univ.; Ont. Scholar; Queen Elizabeth scholarship 1960; Kingswood Scholarship for gen. proficiency in med. (U.W.O.) 1966; Mem., Candn. Public Health Assn.; Assoc. Ed., 'Can. J. of Public Health'; author of over 100 health rsch. articles; Home: 1171 Whitmore Ave., Ottawa, Ont. K2C 2N6; Office: Lab. Ctr. for Disease Control, Health & Welfare Can., Ottawa, Ont. K1A 0L2.

**WILBEE, James J.,** F.C.A.; pension fund executive; b. Toronto, Ont. 21 June 1939; s. John E. and Muriel J. W.; e. C.A. 1965; m. Juliane d. Reinhold and Margarete Reisch 3 Aug. 1963; children: Alexandra Caroline, Simon James; PRES. AND CHIEF EXEC. OFFR. PUBLIC SERVICE PENSION BD. (ONT.) 1990– ; Dir. Retail Sales, Gasoline Motor Fuels and Tobacco Taxes 1979–84; Ont. Supt. of Deposit Instns. 1984–88; Ont. Supt. of Ins. 1988–90; mem. Adv. Ctte. Auditor Gen. Can.; Lectr., York Univ.; Anglican; Home: Toronto, Ont.; Office: Suite 1100, One Adelaide St. E., Toronto, Ont. M5C 2X6.

**WILDE, Alex,** C.A.; insurance executive and consultant; b. Winnipeg, Man. 15 Oct. 1948; s. Richard Lawson and Helen Gertrude (Gill) W.; e. Univ. of Regina, C.A. 1966; CHIEF EXECUTIVE OFFR., WORKERS COMPENSATION BD. OF MANITOBA 1993– and PRES., WIIFM CONSULTING 1991– ; articled with Deloitte, Haskins and Sells, Regina 1966–71; Cooperators Group, Regina 1971–80; joined SGI 1980 serving as Director Bus. Studies, Operational Audit, Claims Support Services and VP Claims, appt'd. President 1985–91; former Dir., Administrative Management Soc. Internat. Bd. 1985–88; City of Regina Economic Development Advisory Ctte. 1985–87; Regina Crime Stoppers 1985–88; Bd. of Dirs., Canada Safety Council 1986–93 (Vice Chrmn. 1989–93); Hospitals of Regina Foundation 1990–92; Investment Corp. of Sask. 1988–92 (Chrmn. 1991–92); Property and Casualty Insurance Compensation Corp. 1991–92; Sask. Crime Stoppers 1988–93; Manitoba Safety Council 1993– ; Workers Compensation Bd. of Manitoba 1993– ; affiliated with various professional and voluntary organizations including: Internat. Insurance Soc.; Mensa Canada; Young President's Organization; Home: 314 – 75 Swindon Way, Winnipeg, Man. R3P 0X2.

**WILDER, William Price,** B.Comm., M.B.A.; financier; b. Toronto, Ont. 26 Sept. 1922; s. William Edward and Marjorie Margaret (Murray) W.; e. Elmhouse Sch. 1934; Upper Canada Coll. 1940 (both Toronto, Ont.); McGill Univ., B.Comm. 1946; Grad. Sch. of Bus. Adm., Harvard Univ., M.B.A. 1950; m. Judith Ryrie, d. Edward W. Bickle, Toronto, Ont. 18 Sept. 1953; children: Martha Helen, William Edward, Thomas Bickle, Andrew Murray; Chrmn., The Consumers' Gas Co. Ltd. 1981–87; Dir., Budd Canada Inc.; Canada Life Assurance Co.; Noranda Inc.; Scotia Synfuels Ltd.; United Corporations Ltd.; mem. Advy. Comte., Energy Internat. N.V.; joined Wood Gundy and Co. Ltd. 1946, Extve. Asst. to Dirs. 1958–61, Extve. Vice-Pres. and Dir. 1961, Pres. and Dir. 1967–72; Chrmn. and C.E.O., Candn. Arctic Gas Study Ltd. 1972–77; Extve. Vice Pres., Gulf Canada Ltd. 1977–79; Pres. & C.E.O., Hiram Walker Resources Ltd. (and predecessor Hiram Walker-Consumers Home Ltd.) 1979–82; Depy. Chrmn., Hiram Walker Resources Ltd. 1982–84; served in 2nd World War; Lt., R.C.N.V.R. on loan to Royal Navy 1941–44; mem. Alpha Delta Phi; United Church; recreations: golf, tennis, skiing, fishing; Clubs: York, Toronto, Toronto Golf, Badminton & Racquet, Cambridge, Queen's (Toronto); Mount Royal (Montreal); Brooks's (London, Engl.); Coral Beach & Tennis (Bermuda); Tadenac Fishing; Osler Bluff Ski; Home: 400 Russell Hill Rd., Toronto, Ont. M4V 2V2; Office: PO Box 105, Scotia Plaza, 40 King St. W., Toronto, Ont. M5H 3Y2.

**WILDMAN, The Hon. C.J. (Bud),** B.A.; politician, educator; b. Ottawa, Ont. 3 June 1946; s. Ernest Jackson and Elizabeth Guilford (Graham) W.; e. Osgoode Twp. H.S. 1962; Carleton Univ. B.A. 1967; m. T. Anne d. Wilbert and Jean Brophy 28 Dec. 1968; children: Robert, Jody, Cary; MINISTER OF ENVIRONMENT AND ENERGY and MINISTER RESPONSIBLE FOR NATIVE AFFAIRS, GOVT. OF ONT. 1993– ; Teacher, Sault Ste. Marie C.I. 1967–75; Head History Dept. 1972; 1st elected to Ont. Legislature as MPP for Algoma Sept. 1975; re-elected 1977, '81, '85, '87, '90; Min. of Natural Resources and Min. responsible for Native Affairs 1990–93; Mem., Ont. Secondary School Teachers Fed.; Mem., N.D.P.; recreations: outdoors, canoeing, reading; Office: 135 St. Clair Ave. W., 12th Floor, Toronto, Ont. M4V 1P5.

**WILDMAN, Sally Ann,** R.C.A., O.S.A.; painter; b. Tynemouth, Eng. 2 Aug. 1939; d. William Caddy and Norah (Taylor) Wildman; e. Ont. Coll. of Art; Goldsmiths Coll. of Art Univ. of London; came to Can. 1953; mem. Ont. Soc. Artists; Royal Candn. Acad. of Artists; rep. in numerous private and pub. colls. Can., USA and Switzerland; Address: 1805 Track St., Claremont, Ont. L1Y 1B8.

**WILDSMITH, Bruce Harris,** B.Sc., LL.M.; educator; lawyer; b. Halifax, N.S. 25 May 1948; s. Alfred Charles and Janet (Vey) W.; e. Fisher Park High Sch. Ottawa 1967; Univ. of Guelph, B.Sc. 1970; Dalhousie Univ. LL.B. 1973; Harvard Law Sch. LL.M. 1978; m. Ardythe d. Harold and Dorothy Walker 16 May 1970; two s. Bruce William, James Walker; PROF. OF LAW, DALHOUSIE UNIV. 1984– and Assoc. Dean 1988–89; called to Bar of N.S. 1974; law practice Stewart, MacKeen & Covert, Halifax 1974–79; Assoc. Prof. of Law present Univ. 1979; lawyer/cons. specializing Indian/Aboriginal Law, Constitutional Law, Administrative Law, Aquaculture & Fisheries Law, Environmental Law; author 'Aquaculture: The Legal Framework' 1982; 'Aboriginal Peoples and Section 25 of the Canadian Charter of Rights and Freedoms' 1988; various scholarly publs.; Dir., Aquaculture Assn. Can. 1985–87; Dir., N.S. Salmon Assn. 1983–87; recreation: salmon angling; Home: 33 Walton Dr., Halifax, N.S. B3N 1X6; Office: Halifax, N.S. B3H 4H9.

**WILES, David McKeen,** M.Sc., Ph.D., F.R.S.C., F.C.I.C.; research chemist; b. Springhill, N.S. 28 Dec. 1932; s. late Prof. Roy McKeen Wiles; e. McMaster Univ. B.Sc. 1954, M.Sc. (Chem.) 1955; McGill Univ. Ph.D. (Chem.) 1957; Leeds Univ. Sir William Ramsay Postdoctoral Fellow 1957–59; m. Valerie Joan d. late Maj. H. E. Rowlands 8 June 1957; children: Gordon Stuart, Sandra Lorraine; PRES., PLASTICHEM CONSULTING 1990– ; Research Offr. Chem. Div. National Research Council of Canada 1959–66, Head, Textile Chem. Sec. 1966–86, Dir. Chem. Div. 1975–90; mem. Engn. Adv. Council Queen's Univ. 1977–79; SCITEC Extve. Comte. and Council 1974–77; Assoc. Grad. Faculty Univ. of Guelph 1967–76; recipient Dunlop Lecture Award 1981; Textile Science Award 1980; Queen's Silver Jubilee Medal 1977; author over 200 publs. incl. 6 book chapters; holds 15 patents polymer and fiber science; Pres. Chem. Inst. Can. 1975–76, Chrmn. of Bd. 1972–74; mem. Inst. Textile Science (Pres. 1973–74); Textile Inst. U.K. (Vice Pres. 1982–85); Candn. High Polymer Forum (Pres. 1967–69); United Church; Home: 3965 Juan de Fuca Terrace, Victoria, B.C. V8N 5W9.

**WILEY, James J.,** B.A., M.D., F.R.S.C.(C); surgeon; educator; b. Kitchener, Ont. 23 Sept. 1929; s. Francis Wilfred and Winnifred (Rohleder) W.; e. Univ. of Toronto B.A. 1950; Univ. of Ottawa M.D. 1955; Diplomate Am. Bd. Orthopaedic Surgs. 1967; m. Therese d. Alfred and Caroline Wintermeyer 7 Jan. 1956; children: James, Martha, Frank, John, Caroline; ORTHOPAEDIC SURG. CHILDREN'S HOSP. OF E. ONT. 1974– , mem. Rsch. Inst. 1987– ; Active and Consulting Staff Ottawa Gen. Hosp. 1963– , mem. Med. Adv. Ctte. 1972–75; Prof. of Surgery (Orthopaedics) Univ. of Ottawa 1987– , Asst. Dean of Post-Grad. Edn. Faculty of Med. 1990–92, Coord. Surgical Training Progs. Med. 1989– ; Med. Internship Univ. of Vt. 1955; Surg. Residency Training Harvard Univ. 1956; Orthopaedic Residency Lahey Clinic, Springfield Shriners, Boston City Hosp. 1957–60; Clin. Rsch. Fellow Univ. of Toronto 1960–62; mem. Bd. Examiners Royal Coll. Test Ctte. 1971–80 and Oral Ctte. 1973–78; Am. Bd. Ortho. Surgs. 1979–83; Ottawa Bd. Rehab Inst. 1972–75; Candn. Bd. Ortho. Found. 1971–88; Internat. Council Ortho. Pres.'s 1988; R.S. McLaughlin Travelling Fellow 1962–63; numerous Visiting Professorships/Lectureships USA and Can.; author 'You Just Can't Hardly Believe It' autobiog. 1989; co-author 'Behaviour of the Growth Plate' 1988; Fellow, Am. Acad. Ortho. Surgs.; mem. Candn. Ortho. Assn. (Bd. 1968–69, Treas. 1978, Sec. 1979–82, Pres. 1988, Historian 1988– ); Dewar Ortho. Soc.; Little Ortho. Soc.; Ont. Ortho. Assn.; Internat. Soc. Ortho. & Trauma; Pediatric Ortho. Soc. N. Am.; Candn. Med. Assn.; Ont. Med. Assn.; R. Catholic; recreations: reading, writing, carpentry; Home: 1558 Featherston Dr. W., Ottawa, Ont. K1H 6P2; Office: 401 Smyth Rd., Ottawa, Ont. K1H 8L1.

**WILK, Martin Bradbury,** B.E., M.S., Ph.D., F.S.S.; retired Canadian public servant; statistician; b. Montreal, Que. 18 Dec. 1922; e. McGill Univ. B.E. (Chem. Engn.) 1945; Iowa State Univ. M.S. (Stat.) 1953, Ph.D. (Stat.) 1955; m. 1stly Thora Sugrue (d); m. 2ndly Dorothy Louise Barrett 3 July 1974; children: Bonnie Rebecca, Carol Nancy Landsman, David Terrence, Teresa Jane McKinley, Kathryn Joan Naugle, Kathleen Schade; Research Chem. Engr. Nat. Research Council of Can. (Atomic Energy Project) 1945–50; Research Assoc., Instr. and Asst. Prof. Iowa State Univ. 1951–55; Research Assoc. and Asst. Dir. Stat. Techniques Group, Princeton Univ. 1955–57; Prof. and Dir. of Research in Stat. Rutgers Univ. 1959–63; mem. Tech. Staff 1956, Head of Stat. and Data Analysis Research Dept. 1963, Head of Stat. Models & Methods Research Dept. 1968, Stat. Dir. Mang. Sciences Research 1969, Bell Telephone Labs.; joined American Telephone and Telegraph Co. 1970 as Dir.-Corporate Modeling Research, Dir.-Corporate Research 1971, Dir.-Planning 1972, Dir.-Corporate Planning 1973, Asst. Vice Pres.-Dir. of Corporate Planning 1976–80; joined Govt. of Canada in 1980 as Chief Statistician of Canada until 1985; Sr. Advisor to Privy Counc. Office 1985–86; Chrmn., Nat. Task Force on Tourism Data 1984–86; Special Adv. to Dir., Bureau of Census 1986–87; Mem., Nat. Stat. Counc. 1986– ; Mem. Rsch. Counc., Candn. Inst. for Advanced Rsch. 1986– ; mem. Adv. Comn. on Pop. Health Res. Prog. of CIAR; Mem. Adv. Ctte. on Human Devel. Res. Prog. of CIAR; Mem., Stats. Can. Adv. Ctte. on Rsch. and Analysis 1986– ; Mem., Stats. Can. Adv. Comn. on Stat. Methods 1987– ; Mem., Stats Can. Adv. Ctte. on Science & Technology Stat. 1993– ; Adjunct Prof. of Statistics, Carleton Univ. 1981– ; mem., National Acad. of Sciences Panel on Foreign Trade Statistics 1989–91; Chrmn., National Task Force on Health Information 1990–91; author or co-author various scient. publs.; rec'd Jack Youden Prize Am. Soc. Quality Control 1972; mem. Census Adv. Comte. 1973–75; Fellow, Am. Stat. Assn. (Chrmn. Sec. on Phys. & Engn. Sciences 1971; Dir. 1973–74, 1980–82; Vice Pres. 1980–82); Fellow, Inst. Math. Stat. (mem. Council 1956–58; Visiting Lectr.1969–70); Fellow, Am. Assn. Advanc. Science; Fellow, N.Y. Acad. Sciences; Hon. Fellow, Royal Stat. Soc.; Hon. Mem., Stat. Soc. of Can.; Pres. Stat. Soc. of Can. 1986–87; el. mem. Internat. Stat. Inst.; Biometric Soc.; Amer. Econ. Assn.; Classification Soc.; Sigma Xi; Phi Kappa Phi; Pi Mu Epsilon; Assoc. Ed. 'Technometrics' 1959–63; Home: P.O. Box 191, R.R. 3, Stittsville, Ont. K2S 1A3; Office: 26th Floor, R.H. Coats Bldg., Tunney's Pasture, Ottawa, Ont. K1A 0T6.

**WILKINS, Gregory C.,** B.Comm.; financial executive; b. Montreal, Que. 2 Feb. 1956; e. Concordia Univ. B.Comm. 1977; EXECUTIVE DIRECTOR, OFFICE OF THE CHAIRMAN, AMERICAN BARRICK RESOURCES CORPORATION and DIRECTOR, THE HORSHAM CORPORATION 1993– ; Chartered Accountant, Peat, Marwick & Mitchell until 1983; Senior Vice-Pres., Finance, Am. Barrick Resources Corp. 1983–91; Executive Vice-Pres. & Chief Financial Offr., American Barrick Resources Corp. 1991–93; Dir., American Barrick Resources Corp.; Mem., Executive/Membership Ctte. and Audit Ctte., The World Gold Council; Office: 24 Hazelton Ave., Toronto, Ont. M5R 2E2.

**WILKINS, Russell,** B.A., B.Ed., M.Urb.; demographer; b. Seattle, Wash. 1 Oct. 1946; s. Albert Warren and Sarah Lucy (Galbreath) W.; e. Univ. of Ore. B.A. 1968; Univ. of N.B. 1968; Univ. de Moncton B.Éd. 1973; Univ. de Montréal M.Urb. 1980; m. Kathryn Charlotte d. Robert Alexander and Tomme Nell Stalker 8 June 1968; children: Claire Kathryn, Carl Leverett, Emily Jane; SR. ANALYST OCCUPATIONAL & ENVIRONMENTAL HEALTH RSCH. SECT. CANDN. CENTRE FOR HEALTH INFO. STATS. CAN. 1988– ; came to Can. 1968; teacher Saint John Vocational Sch. 1968–70 and École Secondaire Polyvalente Louis-Philippe Paré 1971–74; joined Inst. for Rsch. Pub. Policy Montreal 1978–83; Dept. Commmunity Health Montreal Gen. Hosp. 1983–87; mem. Internat. Rsch. Network Health Expectancy; UN/WHO/CICRED Network on Socioecon. Differential Mortality in Industrialized Countries; Inst. Risk Rsch. Univ. of Waterloo; Fellow, Sch. of Community & Pub. Affairs Concordia Univ. 1979–83; author 'Health Status in Canada 1926–1976' 1980; 'Données sur la Pauvreté dans la région métropolitaine de Montréal' 1985; co-author 'Healthfulness of Life' 1983; 'Changes in Mortality by Income in Urban Canada' 1989; 'Birth Outcomes and Infant Mortality by Income in Urban Canada' 1991; mem. Nat. Capital Runners Assn.; Candn. Vintage Motorcycle Group; Assn. des Démographes du Qué. (Vice Pres. 1987–89); Candn. Population Soc.; Candn. Pub. Health Assn.; Internat. Union for the Scientific Study of Population (IUSSP); recreations: running, skiing, tennis; Home: 151 Ruskin St., Ottawa, Ont. K1Y 4B9; Office: RHC-18, Ottawa, Ont. K1A 0T6.

**WILKINSON, Bruce William,** B.Com., M.A. Ph.D.; educator; economist; b. Vanguard, Sask. 10 Apr. 1933; s. William and Florence Mary (Stewart) W.; e. Univ. of Sask. B.Com. 1953; Univ. of Alta. M.A. 1961; Mass. Inst. Technol. Ph.D. 1964; m. Myrna Ellen d. Lawrence Elmer Plewis 8 Oct. 1960; children: Craig William, Glenda Anne, Myrna Lynn; PROF. OF ECON., UNIV. OF ALTA. since 1972; joined Imperial Oil Ltd. 1953–60; Asst. Prof. of Econ. Univ. of Sask. 1964–66; Visiting Asst. Prof. of Econ. Univ. of W. Ont. 1966–67; Assoc. Prof. Econ., Univ. of Alta. 1967–71, Chrmn. of Econ. 1972–77, Prof. of Econ. 1972– ; author 'Studies in the Economics of Education' 1965; 'Canada's International Trade: An Analysis of Recent Trends and Patterns' 1968; 'Canada in the Changing World Economy' 1980; co-author 'Effective Protection in the Canadian Economy' 1968; 'Canada in a Wider Economic Community' 1973; 'Effective Protection and the Return to Capital' 1975; co-author 'Canada's Resource Industries and Water Export Policy' 1986; various articles econ. of educ., Candn. trade, balance of payments, comm. policy and natural resources; mem. Candn. Econ. Assn.; Anglican; recreations: gardening, swimming, reading; Home: 13320 27th Ave., Edmonton, Alta. T5R 3G5; Office: Edmonton, Alta. T6G 2H4.

**WILKINSON, Sir Denys Haigh,** Kt. (1974), M.A., Ph.D., Sc.D., D.Sc., LL.D., Fil.Dr., F.R.S. (1956), F.Inst.P., F.A.P.S.; b. Leeds, Yorkshire, England, 5 Sept. 1922; s. Charles and Hilda (Haigh) W.; e. Cambridge Univ. grad 1943, M.A., Ph.D., Sc.D.; m. 1stly, Christiane Clavier, 20 June 1947; three d.; m. 2ndly, Helen Sommers, 14 June 1967; 2 step-d.; five children; VICE-CHANCELLOR AND PROF. OF PHYSICS, UNIV. OF SUSSEX 1976–87; Fellow of Jesus College, Cambridge 1944–59, Hon. Fellow since 1961; Demonst. and Lect. in Physics 1946–57; Prof. of Exper. Physics 1959–76, Nuclear Physics 1957–59; Head, Nuclear Physics Dept., Oxford Univ., 1962–76; Student of Christ Church 1957–76; Hon. Student since 1979; Pres., Inst. of Physics, 1980–82; Vice Pres. Internat. Union of Pure and Applied Physics 1985– ; awards: Tom W. Bonner Prize (Am. Phys. Soc.) 1974; Comte. d'Honneur du Bontemps de Medoc et des Graves 1973; Goodspeed-Richards Mem. (Univ. of Penn.) 1969; Silliman Mem. (Yale Univ.) 1966; Queen's Lecture (Berlin) 1966; Hughes Medallist (Roy. Soc.) 1965; Graham Young (Glasgow) 1964; Rutherford Mem. 1962; Royal Medal (Roy. Soc.) 1980; Scott Lectures (Cambridge Univ.) 1961; Holweck Medallist of Fr. and Brit. Phys. Socs. 1957; Guthrie Medal of Inst. of Physics 1986; Gold Medal Ettore Majorana Ctr. for Scientific Culture (Erice) 1988; Hon. degree University of Saskatchewan; Utah State Univ.; Uppsala Univ.; Univ. of Guelph; Univ. of Sussex; Queen's Univ., Kingston, Ont.; Coll. William and Mary, Williamsburg; author of 'Ionization Chambers and Counters'; 'Our Universes'; ed., 'Isospin in Nuclear Physics,' 'Mesons in Nuclei' and some 250 articles in learned journs.; Lauritsen Mem. Lect. (Cal. Tech.) 1976; Schiff Mem. Lect. (Stanford) 1977; Racah Mem. Lect. (Jerusalem) 1977; Solly Cohen Mem. Lect. (Jerusalem) 1985; Axel Mem. Lect. (Illinois) 1985; Breit Mem. Lect. (Yale) 1987; W.B. Lewis Mem. Lect. (Chalk River) 1989; Humphry Davy (Acad. d. Sciences Paris) 1990; Rutherford Mem. Lectr. (New Zealand) 1991; mem. Brit.-Candn. Atomic Energy Project 1943–46; Brit. Ornithol. Union; foreign mem., Royal Swedish Acad. of Sciences; recreations: music, ornithology, ancient art; Home: Gayles Orchard, Friston, Eastbourne, E. Sussex, Eng. BN20 0BA; Office: Physics Bldg., Univ. of Sussex, Falmer, Brighton, Eng. BN1 9QH.

**WILKINSON, Frank Cameron,** B.Com.; business consultant; b. Vancouver, B.C. 2 May 1928; s. Joseph William and Marion McGillivray (Cameron) W.; e. St. George's Sch., Vancouver, B.C.; Univ. of British Columbia, B.Com. 1948; London Sch. of Econ., Univ. of London (Post-Grad. work) 1948–49; m. Teresa Ann (King), 16 Mar. 1955; children: Graeme Cameron, Marion Gail, Virginia Ann; Dir., B.C. Sugar Refinery Ltd.; Fletcher Challenge Canada Ltd.; CAE Industries Ltd.; mem. Vancouver Adv. Bd., National Victoria and Grey Trust Co.; Past Dir., Cdn. Steel Serv. Centre Inst.; Duke of Edinburgh's Award in Can.; Vancouver Soc. for Business and the Arts; Vancouver Public Aquarium; Vancouver Playhouse Theatre (hon Life mem. and Past Pres.); Gov., St. George's Sch. for Boys; Alpha Delta Phi; Anglican; recreations: skiing, fishing, riding; Clubs: Shaughnessy Golf; The Vancouver; Saltspring Island Golf; Vancouver Lawn Tennis; Home: 3577 Angus Dr., Vancouver, B.C. V6J 4H4; Office: 700–555 West Hastings St., Vancouver, B.C. V6B 4N5.

**WILLAN, Gordon E.,** B.A.Sc.; retired chemical engineer and executive; b. Toronto, Ont. 3 Oct. 1914; s. Thomas E. and Unite F. (Kirkegaard) W.; e. Univ. of Toronto, B.A.Sc. 1941; m. 1stly, late Mary E., d. late Michael S. White, 1 Feb. 1947; two d., Grace Anne, Karen Edith; 2ndly, Margery Joan, d. late S. G. Renouf, Regina, Sask., 22 June 1963; Mgr., Agricultural Products Dept., BASF Canada Inc., 1973–81; Supvr. of Acid

Dept., Defence Industries Ltd., Transcona, Man., 1941–43; Process Engr. and later Personnel Mgr., Canadian Synthetic Rubber Co. Ltd., Sarnia, Ont., 1943–45; Plant Supt., Dalglish Chemicals Ltd., Toronto, Ont., 1945–47; Plant Supt., Niagara Brand Spray Ltd., 1947; apptd. Gen. Mgr. 1953; resigned as Vice-Pres. & Gen. Mgr., Niagara Chemicals, to join BASF Canada Inc. 1973; Mgr., Agricultural Products Dept. 1973–81; Del. to Gen. Assembly, Groupement Internat. des Assns. Nationales de Fabricants de Pesticides, 1969–73; mem., Assn. of Prof. Engrs. of Ont.; Candn. Agric. Chemicals Assn. (Pres. 1956–57, Life Mem. 1983); Kappa Sigma (G.M.); Master mason, Wellington Sq. Lodge #725 (Burlington, Ont.); Protestant; recreations: gardening, home repairs, Canadian cigarette cards, curling; Club: Lions (Pres. 1967–68); Home: 1287 Fairway Court, Burlington, Ont. L7P 1M5.

**WILLCOCK, Elizabeth,** C.M.; senior citizenship judge; b. Sherbrooke, Que. 12 Oct. 1927; d. Terence Gerard and Mary Irene (Wolf) Walsh; e. Mont Notre Dame Convent; Notre Dame Coll., Francis Robinson Duff Sch. of the Theatre; m. David Noel s. William and May W. 29 July 1950; children: Michael, John, Peter, Shelagh, Mary Kay; SR. CITIZENSHIP JUDGE, DEPARTMENT OF CITIZENSHIP & IMMIGRATION, GOVT. OF CANADA 1987– ; Teacher, Drama & Hist., Notre Dame Sch. 1948–49; Radio announcer/writer/prod., Sherbrooke 1948–49; freelance broadcaster, Toronto 1949–50; Montreal 1950–68; Researcher & interviewer, CBC-TV Pub. Affairs, Winnipeg 1969–71; Dir. of Rsch., Prog. Cons. Party of Man. 1972–76; Extve. Dir., Citizenship Counc. of Man. 1977–84; Chief of Staff, Min. of State for Multiculturalism 1984–85; Citizenship Court Judge 1985; Pres., Nat. Prog. Cons. Women's Caucus; Chrmn., Winnipeg Sch. Div. 1980–83; Pres., Terry Fox Youth Ctr. (Man.) 1980–82; Pres., UN Assn. (Winnipeg) 1986–87; Bd. Mem., St. Paul's Coll. & St. Paul's H.S. 1986–87; Mem., Order of Canada 1991; Home: 409 Waverley St., Winnipeg, Man.; Office: 350 Albert St., Room 310, Constitution Square, Ottawa, Ont. K1A 1K5.

**WILLCOCKS, Allen John;** quantity surveyor; b. Malvern, Eng. 21 July 1941; s. Anthony John and Elizabeth Joyce W.; e. Worcester Royal Grammar Sch. 1957; m. Caroline d. Norton and Eva Bunn 10 June 1967; children: Nicholas Craig, Adrian Neal; PRIN. AND PRES. ROSS WILLCOCKS & ASSOC. LTD. 1972– ; articled Royal Instn. of Chart. Surveyors UK 1958–61; Quantity Surveyor maj. projects incl. first motorways UK 1961–67; Estimator and Chief Estimator maj. constrn. projects Ont. 1967–72; Chrmn. Maritimes Constrn. Devel. Council; Atlantic Region, Candn. Constrn. Mgmt. Inst.; Dir., N.S. Design & Constrn. Inst.; Lectr. Tech. Univ. of N.S. 7 yrs., N.S. Inst. Technol. 6 yrs.; Chrmn. Sch. Trustees Bedford, N.S.; Councillor Pickering, Ont.; Fellow, Candn. Inst. Quantity Surveyors (Past Pres.); mem. Constrn. Assn. N.S.; recreations: sailing, chess, current affairs; Club: Halifax; Home: 66 Golf Links Rd., Bedford, N.S. B4A 2J3.

**WILLCOCKS, R. Paul,** B.A.; newspaper publisher; b. Toronto, Ont. 29 Apr. 1952; s. George Samuel and Barbara Marion (Jones) W.; e. Concordia Univ., B.A. 1974; m. Peigi d. Don and Julietta McGillivray 20 Aug. 1978; children: Rebecca, Samuel; PUBLISHER, VICTORIA TIMES-COLONIST and GROUP PUBLISHER, THOMSON NEWSPAPERS (Vancouver Island) 1993– ; Mng. Ed., Ed., The Red Deer Advocate 1974–78; Publisher 1978–83; Publisher, The Telegraph-Journal and The Evening Times-Globe 1987–91; Pres., New Brunswick Pub. Co. Ltd. 1987–91; Publisher, Peterborough Examiner 1991–93; Vice Chrmn. & Dir., The Canadian Press; Office: Box 300, Victoria, B.C. V8W 2N4.

**WILLE, Stefan,** Ph.D., F.I.C.B.; industrial research executive; b. Quedlinburg, Germany 14 Dec. 1939; s. Ulrich and Liselotte Helene (Mechel) F.; e. H.S. in Switzerland 1960; Univ. of Toronto M.A. 1970; Univ. of Zurich Ph.D. 1971; m. Claire Ann Agnes d. Wilfrid Orlando and Agnes Marion Davis 21 Aug. 1971; children: Allan David, Gordon Edward; nationality: Canadian/Swiss; languages: English, German, French, Italian; PRES./OWNER, AKTRIN RESEARCH INST. 1985– ; Asst. Prof. of Econ., Laurentian Univ. 1971–72; career in internat. banking, Union Bank of Switz. & Candn. Imperial Bank of Commerce (overseas subsidiaries) 1972–81; Chief Admin., Bata Shoe Orgn., Zurich, Switz. 1981; Past Dir., Yonge-Bloor Devel. Corp. (Panama), Toronto; Captain, Swiss Army; Past Trustee, Internat. Primary Sch. of Zurich; Mem., Adv. Ctte., Canadore Coll., North Bay, Ont.; Mem., Maple Leaf Club in Zurich; Swiss Club Toronto; Oakville C. of C.; author: 'The Commercial Printing Industry in Canada' 1986, 'The Publishing Industry in Canada' 1987, 'The Pulp and Paper Industry in Canada' 1988; 'The Commercial Printing Industry in the USA' 1989; 'The Furniture Industry in Canada' 1992; recreations: skiing, hiking, classical music; Home: 2267 Daffodil Court, Oakville, Ont. L6J 5Y2; Office: 151 Randall St., #200, Oakville, Ont. L6J 1P5.

**WILLEMSEN, Richard Martin,** B.A., F.I.I.C.; insurance executive; b. London, Eng., 2 Dec. 1932; s. Verner Rendtorff and Cicely (Jennings) W.; e. Upper Can. Coll., Toronto, Ont.; Amherst Coll., B.A. (cum laude) 1954; m. Aldona, d. Victor Bulzgis, 14 Jan. 1958; two d. Susan and Cynthia; PRESIDENT, INTERNATIONAL INSURANCE CONSULTANTS; with Sterling Offices, Paris, France, 1954–55; Mgr. in Mexico, 1958–60; Secy., Toronto 1960, Vice-Pres. 1965, Extve. Vice Pres. and Dir., 1968; Pres. & Dir., Sterling Offices of Canada Ltd. 1973–85; Chrmn., Sterling Universal Holdings Ltd. 1986–92; former Hon. Consul General of Dominican Republic; Past President, Ins. Institute of Canada; Past Pres., Ins. Inst. of Ont.; Fellow, Ins. Inst. of Can.; Inst. of Directors; Past Chrmn., The Canadian Assoc. of Lloyds Members; Psi Upsilon; Anglican; recreations: golf, squash, scuba diving, bridge; Clubs: Granite; York Downs Golf & Country; Ontario; University; Danish (London, Eng.); Southern Cross (Little Cayman); Home: 12 The Bridle Path, Willowdale, Ont. M2L 1C8.

**WILLER, James Sidney Harold,** B.A.; artist; b. London, England 25 Feb. 1921; s. Sidney Harold and Kathleen Mary (Dowe) W.; e. Ponders End Tech. Coll. (U.K.) 1937; Univ. of Winnipeg, B.A. 1952; studied at Royal Acad., Amsterdam 1955; divorced; children: Kathleen Mary, Xanthe Emily, Sophie Deirdre; exhibitions (since 1953) incl.: 22nd Biennial, Vanc. Art Gall. 1953; Candn. Overseas Award Winners, Nat. Gall. of Can. 1956; Sculpture '67, Toronto City Hall 1967; 3D into the 70's, Art Gall. of Ont. 1970; Art in Winnipeg 1955 to 1959, Univ. of Man. 1982; other galleries 1970– incl.: Portland Art Mus., San Francisco Art Gall.; six solo exhibitions, Bau-Xi Gall. Vanc.; permanent collections incl.: Nat. Gall. of Can.; Winnipeg Art Gall.; Vancouver & Victoria Art Galls.; Petrocanada Calgary; awards & prizes: Candn. Overseas Award to the Netherlands 1954; Can. Counc. Arts Fellowship 1966; Purchase/Prizes, Winnipeg Art Gall. 1954 and Univ. of Manitoba 1960; teacher, Vanc. Sch. of Art 1964–65; Capilano Coll. (extension) 1979–87; Emily Carr Coll. of Art, Outreach Prog. 1981–87; lectures & interviews incl. radio & TV, schools & univs.; moral & tangible support, Western Can. Wilderness Ctte.; Islands Protection Soc.; contbr.: 'Carmanah' & 'Islands at the Edge'; author: 'Paramind' (co-winner, Imperial Tobacco Co. Ltd. Centennial Comp. for Lit. 1967–68) 1973; voluntary juror assignments incl. 'Wood Sculpture of the Americas – '77'; two significant sculptures are, a bas relief 23' x 9' (Red Cross Bldg. Calgary) 1978 and an electronic heliotropic sculpture, 'Photophilos (Lover of Light)' 1974; recreations: travel, hiking, cross-country skiing; Home: R.R. 3 Gambier Harbour Site (C-11), Gibsons, B.C. V0N 1V0; Office: c/o Bau-Xi Gall., 3045 Granville St., Vancouver, B.C. V6H 3J9.

**WILLETT, Dwight A.,** B.Ed., M.B.A., CMC; management consultant; b. Butler, Missouri 20 July 1954; s. James L. and Nina M. (Spears) W.; e. Univ. of Saskatchewan B.Ed. 1977, M.B.A. 1989; m. Janine d. Phil and Marlys Rivard 4 Aug. 1978; children Denae Janine, Kamara Quin; PARTNER RESPONSIBLE FOR TORONTO HUMAN RESOURCE CONSULTING PRACTICE OF SOBECO ERNST & YOUNG, INC. 1992– ; Teacher & Administrator, private secondary schools in Sask. 1978–88; Extve. Search & Human Resources Consultant, Ernst & Young 1988–90; Principal resp. for Mississauga Human Resources Cons. Practice 1991; Certified Management Consultant ICMCO; Former Chair & Treas. & Hon. Life Mem., Saskatchewan Science Centre; recreations: tennis, golf, sailboarding; clubs: Fitness Institute; Royal Cdn. Military Institute; Toronto Bd. of Trade; Home: 2882 Rainwater Dr., Mississauga, Ont. L5N 6K8; Office: Box 251, Ernst & Young Tower, TD Centre, Toronto, Ont. M5K 1J7.

**WILLETT, Terence Charles,** B.Sc., Ph.D.; educator; b. Warwickshire, Eng., 23 Dec. 1918; s. Charles Joseph and Elsie Jane (Allport) W.; e. Greenmore Coll., Eng., 1939; Staff Coll. Camberley, p.s.c. 1951; Univ. of London, B.Sc. 1957; London Sch. of Econ., Ph.D. 1962; m. Winifred, d. Gilbert Small, Providence, R.I., 12 Dec. 1942; children: Mark, Susan; PROFESSOR EMERITUS OF SOCIOLOGY, QUEEN'S UNIV. 1984– ; Sr. Lectr. in Sociol., Royal Mil. Acad. Sandhurst, 1958; Lectr. in Sociol., Univ. of Reading, Berks, UK, 1964; joined Queen's Univ. as Assoc. Prof. of Sociol. 1970, Prof. 1973; served with Royal Regt. of Arty. 1938–58; rank Lt. Col.; awarded T.D.; J.P. for Royal Co. of Berks. 1968–70; Sch. Gov., Camberley (Eng.) Schs.; Visitor, H.M. Borstals; author 'Criminal on the Road' 1964 (runner-up for Denis Carrol Prize, Internat. Soc. Criminol. 1965); 'Drivers After Sentence' 1973; 'A Heritage at Risk: The Canadian Militia as a Social Institution' 1987; also book reviews and various articles on criminol. and sociol. of mil.; Fellow Inter-Univ. Seminar on Armed Forces and Soc. 1976; Anglican; recreations: squash, golf; Office: Dept. of Sociology, Queen's Univ., Kingston, Ont. K7L 3N6.

**WILLIAM, David,** B.A.; actor; director; b. London, England 24 June 1926; s. Eric Hugh and Olwen (Roose) W.; e. Bryanston Sch.; Univ. Coll., Oxford Univ., B.A. 1951; Artistic Director, Stratford Festival 1990–93, principal prodns. there incl. (plays) 'Bacchae', 'The Importance of Being Earnest', 'My Shakespeare', 'Entertaining Mr. Sloane', 'Twelfth Night', 'Merry Wives of Windsor', 'Volpone', 'King Lear', 'Othello', 'Romeo & Juliet', 'Separate Tables', 'Hamlet', 'Treasure Island', 'The Tempest', & many others; played Jaques in 1990 'As You Like It'; Serebryakov in 1992 'Uncle Vanya' (Stratford); Malvolio in 'Twelfth Night' 1994; Productions in U.K. include (plays): 'Dear Daddy' (Ambassadors' Theatre, London), 'Richard II' (National Theatre), 'The Aspern Papers' (Chichester Festival); (operas): World premieres of 'Thérèse' (Royal Opera House, Covent Garden), 'The Lighthouse' (Edinburgh Festival), also 'La Traviata', 'Iphigénie en Tauride', 'Il Re Pastore' & 'Albert Herring' etc., at various international theatres and festivals; Played Richard II in BBC TV series 'An Age of Kings'; author: 'The Tempest on the Stage' 1960, 'Hamlet in the Theatre' 1963; Prof. of Drama, De Paul Univ., Chicago 1987–89; recreations: walking, swimming, zoos; Home: 194 Langarth St., London, Ont. N6C 1Z5.

**WILLIAMS, Adrian J.R.;** graphic communications executive; b. Herts., Eng. 12 Oct. 1929; s. John Albert Stubbs and Minnie W.; e. Christ's Coll. Finchley 1947; R.I.A. 1958; m. Friederike Bister 6 Sept. 1949; children: Daryl, Mark; Pres. & C.E.O., Davis and Henderson Ltd. 1974; Pres. & Dir. Davis and Henderson Systems Ltd.; Acct. Davis and Henderson Ltd. 1957, Sec./Treas. 1959, Vice Pres. Finance 1962; Pres., Reeve Bean Ltd. 1966–70; Dir. & Past President, Candn. Opera Co.; Dir., Ballet Opera House Corp.; Bd. of Govs., Toronto East Gen. Hosp.; recreations: tennis, skiing, golf; Clubs: Donalda; Timberlane; Beacon Hall; Wyndemere C.C.; Home: 512 Quail Ridge Dr., Aurora, Ont. L4G 3G8.

**WILLIAMS, Alan Steven,** B.Sc., M.B.A., C.M.A.; public servant; b. Montreal, Que. 26 June 1948; s. Lionel and Rose (Weinberg) W.; e. McGill Univ. B.Sc. 1969; Univ. of Michigan M.B.A. 1971; C.M.A. 1976; m. Esther d. Lazier and Sarah Caplan 13 June 1971; children: Samuel Zev, Davida Atara; ASST. DEPY. MINISTER, CORPORATE SERVICES, DEPT. OF INDIAN AFFAIRS & NORTHERN DEVEL. 1991– ; various positions, Supply and Services Canada 1972–81; Liaison Offr., Office of the Comptroller General of Canada 1981–87; Director General of Finance, Dept. of Indian Affairs & Northern Devel. 1987–91; Mem., Management Acctg. Practices Ctte., Soc. of Mngt. Accountants; recreations: golf, tennis, reading; Office: 10 Wellington St., Les Terrasses de la Chaudière, Room 2107, Hull, Que. K1A 0H4.

**WILLIAMS, Anne Elizabeth,** B.Mus., L.Mus., B.Ed.; teacher of music, peace educator; b. Montreal, Que. 16 Oct. 1936; d. The Rev. John B. and Mabel C. (Chambers) Bonathan e. McGill Univ. B.Mus. 1959, L.Mus. 1961; Univ. of Lethbridge B.Ed. 1977; m. the late Rev. David Rogers; children: Mark, Sheila, Christopher; TEACHER, of piano and singing; Extve. Sec., 'Can. J. of Philosophy' 1983– ; Organist, Church of St. Mary the Virgin (Lethbridge); Chair, Lethbridge Nuclear Disarmament Coalition 1984– ; served on City of Lethbridge Spec. Council Ctte. on Peace 1986–90; Co-chair, Candn. Fed. of Univ. Women's Sub-Ctte. on Internat. Peace & Security 1984–89; Chair, Anglican Diocese of Calgary Peace & Justice Ctte.; Mem., Consultative Ctte. on Arms Control & Disarmament (adv. body to Canada's Ambassador for Disarmament) 1990–92; YWCA (Lethbridge) 'Women of Distinction' Award for work in peace edn.; Mem., Cand. Fed. of Univ. Women; The Group of 78; The Voice of Women for Peace; Project Ploughshares; Home: 1002 – 15 Street S., Lethbridge, Alta. T1K 1V3.

**WILLIAMS, Bruce MacGillivray,** B.A.; retired diplomat; b. Nipigon, Ont. 31 Jan. 1918; s. Herbert Bruce and Margaret (Hogan) W.; e. Univ. of Toronto, B.A. 1941; joined the Department of External Affairs in 1946 as a Foreign Service Offr.; served with Candn. del. to the U.N., New York, 1946–48; Depy. Permanent Del. of

Can. to European Office of the U.N., Geneva, 1952–53; Counsellor, Office of High Commr., for Can. in India, 1953–56; Candn. Commr. Internat. Supervisory Comn. for Vietnam, 1956–57; High Commr. for Can. in Ghana, 1959–62, and concurrently Ambassador to Togo, Upper Volta, Ivory Coast and Guinea; Ambassador to Turkey, 1962–64; Ass't. Undersecy. of State for External Affairs, 1964–67; Ambassador to Yugoslavia, Bulgaria and Romania 1967–72; High Commr. to India and Ambassador to Nepal 1972–74; Extve. Vice Pres., Candn. International Development Agency, 1974–77; served with Canadian Army in 2nd World War; recreations: golf, bridge; Clubs: University (Montreal); Royal Ottawa Golf; Delhi Gymkhana; Address: 85 Mackay St., Ottawa, Ont. K1M 2E4.

**WILLIAMS, Bryan,** Q.C., B.Com., LL.B.; lawyer; b. Calgary, Alta. 14 Sept. 1932; s. Rupert Norman and Hilda May (Boote) W.; e. Univ. of B.C., B.Com. 1957, LL.B. 1958; Univ. of Victoria, LL.D. 1990; m. Audrey d. Thomas and Mae Downie 19 Sept. 1958; children: Loreen, Jordan, Todd, Shannon; SR. PARTNER, SWINTON & CO.; Dir. Air BC Ltd.; Terra Copia Estates Ltd.; Fellow, Am. Coll. of Trial Lawyers; Hon. Dir., West Coast Environmental Law; Counc. Mem., Internat. Comn. of Jurists; Mem., Internat. Bar Assn.; Duke of Edinburgh Awards Ctte. Counc.; Dir. World Wildlife Fund Can. (mem. Extve. Ctte.); Dir., Laurier Inst.; Dir., The Vancouver Art Gallery; called to the Bar, B.C. 1959, Yukon 1976, NWT 1980; Chrmn. Wilderness Adv. Ctte. (B.C. Prov. Govt.) 1986; Dir. Pub. Interest Advocacy Centre of B.C. 1980–84; Comnr. Law Reform Comn. B.C. 1979–84; Gov. B.C. Law Found. 1979; former Mem. of the B.C. Round Table on the Economy & the Environment; author various articles, papers; Pres. Candn. Bar Assn. 1986–87 (Founding Pres. Law for the Future Fund 1984–86; Nat. Vice Pres. 1985–86; Nat. Treas. 1984–85; Pres. B.C. Br. 1977–78); Chrmn. Legal Aid Soc. B.C. 1977–79; recreations: skiing, tennis; Clubs: Vancouver; Hollyburn Country; Home: 3274 Marine Dr., West Vancouver, B.C. V7V 1M7; Office: Robson Court, 1000 – 840 Howe St., Vancouver, B.C. V6Z 2M1.

**WILLIAMS, (David) Carlton,** M.A., Ph.D., LL.D.; retired educator; b. Winnipeg, Man. 7 July 1912; s. John Andrew and Anna (Carlton) W.; e. Gordon Bell and Kelvin High Schs., Winnipeg, Man.; Univ. of Manitoba, B.A. 1932, LL.D. 1969; Univ. of Toronto, M.A. 1937, Ph.D. 1940, LL.D. 1978; Univ. of Windsor LL.D. 1977; U. Western Ont., LL.D. 1978; m. Margaret Ashwell, d. late William Oliver Carson, 20 Nov. 1943; children: Catherine Ann, David Bruce Carson; Chrmn., Ont. Comm. on Freedom of Information and Individual Privacy 1977–80; Dir. of Research, Toronto Welfare Council, 1940–41; Research Assoc., Nat. Research Council on problems of pilot selection, 1941–42; Special Lectr., Univ. of Toronto 1945–46; Assoc. Prof. of Psychol, Univ. of Manitoba, 1946–48, and Prof. and Head of Dept. of Psychol. there, 1948–49; Prof. of Psychol, Univ. of Toronto, 1949–58; Dir., Divn. of Univ. Extension, 1958–65; Vice Pres., Univ. of Toronto, for Scarborough and Erindale Colls., and Princ. of Erindale Coll., 1965–67, Pres. and Vice Chancellor, Univ. of Western Ont. 1967–77; served in 2nd World War, with Personnel Selection, R.C.A.F. 1942–44, and Aircrew as Pilot, 1944–45; Consultant, Toronto Juvenile Court Clinic, 1951–58; Dir., Addiction Research Foundation of Ont. 1978–84; London Health Assn. (Chrmn., Univ. Hosp. Bd. 1984–86); mem., Robarts Rsch. Inst. Bd.; Ontario Press Council; Chrmn., London Teaching Hospitals Council 1990–93; Fellow, Candn. Psychol. Assn. (Pres. 1954); Fellow Am. Psychol. Assn.; Publications: 'The Arts as Communication' (ed) 1962; 'Public Government for Private People,' 1980; Report of Ont. Comm. on Freedom of Information and Individual Privacy (Chrmn.); United Church; Clubs: York (Toronto); London Hunt & Country; Home: Apt. 407, 1201 Richmond St., London, Ont. N6A 3L6.

**WILLIAMS, Charles Melville,** C.M., Ph.D., F.A.I.C.; educator; b. Regina, Sask. 18 March 1925; s. Edward Percy and Charlotte Alice (Macdonald) W.; e. Univ. of B.C. B.S.A. 1949, M.Sc. 1952; Ore. State Coll. Ph.D. 1955; m. Patricia Jean d. Peter and Lucy Begbie 24 March 1953, div.; children: Allan Begbie, Catherine Ann Greer, Charlotte Lucy Elaine Wass; PROF. EMERITUS OF ANIMAL & POULTRY SCI. UNIV. OF SASK. 1992– ; joined present Univ. 1954, Head of Animal & Poultry Sci. 1975–83; served CUSO 7 yrs. as cons. some 25 countries and as mem. Bd. & Bd. Chrmn.; Chair: Candn. Ctte. Animal Production Services; Expert Ctte. Farm Animal Welfare & Behaviour; Pres. Sask. Inst. Agrols.; Chief Exec. Offr.: Sask. Newstart; Beef Ind. Devels.; mem. Sherbrooke Found.; served with RCNVR WWII; author, ed. various sci. publs.; mem. Candn. C. of C. (Chrmn. Agric. Ctte.); Sask. Lib. Assn. (Pres.); Lib. Party Can. (Vice Pres.); Candn. Soc. Animal Sci. (Cert. of Merit); Candn. Soc. Rural Extension (Hon. Life mem.); Am. Soc. Animal Sci.; Brit. Soc. Animal Prodn.; Sigma Xi; Home: 1 Moxon Cres., Saskatoon, Sask. S7H 3B8; Office: Saskatoon, Sask. S7N 0W0.

**WILLIAMS, Dafydd (Dave) Rhys,** B.Sc., M.Sc., M.D.; Canadian astronaut; b. Saskatoon, Sask. 16 May 1954; e. McGill Univ. B.Sc. 1976, M.Sc., M.D., Master of Surgery 1983; m. Cathy Fraser; CANADIAN ASTRONAUT; Emergency Physician, Sunnybrook Health Sience Centre & Lecturer, Surgery, Univ. of Toronto 1988–89; Emergency Physician, Emergency Assoc. of Kitchener Waterloo and Medical Dir., Westmount Urgent Care Clinic 1989–90; various positions, Sunnybrook Health Science Centre. incl. Staff Emergency Physician, Medical Dir. ACLS Prog., Co-ord. of Postgrad. Training in Emergency Med., Acting Dir., Dept. of Emergency Serv. 1990– ; Asst. Prof. of Surgery and of Med., Univ. of Toronto 1990– ; selected for Canadian Astronaut Program 1992; preparing for Mission Specialist Training, NASA; Commonwealth Cert. of Thanks 1973; Commonwealth Recognition Award 1975; A.S. Hill Bursary 1981, Walter Hoare Bursary 1981, J.W. McConnell Award 1981–93, Faculty Scholar 1983, Univ. Scholar 1983, Psychiatry Prize and Wood Gold Medal and Dean's Honour List 1983 (all McGill Univ.); 2nd Prize for participation in Univ. of Toronto Emergency Med. Rsch. Papers Program 1986, '88, Top Honours 1987; Mem., Coll. of Physicians & Surgeons of Ont.; Ont. Med. Assn.; Coll. of Family Physicians of Can.; Royal Coll. of Physicians & Surg. of Can.; Candn. Assn. of Emergency Physicians; Candn. Aeronautics and Space Inst.; Aerospace Med. Assn.; recreations: flying, parachuting, SCUBA diving, kayaking, canoeing, alpine and nordic skiing; Office: 6767, Route de l'aéroport, Saint-Hubert, Que. J3Y 8Y9.

**WILLIAMS, David,** B.A., M.A., Ph.D.; university professor; b. Souris, Man. 22 June 1945 s. Jack Wilfred and Dorothy (Dahl) W.; e. Univ. of Sask. B.A. (Hons.) 1968; Univ. of Mass. M.A. 1970, Ph.D. 1973; m. Darlene d. Fred and Ann Olinyk 22 July 1967; children: Jeremy, Bryan; PROFESSOR OF ENGLISH, ST. PAUL'S COLLEGE, UNIV. OF MAN. 1983– ; Lectr., Univ. of Man. 1972–73; Asst. Prof. 1973–77; Assoc. Prof. 1977–83; Guest Prof., Workshop on Candn. Studies, M.S. Univ. of Baroda, India 1992; Touring Writer/Lectr., External Affairs, Denmark, Finland, Norway, Sweden 1981; Dir., Intermediate Prose Writing, Sask. Summer Sch. of the Arts 1986; SSHRCC Western Region Selection Ctte., Special M.A. Fellowships 1986; Univ. of Man. Teaching Awards 1986–87, 1989–90; Olive Beatrice Stanton Award for Excellence in Teaching 1992; Univ. of Man. Nominee for Candn. Prof. of Yr., CASE 1993; Rh Inst. Award for Outstanding Rsch. in Humanities 1987; Canada Council Grants 'B' Awards 1977–78, 1981–82; Canada Council Fellow 1969–73; Woodrow Wilson Fellow 1968–69; Bd. of Dir., St. Paul's College (Winnipeg) 1985–87; Univ. of Man. Inst. for Humanities; Mem., The Writers' Union of Canada (Mem. Nat Council 1978–79, 1984–85); Assn. for Candn. College & Univ. Teachers of English; Nordic Assn. for Candn. Studies; author: 'The Burning Wood' 1975, 'The River Horsemen' 1981, 'Eye of the Father' 1985 (novels); 'Faulkner's Women: The Myth and the Muse' 1977, 'Confessional Fictions: A Portrait of the Artist in the Canadian Novel' 1991 (literary criticism); editor: 'To Run With Longboat: Twelve Stories of Indian Athletes in Canada' 1988 (biography); recreations: hockey coach, baseball coach; Home: 39 Kingston Row, Winnipeg, Man. R2M 0S7; Office: Winnipeg, Man. R3T 2M6.

**WILLIAMS, David Malcolm Lewis,** F.R.C.S., F.R.C.S.(C); educator; b. Swansea, Wales 9 June 1932; s. late David Ievan and Gertrude (Jones) W.; e. Gowerton Boys' Grammar Sch. 1951 (Head Boy, Glamorgan Co. Scholarship 1951); Univ. of Sheffield 1951–58; qualified M.R.C.S. Eng., L.R.C.P. London 1958; m. Elizabeth Mary Denise d. late William Thomas Bassett 9 Aug. 1958; children: Paul Bassett, Siân Bassett, Clare Elizabeth; PROF., DEPT. OF MEDICINE, QUEEN'S UNIV.; Head of Otolaryngology, Queens Univ. and Kingston Gen. Hosp. (also Chrmn. Med. Adv. Comte.-Chief of Staff) 1969; House Surg. and House. Phys. Royal Infirmary, Sheffield 1958–59; Sr. House Offr. Wharncliffe Hosp. Sheffield 1959; Sr. House Offr. (Otolaryngol.) Gen. Hosp. Bristol 1959–60; Registrar (Otolaryngol.) The United Sheffield Hosps. 1960–62, 1964–6; Demonst. in anat. Univ. of Sheffield 1962–64; Registrar and Sr. Registrar (Otolaryngol.) Cardiff Hosps. and Welsh Hosp. Bd. 1965–67; Fellow in Otology, Wayne State Univ. Detroit; author or co-author various med. publs., med. film; mem. Candn. Otolaryngol. Soc. (Educ. Comte., Chrmn. Postgrad. Curriculum Comte.); Kingston Acad. Med.; Candn. Standards Assn.; Ont. Med. Assn.; Am. Acad. Otolaryngol.; recreations: music, carpentry, silversmithing; Club: Kingston Yacht; Office: Dept. of Medicine, Queen's Univ., Murray Bldg., Hotel Dieu Hosp., Kingston, Ont. K7L 5G2.

**WILLIAMS, David Ricardo,** Q.C., LL.B., B.A.; author; researcher; b. Kamloops, B.C. 28 Feb. 1923; s. Humphrey David and Mary Elizabeth (Cassady) W.; e. in Vancouver at Bayview Elem. Sch. 1928–34; Kitsilano Jr. High Sch. 1934–35; Queen Mary Jr. High Sch. 1935–36; Lord Byng High Sch. 1936–40; Univ. of B.C., B.A. 1948; LL.B. 1949; m. Laura Ella-Belle, d. Dr. Walter and Ella-Belle Bapty, 29 May 1948; children: Dr. David Bruce; Suzanne Margaret; Harry Bapty; Owen Ricardo; Jonathan Lukyn; ADJUNCT PROFESSOR AND WRITER-IN-RESIDENCE, FACULTY OF LAW, UNIV. OF VICTORIA 1980–94; admitted B.C. Bar 1949; since 1975 has been writing biog. and hist. articles; author: '100 Years at St. Peter's Quamichan' 2nd ed. 1977; 'The Man for a New Country: Sir Matthew Baillie Begbie' 1977 (The Univ. of B.C. Medal for Candn. Biography 1978); 'Matthew Baillie Begbie' 1980; 'Trapline Outlaw: Simon Peter Gun-a-noot' 1982, paperback repr. 1988; 'Duff: A Life in the Law' 1984, B.C. Book Prize (non-fiction) 1985; 'Mayor Gerry: The Remarkable Gerald Grattan McGeer' 1986; 'Ace of Pentacles' 1990; 'Pioneer Parish: The Story of St. Peter's Quamichan' 1991; 'Yesterday To-Day and Tomorrow: A History of Vancouver's Terminal City Club' 1992; 'With Malice Aforethought: Six Spectacular Canadian Trials' 1993; cr. Q.C. 1969; Fellow, Foundation for Legal Research; mem., Law Soc. B.C.; Writer's Union Can.; 9th Circuit Judicial History Soc.; Supreme Court of Canada Legal History Soc.; Oregon Hist. Soc.; B.C. Studies; B.C. Press Council; former mem. Senate, Bd. Govs. Univ. B.C.; former Chrmn. B.C. Forest Museum; King's Daughters Hosp. (Duncan, B.C.); Anglican Church; Clubs: Union B.C.; recreations: squash, reading; Office: 3355 Gibbins Rd., R.R. 2, Duncan, B.C. V9L 1N9.

**WILLIAMS, Major-General Donald Ray,** B.Eng., CMM, CD; armed forces commander; b. Corvallis, Oreg. 6 April 1942; s. Raymond Charles and Hildred Olive (Vancil) W.; e. Riverside Collegiate 1959; Royal Military Coll. B.Eng. 1963; Cdn. Forces Command & Staff Coll. PCSC 1975; Nat. Defence Coll. NDC 1986; m. Bonita d. Lionel and Lilian Smith 9 May 1964; children: Mark Trevor, Ryan Donald; COMMANDER OF FIGHTER GROUP AND CANADIAN NORAD REGION 1992– ; Pilot, Supervisor & Senior Officer, Royal Candn. Force & Candn. Forces 33 years; commanded at Flight, Squadron, Wing & Group levels while accumulating 5200 flight hours on 20 types of aircraft, principally jet fighters & trainers; Staff Officer, NATO, 1 Air Div. H.Q. Lahr Germany 1968–69; Allied forces N. Eur. H.Q. Oslo Norway 1986–88; 4th Allied Tactical Air Force H.Q. Heidelberg Germany 1988–90; NORAD, 23rd NORAD Reg. H.Q. Duluth Minn. 1976–79; Commander of the Order of Military Merit; Candn. Forces Decoration; recreations: sports, reading, financial mgmt., computers; clubs: RMC Ex-Cadet, North Bay Golf & Country, Hylands Golf; Home: 20 Windsor Cres., Hornell Heights, Ont. P0H 1P0; Office: Hornell Heights, Ont. P0H 1P0.

**WILLIAMS, George Ronald,** Ph.D., D.Sc., F.R.S.C.; educator; b. Liverpool, Eng. 4 Jan. 1928; s. George Williams; e. Rawson Rd. Sch. Seaforth 1939; Merchant Taylors' Sch. Crosby 1946; Univ. of Liverpool B.Sc. 1949, Ph.D. 1951, D.Sc. 1969; m. Joyce d. James Mutch 10 May 1952; children: Geoffrey Martin, Glynis Christine, Timothy George; PROF. EMERITUS DIV. OF LIFE SCIENCES, SCARBOROUGH COLL. UNIV. OF TORONTO, 1993– ; Prof. of Biochem. Univ. of Toronto Med. Sch.; Commonwealth Travelling Scholar Worshipful Co. Goldsmiths, Banting & Best Dept. Med. Research Univ. of Toronto 1952–53, Asst. Prof. 1956–61, Assoc. Prof. of Biochem. 1961–66, Chrmn. of Biochem. 1970–77, Prof. Div. of Life Sciences, Scarborough Coll. Univ. of Toronto 1978–93; Chrmn., Div. of Life Sciences, Scarborough Coll. 1978–83; Principal, Scarborough Coll. 1984–89; Fellow, Johnson Foundation, Univ. of Pa. 1953–55; Med. Research Council appt. Sch. of Pathol. Oxford Univ. 1955–56; Sr. Research Fellow Nat. Research Council Can., Royal N. Shore Hosp. of Sydney, Australia 1967–68; Scient. Offr. Med. Research Council Can. 1969–73; Visiting Prof. of Geochem. Lamont-Doherty Geol. Observatory, Columbia Univ. 1977–78; Visiting Prof. of Biochem. & Microbiol., Univ. of Victoria 1989–90; author over 100 articles various scient. journs.; mem. Candn. Biochem. Soc. (Pres. 1971–72); Am. Soc. Biochem. Mol. Biol.; Royal Soc. Can.; United Church; recreations: reading, walking, travel;

Home: 15 Bournville Dr., West Hill, Ont. M1E 1C3; Office: West Hill, Ont. M1C 1A4.

**WILLIAMS, Glen,** M.A., Ph.D.; educator; b. Montreal, Que. 21 Aug. 1947; s. John William and Margaret Christine (Ross) W.; e. York Univ. B.A. 1969, M.A. 1971, Ph.D. 1978; m. Carol-Lynne d. Joseph and May Saad 17 Aug. 1984; one daughter: Anne Zhong Qiu; PROF. OF POL. SCI. CARLETON UNIV. 1991– ; Hist. Teacher Min. of Edn. Zambia (CUSO) 1971–73; Asst. Prof. present Univ. 1976–83, Assoc. Prof. 1983–91; recipient Ont. Grad. Fellowship 1973–75; Can. Council Fellowship 1975–76; author 'Not For Export: Toward A Political Economy Of Canada's Arrested Industrialization' 1983, revised ed. 1986, 3rd ed. 1994; co-ed. 'The New Canadian Political Economy' 1989; 'Canadian Politics in the 1990's' 4th ed. 1994; numerous articles, essay colls.; mem. Candn. Pol. Sci. Assn.; Sec.-Treas. Candn. Coalition Palestinian Human Rights 1988– ; recreation: outdoors; Home: 24 Roslyn Ave., Ottawa, Ont. K1S 4W3; Office: Colonel By Dr., Ottawa, Ont. K1S 5B6.

**WILLIAMS, H. Bruce,** B.A., M.D., F.R.C.S.(C), F.A.C.S.; educator; surgeon; b. New Glasgow, N.S. 20 Sept. 1929; s. Joseph Daniel and Bessie Margaret (Bruce) W.; e. Acadia Univ. B.A. 1951; McGill Univ. M.D. 1955; m. Dorothy d. Robert and Margaret Harris 20 June 1958; two s. Bruce, David; SURGEON-IN-CHIEF, MONTREAL CHILDREN'S HOSPITAL 1992– ; PROF. OF SURGERY AND DIR. PLASTIC & RECONSTRUCTIVE SURGERY, MCGILL UNIV. 1976– ; Dir. of Plastic Surgery Montreal Gen. and Montreal Children's Hosps. 1976– , mem. attending staff Plastic Surgery 1962– ; postgrad. surg. training McGill Univ. teaching hosps. 1955–58; Residency in Pathol. Charlotte (N.C.) Meml. Hosp.; Plastic Surgery residency McGill Univ. 1958–60; Hosmer Teaching Fellow in Surgery Montreal Gen. Hosp. 1961; McLaughlin Travelling Fellowship Eur. and Russia 1962; Visiting Prof.: Univ. of Toronto 1982; Queen's Univ. 1982; Washington Univ. 1981; Univ. of Man. 1982; Univ. of Ottawa 1983; E. Va. Med. Sch. 1984; Univ. of B.C. 1986; Univ. of Western Ont. 1986; Columbia Univ., NY 1988; Keio Univ. Tokyo, Japan 1988; Japanese Soc. of Reconstructive Microsurgery 1988; Columbia Univ. 1989; Queen's Univ. 1990; Univ. of Pittsburgh 1990; Univ. of Toronto 1991; Sao Paulo Medical Sch. 1990; Royal College Lecturer, Candn. Soc. of Plastic Surgeons 1991; Univ. of Mexico 1991; recipient James Barrett Brown Prize Plastic Surgery 1975; awarded Distinguished Service Medal, Acadia Univ. 1992; ed. 'Melanotic Lesions and Vascular Malformations' 1983; 'Transactions of Plastic and Reconstructive Surgery' 1983; 'Peripheral Nerve Surgery, Hand Clinics'; author or co-author over 80 sci. publs. cleft lip surgery, microsurgery, rheumatoid hand surgery, vascular malformations; Past. Chrmn. Royal Coll. Specialty Comte. Plastic Surgery; Past Pres. Que. Soc. Plastic Surgery; Candn. Soc. Plastic Surgery; Ednl. Found. Am. Soc. Plastic & Reconstructive Surgs.; Hist., Am. Assn. Plastic Surgs.; Past Pres., Am. Soc. of Plastic and Reconstructive Surgeons; Past-Pres., Am. Soc. for Reconstructive Microsurgery; Pres.-Elect, Internat. Microsurgery Soc. 1992; Vice Pres., Am. Soc. for Peripheral Nerve; Coordinator, Postgrad. Edn. Am. Soc. Surgery Hand; mem. Am. Bd. Plastic Surgery; Vice Chrmn. Am. Bd. of Plastic Surgery 1985–86; Candn. Med. Assn.; Candn. Soc. Plastic Surgs.; Am. Soc. Surgery Trauma; Internat. Soc. Reconstructive Microsurgery; recreations: golf, travel; Clubs: Royal Montreal Golf; Montreal Badminton & Squash; Home: 26 Edgehill Rd., Westmount, Que. H3Y 1A4; Office: 646F, 1650 Cedar Ave., Montreal, Que. H3G 1A4.

**WILLIAMS, James B.J.,** B.A., M.B.A.; retail electronic company executive; b. Toronto, Ont. 16 Oct. 1945; s. Norman James and Marie (McBride) W.; e. Univ. of Toronto B.A. 1967, M.B.A. 1969; m. Kathleen Fitzgerald 10 May 1969; children: Jason Lawrence, Laura Marie; PRESIDENT & CHIEF EXECUTIVE OFFR., INTERTAN INC. 1992– ; var. operating & admin. positions, Dominion Stores Ltd. ending as Senior Vice-President, Finance & Admin. & Chief Financial Officer 1969–85; Extve. Vice-President, Finance & Administration & Chief Finanancial Officer, Great Atlantic & Pacific Tea Company of Canada Inc. 1985–86; Extve. Vice-President Finance & Administration & Chief Financial Officer, Canadian Tire Corporation, Limited 1986–88; Extve. Vice-President, Marketing, Real Estate, Construction & Distribution 1988–91; Pres. Merchandise Business Group & Corp. Extve. Vice-Pres., Dealer Relations 1991–92; Council of Mktg. Executives, Conference Board of Canada; Home: 15 Bemersyde Dr., Islington, Ont. M9A 2S5; Office: 151 Ferris Lane, Suite 301, Barrie, Ont. L4M 6C1.

**WILLIAMS, James Royal;** engineering executive; b. London, Eng. 24 Feb. 1929; s. Royal Francis and Annie (Cresswell) W.; e. St. Marylebone Grammar Sch. London Sr. Matric.; City & Guilds of London Telecommunications Dip.; Royal Navy, Stanford Rsch. Inst. and Advanced Mgmt. Resch. Inst.; m. Marjorie (Jill) d. Jack and Marjorie Wedge 26 March 1955; three s. Russell Royal, Barry James, Mark Allan; PRES. MIL SYSTEMS ENGINEERING INC. 1987– and of 3 subsidiaries, MSEI Services Inc., MSEI Atlantic and Norris Warming Canada Ltd. 1990; served with Fleet Air Arm RN 1946–54; Tech. Author, De Havilland 1954–57; Flight Test Eng. Canadair Ltd. 1957–59; Design Eng. Computing Devices of Canada 1959–63; Product Line Mgr. Leigh Instruments Ltd. 1963–73; Vice Pres. and Gen. Mgr. Elinca Communications 1973–82; Pres. Itec/Jarowil Corp. 1982–84; Dir. Comm. & Operations MEL Defence Systems 1984–87; author 'The Earl of March' hist. 1975; various tech. papers flight data recording and accident analysis; Assoc. Fellow, Candn. Aeronautics & Space Inst.; Dir., Candn. Maritime Inds. Assn.; mem. Candn. Inst. Marine Engs.; recreations: golf, swimming, alpine skiing; Club: Rideau (Ottawa); Home: 12 Rutherford Cres., Kanata, Ont. K2K 1M9; Office: 1600 Carling Ave., Ottawa, Ont. K1Z 8R7.

**WILLIAMS, John C.,** B.Comm., M.B.A.; retail consultant; b. Rochester, Minn. 24 Feb. 1936; s. Donald H. and Kathleen B. (Crawford) W.; e. Univ. of B.C. B.Comm. 1958; Northwestern Univ. M.B.A. 1959; separated; children: Mark Hemmingson, Michael John, Megan Kathleen, Andrea Louise; FOUNDER & PRESIDENT, JOHN C. WILLIAMS CONSULTANTS (Canada's leading retail cons. firm) 1974– ; Mgr. & Extve., T. Eaton Co. 1959–74; Founder & Pres., Williams Retail (12 stores in Ont.); Founder, Urban Marketing Collaborating Inc. (Canada's leading downtown revitalization firm); frequent writer, columnist for 'Canadian Retailer'; lectr. & speaker on retailing, urban revitalization & shopping centre mktg.; Dir., Internat. Downtown Assn.; Mem., Retail Council of Canada; Nat. Retail Fed.; Internat. Council of Shopping Centres; Internat. Downtown Assn.; author: 'Strategic Retail Marketing' 1986, '89, '92, 'Marketing Main Street' 1989, 'Working with Retailers' 1990; recreations: gardening, travel; clubs: YMCA of Toronto; Office: 584 Church St., Toronto, Ont. M4Y 2E5.

**WILLIAMS, Joseph Kenneth;** Q.C., B.Com.; b. Toronto, Ont. 9 May 1916; s. Harry B. and Myra M. (Hargreaves) W.; e. Runnymede Coll., Toronto, Ont.; Univ. of Toronto, B.Com. 1938; Osgoode Hall, Toronto, Ont. (1939–42); m. Barbara I., d. late Willis D. McLennan, 8 Sept. 1945; one s., Rodney M.; Senior Vice Pres., Gen. Counsel & Secy., The National Life Assurance Co. Of Canada, 1979–81; read law with Arnoldi, Parry & Campbell, Toronto, Ont.; Dir., National Life 1977–86; called to the Bar of Ont., June 1942; cr. Q.C. 1961; Mgr., Property & Legal Dept., Shell Oil Co. of Can. Ltd., Toronto, Ont., 1946–47; The National Life Assnce. Co. of Can., 1947, Secy. 1952, Gen. Counsel and Secy. 1958–67, Vice-Pres. 1967–79; served in 2nd World War with R.C.A.F. as Meteorol. Offr., 1942–45; mem. Law Soc. Upper Can.; Assn. of Life Ins. Counsel; Phi Delta Phi; Protestant; recreations: golf, skiing; Clubs: Mississaugua Golf & Country; Mansfield Ski Club; Empire Club of Canada (Past Dir. & Life Mem.); Home: 25 Widdicombe Hill, Apt. 205, Weston, Ont. M9R 1B1.

**WILLIAMS, Louis Allan,** Q.C., LL.B.; solicitor; b. Glenavon, Sask. 22 May 1922; s. Louis Pomerine and Eula Belle (MacPherson) W.; e. primary and secondary schs. Sask.; Univ. of B.C., LL.B.; m. Marjorie Ruth Lake, Vancouver, B.C. 25 June 1948; children: Louis Ryder, Leslie Ruth, Susan Jane; COUNSEL, DAVIS & COMPANY 1983– ; el. M.L.A. for West Vancouver-Howe Sound prov. g.e. 1966–83; Min. of Labour 1975–79; B.C. Attorney-General 1979–83; served with RCAF, rank Flight Lt.; Social Credit; Protestant; Office: 2800 Park Place, 666 Burrard St., Vancouver, B.C. V6C 2Z7.

**WILLIAMS, Marshall MacKenzie,** B.Eng., M.Eng., Hon. D.Eng.; utilities executive; b. Londonderry, N.S., 11 Dec. 1923; s. late Millard Filmore and late Gladys Christine (MacKenzie) W.; e. Technical Univ. of N.S., B.Eng. (Civil Engn.) 1947, M.Eng. 1949; Banff Sch. of Advanced Mang. 1955; D.Eng. (hon. causa), Technical Univ. of N.S. 1978; m. Joan Atlee Ross, d. late G.W.W. Ross, 6 Sept. 1952; children: Peter, Alex, Stephen, Margot; CORPORATE DIRECTOR, TRANSALTA UTILITIES CORP.; Chrmn., TransAlta Resources Corp. 1981– ; Past Chrmn., Western Regional Ctte., C.D. Howe Inst.; Dir., Canada Northwest Energy Limited; Royal Trustco Ltd.; AEC Power Ltd.; Nfld. Light & Power Co. Ltd. (Past Dir.); Sun Life Assnce. Co. of Can.; Stelco Inc.; Conf. Bd. of Can.; Fortis Inc.; mem. Adv. Bd., Royal Trust (Calgary); Western Centre for Econ. Rsch.; joined Montreal Engineering Company, Limited 1948–54; joined present Co. as Asst. to Gen. Mgr. 1954, Extve. Asst. 1960; Asst. Gen. Mgr. 1966, Extve. Vice Pres. 1968; Dir. 1972; Pres. 1973; Pres. and C.E.O. 1980; Bd. Chrmn., Pres. & C.E.O. 1984; Chrmn. & C.E.O. 1985–89; Chrmn. 1989; mem. Premier's Council on Science & Technology; mem., Assn. Prof. Engrs., Geols. & Geophysicists Alta.; past Pres. and mem., Candn. Elect. Assn.; mem. and past Pres., N.W. Elect. Light & Power Assn.; Vice Pres. & Trustee: The Manning Awards Found.; Jaycee Senator; mem, Bd. of Govs., Com. on Can./U.S. Relations; The Banff Centre; C. of C.; Presbyterian; recreations: skiing, fishing, hiking; Club: The Ranchmen's; Home: #10 – 3231 Rideau Pl. S.W., Calgary, Alta. T2S 2T1; Office: Box 1900, 110 – 12th Ave. S.W., Calgary, Alta. T2P 2M1.

**WILLIAMS, Marty,** B.A.; university administrator; b. Murrayville, B.C. 20 Oct. 1958; s. Frederick Marlowe and Blanche (Prucyk) W.; e. Univ. of Guelph B.A. 1985; MANAGER, STUDENT HOUSING, UNIV. OF GUELPH 1991– ; President, Central Student Assn., Univ. of Guelph 1989–91; Gov., Univ. of Guelph; Chair, Bd. of Dir., Ontarion Inc.; Univ. of Guelph Community Service Award; Rhino Party Candidate for M.P. (Guelph) 1988; author of newspaper articles and Univ. of Guelph chapter in 'The Real Guide to Canadian Universities' 1994; Home: 45 Caledonia St., Guelph, Ont. M1G 2C8; Office: Maritime Hall, Guelph, Ont. N1G 2W1.

**WILLIAMS, Michael Allan,** B.Com., F.C.A.; petroleum executive; b. Vancouver, B.C. 29 May 1933; s. John Samuel and Joyce Winnefred (Cooper) W.; e. Univ. of B.C. B.Com. 1956; m. Daisy Pauline Popoff 18 July 1959; children: Susan, Jennifer, John; CHRMN. & C.E.O., GOBI OIL & GAS LTD. 1993– ; Accounting Clk. Husky Oil & Refining 1956–57; Student and C.A., Peat Marwick Mitchell & Co. 1957–62; various financial and taxation functions Home Oil Co. Ltd. 1962–69; Treas. and Mgr. Accounting, CanDel Oil Ltd. 1969, Vice Pres. Finance & Treas. 1971, Sr. Vice Pres. and Treas. 1974, Extve. Vice Pres. 1975–80, Pres., 1980–81; Extve. Vice Pres., Sulpetro Ltd. 1982–85, Dir. 1983–87, Pres. 1985–87; Mem., Bd. of Govs., Univ. of Calgary 1980–85; Past Pres. Jr. Achievement of S. Alta.; mem. Alta. Inst. C.A.'s; Gov., Acctg. Education Found. of Alta. 1988–93; mem. of Council, Institute of C.A.'s of Alta. 1992– ; Clubs: Calgary Petroleum; Ranchmen's; Bearspaw Golf & Country; Canmore Golf; Home: Box 17, Site 22, R.R. #4, Calgary, Alta. T2M 4L4; Office: Ste. 780, 700 Fourth Ave. S.W., Calgary, Alta. T2P 3J4.

**WILLIAMS, Norah Suzanne;** association executive; b. Vancouver, B.C. 16 Nov. 1934; d. John Guy and Suey Mary (Somers) Henderson; e. Vancouver; Hamilton and Dunnville, Ont.; m. John Thomas Williams 15 Dec. 1956; children: Elizabeth Suzanne Candler, John Guy Westwood; Pres. Nat. Chapter of Can. IODE 1988–90; Home: #2 - 909 Admirals Rd., Esquimalt, B.C. V9A 2P1.

**WILLIAMS, Peter J.,** M.A., Fil.lic., Fil.dr.; educator; b. Croydon, England 27 Sept. 1932; s. John George and Kathleen Emily (White) W.; e. Whitgift Sch. Croydon 1951; Fitzwilliam Coll. Cambridge B.A. 1954, M.A. 1958; Univ. of Oslo 1954–55; Univ. of Stockholm, Fil.lic., Fil.dr. 1969; m. Kari d. Carl Andreas and Else Thams Fuglesang 1 June 1957; children: Eric Dag John, Beatrice Anne, Inger Elisabeth; DIR. GEOTECH. SCI. LABS., CARLETON UNIV. 1978– , Prof. of Geog. 1971– ; Pres. Peter J. Williams and Associates Ltd. 1979– ; Rsch. Offr. Nat. Rsch. Council Can.; 1957–69; Rsch. Fellow Norwegian Geotech. Inst. 1962–65; Assoc. Prof. of Geog. present Univ. 1969; rsch. primarily physics & mechanics freezing soils; guest lectr. various nat. & internat. univs. and instns.; cons. geotech. problems soil freezing; Expert Witness, Berger Inquiry 1975; adv. regulatory agencies, Govt. Can. geotech. problems n. oil & gas megaprojects; author: 'Pipelines and Permafrost: Science in a Cold Climate' 2nd ed. 1986; 'The Surface of the Earth: An Introduction to Geotechnical Science' 1982; (with M.W. Smith) 'The Frozen Earth: Fundamentals of Geocryology' 1989; over 50 sci. papers; co-ed. several monographs; mem. Candn. Geotech. Soc.; Candn. Assn. Geogs.; Internat. Glaciol. Soc.; Candn. Nordic Soc. (Pres. 1986–87); Norwegian Geotech. Soc.; recreations: gardening, languages, people & places; Office: Geotechnical Science Laboratories, Carleton Univ., Ottawa, Ont. K1S 5B6.

**WILLIAMS, Richard D.,** B.A., LL.B.; mining executive; b. Montreal, Que. 9 Apl. 1953; e. Univ. of W. Ont. B.A. 1974; Univ. of Ottawa LL.B. 1978; VICE PRES. REPUBLIC GOLDFIELDS INC. 1988– ; Pres. and Dir.

Western International Explorations Ltd.; Vice Pres. & Sec. Minefinders Corp. Ltd.; Dir. Compania Minera de Santa Gertrudis; recreations: tennis, basketball; Office: 2401, 1 Dundas St. W., Toronto, Ont. M5G 1Z3.

**WILLIAMS, Rupert M.;** banker; b. Green Harbour, N.S. 28 Dec. 1935; s. Donald McKenzie and Penina Angeline (Thorburn) W.; e. Canadian Bankers' Assn. diploma 1957; Queen's Univ. Cost Acctg. 1965–66; Univ. of Toronto, Extve. Mngt. studies 1980; m. Helen Elizabeth d. Pearl and Lauchlin Mackenzie 5 April 1958; children: Jill, Anne, Christopher; VICE-PRESIDENT, FEDERAL BUSINESS DEVELOPMENT BANK; Branch positions, Royal Bank of Canada N.S. & P.E.I. 1954–64; Metropolitan Life Insur. Co. 1964–66; Senior Management & Executive positions, Industrial Devel. Bank/Federal Business Devel. Bank Montreal, Toronto, Winnipeg, & Halifax 1966– ; Mem., Boards of Trade; Chambers of Commerce; Federal Inst. of Management; recreations: travel, fishing, outdoor activities; Home: Summer Gardens, Apt. 505, 1470 Summer St., Halifax, N.S. B3H 3A3; Office: Suite 1400, Cogswell Tower, Scotia Square, Halifax, N.S. B3J 2Z7.

**WILLIAMS, Sharon A.,** LL.B., LL.M., D.Jur., F.R.S.C.; university professor; b. Cardiff, Wales 14 March 1951; d. John Daniel and Honora (Ward) W.; e. Univ. of Exeter, LL.B. 1973; Osgoode Hall Law Sch., LL.M. 1974, D.Jur. 1976; m. Robert W. s. Joseph William and Gertrude Cosman 25 Apl. 1981; children: Sarah Elizabeth Jane Cosman; PROF. OF LAW, OSGOODE HALL LAW SCH. 1990– , ASSISTANT DEAN 1989–91; Mem., Permanent Court of Arbitration, The Hague 1991–97; called to Bar of Ont. 1979; Assoc. Prof. of Law, present Sch. 1981–90; Asst. Prof. of Law McGill Univ. 1976–77, present Sch. 1977–89; Visiting Lectr. Univ. of Toronto 1980, 1986; recipient, David W. Mundell Medal for Law and Letters 1991; author: 'The International and National Protection of Movable Cultural Property: A Comparative Study' 1978; co-author 'An Introduction to International Law, Chiefly as Interpreted and Applied in Canada' 1979, 2nd ed. 1987, French ed. 1982; 'Canadian Criminal Law: International and Transnational Aspects' 1981; various book chapters, articles; Asst. Ed. Candn. Bar Review 1974–83; mem., Institute of Humanitarian Law, San Remo, Italy 1986– ; Am. Soc. Internat. Law (Awards Ctte. 1980–81, 1993–94); Candn. Council Internat. Law (Exec. mem. 1978–82, Vice-Pres. 1992–93); Internat. Comm. Jurists (Nat. Counc. Mem.) 1987–98; Internat. Law Assn. (Extradition Ctte. Mem. 1993– ); L'Association Henri Capitant (Section québecoise); Internat. Assn. of Penal Law; Soc. for the Reform of Criminal Law; recreations: tennis, travel, gardening, cooking, painting; Home: 26 Rose Park Cres., Toronto, Ont. M4T 1P9; Office: Osgoode Hall Law Sch., York University, 4700 Keele St., North York, Ont. M3J 1P3.

**WILLIAMSON, Kenneth Bryce,** B.A.; retired diplomat; b. Winnipeg, Manitoba 1 Nov. 1922; s. Kenneth and Susan Drummond Findlay (Bryce) W.; e. Gordon Bell High Sch. Winnipeg 1940; Univ. of Man., B.A. 1945; Univ. of Toronto Grad. Sch. 1946–47; Univ. of Ottawa, M.A. 1993; m. Patricia d. Keir and Jeanette Bernard 29 Oct. 1947; children: Janet, Susan, Gavin, James; joined Dept. of External Affairs 1947; diplomatic assignments Rome, Prague, Santiago, Berlin and service in Ottawa; Special Asst. to Sec. of State for External Affairs 1965–67; Min. Washington 1970–74; Ambassador Ankara 1974–77; Dir. Gen. Info. Ottawa 1977–80; Ambassador and Perm. Observer to Orgn. Am. States Washington 1980–83; Ambassador Havana 1983–86; Anglican; Home: 150 Sherwood Dr., Ottawa, Ont. K1Y 3V4.

**WILLIAMSON, Moncrieff,** C.M., LL.D., F.R.S.A., F.C.M.A.; author; gallery and museum director; b. East Linton, Scotland 23 Nov. 1915; s. James Watt, J.P., and Gwendoline Pilkington Jackson W.; e. Loretto Sch., Scotland; Michot Mongenast, Brussels; Edinburgh Coll. of Art; LL.D. P.E.I. 1972; m. Pamela Upton, d. Jocelyn Herbert Fanshawe, 30 Sept. 1948; one s. Timothy Malcolm Moncrieff; DIR. EMERITUS CONFEDERATION ART GALLERY AND MUSEUM, 1982– ; Asst. Prof. of Fine Art, Prince of Wales Coll., and Univ. P.E.I. 1966–71; formerly a Dir., Art Exhns. Bureau, London, Eng.; Dir., Art Dept., Glenbow Foundation, Calgary, Alta.; Curator, Art Gallery of Greater Victoria, B.C.; served in 2nd World War, Brit. Army Intelligence Corps in Eng., France, Belgium, Germany; Govt. Communications Dept., Foreign Office; Brit. Air Comn., Washington, D.C.; Publications: 'Four Poems' 1945; 'Fluid Idol' 1952; (Organiser and Catalogue Author) Canadian Fine Crafts Exhbn., Candn. Pavillion, EXPO '67, 'Canadian Fine Crafts' 1967; 'Robert Harris 1849–1919: An Uncoventional Biography' 1971; (Organiser and Catalogue Author) 'Robert Harris' Portraits, Nat. Gallery Can. 1973; 'Through Canadian Eyes' 1976; 'Death in the Picture' (novel) 1982; 'Island Painter' (biography) 1983; 'The Inward Garden' poems selected by Iris Phillips 1990; numerous articles and poems publ. Eng., Germany, U.S., New Zealand, Canada; Pres. (1971–73) Canadian Art Museum Directors Organ.; Fellow Royal Society of Arts; mem., Candn. Museums Assn.; Hon. Life Mem., Am. Art Museum Dirs. Assn. 1976; (Diplôme d'honneur, 1975) Candn. Conf. of the Arts; Commonwealth Assn. of Museums, London; Movable Cultural Property Review Bd., Ottawa (1976–80); Fellow, Candn. Museums Assn. 1980; mem., Candn. Soc. of Decorative Arts 1981; Writers' Union of Canada; Crime Writers of Can.; rec'd Centennial Medal; Silver Jubilee Medal 1977; R.C.A. Medal 1978; Gold Medal, Glenbow Museum Acquisition Soc., Calgary 1986; Anglican; recreations: conversation, reading, swimming; Home: 14 Churchill Ave., Charlottetown, P.E.I. C1A 1Y8; Office: Confederation Centre, Charlottetown, P.E.I.

**WILLINSKY, John Mark,** B.A., M.Ed., Ph.D.; university professor; b. Toronto, Ont. 5 Jan. 1950; s. Jack Mendel and Cecily Valentine (Samuel) W.; e. York Univ. 1969–71; North Bay Teachers Coll., Ont. Teachers cert. 1972; Laurentian Univ., B.A. 1976; Univ. of Toronto, M.Ed. 1979; Dalhousie Univ., Ph.D. 1982; m. Pamela d. Ronald and Gladys Mann 3 June 1972; children: Paul, David, Aaron; PROF. AND DIR., CENTRE FOR THE STUDY OF CURRICULUM AND INSTRUCTION, UNIV. OF B.C. 1990– ; Steelworker, student, taxi driver, farmer, Sault Ste Marie 1969–71; School teacher, Sault Ste Marie Bd. of Edn. 1972–84; Univ. Instr., Dept. of Eng., Algoma Univ. Coll. 1982–84; Prof., Dept. of Curriculum & Instruction, Univ. of Calgary 1984–90; has also taught at Nipissing Univ. Coll. 1980, Dalhousie Univ. 1980–82, Univ. of Sask. 1984; O.I.S.E. 1986; Davies Mem. Scholarship, OPSTF 1980–82; Wilfred R. Wees Diss. Award, CCT 1983; Spencer Fellowship, Nat. Acad. of Edn. (USA) 1988–89; Jewish; mem., CCTE (Task Force Dir. 1986–90); CSSE; NCTE; author: 'The Well-Tempered Tongue' 1984, 'The New Literacy' 1990; 'The Triumph of Literature/The Fate of Literacy' 1991; co-author: '"The Fearful Passage" in the High School' 1989; editor: 'The Educational Legacy of Romanticism' 1990; 'Critical Issues in Curriculum' (series) 1990– ; co-editor: 'Girls, Women and Giftedness' 1990; Book review columnist, OPSTF 'News' 1980–84; Book review ed.: 'Journal of Educational Thought' 1987–90; recreations: classical guitar; Home: 2637 Balaclava St., Vancouver, B.C. V6K 4E3; Office: U.B.C., Vancouver, B.C. V6T 1Z4.

**WILLIS, Clive,** B.Sc., Ph.D., F.C.I.C.; scientific research executive; b. London, Eng. 31 July 1939; s. William H. and Rose Florence (Wilmot) W.; e. Liverpool Univ. B.Sc. 1961, Ph.D. 1964; Carleton Univ. Dip. Pub. Adm. 1980; children: Christopher Peter, Vinca Isobel; VICE-PRESIDENT (PHYSICAL & LIFE SCIENCES), NAT. RESEARCH COUNCIL 1993– ; Post-doctoral Fellow Univ. of Cal. Los Angeles 1964–65; Collaborateur Etranger Centre d'Etudes Nucléaires de Saclay, France 1965–66; Assoc. Rsch. Offr. AECL Chalk River, Ont. 1966–71; Lectr. in Chem., Univ. of W. Indies, Jamaica 1971–73; Sr. Rsch. Offr. Div. Chem. Nat. Rsch. Council 1973–81, Rsch. Council Offr. Prog. Services Secretariat 1981–82, Dir. of Pub. Relations & Info. Services 1982–84; Sec. Gen., Nat. Research Counc. 1984–86; Assoc. Vice Pres. (Science) NRC 1986–87; Vice Pres. (Science) NRC 1987–89; Vice Pres. (Technology) NRC 1989–90; Vice-Pres. (Science) NRC 1990–93; Vice Pres. (Physical & Life Sciences) 1993– ; holds several patents and is author or co-author of many sci. publs. refereed jours.; recreations: reading, travel, cooking for friends, cinema, keeping fit.

**WILLIS, David Lea,** B.Comm., C.A.; petroleum executive; b. Moose Jaw, Sask. 5 Sept. 1931; s. Arthur Henry and Edna Phyllis (North) W.; e. Univ. of Sask., B.Comm. 1955; C.A., Alta. 1961; m. Jean d. Nicholas and Jennie Stronski 10 Nov. 1962; children; Leslie, Michael, Robert; Vice Chrmn., Alta. Petroleum Mktg. Commission 1983, retired; various sr. finan. pos., Imperial Oil 1962–73; Controller, Utility Opns., Northern & Central Gas 1973–75; Controller, Candn. West. Nat. Gas 1975–78; Vice Pres., Admin. & Sr. Finan. Offr., Amerada Minerals of Can. 1978–81; Partner, Corns, Shier & Co. 1981–83; Dir., Financial Execs. Inst., Calgary 1986–90; Petroleum Accts. Soc. of West. Can. 1979–82; Indus. Chrmn., Nat. Adv. Comm. on Petroleum Statistics 1972; mem., Communications and Annual Conference Cttes., Alta. Inst. of Chartered Accountants 1986–89; Dir. & Past Pres., Alta. Theatre Projects 1976–82; Bd. of Dirs., Heritage Park Soc. 1987–91; Former Dir., Calgary Ctr. for Performing Arts; South. Alta. Dir., United Ch., Nat. Ventures in Mission Fund Raising Prog. 1983; several years of activity with United Way; Mem., Calgary C. of C.; Candn. Gas Assn.; Nat. Assn. of Regulatory Utility Comnrs.; recreations: tennis, golf, community groups: soccer coach, cubs; Club: Highwood Golf & Country (Past Mem., Kinsmen, Kiwanis, Toronto Bd. of Trade & Golf, Bayview, Profl.); Home: 14212 Parkside Dr. S.E., Calgary, Alta. T2J 4J5.

**WILLIS, Errick French,** B.A.; business consultant/lobbyist; b. Winnipeg, Man. 22 Aug. 1948; s. Errick French and Louise Isabel (Trimble) W.; e. Univ. of Man., B.A. 1969; m. Ellen d. Paul and Anne Kamarchuk 19 Sept. 1970; children: Christopher, Scott; MANAGING DIR., THE WILLIS CONSULTING GROUP INC. 1989– ; Dir., BDW Ltd.; Pres., Issues Mngt. Group 1980–83; Partner, Policy Concepts Inc. 1983–89; Cons. Assoc., Niagara Inst.; Mem. Bd. of Govs., Trinity College School; Chrmn., Bd. of Trustees Candn. Student Debating Federation; Dir., Etobicoke Lakeshore Progressive Conservative Assn.; Office: 270 Adelaide St. W., Suite 201, Toronto, Ont. M5H 1W7.

**WILLIS, Peter Mercer;** construction equipment executive; b. Toronto, Ont. 9 Oct. 1947; m. Eve Martin d. Brig. Gen. W. Preston and Elizabeth L. (Campbell) Gilbride 7 June 1969; children: Jodie Sean Carmichael, Simon Jeffery Carmichael; VICE-PRES., SEC. & DIR., EQUIPMENT SALES AND SERVICE (1968) LTD. 1973– ; Pres. & Dir., Highway Equipment Rentals Limited 1969– ; Dir., Finlayson Enterprises Limited; Mem., Confrerie des Chevaliers du Tastevin; Dir., Ont. Road Builders Assn.; Clubs: The Tadenac; The Caledon Ski Club; The Muskoka Lakes Golf & Country; Office: 1030 Martingrove Rd., Rexdale, Ont. M9W 4W3.

**WILLIS, Robert D.,** B.Sc., P.Eng.; mining executive; professional engineer; b. New Westminster, B.C. 4 March 1949; s. Leonard and Mary Hazel (Neill) W.; e. Garibaldi S.S. 1967; Univ. of B.C., B.Sc. 1973; m. Marianne Vroom; children: Jeffrey, Kevin, Michael; Pres. & C.E.O., Pioneer Metals Corp. 1983– ; Flotation Operator, Cyrus Anvil Mining Corp. 1970–71; Geol. & Mining Engr., Lornex Mining Corp. 1973–77; Drill Blast Supt., Pit Supt. & Gen. Mine Supvr., Afton Mining Corp./Highmont Mining Corp. 1977–81; Cons. 1981–83; Club: Ridge-Meadows Minor Hockey Assn. (Dir.); Home: 26195 127th Ave., Maple Ridge, B.C. V2W 1C4.

**WILLMENT, Jo-Anne H.,** B.A., M.A.; educator; b. Toronto, Ont. 13 Nov. 1954; d. Irving Frank and Joan D. Willment; e. Albert College SSHGD 1973; Univ. of Waterloo B.A. 1978; Univ. of Guelph M.A. 1982; ADVISOR ON TEACHING & LEARNING, TRACE OFFICE, UNIV. OF WATERLOO 1988– ; Research Co-ord., Niagara College of Applied Arts & Technology 1980–82; Special Projects Officer 1982–87; educational & teaching consultant 1982– ; Doctoral Candidate, Applied Psych., O.I.S.E. 1990– ; Educational Lecturer 1990– ; Pres., Profl. Women's Assn., Univ. of Waterloo 1992–93; Technology Transfer Cons., CIDA, Brazil 1988; Visiting Scholar, Nanjing Normal Univ. China 1987; Steering Ctte., Soc. for Teaching & Learning in Higher Education 1990– ; Mem., Candn. Psych. Assn. 1990– ; ; Am. Assn. for Higher Edn. 1990– ; recreations: music, walking, photography, swimming; Address: Univ. of Waterloo, Waterloo, Ont. N2L 3G1.

**WILLMS, Jon Douglas,** B.E., M.A., M.Sc., Ph.D.; educator; b. Saskatoon, Sask. 11 Sept. 1950; s. the late John L. and Leitha Mary W.; e. Royal Mil. Coll. B.E. 1972; Univ. of B.C. M.A. 1978; Stanford Univ. M.Sc. 1980, Ph.D. 1983; m. Ann d. Randall and Clarice Manuel 28 July 1990; PROF. OF EDN. UNIV. OF B.C. 1993– ; Eng. Offr. Candn. Armed Forces 1972–74; Teacher Maple Ridge Sch. Dist. B.C. 1975–77; Asst. Prof. Univ. of Lethbridge 1978–79, present Univ. 1982– ; Hon. Visiting Rsch. Fellow Edinburgh Univ. 1983–85; Spencer Found. Fellow U.S. Nat. Acad. Edn. 1987; Killam Rsch. Prize 1988; UBC Alumni Award 1991; author 'Monitoring School Performance' 1992; co-ed. 'Pupils, Classrooms and Schools' 1991; recreations: golf, squash, swimming; Home: 3722 Quesnel Dr., Vancouver, B.C. V6L 2W8; Office: 2125 Main Mall, Vancouver, B.C. V6T 1Z4.

**WILLOUGHBY, Bertram Elmore,** B.S.A., P.Ag., F.R.I., C.R.E.; real estate broker; b. Georgetown, Ont. 17 July 1917; s. John Armstrong and Florence Elizabeth (Mothersill) W.; e. Pub. Sch. and N. Toronto Coll. Inst. and Northern Vocational (Matric.) Sch., Toronto, Ont.; Ont. Agric. Coll., B.S.A.; m. Evelyn Boddy 1942 (dec. 1966); children: Diane, Beverly; m. 2ndly Mary Margaret Magee 1971, widow with 3 children: Mark, Libby, David; HON. DIR., ROYAL LePAGE LTD.; Pres., Eglinton Roehampton Ltd.; Bertwill Ltd.; with Canadian

Industries Ltd. as Production Supvr., Shawinigan Falls Works, 1941–45; Past Pres., Ont. Assn. of Real Estate Bds. (1952–53); Toronto Real Estate Bd. (1954–55); Past Pres., Candn. Inst. of Realtors (1960–61); Past Pres., Candn. Assn. of Real Estate Bds. (1964–65); Past Pres., Candn. Chapter, Internat. Real Estate Fed. (1973, 74); mem. Nat. Assn. Realtors; Candn. Real Estate Assn.; Ont. Real Estate Assn.; Toronto Real Estate Bd.; Anglican; recreations: golf, fishing, all sports; Clubs: Rosedale Golf; Board of Trade; Club Metropolitan Toronto; Home: 70 Rosehill Ave., Suite 105, Toronto, Ont. M4T 2W7.

**WILLOUGHBY, Ronald Graeme,** B.Sc., M.Ed.; corporate executive; b. Brantford, Ont. 21 May 1930; s. Gordon Marklyn and Helen Duncan (MacInness) W.; e. Sr. Matric. Brantford Collegiate; Springfield Coll., Mass. B.Sc. 1952, M.Ed. 1954; Darden Graduate Sch. of Business Admin., Univ. of Virginia 1970; m. Susan d. Richard and Katherine Lackey 16 Oct. 1954; children: Katharine Helen, Richard Graeme; PRESIDENT, CORPORATE MANAGEMENT CONSULTANTS INTERNAT. INC.; Dir., Arcanco Inc. (an internat. development corp.); Past Chrmn.: Assn. of Candn. Advertisers; Confedn. of Ch. and Bus. People; Dir., The Studio of Visual Artists' Retirement Home; Adv. Bd., Ont. Craft Counc.; Bd. of Advrs. Sch. of Community and Public Affairs, Concordia Univ.; Dir. Don Valley West Prog. Cons. Assn.; Dir., Citizens Foundation for the Promotion of Police Community Relations in Metro Toronto; recreations: politics, collecting art, farming; Club: Donalda; Home: 25 George St., Toronto, Ont. M5A 4L8; Farm: R.R. #2, Baltimore, Ont. K0K 1C0; Office: 180 Bloor St. W., Suite 303, Toronto, Ont. M5S 2V6.

**WILLOUGHBY, Russell A.,** D.V.M., Ph.D.; university professor; b. Tilston, Man. 7 July 1933; s. J. Wilfred and M. Christena (Young) W.; e. family farm; Univ. of Sask. Sch. of Agric. 1952; Univ. of Toronto, D.V.M. 1957; Cornell Univ., Ph.D. 1965; m. Peggy d. Stan and Florence Ramsey 1 Sept. 1954; children: W. Douglas, Joanne S., Sandra L.; ANIMAL HEALTH CONSULTANT 1990– ; priv. vet. practice, Grenfell, Sask. 1957–61; Asst. Prof., Dept. of Med. & Surg., Ont. Vet. Coll. 1961–62; Rsch. Asst., Dept. of Pathol., Cornell Univ. 1962–65; Assoc. Prof., Ont. Vet. Coll. 1965; Prof. 1967– ; Assoc. Dean Rsch. 1978–83; Chrmn., Dept. Clin. Studies 1983–86; Dir., Equine Rsch. Centre, Univ. of Guelph 1986–90; Am. Coll. Vet. Internal Med., dipl. 1972; Cons., Pharm. & Metalurg. Indus.; Sec., A.C.V.I.M. 1972–80; author of over 50 sci. articles; Home: RR #2, Elora, Ont. N0B 1S0; Office: Equine Research Centre, Univ. of Guelph, Guelph, Ont. N1G 2W1.

**WILLS, Terrance Ingram,** B.Comm.; journalist; b. Toronto, Ont. 12 April 1938; s. Leonard Francis and Bessie Margaret (Ingram) W.; e. Univ. of Toronto Schools 1956; Univ. of Toronto B.Comm. 1960; m. Béatrice d. Arthur and Josephine Dufresne 29 Sept. 1962; children: Marc, Julie, Jennifer; Ottawa Bureau Chief, The Montreal Gazette 1980; City Editor, The Peterborough Examiner 1961–64; Queen's Park Correspondent, The Globe and Mail 1964–68; Washington Correspondent 1968–71; Ottawa Bureau Chief 1971–74; Aide to Hon. Donald Macdonald as Min. of Energy & Min. of Finance 1974–77; Ottawa Bureau Chief, The Toronto Star 1977–80; Canadian Correspondent, Newhouse News Serv. of Washington 1980– ; Former Pilot Officer, Royal Candn. Air Force; Mem., Soc. for the Preservation & Encouragement of Barbershop Singing in America; contbr.: 'Dimensions of Man' and 'The Silver Jubilee Canada'; recreations: squash, skiing; Home: 904 Stanstead Rd., Ottawa, Ont. K1V 6Y5.

**WILLSCHICK, Leonard Julius,** B.A.; marketing executive; b. Toronto, Ont. 31 May 1945; s. Joseph Heinz and Sue (Urovitz) W.; e. Vaughan Rd. C.I. 1964; Univ. of Toronto, B.A. 1967; MGR., MARKET RSCH./SALES FORECASTING, WRIGLEY CAN. INC. 1983– ; Asst. Advtg. Rsch. Mgr., Ted Bates Advtg. Ltd. 1968–71; Advtg. Rsch. Mgr. 1971–73; Mktg. Rsch. Analyst, Kimberly-Clark of Can. Ltd. 1973–83; Part-time Instr., Humber Coll. 1983–86, 1989–94; Mem., Profl. Mktg. Rsch. Soc.; recreations: thoroughbred horse owner/breeder, weight training; Club: Toronto Thoroughbred Racing (Past Dir.); Home: 500 Glencairn Ave., #408, Toronto, Ont. M6B 1Z1; Office: 1123 Leslie St., Toronto, Ont. M3C 2K1.

**WILLSCHICK, William Martin,** B.A., M.B.A.; investment executive; b. Toronto, Ont. 12 Sept. 1951; s. Joseph Heinz and Susan (Urovitz) W.; e. Rutgers Univ., B.A. 1973 (Econ. Hon. Soc., Rutgers Univ. Chapter 1972, 1973; Dean's List); Univ. of Penn., M.B.A. 1975; m. Kathy d. Alfred and Anna Ellis 20 Apr. 1978; children: Elliott Franklin, Aaron Loren; MGR., CAPITAL FINANCING, TREASURY DEPT., MUNICIPALITY OF METRO. TORONTO 1979– ; Auditor/Acct., Arthur Andersen & Co. 1975–77; Fin. Analyst, Toronto Dominion Bank 1977–79; Mem., Urban Fin. Offrs. Assn. of Ont. Investment Sub-Ctte.; Seminar Conductor; Past Pres., Omicron Delta Epsilon; Jewish; author of var. papers; co-author: 'Investment Policy Report – Urban Finance Officers of Ontario' 1983; recreation: aerobics, cross country skiing; Home: 331 Castlefield Ave., Toronto, Ont. M5H 1L4; Office: 55 John St., 14th Floor, Stn. 1143, Toronto, Ont. M5V 3C6.

**WILLSIE, Harry Alford;** writer, investor; b. Jacksonville, MO, USA 20 Dec. 1928; s. late James George and Lillian (Christianson) W.; USMC 1946–48; e. Univ. of Missouri 1948–53; m. 1stly Suzanne Brilliant 1953–70; children: Billie Wayne; Alan Andre; Carol Dean; Debora Marie; 4 grandchildren; m. 2ndly Cleusa Correa of Brazil Oct. 1982; Sports editor, public relation, Quantico, VA Marine Post Newspaper 1946–48; Radio/TV nat. advt. sales rep., Toronto, ON and Montreal, QC 1953–57; founder, Pres. All-Canada Gun Sales Inc., Mtl. 1957–73; Coronet Guns and Gunsmithing Inc., Mtl. 1960–73; Montclair Fuel Oils, Inc., Mtl. 1964–73; Owner, Mgr. real estate comml. and apt. properties, Canada and US 1974– ; Pres., Centre Sportif St. Janvier Inc. and Sportif 2000 Can. Ldt. 1980–82; Dir., Canarico Quarries, Puerto Rico 1974–83; Editor Rod and Gun Magazine 1965–74; Member Holland Soc., Dutch Soc.; SAR; Arctic Circle Club; Mtl. Anglers and Hunters Inc.; Pres., Candn. Skeet Shooting Assn. 1969–76; Life Member Shooting Fed. Can. (Dir. 1963–83); Dir. Quebec Skeet Shooting Federation 1967–83; Dir. Olympic Comm. Conjoint 1974–76; Can. Olympic Assn. (Dir. 1974–82); Life Member National Skeet Shooting Assn., TX (Extve. Comte. 1966–76, 1990–92; Dir. 1966–76, 1984–92); Life member Amateur Trapshooting Assn., OH (Dir. 1959–68); Pres. Candn. Trapshooting Assn. 1963–67; Dir., Quebec Prov. Trapshooting Assn. 1959–67; Author numerous shooting related articles, Columnist/Writer Skeet Shooting Review 1988–92; Columnist Trap & Field Magazine 1990– ; Holder numerous Provincial, Candn., and World records and trophies at Trap and Skeet shooting; Can. rep. 4 Olympic games, 13 World shooting championships, 2 Commonwealth games, several other major champ.; Coach and Manager Candn. skeet shooting team 1977–81; Mgr. Candn. Shooting team Commonwealth Games 1978; Coach and Mgr. Candn. Olympic shooting team 1980; Bronze medal Master games Toronto 1986; NSSA World Champion Sub-Senior Int'l Skeet shooting 1981, 1982, 1984, Sr. Champion 1989, 90; Gold Medal (record) Commonwealth games, New Zealand 1974; Inducted NSSA Hall of Fame 1986; QSSF Hall of Fame 1991; Hobbies: shotgun shooting, photography, fishing, golf, genealogy, birding; Address: 90 Dupuis, Esterel, Que. J0T 1E0.

**WILLSON, John M.,** B.Sc., M.Sc., A.I.M.E., A.R.S.M., M.I.M.M., C.I.M.M.; executive mining engineer; b. Sheffield, England 21 Feb. 1940; s. Jack Desmond and Cicely Rosamond (Long Price) W.; e. Blundell's School (U.K.); Royal School of Mines (U.K.) B.Sc. 1962, M.Sc. 1985; m. Susan d. Arthur and Mary Partridge 31 Oct. 1964; children: Marcus, Carolyn; President, Chief Executive Officer & Director, Pegasus Gold Inc. 1989; son of a mining engineer raised on a mine in Portugal; educated in England; Mining Asst., The African Manganese Co. Ghana 1962–63; var. engr. positions, The Anaconda Co., Butte, Mt. 1964–66; engr. & supervisory positions, Cominco Ltd. 1966–74 (Sullivan Mine, Kimberley, B.C.; Supt. then Mgr., Black Angel Mine, W. Greenland 1970–74); Pres., Garaventa (Canada) Ltd. 1974–81; Vice-Pres. Northern Group, Cominco Ltd. 1981–84; Pres. & Chief Extve. Offr., Western Canada Steel Limited Vancouver 1985–88; Dir., USMX Inc.; Pres., N.W.T. Chamber of Mines 1982–84; Chrmn. & Pres., Western States Public Lands Coalition 1990–91; Dir., Am. Mining Congress; Trustee, Senior Vice-Pres., Northwest Mining Assn.; Mem., Inst. of Mining & Metallurgy, U.K.; Candn. Inst. of Mining & Metal.; Profl. Engrs. of B.C.; of N.W.T.; Soc. for Mining, Metal. & Exploration, U.S.; Assn., Royal School of Mines; Chartered Engineer, U.K.; recreations: sailing, tennis, squash, cycling; Home: 108 W 29th Ave., Spokane, Wa. 99203-1706.

**WILLSON, William Franklin,** B.Com.; b. Fort Erie, Ont. 25 Oct. 1937; s. Harold Erwin and Mary Stewart (Hunter) W.; e. Fort Erie High Sch. 1956; McMaster Univ. B.Com. 1960; m. F. Joanne d. Edward and Gladys Jewson 6 Aug. 1960; children: Douglas, Jennifer, Andrea, Peter; CHRMN. & C.E.O., WILLSON INTERNATIONAL LTD. 1970– ; with Depts. of Finance and Nat. Revenue Ottawa 1960–67; Sr. Consultant Woods Gordon & Co. Toronto 1967–70; Vice Pres. Planning and Devel. Harlequin Enterprises Ltd. 1970–74, Vice Pres. Finance 1974–78, Extve. Vice Pres. Corporate Operations 1978–79, Pres. Harlequin Overseas 1979–81; Extve. Vice Pres. Rupertsland Resources Co. Ltd. 1981–82; Chief Operating Offr. 1982; Vice-Chrmn. and C.E.O. 1982–83; recreations: riding, fishing; Clubs: Toronto and North York Hunt; Caledon Mountain Trout; East Hill; Goodwood; Ocean Reef; Address: 14 Wolf Cres., R.R. 2, Bolton, Ont. L7E 5R8.

**WILSON, Allan,** B.A., M.A., M.D., Ph.D.; university professor; researcher; b. Vancouver, B.C. 24 Feb. 1945; s. George Sidney and Josephine (Richardson) W.; e. Univ. of B.C., B.A. 1967; Univ. of Victoria, M.A. 1971, Ph.D. 1973; Univ. of Man., M.D. 1981; m. Marilyn d. Rachel and Harold Leo Caplan 17 May 1981; PROF. OF PSYCHIATRY AND PSYCHOLOGY, UNIV. OF OTTAWA & DIR., ADDICTIONS SERV., ROYAL OTTAWA HOSP. 1985– ; Dir., Beacon Hill Lodges Ltd. 1987–89; Dir., Beacon Capital Corp. 1987–88; Dir., Digi-Laser Corp. 1988–91; Dir., ADM Network 1991– ; Captain, Royal Candn. Navy 1961–69; Asst. Prof. of Psych. & Rsch. Dir. 1975–83; Prof. 1985; Dir., Chem. Withdrawal Unit, Health Sci. Ctr., Winnipeg 1981–85; Rsch. Dir., Operation Rsch. Assoc. 1974–76; Gov., Alcoholism Found. of Man. 1984–85; Mem., Rsch. Soc. for Alcoholism, N.Y. Acad. of Sci.; Internat. Soc. for Biomed. Rsch. on Alcoholism; Candn. Med. Assn.; author of over 80 sci. pubns.; Clubs: Rockcliffe Park Lawn Tennis; Ottawa Athletic; Home: 40 Mackinnon Rd., Rockcliffe Park, Ont.; Office: 1145 Carling Ave., Ottawa, Ont. K1Z 7K4.

**WILSON, Barry Kenneth,** B.A., B.J., M.A.; journalist; b. Ottawa, Ont. 29 Dec. 1948; s. Kenneth Samuel and Audrey Kathleen (Brown) W.; raised at ancestral home at Low, Quebec: a farm cut out of the Gatineau Hills by his great, great grandfather, his sons & grandsons; e. Hull Protestant H.S. 1965; Carleton Univ. B.A. 1969, B.J. (Hons.) 1974, M.A. 1985; m. Julianne d. Bud and Theresa Labreche 27 Dec. 1988; one d. (from prev. marriage): Cynthia Michelle Holmes; SPECIAL REPORTS EDITOR, OTTAWA BUREAU, COLUMNIST, 'THE WESTERN PRODUCER' 1990– ; Courts, General Reporter, 'Saint John Telegraph-Journal' 1970–71; Edn., Pol., Dist. Ed., 'The Oshawa Times' 1971–73; Politics (Prov. & Fed.), Health Reporter, 'The Saskatoon Star-Phoenix' 1973–76; CJWW Radio News Saskatoon 1976–77; Grains & Transp. Reporter, 'The Western Producer' 1977–79; Nat. Correspondent, Ottawa Bureau 1980; author: 'Politics of Defeat: Decline of the Saskatchewan Liberal Party' 1980, 'Beyond the Harvest: Canadian Grain at the Crossroads' 1981, 'Farming the System: How Farmers & Politicans Influence Agricultural Policy' 1990; recreations: running (incl. marathons), spending as much time as possible in the Gatineau Hills, snowshoeing, walking, canoeing, reading; Home: 15 – 209 Primrose Ave., Ottawa, Ont. K1R 7V5 & Low, Que.; Office: 402 – 150 Wellington St., Ottawa, Ont. K1P 5A4.

**WILSON, Benson Andrus,** B.Sc., D.U.; retired university and government official; b. London, Ont. 12 July 1926; s. Charles Andrus and Pauline (Teeter) W.; e. Univ. of W. Ont. B.Sc. 1948; Oxford Univ. (Rhodes Scholar) B.Sc. 1950; Univ. of Ottawa D.U. 1984; m. Charlotte d. Charles and Blanche Harrington 5 May 1956; children: Benson Andrus, Meredith Jane; Master, Ridley Coll. St. Catharines, Ont. 1950–51; Canadian General Electric Co. Ltd. 1951–55; Mgr. Mfg. Isotope Products Ltd. 1955–56; Contract Adm. Rogers Majestic Electronics Ltd. 1956–57; Analyst, Supr., Co-ordinator, Mgr. Toronto and Calgary British-American Oil Co. Ltd. 1957–68; Dir. Prog. Review Treasury Bd. Ont. 1968–72; Exec. Dir. Prov. Secretariat Resources Devel. 1972–74; Asst. Dep. Min. of Colls. & Univs. 1974–84; Chrmn., Ont. Manpower Comn. 1984–87; Dir., Foundation Gifts, Univ. of Toronto 1987–92; Comnr. Ont.-Que. Perm. Comn. 1975; mem. Ctte. Future Role Univs. in Ont. 1980–81; Leader, Study Team on Education and Research (Federal Task Force on Program Review) 1985; Dir. Toronto Symphony Orchestra 1970–80; Mem. Bd. of Mngmt., Royal Conservatory of Music 1986–90; Lay Trustee, Toronto School of Theology 1992– ; Treas. Candn. Operational Rsch. Soc. 1959–61, mem. Nat. Counc. 1967–68; United Ch. Sun. Sch. Supt., Elder; recreations: tennis, curling; Club: Toronto Cricket Skating & Curling; Home: 812, 80 Front St. E., Toronto, Ont. M5E 1T4.

**WILSON, Bernard R.,** B.Comm., F.C.A.; financial executive; b. Sault Ste. Marie, Ont. 19 Jan. 1943; s. Raymond Alexander and Alice (Duclos) W.; e. St. Mary's Coll. H.S. 1961; St. Francis Xavier Univ., B.Comm.

1965; C.A. 1968; m. Louise d. Joseph and Ida Lefebvre 25 Sept. 1965; children: Scott, Nicole; PARTNER, PRICE WATERHOUSE, TORONTO 1990– ; joined Price Waterhouse 1965; Mng. Partner of Pub. Sector Serv. & Partner-in-Charge (Ottawa area), Price Waterhouse 1985–90; Sr. Vice-Pres., Price Waterhouse Limited; Dir. & Extve. Counc. mem., Ont. c. of c. 1981–87; Founding Chrmn., Outstanding Bus. Achievement Awards; Treas. & Fin. Chrmn. 1982–83; Spec. Events Chrmn. 1983–85; Vice-Pres. 1984–85; Membership Chrmn. 1983–85; Pres. 1986; Chrmn. 1987; Chrmn. and Pres., Computerized Ont. Investment Network 1986–87; Chrmn., Canada Opportunities Investment Network 1987– ; Chrmn., Ontario Chamber Council of Presidents 1986–89; Past Chrmn., Peel West End Creche; Dir., Mississauga Bd. of Trade 1977–81; Past Dir., Toronto West End Creche; Team Leader, Queen of Apostles Retreat Ctr.; Chief Financial Offr., Canadian Chamber of Commerce 1987– ; author: 'The Banker's Guide to Survival' 1979 and mag. articles; co-author: 'Guide to Personal Property Security' 1985; prolific public speaker; recreations: squash, travel, gardening; Club: Rideau; Home: 1296 Catchacoma Court, Toronto, Ont.; Office: 1 First Canadian Place, Box 190, Suite 3300, Toronto, Ont. M5X 1H7.

**WILSON, The Hon. Bertha,** C.C., M.A., LL.B., LL.D., D.Hum.L., D.C.L., D.Litt.S., D.H.L., D.U.; supreme court judge; b. Kirkcaldy, Fife, Scotland 18 Sept. 1923; d. Archibald and Christina (Noble) Wernham; e. Aberdeen Central S.S.; Univ. of Aberdeen, M.A. 1944, LL.D. 1989; Training Coll. for Teachers, Parchment 1945; Dalhousie Univ., LL.B. 1957, LL.D. 1980; Queen's Univ. LL.D. 1983; Univ. of Calgary LL.D. 1983; Mount Saint Vincent Univ. D.Hum.L. 1984; Univ. of Western Ont. D.C.L. 1984; Univ. of Toronto LL.D. 1984; Univ. of Alta. LL.D. 1985; Univ. of Windsor D.C.L. 1985; York Univ. LL.D. 1986; Univ. of B.C. LL.D. 1988; Univ. of Aberdeen LL.D. 1989; Victoria Univ., Univ. of Toronto D.Litt.S. 1990; Chatham Coll., Pittsburg D.H.L.; Univ. of Ottawa, D.U. 1990; Law Soc. of Upper Canada LL.D. 1991; Mount Allison Univ. LL.D. 1991; Carleton Univ. LL.D. 1991; Concordia Univ. LL.D. 1991; Univ. of Victoria LL.D. 1991; elected F.R.S.C. 1991; m. The Rev. John Wilson 1945; COMMISSIONER, ROYAL COMMISSION ON ABORIGINAL PEOPLES 1991– ; Chair, Candn. Bar Assns. Task Force on Gender Equality in the Legal Profession 1991– ; appointed Companion of the Order of Canada 1992; called to N.S. Bar 1957; Ont. Bar 1959; practised law Osler, Hoskin & Harcourt 1958–75 (Partner 1968); Q.C. 1973; Judge, Supreme Court of Canada 1982–91, retired; Mem., Ont. and Nat. Councils of the Candn. Bar Assn 1970–73; Mem., Bd. of Trustees, The Clarke Inst. of Psychiatry 1972–75; The Toronto Sch. of Theology 1975–81 (Extve. Ctte. 1977–81); Chrmn., Rhodes Scholarship Selection Ctte. (Ont.) 1980–84; Mem. Bd. of Govs., Carleton Univ. 1983–85; Mem. Bd. Dir., Candn. Ctr. for Philanthropy 1981– ; Judicial Ctte., United Ch. of Can. 1985– ; Mem. Permanent Court of Arbitration 1984–90; Ont. Court of Appeal 1975; Supreme Court of Canada 1982; Club: Five Lakes; Home: 147 Rideau Terrace, Ottawa, Ont. K1M 0Z4; Office: P.O. Box 1993, Stn. B., Ottawa, Ont. K1P 1B2.

**WILSON, Brian Edward,** B.Com., C.A.; financial executive; b. Brantford, Ont. 12 July 1955; s. John Alexander and Adela Bertha (Schleuter) W.; e. Brantford C.I. 1974; Univ. of Toronto B.Com. 1978; C.A. 1980; m. Anne-Marie d. Mike and Mary (Nolan) Danylkiw Dec. 1985; children: Victoria, Michelle, Lauren, Katherine; SENIOR VICE-PRES. & CHIEF FINANCIAL OFFICER, NATIONAL TRUSTCO INC. & NATIONAL TRUST CO. 1992– ; joined Ernst & Young 1978; Manager (tax specialist) 1982–90; Dir., Taxation, National Trust 1990; Acting Chief Finan. Officer 1991; Lectr. (Acctg.), Univ. of Toronto 1981–82; recreations: skiing, running; clubs: Adelaide; Home: Oakville, Ont.; Office: One Financial Place, 1 Adelaide St. E., Toronto, Ont. M5C 2W8.

**WILSON, Budge Marjorie,** B.A., Dip.Ed.; writer; b. Halifax, N.S. 2 May 1927; d. Mr. Justice Maynard Brown and Helen MacGregor (Dustan) Archibald; e. Halifax schools; Dalhousie Univ. B.A. 1949, Dip. Ed. 1953; Univ. of Toronto 1949–51; m. Alan s. George and Margaret Wilson 31 July 1953; children: Glynis Marie, Andrea Kathryn; teacher, fitness instructor, photographer, illustrator, writer; First Prize, CBC Fiction Awards 1981; Second Prize, Chatelaine Short Story Contest 1983; First Prize, Atlantic Writing Competition (Fiction) 1986; City of Dartmouth Book Award (Fiction) 1991 (for 'The Leaving'); Canadian Library Assn. YA Candn. Book Award 1991 (for 'The Leaving'); Runner-up, Commonwealth Writer's Prize for Best Book Award (Canada-Caribbean Region) 1991 (for 'The Leaving'); Marianna Dempster Award 1992; Ann Connor Brimer Award 1993 (for 'Oliver's Wars'); Mem., Writers' Union of Canada; Candn. Author's Assn.; Writers' Fed. of N.S. (Extve. 1989–91, Vice-Pres. 1990–91, Executive 1992– ); Candn. Soc. of Children's Authors, Illustrators & Performers (Extve. 1987–93, Recording Sec. 1987–89, Atlantic Rep. 1989–93); author: 'The Best/Worst Christmas Present Ever' 1984, 'A House Far From Home' 1986, 'Mr. John Bertrand Nijinsky and Charlie' 1986, 'Mystery Lights at Blue Harbour' 1987, 'Breakdown' 1988, 'Thirteen Never Changes' 1989, 'Going Bananas' 1989, 'Madame Belzile and Ramsay Hitherton Hobbs' 1990, 'Lorinda's Diary' 1991, 'Oliver's Wars' 1992 (children's novels); 'The Leaving' 1990, 'The Courtship' 1994 (adult short stories); 'Birds Horses and Muffins' 1994 (young adult short stories); 'Cassandra's Driftwood' (beginning chapter book) 1994; Home: North West Cove, R.R. 1, Hubbards, N.S. B0J 1T0.

**WILSON, Dean H.,** P. Eng., C.A.E.; professional engineer/association executive; b. Coronation, Alta. 2 Sept. 1938; s. Milton Percy and Helene Faye (Stokes) W.; e. Univ. of Alta., B.Sc. 1962; m. Paulette d. Fernand and Stella Beaudoin 1 Sept. 1966; children: Natalie, Brian; PRES., AUTOMOTIVE IND. ASSN. OF CANADA 1982 to present; RCAF 1958–65; Engr., Montreal Engr. 1965–66; St. Lawrence Seaway Authority 1966–70; Locweld and Forge 1971; Candn. Wood Council 1971–82; Mem., Assn. of Profn. Engrs. of Ont.; Candn. Soc. of Assn. Extves.; Home: 34 Chinook Cres., Nepean, Ont. K2H 7E2; Office: 1272 Wellington St., Ottawa, Ont. K1Y 3A7.

**WILSON, Donald Laurence,** M.D., C.M., M.A., F.R.C.P. (C), F.A.C.P.; physician; university administrator; b. Hamilton, Ont. 2 Oct. 1921; s. Donald Alexander and Laura Louise (Dressel) W.; e. Hamilton (Ont.) Central Coll. 1935–39; Queen's Univ., M.D., C.M. 1944; Fellow in Biochem., Univ. of Toronto 1946–48; M.A. 1948; Fellow in Med., Harvard Med. Sch., 1949–51; m. Mary Isobel, d. late John Wesley Pierce, Peterborough, Ont., 6 Jan. 1945; children: Mary Barbara, Judith Isobel, John Alexander, Peter Pierce, Helen Elizabeth, Donald Bruce; Dean, Faculty of Medicine, Queen's Univ., 1982–88, retired, (Asst. Prof., Dept. of Medicine, 1952–60; Assoc. Prof. 1960–68; Prof. & Head 1976–82); apptd. to Council of Coll. of Phys. & Surg. Ont., 1960 (Pres. 1965–66); served in Can. with R.C.A.M.C., Feb. 1945–Sept. 1946, discharged with rank of Capt.; Publications: many scient. articles to learned journs.; mem., Kingston Acad. Medicine; Ontario Medical Assn. (Pres. 1973–74); Canadian Medical Assn. (Chrmn. 1976–78, Pres. 1979–80); Gov. for Ont., Amer. Coll. of Physicians 1983–87; Conservative; United Church; recreations: fishing, hunting; Home: 1601 Harbour Pl., 185 Ontario St., Kingston, Ont. K7L 2Y7.

**WILSON, Doug,** B.A., M.B.A.; real estate executive; b. Port Dover, Ont. 28 Apl. 1944; s. Thomas Woodrow and Edith Winifred Rose (Kajewski) W.; e. Wilfrid Laurier Univ. B.A. 1967; McMaster Univ. M.B.A. 1970; m. Patricia d. Albert and Ivy Roussel 16 Nov. 1968; one s. Daniel; Sr. Vice Pres., Residential High Rise Bramalea Ltd.; joined Canadian Canners Ltd. 1967–75; Chesebrough Pond's Canada Inc. 1977–87, Vice Pres. Sales & Mktg.; Bramalea Ltd. 1987– , Vice Pres. Sales & Mktg.; Chrmn. Mktg., Media & Merchandizing Adv. Ctte. Ont. Office Sr. Citizens' Affairs; Home: 43 Iroquois Dr., R.R.3, Stouffville, Ont. L4A 7X4.

**WILSON, Douglas Roy,** M.D., FRCP(C); university professor and administrator; b. Toronto, Ont. 19 Feb. 1935; s. Roy Wellington and Dorothy Erica (Holme) W.; e. Univ. of Toronto Schools 1953; Univ. of Toronto M.D. 1959; Royal Coll. of Physicians & Surgeons of Can. Fellowship in Internal Med. FRCP(C) 1964; m. Jane d. Edwin and Bernice Morgan 19 March 1958; children: Karen, Keith, Bruce, Brenda; PROFESSOR OF MEDICINE & DEAN, FAC. OF MEDICINE, UNIV. OF ALBERTA 1984– ; Postgrad. training in Internal Med., Shaughnessy Hosp. Vanc. & Toronto Gen. Hosp. 1959–64; Am. Coll. of Physicians Rsch. Fellow in Nephrology Boston (Harvard) and London 1964–67; Asst. & Assoc. Prof., Dept. of Med., Univ. of Toronto 1967–77; Prof. 1977–84; Co-ord. of Nephrology 1973–79; Sr. Staff Physician, Toronto Gen. Hosp. 1971–84; Active Staff, Univ. of Alta. Hospitals 1984– ; Councillor, Coll. of Phys. & Surg. of Alta. 1984– ; Bd. Mem., Univ. of Alta. Hosps. & Royal Alexandra Hosp. 1984– ; Fellow, Am. Coll. of Phys.; Pres., Candn. Soc. of Nephrology 1976; Councillor, Candn. Soc. of Clin. Investigation 1974–76; MRC 1988– ; Rsch. Grantee, MRC 1967–86; Edit. Bd., 'Kidney Int'l. 1976–85; Gold Medal, Fac. of Med., Univ. of Toronto 1959; Annual Medal in Med., RCPC 1967; Chair, United Way Campaign, Univ. of Alta. 1988–92; author of 122 articles in sci. journals & 9 book chapters; recreations: skiing, bicycling, hiking; Home: 71 Fairway Dr., Edmonton, Alta. T6J 2C2; Office: Edmonton, Alta. T6G 2E1.

**WILSON, Edwin V.;** publisher; b. Toronto, Ont. 12 July 1940; s. Victor H. and Lillian M. (Laccohee) W.; e. Ryerson Polytech. Inst. 1964; m. Maureen d. George and Dorothy O'Rorke 30 Sept. 1967; children: Heather Ellen, Paul Michael; PUBLISHER, MARKETING MAGAZINE, MACLEAN-HUNTER LTD. 1981– ; Production Manager of 2 business publications, Maclean-Hunter Ltd. 1964–66; Sales Rep., Marketing Mag. 1966–74; Sales Mgr., Marketing 1974–77; Publisher, Canadian Premiums & Incentives 1977–80; Dir., Candn. Ad. Benevolent Soc.; Mem., Candn. Bus. Press Assn.; Affil. Mem., Newspaper Ad. Exec. Assoc.; Mem., Candn. Broadcast Extves. Assn.; Mem., Women's Ad. Club of Toronto; Canadian Rowing Champion 1969; Treas., Campus Consolidated Investment Corp.; Dir., Sturgeon Point Golf Club; recreations: rowing, golf, jogging, tennis; clubs: Sturgeon Point Golf, Argonaut Rowing; Home: 20 Holloway Rd., Islington, Ont. M9A 1E8; Office: 777 Bay St., Toronto, Ont. M5W 1A7.

**WILSON, Eric Hamilton,** B.A.; children's author; b. Ottawa, Ont. 24 Nov. 1940; s. Robert Stephen Seymour and Evelyn Maud (Hamilton) W.; e. Univ. of B.C., B.A. 1963; teacher jr. secondary schs. B.C. communities of White Rock, Nanaimo, Campbell River, Blubber Bay, Powell River and Nelson; author children's mysteries: 'Murder on the Canadian' 1976; 'Vancouver Nightmare' 1978; 'Terror in Winnipeg' 1979; 'The Lost Treasure of Casa Loma' 1980; 'The Ghost of Lunenburg Manor' 1981; 'Disneyland Hostage' 1982; 'The Kootenay Kidnapper' 1983; 'Vampires of Ottawa' 1984; 'Summer of Discovery' 1984; 'Spirit in the Rainforest' 1985; 'The Unmasking of "Ksan"' 1986; 'The Green Gables Detectives' 1987; 'Code Red at the Supermall' 1988; 'Cold Midnight in Vieux Québec' 1989; 'The Ice Diamond Quest' 1990; 'The Prairie Dog Conspiracy' 1992; 'The St. Andrews Werewolf' 1993; novel: 'Susie-Q' 1978; estbd. The Eric Wilson Mystery Club, over 22,000 mems.; subject filmstrip and video 'Meet Eric Wilson,' Mead Sound Filmstrips Ltd. Toronto; subject video: 'Eric Wilson's Canada,' Magic Lantern Commn., Oakville, Ont.; Chairman's Award, Crime Writers of Canada 1990; three times recipient of 'El Barco de Vapor' Award from Spain for sales in excess of 100,000 copies; voted 1992 Author of the Year, Candn. Booksellers Assn.; mem. Writers Union Can.; Crime Writers Can.; Mystery Writers Am.; Crime Writers Assn. (UK); Internat. Assn. of Crime Writers; Candn. Assn. Children's Authors, Illustrators & Performers; Address: 801, 620 Toronto St., Victoria, B.C. V8V 1P7.

**WILSON, Fred,** B.Sc., Ph.D.; educator; b. Hamilton, Ont. 27 Dec. 1937; s. Fred and Mary W.; e. McMaster Univ. B.Sc. 1960; Univ. of Iowa Ph.D. 1965; m. Linda d. Dave and Rose Rothman 13 March 1976; children: Carolyn Siobhan, Stephanie Michaela; PROF. OF PHILOS. UNIV. COLL. UNIV. OF TORONTO 1981– ; Asst. Prof. present Univ. 1965, Assoc. Prof. 1969, Assoc. Chair of Philos. 1971–74, Prog. Dir. Univ. Coll. 1975–79, 1982–83, Vice Prin. Univ. Coll. 1982–83, Pres. Faculty Assn. 1987–90; Visiting Asst. Prof. State Univ. of N.Y. Buffalo 1967; Visiting Prof. (Part-time) Glendon Coll. York Univ. 1983–90; author: 'Explanation, Causation and Deduction' 1985; 'Laws and Other Worlds' 1986; 'Psychological Analysis and the Philosophy of John Stuart Mill' 1990; 'Empiricism and Darwin's Science' 1991; co-author: 'Carnap and Goodman: Two Formalists' 1967; co-ed. 'Pragmatism and Purpose: Essays in Honour of T.A. Goudge' 1980; co-editor: 'Hume Studies' 1990–93; Canada Council Leave Fellowship 1974–75; Connaught Leave Fellowship 1993–94; Social Sciences and Humanities Rsch. Council rsch. grant 1993–94; mem. Bd. Ont. Confedn. Univ. Faculty Assns. 1982–86; mem. Bd. Candn. Assn. Univ. Teachers 1984–86, Speaker Council 1985–90, Vice Pres. 1990–91, Pres. 1991–92, Past Pres. 1992– ; mem. Candn. Philos. Assn.; Philos. Sci. Assn.; Hume Soc.; recreation: cooking; Home: 359 Markham St., Toronto, Ont. M6G 2K8; Office: Toronto, Ont. M5S 1Al.

**WILSON, George Wilton,** B.Com., M.A., Ph.D.; educator; b. Winnipeg, Man. 15 Feb. 1928; s. Walter and Ida Jane (Wilton) W.; e. Carleton Univ., B.Com. 1950; Univ. of Ky., M.A. (Econ.) 1951; Cornell Univ., Ph.D. (Econ.) 1955; Inst. of Basic Math. for Application to Business, Harvard Univ., 1959–60; m. Ina Marie (dec. 1986) d. Harold McKinney, Portland, Ont., 6 Sept. 1952; m. Joan Murdock 16 May 1988; children: Ronald Leslie, Douglas Scott, Suzanne Rita; DISTINGUISHED PROFESSOR EMERITUS BUS. ECON., INDIANA UNIV. 1992– ; Prof. Econs. and Business Adm. 1962–92; Dean, Coll. Arts & Sciences 1970–73; Dir., Transportation Res. Center 1990–92; Pres., Transport, Research Forum; Consultant to various pub. and private organs.; Econ., Bd. of Transport Commrs., Ottawa, 1951–52; Teaching Fellow, Cornell Univ., 1952–55; summer session Instr., Carleton Univ., 1955, 1956; Econ., Dept. of Labour, Ottawa, summers 1955, 1956, 1957; Asst. Prof. of Econ., Middlebury (Vt.) Coll., 1955–57; Asst. Prof. of Transport, Ind. Univ., 1957–59, Assoc. Prof. 1959–62; Chrmn. Econ. Dept. there 1966–70; leave of absence to work with Prof. Gunnar Myrdal on S. Asian econ. devel. in Stockholm, 1961; Dir. of study on transport, and econ. devel. for Brookings Inst. and on Can.'s Needs and Resources for Twentieth Century fund; mem. Presidential Task Force on Transport., 1964; mem. Univ. Study Comte., 1965; Dir., study on rail freight rates & devel. W. Can. for Fed.-Prov. Comte. on Western Transport 1974; author of study for Royal Commission on National Passenger Transportation, Canada, 1992; author 'Regulation of Rates of Common Carriers: Does It Need Revision?' 1956; 'Essays On Some Unsettled Questions in the Economics of Transportation' 1962; 'Output and Employment Relationships' 1957; 'Classics of Economic Theory' 1964; 'An Introduction to Aggregative Economics' Part I 1962; co-author: 'Mathematical Models and Methods in Marketing' 1961; 'Road Transportation: History and Economics' Part I 1962; 'Physical Distribution Management' Part I 1963; 'Canada: An Appraisal of Its Needs and Resources' 1965; 'Growth and Change at Indiana University' 1966; 'The Impact of Highway Investment on Development' 1966; 'Asian Drama' 1968; 'Transportation on the Prairies' 1968; 'Transportation and the Economic Development of Indo China' 5 vols. 1973; 'Economic Analysis of Intercity Freight Transportation' 1980; 'Inflation: Causes, Consequences and Cures' 1982; 'U.S. Intercity Passenger Transportation Policy, 1930–1991: An Interpretive Essay' 1992; numerous articles for various prof. journs.; first recipient A. Davidson Dunton Alumni Award, Carleton Univ. 1975; Awarded Disting. Professorship, Indiana Univ., 1978; Distinguished Member Award, Transportation and Public Utilities Group, Am. Econ. Assoc. 1986; Distinguished Transp. Researcher Award, Transp. Rsch. Forum 1990; Salzberg Honorary Medallion, Syracuse, Univ. 1992; mem., Am. Econ. Assn.; recreations: writing, tennis, travel; Home: R.D. #3, Box 1132, Middlebury, VT 05753-8744, USA.

**WILSON, H.T.,** M.A., Ph.D.; university professor; scholar; lecturer; b. Rutland, Vermont 19 Oct. 1940; s. Henry Thomas and Harriet (Mattison) W.; e. Tufts Univ., A.B. (Hon.) 1962 (Scholarship); Rutgers Univ., M.A. 1964, Ph.D. 1968 (Scholarships & Assistantships); PROF., FAC. OF ADMIN. STUDIES, YORK UNIV. & OSGOODE HALL LAW SCH. 1976– ; Instr. & Lectr., Rutgers Univ. 1965–67; Asst. Prof., F.A.S., York Univ. 1967–71; Osgoode Hall 1969–71; Assoc, Prof. 1971–76; Grad. Fac.: Soc. & Pol. Thought 1973– ; Sociology 1974– ; Interdisc. Studies 1975 (numerous M.A. and Ph.D. supervisions in these programmes); Senate Tenure and Promotion Ctte. 1975–78 and numerous cttes. since 1967; Co-Chair, Occupational Ethics Group 1982–87; Chrmn., PLCY Area, F.A.S. 1973, 1974–1978; Radio Broadcasts CBC Ideas, Ryerson Open College; Fellow (1968) and Asst. Master & Acad. Adv., McLaughlin Coll., York Univ. 1984–87; Dir., Social and Political Thought Programme 1988–90; SSHRCC Assessor; freelance cons.; numerous rsch. & travel grants incl. SSHRCC grants; Adjunct Prof., Cork 1973–74; External Examr., Univ. of Bradford 1979– ; Vis. Prof. and Lectr., Holland, Germany, Sweden, Denmark, Belgium, U.K., Ireland, U.S., Australia, Hong Kong, Japan; mem., Internat. Soc. for the Study of European Ideas; European Group for Organization Studies; Candn. Sci. & Technol. Hist. Assn.; Internat. Pol. Sci. Assn.; Australian and Pacific Soc. for Rsch. on Organizations; Ed. Bd.: 'Philosophy of Social Sciences'; 'History of European Ideas'; referee & editor for numerous scholarly jours. & publs.; author: 'The American Ideology' 1977; 'Tradition & Innovation' 1984; 'Political Management' 1985; 'Sex and Gender' 1989; 'Retreat from Governance' 1989; 'Marx's Critical/Dialectical Procedure' 1991; 'No Ivory Tower' 1994; 'The Legitimacy of Capitalism' 1995; Ed. 'The American University and the World of Scholars' 1967; 'Social Change, Innovation and Politics in East Asia' 1980; over 500 articles, monographs, essays, talks and lectures; recreations: swimming, cartography, architecture, nature, hiking, basketball, reading, writing, film, fin de siècle Vienna and middle Europe; Office: 234 McLaughlin Coll., York Univ., North York, Ont. M3J 1P3.

**WILSON, Harry David Bruce,** B.Sc., M.S., Ph.D., F.R.S.C.; geologist; retired university professor; b. Winnipeg. Man. 10 Nov. 1916; s. Frank Ernest and Elizabeth (McFaul) W.; e. Univ. of Man., B.Sc. 1936; California Inst. Tech., M.S. 1939, Ph.D. 1942; m. Marjorie May, d. late William H. Singleton, 1 Oct. 1941; children: Terry Ernest, Wendy Ann, Mary Elizabeth; Consulting Geologist; Geol., Internat. Nickel Co., 1941–47, 1949–51; Asst. Prof. of Geol., Univ. of Man. 1947–49, Assoc. Prof. 1951, Prof. 1956–81, Head of Dept. 1965–72; awarded Barlow Mem. Medal, Candn. Inst. Mining & Metall., 1959; author of numerous papers in scient. journs.; mem. (1969–72) Nat. Research Council Can.; Fellow, Geol. Soc. of Am.; Geol. Assn. Can. (Councillor, 1962–63, Pres. 1965); mem., Candn. Inst. Mining & Metall. (Chrmn., Geol. Div., 1961–62); Soc. Econ. Geols. (Pres. 1976); Assn. Prof. Engrs. Man.; recreation: water sports; Home: 602 - 255 Wellington Cres., Winnipeg, Man. R3M 3V4.

**WILSON, (John Edward) Ian,** P.Eng., A.R.C.S.T., B.Sc.; energy consultant; b. Renton, Scotland 20 April 1936; s. Edward and Mary Turner McLean (Cunningham) W.; e. Royal College of Science & Technology A.R.C.S.T. (Hons.) 1959; Strathclyde Univ. B.Sc. (Hons.) 1959; m. Anne d. Henry and Janet Heggie 5 April 1958; children: Lesley Anne, Stuart Douglas; VICE-PRESIDENT TECHNOLOGY, CANADIAN NUCLEAR ASSOCIATION 1986– ; var. engineering positions relating to energy in the gas, brewing, food and pulp & paper industry 1959–69; Supervising Thermal Studies Engr., Ont. Hydro 1969–72; seconded to Atomic Energy Canada Limited 1972–73; Supervising Process Devel. Engr., Ont. Hydro 1973–76; co-ordinated Ont. Hydro's input to the Royal Comn. on Electric Power Planning 1976–81; Manager of Public Hearings 1981–86; Bates Medal, Candn. Pulp & Paper Assn. 1967; has been a principal public spokesman for Candn. nuclear indus. since 1985; Mem., Candn. Nuclear Soc.; Internat. Assn. for Energy Economics; Assn. of Profl. Engrs. of Ont.; recreations: writing, swimming; Home: 7 Sheldonbury Cres., Scarborough, Ont.; Office: 725, 144 Front St. W., Toronto, Ont. M5J 2L7.

**WILSON, Ian E.,** B.A., M.A.; archivist; b. Montréal, Qué. 2 Apr. 1943; s. Andrew and Marion (Mundy) W.; e. Queen's Univ., B.A. 1967, M.A. 1974; m. Ruth d. Gerhard and Mary Dyck 24 Mar. 1979; ARCHIVIST OF ONT. 1986– ; Dir. General, Information Resource Management Division, Ontario Ministry of Culture and Communications 1990–93; Adjunct Prof., Faculty of Library and Information Science, Univ. of Toronto 1993– ; Univ. Archivist, Queen's Univ. 1970–76; Archivist, City of Kingston 1972–76; Prov. Archivist, Sask. Archives Bd. 1976–86; Chrmn., Sask. Heritage Adv. Bd. 1978–83; Chrmn. Cons. Group on Archives 1978–80, and Adv. Ctte. on Archives 1984–85, Soc. Sci. & Hum. Rsch. Counc. of Can.; Woodrow Wilson Fellowship (hon.) 1967; W. Kaye Lamb Prize 1983; Chrmn., Grace Mennonite Ch. Regina 1981–84; Dir., Sask. Hist. & Folklore Soc. 1982–85; Sask. Mus. Assn. 1985–86; Pres., Ont. Hist. Soc. 1975–76; Sec. & Vice-Pres., Kingston Hist. Soc. 1967–76; Vice Pres. Champlain Society 1991– (Dir. 1989–91); Mennonite; co-author: 'Canadian Archives' 1980, 'Regina Before Yesterday' 1978, 'Heritage Kingston' 1973; editor: 'Kingston City Hall' 1975; recreations: book collecting, hist. rsch.; Home: 249 Woburn Ave., Toronto, Ont. M5M 1L1; Office: 77 Grenville St., Toronto, Ont. M7A 2R9.

**WILSON, J. Carl,** B.A.Sc., P.Eng.; manufacturer; b. Toronto, Ont. 13 July 1914; s. Jonathon A. and Jean (Carmichael) w.; e. Annette St. Pub. Sch. and Humberside Coll. Inst., Toronto; Univ. of Toronto, B.A.Sc. (Elect. Engn.); m. Dorothy A., d. Cecil H. Keys, 17 June 1939; children: Donald K., Kenneth C., Norma L., Debbi E.; PRES., CARL WILSON INDUSTRIES LTD.; Chrmn., J. A. Wilson Display Ltd.; mem. Illuminating Engn. Soc. (rec'd Distinguished Service Award); Assn. Prof. Engrs. Ont.; Delta Tau Delta; Protestant; recreations: golf, fishing, boating; Clubs: Rotary; Boulevard; Great Lakes Cruising; Home: 657 Broadview Ave., Orillia, Ont. L3V 6P1.

**WILSON, James Kenneth,** B.Comm., C.A.; financial executive; b. Calgary, Alta. 13 Jan. 1953; s. Roy I. and Joan G. W.; e. Sir Winston Churchill H.S. 1971; Univ. of Calgary B.Comm. 1976; children: Jeffrey Nathan, Jaclyn Rachel; VICE-PRES., FINANCE & CHIEF FINANCIAL OFFR., CHAUVCO RESOURCES 1990– ; Staff Accountant, Clarkson Gordon Public Accountants 1976–80; Client Manager, Clarkson Gordon 1980–82; Controller & Treas., Precambrian Shield Resources 1982–86; Treas., Mark Resources 1986–88; Vice-Pres. Finance, Mark Resources 1988–90; Mem., Financial Extves. Inst.; Inst. of C.A.s of Alta.; Candn. Petroleum Tax Soc.; Treasury Management Assn. of Canada; recreations: squash; clubs: Calgary Petroleum, Calgary Winter, Country Hills Golf Course; Home: 2133 Edenwold Heights N.W., Calgary, Alta. T3A 3Y2; Office: 2900, 255 – 5 Ave. S.W., Calgary, Alta. T2P 3G6.

**WILSON, James Richard,** B.A., LL.B.; lawyer; b. Ottawa, Ont. 31 May 1948; s. Norman James and Viola Margaret W.; e. Carleton Univ., B.A.; Univ. of Ottawa, LL.B.; m. Denise Rita d. André Chenail 18 Aug. 1973; children: Marc-André, Marie-France, Nicolas; PARTNER, McCARTHY TÉTRAULT, BARRISTERS & SOLICITORS 1981– ; joined firm 1975; Sr. Counsel, Tax Couns. Div., Dept. of Finan. 2 years; Dir., Dai-Ichi Kangyo (Can.) Bank; Sec., Carolyn Sifton Found.; Dir., Miller Brewing of Canada Ltd.; co-author: 'Ontario Estate Practice,' 'Foreign Tax Credits'; co-editor: 'Canadian Estate Planning and Administration Reporter'; Home: 3 Whitney Ave., Toronto, Ont. M4W 2A7; Office: Suite 4700, Toronto Dominion Bank Tower, Toronto-Dominion Centre, Toronto, Ont. M5K 1E6.

**WILSON, James William,** B.A.; legal executive; b. Bracebridge, Ont. 28 June 1944; s. Bernard Francis and Jean Gow (Stevenson) W.; e. Univ. of Toronto B.A. (Hons.) 1964; m. Lynette d. John and Beverly Devlin 19 July 1969; children: Tracy Elizabeth, Michael James; CHIEF OPERATING OFFICER, FRASER & BEATTY 1992– ; Personnel Supvr., Johnson Matthey and Mallory 1964–69; Indus. Relns. Mgr., Molson Indus. Ltd. 1969–71; various positions wtih T. Eaton Co. Ltd. 1971–76; Dir., Indus. Relns., Vice-Pres., Admin., Extve. Vice-Press. & C.O.O., Pres. & C.O.O., Purolator Courier Ltd. 1976–82; Pres. & C.O.O., Purolator Courier Corp. N.Y. 1982–84; President & Chief Executive Officer Toronto 1984–92; Dir., Air Niagara Express Inc.; Jetall Management Corp.; Vice-Chair & Dir., Metro Toronto Home Care Program; recreations: golf, curling, photography: clubs: Mississauga Golf & Country; Office: P.O. Box 100, 1 First Canadian Place, Toronto, Ont. M5X 1B2.

**WILSON, John Arnold (Jack),** B.A.; executive; b. Abington, Pa. 21 Oct. 1942; s. John Arnold and Virginia Lee (Scott) W.; e. Univ. of Colo., B.A. 1968, M.A. (equiv.) 1968; Cornell Univ. Math. Sociol.; m. Prairie Wickens d. Don and Darlene (Wickens) Escallier 18 Aug. 1984; children: Tammy, Tarn, Rima, Tori Escallier; FOUNDER, PRES. AND CHIEF EXEC. OFFR. RSI RESEARCH LTD. 1988– ; Mgr. Applications Programming, The Brookings Instn. Washington, D.C. 1968, Acting Dir. Social Sci. Computation Center 1970–71; Owner, Operator, Marine Salvage & Towing, Vananda, Texada Island, B.C. 1972–76; Dir. Computer Centre, Malaspina Coll. Nanaimo 1976–77; Pres., Co-founder Coast Projects, Victoria 1978–82; Project Mgr. Manipulator Control Systems, ISE International Submarine Engineering Ltd. Vancouver 1982–83; Founder, Pres. & C.E.O., RSI Robotic Systems Internat. Ltd. 1983–89; taught computer sci. courses Camosun Coll. Victoria; mem. Adv. Ctte., Centre for Earth & Ocean Resource; mem., Dir., ASI; mem. Adv. Bd., NSERC Univ. Industry Chair at McGill; Past mem., B.C. Sci. Council; Premier's Adv. Ctte. on Sci. & Tech.; Remote Systems & Robotics in Hostile Environments; recreations: hiking, tennis, go; Home: 6143 Genoa Bay Rd., Duncan, B.C. V9L 1M3; Office: Pacific Marine Technology Centre, 3 - 203 Harbour Rd., Victoria, B.C. V9A 3S2.

**WILSON, John C.,** D.S.L., B.A., C.M.C.; management consultant; b. Oshawa, Ont. 24 Nov. 1925; s. late Charles Edgar and late Dorothy Decima (Jones) W.; e. Univ. of Toronto B.A. 1949; Univ. of Chicago post grad. studies 1950; m. Annita, d. William A. and Kathleen Wecker 8 May 1954; children: David Brian; Heather Lynne; Devon Wecker; Past Chrmn. & Extve. Partner, Woods Gordon 1967–85; Asst. Div. Chief, Aircraft Branch, Dept. of Defence and Defence Production Can. 1951; Gen. Sales Mgr., Avro Aircraft and Candn. Applied Research Divs., Hawker Siddeley Can. Ltd. 1956; joined present firm 1963; mem. Ont. Inst. of Management Consultants; Past Vice Chrmn., Royal Conservatory of Music; Past Mem., Bd. of Regents, Victoria Univ.; Founding Chrmn., Candn. Inst. for Advanced Research; Past Bd. of Management, St. Lawrence Centre for the Arts (Treasr.); awarded 'Medal of Service' by Corp. of City of Toronto; Hon. Doctorate of Sacred Letters (D.S.L.), Victoria Univ. and Univ. of Toronto; recreations: golf; photography; Clubs: Lambton Golf & Country; Ottawa Hunt & Country; University; Club of Toronto; Home: 75 Valecrest Dr., Islington, Ont. M9A 4P5; Office: Box 251, Toronto-Dominion Centre, Toronto, Ont. M5K 1J7.

**WILSON, John Jeffrey;** farmer, association executive; b. Toronto, Ont. 10 June 1953; s. Jack H. and Suzanne H. (Robinson) W.; e. Univ. of Guelph grad. 1976; Advanced Agric. Leadership Program 1985–87; m. Sharon M. s. Neil and Margaret Stewart 5 Jan. 1990; CHAIR, AGCARE 1989– ; Vice-Chair, 'Field to Table' 1992– ;

Dir., Ont. Fed. of Agric. 1988; Candn. Horticultural Council 1984–89 (Mem., Finance/Membership Ctte. 1990– ); Candn. Pesticide Adv. Ctte. 1989– ; Ont. Food Terminal Bd. 1992; Pres., Ont. Fruit & Vegetable Growers' Assn. 1988; Chair, Ont. Asparagus Growers' Mktg. Bd. 1989; W.H.M.I.S. Advisory Bd. Mem., Min. of Consumer & Corp. Affairs 1990; Mem., New Technology Issues Ctte., Univ. of Guelph 1992; Ont. Min. of Agric. & Food's Adv. Ctte. on Envir. Responsibility 1991; Toronto Food Policy Council 1991– ; Co-owner, Birkbank Farms (300 acre fruit and vegetable crops incl. roadside market); Canada's Outstanding Young Farmer of the Year, Great Lakes Region 1992; recreations: skiing, curling, politics; clubs: Caledon Ski, Hillsburgh Curling; Home: R.R. 3, Orton, Ont. L0N 1N0; Office: P.O. Box 1199, Chatham, Ont. N7M 5L5.

**WILSON, John Mackenzie,** M.A.; educator; b. Toronto, Ont. 14 Oct. 1932; s. John Alexander and Barbara Heloise (Kennedy) W.; e. Univ. of Toronto Schs. 1948; Trinity Coll. Sch. Port Hope 1950; Univ. of Toronto B.A. 1957 (Trinity Coll.), M.A. 1960; London Sch. of Econ. & Pol. Sci. 1959–64; m. Sheila d. Rochfort and Barbara Grange 27 Sept. 1958, div. 1988; children: Christopher, Anna, David; PROF. OF POL. SCI. UNIV. OF WATERLOO 1975– ; Asst. Prof. present Univ. 1964, Assoc. Prof. 1969, Chrmn. of Dept. 1973–79; mem. Council Twp. of The Archipelago 1979–82; author 'The Meaning of Socialism: A Community of Friends' 1971; 'The Blackstone Wilderness: The People Speak' 1987; numerous scholarly articles; mem. Candn. Pol. Sci. Assn. (Vice Pres. 1974–76); Candn. Hist. Assn.; Inst. Pub. Adm. Can.; Anglican; NDP; recreations: sailing, walking, chess, painting; Home: 801 – 265 Westcourt Place, Waterloo, Ont. N2L 6E4; Office: Dept. of Pol. Sci., Univ. of Waterloo, Waterloo, Ont. N2L 3G1.

**WILSON, John Montgomery,** B.A.Sc.; mechanical engineer; executive; b. Toronto, Ont. 3 Nov. 1932; s. John Austin and Edith (Montgomery) W.; e. Univ. of Toronto Schs.; Univ. of Toronto B.A.Sc. (Mech. Engn.) 1955; Centre d'Etudes Industrielles, Geneva 1956; m. Nancy d. Paige Rowell 6 Aug. 1955; children: John, Paige, Kate; ADJUNCT PROFESSOR, QUEEN'S SCHOOL OF BUSINESS 1993– ; Works Mgr. Alcan Canada Products, Kingston, Ont. 1968–71; Dir. Kingston Research Centre, Alcan International Ltd. 1971, Dir. Research Centres 1976, Vice Pres. Research & Devel. 1978–80, Vice President, Personnel 1980–82, Vice Pres. Technology 1982–92; Independent Consultant in Manufacturing Management 1992–93; Dir. Alcan International Ltd. 1978–92; Indian Aluminium Co. Ltd. Calcutta, India 1990–93; Dir. & Chrmn., Management of Technology and Innovation Institute, Ancaster, Ont. 1991–92; Chrmn. Major Gifts, Kingston Hospitals Joint Appeal; Dir. Chamber Comm. Kingston; Un. Fund Kingston; mem. and Chrmn. Kingston Indust. Comn.; mem. Bd. Govs. Kingston Gen. Hosp. (former mem. Mang. Comte.); Dir. and Pres. Agnes Hetherington Gallery, Queen's Univ.; Chrmn. Queen's Adv. Council on Engr. 1981–82; Chrmn. Advs. Counc. To Deans of Eng. in Ont. 1985–86; Delta Tau Delta (Pres. Toronto Chapter 1954–55); Protestant; Home: 14 Sydenham St., Kingston, Ont. K7L 3G9; Office: Queen's Univ., Dunning Hall, Kingston, Ont. K7L 3N6.

**WILSON, Keith George,** M.A., Ph.D.; university professor; b. London, Eng. 15 Dec. 1945; s. George Harry and Mabel May (Garwood) W.; e. City of London Sch. 1964; Magdalene Coll. Cambridge B.A. 1967 (Exhn. in Eng. 1964–67), M.A. 1970; Queen's Univ. Kingston M.A. 1969, Ph.D. 1973; m. April Kathleen d. Walter and Kathleen London 11 Feb. 1983; two s. Neil George Douglas, James Andrew London; PROF. OF ENGLISH, UNIV. OF OTTAWA 1990– , mem. Sch. Grad. Studies & Rsch. 1980– ; Lectr. in Eng. The Royal Univ. of Malta 1972–74; Instr. in Eng. Carleton Univ. 1974–76; Asst. Prof. present Univ. 1976, Assoc. Prof. 1982, Dir. Grad. Studies in Eng. 1985–87; recipient Ont. Grad. Fellowship 1969–70; Can. Council Doctoral Fellowship 1970–72; SSHRCC & Univ. of Ottawa Rsch. Grants 1980, 1981, 1986, 1988; author 'Thomas Hardy On Stage' (Macmillan, 1994); numerous articles and reviews 19th and 20th Century lit. various lit. jours.; editorial advisory boards, 'English Literature in Transition' 1990– ; 'English Studies in Canada' 1993– ; newspaper book reviews, Ottawa Citizen, Toronto Globe and Mail; mem. Modern Lang. Assn. Am.; Assn. Candn. Univ. Teachers Eng.; Thomas Hardy Soc.; Victorian Studies Assn.; Soc. for Theatre Research; Cambridge Soc.; Bd. of Dirs., Andrew Fleck Child Centre 1989–93; recreation: family; Home: 74 Glen Ave., Ottawa, Ont. K1S 2Z9; Office: 175 Waller St., Ottawa, Ont. K1N 6N5.

**WILSON, Lawrence J.,** FCIT, CITT; retailing & horticulture management executive; b. Peterborough, Ont. 25 Sept. 1935; s. John and Gwendolyn Elizabeth W.; e. Peterborough Collegiate; York Univ.; m. Geraldine E. d. L.C. Williams 26 May 1962; children: Lisa Elizabeth, Michael Gordon; PRES., SHERIDAN NURSERIES LTD. and PRES., TERMINAL MANAGEMENT LTD.; Past Pres., Candn. Transportation Education Found.; Candn. Inst. of Traffic & Transportation; Dir., Peterborough County Coalition of Cottage Assns.; Fellow, Chartered Inst. of Transport; Office: R.R. 4, Georgetown, Ont. L7G 4S7.

**WILSON, Very Rev. Lois M.,** O.C., O.Ont., D.D., D.C.L., D.Hum.L., LL.D., S.T.D.; minister of religion; b. Winnipeg, Man. 8 Apr. 1927; d. Rev. Edwin Gardiner Dunn and Ada Minnie (Davis) Freeman; e. Kelvin High Sch., Winnipeg; United Coll., Winnipeg B.A. 1947, B.D. 1969; Hon. D.D.: Wycliff, Toronto 1983; United Theological Coll., Montreal 1978; Queen's Univ. 1984; Univ. of Winnipeg 1986; Victoria Univ., Toronto 1978; Mount Allison Univ. 1988; Hon. D.C.L.: Acadia Univ. 1984; Hon. D.Hum.L. Mt. St. Vincent, Halifax 1984; Hon. LL.D. Trent Univ. 1984; Dalhousie Univ. 1989; Ripon College, Wisconsin S.T.D. 1992; m. Rev. Dr. Roy F. s. Peter and Jessie W.; children: Ruth, Jean, Neil, Bruce; 10 grandchildren; National Vice-Pres. UNIFEM 1993– ; Hon. Mem., Candn. Ctte. for 50th Anniversary of United Nations 1993– ; Adv. Bd., Candn. Woman Studies Journal (York Univ./Toronto) 1993– ; Centre for Studies in Religion & Society (Univ. of Victoria, B.C.) 1991– ; Chancellor, Lakehead Univ. 1991– ; Chair, Urban Rural Mission (Canada) 1990– ; Mem., CCIC Team monitoring El Salvador elections (March 20) 1994; Community Assoc. to Social Planning Council, Metro Toronto; o. United Ch. minister 1965; shared pastorates with Rev. Roy Wilson in Winnipeg 1954–60, Thunder Bay 1960–69, Hamilton 1969–78, Kingston 1978–80; first woman Pres. Candn. Counc. of Churches 1976–79; first woman Moderator United Ch. of Canada 1980–82; Co-Dir., Ecumenical Forum of Can. 1983–89; first Candn. Pres. World Counc. of Churches 1983–91; McGeachy Sr. Scholar, The United Church of Canada 1989–91; Candn. rep. Project Ploughshares, U.N. Special Sessions on Disarmament 1978, 1982; Offr. Ont. Human Rights Comn., Niagara Region 1973; Candn. Del. to Washington, D.C. for confs. on Women/Religion/Devel. with women from five world religions 1976; Lectr. on Mission/Ecumenism, Vancouver Sch. of Theol., Queen's Theol. Coll.; author: 'Turning the World Upside Down' 1989; 'Like a Mighty River' 1981; 'Telling Her Story' 1992; 'Miriam, Mary and Me' 1992; documentation on Third World; numerous articles for Internat. Review of Mission 1980–84; 'Town Talk Manual' (for Candn. Assn. of Adult Edn.) 1971; Bible Study booklets (for Candn. Counc. of Churches' 1961–64; Bd. Mem., Amnesty Internat. 1978–88; Bd. mem.: Candn. Inst. for Internat. Peace and Security 1984–88; Candn. Assoc. for Adult Educ. 1986–90; C.A.W. Public Review Bd. 1986– ; Federal Environmental Panel (Concept of the Disposal of Nuclear Waste, Govt. of Canada) 1989– ; Vice Pres., Civil Liberties Assoc. of Can. 1987– ; pioneered use of T.V. in community edn. through 'Town Talk' Thunder Bay, Ont. 1967; United Ch. del. to U.N. Conf. on Human Settlements 1976; extensive travel incl. 3–month teaching assignment India 1975; visits to all continents 1972– ; led study tour for Candn. theological students to USSR 1985, to Uruguay, Argentina, Chile 1986, to China 1987, to Africa 1988; Mem. Group of 78 to devel. alternate foreign policy for Can. 1980; Pres., Candn. Ctte. for Scientists and Scholars, Human Rights Comn. 1984 (Pres. 1985–89); panel mem. Refugee Status Adv. Ctte. 1984–89; Dir. Elizabeth Fry, Hamilton 1976–79; Pres. Thunder Bay Social Planning Counc. 1967–68; Bd. of Regents, Victoria Univ. 1990– ; Patron, New Directions 1989–92; Hon. Pres. Student Christian Movement of Can. 1976–83; Order of Can. 1984; Order of Ontario 1991; World Federalists Peace Award 1985; Pearson Peace Medal, UN Assn. of Can. 1985; Dip. in Production of TV Prog. Ryerson Tech. Inst., Toronto 1974; recreations: skiing, reading, canoeing, skiing; Home/Office: 482 Markham St., Toronto, Ont. M6G 2L3.

**WILSON, Lynton Ronald,** M.A.; executive; b. Port Colborne, Ont. 3 Apr. 1940; s. Ronald Alfred and Blanche Evelyn (Matthews) W.; e. Port Colborne High Sch.; McMaster Univ. B.A. 1962; Cornell Univ. M.A. 1967; m. Brenda Jean d. Dr. J. Howard Black 23 Dec. 1968; children: Edward Ronald, Margot Jean, Jennifer Lyn; CHRMN., PRES. & C.E.O., BCE INC. 1993– ; Chrmn., Montreal Trustco Inc.; Tele-Direct (Pubs) Inc.; HIPAC (Howe Inst. Policy Adv. Ctte.); Dir., BCE Inc., Bell Canada; Northern Telecom Ltd.; BCE Mobile Communications Inc.; BCE Canada Internat. Inc.; Tate & Lyle PLC, London, Eng.; Chrysler Canada Ltd.; Chrysler Corporation; Stelco Inc.; Gov., McGill University; Olympic Trust of Canada; Asst. Comm. Secy. Candn. Embassy Vienna 1963–65; Second Secy. Tokyo 1967–68; Teaching Asst. Cornell Univ. 1968–69; Corporate Econ. John Labatt Ltd., London, Ont. 1969–70, Dir. of Econ. Research 1970–71; Co-ordinator, Indust. R & D Policy, Ministry of State, Science & Technol. Ottawa 1972; Strategic Planning and Devel. MacMillan Bloedel Ltd. Vancouver 1973–74, Vice Pres. and Dir. MacMillan Bloedel Enterprises Inc. Boston, Mass. 1974–77; Extve. Dir. Ministry of Industry & Tourism Ont., Toronto 1977–78, Depy. Min. of Industry & Tourism 1978–81; Pres. & C.E.O. Redpath Industries Ltd. 1981–88; Managing Dir., North Am. Tate & Lyle plc 1986–89; Chrmn. of Bd., Redpath Industries Ltd. 1988–89; Vice Chrmn., The Bank of Nova Scotia 1989–90; Pres. & C.O.O., BCE Inc. 1990–92; Pres. & C.E.O., BCE Inc. 1992–93; recreations: golf, skiing; Clubs: York; Toronto; Toronto Golf; Rideau (Ottawa); Mount Royal; Mount Bruno; University (Montreal); Royal Montreal Golf; Home: 1321 Sherbrooke St. W., Apt. A-110, Montreal, Que. H3G 1J4; Office: 1000, rue de la Gauchetière, Montréal, Que. H3B 4Y7.

**WILSON, Margo Ings,** M.A., Ph.D., M.S.L.; research psychologist; b. Winnipeg, Man. 1 Oct. 1942; d. John Edward Jenner and Edith Helen (Ings) W.; e. Univ. of Alta. B.A. 1964; Univ. of Cal. Davis M.A. 1968; Univ. of London Ph.D. 1972 (Commonwealth Scholar); Univ. of Toronto M.S.L. (Law) 1987; ASSOC. PROF., McMASTER UNIV. 1991– ; Lectr. Univ. of Toronto 1972, Asst. Prof. 1973–75; Visiting Scholar Univ. of Cal. Riverside 1976, Asst. Prof. 1977–78; Asst. Prof. Univ. of S. Cal. 1977; Rsch. Assoc., McMaster Univ. 1978–91; Visiting Scholar Harvard Univ. 1984–85; Fellow, Center for Advanced Study in Behavioral Sci.'s 1989–90; Scholar-in-Residence, Rockefeller Foundation, Bellagio Center 1993; co-author 'Sex, Evolution and Behavior' 1978, 2nd ed. 1983; 'Homicide' 1988; numerous sci. jour. articles; mem. various ed. bds.; mem. Animal Behavior; Am. Soc. Criminols.; Am. Anthrop. Assn.; Internat. Soc. Behavioural Ecology; Human Behavior and Evolution Soc. (mem. Exec.); Law & Soc.; Office: Hamilton, Ont. L8S 4K1.

**WILSON, Marie,** Q.C., B.A., LL.B.; b. Toronto, Ont.; d. Marie (Trotter) and the late Albert Edward Wilson; e. Bishop Strachan Sch., Toronto, Ont.; Univ. of Toronto, B.A.; Osgoode Hall Law Sch., Toronto, Ont.; York Univ. LL.B.; PRES., MARIE WILSON INVESTMENTS INC.; Hon. Dir., Bank of Nova Scotia; mem. Candn. Ladies Golf Assn., Ont. Br. (Past Pres.); Kappa Alpha Theta; P. Conservative; United Church; recreations: golf, music; Clubs: Granite; Rosedale Golf; Canadian; Empire; Windermere Island (Bahamas); Beach Club (Palm Beach, FL); Home: 89 Binscarth Rd., Toronto, Ont. M4W 1Y3.

**WILSON, Michael Clayton,** M.A., Ph.D.; educator and consultant; b. Wellington, Eng. 8 June 1948; s. Cecil Eric and Lucilla (Clayton) W.; e. W. Can. High Sch. Calgary 1965; Banff Sch. of Fine Arts (French) 1965; Univ. of Calgary, B.A. 1969, Ph.D. 1981; Wash. State Univ.; Univ. of Wyo. M.A. 1975; m. Ineke J. Dijks; children (previous marriage): Elisabeth Marie, Robert James Clayton; CONSULTANT & ADJUNCT ASSOC. PROF. OF ARCHAEOLOGY, UNIV. OF CALGARY 1991– ; Archaeol. & Geol. field work in Canada, U.S., Bermuda, Mexico, Cuba, Cameroon, Japan and People's Rep. of China; Field Asst. various agencies incl. Univ. of Calgary, Geol. Survey Can., Prov. Museum & Archives Alta. 1966–71; Field Archaeol. Univ. of Wyo., US Forest Service, 1971–75; Archaeol., Paleontol., Geoarchaeol., Forensic and Land Claims Cons. 1975– ; Instr. in Archaeol. Univ. of Calgary 1979–80, Instr. in Geol. & Geophysics 1980–86; Rsch. Assoc. Museum of the Rockies Bozeman, Mont.; Visiting Prof., Harbin Normai Univ. (China) and Hokkaigakuen Univ. (Japan) 1991–92; Visiting Assoc. Curator, Museum of the Rockies 1993; Main Investigator, Calgary Geoarchaeology Project, 1976–80; Taber Early Man Site excavations Alta. 1978–79; Co-Investigator (with Prof. N. David), Mandara Geoarchaeol. Project Cameroon, W.Africa 1984–86; Rsch. Assoc. Prof. of Archaeol. & Geology, Univ. of Lethbridge 1986; Fletcher Early Man Site project Alta. 1987–91; Gansu Geoarchaeology project, NW China 1987–90; Faunal Analyst, Schmitt Site and Indian Creek Site Projects, Mont. State Univ. 1975–90; Mohler Distinguished Lectr. McPherson Coll. Kans. 1981; Candn. Del. Internat. Geol. Correlation Project (UNESCO); recipient various high sch. prizes; Queen Elizabeth Scholarship Alta. 1965–67; Chevron Standard Centennial Scholarship in Geol. 1967, 1968; Univ. of Calgary 1st Class Standing Prize 1968; Archaeol. Soc. Alta. Award 1969; Woodrow Wilson Fellowship 1969; Hill Scholarship in Geol. Univ. of Wyo. 1972; Izaak Walton Killam Meml. Scholarship 1976–79; S.S.H.R.C. Canada Rsch. Fellowship 1987–1992; Chrmn. 1985–88 and mem. 1983–88 Alta. Paleontol. Adv. Ctte. Alta. Culture; mem. Calgary Zoological Soc. Prehistoric Park design ctte. 1977–82; Adv. Ctte. UNESCO World Heritage Site 1986–90; Can. Soc. Petrol. Geol. Honorary address 1992; CSPG Service Award 1988; author: 'Bibliography of Forensic Science for Fish and Wildlife Law Enforcement' 1979; 'Once Upon a River: Archaeology and Geology of the Bow River Valley at Calgary' 1983; co-author: 'The Big Goose Creek Site: Bison Procurement and Faunal Analysis' 1978; editor: 'Applied Geology and Archaeology: The Holocene History of Wyoming' 1974; 'Alberta Archaeological Review' 1987– ; co-ed. 'Bison Procurement and Utilization: A Symposium' 1978; 'Megaliths to Medicine Wheels: Boulder Structures in Archaeology' 1981; 'Geology of the Calgary Area' 1987; 'The Palliser Triangle: A Region in Space and Time' 1992; editor, Alberta Archaeological Review 1987–92; over 150 articles, reviews, abstracts; Fellow, Geol. Assn. Can.; Fellow, Am. Anthropol. Assn.; Mem., Plains Anthropol. Soc. (Past Pres.); Am. Assn. Adv. Sci.; Candn. Archaeol. Assn. (Past Vice-Pres.); Mont. Archaeol. Soc. (Past Pres., Dir.); Am. Quaternary Assn.; Candn. Quaternary Assn. (Past Vice Pres., Councillor); Candn. Soc. Petrol. Geol.; Soc. Vertebrate Paleontol.; Am. Ornithols. Union and 10 other sci. socs.; Sigma Xi; Phi Kappa Phi; Anglican; recreations: short wave radio, guitar; Office: c/o Dept. of Archaeology, Univ. of Calgary, Calgary, Alta. T2N 1N4.

**WILSON, The Hon. Michael Holcombe,** P.C., M.P., B.Comm.; b. Toronto, Ont. 4 Nov. 1937; s. Harry Holcombe and the late Constance Lloyd W.; e. Upper Canada Coll. 1955; Univ. of Toronto B.Comm. 1959; m. Margaret Catherine d. late Dr. Thomas Hogg and late Marguerite Smellie 17 Oct. 1964; children: Cameron, Geoffrey, Lara; CHRMN., MICHAEL WILSON INTERNATIONAL (internat. business advisory and project finance services); Dir., Amoco Corp., Chicago; Harris & Partners Ltd. 1961–63, 1966–73; Dept. of Finance, Govt. of Can. 1964–65; Exec. Vice-Pres. Dominion Securities 1973–79; el. M.P. Etobicoke Ctr. 26 May 1979; Min. of State, Internat. Trade 1979–80; Opposition Party Spokesman on Industry, Trade & Commerce, for Energy and for Finance; Min. of Finance 1984–91; Min. of Industry, Science and Technology, and Min. for International Trade 1991–93; mem. Exec., Canadian Club 1971–79; Chrmn. and mem. National Exec., Ont. Dist., Investment Dealers Assn. 1973–74; Pres. Metro Toronto Dist. and Campaign Chrmn. Ont. Br., Candn. Cancer Soc. 1973–79; Prog. Conservative; Dir., Canadian Club of Toronto; Trustee, The Aspen Institute, Aspen, Col.; Clubs: The Toronto; Toronto Golf; Badminton & Racquet; Osler Bluff Ski; Albany; Ontario; Office: 181 Bay St., Suite 2370, P.O. Box 875, Toronto, Ont. M5J 2T3.

**WILSON, Michael Paul,** B.A., M.Ed.; university professor; b. Toronto, Ont. 23 Oct. 1943; s. Kenneth Earnest and Ruth Dorothy (Bramley) W.; e. McGill Univ. B.A. 1964; Univ. of Toronto M.Ed. 1980, Ed.D. (forthcoming 1992); m. Nicolina d. Alfredo and Peppina Divito 19 June 1981; children: Gabrielle, Amanda; PROF., THE ARTS, FAC. OF EDN., UNIV. OF OTTAWA 1989– ; Teacher, Lisgar C.I. Ottawa 1977–79; Lectr., Fac. of Edn., Queen's Univ. 1979–81; Head of Arts, Brookfield H.S. Ottawa 1981–87; Co-Chair, Coalition for Arts & Edn.; Bd. Mem., Theatre Ont.; Mem., Candn. Coll. of Teachers; POR; Ont. Council of Drama in Edn.; Candn. Conf. of the Arts; Nat. Arts Centre Orchestra Assn.; author of 37 articles on the arts in education; recreations: skiing, swimming, bicycling, skating; Home: 91 Brighton Ave., Ottawa, Ont. K1S 0T3; Office: Faculty of Education, Univ. of Ottawa, Ottawa, Ont. K1N 6N5.

**WILSON, Paul;** writer; b. Lacombe, Alta. 2 Apl. 1954; s. John Robert (dec.) and Gladys (Hortie) W.; e. high sch. dip. 1972; Lethbridge Community Coll. Cert. in Communications 1974; m. (Common Law) Elizabeth d. Allan and Anna George; two d. Emily, Sarah; LIT. PROG. DIR. SASK. WRITERS GUILD 1981– ; former comm. writer radio Alta. and Sask.; Exec. Asst. present Guild 1979; recipient SWG Lit. Competition 1982, 1986, 1987, 1990; W.O. Mitchell Bursary 1983; Anne Szumigalski Scholarship 1982; author 'The Fire Garden' poetry 1987; 'Dreaming My Father's Body' poetry 1994; co-ed. 'Side Glances: Notes on the Writer's Craft (John V. Hicks) 1987; mem. Writers Union Can.; League Candn. Poets; Regina Guild Folk Arts; recreation: running, volleyball; Home: 2233 Queen St., Regina, Sask. S4T 3C6; Office: P.O. Box 3986, Regina, Sask. S4P 3R9.

**WILSON, Richard Garth,** Ph.D.; provincial civil servant; b. Montreal, Que. 30 July 1945; s. Garth D. and Elizabeth (Morton) W.; e. Sutton High Sch. 1962; McGill Univ. B.Sc. 1966, M.Sc. 1968; McMaster Univ. Ph.D. 1971; m. Susan d. Rupert and Irene Phelps 6 May 1967; two d. Laura Susan, Erica Beth; DIRECTOR OF SUSTAINABLE DEVELOPMENT, B.C. ROUND TABLE ON ENVIRONMENT AND ECONOMY 1990– ; Lectr. and Asst. Prof. Geography McGill Univ. 1970–75; joined B.C. Govt. 1975; Exec. Dir. of Policy and Planning Div., Min. of Environment, B.C. 1989–90; author or co-author various sci. reports and articles profl. jours.; Anglican; recreation: curling, stained glass; Home: 612 Sandra Pl., Victoria, B.C. V9B 4Y2; Office: Suite 229, 560 Johnson St., Victoria, B.C. V8W 3C6.

**WILSON, Robert L.,** B.Com.; manufacturer; b. Montreal, Que. 30 Jan. 1932; s. Robert and Margaret (Neilson) W.; e. Pub. and High Schs., Montreal, Que.; Sir George Williams Univ., B.Com. 1961; m. Dorothy, d. Charles Herring, 2 Oct. 1954; children: Karen Leslie, Robert Graham; Pres. & C.E.O., Dominion Manufacturers Limited 1972; Pres., Rhinekassel Kitchens Ltd. 1988– ; with St. Lawrence Sugar Refineries Ltd. as Vice-Pres., Sales and Marketing, Montreal 1954; Extve. Vice-Pres., and Gen. Mgr., Canadian Electronics Ltd., Edmonton, Alta. 1966; Extve. Asst. to Pres., The Cassidy Group of Cos., Montreal 1967–69;apptd. Gen. Mgr., present Co. 1970; mem. Oakville Chamber Comm.; recreations: golf, music; Clubs: Credit Valley Golf (Mississauga); Bd. of Trade (Mississauga); Bd. of Trade (Toronto).

**WILSON, Roger David,** Q.C.; b. Toronto, Ont. 3 April 1932; s. J.H. Douglas and Beatrice (Avery) W.; e. Chatham (Ont.) Coll. 1950; Queen's Univ. (Econ. and Pol. Sc.) B.A. 1954; Osgoode Hall Law Sch. LL.B. 1958; m. Margaret Macnaughton 11 May 1963; children: Martha, David, Duncan; PARTNER, FASKEN CAMPBELL GODFREY, seconded 1988–91 to Fasken Martineau, London, England; Dir. CT Financial Services Inc. and related Canada Trust cos.; MDS Health Group Limited; and other public and private companies; Secretary, McCain Foods Ltd.; read law with C.C. Calvin, Q.C.; called to the Bar of Ont. June 1958; joined present law firm in 1958, became a Partner 1964; cr. Q.C. 1974; recreations: sailing, skiing, reading; Clubs: Royal Canadian Yacht Club; Toronto Club; Alpine Ski Club; Institute of Directors (London); Home: 68 Heath St. E., Toronto, Ont. M4T 1S3; Office: 42nd Floor, Box 20, T-D Bank Tower, Toronto-Dominion Centre, Toronto, Ont. M5K 1N6.

**WILSON, Roy Gardiner;** real estate executive; b. Coronation, Alta. 4 May 1932; s. Forest Archibald and Florence Mabel (Gardiner) W.; e. Crescent Heights High Sch., Calgary 1950; Olds Coll., Olds, Alta. 1951; Candn. Inst. of Realtors F.R.I. 1962; Advanced Mgmt. Prog., Harvard M.A. 1979; m. Erma d. Clifford and Leila Graham 14 July 1956; children: Keith Roy, Shannon Lee; CHRMN. AND DIR., URBCO INC. 1990– ; Chrmn. & Dir., Mortgage Properties Inc. 1991–93; Pres., Devstar Properties Ltd. 1987–90; mem. founding grp. Carma 1958– ; Dir., Carma 1958–86, Pres. 1971–85; Pres., Chief Exec. Offr. & Dir., Carma Ltd. 1983–85; Alta. Chrmn. National Inst. of Real Estate Brokers 1960; Pres.: Calgary Real Estate Bd. Co-operative Ltd. 1961; Alta. Real Estate Assn. 1965; Co-Chrmn. Property Forum 1975; Chrmn. Residential Devel. Counc., Housing & Urban Devel. Assn. of Can. 1977–78; Pres. N. Calgary Bus. Assn. 1958–59; Pres. Calgary Un. Citizens Assn. 1964–65; mem. City of Calgary Planning Adv. Ctte. 1964–69; M.L.A. 1971–75; Police Comnr. City of Calgary 1976–80; Trustee The Fraser Inst. 1977–78; Chrmn. Olds Coll. Found. 1982–85; Inducted into Olds College Hall of Fame 1988; Home: 136 Scenic Ridge Cres. N.W., Calgary, Alta. T3L 1V3.

**WILSON, Stephanie Ruth,** M.D.; physician; b. Lethbridge, Alta. 24 May 1946; d. Deane Harvey and Ruth Evelyn (Birchill) Smith; e. Univ. of Alta. M.D. 1970; m. Kenneth Foster s. Luela and E. Donald W. 30 May 1970; children: Jessica Alexis, Jordan Deane; HEAD, DIVISION OF ULTRASOUND, TORONTO GENERAL HOSPITAL/THE TORONTO HOSPITAL 1984– ; Head, Div. of Ultrasound, Sunnybrook Medical Center, Toronto 1975–82; Head, Div. of Ultrasound, Walter Mackenzie Health Science Centre Edmonton, Alta. 1982–84; Mem., Candn. Assn. of Radiologists (Chair, Sci. Program Ctte. 1988–91; President 1992–93); Radiologic Soc. of N. Am. (Mem., Sci. Program Ctte.); Am. Roentgen Ray Soc.; Am. College of Radiology; Prof., Dept. of Radiology, Univ. of Toronto; author: 'The Gastrointestinal Tract'; co-author: 'The Liver' in 'Diagnostic Ultrasound' 1991; co-editor: 'Diagnostic Ultrasound' 1991; recreations: golf, tennis, skiing; clubs: Granite, Beacon Hall Golf; Home: 131 Buckingham Ave., Toronto, Ont. M4N 1R5; Office: 200 Elizabeth St., Toronto, Ont. M5G 2C4.

**WILSON, Stephen J.,** B.A.Sc., M.B.A.; bank executive; b. Toronto, Ont. 21 Sept. 1943; s. James D. and Mildred A. (Gausby) W.; e. Univ. of Toronto B.A.Sc. 1966; Univ. of B.C. M.B.A. 1968; F.I.C.B. Toronto 1974; C.S.C. Toronto 1989; m. Margaret d. Bill and Betty Smith 21 Dec. 1968; children: Joanna, Karin; VICE-PRES., CREDIT AND INVESTMENT SERVICES, HONGKONG BANK OF CANADA; Pres., Hongkong-Bank Mortgage Corp.; Pres., Hongkong Bank Securities Inc.; Pres., Toronto-Dominion Leasing Ltd.; Asst. Gen. Mgr., Commercial Banking; Pres., TD Capital Group Ltd. (Venture Capital); Asst. Gen. Mgr., Consumer; Dir., Vancouver Credit Grantors Assn.; Past Dir., Candn. Gen. Capital Corp.; TD Investments Inc.; Derlan Indus.; Past Chrmn., Candn. Bankers Assn., Commercial Affairs Ctte.; recreations: golf, skiing, squash; Clubs: Capilano Golf, Tower Courts, Terminal City; Home: 1075 Eyremont Dr., West Vancouver, B.C. V7S 2B7; Office: 885 West Georgia St., Vancouver, B.C. V6C 3E9.

**WILSON, Thomas Arthur,** A.M., Ph.D., F.R.S.C.; educator; b. Vancouver, B.C. 5 Aug. 1935; s. Victor and Edith (Grange) W.; e. Univ. of B.C., B.A. 1957; Harvard Univ. A.M. 1959, Ph.D. 1961; m. Julia d. Irwin and Loui Dillon 8 Feb. 1958; children: Christine, Arthur; PROF. OF ECON. UNIV. OF TORONTO 1968– ; Instr. Harvard Univ. 1961–62, Asst. Prof. 1962–67; Assoc. Prof. present Univ. 1967–68, Dir. of Econ. 1979–82, Chrmn. of Econ. 1982–85, Dir. Inst. for Policy Analysis 1969–75; Dir. Policy and Econ. Anal. Program 1987– ; Visiting Prof.: Harvard Univ. 1972–73; Univ. of Cal. Berkeley 1975–76; Visiting Sr. Fellow, J.F.K. School of Govt., Harvard Univ. 1986; Visiting Fellow, Wolfson Coll., Univ. of Cambridge 1987; author: 'Fiscal Policy in Canada' 1993; 'Canadian Competition Policy: Essays in Law and Economics' 1979; 'Advertising and Market Power' 1975; and numerous articles in professional and learned journals and government reports; cons. to numerous govt. agencies and non-profit rsch. orgns.; Pres. Candn. Econ. Assn. 1984–85; Office: 140 St. George St., Toronto, Ont. M5S 1A1.

**WILSON, Vincent Seymour,** B.Sc., D.P.A., M.A., Ph.D.; university professor; b. Trinidad, The West Indies 21 Jan. 1937; s. Claude Ellsworth and Lena Jestina (Goodrich) W.; e. Univ. of B.C., B.Sc. 1962; Carleton Univ. D.P.A. 1965, M.A. 1966; Queen's Univ. Ph.D. 1971; m. Marilyn Joyce d. Harold Theodore Ramsey and Mae 5 Oct. 1963; children: Jennifer, Andrew, Timothy; PROF. OF POLITICAL SCIENCE, CARLETON UNIV. 1982– ; Public Servant, Govt. of B.C. 1962–64; Extve. Interchange (Govt. of Can.); Treas. Bd. of Can. 1973–74; Fed.-Prov. Relns. Office 1974–76; Acting Dir., Sch. of Pub. Admin., Carleton Univ. 1976–77; Assoc. Ed., 'Canadian Public Administration' 1979–87; Editor 1987– ; Cons. to various govt. agencies, depts. & comns.; Dir., Harambee Found. of Can. 1985– ; Chrmn., Ctte. on Financial Aid and Attendance Grants to Scholarly Assn., SSHRCC 1985–88; Presbyterian; Sec.-Treas., Candn. Pol. Sci. Assn. 1981–83; Mem., Inst. of Pub. Admin. of Can.; Candn. Pol. Sci. Assn. (Pres. 1992–93); Royal Inst. of Pub. Admin. (U.K.); author: 'Canadian Public Policy and Administration Theory and Environment' 1981; co-author: 'The Biography of an Institution: The Civil Service Commission of Canada 1908–67' 1971, 'Issues in Canadian Public Policy 1977' 1974; recreations: gardening, reading; Home: 966 Killeen Ave., Ottawa, Ont. K2A 2Y2; Office: Loeb Bldg., Rm. D685, Carleton Univ., Ottawa, Ont. K1S 5B6.

**WILSON, William David,** B.Comm., M.B.A.; investment banker; b. Toronto, Ont. 6 Feb. 1945; s. William Robert and Margaret Elizabeth (Lavery) W.; e. Univ. of Toronto B.Comm.; York Univ. M.B.A.; m. Shelagh d. Paul and Evelyn Higgins 14 June 1969; children: Amy Elizabeth, Kathleen Shelagh, Hilary Evelyn; PRESIDENT & DEPUTY CHIEF EXTVE. OFFR., SCOTIAMCLEOD 1993– ; Dominion Securities Corp. 1970–71; Assoc., McLeod Young Weir Ltd. 1971–74; Vice-Pres. & Dir. 1975–78; Vice-Pres., Dir. & Mem., Extve. Ctte. 1978–90; Deputy Chrmn., 1990–93; Dir., Rogers Communications Inc.; National Ballet of Canada; Anglican; recreations: skiing, tennis, golf; clubs: Toronto, Granite, Rosedale Golf, Big Bay Point Golf; Home: 17 Chestnut Park Rd., Toronto, Ont. M4W 1W4; Office: P.O. Box 433, T-D Centre, Toronto, Ont. M5K 1M2.

**WILSON, Honourable Mr. Justice William Ernest,** B.A., LL.B.; Justice, Court of Queen's Bench; b. Edmonton, Alta. 17 June 1933; s. Ernest Brown and Marjorie Doreen (Walker) W.; e. Garneau P.S.; University H.S. Edmonton; Univ. of Alta. B.A. 1955; LL.B. 1956; Chief

Justice Horace Harvey Gold Medal, Law 1956; m. Jean d. Thomas and Elena Lees 3 June 1961; children: William Lee, Thomas Edward Ernest; JUSTICE, ALBERTA COURT OF QUEEN'S BENCH 1991– ; called to Bar of Alta. 1957; Q.C. Alta. 1978; Partner, Bryan & Wilson 1959–91; Mem., Uniform Law Conf. of Canada 1970–81; Mem., Bd. of Dir., Inst. of Law Research & Reform Alta. 1976–86; Chair 1979–86; Bencher, Law Soc. of Alta. 1984–90; recreations: riding, hunting, fishing; Home: Edmonton, Alta.; Office: Law Courts, Edmonton, Alta. T5J 0R2.

**WILSON, William Moore,** C.A.; financial executive; b. Glasgow, Scotland 21 May 1937; e. Edinburgh, Scot.; C.A. (Scot.) 1960; m. Margaret Spalding 20 Oct. 1966; children: Andrew, Alyson, Lorna; CHRMN., ALEXANDER & ALEXANDER EUROPE plc; Dir.: Alexander & Alexander Services Inc., N.Y.; Reed Stenhouse Companies Ltd.; Royal Bank of Scotland Group plc, Edinburgh; Am. Trust plc, Investment Trust, Edinburgh; Noble Grossart Ltd., Merchant Bankers, Edinburgh; Group Acct., Stenhouse Holdings Ltd. 1961, Secy. 1964, Finance Dir. 1966; joined present co. 1973, Dir., Vice Pres. Finance, Chief Financial Offr.; Clubs: Royal Scottish Automobile (Glasgow); Caledonian (London, Eng.); R.C.Y.C.; Toronto.

**WILSON-ROGERS, Robert,** B.A., B.Comm., M.B.A.; marketing executive; b. Toronto, Ont. 29 Dec. 1951; s. George (Ted) and Fern Violet (Hill) R.; e. Trinity Coll. Sch. 1971; Univ. of Guelph B.A. 1974; Univ. of Windsor B.Comm. 1976; M.B.A. 1977; PRES., THE ROGERS GROUP 1986– ; Asst. Prod. Mgr., H.J. Heinz Co. of Can. Ltd. 1977–79; Prod. Mgr., Ralston Purina Can. Inc. 1979–80; Mktg. Dir., RJR Macdonald Inc. 1980–82; Vice-Pres., Mng. Dir., J. Walter Thompson 1982–86; Promotion Instr., Inst. of Candn. Advertisers 1986; Mem., Assn. of Nat. Advertisers (Vice-Pres., Publicity 1984); Mem., Trinity College School, Fund Ctte. 1990–, Ctte. of Convocation 1990–93; Gov., Trinity College Sch. 1992– ; Mem., Sunnybrook Hosp. (Marketing Development Ctte.) 1991; Mem., United Way of Metro Toronto (Marketing Ctte.) 1992; The Candn. National Institute for the Blind (Nat. Council Communications Ctte.) 1993– ; Trinity College School (Bd. of Govs. Nominating Ctte.) 1993– ; Home: 256 St. Germain Ave., Toronto, Ont. M5W 1W3; Office: 365 Bloor St. E., Suite 1601, Toronto, Ont. M4W 3L4.

**WINCH, David Monk,** Ph.D., F.R.S.C.; educator; b. London, Eng. 22 July 1933; s. late Alexander and late Lily Ruth (Monk) W.; e. Co. High Sch. for Boys, Ilford, Eng. 1951; London Sch. of Econ., London Univ. B.Sc. 1954, Ph.D. 1957; Yale Univ. 1955–56; Commonwealth Fellow, St. John's Coll. Cambridge Univ. M.A. 1970; m. Mary Elizabeth d. late Henry Edward Scadding 6 July 1957 (divorced 1973); children: Elizabeth Ann, Alexander David; PROF. EMERITUS OF ECON. McMASTER UNIV. 1989– ; Research Assoc. Univ. of Toronto 1957–58, Visiting Prof. of Econ. 1965–66; Special Lectr. in Econ. Univ. of Sask. 1958–60; Asst./Assoc. Prof. of Econ. Univ. of Alta. 1960–66; Prof. of Econ., McMaster Univ. 1966–89; Chrmn. of Econ. McMaster Univ. 1971–77; mem. Ont. Econ. Council 1973–83; rec'd Killam Award 1970; author 'The Economics of Highway Planning' 1963; 'Analytical Welfare Economics' 1971; 'Microeconomics: Problems and Solutions' 1984; 'Collective Bargaining and the Public Interest' 1989; various articles on econ. theory learned journs.; Fellow, Roy. Soc. of Can.; Home: 661 Holt Dr., Burlington, Ont. L7T 3N4.

**WINDSOR-LISCOMBE, Rhodri,** B.A., Ph.D., F.S.A.; university professor, writer; b. Rhiwbina, Wales 5 Feb. 1992; s. Thomas Mervyn Jones, C.B.E. and Philippa Windsor-Bowen; e. Clifton College 1959–65; Univ. of London Courtauld Inst. of Art B.A. (Hons.) 1968, Ph.D. 1972; m. Suzanne d. Gerald and Lillian Dittrich 29 Dec. 1990; children: Owen Gerald Ernest, Emma Lillian Gretta; PROFESSOR OF FINE ARTS, UNIV. OF B.C.; Lectr., Univ. of London 1970–74; Open Univ. 1971–74; Asst. Prof., McGill Univ. 1974–76; Asst., Assoc., Full Prof., Univ. of B.C. 1976– ; Consultant, Dictionary of Candn. Biography, 'Choice'; Fellow, Soc. of Antiquaires of London 1987– ; Trustee, B.C. Found. for Non-Animal Rsch.; Christian; Anglican Ch. of Canada (Rector's Warden, St. Helen's Ch. 1988–91); Mem., Soc. of Arch. Historians of Am. & G.B.; Walpole Soc.; Soc. for the Study of Arch. in Canada; author: 'Age of Neoclassicism' 1972 (major catalogue), 'William Wilkins, 1778–1839' 1980, 'Arthur Erickson Exhibition' 1985, 'The Church Architecture of Robert Mills' 1985, 'Altogether American. Robert Mills Architect' 1994; co-author: 'Robert Mills Courthouses and Jails' 1982; 'Francis Rattenbury and British Columbia' 1983; num. scholarly & popular articles; recreations: reading, music, walking, swimming, drawing, writing; Home: 4684 West 9th Ave., Vancouver, B.C. V6R 2E4; Office: Dept. of Fine Arts, 403 - 6333 Memorial Rd., Vancouver, B.C. V6T 1Z2.

**WINE, Jeri Dawn,** Ph.D.; university professor; b. Agawam, Okla. 8 Jan. 1939; d. Floyd Ray and Margaret Louise (Ayers) Hubbard; e. Lewis and Clark Coll., B.Sc. 1960; Univ. of Wisc., M.Sc. 1967; Univ. of Waterloo, Ph.D. 1970; children: Wendy, Joanna, Jessica; PROF., DEPT. OF APPLIED PSYCHOLOGY, ONT. INST. FOR STUDIES IN EDN. 1985– ; Asst. Prof., Univ. of Waterloo, 1970–71; Renison Coll. 1971–74; Dir., Student Couns. Servs., Wilfrid Laurier Univ. 1974–75; Assoc. Prof., Dept. of Applied Psych., OISE 1975–85, Prof. 1985– , Chairperson 1985–88; Pres., Candn. Women's Studies Assoc. 1988–89; Pres., Candn. Rsch. Inst. for the Advancement of Women 1990–91; Pres.-elect., Candn. Rsch. Inst. for the Advancement of Women 1989–90; Mem., Bd. of Dirs., Candn. Rsch. Inst. for the Advancement of Women 1987–90; Mem., Ed. Bd., Resources for Feminist Rsch. 1981–91; Head, Centre for Women's Studies in Education 1991–92; Reg. Psych., Ont. Bd. of Examiners in Psych. 1977– ; Office: 252 Bloor St. W., Toronto, Ont. M5S 1V5.

**WINEGARD, Hon. William Charles,** P.C., M.P., B.A.Sc., M.A.Sc., Ph.D.; federal cabinet minister; b. Hamilton, Ont. 17 Sept. 1924; s. William and Hilda W.; e. Univ. of Toronto B.A.Sc. (Hons.) 1949, M.A.Sc. 1950, Ph.D. 1952; m. Elizabeth Latham Jacques 9 Jan. 1947; children: William, Charles, Kathryn; Minister for Science, Fed. Dept. of Industry, Science & Technology (Canada's first) 1990–93; Royal Candn. Navy 1942–45; var. professorial & admin. positions, Univ. of Toronto 1950–64; Asst. Dean, Sch. of Grad. Studies 1964–66; Acting Dean 1966–67; Visiting Prof., Univ. of Cambridge (U.K.) 1959–60; Pres. & Vice-Chancellor, Univ. of Guelph 1967–75; Founder, William C. Winegard & Assoc., Engr. & Mngt. Cons. 1984; 1st elected to Parliament for riding of Guelph-Wellington 1984; Chrmn., House of Commons Standing Ctte. on External Affairs & National Defence 1984–86; on External Affairs & Internat. Trade 1986–88; Parl. Sec. to Min. for Internat. Trade 1988; re-elected for riding of Guelph-Wellington 1988; apptd. Minister of State (Science & Technology) 1989; Chrmn., Council of Ont. Univ. 1973–74; Ont. Council on Univ. Affairs 1977–82; Pres., Candn. Bur., Internat. Edn. 1971–73; Alcan Award, Candn. Inst. of Mining & Metallurgy 1967; Fellow, Am. Soc. for Metals 1970 (Hon. Life Mem. 1985); Honorary LL.D., Univ. of Toronto 1973; Laurentian Univ. 1982; Hon. D.Eng., Memorial Univ. 1977; Fellow, Univ. of Guelph 1970; Gold Medal, Assn. of Profl. Engr. 1989; active in Boy Scouts Movement; P.C.; author of introduction to 'Solidification of Metals' (pub. in French, Japanese, Russian & English); author/co-author of approx. 100 sci. papers in refereed journals; Editor, 'Can. Metallurgical Quarterly' 1965–67; recreations: theatre, art; Office: Room 256, Confederation Bldg., House of Commons, Ottawa, Ont. K1A 0A6.

**WINFIELD, His Excellency David John Sydney,** B.A.; diplomat; b. Chesterfield, Eng. 16 Jan. 1941; s. Harold John and Gladys Margaret (Mousley) W.; e. Burnhamthorpe Coll. Inst. Toronto; W. Can. High Sch. Calgary; Univ. of Alta. B.A. 1963; Univ. of W. Ont. Grad. Studies 1964–65, Dip. Internat. Bus. 1979; m. Carolyn d. Jean and Wilfred McManus 6 Aug. 1966; children: Peter John Roland, Elizabeth Margaret; CANDN. AMBASSADOR TO MEXICO 1989– ; served forest products and petroleum industries W. Can. prior to joining Atty.-Gen.'s Dept. Prov. Alta.; Lectr. in Pol. Sci. Huron Coll. London, Ont. 1964–65; joined Dept. Trade & Comm. as Trade Comnr. 1965 serving in The Hague, Ankara and Tokyo; Dir. Latin Am. Div. Ottawa 1976–80; Min. Counsellor (Econ. Comm.) Mexico 1980–83; Dep. Consul Gen. New York 1983–85; Vice Pres. (Invest. Devel.) Invest. Can. 1985–87; Min. (Econ. Comm.) Tokyo 1987–89; mem. Candn. Soc., N.Y.; St. Andrews Soc., Mexico; Brit. & Commonwealth Soc., Mexico; recreations: sailing, scuba diving, tennis, golf; Club: University (Mexico); Club de Golf Bellavista (Mexico); Office: Schiller 529, Apartado 105-05, 11580 Mexico, D.F.

**WINHAM, Gilbert Rathbone;** university professor; b. Flushing, Long Island, N.Y. 11 May 1938; s. Alfred Rathbone and Margery Rankin (Post) W.; e. Bowdoin Coll., B.A. 1959; Univ. Manchester, Diploma Internat. Law 1965; Univ. North Carolina (Chapel Hill), Ph.D. 1968; m. Linda, d. Elo and Nina Tanner, 11 June 1960; children: Nina Gail; Russell Post; Karla Joyce; ERIC DENNIS MEMORIAL PROF. OF GOVERNMENT AND POLITICAL SCIENCE, DALHOUSIE UNIV. 1992– ; joined Dept. Political Sci., McMaster Univ. 1967; Guest Scholar, Brookings Inst. 1972; Prof., Dept. of Political Sci., Dalhousie Univ. 1975– ; Dir., Centre for Foreign Policy Studies (Dalhousie Univ.) 1975–82; Chairman 1985–88; Visiting Scholar, Harvard Univ. 1979–80; Claude T. Bissell Prof. of Candn.-Am. Studies, Univ. of Toronto 1990–91; Visiting Prof., Colegio de Mexico, May-June 1991; author: 'Trading with Canada: The Canada-U.S. Free Trade Agreement' 1988; 'International Trade and the Tokyo Round Negotiation' 1986; 'The Evolution of International Trade Agreements' 1992; editor, 'New Issues in International Crisis Management' 1987; and articles and edited volumes on diplomacy, negotiation and Candn. economic foreign policy; rec'd. Can. Counc. Leave Fellowship 1973–74; Rockefeller Fellow 1979–80; SSHRCC Leave Fellowship 1982–83; Can. Counc. Killam Rsch. Fellowship 1988–90; served U.S. Navy (Rank Lieut.) 1959–62; Pres., GRW Consultants: negotiation training, lecturing, research services provided to Dept. Ext. Affairs, CIDA, Prov. of Nova Scotia, U.S. State Dept., GATT (Geneva), Internat. Ocean Inst. (Malta) and others; Internat. Trade Adv. Ctte. 1988– ; Chrmn., Nova Scotia Adjustment Adv. Counc. 1988– ; mem., Canada-U.S. Free Trade Agreement dispute settlement panels 1989– ; Ed. Bd., International Journal 1988–92; Visiting Faculty, Internat. Peace Acad. (New York) 1981–85; Research Coordr., Royal Comn. on the Economic Union and Developmental Prospects for Canada 1983–85; mem. Candn. Inst. Internat. Affairs, Toronto (Chrmn., Halifax Branch 1978–82); Candn. Political Sci. Assn. (Bd. Dirs. 1974–76); Candn. Civil Liberties Assn.; recreations: sailing; gentlemen's hockey; Club: Bedford Basin Yacht; Home: 120 Shore Dr., Bedford, N.S. B4A 2E1; Office: Dept. Political Sci., Dalhousie Univ., Halifax, N.S. B3H 4H6.

**WINKLER, Donald;** film director and writer; b. Winnipeg, Man. 20 Apr. 1940; s. Morley and Dorothy (Wire) Winkler; e. Univ. of Man., B.A. 1961; Yale Drama Sch.; joined Nat. Film Bd. 1967; directed: 'Doodle Film' 1970, 'Bannerfilm' 1972; 'In Praise of Hands' 1974, 'Travel Log' 1978, 'Earle Birney: Portrait of a Poet' 1981, 'F.R. Scott: Rhyme and Reason' 1982, 'The Scholar in Society: Northrop Frye in Conversation' 1984, 'Poet: Irving Layton Observed' 1986, 'Al Purdy: "A Sensitive Man"' 1988; 'Winter Prophecies: The Poetry of Ralph Gustafson' 1988; 'Still Waters: The Poetry of P.K. Page' 1990; 'Breaking a Leg: Robert Lepage and the Echo Project' 1992; publications: 'Rose and Thorn: Selected poems of Roland Giguère' (transl.) 1988; Woodrow Wilson Fellow 1961; Home: 3640 Clark St., Montreal, Que. H2X 2S2; Office: P.O. Box 6100, Station A, Montreal, Que. H3C 3H5.

**WINKLER, Warren Keith,** Q.C., LL.M.; lawyer; b. Virden, Man. 10 Dec. 1938; s. Anthony Valentine and the late Eulalia May (Stephenson) W.; e. Univ. of Man. B.A. 1959; Osgoode Hall Law Sch. LL.B. 1962, LL.M. 1964; m. Ruth Eleanor Killam d. of the late Albert J. G. Wilson, Q.C., Toronto, Ont. 8 July 1967; two d. Julia Christine, Janet Lynn; PARTNER, WINKLER, FILION & WAKELY; practice restricted to Labour Relations Law on behalf of management; called to Bar of Ont. 1965; cr. Q.C. 1977; Certified as a specialist in Civil Litigation by the Law Soc. of Upper Can. 1988; Dir. Prepaid Legal Services Program of Can., Faculty of Law, Univ. of Windsor 1979–84; author various publs.; Co-editor, 'Canadian Labour Law Journal'; mem. of the Editorial Advisory Bd., Labour Times 1991– ; mem. Law Soc. Upper Can. (Co-Chrmn. Continuing Educ. Program in Labour Relations Law 1973– ); Participant, Law Society of Upper Canada Special Lectures on Employment Law (1976); Candn. Bar Assn. (Nat. Extve. 1973–75; Extve. Comte. Ont. Br. 1972–74; Past Chrmn. Nat. Labour Relations Sec. 1969–71, Ont. Labour Relations Section 1965–67; Nat. Prepaid Legal Services 1973– ; Founding Chair, Environmental Law Section; Special Comte. on Prepaid Legal Services, Ont. Branch 1973–79; Special Comte. on Judiciary Ont. Br. 1977–79); Ont. Labour Relations Section 1965– ; Mem., Ont. Pensions & Benefits Sect. 1987– ; Mem., Metropolitan Toronto Bd. of Trade Labour Relations Comte., 1966–85; Mem., Assoc. of Pension Lawyers; Advocates' Soc.; County of York Law Assoc.; Chrmn., Bd. of Dirs., Long Point Waterfowl & Wetlands Rsch. Fund 1988– ; Mem., Ontario Labour Relations Act Reform Committee 1991; Life Fellow, Foundation for Legal Research 1992; recreations: shooting, fishing, farming; Clubs: Caledon Mountain Trout; Canard Duck; University; Goodwood; The Bluffs Hunting; Home: 254 Lytton Blvd., Toronto, Ont. M5N 1R6 and Tamarack Farms, R.R. 3, Markdale, Ont.; Office: 390 Bay St., Suite 1800, Toronto, Ont. M5H 2G3.

**WINNETT, William W.,** B.Comm., C.A., R.I.C.; financial consultant; b. Toronto, Ont. 17 Sept. 1931; s. Frederick V. and Margaret J. (Taylor) W.; e. Univ. of

Toronto Schools 1946–51; Carleton Univ. B.Comm. 1955; C.A. 1960; R.I.C. 1982; m. Doreen d. Niilo and Laura 29 Sept. 1962; children: Allison, Andrea, Lesley; PRES., WINNETT MANAGEMENT INC. 1979– ; various financial positions 1960–79; Pres., Pacific Rim Publications Inc. and Dorbert Holdings Ltd. 1979–82; Treas. & Comptroller, B.C. Hydro & Power Authority 1982–92; current: Chief Financial Officer, B.C. Treaty Commission; Pres., Vancouver's Baseball Club Inc.; Past Mem., 9d Adv. Bds. to fed. & prov. govts.; current: Pacific N.W. Econ. Partnership; B.C. Sci. Council Spark Fiscal Adv. Ctte.; Past Dir., Pacific Rim Pub. Inc.; 7 Calif. real estate devel. cos.; Sun Pub. Co. Limited; Candn. Club of Vancouver; B.C. Assn. of Candn. Clubs; B.C. Lions Football Club, Vancouver Canucks Hockey Club, Vancouver's Baseball Club Inc.; Tax Extves. Inst. Inc.; Dorbert Holdings Limited; Inland Pub. Co. Limited; Trove Transp. Limited; Lakeshore Railways Limited; Christmas Fairyland Inc.; Telegram-Maple Leaf Indoor Games Ltd.; frequent public speaker; Gov. Gen. of Canada Commemorative Medal for 125th Anniv. of Confed. of Can. 1993; clubs: Hollyburn Country; Address: 18 – 1925 Indian River Cres., North Vancouver, B.C. V7G 2P7.

**WINNIK, M.A.,** B.A., Ph.D.; professor of chemistry; b. Milwaukee, Wisc. 17 July 1943; s. Donald E. and Sondra (Himmelreich) W.; e. Yale Univ. B.A. 1965; Columbia Univ. Ph.D. 1969; m. Dr. Françoise d. Charlotte and Aimé Walliser 24 Apr. 1980; PROF., DEPT. OF CHEM., UNIV. OF TORONTO 1980– ; Pub. Health Serv. Post-doct. Fellowship, Calif. Inst. of Technol. 1969–70; Asst. Prof., Dept. of Chem., Univ. of Toronto 1970–75; Assoc. Prof. 1975–80; Prof. Associé, Univ. of Bordeaux (France) 1977–78; World Trade Fellow, IBM (San José) 1982; Fellow of the Japan Soc. for the Promotion of Sci., Tokyo Inst. of Technol. 1985–86; Ed. Adv. Bd., 'Macromolecules' 1983–85; 'J. Polym. Sci. Polym. Phys. Ed.' 1991–94; 'Can. J. Chem.' 1991; A.A. Vernon Mem. Lectr., Northeastern Univ., Boston, MA 1983; The Xerox Lectures, Univ. of Victoria 1987; author: 'Photophysical and Photochemical Tools in Polymer Science' 1986 and 200 rsch. pubs.; co-author: (with Y. Wang and F. Haley) 'Latex Film Formation at the Molecular Level: The Effect of Coalescing Aids on Polymer Diffusion' awarded first prize in 1991 Roon Award competition; rsch. activities in polymer sci., spec. in the study of interfaces in high tech. materials; Office: 80 St. George St., Toronto, Ont. M5S 1A1.

**WINNING, David R.;** filmmaker; b. Calgary, Alta. 8 May 1961; s. Martin D. and Fay E. (Rodney) W.; e. William Aberhart H.S. 1978; Univ. of Calgary; began making films at age 10; Film Prod.: 'Canadian Ski Patrol' 1976 Documentary/Industrial, 'Return' 1976, 'The Visitors' 1977, 'In Search of the Last Frame' 1977, 'Game Over' 1978, 'Sequence' 1980 (Can. Counc. grant), 'Rat Patrol' 1980 Commercial; Producer, Dir. & Screenwriter, 'STORM' 1987 (Winner of Five 1986 A.M.P.I.A. Awards incl. Best Prodn. of Festival and Best Feature Drama) expanded to feature length for 1988 U.S. release and 1989 video; 'KILLER IMAGE' 1992, Paramount Feature release (Michael Ironside, M. Emmet Walsh) Finalist, Houston Internat. Film Festival; TV Prod., 'Profile' 1981–82, 1987–88, 'All Star Comedy' 1982, 'Storm: In The Making' 1985 Documentary, 'Screening Room' (Film news) 1988–89, 'The Sweetest Sting' 1989, 'Scarlet Cinema' 1989 and 'Jack In The Box' 1990 (three episodes of Paramount's 'Friday the 13th: The Series' Three nominations: Best Director, 1989 and 1990 Gemini Awards, Canada; Winner of Special Jury Award for Direction, 1989 A.M.P.I.A. Awards; Internat. Television Movie Festival, Mount Freedom, NJ Awards: 'Scarlet Cinema' Best Fantasy/Science Fiction Production Short Subject Award 1989 and 'The Sweetest Sting' Special Merit Award 1989); Two Silver Hugo Awards, 25th Chicago Internat. Film Fest.; Finalist, 1991 New York Festivals for Direction (Friday the 13th Cycle 3); 1991, Episodic Drama; Cannell Films Series 'Street Justice'; Seven 1-hour episodes, 92/93 season. Carl Weathers Syndicated Action Series; Family Drama; 'Neon Rider' 1-hour for Atlantis/AVR; 'MATRIX' 1-hour anthology, USA Network; 'Afraid of the Dark?' 5 episodes, Youth Anthology, NICKELODEON/YTV Canada 1993; Sessional Instr., Film Hist., Univ. of Calgary 1986–87; author: 'Request Line' 1982, 'Storm' 1983, 'Killer Image' 1990 (feature-length motion picture screenplays) and num. short film scripts & children's stories; festivals include: Cannes 1985, 1987, World Film Fest. 1985; Berlin 1986; Vancouver Expo; Banff Television Festival 1988, 1989; Houston Internat. Film Festival 1992; Active Mem., Director's Guild of Can.; Alta. Motion Picture Industries Assoc.; Address: Groundstar Entertainment Corp., Suite 4001, 918 – 16th Ave. N.W., Calgary, Alta. T2M 0K3.

**WINOGRAD, Charles Martin,** B.A., M.B.A., C.F.A.; financial executive; b. Winnipeg, Man. 28 Jan. 1948; s. Neville and Grace (Maza) W.; e. Kelvin H.S.; Univ. of Man., B.A. 1969; Univ. of West. Ont., M.B.A. 1971, C.F.A. 1979; m. Libby Eileen Rosner 27 Aug. 1970; children: Angus, Lev; CHRMN. & CHIEF EXTVE. OFFR., RICHARDSON GREENSHIELDS OF CAN. LIMITED 1987– ; joined Richardson Securities of Can. 1971; Greenshields Inc. 1974; Richardson Securities of Can. 1977; Vice-Pres. & Dir. 1982; Extve. Vice-Pres. & Chief Op. Offr. 1986; Dir., Richardson Greenshields of Canada Limited; Richardson Greenshields Securities Inc.; Sceptre Resources Ltd.; recreations: golf, skiing; Clubs: Winnipeg Squash; Fitness Inst.; The National; Maple Downs Golf & Country; Home: 2 Teakwood Grove, Don Mills, Ont. M3B 2J1; Office: 130 Adelaide St. W., Ste. 1200, Toronto, Ont. M5H 1T8.

**WINSON, Anthony Robert,** M.A., Ph.D.; university professor; b. Asbestos, Que. 15 Oct. 1952; s. Robert William and Dorothy Eileen (Olding) W.; e. Univ. of Western Ont. B.A. (Hons.) 1975 (Dean's Honour List); Univ. of Toronto M.A. 1976 (Ont. Grad. Scholarship), Ph.D. 1982 (Canada Council Doctoral Fellowship); m. Ruth Lesins Dec. 1981; now divorced; one s.: Devin William; ASSOC. PROF. (WITH TENURE), DEPT. OF SOCIOLOGY & ANTHROPOLOGY, UNIV. OF GUELPH 1991– ; SSHRCC post-doct. fellow 1981–82; Visiting Scholar, Ctr. for Rsch. & Investigation of the Agrarian Reform, Managua, Nicaragua 1982; Rsch. Dir., Gorsebrook Rsch. Inst. for Atlantic Canada Studies, Saint Mary's Univ. 1982–85; Asst. Prof., Sociol., Univ. of West. Ont. 1985–86; Asst. Prof., Sociol. & Anthrop., Univ. of Guelph 1986–90; Mem., Candn. Sociol. & Anthrop. Assn.; Rural Sociol. Soc.; Internat. Sociol. Assn. (Extve. Mem., Rsch. Group, Social Practices & Social Transformation of I.S.A. 1990–94); author: 'Coffee and Democracy in Modern Costa Rica' 1989; 'The Intimate Commodity: Food and the Development of the Agro-Industrial Complex in Canada' 1993; and numerous scholarly articles; recreations: canoeing, fishing, photography, sailing; Home: 6 Prospect Ave., Guelph, Ont. N1E 4W6; Office: Guelph, Ont. N1G 2W1.

**WINSOR, Hugh Fraser,** B.A.; journalist; b. Saint John, N.B. 18 Apr. 1938; s. Allan Lacey and Jean Mildred (Townsend) W.; e. Queen's Univ., B.A. 1973; Univ. of Toronto 1969–70; Univ. of Ottawa, french language courses; 1st m. Judith Eubank 1963; children: Christopher, Stephanie, Megan; 2nd m. Christina d. Donald and Bertah Cameron 29 Dec. 1988; NATIONAL POLITICAL EDITOR, THE GLOBE AND MAIL 1985– ; numerous positions at The Globe and The Toronto Telegram over the past 25 years covering Candn. politics; Ottawa Bureau Chief, Globe and Mail 1984; Nat. Affairs Correspondent, 'The Journal' 1982–85; Candn. Correspondent, 'The Independent' newspaper (London, Eng.) 1968– ; Press Training Advr., Min. of Information, Dar es Salaam, Tanzania under the auspices of CUSO 1966–69; member of Globe and Mail Team who won the Michener Award 1972–73; Founding Dir., The North-South Inst.; author of numerous articles and broadcast commentaries (CBC, BBC); co-author: 'The Black Paper, A Response to the Canadian Government's White Paper on Foreign Policy' 1970; recreations: sailing, tennis, skiing; clubs: The National Press, The Kingston Yacht, The Rideau Tennis & Squash; Home: 419 Hinton Ave., Ottawa, Ont. K1Y 1BZ; Office: 165 Sparks St., Ottawa, Ont. K1P 5B9.

**WINSPEAR, Francis George,** O.C. (1967), LL.D., F.C.A., F.C.M.A., F.R.S.A.; b. Birmingham, Eng. 30 May 1903; s. William Willan and Anne Jane (Dewes) E.; e. Pub. and High Schs., Calgary, Alta.; F.C.A., Alta.; Univ. of Alta., Hon. LL.D.; m. late Bessie, d. late Geo. E. Watchorn, Calgary, Alta., 6 Aug. 1927; children: Claude, William; remarried, Harriet Snowball, 26 Mar. 1980; Pres., Winham Investments Ltd.; Pres., The Winspear Foundation; Winham Investments Ltd.; Hon. Dir., Lake Ontario Steel Co. Ltd.; Co-Steel International Ltd.; Sheerness Steel Co. Ltd.; Raritan River Steel Co.; Founding Partner Winspear, Hamilton, Anderson & Co. (Chart. Accts. now amalgamated with Deloitte & Touche); Past Pres., Candn. Chamber of Comm.; former Prof. of Accounting, now Prof. Emeritus, Univ. of Alta.; former mem., Econ. Council Can.; Past Pres., Edmonton Chamber of Comm.; mem., Inst. of Chart. Accts. of Alberta, B.C. and Manitoba; Soc. of Mgmt. Accts. of Alta.; Candn.-Am. C. D. Howe Research Inst.; Care of Can. (Hon. Dir.); mem. Bd. Govs., Edmonton Opera Assn.; Fellow, Royal Soc. for the Encouragement of Arts, Mfrs. & Comm., London; mem., Nat. Advisers of Y.M.C.A.; Delta Upsilon; Freemason; Conservative; Anglican; recreations: golf, photography; Clubs: The Edmonton; Mayfair Golf & Country; Home: Valleyview Manor, 701 - 12207 Jasper Ave., Edmonton, Alta. T5N 3K2.

**WINSTON, Helene;** actress; writer; b. Winnipeg, Man. 16 Sept. 1922; d. Montefiore and Bertha Priscilla (Morris) W.; e. St. John's Tech. High Sch. 1939; m. John Deacon Steiner 8 Sept. 1973; appeared numerous motion pictures M.G.M., Warners, Universal, Disney, Paramount, Columbia, 20th Century Fox, MTM Productions, Nat. Film Bd., Crawley Films and many ind. prodns.; numerous Candn. TV prodns. incl. Wayne & Shuster, 'King of Kensington' (Gladys King) starred in 111 episodes 1975–80; Am. TV appearances incl. 'Twilight Zone,' 'Hill Street Blues,' 'Mary Tyler Moore,' 'Rhoda,' 'Sanford and Son,' 'Tony Orlando and Dawn,' 'Bewitched,' 'The Red Skelton Show,' 'Alfred Hitchcock Presents,' 'The Phil Silvers Show,' 'The Danny Kaye Show'; stage appearances incl. Broadway prodns., Los Angeles Centre Theatre Group, Actors Workshop San Francisco, Stratford (Ont.) Festival, Edinburgh Festival, N.Y. Irish Players, Crest Theatre Toronto, Neptune Theatre Halifax, Rainbow Stage Winnipeg, Man. Theatre Centre; recipient Best Actress Man. Drama Festival 1955; Maurice Rosenfeld Award for Outstanding Newcomer to TV & Films 1956; Best Character Actress Liberty TV Awards 1959, nomination 1960; nomination for 'Gladys King' role 'King of Kensington' 1975–80; author radio plays 1945–55 incl. 'Abel's Girl,' 'The Strange History of the Satisfied Man,' 'Woman With a Shopping Bag,' 'Kelly's Cat,' 'Rosie Leprechaun,' 'Three Men, Some Gold and a Promise,' 'Mr. Winkle and the Boards,' 'Murietta was a Bandit,' 'The Girl in the Red Skirt,' 'Miss Murphy Abroad Among the Mortals'; Founding mem., ACRA (now ACTRA); mem. Candn. Actors Equity (Past Chrmn.); Theatre East Studio City, Cal.; SAG; AEA; AFTRA; recreations: duplicate bridge, gardening, sculpture; Address: 14233 Valerio St., Van Nuys, Cal. 91405.

**WINSTON, Iris Muriel,** B.A. (Hons.), M.A., B.Ed.; association executive; writer; b. London, Eng. 12 Apl. 1943; d. Alexander Bryan and Renée (Raphael) W.; e. Univ. of Wales B.A. (Hons.) 1964; Univ. of London Inst. of Edn. Postgrad. Cert. in Edn. 1965; Univ. of Calgary M.A. 1969, B.Ed. 1971; Univ. of Alta. E.S.L. Dip. 1973; Univ. of Sask. Course Candn. Politics & Govt. 1988; m. Stewart s. Frederick and Charlotte Boston 7 June 1967; children: Alexander Holtby, Sarah Elizabeth; WRITER-IN-RESIDENCE, NATIONAL LIBRARY OF CANADA 1991– ; columnist, theatre and book reviewer, arts writer, reporter: Ottawa Citizen, Calgary Herald, Edmonton Journal, Saskreport, Star-Phoenix, Variety, Southam News, Banff Crag & Canyon since 1976; high sch. teacher Eng. and Hist. N.S., Calgary 1965–67; Instr. S. and N. Alta. Insts. of Technol. 1967–71, 1973–75; Editorialist CBC Radio 1968–76; Publicity Co-ord. World Theatre Mosaic 1979, Banff Centre 1978–79; Communications Dir. Persephone Theatre 1986–88; Host 'Spotlight on Seniors' STV 1987–89; Communications/Promotions Dir. Nightcap Prodns. 1988–89; Promotions Mgr. Mall on Third Ave. 1988–89; Exec. Dir., Candn. Fedn. of Humane Societies 1989–91; recipient Alta. Found. Performing Arts Angle on Arts Award (arts stories) 1985, 1986; Regional Rep. and mem. Ed. Bd. Playwrights Union Can.; author 'Expressions' arts textbook 1979; 'A Province At Work' ind. textbook 1979; 'Moving On' juvenile play 1987; various articles; Home: 1285 Bayview Dr., R.R.1, Woodlawn, Ont. K0A 3M0.

**WINTER, Alan Ernest,** B.Sc., Ph.D.; business executive; b. 6 Feb. 1948; s. David Ernest and Louisa Fredrika (Eves) W.; e. Queen's Univ. (U.K.) B.Sc. (1st class hons.) 1969; Queen's Univ. (Kingston) Ph.D. 1974; m. Carolyn d. George and Reta Stephenson 17 Aug. 1974; one s.: Kyle David; PRES., MPR TELTECH LTD. 1992– ; Project Leader, Dept. of Communication, Communications Rsch. Ctr. 1978; Dir., Telesat Canada 1985; Mem., Assn. of Profl. Engrs. of Ont.; Aerospace Indus. Assn. of Can.; Internat. Adv. Bd., Airshow Canada Symposium; Dir. & Extve. Ctte., PRECARN Assoc. inc.; MPR Teltech Ltd.; Dir., Armed Forces Communications & Electronics Assn.; Candn. Inst. for Telecommunications Rsch.; Trustee & Extve. Ctte., Advanced Systems Inc.; Dir., VISTAR Inc.; CRC Inc.; Fellow, Candn. Aeronautics & Space Inst.; Mem., Internat. Acad. of Astronautics; clubs: Diamond University, Terminal City; Office: 8999 Nelson Way, Burnaby, B.C. V5A 4B5.

**WINTER, Gerald Keith,** B.Sc., M.Sc., Ph.D.; university administrator; b. Moncton, N.B. 19 May 1943; s. Gerald M. and Phyllis Boyd (Baird) W.; e. Prince of Wales Coll. 1960; Mem. Univ. of Nfld., B.Sc. 1965, M.Sc. 1968; Univ. of London (UK) Ph.D 1971; m. June d. Rex and Vera Martin 9 Sept. 1967; children: Christopher, Martin; VICE PRES. (FINANCE & SERVICES),

UNIV. OF CALGARY 1991– ; Asst. Prof. of Chem., Mem. Univ. of Nfld. 1971; Assoc. Prof., Dir. of Gen. Studies, & Assoc. Dean of Arts & Sci. 1975–85; Biotechnol. Cons. 1983–85; Dep. Min., Dept. of Career Devel. & Adv. Studies, Govt. of Nfld. & Labrador 1985–89; Depy. Min., Dept. of Education 1989–91; Mem., Bd. of Gov., Nfld. Inst. of Fisheries & Marine Technol. 1985–87; Cabot Inst. of Applied Arts & Tech. 1987–91; Fisher Inst. of Applied Arts & Technol. 1987–91; Pres., Nfld. & Labrador Track & Field Assn. 1979–81; Vice-Pres., Candn. Track & Field Assn. 1982–87; recreations: tennis, baseball, fishing; Club: Edgemont Raquet; Home: 143 Ranch Estates Rd. N.W., Calgary Alta. T3G 1L4; Office: 2500 University Dr. N.W., A112, Calgary, Alta. T2N 1N4.

**WINTER, Hon. Gordon Arnaud,** O.C. (1974), LL.D., Kst.J.; b. St. John's, Nfld. 6 Oct. 1912; s. Robert Gordon and Ethel Phyllis (Arnaud) W.; e. Bishop Feild Coll., St. John's, Nfld.; Loretto Sch., Musselburgh, Scotland; LL.D., Memorial 1970; m. Millicent, d. Dr. Thomas Anderson, St. John's, Nfld., 2 Sept. 1937; children: Linda, Valda; Chrmn., T. & M. Winter Limited 1959–87; now retired; Hon. Chrmn., The Standard Manufacturing Co. Ltd.; Lieut. Governor of Newfoundland 1974–81; apptd. Vice-Chrmn., Royal Comn. on the Ocean Ranger Marine Disaster 1982; Appt'd. Chrmn., The Roman Catholic Special Commission of Enquiry into Sexual Abuse of Children by Members of the Clergy of the Archdiocese of St. John's, Nfld. 1989; Chairman, Board of Regents, Memorial Univ. of Nfld. 1968–74; Chrmn., St. John's Housing Corp. 1949–50; Pres., Nfld. Bd. of Trade 1946; mem. Adv. Bd., Nfld. Savings Bank 1959–62; Gov., Candn. Broadcasting Corp. 1952–58; apptd. by H.E. the Gov. in Comn., mem. of the Nfld. del. which negotiated and signed on 11 Dec. 1948, the Terms of Union between Nfld. and Can.; apptd. Min. of Finance in first Prov. Govt. of Nfld., 1 Apr. 1949; Anglican; recreations: golfing, curling; Clubs: Bally Haly Golf & Curling; Murray's Pond Fishing; St. John's Curling; Coral Beach and Tennis (Bermuda); Home: 6 Winter Pl., St. John's, Nfld. A1B 1J6.

**WINTER, John Orville,** M.A., C.M.C.; management consultant; b. Belfast, County Antrim, N. Ireland 15 Jan. 1944; s. Louis and Nellie (Gill) W.; e. Sullivan Upper Sch. 1949–60; London Guildhall Sch. of Music & Drama 1960; Queen's Univ. of Belfast B.A. 1964; Univ. of Vienna 1964; Univ. of Toronto M.A. 1965 (Pres. Grad. Students' Union 1968–69; Pres. Lionel Massey Fund 1967–68; Captain Fishing Team 1968); m. Linda Marie, d. John and Adele (Movich) Bernardi; daughter: Courtney Lynn; PRES., JOHN WINTER ASSOCIATES LIMITED 1987– ; Resch. and Teaching Asst., Univ. of Toronto 1964–69; Donship, Univ. Coll. 1968–70; Instr., Ryerson Polytechnical Inst. 1969–70; Lectr. Nipissing Coll. Summer 1970; Cons., Urbanismo e Desenvolvimento S.A., Brazil 1971–73; Teacher, Etobicoke Bd. of Edn. 1973–74; Sr. Cons., Paterson Planning & Rsch. Ltd. 1974–82; Vice-Pres., Clayton Research Associates Ltd. 1982–87; Honour Roll, Inst. of Mgmt. Cons. of Ont.; mem. Exec., Non-Smokers' Rights Assn.; Smoking and Health Action Found. (Treas. 1982–83); Counc., Assn. of Ont. Land Economists; Inst. of Mgmt. Cons.; Candn. Inst. of Planners; Am. Inst. of Cert. Planners; Treas., Massey Coll. Alumni Assoc.; author: 'Retailing in Canada' (subs. newsletter); professional articles published on retailing, free trade, urban economics, planning law, shopping centres, demographics, marketing and merchandising; several short stories and plays for BBC Radio; mem. Ed. Bd. 'The Land Economist'; organized conference 'Ontario in Transition: The Challenge of Economic Development' Nov. 1985; recreations: sailing, tennis, skiing, jogging, jazz piano; Clubs: Royal Commonwealth Soc.; High Park Ski; Home: 54 Maclean Ave., Toronto, Ont. M4E 3A1; Office: Suite 201, 2 Wheeler Ave., Toronto, Ont. M4L 3V2.

**WINTER, Maurice Walcot;** b. St. John's, Nfld. 22 Aug. 1923; s. late Ethel Phyllis (Arnaud) and the late Robert Gordon Winter; e. Bishop Feild Coll., St. John's, Nfld.; Ridley Coll., St. Catharines, Ont.; m. Mary Ethel, d. late Lionel G. Munn, St. John's, Nfld., 29 Sept. 1948; children: Sharon, Susan, Robert; Past Dir., Newfoundland Marine Insurance Co. Ltd.; Past Treas., John Howard Soc. of Can. Ltd. (Nfld. Br.); Past Pres., Newfoundland Game Fish Protection Society Limited; Past President, Newfoundland Board of Ins. Underwriters; Councillor, Newfoundland Bd. Trade 1962–64; Past Dir., Nfld. Transportation Co. Ltd.; Nfld. Containers Ltd.; Newfoundland Marine Holdings Ltd.; Bally Haly Golf & Country Club Ltd.; commenced business career with T. & M. Winter, Ltd., 1942; apptd. a Dir., 1959; apptd. Pres. 1973; retired 1987; served in 2nd World War, 1943–46 as Sgt.-Pilot with RCAF; mem., RCAF Assn.; Roy. Candn. Legion; Life Mem., B.P.O. Elks of

Canada 1989 (PDDGER and Past E.R.); Dir., Past Exalted Rulers Assoc. 1991; mem., Internat. Atlantic Salmon Foundation; Candn. Wildlife Federation; Anglican; recreations: fishing, curling; Clubs: Bally Haly Golf & Curling; Murray Pond Fishing; Home: 168 Elizabeth Ave., Churchill Park, St. John's, Nfld. A1B 1S6.

**WINTER, Nadine,** B.A., M.A.; organization change and human resource management consultant; b. Montreal, Que. 14 Feb. 1949; d. Israel and Sarah (Lefcovitch) Oberfield; e. Concordia Univ. B.A. 1978; York Univ. M.A. 1979, 1979–82; m. Mark Winter 19 Dec. 1970; children: Aaron, Michael; DIR., N. WINTER CONSULTING INC. 1989– ; Grad. Studies Programme, York Univ. 1978–82; The Hay Group 1982–88; Partner, The Hay Group 1987–88; Dir. Job Evaluation Cons. 1987–88; recognized expert in strategic change and alternate reward strategies; Mem., York Alumni Assn.; Assn. of Women Extves.

**WINTERBOTTOM, Richard,** B.Sc., Ph.D.; museum curator; educator; b. Livingstone, Zambia 30 Sept. 1944; s. John Miall and Marjorie Grace (Mash) W.; e. Westerford High Sch. 1962; Univ. of Cape Town B.Sc. 1967; Queen's Univ. Ph.D. 1971; m. Irina d. Alexander and Vera Donskov 23 May 1971; children: Marina, David Alexander; CURATOR, ROYAL ONTARIO MUSEUM 1984– ; post-doctoral fellowships at Smithsonian Inst. 1972, National Mus. of Natural Sci. 1973; teacher J.L.B. Smith Inst. of Ichthyology, Rhodes Univ., S. Africa; joined ROM as Asst. Curator 1978, Assoc. Curator 1979; cross appointed to Dept. of Zoology, Univ. of Toronto as Asst. Prof. 1978, Assoc. Prof. 1986, Prof. 1990; author numerous sci. papers and monographs on fishes and marine biology; leader and participant numerous expdns. to collect fishes in Indo-Pacific region incl. Zululand, Comores, Madagascar, Chagos Archipelago, Great Barrier Reef, Solomon Islands, Cook Islands, Philippines, Society Islands, New Caledonia, Thailand and Fiji 1979–91; mem. Ed. Bds., Syst. Zool., Candn. Jour. of Zoology (1984–87), General Ichthyology Editor, Copeia (Am. Soc. of Ichthyologists and Herpetologists 1991– ) and 'Indo-Pacific Fishes' series of Bishop Mus., Hawaii; cons. various TV documentaries, Government agencies and aquaculture co.'s; member, Am. Soc. of Ichthyologists and Herpetologists (Gov. 1978–83; 1987–92); Soc. of Systematic Zoology; Zoological Soc. of Southern Africa; Willi Hennig Soc.; Soc. for the Study of Evolution; Ichthyological Soc. of Japan; recipient Frederick H. Stoye Award, Am. Soc. of Ichthyologists and Herpetologists; Jessup Award, Acad. of Natural Sci. of Philadelphia; recreations: squash, scuba diving, photography; Home: 314 Indian Rd., Toronto, Ont. M6R 2X8; Office: Dept. of Ichthyology & Herpetology, R.O.M., Toronto, Ont. M5S 2C6.

**WINTERMANS, Jos J.,** LL.B., LL.M., M.B.A.; financial services executive; b. The Netherlands 4 Oct. 1946; s. Jos G. and Catherine M. (Van Dijk) W.; e. Leyden Univ. LL.B. 1967, LL.M. 1972; Queen's Univ. M.B.A. 1972; m. Dr. Eileen d. Joseph and Ray Simon 30 Oct. 1972; PRES., C.E.O. AND DIR. CANADIAN TIRE ACCEPTANCE LTD. 1988– ; Dir., Hamilton Discount Corp. Ltd.; Dir. of Mktg. Standard Brands 1977; Vice Pres. Mktg. Bristol Myers Products 1980; Sr. Vice Pres. Mktg. and Sales, American Express 1982; Pres. Am. Mktg. Assn. Toronto 1981; Hon. Fellowship, Ryerson Polytechnic Univ. 1993; recreations: travel, performing arts; club: Etobicoke Yacht; Welland; Home: 200 Riverside Dr., Toronto, Ont. M6S 4A9; Office: 555 Prince Charles Dr., Welland, Ont. L3C 6B5.

**WIRSIG, Claus A.,** M.A., D.H.A.; retired hospital executive; b. The Pas, Man. 3 Apl. 1933; s. Oscar Adolf and Frida Helene (Renger) W.; e. Univ. of Alta. B.A. 1955, M.A. 1957; Oxford Univ. 1957–59 (Rhodes Scholar); Univ. of Toronto D.H.A. 1968 (Robert Wood Johnson Award 1968); m. Ann d. Harry and Mary Gilleland 29 July 1961; 4 d. Denise, Nadine, Karen, Ingrid; Pres., The Hosp. for Sick Children Foundation 1977–93, Retired; mem. Bd. CyberFluor Inc. 1988–92; Rsch. Ed. Hugh C. Maclean Publications Ltd. 1960; Asst. Ed. Hosp. Adm. in Can. 1960, Ed. 1962–66, Cons. Ed. 1966–73; Adm. Resident Hospital for Sick Children 1967, Adm. Asst. Nursing 1968, Asst. Adm. 1969–71, Dir. Planning & External Relations 1977–86; Exec. Dir.: Univ. Teaching Hosps. Assn. 1971–77, Hosp. Council Metrop. Toronto 1972–77; occasional lectr. and preceptor grad. prog. in Health Adm. Univ. of Toronto; Partner, Sunnyside Campground Westport, Ont. 1972–89; recipient World Univ. Service Travel Scholarship 1956; Kenneth R. Wilson Meml. Award Bus. Journalism 1965; Pres. Bus. Press Eds. Assn. Can. 1965–66; Bd. mem.: Candn. Inst. Child Health 1986– , Vice-Chrmn. of the Bd. 1990–92, Chrmn. 1992– ; Nat. Soc. Fund Raising Execs. Can. 1979–82; Nat. Assn. Children's

Hosps. & Related Instns. (Can. & USA) 1980–84; Pres. and Bd. mem. various univ. alumni brs.; mem. Internat. Hosp. Fedn.; Candn. Coll. Health Service Execs.; Candn. Soc. Fund Raising Execs.; Protestant; recreations: sailing, gardening; Club: University; Home: 96 Ruscica Dr., Toronto, Ont. M4A 1R4.

**WIRTH, Alfred George,** B.A., Dip.Man., D.A.R.; strategic advisor & investment counsellor; b. Vienna, Austria 15 Apl. 1941; s. Manfred F. and Elizabeth A. (Kunerth) W.; e. St. Andrew's Coll. Aurora; e. McGill Univ. B.A. 1962, Dip.Man. 1970; div.; two d. Elizabeth Sheila, Susan Marianne; PRES. & DIR., WIRTH ASSOCIATES INC. 1991– ; Dir., St. Andrew's Coll. Foundation; Vice Pres. Invests., Sun Life Assurance Co. 1981; Vice Pres. & Gen. Mgr., SUNIMCO 1982; Sr. Vice Pres. & Chief Invest. Offr., Crown Life Insurance Co. 1985–91; Past Chrmn.: Am. Council Life Ins. (Invest.); CLHIA (Invests.); Trustee: Inst. for Rsch. Pub. Policy; Heart & Stroke Found.; co-author 'Private Placements' 1984; various mag. articles on business and wine; mem.: Internat. Soc. of Fin. Analysts; N.Y. Soc. Security Analysts; Toronto Soc. Financial Analysts; Advisory Ctte., The Toronto Stock Exchange; Standards Ctte., Pension Invest. Assoc. of Can.; World Future Society; C.I.I.A.; C.D. Howe Inst.; Lutheran; recreations: diving, photography; Clubs: Mount Royal; Granite; Ticker; Chevalier du Tastevin; Commandeur de Bordeaux; Home: 91 Teddington Park Ave., Toronto, Ont. M4N 2C7.

**WISE, Hon. John,** P.C.; former politician; b. St. Thomas, Ont. 12 Dec. 1935; s. Clayton Wesley and Mary (White) W.; e. St. Thomas and Elgin Pub. and High Schs.; Univ. of Guelph grad. 1956; m. Ann Dimora d. George Richardson, St. Thomas, Ont. 18 Oct. 1958; two d. Elizabeth, Susan; Min. of Agriculture, 1984–88; el. to H. of C. for Elgin g.e. 1972, re-el. since; apptd. Chrmn. P. Cons. Caucus Comte. on Agric. 1976; Min. of Agriculture Canada 1979–80; fifth generation dairy farmer; Pres. Elgin Jersey Breeders 1957–58; Dir. Oxford & Dist. Cattle Breeders Assn. 1960, Pres. 1965; formed Elgin Young P. Cons.Assn. and became Charter Pres. 1958; Councillor, Yarmouth Twp. 1960, Depy. Reeve 1965, Reeve 1968; Warden of Elgin Co. and mem. Elgin Co. Council 1969; mem. Prov. Adv. Comte., Mun. Affairs Mins. Ont. 1969; mem. St. Thomas and Suburban Area Planning Bd. 1969; Vice Chrmn. Central Elgin Planning Bd. 1970, Chrmn. 1971–72; Dir. Elgin Co-op. Services 1970; mem. original Talbot Shivaree Comte. 1971; P. Cons. Critic, Min. of Supply & Services 1983–84; Vice Chrmn. Un. Appeal 1961; mem. St. Thomas Elgin Assn. Retarded Children Residence Comte. 1967; has acted as judge numerous occasions Co. and 4-H Dairy shows; rec'd Rotary Club 'Adventure in Citizenship' Award 1954; St. Thomas Jaycees' 'Outstanding Young Man Award' 1967; Freemason; Shriner; P. Conservative; Anglican; Home: #36 County Rd. 45, St. Thomas, Ont. N5R 5T6.

**WISE, Nicholas E.M.,** C.L.U.; b. Rumania 4 Oct. 1923; e. Cambridge Univ. 1941; m. Barbara Golden, 13 July 1945; four children: came to Can. 1947; Pres., Nila Financial & Insurance Services Inc. and Nicholas Insurance Enterprises Inc.; Gen. Agent and Vice-Pres. North West Life Assnce. Co. of Can. 1976; Agent with London Life Insurance Co., 1947–55; Mgr., Northern Life Assurance Co. of Canada, 1955–58; joined Global Life Insurance Co. as Mgr., 1958–63, apptd. Vice-Pres. and Mgr. 1963; served during 2nd World War with Brit. Army in Middle East; discharged with rank of Capt. 1945; mem., Life Underwriters Assn. Montreal (Past Pres.); Ins. Brokers Assn. Prov. Que.; Qualifying & Life mem., Million Dollar Round Table of U.S.; Mem. Top of Table M.D.R.T.; Hebrew; recreations: golf, skiing; Address: 5902 Macdonald Ave., Hampstead, Que., H3X 2X1.

**WISE, Sydney Francis,** B.L.S., M.A.; b. Toronto, Ont. 1924; s. Francis Evelyn and Marjorie Louise (Hutton) W.; e. Bowmore Rd. and Earl Kitchener Pub. Schs.,Toronto; Riverdale Coll. Inst., Toronto; Univ. of Toronto, B.A. (Gold Medalist in Hist.) 1949, B.L.S. 1950; Queen's Univ., M.A. 1953; Univ. of Guelph, LL.D. 1987; m. Verna Isobel, d. Walter Workman Mulholland, Toronto, 5 Sept. 1947; children: John Francis Hutton, Catherine Ellen, Bruce Douglas; DEAN OF GRADUATE STUDIES AND RESEARCH, CARLETON UNIV. 1981–90; Gov. 1980–83; Gen. Ed., Carleton Library Series, 1979–81; Dir., Carleton University Press 1983–90; Lectr. in History, Royal Mil. Coll., 1950–55; with Dept. of Hist., Queen's Univ., 1955–66 (apptd. full Prof. 1964); R. Samuel McLaughlin Research Prof., Queen's Univ., 1964–65; Director, History, Dept. National Defence 1966–73; Visiting Prof., Inst. of Candn. Studies, Carleton Univ., 1964; Prof. of History, 1973; Dir., Inst. of Candn. Studies 1978–81; First Visiting Research Prof., Australian War Memorial, Canberra 1985; served with R.C.A.F. as Pilot, 1943–45, rank Flying Offr.; co-author: 'Men in Arms: a history of the inter-relationships of warfare and western society,' 1956, 2nd ed. 1962, 3rd ed. 1970, 4th ed. 1979, 5th ed. 1991; 'Task Force Report to Fed. Cabinet on Sport for Canadians' 1969; 'Canada's Sporting Heroes: Their Lives & Times' 1974; 'Canadian Airmen in the First World War,' Vol. 1, Official History of the Royal Canadian Air Force, 1980; 'God's Peculiar Peoples Essays in the Political Culture of 19th Century Canada' 1993; and others; has publ. articles and reviews in various journs.; Assoc. Gen. Editor, Carleton Univ. Press 1993– ; Awarded Cruikshank Gold Medal, Ont. Hist. Soc. ('for outstanding service to the cause of history in Ont.'); Fellow, Royal Soc. of Can. 1983; Mem., Order of Canada 1989; Pres., Social Science Research Council Canada 1974–75; mem., Canadian Hist. Assn. (Council 1962–65, Pres. 1973–74); U.N. Assn. Can. (Pres. Kingston Bd., 1963–65); Ont. Hist. Soc. (mem. Extve. 1964–65, Vice Pres. 1966–68, Pres. 1968–69); Chrmn., Archeol. & Hist. Sites Bd. Ont. 1972–74; Vice-Chrmn., Ont. Heritage Fdn., 1975–80; Chrmn., 1980–81, Ont. Heritage Foundation; Chrmn., Conservation Review Bd. of Ont. 1981–83; re-apptd. Dir., Ont. Heritage Found. and Chrmn. Archaeological Comte. 1983; Chrmn. Ont. Counc. on Grad. Studies 1984–86; Vice-Pres. Candn. Assn. of Grad. Schools 1984–85, Pres. 1985–86; Vice Pres., Champlain Society; Executive mem. SCITEC 1972–73; Dir., Friends of Candn. War Museum 1986–91; Chrmn. Adv. Ctte., Firestone Gallery 1985–87; Dir., Battle of Normandy Found. 1992– ; Anglican; Club: Royal Canadian Military Institute; Home: 562 Lisgar St., Ottawa, Ont. K1R 5H5.

**WISEMAN, Christopher Stephen,** M.A., Ph.D.; university professor; writer; b. Hull, England 31 May 1936; s. Stephen and Winifred Agnes (Rigby) W.; e. Manchester Grammar Sch. 1954; Trinity Hall, Cambridge Univ., B.A. (Hons.) 1959, M.A. 1962; Univ. of Strathclyde, Ph.D. 1971; m. Jean d. Ambrose and Marie Leytem 1 Jan. 1963; children: Stephen Robert, Jonathan Christopher; PROF., DEPT. OF ENGLISH, UNIV. OF CALGARY 1980– ; R.A.F. 1954–56; Univ. of Iowa Poetry Workshop 1959–62; Teaching Asst. 1960–62; Lectr. & Founder Mem., Dept. of English Studies, Univ. of Strathclyde 1963–69; Asst. then Assoc. Prof., present univ. 1969–80; visiting writer/reader many schools & univs.; Alta. Achievement Award for excellence in writing 1988; Teaching Excellence Award, Univ. of Calgary 1988; Writers Guild of Alta. Poetry Award 1988; Alta. Culture Poetry Prize 1988, 1989; Poetry ed. 'Dandelion' 1988–91; 'Ariel' 1972–87; Ed. advr., 'Sanscrit'; Bd. Mem., Alta. Foundation for Lit. Arts 1988–91; Mem., Writers Guild of Alta. (past Pres., extve. posts); Humanities Assn. (Past Pres., Calgary Br.); League of Candn. Poets; Victorian Studies Assn. of W. Can.; author: 'Waiting for the Barbarians' 1971, 'The Barbarian File' 1974, 'The Upper Hand' 1981, 'An Ocean of Whispers' 1982, 'Closings' 1986, 'Postcards Home' 1988, 'Missing Persons' 1989 (poetry); 'Beyond the Labyrinth' 1978 (scholarly); recreations: reading, soccer, music; Home: 8 Varwood Pl. N.W., Calgary, Alta. T3A 0C1.

**WISEMAN, Douglas J.;** retired politician; b. Smiths Falls, Ont. 21 July 1930; s. Walter Robert and Beatrice Viola (Garland) W.; e. pub. and high schs. Smiths Falls; Mang. and Sales courses in Shoe Retailing; Animal Husbandry and Judging courses; m. Bernice Emma d. John Holmes Drummond, Toledo, Ont. 26 June 1951; children: Clifford Douglas, Karen Grace; Robert Drummond; Retired from politics 1990; Min. of Govt. Services, Ont. 1979–83; prior to entering politics operated shoe and real estate businesses, private hosp., purebred cattle operation; el. M.P.P. for Lanark 1971, re-el. since; Parlty. Asst. to Min. of Health 1975; Min. without Portfolio 1978; served Perth Pub. Sch. Bd. as mem. then Chrmn. 12 yrs.; former Chrmn. Perth Retail Merchants Assn.; Past Vice Pres. Lanark Co. P. Cons. Assn.; Past Chrmn. E. Ont. Charolais Assn.; mem. of Session and Trustee, St. Paul's Un. Ch. Perth; former mem. Children's Aid Soc.; co-recipient Candn. Shoe Retail Industry Merit Award; rec'd Breeder's Award Candn. Charolais Assn.; P. Conservative; United Church; Home: R.R. 5, Perth, Ont. K7H 3C7.

**WISEMAN, Nelson,** B.A., M.A., Ph.D.; university professor; b. Bucharest, Romania 21 Aug. 1946; s. Joseph and Anna (Shwaid) Waisman; e. Garden City Coll. 1965; Univ. of Man., B.A. (Hons.) 1969; Univ. of Toronto, M.A. 1970, Ph.D. 1975; ASSOC. PROF., DEPT. OF POL. SCI., UNIV. OF TORONTO 1986– ; Cons., Man. Housing & Renewal Corp. 1976, 1982; Govt. of Man. Extve. Counc. 1981, 1982; Canada Mortgage and Housing Corp. 1990; Ont. Min. of Intergovernmental Affairs 1991–92; Vis. Asst. Prof., York Univ. 1977–80; Univ. of Man. 1982; Asst. Prof., present univ. 1980–86; Founding Mem., Man. Children's Mus.; Jewish; mem., Candn. Pol. Sci. Assn.; Inst. of Public Admin. of Can.; author: 'Social Democracy in Manitoba' 1983 and numerous contribs. to books & scholarly journals; editor: 'The City and the Camera' 1980; co-editor: 'Government and Enterprise in Canada' 1985; recreations: photography, swimming; Home: 506 Semple Ave., Winnipeg, Man. R2V 1C6; Office: 100 St. George St., Toronto, Ont. M5S 1A1.

**WISENER, Robert A.,** B.Sc.; merchant banker; b. Toronto, Ont. 8 Feb. 1927; s. late Philip A. and Margaret Jeanne (McLaughlin) W.; e. Toronto Pub. Schs.; Crescent Sch., Toronto; Trinity Coll. Sch., Port Hope, Ont.; Royal Candn. Naval Coll., Royal Roads, B.C.; Univ. of Toronto, B.Sc. 1950; m. (3rd) Patricia, d. Patricia King, Glasgow, Scotland; children: Cynthia, Philip, Lee, Robin, Susan, Joanne, James, Timothy; CHRMN., THE MERBANCO GROUP LIMITED; Chrmn., Canbra Foods Ltd.; Dir., MerBanco Inc.; Mem., Agriculture Food and Beverage SAGIT - Fed. Govt.; Anglican; recreations: sailing, squash, skiing; Home: Site 19, Box 36 S.S. #1, Bearspaw Village Calgary, Alta. T2M 4N3; Office: 720, 999 – 8th St. S.W., Calgary, Alta. T2R 1J5.

**WISMER, William Miller,** Q.C., B.A., LL.B.; retired business executive; b. Jordan Station, Ont. 13 Sept. 1913; s. Philip Henry and Minnie Margaret (Miller) W.; e. St. Catharines Coll. Inst. & Vocational Sch. (Sr. Matric. 1932); Univ. of Toronto (Univ. Coll.), B.A. 1938; Osgoode Hall Law Sch., Toronto, Ont.; m. Margaret Katharine Anna, d. Robert Chalmers, Niagara Falls, Ont., 16 June 1938; one d., Margaret Katharine; read law with Peter White, K.C.; called to the Bar of Ont., 1941; practised law with the firm of White, Ruel & Bristol, Toronto, Ont., 1941–43; Solr. with Ont. Securities Comn.,1945–48; Extve. Secy. and General Counsel, The Broker-Dealers' Assn. of Ont., 1948–56; Vice Pres., The Toronto Stock Exchange 1956–64; Vice-President and Dir., Draper Dobie & Co. Ltd., 1965–72; Pres. and Dir., Canadian Javelin Ltd., 1967–74; Bison Petroleum & Minerals Ltd. 1974–83; Pres. & Dir., URSA Polaris Developments Corp. 1983–91; served in 2nd World War with the R.C.N.V.R. 1943–45 with rank of Lieut.; mem., Toronto Bd. of Trade; Premier of 14th Ont. Older Boys' Parliament, 1934–35; Phi Delta Phi; recreations: reading, walking; Home: Penthouse 1, 50 Prince Arthur Ave., Toronto, Ont. M5R 1B5.

**WITELSON, Sandra F.,** Ph.D.; university professor; b. Montreal, Que. 24 Feb. 1940; e. McGill Univ., B.Sc. 1960, M.Sc. 1962, Ph.D. 1966; m. Henry C. W. June 1960; one d.: Tamar S.; PROF., DEPT. OF PSYCHIATRY MCMASTER UNIV. 1977– ; Lectr., Dept. Edn. Psych., Yeshiva Univ. 1966; NIMH postdoct. fellow, Dept. of Neurology and Psychiatry, New York Univ. 1966–68; Instr., Neuropsychological Lab., Dept. Pediatrics, N.Y. Med. Coll. 1968–69; joined present univ. as Asst. Prof. 1969; Assoc. Mem., Dept. of Psychology 1976– ; Dept. of Biomedical Sciences 1983– ; Morton Prince Award; John Dewan Award; The Clarke Inst. of Psychiatry Rsch. Fund Award; Fellow, C.P.A., A.P.A., A.A.A.S., A.P.S.; Chair, Social Issues, Soc. for Neuroscience 1993–96; Gov., McMaster Univ.; Mem., Candn. & Am. Psych. Assn.; Internat. Neuropsych. Soc.; Am. Assn. for the Advancement of Sci.; Soc. for Neurosci.; Acad. of Aphasia; Internat. Brain Rsch. Orgn.; author of numerous scientific articles; Office: 1200 Main St. W., Hamilton, Ont. L8N 3Z5.

**WITENOFF, Simon,** B.A.; food processing executive; b. Montréal, Qué. 23 Jan. 1950; s. Harry and Anna Pearl (Sammett) W.; e. Sir Winston Churchill High Sch. St-Laurent, Qué. 1967; Sir George Williams Univ. 1967–69; Carleton Univ., B.A. 1973; m. Hester d. Sam and Eva Lieberman 6 June 1972; children: Amy Rose, Noah Lev, Mollie Victoria; PRES. AND CHIEF EXEC. OFFR. MRS. WHYTES PRODUCTS INC. 1984– ; Sec.-Treas. Jaberk Foods Inc. Montréal; bus. career with present family firm; mem. Qué. Food Processors Assn. (AMPAQ), Treas. 1984–85; Candn. Food Processors Assn.; Candn. Restaurant & Food Service Assn.; Hotel & Restaurant Suppliers Assn.; Pickle Packers Internat.; recreations: squash, softball (Exec. Softball League); Club: Cavendish; Office: 196 St. Martin, St. Louis, Que. J0G 1K0.

**WITHERS, Gen. Ramsey Muir,** C.M.M., C.St.J., C.D., B.Sc., D.M.Sc., P.Eng.; public servant; army officer; b. Toronto, Ont. 28 July 1930; s. late William Muir and late Alice Hope Smith (Hannah) W.; e. Royal Mil. Coll. Can., Dipl. 1952; Queen's Univ., B.Sc. 1954; Candn. Army Staff Coll., psc 1961; Jt. Services Staff Coll., Eng., jssc 1963; m. Jean Alison, d. S. F. Saunders, Orillia, Ont., 8 May 1954; children: James Scott, Leslie Susan, Deidre Ann; PRES. & C.O.O., GOVERNMENT CONSULTANTS INTERNATIONAL INC. 1988– ; Chief of Defence Staff, Candn. Armed Forces 1980–83; Depy. Min., Transport Canada 1983–88; served in Korea, Can., Germany and Eng.; Mobile Command H.Q.; CFHQ; N. Region H.Q. presently mem. Assn. Prof. Engrs. Ont.; Chrmn., Consultative Ctte., Candn. War Museum 1988; Commr., Northwest Territories Award for Public Service, 1973; Outstanding Achievement Award, Public Service of Can. 1985; Fellow, Georgian Coll. 1987; Nat. Transportation Award of Excellence 1988; awarded Silver Wolf, Boy Scouts of Canada 1990; Doctor of Military Science (honoris causa) Royal Roads Military College 1992; Trustee, Candn. Museum of Civilization 1990– ; Dir., Candn. Inst. of Strategic Studies 1990– ; Anglican; recreations: boating, curling; Club: Rideau, Ottawa; Address: Suite 1300, 50 O'Connor St., Ottawa, Ont. K1P 6L2.

**WITHERSPOON, Douglas Charles;** executive; b. Toronto, Ont. 8 Sept. 1929; s. Robert James and Hattie Alice (Kelday) W.; e. Bloor Coll. Inst. Toronto 1949; Alexander Hamilton Inst., Business Adm. 1960; Queen's Univ. Business Course 1962; Univ. of W. Ont. Mang. Training Course 1971; m. Barbara June d. Robert Clarke Burns, Toronto, Ont. 15 Sept. 1956; MANAGING DIR., TAYLOR SOAPS AND PERFUMES LTD. 1988– and FOUNDER, CHRMN. & C.E.O., FOOTPRINTS FOOTCARE PRODUCTS LTD. 1990– ; Pres. and Dir., Scholl (Canada) Inc. 1978– ; Pres., Dr. Scholl's Ltd.; Dir. Taylor Soaps-Perfumes Ltd.; Retail Attendant, The Scholl Manufacturing Co. Ltd. Toronto 1949, Sales Rep. Wholesale 1950, Asst. to Mgr.-Retail Div. 1956, Asst. to Sales Mgr. 1958, Asst. to Gen. Mgr. 1960, Gen. Sales Mgr. 1967, Vice Pres.-Marketing 1971, Dir. 1973, Vice Pres. & Gen. Mgr. 1975; Country Gen. Mgr. for Canada, International Consumer Products Div. of Schering-Plough 1981; Dir., Plough Can. Inc. 1982; Vice Pres. and Regional Dir. (Canada, Australia, N.Z. and S. Africa), Internat. Consumer Products Div., Schering-Plough Inc. 1983–88; Past Chrmn., Proprietary Assn. of Can.; mem. Comm. Travellers' Assn. Can. (Past Pres.), Dir., Sales Research Club Toronto (Past Pres.); Candn. Hearing Soc. Found.; Pres., Rotary Club of Toronto 1993–94; Dir., Dr. Scholl Foundation (Chicago, IL); P. Conservative; Protestant; recreations: golf, tennis, swimming, curling, fishing; Clubs: Bd. of Trade of Metro Toronto; Thornhill Golf & Country; Home: 2305 – 7 Concorde Place, Don Mills, Ont. M3C 3N4.

**WITHROW, William J.,** C.M., M.A., M.Ed. C.D., F.C.M.A.; b. Toronto, Ont. 30 Sept. 1926; s. Wilfred Forbes and Evelyn Gertrude W.; e. Univ. of Toronto, B.A. (Art & Archaeol.) 1950; Art Specialist, O.C.E. 1951; B.Ed. 1955, M.Ed. 1958; M.A. (Fine Art) 1961; m. June Roselea Van Ostrom, 1948; 4 children and 6 grandchildren; DIRECTOR EMERITUS, ART GALLERY OF ONTARIO; Dir., Art Gallery of Ont. 1961–90; Art. Dept. Head, Earl Haig Coll. 1951–59; Principal and Research Dir., Ont. Dept. of Educ. 1957–59; Co-Chrmn. Fed. Task Force, Nat. Museums of Can. 1986; served during 2nd World War; discharged with rank of Capt.; author 'Sorel Etrog/Sculpture' 1967; 'Contemporary Canadian Painting' 1972; Member, Order of Canada 1980; Fellow, Candn. Museums Assn.; Life mem., Assn. Art Museum Dirs.; Past Pres., Canadian Art Museum Dir's. Organ.; Clubs: Highland Yacht; University; Home: 7 Malabar Place, Don Mills, Ont. M3B 1A4.

**WITTE, Margaret K. (Peggy),** B.Sc., M.Sc.; mining executive; b. Fallon, Nev. 27 Nov. 1953; d. Kenneth and Gloria (Rosaschi) Kent; e. Univ. of Nevada B.Sc.; Mackay Sch. of Mines M.Sc.; m. William J. 14 Jan. 1976; CHAIR, PRES. & CHIEF EXECUTIVE OFFICER, ROYAL OAK MINES INC.; U.S. Bureau of Mines; Dir., Hydrometallurgy, Ont. Rsch. Found. 1979–81; Founder, Witteck Devel. Inc. 1981; acquired interest in Neptune Resources Ltd. 1986 and developed Colomac Mine (NWT); acquired Royal Oak Resources Ltd., Pamour Inc. and Giant Yellowknife Mines Limited (now Royal Oak Mines Inc.); acquired Hope Brook Mine 1992; regained Colomac Mine 1993; acquired Geddes Resources Limitd 1993; has created more than 1400 jobs in Canada in 12 years; has raised more than $200 million of debt and equity financing and currently manages a company with $115 million of revenue (1992); Mining Man of the Year, The Northern Miner 1991; Address: 1425 W. Pender St., 2nd fl., Vancouver, B.C. V6G 2S3.

**WITTLIN, Curt,** B.A., M.A., Ph.D., F.R.S.C.; educator; b. Basel, Switzerland 13 Apl. 1941; s. Robert and Lina (Schindelholz) W.; e. Humanistisches Gymnasium Basel B.A. 1960; Univ. of Basel M.A., Ph.D. 1965; Univ. of Florence; m. Marie-Louise d. Emil and Josy Vaterlaus 8 Jan. 1966; PROF. OF FRENCH UNIV. OF SASK.

1976– , Head of Dept. 1985–91; recipient rsch. grants Swiss Nat. Funds and Social Sci's & Humanities Rsch. Council Can. for extended studies in Spain; Prof. of Union Coll. Barbourville, Ky. 1965–66; joined present Univ. 1966; ed. medieval texts in Latin, Catalan or Spanish; author over 40 scholarly articles medieval Catalan lit., lang. & civilization, medieval French & Spanish lit., Romance philol.; mem. Candn. Assn. Hispanists (Dir. 1976–81); N. Am. Catalan Soc. (Dir. 1982– ); recreation: mountaineering; Club: Alpine; Home: 1314 – 14th St. E., Saskatoon, Sask. S7H 0A6; Office: Saskatoon, Sask. S7N 0W0.

**WITTY, James Y.;** mayor, insurance broker; b. Toronto, Ont. 26 Aug. 1938; s. Edward Y. W.; e. Parkdale Coll. 1957; m. Anita Marshall 26 Aug. 1964; children: Cheryl Loyst, Kim Richards, Andrea Witty; MAYOR, TOWN OF AJAX 1988– ; elected as Ajax Regional Counc. Nov. 1980–88; Chrmn., Police Services Bd., Region of Durham; Durham Reg. Finan. Chrmn. 1982–88; has served on most major cttes. at town & regional level; Pres., Witty Insur. Brokers Ltd. 1970– ; has worked in gen. insur. business since 1957; Life Mem., Kinsmen Club of Ajax; Past Pres., Ajax K-40 Club; Former Dir., Ajax C. of C.; Durham Reg. Insur. Brokers Assn.; recreations: golf (hole-in-one 3 July 1982), squash; club: Kinsmen of Ajax; Home: 8 Crawford Dr., Ajax, Ont. L1S 3A8; Office: 65 Harwood Ave. S., Ajax, Ont. L1S 2H9.

**WITZEL, Robert A.,** P.Eng., B.Sc., C.A.; financial executive; e. Queen's Univ. B.Sc. 1965; m. Karen; VICE-PRES., FINANCE AND INDUSTRY SERVICES, VANCOUVER STOCK EXCHANGE & PRES., WEST CANADA CLEARING CORP. & WEST CANADA DEPOSITORY TRUST CO. 1983– ; Vice-Pres., Finance, Black & Decker Canada Inc. 1972–78; Dir. of Financial Serv., CanWest Capital Corp. 1978–80; Vice-Pres., Finance and Sec., Sandwell and Co. Limited 1980–83; Pres., West Canada Clearing Corp.; West Canada Depository Trust Co.; Dir., Financial Extves. Inst. Vancouver Chapter; recreations: skiing, sailing, tennis; clubs: Terminal City, Hollyburn Country; Office: Stock Exchange Tower, P.O. Box 10333, 609 Granville St., Vancouver, B.C. V7Y 1H1.

**WOHL, Robert Allen,** B.A., J.D.; industry executive; b. Chicago, Ill. 21 June 1931; s. Max and Frieda (Friedmann) W.; e. Univ. of Wisconsin; San Diego State Univ. B.A. 1952; Univ. of Cal. Sch. of Law; Univ. of San Diego Sch. of Law, J.D. 1960; m. Christine d. Lewis and Margaret Allison 29 March 1974; two d. Melissa, Suzanne; CONSULTANT 1993– ; joined General Dynamics Convair Div. 1956, Mgr. of Contracts 1960, Mgr. Program Control 1962; Asst. to Corporate Vice Pres. General Dynamics Corp. 1963, Corporate Dir. of Contracts 1968; Vice Pres. Adm. Canadair Inc. 1970, Corp. Vice Pres. Adm. and Legal 1979; Extve. Vice Pres. 1988; Pres., Canadair Regional Jet Div. 1989–92; Pres., Bombardier Inc., Bombardier Regional Aircraft Division 1992–93; served as Offr. with U.S. Air Force, Active Service 1952–54, Reserve Service 1954–60, 1st Lt.; admitted to practice law Cal. and U.S. Fed. Bar 1961; Blue Key Nat. Honor Fraternity 1952; Phi Alpha Delta Legal Fraternity (Chapter Pres. 1954); listed in Who's Who in American Colleges and Universities, 1952; Chapter 1st Vice Pres. Nat. Mgmt. Assn.; mem. Candn. Bar Assn.; Am. Bar Assn.; New York City Bar Assn.; Nat. Aeronautic Assn.; Aerospace Industries Assn. of Can. (Past Chrmn. Internat. Trade Comte.); recreations: tennis, golf, skiing; Clubs: Braeside Golf; Wings Club of N.Y.; Aero Club of Southern California; Home: 17 Elmwood Ave., Senneville, Que. H9X 1T5.

**WOHLFARTH, Harry,** M.F.A., Dr.acad., FIACS, FIAL; artist; university professor; b. Oberstdorf, Germany 26 Apr. 1921; s. Kurt Walter and Franziska (Gammel) W.; e. Art Acad. Dresden, Kokoschka, Salzburg; State Univ. of Guanajuato, Mexico, M.F.A. 1968; Roman Acad. Arts and Sciences, Doctoris Academiae 1962; m.; one s., Gunnar; Prof. of Art, Univ. Alta.; one-man exhns. incl.; Banff Sch. Fine Arts 1959; State Univ. Mont. 1960; Univ. of Man. Gallery 1963; Fleet Gallery, Winnipeg, 1964; Jacox Galleries, Edmonton, 1964, 1965; Gallery L'Art de L'Ouest, Montreal, 1968; State Univ. of Guanajuato Gallery, Mexico, 1968; Accademia Tiberina Gallery, Rome, 1970; Environment '71 Calgary; Lefebvre Gallery 1971, 1973 and Latitude 53 Gallery, Edmonton 1975, 1976, 1978; Zurich, Switzerland 1975; Galerie Mauffe, Paris 1976; City Gallerie, Bad Duerrheim 1977; Koenigsfeld 1978; Bad Woerislofen 1978; Gallerie Stern, Villingen (all in Germany) 1978; Burkhardt Academy Gallery, Rome 1980; Friendship Center Gallery, Moscow 1980; Burckhardt Academy Gallery, Rome 1983, 1984; paintings and sculptures in permanent collections include: Banff School of Fine Arts, State Museum Kalkar (Germany), Vatican Collection (Rome), Academia Romana di Science ed Arti, Univ. of Alta., State Univ. of Guanajuato, N. Alta., Jubilee Auditorium, Can. House (New Delhi) and in various private colls.; el. mem. German Acad. of Color Sciences, Bonn, 1961, Pres., 1980–85; el. Fellow, Internat. Inst. Arts & Letters, Geneva, 1961; Senator, Roman Acad. of Arts & Sciences, 1962; mem. Tiberian Acad., Rome, 1968; mem. Internat. Acad. Leonardo da Vinci, Rome, 1970; Hon. Causa mem. Internat. Academy of Letters, Arts and Sciences, Rome 1972; Internat. Burkhardt. Acad., Rome (Gold Medal 1978, 1979, Rennaissance Prize 1979); rec'd. Gold Medal, Tiberian Acad., 1970; Gold Medal, Internat. Acad. 'Leonardo da Vinci' 1971; Cross, Legion d'Oro Honore 1971; Gold Medal, Internat. Acad. Letters, Art & Sciences 1972; Alta. Govt. Achievement Awards 1970, 1972, 1974; City of Edmonton Cultural Achievements Award 1984; Pres., German Acad. of Colorsciences 1980, 1986; author of over 40 scholastic and research publs.; served with Alpine Corps, German Army 1940–45; wounded in action 4 times in Russia; rec'd. Iron Cross, Hand-to-Hand Combat Medal; recreations: climbing, hiking; Club: Alpine; Home: 11025 - 82 Ave., Suite 1101, Edmonton, Alta. T6G 0T1.

**WOJCIECHOWSKI, Jerzy A.,** L.Ph., Ph.D.; educator; b. Brzesc, Poland 30 June 1925; s. Roman and Antonina (Widawska) W.; e. Warsaw, Poland (Sr. Matric.) 1942; Warsaw Tech. Univ. (Mech. Engn.); Inst. Superieur de Philos., Univ. de Louvain, B.Ph. 1949; Univ. Laval, L.Ph. 1951, Ph.D. 1953; m. Cécile, d. late Adrien Cloutier, 27 Dec. 1966; children: Maria, Ewa; PROF. EMERITUS OF PHILOSOPHY, UNIV. OF OTTAWA 1990– ; Adv., program on 'New Communications Technologies and Alternative Development Strategies for Third World Countries,' Communications Studies Area, Center for Economic and Social Studies of the Thrid World in Mexico City 1983– ; Vice Pres., Systems Research Foundation and Dir., Intl. Inst. for Advanced Studies in Systems Research and Cybernetics, 1983– ; came to Can. 1949; Teacher (part-time) Montreal 1952; St. Francis Xavier Univ. 1953; joined present Univ. 1954, Full Prof. since 1965; served in 2nd World War, Polish Underground Army, Mil. Intelligence Div. 1942–45; Offrs. Sch. 1944, took part in Warsaw Insurrection as Cadet-Offr.; twice wounded and decorated; organized 7th Inter-Am. Cong. of Philos.; Pres., Candn. Philos. Assn., 1969–70; Inter-Univ. Comte. on Candn. Slavs; Vice-Pres., Polish Candn. Cong.; Dir., Survey on Status of Philos. in Can.; Chrmn., Organ. Comte., 1st Ottawa Conf. on Conceptual Basis of Classification of Knowledge 1970; mem. (Hon. Life) Candn. Philos. Assn.; mem. Extve. Council, Humanities Research Council Can., 1970–72; Am. Philos. Assn.; Polish Soc. Arts & Sciences Abroad (U.K.); Polish Inst. Arts & Sciences in Am. (N.Y.); elect. mem., Candn. Assoc. for the Club of Rome; Fellow, Internat. Inst. for Advanced Studies in Systems Rsch. and Cybernetics; author 'Survey of the Status of Philosophy in Canada' 1970; Ed., 'Conceptual Basis of the Classification of Knowledge' 1974; co-ed. 'Polonia of Tomorrow' 1977; Mem. Ed. Bd., 'Future Computing Systems' internat. quarterly; and numerous papers and articles in learned and prof. journs.; recipient Systems Research Foundation Award (for contribution to the advancement of systems philosophy and systems studies) 1984; R. Catholic; Home: 80 Pleasant Park Rd., Ottawa, Ont. K1H 5L9.

**WOLEVER, Thomas Matthew Story,** B.A., M.Sc., B.M., B.Ch., M.A., Ph.D., D.M.; university professor; b. Detroit, Mich. 3 July 1953; s. Thomas Harding Story and Eileen Myrtle (Hislop) W.; e. Harvard H.S.; Framlingham Coll. (U.K.); Corupus Christi Coll., Oxford Univ., B.A. 1976, M.Sc. 1978, M.A., B.M., B.Ch. 1980, D.M. 1993; Univ. of Toronto, Ph.D. 1986; m. Judy d. Ralph and Mary Selby 26 July 1985; two s.: David Thomas, Eric William; ASSOC. PROF., DEPT. NUTRITIONAL SCIENCES, UNIV. OF TORONTO 1992– ; House Officer in Surgery, Devonport Hosp. (U.K.) 1980–81; in Medicine, John Radcliffe Hosp., Oxford 1980; Rsch. Fellow, Div. Endocrinol. & Metab., St. Michael's Hosp. 1983–86; Active Staff Mem. 1987– ; Asst. Prof., Dept. Nutritional Sciences, Univ. of Toronto 1987–92; Sci. Dir., Clinical Nutrition & Risk Factor Modification Ctr., St. Michael's Hosp. 1989– ; Anglican; Fellow, Am. Coll. of Nutrition 1986– ; Mem., Candn. Soc. for Nutri. Sci.; Candn. Soc. of Atherosclerosis; Candn. Diabetes Assn.; author of 100 peer-reviewed pubs.; recreations: orienteering (Candn. M35 Orienteering Champion 1989), recorder playing, cycling; Home: 135 Mavety St., Toronto, Ont. M6P 2L8; Office: Dept. Nutritional Sciences, Univ. of Toronto, Toronto, Ont. M5S 1A8.

**WOLF, Jacquelyn Thayer;** see **SCOTT, Jacquelyn Thayer.**

**WOLFE, Bernard M.J.,** M.A., B.M.,B.Ch., M.Sc., F.R.C.P.C; physician; educator; b. Killdeer, Sask. 31 Dec. 1934; s. Jacob John and Leopoldina Anna (Schneider) W.; e. Univ. of Sask. B.A. 1956; Exeter Coll. Oxford (Rhodes Scholar) B.M.,B.Ch. 1963, M.A. 1967; Guy's Hosp. Sch. of Med. London, Eng. 1960–63; McGill Univ. M.Sc. (Exper. Med.) 1967; m. Elene d. John and Irene Dukellis 30 Dec. 1970; one d. Deanna Marion; PROF. OF MEDICINE, UNIVERSITY OF WESTERN ONTARIO 1980– ; Chrmn., Div. of Endocrinology and Metabolism, Fac. of Med, Univ. of Western Ont. 1987–91; Asst. House Surg. and House Phys. Guy's Hosp. London, Eng. 1963–64; Residency and rsch. training Royal Victoria Hosp. and McGill Univ. Clinic, Montreal 1964–68 (Med. Rsch. Counc. Fellow 1965–67); Centennial Fellow Med. Rsch. Counc. Can., Cardiovascular Rsch. Inst. Univ. of Calif. Med. Center, San Francisco 1968–70; Asst. Prof. of Med. present Univ. 1970, Assoc. Prof. 1973; Chief of Endocrinol. and Metabolism Univ. Hosp. London, Ont. 1972–87; mem. Sci. Review Cttes. Candn. Heart Found. 1979–82, Candn. Diabetes Assn. 1982–85; Med. Rsch. Counc. 1988–91; mem., Conf. Organizing Ctte., Candn. Consensus Conf. on Cholesterol, The Government Conf. Ctr., Ottawa Mar. 1988; Mem., Symposium Ctte., Symposium on Diet, Nutrition and Health, sponsored by The Royal Soc. of Can. and The Food and Nutrition Bd. of U.S. Nat. Rsch. Counc., Univ. of West. Ont. May 1987; Pres. Candn. Lipoprotein Conference 1985–86; recipient Robert W. Kramer Scholarship Campion Coll. Regina 1952; Grolier Soc. Award Sask. Teachers' Coll. Moose Jaw 1953; Sask. Teachers Fedn. Scholarship 1955; World Univ. Service Can. Exchange Scholar to Munich Univ. 1956–57; Leonard Lubbock Prize Clin. Pathol. Guy's Hosp. London 1962; author or co-author numerous publs. Candn. and Am. profl. journs.; Charter mem. Candn. Athersclerosis Soc.; Corresponding Mem., Specialty Ctte. in Endocrinology and Metabolism, Royal Coll. of Phys. and Surgs. of Can. 1987–91; mem. Candn. Med. Assn.; Candn. Soc. Clin. Investig.; Candn. Soc. Endocrinol. & Metabolism (Counc. mem., Candn. Soc. Endocrinol. & Metab. for Univ. of W. Ont. and region 1987–93); Am. Heart Assn. (Counc. on Arteriosclerosis); Candn. Diabetes Assn.; recreations: pre-columbian history, choir, farming; Home: 17 Metamora Cres., London, Ont. N6G 1R2; Office: 5 OF 14 University Hospital, London, Ont. N6A 5A5.

**WOLFE, Honourable Jack,** D.V.M.; veterinarian; former politician; b. Rockglen, Sask. 2 May 1955; s. Edmund Carl and Mary Margaret (Mulvena) W.; e. Western Coll. of Vet. Med., Univ. of Sask., D.V.M. (with distinction) 1979; m. Susan Gail d. Dick and Pat Snyder 26 Jan. 1980; children: Patricia Mary, Katharine Leah, Steven Thomas; VETERINARY PRACTITIONER FOR LARGE ANIMALS (with wife Gail) Rockglen, Sask. 1991– ; Chrmn., Legislative Review Ctte.; first el. Assiniboia-Gravelbourg by-election of Dec. 1988, defeated Oct. 1991; Assoc. Min. of Health 1988–90; Min. of Urban Affairs and Min. resp. for Saskatchewan Housing Corp. 1990–91; Min. resp. for Sask. Property Management Corp. 1990–91; Min. of Community Services, Govt. of Sask. 1991; Min. resp. for the Sask. Alcohol and Drug Abuse Commn. and the Health Rsch. Bd.; practised as a vet. in Alta. for 1 year; returned to Rockglen & estab. veterinary clinic with Gail Wolfe (also a vet.) 1980; also practised vet. med. at thoroughbred & standard bred racetracks in Regina & Saskatoon for 5 yrs.; Roman Catholic; Home: Box 130, Rockglen, Sask. S0H 3R0.

**WOLFE, Major-Gen. (retired) John Patterson,** C.D., Q.C., LL.M.; Canadian Forces (retired); b. Winnipeg, Man. 2 May 1924; s. Harold Bertram Wolfe; e. Univ. of Man. LL.B. 1954 (Gold Medal); King's Coll. London LL.M. 1968; m. late Emily Odilla d. late Angelo Borgna 4 Dec. 1976; one s. John Francis, four d. (by previous marriage) Andrea Gail, Catherine Janice, Lorraine Patricia, Leslie Karen; Judge Advocate Gen., Candn. Forces 1976–82; joined Candn. Army 1942–45, Normandy, wounded in action 1944; rejoined 1951, trans. to Legal Br. 1954; called to Bar 1954; cr. Q.C. 1974; loaned to Tanzanian Govt. to assist in drafting defence leg. 1965–66; Depy Judge Advocate Gen. 1972–75; served 6 months Vietnam as Legal Adviser to Internat. Comn. Control & Supervision; Depy. Head, Canadn. Del. to Diplomatic Conf. on Reaffirmation & Devel. of Humanitarian Law Applicable in Armed Conflicts, Geneva 1973–77 and on Possible Restrictions on Use of Certain Conventional Weapons, Geneva 1979; apptd. ad hoc Comnr. Candn. Pension Comn. (CPC) 1984, apptd. Chrmn. CPC 1985; co-author 'Canadian Perspectives on International Law and Organization' 1974; author various journ. articles; mem. Counc. of Candn. Administrative Tribunals; Internat. Soc. Mil. Law & Law of War (past Dir.); R. Catholic; recreations: swimming, cross-country skiing.

**WOLFE, Jonathan A.;** food executive; b. Toronto, Ont. 23 Oct. 1952; e. Swathmore Coll. Philadelphia, Internat. Econ.; PRES. & C.O.O., THE OSHAWA GROUP LTD. 1990– ; Dir., Bank of Nova Scotia; Food Marketing Institute (Washington, DC); IGA Canada; The Oshawa Group Ltd.; National Am. Wholesale Grocers Assn. (NAWGA); Past Chrmn., Candn. Council Grocery Distributors; Dir., Mount Sinai Hosp.; Office: 302 The East Mall, Toronto, Ont. M9B 6B8.

**WOLFE, Leonhard Scott,** M.Sc., Ph.D., M.D., Sc.D., F.R.C.P. & S. (C), F.R.S.C.; educator; physician; researcher; b. Auckland N.Z. 25 March 1926; s. Paul George and May (Kelsall) W.; e. Cornwall Park Elem. Sch. and Auckland Grammar Sch. 1943; Longburn Missy. Coll. Palmerston North, N.Z. 1943–45; Canterbury Univ. Coll. Univ. of N.Z. B.Sc. 1947, M.Sc. 1949; Univ. of N.Z. Scholar; 1951 Univ. Scholar to Univ. of Cambridge; Cambridge Univ. Ph.D. 1952, Sc.D. 1976; Univ. of W. Ont. M.D. 1958; m. Jeanne Mary d. James Saunders 4 Aug. 1959; children: Alexander Paul, Elizabeth Anne: PROF. OF NEUROLOGY & NEUROSURGERY, MONTREAL NEUROLOGICAL INST. since 1970 and Prof. of Biochem. McGill Univ., Dir. Donner Lab. of Exper. Neurochem., Chrmn. McGill-Med. Research Council Biomed. Mass Spectrometry Unit; Assoc. Prof. of Neurol. & Neurosurg. 1965; Visiting Prof. Centre de Neurochimie CNRS Univ. of Strasbourg, Univ. of W. Ont. Med. Sch., Univ. of Sask. Med. Sch.; Career Investigator, Med. Research Council; Counselor, Intramural Program, Nat. Inst. of Neurol. Communicable Disorders & Stroke; Consultant to Research Program, Eunice Kennedy Shriver Center for Mental Retardation; past mem. Bd. of Dir., Douglas Hosp. Research Centre; Assoc. mem., Ctr. for Aging Rsch., McGill; Assoc. mem. McGill Nutrition and Food Science Centre; past mem., Medical Research Council Selection Ctte. on Scientists and Program Grants Ctte.; mem., Sci. Adv. Ctte., Amyotrophic Lateral Sclerosis Soc. of Canada; Med. Adv. Bd., The Gairdner Found.; Profl. Adv. Bd., Batten Disease Support and Rsch. Assoc.; co-author 'Radiation, Radioactivity and Insects' 1963; over 210 articles and chapters scient. journs. and books; Past Chrmn., Publications Comte. Internat. Soc. Neurochem.; Past Deputy Chief Ed. 'Journal of Neurochemistry'; mem. ed. bds. various med. journs.; mem. Corp. Phys. & Surgs. Que.; Montreal Physiol. Soc. (Past Pres.); Candn. Biochem. Soc; Am. Soc.Neurochem.; Am. Soc. Biol. Chems.; Soc. Neurosciences; Internat. Soc. Neurochem.; Internat. Brain Research Organ.; NDP; recreations: music, philately, ceramics, Third world studies and ecology; Club: Oxford & Cambridge; NIH Alumni Assn.; Peripatetic; Home: 4700 Westmount Ave., Montreal, Que. H3Y 1X4; Office: 3801 University St., Montreal, Que. H3A 2B4.

**WOLFE, Rose,** B.A., Dip.Social Work; university administrator; b. Toronto, Ont.; e. Univ. of Toronto B.A. 1938; Dip.Social Work 1939; m. the late Ray D. s. Maurice and Tillie W. 5 July 1940; children: Jonathan, Elizabeth; CHANCELLOR, UNIVERSITY OF TORONTO; Vice-Chair, Univ. of Toronto Found.; Dir., Mount Sinai Hosp.; Dir., McMichael Candn. Art Collection; Mem. Extve. Ctte. of Bd. of Dirs., Candn. Jewish News; Bd. of Advisors, Stratford Chef School; Mem. Joint Community Relations Ctte. and Offr., Candn. Jewish Congress, Ont. Region (former Vice-Pres.); Mem. Extve. Ctte., Candn. Jewish Congress, National; Mem. Extve. Ctte., Jewish Federation of Greater Toronto; Bd. Mem., Canada-Israel Found. for Academic Exchanges; Life Mem., Extve. Ctte. & Bd. of Dirs., Jewish Family and Child Service; former Bd. of Trustees, Banting Rsch. Institute; Hebrew Union College, Cincinnati, USA; former Trustee, Lester B. Pearson Coll. of the Pacific; former mem. Endowment Ctte., Women's Legal Education and Action Fund; professional experience as Case Worker and Supvr. for Jewish Family and Child Services; Protestant Children's Home; and Young Men's Hebrew Assn.; recipient, Order of Ont. 1992; recreations: tennis, golf, swimming, theatre; Home: 89 Bayview Ridge, Willowdale, Ont. M2L 1E3; Office: Suite 100, Simcoe Hall, Univ. of Toronto, Toronto, Ont. M5S 1A1.

**WOLFE, Saul,** B.A., M.A., Ph.D., F.C.I.C., F.R.S.C.; educator; b. Toronto, Ont. 2 July 1933; s. Louis and Freda (Winograd) W.; e. Bruce Pub. Sch., Toronto 1945; Riverdale Collegiate Inst., Toronto 1950; Univ. of Toronto B.A. 1954, M.A. 1955; Univ. of Ottawa Ph.D. 1957; m. Thelma d. Aaron and Rose Organ 16 June 1957; children: Isaac Stewart, Lesley Aviva; UNIVERSITY PROFESSOR, DEPT. OF CHEMISTRY, SIMON FRASER UNIV. 1990– ; Nat. Rsch. Counc. of Can. Postdoctoral Overseas Fellow, Weizman Inst. of Sci., Israel 1957–59; Sr. Rsch. Sci. Bristol Lab., Syracuse, N.Y. 1959–61; Asst. Prof. 1961, Assoc. Prof. 1965, R.S. McLaughlin Rsch. Prof. 1969, Prof. 1970, Chown Rsch. Prof., Dept. of Chem., Queen's Univ. 1978–90; Visiting Prof., Univ. di Bologna 1973–74, Bar Ilan Univ. 1983; Assoc. Ed. Candn. Jour. of Chem. 1974–77; Pacific Northwest Lectr. 1972; Chem. Soc. of France Lectr. 1972; FMC Lectr., Princeton Univ. 1975; JSPS Lectr., Japan 1979; Van Cleave Lectr., Univ. of Regina 1982; Chem. Soc. of Italy Lectr. 1982; Rsch. Triangle Lectr. 1982; KOSEF Lectr., Korea 1992; mem. Am. Chem. Soc.; Fellow: Chem. Inst. of Can. (also Chrmn. Div. of Organic Chem. 1976–77; recipient Merck Sharp and Dohme Award 1972; R.U. Lemieux Award 1992); Royal Soc. of Can.; recipient Prize for Excellence in Rsch., Queen's Univ. 1984; Killam Rsch. Fellow, Canada Counc. 1990; Home: 168 Chadwick Ct., Apt. 1101, North Vancouver, B.C.: Office: Burnaby, B.C. V5A 1S6

**WOLFE, Stuart,** B.A., J.D.; business executive; b. Honolulu, Hawaii 23 March 1947; s. Herbert 'E.' and Ada Nancy (Zablan) W.; e. Punahou Sch. 1965; Michigan State Univ. B.A. 1969; Univ. of Oregon J.D. 1973; m. Corrine d. William S. Richardson 7 March 1975; children: Amy, James; PRES. & CHIEF EXECUTIVE OFFICER, GRAYMONT LIMITED 1991– ; Law Clerk to the Chief Justice of Hawaii 1973–74; Attorney, Woodell, Mukai & Ichiki 1974–76; Pres. & Chief Extve. Offr., Centennial Dredging & Sand Ltd. 1977–85; Fraser River Pile & Dredge Ltd. 1985–91; Extve. Vice-Pres., Graymont Limited 1989–91; Chrmn., Fraser River Pile & Dredge Ltd.; Chrmn. of the Bd., Continental Lime Ltd.; Chrmn., Graybec Calc Inc.; Chrmn., G.U.S. Holdings, Inc.; Dir., Graymont Limited; clubs: The Vancouver, The Royal Vancouver Yacht, The Arbutus; Home: 2427 West 37 Ave., Vancouver, B.C.; Office: 1160 – 999 West Hastings St., Vancouver, B.C. V6C 2W2.

**WOLFF, Terrance Alban,** B.A., B.Comm.; executive; b. Peterborough, Ont.; s. Alban Cecil and Jean (Thorndyke) W.; e. St. Peters Sch., Peterborough; St. Francis Xavier Univ., Antigonish, N.S., B.A. and B.Comm.; m. Irene, d. J.M. Lapoint; children: Bryon, Marc, Jeanne; CHRMN. OF THE BD., PRES. AND CHIEF EXTVE. OFFR., CORPFINANCE INTERNATIONAL LTD.; joined Bank of Nova Scotia as Asst. Acct. Toronto; New Business Mgr. Canadian Acceptance Corp. Ltd.; Br. Mgr. IAC Ltd. Ottawa, Vancouver and Toronto, Regional Mgr. H.O. Toronto, Asst. Vice-Pres.; Pres., Dir. and C.E.O., Scotia Toronto-Dominion Leasing Ltd.; Pres. & C.E.O. Scotia Leasing Ltd.; Bd. Chrmn., Pres. & C.E.O., Corpfinance International Ltd.; Chrmn., C.F.I. Mortgage Brokers Ltd.; Chrmn., C.F.I. Insur. Brokers Ltd.; Chrmn. & Pres., C.F.I. Leasing Ltd. and C.F.I. Lease Trust; Dir., Alzheimers Assoc. of Ont.; mem. and past Chrmn. of Extve. Comte., Equipment Lessors Assn. of Can.; Candn. Assn. of Equipment Distributors; Bd. of Trade of Metrop. Toronto; recreations: golf, skiing, swimming; Club: Donalda; Home: Gormley, Ont.; Office: 151 Yonge St., Suite 601, Toronto, Ont. M5C 2W7.

**WOLFIN, Louis;** mining executive; b. Winnipeg, Manitoba 18 Sept. 1931; s. Samuel and Lillian (Gelfond) W.; e. St. John's H.S. Winnipeg; m. Joan d. Charles and Marie Hutchinson 5 Sept. 1959; children: Leeann, Lisa, Samra, David; PRESIDENT, MINING EXPLORATION; Chair, Berkeley Resources; Pres., Avino Mines & Resources; Coral Gold; clubs: Richmond Golf & Country, Canyon Golf & Country; Home: Ste. 701, 1985 Bellevue Ave., W. Vancouver, B.C.; Office: Ste. 400, 455 Granville St., Vancouver, B.C. V6C 1T1.

**WOLFISH, Norman Morton,** B.Sc., M.D., FRCP(C), FAAP; pediatric nephrologist; b. Toronto, Ont. 19 Aug. 1935; s. William Edward and Hilda Dorothy (Paskowitz) W.; e. Univ. of Toronto B.Sc. 1957, M.D. 1961; Royal College of Physicians FRCP(C) Ped. 1967, Cert. of Special Competence, Ped. Nephrology; Am. Bd. of Pediatrics FAAP Ped. 1967; m. Elaine d. Jack and Lena Gula 26 June 1963; children: Karen, Laila, Daniel; HEAD, NEPHROLOGY SERVICE, CHILDREN'S HOSPITAL OF EASTERN ONTARIO 1974– ; Ped. Nephrology, Head Nephrol. Unit, Ottawa Gen. Hosp. 1968–74; Head, Dept. of Ped. OGH 1970–74; Dir., Ped. Undergrad. Med. Edn. 1974– ; Sec. to Undergrad. Curriculum Ctte. 1982; Mem., Curriculum Revision Ctte. 1987; Curriculum Planning Ctte. 1988; Chair, Faculty Edn. & Devel. Ctte. 1991–93; Ped. Undergrad. Prog. Directors of Can. 1982–88; Sec., Ped. Test Ctte., Medical Council of Canada (MMC) & Royal College of Physicians & Surgeons of Can. 1986– ; Vice-Chair, Central Exam. Ctte., MMC 1993– ; Prof. of Ped., Fac. of Med., Univ. of Ottawa 1989; Sec., Fac. of Med. & Fac. Council 1989; recreations: skiing, sailing, classical music; Office: 401 Smyth Rd., Ottawa, Ont. K1H 8L1.

**WOLFRAME, Daniel Wayne,** CET, CIM, PMgr.; engineering executive; b. Port Arthur, Ont. 30 Sept. 1941; s. Bruce Austin and Grace (Tinsley) W.; e. Lakehead Univ., Engineering Technology Dipl. (Civil) 1963; Candn. Inst. of Management CIM 1977; m. Gwen d. Ruth and Clarence Thrower 13 July 1968; SENIOR SYSTEM PLANNER & DISTRIBUTION ANALYST, THUNDER BAY HYDRO 1980– ; Engineering Technician, Thunder Bay Hydro 1970–72; Engr. Design Supervisor 1972–80; Dir., N.W. Ont. Electrical Assn. 1975–82; Pres., Ont. Assn. of Cert. Engr. Technicians & Technologists 1990–91; Pres. (Elect) 1989; Vice-Pres. 1988–89; Chair, Finance Ctte. 1988; Chapter Affairs & Member Serv. Ctte. 1986–87; Regional Councillor 1983–88; Pres., District 3, Assn. of Municipal Electrical Utilities 1979–81; United Way & Cancer Soc. Fundraiser 1985– ; Dir., Thunder Bay Big Brothers & Big Sisters Assn. 1972–86; Thunder Bay Community Credit Union 1972–87 (Chair, Finance & Admin.; Mem., Bd. of Dir.); Mem., Planning Executives Inst. (Planning Forum) 1983–89; Candn. Inst. of Mngt. 1974– ; The Inst. of Electrical & Electronics Engrs. 1973– ; Internat. Tech. Inst. (Charter Mem.) 1985– ; recreations: golf, curling, automobile restoration, woodworking; clubs: Fort William Curling, Fort William Country; Home: 76 Oak Ave., Thunder Bay, Ont. P7B 4V9; Office: 34 North Cumberland St., Thunder Bay, Ont. P7A 4L4.

**WOLFSON, Joseph Laurence,** M.Sc., Ph.D.; retired educator; b. Winnipeg, Man. 22 July 1917; s. Samuel Wolfson; e. Univ. of Man. B.Sc. 1942, M.Sc. 1943; McGill Univ. Ph.D. 1948; m. Beatrice d. late Aaron Chaifetz 6 Aug. 1944; children: Diana Dell, Jon Gordon; Asst. Research Offr. Atomic Energy of Canada Ltd. 1948–55; Radiation Physicist Jewish Gen. Hosp. Montreal 1955–58; Assoc. Research Offr. Nat. Research Council of Can. Ottawa 1958–64; Prof. 1964–74 and Assoc. Dean 1969–73, Univ. of Sask., Regina; Dean of Science 1974–80 and Prof. of Physics 1974–82, Carleton Univ.; author number of research papers in physics scient. journs.;mem. Candn. Assn. Physicists; Am. Physical Soc.; Jewish; recreation: photography; Home: 951 Blythdale Rd., Ottawa, Ont. K2A 3N9.

**WOLLESEN, Jens T.,** Ph.D., Dr.Phil.; university professor; b. Lübbecke, Germany 19 Jan. 1947; s. Willy Teunis and Erika Solveig (Küntzel) W.; e. Univ. of Hamburg 1970; Univ. of Freiburg 1975; Univ. of Heidelberg Ph.D. 1975; m. Patricia d. Otfried and Guadalupe Stewens; children: Victor, Christina; ASSOC. PROF., DEPT. OF FINE ART, UNIV. OF TORONTO 1985– ; Visiting Asst. prof., Univ. of Calif. at Santa Barbara 1979–80; Wissenschaftlicher Mitarbeiter, Univ. of Munich 1980–85; Guest Prof., Univ. of Gießen 1984–85; Habilitation (Dr. phil. habil), Univ. of Munich 1985; Asst. Prof., Univ. of Toronto 1985; research, Max-Planck Inst. Rome 1976–79; recipient of 4 grants and 4 fellowships; Mem., Univ. of Toronto Faculty Assn. (Chair, Univ. and External Affairs 1991– ); author: 'Die Fresken von San Piero a Grado bei Pisa' 1977, 'Klaus Arnold Pictor' 1985 and numerous articles and lectures; Home: 65 Cavell Ave., Toronto, Ont. M4J 1H5; Office: 100 St. George St., Toronto, Ont. M5S 1A1.

**WONDERS, William Clare,** C.D., B.A., M.A., Ph.D., Fil. Dr.h.c., F.R.S.C.; educator; b. Toronto, Ont. 22 Apr. 1924; s. George Clare and Ann Mary (Bell) W.; e. Univ. of Toronto, Victoria Coll. B.A. 1946, Ph.D. 1951; Syracuse Univ. M.A. 1948; Uppsala Univ. Fil.Dr.h.c. 1981; m. Lillian d. Dr. Franklin and Juliette Johnson 2 June 1951; children: Karen Elizabeth, Jennifer Anne, Glen William; UNIV. PROF., UNIV. OF ALTA. 1983– , Prof. Emeritus of Geog. 1987– ; Lectr. in Geog. Univ. of Toronto 1948–53; Asst. Prof. of Geog., Dept. of Pol. Econ. present Univ. 1953, Assoc. Prof. 1955, Prof. of Geog. 1957–87, Founding Head Dept. Geog. 1957–67, Founding Chrmn. Boreal Inst. for N. Studies 1960–62; Visiting Prof. Univ. of B.C. 1954; Univ. of Okla. 1965–66; St. Mary's Univ./N.S. Land Survey Inst. 1977; Guest Prof. Uppsala Univ. Sweden 1962–63; Rsch. Fellow in Geog. Aberdeen Univ. 1970–71, 1978; Alta. Visiting Fellow, Edinburgh Univ. 1987; Visiting Prof., Univ. of Victoria 1989; J.F. Kennedy Inst. Free Univ. of Berlin 1990; Policy Bd. mem. Candn. Plains Rsch. Centre Univ. of Regina 1975–86; mem. Alta. Historic Sites Bd. 1978–83, (Vice Chrmn. 1982–83); Adv. Bd. Tyrrell Mus. of Palaeontology 1984–89; Chrmn. Atlas of N. Can. Comte. Royal Soc. Can. 1979–83; mem. Adv. Comte. Toponomy Rsch. Candn. Perm. Comte. on Geog. Names 1981– (Comte. Chrmn. 1982–87); mem. Candn. Nat. Comte. Internat. Geog. Union 1953–61, 1964–72; Nat. Adv. Comte. Geog. Rsch. 1965–69; recipient Victoria Coll. Regent's Gold Medal in Geog. 1946; Can. Council Sr. Rsch. Fellowship 1962–63, Leave Fellowship 1969–70, 1977–78; Nuffield Fellowship 1970–71; Sr. Foreign Scientist Fellowship U.S. Nat. Sci. Foundation 1965–66; Service Award Univ. Alta. 1979, 1984; Govt. Alta. Achievement Award (Excel. cat!) 1980; author 'Looking at Maps' 1960; 'Field Guide: Field Tour Ea 1 (The Canadian Northwest)' 1972; 'Junior Atlas of Alberta Teacher's Manual' 1979; 'The Sawdust Fusiliers' 1991; co-author 'Atlas of Alberta' 1969; 'Junior Atlas of Alberta' 1979; 'World Explorers and Discoverers' 1992; ed. and author 'Canada's Changing North' 1971; 'The North' 1972; 'The Arctic Circle' 1976; 'Knowing the North' 1988; over 100 articles prof. jours., book chapters; Fellow, Royal Soc. Can.; Arctic Inst. N.Am.; mem. Candn. Assn. Geogs. (Pres. 1961–62; Councillor 1953, 1955–57; Award for Service 1982); Royal Scot. Geog. Soc.; Candn. Scandinavian Foundation; Candn. Assn. Scot. Studies (Councillor 1974–77); Champlain Soc. (Councillor 1981–86); Mem., The Muttart Found. 1991– (Dir. 1986–93, Vice Pres. 1991–93); Heraldry Soc. Can.; Sigma Xi; Gamma Theta Upsilon (Hon. mem.); recreations: reading, photography, travel, philately, genealogy; Home: Victoria, B.C. V8R 6K3.

**WONG, George Shoung Koon,** M.Sc., Ph.D.; research engineer; b. Hong Kong 21 July 1935; s. Henry Hon Chung and Elizabeth Lai Yung (Lam) W.; e. St. Joseph's Coll. (Hong Kong); Univ. of Manchester, Inst. of Science & Technology, M.Sc. 1963, Ph.D. 1965; m. Emily d. Yee Wah Kong 5 Oct. 1968; children: Patrick Park Ming, David Kar Ming; SR. RSCH. OFFR., NAT. RSCH. COUNC. 1979– ; joined NRC 1966; Assoc. Rsch. Offr. 1970; Convenor (1) & Mem. (4), var. working groups, Internat. Electrotech. Comn.; Chrmn., Tech. Ctte. on Electroacoustics, Candn. Standards Counc. 1985– ; Chrmn., Am. Nat. Standards Ctte., S1, Acoustics 1990– ; Extve. Ctte. Mem., Acoustics & Noise Control, Candn. Standards Assn. 1985– ; Chrmn., Tech. Ctte. on Engineering Acoustics, Acoustical Soc. Am. 1991– ; major rsch. area: acoustical measurements and standards, and the speed of sound in air; Fellow, Acoustical Soc. of Am.; Inst. of Electrical Engrs.; Mem., Inst. of Mech. Engrs.; Assn. of Profl. Engrs. in Ont.; Assoc. ed., Standards News, JASA 1993– ; author of 40 sci. & tech. articles; recreations: photography, reading, swimming; Club: Ottawa Athletic; Home: 26 Whipporwill Dr., Ottawa, Ont. K1J 7J2; Office: N.R.C., Inst. for Nat. Measurement Standards, Ottawa, Ont. K1A 0R6.

**WONG, Gordon Gokleun,** B.Sc., D.Phil.; scientist; b. Vancouver, B.C. 17 Apr. 1956; s. Sang Lok and May (Lee) W.; e. Univ. of B.C., B.Sc. 1978; Oxford Univ. (Rhodes Scholar) D.Phil. 1981; m. Michelle Ann Hallee 1992; SCIENTIFIC FELLOW, GENETICS INST. INC. 1983– ; Merck Postdoctoral Fellow in Molecular Biology, Harvard Univ. 1981–83; recreation: squash; Office: 87 Cambridge Park Dr., Cambridge, Mass. 02140.

**WONG, Jan,** B.A., M.Sc.; journalist; b. Montreal, Que. 15 Aug. 1952; d. Bill and Eva (Chong) W.; e. McGill Univ. B.A. 1974; Peking Univ. cert. 1977; Columbia Univ. M.Sc. 1981; m. Norman V. s. Jack and Lillian Shulman 31 Oct. 1976; children: Ben Wong Shulman, Sam Wong Shulman; BUSINESS REPORTER, CHINA CORRESPONDENT, GLOBE AND MAIL 1987– ; Business Reporter (Shipping), Montreal Gazette 1981–83; Banking Reporter, Boston Globe 1983–85; Financial Services Reporter, Wall Street Journal 1985–87; Mailing Address: 444 Front St. W., Toronto, Ont. M5V 2S9.

**WONG, Milton K.,** B.A.; investment counsel; b. Feb. 1939; e. Univ. of B.C., B.A. 1963; m. Fei Wendy Gee; children: Andrea, Sarah, Elizabeth; CHRMN. & C.E.O., M.K. WONG & ASSOC. LTD. 1980– ; Portfolio Mgr., Nat. Trust Co. 1963–68; Investment Mgr. 1969–80; Chrmn., M.K. Wong Mngt. Ltd.; Bd. Chrmn., Vancouver Gen. Hosp. 1976–78; Adv. Bd., Salvation Army 1983– ; Dir., Science World British Columbia 1984–89; UBC Dean of Comm. Portfolio Mngt. Soc. 1984– ; Bd., Assn. of Candn. Pension Mngt. 1986– ; Mem., Soc. of Fin. Analysts; Mem. Adv. Counc., Fac. of Commerce & Bus. Admin., Univ. of B.C. 1986– ; Mem. of Counc., Duke of Edinburgh's Award in Canada 1986– ; Mem. Bd. of Dirs., The Laurier Inst.; Past Chrmn. & Dir., Candn. Internat. Dragon Boat Festival; recreations: tennis, fishing, skiing; Clubs: Vancouver; Shaunessey Golf & Country; Home: 5010 Cambie St., Vancouver, B.C. V5Z 2Z5; Office: 2520–1066 West Hastings St., Vancouver, B.C. V6E 3X1.

**WONG, Peter,** P.Eng., B.S.C.E.; b. Moose Jaw, Sask. 8 July 1931; s. King and Mary Lee (Chin) W.; e. Radville H.S.; Univ. of Denver, B.S.C.E. 1954; m. Lynn Won d. Wing Wee and May Yee 25 June 1960; children: Nancy Elaine, Eric Douglas; Mayor, City of Sudbury 1983–91; Construction & Design Engr., Ont. Dept. of Highways 1954–65; Highway Engr. (Bangkok Thailand & Toronto), N.D. Lea & Assoc. 1965–68; Roads Engr., Bor. of Etobicoke 1969; Road & Drainage Engr., City of Sudbury 1969–73; City Engr. 1973–82; Dir., Sudbury Reg. Devel. Corp. 1983–91; Dir., Fed. of Candn. Municipalities 1987–91; Dir., Ont. Good Roads Assn. 1988–92; Mem., Recycle North Task Group 1988–91; Dir. & Trustee, Science North 1984–92; Bd. of Gov., Cambrian Coll. 1984–88; Mem., Solid Waste Assn. of North Am. (Extve. Counc. 1980–84; Internat. Pres. 1984; Sec.-Treas., Ont. Chap. 1977– ); Chrmn., Action Sudbury 1984– ; Vice-Chair, Northern Ont. Heritage Fund Corp. 1993– ; Pres., Ont. Community Council on Impaired Driving 1992– ; recreations: alpine skiing, curling, tennis; clubs: Idylwylde Curling, Temple Tennis; Home: 2069 Elderwood Dr., Sudbury, Ont. P3B 2A7.

**WONG, Robert C.,** B.Sc., M.B.A.; executive; b. Fort Erie, Ont. 27 April 1941; e. Univ. of Toronto B.Sc. (Hons. Math & Physics) 1963; York Univ. M.B.A. 1972; Harvard; Univ. of Waterloo; m. Alice Dong, M.D., C.C.B.O.M. 28 Aug. 1971; DEPY. CHRMN., GLEN ARDITH-FRAZER CORPORATION; MPP Ontario Legislature 1987–90; Min. of Citizenship (Min. Resp. for Race Relations, Multiculturalism and the Ontario Human Rights Commn.) 1989–90; Mem., Cabinet Ctte. on Social Policy; Mem., Cabinet Ctte. on Education, Training and Adjustment; Mem., Cabinet Ctte. on Native Affairs; Mem., Cabinet Ctte. on Drug Abuse; Chrmn., Cabinet Ctte. on Race Relations; Mem., Ontario Round Table on Environment and Economy; Chrmn., Toronto Ontario Olympic Ctte. (TOOC) Multicultural Advisory Council; Minister of Energy, Ont. 1987–89; Mem. Cabinet Ctte. on Economic Policy; Mem. Mgmnt. Bd. of Cabinet; Dir. Abico Management Ltd., Winzen Internat. Inc., Confederation Trust Co., World Television Network/Le Reseay Telemonde Inc.; Dir., St. Stephen's Community House; CAA Toronto; former Vice-Chrmn., Dominick & Dominick Securities Inc.; former Vice-Pres., Walwyn Stodgell Cochran Murray; former Chrmn., Goulding, Rose & Turner Ltd.; former Dir., MultiMedia Capital Corp., May Mikkila Inc., Multilingual Television Ltd., Channel 47 Toronto, Canada's first multilingual TV station, Sky Continental Mgmt. Inc.; Spec. Asst. to Min. of National Health and Welfare 1968–70; Spec. Advr. to Canada's first Min. of State for Multiculturalism 1972; former teacher, Asst. Head Mathematics at Northview Heights Collegiate 1964–68; Pres. Ont. Chinese Liberal Assn. 1986; Pres. Toronto and District Liberal Assn. 1974–76; Chrmn. Investment Comte., Liberal Party of Canada (Ont.); author: 'Computing: An Introduction' 1967; co-author 'Algorithms' 1967; estbd. first brokerage office in Toronto's Chinatown; mem. Toronto Soc. Financial Analysts; Analyst of the Year, Financial Times of Canada 1980; Courvoisier Leadership Award 1989; Hon. lifetime membership, Independent Power Producers' Soc. of Ont. 1989; Liberal; United Church; recreation: reading, travelling; Clubs: Ontario; Mandarin; Home: 240 Spadina Rd., Toronto, Ont. M5R 2V1; Office: 4 King St. W., Suite 1310, Toronto, Ont. M5H 1B6.

**WONHAM, Walter Murray,** B.E., Ph.D., F.R.S.C.; educator; b. Montreal, Que. 1 Nov. 1934; s. Walter Richard and Margaret Eileen (Murray) W.; e. Lower Can. Coll. 1952; McGill Univ. B.E. 1956; Univ. of Cambridge Ph.D. 1961; m. Anne d. Forbes and Jane Hale 8 July 1967; two d. Marjorie Jane, Cynthia Margaret; PROF. OF ELECT. ENG. UNIV. OF TORONTO 1972– ; Asst. Prof. Control & Info. Systems Lab. Dept. Elect. Eng. Purdue Univ. 1961–62; Rsch. Sci. Rsch. Inst. Advanced Studies Baltimore 1962–64; Assoc. Prof. Div. Applied Math. and Div. Eng. Brown Univ. Providence 1969; Rsch. Fellow Nat. Acad. Sci's NASA Electronics Rsch. Center Cambridge, Mass. 1967–69, Cons. to Center 1969–89; Assoc. Prof., Univ. of Toronto 1970–72, Prof. 1972– , J. Roy Cockburn Prof. 1991– ; Visiting Lectr. Queen's Univ. Kingston 1962; Mass. Inst. Technol. 1965; Washington Univ. St. Louis 1977, 1979, 1988; Univ. of Bremen W. Germany 1978; Univ. Fed. do Rio de Janeiro 1979; Academia Sinica Beijing 1979; Min. of Defense Bangalore, India 1986; Indian Inst. Technol. Kanpur 1989; Bilkent Univ. Ankara 1989; NATO Advanced Study Inst. 1981, 1987; author 'Linear Multivariable Control: A Geometric Approach' 1974, new eds. 1979, 1985; Fellow, Inst. Elect. & Electronics Engs. (Control Systems Sci. & Eng. Award 1987); Brouwer Medal, Netherlands Mathematical Soc. 1990; recreations: tennis, sailing, travel; Home: 87 Glencairn Ave., Toronto, Ont. M4R 1M7; Office: Toronto, Ont. M5S 1A4.

**WONNACOTT, Ronald Johnston,** Ph.D., F.R.S.C.; university professor; b. London, Ont. 11 Sept. 1930; s. H. Gordon E. and Muriel Smalley (Johnston) W.; e. Univ. of W. Ont., B.A. 1955 (Pres., Univ. Students' Council, 1954–55); Harvard Univ., A.M. 1957, Ph.D. 1959; m. Frances Eloise, d. Jack C. Howlett, London, Ont., 11 Sept. 1954; children: Douglas, Rob, Cathy Anne; PROF. OF ECON., UNIV. OF WESTERN ONT., since 1965 and Chrmn. of Dept. 1969–72; Teaching Fellow, Econ. Dept. and Law School, Harvard Univ., 1956–58; joined present Univ. as Asst. Prof., 1958–61; Assoc. Prof. 1962–65; Visiting Assoc. Prof., Univ. of Minn., 1961–62; served with R.C.N.R; rank Lt.; former mem. Senate, Univ. of W. Ont.; rec'd Woodrow Wilson, Dafoe and Ford Fellowships; also Harvard Univ. Scholarship; author 'Canadian-American Dependence,' 1962; 'Canada's Trade Options' 1975; 'Selected New Developments in International Trade Theory' 1984; 'Aggressive U.S. Reciprocity' 1984; 'The Economics of Overlapping Free Trade Areas and the Mexican Challenge' 1991; co-author; 'Cost of Capital in Canada,' 1962; 'Free Trade Between the United States and Canada,' 1967; 'Introductory Statistics,' 1969; 'Econometrics,' 1970; 'Introductory Statistics for Business and Economics,' 1972; 'Economics' 1979; 'Regression' 1981; 'Statistics: Discovering its Power' 1982; 'Canadian and U.S. Adjustment Policies in a Bilateral Trade Agreement' 1987; other writings incl. articles in learned jounrs; mem., Candn. Econ. Assn. (Pres. 1981–82); Am. Econ. Assn.; Fellow, Roy. Soc. of Can.; Former Dir., Soc. Sci. Fed. of Can. 1982–83; recreations: golf, skiing, tennis; Clubs: London Hunt; The Honourable Company of Edinburgh Golfers; Sunningdale (England); Craigleith Ski; Home: 171 Wychwood Park, London, Ont. N6G 1S1.

**WOOD, Bernard McCarthy,** M.A.; executive; b. Kent, Eng. 6 June 1945; s. Basil McCarthy and Doreen Margaret W.; e. Loyola Coll. High Sch. Montréal; Loyola Coll. Montréal B.A. 1966; Carleton Univ. M.A. 1969; m. Diane Drinkwater 1965; children: Philip Bernard, Margaret Louise; DIRECTOR, DEVELOPMENT CO-OPERATION DIRECTORATE, ORGANIZATION FOR ECONOMIC COOPERATION & DEVELOPMENT (OECD) 1993– ; Dep. Dir. Parlty. Centre for Foreign Affairs & Foreign Trade, Ottawa 1972–76, served as adv. to numerous parlty. cttes. and dels.; Dir. and C.E.O., The North-South Inst. 1976–88; C.E.O. and Mem. Bd. of Dirs., The Canadian Inst. for International Peace and Security (CIIPS) 1989–92; Center Fellow, Center for Internat. Affairs, Harvard Univ. 1992–93; earlier served as official Fed. Dept. Ind., Trade & Comm., univ. teacher and as trust co. offr.; Comm'd 2nd Lt., Cdn. Army (C.O.T.C.) 1964; Special Adv. to Candn. Del. to UN Gen. Assembly 1979, 1982; Candn. mem., UN Sec.-Gen.'s Group of Governmental Experts on Disarmament & Devel. 1980–82; Personal Rep. of Prime Min. of Can. to Commonwealth Heads of Govt. on Southern Africa 1985–86; Canada's Commonwealth Observer for the Election Process in Namibia 1989; Mem., Canada-Japan Forum 2000 1991–93; author, co-author and ed. numerous popular and scholarly articles and books fields of Candn. foreign policy and North-South relations; mem. Candn. Inst. Internat. Affairs; Internat. Institute of Strategic Studies (London); Royal Commonwealth Soc. (London); Office: 2 rue André-Pascal, 75775 Paris, France.

**WOOD, (William) David,** H.B.A., M.B.A., C.A.; investment dealer executive; b. Windsor, Ont. 16 Feb. 1953; s. David Malcolm and Helen (Moffat) W.; e. Univ. of Western Ont. H.B.A. 1976; York Univ. M.B.A. 1980; Inst. of C.A.s of Ont. C.A. 1978; m. Christine Lemee 2 Dec. 1978; DIR. & VICE-PRES., FIRST MARATHON SECURITIES LIMITED and PRES., CORRESPONDENT NETWORK 1989– ; Audit Manager, Clarkson Gordon 1976–80; Dir., Senior Vice-Pres. & Chief Admin. Offr., Midland Doherty 1981–88; Gov., The Toronto Stock Exchange; Dir., Canadian Depository for Securities; Home: 734 Nautalex Court, Mississauga, Ont. L5H 1A7; Office: Suite 3100, 2 First Canadian Place, Box 21, Toronto, Ont. M5X 1J9.

**WOOD, Francis Ian,** B.A.; foreign service officer; b. Québec City, Qué. 12 Feb. 1935; s. Robert and Helen (Elliott) W.; e. Québec H.S.; Ridley Coll.; Univ. of W. Ont., B.A. (Hons.) 1957; Duke Univ., Commonwealth Fellow (post-grad.) 1958; Univ. of Bordeaux 1970; m. Barbara d. Ruth and Robert (Robin) Kindersley 31 Aug. 1957; children: Robin Felicity, Christopher Kindersley, Nicholas Lawson, (Richard) Evan, Jonathan Scott, Jeremy Justin Antony; MANAGING DIR., TAYLOR-WOOD (CANADA) INC.; Foreign Serv. Offr., Govt. of Can. 1957–90; postings in N.Y., Athens, Vienna, Ottawa, Beirut, Paris, Moscow; Exec. Vice-Pres. (Corp. Dev't), Gatoil Internat., Geneva, London, Houston 1979–81; Ambassador to Kuwait, Bahrain, Qatar, Un. Arab Emirates, Sultanate of Oman 1981–85; Corporate-Higher Education Forum 1986–87; Dir. Gen., Dept. of External Affairs 1987–88; Candn. Consul-General, Seattle, Wash.; retired Sept. 1990; Anglican; Delta Upsilon Frat.; recreations: skiing, tennis, golf, travel, reading, music; Clubs: Royal Portrush Golf; Royal Ottawa Golf, Rockcliffe Lawn Tennis; The Meadows Country Club, Sarasota, FL; Residence: Chalet La Maya, CH-3967 Vercorin, Switzerland.

**WOOD, Gerard Edward,** B.Sc.; mineral industry executive; b. Rochdale, England 13 Oct. 1938; s. Charles William and Cora (Cooper) W.; e. Leeds Univ., B.Sc. (Hons.) 1961; m. Jacqueline d. Catherine and George Sharp 21 July 1962; children: Catherine, Louise, Helen; PRES. & C.E.O., AIMCO INCORPORATED 1993– ; Mining Engr., Iron Ore Co. of Can. 1961–63, 1967–69; Cerro Corp. (Peru) 1963–65; First Maritime Mining Corp. 1965–66; Texas Gulf Sulphur Co. 1966–67; Inst. Mining Investment Analyst, Grant Johnson Ltd. & Hector Chisholm Co. Ltd. 1969–74; Min. Econ., Energy Mines & Resources, Ottawa 1974–80; joined Steep Rock Resources Inc. as Devl. Mgr. 1980, Gen. Mgr. of Opns. 1984, Pres., C.E.O. & Dir., 1985–89; Pres., C.E.O. & Dir., Zemex Corporation; Pres., The Feldspar Corp.; Chrmn. Pyron Corp. 1989–93; Profl. Engr. Mem., Candn. Inst. of Mining & Metal.; Bd. Mem., Colburn Gem and Mineral Museum (Asheville, NC); author of var. profl. articles, speeches, rsch. reports & other materials; recreation: glider pilot; Home: 320 Vanderbilt Rd., Asheville, N.C. 28803, U.S.A.

**WOOD, Gordon Walter,** B.Sc. (cl), M.Sc., Ph.D., F.C.I.C.; educator; b. Little River, N.S. 6 Apr. 1933; s. Walter Amos and Marie Ella (Sarson) W.; e. N.S. Teachers Coll. 1951; Mt. Allison Univ., B.Sc. (cl) Hons. 1955; M.Sc. 1956; Syracuse Univ., Ph.D. 1962; m. Marjorie, d. William and Kathleen Fraser, 18 Aug. 1956; children: Michael; Beth; VISITING PROF., ONTARIO INSTITUTE FOR STUDIES IN EDUCATION 1992– ; Volunteer Tutor, East End Literacy, Toronto 1993– ; Principal, Dutch Settlement Sch., Halifax Cty., N.S. 1951–52; Research Chemist, Paints Div., CIL 1956–58; Research Assoc., MIT 1962–63; joined Univ. Windsor 1963 as Asst., then Assoc., Full Prof.; Acting Head, Dept. Chem. 1971–72; Prof. of Chemistry 1975–92; Assoc. Dean, Graduate Studies 1979–82; Dean, Graduate Studies & Research 1982–85; Vice Pres. Acad. 1985–91; Visiting Assoc. Research Scientist, Univ. Calif., Berkeley 1969–70; Chargé de recherche, Univ. Dijon, France 1976–77; Visiting Prof., Florida State Univ. 1991–92; Visiting Prof., Curtin Univ., Australia 1992; co-author of more than 50 publications on chemistry and mass spectrometry since 1965; Bennett Scholar 1952–53; Beaverbrook Scholar, 1953–55; Bristol Fellow 1961–62; elected to Sigma Xi, Phi Lambda Upsilon 1962; elected Fellow, Chem. Inst. Can. 1976; mem. Chem. Inst. Can. (Chrmn., Essex-Kent Sect. 1978–79); Am. Chem. Soc.; Am. Soc. for Mass Spectrometry (Dir. 1984–86); Univ. Windsor Faculty Assn. (Pres. 1968–69); Ont. Confed. Faculty Assns. (Vice-Chrmn. 1971–72); Candn. Assn. Univ. Teachers (Bd. Dirs. 1972–74); Biomedical Mass Spectrometry (Ed. Adv. Bd. 1976–87); Consultant, Mich. Cancer Foundation 1977–78; Counc. Ont. Univ. 1981–82; Ont. Counc. Grad. Studies 1982–85 (Depy. Chrmn. 1984–85); Bd. of Dirs., Inst. Chemical Science & Technology 1987–90; Teacher Education Council, Ont. 1989–91; recreations: alpine skiing; gardening; Home: 92 King St. E., Apt. 1708, Toronto, Ont. M5C 2V8.

**WOOD, James Douglas,** B.Sc., Ph.D., D.Sc.; educator; b. Aberdeen, Scot. 25 Jan. 1930; s. James and Hilda (Johnston) W.; e. Robert Gordon's Coll. Aberdeen 1947; Univ. of Aberdeen B.Sc. 1951, Ph.D. 1954; m. Leila Margaret d. Blake Nephew, Finch, Ont. 29 Dec. 1956; children: Roderick James, Robert Gordon, John Stewart; PROF. OF BIOCHEM., UNIV. OF SASK. since 1968; Research Offr. Can. Dept. Agric. Ottawa 1954–57; Sr. Scient. Fisheries Research Bd. of Can., Vancouver 1957–61; Head, Physiol. Chem. Sec. Defence Research Med. Labs. Toronto 1961–68; Head, Dept. of Biochem., present univ. 1968–87; Asst. Dean of Med. Univ. Sask. 1975–78; mem. Council, Med. Research Council of Can. 1976–82; author over 100 research papers on biochem. and neurochem.; mem. Candn. Biochem. Soc. (Council 1975–78); Internat. Soc. Neurochem.; Am. Soc. Neurochem.; recreations: curling, golf; Home: 318 Sturgeon Dr., Saskatoon, Sask. S7K 4C4; Office: Dept. of Biochemistry, Univ. of Saskatchewan, Saskatoon, Sask. S7N 0W0.

**WOOD, John Denison,** B.A.Sc., M.S., Ph.D.; civil engineer; b. Calgary, Alta. 28 Sept. 1931; s. Ernest William and Ellen Gartshore (Pender) W.; e. Crescent Heights High Sch., Calgary, 1949; Univ. of B.C., B.A.Sc. (Civil Engn.) 1953; Stanford Univ., M.S. (Civil Engn.-Structures) 1954, Ph.D. (Civil Engn. & Engn. Mech.)1956; m. Christena Isabel, d. Charles Visser, Calgary, Alta., 24 July 1953; one d., Donna M.; PRES. & CHIEF EXTVE. OFFR., CANADIAN UTILITIES LTD. 1988– ; Research Asst. in Civil Engn. and Engn. Mech., Stanford Univ., 1953–56; Assoc. Mgr., Dynamics Dept., Engn. Mech. Lab. Space Tech. Labs., Inc., Redondo Beach, Calif. 1956–63; Pres. and Dir., Mechanics Research Inc., El Segundo, Calif. 1963–66; Sr. Vice Pres., Engn. & Research, ATCO Ind. Ltd. 1966–68; Sr. Vice Pres., Eastern Region, ATCO Ind. Ltd. 1968–75; Sr. Vice Pres., Planning ATCO Ind. Ltd.; 1975–77; Pres. and C.E.O., ATCO Industries N.A. Ltd. 1977–82; Pres. and C.E.O., ATCOR Resources Ltd. 1982–84; Pres. and C.O.O., Candn. Utilites Ltd. 1984–88; Chrmn. of the Bd. & C.E.O.: Alberta Power Ltd.; Canadian Western Natural Gas Co. Ltd.; Northwestern Utilities Ltd.; Northland Utilites Enterprises Ltd.; Chrmn. of the Bd., Frontec Logistics Corp.; Dir.: ATCO Ltd.; ATCO Enterprises Inc.; Candn. Utilities Ltd.; ATCOR Ltd.; Thames Power Ltd.; Barking Power Limited; Vencap Equities Alberta Ltd.; Western Orthopaedic & Arthritis Rsch. Foundation; The Council for Canadian Unity; Jr. Achievement of Canada; Bd. of Govs., Junior Achievement of Northern Alberta; co-author, 'Ballistic Missile and Space Vehicle Systems' 1961; awarded Candn. Academy of Engineering Fellowship 1991; Athlone Fellowship; mem., Engn. Inst. of Can.; Scientific Research Soc. of Amer.; President's Club Adv. Ctte. Univ. of Alberta; Mem. of the Calgary Economic Development Authority Advisory Council; Economic Development Edmonton Business Advisory Council; Assn. Prof. Engrs. Alta.; Tau Beta Pi; Sigma Xi; Baptist; recreations: golf, badminton; Clubs: Glencoe; Earl Grey; Calgary Petroleum; Mayfair Golf & Country; Office: 10035 - 105 St., Edmonton, Alta. T5J 2V6.

**WOOD, Neil Cameron Walker;** executive; b. Leeds, Eng. 27 June 1930; s. Dr. James Walker and Minnie (Pennington) W.; e. Moorlands Prep Sch., Leeds, Eng., 1935–42; Bootham Sch., Yorks., Eng., 1942–47; Leeds Engn. Coll., 1947–49 and 1951–52; m. Sue, d. Raymond P. Corby; Children: Stuart Cameron Walker, Charles Cameron Walker, Jane Walker, Kate Walker; PRESIDENT, WALKER WOOD LTD. since 1959; Pres., Camwood Realty Ltd.; Past Chrmn., Fidelity Trust, Fort Gary Trust; served with Brit. Army, REME attached to Edinburgh Univ. 1949–51; comnd. Queen's Own Cameron Highlanders, Candn. Army Reserve 1959; mem. Old York Scholars Assn.; Anglican; recreations: sailing, riding; Clubs: The National; Home: Walker Wood Farms, R.R. #2, Georgetown, Ont. L7G 4S5; Office: 139 John St., Toronto, Ont. M5V 2E4.

**WOOD, Neil R.,** B.Com., M.B.A.; executive; b. Winnipeg, Man. 22 Aug. 1931; s. Reginald and Pearl (Beake) W.; e. Pub. and High Schs., Winnipeg, Man.; Univ. of Man., B.Com. 1952; Harvard Univ., M.B.A. 1955; m. Jean, d. John Hume, 10 Aug. 1957; children: Barbara, David, John, Brian; PRES., C.E.O. & DIR., MARKBOROUGH PROPERTIES INC.; Asst. Mgr., Ont. Real Estate Invest. Office, Great-West Life Assurance Co. 1955–59; Pres. Canadianwide Properties Ltd. 1962; The Fairview Corp. Ltd. and Cadillac Fairview Corp. Ltd. 1959–81; Pres. and Dir. 1971–81; Pres. N. R. Wood Develop. Corp. Ltd. 1982–84; Exec. Vice Pres. and Dir., Campeau Corp. 1985; mem. Bd. Trustees and Past Pres., Internat. Council Shopping Centres; Pres. & Dir., Candn. Inst. of Public Real Estate Cos.; Dir., Roy Thomson Hall; Bd. of Govs., Olympic Trust; recreations: golf, skiing, water sports, music; Clubs: Toronto; Rosedale; Beacon Hall; Loxahatchee; Lost Tree; Craigleith Ski; Beaumaris; Home: R.R. 3, Newmarket, Ont. L3Y 4W1; Office: Suite 2800, One Dundas St. W., Toronto, Ont. M5G 2J2.

**WOOD, Peter Gillard,** M.A.; banker; b. Wolverhampton, Eng., 22 Aug. 1932; s. late Frederick Daniel and Phyllis Marjorie (Hall) W.; e. Primary Sch., Linton, Eng. 1941; Eccleshall 1942; King Edward VI Sch., Stafford, Eng. 1950 (Sch. Cert. 1946, Higher Sch. Cert. 1949, 1950, Co. Maj. Scholar. 1950, Sch. Leaving Scholar, 1950); Queen's Coll., Oxford Univ., M.A. 1955; came to Canada 1955; m. Patricia Jane Laurie, d. late Eric Burns, Ottawa, 1 Aug. 1958; children: Christopher David Gillard, Elizabeth Ann, Sara Laurie, Judith Marjorie; Pres., Peter G. Wood Associates Inc. 1987–89; with J.H. Crang & Co. as Invest. Analyst 1955; Party Chief, ABEM (Canada) Ltd. 1956; Coordinator, Systems Dept., Arvida Works and later Sr. Operations Analyst, Montreal, Aluminum Co. of Canada Ltd. 1957; Mgr., Systems Devel., Canadian Ingersoll-Rand 1965; Functional Dir., P.S. Ross & Partners 1967; apptd. Asst. Dir., Inst. Candn. Bankers, March 1969; Assoc. Dir., Nov. 1969; Dir., Inst. of Candn. Bankers 1971–76; Vice Pres. International Banking, Canadian Commercial and Industrial Bank 1976–81; Pres. & CEO., Wells Fargo Bank Canada 1981–85; Pres. & C.E.O. Oxford Trust Co. Ltd. 1987–89; former Sr. Vice Pres., Barclays Bank; served with Royal Arty. 1950–52; Comnd. 1951, with Terr. Army 1952–55; Chrmn., Council on Prof. and Business Educ.; Inst. Assn. Extves.; mem., Cdn. Ch. of Comm.; recreations: golf, tennis, bridge; Clubs: Canadian; University; St. James's; Edmonton; Univ. of Alta. Faculty; Ranchmen's, Calgary.

**WOOD, Tom,** B.F.A.; actor; playwright; b. Dawson Creek, B.C. 5 May 1950; s. Jessie and Yvette (Bachand) W.; e. Univ. of Alta., B.F.A. 1972; Prin. Actor Stratford Festival 1976–80 and '91, Shaw Festival 1982–86 and '88; Assoc. Dir. Vancouver Playhouse 1980; Writer in Residence and Prin. Actor Phoenix Theatre Edmonton 1982–84; actor most regional theatres in Can.; Acting Teacher, Studio 58, Vancouver and Ryerson Polytech 1990; co-author 'North Shore Live' 1982 (Jessie Award Best New Play); author 'B-Movie' play 1986 (Chalmers Award Best Play 1988); Address: Box 3171, St. Mary's, Ont. N4X 1A7.

**WOOD, W. Donald,** Ph.D.; b. Palermo, Ont. 5 Apr. 1920; s. George Stanley and Ethel (Popplewell) W.; e. McMaster Univ., B.A. 1950; Queen's Univ., M.A. 1952; Princeton Univ., A.M., Ph.D. 1955; m. Constance, d. Wm. Leigh, Scotia Junction, Ont., 25 Aug. 1945; children: Leslie Anne, Sandra Leigh; Emeritus Prof. of Econ. and Dir., Indust. Relations Centre 1960–85 (and first Dir., Sch. of Industrial Relations 1983–85) Queen's Univ.; Dir., Indust. Relations Research Div., Imperial Oil Ltd., Toronto, 1955–60; general merchant and postmaster 1945–48; served with R.C.A.F. during 2nd World War; mem. many public comns. and adv. bds. incl. former Chrmn. Ont. Econ. Council; United Church; recreations: sports; public affairs; Home: 54 Edgehill St., Kingston, Ont. K7L 2T5.

**WOOD, Warren Gregory,** B.A.Sc., M.Eng.Sc., P.Eng.; consulting executive; b. Hamilton, Ont. 11 Oct. 1947; s. John Edward and Marguerite Pearl (Bailey) W.; e. Univ. of Waterloo, B.A.Sc. 1971; Univ. of Melbourne, M.Eng.Sc. 1976; children: Sara Louise, Justine Katherine; PRES., N.D. LEA INTERNAT. LTD. 1990– ; Vice Chrmn., Lea Group; Cons., Project Mgr. (Australia, Venezuela), Alan M. Voorhees & Assoc. 1973–76; Staff Cons., Transp. Devel. Ctr., Montreal 1976–77; Gen. Mgr., Partner, James F. Hickling Mngt. Cons., Ottawa 1977–87; Extve. Dir., Candn. Inst. of Guided Ground Transp., Queen's Univ. 1987–90; Dir., James F. Hickling Mngt. Cons.; Adjunct Prof., Civil Engr., Queen's Univ.; Past Chrmn., Goods Movement Ctte., Roads & Transp. Assn. of Can.; Mem., TAC; Candn. Transp. Rsch. Forum; recreations: skiing, sailing; Home: 24 Cedar Ave., Toronto, Ont.; Office: 251 Consumers Rd., Willowdale, Ont. M2J 4R3.

**WOODBRIDGE, Peter Eric,** B.Sc., M.Sc.; company executive; b. Cheshire, England 21 Feb. 1945; s. Eric James and Margaret Mary (Poustie) W.; e. St. Anselm's Coll. 1960; Univ. of Reading, B.Sc. 1970, Univ. of Bradford, M.Sc. 1971; m. the late Rosemary Ann d. Derek and May Paget 18 Dec. 1982; children: Laura Elizabeth, Michael Andrew, Claire Alexandra, Robert Edward; PRESIDENT, PETER WOODBRIDGE & ASSOCIATES LTD. (forest industry consultants) 1991– ; var. corp. finan. analysis positions in London (U.K.) 1971–74; emigrated to Canada 1974; established cons. practice 1978; acquired F.L.C. Reed & Assoc. 1980; merged with H.A. Simons Ltd. 1985; Vice-Pres. Mktg., H.A. Simons Ltd. 1986; Pres., Woodbridge Reed and Assocs. Ltd. 1980–91; Vice-Pres., Business Planning, H.A. Simons Ltd. 1986–91; Rugby Union: rep. Univ. of Reading 1967–70 (Colours); author: 'B.C. Constraints to Growth' 1983; 'Management in a Climate of Change' 1986; 'Canada's Forest Industry, The Next Twenty Years: Prospects and Priorities' 1988; 'Vision 2010: A Strategic Framework for Growth in B.C.'s Forest Sector' 1992; and var. mag. articles; recreations: climbing, sailing, chess; Home & Office: 1084 Eyremount Dr., West Vancouver, B.C. V7S 2B5.

**WOODCOCK, George,** LL.D., D.Litt., F.R.G.S.; author; editor; b. Winnipeg, Man. 8 May 1912; s. Samuel Arthur and Margaret Gertrude (Lewis) W.; e. Sir William Borlase's Sch.; Morley Coll., London, England; LL.D., Victoria, Winnipeg; D.Litt., Sir George Williams, Ottawa, U.B.C.; m. Ingeborg Hedwig Elisabeth, d. Otto Linzer, Offenbach, Germany, 10 February 1949; Broadcaster (has contributed several hundred talks and scripts of plays and documentaries to CBC programs); Editor of 'NOW,' 1940–47; prof. writer since 1946; first in England to 1949 and afterwards in Can. with interludes of teaching (Univ. of Wash. 1954–55, Univ. of B.C. since 1956, resigning rank of Assoc. Prof. in 1963 to devote more time to writing); Ed., 'Canadian Literature' 1959–77; has travelled greatly in Europe, S.A., the South Pacific and Asia; Guggenheim Fellowship, 1951–52; Candn. Govt. Overseas Fellowship, 1957–58; Can. Council Travel Grants, 1961, 1963, 1965; Gov. General's Award 1967; Can. Council Killam Fellowship 1970–71; Molson Prize 1973;Can. Council Sen. Art Award, 1978; UBC Medal for Popular Biography, 1971 and 1975; C.A.A. Award 1989; Publications: 'The White Island' 1940; 'The Centre Cannot Hold' 1943; 'William Godwin: A Biography' 1946; 'The Incomparable Aphra: A Life of Mrs. Aphra Behn' 1948; 'The Writer and Politics' 1948; 'Imagine the South' 1947; 'The Paradox of Oscar Wilde' 1950; 'A Hundred Years of Revolution: 1848 and After' 1948; 'The Letters of Charles Lamb' 1950; 'The Anarchist Prince' 1950 (later trans. into French); 'Ravens and Prophets: Travels in Western Canada' 1952; 'Pierre-Joseph Proudhon' 1956; 'To the City of the Dead: Travels in Mexico' 1956; 'Incas and Other Men: Travels in Peru' 1959; 'Anarchism' 1962; 'Faces of India' 1964; 'Asia, Gods and Cities' 1966; 'The Greeks in India' 1966; 'A Choice of Critics' 1966; 'The Crystal Spirit' 1966; (Gov. Gen. Award for Eng. Non-fiction); 'Kerala' 1967; 'Selected Poems' 1967; 'The Doukhobors' 1968; 'Canada and the Canadians' 1969; 'The British in the Far East' 1969; 'The Hudson's Bay Company' 1970; 'Odysseus Ever Returning' 1970; 'Gandhi' 1971; 'Dawn and the Darkest Hour: A Study of Aldous Huxley' 1972; 'Herbert Read: The Stream & the Source' 1972; 'The Rejection of Politics' 1972; 'Who Killed the British Empire?' 1974; 'Amor de Cosmos' 1974; 'Gabriel Dumont' 1975; 'Notes on Visitations' 1975; 'South Sea Journey' 1976; 'Peoples of the Coast' 1977; 'Northern Spring' 1977; 'Letter to the Past'; 'Thomas Merton: Monk and Poet' 1978; 'The Kestrel and Other Poems' 1978; 'Faces from History' 1978; 'The Canadians' 1979; 'The World of Canadian Writing' 1980; 'The George Woodcock Reader' 1980; 'The Mountain Road' 1981; 'Confederation Betrayed' 1981; 'Taking it to the Letter' 1981; 'Letter to the Past' 1982; 'The Benefactor' 1982; 'Collected Poems' 1983; 'British Columbia: A Celebration' 1983; 'Orwell's Message' 1984; 'Strange Bedfellows' 1985; 'The Walls of India' 1985; 'The University of British Columbia' 1986; 'Northern Spring' 1987; 'Beyond the Blue Mountain' 1987; 'The Social History of Canada' 1988; 'Caves in the Desert' 1988; 'The Purdy-Woodcock Letters' 1988; 'The Marvellous Century' 1988; 'The Century That Made Us' 1989; 'Powers of Observation' 1989; 'British Columbia: A History of the Province' 1990; 'Tolstoy at Yasnaya Polyana and other poems' 1991; 'The Monk and His Message' 1992; 'Anarchism and Anarchists' 1992; 'Power To Us All' 1992; 'Letter from the Kyber Pass' 1993; 'George Woodcock on Canadian Fiction' 1993; 'George Woodcock on Canadian Poetry' 1993; Home: 6429 McCleery St., Vancouver, B.C. V6N 1G5.

**WOODCOCK, John Robert,** Hons. B.A. Business Administration; business executive; b. Galt, Ont. 30 July 1939; s. Maurice Clifton and Lila Luella (Deyell) W.; e. Grimsby H.S.; North Bay Coll.; Queen's Univ.; Univ. of West. Ont., Hons. B.A. Business Administration; m. Sandra Caryle Lindberg 9 Mar. 1962; children: Kelly, Kimberly; PRES. & CHIEF EXTVE. OFFR., J.R./JANUS MERCHANT BROKERS, INC. 1987– ; Prod. Mgr., Beecham Prod. 1962–64; Acct. Extve., Ogilvy & Mather 1964–66; Mktg. Mgr., Bristol Myers 1966–69; Extve. Vice-Pres., Nat. Student Mktg. Ltd. 1969–70; Partner, Sr. Partner & Pres., Hickling-Johnston Limited 1970–87; Dir., William M. Mercer Limited 1984–87; Mng. Dir., Mercer Meidinger Inc. 1984–87; Dir. & Past Pres., M & A Internat.; Past Pres., Candn. Assn. of Mngt. Cons.; Mem., Inst. of Mngt. Cons. of Ont. (cert. mngt. cons.); XPO; Assn. for Corp. Growth; Assoc. Mem., Candn. Inst. of Chartered Bus. Valuators; recreations: skiing, tennis, fishing; clubs: Alpine Ski, Boulevard, Cambridge, Sigma Chi; Home: 2045 Lakeshore Blvd. W., #4604, Toronto, Ont. M8V 2Z6; Office: 65 Queen St. W., #605, Toronto, Ont. M5H 2M5.

**WOODCOCK, Kathleen Eva,** B.A.; university administrator; b. Petrolia, Ont. 2 June 1955; d. Aldon Clifford and Mary Elizabeth Adaline (Cassan) Stewardson; e. Merlin Dist. H.S. 1974; Wilfrid Laurier Univ. B.A. 1978; m. Robert s. Thomas and Jean Woodcock 27 Aug. 1977; children: Lauren Blakely, Mallory Elayne; ADMINISTRATIVE ASSISTANT, FACULTY OF SOCIAL WORK, WILFRID LAURIER UNIV. 1993– ; Administrative Sec., Admin., Wilfrid Laurier Univ. 1986–89; Field Admin. Asst., Fac. of Social Work 1989–93; Dir., Advanced Detection Systems Inc. 1992– ; Mem., Bd. of Gov., Wilfrid Laurier Univ. 1992– ; Vice-Pres., Confederation of Ont. Univ. Staff Assns. 1992–93, 1993–94; Pres., Wilfrid Laurier Univ. Staff Assn. 1990–91, 1991–92; Vice-Pres. 1989–90; Home: 49 Pinemeadow Cres., Waterloo, Ont. N2T 1A6; Office: 75 University Ave. W., Waterloo, Ont. N2L 3C5.

**WOODFINE, William Joseph,** M.A., Ph.D.; retired university professor; b. Montreal, Que. 21 May 1930; s. Peter Gerard and Mona (McManus) W.; e. St. Francis Xavier Univ., B:A. 1951; McGill Univ., M.A. 1953; Mass. Inst. of Tech., Ph.D. 1959; m. Helen Mary, d. John Macken, Montreal, Que., 15 Aug. 1953; children: Mary, Peter, Jennifer, Paul, Julie, John, Susan; Prof. of Economics, St. Francis Xavier Univ., retired; Consultant, Royal Comn. on Educ., Public Services and Provincial-Municipal Relations; NDP Candidate fed. elections 1979, 1981; Economic Adv., Resch. Dept., Canadian Pacific Ltd., Montreal 1981–83; Instr. Concordia Univ. 1981–83; Sr. Fellow, Can. Council, London Sch. of Econ., U.K. 1967–68; mem. Bd. of Broadcast Govs. 1963–67; mem. Task Force, Structure of Candn. Industry, 1967; Chrmn. (1972) N.S. Task Force on Cost of Prescription Drugs; mem., N.S. Health Council; Candn. Econ. Assn.; mem. Am. Economic Assn.; R. Catholic; Home: Macken Rd., Antigonish Landing, Antigonish, N.S. B2G 2L5.

**WOODLEY, Donald Philip,** B.Comm., M.B.A.; microcomputer manufacturer; b. Saskatoon, Sask. 10 Dec. 1945; s. Philip MacIntyre and Doris Ada (Mahan) W.; e. Univ. of Sask. B.Comm. 1967; Univ. of W. Ont. M.B.A. 1970; m. Janice d. Robert and Lela Turner 15 July 1945; children: Allison, Erin, Sarah; PRES., COMPAQ CANADA INC. 1987; joined Xerox Canada Inc. 1972–84, Mktg. Mgr.; Vice Pres. Sales, Forum Learning Systems 1984–85, Dir. 1984–88 ; Vice Pres. Sales & Mktg. Crowntek Inc. 1985–87; Pres. Olympium Synchronized Swimming Club 1987–88; Club: Brampton Golf; Home: 178 Markland Dr., Etobicoke, Ont. M9C 1P7; Office: 111 Granton Dr., Richmond Hill, Ont. L4B 1L5.

**WOODS, David Ainsley;** writer (poet, playwright), community activist, artist, actor; b. Trinidad, W.I. 21 Aug. 1959; s. Reginald and Rachel Hyacinth (Howe) W.; e. Dartmouth H.S. 1977; Dalhousie Univ. 1977–81; FOUNDER & ARTISTIC DIR., VOICES BLACK THEATRE ENSEMBLE 1991– ; Program Dir., Black United Front of N.S. 1981–82; Founder & Dir., Cultural Awareness Youth Group of N.S. 1982–88; Program Dir., Black Cultural Ctr. of N.S. 1988–89; Program Consultant, Halifax City Regional Libraries regarding Black History & Culture programs; Principal organizer, Black History Month Celebrations, Halifax 1984–92; Mem., Black Artists' Network of N.S.; Candn. Black Artists in Action; author: 'Native Song' (poetry) 1990; 'Part of the Deal' 1991, 'Black Journey' 1992, 'Aunt Jemima Story' 1993 (CBC radio dramas); 'For Elsie Dorrington' 1982, 'Voices' 1984, 'The Dream Continues' 1986, 'The Detention' 1992, 'Talk that Talk' 1993 (stage dramas); Dir., 'Black Loyalists of Nova Scotia' 1991 (video); recipient Nova Scotia Poetry Award 1989; Home: 3 Farthington Place, Apt. 405, Dartmouth, N.S. B3A 2K3.

**WOODS, David James,** B.A., M.B.A., C.A.; advertising executive; b. Toronto, Ont. 24 Aug. 1950; s. Joseph Patrick and Evelyn Mary (Philp) W.; e. Univ. of Toronto B.A. 1972, M.B.A. 1974; m. Karen d. Harry and Lorna Joy 15 July 1972; children: Bryan James, Bradley Christopher, Kristen Leanne; EXECUTIVE VICE-PRESIDENT, MEDIACOM INC. 1992– ; C.A. Thorne Riddell and Co. 1975–77; Controller, Ripley International Limited (owners of 'Ripley's Believe It Or Not') 1977; Vice-Pres. Finance & Dir. 1979–82; Vice-Pres. Systems & Admin., Mediacom Inc. 1982; Vice-Pres. Finance 1983; Sr. Vice-Pres. Finance & Admin. 1989; Sr. Vice-Pres. Sales 1989–92; Dir., Outdoor Advtg. Assn. of Canada & 1st Vice-Chair 1984– ; Dir., Candn. Outdoor Measurement Bureau 1991– ; clubs: Bd. of Trade of Metro Toronto, Boulevard; Home: 898 Kowal Dr., Mississauga, Ont. L5H 3T4; Office: 250 Bloor St. E., Ste. 600, Toronto, Ont. M4W 1G6.

**WOODS, Herbert A.,** B.A.Sc., M.A.Sc.; executive; b. Mount Forest, Ont. 12 Dec. 1947; s. Charles S. and late Elda G. (Winslade) W.; e. Univ. of Waterloo B.A.Sc. 1970, M.A.Sc. 1971; m. Barbara d. Allan and Annabelle Langdon 18 Aug. 1967; children: Krista, Ted; PRES., GANDALF MOBILE SYSTEMS INC., Ottawa, Ont. 1990– ; mem. Sci. Staff Bell-Northern Research, Ottawa 1971–78, voice communication systems, Mgr. Voice & Data Communications Systems Devel.; Vice Pres. Cableshare Inc. London, Ont 1978–84, Electronic Mktg Div., New Bus. Devel.; Vice Pres. Sales & Mktg. Develcon Electronics Ltd., Saskatoon 1984–85, Pres. and Chief Operating Offr. 1985–88; Gen. Mgr., Gandalf Technologies Inc. 1988–90; recreations: curling, golf; Home: 23 Halldorson Cres., Kanata, Ont. K2K 2C6.

**WOODS, John Hayden,** M.A., Ph.D., F.R.S.C.; philosopher; b. Barrie, Ont. 16 March 1937; s. late John Frederick and Gertrude Mary (Hayden) W.; e. St. Mary's Sch., St. Joseph's High Sch. and Barrie (Ont.) & Dist. Coll. Inst.; Univ. of Toronto B.A. 1958, M.A. 1959; Univ. of Mich. Ph.D. 1965; m. Carol Gwendolyn d. late Walter Arnold, Toronto, Ont.; children: Catherine Lynn, Kelly Ann, Michael John; PROFESSOR OF PHILOSOPHY, UNIV. OF LETHBRIDGE, 1979– and ADJUNCT PROF. OF SPEECH, UNIV. OF AMSTERDAM 1988– ; Teaching Asst. Univ. of Toronto 1958–59, Lectr. 1962–64, Asst. Prof. 1964–66 Assoc. Prof. 1966–71 also Assoc. Prof. Centre for Linguistic Studies 1966–71 (Extve. Comte. 1966–67); Toronto and Dist. Rep. Nat. Film Bd. Can. 1958–59; Teaching Fellow, Univ. of Mich. 1959–61, Instr. 1961–62, Assoc. Prof. Summer Inst. of Linguistic Soc. Am. 1967; Visiting Prof. Stanford Univ. summer 1971; Prof. Univ. of Victoria 1971–76, Chrmn. Dept. Philos. 1974–75, Assoc. Dean Faculty of Arts & Science 1975–76; Dean, Faculty of Humanities, Univ. of Calgary and Prof. of Philos. 1976–79; Pres., Vice-Chancellor, Univ. of Lethbridge 1979–86; Visiting Prof., Univ. of Amsterdam 1988–90, 1992–93; Visiting Prof., Univ. of Groningen 1988–89; Fellow, Netherlands Inst. for Advanced Study 1990; rec'd Horace H. Rackham Univ. Fellowship 1961; Can. Council Research Grants 1968–69, 1971; Humanities Research Council Grants 1974, 1976; Social Scis. and Humanities Rsch. Counc. Grants 1986–87 and 1992; recipient Distinguished Rsch. Award, Internat. Soc. for the Study of Argumentation 1991; author 'Proof and Truth' 1974; 'The Logic of Fiction: A Philosophical Sounding of Deviant Logics' 1974; 'Identity and Modality' 1975; 'Engineered Death: Abortion, Suicide, Euthanasia, Senecide' 1978; co-author 'Argument: The Logic of the Fallacies' 1982; 'Fallacies: Selected Papers, 1972–82' 1989; 'Critique de l'Argumentation' 1992; co-ed. 'Necessary Truth' 1969; 'Literature and Formal Semantics' 1979; 'Humanities in the Present Day' 1979; Ed. 'Dialogue: The Canadian Philosophical Review' 1974–81; Ed.-in-Chief, Argumentation; mem. Ed. Bd. Journal of Philosophical Research; Candn. Semiotic Inquiry; Informal Logic; Chrmn., The Berczy Group; Bd. of Dirs., Peter Barrow Communications, Ltd.; mem. Governing Council, Academy II, Royal Society of Canada 1993– ; Ctte. to Elect New Fellows, Royal Society of Canada 1993– ; mem. Candn. Philos. Assn., Bd. of Dirs., 1986–88; Am. Philos. Assn. (Extve. Comte. Pacific Div. 1971–74, Chrmn. of same 1972–73); Soc. for Exact Philosophy; Internat. Soc. for the Study of Argumentation 1986; Extve. Ctte., Candn. Rsch. Group in Argumentation 1991– ; Humanities Research Council Can.; Candn. Federation for the Humanities (Extve. Comte. since 1978, Vice-Pres. 1980–81, Pres. 1981–82); Universities Coordinating Council (Alta.), Extve. Comte. (Chrmn. 1982–86); Humanities Assn. Can.; Candn. Assn. Univ. Teachers; Adv. Comte., Intl. Dev. Office 1979–83; Chrmn., Adv. Bd., CATV Television 1984–88; mem. Exec. Ctte., Candn. Commission for UNESCO; Renaissance Soc. of Amer.; Hon. Fellow, Bretton Hall Coll., Leeds Univ.; Royal Inst. of Philosophy; Hon. Calgary Highlander; mem. The Winston Churchill Soc.; Phi Beta Kappa; Clubs: University (Toronto); Panorama Tennis Club (Invermere, B.C.); Home: 1039 – 16th St. S., Lethbridge, Alta. T1K 1X3.

**WOODS, John Russell;** b. Ottawa, Ont. 10 May 1930; s. Shirley Edwards and Catherine (Guthrie) W.; e. Ashbury Coll. Ottawa; Trinity Coll. Sch. Port Hope; children: James Braden, Jennifer; EXTVE. DIR., STANDARDS COUNCIL OF CANADA 1982– ; past Chrmn. and C.E.O. Scolopax Ltd.; past Chrmn. and Dir. Texada Lime Ltd.; past Dir. ETS Tool Corp. Ltd.; past Chrmn. Cancast Cement Corp. Ltd.; Pres. and Mang. Dir. Holden Mfg. Co. Ltd. Hull, Que. 1954–64; Nat. Dir. of Finance, Lib. Part of Can. 1968–72; Depy. Mayor of Lucerne, Que.; Chrmn. Columbia Lime Products Ltd.; Chrmn. and Chief Financial Offr. Carinex Resources Ltd.; Life Gov. Ashbury Coll.; comnd. 2nd Lt. Gov. Gen.'s Foot Guards 1948; served with Royal Candn. Regt. (co. comdr.) Korea; recipient Repub. of Korea Medal of Mil. Merit; O.St.J., Kt. Comdr. Mil. & Hospitaller Order St. Lazarus Jerusalem; S.E.S. Leo. B. Moore Medal 1989; Dir. Nat. Sporting Frat.; Anglican; recreations: riding, shooting, fishing; Clubs: Rideau; Cavalry & Guards (London, Eng.); Ottawa Valley Hunt; Home: 3 Pine Cone Trail, Stittsville, Ont. K2S 1E1.

**WOODS, Shirley Edwards;** writer; b. Ottawa, Ont. 21 Jan. 1934; s. Shirley Edwards and Catherine Gregor (Guthrie) W.; e. Ashbury Coll., Trinity Coll. Sch., Bishop's Coll. Sch.; m. Sandrea Ruth d. Bartlett and Ruth Oglivie 5 Jan. 1957; children: Victoria Margaret, Julia Ogilvie, Penelope Helen; trainee, S.E. Woods Ltd. 1953–55; Subaltern 2nd Bn. Royal Candn. Reg't. 1956–58; Broker, Royal Securities Ltd. 1958–60; Asst. Mgr., Bongard & Co. 1960–63; Ottawa Office Mgr., Burns Bros. & Denton 1963–70; Co-owner, Devine & Woods Insur. Agency 1970–73; Vice-Pres., Reed Shaw Stenhouse 1973–80; Broker, Burns Fry Ltd. 1980–89; Pres., Holden Mfg. & S.E. Woods Ltd. 1964–66; Fellow, Royal Soc. of Arts (U.K.); Trustee, Am. Mus. of Fly Fishing 1975–77; Founding Pres., Friends of the Nat. Mus. of Nat. Scis. 1980–82; Dir., Ottawa Humane Soc. 1984 (Life Mem.); Candn. Writers' Found. 1984– ; Treas., Victorian Order of Nurses, Lunenburg County Branch 1990–91; Treas., St. Bartholomew's Church 1987–89; Chrmn., Foundation For Youth Support for Lunenburg & Queen's 1990–93; author: 'Cinders & Saltwater' 1992; 'Pip: The Adventures of a Deer Mouse' 1991; 'Her Excellency Jeanne Sauvé' 1986, 'The Money Labyrinth' 1984, 'The Molson Saga' 1983, 'The Squirrels of Canada' 1980, 'Ottawa' 1980, 'Angling for Atlantic Salmon' 1976, 'Gunning for Upland Birds & Wildfowl' 1976; recreations: outdoor activities; Home: 'Hawthorn Hill', Box 540, Mahone Bay, N.S. B0J 2E0.

**WOODSIDE, Bradley Stanford;** politician; b. Fredericton, N.B. 9 Oct. 1948; s. Lewis S. and Gertrude E. (Foster) W.; e. grade 12; business course, Univ. of N.B.; m. Anne d. Neil and Norma Sneyd 3 July 1983; children: Troy, Michael, Carrie; MAYOR, CITY OF FREDERICTON; Mem., Board of Governors, Univ. of N.B.; Home: 25 Carrington Lane, Fredericton, N.B.; Office: City Hall, P.O. Box 130, Fredericton, N.B. E3B 4Y7.

**WOODSIDE, D. Blake,** B.A., M.D., M.Sc., F.R.C.P.C.; psychiatrist; b. Toronto, Ont. 12 Jan. 1957; s. Donald Garth and Sheila Margaret (MacDonald) W.; e. Upper Canada College 1975; Queen's Univ. M.D. 1982; Univ. of Toronto B.Sc. 1978, M.Sc. 1991; Univ. of Western Ont. F.R.C.P.C. 1986; m. M. Anne d. James and Alice Curtis 22 May 1982; children: Laura (dec.), Malcolm, Fraser, Owen; PSYCHIATRIST, THE TORONTO HOSPITAL, DIRECTOR IN-PATIENT EATING DISORDERS PROGRAM & ACADEMIC STAFF, DEPT. OF PSYCH., UNIV. OF TORONTO 1990– ; Fellowship Supervisor Dr. Paul Garfinkel 1986–89; Funded Investigator, Ont. Mental Health Found.; Dir., Centennial Infant & Child Care Centre; Mem., Candn. Med. Assn.; Candn. Psychiatric Assn.; American Psychiatric Assn.; editor: 'Family Approaches in Treament of Eating Disorders' 1991; author: 'Marriage in Eating Disorders' 1993; recreations: sailing, skiing; Clubs: Royal Candn. yacht, Devil's Glen Country; Office: 101 College St., Toronto, Ont. M5G 2C4.

**WOODSIDE, Donald G.,** B.Sc., D.D.S., M.Sc., Ph.D.(h.c.), F.R.C.D.(C), F.A.C.D.; orthodonist; b. Pittsburgh, Pa. 28 Apr. 1927; s. Marshall Leslie and Eleanor (Murchison) W.; e. Dalhousie Univ., B.Sc. 1948, D.D.S. 1952; Univ. of Toronto, M.Sc. (Dent.) 1956; Karolinska Inst., Stockholm, Sweden Ph.D. (h.c.); m. Sheila Margaret, d. Dr. Howard MacDonald, 8 Aug. 1953; three s. Donald Blake, Thane Paul, Scott MacDonald; PROF. EMERITUS, ORTHODONTIC DEPT., UNIV. TORONTO 1993– ; engaged also in private practice; Dept. of Public Health, Gov't. of N.S., 1952–53; Assoc. in Orthodontics, Faculty of Dentistry, Univ. of Toronto, 1956–58, Assoc. Prof., 1958–59, Acting Head of Dept., 1958–59, and 1962, Prof. & Head, Orthodontic Dept. 1962–93; Prof. Emeritus 1993; Assoc. Dean, Faculty of Dent. 1970–73; Alumnus of the Year Award, Faculty of Dentistry, Univ. of Toronto 1989; Ketchum Award, Am. Assn. of Orthodontists 1990; Sheldon Friel Award, European Soc. of Orthodontists 1992; Distinguished Service Award, Candn. Dental Assn. 1992; mem. Great Lakes Soc. Orths.; Am. Assn. Orths.; Charles Tweed Foundation for Orth. Research; Omicron Kappa Upsilon; recreations: sailing, skiing; Clubs: R.C.Y.C.; Devil's Glen Country; Home: 6 May Tree Road, York Mills Valley, Toronto, Ont. M2P 1V8; Office: Suite 104, 219 St. Clair Ave. W., Toronto, Ont. M4V 1R3.

**WOODSWORTH, Anne,** B.F.A., B.L.S., M.L.S., Ph.D.; dean; b. Fredericia, Denmark 10 Feb. 1941; d. Thorvald Ernst and Roma Yrsa Lykke Tideman (Jensen) Lindner; came to Can. 1951; e. Univ. of Man. B.F.A. 1962; Univ. of Toronto B.L.S. 1964, M.L.S. 1969; Univ. of Pittsburgh Ph.D. 1987; one d. Yrsa Anne; DEAN, PALMER SCHOOL OF LIBRARY OF INFORMATION SCIENCE 1991– ; Pres., Anni Lindner Ltd. (Inc.); Dir., Population Research Foundation Toronto; Librarian, Faculty of Educ. Univ. of Man. 1964–65; Reference Librarian, Winnipeg Pub. Lib. 1965–67; Science & Med. Reference Librarian, Univ. of Toronto 1967–68, Adm. Asst. and Head of Reference Dept. 1970–74; Med. Librarian, Toronto Western Hosp. 1969–70; Personnel Dir., Toronto Pub. Lib. 1975–78; Dir. of Libraries, York Univ. 1978–83; Assoc. Provost & Dir. of Univ. Libraries, present univ. 1983–88; Assoc. Prof. of Library Science, Univ. of Pittsburgh 1988–91; rec'd Ont. Arts Council Grant 1974; Can. Council Grant 1974; SSHRC Grant, 1983; UCLA-GLIS Sr. Fellow 1985; Counc. on Library Resources Grant 1986, 1988 and 1991–92; author: 'The "Alternative Press" in Canada' 1973; 'Patterns and Options for Managing Information Technology on Campus' 1991; 'Library Cooperation and Networks' 1991; 'Managing the Economics of Owning, Leasing, and Contracting Out of Information Services' 1993; 'Reinvesting in the Information Job Family' 1993; editor: 'Non-Print Media Problems' 1975; 'Project Progress: A Study of Canadian Public Libraries' 1981; 'Leadership for Research Libraries' 1988; various articles and reports; Candn. Lib. Assn. (Councillor 1977–80); Candn. Assn. Research Libs. (Secy. 1979–80, Pres. 1981–83); Candn. Assn. Special Libs. and Information Services (Treas. 1974–75, Chrmn. 1975–76); Assn. of Research Libraries (Dir. 1981–84, Vice-Pres. and Pres. Elect 1984–85, Pres. 1985–86); mem. Rsch. Libraries Advy. Comte. to O.C.L.C. 1984–87; Bd. of Dirs., Center for Research Libraries 1987–1990; mem. Ctte. on Accreditation, Am. Library Assn. 1990–94; Councillor, Am. Library Assn. 1993–97; Trustee, Long Island Library Resources Council 1993–98; Office: Long Island Univ., C.W. Post Campus, Brookville, NY 11548.

**WOODWARD, Christel A.,** B.S., M.A., Ph.D.; university professor; clinical psychologist; b. Bronx, N.Y. 13 Jan. 1941; d. Frank A. and Charlotte E. G.; e. State Univ. of N.Y. at Potsdam, B.S. 1961; Ohio State Univ., M.A. 1964, Ph.D. 1968; Reg'd. Psycholog. Ont. 1969; ASSOC. PROF. & PROF., DEPT. OF CLIN. EPIDEMIOL. & BIOSTATISTICS, MCMASTER UNIVERSITY 1976– ; Teacher, N.Y. 1961–62; U.S. Pub. Health Serv. Fellow, Psychol., Ohio State Univ. 1964; Psychologist, Harding Hosp. 1967–68, Lakeshore Psychiatric Hosp. 1968–69; Asst./Assoc. Prof., Dept. of Psychiatry, McMaster Univ. 1969–74; Assoc. Prof., Edn. Psychol., Queen's Univ. 1974–76; Psychologist, priv. practice 1969– ; Cons., Candn. Med. Assn.; Health & Welfare Can. 1979–80; Nat. Health Bd. of Finland; Commun. Adv. Bd., Hamilton Psych. Hosp. 1983–88; Chrmn., Clin. Ctte. 1984–86; Dir., March of Dimes (Hamilton reg.) 1978–80; Pres., Hamilton-Niagara Acad. of Psych. 1979–81; Sec. 1981–84; Mem., Health Care Systems Rsch. & Review Ctte., Ont. Min. of Health 1980–86; Senate, McMaster Univ. 1984–89; Associate, Centre for Health Economics and Policy Analysis 1988– ; author of 100 jour. articles & 6 book chaps.; co-author: 'Guide to Questionnaire Construction and Question Writing' 1983, 'Guide to Improved Data Collection in Health & Health Care Surveys' 1982; recreations: swimming, reading, gardening, skiing; Office: Room 3H4, 1200 Main St. W., Hamilton, Ont. L8N 3Z5.

**WOODWARD, Francis William;** insurance executive; b. Winnipeg, Man. 29 Aug. 1931; s. Victor Francis and Mary D. (Meade) W.; e. Notre Dame Coll. 1949; m. Sharon d. Erwin and Kay Seed 10 June 1961; children: Geoffrey, Terri, Shelley, Laurie; PRESIDENT & CHIEF EXECUTIVE OFFICER, FRANSYL GROUP; Dir., Reed Stenhouse Companies Limited 1988– ; Dir.: Comaplex Resources International Ltd.; Comaplex Minerals Corp.; Comstate Resources; Cameco Corporation; IPSCO Inc.; Redfern Resources; United Grain Growers; Saskatchewan Roughrider Football Club; Mem. Adv. Bd., Royal Trust; Sask. Government Insurance Office 1951–56; Sr. Partner Ducketts Ltd., Ins. Brokers 1956–73; Sr Vice-Pres. and Sask. Mgr. present firm 1974, Regional Dir. Mid-West Canada 1976, Exec. Vice Pres. 1984–88; mem. Lloyd's of London; recreations: golf, running, skiing; Club: Assiniboia; Home: 20 Lynn Bay, Regina, Sask. S4S 2W9.

**WOODWARD, Richard Stephen,** B.Sc., M.Sc., Ph.D.; university professor, writer; b. Michigan 25 July 1950; s. William John and Madeline (Kiechlin) W.; e. Univ. of Pennsylvania B.Sc. 1972; London Sch. of Economics M.Sc. 1974; Univ. of Exeter Ph.D. 1981; m. Sharon d. Peter and Stephanie Hugo 31 Dec. 1982; two d.: Sabina Rae, Vanessa Gabrielle; PROFESSOR OF FINANCE, FAC. OF MANAGEMENT, UNIV. OF CALGARY 1986– ; active career in univ. teaching, research, consulting and community service; has taught at universities in the U.K., U.S. & Can.; Pres., Phrenic Resources Ltd.; Bd. of Dir., Adv. Council, Calgary Econ. Devel Authority, Pres. Council, Calgary C. of C., Soc. of Financial Analysts, Polymer Science Corp. and several others; numerous teaching awards; author: 'Gains & Losses from Market Timing' 1986, 'Financial Performance of the U.S. Energy Industry' 1993 and over 50 journal articles; recreations: skiing, tennis, golf, windsurfing; Home: 1305 Riverdale Ave. SW, Calgary, Alta.; Office: Calgary, Alta. T2N 1N4.

**WOODWARD, Roger Francis;** banking executive; b. Peterborough, Ont. 20 Sept. 1931; s. Harry Francis and Estella Dorothy (Skinner) W.; e. Lindsay C.I.; m. Marie d. John R. and Beatrice Falconer 29 June 1957; children: Debra Louise, Brian Grant; PRES., VISA CANADA ASSOCIATION 1989– ; Extve. Vice Pres., VISA International; Dir. & Pres., VISA Canada Association; var. positions, Candn. Imperial Bank of Comm. 1951–89, Vice-Pres. 1984–89; Home: 51 Hedgewood Dr., Unionville, Ont. L3R 6K3; Office: Suite 3710, Scotia Plaza, 40 King St. W., Toronto, Ont. M5H 3Y2.

**WOODWORTH, John Newton,** C.M., B.Arch., Architect; retired architect; b. Vancouver, B.C. 25 July 1924; s. Kenneth Duncan and Violet Mae (Woolner) W.; e. Univ. of B.C. B.Arch. 1952; m. Nancy d. Charles and Violet Bruce 26 June 1946; children: Robin Elizabeth, Carol Vaughn; General Reconnaissance Pilot RCAF (active service) 1942–46; private architectural practice 1952–86; works incl. Kelowna City Hall, Okanagan College Kelowna Campus, Eric Harvie Theatre at the Banff Ctr.; Extve. Sec. (volunteer), Alexander Mackenzie Trail Assn. 1986– ; Soils Conservation Soc. of Am. Honour Award 1981; Heritage Soc. of B.C. Award of Honour 1988; Candn. Parks Serv. Nat. Heritage Award 1988; Order of Canada 1990; Founding Dir. & Chair, Okanagan Similkameen Parks Soc.; Former Trustee & Chair, Nature Conservancy of Canada; Founding Dir., Nature Trust of B.C.; Founding Dir. & Pres., Alexander Mackenzie Trail Assn.; Mem., Royal Architectural Inst. of Can. and MAIBC 1953 until retirement (now AIBC retired assoc.); author: 'The Remodelling Game' 1974, '76, '81, 'Is Everything All Right Up There? 1975, 'Trail Guide: In the Steps of Alexander Mackenzie' 1981, '87 and occasional papers on conservation, parks, nature conservancies, trails; recreations: private pilot (wheels & floats) retired; clubs: Kelowna Rotary; Home: 236 Poplar Point Drive, Kelowna, B.C. V1Y 1Y1.

**WOOLF, Henry,** B.A.; university professor; b. London, England 20 Jan. 1930; s. Caesar Simon and Marie (Brill) W.; e. Hackney Downs Grammar Sch. Exeter; Univ. College, Devon, England B.A. 1955; College of William & Mary, postgrad. 1956; Bristol Univ., postgrad. 1957; m. Susan d. Charles and Marie Williamson 8 Oct. 1968; children: Marie, Sebastian, Hilda, Benjamin; PROF., GREYSTONE THEATRE, DRAMA DEPT., UNIV. OF SASKATCHEWAN 1983– ; directed 1st prod. of Harold Pinter's 1st play 'The Room' at Bristol Univ. Drama Dept. 1957; professional actor/dir. 1957– ; acted with Royal Shakespeare Co. & for Peter Brook in London, Paris (incl. Brook's 1st internat. co. 1968) & N.Y.; in seminal Brook Prodn. of 'The Marat/Sade' in London & on Broadway; created many original roles at Royal Court Theatre (London) & elsewhere; known as 'King of the Avant Garde'; films incl.: 'Gorky Park,' 'The Lion in Winter,' 'The Rocky Horror Picture Show,' 'The Ruttles'; hosted own B.B.C. TV show 'Words and Pictures' 1975–78; Dir., 'The Marriage of Figaro,' Co-opera, Saskatoon 1990, 'The Three Sisters,' Banff Summer School 1983, 'As You Like It,' Shakespeare on the Saskatchewan 1991; Best Actor Award, Edmonton critics 1978 for perf. in 'Hancock's Last Half Hour'; author of 12 produced plays incl. 'Steer Clear of Kafka,' 'A Naval Occasion,' 'Underarm Bowling' and 1 book of poems entitled 'Poems' 1965; Teacher, Univ. of Alberta 1978–80; Artistic Dir., Shakespeare on the Sask. Festival 1991–; subject of various magazine articles; recreations: table-tennis, chess, omniverous reader; Home: 617 Clarence Ave., 5th, Saskatoon, Sask. S7H 2E1; Office: Drama Dept., Univ. of Saskatchewan, Saskatoon, Sask. S7N 0W0.

**WOOLL, Gerald Ray (Gerry);** aviation executive; b. Peterborough, Ont. 15 Sept. 1913; s. Charles Godfrey and Effie Esther (Staples) W.; e. Peterborough (Ont.) Coll. Inst. & Vocational Sch., 1933; Univ. of Toronto and Brock Univ. Extension courses; m. Audrey, d. Samuel Whittaker, Peterborough, Ont., 29 May 1943; three d., Lorraine, Mary, Susan; PRES. AND MANG. DIR., GENAIRE LTD.; Pres., Amaser Ltd.; with Photographic Survey Corp., 1947–48; Kenting Aviation Ltd., 1948–49; Mang. Dir., Field Aviation Co., 1949–51; Leader, Aircraft Industries Trade Mission to Aust., New Zealand with Japan, 1964 and Spain 1969; served with RAF 1939–46 and with RCAF 1946–47; rank Sqdn. Leader; flew 85 operational missions then became Test Pilot for Ministry of Aircraft Production; Councillor, Town of Bowmanville, 1950, Town of Niagara, 1953, and 1954; served on Pub. Sch. Bd. 1955–60 (Chrmn. 2 yrs.); Mayor, Town of Niagara, Niagara-on-the-Lake, 1961–64, Alderman, Town of Niagara-on-the-Lake 1989–92; mem. Planning Bd. for 9 yrs.; Dir., Court House Theatre (Shaw Festival); Charter Pres., Niagara Foundation; chosen 'Citizen of the Year' 1965 by Niagara Town and Township Chamber Comm.; recipient, Queen's Coronation medal; Prov. of Ont. Citizens' medal 1984; 125th Anniversary of the Confederation of

Canada Medal, 1992; Past Dir. and Treas., Rotary International and Rotary Found.; Council of Regents, Colls. of Applied Arts & Tech.; Dir. Ont. International Corp.; Elder, St. Andrew's Presb. Ch.; Fellow, Royal Aero. Soc.; Assoc. Fellow, Candn. Aero. & Space Inst.; Chrmn., Air Industs. Assn. Can.; recreations: community affairs, fishing; Clubs: RAF (London, Eng.); Naval & Military (London, Eng.); Canadian; Niagara Peninsula Armed Forces Inst.; Guild of Air Pilots & Air Navigators (Upper Freeman); Freeman, City of London (Past Master, The Hon. Co. of Freeman of the City of London, N. Am.); Rotary (Past Pres. St. Catharines; Dist. 709 Gov.); Liveryman, Guild of Air Pilots and Air Navigators; Home: 69 Prideaux St., Niagara-on-the-Lake, Ont. L0S 1J0; Office: Box 84, St. Catharines, Ont. L2R 6R4.

**WOOLLEY, Douglas Campbell,** Q.C., B.A.; b. Toronto, Ont. 28 Jan. 1929; s. Harold E. and Dorothy F. P. (Nichol) W.; e. Runnymede Public Sch. and Humberside Coll. Inst., Toronto, Ont.; Queen's Univ., B.A.; Osgoode Hall Law Sch.; children: Campbell, Mardi, Cori; CHRMN., UNITED LANDS CORPORATION LTD. since 1990 and DIGITAL MEDIA NETWORKS CORP. since 1991; Dir. Royaledge Industries Inc.; Koss Limited; Actifund Limited; United Lands Corp. Ltd.; Digital Media Networks Corp.; Barrymore Holding Co. Ltd.; CanAustra Capital Corp.; read law with Daly Thistle Judson & Harvey 1953–54; Assoc. Wm. A. Cobban 1955; Partner, Cobban and Woolley 1957, Cobban Woolley and Dale 1961, Woolley Dale and Stevens 1971; Partner, Woolley, Dale & Dingwall 1971–91; Home: Appleglen, R.R. #2, Erin, Ont. N0B 1T0; Office: 163 Queen St. E., Toronto, Ont. M5A 1S1.

**WOOLLIAMS, Eldon M.,** Q.C., B.A., LL.B.; teacher and lawyer; b. Rosetown, Sask. 12 Apr. 1916; s. Frank and Gertrude (Mattison) W.; e. Univ. of Sask. B.A. 1943, LL.B. 1943; m. Erva Leola, d. Aaron Jones, 1 Sept. 1943; children: Elda Lynn, Brian Mattison; read law with Frank Bastedo, Q.C.; called to Bar of Sask. 1944, of Alta. 1952; cr. Q.C. 1964; former partner in law firm of Van Blaricom, Hamilton & Woolliams, Tisdale, Sask.; the present Firm of Woolliams, Korman, Moore & Wittman created in Calgary with subsequent additions; 1st el. to H. of C. g.e. 1958; el. for Constit. Bow River 1962, 1963, 1965, Calgary North 1968, 1972, 1974, 1978; Delegate to Inter-Parliamentary Group, U.S. and Canada 1959; Candn. Del. & Lectr., U.N. Seminar on Human & Civil Rights, Mexico City 1961; mem. Candn. Del., Inter-Parlty. Union World Conf., Denmark 1964, Lima, Peru 1968; Chrmn. Cons. Caucus on Secy. of State 1963–65; Justice Critic for the Official Opposition since 1968; Justice del. for Can., Conf. on Peace through Law, Yugoslavia 1971, and Washington, D.C. 1975; del. Commonwealth Seminar Conf. London, Eng. 1972; NATO Conf. London, Eng. & Lahr, Germany 1974; Chrmn. P. Cons. caucus comtes. on Secy. State, Justice & Legal Affairs, Manpower & Immigration, and Housing & Urban Affairs; Chrmn., Parl. Standing Cmte. on Justice and Legal Affairs, 1978–79; Vice-Pres., Candn. Jr. Chamber Comm. 1948–50; Freemason (32 Shrine); P. Conservative (Past Sask. Vice Pres. and mem. Nat. Extve.); Anglican; celebrated 50th Anniversary as graduate of Sask. Univ., Saskatoon Sept. 1993; recreations: golf, fishing; Clubs: Calgary Petroleum; Calgary Golf and Country Club (Alta.); Albany (Toronto); Home: 114 Scarboro Ave. S.W., Calgary, Alta. T3C 2H1.

**WOOTTEN, Christopher E.,** B.A., M.B.A.; arts executive; b. Vancouver, B.C. 23 Aug. 1943; s. Philip Alfred and Roberta Eugene (Humphrey) W.; e. Univ. of B.C., B.A. 1965; Harvard Univ. M.B.A. 1967; m. Elizabeth d. Lol and Evelyn Killam 23 Dec. 1967; children: Edward, Nathaniel, Charles, Sarah; GENERAL MANAGER, THE VANCOUVER PLAYHOUSE THEATRE CO. 1992– ; Ford Found. Fellow, Guthrie Theatre Minneapolis 1967–68; Co-Founder New Arts Management New York 1968–71; Founder Vancouver East Cultural Centre 1973–81; Artistic Dir. Vancouver Internat. Children's Festival 1978–81; Producer 'Billy Bishop Goes To War' 1979; Arts Cons. and subsequent Dir. of Prog. EXPO 86 1982–85; Pres. Raven Productions 1986– ; Exec. Dir., Ont. Arts Council 1987–88; Dir., The Owl Centre for Children's Film & Television 1988–90; Producer, Why Not Productions 1990–92; Dir., B.C. Film 1993– ; Dir. B.C. Arts Bd. 1974–77; author: 'Theatre Space in Vancouver' 1977; 'A New Theatre for Vancouver' 1981; recipient Queen's Silver Jubilee Medal 1978; recreation: skiing; Office: 543 West 7th Ave., Vancouver, B.C. V5Z 1B4.

**WOOTTON, Lt. Col. Patrick Alwen;** environmentalist; writer; b. Croydon, Surrey, Eng. 16 Aug. 1919; s. Thomas Sydney and Elizabeth (Alwen Thrale) W.; e. Hazelwood Prep. Sch.; Lancing Coll. Shoreham, Sussex, Eng.; m. Ann Mary d. Edward Arthur and Dorothy Ella Blake 2 Sept. 1954; children: James, Bridget, Louise, Andrew; joined Brit. Army 1938, comnd. 1939, served in Norwegian Campaign, Faröe Island defence, Italy and Greece; estbd. 181 Bgde. Training Centre Khalkis, Greece, later to become 4th Indian Div. Training Sch., promoted Lt. Col. as Commandant 1944; extended service in Greece with Brit. Mil. Mission until 1948; Conservative Cand. for Stoke Newington & Hackney N. 1953–54; moved to Guernsey, Channel Island 1964; founded Island of Lihou Youth Fellowship 1965–82, the ITCL (Internat. Trust for Constructive Living); and the Guernsey Alternative Energy Society; emigrated to P.E.I. 1981; Dir., Constructive Enterprises Ltd. 1983; Candn. Citizen 1987; volunteer counsellor to inmates Provl. Correctional Centre Charlottetown and mem. Chaplaincy Ctte.; author 'Having Fun With Tropical Plants' 1976; 'The Silence Of Lihou Is Wonderful To Listen To' 1980; 'Islands of Silence Touched By The Healing Hand' 1987; 'Silent Are the Footsteps of the Saviour' 1994; Past Pres., P.E.I. Natural Hist. Soc.; Royal Commonwealth Soc. P.E.I. Br.; Chrmn., Justice & Correction Ctte. Charlottetown Christian Council; recreations: cross-country skiing, oil painting, sailing, boating, organic farming; Address: 20 MacDonald Dr., Charlottetown, P.E.I. C1A 7H2.

**WOROBETZ, Hon. Stephen,** O.C., M.C., LL.D., M.D., F.R.C.S. (C); surgeon; b. Krydor, Sask. 26 Dec. 1914; s. Justin and Mary (Boryski) W.; e. Pub. and High Schs., Krydor and Saskatoon, Sask.; Univ. of Sask., B.Sc. 1935; Univ. of Man., M.D. 1940; post grad. work Winnipeg and Philadelphia; m. Michelene, d. late Henry Kindrachuk, 1 May 1949; Gen. Practitioner, Lucky Lake, Sask., 1941–42 and Saskatoon, Sask., 1946–52; Gen. Surg. Saskatoon, 1954–70; Parttime mem., Saskatoon Cancer Clinic, 1976–83; Pres., Med. Staff. St. Paul's Hosp., Saskatoon, 1957–58; mem. Clin. Teacher, Univ. ofSask. Med. Sch., 1955–70; Lt.-Gov. of Sask., 1970–76; served with R.C.A.M.C. in Can., Eng., Italy and Holland, 1942–46; rec'd M.C. while Med. Offr. with P.P.C.L.I. in Italy; Trustee, Separate Sch. Saskatoon, 1950–52; Past Chrmn. St. Joseph's Nursing Home, Saskatoon; Past Pres., P.P.C.L.I. Assn. of Saskatchewan; Candn. Club of Sask. 1977–78; Bd. mem., Candn. Cancer Soc., Saskatoon Unit 1983–90; Dir., Council for Cdn. Unity; Mem. Bd. of Gov., Cdn. Corps of Commissionaires; Sr. Life Mem., Candn. Med. Assn.; Royal Coll. Phys. and Surgs. Can.; mem. Ukrainian Catholic Brotherhood; K.St.J. (1971); Hon. Lt. Col. North Saskatchewan Regiment 1983–89; recipient Century Saskatoon Award 1983; Hon. LL.D. Univ. of Saskatchewan 1984; awarded Commemorative Medal for 125th Anniversary of Candn. Confederation 1992; Officer, Order of Canada 1993; mem. Roy. Candn. Legion; K. of C.; Liberal; Ukrainian Catholic; recreations: fishing, photography, reading; Home: 405 Lake Cres., Saskatoon, Sask. S7H 3A3.

**WORSLEY, John Arthington,** M.A.; investment advisor; b. Hovingham, England 15 July 1928; s. Sir William Arthington and Joyce Morgan (Brunner) W.; e. Eton College; Trinity College, Oxford Univ. M.A. 1951; m. Carolyn d. Viscount Hardinge 16 Jan. 1954; children: Willa, Harry, Jonathan, Dickon, Katie; INVESTMENT ADVISOR, CASSELS BLAIKIE & CO. LIMITED 1985– ; commenced business career with Lazard Brothers & Co. Limited (U.K.); moved to Canada with Royal Trust 1958; career incl. senior executive positions with Ontario Trust & Morgan Trust Co. of Canada; Campaign Chair, United Way of Metro. Toronto 1970; Dir., Uxbridge Cottage Hospital Found.; Pres., Glen Major Angling Club; Anglican; recreations: farming, forestry; clubs: Toronto, Glen Major Angling, Lyford Cay, University Club of Toronto; Home: R.R. 2, Uxbridge, Ont. L9P 1R2; Office: Suite 200, 33 Yonge St., Toronto, Ont. M5E 1S8.

**WORT, Dennis James,** M.Sc., Ph.D.; university professor; b. England 19 July 1906; s. Dennis James and Florence Ann (Dimmer) W.; e. Prov. (Sask.) Normal Sch., 1924–25; Univ. of Sask., B.Sc. (with Great Distinction) 1932, M.Sc. 1934; Univ. of Chicago, Ph.D. 1940; m. Helen Nora, d. D. B. Kinnon, Saskatoon, Sask., 23 June 1936; children: Dennis James, Margaret Helen; PROF. EMERITUS OF PLANT PHYSIOLOGY, UNIV. OF BRIT. COLUMBIA, since 1975; Prof. of Plant Physiology, 1947–72; Research Assoc. 1972; mem. of Ed. Board, 'Northwest Science,' 1950–73; taught high sch. in Sask. for 20 yrs.; Coulter Research Fellow in Botany, Univ. of Chicago 1939 and 1940; Nuffield Foundation Award 1959; Lectr. in Botany and Biol., Univ. of Sask. 1943–45; Assoc. Prof. in Biology and Botany, Univ. of B.C. 1945; Trustee, Northwest Scient. Association 1969–72, Pres. 1973–74, Hon. Life Mem. 1974; author of 'Biology Check Charts' 1940; co-author 'Diversity in Living Things' 1966; 'Physiology and Biochemistry of Herbicides' 1964; 'Handbuch der Pflanzenphysiologie' 1961; 'Tree Growth' 1962; many important papers, mainly on crop plants, chemical control of plant growth and productivity, and cognate subjects; Fellow, Am. Assn. Advanc. Science; mem., Candn. Soc. Plant Physiol.; Am. Soc. Plant Physiol. (Chrmn. Western Sect. 1955); Bot. Soc. of Am.; B.C. Acad. of Sciences (Pres. 1953); Sigma Xi; Protestant; recreation: choral director; Home: 1540 Wesbrook Crescent, Vancouver, B.C. V6T 1V8.

**WORTHINGTON, Capt. Cyril Rupert (Ted);** ocean steamship company executive; b. Liverpool, Eng. 19 March 1931; s. Alfred Ernest and Doris (Erdmann) W.; e. Liverpool Coll.; Nautical Coll. HMS Conway grad. 1949; Liverpool Nautical Coll. Cert. Ocean Going Master Mariner 1957; CHRMN., ATLANTIC PILOTAGE AUTHORITY 1988– ; Brit. Merchant Marine service 1949–59; mgmt. positions Moore-McCormack Lines, Buenos Aires 1959–69; Terminal Operations Mgr. Halterm Ltd. Halifax 1969–72; Regional Mgr. Maritimes, Columbus Line (Canada) Ltd. 1972–88; Pres. Shipping Fedn. of Can. Halifax Dist.; mem. Halifax Port Emergency Ctte.; Chrmn. Halifax Missions to Seaman 1981–83, Bd. mem.; served as Campaign Mgr. and Official Agt. for P. Cons. Prov. Min. of Govt. Services 1978, 1981 and 1983 els.; Treas. and mem. Exec. Halifax W. P. Cons. Assn.; Chrmn. Halifax Visitors & Convention Bureau 1980–82; Pres. Halifax Joseph Howe Festival 1981–83; Founding mem. Soccer N.S. 1972, Exec. Vice Pres. 1973–76; Pres. Clayton Park Residents Assn. 1975–85; Dir. Transp. Ctte. Halifax Bd. of Trade; Club: Halifax; Home: 1354 Queen St., Halifax, N.S. B3J 2H5; Office: Suite 1402, Purdy's Wharf, Tower 1, 1959 Upper Water St., Halifax, N.S. B3J 1N2.

**WORTON, Ronald Gilbert,** C.M., M.Sc., Ph.D.; scientist; educator; b. Winnipeg, Man. 2 Apl. 1942; s. William Keller and Winnifred Pitt (Barber) W.; e. Miles Macdonell Coll. Winnipeg 1960; Univ. of Man. B.Sc. 1964, M.Sc. 1965; Univ. of Toronto Ph.D. 1969; Yale Univ. postdoctoral rsch. 1969–71; Catholique Universite de Louvain, Belgium, Doctorate honoris causa 1991; m. Helen d. Alex and Margaret Dixon 4 June 1966; one s. Scott Robert; GENETICIST-IN-CHIEF, HOSP. FOR SICK CHILDREN 1985– ; Prof. Univ. of Toronto 1984– ; Staff Geneticist and Dir. Chromosome Lab. present Hosp. 1971, Rsch. Sci. 1971–79, Sr. Rsch. Sci. 1980; Asst. Prof. Univ. Toronto 1971, Assoc. Prof. 1980; Med. Rsch. Council Genetics Ctte. 1984–89, Chrmn. 1987–89; recipient King George V Silver Jubilee Award Cancer Rsch. 1967, 1969, 1970; Gairdner Found. Internat. Award 1989; Award of Distinction Muscular Dystrophy Assn. Can. 1989; Centenary Medal Royal Soc. Can. 1990; E. Mead Johnson Award 1991; Distinguished Scientist Award, Can. Soc. for Clin. Investigation; awarded Commemorative Medal for 125th Anniversary of Candn. Confederation; Rutherford Lectr., Royal Society, London; Assoc. Dir. Candn. Network Centers of Excellence, Genetic Basis of Human Disease 1989; frequent guest speaker nat. and internat. meetings, univs. and hosps.; author or co-author over 80 articles profl. jours., 25 review articles, book chapters; Fellow, Candn. Coll. Med. Geneticists (Dir. 1980–84); Fellow, Royal Soc. of Canada 1991– ; Member of the Order of Canada 1994; mem. Candn. Soc. Cell Biol.; Genetics Soc. of Can.; Am. Soc. Human Genetics (Dir. 1989– , Chrmn. Prog. Ctte. 1986); Chrmn. Mgmnt. Ctte., Candn. Genome Analysis and Technology Program; Human Genome Orgn. (Founding Council 1988, Exec. Council 1989, Vice Pres. 1993); recreations: curling, boating; Home: 23 Budgell Terrace, Toronto, Ont. M6S 1B3; Office: 555 University Ave., Toronto, Ont. M5G 1X8.

**WREN, The Hon. Mr. Justice Edward Francis (Ted),** B.A., LL.B.; judge; b. Mlawa, Poland 13 March 1927; e. De La Salle College 1945; St. Michael's Coll., B.A. 1949; Osgoode Hall Law Sch., 1954, LL.B.; m. Jane d. Willis Leonard and Violet Pratt 26 June 1954; children: Paul, Michael, Peter, Patrick, John, Jane; Partner, Kutney & Wren 1954–1970; JUSTICE OF THE ONTARIO COURT OF JUSTICE (GENERAL DIV.) 1990– ; Judge, District Court of Ontario 1970–90; served with Children's Aid Soc., Catholic Settlement House, John Howard Soc. of Toronto; Roman Catholic; emigrated to Canada 1929; recreations: reading, music; Home: 1 Donmac Dr., Don Mills, Ont. M3B 1N4; Office: 361 University Ave., Toronto, Ont. M5G 1T3.

**WRIGHT, Arthur Robert,** M.A.; public servant; b. Kamloops, B.C. 7 Sept. 1939; s. late Arthur Edwin Wright and late Louise Constance Nuyens; e. St. Francis Xavier Univ. B.A. 1960; Carleton Univ. M.A. 1962; Univ. of Pittsburgh Grad. Sch. Pub. & Internat. Affairs

1970–71; m. Sylvia Anne d. Dr. Donald Cameron Bews and Mary Woodsworth, Senneville, Que. 26 Dec. 1972; CANADIAN HIGH COMMISSIONER TO ZIMBABWE AND BOTSWANA AND AMBASSADOR TO ANGOLA AND MOZAMBIQUE 1993– ; Finance Offr., Dept. of Finance Ottawa 1960–62; Diplomat, Dept. of External Affairs 1962–82; served abroad in Nigeria, Malaysia, Thailand, Tanzania and India; High Commr. to Bangladesh and Ambassador to Burma 1979–82; High Commr. to Barbados, Antigua, St. Kitts/Nevis, Dominica, St. Lucia, St. Vincent, Grenada 1987–90; Vice Pres. for Asia, Candn. Int'l. Development Agency 1982–86; Consulting Assoc., The Banff Centre for Mgmt., Banff, Alta. 1986–87; Vice Pres. for Multilateral Programs, CIDA 1990–93; author various publs.; former mem. Bd. of Dir., Asia Pacific Found. of Canada; Soc. Internat. Devel. Rome; Overseas Devel. Council Washington; recreations: sports, photography, natural history, conservation; Office: Canadian High Commission, P.O. Box 1430, Harare, Zimbabwe.

**WRIGHT, Charles James,** M.B., M.Sc., F.R.C.S.C., F.R.C.S.E., F.R.C.S.(Ed.); physician; b. Scotland 3 June 1938; s. Charles James and Mary Dunbar (Adamson) W.; e. Paisley Grammar School 1945–56; Glasgow Univ. M.B., Ch.B. 1956–62; McGill Univ. M.Sc. 1968–70; m. Marilyn d. Joseph and Gertrude Jacobs 21 Jan. 1984; children: Julian, Jonathan, Nigel; VICE-PRES., MEDICAL & ACADEMIC AFFAIRS, VANCOUVER GENERAL HOSPITAL 1989– ; Prof. of Surgery, Univ. of Saskatchewan, Univ. Hosp. 1971–89; Chrmn., Sask. Medical Care Insur. Comn. 1984–88; Chrmn., Dept. of Surgery, Univ. of Sask. & Univ. Hosp. Saskatoon 1987–89; Clinical Prof., Dept. of Health Care & Epidemiology, U.B.C.; Bd. Mem., B.C. Transplant Soc.; Hunter Medal in Surgery, Univ. of Glasgow 1961; Gold Medal in Surgery, Royal College of Physicians & Surgeons of Canada 1971; author of 72 papers in var. med. & sci. jours. & books incl. 'British Med. J.,' 'Can. J. of Surgery,' 'Can. Med. Assn. J.,' etc.; recreations: music & oenology, jazz musician playing clarinet & soprano saxophone semi-professionally; Home: 3053 East Kent Ave., Vancouver, B.C.; Office: 855 West 12th Ave., Vancouver, B.C. V5Z 1M9.

**WRIGHT, Daniel P.,** B.A., M.A., M.B.A.; financial executive; b. Saskatoon, Sask. 3 May 1958; s. Peter Murrell and Vicki Marie (Haidey) W.; e. Univ. of West. Ont. B.A. 1980; Univ. of Toronto M.A. 1982; York Univ. M.B.A. 1982; m. Megan Ward d. Phil and Margaret Ward 12 May 1984; children: Christine Marie, Jennifer Beatrice; VICE-PRESIDENT & CHIEF FINANCIAL OFFICER, ELECTROHOME LTD. 1993– ; Executive Officer, Lloyds Bank Internat. (UK) 1982–84; Assoc., Canada Consulting Group 1984–86; Assoc., Alfred Bunting & Co. Ltd. 1986–88; Sr. Vice-Pres. & C.F.O., Regional Cablesystems Inc. 1988–92; Mem., Maple Grove United Ch.; Finance Ctte., Candn. Crossroads Internat.; recreations: raising two children, sailing, skiing; Home: R.R. 5, Rockwood, Ont. N0B 2K0; Office: 809 Wellington St. N., Kitchener, Ont. N2G 4J6.

**WRIGHT, David Henry,** Q.C., B.A., LL.B.; judge; b. Nipawin, Sask. 26 Oct. 1931; s. David Alexander and Kathleen Winnifred (Mabb) W.; e. public sch.; Tisdale and Nipawin, Sask.; Univ. of Sask., B.A. 1954; LL.B. 1955; m. Lynette, d. T.G.H. Lewis, 4 July 1959; children: Verity Kathleen; Jennifer Corinne; David Lewis; JUSTICE, COURT OF QUEEN'S BENCH, SASK. since 1981; articled Milliken & Milliken (Regina) 1955; admitted to Sask. Bar 1956; joined MacDermid & Co. 1956, progressing to sr. partner by 1960; Chancellor, Diocese Saskatoon (Anglican); Chancellor, General Synod, Anglican Ch. of Can.; Past mem. Counc., Candn. Bar. Assn.; Prov. Pres., Candn. Bar Assn. 1971–72; Past Pres., Saskatoon Club; Dir. Kidney Foundation; Vice-Chrmn., Law Foundation Sask.; recreations: reading; ornithology; Clubs: Saskatoon; Saskatoon Jazz Soc.; Home: 1601 – 415 Heritage Cres., Saskatoon, Sask. S7H 5M5; Office: Law Courts, 520 Spadina Cres. E., Saskatoon, Sask. S7K 3G7.

**WRIGHT, Don (Donald John Alexander),** B.A., D.Mus., L.Mus.; musician; composer; arranger; educator; b. Strathroy, Ont. 6 Sept. 1908; s. Ernest Joel and Mary Jean (Clark) W.; e. Strathroy Pub. and High Schs.; Univ. of W. Ont. Honour Classics '33 (G. Howard Ferguson Trophy); Ont. Coll. of Educ. Toronto 1933–34; m. Lillian Mary Laura d. late Rt. Hon. Arthur Meighen 29 June 1935; children: Timothy A.J., Priscilla J.M., Patrick O.G.; FOUNDER, DON WRIGHT PRODUCTIONS 1950– ; Pres., Castor Lake Holdings Ltd.; Teacher of Classics and Hist. Sir Adam Beck Coll. Inst. London 1934; Dir. of Music for London 1940; Mgr. Radio Stn. CFPL 1946, Don Wright Chorus estbd. (10 yrs. on the air); Don Wright Singers estbd. 1957, many TV and radio appearances incl. Chrysler Festivals; composed, arranged and conducted music various films incl. 'Trail of '98,' 'Opening of Seaway,' 'A Day to Remember,' 'The Unknown Country'; many CBC documentaries; guest speaker many clinics and workshops on The Changing Voice in U.S.A. and Canada; formed Don Wright Charitable Foundation (1966) Scholarships for Music Students Univ. of W. Ont. and 12 other Candn. univs.; composed 'Proudly We Praise' 1966, performed Parlt. Hill 1st July 1967; rec'd Centennial Medal; Presented to the Queen; compiled thesaurus excerpts life's work in music for educ. purposes covering vocal devel. and instrumental arranging 1978–79; donated complete sets 'Fifty Years of Music with Don Wright' to Music Dept. Candn. univs. and teachers' colls. 1980; endowed 34 Don Wright Music Scholarships across Can., endowed each Don Wright Music Scholarship with sufficient funds to make each one perpetual and matching inflation 1985–87; further endowments, Univ. of Western Ont. to the Classics Dept., the Marching Band, Track & Field (with trophies); author 'Collegiate Choir Series' 1938–39; 'Youthful Voices Series' 1940, revised 1964; 'Pre-teen Song Settings' 1960; 'Don Wright Choral Series'; 'Lets Read Music'; served with C.O.T.C. rank Capt., RCAF rank Flying Offr. World War II, wrote all music and dir. orchestra two different units troop shows; rec'd Citation, Althouse Coll. 1981; Award of Merit, Univ. of W. Ont. Alumni (highest honour) 1983; Univ. of W. Ont. Track Meet named in his honour: The Don Wright Invitational, 1983; Doctor of Music (hon. causa), Univ. of Western Ont. 1986; Licentiate in Music (hon. causa) Western Ont. Conservatory of Music 1987; Track & Field, Athletic Hall of Fame, Univ. of Western Ont. 1990; awarded Commemorative Medal for 125th Anniversary of Candn. Confederation; Freemason; Life Mem., ACTRA; Toronto Music Assn.; Charter Mem., CFIB; Delta Upsilon; P. Conservative; Anglican; recreations: music, travel, walking; Address: 77 Chestnut Park Rd., Toronto, Ont. M4W 1W7.

**WRIGHT, Donald John,** Q.C., B.A., LL.B.; b. Toronto, Ont. 5 Oct. 1928; s. Robert Paton and Anita Rosalie (Lyall) W.; e. Univ. of Toronto Schs.; Trinity Coll., Univ. of Toronto, B.A.; Osgoode Hall Law Sch., LL.B.; m. Jane Elizabeth, d. David P. Rogers, 19 June 1953; four children; COUNSEL, LANG MICHENER; Partner, Ridout & Maybee, Barristers & Solicitors; called to Bar of Ont. 1954; cr. Q.C. 1966; mem. Candn. Bar Assn.; Patent and Trade Mark Inst. of Can.; Licensing Exec. Soc. USA/Canada Inc.; Alpha Delta Phi; Clubs: University; Badminton & Racquet; Devil's Glen Country; Home: 60 Rosedale Heights Dr., Toronto, Ont. M4T 1C5; Office: P.O. Box 747, Suite 2500, BCE Place, 181 Bay St., Toronto, Ont. M5J 2T7.

**WRIGHT, Douglas T.,** O.C., Ph.D., P.Eng., D.Eng., LL.D., D.Sc., L.H.D., D.U.; civil engineer; b. Toronto, Ont. 4 Oct. 1927; s. George C. and Etta (Tyndall) W.; e. Univ. of Toronto, B.A.Sc. 1949; Univ. of Ill., M.S. 1952; Cambridge Univ., Ph.D. 1954; Carleton Univ., D.Eng., 1967; Brock Univ., LL.D. 1967; Mem. Univ. of Nfld., D.Sc. 1969; Concordia Univ., LL.D., 1982; Northeastern Univ., Boston, Mass. L.H.D. 1985; Strathclyde Univ. (Glasgow) D.U. 1989; Docteur h.c., Compiègne (France); Univ. de Sherbrooke, Docteur (honoris causa) 1992; Queen's Univ. D.Sc. 1993; McMaster Univ. D.Sc. 1993; Chevalier dans L'Ordre Nationale de Mérite (France) 1993; Officer, Order of Canada 1991; Pres., Univ. of Waterloo 1981–93; Structural Designer, Morrison, Hershfield, Millman & Huggins, consulting engrs., Toronto, 1949 and 1952; Athlone Fellow, Cambridge Univ., 1952–54; successively Lectr., Asst. Prof., Assoc. Prof., Dept. of Civil Engn., Queens Univ., 1954–58; Prof. of Civil Engn., Univ. of Waterloo, 1958, Chrmn., Dept. of Civil Engn., 1958–63, Dean of Engn. 1959–66; Chrmn., Comte. on Univ. Affairs, Prov. of Ont., 1967–72; Chrmn., Comn. on Post Secondary Educ. in Ont., 1969–72; Depy. Prov. Secy. for Soc. Dev., 1972–79; Depy. Minister of Culture and Recreation 1979–80; Chrmn., Task Force on Federal Policies and Programs for Technology Development 1983–84; Prime Minister's Personal Representative to the Council of Ministers of Education 1990–91; Visiting Prof., Instituto de Ingenieria, Universidad Nacional Autonoma de Mexico, 1964, 1966; Université de Sherbrooke 1966–67; Commonwealth Fellow, Australia 1974; consulting engineer on structural problems incl. aseismic design and space-frame structures; consultant, Netherlands and Mexican Pavilions, Expo 67; Olympic Sports Palace, Mexico City, 1968; Ont. Place Dome and Forum,1971; mem. or offr. numerous comtes. concerned with tech. standards under Candn. Standards Assn., Nat. Research Council, Nat. Bldg. Code of Can.; mem., Technical Evaluation Ctte., Toronto Domed Stadium 1984–92; devel. comprehensive theories for structural analysis and design of large reticulated shells; author or co-author of numerous papers on structural engn., engn. educ. and higher educ.; Dir., Assn. Univs. and Colls. of Can., 1965–67; Dir., Electrohome Ltd. 1983– ; Bell Canada 1985– ; Westinghouse Canada 1986– ; Canadian Venture Founders Ltd. 1986– ; Com Dev 1988– ; London Life 1989– ; Geometrica Inc. 1992– ; Visible Decisions Inc. 1992– ; Meloche Monnex Inc. 1993– ; Lac Minerals Ltd. 1993– ; Candn. Inst. of Chartered Accountants 1993– ; Prof'l. Engrs. of Ont. 1993– ; Mem., Premier's Counc. on Science and Technology (Ont.) 1985–91; Mem., Prime Minister's Nat. Adv. Bd. for Sci. and Technol. 1985–91; Mem. of Counc. (representing Can.), Internat. Inst. for Applied Systems Analysis, Laxenburg, Austria; Fellow, Candn. Acad. Engn.; Am. Soc. Civil Engrs.; Engn. Inst. Can.; recipient, Gold Medal, Ont. Assn. of Profl. Engrs. 1990; Gold Medal, Candn. Council of Professional Engrs. 1992; mem., Assn. Profl. Engrs. Ontario; Internat. Assn. Bridge & Structural Engn.; recreations: reading, sailing; Clubs: University (Toronto); RCYC; Westmount (Kitchener); Home: 73 George St., Waterloo, Ont.; Office: Univ. of Waterloo, Waterloo, Ont. N2L 3G1.

**WRIGHT, Edgar,** B.A., M.A., Ph.D.; university administrator; b. London, Eng. 1 Sept. 1920; s. Jack and Minnie (Cohen) W.; e. Upper Latymer Sch., London, Birkbeck Coll.; Univ. London, B.A. 1950; M.A. 1955; Ph.D. 1964; Inst. Education, Diploma in Education, 1951; m. Vera José, d. William and Ellen Scutt, 22 Mar. 1951; children: Geoffrey; John; Prof. of English, Laurentian Univ. retired 1988; Dept. of Eng., Univ. Coll., (Nairobi, Kenya) 1956–66; Head, Eng. Dept., Laurentian Univ. 1966–70; Dean Humanities 1971–74; Dir., Sch. Graduate Studies 1974–85; author of books, articles and reviews on Victorian and African lit.; served as Capt., Brit. Army 1940–45; Home: 54 Birchview Rd., Nepean, Ont. K2G 3G6.

**WRIGHT, Elizabeth Breslin,** B.A., M.B.A.; banker; b. New York, N.Y. 12 June 1945; s. Louis Roscoe and Jane (Franklin) Breslin; e. Smith Coll. B.A. 1967; Univ. of Toronto M.B.A. 1978; m. Joseph Henry s. J.H. W. 27 April 1968; children: Joseph H., Amanda B.; EXECUTIVE VICE-PRES., PRODUCTS, PERSONAL AND COMMERCIAL, CANADIAN IMPERIAL BANK OF COMMERCE 1992– ; Vice-Pres., Chemical Bank of Canada 1978–83; Sr. Vice-Pres. Cash Management, Bank of Montreal 1983–89; Sr. Vice-Pres. Technology Products, CIBC 1988–92; Dir., Children's Oncology Care of Ont.; recreations: tennis, acrobics; club: Royal Canadian Yacht; Office: Commerce Court, W-4, Toronto, Ont. M5L 1A2.

**WRIGHT, Eric,** B.A., M.A.; writer; b. London, England 4 May 1929; e. Univ. of Man., B.A. (Hons.) 1957; Univ. of Toronto, M.A. 1963; m. Valerie Brown 1958; children: Victoria, Jessica; Prof. of English, Ryerson Polytech. Inst. 1958–89; author: 'Death by Degrees' (novel) 1993; 'A Fine Italian Hand' (novel) 1992; 'Final Cut' (novel) 1991; 'A Sensitive Case' 1990 (novel); 'A Question of Murder' 1988; 'A Body Surrounded by Water' 1987; 'A Single Death' 1986 (pub. as 'The Man who Changed his Name' (U.S.); 'Death in the Old Country' 1985; 'Smoke Detector' 1984; 'The Night the Gods Smiled' 1983 (novels); Home: 65 Gormley Ave., Toronto, Ont.

**WRIGHT, George R.;** financial executive; b. Vancouver, B.C. 19 June 1925; e. Candn. Investment Fin. Course I and II; Partners/Directors/Officers Qualifying Exam., Banff Sch. of Advanced Mgmt.; Manitoba Inst. of Mgmt. Course; National Commodity Futures exam.; m. Isabelle Wark 31 July 1948; children: Joseph, Kenneth, Douglas, Roberta, Richard; VICE CHAIRMAN & DIRECTOR, RICHARDSON GREENSHIELDS OF CANADA LTD. 1987– ; Dir., BYG Natural Resources Inc.; CanWest Gas Supply Inc.; Hycroft Resources & Development Corp.; Liberian Iron Ore Ltd.; Pinnacle Resources; served RCAF 1944; joined James Richardson & Sons in security cage 1946, Trader 1951, Registered Rep. 1953, Mgr. Stock Dept. 1959, Asst. Mgr. (Sales) 1960; Resident Mgr. Vancouver Office 1966; Partner, Operations Richardson Securities of Canada, Winnipeg 1974; Sr. Exec. Vice-Pres. Richardson Greenshields of Canada Ltd. 1982; Pres. & C.E.O. 1984–86; past Chrmn.: Vancouver Stock Exchange; Manitoba District Counc., Investment Dealers Assn.; past Pres. B.C. Bond Dealers Assn.; Clubs: Terminal City (Vancouver); Vancouver (Vancouver); Home: 4455 Stone Court, West Vancouver, B.C. V7W 2V4; Office: 500 – 1066 West Hastings St., P.O. Box 129, Stn. A, Vancouver, B.C. V6C 2M4.

**WRIGHT, Graham P.,** B.Sc., Ph.D.; university professor; b. Bexhill-on-Sea, U.K. 13 May 1944; s. Albert Harry and Ruby Dora (Stephens) W.; e. Univ. of Surrey

B.Sc. (1st class hons.) 1967, Ph.D. 1971; ASSOC. PROF., UNIV. OF OTTAWA 1981– ; Rsch. Asst., Royal Aircraft Establishment 1965–67; Mathematics Teacher, Mayfield School 1968–69; Graduate Asst., Univ. of Calgary 1969–70; Asst. Prof., Univ. of Ottawa 1970–81; Extve. Dir., Candn. Math. Soc. 1979– ; Asst. Chief Operating Officer, Internat. Math. Olympiad 1987–95; Managing Ed., CMS Research Journals 1981– ; Council of Ministers of Edn. Canada Numaracy Indicators Project; Candn. C. of C. Mathematics in Canada Report; Most Meritorious Performance in Math. (Univ. of Surrey) 1969; OCUFA Award for outstanding contrib. to univ. teaching 1975; Fellow, Inst. of Math. and its Applications; Mem., Candn. Math. Soc.; Am. Math. Soc.; Math. Assn. of Am.; recreations: squash, tennis, swimming; club: Univ. of Ottawa Health; Home: 41 Maple View, Nepean, Ont. K2G 5J7; Office: 585 King Edward, Ottawa, Ont. K1N 6N5.

**WRIGHT, James Barry,** B.A., LL.B., LL.M., D.Jur.; educator; legal historian; b. United States 15 Feb. 1957 (Candn. citizen); s. William James and Joyce Arlene (Ackroyd) W.; e. Trinity Coll., Univ. of Toronto, B.A. 1980; Osgoode Hall Law Sch., York Univ., LL.B. 1983; The London Sch. of Econ. & Pol. Sci., Univ. of London, LL.M. 1984; Osgoode Hall Law Sch., York Univ., D.Jur. 1990; Canadian citizen; ASSOC. PROF., CARLETON UNIV. 1986– ; Lectr., Sch. of Law, Middlesex Polytech. (UK) 1984–85; Laidlaw Fellowship for Advanced Studies in Law, Osgoode Hall Law Sch. 1985–86; Visiting Fellow, Institute of Advanced Legal Studies, Univ. of London 1993–94; mem., Candn. Assn. of Law Teachers; Osgoode Soc.; Candn. Law & Soc. Assn.; editor (with W.W. Pue), 'Canadian Perspectives on Law and Society: Issues in Legal History' 1988; editor (with F.M. Greenwood) 'Canadian State Trials Project'; recreations: painting, rambles, gardening, environmental concern groups; Office: 1125 Colonel By Drive, Ottawa, Ont. K1S 5B6.

**WRIGHT, James N.,** D.D.S., M.Sc.D., FACD, FICD, MRCD(C); dentist, university professor and administrator; b. Lethbridge, Alta. 29 Sept. 1933; s. James Arthur and Muriel Carley (Simpson) W.; e. Univ. of Alta. D.D.S. 1956; Univ. of Toronto M.Sc.D. 1969; Royal Coll. of Dental Surgeons Ont., cert. periodontics 1970; Nat. Defence Coll. 1981; m. Elaine C. d. Adrian and Blanche Duhamel 28 Nov. 1958; children: Dr. Tamara L., Michele E., Lisa M.; ASSOCIATE DEAN, FACULTY OF DENTISTRY, UNIV. OF MANITOBA 1990– ; Dental Offr., Candn. Forces Dental Serv. 1953–86: Sr. Dental Advr., U.N. Emergency Force Egypt 1957–58; Commandant, Candn. Forces Dental Serv. School 1977–80; Dir., Dental Treatment Serv. 1976–79, 1981–82; Director General, Dental Serv. 1982–86; Prof. & Head of Stomatology, Dentistry, Univ. of Manitoba 1986–90; Mngt. Ctte., Candn. Dental Serv. Plans Inc. 1990– ; Bd. of Dir. 1986–89; Comn. Chrmn., Fed. Dentaire Internat. 1988–90; Vice-Chrmn. 1986–88; OKU Hon. Dental Soc.; Pierr Fauchard Academy; FACD; FICD; Award of Merit CDA; Outstanding Alumnus Univ. of Alta.; Service Award, Ont. Dental Assn.; Queen's Hon. Dental Surgeon; Gold Medal, U.S. Army Inst. of Dental Rsch.; Extve. Council, Candn. Dental Assn. 1984–86; Bd. of Gov. 1981–86; Chrmn., Ctte. on Dental Specialties 1987–90; Ctte. on Salaried Dentists 1982–86; Editor, 'CFDS Quarterly' 1976–77, 1981–82; recreations: golf, photography, curling, travel; clubs: Elmhurst Golf & Country, Granite Curling; Home: 95 Eastwood Dr., Winnipeg, Man. R2E 0C7; Office: 780 Bannatyne Ave., Winnipeg, Man. R3E 0W2.

**WRIGHT, James Valliere,** Ph.D., F.R.S.C.; archaeologist; b. Toronto, Ont. 22 Jan. 1932; s. Milton John and Joyce Marie (Valliere) W.; e. Humbercrest Pub. Sch.; Runnymede Collegiate; Univ. of Toronto, B.A.(Hons.) 1956, M.A. 1957; Univ. of Wisconsin, Ph.D. 1964; m. Dawn, d. Arthur and Elvia Downey, 7 Oct. 1961; 1 d.: Joyce; CURATOR EMERITUS, ARCHAEOLOGICAL SURVEY OF CANADA, CANADIAN MUSEUM OF CIVILIZATION; retired; joined Nat. Museum of Can. as Ontario Archaeol. in 1960, then: Head of E. Can. Sect., Archaeol. Div.; Chief, Archaeol. Survey of Can.; Sr. Archaeol.; Head of Sci. Sect., Archaeol. Survey of Can.; primarily concerned with cultural history, process, and analytical methods, esp. in northeastern N. Am., from 10,000 B.C. to Eur. Contact, and with informing the gen. public about prehistory; Dir., Counc. for Can. Archaeol. 1983–86; founding pres., Can. Archaeol. Assn. 1968–69; mem. of numerous archaeol. bodies; Vis. Assoc. Prof. to Dépt. d'Anthrop., Univ. de Montréal; Vis. Prof. to Dept. of Anthrop., Univ. of Toronto; author and co-author of numerous books and articles, incl.: 'The Ontario Iroquois Tradition' 1966, 'Ontario Prehistory: An 11,000 Year Archaeological Outline' 1972, 'The Shield Archaic' 1972, 'The Nodwell Site' 1974, 'Six Chapters of Canada's Prehistory' 1976, 'The Grant Lake Site, Keewatin District, N.W.T.' 1976, 'Quebec Prehistory' 1979, and a major contributor to the 'Historical Atlas of Canada, From The Beginning To 1800' 1987; recreations: outdoor activities, reading; Home: Box 82, South Mountain, Ont. K0E 1W0; Office: Archaelogical Survey of Canada, Canadian Museum of Civilization, 100 Laurier St., P.O. Box 3100, Stn. B, Hull, Qué. J8X 4H2.

**WRIGHT, The Hon. Mr. Justice John dePencier;** judge; b. Toronto, Ont. 12 Mar. 1940; s. William Lockridge and Margaret Phoebe (Clare) W.; e. Univ. of Western Ont., B.A. 1962; Osgoode Hall Law Sch., LL.B. 1965; m. Elaine d. Edwin and Ada Pearce 29 July 1972; children: Joanne, Peter, Rebecca, Mark; JUDGE, ONTARIO COURT OF JUSTICE (GENERAL DIV.) 1985– ; articles with Fraser & Beatty 1965–66; called to Ont. Bar 1967; Partner, Wishart, Noble 1967–85; Vice Chrmn., Soc. Assistance Review Bd. of Ont. 1970–72; Chrmn. Day Nurseries Review Bd. of Ont. 1976–77; Captain, Office of the Judge Advocate Gen. (Res.) 1985; Senate, Lake Superior Scottish Reg't. 1987– ; Senate, 49th Field Reg't. (R.C.A.) 1991– ; Gold Medal, Huron Coll. 1962; Pres., Algoma Dist. Children's Aid Soc. 1971–76; Pres., Sault Ste. Marie Dist. Counc., Boy Scouts of Can. 1969–72; Mem., Prov. Extve., Boy Scouts of Can. 1969–85; Asst. Prov. Comnr. Boy Scouts 1977–80; Hon. Member, National Council, Scouts Canada 1973– ; Member Prov. Council, Scouts Canada 1985– , Vice-Pres. 1992– ; Pres., Algoma Dist. Law Assn. 1977–78; Dir., Sault Ste. Marie Chapter, John Howard Soc. 1969–71; Sault Ste. Marie Br., Candn. Mental Health Assn. 1970–71; 'Algoway' Boys Home 1970–74; Registrar, Anglican Dioc. of Algoma 1981–83; Chancellor, Dioc. of Algoma 1983–89; Mem., Rules Ctte., Supreme & District Courts of Ont. 1984–85; Candn. Bar Assn.; Advocates Soc.; Criminal Lawyers Assn.; Candn. Judges Conference; Candn. Inst. for the Admin. of Justice; Supreme Court of Appeal, Anglican Church of Canada 1989; Anglican; Mem., United Empire Loyalists Assn.; Champlain Soc.; Selden Soc.; Osgoode Soc.; Supreme Court of Canada Historical Soc.; Candn. Church Historical Soc.; Heraldry Soc. of Can.; Ont. Hist. Soc.; Ecclesiastical Law Soc.; Church Law Assn.; Ont. Genealogical Soc.; Candn. Inst. of Strategic Studies; Lake Superior Reg't (M) Assn.; Conference of Defence Assn. Institute; Candn. Inst. of Internat. Affairs; Commdr., Order of St. Lazarus of Jerusalem; author: 'Division of Matrimonial Assets in Ontario' 1982; numerous articles in scholarly pubs. & mags.; nine legal lectures; recreations: law, Boy Scouts, genealogy; Clubs: Royal Candn. Military Inst., Officers Mess: 49th Field Reg.; Officer's Mess Lake Superior Scottish Reg't.; Office: 277 Camelot St., Thunder Bay, Ont. P7A 4B3.

**WRIGHT, John Elmer,** B.Sc.; executive; b. Leamington, Ont. 12 Jan. 1929; s. Elmer and Dora (Levi) W.; e. Pub. and High Sch., Windsor, Ont.; Queen's Univ., B.Sc. (Mech. Engn.) 1951; m. Bette; children: John, Edward, Mary, Donald, Martha; CHAIRMAN & DIR., TEMPRITE INDUSTRIES LTD. 1961–93, Retired; Pres. and Dir., Applied Thermal Products Co. Ltd., Ackrite Consultants Inc.; Jackson and Brooks Ltd.; began with American Standard Products (Canada) Ltd., Toronto, as Field Engr. 1951–58; apptd. Vice-Pres., R. C. Black & Co. Ltd., Toronto 1958–61; founded and assumed Presidency, Applied Thermal Products Co. Ltd. 1961; mem., Am. Soc. of Heating, Refrigeration & Air Conditioning Engrs.; Assn. Prof. Engrs. of Ont.; Past Dir., Candn. Gas Assn. and Profit Sharing Council of Can.; recreations: skiing, golf, tennis; Clubs: Weston Golf & Country (Past Pres.); Rancho Bernardo Country Club; Address: 11737 Caminito Corriente, San Diego, CA 92128.

**WRIGHT, John Thomas,** B.A., M.A.; civil servant; b. Calgary, Alta. 2 Aug. 1954; e. Univ. of W. Ont. B.A. (Hons.) 1976; Univ. of Alta. M.A. 1977; married with three children; DEPUTY MINISTER OF FINANCE 1990– ; Economist, Taxation and Fiscal Policy, Dept. of Finance, Govt. of Sask. 1977–80; Sr. Economist 1980–82; Sr. Analyst, Budget Bureau, Treas. Bd. Div. 1982–83; Dir. of Social Programs 1983–85; Extve. Dir., Taxation and Economic Policy 1986–89; Assoc. Dep. Min. of Finance, Fiscal Policy and Budget 1989–90; Mem., Bd. of Gov., Univ. of Regina; Univ. of Sask.

**WRIGHT, Joseph Henry III,** B.A.; investment banker; b. New York, N.Y. 17 July 1942; s. Joseph H. Wright II and Barbara Bissell Wright; e. Princeton Univ. B.A. (Magna cum laude) 1964; m. Elizabeth d. Louis R. and Jane F. Breslin 27 April 1968; children: Amanda B., Joseph H. IV; VICE-CHAIR & DIR., INVESTMENT BANKING, BURNS FRY LIMITED 1987– ; Citibank North Am. New York, N.Y. 1964–67, 1972–74; Geneva, Switz. 1968–71; Dir., Corp. Banking, Citibank Canada Toronto 1975–86; recreations: running, fishing, tennis, canoeing; clubs: Royal Candn. Yacht, Badminton & Racquet, Siasconset Casino Tennis; Home: 625 Avenue Rd., Apt. 1804, Toronto, Ont. M4V 2K7; Office: Suite 5000, First Canadian Place, Toronto, Ont. M5X 1H3.

**WRIGHT, Kenneth Osborne,** M.A., Ph.D., D.Sc., F.R.S.C.; astronomer; b. Fort George, B.C. 1 Nov. 1911; s. Charles Melville and Agnes Pearl (Osborne) W.; e. Univ. of Toronto Schs., 1923–29; Univ. of Toronto, B.A. 1933, M.A. 1934; Univ. of Mich., Ph.D. 1940; D.Sc. (Hon.) N. Copernicus Univ., Torun, Poland 1973; m. 1stly Margaret Lindsay, d. Frederick B. Sharp, 25 September 1937 (died 7 June 1969); one d. Nora Louise; 2ndly Jean M. (MacLachlan) Ellis, 21 March 1970; Assistant in Astronomy, University of Toronto, 1933–34; summer Assistant in Astronomy, University of Michigan, 1936; Astron. Assistant Dom. Astrophysical Observatory, 1936–39 and Astrophysicist, 1940–1960; Ass't Dir. 1960–66; Dir. 1966–76; Guest Investigator, 1976–84; Lect. in Physics, Univ. of Brit. Columbia, 1943–44; Visiting Prof., Univ. of Toronto 1960–61; Visiting Foreign Prof., Am. Astron. Soc., Amherst-Mt. Holyoke, 1963; Research Assoc., Mt. Wilson & Palomar Observatories 1962; Hon. Prof. Physics, Univ. Victoria 1965–81, mem. Senate 1973–78, Bd. Govs. 1973–75; Chrmn., National Research Council, Assoc. Comte. on Astron. 1971–74; author of over 70 articles in scient. journals; mem., Royal Astron. Soc. of Can. (Pres. 1964–66); Am. Astron. Soc. (Councillor, 1953–56); Astron. Soc. of the Pacific; Internat. Astron. Union; Royal Astron. Soc.; Candn. Astron. Soc.; Rotary Club; United Church; Home: 202 - 1375 Newport Ave., Victoria, B.C. V8S 5E8.

**WRIGHT, Laurali R. (Bunny);** writer; b. Saskatoon, Sask. 5 June 1939; d. Sidney Victor and Evelyn Jane (Barber) Appleby; e. Univ. of B.C.; Carleton Univ.; Banff Sch. of Fine Arts; Univ. of Calgary; m. John Herbert s. Willis and Mary Wright 6 Jan. 1962; children: Victoria Kathleen, Johnna Margaret; journalist primarily The Calgary Herald 1968–77, free lance writer since 1977; author (novels) 'Neighbors' 1979 (Alta. Novelist Award 1978); 'The Favorite' 1982; 'Among Friends' 1984; 'The Suspect' 1985 (Mystery Writers Am. Edgar Allan Poe Best Novel Award 1986); 'Sleep While I Sing' 1986; 'Love in the Temperate Zone' 1988; 'A Chill Rain in January' 1990 (Crime Writers of Canada Arthur Ellis Best Novel Award 1990); 'Fall From Grace' 1991; 'Prized Possessions' 1993; 'A Touch of Panic' 1994; mem. Writers Union Can.; Authors' Guild (US); International P.E.N.; Mystery Writers of Am.; Crime Writers of Can.; recreations: gardening, reading, movies, theatre, concerts, jogging, travel; Address: 11744 Fraserview St., Maple Ridge, B.C. V2X 8A8.

**WRIGHT, Mary Jean,** M.A., Ph.D.; psychologist; university professor; b. Strathroy, Ont. 20 May 1915; d. Ernest Joel and Mary Jean (Clark) W.; e. Strathroy (Ont.) Coll. Inst., 1935; Univ. of W. Ont. B.A. 1939; Univ. of Toronto M.A. 1940, Ph.D. 1949; LL.D. Brock Univ. 1979; Univ. of Western Ont. 1982; Carleton Univ. 1984; PROFESSOR EMERITA, UNIV. OF WESTERN ONT. 1980; Prof. of Psychol., and Dir. of Lab. Preschool, Univ. of Western Ont. 1973–80, Chrmn. of Dept. 1960–70; Secy., E.J. Wright Central and Affiliated Co.'s, Strathroy 1956–78; Psychol., Prot. Children's Village, Ottawa, 1941–42 and Mental Health Clinic, Hamilton, 1944–45; Instr., Inst. of Child Study, Univ. of Toronto, 1945–46; joined present Univ. as Asst. Prof. 1946–54, Assoc. Prof. 1955–61; Prof. 1962; served overseas with Candn. Children's Service and as Instr., Garrison Lane Nursery Training Sch., Birmingham, Eng., 1942–44; mem. Adv. Bd., Un. Community Services, 1953–59; Retarded Children's Assn. 1954–57; Children's Psychiatric Research Inst., 1966–70; Dir., Un. Appeal, 1956–59; Family Service Bureau 1954–60; Child Guidance Clinic 1960–63; mem. Ont. Comte. on Children 1958–67 (Vice Pres. 1964–65); Candn. Comte. on Early Childhood since 1961; Meals on Wheels, London (Vice-Chair 1984–89); writings incl. articles for prof. journs. and books, co-ed. one book, and author of another; mem., Adv. Acad. Panel, Canada Council, 1976–78; Soc. Sci. and Hum. Research Council of Can. 1978–79; Ont. Bd. Examiners in Psychol. 1970–75 (Chrmn., 1973–74); Ont. Psychol. Assn. (President 1950–51); Fellow, Canadian Psychol. Assn. (Director 1959–62; President 1968–69, Hon. President 1975–76); Fellow, American Psychol. Assn. (Comte. on Internat. Relations, 1977–80); Soc. Research Child Devel. 1949–90; Nursery Educ. Assn. Ont. (Dir. 1956–60; Chrmn., Cert. Bd., 1964–66); Huron Coll. (Extve. Bd. 1983–89); Honorary Fellow 1989; Gamma Phi Beta; P. Conservative; Anglican; recreations: music, travel; Home: 1032 Western Rd., London, Ont. N6G 1G4.

**WRIGHT, Michelle;** recording artist, songwriter; b. Chatham, Ont. 1 July; d. Jack Martin and Monica W.; signed worldwide recording deal with Arista Records 1989; album releases: 'Do Right By Me' (Savannah Records) 1988, 'Michelle Wright' (Arista) 1990, 'Now & Then' (Arista) 1992 (Platinum in Canada, with 2 no. 1 singles 'Take It Like a Man' and 'He Would be Sixteen'); has toured extensively for past 3 years in Canada, U.S. and Europe; Hon. Chairperson, 'Operation C.T. Scan,' St. Joseph's Hosp. (Chatham, Ont.) 1988–93; Awards: Acad. of Country Music: Top New Female Vocalist 1992; Big Country Awards (RPM Mag.): Top Female Vocalist 1989, '91, '92, '93, Artist of the Year 1991, '93, Top Country Album 1993, Top Country Single 1993; Canadian Country Music Awards (CCMA): Entertainer of the Year 1993; Female Vocalist of the Year 1990, '91, '92, '93, Single of the Year 1991, '92, '93, Album of the Year 1991, Video of the Year 1992, '93, Country Music Person of the Year 1992; Juno Award: Country Female Vocalist of the Year 1993; has had 2 TV specials; awarded commemorative medal, 125th anniversary of the Confederation of Canada 1993; Office: 1207 17th Ave. S., Ste. 305, Nashville, Tenn. 37212.

**WRIGHT, Norman George,** B.A.; financial executive; b. Toronto, Ont. 18 Jan. 1931 s. George and Vera (Proctor) W.; e. York Univ. B.A. 1980; m. Constance d. Arthur and Mary McAteer June 1952; children: Murray, Warren; PRESIDENT & CHIEF OPERATING OFFICER, CANADIAN DEPOSITORY FOR SECURITIES 1984– ; Deputy Comnr., Personnel & Public Relns., City of Etobicoke 1958–64; Asst. Gen. Mgr., Personnel & Orgn., Canada Permanent Trust Co. 1964–68; Vice-Pres. Admin. & Mktg. 1968–75; Sr. Vice-Pres. Admin. & Systems 1975–80; Sr. Vice President, Trust Operations 1980–84; Dir., Candn. Depository for Securities; recreations: golf, boating; clubs: Ontario, Markland Woods Golf & Country; Office: 85 Richmond St. W., Toronto, Ont. M5H 2C9.

**WRIGHT, Peter Murrell,** Ph.D.; professor; b. Toronto, Ont. 26 Sept. 1932; s. Gilbert Owen and Ruth Bailey (Cohoe) Murrell-Wright; e. Univ. of Sask. B.E. 1954; M.E. 1961; Univ. of Colorado Ph.D. 1968; m. Vicki d. Mary and Nicholas Haidey 1 Oct. 1955 (div.); children: Daniel, Susan, Laura, Joan; 2ndly m. Dianne Slater 23 Sept. 1989; PROF., FACULTY OF APPLIED SCIENCE & ENGINEERING, UNIV. OF TORONTO 1978– ; Dept. of Civil Engr., Univ. of Sask. 1958–68; Dept. of Civil Engr., Univ. of Toronto 1968– ; major role in devel. of the Candn. Soc. for Civil Engr. 1970–83; Assoc. Dean, Fac. of Applied Sci. & Engr., Univ. of Toronto 1981–85; Acting Dean, Fac. of Arch. & Landscape Arch., during period which incl. an attempted closure of the Fac. 1984–88; Queen's Candn. Silver Jubilee Medal 1977; EIC's J. Stirling Medal 1992; Fellow, Candn. Soc. for Civil Engr. 1983; Mem., Candn. Soc. for Civil Engr. (Pres. 1981–82); Assn. of Profl. Engrs. of Ont.; author/co-author of 14 papers on struc. engr. & engr. edn.; bicycled Saskatoon-Boston-Saskatoon summer 1949; recreations: home renovation; Home: 122A Edgewood Ave., Toronto, Ont. M4L 3H1; Office: 35 St. George St., Toronto, Ont. M5S 1A4.

**WRIGHT, Raymond C.,** B.A., B.L.S.; librarian; b. Winnipeg, Man. 4 May 1917; s. Perce Vancouver and Anna Maud (Lipsett) W.; e. Gordon Bell High Sch., Winnipeg, 1935; Univ. Of Man., B.A. 1939; McGill Univ., B.L.S. 1947; m. (Eileen) Patricia, d. late Robert Collins, 22 Aug. 1942; children: Robert Clifford, Terri Eileen; Chief Librarian, Univ. of Winnipeg, since 1967, now retired; Documents Librarian, Prov. Lib., Govt. of Man., 1947–55; Asst. Librarian, Man. Extension Lib., Univ. of Man., 1955–61; Chief Librarian, United Coll., 1961–67 became Dir. of Libraries when Coll. became Univ. of Winnipeg 1967; served with RCAF 1941–45; Hon. Life Mem., Man. Lib. Assn. (Secy. 3 yrs., Treas. 2yrs., Pres. 2 yrs.); Secy., Comte. Prairie Univ. Librarians, 1972–73; Chrmn., Council of Prairie Univ. Libraries 1981–82 (Secy. 1979–80); Alpha Delta Epsilon; United Church; recreations: reading, watching sports; Home: 488 Queenston St., Winnipeg, Man., R3N 0X2.

**WRIGHT, Richard B.,** B.A.; author; b. Midland, Ont. 4 March 1937; s. Lavern and Laura (Thomas) W.; e. Midland (Ont.) High Sch. 1956; Ryerson Polytech. Inst. Toronto grad. in Radio and TV Arts 1959, Trent Univ. B.A. 1972; m. Phyllis Mary Cotton; two s. Christopher Stephen, Richard Andrew; Journalist and Radio Copywriter 1959–60; Asst. Ed. Macmillan of Canada 1960–65, Trade Sales Mgr. 1966–68; Sales Rep. Oxford University Press 1969–70; Novelist and Freelance Writer 1970–75; Head of Eng., Ridley Coll. St. Catharines, Ont. 1976–79; currently teaching English, Ridley Coll.; author 'Andrew Tolliver' (children) 1965; 'The Weekend Man' 1970; 'In the Middle of a Life' 1973 (Toronto Book Award 1973, Faber Mem. Prize U.K. 1975); 'Farthing's Fortunes' 1976; 'Final Things' 1980; 'The Teacher's Daughter' 1982; 'Tourists' 1984; 'Sunset Manor' 1990; recipient Can. Council Jr. and Sr. Fellowships; Ont. Arts Council Fellowship; recreations: walking, reading, music; editor of 'The Malarkey Review'; Address: 52 St. Patrick St., St. Catharines, Ont. L2R 1K3.

**WRIGHT, Robert J.,** Q.C., LL.B.; barrister and solicitor; b. Toronto, Ont. 25 June 1932; e. Univ. of Toronto Schs.; Trinity Coll. Univ. of Toronto B.A. 1955; Osgoode Hall Law Sch. LL.B. 1961; m. Joan Playfair Jennison 15 Aug. 1957; Dir., Cominco Ltd.; Teck Corporation; Barrister and Solicitor, Lang Michener Lawrence and Shaw 1964–89; Chrmn., Ont. Securities Commission 1989–93; mem. Bar of Ont.; Address: Suite 7000, P.O. Box 170, 1 First Canadian Place, Toronto, Ont. M5X 1G9.

**WRIGHT, Ronald,** M.A., F.R.G.S.; writer; b. 12 Sept. 1948; s. Alan Edward Ashfield and Shirley Phyllis (Wilkinson) W. e. Cambridge Univ. M.A. 1973; m. Janice d. Leigh and Patricia Boddy 1985; author: 'Home and Away' 1993; 'Stolen Continents' 1992; 'Time Among the Maya' 1989; 'Quechua Phrasebook' 1989; 'On Fiji Islands' 1986; 'Cut Stones & Crossroads: A Journey in the Two Worlds of Peru' 1984; numerous articles, broadcasts, lectures, etc.; has travelled extensively doing fieldwork for articles and pubs.; Awards: Gordon Montador Award for 'Stolen Continents' 1993; Trillium Book Award finalist 1993 for 'Stolen Continents,' 1990 for 'Time Among the Maya'; Winner, CBC Lit. Competition 1991 for 'Going to the Wall' (essay); Candn. Sci. Writers' Assn. Award for 'The Lamanai Enigma' 1986; Mem., The Writers' Union of Can.; Internat. P.E.N. (Mem. of Bd. 1989–91); ACTRA; Latin Am. Indian Lit. Assn.; Survival Internat.; Fellow of the Royal Geographical Society; Home: R.R. 1, Campbellcroft, Ont. L0A 1B0.

**WRIGHT, Thomas (Tom) Alan,** B.A., LL.B.; lawyer; b. Hamilton, Ont. 13 June 1948; s. Alan Malcolm and Norma June (Lawson) W.; e. Nelson H.S. Burlington 1967; McMaster Univ. B.A. 1970; Queen's Law School LL.B. 1973; m. Katherine d. Bruce and Verna Elliot 24 July 1970; children: Megan, Amy; COMMISSIONER, INFORMATION & PRIVACY COMN. ONTARIO 1991– ; called to Ont. Bar 1975; private practice with several Ont. law firms 1975–80; sole practitioner, Kincardine, Ont. 1980–85; Senior Lawyer, Min. of the Attorney General, Support & Custody Enforcement Br. 1986–88; 1st Dir. of Legal Services, Information & Privacy Comn. 1988–90; Asst. Comnr. 1990–91; Mem., Law Soc. of U.C.; Candn. Bar Assn.; Candn. Council of Admin. Tribuanals; Council of Govt. Ethics & Laws; Friends of Algonquin Park; recreations: gardening, photography; Office: 80 Bloor St. W., Suite 1700, Toronto, Ont. M5S 2V1.

**WRIGHT, W. Alan,** B.A., M.A., Ph.D.; b. Lachine, Que. 2 March 1946; s. Edwin Percival and Marion Barr (Fleming) Wright; e. Mount Allison Univ. B.A. 1967; McGill Univ. M.A. 1979; Univ. de Montreal Ph.D. 1986; m. Marie-Jeanne d. Jean-Paul and Jeannine Monette 23 June 1984; children: Adam, William, Marianne; FOUNDING EXTVE. DIR., OFFICE OF INSTRUCTIONAL DEVELOPMENT & TECHNOLOGY, DALHOUSIE UNIV. 1988– ; Profl. Devel. Co-ord., Montreal Teachers' Assn. & Prov. Assn. of Protestant Teachers of Que. 1970–72, 1976–79; Assoc. Dir., Curriculum, Prov. of Que. 1972–74; Deputy Dir. Gen., Canada World Youth 1974–75; Assoc. Dean, Undergrad. Studies, Univ. du Qué. à Rimouski 1983–88; active in Profl. & Orgn. Devel. Network (U.S.); Soc. for Teaching & Learning in Higher Edn.; co-author: 'Recording Teaching Accomplishment' 1992; co-editor: 'Learning through Writing' 1992, 'University Teaching and Learning' 1992; recreation: marathon running (40 marathons & ultra-marathons Canada, U.S., France); Home: 6365 Norwood St., Halifax, N.S. B3H 2L2; Office: Halifax, N.S. B3H 3J5.

**WRIGHT, Wayne,** B.Sc., M.B.A.; petroleum industry executive; b. Toronto, Ont. 10 June 1943; s. Archie and Ethel (Majury) W.; e. McGill Univ. B.Sc. 1965; Harvard Graduate School of Business M.B.A. 1970; m. Nancy d. William and Eleanor Hallawell 30 July 1966; children: Heather, Cameron; VICE PRESIDENT, CANADIAN PETROLEUM PRODUCTS INSITUTE 1990– ; Dupont of Canada 1965; Ernst & Young 1970; Sunoco Inc. Planning Director 1972, Director Chemical Marketing 1976, President Sunchem 1979, Vice-Pres. Manufacturing 1981, Vice-Pres. Finance 1985, Corporate Vice-Pres. 1986; Chair, Bd. of Trustees, Nature Conservancy of Canada; Bd. of Dir., Long Point Bird Observatory; Past Co-Chair, UNICEF Greeting Cards; member of var. naturalist & cultural organizations; recreations: skiing, squash, outdoor activities; clubs: Royal Canadian Yacht, Harvard Business School, Board of Trade; Home: 235 Riverside Dr., Toronto, Ont. M6S 4A8; Office: 235 Yorkland Blvd., Suite 510, North York, Ont. M2J 4Y8.

**WRIGHT, Wilfred J.;** company executive; b. Toronto, Ont.; s. John Edward and Sarah Anne (Wright) W.; e. East York Coll. Inst., Toronto, 1946; Univ. of Toronto Extension in conjunction with Soc. Mgmt. Accts., C.M.A. 1955; York Univ., Advanced Advertising Mang. Course, 1960; Univ. of W. Ont., Marketing Mang. Course, 1964; children: Mark, Melody; PRES. & C.E.O., GHANA MINING INC.; former First Vice Pres. and Gen. Mgr. of Operations, The People's Church, Toronto; joined Philco Corp. as Accounting Clerk, 1946; Jr. Acct., Shirriff's Ltd.; 1948; Cost Acct. 1950; Asst. to Comptroller 1952; Adm. Asst. to Extve. Vice-Pres., Shirriff-Horsey, 1956; Controller, Shirriff Div., Salada-Shirriff-Horsey, 1957; Adm. Mgr., Shirriff Div., 1958 and Candn. Div., 1959; Product Mgr., Salada Foods, 1960; Mgr., Corporate Planning, 1962; Gen. Mgr., Snack Foods Div., 1964; Mang. Dir., Chief Extve. Offr. and Dir., Peek Frean (Canada) Ltd. and Langley, Harris & Co. Ltd. 1968; Pres., Chief Extve. Offr. & Mang. Dir., 1970; Pres. and C.E.O., Associated Biscuits of Can. Ltd., 1972–80; Pres. & C.E.O. N. Am. Div. Associated Biscuits 1979–80; Home: 30 Corvus Starway, North York, Ont. M2J 1P3.

**WRIGHT, William Norman;** retired insurance executive; b. Sheffield, Eng. 5 Feb. 1913; s. Samuel and Mary Sarah (Bean) W.; e. King Edward VII Sch. Sheffield, Eng. 1924–30; m. Alice Hildegard Linke 29 Apl. 1935; two s. Stephen, Geoffrey; 9 yrs. service prior to World War II with Royal Insurance Co. Ltd. and affiliated co's in Eng. trans. to Can. 1947 serving in various capacities Toronto, Winnipeg and Montreal incl. Marketing Rep., Asst. Agency Supt., Production Supt., Asst. Br. Mgr., Br. Mgr., Agency Mgr. for Can.; Asst. Gen. Mgr. for Can., Depy. Gen. Mgr. for Can.; Extve. Vice Pres. (Ins. Oper.), retired 1978; Chrmn. Pub. Relations Comte. All-Can. Ins. Fed. 1967–69 (now Ins. Bureau Can.); Commnd. W. Yorks. Regt. (Terr.) March 1939; seconded to Roy. W. African Frontier Force 1940; served W. Africa, India, Burma, rank Lt. Col.; Candn. Army Inf. Reserve, rank Maj.; Assoc. Chart. Ins. Inst.; Councillor, Western Div., British Candn. Chamber of Trade & Commerce; Past Pres., YCC #531; Mem., Royal Commonwealth Soc. (Mainland of B.C. Br.); Hon. Mem., Big Bros. of Can.; Past Pres. St. George's Soc. Toronto; Pres., Soc. of St. George, Vancouver; past Hon. Commandant, Old Fort York; Past Chrmn., Museums Comte., Toronto Historical Bd.; mem. Imperial Officers Assn. of Can. 1979 and Royal United Services Inst. of Vancouver; Mem., Burma Star Assn.; Anglican; recreations: music, reading; Home: 2002 – 6070 McMurray Ave., Burnaby, B.C. V5H 4J3.

**WRIGHT, William Terrence,** B.A., LL.B.; lawyer; b. Winnipeg, Man. 30 Aug. 1945; s. John Robert and Dorothy Louise (MacKechnie) W.; e. Univ. of Manitoba B.A. 1967, LL.B. 1970; m. Melba d. Gissur and Elvera Eliasson 15 Aug. 1969; children: Shannon, Geoffrey, Kimberley, James; Sr. Vice Pres., General Counsel & Secy., Investors Group Inc.; Pitblado & Hoskin 1970–81; United Candn. Shares Limited & the Candn. Indemnity Co. 1981–84; Lawyer, Pitblado & Hoskin 1984–92; Dir., United Candn. Shares Limited; Chrmn., Victoria General Hosp.; Past Chrmn. & Dir., Health Sciences Ctr. Rsch. Found. Inc.; Dir., Royal Winnipeg Ballet; Mem., Candn. Bar Assn.; Law Soc. of Man.; Candn. Tax Found.; Fraser Inst.; Winnipeg C. of C.; recreations: squash, tennis, golf, sailing, cycling, nordic skiing; clubs: St. Charles Country, Winnipeg Winter; Home: 123 Grenfell Blvd., Winnipeg, Man. R3P 0B6; Office: 447 Portage, 18th Floor, One Canada Center, Winnipeg, Man. R3B 2C3.

**WRIGLEY, Robert Ernest,** M.Sc., Ph.D.; museum director; curator; b. Buenos Aires, Argentina 2 May 1943; s. Ernest and Eva (Muir) W.; e. Chambly (Que.) Co. High Sch. 1961; McGill Univ. B.Sc. 1965, M.Sc. 1967; Univ. of Ill. Ph.D. 1970; m. Arlene Dahl 24 May 1986; two s. Mark, Robert; Dir., Oak Hammock Marsh Interpretive Centre 1989– ; Adjunct Prof., Natural Resources Inst., Univ. of Manitoba 1989– ; Museum Dir., Man. Museum of Man and Nature 1980–88, Curator of Mammals and Birds 1970–88, mem. Bd. Govs. 1978–79; Mng. Ed. 'Manitoba Nature Magazine' 1972–82; Assoc. Ed. (Mammalogy) 'Canadian Field Naturalist' 1974–79;

Contbg. Writer, 'TLC for Plants' 1980–91; author: 'Systematics and Biology of the Woodland Jumping Mouse' 1972; 'Small Mammals' Candn. Album Series 1980, 'Large Mammals' 2 vol. 1983, 1985; 'Mammals in North America' 1986; 'Amphibians and Reptiles' 1989; co-author and ed. 'Animals of Manitoba' 1974; co-author 'Manitoba's Big Cat: The Story of the Cougar in Manitoba' 1982; 'The History of Manitoba's Animals' (in 'Manitoba's Natural Heritage') 1984; over 40 articles and 12 books natural hist.; curator of 25 exhibits; mem., Zool. Soc. Man. (Bd. mem. 1970–85); Fort Whyte Center for Environmental Education (Bd. mem. 1983–90); Ducks Unlimited Canada; Candn. Museums Assn.; American Soc. Mammalogists; Manitoba Naturalists Soc.; Friends of the Winnipeg Conservatory (Bd. mem. 1988– ); Manitoba Conservation Awards, Ecological Reserves, and Endangered Species (Adv. Bd. mem. 1982– ); Cactus and Succulent Soc. of Am.; recreations: raising tropical fish and succulent plants, stamp collecting, woodcarving, tennis; Home: 505 Boreham Blvd., Winnipeg, Man.; Office: Oak Hammock Marsh Interpretive Centre, P.O. Box 1160, Stonewall, Man. R0C 2Z0.

**WRIST, Peter E.,** M.A., M.Sc., AMP; pulp and paper executive; b. Mirfield, England 9 Oct. 1927; s. Owen N. and Evelyn (Ellis) W.; e. Cambridge Univ., B.A. 1948, M.A. 1952; London Univ., M.Sc. 1952; Harvard Univ. Business Sch., AMP; Univ. of B.C. D.Sc. (honoris causa) 1993; m. Mirabelle d. Sir Stanley J. and Lady Rhona Harley 3 Sept. 1955; children: Denise E. (Parson), C. Philip, Richard A. (m. Kathryn Idelson), Lydia H. (Schweizer); PRES. & CHIEF EXTVE. OFFR., PULP & PAPER RSCH. INST. OF CAN. 1986– ; Rsch. Physicist, Brit. Paper & Board Indus. Rsch. Assoc. 1949–52; Qué. North Shore Paper Co. 1952–56; Mead Corp. 1956; Assoc. Dir., Rsch. 1960; Dir., Rsch. 1961; Mgr., Rsch. & Engr. 1966; Vice-Pres. 1968; Technol. 1972; Extve. Vice-Pres., Pulp & Paper Rsch. Inst. of Can. 1983–86; Chrmn., Nat. Counc. for Air & Stream Improvement 1972–75; Mem. & Chrmn., Rsch. Adv. Ctte., Inst. of Paper Chem. 1971–83; Tech. Assn. of Pulp & Paper Indus. (TAPPI) Gold Medal 1983; Mem., TAPPI (Bd. mem. 1971–77, Pres. 1977–79); Tech. Assn. CPPA; N.Y. Acad. of Sci.; Gunnar Nicholson Gold Medal Award Selection Ctte.; Chrmn., Marcus Wallenberg Prize Selection Ctte.; recreations: skiing, sailing, tennis, gardening; Clubs: Forest & Stream; Beaconsfield Golf; Baie d'Urfe Yacht; Home: 20722 Gay Cedars, Baie d'Urfe, Qué. H9X 2T4; Office: 570 St. John Blvd., Pointe Claire, Qué. H9R 3J9.

**WRONG, Dennis Hume,** Ph.D.; professor; b. Toronto, Ont. 22 Nov. 1923; s. late Humphrey Hume and late Mary Joyce (Hutton) W.; e. Ecole Internationale, Geneva, 1937–39; Upper Can. Coll., Toronto, 1939–41; Univ. of Toronto, B.A. 1945; Columbia Univ., Ph.D. 1956; m. Jacqueline d. late Earle Conrath, Portland, Ore., 26 March 1966; one s. Terence Hume (by previous m.); PROF. OF SOCIOL. NEW YORK UNIV. since 1963; Instr., Princeton Univ. 1949–50 and Rutgers Univ. 1950–51; Research Asst. to Hon. George F. Kennan, Inst. for Advanced Study, Princeton, 1951–52; Lectr., Dept. of Pol. Econ., Univ. of Toronto, 1954–56; Asst. and Assoc. Prof., Brown Univ., 1956–61; Assoc. Prof., Grad. Faculty, New Sch. for Social Research, 1961–63; joined present Univ. 1963; Chrmn., Dept. of Sociol., Univ. Coll. 1963–65; Visiting Prof., Univ. of Nevada 1965–66; Visiting Fellow, Nuffield Coll., Oxford 1978; Guggenheim Fellow 1984–85; Fellow, The Wilson Center 1991–92; author 'American and Canadian Viewpoints' 1955; 'Population' 1956; 'Population and Society' 1961, 4th ed. 1977; ed. 'Max Weber' 1970; 'Skeptical Sociology' 1976; 'Power: Its Forms Bases and Uses' 1979, 1988; 'Class Fertility Trends in Western Nations' (Sociology Dissertation Series) 1980; 'The Problem of Order' 1994; co-ed. 'Readings in Introductory Sociology' 1967, 3rd ed. 1977; ed. 'Social Research' 1968–64; 'Contemporary Sociology: A Journal of Reviews' 1972–74; mem. Ed. Bd. 'Dissent' 1967– ; 'Partisan Review' 1981–87; other writings incl. numerous articles and reviews in various journs.; mem., Am. Sociol. Assn. (Program Comte. 1970, Nominations Comte. 1971–72, Pub. Comte. 1971–74); E. Sociol. Soc. (Extve. Comte. 1964–66); Home: 144 Drakes Corner Rd., Princeton, N.J. 08540.

**WUBNIG, Judy (Judith),** B.A., M.A., Ph.D.; university professor; b. Brooklyn, N.Y. 12 Jan. 1934; d. Arthur and Sylvia (Lipschitz) W.; e. Washington, D.C. public schools; Central High; Theodore Roosevelt H.S.; Swarthmore College B.A. 1955; Yale Univ. M.A. 1958, Ph.D. 1963; single; ASST. PROF., DEPT. OF PHILOSOPHY, UNIV. OF WATERLOO 1965– ; Instructor/Lecturer various univs. 1960–65; Mem., Am. Philosophical Assn.; Am. Soc. for Pol. & Legal Phil.; Assn. for Informal Logic & Critical Thinking; Candn. Assn .of Univ. Teachers; Candn. Phil. Assn.; Candn. Soc. for Aesthetics; Candn. Soc. for the History & Phil. of Math.; Hume Soc.; Internat. Assn. for Greek Phil.; for Phil. of Law and Social Phil.; Kant Gesellschaft; Metaphysical Soc. of N. Am.; Jacques Maritain Soc.; N. Am. Kant Soc.; N. Am. Soc. for Social Phil.; Nat. Assn. of Scholars; Soc. for Ancient Greek Philosophy; Soc. for Academic Freedom and Scholarship (Bd. of Dir.; Editor of newsletter); Univ. Centres for Rational Alternatives; Jewish; translator & editor: 'Arithmetic and Combinatorics: Kant and His Contemporaries' by Gottfried Martin & appendix: 'Examination of Kant's Criqitue of Pure Reason' by Johann Schultz 1985; author of several articles and reviews; clubs: Univ. of Waterloo Choir; Kitchener-Waterloo Field Naturalists; Home: 188 Lester St., Apt. 28B, Waterloo, Ont. N2L 3W4; Office: Waterloo, Ont. N2L 3G1.

**WUJEC, Tom,** B.Sc.; producer, writer, multimedia designer; b. Winnipeg, Man. 14 July 1959; s. Stanley and Alexandra (Kukuka); e. Univ. of Toronto B.Sc. 1982; m. Susan d. Delbert and Dorothy Seaman 6 Oct. 1984; one d.: Mikayla; SR. AV CONSULTANT, ROYAL ONTARIO MUSEUM; Pres., Synapse Interactive Media 1987– ; Consulting to Royal Ont. Mus., Ont. Mus. Assn., Candn. Mus. Assn., Ministry of Industry, Trade & Technol., Mus. of Sci. & Technol. & many private firms; Producer, McLaughlin Planetarium 1984–92; Mem., Internat. Planetarium Soc.; Planetarium Soc. of Can.; Siggraph; author: 'Pumping Ions: Games and Exercises to Flex the Mind' 1988, 'Feeding the Creative Mind' 1992 (non-fiction/creativity), 'The Book of Mental Exercises' 3 vols. 1992 (non-fiction), 'Envisioning the Universe' forthcoming (astronomy literacy); recreations: Tai Chi, Go, cycling; Home: 63 Hillsview Ave., Toronto, Ont. M6P 1J4; Office: 100 Queen's Park, Toronto, Ont. M5S 1C6.

**WYATT, Donald Edgar,** M.D., C.C.F.P., D.N.B.M.E., L.M.C.C., L.G.M.C.; physician; b. St. John's, Nfld. 7 June 1926; s. the late Herbert Kitchener and late Marion May (Soper) W.; e. Ridley Coll. St. Catharines, Ont.; Mt. Allison Acad. Sackville, N.B.; Mem. Univ. of Nfld.; Mt. Allison Univ.; Dalhousie Univ. M.D. 1963; Certificant in Family Med. Coll. Family Physicians Can.; Certificant in Contact Lens Practice, Nat. Eye Research Foundation U.S.A.; m. Patricia Gladys (Tucker); children (from previous m.): George Robert Herbert, Lorelei Andrea; stepchildren: Shelley Alaine (Yates) Boswell, Liann Carol Yates; private med. practice St. John's, Nfld. 1963– ; Pres. Delta Ltd. 1976– ; Orbit Ltd. 1979– ; DEW Investments Inc. Fla. 1980– ; Mang. Dir. Wyatt's Parts & Service Ltd. 1951–56; Life Underwriter National Life Assurance of Canada 1957–67; Phys., Student Health Services Mem. Univ. of Nfld. 1966–75, Clin. Assoc. Faculty of Med.; Prov. Surg. St. John Ambulance Bgde. 1966–71; Sports Phys. (Staff) XXI Olympic Games Montreal 1976, Candn. Team World Student Games Moscow 1973; mem. Can. Games Council 1974–79, Min.'s Review Comte. Can. Games 1978; mem. St. John's Recreation Comn. 1975–78; Pres. Nfld. and Labrador Amateur Sports Fed. 1973–76; Chrmn. Candn. Council Prov. Sport Feds. 1974–76; Vice Pres. Sports Fed. Can. 1975–76, Dir. 1974–75, 1976–77; mem. Ed. Adv. Bd. Medifacts Ltd. Ottawa 1974–82; served with RCA 1956–63, rank Lt.; RCAMC 1963–(Reserve), rank Capt.; mem., Coll. Family Physicians Can. (Pres. Nfld. Chapter 1974–76, mem. Nat. Extve. Comte. 1974–75); Candn. Med. Assn.; Nfld. Med. Assn. (Extve. Comte. 1967–69); Contact Lens Assn. of Ophthalmologists; Candn. Radio Relay League; Can. Amateur Radio Federation; Soc. of Nfld. Radio Amateurs (Vice Pres. 1990; Pres. 1991, 1992) (Call Sign V01KX); Nfld. Motorsports Fedn. (Treas. 1988–91; Chrmn. 1991, Pres. 1992); Gold Wing Road Riders Assn. Inc.; Chrmn., Nfld. Chapter, Candn. Ride For Sight 1992– (Secy. 1991–92); Office: 207 Lemarchant Rd., St. John's, Nfld. A1C 2H5.

**WYATT, Gerard Robert,** B.A., Ph.D.; biologist; b. Palo Alto, Ca. 3 Sept. 1925; s. Horace Graham and Mary Aimee (Strickland) W.; came to Can. 1935; e. Univ. of B.C. B.A. 1945; Univ. of Ca. Berkeley 1947; Univ. of Cambridge, England Ph.D. 1950; m. late Sarah Silver d. late Arthur Silver Morton 19 Dec. 1951; children: Eve Morton, Graham Strickland, Diana Silver; m. Mary Evelyn d. late Thomas Arthur Rogers 16 Mar. 1985; Prof., Dept. of Biology, Queen's Univ., 1973–94; Scientific Officer, Candn. Agricult. Insect Pathology Lab., 1950; Asst. Prof. Biochem., Yale Univ. 1954; Assoc. Prof. Biol. 1960; Prof. Biol. 1964; Prof. and Head of Biol. Dept., Queen's Univ., 1973–75; Scientific Dir., Insect Biotech Canada 1990–93; author many research papers and scholarly reviews in field of biology, esp. biochemistry and molecular biology of insects; mem., Entomological Soc. Amer.; Candn. Soc. Cell. Biol.; Entomological Soc. Can.; Royal Soc. Can.; Home: 114 Earl St., Kingston, Ont. K7L 2H1.

**WYATT, Harold Edmund;** banker; b. Moose Jaw, Sask. 30 Nov. 1921; s. Edmund Rundle and Zelma Aleta (Turk) W.; e. King George Pub. Sch. and Central Coll. Inst. Moose Jaw, Sask. (Sr. Matric. 1939); m. Isabel Margaret MacDonald, 9 May 1942; children: David MacDonald, Andrea Maureen Shumka, Kathryn Margaret Cottingham; retired Vice Chrmn. & Dir., Royal Bank of Canada; Vice Chrmn. & Dir., Talisman Energy Inc.; Dir., Trimac Ltd.; Industrial Bank of Japan (Canada); The Royal Candn. Geographical Soc.; Chrmn., Advisory Ctte. on Alberta's Economic Future; Chrmn., Senator Stan Waters Memorial Foundation; Mem. Adv. Bd. Marsh & McLennan; Univ. of Calgary Canada/Taiwan Adv. Council; Chrmn., Mount Royal College Foundation, Calgary International Organ Festival; Dir., The Council for Canadian Unity; Past Co-Chrmn., Calgary Economic Development Authority; joined the Royal Bank of Canada 1939; served at several Saskatchewan branches; and held various posts in Sask., Que. and Ont.; Asst. Gen. Mgr., heading the Bank's Central and Northern Ont. districts, Toronto 1965; Depy. Gen. Mgr., responsible for personnel 1967; Gen. Mgr. of Candn. Districts 1970; Vice Pres. & Gen. Mgr. Canada 1971; Vice Chrmn. 1978–86; Past Chrmn., Liquid Carbonic Inc.; Monsanto Canada Inc.; Past Dir. Chrysler Canada Inc.; RCA Canada Inc., Perigo, Asia Pacific Found.; Banff Sch. of Mgmt.; Past Chrmn. & Dir., Candn. Chamber of Commerce; Trustee & Mem.: Am. Mgmt. Assoc.; Calgary Chamber of Comm.; Mem. Adv. Ctte. P.R.I.D.E.; Past Dir. & Mem. of Extve. Ctte. Calgary Philharmonic Soc.; Past Dir., Calgary Winter Festival; Gov., Can. Jaycees; served with R.C.A.F. for 41/2 years during 2nd World War; discharged with rank Flt. Lt.; recipient, Silver Jubilee Medal 1977; Commemorative Medal for 125th Anniversary of Candn. Confederation 1992; United Church; recreations: golf, swimming; Office: Mount Royal College Foundation, City Centre Campus, 3rd Floor, 833 – 4th Avenue S.W., Calgary, Alta. T2P 3T5.

**WYATT, Rachel Evadne;** author; b. Bradford, Eng. 14 Oct. 1929; d. Kenneth Rycroft and Rachel Florence (Brumfitt) Arnold; e. Bradford Girls' Grammar Sch.; m. Alan s. Margaret and Horace Wyatt 1948; children: Antony, Diana, Timothy, Sally; came to Can. 1957; wrote and broadcast talks for CBC, short stories on 'Anthology'; began writing radio dramas 1970, over 75 broadcast by CBC, 30 by BBC (London, Eng.); Playwright-in-Residence, Tarragon Theatre, Toronto 1983–84; Dir., Writing Programme, Banff; teacher, writing, Arctic Coll., Iqaluit, Baffin Island 1986–93; prior to 1962 wrote short features for newspapers and mags. incl. 'The Guardian,' 'Punch,' 'The Sunday Telegraph'; recipient CBC Lit. Prize for 15 minute Drama 1982; author 'The String Box' (novel) 1970; 'The Rosedale Hoax' (novel) 1977; 'Foreign Bodies' (novel) 1982; 'Time in the Air' (novel) 1985; 'Geometry' (stage play, Tarragon Theatre) 1983; 'Chairs and Tables' (stage play, Tarragon Theatre) 1984; mem. Soc. Authors (U.K.); Playwrights Canada; ACTRA; P.E.N. International; recreations: theatre, music, reading, movies; Home: 1217 Tattershall Dr., Victoria, B.C. V8P 1Y8.

**WYATT, Robert Stewart;** foundation executive; b. Hamilton, Ont. 3 June 1952; s. Russell Stewart and Josephine Jennie (Rao) W.; e. Westdale Secondary Sch. Hamilton 1969; Hamilton Coll. Inst. 1970; McMaster Univ.; m. Kathryn Anne d. Dr. Randall E., O.C. and Joan (Broad) Ivany 23 June 1989; children: Joan A.J., Stewart R.; EXEC. DIR. THE MUTTART FOUND. 1989– , Trustee 1986–89; Print and Broadcast Journalist Hamilton, Stratford, Edmonton 1970–79; Pub. Info. Offr. Edmonton Police Service 1979–81; Exec. Asst. to Ombudsman for Alta. 1981–84; Pub. Relations/Govt. Affairs Supr. Alberta Power 1984–87; Dir. of Communications Ont. Min. of Atty. Gen. 1987–89; Asst. to Exec. Dir. Internat. Ombudsman Inst. 1984–85 (delivered paper Helsinki 1984); Lectr. Police-Media Relations Candn. Police Coll. 1981, RCMP 'K' Div. 1974–77; Regional Dir. (Can.) Police Info. Offr. Sect., Internat. Assn. Chiefs of Police 1980; mem., Vice Chair and Chair Pub. Relations Ctte. Candn. Red Cross Soc. Alta. & NWT Div. 1981–86; Dir., Vice Pres. Finance, Sec.-Treas. Edmonton Klondike Days Assn. 1975–81; Mem. Bd. of Govs., Edmonton Club 1993– ; Home: 7520 – 142A St., Edmonton, Alta. T5R 0N4; Office: 530, 9919 – 105 St., Edmonton, Alta. T5K 1B1.

**WYCZYNSKI, Paul,** L. ès L., D.E.S., Ph.D., D.Lit.; educator; b. Zelgoszcz, Poland 29 June 1921; s. Lucjan and Clara W.; e. Univ. de Lille L. ès L. 1949, D.E.S. 1950; Univ. d'Ottawa Ph.D. 1957; Univ. Laurentienne

D.Lit. 1978; Univ. of Guelph D.Lit. 1989; Univ. Laval D.ès.L. 1989; m. Régine d. André Delabit, France 11 Sept. 1951; children: Michel, Isabelle, Rita, Bernard, Marc, Monique, Anne; PROF. TITULAIRE DE RECHERCHE, UNIV. D'OTTAWA since 1970, Prof. agrégé 1960, Prof. titulaire 1964, Dir-fondateur du Centre de recherche en littérature canadienne-française 1958–73; mem. Royal Comn. on Bilingualism & Biculturalism 1963–69; Prof. de l'année Univ. d'Ottawa 1968; fondateur et coordonateur 'Archives des lettres canadiennes'; publs. incl. 'Noc Betlejemska' (théâtre) 1949; 'Emile Nelligan: Sources et Originalité de son oeuvre' 1960; 'Poésie et Symbole' 1965; 'François-Xavier Garneau: Aspects littéraires de son eouvre' 1966; 'Emile Nelligan' 1967; 'François-Xavier Garneau: Voyage en Angleterre et en France ...' 1968; 'Nelligan et la Musique' 1971; 'Albert Laberge – Charles Gill' (catalogue) 1971; 'Bibliographie descriptive et critique d'Émile Nelligan' 1973; 'Dictionnaire pratique des auteurs québécois' (en collaboration) 1976; 'Francois-Xavier Garneau 1809–1866' (catalogue) 1977; 'W slonecznej ciemni' (poetry) 1981; ''La Scouine' d'Albert Laberge' (édition critique) 1986, Prix Champlain 1986; 'Nelligan, biographie' 1987; 'Textes poétiques du Canada français' (en collaboration) vol. 1 1987, vol. 2 1989, vol. 3 1990, vol. 4 1991, vol. 5 1992, vol. 6 1993; 'Dictionnaire des auteurs de langue française en Amérique du Nord' (en collaboration); 'Poésies complètes 1896–1841' d'Émile Nelligan (édition critique en collaboration) 1991; 'Poèmes autographes' d'Émile Nelligan 1991; 'Mowa Korzeni' (poetry) 1991; 'Émile Nelligan, Poésies complètes' (coll. Bibliothèque québécoise, en collaboration) 1992; Killam Research Fellowship 1984; Ordre des francophones d'Amérique 1988; Chevalier de l'ordre des arts et des lettres de France 1990; Officer, Order of Canada 1993; numerous articles various journs.; mem. Royal Soc. Can.; Assn. de littérature comparée; Soc. des écrivains canadiens-français; Soc. française d'histoire d'outre-mer; Inst. polonais des arts et des sciences en Amérique du Nord; Assn. Candn. Profs.; Home: 156 rue Kehoe, Ottawa, Ont. K2B 6A5; Office: Univ. of Ottawa, Ottawa, Ont. K1N 6N5.

**WYKES, Edmund Harold,** LL.B.; lawyer; b. Newcastle-on-Tyne, Eng. 19 July 1928; s. late Cyril Edmund and Sylvia (Glover) W.; e. elem. and sec. sch. Durham, Eng.; Durham Univ. LL.B. 1949; m. Joan d. late Thomas Wilfred Nightingale 1 Oct. 1955; children: Julie Caroline, Christopher John; Vice Pres. and Secy., Imperial Life Assurance Co. of Canada, Retired; held various positions assoc. with legal dept. of Imperial Life from 1957; admitted as Solicitor in Eng. 1953, in Ont. 1958; served with RAF 1949–51; demobilized with rank of Flying Offr.; mem., Eng. Law Soc.; Law Soc. of U.C.; Assn. of Life Assurance Counsel; Am. Soc. of Corp. Secys.; Chrmn. Insurance Law Section, Ont. Br., Candn. Bar Assn., 1979; Anglican; Clubs: University; recreations: music, reading; Home: 86 Wimbleton Rd., Islington, Ont. M9A 3S5.

**WYLIE, (Margaret) Alison,** B.A., M.A., Ph.D.; university professor; b. Swindon, England 26 Aug. 1954; d. Lewis Hutchinson and Margaret Frances (Croll) W.; e. Mount Allison Univ. B.A. (Hons.) 1976; State Univ. of N.Y. at Binghamton M.A. 1978, Ph.D. 1982; m. Samuel Gerszon s. Abraham and Frieda Gerszonowicz 6 July 1983; PROF. (with tenure), DEPT. OF PHILOSOPHY, UNIV. OF WESTERN ONT. 1993– ; Assoc. Prof. 1989–93; many summers spent working on archaeological field projects; post-doctoral (P.D.) fellowships: Visiting P.D. Fellow, Calgary Inst. for the Humanities 1981–82; Univ. P.D. Fellow, Univ. of Calgary 1982–83, 1984–85; Mellon P.D. Fellow, Washington Univ. at St. Louis 1983–84; Visiting Prof., Anthropology, Univ. of Calif. at Berkeley 1989; Visiting Scholar 1990–92; Visiting Fellow, Clare Hall Cambridge 1990 (Life Fellow 1991); Faculty of Arts Rsch. Professorship, U.W.O. 1987–88; Mem., Bd. of Dir., Battered Women's Advocacy Clinic of London 1986–90; Mem., Western's Caucus on Women's Issues (Extve. 1986–90 and 1992–93; Pres. 1989–90); Candn. Soc. for the History & Phil. of Science (Gov. Bd. 1987–90; Extve. 1991–94; Program Chair 1989; Vice-Pres. 1993–95); Candn. Society for Women in Philosophy (Extve. 1992–93); Am. Anthrop. Assn., Arch. Div. (Extve. 1990–92); Co-Chair Ethics Ctte., Soc. for Am. Archaeology; co-editor: 'Critical Traditions in Contemporary Archaeology' 1989; author of scholarly articles in feminist philosophy, philosophy of the social sciences, archaeological theory; recreations: feminist activism; clubs: London Status of Women Action Group, Hags and Crones Feminist Reading Group; Office: Dept. of Philosophy, Univ. of Western Ont., London, Ont. N6A 3K7.

**WYLIE, Barry Kenneth,** B.Com., C.A.; corporate controller; b. Winnipeg, Man. 17 July 1947; s. Kenneth Owen and Grace Eleanor (Emek) W.; e. Gordon Bell High Sch. 1965; Univ. of Man. B.Com. 1969; C.A. Man. 1972 (Silver Medalist); m. Angela d. Paul and Jessie Lungal 17 Aug. 1974; CORPORATE CONTROLLER, NCR CANADA LTD. 1982– ; joined Price Waterhouse Winnipeg 1969, Audit Supr. 1974, Exchange Prog. Dublin, Ireland 1976–77, Audit Mgr. Mississauga 1977, Toronto 1980; recreations: travel, wine; Home: 1189 Rosethorne Rd., Oakville, Ont. L6M 1H5; Office: 6865 Century Ave., Mississauga, Ont. L5N 2E2.

**WYLIE, Betty Jane,** B.A., M.A.; writer; b. Winnipeg, Man. 21 Feb. 1931; d. Jack and (Judith) Inga (Tergesen) McKenty; e. Univ. of Man., B.A. (double Hons.) 1951, M.A. 1952; m. the late William Tennent s. John and Catherine Wylie 7 June 1952; children: Elizabeth, Catherine, John, Matthew; Writer-in-Residence, Humphrey Public Library 1990; Alumni Jubilee Award, Univ. of Manitoba 1989; Bunting fellow, Radcliffe College 1989–90; Chair, The Writers Union of Can. 1988–89 (1st Vice Chair 1987–88); Writer-in-Residence, Burlington Public Library 1987–88; Bd. of Dirs., Investors' Group Mutual Funds, and Investors' Group Trust; TWUC (Counc. 1986–87); Playwrights Union of Can. (Counc. 1986–87, Chair, Women's Caucus 1991) founding member; ACTRA; SOCAN; Dramatists' Guild; paper, reading, Nordic Assn. for Candn. Studies, Oslo 1990 and Turku 1993; recipient, Psychol. Found. Award for Public Educ. 1987; Past Bd. Mem., Bereaved Families of Ont.; patron, Ottawa Chapter; founding mem., Community Contacts for the Widowed; author: 'Men!' 1993; 'Betty Jane's Diary: Holidays' 1991; 'Betty Jane's Diary: Passages' 1991; 'Betty Jane's Diary: Lessons' 1993; 'New Beginnings' 1991; 'Something Might Happen; (poetry) 1989; 'All in the Family' 1988; 'Successfully Single' 1986; 'The Best is Yet to Come' 1985, 2nd ed. 1989; 'Everywomen's Money Book' 1984 (4th ed. 1989); 'The Book of Matthew' 1984, 'Betty Jane's Diary' 1981, 'No Two Alike' 1980, 'Beginnings: A Book for Widows' (in 6 countries) 1977 (3rd ed. in Canada 1989) non-fiction; 'The Betty Jane Wylie Cheese Cookbook' 1984, 'Encore' 1979 (cookbooks); 'John of a Thousand Faces' 1983, 'Tecumseh' 1982 (children's); publ. plays: 'A Place on Earth' (prize winner, prod. in Can., U.S., U.K., N.Z.) 1982, 'The Horsburgh Scandal' 1981, 'Don't Just Stand There – Jiggle!' 1980, 'Mark' 1979, 'Old Woman & Pedlar/Kingsayer' 1978 (plays); 'Double Vision' and 'Time Bomb' 1986; 'Help is on the Way' 1989; 'Veranda' 1990; 'How to Speak Male' 1990; 'A Native of the James Family' 1990; 'Boy in a Cage' 1991; 'Grace Under Pressure' 1992; 'Angel' 1993; record album 'Beowulf' 1985; film (with Donald Martin) 'Coming of Age' 1993; recreations: swimming, theatre; Office: c/o Writers' Union of Canada, 24 Ryerson Ave., Toronto, Ont. M5T 2P3.

**WYMAN, Anna Margaret;** artistic director; choreographer; b. Graz, Austria 29 Apl. 1928; d. Alois and Margareta Schalk; e. Keplerschule Graz, Austria; State Opera House Graz; trained as dancer Eur.; m. Max Wyman (div.); ARTISTIC DIR. & CHOREOGRAPHER, THE ANNA WYMAN STUDIO OF DANCE ART; early career dancer and choreog. Eur.; came to Can. 1968; Artistic Dir. & Choreographer Anna Wyman Dance Theatre Found. 1968–92; toured extensively with present co. to China 1980 (1st invited Candn. dancer), India 1983, 1987, Mexico 1983, New York 1985, Australia 1988; choreog. films 'Klee Wyck: A Ballet for Emily', 'Here in the Eye of the Hurricane', 'Anna in Graz', 'Gala'; video with David Foster and Vancouver Symphony Orch.; served 3 yrs. Adv. Ctte. Can. Council, 15 yrs. grant application juries; 2 yrs. Adv. Council Prov. B.C. Culture; Candn. Rep. Internat. Choreog. Competition London, Eng. 1973; one of top three entries Internat. Choreogs. Competition Cologne, Germany; recipient Women of Distinction Award Arts & Culture 1984; Vancouver Sweney Award Excellence in Arts 1985; named one of W. Vancouver's Outstanding Achievers 1987; Celebration Cert. for hard work and dedication to community 1988; recreations: swimming, cycling, skiing; Home: 319 East 27th St., North Vancouver, B.C. V7N 1B9; Office: 3F, 927 Granville St., Vancouver, B.C. V6Z 1L3.

**WYMAN, William Robert,** B.Comm.; b. Edmonton, Alta. 4 Dec. 1930; s. Robert Andrew and Dora (Joberns) W.; e. Primary Sch. Edmonton, Alta.; Primary Sch., Trinity Coll., Port Hope, Ont.; High Schs. Vancouver, Kelowna & Kamloops, B.C.; Univ. of B.C., B.Comm. 1956, LL.D. (Hon.) 1987; m. Dorothy, d. Charles Taylor, 4 Sept. 1954; children: Timothy, Robyn; Dir., B.C. Telephone Co.; Finning Ltd.; Suncor Inc.; Fletcher Challenge Canada Ltd.; North America Life Ins. Co.; West Coast Energy Inc.; joined Canada Life Assurance Co., Toronto as Analyst, Invest. Dept. 1956; Analyst, Hall Securities Ltd., Vancouver 1957; Registered Rep., Richardson Securities Canada 1960; Mgr. Research Dept., Pemberton Securities Ltd. 1962, Retail Dept. Mgr. and Dir. 1965, Vice-Pres. 1969, Sr. Vice-Pres. 1971, Pres. and C.E.O. 1975, Chrmn. 1982; Chrmn., Finning Ltd.; Vice-Chrmn., Fletcher Challenge Canada Ltd.; Former Chrmn. & C.E.O., B.C. Hydro and Power Authority 1987–92; Former Chrmn. & Dir., Pemberton Securities Inc. (formerly Pemberton Houston Willoughby Bell Gouinlock Inc.) 1987–92; former Vice Chrmn. & Dir., R.B.C. Dominion Securities Inc.; Gov., Univ. of B.C.; Business Counc. of B.C.; Mem., University Adv. Counc.; Past Chancellor, Univ. of B.C.; Past Gov., Montreal Stock Exchange; Past Chrmn.: Invest. Dealers Assn. Can.; Pacific Dist., Investment Dealers Assoc.; Van. Bd. of Trade; Candn. Chamber of Commerce; Wyman Ctte. on Canada Deposit Insurance Corp.; former Dir.: Yorkshire Trust Co.; Koerner Found.; West Vancouver Found.; Crown Forest Industries Ltd.; Insurance Corp. of B.C.; Sunny Hill Hosp. for Children; past mem.: Lortie Ctte. on Inflation and the Taxation of Personal Investment Income; Salvation Army Adv. Ctte.; Anglican; Trustee Killam Estate Trust; recreations: golf, skiing, fishing, swimming; Clubs: Capilano Golf & Country (West Vancouver); Hollyburn Country; Mission Hills Golf & Country; Royal and Ancient Golf Club of St. Andrews; The Vancouver; Address: 2406 Bellevue Dr., West Vancouver, B.C. V7V 1E2.

**WYNANT, Larry,** B.Comm., M.B.A., D.B.A; university professor; b. Winnipeg, Man. 21 Feb. 1946; s. George Frank and Anne (Kacsmar) W.; e. Univ. of Man., B.Comm. 1968; The Univ. of West. Ont., M.B.A. 1972; Harvard Univ., D.B.A. 1977; m. Jessie d. William and Adeline Young 7 June 1969; PROF. AND ASSOC. DEAN, WESTERN BUSINESS SCHOOL, UNIV. OF WEST. ONT.; Money Market Trader, Royal Bank of Can. 1968–70; Vis. Lectr., Univ. of W. Indies (Trinidad) 1972–73; Chrmn., M.B.A. Prog. 1984–88; Instr., Western Exec. Program for Sr. Mgrs. 1981– ; cons. on banking & finan. mngt. to num. Candn. cos.; co-author: 'Chartered Bank Financing of Small Business in Canada' 1982, 'Government Loan Guarantee Programs for Small Business' 1985, 'Canadian Commercial Lending' 1986, 'Canadian Cases in Financial Management' 1986; 'Handbook of Commercial Lending' 1989; 'Banks and Small Business Borrowers' 1991; recreations: fishing, golf; Home: 790 Clearview Cres., London, Ont. N6H 4P7; Office: London, Ont. N6A 3K7.

**WYNDHAM, John David,** P.Eng.; publisher; b. Oakville, Ont. 4 July 1947; s. John S. and Marjorie Anne (Hopper) W.; e. Oakville Trafalgar H.S., Grad. 1967; Univ. of Waterloo B.A.Sc. 1971; m. Lois Margaret d. Wilfred C. Chick 16 Oct. 1982; PRESIDENT, STONE & COX LTD. 1990– ; joined firm of Stone & Cox Ltd. 1980; Mng. Dir., 1987–90; Ed. Annual Publ. 1981; Vice-Pres. 1985; Protestant; recreations: golf, sailing; Home: 2097 Gary Cres., Burlington, Ont. L7R 1T1; Office: 111 Peter St., Suite 202, Toronto, Ont. M5V 2H1.

**WYNDHAM, John Steen;** publisher; b. Oakville, Ont. 21 April 1915; s. William B. and Agnes (Steen) W., e. Oakville High Sch., Grad. 1932; Northern Inst. of Tech., Grad. 1942; m. Marjorie Anne, d. Dr. David A. Hopper, 4 April 1942; CHRMN., STONE & COX LTD. 1986– ; joined firm of Stone & Cox Ltd. 1934; Pres. 1956–86; Ed., year books, 1938; Asst. Ed., Candn. Ins. Law Service, 1938; Ed. of Publs., 1946; served in World War, 1942–45, as Radio Offr. with R.A.F. Ferry Command; Protestant; recreations: golf, curling; Clubs: Oakville Golf; Oakville Curling; Home: 1162 Morrison Heights Drive, Oakville, Ont. L6J 4J1; Office: 111 Peter St., Ste. 202, Toronto, Ont. M5V 2H1.

**WYNN, James Arthur,** Q.C., B.A., LL.B.; lawyer; b. Toronto, Ont. 11 March 1924; s. Arthur Reginald and Marjorie Helen (Galbraith) W.; e. London Sch. of Econ. 1945–46; Univ. of Toronto B.A. 1947; Osgoode Hall Law Sch. grad. & called to Bar June 1950; LL.B. conferred York Univ. June 1991; m. Celia d. William and Celia Tait 24 April 1944; children: Francine, Marcia (Biles), Emily; ASSOC., ROSS & McBRIDE 1989– ; joined law firm of Harley, Sweet, Slemin & Whitbread (Brantford) 1950 & continued until its successor Slemin, Wynn merged with Ross & McBride 1989; general law practice with emphasis on corp. & estate work; Dir., Atkemix Inc.; Sec., Kirkwood Commutators (Can.) Ltd. (also Dir. until 1989); Past Dir. of var. corps.; Gov., Renison College, Univ. of Waterloo until 1986; Past Synod Del. & Extve. Ctte. Mem., Incorp. Synod of the Diocese of Huron; Synod Registrar & Vice Chancellor until 1987; recreations: gardening, tennis, golf, etc.; club: Rotary 1957– ; Home: 15 Wellington St., Brantford, Ont. N3T 2L5; Office: 171 Colborne St., P.O. Box 278, Brantford, Ont. N3T 5M8.

**WYNNE-EDWARDS, Hugh Robert,** O.C., B.Sc., M.A., Ph.D., D.Sc., F.R.S.C.; scientist; b. Montreal, Que. 19 Jan. 1934; s. Prof. Vero Copner and Jeannie Campbell (Morris) W-E.; e. Montreal (Que.) High Sch., 1938–46; Aberdeen (Scot.) Grammar Sch., 1946–51; Univ. of Aberdeen, B.Sc. 1955; Queen's Univ., M.A. 1957, Ph.D. 1959; Memorial Univ., D. Sc. (Hon.) 1975; m. children by former marriages: Robin Alexander, Katherine Elizabeth, Renée Elizabeth Lortie, Krista Smyth, Jeannie Elizabeth, Alexander Vernon; PRES. AND CHIEF EXECUTIVE OFFR., B.C. RESEARCH INC. 1993– and PRES., TERRACY INC. 1989– ; with Geol. Survey of Canada, 1958–59; joined Queen's Univ. as Lectr., 1959–61, Asst. Prof. 1961–64, Assoc. Prof. 1964–68, Secy., Faculty of Arts and Science, 1965–68, Prof. and Head Dept. Geol. Sciences 1968–72; and Prof., Cominco Prof. and Head, Dept. of Geol. Sciences, U.B.C. 1972–77; Asst., Secy., Univ. Branch, Min. of State for Science and Technology, 1977–79; Scientific Dir., Alcan Intl., 1979–80; Vice Pres., Rsch. & Develop., & Chief Scientific Offr., 1980–89; C.E.O., Moli Energy Ltd. 1989–90; Science Adv., Teck Corp. 1989–91; Visiting Prof., Univ. of Aberdeen, 1965–66; State Guest advising Directorate of Geol. and Mining, Uttar Pradesh, India, 1964; Advisor (1968–72), Grenville Project, Que. Dept. Nat. Resources (Co-ordinator of Project, Geol. Survey of Can. 1964–65); Visiting Prof., Univ. of Witwatersrand, Johannesberg, S. Africa 1972; Special Coant, UNDP., 1976; Spendiarov Prize (24th Internat. Geol. Cong. 1972); Pres., Candn. Geoscience Council, 1973–74; Pres., Scitec, 1977; CBC Science Adv. Comte., 1980–84; Conseil de la politique scientifique du Québec, 1981; Dir., Fonds de Recherche en Santé du Québec, 1981; Dir., SOQUIP 1983–87; Dir. and Trustee, Royal Victoria Hosp. 1984–88; Chrmn. Rsch. Inst. Mgmt. Bd. 1984–85; mem. Sci. Council of Can. 1983–90; mem. Nat. Adv. Bd. on Science and Technology 1987–90; Vice Chrmn., Candn. Research Mgmt. Assn. 1982–83, Chrmn. 1984–86, Assn. Medalist 1987; Industrial Liaison Comte., United Nations Centre for Science and Technology in Development 1982– ; 177th Annual Plenary Lectr., The Electro Chemical Soc. 1990; Vice Chrmn., Technology Advisory Group, Business Council for Sustainable Development, Geneva 1991– ; Dir., Candn. Genetic Diseases Network 1990– , Vice Chrmn. 1992– ; Dir., N.R. Network for Neural Regeneration and Recovery 1992–93; Dir., CS Resources Inc. 1993– ; Canada Council Lectr., ASM International 1992–93; Am. Assn. Advanc. Science; apptd. Officer, Order of Canada 1991; United Church; recreations: tennis, skiing, carpentry; Club: University (Montreal); Home: 2030 – 27th Street, West Vancouver, B.C. V7V 4L4.

**WYNNE-JONES, Tim,** B.A., M.F.A.; writer; b. Bromborough Cheshire, Great Britain 12 Aug. 1948; s. Sydney Thomas and Sheila Beryce (Hodgson) W.; e. Ridgemont H.S. 1967; Univ. of Waterloo, B.A. (Hons.) 1974; York Univ., M.F.A. 1979; m. Amanda West d. Laurie and Gary Lewis 25 Sept. 1980; children: Virgil Alexander, Magdalene Beryl, Lewis Arthur; after studying architecture & performing as profl. musician turned to visual art & design before becoming full-time writer in 1980; formerly Visual Art Teacher, Univ. of Waterloo & York Univ.; Creative Writing Teacher, Banff Sch. of Fine Arts, St. Lawrence Coll. & Red Deer Coll. summer writing prog.; Mem., Crime Writers of Can. (Founding Mem. & 1st Sec.); The Writers' Union of Can.; P.E.N. Internat.; Candn. Soc. of Childrens' Authors, Illustrators & Performers; SOCAN; ACTRA; author: 'Odds End' 1981 (Seal First Novel Award), 'The Knot' 1982, 'Fastyngange' 1988 (novels); 'Zoom at Sea' 1983, 'Zoom Away' 1985 (picture books illus. by Ken Nutt); 'Mischief City' (Victor Gad. illus.) 1986, 'I'll Make You Small' (Maryann Kovalski, illus.) 1986, 'The Architect of the Moon' (Ian Wallace, illus.) 1988 (picture books, poetry); 'A Midwinter Night's Dream' book & libretto for an opera, composed by Harry Somers, comnd. by Candn. Children's Opera Chorus; 'Some of the Kinder Planets' (English Children's text) winner of 1993 Governor Gen.'s Literary Award; num. radio plays (ACTRA Award, 'St Anthony's Man') & stories.

**WYNNYCKYJ, Leo G.,** B.A., B.Com., M.B.A., Ph.D., C.M.A., F.C.M.A.; management consultant; b. Jabloniw, Ukraine 21 Feb. 1931; s. Julian Cornelius and Jaroslava (Saturska) W.; e. Concordia Univ. B.Com. 1953, B.A. 1955; Univ. of W. Ont. M.B.A. 1957; Pacific Western Univ. Ph.D. 1985; m. Marta Taissa d. Wasyl and Lydia Wolycky 1 Jan. 1976; children: Levco, Chrystyna, Marco; PRESIDENT, LGW BUSINESS CONSULTANTS LTD. 1977– ; Financial Analyst CIL 1957–60; Mfg. Analysis Mgr. N.A. Operations, Massey-Ferguson Ltd. Toronto; Chief Acct. Pipe Div., Financial Analysis Mgr. Structural Div. CANRON Ltd. Montreal 1960–65; Sr. Cons., Functional Dir. Touche, Ross & Partners Toronto 1966–67; Partner and Pres. RMC Resources Management Consultants Ltd. Toronto 1968–76; Exec. Dir. Strait of Canso Devel. Office Port Hawkesbury, N.S. 1976–77; Pres. Soc. Mgmt. Accts. 1973–74; Fellow, Soc. of Mgmt. Accts. 1984; Address: 1371 Chattaway Ave., Ottawa, Ont. K1H 7S2.

**WYRE, John,** B.Mus.; musician; b. Philadelphia, Pa. 17 May 1941; s. Ross Milan and Edna Myrtle (Sprunger) W.; e. Eastman Sch. of Music, B.Mus. 1963; m. Jean d. John and Mary Donelson 9 Aug. 1977; FOUNDING MEM., NEXUS (Candn. percussion ensemble); timpanist, Marlboro Music Festival 1961–68; Oklahoma City Symphony 1964–65; Milwaukee Symphony 1965–66; Toronto Symphony, 11 seasons 1966–81; Candn. Opera Co. Orchestra 1985–88; Acting Principal Timpanist, Boston Symphony 1987–92; guest soloist, Boston Symphony 1971; percussionist, Contemporary Music Festival, Expo 70, Osaka 1970; teacher, Banff Sch. of the Performing Arts; Nat. Youth Orchestra of Can. 1967–69; Fac. of Music, Univ. of Toronto 1971–74; Queen's Univ. 1974–75; Assoc., Candn. Music Centre; Artistic Dir., World Drums; drum festivals for Toronto Internat. Festival 1984, Expo 86, 1988 Winter and Summer Olympics, Expo 88, Expo 93; composer of commissions for the Festival Singers of Can., Elmer Iseler Singers, Judy Loman, Nat. Youth Orchestra of Can.; works performed by N.Y. Philharmonic, Cleveland Orch., Toronto Symphony, Japan Philharmonic, New Music Concerts (Toronto), Tokyo Philharmonic Choir, Winnipeg Symphony; Address: P.O. Box 100, Norland, Ont. K0M 2L0.

**WYSLOBICKY, Dennis A.,** B.Comm., LL.B., M.B.A.; lawyer; b. Sudbury, Ont. 26 Sept. 1956; s. Michael and Jessie (Sturby) W.; e. McMaster Univ. B.Comm. 1979; York Univ. M.B.A. 1983; Osgoode Hall Law School LL.B. 1983; m. Irene d. Nicholas and Eugenia Kuchtaruk 28 May 1988; PARTNER, THORSTEINSSONS 1991– ; called to Bar of Ontario 1985; Assoc. Lawyer, Blake, Cassels & Graydon 1985; Partner 1991; Mem., Ad Hoc Joint Ctte., Candn. Bar Assn. and Candn. Inst. of C.A.s (CICA) advising Dept. of Finance on implementation of GST legislation; frequent lecturer, CICA In-Depth Sales Tax Course; frequent speaker on commodity tax topics at profl. & other confs. & events incl. Candn. Bar Assn., Ont. meetings and conferences; Mem., Ukrainian Profl. & Business Club, Candn. Property Tax Assn.; author of taxation articles, 'Provincial Sales Tax on Interprovincial Use' (course) 1989; Commentator, 'GST Survival Guide' (audio cassette) 1990; regular contbr., De Boo 'GST & Commodity Tax' newsletter; recreations: tennis, reading; clubs: Toronto Board of Trade; Home: 188 Douglas Ave., Oakville, Ont. L6J 3S1; Office: Canada Trust Tower, P.O. Box 611, Suite 3640, BCE Place, 161 Bay St., Toronto, Ont. M5J 2S1.

**WYSPIANSKI, John O.,** B.A., M.A., Ph.D., C.Psych.; university professor; b. Grudziadz, Poland 15 Feb. 1929; s. Jan Alexander and Catherine (Royko) W.; e. Univ. of Ottawa, B.A. 1958, M.A. 1961, Ph.D. 1963; m. Judy F. B.A., M.Ed. d. Gordon and Alma Gollan; one s.: Peter Howard Alexander; Prof., Univ. of Ottawa 1961–91; Cons. Psychol., St. Vincent Hosp. 1965–77; Chrmn., J.O. Wyspianski & Assoc. Ltd. 1969– ; Chrmn., Leaders' Forum Inc. 1984; Visiting Prof., Stanford Univ. 1977–78, 1989; Cons./Advr., Dept. of Nat. Defence 1978–80; Sr. Vice-Pres., Glaser Bros. Corp. 1980–82; Mem., Bd. of Dirs., Core Mark Int. 1986–87; Advr. to Pres. & Sr. Extves. on Human Organizational Development & Productivity (Can. & U.S.); Mem., Candn. Psychol. Assn.; Am. Psychol. Assn.; N.Y. Acad. of Sci.; author: 'The Canadian Forces Smart Book' 1985; 'Scan for the Future' 1979; recreations: gardening, writing; Clubs: Univ. of Ottawa Faculty Club; Le Cercle Universitaire d'Ottawa; Home: 183 Wilbrod St., Ottawa, Ont. K1N 6L4.

**WYSZECKI, Gunter Wolfgang,** Dr.-Ing.; scientist, b. Tilsit, Germany 8 Nov. 1925; came to Can. 1955; s. Bruno Bernhard and Helene (Goerke) W.; e. Technical Univ. of Berlin Diplom-Ingenieur 1951, Dr.-Ing. Mathematics 1953; m. Ingeborg Christine d. late Karl Rathjens 4 Aug. 1954; children: Wolfgang Michael, Joana Maria; Dir., Institute of Optics, Natl. Rsch. Council of Can.; Pres., Comm. Internationale De l'Eclairage, Adjunct Prof., Sch. of Optometry, Univ. of Waterloo, served with German Navy 1943–45; author of 'Farbsysteme' 1962; co-author 'Color in Business, Science, and Industry' 3rd ed. 1975; 'Color Science' 2nd ed. 1982; over 80 publs. in the field of color science (color vision, colorimetry, photometry, radiometry); rec'd. Judd Gold Medal, Assn. Internat. de la Couleur 1979; Godlove Award, Inter-Society Color Council 1979; Bruning Award, Fed. of Societies of Coating Technologies 1979; Fellow, Royal Society of Canada; Fellow, Optical Soc. of Am.; Fellow, Illuminating Engn. Soc.; mem., Candn. Soc. for Color (Pres. 1972–73); Lutheran; Home: 172 Roger Rd., Ottawa, Ont. K1H 5C8.

# Y

**YACHETTI, Roger Dennis,** B.A., LL.B., Q.C.; lawyer; b. Hamilton, Ont. 14 April 1940; s. Americo and Anna Natalina (Mazza) Y.; e. Univ. of West. Ont. B.A. 1961, LL.B. 1964 (Gold Medalist 1964); m. Cleda d. Edgar and Cleda Bursaw 14 Oct. 1963; children: Aaron, Andrea, Elizabeth; LAWYER, YACHETTI, LANZA & RESTIVO 1967– ; called to Bar 1966; Law Clerk to Chief Justice, High Court of Ont. 1966; Trustee, Hamilton Law Assn. 1975–79; Q.C. 1979; elected Bencher of the Law Soc. of U.C. 1979, '83, '87, '91; Law Soc. Guest Lectr. 1970; Advocates' Soc. Lectr. 1984; Dir., Cath. Youth Orgn. c.1975; Law Soc. of U.C. Treas. Medal 1966; Trustee, Law Found. of Ont. 1990– ; Chair, Bd. of Dir., Hamilton Tiger-Cat Football Club 1992– ; Mem., Candn. Bar Assn.; Hamilton Lawyers' Club (Pres. 1982); The Advocates' Soc. (Dir. 1982–83); The Hamilton Criminal Lawyers' Assn. (Pres. 1978–81); The Judges' Law Clerks' Assn. (Pres. 1967–68); Sons of Italy; Editor, Univ. of W. Ont. Law Review 1964; author of 3 journal articles; recreations: music, antique or restored vehicles, business; club: Hamilton; Home: 6181 Regional Rd. 13 (P.O. Box 62), Binbrook, Ont. L0R 1C0; Office: 154 Main St. E., Ste. 100, Hamilton, Ont. L8N 1G9.

**YACOWAR, Maurice,** M.A., Ph.D.; educator; author; b. Prelate, Sask. 25 March 1942; s. Samuel and Sophie (Gitterman) Y.; e. Central High Sch. Calgary; Univ. of Calgary B.A. 1962; Univ. of Alta. M.A. 1965; Shakespeare Inst. Univ. of Birmingham, Ph.D. (Eng. Lit.) 1968; children: Margaret Mia, Sam Jason Eric; DEAN OF ACADEMIC AFFAIRS, EMILY CARR COLLEGE OF ART AND DESIGN 1989– ; Dean of Humanities, Brock Univ. 1980–87, Prof. of Film Studies 1978–89; Lectr. in Eng. Lethbridge Jr. Coll. 1964–66; Asst. Prof. of Eng. and Drama Brock Univ. 1968, Assoc. Prof. of Drama 1972; film reviewer St. Catharines Standard 1974–89; author 'No Use Shutting the Door' (poems) 1971; criticism: 'Hitchcock's British Films' 1977; 'Tennessee Williams and Film' 1977; 'I Found It At the Movies' 1978; 'Loser Take All: The Comic Art of Woody Allen' 1979 (expanded edition 1991); 'Method in Madness' 1981 (publ. in London 1982 as 'The Comic Art of Mel Brooks'); 'The Films of Paul Morrissey' 1993; Office: 1399 Johnston St., Vancouver, B.C. V6H 3R9.

**YAFFE, Gerald J.;** business executive; b. Toronto, Ont. 10 July 1944; s. David and Lillian Y.; e. Bloor C.I.; Cornell Univ.; m. Elaine d. Irving Schwartz 5 Feb. 1967; children: Jacqueline Adrienne, Samantha Hope; FOUNDER, SAFETY HOUSE OF CAN. LIMITED 1961– ; Founder, Candn. Safety Equipment Distr. Assn. 1978; Pres. & Chief Extve. Offr., Safety House Internat.; Dir., Can.-Israel Securities Ltd.; Former Chrmn., State of Israel Bonds; Former Dir., Ort Can.; Basr-Ilan Univ.; Primrose Club; Toronto Island Yacht Club; Metro. Toronto United Appeal; N.W. Toronto Bus. Region; Dir., Ben-Gurian Univ., CSA Ctte. on Occupational Health & Safety Prod.; Former Dir. & Treas., Arts Can.; House Ctte., Baycrest Hosp.; Clubs: Island Yacht; Primrose; Home: 5 Old Forest Hill Rd., Toronto, Ont. M5P 2P2.

**YAFFE, Leo,** O.C., B.Sc., M.Sc., Ph.D., D.Lett. D.Sc., F.C.I.C., F.R.S.C., F.A.P.S., F.A.A.A.S.; university professor; b. Devil's Lake, N. Dakota 6 July 1916; s. Samuel and Mary (Cohen) Y.; e. Univ. of Manitoba, B.Sc. 1940, M.Sc. 1941; McGill Univ., Ph.D. 1943; D.Lett., Trent Univ.; D.Sc. Univ. of Manitoba; m. Betty, d. Abraham Workman, Montreal, Que., 18 March 1945; children: Carla Joy, Mark John; PROFESSOR EMERITUS, MCGILL UNIV. 1984– ; Vice Principal (Adm. & Prof. Faculties) there 1974–81, Macdonald Professor Chem. 1959–84 (and Chrmn. Dept. 1965–72); Project Leader, Nuclear Chem. and Tracer Research, Atomic Energy of Canada Ltd., Chalk River, Ont., 1943–52; Special Lectr. and Dir. of Radiochem. Lab., Dept. of Chem., McGill Univ., 1952–54; Assoc. Prof. 1955–59; on leave (1963–65) as Dir., Div. of Research & Labs., Internat. Atomic Energy Agency, Vienna, Austria; author of over 150 articles in the field of radiochem.; Fellow, Royal Society of Canada; Chem. Inst. Can.; Am. Phys. Soc.; Am. Assn. for Adv. of Science; recipient, Am. Nuclear Soc. Seaborg Medal 1988; Officer, Order of Canada 1988; Marie-Victorin Prix du Québec 1990; D.Sc. McGill Univ. 1992; Home: 5777 McAlear Ave., Montreal, Que. H4W 2H2.

**YAGER, Barry E.,** C.A., B.Comm.; financial executive; b. Vancouver, B.C. 26 Nov. 1944; s. Ernest F. and Esther V. (Johnson) Y.; e. Univ. of Calgary B.Comm. 1968; Inst. of C.A.s' of Alta. C.A. 1971; L'Ordre des comptables agréés du Québec 1978; m. Beverley Gilbertson 1970; children: Kira, Nicole, Kevin; CHIEF FINANCIAL OFFICER, UTEX CORPORATION 1993– ; Senior Vice-Pres., Finance & Treasurer, Consoltex Inc. 1979–93; Price Waterhouse 1972–79; Clarkson Gordon (Ernst and Young) 1968–72; Past Dir., Canadian Textile Credit Bureau; Forewest Industries Ltd.; Arkwright Mutual Ins. Co. (Candn. Adv. Bd.); recreations: golf, skiing, squash; club: Rockland Squash; Home: 103 Morley Hill, Kirkland, Que. H9J 2M4; Office: 845 Plymouth, Mont-Royal, Que. H4P 1B2.

**YAGER, David Lenard;** publisher / editor; b. Calgary, Alta. 5 Oct. 1953; s. Ernest Fredrick and Esther Viola (Johnson) Y.; e. Salisbury Comp. H.S.; m. Alessandra d. Bruno and Diadora Predolin 30 July 1983; children: Serge, Daniela; Editor & Publisher, 'The Roughneck' 1979; oil industry analyst; Canadian political analyst; Pres., Forewest Industries Ltd. (which owns 'The Roughneck' and four other oil service & manufacturing companies); active in radio, TV & newspaper commentary on petroleum & political issues; recreations: skiing, squash, woodworking; clubs: 400 Club (Secretary); Home: Box 22, Site 19, RR 2, Calgary, Alta. T2P 2G5.

**YALDEN, Janice MacKenzie,** M.A.; b. Kingston, Jamaica 12 Dec. 1931; d. Colin MacKenzie and Cicely Beatrix (Bell) Shaw; e. Univ. of Toronto B.A. 1952; Univ. of Mich. M.A. 1956; m. Maxwell s. Frederick and Marie Yalden 28 Jan. 1952; children: Robert, Cicely (dec. 1990); PROF. OF LINGUISTICS, CARLETON UNIVERSITY 1983– ; joined present Univ. as Lectr. in Spanish 1969, Asst. Prof. 1971, Assoc. Prof. Linguistics 1976, mem. Senate 1974–92, Founding Dir. Centre for Appplied Lang. Studies 1981–84, Dean of Arts 1987–92; Visiting Prof. Univ. de l'Etat à Mons, Belgium 1985–87; author 'The Communicative Syllabus' 1983; 'Principles of Course Design for Language Teaching' 1987; various articles, handbooks, rsch. reports, lang. course materials; Pres. Ont. Modern Lang. Teachers' Assn. 1976–77; Dir.: Candn. Modern Lang. Review 1988; mem. Candn. Assn. Applied Linguistics; Office: Ottawa, Ont. K1S 5B6.

**YALDEN, Maxwell Freeman,** O.C., M.A., Ph.D., D.U.; Canadian public servant; b. Toronto, Ont. 12 Apr. 1930; s. late Frederick George and late Helen Marie (Smith) Y.; e. Victoria Coll., Univ. of Toronto B.A. 1952; Univ. of Mich. M.A. 1954, Ph.D. 1956; D.U. (Univ. of Ottawa) 1982; m. Janice MacKenzie Shaw, d. late Colin MacKenzie Shaw, Tunbridge Wells, Eng., 28 Jan. 1952; children: Robert, and the late Cicely; CHIEF COMMISSIONER, CANADIAN HUMAN RIGHTS COMMISSION, Ottawa 1987– ; joined Dept. of External Affairs 1956; posted to Moscow 1958; CPMUN Geneva 1960; Ottawa 1960–63; First Secy., Paris 1963, becoming Counsellor 1965; Special Asst. for Fed.-Prov. questions Office of Under Secy. of State for External Affairs, Ottawa 1967; apptd. Asst. Under Secy. of State 1969; Depy. Min. of Communications 1973; Commissioner of Official Languages 1977–84; Ambassador of Canada to Belgium and Luxembourg 1984–87; Office: 320 Queen St., 13th Flr., Place de Ville, Tower A, Ottawa, Ont. K1A 1E1.

**YAMADA, Ruth Chizuko,** B.A.; artist; b. Vancouver, B.C. 26 Mar. 1923; d. John Renzo and Teruyo (Kometani) Hagino; e. Kitsilano H.S.; Univ. of Toronto B.A.; m. Sam Isamu 17 May 1947; children: Mark, John, Teri; painting incl. in C.S.P.W. collection sent to Queen Elizabeth's perm. collection, Windsor Castle 1986; painting selected by Office of Prem. Peterson of Ont. as gift to Gov. Xiulian of Jiangsu 1985; introduced Sumi-e (Brush painting), Japanese Candn. Cult. Ctr. 1964 (Head Instr. 19 yrs.); Founder, Sumi-e Artists of Can.; several one-person shows in Can.; awards from Japan 1974, 75, 76; Sumie Soc. of Am. 1985; paintings in corp. collections incl. Sony of Can., IBM Can.; Cons. of Japan, Honda of Can., Confed. Life, Fuji Bank, Sumitomo Bank, Trent Univ.; Donor: John Yamada Mem. Scholarship, Archit. Sch., Univ. of Toronto; mem., All Japan Nanga (Japanese style painting) Soc. 1968– ; Satsuki Kai Soc. (Kyoto) 1968– ; Candn. Soc. of Painters in Watercolours (C.S.P.W.) 1980 (elected); Hon. Mem., Sumie Artists of Can.; Mem., Grace-Church-on-the-Hill 1958– ; illustrator, 'Waves' by Pearl Buck; recreations: skiing, golf; Clubs: Cedarbrae Golf & Country; Health Club; Columbus Ctr.; Home: 20 Glenayr Rd., Toronto, Ont. M5P 3B8.

**YAMAMOTO, Lucas Yasokazu,** M.D.; educator; b. Shibetzu-Shi, Hokkaido, Japan 19 Jan 1928; s. Torimatsu and Chiyo (Ikeda) Y.; e. Shibetzu Primary Sch. and Nayoro Secondary Sch. Hokkaido, Japan 1945; Hoddaido Univ. 1945–48, M.D. 1952; Georgetown Med. Center, Georgetown Univ. Neurosurg, 1954–58; Nuclear Med. and Radiation Research, Med. Research Center, Brookhaven Nat. Lab., L.I., N.Y.; m. Jeanine Marilyn d. Joseph Zollner, River Phillip, N.S. 25 Oct. 1958; children: Ann Marie, Grace, Peter; PROF. OF NEUROL. AND NEUROSURG., DIR. OF NEUROISOTOPE LAB., MCGILL UNIV. AND MONTREAL NEUROLOGICAL INST.; mem. Med. Council Can.; author over 230 articles nuclear med., various med. journs.; mem. Soc. Nuclear Med.; Montreal Neurol. Soc.; Candn. Med. Assn.; Am. Coll. Nuclear Physicians; Candn. Neurol. Soc.; Candn. Assn. Nuclear Med.; Coll. Phys. & Surgs. Que.; Am. Bd. Nuclear Med.; Cert. Specialist Nuclear Med. Que.; R. Catholic; recreations: swimming, skiing; Home: 4861 Parkinson Blvd., Pierrefonds, Que. H8Y 2Z2; Office: 3801 University, Montreal, Que. H3A 2B4 and Medical Arts Bldg. 814, 1538 Sherbrooke St. W., Montreal, Que.

**YANEFF, Chris,** R.C.A.; graphic designer; art dealer; advertising executive; b. Toronto, Ont. 18 May 1933; s. John V. Y.; e. Central Tech. Sch.; Ont. Coll. of Art; m. Kathleen Anna (dec'd) d. William Knowles 1955; children: Gregory Mark, Martha Jane; PRESIDENT AND OWNER, CHRIS YANEFF LTD. 1956– and DIR., YANEFF GALLERY 1975– ; Past Pres. Graphic Designers of Canada (Ont.); Owner, Yaneff Gallery; Advisor, George Brown Coll.; Georgian Coll.; Past Bd. mem., The Toronto Symphony; Past Treas., Lake of Bays Heritage Assoc.; Toronto Island Airport Assoc.; Actifund Ltd.; Art Dir., The Financial Post 1956; former Assoc. Prof. of Visual Arts York Univ.; recipient Design Awards New York, Los Angeles, London (Eng.), Zurich, Hamburg, Tokyo; nat. and internat. graphic design exhns.; author 'Trademarks by Chris Yaneff Ltd.' 1974; Past Dir. & Treas. R.C.A.; mem. Prof. Art Dealers Assn.; original graphic designer for Stratford Shakespearean Festival; Protestant; recreations: antique cars, sailing, flying, painting; Clubs: R.C.Y.C., Toronto; Rotary; Arts & Letters; Office: 119 Isabella St., Toronto, Ont. M4Y 1P2.

**YANG, Stephenson Lok Sang,** B.Sc., M.Sc., Ph.D.; astronomer; b. Hong Kong 13 July 1954; s. Hsin Tsang and Lai Yung (Ma) Y.; e. Univ. of B.C., B.Sc. 1976, M.Sc. 1980, Ph.D. 1986; m. Susan Mary Anne d. David and Anne Hart 26 Aug. 1989; SYSTEM MGR., DEPT. OF PHYS. & ASTRON., UNIV. OF VICTORIA 1989– ; sessional lectr., Univ. of Victoria 1991–94; Royal Roads Military Coll. 1990; Univ. of B.C. 1987–89, 1993–94; post-doctoral fellow, Univ. of B.C. 1986–87; collaborating on project to search for extra-solar planets using the hydrogen fluoride precise radial-velocity technique; mem. Candn. Astron. Soc.; Astron. Soc. Pacific; co-recipient of the Muhlmann Prize; Home: 304 – 1201 Hillside Ave., Victoria, B.C. V8T 2B1; Office: Dept. of Phys. & Astron., Univ. of Victoria, Victoria, B.C. V8W 3P6.

**YANKOVICH, Alex Steven,** B.A.; banking executive; b. Schumacher, Ont. 2 Apr. 1940; s. Steven M. and Katherine (Shish) Y.; e. Colorado Coll., B.A. 1963; Claremont Grad. Sch., Univ. of Calif. at Northridge, UCLA 1965–67; m. Kathleen Clark 24 Aug. 1963; children: Stephanie, Christina; Pres., Dir. & C.E.O., National Westminster Bank of Canada 1986–92; Bank of America (U.S., Greece, U.S.S.R., W. Germany) 1967–79; Bank of Montreal (England, Canada) 1979–86; Mem., Bureau of East-West Trade, U.S. Dept. of Commerce 1977–79; mem. Extve. Ctte., Candn. Bankers' Assn., Schedule II Banks 1990– ; recreations: ice hockey, tennis, golf, skiing, horses; Clubs: Empire Club of Canada; The Canadian; The National Inst. of Corp. Dirs.; Home: Oak Ridge Farm, R.R. 2, Brampton, Ont. L6V 1A1.

**YANOSIK, Hon. Clarence George,** LL.B.; judge; b. Lethbridge, Alta. 20 Apl. 1926; s. George Reginald and Anne (Chollak) Y.; e. St. Basil's Elem. and St. Patrick's High Schs. Lethbridge 1942; Sch. for Veterans Calgary Sr. Matric. 1946; Univ. of B.C. B.A. 1951, LL.B. 1952; m. Cecily Gwyneth d. late Melvin and Marjorie Muir, Vancouver, B.C. 20 Aug. 1954; children: Robert Glen, Larry George, Laurie E.A., Clarence Thomas B. (Tim); JUDGE, COURT OF QUEEN'S BENCH, ALTA. 1979– ; Deputy Judge of the Superior Court of the Yukon Territory 1979– ; Chrmn., Provincial Advisory Bd. for Alberta under the Veteran's Land Act 1979– ; called to Bar of Alta. 1953; Barrister and Solr. 1953–69; Judge, Dist. Court of S. Alta. 1969–75, Dist. Court of Alta. 1975–79; served with RCNVR 1943–45; former Dir. Alta. Lib. Assn.; Past Pres., Lethbridge Lib. Assn.; Lethbridge Bar Assn.; Lib. Cand. Fed. g.e. 1958; mem. Candn. Bar Assn.; Alta. Bar Assn.; R. Catholic; recreations: skiing, golf, fishing, hunting, jogging, weight-lifting; Home: 2818 – 6th Ave. A. South, Lethbridge, Alta. T1J 1H2; Office: Court House, 1010 – 4th Ave. South, Lethbridge, Alta. T1J 4C7.

**YAPP, Michael Anthony;** business executive; b. Alnmouth, Eng. 4 Apr. 1943; s. Derek Sidney and Helen Louise (Manwaring) Y.; e. The Blue Coat Sch. Sonning, Holme Park, Berks. Eng.; Queen's Univ. Exec. Bus. Sch. 1984; m. Ann Marie d. Norman and Margaret Guild 7 Dec. 1985; children: Jonathon Derek, Christopher Seaver; DIR., KUBOTA CANADA LTD. 1975– ; Salesman, Henleys Ltd. 1964–66, Coventry Motor Cars 1966; Salesman, Machine Sales Mgr., Gen. Sales Mgr. W.D. Lynch (Dustbane Distributor) 1968–72; Vice Pres. Brenmac Chemicals Inc. 1972; Regional Sales Mgr. W. Can. Clarke Equipment Canada Inc. and Nat. Sales Mgr. Clarke & Gravely Canada Inc. 1973–75; joined present Co. 1975, Nat. Sales Mgr., Mktg. Mgr., Dir. and Vice Pres.; Past Chrmn. Candn. Farm and Industrial Equipment Inst. 1988, Dir. and Treas.; Past Pres. (1989) & Dir. Candn. Agri-Mktg. Assn.; Past Pres. Ont. Wholesale Farm Equipment Assn.; Past Pres. and Paul Harris Fellow (1984) Unionville S. Markham Rotary; Past Mem. Toronto Rotary; 1991 Charter Pres., The Rotary Club of Lagoon City; recreations: golf, squash, boating; Club: Buttonville Golf; Office: 1495 Denison, Markham, Ont. L3H 5H1.

**YAREMKO, John,** Q.C., LL.B., LL.D., Dr.rer.pol.; b. Welland, Ont. 10 Aug.1918; e. Hamilton (Ont.) Central Coll. Inst. (Sir John Gibson Scholar, Reuben Wells Leonard Scholar, Carter Scholar, Norman Slater Mem. Scholar, W. H. Ballard Gold Medallist, Valedictorian); Univ. of Toronto, Honour Law B.A. 1941 (Dent McCrea Prizeman, Harold G. Fox Prizeman); Osgoode Hall, Toronto, Ont. (Medallist and Christopher Robinson Mem. Prizeman); LL.D. Sir Wilfrid Laurier Univ. 1968; Honourary Doctorate, Dr. Rerum Politicarum, Ukrainian Free Univ., Munich; m. Mary A., Toronto, Ontario, 3 February 1945; read law with Elliot, Hume, McKague & Hume; called to the Bar of Ont. (proxy 1944) 1946; cr. Q.C. 1953; 1st el. to Ont. Leg. for Bellwoods, g.e. 1951; re-el. 1955, 1959, 1963, 1967, 1971; apptd. Min. without Portfolio April 1958; Min. of Transport Dec. 1958–60; Prov. Secy. and Min. of Citizenship 1960; Min. of Pub. Welfare Nov. 1966; Min. of Social & Family Services Nov. 1967; Prov. Secy. and Minister of Citizenship 1971; Solicitor General 1972–74; Chrmn. Liquor Licence, Commercial Registration Appeal Tribunals, Prov. Ont. 1976–85; served as 2nd Lieutenant, Canadian Infantry Corps; Hon. Chrmn., Bellwoods Centres For Community Living Inc.; mem. Advisory Bd., St. Alban's Boys' & Girls' Club; Former Patron, Canadian Psychiatric Research Found.; former mem. Grange Comte. (Bd.), Art Gall. of Ont.; Former mem., Adv. Bd., Candn. Opera Company; mem., Candn. Cultural Property Export Review Board; mem., Candn. Bar Assn.; York Co. Law Assn.; P. Conservative; Ukrainian Orthodox; recreation: Canadiana collector; Clubs: The Lawyers (Past Pres.); Canadian; Empire; The Royal Commonwealth Society; Royal Candn. Institute; Home: 1 Connable Drive, Toronto, Ont. M5R 1Z7.

**YARNELL, John R.,** B.Com., M.B.A.; company executive; b. Montreal, Que. 26 July 1928; s. John E. and M. (Robertson) Y.; ed. Pub. Schs., Winnipeg, Man.; Univ. of Manitoba, B. Com. 1949; Harvard Univ. M.B.A. 1952; m. Elizabeth H. d. S.P. Gemmill, 14 June 1952; children: Sarah, Robert, Ann; CHRMN., YARNELL COMPANIES INC.; Quorum Growth Inc.; YCI Holdings Inc.; Dir.: Colortech Inc.; Norcen Energy Resources Ltd.; DAIWA Bank Canada; Poco Petroleums Ltd.; Presbyterian; recreations: golf, tennis, skiing, hunting; Home: 161 Roxborough Dr., Toronto, Ont. M4W 1X7; Office: Sun Life Tower, 150 King St. W., Suite 1505, P.O. Box 5, Toronto, Ont. M5H 1J9.

**YAROSKY, Harvey W.,** Q.C., B.A., B.C.L.; lawyer, b. Montreal, Que. 8 Dec. 1934; s. late Harry and Rhoda (Kom) Y.; e. Baron Byng High Sch. Montreal 1951; McGill Univ. B.A. 1955, B.C.L. 1961; Univ. of Paris (Inst. d'études Politiques) 1955–56; m. Elaine, d. Irving (Auckie) Sanft 3 July 1962; two d. Karen Anne, Lauren Julie; PARTNER, YAROSKY, LA HAYE, STOBER & ISAACS; read law with Joseph Cohen, Q.C. and Fred Kaufman, Q.C.; called to Bar of Que. 1962; Lectr. in Criminal Law Univ. of Montreal 1970–71; Univ. of Ottawa 1970–72; McGill Univ. 1971–77, 1989– ; Extve. Asst. to Chrmn. Dept. of Justice (Can.) Special Comte. on Hate Propaganda 1965; mem. Govt. of Que. Adv. Council on Justice 1974–78; Counsel to Fed. Comn. of Inquiry (Marin) concerning R.C.M.P. 1974–76; Special Counsel to prov. Comn. of Inquiry on Union activities in Constr. Indust. 1974–75; Dir. John Howard Soc. Que. Inc. 1967–70; mem. Corp. of the Philippe Pinel Inst. of

Montreal (Vice Pres. 1984– ) a Gov. of Portage Program for Drug Dependencies Inc. since 1975; author legal articles; mem. Bar of Montreal (Comte. on Lawyer Referral Service 1968–70, mem. 1968–74 and Chrmn. 1971–74 Comte. on Adm. of Criminal Justice); Bar of Que. (Bd. of Examiners 1968–73, Cmte. on Discipline, 1975–89, Chrmn. Comte. on Adm. Criminal Justice 1972–74); Candn. Bar Assn. (Chrmn. Criminal Justice Sub-Sec. Que. Br. 1970–72, Treas. 1973–74 and Vice Chrmn. Nat. Criminal Justice Sec., 1974–77); American Coll. of Trial Lawyers 1984– ; Jewish; recreations: theatre, music, reading; Club: University; Home: 372 Kitchener Ave., Montreal, Que. H3Z 2E9; Office: 800 René-Lévesque Blvd. W., #2536, Montreal, Que. H3B 1X9.

**YARRILL, Eric Herbert,** M.A., F.I.A.L.; professor; b. Heston Hounslow, Middlesex, Eng., 28 Dec. 1914; s. Herbert George and Amelia Louise (Blackford) Y.; came to Can. 1926; e. Univ. of Toronto, B.A. (Hons.) 1937, M.A. 1938; various Awards at Toronto, Paris and Chicago; Univ. of Paris, Dipl. 1938; Alliance Française de Paris, Cert. and Dipl.; Univ. of Chicago (grad. courses); PROF. EMERITUS OF MODERN LANGUAGES, BISHOPS UNIV. and with Dept. since 1938; Dir., Que. Dept. of Educ. Fr. Specialists/Summer Sch. for 5 yrs.; Visiting Prof. of Fr., Univ. of New Brunswick Summer Session, for 2 yrs.; numerous publications in Can., U.S. and German periodicals; with Reserve Army C.O.T.C., 1940–43, gaz. 2nd Lieut.; R.C.N.V.R., 1943–45, with Directorate of Naval Intel. as Lieut.; with Admiralty on loan to Royal Navy, 1944; Centennial Medal 1967; Life Mem., Sherbrooke Hospital (Gov. 1986) 1990; Gov. Montreal General Hosp. 1990; Anglican; Address: 11 High St., Lennoxville, Que. J1M 1E6.

**YATES, Hon. George,** B.Com., LL.B.; judge; b. Glace Bay, N.S., 24 July 1925; s. Frederick and Mary (Galloway) Y.; e. Dalhousie Univ. LL.B. 1951, B.Com. 1952; widower; served with RCAF 1943–45, Flying Offr. (Aircrew); Clubs: Hamilton; Hamilton Golf & Country (Ancaster); TAMAHAAC; Home: 222 Sulphur Springs Rd., Ancaster, Ont. L9G 4T7; Office: Osgoode Hall, 130 Queen St. W., Toronto, Ont. M5H 2N5.

**YATES, J. Michael,** M.A.; writer, publisher; professor; b. 10 Apr. 1938; s. Joel Hume and Marjorie Diane (Carmichael) Y.; e. Univ. of Mo., B.A. 1961, M.A. 1962; Univ. of Mich., Ph.D. program in Comparative Lit. 1962–64; m. Ann Jean West Yates (div.); presently working for the Dept. of the Attorney General, B.C. Prov. Govt.; Nat. Creative & Promotional Dir., Public Radio Corp., 1961–62; Instr. Creative Writing, Ohio Univ., 1964–65; Special Lectr. Creative Writing, Comparative Lit., Univ. of Alaska, 1965–66; Visiting Asst. Prof. of Creative Writing, Univ. of B.C. 1966–67, Asst. Prof. 1967–69, Assoc. Prof. 1969–71; Pres., The Sono Nis Press and J. Michael Yates Ltd. 1968–76; Visiting Prof. of Eng. & Creative Writing, Univ. of Ark. 1972; Visiting Univ. Prof., Univ. of Texas at Dallas 1976–77; Special Projects, Univ. of B.C. Press 1978; Sales Rep. for Mitchell Press 1979; Public Relations, C.B.C. Vancouver 1980; rec'd Univ. of Kans. City Poetry Prize 1960; Internat. Broadcasting Award 1961, 1962; Maj. Hopwood Award for Poetry and for Drama, 1964; Can. Council Awards 1968, 1969, 1971, 1976 & 1980; Sr. Arts Award 1972–73, 1982–83; The Far Point Contrib. Prize for Poetry 1971; author 'Spiral of Mirrors' 1967; 'Hunt in an Unmapped Interior' 1967; 'Canticle for Electronic Music' (all poetry) 1967; 'Man in the Glass Octopus' (fiction) 1968; 'The Great Bear Lake Meditations' 1970; 'Parallax' (poetry) 1971; 'The Abstract Beast' (fiction & drama) 1971; 'Nothing Speaks for the Blue Moraines' (poetry) 1973; 'Breath of the Snow Leopard' (poetry) 1974; 'Quarks' (drama) 1975; 'The Qualicum Physics' (poetry) 1975; 'Fazes in Elsewhen' (fiction) 1977; 'Fugue Brancusi' 1983; 'Insel' 1984; 'Completely Collapsible Portable Man' (all poetry) 1985; 'Light Like a Summer' 1989; 'Line Screw: My Twelve Riotous Years Working Behind Bars in Some of Canada's Toughest Jail' 1993; Ed., 'Contemporary Poetry of British Columbia' Vol. 1 1970; 'Volvox: Poetry from the Unofficial Languages of Canada in English Translation' 1971; Ed. 'Contemporary Literature in Translation'; Ed. Bd., 'Mundus Artium'; 'Canadian Fiction Magazine'; 'Prism International' (Acting Ed.-in-Chief 1966–67; Poetry Ed. 1967–71); other writings incl. numerous dramas produced in Europe and N. Am., also CBC Radio; papers, reviews, philos. studies for various publs.; mem., Internat. P.E.N. (London Chapter); League Candn. Poets (Extve. 1970–71); Internat. Platform Assn.; Prof. Photog's Am.; Torch & Scroll; Omicron Delta Kappa; Sigma Tau Delta; Alpha Phi Omega; Tau Kappa Epsilon; recreation: fishing.

**YATES, James R.;** steel industry executive; b. Montreal, Que. 15 Feb. 1952; e. Dawson College; Sir George Williams Univ.; m. Gunnel Johansson 7 May 1977; children: Anders, Erika; PRESIDENT, FRANCOSTEEL CANADA 1990– ; Sales Manager, BSC Canada 1974–80; Branch Manager, Intercontinental Metals 1980–82; District Mgr., Francosteel Canada 1982–86; Commercial Director 1986–88; Vice-President 1988–90; Mem., Am. Railroad Engineering Assn.; Am. Iron and Steel Inst.; C. de C. français au Canada; Candn. Steel Importers Assn.; Am. Soc. Metals International; recreations: racquetball, skiing, hiking, bicycling; Office: 5890 Monkland Ave., Suite 300, Montreal, Que. H4A 1G2.

**YATES, Keith,** B.A., M.Sc., Ph.D., D.Phil., F.R.S.C.; university professor; b. Preston, England 22 Oct. 1928; s. Harold and Elizabeth Ann (Wilson) Y.; e. Univ. of B.C., B.A. 1956 (Governor-General's Gold Medal); , M.Sc. 1957, Ph.D. 1959; Oxford Univ., D.Phil. 1961 (NRC & NATO p.d. fellow); m. June d. Alice and Gerald Charter 21 Aug. 1953; children: Alison Elizabeth, Robyn Leslie, Nicola Jane; PROF. EMERITUS OF CHEMISTRY, UNIV. OF TORONTO 1990– ; Asst. Prof., Univ. of Toronto 1961–64; Assoc. Prof. 1964–68; Prof. 1968–90; Asst. Dean, Sch. of Grad. Studies 1967–70; Chrmn. Dept. of Chem. 1974–85; Prof. Emeritus 1990– ; F.R.S.C. 1984; F.C.I.C. 1972; Mem., Chem. Inst. of Can. (Syntex Award 1984); C.I.C. Medal 1991; author: 'Huckel Molecular Orbital Theory' 1978 and approx. 150 sci. articles & reviews; Assoc. Ed., 'Canadian Journal of Chemistry' 1971–75; recreation: bridge; Club: Univ. of Toronto Faculty; Office: Dept. of Chem., Univ. of Toronto, Toronto, Ont. M5S 1A1.

**YATES, (John) Roger,** B.Sc., P.Eng., P.E.; consulting engineer; b. Grimsby, Ont. 25 Sept. 1941; s. Ralph Francis and June Hildegarde (Walker) Y.; e. Trinity Coll. Sch. Port Hope 1960; Queen's Univ. B.Sc. 1964; Univ. of Toronto postgrad. credit Computers 1966; m. Norma Read d. Edward Read and Nancy Adelaide (Hume) Budge 19 Sept. 1964; four s. Barry Read, (Edward) Matthew, Roger Walker, Andrew Budge; VICE PRES., GEN. MGR. & DIR., HATCH ASSOCIATES CONSULTANTS INC. 1989– ; Vice Pres. Eng. & Div. Chief Eng. Ferrco Engineering Ltd. (Co-Steel Group of Co's) 1968–83; Assoc. Hatch Associates Ltd. 1983–89; licensed profl. eng. Texas, Minn., N.J.; reg'd P.Eng. and designated Consulting Eng. Ont.; co-author 'The Mini-Mill Faces New Technologies' 1986; mem. Assn. Iron & Steel Engs.; Iron & Steel Soc. AIME; recreations: skiing, tennis, golf, squash; Club: Las Colinas Sports (Dallas); Home: 3713 Millswood Dr., Irving, Texas 75062; Office: Suite 270, 251 O'Connor Ridge Blvd., Irving, Texas 75038.

**YAWORSKI, Laurie,** B.Sc., B.Com., M.B.A., C.G.A., C.F.A.; credit union executive; b. Invermay, Sask. 29 June 1949; s. Henry Michael and Helen (Shewchuk) Y.; e. Univ. of Sask. B.Sc. 1969, B.Com. 1971; Univ. of B.C. M.B.A. 1973; C.G.A. 1976; C.F.A. 1982; m. Nancy d. John and Margaret Tappin 18 May 1974; children: Scott, Leah, Andrew; SR. VICE PRES., FINANCE AND CHIEF FINANCIAL OFFR. B.C. CENTRAL CREDIT UNION 1986– ; Chairperson, Ethical Funds Inc.; Ethical Funds Investment Services Inc.; Dir., West Canada Depository Trust Co.; self-employed cons. in financial acctg. 1975–86; Asst. Cash Mgr. Crown Zellerbach Canada Ltd. 1973–75; Asst. Treas. Sask. Econ. Development Corp. 1975–77; Lectr. in Introductory Finance Univ. of Sask. 1978–80; Dir. of Acctg. Control & Systems Credit Union Central of Sask. 1977–81, Dir. of Financial Operations 1981–86; mem. C.G.A.'s Assn.; Candn. Tax Found.; Soc. Financial Analysists; Financial Mgmt. Assn.; Financial Execs. Inst.; B.C. Bus. Council Finance Ctte.; Mem., Vancouver Bd. of Trade - B.C. Budget Task Force; recreations: coaching minor sports, golf, Old Timers' hockey, skiing; Home: 10360 St. Johns Pl., Richmond, B.C. V7E 5T5; Office: 1441 Creekside Dr., Vancouver, B.C. V6J 4S7.

**YEATES, Allan Burnside,** B.A.; advertising executive; b. Hamilton, Ont. 7 March 1926; s. Ralph Howard and Helen B. (Reeves) Y.; e. Westdale Secondary Sch., Hamilton, 1944: Univ. of W. Ont., Sch. of Business Adm., B.A. 1948; m. Charlotte E., d. T.S. Farley, Burlington, Ont. 19 May 1948; children: Carolyn Ruth, Jody Helen, Stephen Allan, Peter Gordon, Patricia Charlotte; Chrmn. of the Bd., Comcore Direct (resigned 1992); Business writer and analyst, 'Financial Post,' 1948 and 'Toronto Daily Star,' 1949–51; Asst. Mgr., Pub. Relations and Advertising Dept., Prudential Insurance Co. of America, 1951, Mgr. 1951–53, Asst. Gen. Mgr. and Dir., Pub. Relations and Advertising, 1954–61; joined Spitzer, Mills & Bates Ltd. as Vice Pres., and Account Supvr., 1961–62, Sr. Vice Pres. and Mang. Rep., 1962–64, Extve. Vice Pres. 1964–69, Pres. and Chief Extve. Offr. 1969–72; Pres. & C.E.O., Baker Lovick Ltd. 1973–88; Past Pres., Assn. Candn. Advertisers; Past Chrmn., Candn. Advt. Standards Council; Past Pres. Candn. Advt. Adv. Bd.; Past Chrmn., Inst. of Candn. Advt.; Past Chrmn., Candn. Advt. Foundation; Delta Upsilon; United Church; Home: Willowood, Box 32, R.R. #1, Kettleby, Ont. L0G 1J0.

**YEATES, Maurice,** B.A., M.A., Ph.D., F.R.S.C.; professor; b. Yorkshire, Eng. 24 May 1938; s. Lewis and Rosina (Holmes) Y.; e. Reading Univ., B.A. Hons. 1960; Northwestern Univ., M.A. 1961; Ph.D. 1963; m. Marilynn Snelbaker, 12 Sept. 1962; children: Maurine; Harry; EXTVE. DIR., INT. STUDY CENTRE (QUEEN'S UNIV.) 1994– ; joined Queen's Univ. as Asst. Prof. 1965; Assoc. Prof. 1968; Prof. of Geography 1970– ; Head, Geography Dept. 1973–78; Dean, Grad. Studies and Resch. 1979–84; Extve. Dir., Ont. Council on Grad. Studies 1986–94; author of numerous articles and 14 books, among them 'Main Street' 1975; 'North American Urban Patterns' 1980; 'The North American City' (4th ed.) 1990; 'Land in Central Canada' 1985; rec'd. S.S.H.R.C.C. Leave Award 1971, 1978, 1984; Fellow, Royal Soc. Can. 1980; CAG Award for Scholarly Distinction in Geography, 1982; mem. Candn. Assn. Geographers; Assn. Am. Geographers; Regional Sci. Assn.; recreation: jogging; Home: 185 Ontario St., 1307, Kingston, Ont. K7M 2N4; Office: Herstmonceux Castle, East Sussex, U.K. BN27 1RP.

**YEE, Paul Richard,** M.A., B.A.; author; b. Spalding, Sask. Oct. 1956; s. Gordon Yuen and Gim May (Wong) Y.; e. Univ. of B.C., M.A. 1983, B.A. 1978; married; POLICY ANALYST, ONTARIO MINISTRY OF CITIZENSHIP 1991– ; City of Vancouver Archives 1979–88; Archivist, Archives of Ont. 1988–91; mem., Writers Union of Can.; CANSCAIP; author: 'Teach Me to Fly, Skyfighter' 1983, 'The Curses of Third Uncle' 1986, 'Tales from Gold Mountain' 1989 (fiction); 'Saltwater City: The Chinese in Vancouver, 1886–1986' 1988 (non-fiction); 'Roses Sing on New Snow' 1991 (fiction); Home: 125 Aldwych Ave., Toronto, Ont. M4J 1X8; Office: 77 Bloor St. W., Toronto, Ont. M7A 2R9.

**YELLAND, James J.,** B.Comm.; steel industry executive; b. Montreal, Que. 24 Sept. 1936; s. G.T. James and Ruth (Jack) Y.; m. Elaine Doris d. Roland and Elizabeth Marchand 10 Nov. 1979; children: Leigh, Heather; former Pres., Union Drawn Steel Co. Ltd.; Mem., Steel Indus. Adv. Group; Pres. & Dir., Burlington Art Ctr.; recreations: golf; clubs: Burlington Golf & Country (Dir.), Summit Golf & Country; Home: 764 Cranston Ct., Burlington, Ont. L7T 2Y5.

**YELLOP, William John Patrick;** executive; b. London, Eng. 10 July 1945; s. William John and Constance Josephine (Reynolds) Y.; e. St. Patrick's and Clapham Coll. London, Eng.; Univ. of W. Ont. Executive Program 1985; m. Pamela D. d. George and Lille Shaw 17 May 1975; PRESIDENT, THE ICM GROUP 1992– ; Dir., The ICM Group; The Spruce Goose Brewing Co.; Racing One Stables 88; joined National Westminster Bank London, Eng. 1963; Bank of Montreal 1975 (hired from U.K. Merchant Bank), Vice Pres. Corporate Govt. Banking 1985; Vice Pres. Bank of America, Canada 1987, Sr. Vice Pres. and Head of Corporate Banking 1989–92; speaker and contbr. banking issues Candn. Inst.; mem. Univ. of W. Ont. Toronto Bus. Sch. Club; served Un. Way; Kinsman Clubs; Mem., Candn. Conference Bd.; U.S. Conference Bd.; mem. Bd. Trade Metrop. Toronto; Fellow, Inst. Bankers, UK; mem. Brit.-Candn. Trade Assn. R.Catholic; recreations: golf, horse racing and breeding, reading, running; Clubs: Summit Golf & Country; Adelaide; Home: 72 Gypsy Roseway, Willowdale, Ont. M2N 5Y9; Office: 4936 Yonge St., Suite 162, North York, Ont. M2N 6S3.

**YEO, Leslie James;** actor; producer; writer; director; adjudicator; b. Swindon, Wilts., Eng., 29 May 1915; s. Frederick James and Sybil Annie (Stride) Y.; e. The Coll., Swindon, Wilts.; m. 1stly late Hilary (actress prof. known as Hilary Vernon), d. late Harold Vernon Pagniez, 11 May 1954; one s. Jamie Donald; m. 2ndly Grete Knudsen, d. late Erling Knudsen, Copenhagen, 29 Aug. 1977; actor in over 500 stage roles: in Britain 1939–50; in Can. since 1950 at Playhouse, Vancouver; Citadel, Edmonton; M.T.C., Winnipeg; Theatre plus, Toronto; Theatre Aquarius, Hamilton; Alley Theatre, Houston; Meadowbrook Theatre, Detroit; Shaw Festival, Niagara-on-the-Lake, 1966, 1967, 1976, 1978, 1979; Stratford Shakespearean Festival, 1975, 1977; role of Alan Brooke in world premiere of 'The Soldiers,' Royal Alex, Toronto 1968; first lead in a musical, Pop Fraser in David Warrack's 'Drummer,' Banff Centre, 1980; actor-manager of London Theatre Co. in Maritimes for 6 winter seasons, 1951–57 (brought first Brit. stock co. in 30 yrs.); 1962 stage design consultant & first gen. mgr., Bayview Playhouse; numerous radio and TV roles since 1957 incl. guest star 'Twilight Zone' 1988; guest star 'Adderly' 1987; star 'Littlest Hobo' 1986; feature film roles: Eddy in 'L'Automne Sauvage' 1991; Arthur in Anne Wheeler's 'Bye Bye Blues' 1988; Stephan in 'Dreams Beyond Memory' 1987; Fred Reeves in 'Improper Channels' 1980; Stan Mountain in 'The Luck of Ginger Coffey'; Dir., 'Diary of Anne Frank' Theatre Aquarius, Hamilton 1990; 'Major Barbara' Citadel Theatre, Edmonton 1988; 'The Foreigner' Toronto's Royal Alex. Theatre 1986; 'Noises Off' Vancouver Playhouse and Expo 86; Neptune Theatre, Halifax, 1980, 1981; five prod. at Alley Theatre, Houston, Texas, 1975–78; 'Mrs. Warren's Profession,' Shaw Festival 1976; 49 productions in his own London theatre company, 1951–57; Artistic Dir. Shaw Festival 1978–79 and directed 'The Corn is Green,' 'Blithe Spirit'; wrote and directed 'Cinderella' Hamilton Place 1980; co-producer 'Actually this Autumn,' Dell Theatre, Toronto 1964 and 'Ding Dong at the Dell' 1965; adjudicator, Dom. Drama Festival, CODL Regional Finals 1968 and WODL preliminaries 1967; EODL one-act Festival 1969; prod./dir. over 60 major industrial musicals and conventions since 1966 in Canada, U.S., Jamaica, Mexico, Bahamas, U.K. and Japan; gave Master classes in comedy technique, Banff Centre 1980, 1983, 1984, 1986; Univ. of Alta., Edmonton 1981; Master Class director, 'The Guardsman,' Banff 1981; directed Ryerson graduating class in 'The Government Inspector' 1987; served with RAF in U.K., India and Burma, 1941–46; rank Sgt. on discharge; Vice Pres., Strand Electric (Can.) Ltd., 1957–61; mem., of Bd. and Extve., Candn. Opera Co., 1959–63; Treas. ACTRA, 1969–71; Treas. ACTRA Ins. and Retirement Plan and Fraternal Soc. 1972–82 and 1987–90; Treas., Candn. Actors' Equity Assn., 1976–79; mem., Bd. Comus Music Theatre of Can. 1980–83; mem., Adv. Bd., Theatre Arts Prog., George Brown Coll. 1977–87; mem. Bd., Smile Theatre Co. 1987–91; Awarded Silver Jubilee Medal; Kari Award for best actor as The Esso Man in Candn. Comm. 1986 Bessie's; P. Conservative; Anglican; recreations: golf; Address: 19 Binscarth Rd., Toronto, Ont. M4W 1Y2.

**YEO, Michael Terrence,** B.A., M.A., Ph.D.; educator, writer, philosopher; b. Summerside, P.E.I. 19 Sept. 1956; s. Gerald Collingwood and Eva Louise (Kilbride) Y.; e. York Univ. B.A. 1979; McMaster Univ. M.A. 1981, Ph.D. 1988; m. Barbara d. James and Dorothy Keddie 15 Nov. 1980; children: Alexandra Hannah, Miranda Heather; ASST. PROF., DEPT. OF PHILOSOPHY, BRESCIA COLLEGE, THE UNIV. OF WESTERN ONT. 1993– ; Rsch. Assoc., Westminster Inst. for Ethics and Human Values 1987–93, Assoc. Dir. 1991–93; Lectr., Dept. of Philosophy, Univ. of Western Ont. 1987–91; Fac. of Engr. 1990– ; Mem., Ethics Ctte., College of Family Physicians of Canada; Mem., Ethics Ctte., London Psychiatric Hospital; Ont. Grad. Scholarship 1983–84, 1986–87; Ont. Legis. Internship Scholarship 1984–85; Corp. Sec., Windmill Line Housing Coop. 1984–87; Catholic; Mem., Toronto City Cycling Ctte. 1985–86; Candn. Philosophical Assn. 1986– ; Candn. Bioethics Soc. 1987– ; Candn. Soc. for Hermeneutics & Post-Modern Thought 1986– ; Merleau-Ponty Circle 1989– ; editor: 'Westminster Affairs' 1987–93; chief author: 'Cases and Concepts in Nursing Ethics' 1991; author of var. articles in scholarly books & journals; recreations: tennis, squash, cycling; Home: 47 Cathcart St., London, Ont. N6C 3L8; Office: 361 Windermere Rd., London, Ont. N6G 2K3.

**YEO, Ronald Frederick,** B.L.S.; librarian; b. Woodstock, Ont. 13 Nov. 1923; s. Frederick Thomas and Jugertha Aleda (Vansickle) Y.; e. Univ. of Toronto B.A. 1948, B.L.S. 1967; Univ. of Regina LL.D. (h.c.) 1990; m. Margaret Elizabeth d. Frederick Horsley 12 Oct. 1953; children: Joanne, Peter; CHIEF LIBRARIAN, REGINA PUBLIC LIBRARY 1972–88; mem. Nat. Lib. Adv. Bd. 1982–87 (Chrmn. 1986–87); mem. Adv. Bd. Kelsey Inst. Lib. Program; Chrmn. Steering Comte., Project: Progress (future of pub. libs. in Can.); served with RCAF 1942–45; Mgr. Book Dept., American News Co. Toronto 1948–53; Sales Mgr., Dir., British Book Service, Toronto 1953–63; Mgr. Trade Div. Collier-Macmillan Canada Ltd. Toronto 1963–65; Pub. Services Coordinator, North York Pub. Lib. 1966–1971; rec'd Queen's Silver Jubilee Medal 1977; mem. Candn. Lib. Assn. (Pres. 1978–79), rec'd. Outstanding Service to Librarianship Award 1988; Candn. Assn. Pub. Libs. (Chrmn. 1975–76), rec'd. Outstanding Public Library Service Award 1987; Administrators of Large Pub. Libs. (Chrmn. 1973–74); mem. Sask. Lib. Assn.; Club: Kiwanis; Home: 1453 Parker Ave., Regina, Sask. S4S 4R7; Office: 2311 12th Ave., Regina, Sask. S4P 0N3.

**YEOMAN, Robert G.,** B.Comm., M.Econ.Sc., M.B.A.; executive; b. Limerick, Ireland 1942; s. Richard and Hilda (Tierney) Y.; e. Univ. Coll. Dublin, B.Comm. (1st class honours) 1969, M.Econ.Sc. 1970; Wichita State Univ., M.B.A. 1972; m. Nettie Ann d. Ralph and Mildred Zerger 1973; children: Aisling, Rebecca, Randal; VICE-PRES. FINANCE AND CORPORATE DEVELOPMENT, ANTARES MINING AND EXPLORATION CORP. 1993– ; Asst. Acct. Shannon Diamond and Carbide Ltd. 1961–66; Asst. Div. Mgr. Anglo American Corp. of South Africa 1972–76; Leasing Analyst, Continental Bank of Canada 1976; Mgr. Planning Analysis Noranda Inc. 1977; Sr. Vice Pres. Corporate Devel., Brascan Ltd. 1982–92; Trustee, McLaughlin Earth Sciences Gallery Campaign, Royal Ontario Museum; recreations: mineralogy, ornithology, swimming, travel; Home: 27 Airdrie Rd., Toronto, Ont. M4G 1L8.

**YEOMANS, Donald Ralph,** B.A.Sc., P.Eng., C.M.A., F.C.M.A.; federal public servant; consultant; b. Toronto, Ont. 25 March 1925; s. Ralph and Louise Margaret (Weismiller) Y.; e. Humbercrest Pub. Sch. and Humberside Coll. Inst. Toronto; Univ. of Toronto B.A.Sc. 1947; Urwick Mang. Centre, Slough, 1960; m. Catharine Simpson d. William F. Williams. Toronto, Ont. 13 May 1950; children: Patricia (Mrs. Danyluk), Nancy (Mrs. Love), Jane (Mrs. Charlesworth); CONSULTANT; Design Engr. Eastern Steel Products Ltd. Toronto 1947, Sales Engr. 1948; Field Engr. Canadian Comstock Co. Ltd. 1949, Chief Field Engr. 1951. Coordinator of Operations 1952, Area Supt. 1956; joined Urwick Currie Ltd. as Mang. Consultant 1959, Sr. Consultant 1961; Dir. Organ. Research Group, Royal (Glassco) Comn. on Govt. Organ. 1961; joined Cabinet Secretariat to implement Glassco recommendations 1962, Special Adv. Bureau of Govt. Organ. 1963, Asst. to Secy. to Treasury Bd. 1964, Deputy Secy. to Treasury Bd. in charge of Mang. Improvement Br. 1965; responsible for coordinating all interaction between Expo 67, Privy Council Office and Treasury Bd.; Bicultural Program Quebec City 1968; Special Adv. to Chrmn. Comitée Mineau 1969; Asst. Depy. Min. Dept. Supply and Services 1969, named by Auditor Gen. as mem. Steering Comte. to study Financial Mang. and Controls Govt. Can. 1974, Assoc. Extve. Dir. Anti-Inflation Bd. 1975, Special Adv. Royal Comn. Inquiry Financial Organ. and Accountability in Govt. of Can. (Lambert Comn.) 1977; Asst. Depy. Min. Admin., Dept. of Nat. Health and Welfare, 1977; Commissioner of Corrections, 1978; Chrmn. of the Tariff Bd. 1985–89; Special Advisor, Candn. Judicial Centre 1989–90; has served as mem. numerous adv. comtes. various univs.; rec'd Centennial Medal 1967; Jubilee Medal 1977; Financial Mgmt. Inst. Award 1984; Australian Gov. Commonwealth Visiting Fellow 1985; American Correctional Assn. E.R. Cass Award 1991; Shoaib Memorial Lecturer, Pakistan 1992; Fellow, Soc. of Management Accountants of Can. (F.C.M.A.) 1979; mem. Inst. Pub. Adm. Can. (Pres. 1974); Soc. Indust. Accts. Can. (Pres. 1977); Men's Canadian Club of Ottawa (Pres. 1978); Chrmn., Council of Chrmn. of Ont. Univ.; Chrmn. Bd. of Gov., Carleton Univ. 1989; Assn. of State Correctional Administrators (Pres. 1983); Co-Chrmn. Counc. of Candn. Administrative Tribunals 1986; founding mem. Bd. of Govs., Candn. Comprehensive Auditing Foundation; Beta Theta Pi; United Church; recreation: fishing; Clubs: Five Lakes (Pres. 1975); Home: 310 Clemow Ave., Ottawa, Ont. K1S 2B8.

**YIP, Cecil C.,** B.Sc., Ph.D.; university professor; b. Hong Kong 11 June 1937; s. Sum-Wah and Wai-Yee (Luk) Y.; e. McMaster Univ., B.Sc. 1959; The Rockefeller Univ., Ph.D. 1964; m. Yvette d. Beatrice and Francis Fung 15 Oct. 1960; children: Christopher, Adrian; PROF., BANTING & BEST DEPT. MED. RSCH., UNIV. OF TORONTO 1974– ; Chair of Dept. 1990– ; Vice Dean, Research 1993– ; Charles H. Best Prof. of Med. Rsch. 1987– ; Asst. Prof. 1964–68; Assoc. Prof. 1968–74; Extve. Ctte., Banting & Best Diabetes Ctr., Univ. of Toronto 1979–81, 1987– ; Mem., Grant Rev. Ctte., Med. Rsch. Counc. 1974–77; U.S. Nat. Inst. of Health 1979–84; Juvenile Diabetes Found. 1985–87; Med. Rev. Ctte., Gairdner Found. 1985–92; Vice-Pres., Univ. of Toronto Fac. Assn. 1981; Pres. 1983; The Charles Best Prize 1972; Chrmn., Bd. of Trustees, Walmer Rd. Baptist Ch. 1985–91; Mem., Am. Soc. of Biol. Chems.; Candn. Biochem. Soc.; Candn. Diabetes Assn.; Candn. Soc. of Endocrin. & Metabol.; Am. Assn. for the Advancement of Sci.; Am. Chem. Soc.; Sigma Xi; author & co-author of more than 100 sci. pubns.; Home: 125 Melrose Ave., Toronto, Ont. M5M 1Y8; Office: 112 College St., Toronto, Ont. M5G 1L6.

**YONG, Raymond N.,** Ph.D.; university professor; b. Singapore 10 Apr. 1929; s. Ngim Djin and Lucy (Loh) Y.; e. Washington & Jefferson Coll., B.A. 1950; M.I.T., B.Sc. 1952; Purdue Univ., M.Sc. 1954; McGill Univ., M.Eng. 1958, Ph.D. 1960; m. Florence d. Efim and Anna Lechensky 8 July 1961; children: Raymond T.M., Christopher T.K.; DIR., GEOTECHNICAL RSCH. CTR., MCGILL UNIV. 1976– ; Assoc. Mem., Centre for Medicine, Ethics and Law, McGill Univ.; Adjunct Prof. of Civil Engineering, Univ. of Florida (Gainesville); Adjunct Rsch. Prof. of Civil Engineering, Carleton Univ. (Ottawa); Asst. Prof., McGill Univ. 1959–62; Assoc. Prof. 1962–65; Prof. 1965–73; William Scott Prof. of Civil Engr. & Applied Mechanics 1973– ; Assoc. Dir., Nat. Sci. Found. Summer Inst. for Sr. Univ. Faculty, Univ. of Arizona, summer 1970, 1971; rec'd Charles B. Dudley Award, ASTM 1988; F.E.I.C. 1988; F.R.S.C. 1987; Izaak Walton Killam Prize 1985; Chevalier de l'Ordre nat. du Qué. 1985; Candn. Environmental Achievement Award, Lifetime Achievement 1991; F.CSCE (Fellow of the Candn. Soc. for Civil Engineering) 1989; awarded R.F. Legget Award, Candn. Geotechnical Soc. 1993; Pres., Internat. Soc. for Terrain-Vehicle Systems (ISTVS) 1993– ; mem., Inst. of Civil Engrs.; Order of Engrs. Qué.; Am. Soc. of Civil Engrs.; Candn. Geotech. Soc.; Am. Soc. for Testing & Materials; Soc. of Rheology; Internat. Soc. for Terrain-Vehicle Systems; co-author: 'Introduction to Soil Behaviour' 1966, 'Soil Properties and Behaviour' 1975, 'Vehicle Traction Mechanics' 1984, 'Principles of Contaminant Transport in Soils' 1992, 'Waste Geotechnics' forthcoming; co-editor of several scholary monographs incl. 'Consolidation of Soils' 1985, 'Sedimentation/Consolidation Models' 1984, 'Geological Environment and Soil Properties' 1983; Home: 212 Sherbrooke St., Beaconsfield, Qué. H9W 1P5; Office: 817 Sherbrooke St. W., Montreal, Qué. H3A 2K6.

**YONGE, Keith A.,** M.D., C.M., D.P.M., F.R.C.P.(C), F.R.C.P. (U.K.), F.A.C.P. (U.S.); psychiatrist; educator; b. London, Eng., 22 June 1910; s. Frank Arthur and Alice Maud (Liddle) Y.; e. Tollington Sch., London, Eng., 1928; McGill Univ., M.D., C.M. 1948; Univ. of London, D.P.M. 1952; m. Jane Elizabeth, d. Orval L. Beatty, Victoria, B.C.; 21 June 1948; children: Keith S., Martin B., Devon Anne, Janet E.; Prof. and Chrmn., Dept. Of Psychiatry, Univ. Of Alberta 1957–75; Prof. Emeritus since 1975; Phys., Med. Specialist (Psychiatrist), Univ. Hosp.; Gen. Mgr., Labrador Development Co., 1935–42; Dir., Mental Health Clinic, Moose Jaw, Sask., 1952; Asst. Prof., Dept. Psychiatry, Univ. of Sask., 1954, Assoc. Prof. 1956; rec'd Centennial Medal 1967; author over 60 publs. in prof. and scient. journs.; mem. Alta. Med. Assn.; Candn. Med. scient. journs.; mem. Alta. Med. Assn.; Candn. Med. Assn.; Candn. Psychiatric Assn. (Pres. 1970–71); Am. Psychiatric Assn.; World Psychiatric Assn.; Inter-Am. Council Psychiatric Assn. (Pres. 1973); Candn. Mental Health Assn. (Past Chrmn., Nat. Scient. Planning Council); P. Conservative; Anglican; recreations: hiking, swimming, skiing, tennis, photography; Home: 4345 Kingscote Rd., Cobble Hill, B.C. V0R 1L0.

**YORE, Larry Dean,** B.S., M.A., Ph.D.; university professor; b. Winnegago, Minn. 16 Aug. 1942; s. Leo Michael and Doris Eugene (Campbell) Y.; e. Univ. of Minn., B.S. 1964, M.A. 1968, Ph.D. 1973; m. Sharyl Ann d. Erwin and Doris Sackreiter 1 Oct. 1960; children: Jacklyn Kay, Richard Perry; PROF., FAC. OF EDN., UNIV. OF VICTORIA 1970– ; sch. sci. teacher 1964–70; Univ. of Victoria Bd. of Govs. 1990– ; Chair, Dept. of Social and Natural Sciences 1986–91; Pres., Univ. of Victoria Faculty Assn. 1985–86; Dir., Education Extension 1980–84, 1989–90; Phi Delta Kappa; mem. Candn. Assn. of Univ. Teachers; Nat. Sci. Teachers Assn.; Nat. Assn. for Rsch. in Sci. Teaching; author elementary sch. science textbook series 'Journeys in Science/Science en Marche,' numerous research articles, several curriculum and program guides; recreation: rugby; Home: 2052 Haidey Terrace, R.R. 2, Saanichton, B.C. V0S 1M0; Office: Box 3010, Victoria, B.C. V8W 3N4.

**YORK, Derek,** B.A., D.Phil., F.R.S.C.; educator; writer; b. Normanton, Yorks., Eng. 12 Aug. 1936; s. John and Alice Sylvia (Garfitt) Y.; e. Oxford Univ. B.A. 1957, D.Phil. 1960; m. Lydia d. Joseph and Catherine Senyshyn 16 Dec. 1961; one s. Derek Lionel; PROF. OF PHYSICS UNIV. OF TORONTO 1972– ; monthly sci. columnist Globe and Mail 1980– ; joined present Univ. 1960; recipient Geol. Assn. Can. Past Pres. Medal 1985; Royal Soc. Can. Bancroft Award 1986; author 'Planet Earth' 1976, transl. Jap., Ital.; co-author 'The Earth's Age and Geochronology' 1972, transl. Chinese; mem. Candn. Geophys. Union; Am. Geophys. Union; recreations: tennis, soccer; Home: 29 Kimbark Blvd., Toronto, Ont. M5N 2X6; Office: Toronto, Ont. M5S 1A7.

**YORK, Lorraine Mary,** B.A., M.A., Ph.D.; university professor; b. London, Ont. 21 Nov. 1958; d. Reginald Francis and Margaret Gertrude (Waddell) Y.; e. McMaster Univ., B.A. 1981, M.A. 1982, Ph.D. 1985; m. Michael L. s. Charles and Minnie Ross 23 May 1987; one child: Anna Ross; ASSOC. PROF., DEPT. OF ENGLISH, MCMASTER UNIV. 1991– ; Asst. Prof., English, McGill Univ. 1985–88; Asst. Prof., English, McMaster Univ. 1988–91; SSHRCC Doct. Fellow, 1982–85; McMaster Humanities Teaching Award Winner 1990; Roman Cath.; NDP supporter; mem., Assn. of Candn. Univ. Teachers of English; Assn. for Candn. Studies in the U.S.; Assn. for Candn. Studies; Assn. for Candn. and Québécois Literatures; Modern Languages Assn.; author: 'The Other Side of Dailiness': Photography in the Works of Alice Munro, Timothy Findley, Michael Ondaatje and Margaret Laurence' 1988; 'Front Lines: The Fiction of Timothy Findley' 1991 and several articles; recreations: recorder playing, classical music, biking; Home: 8 Leisure Place, Dundas, Ont. L9H 3X4; Office: Hamilton, Ont. L8S 4L9;

**YOSHIDA, Ken,** Ph.D.; educator; b. Akoh City, Japan 31 Jan. 1931; s. Hirosa and Raku (Okabe) Y.; e. Utsunomiya Univ. Japan B.Sc. 1953; Harvard Sch. of Pub. Health Cert. 1971; Kyoto Univ. Ph.D. 1974; m. Toshiko d. Toshiichi and Toki Inoue 26 Oct. 1957; children: Joe, Midori; Assoc. Prof. of Occupational Hygiene, Univ. of Alta. 1989; Sr. Rsch. Sci. Occupational Hygiene prog. Sask. Rsch. Council 1967; Adjunct Assoc. Prof. of Social & Preventive Med. Univ. of Sask. 1979; Assoc. Prof. of Community Health Sci's Univ. of Calgary 1985; Jt. Occupational Hygienist Dept. Occupational Health & Safety Univ. of Alta. Hosps. Edmonton; Reg'd Occupational Hygienist; Cert. Safety Specialist World Safety Orgn. USA; Visiting Scholar Alta. Heritage Grant Prog. in Occupational Health & Safety 1985; Sustaining mem. Torch Bearers Soc. Calgary; Alta. Children's Hosp.; Guest Lectr. Soviet Acad. Med. Sci. Moscow 1989; jointly conducts rsch. with Soviet sci's; jt. rsch. project Nat. Inst. Occupational Health Budapest; conducts extensive investigs. high technol. areas occupational health and serves as Cons. Inst. Sci. of Labour Japan; reg'd mem. Environmental Experts Nat. Rsch. Council Can.; co-author 'Occupational Exposure to Pesticides: A Guide for its Assessment and Control' forthcoming; author or co-author various articles, book chapters occupational health & hygiene; mem. Am. Ind. Hygiene Assn.; Am. Conf. Govt'al Ind. Hygienists; Candn. Occupational Health Assn.; Candn. Hosp. Engn. Soc.; Am. Soc. Safety Engs.; United Church (sr. choir); recreations: classical music, travel, fitness; Home: 2108 Urbana Rd. N.W., Calgary, Alta. T2N 4B8.

**YOSHIHARA, Toyoshi,** B.A.; business executive; b. Tokyo, Japan 21 June 1937; s. Isamu and Kiwako Y.; e. Waseda Univ. B.A. 1960; m. Ikuko d. Yaeko Tatsuta Aug. 1987; CHAIR & FOUNDER, KOMATSU CANADA LTD. 1972– ; joined Sumitomo Corp. Tokyo Japan 1969; transferred to Vancouver Office to start marketing Japanese construction equipment in Canada 1970; present firm distributes Japanese construction equipment in Canada; Chair, Equipment Fédéral Québec Ltée.; Chair, Coneco Equipment Inc.; Canada Council grant to introduce Canadian theatre to Japan 1989; translator (into Japanese): 'One Thousand Cranes' by Colin Thomas 1985, 'The Tomorrow Box' by Ann Chislett 1986, 'Blood Relations' by Sharon Pollock 1987 (Canadian plays); Home: 108 – 4900 Cartier St., Vancouver, B.C. V6M 4H2; Office: 7500 River Rd., Richmond, B.C. V6X 1X6.

**YOST, Elwy McMurran,** B.A.; television host; author; b. Weston, Ont. 10 July 1925; s. Elwy Honderich and Annie Josephine (McMurran) Y.; e. Weston Coll. & Vocational Sch. 1943; Univ. of Toronto B.A. 1948; m. Lila Ragnhild d. Monrad Melby, North Surrey, B.C. 16 June 1951; two s. Christopher, Graham Boz; EXTVE. PRODUCER AND HOST ('Saturday Night at the Movies,' 'Magic Shadows,' 'Talking Film' and 'The Moviemakers') and Exec. Producer of 'The Movie Show' and 'Film International' TV ONTARIO 1974–87, retired 1987 but still hosting and writing 'Saturday Night at The Movies'; joined Circulation Dept. Toronto Star 1948–52; prof. actor, Jack Blacklock Prodns. in Ont. (summer stock) 'Arsenic and Old Lace,' 'The Man Who Came to Dinner,' 'Mr. Roberts,' 'Angel Street' etc. 1946–53; Human Relations Counselor, Avro Aircraft 1953–59; Eng. Teacher Burnhamthorpe Coll. Inst. 1959–64; Television Panelist, CBC 1959–68, 'Live a Borrowed Life,' 'The Superior Sex' (host), 'Flashback,' 'Passport to Adventure' (host), 'It's Debatable' (Radio host); TV Producer, Metrop. Educ. TV Assn. Toronto 1964–66, Extve. Dir. 1967–70; Supt. of Regional Liaison, TV Ontario 1970–73; served with Candn. Army 1944–45, writer/actor Candn. Army Show 1945; author 'You are the Broadcast: An Anatomy of Television in Education' 1971; 'Magic Moments From The Movies' 1978; 'Secret of the Lost Empire' 1980; 'Billy and the Bubbleship' 1982; 'The Mad Queen of Mordra' 1987; 'A Long Time Till Harry Comes'; 'The Falls of Orellana'; 'The Lost City'; 'The Sound of the Horn,' radio plays CBC; various articles on cinema, TV and educ. and currently writing (since 1987) an adult mystery-adventure novel; nom. for best host-interviewer on tel. at the ACTRA Awards, 1982, 1984; mem. Ont. Secondary Sch. Teachers Fed.; Alliance of Candn. TV & Radio Artists; Protestant; recreations: devising thought experiments and speculating about the meaning of time, space, God, the Universe and self; walking; attending movies, theatres & art galleries; public speaking; reading, loafing, travelling; Club: Sons of the Desert; Office: Elwy Yost Enterprises Inc., 6237 St. Georges Cres., West Vancouver, B.C. V7W 1Z3.

**YOST, Brig. Gen. William John,** C.D., B.A.; consultant; b. Caledonia, Ont. 20 May 1926; s. Arthur William and Rose (Wagner) Y.; e. high sch. Wyoming, Ont.; Univ. of W. Ont., B.A. 1950; Royal Mil. Coll. of Sci. UK; Jt. Services Staff Coll. UK; m. Elizabeth d. Harold and Gertrude Lipscombe 8 July 1953; children: Alison, David; PRES. YOST CONSULTANT SERVICES 1986– ; Vice Pres., CDA Inst.; served with Merchant Navy 1942–43; Candn. Armed Forces 1943–80; comnd. 1951 Royal Candn. Ordnance Corps becoming ammunition and bomb disposal specialist; service UK, Belgium, Germany, Ghana, Egypt and Lebanon; involved with many United Nations peace keeping operations since 1951; headed UN Headquarters Field Operations Mgmnt. Audit in Middle East 1974; Chief Logistics Offr., UNEF, Egypt 1975–76; Chief Internat. Plans and later Coordinator Civil Mobilization, Emergency Preparedness Can. 1980–86; Past Pres. Friends Candn. War Museum; Hon. Chrmn. Royal Candn. Legion Poppy Fund; Past Dir. Defence Assoc's Network; Past Pres., CF Logistics Assn.; Founding Dir. Candn. Defence Preparedness Assn.; author: 'Industrial Mobilization in Canada' 1983; 'Peace Through Security' 1987; ed. 'Dialogue in Peacekeeping' 1979; 'Soviet Union – The Threat to Europe' 1987; 'In Defence of Canada's Oceans' 1988; contbr. 'Peacekeeper's Handbook' 1978; 'Canada's New Field Army' 1989; 'Peacemaking: Canada's Role' 1991; Columnist, Forum Magazine; Exec. Consultant film, 'Reluctant Heroes - Canada's Military Heritage' 1989; Presbyterian; recreations: boating, travel; Home: 1845 Prince of Wales Dr., Ottawa, Ont. K2C 1P2; Office: 601, 100 Gloucester St., Ottawa, Ont. K2P 0A4.

**YOUNES, Ernest Alexander;** aluminum executive; b. Tanta, Egypt 21 Sept. 1917; s. Alexander R. and Rose G. (Kerba) Y.; e. St. Louis Coll., Tanta 1934; York Univ.; m. Yvonne d. Choucri Hamaoui 6 Dec. 1942; children: Mona, Nadia, Adel, Rami, Magda; CHAIRMAN ADVANCED MONOBLOC INC. 1985– ; Dir. 'Al Ahram' newspaper; co-founder and Pres. Advanced Extrusions Ltd. 1968; mem. Candn. Mfrs. Chem. Specialities Assoc.; Candn. Cosmetic, Toiletry & Fragrance Assoc.; Packaging Assoc.; Chem. Specialties Mfrs. Assoc. U.S.A.; past Chrmn. Bd. of Trustees St. George Ch.; mem. Order of St. Ignatus; recreation: swimming; Club: Granite; The Empire Club of Canada; Home: 107 Heathcote Ave., Willowdale, Ont. M2L 2X5; Office: 96 Scarsdale Rd., Don Mills, Ont. M3B 2R7 and 163 Robert St. E., Penetanguishene, Ont. L0P 1K0.

**YOUNG, Cameron Graham,** B.A., M.Ed.; writer; b. Quebec, Que. 25 Feb. 1944; s. Harold Graham and Florence Mary (Armstrong) Young; e. McGill Univ., B.A. 1965; Univ. of Toronto, M.Ed. 1971; m. Anne d. John and Eleanor Wilson 9 Dec. 1967; one d.: Jennifer Ellen; CUSO volunteer, Sarawak, Malaysia 1965–67; Eng. Instr., Sir Sandford Fleming Coll. 1969; Commun. Instr., Vanier Coll. 1971–73; Ed., 'ForesTalk Magazine' 1978–83 Gold Quill Award, Internat. Assn. of Bus. Commun. (IABC) 1981 (N. Am.)); IABC Silver Leaf 1982 (Can.); Media Club of Canada Memorial Award 1990; author: 'The Forests of British Columbia' 1985 (B.C. Book Award best pub. 1986); 'Clayoquot: The Wild Side' 1990; Commun. cons./writer/editor in nat. resources for govt. & envir. orgns. 1983– ; Co-ord., Victoria Chapter of Periodical Writers Assn. of Can. (PWAC) 1985–87, PWAC Regional Dir. 1991, PWAC Vice-Pres. 1992–93, PWAC Pres. 1993–94; Bd. of Dir., Sierra Club of Western Canada 1992–94; Journalism Instr., Univ. of Victoria; recreations: walking, swimming; Club: Sierra Club of West. Can.; Home: 860 Melody Place, R.R. 5, Victoria, B.C. V8X 4M6.

**YOUNG, Christopher Moody,** B.A., M.A.; journalist; b. Accra, Ghana 9 July 1926; s. Norman Andrew Thomson and Mary Grace Holland (Moody) Y.; e. Ravenscourt Sch. Winnipeg 1943; Univ. of Man. B.A. 1947; Balliol Coll. Oxford B.A. 1949, M.A. 1992; m. Florence (dec. 1966) d. John and Ruby Sirett 8 Dec. 1947; m. Ann d. Laurance and Elizabeth Coffin 25 Feb. 1967; children: Alix Harnden, Sheila Evans, Judith, Rachel; POLITICAL COLUMNIST, SOUTHAM NEWS 1989– ; joined Winnipeg Tribune 1949–55, News Ed. 1953–55; Hamilton Spectator, News Ed. 1955–57, Exec. News Ed. 1957–59; Southam News Service (now Southam News), Nat, Corr. Ottawa Bureau 1960–61, Gen. Mgr. 1975–81, Sr. Corr. and London Bureau Chief 1981–84, Nat. Pol. Columnist 1984–86; Sr. Corr. and Moscow Bureau Chief, 1987–89; Ed. Ottawa Citizen 1961–75; radio broadcast commentator, TV script writer and panellist CBC and CTV; recipient Bowater Award for Journalism 1961; Nat. Newspaper Award 1982, 1989; Citation of Merit 1990; Wilderness Award TV Script Writing 1965; Dir. Un. Way Ottawa-Carleton 1966–78, Pres. 1974–76; Chrmn. Inst. Devel. Edn. through the Arts 1977–81; co-ed.: 'A Century of Reporting: The National Press Club Anthology' 1967; recreations: theatre, art, skiing; Clubs: National Press; Wig and Pen (London); Home and Office: 111 Stanley Ave., Ottawa, Ont. K1M 1N8.

**YOUNG, David S.,** B.A.; writer; b. Oakville, Ont. 17 July 1946; s. Samuel Crawford and Winifred (Hodges) Y.; e. Univ. of Western Ont., B.A. 1967; m. Sarah d. Joseph and Gloria Sheard; one s.: Benn; Pres., Coach House Press; Dir., The For/Words Found.; The Writers' Devel. Trust; P.E.N. International (Extve. Ctte.); Theatre Passe Muraille; Baffin Island Writers' Project; A.C.E. Award 1986; Chalmers Award 1989; Dora Mavor Moore Award 1989; Most Promising Screenwriter Award (Genie) 1989; author: 'Incognito' 1982, 'Agent Provocateur' 1976 (novels); 'Love is Strange,' 'Fire' (stage plays) and feature film screenplays as yet unproduced; Office: c/o Theatre Passe Muraille, 16 Ryerson Ave., Toronto, Ont. M5T 2P3.

**YOUNG, David Samuel D'Arcy,** B.A.; writer, screenwriter, playwright, editor; b. Oakville, Ont. 17 July 1946; s. Samuel Crawford and Toto (Winifred Hodges) Y.; e. Univ. of Western Ontario B.A. 1967; one s.: Benn Dashiell Joseph Young; PRES., COACH HOUSE PRESS 1984– ; Founder, The Baffin Island Writers' Project (a High Arctic desktop pub. venture designed to promote literacy & strengthen Inuktitut language in 4 Baffin settlements); Founding Dir., The For/Words Found.; Steering Ctte., The Enow'kin School, Penticton, B.C.; Resident Writer, Candn. Centre for Advanced Film Studies 1990; Bd. of Dir., Theatre Passe Muraille; Extve. Ctte., Internat. P.E.N. 1989; author: 'Agent Provocateur' 1976, 'Incognito' 1982 (novels); 'Love Is Strange' 1988 'Fire' 1990 (4 Dora Mavor Moore Awards & Chalmers/Toronto Drama Branch Award) (plays); 'The Suspect' 1989 (York-Trillium Award, Most Promising Screenwriter) (screenplay); 'Marooned' 1986 (children's book); television: 12 episodes of 'Fraggle Rock' (var. shows won A.C.E. Award, ACTRA Award, International Emmy, Humanitas Prize); editor of a half-dozen books, all with Coach House; Office: 401 (rear) Huron St., Toronto, Ont. M5S 2G5.

**YOUNG, Douglas,** B.A., LL.B., P.C., M.P.; politician; b. Tracadie, N.B. 20 Sept. 1940; s. Douglas and Annie (Wishart) Y.; e. N.B. Teacher's College. Cert. 1957; St. Thomas Univ. B.A. 1972; Univ. of N.B. LL.B. 1975; m. Jacqueline David 9 Dec. 1979; children: Jessica, Alexa, Douglas; MINISTER OF TRANSPORT (CANADA) 1993– ; Radio Announcer, CKBC-Radio 1958–60; Manager, CKNB-Radio 1960–66; Clerk, Centennial Comn., Govt. of Can. 1966–68; Special Asst., Office of the Premier, Legislative Assembly of N.B. 1968–70; Teacher, Sch. Bd. of Fredericton 1972–75; Lawyer, Young, Doiron & Lavoie 1975–87; Member for Tracadie, Legis. Assembly of N.B. 1978–88; Leader of the Opposition 1981–83; Min. of Fisheries & Aquaculture 1987–88; Member for Gloucester, House of Commons 1988–90; Member for Acadie-Bathurst 1990– ; Leadership Candidate, Liberal Party of N.B. 1981 (successful); has held several opposition critic appointments; bilingual; Roman Catholic; recreations: sports, reading, business; Home: P.O. Box 9000, Tracadie, N.B. E0C 2B0; Office: Room 707, Confederation Bldg., House of Commons, Ottawa, Ont. K1A 0A6.

**YOUNG, Earle R.,** B.Sc., D.D.S., B.Sc.D., M.Sc., F.A.D.S.A.; university professor; b. Fredericton, N.B. 26 June 1947; s. Ronald Fletcher and Marjorie Alice (Lynch) Y.; e. Carleton Univ. B.Sc. 1969; Univ. of West. Ont. D.D.S. 1976; Univ. of Toronto B.Sc.D. (Anaesthesia) 1978, M.Sc. (Pharmacology) 1983; Fellowship in Anaesthesia (F.A.D.S.A.) 1986; m. Marg d. Sylvia and Brad Patell 1993; children: Stephen, Lian; ASSOC. PROF. OF ANAESTHESIA, FAC. OF DENTISTRY, UNIV. OF TORONTO 1992– and ACTING HEAD,

DEPT. OF ANAESTHESIA 1990– ; private dentistry practice, Ottawa 1976; private dentistry/anaesthesia practice, Toronto 1978–82 (part-time 1985– ); Asst. Prof. of Anaesthesia, Fac. of Dentistry, Univ. of Toronto 1983–92; Fellow in Anaesthesia, The Wellesley Hosp. 1980–86, Staff 1986– ; Clerkship Tutor & Examiner and Post-Grad. Suprvr., Fac. of Dent.; serves on several fac. cttes.; Consulting Ed., J. Candn. Dental Assn. 1989– ; Dir., YCC #491 (Dir. 1980–86, 1988–92; Vice-Pres. 1986–87, Pres. 1987–88); Omicron Kappa Epsilon – Hon. Dental Soc. Induction 1987; Grad. Class (Fac. of Dent.) Hon. Class Pres., Mem. 1985–94; awarded Dr. Bruce Hord Master Teaching Award 1989; Mem., Med. Staff Assn., The Wellesley Hosp.; Ont. Dental Assn.; Ont. Dental Soc. of Anaesth.; Am. Dental Soc. of Anaesth.; Royal Coll. of Dental Surg. of Ont.; author of num. pubs. & rsch. projects; recreations: swimming, ice skating, cycling, guitar, hockey, baseball; Home: 26 Confederation Way, Thornhill, Ont. L3T 5R5; Office: 124 Edward St., Toronto, Ont. M5G 1G6.

**YOUNG, H. Clifton,** B.S., M.B.A., Ph.D.; university professor; b. Chicago, Ill. 29 Apr. 1929; s. Hume Clifton and Catherine Gladys (Martin) Y.; e. Northwestern Univ., B.S. 1955; Temple Univ., M.B.A. 1962; Northwestern Univ., Ph.D. 1973; ASSOC. PROF., FAC. OF BUSINESS, UNIV. OF ALTA. 1971– ; various positions 1947–59; Gen. Mgr., Heisler Corp. 1959–65; Dir. of Corporate Rsch., Delaware Barrel & Drum Co. 1960–65; Mktg. Area Coord., Univ. of Alta. 1973–77; Extve. Vice-Pres., Treas. & Dir., Rogers & Assoc. 1974–83; Mem., Univ. of Alberta General Appeals Ctte. 1982–84; Mem., Council of the Assn. of The Academic Staff of the Univ. of Alberta 1989–94; Pres. & Dir., Young & Young Planning & Investment Co. Ltd. 1978– ; Partner & Dir., INFODEC 1986– ; instr. for 3 profl. SCUBA Diving assn. 1976– ; Eagle Scout 9 Feb. 1945; Am. Mktg. Assn. Diss. Award Winner 1973; Dir. & First Vice Pres., Am. Mktg. Assn.: N. Alberta 1973–74; Dir., Alta. Advtg. Standards Counc. 1975–77, 1979– ; Dir. & Chrmn., Rsch. & Policy Ctte., Rsch. Dir., Urban Reform Group of Edmonton 1974–75; Dir., Alberta Social Resources Inventory 1978–81; Mem., Intellectual Property Adv. Ctte., Univ. of Alta. 1992–93; Mem., Am. Mktg. Assn. 1955– ; Mem., Prod. Development & Mgt. Assn. 1985– ; Delta Sigma Pi 1954– ; author/co-author several articles, papers, reviews & workshops on new product development and the marketing and management of distance and higher education; recreations: teaching, scuba diving; club: Univ. of Alta. Aikido Soc.; Home: 12904 - 66 Ave., Edmonton, Alta. T6H 1Y7; Office: Edmonton, Alta. T6G 2R6.

**YOUNG, James Hardy;** trust company executive; b. Walkerton, Ont. 28 May 1943; s. Thomas and Phyliss Jean (Nickolson) Y.; e. Walkerton Dist. H.S. 1964; m. Heidi d. Victor and Eileen Willi 27 Nov. 1966; children: James, Darryl; VICE-PRES., RETAIL LENDING, SUN LIFE TRUST COMPANY 1991– ; Dist. Mgr., Transamerica Financial Corp. 1965–76; Regional Vice-Pres. Western Canada, Associates Financial Corp. 1976–80; Extve. Dir. of Opns., Windsor England, Assoc. Capital Corp. 1980–86; Asst. Vice-Pres., Standard Trust Co. 1986–91; recreations: golf, antique sport cars; clubs: Deerfield Golf, Toronto Triumph; Home: 1153 Montrose Abbey Dr., Oakville, Ont. L6M 1A2; Office: 36 Toronto St., Suite 300, Toronto, Ont.

**YOUNG, Joseph Edgar Gerald,** F.I.C.B.; banker; b. Three Rivers, Que. 29 Sept. 1943; s. Thomas and Florianne (LaRose) Y.; e. St. Joseph Coll. 1961; Univ. of W. Ont. grad. mgmt. training course 1981; Candn. Securities Course 1989; m. B. June d. William and Lillian Nuttall 9 Sept. 1967; children: Jason, Nicole, Adam; SR. VICE PRES. ENERGY & COMMODITIES, PARIBAS BANK OF CANADA 1982– ; Dir. SOPEXA (Canada) Ltee; joined Bank of Montreal 1962–76; Bank of B.C. 1976–82; Vice Pres. Corporate Banking present Bank 1982–87; mem. French C. of C.; recreations: music, reading, travel, golf, show jumping, skiing; Clubs: Ontario; Empire; Canadian; Home: 4269 Lakeshore Rd., Burlington, Ont. L7L 1A7; Office: Royal Trust Tower, Ste. 4100, P.O. Box 31, Toronto, Ont. M5K 1N8.

**YOUNG, Lawrence,** B.A., M.A., Ph.D., Sc.D., F.R.S.C.; university professor; b. Hull, England 5 July 1925; s. Herbert and Dora (Padley) Y.; e. Hull Grammar Sch.; Clare Coll., Cambridge Univ., B.A. 1946, Ph.D. 1950, Sc.D. 1963; m. Margaret E.J. d. William and Elizabeth Carr 5 Jan. 1951; EMERITUS PROF., ELECTRICAL ENGR. DEPT., UNIV. OF B.C. 1990– ; Jr. Harwell Rsch. Fellow, Atomic Energy Rsch. Establ., Harwell England 1949–51; post-doct. fellow, Nat. Rsch. Counc. (Ottawa) 1951–52; Asst. Lectr., Imperial Coll. 1952–55; B.C. Rsch. Counc. 1955–63; Prof., Electrical Engr. Dept., Univ. of B.C. 1963–90; Fellow, IEEE; Electrochem. Soc. (Div. Ed. 1967–83); Fellow, Royal Soc. of Canada; Fellow, Royal Soc. of Arts, London; author of one book & over 100 sci. articles; recreations: music (violin & viola), riding; Home: 3226 W. 51st Ave., Vancouver, B.C. V6N 3V7; Office: Univ. of B.C., Vancouver, B.C. V6T 1Z4.

**YOUNG, Leslie Gordon,** B.A., M.Sc.; consultant; b. Compton, Que. 19 Aug. 1934; s. Gordon F. and Lena N. (Cairns) Y.; e. Compton, Waterville and Lennoxville schs.; Park Business Coll. Hamilton; Univ. of Montreal B.A.; Univ. of Mass. M.Sc.; m. Helen G. d. John G. McKirdy, Thunder Bay, Ont. 28 June 1958; two d. Susan L., Mary A.; econ. and business consultant; el. M.L.A. for Edmonton Jasper Place prov. g.e. 1971; Min. of Labour 1979–86; Govt. House Leader 1987–89 & Min. of Technology, Research & Telecommunications, Alta. 1986–89; Extve. Dir., Edmonton Space & Science Centre; Chrmn., Joint Standards Directorate, Consultant; mem. Edmonton Chamber Comm.; P. Conservative; Presbyterian; Home: 509 – 11220 – 99 Ave., Edmonton Alta. T5K 2K6.

**YOUNG, Neil;** song-writer; musician; b. Toronto, Ont. 12 Nov. 1945; s. Scott Young and Edna Ragland; m. Pegi Morton 1978; children: Zeke, Ben, Amber Jean; first performed with rock band Squires' in Man. and N. Ont. 1962–64; performed with Mynah Birds Toronto coffeehouses and later in Detroit; formed rock group Buffalo Springfield, Los Angeles 1966–68; performed with Crosby Stills Nash and Young 1969–74 and with Stills 1976; solo career began 1968 performing alone or with accompanying group Crazy Horse throughout N. Am., Europe and Japan during 1970's; Inducted into Canadian Hall of Fame 14 April 1982; named Best Male Singer and Best Composer 1971 and album 'After the Gold Rush' voted Best Album 1970 by Melody Maker (U.K.) readers; his more than 100 songs incl. 'Expecting to Fly,' 'Broken Arrow,' 'I Am a Child,' 'Country Girl,' 'Helpless,' 'Ohio,' 'Southern Man,' 'Round and Round,' 'Everyone Knows This is Nowhere,' 'Only Love Can Break Your Heart,' 'Tell Me Why,' 'Cinnamon Girl,' 'Heart of Gold,' 'Lotta Love'; rec'd numerous gold record sales awards for albums 1969–86 and million-selling hit song 'Heart of Gold' 1972; various anthols. of songs published; wrote soundtrack autobiographical film 'Journey Through the Past'; documentary 'Rust Never Sleeps' of Young in concert released 1979; Address: c/o Lookout Management, 506 Santa Monica Blvd., Penthouse, Santa Monica, CA 90401.

**YOUNG, Patricia Rose,** B.A.; poet; educator; b. Victoria, B.C. 7 Aug. 1954; d. Walter Bernard and Margaret McAlpine (Love) Barr; e. Univ. of Victoria B.A. 1983; m. Terence s. William Ronald and Clare Young 27 May 1974; children: Clea Fleur, Liam Walter Ashdowne; Lectr. in Creative Writing, Univ. of Victoria 1985–91; recipient various Can. Council Grants; B.C. Fedn. Writers First Prize (poetry) 1988; B.C. Book Prize for Poetry 1988; Nat. Mag. Silver Award for Poetry 1988; C.B.C. Literary Competition 1988 (2nd Prize for Poetry); League of Candn. Poets Nat. Poetry Competition, Co-winner 1989; Pat Lowther Memorial Award for poetry 1990; League of Candn. Poets, Nat. Poetry Competition 1993; nominated for Governor General's Award for Poetry 1993; author (poetry): 'Travelling the Floodwaters' 1983; 'Melancholy Ain't No Baby' 1985; 'All I Ever Needed Was A Beautiful Room' 1987; 'The Mad and Beautiful Mothers' 1989; 'Those Were the Mermaid Days' 1991; 'More Watery Still' 1993; mem. League Candn. Poets; Home: 130 Moss St., Victoria, B.C. V8V 4M3.

**YOUNG, Robert Andrew,** M.A., D.Phil.; educator; b. Toronto, Ont. 16 Nov. 1950; e. McGill Univ. B.A. 1970, M.A. 1974; Univ. of Mich.; Institut d'Etudes politiques Paris; Oxford Univ., D.Phil. 1980; PROF. OF POL. SCI., UNIV. OF WESTERN ONT. 1993– ; Co-Dir., Political Economy Research Group; Lectr. Univ. of N.B. 1976–78; Visiting Asst. Prof., McGill Univ. 1980–81; Asst. Prof. Univ. of Western Ont. Univ. 1981, Assoc. Prof. 1985; Visiting Rsch. Fellow, Institute of Intergovernmental Relations, Queen's Univ. 1991–92; author or co-author monographs, scholarly articles & commentaries federalism, Maritime politics, trade & ind. policy, constitution; recreation: gardening; Office: London, Ont. N6A 5C2.

**YOUNG, Robert Andrew McIntyre,** B.A., LL.B., Q.C.; pipeline executive, lawyer; b. Regina, Sask. 8 July 1939; s. Andrew MacIntyre and Marion J. (Anderson) Y.; e. Univ. of Alberta B.A. 1960; LL.B. 1963; m. Kathy; children: Jason, Graham, Shannon, Jonathan, Samantha; SENIOR VICE-PRES., LAW, TRANSCANADA PIPELINES 1990– ; Lawyer, Walsh Young & predecessor partnerships 1963–90; Partner 1968; Mng. Partner 1978–83; Q.C. 1981; Dir., Western Gas Marketing Ltd.; Alberta Natural Gas Company Ltd.; Loram Corporation; Intermat Holdings Ltd.; Hon. Chief, Kainai Chieftainship 1983; Past Pres., Calgary Exhibition & Stampede; Office: P.O. Box 1000, Stn. M, Calgary, Alta. T2P 4K5.

**YOUNG, Scott Alexander;** journalist; author; b. Glenboro, Man. 14 Apr. 1918; s. Percy Andrew and Jean Ferguson (Paterson) Y.; e. Kelvin Tech. High Sch. Winnipeg; m. Edna B. Ragland June 1940; two s. Robert, Neil; m. Astrid E. Mead May 1961; two d. Deirdre, Astrid; m. Margaret Hogan, May, 1980; Columnist, Globe and Mail, 1971–80 and 1957–69; Pres. Ascot Productions Ltd.; Journalist, Winnipeg Free Press 1936–40; The Candn. Press 1940–43, 1945, Corr. in London 1942–43; Asst. Ed. Maclean's 1945–48; Sports Ed. Toronto Telegram 1969–71; author 40 books and 75 published short stories; rec'd Nat. Newspaper Award 1959; CBC Wilderness Award for TV script 1962; el. NHL Hockey Hall of Fame 1988; Manitoba Hockey Hall of Fame 1992; served with RCNVR 1944–45, Europe, Mediterranean (Italy, Yugoslavia, Greece); Doctor of Letters (honoris causa) Trent Univ. 1990; Fellow, McLaughlin Coll. York Univ.; mem. Candn. War Corr's Assn.; Writers Union Can.; Royal Candn. Mil. Inst.; Protestant; recreations: walking, amateur study flora and fauna; Home and Office: 1 Middleton Dr., Peterborough, Ont. K9J 4Z1.

**YOUNG, Victor L.,** C.A., M.B.A.; executive; b. St. John's, Nfld. 23 June 1945; s. Ross and Maude Y.; e. Memorial Univ., B.Comm (Hons.) 1966; Univ. Western Ont., M.B.A. 1968; m. Eileen Beresford; children: Andrew; Victoria; Michael; Katherine; CHRMN. & C.E.O. FISHERY PRODUCTS INTERNATIONAL LTD. since 1984; Bd. of Dirs., Royal Bank of Canada; McCain Foods; Churchill Falls (Labrador) Corporation (CFLCO); Special Asst. to Deputy-Min. Finance, Prov. Nfld. 1967; Mgmt. Analyst, Prov. Treas. Bd. 1968–69; Deputy-Secy., Treas. Bd. 1970–71; Deputy Min. (Secy.) Treas. Bd. 1972–78; Chrmn. & C.E.O., Nfld. & Labrador Hydro 1978–84; Nfld. & Labrador Fisheries Advisory Council; Bd. of Dirs., Ronald McDonald Children Charities of Canada; Past Pres., Candn. Electrical Assn.; a former Chrmn. of Adv. Bd., Sch. of Business, Memorial Univ.; Mem. of the Premier's Economic Recovery Team; Office: 70 O'Leary Ave., P.O. Box 550, St. John's, Nfld. A1C 5L1.

**YOUNG, William H.;** company executive; b. Hamilton, Ont. 21 Dec. 1918; s. James Vernon and Willmot (Holton) Y.; e. Grove Sch., Lakefield, Ont.; Hillfield Sch., Hamilton, Ont.; Royal Mil. Coll.; Univ. of Toronto; m. Joyce, d. Gordon Ferrie, 4 May 1946; children: Gordon Douglas, Catherine Frances, William James; former Chrmn. & Dir., The Hamilton Group Ltd.; Gore Mutual Insurance Company; worked in textile industry in N.C. 1946–47; joined Hamilton Cotton Co. Ltd. (predecessor firm) 1947; apptd. Gen. Works Mgr. 1951; Dir. 1954; Vice-Pres. and Gen. Mgr. 1956; Pres. 1960; served in 2nd World War with Candn. Army with rank of Maj., 1939–45; Presbyterian; recreation: golf; Clubs: Hamilton Golf & Country; Home: 159 Sulphur Springs Rd., Ancaster, Ont. L9G 4T7.

**YOUNG, William James,** M.B.A., C.A.; executive; b. Hamilton, Ont. 30 Apl. 1954; s. William Holton and Frances Joyce (Ferrie) Y.; e. Univ. of Toronto B.A. 1977; Harvard Grad. Sch. of Bus. Adm. M.B.A. 1981; PRES. HAMILTON GROUP LTD. 1986– ; Sr. Staff Acct. Clarkson & Gordon 1977–79; Chief Financial Offr. Imexa, Mexico City (subsidiary present Co.) 1981–83; Vice Pres. present Co and Chief Operating Offr. Hamilton Computer Sales and Rentals 1983–86; mem. Young Pres.' Orgn.; Home: 471 Sackville St., Toronto, Ont. M4X 1T5; Office: 5985 McLaughlin Rd., Mississauga, Ont. L5R 1B8.

**YOUNG, William James,** B.A.; company executive; b. Windsor, Ont. 10 May 1927; s. late Reginald Sebastien Fruschard and late Mary Janet (Grieves) Y.; e. Walkerville Coll., Windsor 1940–45; Univ. of Toronto, Victoria Coll. B.A. (Hons. Pol. Science and Econs., Gold Medal) 1949; m. Betty Jean, d. late Arthur Robert Davidson, 15 Sept. 1951; children: Robert Scott, Susan; Chrmn. & Dir., Regmar Estates Ltd.; Retired Dir., Exec. Vice-Pres. & C.F.O., Imperial Oil Ltd.; Dir., Interhome Energy Inc. 1982–89; with Ford of Canada 1949–53; Chrysler of Canada 1953–59; The Steel Co. of Canada 1959–61; Imperial Oil Ltd. 1961–89; author: 'The Adventures of Susan and Scott in the Wonderful Land of Piddledeepoo' (children's book); Anglican; recreations: gardening, writing; Clubs: Granite; Office: 8 Suncrest Dr., Don Mills, Ont. M3C 2L2.

**YOUNG, William Lee Jr.,** B.Sc., M.B.A., P.Eng.; business executive; b. Ankara, Turkey 25 Aug. 1954; s. William Lee and Marion Elizabeth (Peers); e. Sydney Church of England Grammar School (Australia) 1972; Queen's Univ. B.Sc. (Hons.) 1977; Harvard Univ. M.B.A. (Distinction) 1981; m. Amanda d. Bill and Thaelia Barclay 9 July 1988; PARTNER, WESTBOURNE MANAGEMENT GROUP 1988– ; Design Engineer, Imperial Oil 1977–79; Partner in European Management Consulting Practice, Bain & Co. (U.K.) 1981–88; Chief Extve. Offr., Consumers Distributing Inc. 1991– ; Bd. of Dirs., The Dellcrest Childrens Centre 1992– ; Trustee, Sedbergh School, Montebello, PQ; Gov., Shaw Festival, Niagara-on-the-Lake; Ontario Profl. Engineering Assn.; recreations: squash, sailing, skiing, pilot; clubs: Rideau, Badminton & Racquet Club of Toronto, Harvard Club of Boston, Harvard Business School Club of Toronto; Home: 143 Hillsdale Ave. E., Toronto, Ont. M4S 1T4; Office: 36 Toronto St., Suite 1100, Toronto, Ont. M5C 2C5.

**YOUNKER, J. Robert;** investment counsel; b. Harrington, P.E.I. 30 June 1936; s. James Stanley and Margaret Kathleen (Rodd) Y.; e. Prince of Wales College, Commercial Cert. 1954; completed I.D.A. courses I & II 1961–62; H & R Block Tax course 1970; Xerox Sales Course 1971; m. Gloria E. d. John Arnold Guest 14 Feb. 1959; children: Katherine E., Janice E., Beverly D.; PRESIDENT, J.R. YOUNKER & ASSOCIATES, INVESTMENT COUNSEL INC.; Advisor, T.D. Greenline Investment Accounts for Nova Scotia; joined Royal Bank of Canada 1954; Eastern Securities (later named Richardson Securities) 1958; Head, Trading Dept., Eastern Securities 1963; joined Investment Dept., Montreal Trust 1972; Asst. Mgr. 1976; Mgr., Atlantic Region 1980; Vice-Pres. & Branch Mgr., Montrusco Assoc. Inc. 1985–87; Pres., Keltic Savings Inv. Mgmnt. Div. 1987–92; won stock selection contest in 'Halifax Herald' 1989, '90; bi-monthly financial broadcast on CJCH & C100 F.M.; Contbr. editor, 'Canadian Money Saver' Magazine; Past Mem., Halifax Toastmasters Club; Past Mem. Halifax Bd. of Trade; Mem., The Atlantic Chapter of the Chartered Financial Analysts Assn.; Royal Commonwealth Soc.; Halifax Curling Club; Investment Ctte., Mount Saint Vincent Univ.; St. Georges Soc.; Maritime Commercial Travellers Assn.; Maritime Fiddlers Assn.; AIESEC Dalhousie (Bd. of Dir.); Past Mem., Neptune Theatre; Host Family Assn.; Candn. Conservatory of Music; recreations: fiddle playing, cards for money, politics, church work at St. Andrew's United, public speaking, stock market, foreign travel, good food & fine wines with candlelight, curling, golf, and his cottage; Home: P.O. Box 213149, 9 Flat Lake Dr., Tantallon, N.S. B0J 3J0; Office: CIBC Bldg., Suite M100, 1809 Barrington St., Halifax, N.S. B3J 3K8.

**YUEN, John H.Y.,** B.A., C.G.A.; company executive; b. Hong Kong 14 Sept. 1946; s. S.C. and H.S. (Chow) Y.; e. Univ. of Toronto B.A. 1971; m. Agnes d. T.Y. and Y.M. (Cheung) Chan 29 Nov. 1972; children: Stacey, Vincent; VICE-PRESIDENT & DIRECTOR, DYNAMIC FUND MANAGEMENT LTD. 1986– ; Financial Analyst, McConnell & Co. Ltd. 1971–72; Senior Manager, Bank of Montreal, Montreal & Toronto 1973–85; Secretary & Founding Dir., Ont. Business Promotion Assn. 1992; Cert. Mem., Cert. Gen. Accts. Assn. of Ont. 1978– ; Vice-Pres. & Dir., Chinese Canadian Greater Toronto P.C. Assn. 1992; recreations: reading, cooking, tea appreciation, cognac collection; Home: 56 Greylawn Cres., Scarborough, Ont. M1R 2V6; Office: 6 Adelaide St. E., 7th Floor, Toronto, Ont. M5C 1H6.

**YUILLE, John C.,** B.A., M.A., Ph.D.; university professor; b. Montreal, Que. 1 Dec. 1941; s. Simpson John and Ivy Florence (Marshall) Y.; e. Univ. of Western Ont. B.A. 1964, M.A. 1965, Ph.D. 1967; m. Judith Daylen d. Dale and Helen Johnson 18 May 1991; CHAIRMAN, FORENSIC PSYCHOLOGY PROGRAM, UNIV. OF B.C.; has conducted research on human memory for over 25 years; during the past 15 years has concentrated on the memory of victims & witnesses of crime; has provided training in interviewing and assessing children in sexual abuse cases in Australia, Canada, the U.K., and the U.S.; Office: 2136 West Mall, Vancouver, B.C. V6T 1Z4.

**YURKO, William J.,** B.Sc., P.Eng., F.C.I.C.; chemical engineer; b. Hairy Hill, Alta. 11 Feb. 1926; s. John and Helen (Hawca) Y.; e. Univ. of Alta. B.Sc. (with distinction) 1950; special summer courses; m. Mary Paul 31 May 1947; children: James, Carol, Janet, Shelley; Chrmn. & C.E.O., Alberta Oil Sands Tech. & Research Authority 1987–93, Retired; Supervisor, Atomic Energy of Canada 1950–56; Sherritt Gordon Mines 1956–60; General Electric 1960–61; Dir., Chemetals, New York 1961–65; Mgr., Bagdad Copper Corp., Arizona 1965–67; own engineering consulting practice 1967–69; Bd. Mem., UNITAR 1987– ; En-Trust 1991– ; 1st elected to Alberta legis. by-election Edmonton 1969; M.L.A. for Edmonton (Goldbar) 1969–79; Min. of Envir. (1st envir. min. in Canada) 1971–75; Min. of Housing & Public Works 1975–78; Energy Ctte., Alta. Cabinet 1971–78; M.P. for Edmonton East 1979–84; Air Force Gunner, RCAF 1944–45, 1949 (6 months); holds several patents; contributes to num. charities; recipient, several recognition awards; extensive involvement in human rights matters; author: 'Parliament and Patriation' and num. papers, reports & speeches; Address: 66 - 303 Twin Brooks Dr., Edmonton, Alta. T6J 6V3.

**YUZBASIYAN, Arto;** artist; b. Istanbul, Turkey (of Armenian parents) 28 Feb. 1948; s. Setrak and Adelina (Yavruyan) Y.; e. studied painting under tutilage of Mrs. Ojeni Telyan 1956–66; Mihitaryan H.S. 1961; Gazi Osman Pasa 1965; fine art sch. under Prof. Mustafa Plevneli 1966–68; travel & study in Eur. 1972–73; m. Veron-Annie d. Garabet and Varsenik Tavityan 20 May 1973; children: Hera, Alex; immigrated to Can. 1973 & began painting immediately; solo exhibs.: Hilda's Gall. Mississauga 1974–75; Gall. of Fine Art Thunder Bay 1976–77; Damkjar Burton Gall. Hamilton 1976; Studio Six Toronto 1977–78; Johnson Gall. Edmonton 1979; Kaspar Gall. Toronto 1980, '82, '83, '85, '90; Kastel Gall. Montreal 1980; Gall. Bernard Desroches Montreal 1987; Univ. of Toronto Erindale Campus Art Gall. 1988; many group exhibs.; Candn. Rep., Seoul Korea Internat. Watercolour Exhib. 1988, 1991; Daegu Internat. Art Bienniel Exhib. 1991; Candn. Artist, Candn. Embassy Washington; public collections: L'Institut Can. de Qué.; Biblio. Gabrielle-Roy; Tilbury Pub. Lib.; Toronto Pub. Lib.; Sunnybrook Hosp.; Univ. of Toronto; Market Gallery; & num. private & corp. collections in Germany, France, Great Britain, Australia, Turkey & U.S.A.; recreations: tennis, photography; clubs: Mayfair Racquet; Home: 50 Lowther Ave., Toronto, Ont. M5R 1C6.

# Z

**ZACHARIAH, Mathew,** Ph.D.; university professor; b. Tiruvalla, Kerala, India 24 May 1935; s. Mannilmalayil Geevarughese and Mary (Mathai) Zacharias; e. Leo XIII English H.S. 1951; Madras Christian Coll., B.A. 1956 (Elizabeth Miller Gold Medal, Eng. Scholarship); Cent. Inst. of Edn., Delhi, B.Ed. 1960 (Cent. Govt. Prize); SUNY, M.S. 1962 (Fullbright grant); Univ. of Colorado, Ph.D. 1965 (Univ. Fellow 1962–65, Phi Delta Kappa scholarship, Internat. Good Will Commendation 1965; Pacesetter Award 1965); m. Saro d. Alexander and Annamma Cherian 29 Jan. 1976; children: Miriam, Benjamin, Philip, Alexander; PROF., FAC. OF EDN., UNIV. OF CALGARY 1973– ; Asst. Master, Bishop Cotton Sch., Simla, India 1956–61 (leave 1959–60); Asst. Prof., State Univ. Coll., New Paltz, N.Y. 1965–66; Asst. Prof., Univ. of Calgary 1966–69; Assoc. Prof. 1969–73; Vis. Rsch. Fellow, Internat. Inst. for Edn. Planning, Paris 1970; Dir., Edn. Evaluation Group, Govt. of Man. 1976; Head, Dept. of Edn. Found., Univ. of Calgary 1976–79; Assoc. Dean, Fac. of Edn. 1982–83, 1993–94; worldwide lectr.; consultant/advisor on multiculturalism and global education; speaks, reads and writes Malayalam; Dir., Shastri Indo-Candn. Inst. 1982–83, 1984–86; 1992 India-Canada Assn. of Calgary Excellence in Professional/Occupational Field Award; 1990 Kappa Delta Pi Educator of the Year (Calgary Chapter) Award; 1989 Alberta Human Rights Award; Stud. Union Superior Teacher Award 1984–85; Killam Resident Fellow 1984, 1989; Annual Fellow, The Calgary Inst. for the Humanities 1981–82; Pres., Comp. & Internat. Edn. Soc. (U.S.) 1978–79; Sec. (Can.) 1967–70; author: 'Revolution Through Reform' 1986 (Indian and Spanish editions 1988, 1989); 'Education and Cultural Transformation in India' 1981; principal author: 'Science for Social Revolution?' 1994; co-ed.: 'Education and the Process of Change' 1987, and approx. 55 scholarly articles and reports mostly on international development and education; principal organizer of several conferences; editor: 'Development Education in Canada in the Eighties' 1983; various ed. pos., 'The Journal of Educational Thought' 1967–72; recreations: tennis, table-tennis; Home: 127 Valhalla Cres. N.W., Calgary, Alta. T3A 1Z7; Office: Fac. of Edn., Univ. of Calgary, Calgary, Alta. T2N 1N4.

**ZACHER, Mark William,** M.A., Ph.D.; educator; b. Boston, Mass. 4 March 1938; s. Frank Xavier and Ruth (Brunnquell) Z.; e. Yale Univ. B.A. 1961; Columbia Univ. M.A. 1963, Ph.D. 1966; m. Carol d. Lloyd and Marjorie Lux 29 Dec. 1962; children: Glenn, Nicole; PROF. OF POL. SCI. UNIV. OF B.C. 1980– , Dir. Inst. Internat. Relations 1971–92; Asst. Prof. present Univ. 1965, Assoc. Prof. 1969–80; recipient Am. Soc. Internat. Law Prize Best Book 1980; Internat. Studies Assn. Prize Best Book Internat. Environmental Issues 1981; Columbia Univ. Prize Best Book Pol. Econ. 1987; author 'Dag Hammarskjold's United Nations' 1970; 'International Conflicts and Collective Security 1946–1947' 1977; co-author 'Pollution, Politics and International Law: Tankers At Sea' 1979; 'Managing International Markets: Developing Countries and the Commodity Trade Regime' 1988; co-ed. 'Conflict and Stability in Southeast Asia' 1974; 'Canadian Foreign Policy and the Law of the Sea' 1977; 'Canadian Foreign Policy and International Economic Regimes' 1992; 'The International Political Economy of Natural Resources' 1992; Ed. Bd. Internat. Orgn.; Fellow, Royal Soc. of Canada; recreations: tennis, skiing; Club: Arbutus; Home: 1721 West 68th Ave., Vancouver, B.C. V6P 2Y9; Office: Vancouver, B.C. V6T 1W5.

**ZACK, Badanna,** B.A., M.F.A., R.C.A.; sculptor; b. Montreal, Que. 22 March 1933; e. Concordia Univ. B.A. 1964; Rutgers Univ. M.F.A. 1967; architectural draughting 1953–62, 1967–68; teaching asst., Rutgers Univ. 1966–67; taught sculpture and associated subjects in the following Ont. Insts.: Georgian Coll., Humber Coll., The Art Gallery of Ont., Guelph Univ. etc. 1969–85; teaching sculpture at Sheridan Coll. Oakville, Ont. since 1980; selected group exhn.: New Jersey Artists, New Jersey State Museum, Trenton N.J. 1967; Art Femme, Montreal, Que. sculpture 1975; Festival of Women in The Arts, Harbourfront Art Gallery Toronto, Ont. sculpture 1975; Rehearsal, Harbourfront Art Gallery Toronto, sculpture 1977; Performance, Harbourfront Art Gallery Toronto, Ont. sculpture 1978; Reflecting a Rural Consciousness, organized by Artspace, Travelling Exhn. Peterborough, Ont. Sudbury, Ont., Toronto, Ont., Rochester, N.Y., Buffalo, N.Y., Paris France, sculpture 1978–80; Toronto International Art Fair, Toronto 1981; Juxtaposition Powerhouse, Montreal, Que. sculpture 1982; Woodstock Livestock, Woodstock, Ont. sculpture 1985; 18th Sculpture Biennial Antwerp Belgium 1985; 12th International Biennial of Tapestry Lausanne, Switzerland 1985; The Perfect Fit, Gairloch Gardens, Oakville, Ont., site specific sculpture 1988; 'Archaeology I' Workscene Gall., Toronto, Ont. 1990; Selected solo Exhns: Thesis exhn. Rutgers Univ. New Brunswick, New Jersey, sculpture, drawings, and prints; Gallery O, Toronto, sculpture 1973; Gallery O, Toronto, sculpture 1975; Burnaby Art Gallery, Burnaby. B.C. sculpture 1977; Gallery O, Toronto, sculpture 1978; The Horse Show, Factory 77, Toronto, sculpture 1981; Autoparts, · Studio Gallery Nine, Toronto, sculpture 1982; From Horse to Horsepower, The Art Gallery of Hamilton, Hamilton, Ont. sculpture 1983–84; Home Sweet Home, Sculpture installation 1985–86, Toronto, Ont.; Travelling Exhbn., Lynnwood Arts Centre, Simcoe Ont.; Kitchener/Waterloo Art Gall.; Oakville Centennial Art Gall.; Tom Thomson Gall., Owen Sound; Lynnwood Arts Centre, Simcoe, Ont. 1990; 'Homage to My Grandfather' Justina Barnick Gall., Univ. of Toronto 1991; 'Homage to My Grandfather' Art Gall. of Algoma, Sault Ste. Marie, Ont. 1991; collections: Douglass Coll, New Brunswick, New Jersey; Rutgers Univ., New Brunswick, New Jersey; Concordia Univ. Montreal, Que.; Art Gallery of Hamilton, Hamilton, Ont.; numerous private collections; publications: Eclectic Eve 1975; Artmagazine (Dec.-Jan.) Canadian Dimension Women Artists' Newsletter 1976; Artnews (Oct.), Artmagazine (June), Toronto Life (Nov.) 1978; Artmagazine (Sept.-Oct.) 1981; Artmagazine (Dec./82, Jan.-Feb./83) 1982; Sculpture Textile (12th International Biennale De La Tapisserie Lausanne 1985) catalogue 1985; Middelheim Automobiennale 18, catalogue 1985; Vie des Arts (Sept.) 1985; Tippett, Maria 'By A Lady' 1992; awards: Canada Council, 1968–69, 1974–75, 1978 & 1985; Ontario Arts Council 1975–85; el. to R.C.A. 1978; rep. in exhns. Can., USA and Europe; Studio and Residence: 83 Elm Grove Ave., Toronto, Ont. M6K 2J2.

**ZAGWŸN, Deborah Turney;** writer; illustrator; painter; b. Cornwall, Ont. 14 Aug. 1953; d. Eugene and Shirley Joan (Johnston) Turney; m. Leo s. Koos and Jakomina Zagwÿn 18 March 1978; children: Sonia Jessica, Graham Lee; toured B.C. craft fair circuit handwoven, hand dyed tapestries 1975–79; five mega-murals comnd. Fraser Valley and Cariboo Region, B.C. 1979–81; four gallery exhns. watercolours, soft-sculpture Seattle 1982–86; two gallery exhns. Harrison Hot Springs book illus. 1987–88, Prince George (B.C.) Art Gallery and Chilliwack (B.C.) exhns. 1989; Maple Ridge Gallery exhn. 1991; finalist Emilia Frances Howard Gibbon Medal Children's book illus. 1986; finalist B.C. Book Awards, Sheila Egoff Children's Prize 1989; illus. 'A

Winter's Yarn' 1986; author-illus. 'Mood Pocket, Mud Bucket' 1988; 'The Pumpkin Blanket' 1990; 'Long Nellie' 1993; mem. CANSCAIP; Candn. Children's Book Centre; Fedn. B.C. Writers; W. Can. Wilderness Cttee.; Children's Lit. Round Table; Writers Union; recreations: cross-country skiing, bicycling, aerobics, reading, gardening, dancing, writing, knitting; Address: P.O. Box 472 Harrison Hot Springs, B.C. V0M 1K0.

**ZAHIR, Muhammad,** M.D., D.Phil., F.R.C.P.(C); pathologist; b. Ludhiana, India 27 Nov. 1936; s. Amin and Haleema (Begum) Z.; e. Univ. of Punjab M.D. 1958; Oxford Univ. (Rhodes Scholar) D.Phil. 1964; m. Maureen Malcouronne 28 Nov. 1964; children: Sara, David, Suzanna; PATHOLOGIST, ROYAL INLAND HOSPITAL 1974– ; Pathol. Radcliffe Infirmary Oxford 1963–65; Asst. Prof. of Pathol. Univ. of Md. Baltimore 1966–72; Pathol., Regional Lab. Moncton, N.B. 1972–74; recreations: tennis, skiing, squash; Home: 2049 Steeple Court, Kamloops, B.C. V2E 2M2; Office: 311 Columbia St., Kamloops, B.C. V2C 2T1.

**ZAID, Frank,** B.A.Sc., LL.B.; lawyer; b. Toronto, Ont. 7 Jan. 1946; s. Irving Oscar and Ruth (Rother) Zaid; e. Univ. of Toronto, B.A.Sc. (Chem. Eng.) 1968; Osgoode Hall Law Sch. York Univ., LL.B. (Hons.) 1971; m. Linda Lester; children: Irwin Michael, Jonathan Robert; PARTNER, OSLER, HOSKIN & HARCOURT 1977– ; called to Bar of Ont. 1973; Assoc. present firm 1973–77; Dir., Alpine Electronics of Canada, Inc.; Norrell Services Inc.; Wee Watch Day Care Systems Inc.; Subway Franchise Systems of Canada, Ltd.; Rent-A-Centre Canada Inc.; Armstrong Medical Industries of Canada Inc.; Revlon Canada Inc.; Noritake Canada Ltd.; Choice Hotels Canada Inc.; past special lectr. Univ. of Windsor and Osgoode Hall Law Sch.; past Lectr. in Trade Practices Ont. Bar Admission Course; General Counsel, Candn. Franchise Assn.; mng. ed. Candn. Franchise Guide; numerous articles and papers franchising, intellectual property & competition law; Candn. contbr. Am. Bar Assn. Compendium Foreign Franchise Laws; mem. various ed. bds.; mem. Oakdale Golf & Country Club; Candn., Am. and Internat. Bar Assns.; Candn. Franchise Assn.; recreations: golf, skiing; Office: P.O. Box 50, First Canadian Place, Toronto, Ont. M5X 1B8.

**ZAITSOFF, Ivan M.,** B.Comm., C.A.; financial executive; b. Saskatoon, Sask. 31 Oct. 1943; e. Univ. of Saskatchewan B.Comm. 1967; COMPTROLLER AND TREASURER, SYNCRUDE CANADA LTD. 1993– ; Accounting, Peat Marwick & Mitchell 1968–75; Staff Acctnt., Syncrude Canada Ltd. 1975–79; Supervisor, Acctg. Div. 1977–78; Fin. Acctg. 1978; Mgr. 1978–81; Asst. Compt. 1981–86; Treas. 1986–90; Compt. 1990–93; Former Bd. Dir., Fort McMurray Family YMCA; Keyano College Found.; Office: Mail Drop 2800, Bag 4023, Fort McMurray, Alta. T9H 3H5.

**ZAKAIB, Lorne John,** B.Eng.; industrial executive; b. Montreal, Que. 11 June 1932; s. Jesse Charles and Rea Yvonne (Brodeur) Z.; e. McGill Univ. B.Eng. 1956, Dip.Bus. 1974; m. Viola d. Louis Kouri 3 Sept. 1961; children: Janice, Jay; EXTVE. VICE-PRES. & CHIEF OPERATING OFFR., CIRCO CRAFT CO.; Operation Mgr., Marine & Land Communications then Program Mgr., FIIID Navigation Systems, Canadian Marconi 1956–73; Site Manager, Bromont Facility, I.B.M. Canada 1973–89; Extve. Vice-Pres., SNC-Lavalin Group and Pres. & Chief Operating Offr., SNC Industrial Technologies Inc. 1990 and its division Simunition TM; Mem., I.E.E.E.; Montreal C. of C.; Order of Engineers; Speaker (Total Quality); I.B.M. President's Award 1984; 'Nouveau Performant' 1986; 3 'Mercuriades' awards; Past Pres., Montreal Assn. for the Mentally Retarded; recreations: squash, tennis, swimming; Home: 421 St-Thomas Cr., St-Lambert, Que. J4R 1Y3; Office: 5 Montée des Arsenaux, Le Gardeur, Que. J5Z 2P4.

**ZALDIN, Arthur H.,** Q.C., LL.B.; lawyer; b. Toronto, Ont. 24 Dec. 1916; s. Nathan and Minnie (Sher) Z.; e. Jarvis C.I. (Hons.) 1936; Univ. of Toronto, Osgoode Hall Law Sch. LL.B. (Hons.) 1940; m. Estelle d. Joseph and Ethel Caplan 3 Dec. 1946; children: Joan (Shapero), Josie (Arbel); LAWYER, ZALDIN AND FINE; served in World War II as Infantry Officer, Captain & Adjutant; Dir., Mem. & Sec. of Audit Cttee., Dylex Limited; Mem., Beth Sholom Synagogue; Home: 625 Avenue Road, #403, Toronto, Ont. M4V 2K7; Office: 111 Richmond St. W., #1012, Toronto, Ont. M5H 2G4.

**ZALESKI, Andrew B.;** business executive; b. Warsaw, Poland 20 Dec. 1938; s. Eligiusz Stanislaw and Joan (Bednarczyk) Z.; e. Sr. Comm. High Sch. and one yr. of Econ. Buenos Aires, Argentina; m. Ursula Maria d. Stefan and Barbara Falkowski 20 Sept. 1961; children: Bohdan, Tamara, Renata; PRESIDENT, TRIMAC TRANSPORTATION SYSTEMS LTD. 1983– ; Acct. Canadian Admiral Corp. Ltd. Port Credit, Ont. 1958, Office Mgr. W. Div. 1962, E.Div. 1963, Gen. Office Mgr. H.O. 1965, Mgr. Mktg. Adm. 1968, Mgr. Br. Operations 1972–73; Asst. Gen. Mgr. Beach Foundry Ottawa, Ont. 1973 (subsidiary of Admiral and subsequently Rockwell Internat.); Gen. Mgr. Beach Appliances (subsidiary of Rockwell International) Ottawa Ont. 1975–78; Pres. White Farm Equipment Canada 1978–82; Vice Pres. and Gen. Mgr. present Co. 1982–83; Home: #2, 3315 Rideau Place S.W., Calgary, Alta. T2S 2T1; Office: 2100, 800 - 5th Ave. S.W., Calgary, Alta. T2P 2P9.

**ZALZAL, Samir Jamil,** B.Sc., P.Eng.; business executive; b. Alexandria, Egypt 28 Sept. 1932; s. Jamil Alexander and Rose (Ackawi) Z.; e. Victoria Coll. (Egypt), Oxford & Cambridge Sch. cert. 1950; Alexandria Univ. B.Sc. 1955; m. Rosette d. Anthony and Saada Farrah 7 Dec. 1958; children: Nayla, Hana, Paul; PRES. & C.E.O., INGERSOLL-RAND CANADA INC. 1992– ; worked for Egyptian govt. 10 years; emigrated to Canada 1966; Tool Group Sales Engr., present firm Montreal, 1967; Tool Group Mgr., E. Reg. 1969–70; Central Reg. Mgr., Tool Group 1970–71; Gen. Mgr. 1971–77; Vice-Pres., Mktg. 1977–92; also resp. for Construc. & Mining Groups 1984; Mem., Assn. of Profl. Engrs.; Candn. Soc. of Profl. Engrs.; Am. Inst. of Plant Engrs.; Mem. Bd. of Dirs., Machinery Equipment Manufacturers Assn. of Can. (MEMAC); Candn. Manufacturers Assn. (Ont.); Pres., Egypt-Can. Bus. Counc.; Canada-Arab Bus. Counc.; recreations: golf; clubs: Donalda Golf, The Fitness Inst.; Home: 43 Haviland Dr., West Hill, Ont. M1C 2T6; Office: 2360 Millrace Court, Mississauga, Ont. L5N 1W2.

**ZAMEL, Noe,** M.D., F.R.C.P.(C); professor of medicine; b. Rio Grande, RS, Brazil 2 April 1935; s. Israel and Blima (Gruszkowsky) Z.; e. Federal Univ. of Rio Grande do Sul Brazil M.D. 1958; m. Regina d. Jacob and Teresa Bekerman 12 Sept. 1959; children: Denis, Andre, Ricardo; DIR., TRIHOSPITAL PULMONARY FUNCTION LABORATORIES, UNIV. OF TORONTO 1972– ; training in pulmonary physiology, Univ. of London, Inst. of Diseases of the Chest, England and Univ. of Calif. at San Francisco, Cardiovascular Rsch. Inst., U.S.A.; Dir., Pulmonary Functions Labs., Univ. of Nebraska 1970–72; present research: smoking, asthma, genetics; Hon. Citizen of Nebraska; Hon. Prof., Fed. Univ. of Rio Grade do Sul; listed in Am. Men & Women of Science; Mem., Am. Physiological Soc.; Am. Thoracic Soc.; Am. Coll. of Chest Physicians; Eur. Respiratory Soc.; Candn. Thoracic Soc.; Candn. Soc. for Clin. Investigation; author of approx. 150 pubns. incl. original rsch. & book chaps. on respiratory diseases; Home: 252 Otonabee Ave., Willowdale, Ont. M2M 2T1; Office: Mt. Sinai Hosp., Rm. 656, 600 University Ave., Toronto, Ont. M5G 1X5.

**ZANN, Lenore E.;** actress/singer/writer; b. Sydney, Australia 22 Nov. 1959; d. Vincent Paul and Janice Rose (Marshall) Z.; e. Cobequid Edn. Ctr. H.S. (Hons.) 1977; York Univ. Theatre Prog. 1978, 1979; m. Ralph Dillon s. Jean and Archie Kerr 26 July 1987; estab. career in 1980 in 'Hey Marilyné'; num. feature films (worldwide) incl. 'Visiting Hours,' 'Def. Con. Four,' 'The Hounds of Notre Dame,' and 'Down Home'; num. stageplays across Can. (mus. & dramas); also played Gittel in 'Two for the See-Saw' (U.K. & Sweden); performed on Rita MacNeil's Gold Album 1988 and various live singing performances; ACTRA radio drama award for Best Actress 1986 for role of Mary Snow in 'Salt Water Moon'; Pantheist; Mem., Performing Artists for Nuclear Disarmament; recreations: music, poetry, art, dance, travel (this world & others), philosophy, quantum physics, psychic phenomena, living Zen Buddhism, life to the fullest; currently writing autobiography.

**ZAOZIRNY, John Brian,** B.Com., LL.B., LL.M., Q.C.; lawyer; b. Calgary, Alta. 26 June 1947; s. John Matthew and Katherine (Nykolychuk) Z.; e. Univ. of Calgary, B.Com. 1969; Univ. of B.C., LL.B. 1972; London Sch. of Econ., LL.M. 1973; m. Elizabeth d. Jack and Bette Marett 20 Apl. 1974; children: John Matthew, Stephen Michael, Andrew Marett; COUNSEL, McCARTHY TÉTRAULT, Vancouver, B.C. and Calgary, Alta. 1987– ; Dir., Alberta Newsprint Co. Ltd.; Alta. Stock Exchange; Anderson Consulting; Barclay's Bank of Canada; Conoco Canada Ltd.; Descon Group; EnServ Corp.; Fording Coal Ltd.; Great Candn. Railtour Co.; Industra Service Corp.; Ipsco Inc.; Mark Resources Inc.; Methanex; Monarch Communications Ltd.; Morrison Middlefield Resources Ltd.; Osprey Energy Inc.; Oxford Properties Canada Ltd.; Pengrowth Gas Corporation; Peters & Co. Ltd.; Standard Life; Trans Mountain Pipe Line Co. Ltd.; UMA Group Ltd.; Vencap Equities Alberta Ltd.; called to Bar of Alta. 1974 and to Bar of B.C. 1986; cr. Q.C. 1984; law practice Gill Cook, later Mason & Co.; estbd. own law firm with John Manolescu, Q.C. 1977; el. M.L.A. Alta. 1979, apptd. Min. of Energy & Natural Resources 1982; named Resource Man of the Year, Alta. Chamb. of Resources 1985; Hon. Chrmn., Alumni Fund Campaign, Univ. of Calgary 1987; rec'd Distinguished Alumni Award, Univ. of Calgary 1987; mem. Candn. Bar Assn.; recreations: skiing, sailing, golfing; Clubs: Calgary Golf & Country; Glencoe (Calgary); Arbutus; Vancouver; Shaughnessy Golf & Country (Vancouver); Home: 4550 Bellevue Dr., Vancouver, B.C. V6R 1E5 and 1906, 1200 - 6 St. S.W., Calgary, Alta. T2R 1H3; Offices: 1300, 777 Dunsmuir St., Vancouver, B.C. V7Y 1K2 and 421 – 7th Ave., Calgary, Alta. T2P 4K9.

**ZARITSKY, John Norman,** B.A.; film producer; director; b. St. Catharines, Ont. 13 July 1943; s. Dr. Michael and Yvonne Joan (White) Z.; e. Denis Morris High Sch. St. Catharines; Univ. of Toronto Trinity Coll. B.A. 1965; m. Virginia d. Jerry and Agnes Storring 24 Dec. 1979; PRES. K.A. PRODUCTIONS INC. 1983– ; Police Reporter 'Hamilton Spectator' 1966; Art Critic 'Kitchener-Waterloo Record' 1967; Pol. Reporter 'Toronto Star' 1968–69; Fellow, Wash. Journalism Center 1970; Investig. Reporter 'The Globe and Mail' 1971–72; Ed. Agence-France Presse Paris 1973; TV Producer-Dir. CBC 'Fifth Estate' 1975–81; independent documentary filmmaker since 1981; recipient Nat. Newspaper Award Spot News 1972; Ohio State Univ. Award of Merit 1981; Acad. Award Best Feature-Length Documentary 1983; ACE Award Acad. Cable Broadcasting 1986; Golden Gavel Award, Am. Bar Assn. 1989; Award of Merit, Robert F. Kennedy Foundation 1991; mem. Acad. Candn. Cinema; recreations: fishing, sailing; Address: 49 Cavell Ave., Toronto, Ont. M4J 1H5.

**ZARUBY, Walter Stephen,** B.A.Sc.; industrialist; b. Vegreville, Alta. 4 March 1930; e. Univ. of Toronto, B.A.Sc. (Engn. and Business) 1952; m. Beth Fargey; children: Stephen, Jeffrey; Pres., Radium Resources Ltd. 1977; Zaruby & Associates Inc.; Industrial Minerals Recovery Inc.; joined The Shell Oil Co. Ltd., various engn. and field operating assignments, Can. and U.S. 1952–65; organized offshore drilling programs, W. and E. Coast Can., Shell Canada Ltd. 1965; Offshore Project Mgr., W. Coast Drilling Program, Shell Canada Ltd. 1967; Offshore Devel. Mgr. 1969; Sr. Vice Pres., Drilling, Westburne International Industries Ltd. 1970, Pres., 1973–76; Pres., Radium Holdings Ltd. 1976–87; Clubs: Calgary Golf & Country; Calgary Petroleum; Glencoe; Home: 1012 Bel-Aire Drive S.W., Calgary, Alta. T2V 2B9.

**ZASLOW, Morris,** Ph.D.; educator; b. Rosthern, Sask. 22 Dec. 1918; s. Isaac and Bessie (Hardin) Z.; e. Edmonton schs., Univ. of Alta., B.A. 1940, B.Ed. 1942; Univ. of Toronto, M.A. 1948, Ph.D. 1957; m. Betty, d. Robert J. Stone, Devon, Eng., 3 Oct. 1945; one s. Jonathan; EMERITUS PROF. OF HIST., UNIV. OF WESTERN ONTARIO, 1984– ; High School Teacher in Alta., 1941–42, 1946–47; Lecturer, Assist. Prof., Assoc. Prof. and Prof., Carleton Univ. 1950–52; Univ. of Toronto 1952–65; Univ. of W. Ont. 1965–84; Visiting Prof., Univ. of Calgary, 1976–77 and 1979–80; author, 'The Opening of the Canadian North 1870–1914' 1971; 'Reading the Rocks: The Story of the Geological Survey of Canada 1842–1972' 1975; 'The Northwest Territories 1905–1980' 1984; 'The Northward Expansion of Canada 1914–1967' 1988; numerous articles mainly upon aspects of Canada's Northern dev.; Ed., 'The Defended Border: Upper Canada and the War of 1812' 1964; 'A Century of Canada's Arctic Islands 1880–1980' 1981; 'Ontario History' 1956–62; 'Issues in Canadian History'; Gen. Ed., Champlain Soc., 1961–71; Adv. Ed., 'Encyclopedia Americana'; awarded Nuffield Foundation Travelling Fellowship in Humanities 1960–61; Killam Sr. Research Fellowships 1973–74 and 1983–84; Canada Confederation, Cruikshank, and Roy. Soc. of Can. Centenary Medals; 'For Purposes of Dominion: Essays in Honour of Morris Zaslow' eds., K.S. Coates and W.R. Morrison 1989; Member Hist. Advisory Committee, Metrop. Toronto and Region Conservation Authority 1958–65; Pres., Ont. Hist. Soc. 1966–67; Hon. Vice-Pres., Champlain Soc.; Fellow, Roy. Soc. of Can.; Chrmn. and organizer of its symposium 'A Century of Canada's Arctic Islands 1880–1980'; Arctic Inst. of North Am.; Hebrew; recreations: stamp collecting; travel; Home: 838 Waterloo St., London, Ont. N6A 3W6.

**ZAYID, Ismail,** M.B., B.S., F.R.C.Path., F.R.C.P.(C); pathologist; b. Beit Nuba, Palestine, 14 March 1933; s. Ibrahim and Othmaneh (Hilweh) Z.; e. Guy's Hosp. Med. Sch., London, M.B., B.S. 1958; Main Hosp., Amman, Jordan; Royal Postgrad. Med. Sch., London 1961–66; m. Greta d. Ernest and Ruby Herbert 20 Aug. 1960; children: Caroline, Dina, Jane, Samira, Omar; PROF. OF PATH., DALHOUSIE UNIV. 1980– and DIR. OF ANAT. PATH., VICTORIA GEN. HOSP. 1985– ; Dir., Dept. of Path., Main Hosp., Amman 1966–69 and 1971–72; Lectr., Royal Postgrad. Med. Sch. and Hon. Cons. Path., Hammersmith Hosp., London 1971–72; Assoc. Prof., Dalhousie Univ. 1972–80; Asst. Path., Victoria Gen. Hosp. 1972–74; Assoc. Path. 1974–85; Dir. of Surg. Path. 1976– ; mem. Gyn. Tumour Panel, mem. Breast Tumour Panel and Dir., Candn. Ref. Centre for Cancer Path.; Ref. Path., Breast Cancer Screening Study, Nat. Cancer Inst. of Can. 1986–90; Pres., Path. Sect., Med. Soc. of N.S. 1980–81; Founding Mem., Internat. Gyn. Cancer Soc.; mem., Internat. Acad. of Path.; Mem., Founding Counc., Univ. of Jordan 1971–72; Pres., Can. Palestine Assn.; Pres., Arab Candn. Assn. of the Atlantic Provs.; Dir. Near East Cultural and Educ. Found., Canada; Muslim; author and co-author of num. publs. and presentations on path. disorders, infertility, the contraceptive pill, breast cancer, fibromatosis, and other topics; first to describe 'Familial Histiocytic Dermatoarthritis' (Zayid-Farraj Syndrome); author: 'Palestine: A Stolen Heritage' 1974; 'Zionism: The Myth and the Reality' 1980; recreations: squash, bridge, reading; Home: 531 Young Ave., Halifax, N.S. B3H 2V4; Office: 1278 Tower Road, Halifax, N.S. B3H 2Y9.

**ZEIDLER, Eberhard Heinrich,** O.C., O.Ont., Dipl. Ing., LL.D., D.Eng., D.Arch., F.R.A.I.C., R.C.A., O.A.A., O.A.Q., Hon. F.A.I.A.; b. Germany; e. Weimar during Bauhaus revival post 1945; Univ. Karlsruhe, summa cum laude 1949; m. Phyllis Jane, d. Robert Abbott, 26 Jan. 1957; children: Margaret, Robert, Kate, Christina; SENIOR PARTNER, ZEIDLER ROBERTS PARTNERSHIP/ARCHITECTS (formerly Craig Zeidler Strong); Since 1951 has been responsible for the design devel. of all projects of firm; Lectr. in Arch., Univ. of Toronto 1953–55; mem. City of Toronto Planning Bd., 1972–75; Dir., Harbourfront Corp., 1978–79; Comte. mem., Candn. Inst. for Advanced Research; Adjunct Prof., Univ. of Toronto 1983– ; some major projects: Ontario Place, Toronto; McMaster Univ. Health Sciences Centre, Hamilton (called obsolescence-proof by 1969 World Hosp. Congress); Detroit Gen. Hosp. & Wayne State Univ. Clinic; Toronto Eaton Centre; Walter C. Mackenzie Health Sciences Centre, Univ. of Alta., Edmonton; Queen's Quay Terminal, Toronto; Yerba Buena Gardens, San Francisco; Canada Place, Vancouver; The Mall, Kuala Lumpur; The Hospital for Sick Children - New Patient Tower, Toronto; Liberty Place - Phase II, Philadelphia; Ontario Pavilion - Expo '86, Vancouver; Candn. Red Cross Soc. National Office, Ottawa; Ottawa Civic Hosp.; MediaPark, Cologne; Cinedom, Cologne; Place Montréal Trust, Montréal; Raymond F. Kravis Center for the Performing Arts, West Palm Beach, Fla.; Pacific Centre, Vancouver; The Gallery at Harborplace, Baltimore; Ont. Cancer Inst./Princess Margaret Hospital, Toronto; Toronto World Trade Centre; North York Performing Arts Centre; Portcullis, London, England; Univ. of Maryland Medical System – Homer Gudelsky Inpatient Bldg., Baltimore; Columbus Center for Marine Research and Exploration, Baltimore; over 80 nat. and internat. awards incl.: Hon. Fellow, Amer. Inst. of Architects 1981; Hon. LL.D., McMaster Univ., Hamilton 1982; Officer, Order of Canada 1984; Royal Arch. Inst. of Canada Gold Medal 1986; D.Eng. (hon. causa) Tech. Univ. of N.S., 1987; Lifetime Achievement Award, Toronto Arts Awards Found. 1987; Order of Ont. 1989; Doctorate of Architecture (hon. causa), Univ. of Toronto 1989; Fellow, Ont. College of Art 1992; Hon. LL.D. York Univ. 1992; awarded Commemorative Medal for 125th Anniversary of Candn. Confederation 1992; Massey Medals and mentioned for outstanding Candn. arch.; Nat. Design Awards 1962, 67, 72; O.M.R. Council Design Awards 1964, 65, 66, 68, 70, 71, 73; Award of Excellence, The Canadian Architect 1969, 70, 71, 74, 75, 86, 88, 91; Eedee Award 1971; Prestressed Concrete Inst. Award 1970; Progressive Arch. Design Award 1972; Am. Iron & Steel Inst. Award 1973; Am. Soc. of Interior Designers (ASID) Internat. Design Award 1975; Am. Soc. of Landscape Architects (ASLA) Internat. Design Award 1975; Ont. Assoc. of Architects, Design Excellence Award, 1976, 1989; l'Ordre des Architectes du Québec 1978; Engineering Soc. of N.Y., Outstanding Achievement Award, 1980; Urban Design Award 1978; Detroit Chapter AIA, Honor Award, 1979; AIA Honor Award, 1980; Urban Design Awards for Excellence, 1980; Governor General's Medals 1982, 86; Urban Land Inst. Award 1983; Builder's Choice Design and Planning Award 1984; Concrete Building Awards, Award of Merit 1984; Commonwealth Association of Architects Award 1985; Credit Foncier Award 1985; Governor General's Cert. of Merit 1986; Modern Healthcare Design Awards (Citation 1986); Excellence on the Waterfront Honor Award 1988, 1989; OAA Design Excellence Award 1989; Am. Concrete Inst. Award 1988, 1989; Internat. Council of Shopping Centres Award 1988, 90; Engineering Award 1990; Arch. Precast Assn. Award 1991; Concrete Constrn. Comte. of Philadelphia Award 1991; Nat. Symposium on Healthcare Design Award 1991; Precast/Prestressed Concrete Inst. Hon. Ment.*1991; Toronto Historical Board Commendation 1991; City of Toronto Urban Design Award 1992; Assn. of Interior Designers of Ont. Award 1992, Ont. Steel Design Award 1992, City of Etobicoke Urban Design Award (Hon. Mention) 1992, Precast/Prestressed Concrete Institute Design Award 1992, 1993; 'Eberhard Zeidler: In Search of Human Space' (Ernst & Sohn 1992) by Christian Thomsen analyses life work; over 350 major articles on work of firm published in leading prof. mags. incl. Domus, Bauen + Wohnen, L'Architecture d'Aujourd'hui, Candn. and Am. journs.; author of 'Healing the Hospital' and 'Multi-Use Architecture in the Urban Context'; served on juries for Candn. Arch. Yearbook Awards 1967; O.M.R. Design Awards 1973; 22nd Progressive Arch. Awards Program 1974; Minnesota Society AIA, Awards Program, 1980; Ohio Chapter AIA Awards Program, 1980; Louis Sullivan Award 1981; Governor General's Medal 1983; Royal Arch. Inst. of Canada National Awards Comte. 1988–90; Canada Council Prix de Rome 1989; has been Guest Lecturer, Nihon Univ. (Japan); Cornell, U.C.L.A.; Univ. of Munich; Columbia Univ.; Univ. of Hanover and others; Clubs: Osler Bluff Ski Club; R.C.Y.C., Toronto; Office: 315 Queen St. W., Toronto, Ont. M5V 2X2.

**ZEIGLER, Earle Frederick,** M.A., Ph.D., LL.D. (Windsor); educator; b. New York, N.Y. 20 August 1919; s. Clarence M. Shinkle and Margaret C. (Beyerkohler) Z.; e. Bates Coll., B.A. (German) 1940; Arnold Coll., Minor Phys. Educ. 1944; Yale Univ. M.A. (German) 1944; Columbia Univ., Grad. Minor Health & Phys. Educ. 1946; Yale Univ., Ph.D. (Educ.) 1951; Univ. of Windsor, Hon. LL.D. 1975; m. Bertha M;, d. Hazen R. Bell 25 June 1941; children: Donald Hazen, Barbara Ann; PROF. EMERITUS, FACULTY OF KINESIOLOGY, UNIV. OF WESTERN ONT. since 1989; Assoc. Phys. and Aquatic Dir., YMCA, Bridgeport, Conn. 1941; Instr. in German, Univ. of Conn. 1943–47, in Phys. Educ. and Coach, Yale Univ. 1943–49; joined present Univ. as Asst. Prof. in Phys., Health & Recreation Educ. and Lectr. in German 1949 (Prof. and Head Dept. Phys., Health & Recreation Educ. 1950–56); Assoc. Prof. of Sch. of Educ. and Supvr. Phys. Educ. & Athletics, Univ. of Mich. 1956–63 (Chrmn. Dept. Phys. Educ. in Sch. of Educ. 1961–63); Prof., Dept. Phys. Educ. for Men, Coll. Phys. Educ., Univ. of Ill. 1963–72 (Head Dept. 1964–68); re-joined present Univ. as Prof., Phys. Educ. 1971 (Dean of Faculty, 1972–77); Fellow, Am. Acad. Phys. Educ. (Pres. 1981–82); Philos. Educ. Soc.; Hon. Fellow, Soc. Mun. Recreational Dirs. Ont.; Am. All. for Health, Phys. Educ., Recreation & Dance; Am. Philos. Assn.; Philos. Soc. for Study of Sport (Pres., 1974); Candn. Assn. Health, Phys. Educ. & Recreation (Vice-Pres. 1955–56, 1983–85); Ont. Recreation Assn. (Vice-Pres., 1955–56); North Am. Soc. for Sport Mgmt. (Past Pres. 1986–87); author of 'Administration of Physical Education and Athletics' 1959; 'Philosophical Foundations for Physical, Health, and Recreation Education' 1964; 'Physical Education: Progressivism or Essentialism?' (with H.J. VanderZwaag) 1966; 'Problems in the History and Philosophy of Physical Education and Sport' 1968; 'Research in the History, Philosophy and Comparative Aspects of Physical Education and Sport' (with Howell and Trekell) 1971; 'A History of Sport and Physical Education to 1900' (ed. & author) 1973; 'Administrative Theory and Practice in Physical Education and Athletics' (with M.J. Spaeth) 1975; 'A History of Physical Education and Sport in the United States and Canada' (ed. & author) 1975; 'Professing Physical Education and Sport Philosophy' 1975; 'Physical Education and Sport Philosophy' 1977; 'A History of Physical Education and Sport' (ed. & author) 1979; 'Issues in North American Sport and Physical Education' 1979; 'Decision-Making in Physical Education and Athletics Administration' 1982; 'Physical Education and Sport: An Introduction' (ed. & author) 1982; 'Management Competency Development in Sport and Physical Education' (with Gary Bowie) 1983; 'Ethics and Morality in Sport and Physical Education' 1984; 'Strategic Market Planning: An Aid to the Evaluation of an Athletic/Recreation Program' (with J. Campbell) 1984; 'Assessing Sport and Physical Education: Diagnosis and Projection' 1986; 'History of Physical Education and Sport' 1988 (ed. & author); 'Change Process in Sport and Physical Education Management' 1988 (with Mikalachki and Leyshon); 'Competency Development in Sport and Physical Education Management: A Primer' 1988 (with Bowie and Paris); 'Introduction to Sport and Physical Education Philosophy' 1989; 'Sport and Physical Education: Past, Present, Future' 1990; 'Applied Ethics for Sport Managers' 1992; also over 425 articles in prof. journs., mags. and newspapers; Hon. Award Soc. Municipal Recreation Directors of Ont., 1956; Hon. Award, Candn. Assn. for Health, Phys. Educ. & Rec. 1975; Scholar-of-the-Year, Am. Alliance for Health, Phys. Educ. & Rec., 1978; Distinguished Service Award from Int'l Relations Council of Am. Alliance for Health, Phys. Ed., and Recreation, 1979; Lansdowne Visiting Scholar, Univ. of Victoria, B.C. 1980; Hon. Award, Am. Alliance for Health, Phys. Ed., Recreation & Dance, 1981; Fellow Award, Candn. Assn. for Health, Phys. Educ. & Rec., 1986; Special Presidential Citation for Health, Phys. Educ. & Rec., 1986; Outstanding Teacher Award., Phys. Educ. Student Counc., Univ. of Western Ont. 1987; Annual Earle Zeigler Lecture estbld., North Am. Soc. for Sport Mgmt. 1988; Distinguished Service & Scholarship Award, Intern. Soc. for Comparative Physical Education and Sport 1988; Hetherington Award, Am. Acad. Phys. Educ. 1989; Gulick Medal, Am. Alliance for Health, Phys. Ed., Recreation & Dance 1990; Annual Earle Zeigler Lecture estbld., Fac. of Kinesiology, Univ. of Western Ont. 1990; elected to Wrestling Wall of Fame, Univ. of Western Ont. 1991; Delta Phi Alpha; Phi Epsilon Kappa; Unitarian; Liberal; recreations: piano, swimming; Home: 25 Berkshire Court, London, Ont. N6J 3N8; Office: London, Ont. N6A 3K7.

**ZEITLIN, Irving M.,** Ph.D.; university professor; b. Detroit, Mich. 19 Oct. 1928; s. Albert and Rose (Goldberg) Z.; e. Wayne State Univ., B.A. 1958, M.A. 1961; Princeton Univ., M.A. 1963, Ph.D. 1964; m. Esther d. Morris and Gertrude Levine 15 Aug. 1950; children: Ruth, Michael, Beth, Jeremy; PROF. OF SOCIOLOGY, UNIV. OF TORONTO 1977– ; Kibbutz Mem. 1950–55; Jr. Supvr., Jewish Community Ctr. (Detroit) 1956–58; Asst. Dir. & Prin., Sholem Aleichem Inst. 1958–62; Prin., Hebrew Sch., Princeton Jewish Ctr. 1962–64; Asst. Prof. of Sociol., Indiana Univ. 1965–68; Assoc. Prof. 1968–69; Vis. Sr. Lectr., Univ. of Leicester, England 1969–70; Prof. of Sociol., Washington Univ. 1970–72; Dept. Chrmn. 1971–72; Prof. & Chair, Sociol., present univ. 1972–77; SSHRCC Sabbatical 1984–85; Vis. Prof., Kwansei Gakuin Univ., Japan; Nat. Sci. Found., postdoct. fellow, Ctr. Nat. de la Rech. Sci., Paris, France 1964–65; Frelinghuysen Fellow 1963; Bobbs-Merrill Award 1963; author: 'Plato's Vision' 1993; 'Jesus and the Judaism of His Time' 1988; 'Ancient Judaism' 1984; 'The Social Condition of Humanity' 1981, '84, Candn. ed. 1991; 'Rethinking Sociology' 1973; 'Liberty, Equality & Revolution in Alexis de Tocqueville' 1971; 'Ideology and the Development of Sociological Theory' 1968, '81, '87, '90, '94; Home: 439 Sumach St., Toronto, Ont. M4X 1V6; Office: 203 College St., Toronto, Ont. M5T 1P6.

**ZELLER, Ludwig;** poet; b. Río Loa, Atacama desert, North of Chile 1 Feb. 1927; s. Guillermo and Rosa Elvira (Ocampo) Z.; m. (recidivist by conviction) Susana d. Jorge and Violeta Wald; children: Harald, Beatriz, Alejo, Javier; selected bibliography: 'Exodo y otras soledades' 1957, 'Del manantial' 1961, 'A Aloyse' 1964, 'Las reglas del juego' 1968, 'Mujer en sueño. Woman in Dream' 1975, 'When the animal rises from the deep the head explodes' 1976, 'In the country of the antipodes' 1979, 'The Marble Head and Other Poems' 1987, 'Salvar la poesía quemar las naves' 1988, 'The Ghost's Tattoos' 1989, 'To Saw the Beloved to Pieces Only When Necessary' 1990 (poems); 'Los placeres de Edipo,' 'Circe's Mirrors. Visions and Wounds. Wanderers in the Mandala' 1978 (poems and collages); 'Alphacollage' 1979, '50 Collages' 1981, 'Espejismos/Mirages' (collages); 'A Perfumed camel never does the tango' 1985 (aphorisms); 'Ludwig Zeller A Celebration' 1987 (his poem 'The White Pheasant' translated into more than 50 languages, illustrated by more than 50 artists on the occasion of his 60th birthday); 'Zeller Free Dream/Zeller Sueno Libre' 1992; many of the above books were illustrated by Susana Wald and/or A.F. Moritz; translations by John R. Colombo, Estela Lorca, A.F. Moritz, Robin Skelton, Susana Wald, Beatriz Zeller; has collaborated with other 'surrealists' (an endangered species) for 30 years; Cons., Visual Arts, Ministry of Education in Chile 16 years; has lived in Canada since 1971; Home: 392 Huron St., Toronto, Ont. M5S 2G6; Office: c/o Mosaic Press, P.O. Box 1032, Oakville, Ont. L6J 5E9.

**ZELMER, Amy E.,** R.N., B.Sc.N., M.P.H., Ph.D.; educator; b. Halifax, N.S. 20 Dec. 1935; d. George T. and Annie C. (Smart) Elliott; e. Ottawa Civic Hosp. Sch. of Nursing R.N. 1956; Dalhousie Univ. Dipl. in Pub. Health Nursing 1957; Univ. of W. Ont. B.Sc.N. 1961; Univ. of Mich. M.P.H. (Master of Pub. Health) 1963; Mich. State Univ. Ph.D. 1973; m. A.C. Lynn s. Hubert and Winona Zelmer 16 Dec. 1969; one d. Jennifer;

PROF., FACULTY OF HEALTH SCIENCES, UNIV. OF CENTRAL QUEENSLAND, Australia 1992– ; held various positions community health and adult educ. agencies N.S. and Alta. 1957–72; Asst. Prof. Sch. of Nursing and Div. of Health Services Adm., Faculty of Med., Univ. of Alta. 1972–74, Dean of Nursing 1976–80, Assoc. Vice Pres. (Acad.) 1980–88; Dean, Faculty of Health Sciences, Univ. of Central Queensland, Australia 1988–92; Health Educ. Specialist S.E. Asia Region World Health Organ. New Delhi 1975–76; Partner, Internat. Communications Inst.; part-time Consultant Candn. Internat. Devel. Agency, Internat. Dev. Prog. Australian Univs. and Assoc. of Commonwealth Univs.; named Nurse of Yr. 1982 Alta. Assn. R.N.'s; mem. Candn. Assn. Univ. Schs. Nursing (Pres. 1980–82); Alta. Pub. Health Assn. (Pres. 1983–84); Edmonton & Dist. Internat. Aid Soc. (March for Millions), Pres. 1980–82; mem. Bd. of Dirs., North-South Inst., Ottawa 1983–88; mem. Bd. of Dirs., Glenrose Rehabilitation Hosp., Edmonton 1985–88; apptd. Mem. Qld. Central Region Health Authority 1991–94; Mem., Rotary Internat.; Home: Box 1414, Main Post Office, Rockhampton, Queensland 4700, Australia; Office: Univ. of Central Queensland, Rockhampton, Queensland 4702, Australia.

**ZEMAN, Jarold Knox,** B.D., D.Theol., D.D. (Bapt.); educator; b. Czechoslovakia, 27 Feb. 1926; e. Charles Univ., Philos. Faculty, Prague, grad. 1948; Hus Theol. Faculty, Prague, Th. Cand. 1948; Knox Coll., Univ. of Toronto, B.D. 1952; Univ. of Zurich, D.Theol. 1966; McMaster Univ. D.D. 1985; m. Lillian, d. James K. Koncicky, Esterhazy, Sask., 18 June 1951; children: Miriam, Dagmar (Mrs. Gary Carter), Timothy, Janice; DIR. OF ACADIA CENTRE FOR BAPTIST AND ANABAPTIST STUDIES, ACADIA UNIV. 1991– ; Prof. of Church History, Acadia Univ. & Acadia Divinity Coll. 1968–91 and Dir. of Conferences there 1981–85; Dir. of Continuing Theol. Educ. Acadia Univ. 1970–81 and 1985–91; Pres., Baptist Federation of Canada, 1979–82; mem., Rel. Advisory Committee, CBC 1979–84; Bapt. Min., Toronto, 1949–55, Villa Nova, Ont., 1955–59; Secy., Dept. of Candn. Missions, Bapt. Conv. Ont., and Que., Toronto, 1959–68; Lectr., Bapt. Theol. Seminary, Ruschlikon, Switzerland 1965, 1984; Atlantic Sch. of Theology, Halifax, 1974; Mennonite Seminary, Elkhart, Ind. 1976–77; Regent College, Vancouver 1979; Gordon-Conwell Seminary, S. Hamilton, Mass. 1983; Moravian Theol. Seminary, Bethlehem, Penn. 1984; Ontario Theol. Seminary, Toronto 1986, 1992; Visiting Lectr. to ten univs. since 1963; author 'God's Mission and Ours' 1963; 'The Whole World at Our Door' 1964; 'Historical Topography of Moravian Anabaptism' 1967; 'The Anabaptists and the Czech Brethren' 1969; 'Baptists in Canada and Co-operative Christianity' 1972; 'The Hussite Movement and the Reformation' 1977; 'Baptist Roots and Identity' 1978; 'Renewal of Church and Society in the Hussite Reformation' 1984; 'Open Doors 1950–1990' 1992; co-author 'Baptists in Canada 1760–1990: A Bibliography' 1989; also articles; co-ed. 'The Believers' Church in Canada' 1979; ed. 'Baptists in Canada' 1980; 'Costly Vision' 1988; mem., Candn. Soc. Ch. Hist.; Am. Soc. Ch. Hist.; Am. Acad. Religion; Soc. Ref. Research; Conf. on Faith and History; Czechoslovak Soc. Arts & Sciences Am.; Address: P.O. Box 164, Wolfville, N.S. B0P 1X0.

**ZEMANS, Joyce Lynn,** B.A., M.A.; art historian; university and arts administrator; b. Toronto, Ont. 21 Apr. 1940; d. Harry and Cecile (Minisman) Pearl; e. Univ. of Toronto, B.A. 1962, M.A. 1966; Courtauld Inst. 1960–61; m. Frederick H. s. Newton and Mozah Zemans 6 June 1960; children: Deborah, David, Marcia; ASSOC. PROF., FACULTY OF FINE ARTS, YORK UNIV. 1992– ; Lectr., Co-Chrmn., Art Hist., Chrmn., Dept. of Liberal Arts Studies, Ont. Coll. of Art 1966–75; Chrmn., Dept. of Visual Arts, York Univ. 1975–81; Assoc. Prof., Art History 1975– ; Dean, Faculty of Fine Arts, York Univ. 1985–88; Dir., The Canada Council 1989–92; Co-Dir., MBA Program in Arts and Media Mngmt., Faculty of Administrative Studies, York Univ. 1994– ; former Bd. mem., Toronto Sculpture Garden; Candn. Assoc. of Fine Arts Deans; Internat. Council of Fine Arts Deans; Univ. Art Assn. of Can. Adv. Bd. Mem., 'The Journal of Canadian Art History'; co-author: 'Kathleen Munn & Edna Tacon: New Perspectives on Modernism in Canada' 1988; author 'Jock Macdonald' 1986, 'Christopher Pratt' 1985, 'J.W.G. Macdonald: The Inner Landscape' 1981, 'Art' 1976; co-author: 'Frederick Varley' 1983; Bd. Mem., Institute for Rsch. on Public Policy 1990–92; Bd. Mem., Laidlaw Foundation 1992– ; Mem., Can. National Ctte., Comité Internat. d'Histoire de l'Art (CIHA); Mem., Canada-Japan Forum 2000 1991–92; Address: Faculty of Fine Arts, York Univ., 4700 Keele St., North York, Ont. M3J 1P3.

**ZERAFA, Boris Ernest,** Dip.Arch., F.R.A.I.C., R.I.B.A., R.C.A., O.A.A., O.A.Q., M.A.A.; architect; b. Cairo, Egypt 20 June 1933; s. Ivan and Velda (Bertelli) Z.; e. Coll. Ste. Famille (Jesuit Fathers), Egypt and France; London Matric. (Eng.) 1950; Kingston Sch. of Arch., Eng., grad. (Sr. Art Award) 1955; children: Lian Anthony, Melanie Ann, Samantha Anne; PARTNER, WEBB ZERAFA MENKES HOUSDEN PARTNERSHIP, ARCHITECTS & PLANNERS; Chief Asst. Arch. with a firm in Eng., 1955–57; came to Can. 1957; formed present Practice in 1961; firm awarded 9 Candn. Architect Awards of Excellence, 2 Candn. Housing Design Council National Design Awards, Candn. Housing Design Council Award for Residential Design, 2 Urban Desigh Awards for Distinguished Urban Design in Calgary, Quebec Order of Architects Award for Distinction in Architecture, Royal Arch. Inst. of Can. Festival of Arch. Award of Merit, 2 Massey Fdn. Massey Medals, 2 Toronto Chapter, Ont. Assn. of Architects Annual Design Awards, 2 Urban Design & Planning Awards of Excellence, Bell System Honour Award, Young Men's Candn. Club of Toronto Apecial Achievement Award (Beautify Toronto Campaign 1963), National Design Council Steel Award, Ont. Masons' Relation Council Design Award, Canadian Council Vincent Massey Award, Pre-stressed Concrete Inst. PCI Award, 4 Masonry Inst. Awards of Excellence; practice extends across Canada with projects in Toronto, Montreal, Ottawa, Calgary, Edmonton, Vancouver, Halifax, Winnipeg, etc. as well as England, France, Italy, Saudi Arabia, Japan and the USA; among their major projects are: Royal Bank Plaza, Hazelton Lanes, Cumberland Court, CN-CP Metro Centre (CN Tower), Eaton Centre Phase II, Lothian Mews, Bell Canada Data Centre (Don Mills), Toronto Star Building, Parkway Place, York Centre, Richmond-Adelaide Centre, Ryerson Polytechnical Inst., Four Seasons Hotel Yorkville, Bristol Place Hotel, Grange Village Residential Complex, A.E. LePage Bldg., Granite Place, The 325 Front St. West Bldg., Sun Life Centre, Continental Bank Bldg., Bank of Nova Scotia Head Office (all in Toronto); Headquarters Elf Aquitaine (Paris, France); The Mandalay Four Seasons Hotel (Dallas, Texas); Exchange Place (Boston, Mass.); Cadillac Fairview Office Complex, Bow Valley Square, Petro-Canada Head Office, Daon Bldg., Calgary City Hall (all in Calgary); Canada Place (Edmonton); Lester B. Pearson Bldg., Dept. of External Affairs (Ottawa); Madeira Hotel (Madeira); Inn-on-the-Park Hotels (Toronto, Vancouver, London (Eng.), Paris, Rome); Arts III Humanities Bldg., Math. & Computer Bldg. and Psychology Bldg., University of Waterloo (Waterloo, Ont.); Hyatt Regency Hotel (Vancouver); Quebec Hilton Hotel (Quebec City); Newport Place (Newport Beach, Calif.); Prudential Assurance Centre (Kitchener, Ont.); Bank of Nova Scotia Tower, Maison des Cooperants, National Bank of Paris (Montreal); King Abdulaziz University (Saudi Arabia); mem., Roy. Inst. of Brit. Architects; Fellow, Roy. Arch. Inst. of Can.; Roy. Candn. Acad. of Arts; Ont. Assn. of Archs.; Que. Assn. of Archs.; Man. Assn. of Archs.; Toronto Soc. of Archs.; Specification Writers Assn. of Can.; Independent; R. Catholic; recreations: music, art collecting; Office: 95 St. Clair Ave. W., Suite 1500, Toronto, Ont. M4V 1N7.

**ZIEGLER, Brig. William Smith,** C.B.E., D.S.O., E.D.; retired company executive; b. Calgary, Alta. 5 Apr. 1911; s. Wm. Geo. and Mary E. (Smith) Z.; e. Schs. of Calgary and Edmonton, Alta.; Univ. of Alberta; m. Mildred E. Dean of Lake Louise and Edmonton, Alta.; one s., Rodney Christopher; joined Candn. Nat. Railways in 1951 and after a series of promotions through various adm. and extve. positions was apptd. Asst. Vice-Pres.-Personnel in Montreal in May 1955; service with Inland Cement Industries Ltd., Edmonton, 1956–73 as Exec. Vice-Pres., Pres. and Chrmn.; served in 2nd World War; joined Candn. Army, 1939, serving Overseas in various theatres in Europe; gaz. Brig. at age 32; awarded D.S.O. (1944), C.B.E. (1945); Golden Aristion Andrias (Greece); Commdr. Order Orange Nassau with Swords (Netherlands); after hostilities served with Brit. Foreign Office (German Sec.) Control Comn. for Germany as Regional Adm. Offr., Land Niedersachsen; mem., Assn. Prof. Engrs. Alta.; Phi Kappa Pi; United Church of Canada; recreations: fishing, shooting, home carpentry; Clubs: Mayfair Golf & Country; Home: 13834 Ravine Drive, Edmonton, Alta. T5N 3M1.

**ZIGMAN, The Hon. Mr. Justice Jerry J.,** B.A., LL.B.; superior court judge; b. Montreal, Que. 24 June 1942; s. Joseph and Ethel (Tendler) Z.; e. Sir George Williams Univ. B.A. 1964; Univ. de Montréal LL.B. 1968; m. Carol d. Eddie and Mary Wolman 26 Aug. 1965; children: Andrew, Marnie; JUDGE, SUPERIOR COURT, PROV. OF QUE. 1987– ; admitted to Bar, Prov. of Que. 1969; Lawyer/Partner, Yarosky, Fish, Zigman, Isaacs and Daviault (spec. in Crim. Law) 1969–87; Mem., Bar of Montreal, Ctte. on the Admin. of Crim. Justice in the Prov. of Que. 1982–85; Spec. Couns., Que. Police Comn. 1986–87; Mem., Candn. Judges Conf. 1988; Lord Reading Law Soc. of Que. 1969; Home: 41 Chatillon Dr., Dollard des Ormeaux, Que. H9B 2B9; Office: 1 est, Notre-Dame, Montreal, Que. H2Y 1B6.

**ZIMMER, Henry B.,** B.A., FCA, CFP; writer; publisher; b. New York, N.Y. 6 Dec. 1943; s. Isaak and Fanny (Vainchel) Z.; e. McGill Univ., B.A. 1964; C.A. (Que.) 1967; CFP 1986; Canadian citizen 1974; Fellow, Institute of Chartered Accountants of Alta. 1994; CO-OWNER/OP. SPRINGBANK PUBLISHING; author/co-publisher: The Wealthy Procrastinator, The Wealthy Paper Carriers, The Wealthy Women, The Money Manager for Canadians, four textbooks on Canadian taxation; former owner/manager CANTAX Corporation Ltd.; Address: 5425 Elbow Dr. S.W., Calgary, Alta. T2V 1H7.

**ZIMMERMAN, Adam Hartley, Jr.,** B.A., F.C.A.; company executive; b. Toronto, Ont. 19 Feb. 1927; s. Adam Hartley and Mary Ethelwyn (Ballantyne) Z.; e. Upper Canada Coll., 1938–40; Ridley Coll., 1940–44; Royal Candn. Naval Coll., 1944–46; Trinity Coll., Univ. of Toronto, 1946–50; m. Janet Digby d. John S. Lewis, Toronto, 19 May 1951; children: Barbara, Thomas, Mary, Kate; Chrm. of the Bd., Noranda Forest Inc. 1987–93, retired 1994; VICE CHRMN., NORANDA INC. 1987– ; Chrmn. & Dir., Confederation Life Ins. Co. 1993– ; Dir., Battery Technologies Inc.; Economic Investment Trust; MacMillan Bloedel Ltd. (Chrmn. 1983–91; Vice-Chrmn. 1991–93); Maple Leaf Foods Inc. (formerly Canada Packers Inc.); Northwood Pulp & Timber Ltd.; The Pittston Co.; Southam Inc.; The Toronto-Dominion Bank; Dir., Roy Thomson Hall; World Wildlife Fund Canada; Chrmn., C.D. Howe Inst. 1990–93; mem. Advisory Bd. Univ. of Toronto, Faculty of Forestry; Hon. Trustee, Hospital for Sick Children Foundation; began as Student-in-Accounts, Clarkson, Gordon & Co., 1950–54; Chart. Acct. 1956; Supv., 1956–58; joined Noranda Inc. as Asst. Comptroller, 1958, Comptroller, 1961–66, Vice President and Comptroller 1966–74, Exec. Vice-Pres. 1974–1982; Pres. & C.O.O. 1982–87; served 6 years in R.C.N.(R); Fellow, Inst. of Chart. Accts. of Ont.; Mining Assn. of Canada; Past Chrmn., Candn. Am. Comte.; Candn. Forest Industries Counc.; Candn. Pulp & Paper Assn.; Zeta Psi; recreations: skiing, sailing, golf; Clubs: York; University; Mount Royal; Vancouver; Toronto Golf; Craigleith Ski; Madawaska; Home: 15 Edgar Ave., Toronto, Ont. M4W 2B1; Office: Suite 500, 1 Toronto St., Toronto, Ont. M5C 2W4.

**ZIMMERMAN, Arthur Maurice,** B.A., M.S., Ph.D.; university professor; b. N.Y. City, N.Y. 24 May 1929; s. Frank and Marion (Ellentuck) Z.; e. New York Univ. B.A. 1950, M.S. 1954, Ph.D. 1956; m. Selma, d. Max Blau, 4 Oct. 1953; children: Susan Ann, Beth Leslie, Robert James; PROF. OF ZOOLOGY; Assoc. Dean, Sch. Of Graduate Studies, 1978–81; Acting Dir., Inst. of Immunology, 1980–81; Prof. of Zoology since 1964; Assoc. Chrm., Univ. of Toronto (1975–78); Research Asst. (1953–55) and Assoc. (1955–56), New York Univ., Instr., Newark State Coll., 1956 (rec'd. Lalor Research Award, Marine Biol. Lab., Woods Hole, (Mass.); Research Fellow, Nat. Cancer Inst., Univ. of Cal., Berkeley 1956–58; Instr. of Pharmacol., State Univ. of N.Y., Downstate Med. Center, N.Y. 1958–60, and Asst. Prof. there 1960–64; Ed. 'Canadian Journal of Biochemistry and Cell Biology' 1984–93; N. Amer. Ed. 'Cell Biology International' 1985–94; Consulting Ed. 'Cytobios,' 'Microbios' 1980– ; Ed. Bd. Mem. 'Experimental Cell Research' 1983–92; Publications: over 200 scient. papers in tech. journs.; Fellow Am. Assn. Advanc. Science; mem. Candn. Soc. Cell Biols. (Pres. 1976–77); Am. Soc. Cell Biols. (Treas. 1974–80); Internat. Fed. for Cell Biology (Secy.-Gen. 1985–92); Home: 8 Barksdale Ave., North York, Ont. M3H 4S3.

**ZIMMERMAN, David,** B.A., M.A., Ph.D.; university professor; b. New York, N.Y. 19 Feb. 1959; s. Eugene H. and Elaine G. (Green) Z.; e. Jarvis C.I. 1977; Univ. of Toronto, B.A. 1981; Univ. of N.B., M.A. 1983, Ph.D. 1987; ASSOC. PROF., DEPT. OF HISTORY, UNIV. OF VICTORIA 1987– ; author: 'The Great Naval Battle of Ottawa' 1989, 'Coastal Fort: A History of Fort Sullivan, Eastport, Maine' 1985 and several scholarly articles; Office: Victoria, B.C. V8W 2Y2.

**ZIMMERMAN, G. Douglas,** B.A.Sc.; industrialist; b. Toronto, Ont. 8 May 1918; s. Dr. George Foster and Evelyn Pearl (Thompson) Z.; e. Univ. of Toronto, B.A.Sc. (Chem. Engn.) 1943; m. Mary, d. Walter R. McConnell, Toronto, Ont. 28 Aug. 1942; children: Judith Anne, Stephen Michael, Richard Donald, Susan

Mary, Virginia Lynn, William Paul; Instrument Engr., Canadian Synthetic Rubber Ltd., Sarnia, Ont., 1943–45; Field Engr., Fischer & Porter (Can.) Limited, 1949–56, & President, 1956–59; Executive Vice President and Director, Candn. Curtiss-Wright Limited, 1959–60; Pres., Industrial Wire & Cable Ltd. 1960–74; member, Association of Professional Engrs. of Ontario; Gov., Etobicoke Gen. Hosp.; Presbyterian; recreation: swimming; Clubs: Toronto Board of Trade; Ont. Jockey Club (Trustee); Caledon Mountain Trout; Home: Domarr Farm, R.R. No. 1, Kleinburg, Ont. L0J 1C0.

**ZIMMERMAN, John Murr,** B.A., D.D.; Lutheran clergyman; b. Milverton, Ont. 25 Dec. 1922; s. late John and late Louise (Murr) Z.; e. Milverton Pub. and High Schs.; Waterloo Coll. (Univ. of W. Ont.) B.A. 1944; Waterloo Lutheran Semy. grad. 1947; Waterloo Lutheran Univ. D.D. 1973; m. Alma Elizabeth d. late William Wolff 8 May 1948; children: Mark, Joel, Thomas, Peter, Paul; Pastor, Christ Lutheran Church, Peterborough 1985–88; retired 1988; Parish Pastor, Pembroke, Ont. 1947–59; Kitchener, Ont. 1959–62; Spruce Grove, Alta. 1970–73; Extve. Secy., Lutheran Ch. in Amer., Candn. Sec. 1973–84; Pres. Western Can. Synod, Lutheran Ch. in Am. 1962–70; mem. Pembroke & Dist. High Sch. Bd. 1957–59; mem. and Pres. Bd. of Govs. Waterloo Lutheran Univ. 1959–62; NDP; Lutheran; recreations: gardening, music; Home: Round Lake Centre, Ont. K0J 2J0.

**ZIMMERMAN, Oscar,** B.Sc., F.S.A., F.C.I.A., M.A.A.A.; insurance executive; b. Montreal, Que. 24 April 1952; s. Isreal and Lucy Z.; e. McGill Univ. B.Sc. 1974; m. Anna d. Hy and Leah Day 15 March 1976; children: Daniel, Jodie, Michelle; SENIOR VICE-PRESIDENT, INSURANCE, BANK OF NOVA SCOTIA 1992– ; joined Crown Life 1974; Sr. Vice Pres. Managed Assets Operation, Crown Life Insurance Co. 1990–92; Pres., Crown America Life Insur. Co. 1991–92; Pres., Crown Am. Series Fund 1991–92; Pres., Crown Life Employees Credit Union 1986–92; recreations: tennis, squash; clubs: Fitness Institute; Home: 161 Old Forest Hill Rd., Toronto, Ont. M6C 2G7; Office: 44 King St. W., Toronto, Ont. M5H 1H1.

**ZIMMERMAN, William Martin,** M.S.W.; social service executive; b. Winnipeg, Man. 11 Feb. 1930; s. Walter Harry and Elizabeth (Gillies) Z.; e. Univ. of Man., B.A. 1952, B.S.W. 1953, M.S.W. 1957; m. Sheila d. Norman and Grace Young 1955; children: Katherine, John, Frances; Extve. Dir., United Way of Ottawa-Carleton 1980; Chief Probation Offr. Winnipeg Juvenile Court 1957–64; Exec. Dir. Social Planning Council of Ottawa-Carleton 1974–80; former lectr. Carleton Univ. Sch. of Social Work and Candn. Police Coll.; former Visiting Prof. Univ. of Ottawa, Dept. of Criminol.; Past Dir.,: Sir Hugh John Macdonald Meml. Hostel Winnipeg; Indian & Métis Friendship Centre Winnipeg; Neighbourhood Service Centres Winnipeg; Civic Hosp. Ottawa; recognized by Ottawa St. Citizens' Council for contributions to older people of Ottawa 1982; wrote original project proposals Fed. Govt.'s New Horizons prog. for elderly; former Assoc. Ed. Candn. Jour. Criminol., The Social Worker; mem. Candn. Assn. Social Workers; Assn. Candn. TV & Radio Artists; Actors' Equity; recreation: basketball; Home: 26 Alexander, Ottawa, Ont. K1M 1M9.

**ZIMMERMANN, Ernest Robert,** B.A., Ph.D.; educator; b. Cologne, Germany 18 June 1931; s. Josef and Katharina (Frauenrath) Z.; e. Volksschule, Gymnasium; Stratford (Ont.) Coll. Inst. 1957; McMaster Univ. B.A. 1961; Sch. of Slavonic & E. Eur. Studies Univ. of London Ph.D. 1968; children: Stephen Andrew, Susan Elizabeth; ASSOC. PROF. OF HISTORY, LAKEHEAD UNIV. 1976– ; Lectr. Univ. of Sask. 1965–67; Lectr. present Univ. 1967, Asst. Prof. 1968, Dean of Arts 1978–83, Chrmn. of Hist. 1977–78, Pres., Faculty Assn. 1973–74, Vice Pres., 1986–88, Pres. 1988–89, Mem. Bd. of Govs. 1991– ; Commonwealth Scholar 1961–64; Woodrow Wilson Fellow 1961; Dir. Thunder Bay Hist. Museum Soc. and Thunder Bay Nat. Exhbn. Centre and Centre for Indian Art 1979–83; Pres. Port Arthur Riding Assn. NDP 1969–71, 1976–81; mem. Candn. Hist. Assn.; AAASS; CAS, LUFA, CAUT; Unitarian; Home: 159 Hogarth St., Thunder Bay, Ont. P7A 7H1; Office: Oliver Rd., Thunder Bay, Ont. P7B 5E1.

**ZINGG, Walter,** M.D., D.Sc. (Hon.), M.Sc., FRCSC, FACS, FACC; surgeon; educator; b. Kloten, Switzerland 29 Mar. 1924; s. late Ernst J. and late Ida (Haab) Z.; e. Univ. of Zurich, Fac. of Med. Staatsexamen 1948; Dr. Med. 1951; Univ. of Man. M.Sc. 1952; D.Sc. (Hon.) Université Laval 1986; m. Regula L. (dec.) d. Ernst F. (dec.) and Lydia L. Zollinger (dec.) 25 June 1949; children: Claudia E., Jeannette R., Esther A., David W., Tracy Bill; PROF. EMERITUS, UNIV. OF TORONTO 1990– ; Dir., Univ. of Toronto Inst. of Biomedical Engineering 1983–89; Lectr. in Physiology, Univ. of Manitoba 1956–57; Lectr. to Assoc. Prof. of Surgery and Dir. Surgical Research, Univ. of Man. 1957–64; Asst. Prof. to Prof. of Surgery, Univ. of Toronto 1964–90; Chief Div. Surgical Res. Hosp. for Sick Children Rsch. Inst. 1964–88; Ed. 'Microcirculation' 1976; 'Biomedical Materials' 1986; Vice Pres. (Medical Affairs) Pharma Patch, plc; Chrmn. Conn Smythe Rsch. Found. for Crippled Children 1980–84; Pres. Candn. Biomaterials Soc. 1979–81; Pres. Candn. Med. and Biological Engineering Soc. 1984–88; Fellow, Candn. Medical and Biological Engineering Soc. 1989; Sr. Fellow Massey Coll. Univ. of Toronto 1975– ; Home: 3255 Niagara Parkway, Stevensville, Ont.; Office: Univ. of Toronto, Toronto, Ont. M5S 1A4.

**ZIPURSKY, Alvin,** B.Sc., M.D.; university professor; physician; b. Winnipeg, Man. 27 Sept. 1930; s. Isaac and Doris Z.; e. St. John's Tech. H.S. 1947; Univ. of Manitoba B.Sc.(Med.) 1953, M.D. 1953; m. Freda d. Harry and Rose Cohen 16 June 1953; children: Steven Lawrence, Robert Baruch, Benjamin Charles; PROFESSOR, FACULTY OF MEDICINE, UNIV. OF TORONTO 1981– ; Asst. Prof., Ped., Univ. of Manitoba 1962–64; Assoc. Prof. 1964–67; Prof., Ped., McMaster Univ. 1966–81; Chair 1966–72, 1978–81; Head, Hematology-Oncology, Hosp. for Sick Children 1981–91; Med. Dir., Blood Transfusion Serv., Candn. Red Cross Soc. 1960–66 (Chair, Sci. Adv. Ctte. 1976–80); Dir., Clin. Investigation & Rsch. Unit, Children's Hosp. of Winnipeg 1965–66; Attending Physician, Winnipeg Gen. Hosp. & Children's Hosp. of Winnipeg 1957–67; Edit. Bd. Mem., 'Paed.,' 'Clin. & Lab. Invest.,' 'Early Human Devel.,' 'Am. J. of Paed. Hem./Oncol.,' 'Ped. Hem./Oncol.'; Pres., Candn. Soc. for Clin. Invest. 1975–76; Candn. Haem. Soc. 1974–76; Chair & Extve., Paed. Oncol. Group of Ont. 1983–91; Office: Toronto, Ont. M5S 1A1.

**ZIRALDO, Donald J.P.,** B.Sc.; executive; b. St. Catharines, Ont. 13 Oct. 1948; s. Frederick and Irma (Schiratti) Z.; e. Denis Morris H.S., St. Catharines, Ont. 1967; Univ. of Guelph B.Sc. Agric. 1971; PRESIDENT, INNISKILLIN WINES INC. 1974– ; Pres., Inniskillin Napa Vineyards Inc. 1988– ; Pres. (1971) Ziraldo Farms and Nurseries; Chrmn., Vintners Quality Alliance (1988); Vice-Pres., Peninsula Travel Ltd.; Dir., Canadian Wine Inst.; Past Bd. of Govs., Shaw Festival Theatre; mem.: Am. Wine Soc.; Vinifera Wine Growers Assn.; Ont. Inst. of Agrologists; Business Achievement Award; Stratford Chef School, Stratford, Ont.; recipient, Citadell D'or Award, Bordeaux, France 1991; 1991's 'Men of the Year' (with partner Karl J. Kaiser, Foodservice & Hospitality Magazine, Ontario Hostelry Institute Chairman's Award; Marketer of the Year, Toronto Chapter Am. Marketing Assn. 1993; Order of Ontario 1993; Distinguished Achievement Award, Wineries Unlimited & Vineyard & Winery Mngmt. Magazine 1994; Business Person of the Year Award, St. Catharines Advertising & Sales Assn. 1994; Address: R.R. #1, Niagara-on-the-Lake, Ont. L0S 1J0.

**ZITZERMAN, Saul B.,** B.A., LL.B.; business consultant and financier; barrister and solicitor; b. Winnipeg, Man., 16 Feb. 1936; s. Harry and Minnie (Daitchman) Z.; e. Univ. of Manitoba, B.A. 1956; Manitoba Law Sch. LL.B. 1960; m. Zelma, d. late Myer Goldberg, 2 Sept. 1956; children: David, Mira; Pres., Cancorp Seniors Inc., Counsel Management Ltd.; Chrmn., Flavex Industries Ltd.; Bio Nova Industries Inc.; Sr. Partner, Buchwald, Asper, Henteleff, Zitzerman, Greene & Shead, 1970; Dir., A & M Distributors Ltd.;r ead law with late L. S. Matlin, Q.C., called to Bar of Man. 1960; Partner, Matlin, Buchwald, Zitzerman, Kushner & Abbott 1961; Buchwald, Henteleff & Zitzerman 1965; Chrmn. Bd. Trustees,Talmud Torah Foundation; Pres. Bd. Dirs., Winnipeg Hebrew Sch.; Joseph Wolinsky Coll.; Dir., Winnipeg Jewish Community Council; Pres., Jewish Nat. Fund of Canada; Counsel to Bank of Nova Scotia 1970–74; Gen. Counsel to Imperial Group 1960–74, Pres., 1974–79; Past Vice-Pres., Liberal Party of Man.; Past Pres., Univ. Student Libs.; mem. Candn. Bar Assn. (Lect. in Taxation, Man. Sec.); Man. Bar Assn.; Law Soc. of Man.; Medico-Legal Assn.; Internat. Comn. of Jurists; Candn. Tax Foundation; Hebrew; Liberal; Zeta Beta Tau; recreations: golf, bowling, reading.

**ZLOTKIN, Stanley Howard,** B.Sc., M.D., Ph.D., F.R.C.P.(C); paediatrician; medical nutritionist; b. Toronto, Ont. 5 Feb. 1948; s. Michael and Nina (Kendall) Z.; e. Univ. of Toronto B.Sc. 1971, Ph.D. 1981; McMaster Univ. M.D. 1974; m. Judith Wolfson 7 June 1970; three s. Julian, Alexander, Nathaniel; ATTENDING STAFF DIV. OF CLIN. NUTRITION THE HOSP. FOR SICK CHILDREN 1980– ; Active Staff, Cons. in Paediatrics Hugh MacMillan Centre Toronto 1982– ; Cons. in Paediatrics Women's Coll. Hosp. 1984– ; Prof. of Nutrition & Paediatrics Univ. of Toronto 1993– , Full mem. Sch. Grad. Studies 1985– , Staff Phys. Health Service 1977–80, Lectr. in Continuing Studies 1978–79, Asst. Prof. of Nutrition & Paediatrics 1980–87; Resident in Paediatrics Montreal Children's Hosp. 1974–77; Attending Phys. Clinique de Jenuesse de Montréal 1975–77; Med. Rsch. Council Can. Fellow 1977–80; Cons. Drug Benefit Prog. Min. of Health Ont.; mem. Task Forces Prevention of Obesity, Treatment of Obesity, Assistive Devices Prog. Min. Health Ont.; mem. Sci. Review Ctte. Revision Recommended Nutrient Intakes for Candns. Health & Welfare Can.; author or co-author numerous profl. publs.; recipient, Borden Award in Nutrition, Candn. Soc. for Nutritional Sciences 1992; Colin R. Woolf Continuing Education Award, Univ. of Toronto, Faculty of Medicine; mem. Candn. Paediatric Soc. (Chrmn. Nutrition Ctte.); Candn. Soc. Nutritional Sci's (Past Pres.); Am. Soc. Clin. Nutrition; Am. Council Sci. & Health; Clin. Rsch. Soc. Toronto; Candn. Soc. Med. Bioethics; Soc. Pediatric Rsch.; Office: 555 University Ave., Toronto, Ont. M5G 1X8.

**ZNAIMER, Moses,** M.A.; producer; b. Kulab, Tajikistan; s. Aron and Helen (Apfelzweig) Z.; e. McGill Univ. B.A. (Hons., Phil. and Politics) 1963; Harvard Univ. M.A. (Govt.) 1965; PRES. & EXECUTIVE PRODUCER, CITYTV; came to Can. 1948; joined CBC as Producer Pub. Affairs Radio, Toronto and Montreal 1965; specialized in pol. commentary and documentary, co-created world's first Nat. Open Line Phone-In ('Cross Canada Check-Up'); Producer/Dir. 'Revolution Plus Fifty'; Co-Host CBC 'Take Thirty' and 'The Way It Is'; Vice Pres. Helix Investments and T'ang Management, Venture Capital Fund 1969; co-founder, Pres., Extve. Producer CITYTV 1972; creates and supervises as exec. producer all CITYTV programs, incl.: 'CityLine'; 'CityPulse'; 'Breakfast Television'; 'Lunch Television'; 'MT-Movie Television'; 'FT-Fashion Television'; 'NewMusic,' MediaTelevision; 'The Originals'; 'Electric Circus'; Patrick Watson's 'Titans'; Leonard Cohen's 'I am a Hotel' and 'Toronto Trilogy'; freelance theatrical producer: 'Miss Margarida'; 'Travesties'; 'Tamara,' Los Angeles, Buenos Aires, Sao Paolo; actor: 'Atlantic City'; 'The Best Revenge'; 'Misdeal'; 'Love'; Pres. Exec. Prod., 'Tour of the Universe,' 'InterActive Entertainment Inc.'; co-founder, Pres., Extve. Producer 'MUCHMUSIC' (the nation's English satellite music stn.) 1984; 'MUSIQUEPLUS' (the nations' French satellite music station) 1986; speaker/writer; mem. ACTRA; recreations: running, squash; Office: 299 Queen St. W., Toronto, Ont. M5V 2Z5.

**ZOLF, Larry,** B.A.; journalist and writer; b. Winnipeg, Man. 19 July 1934; s. Falek Yoshua (Western Can.'s best-known Yiddish writer) and Freda Rachel (Pasternak) Z.; e. Univ. of Man. B.A. 1956; Osgoode Hall Law Sch. Toronto; Univ. of Toronto; Winner of Isbister, Marcus Hyman Principal Sparling, A.A. Baird Scholarships for Academic Excellence; children: David, Rachel; WRITER, NEWS AND CURRENT AFFAIRS REPORTER, PRODUCER, CONSULTANT CBC TORONTO 1962– ; author 'Dance of the Dialectic' 1973; 'Survival of the Fattest: An Irreverent View of the Senate,' and 'Just Watch Me: Remembering Pierre Trudeau' 1984; 'The Good Humour Man' (Manitoba Humour Anthology) 1987; 'Scorpions for Sale' (fiction) 1989 (nominated for Leacock Award for Humour); contrib. various mags. and newspapers; essays and articles anthologised in 'The New Romans' 1968; 'The Peaceable Kingdom' 1969; 'Gordon to Watkins to You' 1970; 'Mordecai Richler' 1971; 'Columbo's Canadian Quotations' 1974; 'Book of Insults' 1980; 'The Spice Box' 1981; Govt. Archivist Prov. Ont. 1958–59; pub. relations rep. Toronto Labour Council 1959–61; film critic Macleans Magazine 1966–67; Lectr. Carleton Univ. 1972–73; political Columnist Weekend magazine 1977–79; mem. Queen's Park Legislative Press Gall. 1977–86; rec'd Wilderness Award TV journalism 1965; Brussels Internat. Labour Film Festival Prize 1966; nominee, Gordon Sinclair Award 1983; nominee, Gemini Awards 1994; Dir., Parliamentary Press Gall. 1972; Toronto Press Club 1974–77; John G. Diefenbaker Memorial Found. 1982– ; Dir., Cecil Community Centre 1991– ; mem., Writers Guild of Canada; Writers Union of Canada; Caveat Reginam.

**ZSOLT, Andrew,** P.Eng.; executive; b. Budapest, Hungary 8 Apr. 1923; s. Ernest and Josephine (Pfeifer) Z.; e. high sch. Budapest; Tech. Univ. Budapest and Munich, Degree in Civil Engn. 1948; m. Jean Ann d. Murray and Doris Shaver 1 Aug. 1980; children: Katherine, Andrew, Tom, John, JoAnne McManus, Michael McManus, John

McManus. Patrick McManus; PRES., EDEVCO MANAGEMENT LIMITED 1992– ; Field Engr. 1949, Structural Engr. 1950–53, Foundation Co. of Ontario Ltd. Toronto; Supervising Structural Engr. Fenco 1954–59; Pres., Codeco Ltd. Toronto 1959; Inducon Engineering Ltd. 1962; Inducon Construction (Eastern) Ltd. and subsidiaries Can. and U.S. 1962; Inducon Holdings Ltd. 1968; Chrmn. & C.E.O., Inducon Development Corp. 1977–92; Founder, Inducon Group of Companies specializing in 'turn-key' method of contracting and real estate development; author various papers; mem. Assn. Prof. Engrs. Prov. Ont.; Engn. Inst. Can.; Bd. Trade Metrop. Toronto; recreations: sailing, skiing, scuba diving; Club: Lagoon City Yacht; Office: 3800 Yonge St., PH 5, Toronto, Ont. M4N 2N6.

**ZUCCHET, Norris Thomas Paul,** B.A.Sc., P.Eng.; public utility executive; b. Toronto, Ont. 7 Oct. 1950; s. Domenic and Santina (Biasotto) Z.; e. York Memorial Collegiate; Univ. of Waterloo 1975; m. Daniela d. Frank and Maria Zussino 13 Aug. 1977; children: Ashley Anne, Nolan Elliot; Pres., The Parking Authority of Toronto 1991; Transportation Engr., Proctor & Redfern Cons. Engr. 1975–77; Transp. Planner, Metro. Toronto 1977–81; Sr. Transp. Planner, Region of Peel 1981–85; Devel. & Transp. Coord., City of Toronto 1985–88; Vice-Pres., Devel., The Parking Authority of Toronto 1988–91; Mem., Assn. of Profl. Engrs. of Ont.; Inst. of Transp. Engrs.; Candn. Parking Assn.; Inst. & Mun. Parking Congress; recreations: golf, tennis, squash, music; clubs: Toronto Cricket, Skating & Curling; Home: 122 Brooke Ave., Toronto, Ont. M5M 2K4.

**ZUCKER, Steven Warren,** M.Eng., Ph.D.; educator; b. Philadelphia, Pa. 20 Apr. 1948; s. Samuel and Evelyn (Naselow) Z.; e. Carnegie-Mellon Univ. Pittsburg B.Eng. 1969; Drexel Univ. Philadelphia M.Eng. 1972, Ph.D. 1975; m. Judith d. Ernest and Betty Schwartz 26 Dec. 1974; children: Lauren Jessica, Jonathan Michael; PROF. OF ELECT. ENG. McGILL UNIV. 1985– ; Fellow, Candn. Inst. for Advanced Rsch. 1983– ; Fellow, IEEE 1988; Postdoctoral Fellow Univ. of Md. 1974, Rsch. Assoc. Computer Sci. 1975; Asst. Prof. of Elect. Eng. present Univ. 1976, Assoc. Prof. 1980; author or co-author over 150 publs. sci. jours., confs., books; Home: 338 Metcalfe Ave., Westmount, Qué. Office: 3480 University St., Montréal, Qué. H3A 2A7.

**ZUKOTYNSKI, Stefan;** educator; b. Warsaw, Poland 26 Feb. 1939; s. Julian and Krystyna Z.; e. TPD 1 (Warsaw) 1956; Warsaw Univ., Magister 1961; Ph.D. 1966; m. Susan, d. Michael and Irene Nirenberski, 2 Jan. 1968; child: Katherine; PROF., UNIV. TORONTO since 1981; N.R.C. Post-Doctoral Fellow, Univ. Alta. 1966–68; joined present univ. as staffmember, Dept. Electrical Engineering 1968; Consultant, Elec. Eng. Consociates Ltd. 1971– ; Resident Visitor, Bell Labs (Murray Hill, N.J.) 1977–78; Pres., Torion Plasma Corp. 1990– ; author numerous scientific papers; mem., APEO; CAP: IEEE: APS: Home: 32 Maryvale Cres., Richmond Hill, Ont. L4C 6P8; Office: Dept. Electrical Engineering, Univ. Toronto, Toronto, Ont. M5S 1A4.

**ZUMTHOR, Paul Joseph,** Dr., F.R.S.C.; chercheur et écrivain; né Genève, Suisse, 5 mars 1915; f. Albert Franz et Léontine Alexandrine (Marin) Z.; é. lycée à Orléans (France); univ. de Paris, fac. de droit et de lettres, L. ès L. 1935, dip. d'études supérieures des lettres 1936; univ. de Genève, D. ès L. 1943; ép. Marie Lépine 1942, Colette Pachoud 1946, Marie-Louise Ollier 1976; enfants: Bernard, Claire, Dominique, Aliette, Pernette; PROFESSEUR D'UNIVERSITE (retraité 1980); prof. univ. de Groningen (Pays-Bas) 1948–51; prof. univ. d'Amsterdam 1952–71; prof. univ. de Montréal 1972–80; collaborateur régulier de diverses revues; H. prés. de la Féd. Internat. des Langues et Littératures Modernes; chevalier de la Légion d'Honneur (France); officier du Mérite (Italie); Chevalier, Ordre National du Québec; Académie royale des sciences des Pays-Bas; Société Royale du Canada; auteur de plusieurs livres, les principaux: 'Les hautes eaux' (roman) 1958, 'La vie quotidienne en Hollande au temps de Rembrandt' 1960 et 1990, 'Guillaume le Conquérant et la civilisation de son temps' 1964 et 1978, 'Le puits de Babel' (roman) 1969, 'Essai de poétique médiévale' 1972, 'Le masque et la lumière' 1978, 'Parler du moyen âge' 1980, 'Introduction à la poésie orale' 1983; 'La lettre et la voix' 1987; 'La fête des fous' (roman) 1987; 'Les contrebandiers' (nouvelles) 1989; 'Point de fuite' (poémes) 1989; 'Ecriture et nomadisme' (entretiens) 1990; 'La traversée' (roman) 1991; 'La mesure du monde' 1993; récréations: bricolage, natation, marche; Résidence: 4874 avenue Victoria, Montréal, Qué.

**ZUNENSHINE, Jeffrey S.,** B.A., M.B.A.; printing executive; b. Montreal, Que. 2 May 1951; s. Irving and Ruth (Rottenberg) Z.; e. Bar-Ilan Univ. B.A.; Concordia Univ. M.B.A.; m. Denise Goldman 2 Jan. 1975; children: Mindy, Michael, Jaime; PRESIDENT, DATAMARK INC.; Dir., Metrographic; Champion Packaging; Office: 700 McCaffrey, St-Laurent, Que. H4T 1N1.

**ZUPPINGER, Walter Urs,** B.A., M.B.A.; food services executive; b. Zurich, Switzerland 6 Sept. 1943; s. the late Walter Ernst and Charlotte Fanny (De Vigier) Z.; e. Mitchell (Ont.) Dist. High Sch. 1964; Univ. of W. Ont. B.A. 1968, M.B.A. 1970; m. Alexandra Catherine d. Henry and Virginia Koury 26 Sept. 1981; children: Max Walter, Zoey Alexandra; CHRMN. & C.E.O., DOMCO FOODSERVICES LTD. 1977– ; Dir. Eastern Catering Ltd.; Les Alimentations Domco Ltée; Domco Foodservices Inc. Seattle; Sec.-Treas. Restaurant Div. present Co. 1970, Vice Pres. Finance 1973, Pres. 1975; United Church; recreations: collecting lead soldiers, rare books; Clubs: University; The Toronto Lawn Tennis; Home: 12 Dale Ave., Toronto, Ont. M4W 1K4; Office: 1 Concorde Gate, Suite 808, Don Mills, Ont. M3C 3N6.

**ZURBRIGG, Homer Franklin,** B.Sc., M.Sc., P.Eng., U.E.; retired mining executive; b. Markham, Ont. 8 July 1909; s. Albert Henry and Mabel (Hutchison) Z.; e. Queen.s Univ., B.Sc. 1931,M.Sc. 1933; m. Helen, d. late Alexander McLean, 2 May 1936; children: Ronald Benson (dec'd), Janet Elizabeth, John Robert; began as Geol. with International Nickel Co. of Canada Ltd., Copper Cliff, Ont., 1933, Chief Geol. (Creighton Mine) 1935, Geologist then Chief Mines Geologist 1937–40, Chief Geologist 1956 and transf. to Toronto, Ont. 1962; apptd. Asst. Vice Pres. and Chief Geol., 1964; Pres. and Dir., Canadian Nickel Co. 1965; Vice President, Exploration, International Nickel Co. of Canada Ltd. 1968–74; Vice Pres., International Nickel Co. Inc. 1970–74; retired 1974; mem. Geol. Soc. of America; Canadian Inst. Mining & Metall.; Am. Inst. Mining, Metall. & Petroleum Engrs., Soc. of Econ. Geol.; Prof. Eng., Prov. of Ontario; Mining & Metall. Soc. of Am.; Am. Inst. of Professional Geologists; Protestant; Clubs: Bd. of Trade; Lambton; Home: 21 Valecrest Drive, Islington, Ont. M9A 4P4.

**ZUSSMAN, David R.,** B.Sc., M.Sc., Ph.D.; b. Montreal, Que. 24 Jan. 1947; s. Saul and Anne (Handman) Z.; e. McGill Univ. B.Sc. 1968; Florida State Univ. M.Sc. 1970; McGill Univ. Ph.D. 1975; m. Sheridan d. George and Jean Scott 28 May 1975; children: Richard, Julianne; PRES., ENVIRONICS-DRZ 1992– ; Asst. Prof., Sch. of Public Admin., Univ. of Victoria 1978–81; Commun. Sec., Privy Counc. Office, Govt. of Can. 1981–82; Policy Advr. to Min. of Energy, Mines & Resources 1982–84; Sr. Dept. Policy Advr. to Min. of State for External Affairs & the Dep. Prime Min. 1984; Assoc. Prof. of Public Policy & Mngt., Fac. of Admin., Univ. of Ottawa 1984– ; Asst. Dean, Grad. Prog. 1985–88; Dean, Fac. of Admin. 1988–92; publications: 'The Vertical Solitude: Managing in the Public Sector' (with J. Jabes); 'Shifting Sands: Managing People in Public Bureaucracies: Summary of Discussions'; 'The Image of the Public Service in Canada' 'Bonuses and Performance in the Public Sector'; 'Organizational Culture in Public Bureaucracies'; (with Rodney Dobell) 'An Evaluation System for Government: If Politics is Theatre, then Evaluation is (mostly) Art'; 'Motivation, Rewards, and Satisfaction in the Candn. Federal Public Service'; 'Government Service to the Public'; Mem., Bd. of Govs., Candn. Comprehensive Audit Foundation; Mem., Inst. of Public Admin.; Candn. Psychol. Assn.; Board of Dirs. (interim), World Trade Centre (Ottawa); recreations: squash, tennis; club: Rideau; Cercle Univ.; Address: 749 Island Park Dr., Ottawa, Ont. K1Y 0B9.

**ZWAIG, Melvin C.,** B.Comm., F.C.A.; financial executive; b. Montreal, Que. 8 Dec. 1936; e. Sir George Williams Univ. B.Comm. 1959; PRES., ARTHUR ANDERSEN INC.; articled with Riddell Stead; admitted to Que. Order of Chartered Accountants 1961 (F.C.A. 1984); Ont. Inst. 1964 (F.C.A. 1985); Alta. Inst. 1983; Lectr., Extension Dept., McGill Univ. 1962–68; Partner, Riddell Stead, 1968–74; Partner & National Director, Receivership and Insolvency, Thorne Riddell; Pres., Thorne Riddell Inc. 1974–84; Executive Partner, Spicer MacGillivray 1984–86; Adv. on insolvency legislation, Senate Ctte. on Banking, Trade and Commerce; Adv. to Min. of Consumer and Corporate Affairs on amendments to the Bankruptcy Act.; Affil.: Candn. Insolvency Assn. (Chrmn. of Professional Standards Ctte. 1983); Certified Public Accountants of Israel (Associate Internat. Mem.); Inst. of Candn. Bankers (Mem., Academic Ctte. 1975–77); Montreal Bd. of Trade (Mem., Insolvency Ctte. 1971–74); Commercial Law League of America (Mem., Bankruptcy Ctte. and Candn. Membership Ctte. 1971–74); Candn. Inst. of Chartered Accountants (Chrmn., Bankruptcy Study Group 1969–74); Que. Order of Chartered Accountants (Mem., Extve. Ctte., newsletter editor and Summer evening sch. lectr., Students' Soc., 1962–64); Ben-Gurion Univ. of the Negev, Israel (Vice-Chrmn., Bd. of Govs. and Mem., Extve. Ctte.); Candn. Associates of the Ben-Gurion Univ. of the Negev (Pres., Montreal Branch and Nat. Treas. 1978–81, Nat. Pres., 1981–85); Nat. Treas., Candn. Assocs; Mem. Bd. of Govs., Montreal Israel Bond Orgn. (Dir.); Comité Quebec-Israel, Montreal (Dir.); Candn. Liver Found. (Chrmn.); Junior Achievement, Metro-Toronto (Mem., Bd. of Govs. and Chrmn., Gen. Campaign, 1986–87); Chrmn., Capital Funds Campaign 1989–90; Jewish Public Library, Montreal (Gov.); Order of St. John (Hon. Mem. of Council, Quebec Counc.); Candn. Friends of Haifa Univ. (Nat. Bd. Mem.); Concordia Univ., Montreal (Mem. Adv. Bd.); Mount Royal Lodge, B'Nai B'Rith, Montreal (Mem.); Canada Lodge (Mem.); Canada-Israel Chamber of Commerce, (Hon. Vice Pres.; Pres. 1984–85); Club Laurier (Depy. Chrmn.); Laurier Club 1988, 1989, 1990 (Co-Chrmn.); Dir., Beth Halochem; Shaare Zedek Congregation, Montreal (Dir., 1983–84); Adventure Place, Toronto (Treas. 1982, Dir. 1984); Assn. of Alumni, Sir George Williams Univ. (Pres. 1972–74); Student Zionist Orgn. (Pres. 1958–59); B'Nai B'Rith Hillel, Sir George Williams Univ. (Pres. 1956–57); co-author: 'The Proposed Bankruptcy Act, 1975 (C-60)'; 'The Proposed Bankruptcy Act, 1978 (Bill S-11)'; Clubs: Bayview Golf and Country; Ontario; Fitness Inst. (all of Toronto); Faculty Club, Concordia Univ.; Montefiore (both of Montreal); Residence: #2502 – 65 Harbour Square, Toronto, Ont. M5J 2L4; Office: 79 Wellington St. W., 19th Flr., IBM Tower, Toronto-Dominion Centre, Toronto, Ont. M5K 1H1.

**ZWELLING, Marc,** B.Sc.; strategist; b. Cleveland, Ohio 19 Sept. 1946; s. Karl and Rose Lee (Feldman) Z.; e. Northwestern Univ. B.Sc. (Jour.) 1968; m. Judith Marsh d. Dorothy Asher Adam 1 May 1978; children: Brendan, Arden; FOUNDER AND PRES. VECTOR RESEARCH + DEVELOPMENT INC. 1980– ; Dir. of Forecasting and Facilitator, Intercorporate Futures Group (national network for corporate planners) 1983– ; Reporter for United Press Internat. Chicago, Candn. Press Toronto, Toronto Telegram; Staff Rep. Dist. 6 Un. Steelworkers Am., Dept. Head Pub. Relations Nat. Office Toronto 1979; created Union Operations seminars for sr. execs. Niagara Inst., Niagara-on-the-Lake, Ont.; designed training package forecasting techniques for non-tech. mgr.; lectr. opinion rsch. strategy Can. and USA; Lectr., Candn. Forces Staff College 1992– ; Candn. Centre for Management Development 1991; recipient Medill Scholarship 1964–65; Founder: 'Vector Union Report'; Rsch. Dir., 'Vector Public Opinion Report'; monthly monitor of polls; Publisher and contributor: 'John Kettle's FutureLetter' (monthly forecasting service) 1982– ; contbr.: 'The Media Game' anthol.; 'Content' mag.; Ed., 'Sustainable Farming: Possibilities 1990–2020' Science Council of Canada; 'Science for the Future, 1990–2016' Science Council of Canada; Author, 'Futurology,' 'Harrowsmith' magazine, Nov.-Dec. 1991; 'Desktop Farms... Alternative Futures for Sustainable Agriculture,' 'The Futurist' magazine July-Aug. 1992; mem. Profl. Mktg. Rsch. Soc.; World Futures Soc.; Am. Assn. for Public Opinion Rsch.; Toronto Newspaper Guild (Past Pres.); recreations: jogging, reading; Home: 101 Gordon Rd., North York, Ont. M2P 1E5.

**ZWICKER, Barrie Wallace;** publisher; media critic; b. White Head, N.S. 5 Nov. 1934; s. Wilfred Grenfell and Norah (Hall) Z.; e. Russell (Man.) Coll. Inst. 1951; Ryerson Inst. of Technol. Cert. in Journalism 1958 (winner Maclean-Hunter Gold Watch for top standing grad. yr.); Univ. of Mich. (Press Club Co-op. Journalism Fellowship) 1959–61; m. Jean d. Charles and Adie Muzzell 1 Feb. 1964; children: Xena-Linda Yalina, Gren-Erich Charles; FOUNDER AND PUBLISHER, SOURCES 1977– ; joined Russell (Man.) Banner 1950; served weeklies Sask. and B.C. to 1955; Candn. and U.S. daily newspapers 1958–69 incl. The Globe and Mail 1961–68 and The Toronto Star (Edn. Ed.) 1969; taught Media & Soc. and Media, Ethics & the Law courses Ryerson 1970–75, 1980–83; purchased 'content' mag. 1974, Publisher 7 yrs.; conducted numerous print and broadcast commentaries, interviews and lectures critiquing media performance; exec. producer first prog. 'CANADAthon 72' CITY-TV 1972; syndicated commentator 'Facing the Fourth Estate' CBC Radio 1981–85; commentator 'Media Seen' 1988–90; 'Arts Express' VISION-TV 1991–93; recipient top 3 awards (nat., provl. (state) & local coverage) Education Writers Assn. of Am. 1966; author 'War, Peace and the Media' 1983; co-author, ed. 'Increasing the Commercial Revenue of the Special-Interest Magazine' 1973; 'The News. Inside the Canadian Media' 1982; adv. ctte. Esprit Orch.; exec. co-ord. Candn. Periodical Pubs. Assn. 1974 and bd. mem. 3 yrs.;

Hon. Life Mem., Media Club Can.; mem. ACTRA; Candn. Assn. Journalists; Toronto Press Club; Alliance Non-Violent Action; Council of Candns.; Humanist Assn. Can.; World Federalists Can.; Corp. mem. Recycling Council Ont.; NDP; recreations: theatre, music, tennis, skiing; Home: 91 Raglan Ave., Toronto, Ont. M6C 2K7.

**ZWICKER, Sherman Fenwick Homer,** B.A.; executive; b. Halifax, N.S. 10 Feb. 1930; s. Fenwick Homer and Marion Louise (Dearborn) Z.; e. Lunenburg Co. Acad., 1935–44; Rothesay (N.B.) Coll. Sch., 1944–47; Dalhousie Univ. B.A. 1950; (Pres. Students' Council 1949–50); m. Elinor Barbara, d. Dr. Samuel Marcus, Bridgewater, N.S., 30 June 1956; children: Peter Sherman, Lisa Ann, Andrea Barbara; Exec. Dir., Union of Nova Scotia Municipalities, (retired Sept. 1990); Mem. Adv. Bd., Royal Trust Co., N.S.; Pres. & Mang. Dir.,

Zwicker & Co. Ltd., (Estbd. 1789) since 1960; joined family firm as Secy.-Treas. 1953; Exec. Dir. Union of Nova Scotia Municipalities, March 1980–90; Pres. local Br. of Candn. Red Cross, 1961–63; Secy., Lunenburg Bd. Trade, 1953–56; mem. Bd. of Mgmt., Lunenburg-Queen's Mental Health Assn. 1962; Past Dir., Fisheries Council of Can.; Pres., Candn. Atlantic Salt Fish Exporters Assn. 1956–58, 1967–70; Pres. Union of Nova Scotia Municipalities 1977–78; Pres., Lunenburg-Queen's Br. and mem. Prov. Extve., Candn. Mental Health Assn. 1969–70; Councillor, Town of Lunenburg 1958–66; el. Mayor, Town of Lunenburg 1971–79; Dir., Lunenburg Heritage Soc. and Marine Museum Soc.; Gov., Dalhousie Univ. 1983–89 and 1990–93; Mem., Provincial Electoral Boundaries Commn.; Alpha Mu; Zeta Psl; Anglican; Clubs: Bluenose Golf, (Pres. 1958–60); Lunenburg Yacht (Secy. 1958–60, 1967–70); Lunenburg Curling; R.N.S.Y.S.; Home: 101 Mason's Beach Rd.,

Lunenburg, N.S. B0J 2C0; Mailing Address: P.O. Box 940, Lunenburg, N.S. B0J 2C0.

**ZWICKY, Jan,** B.A., M.A., Ph.D.; poet, philosopher, essayist; b. Calgary, Alta. 10 May 1955; d. Robert William and Jean Nellie (Keeley) Z.; e. Univ. of Calgary B.A. 1976; Univ. of Toronto M.A. 1977, Ph.D. 1981; teaching positions in philosophy, in humanities, and/or in envir. studies: Univ. of Waterloo 1981, '84, '85, Princeton Univ. 1982, Univ. of W. Ont. 1989, Univ. of Alta. 1992; freelance violinist; independent scholar; Editor, Brick Books; Book Review Editor, 'The Fiddlehead'; recipient of Canada Council, SSHRCC & num. other grants for creative & scholarly work; author: 'Wittgenstein Elegies' 1986, 'The New Room' 1989, 'Lyric Philosophy' 1992; Mailing address: Box 1149, Mayerthorpe, Alta. T0E 1N0.

**EADIE, Thomas Michael,** B.A., M.A., M.L.S.; librarian; b. Halifax, N.S. 21 April 1941; s. James Thomas and Margaret Patricia E.; e. Trinity College School 1960; Queen's Univ. B.A. 1968, M.A. 1971; Univ. of Western Ont. M.L.S. 1972; m. Joan d. Jack and Bessie Amos 28 Dec. 1965; children: Katherine Jennifer, Beverley Anne; DIRECTOR OF LIBRARIES, UNIV. OF CALGARY 1992– ; Copywriter, Simpsons-Sears 1963; Textile Worker, DuPont 1964–65; Tutor, McArthur Coll. of Edn. 1968; Tutor, Phil. Dept., Queen's Univ. 1968–70; Librarian, Info. & Orientation, Univ. of B.C. 1972–74; Head Ref. & Collection Devel., Porter Lib., Univ. of Waterloo 1974–87; Univ. Lib., Mt. Allison Univ. 1987–92; Cons., Library Review, Univ. of P.E.I. 1992; Brandon Univ. 1989; Bd. of Dir., Anchorage Press 1991– ; Dir. of Mktg., Binkley Communication Serv. 1990–92; Editor, Quarry and Quarry Press 1962–68; Mem., Candn. Lib Assn. (Councillor 1991–94); Candn. Assn. Coll & Univ. Lib.; Candn. Assn. Univ. Teachers; Candn. Parents for French; Atlantic Prov. Lib. Assn.; Council of Head Libn's N.B.; Assn. of Atlantic Univ. Lib. Council; Candn. Assn. of Small Univ. Lib.; Humanities Assn. of Can.; N.B. Assn. for Cont. Ed.; Bibliographical Soc. of Can.; Candn. Assn. of Rsch. Libs; Library Assn. of Alta.; several past executive assn. appointments; author: 'The Beast With Three Backs' (poetry) 1965 and several articles and occasional papers; Home: 39 Hawkhill Mews NW, Calgary, Alta. T3G 3A3; Office: Calgary, Alta. T2N 1N4.

**EAGLES, Stuart Ernest,** B.Sc.; executive; b. Saint John, N.B. 29 July 1929; s. Ernest Lyle and Evelyn Gertrude (Feltmate) E.; e. Summerside Acad. P.E.I.; Acadia Univ. B.Sc. 1949, D.C.L. (Honorary) 1992; m. Margaret Anne Gulliver 30 Sept. 1952; children: James Stuart, Patricia Anne, Mark Edward Ernest; PRES. AEGEAN DEVELOPMENTS INC.; Dir. AGF Trust Co.; Hardit Corp.; The Ont. Chamber of Commerce; Jr. Achievement; Past Trustee and Dir. Internat. Council Shopping Centres; Past Pres. & Dir. Candn. Inst. Pub. Real Estate Co's; Clubs: National (Past Pres. & Dir.); Canadian; Empire; Office: 130 Adelaide St. W., Ste. 1714, Toronto, Ont. M5H 3P5.

**EAGLESON, R. Alan,** O.C., Q.C., B.A., LL.B.; b. St. Catharines, Ont. 24 Apr. 1933; s. James Allen E.; e. Mimico (Ont.) High Sch.; Univ. of Toronto, B.A. 1954, LL.B. 1957; Osgoode Hall Law Sch., 1959; m. Nancy, d. Melvin Fisk, 1960; children: Trevor Allen, Jill Anne; read law with J.D.W. Cumberland, Q.C.; called to Bar of Ont. 1959; cr. Q.C. 1972; Extve. Dir., Nat. Hockey League Players' Assn. 1967–91; directed formation of above Assn. 1967; Chief Negotiator for Canada's Internat. Hockey Programme 1974–93; helped form and direct, Team Canada, World Hockey Champions 1972; Chrmn. Canada Cup of Hockey 1976, 1981, 1984, 1987, 1991; el. M.P.P. for Toronto Lakeshore in prov. g.e. 1963; el. Pres., Ont. Progressive Conservative Assn. 1968–76; Dir.: Teledyne Canada Limited; Hockey Canada; Big Bros. Metrop. Toronto; Gov., Queensway Gen. Hosp.; Etobicoke Gen. Hosp.; Vanier Award Winner 1968; Lester B. Pearson Peace Award Winner 1987; el. Member, Canada Sports Hall of Fame 1988; el. Hockey Hall of Fame 1989; Officer, Order of Canada 1989; mem., Law Soc. Upper Can.; York Co. Law Assn.; recreations: golf, skiing, tennis; Clubs: Albany; Empire; Lambton Golf & Country; Toronto Lawn Tennis; Craigleith Ski; Home: Toronto, Ont.; Office: Maitland House, 37 Maitland St., Toronto, Ont. M4Y 1C8.

**EALES, John Geoffrey,** B.A., M..Sc., Ph.D., F.R.S.C.; educator; b. Wolverhampton, Eng. 9 Sept. 1937; s. John Gordon and Marion (Phipps) E.; e. Dudley Grammar Sch. Eng. 1956; Oxford Univ. B.A. 1959; Univ. of B.C. M.Sc. 1961, Ph.D. 1963; m. Sachiko d. Hyozo and Shizu (Hamaguchi) Tabata 25 May 1963; children: John David, Carol Ann; DISTINGUISHED PROF. UNIV. OF MAN. 1989– , Prof. of Zool. 1973– ; Asst. Prof. Univ. of N.B. 1963–67; Asst. Prof. present Univ. 1967, Assoc. Prof. 1969, Assoc. Dean Grad. Studies 1978–79, Dir. Biol. Teaching Unit 1979–80; recipient Olive Beatrice Stanton Award for excellence in undergrad. teaching 1974; Rh Award for Rsch. Excellence 1983; Killam Rsch. Fellow 1989; Candn. Track Champion and Winner Candn. Olympic Trials 1500 m and 5000 m 1960; author over 100 rsch. articles, monographs and reviews fish endocrinol.; ed. Candn. Jour. Zool. 1988– ; ed. bd. Gen. & Comparative Endocrinol. 1974– ; mem. Candn. Soc. Zools.; Am. Soc. Zools.; NSERC Cttes. (Postdoctoral Fellowships; Animal Biol. Grant Selection; Adv. Ctte. Life Sci's); recreations: running, flyfishing, cottage building; Home: 75 Fordham Bay, Winnipeg, Man. R3T 3B8; Office: Winnipeg, Man. R3T 2N2.

**EARL, Allan E.,** B.Sc., M.Sc., Ph.D.; food industry executive; b. Kingston, Ont. 19 Sept. 1939; s. Robert Cecil and Charlotte Elizabeth (Fair) E.; e. Queen's Univ. B.Sc. 1961, M.Sc. 1963; Univ. of Alberta Ph.D. 1968; m. Elizabeth d. Harriet and Don Stratton 29 Dec. 1961; children: Kelly Anne, Robert Donald, Graham Allan; CHIEF EXECUTIVE OFFICER, B.C. TREE FRUITS 1988– ; Senior Scientist, Labatt Breweries of Canada 1968–74; Engineer, Food Product Devel., Dept. of Industry & Commerce, Govt. of Manitoba 1975–76; Dir., Candn. Food Products Devel. Ctr., Portage La Prairie, Man. 1977–78; Pres., Canola Council of Canada (Winnipeg) 1978–88; Former Dir., POS Pilot Plant Saskatoon; Fellow, Chem. Inst. of Canada; Mem., Unitarian Ch. (Mem. of Bd. at London, Winnipeg & Kelowna; Pres. at Kelowna); Home: 2211 Shannon Way, Westbank, B.C. V4T 1S2; Office: 1473 Water St., Kelowna, B.C. V1Y 1J6.

**EARLE, Arthur Frederick,** B.Sc., Ph.D.; economic and management consultant; b. Toronto, Ont. 13 Sept. 1921; s. Frederick Charles and Hilda Mary (Brown) E.; e. Univ. of Toronto; London Sch. of Econ., B.Sc. (Econ.), Ph.D.; m. Vera Domini, d. late Harry G. Lithgow, 16 Nov. 1946; children: Timothy Arthur Frederick, Michael Nelson Lithgow, Wendy Jacqueline; Dir. Rio Algom Ltd. (to 1992); with Canada Packers Limited 1946–48; joined Aluminium Limited, British Guiana, West Indies, and Canada 1948–53; became Treas., Alumina Jamaica Limited 1953–55; Sales Executive, Aluminium Union, London 1955–58; apptd. Vice Pres., Aluminium Ltd. Sales Inc., New York 1958–61; joined Hoover Ltd., Eng., as Depy. Chrmn. and Mang. Dir. (from 1963) 1961–65; first Principal, London (U.K.) Grad. Sch. of Business Studies 1965–72; Pres. International Investment Corp. for Yugoslavia, S.A. (World Bank) 1972–74; Pres., Boyden Consulting Group Ltd. 1974–82; Sr. Vice Pres. of (parent Co.) Boyden Associates, Inc., Nov. 1980–82; Advisor to the Pres., Canada Development Investment Corp. 1983–86; served with R.C.N., rising from Rating to Lieut. Commander 1939–46; Dir., Nat. Ballet of Canada 1982–85; Gov. Ashridge Mang. Coll., Eng. 1962–65; mem., Council of Industrial Design; Gov., The National Institute of Econ. and Social Research; Fellow, Brit. Inst. of Management; mem. Consumer Council 1963–68; Econ. Devel. Comte., Elect. Indust. 1965–71; N.E.D.O. Comte. on Mgmt. Educ., Training & Devel. 1967–69; Council of Mgmt., The Ditchley Foundation; Gov. and Hon. Fellow, London Sch. of Econ.; Chrmn., Candn. Assn. of Friends of L.S.E.; Fellow, The London Grad. Sch. of Business Studies, London, Eng. 1988; Sr. Rsch. Fellow, NCMRD (Nat. Centre for Mgmt. Rsch. and Devel.), Sch. of Bus. Admin., Univ. of Western Ont. 1988–90; Anglican; recreation: hill climbing; Club: The Royal Candn. Mil. Inst.; Home: 1234 Rushbrooke Dr., Oakville, Ont. L6M 1K9.

**EARLE, Arthur Percival,** B.E., F.E.I.C.; textile manufacturer; b. Montreal, Que. 23 Apr. 1922; s. Arthur P. and Bernadette (Gosselin) E.; e. Westmount (Que.) High Sch.; Trinity Coll. Sch. Port Hope, Ont.; McGill Univ. B.E. 1949; Harvard Business Sch. Dipl. Business Adm.; m. Muriel Elizabeth d. John G. Vining, Cap-de-la-Madeleine, Que. June 1946; children: Arthur, Richard, Janet; BD. CHRMN., AEROPORTS DE MONTREAL 1989– ; joined Shawinigan Water & Power Co. 1949–63 serving as Engr., Supt., Asst. Mgr. Production Plant Dept.; joined Dominion Textile Inc. as Asst. Chief Engr. 1963, became Chief Engr. 1965, Vice Pres. 1969, Group Vice Pres. 1971, Sr. Vice Pres. 1978–88, Corporate Affairs Consultant 1988–90; Past Pres., Fireside Fabrics; Lana Knit; Elpee Yarns; Jaro Ltd.; Fiberworld Ltd.; Past Chrmn., Penmans Ltd.; Bd. Chrmn., Foresbec Inc. 1990–92 (Bd. of Dir. 1988–93, Chrmn. 1990); Bd. of Dir. & Chrmn. Stella-Jones Inc. 1993– ; Bd. of Dir., Hubbard Dyers Ltd. 1986–94; Shermag 1989– ; Avec Technologies 1987– ; President, Montreal Bd. Trade 1980–81, Chairman 1981–82; Pres., Cham. de Comm. du Qué. 1983–84, Pres. Honoraire 1984–85; Pres. Les Mercuriades 1985; mem. of Bd., Ecole de Technologie Supérieure de l'Université du Qué. 1978–84, Exec. Ctte. 1981–84, Vice Pres. 1982–84; Bd. of Dir., Centraide Montreal 1982–88, Exec. Ctte. 1985–88, Vice-Pres. 1987–88; Chrmn. Exec. Ctte., Phoenix Found. 1985–89; Nat. Treas., Engn. Ins. Can. 1986–88, Sr. Vice Pres. 1988–89, Pres. 1989–90; Chrmn., Le Conseil de l'Aeroport International de Montréal 1987–89; mem. Bd. of Dirs., Lakeshore Gen. Hosp. 1987– , Vice Chair 1989– ; Pres., Lakeshore Gen. Hosp. Corp. 1991– ; Chrmn. & Pres., Aeroports de Montréal 1989–90, Chrmn. 1990– ; Chrmn. & Pres., La Société de Promotion de l'Aeroport de Montreal 1989– ; mem. Bd. of Dirs., Candn. Airports Council 1990, Chrmn. 1990–93; served with RCAF 1941–45; Pilot Offr.; Fellow, Engr. Inst. of Can. 1988; recipient, Award of Distinction for Exceptional Service to the Community, Concordia Univ. 1989; Hon. Bd. Chrmn., Phoenix Found. 1991– ; mem. Inst. Elect. & Electronic Engrs. (Past Sec. Chrmn.); mem., Engn. Inst. Can.; Assn. Prof. Engrs. Prov. Ont.; Ordre des Ingénieurs du Qué.; Anglican; recreations: golf, curling, fishing; Clubs: Mt. Stephen; Royal Montreal Golf; Montreal Thistle Curling (Past Pres.); M.A.A.A.; Home: 63 White Pine Dr., Beaconsfield, Que. H9W 5E4; Office: 1100 René Levesque Blvd., Ste. 2100, Montreal, Que. H3B 4X8.

**EARLE, Eric Davis,** B.Sc., M.Sc., D.Phil.; scientist; b. Carbonear, Nfld. 26 Nov. 1937; s. Eric Guy and Mildred Hannah (Davis) E.; e. Memorial Univ. of Nfld. B.Sc. 1958; Univ. of B.C., M.Sc. 1960; Oxford Univ. D.Phil. 1964; Rhodes Scholar 1960–63; m. Kerstin Bjarbo 1 Aug. 1977; children: Mark Davis, Simon Joseph, Steven Philip; SCIENTIFIC OFFR., ATOMIC ENERGY OF CANADA LTD. 1964– ; specializing in nuclear physics; Assoc. Dir., Sudbury Neutrino Observatory collaboration; mem. Candn. Assn. of Physics; recreations: skiing, canoeing; Home: Box 1302, Deep River, Ont. K0J 1P0; Office: Stn. 18A, CRNL, AECL, Chalk River, Ont. K0J 1J0.

**EARP, Alan,** O.C. (1987), M.A., M.Litt., LL.D.; educator; b. Toronto, Ont. 18 Feb. 1925; s. Rev. William Arthur and Laura (Sloan) E.; e. Cheam Sch., Eng.; Marlborough Coll., Eng.; Trinity Coll., Univ. of Toronto, B.A. 1948; Univ. of Cincinnati (Teaching Fellow), M.A. 1950; Jesus Coll., Cambridge Univ., M.Litt. 1952; Univ. of N.B., LL.D. 1968; Trent Univ., LL.D. 1987; Brock Univ. LL.D. 1990; two s., Stephen, Jonathan; PRES. EMERITUS, BROCK UNIV.; joined Univ. of Manchester as Asst. Lectr. 1952–53; Univ. Coll. of N. Staffordshire (now Keele Univ.) 1953–54; Lectr., Univ. of W. Indies, 1954–55; Dean of Men, Registrar and Assoc. Prof. of Classics, Trinity College, Univ. of Toronto 1955–64; Registrar and Prof. of Classics, Carleton Univ. 1964–65; Princ. and Vice. Chancellor, Univ. of Guyana, 1965–68; Provost and Vice-Pres., Brock Univ. 1968–73, Pres. and Vice-Chancellor 1973–88; served with Argyll & Sutherland Highlanders of Can., 1943–45; N.W. Europe; rank Lt.; author of various articles; Pres., Candn. Bureau Internat. Educ. 1977–79; Pres., Assoc. Univ. and Coll. of Canada, 1979–81; Chrmn., Counc. of Ont. Univs. 1985–87; Hon. Senator, Albert-Ludwig's Universitat, Freiburg, Germany 1988; Hon. Lt. Col., Lincoln and Welland Regiment 1989; Anglican; Home: 248 Palatine Place, Niagara-on-the-Lake, Ont. L0S 1J0.

**EASSON, Alison Christine Harle,** B.A., M.A.; curator, archaeologist; b. Seahouses, Northumberland, England 12 April 1941; d. James Alfred and Constance (Balfour) Harle; e. Univ. of Alberta B.A. 1961; Univ. of Toronto M.A. 1968; m. Bruce Albert s. Albert and Ethel E.; ASSOCIATE CURATOR IN CHARGE, GREEK & ROMAN DEPT., ROYAL ONTARIO MUSEUM 1988– ; Curatorial Asst., Greek & Roman Dept., Royal Ont. Mus. 1962–68; Asst. Curator 1968–86; Assoc. Curator 1986– ; Fellow, Soc. of Antiquaries of London (UK); Mem., Archaeological Inst. of Am.; Am. Numismatic Soc.; London & Middlesex Arch. Soc. (UK); Study Group for Roman Pottery (UK); author: 'Central and East Gaulish Mould-Decorated Samian Ware in the Royal Ontario Museum' 1988 and articles; recreation: needlework; Home: 147 Kenilworth Ave., Toronto, Ont. M4L 3S7; Office: 100 Queen's Park, Toronto, Ont. M5S 2C6.

**EASTCOTT, Donald R.;** strategic management consultant; socio-economic philosopher; futurist; b. Rossland, B.C. s. Wilbert Franklin and Christie Ann (McLeod) E.; e. Univ. of Notre Dame, Univ. of B.C., Univ. of Alta., Univ. of Boston, Dips. in Bus. Adm., Pub. Relations, Personnel Adm., Real Property Adm., Interpersonal Skills; m. Marie Elizabeth; 3 children; PRES., EADON COMPANIES GROUP 1974– ; MNG. DIR. & CORPORATE SEC., CANDN. ORGN. SMALL BUS. INC. 1987– ; journalist, lecturer, editor and businessman 1962–67; bus. cons. and small bus. owner and psychology researcher, adult student Univ. of Alta. 1967–69; Asst. to Dean of Pharm. Univ. of Alta. 1969–74; Pres., Alberta Country; Pres., North Glenora Community League; Chrmn. Adv. Bd., Enviro-cycle Expediting Ltd.; mem. Am. Legis. Exchange Council; Soc. of Mfg. Engrs.; Northern Alta. Economic Soc.; Alta. Found. for Economic Educ.; The Conf. Soc. of Alta.; The Planning Forum; Pres., Progressive Savings & Credit Union; Alberta Country; North Glenora Community Leagues; Chrmn. Advisory Bd., Envirocycle Expediting Ltd.; Mem. Bd. of Dirs., numerous business orgns.; active in several community organizations; serves as mem. of several govt. adv. cttes. and bds.; named Family of Yr.; twice runner-up Citizen of Yr.; nominee finalist Gov. Gen.'s Award Outstanding Young Candn.; Office: P.O. Box 11246, Edmonton, Alta. T5J 1L6.

**EASTCOTT, Robert Wayne,** R.C.A.; artist; b. Trail, B.C. 20 July 1943; s. George Rowland and Annie Spence (Johnson) E.; e. Robson and Rossland, B.C. elem. and high schs.; Vancouver Sch. of Art 1962–66; m. Shirley Lydia d. John Thomas Place, Burnaby, B.C. 6 July 1968; one d. Elizabeth Rose; Lectr., Capilano Coll. N. Vancouver since 1973 (estbd. Print Making Dept. 1975 and The Art Inst. 1981); Graphic Artist, KVOS-TV 12 Vancouver 1967–70; Cascade Electronics 1972; Instr. Vancouver Sch. of Art 1965–74; solo exhns. incl. Mary Frazee Vancouver 1969; Pollock Gallery Toronto 1971; Priestlay Gallery (Equinox) Vancouver 1971; Gallery Pascal Toronto 1975; Gallery Graphics Ottawa 1976; Fleet Gallery Winnipeg 1977, 1980; Kabutoya, Tokyo 1979; Crown Gallery, Vancouver B.C. 1985, 1987; Burnaby Art Gallery 1988, Okui Assoc., Tokyo, Japan 1989; Outlook Gallery, Regent Coll., Vanvoucer, B.C. 1990; Patrick Doheny & Assoc. Fine Art Ltd. 1991; rep. in group exhns. Can., USA, S.Am., Europe, Japan and Hawaii since 1965; rep. in various perm. colls. Can., Japan and USA incl. Can. Council Art Bank, Nat. Gallery Can.; rec'd Can. Council Grant 1968 for research in Print Making utilizing xerox equipment; since 1979 involved in Japanese Print community with extended study/exhibition trips in 1979, 1983, 1989; cited numerous bibliogs.; represented by Okai Assn., Tokyo, Japan and Patrick Doheny & Assoc. Fine Art Ltd., Vancouver, B.C.; mem. Soc. Candn. Artists; Dundarave Print Workshop (Founding mem., Pres. 1972–77); Malaspina Print Soc.; Print & Drawing Council Can.; World Print Council; Presbyterian; recreations: camping, winemaking.

**EASTER, Wayne Arnold,** M.P.; farmer; union executive; b. Charlottetown, P.E.I. 22 June 1949; s. A. Leith and Hope (MacLeod) E.; e. Charlottetown Rural H.S. 1969; N.S. Agric. Coll. Dip. 1970; Hon. LL.D., Univ. of P.E.I. 1988; m. Helen Arleighn Laird 25 July 1970; children: Kimberley Ann, Jamie Neil; MEMBER OF PARLIAMENT FOR MALPEQUE, 1993– ; Owner Easterhaven Farms (dairy, beef & grain); Nat. Jr. Pres. Union 1973, Regional Coordr. (Maritimes) 1978–80, Nat. Vice Pres. 1980–81, mem. P.E.I. Family Farm Adv. Ctte. 1976; North Wiltshire Community Improvement Ctte. 1976–78; Pres. and C.E.O., National Farmers Union 1982–93; Nat. Bd. and Extve. Mem., Counc. of Canadians 1992; Del. with Min. of Agric. F.A.O. Rome 1982; Adv. to fed. agency Canagrex 1983; chosen del. 1983 Gov. Gen. Conf.; Del. Farm. Peace Mtg., Sofia, Bulgaria 1986; European Economic Community E.C.V.P. 1987, examining agric. policy in Germany, France, Belgium, Denmark; mem. Holstein Assn. Can.; United Church; awarded Commemorative Medal for 125th Anniversary of Candn. Confederation; recreations: skating, golf; Home: North Wiltshire, P.E.I. C0A 1Y0; Office: 466W, House of Commons, Ottawa, Ont. K1A 0A6.

**EASTERBROOK, James Arthur,** M.A., Ph.D.; educator; psychologist; b. Spooner (E. Beaudette), Minn. 10 Apr. 1923; s. William James Arthur and Bertha Lillian (Amorde) E.; e. Dauphin, Man. pub. schs. 1940 (Gov. Gen.'s Medal); St. Mary's Priory; Univ. of Man. sr. matric. 1941; Queen's Univ. B.A. 1949, M.A. 1954; Univ. of London Ph.D. 1963; m. Margaret Pamela Edith d. late James Evans 19 Nov. 1944; children: Christine Susan (Tricoteux), Anthony James, Pamela Jane (Nadeau), Laurence Arthur, Margaret Ann; Professor Emeritus 1990, Prof. of Psychol., Univ. of N.B. 1967–88, Head of Dept. 1967–73; Reporter, Dauphin Herald & Press 1940–41; Partner, J. A. Easterbrook & Co., retail trade Dauphin, Man. 1946–49; News Ed. and Assoc. Ed. Queens Journal 1946–49; Research Offr. Inst. Aviation Med. RCAF 1949; Lectr. in Psychol. Queen's Univ. 1949–50; Defence Research Scient. Offr. Fort Churchill, Edmonton, Halifax 1950–57; Research Asst. Inst. of Psychiatry, London, Eng. 1958; Research Psychol. Burden Neurol. Inst. Bristol, Eng. 1959–61; Asst. Prof. of Psychiatry Univ. of Alta. 1961–67; Visiting Lectr. Massey Univ., N.Z. 1976, 1987; recipient J. McBeth Milligan Fellowship in Philos. 1949–50; Social Sciences & Humanities Research Council Can. Research Fellowship 1979–80; 'Citation Classic,' Current Contents, 1982; Chrmn. and Dir. Research Jt. Consultative Comte. Phase Down Coal Mining, Minto, N.B. 1968–72; Dir. Social Science Research Inst. N.B. 1970–72; Consultant N.B. Newstart Inc. 1971–74; author 'Determinants of Free Will' 1978; over 56 research reports defence science and psychol.; contrib. to various scient. publs.; served with RCAF 1941–45, attached RAF 1942–45, rank Flight Lt.; mem. Brit. Psychol. Soc.; Coll. Psychols. N.B.; Assn. Univ. N.B. Teachers (local Vice Pres. 1973–74); N.B. Bd. Examiners Psychol. 1973–79 (Chrmn. 1978–79); United Church; recreations: swimming, gardening, genealogical research; Home: R.R. 5, Fredericton, N.B. E3B 4X6.

**EASTMAN, Barbara Christina,** M.A., D.Phil.; writer; company director; b. Toronto, Ont.; d. John Morgan and Kathleen (McGuire) E.; e. Bishop Strachan Sch. 1965; Univ. of Toronto Trinity Coll. B.A. 1968; York Univ. M.A. 1971; St. Hilda's Coll. Oxford D.Phil. 1978;

SECY.-TREAS. & DIR., PROBYN & CO. LTD.; Pres., Rostand Inc. 1990– ; Treasurer, Cochrane Power Corp. 1992– ; Kirkland Lake Power Corp. 1992– ; Whitecourt Power Corp. 1992– ; Chapais Electrique Ltée 1993– ; Dir., Enserve Power Corp.; joined Sir Thomas Browne Institute, Rijksuniversiteit te Leiden, Netherlands 1978–79; European Space Agency, Netherlands 1979–80; Imperial Oil Ltd. Toronto 1981–82; The Royal Bank of Canada, Toronto 1982–89; Dir.-Gen. Prov.-Mun. Secretariat 1988 Toronto Economic Summit; Dir. and Chrmn. Legis. Cttte. Candn. Assn. Women Execs. 1982–84; mem. Bd. Trade Metrop. Toronto (Exec. Forum Ctte. 1983–88); Exec. Council Inst. Pol. Involvement 1986–89; Dir. Addiction Rsch. Found. Toronto 1985–88; Dir. Couchiching Inst. Pub. Affairs 1985– , Pres. 1988–90; mem. National Comm., Campaign for Oxford 1989– ; Guest Lectr. Univ. of Cal. Berkeley 1977; Can. Council Doctoral Fellow 1972–75; Prov. Ont. Grad. Scholar 1970–72; York Univ. Postgrad. Fellow 1970–72; Hon. mem. Sr. Common Room Trinity Coll. Toronto 1987–89; author 'Ezra Pound's Cantos: The Story of the Text' 1977; mem., Oxford Soc. S.W. Ont. (Mem.'ship Sec. 1987–89); recreation: painting; club: RCYC; Home: 70 Rosehill Ave., Toronto, Ont. M4T 2W7; Windjammer Landing, St. Lucia, W.I.; Office: 95 King St. E., 2nd Floor, Toronto, Ont. M5C 1G4.

**EASTMAN, Donald Nial, Jr.,** B.A.; economist, grape growr; b. Listowel, Ont. 3 Oct. 1942; s. Donald Nial and Jessie Mary (Turbitt) E.; e. McMaster Univ. B.A. 1967; m. Beatrice d. Rose and Tom Harasen 28 Nov. 1964; one s.: Dunestan William Nial; OWNER, EASTMAN VINEYARD 1986– ; joined Dofasco Inc. 1967; seconded to B.C. Govt. as Steel Consultant 1975–76; Manager, Commercial Research 1976–90; Sr. Manager 1990–92; Vice-Pres., Policy, Ont. C. of C. 1992, '93; Dir., Extve. Council 1989–93; Chair, Economic Policy 1989–93; Mem., Nat. Statistics Council; recreations: wine and beer making, orchid growing, nordic skiing; club: Wentworth West Zymologists; Home: R.R. 1, Binbrook, Ont. L0R 1C0.

**EASTMAN, Harry Claude MacColl,** A.M., Ph.D.; former university professor; b. Vancouver, B.C., 29 July 1923; s. Samuel Mack and Antonia Françoise (Larribe) E.; Univ. of Toronto B.A. 1947; Univ. of Chicago, A.M. 1949, Ph.D. 1952; m. Sheila Baldwin, d. W. N. MacQueen, Toronto, Ont., 9 July 1949; three d. Julia, Alice, Harriet; CHRMN., PATENTED MEDICINE PRICES REVIEW BD. 1987– ; Prof. of Economics, Univ. of Toronto 1963–89 and Vice Pres. Research and Planning 1977–81; mem. of Candn. Nat. Comn. for UNESCO, 1957–60; mem., Candn. Pol. Science Assn. (Secy.-Treas. 1955–65); Internat. Econ. Assn. (mem. of Extve. Comte. 1968–74); Candn. Economics Assn. (Pres. 1971–72); Comnr., Comn. of Inquiry on the Pharm. Indus. 1984–85; elected Fellow, Royal Soc. of Canada 1974– ; served in 2nd World War with R.C.A.F., 1943–45; Home: 11 Maclennan Ave., Toronto, Ont. M4W 2Y4; Office: 6th Flr., Trebla Bldg., 473 Albert St., Ottawa, Ont. K1A 0C9.

**EASTON, David,** M.A., Ph.D., LL.D., F.R.S.C., F.A.A.A.S.; educator; b. Toronto, Ont. 24 June 1917; e. Univ. of Toronto B.A. 1939, M.A. 1943; Harvard Univ. Ph.D. 1947; McMaster Univ. LL.D. 1970; Kalamazoo Coll. LL.D. 1972; m. Sylvia Johnstone; one s. Stephen Talbot; DISTINGUISHED PROFESSOR OF POLITICAL SCIENCE, UNIV. OF CALIFORNIA 1982– ; Teaching Fellow in Govt. Harvard Univ. 1944–47; Asst. Prof. of Pol. Science Univ. of Chicago 1947, Assoc. Prof. 1953; Prof. 1955; Andrew MacLeish Distinguished Service Prof. 1969; Emeritus (1982); Sir Edward Peacock Prof. of Pol. Science Queen's Univ. 1971–80; Ford Prof. of Govt.'al Affairs 1960–61; Pres. Internat. Comte. on Social Science Documentation 1969–71, mem. Extve. Comte. 1965–69; Chrmn. Comte. on Information Behavioral Sciences, Nat. Acad. Sciences, Nat. Research Council 1966–70; mem. Extve. Comte. Social Science Educ. Consortium 1962–64, Inter-Univ. Consortium Pol. Research 1962–64; Consultant, Brookings Inst. 1953; Mental Health Research Inst. Univ. of Mich. 1955–56; Royal Comn. Bilingualism & Biculturalism Can. 1965–67; Comn. Examiners Grad. Record Examination Pol. Science, Educ. Testing Service Princeton 1966–68; Fellow, Center Advanced Study Behavioral Sciences Stanford, Cal. 1957–58; author 'The Political System: An Inquiry into the State of Political Science' 1953, 2nd ed. 1971; 'A Framework for Political Analysis' 1965; 'A Systems Analysis of Political Life' 1965; 'The Analysis of Political Structure' 1990; co-author 'Children in the Political System' 1969; ed. 'Varieties of Political Theory' 1966; co-editor 'Divided Knowledge: Academic Experiences in Contemporary Perspective' 1991; 'The Development of Political Science: A Comparative Survey' 1991; author various reports, articles; mem. Bd. Eds. various publs.; mem. Am. Pol. Science Assn. (Pres. 1968–69, Chrmn. Comte. Scient. Information Exchange 1970–73, mem. Council 1964–66); Am. Acad. Arts & Sciences (Chrmn. Comte. Research & Planning 1979–82, mem. Extve. Bd. 1978–82, Nat. Council 1975–83, Chrmn., Talcott Parsons Prize Comte. 1983–86); Vice Pres., American Academy of Arts & Sciences 1984–90; Co-Chrmn., Western Centre, Am. Acad. of Arts & Sci. 1984–90; Chair, People's Republic of China Exchange Program 1984– ; Candn. Pol. Science Assn. (Comte. Ethics & Research Policy 1976–77); Internat. Pol. Sci. Assn.; Office: School of Social Sciences, University of California, Irvine, Calif. 92717 USA.

# ABBREVIATIONS

Short forms of common words, positions, and place-names are used throughout the text where these are free of ambiguity and permit additional information within the space available. However, many other abbreviations, particularly ones relating to academic degrees, honours, and awards, also necessarily appear in the course of the biographies, and the following list of meanings is offered for the convenience of users of the *Canadian Who's Who*.

| | | | | | |
|---|---|---|---|---|---|
| A.A.A. | Amateur Athletic Association | B.A.O. | Bachelor of Obstetrics | B.S.M.E. | Bachelor of Science in Mechanical Engineering |
| A.A.G. | Assistant-Adjutant-General | B.Arch. | Bachelor of Architecture | | |
| A.A.O.N.M.S. | Ancient Arabic Order of the Nobles of the Mystic Shrine | Bart. | Baronet | B.S.P. | Bachelor of Science of Pharmacy |
| A.A. & Q.M.G. | Assistant Adjutant and Quartermaster General | B.A.S. | Bachelor in Agricultural Science | B.S.S. | Bachelor of Social Sciences |
| | | B.A.Sc. | Bachelor of Applied Science | B.S.W. | Bachelor of Social Work |
| A.B. | Bachelor of Arts (U.S.) | Batty. | Battery | Bt. | Brevet |
| A.C.A. | Associate of the Institute of Chartered Accountants (England) | B.B.A. | Bachelor of Business Administration | B.T., B.Th. | Bachelor of Theology |
| A.C.B.A | Associate of the Canadian Bankers Association | B.B.C. | British Broadcasting Corporation | Bucks. | Buckinghamshire |
| | | B.C.D. | Bachelier en Chirurgie Dentale | B.V.Sc. | Bachelor of Veterinary Science |
| Acad. | Academy; Academician; Academic | B.C.L. | Bachelor of Civil (or Common) Law | B.W.I. | British West Indies |
| A.C.C.O. | Associate of the Canadian College of Organists | B.Ch., B.Chir. | Bachelor of Surgery | (C). | Canada |
| | | B.Com. | | C.A. | Chartered Accountant |
| A.C.D. | Archaeologiae Christianae Doctor (See Doct. Arch.) | (B.Comm.) | Bachelor of Commerce | C.A.D.C. | Canadian Army Dental Corps |
| | | B.C.S. | Bachelor of Commercial Science | Cambs. | Cambridgeshire |
| A.D.C. | Aide-de-Camp | B.D. | Bachelor of Divinity | C.A.M.C. | Canadian Army Medical Corps |
| Ad eund. | Ad eundem gradum (admitted to the same degree) | B.D.C. | Bachelor of Canon Law (Bacc. Droit Canonique) | Cantab. | Pertaining to Cambridge University, England |
| Adj (t). | Adjutant | B.E. | Bachelor of Engineering | C.A.P.C. | Canadian Army Pay Corps |
| A.D.M.S. | Assistant Director of Medical Services | B.Ed. | Bachelor of Education | C.A.S.C. | Canadian Army Service Corps |
| | | Beds. | Bedfordshire | C.B. | Companion of the Bath; Cape Breton |
| A.F. & A.M. | Ancient Free and Accepted Masons | B.E.E. | Bachelor of Electrical Engineering | | |
| | | B.E.F. | British Expeditionary Force | C.B.C. | Canadian Broadcasting Corporation |
| A.F.C. | Air Force Cross | B. en Ph. | Bachelier en Philosophie | | |
| A.F.L. | American Federation of Labour | B.en Sc.Com. | Bachelier en Science Commerciale | C.B.E. | Commander Order of the British Empire |
| A.F.R.Ae.S. | Associate Fellow Royal Aeronautical Society | | | C.C. | Companion of the Order of Canada; Compagnon de l'Ordre du Canada |
| | | Berks. | Berkshire | | |
| Ag. de l'U (Paris) | Agrégé de l'Université (Paris) | B.ès A. | Bachelier ès Arts | | |
| | | B.ès L. | Bachelier ès Lettres | C.C.L. | Canadian Congress of Labour |
| Ag. de Phil. | Agrégé de Philosophie | B.ès Sc. | Bachelier ès Science | C.D. | Canadian Forces Decoration |
| Agron. | Agronomy; Agronomist | B.ès Sc.App. | Bachelier ès Science Appliqué | C.E. | Civil Engineer |
| A.I.A. | Associate of the Institute of Actuaries (England) | B.F. | Bachelor of Forestry | Cer.E. | Ceramic Engineer |
| | | Bgde. | Brigade | C.E.F. | Canadian Expeditionary Force |
| A.I.C.B. | Associate of the Institute of Canadian Bankers | B.J. | Bachelor of Journalism | Cert. | Certificate; Certified |
| | | B.J.C. | Bachelor in Canon Law | C.E.S. | Certificat d'études Secondaires (La Sorbonne) |
| A.I.C.E. | Associate of the Institute of Engineers (England) | B.L. | Bachelor in Literature (or of Laws) | | |
| | | | | C.F.A. | Canadian Field Artillery |
| A.I.I.A. | Associate Insurance Institute of America | B.Litt. | Bachelor of Letters (or of Literature) | C.H. | Companion of Honour |
| A.I.S.A. | Associate of the Incorporated Secretaries' Association | B.L.S. | Bachelor of Library Science | Ch.B. | Bachelor of Surgery |
| | | B.M. | Bachelor of Medicine | Chev. | Chevalier |
| A.L.A. | Associate of the Library Association (England); American Library Association | B.Mus. | Bachelor of Music | Chim. | Chimie; Chimique; Chimiste |
| | | B.M.V. | Bachelier en Médicine Vetérinaire | Chirurg. | Chirurgical; Chirurgien |
| | | | | Ch.M. | Mastery of Surgery |
| | | Bn. | Battalion | Chrmn. | Chairman |
| A.M. | Master of Arts; Albert Medal | B.N.A. | British North America | Cie. | Compagnie |
| A.M.C. | Army Medical Corps | Bot. | Botany; Botanist; Botanical | C. in C. | Commander-in-Chief |
| Anat. | Anatomy; Anatomical; Anatomist | B.Paed.(Péd.) | Bachelor of Pedagogy | C. of E. | Church of England |
| A.O.C. | Air Officer Commanding | B.P.A. | Bachelor of Public Administration | C.L.C. | Canadian Labour Congress |
| A.O.C.-in-C. | Air Officer Commanding-in-Chief | B.P.E. | Bachelor of Physical Education | C.L.J. | Commander of the Order of St. Lazarus of Jerusalem |
| A.Q.M.G. | Assistant-Quartermaster-General | B.Ph. | Bachelor of Philosophy | | |
| A.R.A. | Associate of the Royal Academy | B.P.H.E. | Bachelor of Physical and Health Education | Clin. | Clinical; Clinic |
| A.R.A.M. | Associate of the Royal Academy of Music | | | Clk. | Clerk |
| | | Brig. | Brigadier | C.L.U. | Chartered Life Underwriter |
| A.R.C.A. | Associate of the Royal Canadian Academy of Arts; Associate Royal College of Art | B.S. | Bachelor of Science (U.S.) | C.M. | Canada Medal; Member of the Order of Canada; Membre de l'Ordre du Canada; Master in Surgery |
| | | B.S.A., B.Sc.A. | Bachelor of Science in Agriculture | | |
| A.R.I.B.A. | Associate of the Royal Institute of British Architects | B.Sc. | Bachelor of Science | | |
| | | B.Sc.Com. | Bachelor of Commercial Science | C.M.G. | Companion of St. Michael and St. George |
| Arty. | Artillery | B.Sc.F. | Bachelor of Science in Forestry | | |
| A.S.A. | Associate of the Society of Actuaries | B.Sc.Soc. | Bachelor of Social Science | C.M.M. | Commander of the Order of Military Merit |
| | | B.S.C.E. | Bachelor of Science in Civil Engineering | | |
| Atty. | Attorney | | | C.N.I.B. | Canadian National Institute for the Blind |
| | | B.S.Ed. | Bachelor of Science in Education | | |
| | | B.S.E.E. | Bachelor of Science in Electrical Engineering | C.N.R. | Canadian National Railways |
| b. | Born | | | C.O. | Commanding Officer |
| B.A.I. | Bachelor of Engineering | B.S.F. | Bachelor of Science in Forestry | Co. | County; Company |

| | |
|---|---|
| C.O.F. | Canadian Order of Foresters; Catholic Order of Foresters |
| Coll. | College; Collegiate |
| Cons. | Conservative; Conservateur |
| C.O.T.C. | Canadian Officers' Training Corps |
| C.P.A. | Certified Public Accountant |
| Cpl. | Corporal |
| C.P.R. | Canadian Pacific Railway |
| C.R. | Conseil de la reine |
| cr. | Created; Créé |
| C.S.I. | Companion of the Order of the Star of India |
| C.St.J. | Commander of the Order of St. John of Jerusalem |
| C.V.O. | Companion of the Royal Victorian Order |
| Cytol. | Cytology; Cytological; Cytologist |
| d. | Daughter; Died |
| D.A. | Doctor of Archaeology (Laval) |
| D.A.A.G. | Deputy Assistant-Adjutant-General |
| D.A.A. & Q.M.G. | Deputy Assistant-Adjutant and Quartermaster-General |
| D.Adm. | Doctor of Administration |
| D.A.D.M.S. | Deputy Assistant Director of Medical Services |
| D.A.G. | Deputy Adjutant-General |
| D.A.Q.M.G. | Deputy Assistant-Quartermaster-General |
| D.A.Sc. | Doctor in Agricultural Sciences |
| D.B.A. | Doctor of Business Administration |
| D.C.L. | Doctor of Common Law (or Civil Law) |
| D.C.M. | Distinguished Conduct Medal |
| D.C.T. | Doctor of Christian Theology |
| D.Cn.L. | Doctor of Canon Law |
| D.D. | Doctor of Divinity |
| D.D.C. | Docteur en Droit Canonique |
| D.de l'Un. | Doctorat de l'Université |
| D.D.M.S. | Deputy Director of Medical Services |
| D.D.S. | Doctor of Dental Surgery |
| D.D.Sc. | Doctor of Dental Science |
| def. | Defeated; Défaite |
| D.Eng. | Doctor of Engineering |
| D.en Méd. Vet. | Docteur en Médicine Vétérinaire |
| D.en Ph. | Docteur en Philosophie |
| Dent. | Dentist; Dental; Dentistry |
| D.ès L. | Docteur ès Lettres (Doctor of Letters) |
| D.F.A. | Doctor of Fine Arts |
| D.F.C. | Distinguished Flying Cross |
| D.F.S. | Doctor in Forest Science (Laval) |
| D.F.Sc. | Doctor of Financial Science (Laval) |
| D.G.M. | Deputy Grand Master |
| D.Gén. | Doctorat en Génie |
| D.H.L. | Doctor of Hebrew Literature |
| D.Hum.Litt. | Doctor of Humane Letters |
| D.I.C. | Diploma of Imperial College |
| D.J.C. | Doctor of Canon Law |
| D.L. | Doctor in Civil Law |
| D.Lit. or D.Litt. | Doctor of Literature; also Letters |
| D.L.S. | Dominion Land Surveyor |
| D.Litt.S. | Doctor of Sacred Literature |
| D.M. | Doctorate Médecine |
| D.Man.Sc. | Doctor of Management Sciences |
| D.Mus. | Doctorat en musique |
| D.O. | Doctor of Osteopathy |
| D.O.C. | District Officer Commanding |
| Doct.Arch. | Doctor of Christian Archeology (Pontifical Institute, Rome) |
| Dom. | Dominion |
| D.Paed.(Péd.) | Doctor of Pedagogy |
| D.P.H. | Doctor (or Diploma) of Public Health |
| D.Phil., D.Ph. | Doctor of Philosophy |
| D.P.Sc. | Doctor of Political, Social and Economic Sciences |

| | |
|---|---|
| Dr.Com.Sc. | Doctor of Commercial Science |
| Dr. de l'U. (Paris) | Doctor of the University (Paris) |
| Dr. ès Lettres | Doctor of Letters (History of Literature) |
| Dr.jur. | Doctor Juris |
| Dr.rer.pol. | Doctor of Political Economy (Dr. Rerum Politicarum) |
| D.S.A. | Docteur ès Science Agricole |
| D.S.C. | Distinguished Service Cross |
| D.Sc. | Doctor of Science |
| D.Sc.Adm. | Doctor in Administrative Sciences |
| D.Sc.C(om). | Doctor of Commercial Science |
| D.Sc.Fin. | Doctor of Financial Science |
| D.Sc.Nat. | Doctor of Natural Science |
| D.Sc.P. | Doctor of Political Science |
| D.Sc.Soc. | Doctor of Social Science |
| D.S.O. | Companion of the Distinguished Service Order |
| D.S.S. | Doctor of Sacred Scripture |
| D.Th., D.Theol. | Doctor of Theology |
| D.U. | Docteur d'Université |
| D.Univ.(Paris) | Doctor of the University (Paris) |
| D.V.M. | Doctor of Veterinary Medicine |
| D.V.Sc. | Doctor of Veterinary Science |
| E. | East; Eastern |
| e. | Educated; Eldest; Elder |
| é. | Eduqué; Education |
| Ecol. | Ecology; Ecological; Ecologist |
| Econ. | Economy; Economics; Economical; Economist |
| E.D. | Efficiency Decoration |
| Ed.D. | Doctor of Education |
| Ed.M. | Master of Education (Harvard) |
| E.E. | Electrical Engineer |
| el. | Election; Elected; Electoral |
| ép. | Epous; Epouse; Epousé(e) |
| Epis. | Episcopal; Episcopalian |
| Ethnol. | Ethnology; Ethnological; Ethnologist |
| f. | Fils; Fille |
| F.A.A.A. | Fellow of the American Academy of Allergy |
| F.A.A.A.S. | Fellow of the American Association for the Advancement of Science |
| F.A.A.S. | Fellow of the American Academy of Arts and Sciences |
| F.A.C.D. | Fellow of the American College of Dentistry |
| F.A.C.H.A. | Fellow of the American College of Health Administrators |
| F.A.C.P. | Fellow of the American College of Physicians |
| F.A.C.S. | Fellow of the American College of Surgeons |
| F.A.E. | Fellow of the Accountants' and Executives' Corporation of Canada |
| F.A.G.S. | Fellow of the American Geographical Society |
| F.A.I.A. | Fellow of the American Institute of Architects |
| F.A.P.H.A. | Fellow of the American Public Health Association |
| F.A.P.S. | Fellow of the American Physical Society |
| F.B.A. | Fellow of the British Academy |
| F.B.O.A. | Fellow of the British Optical Association |
| F.B.O.U. | Fellow of the British Ornithologists Union |
| F.Brit.I.R.E. | Fellow of the British Institution of Radio Engineers |
| F.B.Ps.S. | Fellow of the British Psychological Society |
| F.B.S.C. | Fellow of the British Society of Commerce |

| | |
|---|---|
| F.C.A. | Fellow of the Institute of Chartered Accountants |
| F.C.A.S.I. | Fellow of the Canadian Aeronautics and Space Institute |
| F.C.B.A. | Fellow of The Canadian Bankers' Association |
| F.C.C.O. | Fellow of The Canadian College of Organists |
| F.C.I. | Fellow of the Canadian Credit Institute |
| F.C.I.A. | Fellow of the Canadian Institute of Actuaries |
| F.C.I.C. | Fellow of the Chemical Institute of Canada |
| F.C.I.I. | Fellow of the Chartered Insurance Institute |
| F.C.I.S. | Fellow of the Chartered Institute of Secretaries |
| F.C.S. | Fellow of the Chemical Society |
| F.C.W.A. | Fellow of the Institute of Cost and Works Accountants |
| F.E.I.C. | Fellow of the Engineering Institute of Canada |
| F.E.S. | Fellow of the Entomological Society; Fellow of the Ethnological Society |
| F.F.A. | Fellow of the Faculty of Actuaries (Scotland) |
| F.F.P.S. | Fellow of the Royal Faculty of Physicians and Surgeons (Glasgow) |
| F.F.R. | Fellow of the Faculty of Radiologists |
| F.G.A. | Fellow of Gemmological Association |
| F.G.S. | Fellow of the Geological Society |
| F.G.S.A. | Fellow of the Geological Society of America |
| F.I.A. | Fellow of the Institute of Actuaries (London) |
| F.I.A.I. | Fellow of the International Institute of Arts and Letters |
| F.I.Ae.S. | Fellow of the Institute of Aeronautical Sciences |
| F.I.A.S. | Fellow of the Institute of Aeronautical Sciences (U.S.) |
| F.I.C. | Fellow of the Institute of Commerce |
| F.I.C.B. | Fellow of the Institute of Canadian Bankers |
| F.I.C.D. | Fellow of the International College of Dentists |
| F.I.E.E. | Fellow of the Institute of Electrical Engineers |
| F.I.I.A. | Fellow of the Institute of Industrial Administration |
| F.I.I.C. | Fellow of the Insurance Institute of Canada |
| F.I.Inst. | Fellow of the Imperial Institute |
| F.I.L.A. | Fellow of the Institute of Landscape Architects |
| F.I.M. | Fellow of the Institute of Metals |
| F.I.M.C. | Fellow of the Institute of Management Consultants |
| F.Inst.P. | Fellow of Institute of Physics |
| F.Inst.Pet. | Fellow of the Institute of Petroleum |
| F.I.R.E. | Fellow of the Institution of Radio Engineers |
| F.I.S.A. | Fellow of the Incorporated Secretaries' Association |
| F.L.A. | Fellow of the Library Association (England) |
| F.L.C.M. | Fellow of the London College of Music |
| F.L.S. | Fellow of the Linnean Society |
| F.M.S.A. | Fellow of the Mineralogical Society of America |
| F.P.S. | Fellow of Philosophical Society; also Pathological Society of Great Britain |
| F.Phys.S. | Fellow of the Physical Society |
| F.R.Ae.S. | Fellow of the Royal Aeronautical Society |

| | | | | | |
|---|---|---|---|---|---|
| F.R.A.I. | Fellow of the Royal Anthropological Institute | F.Z.S. | Fellow of the Zoological Society | K.C.M.G. | Knight Commander of St. Michael and St. George |
| F.R.A.I.C. | Fellow of the Royal Architectural Institute of Canada | Gaz. | Gazetted | K.C.S.G. | Knight Commander of St. Gregory |
| F.R.A.M. | Fellow of the Royal Academy of Music (London) | G.B.E. | Knight Grand Cross, Order of the British Empire | K.C.S.I. | Knight Commander of the Star of India |
| F.R.A.S. | Fellow of the Royal Astronomical Society; also Fellow of the Royal Asiatic Society | G.C. | George Cross | K.C.V.O. | Knight Commander of the Royal Victorian Order |
| | | G.C.I.E. | Knight Grand Commander of the Indian Empire | | |
| F.R.B.S. | Fellow of the Royal Botanic Society; Fellow of the Royal Society of British Sculptors | G.C.M.G. | Knight Grand Cross of St. Michael and St. George | K.G. | Knight Commander of the Garter |
| | | | | K.St.J. | Knight of Grace, Order of St. John of Jerusalem |
| | | G.C.S.I. | Knight Grand Commander of the Star of India | K.H.S. | Knight of the Holy Sepulchre |
| F.R.C.D.(C). | Fellow of the Royal College of Dentists (Canada) | G.C.V.O. | Knight Grand Cross of the Royal Victorian Order | K.St.J. | Knight of Justice, Order of St. John of Jerusalem |
| F.R.C.M. | Fellow of the Royal College of Music | g.e. | General Election | K.T. | Knight of the Order of the Thistle; Knight Templar |
| F.R.C.O. | Fellow of the Royal College of Organists | Geneal. | Genealogy; Genealogist; Genealogical | Kt. | Knight; Knight Bachelor |
| F.R.C.O.G. | Fellow of the Royal College of Obstetricians and Gynaecologists | Geol. | Geology; Geological; Geologist | Lancs. | Lancashire |
| | | G.H.Q. | General Headquarters | L.Ch. | Licentiate in Surgery |
| F.R.C.P. | Fellow of the Royal College of Physicians | Glos. | Gloucestershire | L.D.C. | Licentiate Droit Canonique |
| | | G.M. | George Medal | L.Div. | Licentiate in Divinity |
| F.R.C.P.(C). | Fellow of the Royal College of Physicians (Canada) | G.O.C. | General Officer Commanding | Ldr. | Leader |
| | | G.S.O. | General Staff Officer | L.D.S. | Licentiate in Dental Surgery |
| F.R.C.S. | Fellow of the Royal College of Surgeons | | | L.ès. D. | Licencié ès Droit |
| | | H. of C. | House of Commons | L.ès. L. | Licencié ès Lettres |
| F.R.C.S.(C). | Fellow of the Royal College of Surgeons (Canada) | Hants. | Hampshire | L.ès. Sc. | Licencié ès Sciences |
| | | H.E. | His (or Her) Excellency; His Eminence | Lic. | Licentiate; Licencié |
| F.R.C.V.S. | Fellow of the Royal College of Veterinary Surgeons | | | Lic.Med. | Licentiate in Medicine |
| | | Herts. | Hertfordshire | Lit.hum. | Litterae humaniores (classics) |
| F.R.E.S. | Fellow Royal Empire Society; Fellow of the Royal Entomological Society; Fellow of the Royal Economic Society | Histol. | Histology; Histological; Histologist | Litt. | Littérateur; Littéraire |
| | | | | Litt.B. | Bachelor of Letters |
| | | H.M. | His (or Her) Majesty | Litt. D. | Doctor of Letters; Doctor of Literature |
| | | H.M.C.S. | Her Majesty's Canadian Ship | | |
| F.R.G.S. | Fellow of the Royal Geographic Society | H.M.S. | Her Majesty's Ship | L.J.C. | Licentia Juris Canonici |
| | | H.O. | Head Office | LL.B. | Bachelor of Laws |
| F.R.G.S.(C). | Fellow of the Royal Geographic Society (Canada) | Homoeo. | Homoeopathy; Homoeopathic; Homoeopath | LL.D. | Doctor of Laws |
| | | | | LL.L. | Licentiate of Laws |
| F.R.H.S., F.R.Hist.S. | Fellow of the Royal Historical Society | Hortic. | Horticulture; Horticultural; Horticulturist | LL.M. | Master of Laws |
| | | | | L.M.C.C. | Licentiate of Medical College of Canada |
| | | H.Q. | Headquarters | | |
| F.R.Hort.S. | Fellow of the Royal Horticultural Society | H.R.H. | His (or Her) Royal Highness | L.O.L. | Loyal Orange Lodge |
| | | Hts. | Heights | L.Péd. | Licence en Pédagogie |
| F.R.I.B.A. | Fellow of the Royal Institute of British Architects | Hunts. | Huntingdonshire | L.Ph. | Licence en Philosophie |
| | | | | L.Psych. | Licencié en Psychologie |
| F.R.I.C. | Fellow of the Royal Institute of Chemistry | i/c | In Charge | L.R.A.M. | Licentiate of the Royal Academy of Music, London |
| | | I.C.A.O. | International Civil Aviation Organization | | |
| F.R.I.P.H.H. | Fellow of the Royal Institute of Public Health and Hygiene | | | L.R.C.P. | Licentiate of the Royal College of Physicians |
| | | I.L.O. | International Labour Office | | |
| F.R.M.S. | Fellow of the Royal Microscopical Society | Inf. | Infantry | L.R.C.S. | Licentiate of the Royal College of Surgeons |
| | | Ins. | Insurance | | |
| F.R.Met.S. | Fellow of the Royal Meteorological Society | Inspr. | Inspector | L.R.C.T. | Licentiate of the Royal Conservatory of Toronto |
| | | Inst. | Institute; Institution; Institut | | |
| F.R.N.S. | Fellow of the Royal Numismatic Society | Inst(r). | Instructor; Instruction | L.R.C.V.S. | Licentiate of the Royal College of Veterinary Surgeons |
| | | Invest. | Investment; Investissement | | |
| F.R.P.S.L. | Fellow of the Royal Philatelic Society, London | Investig. | Investigation | L.S.A. | Licentiate in Agricultural Science |
| | | I.O.D.E. | Independent Order Daughters of the Empire | L.Sc.Comm. | Licentiate in Commercial Science |
| F.R.S. | Fellow of the Royal Society | | | L.S.Sc. | Licentiate in Sacred Scriptures |
| F.R.S.A. | Fellow of the Royal Society of Arts | I.O.F. | Independent Order of Foresters | L.Sc.Soc. | Licence in Social Science |
| | | I.O.O.F. | Independent Order of Oddfellows | L.Th. | Licentiate in Theology |
| F.R.S.C. | Fellow of the Royal Society of Canada | I.S.O. | Imperial Service Order | | |
| F.R.S. Chem. | Fellow of the Royal Society of Chemistry | | | m. | Married; Marié |
| | | J.C.B. | Bachelor of Canon Law | M.A. | Master of Arts |
| F.R.S.E. | Fellow of the Royal Society of Edinburgh | J.C.D. | Juris Canonici Doctor (Doctor of Canon Law) | M.A.A.A. | Montreal Amateur Athletic Association |
| | | | | | |
| F.R.S.H. | Fellow of the Royal Society of Health | J.C.L. | Juris Canonici Licentiatus (Licentiate in Canon Law) | M.A.I. | Master of Engineering |
| | | | | M.A.L.S. | Master of Arts in Library Science |
| F.R.S.L. | Fellow of the Royal Society of Literature | J.D. | Doctor of Jurisprudence | M.A.N. | Membre de l'Assemblée Nationale |
| | | J.D.S. | Doctor of Juridical Science | M.A.O. | Master of Obstetric Art |
| F.R.S.M. | Fellow of the Royal Society of Medicine | Jos. | Joseph | M.Arch. | Master of Architecture |
| | | J.P. | Justice of the Peace | M.A.Sc. | Master of Applied Science |
| F.R.S.T.M.&H. | Fellow of the Royal Society of Tropical Medicine and Hygiene | Jt. | Joint | M.B. | Bachelor of Medicine |
| | | J.U.L. | Licentiate of Law in Utroque (both Civil and Canon Law) | M.B. | Medal of Bravery (Canadian) |
| F.S.A. | Fellow of the Society of Antiquaries; Fellow of the Society of Actuaries (U.S.) | | | M.B.A. | Master in Business Administration |
| | | Jur.utr.Dr. | Juris utriusque doctor (equivalent to LL.D.) | | |
| F.S.A.A. | Fellow of the Society of Incorporated Accountants and Auditors | | | M.B.E. | Member of the Order of the British Empire |
| | | K.B.E. | Knight Commander of the British Empire | M.C. | Military Cross |
| F.S.E. | Fellow of the Society of Engineers | K.C. | King's Counsel | M.C.E. | Master of Civil Engineering |
| F.S.S. | Fellow of the Royal Statistical Society | K.C.B. | Knight Commander of the Bath | M.Ch., M.Chir. | Master in Surgery |
| | | | | M.Com. | Master of Commerce |

| | |
|---|---|
| M.D. | Doctor of Medicine |
| | Military District |
| M.du C. | Canada Medal |
| M.E. | Mining Engineer; Mechanical Engineer |
| M.Ed. | Master of Education |
| Mem. | Memorial |
| M.Eng. | Master of Engineering |
| Meth. | Methodist |
| Metrop. | Metropolitan |
| M.F.A. | Master of Fine Arts |
| M.H.A. | Member of House Assembly |
| M.H.L. | Master of Hebrew Letters |
| Mil. | Military; Militia |
| Min. | Minister |
| Missy. | Missionary |
| M.L.A. | Member of the Legislative Assembly |
| M.M. | Military Medal |
| M.M.M. | Member of the Order of Military Merit |
| M.N.A. | Member of the National Assembly |
| M.P. | Member of Parliament |
| M.P.P. | Member of Provincial Parliament |
| M.S. | Master of Surgery; Master of Science (U.S.) |
| M.S.A. | Master of Science in Agriculture |
| M.S.C. | Meritorious Service Cross (Canadian) |
| M.Sc.Com. | Master in Commercial Sciences |
| M.Sc.F. | Master of Science in Forestry |
| M.S.Ed. | Master of Science in Education (U.S.) |
| Msgr. | Monseigneur |
| M.S.S. | Master of Social Science |
| M.S.W. | Master of Social Work |
| Mun. | Municipality; Municipal |
| M.U.Dr. | Medecinae Universae Doctor (Prague) (Dentistry and Medecine) |
| Mus.B(ac). | Bachelor of Music |
| Mus.D(oc). | Doctor of Music |
| Mus.M. | Master of Music |
| M.V.O. | Member of Royal Victorian Order |
| Mycol. | Mycology; Mycological; Mycologist |
| | |
| n. | né(e) |
| N.A.T.O. | North Atlantic Treaty Organization |
| N.D.G. | Notre Dame de Grace |
| N.D.P. | New Democratic Party |
| Neurol. | Neurology; Neurological; Neurologist |
| No. | Number; Nombre |
| Notts. | Nottinghamshire |
| N.P. | Notaire Publique |
| N.P.A.M. | Non Permanent Active Militia |
| N.S.W. | New South Wales |
| Numis. | Numismatic |
| N.Z. | New Zealand |
| | |
| o. | Ordained; Ordiné |
| O.B.E. | Officer Order of the British Empire |
| O.C. | Officer of the Order of Canada; Officier de l'Ordre du Canada; Officer Commanding |
| Offr. | Officer |
| O.F.M. | Franciscan Fathers |
| O.M. | Order of Merit |
| O.M.M. | Officers of the Order of Military Merit |
| O.M.I. | Oblate of Mary Immaculate |
| Ophthal(mol). | Ophthalmology; Ophthalmic; Ophthalmologist |
| Organ. | Organization; Organized |
| Ornithol. | Ornithology; Ornithological; Ornithologist |
| O.S.A. | Ontario Society of Artists |
| O.St.J. | Officer of Order of St. John of Jerusalem |
| Otol. | Otology; Otological; Otologist |
| Oxon. | Oxfordshire; of Oxford |

| | |
|---|---|
| P. | Progressive |
| Pac. | Pacific |
| Path(ol). | Pathology; Pathological; Pathologist |
| P.C. | Privy Council; Privy Councillor |
| P.D.D.G.M. | Past District Deputy Grand Master |
| P.Eng. | Professional Engineer |
| Perm. | Permanent |
| P.G.M. | Past Grand Master |
| P.G.Z. | Past Grand Z |
| Ph.B. | Bachelor of Philosophy |
| Ph.C. | Philosopher of Chiropractic |
| Ph.D. | Doctor of Philosophy |
| Philol. | Philology; Philological; Philologist |
| Philos. | Philosophy; Philosophical |
| Phm.B. | Bachelor of Pharmacy |
| Phys. | Physical; Physician |
| Physiol. | Physiology; Physiological; Physiologist |
| Phytopath(ol). | Phytopathology; Phytopathological; Phytopathologist |
| P.M. | Past Master |
| Pol. | Political |
| Polytech. | Polytechnic; Polytechnique |
| Pomol. | Pomology; Pomological; Pomologist |
| P.O.W. | Prisoner of War |
| P.P.C.L.I. | Princess Patricia's Canadian Light Infantry |
| Prep. | Preparatory |
| Presb. | Presbyterian |
| Presby. | Presbytery |
| Prop. | Proprietor; Proprietaire |
| Prot. | Protestant |
| p.s. | Passed School of Instruction (Officers) |
| p.s.a. | Graduate of R.A.F. Staff College |
| p.s.c. | Passed Staff College |
| P.S.G.M. | Past Supreme Grand Master |
| Psychol. | Psychology; Psychological; Psychologist |
| Pte. | Private (soldier) |
| Pty. | Proprietary |
| P.Z. | Past Z |
| | |
| Q.C. | Queen's Counsel |
| Q.H.S. | Queen's Honorary Surgeon |
| Q.M. | Quartermaster |
| Q.M.G. | Quartermaster-General |
| Q.O.R. | Queen's Own Rifles |
| | |
| R.A. | Royal Artillery |
| | Royal Academician |
| R.A.F. | Royal Air Force |
| R.A.M. | Royal Academy of Music; Royal Arch Mason |
| R.A.M.C. | Royal Army Medical Corps |
| R.B.A. | Royal Society of British Architects |
| R.C.A. | Royal Canadian Artillery; Royal Canadian Academy of Arts |
| R.C.A.C. | Royal Canadian Armoured Corps |
| R.C.A.F. | Royal Canadian Air Force |
| R.C.A.M.C. | Royal Canadian Army Medical Corps |
| R.C.D. | Royal Canadian Dragoons |
| R.C.E. | Royal Canadian Engineers |
| R.C.E.M.E. | Royal Canadian Electrical and Mechanical Engineers |
| R.C.F.A. | Royal Canadian Field Artillery |
| R.C.G.A. | Royal Canadian Garrison Artillery |
| R.C.M.P. | Royal Canadian Mounted Police |
| R.C.N. | Royal Canadian Navy |
| R.C.N.V.R. | Royal Canadian Naval Volunteer Reserve |
| R.C.O.C. | Royal Canadian Ordnance Corps |
| R.C.R. | Royal Canadian Regiment |
| R.C.Y.C. | Royal Canadian Yacht Club |
| R.E. | Royal Engineers |

| | |
|---|---|
| Regt. | Regiment |
| Res. | Resident |
| R.F.A. | Royal Field Artillery |
| R.F.C. | Royal Flying Corps |
| Rhinol. | Rhinology; Rhinological; Rhinologist |
| R.I.A. | Registered Industrial and Cost Accountant |
| R.M.C. | Royal Military College (Canada) |
| R.N. | Royal Navy; Registered Nurse |
| R.N.S.Y.S. | Royal Nova Scotia Yacht Squadron |
| R22eR | Royal 22e Régiment |
| R.O. | Reserve of Officers |
| Röntgenol. | Röntgenology; Röntgenological; Röntgenologist |
| R.P.F. | Registered Professional Forester |
| R.R. | Rural Route |
| | |
| s. | Son |
| Salop. | Shropshire |
| Sask. | Saskatchewan |
| S.B. | Bachelor of Science |
| S.C. | South Carolina |
| S.C. | Star of Courage (Canadian) |
| Sc.D. | Doctor of Science |
| Sc.L. | Licence ès Sciences |
| Sc.Soc.B. | Bachelier Science Sociale |
| Sc.Soc.D. | Doctor of Social Science |
| Sc.Soc.L. | License in Social Science |
| S.D. | Doctor of Science |
| Sec. | Section |
| Sém. | Seminaire; Seminarien |
| Semy. | Seminary |
| S.J. | Society of Jesus (Jesuits) |
| S.J.D. | Doctor of Juristic Science |
| S.M. | Master of Science |
| Soc. | Society; Société |
| Sociol. | Sociology; Sociological; Sociologist |
| Solr. | Solicitor |
| Sqdn. | Squadron |
| Sr. | Senior |
| S.S.B. | Bachelier en Science Sacrée |
| S.S.L. | Licentiate in Sacred Scripture |
| Stat. | Statistical; Statistics; Statistician |
| S.T.B.(S.Th.B.) | Bachelor of Sacred Theology |
| S.T.D.(S.Th.D.) | Doctor of Sacred Theology |
| S.T.L.(S.Th.L.) | Licentiate in Sacred Theology |
| S.T.M. | Master of Sacred Theology |
| | |
| Th.B. | Bachelor of Theology |
| Theol. | Theology; Theological; Theologian |
| Theos. | Theosophy; Theosophical; Theosophist |
| Th.L. | Theological Licentiate |
| Topog. | Topography; Topographical; Topographer |
| Toxicol. | Toxicology; Toxicologist |
| Twp. | Township |
| | |
| U.E.L. | United Empire Loyalist |
| U.K. | United Kingdom |
| U.M.W.A. | United Mine Workers of America |
| Un. | United; Unis |
| U.N. | United Nations |
| U.N.E.S.C.O. | United Nations Educational, Scientific and Cultural Organization |
| U.N.I.C.E.F. | United Nations International Chidren's Emergency Fund |
| unm. | Unmarried |
| U.N.O. | United Nations Organization |
| U.N.R.R.A. | United Nations Relief and Rehabilitation Administration |
| Urol. | Urology; Urological; Urologist |
| U.S.N. | United States Navy |
| | |
| V.C. | Victoria Cross |
| V.D. | Volunteer Officers' Decoration |
| Ven. | Venerable (of an Archdeacon) |
| Very Rev. | Very Reverend (of a Dean) |

| | |
|---|---|
| **Vet.** | Veterinary; Veterinarian |
| **Vol.** | Volunteer; Voluntary; Volume |
| **V.Q.M.G.** | Vice-Quartermaster-General |
| | |
| **W.P.T.B.** | Wartime Prices and Trade Board |
| **W.C.T.U.** | Women's Christian Temperance Union |
| **W.F.** | White Fathers |
| **Wilts.** | Wiltshire |
| **W.O.W.** | Woodmen of the World |
| | |
| **y.** | youngest |
| **Y.M.C.A.** | Young Men's Christian Association |
| **Y.M.H.A.** | Young Men's Hebrew Association |
| **Yorks.** | Yorkshire |
| **Y.W.C.A.** | Young Women's Christian Association |